WHO WAS WHO

VOL. V

1951-1960

WHO'S WHO

AN ANNUAL BIOGRAPHICAL DICTIONARY

FIRST PUBLISHED IN 1849

WHO *WAS* WHO

VOL. I. 1897–1915

VOL. II. 1916–1928

VOL. III. 1929–1940

VOL. IV. 1941–1950

VOL. V. 1951–1960

VOL. VI. 1961–1970

VOL. VII. 1971–1980

A CUMULATED INDEX 1897–1980

PUBLISHED BY

ADAM & CHARLES BLACK

WHO WAS WHO. VOL. V

WHO WAS WHO
1951-1960

A COMPANION TO

WHO'S WHO

CONTAINING THE BIOGRAPHIES
OF THOSE WHO DIED DURING
THE DECADE 1951-1960

ADAM & CHARLES BLACK
LONDON

FIRST PUBLISHED 1961
SECOND EDITION 1964
THIRD EDITION 1967
FOURTH EDITION 1984

A. AND C. BLACK (PUBLISHERS) LIMITED
35 BEDFORD ROW, LONDON WC1

ISBN 0-7136-2598-8

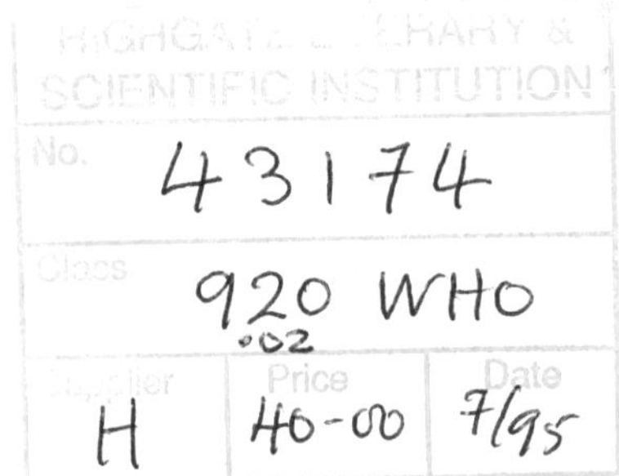

PRINTED IN GREAT BRITAIN

PREFACE TO THE FOURTH EDITION

THIS volume contains the entries, as they appeared in *Who's Who* for the last time, of those who died during the years 1951–1960, brought up to date and with the date of death added. The number of children shown in an entry is the number living at the date of the last issue of *Who's Who* in which the entry appeared.

When this volume was first published in 1961 a certain number of entries were omitted as it was not then known to the publishers that those concerned had died. In subsequent editions such entries have been included in an enlarged Addenda on pages xxvii-xxxii.

In 1981 an index to all the current volumes of *Who Was Who* was published for the first time, giving the names shown in *Who Was Who* from the first volume, with deaths from 1897 onwards. It is hoped that this will make the use of *Who Was Who* a great deal easier for researchers, since it is no longer necessary to search from volume to volume if the year of death is not known.

CONTENTS

	PAGE
PREFACE	v
ABBREVIATIONS USED IN THIS BOOK	ix
ADDENDA	xxvii
BIOGRAPHIES	1

ABBREVIATIONS USED IN THIS BOOK

A

A.A. . . Anti-Aircraft; Automobile Association; Architectural Association; Augustinians of the Assumption.
A.A.A.. . Amateur Athletic Association.
A.A. & Q.M.G. Assistant Adjutant and Quartermaster-General.
A.A.A.S. . American Association for Advancement of Science.
A.A.C.C.A.. Associate of the Association of Certified and Corporate Accountants.
A.A.F. . . Auxiliary Air Force (now R. Aux. A.F.).
A.A.G.. . Assistant-Adjutant-General.
A.A.I. . . Associate of Chartered Auctioneers' and Estate Agents' Institute.
A.A.M.C. . Australian Army Medical Corps.
A. & A.E.E. Aeroplane and Armament Experimental Establishment.
A.A.S.A. . Associate of Australian Society of Accountants.
A.A.U.Q. . Associate in Accountancy, University of Queensland.
A.B. . . Bachelor of Arts (U.S.); able-bodied seaman.
A.B.A. . . Amateur Boxing Association.
A.B.C. . . Australian Broadcasting Commission.
A.B.C.F.M.. American Board of Commissioners for Foreign Missions.
Aber. . . Aberdeen.
Abp. . . Archbishop.
A.C. . . *Ante Christum* (before Christ).
A.C.A. . . Associate of the Institute of Chartered Accountants.
Acad. . . Academy.
A.C.A.S. . Assistant Chief of the Air Staff.
A.C.C.S. . Associate of Corporation of Secretaries (formerly of Certified Secretaries).
A.C.F. . . Army Cadet Force.
A.C.G. . . Assistant Chaplain-General.
A.C.G.I. . Associate of City and Guilds of London Institute.
A.C.I.I. . Associate of the Chartered Insurance Institute.
A.C.I.S. . Associate of the Chartered Institute of Secretaries.
A.C.S. . . Additional Curates Society.
A.C.S.E.A. . Allied Command S.E. Asia.
A.C.S.M. . Associate of the Camborne School of Mines.
A.C.T. . . Australian Capital Territory; Australian College of Theology; Associate of the College of Technology.
A.D. . . *Anno Domini.*
A.D.C. . . Aide-de-camp.
A.D.C.M. . Archbishop of Canterbury's Diploma in Church Music.
A.D. Corps. Army Dental Corps.
Ad eund. . *Ad eundem gradum* (admitted to the same degree); and *see under* a.e.g.
A.D.F.W. . Assistant Director of Fortifications and Works.
A.D.G.B. . Air Defence of Great Britain.
A.D.G.M.S. Assistant Director-General of Medical Services.
A.D.H.. . Assistant Director of Hygiene.
Adj. . . Adjutant.
A.D.J.A.G.. Assistant Deputy Judge Advocate General.
Adm. . . Admiral.
A.D.M.S. . Assistant Director of Medical Services.
A.D.O.S. . Assistant Director of Ordnance Services.
A.D.P.R. . Assistant Director of Public Relations.
A.D.S. & T. Assistant Director of Supplies and Transport.
Adv. . . Advocate.
A.D.V.S. . Assistant Director of Veterinary Services.
Advt. . . Advertisement.
A.D.W.E. & M. Assistant Director of Works, Electrical and Mechanical.
A.E.A. . . Air Efficiency Award.
A.E.A.F. . Allied Expeditionary Air Force.
A.E.C. . . Army Educational Corps (now R.A.E.C.).
A.E.F. . . American Expeditionary Forces.
a.e.g. . . *ad eundem gradum* (to the same degree—of the admission of a graduate of one university to the same degree at another without examination).
A.E.I. . . Associated Electrical Industries.
A.E.M.. . Air Efficiency Medal.
A.E.R. . . Army Emergency Reserve.
A.E.R.E. . Atomic Energy Research Establishment (Harwell).
Æt., Ætat. . *Ætatis* (aged).
A.E.U. . . Amalgamated Engineering Union.
A.F.A. . . Amateur Football Association.
A.F.C. . . Air Force Cross.
A.F.H.Q. . Allied Force Headquarters.
A.F.I.A. . Associate of Federal Institute of Accountants (Aust.).
A.F.I.A.S. . Associate Fellow Institute of Aeronautical Sciences (U.S.).
A.F.R.Ae.S. Associate Fellow Royal Aeronautical Society.
A.F.V. . . Armoured Fighting Vehicles.
A.G. . . Attorney - General; Adjutant-General.
A.G.I. . . Associate of the Institute of Certificated Grocers.
A.G.S.M. . Associate of Guildhall School of Music.
A.H.Q.. . Army Headquarters.
A.H.W.C. . Associate of Heriot-Watt College, Edinburgh.
A.I.A. . . Associate of the Institute of Actuaries; American Institute of Architects.
A.I.A.E. . Associate of the Institute of Automobile Engineers.
A.I.A.L. . Associate Member of the International Institute of Arts and Letters.
A.I.B. . . Associate of the Institute of Bankers.
A.I.B.D. . Associate of the Institute of British Decorators.
A.I.B.P. . Associate of the Institute of British Photographers.
A.I.C. . . Agricultural Improvement Council.
A.I.C.A. . Associate Member Commonwealth Institute of Accountants.
A.I.C.E. . Associate of the Institution of Civil Engineers.
A.I.E.E. . Associate Institution of Electrical Engineers.
A.I.F. . . Australian Imperial Forces.
A.I.G. . . Adjutant-Inspector-General.

A.I.I.A. . Associate Insurance Institute of America.
A.I.L. . . Associate of the Institute of Linguists.
A.I.L.A. . Associate of the Institute of Landscape Architects.
A.I.Loco.E. Associate of Institute of Locomotive Engineers.
A.I.Mar.E. . . Associate of the Institute of Marine Engineers.
A.I.O.B. . Associate of the Institute of Builders.
A.Inst.P. . Associate of Institute of Physics.
A.Inst.P.I. . . Associate of the Institute of Patentees (Incorporated).
A.I.S.A. . Associate of the Incorporated Secretaries' Association.
A.J.A.G. . Assistant Judge Advocate General.
A.K.C. . Associate of King's College (London).
A.L.A. . . Associate of the Library Association.
Ala. . . Alabama (U.S.).
A.L.A.S. . Associate Land Agents Society.
A.L.C.D. . Associate of London College of Divinity.
A.L.C.M. . Associate London College of Music.
A.L.F.S.E.A. Allied Land Forces South-East Asia.
A.L.I. . . Argyll Light Infantry.
A.L.S. . . Associate of the Linnæan Society.
Alta. . . Alberta.
Am. . . American.
A.M. . . Master of Arts (U.S.); Alpes Maritimes; Albert Medal.
A.M.A. . Associate of the Museums Association.
Amb. . . Ambulance.
A.Met. . . Associate of Metallurgy (Sheffield University).
A.M.F. . . Australian Military Forces.
A.M.G.O.T. Allied Military Government of Occupied Territory.
A.M.I.A.E. . . Associated Member of Institute of Automobile Engineers.
A.M.I.C.E. . . Associate Member of Institution of Civil Engineers.
A.M.I.Chem.E. Associate Member of Institution of Chemical Engineers.
A.M.I.E.A. . . Associate Member of Institute of Engineers, Australia.
A.M.I.E.E. . . Associate Member of Institution of Electrical Engineers.
A.M.I.E. (Ind.) Associate Member, Institution of Engineers, India.
A.M.I.Mech.E. Associate Member Institution of Mechanical Engineers.
A.M.I.Min.E. Associate Member of Institution of Mining Engineers.
A.M.Inst.B.E. Associate Member of the Institution of British Engineers.
A.M.Inst.C.E. Associate Member of Institution of Civil Engineers (changed 1946 to A.M.I.C.E.).
A.M.Inst.R. Associate Member of Institute of Refrigeration.
A.M.Inst.T. Associate Member of the Institute of Transport.
A.M.I.Struct.E. Associate Member of the Institution of Structural Engineers.
A.M.R.I.N.A. Associate Member of Royal Institution of Naval Architects.
A.M.S. . . Assistant Military Secretary; Army Medical Service.
A.M.T.P.I. . . Associate of Town Planning Institute.
A.N.A. . . Associate National Academician (America).
Anat. . . Anatomy; Anatomical.
A.N.E.C. Inst. Associate of N.E. Coast Institution of Engineers and Shipbuilders.
Anon. . . Anonymously.
A.N.Z.A.A.S. Australian and New Zealand Association for the Advancement of Science.
A.O.A. . . Air Officer in charge of Administration.
A.O.C. . . Air Officer Commanding.
A.O.C.-in-C. Air Officer Commanding-in-Chief.
A.O.D. . . Army Ordnance Department.
A.O.E.R. . Army Officers Emergency Reserve.
A.P.D. . . Army Pay Department.
A.P.S. . . Aborigines Protection Society.
A.Q.M.G. . Assistant-Quartermaster-General.
A.R. . . Associated Rediffusion (Television).
A.R.A. . Associate of the Royal Academy.
A.R.A.D. . Associate of the Royal Academy of Dancing.
A.R.Ae.S. . Associate of the Royal Aeronautical Society.
A.R.A.M. . Associate of the Royal Academy of Music.
A.R.A.S. . Associate of the Royal Astronomical Society.
A.R.B.C. . Associate Royal British Colonial Society of Artists.
A.R.B.S. . Associate Royal Society of British Sculptors.
A.R.C. . . Architects' Registration Council; Agricultural Research Council.
A.R.C.A. . Associate Royal College of Art; Associate Royal Canadian Academy.
A.R.Cam.A. Associate Royal Cambrian Academy (formerly A.R.C.A.).
A.R.C.E. . Academical Rank of Civil Engineers.
Archt. . Architect.
A.R.C.M. . Associate Royal College of Music.
A.R.C.O. . Associate Royal College of Organists.
A.R.C.O.(CHM) Associate Royal College of Organists with Diploma in Choir Training.
A.R.C.S. . Associate Royal College of Science.
A.R.C.S.T. . Associate Royal College of Science and Technology (Glasgow).
A.R.C.V.S. . Associate of Royal College of Veterinary Surgeons.
A.R.E. . . Associate of Royal Society of Painter Etchers.
A.R.I.B.A. . Associate of the Royal Institute of British Architects.
A.R.I.C. . Associate of the Royal Institute of Chemistry.
A.R.I.C.S. . Professional Associate of the Royal Institution of Chartered Surveyors.
Ark. . . Arkansas (U.S.).
A.R.M.S. . Associate of the Royal Society of Miniature Painters.
A.R.P. . . Air Raid Precautions.
A.R.P.S. . Associate of the Royal Photographic Society.
A.R.R.C. . Associate of the Royal Red Cross.
A.R.S.A. . Associate Royal Scottish Academy.
A.R.S.M. . Associate Royal School of Mines.
A.R.T.C. . Associate Royal Technical College (Glasgow) (name changed) *see under* A.R.C.S.T.
A.R.V.I.A. Associate Royal Victorian Institute of Architects.
A.R.W.A. . Associate Royal West of England Academy.
A.R.W.S. . Associate Royal Society of Painters in Water-Colours.
A.S. . . Anglo-Saxon.
A.S.A.A. . Associate of the Society of Incorporated Accountants and Auditors.
A.S.A.M. . Associate of the Society of Art Masters.
A.S.C. . . Army Service Corps.

A.S.E. Amalgamated Society of Engineers.
A.S.L.I.B. Association of Special Libraries and Information Bureaux.
Assoc. I.N.A. Associate of the Institution of Naval Architects.
Assoc. I.S.I. Associate of Iron and Steel Institute.
Assoc.M.C.T. Associateship of Manchester College of Technology.
Assoc.M.I.Ae.E. Associate Member Institution of Aeronautical Engineers.
Assoc. Sc. Associate in Science.
Asst. Assistant.
Astr. Astronomy.
A.S.W. Association of Scientific Workers.
A.T.A. Air Transport Auxiliary.
A.T.C. Air Training Corps.
A.T.C.L. Associate of Trinity College of Music, London.
A.T.D. Art Teachers' Diploma.
Ath. Athabasca (Canada).
A.T.I. Associate of the Textile Institute.
A.T.S. Auxiliary Territorial Service.
A.T.V. Associated TeleVision.
A.U.S. Army of the United States.
Av. Avenue.
A.V.D. Army Veterinary Department.

B

b. born; brother.
B.A. Bachelor of Arts.
B. & F.B.S. British and Foreign Bible Society.
B.A.F.O. British Air Forces of Occupation.
B.A.I. Bachelor of Engineering (*Baccalarius in Arte Ingeniaria*).
B.A.O. Bachelor of Obstetrics.
B.A.O.R. British Army of the Rhine (formerly *on* the Rhine).
Barr. Barrister.
Bart. or **Bt.** Baronet.
B.A.S. Bachelor in Agricultural Science.
B.A.Sc. Bachelor of Applied Science.
Batt. Battery.
B.B. & C.I.Rly. Bombay, Baroda and Central India Railway.
B.B.C. British Broadcasting Corporation.
B.C. Before Christ; British Columbia.
B.Ch. or **B.Chir.** Bachelor of Surgery.
B.C.L. Bachelor of Civil Law.
B.C.M.S. Bible Churchmen's Missionary Society.
B.C.O.F. British Commonwealth Occupation Force.
B.Com. Bachelor of Commerce.
B.C.S. Bengal Civil Service.
B.C.U.R.A. British Coal Utilisation Research Association.
B.D. Bachelor of Divinity.
Bd. Board.
B.D.A. British Dental Association.
Bde. Brigade.
B.D.S. Bachelor of Dental Surgery.
B.E. Bachelor of Engineering; British Element.
B.E.A. British East Africa; British European Airways.
B.Ec. Bachelor of Economics (Australian).
Beds. Bedfordshire.
B.E.E. Bachelor of Electrical Engineering.
B.E.F. British Expeditionary Force.
B.E.M. British Empire Medal.
Berks. Berkshire.
B.F.P.O. British Forces Post Office.
B.G.S. Brigadier General Staff.
B.I.F. British Industries Fair.
B.I.S.R.A. British Iron and Steel Research Association.
B.L. Bachelor of Law.
B.L.A. British Liberation Army.
B.L.E. Brotherhood of Locomotive Engineers.
B.Litt. Bachelor of Letters.
B.M.A. British Medical Association.
B.M.J. British Medical Journal.
Bn. Battalion.
B.N.A.F. British North Africa Force.
B.N.C. Brasenose College.
B.N.O.C. British National Opera Company.
B.O.A.C. British Overseas Airways Corporation.
Bom. C.S. Bombay Civil Service.
Bom. S.C. Bombay Staff Corps.
Bot. Botany; Botanical.
Bp. Bishop.
B.Pharm. Bachelor of Pharmacy.
B.R. British Railways.
B.R.A. Brigadier Royal Artillery.
B.R.C.S. British Red Cross Society.
Brig. Brigadier.
Brit. I.R.E. British Institution of Radio Engineers.
B.S. Bachelor of Surgery; Bachelor of Science.
B.S.A. Bachelor of Scientific Agriculture; Birmingham Small Arms.
B.S.A.A. British South American Airways.
B.S.A.P. British South Africa Police.
B.S.C. Bengal Staff Corps.
B.Sc. Bachelor of Science.
B.Sc. (Dent.) Bachelor of Science in Dentistry.
B.S.E. Bachelor of Science in Engineering (U.S.).
B.S.F. British Salonica Force.
B.S.J.A. British Show Jumping Association.
B.S.I. British Standards Institution.
Bt. Baronet; Brevet.
B.T.A. British Troops, Austria.
B.T.C. British Transport Commission.
B.T.E. British Troops in Egypt.
B.Th. Bachelor of Theology.
B.V.M. Blessed Virgin Mary.
Bucks. Buckinghamshire.
B.W I. British West Indies (now W.I.: West Indies).
B.W.M. British War Medal.

C

(C.) Conservative; 100.
c. Child; cousin.
C.A. Central America; County Alderman; Chartered Accountant (Scotland).
C.A.C.T.M. Central Advisory Council of Training for the Ministry.
Cal. California (U.S.).
C.A.L.E. Canadian Army Liaison Executive.
Cambs. Cambridgeshire.
C.A.M.C. Canadian Army Medical Corps.
C.A.M.W. Central Association for Mental Welfare.
Cantab. Of Cambridge University.
Capt. Captain.
C.A.S. Chief of the Air Staff.
Cav. Cavalry.
C.B. Companion of the Bath.
C.B.E. Commander Order of the British Empire.
C.B.S.A. Clay Bird Shooting Association.
C.C. City Council; County Council; Cricket Club; Cycling Club; County Court.
C.C.C. Corpus Christi College; Central Criminal Court.
C.C.F. Combined Cadet Force.
C.C.G. Control Commission Germany.
C.C.P.R. Central Council of Physical Recreation.
C.C.R.A. Commander Corps Royal Artillery.
C.C.S. Casualty Clearing Station Ceylon Civil Service.

C.D. . . Canadian Forces Decoration.
Cdre. . . Commodore.
C.E. . . Civil Engineer.
C.E.F. . . Canadian Expeditionary Force.
C.E.M.A. . Council for the Encouragement of Music and the Arts.
C.E.M.S. . Church of England Men's Society.
C.E.T.S. . Church of England Temperance Society.
C.F. . . Chaplain to the Forces.
C.F.A. . . Canadian Field Artillery.
C.F.E. . . Central Fighter Establishment.
C.F.S. . . Central Flying School.
C.G.I.A. . City and Guilds of London Insignia Award.
C.G.S. . . Chief of General Staff.
C.H. . . Companion of Honour.
Chanc. . Chancellor; Chancery.
Chap. . . Chaplain.
Chap. St. J. Chaplain of Order of St. John of Jerusalem (now Ch.St.J.).
Ch.B. . . Bachelor of Surgery.
Ch.Ch. . Christ Church.
Ch. Coll. . Christ's College.
(CHM). . *See under* A.R.C.O.(CHM), F.R.C.O.(CHM).
Ch.M. . . Master of Surgery.
Chm. . . Chairman.
Ch.St.J. . Chaplain of Order of St. John of Jerusalem.
C.I. . . Imperial Order of the Crown of India; Channel Islands.
C.I.A.D. . Central Institute of Art and Design.
C.I.A.L. . Corresponding Member of the International Institute of Arts and Letters.
C.I.D. . . Criminal Investigation Department.
C.I.E. . . Companion of the Order of the Indian Empire.
C.I.G.S. . Chief of the Imperial General Staff.
C.I.Mar.E. . Companion of the Institute of Marine Engineers.
C.I.Mech.E. Companion of the Institution of Mechanical Engineers.
C.-in-C. . Commander-in-Chief.
Cir. . . Circus.
C.I.V. . . City Imperial Volunteers.
C.J. . . Chief Justice.
C.J.M. . Congregation of Jesus and Mary (Eudist Fathers).
C.L. . . Commander of Order of Leopold.
Cl. . . Class.
C.M. . . Congregation of the Mission (Vincentians); Master in Surgery; Certificated Master; Canadian Militia.
C.M.A.. . Canadian Medical Association.
C.M.B. . . Central Midwives' Board.
C.M.F. . . Commonwealth Military Forces; Central Mediterranean Force.
C.M.G.. . Companion of St. Michael and St. George.
C.M.S. . . Church Missionary Society.
C.N.R. . . Canadian National Railways.
C.O. . . Commanding Officer; Colonial Office; Conscientious Objector.
Co. . . County; Company.
C. of E. . Church of England.
C. of S. . Chief of Staff.
Co. L. or **Coal. L.** Coalition Liberal.
Col. . . Colony; Colonel.
Coll. . . College; Collegiate.
Colo. . . Colorado (U.S.).
Col.-Sergt.. Colour-Sergeant.
Com. . . Communist.
Comd. . . Command.
Comdg. . Commanding.
Comdr. . Commander.
Comdt. . Commandant.
Commn. . Commission.
Comp.I.E.E. Companion of the Institution of Electrical Engineers.
Comr. . . Commissioner.
Comy.-Gen. Commissary-General.
Conn. . . Connecticut (U.S.).
Corp. . . Corporation; Corporal.
Corr. Mem. or **Fell.** Corresponding Member or Fellow.
C.O.S. . Charity Organisation Society.
C.O.S.S.A.C. Chief of Staff to Supreme Allied Commander.
Co. U. or **Coal. U.** Coalition Unionist.
C.P. . . Central Provinces; Cape Province.
C.P.A. . . Certified Public Accountant (Canada).
C.P.R. . . Canadian Pacific Railway.
C.P.R.E. . Council for the Preservation of Rural England.
C.R. . . Community of the Resurrection.
cr. . . created or creation.
C.R.A. . . Commander, Royal Artillery.
C.R.A.S.C. . Commander, Royal Army Service Corps.
C.R.E. . . Commander, Royal Engineers.
Cres. . . Crescent.
C.R.O. . . Commonwealth Relations Office; Chief Recruiting Officer.
C.S. . . Civil Service.
C.S.C. . . Conspicuous Service Cross.
C.S.I. . . Companion of the Order of the Star of India.
C.S.I.R. . Commonwealth Council for Scientific and Industrial Research (re-named: Commonwealth Scientific and Industrial Research Organisation; *see* below).
C.S.I.R.O. . Commonwealth Scientific and Industrial Research Organisation (and *see* above).
C.S.O. . . Chief Signal Officer.
C.S.P. . . Chartered Society of Physiotherapists; Civil Service of Pakistan.
C.SS.R. . Congregation of the Most Holy Redeemer (Redemptorist Order).
C.St.J. . . Commander of the Order of St. John of Jerusalem.
C.T.A. . . Chaplain Territorial Army.
C.T.C. . . Cyclists' Touring Club.
C.T.R. (Harwell) Controlled Thermonuclear Research.
C.U. . . Cambridge University.
C.U.A.C. . Cambridge University Athletic Club.
C.U.A.F.C. . Cambridge University Association Football Club.
C.U.B.C. . Cambridge University Boat Club.
C.U.C.C. . Cambridge Univ. Cricket Club.
C.U.H.C. . Cambridge University Hockey Club.
C.U.R.F.C. . Cambridge University Rugby Football Club.
C.V.O. . . Commander of the Royal Victorian Order.

D

D. . . . Duke.
d. . . . Died; daughter.
D.A. . . Diploma in Anaesthesia.
D.A.(Edin.) Diploma of Edinburgh College of Art.
D.A.A. & Q.M.G. Deputy Assistant Adjutant and Quartermaster-General.
D.A.A.G. . Deputy - Assistant - Adjutant - General.
D.A. & Q.M.G. Deputy Adjutant and Quartermaster-General.
D.A.C.G. . Deputy Assistant Chaplain-General.
D.A.D. . . Deputy Assistant Director.
D.A.D.M.S. Deputy Assistant Director of Medical Services.
D.A.D.O.S. . Deputy Assistant Director of Ordnance Services.
D.A.D.Q. . Deputy Assistant Director of Quartering.
D.A.D.S.T. . Deputy Assistant Director of Supplies and Transport.

D.A.G. . . Deputy-Adjutant-General.
D.A.M.S. . Deputy Assistant Military Secretary.
D.A.Q.M.G. Deputy - Assistant - Quarter - master-General.
D.A.Sc. . Doctor in Agricultural Sciences.
D.B.E. . . Dame Commander Order of the British Empire.
D.C. . . District of Columbia (U.S.).
D.C.A.S. . Deputy Chief of the Air Staff.
D.C.G. . . Deputy Chaplain-General.
D.C.G.S. . Deputy Chief of the General Staff (on the Field).
D.Ch. . . Doctor of Surgery.
D.C.H. . . Diploma in Child Health.
D.C.I.G.S. . Deputy Chief of the Imperial General Staff.
D.C.L. . . Doctor of Civil Law.
D.C.L.I. . Duke of Cornwall's Light Infantry.
D.C.M. . . Distinguished Conduct Medal.
D.Cn.L. . Doctor of Canon Law.
D.C.S. . . Deputy Chief of Staff; Doctor of Commercial Sciences.
D.C.T. . . Doctor of Christian Theology.
D.C.V.O. . Dame Commander of Royal Victorian Order.
D.D. . . Doctor of Divinity.
D.D.L. . . Deputy Director of Labour.
D.D.M.E. . Deputy Director of Mechanical Engineering.
D.D.M.I. . Deputy Director of Military Intelligence.
D.D.M.S. . Deputy Director of Medical Services.
D.D.M.T. . Deputy Director of Military Training.
D.D.N.I. . Deputy Director of Naval Intelligence.
D.D.O. . . Diploma in Dental Orthopædics.
D.D.P.R. . Deputy Director of Public Relations.
D.D.P.S. . Deputy Director of Personal Services.
D.D.R.A. . Deputy Director Royal Artillery.
D.D.S. . . Doctor of Dental Surgery; Director of Dental Services.
D.D.Sc. . Doctor of Dental Science.
D.D.S.D. . Deputy Director Staff Duties.
D.D.S.T. . Deputy Director of Supplies and Transport.
D.D.W.E. & M. Deputy Director of Works. Electrical and Mechanical.
D.E. . . Doctor of Engineering.
Decd. . . Deceased.
D.Econ.Sc. . Doctor of Economic Science.
deg. . . Degree.
Del. . . Delaware (U.S.).
Deleg. . . Delegate.
D.Eng. . Doctor of Engineering.
D. en M. . Docteur en Médecine.
D.E.O.V.R. Duke of Edinburgh's Own Volunteer Rifles.
Dep. . . Deputy.
Dept. . . Department.
D. ès L. . Docteur ès lettres.
Des. R.C.A. Designer of the Royal College of Art.
D.F.C. . . Distinguished Flying Cross.
D.G. . . Dragoon Guards.
D.G.A.M.S. Director-General Army Medical Services.
D.G.M.S. . Director-General of Medical Services.
D.G.M.W. . Director - General of Military Works.
D.G.P. . . Director-General of Personnel.
D.G.St.J. . formerly Dame of Grace, Order of St. John of Jerusalem (now D.St.J.).
D.H.L. . . Doctor of Hebrew Literature.
D.H.Q. . District Head Quarters.
D.I.C. . . Diploma of the Imperial College.
D.I.G. . . Deputy Inspector-General.
D.I.H. . . Diploma in Industrial Health.
Dioc. . . Diocese; Diocesan.
Dip.C.D. . Diploma Civic Design.
Dis. T.P. . Distinction Town Planning.
Div. . . Division; Divorced.
D.J.A.G. . Deputy Judge Advocate General.
D.J.St.J. . formerly Dame of Justice of St. John of Jerusalem (now D.St.J.).
D.L. . . Deputy-Lieutenant.
D.L.C. . . Diploma Loughborough College.
D.L.I. . . Durham Light Infantry.
D.Litt. or **D.Lit.** Doctor of Literature; Doctor of Letters.
D.L.O. . . Diploma in Laryngology and Otology.
D.M. . . Doctor of Medicine.
D.M.D. . Doctor of Medical Dentistry (Australia).
D.M.E. . Director of Mechanical Engineering.
D.M.I. . . Director of Military Intelligence.
D.M.R. . Diploma in Medical Radiology.
D.M.R.E. . Diploma in Medical Radiology and Electrology.
D.M.S. . . Director of Medical Services.
D.Mus. . Doctor of Music.
D.M.T. . Director of Military Training.
D.N.B. . . Dictionary of National Biography.
D.N.E. . . Director of Naval Equipment.
D.N.I. . . Director of Naval Intelligence.
D.O. . . Diploma in Ophthalmology.
D.O.C. . . District Officer Commanding.
Doc. Eng. . Doctor of Engineering.
D.O.L. . . Doctor of Oriental Learning.
Dom. . . *Dominus*.
D.O.M.S. . Diploma in Ophthalmic Medicine and Surgery.
D.O.S. . . Director of Ordnance Services.
Dow. . . Dowager.
D.P.A. . . Diploma in Public Administration; Discharged Prisoners' Aid.
D.P.Ec. . Doctor of Political Economy.
D.P.H. . . Diploma in Public Health.
D.Ph. or **D.Phil.** Doctor of Philosophy.
D.P.M. . Diploma in Psychological Medicine.
D.P.R. . . Director of Public Relations.
D.P.S. . . Director of Personal Services; Director of Postal Services.
D.Q.M.G. . Deputy Quartermaster-General.
Dr. . . Doctor.
D.R.A.C. . Director Royal Armoured Corps.
Dr.Ing. . Doctor of Engineering (Germany).
Dr.Œc. Pol. Doctor Œconomiæ Politicæ.
D.S.C. . . Distinguished Service Cross.
D.Sc. . . Doctor of Science.
D.Sc.A. . Docteur en sciences agricoles.
D.S.D. . . Director Staff Duties.
D.S.I.R. . Dept. of Scientific and Industrial Research.
D.S.M. . . Distinguished Service Medal.
D.S.O. . . Companion of the Distinguished Service Order.
D.S.P. . . Director of Selection of Personnel; *Docteur en sciences politiques* (Montreal).
d.s.p. . . *decessit sine prole* (died without issue).
D.S.S. . . Doctor of Sacred Scripture.
D.S.T. . . Director of Supplies and Transport.
D.St.J. . . Dame of Grace, Order of St. John of Jerusalem; Dame of Justice, Order of St. John of Jerusalem; and *see* G.C.St.J.
D.T.D. . . Dekoratie voor Trouwe Dienst (Decoration for Devoted Service).
D.T.H. . Diploma in Tropical Hygiene.
D.Theol. . Doctor of Theology.
D.Th.P.T. . Diploma in Theory and Practice of Teaching (Durham University).
D.T.M. . Diploma in Tropical Medicine.
D.U.P. . . Docteur de l'Université de Paris.
D.V.H. . Diploma in Veterinary Hygiene.
D.V.S.M. . Diploma in Veterinary State Medicine.

E

E. . . . East; Earl.
e. . . . eldest.
E.A.P. . . East Africa Protectorate.
Ebor. . . (*Eboracensis*) of York.
E.C. . . East Central (postal district); Emergency Commission.
E.C.A. . . Economic Co-operation Administration.
E.C.A.F.E. . Economic Commission for Asia and the Far East.
E.C.S.C. . European Coal and Steel Community.
E.C.U. . . English Church Union.
E.D. . . Efficiency Decoration; Doctor of Engineering (U.S.).
Edin. . . Edinburgh.
Edn. . . Edition.
Educ. . . Educated.
Educn. . Education.
E.E.F. . . Egyptian Expeditionary Force.
E.E.T.S. . Early English Text Society.
E.F.T.A. . European Free Trade Association.
e.h. . . *ehrenhalber*; see under *h.c.*
E.I. . . East Indian; East Indies.
E.I.C.S. . East India Company's Service.
E.-in-C. . Engineer-in-Chief.
E.M.S. . . Emergency Medical Service.
Ency. Brit. Encyclopædia Britannica.
Eng. . . England; Engineer.
E.N.S.A. . Entertainments National Service Association.
E.N.T. . . Ear, Nose and Throat.
er. . . elder.
E.R. . . Eastern Region (B.R.).
E.R.D. . . Emergency Reserve Decoration (Army).
esp. . . especially.
E.S.U. . . English-Speaking Union.
Ext. . . Extinct.

F

F.A. . . Football Association.
F.A.A. . . Fellow Australian Academy of Science; Fleet Air Arm.
F.A.A.S. . Fellow of the American Academy of Arts and Sciences.
F.A.C.C.A. . Fellow of the Association of Certified and Corporate Accountants.
F.A.C.D. . Fellow of the American College of Dentistry.
F.A.C.E. . Fellow of the Australian College of Education.
F.A.C.I. . (Changed to) F.R.A.C.I.
F.A.C.P. . Fellow of American College of Physicians.
F.A.C.R. . Fellow of American College of Radiology.
F.A.C.S. . Fellow of American College of Surgeons.
F.A.G.S. . Fellow American Geographical Society.
F.A.I. . . Fellow of Chartered Auctioneers' and Estate Agents' Institute.
F.A.I.A. . Fellow of American Institute of Architects.
F.A.I.M. . Fellow of the Australian Institute of Management.
F.A.M.S. . Fellow of the Ancient Monuments Society.
F.A.N.Y. . First Aid Nursing Yeomanry.
F.A.O. . . Food and Agriculture Organisation.
F.A.P.H.A. Fellow American Public Health Association.
F.A.S. . . Fellow of the Antiquarian Society.
F.A.S.A. . Fellow of Australian Society of Accountants.
Far E.L.F. . Far East Land Forces.
F.B.A. . . Fellow of the British Academy.
F.B.H.I. . Fellow of the British Horological Institute.
F.B.I. . . Federation of British Industries.
F.B.I.M. . Fellow of the British Institute of Management (formerly F.I.I.A.: Fellow of the Institute of Industrial Administration).
F.B.O.A. . Fellow of British Optical Association.
F.B.O.U. . Fellow British Ornithologists Union.
F.Brit.I.R.E. Fellow of British Institution of Radio Engineers.
F.B.Ps.S. . Fellow of British Psychological Society.
F.B.S. . . Fellow Building Societies Institute.
F.B.S.I. . Fellow of Boot and Shoe Industry.
F.B.S.M. . Fellow of the Birmingham School of Music.
F.C.A. . . Fellow of the Institute of Chartered Accountants.
F.C.C.S. . Fellow of Corporation of Secretaries (formerly of Certified Secretaries).
F.C.G.I. . Fellow of City and Guilds of London Institute.
F.C.H. . . Fellow of Coopers Hill College.
F.Ch.S. . Fellow of the Society of Chiropodists.
F.C.I.C. . Fellow Chemical Institute of Canada (formerly Canadian Institute of Chemistry).
F.C.I.I. . Fellow of the Chartered Insurance Institute.
F.C.I.P.A. . Fellow of the Chartered Institute of Patent Agents.
F.C.I.S. . Fellow of the Chartered Institute of Secretaries.
F.C.P. . . Fellow College of Preceptors.
F.C.P.(So. Af.) Fellow of the College of Physicians, South Africa.
F.C.S. . . Fellow of the Chemical Society.
F.C.S.(So.Af.) Fellow of the College of Surgeons, South Africa.
F.C.S.T. . Fellow of the College of Speech Therapists.
F.C.T. . . Federal Capital Territory (now A.C.T.).
F.C.T.B. . Fellow of the College of Teachers of the Blind.
F.C.U. . . Fighter Control Unit.
F.C.W.A. . Fellow of the Institute of Cost and Works Accountants.
F.D.S. . . Fellow in Dental Surgery.
F.E.A.F. . Far East Air Force.
F.E.I.S. . Fellow of the Educational Institute of Scotland.
F.E.S. . . Fellow of the Entomological Society; Fellow of the Ethnological Society.
F.F. . . Field Force.
F.F.A. . . Fellow of Faculty of Actuaries (in Scotland).
F.F.A.R.A.C.S. Fellow of Faculty of Anæsthetists, Royal Australian College of Surgeons.
F.F.A.R.C.S. Fellow of Faculty of Anæsthetists, Royal College of Surgeons.
F.F.A.S. . Fellow of Faculty of Architects and Surveyors, London.
F.F.F. . . Fighting French Forces.
F.F.Hom. . Fellow of Faculty of Homœopathy.
F.F.I. . . French Forces of the Interior.
F.F.P.S. . Fellow of the Royal Faculty of Physicians and Surgeons (Glasgow).
F.F.R. . . Fellow of Faculty of Radiologists.
F.G.A. . . Fellow Gemmological Association.
F.G.I. . . Fellow of the Institute of Certificated Grocers.
F.G.S. . . Fellow of the Geological Society.
F.G.S.M. . Fellow of Guildhall School of Music.
F.H.A. . . Fellow of the Institute of Hospital Administrators.

F.H.A.S. . Fellow of Highland and Agricultural Society of Scotland.
F.H.W.C. . Fellow of Heriot-Watt College, Edinburgh.
F.I.A. . . Fellow of Institute of Actuaries.
F.I.A.A. & S. Fellow of the Incorporated Association of Architects and Surveyors.
F.I.A.L. . Fellow of the International Institute of Arts and Letters.
F.I.Arb. . Fellow of Institute of Arbitrators.
F.I.A.S. . Fellow Institute of Aeronautical Sciences (U.S.).
F.I.B. . . Fellow of Institute of Bankers.
F.I.B.D. . Fellow of the Institute of British Decorators.
F.I.B.P. . Fellow of the Institute of British Photographers.
F.I.C. . . *See* F.R.I.C.
F.I.C.A. . Fellow of the Commonwealth Institute of Accountancy.
F.I.C.D. . Fellow of the Indian College of Dentists.
F.I.C.I. . Fellow of the Institute of Chemistry of Ireland; Fellow of the International Colonial Institute.
F.I.C.S. . Fellow of Institute of Chartered Shipbrokers; Fellow of the International College of Surgeons.
F.I.E.S. . Fellow of Illuminating Engineering Society.
F.I.G.C.M. . Fellow Incorporated Guild of Church Musicians.
F.I.I.A. . Fellow of Institute of Industrial Administration (now F.B.I.M: Fellow of the British Institute of Management).
F.I.Inst. . Fellow of the Imperial Institute.
F.I.L. . . Fellow of the Institute of Linguists.
F.I.L.A. . Fellow of Institute of Landscape Architects.
F.I.M. . . Fellow of the Institution of Metallurgists.
F.I.M.I. . Fellow of the Institute of the Motor Industry (formerly F.I.M.T.: Fell. Inst. of Motor Trade).
F.I.M.I.T. . Fellow of the Institute of Music Instrument Technology.
F.I.M.T.A. Fellow of the Institute of Municipal Treasurers and Accountants.
F.I.N. . . Fellow of the Institute of Navigation.
F.Inst.D. . Fellow of Institute of Directors.
F.Inst.F. . Fellow of Institute of Fuel.
F.Inst.Met. Fellow of Institute of Metals.
F.Inst.P. . Fellow of Institute of Physics.
F.Inst.Pet. . Fellow of the Institute of Petroleum.
F.Inst.P.I. . Fellow of the Institute of Patentees (Incorporated).
F.Inst.W. . Fellow of the Institute of Welding.
F.I.O. . . Fellow of the Institute of Ophthalmic Opticians.
F.I.O.B. . Fellow of Institute of Builders.
F.I.P.A. . Fellow of the Institute of Public Administration.
F.I.R.A.(Ind.) Fellow of Institute of Railway Auditors and Accountants (India).
F.I.R.E. . Fellow of the Institution of Radio Engineers.
F.I.R.I. . Fellow of the Institution of the Rubber Industry.
F.I.S. . . Fellow of the Association of Incorporated Statisticians.
F.I.S.A. . Fellow of the Incorporated Secretaries' Association.
F.I.S.E. . Fellow Institution of Sanitary Engineers.
F.I.W.M. . Fellow of the Institution of Works Managers.
F.I.W.Sc. . Fellow of the Institute of Wood Science.
F.J.I. . . Fellow of Institute of Journalists.
F.K.C. . . Fellow of King's College (London).
F.L.A. . . Fellow of Library Association.
Fla. . Florida (U.S.).
F.L.A.S. . Fellow of the Land Agents Society.
F.L.C.M. . Fellow of the London College of Music.
F.L.H.S. . Fellow of the London Historical Society.
F.L.S. . . Fellow of the Linnæan Society.
Flt. . . Flight.
F.M. . . Field-Marshal.
F.M.A. . . Fellow of the Museums Association.
F.M.S. . . Federated Malay States.
F.N.I. . . Fellow of National Institute of Sciences in India.
F.N.Z.I.A. . Fellow of the New Zealand Institute of Architects.
F.N.Z.I.C. . Fellow of the New Zealand Institute of Chemistry.
F.O. . . Foreign Office; Field Officer; Flying Officer.
F.O.I.C. . Flag Officer in charge.
F.P.S. . . Fellow of the Pharmaceutical Society.
F.Ph.S. . Fellow of the Philosophical Society of England.
F.Phys.S. . Fellow of the Physical Society.
F.R.A.C.I. . Fellow of the Royal Australian Chemical Institute (formerly F.A.C.I.).
F.R.A.C.P. . Fellow of the Royal Australasian College of Physicians.
F.R.A.C.S. . Fellow of the Royal Australasian College of Surgeons.
F.R.A.D. . Fellow of the Royal Academy of Dancing.
F.R.Ae.S. . Fellow of the Royal Aeronautical Society.
F.R.A.H.S. . Fellow Royal Australian Historical Society.
F.R.A.I. . Fellow of the Royal Anthropological Institute.
F.R.A.I.A. . Fellow of the Royal Australian Institute of Architects.
F.R.A.I.C. . Fellow of the Royal Architectural Institute of Canada.
F.R.A.M. . Fellow of the Royal Academy of Music.
F.R.A.S. . Fellow of the Royal Astronomical Society; Fellow of the Royal Asiatic Society.
F.R.A.S.B. . Fellow of Royal Asiatic Society of Bengal.
F.R.B.S. . Fellow of Royal Society of British Sculptors; Fellow of the Royal Botanic Society.
F.R.C.M. . Fellow of the Royal College of Music.
F.R.C.O. . Fellow of the Royal College of Organists.
F.R.C.O. (CHM) Fellow of the Royal College of Organists with Diploma in Choir Training.
F.R.C.O.G. . Fellow of the Royal College of Obstetricians and Gynæcologists.
F.R.C.P. . Fellow of the Royal College of Physicians.
F.R.C.P.(C.) Fellow of the Royal College of Physicians of Canada.
F.R.C.P.E. and F.R.C.P.Ed. Fellow of the Royal College of Physicians of Edinburgh.
F.R.C.P.I. . Fellow of the Royal College of Physicians in Ireland.
F.R.C.S. . Fellow of the Royal College of Surgeons.
F.R.C.S.E. and F.R.C.S.Ed. Fellow of the Royal College of Surgeons of Edinburgh.
F.R.C.S.I. . Fellow of the Royal College of Surgeons in Ireland.
F.R.C.V.S. . Fellow of the Royal College of Veterinary Surgeons.
F.R.Econ.S. Fellow of Royal Economic Society.

F.R.E.S. . Fellow of Royal Entomological Society of London.
F.R.F.P.S.(G.) Fellow of Royal Faculty of Physicians and Surgeons (of Glasgow).
F.R.G.S. . Fellow of the Royal Geographical Society.
F.R.H.S. . Fellow of the Royal Horticultural Society.
F.R.Hist.S. Fellow of Royal Historical Society.
F.R.I. . . Fellow of the Royal Institution.
F.R.I.A.S. . Fellow of the Royal Incorporation of Architects of Scotland.
F.R.I.B.A. . Fellow of the Royal Institute of British Architects.
F.R.I.C. . (formerly F.I.C.) Fellow of Royal Institute of Chemistry.
F.R.I.C.S. . Fellow of the Royal Institution of Chartered Surveyors.
F.R.I.H. . Fellow of Royal Institute of Horticulture (N.Z.).
F.R.I.P.H.H. Fellow of the Royal Institute of Public Health and Hygiene.
F.R.M.C.M. Fellow of Royal Manchester College of Music.
F.R.M.S. . Fellow of the Royal Microscopical Society.
F.R.Met.S. . Fellow of the Royal Meteorological Society.
F.R.N.S. . Fellow of Royal Numismatic Society.
F.R.N.S.A. . Fellow Royal School Naval Architecture.
F.R.P.S. . Fellow of the Royal Photographic Society.
F.R.P.S.L. . Fellow of the Royal Philatelic Society, London.
F.R.S. . . Fellow of the Royal Society.
F.R.S.A. . Fellow of Royal Society of Arts.
F.R.S.A.I. . Fellow of the Royal Society of Antiquaries of Ireland.
F.R.San.I. . Fellow of Royal Sanitary Institute (*see* F.R.S.H.).
F.R.S.C. . Fellow of the Royal Society of Canada.
F.R.S.E. . Fellow of the Royal Society of Edinburgh.
F.R.S.G.S. . Fellow of the Royal Scottish Geographical Society.
F.R.S.H. . Fellow of the Royal Society for the Promotion of Health (formerly F.R.San.I.).
F.R.S.L. . Fellow of the Royal Society of Literature.
F.R.S.M. or **F.R.Soc.Med.** Fellow of Royal Society of Medicine.
F.R.S.N.Z. . Fellow of Royal Society of New Zealand.
F.R.S.S.A. . Fellow of Royal Society of South Africa.
F.R.S.T. . Fellow of the Royal Society of Teachers.
F.R.S.T.M. & H. Fellow of Royal Society of Tropical Medicine and Hygiene.
F.R.V.I.A. . Fellow Royal Victorian Institute of Architects.
F.R.Z.S.Scot. Fellow of the Royal Zoological Society of Scotland.
f.s. . Graduate of Royal Air Force Staff College.
F.S.A. . . Fellow of the Society of Antiquaries.
F.S.A.A. . Fellow of the Society of Incorporated Accountants and Auditors.
F.S.A.M. . Fellow of the Society of Art Masters.
F.S.Arc. . Fellow of Society of Architects (merged with the R.I.B.A., 1925).
F.S.A.Scot. Fellow of the Society of Antiquaries of Scotland.
F.S.A.S.M. . Fellow of the South Australian School of Mines.
F.S.D.C. . Fellow of Society of Dyers and Colourists.
F.S.E. . . Fellow Society of Engineers.
F.S.G. . . Fellow of the Society of Genealogists.
F.S.G.T. . Fellow Society of Glass Technology.
F.S.I. . . Fellow of Royal Institution of Chartered Surveyors (changed Aug. 1947 to F.R.I.C.S.).
F.S.I.A. . Fellow of Society of Industrial Artists.
F.S.M.A. . Fellow Incorporated Sales Managers' Association.
F.S.M.C. . Fellow of the Spectacle-Makers' Company.
F.S.S. . . Fellow of the Royal Statistical Society.
F.T.C.D. . Fellow of Trinity College, Dublin.
F.T.C.L. . Fellow of Trinity College of Music, London.
F.T.I. . . Fellow of the Textile Institute.
F.T.S. . . Flying Training School.
F.Z.S. . . Fellow of the Zoological Society.
F.Z.S.Scot. (Changed to) F.R.Z.S.Scot.

G

Ga. . . Georgia (U.S.).
G.A.T.T. . General Agreement on Tariffs and Trade.
G.B.A. . . Governing Bodies Assoc.
G.B.E. . . Knight or Dame Grand Cross Order of the British Empire.
G.C. . . George Cross.
G.C.B. . . Knight Grand Cross of the Bath.
G.C.H. . . Knight Grand Cross of Hanover.
G.C.I.E. . Knight Grand Commander of the Indian Empire.
G.C.M.G. . Knight Grand Cross of St. Michael and St. George.
G.C.S.I. . Knight Grand Commander of the Star of India.
G.C.St.J. . Bailiff or Dame Grand Cross of the Order of St. John of Jerusalem.
G.C.V.O. . Knight Grand Cross of Royal Victorian Order.
Gdns. . . Gardens.
Gen. . . General.
Ges. . . Gesellschaft.
G.F.S. . . Girls' Friendly Society.
g.g.s. . . Great grandson.
G.H.Q. . . General Headquarters.
Gib. . . Gibraltar.
G.I.Mech.E. Graduate Institution of Mechanical Engineers.
G.L. . . Grand Lodge.
Glos. . . Gloucestershire.
G.M. . . George Medal.
G.M.C. . . Guild of Memorial Craftsmen.
G.M.I.E. . Grand Master of Indian Empire.
G.M.S.I. . Grand Master of Star of India.
G.O.C. . . General Officer Commanding.
G.O.C.-in-C. General Officer Commanding-in-Chief
G.O.E. . . General Ordination Examination.
Gov. . . Governor.
Govt. . . Government.
G.P. . . General Practitioner.
G.P.D.S.T. . Girls' Public Day School Trust.
G.P.O. . . General Post Office.
G.Q.G. . . Grand Quartier Général (French G.H.Q.).
Gr. . . Greek.
Gram.Sch. Grammar School.
G.R.S.M. . Graduate of the Royal Schools of Music.
G.S. . . General Staff.
g.s. . . Grandson.
G.S.M. . . Guildhall School of Music.
G.S.O. . . General Staff Officer.
G.T.S. . . General Theological Seminary (New York).
G.W.R. . Great Western Railway (*see* B.R.).

H

H.A.A. . Heavy Anti-Aircraft.
H.A.C. . . Honourable Artillery Company.
Hants. . . Hampshire.

Harv. . . Harvard.
H.B.M. . His (or Her) Britannic Majesty (Majesty's).
h.c. . . *honoris causa*.
H.C.F. . . Hon. Chaplain to the Forces.
H.D.D. . Higher Dental Diploma.
H.E. . . His Excellency; His Eminence.
H.E.H. . His Exalted Highness.
H.E.I.C. . Honourable East India Company.
H.E.I.C.S. . Honourable East India Company's Service.
Heir-pres. . Heir-presumptive.
Herts. . . Hertfordshire.
H.F.A.R.A. Honorary Foreign Associate of the Royal Academy.
H.F.R.A. . Honorary Foreign Member of the Royal Academy.
H.G. . . Home Guard.
H.H. . . His (or Her) Highness; His Holiness.
H.I.H. . . His (or Her) Imperial Highness.
H.I.M. . . His (or Her) Imperial Majesty.
H.L.I. . . Highland Light Infantry.
H.M. . . His (or Her) Majesty, or Majesty's.
H.M.C. . Headmasters' Conference.
H.M.H.S. . His (or Her) Majesty's Hospital Ship.
H.M.I. . His (or Her) Majesty's Inspector.
H.M.O.C.S. His (or Her) Majesty's Overseas Civil Service.
H.M.S. . His (or Her) Majesty's Ship.
H.M.S.O. . His (or Her) Majesty's Stationery Office.
Hon. . . Honourable; Honorary; Honour.
H.P. . . House Physician.
H.Q. . . Headquarters.
(H.R.) . . Home Ruler.
H.R.C.A. . Honorary Royal Cambrian Academician.
H.R.H. . His (or Her) Royal Highness.
H.R.H.A. . Honorary Member of Royal Hibernian Academy.
H.R.I. . . Honorary Member of Royal Institute of Painters in Water Colours.
H.R.O.I. . Honorary Member of Royal Institute of Oil Painters.
H.R.S.A. . Honorary Member of Royal Scottish Academy.
H.R.S.W. . Honorary Member of Royal Scottish Water Colour Society.
H.S. . . House Surgeon.
H.S.H. . . His (or Her) Serene Highness.
Hum. . . Humanity, Humanities (Latin).
Hunts. . Huntingdonshire.
Hy. . . Heavy.

I

I. . . . Island.
Ia. . . Iowa (U.S.).
I.A. . . Indian Army.
I.A.E. . . Institute of Automobile Engineers.
I.A.F. . . Indian Air Force; Indian Auxiliary Force.
I.A.H.M. . Incorporated Association of Headmasters.
I.A.M.C. . Indian Army Medical Corps.
I.A.O.C. . Indian Army Ordnance Corps.
I.A.R.O. . Indian Army Reserve of Officers.
I.A.S. . . Indian Administrative Service.
I.A.T.A. . International Air Transport Association.
Ib. or **Ibid.** *Ibidem* (in the same place).
i/c. . . In charge.
I.C.A.A. . Invalid Children's Aid Association.
I.C.A.O. . International Civil Aviation Organisation.
Icel. . . Icelandic.
I.Chem.E. . Institution of Chemical Engineers.
I.C.F.T.U. . International Confederation of Free Trade Unions.
I.C.I. . . Imperial Chemical Industries.
I.C.R.C. . International Committee of the Red Cross.
I.C.S. . . Indian Civil Service.
I.C.T. . . International Computers and Tabulators.
Id. . . Idaho (U.S.).
i.d.c. . . Completed a Course at, or served for a year on the Staff of, the Imperial Defence College.
I.E.E. . . Institution of Electrical Engineers.
I.E.S. . . Indian Educational Service; Illuminating Engineering Society.
I.F.S. . . Irish Free State; Indian Forest Service.
I.H.S. . . *Iesus Hominum Salvator* (Jesus the Saviour of Mankind).
Ill. . . Illinois (U.S.).
I.L.O. . . International Labour Office.
I.L.P. . . Independent Labour Party.
I.M.A. . . International Music Association.
I.M.E. . . Institution of Mining Engineers.
I.M.E.A. . Incorporated Municipal Electrical Association.
I.Mech.E. . Institution of Mechanical Engineers.
I.M.M.T.S. . Indian Mercantile Marine Training Ship.
Imp. . . Imperial.
I.M.S. . . Indian Medical Service.
I.N. . . Indian Navy.
Inc. . . Incorporated.
Incog. . . *Incognito* (in secret).
Ind. . . Independent; Indiana (U.S.).
Insp. . . Inspector.
Inst. . . Institute.
Inst.C.E. . Institution of Civil Engineers.
Inst.M.M. . Institution of Mining and Metallurgy.
Instn. . . Institution.
I.O.D.E. . Imperial Order of the Daughters of the Empire.
I. of M. . Isle of Man.
I.O.G.T. . International Order of Good Templars.
I.O.M. . . Isle of Man; Indian Order of Merit.
I.O.O.F. . Independent Order of Oddfellows.
I.O.P. . . Inst. Painters in Oil Colours.
I.o.W. . . Isle of Wight.
I.P.I. . . International Press Institute.
I.P.S. . . Indian Police Service.
I.R.A. . . Irish Republican Army.
I.R.O. . . International Refugee Organisation.
Is. . . . Island(s).
I.S. . . . International Society of Sculptors, Painters and Gravers.
I.S.C. . . Indian Staff Corps.
I.S.E. . . Indian Service of Engineers.
I.S.M.R.C. . Inter-Services Metallurgical Research Council.
I.S.O. . . Imperial Service Order.
I.T. . . . Indian Territory (U.S.).
Ital. or **It.** . Italian.
I.T.O. . . International Trade Organisation.
I.U.C.W. . International Union for Child Welfare.
I.W. . . Isle of Wight.
I.W.G.C. . Imperial War Graves Commission.
I.Y. . . Imperial Yeomanry.
I.Z. . . I Zingari.

J

J.A. . . Judge Advocate.
J.A.G. . . Judge Advocate General.
Jas. . . James.
J.C.B. . . *Juris Canonici Bachelor* (Bachelor of Canon Law).

J.C.D. . . *Juris Canonici Doctor* (Doctor of Canon Law).
J.C.S. . . Journal of the Chemical Society.
J.D. . . Doctor of Jurisprudence.
Jes. . . Jesus.
J.Inst.E. . Junior Institution of Engineers.
jls. . . Journals.
Joh. or **Jno.** John.
J.P. . . Justice of the Peace.
j.s.c. . . Qualified at a Junior Staff Course, or the equivalent, 1942–46.
j.s.s.c. . . Joint Services Staff Course.
J.U.D. . . *Juris Utriusque Doctor*, Doctor of Both Laws (Canon and Civil).
Jun. . . Junior.
Jun. Opt. . Junior Optime.

K

Kans. . . Kansas (U.S.).
K.A.R. . . King's African Rifles.
K.B.E. . . Knight Commander Order of the British Empire.
K.C. . . King's Counsel.
K.C.B. . . Knight Commander of the Bath.
K.C.C. . . Commander of Order of Crown, Belgian and Congo Free State.
K.C.H. . . King's College Hospital; Knight Commander of Hanover.
K.C.I.E. . Knight Commander of the Indian Empire.
K.C.L. . . King's College, London.
K.C.M.G. . Knight Commander of St. Michael and St. George.
K.C.S.G. . Knight Commander of St. Gregory.
K.C.S.I. . Knight Commander of the Star of India.
K.C.S.S. . Knight Commander of St. Silvester.
K.C.V.O. . Knight Commander of the Royal Victorian Order.
K.D.G. . . King's Dragoon Guards.
Keb. . . Keble College, Oxford.
K.E.H. . . King Edward's Horse.
K.G. . . Knight of the Order of the Garter.
K.G.St.J. . formerly Knight of Grace, Order of St. John of Jerusalem (now K.St.J.).
K.H. . . Knight of Hanover.
K.H.C. . . Hon. Chaplain to the King.
K.H.D.S. . Hon. Dental Surgeon to the King.
K.H.N.S. . Hon. Nursing Sister to the King.
K.H.P. . Hon. Physician to the King.
K.H.S. . . Hon. Surgeon to the King; Knight of the Holy Sepulchre.
K.-i-H. . Kaisar-i-Hind.
K.J.St.J. . formerly Knight of Justice, Order of St. John of Jerusalem (now K.St.J.).
K.O.R.R. . King's Own Royal Regiment.
K.O.S.B. . King's Own Scottish Borderers.
K.O.Y.L.I. . King's Own Yorkshire Light Infantry.
K.P. . . Knight of the Order of St. Patrick.
K.R.R.C. . King's Royal Rifle Corps.
K.St.J. . . Knight of Order of St. John of Jerusalem; and *see* G.C.St.J.
K.S. . . King's Scholar.
K.S.G. . . Knight of St. Gregory.
K.S.L.I. . King's Shropshire Light Infantry.
K.S.S. . . Knight of St. Silvester.
K.T. . . Knight of the Order of the Thistle.
Kt. or **Knt.** Knight.
Ky. . . Kentucky (U.S.).

L

(L.) . . Liberal.
L.A. . . Literate in Arts; Liverpool Academy.
La. . . Louisiana (U.S.).
(Lab.) . . Labour.
L.A.C. . . London Athletic Club.
L.-Corp. or **Lance-Corp.** Lance-Corporal.
Lancs. . . Lancashire.
L.C.C. . . London County Council.
L.Ch. . . Licentiate in Surgery.
L.C.J. . . Lord Chief Justice.
L.C.P. . . Licentiate of the College of Preceptors.
L.Div. . . Licentiate in Divinity.
L.D.S. . . Licentiate in Dental Surgery.
L.D.V. . . Local Defence Volunteers.
L. ès L. . Licencié ès lettres.
L.H. . . Light Horse.
L.H.D. . . (*Literarum Humaniorum Doctor*) Doctor of Literature.
L.I. . . Light Infantry; Long Island.
Lic. Med. . Licentiate in Medicine.
Lieut. . . Lieutenant.
Lincs. . . Lincolnshire.
Lit. . . Literature; Literary.
Lit.D. . . Doctor of Literature; Doctor of Letters.
Lit. Hum. . *Literæ Humaniores* (Classics).
Litt.D. . . Doctor of Literature; Doctor of Letters.
Liv. . . Liverpool.
L.J. . . Lord Justice.
L.L.A. . . Lady Literate in Arts.
LL.B. . . Bachelor of Laws.
L.L.C.M. . Licentiate London College of Music.
LL.D. . . Doctor of Laws.
LL.L. . . Licentiate in Laws.
LL.M. . . Master of Laws.
L.M. . . Licenciate in Midwifery.
L.M.B.C. . Lady Margaret Boat Club.
L.M.C.C. . Licentiate of Medical Council of Canada.
L.M.R. . London Midland Region (B.R.).
L.M.S. . . London, Midland and Scottish Railway (*see* B.R.); London Missionary Society.
L.M.S.S.A. . Licentiate in Medicine and Surgery, Society of Apothecaries.
L.Nat. . . Liberal National.
L.N.E.R. . London and North Eastern Railway (*see* B.R.).
L. of C. . Lines of Communication.
L.P.T.B. . London Passenger Transport Board.
L.R.A.D. . Licentiate of the Royal Academy of Dancing.
L.R.A.M. . Licentiate of the Royal Academy of Music.
L.R.C.P. . Licentiate of the Royal College of Physicians.
L.R.C.P.E. . Licentiate Royal College of Physicians, Edinburgh.
L.R.C.S. . Licentiate of the Royal College of Surgeons.
L.R.C.S.E. . Licentiate of the Royal College of Surgeons, Edinburgh.
L.R.F.P.S. . Licentiate of the Royal Faculty of Physicians and Surgeons.
L.R.I.B.A. . Licentiate Royal Institute of British Architects.
L.S.A. . . Licentiate of the Society of Apothecaries.
L.S.E. . . London School of Economics.
Lt. . . Light (*e.g.* Light Infantry).
Lt. or **Lieut.** Lieutenant.
L.T. . . Licentiate in Teaching.
L.T.C.L. . Licentiate of Trinity College of Music, London.
Lt.-Col. . Lieutenant-Colonel.
Lt.-Gen. . Lieutenant-General.
L.Th. . . Licentiate in Theology.
(L.U.) . . Liberal Unionist.
L.U.O.T.C. . London University Officers' Training Corps.
LXX. . . Septuagint.

M

M. . . . Marquess; Member; Monsieur.
m. . . . married.
M.A. . . . Master of Arts.
M.A.A.F. . Mediterranean Allied Air Forces.
M.A.A.S. . Member of the American Academy of Arts and Sciences.
M.A.C.E. . Member of the Australian College of Education.
M.A.C.S. . Member of the American Chemical Society.
M.A.E.E. . Marine Aircraft Experimental Establishment.
Mag. . . Magnetism or Magazine.
Magd. . . Magdalen; Magdalene.
M.A.I. . . Master of Engineering (*Magister in Arte Ingeniaria*).
M.A.I.Ch.E. Member of the American Institute of Chemical Engineers.
Maj.-Gen. . Major-General.
Man. . . Manitoba (Canada).
M.A.O. . Master of Obstetric Art.
M.A.O.U. . Member American Ornithologists' Union.
M.A.P. . Ministry of Aircraft Production.
M.Arch. . Master of Architecture.
Marq. . . Marquess.
M.A.S.C.E. . Member American Society of Civil Engineers.
M.A.S.M.E. Member American Society of Mechanical Engineers.
Mass. . . Massachusetts (U.S.).
Math. . . Mathematics; Mathematical.
M.B. . . Bachelor of Medicine.
M.B.E. . Member of the Order of the British Empire.
M.B.I.M. . Member of the British Institute of Management (formerly M.I.I.A.: Member of the Institute of Industrial Administration).
M.B.O.U. . Member British Ornithologists' Union.
M.Brit.I.R.E. Member British Institute of Radio Engineers.
M.C. . . . Military Cross; Master of Ceremonies.
M.C.C. . . Marylebone Cricket Club.
M.C.E.(Melb.) Master of Civil Engineering (Melbourne Univ.).
M.Ch. or **M.Chir.** Master in Surgery.
M.Ch.Orth. Master of Orthopædic Surgery.
M.C.M.E.S. Member of Civil and Mech. Engineers' Society.
M.Com. . Master of Commerce.
M.Cons.E. . Member of Association of Consulting Engineers.
M.C.P. . . Master of City Planning (U.S.).
M.C.P.A. . Member of the College of Pathologists of Australia.
M.C.P.S. . Member College of Physicians and Surgeons.
M.C.S. . . Madras Civil Service; Malayan Civil Service.
M.D. . . Doctor of Medicine; Military District.
Md. . . Maryland (U.S.).
M.D.S. . . Master of Dental Surgery.
Me. . . . Maine (U.S.).
M.E. . . . Mining Engineer.
M.E.A.F. . Middle East Air Force.
M.E.C. . . Member of Executive Council.
Mech. . . Mechanics; Mechanical.
Med. . . Medical.
M.E.F. . . Middle East Force.
M.E.I.C. . Member Engineering Institute of Canada.
M.E.L.F. . Middle East Land Forces.
M.Eng. . Master of Engineering.
Met.R. . . Metropolitan Railway.
M.F.G.B. . Miners' Federation of Great Britain.
M.F.H. . Master of Foxhounds.
M.G.A. . Maj.-Gen. i/c Administration.
M.G.C. . . Machine Gun Corps.
M.G.G.S. . Major-General, General Staff.
M.G.I. . . Member of the Institute of Certificated Grocers.
Mgr. . . Monsignore.
M.H.A. . Member of House of Assembly.
M.H.R. . Member House of Representatives.
M.I. . . Military Intelligence.
M.I.A.E. . Member of the Institution of Automobile Engineers.
M.I.Ae.E. . Member Inst. of Aeronautical Engineers.
M.I.A.S. . Member Institute of Aeronautical Science (U.S.).
M.I.B.F. . Member Inst. British Foundrymen.
M.I.British E. Member Institute of British Engineers.
M.I.C.E. . Member of Institution of Civil Engineers.
M.I.C.E.I. . Member of Institution of Civil Engineers of Ireland.
Mich. . . Michigan (U.S.).
M.I.Chem.E. Member of the Institution of Chemical Engineers.
M.I.E.Aust. Member Institution of Engineers, Australia.
M.I.E.E. . Member of Institution of Electrical Engineers.
M.I.E.I. . Member of Institution of Engineering Inspection.
M.I.E.(Ind.) Member Institution of Engineers, India.
M.I.E.S. . Member Institution of Engineers and Shipbuilders, Scotland.
M.I.Ex. . Member Institute of Export.
M.I.H.V.E. Member Institution Heating and Ventilation Engineers.
M.I.I.A. . Member of the Institute of Industrial Administration (now M.B.I.M.: Member of the British Institute of Management).
Mil. . . Military.
M.I.Loco.E. Member of Institution of Locomotive Engineers.
M.I.Mar.E. Member of the Institute of Marine Engineers.
M.I.Mech.E. Member Institution of Mechanical Engineers.
M.I.M.I. Member of Institute of Motor Industry.
M.I.Min.E. Member of the Institution of Mining Engineers.
M.I.M.M. . Member Institution of Mining and Metallurgy.
M.I.Mun.E. Member Institution of Municipal Engineers.
Min. . . Minister; Ministry.
M.I.N. . . Member of the Institute of Navigation.
Minn. . . Minnesota (U.S.).
M.Inst.C.E. Member of Institution of Civil Engineers (changed Feb. 1946 to M.I.C.E.).
M.Inst.F. . Member of Institute of Fuel.
M.Inst.Gas E. Member Institution of Gas Engineers.
M.Inst.H.E. Member of the Institution of Highway Engineers.
M.Inst.M.E. Member of Institution of Mining Engineers.
M.Inst.Met. Member of the Institute of Metals.
M.Inst.Pet. Member of the Institute of Petroleum.
M.Inst.P.I. Member of the Institute of Patentees (Inc.).
M.Inst.R.A. Member of the Institute of Registered Architects.
M.Inst.T. . Member of the Institute of Transport.
M.Inst.W. . Member Institute of Welding.
M.Inst.W.E. Member of the Institution of Water Engineers (now M.I.W.E.).
M.I.P.R. . Member of the Institute of Public Relations.
M.I.Prod.E. (formerly M.I.P.E.) Member of the Institution of Production Engineers.
M.I.R.E. . Member of the Institution of Radio Engineers.
M.I.R.T.E. . Member of Institute of Road Transport Engineers.

M.I.S. (India) Member of the Institution of Surveyors of India.
M.I.S.I. . Member of Iron and Steel Institute.
Miss. . . Mississippi (U.S.).
M.I.Struct.E. Member of the Institution of Structural Engineers.
M.I.W.E. . Member of the Institution of Water Engineers.
M.J.I. . . Member of Institute of Journalists.
M.J.I.E. . Member of the Junior Institute of Engineers.
M.J.S. . . Member of the Japan Society.
M.L. . . Licentiate in Medicine; Master of Laws.
M.L.A. . Member of Legislative Assembly.
M.L.C. . . Member of Legislative Council.
Mlle. . . *Mademoiselle* (Miss).
M.L.O. . . Military Liaison Officer.
M.L.S. . . Member of the Linnæan Society.
M.M. . . Military Medal.
M.Mech.E. . Master of Mechanical Engineering.
Mme. . . Madame.
M.Met. . Master of Metallurgy.
M.M.G.I. . Member of the Mining, Geological and Metallurgical Institute of India.
M.M.S.A. . Master of Midwifery Society of Apothecaries.
M.N.A.S. . Member of the National Academy of Sciences (U.S.).
M.O. . . Medical Officer.
Mo. . . Missouri (U.S.).
Mods. . . Moderations (Oxford).
M.O.H. . Medical Officer(s) of Health.
M.O.I. . . Ministry of Information.
Mon. . . Monmouthshire.
Mont. . . Montana (U.S.); Montgomeryshire.
M.O.P. . Ministry of Power.
Most Rev. Most Reverend.
M.P. . . Member of Parliament.
M.P.P. . Member of Provincial Parliament.
M.P.S. . . Member of Pharmaceutical Society.
M.R. . . Master of the Rolls; Municipal Reform.
M.R.A.I.C. . Member Royal Architectural Institute of Canada.
M.R.A.S. . Member of Royal Asiatic Society.
M.R.C. . . Medical Research Council.
M.R.C.O.G. Member of Royal College of Obstetricians and Gynæcologists.
M.R.C.P. . Member of the Royal College of Physicians.
M.R.C.P.E. Member of the Royal College of Physicians, Edinburgh.
M.R.C.S. . Member Royal College of Surgeons.
M.R.C.S.E. . Member of the Royal College of Surgeons, Edinburgh.
M.R.C.V.S. Member of the Royal College of Veterinary Surgeons.
M.R.Emp.S. Member of the Royal Empire Society.
M.R.I. . . Member of the Royal Institution.
M.R.I.A. . Member of the Royal Irish Academy.
M.R.I.A.I. . Member of the Royal Institute of the Architects of Ireland.
M.R.I.N.A. Member of Royal Institution of Naval Architects.
M.R.San.I. . Member of Royal Sanitary Institute (*see* M.R.S.H.).
M.R.S.H. . Member of the Royal Society for the Promotion of Health (formerly M.R.San.I.).
M.R.S.T. . Member of Royal Society of Teachers.
M.R.U.S.I. . Member of the Royal United Service Institution.
M.S. . . Master of Surgery: Master of Science (U.S.).
MS., MSS. . Manuscript, Manuscripts.
M.S.A. . Master of Science, Agriculture (U.S.).
M.S.A.E. . Member of the Society of Automotive Engineers (U.S.).
M.S.A.I.C.E. Member of South African Institution of Civil Engineers.
M.S. & R. . Merchant Shipbuilding and Repairs.
M.S.Aut.E. Member of the Society of Automobile Engineers.
M.S.C. . . Madras Staff Corps.
M.Sc. . . Master of Science.
M.Sc.D. . Master of Dental Science.
M.S.E. . . Master of Science in Chemical Engineering (U.S.).
M.S.H. . . Master of Stag-Hounds.
M.S.I.A. . Member Society of Industrial Artists.
M.S.I.T. . Member Society of Instrument Technology.
M.S.M. . Meritorious Service Medal.
M.S.R. . . Member Society of Radiographers.
Mt. . . Mountain.
M.T. . . Mechanical Transport.
M.T.C.A. . Ministry of Transport and Civil Aviation.
M.T.P.I. . Member of Town Planning Institute.
Mus.B. . Bachelor of Music.
Mus.D. . Doctor of Music.
Mus.M. . Master of Music.
M.V. . . Merchant Vessel, Motor Vessel (naval).
M.V.O. . Member of the Royal Victorian Order.
Mx. . . Middlesex.

N

(N.) . . Nationalist; Navigating Duties.
N. . . . North.
n. . . . Nephew.
N.A. . . National Academician (America).
N.A.A.F.I. . Navy, Army and Air Force Institutes.
N.A.B.C. . National Association of Boys' Clubs.
N.A.L.G.O. (Nalgo) National and Local Government Officers' Association.
N.A.P.T. . National Association for the Prevention of Tuberculosis.
N.A.T.O. . North Atlantic Treaty Organisation.
Nat. Sci. . Natural Sciences
N.B. . . New Brunswick.
N.B.A. . . North British Academy.
N.B.C. . . National Book Council (now National Book League); National Broadcasting Company (of America).
N.B.L. . . National Book League (formerly National Book Council).
N.C. . . North Carolina (U.S.).
N.C.B. . . National Coal Board.
N.C.L.C. . National Council of Labour Colleges.
N.C.U. . . National Cyclists' Union.
N.D.A. . . National Diploma in Agriculture.
N. Dak. . North Dakota (U.S.).
N.D.D. . . National Diploma in Dairying; National Diploma in Design.
N.D.H. . . National Diploma in Horticulture.
N.E. . . North-east.
N.E.A.C. . New English Art Club.
Neb. . . Nebraska (U.S.).
N.E.C.Inst. North-East Coast Institution of Engineers and Shipbuilders.
Nev. . . Nevada (U.S.).
New M. . New Mexico (U.S.).
N.F.S. . . National Fire Service.
N.F.U. . . National Farmers' Union.
N.F.W.I. . National Federation of Women's Institutes.
N.H. . . New Hampshire (U.S.).

N.I. . . Northern Ireland; Native Infantry.
N.I.A.B. . National Institute of Agricultural Botany.
N.I.D. . . Naval Intelligence Division; National Institute for the Deaf; Northern Ireland District.
N.J. . . New Jersey (U.S.).
N.L. . . National Liberal.
N.L.F. . . National Liberal Federation.
Northants. Northamptonshire.
Notts. . . Nottinghamshire.
N.P. . . Notary Public.
N.R.A. . . National Rifle Association; National Recovery Administration.
N.R.D. . . National Registered Designer.
N.S. . . Nova Scotia; New Style in the Calendar (in Great Britain since 1752); National Society.
n.s. . . Graduate of Royal Naval Staff College, Greenwich.
N.S.A. . . National Skating Association.
N.S.P.C.C. . National Society for Prevention of Cruelty to Children.
N.S.W. . New South Wales.
N.T. . . New Testament; Northern Territory of South Australia.
N.U.I. . . National University of Ireland.
N.U.P.E. . National Union of Public Employees.
N.U.R. . National Union of Railwaymen.
N.U.T. . . National Union of Teachers.
N.U.T.N. . National Union of Trained Nurses.
N.U.W.W. National Union of Women Workers.
N.W. . . North-west.
N.W.F.P. . North-West Frontier Province.
N.W.P. . North-Western Provinces.
N.W.T. . North-Western Territories.
N.Y. . . New York—City or State.
N.Y.C. . . New York City.
N.Z. . . New Zealand.
N.Z.E.F. . New Zealand Expeditionary Force.

O

O. . . . Ohio (U.S.).
o. . . . only.
O.A. . . *Officier d'Académie.*
O.A.S. . . On Active Service.
O. & E. . Operations and Engineering (U.S.).
O. & O. . Oriental and Occidental (Steamship Co.).
ob. . . died.
O.B.E. . . Officer Order of the British Empire.
O.B.I. . . Order of British India.
o.c. . . . only child.
O.C. and o/c Officer Commanding.
O.C.F. . . Officiating Chaplain to the Forces.
O.C.T.U. . Officer Cadet Training Unit.
O.E.E.C. . Organisation for European Economic Co-operation.
O.F.M. . Order of Friars Minor.
O.F.S. . . Orange Free State.
O.H.M.S. . On His (or Her) Majesty's Service.
O.L. . . Officer of the Order of Leopold.
O.M. . . Order of Merit.
O.M.I. . . Oblate of Mary Immaculate.
Ont. . . Ontario.
O.P. . . *Ordinis Prædicatorum*=of the Order of Preachers (Dominican Ecclesiastical Title); Observation Post.
O.R.C. . . Orange River Colony.
Ore. . . Oregon (U.S.).
O.S. . . Old Style in the Calendar (in Great Britain before 1752).
o.s. . . only son.
O.S.A. . . Ontario Society of Artists.
O.S.B. . . Order of St. Benedict.
O.S.F.C. . Franciscan (Capuchin) Order.
O.S.N.C. . Orient Steam Navigation Co.
O.S.R.D. . Office of Scientific Research and Development.
O.St.J. . . Officer of Order of St. John of Jerusalem.
O.T. . . Old Testament.
O.T.C. . . Officers' Training Corps.
O.U. . . Oxford University.
O.U.A.C. . Oxford University Athletic Club.
O.U.A.F.C. . Oxford University Association Football Club.
O.U.B.C. . Oxford University Boat Club.
O.U.C.C. . Oxford University Cricket Club.
O.U.D.S. . Oxford University Dramatic Society.
O.U.R.C. . Oxford Union Rifle Club.
O.U.R.F.C. . Oxford University Rugby Football Club.
Oxon. . . Oxfordshire; of Oxford.

P

P.A. . . Pakistan Army.
Pa. . . Pennsylvania (U.S.).
p.a.c. . . passed the final examination of the Advanced Class, The Military College of Science.
P.A.S.I. . Professional Associate Chartered Surveyors' Institution (changed August 1947 to A.R.I.C.S.).
P.C. . . Privy Councillor; Police Constable; Perpetual Curate; Peace Commissioner (Irish Free State).
p.c. . . *per centum* (by the hundred).
P.C.M.O. . Principal Colonial Medical Officer.
P.E.I. . . Prince Edward Island.
P.E.N. . . (Name of Club: Poets, Playwrights, Editors, Essayists, Novelists.)
P.E.P. (PEP). . Political and Economic Planning.
P.F. . . Procurator-Fiscal.
p.f.c. . . Graduate of R.A.F. Flying College.
Ph.B. . . Bachelor of Philosophy.
Ph.C. . . Pharmaceutical Chemist.
Ph.D. . . Doctor of Philosophy.
Phil. . . Philology, Philological; Philosophy, Philosophical.
Phys. . . Physical.
P.I.C.A.O. . Provisional International Civil Aviation Organisation.
pinx. . . (He) painted it.
Pl. . . Place; Plural.
Plen. . . Plenipotentiary.
P.M.G. . Postmaster-General.
P.M.N. . . *Panglima Nangku Negara* (Malayan Honour).
P.M.O. . Principal Medical Officer.
P.M.R.A.F.N.S. Princess Mary's Royal Air Force Nursing Service.
P.M.S. . . President Miniature Society.
P.N.E.U. . Parents' National Educational Union.
P. & O. . Peninsular and Oriental Steamship Co.
P. & O.S.N.Co. Peninsular and Oriental Steam Navigation Co.
P.O. . . Post Office.
Pop. . . Population.
P.O.W. . Prisoner of War; Prince of Wales's.
P.P. . . Parish Priest; Past President.
Pp. . . Pages.
P.P.C.L.I. . Princess Patricia's Canadian Light Infantry.
P.P.E. . . Philosophy, Politics and Economics (Oxford Univ.).
P.P.R.A. . Past President of the Royal Academy.
P.P.R.B.A. . Past President of the Royal Society of British Artists.

P.P.T.P.I. . Past President Town Planning Institute.
P.Q. . . Province of Quebec.
P.R.A. . President of the Royal Academy.
P.R.C.S. . President of the Royal College of Surgeons.
Preb. . . Prebendary.
Pres. . . President.
P.R.I. . . President of the Royal Institute of Painters in Water Colours.
P.R.I.A. . President of the Royal Irish Academy.
Prin. . . Principal.
Proc. . . Proctor; **Proceedings.**
Prof. . . Professor.
P.R.O.I. . President of the Royal Institute of Oil Painters.
Pro tem. . *Pro tempore* (for the time being).
Prov. . . Provost.
Prox. . . *Proximo* (next).
Prox. acc. . *Proxime accessit* (next in order of merit to the winner, or a very close second).
P.R.S. . . President of the Royal Society.
P.R.S. . . Performing Right Society Ltd.
P.R.S.A. . President Royal Scottish Academy.
P.R.S.E. . President of the Royal Society of Edinburgh.
P.R.U.A.A. President Royal Ulster Academy of Arts.
P.R.W.S. . President Royal Society of Painters in Water Colours.
P.S. . . Pastel Society.
p.s. . . passed School of Instruction (of Officers).
p.s.a. . . Graduate of R.A.F. Staff College.
p.s.c. . Graduate of Staff College († indicated Graduate of Senior Wing Staff College).
p.s.m. . . Certificate of Royal Military School of Music.
P.S.M.A. . President of Society of Marine Artists.
P.S.N.C. . Pacific Steam Navigation Co.
Pte. . . Private (soldier).
Pty. . . Proprietary.
P.W.D. . Public Works Department (roads, buildings, Govt. railways, telegraphs, etc.).
P.W.O. . Prince of Wales's Own.

Q

Q. . . . . Queen.
Q.A.I.M.N.S. Queen Alexandra's Imperial Military Nursing Service.
Q.A.L.A.S. . Qualified Associate Land Agents' Society.
Q.A.R.A.N.C. Queen Alexandra's Royal Army Nursing Corps.
Q.A.R.N.N.S. Queen Alexandra's Royal Naval Nursing Service.
Q.C. . . Queen's Counsel.
Q.H.C. . Queen's Honorary Chaplain.
Q.H.D.S. . Queen's Honorary Dental Surgeon.
Q.H.N.S. . Queen's Honorary Nursing Sister.
Q.H.P. . . Queen's Honorary Physician.
Q.H.S. . . Queen's Honorary Surgeon.
Qld. . . Queensland.
Q.M.A.A.C. Queen Mary's Army Auxiliary Corps.
Q.M.C. . . Queen Mary College (London).
Q.M.G. . Quartermaster-General.
Q(ops.) . Quartering (operations).
Qr. . . Quarter.
Q.S. . . Quarter Sessions.
q.s. . . R.A.F. graduates of the Military or Naval Staff College (symbol omitted if subsequently qualified p.s.a.).
Q.U.B. . . Queen's University, Belfast.
Q.U.I. . . Queen's University in Ireland.
q.v. . . *quod vide* (which see).

R

(R.) . . **Radical; Reserve.**
r. . . . right.
R.A. . . Royal Academician; Royal Artillery.
R.A.A.F. . Royal Australian Air Force.
R.A.A.M.C. Royal Australian Army Medical Corps.
R.A.C. . . Royal Automobile Club; Royal Agricultural College; Royal Armoured Corps.
R.A.C.P. . Royal Australasian College of Physicians.
R.A.C.S. . Royal Australasian College of Surgeons.
R.A.D.A. . Royal Academy of Dramatic Art.
R.A.E. . . Royal Australian Engineers; Royal Aircraft Establishment.
R.A.E.C. . Royal Army Educational Corps.
R.Ae.S. . Royal Aeronautical Society.
R.A.F. . . Royal Air Force.
R.A.F.O. . Reserve of Air Force Officers (now Royal Air Force Reserve of Officers).
R.A.F.R.O. Royal Air Force Reserve of Officers.
R.A.F.V.R. Royal Air Force Volunteer Reserve.
R.A.I.A. . Royal Australian Institute of Architects.
R.A.I.C. . Royal Architectural Institute of Canada.
R.A.M. . Member of Royal Academy of Music.
R.A.M.C. . Royal Army Medical Corps.
R.A.N. . Royal Australian Navy.
R.A.N.V.R. Royal Australian Naval Volunteer Reserve.
R.A.O.C. . Royal Army Ordnance Corps.
R.A.P.C. . Royal Army Pay Corps.
R.A.R.O. . Regular Army Reserve of Officers.
R.A.S. . . Royal Astronomical or Asiatic Society.
R.A.S.C. . Royal Army Service Corps.
R.A.S.E. . Royal Agricultural Society of England.
R.Aux.A.F. Royal Auxiliary Air Force.
R.A.V.C. . Royal Army Veterinary Corps.
R.B. . . Rifle Brigade.
R.B.A. . . Member Royal Society of British Artists.
R.B.C. . . Royal British Colonial Society of Artists.
R.B.S. . . Royal Society of British Sculptors.
R.B.S.A. . Royal Birmingham Society of Artists.
R.C. . . Roman Catholic.
R.C.A. . . Member Royal Canadian Academy; Royal College of Art.
R.C.A.F. . Royal Canadian Air Force.
R.Cam.A. . Member Royal Cambrian Academy (formerly R.C.A.).
R.C.M. . Royal College of Music.
R.C.N. . . Royal Canadian Navy.
R.C.N.C. . Royal Corps of Naval Constructors.
R.C.N.V.R. Royal Canadian Naval Volunteer Reserve.
R.C.O. . . Royal College of Organists.
R.C.O.G. . Royal College of Obstetricians and Gynæcologists.
R.C.P. . . Royal College of Physicians.
R.C.S. . . Royal College of Surgeons; Royal Corps of Signals; Royal College of Science.
R.C.S.(I.) . Royal College of Surgeons (of Ireland).
R.C.V.S. . Royal College of Veterinary Surgeons.
R.D. . . Rural Dean; Royal Naval Reserve Decoration.
Rd. . . Road.
R.D.C. . . Rural District Council.
R.D.F. . . Royal Dublin Fusiliers.
R.D.I. . . Royal Designer for Industry (Royal Society of Arts).

R.D.S. . . Royal Dublin Society.
R.E. . . Royal Engineers; Fellow of Royal Society of Painter Etchers.
Rear-Adm. Rear-Admiral.
R.Econ.S. . Royal Economic Society.
Rect. . . Rector.
Reg. Prof. . Regius Professor.
Regt. . . Regiment.
R.E.M.E. . Royal Electrical and Mechanical Engineers.
R.E.R.O. . Royal Engineers Reserve of Officers.
R.E.S. . . Royal Empire Society (now Royal Commonwealth Society).
Res. . . Resigned; Reserve; Resident; Research.
Rev. . . Reverend.
R.F.A. . . Royal Field Artillery.
R.F.C. . . Royal Flying Corps (now R.A.F.).
R.F.P.S.(G.) Royal Faculty of Physicians and Surgeons (of Glasgow).
R.G.A. . Royal Garrison Artillery.
R.G.S. . . Royal Geographical Society.
R.H.A. . Royal Hibernian Academy; Royal Horse Artillery.
R.H.B. . Regional Hospitals Board.
R.H.G. . Royal Horse Guards.
R.H.R. . Royal Highland Regt.
R.H.S. . Royal Horticultural Society; Royal Humane Society.
R.I. . . Member Royal Institute of Painters in Water Colours; Rhode Island.
R.I.A. . . Royal Irish Academy.
R.I.A.M. . Royal Irish Academy of Music.
R.I.A.S.C. . Royal Indian Army Service Corps.
R.I.B.A. . Royal Institute of British Architects.
R.I.B.I. . Rotary International in Great Britain and Ireland.
R.I.C. . . Royal Irish Constabulary.
R.I.E. . . Royal Indian Engineering (Coll.).
R.I.F. . . Royal Irish Fusiliers.
R.I.I.A. . Royal Institute of International Affairs.
R.I.M. . . Royal Indian Marine.
R.I.N. . . Royal Indian Navy.
R.I.N.A. . Royal Institution of Naval Architects.
R.M. . . Royal Marines; Resident Magistrate.
R.M.A. . Royal Marine Artillery; Royal Military Academy, Sandhurst (now incorporating Royal Military Academy, Woolwich).
R.M.C. . Royal Military College, Sandhurst (now Royal Military Academy).
R.M.C.S. . Royal Military College of Science.
R.Met.S. . Royal Meteorological Society.
R.M.F.V.R. Royal Marine Forces Volunteer Reserve.
R.M.L.I. . Royal Marine Light Infantry.
R.M.O. . Resident Medical Officer(s).
R.M.P.A. . Royal Medico - Psychological Association.
R.M.S. . Royal Microscopical Society; Royal Mail Steamer; Royal Society of Miniature Painters.
R.N. . . Royal Navy; Royal Naval.
R.N.A.S. . Royal Naval Air Service.
R.N.C. . . Royal Naval College.
R.N.E.C. . Royal Naval Engineering College.
R.N.L.I. . Royal National Life-boat Institution.
R.N.R. . . Royal Naval Reserve.
R.N.V.R. . Royal Naval Volunteer Reserve.
R.N.V.S.R. Royal Naval Volunteer Supplementary Reserve.
R.O.C. . . Royal Observer Corps.
R.O.F. . . Royal Ordnance Factories.
R. of O. . Reserve of Officers.
R.O.I. . . Royal Institute of Oil Painters.
(Rot.) . . Rotunda Hospital, Dublin (after degree).
Roy. . . Royal.
R.P. . . Member Royal Society of Portrait Painters.
R.P.C. . . Royal Pioneer Corps.
R.P.S. . . Royal Photographic Society.
R.R.C. . . Royal Red Cross.
R.S.A. . . Royal Scottish Academician; Royal Society of Arts.
R.S.A.I. . Royal Society of Antiquaries of Ireland.
R.San.I. . *See* R.S.H.
R.S.C. . . Royal Society of Canada.
R.S.C.M. . Royal School of Church Music.
R.S.C.N. . Registered Sick Children's Nurse.
R.S.E. . . Royal Society of Edinburgh.
R.S.F. . . Royal Scots Fusiliers.
R.S.F.S.R. . Russian Socialist Federated Soviet Republic.
R.S.G.S. . Royal Scottish Geographical Society.
R.S.H. . . Royal Society for the Promotion of Health (formerly Royal Sanitary Institute).
R.S.L. . . Royal Society of Literature.
R.S.M. . . Royal Society of Medicine; Royal School of Mines.
R.S.O. . . Rural Sub - Office; Railway Sub-Office.
R.S.P.B. . Royal Society for Protection of Birds.
R.S.P.C.A. . Royal Society for Prevention of Cruelty to Animals.
R.S.S.A.I.L.A. Returned Sailors, Soldiers and Airmen's Imperial League of Australia.
R.S.W. . Member Royal Scottish Water Colour Society.
Rt. Hon. . Right Honourable.
R.T.O. . . Railway Transport Officer.
R.T.R. . . Royal Tank Regiment.
Rt. Rev. . Right Reverend.
R.T.S. . . Religious Tract Society; Royal Toxophilite Society.
R.U. . . Rugby Union.
R.U.I. . . Royal University of Ireland.
R.U.S.I. . Royal United Service Institution.
R.W.A. (R.W.E.A.) Member of Royal West of England Academy.
R.W.F. . Royal Welch Fusiliers.
R.W.S. . Member Royal Society of Painters in Water Colours.
R.Y.A. . Royal Yachting Association.
R.Y.S. . . Royal Yacht Squadron.

S

(S) . . . (in Navy) Paymaster.
S. . . . Succeeded; South; Saint.
s. . . . Son.
S.A. . . South Australia; South Africa; *Société Anonyme.*
S.A.A.F. . South African Air Force.
S.A.C.S.E.A. Supreme Allied Command, S.E. Asia.
S.A.D.G. . *Société des Architectes Diplômés par le Gouvernement.*
Salop . . Shropshire.
S.A.M.C. . South African Medical Corps.
Sarum . Salisbury.
S.A.S. . . Special Air Service.
S.A.S.O. . Senior Air Staff Officer.
S.B. . . Bachelor of Science (U.S.).
S.B.A.C. . Society of British Aircraft Constructors.
S.B.St.J. . Serving Brother, Order of St. John of Jerusalem.
S.C. . . Senior Counsel (Eire); South Carolina (U.S.).
s.c. . . Student at the Staff College.
S.C.A.O. . Senior Civil Affairs Officer.
S.C.A.P.A. Society for Checking the Abuse of Public Advertising.
Sc.D. . . Doctor of Science.
S.C.F. . . Senior Chaplain to the Forces.
Sch. . . Scholar.

S.C.L. . . Student in Civil Law.
S.C.M. . . State Certified Midwife; Student Christian Movement.
Sculpt. . Sculptor.
S.Dak. . South Dakota (U.S.).
S.D.B. . . Salesian of Don Bosco.
S.D.F. . . Sudan Defence Force; Social Democratic Federation.
S.E. . . South-east.
S.E.A.C. . South-East Asia Command.
S.E.A.L.F. . South-East Asia Land Forces.
S.E.A.T.O. . South-East Asia Treaty Organisation.
Sec. . . Secretary.
Selw. . . Selwyn College, Cambridge.
S.E.S.O. . Senior Equipment Staff Officer.
S.G. . . Solicitor-General.
S.G.A. . . Member Society of Graphic Art.
Sgt. . . Sergeant.
S.H.A.E.F. . Supreme Headquarters, Allied Expeditionary Force.
S.H.A.P.E. . Supreme Headquarters, Allied Powers, Europe.
S.J. . . Society of Jesus (Jesuits).
S.J.A.B. . St. John Ambulance Brigade.
S.J.D. . . Doctor of Juristic Science.
S.L. . . Serjeant-at-Law.
S.M. . . Master of Science.
S.M.A. . . Society of Marine Artists.
S.M.E. . . School of Military Engineering.
S.M.I.R.E. . Senior Member Institution of Radio Engineers (New York).
S.M.O. . . Senior Medical Officer.
S.N.C.F. . Société Nationale des Chemins de Fer Français.
S.O. . . Staff Officer.
S.O.A.S. . School of Oriental and African Studies.
Soc. . . Society.
s.p. . . *sine prole* (without issue).
S.P.C.K. . Society for Promoting Christian Knowledge.
S.P.D. . . Salisbury Plain District.
S.P.G. . . Society for the Propagation of the Gospel.
S.P.R.C. . Society for Prevention and Relief of Cancer.
Sq. . . Square.
S.R. . . Special Reserve; Southern Railway (*see* B.R.); Southern Region (B.R.).
S.R.M.C. . Southern Rhodesia Medical Corps.
S.R.N. . . State Registered Nurse.
S.R.O. . . Supplementary Reserve of Officers.
SS. . . Saints.
S.S. . . Straits Settlements; Steamship.
S.S.A. . . Society of Scottish Artists.
S.S. & A.F.A. Soldiers, Sailors, and Airmen's Families Association.
S.S.C. . . Solicitor before Supreme Court (Scotland); Sculptors Society of Canada.
S.S.J.E. . Society of St. John the Evangelist.
S.S.M. . . Society of the Sacred Mission.
S.S.O. . . Senior Supply Officer.
S.S.St.J. . Serving Sister, Order of St. John of Jerusalem.
St. . . Street; Saint.
S.T.B. . . *Sacræ Theologiæ Bachelor* (Bachelor of Sacred Theology).
S.T.C. . . Senior Training Corps.
S.T.D. . . *Sacræ Theologiæ Doctor* (Doctor of Sacred Theology).
Stip. . . Stipend; Stipendiary.
S.T.L. . . *Sacræ Theologiæ Lector* (Reader or a Professor of Sacred Theology).
S.T.M. . . *Sacræ Theologiæ Magister.*
S.T.P. . . *Sacræ Theologiæ Professor* (Professor of Divinity, old form of D.D.).
S.T.S.O. . Senior Technical Staff Officer.
Supp. Res. Supplementary Reserve (of Officers).
Supt. . . Superintendent.
Surg. . . Surgeon.
Surv. . . Surviving.
S.W. . . South-west.
Sx. . . Sussex.
Sy. . . Surrey.
Syd. . . Sydney.

T

T. . . Telephone; Territorial.
T.A. . . Telegraphic Address; Territorial Army.
T.A.A. . . Territorial Army Association.
T.A.F. . . Tactical Air Force.
T. & A.F.A. Territorial and Auxiliary Forces Association.
T.A.N.S. . Territorial Army Nursing Service.
T.A.R.O. . Territorial Army Reserve of Officers.
Tasm. . . Tasmania.
T.C.D. . . Trinity College, Dublin.
T.C.F. . . Temporary Chaplain to the Forces.
T.D. . . Territorial Decoration; (Tealta Dail) Member of the Dail, Eire.
T.E.D. . . Territorial Efficiency Medal.
Temp. . . Temperature; Temporary.
Tenn. . . Tennessee (U.S.).
Ter. or **Terr.** Terrace.
Tex. . . Texas (U.S.).
T.F. . . Territorial Forces.
T.F.R. . . Territorial Force Reserve.
Th.L. . . Theological Licentiate.
T.P. . . Transvaal Province.
T.P.I. . . Town Planning Institute.
Trans. . . Translation, Translated.
Transf. . Transferred.
T.R.C. . . Thames Rowing Club.
T.R.H. . . Their Royal Highnesses.
Trin. . . Trinity.
t.s.c. . . passed a Territorial Army Course in Staff Duties.
T.S.D. . . Tertiary of St. Dominick.
T.U.C. . . Trades Union Congress.
TV . . Television.
T.Y.C. . . Thames Yacht Club.

U

(U.) . . Unionist.
u. . . Uncle.
U.A.B. . . Unemployment Assistance Board.
U.C. . . University College.
U.C.H. . . University College Hospital (London).
U.C.L. . . University College, London.
U.C.W. . . University College of Wales.
U.D.C. . . Urban District Council.
U.D.F. . . Union Defence Force.
U.F. . . United Free Church.
U.G.C. . . University Grants Committee.
U.J.D. . . *Utriusque Juris Doctor*, Dr. of both Laws (Dr. of Canon and Civil Law).
U.K. . . United Kingdom.
U.K.A.E.A. United Kingdom Atomic Energy Authority.
U.N. . . United Nations.
U.N.A. . . United Nations Association.
U.N.C.I.O. . United Nations Conference on International Organisation.
U.N.E.S.C.O. (Unesco). United Nations Educational, Scientific and Cultural Organisation.
Univ. . . University.
U.N.O. . . United Nations Organisation.
U.N.R.R.A. United Nations Relief and Rehabilitation Administration.
U.N.R.W.A. United Nations Relief Works Agency.
U.P. . . United Provinces; United Presbyterian.
U.S. . . United States.
U.S.A. . . United States of America.
U.S.A.A.F. . United States Army Air Forces.

U.S.M.A. . United States Military Academy.
U.S.N. . . United States Navy.
U.S.N.R. . United States Naval Reserve.
U.S.S. . . United States Ship.
U.S.S.R. . Union of Soviet Socialist Republics.
U.T.C. . . University Training Corps.
(U.U.) . . Ulster Unionist.

V

V. . . . Five (Roman numerals); Version; Vicar; Viscount; *Vice.*
v. . . . *Versus* (against).
v. or **vid.** . *Vide* (see).
V.A. . . Victoria and Albert.
Va. . . Virginia (U.S.).
V.A.D. . Voluntary Aid Detachment.
V.C. . . Victoria Cross.
V.C.A.S. . Vice-Chief of the Air Staff.
V.D. . . Royal Naval Volunteer Reserve Officers' Decoration (now V.R.D.); Volunteer Officers' Decoration; Victorian Decoration.
V.D.C. . . Volunteer Defence Corps.
Ven. . . Venerable (of an Archdeacon).
Very Rev. Very Reverend (of a Dean).
Vet. . . Veterinary.
V.H.S. . . Hon. Surgeon to Viceroy of India.
Vic. . . . Victoria; *see also* Vict.
Vice-Adm. Vice-Admiral.
Vict. . . Victoria; *see also* Vic.
Visc. . . Viscount.
V.M. . . Victory Medal.
V.M.H. . Victoria Medal of Honour (Royal Horticultural Society).
Vol. . . Volume; Volunteers.
V.P. . . Vice-President.
V.Q.M.G. . Vice-Quartermaster-General.
V.R. . . *Victoria Regina* (Queen Victoria).
V.R.D. . Royal Naval Volunteer Reserve Officers' Decoration.
Vt. . . . Vermont (U.S.).

W

W. . . . West.
W.A. . . West Australia.
W.A.A.F. . Women's Auxiliary Air Force (now W.R.A.F.).
Wadh. . Wadham.
Wash. . Washington State (U.S.).
W/Cdr. . Wing Commander.
W.E.A. . Workers' Educational Association; Royal West of England Academy.
W.E.U. . Western European Union.
W.H.O. . World Health Organisation.
Wh.Sch. . Whitworth Scholar.
W.I. . . West Indies (formerly B.W.I.: British West Indies).
Wilts. . . Wiltshire.
Wis. . . Wisconsin (U.S.).
W.L.A. . Women's Land Army.
W.L.F. . Women's Liberal Federation.
Wm. . . William.
W.O. . . War Office.
Worcs. . Worcestershire.
W.O.S.B. . War Office Selection Board.
W.R. . . West Riding; Western Region (B.R.).
W.R.A.C. . Women's Royal Army Corps.
W.R.A.F. . Women's Royal Air Force (formerly W.A.A.F.).
W.R.N.S. . Women's Royal Naval Service
W.S. . . Writer to the Signet.
W.S.P.U. . Women's Social and Political Union.
W. Va. . West Virginia (U.S.).
W.V.S. . Women's Voluntary Services.
Wyo. . . Wyoming (U.S.).

X

X. . . Ten (Roman numerals).

Y

y. . . . youngest.
Yeo. . . Yeomanry.
Y.H.A. . Youth Hostels Association.
Y.M.C.A. . Young Men's Christian Association.
Yorks. . Yorkshire.
yr. . . . younger.
yrs. . . . years.
Y.W.C.A. . Young Women's Christian Association.

ADDENDA

The following biographies are of those whose deaths occurred before 31st December 1960, but which were not reported until after the body of this book went to press.

ACKERMANN, Gerald, R.I., water-colour painter; *b.* Blackheath, 1876; *s.* of Arthur Ackermann. *Educ.:* New College, Eastbourne. Studied at Heatherley's and Royal Academy Schools; while there won the Creswick prize and Landseer scholarship; exhibited at the Royal Academy and held exhibitions at the Leicester Galleries and the Fine Art Society. Official purchases: Wellington (N.Z.), New South Wales, and provincial galleries in England. Enlisted in the Artists Rifles O.T.C. and held commission in the Royal Air Force. *Recreation:* walking. *Address:* Santa Claus, Blakeney, Norfolk. *Club:* Chelsea Arts. [*Died* 27 *Dec.* 1960.

ALFORD, (Edward) John (Gregory); *b.* 3 April 1890; *s.* of late Sir Edward Fleet Alford and Jane Eliza Helen Nathalie Shand; *m.* 1st, 1917, Margherita Gabriella, *d.* of Carlo Ascanio Tealdi of Cesanello, Pisa; two *s.* one *d.*; 2nd, 1945, Roberta, *d.* of Robert I. Murray, New York and Chappaqua, N.Y.; became an American citizen, 1950. *Educ.:* Tonbridge School; King's College, Cambridge. Assistant Editor to Harold Monro on Poetry and Drama; war service with British Red Cross Society and B.E.F. in Italy, 1915-19; much abroad, principally in Italy and France studying art; resident Toynbee Hall, 1921-22; manager to Christophers (publishers), 1922-24, and some experience of furnishing trade; lecturer at the Institute of Education and the Courtauld Institute of Art, University of London; first holder of Professorship of Fine Art, University of Toronto, 1934-45; Professor of Aesthetics, 1945, and Head, Dept. of Hist. of Art, 1945-53, Rhode Island School of Design; a director of College Art Association of America, 1940-46; Bollingen Foundation Fellowship, 1951, 1952; N.Y. Foundation Visiting Professor: Middlebury Coll., 1954-1955; Birmingham-Southern Coll., 1956; Visiting Prof. of Philosophy, Indiana Univ., 1957-58; Trustee, Amer. Soc. for Aesthetics, 1955. *Publications:* some poetry, represented in various anthologies; numerous articles in educational, learned and technical journals; responsible with J. C. Dale for English version of Meresjkowsky's Paul I produced at Court Theatre, London, 1927. *Address:* R.F.D.2, East Chatham, N.Y., U.S.A. [*Died Feb.* 1960.

BANERJEA, Pramathanath, M.A.; D.Sc. Econ.; Patron, Calcutta Assoc. for the United Nations; President: Indian Economic Soc.; Indian Inst. of Political Science; Federation Hall Society; Vice-President, Indian Statistical Institute; Hon. Director Indian Cultural Institute; Leader, Nationalist Party, Central Legislative Assembly, 1942-45; Barrister-at-law; Pres., Indian Economic Conference, 1931; Pres., Indian Political Science Conference, 1940; Minto Professor of Economics, Calcutta University, 1920-35; formerly President, Council of Post-Graduate Teaching in Arts, Calcutta University, India; *b.* 1881; *s.* of Nanilal Banerjea; *m.* 1901; no *c.* (one adopted *d.*). *Educ.:* Presidency College, Calcutta; School of Economics, London. Worked as Professor in Colleges of the Calcutta University; Member of the Senate, Calcutta University, 1923-53; Member of the Syndicate, 1924-53; Dean of the Faculty of Arts, Calcutta University, 1929-30; President of the Boards of Studies in Economics and Commerce; represented the University at the Congress of the Universities of the British Empire at Oxford, 1921; Mem. Bengal Legislative Council, 1923-30; Pres., Federation Hall Soc. *Publications:* A Study of Indian Economics, 7th edn., 1954; Public Administration in Ancient India; Fiscal Policy in India; Indian Finance in the Days of the Company; A History of Indian Taxation; Provincial Finance in India; The Future of Finance in India; Industry in India, etc. *Address:* 4/1A Vidyasagar Street, Calcutta, India. *Club:* Calcutta University Institute (Calcutta). [*Died* 5 *Nov.* 1960.

BARTHOLOMEW, James Rankin, C.M.G. 1946; *b.* Airdrie, Scotland, 29 May 1887; *s.* of Thomas Bartholomew; *m.* 1910, Ellen Martin; three *d.* *Educ.:* Otago Boys' High School; Otago University (LL.B.). Barrister and Solicitor, 1902-09; Stipendiary Magistrate, Dunedin, 1909-46. *Recreation:* golf. *Address:* 205 Forbury Road, St. Clair, Dunedin, New Zealand. *Club:* Otago (Dunedin). [*Died* 22 *April* 1951.

BEDELL, Frederick; Professor Emeritus of Physics at Cornell University since 1937; *b.* Brooklyn, New York, 1868; *m.* 1st, 1896, Mary L. Crehore (*d.* 1936) (author of Modern Gypsies) of Cleveland; two *d.*; 2nd, 1938, Mrs. Grace E. Wilson. *Educ.:* Yale Univ., A.B. 1890; Cornell Univ., Ph.D. 1892. Assist. Profesor of Physics, Cornell Univ., 1893-1904; Professor of Applied Electricity, 1904-37; has made many contributions to the proceedings of scientific societies on alternating currents of electricity; has made many electrical inventions; his researches on bone conduction revolutionized hearing aids; Vice-President of the American Institute of Electrical Engineers, 1917-18; Fellow American Physical Society; former member International Electrotechnical Commission; past General Secretary American Association for the Advancement of Science; pioneer member Aeronautical Society of America; member Aero Club of America; editor of the Physical Review, 1893-1922. *Publications:* A Treatise on Alternating Currents (with Dr. A. C. Crehore), 1892; The Principles of the Transformer, 1896; Direct and Alternating Current Testing, 1909; Airplane Characteristics, 1918; The Air Propeller, 1919; The Airplane, 1920. *Address:* 1147 Lura Street, Pasadena 5, California, U.S.A. [*Died* 5 *May* 1958.

BLACK, William Charles, C.B.E. 1954; *b.* 21 Aug. 1890; *s.* of Thomas Black, Newspaper Editor and Manager, Barnsley; *m.* 1913, Emma MacFarlane; one *d.* *Educ.:* Sheffield. Trained as Builder; in business on own account since 1924. Entered Dundee

Town Council, Nov. 1935; Lord Provost of the City of Dundee, 1952-54. *Recreation:* golf. *Address:* Arnhall, Perth Road, Dundee. *T.:* Dundee 68472. [*Died Feb.* 1959.

BLANKENBERG, Sir Reginald Andrew, K.B.E., *cr.* 1920 (O.B.E. 1919); *b.* 25 Dec. 1876; s. of late Charles Andrew Blankenberg; *m.* 1903, Laura Veryan (*d.* 1932), *d.* of late John Truscott, Fowey, Cornwall. Official Secretary, Office of High Commissioner for Union of South Africa, 1918-25. [*Died July* 1960.

BOTTOMLEY, John Mellor, C.I.E. 1937; M.A.; *b.* Taradale, New Zealand, 21 March 1888; *m.* 1917, Maude Millicent, *d.* of late Lt.-Col. G. R. Row, I.A.; one *d.* *Educ.:* Merchant Taylors' School, Crosby; Christ Church, Oxford. Appointed to Indian Educational Service, 1911; Director of Public Instruction, Bengal, 1933-43. *Recreations:* golf and billiards. *Address:* Rest-harrow, Shillong, Assam. *Clubs:* Oxford and Cambridge; Tollygunge (Calcutta). [*Died* 3 *Aug.* 1960.

BURT, Rev. Henry Chadwick, M.A.; Hon. D.C.L.; Professor of Philosophy and Economics, and Lecturer in Apologetics and Church History, University of Bishop's College, Lennoxville, 1910-42; Professor Emeritus in Philosophy since 1942; *b.* Perth, Lanark Co., Ont., 5 Dec. 1871; parents from Birmingham; *m.* M. H. Kerr; two *s.* three *d.* *Educ.:* Trinity College, Toronto University; First-Class Honours in History; 1st Prizeman in Arts and Theology, 1897; Rector of St. Paul's Church, Mt. Forest, Ontario, 1897-1904; Rector of St. Paul's, Quebec City, Bishop's Chaplain, Editor of Diocesan Gazette, 1904-07; Lecturer in University of Bishop's College, Lennoxville, 1907-10; elected Prof. of Phil. and Econ., 1910; retired, 1942. *Recreations:* golf, cricket, curling. *Address:* P.O. Box 52, Lennoxville, Quebec, Canada. [*Died March* 1959.

CAMERON, Lieut.-Colonel Sir Donald Charles, K.C.M.G., *cr.* 1932 (C.M.G. 1919); D.S.O. 1917; V.D., *b.* Brisbane, 19 Nov. 1879; *s.* of John Cameron, Longreach, Queensland; *m.* 1914, Evelyn Stella, *d.* of late Alexander Jardine, Brisbane. Served S. Africa, 1900-02 (despatches, Queen's medal with two clasps); European War, 1915-19 (despatches thrice, D.S.O., Order of the Nile); an Australian Delegate, League of Nations Assembly, Geneva, 1923 and 1932; Member House of Representatives, Commonwealth of Australia, 1919-31 and 1934-37. *Address:* 4 Rosemont Avenue, Woollahra, N.S.W. *Clubs:* Queensland (Brisbane); Union (Sydney). [*Died* 18 *Nov.* 1960.

CAMMIDGE, Percy John, M.D. (Lond.) 1908; M.R.C.S., L.R.C.P. (Lond.) 1898; D.P.H. (Camb.) 1903; *b.* York, 1872; *s.* of John Cammidge; *m.* Agnes Jane, 2nd *d.* of late John Staniland Gainsborough; one *s.* *Educ.:* Edward VI. Grammar School, E. Retford; University of Leeds; St. Bartholomew's Hospital, London. Demonstrator of Biology, St. Bartholomew's Hospital; Lecturer in Biology, E. London Polytechnic; Treasurer's Research Student, St. Bartholomew's Hospital; Path. Curator, General Infirmary, Leeds; County Bacteriologist, West Riding, Yorks; Arris and Gale Lecturer, Royal College of Surgeons, 1904. *Publications:* The Pancreas: its Surgery and Pathology; Gallstones and their Treatment; Glycosuria and Allied Conditions; Diabetic Dieting and Cookery; The Fæces of Children and Adults; New Views on Diabetes Mellitus; The Insulin Treatment of Diabetes Mellitus; contributions to current medical literature. *Recreations:* architecture, photography. *Address:* The Grange Hotel, Salisbury, Wilts. [*Died* 30 *June* 1956.

CAMPBELL, Percy Gerald Cadogan, M.A. (Oxford); Docteur de l'Université de Paris; Hon. LL.D. (Queen's); Prof. Emeritus of French, Queen's Univ., Canada; *b.* 8 Jan. 1878; *e. s.* of Rev. C. Cadogan Campbell; *m.* 1910, Evelyn Amy, *d.* of Frank Jessup Rogers; two *s.* *Educ.:* France; Rossall; Balliol College, Oxford, Chancellor's Essay, 1902; University of Paris. Went to Queen's University on taking B.A. at Oxford, 1902; Commandant Fort Henry Internment Station, 1915-1916; O.C. 253rd Battalion, C.E.F., 1916-17; Seconded to Imperial Forces in France, 1917-18; O.C. Queen's C.O.T.C., 1928-32. Treasurer of Diocese of Ontario, 1933-59. *Publication:* L'Epitre d'Othéa de Christine de Pisan. *Address:* 420 Earl Street, Kingston, Ontario, Canada. [*Died* 1960.

CARTON DE WIART, Count Edmund, K.B.E. (hon.); Grand Maréchal (hon.) de la Cour de Belgique; Président de la Commission Royale des Monuments de Belgique; *b.* Brussels, 4 Jan. 1876; *s.* of Constant Carton de Wiart, Brussels; *m.* 1910, Louise, *d.* of Baron de Moreau, former Minister of Foreign Affairs of Belgium; one *d.* *Educ.:* Louvain; Paris; Oxford; Berlin. Doctor of Law and Social Sciences. Secretary of Mr. Beernaert, former Prime Minister, 1897-1901; Professor Louvain University, 1897-1901; Political Secretary of King Leopold, 1901-09; Belgian Plenipotentiary at several conferences; Financial Delegate of the Belgian Government in England during the War. Great Cross of Belgian Orders, Grand Officier of Légion d'Honneur, Great Cross, etc. *Publications:* The British Chartered Companies in the 19th Century; Leopold II, a Biography, etc. *Address:* Avenue de Tervueren 177, Brussels; Château de Brumagne, Namur, Belgium. [*Died* 2 *Dec.* 1959.

CHRISTIE, James, C.M.G. 1934; LL.M.; On Staff N.Z. Law Drafting Office, 1907-45; Law Draftsman, 1918-38; Counsel to Law Drafting Office, 1938-45; retired, 1945; Judge (temp.) of Supreme Court of New Zealand, 1947-49. *Address:* Jubilee Road, Khandallah, Wellington, N.5, N.Z. [*Died* 26 *Dec.* 1960.

COPEMAN, Constance Gertrude, A.R.E. 1895; *b.* Liverpool; *d.* of C. R. Copeman, solicitor; unmarried. *Educ.:* private schools, Liverpool and London. Studied Art under John Finnie, R.E., at the School of Art, Liverpool; Silver Medallist; 1st special Queen's Prize for Figure Composition, National Competition, 1892; Member of the Liverpool Academy and an exhibitor at the Royal Academy and provincial galleries; pictures in the permanent collections at Liverpool and Preston; Figure painter chiefly, in oil and pastel; Toy Designer. *Address:* 158 Upper Parliament Street, Liverpool 8. [*Died* 1953.

de SILVA, Sir Albert Ernest, Kt., *cr.* 1946; *b.* 26 Nov. 1887; *s* of Albert Emmanuel de Silva; *m* 1913, Evadne Lukshmini, *d.* of S. D. S. Gunasekera; two *s.* four *d.* *Educ.:* Royal College, Colombo, Clare College, Cambridge. B.A. (Cantab.) 1910; Barrister-at-Law, Inner Temple, 1912. Chairman, Bank of Ceylon, since 1939; Chairman, State Mortgage, Bank of Ceylon, since 1935. *Recreations:* billiards; stamp collecting. *Address:* Sirimethipaya, Flower Road, Colombo, Ceylon. *Clubs:* Orient, Ceylon Turf (Colombo). [*Died* 9 *May* 1957.

DOMVILLE-FIFE, Charles William; author, explorer, journalist; Editor, The Seagoer; *b.* 15 March 1887; *s.* of Captain George Domville-Fife and Elizabeth Archer-Waythe; *m.* 1916, Doris Mary Tozer. *Educ.:* privately, and for the Navy. Pioneer of submarine boat construction in England, and with Rear Admiral Charles Windham, C.V.O.

designed and developed two types of war vessels; Special Correspondent of the Times in S. America, 1910; War Correspondent in Paraguay, 1912; exploring work in Amazon region, 1912-22; commanded various anti-submarine craft in North Sea, 1916-17; commanded early type of Q. boat, 1917; General Staff, Mining School, 1918-19; founded and edited the first Encyclopaedia of the British Empire; Special Commissioner of the Graphic in S. America, 1928-29; in West Indies, 1929-30; in the Far East, 1930-31; established course in Imperial History, Geography and Economics, since adopted in schools throughout the Empire; travelled extensively on a variety of missions in S. America, Central America, Africa, Burma, India, China, the Arctic, and almost every part of the world; has acted as adviser to several Colonial Governments. *Publications:* Naval: Submarine Engineering, 1912; The Submarine Mine and Torpedo in the War (Daily Telegraph War Book); Submarines and Sea Power, 1919; Exploration and Travel: The United States of Brazil, 1909; The Great States of S. America, 1910; Through Guatemala and Central America, 1912; The Real South America, 1922; Among Wild Tribes of the Amazons, 1922; Things seen in Switzerland in Winter, 1925; Savage Life in the Black Sudan, 1927; Modern South America, 1932; World Travels (six vols.), 1934; The King and His Empire (3 vols.), 1935; This is Germany, 1939; Evolution of Sea Power, 1939; Canada with Pen and Camera, 1939; I Tell of the Seven Seas, 1942; Epics of the Square-rigged Ships, 1958; most of the above translated into several foreign languages. *Address:* c/o Seeley Service & Co., Ltd., 196 Shaftesbury Avenue, W.C.2.
[*Died* 10 *Oct.* 1960.

FAWSITT, Charles Edward, D.Sc. (Edinburgh), B.Sc. (London), Ph.D. (Leipzig); Professor of Chemistry, University of Sydney, 1909-46; Dean of the Faculty of Science, University of Sydney, 1923-29; *b.* Glasgow, 1878; *s.* of late Charles Albert Fawsitt, chemical manufacturer, Glasgow; *m.* 1909, Lena Gertrude, *e. d.* of late Rev. Matthew Gardner, D.D., formerly of Hyndland Church, Glasgow; one *d.* *Educ.:* High School, Glasgow; Universities of Birmingham, Edinburgh, Leipzig, and London; Technische Hochschule, Aachen. Hope Prize Scholar and Gunning Victoria Jubilee Prizeman at Edinburgh University; 1851 Exhibition Scholar, 1900-02; Carnegie Research Fellow, 1903-04; Assistant to Professor of Chemistry, Edinburgh University, 1902-04; Assistant to Professor of Chemistry, Glasgow University, 1904-07; Lecturer on Metallurgical Chemistry, Glasgow University, 1904-08; President, Royal Society of N.S.W., 1919-20. *Publications:* Tables for Students of Quantitative Chemical Analysis, 1903; also research papers in Proc. Roy. Soc., etc. *Recreations:* music, golf. *Address:* 14A Darling Point Road, Edgecliff, Sydney, N.S.W.
[*Died* 16 *Nov.* 1960.

FITZGERALD, Sir John Joseph, 2nd Bt., *cr.* 1903; *b.* 20 Feb. 1876; *s.* of 1st Bt. and Anne, *d.* of John O'Donoghue, Cork; *S.* father 1927; *m.* 1911, Mary Thomasine, *d.* of John Burke, Bandon, Co. Cork; three *s.* *Heir:* *s.* Rev. Edward Thomas Fitzgerald *b.* 7 Mar. 1912 (who did not claim; Btcy. now *abeyant*).
[*Died* 1957.

FRY, Henry Kenneth, D.S.O. 1917; B.Sc., M.D. (Adelaide); B.Sc., D.P.H., Diploma Anth. (Oxon); F.R.A.C.P.; Medical Officer of Health, City of Adelaide, from 1938; *b.* 25 May 1886; *s.* of Henry Thomas Fry; *g.s.* of Rev. Henry Fry; *m.* Dorothy Editha Deeley; one *s.* one *d.* *Educ.:* Prince Alfred College; Univ. of Adelaide; Rhodes Scholar, Balliol College, Oxford. A.A.M.C., A.I.F., 1914-19. Lecturer in Materia Medica and Therapeutics, University of Adelaide, 1920-39; Hon. Physician, Adelaide Hospital, 1935-46. *Publications:* An Introduction to General Therapeutics, 1935; Medical and Anthropological papers to various journals. *Address:* Waverley Ridge, Crafers, South Australia.
[*Died* 22 *July* 1959.

GANDHI, Prof. Nagardas P., M.A., B.Sc., A.R.S.M., D.I.C., F.I.M., M.I.E. (Ind.) M.Inst. M.M., M.Inst.Met., M.I.S.I.; Consulting Mining Engineer and Metallurgist, Bombay; Director, Industrial Research Laboratory, Devlali, since 1947; *b.* 22 Dec. 1886; *m.* Shiv Kunvar; four *s.* *Educ.:* Bahauddin College, Junagad; Wilson Coll., Bombay; Royal School of Mines (Imperial College of Science and Technology), London. General Manager, Tata Sons' Wolfram and Tin Mines, Tavoy, Burma, 1916-19; Head of the Department of Mining and Metallurgy, Benares Hindu University, 1919-42; President, Geology Section, Indian Science Congress, 1933; President, Geological, Mining and Metallurgical Society of India, 1935-36. President, Bombay Metallurgical Society, 1945-48; Corr. Mem. for India of Inst. of Metals, London, 1942-55; Chairman of Indian Non-ferrous Metals Standardization Cttee., 1948-51; Hon. Mem. Indian Inst. of Metals, 1954. Hon Mem., Bombay Metallurgical Soc., 1957. *Recreations:* tennis, cricket and photography. *Address:* Kennaway House, Proctor Rd., Girgaon, Bombay, 4. *T.:* 70845; 183 Lam Road, Devlali, India.
[*Died* 26 *June* 1960.

GIBSON, Alexander James, M.E. (Hon. Queensland), M.Inst.C.E., M.I.E. Aust.; Consulting Engineer; *b.* 18 Dec. 1876; *s.* of E. Morris Gibson, Solicitor, Sutton, Surrey; *m.* 1902, Marion Helen (*d.* 1947), *d.* of T. J. Hitchman, Sydney, N.S.W.; two *s.* two *d.*; *m.* 1954, Ann Muriel, (*d.* 1957), *d.* of A. C. Dent, Rockhampton, Qld. *Educ.:* Dulwich College. Apprentice, Thames Ironworks and Shipbuilding Co., Ltd., Blackwall, London; Eng. Draftsman, S. C. Farnham & Co., Shanghai, China; Public Works Dept. N.S.W., 1900-03; Lecturer, Engineering Design, Univ. of Sydney, 1903-10; Prof. of Engineering, University of Queensland, 1910-18; Commonwealth Defence Department, Munitions Service, England, 1917; Acting General Manager, Chief Engineer, Commonwealth Arsenal, 1918; Superintendent of Construction, Broken Hill Pty. Co., Ltd., Steel Works, Newcastle, N.S.W., 1919-22; Past Chm. Standards Assoc. of Australia, 1940-48; Past President Institution of Engineers, Australia; P.N. Russell Medal; Fellow of Senate of University of Sydney, 1934-39; Past Chm. of Advisory Council, Sydney Central Technical Coll., 1936-42; Past Mem. of Council and Chm. of Advisory Cttee., N.S.W., Council for Scientific and Industrial Research. *Address:* Julius, Poole & Gibson, Consulting Engineers, 906 Culwulla Chambers, Castlereagh Street, Sydney, N.S.W. *T.A.:* Jupag, Sydney.
[*Died* 2 *Dec.* 1960.

GILL, Robert Carey Chapple; High Sheriff, Montgomeryshire, 1924; senior partner, R. & C. Gill, Liverpool; Member of Liverpool and New York Cotton Exchanges; *b.* 19 July 1875; *s.* of late Chapple Gill, of Lower Lee, Woolton; *m.* 1908, Mildred, 3rd *d.* of William Pretty, The Goldrood, Ipswich; two *s.* one *d.* *Educ.:* private. Formerly: Chairman of the Liverpool Committee of Lloyds Bank; Deputy Chairman, Thos. Taylors, Ltd., Wigan; Trustee Blue Coat Hospital, Liverpool; Director: Liverpool Storage Company; Liverpool Warehousing Co. Ltd.; The Sandon Motor Co. Ltd. *Recreations:* shooting, hunting and general. *Address:* Brynderwen, Bwlch-y-Cibau, Montgomeryshire: Ford House, Bath Street, Southport. *T.A.:* Chesterlie, Liverpool. *T.:* Llanfyllin 226; Cent. Liverpool 3129. Southport 4770. *Club:* Old Hall (Liverpool).
[*Died* 5 *Nov.* 1960.

GOOLD, Sir (George) Patrick, 5th Bt., *cr.* 1801; *b.* 9 July 1878; *s.* of 4th Bt.; *m.* 1900, Mary, *d.* of Nicholas Brown; two *s.*; *S.* father, 1926. *Heir: s.* George Ignatius, *b.* 29 April 1903. *Address:* Solomontown, Port Piri, S. Australia.

[*But his name never appeared on the official Roll of Baronets.* [*Died* 13 *Jan.* 1954.

GOWEN, Rev. Herbert H., D.D., F.R.G.S.; Professor Oriental Languages and Literature, Univ. of Washington, 1914; Prof. Emeritus, 1944; *s.* of late H. C. Gowen, Great Yarmouth, England; *m.* 1892, Annie Kate Green of Great Yarmouth; three *s.* two *d.* *Educ.:* Priory School, Great Yarmouth; S. Augustine's College, Canterbury. Missionary in Honolulu and in charge of Chinese Church in this city, 1886-90; Curate at S. Nicholas', Gt. Yarmouth, 1891-92; Rector of S. Barnabas', New Westminster, B.C., 1892-96; Trinity, Seattle, Wn., 1896-1914; Priest in charge of S. Mark's Parish, 1919-20; Priest-in-charge Memorial Chapel, Seattle; Associate Editor Anglican Theological Review; retired from Parochial work, 1936; Hon. Canon St. Mark's Cathedral, Seattle, 1950. President Washington State Philological Association; American Or. Soc., Society for Oriental Research, Japan Society of New York, R.G.S., Royal Asiatic Society, etc. *Publications:* Temperantia, 1891; The Paradise of the Pacific, 1892; The Kingdom of Man, 1893; Biography of Bishop Sillitoe, 1899; Idylls of Love and Death in Hawaii, 1908; The Revelation of S. John the Divine, 1910; Stella Duce, 1911; The Day of His Coming, 1907; The Revelation of the Things that Are, 1908; Sonnets for the Sundays, 1916; The Book of the Seven Blessings, 1919; An Outline History of China, 1914; The Napoleon of the Pacific, 1919; Sonnet Stories from the Chinese, 1920; Christ and Colosse, 1922; The Universal Faith, 1926; Asia: a Short History, 1926; An Outline History of Japan, 1927, French Edition, Spanish Edition, 1939; The Little Grey Lamb, and other Christmas Poems, 1928; The Psalms, or Book of Praises, 1929; A History of Indian Literature, 1931; A History of Religion, 1934; Five Foreigners in Japan, 1936; Asia, a Short History, revised and enlarged edition, 1936, French edition, 1937. *Recreations:* botanising, walking, gardening. *Address:* 2205, 74th Ave., S.E. Mercer Is., Washington, U.S.A. *Clubs:* Authors'; University Faculty, Monday, University (Seattle). [*Died* 6 *Nov.* 1960.

GRIEVE, Edward William Lawrence, R.D.I. 1940; F.R.S.A.; Manager of Display for Harrods, Ltd., 1932-53, resigned; joined Merchant Navy, Royal Mail Lines, 1956; *b.* Kirkliston, Scotland, 9 July 1902; 2nd *s.* of William Osburn Grieve, J.P., late of the Square, Kirkliston, and Jemima Noble Lawrence; *m.* 1951, Madame Virginia Christine de la Torre (marr. diss., 1957), *d.* of Edouardo Perez - Triana, Colombia. *Educ.:* George Heriot's School, Edinburgh. Started career as student of merchandising with Sir Robert Maule, Princes Street, Edinburgh; responsible for the décor of the Hall of Fashion at British Industries Fair, Earl's Court, London, 1939; from outbreak of War, designed and organised propaganda exhibitions at Harrods in connection with the War effort—arranged in collaboration with Government Ministries and the Governments of our Allies; staged dramatic presentation of Victorian settings in 40 display windows and in Central Hall (Harrod's Centenary, 1949); staged exhibition, 1951, at St. James's Palace (in collaboration with Principals of Roy. School of Needlework), of Roy. Coronation Robes and other historic pieces of needlework. Lived in Estoril, Portugal, 1954-56. *Address:* c/o Midland Bank, 50 Leicester Square, W.C.2. [*Died* 12 *Dec.* 1960.

GUNN, Col. John Alexander, C.B. 1919; O.B.E. 1918; Consulting Surgeon, Winnipeg General Hospital and St. Boniface Hospital; Emeritus Prof. of Surgery, Manitoba University; *b.* 1878; *m.* 1920, Armorel M. Thomas; two *s.* Served European War, 1914-19 (despatches twice, O.B.E., C.B., 1914-15 Star, two medals). Retired, 1953. *Address:* 1 Rossmore Apts., Winnipeg 1, Canada. *Club:* Manitoba (Winnipeg). [*Died Aug.* 1960.

HAGUE, Professor Bernard, Ph.D.; D.Sc.; Professor of Electrical Engineering, The University of Glasgow, since 1946; *b.* Barnsley, Yorks., 7 July 1893; *s.* of Joe and Amy Florence Hague; *m.* 1922, Muriel Thorne Grose; one *d.* *Educ.:* Grammar School, Eccles; Central Higher Grade School, Rochdale; City and Guilds College, South Kensington. Ph.D. (Glasgow) 1926, D.Sc. (London) 1927; F.C.G.I. 1936; M.I.E.E. 1929; M.Amer.I.E.E. 1930. Workshop training, Carter Bros., Rochdale, 1908-10; drawing office, Ferranti Ltd., Hollinwood, 1911-13; City and Guilds Coll., London, 1913-16; technical asst., Royal Aircraft Establishment, 1916-20; City and Guilds Coll., Lecturer, 1920-23; Univ. of Glasgow, Lecturer, 1923-29; Visiting Prof., Polytechnic Institute, Brooklyn, N.Y., 1929-30; Univ. of Glasgow, Senior Lecturer, 1930-46. *Publications:* Alternating Current Bridge Methods, 1st edn., 1923, revised 6th edn. 1957; Electromagnetic Problems in Electrical Engineering, 1929; Instrument Transformers, 1936; Introduction to Vector Analysis, 1st edn. 1939; 5th edn. 1951. Some 24 papers in Jl.I.E.E., Electrician, World Power, Engineering; numerous reviews and abstracts. *Recreations:* orchestral music (oboe); handicrafts in wood and metal. *Address:* 1 Princes Terrace, Glasgow, W.2. *T.:* Western 3354. *Club:* Authors'. [*Died* 29 *Sept.* 1960.

HARRIS, John Redford Oberlin; Headmaster, Hutchins School, Hobart, 1929-1942, retired 1942; *b.* 4 Dec. 1877; *s.* of Rev. John Oberlin Harris and Mary Hunt; *m.* 1917, Helen Mackenzie; two *d.* (one *s.* killed in action with R.A.A.F., 1942). *Educ.:* Christ's Coll. and Hutchins School, Hobart; Univ. of Tasmania (Classical Scholar). B.A. 1898, 1st Class Hons. in Classics; M.A. 1900. Junior Master, Hutchins School, 1895 and 1897; Classical Master at Launceston Church Gram. Sch., 1899-1902; Master at Melbourne Gram. Sch., 1903; Church of England Gram. Sch., Sydney, 1904-29; served with the A.I.F. in Egypt, France, and Belgium, 3rd Bn. Inf., rank of Major, 1915-18 (despatches); promoted Lt.-Col. on retirement, 1937. Member, Council, Univ. of Tasmania; an examiner to Univ. of Melbourne. Chief State Comr. of Boy Scouts, Tas. *Address:* 9 Lysterville Av., Malvern S.E.4, Melbourne, Vic., Australia. [*Died* 8 *Aug.* 1960.

HYDE, James Hazen; *b.* New York City, 6 June 1876; *s.* of Henry Baldwin Hyde (founder and late President Equitable Life Assurance Society of the United States) and Annie Fitch Hyde; one *s.* *Educ.:* Cutler's School, New York; A.B. Harvard Univ., 1898; Hon. M.A. Princeton University, 1903; Dr. *h.c.* Rennes University, France, 1920; Hon. LL.D. Skidmore Coll., 1956. Vice-President Equitable Life Assurance Society, U.S., 1899-1905; founder (1902) and First President of the Fédération des Alliances Françaises aux Etats-Unis (now Hon. Pres. and Mem. Exec. Cttee.); Fellow R.S.L. and R.S.A., London; Grand Croix of the Légion d'Honneur; Member of Académie des Sciences Morales et Politiques (Institut de France) since 1938. Chm. of Board, French Institute (New York); Vice-Pres. New York France-America Soc.; Hon. mem. Com. Amer. Field Service Fellowships, N.Y.;

Fellow, Metropolitan Museum of Art, N.Y. City; Member: American Geographical Soc., N.Y.; N.Y. Historical Soc.; Exec. Committee, American Society of French Legion of Honor; Life Fellow Cleveland Museum of Art (Ohio.) Capt. and Aide to High Comr., Amer. Red Cross in Paris during European War, 1914-18; organized Conreid Metropolitan Opera Co., N.Y., 1903; one of sponsors of New Theatre, N.Y., 1909. *Publications:* articles and lectures. *Recreations:* reading, collecting art objects on the allegorical representations of the Four Parts of the World. *Address:* Savoy Hilton Hotel, New York, N.Y. *T.A.:* Hazenhyde, New York. *Clubs:* Century Association, Meadow Brook (hon. mem.), Harvard, Knickerbocker, University, Union (New York); University (Albany). [*Died* 26 *July* 1959.

INCE, Sir Godfrey Herbert, G.C.B., *cr.* 1951 (K.C.B., *cr.* 1946 ; C.B. 1941) ; K.B.E., *cr.* 1943 ; B.Sc. ; Hon. LL.D. (London) ; Permanent Secretary, Ministry of Labour and National Service, 1944-Jan. 1956 ; Member of Economic Planning Board, 1947-Jan. 1956, retd. ; Chairman of Cable and Wireless, Ltd., and its associated companies, since 1956 ; Member of Senate of London University ; *b.* 25 Sept. 1891 ; *er. s.* of G. A. R. Ince, J.P., Reigate, Surrey ; *m.* 1918, Doris, 2nd *d.* of late C. Maude, Northallerton, Yorkshire ; three *d.* *Educ.:* Reigate Grammar School ; University College, London (Surrey County Scholar), Sherbrooke University Scholar (Mathematics), 1912 ; Mayer de Rothschild Scholar (Pure Mathematics), 1913 ; Ellen Watson Memorial Scholar (Applied Mathematics), 1913 ; Joseph Hume Scholar (Political Economy), 1914 ; Senior Mathematics Prizeman, 1913, Senior Physics Prizeman, 1914, at University College ; B.Sc. First Class Hons. Mathematics, 1913 ; served European War, 1915-19, Commission in Yorkshire Regt., 1915 ; transferred to East Lancashire Artillery ; service in France attached to Royal Engineers, Field Survey (wounded) ; entered Ministry of Labour as Assistant Principal, 1919 ; Private Secretary to Sir David Shackleton (Chief Labour Adviser), 1920-23 ; Principal Private Secretary to Ministers of Labour, 1930-33 ; Assistant Secretary, Ministry of Labour, 1933 ; Chief Insurance Officer under Unemployment Insurance Acts, 1933 - 37 ; Adviser to the Commonwealth of Australia on Unemployment Insurance, 1936-37 ; also visited New Zealand to advise N.Z. Government, 1937 ; Principal Assistant Secretary, Ministry of Labour, 1938 ; Under Secretary, Ministry of Labour and National Service, 1940 ; seconded to offices of War Cabinet, to take charge of Production Executive Secretariat, Jan. 1941 ; Director-General of Man Power, Ministry of Labour and National Service, June 1941-44 ; Deputy Secretary, 1942. *Publications:* Report on Unemployment Insurance in Australia, 1937 ; Ministry of Labour and National Service, 1960 ; papers on Manpower in Gt. Britain, in Proc. Manchester Statistical Soc., 1945 and 1953. *Recreations:* cricket, lawn tennis, association football. *Address:* The Witterings, 138 Copse Hill, Wimbledon, S.W.20. *T.:* Wimbledon 1713. *Clubs:* Athenæum, Royal Commonwealth Society. [*Died* 20 *Dec.* 1960.

INSH, George Pratt, C.B.E. 1944; B. Litt.; Historian; *b.* 17 Oct. 1883; *s.* of George Pratt Insh of Longside, Aberdeen, and Isabella Forbes Smith of Inverurie; *m.* 1911, Alice Louisa Dummer (*d.* 1952); one *s.* one *d.* *Educ.:* Crossmyloof School; Queen's Park School; Glasgow Univ. M.A. Glasgow, 1906; Carnegie Essay Prize of £100, 1921; D.Litt. 1922; Research Fellow, History, 1922; Teacher Glasgow Elementary Schools, 1904-1910; History Master, Hutchesons' Grammar School, 1910-23; Prin. Lect. History, Jordanhill Training College, 1923-45. President Educational Inst. of Scotland, 1938-39. Member Advisory Council Scottish Records, 1944; Historical Section of Cabinet, 1945-1946. President, The Forty-Five Association, 1955. Rifleman 1st Lanark R.V., 1902-5; Rifleman Cameronians, Captain Highland Light Infantry, 1914-19; Captain and Adjt. 11th Cameronians Sept. 1939-Dec. 1940, Staff Capt. (Educ.), Scottish Command, 1941, Instructor (Major) Army School of Education; Wakefield, 1941-42; Staff Officer (Educ.); Major, Galloway Area and Lothian and Border District, 1943. *Publications:* Scottish Colonial Schemes, 1922; Darien Shipping Papers (Scottish Hist. Soc.), 1924; School Life in Old Scotland, 1925; Carmina Glottiana: Poems of Avondale and Clydeside, 1928; Educational Values, 1932; The Company of Scotland trading to Africa and the Indies, 1932; The Study of Local History and other Essays, 1932; Scotland and the Modern World, 1932; The Clyde, the Elusive River, 1933, 3rd edition, 1946; Scotland, an Essay in Interpretation, 1936; Lanarkshire, 1937; Historian's Odyssey, 1938; The Challenge to Education, 1939; A Richard Jefferies Anthology, 1945; Thomas Henderson: an Appreciation, 1946; The Darien Scheme, 1947; Men, Moods and Movements, 1947; The Scottish Jacobite Movement: A Study in Economic and Social Forces, 1952; The Wartime History of the Scottish Red Cross, 1952. *Recreations:* walking, travel, historical research. *Club:* Literary (Glasgow). [*Died* 19 *March* 1956

JAMESON, Ven. Francis Bernard ; Archdeacon of Waterford and Lismore since 1955 ; Examining Chaplain to Bishop of Cashel ; *b.* 14 July 1889 ; 4th *s.* of Rev. Thomas Edward Jamieson ; *m.* 1921, Dorothy Elizabeth Sayers ; two *s.* one *d.* *Educ.:* Leeds Grammar School ; University Coll., Durham ; St. Augustine's College, Canterbury. S. Michael's Church, Wakefield, 1914-17 ; S.P.G. Missionary and Chaplain, Tinnevelly Diocese, Madras, 1917-33 ; Rector Aughrim, Diocese Clonfert, 1934-39 ; Dunmore East, Diocese of Waterford, 1939 ; Precentor and Prebenda y of Corbally, 1942. *Address:* Dunmore East Rectory, Co. Waterford. *T.:* Dunmore East 7329. [*Died* 25 *Oct.* 1960.

JONES, Rev. Gilbert Basil ; Incumbent of Trinity Church, St. Agathe des Monts, P.Q., Canada, since 1950 ; *b.* 7 Oct. 1894 ; *s.* of Rev. Thomas Jones, Vicar of Penbryn, Cardiganshire ; *m.* 1921, Katherine, *d.* of William Douglas, Baldovan, Perthshire ; one *d.* *Educ.:* St. Andrew's, Tenby ; Lancing College ; University London ; Balliol College, Oxford ; B.A. (Lond.), 1st Class Hons. in Philosophy, 1917 ; B.A. Oxon, 1st Class Hons. in Theology, 1920 ; M.A. 1925 ; D.C.L. (Bishop's University), 1941. Deacon, 1918 ; Priest, 1919 ; Chaplain and Tutor, St. Edmund Hall, Oxford, 1919-20 ; Sub-Warden of St. Michael's College, Llandaff, 1921-22 ; Warden of Church Hostel, Bangor, 1923-30 ; Examining Chaplain to Bishop of Bangor, 1922-30 ; Special Lecturer in Philosophical Theism, Univ. College of N. Wales, 1923-30 ; Warden of the Central Society of Sacred Study (Bangor Diocese), 1923-30 ; Welsh Church Scholarship Examiner, 1925-31 ; Examiner for first B.D. (Wales) 1925-31 ; Rector of South Luffenham, Rutland, 1931-36 ; Dean of Divinity, and Harold Professor, Bishop's Univ., Lennoxville, Que., 1936-49 ; Vice-Principal, 1941. General Ordination Examiner of English Church Assembly, 1933-34. *Publication:* Church Ceremonial: Four Addresses, 1942. *Recreations:* travelling, golf. *Address:* St. Agathe des Monts, P.Q., Canada. [*Died Oct.* 1958.

JONES, William Ernest, C.M.G. 1935 ; J.P. ; *b.* 1867 ; *s.* of Alfred Jones, Dudley, Worcestershire ; *m.* 1905, Kathleen Mary Mahony, Melbourne ; one *s.* one *d.* *Educ.:* Epsom College. Middlesex Hospital, 1884-1889 ; Newcastle on Tyne Medical School ; Medical Officer, Earlswood, Leicestershire, Rutland, and Northampton Co. Asylums ; 1st Medical Superintendent, Brecon and Radnor Counties Asylum, 1900 ; Director of Mental Hygiene, Victoria (Inspector-General of Insane), 1905-37 ; retired, 1937 ; Beattie

Smith Lecturer, 1938. Lt.-Col. A.A.M.C. *Publications:* Ann Mackenzie Oration, 1934; and other publications on Psychiatric problems. *Recreation:* golf. *Clubs:* Melbourne, Royal Melbourne Golf (Melbourne). [*Died Sept.* 1957.

KING, Lt.-Col. Giffard Hamilton Macarthur, C.M.G. 1915; D.S.O. 1918; V.D.; late 1st Field Artillery Brigade, Australian Imperial Force; Accountant Taxation Dept., New South Wales; *b.* 15 Jan. 1885; *m.* Frankun, *d.* of E. P. Pearce, Parramatta, N.S.W. Served European War (Dardanelles), 1914-18 (despatches, C.M.G., D.S.O.). *Address:* 13 Olova Avenue, Vaucluse, Sydney, N.S.W. [*Died* 12 *Oct.* 1956.

KUKDAY, Col. Sir Krishnaji Vishnoo, Kt., *cr.* 1939; C.I.E. 1926; Indian Medical Service, retired; Retired Inspector General of Civil Hospitals, Central Provinces India; *b.* 1870; *m.* 1886, Mainabai Gandhi; one *s.* two *d.* *Educ.:* Grant Medical College, Bombay; Edinburgh; London. Served British East Africa; European War, 1914-19 (despatches). *Address:* Maharajbag Club, Nagpur, C.P., India. [*Died* 4 *May* 1958.

LEE, Joseph Johnston; Author and Artist; *b.* Dundee, 1876; *s.* of David Alexander Lee and Christina Easson Blair; *m.* 1924, Dorothy Havercroft (A.R.A.M.), *d.* of George Barrie. Studied art at Heatherley's and Slade; during War served with the Black Watch from private to sergeant, later as Lieut. in K.R.R.C. *Publications:* Tales o' our Town, 1910; Fra Lippo Lippi, 1914; Ballads of Battle, 1916; Work-a-day Warriors, 1917; A Captive at Carlsruhe, 1920. *Recreations:* reading; "Going to and fro in the earth, and walking up and down in it." *Address:* Argyle Place, Thomson St., Dundee. [*Died* 1954.

LEVER, Richard Hayley, N.A., R.B.A., R.W.A. 1908; *b.* Adelaide, South Australia, 28 Sept. 1876; *s.* of Albion and Catherine Lever; *m.* 1906, Aida Smith Gale (*d.* 1949), St. Austell, Cornwall, England; one *s.* *Educ.:* Prince Alfred College, Adelaide. Came to St. Ives, Cornwall, 1899; Exhibitor, Venice International, Pittsburg International, Nice International, and Great White City Exhibitions, London; Royal Academy, New York Academy, Philadelphia Academy, International Exhibition, Toronto, New Salon, and Old Salon, Paris, etc. Represented in many galleries and museums in Australia, England and America, including Schumann Collection, Boston, Mass., Hon. Mention International Exhibition, Carnegie Institute, Pittsburgh, 1913; $500 Carnegie Prize, National Academy, New York, 1915; Silver Medal, National Arts Club, New York, 1914, and Gold Medal, 1916; Gold Medal, San Francisco Exp. 1915; Sesnam Gold Medal, Philadelphia Academy, U.S.A.; Temple Gold Medal, Pennsylvania Academy of Fine Arts, 1925; Bronze Medal, Philadelphia Sequistennial, 1926; Philadelphia Water-colour Prize, 1918, Bronze Medal Amsterdam Olympic Exhibition; Montclair Art Medal, New Jersey, 1930; Potter Palmer Marine Prize, National Academy, New York, 1936 and 1938; Newark (New Jersey) Art Club Marine Prize, Special Exhibition, Newark Centenary, 1936; 1st Hon. Mention Internat. Exhib. of Water Color, Chicago Inst., 1940; Instructor, Art Students' League (Hon. Life Member), New York; Instructor, Newark Art Club, N.J.; Hon. Member of Mt. Vernon Art Association, 1957-. 1st Award $1000 Annual Exhib. of Contemporary Amer. Artists, Studio Club Galleries, 1949; 1st Prize Westchester Art Centre, N.Y., 1953. *Recreations:* cricket, fishing, yachting. *Address:* National Arts Club (Life Mem.), Gramercy Park, N.Y., U.S.A. [*Died* 6 *Dec.* 1958.

LUXTON, Brig. Daniel Aston, C.M.G. 1918; D.S.O. 1917; V.D.; commanded 3rd Military Training Depot, Victoria, 1941-45; *b.* 22 June 1891; *s.* of Samuel J. Luxton, Melbourne. Served European War, 1914-18 (wounded, despatches, D.S.O., C.M.G.). *Address:* 8 Palm Avenue, Caulfield, Melbourne, S.E.7, Australia. [*Died* 17 *Dec.* 1960.

MACAN-MARKAR, Hadji Sir Mohamed, Kt., *cr.* 1938; Director of the Bank of Ceylon; Merchant; Governing Director in the firm of O. L. M. Macan Markar Ltd., Colombo; Director of Macan Markar Buildings Ltd.; Member of The Ceylon Senate; Director of Moslem Educaional Society Ltd.; Director of the Galle-Face Land and Building Co., Ltd.; *b.* 7 Sept., 1879; *e. s.* of late Osuman Lebbe Marikar Macan Markar, and of Aamina Umma, *d.* of Mudallyar Cassile Bronc. Cassie Lebbe Marikar; *m.* 1910, Noorul Neima (*decd.*), *e. d.* of late S. L. Naina Marikar Hadjiar; three *s.* four *d.* *Educ.:* Wesley College, Colombo. Consul for Turkey, 1903-15; member of Galle Municipal Council, 1906-31; returned as the first Muslim member to Ceylon Legislative Council, 1924-30; member for Batticoloa South seat, State Council, 1931-36; Minister of Communication and Works, 1931-1936; Chairman of now defunct Ceylon Electricity Board, 1966-67. *Recreations:* played for the Wesley College Cricket Eleven, 1898 and 1899; cricket and walking. *Address:* Muirburn, Turret Road, Cinnamon Gardens, Colombo; G.O.H. Buildings, Fort, Colombo. *T.A.:* Macan, Colombo. *T.:* 4897 and 4975. [*Died* 11 *May* 1952.

MACKAWEE, Khan Bahadur Sir Mahomed Abdul Kader, K.B.E. 1949 (O.B.E. 1933); Member Legislative Council; *b.* 1875; *s.* of Khan Bahadur Abdul Kader Mahomed Mackawee. *Educ.:* privately. Merchant and contractor for constructional works. Khan Bahadur, 1925. *Publication:* Anglo-Arabic Primer, 1904. *Recreations:* tennis and walking. *Address:* Camp, Aden, S. Arabia. [*Died* 1954.

McKENDRICK, Archibald, J.P., F.R.C.S.Ed., D.P.H., L.D.S.Ed., F.R.S.Ed.; Consulting Radiologist, Edin. Royal Infirmary, Medical Referee for the Lothians and Peebles under Workmen's Compensation Acts; *b.* 1 June 1876; *s.* of Jas. D. McKendrick, Dental Surgeon, Kirkcaldy; *m.* 1906, Gertrude Maud Smith; two *s.* Medals in Surgery, Medicine, Midwifery, Chemistry, Materia Medica, Physiology, Medical Jurisprudence and Public Health; Late Demonstrator in Anatomy, Out-Patient Resident Surgeon, Resident Gynæcological Surgeon, Clinical Asst. Ear and Throat wards, Lock wards, and Surgeon in Charge X-Ray Department, Edinburgh Infirmary; Lecturer in Medical Physics; Examiner for Royal College of Surgeons, Edinburgh. *Publications:* Public Health Law and Vital Statistics Book; Volumes on Malingering, Back Injuries, and Medico-legal Injuries, X-Ray Atlas; Numerous publications in Medical Journals. *Recreations:* golf, shooting, and fishing. *Address:* 24 Murrayfield Gardens, Edinburgh 12. *T.:* Donaldson 4955. [*Died* 2 *Nov.* 1960.

MAGUIRE, Maj.-Gen. Frederick Arthur, C.M.G. 1933; D.S.O. 1918; V.D.; M.D., Ch.M. (Sydney); F.R.C.S. (England); F.R.A.C.S.; F.A.C.S. (1947); F.R.C.O.G.; Fellow of College of Radiology (Austr. and N.Z.); Hon. Lecturer in Anatomy and Pathology, University of Sydney; Post-Graduate Lecturer in Gynæcology, University of Sydney; late Lecturer in Gynæcology, University of Sydney; Hon. Surgeon for Diseases of Women, Royal Prince Alfred and Prince Henry Hospital, Sydney; Hon. Cons. Surgeon, Diseases of Women, St. Vincent's Hospital, Sydney; Hon. Cons. Gynæc. Surgeon, Royal North Shore Hospital, Sydney; Chairman Regional Council in Australia of Royal College of Obstetricians and Gynæcologists; Alderman of Council of City of Sydney, 1949; Member Board of Directors Royal Prince Alfred Hospital; former Member of National Health and Medical Research Council of Australia; *b.* Cobar, N.S.W., 1888; *s.* of G. F. Maguire; *m.* 1st, 1913, Alma Myee (*d.* 1919); one *s.*; 2nd, 1922, Beatrice Macel; one *d.* *Educ.:* Sydney Grammar School; Sydney University; London and Middlesex Hospitals. Served European War, 1914-18 (despatches four times, D.S.O.); Acting Professor of Anatomy, University of Sydney, 1920-22, and 1924-25; Hon. Surgeon to Governor-General of Commonwealth of Australia, 1935-1939; Director-General Medical Services of the Commonwealth, 1941-42; Fellow of Senate, University of Sydney, 1933-38. Edward Stirling Orator, 1952, Listerian Orator, 1933, University of Adelaide. Hospitaller and Almoner of Priory of St. John of Jerusalem in Australia. Grand Master, Grand Lodge of Freemasons, N.S.W., 1933-1935, 1944-45. C.St.J. 1947; K.St.J. 1953. *Publications:* The Anatomy of the Female Pelvis, 4th Edn. 1949; The Anatomy of Procidentia Uteri, 1924; A Critical Survey of the Anatomy of the Female Pelvis, 1925; The Anatomy of the Bony Pelvis and Pelvic Floor, in Modern Trends in Gynæcology and Obstetrics, 1950. *Address:* 193 Macquarie Street, Sydney, N.S.W. *Clubs:* Authors'; Union, Royal Sydney Golf, Elanora Country (Sydney); Melbourne (Melbourne). [*Died* 10 *June* 1953.

McLEISH, Donald Alexander Stewart, O.B.E. 1957; LL.D.; Professor of Conveyancing, Glasgow University, 1946-55, retired 1955; *b.* 5 Oct. 1893; *s.* of James Alexander McLeish, solicitor, Glasgow, and Jane Little McLeish (*née* Smith); *m.* 1928, Margaret Lowson Inverwick Thomson; two *d.* (and one *d.* decd.). *Educ.:* Uddingston Grammar School; Glasgow Univ. M.A. 1913, LL.B. 1917, Glasgow. Qualified solicitor, 1917; Lectr. on Evidence and Procedure, Glasgow Univ., 1931-46. Partner of McLeish Thomson & Co., solicitors, Glasgow. Joint Hon. Sec. Scottish Unionist Assoc. 1947. *Recreations:* none. *Address:* (home) 40 Newark Drive, Glasgow. *T.:* Pollok 1826; (business) 163 Hope St., Glasgow. *T.:* City 6522. *Clubs:* Conservative (Glasgow and Edinburgh); New (Glasgow). [*Died* 26 *June* 1958.

MARCUS, Michael; Barrister-at-Law of the Middle Temple; Chairman Finsbury, Shoreditch Rent Tribunal, Oct. 1946-Oct. 1952; *b.* 9 Nov. 1894. *Educ.:* St. Leonard's Public Board School; George Heriot's School, Edinburgh; Edinburgh University, LL.B. Elected to Edinburgh Town Council for St. Leonard's Ward, 1926; formerly solicitor in practice in Edinburgh; election agent for late Rt. Hon. Wm. Graham, 1923-28; Hon. Solicitor to Edinburgh Trades and Labour Council, 1926-30; M.P. (Lab.) Dundee, 1929-31; Parliamentary Private Secretary to Mr. J. Westwood, M.P., Under-Secretary of State for Scotland, 1931; contested Dundee in Labour interest in Parliamentary elections of 1931 and 1935; joined Edinburgh Central Branch of I.L.P., 1918 (Chairman, 1919); served on numerous parliamentary and political committees; Member of British Institute of Philosophy. *Publications:* Legal Aspects of Trade Unionism; numerous articles on economic, social, political, and philosophical subjects. *Recreations:* books, walking, tennis, gardening. *Address:* 42 Glenloch Road, Hampstead, N.W.3. [*Died Nov.* 1960.

MASON, Thomas Godfrey, F.R.S. 1937; Physiologist, Cotton Research Station, Trinidad, W.I., since 1926; *b.* 24 July 1890; Irish. *Educ.:* Cheltenham College; Trinity College, Dublin. Army, 1914-18; Lecturer Botany, Alberta, 1919-20; Botanist, Barbados, 1920-22; Professor of Botany, Imperial College of Tropical Agriculture, Trinidad, 1922-23; Senior Botanist, Nigeria, 1924-1925. *Publications:* mainly on Movement of Food Materials in Plants, in Annals of Botany. *Address:* Cotton Research Station, Trinidad, W.I. [*Died* 22 *Oct.* 1959.

MURSHIDABAD, Nawab Bahadur of, K.C.S.I., *cr.* 1910; K.C.V.O., *cr.* 1912; H. H. Ehteshamul-Mulk, Rais-ud-Dowla, Amir-ul-Omrah, Nawab Asif Quadar Sir Syed Wasif Ali Meerza, Khan Bahadur, Mahabut Jung, premier noble of Bengal, Behar, and Orissa; 38th in descent from the Prophet of Arabia; *b.* 7 Jan. 1875; *s.* of Ihtisham-ul-Mulk, Rais-ud-Dowla, Amir-ul-Omrah, Nawab Sir Syud Hussan Ali Meerza Khan Bahadur, Mahabut Jung, G.C.I.E., late Nawab Bahadur of Murshidabad and Nawab Kulsumunnisa Begum Saheba; *m.* 1898, Nawab Sultan Dulin Fugfoor Jahan Begum Saheba. *Educ.:* in India, under private tutors in English, Arabic, Persian, and Urdu; and in England, at Sherborne, Rugby, and Oxford; *S.* father with hereditary titles of Nawab Bahadur of Murshidabad, Amir-ul-Omrah, 1906; has eight times been a Member of Bengal Legislative Council; has taken great interest in Municipal matters; was selected to represent Bengal at King's Coronation in London; attended the Delhi Coronation Durbar of 1st Jan. 1902 as a guest of Government of Bengal; as premier noble of Bengal had the honour of receiving King-Emperor George V. in Calcutta; Patron of the Calcutta Historical Society and Anjuman-e-Musalmanan-e-Bangala; founder President of the Hindu Muslim Unity Assoc.; is reputed for the efficient management of his estates and public charities; is also well known for his English and Urdu Poems. *Recreations:* an athlete, keen at all kinds of sports; polo, shooting, billiards. *Address:* 85 Park St., Bengal, India. [*Died Oct.* 1959.

NAIRAC, Sir (George) Edouard, Kt., *cr.* 1938; Q.C.; *b.* 15 March 1876; *s.* of Edouard Nairac and Laurence Couve; *m.* 1904, Marie Pauline Eva Rousset; six *s.* two *d.* *Educ.:* Royal College, Port Louis, Mauritius (Scholar). Called Bar, Middle Temple, 1898; Practised Mauritius Bar, 1898-1927; Member Legislative Council, 1911-27; Mayor of Port Louis, 1913, 1921, 1922; K.C. 1926; Procureur and Advocate General, 1927; M.E.C., 1927-36; Acting Colonial Secretary, 1929; Acting Chief Judge, 1930; Chief Justice, Mauritius, 1936-39; Pres., Fighting French Committee in Mauritius. *Publications:* Mauritius Law Reports, 1906-39; Digest of the Mauritius Law Reports, 1902 to 1925; Editor, Vol. IX, of Revised Laws of Mauritius (1930 to 1935); Causeries du Mercredi (Radio Talks in 1941 and 1942). *Address:* Schifanoia, Vacoas, Mauritius. *T.A.:* Vacoas Mauritius. [*Died* 1960.

PAINE, Brig. Douglas Duke, C.B.E. 1941; D.S.O. 1918; V.D.; Chairman, Trotting Control Board of Victoria, since 1957; *b.* 26 May 1892; *s.* of William Louis Paine and Nellie Brown; *m.* 1914, Freda Alice McClintock; one *s.* two *d.* *Educ.:* Melbourne High School. 2nd Lt. A.A.S.C., Australian Military Forces, 1911; Lieut. 1st Australian Divisional Train, A.I.F., 1914; Captain, 1915; Major S.S.O., 1917; A.D.S.T. 3rd Military District, 1919; Lieut.-Colonel C.A.S.C. 3rd Division, A.M.F., 1921-35; served European War, 1915-18 (D.S.O., despatches twice, 1914-15 star, two medals); Middle East, 1941 (C.B.E.); General Secretary, Victorian and Melbourne Centenary Celebrations Council, 1933-35; Comptroller of Stamps for Victoria, Australia, 1936; Assistant Director of Supply and Transport, Southern Command, Australian Military Forces, 1939; went abroad with

A.I.F. as Deputy Director of Supplies and Transport, 1940; served in Libya, Greece and Syria; recalled to Australia, 1942, and appointed Deputy Q.M.G., A.M.F.; Chairman Public Service Board of Victoria, 1944-1957. *Address:* 5 Gordon Grove, South Yarra, Melbourne, S.E.1, Australia. [*Died* 27 *Feb.* 1960.

PAKENHAM-WALSH, Rt. Rev. Herbert Pakenham, D.D. (Dub.); *b.* Dublin, 22 Mar. 1871; 3rd *s.* of late Rt. Rev. William Pakenham-Walsh, Bishop of Ossory, and Clara Jane Ridley; *m.* 1916, Clara Ridley, *y. d.* of late Rev. F. C. Hayes. *Educ.:* Chard Grammar School; Birkenhead School; Trinity College, Dublin. Deacon, 1896; worked as a member of the Dublin University Brotherhood, Chhota Nagpore, India, 1896-1903; Deacon, Priest, 1896; 1902; Principal S.P.G. College, Trichinopoly, 1904-07; Head of the S.P.G. Brotherhood, Trichinopoly—moved to Bangalore, 1907-14; Bishop in Assam, 1915-23; Principal of Bishop's College, Calcutta, 1923-35; Delegate to the Pan-Anglican Conference, 1908; Warden Bishop Cotton School, Bangalore, 1907-13; Organising Secretary C.E.M.S. for S. India, 1914. *Publications:* Lights and Shades of Christendom, Vols. I., II. and III.; A Devotional Study of the Holy Communion; With Christ in the Upper Room. *Address:* Christa Sishya Ashram, Tadagam, Coimbatore, India. [*Died* 9 *Jan.* 1959.

PARSONS, Rt. Rev. Edward Lambe, D.D., LL.D.; *b.* 18 May 1868; *s.* of Arthur W. Parsons and Helen C. White; *m.* 1897, Bertha de Forest Brush (decd.); two *d.* (one *s.* decd.). *Educ.:* Yale Univ.; Union Theol. Sem., N.Y.; Univ. of Berlin; Episcopal Theological School, Cambridge, Mass. Hon. D.D. Pac. Sch. Rel.; Yale; Epis. Theol. Sch., Cambridge, Mass.; LL.D., Univ. of California, Mills College; Asst., Grace Church, N.Y., 1894-95; Rector, Trinity Church, Menlo Park, California, 1896-1900; St. Matthew's San Mateo, 1900-04; St. Mark's, Berkeley, 1904-19; Bishop Coadjutor of California, 1919; Bishop of California, 1924-1940; Instructor in Philosophy, Stanford University, 1897-1902; Lecturer in Philosophy of Religion, Church Divinity School of the Pacific; Chairman, Earthquake Relief Com., Berkeley, 1906; Pres. War Work Council, 1917-18; Trustee, Church Div. School of the Pacific, Rosenberg Foundation and other like agencies; Delegate to Faith and Order Conference, Lausanne, 1927, Edinburgh, 1937; Chm. Liturgical Commission Prot. Episcopal Church, 1930-46; Chm. Commission on Approaches to Unity, 1928-1943; member of various others; Pres. Church League for Industrial Democracy, 1923-50; Vice-Chm. Amer. Civil Liberties Union. *Publications:* What is the Christian Religion?; The American Prayer Book (with B. H. Jones); Victory with Christ; essays, sermons and contributions to various books such as Episcopacy, Ancient and Modern, and the Anglican Communion, 1948. *Address:* 2901 Broderick St., San Francisco, California, U.S.A. *Clubs:* University, Commonwealth (San Francisco). [*Died* 18 *July* 1960.

PICKERING, Loring, F.R.G.S.; retired; *b.* San Francisco, 1888; *s.* of Loring Pickering, San Francisco, and Rose Crothers, Montreal; *m.* 1916, Harriett Alexander; two *s.*; divorced 1938; *m.* 1940, Chouteau Scott. *Educ.:* Stanford University; Chicago Law School; Oxford; Sorbonne. Captain and Major (pilot), Air Service, U.S. Army, 1917; Editor of the Bulletin, San Francisco, 1919-1921; organised The North American Newspaper Alliance, a co-operative association of one hundred and fifty daily newspapers in all parts of the world, and with offices in London, Paris, New York, etc., 1922; Managing Director of the North American Newspaper Alliance, 1922; Lieut.-Col., Air Corps, U.S.A., Jan. 1942; organised Army Courier Service, 1942; Col. 1943; Air Staff, 1944-46. Member of the Society of Colonial Wars; Charter Member of the American Society of Newspaper Editors; Fellow, American Geographical Society and Member, New England Historic Genealogical Society; organised the Wilkins North Pole Expedition; General Manager of the North American Newspaper Alliance. *Recreations:* shooting, fishing. *Address:* Todos Bancos, Woodside, California, U.S.A. *Clubs:* Savile; Players' (New York); Army and Navy (Washington); Pacific-Union (San Francisco); Burlingame (California); Peking (Peiping). [*Died* 11 *March* 1959.

POLLARD, Captain Alfred Oliver, V.C. 1917; M.C., D.C.M.; late R.A.F.; *s.* of J. A. Pollard, Tidbury, Wallington, Surrey; *b.* 4 May 1893; *m.* 1st, 1918, Mary, *d.* of Mr. Ainsley, Trefilan, Purley; 2nd, 1925, Violet Irene, *yr. d.* of R. A. Swarbrick, Elbury, Craven Avenue, Ealing, W. *Educ.:* Merchant Taylors' School. Served European War, 1914-18 (M.C. and bar, D.C.M., V.C.). *Publications:* Pirdale Island; Rum Alley; Murder Hide-and-Seek, 1931; Fire Eater; The Memoirs of a V.C., 1932; The Death Flight, 1932; The Riddle of Loch Lemman, 1933; The Phantom Plane, 1934; The Royal Air Force, 1934; Murder in the Air, 1935; The Secret of Castle Voxzel, 1935; Unofficial Spy; Boy's Romance of Aviation, 1935; The Death Game; Hidden Cipher, 1936; Romantic Stories of Air Heroes, 1936; The Murder Germ; Flanders Spy, 1937; Black-out; Air Reprisal, 1938; The Secret Formula; Murder of a Diplomat, 1939; The Secret Pact; A.R.P. Spy; Epic Deeds of the R.A.F., 1940; Bombers Over the Reich, 1941; Secret Weapon, 1941; Wanted by the Gestapo, 1942; Invitation to Death, 1942; The Death Squadron, 1943; Gestapo Fugitive, 1944; The Fifth Freedom, 1944; Blood Hunt, 1945; Double Cross, 1946; A Deal in Death, 1947; The Iron Curtain, 1947; The Death Curse; David Wilshaw investigates; The Secret Vendetta; Dead Man's Secret; Red Hazard, 1950; The Poisoned Pilot, 1950; The Death Parade, 1951; The Golden Buddha, 1951; Death Intervened, 1951; Counterfeit Spy, 1952; Criminal Airman, 1953; The Dead Forger, 1952; The Buckled Wing, 1953; Homicidal Spy, 1954; The Missing Diamond, 1955; Sinister Secret, 1955; Smugglers' Buoy, 1958; Wrong Verdict, 1960. *Address:* Linkwood, 18 Queen's Park Gardens, Bournemouth. [*Died* 4 *Dec.* 1960.

RENNIE, John, M.D., Aberdeen; D.P.H., Sheffield; late Medical Officer of the City of Sheffield; retired, 1947; Professor of Public Health, Sheffield University, 1930-47. *Address:* Blairmaud, Stonehaven, Kincardineshire. [*Died* 15 *Nov.* 1960.

ROBIQUET, Jean; French art historian and essayist; Honorary Keeper of Musée Carnavalet and of Musée of Ile-de-France; *b.* Meudon (Seine-et-Oise), 6 July 1874; *s.* of late Paul Robiquet, Officer, Legion of Honour, and late Marie Lombard; *m.* 1908, Raymonde Berthelot; no *c.* *Educ.:* Lycée Henri IV; Faculté des Lettres, Paris (Licencié ès Lettres). Entered Musée Carnavalet, 1897, Keeper, 1919-34; helped to organise exhibitions in Paris, 1900, Turin, 1911, Gand, 1912, Wiesbaden, 1921, Liege, 1930, Paris, 1937; organised many exhibitions at the Orangerie des Tuileries and Musée Carnavalet. Hon. Pres., Association de la Presse artistique française; Hon. Pres., French Assoc. of Museum Conservators. Officer, Legion of Honour. *Publications:* L'Œuvre inédit de Gavarni, 1912; Les Vieux Hôtels du Marais, 1927; Louis XIV et la Faculté; La Révolution de 1789; La Femme dans la peinture française, 1938; La Vie quotidienne pendant la Révolution, 1938; La Vie quotidienne au temps de

Napoléon 1er, 1943; L'Impressionnisme vécu, 1948, etc. *Address:* c/o Musée Carnavalet, 23 rue de Sévigné, Paris III, France. *Club:* Cercle des Escholiers (Hon. Pres.)

[*Died* 10 *Oct.* 1960.

RONAN, Very Rev. Myles V., D.Litt., M.R.I.A., F.R.Hist.S.; Parish Priest, St. Michan's, Dublin; *b.* 19 July 1877; *s.* of Myles and Margaret Ronan, Dublin. *Educ.:* Holy Cross College, Clonliffe; Propaganda College, Rome. Exhibitioner and prizewinner in the Intermediate Examinations, 1892, 1893; Medallist in Dogmatic Theology and Gregorian Chant, Rome, 1899; Ordained at Rome, 1900; Curate in Rathdrum, Co. Wicklow, 1901; St. Michan's, 1902; Pro-Cathedral, Dublin, 1904; Dun Laoghaire, 1923; for some years Secretary to Archbishop Walsh; Hon. Treasurer, Leinster College of Irish; Vice-President of Academy of Christian Art; Chairman, Literary Committee, Aonach Tailteann; Trustee of the National Library of Ireland; Vice-President of the Royal Society of Antiquaries, Ireland; Aonach Tailteann Gold Medallist for English Prose, 1928 and 1932. *Publications:* The Reformation in Dublin, 1536-1558; The Reformation in Ireland under Elizabeth, 1558-1580; The Irish Martyrs of the Penal Laws; St. Anne; Her Cult and Her Shrines; Catholic Emancipation Centenary Record, 1929; An Apostle of Catholic Dublin—Father Henry Young, 1786-1869; Several booklets on Ecclesiastical History; contributor to Irish Ecclesiastical Record, Catholic Historical Review (Washington Univ.), Journal, Roy. Soc. of Antiquaries, Ireland, Proceedings, Royal Irish Academy, Encyclopædia Britannica (1929 edition), Encyclopædia Americana (1953). European Civilisation (Eyre, Vol. IV.); Archivium Hibernicum (Maynooth Record Society); Ed. Jl. Acad. Christian Art, etc. *Recreations:* music, golf. *Address:* Presbytery, Halston Street, Dublin. *T.:* Dublin 441561.

[*Died* 7 *April* 1959.

ROW, Brigadier Robert Amos, D.S.O. 1918; Bar to D.S.O. 1944; New Zealand Staff Corps; *b.* 30 July 1888; *s.* of Frederick Ley Row and Emily Elizabeth Amos; *m.* 1913, Aimée Olga Stewart; three *s.* two *d.* *Educ.:* Christchurch Boys' High School; Canterbury College, N.Z. First Commission, 1909; served European War, 1914-19; commanded 1st Bn. Canterbury Regt. and 3rd Bn. Canterbury Regt.; Brigade Major 3rd N.Z. Mounted Rifles Brigade; A.A. and Q.M.G. Southern Military Command; General Staff Officer, 1st Grade, Central Military Command; Quartermaster-General N.Z. Military Forces, 1936-39; O.C. Field Troops, 2nd (Central) Military District, 1940; commanded Northern Field Force (1st Mil. District, Auckland), 1940-42; commanded 8 Bde. 3 N.Z. Div. in Pacific, 1942-1944. Legion of Merit (U.S.A.), 1944. *Address:* 6 Lockett St., Lower Hutt, Wellington, N.Z. [*Died* 7 *Jan.* 1959.

SANDERS, Henry Arthur; Professor of Latin, University of Michigan, 1911-Feb. 1939, Emeritus from 1939; Chairman of the Dept. of Speech and General Linguistics since 1932; Visiting Professor of Latin, University of Illinois, 1942; *b.* Livermore, Maine, U.S.A., 22 Oct. 1868; *s.* of John Sanders and Luretta Gibbs; *m.* 1913, Charlotte Ione Poynor; one *d.* *Educ.:* University of Michigan (A.B. 1890, A.M. 1894); University of Berlin, 1895-96; University of Munich (Ph.D. 1897); Hon. L.H.D. Colby, 1940. Teacher of Latin, Central High School, Minneapolis, 1890-2; and Greek, Kansas City, 1892-93; Instructor, University of Michigan, 1893-95; Minnesota, 1897-99; Michigan, 1899-1902; Assistant Professor, 1902-8; Junior Professor, 1908-11; Acting Director of the School for Classical Studies in the American Academy in Rome, 1915-16; Professor in charge of the School of Classical Studies of American Academy in Rome, 1928-31; Member, Amer. Editorial Board of Internat. Project to Establish a Critical Apparatus of the Greek New Testament, 1948-; Member: Amer. Philosophical Soc., Archeological Soc. of Amer., Philological Society, Society Biblical Research and Exegesis, Oriental Society, American Academy of Arts and Sciences, Council of several learned societies. *Publications:* Præfatio zu den Quellencontamination im xxi. xxii. Büche des Livius (The Lost Epitome of Livy), Berlin, 1897; Die Quellencontamination im xxi. xxii. Büche des Livius, Berlin, 1898; University of Michigan Studies, Vol. I. Roman Historical Sources, 1904; IV. Roman History and Mythology, 1908; VIII. I. Washington MS. of Deuteronomy and Joshua, 1910; II. Washington MS. of the Psalms, 1917; IX. I. Washington MS. of the Four Gospels, 1912; II. Washington MS. of the Epistles of Paul, 1917; XXI. Minor Prophets in the Freer Collection and Berlin Fragment of Genesis, 1927; XXXVIII. A Third Century Papyrus Codex of the Epistles of Paul, 1935; XLVIII. (P.Mich. Vol. VII.) Latin Papyri in the University of Michigan Collection, 1947. Facsimile of the Washington MS. of Deuteronomy and Joshua, 1910; Facsimile of the Washington MS. of the Four Gospels, 1912; Facsimile of the Minor Prophets in the Freer Collection and of the Berlin Fragment of Genesis, 1927; Hugo Grotius, The Law of War and Peace, translated by Francis W. Kelsey, Henry A. Sanders, and Arthur E. Boak, Carnegie Peace Foundation, Washington, 1927; Beati in Apocalipsin Libri Duodecim, Papers and Monographs of the American Academy in Rome, vol. vii, 1929. *Address:* 2037 Geddes Avenue, Ann Arbor, Michigan, U.S.A. *Clubs:* University, Golf (Ann Arbor).

[*Died* 16 *Nov.* 1956.

SMITH, Theodore Clarke; Professor of American History, Williams College, Mass., 1904-38, Emeritus since 1938; Member Mass. Hist. Soc.; *b.* 18 May 1870; *s.* of Azariah Smith and Sophia Elizabeth Van Duzer. Unmarried. *Educ.:* Roxbury Latin School, Boston, Mass.; Harvard (B.A. 1892; M.A. 1893; Ph.D. in Political Science, 1896). Assistant in History at Harvard, 1893-94; Fellow in History at University of Wisconsin, 1895; studied, as holder of a travelling fellowship from Harvard, at University of Paris, 1896-97, and University of Berlin, 1897; Instructor at University of Michigan, 1898; Instructor at Vassar College, 1899-1900; Assistant-Professor at Ohio State University, 1902-3. *Publications:* The Free Soil Party in Wisconsin, 1895; The Liberty and Free Soil Parties in the North-West, 1898; Expansion after the Civil War, 1902; Political Reconstruction, in Cambridge Modern History, vol. vii.; Politics and Slavery, 1951-59, 1906; Wars Between England and America, 1914; Life and Letters of James Abram Garfield, 1925; United States as a Factor in World History, 1941. *Address:* Williams College, Williamstown, Mass.

[*Died* 19 *Nov.* 1960.

SOUNDY, Hon. Sir John, Kt., *cr.* 1954; C.B.E. 1943; *b.* Dorchester, England, 14 November 1878; *s.* of J. T. Soundy; *m.* 1907, Edith, *d.* of Rev. George Wainwright; two *s.* five *d.* *Educ.:* Friends' School, Hobart. Lived in South Africa, 1903-7; returned to Tasmania and went into business (drapery and furnishings). Coroner to Hobart, 1911; M.H.A. for Hobart, 1925-1946; Alderman of Hobart City Council, 1917; Mayor of the City of Hobart, 1924 and 1929, elected by fellow Aldermen; first Mayor elected by Citizens, 1930-32; Lord Mayor of Hobart, 1938-46; M.L.C. 1946; J.P. Tasmania; retired from public affairs,

1952. O.St.J. *Recreations:* fishing, shooting, and bowls. *Address:* 92 Newdegate Street, Hobart, Tasmania. *T.:* Res. 31345 and Business 33268. [*Died* 25 *Oct*. 1960.

STRONG, Rev. Canon Edward Herbert, M.A., B.Litt.; Canon-Emeritus, St. Peter's Cathedral, Hamilton, N.Z., 1941; Officiating Priest, Diocese of Dunedin; *b.* Winscombe, Somerset; *s.* of late Samuel Herbert and Mary Strong; unmarried. *Educ.:* Nelson College; University College, Auckland; St. John's College, Oxford; Cuddesdon Theological College. Deacon, 1906; Priest, 1907; Assistant Curate St. Barnabas, Balsall Heath, Birmingham, 1907-8; Sub-Warden St. John's College, Auckland, 1909-14; Chaplain King's College, Auckland, 1914-19; Vice-Principal Wells Theological College, 1919-20; Archdeacon of Tonga, 1920-22; Chaplain Boys' High School, New Plymouth, N.Z., 1922-32; Vicar of St. Mary's, New Plymouth, 1927-32; Warden of St. John's College, Auckland, 1932-38; Canon of Auckland Cathedral; P. in C. Dunedin Cathedral, 1939; Rector and Canon, Rockhampton Cathedral, 1940; Member of General Synod of N.Z., 1910, 1925, 1928, 1931, 1937, 1940, 1943, 1946, 1949, 1952; Commissary to Bishop of Melanesia since 1935. *Recreations:* golf and tennis. *Address:* c/o Diocesan Office, Stuart Street, Dunedin N.Z. [*Died* 6 *Nov*. 1960.

THUMBOO CHETTY, Amatyasiromani Sir Bernard T., Kt., *cr.* 1946; O.B.E. 1935; *b.* 18 Aug 1877; *s.* of Rajadharmapravina late T. R. A. Thumboo Chetty, C.I.E.; *m.* Gertrude, *d.* of S. Rajaratna Chetty, Madras; two *d. Educ.:* St. Joseph's College and Central College, Bangalore; B.A. Madras University. Joined Mysore Civil Service, 1904, as Assistant Commissioner; Assistant Secretary to the Maharaja, 1914; Deputy Commissioner, 1921; Huzur Secretary to the Maharaja, 1922; given status of Member of Executive Council, 1929; Private Secretary to Maharaja of Mysore, 1942-49; retired, 1949. Titles of Rajasabhabhushana, 1928, and Amatyasiromani, 1942, from the Maharaja; K.S.G. 1938, K.C.S.G. 1946. *Publications:* articles on St. Philomena and other subjects in Catholic journals. *Recreations:* tennis and photography. *Address:* Alphonsa Manor, No. 6 Cunningham Road, Bangalore, India. [*Died* 20 *May* 1952.

WADDELL, Hon. Sir (Charles) Graham, K.B.E., *cr.* 1927; M.L.C., New South Wales, 1936-49; *b.* 7 Jan. 1877; *s.* of Col. G. W. Waddell, Green Hills, Adelong, N.S.W.; *m.* 1909, Alison Lyall, *d.* of G. F. Simpson, Jerilderie, N.S.W.; two *d. Educ.:* Sydney Grammar School. Pres., Graziers' Association of N.S.W., 1925-28; Chairman, Australian Woolgrowers' Council, 1925-35; Member Central Council of Country Party of New South Wales; Director: Associated Newspapers, Colonial Mutual Life Assce. Co., Union Trustee Co., F. W. Williams & Co. Pty. Ltd., Australian Sisal-Kraft Co., McGarvie Smith Institute. *Address:* Glen Iris, Bethungra, N.S.W. *Clubs:* Australian, Union, Royal Sydney Golf (Sydney); Pioneers of Australia. [*Died* 7 *April* 1960.

WALMSLEY, Ben, C.B.E. 1920; *b.* 1871; *m.* 1906, Laura W. Champernowne, *d.* of late Rev. John Willington, Fen End House, Knowle. Was a Section Director (Pig Iron), a Director Iron and Steel Contracts, and Controller Ferrous Metals, Ministry of Munitions. 1916-19. *Address:* Stone Cottage, Halse, nr. Taunton. *T.:* Bishops Lydeard 203. [*Died* 19 *Dec*. 1960.

WALTON, Lieut.-Col. Robert Henry, C.B.E. 1919; M.D., F.R.C.S.; *b.* 1877; *s.* of Richard Walton; *m.* 1925, Eva Beatrice, *er. d.* of Thos. G. Gummer, Auckland; one *s. Educ.:* Grammar School and University, Auckland; Edinburgh University. Served European War, 1914-19 (despatches, C.B.E.). *Address:* Fairmount, 625 Mount Eden Road, Auckland, N.Z. *Club:* Northern (Auckland). [*Died* 10 *Nov*. 1959.

WILLIAMS, David Davey, J.P., F.H.A.S., M.R.A.S.; *b.* 1 Jan. 1874; *s.* of Alderman D. J. Williams, J.P.; *m.* 1908; two *c. Educ.:* The Grammar School and University College, Aberystwyth. Lecturer at Aspatria Agricultural College, 1895-98; Lecturer U.C.W. Aberystwyth, 1898-1914; Divisional Live Stock Officer, Ministry of Agriculture, 1914-34; High Sheriff of Cardiganshire, 1935-36. *Publications:* Agriculture for Welsh Farmers and numerous Bulletins. *Recreations:* shooting, gardening, and golf. *Address:* Argoed Hall, Tregaron, Cardiganshire. *T.:* 21. [*Died* 5 *July* 1954.

WOODS, Walter Sainsbury, C.M.G. 1946; LL.D. (British Columbia Univ.), 1947; *b.* 16 July 1884; *s.* of W. J. Sainsbury Woods and Elizabeth Barnes (both English); *m.* 1919, Elene Fawk; two *s. Educ.:* private and grammar schools in Great Britain. Superintendent Soldier Settlement, Central Saskatchewan and Southern Alberta, 1919-30; Chairman War Veterans Allowance Board, 1930-41; Associate Deputy Minister, Dept. Pensions and National Health in Charge of Rehabilitation, 1941-44; Deputy Minister, Department of Veterans Affairs, Dominion of Canada, 1944-50. *Recreations:* reading and gardening. *Address:* 1221 Devonshire Crescent, Vancouver, British Columbia, Canada. [*Died* 11 *Nov*. 1960.

WORLEY, Frederick Palliser, M.A., M.Sc. (N.Z.); D.Sc. (London); D.I.C., F.N.Z.I.C.; Professor emeritus; *b.* Nelson, N.Z., 5 Oct. 1880; *e. s.* of William Frederick Worley; *m.* 1919, Doris, *d.* of late Walter James Payne; two *s.* one *d. Educ.:* Nelson College; Auckland Univ. College; City and Guilds (Engineering) College, South Kensington. Acting Professor of Chemistry, Auckland University College, 1907; Leathersellers' Company's Research Fellow, City and Guilds (Engineering) College, S. Kensington, 1908-12; Professor of Chemistry, Auckland Univ. Coll., 1914-48; Foundation Member, Past Pres. and Hon. Fell., N.Z. Inst. Chem.; Pioneer of modern forensic ballistics. *Publications:* various original papers to Proc. Roy. Soc. and scientific journals. *Recreations:* golf, sketching. *Address:* Hollywood Avenue, Titirangi, Auckland, New Zealand. *Club:* Northern (Auckland). [*Died* 8 *Dec*. 1960.

WRIGHT, William Hammond; Director Emeritus of Lick Observatory since 1942; *b.* 4 Nov. 1871; *s.* of Selden Stuart Wright and Joanna Shaw; *m.* 1901, Elna W. Leib. *Educ.:* San Francisco Public Schools; University of California. Assistant Astronomer, Lick Observatory, 1897-1908; in charge Lick Observatory's Expedition to the Southern Hemisphere, 1903-06, Astronomer, 1908-44, Director, 1935-42; Captain, Ordnance, U.S.A., 1918-19; Associate, Royal Astronomical Society, London (George Darwin Lectureship, 1928; annual medal, 1938); Member: National Academy; American Philosophical Society. Holds hon. degrees and various scientific medals from U.S. and Europe. *Publications:* contributions to astronomical publications. *Address:* 60 North Keeble Avenue, San José 26, Cal., U.S.A. [*Died* 16 *May* 1959.

WURTH, Wallace Charles, C.M.G. 1941; LL.B.; Chairman of Public Service Board, New South Wales, since 1939; President, now Chancellor, University of New South Wales, since 1949; President, Australian Museum; *b.* 1896. Served A.I.F. abroad in European War, 1914-

1918; Assistant Under-Secretary and Industrial Registrar, Department of Labour and Industry, New South Wales, 1932; Member, Public Service Board, 1936; Director General of Man Power (Commonwealth), 1942-44; Chm., War Commitments Cttee., 1943-44. Hon. LL.D. (Sydney). ***Address:*** **19 O'Connell Street, Sydney, New South Wales.**
[*Died* 16 *Sept*. 1960.

YATES, Lt.-Col. Donald, C.M.G., 1943; M.C.; Consulting Engineer; *b*. 27 Feb. 1893; *s*. of Thomas Yates, Adelaide; *m*. 1916, Norah, *d*. of J. H. Crowe, Adelaide; one *s*. one *d*. *Educ.:* St. Peter's School Collegiate, Adelaide; Adelaide University (B.E.); School of Mines, Adelaide (F.S.A.S.M.). Served European War, 1st Tunnelling Co., A.I.F., Capt. (M.C.); B.H.P. Pty. Ltd., Newcastle, 1919-27; B.H.A.S. Pty Ltd., Port Pirie, 1927-44; War of 1939-45; rejoined 2/A.I.F. Sept. 1942, Lt..-Col. S.O.R.E.; V.D.C. Bn. Comdr. (Home Guard), 1940-42. Sen. Mem., Australasian Institute of Mining and Metallurgy (Pres. 1937). *Recreations:* rowing, football in former years; golf and tennis. *Address:* 224 Young St., Unley, South Australia. *T:* UA 7827. *Clubs:* Adelaide, Naval and Military (Adel.).
[*Died* 22 *Nov*. 1960.

WHO WAS WHO, 1951-60

A

ABBOTT, Arthur, C.B.E. 1933; *b.* 19 June 1879; *s.* of late Robert Lamb Abbott, M.A.; *m.* 1906, Cecile, *d.* of late Abraham Auret. *Educ.:* St. Edward's, Oxford; privately. Vice- and Acting Consul at Munich, 1911; Consul at São Paulo, Brazil, 1919; Consul-General, São Paulo, 1928-39; Press Attaché, Rio de Janeiro, 1939-1941; retd., 1941. *Recreations:* golf, motoring, and travel. *Club:* Junior Carlton.
[*Died* 17 *May* 1955.

ABBOTT, Hon. Sir Charles (Arthur Hillas) Lempriere, Kt. 1960; Q.C. (Aust.); J.P.; B.A., LL.B.; Chairman, Public Libraries Board of South Australia; one of H.M. Judges of the Supreme Court of South Australia, 1944-59; *b.* Wagga Wagga, N.S.W., 31 Oct. 1889; *er. s.* of Charles Thomas Abbott, M.D., and Susie Evelyn Abbott; *m.* 1917, Gladys Rose De Lany; two *s.* one *d.* *Educ.:* Trinity School, San Francisco; University of California; University of Adelaide. Admitted to the Bar, 1914; apptd. by Univ. of California as its Representative at Jubilee Celebrations of Univ. of Adelaide, 1926. M.P. for East Torrens, 1933-38, and for Burnside, 1938-46; K.C. 1943; Attorney-General, Minister of Education, and Minister of Industry in Playford Govt., 1944-46. Chairman: Road Traffic Act Revision Cttee., 1935-36; State Traffic Cttee., 1936-44; Industries Development Cttee., 1942-44. Mem. Council of Law Society of S.A. Inc., 1925-45; Pres. Law Society, 1943-45; Mem. Statutory Cttee., 1931-44; Vice-Pres., Australian Law Council, 1944; Mem. Council, Univ. of Adelaide, 1938-44; Acting Dean of Faculty of Law, 1943-44; Pres. Australian-American Assoc., 1946-47; (twice) Pres. Aust. Lacrosse Council, 1936-39, 1953-56; Pres. S.A. Lacrosse Assoc., 1934-; Pres. Royal Life Saving Soc., 1950-. *Recreations:* reading, gardening. *Address:* Shelton, 53 Park Terrace, Parkside, South Australia. *T.:* 71.22.33. *Clubs:* Adelaide (Adelaide); Naval, Military and Air Force (Adelaide).
[*Died* 14 *Sept.* 1960.

ABBOTT, Charles Theodore; Puisne Judge, Malaya, since 1950; *o.s.* of late John Theodore Abbott, F.R.C.S., and late Mrs. W. E. Reynolds; *step-s.* of late Dr. William Edward Reynolds, M.D.; *m.* 1921, Constance Mary, *o. d.* of late W. W. Smithett, F.G.S.; one *s.* *Educ.:* Portora Royal School, Enniskillen. Able Seaman, Royal Navy, 1914-15; Lieut., The Middlesex Regiment, 1915-19; India, Mesopotamia, Salonika; called to Bar, Gray's Inn, 1921; Crown Counsel and Resident Magistrate, Kenya Colony and Protectorate, 1930; President, District Court, Cyprus, 1932; Solicitor-General, Sierra Leone, 1938; acted as Chief Justice of Aden in 1940-41; Puisne Judge, Nigeria, 1944-50; acted as Chief Justice of Malaya, 1951; member of the Central Criminal Court, and South Eastern Circuit; a foundation member of Haldane Club. *Address:* c/o Supreme Court, Kuala Lumpur, Malaya.
[*Died* 13 *Jan.* 1956.

ABBOTT, Percival William Henry, B.A. (Lond.); *b.* 7 June 1869; *s.* of J. S. Abbott; *m.* Isobel M. Lucy; one *d.* *Educ.:* privately; London University. Mathematical master, The Polytechnic, and Head of the Mathematical Dept., 1895-1919; Headmaster, Polytechnic School, Regent Street, W.1, 1919-34; Member I.A.H.M.; formerly Hon. Secretary and President, Association of Teachers in Technical Institutions; Member Consultative Committee; Board of Education, 1920-26; Member Secondary Schools Examination Council, 1916-28; Member Teachers' Registration Council and Chairman of Technical Section, 1912-26; Leader of the Technical Panel, Burnham Committee, 1919-22; formerly Hon. Secretary of the Teaching Committee, Mathematical Association. *Publications:* Mathematical Tables and Formulae, 1918; Numerical Trigonometry, 1918; Exercises in Arithmetic and Mensuration, 1913; National Certificate Mathematics (3 vols.), 1938; Teach yourself Trigonometry, 1940; Teach yourself Mechanics, 1941; Teach yourself Algebra, 1942; Teach yourself Calculus, 1946; Teach Yourself Geometry, 1947. Editor Technical College Series. Formerly Editor, The Technical Journal. *Recreations:* music, travel. *Address:* West Winds, Church Lane, Sarratt, Herts. *T.:* Kings Langley 7844. [*Died* 29 *Jan.* 1954.

ABELL, Lt.-Col. Robert Lloyd, D.S.O. 1919; M.C.; *b.* 1889; *s.* of late G. F. Abell, J.P. of Grafton Manor, Bromsgrove, Worcestershire. *Educ.:* Repton. Formerly Major Royal Field Artillery; served European War, 1914-19 (thrice wounded, despatches, M.C., D.S.O., Italian Croix de Guerre); Royal Artillery and General Staff, 1940-46. *Recreations:* hunting, shooting. *Address:* Foxcote Manor, Andoversford, Glos. *T.:* Andoversford 223.
[*Died* 2 *Feb.* 1957.

ABELL, Thomas Bertrand, O.B.E. 1920; M.Eng. (Liv.); R.C.N.C., retired; *b.* March 1880; 2nd *s.* of Thomas Abell, M.B.E., J.P.; *m.* Gertrude (*d.* 1930), *d.* of late Edwin F. Brook. *Educ.:* West Buckland School; Royal Naval Engineering College, Devonport; Royal Naval College, Greenwich. Appointed to Royal Corps of Naval Constructors, 1903; Admiralty Experiment Tank, 1904-8; Instructor in Naval Architecture, Royal Naval College, 1910-14; Lecturer at Royal Naval War College, Portsmouth. Temporary Constructor, Admiralty, 1916; Assistant Director of Designs, Admiralty, and Ministry of Shipping, 1917-19; Professor of Naval Architecture, University of Liverpool, 1914-40; Pro-Vice-Chancellor, 1935-40; Professor Emeritus, 1940; Vice-President Inst. Naval Architects, 1940; Portreeve of Ashburton, 1943-44. *Publications:* Stability and Seaworthiness of Ships; papers on subjects relating to Naval Architecture. *Address:* Priestaford House, Ashburton, Devon. *T.:* Ashburton 336. [*Died* 26 *July* 1956.

ABEND, Hallett; book and magazine writer and lecturer on international affairs; *b.* 15 Sept. 1884; *s.* of Alexander Abend and Kittie Hallett; unmarried. *Educ.:* University of Illinois; Stanford University, California. Began newspaper work at

Spokane, 1906; bought farm in B.C., 1912; City Editor Star-Bulletin, Honolulu, 1915; Managing Editor Idaho Daily Statesman, 1916; City Editor Los Angeles Times, and Editor Preview, motion picture weekly, 1920. Two years with Norma and Constance Talmage, working on screen stories. Went to China, for North American Newspaper Alliance, 1926; chief of Far East Bureau, in China, for New York Times, 1927-41; since then, free lancer; now makes home on farm in New York State, in house built 1776. *Publications:* Tortured China, 1930; Can China Survive?, 1936; Chaos in Asia, 1939; Japan Unmasked, 1941; Ramparts of the Pacific, 1942; My Life in China, 1943; Pacific Charter, 1943; Treaty Ports, 1944; Reconquest, its Results and Responsibilities, 1946; The God from the West (Biog. of Frederick Townsend Ward), 1947; Half Slave Half Free, 1949; Contributor, Saturday Evening Post, Reader's Digest, American Mercury, Cosmopolitan, Coronet, etc. *Recreations:* trout fishing, golf, gardening. *Address:* R.F.D., Buskirk, New York, U.S.A. *T.A.:* Abend, Buskirk, New York. *T.:* Cambridge 3745. *Clubs:* Spokane (Washington); Shanghai (Shanghai); Peking (Peking); Nanking (Nanking); Seekingjao Golf; Hungjao Golf.
[*Died* 27 *Nov.* 1955.

ABERCONWAY, 2nd Baron, *cr.* 1911, of Bodnant in the county of Denbigh, **Henry Duncan McLaren,** Bt., *cr.* 1902; C.B.E. 1918; LL.D. 1949; J.P. Denbighshire, Chairman Quarter Sessions; Hon. A.R.I.B.A.; Chm.: John Brown Ltd., Tredegar Iron and Coal Co., Ltd., Yorkshire Amalgamated Collieries, Sheepbridge Coal and Iron Co. Ltd., English Clays Lovering Pochin & Co.; a director: National Provincial Bank; London Assurance; *b.* 16 April 1879; *e. s.* of 1st Baron and Laura, Lady of Grace of Order of St. John of Jerusalem, C.B.E. (*d.* 1933), *o. d.* of late Henry Pochin, M.P., Bodnant, Denbighshire; *S.* father 1934; *m.* 1910, Christabel, *y. d.* of late Sir Melville Macnaghten, C.B.; two *s.* two *d.* (and one *s.* decd.). *Educ.:* Eton (Captain of the Oppidans, 1897-98); Balliol Coll., Oxford. Barrister of Lincoln's Inn; M.P. (L.) West Staffs., 1906-10; (C.L.) Bosworth Division, Leicester, 1910-22; Parliamentary Private Secretary to the Chancellor of the Exchequer, 1908-10; President of the Royal Horticultural Society since 1931. *Recreations:* shooting, gardening, motoring. *Heir: s.* Hon. Charles Melville McLaren. *Address:* Bodnant, Tal-y-cafn, Denbighshire. *T.:* Tynygroes 200; 12 North Audley St., W.1. *T.:* Grosvenor 3320. *Club:* Brooks's.
[*Died* 23 *May* 1953.

ABERCORN, 3rd Duke of (*cr.* 1868), **James Albert Edward Hamilton;** K.G. 1928; P.C. 1945; K.P. 1923; P.C. (N.I.), 1922; Royal Victorian Chain, 1945; Baron of Paisley, 1587; Baron Abercorn, 1603; Baron Hamilton and Earl of Abercorn, 1606; Baron of Strabane, 1617; Viscount of Strabane, 1701; Viscount Hamilton, 1786; Marquess of Abercorn, 1790; Marquess of Hamilton, 1868; *b.* 30 Nov. 1869; *s.* of 2nd Duke and Lady Mary Anna Curzon, *d.* of 1st Earl Howe; *S.* father, 1913; *m.* 1894, Lady Rosalind Cecilia Caroline Bingham, D.B.E., *cr.* 1936, *o. d.* of 4th Earl of Lucan; two *s.* three *d.* *Educ.:* Eton. Treasurer to H.M. Household, 1903-05; M.P. (U.) City Londonderry, 1900-13; entered army, 1st Life Guards, 1892; resigned, 1903; late Major North Irish Horse; Lord-Lieut. of Tyrone since 1917; a Senator of Northern Ireland, 1921; Governor of Northern Ireland, 1922-45. *Heir: s.* Marquess of Hamilton. *Address:* 68 Mount Street, W.1. *T.:* Grosvenor 1014; Barons Court, Co. Tyrone, Ireland. *Club:* Carlton.
[*Died* 12 *Sept.* 1953.

ABERCORN, Dowager Duchess of (Rosalind Cecilia Caroline), D.B.E., *cr.* 1936; LL.D.; *b.* 26 Feb. 1869; *o. d.* of 4th Earl of Lucan, K.P.; *m.* 1894, as Lady Rosalind Bingham, 3rd Duke of Abercorn, K.G., K.P., P.C. (*d.* 1953); two *s.* three *d.* *Educ.:* privately. Hon. LL.D. (Belfast). *Address:* 44 Mount Street, W.1. *T.:* Grosvenor 1014. *Club:* Ladies' Empire.
[*Died* 18 *Jan.* 1958.

ABERCROMBIE, Sir John Robertson, K.B.E., *cr.* 1946; Kt., *cr.* 1935; M.C.; retired; *b.* 11 June 1888; *s.* of Alexander and Emily Constance de Laurensart Abercrombie; *m.* 1915, Elsie Maude, *d.* of E. W. Collin, I.C.S.; (one *s.* decd.). *Educ.:* Cheltenham College. Served with 18th. K.G.O. Lancers in France and Palestine (despatches, M.C.); Pres. Bombay Chamber of Commerce, 1930 and 1935; Chairman Bombay Branch European Association, 1931-32, 1934; Member Bombay Legislative Council, 1925-26, 1930-31. *Recreations:* golf and fishing. *Address:* 201 Raleigh House, Dolphin Sq., S.W.1. *Club:* Flyfishers'.
[*Died* 11 *Sept.* 1960.

ABERCROMBIE, Sir (Leslie) Patrick, Kt., *cr.* 1945; M.A.; Hon. D.Lit., LL.D.; F.R.I.B.A., F.S.A.; Professor Emeritus of Town Planning in the University of London; Hon. Fellow of St. Catharine's College, Cambridge; Officier de la Couronne, of Belgium; Member of Royal Commission on the Location of Industry; Chairman of C.P.R.E.; Chm. of Housing Centre; Pres., International Union of Architects; Pres. Franco-British Union of Architects; *b.* 1879; *s.* of late William Abercrombie; *m.* Emilia Maud (*d.* 1942), *d.* of Robert Gordon; one *s.* one *d.* *Educ.:* Uppingham. Professor of Civic Design, University of Liverpool, 1915-35; Professor of Town Planning, University College, London, 1935-46; Past President of Town Planning Institute; ex-Mem. Royal Fine Art Commission. Won first premium (in partnership with Sydney A. Kelly, F.S.I.) in international competition for replanning Dublin, 1913. Present consultant to Dublin Corporation. Prepared post-war schemes for rebuilding and planning London (L.C.C. and Greater), Edinburgh, Plymouth, Hull, Warwick, Bournemouth, the Clyde and W. Midlands Regions; architect (with A. C. Holliday) for the new University of Ceylon; reports for Colonial Office on Hong Kong and Cyprus. Howard Memorial Medal, 1943; Royal Gold Medal for Architecture, 1946; Gold Medal of American Institute of Architects, 1949. *Publications:* Reports and Plans on the following Regions and Towns: Doncaster (with T. H. Johnson); East Kent Coalfield (with J. Archibald); East Suffolk, Sheffield District and Cumberland (with S. A. Kelly); Cærnarvonshire; Bath and Bristol (with B. F. Brueton); Stratford-on-Avon (with Lascelles Abercrombie). Sheffield Civic Survey; Dublin of the Future (with S. A. Kelly); County of London Plan, 1943 (with J. H. Forshaw); Greater London; A Plan for Plymouth, 1943 (with J. Paton-Watson); Edinburgh (with D. R. Plumstead); Clyde Valley (with R. H. Matthew); Hull (with Sir Edwin Lutyens); Town and Country Planning (Home Univ. Library); the Preservation of Rural England. *Address:* Red House, Aston Tirrold, Berks; Penrhos Bach, Holy Island, Anglesey. *T.:* Blewbury, Berks 207. *Club:* Brooks's.
[*Died* 23 *March* 1957.

ABERDARE, 3rd Baron (*cr.* 1873), of Duffryn, **Clarence Napier Bruce;** G.B.E. *cr.* 1954 (C.B.E. 1949); *b.* 2 Aug. 1885; *e. surv. s.* of 2nd Baron and Constance Mary (*d.* 1932), *d.* of Hamilton Beckett and Hon. Mrs. Beckett, 2nd *d.* of Lord Lyndhurst; *S.* father, 1929; *m.* 1912, Margaret Bethune (Betty) (*d.* 1950), *o. d.* of late Adam Black; two *s.* two *d.*; *m.* 1957, Griselda, *d.* of late Dudley Hervey, Aldeburgh. *Educ.:* Winchester; New Coll., Oxford (B.A.). Called to Bar, Inner Temple,

1911; Capt. 2/1 Glamorgan Yeo.; Lieut. (temp.) 2nd Life Guards; later 2nd Batt. Guards Machine Gun Regt.; demobilised with rank of Capt., 1919; Major 11th Batt. Surrey Home Guard, 1940-45. Chairman of late National Advisory Council for physical training and recreation, 1937-39; Member of National Youth Cttee., Board of Education, 1939-42; Member Miners Welfare Commission, 1931-46; Hon. Col. 77th (Welsh) A.A. Bde. R.A. (T.), now 282 (Welsh) Heavy A.A. Regt. R.A., T.A., 1930-52. President: Welsh National School of Medicine, Univ. of Wales; Lansdowne Club, Five Million Club, 1942-51; British Prisoners of War (Books and Games) Funds, 1941-46; Junior Lawn Tennis Club, 1937-55; New College Society, 1952-54; Sixth British Empire and Commonwealth Games, 1958. Hon. Adviser J. A. Rank Org. on Children's Cinema Clubs, 1948. Prior of Order of St. John of Jerusalem (Priory for Wales). Chairman: Nat. Assoc. of Boys' Clubs; British Sportsman's Club; Fortnightly Review, Ltd., 1938-55; International Congress on Physical Education (1948); Queen's Club Ltd., 1926-54; Queen's Institute of District Nursing. Member: Joint Committee Order of St. John of Jerusalem and B.R.C.S.; International Olympic Committee (Exec. 1931-51), National Trust and Standing Conf. of Nat. Voluntary Youth Organisations; Executive of Army Cadet Force Assoc., British Olympic Assoc., Central Council of Physical Recreation, and Organising Cttee. for Olympic Games, London, 1948, National Playing Fields Assoc. (Mem. Council), Research Board for Correlation of Medical Science and Physical Recreation, Standing Cttee. on National Parks, Academic Advisory Council F.O. (German Section), 1949, Independent Television Authority, 1954-56. Hon. LL.D. Wales, 1953. K.St.J. *Publications:* First Steps to Rackets (with E. B. Noel), 1926; (Editor) Rackets, Squash Rackets, Tennis, Fives and Badminton, 1933 and contributor to Chambers's Encyclopædia of Sport, Tennis, Rackets and Squash Rackets, and to Encyclopædia Britannica, Tennis and Rackets. *Recreations:* cricket, rackets (Amateur Champion, 1922 and 1931; 10 times Doubles Champion, and Champion of U.S.A. Doubles, 1928, 1930; Singles Champion of Canada, 1928, 1930, and Doubles Champion of Canada, 1930; Open Champion, British Isles, 1931); tennis (Amateur Champion, U.S.A., 1930, British Isles, 1932 and 1938); 3 times winner of Inter-Club Tennis Doubles (Bailey Cup) for Queen's Club; 5 times winner of M.C.C. Gold Prize, and 9 times winner of M.C.C. Silver Prize; 18 times representative of Great Britain in the Bathurst Cup, 6 times winner of Coupe de Paris), golf, shooting, and lawn tennis. *Heir: s.* Capt. (temp. Major) Hon. Morys George Lyndhurst Bruce [Welsh Guards, 1940; H.Q. 12th Corps, 1944; *b.* 16 June 1919; *m.* 1946, Sarah, *o. d.* of Sir John Dashwood, 10th Bt.; two *s.* *Educ.:* Winchester; New College, Oxford]. *Address:* Danescross, Hook Heath, Woking. *T.:* Woking 508. *Clubs:* Hampton Court Royal Tennis, Lansdowne (Chm.), M.C.C.

[*Died* 4 *Oct.* 1957.

ABERGAVENNY, 4th Marquess of (*cr.* 1876); **Major Guy Temple Montacute Larnach-Nevill;** Baron Abergavenny, 1450; Earl of Abergavenny and Viscount Nevill, 1784; Earl of Lewes, 1876; D.L., J.P.; Director of Sun Insurance Office Ltd. and Sun Life Assurance Society; *b.* 15 July 1883; *s.* of late Lord George Montacute Nevill and Florence Mary, C.B.E. (*d.* 1929), *d.* of late Temple Soames; *S.* uncle, 1938; *m.* 1909, Isabel Nellie (*d.* 1953), *d.* of late James Walker Larnach, and late Lady Isabel Larnach, *d.* of 9th Earl of Cork and Orrery; two *s.* one *d.* *Heir: s.* Earl of Lewes. *Address:* Eridge Castle, Tunbridge Wells; 10 Lowndes Square, S.W.1. *T.:* Sloane 7486. *Clubs:* Turf, Buck's.

[*Died* 29 *March* 1954.

ABRAHALL, Bennet; *see* Hoskyns-Abrahall.

ABRAHAM, Ashley Perry; photographic artist, journalist and lecturer; *b.* Keswick, 20 Feb. 1876; *m.* 1902; three *s.* one *d.* *Educ.:* Blackman's School. Pioneer of mountaineering photography, discoverer of many new rock and snow climbs in English Lakeland, Wales, Scotland and Switzerland; authority on rock-climbing and mountaineering; First President Fell and Rock-climbing Club. *Publications:* Rock-climbing in Skye; Rock-climbing in North Wales; Beautiful Lakeland; Beautiful North Wales; The Lake Poets; various magazine and Press articles. *Recreations:* mountaineering, golf, swimming, billiards and chess (Cumberland County Chess Champion, 1932 and 1939). *Address:* The Screes, Keswick, Cumberland. *Clubs:* Fell and Rock; English Climbers; several golf.

[*Died* 9 *Oct.* 1951.

ABRAHAM, Edgar Gaston Furtado, C.B. 1920; I.C.S. Punjab Commission, retired; *b.* 1880; *m.* Ruth, *d.* of Rev. Gerald S. Davies, late The Master of The Charterhouse, London; one *s.* *Educ.:* St. Paul's School; Corpus Christi Coll., Oxford. Entered I.C.S. Punjab Commission, 1904; served European War in France, R.G.A.; Asst. Secretary, War Cabinet, Jan. 1918; Supreme War Council, Versailles, May 1918, and Supreme Council Peace Conference, Jan. 1919-20. *Address:* Mangerton House, Nr. Bridport, Dorset. *T.:* Powerstock 217.

[*Died* 17 *Feb.* 1955.

ABRAHAM, Rt. Rev. Philip Selwyn; Bishop of Newfoundland since 1942; *b.* Lichfield, 29 July 1897; 5th *s.* of late Charles Thomas Abraham; *m.* 1923, Elizabeth Dorothy Cicely, *o. d.* of late Sir John Marriott; three *s.* one *d.* *Educ.:* Eton College (King's Scholar); New College, Oxford. Commissioned Service in 35th Division R.A., France, 1915-19, Captain R.A. IV Corps; Deacon, 1922; Priest, 1923; Curate of Daybrook, Notts, 1922-25; Curate of S. Mary Redcliffe, Bristol, and Chaplain to Bristol Division, R.N.V.R., 1925-28; Precentor of Quebec Cathedral, 1928-31; Vicar of Romford, Essex, and Member of Essex C.C. Education Committee, representing Oxford University, 1931-37; Coadjutor Bishop of Newfoundland, 1937-42. *Address:* Bishopscourt, St. John's, Newfoundland. *T.:* 3887. [*Died* 22 *Dec.* 1955.

ABRAHAMS, Rt. Hon. Sir Sidney Solomon, P.C. 1941; Kt., *cr.* 1936; Member of Judicial Cttee. of Privy Council since 1941; Senior Legal Assistant, Commonwealth Relations Office and Colonial Office; *b.* Birmingham, 11 Feb. 1885; *s.* of Isaac Abrahams; *m.* 1914, Ruth, *d.* of late L. G. Bowman, one *s.* one *d.* *Educ.:* Bedford Modern School. Emmanuel College, Cambridge, B.A., LL.B., 1906. Barrister-at-law, Middle Temple, 1909; Hon. Bencher, 1948; Town Magistrate, Zanzibar, 1915; seconded to Mesopotamia Civil Administration, 1920; Advocate-General, Baghdad, 1920; President, Civil Courts, Basrah, 1921; Attorney-General, Zanzibar, 1922; Uganda, 1925; Gold Coast, 1928; Chief Justice of Uganda Protectorate, 1933-34; Vice-President, H.M. Court of Appeal for Eastern Africa; Chief Justice, Tanganyika, 1934-36; Chief Justice of Ceylon, 1936-39; Order of Brilliant Star of Zanzibar, Second Class, 1924; K.C. for the Gold Coast, 1930. *Publications:* edited (with A. Abrahams) Dagens Nyheter Stadion Edition, 1912; various contributions to journalism on track Athletics and legal subjects. *Recreations:* Represented Cambridge against Oxford in long jump, 1904, 5, and 6, and in 100 yds., 1906; represented Great Britain in Olympic Games, Athens, 1906, in 100 metres and long jump, and at Stockholm 1912 in long jump; Amateur Long Jump Champion, 1913; Pres. London Athletic Club, 1947-48; Hon. Legal

Adviser, Amateur Athletic Association. *Address:* 5 Pump Court, Temple, E.C.4. *T.:* Central 5711. *Clubs:* Royal Empire Society, London Athletic, Achilles.
[*Died* 14 *May* 1957.

ACHARYA, Sir Vijaya Ragahava, K.B.E., *cr.* 1926, Diwan Bahadur; Member Indian Legislative Assembly, Delhi, 1925; *b.* Karur, Southern India, 1875; *m.* Janaki Ammal of Kodavasal; one *s.* three *d.* *Educ.:* Presidency College, Madras. Entered the Madras Civil Service, 1898; served as District Officer till 1912; on the Madras City Corporation. 1912-17; Secretary to Board of Revenue and Deputy Director of Industries, 1917-19; organised the Madras Exhibitions of 1915 and 1917; Diwan (Prime Minister) of Cochin State, 1919-1922; Comr. for India at Wembley, 1922-25; Director of Industries, Madras, 1926; Member, Public Service Commission, India, 1926; Vice-President of Agricultural Research Council of India, 1929-35; opened Canadian National Exhibition, Toronto, 1926; Prime Minister, Udaipur, 1940-47; Chairman F.A.O. Forestry Conference for Asia and the Pacific, Mysore, 1949. *Recreations:* conversation and travel. *Address:* Riverside, Adyar, Madras, India. *Clubs:* National Liberal, British Empire, Overseas; London and Cosmopolitan (Madras). [*Died* 28 *Feb.* 1953.

ACHESON, Andrew Basil, C.M.G. 1942; C.B.E. 1958; H.M. Civil Service, retd.; *b.* 8 January 1895; *s.* of late John Fleetwood Acheson; *m.* 1920, Barbara, *o. d.* of Ramos and Kate Appleyard, Harrogate, Yorks. *Educ.:* Dulwich College; Keble College, Oxford (Scholar). Entered Colonial Office, 1920; Private Secretary to Permanent Under-Secretary, 1923; Principal, 1926; Assistant Secretary, 1938; Assistant Secretary, Offices of the Cabinet, 1948-57. *Recreations:* fishing, photography. *Address:* 22 Beech Grove, Harrogate, Yorkshire.
[*Died* 12 *May* 1959.

ACHESON, Hon. Patrick (George Edward Cavendish-), D.S.O. 1915; M.V.O. 1904; Captain R.N., retired; *b.* 30 June 1883; 2nd *s.* of 4th Earl of Gosford; *m.* 1915, Norah, *d.* of Alfred Jones, Halifax, Canada; (two *s.* killed in action, 1941 and 1944 respectively) one *d.* Served European War, 1914-18 (D.S.O. for distinguished conduct on H.M.S. Inflexible when struck by a mine at the Dardanelles); in command Rhine Flotilla, Cologne, 1919-1921; retired list, 1922. Croix de Guerre avec Palme, 1915. *Address:* 38 The Avenue, Branksome Park, Bournemouth, Hants. *Club:* United Service.
[*Died* 30 *Aug.* 1957.

ACKERLEY, Rev. Frederick George; *b.* Mitton, Yorks, 12 Nov. 1871; *s.* of Rev. George Biglands Ackerley, vicar of Mitton, and Patty Elizabeth, *d.* of Frederick Oxley, Liverpool; *m.* 1902, Vera Mary (*d.* 1947), *d.* of Charles James Hill, H.B.M. Vice-Consul, Libau, Russia; no *c.*; *m.* 1948, Phyllis (*née* Ray), *widow* of Fred Ransley. *Educ.:* Rossall School; Jesus College, Oxford, M.A. Deacon, 1897; Priest, 1898; Curate of Keighley, 1897; of Eccles, nr. Manchester, 1898; of Washington, Durham, 1899; Chaplain to British residents at Libau, 1901; Vicar of Grindleton, near Clitheroe, 1905-25; Vicar of Mitton, 1925-29; Rector of Carleton-in-Craven, 1929-36; Vicar of Mitton, 1936-1945; a Surrogate in the Diocese of Bradford, Rural Dean of Bolland, 1920-29; Hon. Canon, Bradford Cathedral, 1921; Canon Emeritus, 1951; Archdeacon of Bradford, 1932-34; Archdeacon of Craven, 1934-49. Editor, Journal of Gypsy Lore Society, 1935; Prolocutor of Lower House, York Convocation, 1936-43; F.R.S.A. 1936; D.D. (Lambeth) 1943. *Publications:* A Rumanian Manual, 1916; History of Mitton, 1948; contributions to Journal of Gypsy Lore Society. *Recreation:* learning languages. *Address:* Westfield, Waddington, Clitheroe. *T.:* Clitheroe 21. [*Died* 21 *Oct.* 1954.

ACLAND, F. A.; *b.* Bridgwater, England, 1861; *m.* 1888, Elizabeth Adair, Toronto; one *s.* one *d.* *Educ.:* Bridgwater. Engaged in journalism, various cities England, United States, Canada, 1880-90; Assistant Editor Globe, Toronto, Ont., 1890-1902; various literary work, London, Philadelphia, and Western Canada, 1902-7; Secretary Dept. of Labour, 1907; Deputy Minister of Labour for Canada, 1908-23; King's Printer, 1921; retired 1933; was also charged as registrar with administration of Industrial Disputes Investigation Act 1907, commonly known as Lemieux Act; represented Government of Canada at meetings in Paris and London, 1920, Copenhagen and Stockholm, 1921, and Geneva, 1924, of Governing Body of International Labour Office. *Address:* c/o Bank of Montreal, Ottawa, Canada.
[*Died* 1 *Sept.* 1950.
[*But death not notified in time for inclusion in Who Was Who 1941–1950, first edn.*

ACLAND, Col. Sir Hugh Thomas Dyke, Kt., *cr.* 1933; C.M.G. 1917; C.B.E. 1919; F.R.C.S.; F.R.A.C.S.; Assistant Director of Medical Services, Southern Military District, New Zealand, 1940-48, retd.; Hon. Consulting Surgeon to Christchurch Hospital; *b.* 10 Sep. 1874; *s.* of late Hon. John Barton Arundel Acland and Emily Weddell, *d.* of Most Rev. H. J. C. Harper, D.D., Primate of New Zealand and Bishop of Christchurch, N.Z.; *m.* 1903, Evelyn Mary, *d.* of late J. L. Ovans, East Sheen; three *s.* one *d.* *Educ.:* Christ's College, Christchurch, N.Z.; Otago University; St. Thomas's Hospital, London. Served South African War, 1900-1; European War, 1914-18; Consulting Surgeon, N.Z.E.F., 1916-19 (despatches, C.M.G.); Hon. Surgeon to Governor-General, 1930-35; a member of Christchurch City Council, 1936-41. *Address:* 51 Brown's Road, Christchurch, N.1, New Zealand.
[*Died* 15 *April* 1956.

ACLAND, Rt. Rev. Richard Dyke, M.A.; *b.* 1881; *y. s.* of late Rev. H. D. Acland, M.A. *Educ.:* Bedford School; Keble College, Oxford; Cuddesdon College. Deacon, 1905; Priest, 1906; Curate St. Mary's, Slough, 1905-10; Missionary S.P.G. Ahmednagar, Kolhapur, Dapoli, Bombay, 1911-29; Bishop of Bombay, 1929-47. Kaisar-i-Hind Gold Medal, 1947. *Publications:* Bombay Verses; Bible Readings and Prayers for Every Day in Lent; Suggested Lectionary for Sundays; Ninety-Four Collects for the Christian Year; Private Prayers (A Communicant's Manual); So Great a Cloud (Notes on the Minor SS. and Holy Days). *Recreations:* fishing, sketching, botany, and birds. *Address:* 15 Ashley Road, Taunton.
[*Died* 4 *Jan.* 1954.

ACLAND, Rev. Theodore William Gull, M.A., A.R.I.C.; Hon. Curate, St. Luke, Stanmore, Winchester, since 1955; Member The Council, Missions to Seamen; Member Board: Church Army; Christian Evidence Society; St. Thomas's Hospital's representative on Governing Body of St. Olave's and St. Saviour's Grammar School Foundation; Member Standing Committee, National Society; *b.* London, 7 November 1890; *o. s.* of late Theodore Dyke Acland, M.D., Oxon., F.R.C.P., and Caroline Cameron Gull, *g.s.* of Sir Henry Acland, Bt., M.D., F.R.S., and of Sir William Gull, Bt., M.D., F.R.S.; *m.* 1944, Mary Maxwell, *y. d.* of late Robert Maxwell Moffat, M.D. *Educ.:* Gresham's School, Holt; King's Coll., Cambridge (Exhibitioner); Univ. of Berlin. 1st Cl. Nat. Sci. Tripos, Part I, 1912; 1st Cl. Nat. Sci. Tripos (Chemistry), Part II, 1913; Commission, London Electrical En-

ACKERMANN, Gerald. See page xxvii.

gineers, 1914; seconded for technical duties with Department of Explosives Supplies and subsequently with Munitions Inventions Dept., 1915; on technical staff of Brunner, Mond & Co., 1920-22, and of Garton & Co., 1922-23; Asst. Master, Stowe School, Buckingham, 1923-30; House Master, 1924-30; Headmaster of King Edward VI School, Norwich, 1930-43; Member Court of Governors, St. Thomas's Hosp., 1931-48, and of Grand Cttee., 1945-; Hon. Secretary, Clergy Widows' Fund (London Diocese), and Diocesan Officer, 1944-46; Member: Standing Cttee., S.P.C.K., 1946-52; Board of Governors, Univs. Fed. for Animal Welfare, 1946-1951; Council, S. Katharine's Training College, Tottenham, 1945-48; London Diocesan Conference, 1946-49; Cent. Advisory Council of Training for the Ministry, 1943-1953; Cent. Council for Women's Church Work, 1948-53; Mem. Council of Bishops' Coll., Cheshunt, 1946-59; ordained Deacon, 1953; Priest, 1957; Hon. Curate, St. Bartholomew, Hyde, Winchester, 1953-55. *Recreation:* travelling. *Address:* Becton Lodge, Bereweeke Road, Winchester. *T.:* Winchester 5679. *Clubs:* Athenæum, Royal Commonwealth Society.
[*Died* 13 *Oct.* 1960.

ADAM, Mrs. George (H. Pearl); *b.* 25 Apr. 1882; *d.* of late J. A. Humphry and late Mrs. Humphry, Madge of Truth; *m.* 1909, George Jefferys Adam (*d.* 1930). *Educ.:* privately. Started journalism at age of seventeen; contributor to Truth, Fortnightly Review, Observer, Farmers' Weekly, Textile trade papers, Home and Country, Sunday Times, Radio Times, Girls' Own Paper, etc. *Publications:* International Cartoons of the War, 1916; Paris Sees it Through, 1919; (with G. J. Adam) A Book about Paris, 1927; Kitchen Ranging, 1929; British Leather: A Record of Achievement, 1946. *Address:* 2E Oxford and Cambridge Mansions, Marylebone Road, N.W.1. *T.:* Paddington 4305.
[*Died* 2 *Jan.* 1957.

ADAM, John Hunter, C.I.E. 1933; C.B.E. 1946 (O.B.E. 1918); *b.* 1 June 1882; *s.* of William Adam and Jane Blane; *m.* 1910, Mary Dorothy Burman; one *s.* one *d.* *Educ.:* Glasgow. Joined Indian Police, 1902; Inspector General of Police, North West Frontier Province, 1930-35; Lieut.-Colonel G.S. (T.A.R.O. Sp. List), 1939; Col. 1943; retired Dec. 1945. *Club:* East India and Sports. [*Died* 9 *July* 1958.

ADAMI, Sir Leonard Christian, Kt., *cr.* 1929; Indian Civil Service, retired; *b.* 15 Mar. 1874; *s.* of late John George Adami and Mrs. S. A. E. Adami, of Ashton-on-Mersey, Cheshire; *m.* 1899, Elisabeth Shaw, *d.* of late Graham Hardie Thomson, of Glasgow; one *s.* *Educ.:* St. Edmund's School, Hunstanton; Cheltenham College (Scholar); Jesus College, Cambridge (Scholar); Second Class Classical Tripos, 1895, B.A.; passed into the Indian Civil Service 1896; Assistant Magistrate at Dacca and Bhagalpur in the Province of Bengal; Secretary to the Bengal Council and Assistant Secretary in the Legislative Department, Government of Bengal, 1904-8; District Judge, Cuttack, 1909; Superintendent and Remembrancer of Legal Affairs to the Government of Bihar and Orissa, 1913-17; a Puisne Judge of the High Court at Patna, Bihar and Orissa, India, 1919-31; retired, 1931. *Address:* Devonshire House, Shortlands, Kent. *T.:* Ravensbourne 0300. *Clubs:* Royal Empire; United Service (Calcutta).
[*Died* 23 *March* 1952.

ADAMIC, Louis; Writer; *b.* 23 March 1899; *s.* of Anton and Ana Adamic, Slovenian peasants; *m.* 1931, Stella Sanders, New York; no *c.* *Educ.:* formal education ended in second year of Gymnasium in Ljubljana, Slovenia (then in Austria). Came to U.S. as 14½-year-old immigrant, 1913; worked at odd jobs in N.Y. until 1917 when joined U.S. Army and served beyond end of European War until 1919. Worked in coal mines, steel factories, etc., on farms, docks and ships till late 1920's, roving about U.S. and other parts of the world, reading in libraries between jobs. Began to write in English late 1920's, publishing stories and narratives in H. L. Mencken's American Mercury from 1928. Member of several American associations. Order of National Unity, Yugoslavia, 1944. *Publications:* Dynamite, 1931; Laughing in the Jungle, 1932 (awarded Guggenheim Fellowship to spend a year in Yugoslavia); The Native's Return, 1934; Grandsons, 1935; Cradle of Life, 1936; The House in Antigua, 1937; My America, 1938; From Many Lands, 1940; Two-Way Passage, 1941; What's Your Name?, 1942; My Native Land, 1944; A Nation of Nations, 1945; Dinner at the White House, 1946; The Eagle and the Root, 1950. *Recreations:* working on his farm, walking. *Address:* Mountain View Farm, Milford, N.J., U.S.A.
[*Died* 4 *Sept.* 1951.

ADAMS, 1st Baron, *cr.* 1949, of Ennerdale; **John Jackson Adams,** O.B.E. 1944; J.P. 1934; M.A. (h.c.) Durham 1948; Director and General Manager (Vice-Chairman 1950), West Cumberland Industrial Development Co. Ltd., Whitehaven, since 1937; *b.* 12 Oct. 1890; *m.* 1914, Agnes, *o. d.* of T. Birney; (one *s.* decd.). *Educ.:* Arlecdon Council School. Chairman, Arlecdon and Frizington U.D.C., 1919-23; Chairman, Workington Borough Health and Education Committees, 1923-31; Alderman, Cumberland County Council, 1931-; Secretary, Cumberland Development Council Ltd., 1935-; Chairman, Health Committee, Cumberland County Council, 1942-48; Chairman of Governors, Whitehaven Grammar School, 1942-; Member of the B.B.C. Advisory Panel, N.W. Area, 1944-49; Dep. Regiona Controller, Board of Trade (Cumberland and Westmorland Sub Region), 1944-48; Mem. N. Regional Gas Bd., 1949-; N. & C. Div. Nat. Coal Bd., 1950-54. *Recreations:* football, reading. *Heir:* none. *Address:* Wybrow Terr., Workington, Cumberland. *T.:* Workington 597.
[*Died* 23 *Aug.* 1960 (*ext.*).

ADAMS, Alexander Annan, C.B.E. 1935; *b.* 29 Jan. 1884; *s.* of Alexander Annan Adams and Margaret Lamb; *m.* 1st, 1910, Berenice (*d.* 1946), *d.* of William de Schrader, Sheboygan, Wisconsin, U.S.A.; no *c.*; 2nd, 1951, Thomasina Cunningham, *d.* of James Miller, Edinburgh. *Educ.:* Vienna; London. Entered Consular Service in 1908; served in U.S.A., South America, Roumania and France; Assistant Director (in charge of Latin Section) Department of Overseas Trade, 1919; Commercial Secretary, with rank of First Secretary in the Diplomatic Service, and posted to the British Legation in Bucharest, 1919; Prague, 1924; Madrid, 1927; local rank of Commercial Counsellor, 1933; Commercial Counsellor, British Legation, Bucharest, Roumania, 1935-41, and Ankara, 1941; employed on special duties in Egypt and S. Africa, 1941-42; employed in Dept. of Overseas Trade, 1942-44; Secretary of Committee of Council for Europe of U.N.R.R.A., 1944-45. *Publications:* Plateau Peoples of South America, 1915; article on Economic Conditions in Spain for Encyclopædia Britannica. *Recreations:* motoring in Europe, golf. *Address:* The Nuttery, Seal Chart, Kent. *T.:* Sevenoaks 61045. *Club:* Athenæum.
[*Died* 7 *Oct.* 1955.

ADAMS, Dartrey; *see* Adams, H. D. C.

ADAMS, Frederick James, C.I.E. 1946; retired; *b.* 18 Feb. 1885; *m.* 1912, Cecilia

Mary, *d.* of Roman Basche, London; one *s.* two *d.* (and one *d.* decd.). *Educ.:* Ardingly. Entered India Office, 1905; transferred to Office of High Commissioner for India, 1922; Secretary, General Dept., 1938; retired 1945. *Recreation:* music. *Address:* Fairmile, Chipstead, Surrey. [*Died* 31 *Aug.* 1957.

ADAMS, Henry Charles; Consulting Engineer, M.Inst C.E., M.I.Mech.E., F.R.San.I., M.Inst.W.E., F.I.S.E.; *b.* 31 Oct. 1873; *e. s.* of late Prof. Henry Adams; *m.* 1899, Madeline Alice, *d.* of Edmund Green, Moseley, Birmingham; one *d.* *Educ.:* Cranleigh; City Lond. Coll.; Crystal Palace School of Engineering; served articles with father; passed technical examinations of Surv. Inst., Roy. San. Inst., Inst. M. and Cy. Eng. etc., Miller Prizeman Inst. C.E., 5 years Hon. Sec. B'ham. Assocn. of Inst.C.E., Hon. Sec. B'ham. and Mid. Inst. Scientific Soc.; Acting Prof. of Engineering Hollesley Bay Colonial Coll. 1893; Public Works Dept. Birmingham, 1898; Chief Engineer and Manager of Birmingham Office of Pritchard, Green and Co., Consulting Engineers, 1900; in partnership with Prof. Henry Adams, 1909-28; Engineer and Manager Holyhead Water Works Co., 1937-44; Member of Panel I of Civil Engineers appointed by Home Secretary under Reservoirs (Safety Provisions) Act, 1930; President Institution Sanitary Engineers, 1932 and 1933; Chairman Exam. Bd., 1934; Pres. Society Engineers, 1917; President Inst. Mun. E., 1915; Member Council Royal Sanitary Institute, 1936; Hon. Member Junior Inst. Eng.; Hon. Member Inst. Eng. in Charge; Active Craft and R.A. Freemason; Orpington Rotary Club. *Publications:* Sewerage of Sea Coast Towns; Waterworks for Urban and Rural Districts; Domestic Sanitation, etc. *Address:* Mona, 52 Princes Ave., Petts Wood, Orpington, Kent. *T.:* Orpington 6805. [*Died* 29 *Feb.* 1952.

ADAMS, Capt. Henry George Homer, C.B.E. 1919; late R.N.; *b.* 10 Apr. 1879; *yr. s.* of Rev. C. E. Adams; *m.* 1907, Emma Florence Craig; three *s.* *Educ.:* Oxford Preparatory School. Served in war as Commander (N.) in H.M.S. Russell, flagship of the 6th Battle Squadron, until July 1915, and as Commander (N.) and Captain (N.) in H.M.S. Barham, flagship of the 5th Battle Squadron, under Vice-Admiral Sir Hugh Evan Thomas (Order of St. Stanislas, C.B.E.); promoted Captain, June 1918; retired list, 1922. *Address:* Pen-y-Maes, Hay, Hereford. [*Died* 28 *Feb.* 1960.

ADAMS, Herbert; *b.* 1874; *s.* of William Adams, L.C.C., and Clara Simkin; *m.* 1900, Jessie Louise Cooper (*d.* 1952); three *s.* *Educ.:* City of London School. Member Surveyors Institute and practised for some years; then turned to literature. *Publications:* over fifty novels, including The Writing on the Wall, Welcome Home, Diamonds are Trumps, Crime Wave at Little Cornford, The Dean's Daughters, The Sleeping Draught, Exit The Skeleton, The Spectre in Brown, Slippery Dick, The Judas Kiss, Death on the First Tee. *Address:* Savoy Hotel, Bournemouth. [*Died* 24 *Feb.* 1958.

ADAMS, (Howard) Dartrey (Charles), C.M.G. 1947; LL.B. (N.Z.); New Zealand Parliamentary Law Draftsman since 1938; Compiler of Statutes since 1953; *b.* 12 Oct. 1897; *s.* of late Dr. Charles Edward Adams and Eleanor Robina Jacobson; *m.* 1921, Eliza Veitch Duncan (marriage dissolved, 1956); two *s.* one *d.*; *m.* 1956, Nancy Rose Cowper (*née* Hume). *Educ.:* Wellington College and Victoria University College, Wellington, New Zealand. Employed as barrister and solicitor by Chapman, Skerrett, Tripp and Blair of Wellington, 1918-22; Partner in Tudhope and Adams, of Hamilton, 1922-29; Public Trust Office, Wellington, 1929-30; Asst. Parl. Law Draftsman, 1930-34; Crown Solicitor, Crown Law Office, 1934-35; First Asst. Law Draftsman, 1935-38. Member: N.Z. Law Revision Cttee. *Publications:* assisted in Reprint of Public Acts of New Zealand, 1932; edited new edns. of Joliffe's Local Government in Counties and Local Government in Boroughs, 1934. *Recreations:* theatre and music. *Address:* 1 Hobson St., Wellington, N.1, New Zealand. *T.:* 42-383. [*Died* 3 *July* 1958.

ADAMS, Katharine; *see* Webb, Katharine.

ADAMS, Marcus Algernon, F.R.P.S. (Hon.); Life director Marcus Adams Ltd.; retired from active work, 1957; *b.* 16 May 1875; 5th *s.* of Arthur Walton and Annie Adams; *m.* 1904, T. Lillie Maud Farr; one *s.* *Educ.:* York House School; studied art at Reading University. Began photography, 1889, in Reading; formed Marcus Adams Co. Ltd., 1919; opened Children's Studio in London where royal pictures made, 1926-. Member Council of Royal Photographic Soc. for many years; Hon. Fell. Inst. British Photographers; Member or Hon. Member of various photographic and art societies in Britain and U.S.A. Has exhibited paintings and photographs, and lectured in many countries. *Publications:* Rhythm of Children's Features; many articles on art and photography. Royal pictures published all over the world. *Recreations:* travelling, gardening, motoring, carpentry, painting; study of Ancient History. *Address:* Lavender Cottage, Wargrave-on-Thames. *T.:* Wargrave 446. *Club:* Overseas League. [*Died* 9 *April* 1959.

ADAMS, Colonel Noel Percy, C.M.G. 1917; J.P.; *b.* 1882; *s.* of Percy Bolland Adams of Inner Temple and Nelson, New Zealand; *m.* 1910, Eileen, 3rd *d.* of George Henry Raw of Sunningdale, Berks. *Educ.:* Nelson College, N.Z.; Trinity Hall, Cambridge, M.A. Commanded Cambridge Mounted Infantry, 1902-4; Barrister Inner Temple, 1904; member North-eastern Circuit and N.Z. Bar; King Edward's Horse, 1904-10; N.Z. Field Artillery, 1910; Headquarters Staff N.Z. Military Forces, 1914-1918 (despatches); Commandant N.Z. Training Camp, 1916-18. *Address:* Matingarahi, Private Bag, Clevedon, New Zealand. *Club:* Northern (Auckland). [*Died* 1 *March* 1954.

ADAMS, Samuel Vyvyan Trerice; Political Researcher since 1946; *b.* 22 April 1900; *s.* of late Reverend Canon Samuel Trerice Adams, Hon. Canon of Ely and Rural Dean of Cambridge; *m.* 1925, Mary Grace Campin, *d.* of late Edward Bloxham Campin; one *d.* *Educ.:* King's School, Cambridge; Haileybury (Senior Scholar); King's Coll., Cambridge (Senior Exhibitioner). M.A., Winchester Prizeman, President of the Union; Classical Tripos, Parts I and II; called to Bar (Inner Temple), 1927; M.P. (Conservative) West Leeds, 1931-45; Parl. Candidate (C.) East Fulham, 1947-50; President Hardwicke Society, 1932; Member of Executive, League of Nations Union, 1933-1946 and of United Nations Association since 1948; Vice-President New Commonwealth Society; Army, War of 1939-45, Major D.C.L.I., D.A.A.G., 1940-46. *Publications:* Right Honourable Gentlemen, 1939; What of the Night? 1940; Churchill: Architect of Victory, 1940 (all under pen-name of Watchman); A Letter to a Young Politician, 1946; The British Co-operative Movement, 1948; articles and reviews. *Address:* 3 Gloucester Gate, Regent's Park, N.W.1. *T.:* Welbeck 5337. *Club:* Athenæum. [*Died* 13 *Aug.* 1951.

ADAMS, Most Rev. Walter Robert, M.A., D.D.; formerly Metropolitan of the Province of British Columbia; *b.* 1 Sept. 1877; *s.* of Robert John Adams, Wandsworth Common, S.W.; *m.* Elizabeth Mary (*d.* 1954), *e. d.* of John Whiteman, Woldingham, Surrey, formerly of Northampton; one *s.* two *d.* *Educ.:* Ardingly and Hurst Colleges (Woodard Schools); Durham University (Scholar),

B.A., 1st Class Math. Honours; Fellow of the University, 1901-09; Hon. D.D. 1925; President of Union, 1899; President of the Boats, 1900. Deacon, 1901; Priest, 1902; Curate of Croxdale, Co. Durham, 1901-04; Senior Curate of Lambeth Parish Church, 1904-07; Missionary at Baring; Vicar of Whitewood; Rector of Indian Head, all in Sask., Canada, 1907-12; Chaplain and Hon. Captain of the 16th Light Horse (Canadian Militia), 1910-12; Assistant with Archbishops' W. Canada Fund, 1912-14; Assistant Chaplain and Lecturer, St. Katharine's Training College, Tottenham, 1915-19; Senior Diocesan Inspector of Schools, Southwark, 1919-25; Examiner Durham University Schools Examinations, 1919-25; Bishop of Cariboo, 1925-34; Bishop of Kootenay, 1933-47; Bishop of Yukon, 1947-52. *Recreations:* chess, mathematics. *Address:* Sullivan Station, B.C. [*Died* 26 *July* 1957.

ADAMS, Walter Sydney, A.M., D.Sc., LL.D., retd.; *b.* Antioch, N. Syria, 20 Dec. 1876; *s.* of Lucien H. Adams; *m.* 1st, 1910, Lillian M. Wickham (*d.* 1920); 2nd, 1922, Adeline L. Miller; two *s.* *Educ.:* Dartmouth College; Univ. of Chicago; Univ. of Munich. Assistant, Yerkes Observatory, 1901-3; Instructor, 1903-4; Assistant Astronomer Mount Wilson Observatory, 1904-9; Acting Director, 1910-11; Assistant Director, 1913-23; Director, 1923-46; Research Associate, Carnegie Institution of Washington, 1946-48; Research Associate, California Institute of Technology, 1947-48. Member Astronomical Society of America (President, 1931-34); Member Astronomical Society of the Pacific (President, 1923); Fellow and Associate R.A.S., gold medal, 1917; Member Société Astronomique de France; Member Royal Society of Sciences, Uppsala; Member American Philosopical Society; Member National Acad. of Sciences, Foreign Associate Paris and Royal Swedish Academies of Sciences; Foreign Member Royal Society; Vice-Pres. Internat. Astronomical Union, 1935-49; Draper Medal of National Academy of Sciences, 1918; Prix Janssen of the Société Astronomique de France, 1926; Bruce Medal of the Astronomical Society of the Pacific, 1928; Janssen Medal of the Académie des Sciences, 1935. *Publications:* numerous papers on stellar spectroscopy, radial velocities and stellar parallaxes. *Address:* Pasadena, California. *T.:* Sycamore 4-1097. *Clubs:* Twilight, Athenæum (Pasadena). [*Died* 11 *May* 1956.

ADAMS, Wm. Dacres; Artist; Associate Société Nationale des Beaux Arts; *b.* 1864; *s.* of Rev. William Fulford and Catherine M. Adams; *m.* 1st, Regina E. Houghton (*d.* 1940), New York; one *s.* one *d.*; 2nd, 1940, Millicent Etheldreda, *d.* of Col. H. W. Gray, V.D., J.P., of Kensington. *Educ.:* Radley College; Exeter College, Oxford. Studied at Bushey under Prof. Sir Hubert von Herkomer, and at Munich. *Address:* 90 High St., Lewes, Sussex. *T.:* 747. [*Died* 17 *Aug.* 1951.

ADAMSON, Horatio George, M.D.Lond., F.R.C.P. Lond.; Consulting Physician for Diseases of the Skin at St. Bartholomew's Hospital, E.C.; *b.* 1865; *m.* Mabel, *y. d.* of Henry Valentine Draper. Hon. Fellow Royal Society of Medicine; Past President Dermatological Section; President British Association of Dermatology and Syphilology (1924); Membre Correspondant Étranger de la Société Française de Dermatologie; Corresponding Member Danish Dermatological Association; Hon. Member, New York Dermatological Society; American Dermatological Society; American Dermatological Association; corresponding member of Dermatological Association of Hungary; Goulstonian Lecturer, Royal College of Physicians, 1912. *Publications:* contributions to medical journals. *Address:* The Abbey, Bourne End, Bucks. *T.:* Bourne End 58. [*Died* 6 *July* 1955.

ADDISON, 1st Viscount, *cr.* 1945, of Stallingborough; 1st Baron, *cr.* 1937; **Christopher Addison,** K.G. 1946; P.C. 1916; M.D. B.S. Lond., F.R.C.S. Eng.; Lord President of the Council, March-Oct. 1951; Chm. Medical Research Council, 1948; Leader of House of Lords, 1945-51; *b.* Hogsthorpe, Lincs., 19 June 1869; *s.* of Robert and Susan Addison; *m.* 1st, 1902, Isobel (*d.* 1934), *d.* of late Archibald Gray; two *s.* two *d.*; 2nd, 1937, Dorothy, *d.* of J.P. Low. *Educ.:* Trinity Coll., Harrogate; St. Bartholomew's Hosp. Hunterian Prof. (1901) and Examiner in Anatomy, Univs. of Cambridge and London; Menber of Faculty of Medicine; Chm. of Board of Intermediate Medical Studies; and Member of Board of Human Anatomy and Morphology, University of London; late Sec. Anatomical Society of Great Britain and Ireland, etc.; late Professor of Anatomy, University Coll., Sheffield; formerly Lecturer on Anatomy, St. Bartholomew's Hospital; late editor of the Quarterly Medical Journal, etc.; M.P. (L.) Hoxton Division, Shoreditch, 1910-22; M.P. (Lab.) Swindon Division of Wilts, 1929-31 and 1934-35; Parliamentary Sec. to the Board of Education, 1914-15; to the Office of Munitions, 1915-16; Minister of Munitions, 1916-17; Minister in Charge of Reconstruction, 1917; President of the Local Government Board, 1919; First Minister of Health, 1919-21; Minister without Portfolio, 1921; Parliamentary Secretary Ministry of Agriculture, 1929-30; Minister of Agriculture and Fisheries, 1930-1931; Secretary of State for Commonwealth Relations, 1945-47; Paymaster-General, 1948-49; Lord Privy Seal, 1947-51; Hon. D.Sc. Cantab., D.C.L. Oxon., LL.D., Sheffield. *Publications:* The Betrayal of the Slums, 1922; Politics from Within, 2 vols., 1924; Practical Socialism, 2 vols., 1926; Four and a Half Years, Vols. I and II, 1934; A Policy for British Agriculture, 1939; Editor of Ellis's Demonstrations of Anatomy, 12th ed.; Joint Author (with Major J. W. Jennings), With the Abyssinians in Somaliland; On the Topographical Anatomy of the Pancreas and Adjoining Viscera—memoir published by University College, Sheffield; On the Topographical Anatomy of the Abdominal Viscera in Man, etc., Proceedings of the Royal Society, 1898, vol. lxiv. (abstract); detailed work on the same subject; The Journal of Anatomy and Physiology, in four parts. vols. xxxiii, xxxiv. xxxv.; and various papers in Med. Journals. *Heir:* *s.* Major Hon. Christopher Addison [*b.* 8 Dec. 1904; *m.* 1928, Brigit Helen Christine, *d.* of Ernest Edwin George Williams, Wimbledon; two *d.* *Educ.:* University Coll. Sch.; Newton Coll., Newton Abbot]. *Address:* Radnage, West Wycombe, Bucks. [*Died* 11 *Dec.* 1951.

ADDISON, Admiral Sir (Albert) Percy, K.B.E., *cr.* 1931; C.B. 1924; C.M.G. 1917; *b.* 8 Nov. 1875; *s.* of Albert Addison, Solicitor, Portsmouth; *m.* 1908, Mary Harriet (*d.* 1947), *d.* of W. Kellett, Southport; one *s.* one *d.*; *m.* 1948, Vera Louise Wilson Hughes. Served European War, 1914-1919; (C.M.G., Legion of Honour, Croix de Guerre, Order of Savoy, Italy; Order of Rising Sun, Japan; Bronze and Silver Humane Society Medals); Rear-Admiral, 1923; Commodore and Rear-Admiral commanding Australian Fleet, 1922-24; Rear-Admiral Commanding Destroyer Flotillas, Mediterranean Fleet, 1924-26; Director of Dockyards. Admiralty, 1928-37; Vice-Adm., 1929; retired list, 1929; Admiral, retired, 1933. *Address:* Sutherland, Lymington, Hants. [*Died* 13 *Nov.* 1952.

ADDISON, D'Arcy Wentworth, C.M.G. 1928; M.V.O. 4th class, 1927, 5th class, 1920;

I.S.O. 1920; J.P.; *b.* Hobart, 10 Dec. 1872; *s.* of late Captain J. E. Addison, 5th Royal Irish Lancers; *m.* 1919, Una Stella, *widow* of Sir John Downer, K.C.M.G., K.C., South Australia. *Educ.:* Scotch College, Hobart. Secretary to Premier, Tasmania, 1902-26; Clerk, Executive Council, 1903-30; Secretary to the Agent - General, 1908-09; Under - Sec. for Tasmania, 1914 - 30; Chief Electoral Officer, 1914-30; Agent-General for Tasmania, 1930-1931; Administrator of Charitable Grants, 1914 - 19; Secretary, Neglected Children, 1914-19; State Organiser Royal Visit, 1920; Hon. Private Secretary to the Administrator of the Government, 1922-23; Chairman Tasmanian State Executive, British Empire Exhibition; Organising Secretary, State Development Board, 1924-25; Hon. Corresponding Secretary Royal Empire Society, 1900 - 30; State Director, Royal visit, 1927. *Recreations:* golf, yachting, motoring. *Address:* St. George's Terrace, Hobart, Tasmania. *Clubs:* Tasmanian (Hobart); Adelaide (Adelaide).

[*Died* 28 *Aug.* 1955.

ADDISON, Sir Joseph, K.C.M.G., *cr.* 1933 (C.M.G. 1924); *b.* 1879. Entered Foreign Office, 1903; Second Secretary at Peking, 1908; Private Secretary to Mr. McKinnon Wood, Under-Sec. of State for Foreign Affairs, 1911; and later to Mr. F. D. Acland; resigned Foreign Office, 1913; temporary Secretary to Ambassador in Paris, 1916; Commercial Counsellor, 1918; Counsellor of Embassy in Berlin, 1920; Chargé d'Affaires on several occasions; Envoy Extraordinary and Minister Plenipotentiary at Riga, Reval and Kovno, 1927 - 30; at Prague, 1930-36; retired 1936.

[*Died* 24 *Nov.* 1953.

ADDISON, Adm. Sir Percy; *see* Addison, Sir A. P.

ADDISON - SMITH, Chilton Lind, C.B.E. 1928 (O.B.E. 1919); Commander of the Order of Wen-Hu (Striped Tiger), China; Commander of Saxe - Coburg; D.L. Edinburgh; Registrar of Friendly Societies for Scotland, formerly Assistant, retired 1953; *b.* 27 April 1875; 3rd *s.* of late Robert Addison-Smith, C.V.O., Edinburgh, and late Isabella Mary, *y. d.* of David Lind; *m.* 1927, Katharine Lushington, *o. d.* of John Ewart, W.S., and Catherine Helen, *d.* of Colonel Charles May Allan Morant. *Educ.:* Craigmount House School; Edinburgh University. Writer to His Majesty's Signet, 1899; senior partner of the firm of R. Addison-Smith & Co., W.S., Edinburgh; H.M. Commissioner Queen Victoria School, Dunblane (for sons of soldiers, sailors and airmen); joined 3rd Battalion The Seaforth Highlanders (Ross-shire Buffs, The Duke of Albany's) 1896; served South African War, 1899-1901 (Queen's medal); one of founders and Chairman, Scottish Naval, Military and Airmen's Veterans' Residences, Edinburgh and Broughty Ferry; raised the Veteran Reserve, 1911; Member of the Advisory Committee of the Army Council of the National Reserve, 1911; Member of the War Office Consultative Committee on Employment of Soldiers, etc., 1913; Member of Scottish Savings Committee; Chairman of Scottish Branch of Regular Forces Employment Association; served European War; promoted temp. Lieutenant-Colonel, 1 Dec. 1914; raised and commanded 10th Batt. The Seaforth Highlanders (despatches, medals, O.B.E.); promoted Lt.-Col. in the Army and appointed to command 3rd Batt. The Seaforth Highlanders; Deputy Chairman and Hon. Treasurer The Seaforth Highlanders Association, 1905. King's Jubilee Medal, 1935; Coronation Medal, 1937. *Address:* 19 and 29 Heriot Row, Edinburgh. *Clubs:* United Service; Scottish Conservative, Caledonian United Service (Edinburgh).

[*Died* 28 *May* 1955.

ADEY, William James, C.M.G. 1935; *b.* 27 May 1874; *s.* of Charles George Adey and Ann Donaldson Ritchie; *m.* 1st, 1910, late Mabel Edith Dyer; 2nd, 1921, Constance Margaret Weston; two *s.* one *d.* *Educ.:* Teachers Training College and University of Adelaide. Principal Adelaide High School, 1908-20; Superintendent Secondary Education, 1920-29; Director of Education, South Australia, 1929-39; Chm. Soldiers' Children Educ. Bd., 1928-. During War of 1939-45 engaged in Y.M.C.A. Military Service, and War Loan Organisation in South Australia. *Publications:* various educational articles. *Recreations:* cricket, tennis, golf. *Address:* Cockenzie, High St., Burnside, S. Australia. *Clubs:* Commonwealth, Royal Adelaide Golf (Adelaide).

[*Died* 23 *May* 1956.

ADKIN, Rev.W. K. K.; *see* Knight-Adkin.

AERON - THOMAS, Gwilym Ewart, C.B.E. 1950 (O.B.E. 1944); D.L., J.P.; M.I.M.E., M.A., LL.B.; *b.* 5 Nov. 1885; *s.* of late John Aeron-Thomas, J.P., Dolgoy, West Cross, Swansea; *m.* 1919, Cicily Mary, *d.* of T. Baker-Jones, Newport, Mon.; two *s.* *Educ.:* Clifton; Caius College, Cambridge. Barrister Inner Temple, 1910. Served European War, 1914-18, Royal Artillery (despatches four times); Hon. Col. R.A. 1941; Lt.-Col. Commanding 28 Home Guard A.A. Regiment; Hon. Col. R.A.S.C. 1949. D.L. Glamorgan, 1936; J.P. Swansea, 1939 (Chm. Justices). Member Swansea Corp., 1945-47. Past President Swansea Chamber of Commerce, now Hon. Treasurer. Director of a number of Industrial concerns, including: Lime Firms Ltd., etc., Wales & Mon. Industrial Estates Ltd. Member: Special Areas Reconstruction Panel, 1935-1946; Advisory Committee to Board of Trade representing Coal Industry, 1936-39; Council for Wales and Monmouthshire, 1949-53; Chairman: South Wales Argus, Newport; South Wales Executive Board under Coal Mines Act, 1930, 1936-46; South Wales Brattice Cloth & India Rubber Co. Ltd., Newport (Mon.); Unifloc Ltd.; Swansea Foundry & Engineering Ltd.; Emlyn Brick Co. Ltd.; Vice-Pres. Central Council under Coal Mines Scheme, 1944-46; Chm. Exports Cttee. of Central Council, 1936-46; Deputy Chairman, S.W. Divisional Coal Board, 1946-48, Chairman, 1948-52; Vice-President: South Wales Institute of Engineers, 1953-56; Past-Pres. Institute of Directors for Wales, 1956-57. Old Cliftonian Society. Member Export Committee of F.B.I. and Internat. Chamber of Commerce; Member Exec. Council of Industrial Assoc. of Wales and Mon., 1936-; Pres., British Legion (Swansea Branch), 1946. K.St.J. *Recreations:* tennis, golf. *Address:* Dolgoy, West Cross, Swansea. *T.:* Mumbles 66050. *Clubs:* Oxford and Cambridge; Cardiff and County (Cardiff); Newport County (Newport).

[*Died* 8 *June* 1958.

AGA KHAN (III), H.H. Rt. Hon. Aga Sultan Sir Mahomed Shah, P.C. 1934; G.C.S.I., *cr.* 1911; G.C.M.G., *cr.* 1955; G.C.I.E., *cr.* 1902 (K.C.I.E., *cr.* 1898); G.C.V.O., *cr.* 1923; LL.D. hon. Camb.; *b.* 1877; *m.* 1st, 1908; one *s.* (*see* Aly Khan); 2nd, 1929, Andrée Carron (decree of divorce granted, Geneva, 1943); one *s.* (Sadruddin); 3rd, Yvette Labrousse. Brilliant Star of Zanzibar, 1900, 1st class; 1st class Prussian Order of Royal Crown, 1901; Head of Ismaili Mahomedans; founded the Moslem University, Aligarh, 1910; Member of the Viceroy's Council, 1902-04; led Moslem deputation to Lord Minto, 1906; attended Coronation, 1937, as British India's first representative; salute of 11 guns in recognition of loyal services during European War; Chairman of British Indian Delegation to the Round Table Conference, London, 1930 and 1931; represented India at World Disarmament Conference, Geneva, 1932; led Indian Delegation to League of Nations Assembly,

1932, 1934, 1935, 1936 and 1937; also to special meetings for Paraguay-Bolivia and Manchurian disputes, and meeting, 1937, when Egypt became member of League of Nations; President of League of Nations Assembly, Geneva, 1937; won the Derby with Blenheim, 1930; won the Two Thousand Guineas, Derby and St. Leger (Triple Crown) with Bahram, 1935, and the Derby with Mahmoud, 1936, with My Love, 1948, with Tulyar, 1952. Hon. Member of Jockey Club. *Publications:* India in Transition, 1918; The Memoirs of Aga Khan, 1954. *Recreations:* golf, racing, motoring, travel. *Heir:* (nominated in his will) *g. s.* Karim [*b.* 1937; *er. s.* of Aly Khan, *q.v.*]. *Address:* Villa Barakat, Versoix, Canton of Geneva, Switzerland; Yakymour, Le Cannet-Cannes, France.

[*Died* 11 *July* 1957.

AGAR, Lt.-Col. John Arnold Shelton, D.S.O. 1918; *m.* 1923, Kathleen Douglas, *o. d.* of H. Douglas Robertson, Indian Police, retired; two *s.* Served European War, 1914-18 (despatches, D.S.O., Bt. Lt.-Col.). *Address:* c/o Lloyds Bank, Ltd., Bexhill-on-Sea, Sussex.

[*Died* 6 *March* 1951.

AGAR, Wilfred Eade, C.B.E. 1948 (O.B.E. 1939); F.R.S. 1921; Emeritus Professor of Zoology, University of Melbourne; *b.* 27 Apr. 1882; *s.* of Edward Larpent Agar, of Milford House, near Lymington, Hants; *m.* 1908, Elizabeth, *y. d.* of David MacDonald, Glasgow; two *s.* three *d.* *Educ.:* Sedbergh; King's College, Cambridge (Fellow, 1907-13). Lecturer in Zoology, University of Glasgow; Captain, 5th Batt. Highland Light Infantry, Oct. 1914-Apr. 1918. *Publications:* Cytology, 1920; The Theory of the Living Organism, 1943; contributions to various scientific journals on biological subjects. *Address:* c/o The University, Melbourne, Australia.

[*Died* 14 *July* 1951.

AGNEW, Sir Andrew, Kt. *cr.* 1938; C.B.E. 1918; Managing Director, Shell Transport and Trading Co. Ltd.; Director: Anglo-Saxon Petroleum Co. Ltd.; Shell Petroleum Co. Ltd.; *b.* 28 Feb. 1882; *s.* of Andrew Agnew, Greenock; *m.* 1912, Belle, *d.* of James McClymont, Girvan; two *s.* *Educ.:* Holmscroft Sch., Greenock. Formerly Chm., Elba Tinplate Co. Ltd., and Straits Settlements River Craft Cttee.; Mem. Singapore Harbour Bd., 1911-19, and M.L.C. Straits Settlements; Comdt. Singapore Civil Guard, 1915-18. Holds several foreign decorations. *Address:* Glenlee Park, New Galloway, Kirkcudbrightshire. *Club:* Caledonian.

[*Died* 4 *March* 1955.

AGNEW, Sir John Stuart, 3rd Bt., *cr.* 1895; T.D.; D.L.; *b.* 16 Sept. 1879; *e. s.* of Sir George Agnew, 2nd Bt., and Fanny (*d.* 1937), *y. d.* of late John Stuart Bolton of Oulton Hall, Aylsham, Norfolk; *S.* father, 1941; *m.* 1910, Kathleen, 3rd *d.* of late T. W. White of Meanwood, Leeds; three *s.* *Educ.:* Rugby; Trinity College, Cambridge. Major late Suffolk Yeomanry (T.A.); served European War, 1914-18. High Sheriff of Suffolk for 1946-47. *Heir:* *s.* John Anthony Stuart, *b.* 25 July 1914. *Address:* Rougham, Bury St. Edmunds, Suffolk. *Clubs:* Cavalry, Boodle's.

[*Died* 27 *Aug.* 1957.

AGNEW, Vice-Adm. (retd.) Sir William Gladstone, K.C.V.O., *cr.* 1947 (C.V.O. 1943); C.B. 1941; D.S.O. 1943 (and Bar 1944); *b.* 1898; *s.* of late Charles Morland Agnew, O.B.E., and Evelyn Mary, *d.* of William Naylor; *m.* 1930, Patricia Caroline, *d.* of late Col. Alfred William Bewley, C.M.G. Served European War, 1914-18, and War of 1939-45. Commanded H.M.S. Vanguard during royal tour of South Africa. Director of Personal Services and Deputy Chief of Naval Personnel, Admiralty, 1947-1949; retired Jan. 1950; Vice-Admiral (retd.), 1950. General Secretary of the National Playing Fields Association, 1950-1953. *Address:* Glentimon, Palmerston Way, Alverstoke, Hants.

[*Died* 12 *July* 1960.

AGRON, Gershon (formerly **Gershon Agronsky**); elected Mayor of Jerusalem, Sept. 1955, for four-year term; Founder and Editor, Palestine Post (renamed Jerusalem Post); *b.* Ukraine, 1893; *m.* 1921, Ethel Lipschutz; one *s.* two *d.* Immigrated U.S.A., 1906. *Educ.:* Mishkan Israel Talmudic School, Brown Preparatory School, Temple University, Philadelphia; began journalism on Jewish World, 1915; editor Das Juedische Volk, 1917; joined Jewish Regt., Egyptian Expeditionary Force, for Palestine front, 1918; headed Press Bureau of Zionist Commission to Palestine, 1921; editor Jewish Telegraphic Agency, New York, 1921-24; Dir. Press Bureau, Zionist Exec., Jerusalem, 1924-1927; acted for number of years as Jerusalem Correspondent for Christian Science Monitor, United Press, Daily Telegraph, Exchange Telegraph, etc.; represented Zionist Organisation at International Reclamation Conference, Honolulu, 1927; special commissions to study conditions in relation to Palestine, in Salonica, Aden, India, Iraq, and Rumania; edited Palestine Bulletin, 1931-32; Director, Information Services, State of Israel, 1949-51; led two campaigns for Joint Palestine Appeal in Britain, 1948; took part in drives in U.S.A. and Canada, for United Jewish Appeal, 1951, and Israel Independence Loan, 1952, 1953 and 1956. Delegate International Zionist Congresses. *Address:* 4 Rashba Road, Rehavia, Jerusalem, Israel. *T.A.:* Agronews.

[*Died* 1 *Nov.* 1959.

AHMAD, Maulvi Sir Nizam-ud-Din-Nawab Nizamat Jung Bahadur, Kt., *cr.* 1929; C.I.E. 1924; O.B.E. 1919; late of Political Dept., H.E.H. the Nizam's Government; retired, 1930; *b.* 1871. *Educ.:* Hyderabad; Trinity College, Cambridge. B.A., LL.B. 1891; M.A. 1896. Called to Bar, Inner Temple, 1895. *Address:* Hyderabad, Deccan, India.

[*Died Dec.* 1955.

AHMAD, Maulvi Sir Rafiuddin, Kt., *cr.* 1932; Barrister-at-law; *b.* 1865. Minister for Education, Bombay, 1928-32. One of Founders of All India Muslim League, 1906. *Address:* Ganeshkind Road, Poona 5, India.

[*Died* 8 *March* 1954.

AIKENHEAD, Brigadier David Francis, D.S.O. 1940; M.C.; Royal Horse Artillery (retd.); *b.* 29 June 1895; *yr. s.* of Lt.-Col. Frank Aikenhead, R.A., and Mabel Louisa Aikenhead; *m.* 1917, Margaret Clotilda Bayne; one *s.* one *d.* *Educ.:* Cheltenham College; R.M.A., Woolwich. Commissioned on outbreak of war, 1914; served continuously in France until 1919, (twice wounded, M.C., despatches); proceeded to India, Afghan war of 1919, and then to Mesopotamia and Iraq rebellion of 1920; much service in Egypt, commanding J Battery R.H.A. at outbreak of war, 1939; proceeded to France early 1940, commanding 2nd Regt. R.H.A., evacuated from Dunkirk (D.S.O.); with same Regt. to Egypt in Oct. 1940; evacuated from Greece, April 1941; Brig. Oct. 1941; C.C.R.A. of 30th Corps in Libya; served at home, 1942-44; Palestine and Italy, June-Oct. 1944; C.C.R.A. 3rd Corps in Greece, Oct. 1944 (despatches thrice); retired, 1947. *Address:* Great Elm, Frome, Somerset. *T.A.:* Mells. *T.:* Mells 332. *Club:* Naval and Military.

[*Died* 19 *May* 1955.

AILSA, 5th Marquess of (*cr.* 1831), **Charles Kennedy;** Baron Kennedy, 1452; Earl of Cassillis, 1509; Baron Ailsa (U.K.), 1806; *b.* 10 April 1875; 2nd *s.* of 3rd Marquess and Hon. Evelyn Stuart (*d.* 1888), *d.* of 12th Lord Blantyre; *S.* brother 1943; *m.* 1st, 1925,

Constance Barbara (*d.* 1931), *widow* of Admiral Sir John Baird, K.C.B.; 2nd, 1933, Helen Ethel, *widow* of Richard John Cuninghame, M.C., F.Z.S., and *o. d.* of late James McDouall, J.P., D.L., of Logan, Wigtownshire. *Educ.:* Eton: Royal Agricultural College, Cirencester (Diploma and Goldstand Silver Medallist). Served South African War, 1900-1 (Queen's medal with two clasps). *Recreations:* farming, astronomy, shooting, and fishing. *Heir:* *b.* Lord Angus Kennedy (*see under* 6th Marquess of Ailsa). *Address:* Hensol, Mossdale, Castle-Douglas. *T.A.:* Mossdale, Castle-Douglas. *T.:* Laurieston 207. *Club:* New (Edinburgh).
[*Died* 1 *June* 1956.

AILSA, 6th Marquess of (*cr.* 1831), **Angus Kennedy;** Baron Kennedy, 1452; Earl of Cassillis, 1509; Baron Ailsa (U.K.), 1806; *b.* 28 Oct. 1882; 3rd *s.* of 3rd Marquess of Ailsa and Hon. Evelyn Stuart (*d.* 1888), *d.* of 12th Lord Blantyre; *S.* brother 1956; *m.* 1922, Gertrude Millicent Cooper; one *s.* *Educ.:* Eton. Trained as Naval Architect; served as Sub-Lieutenant R.N.R., Lieutenant R.N.V.R., Captain R.A.F. (Tech.), during European War; represented Baird Television in South Africa, 1929; Liveryman of Worshipful Company of Shipwrights and Freeman of City of London. *Heir:* *s.* Earl of Cassillis. *Address:* c/o Cassillis and Culzean Estates, Maybole, Ayrshire.
[*Died* 31 *May* 1957.

AINLEY-WALKER, Ernest William, M.A., D.Sc., D.M., B.Ch. Oxon.; late Dean of the School of Medicine, University of Oxford; Fellow Emeritus of University College, Oxford; late Univ. Reader in Pathology, Oxford; late Member of the Court of Assistants of the Worshipful Soc. of Apothecaries of London; Junior Warden, 1940-41; *b.* 27 Jan. 1871; *s.* of Rev. William Henry Walker and Louisa Shepherd, *d.* of late James Taylor of Barnsley and later of Brentwood; *m.* 1st, 1909, Emily Hilda (*d.* 1917), *e. d.* of late Sir Edward Bagnall Poulton, F.R.S.; 2nd, 1919, Inez Elizabeth, *o. surv. c.* of late Rev. Canon J. H. Skrine, D.D.; one *s.* two *d.* *Educ.:* Kingswood School, Bath; Rydal School; Christ Church, Oxford (Scholar). Goldsmiths' Exhibitioner, 1891-94; honours; 1st Class Final Honour, School of Physiology, 1894; B.A. 1894; Assistant Demonstrator of Physiology, Oxford, 1895-96; Price Entrance Scholar of the London Hospital, 1896; Sutton Scholar of the London Hospital, 1898; M.A., M.B., B.Ch., 1899, Oxford; Radcliffe Travelling Fellow, Oxford, 1899-1902; D.M. Oxford, 1900; House Physician and House Surgeon, London Hosp.; Gordon Lecturer in Experimental Pathology and Director of the Pathological Department, Guy's Hospital, 1902; Member, and Gillson Research Scholar in Pathology of the Society of Apothecaries of London, 1905; Member of Pathological Society of Great Britain and Ireland; late Examiner in Pathology in the Universities of Oxford, Cambridge, Sheffield, and Leeds. *Publications:* contributions to Journal of Pathology and Bacteriology, and many other scientific writings and communications. *Recreations:* gardening, fishing, travel. *Address:* St. Cuthberts, Upavon, Wiltshire. *T.:* Upavon 34. [*Died* 15 *Aug.* 1955.

AINSLIE, Charlotte, O.B.E. 1929; B.A. (Lond.); Hon. LL.D. Edin.; *b.* Edinburgh, 15 Feb. 1868; 2nd *d.* of late William Ainslie, Edinburgh. *Educ.:* George Watson's Ladies' Coll., Edinburgh; Germany; Switzerland; read for Arts degree of the University of London, at Bedford Coll. (Reid Scholar, Gilchrist Scholar). Assistant Mistress at Skinners' School for Girls, Stamford Hill, London, 1896-1900; lecturer in Psychology and Education at Cambridge Training College, 1901-2; Headmistress of George Watson's Ladies' College, Edinburgh, 1902-26; lectured on Methods of Teaching Modern Languages, at Cambridge University Extension Summer Meeting, 1902; President of the Secondary Education Association of Scotland, 1912-13. *Publications:* essays and reports on educational subjects. *Recreation:* travelling. *Address:* 12 Mayfield Terrace, Edinburgh.
[*Died* 24 *Aug.* 1960.

AINSWORTH, Alfred Richard, C.B. 1934; *b.* 1879; *s.* of John Duxbury Ainsworth. *Educ.:* Ipswich Grammar School; Dulwich; King's College, Cambridge. Lecturer Manchester University, 1902-3, Edinburgh University, 1903-7. Joined Board of Education, 1908; Principal Assistant Secretary, 1931; Deputy Secretary, 1939; retired, 1940. *Address:* Barbary, King's Thorn, Herefordshire. [*Died* 25 *Dec.* 1959.

AINSWORTH, Bt. Col. Charles; Chairman and Managing Director, Charles Ainsworth and Co. Ltd.; *b.* Ingol, nr. Preston, 25 Feb. 1874; *s.* of late Hargreaves Ainsworth, Windermere; *m.* 1902, Clara H., *d.* of late H. R. Middlemost, Huddersfield; two *s.* one *d.* *Educ.:* privately. Served with Lancs. Fusiliers, 1914-18; Egypt, 1914; Turkey, 1915; Lt.-Col. Commanding 5th Bn. Lancs. Fusiliers, 1928-33; Bt.-Col., 1932; Member of the National Assembly, Church of England, 1919-29; interested in farming and horse-breeding; Master Holcombe Hunt, 1926-31; M.P. (C.) Bury, Lancashire, Dec. 1918-35. *Address:* Redisher, Holcombe Brook, Lancashire. *T.:* Ramsbottom 2233. *Club:* Carlton.
[*Died* 10 *April* 1956.

AINSWORTH, Major-General Sir Ralph Bignell, Kt., *cr.* 1946; C.B., 1935; D.S.O. 1916; O.B.E. 1923; Knight of Grace Order of St. John of Jerusalem; late R.A.M.C. and Dir. of Medical Services Joint Cttee. of B.R.C.S. and Order of St. John; late Inspector of Hospitals in the Emergency Medical Service, Ministry of Health; late Comdt. Royal Army Medical College, Hon. Physician to the King; D.D.M.S. Scottish Command, Prof. of Hygiene, Royal Army Medical College, and Assistant Director-General Medical Services, War Office; *b.* 26 Sep. 1875; 2nd *s.* of late Capt. W. Ainsworth, Spotlands, Lancashire; *m.* 1903, Florence, *o. d.* of late Imre Kiralfy, Washington Square, New York; two *d.* *Educ.:* St. Paul's School. Entered St. George's Hospital, 1893; M.R.C.S. Eng., L.R.C.P. London, 1899; joined Royal Navy as Surgeon, 1900; retired, 1902; Lieut. R.A.M.C., 1902; Captain, 1906; Major, 1914; Lt.-Col. 1924; Colonel, 1930; Major-General, 1932; retired pay, 1935; Special Sanitary Officer, 6th Division (Poona), 1908; Salisbury Plain, 1910-1914; with Exped. Force to France, Aug. 1914, and N. Russia E. F., 1919 (despatches thrice, D.S.O.); Bt. Lt.-Col., médaille des Epidémies (in vermeil) from French Government. Officer Legion of Honour, Czechoslovak Order of the White Lion and Military Medal of Merit; Governor Queen Mary's (Roehampton) Hosp. and British Hosp., Port Said. *Publications:* The House Fly as a Disease Carrier, 1908; Sanitation in War, 1915. *Address:* The Ivy House, Hampton Court. *Clubs:* Junior United Service, Royal Automobile.
[*Died* 27 *Jan.* 1952.

AIREDALE, 3rd Baron, of Gledhow, *cr.* 1907; **Capt. Roland Dudley Kitson,** Bt., *cr.* 1886; D.S.O. 1918; M.C.; J.P., West Riding; High Sheriff of County of London since 1928; late 1/8 West Yorks Regiment; Director: Ford Motor Co. Ltd.; London Assurance Corporation; John Dickinson & Co. Ltd.; Lieutenant of City of London; *b.* Leeds, 19 July 1882; *y. s.* of 1st Baron and Mary Laura (*d.* 1939), *o. d.* of Edward Fisher Smith, The Priory, Dudley; *S.* half-brother 1944; *m.* 1st, 1913, Sheila Grace (*d.* 1935), *y. d.* of late F. E. Vandeleur; one *s.* one *d.*; 2nd, 1937, Dorothy Christobel Rowland, *d.* of late Canon Raymond Pelly. *Educ.:* Westminster; Trinity Coll., Cambridge, B.A. Served European War (D.S.O.,

M.C., despatches). Director, Bank of England, 1923-47. *Heir:* *s.* Maj. Hon. Oliver James Vandeleur Kitson, The Green Howards, *b.* 22 April 1915. *Address:* Ufford Hall, Stamford, Northants. *Clubs:* Brooks's, Reform. [*Died* 20 *March* 1958.

AIREY, Sir Edwin, Kt., *cr.* 1922; Governing Director of W. Airey & Son (Leeds), Ltd.; *b.* 7 Feb. 1878; *s.* of late William Airey; *m.* 1904, Edith, *d.* of late Wm. Greaves; one *s.* four *d.* *Educ.:* Central High School and Yorkshire College, Leeds. Lord Mayor of Leeds, 1923-24; Pres. United Kingdom Commercial Travellers' Association, 1923-24; Chairman of Board, Leeds Public Dispensary, 1922-29; Chairman of Directors, Leeds Cricket, Football, and Athletic Co., Ltd.; President of the National Federation of Building Trade Employers, 1930-1931; High Sheriff of Yorkshire, 1944; Fellow of the Institute of Builders; M.I.Struct.E. Commander of the Order of Orange-Nassau. *Recreations:* music, chess, travel, motoring. *Address:* Oakwood Grange, Leeds. *T.A.:* Duo, Leeds. *T.:* Leeds 21573, Roundhay 65-8206. [*Died* 14 *March* 1955.

AIRLIE, Mabell, Countess of, G.C.V.O., *cr.* 1953; G.B.E., *cr.* 1920; Hon. LL.D., St. Andrews; J.P.; formerly Lady of the Bedchamber to H.M. Queen Mary; *b.* 10 Mar. 1866; *e. d.* of 5th Earl of Arran; *m.* 1886, David William Stanley, 10th Earl of Airlie, who was killed in action at Diamond Hill, Pretoria, 11 June 1900; three *s.* three *d.* *Publications:* In Whig Society, 1775-1818, 1921; Lady Palmerston and her Times, 1922; With the Guards We Shall Go, 1933. *Address:* Airlie Castle, Kirriemuir, Angus, Scotland. *T.:* Craigton 206. [*Died* 7 *April* 1956.

AITCHISON, George; Former Editor Brighton and Hove Herald; *b.* 6 June 1877; *s.* of John Aitchison and Clara Maynard; *m.* 1st, 1907, Edith Mary (*d.* 1943); no *c.*; 2nd, 1946, Gladys Marie, *widow* of Herbert Bailey, journalist. *Educ.:* Brighton Grammar School. Apprenticed to Brighton Herald, 1893; actively engaged on that paper all his life; now Director; lecturer on literary, travel and local subjects. F.J.I. and Hon. Member Critics Circle. *Publications:* Unknown Brighton, 1926; Sussex, 1936; minor historical or topographical papers, etc. *Recreation:* gardening. *Address:* 8 Adelaide Crescent, Hove 3, Sussex. *T.:* Hove 38641. [*Died* 30 *April* 1954.

AITCHISON, Sir Stephen Charles de Lancey, 3rd Bt. *cr.* 1938; Chairman and Managing Director: Walter Willson Ltd., De Lancey Lands Ltd., etc.; *b.* 10 Mar. 1923; *e. s.* of Walter de Lancey Aitchison, 2nd Bt., of Lemmington and Coupland Castle, Wooler, Northumberland, and Shena Lennox, *d.* of Dr. C. L. Fraser, T.D., J.P., Berwick-upon-Tweed; *S.* father 1953; *m.* 1950, Elizabeth Anne Milburn, *er. d.* of Lt.-Col. Edward Reed, Ghyllheugh, Longhorsley, Northumberland; two *s.* *Educ.:* Rugby; University College, Oxford. Served R.T.R. and 13th/18th Royal Hussars, 1942-47, Major. *Heir:* *s.* Charles Walter de Lancey, *b.* 27 May 1951. *Address:* Coupland Castle, Wooler, Northumberland. *T.:* Morpeth 3327. *Club:* Union (Newcastle upon Tyne). [*Died* 12 *May* 1958.

AITCHISON, Sir Walter de Lancey, 2nd Bt., *cr.* 1938; M.A.; F.S.A.; Chairman and Governing Director of de Lancey Lands Ltd., Walter Willson Ltd., Kirklinton Park Estates Ltd., etc.; *b.* 14 May 1892; *s.* of Sir Stephen Aitchison, 1st Bt., J.P., and Alice Mary (*d.* 1932), *d.* of Walter de Lancey Willion, J.P., Kirklinton Park, Cumberland; *S.* father 1942; *m.* 1922, Shena Lennox, *er. d.* of C. L. Fraser, F.R.C.S., F.R.C.P., T.D., J.P., Berwick-on-Tweed; three *s.* one *d.* *Educ.:* Repton; University College, Oxford. Served European War, Overseas, 1914-18, Capt., N. Staffordshire Regt. *Heir:* *s.* Stephen Charles de Lancey (*see under* Sir Stephen Aitchison, 3rd Bt.). *Address:* Coupland Castle, Wooler, Northumberland. [*Died* 14 *Oct.* 1953.

AITKEN, Cecil Edward, C.I.E., 1941; B.Sc.; *b.* 8 Oct. 1888; *s.* of E. H. Aitken; *m.* 1923, Jessie Olive Yuille (*d.* 1949), one *s.* one *d.* Joined Indian Service of Engineers, 1911; Chief Engineer and Secretary to Govt., P.W.D., Bombay, 1938; retd., 1943. *Address:* Ballachrink, West Baldwin, I. of M. [*Died* 4 *Oct.* 1959.

AITKEN, James Hume; journalist; Glasgow Correspondent of the Times since 1914; *b.* 17 Nov. 1890; *s.* of James Hume Aitken and Mary Hogg; *m.* 1913, Mary Wilson; one *s.* one *d.* *Educ.:* Harris Academy, Dundee. President National Union of Journalists, 1933-34; President of Glasgow Press Club, 1928-1935. *Recreation:* golf. *Address:* 14 Firwood Drive, Cathcart, Glasgow, S.4. *T.:* Merrylee 1558. *Club:* Press (Glasgow). [*Died* 14 *Sept.* 1955.

AITKEN, John E., R.S.W.; R.C.A.; A.R.W.A.; A.R.B.C.; Artist; *s.* of James Aitken, marine painter and Mary Aitken. Studied art at the studio of his father, also at the Schools of Art of Liverpool, Manchester and Wallasey; pictures exhibited in Royal Academy, Royal Scottish Academy, Royal Institute, Glasgow Institute, Walker Art Gallery, Liverpool, Manchester and many other galleries; pictures in permanent Collections of Birkenhead, Wakefield and Douglas; has painted in Holland, France, Belgium, Switzerland and Italy. *Publications:* Several colour prints. *Address:* Gullane, Port St. Mary, Isle of Man. [*Died* 15 *June* 1957.

AITKEN, Robert Grant; *b.* Jackson, Amador Co., California, U.S.A., 31 Dec. 1864; *s.* of Robert Aitken and Wilhelmina Depinau; *m.* 1888, Jessie, *d.* of Capt. W. R. Thomas and Nellie Wells; three *s.* one *d.* *Educ.:* Elementary schools, Jackson, the Oakland High School, and Williams College, Mass. Studied astronomy under Truman H. Safford, A.B. degree, 1887; M.A., 1892; Hon. Sc.D., 1917; Hon. Sc.D., College of the Pacific, 1903; University of Arizona, 1923; Hon. LL.D. University of California, 1935. Professor Mathematics and Astronomy, College of the Pacific, 1891-95; Assistant Astronomer, Lick Observatory, 1895-1907; Astronomer 1907-35; Associate Director, 1923-30; Director 1930-35; Emeritus Director and Astronomer, 1935; Member National Academy of Sciences (Chairman, Section of Astronomy, 1929-32), American Astronomical Society (Vice-President, 1928-30, President, 1937-40), American Philosophical Society, Astronomical Society of the Pacific, Fellow of the American Association for the Advancement of Science (Vice-President Section D., 1926-27; President, Pacific Division, 1925-26); Associate Royal Astronomical Society; Mem. Internat. Astron. Union; hon. mem. Calif. Acad. Sci.; awarded Laland Gold Medal, Paris Academy of Sciences, 1906, for double star discoveries; Bruce Gold Medal, Astronomical Society of the Pacific, for distinguished services to Astronomy, 1926; Gold Medal, Royal Astronomical Society, 1932, for work on double stars; appointed George Darwin Lecturer before the Society for 1932. *Publications:* Observations of Double Stars. Lick Observatory Publications, vol. xii., 1914; The Binary Stars, 1918; 2nd edition, 1935; New General Catalogue of Double Stars within 120° of the North Pole, 1932; numerous papers in various astronomical and other scientific journals. Has discovered 3108 double stars, computed many orbits of double stars and of comets. Is continuing researches on double stars. *Address:* 1109 Spruce Street, Berkeley 7, California, U.S.A. [*Died* 29 *Oct.* 1951.

AIYAR, Hon. Mr. Justice N. Chandrasekhara, B.A., B.L.; **Rao Bahadur**; *b.* 25 Jan. 1888; *s.* of N. Kuppu-Swami Aiyar and Srimathi Lakshmiammal; *m.* 1904, Srimathi Sitalakshmi, *d.* of Dewan Bahadur C. V. Muniswami Iyer, Chief Reporter, Madras Mail; no *c.* *Educ.:* Madras Christian College; Law College, Madras. Law apprentice under late Hon. Mr. V. Krishmaswami Aiyar, and Sir C. P. Ramaswami Aiyar; Vakil, Madras High Court, 1910; City Civil Judge, July 1927; District Judge, Dec. 1927; Additional Judge, High Court, 1941; Judge, High Court, Madras, 1943-48; retired 1948. India's representative on the Indo-Pakistan Boundaries Commission. Judge, Supreme Court, New Delhi, Sept. 1950. Chairman Delimitation Commission, India, 1953. *Publications:* Mayne's Hindu Law (11th edn.); Life of Anjaneya; (trans.) Valmiki Ramayana. *Recreations:* cricket, tennis, volley ball. *Address:* Sri Sadma, 96 Mount Road, Madras. *T.:* 88011. *Clubs:* Cosmopolitan (Madras); Mylapore (Mylapore); Union (Madura). [*Died* 31 *March* 1957.

AKERS, Sir Wallace Alan, Kt., *cr.* 1946; C.B.E. 1944; F.R.S. 1952; F.R.I.C.; F.R.S.A.; retired as research director of I.C.I.; Trustee of the National Gallery; *b.* 9 Sept. 1888; *s.* of Charles Akers, London; *m.* 1953, Bernadette La Marre, Landerneau and Bracieux, France. *Educ.:* Lake House School, Bexhill; Aldenham School; Christ Church, Oxford. Brunner Mond & Co., 1911-1924; Borneo Co. Ltd., 1924-28; Imperial Chemical Industries Ltd., 1928-53. Director of Atomic Energy Research, under Dept. of Industrial and Scientific Research, Dec. 1941-Feb. 1946. Fellow: Soc. of Chemical Industry; Chemical Soc.; Member: Faraday Society; Biochemical Society; Advisory Council, D.S.I.R., 1952-. Hon. D.Sc. (Durham), 1949; Hon. D.C.L. (Oxon.); Hon. Assoc. M.C.T., 1953. *Address:* Yledyn, King's Road, Alton, Hants. *T.:* Alton 2174. *Clubs:* Athenæum, Leander, Royal Thames Yacht. [*Died* 1 *Nov.* 1954.

ALABASTER, Sir Chaloner Grenville, Kt., *cr.* **1942; O.B.E. 1918; K.C. 1922;** *o. surv. s.* **of late Sir Chaloner Alabaster, K.C.M.G.;** *m.* **1909, Mabel Winifred Mary, M.B.E. (*d.* 1951), *d.* of late Col. E. P. Mainwaring, Indian Army; one *d.* *Educ.:* Tonbridge. Called to Bar, Inner Temple, 1904; Western Circuit; Acting Attorney-General, Hong-Kong, 1911, 1912, 1928; unofficial member Legislative Council, 1919, 1924, 1925; Attorney-General of Hong-Kong, 1930-46; Acting Chief Justice, 1937. Interned by Japanese in Stanley Camp, Hong-Kong, 1942-45. *Publication:* Editor of Laws of** Hong-Kong, 1844-1912. *Address:* Lysways, Bransgore, Hants. *Clubs:* Royal Commonwealth Society; Hong-Kong. [*Died* 10 *Sept.* 1958.

ALAGAPPA CHETTIAR, **Sir Ramanatha,** Kt., *cr.* 1946; M.A., D.Litt., LL.D.; Barrister-at-Law; *b.* April 1909; *s.* of late K. V. Al. Ramanathan Chettiar; *m.*; one *d.* *Educ.:* Presidency College, Madras; Middle Temple, London. Managing Director, Alagappa Textiles (Cochin) Ltd.; Umayal Weaving Establishment Ltd. Director of several Joint Stock Companies and Indian Bank Ltd. Life Member, Madras and Annamalai Universities. Donated over five million rupees to charitable and educational institutions, including Rs. 15 lakhs to the Electro-Chemical Research Institute, Karaikudi, foundation-stone laid by Pandit Jawaharlal Nehru, Prime Minister; also to Thakkar Bapa Vidyalaya (Harijan Industrial School), foundation-school laid by Mahatma Gandhi; and to Dr. Alagappa Chettiar College of Technology at Annamalainagar and Madras. Founder, Dr. Alagappa Chettiar College, Karaikudi. Member, Governing Body of Council of Scientific and Industrial Research; Indian Peoples' Famine Trust, Government of India. *Address:* Krishna Vilas, Vepery, Madras. [*Died* 5 *April* 1957.

ALBA, 17th Duque de, (and 10th Duke of Berwick but for Act of Attainder, W. & M., 1695); (Jacobo Maria del Pilar Carlos Manuel) **Fitz-James Stuart;** Member of the Royal Spanish Academy; Director of the Royal Academy of History; Member of the Royal Academy of Fine Arts of San Fernando; Member of the Patronato del Museo del Prado; Hon. D.C.L. of Oxford and Trinity College, Dublin; Corresponding Member of the British Academy; *b.* Madrid, 17 Oct. 1878; *e. s.* of Carlos, 16th Duke of Alba, 9th Duke of Berwick, and Maria del Rosario Falcó y Osorio, 22nd Condesa de Siruela; *m.* 1920, Maria del Rosario de Silva y Gurtubay, Marquesa de San Vicente del Barco (*d.* 1934), *d.* of Duke of Aliaga. *Educ.:* Beaumont. Minister of Education, Spain, 1930; Foreign Minister Spain, 1930-31; Spanish Ambassador to Great Britain, 1939-45. *Publications:* El Embajador Gómez de Fuensalida; Catálogo de la Coleccion de Pinturas de la Casa de Alba; Noticias históricas y genealógicas de las Casas de Montijo y Teba; Discourse on Entrance to Academy of History; Biblia de la Casa de Alba; Discourse on Entrance to Academy of San Fernando; Discourse on Entrance to the Royal Spanish Academy, El Mariscal de Berwick; Miniaturas de la Casa de Alba; La Música en la Casa de Alba; Lettres familières de l'Impératrice Eugénie; Lettres intimes de Prosper Mérimée à la Comtesse de Montijo; Discurso de Don Sancho de Londoño; Epistolario del III Duque de Alba. *Recreations:* shooting, ski-ing, motoring, polo, golf. *Heir:* *d.* Maria del Rosario Cayetana Fitz-James Stuart y de Silva, Duquesa de Montoro, Marquesa de San Vicente del Barco [*b.* Madrid, 28 March 1926; *m.* 1947, Don Luis Martinez de Irujo, *s.* of Duke of Sotomayor; one *s.* Catholic.] *Address:* Martires de Alcala 4, Madrid. *Clubs:* Marlborough-Windham, St. James', Beefsteak; Jockey (Paris). [*Died* 24 *Sept.* 1953.

ALCOCK, Rev. Preb. John Mark; Prebendary of Warminster in Wells Cathedral since 1913; Canon Residentiary of Wells Cathedral, 1915-51; *s.* of late Rev. J. P. Alcock, Rector of Southfleet, Kent; *m.* 1898, Marion (*d.* 1947), *d.* of Oswald Rufus Milne of Werneth, Lancs. *Educ.:* King's School, Canterbury; Oriel College, Oxford, M.A. 1891. Ordained, 1889; Curate of West Wickham, 1889-91; Evershot, 1891-1896; Tolpuddle, 1896-1900; Vicar of Godney, 1900-15; Rural Dean of Glastonbury, 1912-15; Chaplain and Secretary to Bishops of Bath and Wells, 1908-42. *Address:* The North Liberty, Wells, Som. [*Died* 6 *Sept.* 1955.

ALDAM, Col. William St. A. W.; *see* Warde-Aldam.

ALDANOV, Mark; author; *b.* 7 Nov. 1889; *m.* **1922, Tatiana Saltzov; no *c.* *Educ.:* Russian University (faculties of law and science). Lived in St. Petersburg (now Leningrad); Emigré since 1919. Some of his books have been translated into 24 languages. *Publications:* (in English) novels: The Ninth Thermidor, 1925; The Devil's Bridge, 1926; St. Helena, 1928; The Key, 1930; The Fifth Seal (Book of the Month, U.S.), 1943; For Thee the Best, 1945; Before the Deluge (Book Society choice, Great Britain), 1948; The Tenth Symphony, 1949; The Escape, 1950. Five books of essays; three books of chemistry. *Address:* 109 West 84 Street, New York 24. *T.:* TR 79569.** [*Died* 24 *Feb.* 1957.

ALDER, Professor Kurt; Dr.phil.; Dr.med.*h.c.*, Köln, 1950; Dr. *h.c.* Salamanca, 1954; Director of Chemical Institute of University of Cologne since 1940; *b.* 10 July 1902; *s.* of Joseph and Maria Alder. *Educ.:* Königshütte; Berlin; Kiel. Kiel: Dr. phil., 1926; Dozent, 1930; Prof., 1934. Prof., Köln, 1940. (Jointly) Nobel prize for Chemistry, 1950. Hon. mem. Real Sociedad Española de Física y Química, 1953; hon. adviser, Consejo Superior de Investigaciones Científicas, Madrid, 1953. Corresp. mem. Mathematisch-naturwissenschaftliche Klasse, Bayerische Akademie der Wissenschaften, München. 1955. *Publications:* Essays in chemical journals. *Recreations:* music, literature, fishing. *Address:* 47 Zülpicher St., Cologne, Germany. [*Died* 20 *June* 1958.

ALDERSON, Sir Edward Hall, K.C.B., *cr.* 1931 (C.B. 1919); K.B.E., *cr.* 1925; J.P.; *b.* 1864; *s.* of late Francis J. Alderson, and *g.s.* of late Sir Edward Hall Alderson, a Baron of the Exchequer; *m.* 1900, Mary Emily (*d.* 1935), *d.* of Sir H. Cosmo Bonsor, 1st Bt.; one *s.* one *d.* *Educ.:* privately; Brasenose College, Oxford (B.A.). Called to Bar, Inner Temple, 1890; S.E. Circuit and C.C.C.; Private Secretary to Lord Chancellor (E. Halsbury), and Secretary of Commissions, 1895-1900; Reading Clerk and Clerk of Outdoor Committees, House of Lords, 1900-1917; Clerk Assistant of the Parliaments, 1917-1930; Clerk of the Parliaments, 1930-34. *Recreations:* riding, tennis, golf, play-acting. *Address:* The Hall, Tunstall, Woodbridge, Suffolk. *Clubs:* Travellers', Beefsteak. [*Died* 7 *March* 1951.

ALDRICH, Mrs. Richard Stoddard; *see* Lawrence, Gertrude.

ALDRIDGE, Leonard, C.B.E. 1946; F.G.S.; Founder and Chairman Anglo-French Consolidated Investment Corp. Ltd.; Chm. Mitchell Cotts & Co. Ltd.; Chm. or Director of some 50 Cos., constituting Anglo-French-Mitchell Cotts Group covering inter-Empire trading, including shipping, coal, steel, engineering, industrial and base metal mining interests; Director Goodlass Wall & Lead Industries Ltd., Natal Navigation Colleries & Estate Co. Ltd., Transvaal Navigation Collieries & Estate Co. Ltd., etc.; a firm believer in British Empire, in which he has travelled extensively; has initiated or taken part in creation of various industrial and other undertakings contributing to strengthening of economic and trade links within the Empire and fostering of relations between the Empire and other countries; *b.* 12 Nov. 1892; *s.* of Richard Aldridge; *m.* 1st; one *d.*; 2nd, 1936, Marguerite, *y. d.* of Louis Laroque, Montmezeri, Haut Vienne, France. Chm. of Council Pilgrim House Settlement, Old Ford and Poplar, E.; Hon. Colonel 1st City of London Cadet Regt.; Freeman City of London; Liveryman Company of Coopers, Company of Paviors. Held number of hon. civilian and para-military Government appts. during War of 1939-45, including: in the Levant: Economic Adviser to H.B.M.'s Minister, Levant States; Economic Adviser, Spears Mission to Syria and the Lebanon; British Govt. Representative, Office des Céréales Panifiables (O.C.P.); Member Levant Ports and Transit Cttee.; Chief Rep., Middle East Supply Centre, Levant States; in Egypt: Member Lord Moyne Man-Power Cttee. for Middle East; in Persia: Economic Adviser and Special Representative in Persia to Middle East Supply Centre; Adviser to Food Dept. of Milspaugh (American) Economic Mission, Teheran, on the collection and distribution of Cereals; in India: Additional Commissioner and Director-General, Transportation and Storage, Dept. of Civil Supplies, Govt. of Bengal. *Recreations:* practical geology. During earlier years took part in field surveys in Africa, Australia, some Pacific Islands and Portugal. *Address:* 2 Queen Anne's Gate, Westminster, S.W.1; also Khartoum, Johannesburg and Paris. *Clubs:* Royal Societies, Junior Carlton, Royal Aero, Public Schools, Hurlingham; Turf (Cairo); Muthaiga (Nairobi); City (Cape Town); Bengal (Calcutta). [*Died* 8 *June* 1952.

ALEXANDER, Edward Bruce, C.M.G. 1925; V.D.; late Ceylon Civil Service; *b.* 3 March 1872; *s.* of R. Dundas Alexander, I.C.S.; *m.* 1899, Mabel Eleanor, *d.* of W. D. Bosanquet, Ripsley House, Liphook, Hants; two *s.* one *d.* *Educ.:* Forest School; Trinity College, Oxford. Retired as Controller of Revenue, Ceylon, 1927; acted as Colonial Secretary, 1925-27, and as Governor, Oct.-Nov. 1925; represented Ceylon at the Colonial Office Conference, 1927; representative of Govt. of Ceylon on the International Tea Committee since 1933, and on the International Rubber Regulation Committee, 1934-44; served European War, 1914-18; Hon. Lt.-Col. late Ceylon Mounted Rifles; Grand Officer, Order of the Crown of Belgium. Member of Toc H since its foundation and of Exec. Cttee. of Brit. Emp. Leprosy Relief Assoc. *Recreations:* Association football blue at Oxford, Corinthians, Authentics; played cricket for Ceylon, etc. *Address:* c/o Chartered Bank of India, Australia, and China, 38 Bishopsgate, E.C.2. *Clubs:* Oxford and Cambridge, M.C.C., Queen's. [*Died* 21 *March* 1955.

ALEXANDER, Lieut.-Col. Francis David, C.B.E. 1925; *b.* 2 June 1878; *s.* of D. T. Alexander, Dinas Powis, Cardiff; *m.* Dorothy, *d.* of A. J. Robarts, Tile House, Buckingham; two *d.* *Educ.:* Haileybury College; Trinity College, Cambridge. Joined 19th Hussars, 1900; served S. African War and European War with 19th Hussars; joined Remount Service, 1918. Rejoined the army Sept. 1941 and retired Apr. 1945. *Address:* Manton, Oakham. *Club:* Cavalry. [*Died* 2 *Nov.* 1956.

ALEXANDER, Sir Frank (Samuel), 1st Bt., *cr.* 1945; Kt., *cr.* 1942; Alderman of Aldgate Ward in City of London; *b.* London, 17 June 1881; *s.* of Edward Alexander, Highgate; *m.* 1922, Elsa Mary (*d.* 1959), *d.* of Sir Charles Collett, 1st Bt.; two *s.* two *d.* *Educ.:* Highgate School. Shipbroker and shipowner; Partner in Capper, Alexander & Co.; Director of Alexander Shipping Co., Ltd., Yorkshire Insurance Co., Ltd., Houlder Line, Ltd., Waxed-Papers, Ltd.; Chairman of Baltic Mercantile and Shipping Exchange, 1939-46; Sheriff for the City of London, 1940-1941; Lord Mayor of London, 1944-45. Capt. and Adjutant of 72nd Heavy Artillery Brigade in European War, 1914-18. *Recreations:* tennis, golf, swimming. *Heir:* *s.* Charles Gundry, *b.* 5 May 1923. *Address:* Norsted Manor, Farnborough, Kent. *T.:* Knockholt 2288. *Clubs:* Royal Automobile, City Livery, United Wards. [*Died* 18 *July* 1959.

ALEXANDER, Frederick Matthias; during past 60 years has been an explorer in the previously unexplored field of human biology; *b.* 20 Jan. 1869; *s.* of John and Betsy Alexander-educated. *Educ.:* privately; more or less self-educated. With mining company in Tasmania; secretary in Melbourne; professional reciter; trouble developed in voice and throat and as orthodox treatment failed to help him he began a series of experiments upon himself as set down in The Use of the Self, which led to his discovery of a primary control of the use of the self and to the evolution of a technique for its employment; relinquished the career of a reciter to teach this technique, first in Melbourne and then in Sydney with the support of many medical men; came to London in 1904; in 1940 evacuated the F. Matthias Alexander Trust Fund School to Stow, Mass. After arranging for the carrying on of the work in U.S.A. he returned to London, 1943; formerly Director of the F. Matthias Alexander Trust Fund School at Penhill, near Bexley. *Publications:* Man's Supreme Inheritance, 1910 (revised, 1918); Conscious Control, 1912; Constructive Conscious Control of the Individual, 1923; The Use of the Self, 1932; The Universal Constant in Living, 1941; Treatise: Respiratory Re-education, 1906. *Recreations:* riding, shooting, theatre. *Address:* 16 Ashley Place, S.W.1. *T.:* Victoria 1863. [*Died* 10 *Oct.* 1955.

ALEXANDER, Gilchrist Gibb, M.A.; *b.* 5 Oct. 1871; *s.* of Wm. Alexander, Clarkfield, Partick, Glasgow; *m.* Jenny (*d.* 1952), *e. d.* of John White, J.P., 1 Prince's Gardens, Glasgow, W.; two *d. Educ.:* Glasgow Academy and Glasgow University. M.A. with first-class honours in Mental Philosophy, 1893; awarded Thomas Logan Memorial Gold Medal as most distinguished graduate in Arts of that year, Gartmore Gold Medal for University Essay and Eglinton Fellowship. Called to Bar, Middle Temple, 1896; practised in London until 1907; from 1907-20 (with interval of two years for service with Imperial Army) acted in Fiji and Western Pacific as Chief Police Magistrate, Attorney-General, Chief Justice, and Chief Judicial Commissioner, in the New Hebrides as British Judge in the Joint Court of the Condominium, and in the Solomon Islands as Lands Commissioner to deal with land disputes; Chairman of Commission to investigate shipping conditions, Fiji; Senior Puisne Judge, High Court, Tanganyika, East Africa, and Member Court of Appeal for Eastern Africa, 1920-25; acting Chief Justice, 1921-22, 1923-24; retired, 1925. *Publications:* From the Middle Temple to the South Seas, 1927; Tanganyika Memories; A Judge in the Red Kanzu, 1936; The Temple of the Nineties, 1938; After Court Hours, 1950; many contributions to Law Times. *Recreation:* golf. *Address:* 25 Platt's Lane, Hampstead, N.W.3. *T.:* Hampstead 0220; Fountain Court, Temple, E.C. [*Died* 24 *Nov.* 1958.

ALEXANDER, Sir Lionel Cecil William, 6th Bt., *cr.* 1809; D.S.O. 1916; late Major 23rd Batt. London Regiment; late Lieut. Grenadier Guards; *b.* 23 Sept. 1885; *S.* father, 1896; *m.* 1st, 1908, Nooroux Weston (marriage dissolved, 1923), *e. d.* of 1st Baron Cable; one *s.*; 2nd, 1924, Hope, *yr. d.* of late Capt. Hurrell, Aberdeen; one *s.* Served European War, 1914-18 (D.S.O., Croix de Guerre avec Palmes); High Sheriff of Cambridgeshire and Huntingdonshire, 1929. *Heir: s.* Desmond William Lionel Cable-Alexander [*b.* 4 Oct. 1910; *m.* 1st, 1935, Mary Jane O'Brien (marriage dissolved, 1941) one *s.*; 2nd, Margaret Wood, *d.* of late John Burnett, Dublin; two *d*]. *Address:* Mill Lane House, Crondall, Hants. [*Died* 6 *Aug.* 1956.

ALEXANDER, Brigadier-General Sir William, K.B.E., *cr.* 1920; C.B. 1919; C.M.G. 1918; D.S.O. 1916; T.D. 1919; 6th Black Watch (T.F.R.); *b.* Glasgow, 4 May 1874; *s.* of late Thomas Alexander of Brentham Park, Stirling; *m.* 1st, 1911, Beatrice Evelyn (*d.* 1928), *y. d.* of late John Ritchie of Bingham, Paramatta, N.S.W.; four *s.*; 2nd, 1930, Ruby Mary (*d.* 1951), *widow* of Comdr. Patrick Spencer, R.N., and *e. d.* of late John Ritchie, Bingham, Paramatta. *Educ.:* Kelvinside Academy; Glasgow University; Göttingen. Lieut. T.F., 1899; Capt. 1906; Major, 1915; Brig.-Gen. 1917; served European War, 1914-18 (D.S.O., despatches, Bt. Lt.-Col., Temp. Brig.-Gen., Legion of Honour, Officer of St. Maurice and St. Lazarus); Director of Administration National Explosives Factories, Ministry of Munitions, 1916-17; Controller of Aircraft Supply and Production, 1917-19; Director-General of Purchases, 1919-20; M.P. (U.) Central Glasgow, 1923-45. *Address:* Grey Gables, St. Aubin, Jersey, C.I. *T.:* Southern 80. [*Died* 29 *Dec.* 1954.

ALEXANDER, Lieutenant-Colonel William Nathaniel Stuart, D.S.O. 1915; late the Connaught Rangers; *b.* 8 May 1874; *m.* 1914, Kathleen Marguerite, *d.* of Lt.-Col. H. N. Hilliard, Indian Army. *Educ.:* Rugby. Entered army, 1894; Captain, 1901; Major, 1914; Lt.-Col. 1921; served S. Africa, 1902 (Queen's medal 3 clasps); European War, 1914-1918 (D.S.O. and bar); 3rd Afghan War, 1919 (medal and clasp); retired pay, 1923. *Address:* Winton Lodge, Gordon Rd., Camberley, Surrey. *T.:* Camberley 548. [*Died* 7 *March* 1956.

ALFORD, Lieut.-Colonel Henry; late Gordon Highlanders; traveller; *b.* London; *s.* of late Lewis Alford and Florence, *e. d.* of late Colonel Henry Stamford, Bombay Horse Artillery; unmarried. *Educ.:* Harrow; R.M.C., Sandhurst. Travelled extensively in Africa, 1896-1901; served under Lord Kitchener as Lieut. on Transport Staff, Sudan, 1896 (Queen's and Khedive's medals with clasp); as Lieut. Royal Scots Fusiliers and on Staff in S. African War, 1899-1901 (medal with five clasps); retired with rank of Captain, 1902, and joined Reserve of Officers; travelled in India, Far East, and Canada, 1902-4; visited every country in Europe (including Iceland) and every State in U.S.A., 1905-10; was in Mexican Revolution, 1910; raised and commanded 11th Batt. Gordon Highlanders in European War, 1914-17; mentioned for valuable services (medal); on demobilisation in 1920 was granted rank of Lt.-Col.; War of 1939-45: Civil Defence (medal); Jubilee Medal, 1935; Coronation Medals, 1911, 1937, 1953; Member of the Queen's Bodyguard for Scotland (Royal Company of Archers). F.G.S., F.R.G.S., F.Z.S. *Publication:* The Egyptian Sudan, its Loss and Recovery, 1898. *Recreation:* foreign travel. *Clubs:* Travellers', Shikar. [*Died* 31 *July* 1955.

ALI, Abdullah Yusuf, C.B.E. 1917; M.A., LL.M. (Cantab.); F.R.S.L.; F.R.Empire S.; M.R.A.S.; Barrister-at-law, of Lincoln's Inn; *b.* 4 Apr. 1872; *s.* of late Khan Bahadur Yusuf Ali. *Educ.:* Wilson College, Bombay; Bombay University; St. John's College, Cambridge. Joined I.C.S., 1895; Assistant Magistrate, 1896; Joint Magistrate, 1899; Assistant Sessions Judge, 1902; subsequently Deputy Commissioner and District Magistrate; Under-Secretary to Government of India, Finance Department, 1907; acted as Deputy Secretary, 1911-12; retired from Indian Civil Service, 1914; President, U.P. Industrial Conference, Agra, 1909; President, All-India Muhammadan Educational Conference, Nagpur, Dec. 1910; Lecturer on Hindustani, Hindi, and Indian Religions, Manners, and Customs, School of Oriental Studies, London University, 1917-1919; Chairman of special committees and Member of the Committee on India, Imperial Institute, 1916-19; President of Indian Students Prisoners of War Fund, 1916; Lecture Tour in Denmark, Sweden, and Norway, Apr.-May 1918, and in Holland, Oct.-Nov. 1920; Sarf-i-Khas Counsel, Hyderabad, Deccan, 1919-20; Revenue Minister, Hyderabad, Deccan, 1921-22; Lucknow Bar, 1922-24; Principal, Islamia College, Lahore, 1925-27; Fellow and Syndic, Punjab University, 1925-28; Member of Court, Aligarh University; Educational tour through the Near East; one of India's representatives to the 9th Assembly of the League of Nations, 1928; world tour, through America, Hawaian Islands, Japan, China, Philippines, Straits Settlements, Ceylon and India, 1929-30; through Canada from Halifax to Victoria as guest of National Council of Education, 1932; Executive Committee of World Conference for International Peace through Religion; President Sind Azad Conference, 1932; President All India Muslim Conference, Calcutta, 1932; Member Punjab University Enquiry Committee, 1932-33; Principal, Islamia College, Lahore, 1935-37; and Fellow of the Panjab University, 1935-39; Lecture Tour through Canada, 1938-39. *Publi-*

ALFORD, (Edward) John (Gregory). See page xxvii.

cations: Silk Fabrics in the North-Western Provinces and Oudh, 1900; Life and Labour in India, 1907; The Indian Muhammadans, 1907; Mestrovic and Serbian Sculpture, 1916; Indian Section in Expansion of the Anglo-Saxon Nations, 1920; 6th ed. Wilson's Anglo-Muhammadan Law, 1930; Muslim Educational Ideals, 1923; Making of India, 1925; Islam as a World Force, 1926; India and Europe, 1926; Three Travellers to India, 1927; Social and Economic Conditions in Mediaeval India (in Urdu), 1928; Fundamentals of Islam, 1929; Personality of Muhammad the Prophet, 1929; Moral Education: Aims and Methods, 1930; Personality of Man in Islam, 1931; Imam Husain and his Martyrdom, 1931; Medieval India, 1932; Religious Polity of Islam, 1933; English Translation and Commentary on the Quran, 1934-38; revised ed., 1939-40; Life and Literature, 1936; Religion and Social Equality, 1936; Islamic History, its scope and content, 1936; Idea of Salvation in Islam, 1939; The Message of Islam, 1940; articles in Indian and English magazines and papers. *Recreations:* walking, riding, travel, tennis, chess. *Club:* National Liberal. [*Died* 10 *Dec.* 1953.

ALI-RAJPUR, Chief, H.H. Raja Sir Pratap Singhji, Raja of, K.C.I.E., *cr.* 1933 (C.I.E. 1915); *b.* 1881; *S.* 1891; State covers 836 square miles and has a population of 89,364. *Grandson and Heir:* Surendra Sinhji. The Raja receives a hereditary salute of eleven guns. *Address:* Ali-rajpur (*via* Dohad, B.B. and C.I.), Southern States, Central India. [*Died* 1948.

[*But death not notified in time for inclusion in Who Was Who 1941–1950, first edn.*

ALINGTON, Adrian Richard; Author; *b.* 19 April 1895; *s.* of Rev. E. H. Alington, Oxford; *m.* 1928, Lucy Wilson (*d.* 1957). *Educ.:* Marlborough College; Magdalen Coll., Oxford; Served European War, 1914-18, Wiltshire Regt.; France 1915-18 (wounded); final rank, Captain, 1918; Cipher Officer, Supreme War Council, Versailles. War of 1939-45, Private, Home Guard. *Publications:* Slowbags and Arethusa; The Career of Julian Stanley-Williams; Mr. Jubenka: Chaytor's; Ann and Aurelia; Donaldson; Moss is the Stuff; Waiting for Joanna; The Vanishing Celebrities; The Amazing Test Match Crime; The Boy King; These, our Strangers; Sanity Island; Those Kids From Town Again; Rosie Todmarsh; edited John Buchan's Episodes of the Great War; various film and radio scripts, etc. *Address:* 33B Marloes Road, W.8.
[*Died* 30 *Oct.* 1958.

ALINGTON, Hon. Mrs. Cyril, (Hester Margaret), C.B.E. 1949; *b.* 26 Dec. 1874; *y. d.* of 4th Baron Lyttelton, P.C.; *m.* 1904, Very Rev. Cyril Alington, D.D. (*d.* 1955); three *d.* (and one *s.* killed on active service, 1943, one *s.* one *d.* decd.). *Address:* Treago, St. Weonard's, Hereford.
[*Died* 26 *March* 1958.

ALINGTON, Very Rev. Cyril Argentine, D.D. (Oxon.) Hon. D.C.L. Durham; Dean of Durham, 1933-51, Dean Emeritus since 1951; Hon. Fellow of Trinity College, Oxford, 1926; *b.* 1872; *s.* of late Rev. H. G. Alington of Candlesby, Lincolnshire; *m.* 1904, Hon. Hester Margaret, *y. d.* of 4th Baron Lyttelton, P.C.; one *s.* three *d.* (and one *s.* killed on active service, 1943, one *d.* decd.). *Educ.:* Marlborough; Trinity College, Oxford. 1st Class Classical Moderations, 1893; 1st Class Literæ Humaniores, 1895. Fellow of All Souls; Assistant Master at Marlborough and Eton; Headmaster, Shrewsbury School, 1908-16; Headmaster of Eton College, 1916-33; Chaplain to the King, 1921-33; Select Preacher to University of Oxford, 1909-10, 1928-29, and 1945-46; sometime Examining Chaplain to Bishop of Lichfield; Chairman Headmasters' Conference, 1924-25. Hon. Freeman of City of Durham, 1949. *Publications:* A Schoolmaster's Apology, 1914; Shrewsbury Fables, 1917; Twenty Years, 1921; Eton Fables, 1921; Strained Relations, 1922; Mr. Evans: a Cricketo-Detective Story, 1922; Why we Read the Old Testament, 1923; King Harrison and Others, 1923; An Eton Poetry Book, 1925; The Count in Kensington, 1926; Tommy's Uncle, 1927; Elementary Christianity, 1927; More Eton Fables, 1927; Doubts and Difficulties, 1929; The Abbot's Cup, 1930; The Task of Happiness, 1931; Christian Outlines, 1931; The Fool Hath Said, 1933; Final Eton Fables, 1933; Eton Faces—Old and New, 1933; Lionel Ford, 1934; Things Ancient and Modern, 1936; A New Approach to the Old Testament, 1937; The New Testament: A Reader's Guide, 1938; Crime on the Kennet, 1939; The Kingdom of God, 1940; Poets at Play, 1941; In Shabby Streets, 1942; Fables and Fancies, 1943; Edward Lyttleton, 1943; Ten Crowded Hours, 1943; Good News, 1945; Archdeacons Afloat, 1946; Europe: A Personal and Political Survey, 1946; The Life Everlasting, 1947; Archdeacons Ashore, 1947; Midnight Wireless, 1947; Durham Cathedral, 1948; Sense and Non-sense, 1949; Blackmail in Blankshire, 1949; Gold and Gaiters, 1950; The Nabob's Jewel, 1952; A Dean's Apology, 1952. *Address:* Treago, St. Weonard's, Hereford. [*Died* 16 *May* 1955.

ALISON, David, R.S.A. 1922 (A.R.S.A. 1916); R.P.; *b.* Dysart, Fife; *m.* 1913, Mary, 2nd *d.* of Charles Bearsley, M.A., Old Meldrum; one *s.* one *d.* *Educ.:* Kirkcaldy High School. Studied Glasgow School of Art, Paris, Italy. Gained Haldane Travelling Scholarship, Glasgow, also Carnegie Travelling Scholarship of Royal Scottish Academy. Exhibits Royal Academy, Royal Portrait Society, Royal Scottish Academy, Glasgow Institute; Paris Salon, Société des Artistes Français (Silver Medal, 1931). Represented in public collections, Liverpool, Leamington, Paisley, Edinburgh. Served 5th Royal Scots, 1914-18. *Address:* 78 Queen Street, Edinburgh. *T.:* Edinburgh 23458. *Club:* Chelsea Arts. [*Died* 14 *Jan.* 1955.

ALISON, John, M.A., LL.D., F.R.S.E.; *b.* Kirkcaldy, Fife, 28 Feb. 1861; *s.* of late Peter Alison, schoolmaster, Gallatown; *m.* 1888, Margaret, *e. d.* of S. K. Orr, Edinburgh; three *d.* *Educ.:* Edinburgh University. Pupil Teacher; Queen's Scholar and Teacher in Moray House Training College; Mathematical Master in Edinburgh Academy, 1884-86; in George Watson's College till 1902; Principal of Glasgow U.F.C. Training College till 1904; Headmaster, George Watson's College, Edinburgh, till 1926, when he retired. *Publication:* (Joint) Arithmetic for Schools and Colleges. *Address:* 126 Craiglea Drive, Edinburgh.
[*Died* 21 *March* 1952.

ALLAN, Archibald Russell Watson, R.S.A. 1937 (A.R.S.A. 1931); Artist in Oil, Watercolour, and Pastel; *b.* Glasgow, 6 March 1878; *s.* of A. R. Allan, J.P. and Margaret Hunter; *m.* 1913, Alice, 3rd *d.* of William Young and Margaret Robertson. *Educ.:* Collegiate School, Glasgow; Greenock Academy. First studies in Art under John Spiers, portrait painter, Glasgow; thereafter at Glasgow Athenæum School of Art, Julian's Colarossis, Glasgow School of Art (Diploma); principal works: The Aeroplane, The Top of the Hill (Glasgow Corporation); Noon (Paisley Corporation); The Rebel (Smith Institute, Stirling). *Recreations:* gardening, reading and the study of Scottish Gaelic. *Address:* Kilmichael, Randolph Road, Stirling. *Club:* Glasgow Art. [*Died* 24 *April* 1959.

ALLAN, Sir Harold Egbert, Kt., *cr.* **1948; O.B.E. 1942; P.C. Jamaica 1942; Minister of Finance, Jamaica, B.W.I., since**

1945, and Leader of House of Representatives; *b.* Port Antonio, Jamaica, 15 Mar. 1894; *s.* of Patrick Kerr and Elizabeth Allan; *m.* 1941, Edris Elaine Trottman; no *c.* *Educ.:* Mico College, Jamaica, and by private tuition. Has been businessman, planter, legislator; Head Master Titchfield Upper School. J.P. 1930; M.L.C. 1935; Founder Assoc. of Elected Members of Jamaica Legislature, 1935; Chm. B.W.I. Deleg. to World Trade Confs., London and Geneva, 1947; rep. B.W.I. at World Trade Conf., Havana, 1948. Founder Benevolent Societies and Literary Clubs. Mico College Gold Medal for meritorious public service, 1942. *Recreations:* cricket, swimming. *Address:* Half Way Tree, Jamaica, B.W.I. *T.A.:* Kingston, Jamaica, British West Indies. *T.:* 6209. *Clubs:* Manchester Country (Mandeville); Kingston Polo, Kingston Cricket (Kingston).
[*Died* 18 *Feb.* 1953.

ALLAN, Sir Henry S. M. H., Bt.; *see* Havelock-Allan.

ALLAN, Colonel Sir Hugh Montagu, Kt., *cr.* 1904; C.V.O. 1907; Order of Rising Sun of Japan (3rd class), 1907; E.D. 1932; retired; Hon. Colonel Black Watch (Royal Highlanders) of Canada; Lt.-Col. Canadian Expeditionary Forces; *b.* Montreal, 13 Oct. 1860; 2nd *s.* of late Sir Hugh Allan of Ravenscrag, Montreal, Canada, and Matilda Caroline, *d.* of late John Smith, Montreal; *m.* 1893, Marguerite Ethel, *d.* of late Hector Mackenzie of Montreal. *Educ.:* Bishop's College School, Lennoxville, Province of Quebec; Paris. *Address:* The Chateau, 1321 Sherbrooke Street, W., Montreal. *Clubs:* Canada; St. James's, Mount Royal (Montreal).
[*Died* 26 *Sept.* 1951.

ALLAN, John, C.B. 1948; M.A., F.B.A., F.S.A. (London and Scotland); LL.D. (Edin.); Lecturer in Sanskrit, University of Edinburgh; Keeper of the Dept. of Coins and Medals, British Museum, 1931-49; *e. s.* of late J. G. Allan, Longniddry; *m.* Ida, *y. d.* of late J. C. Law, Dundee; one *s.* one *d.* *Educ.:* Royal High School, Edinburgh; Univs. of Edinburgh and Leipzig. Entered British Museum, 1907; Deputy Keeper, 1924-31; Lecturer in Sanskrit, University Coll., 1909-17, and at the School of Oriental Studies, 1920-22; Examiner in Indian subjects in British and Indian Universities; in Military Intelligence Department of War Office, 1915-18; Secretary of the Royal Numismatic Society, 1909-48; an Editor of the Numismatic Chronicle, 1921-50; Secretary of the Royal High School Club in London, 1920-49 and President, 1932; Medallist of the Numismatic Society of India, 1928 and 1937, of the Royal Numismatic Society, 1936, and of the American Numismatic Society, 1936; Vice-Pres. Soc. Antiquaries, 1949-54; Pres., Berwickshire Naturalists' Club, 1955. Hon. Vice-President Royal Archæological Institute. Corresp. Member: Kungl. Vitterhets Akad. of Sweden; Archæological Soc. of Finland. Hon. Member: Yorkshire Philosophical Soc.; Société Française de Numismatique and of the Vienna, American, Indian, Czecho-Slovak and Zagreb Numismatic Societies. *Publications:* two volumes of British Museum Catalogue of Indian Coins; The Inscriptions of Ajanta; edited Catalogue of Coins in the Indian Museum, vol. iv.; joint author of the Cambridge Shorter History of India; contributions to encyclopædias and Oriental and archæological periodicals. *Recreations:* walking and fishing. *Address:* The University, Edinburgh. [*Died* 26 *Aug.* 1955.

ALLAN, Maud; dancer, actress, pianist, writer; *b.* Toronto; *d.* of Dr. William Allan and Dr. Isabell M. Allan, *née* Hutchinson; unmarried. *Educ.:* San Francisco; Vienna; Royal Academy of Music, Berlin. Originally intended to be a pianist, studied under Busoni in his master-class; graduated with honours at the Royal Academy of Music, Berlin; decided, after studying classical sculpture and painting in Italy, to revive the lost art of the classic dance; made début as a dancer in Vienna, 1903, and subsequently appeared in the leading Continental cities; performed at the Palace Theatre, London, in 1908, with classical dances and the Vision of Salome; appeared at that theatre without a break until Nov. 1908; reappeared there Feb. to May 1909, after touring provinces; returned to perform there throughout the summer, 1909; in Dec., same year, appeared in Petrograd and Moscow; Jan. 1910, proceeded to America and made first appearance in the Carnegie Hall, New York; returned to Palace Theatre, London, 1911; toured South Africa, India, Malay Straits, Burma, China, Manilla, Australia, New Zealand, Tasmania, and United States of America; after several reappearances and provincial tours in England, proceeded again to America, and subsequently toured Argentine, Chili, and Brazil; returned, and performed at London Palladium, Coliseum, and Alhambra; in 1923 toured Egypt, Malta, and Gibraltar; was in London, Paris, and United States, 1924-25; returned to England 1928 since when has devoted much time to teaching very poor children and n preparing material for new work on her life; played the Abbess in the Miracle at Lyceum, 1932. *Publications:* My Life and Dancing, 1908; miscellaneous articles in the Press. *Recreations:* sculpture and architectural design, and wood-carving.
[*Died* 7 *Oct.* 1956.

ALLANSON, Harry Llewelyn Lyons, C.I.E. 1926; I.C.S. (retired); *b.* 16 April 1876; *s.* of late J. B. Allanson; *m.* 1913, Helen (*d.* 1950), *d.* of Col. J. R. Wilmer; one *s.* *Educ.:* Bedford School; Exeter College, Oxford, B.A. 1st Cl. Hon. Mod.; 1st Cl. Litt. Hum.; passed into I.C.S. 1899; Asst. Mag. and Coll., Bengal, 1900; Settlement Officer, Santal Parganas, 1905-10; Deputy Commissioner, Santal Parganas, 1910-12; transferred to Bihar and Orissa, 1912; District and Sessions Judge, 1916; Judicial Sec. to Govt. and Legal Remembrancer, 1921-24; Acting Judge, High Court, Patna, 1927-28; retired 1932. *Publication:* Final Report of Survey and Settlement Operations (1906-10), Santal Parganas. *Address:* Dinas, Bathampton, Bath. *T.:* Bath 88298.
[*Died* 6 *Jan.* 1955.

ALLARD, Sir George Mason, Kt., *cr.* 1926; a Vice-Pres. Royal Empire Society, N.S. Wales Branch; *b.* London, 28 Dec. 1866; *s.* of George Allard; *m.* 1895, Emma Victoria Oliver; one *s.* one *d.* *Educ.:* United Westminster Schools. Representative of Government of Commonwealth of Australia on and Chairman of the Amalgamated Wireless Co. Ltd., 1922-31; President, The Institute of Chartered Accountants in Australia, 1932-41. *Address:* Yarwood Vane & Co. with G. Mason Allard, Chartered Accountants (Aust.), Box 243 D., G.P.O., Sydney. *T.:* BW 8203; 28 and 30 O'Connell Street, Sydney, N.S.W.; Bundarra, Woonona Avenue, Wahroonga, Sydney, N.S.W. *Club:* Union (Sydney). [*Died* 1 *May* 1953.

ALLARDYCE, Robert Moir, C.B.E. 1943 (O.B.E. 1936); M.C., J.P.; LL.D. Glasgow, 1943; M.A., LL.B.; *b.* Rothiemay, Banffshire, 22 May 1882; *er. s.* of Rev. William Allardyce, M.A.; *m.* 1912, Clementina, *y. d.* of Peter Hendry, Hillockhead, Huntly; one *s.* one *d.* *Educ.:* Gordon's College, Aberdeen; Aberdeen University. Classical Master in Elgin Academy, 1902-5; in the High School of Glasgow, 1905-12; Organising Secretary and later Clerk and Treasurer to the Renfrew County Committee on Secondary Education, 1912-19; Director of Education Clackmannan County Education Authority, 1919-25, with Kinross additional; Depute Director of Education Authority of Glasgow,

1925-29; Director of Education, Glasgow, 1929-1944; temp. Assistant Secretary in Scottish Education Dept. (Further Education and Training Scheme), 1944-49; retired, 1949. *Publications:* New Latin Course, 1910; Something about Education (Army Lectures), 1919; Latin for Beginners, 1929. *Address:* 6 Campbell Road, Edinburgh 12. *T.:* Edinburgh 61355.
[*Died* 22 *Jan.* 1951.

ALLASON, Brig.-Gen. Walter, D.S.O. 1915; Retired Pay; late the Bedfordshire and Hertfordshire Regiment; *b.* 18 March 1875; *m.* 1908, Katharine Hamilton, *d.* of late Vice-Admiral James A. Poland; one *s.* one *d.* Entered army, 1896; Capt. 1902; Major, 1918; Lieut.-Colonel, 1921; Colonel, 1923; served S. Africa, 1899-1900 (Queen's medal 2 clasps); European War, 1914-19; commanded 52nd Infantry Brigade, April 1918-April 1919, then 51st Bedf. Regt. on the Rhine (wounded four times, despatches five times, D.S.O. and bar, Bt. Lt.-Col.); commanded 1st Bedfordshire and Hertfordshire Regt., 1922-25; 156th (West Scottish) Inf. Bde. T.A., 1927-31; retired pay, 1931. *Publication:* Military Mapping and Reports, 1940, now in 6th edition. *Recreations:* formerly swimming (Plunging Championship of England, 1896 and 7, 1902, 1908 and 9, 1922, also rep. Army v. Navy, 1924-27, 1929 and 1930; gold shamrock medals Irish swimming Championship, 1899); won Aldershot Comd. Officers Shooting Challenge Cup, 1912. *Address:* 29 Alexandra Court, Queen's Gate, S.W.7. *Club:* United Service. [*Died* 11 *Jan.* 1960.

ALLCOTT, Walter Herbert, R.W.A. 1920; R.B.S.A. 1921; landscape painter, water-colours; *b.* Birmingham, 21 Jan. 1880; *s.* of Henry Allcott and Emily Jane Herbert; *m.* 1913, Maud, *d.* of Major Herbert H. Bird of Erdington; no *c.* *Educ.:* privately; Birmingham Municipal School of Art. Formerly a painter of portraits and subject pictures in oils; exhibited first in 1898; obliged by ill-health to give up living in towns; settled in Chipping Campden, Glos., 1919, where he painted landscapes in water-colours; visited and painted all the principal Italian cities, 1922-23; Venice and Verona, etc., 1924-25; Spain and Mallorca, 1926; regular exhibitor R.A., R.I., and most provincial galleries. *Address:* Electra House, Haslemere, Surrey.
[*Died* 13 *Jan.* 1951.

ALLDERIDGE, Charles Donald, D.S.O. 1917; T.D.; F.R.I.B.A., A.M.I.Struct.E.; Bt. Col., R.A. (T.); late O.C. East Riding Heavy Brigade R.A.; Hon. Col. 676 H.A.A. Regt. R.A. since 1949; architect surveyor and valuer; Inspectorate Division (London), established civil servant, Ministry of Local Govt. and Planning; President Hull Guild of Building, 1934; Vice-President of York and E. Yorkshire Architectural Society; *b.* Ripley, Derbyshire, 25 Nov. 1889; *s.* of Rector of Routh, E. Yorks; *m.* Dorothy Gravill (*d.* 1937), L.R.A.M.; one *s.* one *d.*; *m.* 1942, Mabel Beatrice Smith (*d.* 1945). *Educ.:* Hymers College, Hull. Architect-pupil Brodrick, Lowther & Walker, F.R.I.B.A., 1908-11; Assistant Valuer Land Valuation Dept. Inland Revenue, 1912-14; served European War in R.G.A., 1914-19; in France, 1916-19, and rose to command of a Brigade of Artillery; joined Territorial Force 1909; Adjutant, East Riding Heavy Brigade R.A. (T.A.), 1923-26; Officer cmdg. troops in Falkland Islands and South Georgia and reorganised coastal Defences, 1941-42; Member of Hull City Council (Botanic Ward), 1927-33; Architect to E. Riding Terr. Army and Air Force Assoc., 1942; Chief Special Constable of Hull, 1938-41. *Works:* large hosp., schools, housing schemes, etc., 1920-23; houses, Hull, Grimsby, Howden, and E. Yorks generally; Roman Catholic Church Hall, several Parish Halls; dilapidation surveys and large alteration schemes; J.P. Falkland Is. *Recreation:* golf. *Address:* Flat No. 2, 121 Palace Road, S.W.2.
[*Died* 21 *Jan.* 1958.

ALLEN, A. Stuart; Chairman and Managing Director of the Anglo Transvaal Trustees Ltd. since 1948; *b.* 12 May 1890; *s.* of William and Elizabeth Allen; *m.* 1919, Hilda Winifred, *d.* of William Stokes; two *d.* *Educ.:* University College School. Inland Revenue, 1909-16; Clerk to Commissioners, 1916; Senior Partner, Allen, Baldry, Holman & Best, Incorporated Accountants, London, 1927-48; President, Society of Incorporated Accountants, 1949-51. *Address:* Turknell Cottage, Streatley, Berkshire. *T.:* Goring 162. *Club:* Devonshire.
[*Died* 11 *Aug.* 1957.

ALLEN, Sir (Albert) George, K.C.V.O., *cr.* 1952; D.S.O. 1919; M.C.; solicitor; retired; First Class Honours; Law Society prizeman; Joint founder of firm of Allen & Overy, London, 1930; *b.* 1888; 2nd *s.* of Alfred Allen and Fanny Parsons; *m.* 1917, Florence, *d.* of Thomas Walton Tarn; one *s.* *Educ.:* North Malvern School. Served European War, 1914-19, in France as Captain, 8th South Staffordshire Regiment, and Brigade Major, 51st Infantry Brigade (D.S.O., M.C., despatches twice). Private Solicitor to King Edward VIII, 1936. Chairman, Law Debenture Corporation Ltd.: Director English & Scottish Investors Ltd., The Australian Estates Co. Ltd., Lewis and Peat Ltd., Hindley & Co. Ltd.; Safeguard Industrial Investments Ltd. *Address:* 113 Mount St., W.1. *Club:* White's. [*Died* 10 *Aug.* 1956.

ALLEN, Major-Gen. Arthur Samuel, C.B. 1941; C.B.E. 1941; D.S.O. 1917; V.D.; F.C.A. (Aust.); practising as A. S. Allen & Co., Chartered Accountants (Aust.), 4 Balmoral Ave., Mosman, N.S.W.; Director of companies; *b.* Sydney, N.S.W., 10 March 1894; *s.* of late John Allen, Hurstville, N.S.W.; *m.* 1921, Agnes Mona Blair, *d.* of late Robert Mackay, Kempsey, N.S.W.; two *s.* *Educ.:* private study. Served European War, 1914-18; enlisted A.I.F.; 2nd Lt., Middle East and France, Lt.-Col. 1917 (despatches twice D.S.O., French Croix de Guerre). Served A.M.F., 1919-39; Col. 1931, Brig. 1937; Chartered Accountant, partner Truman, Allen & Co., Sydney, 1922-45; War of 1939-45; left Australia, 1940, comdg. 16th Aust. Inf. Bde. for First Lybian Campaign, Battles of Bardia and Tobruk (despatches, C.B.E., C.B.), and for Greek Campaign (despatches, Greek Mil. Cross, 1st Cl.); Maj.-Gen. 1941; comdg. 7th Aust. Div. for Syrian Campaign (despatches), Java, and New Guinea (Aug. 1942-Mar. 1943), defence of Moresby, Owen Stanley Range Campaign and battles Imita Ridge to Kokoda; G.O.C. Northern Territory Force (March 1943-Oct. 1944); now R. of O. *Recreations:* golf, bowls. *Address:* 4 Balmoral Avenue, Mosman, Sydney, N.S.W. *T.:* XM 5252. *Club:* Union (Sydney). [*Died* 25 *Jan.* 1959.

ALLEN, Rear-Admiral Sir Bertram Cowles, K.C.B., *cr.* 1929 (C.B. 1919); M.V.O. 1912; *b.* 29 Nov. 1875; *s.* of late Staff Commander G. H. Allen, R.N.; *m.* 1908, Edith Mary, 3rd *d.* of Sir R. W. Perks, 1st Bt.; two *d.* *Educ.:* Christ's Hospital. Entered Navy, 1893; served Naval Brigade, S.A. War, 1899-1900 (clasps for Belmont, Modder River, Driefontein, and Paardeberg), specially promoted to paymaster, 1900; fleet paymaster of H.M.S. Medina during voyage of King to India; Paymaster Captain, 1921; Secretary to Fourth Sea Lord; Paymaster Director-General, 1926-29; retired list, 1929. *Address:* Channel View, Seaford. *Club:* Army and Navy. [*Died* 11 *Feb.* 1957.

ALLEN, Charles Turner, C.I.E. 1920; farming, Sussex; *b.* 1877; *s.* of late Sir George Allen, K.C.I.E.; *m.* 1905, Gladys Mabel, *d.* of late Col. St. George Corbet Gore, C.S.I.; two *s.* two *d.* *Educ.:* Eton; Magdalen College, Oxford. *Recreations;* athletics of every kind and sport. *Address;* Kidborough Farm, Dane Hill, Sussex. *T.:* Dane Hill 316. *Clubs:* Royal Empire Society, M.C.C., Free Foresters, I Zingari, etc. [*Died* 18 *March* 1958.

ALLEN, Clarence Edgar; Editor and Director of Machinery; Chartered Mechanical Engineer; Chartered Electrical Engineer; *b.* 21 Nov. 1871; *e. s.* of late David Allen of Long Buckby, Northants. *Publications:* The Modern Locomotive; Screw Threads, etc. *Recreations:* music; flute playing and idling. *Address:* Tolverne, The Parade, Greatstone, New Romney, Kent. *T.:* Littlestone 262. *Clubs:* Press, St. Stephen's; Coventry and County (Coventry). [*Died* 24 *Dec.* 1951.

ALLEN, Ernest Joshua, C.B.E. 1918; M.I.Mech.E.; *b.* 1871; *s.* of J. Allen; *m.* 1899 Maud Lilian (*d.* 1936), *d.* of late J. E. Randell, Hereford; one *s.* (and one *d.* decd.). Late Director Railway Materials, Ministry of Munitions. *Address:* Waldronhyrst Hotel, South Croydon, Surrey. [*Died* 4 *June* 1955.

ALLEN, Frederick Lewis; Director of Harper & Bros., publishers (formerly Vice-President), and Consulting Editor of Harper's Magazine since 1953 (Editor, 1941-53); *b.* 5 July 1890; *s.* of Rev. F. B. Allen; *m.* 1st, 1918, Dorothy Penrose Cobb; one *s.* (one *d.* decd.); 2nd, 1932, Agnes Rogers. *Educ.:* Harvard. Asst. in English, Harvard Univ., 1912-14; Asst. Editor Altantic Monthly, 1914-16; Managing Editor Century Magazine, 1916-17; Secretary to the Corporation, Harvard Univ., 1919-23; Overseer, Harvard University, 1942-48, 1950-. Trustee, Ford Foundation. Associated with Harper's Magazine since 1923. *Publications:* Only Yesterday, 1931; The Lords of Creation, 1935; Since Yesterday, 1940; The Great Pierpont Morgan, 1949; The Big Change, 1952; (with Agnes Rogers): The American Procession, 1933; Metropolis, 1934; I Remember Distinctly, 1947. *Address:* 121 E. 35 St., New York, N.Y., U.S.A. [*Died* 13 *Feb.* 1954.

ALLEN, Sir George; *see* Allen, Sir A. G.

ALLEN, Rt. Rev. Gerald Burton, D.D.; Emeritus Student of Christ Church, Oxford, since 1952; Assistant Bishop of Oxford since 1952; *b.* Cheltenham, 9 Jan. 1885; *e. s.* of late Rev. T. K. Allen, formerly Rector of Weyhill, Hants. *Educ.:* Cheltenham College; Wadham College, Oxford (Scholar); 1st Class Hon. Theol. 1908; Wells Theological College, 1908; Deacon, 1908; Chaplain of Wadham College, 1908; Priest, 1909; Denyer and Johnson Theological Scholar, 1910; Ellerton Prize Essay, 1910; Fellow, Dean and Chaplain of Pembroke College, 1910-20; Theological Lecturer, 1911; Tutor, 1912; T.C.F., 1917-18; Chaplain, R.A.F., 1918-19; Senior Proctor, 1920-21; Principal of St. Edmund Hall, 1920-28; Bishop Suffragan of Sherborne, 1928-36; Prebendary of Fordington in Salisbury Cathedral, 1927-36; Assistant Bishop of Oxford, 1936-39; Archdeacon of Oxford and Canon of Christ Church, 1936-1952; Bishop Suffragan of Dorchester, 1939-1952; Select Preacher at Oxford, 1920-23; Cambridge, 1926 and 1932; Examining Chaplain to the Bishop of Salisbury, 1911-31; to the Bishop of Carlisle, 1921-28; Member of Hebdomadal Council, 1923-28; Member Cheltenham College Council, 1923-51; President of Cheltenham Coll., 1939-51; Life Governor of Marlborough College; Hon. Fellow of Pembroke College, 1934, and of St. Edmund Hall, 1942. *Address:* Dorchester Lodge, Cheltenham. [*Died* 27 *March* 1956.

ALLEN, Harry Epworth, R.B.A. 1934; *b.* 27 Nov. 1894; *s.* of Henry Allen and Elizabeth, *d.* of Samuel Blacktin; *m.* 1925, Lucy, *d.* of T. O. Hodder, Southampton. *Educ.:* King Edward VII School, Sheffield; Sheffield College of Art. Member Royal Society of British Artists and Pastel Society. Exhibitor: Royal Academy and principal provincial galleries. Official purchases; National Gallery of South Australia; Newcastle upon Tyne; Leeds; Hull; Wakefield; Stoke-on-Trent; Swansea; Derby; Preston; Batley; Newport (Mon.); Sheffield; Napier (N.Z.). *Address:* 67 Banner Cross Road, Sheffield. [*Died* 25 *March* 1958.

ALLEN, Herbert Stanley, F.R.S. 1930; Professor of Natural Philosophy, 1923-44, and Director of Physics Research Laboratory, University of St. Andrews; *b.* Bodmin, Cornwall, 29 Dec. 1873; *s.* of late Rev. R. Allen; *m.* 1907 Jessie, *d.* of late Rev. A. Macturk; one *s.* one *d.* *Educ.:* Kingswood School, Bath; Trinity College, Cambridge (Foundation Sizar). Tenth Wrangler in Mathematical Tripos, 1896; 1st Cl. Part II., Nat. Sci. Tripos, 1897; M.A. Camb.; D.Sc. Lond.; Hon. LL.D. St. Andrews; Supt. of Blythswood Laboratory, Renfrew, 1900; Lecturer in Physics, King's College, London, 1905; Reader in Physics, University of London and afterwards in University of Edinburgh; F.R.S.E.; F.Inst.P. *Publications:* Photo-electricity: the Liberation of Electrons by Light; Text-book of Practical Physics (with H. Moore), 3rd ed. revised and reset, 1948; The Quantum and its Interpretation; Electrons and Waves; Text-book of Heat (with R. S. Maxwell); Scientific Papers in Proceedings of Royal Societies of London and Edinburgh. *Address:* Manse of Resolis, by Conon Bridge, Ross-shire. [*Died* 27 *April* 1954.

ALLEN, Vice-Admiral John Derwent, C.B. 1914; *b.* 28 Mar. 1875; *m.* 1906, Ruth, *e. d.* of late Admiral Sir George Atkinson Willes, K.C.B.; one *s.* two *d.* Served Somaliland, 1902-4 (clasp); commanded H.M.S. Kent, battle of Falklands, 1914 (C.B.); retired list, 1924. *Address:* The Old Rectory, Southease, Sussex. *T.:* Newhaven 39. [*Died* 23 *May* 1958.

ALLEN, Sir Oswald Coleman, Kt., *cr.* 1950; C.B. 1944; C.B.E. 1920; U.K. Rep. on Social Commission of U.N. since 1947; Trustee of Imperial War Museum since 1946; Barrister-at-law, Middle Temple; *b.* 13 April 1887. Appointed Board of Trade, 1912; Ministry of Munitions, 1915; Mission Anglaise de l'Armement (Paris), 1918; Ministry of Labour, 1919; Home Office (A.R.P. Dept.), 1939; Under-Secretary, acting Deputy Sec., Ministry of Home Security, 1944-45; Principal Assistant Under-Secretary of State, Civil Defence Dept., Home Office, 1945-48. Officer Crown of Italy; Chevalier Legion of Honour; Gold Medal of Riksluftskyddsförbundet (Sweden). *Club:* Reform. [*Died* 4 *May* 1959.

ALLEN, Sir Richard William, Kt., *cr.* 1942; C.B.E. 1918; D.L. County of Bedford; Chairman of W. H. Allen, Sons & Co., Ltd., Bedford; *b.* 1867; *e. s.* of late W. H. Allen, Bromham, Bedfordshire; *m.* Geraldine Agnew (*d.* 1948), *d.* of William Joseph Fedden, Clifton, Bristol; two *d.* (one *s.* killed in R.F.C., 1917). Member of the Institution of Civil Engineers; Past President of the Institution of Mechanical Engineers; M.I.N.A.; M.I.Mar.E.; F.R.Hort.S.; Fellow R. Empire Soc.; etc.; Governor of the Royal Agricultural Society; Trustee Engineering and Allied Employers National Federation; Member the Pilgrims Anglo-Egyptian Soc.; High Sheriff for the County of Bedford, 1921. Order of the Sacred Treasure, Japan. *Publication:* The Air Supply to Boiler Rooms for Modern Ships of War (3rd edition). *Address:* Hurst

Grove, Bedford; 75 Victoria Street, Westminster, S.W.; Homelea, 8 Linnell Drive, N.W.11. *Clubs:* Carlton, Royal Automobile, M.C.C. [*Died* 17 *July* 1955.

ALLEN, William Philip, C.B.E. 1946; Manpower Advisor, British Transport Commission, since 1955; *b.* 11 Nov. 1888; Gen. Secretary Assoc. Soc. Locomotive Engineers and Firemen, 1940-47; Member of the Railway Executive, 1948-53; Chief of Establishment and Staff, British Transport Commission, 1953. *Address:* Hilldene, 31 Furness Road, West Harrow, Middlesex. *T.:* Byron 2593. [*Died* 4 *May* 1958.

ALLEN, Rev. Willoughby Charles; late Chaplain-Fellow, Lect. in Theology and in Hebrew at Exeter College, Oxford; *b.* 7 Oct. 1867; *m.* Catherine Ellen, *d.* of W. F. Green, of Wroxham; three *s.* *Educ.:* Exeter College, Oxford (Hasker Scholar). 1st class Hon. Theol. 1890; 1st class Oriental Studies, 1892; Pusey and Ellerton Scholar, 1890; Houghton Syriac Prize, 1892; Junior Kennicott Scholar, 1892; Prin. of Egerton Hall, Manchester, 1908-15; Archdeacon of Manchester, 1909-16; Archdeacon of Blackburn, 1916-20; Rector of Chorley, 1916-22; Rector of Saham Toney, Norfolk, 1922-32; Public Examiner in Hon. Theol. 1898-1900, 1904-6; in Oriental Studies, 1902; Examining Chaplain to the Bishop of Lichfield, 1905-8; Junior Proctor, Oxford, 1907-8; Exam. Chaplain to Bishop of Manchester, 1908. *Publications:* St. Matthew in International Critical Commentary; St. Mark in Oxford Church Biblical Commentary; The Christian Hope; (with L. W. Grensted) Introduction to Books of New Testament; Contributor to Dictionary of Bible, Encyclopædia Biblica, and to Contentio Veritatis, 1902. *Address:* 65 St. James Road, Sutton, Surrey. [*Died* 10 *Feb.* 1953.

ALLENDALE, 2nd Viscount, *cr.* 1911, **Wentworth Henry Canning Beaumont,** K.G. 1951; C.B. 1948; C.B.E. 1943; M.C.; Baron (*cr.* 1906); a Lord-in-Waiting to the Queen since 1954; Bt. Colonel, late Northumberland (Hussars) Yeomanry; Hon. Col. Northumberland Hussars (Yeomanry), 1955; *b.* 6 August 1890; *e. s.* of 1st Viscount and Lady Alexandrina Louisa Maud (Aline) Vane-Tempest (*d.* 1945), *d.* of 5th Marquess of Londonderry; *S.* father, 1923; *m.* 1921, Violet, *d.* of Sir Charles Seely, 2nd Bt.; five *s.* one *d.* *Educ.:* Eton; Trinity College, Cambridge. 2nd Life Guards, 1912; Capt., 1915-22. Chairman W. R. Unemployment Centres, 1936-41; Jt. Master Badsworth Hounds, 1936-45; Steward of the Jockey Club, 1947; Pres. Northern Liberal Federation, 1925-49; H.M. Lieutenant for County of Northumberland, 1949-56; a Lord-in-Waiting, 1931-32 and since 1937. *Heir:* *s.* Hon. Wentworth Hubert Charles Beaumont [*b.* 12 Sept. 1922; *m.* 1948, Hon. Sarah Ismay, *d.* of 1st Baron Ismay, K.G., P.C., G.C.B., C.H., D.S.O.; three *s.*]. *Address:* 30 Hyde Park Street, W.2. *T.:* Ambassador 6235; Bywell Hall, Stocksfield-on-Tyne. *T.:* Stocksfield 3169. *Club:* Turf. [*Died* 16 *Dec.* 1956.

ALLFREY, Major Edward Mortimer, D.S.O. 1917; *b.* 1886; *yr. s.* of late Walter Mortimer Allfrey, Farley Castle, Swallowfield, Reading; *m.* 1925, Ellen Kathleen, *y. d.* of late A. E. Huggins, Hare Hatch House, Twyford, Berks; one *d.* Formerly Major Royal Berkshire Regt. Served European War, 1914-17 (despatches twice, D.S.O.). *Club:* Junior Carlton. [*Died* 28 *March* 1957.

ALLGOOD, Brig.-Gen. William Henry Loraine, C.B. 1925; C.M.G. 1918; D.S.O. 1917; late K.R.R.C.; *b.* 1868; *s.* of Rev. J. Allgood, of Nunwick, Humshaugh, Northumberland; *m.* 1914, Sophia Beryl Sheila (*d.* 1957), *d.* of late Col. J. H. G. Holroyd Smyth, C.M.G., and Lady Harriette Holroyd Smyth of Ballynatray, Youghal, co. Waterford. *Educ.:* Eton. Served Burma Expedition, 1891-92; South African War, 1899-1900 (Queen's medal three clasps); European War, 1914-18 (despatches four times, C.M.G., D.S.O., Legion of Honour); retired pay, 1925. *Address:* Charlcot, Ripon, Yorkshire. *T:* Masham 385. [*Died* 27 *Dec.* 1957.

ALLHUSEN, Lieut.-Colonel Frederick Henry, C.M.G. 1918; D.S.O. 1916; retired pay, 9th Lancers; Lovat Scouts; *b.* 24 Jan. 1872: *s.* of late Henry Christian Allhusen, of Stoke Court, Bucks; *m.* 1908, Enid (*d.* 1948), *d.* of Comdr. Harold W. Swithinbank; two *s.* *Educ.:* Cheltenham College. Served South Africa, 1899-1900 (despatches, Queen's medal 4 clasps); European War (Gallipoli, Egypt and France), 1914-19 (despatches twice, C.M.G., D.S.O.); County Councillor, Bucks., 1934-49; rep. on Thames Conservancy Board; High Sheriff of Buckinghamshire, 1932. *Address:* Fulmer House, Fulmer, Bucks. *Club:* Carlton. [*Died* 13 *Jan.* 1957.

ALLINSON, Adrian Paul, P.S.; R.B.A.; artist (painter and sculptor); *b.* 9 Jan. 1890; *s.* of Thomas Richard Allinson, L.R.C.P.; *m.* Clarke Buckland; one *s.* *Educ.:* Wycliffe; Wrekin; Slade. Slade Scholarship; scenic designer to Beecham Opera Co.; ex-teacher of drawing and painting, Westminster School of Art; exhibitor R.A., N.E., Zürich, Munich, Toronto, etc. Poster Designer to British Railways (Southern Region). *Recreations:* ski-ing, climbing, swimming and music. *Address:* Studio, 87A., Clifton Hill, N.W.8. *T.:* Maida Vale 1246. [*Died* 20 *Feb.* 1959.

ALLISON, James, C.B.E. 1920; M.A. (St. Andrews), LL.B. (Edinburgh); Solicitor in Dundee; Reader in Scots Law, Univ. of St. Andrews, till 1945, and one of the Board of Examiners under the Law Agents (Scotland) Acts, 1912-33, and an Examiner under the Solicitors (Scotland) Act, 1933-41; *b.* 27 April 1865; *s.* of Matthew Allison, Dundee; *m.* 1897, Kate Constable, *d.* of Peter Young, Dundee; two *d.* *Educ.:* St. Andrews and Edinburgh Universities. Graduated in Arts at St. Andrews (M.A.), 1884, and in Law at Edinburgh (LL.B. with distinction), 1888; qualified as Law Agent, 1888; commenced practice of profession of solicitor at Dundee, 1888; Searcher of the Burgh Register of Sasines, Dundee, 1893 to close of register in 1929; Burgh Prosecutor of Newport, 1896-1949; Chairman of the Court of Referees for the Dundee District of Scotland under the Unemployment Insurance Acts, 1913-37; Dean of the Faculty of Procurators and Solicitors in Dundee, 1925-27; Hon. Sheriff-Substitute of Forfarshire since 1926 and now of the Counties of Perth and Angus; Chairman Local Munitions Tribunal Dundee District, 1914-18. *Recreations:* walking and gardening. *Address:* Craiglea, East Newport, Fife. *T.:* Dundee 3932; Newport, Fife, 3189. [*Died* 27 *March* 1951.

ALLISON, Sir Richard (John), Kt., *cr.* 1927; C.V.O. 1934; C.B.E. 1920 (O.B.E. 1918); F.R.I.B.A. (retired), 1919; *b.* 8 Jan. 1869; 2nd *s.* of Joseph Charles Allison; unmarried; *Educ.:* Private Choir School. Entered H.M. Office of Works, 1889; employed on temporary Architectural staff for 12 years; Assistant Architect, 1901; Architect, 1911; Principal Architect, 1914 (Art and Science Buildings, Diplomatic and Consular Buildings, etc.); Chief Architect H.M. Office of Works, 1920-34. *Works:* New Science Museum, South Kensington; H.M. New Stationery Office; British Legations, Stockholm, etc. *Address:* 63 Hornsey Lane, Highgate, N.6. *T.:* Mountview 2614. *Club:* Arts. [*Died* 28 *Sept.* 1958.

ALLMAND, Arthur John, M.C.; F.R.S. 1929; F.R.I.C.; Emeritus Professor of Chemistry, Univ. of London, since 1950; Fellow of King's College; *b.* Wrexham, 1885; *s.* of Frank Allmand, Wrexham; *m.* Marguerite, *d.* of Leonor Malicorne, St. Lô and St. Mandé, France; one *s.* (and one *s.* killed in action, 1944, awarded posthumous V.C.) one *d.* *Educ.:* Univ. of Liverpool; Technical High Schools of Karlsruhe and Dresden, D.Sc. (Liv.) 1910; studied in Germany, 1910-12; Asst. Lecturer and Demonstrator, Univ. of Liverpool, 1913; Professor of Chemistry, King's College, 1919-1938; Daniell Professor of Chemistry, King's College, 1938-50; Asst. Principal of King's College, 1937-43; served European War, 1915-19; finally Major and Chemical Adviser successively to Fourth and Second Army H.Q. (M.C.). Pres. of Faraday Society, 1947-48. *Publications:* Principles of Applied Electro-Chemistry, 1912, revised edition, 1925; Papers in scientific journals. *Address:* 5 North Square, N.W.11. [*Died* 4 *Aug.* 1951.

ALLSEBROOK, His Honour George Clarence; J.P. Cumberland and Westmorland; *b.* 12 August 1877; 5th *s.* of late William Pole Jones Allsebrook, J.P., Wollaton, Nottinghamshire; *m.* 1917, Dorothy Allnutt (*d.* 1938), 3rd *d.* of late Major Vicessimus Knox, J.P., Spring Hill, Moreton-in-Marsh, Glos.; one *s.* (and one killed in action, 1943) two *d.* *Educ.:* Nottingham High School; Trinity College, Oxford, M.A. Mining Engineer, 1896-1909; agent and manager of collieries in Derbyshire and Notts, 1903-9; Trinity College, Oxford, 1910-1914; called to Bar, Inner Temple, 1913 and joined Midland Circuit; embodied with Derbyshire Yeomanry 5 Aug. 1914; served in Egypt and Greece; Captain; seconded to Ministry of Munitions of War; became a director of the Labour Regulation Dept.; disembodied, 1919; British Arbitrator in La Commission Arbitrale des Litiges Miniers au Maroc, 1919-21; Independent Chairman of Derbyshire District Wages Board (exclusive of S. Derbyshire), 1930-42; Judge of County Courts circuit No. 3, 1934-50; Chm. of Cumberland Quarter Sessions, 1945-53. Member of Royal Commission on Safety in Coal Mines, 1936-39. *Address:* The Green, Cark-in-Cartmel, Lancashire. *T.:* Flookborough 258. [*Died* 2 *Dec.* 1957.

ALLSOP, Lieut.-Col. William Gillian, C.M.G. 1919; D.S.O. 1917; V.D.; *b.* 31 Jan. 1874; *s.* of William Allsop, Clifton, England; unmarried. *Educ.:* People's College, Warrington. Served European War, 1915-18 (despatches, D.S.O., C.M.G.). *Address:* Hillcroft, Dornoch Terrace, Highgate Hill, South Brisbane, Queensland. *Club:* United Service (Brisbane). [*Died* 1 *June* 1951.

ALLWARD, Walter Seymour, C.M.G. 1944; LL.D., R.C.A.; F.R.I.A.C.; Sculptor; *b.* Toronto, 18 Nov. 1876; *s.* of John Allward and Emma Hart Pitman, Newfoundland; *m.* 1898, Margret, *d.* of Angus Kennedy and Margret MacGillivray, Oban, Scotland; one *s.* *Educ.:* Toronto Public Schools. Studied Architecture from the ages of 15-20; then went in for Sculpture; went to London and Paris; on return to Canada, executed following commissions: National South African Memorial, Toronto; monuments to John Graves Simcoe, Sir Oliver Mowat, Sandfield McDonald, North West Volunteers, all in Toronto; allegorical memorial to inventor of the Bell telephone, in Brantford; War memorials in Stratford and Peterborough; Baldwin Lafontaine Memorial in Ottawa. In 1921 won the competition in British Empire for Canadian National Memorial for Vimy Ridge in France; went to Europe in 1922 and lived in studio built by Alfred Gilbert at 16 Maida Vale, London; in this studio all sculptures for Vimy Ridge Memorial were executed; on completion of this memorial, 1936, returned to Toronto to complete memorials to King Edward VII and to William Lyon MacKenzie, and various other idealistic designs. Now working on a Memorial to Sir Frederick Banting. *Recreation:* music. *Address:* The Studio, Old Yonge Street, York Mills, Ontario, Canada. *T.:* Hudson 4879. *Club:* Arts and Letters (Toronto). [*Died* 24 *April* 1955.

ALNESS, 1st Baron, *cr.* 1934; **Rt. Hon. Robert Munro,** P.C. 1913; G.B.E., *cr.* 1946; a Lord-in-Waiting, 1940-45; Chairman: the Select Committee of the House of Lords on the prevention of road accidents; Chinese Bond-holders' Committee appointed by Governor of Bank of England; Home Office Night Baking Committee, 1936; Executive Committee of the Child Guidance Council; National Council for Mental Hygiene; Scottish Office Committee on Grants to the Scottish Universities; Departmental Committee on Nursing (Scotland); President: Magna Carta Society; Sons of the Manse Society (London); Trustee of the Carnegie Trust; Vice-President: Building Societies Assoc.; Royal Scottish Corp.; Bournemouth Trustee Savings Bank; President of Bournemouth Association for Mental Health and Bournemouth Savings Committee; *b.* 28 May 1868; *s.* of a Ross-shire Free Church minister; *m.* 1st, 1898, Edith Gwladys (*d.* 1920), *d.* of Rev. Llewellyn Evans, The Parsonage, Peebles; 2nd, 1921, Olga Marie, *o. d.* of J. G. Grumler, Woodgarth Kent Avenue, Harrogate. *Educ.:* Edinburgh University. M.A., LL.B., LL.D. 1919; F.E.I.S. 1919; Counsel to Inland Revenue, Advocate-Depute, and Lord Advocate in succession, 1913; Secretary for Scotland, 1916-22; M.P. (L.) Wick Burghs, Jan. 1910-Dec. 1918, and (Co. L.) Roxburgh and Selkirk, Dec. 1918-22; Lord Justice-Clerk, 1922-33; and took his seat on the Bench with the judicial title of Lord Alness; Hon. Bencher of Lincoln's Inn; Freeman of the City of Edinburgh, of Dingwall and of Peebles; formerly Chm. of Joint Exchequer Board; Hon. Member of the Edinburgh Merchant Company; D.L. Edinburgh; LL.D. of Edinburgh, St. Andrews and Aberdeen Universities. President and Chairman of Scottish Savings Committee, 1941-45; Chairman of Agricultural Education Committee (Scotland); President of the Grotius Society, 1936-38; Chief of the London Ross-shire and Sutherland Association, 1936-37; Chief of the St. Andrews Society (London), 1937-38; President of the Burns Club of London, 1938-39. *Publication:* Looking Back: Fugitive Writings and Sayings, 1930. *Address:* Durley Dean Hotel, Bournemouth. [*Died* 6 *Oct.* 1955 (*ext.*).

ALPE, Frank Theodore; Recorder of Borough of Great Yarmouth since 1951. Called to the Bar, Middle Temple, 1925, South Eastern Circuit; Judge, Norwich Guildhall Court of Record. *Address:* 3 Hare Court, Temple, E.C.4. *T.:* Central 7742; 39 Exchange Street, Norwich, Norfolk. *T.:* Norwich 26158. [*Died* 25 *Jan.* 1952.

ALSTON, Rt. Rev. Arthur Fawssett, M.A.; *b.* Sandgate, Kent, 30 Dec. 1872; *s.* of late Surgeon-Major W. E. Alston, M.D., J.P., and late Mrs. E. R. Alston, Sydney, N.S.W.; *m.* 1900; three *s.* two *d.* *Educ.:* Clare College, Cambridge; Ridley Hall, Cambridge. Ordained, 1896; Curate of St. Katherine, Northampton, 1896-98; Faringdon, 1898-1905; St. Simon, Southsea, 1905-7; Vicar of St. Matthew, Hull, 1907-15; St. George's, Leeds, 1915-18; All Saints, Bradford, 1918-20; Rector of St. Leonards-on-Sea, 1920-29; Rural Dean of Hastings, 1926-29; Archdeacon of Hastings, 1928-38; Suffragan Bishop of Middleton and Residentiary Canon of Manchester, 1938-43. *Recreation:* golf. *Address:* 18 West Hill, St. Leonards-on-Sea. *T.:* Hastings 2083. [*Died* 20 *Feb.* 1954.

ALSTON, Leonard; *b.* Australia, 1875. Thrice Univ. prizeman, Camb.; Deputy Prof. of History and Political Economy, Elphinstone Coll., Bombay, 1904-5; University Lecturer, in Economics, Cambridge, 1926-40; Litt.D., Melbourne, 1908. *Publications:* Modern Constitutions in Outline, 1905; The Obligation of Obedience to the Law of the State, 1905; Stoic and Christian in the Second Century, 1906; Sir Thomas Smith's De Republica Anglorum, 1906; The White Man's Work in Asia and Africa, 1907; Education and Citizenship in India, 1910; Elements of Indian Taxation, 1910; The Functions of Money, 1932. *Address:* 23 Warkworth Street, Cambridge.
[*Died* 4 *Dec.* 1953.

ALTON, Ernest Henry, M.C., M.A., Litt.D., M.R.I.A., Hon. D.Litt. (Oxon.), Hon. Dott. Univ. (Padua); Provost of Trinity Coll., Dublin, since 1942; *e. s.* of late James Poë Alton, Limerick, and late Marguerite Keely; *m.* 1915, Ethel Marjory, *d.* of late Col. Sir Charles Hughes-Hunter, Bt., D.L., J.P., of Anglesey; two *s.* one *d.* *Educ.:* The High School, Dublin; Trinity College, Dublin (1st Classical Schol., 1894; Wray Prize, Berkeley Medal, Vice-Chancellor's Medal, 1895; 1st Senior Moderatorship in Classics, Sen. Moderatorship in Philosophy, Classical Studentship and Vice-Chancellor's Prize, 1896). Tried journalism for a time, but returned to read for Fellowship; Madden Prize, 1903; Fellowship, 1905; became Tutor, Lecturer in Classical Composition, Special Lecturer in Classics, Lecturer in Hebrew; Professor of Latin, 1927-42; Senior Proctor, 1937-38; Capt., D.U.O.T.C., 1915; retd., 1920; Vice-Pres., Royal Irish Academy, 1942, and Member of Council; Fellow St. Columba's College, Rathfarnham; and Chairman of Board of Erasmus Smith Schools; Member of Greater Dublin, and other Commissions; formerly Member of Film Censor's Appeal Board, I.F.S.; ex.-Pres. Classical Assoc. of Ireland; Vice-Pres. Classical Assoc. of England; Member of Southern Ireland Parliament, 1922; Representative of Dublin Univ. in Dail Eireann, 1923-37; Member of Irish Senate, 1938-43. *Publications:* Editor of Hermathena, 1921-37; compiled (with Dr. Goligher) the Roman volume in Herbert Spencer's Sociological Data Series; contributor of various articles to Hermathena, Kottabos, Cambridge Classical Companion, Classical Review, Classical Quarterly, The Year's Work in Classics (Latin Literature), and other papers and encyclopedias. *Recreations:* formerly travel and Rugby football; now reading and walking. *Address:* Provost's House, Trinity College, Dublin. *T.:* Dublin 73888. *Clubs:* Savage; University (Dublin); Royal St. George Yacht (Kingstown).
[*Died* 18 *Feb.* 1952.

ALTRINCHAM, 1st Baron, *cr.* 1945, of Tormarton; **Edward William Macleay Grigg,** P.C. 1944; K.C.M.G., *cr.* 1928 (C.M.G. 1919); K.C.V.O., *cr.* 1920 (C.V.O. 1919); D.S.O. 1918; M.C.; Chevalier of the Order of Leopold II; Officier de la Légion d'Honneur; Editor, National Review, since 1948, amalgamated with English Review Magazine as National and English Review, 1950; *b.* 8 Sept. 1879; *o. s.* of late Henry Bidewell Grigg, C.I.E., I.C.S., and Elizabeth, *e. d.* of Sir Edward Deas-Thomson, Colonial Secretary of New South Wales; *m.* 1923, Hon. Joan Poynder, *o. c.* of 1st Baron Islington, P.C., G.C.M.G., G.B.E.; two *s.* one *d.* *Educ.:* Winchester (Scholar); New College, Oxford (Scholar); 2nd Class in Mods., 1900; 3rd in Lit. Hum., 1902; Gaisford Greek Verse Prize, 1902. Joined editorial staff of The Times, 1903; Assist. Editor of the Outlook, 1905-6; travelled, 1907-8; rejoined editorial staff of The Times, 1908, resigned 1913; joined Grenadier Guards, 1914; became G.S.O. 1 of the Guards Division; Military Secretary to Prince of Wales, Canada, 1919, Australia, and New Zealand; relinquished Commission with rank of Lt.-Col., 1921; Private Secretary to Mr. Lloyd George, 1921-22; M.P. (N.L.) Oldham, 1922-25; Secretary to the Rhodes Trustees, 1923-25; Governor and Commander-in-Chief and High Commissioner for Transport, Kenya Colony, 1925-31; Chairman of Milk Reorganisation Commission, 1932; M.P. (Nat. C.) Altrincham, 1933-45; Parliamentary Secretary to Ministry of Information, 1939-40; Financial Secretary, War Office, 1940; Joint Parliamentary Under-Secretary of State for War, 1940-42; Minister Resident in the Middle East, 1944-45. D.L. Gloucestershire, 1950-. *Publications:* The Greatest Experiment in History, 1924; Three Parties or Two, 1931; The Faith of an Englishman, 1936; Britain Looks at Germany, 1938; The British Commonwealth, 1943; British Foreign Policy, 1944. *Heir:* *s.* Hon. John Edward Poynder Grigg, *b.* 15 April 1924. *Address:* 47 Lowndes Square, S.W.1. *T.:* Sloane 3724; Tormarton Court, Badminton. *Clubs:* Guards, Beefsteak.
[*Died* 1 *Dec.* 1955.

ALVAREZ de Rocafuarte; *see* D'Alvarez, Madame.

ALVINGHAM, 1st Baron, *cr.* 1929, of Woodfold; **Major Robert Daniel Thwaites Yerburgh;** *b.* 10 Dec. 1889; *e. s.* of late Robert Armstrong Yerburgh, D.L., 27 years M.P. for Chester, of Caythorpe Court, Lincs, and of Elma Amy (*d.* 1946), of Woodfold Park, Lancs, *o. d.* of D. Thwaites, D.L., for some years M.P. for Blackburn; *m.* 1st, Dorothea Gertrude (*d.* 1927), *d.* of late J. Eardley Yerburgh; one *s.* two *d.*; 2nd, 1936, Mrs. M. L. G. Bright. *Educ.:* Harrow; University College, Oxford. In Army, European War, 1915-19 (Bt. Major); M.P. (U.) South Dorset, 1922-29. *Heir:* *s.* Hon. Robert Guy Eardley Yerburgh, Capt., Coldstream Guards [*b.* 16 Dec. 1926; *m.* 1952, B. E. Williams; one *d.*]. *Address:* Shottersley, Haslemere, Surrey. *Club:* Carlton.
[*Died* 27 *Nov.* 1955.

ALY KHAN, Shah; Ambassador and Permanent Representative of Pakistan to the United Nations since 1958; Chairman, Pakistan Delegation and Vice-Pres. 13th Session, General Assembly; Vice-Chm. U.N. Peace Observation Commission from 1959; Representative of Pakistan to Geneva Office of U.N.; *b.* 13 June 1911; *e. s.* of Mohammed Shah, H.H. Aga Khan, P.C., G.C.S.I., G.C.M.G., G.C.I.E., G.C.V.O., LL.D. (*d.* 1957); *m.* 1st, 1936, Hon. Joan Barbara, *e. d.* of 3rd Baron Churston (marriage dissolved, 1949); two *s.* (*er. s.* H.H. Aga Khan IV); 2nd, 1949, Margarita Cansino (Rita Hayworth) (marriage dissolved, 1953); one *d.* Was a secretary to the British Indian Delegation at the Second Round Table Conference, 1931. 2nd Lt. Foreign Legion, 1939; transferred to Royal Wilts. Yeomanry, 1940; Lt.-Col. 1945; Legion of Honour (Officer); Croix de Guerre with palms; Bronze Star Medal (U.S.A.). Col. Comdt. of Fourth Cavalry, Pakistan Army. *Recreations:* racing, flying, riding, shooting, hunting. *Address:* Château de l'Horizon, Golfe Juan, Alpes Maritimes, France. *Club:* Athenæum.
[*Died* 12 *May* 1960.

AMBEDKAR, Bhimrao Ramji, M.A., Ph.D., D.Sc., LL.D.; Barrister-at-Law; Minister for Law, India, 1947, resigned, 1951; late Member Governor-General's Executive Council; *b.* 14 April 1893; Untouchable by caste; *s.* of Ramji Maloji. Subhedar in the 7th Pioneer, and Bhimabai; *m.* 1948, Dr. Sharda Kabir, Brahmin by caste, of Bombay. *Educ.:* Elphinstone College, Bombay; Columbia University, New York; School of Economics, London; Gray's Inn. Professor of Political Economy, Sydenham College of Commerce, Bombay; Practising Lawyer High Court, Bombay; Fellow of Univ. of Bombay; Univ. Examiner in Economics and Law; ex-member Bombay Legislative Assembly; President I.L.P.;

delegate to Indian Round Table Conference; member Bombay (Simon Commission) Provincial Committee and Lothian Committee on Indian Franchise; architect of Free India's Constitution and other important Social legislatures. Many books on origin of Sudras (untouchables) and caste, and on what Gandhi and Congress have done for untouchables, etc. Keen student and research worker in religion, philosophy, finance, politics, etc.; only recognised leader of all untouchables in India. *Publications:* Problem of the Rupee, 1923; Provincial Finance in British India, 1924; Annihilation of Caste, 1937; Federation versus Freedom, 1939; Thoughts on Pakistan, 1941; Ranade, Gandhi and Jinnah, 1943, etc. *Address:* 26 Alipore Road, Delhi. *T.:* 23613.
[*Died* 6 *Dec.* 1956.

AMCOTTS, Lt.-Comdr. John; *see* Cracroft-Amcotts.

AMERY, Rt. Hon. Leopold Stennett, P.C. 1922; C.H. 1945; Hon. D.C.L. Oxford, 1943, Durham, 1950; LL.D. Cambridge, 1952; M.P. (U.) Sparkbrook (formerly South) Division of Birmingham, 1911-45; *b.* 22 Nov. 1873, Gorakhpur, U.P., India; *e. s.* of late Charles F. Amery, of Middle Coombe, Lustleigh, S. Devon, and of the Indian Forest Department, and Elizabeth Leitner; *m.* 1910, Florence (C.I. 1945), *d.* of late John Hamar Greenwood, of Whitby, Ont., and *sis.* of 1st Viscount Greenwood, P.C., K.C.; one *s.* *Educ.:* Harrow; Balliol College, Oxford (exhibitioner). 1st class in Mods. 1894; 1st in Lit. Hum. 1896; private secretary to Rt. Hon. L. H. Courtney, M.P., 1896-97; elected Fellow of All Souls College, Oxford, 1897; Hon. Fellow of Balliol College, Oxford, 1946; on The Times editorial staff, 1899-1909; organised The Times war correspondence in South Africa, 1899-1900; Barrister, Inner Temple, 1902; contested Wolverhampton (East), as Unionist and Tariff Reformer, 1906, 1908, and January 1910; Bow and Bromley, December 1910; served in Flanders and the Near East, 1914-16; Assistant Secretary War Cabinet and Imperial War Cabinet, 1917; on the staff of the War Council, Versailles, and on personal staff of Secretary of State for War, 1917-18; temp. Lt.-Col. on General Staff; Parliamentary Under-Sec. for the Colonies, 1919-21; Parliamentary and Financial Secretary to the Admiralty, 1921-22; First Lord of the Admiralty, Oct. 1922-Feb. 1924; Secretary of State for the Colonies, Nov. 1924-June 1929; Secretary of State: for Dominion Affairs, July 1925-June 1929; for India and for Burma, 1940-45; has travelled extensively in the Near East and in all the British Dominions. *Publications:* Times History of the S. African War, 7 vols. completed 1909; The Problem of the Army, 1903; Fundamental Fallacies of Free Trade, 1906; The Great Question, 1909; Union and Strength, 1912; The Empire in the New Era, 1928; Empire and Prosperity, 1930; A Plan of Action, 1932; The Stranger of the Ulysses, 1934; The Forward View, 1935; The German Colonial Claim, 1939; Days of Fresh Air, 1939; India and Freedom, 1942; The Framework of the Future, 1943; The Washington Loan Agreements, 1946; In the Rain and the Sun, 1946; Thoughts on the Constitution, 1947; The Awakening, 1948; The Elizabethan Spirit, 1948; My Political Life: Vol. I, 1953: England Before the Storm; Vol. II, 1953: War and Peace; Vol. III, 1955: The Unforgiving Years; A Balanced Economy, 1954. *Recreations:* travelling, mountaineering, ski-ing, sailing. *Address:* 112 Eaton Square, S.W.1. *Clubs:* Alpine, Athenæum, Carlton.
[*Died* 16 *Sept.* 1955.

AMERY, William Bankes, C.B.E. 1920; United Kingdom Member, Board of British Phosphate Commissioners, since 1946; *b.* 26 Oct. 1883; *e. s.* of Thomas Arthur Amery of Norwell, Newark, Notts.; *m.* 1940, Edna Mary, *d.* of late Mrs. Maria Truman, Fairlight, Sussex. *Educ.:* Christ's Hospital. Assist.-Secretary, War Trade Dept., 1916-19; Establishment Officer, Ministry of Transport, 1919-22; Finance Officer, Oversea Settlement Dept. of the Dominions Office, 1922-25; Representative of the United Kingdom Government in Australia under the Empire Settlement Act 1925-28; Assistant Secretary, Dominions Office, 1937; Controller Export Licensing Dept. Board of Trade, 1939; Asst.-Sec. Ministry of Food, 1940; Head of U.K. Food Mission to Australia, representing Ministry of Food, 1942-45. *Address:* British Phosphate Commission, 2 Grosvenor Gardens, S.W.1. *Club:* Savile.
[*Died* 26 *Nov.* 1951.

AMES, Sir Herbert (Brown), Kt., *cr.* 1915; *b.* Montreal, 27 June 1863; *m.* 1890, Louise Marion, *d.* of late Sir John Kennedy. *Educ.:* Public Schools, Montreal; Amherst Coll., Mass. (LL.D.). President of the Volunteer Electoral League; Alderman, 1898-1906; Chairman Municipal Board of Health, 1900-4; Member House of Commons, Montreal, 1904-21; Chairman Select Standing Committee on Banking and Commerce, 1911; Hon. Secretary Canadian Patriotic Fund, 1914-19; Chairman Special Committee of the House of Commons *in re* care and treatment of returned soldiers, 1917; Financial Director of League of Nations Secretariat, 1919-26; LL.D. Amherst College; Lecturer for the Carnegie Endowment for International Peace, 1929-38. *Address:* c/o Montreal Convalescent Hospital, 3001 Kent Avenue, Côte des Neiges, Montreal 26, Canada.
[*Died* 31 *March* 1954.

AMMON, 1st Baron, *cr.* 1944, of Camberwell, **Charles George Ammon,** P.C. 1945; D.L., J.P.; Past President International Arbitration League; Vice-President Royal National Lifeboat Institution; Assoc. of Building Societies and Metropolitan Association of Building Societies; Governor London School of Economics, Dulwich College; late Chm. Trustees of Crystal Palace; Member Channel Islands Commn., 1947; director: Municipal Mutual Insurance; Atlas Building Society; *s.* of Charles George and Mary Ammon; *m.* Ada Ellen (*d.* 1958), *d.* of David May, Walworth, London; two *d.* *Educ.:* Public Elementary Schools and private study. In Post Office Service for twenty-four years; London County Councillor for North Camberwell, 1919-25 and 1934-1946; Chairman L.C.C., 1941-42; contested North Camberwell for Parliament, 1918 and 1931; M.P. (Lab.) North Camberwell, 1922-31 and 1935-44; Labour Party Whip, 1923; member Nat. Executive Labour Party, 1921-26; Parliamentary Sec. to the Admiralty, 1924 and 1929-31; National President Brotherhood Movement, 1929 and 1945; Member West African Mission, 1938-1939; Member Select Committee on National Expenditure, 1939-44; Chairman Mission to Newfoundland, 1943; Temp. Chairman of Committees, 1943; Chairman Parl. Mission to China, 1947; Captain of the Gentlemen-at-Arms, 1945-49; lately Govt. Chief Whip; a Deputy Speaker, House of Lords, 1945-58; Chairman National Dock Labour Corp. Ltd., 1944-50; Alderman Camberwell Borough Council, 1934-53; Mayor of Camberwell, 1950-51. Freedom of Borough of Camberwell, 1951. Past-Pres. U.K. Band of Hope Union; Methodist Local Preacher. *Publications:* Christ and Labour; Newfoundland: the Forgotten Island; pamphlets, articles in reviews, periodicals, etc. *Recreations:* reading, walking. *Address:* 70 Ferndene Road, S.E.24. *T.:* Brixton 4828.
[*Died* 2 *April* 1960 (*ext.*).

AMPTHILL, The Dowager Lady; Margaret, C.I. 1899; G.C.V.O., *cr.* 1946; G.B.E., *cr.* 1918; formerly Lady-in-Waiting to Queen Mary; *b.* 8 Oct. 1874; *d.* of 6th Earl Beauchamp; *m.* 1894, 2nd Baron Ampthill, G.C.S.I., G.C.I.E. (*d.* 1935); four *s.* one *d.* *Address:* 55 Chester Square, S.W.1. *T.:* Sloane 4927. *Club:* V.A.D. Ladies. [*Died* 12 *Dec.* 1957.

ANCASTER, 2nd Earl of (*cr.* 1892), **Gilbert Heathcote-Drummond-Willoughby,** G.C.V.O. *cr.* 1937; T.D.; Baron Willoughby de Eresby, 1313; Baron Aveland, 1856; *b.* 29 July 1867; *e. s.* of 1st Earl of Ancaster and Evelyn, *d.* of 10th Marquess of Huntly; *S.* father, 1910; *m.* 1905, Eloise, *e. d.* of late W. L. Breese of New York; two *s.* two *d.* *Educ.:* Eton; Trinity College, Cambridge (M.A.). Lt.-Col. O.C. Lincolnshire Yeomanry, 1911-15; M.P. (C.) Horncastle Division of Lincolnshire, 1894-1910; Parliamentary Secretary to the Ministry of Agriculture, 1921-23; Chairman of Quarter Sessions, Kesteven, Lincs, 1911-1936; Chairman of Rutland County Council, 1922-37; Lord Great Chamberlain of England, 1937-50; Lord Lieutenant County Rutland, 1921-51. *Recreations:* hunting, shooting. *Heir:* *s.* Lord Willoughby de Eresby. *Address:* Grimsthorpe, Bourne, Lincs; Drummond Castle, Crieff. *T.:* Edenham 222. *Clubs:* Carlton, Turf. [*Died* 19 *Sept.* 1951.

ANDERSON, Sir Alan Garrett, G.B.E., *cr.* 1934 (K.B.E., *cr.* 1917); Commander Order of Crown of Italy; Officer Legion of Honour; Commander Order of White Rose of Finland; Captain (Hon.) R.N.R.; Hon. Fellow Trinity College, Oxon.; *b.* 9 Mar. 1877; *s.* of J. G. S. and Elizabeth Garrett Anderson, M.D.; *m.* 1903, Muriel Ivy Duncan; two *s.* two *d.* *Educ.:* Elstree; Eton (King's Scholar); Trinity College, Oxon. Director, Orient P. & O. & B.I.; Director, Suez Canal Company; President of Hospital Saving Association; Hon. President International Chamber of Commerce; Deputy-Lieutenant of City of London; High Sheriff of County of London, 1922; M.P. (C.) City of London, 1935-40; Controller of Railways, Ministry of War Transport, 1941-45; Chairman of Railway Executive, 1941-45; President of the Chamber of Shipping of the United Kingdom, 1924-25; Pres. Institute of Marine Engineers, 1928; Pres. Association of Chambers of Commerce, 1933-34. *Address:* 105 Park Lane, W.1; Notgrove Manor, Glos. *Clubs:* Brooks's, City of London, Royal Cruising, Cruising Association; Royal Yacht Squadron (Cowes); Royal Irish Yacht (Kingstown). [*Died* 4 *May* 1952.

ANDERSON, Alan Orr, M.A., LL.D. (Edin.); Hon. F.S.A. Scot.; *b.* 1879; *s.* of Rev. John Anderson, B.D., and Ann, *d.* of Rev. John Masson; *m.* 1932, Marjorie Ogilvie, *d.* of James Cunningham, LL.D. *Educ.:* Royal High School and University, Edinburgh. *Publications:* Scottish Annals from English Chroniclers, 1909; Early Sources of Scottish History, 1922; Prophecy of Berchan, 1929; Prospects of the Advancement of Knowledge in Early Scottish History, 1940; (with his wife) Introduction to the Chronicle of Melrose, facsimile edition, 1936, and a Historical Edition of Adomnan's Life of Columba, 1961; contributions to his wife's edition of the Chronicle of Holyrood, 1938. *Address:* 24 Bruce Road, Downfield, Dundee. *T.:* Dundee 85000. [*Died* 9 *Dec.* 1958.

ANDERSON, Alexander; M.P. (Lab.) Motherwell Division of Lanarkshire since 1945; M.A.; J.P. (Lanark); Member Nature Conservancy since 1949; *b.* Wick, Caithness, 12 April 1888; *s.* of Thomas Anderson and Ina Manson, Wick; *m.* 1922, Margaret Pyper Craig Sinclair; one *s.* one *d.* *Educ.:* Pulteneytown Academy, Wick; Edinburgh University (M.A. 1910). English Master various schools, Wishaw High School, 1921-1945. Member Motherwell Town Council, 1929-45; Hon. Treasurer, 1935-45. *Recreations:* angling, yachting, gardening, reading thrillers. *Address:* 31 Kenilworth Avenue, Wishaw. *T.:* Wishaw 554. [*Died* 11 *Feb.* 1954.

ANDERSON, Alexander Knox, M.A., F.R. Hist. Soc.; Principal, The Scots College, Bellevue Hill, Sydney, N.S.W., Australia, since 1935; *b.* 12 Jan. 1892; *s.* of James Robert and Margaret Anderson; *m.* 1917, May Synnitt Irvine; one *d.* *Educ.:* Port Chalmers District High School; Dunedin Teachers' Training College; Otago University; Canterbury University College, N.Z. B.A., 1914; M.A. 1915 (First Class Honours in History); Assistant Master, Waitaki Boys' High School, 1912-16; Assistant Master Otago Boys' High School, 1916-20; Lecturer on Advanced and Honours History, Otago University, 1918-20; Rector, St. Andrew's College, Christchurch, 1920-1934; External Examiner in B.A. History to University of New Zealand, 1921-25; President of Association of Principals of Registered Secondary Schools of New Zealand, 1933-34; Chairman Great Public Schools' Headmasters' Assoc., 1940 and 1946; Pres. Teachers' Guild of N.S.W., 1945-46; Chairman Headmasters' Conference (N.S.W.), 1949-54; Member State Standing Cttee., 1948-54. Board of Secondary School Studies, 1949-55, and of National Trust, 1948-49. Coronation Medal, 1937. *Recreations:* rifle shooting (tied South-land Championship, N.Z., 1916, second Otago Championship, 1916), cricket, hockey, tennis, golf. *Address:* The Scots College, Bellevue Hill, Sydney, N.S.W. *T.:* F.M. 2186 Sydney. [*Died* 6 *Jan.* 1955.

ANDERSON, Sir Athol Lancelot, K.C.B., *cr.* 1939 (C.B. 1936); *b.* 17 Jan. 1875; *s.* of William Curling Anderson and Sophia Griffiths; *m.* 1901, Alice Mabel Ann Emmott (*d.* 1954); no *c.* *Educ.:* Cheltenham Coll. Articled to Sir James Lemon, M.Inst.C.E., Southampton and Westminster; served under Civil Engineer in Chief, Admiralty at Portsmouth, Malta, Rosyth, Hong Kong, Simonstown, Jamaica, Heligoland and at Singapore; also various periods of service at the Admiralty; Civil Engineer-in-Chief, Admiralty, 1934-40; a member of the Commission des Travaux of the International Commission of the Canal Maritime de Suez. *Address:* 3 Furze Croft, Hove, Sussex. *T.:* Hove 34800. [*Died* 7 *June* 1955.

ANDERSON, Major Charles, D.S.O. 1918; M.C.; J.P.; Hon. Sheriff Substitute for County of Roxburgh; Writer to the Signet; Partner Charles and R. B. Anderson, W.S., Jedburgh; Clerk to Commissioners of Income Tax for Roxburghshire; *b.* 30 July 1886; *e. s.* of late R. B. Anderson of Glenburn Hall, Jedburgh, Roxburghshire; *m.* 1921, Maimie, *y. d.* of Dr. G. Gunn Bannerman, Hawick; two *s.* one *d.* *Educ.:* Edinburgh Academy; Edinburgh University. Writer to the Signet, 1910; served France, 1916-1919 (M.C., D.S.O., despatches twice, G.S. and Victory medals); demobilised 1919. *Address:* Glenburn Hall, Jedburgh, Scotland. *Club:* New (Edinburgh). [*Died* 25 *June* 1954.

ANDERSON, Charles Buxton, C.M.G. 1944; I.S.O. 1937; M.Inst.C.E.; M.I.E.A.; *b.* 19 Aug. 1879; *s.* of late John Anderson, Adelaide, S. Australia; *m.* 1902, Eva, *d.* of late J. B. Scott; five *d.* *Educ.:* Glenelg Collegiate School; S. Australian School of Mines. Joined S.A. Public Works Dept., 1898, as Draughtsman; successively, Surveyor, Resident Engineer, Railways; General Supt., Railways; Railways Commissioner for State of S. Australia, 1930-46; a Comr. S. Australian Harbours Bd., 1946-51, Dep. Comr., 1951, Actg. Chm. 1952; retired, Oct. 1952. O.St.J.; late Hon. Col. Engineering and Railway Staff Corps. *Address:*

88 First Avenue, St. Peters, S. Australia. *T.:* FY2513. *Clubs:* Adelaide, Commonwealth (Adelaide). [*Died* 12 *Dec.* 1953.

ANDERSON, Sir David, Kt., *cr.* 1951; LL.D., B.Sc., M.I.C.E.; Senior Partner in firm of Mott, Hay & Anderson; *b.* 6 July 1880; *m.* 1st, 1907; 2nd, 1935; no *c.* *Educ.:* High School, Dundee; St. Andrews University. Assistant Engineer to late Sir Benjamin Baker, K.C.B.; Resident Engineer, Blackfriars Bridge Widening and Reconstruction of Rochester Bridge; Chief Assistant and then partner with the late Sir Basil Mott, Bt., and late Mr. David Hay; responsible with his partners for the design and construction of Southwark Bridge, Tyne Bridge, Wearmouth Bridge, Tees Bridge, Londonderry, and many other bridges; construction and design of Mersey Tunnel; with his partner, Consulting Engineer to Central London Railway and City & South London Railway; Joint Consulting Engineer for London Passenger Transport Board (now London Transport Executive), and responsible for Central London Railway Realignment, extension to Newbury Park, Ilford; Joint Engineer for Dartford Tunnel for Ministry of Transport; Consulting Engineer, Mersey Tunnel Joint Cttee.; Engineer for Tyne Tunnels; served European War as Captain, Royal Engineers, and then transferred to Royal Marine Engineers; President (1943-44) of Institution of Civil Engineers; M.Am.Soc.C.E. *Publications:* Technical papers to Institution of Civil Engineers: Tyne Bridge, Newcastle, Widening of Blackfriars Bridge, Mersey Tunnel. *Recreation:* yachting. *Address:* 9 Iddesleigh House, Caxton Street, Westminster, S.W.1. *T.A.:* Lydonist Sowest London. *T.:* Abbey 1631. *Clubs:* St. Stephen's; Medway Yacht (Rochester). [*Died* 27 *March* 1953.

ANDERSON, David Martin, C.B.E. 1920; Knight of the Crown of Italy; Director R. D. Nicol and Co., Ltd., Sheffield; *b.* 1880; 2nd *s.* of late James Anderson and Mrs. Anderson, Glasgow; *m.* 1927, Isabella, *d.* of late Alexander Pearson and Mrs. Pearson, 3 Craigholm Crescent, Burntisland. Controller, Forgings, Castings, and Stamping Department, Ministry of Munitions, 1914-19. *Clubs:* Junior Carlton; Sheffield (Sheffield). [*Died* 4 *April* 1955.

ANDERSON, Lady, D.B.E. *cr.* 1937, **Edith Muriel;** *d.* of late William H. Teschemaker; *m.* 1908, Admiral Sir (David) Murray Anderson (*d.* 1936), K.C.B., K.C.M.G., M.V.O., late Governor of Newfoundland and of New South Wales. *Address:* 4 Parkmead, Roehampton, S.W.15. [*Died* 5 *Sept.* 1958.

ANDERSON, Colonel Eric Litchfield Brooke, C.B.E. 1941 (O.B.E. 1936); D.S.O. 1914; late R.F.A.; *b.* 10 Sept. 1889; *s.* of Col. E. B. Anderson, late Indian Army; *m.* 1926, Betty, *d.* of Mrs. A. H. Etherington, Seal Chart; three *d.* *Educ.:* Clifton Coll.; R.M.A. Woolwich. Entered army, 1909; Capt. 1915; served European War, 1914-17 (desp., D.S.O., order of Danilo); retired 1920, with hon. rank of Lieut.-Col. War of 1939-45, Director of Pioneers and Labour, E. Africa Command (despatches, C.B.E.), rank, Colonel; Kenya Administration, 1919-1950 (retired). *Club:* East India and Sports. [*Died* 13 *June* 1959.

ANDERSON, Frank; M.P. (Lab.) Whitehaven Division of Cumberland since 1935; *b.* 21 Nov. 1889; *s.* of Thomas and Nancy Anderson; *m.* 1919, Mary Elizabeth Thompson; no *c.* *Educ.:* Greenmount Elementary School. Railway Clerk until elected to House of Commons, English Whip, 1937-40. *Address:* House of Commons, S.W.1. [*Died* 25 *April* 1959.

ANDERSON, Lieut.-Col. Frederick Jasper, C.I.E. 1939; M.C. 1916; I.M.S., retired; Hon. Surgeon to Governor of Bengal; Late Prof. of Surgery, Medical College, Calcutta; *b.* 10 March 1886; *s.* of Alfred Jasper Anderson, Cape Town. *Educ.:* Epsom College; South Africa College; London University. M.B., B.S., 1912; F.R.C.S. Eng. 1922; Lt. I.M.S., 1912; Capt. 1915; Major, 1923; Lt.-Col. 1931; served European War, 1914-19 (despatches twice, M.C.). *Recreation:* racing. *Address:* 5 Pretoria Street, Calcutta 16, India. *Club:* Naval and Military. [*Died* 28 *Nov.* 1957.

ANDERSON, George Henry Garstin, C.B.E. 1946; D.S.O. 1918; M.C.; *b.* 22 April 1896; *s.* of late James Drummond Anderson, Litt.D., I.C.S., and Frances Louisa Cordue; *m.* 1924, Doris Constance (*d.* 1954), *d.* of late E. J. Gross, President of Gonville and Caius Coll., Cambridge; four *d.* *Educ.:* Perse School, Cambridge. Joined Rifle Brigade, 1915; served European War; operations in France and Belgium, 1915-18 (despatches, D.S.O., M.C. and bar); Adjutant, 2nd Battalion Rifle Brigade, 1918-1921; entered Indian Civil Service, 1921; served as Personal Assistant to Chief Commissioner, Delhi; Asst. Principal, India Office, 1925; Principal, 1930: Asst. Secretary, Ministry of Labour, 1939; Principal Officer, Eastern (Civil Defence) Region, 1939-44; Ministry of Labour, 1944-45; Director of Recruiting, Control Office for Germany and Austria, 1945-46; Director of Overseas Staff, Foreign Office (German Section), 1947-49, and Establishment Officer, 1950-51); Asst. Secretary, Home Office, 1951-58. *Address:* c/o National and Grindlay's Bank, 54 Parliament St., S.W.1. [*Died* 22 *Sept.* 1959.

ANDERSON, Col. James, C.M.G. 1918, D.S.O. 1916; D.L., J.P.; late H.L.I.; *b.* 1872; *m.* 1914, Elsie Mary, *d.* of J. E. Corby, Rowley Bank, Arkley. Served European War. 1914-18 (wounded, despatches five times, D.S.O. and 2 bars, C.M.G.). *Address:* The Elms, Milliken Park, Renfrewshire. *Club:* New (Glasgow). [*Died* 18 *Dec.* 1955.

ANDERSON, John George Clark, M.A., Hon. LL.D. (Aberdeen); Honorary Fellow of Lincoln College, Oxford; Member of the German Archæological Institute; a Vice-President, Society for Promotion of Roman Studies; *b.* 6 Dec. 1870; *s.* of Rev. Alexander Anderson, D.D., Edinkillie, Morayshire. *Educ.:* Aberdeen University; Christ Church, Oxford. Craven Fellow, 1896; Fellow of Lincoln College, Oxford, 1897-1900; travelled widely in Asia Minor for archæological purposes, 1896-1900, 1912; Senior Student and Tutor of Christ Church, 1900-27; Junior Censor, 1907-8; Senior Censor, 1908-11; Conington Prize, 1903; University Lecturer in Roman Epigraphy (appointed 1914), 1919-27; Reader in Roman Epigraphy, 1927; Camden Professor of Ancient History in the University of Oxford and Fellow of Brasenose College, 1927-36. *Publications:* Numerous papers in Journal of Hellenic Studies, Journal of Roman Studies, other learned periodicals; contributions to Studies in the Eastern Roman Provinces, 1906, Anatolian Studies pres. to Ramsay, 1923, and to Buckler, 1939; Map of Ancient Asia Minor, 1903; The Students Gibbon, Pt. II. (A.D. 565-1481), 1901 and 1911; Studia Pontica, jointly with F. Cumont, since 1903; The Agricola of Tacitus, 1922 (2nd impression, with corrections, 1929); contributions to Cambr. Anc. Hist. Vol. X, 1934; The Germania of Tacitus, 1938. *Recreations:* golfing, gardening, motoring. *Address:* 25 Charlbury Road, Oxford. *T.:* Oxford 5609. [*Died* 31 *March* 1952.

ANDERSON, General Sir Kenneth Arthur Noel, K.C.B., *cr.* 1943 (C.B. 1940): M.C.; *b.* 25 Dec. 1891; *m.* 1918, Kathleen Lorna Mary, *d.* of late

Sir Reginald Gamble; one *s.* (killed in action), one *d.* (decd.). *Educ.:* Charterhouse; R.M.C., Sandhurst. 2nd Lieutenant Seaforth Highlanders, 1911; Captain, 1915; Major, 1923; Bt. Lieut.-Col. and Lieut.-Col. 1930; Col. 1934; Maj.-Gen. 1940; Lt.-Gen. 1943; General 1949; Staff Coll., 1926-28; O.C. British Troops, Palestine, 1930-32; 11 Inf. Bde., 1938-40; served European War, 1914-18 (wounded, M.C.); N.W. Frontier of India, 1930-31 (despatches); War of 1939-45 (despatches, C.B., K.C.B.); Comd. 11 Inf. Bde. in France and Flanders; 3 Div. Dunkirk; 1 Div. 8 Corps, 2 Corps, 1st Army Aug. 1942 throughout North African campaign to victorious end in May 1943; 2nd Army in U.K., June 1943-Jan. 1944; Eastern Command, Jan.-Dec. 1944; G.O.C.-in-C. East Africa Command, Jan. 1945 - Oct. 1946; Governor and Commander-in-Chief, Gibraltar, 1947-52; retired 1952. Chief Commander U.S. Legion of Merit; Commander French Legion of Honour; Croix de Guerre with palm; Grand Cordon Moroccan Ouissam Alaouite; Grand Cordon Tunisian Nisham Iftikar; Grand Cordon Star of Ethiopia; K.St.J., 1952. *Address:* Villa Bellocchio, 83 Boulevard de Garavan, Menton (A-M), France. *Club:* Army and Navy. [*Died* 29 *April* 1959.

ANDERSON, Maxwell; Playwright; *b.* 15 Dec. 1888; *s.* of William Lincoln Anderson and Premily Stephenson; *m.* 1st, 1911, Margaret Haskett (*d.* 1931); 2nd, 1933, Gertrude Maynard (*d.* 1953); three *s.* one *d.* *Educ.:* Univ. of North Dakota (B.A.); Stanford University (M.A.). *Plays produced in New York City:* White Desert, What Price Glory? (Collab.), Outside Looking In, The Buccaneer (Collab.), First Flight (Collab.), Saturday's Children, Gods of the Lightning (Collab.), Gypsy, Elizabeth the Queen, Night Over Taos, Both Your Houses (Pulitzer Prize Play), Mary of Scotland, Valley Forge, Winterset (Critics' Prize Play), The Wingless Victory, High Tor (Critics' Prize Play), The Masque of Kings, The Star-Wagon, Knickerbocker Holiday (with music by Kurt Weill), Key Largo, Journey to Jerusalem, The Eve of St. Mark; Storm Operation; Truckline Cafe; Joan of Lorraine; Anne of the Thousand Days; Lost in the Stars (with music by Kurt Weill); Barefoot in Athens; The Bad Seed (produced London 1955). *One Act Plays:* The Feast of Ortolans, Second Overture, Miracle of the Danube. *Poems:* You Who Have Dreams. *Books of Essays:* The Essence of Tragedy; Off Broadway. *Address:* New City, New York. *Club:* Century (New York). [*Died* 28 *Feb.* 1959.

ANDERSON, Captain Sir Maxwell Hendry Maxwell-, Kt., *cr.* 1934; C.B.E. 1919 (O.B.E. 1918); K.C.; Royal Navy (retired); *b.* 1879; *e. s.* of late Rev. J. H. Anderson, Rector of Tooting; *m.* 1913, Mildred (*d.* 1945), *e. d.* of late Rev. I. H. Jones, Rector of Nevern, Pembroke; one *d.* *Educ.:* privately; H.M.S. Britannia. Various commissions abroad; while Navigating Officer of Flora thanked by Admiralty for valuable series of Magnetic Observations in Pacific Ocean; Younger Brother Trinity-House, 1910; called to Bar, 1909; retired from R.N. to practise at Bar, 1912; rejoined R.N. on outbreak of war; served in Trade Division A.W.S. for special service at Admiralty; Councillor for Tooting, Wandsworth Boro' Council, 1913-18; Government Member Central Unemployed Body for London, 1914; retired Captain, April 1919; Liberal Candidate for Parliament, Balham, Tooting, Dec. 1918; Attorney-General of Gibraltar, 1919-29; Chief Justice of the Supreme Court of Fiji and Judicial Commissioner for the Western Pacific, 1929-36. *Publications:* Elements of Pilotage and Navigation, 1908-16; the Navy and Prize, 1916; various articles on Prize and kindred matters. *Clubs:* United Service; Union (Malta). [*Died* 9 *June* 1951.

ANDERSON, Venerable Nicol Keith; Archdeacon Emeritus since 1953; *b.* 10 June 1882; *s.* of William Richard and Edith Anderson; *m.* 1913, Kathleen Irene Duffin; one *s.* (and one killed on active service). *Educ.:* Marlborough; Oriel College, Oxford (Exhibitioner). Assistant Curate, St. Pancras Parish Church, 1908-11; Chaplain, Indian Ecclesiastical Establishment, Rangoon, 1911-1934; Archdeacon of Rangoon, 1930 (resigned) 1934,; Secretary, South London Church Fund and Southwark Diocesan Board of Finance, 1935-52; Canon Residentiary, Southwark Cathedral, 1937-50; Archdeacon of Kingston-upon-Thames, 1946-1952; Silver Jubilee Medal, 1935. *Address:* Marywood, Copt Hill Lane, Tadworth, Surrey. [*Died* 1 *Sept.* 1953.

ANDERSON, Peter Corsar, C.B.E. 1947; M.A., J.P.; Prin. of Scotch Coll. Swanbourne, W. Australia, 1904-45; *b.* 16 Feb. 1871; *s.* of M. L. Anderson, M.A., D.D., and Jane Corsar; *m.* Agnes Henrietta Macartney; six *s.* six *d.* *Educ.:* Madras College, St. Andrews, St. Andrews University. M.A. St. Andrews, 1893; won Amateur Golf Championship at Prestwick, 1893; Licentiate of Church of Scotland, 1895; Master at Geelong Grammar School, 1898; Silver Jubilee medal 1935; Coronation medal 1937. *Recreations:* bowls, golf, shooting. *Address:* 33 Congdon Street, Swanbourne, W. Australia. *Club:* Cottesloe Golf. [*Died* 26 *Aug.* 1955.

ANDERSON, Brig.-General Stuart Milligan, D.S.O. 1917; late R.A.; a Director The Exchange Telegraph Co., Ltd.; *b.* 1879; *m.* 1914, Alexandra Helen Ganesco, Bucharest; one *s.* one *d.* Served South African War; European War, 1914-19 (D.S.O., Legion of Honour, American D.S.M.). *Address:* Harry Warren House, Studland, Dorset. [*Died* 23 *May* 1954.

ANDERSON, Thomas Alexander Harvie, C.B. 1917; T.D.; *o. s.* of late Harvie Anderson of Quarter and Shirgarton, Stirlingshire; *m.* Nessie Wilson (*d.* 1938), *d.* of late Sir John Shearer, D.L. Glasgow; one *d.* *Educ.:* Glasgow Academy and University. M.A., B.L., LL.B.; Solicitor and Partner of firm of Anderson, Fyfe, Littlejohn & Co., solicitors, Glasgow; formerly Secretary Glasgow Territorial Army Association; late Hon. Col. The Glasgow Highlanders Highland Light Infantry; Sec. and Treas. Princess Louise Hospital for Limbless Sailors and Soldiers, Erskine; D.L., J.P. City of Glasgow. *Address:* Quarter, by Denny, Stirlingshire. [*Died* 1 *May* 1953.

ANDERSON, Col. Thomas G. G.; *see* Gayer-Anderson.

ANDERSON, William, M.A.; Professor of Philosophy, Auckland University College, since 1921; *b.* Kirkmaiden, Scotland, 21 Dec. 1889; *s.* of Alexander Anderson, M.A.; *m.* 1919, Margaret W. Summers; one *s.* two *d.* *Educ.:* Hamilton Academy; Glasgow Univer. (Scholar). Graduate with Honours (1st Class) in Philosophy, 1911; Lecturer in Logic, Glasgow, 1912-1920. Served European War, 1917-18; Temporary Assistant to Professor of Moral Philosophy, Glasgow, 1919; President, Australian Association of Psychology and Philosophy, 1930. *Publications:* articles and reviews. *Recreations:* golf, walking. *Address:* 1 Grand View Road, Remuera, Auckland, N.Z. [*Died* 7 *Aug.* 1955.

ANDERSON, Major-Gen. William Beaumont, C.M.G. 1919; D.S.O. 1917; O.St.J. 1945; *b.* Ottawa, 9 Sept. 1877; *s.* of late Col. Wm. P. Anderson, C.M.G., V.D.; *m.* 1st, 1903, Lois Winnifred Taylor; one *s.*; 2nd, 1951, Mary Johnston Wood. *Educ.:* Royal Military College, Kingston; McGill Univ. Montreal. First Commission in R.C.E.; Captain, 1905; Intelligence Staff Officer, 1903-6; Assistant Director of Surveys at Militia Headquarters, Ottawa, 1906-8; Staff College, Camberley, 1909-10; G.S.O. Halifax Fortress, 1911; Director of Military Training, Canada, 1912-13; G.S.O. 4th Division, Montreal, 1913 to outbreak of War; D.A.A. and Q.M.G. Canadian Corps, 1915-16; A.Q.M.G. 1916-19; G.S.O., M.D. No. 6, Halifax, 1919-24; D.O.C. Military District No. 7, St. John, 1924–28; D.O.C. Military District No. 3, Kingston, 1928-1938; Retired, 1938; Bachelor of Applied Science; Ontario Land Surveyor; Dominion Land Surveyor. *Address:* 645 Dunn Ave., Lancaster, N.B., Canada. [*Died* 14 *May* 1959.

ANDERSON, William Blair, D.Litt. Hon.LL.D. (Aberdeen); M.A. Cambridge and Manchester; Kennedy Professor of Latin, Cambridge Univ. 1936-42, now Emeritus Professor; Fellow of St. John's College; *b.* Aberdeen, 28 July 1877; *e. s.* of William B. Anderson. *Educ.:* Gordon's College and University of Aberdeen; Trin. College, Cambridge. Assistant Lecturer in Classics, Victoria University of Manchester, 1903-6; Professor of Latin, Queen's University, Kingston, Canada, 1906-13; Professor of Imperial Latin, University of Manchester, 1913-29; Hulme Professor of Latin, 1929-36. *Publications:* Livy, Book IX., edited with introduction, notes, etc., 1909; third edition, 1928; The Works of Apollinaris Sidonius (Loeb Series), Vol. I 1936; contributions to classical and other periodicals. *Address:* St. John's College, and Beaufort Lodge, Hinton Av., Cambridge. *T.:* 87822. [*Died* 9 *Dec.* 1959.

ANDERSON, Brigadier William Henniker, C.B.E. 1925; Indian Army, retired; Director Upend Stud Ltd., Newmarket, retired; *b.* 17 April 1880; *s.* of Col. John Anderson; *m.* 1st; one *s.* (and one *s.* decd.); 2nd, 1935, Joceleyn Frances Ruthven Jackson (*née* Prevost); one *s.* *Educ.:* The Mount, Chesterfield. Joined Royal Norfok Regiment, 1899; transferred to 33rd (Q.V.O.) Light Cavalry Indian Army, 1903; served European War, 1914-18, Army Headquarters India and in Mesopotamia (despatches thrice, Brevet Lt.-Col. 1926); in Irak (Arab Rebellion), 1920; Assistant Director Remounts, 1914; Deputy Director Remounts and Director Remounts, 1918-20, M.E. Force; Deputy Director Remounts, A.H.Qrs., India, 1922-26; Director Remounts A.H.Qrs., India, 1926-30. Polo Manager Hurlingham Club, 1936-39; Secretary of the Arab Horse Society of England, 1934-51. Group Commander Essex Home Guard, War of 1939-45. *Recreations:* polo, hunting, and racing. *Address:* Lloyds Bank Ltd., Cox and King's Branch, 6 Pall Mall, S.W.1. *Club:* Cavalry. [*Died* 4 *April* 1958.

ANDERSON, Very Rev. W(illiam) White, M.C. 1917; V.R.D. 1943; M.A. (Glasg.) 1911, Hon. D.D. (Glasg.) 1943; Moderator, General Assembly of the Church of Scotland, 1951; Minister of St. Cuthbert's Parish Church, Edinburgh, since 1931; Chaplain to the Queen in Scotland since 1952; *b.* 17 March 1888; *s.* of Johan Anderson and Annie White. *Educ.:* Bo'ness Academy; Glasgow University. Missioner, New Brunswick, Canada, 1912. European War, 1914-18, C.F.; Senior Chaplain (9th Div.); Army of Occupation, Germany, Senior Chaplain Lowland Div. Chap. R.N.V.R., 1926. War of 1939-45, served with Royal Navy. Bellahouston Parish Church, Glasgow, 1919-26; New Kilpatrick Parish, Bearsden, 1926-31; translated to St. Cuthbert's, Edinburgh, 1931 as Jun. Minister; Sen. Minister, 1937. Declined calls to St. Andrew's, Ottawa, and Central Presbyterian, Hamilton, Ont., 1925. Convener Home Board of Church of Scotland, 1942-47; Vice-Convener Business Cttee. Gen. Assembly, 1946-49; Convener Business Cttee., 1950-54; Convener Nomination Cttee., 1949-51; Convener General Administration Cttee., 1952; Moderator Presbytery of Edinburgh, 1942; Pres. Scottish Church Soc., 1943; Chaplain to King George VI in Scotland, 1949-52. Chairman Donaldson Trust for Education of Deaf and Dumb Children; Director Society for Teaching Outdoor Blind to read in their own Homes; Member Committee Roy. Soc. for Relief of Indigent Gentlewomen; Gov. Fettes College, Edinburgh; Director Edinburgh Concert Soc. *Recreations:* golf, curling. *Address:* 12 Garscube Terrace, Edinburgh 12. *T.:* 63820. *Club:* Scottish Conservative (Edinburgh). [*Died* 17 *Dec.* 1956.

ANDREW, George, C.B.E. 1937; M.A.; F.R.S.E.; *b.* 28 Nov. 1873; *s.* of A. R. Andrew, LL.D.; *m.* 1924, Kathleen Sturton, *d.* of Alfred Lunn, C.E. *Educ.:* Keith Grammar School; Aberdeen University; Christ Church, Oxford. Classical Master, Hillhead High School, Glasgow; Junior Inspector of Schools, Scottish Education Department; H.M. Inspector in charge of (a) Lanarkshire, (b) Dundee and Forfarshire, (c) Glasgow; H.M. Chief Inspector in charge of (a) Highland Division, (b) Western Division; H.M. Senior Chief Inspector of Schools in charge of (a) Western Division, (b) Training of Teachers; retired, 1938; Deputy Chief Divisional Food Officer for Scotland, 1939-44. *Publications:* Various official reports. *Recreation:* golf. *Address:* 43 Cluny Drive, Morningside, Edinburgh. [*Died* 4 *July* 1956.

ANDREW, Samuel Ogden, M.A. Oxon; *b.* 8 Jan. 1868; *e. s.* of Samuel Andrew and Mary Ogden; *m.* Lilian, *y. d.* of William Pullinger; one *s.* two *d.* *Educ.:* Manchester Grammar School; Oriel Coll., Oxford (Scholar). First-class Classical Mods. 1888; First-class Lit. Hum. 1890; a year in Germany studying psychology; Master at Llandovery College, 1892-95; Headmaster of Oldham Grammar School, 1895-1902; Headmaster, Whitgift School, Croydon, 1903-28. *Publications:* Greek Prose Composition; Greek Versions; articles on Greek Life and Thought and Old English: Sir Gawayne and the Greene Knight; The Wrath of Achilles (translation of Homer's Iliad); Syntax and Style in Old English; Homer's Odyssey; Postcript on Beowulf. *Recreations:* walking, tennis. *Address:* The Hey, Sanderstead, Surrey. *T.:* Sanderstead 1445. [*Died* 10 *April* 1952.

ANDREWS, Lieut.-Col. Cecil Rollo Payton, J.P., M.A.; D.Litt. (Hon.) University of Western Australia, 1929; *b.* London, 2 Feb. 1870; *s.* of Rev. J. M. Andrews (Vicar of St. Jude's, Gray's Inn Road, and subsequently Vicar of Highgate); *m.* 1900, Bertha Arnold, *d.* of T. H. Agnew, Guernsey; one *s.* two *d.* *Educ.:* Merchant Taylors' School, London; St. John's College, Oxford (Classical Scholar). 1st Class Honours, Classical Moderations, 1890; 2nd Class Honours, Literæ Humaniores, 1892; B.A., 1892; M.A., 1898; Assistant Master, Highgate School, 1893-94; Sixth Form Master, Forest School, 1894-96; Resident Tutor, St. John's Training College, Battersea, 1896-1900; Principal of Training College, Claremont, Western Australia, 1901-3; Head of Education Department, 1903-29; Officer Commanding Cadets, Commonwealth Military Forces, W.A., 1906-12; Major, 1906; Lieut.-Col., 1910; Member of University Senate and Pro-Chancellor, 1912-1929; represented Western Australia at Imperial Education Conference, London, 1911. *Recreations:* gardening, walking. *Address:* Argyll, Rosebery Rd., Cheam, Surrey. *T.:* Vigilant 1823. [*Died* 14 *June* 1951.

ANDREWS, Rt. Hon. Sir James, 1st Bt. *cr.* 1942; P.C. Northern Ireland, 1924; Lord Chief Justice of Northern Ireland since 1937; *b.* 3 Jan. 1877; *s.* of late Rt. Hon. Thomas Andrews, D.L., of Ardara,

Comber, and Eliza Pirrie; *m.* 1922, Jane Lawson Haselden, *widow* of late Captain Cyril Haselden, R.E., and *d.* of late Joseph Ormrod, Bolton. *Educ.:* Royal Academical Institution, Belfast; Stephen's Green School, Dublin; Trinity College, Dublin (Mod., B.A. 1st cl. hons. in Logics and Ethics, 1st cl. hons. in Modern Literature, hons. in Mathematics, Senior Exhibitioner; Auditor, Gold Medallist, Hon. Member, and Vice-Pres. of College Historical Society; Prizeman in Law). Called to Irish Bar, King's Inns, Dublin, 1900 (Prizeman in Law); K.C. 1918; Lord Justice of Appeal for Northern Ireland, 1921-37; a Bencher of King's Inns, 1920; a Bencher of Inn of Court of Northern Ireland, 1926; Senior Pro-Chancellor of Queen's University, Belfast; D.L. Co. Down, 1928; Hon. LL.D. Dublin, 1938; Chairman Ulster Savings Committee, 1939-46, President 1946; Hon. Member of Chartered Surveyors' Institution, 1940. Senior Lord Justice for Government of Northern Ireland during absence of the Governor. *Recreations:* cricket, sailing, shooting, and golf. *Address:* Eusemere, Comber, Co. Down. *T.:* Comber 210. *Clubs:* Ulster (Belfast); Royal Ulster Yacht (Bangor). [*Died* 18 *Feb.* 1951 (*ext.*).

ANDREWS, Rt. Hon. John Miller, P.C. Northern Ireland, 1922; C.H. 1943; D.L.; LL.D.; M.P. (Unionist) Co. Down, Parliament of Northern Ireland, 1921-29, Mid-Down and Down, 1929-53; flax spinner; landowner; *b.* 17 July 1871; *e. s.* of late Rt. Hon. Thomas Andrews, D.L., of Ardara, Comber, Co. Down, and Eliza, *d.* of James Alexander Pirrie, Belfast; *m.* 1902, Jessie (*d.* 1950), *e. d.* of Joseph Ormrod, Morelands, Heaton, Bolton; one *s.* two *d.* *Educ.:* Royal Academical Institution, Belfast. High Sheriff for Co. Down, 1929; Member of County Council of Down, 1917-37; President of Ulster Unionist Labour Association; Patron Ulster Unionist Council; President Belfast Chamber of Commerce, 1936; Minister of Labour in Cabinet of Northern Ireland, 1921-1937; Minister of Finance, Northern Ireland, 1937-40; Prime Minister of Northern Ireland, 1940-43; Grand Master: Orange Institution of County Down since 1941; Orange Institution of All Ireland, 1948-54; Imperial Grand Council of World, 1949-54. Hon. Col. R.A.O.C. since 1941. Freeman City of Londonderry, 1943. *Recreations:* hunting, yachting, golf. *Address:* Maxwell Court, Comber, Co. Down, N. Ireland. *Clubs:* Ulster, Ulster Reform (Belfast); Strangford Lough Yacht (Co. Down). [*Died* 5 *Aug.* 1956.

ANDREWS, Roy Chapman, M.A. Sc.D.; Hon. Director, American Museum Natural History, New York; leader of Asiatic Expeditions; *b.* Beloit, Wis., U.S.A., 26 Jan. 1884; *s.* of Chas. E. Andrews and Cora M. Chapman; *m.* 1st 1914, Yvette Borup; two *s.*; 2nd 1935, Wilhelmina A. Christmas. *Educ.:* Beloit College, A.B.; Columbia University, A.M.; Hon. Sc.D. Brown University and Beloit College. Explored in Alaska, 1908; special naturalist U.S.S. Albatross on voyage to Dutch E.I., Borneo, Celebes, 1909-1910; explored N. Korea, 1911-12; Borden Alaska Expedition, 1913; leader 1st Asiatic Expedition of American Museum Natural History to S.W. China, 1917; 2nd Expedition to Mongolia, 1919; 3rd Expedition to Central Asia and Mongolia, 1921-30. In U.S. Intelligence Service, 1917-18; The Central Asiatic Expeditions; discovered great fossil fields in Mongolia; found the first dinosaur eggs known to science, mapped large unknown areas of Gobi Desert; did much work in palæontology, archæology, botany, zoology, geology, topography; Elisha Kent Kane Gold Medal, Philadelphia Geographical Society; Hubbard Gold Medal, National Geographical Society; Explorers Club Medal, New York City; Charles P. Daly Gold Medal, American Geographical Society; Vega Medal, Royal Swedish Geographical Society; Loczy Medal of Royal Hungarian Geographical Society. *Publications:* Whale Hunting with Gun and Camera; Camps and Trails in China; Across Mongolian Plains; On the Trail of Ancient Man; Ends of the Earth; The New Conquest of Central Asia; This Business of Exploring, 1935; Exploring with Andrews, 1938; This Amazing Planet, 1941; Under a Lucky Star, 1943; Meet your Ancestors, 1945; scientific publications; many papers and two monographs on water mammals. *Recreations:* fly fishing, bird shooting. *Address:* Carmel Valley, California, U.S.A.; American Museum Natural History, N.Y. *Clubs:* Explorers, Boone and Crockett, Dutch Treat (N.Y.); Doolittle (Conn.); Peking (Peking). [*Died* 11 *March* 1960.

ANDREWS, William Horner, D.Sc. (Lond.); M.R.C.V.S.; Animal Health Division, Ministry of Agriculture and Fisheries; *b.* 22 June 1887; *s.* of Major H. G. Andrews, late A.O. Dept.; *m.* 1916, Doris, 2nd *d.* of late H. Burls, Christiana, Transvaal; one *s.* one *d.* *Educ.:* Mathematical School, Rochester; Royal Veterinary College, London; Institut Pasteur, Paris. Assistant Government Veterinary Bacteriologist, Transvaal, 1909; Veterinary Research Officer, Union of South Africa, 1912; Captain, South African Veterinary Corps, German South-West Africa, 1914-15; Senior Veterinary Research Officer, 1918; Professor of Physiology, Transvaal University College, Pretoria, 1920; Research Assistant, Research Institute in Animal Pathology, London, 1924; Director, Veterinary Laboratory, Weybridge, 1927-41, and of Imperial Bureau of Animal Health, 1929-41. *Publications:* various technical articles in scientific journals relating especially to plant poisoning. *Recreation:* gardening. *Address:* Animal Health Division, Ministry of Agriculture and Fisheries, 99 Gresham St., E.C.2. [*Died* 19 *March* 1953.

ANDRUS, Brig.-Gen. Thomas Alchin, C.M.G. 1916; J.P.; *b.* 1872; *s.* of Capt. Thomas Alchin Andrus (Militia) of Scadbury Manor, Southfleet, Kent; *m.* 1913, Loveday, 2nd *d.* of late Adm. Alfred Arthur Chase Parr, R.N., Bickley, Kent; one *s.* one *d.* Joined 1st Batt. Prince of Wales North Staffordshire Regt. 1893; served Sudan campaign, 1896 (British medal, Khedive's Sudan medal); Indian N.-W. Frontier campaign, 1897-98, with the Malakand Field Force and the Utman Khel Column; also Buner Field Force in the attack and capture of the Tanga Pass (Indian medal and clasps); European War, 1914-18; raised the 7th Service Batt. North Stafford Regiment, and commanded it throughout, Aug. 1914-July 1916; Brigadier-General, July 1916, and commanded the 39th Inf. Brigade until March 1919 in Mesopotamia, Persia, and the Caucasus (severely wounded Aug. 1915 in the attack on Sari Bair in Gallipoli, despatches thrice, Bt. Lt.-Col., C.M.G.; Imp. Order of St. Anne of Russia, 2nd class, with swords; 1914-15 Star; British and Victory war medals); Colonel, 1920; Temp. Colonel Commandant in Ireland, 1921-22; retired, 1923; J.P. Kent. *Address:* Scadbury Manor, Southfleet, Kent. *T.:* Southfleet 397. *Club:* Army and Navy. [*Died* 19 *Nov.* 1959.

ANGEL, John, N.A. 1948 (A.N.A. 1944); Litt.D., F.R.B.S.; Sculptor; *b.* Newton Abbot, England, 1 Nov. 1881; *s.* of Samuel Angel and Hannah Maria Bearne; *m.* 1914, Elizabeth D. (*d.* 1942), *d.* of Prof. Thomas Day Seymour, Yale University; two *s.* *Educ.:* Exeter College of Art; Lambeth Art School; Royal Academy Schools, London. After 7 years apprenticeship carving marble, stone and wood, and study in Exeter and at Lambeth Schools, entered Royal Academy Schools, 1906; Landseer Scholarship, Armitage diploma, two first silver medals, gold medal, 1911; studied in Rome and Athens, 1912; assisted Sir George Frampton 4 years; exhibited at Royal Academy, 1912-27; designed and executed Exeter and Bridgwater War Memorials and statue of St. George at Rotherham; statuettes and busts in various collections, including Institute of Fine Arts, Glasgow, and Albert Memorial Museum, Exeter; busts of Sir John Biles, Sir Philip Watts, etc.: left England for U.S.A. 1925; made most of statuary on Cathedral of St. John the Divine, New York (Ralph Adams Cram Architect); statuary on Altar St. Patrick's Cathedral, New York, also marble statue of Saint Patrick in its choir; statues of William M. Rice, Rice Institute, Texas, Francis Vigo, (granite) at Vincennes, Ind., Alexander Hamilton, Chicago, also a bronze statue of Stephen Fuller Austin, for Austin, Tex., St. Paul at Concord, N.H., Last Supper group (marble) for East Liberty Church, Pittsburgh, Crucifixion group, St. Louis, Mo., Majestas group, and The Annunciation group, Princeton Univ. Chapel, Christ in the Temple (marble panel), St. Paul's School, Concord, N.H., Madonna and Child (marble panel), Chatham Hall School, Chatham, Va. Bronze Doors, Central Portal, West Front, St. Patrick's Cathedral, New York. statue Christ the Teacher (bronze) for Catholic Central High School, Braintree, Mass.; statuary reredos, St. John's Church, Youngstown, Ohio. Present work: additional sculpture on Cathedral of St. John the Divine; Sculpture for National Shrine of Immaculate Conception, Washington, D.C.; four twelve-foot marble statues of Saints for Cathedral of St. Paul, St. Paul, Minnesota, etc. Bust of Judge John Munro Woolsey, Phillips Acad., Andover, Mass.; designed William Edward Parsons Memorial Medal for Yale University; designed 1956 medal for Medallic Art Society. Hon. Litt.D. Columbia Univ., 1936; member Mediæval Academy of America, Architectural League, National Sculpture Soc. of America, National Acad. of Design. Fell. of Internat. Inst. of Arts and Letters, 1956. Has lectured at Yale Univ., Metropolitan Museum, New York, etc. *Recreations:* billiards and photography. *Address:* Old Mill Road, Sandy Hook, Conn. *T.:* Garden 6.4159. *Club:* Century (New York). [*Died* 16 *Oct.* 1960.

ANGERS, The Hon. Eugène-Réal; Judge of the Exchequer Court of Canada, 1932-53; *b.* 1 Oct. 1883; *s.* of Réal Angers and Joséphine Trudel; *m.* 1909, Germaine Tousignant; four *s.* three *d.* *Educ.:* High School, St. Mary's College (B.A.) and Laval University (LL.L.), Montreal. Admitted to Bar, Province of Quebec, 1907; Practised law in Montreal, 1907-1932; K.C., 1930; Hon. LL.D.: Ottawa Univ., 1937; Univ. of Montreal, 1950. *Address:* 188 Durocher, Hull, Quebec, Canada. [*Died* 27 *Jan.* 1956.

ANGLESS, Violet; *see* Brunton-Angless.

ANGLIN, Arthur Whyte, Q.C. (Can.) 1908; Member of firm of Blake, Anglin, Osler & Cassels, Toronto; *b.* St. John, N.B., 10 Jan. 1867; *s.* of late Hon. T. W. Anglin, Speaker, Canadian House of Commons; *m.* 1894, Madeleine St. George (*d.* 1929), *e. d.* of late Sir Glenholme Falconbridge; five *s.* six *d.* *Educ.:* St. Mary's College, Montreal; Ottawa University; Law Society, Upper Canada; First scholarship, 1888 and 1889; gold medal, 1890. Called to Ontario Bar, 1890. *Address:* 71 Clarendon Avenue, Toronto. [*Died* 18 *March* 1955.

ANGLISS, Hon. Sir William Charles, Kt., *cr.* 1939; M.L.C. Victoria for Southern Province, Australia, 1912-52, retired. Chairman: Investors Pty. Ltd., Bluff Downs Pastoral Co. Pty. Ltd., Miranda Downs Pastoral Co., Queensland Stations Pty. Ltd., Vanrook Pastoral Co. Pty. Ltd. Benbow Mills Pty. Ltd., Premier Printing Co. Pty. Ltd.; Director of many other Companies; *b.* Dudley, England, 29 Jan. 1865; *s.* of William and Eliza Angliss; *m.* 1919, J. Grutzner, C.B.E. 1949; (one *d.* decd.). *Address:* Benbow, Harcourt St., Hawthorn, Melbourne, Australia. [*Died* 15 *July* 1957.

ANGUS, Alfred Henry, B.Sc. (Vict.); F.C.I.S.; founder and first Editor, The British Advertiser; *b.* Hutton Lowcross, Guisborough, Yorks, 29 May 1873; *s.* of G. H. Angus and E. Calvert; *m.* 1st, 1900, Nellie, *d.* of Joseph Unsworth, Liverpool; one *s.* one *d.*; 2nd, 1936, Selina Jane Arnott, *e.d.* of late James Treble, Assistant Director, Education, Northumberland. *Educ.:* Sir Joseph Pease's School, and Univ. College, Liverpool. History Lecturer, Leeds Pupil Teachers' Centre, 1895-6; House Master, Harrogate College, 1896-1900; Second Master and Chief Mathematical Master, Central Secondary School, Birmingham, 1901-6; Headmaster, George Dixon Secondary School, Birmingham, 1906-13; Principal, Hon. Secretary and Hon. Chaplain, Tettenhall Coll., Staffordshire, 1913-25. *Publications:* Introduction to Differential and Integral Calculus; Manual of Slide Rule; Ideals in Teaching; numerous articles in Educational Journals. *Recreations:* golf, shooting, motoring. *Address:* 4 Beechey Road, Bournemouth. [*Died* 11 *Jan.* 1957.

ANGWIN, Col. Sir (Arthur) Stanley, K.C.M.G. 1957; K.B.E. 1945; Kt. 1941; D.S.O. 1917; M.C. 1917; T.D. 1923; *b.* 11 December 1883; *s.* of George William Angwin; *m.* 1921, Dorothy Gladys Back; three *s.* one *d.* *Educ.:* East London College. Pupil of Messrs. Yarrow & Co., Shipbuilders and Engineers; subsequently entered Post Office Engineering Dept.; B.Sc. (Eng.) London; Whitworth Exhibitioner; served European War, Gallipoli, Egypt, France; Commanded 52nd (Lowland) Divisional Signals; after war commanded 44th Div. Sigs.; later Deputy Chief Signal Officer (Supplementary Reserve); President Institution of Electrical Engineers, 1943-44; Member of Television Committee, 1934 and 1943, and Television Advisory Committees, 1939 and 1945; Engineer-in-Chief, General Post Office, 1939-46; Chairman of Cable and Wireless Ltd., 1947-1951; Chairman Radio Research Board, 1947-52; Chairman Commonwealth Telecommunications Board, 1951-56. Fellow Queen Mary College, 1946. Faraday Medallist, I.E.E., 1953; Hon. M.I.E.E. 1956. D.Sc. (Lond.). *Address:* 32 Guessens Road, Welwyn Garden City, Herts. *T.:* Welwyn Garden 485. [*Died* 21 *April* 1959.

ANLEY, Brigadier-General Barnett Dyer Lempriere Gray, C.B. 1925; C.M.G. 1917; D.S.O. 1900; *b.* 22 Aug. 1873; *e. s.* of Col. Barnett N. Anley; *m.* 1902, Gwendolyn, *e. d.* of Major Leigh Gwatkin, J.P. Entered Army, 1894; served South Africa, 1899-1900 (despatches twice); European War, 1914-18 (despatches six times, Bt. Lt.-Col. and Col., C.M.G., Chevalier Légion d'Honneur); Commanded 183rd Infantry Brigade; G.S.O.1. Staff College, 1919; commanded 1st Batt. K.O.R.R., 1919-20; commanded 3rd London Infantry Brigade, 1920-1921; Commandant Senior Officers' School, Sheerness, 1921-25; Commanded 125th (Lancs. Fusiliers) Infantry Brigade T.A., 1926-28; retired pay, 1928. *Address:* St. George's, Wych Hill Lane, Woking. *T.:* Woking 868. [*Died* 3 *Dec.* 1954.

ANLEY, Major Philip Francis Ross, C.B.E. 1927; *b.* 1874; *s.* of Col. B. N. Anley; *m.* 1911, Adeline Ellen (*d.* 1932), *d.* of late General Sir William Sherbrook Ramsay Norcott, K.C.B. Served S. Africa, 1899-1901 (wounded, despatches twice, Queen's medal with five clasps); European War, 1914-18. *Address:* St. George's, Wych Hill Lane, Woking, Surrey. [*Died* 27 *April* 1956.

ANNAN, William, M.A., C.A., F.C.W.A., F.R.S.E.; Partner of Graham Smart and Annan,

C.A., Edinburgh and London; Emeritus Prof. of Accounting and Business Method, Edinburgh University; *b.* Lochee, Dundee, 23 Aug. 1872; *s.* of David Annan and Jane Wilkie; *m.* 1897, Margaret Letts Munro; no *c.* *Educ.:* High School, Dundee. *Recreation:* golf. *Address:* 22 Charlotte Square, Edinburgh. *T.:* Edinburgh 26253. *Club:* University (Edinburgh).
[*Died* 13 *Aug.* 1952.

ANNE, George Charlton, O.B.E.; *b.* 1886; *e. s.* of late Ernest Anne of Burghwallis and Edith, *d.* of Sir Thomas George Augustus Parkyns, 6th Bart.; *m.* 1st, Amy Violet (*d.* 1935), *d.* of late James Montagu of Melton Park and Hon. Mrs. Lindley Wood; three *s.* one *d.*; 2nd, 1938, Constance, *d.* of Alfred Dagnell. *Educ.:* Oratory School; Exeter College, Oxford. Major, late R.F.C. and R.A.F.; formerly Capt. K.O.Y.L.I.; A.D.C. to Governor of Gold Coast, 1909-10; served throughout European War, 1914-18 (despatches); founded Wire Fox Terrier Association, 1912; Secretary R.A.F. Boxing Association, 1924-27; a pioneer of the Totalisator form of Betting in England and Scotland; Manager, North District Racecourse Betting Control Board, 1929-32; General Manager, Tote Investors Ltd., 1932-39; Life Member (Hon.) National Playing Fields Association. Patron of one living. *Address:* Draycott House, Roedean Way, Brighton 7. *T.:* Brighton 61654. [*Died* 14 *Feb.* 1960.

ANNESLEY, 8th Earl (*cr.* 1789), **Beresford Cecil Bingham Annesley;** Baron Annesley, 1758; Viscount Glerawly, 1766; late Lieut. 6th Batt. Royal Fusiliers; Pilot Officer in R.A.F.V.R., 1941; *b.* 4 Apr. 1894; *o. s.* of 7th Earl and Maud Fleming (*d.* 1923), *d.* of Haynes Bingham Higginson, Rock Ferry, Cheshire; *S.* father, 1934; *m.* 1st, 1921, Edith (who obtained a divorce, 1940; she *d.* 1950), *o. d.* of Maj. Rawlinson, late of 4 Aldford St., W.; 2nd, 1945, Josephine Mary, *widow* of Capt. G. J. S. Repton, 29 Curzon St., W. and of Irish Guards, *d.* of late Phillip Brandell, New York City. *Heir: kinsman,* Robert Annesley, *b.* 20 Feb. 1900. *Address:* Palais St. James, Monte-Carlo. *Clubs:* Union; Metropolitan (New York).
[*Died* 29 *June* 1957.

ANNETT, Henry Edward, M.B.E.; M.D., D.P.H.; retired; Turner Research Fellow (Cancer), 1931-38; Hon. Lecturer Pathology of Meat, etc., University of Liverpool, 1922-25; Lecturer in Animal Pathology, University of Liverpool, 1922-28; Cancer Researcher, University of Liverpool, 1923-30; Superintendent, Research Laboratories, Higher Runcorn, 1911-1922; Professor of Comparative Pathology, University of Liverpool, 1906-11; *b.* 5 June 1871; *m.* 1906, E. L., *d.* of George Bell. *Educ.:* University College, Liverpool; Victoria University, Manchester. Graduated with honours, 1894. Lecturer on Comparative Pathology, University, Liverpool, 1903; Superintendent, Incorporated Liverpool Institute of Comparative Pathology since 1902; member of first expedition sent out by Liverpool School of Tropical Medicine to West Africa, 1891; directed second expedition, 1900; Director Animal Diseases Expedition to Uruguay, 1905, and of Colonial Office Expedition to W. Indies, 1906-7; M.O.H. Runcorn Urban District, 1913-1923; Acting M.O.H. Widnes Borough District, 1915-19; M.O. in command Runcorn Vicarage Military Hospital; Joint Author—Report of Malaria Expedition to Sierra Leone, 1899; Report of Expedition to Nigeria (Malaria), 1900; Report of Expedition to Nigeria (Filariasis), 1900. *Address:* 143 Highfield Road, Rock Ferry, Cheshire. *T.:* Rock Ferry 518.
[*Died* 10 *April* 1945.
[*But death not notified in time for inclusion in Who Was Who 1941–1950, first edn.*

ANREP, Gleb V., F.R.S. 1928; Professor of Physiology, Fouad I University, Cairo, 1931; *b.* Petrograd, 1891; *s.* of Basil von Anrep; *m.* Annie Wieninger; (one *s.* of previous marriage). *Educ.:* Medical Academy, Petrograd; University College, London. M.B. 1914; joined the Russian Army as a medical officer, 1914, till the end of the participation of Russia in European War, 1917; M.D. Medical Academy and Lecturer in the Institute of Experimental Medicine, Petrograd; joined the forces of General Denikine against the Bolsheviks, 1918; settled in England in 1920; naturalised, 1925; first Assistant at University College, London, then Lecturer at Cambridge University; M.Sc. and D.Sc., London; M.A. Cantab.; Fellow of University College; Sharpey-Schafer prize, W. Mickle prize, Sydney Ringer Lecturer; Cooper Lane Lecturer, Stanford Univ., San Francisco, U.S.A.; engaged in research work since 1912. Member: Academy of Medicine, Roumania; Academy of Science, Vienna. *Publications:* in various Physiological Journals, chiefly on circulation and conditioned reflexes. *Recreations:* anything which comes along. *Address:* Physiological Laboratory, Fouad I University, Cairo, Egypt. *T.A.:* Maadi, Cairo. *T.:* Maadi 53479. *Clubs:* Gezira Sporting, Turf (Cairo).
[*Died* 9 *Jan.* 1955.

ANSELL, Rev. Preb. George Frederick James; Prebendary of S. Paul's Cathedral since 1948; Rural Dean of Poplar since 1941; Rector of S. Mary, Bow, E.3, since 1932; *b.* 11 Feb. 1886; *s.* of George and Mary Fiddy Ansell; *m.* 1912, Alice Martha Smith, S.R.N.; two *s.* one *d.* *Educ.:* King's College, London University. A.K.C. 1916; Deacon, 1916; Priest, 1917; Curate S. Michael, London Fields, 1916-26 (in charge of S. Martin, 1918-26); Vicar S. Michael, London Fields, 1926-32; President of Sion College, E.C., 1947-48. *Address:* Bow Rectory, Fairfield Road, E.3. *T.:* Advance 1721. [*Died* 3 *May* 1951.

ANSELL, William Henry, C.B.E. 1955; M.C.; architect; F.R.I.B.A. (Past Pres. R.I.B.A.); F.S.A., Hon. A.R.E.; *b.* Nottingham, Nov. 1872; *m.* 1902, Florence Leman (*d.* 1946), Chipping Norton, Oxon. *Educ.:* Derby. Articled to firm of architects in Derby; commenced practice in London as an architect, 1900; principal works: hospitals, Westbury, Sevenoaks; country houses, Surrey, Derbyshire, Devonshire; churches, Liverpool, London, and Suffolk; Head Offices, National Deposit Friendly Society, London; Butchers' Charitable Institution, Hounslow; Convalescent Homes, Skegness, St. Margaret's Bay, Everleigh, Banstead Surrey; Greshams School Holt Sanatorium. Etcher of architectural subjects. Served European War, Oct. 1915-18 (M.C., despatches twice); President Architectural Association, 1928; Chairman Board of Architectural Education, 1931-33; Vice-President Royal Institute of British Architects, 1933-35, President 1940-43; Vice-Chairman National Buildings Record; Master Art Workers Guild, 1944. *Address:* 12 Gray's Inn Square, Gray's Inn, W.C.1. *T.:* Chancery 8169; Little Paddock, Seal, Sevenoaks. *T.:* Sevenoaks 61568. *Club:* Athenæum. [*Died* 11 *Feb.* 1959.

ANSON, Viscount; Thomas William Arnold Anson; Lt.-Col. Grenadier Guards, retired; *b.* 4 May 1913; *s.* of 4th Earl of Lichfield; *m.* 1938, Anne Ferelith (marriage dissolved, 1948; she *m.* 2nd, 1950, Prince Georg of Denmark), *d.* of late Hon. John Bowes-Lyon; one *s.* one *d.*; *m.* 1955, Mrs. Monica Inglis, *d.* of late Comdr. Ralph Neville, R.N., and Hon. Mrs. Pearson Gregory. *Educ.:* Harrow. *Address:* Shugborough Park, Stafford. *T.:* Milford (Staffs.) 22; 17 Eaton Mews North, Eaton Place, S.W.1. *T.:* Sloane 6370. *Clubs:* Guards, Boodle's, Pratt's. [*Died* 18 *March* 1958.

ANSON, Sir Edward (Reynell), 6th Bt., *cr.* 1831; *b.* 31 Jan. 1902; *o. surv. s.* of late Rear-Adm. Algernon Horatio Anson, 4th *s.* of 2nd Bt., and Hon. Adela Vernon, *d.* of 6th Baron Vernon; *S.* brother, 1918; *m.* 1923, Alison, *o. d.* of Hugh Pollock, Crossways, South Chard, Somerset; two *s.* *Educ.:* Royal Naval Colleges, Osborne and Dartmouth; Trinity College, Cambridge. Joined R. Navy, 1915; retired, 1919; served in Royal Artillery, 1939-45 (Lt.-Col). *Publication:* The Owner-Gardener, 1934; The Small Garden, 1936. *Recreations:* gardening and fishing. *Heir:* *s.* Peter Anson, *b.* 31 July 1924. *Address:* Meadows, Hatch Beauchamp, Taunton, Somerset. *T.:* Hatch Beauchamp 202. *Club:* St. James'.
[*Died* 26 *June* 1951.

ANSON, George H., M.C., T.D., D.L.; late commanding Staffs. Yeomanry; J.P. Derbyshire; *e. s.* of Henry Anson Horton, of Catton Hall, Co. Derby; *m.* 1st, 1926, Barbara Mary (*d.* 1939), *o. d.* of Algernon H. P. Strickland, of Apperley Court, Gloucestershire; 2nd, 1941, Magdalen Luker, Park Lodge, Kedleston. *Educ.:* Eton; New College, Oxford. B.A. Barrister Inner Temple, 1912; served in Egypt and Palestine and Syria, 1914-19; Master S. Staffs. Hounds, 1920-27; Sheriff of Derbyshire, 1941. *Address:* Catton Hall, Burton-on-Trent. *T.:* Barton-under-Needwood 222. *Club:* Bath.
[*Died* 21 *Sept.* 1957.

ANSON, Rev. Harold, M.A.; Master of the Temple since 1935; Hon. Canon of Southwark, 1933; *b.* 1867; *s.* of Rev. Frederick Anson, Canon of Windsor, and Caroline, *e. d.* of 5th Lord Vernon; *m.* 1st, 1894, Gwenllian (*d.* 1935), *d.* of Henry Langridge; two *s.* one *d.*; 2nd, 1944, Lally Anne, *d.* of T. Sydney Walker, Edgbaston. *Educ.:* Clifton; Christ Church, Oxford. Deacon, 1890; Priest, 1891; Curate of St. Pancras, 1890-94; Rector of Whitton, 1894-97; Vicar of Hawera, N.Z., 1897-1902; Warden of St. John's College, Auckland, N.Z., 1902-5; Rector of Badsworth, 1906-10; Rector of Birch-in-Rusholme, 1910-19; Curate of St. Mary's, Primrose Hill, 1919-22; of St. Martin in the Fields, 1922-28; Examining Chaplain to Bishop of Lincoln, 1920-25; Select Preacher, Cambridge, 1918 and 1938; Vicar of Tandridge, 1928-35; Rural Dean of Godstone, 1930-35. *Publications:* Spiritual Healing; A Practical Faith; Thinking Aloud; Looking Forward, 1938; The Truth about Spiritualism; Life of T. B. Strong, 1949. *Address:* Temple Cottage, Ide Hill, Sevenoaks. *T.:* Ide Hill 221.
[*Died* 1 *April* 1954.

ANSTEY, Most Rev. Arthur Henry, C.B.E. 1944; Hon. D.D. Oxford and Durham. *Educ.:* Keble College, Oxford. Ordained, 1898; Curate at Aylesbury and Bedminster; Principal of St. Boniface Missionary College, Warminster, 1904-10; Examining Chaplain to Bishop of Barbados, 1911-18; Bishop of Trinidad, 1918-45; Archbishop of the West Indies, 1943-45. *Address:* c/o S.P.G., 15 Tufton St., S.W.1.
[*Died* 13 *Nov.* 1955.

ANSTEY, Brig. Edgar Carnegie, D.S.O. 1919; late R.A.; *b.* 1882; *s.* of H. Anstey; *m.* 1st, 1923, Laura Samsonov (*d.* 1946); 2nd, 1951, Millicent Anfield Campbell, *d.* of late Comtesse de Prologue. *Educ.:* Wellington College and R.M.A. Served European War, 1914-18 (despatches, D.S.O., Légion d'Honneur, Croix de Guerre); Chief Staff Officer, Armaments Sub-Commission of the Inter-Allied Commission of Control in Germany, 1920-22; Instructor, Senior Officers Sch., Belgaum, India, 1925-28; Brig., R.A., Western Command, India, 1931-1932; Brigadier, General Staff, Western Command, India, 1932-35; retired pay, 1935; Passive Air Defence Officer, London District, 1938-40; Special employment, Southern Command, 1940; Member of Historical Section, Offices of the Cabinet, 1940-1942; Military Correspondent, Daily Sketch and Sunday Times, 1942-44, and of Daily Despatch and Sunday Chronicle, 1944-45. *Publications:* The Vanishing Yacht, 1936; The Mystery of the Blue Inns, 1937; Peace in Our Time, 1945. *Address:* 11 Thurloe Square, S.W.7. *T.:* Kensington 2958.
[*Died* 6 *Nov.* 1958.

ANSTRUTHER, Colonel Philip Noel, D.S.O. 1916; M.C.; *b.* 2 Sept. 1891; *o. s.* of late Admiral Robert H. Anstruther, C.M.G.; *n.* of Sir Ralph Anstruther, 6th Bart. of Balcaskie, Fife; *m.* 1920, Hope Lewin (who obtained a divorce, 1931); one *s.* one *d.*; *m.* 1952, Mrs. Marion Secretan, *d.* of late Capt. I. Gregor Macgregor, R.N.R., and of Mrs. Macgregor. *Educ.:* Sherborne Sch.; R.M.C., Sandhurst. Commn. in Regular Army, 1911; served in India till Jan. 1914; Adj. and actg. Lt.-Col. commanding 7th Bn. of Royal West Kent Regt. during European war, 1914-18 (M.C., D.S.O., despatches twice, seriously wounded); India, 1921-26; graduated Staff College, Quetta, 1926; Staff Captain, Malta, 1928-29; Brigade Major, Canal Brigade, Egypt, 1930-32; India, 1932-37; commanded 1st Bn. The Queen's Own Royal West Kent Regiment, 1937-40; Temp. Col. 1940; Admiralty Ferry Crew Skipper, 1945-1946. *Recreations:* sailing and music. *Address:* Park House, Pittenweem, Fife. *Clubs:* Little Ship, R.N.V.R.
[*Died* 26 *Feb.* 1960.

ANSTRUTHER-GOUGH-CALTHORPE, Sir FitzRoy Hamilton, 1st Bt., *cr.* 1929; J.P.; *b.* 1872; *m.* 1898, Hon. Rachel Gough-Calthorpe (*d.* 1951), *e. d.* of 6th Baron Calthorpe; one *s.* two *d.* *Educ.:* Harrow. Permanent Staff Officer i/c Army Motor Reserve. Served European War on General Staff, 1914-19; Military Order of Avis, Portugal. *Heir:* *s.* Brigadier Richard Hamilton Anstruther-Gough-Calthorpe, C.B.E. *Address:* Star Hill, Hartford Bridge, Basingstoke. *T.:* Hartley Wintney 148. *T.A.:* Hartley Wintney. *Clubs:* Royal Thames Yacht; Royal Yacht Squadron.
[*Died* 29 *Sept.* 1957.

ANWYL, Rev. John Bodvan; *b.* Chester, 1875; 4th *s.* of John and Elen Anwyl; *b.* of late Sir Edward Anwyl. Minister of Elim Welsh Congregational Church, Carmarthen, 1899-1901; Superintendent of the Glamorgan Mission to the Deaf and Dumb, 1904-19; Cataloguer at the National Library of Wales, Aberystwyth, 1919-21; Dictionary Secretary to the Board of Celtic Studies of the Univ. of Wales, 1921-35; winner of prize offered by Mr. William George for best rendering of National Insurance Act terms into Welsh. *Publications:* Spurrell's Welsh-English Dictionary, editions 1914, 1915, 1918, 1920, 1925, 1930, 1934, 1937; Spurrell's English-Welsh Dictionary, editions 1916, 1922, 1926, 1932, 1937; Spurrell's Pocket Dictionary, Welsh-English and English-Welsh, 1919, 1929, 1930, 1937, 1948; Y Pulpud Bach, 1924; Y Bardd Cwsg (rev. edn.), 1927; Drych y Prif Oesoedd (rev. edn.), 1932; Englynion, 1933; Fy Hanes i fy Hunan, 1933; Yr Arian Mawr, 1934; has translated about a dozen volumes into Welsh; has written numerous articles, stories, essays, and poems, chiefly in Welsh. *Recreations:* gardening, etc. *Address:* Bryn Bodfan, Llangwnadl, Pwllheli, Caernarvonshire.
[*Died* 22 *July* 1949.
[*But death not notified in time for inclusion in Who Was Who 1941–1950, first edn.*

ANWYL-PASSINGHAM, Colonel Augustus Mervyn Owen, C.B.E. 1942 (O.B.E. 1918); D.L. 1927; J.P. Middlesex; Knight of St. John of Jerusalem; Officer Crown of Italy; Member Chapter General, Order of St. John of Jerusalem; *b.* 31 Aug. 1880; *y.* and *o. surv. s.* of late Major Robert T. Anwyl-Passingham, Bryn-y-Groes, Bala, Merioneth, D.L., J.P., and Lucy Emma, *er. d.* and co-heiress of late Jeffreys Badger of Kingsland, Salop; *m.* 1909, Margaret, 4th *d.* of late C. J. Radclyffe, D.L.,

J.P., Hyde House, Wareham, Dorset and Foxdenton Hall, Lancs; one *d.* *Educ.:* Dover College. Commissioned Middlesex Regiment, 1901; Major 1916; Colonel in the Army, 1916; retired, 1922; Secretary, Middlesex Territorial Army and Air Force Association, 1924-45; County Welfare Officer, County of Middlesex, 1940-45; a Vice-President T.A. Sports Assoc., 1951; served South African War, 1900-2; Northern Nigeria with Mounted Infantry, Hadeija and Sokoto Expeditions, 1906; Belfast Riots, Ireland (severely wounded); European War, 1914-18 (O.B.E., despatches twice); Upper Silesia, 1919-21; Assistant Inspector Recruiting, War Office; Director of Recruiting for Wales; Special Service, Italy; British Empire Exhibition, Wembley; High Sheriff County of Middlesex, 1938. *Recreations:* Rugby football, boxing, riding, shooting, fishing. *Address:* Orchard Lea, Priory Road, Ascot. *T.:* Winkfield Row 3230. *Clubs:* Army and Navy; Sandown Park (Esher); Kempton Park (Sunbury-on-Thames).
[*Died* 22 *Nov.* 1955.

APLIN, Harold D'Auvergne, C.M.G. 1930; *b.* 1879; *s.* of Capt. P. H. P. Aplin, the Buffs; *m.* 1931, Marion Sylvester Bostock. *Educ.:* United Services College, Westward Ho. Secretariat, Nyasaland, 1901; Provincial Commissioner, 1921; Senior Provincial Commissioner, 1928; Sec. for Native Affairs, 1931; retd. 1933. *Address:* c/o Standard Bank of S. Africa, Ltd., Salisbury, S. Rhodesia.
[*Died* 17 *July* 1958.

APPERLEY, (George Owen) Wynne, R.I. 1913; figure and landscape painter; *b.* Ventnor, 17 June 1884; *s.* of William Wynne Apperley, who was *g.s.* of C. J. Apperley, the author, known as Nimrod, and Margaret Tremenheere; *m.* 1st, 1907, Hilda May Pope; one *s.* one *d.*; 2nd, Enriqueta Contreras; two *s.* *Educ.:* Uppingham. Studied art under Herkomer; first exhibited at Royal Academy, 1905; one-man exhibitions in London, 1906, 1908, 1910, 1912-15; exhibited also at Paris Salon, Venice International, etc.; one-man exhibns abroad — Madrid, 1919, 1928, 1944, 1951; Buenos Ayres, 1924, Granada, 1931, 1953, Tangier, 1940, 1944, Malaga, 1951; Barcelona, 1955; elected member of Real Academia de San Telmo; one of his pictures bought by the Spanish Government, and is now in the Modern Art Gallery, Madrid; represented at Victoria and Albert Museum, Lever Art Gallery, Hull Art Gallery, etc. Given: Order of the Mehdauia by the Jalifa of Tetuan, 1938; Order of Alfonso X el Sabio by Spanish Govt., 1945. *Publications:* Series of Chapters on Water Colour painting published in Drawing, 1914-15; articles in The Studio and in daily press. *Recreation:* music. *Address:* Villa Apperley, Tangier, Morocco; Plaza San Nicholas, Granada, Spain.
[*Died* 10 *Sept.* 1960.

APPLEBY, Sir Alfred, Kt., *cr.* 1923; J.P.; *b.* 1866; *m.* 1897, May Crandon, *o. d.* of Edward Orams, of The Elms, Norwich; one *s.* one *d.* Formerly Head of firm of Appleby & Lisle, solicitors, retired, 1951; H.M. Coroner for City and County of Newcastle-upon-Tyne, 1906-51. *Address:* Catfield Hall, Great Yarmouth, Norfolk. *T.:* Stalham 220. [*Died* 12 *Feb.* 1952.

APPLETON, Sir William, Kt., *cr.* 1950; Company Director, New Zealand; *b.* Alexandra, N.Z., 3 Sept. 1889; *s.* of Edwin Appleton, Yorkshire, and Margaret Bruce, Scotland; *m.* 1st, 1913, Helen (*decd.*), *d.* of William Munro; two *s.*; 2nd, 1919, Rose, *d.* of James Hellewell; two *s.* one *d.* *Educ.:* Alexandra Public School; Wellington Technical College; Victoria University College, Wellington. Spent 6 years in Government service, and 25 years in advertising (Haines). Member: Onslow Borough Council, 1915-19; Wellington Hospital Board, 1923-29; Wellington City Council, 1931-44; and Wellington Harbour Board, 1938-. Contested Wellington South (Coalition United), 1931; Otaki (Independent), 1935; Wellington Central (National), 1938, 1949; Mayor of Wellington, 1944-50. Qualified Accountant; Ex-Pres. Incorp. Accountants Inst. of N.Z. and Life Member N.Z. Soc. of Accountants. *Recreations:* football and bowls. *Address:* 10 Oriental Terrace, Wellington, C.4, N.Z.; 154 Featherstone Street, Wellington, N.Z. *Clubs:* Wellington, Wellesley (Wellington).
[*Died* 22 *Oct.* 1958.

APPLIN, Lieut.-Col. Reginald Vincent Kempenfelt, D.S.O. 1902, O.B.E. 1919; *b.* 11 April 1869; *e. s.* of late Capt. V. J. Applin, late R.M.T.; *m.* 1st, 1902, Beatrice Caroline Buchan, *née* Bather (*d.* 1933), of Wroxeter, Salop; 2nd, 1935, Daisy B. Rogers, *née* Fifield. *Educ.:* Newton College; and Sherborne. Entered British North Borneo Service as cadets 1889; served through Syed and Mat Salleh Rebellions, 1895-97 (medal and clasp); served through South African War, 1899-1901; District Commissioner, Bloemfontein (medal, four clasps, despatches twice, D.S.O.); Battles Messines and Passchendaele, 1917 (despatches twice, Brevet Lt.-Col., O.B.E.); commanded 14th King's Hussars, 1919-22; M.P. (C.) Enfield Division, 1924-29 and 1931-35. *Publications:* Across the Seven Seas; Machine-gun Tactics. *Recreations:* shooting, fishing. *Address:* c/o Lloyd's Bank, 6 Pall Mall, S.W.1; Howick, Natal, S. Africa. *T.:* Howick 145.
[*Died* 3 *April* 1957.

APPS, Rear-Admiral Edgar Stephen, C.B.E. 1948; *b.* 1893; *s.* of late Engineer Lieut.-Comdr. H. E. G. Apps, R.N.; *m.* 1920, Alice Muriel Loyd, *d.* of late Rev. W. Loyd Protheroe, Llanasa, Flintshire; one *d.* Joined R.N., 1910; served European War, 1914-18; Paymaster-Comdr. 1931; served war of 1939-45: H.M.S. King George V, 1940-42; H.M.S. Victory, 1943; on staff of Flag Officer i/c, Greenock, 1944; H.M.S. Pembroke, 1945; Rear-Adm. (S) 1946. *Address:* 31 Hurn Way, Christchurch, Hants. *T.:* Christchurch 1760. *Clubs:* Goat; Royal Naval (Portsmouth).
[*Died* 30 *April* 1958.

ARBER, Agnes (Mrs. E. A. Newell Arber), F.R.S. 1946; F.L.S.; M.A., D.Sc.; *b.* 1879; *e. d.* of H. R. Robertson; *sister* of Professor Donald Struan Robertson, M.A.; *m.* 1909, Dr. E. A. Newell Arber (*d.* 1918); one *d.* *Educ.:* North London Collegiate School; University College, London; Newnham College, Cambridge. Linnean Medal, 1948. *Publications:* Herbals, 1912; 2nd edition, 1938; reimp. 1953; Water Plants, 1920; Monocotyledons, 1925; The Gramineae: a Study of Cereal, Bamboo and Grass, 1934; The Natural Philosophy of Plant Form, 1950; The Mind and the Eye, 1954; The Manifold and the One, 1957; author or jt. author of about 80 memoirs on botany and hist. of botany in scientific jls. *Address:* 52 Huntingdon Rd., Cambridge. *T.:* 3144.
[*Died* 22 *March* 1960.

ARBUTHNOT, Admiral Sir Geoffrey Schomberg, K.C.B., *cr.* 1942 (C.B. 1938); D.S.O. 1919; R.N. (retd.); *s.* of late Admiral C. Arbuthnot and late Emily Caroline, *d.* of Rear-Admiral C. F. Schomberg; *b.* 1885; *m.* 1913, Jessie Marguerite (*d.* 1947), *d.* of Wm. Henderson of Berkley House, Frome; one *s.* one *d.* (and one *s.* killed in action). Served European War (D.S.O., Chevalier Legion of Honour); Naval Member of the Ordnance Committee at Woolwich, 1927-1929; commanding cruiser Suffolk, 1929-1931; Deputy Director of Training, 1932-33; Director of Training and Staff Duties, Admiralty, 1933-34; commanded destroyer flotillas, Home Fleet, 1934-35; commanded H.M.S. Valiant, 1935-37; Fourth Sea Lord and Chief of Supplies and Transport, 1937-

1941; C.-in-C. East Indies, 1941-42; Chm. Honours and Awards Cttee., 1942-45; retired, 1944. *Address:* Northend House, Heyshott, Sussex. *T.:* Midhurst 69. *Clubs:* United Service; Royal Naval (Portsmouth).
[*Died* 4 *Oct.* 1957.

ARBUTHNOT - LESLIE, of Warthill, William; landed proprietor; *b.* 1878; *s.* of George Arbuthnot (Royal Scots Greys) and Mary Rose Leslie, heiress of Warthill, whom he succeeded 1900; *m.* 1st, 1921, Madame de Mier (from whom he obtained a divorce 1944, *e. d.* of Don Guillermo de Landa y Escandon; one *d.*; 2nd, 1944, Georgiana Nutter, *widow* of Capt. A. B. Urmston, Gordon Highlanders, of Glen Morven, Argyll. *Educ.:* Eton. Served with Gordon Highlanders, South African War (Queen's medal with three clasps); transferred to Scots Guards; A.D.C. to Governor and Commander-in-Chief, Hong Kong, 1904-6; invalided from Army, 1912. Member Queen's Body Guard for Scotland (Royal Company of Archers). *Address:* Warthill, Aberdeenshire. *Club:* Carlton.
[*Died* 27 *Oct.* 1956.

ARBUTHNOTT, 14th Viscount of, *cr.* 1641; **John Ogilvy Arbuthnott;** Lord Lieutenant of Kincardineshire; President County of Kincardine Territorial Association; Convener Kincardineshire County Council; *b.* 15 Sept. 1882; *s.* of 13th Viscount and Emma Marion Hall (*d.* 1930), *d.* of Rev. J. H. Parlby; *m.* 1914, Dorothy, O.B.E. 1951, *d.* of Adm. Charles L. Oxley, The Hall, Ripon; *S.* father, 1920. A representative Peer for Scotland, 1945-55. *Heir: cousin,* Maj.-Gen. Robert Keith Arbuthnott, C.B. *Address:* Arbuthnott House, Fordoun, Kincardineshire. *Club:* New (Edinburgh).
[*Died* 17 *Oct.* 1960.

ARCEDECKNE-BUTLER, Major-General St. John Desmond, C.B.E. 1946; F.R.S.A.; retired; *b.* 30 Nov. 1896; *s.* of late St. John Henry Arcedeckne-Butler, Dangtein, Petersfield, Hants; *m.* 1929, Ethel Helen (*d.* 1953), *d.* of late Lt.-Col. R. Selby-Walker, R.E.; two *s.* one *d.* *Educ.:* U.S.A., Switzerland; R.M.C., Sandhurst; École Supérieure d'Électricité, Paris (Diploma of Radio-Electric Engineer). 2nd Lt. Royal Munster Fusiliers, 1915; served in France and Belgium. Transferred to Royal Sussex Regt. 1922; to Royal Corps of Signals, 1923; at École Supérieure d'Électricité, 1928-29; Superintendent Signals Experimental Establishment, 1934-39; Col. 1938; France, Sept. 1939; Col. Gen. Staff, War Office, 1940; Temp. Maj.-Gen. (Deputy Director-General), Ministry of Supply, 1941-46; late Member of Radio Board and of Television Advisory Committee and Broadcasting Advisory Committee (Eire). *Recreations:* tennis, golf, winter sports. *Address:* Fairfields, Killinick, Co. Wexford, Eire. *Club:* Army and Navy.
[*Died* 4 *Feb.* 1959.

ARCHDALE, Rev. Canon Eyre William Preston; *b.* 26 Feb. 1871; *s.* of late Rt. Rev. M. Archdale, Bishop of Killaloe, and Henrietta, *d.* of Eyre W. Preston, Clontarf; *m.* Edith Gladys Jeannette, *d.* of late R. de Ros Rose, of Ardhu and Aghabeg, Co. Limerick; one *s.* one *d.* *Educ.:* Trinity College, Dublin (M.A.). Curate of Magherafelt, 1894-96; Shankhill, Lurgan, 1896; Ballywillan, Portrush, 1896-1900; Chaplain, Loretto School, 1900-1; Curate of St. Mary's Cathedral, Limerick, 1901-5; Precentor, 1905-8; Rector of Killaloe, 1908; Canon of Killaloe, 1908; Chaplain to Bishop of Killaloe; Vicar of Stockland-Bristol, 1922-45; retired, 1945. *Recreations:* motoring, shooting, fishing. *Address:* Alcombe Cottage, Alcombe, near Minehead, Som. *T.:* Minehead 454. [*Died* 8 *July* 1955.

ARCHDALE, Vice - Adm. Sir Nicholas Edward, 2nd Bt., *cr.* 1928; C.B.E. 1920; *b.* 11 June 1881; *e. s.* of Right Hon. Sir Edward M. Archdale, 1st Bt.; *S.* father 1943; *m.* 1920, Gerda, 2nd *d.* of late F. C. Sievers, Copenhagen; one *s.* one *d.* *Educ.:* Royal Academy, Gosport; H.M.S. Britannia. Midshipman, 1897; Sub-Lieut. 1900; obtained 4 first-class certificates; Lieut 1902; joined Submarine Service, 1902; qualified in Torpedo, 1904; Staff of H.M.S. Vernon, 1905; employed with minelayers and destroyers till 1908, when rejoined Submarine Service; Commander, 1913, when in command of China S.M. Flotilla; employed with submarines during European War; Captain 1918; Naval A.D.C. to the King, 1929; Rear-Adm., 1929; retired list, 1930; General Inspector under Ministry of Home Affairs, Northern Ireland, 1931-46; Vice-Adm., retired list, 1935. *Recreations:* shooting and golf. *Heir: s.* Edward Folmer, *b.* 8 Sept. 1921. *Club:* Ulster (Belfast).
[*Died* 28 *July* 1955.

ARCHER, Admiral Sir Ernest Russell, K.C.B. *cr.* 1948 (C.B. 1945); C.B.E. 1942; *b.* 14 Sept. 1891; 2nd *s.* of late Col. Archer, Lydd, Kent; *m.* 1917, Margaret Elizabeth Hope, *d.* of Reginald Bewes, Plymouth; three *d.* *Educ.:* Royal Naval Colleges, Osborne and Dartmouth. Entered R.N. 1904; Rear-Adm. 1943; Vice-Adm. 1947; Adm. 1950. Served European War, 1914-19, in Destroyers (despatches); War of 1939-45 (despatches); commanded H.M.S. Revenge, 1939; Commodore Royal Naval Barracks, Portsmouth, 1941; Senior British Naval Officer, North Russia, 1943; head of Joint Military Mission to U.S.S.R., 1944; Rear-Adm. (Destroyers) British Pacific Fleet, 1945; Flag Officer, Gibraltar, 1947; Flag Officer Commanding Scotland and Northern Ireland, 1948-50; retired list, 1950. A.D.C. to King George VI, 1942-1943. Order of St. Stanilaus (Russia old Regime); Liberty Cross (Norway); Order of the Oaken Crown (Luxembourg). *Address:* The Cottage, Easton, Nr. Winchester, Hants. *T.:* Itchen Abbas 300. *Club:* United Service.
[*Died* 17 *Dec.* 1958.

ARCHER, George, C.M.G. 1945; Director, Mond Nickel Co. Ltd. (Chairman, 1959); *b.* 5 May 1896; *s.* of Thomas S. Archer, Lytham St. Annes; *m.* Winifred May, *d.* of John Nelson King, S. Norwood; two *d.* *Educ.:* King Edward VII School, Lytham. Entered Civil Service, 1913; served in various Departments, including Customs and Excise, Import Duties Advisory Cttee., and Min. of Supply (Under-Sec.); Sec.-Gen. Br. Raw Materials Mission, Washington, 1942-44, Head of Mission, 1945; U.K. Sec. Combined Raw Materials Board, 1942-45. *Address:* 4A Woodcote Park Avenue, Purley, Surrey. *Club:* Union.
[*Died* 20 *Sept.* 1960.

ARCHER, Richard Lawrence, M.A. (Oxon.); Hon. D.Litt. (Wales); Emeritus Professor of Education, University College of North Wales, Bangor (Professor, 1906-42); *b.* 1874; unmarried. *Educ.:* Leamington College; Wadham College, Oxford (Scholar). 1st class Classical Moderations, 1895; 1st class Litt. Hum., 1897; Classical Master in secondary schools, 1897-1904; Assistant Lecturer in Education, Cambridge University Day Training College, 1904-6. *Publications:* The Teaching of Geography in Elementary Schools, 1910; The Teaching of History in Elementary Schools, 1916; The Passman, 1918; Secondary Education in the Nineteenth Century, 1921. *Address:* 15 Menai View Terrace, Bangor.
[*Died* 24 *Oct.* 1953.

ARCHIBALD, Raymond Clare; Professor of Mathematics, Brown University, Providence, R.I., 1923-43; Professor of Mathematics Emeritus, 1943; *b.* Colchester Co., Nova Scotia, 7 Oct. 1875; *s.* of Abram Newcomb Archibald and Mary Mellish; unmarried. *Educ.:*

Mount Allison University, Sackville, N.B., B.A.; Harvard University, B.A. and M.A.; University of Berlin; University of Strasbourg, Ph.D.; University of Paris; University of Rome; Mount Allison Conservatory of Music, diplomas as graduate in violin playing, 1894 and 1895; Professor of Mathematics, Librarian, and Head of the violin department, Mount Allison Ladies' College, Sackville, N.B., 1900-7; Professor of Mathematics, Acadia University, Nova Scotia, 1907-8; at Brown University, Instructor in Mathematics, 1908-11, Assistant-Professor, 1911-17; Associate Professor, 1917-23; lecturer at University of California, 1924; at Harvard University, 1931; and at Columbia University, 1939-40; F.A.A.S. 1918; Hon. Member Harvard University Chapter of Phi Beta Kappa Society, 1921; Hon. Member of English, Czech, Polish and Rumanian scientific societies; delegate to congresses at Padua, London, Athens, Bologna, Cambridge (Mass.), Oslo, Zurich; Hon. Doctor University of Padua, 1922; Hon. LL.D. Mount Allison University, 1923; Associate Editor of Revue Semestrielle des Publications Mathématiques, Amsterdam, 1923-34; Associate Editor, Isis, 1924-53; Associate Editor, Scripta Mathematica, since 1932; Editor-in-chief of American Mathematical Monthly, 1919-21; Associate Editor of Eudemus, 1939; President of the Mathematical Association of America, 1922; Librarian of the American Mathematical Society, 1921-41; member of the American Section of the International Mathematical Union, 1924-28; Member International Commission on Mathematical Bibliography, 1924-1928; Vice-Pres. of American Association for Advancement of Science, 1928, 1937; Member of Division of Mathematical and Physical Sciences of National Research Council, 1928-31, 1940-43, 1944-47; Member of Executive Committee, 1941-43; Founder and Joint Editor of its Mathematical Tables and other Aids to Computation (quarterly journal), 1943-49; Founder, 1905-55, Mary Mellish Archibald Memorial Library, of English and American Poetry and Drama, Mount Allison University. *Publications:* Carlyle's First Love, Margaret Gordon, Lady Bannerman, 1910; Euclid's Book on Divisions of Figures with a Restoration, 1915; The Training of Teachers of Mathematics, 1918; Benjamin Peirce, 1809-1880, Biographical Sketch and Bibliography, 1925; Bibliography of Egyptian and Babylonian Mathematics, 1927-29; Editor of second English edition of F. Klein's Famous Problems of Elementary Geometry, 1930; Outline of the History of Mathematics, 1932 (6th edition, 1949); Unpublished Letters of James Joseph Sylvester, 1936; The scientific achievements of Nathaniel Bowditch, 1937; A Semicentennial History of the American Mathematical Society 1888-1938, 1938; Mathematical Table Makers; Portraits, Paintings, Busts, Monuments. Bio-bibliographical Notes, 1948; Introduction and Notes to an English translation of J. Steiner, Constructions with a Ruler, given a Fixed Circle with its Centre, 1950; articles in Encyclopædia Britannica, 14th ed., 1929, and Dictionary of American Biography, 1929-36, 1944; extensive contributor to mathematical journals and reviews of Europe and America. *Recreations:* music, library work. *Address:* Brown University, Providence, Rhode Island. *Club:* Faculty (Providence).

[*Died* 26 *July* 1957.

ARCHIBALD, Sir Robert George, Kt., *cr.* 1934; C.M.G. 1928; D.S.O. 1917; M.D.; R.A.M.C., retired; Professor of Bacteriology, Farouk University, Alexandria, 1947; of Parasitology since 1949; Pathologist, County Laboratory, Poole, Dorset; Medical Superintendent, Leper Settlement, Trinidad, West Indies; J.P. County St. George, Trinidad; *b.* 1880; *s.* of Rev. W. F. Archibald, C.F.; *m.* 1919, Olive Chapman, *o. c.* of Arthur Cant, Claremont House, Colchester; two *d.* *Educ.:* Dollar Academy; Edinburgh University. M.B., Ch.B. 1902; corresponding member Société Pathologie Exotique, 1920; Member of Council Section of Tropical Diseases and Parasitology, Royal Society of Medicine; President Sudan Branch British Medical Association, 1935-36; entered Royal Army Medical Corps, 1906; Pathology Prizeman, Army Medical College, 1906; Ambulance Surgeon, Northern Hospital, Liverpool; Assistant Medical Officer, Rainhill Asylum; House Surgeon, St. Mary's Hospital for Women and Children, Plaistow; seconded for Sleeping Sickness Commission, Uganda, 1907; attached Egyptian Army, 1908; Blue Nile Operations, 1908 (despatches); Mediterranean Expeditionary Force, Dardanelles, 1915 (despatches); Darfur Expedition (despatches), Sudan, 1916 (Order 4th Class Medjidieh, Order 2nd Class Nile, and D.S.O.); Director Wellcome Tropical Research Laboratories, Khartum, 1920; Director Stack Medical Research Laboratories, 1928; retired, 1936. *Publications:* Reviews of Recent Advances in Tropical Medicine, Supplements to Reports, Wellcome Research Labs. (with Dr. Andrew Balfour); Editor (with W. Byam) Practice of Medicine in the Tropics; contributor Oxford Index of Therapeutics, 1921; many contributions to medical and scientific journals. *Recreations:* riding, shooting, golfing, fishing. *Address:* c/o Holt & Co., Kirkland House, Whitehall, S.W.1. *Clubs:* Athenæum, Caledonian; Union (Alexandria, Egypt).

[*Died* 2 *May* 1953.

ARCOT, Prince of (Omdatul-Omara, Amir-ul-umara, Sirajul Omara, Madar-ul-Mulk, Omdatul Mulk, Azimud Dowlah, Asadud Dowlatul Ingleez, Nawab Azim Jah, H.H. Sir Ghulam Muhammad Ali Khan Bahadur, Amir-i-Arcot), G.C.I.E., *cr.* 1917 (K.C.I.E., *cr.* 1909); *b.* 26 Feb. 1882; *S.* father (Sir Muhammad Munawar Khan Bahadur, K.C.I.E.), 1903. Premier Mahomedan nobleman of Southern India, being the direct male representative of the Sovereign Rulers of the Carnatic; acknowledged leader of Muslim community of Madras Presidency; two *d.* *Educ.:* Newington Institution, Madras, under C. Morrison, M.A.; received title of Khan Bahadur in 1897; Member of Madras Legislative Council, 1904-6; Member of the Imperial Legislative Council (Mahomedan Electorate) of the Madras Presidency, 1910-13; Member of the Madras Legislative Council by nomination, 1916; Patron Cosmopolitan Club, Madras; Life Member South Indian Athletic Association; President All India Muslim Association, Lahore; Life Member Lawley Institute, Ootacamund; celebrated Silver Jubilee, 1928; Distinction of Highness conferred, 1935. *Address:* Amir Mahal, Madras. *T.:* 3679. *Club:* Gymkhana (Madras).

[*Died* 17 *July* 1952.

ARDEN-CLOSE, Colonel Sir Charles (Frederick), K.B.E., *cr.* 1918; C.B. 1916; C.M.G. 1899; F.R.S. 1919; Hon. Sc.D. (Cantab.), 1928; R.E.; Officier de l'Ordre de Léopold; *b.* 10 Aug. 1865; *s.* of late Maj.-Gen. Frederick Close of Shanklin; changed surname to Arden-Close, 1938; *m.* 1913, Gladys Violet, *d.* of late Theodore Percival, Shanklin; one *s.* one *d.* Entered army, 1884; served on Balloon Det., 1887-88; Survey of India, 1889-93; in charge Niger Protectorate—Kamerun Boundary Survey, 1895; British Commissioner on the Nyasa-Tanganyika Boundary Commission, 1898; served in South African War, 1899-1900; Head of the Geographical Section, General Staff, 1905-11; Director-General Ordnance Survey, 1911-22; Halley Lecturer, Oxford, 1914; retired pay, 1922; Delegate at Conference on Frontiers between Uganda, German E. Africa, and Congo, Brussels, 1910; Boundary Commissioner under Representation of the People Bill, 1917; President S.E. Union of Scientific Societies, 1922; President Geographical Association, 1927; President Royal Geographical Society,

1927-30; President International Population Union, 1931-37; President Hants Field Club, 1929-32, 1935-36; President International Geographical Union, 1934-38; Chairman Palestine Exploration Fund, 1930-45; Victoria Research Medal, R.G.S., 1927; Hon. Mem. Soc. Royale Belge de Géographie; Hon. Mem. K. Nederland Aardsijk. Gen Amsterdam; Hon. Corr. Mem. Geographical Soc., Madrid; Hon. Mem. Geog. Soc. of Russia. *Publications:* Text Book of Topographical Surveying; The Early Years of the Ordnance Survey, 1926; The Map of England, 1932; Geographical By-ways, 1947; various technical papers. *Address:* 22 Christchurch Road, Winchester.
[*Died* 19 *Dec.* 1952.

ARENDZEN, Rev. John, M.A. Cantab.; D.D., D.Ph.; retired; Spiritual Director of St. Edmund's College, Ware, from 1937; a Canon of Metropolitan Chapter of Westminster from 1938; Member of Catholic Missionary Society since 1902; *b.* Amsterdam, 6 Jan. 1873; *s.* of P. J. Arendzen, Dutch Etcher, Assoc. Royal Academy of Belgium, who settled in England, and E. Stracké, of Belgian parentage; unmarried. *Educ.:* Christ's College, Cambridge (Research degree). Theological course at Oscott College, 1891-95; Holy Orders in 1895; at Bonn University, 1895-97; Doctor of Philosophy (Semitic Philology), 1897; Munich University, 1900, Doctor of Theology. *Publications:* Theodori Abu Kurra Libellus de Cultu Imaginum (Arabic-Latin), 1897; Gospels—Fact, Myth or Legend?; Prophets, Priests and Publicans; What becomes of the Dead?; Whom do you say?; Men and Manners in the Days of Christ; articles in Catholic Encyclopædia, Journal of Theological Studies, Jewish Quarterly, etc. *Recreation:* chess. *Address:* 14 Quex Road, N.W.6. [*Died* 21 *July* 1954.

ARIFF, Sir Kamil Mohamed, Kt., *cr.* 1956; C.B.E. 1951; Malayan Certificate of Honour, 1940; J.P.; State Councillor, Penang, since 1948; Medical Practitioner since 1918; *b.* 9 July 1893; *s.* of Kadir Mastan, I.S.O. and Hajji Bee; *m.* 1918, Rahiman Bee binti Fakir Mohiaddin; two *s.* two *d.* *Educ.:* St. Xavier's Institution, Penang; King Edward VII College of Medicine, Singapore (graduated 1917). Member of Committee, Penang Mercantile Marine Fund, 1932-1954; Municipal Commissioner, 1940-54; Federal Legislative Councillor, 1948-55; Member of the Nominated Council Penang, 1948-56. Commissioner (now Chm.), Muslim & Hindu Endowments Board, 1946-; Chm., Muslim Advisory Board, 1949-59; Chm. Muslim Welfare Assoc., 1956-; Chm., Muslim Orphanage, 1946-; Mem. of Exec. Cttee., Penang & Province Wellesley, Red Cross Branch, and of Penang Boy Scouts Assoc. J.P. (Malaya), 1930. *Recreations:* reading, tennis and billiards. *Address:* (Residence) Barkat, 180 Burmah Road, Penang. *T.:* Penang 63229; (Office) 12 Beach Street, Penang, Federation of Malaya. *T.:* 60027. *Clubs:* Penang Malay Association; Rotary International. [*Died* 11 *Aug.* 1960.

ARIS, Major Herbert, M.A., F.R.G.S., J.P. Hants; *b.* 1868; *s.* of late John Aris, of Lois Weedon House, Northants; *m.* 1915, Sydney Dorothy, *d.* of late John Thomas Arundel; one *s.* one *d.* *Educ.:* Rossall; King's College, Cambridge. House Master, Winchester College, 1911-20; O.C. Winchester Coll. O.T.C., 1908-18; Member of Council of Central Landowners' Association, 1921-30; Verderer of New Forest, 1936; Governor of University College, Southampton; High Sheriff for County of Southampton, 1940. *Recreations:* hunting and shooting. *Club:* Royal Societies.
[*Died* 14 *April* 1952.

ARKELL, Reginald; Author and Dramatist; *s.* of late Daniel Arkell, Lechlade, Gloucestershire; *m.* Elizabeth Evans; one *s.* *Educ.:* Burford Grammar School. Trained as a journalist until outbreak of war (1914-1918); has written many revues and musical comedies, including libretto or lyrics for Jumble Sale, 1920; Now and Then, 1921; The Last Waltz, 1922; Catherine, 1923; Our Nell, 1924; Frasquita, 1924; Blue Train, 1927; Chelsea Follies, 1930; Savoy Follies, 1932; Listeners' Inn, 1932; 1066 and All That, 1935; Gay Deceivers, 1935; Kingdom for a Cow, 1935; Paganini, 1937; Laughing Cavalier, 1937; Moonshine, 1940; More 1066 and All That, 1942; film of Charley Moon, 1955; lyrics for Mr. Brown of London Town, Big Ben and other popular songs; has broadcast on many occasions; wrote East is East and West is West, two Kipling broadcasts, 1942; Compère and contributor to Country Magazine and Transatlantic Call, 1945. *Publications:* Colombine and Other Verses, 1912; Tragedy of Mr. Punch, 1920; Meet These People, 1928; Winter Sportings, 1929; Richard Jefferies, 1933; A Cottage in the Country; Bridge Without Sighs; Green Fingers, 1934, (America) 1951; Playing the Games, 1935; Pedlar's Pack; More Green Fingers, 1938; War Rumours, 1939; Green Fingers Again, 1942; Old Herbaceous, 1950, (America) 1951; And a Green Thumb, 1950; Come to the Ball (with A. P. Herbert), 1951; Charley Moon, 1953; Flowers for Lady Charteris, (Germany) 1954; In an English Garden, (France) 1955; Trumpets Over Merriford, 1955; The Lady and the Gardener (Italy); Collected Green Fingers, 1957; New Gods and Old Bells (Germany); The Round House, 1958; Farmer's Boy, 1960. *Recreations:* I always like to call a slam; That is the sort of fool I am. *Address:* Marston Meysey, Cricklade, Wilts. *T.:* Kempsford 217. *Clubs:* Savage; Dramatists'. [*Died* 1 *May* 1959.

ARKELL, William Joscelyn, F.R.S., 1947; M.A., D.Sc.; Fellow of Trinity College, Cambridge; *b.* 9 June 1904; *y. s.* of James Arkell, Redlands Court, Highworth, Wilts.; *m.* 1929, Ruby Lillian Percival; three *s.* *Educ.:* Wellington Coll., Berks.; New Coll., Oxford. B.A. (1st Class Honours in Natural Science), 1925; Burdett-Coutts Scholar, 1925-27; B.Sc., 1927; M.A., D.Phil., 1929; D.Sc., 1934 (Oxford); engaged in research on palæontology, stratigraphy and tectonics. Associate of the Prehistoric Survey of the University of Chicago, investigating the geology and prehistoric archæology of the Nile Valley in Egypt, 1926-30; Lecturer in Geology, New College, Oxford, 1929-33; Fellow, 1933-40; Ministry of War Transport, 1941-43; Thompson Gold Medallist, National Academy of Sciences, Washington, 1944; Lyell Medallist, Geological Society of London, 1949; von Buch Medallist, German Geol. Soc., 1953. Hon. Mem. or Corresp.: Geol. Socs. of France, Germany, Belgium and Egypt; Paleontological Soc. of America; Linnean Soc. of Normandy; Dorset Nat Hist. and Archæol. Soc. *Publications:* The Jurassic System in Great Britain; The Geology of Oxford; Oxford Stone; The Geology of Weymouth, Swanage, Corfe, and Lulworth (Geological Survey); Jurassic Geology of the World; three monographs of the Palæontographical Society; English Rock Terms, etc. *Address:* 14 Cranmer Road, Cambridge. *T.:* Cambridge 57646.
[*Died* 18 *April* 1958.

ARKWRIGHT, Sir John Stanhope, Kt., *cr.* 1934; M.A., F.L.S.; D.L., J.P., Barrister-at-law; *b.* 1872; *m.* 1905, Helen Muriel Stephanie (*d.* 1947), *y. d.* of Stephen Robinson of Lynhales, Kington; one *s.* *Educ.:* Eton; Christ Church, Oxford; Newdigate Prizeman, 1895; M.P. (C.), Hereford, 1900-12. *Publications:* The Last Muster; The Supreme Sacrifice, and other poems in time of War. *Address:* Kinsham Court, Presteigne, Radnorshire.
[*Died* 19 *Sept.* 1954.

ARLEN, Michael (name changed by deed poll from Dikran Kouyoumdjian); author; *b.* Roustchouk, Bulgaria, 16 Nov. 1895, of Armenian parents; naturalised British subject, 1922; *m.* 1928, Atalanta, *d.* of Count Mercati; one *s.* one *d.* *Educ.:* Malvern College. *Publications: novels and short stories:* The London Venture; The Romantic Lady; Piracy; These Charming People; The Green Hat; May Fair; Young Men in Love; Lily Christine; Babes in The Wood; Men Dislike Women, 1931; Man's Mortality, 1933; Hell! said the Duchess, 1934; The Crooked Coronet, 1937; Flying Dutchman, 1939; *plays:* The Green Hat; These Charming People; (with Walter Hackett), Good Losers. *Address:* 23 E. 74th St., New York 21, U.S.A. *Clubs:* Garrick, Savage.
[*Died* 23 *June* 1956.

ARLISS, Vice-Adm. Stephen Harry Tolson, C.B. 1949; D.S.O. 1941; *b.* 11 July 1895; 2nd *s.* of Edward and Florence Helena Arliss, New Lodge, Hanbury, Burton-on-Trent; *m.* 1926, Alice Dugdale Greenwood; one *s.* *Educ.:* Bramcote, Scarborough; R.N.C., Osborne and Dartmouth. Served European War, 1914-18; Midshipman H.M.S. Hercules, 1913-15; Sub-Lieut. H.M.S. Snowdrop, 1915-16; Lance and Miranda, 1917; Lt. (First) H.M.S. Viking, 1917, Speedwell, 1918; Lt.-in-command H.M.S. Saltburn, 1918-19; Lt. (First) H.M.S. Leamington, 1920, Wisteria, 1920-23, Wivern, 1923-25; Lt.-Comdr. in command H.M.S. Stirling, 1926-29, Waterloo, 1929-31; Commander H.M.S. Waterhen, 1931, Thruster, 1932-33, Effingham, 1933-34, Delight, 1934, Wild Swan, 1934-36, Hero, 1936-37; Capt. H.M.S. Hero, 1937; served War of 1939-45; naval attaché West Coast, South America, 1938-40; Capt. D Napier, 7th Destroyer Flotilla, 1940-1942; Commodore D, Eastern Fleet, 1942-1944; Capt. Berwick, 1944-46; Flag Officer commanding British Naval Forces, Germany, 1947-49; retired list, 1949. *Recreations:* riding, shooting, fishing, polo. *Address:* Arden, Kingswood, Surrey; Robin's Oak, Oljoro Orok, Kenya. *T.:* Mogador 2745. *Club:* United Service.
[*Died* 6 *Nov.* 1954.

ARMBRUSTER, Charles Hubert, O.B.E. 1919; M.A. (Camb.); *b.* London, 1874; 2nd *s.* of late C. Armbruster, Musical Adviser to London County Council, and Jeanie, 2nd *d.* of F. A. Ford; *m.* Stefana, *widow* of F. Knobel. *Educ.:* Christ's Hospital (Senior Grecian, 1893; Lamb, Pitt, and Thomson medals; Pitt Club Exhibitioner); King's College, Cambridge (Minor Scholar); B.A. (Classical Honours), 1896. Assistant Collector and Judicial Officer in British Central Africa Protectorate Administration, 1897; transferred by Lord Cromer to Sudan, 1900; served in Dongola and Kasala; accompanied as Political Officer expedition into Abyssinia against Haila Maryam, 1906; sent by Sudan Govt. on political missions to Abyssinia, 1907, 1908; accompanied the Sirdar (Gen. Sir R. Wingate) on his mission to Somaliland as Intelligence Officer, and sent on political mission to Addis Ababa, 1909; Examiner in Amharic for Civil Service Commissioners, 1910, 1911, for Sudan Govt., 1922, and in Arabic for Sudan Govt., 1911, 1912; Senior Inspector in the Legal Department, Sudan Govt., 1909-12; H.M. Consul for North-West Ethiopia, 1912-19; retired from Sudan Political Service, 1926; temp. Lieut., Intelligence Corps, Force in Egypt, 1915; Egyptian Expeditionary Force, 1916-19 (1914-15 Star, despatches four times, O.B.E.); Local Major and General Staff Officer, 2nd Grade, 1918; 4th class Medjidieh, 1909; 3rd class Nile, 1917; Commander, Star of Ethiopia, 1932. *Publications:* Initia Amharica: Amharic Grammar, 1908 (awarded £100 by Prime Minister); English-Amharic Vocabulary, 1910; Amharic-English Vocabulary, 1920; in map of Africa 1:250,000: Qavtya, Wolqait (56-I, J), Wogera, Simyen (56-J, N), Gondar, Dembya, Saqqalt (56-M). *Recreations:* music, remembering. *Address:* Marmacén, Puerto de Andraitx, Mallorca, Spain. *Club:* Athenæum.
[*Died* 17 *April* 1957.

ARMFELT, Roger Noel; Professor of Education, Leeds University, since 1949; *b.* 24 Dec. 1897; *s.* of Paul Alexander Cumming Armfelt and Isabel Bertram; *m.* 1926, Mona Adele Ward, *d.* of Col. A. J. Thompson, D.S.O.; two *s.* three *d.* *Educ.:* Cranleigh School; King's College, Cambridge. Assistant Master, Dulwich College, 1923-24; Inspector, Kent Education Cttee. 1925-28; Asst. Sec., Bucks Education Cttee., 1928-30; Sec., Devon Education Cttee., 1930-41; Asst. Controller (Home Division), B.B.C., 1941-45. Secretary of School Broadcasting Council, 1945-49, and Educational Adviser to B.B.C. *Publications:* County Affairs, 1945; Village Affairs, 1946; Shapton Affairs, 1948; Education: New Hopes and Old Habits, 1949; Our Changing Schools; The Structure of English Education, 1955; articles in Times Educational Supplement and other educational journals. *Recreation:* fishing. *Address:* 521 Shadwell Lane, Moortown, Leeds.
[*Died* 3 *Dec.* 1955.

ARMITAGE, Cecil Henry, C.B.E. 1918; D.L., J.P. Derbyshire; *b.* 1877; *s.* of late Frederick Armitage, North Allerton; *m.* 1902, Mary Marchent, *d.* of late John Edwards, Taunton; one *s.* one *d.* *Educ.:* King William's College, I.O.M. *Recreations:* hunting and gardening. *Address:* Longstone Grange, nr. Bakewell, Derbyshire. [*Died* 20 *April* 1955.

ARMITAGE, Major Charles Leathley, D.S.O. 1915; O.B.E. 1918; late 6th Batt. Worcestershire Regt.; *b.* 6 Mar. 1871. Entered Army, 1892; Captain, 1900; retired Liverpool Regt., 1907; joined 6th Batt. Worcestershire Regt. 1914; served European War, 1914-15 (D.S.O. for assault on the German lines at Richebourg). Chief Constable of Southport, 1907-19. *Address:* Maple Bay, Duncan, V.I., B.C. [*Died* 17 *Sept.* 1951.

ARMITAGE, Francis Paul, C.B.E. 1933; M.A. Oxon.; Director of Education for the City of Leicester, 1919-40 (retired); *b.* 21 April 1875; *s.* of Rev. William Armitage, Vicar of Scotforth, Lancaster and Margaret Robinson; *m.* 1907, Louise (*d.* 1950), *d.* of Lt.-Col. J. W. Wilson, J.P., Trinidad; two *s.* one *d.* *Educ.:* Royal Grammar School, Lancaster; Magdalen College, Oxford; Bonn University. Assistant Master at St. Paul's School, London, 1898-1918 (Head of Modern Side from 1910; Housemaster); Jubilee Medal, 1935; Coronation Medal, 1937. *Publications:* A History of Chemistry, 1906; Chemistry, Part I (1915); Part II (1916); Diet and Race, 1922; Leicester, 1914-18, 1933. *Recreations:* gardening, tapestry. *Address:* Red Roses, Barton Court Road, New Milton, Hants. *T.:* New Milton 309.
[*Died* 27 *June* 1953.

ARMITAGE, Frank, C.I.E. 1927; retired; *b.* 19 Jan. 1872; *s.* of late Arthur Armitage, J.P., D.L., of Dadnor, Ross, Herefordshire; *m.* 1905, Muriel, *d.* of late Rev. Frederic Louis Byrde; two *s.* *Educ.:* Marlborough College. Entered Police Department, Madras, 1890; Commissioner of Police, Madras City, 1910-1920; Inspector-General of Police, Madras Presidency, 1921-27. *Address:* Nynehead Court, Wellington, Somerset.
[*Died* 6 *Sept.* 1955.

ARMITAGE, Rev. Robert, D.S.O. 1902; M.A.; Preb. of Hereford, 1932-39, now Preb. Emeritus; *b.* 5 March 1857; *e. s.* of Arthur Armitage of Bridstow, Co. Hereford. *Educ.:* Marlborough; Magdalen College, Oxford. Deacon, 1880; Priest, 1882; Curate of Llandingat, 1880-82; Chaplain, Oxford Military College, 1882-84; Curate of St. John Baptist, Leamington, 1884-86; served Aldershot, 1886-90; Wellington Barracks, 1890-94; Barbados, 1894-

1898; Woolwich, 1898-99; Cape of Good Hope, 1899-1902; served South Africa, 1899-1902; Woolwich, 1902-7; C.F., Cairo, 1907-11; Plymouth, 1911-12; Vicar of St. Chad's, Tushingham, 1912-15; Bunbury, 1915-22; Vicar of Stanton Lacy, 1922-45; Rural Dean of Ludlow, 1931-35. *Address:* 15 Meyrick Street, Hereford.
[*Died* 29 *May* 1954.

ARMS, John Taylor, A.R.E. 1934; N.A. 1933 (A.N.A. 1930); Etcher; President, The Society of American Graphic Artists; President, Tiffany Foundation; *b.* Washington, D.C., U.S.A., 1887, of American parentage; *m.* 1913, Dorothy Noyes; two *s.* one *d.* *Educ.:* Princeton Univ., Massachusetts Inst. of Technology, S.B. 1911; S.M. 1912. Architect until 1917; Etcher; represented in the Permanent Collections of: New York Public Library, Congressional Library, Museum of Fine Arts (Boston, Mass.), United States National Museum (Washington, D.C.), Bibliothèque Nationale (Paris), The British Museum, Victoria and Albert Museum, etc.; Hon. M.A. Wesleyan Univ. 1939; Hon. Litt.D. Hobart College, 1940; Hon. M.A. Princeton Univ., 1947. Member: National Institute of Arts and Letters, 1932; American Academy of Arts and Letters, 1947. Chevalier de la Légion d'Honneur (France), 1933, Officier, 1951. Gold Medal from Holland Soc. of New York, 1952. *Publications:* Handbook of Print Making and Print Makers, 1934; (with wife) Design in Flower Arrangement, 1937; illustrated Churches of France and Hill Towns and Cities of Northern Italy, by Dorothy Noyes Arms. *Address:* Mill Stones, Greenfield Hill, Fairfield, Connecticut, U.S.A. *T.:* Fairfield 9-0477. *Clubs:* Century, Lotos, Grolier, National Arts (Life Member), Salmagundi, Princeton (New York); Kiwanis (Bridgeport).
[*Died Oct.* 1953.

ARMSTRONG, David; *see* Clewes, Winston.

ARMSTRONG, Lieut.-Col. Edward, C.M.G. 1918; D.S.O. 1917; *b.* 1869; 2nd *s.* of late C. E. Armstrong, of Staunton Wyville, Leicestershire; *m.* 1907, Constance E., 2nd *d.* of late A. R. Tull, D.L., J.P., of Crookham House, near Newbury; one *d.* *Educ.:* Haileybury. Entered H.L.I. 1892; retired as Lieut.-Colonel, 1919; served N.W. Frontier of India, 1897-8 (medal with clasp); South African War, 1901-2 with Mounted Infantry (despatches Queen's medal three clasps; Brevet Major); European War, 1914-19 (despatches, C.M.G., D.S.O.). *Address:* Lock's Lane House, Sparsholt, near Winchester, Hants. *Club:* Army and Navy.
[*Died* 8 *Sept.* 1951.

ARMSTRONG, Brigadier John Cardew, C.B.E. 1942; M.C.; *b.* 3 June 1887; *s.* of late Henry George Armstrong, M.R.C.S., L.S.A.; *m.* 1916, Winifred Helen, *yr. d.* of late Maj.-Gen. A. A. Sutton, C.B., D.S.O.; one *s.* two *d.* *Educ.:* Wellington; Gonville and Caius College, Cambridge (B.A. 1910). Entered R.A.S.C., 1910; Lieut. 1912; Capt. 1915; Major 1929; Lt.-Col. 1935; Col. 1939; (Temp.) Brig. 1941. Served with B.E.F., France, 1914-16 and 1918-19 (despatches, M.C.); with Middle East Force, 1939-42; A.D.S.T., Egypt, 1939; D.D.S.T., Western Desert Force, 1940; D.D.S.T., Ninth Army, 1941-42 (despatches twice, C.B.E.); retired, 1944. *Address:* 109A Shooters Hill Road, Blackheath, S.E.3. *T.:* Greenwich 1065.
[*Died* 3 *Oct.* 1953.

ARMSTRONG, His Honour John Warneford Scobell, C.B.E. 1920; Officier d'Académie; *b.* 1 March 1877; *o. s.* of late John and late Fanny Scobell Armstrong, of Nancealverne, nr. Penzance; *m.* 1926, Winifred Amy, *yr. d.* of Rev. Douglas Hamilton, of Renhold, near Bedford; one *s.* *Educ.:* Abroad. Called to Bar, Inner Temple, 1905; member of Western Circuit; Assistant Postal Censor, 1914-15; in charge of sub-section of Directorate of Military Intelligence, War Office, 1915-19; Assistant Legal Adviser to the Foreign Office, 1919-20; Legal Adviser to Reparation Claims Department, Board of Trade, 1920-22. Judge of Circuit No. 59, Cornwall, Plymouth, etc., 1940-50. Chairman of Cornwall Quarter Sessions, 1945-53. *Publications:* The Trade Continuation Schools of Germany, 1913; War and Treaty Legislation, 1914-21; The Taxation of Profits, 1937; Victorian Verses, 1950; Yesterday, 1955. *Address:* Nancealverne, Penzance. *T.:* Penzance 3101. *Clubs:* St. James', M.C.C.
[*Died* 2 *March* 1960.

ARMSTRONG, Sir Nesbitt William, 4th Bart., *cr.* 1841; *b.* 3 July 1875; *s.* of 2nd Bart. and Alice, *d.* of W. W. Fisher; *S.* brother, 1922; *m.* 1910, Clarice Amy, *d.* of John Carter Hodgkinson, Maryborough, Victoria, Australia, one *s.* one *d.* *Heir:* *s.* Andrew St. Clare, *b.* 27 Dec. 1912. *Address:* 11 Ruihi Street, Rotorua, N.Z.
[*Died* 23 *Sept.* 1953.

ARMSTRONG, General St. George Bewes, C.B. 1919; C.M.G. 1919; *b.* 23 May 1871; *s.* of Col. W. G. Armstrong, R.M.L.I., and Augusta Annie, *d.* of Augustus Bewes; *m.* 1914, Constance Dorothy Christian, *d.* of J. E. Friar, of Duddo, Co. Northumberland; one *s.* (*d.* 1931). *Educ.:* Mannamead School, Plymouth. 2nd Lieut. Plymouth Div. R.M.L.I. 1889; Major-General, 1923; Lt.-Gen. 1925; General, 1926; Naval Intelligence Department, 1899-1904; p.s.c. 1907; Staff R.N. War College, 1907-10; G.S.O. 2 Western Coast Defences, 1913; A.A. and Q.M.G., H.Q. L. of C. Mediterranean Expeditionary Force, 1915; after evacuation of Gallipoli held various staff appointments in Egyptian Expeditionary Force, including A.A. and Q.M.G. 54 Div. 1917 and D.A. and Q.M.G. (temp. Brig.-General) 21st Army Corps and North Force, 1917-20 (Brevet Colonel, C.M.G., C.B., 3rd Class Nile, Croix de Guerre, despatches 5 times); Commandant, Portsmouth Division Royal Marine Light Infantry, 1920-23; retired list, 1927; Hon. Colonel Commandant, Chatham Division R.M., 1934-41; L.D.V. and H.G., 1940-1945. *Address:* c/o Lloyds Bank Ltd., Jersey, C.I. *Club:* United Service.
[*Died* 22 *May* 1956.

ARMSTRONG, Samuel, C.B.E. 1937; J.P.; Chairman since 1937 and Managing Director since 1908 of Cranfield Bros. Ltd., Flour Millers, Ipswich; Director of: Purchase Finance Co. Ltd.; British Millers' Mutual Pool, Ltd.; *b.* 1878; *s.* of late Samuel Armstrong, Shingay, Cambridgeshire; *m.* 1903, Florence Eva (*d.* 1954), *d.* of late Thomas Dixon, Chelmsford; two *s.* one *d.* *Educ.:* Kent College, Canterbury. Commenced business at Cranfield Bros., 1893; Member of Council of National Association British and Irish Millers since 1914; Member of Executive Committee, 1917-51; President, 1920-21; Member of Board of Millers Mutual Association since 1930; Member of Ipswich Dock Commission since 1909; Chairman since 1949; Member of Harwich Harbour Conservancy Board; Member of Wheat Commission, 1932-57; Member of Ipswich Town Council, 1945-53; Member of Board Alliance Assurance Co., Ipswich Branch. *Recreations:* golf, tennis, shooting. *Address:* Barncroft, Stone Lodge Lane, Ipswich, Suffolk. *T.A.* and *T.:* Ipswich 53331. *Club:* County (Ipswich).
[*Died* 27 *March* 1959.

ARMSTRONG, William, C.B.E. 1951; M.A.; *b.* Edinburgh, 30 Nov. 1882. *Educ.:* George Heriot's School and University, Edinburgh. Studied for the musical profession, and was for some years a schoolmaster; studied for stage under F. R.

Benson; first appearance on London stage in 1909 with Beerbohm Tree's company; acted in Germany, America, and in London under the management of Arthur Bourchier, J. B. Fagan, Matheson Lang and others; for many years acting with various Repertory Theatre Companies in Glasgow, Liverpool, Birmingham, and Everyman Theatre; played leading parts with Mrs. Patrick Campbell; appointed Producer to the Liverpool Repertory Theatre, 1922, and was Director of the Theatre, 1923-44; produced for the O.U.D.S. in 1925; Shute Lecturer in the Art of the Theatre at Liverpool University, 1929; worked in an administrative capacity with ENSA at Drury Lane Theatre, London, 1941-42. Has directed several West End productions including Van Druten's Old Acquaintance and Somerset Maugham's The Circle; Assistant Director to Sir Barry Jackson, Birmingham Repertory Theatre, 1945-47. Hon. M.A. Liverpool Univ., 1930. *Publications:* Collaborated in a children's play, King of the Castle, with A. P. Herbert, and with Francis Brett Young in the play entitled The Furnace; has edited several volumes of One-Act Plays. *Address:* 176 Oaktree Lane, Bournville, Birmingham 30. *Clubs:* Garrick; University (Liverpool).
[*Died* 5 *Oct.* 1952.

ARMYTAGE, Rev. Canon Duncan, M.A.; Canon of St. George, Windsor, since 1947; *b.* 22 Aug. 1889; *s.* of William Kaye Lewis Armytage and Florence Beatrice Daniel; *m.* 1940, Pleasaunce Elizabeth Hope, *yr. d.* of late H. B. Napier, Long Ashton, Bristol. *Educ.:* Leeds Grammar School; St. Edmund Hall, Oxford; Cuddesdon Theological College. Asst. Curate, St. Peter's, Plymouth, 1913-17; Asst. Master, St. Cuthbert's School, Worksop, and Licensed Preacher in the diocese of Southwell, 1917-18; Asst. Curate, The Annunciation, Chislehurst, 1918-19; Asst. Curate, St. James', Devonport, in charge of the Kelly College Mission, 1919-23; Vice-Principal, Dorchester Missionary College, 1923-27; Warden of St. Anselm Hall, University of Manchester, 1927-34; Canon of Southwark and Diocesan Missioner; Warden of the College of St. Saviour, and Warden of the Southwark Diocesan House, Warlingham, Surrey, 1934-1947; Examining Chaplain to the Bishop of Southwark, 1932-48; Hon. Chaplain to Bishop of Hereford, 1941-48. *Publications:* Christianity in the Roman World; Firmly I believe; One Sufficient Sacrifice. *Recreations:* golf, etc. *Address:* 6 The Cloisters, Windsor Castle. *T.:* Windsor 313. *Club:* Authors'.
[*Died* 14 *Feb.* 1954.

ARMYTAGE, Brig.-Gen. Sir George (Ayscough), 7th Bt., *cr.* 1738; C.M.G. 1918; D.S.O. 1917; *b.* 2 Mar. 1872; *s.* of 6th Bt. and Ellen (*d.* 1890), *d.* of Rev. A. Fawkes of Farnley Hall, Yorkshire; *S.* father, 1918; *m.* 1899, Aimée, 3rd *d.* of Sir Lionel Milborne Swinnerton-Pilkington, 11th Bt.; two *s.* one *d.* J.P., W. Riding of Yorkshire; formerly Lt.-Col. K.R.R.C., and Col. commanding 2nd West Riding Inf. Brig., T.A., 1921-22 (now Hon. Brig.-Gen.); European War, 1914-18. Brig.-Gen. commanding an Infantry Brigade, 1916-18 (despatches four times, Bt. Lt.-Col., D.S.O., C.M.G., Col., Croix de Guerre). *Heir: s.* John Lionel [*b.* 23 Nov. 1901; *m.* 1st, 1927, Evelyn Mary Jessamine (marriage dissolved, 1946), *d.* of Edward Herbert Fox, of Adbury Park, Newbury; one *s.* one *d.*; 2nd, 1949, Maria Margarete, *o. d.* of Paul Tenhaeff, Bruenen, Niederrhein. *Educ.:* Eton; R.M.C., Sandhurst. Capt. King's Royal Rifle Corps]. *Club:* Carlton. [*Died* 15 *Aug.* 1953.

ARNAUD, Yvonne, Actress; *b.* Bordeaux, 20 Dec. 1895; *d.* of Charles Léon Arnaud and Antoinette de Montégu; *m.* 1920, Hugh McLellan. *Educ.:* Paris. Début as Princess Mathilde in The Quaker Girl at the Adelphi, 1911; parts include Suzanne in The Girl in the Taxi, 1912 and numerous revivals; Noisette in Oh, be Careful! 1915; Kitty Pearson in Jerry, 1916; Georgette St. Pol in Kissing Time, 1919; Chiquette in The Naughty Princess, 1920; Louise Allington in Tons of Money, 1922-24; Marguerite Hickett in A Cuckoo in the Nest, 1925; Mrs. Pepys in And so to Bed, 1926, and same part in New York, 1927; Elizabeth in By Candle Light, 1928; Elma Melton in Canaries Sometimes Sing, 1929, and same part in New York, 1930; Duchess of Tann in The Improper Duchess, 1931; Louise in Will you love me always? 1932; Hélène Lorimer in Doctor's Orders, 1933; Princess Katharine in Henry V., 1934; Mrs. Val Shannon in Tread Softly, 1935; also in Plan for a Hostess, 1938; What Say They, 1939; In Good King Charles's Golden Days, 1940 (also at Malvern Festival, 1939); The Nutmeg Tree, 1941; Love for Love, 1943; The Circle, 1944; Jane, 1947; Travellers' Joy, 1948-50; Dear Charles, 1952; Mrs. Willie, 1955; Six Months Grace, 1957. Entered films 1924 and has appeared in Desire, On Approval, Tons of Money, Canaries Sometimes Sing, A Cuckoo in the Nest, Stormy Weather, The Improper Duchess, Neutral Port, To-morrow we Live, etc. *Address:* Banks Way Farm, Effingham Common, Surrey. *T.:* Bookham 350.
[*Died* 20 *Sept.* 1958.

ARNOLD, Bening Mourant, D.S.O. 1918; M.A.; M.I.N. 1951; *b.* 4 Aug. 1884; *s.* of late Bening Arnold and Emilie Mourant; *m.* 1914, Elsie Kate, *e. d.* of Rev. J. D. Best of Sandon Rectory, Chelmsford; two *s.* three *d.* *Educ.:* St. Paul's School; Jesus College, Cambridge; B.A. degree in mech. sciences; six years practical experience at Thornycroft's and Woolwich Arsenal. Commanded L. Anti-aircraft Battery, B.E.F., 1916-18 (despatches, D.S.O.); Major Instructor in A.A. gunnery, 1918-19; Assistant Master, Bradfield College, 1920, House Master, 1926-1940; a skipper, Admiralty Ferry Crew Service, 1941-45; Sub. Lt. (temp.) R.N.V.R., 1943. *Recreation:* cruising (Riduna III). *Address:* Loxley, Kingswood, Sutton Valence, Maidstone. *T.:* Ulcombe 340. *Clubs:* Leander, Royal Cruising, Little Ship.
[*Died* 20 *May* 1955.

ARNOLD, Ivor Deiniol Osborn, M.A., Doctor of University of Strasbourg; Professor of Old French Language and Literature, University of Leeds, 1938-52; *b.* 8 Dec. 1895; *s.* of Edward Vernon Arnold and Violet Osborn; *m.* 1924, Inger Margrethe Ellgaard; no *c.* *Educ.:* Friars School, Bangor; Perse School, Cambridge; Universities of Wales and Strasbourg. Served European War, France, Salonika, Malta, Turkey, 1914-20; Assistant Lecturer, University of Manchester, 1924-27; Independent Lecturer in Mediæval French, University of Belfast, 1927-38. *Publications:* Edition of L'Apparicion Maistre Jehan de Meun, by Honoré Bonet, 1926; edition of Wace's Brut, vol. 1. 1938, vol. 2. 1940; articles on Old French literature in Romania and Medium Aevum. *Address:* 420 Otley Road, Leeds 6. [*Died* 5 *June* 1952.

ARNOLD-FORSTER, Rear-Adm. Forster Delafield, C.M.G. 1918; R.N., retd.; *b.* 1876; *s.* of late Edward Penrose Arnold-Forster, J.P., D.L., and Edith Mary, *d.* of late William Ford, C.S.I.; *m.* 1907, Georgina Mary (*d.* 1952), *d.* of Alfred Tucker; one *d.* H.M.S. Britannia, 1890; Comdr., 1908; served in European War, 1914-18; Captain R.N., 1916; served Admiralty Anti-Submarine Division, 1918-19; Captain-in-Charge, Simonstown Dockyard, 1921-23; retired pay, 1923; officer St. Maurice and St. Lazarus (Italy), 1916. *Publication:* The Ways of the Navy, 1931; At War with the Smugglers, 1936. *Address:* Woodpecker Cottage, Iwerne Minster, Blandford, Dorset. *T.:* Fontmell Magna 385.
[*Died* 21 *April* 1958.

ARNOLDI, Colonel Frank Fauquier, D.S.O. 1917; *b.* Toronto, 7 July 1889; *s.* of late Frank Arnoldi, K.C. *Educ.:* Upper Canada College and Royal Military College, Canada. Went into civil life; Subaltern 15th Battery Canadian Field Artillery, C.E.F. Dec. 1914; served European War, France, 1915-17 (D.S.O.); North Russia, 1918-19 (bar to D.S.O., Order ofSt. Stanislas, Russia). Commanded 7th (R.) Toronto Regiment, R.C.A. until Sept. 1944; Hon. Col. 7th (R.) Toronto Group, R.C.A. 1944. *Club:* National (Toronto). [*Died* 5 *Aug.* 1953.

ARNOTT, Sir Lauriston John, 3rd Bt., *cr.* 1896; Director Irish Times since 1919, Managing Director, 1940-54; *b.* 27 Nov. 1890; *e. s.* of Sir John A. Arnott, 2nd Bt., and Caroline, D.B.E. (*d.* 1933), *e. d.* of Sir F. M. Williams, 2nd Bt. of Tregullow; *S.* father, 1940. *Educ.:* Wellington College; Royal Military Academy, Woolwich. Commissioned Cameronians, 1910; retired, 1914; served European War, 1914-18 (wounded twice), 3rd Royal Irish Rifles. *Heir: b.* Robert John [*b.* 19 Aug. 1896; *m.* 1926, Emita Amelia, *d.* of Francis James, formerly of Royston, Herts.; two *s.*]. *Address:* Shearwater, Baily, Co. Dublin. *Clubs:* Army and Navy; Kildare Street (Dublin). [*Died* 2 *July* 1958.

ARONSON, Victor Rees, C.B.E. 1950; K.C. 1949; *b.* 5 Dec. 1880; *s.* of S. P. Aronson; *m.* 1911, Annie Elizabeth Fraser (*d.* 1945); two *s.* three *d.* *Educ.:* Clifton; Merton College, Oxford. Called to bar, Inner Temple, 1904; a Chm. Industrial Court; Standing Counsel to Board of Trade in Bankruptcy cases, 1937-49; District Referee, Somerset Coalfield; Dep. Chm., Road Haulage Wages Council; Bakery Trade Wages Council; Fur Trade Wages Council. Chairman, Commission of Inquiry into Rubber-proofed Garments Industry, 1949; Chairman, Negotiating Cttee. of Cotton Spinning Industry, 1947. *Publications:* Editor, 12th Edn. Russell on Arbitration, 1931; Editor, 9th Edn. Chalmers and Hough on Bankruptcy, and 16th Edn. Williams on Bankruptcy. *Address:* 11 Ranelagh Avenue, S.W.13. *T.:* Prospect 1697; 3 King's Bench Walk, Temple, E.C.4; *T.:* Central 5482. *Clubs:* Oxford and Cambridge, Roehampton. [*Died* 1 *Jan.* 1951.

ARRAN, 6th Earl of (*cr.* 1762), **Lt.-Col. Arthur Jocelyn Charles Gore,** K.P. 1909; P.C. (Ire.) 1917; Bt. 1662; Viscount Sudley, Baron Saunders, 1758; Earl of Arran of the Aran Islands, Co. Galway, 1762; Baron Sudley (U.K.) 1884; Lord-Lieut. Co. Donegal, 1917-1920; late Brev. Major and Adjutant Royal Horse Guards; *b.* 14 Sept. 1868; *s.* of 5th Earl and Hon. Edith, *d.* of Viscount Jocelyn; *S.* father, 1901; *m.* 1st, 1902, Maud (*d.* 1927), *o. d.* of Baron Huysson de Kattendyke of The Hague; two *s.*; 2nd, 1929, Lilian Constance, *widow* of Francis Brown. Served in Egyptian Cavalry (Order of Medijeh, invalided); comd. R.H.G. Squadron, Household Cavalry, South African War (Bt. Major, medal with 4 clasps); Hon. Sec. Liberal League; late Brigadier commanding all Officers' Training Corps in Ireland, 1909-12; Brevet Major Royal Horse Guards, 1914, invalided; raised and commanded St. Mawes Home Guard; Chm. Royal Westminster Ophthalmic Hospital, 1907-34; Hon. Treasurer Children's Country Holiday Fund, 1904-34; D.L., J.P. Herts, Donegal, Louth, Mayo. *Publications:* articles in Nineteenth Century, Punch, National Review, English Review, Daily News. *Heir: s.* Viscount Sudley (*see under* 7th Earl of Arran). *Address:* St. Mawes, Cornwall. *Clubs:* Turf, Travellers', Beefsteak; Royal Yacht Squadron. [*Died* 19 *Dec.* 1958.

ARRAN, 7th Earl of, *cr.* 1762; **Arthur Paul John Charles James Gore;** Bt. 1662; Visc. Sudley, Baron Saunders, 1758; Earl of Arran of the Aran Islands, Co. Galway, 1762; Baron Sudley (U.K.) 1884; *b.* 31 July 1903; *er. s.* of 6th Earl of Arran, K.P., P.C.; *S.* father 1958. *Educ.;* Winchester; New College, Oxford. A.D.C. to Governor-General of South Africa, 1931-32. *Publications:* William, a Satire, 1933 (reprinted 1955). Edited and translated Lieven-Palmerston Correspondence, 1943; *translations:* Tibetan Venture, 1947; Jesuits Go East, 1948; Know Your Germans, 1949; The Three Musketeers (Penguin Classics), 1950; The Story of Axel Munthe, 1953; Enough, No More, etc.; Occasional articles in The Times, Daily Telegraph, Manchester Guardian, etc. *Heir: b.* Hon. Arthur Kattendyke Strange David Archibald Gore [*b.* 5 July 1910; *m.* 1937, Fiona Bryde, *d.* of Sir Iain Colquhoun, 7th Bt., K.T., D.S.O.; two *s.*]. *Club:* Travellers'. [*Died* 28 *Dec.* 1958.

ARTHUR, Colonel Sir Charles Gordon, Kt., *cr.* 1937; M.C.; V.D.; *b.* 24 Oct. 1884; *s.* of late John William Arthur, J.P., Glasgow; *m.* 1914, Dorothy Grace, *d.* of late Sir William Henry Hoare Vincent, G.C.I.E., K.C.S.I.; one *s.* (and one killed Iraq, 1941) one *d.* *Educ.:* Glasgow Academy. Served European War, 1915-19, R.F.A. in France and Belgium; Col. Calcutta Light Horse, 1922-1928; Hon. A.D.C. to Viceroy of India, 1924-1928; Pres. Imperial Bank of India (Calcutta), 1935; Sheriff of Calcutta, 1936; Vice-President Bengal Chamber of Commerce, 1935-37; M.L.C. Bengal Legislative Council, 1935; Member Council of State, Government of India, 1936-37. *Address:* St. Michaels Manor, St. Albans, Herts. *T.:* St. Albans 254. *Clubs:* Oriental; Royal Calcutta Turf (Calcutta). [*Died* 22 *Jan.* 1953.

ARTHUR, Colonel John Maurice, C.M.G. 1918; D.S.O. 1915; T.D.; Officer of the Order of the Crown of Belgium; D.L., Lanarkshire; J.P.; Architect; F.R.I.B.A., with extensive practice in Scotland; Past President of Glasgow Institute of Architects; *b.* 1877; *s.* of George Arthur, Airdrie; *m.* 1905, Katharine Adam Stevenson, *d.* of Andrew Hutton; two *s.* one *d.* Served European War (D.S.O.). *Address:* Glentore, Airdrie, Lanarkshire. [*Died* 8 *May* 1954.

ARTHUR, Colonel Lionel Francis, D.S.O. 1917; O.B.E. 1920; Indian Army, retired; *b.* London, 14 March 1876; 3rd *s.* of late Edward Jenkins, author of Ginx's Baby, M.P., Dundee, etc.; one *s.* one *d.*; *m.* 2nd 1934, Muriel Irene, *e. d.* of late Sir G. Tilley, and *widow* of Lieut.-Col. S. G. C. Murray, C.I.E., I.A.; one *s.* *Educ.:* St. Paul's; Neuenheim College, Heidelberg; R.M.C., Sandhurst. First commission, Indian Unattached List, 1896; Russia, 1905-1906; Qualified Interpreter; Staff, A.H.Q., Simla, 1907-9; Staff Coll., Camberley, 1911-12; p.s.c.; Brig.-Maj., Bangalore Brigade, 1914; Brig.-Maj., Imperial Service Cavalry Brigade, Egypt, Sep. 1914; D.A.Q.M.G. H.Q. Force in Egypt, Jan. 1916; Gen. Staff, Feb. 1916 (despatches); Gen. Staff, Australian Imperial Force, Mar. 1916; B.E.F., France, 1916-17 (despatches, D.S.O.); Assist. Comdt. Cadet College, Quetta, 1917-19; 3rd Afghan War, 1919, G.S.O. (1), Waziristan Force (despatches, O.B.E.); Comdt. Royal Deccan Horse, 1920; A.Q.M.G. Eastern Command, India, 1921-26; A.A.G., A.H.Q., India, 1927-30; retired 1930. *Recreations:* golf, tennis. *Address:* Yockley House, near Camberley, Surrey. [*Died* 29 *Jan.* 1952.

ASCH, Sholem; Officer, Order of Polonia Restituta (Poland); author; *b.* Kutno, Poland, 1 Nov. 1880; *s.* of Moishe Asch and Malka (*née* Wydawski); *m.* 1901, Mathilda Spiro; three *s.* one *d.* *Educ.:* Hebrew schools and Rabbinical College, Poland. Hon. D.H.L., Inst. Jewish Religion, N.Y. City; Hon. mem. P.E.N., London; Hon. pres., Jewish P.E.N., Buenos Aires, Argentina. *Publications:* Three Cities, 1933; Salvation, 1934; Mottke the Thief, 1935; In the Beginning, 1935; The Mother, 1937; The War Goes On, 1937; Three Novels, 1938; Song of the Valley, 1939; The Nazarene, 1939; What I Believe, 1941; Children of Abraham, 1942; The Apostle, 1943; One Destiny, 1945; East River, 1946; Tales of My People, 1948; Mary, 1949; Moses, 1951; Salvation, 1953; A Passage in the Night, 1954; The Prophet, 1955; From Many Countries, 1958. *Address:* c/o G. P. Putnam's Sons, 210 Madison Avenue, New York 16, N.Y., U.S.A. [*Died* 10 *July* 1957.

ASCOLI, Frank David, C.I.E. 1925; F.I.R.I.; Rubber Expert; retired; Underwriting Member of Lloyds; *b.* 10 August 1883; *s.* of late E. Ascoli; *m.* 1912, Mary Isobel, *d.* of late J. Morrison Anderson; two *s.* *Educ.:* Manchester Grammar School; Exeter College, Oxford. 1st class Lit. Hum., 1906; entered Indian Civil Service, 1907; Secretary, Board of Revenue, Bengal, 1917-20; President, Boiler Laws Cttee., India, 1920-21; Deputy Secretary, Government of India; Department of Industries and Labour, 1921-22; Controller, Printing, Stationery and Stamps, India, 1923-25; retired from Indian Civil Service, 1926; Controller of Rubber, Ministry of Supply, 1942; Director of Rubber, Ministry of Supply, 1943-45; Chairman Rubber Growers Assoc., 1946-47; President, Institution of the Rubber Industry, 1948-49, Hancock Medallist, 1954. *Publications:* Early Revenue History of Bengal, 1917; Revenue History of the Sunderbans, 1919. *Recreation:* gardening. *Address:* Beeches, Manor Rd., Penn, Bucks. *T.:* Penn 3175. *Clubs:* East India and Sports; Royal Calcutta Turf (Calcutta). [*Died* 14 *Feb.* 1958.

ASCROFT, Sir William (Fawell), Kt., *cr.* 1939; D.L., J.P. (Lancs.); *b.* 1 Oct. 1876; *s.* of late Sir William Ascroft, J.P., Preston; *m.* 1906, Eve Mary, *d.* of John Thomas Belk, Middlesbrough, Yorks; two *d.* (one *s.* decd.). *Educ.:* Rugby; Corpus Christi College, Oxford. High Sheriff Lancs., 1943; Chairman of: Preston Employment Cttee., Preston and District Disablement Cttee. and Harris Inst. Trustees; H.M. Prison (Preston) Bd. of Visitors; Hon. Treas. of N.W. Partially-sighted School; General Commissioner of Income Tax; formerly Vice-Chm. of Standing Jt. Cttee. of Lancashire; Ex-chairman of Preston Royal Infirmary; Lancs. Branch of C.P.R.E., British Hospitals Assoc. N.W. Area; served European War, Brevet-Major, 1919. *Recreations:* formerly cricket, Rugby football, mountaineering, and fell walking; ex-President of Preston Grasshoppers R.F.C. *Address:* Gleadale, Longridge, Preston, Lancs.; The Wyke, Grasmere. *Club:* Winckley (Preston). [*Died* 7 *May* 1954.

ASH, Audrey B.; part-time Voluntary Worker at W.V.S. *Educ.:* The Laurels, Rugby; Dartford Physical Training College. Physical Training Lecturer, Glasgow University and Training College, 1908-17; H.M. Inspector Physical Training, Board of Education, 1917-30 (resigned Sept. 1930); Principal St. Michael's, Grove Park, S.E.12 (a hall of residence for women students of Goldsmiths' College), 1931-39. War of 1939-1945, full-time Voluntary Worker, W.V.S. *Address:* Maddagedera, 6 Bell Hill, Petersfield, Hants. *T.:* 127. *Club:* Cowdray. [*Died* 6 *April* 1958.

ASH, Rt. Rev. Fortescue Leo; Commissioner of Australian Board of Missions Centenary Appeal, 1947-52; actg. Rector of St. Anne's, Strathfield; *b.* 26 Aug. 1882; *m.* 1st, 1919, *d.* of late James Page, of Eton Vale Station, Queensland; three *c.*; 2nd, 1941, *d.* of late Nugent Wade Brown, Ban Ban Station, Gayndah, Queensland, and *widow* of Ernest Holland Watts, Jarvisfield, Winton, Queensland. *Educ.:* St. Paul's College, Sydney, B.A. Deacon, 1908; Priest, 1910; Curate St. Anne, Strathfield, N.S.W., 1908-1911; Holy Trinity, South Wimbledon, 1911-14; Rector of Ravenswood, 1914-16; Bowen, 1916-18; Chaplain A.I.F., 1918-19; Rector of Mackay, Queensland, 1919-27; of Warwick, 1927-28; Bishop of Rockhampton, 1928-46. *Address:* 77 The Boulevarde, Strathfield, N.S.W. *Club:* University (Sydney, N.S.W.). [*Died* 22 April 1956.

ASHBURNHAM, Sir Fleetwood, 11th Bt., *cr.* 1661; *b.* 2 March 1869; *s.* of Sir Anchitel Ashburnham, 8th Bt., and Isabella, *e. d.* of late Capt. G. B. Martin, C.B., R.N.; *S.* brother 1944; *m.* 1908, Elfrida, *d.* of late James Kirkley; one *s.* one *d.* (and one *s.* decd.). *Educ.:* Blackheath. *Recreation:* shooting. *Heir:* *s.* Denny Reginald [*b.* 24 March 1916; *m.* 1946, Mary F. Mair; one *s.* two *d.*]. *Address:* Manor House, Brede, Rye, Sussex. *T.:* Brede 97. [*Died* 5 *March* 1953.

ASHBY, Arthur Wilfred, C.B.E. 1946; M.A.; J.P.; Director of Inst. for Research in Agricultural Economics, Oxford Univ., 1946-1952; *b.* 19 Aug. 1886; *e. s.* of late Joseph Ashby, J.P., Tysoe, Warwick; *m.* Rhoda Dean, *e. d.* of late John Dean and Rhoda Bland; one *s.* *Educ.:* Ruskin Coll., Oxford; Univ. of Wisconsin, U.S.A. Diploma (with Honours) in Economics and Political Science, University of Oxford, 1911; Ministry of Agriculture Research Scholar in Agricultural Economics, 1912-15 (first holder of scholarship); Honorary Fellow in Political Economy, Univ. of Wisconsin, U.S.A., 1915; Food Production Dept., 1917-18; M.A. (hon.) Oxon, 1923; M.A. Oxon, 1946. Senior Research Assistant, Agricultural Economics Research Institute, Oxford, 1920-24; Member of Royal Commission on Agriculture, 1919; Member of (Linlithgow) Departmental Committee on Prices of Farm Produce, 1923-24; Appointed (Impartial) Member of National Agricultural Wages Board, 1924; Member of Council of Agriculture for England, 1920-46, and Chairman, 1939-40; Member of Standing Committee of Council of Agriculture for England, 1924-46; Member of Advisory Committee, Ministry of Agriculture, from 1924; Member of Council of Agriculture for Wales, 1927-46, and Chairman, 1944-45; President Agricultural Economics Society, 1934-35 and 1952-53; Vice-Pres. International Conference of Agricultural Economists, 1949-1952; Advisory Lecturer in Agric. Economics, 1924, Prof. of Agricultural Economics, 1929-45, Univ. Coll. of Wales, Aberystwyth; Foreign Mem. Roy. Swedish Acad. of Agriculture, 1951; Mem. Scientific Agric. Soc. of Finland, 1953. *Publications:* One Hundred Years of Poor Law Administration; Oxford Studies in Social and Legal History edited by P. Vinogradoff, 1912; Allotments and Small Holdings in Oxfordshire, 1917; (with P. G. Byles) Rural Education, 1923; (with I. L. Evans) The Agriculture of Wales, 1944; contributions to scientific Journals and Reviews. *Recreations:* gardening, motoring. *Address:* 6 Frenchay Road, Oxford. *T.:* 55419. [*Died* 9 *Sept.* 1953.

ASHBY, Hugh Tuke, B.A., M.D., C.B. (Camb.), F.R.C.P. (London); Physician to the Manchester Children's Hospital, Hon. Physician to Salford Royal Hospital, Consulting Physician Princess Christian College; Lecturer Diseases of Children, Univ. of Manchester; Physician for Children to the Manchester Public Health Committee; *b.* 16 Sept. 1880; *s.* of late Henry Ashby, M.D., F.R.C.P. *Educ.:* Clifton College; Cambridge, Marburg, and Manchester Universities. Late House Surgeon, Royal Infirmary, Manchester; late Senior and Junior Resident Medical Officer Manchester Children's Hospital; late Senior Medical Officer to Out-patients Manchester Children's Hospital. President British Paediatric Assoc. *Publications:* Diseases of Children, Medical and Surgical, with

C. Roberts, F.R.C.S., 1922; Infant Mortality 1914 and 1922; revised and re-written Notes on Physiology, by late H. Ashby; Post-Anæsthetic Acidosis Medical Chronicle, 1908; The Leucocytosis of Whooping-Cough, B.M.J., 1908; Headache in Children, Clinical Journal, 1911; Anæmia of Rickets, Splenic Anæmia, Practitioner, 1911. *Recreations:* golf, tennis. *Address:* 13 St. John Street, Manchester. *T.:* Blackfriars 0206; 3 Lancaster Rd., Didsbury, Manchester 20. *T.:* 3107 Didsbury. *Club:* Clarendon (Manchester).

[*Died* 9 *Oct.* 1952.

ASHDOWN, Arthur Durham, C.I.E. 1925; Lt.-Col. I.A.R.O.; retired; *b.* 7 Aug. 1872; *s.* of John Ashdown, late of East Molesey; *m.* 1st, 1898, Anne Florence Clifford (*deceased*); one *s.* five *d.*; 2nd, 1931, Muriel Kathleen, *widow* of Capt. R. H. Gwyn-Williams, O.B.E., M.C., and *y. d.* of W. H. Phelps, Calcutta. *Educ.:* Heidelberg College. Joined Indian (Imperial) Police, 1893; District Superintendent Police, Cawnpore, Meerut, Jhansi, etc.; Principal, Police Training School, 1911-16; Deputy Inspector General of Police, 1917; Lt.-Col. I.A.R.O., 1918; Inspector General, Government Railway Police and Police Assistant to Agent to Governor General, Rajputana, 1920-23; Inspector General of Police, United Provinces, 1923; King's Police Medal, 1924; Member of U.P. Legislative Council, 1923; President St. John's Ambulance Association, U.P., 1924; retired 1927. *Recreations:* shooting, fishing, travel, motoring, winter sports, etc. *Address:* St. Cergue, St. Martin's, Guernsey, C.I. *T.:* Guernsey 8978.

[*Died* 11 *June* 1953.

ASHFORD, Sir Cyril Ernest, K.B.E., *cr.* 1927; C.B. 1919; M.V.O. 1911; Hon. LL.D. Edin.; M.A.; *b.* 17 June 1867; *y. s.* of W. W. Ashford of Edgbaston, Birmingham, and Eliza, *d.* of Thos. Lowe; *m.* 1899, Leila (*d.* 1913), *e. d.* of Alfred Allhusen of Beadnell Tower, Northumberland; three *d.* *Educ.:* King Edward's School, Birmingham; Trinity Coll., Camb. (scholar); 11th Wrangler, 1889; 1st class in Part I. Natural Sciences Tripos, 1890; Assistant Demonstrator at Cavendish Laboratory; Assistant Master at Clifton College, 1892-94; Senior Science Master at Harrow till 1903; Headmaster R.N. College, Osborne, till 1905; Headmaster R.N. College, Dartmouth, 1905-27; Chairman of Oxon Education Committee, 1938-46. *Address:* Old Barn, Kidmore End, near Reading. *T.:* Kidmore End 2118. *Club:* Oxfordshire (Oxford).

[*Died* 29 *April* 1951.

ASHMORE, Major-General Edward Bailey, C.B. 1918; C.M.G. 1916; M.V.O. 1911; *b.* 20 Feb. 1872; *s.* of late Fitzroy Paley Ashmore, barrister; *m.* Betty, *d.* of Rev. F. W. Parsons, Vicar of Tandridge, Surrey. *Educ.:* Eton; Woolwich. Entered R.A. 1891; served South Africa with "Q" Battery R.H.A.; severely wounded, Sanna's Post, 31 March 1900; Adj. R.H.A. 1904; Staff Coll. 1906-7; General Staff in the War Office, 1908-12; Military Secretary to the Inspector-Gen. of the Oversea Forces, 1913-14; European War, 1914-17; Commanded a Brigade R.F.C. 1916 (C.M.G., Bt.-Col., Commander of the Legion of Honour); G.O.C. Air Defences of London, 1917; Commander 1st Air Defence Brigade, 1920-24; G.O.C. Territorial Air Defence Brigades and Inspector Anti-Aircraft, 1924-1928; founded the Observer Corps; retired pay, 1929. Raised and commanded a battalion of the Home Guard. *Publication:* Air Defence, 1929. *Recreations:* languages, music; is a Fellow of the Philharmonic Soc. *Address:* 30 Maltravers Street, Arundel, Sussex. *T.:* Arundel 2127. [*Died* 5 *Oct.* 1953.

ASHMORE, Major Edwin James Caldwell, D.S.O., M.C.; late 3/20th Burma Rifles; *b.* 11 July 1893; *s.* of late W. C. Ashmore, C.I.E.; *m.* 1919, Dulcie Marguerite, *y. d.* of late Frederick Dransfield of Longsight House, Darton; (one *s.* killed in Burma, 1944). *Educ.:* United Services College, Windsor; R.M.C. Sandhurst. Entered Indian Army, 1913; attached 1st P.O.W. Leinster Regiment; posted 10th Gurkha Rifles, 1914; transferred Burma Rifles, 1921; served European War, France, 1914-15 (wounded); Gallipoli, 1915; Palestine, 1917-18 (M.C., D.S.O., despatches); Malabar, 1921-22 (medal and bar); Burma Rebellion, 1930-32 (bar); retired 1933. *Address:* Rose Cottage, Chideock, Dorset.

[*Died* 23 *July* 1959.

ASHTON, Lieut.-General Ernest Charles; C.B. 1935; C.M.G. 1918; V.D., M.D.; C.M.; retired; *b.* Brantford, Ontario, 28 Oct. 1873; *s.* of Rev. Robert Ashton, Principal, Mohawk Inst.; *m.* 1907, Helen M. Weir; one *d.* *Educ.:* Trinity University, Toronto. Graduated in Medicine, 1898; Medallist and Hon. Graduate Trinity University, 1898, and Trinity Medical College, 1898: College of Physicians and Surgeons Ontario, 1899; House Surgeon, Hospital Sick Children, Toronto, 1898-99; Medical Superintendent, Muskoka Cottage Sanatorium, 1899-1901; Staff Surgeon, Brantford General Hospital, 1901-15; Member of Board of Governors, Brantford General Hospital, Brant Sanatorium, Brantford; Lieut. Dufferin Rifles of Canada, 1893: Captain 1896; Major, 1902; Lieut.-Colonel, 1907-12; organised and commanded 32nd Battery C.F.A., 1913, and 36th Battalion C.E.F., 1915; Colonel, C.M., 1916; Commanded Canadian Training Brigade, 1915-16; Division, 1916-17; 15th Canadian Infantry Brigade, 1917; Brig.-General, 1917; Adjutant-General C.M. (temp.), 1918; C.M. 1919-20; Quartermaster-General C.M., 1920-22; N.D. 1923; D.O.C. M.D. 2, 1930-33; District Officer Commanding M.D. No. XI., Esquimault, B.C., 1933-35; Chief of Canadian General Staff, 1935-1938; Inspector General Military Forces in Canada, 1939-41; Major-General, 1918; Lt.-Gen. on retirement, 1941; three times mentioned for valuable services in war (overseas). *Address:* 3450 Upper Tce., Victoria, B.C. *Clubs:* Rideau (Ottawa); Union (Victoria).

[*Died* 19 *Aug.* 1957.

ASHTON, Harry, M.A., Litt.D. (Cantab.); D.Litt. (Birmingham); D.Litt. (Paris); Hon. LL.D. (B.C.); Officier de l'Instruction Publique; Chevalier de la Légion d'honneur; retired; *b.* Bury, Lancs, 31 January 1882; *s.* of Edwin Ashton and Priscilla Wrigley, Middleton; *m.* 1934, Mrs. Anne Venner Earle, *d.* of late William Venner Marriner and Mrs. Ernest Staines. *Educ.:* Bury Grammar School; Saltley College, Birmingham; Gonville and Caius College, Cambridge; University of Paris. Lecturer, University of Birmingham, 1913-1915; Professor and Head of Modern Language Department, University of British Columbia, 1915-33; Lecturer in French, University of Cambridge, 1933-46; Professor of French Literature, University of British Columbia, 1946-48. *Publications:* Du Bartas en Angleterre, 1908; Mme de La Fayette sa vie et ses œuvres, 1922; Lettres de Mme de La Fayette et de Gilles Ménage, 1924; A Preface to Molière; La Princesse de Clèves; The French Novel, Molière; etc. *Address:* 3625 Galiano Road, Vancouver, B.C., Canada.

[*Died* 12 *July* 1952.

ASHTON, Helen (Mrs. Arthur Jordan); Novelist; *b.* London, 18 Oct. 1891; *d.* of late Arthur J. Ashton, K.C.; *m.* 1927, Arthur Edward North Jordan, barrister-at-law of Gray's Inn and the Oxford Circuit. *Educ.:* London University; M.B., B.Ch. *Publications:* A Lot of Talk, 1927; Far Enough, 1928; A Background for Caroline, 1929; Doctor Serocold, 1930; Mackerel Sky, 1930; Bricks and Mortar, 1932; Belinda Grove, 1932; Family Cruise, 1934; Hornet's Nest, 1935; Dust over the Ruins, 1936; People in Cages, 1937; William and

Dorothy, 1938; The Swan of Usk, 1939; Tadpole Hall, 1941; Joanna at Littlefold, 1943; Yeoman's Hospital, 1944 (filmed as White Corridors, 1951); The Captain Comes Home, 1947; Parson Austen's Daughter, 1949; Letty Landon, 1951; Footman in Powder, 1954; The Half-Crown House, 1956; Return to Cheltenham, 1958. *Address:* Broadwell Old Manor, Lechlade, Glos. *T.:* Filkins 216. *Club:* Sesame.
[*Died* 27 *June* 1958.

ASHTON, Captain Henry Gordon Gooch, D.S.O. 1916; F.R.G.S.; late Welsh Guards; *b.* 25 Nov. 1870; 2nd *s.* of late Lt. James Walter Ashton, Royal Navy; *m.* 1906, Gladys Mary Letitia (served European War with French Red Cross, Medaille de l'Union des Femmes de France, 1915), *d.* of late J. M. Phillips, M.D., J.P., Pembrokeshire. Associate of the Institution of Naval Architects; holds the Shipwreck and Humane Society's Silver Medals and Certificates for saving life at sea; has travelled extensively all over the world; served European War, 1914-18 (despatches twice, D.S.O. (immediate award), seriously wounded Sept. 1916). High Sheriff of Pembrokeshire, 1944. *Recreations:* shooting, yachting (Board of Trade Master's Certificate), and painting. *Address:* Welston Court, Milton, Tenby, S. Wales. *T.:* Carew 227. *Club:* Guards'.
[*Died* 15 *Feb.* 1951.

ASHTON, Engineer Rear-Admiral James, D.S.O. 1918; R.N. retired; *b.* 1883; *m.* 1929, Florence Mary, *widow* of Dr. Sinclair Mason, Sutton Coldfield. *Educ.:* Bedford Grammar School; Royal Naval Engineering College, Devonport. Served European War, 1914-18 (despatches, D.S.O.); A.D.C. to the King, 1936; Eng. Rear-Adm. 1936; retired list, 1936; served at Admiralty, 1939-45. *Address:* Tullagh, Fernhill Road, New Milton, Hants. *T.:* New Milton 377. *Club:* Junior Army and Navy.
[*Died* 30 *Dec.* 1951.

ASHWELL, Lena, O.B.E. 1916; 3rd *d.* of Commander Pocock, R.N.; *m.* 1908, Sir Henry Simson, K.C.V.O. (*d.* 1932). Hon. Organiser of Lena Ashwell Concerts at the Front, 1914-1920; and Chairman Lena Ashwell Players. *Principal parts:* Mrs. Dane in Mrs. Dane's Defence, 1900; Ellen Farndon in Chance the Idol, 1902; Katusha in Resurrection; Pia and Gemma in Dante; Yo San, Darling of the Gods; Leah Kleschna; Bond of Ninon; Deborah in The Shulamite; Iris in Iris Intervenes. Manager Kingsway Theatre, produced Diana of Dobson's and Irene Wycherley. *Publications:* Modern Troubadours, also Reflections from Shakespeare; The Stage; Myself a Player, Autobiography, 1936. *Address:* 5 Belgrave Mews West, S.W.1. *T.:* Sloane 2977.
[*Died* 13 *March* 1957.

ASKE, Sir Robert William, 1st Bt., *cr.* 1922; Kt., *cr.* 1911; Q.C. 1934; *b.* 1872; *s.* of Edward Aske; *m.* 1st, 1899, Edith (*d.* 1900), *d.* of Charles McGregor; 2nd, 1909, Edith (*d.* 1918), *d.* of late Sir W. H. Cockerline; two *s.* two *d.* Received LL.D. from London University and gold medal of the University, 1900; contested Central Hull (L.), 1910 and 1911; M.P. (L.) Newcastle E., 1923-24 and 1929-45 (L. Nat., 1931-45). Lt.-Col. 1/5th Batt. East Yorks Regt. (R.); T.D.; Deputy-Sheriff of Hull three times; J.P. Surrey. *Publication:* The Law of Customs of Trade. *Heir:* *s.* Conan, *b.* 22 April 1912. *Address:* 5 Paper Buildings, Temple, E.C.4; Clevehurst, St. George's Avenue, Weybridge, Surrey. *Club:* National Liberal.
[*Died* 10 *March* 1954.

ASKURAN, Sir Shantidas, Kt., *cr.* 1942; Chairman and Director of several Mills and Concerns; ex-Member Council of State; *b.* 1882; *m.* Manibal; one *s.* two *d.* *Educ.:* at Cutch. Sheriff of Bombay, 1944. Has visited Europe nine times. *Recreations:* racing, cards, billiards. *Address:* Mahendra Bhuvan, Nepean Sea Road, Bombay 6. *T.A.:* Ravishant, Bombay. *T.:* Bombay 40288. *Clubs:* Royal Western Indian Turf, Willingdon, Orient, Cricket Club of India, Bombay Flying (Bombay); Roshanara, Chelmsford (Delhi).
[*Died* 21 *Dec.* 1950.
[*But death not notified in time for inclusion in Who Was Who 1941–1950, first edn.*

ASLIN, Charles Herbert, C.B.E. 1951; F.R.I.B.A.; *b.* 1893; *s.* of Arthur William Aslin; *m.* 1920, Ethel Fawcett Armitage; one *d.* Formerly: architect to County Borough of Rotherham; deputy county architect of Hampshire; borough architect of Derby; County Architect for Hertfordshire. Works include: Derby Central Improvement scheme; Templewood School, Welwyn Garden City (Royal Institute of British Architects Bronze Medal, 1951). F.R.S.A. 1955. Pres. Royal Institute of British Architects, 1955-56. *Address:* New Place, Queen's Road, Hertford.
[*Died* 18 *April* 1959.

ASPINALL, Sir Algernon (Edward), K.C.M.G., *cr.* 1939 (C.M.G. 1918); Kt., *cr.* 1928; C.B.E. 1926; Officer, Order of St. John of Jerusalem, 1930; Consultant Imperial College of Tropical Agriculture, 1940-49, Secretary, 1921-1940; Vice-Pres., the West India Cttee., Secretary, 1898-1938; President, W. Indian Club; Chairman, West Indian Produce Association and Davison, Newman & Co.; *b.* 1871; *y. s.* of late Robert Augustus Aspinall, J.P., D.L. and Isabella, *d.* of R. W. Selby Lowndes, Elmers, Bletchley; *m.* 1907, Kathleen, *y. d.* of late William Augustus Mason. *Educ.:* Eton; Magdalen College, Oxford (Honours Law). B.A. 1894; called to Bar, Inner Temple, 1897; A.B. in R.N.V R. Anti-Aircraft Corps, 1914-18 (Royal Humane Society's Medal, 1916); Secretary, the West Indian Contingent Committee, 1915-1919; Original Member of Council, British Cotton-growing Assoc.; Chm., Cocoa Assoc. of London, 1930-31; Hon. Sec., British Guiana Colonisation Deputation, 1919; Member West Indian Shipping Committee, 1918-19, Committee on Colonial Blue-books, 1917, Tropical Agricultural College Committee, 1919 (Hon. Sec.), West Indian Currency Committee, 1923, and West Indian Air Transport Committee, 1926; Hon. Commissioner for West Indian and Atlantic Group, British Empire Exhibition, 1924-25 (C.B.E.). *Publications:* The Pocket Guide to the West Indies; West Indian Tales of Old; A Wayfarer in the West Indies. *Recreation:* travel. *Address:* c/o Westminster Bank Ltd., 21 Hanover Square, W.1. *Clubs:* West Indian, Corona.
[*Died* 6 *May* 1952.

ASPINALL, Lt.-Col. Robert Stivala, C.I.E. 1936; F.R.C.S. Edinburgh; late I.M.S.; Chief Medical Officer, Western India States Agency and Residency Surgeon, Rajkot; *b.* 5 Feb. 1895. Civil Surgeon Ajmer-Merwara and Chief Medical Officer, Rajputana, 1935; Civil Surgeon, Sibi, 1936; retired, 1949. *Address:* Rajkot, India.
[*Died* 25 *Dec.* 1954.

ASPINALL-OGLANDER, Brig.-Gen. Cecil Faber, C.B. 1919; C.M.G. 1916; D.S.O. 1917; D.L.; *b.* 8 Feb. 1878; *m.* 1st, 1902, Frances Maud (marriage dissolved), *e. d.* of Percival Huth, Freshford Manor, Somerset; 2nd, 1927, Florence Joan, A.R.R.C. 1918 (despatches twice), *o. d.* of late J. H. Oglander, J.P., D.L., Nunwell, Isle of Wight. *Educ.:* Rugby. Entered Army (Royal Munster Fusiliers), 1900; Captain, 1908; Major, 1915; Lt.-Col. 1916; Brig.-Gen. 1917; retired with rank of Brig.-Gen. 1920; passed Staff College, 1908; employed General Staff, India, and at War Office, 1909-14; served in operations in Ashanti, 1900 (despatches, medal); South African War, 1901-2 (medal and 4 clasps); Mohmand Expedition 1908 (medal and clasp); European War, 1914-18, was chief general staff officer Dardanelles army during the evacuation of Gallipoli (despatches 10 times, Bt. Maj., Bt. Lt.-Col., C.B., C.M.G., D.S.O., Legion of Honour, White Elephant of Siam). Raised and commanded 20th (Nunwell) Bn. Hamps. Home Guard, 1940-44; also the 1st (Princess Beatrice's) Wight Cadet Bn., A.C.F. *Publications:* Military Operations, Gallipoli, vol. i. 1929, vol. ii. 1932; Admiral's Wife, 1940; Admiral's Widow, 1942; Nunwell Symphony, 1945; Roger Keyes, 1951; Freshly Remembered: the story of Lord Lynedoch, 1956. *Address:* Carrington House, Hertford Street, W.1. *T.:* Grosvenor 3787; Nunwell, Brading, Isle of Wight. *T.:* Brading 244. *Club:* United Service. [*Died* 23 *May* 1959.

ASQUITH OF BISHOPSTONE, Baron (Life Peer), *cr.* 1951, of Bishopstone, Sussex; **Cyril Asquith,** P.C. 1946; Kt., *cr.* 1938; a Lord of Appeal in Ordinary since 1951; 4th *s.* of 1st Earl of Oxford and Asquith; *b.* 1890; *m.* 1918, Anne Stephanie, *d.* of late Sir A. D. W. Pollock, K.C.M.G.; two *s.* two *d.* *Educ.:* Winchester (Sch.); Balliol Coll., Oxford (Sch.). 1st class mods.; Hertford, Craven and Ireland Scholarships, 1911; 1st Cl. Lit. Hum., Eldon Scholar, and Fellow of Magdalen Coll., Oxford, 1913; Hon. Fellow Balliol College, 1947; served in Queen's Westminster Rifles, 1914-19 (Capt.); Bar, Inner Temple, 1920; K.C. 1936; Assistant Reader in Common Law to Council of Legal Education, 1925-38, and Member of the Council, 1938-53; Recorder of Salisbury, 1937-38; Judge of High Court of Justice, King's Bench Division, 1938-46; a Lord Justice of Appeal, 1946-51; Member of the Lord Chancellor's Law Revision Committee since 1934; High Court Judge attached to General Claims Tribunal, 1939; Chairman of the Commission on Higher Education in the Colonies, 1943-44; Chairman Royal Commission on Equal Pay for Equal Work, 1944-46; Chm. Political Honours (Scrutiny Cttee.), 1952-; Member Lord Chancellor's Law Reform Cttee., 1952. Member of The Club, The Other Club; and of the Literary Society. *Publications:* Trade Union Law for Laymen, 1927; Versions from A Shropshire Lad, 1930; Life of Herbert Henry Asquith, Lord Oxford and Asquith (with J. A. Spender), 1932. *Address:* 1 Sloane Gardens, Sloane Sq., S.W.1. *Club:* Brooks's. [*Died* 24 *Aug.* 1954.

ASQUITH, Lady Cynthia; *d.* of 11th Earl of Wemyss; *m.* 1910, Hon. Herbert Asquith (*d.* 1947), *s.* of 1st Earl of Oxford and Asquith; two *s.* (and one *s.* decd.). *Educ.:* home. Secretary to J. M. Barrie, 1918-37. *Publications: novels:* The Spring House; One Sparkling Wave; *short stories:* What Dreams May Come; *biography:* Queen Elizabeth; The King's Daughters; *anthology:* She Walks in Beauty; *for children:* I wish I were You, etc.; *reminiscences:* Haply I Remember; Remember and be Glad; Portrait of Barrie. Editor: many books for children; The Ghost Book, etc. *Address:* 15 Queen's Gate Gardens, S.W.7. [*Died* 31 *March* 1960.

ASSHETON, Sir Ralph Cockayne, 1st Bt., *cr.* 1945; *b.* 13 Sept. 1860; *s.* of late Ralph Assheton, M.P., and Emily Augusta, *d.* of late Joseph Feilden, M.P., Witton Park, Blackburn, and *g.s.* of William Assheton and Frances Annabella, *d.* of Hon. William Cockayne of Rushton Hall, Co. Northampton; *m.* 1898, Mildred Estelle Sybella (*d.* 1949), C.B.E. 1934, J.P. Lancs, *d.* of late John Henry Master, Petersham, Sy.; one *s.* three *d.* *Educ.:* Eton; Jesus College, Cambridge. J.P., W. Riding, Yorks., 1888-, Lancs., 1890-; High Sheriff of Lancs., 1919; is a D.L. County of Lancaster; Lancs C.C., 1892-1949; lord of the Manor of Downham. *Heir:* *s.* 1st Baron Clitheroe, P.C. *Address:* Downham Hall, Clitheroe. *Club:* Carlton. [*Died* 21 *Sept.* 1955.

ASTBURY, Lieutenant-Commander Frederick Wolfe, J.P.; *b.* Holton Park, Prestwich, 1872; *m.* 1903, Beatrice, *d.* of C. W. Bayley. *Educ.:* privately. Entered Naval Service, 1915; hon. recruiting officer for Manchester and East Lancashire; M.P. (U.) West Salford, Dec. 1918-23, 1924-29, and 1931-35. [*Died* 28 *Dec.* 1954.

ASTLEY, Major Delaval Graham L'Estrange, C.B. 1941; D.L., J.P., Norfolk; Alderman Norfolk County Council; *b.* 7 Dec. 1868; *e. s.* of Frederick Bernard Astley; *m.* 1897, Kate, *d.* of J. Kerr-Clark; two *d.* *Educ.:* Rugby. Lieut. Welch Regt.; Major North Somerset Yeomanry Cavalry. *Recreations:* shooting, fishing, yachting. *Address:* Wroxham Cottage, Wroxham, Norfolk. *T.:* Wroxham 13. *Clubs:* Army and Navy; Royal Norfolk and Suffolk Yacht (Lowestoft); Norfolk (Norwich). [*Died* 17 *May* 1951.

ASTON, Rev. Canon Basil, D.S.O. 1916; M.A.; Hon. Canon of Salisbury Cathedral, 1950; *b.* 1880; *s.* of Rev. E. H. Aston, Rector of Codford St. Mary, Wilts; *m.* 1924, Erica, *o. d.* of late Ven. Eric J. Bodington. *Educ.:* St. John's College, Oxford. Served as Chaplain to the Forces, European War, 1915-19 (wounded, despatches twice, D.S.O.); Vicar of Melksham, Wilts, 1919-33; St. Mark's, North End, Portsmouth, 1933-37; Rector of Havant, 1937-43; Rural Dean of Havant, 1938-43; Vicar of Alderbury, 1943-1954; Rural Dean of Alderbury, 1944-53. *Address:* Long St., Sherborne, Dorset. [*Died* 9 *May* 1957.

ASTON, Bernard Cracroft, C.B.E. 1949; F.R.I.C., F.R.S.N.Z.; late Chief Agricultural Chemist (N.Z. Government); *b.* Beckenham, Kent, 1871; *e. s.* of Murray Aston; unmarried. *Educ.:* Otago University; Victoria University College. Entered service of N.Z. Department of Agriculture as chemist, 1899; retired, 1937; continuously engaged in chemical research into agricultural problems, especially regarding bush sickness in ruminants proved by him to be due to iron starvation; Hon. Sec. N.Z. Institute, 1909-1925; President, 1926-28; Vice-Pres., 1931-1934; Vice-Pres., Roy. Soc. of N.Z., 1935; President N.Z. Science Congress, 1929; awarded Hector Prize and Medal for Chemical Research, 1925; Director Empire Marketing Board's Grant for Mineral Content of New Zealand Pastures Research, 1928-33; Vice-Pres. N.Z. Forest and Bird Protection Soc., 1934, Pres. 1946 and 1947; Hon. Memb. Soc. Pub. Analysts, 1936. *Publications:* Papers on N.Z. botanical and agricultural matters. *Recreations:* gardening and botanical exploration. *Address:* (Box 40 G.P.O. C.1), Wellington, N.Z. *T.:* 26636. [*Died* 31 *May* 1951.

ASTOR, 2nd Viscount, *cr.* 1917, of Hever Castle; **Waldorf Astor;** Baron, *cr.* 1916; *b.* 19 May 1879; *e. s.* of 1st Viscount Astor and Mary Dahlgren (*d.* 1894), *d.* of James W. Paul, Philadelphia, Pennsylvania, U.S.A.; *S.* father, 1919; *m.* 1906, Nancy Witcher (Viscountess Astor, C.H., M.P.), *d.* of Chiswell Dabney Langhorne; four *s.* one *d.* *Educ.:* Eton (captain of the boats); New Coll., Oxford (represented the University against Cambridge in polo, steeplechasing, and sabres); took degree in history. Chm. of the Departmental Committee on Tuberculosis; Chm. of the State Medical Research Committee; M.P. (C.) Plymouth, 1910-19; Inspector of Quartermaster General Services, October 1914-January 1917 (despatches); Parliamentary Secretary to the Prime Minister, 1918, to Ministry of Food, 1918, and to Ministry of Health, 1919-21; a British delegate to the League of Nations Assembly, 1931; Master Worshipful Co. of Musicians, 1934-35; Chairman of League of Nations Committee on Nutrition, 1936 and

1937; Chairman of Directors of the Observer; Chairman Royal Institute of International Affairs, 1935-49; Pres. South Western Division Y.M.C.A.; late Hon. Col. Devon and Cornwall Heavy Brigade (T.); Lieut. City of London; Hon. Freeman City of Plymouth, Lord Mayor of Plymouth, 1939-44; High Steward of Maidenhead. *Publication:* (with Keith A. H. Murray) Land and Life, 1932, and The Planning of Agriculture, 1933; (with B. Seebohm Rowntree and others) British Agriculture, 1938; Mixed Farming and Muddled Thinking, 1946. *Heir:* *s.* Hon. William Waldorf Astor. *Address:* Cliveden, Taplow, Bucks; 35 Hill Street, W.1. *Clubs:* Carlton; Jockey (Newmarket); Knickerbocker (New York). [*Died* 30 *Sept.* 1952.

ATCHERLEY, Air Vice-Marshal David Francis William, C.B. 1950; C.B.E. 1946; D.S.O. 1944; D.F.C. 1942; Air Officer Commanding No. 205 Group, Middle East Air Force, since 1952; *b.* 12 Jan. 1904; *s.* of Major-General Sir Llewellyn Atcherley, *q.v.*; unmarried. *Educ.:* Oundle; R.M.C. Sandhurst. E. Lancs. Regt. 1924; No. 5 Flying Training School, R.A.F., Sealand, 1927; No. 2 Sqdn. R.A.F. 1928; R.A.F. College, Cranwell (Flying Instructor), 1929-1931; 28 Sqdn., 1932-33; 20 Sqdn., 1933-34; R.A.F. Staff College, 1935; H.Q. 16 Group (Coastal Command), 1936; C.O. 85 Fighter Sqdn., 1938; C.O. R.A.F. Station, Castletown, 1940; C.O. 25 Night Fighter Sqdn., 1941; C.O. R.A.F. Station, Hawarden, 1941-1942; C.O. R.A.F. Station, Fairwood Common, 1942; C.O. 325 Wing (N. African Campaign), 1943; S.A.S.O. 2 Group (2nd T.A.F.), 1944; A.O.C. 47 Group (Transport Comd.), 1946; Director of Air Support and Transport Ops. (Air Ministry), 1947; Commandant, Central Fighter Establishment, 1948-50; S.A.S.O., Fighter Command, 1950-52. *Recreations:* usual games and recreations; flying. *Address:* Fulford Villa, York. *T.:* York 77120. *Club:* Royal Air Force. [*Died* 8 *June* 1952.

ATCHERLEY, Colonel, Hon. Maj.-Gen., Sir Llewellyn William, Kt., *cr.* 1925; C.M.G. 1916; C.V.O. 1918 (M.V.O. 1912); *b.* 1 Mar. 1871; *y. s.* of late Lieut.-Col. F. T. Atcherley, 30th Regiment Foot of Marton, Salop; *m.* 1897, Eleanor Frances, *y. d.* of Richard Micklethwait, J.P., D.L., Ardsley House, Barnsley, Yorks; one *s.* two *d.* (and one *s.* decd.). *Educ.:* Oundle. Entered army (East Lancs Regt.) 1890; Army Service Corps, 1894; Captain, 1898; Bt. Major, 1900; Major, 1905; served Ashanti, 1895-96 (star, despatches); S. African War, 1899-1902 (despatches twice, Queen's medal 6 clasps, King's medal 2 clasps); European War, 1914-16 (despatches twice, C.M.G.); Chief Constable of Shropshire, 1905-8; Chief Constable West Riding, Yorks, 1908-19; H.M. Inspector of Constabulary, 1919-36; re-employed as H.M.I., 1940-45. *Address:* Fulford Villa, Fulford, York. *T.:* Fulford 77120. *Club:* Army and Navy. [*Died* 17 *Feb.* 1954.

ATHERTON, Ray; retired alternate U.S. Representative to U.N. General Assembly; *b.* Brookline, Mass., U.S.A., 1885; *m.* 1928, Maude Hunnewell; one *s.* one *d.* *Educ.:* Harvard College. Counsellor U.S. Embassy, London, 1927; U.S. Minister to Bulgaria, 1937; U.S. Minister to Denmark; Chief, Division of European Affairs Dept. of State, Washington, 1940; U.S. Ambassador to Canada, 1943-48. *Recreation:* golf. *Address:* 3017 O. Street N.W., Washington, D.C., U.S.A. [*Died* 16 *March* 1960.

ATHILL, Lieut.-Col. Francis Remi Imbert, C.M.G. 1918; O.B.E. 1945; D.L. Northumberland, 1946; late Northumberland Fusiliers; Sec., T.A. Assoc. of the County of Northumberland, 1928-45; *b.* 1880; *e. s.* of late Rev. Herbert Athill, M.A., formerly Rector of Digswell, Welwyn; *m.* 1912, Olive Margaret, *er. d.* of late Sir David Drummond, C.B.E.; two *d.* *Educ.:* Wellington College; Trinity College, Cambridge. Served South African War, 1902 (Queen's medal 3 clasps); European War, 1914-18 (despatches, 1914-15 Star, C.M.G.), D.A.A.G. War Office, 1916; Member of British Mission to U.S.A., 1917-18; D.A.A.G., Egypt, 1920-24; retired pay, 1926. *Address:* Harbottle Castle, Harbottle, Northumberland. [*Died* 5 *Sept.* 1958.

ATHLONE, 1st and last Earl of, *cr.* 1917; **Alexander Augustus Frederick William Alfred George Cambridge;** K.G. 1928; P.C. 1931; G.C.B. 1911; G.M.M.G. 1936 (G.C.M.G. 1923; C.M.G. 1917); G.C.V.O. 1904 (K.C.V.O. 1898; C.V.O. 1897); D.S.O. 1900; Royal Victorian Chain, 1935; F.R.S. 1937; Viscount Trematon; Personal A.D.C. to the Queen since 1953 (to King George VI, 1919-52); Hon. Maj.-Gen., retired; Bailiff G.C. St. John of Jerusalem; Governor of Windsor Castle since 1931; Chancellor of London University, 1932-55; Chancellor of Order of St. Michael and St. George, 1934-36; Grand Master since 1936; *b.* Kensington Palace, 14 Apr. 1874; 3rd *s.* of late Duke of Teck and late Princess Mary Adelaide; *m.* 1904, Princess Alice of Albany, G.C.V.O. 1948, G.B.E. 1937; one *d.* *Educ.:* Eton; R.M.C., Sandhurst. Late Captain 7th Hussars and Royal Horse Guards, and 2nd Life Guards; served Matabeleland, 1896 (despatches, medal); South Africa, 1899-1900 (despatches, Queen's medal 5 clasps, D.S.O.); European War, 1914-19 (despatches twice, C.M.G.); Governor-General of The Union of South Africa, 1923-31; Governor-General of Dominion of Canada, 1940-46. *Heir:* none. *Address:* Kensington Palace, W.8. *T.:* Western 5868. [*Died* 16 *Jan.* 1957.

ATHOLL, 9th Duke of, *cr.* 1703; **James Thomas Stewart-Murray,** Lord Murray of Tullibardine, 1604; Earl of Tullibardine, Lord Gask and Balquhidder, 1606; Earl of Atholl, 1629; Marquess of Atholl, Viscount Balquhidder, Lord Balvenie, 1676; Marquess of Tullibardine, Earl of Strathtay, Earl of Strathardle, Viscount Glenalmond, Viscount Glenlyon, 1703—all in the Peerage of Scotland. Lord Strange of Knockyn (England), 1628; Lord Percy (by writ), 1722; Earl Strange and Lord Murray of Stanley, 1786—all in the Peerage of Great Britain. Lord Glenlyon of Glenlyon (U.K.), 1821; formerly Major Queen's Own Cameron Highlanders; *b.* 18 Aug. 1879; *s.* of 7th Duke of Atholl and Louisa (*d.* 1902), *d.* of Sir Thos. Moncreiffe of Moncreiffe, 7th Bt.; *S.* brother, 1942. *Educ.:* Eton. Served S. Africa, 1900-2 (Queen's medal 4 clasps, King's medal 2 clasps); European War, 1914 (wounded, prisoner). *Heir:* *kinsman*, George Iain Murray, *b.* 19 June 1931. *Address:* Blair Castle, Blair Atholl, Perthshire. *Clubs:* Caledonian; New (Edinburgh). [*Died* 8 *May* 1957.

ATHOLL, Duchess of (Katharine Marjory), D.B.E., *cr.* 1918; Hon. D.C.L. (Oxford, Durham); Hon. LL.D. (Glas., Man., Leeds, McGill (Canada) and Columbia (New York) Universities); F.R.C.M.; *d.* of Sir James Henry Ramsay, 10th Bart. of Bamff, Perthshire; *m.* 1899, 8th Duke of Atholl, K.T., G.C.V.O., C.B., D.S.O. (*d.* 1942). *Educ.:* Wimbledon High School; Royal College of Music (Hon. Scholar and A.R.C.M., piano). M.P. (U.) Kinross and West Perth, 1923-38; Parliamentary Sec., Board of Education, 1924-29; President Perthshire Branch British Red Cross Society, 1909-45; member of Departmental Committee on Medical and Nursing Services in Highlands and Islands of Scotland, 1912; Member of Departmental Committee on Scottish Tinkers, 1917-18; Commandant Blair Castle Auxiliary Hospital, 1917-19; Member of Central Agricultural Wages Com-

mittee for Scotland, 1918-20; Member of Perthshire Education Authority and Vice-Pres. Association of Education Authorities in Scotland, 1919-24; Chm. of Scottish Board of Health's Consultative Council for Highlands and Islands, 1920-24; a substitute Delegate to Assembly of League of Nations, 1925; Member of the Royal Commission on the Civil Service, 1929-31; Chairman British League for European Freedom since 1944. *Publications:* Song-Flowers from A Child's Garden of Verses; Songs of Travel (three settings from R. L. Stevenson); edited and contributed to A Military History of Perthshire, 1660-1902 (two vols.), 1908; Women and Politics, 1931; The Conscription of a People, 1931; Searchlight on Spain, 1938; The Tragedy of Warsaw, 1945; Working Partnership, 1958. *Recreation:* music. *Address:* 58 India Street, Edinburgh; Blair Castle, Blair Atholl. *Clubs:* Forum; Queen's (Edinburgh).
[*Died* 21 *Oct.* 1960.

ATKEY, Oliver Francis Haynes, C.M.G. 1929; M.B., B.S. London, 1904; F.R.C.S. 1905; late Director Sudan Medical Service. *Educ.:* Highgate School; King's College Hospital. Order of Nile, 2nd class. *Address:* 15 Latymer Court, W.6. *Club:* Bath.
[*Died* 11 *Feb.* 1960.

ATKINS, Dr. Charles Norman, C.M.G. 1949; E.D. 1935; M.B., Ch.B. (Melb.); D.P.H. (Oxon.); Retired Medical Practitioner; lately City Health Officer, Hobart; *b.* Tasmania, 29 Jan. 1885; *s.* of Charles James Atkins, Coventry, England, and Kate Elizabeth Shoobridge; *m.* 1917, Marjorie Maybelle Walker, Hobart; three *d.* *Educ.:* Hutchins School, Hobart; Trinity College, Melbourne University; Oxford University. Served European War, 1914-18, Capt. Army Medical Corps (Australian); present Gallipoli Landing; War of 1939-45, Director Hygiene, Southern Command, H.Q., Melbourne; retired 1943, rank of Lt.-Col. City Health Officer, Hobart, 1931; retired, 1949. Pres. Tasmanian Cricket Assoc. since 1945; Chairman, Sailors' Home, Hobart, 1944-45; F.R.San.I., London, 1940. Health Broadcasts, Australian Broadcasting Commission, 1934-39; Health Broadcasts to all Australia for School Children, 1940. Member House of Assembly, Tasmanian Parl., 1941-46; Dep. Leader Opposition, 1945-46. J.P. King's Jubilee Medal, 1935; Coronation Medal, 1937; Gallipoli Star, 1915. *Publication:* Hygiene in Simple Language, Military and Civil (Melbourne), 1941. *Recreations:* cricket, Royal tennis, trout fishing, yachting. *Address:* Kingston Beach, Hobart, Tasmania. *Clubs:* Tasmanian, Naval and Military, Royal Yacht (Hobart); Melbourne (Melbourne).
[*Died* 25 *Oct.* 1960.

ATKINS, Col. Ernest Clive, C.B. 1945; D.L.; J.P. Leicestershire; *b.* 13 Feb. 1870; *e. s.* of late Arthur Atkins, Middlefield, Hinckley; *m.* 1900, Agnes, *d.* of late Rev. Benjm. Pidcock, Easton, Hants; three *s.* one *d.* *Educ.:* Bedford. Lt.-Col. late 4th Bn. Leicestershire Regt.; Chairman, 1938, Leicestershire Territorial Assoc. Served European War, 1914-17; commanded 2/5th Bn. Leicestershire Regt.; Hon. Col. 1940. High Sheriff Leicestershire, 1931. *Address:* Stretton House, Stretton Baskerville, nr. Hinckley, Leics. *T.:* Burbage 219.
[*Died* 9 *Jan.* 1953.

ATKINS, Sir Ivor Algernon, Kt., *cr.* 1921; Mus.Doc. Oxon; F.S.A.; Hon. R.A.M. 1910; F.R.C.O.; Organist and Master of the choristers of Worcester Cathedral, 1897-1950; retd. 1950; Cathedral Librarian; *b.* Llandaff, 29 November 1869; *s.* of late Frederick Pyke Atkins; *m.* 1899, *o. d.* of late Rev. Edward Butler of Llangoed Castle, Breconshire; one *s.* *Educ.:* Roath and privately. Assistant Organist of Truro Cathedral, 1885-86; of Hereford Cathedral, 1890-93; Organist Collegiate Church of Ludlow, 1893-97; Conductor of Festivals of the Three Choirs at Worcester, 1899, 1902, 1905, 1908, 1911, 1920, 1923, 1926, 1929, 1932, 1935, and 1938; President, Royal College of Organists, 1935, 1936; External Examiner in Music, London University, 1932-36; Fellow St. Michael's College, Tenbury; formerly Conductor of Festival Choral Society, Worcestershire Orchestral Society, Worcs. Ladies' Choral Society, etc. *Compositions:* Cantata, Hymn of Faith (libretto arranged by Sir Edward Elgar), Worcester Festival, 1905; Edited with Sir Edward Elgar Bach's 'St. Matthew' Passion 1911; Edited 'St. John' Passion 1929; Festival settings of Magnificat and Nunc Dimittis for Chorus and Orchestra, opening of Hereford and Gloucester Festivals, 1903 and 1904; revised edition of 'St. Matthew' Passion (Bach), 1938; 'St. John' Passion (1704) Handel, 1940; Anthems, Part-Songs, Songs. *Publications:* The Organists of Worcester Cathedral (Wor. Hist. Soc.), 1918; An Investigation of Two Anglo-Saxon Kalendars, 1928; Patrick Young's Catalogus Librorum Manuscriptorum Bibliotheca Wigorniensis (with Neil R. Ker), 1944; The Worcester Psalter, 1950; Articles in English Historical Review, Archaeologia, etc. *Recreation:* travelling. *Address:* College Yard, Worcester. *T.:* 2473. *Club:* Athenæum.
[*Died* 26 *Nov.* 1953.

ATKINS, John Black, M.A.; Founder of A Committee for Verse and Prose Recitation (known as "Poetry and Plays in Pubs"); Chm., I.E. Co-operative Wine Society, 1939-1953; *b.* 5 Nov. 1871; *y. s.* of Capt. James Bucknell Atkins, Elder Brother of Trinity House, and Mary Colquhoun; *m.* 1st, 1899, Muriel (*d.* 1931), *e. d.* of C. E. Thornycroft, Thornycroft Hall, Cheshire; two *d.* (one *s.* decd.); 2nd, 1934, Eileen, *yr. d.* of late Lt.-Gen. Rt. Hon. Sir William Butler, G.C.B., and *widow* of 15th Viscount Gormanston. *Educ.:* Marlborough; Pembroke College, Cambridge. Special correspondent of the Manchester Guardian in Turco-Greek War, 1897; Spanish-American War, 1898; South African War, 1899-1900; London Editor, Manchester Guardian, 1901-5; Asst. Editor of the Spectator, 1907-26; Editor of the Guardian, 1931-36; Editor of A Monthly Bulletin, a magazine which he founded for the improvement of public houses, 1931-48; Member of Council, Life and Liberty Movement, 1921-1925; Member of Executive, Imperial War Relief Fund, 1922-25. President Society for the Study of Addiction, 1947-49. *Publications:* The Relief of Ladysmith; Side Shows: The Life of Sir W. H. Russell; A Floating Home (with C. C. L. Ionides); Further Memorials of the Royal Yacht Squadron; Incidents and Reflections, etc.; contrib. to D.N.B., etc. *Recreation:* yachting. *Address:* 3 Burford Lodge, Elstead, Surrey. *T.:* Elstead 2255. *Clubs:* Travellers'; Royal Yacht Squadron (Cowes); Colne Yacht.
[*Died* 16 *March* 1954.

ATKINS, John William Hey; *b.* 22 Oct. 1874; *s.* of Lewis and Mary Atkins, Swansea; *m.* Fanny Winifred, 3rd *d.* of Frederic Charles Winfield of Stoke Ferry, Norfolk. *Educ.:* University College of Wales, Aberystwyth; St. John's College, Cambridge. Foundation Scholar and Wright's Prizeman; B.A. University of London; English Exhibitioner; First Class (with special distinction) in the English sections of Medieval and Modern Languages Tripos, Cambridge; Hughes Prizeman; M.A. (Lond.); Lecturer in English at University of Manchester, 1903-6; Rendel Professor of English Language and Literature, University College of Wales, Aberystwyth, 1906-40; Emeritus Professor, 1940; Fellow of St. John's College, Cambridge, 1905-11. Hon. Litt.D., Manchester, 1946. *Publications:* Contribution to Cambridge History of English Literature (vols. i. and iii.); an edition of The Owl and the Nightingale, 1922; Literary Criticism in Antiquity, 2 vols, 1934; English Literary Criticism, Medieval,

1943; English Literary Criticism: the Renascence, 1947; English Literary Criticism: 17th and 18th Centuries, 1951. *Address:* Islwyn, Aberystwyth, Cards.
[*Died* 10 *Sept.* 1951.

ATKINS, Malcolm Ramsay, C.B.E. 1935; B.Sc. (Eng.) London, M.I.C.E., M.T.P.I.; Part-time Inspector, Ministry of Housing and Local Government; *b.* 17 Mar. 1881; *s.* of late Ramsay Atkins; *m.* 1908, Susan May Sinclair Laing (*d.* 1944); two *s.* one *d.*; *m.* 1949, Elizabeth Muriel Graham (*née* Grazebrook). *Educ.:* Whitgift; University College, London. Engaged on civil engineering construction in England and Ceylon, 1901-19; Chief Engineer Calcutta Improvement Trust, 1919-36. *Address:* 29 Ovington Court, Brompton Road, S.W.3. *T.:* Kensington 1815.
[*Died* 28 *Aug.* 1960.

ATKINS, William Ringrose Gelston, C.B.E. 1951 (O.B.E. 1919); F.R.S. 1925; Boyle Medal, Roy. Dublin Soc. 1928; Head of Dept. of General Physiology, Marine Biological Association's Laboratory, Plymouth, Devon, 1921-55; *b.* 4 Sept. 1884; *e. s.* of late Thomas Gelston Atkins, M.D., Cork, and (Nenone) Mary Eliza, *d.* of Very Rev. George Mignot Innes, D.D., Dean of St. Paul's, London, Ontario; *m.* 1922, Ingaborg Jackson, *d.* of late George Miller, J.P.; one *s.* *Educ.:* Friends School, Newtown, Waterford; Grammar School, Cork; Trinity College, Dublin, Senior Moderatorships in Experimental and in Natural Science, T.C.D. 1906; M.A., Sc.D. (stip. con.), F.R.I.C.; F.Inst.P.; asst. to Univ. Professor of Chemistry, T.C.D., 1906-11; asst. to University Professor of Botany, T.C.D., 1911-20; 2nd Lt. R.F.C., 1916; i/c Experimental Section X Aircraft Depôt, Egypt; Major, 1917 (despatches twice); Lt. Home Guard, 1941; Capt. R.A.M.C., 1942; Indigo Research Botanist, Imperial Department of Agriculture, India, 1920; Meteorological Office, Air Ministry, 1943-45. *Publications:* Some Recent Researches in Plant Physiology, 1916; papers in Journal Chemical Society, Biochem. Journal, Sci. Proc. R. Dublin Soc., Reports of Advisory Committee for Aeronautics and of Agric. Research Inst., Pusa, India, J. Marine Biol. Assoc., Proc. and Philos. Trans. Roy. Soc., Automobile Engineer, Trans. Faraday Soc., etc. *Recreation:* gardening. *Address:* Old Vicarage, Antony, Torpoint, Cornwall. *T.:* Torpoint 84.
[*Died* 4 *April* 1959.

ATKINSON, Major Sir Arthur Joseph, K.B.E., *cr.* 1929; J.P.; Director of William Brown Atkinson & Co., Ltd., and of Sea Steamship Co. Ltd., of Hull; *s.* of Joseph Atkinson, J.P., of Elloughton Rise, E. Yorks; *m.* 1891, Bertha (*d.* 1948), *d.* of David Haughton, J.P. of Sutton Hall, E. Yorks; one *s.* one *d.* *Educ.:* Leys School, Cambridge. Entered father's offices, 1880; Sheriff of Hull, 1917-18; Pres., Hull Chamber of Commerce and Shipping, 1928-1929; Knight of Grace of Order of St. John of Jerusalem; Hon. Brother of the Hull Trinity House; Chairman of United Charities of Hull; raised and commanded East Riding Motor Volunteers, M.T., A.S.C.; was also Chairman, Hull Tribunal, etc. *Recreations:* motoring, travelling. *Address:* Ferriby Lodge, North Ferriby, E. Yorks. *T.A.:* Arthur Atkinson, North Ferriby. *T.:* Ferriby 5.
[*Died* 17 *Feb.* 1959.

ATKINSON, Cecil Hewitt, M.C.; physician; *b.* 28 June 1894; *s.* of Frederick Benjamin Atkinson and Elvina Percival Hewitt; *m.* Edith Marjorie Haynes; one *s.* two *d.* *Educ.:* Haileybury College; Guy's Hospital. Gazetted to the Royal Field Artillery, 18th Division, 1914; Major, 1918; commanded battery of Field Howitzers (D Battery, 83rd Brigade) (M.C. with two bars); demobilised with hon. rank of Major, 1919; returned to Guy's Hospital; appointments previously held, Out-Patient Officer, and later Clinical Assistant National Hospital for Diseases of the Heart; Neurological Registrar and Chief Clinical Assistant in Psychological Medicine, Guy's Hospital; Chief Clinical Assistant Medical Out-Patients, Guy's Hospital; served in R.A.M.C. as Registrar of General Hospital in France and at home with rank of Major up to Oct. 1941; Fellow Royal Society of Medicine; Member of Council of the York Clinic, Guy's Hosp. *Recreations:* shooting, golf. *Address:* 53 Green Street, Park Lane, W.1. *T.:* Mayfair 6080 and 2444; Thames Cottage, Flackwell Heath, nr. Bourne End, Bucks. *T.:* Bourne End 877. *Clubs:* Guy's; Flackwell Heath Golf (High Wycombe).
[*Died* 31 *Aug.* 1954.

ATKINSON, Sir Edward Hale Tindal, K.C.B., *cr.* 1932; C.B.E. 1919; Director of Public Prosecutions, March 1930-Sept. 1944; Chm. Central Price Regulation Committee, Jan. 1945-April 1953; *b.* 1878; *o. s.* of Henry Tindal Atkinson, Judge of County Courts. *Educ.:* Harrow; Trinity College, Oxford (B.A.). Called to bar, Middle Temple, 1902; Bencher, 1929; Treasurer, 1948; S.E. Circuit and Herts and Essex Sessions; sometime Member of the Bar Council; during war Lieut. R.N.V.R.; Major R.A.F. (Administrative); member Air Section, British Delegation, Peace Conference, Paris, 1919; British Secretary, International Air Commission, Paris, 1919; first Recorder of Southend-on-Sea, 1929-30; Chevalier Légion d'Honneur, 1919. *Address:* 66 Oakley Street, Chelsea, S.W.3. *Club:* Athenæum.
[*Died* 26 *Dec.* 1957.

ATKINSON, Frank Buddle, J.P.; M.F.H. Morpeth, 1902-37; *b.* 1866; *m.* 1st, 1889, Clara (*d.* 1929), *d.* of J. F. Draper, St. Heliers, Jersey; one *s.* four *d.*; 2nd, 1936, Mrs. Philip Noble, *d.* of late Percy G. B. Westmacott. *Educ.:* Eton; R.M.C., Sandhurst. Served European War, 1914-19; High Sheriff of Northumberland, 1941-42. *Address;* Gallowhill Hall, Morpeth. *T.:* Belsay 3. *Club:* Cavalry.
[*Died* 1 *Dec.* 1953.

ATKINSON, Robert, O.B.E. 1951; F.R.I.B.A.; *b.* Wigton, Cumberland, 1 Aug. 1883. *Educ.:* University College and School of Art, Nottingham. Studied in Italy, Paris, and America; Tite Prizeman, R.I.B.A., 1904; Principal, Architectural Association Schools of Architecture, 1913; Director of Education, Architectural Association Schools of Architecture, 1920-29; Architect for the Bath Improvement Scheme, Saint Catherine's Church, Hammersmith, W., The Regent Theatre, Brighton, The Picture House, Edinburgh, Gresham Hotel, Dublin, and many private and other works. *Recreations:* gardening and collecting. *Address:* 13 Manchester Square, W.1. *T.:* Welbeck 4147. *Club:* Arts.
[*Died* 26 *Dec.* 1952.

ATKINSON, Vivian Buchanan, C.B.E. 1943; *b.* 12 Dec. 1886; *s.* of late Sir William Nicholas Atkinson, I.S.O., LL.D.; *m.* 1923, Emily Etheldred (*d.* 1946), *d.* of H. L. Atkinson; one *d.* *Educ.:* Shrewsbury School. Pupil to C. J. Crosbie Dawson, Chief Engineer, North Staffs Rly., 1904-7; Asst. Engineer, North Staffs Rly., 1907-12; Asst. Engineer, Uganda Rly., 1912-20; District Engineer, Tanganyika Rlys., 1920-1930; Asst. Chief Engineer, Kenya and Uganda Rlys. and Harbours, 1930-42; Chief Engineer, Kenya and Uganda Railways and Harbours, 1942-46; retired, 1946. *Address:* Firle Farm, Limuru, Kenya Colony.
[*Died* 26 *Oct.* 1960.

AUBREY, Brigadier Herbert Arthur Reginald, O.B.E. 1919; M.C. 1915; *b.* 30 July 1883; *s.* of J. B. and F. G. Aubrey; *m.* 1920, Marion, *d.* of late J. Brooke Houghton; one *d.* *Educ.:* private; R.M.C. Sandhurst. Commanded 1st K.S.L.I., 1930-

1934: Commander 146th Infantry Brigade, 1934-38; retired pay, 1938; served War of 1939-45, Commander 212th Infantry Briagde, 1940-41; Commander North West London Sub-District, 1941-45. *Recreations:* fishing, shooting. *Address:* The Moat Farm House, Rougham, near Bury St. Edmunds, Suffolk. [*Died* 22 *Nov.* 1954.

AUBREY, Rev. Melbourn Evans, C.H. 1937; B.A., University of Wales; M.A. Oxon. and Cantab.; Hon. D.C.L. (Acadia Univ., Nova Scotia); Hon. LL.D. (McMaster Univ., Ont.); General Secretary of the Baptist Union of Great Britain and Ireland, 1925-51; *b.* 21 April 1885; *e. s.* of late Rev. Edwin Aubrey; *m.* 1912, Edith Mary Moore; one *s.* one *d.* *Educ.:* Taunton School; University of Wales; Mansfield College, Oxford; Trinity Hall, Cambridge. Minister of Victoria Road Baptist Church, Leicester, 1911-13; Minister of St. Andrew's Street Baptist Church, Cambridge, 1913-25; Moderator of the Federal Council of the Evangelical Free Churches of England, 1936-38; Select Preacher, Univ. of Cambridge, 1946; Chairman of United Navy, Army and Air Force Board, 1925-51; Member: Royal Commission on the Press, 1947; Central Committee of World Council of Churches; Vice-Pres. of British Council of Churches, 1948-50; Chm. United Cttee. of Churches for Christian Reconstruction in Europe, 1943-50; President of Baptist Union of Great Britain and Ireland, 1950-51. *Publications:* A Manual for Free Church Ministers, 1926; The Work of a Minister, 1929; various articles and sermons. *Address:* Maryland, The Drive, Godalming, Surrey. *Clubs:* Athenæum; Union (Cambridge). [*Died* 18 *Oct.* 1957.

AUCKLAND, 7th Baron (*cr.*—Irish barony, 1789; British, 1793), **Capt. Geoffrey Morton Eden,** M.B.E. 1919; Governor Star and Garter Home, Richmond; *b.* 17 Feb. 1891; *s.* of Hon. George Eden and Amy V. P. Hay; *S.* cousin, 1941; *m.* 1919; two *d.* *Educ.:* Eton. Army, 1914-22 and 1939-41; with an Engineering Company, 1923-34. *Heir:* *b.* Major Hon. Terence Eden (*see under* 8th Baron Auckland). *Address:* Wavertree, St. Peter's Road, St. Margarets on Thames, Mx. *T.:* Popesgrove 4787. [*Died* 21 *June* 1955.

AUCKLAND, 8th Baron (*cr.*—Irish barony, 1789; British, 1793), **Terence Eden,** M.C. 1917, and Bar 1918; Member of London Stock Exchange since 1922; *b.* 3 Nov. 1892; *s.* of Hon. George Eden (*d.* 1924), 3rd *s.* of 4th Baron and Amy V. P. Hay (*d.* 1926); *S.* brother 1955; *m.* 1925, Evelyn Vane, *d.* of late Colonel Arthur William Hay-Drummond; two *s.* *Educ.:* Eton. Served European War, 1914-18, King's Own Royal Lancaster Regt. and Motor Machine-Gun Corps; War of 1939-45, Major 4th County of London Yeo.; retired, 1941. *Recreation:* shooting. *Heir:* *s.* Hon. Ian George Eden [*b.* 23 June 1926; *m.* 1954, Dorothy Margaret, *d.* of H. J. Manser; one *d.*]. *Address:* 52 Onslow Gardens, S.W.7. *T.:* Kensington 4095. *Clubs:* Pratt's, Gresham, Royal Automobile. [*Died* 14 *Sept.* 1957.

AUDEN, George Augustus, M.D., M.A., B.C. (Cantab.); F.R.C.P. (Lond.); Ph.D. (Birmingham); D.P.H. (Camb.); *b.* 27 Aug. 1872; *s.* of Rev. John Auden, M.A., Horninglow, Burton on Trent and Eliza, *d.* of W. Hopkins; *m.* 1899, Constance Rosalie (*d.* 1941), *d.* of Rev. R. H. Bicknell, M.A., Wroxham, Norfolk; three *c.* *Educ.:* Repton; Christ's Coll., Camb. (Natural Science Scholar, Porteous Gold Medallist, First Class Nat. Science Tripos); St. Bartholomew's Hospital (Kirkes Scholar and Gold Medal, Lawrence Scholar and Gold Medal); Continent. School Medical Officer, City of Birmingham, 1908-37; formerly: Prof. Public Health and Medical Officer, Birmingham Univ., Hon. Psychologist, Children's Hosp., Birmingham; Sanitary Adviser to Governors Rugby School; Physician to outpatients and Resident Med. Officer, General Lying-in Hosp., Lambeth; Hon. Physician, York County Hosp. Lectr. Ontario Bd. of Educ., Ann Arbor Univ., Michigan and Columbia Univ., N.Y. Fellow Society Antiquaries, London; Foreign Member Society Northern Antiquaries, Copenhagen. R.A.M.C. (T.F.) Egypt, Gallipoli and France, 1914-19. *Publications:* translation, Rathgen, Preservation of Antiquities; translation, Guide to Prehistoric Collections Nat. Mus. Copenhagen (Official English edition); editor, Historic and Scientific Survey York and district and Handbook to Birmingham; various papers on psychological and archaeological subjects. *Address:* Repton, Derby. [*Died* 3 *May* 1957.

AUSTIN, Vice-Admiral Sir Francis Murray, K.B.E., *cr.* 1942; C.B. 1933; *b.* 1881; *m.* Marjorie Jean Stewart, *d.* of late Maj.-Gen. J. Stewart S. Barker, R.A., C.B.; two *s.* *Educ.:* H.M.S. Britannia. Served European War, 1914-19; Rear-Admiral in Charge and Admiral Superintendent, H.M. Dockyard, Gibraltar, 1932-35; Vice-Adm. and retired list, 1936. *Address:* 8 Cardinal Mansions, Carlisle Place, S.W.1. *Club:* United Service. [*Died* 19 *June* 1953.

AUSTIN, Frederic, Hon. R.A.M.; baritone and composer; Artistic Director, late British National Opera Company; *b.* London, 1872. Sang at Gloucester Festival, 1904; subsequently Birmingham, Norwich, Hereford, Worcester, Lincoln and other festivals; Royal Opera, Covent Garden; English Ring, Covent Garden; principal baritone Beecham Opera Company. Pres. Inc. Society of Musicians, 1941-42. *Compositions:* the new version (Hammersmith) of the Beggar's Opera, and its sequel, Polly; music to the Knight of the Burning Pestle, the Insect Play, The Way of the World, and other plays; Pervigilium Veneris, Leeds Festival, 1931; miscellaneous orchestral works, songs, pianoforte music, etc. *Club:* Garrick. [*Died* 10 *April* 1952.

AUSTIN, Brig.-Gen. John Gardiner, C.B. 1920; C.M.G. 1915; late R.A.O.C.; *e. s.* of John Gardiner Austin of Barbadoes, W.I.; *m.* Margaret Drew, 2nd *d.* of late Rev. Charles Moir, M.A., Glasgow; one *s.* *Educ.:* privately; R.M. Academy, Woolwich. Obtained a commission in the R.A., 1891; transferred to the Army Ordnance Department, 1909; subsequently served at the War Office and as Director of Ordnance Services to the Commonwealth of Australia; on the Staff of the 1st Australian Division at the landing and evacuation of Anzac (despatches, Bt.-Col., C.M.G., C.B., Croix de Guerre); Inspector of Army Ordnance Services, 1926-28; retired pay, 1928. *Recreations:* cricket and golf. *Address:* 800 St. Charles St., Victoria, B.C. *Clubs:* M.C.C.; I Zingari, Free Foresters. [*Died* 2 *Nov.* 1956.

AUSTIN, John Langshaw, O.B.E. 1945; F.B.A. 1958; White's Prof. of Moral Philosophy, University of Oxford and Fellow of Corpus Christi College, since 1952; *b.* 26 March 1911; *s.* of Geoffrey Langshaw Austin and Mary Bowes-Wilson; *m.* 1941, Jean, *d.* of late C. R. V. Coutts; two *s.* two *d.* *Educ.:* Shrewsbury Sch. (Classical Schol.). Balliol Coll., Oxford (Classical Schol.). Fellow of All Souls College, Oxford, 1933; Official Fellow and Tutor in Philosophy, Magdalen College, Oxford, 1935; War of 1939-45, Intelligence Corps, Lt.-Col. Junior Proctor of the University, 1949-50; William James Lecturer, Harvard Univ., 1955; Visiting Professor, Univ. of California, 1958. Officer, Legion of Merit, 1945; Croix de Guerre, 1945; *Publications:* Frege's Foundations of Arithmetic, 1950. Articles and reviews in Mind, Proc. Aristotelian Soc., etc. *Address:* Walnut Tree House, Old Marston, Oxford. *T.:* Oxford 2799. [*Died* 8 *Feb.* 1960.

AUSTIN, Roland, hon. M.A. (Bristol); F.S.A.; *b.* 18 April 1874; *s.* of late Benjamin James Austin, Reading; *m.* Anne Elizabeth Austin. Librarian of Gloucester Public Library, 1900-36; formerly of Reading and Southwark Public Libraries; Hon. Sec. Cotteswold Naturalists Field Club, 1916-19; Hon. Sec. Bristol and Gloucestershire Archæological Society, 1917-28, editor, 1923-48, Chm. of Council, 1936-39, and Pres., 1939-45; Records Officer, Gloucestershire County Council, 1936-1948; Joint Editor of the quarterly Review of Archæology, Antiquity, 1927-48. *Publications:* Some Gloucestershire Books and their Writers, 1911; Joint Author of Supplement to the Bibliographer's Manual of Gloucestershire Literature, 2 vols., 1915-16; Bibliography of George Whitefield, 1916; Bicentenary History of the Gloucester Journal, 1922; Catalogue of the Gloucestershire Collection in Gloucester Public Library, 1928; The Crypt School, Gloucester, 1539 to 1939; papers in Transactions of the Bristol and Gloucestershire Archæological Society and compiler of general indexes, vols. 21-60; contributions in Proceedings Cotteswold Naturalists Field Club, Proceedings Wesley Historical Society, Notes and Queries, The Library. *Recreations:* the study of local history, bibliography. *Address:* c/o 157 Lake Road West, Cardiff. [*Died* 8 *April* 1954.

AVELING, Arthur Francis, C.M.G. 1937; C.B.E. 1920; *b.* 10 Aug. 1893; *s.* of late T. L. Aveling, J.P., of Pettings Court, Wrotham. *Educ.:* Harrow. 3rd Secretary H.M. Legation, Prague, 1920-22; transferred to Foreign Office, 1922. 2nd Secretary, 1923; transferred to H.M. Legation, Peking, 1927; 1st Secretary, 1929; transferred to Foreign Office, 1932; appointed to Imperial Defence College, London, 1933; transferred to H.M. Embassy, Warsaw, 1934; Acting Counsellor, 1935-37; Counsellor H.M. Embassy, Brussels, 1937-40; Chargé d'Affaires to Belgian and Luxembourg Govts. in France and London, 1940-41; retired from Foreign Service, 1946. *Address:* c/o Barclay's Bank Ltd., High Street, Rochester, Kent. *Club:* Royal St. George's Golf (Sandwich). [*Died* 21 *Sept.* 1954.

AVELING, Charles, C.B.E. 1941 (O.B.E. 1933); J.P.; *b.* 8 August 1873; *s.* of William Aveling, Whittlesey, Isle of Ely; *m.* 1899, Edith Sherwood, Stainton-in-Cleveland, Yorkshire; no *c.* *Educ.:* Whittlesey. Member of County Borough of Southport, 1910-49, Alderman, 1923-49, Mayor, 1923, Hon. Freeman, 1940; Member of Company of Feltmakers, 1924; Freeman City of London, 1924; President Southport Chamber of Trade, 1911; President National Chamber of Trade, 1916, 1917; Chairman of Licensing Bench, 1927-48; Chm. Southport and District Hospital Management Cttee., 1948-57; Member Lancashire River Board, 1951; N.W. Tribunal Conscientious Objectors under National Service and Armed Forces Act, 1939-54. *Recreations:* motoring, gardening. *Address:* Balfour Road, Southport, Lancs. *T.:* 5332. *Club:* Royal Automobile. [*Died* 22 *Dec.* 1959.

AVENOL, Joseph Louis Anne, K.B.E. (Hon.) 1921; *b.* 1879; *s.* of Ernest Avenol and Renée de Hansy. *Educ.:* Poitiers; École des Sciences Politiques, Université de Paris. French Treasury, 1905; Inspecteur Général des Finances; Financial Delegate of the French Government, London, 1916-23; Deputy Secretary General, League of Nations, 1923-32; Secretary General League of Nations, 1933-1940. Hon. D.C.L. Oxford, 1936. *Publication:* L'Europe Silencieuse, 1944. *Address:* Duillier sur Nyon, Vaud, Suisse. [*Died* 2 *Sept.* 1952.

AVERILL, Most Rev. Alfred Walter, C.M.G. 1957; D.D.; Sub-Prelate Order of St. John of Jerusalem in England since 1924; Episcopal Canon (Pisgah) in St. George's Collegiate Church, Jerusalem, since 1936; *b.* 1865; *s.* of late Henry Averill, Stafford; *m.*; two *s.* one *d.* (and two *s.* decd.). *Educ.:* King Edward VI. School, Stafford; private tuition; St. John's College, Oxford (2nd class Hons. Theology); Ely Theological College. Ordained 1888; Curate of St. George's, Hanover Square, 1888-91; Curate of Holy Trinity, Dalston, 1891-94: went to New Zealand in latter year; Vicar of St. Michael, Christchurch, N.Z., 1894-1909; Archdeacon, Akaroa, 1903-9; Hon. Canon Christchurch Cathedral, 1903-9; Archdeacon of Christchurch, 1909; Bishop of Waiapu, 1910-1914; Bishop of Auckland, 1914-40; Primate and Archbishop of New Zealand, 1925-40. *Publication:* Fifty Years in New Zealand: Recollections and Reflections. *Address:* 8 Chapter St., St. Alban's, Christchurch, N.Z. [*Died* 6 *July* 1957.

AVERY, Major Leonard, D.S.O. 1918; T.D.; *b.* Queensland, Australia; *m.*; one *s.* one *d.* *Educ.:* Queensland; Wadham College, Oxford. St. George's Hospital (House Surgeon and House Physician). Started general practice in London, 1900; joined the Loyal Suffolk Hussars as Medical Officer, 1902; transferred to the Westminster Dragoons, 1913; went with them to Egypt at the outbreak of war; served in Egypt, Gallipoli, the Senousi Campaign and through Palestine (D.S.O., despatches, Order of the Nile); O.C. Officers Hospital Nasvieh, Cairo, 1919-20; D.A.D.M.S., 54th Division, 1920-1921; Member of British Colonial Film Co.'s Expedition, Kenya and Tanganyika, 1928; Member of British Museum Expedition to Belgian Congo, 1930; designer of the Rapid Transit Galloping Ambulance. *Recreations:* hunting, shooting, polo, golf. [*Died* 30 *Oct.* 1953.

AYDELOTTE, Frank, K.B.E. (Hon.) 1953; American Secretary to Rhodes Trustees, 1918-53; *b.* 16 Oct. 1880; *m.* 1907, Marie Jeannette (*d.* 1952), *d.* of George L. Osgood; one *s.* *Educ.:* Indiana University (B.A. 1900); Harvard (M.A. 1903); Brasenose, Oxford (Rhodes Scholar, B. Litt. 1908). Hon. Fellow of Brasenose College; Associate Professor of English, Indiana University, 1908-1915; Prof. of English, Massachusetts Inst. of Technology, 1915-21; Pres. Swarthmore Coll., 1921-40; Chm. Educl. Advisory Bd., Guggenheim Foundation, 1925-50, now Emeritus; Director of Institute for Advanced Study at Princeton, New Jersey, 1939-47, now Emeritus. Member, Committee on Education and Special Training U.S. War Dept., 1918; Chairman Committee on Scientific Personnel O.S.R.D., 1942; Chairman, New Jersey Enemy Alien Hearing Board, 1941-42; Member, Anglo-American Palestine Commission, 1945-46; Trustee Carnegie Foundation for the Advancement of Teaching, 1922-1953; Trustee, Teachers Insurance and Annuity Association, 1923-27; Trustee, Inst. of International Educ., 1925-41; Pres., Association of American Colleges, 1925; Trustee World Peace Foundation since 1927; Institute for Advanced Study since 1930; Member Board of Directors American Friends Service Cttee., 1940-46; Life Member Board of Managers, Swarthmore Coll.; Director and V. Pres. Phi Beta Kappa Associates, 1946-; LL.D. Allegheny Coll., 1923; Yale, 1928; Indiana Univ., 1937; New York Univ., Dickinson Coll., 1940; Pomona, Iowa, 1941; California, 1942; L.H.D. Univ. of Pennsylvania, 1924; Swarthmore Coll., 1940; D.Litt., Univ. of Pittsburgh, 1925; Oberlin Coll., 1926; Hon. D.C.L. Oxford, 1937; University of the South, 1949; member of Phi Beta Kappa (Senator, 1931-49), and American Philosophical Society (Vice-President, 1941-43); Modern Language Association of America; Am. Hist. Assoc. Council on Foreign Relations; Hon. Member American Association of University Professors; President Assoc. of American Rhodes Scholars since 1930; Member Board of Electors, George

Eastman Professorship, since 1929; Marfleet Lecturer, University of Toronto, 1938; Sachs Lecturer, Columbia University, U.S.A., 1939. *Publications:* The Oxford Stamp, 1917; College English, 1913; Materials for the Study of English Literature and Composition, 1914; Elizabethan Rogues and Vagabonds, 1913; English and Engineering, 1917; Oxford of To-day, with L. A. Crosby and A. C. Valentine, 2nd ed. 1927; Honours Courses in American Colleges and Universities, 2nd ed. 1925; Breaking the Academic Lock Step, 1944; The American Rhodes Scholarships, A Review of the First Forty Years, 1946; English Edition, The Vision of Cecil Rhodes, 1946; many articles on educational subjects. *Recreation:* golf. *Address:* Institute for Advanced Study, Princeton, N.J., U.S.A.; (home) 88 Battle Road, Princeton. *T.:* Princeton 1-0185. *Clubs:* Athenæum; Cosmos (Washington); Harvard, Century (New York); Harvard (Boston); Franklin Inn, University (Philadelphia); Nassau Princeton); Thames (New London). [*Died* 17 *Dec.* 1956.

AYLES, Walter Henry; *b.* London, 24 March 1879; *s.* of late Percy Ayles; *m.* 1904, Bertha Winifred (*d.* 1942), *d.* of Abraham Batt, Worle, Somerset; (one *s.* killed in action 1943); *m.* 1944, Jean Ogilvie, *d.* of William Middleton, Stonehaven, Kincardineshire. M.P. (Lab.) North Bristol, 1923-24, and 1929-31; M.P. (Lab.) Southall, 1945-50, Hayes and Harlington, 1950-53; resigned through ill health, Jan. 1953. *Address:* Brookwood, Kingussie, Inverness-shire. [*Died* 6 *July* 1953.

AYLESFORD, 10th Earl of (*cr.* 1714), **Charles Daniel Finch-Knightley;** Baron of Guernsey, 1703; Capt., Rifle Brigade; *b.* 23 Aug. 1886; *s.* of 8th Earl and Ella Victoria, *d.* of John Ross, Benena; assumed additional surname of Knightley, 1912; *S.* nephew, 1941; *m.* 1918, Aileen Jane Charters, *d.* of W. M. Boyle; two *s.* *Heir:* *s.* Lord Guernsey. *Address:* Packington Hall, Coventry; Diddington Hall, Coventry. *Club:* Lansdowne. [*Died* 20 *March* 1958.

AYLESWORTH, Hon. Sir Allen Bristol, K.C.M.G., *cr.* 1911; Senator, Canada, 1923; *b.* Newburgh, Ont. 27 Nov. 1854; *e.s.* of John Bell Aylesworth; *m.* 1878, Adelaide Augusta, *d.* of C. H. Miller; *o. s.* died 1919 after return from War. *Educ.:* Newburgh High School; Toronto Univ., M.A. 1875. A Liberal; called to the Bar, 1878; Q.C. 1889; Bencher Law Society, Upper Canada, since 1891; Member Alaska Boundary Tribunal, 1903; Member Canadian House of Commons, 1905-11; Postmaster-General and Minister of Labour, 1905; Minister of Justice, Canada, 1906; British Agent before the Hague Tribunal (North Atlantic Fisheries), 1910. *Address:* 21 Walmer Road, Toronto 4. *Club:* Rideau (Ottawa). [*Died* 13 *Feb.* 1952.

AYRE, Sir Amos Lowrey, K.B.E., *cr.* 1943 (O.B.E. 1918); Kt., *cr.* 1937; Hon. D.Sc. Durham, 1946; Chairman, The Shipbuilding Conference; *b.* South Shields, 23 July 1885; *er. s.* of late A. L. Ayre, J.P.; *m.* Susan Alice, *d.* of late Henry Woolgar, South Shields; two *s.* one *d.* *Educ.:* Armstrong College, Newcastle on Tyne; King's Prizeman in naval architecture, 1904-5; honours medal in naval architecture, 1905-6. Pres., Institute of Marine Engineers, 1946-48; Vice-Pres. Institution of Naval Architects; Hon. Fellow N.E.C. Inst.; represented British Shipbuilding and acted as chairman of League of Nations Committee to deal with International shipbuilding statistics, 1928; represented shipbuilding on British delegation to International Conference on Safety of Life at Sea, 1929; Pres. of Shipbuilding Employers Federation, 1930-31; Pres., National Confederation of Employers' Organisations, 1934; Chm. Board of Trade Advisory Cttee. on Merchant Shipping until 1939; Member Unemployment Insurance Statutory Committee until 1938; Member Falmouth Committee on Oil from Coal (Committee of Imperial Defence), 1937-38; Chairman Committee on Hydro-Carbon Oil Duties, 1944-45; Supervisor of Fleet Coaling, Firth of Forth, 1914-16, and District Director for Shipbuilding (Scotland) for the Admiralty during Great War; Chairman Burntisland Shipbuilding Co., Ltd., Burntisland, Fife, until 1936; Director of Merchant Shipbuilding and Repairs Division Ministry of Shipping, 1939-40; Deputy Controller of Merchant Shipbuilding and Repairs, and Director of Merchant Shipbuilding, Admiralty, 1940-44; Prime Warden, Company of Shipwrights, 1946-47; Officer of the Order of Orange Nassau, 1947; Commander of the Order of St. Olav, 1949. *Address:* The Shipbuilding Conference, 21 Grosvenor Place, S.W.1.; 6 Shrewsbury House, Cheyne Walk, Chelsea, S.W.3. *T.:* Flaxman 3807. *Club:* Athenæum. [*Died* 13 *Jan.* 1952.

AYRES, Ruby Mildred; *b.* Jan. 1883; *m.* 1909, Reginald William Pocock; no *c.* Wrote fairy stories as a child, started other stories when about twenty-five years old; wrote serials for Daily Chronicle and Daily Mirror; since then for almost every newspaper and magazine, stories afterwards published as novels; has also done work for Films in London and America. *Publications:* Richard Chatterton, V.C.; The Remembered Kiss; Castles in Spain; The Road that Bends; The Scar; The Littl'st Lover; The Bachelor Husband; The Street Below; The Romance of a Rogue; Candle Light, Spoilt Music; Life Steps In; In the Day's March; The Big Fellah; Man Made The Town; Compromise; The Tree Drops a Leaf; By The World Forgot; So Many Miles; Return Journey; Little and Good; Silver Wedding (play produced 1932); Sometimes Spring is Late; Sunrise for Georgie; Still Waters; The Lady from London; The Dreamer Wakes; Where are You Going?; Missing the Tide; Steering by a Star; Young Shoulders; The Man from Ceylon; The Man who lived alone. *Address:* Rest Harrow, St. George's Hill, Weybridge. *T.:* Weybridge 904. [*Died* 14 *Nov.* 1955.

AYRTON, (Ormrod) Maxwell, F.R.I.B.A.; Architect, now in partnership with Courtenay Theobald, B.A., F.R.I.B.A.; *m.* 1902, Elsa Marie, *e. d.* of Sir Ernest Waterlow, R.A.; one *d.* (one *s.* decd.). Principal Works: British Empire Exhibition and Stadium, Wembley; Bedford College for Women, Tuke, Oliver, Herringham and Darwin Buildings; National Institute for Medical Research, Mill Hill; Central Public Health Laboratories, Colindale, for M.R.C.; Royal Free Hospital School of Medicine Teaching and Research Labs.; Presbyterian Church of England Church House, W.C.1; St. Andrew's Church, Cheam, Sy. Bridges and road works: Twickenham, Lea Valley, Wansford, Slough Southern By-pass, bridges on road Perth to Inverness, etc. *Publication:* Wrought Iron and its Decorative Uses. *Recreations:* sketching and travelling. *Address:* 9 Church Row, Hampstead, N.W.3. *Club:* Arts. [*Died* 18 *Feb.* 1960.

B

BABB, S. Nicholson, F.R.B.S., sculptor; *b.* Plymouth, 1874; *s.* of William and Amelia Babb; *m.* Emily, *d.* of H. Pollington Hearder, Plymouth. *Educ.:* Plymouth College. Studied Art at Plymouth; National Art Training School; Kensington Royal Academy Schools; Gold Medal and Travelling Scholarship Royal Academy, 1901-2; travelled in Italy; has exhibited regularly at R.A. since 1898; executed Boer War Memorial, Grahamstown, South Africa; Memorial to Capt. Scott and Antarctic

Party, St. Paul's Cathedral; Memorial to late Professor Maitland, Downing College, Cambridge; Figures of Gainsborough and Romney, Victoria and Albert Museum; Decorative Light Standards, Horse Guards Parade; War Memorials at Bridlington (Yorks.), Tunbridge Wells, Messrs. Coutts (Strand), etc.; ideal works: The Coming of Spring, 1910; Love and the Vestal, 1912; Leds. 1913, etc. *Address:* 139 Milton Street, Brixham, Devon.
[*Died* 16 *Sept.* 1957.

BABER SHUM SHERE JUNG BAHADUR RANA, General, G.C.V.O. (Hon.), *cr.* 1946; G.B.E. (Hon.), *cr.* 1919; K.C.S.I. (Hon.), *cr.* 1919; K.C.I.E. (Hon.), *cr.* 1916; Hon. Colonel British Army, 1927; First Class of Nepalese Orders of the Star of Nepal, 1918, of the Gurkha Right Hand, 1934, of the Trisakti Patta, 1939, of Om Rama and the American Legion of Merit 1st Class, 1946; *b.* Katmandu, Nepal, 27 Jan. 1888; 2nd *s.* of His late Highness Hon. General Maharaja Chandra Shum Shere Jung, G.C.B., G.C.S.I., G.C.M.G., G.C.V.O., etc., of Nepal and H.H. Bada Maharani Chandra Lokabhakta Lakshmi Devi; *m.* 1903, Bada Rani Deva Vakta Lakshmi Devi; two *s.* two *d.* Maj.-Gen. 1901; Lieut.-Gen. 1903; Gen. 1914; Director-General Police Forces, Katmandu, 1903-29; Director-General Medical Department, Nepal, 1932-1945; Commanding General, Eastern Division, 1934; Adjutant General, 1934-48; Director-Gen. Army Provident Fund, 1934-1948; in charge of Provinces, Eastern Terai, Nepal, 1939-45; Senior Commanding General and Q.M.G., 1945-48; Minister and Commander-in-Chief of Nepal, 1948-51; Defence Minister, Feb.-June 1951. Was present at the Delhi Durbar, 1903; visited Europe, 1908; was in charge of shooting arrangements during King George V's shoot in the Nepal Terai, December 1911; and of Police arrangements during the shoot of Prince Edward of Wales, 1921; attached to the Army Headquarters, India (March 1915 to February 1919) as Inspector-Gen. of Nepalese Contingents in India during the Great War (despatches, thanks of C.-in-C. in India, K.C.I.E., K.C.S.I., for meritorious service, 1st Class Order of the Star of Nepal, Sword of Honour); European War (Waziristan Field Force, 1917) (despatches: special mention by Commander-in-Chief in India and Governor-General in Council; the Nepalese military decoration for bravery; British War and Victory Medals); at Army Headquarters, India, as Inspector-General of Nepalese Contingent during Afghan War, 1919 (despatches, G.B.E.; India General Service Medal, with clasp). Represented Nepal at Northern Command Manoeuvres, Attock, 1925; Leader of the Nepalese Contingent to the Victory Parade in London, 1946; head of Goodwill Mission to the U.S.A. and Special Mission to bestow hon. rank of Comdg. Gen. in Nepalese Army on King George VI and to present decorations to Queen Elizabeth, 1946. *Address:* Baber Mahal, Katmandu, Nepal, via India.
[*Died* 12 *May* 1960.

BABINGTON, Very Rev. Richard, M.A.; Dean of Cork, 1914-51; *b.* Londonderry, 4 Feb. 1869; *s.* of Rev. Canon R. Babington of Londonderry; *m.* 1899, Catherine Lessingham (*d.* 1934), *d.* of Rev. Robert Hamilton, Drumcree, Co. Tyrone; one *s.* *Educ.:* Foyle College, Londonderry; Trinity College, Dublin. Ordained 1892 Curate of Drumragh, Omagh, 1892-99; Rector of Moville, Co. Donegal, 1899-1905; Rector of Drumragh, Omagh, 1905-14; Canon of Derry Cathedral, 1911. *Recreations:* fishing, gardening. *Clubs:* County (Cork); Friendly Brothers House (Dublin).
[*Died* 11 *Dec.* 1952.

BABINGTON, Colonel Stafford Charles, C.M.G. 1919; D.S.O. 1918; *b.* 1866. Entered R.E. 1886; Col., 1916; retired, 1921; a Deputy Chief Engineer at War Office, 1920-21; served European War, 1914-18 (despatches, D.S.O., C.M.G., Belgian Croix de Guerre). *Address:* White Lodge, Springfield Road, Camberley, Surrey. *Club:* United Service.
[*Died* 19 *Nov.* 1951.

BACCHUS, Captain Roy, D.S.O. 1916; *b.* 24 April 1883; *y. s.* of late Col. R. S. Bacchus, Little Winters, Uplyme, Devon; *m.* 1910, Gertrude M. Fienberg, South Africa; one *s.* *Educ.:* Haslewood, Limpsfield; H.M.S. Britannia. Sub.-Lieut. 1903; Lieut. 1905; Lieut.-Commander, 1913; in command of the Grampus, served at Gallipoli, April 1915, during landing of Expeditionary Force; also engaged in mine-sweeping in the Dardanelles (despatches, D.S.O.); commanded H.M.S. Napier, 12th Flotilla, Grand Fleet; retired list, 1922; Inspector H.M. Coastguard S.W. Division; invalided and retired, 1943. *Address:* Collaton Way, Paignton, Devon. *T.:* Paignton 5500.
[*Died* 23 *June* 1951.

BACHELLER, Irving; author; *b.* Pierpont, N.Y., 26 Sept. 1859; *s.* of Sanford Paul Bacheller and Achsah Ann Buckland; *m.* 1883, Anna Detmar Schultz. *Educ.:* Canton, N.Y., Academy; St. Lawrence University; B.S., 1882, M.S., 1892; A.B., 1901; A.M., 1903; D.H.L., 1911; Middlebury College, Litt.D., 1910; LL.D. Rollins Coll., 1941. *Publications:* The Master of Silence, 1890; The Still House of O'Darrow, 1894; Eben Holden, 1900; D'ri and I, 1901; Darrell of the Blessed Isles, 1903; Vergilius, 1904; Silas Strong, 1906; Cricket Heron, 1909; The Master, 1910; Keeping up with Lizzie, 1911; Charge It, 1912; The Turning of Griggsby, 1913; The Marryers, 1915; The Light in the Clearing, 1917; Keeping up with William, 1918; Man for the Ages, 1919; The Prodigal Village, 1920; In the Days of Poor Richard, 1921; The Scudders, 1923; Father Abraham, 1925; Dawn, 1927; Coming up the Road, 1928; The House of the Three Ganders, 1929; A Candle in the Wilderness, 1930; The Master of Chaos, 1932; Uncle Peel, 1933; The Harvesting, 1935; The Oxen of the Sun, 1936; A Boy for the Ages, 1938; From Stores of Memory, 1938; Winds of God, 1941. *Clubs:* Century, Authors' (New York).
[*Died* 24 *Feb.* 1950.
[*But death not notified in time for inclusion in Who Was Who 1941–1950, first edn.*

BACK, Ivor, M.A., M.B., B.C. (Cantab.), F.R.C.S. (Eng.); Consulting Surgeon to St. George's Hospital; Surgeon to the Grosvenor Hospital for Women; late Examiner in Surgery to the University of Cambridge; *e. s.* of late Francis Formby Back; *m.* Barbara, *d.* of F. H. O. Nash of Battle, Goring, Oxon; one *s.* *Educ.:* Marlborough College (Classical Scholar); Trinity Hall, Cambridge (Classical Scholar); St. George's Hospital (University Scholar). Travelled round the world as A. K. Travelling Fellow, 1911-12. Served European War, 1914-18, R.A.M.C. *Publications:* Round the World—and Back (privately), 1913; (with A. Tudor Edwards) Synopsis of Surgery, 1921; various contributions to contemporary medical literature. *Recreation:* fly-fishing. *Address:* 8 Connaught Place, Marble Arch, W.2. *Clubs:* Savile, Flyfishers'.
[*Died* 13 *June* 1951.

BACKHOUSE, Thomas Mercer; His Honour Judge Backhouse, O.B.E. 1945; T.D. 1943; Judge of County Courts, Circuit 18, since 1953; *b.* 2 Oct. 1903; 2nd *s.* of Henry Backhouse, Balderstone, nr. Blackburn, Lancs.; *m.* 1935, Audrey Ursula Heppard, 2nd *d.* of Frank L'Estrange Heppard, Blackburn; one *s.* two *d.* *Educ.:* Denstone; Selwyn College, Cambridge. Open History Schol., Selwyn, 1922; B.A. (1st Cl. Hons.), 1925. Called to Bar, Gray's Inn, 1926; Northern Circuit, 1926-53. Commissioned 4/5 East Lancashire Regt., 1926. Judge Advocate General's Branch, 1939-45 (de-

spatches twice, O.B.E.): France, 1939-40; France, Belgium, Germany, 1944-45; Officer-in-charge, War Crimes Section, B.A.O.R., 1945; Chief Prosecutor, Belsen Trial, 1945. Colonel, 1945; Hon. Col., 42 (Lancashire) Infantry Div., R.A.O.C., T.A., 1950. *Address:* Newstead Abbey, Nottinghamshire. *Clubs:* Lansdowne; Leander; Yorkshire (York); Nottinghamshire (Nottingham).
[*Died* 16 *Sept.* 1955.

BADDELEY, Hon. John Marcus; Director of State Coal Mines, N.S.W., since 1949; *b.* Burslem, Staffordshire, 21 Nov. 1881. *Educ.:* Newcastle South Public School. President Coal & Shale Employees Federation, 1914. M.L.A. for Newcastle, 1920-27, and for Cessnock, 1927-49. Minister for Mines, Labour and Industry and Deputy Premier, 1925, 1927 and 1930-32; Chief Secretary, Minister for Mines and Deputy Premier, 1941-49. *Address:* Box 4117, G.P.O., Sydney, N.S.W.
[*Died* 2 *July* 1953.

BADDELEY, Sir (John) William, 2nd Bt., *cr.* 1922; J.P.; *b.* 24 Aug. 1869; *e. s.* of 1st Bt. and Mary, *d.* of William Locks, Hackney; *S.* father, 1926; *m.* 1892, Kate, *d.* of Matthew Shaw, Clapton; two *s.* one *d.* (and one *d.* decd.). *Heir: er. s.* John Beresford, [*b.* 23 Nov. 1899; *m.* 1929, Nancy Winifred, *d.* of Thomas Wolsey; one *s.* two *d.*]. *Address:* Heath Farm House, Walton Heath, Tadworth, Surrey.
[*Died* 28 *Dec.* 1951.

BADDELEY, Rt. Rev. Walter Hubert, D.S.O. 1919; M.C.; D.D. (Lambeth), S.T.D. (Columbia, N.Y.); Bishop of Blackburn since 1954; *b.* 22 March 1894; *m.* 1935, Mary Katharine Thomas, *yr. d.* of late Rt. Rev. Arthur Nutter Thomas, sometime Bishop of Adelaide; one *s.* three *d.* *Educ.:* Varndean Grammar Sch., Brighton; Keble Coll., Oxford (M.A.); Cuddesdon Coll. Royal Sussex Regt. and East Surrey Regt. on Western Front, 1914-19 (despatches four times, M.C. and bar, D.S.O.); Curate at Armley, Leeds, 1921-24; Vicar of South Bank, Yorks, 1924-32; Bishop of Melanesia, 1932-47; Bishop of Whitby, 1947-54; Proctor in Convocation for Archdeaconry of Cleveland, 1929-32. Hon. Chaplain R.N.Z.N.V.R., S. Pacific, 1942-45 (U.S. Medal of Freedom with palm). Grand Chaplain, United Grand Lodge of Masons (England), 1949-50; Prov. Grand Chaplain (N. & E. Ridings), 1950. Sub-Prelate Order of St. John of Jerusalem, 1955-. *Recreation:* walking. *Address:* Bishop's House, Clayton-le-Dale, Blackburn. *T.:* Blackburn 48234.
[*Died* 11 *Feb.* 1960.

BADELEY, 1st Baron, *cr.* 1949, of Badley; **Henry John Fanshawe Badeley,** K.C.B. *cr.* 1935; C.B.E. 1920; R.E. 1914; F.S.A.; *b.* Elswick, 27 June 1874; *s.* of late Capt. Henry Badeley of Guy Harlings, Chelmsford, and Blanche, *d.* of late Christian Allhusen of Stoke Court, Stoke Poges, Bucks. *Educ.:* Radley College; Trinity College, Oxford. Clerk of the Parliaments, 1934-49. Hon. Fellow of Trinity Coll., Oxford, 1948. Hon. Secretary, Royal Society of Painter-Etchers and Engravers, 1911-1921; County Director (T.F.A.) Voluntary Aid Organisation of County of London, 1917-19; President County of London Branch British Red Cross Society, 1919-23. Represented Oxford in University sports *v.* Cambridge, 1895, 1896, 1897; won Parliamentary Golf Handicap, 1901. *Recreations:* golf; line engraving. *Heir:* none. *Address:* 2 Morpeth Terrace, S.W.1. *T.:* Victoria 3403. *Club:* Brooks's.
[*Died* 27 *Sept.* 1951 (*ext.*).

BADHAM-THORNHILL, Colonel George, C.M.G. 1932; D.S.O. 1917; *b.* 1876; *s.* of late Lt.-Col. L. Badham-Thornhill of Ballinasloe, Co. Galway, Ireland; *m.* 1913, Kathleen (*d.* 1944), *d.* of late Barry Mann, Monkstown, Co. Dublin; two *s.*; *m.* 1948, Mrs. Kathleen Wastall. Served China, 1900 (medal with clasp); European War, 1914-18, France and Italy, 1915-18 (despatches 6 times, D.S.O., Italian Croce di Guerra, Brevet Lt.-Col.); Military Attaché, Peking, 1928-32; G.S.O.1. China (temp.) 1932; retired pay, 1932. *Address:* Harleyford, Crowthorne, Berks. *T.:* Crowthorne 2066.
[*Died* 30 *April* 1958.

BAERLEIN, Henry; *b.* Manchester, 1 April 1875. *Educ.:* Charterhouse; Trinity College, Cambridge. *Publications:* In Pursuit of Dulcinea, 1904; The Shade of the Balkans, 1904; The Diwan of Abu'l Ala, 1908; Yrivand, 1908; On the Forgotten Road, 1909; The Singing Caravan, 1910; Mexico the Land of Unrest, 1913; Abu'l Ala the Syrian, 1914; London Circus, 1914; Windrush and Evenlode, 1915; Rimes of the Diables Bleus, 1917; A Difficult Frontier, 1922; The House of the Fighting Cocks, 1922; Under the Acroceraunian Mountains, 1922; The Birth of Yugoslavia, 1922; Box o' Lights, 1923; The Raft of Love, 1923; Over the Hills of Ruthenia, 1923; Mariposa, 1924; Here are Dragons, 1925; The March of the Seventy Thousand, 1926; Memoirs of the Marquise de Keroubec, 1927; Mariposa on the Way, 1927: Heine: The Strange Guest, 1928; In Search of Slovakia (called in America Dreamy Rivers), 1929; Spain: Yesterday and To-morrow, 1930; And Then To Transylvania, 1931 (called in America Enchanted Woods); The Endless Journey, 1933; Belmonte the Matador, 1934; Bessarabia and Beyond 1935; No Longer Poles Apart, 1936; In Czechoslovakia's Hinterland, 1938; In Old Romania, 1940; Travels without a Passport, 1941; Travels without a Passport (second series), 1942; Baltic Paradise, 1943; The Caravan Rolls On, 1945; Leaves in the Wind, 1946; The Romanian Scene, 1945; So Many Roads, 1947; Romanian Oasis, 1948; The Problem of South Slesvig, 1948; Landfalls and Farewell, 1949; All Roads lead to People, 1951; The Squire of Piccadilly, 1951; Laugh, and the ghosts laugh with you . . ., 1951; Today in Greece, 1954; Travel News: Madeira, Luxembourg, 1955; Denmark, Land of Islands, 1956; Finland, Land of a Thousand Lakes, 1957; Malta, the British Riviera, 1957; Portugal the Land of Wine and Sunshine, 1958. *Recreations:* primitive pleasures.
[*Died* 9 *Dec.* 1960.

BAGNALL, Sir John, Kt., *cr.* 1936; unofficial member of Executive, 1935-42, and Legislative, 1926-39, Councils of the Straits Settlements; late Chairman and Managing Director of The Straits Trading Co., Ltd., Singapore; *b.* 23 May 1888; *s.* of late Albert Edward Bagnall, Liverpool; *m.* 1934, Lynn, *widow* of Major Alan Turnbull, D.S.O., M.C.; no *c*: *Educ.:* Liverpool Institute, Liverpool. *Address:* Bretton Woods, Killarney, Johannesburg, S. Africa.
[*Died* 29 *Sept.* 1954.

BAGNALL-WILD, Brig.-Gen. Ralph Kirkby, C.M.G. 1918; C.B.E. 1919; D.L., J.P. Notts; R.A.F., retired; *b.* 18 Aug. 1873; *s.* of late Ralph Bagnall Bagnall-Wild; *m.* 1897, Maida Devereux (*d.* 1928); one *s.* *Educ.:* Hermitage School, Bath; Royal Military Academy, Woolwich. Commission Royal Engineers, 1893; Director Aeronautical Inspection, Air Ministry, 1919-21; Director of Research, Air Ministry, 1921-24. Past Pres. Institution Automobile Engineers; Past Chairman Royal Aeronautical Soc. *Address:* 35 Florence Rd., West Bridgford, Notts. *T.:* Nottingham 89542.
[*Died* 12 *Oct.* 1953.

BAGSHAWE, Edward Leonard, C.I.E. 1916; D.S.O. 1918; O.B.E. 1919; *b.* 15 Nov. 1876; 3rd *s.* of late C. W. Bagshawe; *m.* 1919, Anne Josephine Lambart, *y. d.* of late Lt.-Col. J. Sladen, and late Lady Sarah Sladen. *Educ.:* St. Cuthbert's College, Ushaw; Dover College; R.I.E. College, Coopers Hill. Entered Telegraph Service, 1897;

Chief Engineer, Indian Telegraph Dept., 1925-1930; retired, 1930; served European War (temp. R.E.), (Mesopotamia), 1915-19 (C.I.E., D.S.O., O.B.E., despatches seven times, granted rank of Lieut.-Colonel). *Address:* The Old Rectory, Tarrant Keynston, Blandford, Dorset. *T.:* Blandford 319. [*Died* 16 *Dec.* 1955.

BAGSHAWE, Francis John Edward, C.M.G. 1937; M.B.E. 1919; Commander Order of St. Sylvester; farmer; *b.* 3 Sept. 1877; *s.* of late Judge W. H. G. Bagshawe, Q.C.; *m.* 1903, Maud Edith, *d.* of late Tallis Hurly; three *s.* five *d.* *Educ.:* Beaumont College. Matabele and Mashona Campaign, 1896-97; Boer War, 1899-1902; European War, 1914-18; Rhodesian Mounted Police, 1896-97; South African Constabulary, 1901-3; Magistrate Orange River Colony, 1903-4; farmer, Orange Free State, 1903-13; Editor, Farmer's Weekly, O.F.S., 1913-14; 5th Mounted Bde., 1914-15; 1st Cape Corps, 1915-17; Army Intelligence and Political Officer, 1917-18; Civil Servant, Tanganyika Territory, 1918-37; Senior Provincial Commissioner, Tanganyika Territory, 1926-37; Major S.R. Internment Camp Corps, 1941-46; Permanent Out-Pensioner Chelsea Hospital since 1907. *Publications:* numerous reports on native affairs, economics, land and ethnology in East Africa. *Recreations:* shooting, golf. *Address:* Oakes, Ruwa Siding, Box 1222, Salisbury, Southern Rhodesia. [*Died* 23 *July* 1953.

BAILEY, Arthur Charles John, C.I.E. 1931; *b.* 2 Oct. 1886; *s.* of late J. C. Bailey; *m* 1916, Heather Mary Halliday Hickie; two *s.* *Educ.:* St. Andrew's College and King's Hospital, Dublin. Joined Indian Police, 1906; Inspector General of Police, Bombay Presidency, 1940-42; retired, 1942; King's Police Medal, 1920. *Address:* Bere Hill Flat, Whitchurch, Hants. *T:* 2119 Whitchurch (Hants). [*Died* 10 *July* 1951.

BAILEY, Cyril, C.B.E. 1939 (M.B.E. 1918); F.B.A.; M.A.; D.Litt. (Oxford, Durham, and Univ. of Wales); LL.D. (Glas.); D.L. (Calif.); Hon. Fell. of Balliol Coll. and of Lady Margaret Hall, Oxford; *b.* 13 April 1871; *e. s.* of late Alfred Bailey, M.A., barrister, formerly Fellow of Univ. Coll., Oxford; *m.* 1912, Gemma, *d.* of late Dr. Creighton, Bishop of London; one *s.* three *d.* *Educ.:* St. Paul's School, London (Scholar); Balliol Coll., Oxford (Scholar). Hertford and Craven (University) Scholarships, 1891; Fellow of Exeter College, 1894-1902; Fellow and Classical Tutor of Balliol College, 1902-1939; Jowett Fellow, 1916-32; Jowett Lecturer, 1932-39; Public Orator, Oxford University, 1932-39; Governor of St. Paul's School, 1901-54; President, Old Pauline Club, 1919-30; President of the Classical Association, 1934; Mem. Berkshire Educ. Cttee., 1943-52; Member of Council of Lady Margaret Hall, Oxford, 1915-54; Governor of Wantage School; Delegate of the University Press, 1920-46; Ministry of Munitions (Labour Department), 1915-18. *Publications:* Text of Lucretius (Bibliotheca Oxoniensis), 1898; Religion of Ancient Rome, 1907; Translation of Lucretius, 1910; Ovid, Fasti III., 1921; edited The Legacy of Rome, 1925; Epicurus, the extant remains, 1926; The Greek Atomists and Epicurus, 1928; Phases in the Religion of Ancient Rome, 1932; Religion in Virgil, 1935; Francis Fortescue Urquhart, 1936; Commentary on Lucretius, 1947; Hugh Percy Allen, 1948. *Recreations:* cricket, mountaineering, walking, bicycling. *Address:* The Mulberries, East Hanney, Wantage. *T.:* West Hanney 231. *Club:* Alpine. [*Died* 5 *Dec.* 1957.

BAILEY, Ernest Edmond, C.B. 1951; C.B.E. 1946; Principal Finance Officer, Ministry of Food, from 1947; *b.* 29 May 1907; *e. s.* of late Ernest Aston Bailey and of Frances Eileen Bailey, J.P., Otahuhu, Auckland, N.Z.; *m.* 1933, Helen Margaret, *o. d.* of late Sir Robert Laurie Morant, K.C.B.; two *s.* two *d.* *Educ.:* Sacred Heart College, Auckland; Auckland University College (LL.M. and Senior Scholar); Magdalen College, Oxford (D.Phil.). Barrister and Solicitor, Supreme Court of N.Z., 1928; Rhodes Scholar, 1929; Solicitor (England), 1936; Barrister, Middle Temple, 1945. Served War of 1939-45 : Deputy Director General, Middle East Supply Centre, Cairo, 1942-44; Director General, 1945; Principal Assistant Secretary, Minister Resident's Office, Cairo, 1945. Under Secretary (Finance), Ministry of Food, 1946. *Recreations:* gardening, travelling. *Address:* Chinthurst, Shalford, Surrey. *T.:* Guildford 61187. *Club:* Travellers'. [*Died* 30 *April* 1956.

BAILEY, Lt.-Col. Frederick George Glyn; R.A., Retired; *b.* 1880: 2nd *s.* of Sir Jas. Bailey, M.P., D.L., J.P.; *m.* 1908, Janet L. Mackay, 2nd *d.* of 1st Earl of Inchcape, G.C.S.I., G.C.M.G., K.C.I.E.; two *s.* (*e. s.* killed in Italy, May 1944), two *d.* *Educ.:* Harrow; Cambridge. Served S. African war, 1900-1, with Imperial Yeomanry; direct commn. R.F.A., 1900; served European War, 1914-19, with 2 divn. B.E.F. in France and Belgium; and in Syria; Brevet Lt.-Col. 1915; retired, 1919; High Sheriff Wilts. 1937 and 1941. *Address:* Lake House, Salisbury, Wilts. *T:* Amesbury 2138. *Clubs:* Cavalry, Boodle's. [*Died* 26 *Oct.* 1951.

BAILEY, Sir George Leader, K.B.E., *cr.* 1952 (C.B.E. 1937); Resident Director in Greece of Lake Copais Co. Ltd.; *b.* 8 June 1882; *s.* of late Benjamin Charles Bailey, Superintendent Indian Telegraphs; *m.* 1914, Alice Mary, *d.* of Rev. Canon Henry Andrew; one *s.* *Educ.:* Ardingly College. Lieutenant 3rd Battn. Suffolk Regiment, 1899-1903; South African War, 1901-2 (Queen's medal with four clasps); served as British Delegate on Inter-Allied Commission to report on agricultural development of land behind the fighting lines in Macedonia, 1917; acted as Hon. Adviser and Inspector General to Commission appointed by Greek Government for concentration of foodstuffs in Greece during European War; Chevalier of Royal Order of Redeemer of Greece, 1917. Agricultural Adviser to Office of Minister of State, Middle East, and to Middle East Supply Centre, 1942-44; Hon. Agricultural Adviser to British Economic Mission to Greece, 1946-47. *Address:* c/o The Lake Copais Co., Winchester House, Old Broad St., E.C.2.; Aliartos, Greece. *Clubs:* Travellers', Royal Automobile. [*Died* 12 *Jan.* 1953.

BAILEY, Miss (Irene) Temple; author; *b.* Petersburg, Va.; *d.* of Milo Varnum Bailey and Emma Sprague; unmarried. *Educ.:* Mrs. English's School, Richmond, Va.; College courses. Presbyterian. *Publications:* Glory of Youth, 1913; Contrary Mary, 1915; Mistress Anne, 1917; Adventures in Girlhood, 1917; The Tin Soldier, 1919; The Trumpeter Swan, 1920; The Gay Cockade, 1921; The Dim Lantern, 1923; Peacock Feathers, 1924; The Holy Hedge, 1925; The Blue Window, 1926; Wallflowers, 1927; Silver Slippers, 1928; Burning Beauty, 1929; Wild Wind, 1930; So This is Christmas, 1931; Little Girl Lost, 1932 ; Enchanted Ground, 1933; Fair as the Moon, 1934; The Radiant Tree, 1935; I've been to London, 1937; Tomorrow's Promise, 1938; Blue Cloak, 1941; Pink Camellia, 1942; Red Fruit, 1945; short stories, serials, and essays to leading magazines. *Clubs:* Chevy Chase, Arts, Washington (Washington); Authors' (Boston). [*Died* 6 *July* 1953.

BAILEY, John, C.M.G. 1938; *b.* 20 May 1889; *s.* of late John Bailey, Parkside, Salop; *m.* 1921, Eileen, *e. d.* of Brigadier-General R. C. Stevenson, R.A. *Educ.:*

Petersfield (Churcher's College); Bonn. Student Interpreter in Siam, 1907; served in various consular capacities in Siam and Netherlands-India; H.M. Consul General, Bangkok, 1933-38; worked in Aliens Dept., Home Office, 1939-40; Deputy Organizer, Exmouth A.R.P., 1941; Assisted Siamese Editor, B.B.C., 1942-44; Siamese Editor, B.B.C., 1944-45. *Address:* 16 Stanford Court, Cornwall Gardens, S.W.7. *T.:* Western 4006. [*Died* 15 *July* 1957.

BAILEY, John E., J.P.; Farmer and Property Owner; M.P. for West Down, Northern Ireland, since 1938; Junior Whip, N. Ireland Govt. since 1946; Parliamentary Secretary to Minister of Agriculture, N.I., since Oct. 1956; *b.* 1897; *s.* of Matthew and Rebecca Bailey; *m.* 1918, Martha Smith; one *s.* four *d.* *Educ.:* Private School. Practical Farmer and has always been interested in the mechanisation of agriculture. *Recreations:* motoring, golf, and reading. *Address:* Fort House, Moybrick, Dromara, Co. Down. *T.:* Dromara 205. [*Died* 14 *Nov.* 1958.

BAILEY, Rev. J(ohn) H(enry) Shackleton, D.D. (Oxon); Vicar of St. Michael's-on-Wyre, 1938-52; *b.* 1875; *e. s.* of W. de V. Bailey; *m.* 1904, Rosamond Maud (*d.* 1949), *y. d.* of late W. Giles, Necton, Norf.; three *s.* one *d.* *Educ.:* St. Paul's School; Worcester College, Oxford. 1st Class Hons. in Maths., Oxford, 1897; ordained 1898; Chaplain and Naval Instructor, Royal Navy, 1900-9; First Chaplain of H.M.S. Dreadnought; served also in H.M.S. King Edward VII., Good Hope, etc.; Head of Modern Side, Rossall School, 1909-12; Headmaster, Lancaster Royal Grammar School, 1912-39; Rural Dean of Garstang, 1947-50; Vice-President and Chairman of Council of Westfield War Memorial Village, 1934-49; Provincial Grand Chaplain, W. Lancs, 1919. *Publication:* Elementary Analytical Conics, 1936. *Recreations:* motoring, chess. *Address:* Holmwood, 37 Upper Olland St., Bungay, Suffolk. [*Died* 13 *April* 1956.

BAILEY, Kenneth Claude; Fellow of Trinity College, Dublin, since 1926; Registrar of University of Dublin since 1942; *b.* 9 May 1896; *s.* of late C. W. Bailey; *m.* 1923, Dorothy, *d.* of F. B. Lavelle, Senior Inspector of National Schools, Ireland; one *d.* *Educ.:* St. Andrew's College, Dublin; Trinity College, Dublin (Classical Scholar); University of Toulouse. Served European War, 1915-19; Studentship and double Senior Moderatorship, T.C.D., 1921; M.A. (Dublin) 1922; Docteur de l'Université de Toulouse, 1922; Member of the Royal Irish Academy, 1925; Sc.D. (Dublin), 1925; Litt.D. (Dublin), 1929; Junior Dean, 1931-42, Professor of Physical Chemistry, 1935-47, in University of Dublin. *Publications:* Etymological Dictionary of Chemistry and Mineralogy (with Dr. Dorothy Bailey), 1929; The Elder Pliny's Chapters on Chemical Subjects, Vol. I. 1929, Vol. II. 1932; The Retardation of Chemical Reactions, 1937; History of Trinity College, Dublin from 1892 to 1945, 1947; Papers on the inhibition of chemical reactions and other chemical subjects, in the scientific publications of the Chemical Society, the Royal Dublin Society, the Royal Irish Academy, l'Académie Française, etc.; Notes on the Natural History of Pliny in Hermathena, 1926 and 1931. *Recreations:* golf, philately. *Address:* Trinity College, Dublin. *T:* Dublin 92448. [*Died* 18 *Sept.* 1951.

BAILEY, Liberty Hyde; botanist, horticulturist, and author; *b.* S. Haven, Mich., 15 Mar. 1858; *s.* of Liberty Hyde Bailey and Sarah Harrison; *m.* 1883, Annette Smith (*d.* 1938); one *d.* (and one *d.* decd.). Professor of Horticulture, Cornell Univ., 1888-1903; dean and dir., Coll. of Agriculture, 1903-13; Director Bailey Hortorium of Cornell University, 1935-51. *Publications:* Annals of Horticulture, 1889-93 (5 vols.); Manual of Cultivated Plants; The Holy Land; many books on farming, gardening, horticulture, and social problems. Editor, Rural Science Series; Rural Manual Series, Cyclopedia of American Agriculture, 4 vols., Standard Cyclopedia of Horticulture, 3 vols., etc. *Address:* Ithaca, N.Y. [*Died* 25 *Dec.* 1954.

BAILEY, Sir Reginald (Greenwood), Kt., *cr.* 1949; C.B.E. 1944; Adviser to the Board of Trade on Wool Exports since 1939; *b.* 1 June 1894; *s.* of late Greenwood Bailey, Bradford, and Hannah (*née* Clough); *m.* 1919, Hjördis Maria Fredrikson; one *s.* one *d.* *Educ.:* Belle Vue High School, Bradford; Bradford Technical Coll. Exec. Member and Past Pres. British Wool Federation; Exec. member, Wool Textile Delegation; Member of the Council, Bradford Chamber of Commerce; Past Pres., Bradford Textile Society; Hon. Consul for Sweden; Hon. Vice-Consul for Finland; F.T.I.; F.R.G.S.; M.I.Ex. *Address:* Glenholme, Shipley, Yorkshire. *T.:* Shipley 54626. [*Died* 9 *Feb.* 1953.

BAILEY, Richard William, F.R.S. 1949; D.Sc.(Eng.); M.I.Mech.E.; Consulting Research Engineer, Research Department, Metropolitan Vickers Electrical Co. Ltd., Trafford Park, Manchester; *b.* 6 Jan. 1885; *s.* of James William Bailey and Ann (*née* Durley); *m.* 1909, Mary Florence Dormer Alderman; two *d.* Whitworth Scholar; A.M.I.Mech.E. 1922; M.I.Mech.E. 1936; Member of Council of Institution of Mechanical Engineers (Vice-Pres. March 1949, President 1954). Hon. Assoc. Manchester College Technology; Fellow, Queen Mary College (London Univ.). *Address:* 20 Grange Avenue, Hale, Altrincham, Cheshire; Metropolitan Vickers Electrical Co. Ltd., Trafford Park, Manchester. [*Died* 4 *Sept.* 1957.

BAILEY, Miss Temple; *see* Bailey, Miss I. T.

BAILIE, Thomas; J.P. Co. Down; *b.* Boston, U.S.A., 15 July 1885. British parentage; *s.* of William Baillie and Margaret Crooks, Newtonards, Co. Down; *m.* 1908, Jean Fowler, Bangor; one *s.* four *d.* *Educ.:* Ward School, Bangor, Co. Down. Member Bangor Borough Council, 1913-53; Alderman, 1931; subseq. Mayor. Formerly M.P. (U.) for North Down in N. Ireland Parliament; Dep. Speaker and Chm. of Cttees., 1945-48. Chairman of the Hospital Management Cttee. for North Down; Member N. Ireland Hospitals' Authority, 1948-. Freeman of Bangor. *Recreations:* golfing and bowling. *Address:* Ardmara, 99 Clifton Road, Bangor, Co. Down. *T.A.:* Alderman Bailie, Bangor, Down. *T.:* Bangor 666. [*Died* 22 *Nov.* 1957.

BAILLIE, Rev. Albert Victor, K.C.V.O., *cr.* 1932 (C.V.O. 1921); D.D.; M.A.; a Chaplain to the Queen since 1952 (to King George VI, 1944-52); *b.* 5 Aug. 1864; 3rd *s.* of late Evan Peter Montagu Baillie; *m.* 1898, Hon. Constance Elizabeth Hamilton-Russell (*d.* 1924), 5th *d.* of 8th Viscount Boyne; one *s.* *Educ.:* Marlborough; Trinity College, Cambridge. Formerly Domestic Chaplain to the Bishop of Rochester; Chancellor and Hon. Canon Collegiate Church, Coventry, 1908; Rural Dean and Rector of Rugby, 1898-1912; Vicar of St. Michael, Coventry, 1912-17; Hon. Canon of Worcester, 1905-8; Dean of Windsor, 1917-44; Domestic Chaplain to the King, 1917-44. *Publications:* (with Hector Bolitho): Editor of Letters of Lady Augusta Stanley, 1927, and Later Letters of Lady Augusta Stanley, 1929; A Victorian Dean: A Memoir of Arthur Stanley, 1930; My First Eighty Years (autobiography), 1951. *Address:* St. Mary's, Baldock, Herts. *T.:* Baldock 3. [*Died* 3 *Nov.* 1955.

BAILLIE, Rev. Professor Donald Macpherson, M.A., D.D.; Professor of Systematic Theology in the University of St. Andrews since 1935; *b.* 5 Nov. 1887; *s.* of Rev. John Baillie and Annie Macpherson. *Educ.:* Inverness Royal Academy; Universities of Edinburgh, Marburg and Heidelberg; New College, Edinburgh. M.A. (Edin.), 1909 with first class honours in Mental Philosophy; J. E. Baxter Scholar of Edinburgh University, 1910-12; Hamilton Fellow of Edinburgh University, 1912-15; Assistant to the Professor of Moral Philosophy, 1911-14; Ordained, 1918; Minister of Bervie United Free Church, 1918-23; St. John's, Cupar, 1923-30; St. Columbia's, Kilmacolm, 1930-1934; Examiner in Divinity and Ecclesiastical History to St. Andrews University, 1921-24; Examiner in Divinity to Edinburgh University, 1933-35; Kerr Lecturer in Glasgow, 1926; Hon. D.D. St Andrews, 1933; lectured in America, 1924 and 1933; Forwood Lecturer in the Philosophy of Religion in Liverpool University, 1947; Moore Lecturer in San Francisco Theological Seminary, 1952. *Publications:* The Christian Faith in Outline, by Friedrich Schleiermacher, translated from the German with the two editions on opposite pages, 1922; Faith in God and its Christian Consummation (Kerr Lectures), 1927; God was in Christ: an Essay on Incarnation and Atonement, 1948; co-operated in the translation of Schleiermacher's The Christian Faith, 1928; various lectures and articles in composite works and in journals. *Address:* The Crask, St. Andrews, Fife. *T.:* 789.

[*Died* 31 *Oct.* 1954.

BAILLIE, Very Rev. John, C.H.1957; M.A., D.Litt., D.D., S.T.D.; LL.D.; An Extra Chaplain to the Queen in Scotland since 1956; Chaplain to the Queen in Scotland, 1952-56 (to King George VI, 1947-52); Principal of New College, Edinburgh and Dean of the Faculty of Divinity, 1950-56; Professor of Divinity in the University of Edinburgh, 1934-56; Pres., Univ. of Edinburgh Graduates Assoc., 1958-; *b.* Gairloch, Scotland, 26 March 1886; *e.s.* of late Rev. John Baillie and late Annie Macpherson; *m.* 1919, Florence Jewel, *e. d.* of late Richard Fowler, Mount Vernon, Caterham; one *s.* *Educ.:* Inverness Royal Academy (Gold Medallist in Classics); Edinburgh University (M.A. with First Class Hons. in Mental Philosophy, 1908; D.Litt. 1928; Hon. D.D. 1930); New College, Edinburgh; Universities of Jena and Marburg; Vans Dunlop Scholar, Rhind Scholar, and Baxter Scholar at Edinburgh University; Bruce of Grangehill Prizeman; Assistant in Philosophy, Edinburgh University, 1909-12; Examiner in Philosophy, Edinburgh University, 1917-19; Assistant Minister, Broughton Place Church, Edinburgh, 1912-14; served under Y.M.C.A. with British Armies in France, 1915-19; Assistant Director of Education on Lines of Communication, 1917-19 (despatches); Richards Prof. of Christian Theology in Auburn Theological Seminary, U.S.A., 1919-27; Prof. of Systematic Theology, Emmanuel College, Univ. of Toronto, 1927-30; Roosevelt Professor of Systematic Theology in Union Theological Seminary, New York City, 1930-34. *Hon. degrees:* D.D.: Victoria Univ., Toronto, 1930; Yale Univ., 1934; Princeton, 1948; LL.D. Muhlenberg Coll., U.S.A., 1948; L.H.D., Wooster Coll., Ohio, 1954; S.T.D. Dickinson College, U.S.A., 1933; D.Theol., Strasbourg, 1956; D.Theol., Budapest, 1956; D.Theol., Jena, 1958; Ely Lecturer Union Theological Seminary, New York, 1929; Dudleian Lectr., Harvard Univ., 1931; Deems Philosophical Lecturer in New York Univ., 1931-1932; Ayer Lecturer in Rochester-Colgate Theological Seminary, 1932; Swander Lecturer in Theological Seminary of the Reformed Church, Lancaster, U.S.A., 1932, and 1934. Gunning Lecturer in Edinburgh University, 1934-36; Nathaniel Taylor Lecturer in Yale University, 1936; Special Lecturer in King's College, London, 1937; Stone Lecturer in Princeton Seminary, U.S.A., 1941; Robertson Lecturer in Glasgow University, 1941; Riddell Lecturer in Durham University, 1945; Bampton Lectr., Columbia Univ., N.Y., 1954; Birks Lectr., McGill Univ., Montreal, 1954; Fosdick Visiting Professor, Union Theological Seminary, New York, 1956-57; Gifford Lectr. Univ. of Edinburgh, 1960-62. Member Edinburgh University Court, 1946-50; Examiner in Theology, Glasgow University, 1935-38; Director of Religious and Educational Activities with Y.M.C.A. with B.E.F. 1940; visited United States, Feb. and March 1941, speaking about the War. Convener of Church of Scotland Commission on the Interpretation of God's Will in the Present Crisis, 1940-45; Moderator of the General Assembly of the Church of Scotland, 1943-1944; Co-Pres., World Council of Churches, 1954-. Mem. Amer. Philosophical Assoc.; Mem. Amer. Theological Soc. (Pres. 1930-1931); Hon. Pres. Soc. for the Study of Theology, 1952-54. *Publications:* The Roots of Religion in the Human Soul, 1926; The Interpretation of Religion, 1929; The Place of Jesus Christ in Modern Christianity, 1929; And the Life Everlasting, 1934; A Diary of Private Prayer, 1936; Our Knowledge of God, 1939; Invitation to Pilgrimage, 1942; The Prospects of Spiritual Renewal, 1943; What is Christian Civilization, 1945; Belief in Progress, 1950; The Human Situation, 1950; contributed to Contemporary American Theology, vol. II., 1933; Co-editor of Revelation, 1937; Natural Science and the Spiritual Life, 1951; A Diary of Readings, 1955; The Idea of Revelation in Recent Thought, 1956. *Recreations:* angling, travel, chess, collecting engravings, etc. *Address:* 9 Whitehouse Terrace, Edinburgh. *T.:* 42647. *Clubs:* Authors'; New (Edinburgh).

[*Died* 29 *Sept.* 1960.

BAILLIE, John Gilroy; *b.* 3 Sept. 1896; *m.* 1927; one *s.* one *d.* Asst. Clerk, H.M. Office of Works, 1914; served European War, 1914-19; returned to Office of Works; transferred to F.O., Nov. 1919; to Consular Service and Appt. Probationer Vice-Consul in the Levant, 1924; served in Constantinople (now Istanbul), Athens, Piraeus, Smyrna, Bushire, Ahwaz, Tabriz, Buenos Aires. Acting Consul-General at Buenos Aires, Apr.-Dec. 1937; Consul at Tabriz, 1938; Ahwaz, 1942; Baghdad, 1943; Vienna, 1947; Minister to Republic of Liberia, 1949-51; Consul-General, Gothenburg, 1951-55, retired 1955. *Address:* c/o Lloyds Bank Ltd., Pall Mall, S.W.1.

[*Died* 7 *March* 1960.

BAILLON, Major-General Joseph Aloysius, C.B. 1948; C.B.E. 1943 (O.B.E. 1941); M.C. 1918; p.s.c.; Director of Messrs. Beamish and Crawford Ltd., Brewers, Cork, since 1949; *b.* 6 Oct. 1895; 7th *s.* of late Louis Augustin and Mary Julia Baillon, at one time of the Falkland Islands; *m.* 1925, Gertrude Emily, *d.* of A. B. Fellowes Prynne, Plymouth; two *s.* one *d.* *Educ.:* King Edward's School, Birmingham; St. Bede's College, Lancashire; Staff College, Camberley. Served European War, 1914-19, with South Staffordshire Regt. 2nd Lt. 1915; Bt. Major, 1936; Bt. Lt.-Col., 1939; Col., 1942; Brig. 1942; C.G.S., Persia and Iraq, 1942; C.G.S., M.E.F., 1943; Maj.-Gen. (Temp.), 1942, (Subst.) 1944; Director of Organisation, War Office; G.O.C. Aldershot District, 1946-48; retired pay, 1949. *Recreations:* all outdoor pursuits; flying. *Address:* c/o Midland Bank, Ltd., 3 Wood Hill, Northampton. *Clubs:* Army and Navy, United Hunts; Kildare Street (Dublin).

[*Died* 11 *April* 1951.

BAINBRIDGE, Brig.-Gen. William Frank, C.B. 1924; C.M.G. 1915; C.B.E. 1920; D.S.O. 1900; late 54th Sikhs; *b.* 15 Jan. 1873; *e. s.* of late Major-Gen. F. T. Bainbridge; *m.* 1902,

Violet Maud (*d.* 1945), *e. d.* of Captain J. Henderson of Rylstone, Yorks, and Rylstone House, Cheltenham; one *s.* *Educ.:* Cheltenham College. Commander Jullundur Brigade Area, 1920-1923; retired, 1924; served N.W. Frontier, 1897-98 (Tochi); China, 1900 (despatches, medal, D.S.O.); European War, 1915 (C.M.G., Officer Legion of Honour); Afghan War, 1919 (C.B.E.); Waziristan, 1920-21; Order of the Nile, 4th Class. *Address:* c/o Lloyds Bank, 6 Pall Mall, S.W.1. *Club:* United Service.
[*Died* 24 *March* 1953.

BAINES, Ven. Albert; Archdeacon and Canon Emeritus since 1946; *m. d.* of James Harrison, Mossley Hill, Liverpool; two *s.* one *d.* *Educ.:* St. John's College, Cambridge. Curate of All Saints', Sheffield; Vicar of St. George's, Newcastle-under-Lyme; of St. Helens, Lancashire; Diocesan Canon Liverpool, 1917-25; Vicar and Rural Dean of Huddersfield, 1925-35; Archdeacon of Halifax, 1935-46; Examining Chaplain to the Bishop of Wakefield, 1935-46; Hon. Canon Wakefield Cathedral, 1925-37; Canon of Wakefield, 1937-46; Proctor in Convocation. *Recreations:* represented College in football, lawn tennis, lacrosse, and athletics; skating, climbing. *Address:* Westwood, Knaresbro. [*Died* 14 *Jan.* 1951.

BAINES, Hubert, C.B.E. 1920 (O.B.E. 1918); late Chief Electrical and Mechanical Engineer, H.M. Office of Works; *b.* 29 June 1874. Retired 1936. *Address:* Alicon, Trapps Hill, Loughton, Essex. *T.:* Loughton 30. [*Died* 1 *Nov.* 1953.

BAINES, William Henry, C.B.E. 1944; LL.M.; *b.* 17 Mar. 1879; *e. s.* of Henry and Mary Elizabeth Baines; *m.* 1904, Elizabeth Ann Senior; one *d.* *Educ.:* Liverpool. Solicitor; Deputy Town Clerk of Liverpool for ten years; Town Clerk of Liverpool and Clerk to the Mersey Tunnel Joint Committee, 1936-47; retd. 1947; Civil Defence Controller for City and other appts. during the War. *Recreation:* golf. *Address:* Birch Lodge, Bramley, Guildford, Surrey.
[*Died* 4 *Oct.* 1958.

BAINTON, Edgar Leslie, D.Mus. Dunelm; F.R.C.M.; Hon. R.A.M.; *b.* 14 Feb. 1880; 2nd *s.* of Rev. George Bainton; *m.* 1905, Ethel F. Eales; two *d.* *Educ.:* King Henry VIII School, Coventry; Royal Coll. of Music, London. Prof. of Piano and Composition, 1901, Principal, 1912-34, Conservatoire of Music, Newcastle upon Tyne; Conductor, Newcastle Philharmonic Orchestra, 1911-34; interned at Ruhleben, 1914; interned in Holland, March-Dec. 1918; conducted 2 concerts of British Music with Mengelberg Orchestra, Amsterdam, and The Hague, 1918; Examiner to the Associated Board, Royal Schools of Music, London; Adjudicator at principal musical competitive festivals in Great Britain and Canada; conducted 2 pieces for Orchestra, Queen's Hall, London, Sept. 1919; 3 pieces for Orchestra, Hereford Festival, 1921; Concerto-Fantasia, Royal Philharmonic Concert, Jan. 1922; Rhapsody: Epithalamion, for Orchestra, Three Choirs Festival, Worcester, Sept. 1929; Director N.S.W. State Conservatorium of Music, Sydney, 1934-46. *Publications:* an opera, The Pearl-Tree; Choral Symphony, Before Sunrise; Concerto-Fantasia for Piano and Orchestra, Carnegie Trust Publications; The Tower, for chorus and orchestra, 1924; A Hymn to God the Father, for chorus and orchestra, 1926; The Blessed Damozel; A Song of Freedom and Joy; The Vindictive Staircase; The Dancing Seal, for chorus and orchestra Symphony in D minor; Epithalamion for full orchestra; songs, part-songs, and piano-pieces. *Recreations:* walking, swimming, reading. *Address:* Longworth Avenue, Point Piper, Sydney, N.S.W.
[*Died* 8 *Dec.* 1956.

BAIRD, Brig.-Gen. Edward William David, C.B.E. 1919; D.L., J.P.; member of Jockey Club since 1894; *b.* 1864; 6th *s.* of late William Baird of Elie; *m.* 1st, 1893, Millicent Bessie (*d.* 1936), 2nd *d.* of late Major-General Sir Stanley Clarke, G.C.V.O., C.M.G.; three *s.* three *d.*; 2nd, 1939, Cicely, *widow* of Captain A. E. Butter. *Educ.:* Eton. Formerly Capt. 10th Hussars; served with Imp. Yeo. South African War, 1900; Hon. Major in the Army, 1901; Lt.-Col. commanding (Hon. Col., 1906) Suffolk Hussars I.Y., 1901-6; served European War, 1914-17; Brig.-Gen. 1916; lately Ensign Royal Company of Archers (King's Bodyguard for Scotland); won St. Leger with Woolwinder, 1907. *Address:* Kelloe, Edrom, Berwickshire. *Club:* Turf. [*Died* 8 *Aug.* 1956.

BAIRD, Percy Johnstone, C.B.E. 1941 (O.B.E. 1925); F.R. Empire Soc.; *b.* 29 Nov. 1877; *s.* of Andrew Johnstone Baird, Blackford, Lockerbie; *m.* 1906, Mary Evelyn Baird; two *d.* *Educ.:* Grammar School Dudley; Masons College, Birmingham A.C.A. 1902; Chief Accountant, Administration of North Eastern Rhodesia, 1906; Treasurer, Administration of Northern Rhodesia, 1908; Chief Accountant, British South Africa Co., London, 1913; Secretary, British South Africa (Chartered) Co., 1928-45, a Director, 1945-51. *Address:* Cantelupe Hotel, Bexhill. *Clubs:* All England Lawn Tennis; New (Bexhill). [*Died* 21 *July* 1956.

BAIRD, Major Sir William, Kt., *cr.* 1947; D.L., J.P. Belfast City; Director, Belfast Telegraph; retired as Chairman and Managing Director of W. and G. Baird Ltd., publishers of the Belfast Telegraph and allied newspapers, 1951; *b.* 1874; *m.*; two *d.* (one *s.* decd.). *Educ.:* Belfast Royal Academy; Royal Belfast Academical Institution; Queen's College, Belfast. Served European War, 1914-18. Retired with rank of Major. D.L. 1934. President, Northern Ireland Amateur Athletic Association, and of Irish Bowling Association. *Address:* Glynn Park, Carrickfergus, Co. Antrim, N. Ireland; Belfast Telegraph, Royal Avenue, Belfast.
[*Died* 10 *Jan.* 1956.

BAIRD-SMITH, David, C.B.E. 1920; LL.D., Officier de la Légion d'Honneur; solicitor, Glasgow; 2nd *s.* of late J. Baird-Smith, solicitor, Glasgow, and Mary, *d.* of Rev. Alex. MacEwen, D.D.; *m.* Jessica, *o. c.* of late T. D. Jameson, Inspector-General Burma Police; one *s.* *Educ.:* Glasgow University; M.A., LL.B., Hon. LL.D. Crown Trustee and Vice-Chairman of National Library of Scotland; Member Advisory Council under Public Records (Scotland) Act; Chairman of Council, Stair Society; member of Discipline Committee under Solicitors (Scotland) Act; Ex-Dean of the Faculty of Procurators in Glasgow; Member of War Executive, Scottish Branch B.R.C.S. and of British Committee, French Red Cross, 1914-20 (C.B.E., Legion of Honour); Chairman of Executive of Scottish Branch, B.R.C.S., and Member of Council of B.R.C.S., 1920-30; President, Scottish Text Society, 1927-30; Member Court of Glasgow University, 1928-46; Corresponding Member, Académie de Rouen; Vice-Chairman, Central Advisory Committee of Distress in Mining Areas (Scot.) Fund, 1929-1930. *Publications:* articles in Scottish Historical Review, Revue du Seizième Siècle, Juridical Review, etc.; Ex-General Editor Scottish Text Society. *Recreation:* travel. *Address:* 5 Kirklee Terrace, Glasgow, W.2. *Clubs:* Athenæum; Western (Glasgow).
[*Died* 22 *Feb.* 1951.

BAIRNSFATHER, Capt. Bruce; artist and journalist; *b.* Murree, India, July 1888; *s.* of late Major T. H. Bairnsfather and late A. J. E. Bairnsfather (*née* Every); *m.* 1921, Hon. Mrs. M. Scott; one *d.* *Educ.:* United Services College, Westward Ho! Served in Warwickshire Militia prior

to the war, 1911-14; after which, Civil Engineer; at outbreak of war returned from abroad and rejoined the Royal Warwickshire Regt.; went to France Nov. 1914, and served with the 1st Batttalion Royal Warwicks; Captain, July 1915; served in France till Dec. 1916; afterwards attached War Office for work abroad; Official War Cartoonist attached to U.S. Army, European Theatre of War, 1942-44; has concluded eleventh tour of United States and Canada; contributed weekly to Tatler and many magazines and papers in America, Australia, etc. *Publications:* Fragments from France (6 volumes); The Better 'Ole; Bullets and Billets; From Mud to Mufti; Old Bill, M.P. 1; Wide Canvas, 1939; Old Bill Stands By, 1939; Old Bill does it again, 1940; Jeeps and Jests, 1943; No Kiddin', 1944; also illustrations to several war-books, including C'est pour la France, Back to Blighty. *Address:* Littleworth, Norton, Worcester.
[*Died* 29 *Sept.* 1959.

BAJPAI, Sir Girja Shankar, K.C.S.I., *cr.* 1943; K.B.E., *cr.* 1935 (C.B.E. 1922); C.I.E. 1926; Governor of Bombay since 1952; *b.* 1891; *s.* of late Rai Bahadur Sir S. P. Bajpai, C.I.E.; *m.* Rajni Misra, of Cawnpore; three *s.* four *d.* *Educ.:* Muir Central College, Allahabad; Merton College, Oxford. Entered I.C.S. 1914; served as Under-Secretary to Government of United Provinces and as Secretary for India at Imperial Conference, 1921, and at Conference for Limitation of Armaments, Washington, 1921-22; deputed to visit Canada, New Zealand, and Australia to investigate status of Indians, 1922; Under-Sec. to Govt. of India, Education, Health and Lands Department, 1923; officiating Deputy Secretary, 1924; was Secretary to Indian Deputation to South Africa, 1925-26, and to Round Table Conference on Indian Question in South Africa, 1926-27; also adviser to Indian Delegation, Imperial Conference, 1926; Secretary to the Government of India, Department of Education, Health and Lands, 1927-29; Adviser to Indian Delegations to 10th Assembly of the League of Nations and to Conference on Dominion Legislation, 1929; Joint Secretary to the Government of India, Department of Education, Health and Lands, 1929; Adviser to Indian Delegations to 11th Assembly of the League of Nations and to the Imperial Conference, 1930; Joint Secretary to the British India Delegation to the Indian Round Table Conference, first and second session; Member-Secretary of the Government of India Delegation to the Second Round Table Conference with representatives of the Government of the Union of South Africa, 1932; Temporary Member of Executive Council of Governor-General of India, Sept. 1935-Jan. 1936; Secretary to Government of India Dept. of Education, Health, and Lands, 1932-40; Member, 1940-41; Agent-General for India, Washington, D.C., 1941-47; Secretary-General of Ministry of External Affairs, Government of India, 1947-52; adviser to Prime Minister of India, Conf. of Commonwealth Prime Ministers, 1948, and meetings of Commonwealth Prime Ministers, 1949 and 1951; Representative of India, Kashmir Negotiations under U.N. 1953. *Address:* Government House, Bombay, India.
[*Died* 5 *Dec.* 1954.

BAKER, Lt.-Col. (Bernard) Granville, D.S.O. 1918; J.P.; F.R.G.S.; F.R.Hist.S.; *b.* Poona, 23 Oct. 1870; *s.* of Montagu Bernard Baker, I.C.S. (Bombay), and Harriet Fanny Bangh; *m.* 1897, Lorina (*d.* 1942), *d.* of Rev. A. O. Hartley; no *c.* *Educ.:* Winchester; Military College, Dresden. Served with 21st Hussars (India, detached to Q.M.G. Branch, Upper Burma), 1890-1894 9th Prussian Hussars, 1894-1900; Captain and Adj. Imperial Yeomanry, S. Africa, 1900-1901 (despatches twice, Queen's medal 3 clasps); joined Indian Corps Staff at Marseilles, 1914; 1st Army Staff, France, 1915; 2nd in command 20th Battalion, Middlesex Regiment, 1918; Lieut.-Col. commanding 13th Battalion the Yorkshire Regiment, 1916; British Commissioner for Propaganda in Enemy Countries, Italian and Salonika Fronts, 1918; Supreme Economic Councils' Mission to Central Europe, 1919; retired Dec. 1919 (D.S.O., despatches twice). *Publications:* The Walls of Constantinople; The Danube with Pen and Pencil; A Winter Holiday in Portugal; The Passing of the Turkish Empire in Europe, illustrated by author; The German Army from Within; From a Terrace in Prague, 1923; Waveney, 1928; Blithe Waters, 1931; Old Cavalry Stations, 1938. *Recreation:* travel. *Clubs:* Press, Savage, English-Speaking Union.
[*Died* 12 *March* 1957.

BAKER, Charles Henry Collins, C.V.O. 1934; *b.* 24 Jan. 1880; *s.* of John Collins Baker, Ilminster, Som.; *m.* 1903, Muriel Isabella (*d.* 1956), *d.* of H. R. T. Alexander, Supreme Court Taxing Master; one *d.* *Educ.:* Berkhampstead; Royal Academy Schools. Hon. Sec. New English Art Club, 1921-25; Art Critic, successively on the Outlook and Saturday Review; Private Assist. and Sec. to the Director of the National Gallery, 1911; Keeper and Secretary of the National Gallery, 1914-32; Member of Research Staff at the Huntington Library, California, 1932-49; Surveyor of the King's Pictures, 1928-34. *Works:* In the Manchester, Leeds, and Huddersfield Public Galleries. *Publications:* Lely and the Stuart Portrait Painters, 1912; Crome, 1921; P. de Hooch, 1925; Dutch Painting of XVIIth Century, 1926; Catalogue of Hampton Court Picture Gallery, 1929; (in collaboration) Engl. Malerei des 16. und 17. Jahrhunderts, 1930; British Painting, 1933; Catalogue of the Principal Pictures at Windsor Castle, 1937; (in collaboration with Muriel I. Baker) James Brydges, Duke of Chandos, Patron of the Liberal Arts, 1949; and catalogues of several collections, including the Huntington Art Gallery. *Address:* 8 Holyoake Walk, N.2.
[*Died* 3 *July* 1959.

BAKER, Charles Maurice, C.I.E. 1921; late I.C.S.; *b.* Cobham, Kent, 1872; *s.* of Thomas Henry Baker, J.P.; *m.* 1902, Mabel (*d.* 1928), *d.* of Major-General Henry Edmeades of Nurstead Court, Kent; two *s.* one *d.* *Educ.:* Tonbridge; Trinity College, Oxford. Commissioner; Member Council of State; Revenue Officer, Sukkur Barrage; retired, 1927. *Recreation:* beagling. *Address:* Green Farm, Meopham, Kent. *T.:* Meopham 2161. *Club:* East India and Sports.
[*Died* 16 *March* 1952.

BAKER, Edmund Wilfrid, I.S.O. 1912; late Registrar, Government of India Finance Department; *b.* 28 Aug. 1869; *e. s.* of late Alexander Baker and Isabel Jervis; *m.* 1890, Melvina Constance (*d.* 1933), *e. d.* of late John Grieff, chief engineer, River Steam Navigation Co.; three *s.* four *d.* *Educ.:* St. Xavier's Coll., Calcutta. Entered the Service of the Government of India, Finance Department, 1887; ret. 1924. *Recreations:* athletics, cricket, football, shooting, riding. *Address:* c/o Lloyds Bank Ltd., 6 Pall Mall, S.W.1.
[*Died* 24 *Jan.* 1953.

BAKER, Francis Douglas, C.B.E. 1942 (O.B.E. 1934); M.C.; *b.* 15 Sept. 1884; *s.* of late A. de Winter Baker, M.R.C.S., L.R.C.P., and Margaret Charlotte Kirby, *d.* of late Francis Barrow, Recorder of Rochester; *m.* 1925, Nevart, *d.* of late A. Mavian of Istanbul and Cairo. *Educ.:* Allhallows, Honiton; Westminster School. Egyptian Government service, 1920-46; served with R. 1st Devon Yeomanry, Gallipoli 1915 (M.C., despatches twice) and with G.S. Intelligence, G.H.Q., Egypt Western Desert, Palestine and Syria, 1917-20; Order of Ismail 3rd Class; Order of Nile 3rd Class; Commander Crown of Italy; Greek

Distinguished Service Medal; Commander Crown of Roumania; Egyptian Gold Medaille du Devoir. Afghan Order of Astaur, 2nd Class; Iranian Order of Humayuni, 3rd Class. *Recreation:* billiards. *Address:* 305 Ave. Fouad I, Alexandria, Egypt. *T.:* Alexandria 72265. *Clubs:* Turf, Cairo, Union (Alexandria). [*Died* 29 *Jan.* 1958.

BAKER, George Edwin, C.B.E. 1925; F.R.G.S.; ex-Assistant Secretary, Board of Trade; retired, 1937; *b.* 1876; *s.* of Thomas Baker; *m.* 1st, 1907, Gertrude Robinson; two *d.*; 2nd, 1929, Helena Thomson. *Address:* 40 Parkway, Willingdon, Eastbourne, Sussex. [*Died* 3 *Sept.* 1960.

BAKER, George Philip; F.R.Hist.S., author and artist; *b.* 21 May 1879; *s.* of Philip Baker and Emily, *d.* of Charles Baker, Plumstead, Kent; *m.* 1910, Josephine, *d.* of Joseph Garthwaite, Durham; no *c.* *Educ.:* private tuition. Lost hearing after serious illness at age of eight; entered Royal Carriage Department, Woolwich Arsenal, 1895, in continuation of family service since 1805; left in 1922 to devote whole time to historical study and literary activities. *Publications:* Magic Tale of Harvanger and Yolande, 1914; Romance of Palombris and Pallogris, 1915; Religion and Art (Hibbert Journal, July 1922); Sulla the Fortunate, 1927; Tiberius Caesar, 1929; Hannibal, 1930; Constantine the Great, 1931; Fighting Kings of Wessex, 1931; Justinian, 1932; Charlemagne, 1933; Twelve Centuries of Rome, 1934; A Book of Battles, 1935; Augustus: The Golden Age of Rome, 1937; edited (with G. E. Bryant) A Quaker Journal, 1934. *Recreations:* in youth, cricket and Rugby football; more recently, genealogical and archæological research and playing patience. *Address:* Marigold Corner, Elmer Sussex. *T.:* Middleton-on-Sea 364. [*Died* 19 *April* 1951.

BAKER, Lt.-Col. Granville; *see* Baker, Lt.-Col. B. G.

BAKER, Right Hon. Harold Trevor, P.C. 1915; Fellow of Winchester College, 1933, Warden, 1936-46; *b.* 22 Jan. 1877; *s.* of late Sir John Baker, M.P. for Portsmouth; unmarried. *Educ.:* Winchester, New College, Oxford. Scholar and Fellow, 1896-1907; Craven Scholar; Hertford Scholar; Gaisford Prizeman; Eldon Scholar; President of the Union. Called to Bar; Secretary to Royal Commission on War Stores in S. Africa; M.P. (L.) Accrington Division, Lancs, 1910-18; Financial Secretary to the War Office, 1912-13; Member of H.M.'s Army Council, European War, 1914; Inspector of Quartermaster-General Services, 1916. *Publication:* Manual of the Territorial Force. *Address:* Crabwood, Pitt, Winchester. *Clubs:* Athenæum, Brooks's. [*Died* 12 *July* 1960.

BAKER, Henry Frederick, F.R.S. 1898; Sc.D.; Hon. LL.D. Edin.; Lowndean Professor of Astronomy and Geometry, Cambridge, 1914-36. *Educ.:* Perse School; St. John's College, Cambridge. Fellow of St. John's College. *Publications:* Abel's Theorem and Theta functions, 1897; Multiply-periodic functions, 1907; Principles of Geometry, six vols. 1922-33; Plane Geometry, 1943; editor of Sylvester's Mathematical Papers, four vols., 1904-12. *Address:* Walcott, 3 Storey's Way, Cambridge. [*Died* 17 *March* 1956.

BAKER, Rev. James F. B.; *see* Bethune-Baker.

BAKER, Lieut.-Gen. James Mitchell, C.B. 1944; C.B.E. 1919; D.S.O. 1916; *b.* 14 Feb. 1878; *s.* of late Leonard Baker, Stirlingshire; *m.* 1915, Lilia Theta, *d.* of late Captain J. M. Poynter, Eltham, New Zealand; two *s.* *Educ.:* Stirlin High School; Glasgow University. Entered army, 1899: resigned Imperial Commission, 1902, and entered Transvaal service; Captain, 1908; Major, 1914; Lt., Col., 1918; Col. 1929; served S. African War, 1899-1902 (despatches, King's and Queen's S.A. Medals); served European War, G.S.W. Africa, Egypt. France, Flanders, 1914-18 (despatches five times, D.S.O., Bt. Lt.-Col.); retired, 1933; recalled, 1939; A.D.C. to King, 1922-48; Brig.-Gen. 1940; Maj.-Gen. 1942; Lieut.-Gen. 1947; retired, 1948. *Recreation:* fishing. *Address:* Mitchiesrus, Fernridge, George, Cape, S.A. *Club:* Pretoria (Pretoria). [*Died* 14 *Dec.* 1956.

BAKER, John Alfred, C.I.E. 1927; M.Sc.; late Chief Engineer, Public Works Dept., Central Provinces, India; *b.* 14 May 1882; *s.* of Alfred Baker, Ilminster; *m.* 1907, Dorothy Anstice Prideaux; two *s.* one *d.* *Educ.:* R. I. E. C., Coopers Hill. Entered Indian Service of Engineers, 1904; retired 1935. *Address:* Roscoff, Warren Edge Road, Southbourne, Bournemouth. *T.:* Southbourne 650. [*Died* 18 *Dec.* 1957.

BAKER, Julian Levett, F.C.G.I., F.R.I.C.; technical chemist (retired); editor of the Journal of the Institute of Brewing, 1920-49; editor of the Analyst, 1907-20; *b.* 24 Feb. 1873; *s.* of G. L. Baker, A.K.C., Worthing, Sussex; *m.* 1901, Eveleen (*d.* 1945), *d.* of H. A. Daniels, J.P., Fermoy, Co. Cork; two *s.* one *d.*; *m.* 1948, Catherine St. Paul (*d.* 1956). *Educ.:* City of London School and Finsbury Tech. Coll. Vice-Pres. of Inst. of Brewing; late Vice-Pres. of Soc. of Chemical Industry, late Chairman, London Section of the Society of Chemical Industry; late member of Council of Chemical Society, of the Royal Institute of Chemistry; Hon. Sec. of the Institute of Brewing, 1909-1918; Hon. Secretary, London Section Society of Chemical Industry, 1903-9; Examiner to Birmingham University (Malting and Brewing), 1928-31, and the City and Guilds of London Institute (Brewing), 1908-1911; Horace Brown Medallist, Institute of Brewing, 1948. *Publications:* Brewing Industry, 1905; contributions (83) to Journal of the Chemical Society, the German Chemical Society, the Society of Chemical Industry, the Institute of Brewing, the Analyst, the Bio-Chemical Society, and the Encyclopædia Britannica, etc. *Recreations:* fishing, golf. *Address:* Dial Cottage, Cookham Road, Maidenhead. *T.:* Maidenhead 588. *Club:* Savage. [*Died* 29 *Jan.* 1958.

BAKER, Lt.-Col. Sir Randolf Littlehales, 4th Bt. of Ashcombe; *cr.* 1802; D.S.O. 1918; *b.* 20 July 1879; *s.* of 3rd Bt. and Amy, *d.* of Lieut.-Col. Marryat; *S.* father, 1900; *m.* 1920, Elsie (*d.* 1955), *widow* of Major Boyd Cuninghame and *d.* of late Robert George Burrell; one *d.*; *m.* 1955, Mary Caroline, *widow* of Lt.-Col. Frank Preedy, D.S.O., M.C. and *d.* of late A. S. Orlebar, M.A. M.P.(U.) North Dorset, 1910-1918; served European War, 1914-18 (twice wounded, D.S.O. and bar); J.P.; D.L. *Heir:* none. *Address:* Ranston, Blandford, Dorsetshire. *T.:* Childe Okeford 220. *T.A.:* Iwerne Courtney. *Club:* Carlton. [*Died* 23 *July* 1959 (*ext.*).

BAKER WILBRAHAM, Sir P. W.; *see* Wilbraham.

BAKKER, Cornelis Jan; Director General European Organization for Nuclear Research (C.E.R.N.), in Geneva, since 1955; Extraordinary Professor of Physics, Univ. of Amsterdam, since 1955; *b.* Amsterdam, 11 March 1904; *m.* 1933, Anna Margaretha Herwig; one *s.* two *d.* *Educ.:* University of Amsterdam (Doctor of Physics, 1931). Member of Scientific Staff of Physical Laboratory of Philips, Eindhoven, 1933-1946; Professor of Physics, University of Amsterdam, Director of Zeeman-laboratory and Director of Institute for Nuclear Research, Amsterdam, 1946-55. Member of

Royal Netherlands Academy of Sciences, 1952. Dr. *h.c.* Univ. of Geneva, 1957. *Publications:* publications on spectroscopy, physical problems in radio, nuclear physics. *Address:* 12 Chemin du Velours, Geneva.
[*Died* 23 *April* 1960.

BALD, Lt.-Col. John Arthur, C.M.G. 1916; C.B.E. 1925; late 1/1 Madras Pioneers (King George's Own), Indian Army; *b.* 20 July 1876; *e. s.* of late Arthur Bald, Liverpool; *m.* 1924, Viola E. M., *y. d.* of late John Howard, and *widow* of Peter Tarbet, M.R.C.S. Served China, 1900 (medal with clasp, Relief of Pekin); European War, 1914-18 (C.M.G., despatches); Waziristan, 1923 (C.B.E.); retired, 1925. *Address:* The Long House, Finchampsted, Berks.
[*Died* 18 *April* 1960.

BALDERSTON, John Lloyd; lecturer in drama in the University of Southern California since 1952; *b.* Philadelphia, U.S.A., 1889; *s.* of Dr. Lloyd Balderston and Mary F., *d.* of Prof. Samuel Alsop, jun.; *m.* 1921, Marion Rubincam, New York; one *s.* *Educ.:* Columbia Univ., New York. War correspondent McClure Newspaper Syndicate in Europe, 1914-18; Director of Information for Great Britain, U.S. Govt. Committee on Public Information, 1918-19; Chairman New Outlook Co. Ltd., 1921-23, and editor The Outlook, 1920-24; chief correspondent in London, New York World, 1923-31; official Washington observer, Committee to Defend America by Aiding the Allies, 1940; author seven so-called Balderston Demands for assistance to Britain, Sept. 1940, for which denounced by isolationists in Senate and elsewhere; Member Council on Foreign Relations, New York; author Berkeley Square, play produced London, 1926-27, revived in West End, 1929, 1940-41 and 1945, produced New York, 1929-30, and in various theatres throughout the world; Co-author, Red Planet, play produced New York, 1932; Farewell Performance, play produced London, 1936; Goddess and God, 1952, various original screen plays and adaptations for motion pictures, including Lives of a Bengal Lancer, Prisoner of Zenda, etc. *Publications:* A Goddess to a God, The Cleopatra-Caesar Correspondence; Berkeley Square; Genius of the Marne: A Morality Play for the Leisure Class; Chicago Blueprint. *Recreations:* aviation, numismatics, book-collecting. *Address:* 615 North Rodeo Dr., Beverly Hills, California. *T.:* Crestview 6-9016. *Clubs:* Athenæum, Savile; Century (New York).
[*Died* 8 *March* 1954.

BALDWIN of Bewdley, 2nd Earl, *cr.* 1937; Viscount Corvedale, *cr.* 1937, of Corvedale; **Oliver Ridsdale Baldwin,** F.R.G.S., F.G.S. (America); author and politician; *b.* 1 March 1899; *s.* of 1st Earl Baldwin of Bewdley, K.G., P.C., F.R.S., and Lucy, G.B.E., *cr.* 1937 (*d.* 1945), *e. d.* of late E. L. J. Ridsdale, Rottingdean; *S.* father 1947. *Educ.:* in football at Eton; in other things, beginning to learn. Served European War, 1916-19; acting Vice-Consul, Boulogne, 1919; Armeno-Turkish War, 1920; Armeno-Russian War, 1921; imprisoned by Bolsheviks and Turks, 1921; correspondent in East Africa, 1922; served 1940-45; Parliamentary Labour candidate for Dudley, 1924; Chatham, 1931; Paisley, 1935; M.P. (Lab.) Dudley, 1929-31; M.P. (Lab.) Paisley, 1945-1947; Governor and C.in-C. Leeward Islands, 1948-50. *Publications:* Konyetz; Six Prisons and Two Revolutions; Socialism and the Bible (translated); Conservatism and Wealth (with R. Chance); The Questing Beast; Unborn Son; The Coming of Aissa; Oasis. *Plays:* From the Four Winds; The Wrong Bus (Radio). *Recreations:* music, walking, conversation. *Heir:* *b.* Hon. (Arthur) Windham Baldwin [*b.* 22 March 1904; *m.* 1936, Joan Elspeth, *d.* of late C. Alexander Tomes, New York; one *s.*]. *Clubs:* Bath, Savage, Press.
[*Died* 10 *Aug.* 1958.

BALDWIN, Eng.-Rear-Adm. George William, C.B. 1926; C.B.E. 1922; R.N., retired; *b.* 1871; *s.* of late Thomas Baldwin, Gosport, Hants; *m.* Maud Edith, *er. d.* of late R. Clover, J.P., Southsea, Hants; no *c.* *Educ.:* Portsmouth; R.N. Engineering College, Devonport; R.N. College, Greenwich. Served Benin Expedition, 1897; European War, 1914-16; Chief Engineer, Invergordon Dockyard, 1917-1918; Malta Dockyard, 1919-22; Engineer-Manager Devonport Dockyard, 1922-26. *Address:* Gorselands, Glenmoor Road, Ferndown, Dorset. *Clubs:* South Hants Automobile; Ferndown Golf.
[*Died* 18 *Dec.* 1955.

BALFOUR, Brigadier Edward William Sturgis, C.V.O. 1943; D.S.O. 1915; O.B.E. 1919; M.C. 1917; *b.* 6 Dec. 1884; *o. surv. s.* of late Edward Balfour, J.P., D.L., of Balbirnie, Markinch; *m.* Lady Ruth, C.B.E. 1941, M.B., B.S., M.R.C.S., L.R.C.P., *d.* of 2nd Earl of Balfour, P.C.; two *s.* two *d.* *Educ.:* Eton; Royal Military Academy, Woolwich. Entered R.A., 1904; Captain, 5th Dragoon Guards, 1912; Major, 1918; Staff College, 1919; Major, Scots Guards, 1921; Lieut.-Col., 1929; Col., 1933; served European War, 1914-18 (D.S.O., O.B.E., M.C.); commanded 1st Batt. Scots Guards, 1929-33; Officer Commanding Scots Guards Regt. and Regimental District, 1934-38 and 1939-43; retired pay, 1938. *Address:* Balbirnie, Markinch, Fife. *Clubs:* Turf, Guards, Travellers'; New (Edinburgh).
[*Died* 23 *Dec.* 1955.

BALFOUR, Hon. James Moncreiff, O.B.E. 1919; F.S.A.; *b.* 6 July 1878; 2nd *s.* of 1st Baron Kinross; *m.* 1908, Madeline Maude, *d.* of late James Graham Watson. *Educ.:* Edinburgh Academy; Cheltenham; Balliol College, Oxford. B.A. (2nd Class Honours History), 1901; W.S. 1904; Captain Scottish Horse and a Staff Captain, 1914-17; Assistant Secretary Ministry of National Service, 1917-1918; General Secretary of Commission for Revision of Civil Service Exemptions, 1918; Chief Assistant to Financial Adviser to Persian Government, 1920-21; formerly partner in Shepherd and Wedderburn, W.S., Edinburgh, and in banking firm of Guinness, Mahon & Co.; and Dir. of many Trust Cos.; now retired. Knight of Justice of Order of St. John of Jerusalem. *Publication:* Recent Happenings in Persia, 1922. *Recreations:* golf, travel. *Address:* Flat 2, 26 Gloucester Sq., W.2. *T.:* Paddington 1949. *Club:* Carlton.
[*Died* 30 *April* 1960.

BALFOUR, Colonel John Edmond Heugh, C.M.G. 1918; D.S.O. 1900; J.P. and D.L. Devon; late Capt. 11th Hussars; Lt.-Col. and Hon. Col. R. 1st Devon Imp. Yeo.; *b.* 1863; *s.* of George Edmond Balfour, Sidmouth Manor; *m.* 1910, Evelyn, 2nd *d.* of late Hon. R. J. Gerard-Dicconson; one *d.* *Educ.:* Eton, Served S. Africa, 1899-1900 (despatches, medal with six clasps, D.S.O.); European War, 1914-18 (C.M.G., despatches twice); High Sheriff, Devon, 1922. *Address:* Sidmouth Manor, Devon. *Club:* Carlton.
[*Died* 5 *Oct.* 1952.

BALFOUR, Lieutenant-Colonel, Oswald Herbert Campbell, C.M.G. 1923; O.B.E. 1944; Chairman of: Peco, Ltd.; High Grade Steels Ltd.; Hall Green Non-Ferrous Metals Ltd.; Director, Anglo-Scottish Amalgamated Corporation Ltd., Anglo-Scottish Securities Ltd., Scottish Fine Steels Ltd.; *s.* of late Colonel Eustace Balfour, and late Lady Frances Balfour; unmarried. *Educ.:* Westminster; R.M.C. 2nd Bt. K.R.R.C., 1914 (wounded, despatches); 3rd Batt. K.R.R.C.; 1915 (wounded); served in Egypt, 1916; Salonica, 1916-18; with the 60th Rifles and General Staff 26th Division; 2nd in command the 18th K.R.R.C., 1919; A.D.C. to the Governor-General of Canada, Jan.-Oct. 1920; Mil. Sec. to Governor-General, 1920-23.

Address: White House, Landermere, Thorpe-le-Soken, Essex. *T.:* Thorpe-le-Soken 284. *Clubs:* Naval and Military, Royal Automobile; India House (New York). [*Died* 16 *Oct.* 1953.

BALIOL SCOTT, Napier; Under Secretary, Ministry of Supply; *b.* 25 December 1903; *s.* of Edward Baliol Scott. *Educ.:* Westminster School; Christ Church, Oxford. Management Research Group, 1927; Wallace Clark & Co. (American management engineers), 1929; Harrods Ltd., Director of Research and Planning, 1934; H.M. Treasury, 1939-44; Minister of State's Office, Cairo, 1942; Bengal Admin. Enquiry Cttee., 1948; Under Sec. (Temp.) Treasury, 1948; Director of Organization and Methods, Ministry of Supply, 1952. *Recreations:* music, gardening, chess, golf. *Address:* Hazards, Ide Hill, nr. Sevenoaks, Kent. *Club:* Reform. [*Died* 18 *Sept.* 1956.

BALL, Major George Joseph, C.B.E. 1922 (O.B.E. 1917); barrister; *b.* 1880; *s.* of late George Ball, Ballsgrove, Drogheda and Belfield, Raheny, Ireland; *m.* 1925, Evelyn Jane Florence, *d.* of late Frederick Kennedy, Frescati, Blackrock, Co. Dublin. Appointed to War Office, 1911, and attached Headquarters Irish Command; served European War, 1914-18; Captain, 1914; with B.E.F. France and Belgium, 1915 (despatches); Headquarters Irish Command, 1916; Major, 1917; transferred to Regular Army Reserve of Officers, Royal Engineers, 1921; transferred to War Office, 1922; Headquarters British Army of Rhine, 1926-27; retired from Army, 1928; Professional Legal Officer Director of Public Prosecutions Dept., 1929-46. Member of Lord French's Central Advisory Committee for resettlement of Ex-Service Men in Ireland, 1919-22; called to Bar, Middle Temple, 1929. *Recreations:* motoring (was one of the first owners of motors, 1899); golf. *Address:* 1 Essex Court, Temple, E.C.4; Woodcot, Woldingham, Sy. *T.:* 3253. [*Died* 3 *Oct.* 1952.

BALL, Sir William Valentine, Kt., *cr.* 1946; O.B.E. 1918; F.G.S.; M.A. Cantab., Barrister-at-law; Master of the Supreme Court, King's Bench Division, 1921-43, Senior Master and King's Remembrancer, 1943-47; Bencher Lincoln's Inn, 1945; *b.* Wellington Place, Dublin, 10 Feb. 1874; 2nd *s.* of Sir Robert Stawell Ball, LL.D., F.R.S., Lowndean Prof. of Astronomy at Cambridge, and Frances Elizabeth, *d.* of W. Steele, M.D.; *m.* 1903, Kathleen Mary (*d.* 1957), *d.* of George Butt, Bengal Civil Service; no *c.* *Educ.:* Tonbridge School; King's Coll., Cambridge. 2nd Class Natural Sciences Tripos, 1895; called to Bar, Lincoln's Inn, 1897; Examiner of the Court, 1917, Master of Worshipful Company of Clockmakers, 1953; Past Grand Registrar Supreme Grand Chapter. Senior Fellow of the Geological Society. *Publications:* The Law of Libel and Slander (2nd edn.), 1936; Bankruptcy, Deeds of Arrangement and Bills of Sale; editor of Emden's Building Contracts (4th ed.); Lincoln's Inn, its History and Traditions; editor of the Annual Practice, 1924-47; editor of the Letters and Reminiscences of Sir Robert Ball. *Recreations:* mechanics, carpentry. *Address:* 18 Holland Street, W.8. *T.:* Western 5929. *Club:* Athenæum. [*Died* 25 *Nov.* 1960.

BALLANTYNE, Arthur James, M.D., Ch.B., F.R.F.P.S., Glasgow; LL.D., Univ. of Glasgow; Emeritus Professor of Ophthalmology, Glasgow University; Hon. Consulting Opthalmic Surgeon, Glasgow Royal Maternity and Women's Hospital and Glasgow Eye Infirmary; F.R.S.M.; late President Ophthalmological Section; Member (President, 1946-48) Opthalmological Soc. of United Kingdom; late President Scot. Oph. Club; Member B.M.A., late Pres. Ophthalmological Sect.; Hon. Mem. Irish Ophthalmological Soc.; Hon. Member Ophthalmological Soc. Chicago, U.S.A.; *b.* 1876; *s.* of Thomas Ballantyne and Jane Chalmers; *m.* Jessie Snodgrass (*d.* 1928). *Educ.:* Glasgow Board School; Universities of Glasgow and Vienna. House Surgeon, Glasgow Royal Infirmary, 1899; House Physician, 1899-1900; House Surgeon, Glasgow Eye Infirmary, 1900-01; Assistant Surgeon, 1902-09; Surgeon, 1909-35; Professor of Physiology, Anderson College of Medicine, Glasgow, 1909-14; Professor of Ophthalmology, St. Mungo's College, Glasgow, 1914-15, and The Anderson College of Medicine, Glasgow, 1915-20; Lecturer in Ophthalmology, University of Glasgow, 1920-1935; Mackenzie Memorial Medal, Ophthalmology; Montgomery Lecturer, Dublin, 1943; Doyne Lecturer, Oxford, 1946; Nettleship Prize, Ophth. Soc. of U.K. 1950; Hon. D.Sc. Roanoke Coll., Virginia, U.S.A. *Publications:* A Pocket Book of Ophthalmology; numerous contributions to ophthalmological journals and proceedings of societies. *Address:* Brackenrigg, Killearn, Stirlingshire. *T.:* Killearn 350. *Clubs:* English-Speaking Union; Royal Scottish Automobile, College (Glasgow). [*Died* 9 *Nov.* 1954.

BALLANTYNE, Horatio; F.R.I.C., F.C.S.; an advisory Director of Unilever, Ltd.; *b.* 1871; *s.* of Thomas Ballantyne and Jane Chalmers, Glasgow; *m.* 1899, Katherine I. Russell; three *d.* *Educ.:* Garnethill School; Glasgow and West of Scotland Technical College; Athenæum, Glasgow. Assistant to City Analyst, Glasgow, 1886-96; Consulting Chemist, London (chiefly on patents, inventions, and chemical manufactures), 1896-1928; Vice-President, Institute of Chemistry, 1918 and 1920-22; Member of Committee, Technical Institutions' Conference on Patent Law Amendment, 1918-19; Member of Inter-Departmental Committee on methods of dealing with inventions made by Government servants, etc., 1922; Member of Board of Trade Committee on Patent Law and Practice, 1929. *Publications:* various papers and lectures on chemical subjects. *Address:* Copt Hill Court, Burgh Heath, Tadworth, Surrey. *T.:* Burgh Heath 3. *Club:* Athenæum. [*Died* 25 *Jan.* 1956.

BALLANTYNE, John Andrew, M.B.E. 1945; M.A. (Cantab.); Headmaster of Cranbrook School since 1960; *b.* 3 May 1912; *s.* of John George Ballantyne, Glasgow, and Marguerite Vander Meersch, Bruges; *m.* 1938, Joyce, *o. c.* of Arthur Mulley, Spalding, Lincs.; one *s.* one *d.* *Educ.:* Ayr Academy; Edinburgh University; St. John's College, Cambridge (Scholar). M.A., 1st cl. Hons. in Classics, Edin. Univ., 1934; Rhind Research Scholar, 1935; Classical Tripos: 1st cl. in Part I, 1935; 1st cl. in Part II, 1936; Graves Prize, St. John's Coll., Camb., 1936. Asst. Lectr. in Ancient History, Manchester Univ., 1936-37; Asst. Master: Dulwich Coll., 1937; Cranbrook Sch., 1938; Bedford Sch., 1938; Sixth Form Classical Master, St. Olave's Sch., London, 1938-40. Served War of 1939-45 (M.B.E.): 2nd Lt. North Irish Horse, 1941, Lt. 1942; N. Africa, 1943 (wounded, P.O.W.); Staff Captain, 21 Tank Bde., 1945. Asst. Director of Education: Norfolk Educ. Cttee., 1946-47; Cheshire Educ. Cttee., 1947-1948; Headmaster, St. Bartholomew's Grammar School, Newbury, 1948-60. *Recreations:* reading, motoring, golf, watching Rugby football. *Address:* School House, Cranbrook, Kent. *T.:* Cranbrook 2163. [*Died* 7 *Nov.* 1960.

BALLARD, Rev. Frank Hewett, M.A. Cantab.; Minister of Religion; retired; *y. c.* of late Charles and Eliza Ballard, Spencers Wood, Berks; *m.* 1921, Isabel Gertrude, *e. d.* of late Dr. John Oman, Principal of Westminster College, Cambridge; two *s.* one *d.* *Educ.:* Kendrick

School; Paton College; Jesus College, Cambridge. Ordained, 1911, Knutsford Congregational Church; Chaplain to Forces (Egypt and Salonica), 1915-17; Minister Victoria Road Church, Cambridge, 1917-1921; Highbury Church, Bristol, 1921-33; Hampstead Garden Suburb Free Church, 1933-51; Minister Emeritus, 1951-; Resident Minister, Linton, Cambridge, 1952-59; Moderator, Nat. Free Church Federal Council, 1946-47; President Speedwell Housing Soc. *Publications:* In the Form of a Servant; Spiritual Pilgrimage of St. Paul; Undying Wisdom; The Desire of all Nations; The Return to Religion; Does War Shake Faith; The Churches Face the Challenge; Crossing the Bar; Exposition of Psalms 90-150 in Interpreter's Bible; Edited: The Christian Layman Looks Ahead; Heroes of the Faith; A Dialogue with God, etc. *Address:* 10 St. Paul's Road, Cambridge. *Club:* Union (Cambridge). [*Died* 18 *May* 1959.

BALLS, William Lawrence, C.M.G. 1944; C.B.E. 1934; F.R.S. 1923; Sc.D.; Hon. Fell., St. John's College Cambridge, 1955; Hon. F.T.I. 1943; Hon. Assoc. Manchester College of Technology, 1949; D.Sc. (Hon.) Manchester, 1952; *b.* Garboldisham, Norfolk, 3 Sept. 1882; *o. s.* of William Balls, Oulton Broad, and Emma Mary Lawrence; *m.* 1909, Florence Edith, *d.* of A. Tyrrell; one *s.* *Educ.:* King Edward VI. School, Norwich; St. John's College, Cambridge (Fellow, 1909-13); Walsingham Medal, 1906; Membre de l'Institut Egyptien, 1910; Botanist Khedivial Agricultural Society, 1904-10, and Egyptian Government Dept. of Agriculture, 1911-13 and 1927-33; Designer and Head of Experimental Department, Fine Cotton Spinners' Association, at Bollington, 1915-26; Cotton Technologist to Egyptian Ministry of Agriculture, 1934-47. Studied effect of subsoil water in causing deterioration of cotton crop; designed the Giza Cotton Exp. Station and system of pure seed supply for Egyptian cotton; Provisional Committee for Research in Cotton Industry, 1916; Board of Trade's Empire Cotton Committee, 1917; President of Trustees of Alexandria Testing House, 1935; Chairman Scientific Advisory Committee to C.-in-C., G.H.Q. Middle East, 1940-46; Battersea Polytechnic governing body, 1949. Orders of: Medjidieh, 3rd Class, 1914; Ismail, 3rd Class, 1936; Ziraa, 1st Class, 1947. *Publications:* The Cotton Plant in Egypt; The Development of Raw Cotton; Egypt of the Egyptians; Spinning Tests for Cotton Growers; Studies of Quality in Cotton; The Yields of a Crop; many original papers on growth, heredity, irrigation, instruments, etc., relating to cotton in scientific and other journals. *Address:* The Crossways, Fulbourne, Cambridge. *T.A.:* Fulbourne. *T.:* Fulbourne 291. *Club:* Royal Commonwealth Society. [*Died* 18 *July* 1960.

BALME, Harold, O.B.E. 1942; M.D., F.R.C.S.; Consultant Adviser on Rehabilitation to U.N., World Health Organization, World Veterans Federation. *Educ.:* King's Coll. Hosp., St. Bartholomew's Hosp. M.D. Durham, 1928; F.R.C.S. (Eng.) 1905; M.R.C.S. (Eng.), L.R.C.P. (Lond.), 1903; D.P.H. 1913. Med. Missionary work in China for 11 years; initiated rehabilitation centres for disabled refugees, as Adviser to Internat. Refugee Organization. Formerly: Cons. Adviser on Rehab., Min. of Health; Dir. Welfare Services, B.R.C.S.; Dean of Sch. of Medicine, Cheeloo Univ., China. Has visited Europe, Egypt, and U.S. to advise on problems of rehab.; has broadcast, and directed courses for Brit. Council, on this subject. *Publications:* A Criticism of Nursing Education with Suggestions for Constructive Reform, 1937; The Relief of Pain: Handbook of Modern Analgesia, 2nd edn., 1939. *Address:* 64 Copers Cope Rd., Beckenham, Kent. *T.:* Beckenham 4455. [*Died* 13 *Feb.* 1953.

BAMBRIDGE, Henry James, O.B.E. 1946; J.P.; Chairman Leeds Regional Hospital Board since 1949; Chairman West Riding County Council since 1955 (Chairman West Riding County Council Finance Committee, 1952-55); *b.* 11 March 1881; *m.* 1904, Annie Richardson; two *s.* two *d.* *Educ.:* Westgate Council School, Otley. Wharfedale Board of Guardians, 1910-30; Otley U.D.C., 1923-36; West Riding C.C., 1919-22 and 1931-; Leeds Regional Hospital Board, 1948-55; Member County Councils Assoc., 1945-. *Recreations:* no time. *Address:* 290 Bradford Road, Otley, Yorkshire. *T.:* 2086 Otley. [*Died* 16 *March* 1956.

BAMFIELD, Maj.-Gen. Harold John Kinahan, C.B. 1925; D.S.O. 1917; I.M.S., retired; *s.* of S. Bamfield, Deputy Inspector-General of Hospitals and Fleets; *m.* 1898, Katharine Basset Witherby; one *s.* *Educ.:* King's School, Rochester; St. Mary's Hospital. Entered Indian Medical Service, 1894; served N.W. Frontier, 1897-98; Mohmand Campaign, 1908; European War, France, Egypt, Syria; Moplah Rebellion, 1922; retired, 1928. *Publication:* (with S. E. Palmer) The Art of Sailing, 1933. *Address:* Peaslake, Surrey. *T.:* Abinger 53. [*Died* 8 *March* 1959.

BAMFORD, Sir Eric St. John, K.C.B., *cr.* 1949 (C.B. 1942); K.B.E., *cr.* 1946; C.M.G. 1936; M.A. (Oxon); *b.* 14 Oct. 1891; *s.* of late Frederick Linwood Bamford; *m.* 1920, Alice May, *d.* of late George William Dennistoun Scott; two *s.* one *d.* *Educ.:* Wimbledon; Stonyhurst; Corpus Christi College, Oxford (Scholar). 2nd Mods. 1912; 1st Modern History, 1914; M.A. 1930; Hon. Fellow, Corpus Christi College, 1948; entered Secretary's Office, G.P.O. 1914; H.M. Treasury, 1919; Private Secretary to Financial Secretary, 1919-21; Principal, H.M. Treasury 1921; Secretary to Trade Facilities Act Advisory Committee and other Committees, 1926-1933; Secretary Imperial Communications Advisory Committee, 1933-38; Assistant Secretary, H.M. Treasury and Treasury Representative on Select Committee on Estimates, 1938-39; Ministry of Information, 1939; Controller, 1940; Deputy Director-General, 1941; Director-General, 1945; and Director-General, Central Office of Information, April-June 1946; Third Secretary H.M. Treasury, July 1946-Aug. 1938; Chairman, Board of Inland Revenue, 1948-55; retired 1955. Served European War with Rifle Bde., 1914-19 (twice wounded); invalided, 1919, with rank of Captain. *Address:* Linksfield, Red Lane, Claygate, Surrey. *T.:* Esher 2569. *Club:* Union. [*Died* 13 *April* 1957.

BAMFORD, Percival Clifford, C.I.E., 1931; Indian Police, retired; *b.* 1886; *s.* of Rev. Frederick William Bamford; *m.* 1919, Geraldine Beatrice, *d.* of late F. C. French, C.S.I.; one *d.* Joined the Indian Police, 1906; retired, 1941. *Address:* Debenhurst, Woodbridge, Suffolk. *T.:* Woodbridge 517. [*Died* 11 *March* 1960.

BANCROFT, George Pleydell; Clerk of Assize for the Midland Circuit, 1913-46; retired; *b.* London, 1 Nov. 1868; *s.* of late Sir Squire Bancroft and late Marie Effie Wilton; *m.* 1893, Effie Lucy (*d.* 1934), *e. d.* of late Sir John Hare; three *d.* *Educ.:* Eton; Brasenose College, Oxford; Honours in Law; M.A. Called to Bar, Inner Temple, 1893. *Publications:* The Ware Case, 1913; Stage and Bar, Recollections, 1939, etc. *Dramatic Works:* Teresa, 1898; The Ware Case, 1915, etc. *Address:* Elibank House, Taplow, Bucks. *T.:* Maidenhead 747. *Club:* Garrick. [*Died* 1 *March* 1956.

BANDARANAIKE, Solomon West Ridgeway Dias; Prime Minister of Ceylon since 1956; *b.* 8 Jan. 1899; *o. s.* of late Maha Mudaliyar, Sir Solomon Dias Bandaranaike, K.C.M.G.; *m.* 1940, Sirimawo

Ratwatte; one *s.* two *d.* *Educ.:* St. Thomas' Coll., Mount Lavinia, Ceylon; Christ Church, Oxford (B.A.). Barr.-at-law, Inner Temple. Member State Council, 1931; Minister of Local Administration, 1937; Minister of Health and Local Government and Leader of the House of Representatives, 1947; Leader of the Opposition, 1952-56. *Recreations:* tennis, billiards, riding; is a great lover of dogs. *Clubs:* Orient (Colombo); Tennis (Bandarawela).
[*Died* 26 *Sept.* 1959.

BANKART, Arthur Sydney Blundell, M.A., M.Ch. Cantab., F.R.C.S. Eng.; Consulting Orthopædic Surgeon to the Middlesex Hospital and Royal National Orthopædic Hospital; Consulting Surgeon Hospital for Epilepsy and Paralysis, Maida Vale and Queen's Hospital for Children; *b.* 1879; *o. s.* of late James Bankart, F.R.C.S., of Exeter; *m.* Beryl Winifred, *o. d.* of A. S. Moss-Blundell of Sparsholt, nr. Winchester; one *d.* *Educ.:* Rugby School; Trinity College, Cambridge; Guy's Hospital. Fellow, Royal Society of Medicine, Ex-President Orthopædic Section; ex-President British Orthopædic Association; Fellow Association of Surgeons of Great Britain and Ireland; Hon. Member Société Française d'Orthopédie; Member Society British Neurological Surgeons; Member Société Internationale de Chirurgie Orthopédique. *Publications:* various papers in medical journals. *Address:* 95 Harley Street, W.1. *T.:* Welbeck 4772.
[*Died* 8 *April* 1951.

BANKS, Leslie James, C.B.E. 1950; Actor, Producer; F.R.S.A.; *b.* West Derby, 9 June 1890; *s.* of George and Emily Banks; *m.* 1915, Gwendoline Haldane Unwin; three *d.* *Educ.:* The Leas, Hoylake, Cheshire; Trinity Coll., Glenalmond (Classical Scholarship); Keble Coll. Oxford (Classical Scholar). First stage appearance Brechin Town Hall, Oct. 1911, as Old Gobbo in The Merchant of Venice, F. R. Benson's Company; first New York appearance Garrick Theatre, Jan. 1914, as the Porter in Eliza Comes to Stay; first London appearance Vaudeville, May 1914, as Lord Murdon in The Dangerous Age; Essex Regt. 1914-18; Birmingham Repertory Co. 1919; Lena Ashwell's Repertory Co 1919-20; Everyman Theatre, Hampstead, 1921; Captain Hook in Peter Pan, New York, 1924; also appeared in America, 1930 and 1931; Gabriel Service in Service, Wyndhams, 1932-33; Nicholas in This Inconstancy, Wyndhams, 1933; Robert Clive in Clive of India, Wyndhams, 1934; James Brett in Man of Yesterday, St. Martin's, 1935; Geoffrey Carroll in The Two Mrs. Carrolls, St. Martins, 1935; Robert Morrison in Till the Cows Come Home, St. Martin's, 1936; Petruchio in The Taming of the Shrew, New, 1937; appeared in America, 1937-38; Sanders in The Sun Never Sets, Drury Lane, 1938; Mr. Chips in Goodbye, Mr. Chips, Shaftesbury, 1938; John Thackeray in The Man in Half Moon Street, New, 1939; Cottage to Let, 1940-41; The Duke in the Duke in Darkness, 1942-43; Mr. Tattle in Love for Love, 1943-44; Claudius in Hamlet, 1944; Lord Porteous in the Circle, 1945; Bottom in Midsummer Night's Dream, 1945; Gerald Coates in Grand National Night, Apollo Theatre, 1946. Father in Life with Father, Savoy Theatre, 1947; Sir Edward in Home is To-morrow, 1948; in A Woman's Place, Vaudeville, 1949; Aubrey Tanqueray in The Second Mrs. Tanqueray, Haymarket, 1950; producer since 1936, Crime and Punishment, The Lady with the Lamp, etc.; appeared in films since 1932. *Recreations:* golf, painting. *Address:* 27 South Terrace, S.W.7. *T.:* Kensington 9965. *Clubs:* Garrick, Beefsteak, Green Room, Stage Golfing Society.
[*Died* 21 *April* 1952.

BANNATYNE, Sir Robert Reid, Kt., *cr.* 1944; C.B. 1919; *b.* 1875; *s.* of Mark Bannatyne, Glasgow; *m.* 1913, Rose Emma, *d.* of late Hon. John Donohoe Fitzgerald, K.C.; two *d.* *Educ.:* Rugby School (Scholar); New College, Oxford (Scholar, 1st Class Mods., 1st Class Lit. Hum.). Resident Toynbee Hall, 1900-03. Late Assistant Under Secretary of State, Home Office; retired, 1939; rejoined Home Office, June 1940; transferred to Ministry of National Insurance, March 1945 - June 1948; Member Industrial Health Research Board; a British Government delegate to International Labour Conference at Geneva, 1925; Member of Royal Commission on Workmen's Compensation, 1938; Chairman (acting) of State Management Districts Council, 1940-45; Member of Beveridge Committee on Social Insurance, 1941-42; Tomlinson Committee on Rehabilitation of Disabled Persons, 1942; Monckton Committee on Alternative Remedies, 1944-46. *Address:* 5 Hickman's Close, Lindfield, Sussex. *T.:* Lindfield 2258.
[*Died* 8 *April* 1956.

BANNERMAN, Lt.-Col. Sir Arthur D'Arcy Gordon, 12th Bart., *cr.* 1682; K.C.V.O., *cr.* 1928 (C.V.O. 1911); C.I.E. 1903; Extra Gentleman Usher to the Queen since 1952 (to King George VI, 1936-1952); *b.* 20 Feb. 1866; *s.* of late Col. Patrick W. Bannerman; *S.* cousin, 1934; *m.* 1st, 1898, Virginia Emily (*d.* 1915), *d.* of late Surgeon-Major W. J. G. Bedford, General Staff, N.S.W., of Doddington, Cambs.; one *s.* one *d.*; 2nd, 1918, Philippa (*d.* 1949), wife of Lt.-Col. Vores, R.H.A. *Educ.:* Harrow; R.M.C., Sandhurst. Entered Army, 1885; Captain, 1896; Major, 1903; Lt.-Col., 1911; Indian Political Department, 1893; Resident, Kashmir, 1917-21; Political A.D.C. to Secretary of State for India, 1921-28; Gentleman Usher to the King, 1928-36. *Heir:* *s.* Lt.-Col. Donald Arthur Gordon Bannerman [Cameron Highlanders, *b.* 2 July 1899; *m.* 1932, Barbara Charlotte *d.* of late Lt.-Col. A. Cameron, O.B.E., Indian Medical Service, of Southwold, Suffolk; two *s.*, twin *d.* *Educ.:* Harrow; R.M.C. Sandhurst. Served N. Russia, 1919; War of 1939-45, in Egypt]. *Address:* c/o Lloyds Bank, 6 Pall Mall, S.W.1.
[*Died* 27 *April* 1955.

BANNISTER, Prof. Charles Olden, M. Eng., A.R.S.M., F.R.I.C.; Professor Emeritus of Metallurgy in the University of Liverpool; Member Institution of Mining and Metallurgy, Institute of Metals, etc.; *b.* 1876; *s.* of late Thomas and Frances Bannister; *m.* 1904, Alice Edith, *e. d.* of late Charles and Alice Burr, London; one *s.* one *d.* *Educ.:* Stourbridge Grammar School; Royal School of Mines. Bessemer Medallist, Matthey Prizeman and Honours Associate of the School; Head of Metallurgy Department, Sir John Cass Technical Institute, London, 1903-1919; practised as Consulting Metallurgist with Messrs. Edward Riley and Harbord, Westminster, 1913-20; Professor of Metallurgy, University of Liverpool, 1920-41. *Publications:* numerous researches and papers on metallurgical subjects in the proceedings of the Institution of Mining and Metallurgy; Journals of the Iron and Steel Institute; Institute of Metals, etc. *Address:* Northstead, New Brighton. *T.:* Wallasey 1974. *Club:* University (Liverpool).
[*Died* 22 *Feb.* 1955.

BANSDA, ex-Maharaja Saheb of; Maharawalji Shri Sir Indrasinhji Pratapsinhji, K.C.I.E., 1937; *b.* 16 Feb. 1888; acceded to Gadi, 1911; abdicated 1947; *m.* A. S. Anandkunverba Sahiba, *d.* of late Raolji Shri of Mansa; one *s.* six *d.* *Educ.:* Rajkumar College, Rajkot. Area of State, 215 sq. miles; Population 54,764; Salute, 9 guns. Free education, secondary and primary; fully equipped hospitals for men, women and children, and dispensaries giving free medical relief. Contributed over Rs. 216,000/- to various War Purposes; Anand Bhuwan Palace at Bombay was given for use of Officers of the three war Services. *Address:* Bansda State, Gujarat, India.
[*Died* *November* 1951.

BANERJEA, Pramathanath. See page xxvii.

BANSWARA, Maharawal of, H.H. Rayan Rai Maharadhiraj Maharawalji Sahib Shree Sir Pirthi Singhji Bahadur, K.C.I.E., *cr.* 1933; *b.* 15 July 1888; *S.* 1914; *m.*; two *s.* Area, including Patta Kushalgarh, 1946 square miles, and population 260,670. *Heir:* Maharaj Raj Kumar Sahib Shree Chandra-Veer Singhji. *Address:* Banswara, Rajputana, India.
[*Died* 28 *July* 1944.
[*But death not notified in time for inclusion in Who Was Who 1941–1950, first edn.*

BANTA, Arthur Mangun, B.S., M.A., Ph.D.; Zoologist; Prof. of Experimental Zoology, 1929-30, Research Prof. of Biology, 1930-45, Prof. Emeritus since 1945, Brown Univ., U.S.A.; *b.* 31 Dec. 1877; *s.* of J. H. Banta and Mary Mangun; *m.* 1906, Mary Charlotte Slack; one *s.* two *d.* *Educ.:* Indiana and Harvard Univs. Resident Investigator Carnegie Experimental Evolution Station, 1909-30. Associate Carnegie Inst. of Washington, 1930-32 and 1936-37. *Publications:* The Fauna of Mayfield's Cave, 1907; Selection in Cladocera on the Basis of a Physiological Character, 1921; Physiology, Genetics and Evolution of some Cladocera, 1939; contrib. to biol. journals. *Address:* 168 Medway Street, Providence, R.I., U.S.A.
[*Died* 1 *July* 1946.
[*But death not notified in time for inclusion in Who Was Who 1941–1950, first edn.*

BARBER, Arthur Vavasour, B.A., F.I.B., F.R.E.S.; late partner Glyn, Mills & Co.; *e.s.* of late Rev. Robt. W. Barber, M.A.; *m.* Kathyrna, *e. d.* of Prof. G. Speransky; two *d.* *Educ.:* Uppingham; Oxford Univ. *Publications:* Many articles in U.K. and U.S.A. upon Banking, Currency, Education, etc.; *Recreation:* music. *Address:* The Hey, Throwleigh, Nr. Okehampton, Devon; Roseau, Domenica, B.W.I. *Club:* Union.
[*Died* 24 *Aug.* 1957.

BARBER, Donald, C.B.E. 1949 (O.B.E. 1944); Director, Retail Distributors' Association Incorporated, since 1935; *b.* 9 April 1905; *s.* of Cecil Walter and Mary Ann Barber; *m.* 1929, Henrietta Mary Evelyn, *née* Dunne (marriage dissolved, 1947); one *s.* one *d.*; *m.* 1947, Mrs. Muriel Irene Frith (*née* Jex). *Educ.:* Christ's Hospital; Trinity College, Cambridge (Scholar). 1st Class, Mathematical Tripos Part I, 1924; 1st Class, Economics Tripos Part II, 1926; Adam Smith Prizeman, Wrenbury Scholar, University of Cambridge. *Address:* 12 Paxton Gardens, Woodham Lane, Woking, Surrey.
[*Died* 31 *May* 1957.

BARBER, Sir (Edward) Fairless, Kt., *cr.* 1918; late Additional Member of Legislative Council, Government of Madras; *b.* 19 Sept. 1873; 2nd *s.* of William Barber, Q.C., Judge Derby County Court; *m.* 1st, 1897, Beatrice Annie (*d.* 1930), *d.* of Robert Baldwin Hayward, F.R.S., Harrow; two *d*; 2nd, 1931, Eileen M., *d.* of William Holt. *Educ.:* Evelyns; Marlborough. *Address:* Orchards, Templewood Lane, Farnham Common, Bucks. *T.:* Farnham Common 27. [*Died* 15 *July* 1958.

BARBER, Maj.-Gen. George Walter, C.B. 1919; C.M.G. 1918; D.S.O. 1917; V.D. 1920; *b.* 20 Nov. 1868; *s.* of Charles Worthington Barber and Isabella Loughborough; *m.* 1896, Janet Watson Salmond; one *s.* three *d.* *Educ.:* H.M.S. Conway; Whitgift Grammar School; Middlesex Hospital Medical School. Served European War, 1914-18 (C.B., C.M.G., D.S.O., despatches, Croix de Guerre avec Étoile); Director-General of Medical Services, Australian Military Forces, 1925-34, and Royal Australian Air Force, 1927-34, and Civil Aviation, 1930-34; retired list, 1934. *Address:* Central Road, Kalamunda, Western Australia. *Club:* Weld (Perth, Western Australia).
[*Died* 24 *July* 1951.

BARBER, Harold Wordsworth, M.A., M.B. (Cantab.); F.R.C.P. London; Consulting Physician to the Skin Department, Guy's Hospital; Ex-Pres. British Assoc. of Dermatology; Ex-Pres. Dermatological Section, Royal Soc. of Medicine; Consulting Dermatologist to Royal Navy; *b.* Nottingham, 13 May 1886; *s.* of Robert Barber, Solicitor, Nottingham; *m.* Juliette Louise, *d.* of Madame Veuve Champrenaud, Paris; no *c.* *Educ.:* Repton School; Clare College, Cambridge (Natural Science Scholar); Guy's Hospital. B.A. (First Class Natural Science Tripos), 1908; M.A., M.B., B.C. Cambridge, 1911; F.R.C.P. (Lond.), 1922. Arthur Durham Travelling Scholarship, Guy's Hospital, 1913; studied Dermatology in Paris, and with Professor Unna in Hamburg during tenure of Scholarship; during European War served in R.A.M.C. in India, Mesopotamia, German East Africa, and France; Medical Registrar at Guy's, 1913-15 and 1919; Lettsomian Lecturer, 1929. *Publications:* Diseases of the Skin: Taylor and Poulton's Medicine; numerous papers on dermatological and medical subjects. *Recreation:* ornithology. *Address:* 58 Harley Street, W.1. *T.:* Welbeck 9727.
[*Died* 14 *Jan.* 1955.

BARBER, Percival Ellison, B.A., M.R.C.S., L.R.C.P. Lond.; Ch.M. Sheffield (Hon.); T.D.; retired; Major R.A.M.C. (T.F.) attached West Riding R.H.A. (Retired); Hon. Consulting Surgeon, Jessop Hospital, Sheffield. *Educ.:* Cambridge; St. Bartholomew's Hospital. Was demonstrator of anatomy, University College, Sheffield; Professor of Midwifery, Sheffield University, 1911; House Surgeon, Royal Hospital, Jessop Hospital and Cancer Hospital, Brompton. Asst. County Director, Red Cross, Derbyshire; Patron, Ashford Branch of British Legion. *Recreation:* cricket for Caius College, United Hospitals and St. Bartholomew's. *Address:* Riverside Ashford, near Bakewell, Derbyshire.
[*Died* 24 *April* 1959.

BARBER, Rev. Thomas Gerrard, M.A., Vicar of Hucknall, Notts, 1907-46; Rural Dean of Bulwell, 1915; Canon of Southwell, 1919, Emeritus, 1946; Chaplain to the R.A.F.; Member of the I.O.F.; *s.* of Robert Barber, solicitor, Nottingham; *m.* Gertrude M. Palmer, Horwich, Lancs; one *s.* three *d.* *Educ.:* Repton School; Trinity Coll., Cambridge; Ridley Hall, Cambridge. Deacon, 1898; Priest, 1899; Curate, Doncaster Parish Church, 1898; Beeford, Yorks, 1901; St. James', Bath, 1902; Curate in charge of St. Peter's, Hucknall, 1904; A Knight of Greek Order of the Redeemer, 1924. *Publications:* Hucknall Torkard Church and its Byron Associations; Byron—and where he is buried; How the Church came to Hucknall; The Children's Pilgrimage; How the Church came to Spondon. *Recreations:* fishing, shooting, tennis. *Address:* The Vicarage, Spondon, Derby. *T.:* Derby 55573. [*Died* 15 *Oct.* 1952.

BARBER, William David, O.B.E. 1919; I.S.O. 1912; Hon. Treasurer of Civil Service Widows' and Orphans' Annuities Assurance Society, and Civil Service Insurance Society; late Chief Civil Assistant to the Hydrographer of the Navy, Admiralty. *Address:* 7 Bishopsthorpe Rd., S.E. 26.
[*Died* 19 *Aug.* 1952.

BARBER, W(illiam) Edmund; formerly Capt. 4th Bn. Seaforth Highlanders; *o. s.* of W. H. Barber, L.L.D., Emsworth, Hants. *Educ:* Bradford; Christ's College, Cambridge (Scholar and Exhibitioner). For one year assistant master at Felsted School; Literary Editor of the Morning Post, 1910; enlisted London Regt. Aug. 1914; 2nd Lieut. Seaforth Highlanders, 1915; Intelligence Corps, War Office, 1916-18; Admiralty, 1918; Chief Resettlement Officer

for Scotland and North England, 1918-19; Editor of the Economic Review, 1919-22; Foreign Correspondent of the Morning Post in the Rhineland, etc., 1922-24; Diplomatic Correspondent of the Morning Post, 1924-25; Editor of Country Life, 1925-32; Press Officer, Ministry of Labour, 1935-36. *Address:* 40 St. Ann's Crescent, Lewes, Sussex.
[*Died* 13 *Oct.* 1958.

BARBOUR, Rt. Hon. Sir John Milne, of Hilden, Co. Antrim, 1st Bt., *cr.* 1943; P.C. (N. Ire.), 1925; J.P., D.L.; *b.* The Fort, Lisburn, Co. Antrim, 1868; 2nd *s.* of late John D. Barbour, J.P., D.L., of Conway, Dunmurry, Co. Antrim, and Elizabeth Law, *e. d.* of late John Milne, J.P., of Trinity Grove, Edinburgh; *m.* 1899, Eliza (*d.* 1910), *e. d.* of late Robert Barbour of Paterson, New Jersey; three *d. Educ.:* Elstree; Harrow; Brasenose, Oxford (M.A.). Hon. LL.D. Queen's University, Belfast; M.P. Co. Antrim, Northern Parliament, Ireland, 1921-29; South Antrim since 1929; Parliamentary and Financial Secretary to Ministry of Finance of Northern Ireland, 1921-40; Minister of Commerce Northern Ireland, 1925-41; Minister of Finance, Northern Ireland, 1941-43. High Sheriff Co. of Antrim, 1905; Co. of Down, 1907; President of the Belfast Chamber of Commerce, 1911; Pres. of the Royal Ulster Agricultural Society, 1925-30, and since 1931; Member of general synod of Church of Ireland. Member of Belfast Harbour Commissioners, 1914-50; served for some years on the Senate of the Queen's University of Belfast; Director Linen Thread Co., Ltd., Glasgow; and of several other companies; President of Scottish Amicable Life Assurance Society; President Royal Victoria Hospital, Belfast; Member of South Antrim Hospital Committee (Lisburn); Pres. Northern Ireland Scout Council; takes an active interest in Freemasonry, being Sovereign Grand Commander Supreme Council 33°. (Irish Constitution), Grand King, Supreme Grand Royal Arch Chapter of Ireland and has served as Provincial Senior Grand Warden of Antrim. *Recreations:* rowed in the Brasenose College Boat; head of the River Torpids, 1888; VIII.'s 1889, and played in the College Association Football XI. *Address:* Conway, Dunmurry, Co. Antrim, Ulster. *T.A.:* Barbour, Conway, Dunmurry. *T.:* 2281 Dunmurry. *Clubs:* Bath, Royal Automobile, Overseas League; Ulster (Belfast); Western (Glasgow); Kildare Street (Dublin); Royal Ulster Yacht (Bangor).
[*Died* 3 *Oct.* 1951 *(ext.).*

BARCLAY, Rev. Humphrey Gordon, C.V.O. 1946; M.C.; Rector of Southrepps since 1946; Chaplain to the Queen since 1952 (formerly to King George VI); *e. s.* of late Col. H. A. Barclay, C.V.O.; *m.* Beatrice Eremar, 2nd *d.* of late Benjamin Bond Cabbell, Cromer Hall; two *s.* three *d.* *Educ.:* Eton; Trinity Hall, Cambridge. Ordained, 1905; Mission to Seamen, Poplar, 1905-8, Calcutta, 1908-9, Middlesbrough, 1910-14; C.F., European War, 1914-18; Rector of Carlton Forehoe, 1918-20; of Southrepps, 1920-25, of Tittleshall, 1925-39; Domestic Chaplain to the King, Royal Chapel, Windsor Gt. Park, 1939-46. *Recreations:* sports and games. *Address:* Southrepps, Norwich.
[*Died* 2 *Oct.* 1955.

BARCLAY, Sir (Robert) Noton, Kt., *cr.* 1936; J.P. Manchester; *b.* 1872; *m.* 1898, Helena Margaret Bythell; two *s.* two *d. Educ.:* Uppingham; Manchester University. Export shipping merchant, Robert Barclay & Co., Ltd., Manchester; Lord Mayor of Manchester, 1929-1930; Alderman of City of Manchester; Pres. of Manchester Chamber of Commerce, 1914-16; M.P. (L.) Manchester (Exchange), 1923-24; High Sheriff for Cheshire, 1937-38; formerly Dir. of District Bank (Chm., 1936-46); Dir. of National Boiler Insurance Co. and of Manchester Ship Canal; Chairman of Manchester Y.M.C.A. *Address:* Far Hills, Alderley Edge, Manchester. *T.:* Alderley Edge 2197. *Clubs:* Reform, Clarendon (Manchester).
[*Died* 24 *Nov.* 1957.

BARCLAY, Robert Wyvill; *b.* 23 Nov. 1880; *e. s.* of late Robert Barclay, J.P., D.L., of Bury Hill, Dorking, and Laura Charlotte Rachel, *d.* of late Marmaduke Wyvill, M.P., of Constable Burton, Yorkshire; *m.* 1904, Elsa Mary, *o. d.* of late Sir Edward Bray; three *s.* one *d. Educ.:* Privately; Trinity College, Cambridge. Lieut.-Colonel (retired) Surrey (Queen Mary's Regiment) Yeomanry, late Temp. Captain 2nd Life Guards; Patron of one living; J.P., D.L. Surrey; High Sheriff of Surrey, 1923-24. *Recreations:* shooting, fishing. *Address:* Bury Hill House, Dorking, Surrey. *Club:* Bath.
[*Died* 19 *Nov.* 1951.

BARCROFT, John Coleraine Hanbury, C.M.G. 1957; Financial Secretary, Government of Sarawak, since 1955; *b.* 2 Aug. 1908; *s.* of Lt.-Col. J. H. P. Barcroft, Kensington Close, W.8, and Mrs. Barcroft, Marchwood, Hants. *Educ.:* Weymouth Coll., Dorset; on Continent. Sarawak C.S., 1930; Colonial Administrative Service, 1947; Brit. Adviser to Sultan of Brunei, 1952. Star of Sarawak, 1946. *Recreations:* fishing, shooting, sailing, photography. *Address:* Hangers, Nr. Marchwood, Hants. *T.:* Hythe 2198. *Clubs:* Bath; Sarawak Turf (Sarawak); Royal Brunei Yacht (Borneo); Singapore (Singapore). [*Died* 6 *June* 1958.

BARDOUX, Jacques, M.C., Commandeur de la Légion d'Honneur, Croix de guerre, etc., Hon.D.Litt., Oxf.; Sénateur du Puy-de-Dôme; France, 1938-45; late lecturer on Diplomatic History at École Supérieure de Guerre and École des Sciences politiques de Paris; Member Acad. des Sciences morales et politiques, 1925; Acad. des Sciences Coloniales, 1938; one of the Directors of the French Committee, Institute for Intellectual Co-operation; Dep. Chm. of le Rassemblement Républicain, 1945; Député à l'Assemblée Nationale, 1945, 1946, 1951; Chm. of Foreign Affairs committee of l'Assemblée Nationale, 1952; *b.* Versailles, 27 May 1874; *s.* of A. Bardoux, Senateur inamovible, Membre de l'Institut, *n.* of Louis Blanc; *m.* Geneviève, *d.* of Georges-Picot, historian, Membre de l'Institut, *g.d.* of Comte de Montalivet, Minister of Napoleon I.; one *s.* four *d. Educ.:* Lycées Janson de Sailly and Condorcet; Oxford, unattached student; Sorbonne. Doctor in letters (Sorbonne), 1901; Foreign Editor of Journal des Débats, 1901; French Editor of Queen Victoria's letters, 1907; Foreign Editor of L'Opinion, 1908; Lecturer at École Libre des Sciences politiques, 1908; Aug. 1914 volunteered as N.C.O. in French infantry unit; Apr. 1915, attached as liaison officer to the British Army; Nov. 1918-Mar. 1919, Private Secretary to Marshal Foch; Lecturer at École Supérieure de Guerre, 1919; French Expert to Genoa Conf., May 1922; French Delegate to the League of Nations, July 1923, to U.N.O., 1952; candidate as Republican in the Dep. of Puy-de-Dôme, Nov. 1919, May 1924, and April 1928, and for the Senate, Jan. 1927 and October 1935; Hon. Sec. of the Groupe des Résistants du Sénat, 1942-45; Membre of Assemblée Nationale Constituante, 1945 and 1946; French delegate at the European Assembly, Strasburg, 1949; 1924 contributor to Le Temps; Administrator of Cie générale du Maroc, Cie des Étains d'Extrême Orient, etc. *Publications:* Souvenirs d'Oxford; Walter Map; John Ruskin; Essai d'une psychologie de l'Angleterre contemporaine, 7 vols.; La Reine Victoria; Le Socialisme en Angleterre; La Reine Victoria (pages choisies de sa correspondance); Silhouettes d'Outre-Manche; Silhouettes royales d'outre-Manche; Croquis d'Outre-Manche; La Marche à la guerre; L'Ouvrier anglais d'aujourd'hui; D. Lloyd George et la France; J. Ramsay Macdonald; Hors du marais: la

Route de France; Le dialogue Edouard Herriot—J. R. Macdonald; L'Ile et l'Europe: la Politique Anglaise, 1930-32; Le drame français: refaire l'Etat ou subir la force, 1934; La France de demain, 1936; Les Soviets contre la France; J'accuse Moscou; Le Chaos Espagnol; éviterons-nous la contagion?, 1937; Staline contre l'Europe: les preuves du complot Communiste; Ni communiste, ni hitlérienne: la France de demain: un plan, 1937; L'ordre Nouveau: face au communisme et au racisme, 1939; Destin de France: le rythme des Invasions, 1945; Les Origines du Malheur Européen: l'aide anglo-française à la domination prussienne, 1949; Paix, Ordre, Liberté: Treize années du Mandat, 1951. Quand Bismarck dominait l'Europe, 1952; La défaite de Bismarck; l'Empire français et l'Alliance russe, 1953; Journal d'un témoin de la IIIe République, I, Paris, Bordeaux, Vichy (1938-40); II; La délivrance de Paris: délibérations et négociations clandestines (Sept. 1943-Sept. 1944); III, Le second Royaume de Bourges sous Jeanne d'Arc: Vichy. *Recreation:* tennis. *Address:* 11 rue Mérimée, Paris (XVI). *T.:* Passy 49-65; Saint Saturnin, Puy-de-Dôme. *Clubs:* Union Interalliée, France-Amérique, France-Grande-Bretagne, Académie Diplomatique Internationale. [*Died* 15 *Aug.* 1959.

BARDSLEY, Robert Vickers, C.M.G. 1933; O.B.E. 1927 (M.B.E. 1919); *b.* 28 June 1890; *o. s.* of late Alexander Bardsley, Manchester, and Lucy Vickers; *m.* 1926, Agnes Margaret, *y. d.* of late H. T. Parke, Withnell Fold, nr. Chorley; one *s.* one *d.* *Educ.:* Shrewsbury; Merton College, Oxford (Classical Exhibitioner). Joined Sudan Political Service, 1913; District Commissioner in Khartoum and Blue Nile Provinces; Assistant Private Secretary (1920) and Private Secretary (1924) to the Governor-General, also Secretary to his Council; Assistant Civil Secretary, 1926; Deputy Governor (1927) and Governor (1928) of the Blue Nile Province; retired, 1932; Order of the Nile, 4th Class, 1924; 3rd class, 1931. *Recreations:* cricket, golf, shooting. *Address:* Coldwaltham Lodge, nr. Pulborough, Sussex. *Club:* Boodle's. [*Died* 26 *July* 1952.

BAREA, Arturo, Cross of Military Merit with Red Ribbon (Spain), 1923; Spanish writer (free-lance) and broadcaster; British subject by naturalisation, 1948; *b.* Badajoz, Spain, 20 Sept. 1897; *s.* of Miguel Barea and Leonor Ogazón; *m.* 1st, 1924, Aurelia Grimaldos; two *s.* two *d.*; 2nd, 1938, Ilsa Pollak-Kulcsar. *Educ.:* Escolapians, Madrid. Clerical posts in bank and commerce, 1911-20. Military service Spanish Army in Morocco, 1920-23. Technical man, manager for patent-agent, 1924-36. Foreign Press Censor, Madrid, 1936-37; Broadcaster, Madrid, 1937. Emigrated to France with wife, Ilsa, 1938; resident England, 1939-. Commentator B.B.C. Latin-American Service, 1940-. Visiting Prof., Pennsylvania State Coll., 1952. London correspondent of La Nacion, Buenos Aires, 1956-. Writer (autobiography, fiction, essays), 1937-; writes in Spanish (translations into English by wife). *Publications:* Valor y Miedo, 1938; The Forge, 1941; Struggle for the Spanish Soul, 1941; The Track, 1943; Lorca, 1944; The Clash, 1946; The Broken Root, 1951; Unamuno, 1952; short stories and literary essays. Has been translated into 9 languages. *Recreations:* carpentering, clock-mending, mechanical repairs. *Address:* Middle Lodge, Eaton Hastings, Faringdon, Berks. *T.:* Faringdon 2185. *Club:* P.E.N. [*Died* 24 *Dec.* 1957.

BARGONE, Frédéric C.; *see* Farrère, Claude.

BARHAM, Col. Arthur Saxby, C.M.G. 1918; V.D.; J.P.; Col. T. F. (ret.); director of United Dairies Ltd., Sir George's Trust Ltd., and de Berhams Ltd.; *b.* 17 July 1869; *y. s.* of late Sir George Barham, J.P., of Wadhurst, Sussex; *m.* 1st, 1893, Annie Gertrude (*d.* 1939), *d.* of late E. H. Edwards; one *s.*; 2nd, 1940, Anna Marie (*d.* 1941), *d.* of late Conrad Schaufelberger, Zürich. *Educ.:* University College School. Served with 19th Middlesex (Bloomsbury) V.R., 1888-1908; commanded that Battalion 1904-08; rejoined Sept. 1914 to Queen Victoria's Rifles; appointed to command 2/12th London (The Rangers), Feb. 1915; served with that Battalion in France and Flanders (despatches, C.M.G.); Member of Kent County Council since 1925; Alderman, 1937-49. *Address:* Hole Park, Rolvenden, Kent. *T.:* Rolvenden 304. [*Died* 16 *July* 1952.

BARING, Sir Godfrey, 1st Bt., *cr.* 1911; K.B.E., *cr.* 1952; J.P., D.L.; High Sheriff of Hampshire, 1897; Chairman of Isle of Wight C.C. since 1898; late Alderman of the London County Council; *b.* 18 Apr. 1871; *s.* of late Lt.-Gen. Charles Baring (Coldstream Guards) and Helen, 3rd *d.* of Rt. Hon. Sir Jas. Graham, 2nd Bt., of Netherby; *m.* 1st, 1898, Eva Hermione (*d.* 1934), M.B.E., J.P., *d.* of late Mackintosh of Mackintosh, Moy-Hall, Inverness; two *s.* two *d.*; 2nd 1937, Brenda Margery (*d.* 1953), *yr. d.* of late Canon J. S. Blake. *Educ.:* Eton. Contested (L.) Isle of Wight, 1900; Stoke-on-Trent, 1900; M.P. (L.) Isle of Wight, 1906-10; Barnstaple Division, Devonshire, 1911-19; contested Devonport, 1910; Chm., Royal Nat. Lifeboat Institute, 1923-56; Mem. of the Board of Visitors for Parkhurst Convict Prison and Advisory Committee of Camp Hill Prison. *Recreations:* shooting, yachting, cricket, tennis, motoring. *Heir:* *s.* Charles Christian, *b.* 16 Dec. 1898. *Address:* Nubia House, Cowes, Isle of Wight. *T.:* Cowes 27. *Clubs:* Brook's, Turf, National Liberal; Royal Yacht Squadron (Cowes). [*Died* 24 *Nov.* 1957.

BARKER, Sir Alport; *see* Barker, Sir T. W. A.

BARKER, Sir Ernest, Kt., *cr.* 1944; F.B.A.; D.Litt. Oxf. and (*ad eundem*) Cantab.; Hon. LL.D., Edinburgh, Harvard, Calcutta, Dalhousie (Canada) and Salonica; Hon. Ph.D., Oslo; Hon. Fellow of Merton College, Oxford, and Peterhouse, Cambridge; Life Governor of King's College and Hon. Fellow of Westfield College, London; Officier de la Légion d'Honneur; Grosse Verdientskreuz (Germany); Kt. Commander Order of George I (Greece), Commander Order of the Crown (Belgium), Order of Orange-Nassau (Netherlands), and Order of the White Lion (Czechoslovakia); King Haakon VII Liberty Cross (Norway); *b.* 23 Sept. 1874; *s.* of George Barker of Woodley, Cheshire; *m.* 1st, 1900, Emily Isabel (*d.* 1924), *d.* of Rev. R. Salkeld, Vicar of St. Mark's, Dukinfield, Cheshire; one *s.* two *d.*; 2nd, 1927, Olivia Stuart, *o. d.* of John Stuart Horner, Mells, Somerset; one *s.* one *d.* *Educ.:* Manchester Grammar School; Balliol College, Oxford (Classical Scholar). Fellow (Classical) of Merton Coll., 1898-1905; Lecturer in modern history at Wadham College, 1899-1909; Fellow and Lecturer, St. John's College, 1909-13; Fellow and Tutor, New College, 1913-20; Princ. of King's Coll., London, 1920-27; Prof. of Political science, and Fellow of Peterhouse, Cambridge, 1928-39; Professor of Political Science, Univ. of Cologne, 1947-48. *Publications:* The Political Thought of Plato and Aristotle, 1906; Political Thought in England from Herbert Spencer to To-day, 1915 (revised edition, 1947); National Character, 1927 (revised ed. 1948); Reflections on Government, 1942; Britain and the British People, 1942 (revised ed. 1955); Translation of Aristotle's Politics, 1946 (shorter edn., 1948); ed. Character of England, 1947; Traditions of Civility, 1948; Principles of Social and Political Theory, 1951; Age and

Youth (memories), 1953; (joint ed.) The European Inheritance, 1954; From Alexander to Constantine, 1955; Social and Political Thought in Byzantium, 1957. *Address:* 17 Cranmer Road, Cambridge. *T.:* Cambridge 4394. *Club:* Athenæum. [*Died* 17 *Feb.* 1960.

BARKER, Lieut.-Colonel Frederic Allan, C.I.E., 1938; O.B.E., 1918; M.A., M.D., B.C.; I.M.S., retd.; Medical Practitioner, retd.; *b.* Gosforth, Cumberland, 17 October 1882; *s.* of Rev. H. A. Barker; *m.* 1908, Amy Helen Clarke; one *d.* (and one *s.* decd.). *Educ.:* Repton; Cambridge Univ.; Guy's Hospital. Joined I.M.S., 1907; military duty till 1910; then Civil Surgeon and Superintendent Jails, Andaman Islands; Supt. Borstal Institution, Lahore, 1912-14; on active service in Egypt, M.E.F., Gallipoli and Palestine (despatches, O.B.E.), 1914-20; S.M.O. and Civil Surgeon, Port Blair, Andamans, 1920-25; I.G. Prisons, Central Provinces, 1926-27; Inspector-Gen. of Prisons, Punjab, 1927-39; Deputy D.G.I.M.S., 1935; military employ, Quetta, 1936; retired 1939; C.M.O. Alien Internment Camps, Isle of Man, 1940-45. O.St.J. *Publications:* Borstal Training for Indian Prisoners; Imprisonment; Modern Prison System of India, 1944. *Address:* Silver Stream, Headbourne Worthy, Nr. Winchester, Hants. *T.:* Winchester 5227. [*Died* 30 *June* 1959.

BARKER, Lieut.-Colonel Frederick George, C.B.E. 1919; *b.* 27 Oct. 1866; *s.* of Rev. Alfred Gresley Barker and Agnes, *d.* of Rev. Comyns Tucker, Rector of Washford, Devon; *m.* 1895, Lucile Mary (*d.* 1945), *d.* of Cartmell Harrison of Bramley, Hants; four *s.* one *d.* *Educ.:* Eton; Brasenose, Oxford (M.A.). Called to bar, Inner Temple, 1894; Western Circuit; gazetted 3rd Royal Berkshire Regiment (Militia), 1887; served during South African War; commanded Regiment, 1909-1917; went to France on the Staff, served till 1920 (despatches, C.B.E.); D.L., J.P. Berkshire; Alderman of County Council for Berks; Chairman of the Wokingham County Bench, 1931-1944; Member of Thames Conservancy Board; Commissioner of Income Tax; Patron of the living of Sherfield-on-Loddon, Hants. *Recreations:* played cricket a good deal, hunting all his life, Secretary Vine Hunt 10 years, Master of Garth Fox Hounds, 1927-30, fishing, shooting. *Address:* Stanlake Park, Twyford, Berks. *T.:* Twyford 5. *Club:* Oxford and Cambridge. [*Died* 18 *Nov.* 1951.

BARKER, Rev. Canon Gilbert David M.A.; Canon Residentiary and Chancellor of Southwark Cathedral since 1936; *b.* 25 July 1882; *s.* of T. D. Barker; *m.* 1909, Helen Mary, *d.* of W. F. Atkinson. *Educ.:* St. Peter's College, Cambridge. Ordained, 1905; Curate, St. Mary Bishophill Senior, York, 1905-9; Bowdon, 1909-12; Hessle, 1912-14; Domestic Chaplain to Bishop of Lichfield, 1914-16; temp. C.F., 1914-16; Vicar of St. Paul's, Stafford, 1916-1919; Rector of St. Mary Bishophill Senior, York, 1919-28; Canon of York, 1928; Superintendent of Religious Education, Diocese of York, 1928-33; Territorial Chaplain, 4th class, 1915; Senior Chaplain to Territorial Army, Northern Command, 1924-1933; Director of Religious Education, Dioceses of London and Southwark, 1933-1949; Hon. Chaplain to the King, 1928-1942; Hon. Canon of Southwark, 1933-36; Secretary to Clergy Orphan Corporation, 1940-54. *Publications:* A Guide for Church School Managers: A New Guide for Church School Managers, Governors and others interested in Church Day Schools. *Address:* 38 Danecroft Road, Herne Hill, S.E.24. *T.:* Brixton 1009. [*Died* 1 *Nov.* 1958.

BARKER, Lt.-Col. John Stafford, M.V.O. 1911; late R.E.; *b.* Bangalore, 6 Sept. 1879; *s.* of late J. Pinder Barker, Mysore Revenue Survey; *m.* 1906, Mary Gertrude, *o. d.* of late H. L. Moysey, I.S.O.; three *s.* *Educ.:* Bedford Grammar School. Entered Royal Military Academy, 1896; Commission in R.E., 1898; Capt., 1907; Major, 1915; Lt.-Col. 1924; served in Ceylon, 1900, 1904; India, 1905-29; retired, 1929; Electrical Engineer, Coronation Durbar, Delhi, 1911; served European War; Field Engineer, Garrison Kut-el-Amara (despatches); P.O.W. Turkey. *Address:* 2 Oast House Road, Icklesham, Nr. Winchelsea, Sussex. [*Died* 10 *Aug.* 1959.

BARKER, Dame Lilian Charlotte, D.B.E., *cr.* 1944 (C.B.E. 1917); J.P.; *b.* London, 1874; *d.* of James Barker, Sweffling, Suffolk. *Educ.:* Whitelands College, Chelsea. Elementary teacher under L.C.C.; Principal of Cosway Street L.C.C. Women's Institute, Marylebone; 1st Commandant of the Women's Legion Cookery Section under Lady Londonderry; Lady Superintendent, Royal Arsenal, Woolwich; Principal Officer, Training Section, Ministry of Labour; Secretary of the Central Committee Women's Training and Employment; Governor of H.M. Borstal Institution for Girls, Aylesbury, 1923-35; Assistant Commissioner and Inspector of H.M. Prisons, 1935-43; Director of Aylesbury Association for after-care of Borstal Girls and Convicts, 1928-43; retired, 1943. *Recreation:* gardening. *Address:* Charcroft, Wendover Dean, Bucks. *T.:* Wendover 2204. *Club:* Forum. [*Died* 20 *May* 1955.

BARKER, Louis William, D.S.O. 1919; V.D.; Vice-President and Director (retd. 1948), National Drug and Chemical Co. of Canada Ltd.; *b.* St. John, N.B., 1 Oct. 1879; *s.* of Henry Ward Barker and Anna Christie; *m.* 1st, Gladys Troop McLauchlan (*d.* 1931); one *d.*; 2nd, 1936, Mary Ainslie. *Educ.:* Rothesay Collegiate School; University of New Brunswick. Entered wholesale drug business of T. B. Barker & Son, Ltd., St. John, N.B., 1898; Officer in 3rd N.B. Garrison Artillery, 1898-1912; moved to Montreal as manager of branch of National D. and C. Co. Ltd., 1912; overseas as O.C. 4th Canadian Siege Battery, 1915-19 (D.S.O., V.D.); President, Royal Montreal Curling Club, 1929-31; President, Kanawaki Golf Club, 1932-33; President, Province of Quebec Golf Association, 1934. *Recreations:* curling and golf. *Address:* 3980 Côte des Neiges Rd., Montreal, P.Q. Canada. *Clubs:* Montreal Canadian, Royal Montreal Curling (Montreal). [*Died* 28 *April* 1954.

BARKER, Lt.-Gen. Michael George Henry, C.B. 1937; D.S.O. 1917; D.L.; Colonel of the York and Lancaster Regt., 1936-46; a Deputy Regional Commissioner for Civil Defence, London Region, 1941; *b.* 1884; *s.* of E. V. P. Barker, of the Priory, Glastonbury; *m.* 1914, Barbara Maude Bentall; one *s.* *Educ.:* Malvern. Served S.A. War, 1902 (Queen's medal two clasps); European War, 1914-18 (despatches, D.S.O. and bar; Bt. Maj. Legion of Honour, Bt. Lt.-Col.); Director of Recruiting and Organization, War Office, 1936-38; General Officer Commanding, British Forces in Palestine and Transjordan, 1939-40; G.O.C.-in-C. Aldershot Command, 1940; retired pay, 1941. D.L., Essex, 1946. *Address:* Lexden R'se, Colchester. [*Died* 21 *May* 1960.

BARKER, Sir Robert (Beacroft), Kt., *cr.* 1950; O.B.E. 1944; Minister without portfolio, Jamaica, Nov. 1957-Dec. 1958 (resigned); *b.* 18 May 1890; *s.* of John and Hannah Barker, Yorks., England; *m.* 1919, Nina Gladys (*née* Alexander); one *s.* *Educ.:* Blackburn Gram. School; Victoria Univ. of Manchester. B.A. 1911, M.A. 1912. Commissioned in Royal Garrison Artillery European War, 1914-19. Settled in Jamaica, 1919; Nominated Member Legislative Council, Jamaica, 1942-45; Nominated Member Legislative Council, Jamaica (New Con-

stitution), 1945-58 (resigned); Member Executive Council 1945-57. *Address:* 5 Devon Road, Half-Way-Tree, Jamaica. *Clubs:* Jamaica, Liguanea (Jamaica).
[*Died* 11 *Dec.* 1960.

BARKER, Captain Roland Auriol, C.B.E. 1947; M.V.O. 1936; Under Secretary Ministry of Works, since 1952, and Secretary Osborne House Committee since 1938; a Crown Estate Paving Commissioner since 1948; *b.* 13 Sept. 1892; *y. s.* of late Rev. H. A. Barker; *m.* 1922, Ethel Grace Marjorie, *o. d.* of J. E. Layton, Bromley, Kent; two *d.* *Educ.:* Rugby School; Sidney Sussex College, Cambridge. Tutor at Cheltenham College to the sons of Yuan Shai Kai, Emperor of China, 1913; 2nd Lieut. 3rd Loyal (N. Lancashire) Regt. 1914; Capt. 1915; served in France 1915-16 (twice wounded); transferred to 3rd Gurkha Rifles, I. A. 1917; Staff Officer, Nepalese Contingent in India, 1918-19; Asst. Principal H.M. Office of Works, 1920; Private Secretary to Sir Lionel Earle, 1926, to First Commissioners of Works, Lord Londonderry, 1929 and 1931, George Lansbury, 1929, W. Ormsby-Gore, 1931; Principal, 1933; Asst. Secretary, 1940. *Address:* Dore, Englefield Green, Surrey. *T.:* Egham 148. *Club:* United Service.
[*Died* 12 *April* 1954.

BARKER, Sir Ross; *see* Barker, Sir W. R.

BARKER, Sir (Thomas William) Alport, Kt., *cr.* 1951; C.B.E. 1946; Publisher Fiji Times and Herald since 1901; *b.* Akaroa, N.Z.; *s.* of late Thomas William Barker; *m.* 1st, 1909, Evelyn May (decd.), *er. d.* of late James Burton Turner; one *d.* 2nd, May Winifred Watson, Auckland. *Educ.:* West Christchurch (N.Z.) High School; Grammar School, Suva, Fiji. Elected Member: Fiji Legislative Council, 1922-43, 1950-53; Fiji Executive Council, 4 years previously, and 1950-53. Mayor of Suva, 1931, 1934, 1935; Chm. Suva Town Board, 1942-48; Mayor of Suva (Suva Town Council), 1949, 1950, 1951. President: Suva Chamber of Commerce, 1948-52; Suva Rugby Union for 20 years, up to 1952; Suva Swimming Club; Chairman Board of Trustees, Fiji Museum; President: Fiji Show Assoc.; Fiji branch of Roy. Life Saving Soc.; Director of W. R. Carpenter & Co. (Fiji) Ltd., Fiji Investment Trust (Ltd.), Suva Motors (Ltd.), Fiji Transport Co., Ltd.; Proprietor Fiji Times and Herald (only daily in South Seas) and Shanti Dut (Hindi Weekly). *Recreations:* yachting, football. *Address:* Suva, Fiji. *T.:* 22. *Clubs:* Defence (Fiji); Northern (Auckland, N.Z.).
[*Died* 13 *June* 1956.

BARKER, Sir (Wilberforce) Ross, K.C.I.E., *cr.* 1930; C.B. 1919; *b.* 19 Sept. 1874; *e. s.* of Very Rev. William Barker, late Dean of Carlisle, and Anne, *o. d.* of Adm. Sir James Ross; *m.* Helen May (*d.* 1953), *d.* of Matthew Chadbourne; two *s.* one *d.* *Educ.:* Marlborough Coll.; Worcester Coll., Oxford; Chancellor's English Essay Prize, 1899. Barrister, Gray's Inn, 1897; served in Board of Education, 1903-25, as Legal Adviser, 1918-25; Chairman of the Indian Public Service Commission, 1926-32; Member Royal Commission, University of Durham, 1934; President, Royal Society of Teachers, 1936-1948. *Publications:* The Superannuation of Teachers in England and Wales; (joint) History of Worcester College; Editor, Owen's Education Acts; contributor to the Nineteenth Century, Edinburgh Review, etc. *Address:* Verrall's Oak, Egerton, Kent.
[*Died* 4 *Oct.* 1957.

BARKLEY, Alben William; United States lawyer, and formerly Senator; *b.* Graves County, Kentucky, 24 Nov. 1877; *m.* 1903, Dorothy Brower; one *s.* two *d*; *m.* 1949, Mrs. Carleton S. Hadley. *Educ.:* Marvin College, Clinton, Ky. (A.B.); Emory College, Oxford, Georgia; Univ. of Virginia Law School. Admitted to Kentucky Bar, 1901; Prosecuting Attorney, McCracken County, Ky., 1905-9; Judge, McCracken County Court, 1909-13. Member of Congress for First Kentucky District, 1913-27. U.S. Senator, 1927-51; Leader of Democratic Party in Senate. Temporary Chairman of Democratic National Convention, 1932-36; permanent Chairman, Chicago, 1940; temp. Chm., and keynote speaker, Philadelphia, 1948; Vice-President of the U.S., 1949-53. *Publication:* That Reminds Me. *Address:* Paducah, Kentucky, U.S.A.
[*Died* 30 *April* 1956.

BARKLEY, Colonel Macdonald, C.B. 1942; D.L., J.P.; B.A.; Agent to Earl of Sandwich; Managing Director, Huntingdon Steeplechases; *b.* 1871; *s.* of Henry Charles Barkley; *m.* 1907, Hilda W., *d.* of late W. Coote; one *d.* *Educ.:* Haileybury; Lincoln College, Oxford. Served as a Lieut. Imperial Yeomanry in S. Africa, 1899-1902 (severely wounded); in Huntingdonshire Cyclist Bn. in European War, 1914-19, attached to 7th Sherwood Foresters in France (despatches); Commanded 5 (Huntingdonshire) Bn. Northamptonshire Regt., 1919-24; Zone Commander, Hunts H.G., 1940-42; Asst. Sec. T.A. Assoc., Northampton, 1942-1944. *Recreations:* formerly hunting, shooting, and fly-fishing. *Address:* George Hotel, Huntingdon.
[*Died* 8 *July* 1956.

BARLEE, Sir Kenneth William, Kt., *cr.* 1937; *s.* of late Arthur Lee Barlee, Dublin, and Mary, *d.* of Rev. William Attwood, Gosbeck, Suffolk; *m.* Mary, *d.* of Edward Neale, Indian Navy; one *d.* *Educ.:* Warwick School; Dublin University. Entered I.C.S., 1900; served in Bombay Presidency, Kathiawar and Sind, 1901-30; Puisne Judge, High Court, Bombay, 1931-37. *Address:* Great Cornard, Sudbury, Suffolk.
[*Died* 18 *June* 1956.

BARLING, Lt.-Col. Seymour Gilbert, C.M.G. 1919; M.S. Lond.; F.R.C.S.; Past Chairman South Worcestershire Hospital Management Committee; Emeritus Professor of Surgery, University of Birmingham; Hon. Consulting Surgeon, Birmingham United Hospital; Consulting Surgeon, Birmingham and Midland Hospital for Sick Children; President, Association of Surgeons of Great Britain and Ireland, 1934; formerly Member of Council of R.C.S. of England; past Member of Radium Commission; past Member Court of Examiners R. Coll. Surgeons (England); *m.*; two *s.* one *d.* Served European War, 1914-19 (despatches, C.M.G.). *Address:* St. Mary's, Alfrick, Worcester. *T.:* Suckley 218.
[*Died* 4 *July* 1960.

BARLOW, Rt. Hon. Sir Anderson M.; *see* Montague-Barlow.

BARLOW, Horace M.; Secretary, Royal College of Physicians of London, 1923-44; *b.* 1884; *m.* 1st, 1912, Eleanor (*d.* 1914), *d.* of late John Hamilton, Dromore, Co. Down; 2nd, 1924, Elva, *d.* of late Edward Watson. Assistant Librarian, Royal College of Physicians, 1907-23. *Publications:* Old English Herbals (1525-1640), 1913; Catalogue of the Library of the Royal College of Physicians, 1912; Catalogue of Engraved Portraits in the Royal College of Physicians, 1918; A Descriptive Catalogue of Legal and other Documents in the Archives of the Royal College of Physicians, 1924; The Quarterly Journal of Medicine (1907-19) Index, 1921; various contributions to professional and other papers. *Recreations:* golf, collector of medical ex-libris. *Address:* 12A Romney Court, Worthing. *T.:* Worthing 5505. *Club:* National Liberal.
[*Died* 21 *June* 1954.

BARLTROP, Ernest William, C.M.G. 1950; C.B.E. 1947 (O.B.E. 1938); D.S.O. 1919;

Labour Adviser to Sec. of State for Colonies since 1947; *b.* London, 27 July 1893; *s.* of William James Barltrop, London; *m.* 1917, Ethel Alice Lucy Baker; two *s.* three *d.* *Educ.:* Sir John Cass Foundation School; King's College, London. Entered Civil Service as Second Division Clerk, 1912; Assist. Principal at Ministry of Labour Headquarters, 1920; First Class Officer, 1928; Deputy Divisional Controller, 1932; Chief Instructions Officer, 1938; Regional Controller, Birmingham, 1939; Leeds, 1942; served with the Civil Service Rifles and the 9th Batt. Essex Regt., 1914-18 (demobilised with rank of Captain, despatches, and D.S.O.). *Recreations:* music, golf, chess. *Address:* 68A Addiscombe Road, Croydon, Surrey. *T.:* Addiscombe 6944. [*Died* 26 *Nov.* 1957.

BARNARD, Leonard William, F.R.I.B.A., Architect; *b.* 1870; *s.* of Major R. C. Barnard; *m.* F. H. Thiselton Dyer; one *s.* Served in ranks of C.I.V. and in World War as Captain in the R.E.; architect to several churches, schools, including Umtata Cathedral. *Recreation:* archæology. *Address:* 13 Imperial Square, Cheltenham. *Club:* Rotary. [*Died* 18 *Jan.* 1951.

BARNARD, Hon. William Edward, C.B.E. 1957; Barrister and Solicitor, Tauranga, New Zealand; *b.* 29 Jan. 1886; *s.* of Charles Leonard Barnard and Ellen Banks; *m.* 1921 Elfreda Helen Eames; one *d.* *Educ.:* Levin State School; Victoria University College Wellington. Solicitor, 1908; Barrister, 1925 Served European War, 1916-19, as Private in R.A.M.C.; Gunner in R.F.A.; joined N.Z. Labour Party, 1923; M.P. Napier, N.Z., 1928-1943; Speaker, House of Representatives, N.Z., 1936-44; resigned N.Z. Labour Party, 1940; declared himself non-party, 1943; active in Ecumenical Movement. Mayor, Tauranga, 1950-52. Order, Brilliant Star (China), 1948; Coronation medals, George VI, Elizabeth II, Jubilee medal, George V and Queen Mary. *Recreations:* gardening, bowls. *Address:* Tauranga, New Zealand. [*Died* 12 *March* 1958.

BARNARD, William George, C.B.E. 1953; F.R.C.P.; Professor of Pathology in University of London at St. Thomas's Hosp. Medical School, since 1939; Director of Pathology, St. Thomas's Hosp.; Dean of St. Thomas's Hosp. Medical School; Examiner in Pathology, and Mem. of Senate, London Univ.; Treasurer Royal College of Physicians; *b.* Tangier, Morocco, 1892; 2nd *s.* of late E. U. Barnard, Bath, missionary, and Sarah P. Brown, Bristol; *m.* 1930, Margaret Roscoe Osler; one *s.* *Educ.:* Privately; London Hospital. Lieut., Capt., R.F.A. (T.) France, 1915-17; Captain, London Hospital, R.F.C., 1919-20; Clinical Assistant to Surgical Out-Patients, London Hospital, 1920; Junior Assistant Director, Pathological Institute, London Hospital, 1921-23; Voluntary Assistant to Professor L. Aschoff, Freiburg i/B., 1927; Pathologist to University College Hospital; Lecturer in Morbid Anatomy and Curator of Museum, University College Hospital Medicine School, 1923-31; Consultant Histologist to the Public Health Department, London County Council, 1931-39; Fellow of Royal Society of Medicine, Pathological Society of Great Britain and Ireland, and Medico-Legal Society. *Publications:* Elementary Pathological Histology; Kettle's Tumours; The Nature of the Oat-Celled Sarcoma of the Mediastinum, and other articles. *Recreations:* painting and carving. *Address:* Beckhams, Chiddingfold, Surrey. *Clubs:* Royal St. George's Golf (Sandwich); Royal Cinque Ports Golf (Deal). [*Died* 20 *Dec.* 1956.

BARNE, Rt. Rev. George Dunsford, C.I.E. 1923; O.B.E. 1919; D.D.; M.A.; V.D.; Rector of Harthill, nr. Sheffield, since 1949; Hon. Canon of Sheffield Cathedral since 1951; *b.* Jamaica, 6 May 1879; *s.* of late Capt. W. C. Barne, 14th Foot (P.W.O. West Yorks. Regt.); *m.* 1907, Dorothy Kate, M.B.E. 1919, Kaisar-i-Hind Gold Medal, 1941, 3rd *d.* of William Savage Akerman, of The Mount, Burnham, Somerset; no *c.* *Educ.:* Clifton College; Oriel College, Oxford. Assistant Master, Summer Fields, Oxford, 1902-8; Assistant Curate, S. John Baptist, Summertown, Oxford, 1904-8; Curate of Simla, India, 1908-10; Chaplain Indian Ecclesiastical Establishment, 1910; Principal of the Lawrence Royal Military School, Sanawar, India, 1912-32; Canon of Lahore Cathedral, 1928; Bishop of Lahore, 1932-49; resigned, 1949. *Address:* c/o Lloyds Bank, 6 Pall Mall, S.W.1. *Club:* Athenæum. [*Died* 18 *June* 1954.

BARNE, Brigadier William Bradley Gosset, C.B.E. 1920; D.S.O. 1918; Knight of Order of St. John; late Royal Artillery; *b.* 1880; *s.* of late Capt. William Charles Barne, 14th Regt.; *m.* 1908, Dorothy Isabel, *d.* of late Col. Edward Donald Malcolm, C.B., of Poltalloch, Argyll; one *s.* four *d.* *Educ.:* Gore Court, Sittingbourne; Clifton College; R.M. Academy, Woolwich. Staff College, 1910-1911; served European War, 1914-19 (despatches, D.S.O., Croce di Guerra); British Military Mission to Russian Volunteer Army (despatches, C.B.E., Order of St. Vladimir); Commanded Royal Artillery, Gibraltar, 1930-1934; Brigadier, R.A., Eastern Command, 1934-37; retired, 1937; M.F.H. Royal Calpé Hunt, 1933-34. *Address:* c/o Lloyds Bank (Cox & King's Branch), 6 Pall Mall, S.W.1. *Club:* United Service. [*Died* 7 *Oct.* 1951.

BARNES, Alfred Edward, M.B., F.R.C.P.; *b.* Sheffield, 3 June 1881; *s.* of Josiah Barnes; *m.* 1911, Jessie Morrison; two *s.* *Educ.:* Grammar School and University College, Sheffield. Capt. R.A.M.C.T.; O. i/c Med. Div. 37th General Hospital, Salonika. Professor of Medicine, University of Sheffield, 1936-46; Cons. Physician to Royal Infirmary, Sheffield. *Recreation:* garden. *Address:* 25 Suffolk St., Helensburgh, Dunbartonshire. [*Died* 23 *Oct.* 1956.

BARNES, Rev. Canon Arthur Hubert, M.A.; Vicar of Tisbury, Wilts., 1934-51; Hon. Canon of Chester Cathedral, 1922-34; Canon Emeritus since 1934; Fellow of St. Michael's College, Tenbury, since 1922; *s.* of late Rev. W. Miles Barnes, Rector of Monkton, Dorchester; *g.s.* of Rev. William Barnes, the Dorset Poet; unmarried. *Educ.:* Keble College, Oxford. Ordained, 1900; Priest, 1901; Curate, Woodstock, Oxon; Curate, St. Peter's, Stockport, 1906; Vicar of St. Peter's, Stockport, 1908-34. *Address:* c/o The Vicarage, Dilton Marsh, Westbury, Wilts. [*Died* 2 *Aug.* 1952.

BARNES, Arthur Kentish; late Treasurer and Director of Liverpool Cotton Association; *b.* 30 May 1872; *s.* of late Edward Kentish Barnes, R.N.; *m.* 1898, Melita, *d.* of Rev. J. M. Hillyar; three *s.* one *d.* *Educ.:* Royal Naval School, New Cross. Late senior partner in the firm of Mellor & Fenton, cotton merchants, Liverpool; late Chairman The Royal Insurance Co. and Liverpool London & Globe Insurance Co.; Director British and Foreign Marine Insurance Co.; The Thames and Mersey Marine Insurance Co.; Royal Insurance Co.; Liverpool and London and Globe Insurance Co.; Pres. of Liverpool Cotton Association, 1916-1917. *Recreations:* fishing, golf. *Address:* Dawstone, Heswall, Cheshire. [*Died* 9 *Sept.* 1954.

BARNES, Air Commodore Eric Delano, C.B. 1949; A.F.C. 1931; p.s.a.; R.A.F., retired; *b.* 1900; *s.* of A. A. Barnes, Highgate; *m.* 1935, Ena Elizabeth, *d.* of late H. C. Sheffield, Branksome Park, Bournemouth; one *s.* one *d.* Joined R.F.C., 1918; R.A.F. General Duties Branch; served War of 1939-45 in Bomber Command and S.W. Pacific; Commandant, Empire Flying School, 1947-49; Group Captain, 1946; Air Commodore, 1947; retired, 1949. *Club:* R.A.F. [*Died* 4 *Dec.* 1957.

BARNES, Rt. Rev. Ernest William, F.R.S., Sc.D., Hon. D.D. (Aberdeen and Edinburgh); Hon. LL.D. (Glasgow); *b.* 1 April 1874; *e. s.* of John Starkie Barnes; *m.* 1916, Adelaide Caroline Theresa, *o. d.* of late Sir Adolphus W. Ward, Litt.D., F.B.A., Master of Peterhouse, Cambridge; two *s.* *Educ.:* King Edward's School, Birmingham; Trinity College, Cambridge (Scholar). Bracketed 2nd Wrangler, 1896; President of the Union, 1897; First Class First Division of the Mathematical Tripos, part ii. 1897; first Smith's Prizeman, 1898; Fellow of Trinity College, 1898-1916; M.A. 1900. Ordained, 1902; Assistant Lecturer Trinity Coll., 1902; Junior Dean, 1906-8; Tutor, 1908-15; Master of the Temple, 1915-19; Canon of Westminster, 1918-24; Bishop of Birmingham, 1924-53; Examining Chaplain to Bishop of Llandaff, 1906-20; a Governor King Edward's Sch., Birmingham, 1907-53; F.R.S. 1909; Select Preacher, Cambridge, 1906, etc., and Oxford, 1914-16, etc.; Fellow of King's College, London, 1919; Gifford Lecturer, Aberdeen, 1927-29. *Publications:* Memoirs and Papers on pure mathematics; contributor to a number of volumes of theological essays; numerous sermons; Should such a Faith Offend?, 1927; Scientific Theory and Religion (Gifford Lectures), 1933; The Rise of Christianity, 1947; Religion Amid Turmoil (Rede Lecture, Cambridge), 1949. *Address:* Hampton Lodge, Hurstpierpoint, Sussex. *Club:* Athenæum. [*Died* 29 *Nov.* 1953.

BARNES, Frank, M.B., M.S. Lond., F.R.C.S. Eng., etc.; LL.D.; Captain, R.A.M.C., 1st Southern General Hospital; Lecturer in Operative Surgery, Birmingham University; Examiner in Surgery to University of Birmingham; Member of Court of Governors, University of Birmingham. *Educ.:* Birmingham University Coll.; St. Bartholomew's Hospital. Medical education commenced at Mason Science College, Prizeman in Anatomy, Physiology, Pathology; Prosector of Anatomy and afterwards Demonstrator of Anatomy and Lecturer in Osteology; House Surgeon at the Children's Hospital and Great Northern Central Hospital; Resident Surgical Officer, General Hospital, and later, Surgical Casualty Officer; late Hon. Surgeon Orthopædic Hospital and Hon. Surgeon to the General Hospital, Birmingham; late President of Midland Medical Society; late President of Central Division, B.M.A. Hon. LL.D. Birmingham, 1957. *Publications:* Congenital Dislocation of the Hip; Infantile Paralysis; Acute Perforations of the Duodenum. *Recreations:* golf, fishing. *Address:* The Briars, 138 Monyhull Hall Road, Kings Norton, Birmingham. *T.:* 1875 Kings Norton. *Club:* Clef (Birmingham). [*Died* 18 *Feb.* 1960.

BARNES, Colonel Frank Purcell, D.S.O. 1916; O.B.E. 1918; M.I.M.E.; late Indian Army; *b.* 2 Oct. 1880; *s.* of Rev. Canon I. P. Barnes, Incumbent of Ballycastle Church; *m.* 1st, 1910, Florence Alice (*d.* 1915), *d.* of late C. P. Beck, Bloemfontein, South Africa; one *s.*; 2nd, 1921, Ethel Mary, *d.* of late J. R. Harding, Sellarsbrook, Monmouth; one *s.* *Educ.:* Bilton Grange, Rugby; Tonbridge School (Scholar); Magdalene College, Cambridge. Double Exhibitioner; took Classical Tripos in second year of residence, and History Special in 3rd year; in College boat for 3 years; joined A.S.C. as University Candidate, 1904; in South Africa, 1905-11; took up Mechanical Transport on return to England and became Senior M. T. Instructor, Jan. 1914; formed Base M. T. Depot on mobilisation; served European War, 1914-19 (D.S.O., O.B.E.); Chief Instructor Mechanical Transport School, Aldershot, 1920-23; Chief Instructor at Boys' Technical School, Chepstow, 1923-26; O.C. R.A.S.C., Ceylon; transferred to Indian Army, 1928; A.D.T., Army Headquarters, India, 1929-30; Mechanical Transport Adviser, India Office, 1930-35; Col. 1934; Deputy Director of Transport, Army Headquarters, India, 1936-37; retired 1937; re-employed 1939-41. *Recreation:* fly-fishing. *Address:* The Cottage, Frensham, Surrey. [*Died* 29 *March* 1956.

BARNES, Sir George (Reginald), Kt., *cr.* 1953; Principal of the University College of N. Staffordshire since Sept. 1956; *b.* 13 Sept. 1904; *s.* of late Hugh Shakespear Barnes, K.C.S.I., K.C.V.O., and Edith Helen Barnes; *m.* 1927, Dorothy Anne, *d.* of Henry Bond, LL.D.; one *s.* *Educ.:* R.N. Colleges, Osborne and Dartmouth; King's College, Cambridge. Asst. Master R.N. College, Dartmouth, 1927-1930; Asst. Secretary Cambridge University Press, 1930-35; B.B.C. Talks Department, 1935, Director of Talks, 1941; Head of the Third Programme, 1946-48; Director, The Spoken Word, B.B.C., 1948-50; Director of Television, B.B.C., 1950-56. Member Council Royal College of Art, 1954-56; Governor of British Film Institute, 1952-58; Member, Standing Commission on Museums and Galleries, 1959-; Council of Industrial Design, 1959-. Chm. The Wedgwood Soc. 1955; Pres. The Television Soc., 1958. Lord High Steward, Newcastle-under-Lyme, 1958. Hon. D.C.L. Durham, 1956. *Publication:* (with Commander J. H. Owen) The Private Papers of John, 4th Earl of Sandwich, 4 vols., 1932-38. *Recreations:* sailing, music. *Address:* The Clock House, Keele, Staffs. *T.:* Keele Park 301. *Club:* Oriental. [*Died* 22 *Sept.* 1960.

BARNES, Sir (James) Sidney, K.B.E., *cr.* 1937 (O.B.E. 1918); C.B. 1928; M.A.; *b.* 1881; *y. s.* of late Starkie Barnes; unmarried. *Educ.:* King Edward's School, Birmingham; Trinity Coll., Cambridge (Scholar); Bracketed Third Wrangler, 1903. Private Secretary to Second and First Sea Lords, 1910-14; Private Secretary to First Lord, 1919-21; a Principal Assistant Secretary Admiralty, 1932-35; Deputy Secretary, Admiralty and Accountant General of the Navy, 1936-44; Director of Greenwich Hospital, 1944-48; *Address:* 15 Hay Hill, W.1. *Club:* United University. [*Died* 28 *Nov.* 1952.

BARNES, Sir Kenneth Ralph, Kt., *cr.* 1938; Principal of the Royal Academy of Dramatic Art, 1909-55; *b.* 11 Sept. 1878; *s.* of Rev. Prebendary R. H. Barnes; *m.* 1925, Daphne (Wing Officer in the W.A.A.F.), *d.* of Sir Richard Graham, 4th Bt.; (one *s.* decd.). *Educ.:* Westminster; Christ Church, M.A. Journalist and dramatic critic, 1903-09; adapted Hervieu's Connais Toi, produced as Glass Houses, Globe Theatre, 1909; served India, Mesopotamia, Siberia, 1914-19 (despatches); Captain 1/9 Hants Regt.; Trustee Shakespeare Memorial Fund; Member: Council Anglo-French Soc.; Advisory Cttee. on Diploma in Dramatic Art of the Univ. of London; Exec. Cttee. of Royal Academy of Dancing; Joint Council of National Theatre and Old Vic; Vice-President of Actors' Church Union. *Plays:* Undercurrents, produced R.A.D.A. Players, 1922; The Letter of the Law, produced Grand Theatre, Fulham, 1924, and in the provinces. *Publication:* (Autobiography) Welcome, Good Friends (posthumous), 1958. *Recreation:* building. *Address:* Spring Tide, Kingston Gorse, East Preston, Sussex. *T.:* Rustington 1113. *Clubs:* Garrick, M.C.C., Green Room. [*Died* 16 *Oct.* 1957.

BARNES, Sir Sidney; *see* Barnes, Sir J. S.

BARNES, Stanley, M.D., D.Sc., F.R.C.P., Hon. LL.D. (Birmingham); President, Warwickshire County Cricket Club, since 1955; Chairman, Birmingham Hospitals Centre; late Pres. of Assoc. of British Neurologists; late Dean of the Faculty of Medicine, University of Birmingham; late Fire Prevention Executive Officer, Midland Region; Consulting Physician to the Queen Elizabeth Hospital, Birmingham; to the Guest Hospital, Dudley, and Eye Hospital, Birmingham; ex-President Neurological Section, Royal Society of Medicine; of Birmingham Medical Benevolent Society; of Midland Medical Society and of Queen's Medical Society; *b.* 1875; *s.* of Starkie Barnes, Birmingham; unmarried. *Educ.:* King Edward's School (Camp Hill), and Mason College, Birmingham; University of London. Resident Medical Officer, National Hospital for the Paralysed and Epileptic, 1901; Pathologist, Queen's Hospital, Birmingham, 1903. *Publications:* chiefly on Neurological Subjects, in Brain, Journal of Neurology and Psychiatry, Quarterly Journal of Medicine, and other medical publications, 1904-33; The Middlemore Lecture on Ocular Paralysis, 1912; Anglers Knots in Gut and Nylon (2nd Edn.), 1951; The Birmingham Hospitals Centre, 1952. *Recreations:* golf, fishing, photography. *Address:* C 8 Kenilworth Court, Hagley Road, Edgbaston, Birmingham, 16. *Club:* Clef (Birmingham). [*Died* 11 *Aug.* 1955.

BARNES, Air Vice-Marshal William Edward, ret.; C.B.E. 1951; *b.* 24 July 1897; *s.* of late William Albert Barnes, Crouch End, Finchley; *m.* 1923, Kathleen Mary, *d.* of late Peter King, Lucan, Co. Dublin; one *s.* *Educ.:* University College School and Hospital, London. Served European War, 1914-19, with R.F.A.; with R.A.M.C., 1921-22; transferred to R.A.F. (Medical Branch), 1922; War of 1939-45, France and S.E. Asia. K.H.S. 1951; Q.H.S. 1952; Principal M.O., Home Command, 1950-1953. Croix de Guerre (France), 1918. *Address:* 44 Surrenden Crescent, Brighton 6, Sussex. *Club:* R.A.F. [*Died* 28 *July* 1958.

BARNETT, Lieut.-Colonel Alfred George, C.B.E. 1919; Comptroller of Accounts, Ministry of Works, 1929-45; *b.* 23 June 1883; *e. s.* of late James Barnett; *m.* 1919, Mabel Lilian Beatrice (*d.* 1939), 4th *d.* of late H. O. Strong, Bristol. *Address:* 13 Elm Grove, Rhyl. [*Died* 11 *March* 1955.

BARNETT, Cecil Guy, C.I.E. 1923; F.C.H.; retd.; *b.* 7 Nov. 1881; *s.* of late C. W. Barnett, Penang, S.S.; *m.* 1906, Norah (*d.* 1946), *d.* of A. Sullivan, Ealing; two *s.* *Educ.:* Dollar Academy; Coopers Hill. Assistant Engineer, India, P.W.D., 1902; Executive Engineer, 1910; Superintending Engineer, 1918; served in Burma, 1902-13; New Capital Works, Delhi, 1913-20; Chief Engineer Buildings and Secretary to Government of Burma, P.W.D., 1926; retired, 1930; Regional Technical Adviser, A.R.P. Dept., Home Office, 1939; Assist. Chief Engineer, Ministry of Home Security, 1940; Deputy Chief Engineer, Home Office, 1944-49. *Address:* c/o National and Grindlays Bank Ltd., 26 Bishopsgate, E.C.2. [*Died* 15 *July* 1959.

BARNETT, Rev. Ernest Judd; Rural Dean of Sherborne, 1937-50; resigned, 1950; *b.* 1859; *m.* Lillias Sara, *d.* of William John Digby of Moat Lodge, Co. Galway. *Educ.:* Trinity College, Melbourne Univ. (Rupertswood Scholar). Bromby Prizeman in Greek, 1885; in Hebrew, 1886; B.A. 1885; M.A. 1887; Deacon, 1885; Priest, 1886; Curate, Holy Trinity, Kew, Melbourne 1885-86; St. Mary's, N. Melbourne, 1886-88; Headmaster Caulfield Grammar School, Victoria, 1888-96; Secretary of Church Missionary Association, Victoria, 1896-1902; Warden S. Stephen's College, Hong-Kong, 1902-14; Secretary C.M.S. in S. China, 1909-25; Archdeacon of Hong Kong, 1910-25; Rector of Beer Hackett, 1925-33, of Thornford with Beer Hackett, 1933-42. *Address:* 30 Albert Road West, Moonah, Tasmania. [*Died* 20 *May* 1955.

BARNETT, Lt.-Col. Henry N.; *see* Norman Barnett.

BARNETT, Lionel David, C.B. 1937; F.B.A. 1936; M.A., Litt.D.; late Keeper of Dept. of Oriental Printed Books and Manuscripts, British Museum; *b.* 1871; *e. s.* of B. Barnett, Liverpool; *m.* Blanche (*d.* 1955), *d.* of Rev. B. Berliner; one *s.* one *d.* *Educ.:* High School, Liverpool Institute; Liverpool University; Trinity College, Cambridge. Classical Tripos, Class I. Div. I. in Part I. (1894), Class I. in Part II. (1896). *Address:* 33 West Heath Drive, N.W.11. [*Died* 28 *Jan.* 1960.

BAROJA NESSI, Pio; (Don Pio Baroja); Spanish writer, painter and etcher; *b.* Vera del Bidasoa (Basque country), 28 Dec. 1872; *s.* of Serafin Baroja Zornorza and Carmen Nessi Goñi; unmarried. *Educ.:* Valencia; Madrid (Doctor of Medicine). In practice for a short time; then in business and the Arts, in Madrid. Member of Spanish Royal Academy, 1935-. *Publications:* about 100 volumes of novels, short stories and essays: novels include: Zalacain el aventurero, Idilios vascos, La cuidad de la niebla, Las inquietudes de Shanti Andía, La dama errante, Mala hierba, Paradox Rey, El árbol de la ciencia; historical series: Memorias de un hombre de acción, in 17 volumes; memoirs (also published by instalments) From the Last Bend in the Road (Desda la última vuelta del camino); contributions to newspapers. *Recreation:* bibliophile. *Address:* Ruiz de Alarcón 12, Madrid. [*Died* 30 *Oct.* 1956.

BARR, Sir George (William), Kt., *cr.* 1951; C.B.E. 1945; Chairman, Liverpool and North Wales S.S. Co. Ltd.; *b.* 8 Nov. 1881; *m.* 1907, Annie, *d.* of late John Field; two *s.* *Address:* Woodlea, Grange over Sands, Lancs. [*Died* 5 *Aug.* 1956.

BARR, Sir James, Kt., *cr.* 1949; F.R.I.C.S.; Chartered Surveyor; Senior Partner, James Barr & Son, Surveyors and Valuers, 213 St. Vincent Street, Glasgow, C.2; *b.* 1884; *e. s.* of late James Barr, Surveyor, Glasgow; *m.* 1912, Mary W., *o. d.* of late Dr. W. A. McLachlan, Dumbarton; two *s.* one *d.* *Educ.:* Glasgow Academy and Technical College, Glasgow. Pres. R. Inst. Chartered Surveyors, London, 1944; Member Uthwatt Cttee. to report on Compensation and Betterment, 1941-42; Deputy Comr. under War Damage Act 1941 for Scotland, and Member Emergency Services Organisation for West of Scotland; Member Cttee. on Housing, Scotland, 1934; Chm. Cttee. on House Building costs, Scotland, 1939; Member Administrative Cttee. and Convener of Sites and Buildings Cttee., Empire Exhibition, Glasgow, 1938; Chm. Cttee. on Mid-Scotland Ship Canal, 1946; Member Cttee. of Scottish Development Council and Director of Building Centre (Scotland) Ltd.; Member Price Regulation Cttee., Board of Trade, for Glasgow and West of Scotland during War of 1939-45; Member Panel under War Damage to Land (Scotland) Act, 1941. *Recreations:* golf and motoring. *Address:* Ranfurly House, Bridge of Weir, Renfrewshire. *T.:* 16. *Clubs:* Royal Scottish Automobile (Glasgow); Ranfurly Castle Golf (Bridge of Weir); Machrihanish Golf (Argyllshire). [*Died* 6 *Oct.* 1952.

BARRACLOUGH, Sir (Samuel) Henry (Egerton), K.B.E., *cr.* 1920 (C.B.E. 1919); V.D.; M.Inst.C.E., M.I.Mech.E.; Professor of Mechanical Engineering, University of

Sydney, 1915-42; *b.* 25 Oct. 1874; *m.* 1927, Mona Rossiter. Was in charge of Australian Munitions Workers. Served European War, 1914-19 (despatches, C.B.E.); Dean of the Faculty of Engineering, 1924-33, and from 1936; President of Australian Institution of Engineers, 1935-36. *Address:* c/o The University, Sydney, Australia. *Clubs:* Australian, Royal Sydney Golf (Sydney). [*Died* 30 *Aug.* 1958.

BARRAN, Sir John (Nicholson), 2nd Bt., *cr.* 1895; *b.* 16 Aug. 1872; *s.* of John Barran, *e. s.* of 1st Bt. and Eliza Henrietta, *d.* of late Edward Nicholson; *S.* grandfather, 1905; *m.* 1902, Alice Margarita (*d.* 1939), *d.* of Rev. Leighton Parks, D.D., New York City; three *s.* one *d.*; *m.* 1946, Esther Fisher, *e. d.* of Hon. F. M. B. Fisher, *q.v.* *Educ.:* Winchester; Trinity College, Cambridge (B.A.); M.P. (L.) Hawick Burghs, 1909-18; Parliamentary Secretary (unpaid) to Postmaster-General, President of Local Government Board, Home Secretary, Foreign Secretary and Prime Minister, 1909-16; to Rt. Hon. H. H. Asquith, M.P., 1916-18; Chairman Port and Transit Executive, 1920-1922; J.P., West Riding, Yorks. *Heir: s.* John Leighton, Commander R.N.V.R. [*b.* 24 Mar. 1904; *m.* 1929, Hon. Alison Mary Ruthven, 3rd *d.* of 9th Baron Ruthven, *q.v.*; one *s.*]. *Address:* Sawley Hall, Ripon, Yorks. *T.:* Sawley 202; 22 Little Boltons, S.W.10. *T.:* Fremantle 9837. *Club:* Brooks's. [*Died* 8 *July* 1952.

BARRATT, Colonel Herbert James, C.I.E. 1918; retired, Army Medical Service; *b.* 1858; *s.* of James Barratt of Hanslope, Bucks; *m.* 1894, Edith Violet, *d.* of late A. W. Stogdon, I.C.S.; one *d.* *Educ.:* Bedford; St. Bartholomew's Hospital. M.R.C.S., L.R.C.P., D.P.H., London; served South African War, 1899-1902 (Queen's medal five clasps); European War, 1914-18 (C.I.E.); A.D.M.S. Meerut Division, India. *Address:* 193 Leckhampton Road, Cheltenham. [*Died* 10 *June* 1952.

BARRATT, John Oglethorpe Wakelin, M.D., D.Sc. Lond., F.R.C.S. Eng. F.R.C.P. Lond.; (retired); late Research Worker Lister Institute of Preventive Medicine; Past-master, Society of Apothecaries of London; Capt., late Royal Army Medical Corps (T.A.); *b.* Birmingham, 1862; *s.* of late Dr. O. W. Barratt of Birmingham; *m.* 1913, Mary Muter, *d.* of J. H. Gardner, Stonehouse, Lanarkshire. *Educ.:* University College, Lond.; Universities of Göttingen and München. Engaged in experimental work in physiology and pathology at University College, London, 1893-96; Research worker in Neuropathology, London County Asylums Laboratory, 1897-99; Pathologist to West Riding Asylum, Wakefield, 1899-1902; British Medical Association Research Student, 1903-5; Assistant Bacteriologist, Lister Institute of Preventive Medicine, 1905-6; Research Worker, Dept. of Cytology and Cancer Research, University of Liverpool, 1906-7; senior member of Blackwater Fever Expedition (Nyasaland) of Liverpool School of Tropical Medicine, 1907-8; Director of Cancer Research Laboratory, The University, Liverpool, 1909-13; Beit Research Fellow, 1914-15 and 1919-20; Captain 1st London (City of London) Sanitary Company, Royal Army Medical Corps (T.), 1915-18. member of Medical Research Club. *Publications:* Contributions to British and foreign scientific journals. *Recreations:* walking, sketching, photography. *Address:* 56 Alfriston Road, S.W.11. *Club:* Authors'. [*Died* 1 *Dec.* 1956.

BARRATT, Rev. Thomas H., B.A.; *b.* St. Austell, Cornwall, 1870; *s.* of Rev. R. C. Barratt; *m.* 1898, Edith Chester of Loughborough; one *s.* two *d.* *Educ.:* Kingswood School, Bath; London University; Handsworth College. Master at Woodhouse Grove School, 1890-93; entered Wesleyan Ministry, 1894; ministered mainly in Birmingham and London; Principal and Tutor in Pastoral Theology, Didsbury College, 1919-39; retired, 1939. *Address:* Arden Hotel, Leamington Spa. [*Died* 5 *Sept.* 1951.

BARRATT, William Donald; D.L.; Manager and Director, Hodbarrow Mining Co. Ltd.; *b.* 1883; *s.* of late William I. Barratt; *m.* 1st, 1911, Olive (*d.* 1921), *d.* of late Canon T. P. Monnington; four *s.*; 2nd, 1930, Dorothy, *d.* of late J. T. Marshall; two *s.* *Educ.:* Harrow; Trinity College, Cambridge. Member of Millom U.D.C. 1911-34, Chairman 1928-30; Member of Millom R.D.C. since 1934; member of Cumberland C.C. since 1922; County Alderman since 1933; J.P., Cumberland, 1921; High Sheriff of Cumberland, 1944-45; D.L. Cumberland. Served with 4th Bn. King's Own Royal Regt. (T.F.), 1906-23; served on Western Front, 1915-1916. *Recreations:* fishing and shooting. *Address:* Hazel Mount, Thwaites, Millom, Cumberland. *T.:* Millom 215. [*Died* 1 *Oct.* 1955.

BARRETT, Major Alexander Gould, J.P.; *b.* 1866; 3rd *surv. s.* of late Major William Barrett, J.P., D.L. of Moredon, North Curry, Somerset; *m.* 1909, Dorothy (*d.* 1948), 2nd *d.* of Rev. A. R. Cartwright, Hornblotton Rectory, Somerset. *Educ.:* Eton; Oxford. West Somerset Yeomanry, retired. *Recreations:* Secretary, Taunton Vale Foxhounds; President, Somerset County Cricket Club, 1931 and 1932. *Address:* Eastbrook House, near Taunton, Somerset. *T.A.:* Trull. *T.:* Taunton 509. [*Died* 12 *March* 1954.

BARRETT, Frank Ashley, C.B. 1922; *m. d.* of late G. W. T. Omond. Assistant Secretary, Board of Inland Revenue, 1912; Commissioner and Secretary, 1919-38. *Address:* Laddingford House, Yalding, Kent. [*Died* 8 *April* 1954.

BARRETT, Rev. Hugh S.; *see* Scott-Barrett.

BARRETT, Very Rev. William Edward Colvile, M.A. (Cantab.); H.C.F.; *b.* 27 April 1880; *s.* of Sir William Scott Barrett and Julia Louisa Colvile; *m.* 1920, Hilda Agneta Bertha Stanley-Adams; one *s.* two *d.* *Educ.:* Aldenham School; Pembroke College, Cambridge; Leeds Clergy School. Assistant Curate, Kirkburton, nr. Huddersfield, 1903-06; Charleville Bush Brotherhood, Diocese of Brisbane, 1906-12; Vicar of Gildersome, nr. Leeds, 1913-19; Chaplain to the Forces, B.E.F., 1917-19; Organising Secretary for S.P.G., Dioceses of Liverpool, Chester, and Sodor and Man, 1919-21; Rector of Sherwood, Brisbane Diocese, 1922-1930; Warden of St. John's Coll., Univ. of Queensland, 1930-32; Dean of St. John's Cathedral, Diocese of Brisbane, 1932-52; resigned, 1952, now Dean Emeritus. *Recreations:* golf, fishing. *Address:* 13 John's St., Redcliffe, Queensland, Australia. *T.:* Redcliffe 978. [*Died* 29 *June* 1956.

BARRIE, Alexander Baillie, C.B.E. 1949; M.A.; C.A.; Partner in McClelland, Ker & Co., Chartered Accountants, 23 Lawrence Lane, Cheapside, E.C.2 and 120 St. Vincent St., Glasgow; Advisory Accountant to Raw Materials Dept., Board of Trade, since 1946; Member Development Areas Treasury Advisory Cttee. since 1947 (Chairman since 1948); Member, Hotel Grants Advisory Cttee., 1950-51; *b.* 4 July 1906; 2nd *s.* of David Watson Barrie and Margaret S. Dewar; *m.* 1935, Betty Nicoll McLaren. *Educ.:* Dundee High School; St. Andrew's University. Admitted member of Institute of Accountants and Actuaries in Glasgow, 1933. Controller of Raw Materials Accountancy, Ministry of Supply, 1940-45. *Recreation:* golf. *Address:* Yew Tree Cottage, Silverstead Lane, Westerham Hill, Kent. *T.:* Biggin Hill 289. *Club:* Caledonian. [*Died* 14 *Feb.* 1957.

BARRINGTON, 10th Viscount (*cr.* 1720), **William Reginald Shute Barrington,** Baron Barrington, 1720; Baron Shute (U.K.) 1880; late Captain 3rd Batt. Oxford Light Infantry; *b.* 23 July 1873; *e. s.* of 9th Viscount and Mary Isabella (*d.* 1903), *d.* of Rev. Richard Bogue; *S.* father, 1933. *Educ.:* Trin. Hall, Camb. *Heir: n.* Patrick William Daines Barrington [*b.* 29 Oct. 1908. *Educ.:* Eton; Magdalen College, Oxford (B.A.). Barrister-at-law, Inner Temple, 1940. Late 2nd Lieut., R.A. Formerly Hon. Attaché, H.B.M.'s Embassy, Berlin, and sometime in Foreign Office]. *Address:* Hurstlands, Hart Lane, Hartfield, Sussex. *T.:* Coleman's Hatch 53. *Club:* Carlton. [*Died* 4 *Oct.* 1960.

BARRINGTON, Hon. Bernard; *see* Barrington, Hon. W. B. L.

BARRINGTON, Claud; Member Board of Management British Road Services (part-time) since 1960; Chairman, The Atlantic Steam Navigation Co. Ltd.; Chairman, Frank Bustard & Sons, Ltd.; Chairman, B.R.S. (Pickfords), Ltd.; *b.* Portishead, Somerset, 30 Jan. 1893; parents English (both deceased). *Educ.:* Colston School, Bristol. Served European War, 1914-18; joined 12th Bn. Glos'ter Regt. (Bristol Bn.) as 2nd Lt., 1914, from Bristol Univ. O.T.C.; after being wounded, Somme, 1916, became Chief Road Inspector for Scotland for Inland Waterways and Docks Dept. of R.E. Started in Road Haulage in Bristol, 1921, and later extended activities to London and Birmingham; instrumental in formation of Transport Services, Ltd., 1936 (was sold to British Transport Commission, 1948); was Managing Director from its formation. Early in 1941, joined Ministry of War Transport, as Chief Road Haulage Officer, and later became Director of Road Haulage. Underwriting Member of Lloyd's. M.I.Mech.E., M.Inst.T. *Recreations:* billiards, bowls and gardens. *Address:* 27 Courtenay Gate, Hove, Sussex. [*Died* 31 *Oct.* 1960.

BARRINGTON, Hon. (Walter) Bernard (Louis); 2nd *s.* of 9th and heir presumptive to 10th Viscount Barrington; *b.* 15 May 1876; *m.* 1901, Eleanor Nina (*d.* 1947), *d.* of late Sir Thomas William Snagge, K.C.M.G., J.P., D.L., Judge of County Courts; one *s.* two *d.* *Educ.:* Cheam; Charterhouse. Admitted solicitor, 1900; partner in the firm Norton, Rose, Barrington & Co., 1904-19; member of Council of Law Society, 1909-11; retd. from legal profession, 1919, becoming a Director of Helbert, Wagg & Co. Ltd., Investment Bankers; is Director of Gresham Life Assurance Society Ltd., Gresham Fire and Accident Insurance Society Ltd. President Legal and General Assurance Society Ltd., 1958. *Recreations:* shooting, fishing and gardening. *Address:* Poplar Farm, Hollesley, Suffolk. *T.:* Shottisham 38. *Club:* Carlton. [*Died* 12 *May* 1959.

BARRINGTON-WARD, Sir Lancelot Edward, K.C.V.O., *cr.* 1935; Ch.M. Edin.; F.R.C.S. Edin.; F.R.C.S. England; Grand Cross Order of St. Olav; Order of St. Sava; Extra Surgeon to the Queen since 1952 (Surgeon to King George VI, 1936-52); Consulting Surgeon to Royal Northern Hospital and to Hospital for Sick Children, Great Ormond Street, and Wood Green Hospital; formerly Pres. Surrey Agricultural Assoc.; *b.* Worcester, 4 July 1884; 2nd *s.* of late Canon M. J. Barrington-Ward, D.D.; *m.* 1st, 1917, Dorothy Anne (*d.* 1935), 2nd *d.* of late T. W. Miles, P.W.D., India, of Caragh, Co. Kerry; three *d.*; 2nd, 1941, Catherine, *o. d.* of late E. G. Reuter, Harrogate; one *s.* *Educ.:* Westminster (Classical Scholar); Bromsgrove (Classical Scholar); Edinburgh University; Worcester College, Oxford (Classical Exhibition). M.B., Ch.B. Honours, Edinburgh University, 1908; M.Ch. Honours, 1913; Chiene Medal in Surgery, 1913; Examiner in Surgery, Univ. of St. Andrews and Edinburgh Univ.; Hunterian Professor, R.C.S., 1952. Surgeon-in-Chief, Lady Wimborne's Hospital, Uskub, Serbia, 1915. *Publications:* Abdominal Surgery of Children; Editor Royal Northern Operative Surgery; numerous articles and communications to surgical journals. *Recreations:* formerly Rugby football; played for Edinburgh University (Captain, 1908) six years; played for England (International) on four occasions; shooting. *Address:* Hawkedon House, Bury St. Edmunds. [*Died* 17 *Nov.* 1953.

BARROW, General Sir George de Symons, G.C.B., *cr.* 1928 (K.C.B., *cr.* 1919; C.B. 1915); K.C.M.G., *cr.* 1918; Indian Army, retd.; late Colonel 14th/20th Hussars; and 14th P.W.O. Scinde Horse; *b.* 25 Oct. 1864; *s.* of late Major-General de Symons Barrow; *m.* 1902, Sybilla, *d.* of late Colonel G. Way, C.B.; one *d.* Entered Army, Connaught Rangers, 1884; I.S.C. 1886; Captain, 1895; Major, Indian Army, 1902; Lieut.-Colonel, 1910; Lieut.-Gen. 1921; General, 1925; A.D.C. to C.-in-C., East Indies, 1899; D.A.Q.M.G., India, 1903; D.A.A.G., Staff College, 1908; General Staff Officer, 1914; served Waziristan, 1894-95; China, 1900 (medal with clasp); European War, 1914-18 (despatches, C.B., prom. Maj.-Gen.), including Capture of Jerusalem (K.C.M.G., K.C.B.); Afghan War, 1919; G.O.C. Peshawar District, 1919-23; Adjt.-Gen. in India, 1923; G.O.C.-in-Chief, Eastern Command, India, 1923-28; A.D.C.-General to the King, 1924-28; retired, 1929; Comm. Legion of Honour, 1917; 2nd Class Order of the Nile, 1918. *Publications:* The Life of Gen. Sir Charles Carmichael Monro, G.C.B., G.C.M.G., 1931; The Fire of Life; Life of David Shepherd, Warrior, King; India—our finest monument; The Broad Swathe. *Address:* Concord, Long Bennington, Nr. Newark, Notts. *T.:* Long Bennington 308. *Club:* Cavalry. [*Died* 28 *Dec.* 1959.

BARROW, Major-General Harold Percy Waller, C.B. 1929; C.M.G. 1917; D.S.O. 1918; O.B.E. 1919; D.P.H., D.T.M.; M.R.C.S., L.R.C.P. London; R.A.M.C.; Colonel Commandant, 1941-46; *b.* 30 June 1876. *Educ.:* Guy's Hosp. Surgeon-on-Probation, R.A.M.C. 1898; Lieut., 1899; Capt., 1902; Major, 1910; Lt.-Colonel, 1915; Colonel, 1922; Major-General, 1926; Adjutant, Vols. 1907-8, T.F. 1908-10; D.A.D.G.A.M.S. 1914-16; Director Hygiene and Pathology, Army Headquarters, India, 1919-22; Hon. Surgeon to the Viceroy of India, 1919-23; D.D.M.S. Western Command, Chester, 1923-24; Director of Hygiene, War Office, 1924-30; Hon. Surgeon to the King, 1926-30; retired pay, 1930; Health Officer, Antigua, B.W.I.; Member of Federal Executive Council of the Leeward Islands and of Executive Council of Antigua, 1930-33; a Commissioner of the Royal Hospital, Chelsea, 1943-52. Served S. Africa, 1900-2 (Queen's medal 3 clasps, King's medal 2 clasps); European War, 1914-1918 (C.M.G., D.S.O., O.B.E.); 3rd Afghan War, 1919; Officier de l'ordre de la Couronne Belge; 2nd Class of Order Crown of Siam. *Address:* c/o Glyn, Mills & Co., Holt's Branch, Whitehall, S.W.1 [*Died* 20 *Dec.* 1957.

BARROW, Walter, LL.M.; *b.* Birmingham, 1867; 2nd *s.* of Richard Cadbury Barrow (Mayor of Birmingham 1888); *m.* 1895, Agnes Ann Smithson (*d.* 1950); one *d.* *Educ.:* Oliver's Mount School, Scarborough; Lycée de Lille, France. Solicitor 1889; formerly Member of firm of Wragge and Co., Birmingham; a managing director of

Cadbury Brothers Ltd., 1918-36; Member of Birmingham City Council, 1898-1904; Governor of King Edward Schools, Birmingham 1905-18; Pro-Chancellor of University of Birmingham, 1933-39; President of Birmingham Law Society 1908-10 and of Birmingham Chamber of Commerce, 1929; F.S.A. 1928. *Publications:* various papers in the Transactions of the Birmingham Archæological Society, e.g. Birmingham Markets and Fairs. *Recreations:* golf, mountaineering, archæology, photography. *Address:* Willersey Hill, nr. Broadway, Worcs. *T.:* Broadway 3122. *Clubs:* Alpine; Union (Birmingham). [*Died* 21 *June* 1954.

BARROW, Sir Wilfrid (John Wilson Croker), 5th Bt., *cr.* 1835; Major; F.R.Hist.S.; F.R.G.S., F.Z.S.; *b.* 28 Dec. 1897; *s.* of Sir Francis Laurence John Barrow, 4th Bt., and Winifred Sarah (*d.* 1932), 2nd *d.* of William C. Steward, Whitehaven; *S.* father 1950; *m.* 1926, Patricia, *o. surv. d.* of late R. G. FitzGerald Uniacke, F.S.A., F.R.A.S. (Irel.); one *s.* three *d.* *Educ.:* Stonyhurst; Oxford; R.M.C. Sandhurst; Middle Temple. Served European War, 1914-19; Afghan campaign, 1919-20; Capt. Royal Fusiliers, 1918, Major, 1918; A.D.C. to Earl of Ronaldshay, Bengal, 1920; Temp. King's Messenger, 1923; apptd. Mil. Sec. to Governor of Uganda, 1924; retired, 1929. Regional Officer, Ministry of Home Security, 1941; Dep. Senior Regional Officer, 1943-44. Contested (L.) Carshalton Div. of Surrey, 1945. *Heir:* *s.* Richard John Uniacke, Captain 1st Bn. Irish Guards; *b.* 2 Aug. 1933. *Address:* Wharf House, Bures St. Mary, Suffolk. *T.:* Bures 337. [*Died* 11 *Jan.* 1960.

BARRY, Admiral Sir Claud Barrington, K.B.E., *cr.* 1948; C.B. 1945; D.S.O. 1918; Director of Dockyards, 1946-51; *b.* 1891; *e. s.* of C. E. Barry, Clifton; *m.* 1921, Marsali Campbell, Geelong, Australia; one *s.* *Educ.:* Cordwalles, Maidenhead; R.N. Colleges, Osborne and Dartmouth. Midshipman, 1909; Sub.-Lieut., 1912; Lieut., 1914; Lieut.-Comdr., 1922; Commander, 1926; Capt., 1933; Rear-Adm., 1943; Vice-Adm. 1946; entered Submarine Service, Jan. 1914; served in submarines during war; Admiral, Submarines, 1942-44. Naval Secretary to the First Lord of the Admiralty, 1945-46; retired, promoted Adm., and re-employed, 1950. *Clubs:* United Service, Lansdowne. [*Died* 27 *Dec.* 1951.

BARRY, David Thomas, M.D., D.Sc., F.R.C.S. Eng., D.P.H.; Professor of Physiology, University College, Cork, 1907-42, emeritus since 1942; Chevalier de la Légion d'Honneur, 1929; *b.* Ballyannhan, County Cork, 1870; *e. s.* of late Thomas Barry; *m.* 1908, Yvonne, *d.* of Felix Boiret, architect, Paris; two *s.* *Educ.:* Cork, Berlin, etc. In medical practice at Rock Ferry, Cheshire, 1900; gave up general practice after taking primary Fellowship; during the following years studied at Berlin, Heidelberg, and Paris. F.R.C.S. 1907. *Publications:* The Passing of Valois; numerous scientific publications on heart perfusion, etc. *Recreations:* chess, bridge. *Address:* 7 Lancaster Gate, W.2. *Club:* English-Speaking Union. [*Died* 15 *April* 1955.

BARRY, Lt.-Col. Edward, C.M.G. 1949; O.B.E. 1942 (M.B.E. 1936); H.M. Consul, Mogadishu, Somaliland, 1950-52; *b.* 16 Jan. 1896; *s.* of James Barry and Elizabeth Anne Dewhurst, Preston, Lancs. *Educ.:* Mount St. Mary's. Served European War, 1914-18, France, Mesopotamia, Palestine (despatches). Left Army and joined Somaliland Administration, 1928. War of 1939-45, Somaliland and Ethiopian campaigns (despatches), Somalia and Somaliland, 1939-46. Commissioner for Native Affairs, British Somaliland, 1946; Chief Secretary, Somaliland Protectorate, 1947-50. Acted as Military Governor of Somaliland in 1947 and in 1948. *Publication:* An Elementary Somali Grammar, 1939. *Address:* c/o Lloyd's Bank Ltd., 6 Pall Mall, S.W.1. *Club:* Army and Navy. [*Died* 22 *Aug.* 1952.

BARRY, William James; *b.* 18 Mar. 1864; 4th *s.* of Sir Francis Tress Barry, 1st Bt.; *m.* 1896, Lady Grace Murray, 3rd *d.* of 7th Earl of Dunmore; two *s.* two *d.* *Educ.:* Harrow; Oxford. J.P. Norfolk; Sheriff, 1912. *Heir:* *er. s.* Captain Gerald Barry, M.C., late Coldstream Guards [*m.* 1923, Lady Margaret Pleydell-Bouverie, 4th *d.* of 6th Earl of Radnor]. *Address:* Witchingham Hall, Norwich. *Club:* Marlborough-Windham. [*Died* 2 *July* 1952.

BARRYMORE, Ethel; stage and film actress; *b.* Philadelphia, 15 Aug. 1879; *d.* of late Maurice Barrymore and Georgie Drew; *m.* Russell Griswold Colt (marriage dissolved, 1923); two *s.* one *d.* First appearance on stage, New York, 1894; début on London stage, Adelphi, 1897; later appeared in leading rôles with Henry Irving; returned to America, 1898, and subsequently made occasional appearances on the London stage; played star rôles in New York theatres since 1901; has toured in America and England. Opened the Ethel Barrymore Theatre in New York, 1928. Began film career in 1914 and has appeared in many films. *Publication:* Memories, 1956. *Address:* Mamaroneck, N.Y., U.S.A. [*Died* 18 *June* 1959.

BARRYMORE, Lionel; Actor; *b.* Philadelphia, 28 April 1878; *s.* of Georgie Drew and Maurice Barrymore; *m.* 1924, Irene Fenwick (*decd.*) *Educ.:* Seton Hall College, S. Orange, N.J. Acting since 1893; travelled all over world in plays and stock companies; studied art in Paris; became illustrator in New York City; at persuasion of brother, John Barrymore, returned to stage in The Copperhead and the Claw; first on screen in Friends, 1909; alternated between stage and screen in silent pictures; at start of talking pictures, became Director for Metro-Goldwyn-Mayer Studios; returned to acting in A Free Soul, which won him the Academy of Motion Picture Arts and Sciences Award; signed by Metro-Goldwyn-Mayer; has appeared in Mata Hari, Washington Masquerade, Grand Hotel, Rasputin and the Empress, Dinner at Eight, David Copperfield, Ah Wilderness, Captains Courageous, Saratoga, A Yank at Oxford, Test Pilot, You Can't Take It with You, On Borrowed Time, Dr. Gillespie Series, Duel in the Sun, Down to the Sea in Ships. *Recreations:* etching, piano. *Address:* Metro-Goldwyn-Mayer Studios, Culver City, California; Chatsworth, California. *Club:* Players (New York). [*Died* 15 *Nov.* 1954.

BARSTOW, Major-General Henry, C.B. 1928; C.B.E. 1919; *b.* 14 Nov. 1876; *s.* of late H. C. Barstow, formerly of I.C.S.; *m.* 1906, Louise Mélanie (*d.* 1943), *d.* of Capt. H. F. Crohan, R.N. *Educ.:* Clifton College; R.M.C., Sandhurst. First Commission, 1896; served N.W. Frontier of India, Mohmand, 1897-1898; N.W. Frontier of India, Waziristan, 1901-2; European War, 1914-19; operations in France and Belgium (despatches, Brevet Lt.-Col., C.B.E.); Maj.-Gen., 1927; retired, 1929. *Address:* The Cedars, Crondall, Hants. *T.:* Crondall 212. *Club:* Army and Navy. [*Died* 23 *Oct.* 1952.

BARTER, Capt. Frederick, V.C. 1915; M.C.; Indian Army, retired; late 3rd Batt. Royal Welsh Fusiliers. Served in ranks (prom. Lieut.), European War, 1914-18 (V.C.); retired, 1922. Labour superintendent, A.E.C. Southall, Middx., 1927-53, retired. *Address:* Westminster Bank, Ealing Common, W.5. [*Died* 15 *May* 1953.

BARTER, Geoffrey Herbert, C.M.G. 1950; Fellow and Bursar of Exeter College, Oxford, 1949, resigned 1952; *b.* 25 April 1901; *s.* of late Rev. Canon H. F. T. Barter; *m.* 1926, Elsie Margaret Myers; one *d.* *Educ.:* Marlborough; Exeter College, Oxford. B.A.(Hons.) Lit.Hum., 1924; M.A. 1941. Entered Sudan Political Service as Asst. District Comr., 1924; District Comr., 1934; Asst. Financial Secretary, 1942; Director of Establishments, 1943; retired, 1949. Order of the Nile, 4th Cl., 1936. *Address:* 9 Norham Gardens, Oxford. *T.:* Oxford 48549. *Club:* Leander (Henley on Thames). [*Died* 5 *April* 1952.

BARTLETT, Lt.-Col. Alfred James Napier, D.S.O. 1918; O.B.E. 1946; *b.* 1884; *s.* of late J. E. Bartlett Peverel Court, Aylesbury, Bucks; *m.* 1909, Hilda (*d.* 1949), *d.* of late John Barran, Weetwood, Leeds; one *s.* two *d.* *Educ.:* Rugby; Sandhurst. Entered 52nd (Oxfordshire) Light Infantry, 1903; retired, 1922; Commanded 4th Batt. Oxfordshire and Buckinghamshire Light Infantry during War (D.S.O. and bar, despatches four times). Secretary Oxford Territorial Army Assoc., 1927-46. *Address:* The Red House, Iffley, Oxford. *Club:* United Service. [*Died* 2 *Feb.* 1956.

BARTLETT, Sir Charles (John), Kt., *cr.* 1944; Managing Director, Vauxhall Motors Ltd. (Chairman, 1953-54); *b.* 12 Dec. 1889; *m.* 1925, Emily May Pincombe; no *c.* *Educ.:* Bibury, Glos.; Bath Technical Coll. Served in Devonshire and Dorsetshire Regts., 1914-19. Took up commercial and industrial work, 1920; Managing Director, General Motors Ltd., 1926. *Recreations:* horticulture and sport of any kind. *Address:* Whitewalls, Kinsbourne Green, Harpenden, Herts. *T.:* Harpenden 124. *Clubs:* Reform, Royal Automobile. [*Died* 10 *Aug.* 1955.

BARTLETT, Humphrey Edward Gibson, C.M.G. 1934; *b.* 16 Jan. 1880; *s.* of late Edward Henry Bartlett and late Katharine, *d.* of late Rev. J. D. Gibson, Chaplain H.E.I.C.S., Bombay; *m.* 1920, Grace Enid Margaret, *e. d.* of late Arthur Maltby, The Madras Survey; one *d.* *Educ.:* Winchester; Trinity College, Oxford (M.A.). Solicitor, 1906; Colonial Service, Gold Coast Colony; Assistant District Commissioner, 1909; District Commissioner, 1913; Deputy Provincial Commissioner, 1921; Provincial Commissioner, 1923; Commissioner of Lands, 1930; Official Member of Legislative Council, 1923-33; Retired, 1933. *Address:* c/o The Crown Agents for the Colonies, 4 Millbank, S.W.1. [*Died* 29 *Aug.* 1951.

BARTLEY, Sir John, Kt., *cr.* 1945; C.S.I. 1941; C.I.E. 1936; *b.* 2 Mar. 1886; *s.* of Charles Bartley and Louisa Murray; *m.* 1913, Constance Edith, 3rd *d.* of A. T. Collins, Dublin. *Educ.:* Campbell College, Belfast; Dublin University (Scholar, Senior Moderator in Classics and in Modern Literature). B.A. 1908; M.A. 1919; LL.B. 1923; Barrister-at-Law, Lincoln's Inn, 1923; entered Indian Civil Service, 1909; posted to Bengal, 1910; Political Agent, Hill Tippera State, 1915-19; Political Officer, Sikkim, 1920; District and Sessions Judge, 1921-23; Secretary to Government of Bengal in Legislative Department and Secretary to Bengal Legislative Council, 1924-31; Joint Secretary to the Government of India, Legislative Department, 1932, Additional Secretary, 1938-45; Adviser to Indian Delegation to United Nations Conference, San Francisco, 1945, and to United Nations Preparatory Commission and First General Assembly, London, 1945-1946. *Publications:* General Clauses Act (India), 1897, Fourth Edn., with appendices on statutory drafting, 1940 *Recreations:* photography, model engineering. *Address:* The Priory, Shaldon, Teignmouth, S. Devon. *T.:* Shaldon 176. *Club:* East India and Sports. [*Died* 9 *July* 1954.

BARTLEY, Patrick; M.P. (Lab.) Chester-le-Street Division of Durham, since 1950; *b.* 24 March 1909; British; *s.* of James and Maria Bartley; *m.* 1938, Edith Wood; one *s.* *Educ.:* St. Joseph's Elementary School, Washington; Catholic Workers' College, Oxford. Coalminer, 1923-42; Catholic Workers' College, 1930-32; National Union of Mineworkers Branch Secretary, 1933-42. Member, Washington U.D.C., 1934-37; C.C., Durham, 1937-49; Asst. Labour Director, Ministry of Fuel and Power, Northern "B" Region, 1942-46; Conciliation Officer, National Coal Board (Northern Division), 1947-50. *Address:* Barwood, 29 Oxford Avenue, Washington, Co. Durham. [*Died* 25 *June* 1956.

BARTLEY-DENNISS, Lieutenant-Colonel Cyril Edmund Bartley, D.S.O. 1917; late Royal Artillery; *b.* Hendon, 4 March 1882; *o. surv. s.* of late Sir Edmund R. B. Bartley-Denniss, K.C.; *m.* 1916, Maud, *o. d.* of late Captain Arthur Kent, of Ashford House, Barnstaple; one *s.* one *d.* *Educ.:* Elstree; Harrow; R.M. Academy, Woolwich. 1st Commission R.F.A. 1900; Captain, 1913; Major, 1915; Lt.-Col. 1929; served European War, 1916-18 (D.S.O., despatches); retired pay, 1932; Deputy Director Passive Air Defence, Ministry of Supply, 1939-45; D.L. (Devon), 1938-45. Secretary, Jamaica Legion, British Empire Service League, 1950. *Recreation:* fishing. *Address:* Oak Cottage, Eversley, Hants. *T.:* Eversley 3132. *Clubs:* Army and Navy, Royal Empire Society. [*Died* 6 *Jan.* 1955.

BARTON, Major Basil Kelsey, M.C.; solicitor; *b.* 1879; *s.* of late Major Bernard Barton. *Educ.:* Oundle. Served European War, 1914-19 (M.C.) and 2nd European War, 1939-45; M.P. (U.) Kingston-upon-Hull Central Division, 1931-35. *Address:* Thornleigh, Brough, E. Yorks. *T.:* Brough 32. [*Died* 2 *July* 1958.

BARTON, Clarence; *b.* Pudsey, Yorks, 21 June 1892; *m.* 1917, Jennie, *yr. d.* of W. F. Blackett, Bradford, Yorks (only child, Kenneth Noel, killed on Active Service, 21 Dec. 1943). *Educ.:* Greenside Elementary, Pudsey, Yorks; Hanson Memorial Secondary, Bradford, Yorks. Formerly Clerk, London Goods Accountant, British Transport Commission (E.R.). 15 years Member Wembley Borough Council; Alderman, 1942-49; Mayor of Wembley, 1942-43; J.P., Middlesex, 1944-52; M.P. (Lab.) Wembley (South), 1945-50. Member Transport Salaried Staff Assoc. since 1912; Pres., 1944, and Member of Exec. Cttee. of Nat. Assoc. of Divisional Executives for Education. *Recreations:* photography and swimming. *Address:* Aysgarth, Westfield Avenue, Saltdean, Sussex. *T.:* Rottingdean 3654. [*Died* 15 *Sept.* 1957.

BARTON, Edwin Alfred, L.R.C.P., M.R.C.S.; retired; *b.* 12 July 1863; *s.* of Dr. Alfred Bowyer Barton and Editha Helen Howell; *m.* 1895, Margaret Ellen Pittis; one *d.* *Educ.:* Harrow; University College Hospital. Forty years medical practice in Kensington; Medical Officer Child Welfare Dept., University College Hospital 15 years; Fellow R. Photographic Society (Medallist, 1913); Vice-President Flyfishers' Club. *Publications:* Essentials of Infant Feeding, 1925; Chalk Streams and Water Meadows, 1933; A Doctor Remembers, 1941; Running Water, 1944; An Album of the Chalk Streams, 1946. *Recreations:* photography, fishing, ornithology, water-colours. *Address:* 26 Lytton Grove, Putney Hill, S.W.15. *T.:* Putney 2482. *Club:* Flyfishers'. [*Died* 10 *Feb.* 1953.

BARTHOLOMEW, James Rankin, C.M.G. See page xxvii.

BARTON, Lieut.-Col. Sir Henry Baldwin, Kt., cr. 1921; b. 1869; s. of Henry Barton, 9 Lordship Lane, Wood Green, N.; m. 1892, Fannie, d. of George Revell, Kensington; three s. one d. Lieut.-Col., retired; Mayor of Finsbury, 1911-21. *Address:* 15 Park Avenue North, Hornsey, N.8.
[*Died* 24 *June* 1952.

BARTON, Joseph Edwin, M.A. (Oxon.); b. 1875; s. of Rev. J. E. Barton; m. 1905, Bertha, d. of George Speight, Bradford; one s. *Educ.:* Crypt School, Gloucester; Pembroke College, Oxford (Scholar). First Class Classical Mods., 1896; Newdigate Prize, 1897; First Class Lit. Hum., 1898; Senior Classical Master, Bradford Grammar School, 1900-1906; Headmaster, Crypt School, Gloucester, 1906-1910; Wakefield Grammar School, 1911-16; Bristol Grammar School, 1916-38; President Incorporated Association Head Masters, 1932; Dominion Lecturer in Art for National Gallery of Canada, 1935 and 1940; Lecturer for British Council; Hon. A.R.I.B.A., 1938. *Publications:* The Poetry of Thomas Hardy (with Lionel Johnson's Art of Thomas Hardy, 1923 ed.); Introduction to Dening's Eighteenth Century Architecture of Bristol, 1923; Modern Art (B.B.C. booklet), 1932; Purpose and Admiration, enlarged edn., 1948; numerous articles on literary subjects in Saturday Review and other periodicals. *Recreations:* Art, antiques, travel, golf. *Address:* 86 Quantock Road, Weston-super-Mare.
[*Died* 6 *June* 1959.

BARTON, Lt.-Col. Leslie Eric, C.I.E. 1941; Indian Political Service, retired; Assistant Chief Constable, War Department Constabulary, since 1944; b. 3 Feb. 1889; y. s. of late William Barton; m. Mary Frances (d. 1946), d. of M. D. Daly, J.P. of County Cork; one s. *Educ.:* Onslow Hall, Richmond; R.M.C., Sandhurst. Entered Army 1909, attached to R. Warwicks. Regt.; transferred 30th Punjabis I.A., 1910. Served European War, 1914-18, Operations on N.W. Frontier, 1915-16; Mohmand Expedition, 1916-17; Afghan War, 1919; Waziristan, 1919-21 and 1921-23. Entered Political Service, 1919; amongst other appts. held those of Deputy Commissioner, Dera Ismail Khan, 1921-22, Kohat, 1925, and Bannu, 1926-27; Political Agent, Haraoti and Tonk, 1928-32; Resident in Jaipur, 1934-35; Political Agent, Bundelkhand, 1936-37; Resident in Udaipur, 1938; Resident in Eastern States, 1939-41; Resident in Kashmir, 1941-43; retired, 1944. *Address:* 68 Park Mansions, Knightsbridge, S.W.1. *T.:* Kensington 6670. *Club:* East India and Sports.
[*Died* 28 *Feb.* 1952.

BARTON, Samuel Saxon, O.B.E., F.S.A.Scot., F.R.F.P.S. Glasgow, L.R.C.P.; M.R.C.O.G.; Hon. R.C.A. 1946; Gynæcological and Obstetrical Surgeon; Honorary Secretary Fellowship of the White Boar; s. of Samuel Saxon Barton, The Beach, St. Michael's Hamlet, Liverpool, and Jessie, d. of John Latimer, Sandfield Hall, Wallasey, Cheshire; m. Dorothy Atherton, M.B., Ch.B., D.O.M.S., d. of S. R. Williams, The Chart, Caldy, Cheshire; three s. *Educ.:* Greenbank School, Liverpool; Loretto School. Musselburgh; Universities of Liverpool and Edinburgh. House Surgeon, Hospital for Women, Liverpool; House Physician, Northern Hospital, Liverpool; Temp. Surgeon-Lt. R.N. in charge of H.M.S. Dwarf in Cameroons and West Coast of Africa; O.B.E.; Tropical Specialist, Ministry of Pensions Medical Boards, Liverpool; Hon. Clinical Assistant Hospital for Women, Liverpool; Hon. Assistant Surgeon Liverpool and Samaritan Hospital for Women; F.R.S.M.; Vice-President, Historic Society of Lancashire and Cheshire. *Publications:* papers in medical journals; A Yorkshire Royal Mystery, Yorkshire Herald; Songs before Sunset; Songs by the Wayside; Songs by the Fireside. *Recreations:* antiquarian research, motoring, painting. *Address:* 88 Rodney Street, Liverpool, 1. *T.:* Royal 3560; Sandford, Gladdeath Avenue, Llandudno. *T.:* Llandudno 6109. *Club:* Royal Automobile.
[*Died* 17 *Feb.* 1957.

BARTON, Rev. Walter John, M.A.; F.R.G.S.; Canon Emeritus of Salisbury Cathedral; Treasurer of Salisbury Cathedral and Prebendary of Calne since 1949; resigned Treasurership to be Chaplain-in-charge of St. Paul's Anglican Cathedral, Valetta, Malta, for six months, Dec. 1954; m. 1918, Dorothea Margaret, d. of late Adolf Zimmern. *Educ.:* Winchester (scholar); New College, Oxford (scholar), 1st class Mods. and Lit. Hum.; University Scholar in Geography, 1904. Asst. Master, R.N. College, Osborne, 1905; Winchester College, 1907-13; Ordained, 1909; Headmaster Epsom College, 1914-22; Headmaster of Portsmouth Grammar School, 1926-1936; Examining Chap. to the Lord Bishop of Portsmouth, 1928-36; to Bishop of Salisbury, 1936-46; Hon. Canon of Portsmouth, 1931; Canon Res. of Salisbury Cathedral, 1944-1951; Recorder of geographical section of British Association, 1910-13; Vice-President, 1916. *Address:* 20 The Close, Salisbury. *T.:* Salisbury 2983. *Club:* Athenæum.
[*Died* 21 *March* 1955.

BARTON, Wilfred Alexander, Q.C. 1937; Practising Barrister; b. 9 Oct. 1880; 2nd s. of late Rt. Hon. Sir Edmund Barton, G.C.M.G., P.C., first Prime Minister of Commonwealth of Australia and late Lady Barton, Sydney, New South Wales; m. 1926, Marjorie, d. of R. I. Hall, Frines Kraal, Ladysmith, Natal; one s. one d. *Educ.:* Sydney Grammar School; Sydney University (Coutts Classical Scholar, University Gold Medallist for Classics); Magdalen College, Oxford (Rhodes Scholar, Vinerian Scholar, B.A., 1st Class School of Jurisprudence, Bairstow Law Scholar). Called to Bar Gray's Inn 1908, Inner Temple 1928; served European War, King's Liverpool Regt., Captain, and at G.H.Q. (despatches). *Recreations:* tennis, golf and motoring. *Address:* 3 Dr. Johnson's Buildings, Temple, E.C.4. *T.:* Cunningham 2824. *Club:* Oxford and Cambridge.
[*Died* 18 *March* 1953.

BARTON, Sir William, Kt., cr. 1917; b. 5 Aug. 1862; s. of late Robert Barton and Annie Gray; m. 1st, 1895, Jessie Cuthbertson (d. 1915), d. of late James Boyd, Merchant, Manchester; one d.; 2nd, 1918, Olive Ruth Bryson (d. 1956), Matron of Balmoral Red Cross Hospital, Flanders, d. of late Oliver Bryson, The Haw, Lifford; one d. *Educ.:* High School and Univ. of Glasgow. Presbyterian; F.R.S.A.; Vice-Pres. British Cotton Growing Assoc.; J.P. County of Lancaster; Director, Manchester Athenæum, 1903-9; Member Manchester City Council, 1906-9; M.P. (L.) Oldham, 1910-18, (Coal.L.) 1918-22. *Address:* Goatfell, Upper Colwyn Bay, North Wales. *T.:* Colwyn Bay 2700.
[*Died* 9 *July* 1957.

BARTON, Sir William (Pell), K.C.I.E., cr. 1927 (C.I.E. 1914); C.S.I. 1920; late Indian Political Department; b. 1871; m. 1918, Evelyn Agnes, d. of J. C. T. Heriz-Smith, of Slade, Bideford; two d. *Educ.:* Bedford Modern School; Worcester College, Oxford; University College, London. Entered I.C.S. 1893; Agent on special duty, Kurram, 1899-1902; Assistant Commissioner N.W. Frontier Province, 1903; Deputy Commissioner, 1904; Divisional Judge, Peshawar, 1907; Deputy Commissioner, Dera Ismail Khan, 1907; Kohat, 1908; Political Agent, Dir, Swat and Chitral, 1910; Officiating Revenue Commissioner, 1911; Judicial Commissioner at Peshawar, 1915-18; Resident in Baroda, 1919; served Afghan War, 1919 (C.S.I.); Resident Mysore, 1920-25; Resident at Hyderabad, 1925-30; went to India with the Ministry of Supply Mission, 1940-41. *Publications:* The Princes of India, 1934; India's North-West Frontier, 1939; India's Fateful

Hour, 1942. *Address:* Lower Lodge, Ardingly, Sussex. *Club:* East India and Sports.
[*Died* 28 *Nov.* 1956.

BARWELL, Harold Shuttleworth, M.B. Lond., F.R.C.S. Eng.; L.R.C.P. Lond.; retired; Consulting Surgeon for Diseases of the Throat and Ear, St. George's Hospital; Past-Pres. Laryngological Section, Royal Society of Medicine: *b.* London, 1875; *s.* of late Richard Barwell, F.R.C.S., Consulting Surgeon to Charing Cross Hospital, and Mary Diana Shuttleworth, of Preston, Lancashire; *m.* 1907, Evelyn, 2nd *surv. d.* of Dr. J. Foster-Palmer of Chelsea; two *s.* *Educ.:* Westminster School (Bishop Williams' Exhibition); St. George's Hospital (£145 Scholarship); Johnson Prize in Anatomy; 2nd Year's Proficiency Prize; Brackenbury Prize in Surgery; Brown £100 Exhibition; M.R.C.S., L.R.C.P. 1899; M.B. (Lond), F.R.C.S. (Eng.), in 1901; House Surgeon, House Physician, Assist. in Ophthalmic, Dental, and Throat Departments, St. George's Hospital; Senior Clinical Assistant for two years at Hospital for Diseases of the Throat, Golden Square; and Assistant Surgeon to the Metropolitan Ear, Nose, and Throat Hospital; Laryngologist to Mount Vernon Hospital for Diseases of the Chest; Surgeon to the Throat and Ear Department, Hampstead General Hospital; Laryngologist, St. John Clinic; Surgeon for and Lecturer on Diseases of Throat and Ear, St. George's Hospital; Vice-President, Section of Oto-Rhino-Laryngology, B.M.A.; Hon. Secy., Laryngological Section, Roy. Soc. of Med. *Publications:* Diseases of the Larynx, 1907; 3rd edition, 1928; Editor of Laryngeal Phthisis (Lake and Barwell), 2nd edition, 1905. *Articles:* Nose and its Accessory Sinuses, Choyce's System of Surgery, 1928; Larynx, Pharynx, and Nose, Latham and English's System of Treatment, 1912; Nose and Throat, Price's Practice of Medicine, 1944; Laryngeal Tuberculosis, Edin. Medical Journal, 1905; Laryngeal Paralyses, Lancet, 1905, etc. *Address:* Fincham End, Crowthorne, Berks. *T.:* Crowthorne 2780.
[*Died* 27 *May* 1959.

BARWELL, Hon. Sir Henry Newman, K.C.M.G. 1922; former Premier and Attorney-General of South Australia, and former Agent-General; Chairman of Commissioners of Charitable Funds in South Australia; Member of South Australia Housing Trust; of Board of Management of Royal Adelaide Hospital; of Council of S.A. Institute of Medical and Veterinary Science; *b.* Adelaide, 26 February 1877; *s.* of late Henry Charles Barwell, Adelaide; *m.* 1902, Anne, *d.* of late Canon Webb, Rector of Clare, S. Australia; one *s.* three *d.* *Educ.:* Whinham Coll., Adelaide; St. Peter's Coll., Adelaide; Adelaide University (LL.B. 1899). Admitted to S.A. bar, 1899; practised at the bar from 1899; President of Port Pirie (S.A.) School of Mines, 1900-15; entered Parliament as Liberal representative for district of Stanley, 1915; Attorney-General and Minister of Industry, South Australia, 1917, and 1918-1920; Premier and Attorney-General of South Australia, 1920-24; Leader of the Opposition, 1924-25; Member of Commonwealth Senate, 1925-28; Agent-General for South Australia, 1928-33; Member of Church of England, Church Advocate, 1916-19. Permitted to retain the title of Honourable, 1924. *Recreations:* bowls, billiards, motoring. *Address:* 3 Ashleigh Grove, Unley Park. South Australia. *T.:* M3868.
[*Died* 30 *Sept.* 1959.

BARWICK, Sir John Storey, 2nd Bt., *cr.* 1912; coal-owner; *b.* 4 Aug. 1876; *s.* of 1st Bt. and Margaret (*d.* 1908), *d.* of late George Short of Pallion; *S.* father, 1915; *m.* 1st, 1907, Gwladys Jessie (*d.* 1949), 3rd *d.* of George William Thomas, of Ystrad Mynach, Glamorgan; one *s.* two *d.* (and one *s.* decd.); 2nd, 1950, Evelyn Maude, *d.* of late Charles Turner. *Heir:* *s.* Richard Llewellyn [*b.* 4 Nov. 1916; *m.* 1948, Valerie Maud Ward (*née* Skelton); one *d.* *Address:* Thimbleby, Northallerton, Yorks.
[*Died* 26 *March* 1953.

BASKERVILLE, Beatrice; *see* Guichard Beatrice C.

BASKETT, Charles H.; R.E. 1918; Principal Chelmsford School of Science and Art, 1905-32, retd.; *b.* 25 Mar. 1872; *s.* of C. E. Baskett, A.R.E. *Educ.:* Colchester Grammar School. Painter and etcher; exhibited etchings, Royal Academy, Salon, International, Liverpool, Glasgow, Birmingham. *Publications:* numerous etchings and aquatints. *Recreations:* yachting and motoring. *Address:* The White Cottage, Sarisbury Green, Southampton.
[*Died* 10 *Oct.* 1953.

BASS, His Honour Judge John Stuart, M.B.E. 1945; T.D. 1950; Additional Judge, Mayor's and City of London Court since 1953; *b.* 9 Jan. 1905; *s.* of John Bass and Catharine Agnes Kingston; *m.* 1929, Eunice Louise Arber; two *s.* one *d.* *Educ.:* Forest School Walthamstow; Hertford College, Oxford. Barrister-at-Law, Lincoln's Inn, 1929. Commissioned 2nd Lieut. 54th (East Anglian) Divisional R.A.S.C. (T.A.), 1939; D.A.A.G. H.Q. Lines of Communication, 21st Army Group, British Liberation Army, 1944; demobilized, 1945, with hon. rank of Major. Third Junior Prosecuting Counsel to the Crown at the Central Criminal Court, Nov. 1945, Second Junior, Jan. 1950, First Junior, 1950-53; Recorder of Great Yarmouth, 1952-53. *Recreation:* sailing. *Address:* Ruthwell, Lucton's Avenue, Buckhurst Hill, Essex.
[*Died* 16 *Sept.* 1954.

BASS, Sir William (Arthur Hamar), 2nd Bt., *cr.* 1882; *b.* 24 Dec. 1879; *e. s.* of late H. A. Bass, M.P.; *S.* uncle, 1909; *m.* 1903, Lady (Wilmot Ida) Noreen Hastings (*d.* 1949), *d.* of 13th Earl of Huntingdon. *Educ.:* Harrow. Formerly Lieut. 3rd Batt. East Surrey Regt.; joined 10th Hussars, 1899; served in South Africa, 1900-1902. *Recreations:* horse-racing, hunting, shooting, fishing, motoring. *Heir:* none. *Address:* 71 Park Street, W.1. *T.:* Grosvenor 1803; Byrkley Lodge, Burton-on-Trent. *Clubs:* Jockey, Turf, White's.
[*Died* 28 *Feb.* 1952 (*ext.*).

BASSET, Maj.-Gen. Richard Augustin Marriott, C.B. 1945; C.B.E. 1940; M.C. 1917; *b.* 10 Feb. 1891; *s.* of Rev. William Basset, Rector of Frimley, Surrey; *m.* 1914, Eileen, *d.* of George Wale; one *s.* one *d.* *Educ.:* Marlborough College. 2nd Lt. The Queen's Regt. 1911; Capt. 1915; Bt. Major, 1918; Major, 1927; Bt. Lt.-Col. 1931; Lt.-Col. 1933; Col. 1937; Temp. Maj.-Gen. 1943. Served European War in France and Belgium, 1915-18 (despatches twice, Bt. Major, M.C.); War of 1939-45 (despatches twice, C.B.E.); A.D.C. to the King, 1942-46; retired pay, 1946. *Address:* West Barn, Frimley, Surrey.
[*Died* 7 *Jan.* 1954.

BASTARD, Bt. Colonel Reginald, D.S.O. 1915; D.L., J.P.; late Lincs Regt.; *b.* 2 Oct. 1880; *o. s.* of late John Algernon Bastard; *m.* 1919, Lilias, *d.* of late J. W. Summers, M.P., and *widow* of Capt. C. G. V. Wellesley; one *s.* *Educ.:* Eton. Entered army, 1900; Captain, 1912; Bt. Col. 1933; served South Africa, 1899-1902 (Queen's medal 3 clasps, King's medal 2 clasps); European War, 1914-18 (D.S.O. and bar), Sector Commander, Plymouth Home Guard, 1940-45; Hon. Air Commodore of No. 934 Squadron, Balloon Cmd., R.A.F., 1939-45, High Sheriff of Devon, 1934. *Address:* Kitley. Yealmpton, Devon. *T.A.:* Yealmpton. *T.:* 401. *Club:* Beefsteak.
[*Died* 20 *May* 1960.

BASTIN, Major-General George Edward Restalic, C.B. 1955; O.B.E. 1943; Assistant Master-General of the Ordnance since November 1959; *b.* 14 October 1902; *s.* of late Edward Mathew Bastin and Alice Marie (*née* Widiez); *m.* 1933, Frances Gwendoline Ursula Venning; one *s.* one *d.* *Educ.:* Sherborne Sch.; R.M.A., Woolwich. Joined Royal Artillery as 2nd Lieut., 1923; Capt., 1936; p.s.c. 1937; Maj., 1940; Commander, 29 Inf. Bde., 1945; Brigadier, General Staff, 14th Army, 1945; Brig. i/c Administration, Italy, 1946-48; Dep. Dir., Weapons Development, War Office, 1948-49; i.d.c. 1950; Comdr., 65 Anti-Aircraft Bde., 1951-53; U.K. and Commonwealth Rep., U.N. Armistice Commn., Korea, 1953-54; Major-General in Charge of Administration, G.H.Q., M.E.L.F., 1954-56; Dir. Weapons Development, W.O., 1956-58; Asst. Controller of Munitions, Ministry of Supply, 1958-59. *Address:* War Office, Whitehall, S.W.1; Dunmoorland, Dunmow Hill, Fleet, Hants. *T.:* Fleet 110. *Club:* Army and Navy. [*Died* 2 *Aug.* 1960.

BATCHELOR, Lieut.-Colonel Vivian Allan, D.S.O. 1917; J.P., Somerset; late Royal Artillery; *b.* 24 Aug. 1882; *o. s.* of G. B. Batchelor, Combe Florey House, Taunton, and Mary, *d.* of E. M. Lewis, J.P., of The Maindee, Newport, Mon.; unmarried. *Educ.:* Rugby; Royal Military Academy, Woolwich. Commissioned in R.H. and R.F.A. 1900; served in The Chestnut Troop, R.H.A., 1908-1914; Captain, 1913; Major, 1915; Lieut.-Col., 1929; left India Oct. 1914 with the Lahore Division; served in France and Flanders, 1914-19, also Suvla Bay and Egypt; acting Lieut.-Colonel commanding the 64th (Army) Brigade R.F.A., 1918-19 (wounded four times, despatches three times, D.S.O. and bar, 1914 Star, Belgian Croix de Guerre); retired pay, 1932; Lord of the Manor of Combe Florey. *Recreations:* hunting, shooting. *Address:* Combe Florey House, Taunton. *T.A.:* Combe Florey. *T.:* Bishop's Lydeard 297. [*Died* 24 *Oct.* 1960.

BATE, Captain Claude Lindsay, C.B.E. 1945; D.S.O. 1920; R.N., retired; *o. surv. s.* of late Col. T. E. L. Bate, C.I.E., C.B.E.; *m.* 1913, Julia, *yr. d.* of late Surgeon Major G. Duncan, 42nd Regt. *Educ.:* Wellington College; H.M.S. Britannia. Joined Navy, 1898; served European War, Jutland (despatches); Baltic Operations (despatches, D.S.O.); retired list 1929; served War of 1939-46. *Address:* Padiss Corner, Fordingbridge, Hants. [*Died* 5 *Sept.* 1957.

BATEMAN, Arthur Leonard; *b.* County of London, 1879; *m.*; one *d.* *Educ.:* privately. Member of the Worshipful Coy. of Basketmakers, and Freeman, City of London; Councillor Borough of Camberwell, 1922-31; ex-Mayor of Camberwell; M.P. (U.) North Camberwell, 1931-35; Hon. Organizer and Founder Camberwell Children's Christmas Treat and Summer Holiday Camp Fund; ex-Member L.C.C. for Peckham; Member Warwick County Borough Council, 1946-51. Guild of Freemen, City of London and Metropolitan Mayors Association, London. *Recreations:* fishing and motoring. *Address:* The Woodlands, Cliffe Hill, Warwick. *T.:* Warwick 223. *Clubs:* Bartholomew, City Livery, Farringdon Ward; Sussex Motor Yacht (Brighton); Worthing Sailing; Brookhurst Golf. [*Died* 8 *May* 1957.

BATEMAN, James, R.A. 1942 (A.R.A. 1935); *s.* of Miles and Frances Jane Bateman; *m.* 1918, Eleanor Vera Grant; two *s.* one *d.* *Educ.:* Royal College of Art; Slade School. Painter; subjects mostly pastoral; also paints portraits and mural decorations; works in Tate, British Museum, Vancouver, Adelaide, Sydney, Newcastle upon Tyne, Leeds, Cheltenham, Southampton, etc. *Recreations:* various. *Address:* 3 Chelsea Manor Studios, Flood St., Chelsea, S.W.3. *Club:* Chelsea Arts. [*Died* 2 *Aug.* 1959.

BATES, Brig.-Gen. Sir (Charles) Loftus, K.C.M.G., *cr.* 1919 (C.M.G. 1916); C.B. 1918; D.S.O. 1900; late Hon. Colonel Northumberland Hussars Yeomanry (late Capt. King's Dragoon Guards); *b.* 2 Aug. 1863; *s.* of Thomas Bates of Aydon, Northumberland; *m.* 1892, Katharine (*d.* 1937), *d.* of Edward Leadbitter, The Spital, Northumberland; one *s.* *Educ.:* Eton. Served South Africa (severely wounded, despatches, D.S.O.); European War, France 1914-15, Egypt 1916-1919 (K.C.M.G., C.B., White Eagle of Servia, despatches four times); Director of Remounts 1915-19; contested (C.) Hexham, 1910; late Chairman of Racecourse Owners Assoc.; J.P., D.L. Northumberland; late Deputy Chairman, Quarter Sessions. *Address:* The Spital, Hexham. *T.A.:* 40 Hexham. *T.:* 40. *Clubs:* Army and Navy; Northern Counties (Newcastle); County (Carlisle). [*Died* 9 *March* 1951.

BATES, Brig.-Gen. Francis Stewart Montague, C.B. 1919; C.M.G. 1918; D.S.O. 1917; *b.* 8 Feb. 1876; *s.* of late Henry Montague Bates, of Manaccan, Cornwall. Served Lumsden's Horse; 2nd Lt. East Surrey Regt., 1900; Captain, 1909; Major, 1915; Brevet Lieutenant-Colonel, 1916; Brevet Colonel, 1926; Colonel 27 Dec. 1927, with seniority 3rd June 1920; employed S.A. Constabulary, 1902-6; with Canadian Forces, 1910-12; Adjt. T.F. 1914; served S. Africa, 1899-1901 (Queen's medal and 4 clasps); European War, 1914-18 and Post Wars, 1918-20 (despatches six times, C.B., C.M.G., D.S.O., and Bt. Lt.-Col., French Legion of Honour, Croix de Guerre avec Palme, Commander Order of Redeemer, Greece); Brigade-Commander, Sep. 1916-Oct. 1920; G.O.C. troops Ismid, 1920; Commanded 141st (5th London) Infantry Brigade T.A., 1928-32; retired, 1932; Home Guard, 1940-41. *Publication:* The Infantry Scout. *Address:* Manaccan, Cornwall. [*Died* 21 *June* 1954

BATES, Frederic Alan, M.C., A.F.C.; D.L.; *b.* 16 Aug. 1884; 4th *s.* of late Sir E. P. Bates, Bt., and Constance, *d.* of late S. R. Graves, M.P. for Liverpool; *m.* 1932, Barberie, *d.* of late Thomas Fair of Clifton Hall, Preston. *Educ.:* Winchester; Trinity College, Cambridge. Served European War, 1914-19 (M.C., A.F.C., despatches four times); late Major R.A.F. and Capt. Denbigh Yeo.; D.L. Flints. (Sheriff 1935); Director of Cunard S.S. Co., T. and J. Brocklebank Ltd., Cunard White Star Ltd., Martin's Bank, Port Line Ltd., Cunard House Ltd., Edward Bates & Sons Ltd. *Publication:* Dingle Stalk, 1960 (Posthumous). *Address:* Cunard Building, Liverpool. [*Died* 24 *June* 1957.

BATES, Henry Thomas Roy; Chief Inspector of Audit, Ministry of Housing and Local Government, since 1958; *b.* 13 April 1902; *s.* of late Henry Wilberforce Bates, Plymouth, Devon; *m.* 1930, Kathleen Stewart, *d.* of C. E. W. Wilmot, M.D.; three *s.* *Educ.:* Plymouth College; Imperial College of Science and Technology. B.Sc. London, 1923; Associate of Royal College of Science, 1923; Assistant District Auditor, Ministry of Health, 1924; District Auditor (Cardiff), 1949-52; Deputy Chief Inspector of Audit, 1952-58. *Recreations:* gardening, walking, golf. *Address:* 27 Green Lane, Purley, Surrey. *T.:* Uplands 9024. [*Died* 14 *Oct.* 1958.

BATES, Sir Loftus; *see* Bates, Sir (C.) L.

BATES, Thorpe, F.R.A.M.; F.G.S.M.; Professor of Singing, Trinity College, London; actor-singer; *b.* London, 11 Feb. 1883; *s.* of Frederick and Elizabeth Bates, London; *m.* 1907, Edith Helena Leech; one *s.* one *d.* *Educ.:* Royal Academy of Music. Started career as a concert singer after leaving Royal Academy of Music, where he studied with Dr. Theo. Lierhammer; has sung at the

Musical Festivals of Leeds, Sheffield, Birmingham Hereford, etc., Royal Choral Society; made debut on stage at Daly's Theatre in The Happy Day (May 1916); played in The Maid of the Mountains (Beppo), The Shop Girl, The Rebel Maid, The Golden Moth, and The Yankee Princess. *Recreation:* golf. *Address:* 17 Burgess Hill, Hampstead, N.W.2. *T.:* Hampstead 8240. [*Died* 23 *May* 1958.

BATESON, Colonel John Holgate, C.M.G. 1919; D.S.O. 1917; late Royal Artillery, *b.* 1880; *s.* of Henry Bateson, Farnworth, Lancs; and *g.s.* of Rev. Christopher Bateson, Westhoughton, Lancs; *m.* 1st, 1908, Mary Elizabeth, 3rd *d.* of J. Prestwich, Eccles; one *d*; 2nd, 1915, Madeline de Vere, *d.* of late Major-General William Walter Hopton Scott, C.B., XIth Lancers, Indian Army. *Educ.:* privately in Edinburgh; Manchester University. After studying Medicine for three years joined the Royal Artillery as a University Candidate, 1900; served principally in India on the N.W. Frontier, where he obtained an intimate knowledge of the people, and participated in the Mohmand Campaign, 1908; during European War served on the General Staff and on the Staff of the Heavy Artillery (D.S.O., C.M.G., Bt Lt.-Col., despatches); retired pay, 1936. *Recreations:* sailing and shooting. [*Died* 12 *Sept.* 1956.

BATH, Hon. Thomas Henry, C.B.E. 1948; J.P.; *b.* Hill End, New South Wales, 21 Feb. 1875; *s.* of T. H. Bath, Cornwall, England; *m.* 1904, Elizabeth Fensome (*d.* 1931); one *s.* two *d.* *Educ.:* Public School, Hill End. Left N.S.W. for Western Australia, 1896; followed various callings, mining, and journalism; closely identified with labour and reform movements in State; Member of State Parliament, 1902; Chairman of Committees and Deputy Speaker, 1904; Minister for Lands and Education, 1905; Leader of Labour Opposition in State Parliament, 1906-10; Acting Premier during 1913 and 1914; Minister for Lands and Agriculture, Western Australia, 1911-14; retired from political life and engaged in farming pursuits, 1914; Member of Royal Commission appointed under Control of Trade in War Time Act, W. Australia, 1915; Member of Honorary Royal Commission on the Establishment of University for Western Australia; Member of the University Senate until 1918; J.P. for whole State; associated with Co-operative movement, Trustee Wheat Pool of Western Australia, 1925-54; Vice-Chairman Co-operative Federation of W.A.; Chairman Co-operative Bulk Handling, Ltd., 1943-48; Member Transport Co-ordination Board of W.A., 1934-46; wartime activities for Commonwealth of Australia; member Liquid Fuel Control Board W.A. and Cargo Control Committee W.A. etc. *Recreations:* bowls, gardening, literary studies. *Address:* 74 Farnley Street, Mount Lawley Perth, W. Australia. [*Died* 6 *Nov.* 1956.

BATHO, Cyril, D.Sc., M.Inst.C.E.; Emeritus Professor, University of Birmingham; Beale Professor of Civil Engineering, University of Birmingham, 1924-50; *b.* Liverpool, 21 June 1885; *s.* of late Robert James Batho, Liverpool; unmarried. *Educ.:* Liverpool College; Liverpool University; Charlottenburg. B.Eng. (1st Hons.) 1904, B.Sc. (Mathematics, 1st Hons.) 1905, Liverpool; University Scholar and Fellow, Liverpool University; Lecturer in Civil Engineering, McGill University, 1908; studied in Berlin and Charlottenburg, 1910-11; Assistant Professor, McGill University, 1911; Assistant Designing Engineer on New Quebec Bridge, 1912-13; D.Sc. McGill, 1917; Research Officer, Canadian Machine Gun Corps, 1918; Technical Assistant, Royal Aircraft Establishment, 1918-1919; Lecturer in Trinity College, Cambridge, 1919; Associate-Professor of Applied Mechanics and Hydraulics, McGill University, 1919; Member of Steel Structure Research Committee, 1929-36. M.I.Struct.E., 1931-50. *Publications:* various research papers on Elasticity, Structural Engineering, and Thermodynamics in British and American Journals and Reports of the Dept. of Scientific and Industrial Research. *Recreations:* books, art and music travel. *Address:* 7 George Road, Edgbaston Birmingham 15. [*Died* 23 *March* 1951.

BATHURST, Major Sir Frederick Edward William Hervey-, 5th Bt., *cr.* 1818; D.S.O. 1917; late Grenadier Guards; *b.* 11 Feb. 1870; *s.* of 4th Bt. and Ada, *d.* of Sir J. Ribton, 4th Bt.; *m.* 1st, 1901, Hon. Moira O'Brien (whom he divorced, 1912), 2nd *d.* of 14th Baron Inchiquin; one *s.*; 2nd, 1919, Katharine, O.B.E., *d.* of late Alexander Dick-Cunyngham and *widow* of J. H. Nevill, Grenadier Guards; one *s.* *Educ.:* Eton. Served through Egyptian Campaign; also through war in South Africa (despatches twice); European War, 1914-19 (despatches three times, D.S.O.). *Heir:* *s.* Frederick Peter Methuen [*b.* 26 Jan. 1903; *m.* 1933, Maureen, *e. d.* of Charles Gordon, Boveridge Park, Salisbury; one *s.* (Frederick John Charles Gordon, *b.* 23 Apr. 1934) one *d.* *Educ.:* Eton]. *Address:* Sombourne Park, Stockbridge, Hants. *Club:* Guards. [*Died* 16 *April* 1956.

BATLEY, Mrs. R. C.; *see* Lewis, Mabel Terry.

BATT, Rear-Admiral Charles Ernest, C.M.G. 1918; late Royal Navy; *b.* 2 Oct. 1874; *s.* of Captain Robert Barrie Batt, Royal Navy; *m.* Olive Valentine, (*d.* 1957), *y. d.* of William M. Cunningham, Writer, Glasgow; one *s.* one *d.* *Educ.:* Christ's Hospital. Served on Australian Station, 1891-1895; Channel Fleet, 1896-97; Australian Station (Flagship), 1898-1901; Staff of Commander-in-Chief, Portsmouth, 1901-3; Secretary to Commodore in Charge, Hongkong, 1904-1905; to Rear Admiral, Channel Fleet, 1907; Royal Naval War College, 1907-8; to Rear Admiral Commanding 2nd Cruiser Squadron, 1908-1910; to Commander-in-Chief, Coast of Scotland, 1913-17; to Admiralty Reconstruction Committee, 1918; to Vice-Admiral Commanding Light Cruiser Force, Grand Fleet, 1918-19; to Commander-in-Chief, North America and West Indies Station, 1920; Coastguard Paymaster, Scottish Command and Admiralty, 1921-24; Paymaster Captain of H.M.S. Excellent, 1924-26, and R.N Barracks, Portsmouth, 1926-29; Retired list, 1929. *Address:* The Mount, 57 Pashley Road, Eastbourne. *T.:* Eastbourne 649. [*Died* 5 *March* 1958.

BATT, Lt.-Col. Reginald Cossley, C.B.E. 1919; M.V.O. 1906; *b.* 29 Oct. 1872; *y. s.* of late William Forster Batt of Cae Kenfy, Abergavenny; *m.* 1st, 1903, Violet (*d.* 1910), *y. d.* of Robert Millington Knowles, J.P., D.L., of Colston-Bassett Hall, Notts; one *s.* (and three *s.* decd.); 2nd, 1913, Eileen Augusta (*d.* 1924), *o. d.* of Henry William Russell Domvile, Pentre Cottage, Abergavenny; 3rd, 1931, Violet Frances Mary Owen (*d.* 1951), *o. d.* of late Captain F. B. Cole, J.P., D.L. Denbighshire. *Educ.:* Wellington; Sandhurst. Entered Army, 1892; Captain Royal Fusiliers, 1899; Adjutant, 1900-4; Adjutant, 3rd Vol. Batt. Norfolk Regiment, 1905-7; retired, 1907; Lieut.-Col. commanding 6th Batt. Royal Fusiliers, 1913; patron of the livings of North Barningham and Ingworth; Lord of the Manors of Banningham, Colby, Ingworth, Tuttington with Crackford, East Beckham Isaacs, East Beckham Marriots, Norwood Barningham, Runton Hayes, Dilham. *Address:* Gresham Hall, Norfolk. *Club:* Army and Navy. [*Died* 30 *Dec.* 1952.

BATTEN, (Harry) Mortimer; author, inventor, and lecturer; *b.* 4 Feb. 1888; *s.* of Wm. Townshend Batten, M.I.C.E.; *m.* 1918, Ivy Kathleen, *d.* of John William Godfrey, J.P.,

Barkingside; one *s.* two *d.* *Educ.:* Oakham. Studied natural history and game preservation in Canada and British Columbia. War service, 1914-18, dispatch rider, and French Army (Croix de Guerre); dispatch rider, 1940-1942. *Publications:* Habits and Characters of British Wild Animals; Wandering Otter; The Badger Afield and Underground; Romances of the Wild; The Grey Fox of Bennan; Prints from Many Trails; Nature from the Highways: Nature Jottings of a Motorist; Wild Animals and their Tracks, official publication of the Boy Scouts Association; Dramas of the Wild Folk; 2 L.O. Animal Stories; 2 L.O. Bird Stories; Forth from the Wilderness; How to Feed and Attract the Wild Birds; Muskwa the Trailmaker; Starlight; Electricity and the Camera; Ray of the Rainbows; British Wild Animals Illustrated, etc.; nature stories and articles to various periodicals, technical contributions to motoring and engineering press. Left Great Britain April 1954 on five years' expedition to British Columbia and Alaska to write up sea-faring fish of Canadian Pacific Coast. *Recreations:* fishing, shooting, motoring, and wild life photography. *Address:* Le Jeune Lodge, Box 8 Kamloops, B.C.; c/o Messrs. Charles Lavell Ltd., Abbey Gardens Mews, St. John's Wood, N.W.8. *Club:* New (Edinburgh).

[*Died* 3 *Jan.* 1958.

BATTERSHILL, Sir William Denis, K.C.M.G., *cr.* 1941 (C.M.G. 1938); K.St.J.; *b.* 29 June 1896; *m.* 1924, Joan Elizabeth, *e. d.* of late Maj.-Gen. Sir John Gellibrand, K.C.B., D.S.O.; two *d.* On war service Aug. 1914-19, India and Iraq, with the 6th Bn. The East Surrey Regt. and the 2nd Bn. The Queen's Own Royal West Kent Regt.; Cadet Ceylon Civil Service, 1920; 2nd Assistant Secretary, and Clerk Legislative Council, 1928; Assistant Colonial Secretary, Jamaica, 1929-35; Colonial Secretary Cyprus, 1935-37; Chief Secretary to Government of Palestine, 1937-39; Governor and Commander-in-Chief of Cyprus, 1939-41 (despatches); Asst. Under-Sec. of State, Colonial Office, 1941-42; Deputy Under-Sec. of State, 1942-45; Governor and C.-in-C. Tanganyika Territory, 1945-49. *Recreations:* fishing, riding. *Address:* Livas, Kyrenia, Cyprus. *Club:* East India and Sports.

[*Died* 11 *Aug.* 1959.

BATTLEY, John Rose; Governing Director of the firm of Battley Bros. Ltd., printers; F.R.S.A.; J.P.; *b.* 26 Nov. 1880; *s.* of George Battley, Clapham; *m.* 1933, Dorothy Sybil, *d.* of Stanley Alchurch, Cheam, Surrey; two *s.* Member L.C.C. (Clapham), 1938; J.P. London, 1940. M.P. (Lab.) Clapham Division of Wandsworth, 1945-50. *Publication:* A visit to the Houses of Parliament with John Battley, M.P. *Address:* 94 Clapham Park Road, Clapham, S.W.4.

[*Died* 1 *Nov.* 1952.

BATTY, Rt. Rev. Basil Staunton, O.B.E. 1918; D.D., F.R.A.S.; Honorary Assistant Bishop of London since 1946; Rector of St. Anne and St. Agnes, Gresham Street, E.C., since 1933; *s.* of late Rev. W. E. Batty; *m.* 1903, Kathleen, *d.* of late Martin J. Sutton, J.P.; two *s.* one *d.* *Educ.:* St. Paul's; Selwyn College, Cambridge. Ordained, 1896; Curate of St. Clement's, Yorks, 1896-98; Vicar of Medmenham, 1898-1906; Bolsover, 1906-11; Wargrave, 1911-14; Rector of South Hackney, 1914-18; Vicar of St. Gabriel's, Warwick Square, 1918-24; Vicar of Christ Church, Mayfair, 1924-26; First Bishop of Fulham, 1926-46 (Suffragan Bishop in the Diocese of London, with charge of the Chaplaincies in North and Central Europe); Chm. of the Bishop of London's Council for Work in Munition Centres, 1916-18; Member of the Executive Board of the Church Army; Select Preacher at Cambridge, 1936; Officer of Crown of Italy, 1920; Royal Order of the Dannebrog, Denmark, 1st Class, 1929; Grand Order of Star of Roumania, 1st class, 1935. *Publications:* Conversion: Why we should preach it; pamphlets on theological and astronomical subjects. *Recreations:* cricket, tennis, shooting, rowing. *Address:* Riseholme, Horsell, Woking. *T.:* Woking 818. *Clubs:* Oxford and Cambridge, Leander, M.C.C.

[*Died* 19 *March* 1952.

BATTYE, Brigadier Ivan Urmston, C.B. 1930; D.S.O. 1916; *b.* Abbottabad, India, 5 March 1875; 5th *s.* of late Major Legh Richmond Battye, 5th Gurkha Rifles; *m.* 1897, Marie, 4th *d.* of late Colonel John Robertson, C.I.E., of Liddington Hall, nr. Guildford, Surrey; two *d.* *Educ.:* Launceston, Tasmania; Combe Down School, Bath; Sandhurst. Entered Indian Army, 1895; Lieutenant, 1897; Captain, 1904; Major, 1913; Lieut.-Colonel, 1921; Colonel, 1923; Brigade Major, Secunderabad Infantry Brigade, 1913-15; Acting Lt.-Colonel Commanding 1/8th Gurkha Rifles, 1917-21; Commandant Q.V.O. Corps of Guides, Infantry, 1921-25; Comdt. Small Arms School, India, 1925-27; served N.W. Frontier of India, 1897-98; Reliefs of Malakand and Chakdara, Malakand; operations in Bajaur, Utman Khel, Buner (medal with 2 clasps); N.W. Frontier of India, 1915 (dangerously wounded, despatches, D.S.O.) and 1916-17; Mesopotamia, 1917; Palestine and Syria, 1918 (despatches); Syria, 1919 (despatches, Bt. Lt.-Col.); Q.V.O. Corps of Guides (Frontier Force); Commanded Ferozepore Brigade Area, 1927-1930; retd. from Indian Army with rank of Brigadier, Nov. 1930; Game Warden, Tanganyika Territory, Nov. 1930-March 1932. *Recreations:* polo, tennis, big-game shooting, travel. *Address:* Karen, Box 4955, Ngong, Kenya; c/o Standard Bank of South Africa Ltd., Nairobi, Kenya.

[*Died* 30 *Aug.* 1953.

BATTYE, James Sykes, C.B.E. 1950; B.A., LL.B., Litt.D.; Principal Librarian and Secretary, Public Library, Museum and Art Gallery of Western Australia since 1911; Principal Librarian, Public Library, Perth, since 1894; *b.* Geelong, 14 Nov. 1871; *s.* of Dan. Battye, Geelong, Vic.; *m.* 1895, May, *e. d.* of Edwin Jenkins, Melbourne; two *s.* three *d.* *Educ.:* State Schools; Geelong College; Melbourne University (State Scholar). Exhibition, 1884, B.A. 1891, LL.B. 1893, Litt.D. 1922; Hon. LL.D. 1943. Asst., Melbourne Public Library, 1889-94; Chm. Bd. of Governors, High School, Perth, 1911-1923; Hon. Sec. of Roy. Commn. on establishment of a University in W.A., 1909-11, and of University Site Cttee., 1912; member Univ. Senate since 1912; Warden of Convocation, 1920, 1922-23; Pro-Chancellor, 1931-36; Chancellor, 1936-43. Pres., Children's Hosp., Perth, 1911-13; Dep. Grand Master, Grand Lodge of Freemasons of W.A., 1908-15, and 1918-19, Grand Master, 1936-1952; First Grand Principal, Royal Arch Masons, 1910-21, 1922-43. Chm.: Country Free Lending Libraries Cttee., 1944-; Nomenclature Adv. Comm. Lands Dept., 1938-. *Publications:* History of Western Australia, 1924; (Editor) Encyclopædia of W.A., and History of the North-West. *Recreations:* bowling, reading. *Address:* Public Library, Perth, W. Australia. *T.:* B2756, BA 4329. *Club:* Freemasons' (Perth).

[*Died* 15 *July* 1954.

BATTYE, Major Richmond Keith Molesworth; Colonial Administrative Service; late Indian Political Service; *b.* 30 Aug. 1905; *s.* of late Lieut.-Colonel W. R. Battye, D.S.O.; *m.* 1937, Amy Joan, *d.* of Sir Robert Reid, K.C.S.I.; one *s.* two *d.* *Educ.:* Marlborough; R.M.A., Woolwich. Commissioned in Royal Artillery, 1925; served in 27th F. Brigade R.A. till 1929; transferred to Hodson's Horse, I.A.; operations N.W.F.P. 1930-31; seconded to Foreign and Political Dept. Govt. of India. *Publications:*

A Halbi Grammar; Short Stories in Cavalry Journal: A right and left in Tigerland; The Cream of Sport. Bombay Natural History Society: Notes on some birds observed between Yatung and Gyantse, Tibet; articles in Field, and Roy. Central Asian Society Jl. *Recreations:* big and small game shooting, fishing, polo, pig-sticking. *Address:* c/o The Secretariat, Dar-es-Salaam E. Africa. *Clubs:* Army and Navy; Quetta; Dar-es-Salaam. [*Died* 22 *Oct.* 1958.

BATY, Thomas, D.C.L., LL.D.; 2nd Class, Order of the Sacred Treasure; Barrister-at-Law (Inner Temple); Legal Adviser to Imperial Japanese Foreign Office, 1916-41 and since 1952; Vice-President, Vegetarian Society (U.K.); *b.* Stanwix, Cumberland, 8 Feb. 1869; *e. c.* of late William Thomas Baty, and Mary, *o. d.* of William Matthews of Penrith; unmarried. *Educ.:* High School, Carlisle; Queen's College, Oxford; Trinity College, Cambridge (Whewell Scholar). Civil Law Fellow, University College, Oxford; Bar, 1898; Hon. General Secretary, International Law Association, 1905-16; junior counsel in Zamora case. Assoc. Mem. Institut de Droit International, 1921-. *Publications:* The Laws of Law, 1899; First Elements of Legal Procedure, 1900, 2nd edit. 1927; International Law in South Africa, 1900; International Law, 1909; Britain and Sea Law, 1911; (trans.) Jellinek's Rights of Minorities (with A. M. Baty), 1912; Polarized Law (Private International Law), 1914; War and its Legal Results (jointly with Prof. Morgan), 1915; Vicarious Liability, 1916; Notes on Hire and Loan, 1918; Canons of International Law, 1930; Academic Colours, 1933; International Law in Twilight; articles in Quarterly Review, etc. *Recreations:* music, heraldry, the sea; extreme feminist, would abolish all sex distinctions; conservative; vegetarian. *Address:* 3 Paper Buildings, Temple E.C.; Itinomiya, Tiba, Japan. [*Died* 9 *Feb.* 1954.

BAUGH, Charles Herbert, Commissioner; retired from Command of the Salvation Army in Canada, 1951; *b.* 3 Jan. 1881; *m.* 1906, Nellie Stewart; one *s.*; Chief of the Staff and Second in Command of the International Salvation Army, 1943-46. *Address:* Salvation Army Headquarters, Queen Victoria St., E.C.4. [*Died* 24 *April* 1953.

BAUM, Vicki; novelist, play and scenario writer; *b.* Vienna, 24 Jan. 1896; *d.* of Herman and Mathilda Baum; *m.* Richard Lert, conductor; two *s.* *Educ.:* High School of Music, Vienna. *Publications:* Grand Hotel, play and novel; And Life goes on, novel; The Divine Drudge, play; Martin's Summer, Secret Sentence, Helene, Falling Star, Men Never Know, Career, A Tale from Bali, Nanking Road, 1939, Central Stores, 1940, The Ship and the Shore, 1941, Grand Opera, 1942; Marion Alive, 1943; The Weeping Wood, 1943; Berlin Hotel '43, 1944; Headless Angel, 1948; Danger from Deer, 1951, novels and short stories; The Mustard Seed, 1953; Written on Water, 1957, Ballerina, 1958. *Recreations:* gardening, playing with children, travelling. *Address:* 2477 Canyon Oak Drive, Hollywood, Los Angeles, Calif., U.S.A. [*Died* 29 *Aug.* 1960.

BAX, Sir Arnold Edward Trevor, K.C.V.O., *cr.* 1953; Kt., *cr.* 1937; D.Mus. (Hon.) Oxon 1934, Durham 1935, N.U.I. 1947; Master of the Queen's Musick since 1952 (Master of the Musick to King George VI, 1942-52); *b.* 8 Nov. 1883; *s.* of late Alfred Ridley Bax, F.S.A., and Charlotte Ellen Lea. *Educ.:* privately; Royal Academy of Music. First public appearance as composer, St. James's Hall, July 1903; gave recital of own works, July 1908; since then works have appeared frequently in programmes of the Philharmonic Society and other principal London concerts; with Madame Karsavina and Sir J. M. Barrie produced The Truth about the Russian Dancers, 1920; Gold Medallist of the Royal Philharmonic Society and of the Worshipful Company of Musicians, 1931. *Publications:* A Celtic Song-Cycle; choral works, Enchanted Summer; cantata, Fatherland; To the Name above every Name; St. Patrick's Breast-Plate; Walsinghame; The Morning Watch; and unaccompanied Motets; 3 String Quartets; Sonata in E, Violin and Piano; Piano Quintet; 2nd Sonata for Violin and Piano; 3rd Sonata for Violin and Piano; four Piano Sonatas, Viola Concerto; Cello Concerto; Violin Concerto; Sonata, Viola and Piano; Sonata for Viola and Harp; Sonata, Cello and Piano; Sonata for Two Pianos; Sonata for Clarinet and Piano; Symphonic Poems, November Woods, The Garden of Fand; Tintagel; In the Faery Hills; The Tale the Pine-trees knew; Seven Symphonies; Winter Legends for Piano and Orchestra; Romantic Overture; The Happy Forest; Overture to Adventure; London Pageant, 1937; Farewell my Youth (Reminiscences), 1943; piano pieces, songs, other chamber works. *Recreations:* walking; specially interested in every aspect of Celtic life and history. *Address:* White Horse Inn, Storrington, Sx. [*Died* 3 *Oct.* 1953.

BAXENDALE, Col. Joseph Francis Noel, C.B. 1930; T.D.; *b.* 1877; *o. s.* of J. W. Baxendale; *m.* 1906, Margaret, *y. d.* of late Rev. G. V. Heathcote; three *d.* *Educ.:* Eton; Oxford. *Address:* Froxfield Green, Petersfield, Hants. *Clubs:* Cavalry, Royal Cruising, Royal Yacht Squadron (Cowes). [*Died* 29 *Jan.* 1957.

BAXTER, Commodore Sir Arthur James, K.B.E., *cr.* 1945; D.S.C. 1918; R.D.; R.N.R.; *b.* 28 Feb. 1890; *s.* of George Baxter, Norwich; *m.* 1916, Zoë Cruice (*d.* 1948); two *s.* *Educ.:* Great Yarmouth Grammar School. Commenced seafaring career as cadet in Merchant Navy, 1904; joined R.N.R. 1913; served in R.N. in command of Destroyers during European War, 1914-18 (D.S.C.). Commodore of Ocean Convoys, 1940-45 (despatches). A.D.C. to the King, 1944-45. Commodore of Orient Line Fleet, 1948-49; retired 1949. *Address:* 6a Lauderdale Drive, Petersham, Surrey. *T.:* Richmond 0995. [*Died* 27 *Dec.* 1951.

BAXTER, Sir Thomas, Kt., *cr.* 1943; *b.* Jan. 1878; *s.* of Thomas Baxter, Dutton Hall, Warrington; *m.* 1903, Mabel Hilda Clare; two *s.* two *d.* *Educ.:* Turton Hall College, Gildersome. Farming career. President N.F.U., 1927; Chairman, Milk Marketing Board, 1933-49, retired. *Recreations:* tennis, shooting. *Address:* 46 Somerville Road, Sutton Coldfield. *T.A.:* Beverley, Sutton Coldfield. *T.:* Sutton Coldfield 1712. *Club:* Constitutional. [*Died* 14 *April* 1951.

BAYES, Gilbert, R.B.S. (President, 1938-43); H.R.I.; sculptor; *b.* London, 1872; *s.* of A. W. Bayes, R.E., and Emily Bayes; *m.* 1906, Gertrude Smith; one *s.* one *d.* Gold medal and travelling scholarship, Royal Academy, 1899; hon. mention Paris International Exhibition, 1900; Hon. mention Salon, 1922; Bronze Medal, Salon, 1929; Diplome d'honneur and gold medal Ex. Int. Dec. Art, Paris, 1925; hon. mention and bronze medal Société des Artistes Françaises (salon); gold medal and diplôme d'honneur, International Exhibition, Paris, 1925; Royal Society of British Sculptors silver medal, 1931, best work of the year; work purchased Dresden National Museum, 1900; Chantrey Bequest, 1910; Liverpool, 1921; Preston, 1920; Dunedin, 1926; Liveryman of the Worshipful Co. of Glaziers. *Other works:* The Great Seal; His Majesty King George V; work for Art Gallery, Sydney, N.S.W.; figures of Sir Charles Barry and Sir W. Chambers for the Victoria and Albert Museum, South Kensington; memorials to late

Lord Chesterfield, Lord Nunburnholme, Hon. Gerald Wilson, Dr. Yellowlees, LL.D., Glasgow; Dr. Adamson, LL.D., Glasgow and Manchester; Prof. Sidgwick, Cambridge; Sir W. Moore, Bombay; late Constant Coquelin for the Comédie Française; Bronze Equestrian Statues War and Peace for National Art Gallery, Sydney; the King's Police Medal; Gold Medal given by R. Geographical Society to Captain Scott, and also that to Sir E. Shackleton; Queen Mary Medal; Segrave Trophy; Saville Theatre Frieze; Selfridge Great Clock; Sports Frieze at Lords; London Fire Brigade Memorial. Law Soc. War Memorial; Gold Coast War Memorial; Medal, Knights of St. John. *Address:* 4 Greville Place, N.W.6. *T.:* Maida Vale 2927. *Clubs:* Arts, Athenæum. [*Died* 4 *April* 1952.

BAYES, Walter, R.W.S., 1931; painter and writer on artistic subjects; Founder-member of Camden Town Group and London Group; Lecturer in Perspective, Royal Academy of Arts, and Slade School for a period of years in each case; *b.* London, 31 May 1869; *m.* 1904, Kitty Telfer; two *s.* Contributed articles to the Outlook, Saturday Review, Studio, Art Journal, Architectural Review, etc.; art critic on the Athenæum, 1906-16; Headmaster, Westminster Art School, 1918-34; organiser and director of Painting School, Lancaster School of Arts and Crafts, 1944-49; large oil painting, The Top of the Tide, purchased for the city of Liverpool, 1900; decoration The Underworld, R.A. 1918, purchased by the Imperial War Museum; Survivors from a Torpedoed Ship, and a Design for Tapestry, purchased by the Imperial War Museum, 1919; The Ford and Under the Candles acquired by Tate Gallery 1930 and 1934 respectively; Pulvis et Umbra, R.A. 1919; Oratio Obliqua, R.A. 1920; series of Recording Britain drawings for Pilgrims' Trust, 1941-42; one-man shows at Leicester Galls., 1919, 1920, 1951; representative Exhibition of pictures at Salford, 1948. *Publications:* The Art of Decorative Painting, 1926; Turner, a speculative portrait, 1931; A Painter's Baggage, 1932. *Address:* 54 Fitzjohns Avenue, N.W.3. [*Died* 21 *Jan.* 1956.

BAYFORD, Robert Frederic, O.B.E.; K.C. 1919; Recorder of Portsmouth, 1929-44; *b.* 24 Sept. 1871; *e. s.* of late Robert Augustus Bayford, K.C.; *m.* 1900, Catharine Mary (*d.* 1951), *d.* of Henry Goodenough Hayter; two *s.* two *d.* *Educ.:* Eton College; Trinity Hall, Cambridge (B.A.). Called to Bar, Inner Temple, 1895; Bencher Inner Temple, 1925; Deputy Chairman Hampshire Quarter Sessions, 1938-1947, resigned 1947. *Recreations:* shooting, fishing, golf; Cambridge Eight, 1893; won University Fours, 1894; Head of the River, 1892 and 1894. *Address:* Ashridge, Compton, near Winchester. *T.:* Twyford 2104. *Club:* Oxford and Cambridge. [*Died* 5 *June* 1951.

BAYLAY, Brig.-Gen. Sir Atwell Charles, Kt., *cr.* 1947; C.B.E. 1943; D.S.O. 1917; 4th Class White Eagle (Serbia); *b.* 1 Sept. 1879; *s.* of late Col. F. G. Baylay, R.A.; *m.* 1904, Maria Edmondson (*d.* 1947), *d.* of late Governor J. B. Groome, Maryland, U.S.A.; one *d.* *Educ.:* Cheltenham College; R.M. Academy, Woolwich. 2nd Lieut. R.E. 1898; Lieut. 1901; Capt. 1907; Major, 1915; Bt. Lt.-Col. 1918; Brig.-Gen. 1918; served European War, 1915-18; retired, June 1919. *Address:* The Grange, Radford Semele, Leamington Spa. [*Died* 6 *Oct.* 1957.

BAYLAY, Brig.-Gen. Frederick, C.B.E. 1919; *b.* 1865; *s.* of Col. F. G. Baylay, R.A., of Blackheath; *m.* Marion Kirkpatrick (*d.* 1953), *d.* of George Young, Helensburgh. *Educ.:* Westward Ho; R.M.A. Joined R.E. 1884; served European War, 1914-19 (C.B.E.); retired, 1919. *Address:* c/o Lloyds Bank, Cox's and King's Branch, 6 Pall Mall, S.W.1. [*Died* 28 *Nov.* 1956.

BAYLEY, Brig.-General Gerald Edward, C.M.G. 1918; D.S.O. 1915; late 2nd Batt. the York and Lancaster Regt.; *b.* 6 Mar. 1874; *s.* of late Capt. Francis Bayley; *m.* 2nd, 1917, Marjorie Singleton, *e. d.* of H. S. Powell, Pocklington; two *d.*; 3rd, 1929, Edna Jean, *yr. d.* of J. Joynt, Sheen Lodge, Limerick. *Educ.:* Rugby School. Entered army from 3rd York and Lancaster Regiment, 1894; Capt., 1902; Major, 1912; with Ceylon Volunteers, 1902-8; served European War, 1914-18 (despatches 5 times, C.M.G., Officer of Order of St. Maurice and St. Lazarus, D.S.O., Col.); retired pay, 1923; Lieut. 13th Bn. Loyal N. Lancashire H.G., 1941-44; Medals—Royal Humane Society, 1914 Star, War and Victory Medals, Iraq and North-West Persia bar, King George V Coronation. *Address:* Forthill, Ballymaconnell Road, Bangor, Co. Down, N. Ireland. [*Died* 12 *Feb.* 1955.

BAYLEY, Sir John, Kt., *cr.* 1928; Vice-President of British and Foreign School Society; Director of Park Lane Hotel, London; Councillor and Alderman for 43 years (Salop C.C.); *b.* 21 Dec. 1852; *m.* 1877, Emily Susannah (*d.* 1928), *d.* of late T. W. Butler, Warehorne, Ashford, Kent. Trained Teacher, Boro Road College, London; organised Wellington Parliamentary Div., 1883-1910; contested (Coal.) Wrekin Division of Shropshire, 1920. Founder of the Public School Wrekin College; Headmaster of Wellington (now Wrekin College), 1880-1920; retired from active scholastic work in 1921; interested in work in Schools and in choice and training of young teachers. *Address:* East Court, Ramsgate. [*Died* 28 *April* 1952.

BAYLY, Lieut.-Colonel Abingdon Robert, D.S.O., O.B.E., R.F.A.; retired; *b.* 7 March 1871; *s.* of late General A. A. Bayly, Col. Commandant, R.A.; *m.* 1912; one *d.* *Educ.:* Marlborough College; R.M.A., Woolwich. Joined R.F.A. in India, 1890; Captain, 1900; Major, 1907; Lt.-Col. 1914; served European War in 1st Division, 1914-18 (despatches, D.S.O.); attached British Legation, Berne, 1918 (despatches, O.B.E.); retired pay, 1923. *Address:* Châlet des Lauriers, La Tour de Peilz, (Vaud) Switzerland. *Club:* Royal Automobile. [*Died* 13 *Feb.* 1952.

BAYLY, Major Edward Archibald Theodore, D.S.O. 1917; late Royal Welch Fusiliers; *b.* 19 June 1877; *e. s.* of late Col. E. R. Bayly, D.L., of Ballyarthur, Woodenbridge, Co. Wicklow; *m.* 1921, Ileene Caroline Ethel Otway, *d.* of late Major A. H. Inglefield of Old Church House, Beckington, Bath; one *s.* two *d.* *Educ.:* Radley College; University College, Oxford. 2nd Lieut. Royal Welch Fusiliers, 1899; Capt. 1907; Major, 1915. Attached Egyptian Army, 1908-18; served S. African War, 1899-1902; Relief of Ladysmith, actions at Colenso, Tugela Heights, Pieter's Hill, operations in Transvaal and Cape Colony; (severely wounded; Queen's medal with 5 clasps; King's medal with 2 clasps); Sudan, 1908 (10th Sudanese); operations in Jebel Nyima District of S. Kordofan (Egyptian medal with clasp); Sudan, 1910; operations in S. Kordofan (Sudan medal with clasp); 13th Sudanese in Command; Sudan, 1916; conquest of Darfur (despatches, clasp to Sudan medal, D.S.O.); O.C. Sobat Pibor District, 1916-18; Sudan, 1917; operations against Lau Nuers (in command; despatches, 3rd class Order of the Nile clasp to Sudan medal); Palestine, 1918; Western Desert Province, Frontiers Administration, Egyptian Govt., 1919-30; Governor Western Desert Province, 1924-30; Member of Egyptian-Italian Western Frontier Delimitation Commission; Commander of the Crown of Italy, 1927. *Address:* Ballyarthur, Woodenbridge, Co. Wicklow. *T.:* Avoca 10. *Club:* Royal Irish Automobile (Dublin). [*Died* 10 *Dec.* 1959.

BAYNE, Charles S.; Editor of Little Folks, 1908-15, and all Cassell & Co.'s book publications for young people; *b.* 26 Nov. 1876; 2nd *s.* of late Thomas Bayne, Headmaster of Larchfield Academy, Helensburgh, Scotland; unmarried. *Educ.:* Larchfield Acad., Helensburgh. Began business as a papermaker, but soon drifted into journalism and printing; originated Cassell's Annual, 1909; The British Boy's Annual, 1910; The British Girl's Annual, 1910; Editor The Girl's Realm, 1909-13; Editor The London Naturalist, 1922-30. *Publications:* Getting to know the Birds, 1944; Exploring England (new edn.), 1945; The Call of the Birds (new edn.), 1945; many books and short stories for children; literary, political, and general articles. *Recreations:* walking, natural history, music. *Club:* Savage. [*Died* 28 *June* 1952.

BAYNE-JARDINE, Brigadier Christian West, C.B.E. 1944; D.S.O. 1917; M.C.; *b.* 25 July 1888; 3rd *s.* of late Rev. D. Bayne-Jardine, Keir Manse, Thornhill, Dumfriesshire; *m.* 1930, Isabel, *yr. d.* of late Charles Forman, C.E.; one *s.* two *d.* *Educ.:* Marlborough College; R.M.A., Woolwich. Commissioned, 1909; served European War, France, 1914-17; Italy, 1918-19 (four times wounded, despatches thrice); retired pay, 1945. *Address:* Humbie House, Humbie, East Lothian. *Clubs:* Army and Navy; New (Edinburgh). [*Died* 22 *March* 1959.

BEACH, Colonel Gerald, C.B. 1930; O.B.E. 1925; T.D.; Officer Order of the Hospital of St. John of Jerusalem; D.L. County of Middlesex; J.P.; County Army Welfare Officer, 1949; Territorial Army, retired; Member Middlesex C.C.; County Alderman; *b.* 30 May 1881; *s.* of late William James Beach; unmarried. *Educ.:* Cheltenham College; 2nd Lt. 5th West Middlesex V.R.C., 1900; Capt. 1904; 9th Batt. The Middlesex Regt., D.C.O., 1908, on formation T.A.; proceeded India and Mesopotamia with Batt., 1914-18; Major, 1916; Lt.-Col. on Staff 3rd Afghan War; Lt.-Col. Commanding 9th Batt. Middlesex Regt., 1922; despatches twice; Brevet-Col. 1926; Sub.-Col. 1929-44; Col. Commandant Army Cadet Force, County of Middlesex, 1929-43; Army Welfare Officer, 1939; Hon. Col. Royal Artillery, 1939-51. *Address:* 81 Hendon Lane, Finchley, N.3. *T.:* Finchley 4481. *Club:* United Service. [*Died* 25 *Dec.* 1955.

BEACH, Maj.-Gen. William Henry, C.B. 1919; C.M.G. 1917; D.S.O. 1916; *b.* 7 June 1871; *s.* of Rev. Canon W. R. Beach; *m.* 1914, Constance Maude, *d.* of late A. A. Cammell, 14th Hussars, of Brookfield Manor, Derbyshire; one *s.* Commissioned in R.E. 1889; served till 1894 in England and Ireland; thence onwards, until War of 1914-18, mostly in India, with Sappers and Miners and on Staff; served Mohmand Campaign, India, 1908; European War, 1915-18 (despatches, C.B., C.M.G., D.S.O., Bts. of Lt.-Col. and Col.); subsequent to European War served at Army H.Q., India, and commanding Infantry Brigade, and finally, 1929-1932, in England in command of 42nd East Lancs Division; A.D.C. to the King, 1926-28; Major-General, 1928; retired, 1932; Col. Comdt. R.E., 1936-41; late Chairman R.E. Old Comrades' Association; late Council of Regular Forces Employment Association; late Council of V.A.D. *Address:* Bradstones, Camberley, Surrey. *Club:* United Service. [*Died* 22 *July* 1952.

BEADON, Lt.-Col. Henry Cecil, C.I.E. 1919; Indian Army (retired); *b.* 1869; *s.* of late Col. Cecil Beadon; *m.* 1st, Marion A.; 2nd, Dorothy A., *d.* of H. E. Brown of Barton Hall, Kingskerswell, Devon; one *d.* *Educ.:* Cheltenham College. In military employ, 1890-95, and subsequently in civil employ; Deputy Commissioner, Delhi, 1912-19; Chief Commissioner, Andaman and Nicobar Islands, 1920-23. *Address:* Holderness, Exmouth, Devon. [*Died* 4 *July* 1959.

BEALE, Peyton Todd Bowman, F.R.C.S. Eng., L.R.C.P. Lond.; L.S.A. Lond.; Consulting Surgeon, King's College Hospital, Royal Northern Hospital and Milford-on-Sea Cottage Hospital; Fellow, King's College, London; *b.* 20 June 1864; *s.* of Lionel S. Beale, F.R.S., F.R.C.P.; *m.* 1892, Gertrude (*d.* 1949), *d.* of Henry Attwell, K.O.C., Barnes; two *d.* *Educ.:* Westminster School; King's College, London (Scholar and Prizeman); King's College Hospital. Was Surgeon and Dean, King's College Hospital; Surgeon, Royal Northern Hospital and City Dispensary; examiner in surgery, Society of Apothecaries, London; Senior Demonstrator of Physiology and Histology for twelve years, and Lecturer on Biology, King's College, London; Prosector, Royal College of Surgeons; Lecturer on Nursing, etc., Women's Department, King's College; late additional examiner in surgery, Glasgow University; Examiner in Biology, Royal College of Surgeons, and in Physiology and Surgery, Society of Apothecaries; President N. Lond. Med. Chir. Society; Fellow of Medical, Microscopical, and Member of other learned Societies; Member Medical Faculty, Univ. of London; Dean, King's Coll. Hospital. *Publications:* numerous papers on treatment of wounds, appendicitis, and other professional subjects; books on physiology and biology. *Recreations:* microscopy and botany, mechanical work of all kinds in metal and wood, music. *Address:* Lymore End, near Lymington, Hants. *T.:* Milford-on-Sea 91. [*Died* 24 *Dec.* 1957.

BEALE-BROWNE, Brig.-Gen. Desmond John Edward, D.S.O. 1916; *b.* 4 July 1870; *s.* of late John Beale-Browne, J.P., D.L., of Salperton Park, Glos., and Crotta House, Kilflyn, Co. Kerry, and Charlotte Sophia, *d.* of late J. H. Cancellor; *m.* 1916, Ethel Alexander (*d.* 1933), *d.* of Mrs. E. F. Jowers of Birch House, Hayward's Heath; one *d.* *Educ.:* Eton; Trinity Hall, Cambridge. Joined 9th Lancers, 1891; served South African War on Staff of Sir F. Forestier Walker (Queen's medal 4 clasps, King's medal 2 clasps); Lt.-Col. of 9th Lancers, served European War, 1914-18 (despatches twice, Lt.-Col., D.S.O., Commander Crown of Belgium); Temp. Brig.-Gen. October 1915; Brig.-Gen. Commanding 2nd Cavalry Brigade; retired pay, 1920; J.P., Sussex, 1925; High Sheriff, 1932; D.L., 1937; Colonel of 9th Lancers, 1936-40. *Recreations:* all forms of sport. *Address:* Middleham, Ringmer, Sussex. *T.:* Ringmer 42. *Clubs:* Cavalry; Royal Yacht Squadron (Cowes). [*Died* 26 *Jan.* 1953.

BEAMISH, Rear-Adm. Tufton Percy Hamilton, C.B. 1917; R.N.; D.L.; *b.* 1874; *s.* of Rear-Adm. H. H. Beamish, C.B.; *m.* 1914, Margaret, *d.* of late Henry Simon and Mrs. Simon of Lawnhurst, Didsbury; one *s.* two *d.* (and one *s.* killed in action, 1945). Served in East Africa, 1896, and Benin Expedition, 1897 (medal and clasp); Flag Comm. to Vice-Adm. Prince Louis of Battenberg, 1908-10; at Admiralty as Assist. to Chief of War Staff, 1912-13; Capt., June 1914; Naval Assistant to First Sea Lord, Aug.-Nov. 1914; commanded H.M.S. Invincible Nov. 1914-March 1915; Battle of the Falklands; commanded H.M.S. Cordelia, Apr. 1915-May 1917; Battle of Jutland; at Admiralty, Sept. 1917-Aug. 1919; retired, 1922; Rear-Adm. retired, 1925; M.P. (U.) Lewes, 1924-31 and 1936-45. *Address:* Chelworth, Chelwood Gate, Haywards Heath. *T.:* Chelwood Gate 13. *Clubs:* United Service, Carlton. [*Died* 2 *May* 1951.

BEANE, Sir Francis Adams, Kt., *cr.* 1939; *b.* 1872; 2nd *s.* of late William Beane, Alsager, Cheshire; *m.* Irene, *e. d.* of A. J. Haggie, The Manor House, Long Benton, Northumberland; (two *s.* killed War of 1939-45). *Address:* Willington, Silverdale Avenue, Walton-on-Thames. *T.:* Walton 2807. [*Died* 13 *Feb.* 1959.

BEARDSWORTH, Air Vice-Marshal George Braithwaite, C.B. 1947; M.I.Mech.E.; M.Inst.T.; F.R.Ae.S.; Senior Air Staff Officer of Technical Training Command since 1957; *b.* Queensland, 10 Feb. 1904; *m.* 1934, third *d.* of late William Seager of Broomfield, Kent. *Educ.:* Christ's Hospital; Royal Air Force College, Cranwell. Commanded 36 Squadron, Far East, 1936-38; served war, 1939-45, in U.K. (despatches), Canada, and Middle East. Senior Technical Staff Officer: Fighter Command, 1949-51, Far East Air Force, 1952-53; Director of Aircraft Engineering, Air Ministry, 1954-55; Commanding No. 24 Group, R.A.F., 1955-57. *Address:* Ford Cottage, Abbotsbrook, Bourne End. *T.:* Bourne End 64. *Club:* Royal Air Force. [*Died* 5 *Aug.* 1959.

BEARE, Ernest Edwin, C.B.E. 1924; *b.* 14 Jan. 1877; *s.* of late William Thomas Beare; *m.* 1903, Beatrice Mary, *d.* of late Nathaniel Coombs; one *d.* Entered Inland Revenue Department, 1896; Private Secretary to Earl of Crawford and Balcarres (as Chairman of Royal Commission on Wheat Supplies), 1920; Secretary, Government Hospitality, 1922-29; Curator, Milton's Cottage, 1945-54. *Address:* St. Cross Grange, Winchester. *T.:* Winchester 314211. [*Died* 2 *Sept.* 1956.

BEASLEY, Cyril George, C.M.G. 1950; Economic Adviser to the Comptroller, Development and Welfare Organisation, British West Indies, since 1946; *b.* 5 April 1901; *o. s.* of late George Beasley, Greenford, Mx.; *m.* 1st, 1924, I. M. Girdwood; 2nd, 1940, Doreen Commins; three *d.* *Educ.:* Kilburn Grammar School; University College, London. B.A. (1st Cl. Hons.) 1921; M.A. 1925. Senior lecturer in Geography, University College, Nottingham, 1922; Professor of Geography and Geology, University of Rangoon, 1931; Statistical Adviser, Commerce Dept. of Govt. of Burma, 1937; Member Fiscal and Tariff Committees, 1938; Adviser to Govt. of Burma for trade negotiations with India, 1940-41; Secretary-Adviser, Burma delegation, Eastern Group Supply Conference, Delhi, 1941; Member War Risks Insurance Board, Burma; Chief Administrative Officer, University of Rangoon; with Government of Burma at Simla, 1942-45; Adviser at Montego Bay Conference on Closer Association of West Indian colonies; Member Evans Commission on Settlement of British Guiana and British Honduras. Chm. Regional Economic Cttee., British West Indies. *Recreations:* golf, chess, bridge. *Address:* Hastings House, Barbados, British West Indies. *Clubs:* East India and Sports; Royal Yacht, Bridgetown (Barbados). [*Died* 8 *Aug.* 1956.

BEASLEY, Sir (Horace) Owen (Compton), Kt. 1930; C.B.E. 1958 (O.B.E. 1919); President Pensions' Appeal Tribunals, 1947-58, retired; Chairman, Pensions' Appeal Tribunal, 1943-47; *b.* 2 July 1877; *o. surv. s.* of late Ammon Beasley, and late L. A. Beasley, of Lindens, Penarth, Glamorganshire; *m.* 1909, Evelyn Augusta Atherton; two *s.* *Educ.:* Westminster School; Jesus College, Cambridge, B.A., 1899. Called to Bar, Inner Temple, 1902; South Wales Circuit; then a Judge, High Court of Burma, 1923-24; a Judge in the High Court of Madras, 1924-29; Chief Justice of Madras, 1929-37; served European War, 1914-19; Western Front, 1916-19 (Major, O.B.E., despatches). Served with his wife in the Y.M.C.A. with the B.E.F. in France in 1940. *Recreations:* motoring; Cambridge University Association Football XI., 1896-99 (Captain, 1898-99); Corinthian Football Club; played cricket for Glamorganshire. *Address:* 25A Gwendolen Avenue, Putney, S.W.15. *Clubs:* Oxford and Cambridge; Madras (Madras). [*Died* 1 *Jan.* 1960.

BEATTIE, Lieut.-Colonel Alexander Elder, C.M.G. 1933; C.B.E. 1920; M.C.; Officer of the Order of St. John of Jerusalem; Commander of the Order of the Khalifa (Morocco); late the Queen's Royal Regiment; *b.* Stirling Castle, 25 Jan. 1888; *e. s.* of late Maj. Alexander Beattie, 93rd Highlanders; *m.* 1917, Janet Dunbar, *d.* of late Thomas Kirkcaldy; two *s.* *Educ.:* abroad; Stirling. Enlisted Argyll and Sutherland Highlanders, 1906; commissioned the Queen's Regiment, 1908; served in Aden, India, and United Kingdom; Lieut., 1911; seconded West African Frontier Force, 1911; Assistant-Adjutant, Southern Nigeria Regt., 1912; Actg. Regimental Adjutant, Southern Nigeria Regt., 1913; Adjutant, 4th Batt. Nigeria Regt., 1914; served operations on Nigeria-Cameroons Frontier and in Cameroons, 1914-15 (Staff-Officer to Field Columns, despatches); Captain, 1915; severely wounded, 1915; M.C., 1915; Staff Officer, West African Frontier Force, 1916; Brevet Major, 1918; temp. Lt.-Col., 1918; retired with rank Lt.-Col. R.A. R. of O, 1922; appointed to Colonial Administrative Service; Asst. Secretary, Gibraltar, 1922; Clerk of Executive Council, etc., Gibraltar, 1922; Colonial Secretary, Falkland Islands, 1925; Acting Governor and Commander-in-Chief 1926-27; Chief Assistant Secretary to the Government of Cyprus, 1927-30; acting Colonial Secretary on nine occasions, 1927-29; Colonial Secretary, Gibraltar, 1930-41; Administrator of St. Vincent, 1941-44; Governor's Deputy, Windward Islands, 1943; Colonial Office Regional Welfare Officer, Scotland and N.E. England, 1944-47; temporarily re-employed in Colonial Office on special duty, 1949. *Recreations:* shooting, fishing, golf, etc. *Address:* c/o Crown Agent for the Colonies, 4 Millbank, S.W.1. *Clubs:* Royal Automobile, Royal Empire Society, Overseas. [*Died* 14 *April* 1951.

BEATTIE, Charles Innes, M.A.; Director, Associated Newspapers, Ltd., 1915-26; *b.* Aberdeen, 29 Jan. 1875; *e. s.* of John Beattie; *m.* 1908, Katharine Frances, *e. d.* of late E. Ashworth Briggs, Barrister; one *s.* one *d.* *Educ.:* Robert Gordon's College, Aberdeen; Aberdeen University. Joined Daily Mail staff, 1905; retired, 1930. *Address:* The Quillot, Burwood, Walton-on-Thames. *T.:* Walton-on-Thames 1400. *Clubs:* Devonshire; Burhill Golf (Walton-on-Thames). [*Died* 23 *Oct.* 1952.

BEATTIE, Dr. James Martin; Major R.A.M.C. (T.) (retired); M.A. N.Z.; M.D. Edinburgh; D.Sc. (Hon.), National University, Ireland; *b.* 31 May 1868; *m.* Margaret, 2nd *d.* of late Thomas Kettle, Kilmarnock; one *s.* one *d.* (and one *d.* decd.). *Educ.:* Univ. of Otago; Univ. of Edinburgh; Univ. College, Lond. M.R.C.S. Eng.; L.R.C.P. Lond.; M.A. with First Class Honours, and Senior Scholar in Nat. Hist., Univ. of New Zealand; M.B.C.M. with First Class Honours; M.D. (Gold Medallist) Univ. of Edinburgh. Sen. Asst. to the Professor of Pathology, and Lecturer in Pathological Bacteriology, University of Edinburgh, 1901-7; Assistant Pathologist, Royal Infirmary, Edinburgh, 1902-5; Professor of Pathology and Bacteriology and Dean of Medical Faculty, University of Sheffield, 1907-12; Professor of Bacteriology, University of Liverpool, 1912-1934; Dean of the Medical Faculty, 1914-1917; Professor Emeritus since 1935; City Bacteriologist, Liverpool, 1912-34; Hon. Sec. Committee of Clinical Studies, University of

Sheffield, 1910-12; Hon. Pathologist Sheffield Royal Infirmary and Sheffield Royal Hospital, 1908-12. Formerly Examiner in Pathology, National University of Ireland, Universities of Edinburgh, Glasgow, Aberdeen, St. Andrews, Birmingham, Bristol, London, Belfast, Durham, and Trinity College, Dublin. *Publications:* Textbook of General Pathology; Textbook of Special Pathology; Post Mortem Methods; Pathological Editor of a System of Surgery by C. C. Choyce; Papers in the various scientific journals on the Bacteriology of Acute Rheumatism, the Cells of Inflammatory Exudations, Electrical Sterilisation of Milk, etc. *Address:* Sefton, Barkfield Avenue, Formby, Liverpool. *T.:* Formby 473. *Clubs:* University Union (Edinburgh); University (Liverpool). [*Died* 10 *Oct.* 1955.

BEATTIE, John; M.P. (Lab.) Belfast West, House of Commons, 1943-50, and 1951-55; Member of Northern Ireland Parliament for East Belfast, 1925-29, Pottinger Division of Belfast, 1929-49; late Leader of Parliamentary Labour Party in Northern Ireland; J.P. *Address:* 83 High Street, Belfast, Ireland. [*Died* 9 *March* 1960.

BEATTIE, Rt. Rev. Philip Rodger, D.D.; Bishop of Kootenay since 1955; *b.* Barrie, Ontario, 26 March 1912; *s.* of James Campbell Beattie. *Educ.:* University College, Toronto; Wycliffe College, Toronto. Secretary, S.C.M., Canada, 1936-40; Rector of Sudbury, Ont., 1940-48; Chaplain, R.C.A.F., 1943-46; Hon. Canon, Algoma, 1947-48; Rector, St. George's, St. Catharine's, Ont., 1948-52; Hon. Canon, Niagara, 1950-52; Chaplain to Bishop of Niagara, 1950-52; Rector of Christ Church Cathedral, Victoria, B.C., and Dean of Brit. Columbia, 1952-55. Hon. D.D. Wycliffe College, Toronto, 1952. *Address:* Bishop's House, 2136 Abbott Street, Kelowna, British Columbia. [*Died* 9 *Sept.* 1960.

BEATTY, Maj.-Gen. Sir Guy Archibald Hastings, K.B.E. *cr.* 1931; C.B. 1923; C.S.I. 1921; C.M.G. 1919; D.S.O. 1917; Indian Army, retired; *b.* Poona, 22 June 1870; *s.* of Surgeon-General Thomas Berkely Beatty and Augusta Sarah Ellis; *m.* 1905, Mabel (*d.* 1954), *d.* of William Reynolds. *Educ.:* Newton Coll.; Charterhouse. 18th Royal Irish Regiment, 1889-1892; 9th Bengal Lancers, 1892-1920; commanded 9th Hodson's Horse, France, 1914-17; Lucknow Cavalry Bde., France, Egypt, 1918; raised 13th Mounted Bde., Quetta, 1918; British Forces N.E. Persia and Transcaspia, 1919 (despatches, C.M.G., 1st Class Order of the Golden Star of Bokhara); 6th Inf. Brigade, Khyber Operations, 1919 (despatches, medal and clasp, Bt.-Col.); 75th Bde., Mesopotamia Operations, 1920-21 (despatches, C.S.I.); served N.W. Frontier, 1897 (medal and clasp); Boxer Expedition, China, 1900 (despatches, medal); European War, 1914-18 (D.S.O. and bar, despatches); Colonel Commandant 1st Indian Cavalry Brigade, 1921-25; A.D.C. to the King, 1925; Maj-Gen., 1926; Military Adviser-in-Chief, Indian State Forces, 1927-31; retired 1931. *Recreations:* all sports and pastimes. *Address:* c/o Lloyds Bank, 6 Pall Mall, S.W.1; Sea Haven, Budleigh Salterton, Devon. [*Died* 22 *May* 1954.

BEAUCHESNE, Arthur, C.M.G. 1934; Q.C. (Can.) F.R.S.C.; F.C.I.S. 1949; M.A., LL.D., Litt.D.; Clerk of the House of Commons of Canada, 1925-49, retd. 1949; Hon. Officer of House of Commons (by resolution), 1949; *b.* Carleton, Quebec, 15 June 1876; *s.* of P. C. Beauchesne and Caroline Lefebvre de Bellefeuille; *m.* 1916, Florence Le Blanc (*d.* 1941); twin *d.* *Educ.:* St. Joseph's Univ., New Brunswick, B.A., M.A., Litt.D.; Laval Univ., Montreal. Secretary to Speaker of Legislature in Quebec, 1896-97; to Lieut.-Governor Sir J. A. Chapleau; admitted to Quebec Bar, 1904; K.C. 1914; journalist, 1897-1904; reporter on Montreal Gazette and Montreal Daily Star; also on La Presse; Managing Editor of Le Journal, Montreal; contested Bonaventure, 1908 and 1912; Legal Adviser, Department of Justice, 1913-16; Clerk-Assistant of the House of Commons, 1916; Secretary of the Commonwealth Parliamentary Assoc. (Canadian Branch); President Canadian Club, Ottawa, 1931; President National Council of Education (Ottawa Branch), 1932-33 and 1936-39; Member of Executive Committee, 1939; Vice-Pres. Association of Canadian Clubs, 1930-31-32; President Federal District Centre of St. John Ambulance Association, 1940-47; Fellow of Chartered Institute of Secretaries; President Association des Juristes de Langue française; Life Member Institut Canadien français d'Ottawa; Hon. Member of the Bar of Haiti; LL.D. Ottawa, 1931; F.R.S. Canada and Hon. Secretary, 1935-40; Officer of Order of Hospital of St. John of Jerusalem (Hon. Patron, 1949); on board of directors of Canadian Geographical Society; Constitutional Adviser to Quebec Govt., 1950-53. *Publications:* pamphlets, etc. *Recreation:* golf. *Address:* 417 Laurier Avenue East, Ottawa, Canada. *Clubs:* Royal Ottawa Golf, Rideau, Canadian, Institut Canadien-Français (Ottawa). [*Died* 1959.

BEAUCLERK, Lord William de Vere; *b.* 16 Aug. 1883; 3rd *s.* of 10th Duke of St. Albans (*d.* 1898); *b.* and *heir-pres.* of 12th Duke of St. Albans. *Educ.:* Eton. *Address:* Newtown Anner, Clonmel, Co. Tipperary, Eire. [*Died* 25 *Dec.* 1954.

BEAUFOY, Henry Mark; J.P.; *b.* 14 Aug. 1887; *s.* of late Mark Hanbury Beaufoy, M.P., J.P., and late Mildred Scott Tait; *m.* 1911, Gwendolyn Wood (*d.* 1956); one *d.* *Educ.:* Eton; Trinity Coll., Cambridge. High Sheriff of Oxfordshire, 1944. *Recreations:* hunting, shooting, racing. *Address:* Hill House, Steeple Aston, Oxon. *T.:* Steeple Aston 247. *Club:* United University. [*Died* 8 *Feb.* 1958.

BEAUMONT, Michael Wentworth, T.D.; *b.* 8 Feb. 1903; *m.* 1st, 1924, Hon. Faith Muriel Pease (*d.* 1935), *yr. d.* of 1st Baron Gainford; one *s.*; 2nd, 1935, Doreen Christian, *d.* of late Sir Herbert Davis-Goff. *Educ.:* Eton; Oundle; R.M.C., Sandhurst. 2nd Lieut. Coldstream Guards, 1923-24; Lieut. 99th (Bucks and Berks Yeomanry) Field Brig. R.A. 1925; Capt. 1931; Major, 1939; T.D. 1943; M.P. (C.) Aylesbury Division of Bucks, 1929-1938; C.C. 1925-34; J.P. 1927, Buckinghamshire; D.L. 1938. M.F.H. Bicester and Warden Hill, 1945-47; Kildare, 1948. *Recreations:* hunting and shooting. *Address:* Harristown House, Brannockstown, County Kildare, Eire. *T.:* Brannockstown 3. *Clubs:* Buck's; Kildare Street (Dublin). [*Died* 19 *Dec.* 1958.

BEAUMONT, W(illiam) Comyns; journalist, author, and lecturer; (writes as Comyns Beaumont); *b.* 1879; *s.* of late Harry Beaumont, Whaddon, Cambridgeshire, and late Emily, *d.* of Charles Muriel Bidwell, Ely, Cambs.; *m.* Ida (*d.* 1945), *d.* of Wilfred Gibson, Hexham; one *s.* three *d.* *Educ.:* Cheltenham. First joined New York Herald under James Gordon Bennett; created and edited the Bystander, later edited the Graphic; joined late Lord Northcliffe and edited London Magazine and various journals; created and edited Passing Show, 1915; Pan, 1920; editor of the Bystander (for second time), 1928-32; editor of the National Graphic, 1932; Editor on Odham's Press, 1936; Literary Editor, Illustrated London News, 1940. *Publications:* The Mysterious Comet; Britain, Mother of Civilisation; The Riddle of Prehistoric Britain; The Private Life of the Virgin Queen; A Rebel in Fleet Street; Britain—

The Key to World History; The Great Deception. *Recreations:* travel, archæology, metaphysics. *Address:* Lodge House, Puckane, nr. Nenagh, Co. Tipperary, Eire. [*Died* 30 *Dec.* 1955.

BEAUREPAIRE, Sir Frank, Kt., *cr.* 1942; Founder and Chairman, Olympic Consolidated Industries Ltd. (comprising The Olympic Tyre & Rubber Co. Pty. Ltd., Olympic Cables Pty. Ltd., Olympic General Products Pty. Ltd., and Beaurepaire Tyre Service Pty. Ltd.); Member Melbourne City Council since 1928; Lord Mayor of Melbourne, 1940-42; *b.* 1891; *m.* 1915, Myra McKay; one *s.* one *d.* *Educ.:* Albert Park School; Wesley Coll., Melbourne. Former World's Champion Swimmer; winner of over 200 senior swimming championships in all parts of the world; former World's Record holder for several distances, 1910-21; former M.P. for Monash Prov. in Victorian Parl. for almost 10 years. Gold Medal of Royal Humane & Shipwreck Society. Served with Australian Army in Egypt, France, and England, 1915-17. *Address:* Fordholm Road, Hawthorn, Melbourne, Australia. [*Died* 29 *May* 1956.

BEAZLEY, Sir (Charles) Raymond, Kt., *cr.* 1931; D.Litt. (Oxon); J.P. Birmingham; Emeritus Professor, Birmingham; Hon. Vice-Pres., Royal Historical Society; F.R.G.S.; Corr. Fellow of Lisbon Academy of Sciences and of Lisbon Geographical Society, of American Geographical Society, and of Hispanic Society of America; formerly on Council of R.G.S. and of Hakluyt and African Societies; a former member of the Church Assembly and of Council of National Society; *b.* Blackheath, 3 April 1868; *y. s.* of Rev. J. Beazley; *m.* 1901, Gladys, *e. d.* of Rev. Morlais Jones, *niece* of Lord Rhayader. *Educ.:* St. Paul's School; King's College, London; Balliol College, Oxford. Scholar of Balliol (Brakenbury History), 1885; Prize Fellow of Merton College, 1889-1896; Research Fellow, 1897-1910; Sub-Warden, 1906-8; proxime Stanhope, 1888; proxime Arnold, 1892; Lothian Essay, 1889; Oxford Geographical studentship, 1894; 1st class History, 1889; B.A. 1890; M.A. 1893; D.Litt. 1908; Hon. Ph.D., Breslau, 1937; Professor of History, University of Birmingham, 1909-33; Ilchester Lecturer (Russian History), Oxford, 1913; Lowell Lecturer, Boston, Mass., 1908; lectured at Yale, Wisconsin, Chicago, North-Western, and other U.S. universities; lectured on British front in France, 1918; member of University Delegations to France, 1919, 1921; lecturing visits to Germany, 1930, 1931, 1933, 1934, 1937, etc.; visits to Saar, 1934. *Publications:* James of Aragon, 1890; Henry the Navigator, 1895; Dawn of Modern Geography (vol. i. 1897, vol. ii. 1901, vol. iii. 1906; for this, Gill Memorial of Royal Geographical Society, 1907); John and Sebastian Cabot, 1898; Azurara's Discovery of Guinea (with colleague: vol. i. 1896, vol. ii. 1899); Voyages and Travels (16th-17th cents.), 2 vols. 1902; Carpini and Rubruquis, Friar Travellers, 1245-1255, 1903; Elizabethan Seamen, 1907; Directorium transmarinum, 1907; Notebook of Mediaeval History, 1917; History of Russia (with colleagues), 1918; Introduction to Chronicle of Novgorod, 1915; Nineteenth Century Europe, 1922; The Road to Ruin in Europe, 1932; Beauty of the North Cotswolds, 1946; contributions to Social England, 1894-96; to Encyclopædia Britannica; to Dictionary of National Biography; to Contemporary Review, Quarterly Review, etc. *Address:* 6 Arthur Road, Edgbaston, Birmingham. *T.:* Edgbaston 1062. [*Died* 1 *Feb.* 1955.

BECHER, Lt.-Col. Henry Wrixon-, D.S.O.; *b.* 27 July 1866; 3rd *s.* of late Sir J. W. Wrixon-Becher, 3rd Bart., and late Lady Emily Catherine Hare, 2nd *d.* of 2nd Earl of Listowel; unmarried. *Educ.:* Harrow. Joined army; Duke of Wellington's West Riding Regt. 1886; retired 1907; served in Bermuda, Canada, West Indies, South Africa, and India; South African War 1900-2 (despatches, Bt. Major, Queen's and King's medals); rejoined Army, 5 Aug. 1914; commanded 12th Bn. Yorkshire Regt. and 17th Bn. Worcestershire Regt. in B.E.F. (despatches twice, D.S.O., wounded). *Recreation:* shooting. *Address:* Killetra, Mallow, Co. Cork. *Club:* County of Cork (Cork). [*Died* 9 *June* 1951.

BECK, Diana Jean Kinloch, F.R.C.S.; Consultant Neurosurgeon to Middlesex Hospital, London, W.1; *b.* 1902; *o. d.* of late James and Margaret Beck, Chester. *Educ.:* Queen's School, Chester; Royal Free Hospital School of Medicine. M.B., B.S. (Lond.) 1925; F.R.C.S. 1931; F.R.C.S.E. 1930. Late Surgical Registrar and Hon. Neurosurgeon, Royal Free Hospital; late Asst. to Sir Hugh Cairns, Oxford; late Consultant Adviser in Neurosurgery to South-West Region (Ministry of Health). *Publications:* papers on surgical and neurosurgical subjects in B.J.S., Jl. of Neurosurg. Brain, etc. *Recreations:* embroidery, painting, music, travel. *Address:* 55 Harley House, Regent's Park, N.W.1. *T.:* Welbeck 1645. [*Died* 3 *March* 1956.

BECK, Sir Raymond, Kt., *cr.* 1911; J.P. Co. Devon; *b.* 31 May 1861; *y. s.* of Morris Beck of Lloyd's; *m.* 1912, Elsie Mary, 2nd *d.* of C. J. Whittington, of Pauntley, Sidmouth; two *s.* *Educ.:* Lancing College. Entered Lloyd's, 1879; Underwriting Member, 1888; Chairman, 1910-11, 1915-17; Dep. Chm., 1912-14. *Address:* Castle Point, Salcombe, Devon. [*Died* 17 *Sept.* 1953.

BECK, Very Rev. William Ernest; Dean of Worcester since 1949; *b.* 4 Oct. 1884; *s.* of Bessey and Jane Beck; *m.* 1911, Grace Evelyn Sayers; one *s.* one *d.* *Educ.:* Great Yarmouth Grammar School. Theological, Newby (Classical) and Hebrew Scholar, 1st Class Hons. Theology, Univ. of Durham; B.A. Univ. of London, 1904; M.A. Univ. of Durham; Hon. M.A. 1948; Hon. D.Litt. 1949, Univ. of Bristol. Tutor, St. Aidan's Theological College, Birkenhead, 1908-9; Chaplain, 1909-12; Vice-Principal, 1912-15; Vicar of St. Anne's, Birkenhead, and Lecturer at St. Aidan's, 1915-21; Chaplain to the Forces, 1918-19, now Hon. C.F.; Examining Chaplain to the Bishop of Truro, 1919-23, to the Bishop of Chelmsford, 1923-29, to the Bishop of Manchester, 1929-47, to the Bishop of Gloucester, 1929-49; Principal of St. Paul's Training College, Cheltenham, 1921-49; Proctor in Convocation, 1936-49; Hon. Canon of Gloucester, 1942-49. *Publications:* Adventurers for God; Signposts; St. Luke's Gospel; The Acts of the Apostles; St. Mark's Gospel. *Recreation:* fly-fishing. *Address:* The Deanery, 15 College Green, Worcester. [*Died* 22 *May* 1957.

BECK, William Hopkins; *b.* Washington, D.C., 8 Sept. 1892; *m.* 1923, Mae Edwards Norwood, Washington, D.C.; one *d.* (and one *d.* decd.). *Educ.:* Eastern and Business High School, Washington, D.C. Sec. to Member of Congress 1½ years; Institute of Industrial Research 3½ years; National Geographic Society 2 years; U.S. Army, 1917-20 overseas service; detailed to American Commission to negotiate peace, Paris, 1919; Private Secretary to the Secretary of State, 1920; detailed to accompany the Secretary of State on mission to S. America, 1920, and to Rio de Janeiro, 1922; detailed to accompany the Secretary of State on mission for signature of Pact for Renunciation of War, Paris, 1928; Secretary of London Naval Conference, 1930; Consul General and Secretary in Diplomatic Service, 1931; Consul-General

of the U.S.A. at Ottawa. Canada. 1931-35; Oslo, Norway, 1936-39; Hamilton, Bermuda, 1940-45; Southampton, 1945-50; retired from Foreign Service, 1951. Rejoined staff of National Geographic Society, Washington 6, D.C., Oct. 1951. *Recreation:* fishing. *Address:* 2921 Bellevue Terrace, N.W. Washington 16, D.C., U.S.A.
[*Died* 30 *March* 1957.

BECKER, Neal Dow; Chairman Intertype Corporation, New York, and Intertype Ltd., London; former Chairman Board of Trustees, Cornell University, and Trustee since 1934; *b.* 13 February 1883; *s.* of William E. and Eva Kenyon Becker; *m.* 1st, 1909, Ivah E. Smith (*d.* 1951); two *d.*; 2nd, 1954, Charlotte Dawn Allen. *Educ.:* Cornell Univ. (A.B., LL.B.). Hon. LL.D. Dickinson Coll. Practised law in New York as member of firm of Kelley and Becker, 1910-35; Director: Consolidated Edison Co. of New York Inc., New York Dock Co. and various other corporations; Member: Nat. Industrial Conf. Bd. (Ex-Chm.); Council on Foreign Relations; Assoc. of Bar of City of New York; Delta Chi; Ex- Pres. Commerce and Industry Assoc. of New York, Inc. *Recreation:* golf. *Address:* 340 Park Avenue, New York 22, N.Y. *T.:* Eldorado 5-2422. *Clubs:* American; Sunningdale Golf (Eng.); Royal and Ancient Golf (St. Andrews); University, Cornell, Racquet and Tennis (New York). [*Died* 16 May 1955.

BECKETT, Harold, C.M.G. 1941; retired; *b.* 9 Oct. 1891; *y. s.* of John Fellows and Clara Beckett. *Educ.:* Monmouth Grammar School; Wadham College, Oxford (exhibitioner, Symons exhibitioner). 1st Class Classical Mods. 1912; 3rd class Lit. Hum. 1914; entered Colonial Office, 1914; member West Indies Currency Committee, 1923; went to Mauritius, 1925, to report on questions of currency and exchange; Assistant Secretary, 1931; visited Bermuda, Bahamas, Jamaica, British Honduras, 1939; retired, 1951. *Address:* 3 Christchurch Hill, N.W.3.
[*Died* 30 *Sept.* 1952.

BECKETT, Hon. Rupert (Evelyn); late Major, Yorkshire Hussars; J.P., D.L. West Riding of York; Director Westminster Bank, Ltd. since 1921 (Chm., 1931-50); Director of Yorkshire Penny Bank, Ltd.; *b.* 2 Nov. 1870; 3rd *s.* of late William Beckett, M.P.; *m.* 1896, Muriel Helen Florence (*d.* 1941), C.B.E., *d.* of Lord Berkeley Paget; two *d.* (and two *d.* decd.). *Educ.:* Eton; Trinity College, Cambridge. Chm. Yorkshire Post, 1920-50; late Director: L. and N.E. Railway; Aire and Calder Navigation. Hon. Freedom of Leeds, 1931; Hon. LL.D. Leeds, 1938. *Address:* Stone House, Moor Allerton, Leeds; 28 Hyde Park Gardens Mews, W.2. *Clubs:* Carlton, Turf, St. James', White's; Royal Yacht Squadron (Cowes).
[*Died* 25 *Apr.* 1955.

BECKETT, Brig.-Gen. William Thomas Clifford, C.B.E. 1919; D.S.O. 1918; V.D.; *b.* 1862; *s.* of Col. W. H. Beckett, Indian Army; *m.* 1889, Bessie (*d.* 1947), *d.* of Maj.-Gen. C. S. Thomason, R.E. *Educ.:* Tonbridge. Served European War, 1914-18, Siberia, 1919-20, Manchuria, 1920-23, commanding British Military Railway Mission (despatches four times, D.S.O., C.B.E., Order of Chia Ho, China and Order of Rising Sun, Japan); British representative on Inter-Allied Technical Board. *Address:* Umaria, Grantown-on-Spey, Scotland.
[*Died* 4 *March* 1956.

BECKLES, Gordon; Editor and writer; *b.* 21 Oct. 1901; *e. s.* of late Lt.-Col. Beckles Willson, and Ethel Grace Willson, of Colborne, Ontario; *m.* 1st, 1925, Patricia Donnelly (*d.* 1934), Co. Tyrone; one *s.* two *d.*; 2nd, 1939, Denise Helene, *er. d.* of Paul Planquart, Le Touquet, France. *Educ.:* privately; Royal Navy (Canada), 1916-19. Staff Daily Graphic, 1923-26; Assistant Editor, Sunday Dispatch, 1926-28; Staff Daily Express, 1928-38 (except 1932, Assistant Editor, Daily Herald); Assistant and Deputy Editor, Daily Mail, 1938-40. *Publications:* Tankard Travels, 1936; Dunkirk and After, 1940; Birth of a Spitfire; Canada Comes to England, 1941; Tanks Advance, 1942; articles to leading magazines; diarist of Tatler and Bystander since 1947. *Recreations:* travel and talk. *Address:* 42 Chesterfield House, Mayfair, W.1. *Club:* Savage.
[*Died* 5 *Aug.* 1954.

BEDDINGTON, Gerald Ernest, C.B.E. 1921; formerly member of firm of Chas. Balme & Co.; *b.* 23 May 1867; *s.* of late John Henry Beddington, 16 Sussex Pl., Regent's Park; *m.* 1st, 1892, Alice Mary (*d.* 1950), *d.* of late M. A. Goldschmidt, 66 Mount Street, Park Lane; three *s.*; 2nd, 1953, Mrs. Catherine Hope Mansfield, widow of Captain Frank Mansfield, M.C., R.E., and *d.* of late W. S. Godfrey, Chevington, Suffolk. *Educ.:* Clifton; Trinity College, Cambridge, M.A. Member of the Board of Control of Committee of London Wool Brokers, 1917-1921; Chairman Wool Transport and Storage Advisory Committee, 1919-20; Member of the Wool Council, 1919; Vice-Chairman Associated London Selling Wool Brokers, 1919-21. *Address:* Court, Crondall (Hants), nr. Farnham, Sy. *T.:* Crondall 220. *Clubs:* Carlton, Boodle's, Portland.
[*Died* 23 *Dec.* 1958.

BEDDINGTON, Jack, C.B.E. 1943; Hon. F.S.I.A., Hon. F.R.C.A.; Deputy Chairman of Colman, Prentis & Varley; *b.* 30 January 1893; *s.* of Charles and Stella Beddington; *m.* 1918, Olivia Margaret Streatfeild; one *s.* one *d.* *Educ.:* Wellington College; Balliol College, Oxford. K.O.Y.L.I., 1914-19 (wounded); China, 1919-27; Shell-mex and B.P. Ltd., 1927-46; Director of Films Division, M.O.I., 1940-46. *Address:* Little Place, Bampton, Oxon. *Club:* Bath.
[*Died* 13 *April* 1959.

BEDFORD, 12th Duke of (*cr.* 1694), **Hastings William Sackville Russell;** Marquess of Tavistock, 1694; Earl of Bedford, 1550; Baron Russell of Chenies, 1539; Baron Russell of Thornhaugh, 1603; Baron Howland of Streatham (England), 1695; *b.* 21 Dec. 1888; *o. c.* of 11th Duke and Mary du Caurroy (*d.* 1937), *d.* of late Ven. W. H. Tribe, Archdeacon of Lahore; *S.* father, 1940; *m.* 1914, Louisa Crommelin Roberta, *y. d.* of late Robert Jowitt Whitwell; two *s.* one *d.* *Educ.:* Balliol College, Oxford. *Publications:* The Road to Real Success; Poverty and Over-taxation—the Way Out; Parrots and Parrot-like Birds in Aviculture. *Heir: s.* Marquess of Tavistock. *Address:* Woburn Abbey, Bedfordshire; Cairnsmore, Newton Stewart, Wigtonshire. [*Died* 9 *Oct.* 1953.

BEDFORD, James Douglas Hardy, C.S.I. 1938; *b.* 1 June 1884; *m.* 1932, Helen Beatrice, *d.* of W. Beaumont; one *s.* four *d.* *Educ.:* St. Mark's School, Windsor; Cooper's Hill. Joined Indian Service of Engineers, 1905; Superintending Engineer for the construction of various canals, 1927; Chief Engineer (Constructional) and Secretary to the Governor of the Punjab, making irrigation projects, 1932-39; retired, 1939. *Address:* Cribden, Wharncliffe Road, Highcliffe-on-Sea, Hants. [*Died* 25 *Jan.* 1960.

BEDWELL, Horace, C.M.G. 1913; *b.* 19 Oct. 1868; *m.* 1st, Constance Brodie (*d.* 1901), *d.* of Dr. Bransby Roberts, Eastbourne; one *d.*; 2nd, 1911, Edith Isabel (*d.* 1949), *d.* of George James Caple, London. *Educ.:* Sedbergh; private; Jesus College, Cambridge. Assistant District Commissioner, Nigeria, 1896; District Commissioner, Warri, 1898; Asaba, 1899-1900; Asst. Secretary, 1901-6; Deputy High Commis-

BEDELL, Frederick. See page xxvii.

sioner, 1906; Provincial Commissioner and Resident (1st Class), Nigeria, 1906-18; retired, Oct. 1918. *Address:* c/o Lloyds Bank, Littlehampton, Sussex. [*Died* 17 *Feb.* 1954.

BEEDING, Francis; *see* Saunders, H.A.St.G.

BEEMAN, Brigadier William Gilbert, D.S.O. 1917; retired; *b.* Centreville, Ontario, 28 June 1884; *s.* of M. I. Beeman, M.B., and Lilian Louise Henault; *m.* Kathleen Burpee Carruthers; three *s.* one *d.* *Educ.:* R. Military College, Kingston. *Recreations:* fishing, shooting. *Address:* Portsmouth, Ontario, Canada. [*Died* 18 *March* 1953.

BEER, Sir Frederick T. T.; *see* Tidbury-Beer.

BEERBOHM, Sir Max, Kt., *cr.* 1939; Hon. D.Litt. (Oxon); Hon. LL.D. (Edin.); Hon. Fellow of Merton; *b.* London, 24 Aug. 1872; *y. s.* of Julius E. Beerbohm and Eliza Draper; *m.* 1910, Florence Kahn (*d.* 1951), of Memphis, Tennessee, U.S.A.; *m.* 1956, Elisabeth Jungmann. *Educ.:* Charterhouse; Merton Coll., Oxford. *Publications:* The Works of Max Beerbohm; More; Yet Again; And Even Now; A Christmas Garland; The Happy Hypocrite; Zuleika Dobson; Seven Men; The Dreadful Dragon of Hay Hill; Lytton Strachey (Rede Lecture, 1943); Mainly on the Air, 1946; Caricatures of Twenty-Five Gentlemen; The Poet's Corner; A Book of Caricatures; The Second Childhood of John Bull; Fifty Caricatures; A Survey; Rossetti and his Circle; Things New and Old; Observations; Around Theatres, 1953. *Relevant Publications:* Max's Nineties, 1958; Selected Essays, 1958; Conversation with Max (by S. N. Behrman), 1960. *Address:* Villino Chiaro, Rapallo, Italy. *Clubs:* Athenæum, Savage. [*Died* 20 *May* 1956.

BEGBIE, Ven. Herbert Smirnoff; Archdeacon of Parramatta, 1935-41, of Cumberland since 1941; Canon of St. Andrew's Cathedral, Sydney, since 1927; Minister i/c St. Philip's Church, Sydney, 1940-44; *b.* 3 April 1871; *s.* of Alfred Daniel Campbell Begbie and Sarah Matilda Cooper; *m.* 1893; four *s.* five *d.* *Educ.:* Sydney Grammar School. For eight years followed banking; theological course Moore Theological College, Sydney (graduated first class); Oxford and Cambridge Prelim. (first class); curacies at Marrickville, Sydney, and Bendigo (Vic.); Rector of St. Mark's, Picton, 1902-5; St. Mary's, North Melbourne, 1905-8; Bairnsdale (Vic.), 1908-9; All Souls, Leichhardt (Sydney), 1900-14; St. Stephen's, Newtown, N.S.W. 1914-21; St. Stephen's, Willoughby, N.S.W. 1921-36; Chaplain Deaconess Institution, 1915-36; Rector of St. John's Church, Parramatta, 1936-40; Commissary Bishop of Bendigo, 1917; Deputy Commissary for Archbishop of Sydney, 1938-39. *Recreations:* gardening, music. *Address:* Grey Rocks, Fleming Street, Northwood, N.S.W. *T.:* JB 1591. [*Died* 8 *Sept.* 1951.

BEHAN, Sir John (Clifford Valentine), Kt., *cr.* 1949; M.A., LL.D. (Melb.), M.A., B.C.L. (Oxon.); of the Middle Temple, Barrister-at-Law; General Secretary in Australia for the Rhodes Scholarships Trust 1922-52; *b.* 8 May 1881; *s.* of late William Behan of Sydney, N.S.W.; *m.* 1907, Violet Greta, *y. d.* of late Robert Caldwell, M.L.A., Melbourne. *Educ.:* Caulfield Grammar School; Trinity College, Melbourne (Exhibitioner and Scholar); Hertford College, Oxford. First-class final honours and final scholarships in the Schools of Philosophy, History and Law, University of Melbourne; Cobden Club Medal; Supreme Court Prize; First Rhodes Scholarship for the State of Victoria, 1904; Vinerian Law Scholarship, 1906; Honorary Scholar of Hertford College, Oxford, 1906; Eldon Law Scholarship, 1906; 1st Class in Law Finals, B.C.L. and Bar Exam., 1906; Stowell Civil Law Fellow of University College, Oxford, 1909; Lecturer in Law at University College, 1907; Dean of University College, 1914-17; Ministry of Munitions, 1915; Ministry of Food, 1917; Munitions, 1915; Ministry of Food, 1917; Warden of Trinity College in the University of Melbourne, 1918-46. *Publication:* The Use of Land as affected by Covenants and Obligations not in the Form of Covenants, 1924. *Recreation:* tennis. *Address:* Silvermist, Olinda, Victoria, Australia. [*Died Sept.* 1957.

BEHARRELL, Sir (John) George, Kt., *cr.* 1919; D.S.O. 1917; Hon. Consultant (lately President) Dunlop Rubber Co. Ltd.; *s.* of George Beharrell of Almondbury, Yorks, and Elizabeth, *d.* of John Dalby, York; *b.* 11 March 1873; *m.* 1898, Kate, *o. d.* of Jos. Ripley, Sheffield; three *s.* one *d.* *Educ.:* King James's School, Almondbury; privately; Leeds University. Assistant to General Manager N.E. Ry.; Assistant Goods Manager and Commercial Agent N.E. Ry.; Director of Stats. and Requirements, Ministry of Munitions; Assistant Director-General of Transportation, France; Assistant Inspector-General Transportation, all theatres of war; rank, Lt.-Col.; Director of Statistics, Admiralty; attached to Geddes Committee on National Expenditure, 1921-22; Director-General of Finance and Statistics, Ministry of Transport, 1919-22; Man. Dir. Dunlop Rubber Co., Ltd., 1923, Chairman, 1937-49, President, 1949-57; President India Rubber Manufacturers' Association, 1926-28; President Soc. of Motor Manufacturers and Traders 1927-28, 1928-29; Pres. Federation of British Industries, 1932-33; President Institution of Rubber Industry, 1933-34-35-36; Chairman Sixth International Congress for Scientific Management, 1935; Member of Advisory Panel representing Manufacturers to International Rubber Regulation Committee, 1934-43; Member of Primein Mister's Advisory Panel of Industrialists, 1938; Commander of Orders of: Crown of Belgium; S. Maurizio and S. Lazarro; Orange Nassau. *Address:* St. Andrews, Southdown Road, Harpenden, Herts. *T.:* Harpenden 3240. *Club:* Reform. [*Died* 20 *Feb.* 1959.

BEITH, Maj.-Gen. John Hay, C.B.E. 1918; M.C.; novelist and playwright (pen-name, Ian Hay); Director of Public Relations at the War Office, 1938-41; *b.* 17 April 1876; *s.* of late John A. Beith, of Manchester and Altnacraig, Oban; *m.* 1915, Helen Margaret, *o. d.* of late P. A. Spiers, of Polmont Park, Stirlingshire. *Educ.:* Fettes College; St. John's College, Camb. 2nd Class, Classical Tripos, 1898. Served (with rank of Capt.) in the Argyll and Sutherland Highlanders, Ninth Division, B.E.F. (despatches, M.C.); Member British War Mission to U.S.A., 1916-17-18; Member of the Royal Company of Archers, the Queen's Bodyguard in Scotland; Officer of the Order of S. John of Jerusalem; for twenty-four years a Governor of Guy's Hospital; President, The Dramatists' Club. For ten years Chairman Society of Authors. *Publications:* Pip, 1907; The Right Stuff, 1908; A Man's Man, 1909; A Safety Match, 1911; Happy-Go-Lucky, 1913; A Knight on Wheels, 1914; The Lighter Side of School Life, 1914; The First Hundred Thousand "K (1)," 1915; Carrying On, 1917; The Last Million, 1918; The Willing Horse, 1921; The Lucky Number, 1923; The Shallow End, 1924; Paid, with Thanks, 1925; Half-a-Sovereign, 1926; The Poor Gentleman, 1928; The Middle Watch, 1930; Their Name Liveth, 1931; The Midshipmaid, 1932; The Great Wall of India, 1933; David and Destiny, 1934; Lucky Dog, 1934; Housemaster, 1936; The King's Service, 1938; Stand at Ease, 1940; Little Ladyship, 1941; America Comes Across, 1942; The Unconquered Isle (Malta, G.C.), 1943; The Post Office went to War, 1946; Peaceful Invasion, 1946; R.O.F., the Story of the Royal Ordnance Factories, 1948; Arms and the Men, 1939-45: The History of the King's Bodyguard for Scotland

(1676-1950); (posthumous); 100 years of Army Nursing, 1953; Cousin Christopher, 1953; *plays:* Tilly of Bloomsbury, 1919; A Safety Match, 1921; The Happy Ending, 1922; Good Luck (with Seymour Hicks), 1923; The Sport of Kings, 1924; A Damsel in Distress (with P. G. Wodehouse), 1928; Baa, Baa, Black Sheep (with P. G. Wodehouse), 1929; The Middle Watch (with Stephen King-Hall), 1929; A Song of Sixpence (with Guy Bolton), 1930; Leave it to Psmith (with P. G. Wodehouse), 1930; Mr. Faint-Heart, 1931; The Midshipmaid (with Stephen King-Hall), 1931; Orders are Orders (with Anthony Armstrong), 1932; A Present from Margate (with A. E. W. Mason), 1933; Admirals All (with Stephen King-Hall), 1934; The Frog (from novel by Edgar Wallace), 1936; Housemaster, 1936; The Gusher, 1937; Little Ladyship, 1939; Off the Record (with Stephen King-Hall), 1947; The White Sheep of the Family (with L. Du Garde Peach), 1951. *Address:* 49 Hill Street, W.1. *Clubs:* Beefsteak, Garrick, Caledonian; Royal and Ancient (St. Andrews).
[*Died* 22 *Sept.* 1952.

BELCHER, Captain Douglas Walter, V.C. 1915; *b.* Surbiton, 15 July 1889; *m.* 1917, Emily F. Luxford (whom he divorced, 1935), Surbiton; two *c.*; *m.* 1941, Gertrude E. Brine. *Educ.:* Tiffins School, Kingston-on-Thames. Was with Waring & Gillow, Ltd., Oxford St., W.; joined Volunteer Force, 1906-8, and transferred to Territorial Force, 1908. Served European War, 1914-18; went to France with the London Rifle Brigade Nov. 1914, and gained the V.C. 13 May 1915 as a Sergt.; was first Territorial ranker to win the V.C.; commission in the Queen Victoria's Rifles (9th London T.F.), 1916; 6th Gurkha Rifles, I.A., 1918-22; retired from I.A., 1922. Served War of 1939-45, London Rifle Bde., National Defence Coy. and 7th Bn. Rifle Bde., 1939-40, and R.A.P.C. and P.O.W. Duties, 1941-43. *Address:* Tera, 16 Rythe Road, Claygate, Surrey.
[*Died* 3 *June* 1953.

BELISHA, 1st Baron Hore-; *see* Hore-Belisha.

BÉLIVEAU, Most Rev. Arthur; Archbishop of St. Boniface (R.C.) since 1916; *b.* 1870. *Educ.:* St. Boniface College; Grand Seminary, Montreal; Canadian College, Rome. Priest, 1893; Chancellor of Diocese of St. Boniface, 1905-13; Administrator of the Cathedral, 1913; Auxiliary to Archbishop of St. Boniface and titular Bishop of Domitianopolis, 1913. Owing to the Archbishop's illness, the Archdiocese had been administered by a Coadjutor-Archbishop with right of succession from 1933. The Apostolic Administrator and Coadjutor Archbishop, from 1952, was Most Rev. Maurice Baudoux. *Address:* Archbishop's Residence, 151 Cathedral Ave., St. Boniface, Man., Canada. [*Died* 14 *Sept.* 1955.

BELK, Lieut.-Col. William, C.M.G. 1917; Order of St. John; late 4th Dragoon Guards; *s.* of late J. T. Belk, J.P., Middlesborough and Grasmere, Westmorland; *b.* 14 May 1869; *m.* 1st, 1911, Mary Eliza (*d.* 1930), *d.* of late John Waddington, Leeds; 2nd, 1936, Irene May, *d.* of late H. W. Marston. *Educ.:* Aysgarth and Giggleswick Schools; R.M.C., Sandhurst. Commissioned 4th Dragoon Guards, 1889; retired, 1911; ordained Priest in Liberal Catholic Church, 1935. *Address:* c/o National Provincial Bank, Ltd., Middlesbrough.
[*Died* 25 *March* 1952.

BELL; *see* Morrison-Bell.

BELL, Lieut.-Commander Archibald Colquhoun, R.N., retired; 2nd *s.* of Alexander Montgomerie Bell; *m.* Violet, *y. d.* of Rev. Canon Langbridge of St. Mary's, Limerick. *Educ.:* Blundell's School, Tiverton. Entered the Navy, 1902; Hydrographic Survey; Naval Assistant to the Hydrographer, 1911; transferred to the historical section of the Committee of Imperial Defence, 1919; Secretariat the Council of Five, Paris, 1919; Naval Assistant to Official Historian of Naval Operations in European War; employed by Foreign Office to write a confidential history of the blockade of Germany for official reference, 1931-37; awarded the Julian Corbett prize for research in naval history by the University of London, 1930; later appointed F.R.Hist.S.; joined Intelligence Division R.A.F. 1939; served as 15 Group Intelligence Officer, Jan.-April 1940; H.Q. Fighter Command, July 1940-Jan. 1941; subsequently R.A.F. Intelligence Officer H.Q. Western Command. *Publications:* Sea Power and the Next War, 1938; articles on trade defence to the Edinburgh Quarterly and Brassey's Naval Annual under the pen-name of Archibald Colbeck. War History of the Manchester Regiment, 1954. *Recreation:* beekeeping. *Address:* Wrawby Cottage, Wivenhoe, Essex.
[*Died* 18 *Feb.* 1958.

BELL, Maj.-Gen. Arthur Henry, C.M.G. 1918; D.S.O. 1917; *b.* 1871; *s.* of Rev. Joseph S. Bell, Canon of St. Patrick's Cathedral, Dublin; *m.* 1911, Ellen, *d.* of Bernard Claffy, Ottawa. Served Matabele Rebellion, 1896 (medal); S. Africa (Queen's medal with three clasps, King's medal with two clasps); European War, 1914-18 (wounded, despatches six times, D.S.O., C.M.G., Croix de Guerre, 1914-15 Star, two medals). Adjutant General, Canadian Militia, 1930-33; *Address:* Roxborough Apts., Ottawa, Canada.
[*Died* 23 *Nov.* 1956.

BELL, Sir (Bernard) Humphrey, K.B.E., *cr.* 1937 (C.B.E. 1923); *s.* of late Rev. J. T. Bell, Headmaster of Christ's Hospital, Hertford; *m.* 1912, Lilian Constance Bagot (*d.* 1959), *d.* of late Rev. G. P. Dew, Rector of Shirenewton, Monmouthshire, and late Lady Mary Dew. *Educ.:* Christ's Hospital; Trinity College, Cambridge (scholar); B.A., 1906; Fourth Wrangler. Sudan Political Service, 1907; Barrister, Gray's Inn, 1917; President, Court of First Instance, Bagdad, 1918-20; President, Court of Appeal, Bagdad, 1920-22; Judge of High Court, Khartoum, 1923-26; Chief Justice of the Sudan, 1926; Legal Secretary to the Sudan Government, 1930-1936; Assistant Legal Adviser, Home Office, 1939-45. *Address:* Restormel, Pennington, Hants. [*Died* 7 *Dec.* 1959.

BELL, Rev. Canon Charles Carlyle, M.A.; Canon Residentiary of York Minster, 1914-53; Precentor of York, 1925-53; Vicar of St. Martin's, Coney Street, York, 1920-53; *b.* Titchfield, Hants, 1868; *e. s.* of William Warden Bell, E.I.C.S., and Mary Brace, of Catisfield, Fareham, Hants; *m.* 1897, Gertrude, *y. d.* of James Francis Doyle of Childwall near Liverpool; one *s.* three *d.* *Educ.:* Tonbridge School; Keble College, Oxon; Cuddesdon Theological College. Deacon, 1891; Priest, 1892; Assistant Curate of St. Pancras Parish Church, London, 1891-96; Minor Canon and Sacrist of Carlisle Cathedral, 1896-1901; Vicar of Carleton, Pontefract, Yorks, 1901-06; Vicar of St. Olave-with-St. Giles, City of York, 1906-15; Canon Missioner of Diocese of York, 1914-1924. *Publications:* The Work of an Evangelist; The Sower; The Children's Book of Church and Sacraments; The Story of Fountains Abbey, 1932. *Address:* 7 Minster Yard, York. *T.:* York 2976.
[*Died* 4 *Sept.* 1954.

BELL, Cyril Francis, C.I.E. 1938; *b.* 23 Feb. 1883; two *d.* Joined Indian Forest Service, 1905, Chief Conservator of Forests, C.P., 1935-38; retired, 1938. *Address:* 7 Egliston Road, Putney, S.W.15.
[*Died* 27 *Dec.* 1957.

BELL, Sir Eastman, 2nd Bt., *cr.* 1909; M.C.; Director Liebigs Extract of Meat Co.; *b.* 27 July 1884; *s.* of 1st Bt. and Lizzie French (*d.* 1895), *d.* of T. C. Eastman, New York; *S.* father 1931. *Educ.:* Winchester; University College, Oxford. Called to Bar, Inner Temple, 1909; served European War, 1914-19 (despatches, M.C.). *Heir:* none. *Address:* Fosbury Manor, Marlborough. *Clubs:* Carlton, Cavalry, Bath. [*Died* 19 *Dec.* 1955 (*ext.*).

BELL, Edward Allen, M.A.; Oxford Group since 1935; *b.* 8 May 1884; *s.* of late Canon J. Allen Bell, Canon of Norwich. *Educ.:* Westminster; Christ Church, Oxford. Assist. Master at Giggleswick, 1910-18; Lieut. The Norfolk Regiment, 1918; Major and Chief Instructor, Army General College, Cologne, B.E.F., 1919; Assistant Master at Eton College, 1921-26; Headmaster St. Bees School, Cumberland, 1926-35. A Governor of the College of the Good Road, 1949-50. *Publications:* History of Giggleswick School (1499-1912), 1912; Poems, 1926; Poems, 1949. *Recreation:* fencing. *Address:* 2 St. Barnabas Houses, Newland, Malvern. Worcs. [*Died* 9 *July* 1959.

BELL, Sir (Edward) Peter (Stubbs), Hon. Mr. Justice Bell, Kt., *cr.* 1954; Chief Justice, Northern Rhodesia, since 1955; *b.* 10 May 1902; *e. s.* of late Lieut.-Colonel Edward Bell, O.B.E., and of Elizabeth Alice Bell, Dunmore East, Co. Waterford, Ireland, and British West Indies; *m.* 1947, Geneviève Marie-Antoinette, *d.* of Albert William Scott, United States Foreign Service; one *s.* Secretariat, Antigua, Leeward Islands, 1920; Magistrate, Dominica, 1931; St. Kitts-Nevis, 1934; called to Bar, Inner Temple, 1934; Attorney-General, St. Lucia, 1935; Crown Counsel, Palestine, 1938; Legal Secretary, Malta, 1941-45; Chm. Malta War Damage Commission, 1943-45; Solicitor-General, Malaya, 1946; K.C. Malaya, 1948; Puisne Judge, Tanganyika, 1949; Chief Justice, British Guiana, 1951-55; C.St.J. 1955. *Recreations:* lawn tennis, bird watching. *Address:* High Court, Lusaka, Northern Rhodesia; c/o Barclays Bank (D.C. & O.), Oceanic Building, Cockspur St., S.W.1. *Club:* National. [*Died* 18 *June* 1957.

BELL, Eric Temple, Ph.D. Columbia; Professor of Mathematics, California Institute of Technology, Pasadena, since 1926; *b.* 7 Feb. 1883; *y. s.* of James Bell, Aberdeen; *m.* 1910, Jessie Brown (*d.* 1940); one *s.* *Educ.:* Bedford; Universities: Stanford, Washington, Columbia. Instructor-Professor of Mathematics, Univ. of Washington, 1912-1926; Prof., Summers, Univ. of Chicago, 1924-29; Prof., Harvard (visiting), 1926. Pres. Mathematical Association of America, 1931-33; Vice-Pres., American Mathematical Society, 1926; Bôcher prize for mathematical research, 1921; Member, National Academy of Sciences (U.S.A.), American Philosophical Society. *Publications:* The Queen of the Sciences, 1931; Numerology, 1933; The Search for Truth, 1934; Handmaiden of the Sciences, 1937; Man and His Lifebelts, 1938; The Development of Mathematics, 1940, 2nd ed. 1945; Men of Mathematics, 1937; The Magic of Numbers, 1946; Mathematics, Servant of Science, 1950; fifteen science fiction novels (pseud. John Taine); papers in various mathematical periodicals. *Recreations:* gardening, cats. *Address:* California Institute of Technology, Pasadena, California. [*Died* 21 *Dec.* 1960.

BELL, Sir Ernest Albert Seymour, Kt., *cr.* 1923; C.I.E. 1919; M.Inst.C.E.; formerly: Chairman and Man. Dir., South Indian Railway and other Indian Railways; Member Railway Board, Govt. of India; *m.* 1st, 1902, Amie (*d.* 1941), *y. d.* of late E. B. Loynes, Solicitor, Wells, Norfolk; three *s.* one *d.*; 2nd, 1943, Lena Jones, The Grange, Ascott-under-Wychwood, Oxford. *Address:* 6 Fairacres, Roehampton Lane, S.W.15. *T.:* Prospect 2461. [*Died* 8 *Jan.* 1955.

BELL, Eva Mary, O.B.E. 1919; novelist, journalist, and lecturer; *d.* of Robert Craigie Hamilton and Charlotte Lewis, *d.* of Archbishop of Ontario; *m.* Lt.-Col. George Henry Bell (*d.* 1916), 27th Punjabis; no *c.* *Educ.:* St. Winifreds, Eastbourne. Spent about thirteen years in India and made a special study of the problems and outlook of the women of the martial classes; selected to go to India as a member of the Church's Mission of Help; is the only woman to have lectured at the Staff College, Quetta; Subject: The Problems of the Women of the Martial Classes in India; gave an address in the India Office, 1919; wrote the inscription on the All India Memorial to King Edward VII. at Delhi; a delegate (India) to the Imperial Press Conference, 1930; Kaiser-i-Hind Gold Medal, 1941. *Publications:* a contributor to the World Call to the Church (India and Ceylon chapter), and to leading journals and reviews. *Novels:* Sahiblog; In the World of Bewilderment; Second Nature; A Servant when he Reigneth; The Mortimers; In the Long Run; Those Young Married People; Jean, A Halo and Some Circles; Safe Conduct; The Foreigner (translated into Dutch); Hot Water; Comrades-in-Arms (a text-book for Indian Schools); The Hamwood Papers of the Ladies of Llangollen and Caroline Hamilton. *Address:* Hampton Court Palace. [*Died* 11 *Feb.* 1959.

BELL, Lt.-Col. Frederick William, V.C. 1900; late West Australian Mounted Infantry and 4th Reserve Regiment of Cavalry; *m.* Mabel MacKenzie Skinner (*d.* 1944); *m.* 1945, Mrs. Brenda Margaret Cracklow. Served South Africa, Somaliland, European War; Commandant, Embarkation Camps, Plymouth; Administrative Officer, British Somaliland, Northern Nigeria and Kenya Colony; retired from Colonial Service, 1925. *Address:* 89 Stoke Lane, Westbury-on-Trym, Bristol. [*Died* 28 *April* 1954.

BELL, Rev. Canon George Fancourt, M.A.; Hon. Canon of Rochester, 1928; *b.* 21 May 1874; *o. s.* of Adolphus William George Bell and Louise Clarisse, 4th *d.* of G. W. M. Reynolds; *m.* 1900, Annie Muriel (*d.* 1950), 3rd *d.* of Thomas Backhouse of Holgate House, York; two *s.* one *d.* *Educ.:* privately; University College, Durham (organ exhibitioner); Ely Theological College. Deacon, 1898; Priest, 1899; Assistant Curate, Penzance, St. John's, Upper Norwood, and Folkestone; Vicar of Riverhead, 1905-46; Rural Dean of Sevenoaks, 1924-42; Surrogate, 1929. *Address:* c/o St. J. Fancourt Bell, Esq., Byeways, Haywards Heath, Sussex. [*Died* 17 *March* 1952.

BELL, Rt. Rev. George Kennedy Allen, D.D.; *b.* Hayling Island, 4 Feb. 1883; *e. s.* of late Rev. Canon J. Allen Bell; *m.* 1918, Henrietta Millicent Grace, *e. d.* of late Rev. Canon R. J. Livingstone and Hon. Mrs. Livingstone; no *c.* *Educ.:* Westminster; Christ Church, Oxford (scholar); Wells Theological College; 1st Class in Classical Moderations, 1903; Newdigate Prize, 1904; 2nd Class in Lit. Hum., 1905; D.D. (Oxon. by decree), 1924; Hon. D.D. (Glasgow), 1939. Hon. D.Th. (Basle), 1939; Hon. LL.D. (Southern California), 1945; Hon. D.Theol. (Göttingen and Münster), 1949; Hon. D.D. (Wycliffe Coll., Toronto Univ.), 1950; Hon. S.T.D., Northwestern Univ., U.S.A., 1954; Hon. Student, Christchurch, Oxford, 1952. Ordained, 1907; Curate at Leeds, 1907-10; lecturer (Classics and English) and tutor, Christ Church, Oxford, 1910-14; student of Christ Church, 1911-14; examining chaplain to the Bishop of Wakefield, 1910-16; resident chaplain to the Archbishop of Canterbury, 1914-24; Dean of Canterbury, 1924-29; Bishop of Chichester, 1929-58. Assistant Secretary Lambeth Conference, 1920; Episcopal Secretary, Lambeth Conference, 1930; Member of Archbishops' Committee on Social and Industrial Problems, 1917; Member of Royal Institute of International Affairs, 1923; Chairman of the Governing Body, King's School, Canterbury, 1924-29; Chairman of the Governors, Simon Langton Schools, Canterbury, 1924-29; Chairman of the Advisory Committee for Juvenile Employment, Canterbury, 1924-29; Chairman of Council of Bishop Otter Training College for Teachers, Chichester, 1929-58; Examining Chaplain to Archbishop of Canterbury, 1924-29; President Religious Drama Society of Great Britain, 1929-; Chm. of Universal Christian Council for Life and Work, 1934-36; Chm. of Church of England Committee for Non-Aryan Christians, 1937; Vice-Chairman Christian Council for Refugees, 1938; Select Preacher, Cambridge, 1923, 1933, 1941, 1946 and 1951; Olaus Petri Lecturer, Upsala, 1925 and 1946; Select Preacher, Oxford, 1926 and 1946; Busby Trustee, 1932; Chairman Famine Relief Committee, 1942-45; Hon. Life Associate of Central Institute of Art and Design, 1941; President of Sussex Churches Art Council, 1942; Member of Council of Royal Academy of Dramatic Art, 1936; Chm. Church of England Council on Foreign Relations, 1945; Chm., Central Cttee. of World Council of Churches, 1948-1954; Hon. Pres. World Council of Churches, 1954. King Haakon VII Liberty Cross, 1947. Hon. Freeman, City of Chichester, 1954. Hon. Mem. N.U.P.E., 1952. *Publications:* Editor—Golden Anthologies, 1906, etc.; The War and the Kingdom of God, 1915; The Meaning of the Creed, 1917; Documents bearing on the Problem of Christian Unity and Fellowship, 1916 - 20, 1920; Documents on Christian Unity, 1920-24, 1924; Second Series, 1924-30, 1930; Third Series, 1930-48, 1948; Fourth Series, 1948-58, 1958; The Stockholm Conference on Life and Work, 1925, 1926; The Modern Parson, 1928; A Brief Sketch of the Church of England, 1929 (trans. into French, German, and Greek); Joint Editor of Mysterium Christi, 1931; Randall Davidson, Archbishop of Canterbury, 1935; Common Order in Christ's Church, 1937; Christianity and World Order, 1940; The English Church, 1942; The Church and Humanity, 1946; Christian Unity, The Anglican Position, 1948; Editor, With God in the Darkness, by Bishop Berggrav (Oslo), 1943; The Word and the Sacraments, 1952; The Kingship of Christ, 1954. *Recreation:* walking. *Address:* 1 Starr's House, The Precincts, Canterbury. *Club:* Athenæum. [*Died* 3 *Oct.* 1958.

BELL, Lt.-Col. Sir Harold W.; *see* Wilberforce-Bell.

BELL, Henry McGrady, C.V.O. 1934; C.B.E. 1920; Commander First Class White Rose of Finland; Chairman of Bell and Sime, Ltd., Dundee; Hon. Consul-General for Finland, 1931-39, and since 1948; *b.* Dundee, 25 Oct. 1880; *s.* of James Bell, Dundee; *m.* Wilhelmine Basilike, *d.* of Professor Schwappach; two *d.* *Educ.:* Dundee High School; Morrison's Academy, Crieff; abroad. Conducted negotiations with Russian Government in Petrograd for British Embassy in connection with requisitioned Timber Claims, 1916-17; purchased Sulphur Pyrites in Norway for Ministry of Munitions, 1918; acting Consul at Helsingfors, 1918; acting Chargé-d'affaires in Finland, 1919; Delegate to Economic Council, League of Nations, Geneva, on behalf of Timber Trades Federation of the United Kingdom, 1932; negotiated with Roumanian Government (Forestry Dept.) with a view to Barter arrangement, 1939; Representative of the Finland Fund in Finland, 1940-41. *Publication:* Land of Lakes—Memories Keep Me Company, 1950. *Recreations:* golf, ski-ing. *Address:* 6 Bridge Road, Cranleigh, Surrey. *T.:* Cranleigh 312. *Clubs:* Caledonian, Royal Automobile. [*Died* 15 *March* 1958.

BELL, Sir Hesketh, G.C.M.G., *cr.* 1925 (K.C.M.G., *cr.* 1908; C.M.G. 1903); *b.* Dec. 1864. Entered Colonial Civil Service, 1883; held various junior appointments in West Indies till 1889, when transferred to Gold Coast; Chief Assistant Treasurer, 1891; Receiver-General of the Bahamas, 1894; Member of Executive Council; represented Harbour Island in House of Assembly, 1895-1896; Administrator of Dominica, West Indies, 1899-1905; Commissioner of Uganda, 1905, and in 1907 was made first Governor of the Protectorate; for special services rendered in Uganda was created a K.C.M.G.; and in 1909 was appointed Governor and Commander-in-Chief of Northern Nigeria; Governor of Leeward Islands, 1912-15; Governor of Mauritius, 1915-24; retired, 1925. *Publications:* Obeah; A Witch's Legacy; Love in Black; Foreign Systems of Colonial Administration in the Far East, 1928; Glimpses of a Governor's Life, 1946; Witches and Fishes, 1948. *Clubs:* Athenæum, Bath, West Indian. [*Died* 1 *Aug.* 1952.

BELL, Sir Humphrey; *see* Bell, Sir B. H.

BELL, James, J.P.; *s.* of John Bell, a miner; *b.* Darlington, 1872; *m.* 1895, Elizabeth Hannah, *d.* of Cowling Heaton. M.P. (Lab.) Ormskirk Div. of Lancs, Dec. 1918-22. *Address:* 597 Altrincham Road, Northenden, Manchester. [*Died* 28 *Dec.* 1955.

BELL, John, M.A.; Headmaster, King Edward VII School, Lytham, 1942-57, retd.; *b.* 4 Nov. 1890; *e. s.* of late Rev. Preb. H. H. Bell; *m.* 1931, Mary Kathleen Pickles; two *d.* *Educ.:* Marlborough (Scholar); Balliol College, Oxford (Scholar and Jenkyns Exhibitioner). Craven University Scholar, 1910; 1st class in classical moderations, 1911; *Proxime Accessit*, Ireland and Hertford Scholarships, 1911; 1st class in Lit. Hum., 1913; John Locke University Scholar, 1913; Fellow (1914-27), Tutor and Dean, Queen's College, Oxford, Supernumerary Fell., 1954; High Master of St. Paul's School, 1927-38; Headmaster of Cheltenham College, 1938-40; Assistant Master at Eton College, 1940-42; served in 2/5 Somerset L.I. (T.F.) in Burma and India, 1914-19; Capt. and Adjt., 1918; Classical Moderator, 1923-24; President Headmasters' Association, 1946. *Publications:* contributions to The Mind of Rome, 1926; and to Great Tudors, 1935. *Recreations:* walking, travel. *Address:* 37 Chalfont Road, Oxford. *Club:* Royal Empire Society. [*Died* 7 *May* 1958

BELL, Rev. Kenneth Norman, M.A., M.C.; Vicar of Binley Coventry, 1940-51; *b.* 3 Sept. 1884; *e. s.* of late A. G. Bell (*d.* 1916), landscape painter, and Nancy Bell (*d.* 1933), authoress; *m.* 1909, Esther *d.* of Lt.-Col. Sydney Bell; three *s.* five *d.* *Educ.:* Berkhamsted School; Balliol College, Oxford (Brackenbury Scholar). Fellow of All Souls College, Oxford, 1907-14; Lecturer in History, Toronto University, 1909-11; Director of G. Bell & Sons, publishers, 1912-14; Commissioned 1/1st London R.G.A. (T.), 3 Aug. 1914; commanded 130 Heavy Battery, 329 Siege Battery, and 99 Siege Battery (M.C.); Fellow and Tutor, Balliol College, 1919-41; Jowett Fellow, 1931-41; Senior Proctor, 1926-1927; Beit Lecturer in Colonial History, 1924-1927; Chairman of Modern History Examiners, 1933; Supervisor, L.C.C. Rest Centre Service, 1942-43; ordained 1946. *Publications:* (with W. P. Morrell) Select Documents in British Colonial History, 1830-60, 1928. *Address:* The Rectory, Boddington, Northants. [*Died* 13 *Oct.* 1951.

BELL, Oliver, M.A.; J.P.; Secretary-General, Magistrates Association, since 1949; *b.* 9 Jan. 1898; *s.* of late E. A. and Emmeline Bell; *m.* 1923, Constance K., *d.* of William Phipps, Oxford; no *c.* *Educ.:* Marlborough; University Coll., Oxford. R.F.C. 1916-19 (despatches); on staff of League of Nations Union, 1923-34; Press Officer Conservative Central Office, 1934-36; Director British Film Institute, 1936-49; Vice-Chm. of Films Cttee., British Council, 1940-46; Member of Films Sub-Cttee., International Intellectual Co-operation Organisation of League of Nations, 1937-45; Secy. of the Audio-Visual Aids Commission of the Conference of Inter-allied Ministers of Education, 1943-45; Member of Advisory Council on Children's Entertainment Films, 1943-49; Vice-chairman S.P.C.K. and of Films Committee; Chairman Pilgrim Players; Member of Council Religious Drama Society. *Address:* Tavistock House South, W.C.1; 2A Aylward Road, Merton, S.W.20. *T.:* Euston 2302, Liberty 3042. *Clubs:* Oxford and Cambridge, R.A.F. [*Died* 8 *Feb.* 1952.

BELL, Sir Peter; *see* Bell, Sir E. P. S.

BELL, Sir Robert Duncan, K.C.S.I., *cr.* 1935 (C.S.I. 1932); C.I.E. 1919; *b.* Edinburgh, 18 May 1878; *s.* of late William Bell; *m.* 1st, 1901, Jessie Spence (*d.* 1934); two *s.* two *d.*; 2nd, 1940, Marjorie, *d.* of Lt.-Col. A. H. Dobbs, I.A., of Co. Antrim, and *widow* of Major H. G. Dewey, M.C., R.A. *Educ.:* George Heriot's School, Edinburgh; Edinburgh University; Trinity College, Cambridge. Joined Indian Civil Service, 1902; on special duty in connection with destruction of locusts, 1904; prepared revised edition of the Statistical Atlas of the Bombay Presidency; Assistant Collector and Magistrate, 1905-9; Under-Secretary to the Government of Bombay, Revenue and Financial Departments, 1909-12; Assistant Settlement Officer, Poona, 1913-16; Acting Settlement Commissioner and Director of Land Records 1916; Secretary, Indian Industrial Commission, 1916-18; served under Indian Munitions Board as Controller, Industrial Intelligence, and Controller, Oils and Paints, 1917-19; Director of Industries, Bombay, 1919-24; Controller of Munitions, Bombay, 1919-21; Member Imperial Legislative Assembly, 1924; Secretary to Government Development Department and Commissioner, Bombay Suburban Division, 1924-30; Chief Secretary to Government, 1930-1932; Member of Executive Council of Governor of Bombay, 1933-37; acting Governor of Bombay, 1936; retired 1937; Commissioner to enquire into Financial Position and Development of Nyasaland, 1937-38. *Address:* The Platt, Crondall, nr. Farnham, Surrey. *T.:* Crondall 288. *Club:* East India and Sports. [*Died* 24 *May* 1953.

BELL, Sir Thomas, K.B.E., *cr.* 1917; late Director John Brown & Co., Ltd.; *b.* Sirsawa, British India, 1865; *e. s.* of late Imrie Bell, M.Inst.C.E.; *m.* 1900, Helen (*d.* 1926), *d.* of Malcolm Macdonald; one *d.* *Educ.:* King's College School; Royal Naval Engineering College, Devonport. Entered in 1886 the engineering and shipbuilding works of James and George Thomson, Clydebank, which were subsequently purchased by John Brown & Co., Ltd., of Sheffield and Clydebank; Resident Director in charge, 1909-35; Deputy Controller of Dockyards and Shipbuilding at Admiralty, May 1917-Dec. 1918; A Vice-President of Institution of Naval Architects; M.I.C.E. and member of other technical Societies. *Recreation:* gardening. *Address:* Furzecroft, Helensburgh, Dumbartonshire. *T.:* Helensburgh 78. [*Died* 9 *Jan.* 1952.

BELL, Rev. Canon William Godfrey, M.A.; Rector of Bexhill and Rural Dean of Battle and Bexhill since 1941; *b.* 2 Nov. 1880; *s.* of William Middlewick Bell and Frances Fifield; *m.* 1907, Madeline, *d.* of Charles Houghton Robinson; one *s.* two *d.* *Educ.:* private schools; Peterhouse, Cambridge. Deacon, 1904; Priest, 1905; Curate All Saints', Stranton, West Hartlepool, 1904-6; Stretham with Thetford, 1906-7; St. Leonard's, Streatham, 1907-14; Chaplain T.F. attached 2nd City of London Regt. (Royal Fusiliers), 1908-18; Vicar, Christ Church, Streatham, 1914-19; Clerical Secretary Southwark Diocese, 1919-21; First Editor of Southwark Diocesan Magazine and Gazette, 1921-23; Secretary of Chichester Diocesan Fund and Board of Finance (Incorporated), 1923-41; Secretary of Chichester Diocesan Conference and Diocesan Synod since 1923; Secretary Theological College, Ltd., 1923-1946; Proctor in Convocation, 1929-45; Assistant Grand Chaplain of England in Freemasonry 1933; Canon and Prebendary of Woodhorn in Chichester Cathedral, 1933; Member of the Home Office Probation Advisory Committee 1937-43; Chaplain, Roedean School, Brighton 1939-40; Member of Central Board of Finance of Church of England, 1940-44; O.C.F. 1943-1946. *Publications:* History of St. Leonard' Church, Streatham, 1916; Editor of Chichester Diocesan Directory, 1923-41. *Recreations* Freemasonry, motoring. *Address:* Church Farm House, Bexhill-on-Sea, Sussex. [*Died* 14 *Jan.* 1953.

BELLAIRS, Commander Carlyon R.N.; *b.* 15 March 1871; *s.* of late Lieut.-General Sir William Bellairs, K.C.M.G., C.B.; *m.* 1911 Charlotte (*d.* 1939), *d.* of late Col. H. L. Pierson of Laurence, Long Island, U.S.A. *Educ.:* H.M.S. Britannia and R.N. College. Entered R.N 1884; Midshipman, 1886; Lieut. 1891 (specially promoted, having obtained 1st class certificates at all examinations; inventor of certain adopted naval devices; retired on failure of eye sight, 1902; M.P. (L.) King's Lynn, 1906-9, and (U.) 1909-10; Maidstone, 1915-18, Maidstone div., 1918-31; Member for Lewisham on L.C.C. 1913-15; sometime Lecturer for War Course o Senior Officers at R.N. College; presented with Silver Medal of Society of Arts; late President of the Poetry Society; objects to political honours and declined a baronetcy in 1927. In 1954 founded and completely endowed, in memory of his wife, the Biological Institute of McGill Univ. *Publications:* The Battle of Jutland: The Sowing and the Reaping 1919; (poems) The Ghosts of Parliament Poems, 1929; contrib. to various publications. *Address:* Bellairs Research Institute St. James, Barbados, B.W.I. *T.A.:* Bellairs Barbados. *T.:* Barbados 0165. [*Died* 22 *Aug.* 1955

BELLAIRS, Rear-Admiral Roger Mowbray, C.B. 1930; C.M.G. 1919; C.B.E. 1957; Head of Historical Section, Admiralty 1948-56; *b.* 9 Aug. 1884; *s.* of late Lieut.-General Sir William Bellairs, K.C.M.G., C.B.; *m.* 1909, Veronica Beatrice (*d.* 1957), *d.* of late Colonel A. H. Wavell, Welch Regiment; two *d.* *Educ.:* H.M.S. Britannia. Entered Royal Navy, 1900; five first-class certificates and promotion marks, R.N. College, Greenwich, 1904; Lieutenant, 1904; Commander, 1916; Captain, 1920; Rear-Adm., 1932; passed Staff Course, 1913; Torpedo Officer on Staff of C.-in-C. Grand Fleet, 1914-16; War Staff Officer to C.-in-C. Grand Fleet, 1916-19 (despatches); Naval Assistant 1st Sea Lord, Admiralty, 1919-25; Chief of Staff and Flag Capt. H.M.S. Effingham, East Indies Station, 1925-27; Director of Plans Division, Admiralty, 1928-30; commanded H.M.S. Rodney, 1930-32; retired list, 1932; Representative on League of Nations Permanent Advisory Commission, 1932-39; Admiralty, 1939-46. Chevalier of Legion of Honour, 1916. *Address:* Wyvenhoe, Farnham Royal, Bucks. *T.:* Farnham Common 127. *Club:* United Service. [*Died* 26 *April* 1959.

BELLARS, Rear-Admiral Edward Gerald Hyslop, C.B. 1944; *b.* 10 July 1894; *s.* of Rev. William and Charlotte

Agatha Bellars; *m.* 1st, Ethel Marion Hollins (marriage dissolved, 1945); two *s.* one *d.*; 2nd, Beatrice Maude Watson (*d.* 1949). *Educ.:* King's School, Canterbury; R.N.C., Osborne and Dartmouth. Cadet, 1907; Midshipman, 1912; Lieut. 1916; European War H.M.S. Britannia, 1914, Albemarle, 1915, Barham, 1915-19 (Jutland, 1916); qualified in Gunnery, 1919-1921; Gunnery Officer, H.M.S. Repulse, 1922-23; Experimental, Whale Is., 1923-1926; Gunnery Officer H.M.S. Nelson (1st commission), 1926-28; Commander 1928; Staff College, Greenwich, 1929; Admiralty (D.N.O.), 1930-32; H.M.S. Nelson (Fleet Gunnery Officer), 1932-33; Executive Officer H.M.S. Cornwall, 1933-35; Capt. 1935; Tactical Division, Admiralty, 1936-38; commanded H.M.S. Galatea, 1938-40; Plans Division, Admiralty, 1940-42; commanded H.M.S. Norfolk, 1942-43; Chief of Staff, Portsmouth, 1944-45; Assistant Chief of Naval Staff (Foreign), 1945; invalided 1946; Rear-Adm. (Retd.) 1946. *Recreations:* drawing, painting, heraldry. *Address:* c/o National Provincial Bank Ltd., 69 Baker Street, W.1. [*Died* 4 *Oct.* 1955.

BELLINGHAM, Brig.-Gen. Sir Edward (Henry Charles Patrick), 5th Bt. (2nd creation); *cr.* 1796; C.M.G. 1918; D.S.O. 1916; late Major (Bt. Lieut.-Colonel) The Royal Scots; Lieutenant of Co. Louth; *b.* 26 Jan. 1879; *e. s.* of Sir Henry Bellingham, 4th Bt., and Lady Constance Julia Eleanor Georgiana Noel (*d.* 1891), *d.* of 2nd Earl of Gainsborough; *S.* father, 1921; *m.* 1904, Charlotte Elizabeth, *d.* of Alfred Payne and *widow* of Frederick Gough; one *d.* *Educ.:* The Oratory School; R.M.C., Sandhurst. Late Clerk and British Vice-Consul British Legation, Guatemala; served South African War, 1899-1902 (King's medal and Queen's medal, 3 clasps); European War, 1914-18 (wounded, despatches thrice, D.S.O., C.M.G., Bt. Lt.-Col.); War of 1939-45; Squadron Ldr., R.A.F. Regt., 1939-1944; Commission of Control in Germany, 1945-47. Member of the Senate of the Irish Free State, 1925-36; breeder of pedigree pigs and Aberdeen-Angus cattle. *Heir:* *n.* Roger Carroll Patrick Stephen, *b.* 28 April 1911. *Address:* Castle Bellingham, Co. Louth. *T.A.:* Castlebellingham. *Club:* Kildare Street (Dublin). [*Died* 19 *May* 1956.

BELLOC, (Joseph) Hilaire (Pierre); *b.* St. Cloud, France, 27 July 1870; *s.* of Louis Swanton Belloc and Bessie Rayner Parkes; *m.* 1896, Elodie Agnes Hogan (*d.* 1914), of Napa, California; one *s.* two *d.* (and *e. s.* killed in action, 1918, *y. s.* died O.A.S., 1941). *Educ.:* The Oratory School, Edgbaston; Balliol College, Oxford; Brackenbury History Scholar, and 1st Class in Honour History Schools, 1895. On leaving school served as a driver in the 8th Regiment of French Artillery at Toul Meurthe-et-Moselle; matriculated at Balliol, January 1893; took final schools, June 1895. Became a naturalised British subject in 1902. M.P. (L.) S. Salford 1906-10; Knight Commander with Star Order of St. Gregory the Great, 1934. *Publications:* Verses and Sonnets, 1895; The Bad Child's Book of Beasts, 1896; More Beasts for Worse Children, 1897; The Modern Traveller, 1898; The Moral Alphabet; Danton, 1899; Lambkins Remains, 1900; Paris, 1900; Robespierre, 1901; Path to Rome, 1902; Caliban's Guide to Letters, 1903; Avril, 1904; Mr. Burden, 1904; The Old Road, 1905; Esto Perpetua, 1906; Hills and the Sea, 1906; The Historic Thames, 1907; Cautionary Tales, 1907; On Nothing, 1908; Mr. Clutterbuck's Election, 1908; The Pyrenees, 1909; On Everything, 1909; A Change in the Cabinet, 1909; Marie Antoinette 1910; On Anything, 1910; Verses, 1910; The Girondin, 1911; More Peers (with Lord Basil Blackwood), 1911; The Party System (with Mr. C. Chesterton), 1911; On Something, First and Last, Blenheim, Malplaquet, 1911; Waterloo, The Four Men, The Green Overcoat, 1912; The Servile State, 1912; The River of London, This and That, Crecy, The Stane Street, Tourcoing, 1913; The Book of the Bayeux Tapestry, 1913; A Continuation of Lingard's History to the death of Edward VII., 1914; General Sketch of the European War, 1st Phase, 1915; The Last Days of the French Monarchy, 1916; General Sketch of the European War, 2nd Phase (The Battle of the Marne), 1916; The Free Press, 1917; Europe and the Faith, 1920; The House of Commons and Monarchy, 1920; The Jews, 1922, 2nd ed. 1937; The Mercy of Allah, 1922; On, 1923; The Contrast, 1923; Verses and Sonnets, 1924; History of England, Vols. I. and II.; The Cruise of the Nona, 1925; Mr. Petre, 1925; Miniatures of French History, 1925; The Emerald of Catharine the Great, 1926: a companion to Mr. Wells' History of the World, 1926; History of England, Vol. III., James II.; Many Cities, 1928; But Soft, We are Observed, 1928; A Conversation with an Angel, 1928; Belinda, 1928; Survivals and New Arrivals, 1929; Joan of Arc, 1929; The Missing Masterpiece, 1929; Richelieu, 1930; Wolsey, 1930; The Man who made Gold, 1930; New Cautionary Tales, 1930; A Conversation with a Cat, 1931; Essays of a Catholic Layman in England, 1931; History of England, Vol. IV., 1525-1612, 1931; Cranmer 1931; Six British Battles, 1931; The Postmaster-General, 1932; Napoleon, 1932; The Tactics and Strategy of the Great Duke of Marlborough, 1933; William the Conqueror, 1933; Charles I, 1933; Cromwell, 1934; A Shorter History of England, 1934; Milton, 1935; The Battle-Ground, 1936; The County of Sussex, 1936; Characters of the Reformation, 1936; The Hedge and the Horse, 1936; An Essay on the Nature of Contemporary England, 1937; The Crusade, 1937; The Crisis of Our Civilisation, 1937; The Question and the Answer, 1938; Monarchy: A Study of Louis XIV, 1938; Return to the Baltic, 1938; The Great Heresies, 1938; The Last Rally, 1940; On the Place of Gilbert Chesterton in English Letters, 1940; The Silence of the Sea and Other Stories, 1941; Places, 1942; Selected Essays, 1948; On Sailing the Sea, 1951. *Relevant publication:* (posthumous) The Life of Hilaire Belloc, by Robert Speaight, 1957. *Address:* King's Land, Shipley, Horsham. *Club:* Reform. [*Died* 16 *July* 1953.

BELMORE, 7th Earl of (*cr.* 1797), **Galbraith Armar Lowry-Corry;** Baron Belmore, 1781; Viscount Belmore, 1789; Major, late Royal Inniskilling Fusiliers; D.L. County Fermanagh; *b.* 14 April 1913; *s.* of Major Adrian Lowry-Corry (*d.* 1921) and Geraldine (*d.* 1944), *d.* of late William Thomas Hartcup; *S.* cousin 1949; *m.* 1939, Gloria Anthea, *d.* of late Herbert Bryant Harker, Melbourne; one *s.* two *d.* *Educ.:* Lancing College; R.M.C., Sandhurst. 2nd Lt. Royal Inniskilling Fusiliers, 1933; served War of 1939-45, Burma, 1942-1943 (wounded); N.W. Europe, 1945; Major, 1942. *Heir:* *s.* Viscount Corry. *Address:* Castlecoole, Enniskillen, Northern Ireland. *Club:* Army and Navy. [*Died* 20 *July* 1960.

BELPER, 3rd Baron (*cr.* 1856) **Algernon (Henry) Strutt;** late 2nd Life Guards; *b.* 6 May 1883; *s.* of 2nd Baron Belper, and Lady Margaret Coke, *d.* of 2nd Earl of Leicester; *S.* father, 1914; *m.* 1st, 1911, Hon. Eva (Isabel Mary) Bruce (who obtained a divorce, 1922; she *m.* 2nd, 1924, 6th Earl of Rosebery), 2nd *d.* of 2nd Baron Aberdare; one *s.* one *d.*; 2nd, 1923, Angela Mariota, *y. d.* of late Hon. D. Tollemache; two *s.* *Educ.:* Harrow; Trinity College, Cambridge. Entered army, 1908; Captain 1910. Owns over 5000 acres. *Heir:* *s.* Maj. Hon. Alexander Ronald George Strutt [late Coldstream Guards; *b.* 23 April 1912; *m.* 1940, Zara, *y. d.* of late Sir Harry Mainwaring]. *Address:* Kingston Hall, Derby. [*Died* 20 *March* 1956.

BELSTEAD, 1st Baron, *cr.* 1938, of Ipswich; **Lt.-Col. Francis John Childs Ganzoni;** 1st Bt., *cr.* 1929; Kt., *cr.* 1921; M.A., F.R.G.S.; a Chairman Private Bills Cttees., House of Lords, since 1940; *b.* London, 19 Jan. 1882; *o. s.* of Julius Charles Ganzoni (*d.* 1949) and late Mary Frances, *o. d.* of Major James Childs; *m.* 1930, Gwendolen Gertrude, *er. d.* of late Arthur Turner, Ipswich; one *s.* one *d.* *Educ.:* Tonbridge School; Christ Church, Oxford, M.A. Called to Bar, 1906; joined South-Eastern Circuit; also practised in Admiralty Court, at the Sussex Sessions and Central Criminal Court; served with British Expeditionary Force, 4th Bn. Suffolk Regiment, France 1914-18; Local Army Welfare Officer; Ipswich, 1939-42; County A.W.O., Suffolk, rank of Lt.-Col., 1942-49; has travelled extensively the British dominions—West Indies, South Africa, New Zealand, Australia, Egypt; also Central and South America and most of Europe; Parliamentary Private Sec. to P.M.G., 1924-29; M.P. (U.) Ipswich, 1914-23, and 1924-37; Temporary Chairman of Committees of House of Commons, 1932-35; Chairman of Private Bills Committees, 1923-37; Chairman Kitchen Committee, 1932-37; member of the Lawn Tennis Council, 1910-23; D.L. Suffolk, 1937; J.P. Suffolk, 1943. *Publications:* various articles and verses. *Recreations:* lawn tennis, cricket, golf, etc. *Heir:* *s.* Hon. John Julian Ganzoni, *b.* 30 Sept. 1932. *Address:* Stoke Park, Ipswich. *T.:* Ipswich 52860. *Clubs:* Carlton, M.C.C., All England Lawn Tennis; County (Ipswich).

[*Died* 15 *Aug.* 1958.

BENAVENTE, Jacinto; Spanish dramatist and poet; Nobel Prize for Literature, 1922; *b.* 1866. *Works:* El teatro fantastico; El nido ajeno, 1894; Gente conocida, 1896; La comida de las fieras, 1898; La gata de Angora, 1900; Lo cursè, 1901; La gobernadora, 1901; Noche del Sabado, 1903; El hombrecito, 1903; Rosas do Otono, 1905; Los intereses creados, 1907; El principe que todo lo aprendio en los libros, 1909; La Malquerida, 1913; The Fabricated Truth, 1933; El Pan Comido en la Mano, 1934, Ni Al Amor Ni Al Mar, 1935, etc. Some of his plays were produced, in translation, on the London stage, 1912-29. Three new plays produced on Madrid stage, 1951. Translated King Lear into Spanish. Grand Cross of Alfonso the Wise, 1944; Medal of Labour, 1950; El Marido de Bronze, 1953. *Publications:* De Sobremesa, etc.; vols. in Colección Austral. *Address:* Madrid. [*Died* 14 *July* 1954.

BENDA, Wladyslaw Theodor; illustrator, painter; *b.* Poznan, Poland, 15 Jan. 1873; *s.* of Jan. S. Benda, pianist and composer; *m.* 1920, Romola Campfield, New York; two *d.* *Educ.:* School of Technology, and Academy of Fine Arts, Cracow; Art Schools in Vienna, San Francisco, New York. Went to California, 1900, where he taught art; New York, 1902; naturalised, 1911; illustrates for most of the leading American periodical publications, Century Magazine, Scribner's, Collier's Weekly, Cosmopolitan Liberty, Harper's Bazaar, and others; also does mural painting; creator of Benda Masks used on the stage in Europe and America; Member of Society of Illustrators, Architectural League, Society of Mural Painters; Chevalier d'ordre Polonia Restituta. *Publication:* Article on Modern Masks in new edition of Encyclopædia Britannica. *Address:* 27 West 67th Street, New York City. *T.:* Susquehanna 7-3750. *Clubs:* Players, Coffee House, Dutch Treat (New York). [*Died* 30 *Nov.* 1948.

BENDALL, Col. Frederic William Duffield, C.M.G. 1918; M.A.; London Regiment; *b.* Manningtree, 6 July 1882; *s.* of late F. J. Bendall, Manningtree, Essex. *Educ.:* Ipswich School; Selwyn College, Cambridge (Senior Classical Scholar). Singh Prizeman; Honours (2nd class), Classical Tripos, 1904; C.U.A.F.C. 1901-2; admitted to Freedom of City of London, 1909; Commission T.F. (O.T.C.) 1910; promoted from Capt. to Lt.-Col., and appointed to Command a Batt. Lond. Regt. Sept. 1914; O.C. British Troops, Khartoum. 1915; War service in Malta, the Sudan, Gallipoli. France (wounded, despatches twice, C.M.G., promoted Colonel); H.M.I. Board of Education; Director of Army Education at War Office, 1940-42. *Recreation:* rock gardening. *Address:* Fir Cottage, Bighton, Alresford, Hants. *T.:* Alresford 2272.

[*Died* 13 *Dec.* 1953.

BENIANS, Ernest Alfred, M.A.; Hon. Litt.D., Trinity College, Dublin, 1939, Hon. Fellow, 1947; Master of St. John's College, Cambridge, since 1933; *b.* Oct. 1880; *s.* of late W. A. Benians of Goudhurst, Kent; *m.* 1918, Sylvia Mary, *d.* of J. Theodore Dodd, St. Giles', Oxford; one *s.* two *d.* *Educ.:* St. John's College, Cambridge. Lightfoot Scholarship, 1903; Allen Scholarship, 1905; Adam Smith Prize, 1906; "A. K." Travelling Fellowship, 1910; Local Adviser to Indian Students, University of Cambridge, 1913-19; Fellow, 1906, Lecturer, 1910, Tutor, 1918 and Senior Tutor, 1927, St. John's College; University Lecturer in History, 1926-34; Vice-Chancellor of the University, 1939-41. *Publications:* Contributions on Colonial History to the Cambridge Modern History; Assistant Editor of the Cambridge Modern History Atlas; Joint Editor of the Cambridge History of the British Empire; The United States, an historical sketch. *Address:* The Master's Lodge, St. John's College, Cambridge.

[*Died* 13 *Feb.* 1952.

BENJAMIN, Arthur; composer of musical works; *b.* Sydney, Australia, 18 Sept. 1893; *s.* of Abram and Amelia Benjamin. *Educ.:* Bowen House Preparatory School and Brisbane Grammar School, Brisbane, Queensland. Began career as pianist at age of 6, since when his travels as pianist, conductor and composer have been world-wide. Won scholarship at Royal College of Music, London, 1912. Served European War, 1914-18, Royal Fusiliers and R.A.F. Professor at Sydney Conservatorium of Music, 1919-21, and at Royal College of Music, 1925-53, except for an interval, 1938-45, when he conducted the C.B.R. Symphony Orchestra in Vancouver, Canada. Now spends all his time as composer only. *Publications:* opera, symphony, chamber music, vocal music, children's educational music. *Recreations:* theatre, cooking, bridge, sun-bathing, reading. *Address:* 15 Ranulf Road, Hampstead, N.W.2. *Club:* Savile. [*Died* 10 *April* 1960.

BENN, Sir Ernest John Pickstone, 2nd Bt., *cr.* 1914; C.B.E. 1918; Publisher; *b.* 25 June 1875; *e. s.* of late Sir John Williams Benn, 1st Bt., and Elizabeth, 4th *d.* of late John Pickstone of Silver Hill, Hyde, Cheshire; *S.* father, 1922; *m.* 1903, Gwendoline, *d.* of F. M. Andrews, of Edgbaston; two *s.* (3rd *s.* killed in action) two *d.* *Educ.:* City Central Foundation School, London. High Sheriff, County of London, 1932; Freeman of City of London; Chairman, Benn Brothers Ltd., 1922-41, and Ernest Benn, Ltd., 1924-45; Chm. United Kingdom Provident Institution, 1934-49; Pres. John Benn Boys' Hostels' Assoc. 1926-37; Vice-Chm. Building Societies Assoc.; Pres. National Advertising Benevolent Soc., 1928-29; Pres. Readers' Pension Corporation, 1933-34; Pres., Institute of Export, 1933; President Commercial Travellers' Schools, 1935; Advertising Association, 1936; President Society of Individualists, 1942; Mem. of Council King George's Fields Foundation. *Publications:* Founder and Editor, The Independent; Prosperity and Politics, 1924;

The Confessions of a Capitalist, 1925; If I were a Labour Leader, 1926; Letters of an Individualist, 1927; Trade, 1927; The Return to Laisser Faire, 1928; Producer *v.* Consumer, 1928; The Case of Benn *v.* Maxton, 1929; About Russia, 1930; Account Rendered, 1900-1930, 1930; Honest Doubt, 1931; This Soft Age, 1933; Modern Govern- 1936; Debt, 1938; The Murmurings of an Individualist, 1941; Benn's Protest, 1945; Happier Days, 1949; The State the Enemy, 1953; *pamphlets:* The Political Method, 1940; The Profit Motive, 1940; The B.B.C. Monopoly, 1941; The Educational Revolution, 1941; Hard Times Ahead, 1942; The Beveridge Plan, 1943; The "City's" Foundations, 1944; The Deathbed of the Nation, 1945; Mind Your Own Business, 1946; Can Britain Survive?, 1947; Governed to Death, 1948. *Recreation:* golf. *Heir:* *s.* John Andrews Benn. *Address:* Morven, Oxted, Surrey; Bouverie House, Fleet Street, E.C. *T.:* Central 3212. *Club:* Reform.
[*Died* 17 *Jan.* 1954.

BENN, Ion Bridges Hamilton; Lieut.-Colonel (Bt. Col.); *b.* 14 June 1887; *o. s.* of Captain Sir Ion Hamilton Benn, 1st Bt., C.B., D.S.O., T.D.; *m.* 1916, Theresa Dorothy, *d.* of Maj. F. H. Blacker, 4th Hussars, Johnstown, Co. Kildare; one *s.* one *d.* *Educ.:* Rugby; New College, Oxford. Gazetted to Duke of Cornwall's L.I., Jan. 1909; retired, 1920, with rank of Major. Served European War, 1914-18 (despatches); joined 4th Bn. Royal Norfolk Regt., 1920; Lieut.-Colonel, 1930; Brevet Colonel, 1934. Rejoined the Army as Major, D.C.L.I., and served War of 1939-45, 1940-41. J.P. for County of Norfolk, 1928. High Sheriff of Norfolk, 1949. *Address:* Broad Farm, Rollesby, Norfolk. *T.:* Martham 221.
[*Died* 4 *Aug.* 1956.

BENNET, Sir Edward, Kt., *cr.* 1939; *b.* 26 Oct. 1880; *s.* of Edward McClelland and Helen Mary Bennet; *m.* 1920, Margaret Thérèse, *d.* of Major Edwin William Allum; no *c.* *Educ.:* Campbell College, Belfast; Trinity College, Dublin; Inner Temple, London. Trinity College; Senior Moderator and Gold Medallist, LL.B. & LL.D. 1904; Barrister-at-Law, Inner Temple; Indian Civil Service, 1904; Served in United Provinces as asst. and joint magistrate, 1904-14; district and sessions judge, 1914-28; legal remembrancer to govt., 1924; Judge, High Court, Allahabad, 1929-40. *Publications:* Idylls of the East, 1911; Shots & Snapshots in British East Africa, 1914. *Recreations:* golf, shooting, farming in Kenya Colony. *Address:* Riverside, P.O. Rongai, Kenya Colony. *T.A.:* Bennet Rongai. *T.:* Rongai 9Y5. *Club:* Rift Valley Sports.
[*Died* 15 *May* 1958.

BENNETT OF EDGBASTON, 1st Baron, *cr.* 1953, of Sutton Coldfield; **Peter Frederick Blaker Bennett,** Kt., *cr.* 1941; O.B.E.; Hon. LL.D.; J.P.; Joint Managing Director, Joseph Lucas Industries, Ltd.; Past Pres.: Federation of British Industries, Society of Motor Manufacturers and Traders; Birmingham Chamber of Commerce; County Pres. Birmingham and District Assoc. of Boy Scouts; President of Birmingham Y.M.C.A.; *b.* 1880; *s.* of late F. C. Bennett; *m.* 1905; no *c.* *Educ.:* King Edward's School, Five Ways, Birmingham. Member of Prime Minister's Panel of Industrial Advisers, 1938-39; Dir.-Gen. of Tanks and Transport, Min. of Supply, 1939-40; M.P. (U.) Edgbaston Division of Birmingham, 1940-53; Dir.-Gen. of Emergency Services Organization, M.A.P., 1940-41; Chm. Automatic Gun Board, 1941-44. Parliamentary Sec., Min. of Labour, 1951-52. Formerly: Chairman of British Productivity Council (Pres. 1955-); Member of Anglo-American Productivity Council: Director of I.C.I. Ltd.; Director of Lloyds Bank, Ltd.; Member of Council of International Chamber of Commerce. Pres. Warwickshire County Cricket Club, 1956-. Hon. LL.D. Birmingham University, 1950. *Recreations:* walking, golf. *Address:* Ardencote, Luttrell Road, Four Oaks, Warwickshire. *T.:* Four Oaks 107. *Clubs:* Carlton, Royal Automobile; Union (Birmingham).
[*Died* 27 *Sept.* 1957 (*ext.*).

BENNETT, Lt.-Col. Sir C(harles) Wilfrid, 2nd Bt., *cr.* 1929; T.D.; London Metropolitan Police Court Magistrate since 1946; *b.* 15 March 1898; *s.* of Sir Albert James Bennett, 1st Bt.; *S.* father 1945; *m.* 1927, Agnes Marion, *d.* of late James Somervell, and adopted *d.* of late Edwin Sandys Dawes; one *s.* one *d.* *Educ.:* Charterhouse; R.M.C., Sandhurst; Trinity College, Oxford. Commissioned as Regular Officer 9th (Q.R.) Lancers, 1916; served European War, France and Germany, 1917-1919; retired to Special Reserve 9th Lancers, 1919; commissioned Nottinghamshire (Sherwood Rangers) Yeomanry, 1920; mobilised, 1939; served Palestine, Middle East, Persia and Iraq, 1939-43 (despatches); War Office, 1943-46; invalided out, 1946. Called to Bar, Inner Temple, 1924; practised Midland Circuit and London until War. *Recreations:* hunting, shooting, fishing. *Heir:* *s.* Ronald Wilfrid Murdoch, *b.* 25 March 1930. *Address:* 40 Cheyne Court, Flood Street, Chelsea, S.W. *T.:* Flaxman 5026. *Club:* Garrick.
[*Died* 25 *April* 1952.

BENNETT, F. H. D. C.; *see* Curtis-Bennett.

BENNETT, George Macdonald, C.B. 1948; F.R.S. 1947; M.A., Sc.D. (Cantab.), B.A., Ph.D. (Lond.), F.R.I.C.; Government Chemist since 1945; *b.* 25 Oct. 1892; 2nd *s.* of Rev. J. E. Bennett, of the Thomas Cooper Memorial Chapel, Lincoln; *m.* 1918, Doris, (*d.* 1958), *d.* of J. Laycock; no *c.* *Educ.:* Private School; Queen Mary College, London (Exhibitioner and Scholar); St. John's College, Cambridge (Exhibitioner and Scholar); Fellow of St. John's College, Cambridge, 1917-23; Fellow of Queen Mary College, London, 1939; Demonstrator in Chemistry, Guy's Hospital Medical School; Lecturer in Organic Chemistry University of Sheffield, 1924-31; Firth Professor of Chemistry, University of Sheffield, 1931-38; University Professor of Chemistry at King's College, London, 1938-45; Hon. Sec. Chemical Society, 1939-46. *Publications:* Papers in Journal of the Chemical Society and other scientific periodicals. *Address:* The Government Laboratory, Clement's Inn Passage, W.C.2
[*Died* 9 *Feb.* 1959.

BENNETT, Lt.-Col. Sir Wilfrid; *see* Bennett, Lt.-Col. Sir C. W.

BENSKIN, Col. Joseph, D.S.O. 1916; O.B.E. 1919; D.L. Sussex; J.P.; late R.E.; Hon. rank of Col., 1942; *b.* 1883; *e. surv. s.* of late Thomas Benskin, Watford; *m.* 1919, Gladys Sheffield, C.B.E., *d.* of late M. P. Grace, and *widow* of Major R. S. Hamilton-Grace. *Educ.:* Harrow. Served European War, 1914-16 (despatches, D.S.O., O.B.E.); retired pay, 1924; L.C.C., 1928-34; Mil. Mem. Board of N.A.A.F.I., 1940-42; E. Sussex County Council, 1934-46. *Address:* Knowle, Frant, Sussex; 40 Belgrave Square, S.W.1. *Clubs:* Army and Navy, Carlton.
[*Died* 14 *July* 1953.

BENSON, Air Cdre. Constantine Evelyn, C.B.E. 1946; D.S.O. 1917; Air Cdre., A.A.F.; Director of Robert Benson, Lonsdale and Co. Ltd., Aldermanbury House, E.C.2, Merchant Bankers; Dir. Lloyds Bank Ltd., etc.; *y.s.* of late R. H. Benson; *m.* 1921, Lady Morvyth Ward (*d.* 1959), 2nd *d.* of 2nd Earl of Dudley; one *d.* *Educ.:* Eton; Balliol Coll., Oxford. Late Gren. Guards (Capt.); served European War, 1914-18 (wounded, despatches, D.S.O.). *Address:* Chenies Place, Chenies, Bucks. *Club:* White's.
[*Died* 20 *Sept.* 1960.

BENSON, Sir Frank, Kt., *cr.* 1942; C.V.O. 1941; C.B.E. 1918; *b.* 1878; *s.* of late Rev. W. J. Benson; *m.* 1906, Stephana Rose, *d.* of late Rev. J. G. Pooley, J.P., Rural Dean; two *d.* *Educ.:* Haileybury. General Manager of the Canteen and Mess Co-operative Society, Limited, 1912; on the outbreak of War, 1914, undertook the organisation of Expeditionary Force Canteens and was General Manager thereof; later Deputy Controller on the War Office Staff, with the rank of Colonel; Director of the Navy-Army Canteen Board, with a seat on the Council, 1917; active service in France and Italy (despatches); General Manager Navy, Army, and Air Force Institutes, 1923-42; Board of Management, 1942. *Address:* Down Lodge, Wrotham, Kent. *T.:* Fairseat 73. *Club:* Knole Park (Sevenoaks).
[*Died* 30 *Oct.* 1952.

BENSON, Frank Weston, M.A. Tufts College, 1930; painter, etcher, and teacher; Hon. President, Society of American Etchers; *b.* Salem, Mass., U.S.A., 24 March 1862; *s.* of George W. Benson and Elizabeth F. Poole; *m.* 1888, Ellen Perry Peirson; one *s.* three *d.* *Educ.:* Boston Art Museum; Boulanger and Lefebre, Paris. Member of National Academy of Design, 1905 (Associate, 1897); Ten American Painters; National Institute of Art and Letters; Chicago Society of Etchers; Brooklyn Society of Etchers; Guild of Boston Artists (President); awarded many medals and prizes since 1889; Gold Medal of Honour, Pennsylvania Academy Fine Arts, 1926; Joseph Pennell Memorial Medal, Philadelphia, 1929; Gold Medal (for group of Water-colours) Sesquicentennial International Exposition at Philadelphia, 1926; Represented in the Art Institute of Chicago; Museum of Fine Arts, Boston; Metropolitan Museum of Art, New York; and other art museums and galleries. *Address:* 14 Chestnut Street, Salem, Mass., U.S.A. *Club:* Tavern (Boston).
[*Died* 14 *Nov.* 1951.

BENSON, Brig. Robert, D.S.O.; *b.* 1881; *m.* 1907, Gertrude, *d.* of W. Fell Smith, Deer Park, Honiton; one *s.* one *d.* *Educ.:* Eton. Served European War, 1914-17 (D.S.O., 1917, despatches, wounded); served in North Russia, 1918. Commander, Royal Artillery 51st (Highland) Division T.A., 1934-38; retired pay, 1938; re-employed until 1941. *Address:* Applecombe, Wild Oak Lane, Taunton. [*Died* 24 *Oct.* 1952.

BENSON, Colonel Wallace, C.B.E. 1935; D.S.O. 1917; B.A., M.B., B.Ch., B.A.O. Dub.; late R.A.M.C. Late House Surgeon, Birkenhead Hosp., and Civil Surg., Station Hosp., Curragh Camp; served N.W. Frontier, India, 1908 (medal with clasp); European War, 1914-1917 (D.S.O.); retired pay, 1935. O.C. Queen Alexandra Military Hospital, Millbank, 1929-1943. *Address:* Glyn, Mills & Co., Kirkland House, Whitehall, S.W. *Clubs:* Army and Navy; Oxford and Cambridge Musical.
[*Died* 28 *Dec.* 1951.

BENSON, Col. William George Sackville, C.B. 1918; late Army Pay Department; *b.* 1861; *s.* of W. R. Benson, B.C.S.; *m.* 1896, Maude Emmeleen, *er. d.* of Major-Gen. J. B. Dennis, late R.A. Served Sudan, 1884-85 (medal and clasp, bronze star); retired pay, 1919. *Address:* Larchfield, Kilkenny, Ireland.
[*Died* 8 *Nov.* 1954.

BENSON, William Noël, F.R.S. 1941; M.A., D.Sc., William Evans Professor of Geology, 1950, Emeritus Professor of Geology since 1951, University of Otago, Dunedin; *b.* London, 26 Dec. 1885; *s.* of William Benson, Shipping Manager; *m.* 1923, Gertrude Helen Rawson, M.A., Professor of Home Science, University of Otago, Dunedin; no *c.* *Educ.:* Friends' High School, Hobart, Tasmania; University of Sydney; Cambridge University. B.Sc. Sydney, 1907; Acting Lecturer Mineralogy, Adelaide University, 1908; Demonstrator in Geology, Sydney Univ., 1909-10; 1851 Science Research Scholar from Sydney University at Cambridge, 1911-13, and at various European Universities, 1913-14; B.A. (Research) Cambridge, 1913; Linnean Macleay Research Fellow, Sydney, 1914-15: D.Sc. Sydney, 1916; Hon. D.Sc. N.Z., 1951; M.A. Cantab., 1954; Actg. Lectr. in Geology, Sydney, 1916; Prof. of Geology and Mineralogy, the University of Otago, Dunedin, 1917-50. Lyell Fund, Geological Society of London, 1923; Hector Medallist, Royal Society of New Zealand, 1933; Carnegie Grant for Research in England, 1933-34; Lyell Medallist, Geological Soc. London, 1939; Hutton Medallist, Royal Society of N.Z., 1944; Clarke Medallist, Royal Soc. of N.S.W., 1945; Mueller Medallist, Australian and N.Z. Assoc. Advancement of Science, 1951; Fellow: Geol. Soc., London; Roy. Geographical Soc.; Roy. Soc., New Zealand; Austr. and N.Z. Assoc. Adv. Sci.; Hon. Member of the Mineralogical Soc.; Linnean Soc. of N.S.W., etc.; Correspondent, Geol. Soc., America: President: Geology Section, Australasain Assoc. Advancement of Science, 1921; Roy. Soc. of N.Z., 1945-47; Sixth Roy. Soc. of N.Z. Science Conf., 1947. *Publications:* many geological papers since 1907. *Address:* 54 Warden Street, Dunedin, N.E.1, N.Z. *T.A.:* University, Dunedin, N.Z. *Club:* University (Dunedin).
[*Died* 20 *Aug.* 1957.

BENSUSAN, Samuel Levy, J.P.; *b.* 29 Sept. 1872. *Educ.:* City of London School; Great Ealing School. Literary Adviser to Theosophical Publishing House, and Editor of the Theosophical Review, 1925-28. Editor of Jewish World, 1897-98; Special Correspondent in Morocco, Spain, Portugal, Italy, Germany, and Canada; sometime musical critic Illustrated London News, Sketch, and Vanity Fair; Editor of the Homes and Haunts Library and Twentieth Century Cities Library; Adviser to Publications Branch of Ministry of Agriculture, and to Ministry of Transport, 1919-21. *Publications:* Morocco, 1904; The Man in the Moon, 1906: A Countryside Chronicle, and Wild Life Stories, 1907; The Heart of the Wild, 1908; The Children's Bee Book, 1909; Home Life in Spain, 1910; Father William, 1912; The Makers of the Renaissance (with J. D. Symon); Coleridge (People's Books Library); May Magic, 1913; The Furriner, a three-act dialect comedy, 1914; Some German Spas: A Holiday Record, 1925; Village idylls, 1926; Latter-day Rural England, 1928; A Tale That is Told, 1928; Comment from the Countryside, 1928; April (Verse), 1928; On the Tramp in Wales, 1929; Dear Countrymen, 1931; A Child of Chance, 1932; Joan Winter, 1933; Maurice Dravidoff (sequel to Joan Winter), 1934; At the Sign of the Wheatsheaf, 1934; The Annals of Maychester, 1936; The Wise Woman, and Joshua (One Act Comedies); Marshland Echoes, 1937; Marshland Calling, 1938; Tales from the Saxon Shore and 4 One Act Plays, 1939; Back o' Beyond, and Fireside Papers, 1945-1946; Woodland Friends, 1947; These from God's Own County, 1947; Salt of the Marshes, 1948; Right Forward Folk, 1949; Quiet Evening, 1950; Late Harvest, 1950; A Marshland Omnibus, 1954; Marshland Voices, 1955. *Recreation:* travelling. *Address:* Godfrey's, Langham, Colchester. *T.:* Dedham 3183. [*Died* 11 *Dec.* 1958.

BENT, Colonel Charles Edward, C.M.G. 1918; D.S.O. 1917; Canadian Infantry, Ontario Regiment; *b.* Pugwash, Nova Scotia, 2 Jan. 1880; *m.* 1907, Lyda Catherwood Cutting; three *s.* Mil. trg., Roy. Sch. of Infty., Fredericton, N.B. Served European War, 1914-18 (despatches 6 times, D.S.O. and Bar, C.M.G.). *Address:* Lawrencetown, Annapolis Co., Nova Scotia. [*Died* 27 *Oct.* 1955.

BENTINCK, Lt.-Col. Lord Charles; *see* Cavendish-Bentinck.

BENTINCK, Rev. Sir Charles Henry, K.C.M.G., *cr.* 1937 (C.M.G. 1923); Chaplain of Christ Church, Brussels, and Hon. Chaplain to H.M.'s Embassy, Brussels, since 1946; is a Count of the Holy Roman Empire, Creation 1732 by the Emperor Charles VI.; Royal Licence granted by Queen Victoria in 1886 to bear the title in England; *b.* 23 April 1879; 2nd *s.* of late Lieut.-Colonel Count Hy. C. A. F. W. A. Bentinck and of late Countess Aldenburg Bentinck, formerly McKerrell; *m.* 1922, Lucy Victoria, *d.* of late Sir T. F. V. Buxton, Bt., and Lady Buxton, Warlies, Waltham Abbey. *Educ.:* Trinity College, Cambridge; Wycliffe Hall, Oxford. Entered the Diplomatic Service, 1904; was employed in the Foreign Office until 1905; Attaché to Berlin, 1905; 3rd Secretary, 1906; transferred to St. Petersburg, 1906; The Hague, 1908-14, where he acted as Secretary in charge of Commercial matters, and acted as Chargé d'affaires upon several occasions; 2nd Secretary, 1910; Tokio, 1914-19; 1st Secretary, 1917; employed at Foreign Office, 1919-20; transferred as Counsellor to Athens, 1920, acted as Chargé d'affaires for a considerable period; and was British Delegate on the International Financial Commission; Consul-General at Munich, 1924; British Minister and Consul-General in Ethiopia, 1925; British Minister to Peru and Ecuador, 1929-33; to Bulgaria, 1934-36; to Czechoslovakia, 1936-37; H.M. Ambassador, Santiago, 1937-40; retired from Diplomatic Service 1941; ordained, 1941; Vicar of West Farleigh, Kent, 1941-46; Officiating Chaplain to R.A.F. Delegation, 1946-49, and to H.M. Forces in Belgium, 1947-48. *Recreations:* formerly riding, swimming, music. *Address:* Christ Church Chaplaincy, 29 Rue Crespel, Brussels. *T.:* 11.71.83. *Clubs:* St. James', National. [*Died* 26 *March* 1955.

BENTINCK, Baron (Dutch title, *cr.* 1550) **Walter Guy,** C.M.G. 1912; C.B.E. 1919; D.S.O. 1902; late Lt.-Col. Rifle Brigade; *b.* 5 Nov. 1864; *s.* of late W. Bentinck (13th Baron), 15th Hussars; *m.* 1904, Anne Elizabeth (*d.* 1934), *d.* of late Colonel Burnett-Ramsay, Rifle Brigade, of Banchory; one *s.* [W. T. B. R. Bentinck, late Lt. 5/7 The Gordon Highlanders. *Educ.:* Eton; R.M.C., Sandhurst.] *Educ.:* Marlborough College; R.M.C., Sandhurst. Rifle Brigade, 1885; Captain, 1894; Major, 1902; Lieut.-Colonel, 1915; served South Africa, 1899-1902 (wounded, despatches, D.S.O., Queen's medal 6 clasps, King's medal 2 clasps); District Commissioner, Vereeniging, 1900-1; special service, S.A. Peace Conference, 1902; Resident Magistrate, District Wakkerstroom, Transvaal, 1901-7; Assistant Imperial Secretary to the High Commissioner, South Africa, 1907-11; Union of South Africa, King's medal, 1911; served European War, 1914-20, G.S.O. War Office (despatches); D.L., J.P. Kincardineshire. *Recreation:* travel. *Address:* Balmain, Banchory, Kincardineshire. *T.:* Banchory 101. [*Died* 7 *July* 1957.

BENTLEY, Edmund Clerihew; Writer; *b.* 10 July 1875; *e. s.* of late J. E. Bentley and M. R. Clerihew; *m.* 1902, Violet (*d.* 1949), *d.* of Gen. N.E. Boileau, Bengal Staff Corps; two *s.* *Educ.:* St. Pauls School; Merton College, Oxford (scholar, B.A.). President Oxford Union Society, 1898; called to Bar, Inner Temple, 1901; joined staff of Daily News in 1902; leader-writer on Daily Telegraph, 1912-34; rejoined staff, 1940; writer of detective novels and short stories since 1912; contributor of prose and verse to many periodicals since 1896. *Publications:* Biography for Beginners, 1905; Trent's Last Case, 1912; More Biography, 1929; Trent's Own Case (with H. Warner Allen), 1936; Trent Intervenes, 1938; Baseless Biography, 1939; Those Days, 1940; Elephant's Work, 1950; Clerihews Complete, 1951. *Address:* 10 Porchester Terrace, W.2. [*Died* 30 *March* 1956.

BENTLIFF, Hubert David; *b.* 28 May 1891; *e. s.* of late Walter D. Bentliff and of Margaret Bentliff; *m.* 1919, Barbara (*d.* 1922), *d.* of George Brown, London, Ontario. *Educ.:* Dulwich College; Trinity College, Cambridge. B.Sc. (London), 1910; M.A. (Cantab.), 1917; called to Bar, 1920, Inner Temple; member Northern Circuit. Served European War, 1914-19, retired as Captain, Essex Regt. Under-Secretary, National Assistance Board, 1946-50. Contested (L.) Southport, Gen. Election, 1951, Bye-Election, Feb. 1952. *Recreations:* music and sitting in the sunshine. *Address:* 10 Lord Street West, Southport, Lancs. *T.:* Southport 55744. *Club:* National Liberal. [*Died* 21 *April* 1953.

BENYON, Sir Henry Arthur, 1st Bt., *cr.* 1958; D.L., J.P.; Lord Lieutenant of Berkshire since 1945; *b.* 9 Dec. 1884; *s.* of James Herbert Benyon, Lord Lieutenant of Berkshire, 1901-35, and Dame Edith Benyon, G.B.E., 1919, *d.* of Sir John Walrond, 1st Bart.; *m.* 1915, Violet Eveline, C.B.E. 1946, President Berkshire Branch, B.R.C.S., C.C. 1934 and C.A. 1949, Berkshire, *d.* of Sir Cuthbert Peek, 2nd Bart., and Hon. Lady Peek, Rousdon, Devon. *Educ.:* Eton; Trinity Hall, Cambridge. Joined Berkshire Yeomanry, 1910, served in Egypt in European War, 1914-18; Member of Berks County Council, 1922-49; County Alderman, 1935, Vice-Chm., 1938; Chm., 1948-49; High Sheriff of Berkshire, 1925; Chm. Berks. Agric. Exec. Cttee., 1944-57; Dep.-Pres. Roy. Agric. Soc., 1954; Pres. Berks. T.A. *Recreation:* shooting. *Heir:* none. *Address:* Englefield House, Berkshire. *T.:* Theale 221. *Club:* Cavalry. [*Died* 15 *June* 1959 (*ext.*).

BENZIGER, August; artist, portrait painter, retired; *b.* Einsiedeln, Switzerland, 2 Jan. 1867; *s.* of Adelrich (head of firm Benziger Bros., publishers, Einsiedeln, Switerland, and New York; Cincinnati, Ohio; Chicago, Ills.; and St. Louis, Mo., U.S.A.) and Marie Koch; *m.* 1898, Gertrude Lytton; three *d.* *Educ.:* Downside College (England); Brussels, Geneva, Munich, Vienna, Académie Julien and Beaux Arts, Paris. Painted portraits of Presidents of the U.S.A., Switzerland, etc., three Popes, and many well-known people in France, Switzerland, England, and America; Commandeur de l'ordre du Christ, officier de l'ordre St. Jacques. *Recreations:* one of the first automobilists of Switzerland, and formerly an enthusiastic horseman. *Address:* 1 East 66th Street, New York 21, N.Y., U.S.A. *T.:* Trafalgar (N.Y.) 9-3900. *Clubs:* Automobile Suisse; A.A.A. (New York). [*Died* 13 *April* 1955.

BEOKU-BETTS, Sir Ernest (Samuel), Kt. 1957; M.B.E. 1934; *b.* 1895; Speaker of the House of Representatives, Sierra Leone, since 1957; Vice-President of the Legislative Council, 1954. *Educ.:* Educational Institute, Sierra Leone; Fourah Bay College, Sierra Leone. Barrister-at-Law, Middle Temple, London. Police Magistrate, Sierra Leone, 1937; Crown Counsellor, 1937; Puisne Judge, 1945; retired, 1954. Editor of Sierra Leone Law Recorder, Vols. I, II and III. *Address:* The House of Representatives, Freetown, Sierra Leone. [*Died* 11 *Sept.* 1957.

BERENSON, Bernhard; *b.* 26 June 1865; *e. s.* of Albert Berenson of Boston, U.S.A.; *m.* 1900, Mary Logan Costelloe, *e. d.* of Robert Pearsall Smith of Philadelphia, U.S.A. *Educ.:* Boston Latin School; Harvard University. Member of American Academy of Arts and Letters; For. Member of Italian Lincei and Venetian Ateneo;

Associate of Belgian Academy; Foreign Member of Norwegian Academy. British Academy Serena medal for Italian studies. Honorary citizen of Florence. Hon. Dr. Paris and Florence Universities. *Publications:* Venetian Painters of the Renaissance, 1894; Lorenzo Lotto, an Essay in Constructive Art Criticism, 1895 (new edition, 1953, revised edition, 1956); Florentine Painters of the Renaissance, 1896; Central Italian Painters of the Renaissance, 1897; The Study and Criticism of Italian Art, 1901; second series, 1902; third series, 1916; The Drawings of the Florentine Painters, 1903; 2nd edit. revised and enlarged 1938; North Italian Painters of the Renaissance, 1907; Sienese Painter of Franciscan Legend, 1910; Catalogue of the Italian Masters in the J. G. Johnson Collection, Philadelphia, 1913; Fifteenth-Century Venetian Painting in America, 1916; Essays in the Study of Sienese Painting, 1918; Catalogue of the Italian Masters in the Widener Collection, Philadelphia; Three Essays in Method, 1927; Catalogue of the Italian Masters in the Michael Friedsam Collection, New York; Studies in Medieval Painting, 1930; The Italian Painters of the Renaissance, 1932 (Edn. 1952 with new Preface and 400 illus.); Italian Pictures of the Renaissance, 1932; Aesthetics, Ethics and History, 1948; Sketch for a self Portrait, 1949; Rumour and Reflection, 1949; Piero della Francesca and the Ineloquent in Art, 1950; Caravaggio, 1951; Seeing and Knowing, 1951; The Arch of Constantine and its Reliefs, 1952; Catalogue of Venetian Paintings, 1300–1600, 1957; Essays in Appreciation, 1958; The Passionate Sightseer, 1960 (Posthumous). *Address:* I Tatti, Florence, Italy. [*Died* 6 *Oct.* 1959.

BERESFORD-PEIRSE, Lieut.-Gen. Sir Noel Monson de la Poer, K.B.E., 1941; C.B. 1943; D.S.O. 1918; Col. Comdt. R.A. since 1944; *b.* 22 Dec. 1887; *s.* of late Col. William John de la Poer Beresford-Peirse and Mary, *d.* of Thomas Chambers of Aberfoyle, Co. Derry; *m.* 1st, 1912, Hazel Marjorie (whom he divorced), 1924), *d.* of late J. A. Cochrane, Riverina, Australia; 2nd, 1925, Jean (*d.* 1926), *o. c.* of late Surgeon-Captain R. D. Jameson, C.M.G., R.N.; 3rd, 1929, Katharine Camilla, *d.* of late Col. J. M. C. Colvin, V.C. *Educ.:* Wellington; R.M.A., Woolwich; Staff College, Camberley. Served European War, 1914–18 (D.S.O.); War of 1939–45 (K.B.E.); Commander 4 Indian Division, 1940–41; Commander Western Desert Force, April-Sept., 1941; G.O.C. Sudan, Sept. 1941-April, 1942; Commander 15 Indian Corps, 1942; G.O.C.-in-C. Southern Army, India, 1942–45. Lt.-Col. 1935; Col. 1937; Maj.-Gen., 1938; Acting Lt.-Gen. 1941; Lt.-Gen. 1942; Welfare General in India, 1945–47; retired pay, 1947. *Recreation:* fishing. *Address:* Watergate House, Bulford, Wiltshire. *T.:* Bulford, 2144. [*Died* 14 *Jan.* 1953.

BERESFORD-PEIRSE, Rev. Richard Windham de la Poer, M.A., Prebendary of St. Paul's since 1933; Vicar of Christ Church, Lancaster Gate, 1921–48; Rural Dean of Paddington since 1930; *b.* 6 Aug. 1876; 2nd *s.* of Sir H. M. De la P. Beresford-Peirse, 3rd Bt.; *m.* 1st, 1910, Lady Lilian Katharine Campbell (*d.* 1918), 3rd *d.* of 3rd Earl Cawdor; one *s.* three *d.*; 2nd, 1924, Katherine, *er. d.* of Mr. Scarlett, Fyfield House, Andover. *Educ.:* Eton; Trinity College, Oxford. Ordained 1901; curate of Leeds, 1901–7; vicar of St. Mary's of Eton, Hackney Wick, N.E., 1907–12; St. John's, Middlesbrough, 1912–21. *Address:* The Cottage, Hambledon, Henley-on-Thames. [*Died* 13 *March* 1952.

BERKELEY, Lt.-Col. Christopher Robert, C.M.G. 1917; D.S.O. 1900; O.B.E. 1919; late Welch Regt.; *b.* 18 Jan. 1877; *s.* of late Major Henry Wm. Berkeley; *m.* 1919, Nest, *y. d.* of late Col. Sir Joseph A. Bradney, C.B., Talycoed Court, Monmouth; three *s.* *Educ.:* Oratory School; Sandhurst. Entered Army, 1897; Capt., 1904; Major, 1915; Bt. Lt.-Col., 1916; Lt.-Col., 1922; served South Africa, 1899–1900 (severely wounded, despatches twice, D.S.O.); European War, 1914–18 (wounded, despatches six times, Bt. Lt.-Col., C.M.G., O.B.E., Légion d Honneur, Croix de Guerre (avec palmes); Indian Frontier, Waziristan, 1923; retired pay, 1927. *Address:* c/o Lloyds Bank, Ltd., Cox's and King's Branch, 6 Pall Mall, S.W.1. *Club:* Army and Navy. [*Died* 27 *April* 1959.

BERNARD, Professor Albert Victor, C.M.G. 1945; C.B.E. 1941 (O.B.E. 1928); M.D. (Malta); D.P.H. (Liverpool); D.T.M. & H. (Eng.); *b.* 1885. Asst. Resident M.O., Malta Govt. Hospital, 1909; M.O.H. 1912; Professor of Hygiene and Preventive Medicine, Malta Univ., 1921; Asst. Supt. Public Health, 1929; Chief Govt. Medical Officer, 1936–45, retd. *Address:* 195 Main St., St. Julian's, Malta. [*Died* 21 *June* 1955.

BERNARD, Andrew M.; *see* Fleming-Bernard.

BERNARD, Lt.-Gen. Sir Denis Kirwan, K.C.B. *cr.* 1939 (C.B. 1935); C.M.G. 1918; D.S.O. 1917; *b.* 22 Oct. 1882; *s.* of Percy B. Bernard and Mary, *d.* of Denis Kirwan, Castle Hacket, Co. Galway; unmarried. *Educ.:* Eton; Sandhurst. 2nd Lieut. Rifle Brigade, 1902; Capt. 1912; served European War (France, Gallipoli, Salonica, and Egypt) 1914–18 (despatches, C.M.G., D.S.O., Bt. Major, Bt. Lt.-Col., Croix de Guerre, wounded); General Staff Officer, March 1915 till end of war; Brevet-Col. 1923; Lt.-Col. 1927; Col. 1930; Maj.-Gen. 1933; Lieut.-Gen. 1939; commanded 1st Batt. Royal Ulster Rifles, 1927–30; Brigadier, General Staff, Northern Command, India, 1930–1934; Director of Recruiting and Organization, War Office, 1934–36; Commander of 3rd Division, 1936–39; Governor and Commander-in-Chief of Bermuda, 1939–41; Colonel of the Royal Ulster Rifles, 1937–47; D.L. Co Galway. *Address:* Castle Hacket, Galway, Ireland. *Clubs:* Army and Navy; Kildare Street (Dublin). [*Died* 25 *Aug.* 1956.

BERNARD, Col. Joseph Francis, C.M.G. 1916; D.S.O. 1918; late Royal Army Ordnance Corps; *s.* of late Colonel Count Bernard; *b.* 24 Oct. 1871; *m.* 1924, Hermione, *d.* of late C. G. Hawdon of Hove. Entered Royal Malta Artillery, 1891; Captain, 1896; Adjutant, 1897–99; Major A.O.D. 1907; Lt.-Col. 1914; has 3rd class Medjidie and 1914 Star; served S. Africa, 1900–02 (Queen's medal 3 clasps, King's medal 2 clasps); European War, 1914–18 (despatches five times, C.M.G., D.S.O.); retired with rank of Colonel, 1922. *Club:* United Service. [*Died* 27 *July* 1953.

BERNEY, Sir Henry, Kt., *cr.* 1937; J.P., D.L.; architect; *b.* 1862; *s.* of John Berney, Croydon; *m.* 1896 (wife *d.* 1949). J.P. Croydon; D.L. Surrey. *Address:* 37 South Park Hill Rd., Croydon. *T.:* Croydon 0208. [*Died* 26 *Dec.* 1953.

BERNSTEIN, Henri; dramatist; *b.* Paris, 1876. *Educ.:* Cambridge. After War of 1914–18 became Manager of the Gymnase. Lived in New York, 1940–46. *Works:* Le Marche; Joujou; Le Détour; Le Bercail; La Rafale (Eng. adaptation, The Whirlwind); La Griffe; Le Voleur; Samson; Israël; Après Moi; L'Assaut; Le Secret; Judith; La Galerie des Glaces; Félix; Le Venin; Mélo; Le Bonheur; Le Messager; Espoir; Le Coeur; Le Voyage; Le Camp des Tempêtes; Elvire, 1940, at Théâtre des Ambassadeurs (his own theatre, where there were notable productions of his works, especially in 1946, and 1950); Rose Burke (in English) with Katharine Cornell in leading part, San Francisco, 1942. *Address:* Théâtre des Ambassadeurs, 1 Avenue Gabriel, Paris. [*Died* 27 *Nov.* 1953.

BERRY, Henry, C.B.E. 1951; M.I.Mech.E., A.I.Struct.E.; F.R.S.A.; *b.* Woolwich, 7 Jan. 1883; *s.* of Benjamin and Elizabeth Ann Berry; *m.* 1906, Mary Winifred Startup (*d.* 1945); one *s.* three *d.* *Educ.:* Woolwich; Woolwich Polytechnic; Goldsmiths' College. Engineering Apprentice, Siemens, Woolwich; Junior Engineer and Draughtsman, Hoe and Co.; Mechanical Superintendent, Amalgamated Press Ltd.; London Manager, Moon Bros. Ltd.; Consulting Engineer; Member Woolwich Boro' Council, 1922-45; M.P. (Lab.) West Woolwich, 1945-50. London County Council, 1928-55; Metropolitan Water Board since 1923 (Chairman, 1940-1946); Mayor of Woolwich, 1935-36; Vice-Chairman L.C.C., 1940-41; Treasurer, National Allotments Society Ltd., 1922-; Member Central Allotments Advisory Cttee., 1922-51; Pres. Internat. Allotments Organisation, 1947-49; President British Waterworks Association, 1948; Member Central Water Advisory Committee since 1946; Member Thames Conservancy since 1940; Hon. Member American Water Works Association, 1949. *Address:* 10 Greenholm Road, Eltham, S.E.9. *T.:* Eltham 4090. [*Died* 14 *Feb.* 1956.

BERRYMAN, Sir Frederick Henry, Kt., *cr.* 1932; V.L., J.P.; *b.* 1869; *s.* of Frederick Berryman, Shepton Mallet. Called to Bar, Middle Temple, 1902; Chairman of Somerset County Council, 1927-32; Vice-Lieut. Somerset, 1939; High Sheriff, 1939; Capt. Cardigan R.A. (M.), 1897-1909; Reserve of Officers since 1909; Major, R.G.A., 1914-19. *Address:* Field House, Shepton Mallet. *T.:* Shepton Mallet 6. *Clubs:* Athenæum, Junior United Service. [*Died* 22 *Dec.* 1952.

BERTENSHAW, Eric Strickland, C.B. 1949; C.B.E. 1942; B.A. (London), 1909; *b.* 1888; *s.* of T. H. Bertenshaw, some time master at City of London School; *m.* 1916, Jessie Milne, *d.* of late John Lindsay Mackie, C.B.E.; one *s.* one *d.* *Educ.:* City of London School; on the Continent. Entered Secretaries' Office, H.M. Customs and Excise, 1911; Asst. Sec., 1926-43; Commissioner of Customs and Excise, 1943-49, retd. 1949. Writes articles for trade journals. *Address:* 121 Princes Park Avenue, N.W.11. *T.:* Speedwell 3080. *Clubs:* Wine Trade: Finchley Golf. [*Died* 26 *Feb.* 1957.

BERTHOUD, Edward Henry, C.I.E. 1928; O.B.E. 1919; *b.* 13 Sept. 1876; *s.* of A. H. Berthoud, 42 Bramham Gardens, S.W.; *m.* Phyllis Hamilton, *d.* of G. W. S. Cox, Indian Police; one *d.* *Educ.:* Uppingham; New College, Oxford. Joined Indian Civil Service, 1900; served as Assistant Magistrate, Joint Magistrate, Collector, Deputy Commissioner, Commissioner of Excise, Inspector-General of Registration, and Commissioner of Chota Nagpur in Bihar and Orissa; retired, 1932. *Address:* Pentland, 87 Cooden Drive, Bexhill, Sussex. [*Died* 25 *June* 1955.

BERTIE OF THAME, 2nd Viscount, *cr.* 1918; **Vere Frederick Bertie;** Baron, *cr.* 1915; *b.* 20 Oct. 1878; *s.* of 1st Visc. and Lady Feodorowna Cecilia (*d.* 1920), *d.* of 1st Earl Cowley, K.G.; *m.* 1901, Nora, *e. d.* of late Frederick Webb; *S.* father, 1919. *Educ.:* Eton; Christ Church, Oxford; Trinity Hall, Cambridge. Called to Bar, Inner Temple, 1902. *Heir:* none. *Address:* Shirburn Lodge, nr. Watlington, Oxfordshire. *T.:* Watlington 59. *Club:* Carlton. [*Died* 29 *Aug.* 1954 (*ext.*).

BERTIE, Major Hon. Arthur Michael, D.S.O. 1917; M.C.; late Rifle Brigade; *b.* 29 Sept. 1886; 2nd *s.* of 7th Earl of Abingdon (*d.* 1928) and *heir-pres.* to Earl of Lindsey and Abingdon; *m.* 1st 1929, Aline Rose (*d.* 1948), *d.* of late George Arbuthnot-Leslie, and *widow* of Hon. Charles Fox Maule Ramsay; one *s.*; *m.* 2nd 1949, Lilian, *d.* of late Charles Cary-Elwes, and *widow* of Lt.-Comdr. F. Crackanthorpe, R.N. *Educ.:* Austria; Balliol College, Oxford. Honorary attaché at Petrograd Embassy, 1906-07; served European War, 1914-18 (twice wounded, D.S.O., M.C., despatches twice); attached to British Armistice Commission, Spa, 1918-19; Inter-Allied Military Control Commission in Germany, 1920-23; Secretary to the High Commissioner of the League of Nations for Danzig Free State, 1923-25. Served War of 1939-45, in S. African Defence Force, 1940-44; C.C.G., 1945-48. *Address:* Crepping Hall, Stutton, Ipswich. [*Died* 1 *Feb.* 1957.

BERTRAM, Lady; (Edith), C.B.E. 1919; *widow* of Sir Anton Bertram (*d.* 1937), late Chief Justice of Ceylon; 2nd *d.* of Rees Jones, Porthkerry, Glam. *Address:* Hampton Court Palace, Middlesex. [*Died* 6 *Feb.* 1959.

BERWICK, 9th Baron (*cr.* 1784), **Charles Michael Wentworth Noel-Hill;** late Lieut. K.S.L.I.; *b.* 4 March 1897; *o. s.* of late Rev. Charles Noel-Hill and late Edith Mary, *d.* of late Rev. R. G. Benson; *S.* cousin 1947. *Educ.:* Wellington; Royal Military College, Sandhurst. Rifle Brigade, 1916-22; A.D.C. to Viceroy of India, 1921-1924. *Heir:* none. *Address:* c/o Frogmore, Upton Magna, nr. Shrewsbury. [*Died* 27 *Jan.* 1953 (*ext.*).

BESANT, Arthur Digby, B.A., F.I.A.; General Manager of Clerical, Medical and General Life Assurance Soc., 1906-33, Director, 1933-57; *b.* Cheltenham, 16 Jan. 1869; *o. s.* of Rev. Frank (*d.* 1917) and Mrs. Annie Besant (*d.* 1933); *m.* 1894; one *d.* (and one *s.* decd. and one *d.* decd.). *Educ.:* Portsmouth Grammar School; University College, London. Fellow and Joint-Treas. of Univ. Coll. 1924-48; Fellow of the Institute of Actuaries, 1895; Vice-President, 1916-19; President, 1924-26; Chairman of the Life Offices' Association, 1923-24; Member of Royal Commission on National Health Insurance, 1924-26. Director of Employers Liability Assurance Corporation, 1921-52; Director of Merchants' Marine Co., 1928-52, and of Clarendon Property Company, 1933; member Unemployment Insurance Statutory Committee, 1934-39; a Senator of University of London, 1944-48. *Publications:* Notes on Canadian Mortgages as Investments, 1914; Our Centenary, the history of the first hundred years of the Clerical, Medical and General Life Assurance Society, 1924; The Besant Pedigree, 1930; The Gallio Club, 1903-1953, 1953; contributions on actuarial subjects. *Recreations:* mountain walking, philately. *Address:* 9 Hampstead Hill Gardens, N.W.3. *T.:* Hampstead 4603. *Clubs:* Athenæum, Reform. [*Died* 29 *April* 1960.

BESSBOROUGH, 9th Earl of (*cr.* 1739), Earl (U.K.), *cr.* 1937; **Vere Brabazon Ponsonby,** P.C. 1931; G.C.M.G., *cr.* 1931 (C.M.G. 1919); Baron of Bessborough; Viscount Duncannon, 1723; Baron Ponsonby, 1749; Baron Duncannon (U.K.), 1834; J.P., D.L., Co. Kilkenny; Captain, Territorial Force Reserve; Knight of Justice of St. John of Jerusalem; *b.* 27 Oct. 1880; *e. s.* of 8th Earl of Bessborough and Blanche Vere, C.B.E. (*d.* 1919), *d.* of Sir John Guest, 1st Bart.; *S.* father, 1920; *m.* 1912, Roberte de Neuflize, Dame Grand Cross of Order of St. John of Jerusalem, *d.* of late Baron Jean de Neuflize; one *s.* one *d.* (and two *s.* decd.). *Educ.:* Harrow; Trinity College, Cambridge (B.A.); Hon.

LL.D. MacGill, Toronto Univs. 1931; Hon. F.R.I.B.A. Called to Bar, Inner Temple, 1903; late Lieut. Bucks Yeomanry; contested Carmarthen Boroughs (U.), 1906; M.P. (C.) Cheltenham, Jan.-Dec. 1910; Dover, 1913-20; L.C.C. (M.R.), Marylebone East, 1907-10; served in Gallipoli, 1915, and in France on the Staff 1916-18; Governor-General of Canada 1931-35; Pres. of Council of Foreign Bondholders, 1936; Chm. League Loans Cttee., 1937; Chm., Cheltenham Ladies' Coll., Chichester Diocesan Fund, Church of England Council for Commonwealth and Empire Settlement; Hotels and Restaurants Assoc., Franco-British Soc.; Rio Tinto Co.; Grand Cross of Legion of Honour; holds orders of: St. Anne, Russia; Leopold II., Belgium; SS. Maurice and Lazarus, Italy; and Redeemer, Greece. *Publications:* Ed. (with A. Aspinall) Lady Bessborough and her Family Circle, 1940; ed. The Diaries of Lady Charlotte Guest, 1950; ed. The Diaries of Lady Charlotte Schreiber, 1952; (ed.) The Diaries of Georgiana, Duchess of Devonshire, 1955. *Heir: s.* Viscount Duncannon. *Address:* Stansted Park, Rowlands Castle, Hants. *Club:* Turf.

[*Died* 10 *March* 1956.

BEST, George Percival, C.B.E., 1937; *b.* London, 15 April 1872; *s.* of G. H. Dukes Best. Entered Civil Service, 1896; Office of H.M. Woods, Forests and Land Revenues (now Office of the Commissioners of Crown Lands); Assistant Commissioner of Crown Lands, 1935-37. *Publications:* The Civil List and the Hereditary Revenues of the Crown (under name of G. Percival), Fortnightly Review, March 1901, and contributions to the Bulletin des Amis de Montaigne, Paris, of which society he is a Life Member and a Vice-Pres.; Member Société des Bibliophiles de Guyenne, Bordeaux. *Recreations:* travel in France and critical researches *re* biography and essays of Montaigne. *Club:* Reform. [*Died* 29 *June* 1953.

BEST, Captain Humphrey Willie, C.B.E. 1944; D.S.O. 1918; R.N.; Sea Transport Service; *b.* 2 July 1884; 2nd *s.* of late Major Hon. T. W. Best; *m.* 1914, Helen Grace Meakin; two *s.* one *d.* *Educ.:* Littlejohns; H.M.S. Britannia. R.N. till 1923. Served European War, 1914-18 (D.S.O. in 1918 for action with enemy submarine, UB 68, commanded by Doenitz). Retired in 1923 and rejoined July 1939 for service in Sea Transport. C.B.E. for work in planning of landing operations in Normandy, 1944. *Address:* Harewood, Marlpit Lane, Seaton, Devon. *T.:* Seaton 293. [*Died* 29 *April* 1959.

BEST, Hon. James William, O.B.E.; J.P. Dorset; farmer; *b.* 3 May, 1882; *y. s.* of 5th Baron Wynford; *m.* Florence Mary Bernarda, *e. d.* of Sir Elliot Lees, Bt., D.S.O.; four *s.* two *d.* *Educ.:* Wellington College; Royal Indian Engineering College, Coopers Hill. India Forest Service, 1904-25; served in the Central Provinces of India; Conservator of Forests, Jubblepur, 1922; first Sylviculturist to the C. P. Government, 1923; was Captain in 2nd Nagpur Rifles, Indian Auxiliary Force. Volunteer Decoration, 1923. *Publications:* Indian Shikar Notes; Tiger Days; The Marked Maneater; Forest Life in India, 1935. *Recreations:* shooting and fishing. *Address:* Hincknowle, Melplash, Bridport, Dorset. *T.A.:* Netherbury. *T.:* Netherbury 221. *Club:* Junior Carlton.

[*Died* 16 *July* 1960.

BEST, Richard Irvine, Litt.D.; *b.* 1872; *s.* of Henry Best and Margaret Jane Irvine; *m.* 1906, Edith Oldham (*d.* 1950), A.R.C.M. and Hon. A.R.C.M. Dir., National Library of Ireland, 1924-40; Assist. Librarian, 1904; Sen. Prof., School of Celtic Studies in Dublin Institute for Advanced Studies, 1940-1947. Chairman of the Irish MSS. Commission, 1948-56; Hon. Sec., School of Irish Learning, 1903-24; Pres. of the Roy. Irish Acad., 1943-46; Leibniz Medal, Roy. Prussian Academy, 1914; Commemoration Medal of Pontifical Academy of Sciences, 1937; Hon. D.Litt. National University of Ireland, 1920; Hon. Litt.D., Dublin Univ., 1923; Hon. Member of Modern Language Assoc. of America, 1947. *Publications:* Bibliography of Irish philology and printed Irish Literature, 1913, 1942; Lebor na Huidre, or Book of the Dun, text with Introduction, edited in collaboration with Osborn Bergin, Litt.D., 1929; The Book of Leinster, text ed. in collaboration with M. A. O'Brien, Ph.D., Vol. I, 1954, Vol. II, 1956, Vol. III, 1957; Irish MS. 23 N10, R.I.A.: Collotype Facsimile with Introd., 1955. The Martyrology of Tallaght, ed. in collaboration with Very Rev. H. J. Lawlor, D.D., for Henry Bradshaw Society, 1931; The Annals of Inisfallen, Rawl. B. 503 published in Facsimile, with Introduction 1933; The Commentary on the Psalms, with Glosses in Old-Irish, preserved in the Ambrosian Library (C 301 Inf.). Collotype Facsimile with Introduction, 1936; Ancient Laws of Ireland, Senchas Mār, Facsimile, with Introduction, of the oldest fragments, 1931, The Irish Mythological Cycle and Celtic Mythology (translated from the French of H. D'Arbois de Jubainville, with additional notes), 1903; Whitley Stokes (1830-1909): A memorial discourse, 1951. Editions and translations of various Middle-Irish texts, palæographical and bibliographical papers, contributed to Eriu. Zeitschrift für Celtische Philologie, Hermathena, Celtica, Journal of Celtic Studies, Anecdota from Irish MSS. (Joint Editor), Proceedings of the Royal Irish Academy, etc. *Address:* 57 Upper Leeson Street, Dublin.

[*Died* 25 *Sept.* 1959.

BETHELL, Colonel Alfred Bryan, C.M.G. 1918; D.S.O. 1915; late R.A.; D.L.; *b.* 25 April 1875; *s.* of late Alfred Bethell, M.R.C.S., Bridgnorth, Shropshire; *m.* 1913, Caroline Patience Nangle (*d.* 1955), *d.* of late W. E. Wilson, D.Sc., F.R.S., Daramona, Westmeath; (one *s.* killed Palestine, 1946). Entered army, 1895; Captain, 1901; Major, 1911; Col., 1921; employed with Egyptian Army, 1901-11; South Africa, 1900-01 (despatches, Queen's medal 4 clasps); Sudan, 1905 (despatches, Egyptian medal with clasp); served European War, 1914-18 (D.S.O., Legion of Honour; C.M.G.); retired pay, 1921.

[*Died* 23 *Nov.* 1956.

BETHELL, Sir Thomas Robert, Kt., *cr.* 1914; *s.* of late George Bethell, South Woodford; *m.* 1925, Edith Lillie (*d.* 1957), *d.* of late George Tabor, Highbury. *Educ.:* Heversham Grammar School. Called to Bar, Middle Temple, 1897; M.P. (L.) Maldon Division, Essex, 1906-10; contested (L.) Suffolk, E., Eye Div., Oct. 1924; was Deputy-Chairman of County of London Electric Supply Co. Ltd., and a Director of other Associated and Subsidiary Companies until those Companies were Nationalised. *Address:* 169 Queen's Gate, S.W.7. *T.:* Kensington 3316; 2 Harcourt Buildings, Temple, E.C.4. *T.:* Central 8415. *Clubs:* Reform, Hurlingham.

[*Died* 23 *Dec.* 1957.

BETHUNE, Francis John, Q.C.; retired from active practice; *b.* Dec. 1860; *y. s.* of late Admiral C. R. D. Bethune, C.B., of Balfour, Fife; *m.* 1894, Helen Marian, *d.* of late Edward K. Crace of Gungahleen, N.S.W.; one *d.* *Educ.:* Harrow; Trinity College, Cambridge. Called to Bar, 1887; joined N.E. Circuit; read in the Chambers of late Lord Robson, and began practice in London; left London for Sydney, N.S.W., 1894, and admitted to the N.S.W. Bar; K.C. 1922. *Recreations:* reading, music. *Address:* Windyriggs, Moss Vale, N.S.W. *Club:* Marlborough-Windham.

[*Died* 25 *Feb.* 1954.

BETHUNE, Rev. John Walter, C.B.E. 1927; M.A. Cantab.; *b.* 5 Nov. 1882; *s.* of

John Charles Bethune, LL.B. (Cantab.), and Annie Emily Pogson; unmarried. *Educ.*: Church Grammar School, Launceston; Hutchins School, Hobart; Selwyn College, Cambridge. Deacon, 1905; Priest, 1906; Curate St. David's Cathedral, Hobart, 1905-1907; Rector of St. Paul's Launceston, 1908-15, and Chaplain to Hospital; Chaplain A.I.F. Troops, Claremont Camp, 1915-18; Headmaster Launceston Church Grammar School, Tasmania, 1919-28; Priest in charge of Wynward, Tasmania, 1929-40; Actg. Supt. Seamen's Mission, Hobart, 1941-42; Prisoners' Chaplain, H.M. Gaol, 1944-51; Chm. Aid Soc., Hobart, 1944-51; retired, 1952. *Publication:* Feed my Lambs, 1935. *Recreations:* Won quarter-mile Selwyn College, 1903, 1904; cricket, tennis, golf. *Address:* c/o Diocesan Office, Hobart, Tasmania. [*Died* 2 *Oct.* 1960.

BETHUNE-BAKER, Rev. James Franklin, D.D.; F.B.A.; Fellow of Pembroke College, Cambridge, since 1891; Hon. Chaplain to Bishop of Birmingham; *b.* 23 Aug. 1861; *s.* of late Alfred Baker, F.R.C.S., of Birmingham, and Emmeline Bethune, *d.* of George Armitage; assumed the additional name Bethune 1884; *m.* 1891, Edith (*d.* 1949), *d.* of Furneaux Jordan, F.R.C.S.; (one *s.* decd.). *Educ.*: King Edward's School, Birmingham; Pembroke College, Cambridge. 1st class Classical Tripos, 1884, and Theological Tripos, Part II., 1886; George Williams Prize, 1886; Burney Prize, 1887; Norrisian Prize, 1888; B.D. 1901; D.D. 1912. Headmaster's Assistant King Edward's School, Birmingham, and Curate St. George's, Edgbaston, 1888-90; Dean of Pembroke College, 1891-1906; Examining Chaplain to the Bishop of Rochester, 1905-14; Editor, Journal of Theological Studies, 1903-35; Lady Margaret's Professor of Divinity, Cambridge, 1911-35; Examining Chaplain to the Bishop of Birmingham, 1924-35. *Publications:* The Influence of Christianity on War, 1888; The Sternness of Christ's Teaching, 1889; The Meaning of Homoousios in the Constantinopolitan Creed, 1901; An Introduction to the Early History of Christian Doctrine, 1903; essay on The Ethical Significance of Christian Doctrines, in Cambridge Theological Essays, 1905; Nestorius and his Teaching, 1908; The Faith of the Apostles' Creed, 1918; The Way of Modernism, and other Essays, 1927; Early Traditions about Jesus, 1929; (with W. Grierson) The New View of Christianity, 1930. *Recreation:* gardening. *Address:* 7 Chaucer Road, Cambridge. *T.:* Cambridge 54828. [*Died* 13 *Jan.* 1951.

BETT, Rev. Henry, Litt.D., M.A.; *b.* 23 March, 1876; *s.* of Wingate Bett; *m.* 1st, Margaret Turnbull (*d.* 1930); 2nd, Sarah Annie Burgin (*d.* 1951); one *s.* two *d.* *Educ.*: Headingley Coll., Leeds; Univ. of Manchester. Methodist Minister at Sunderland, Rugby, Darlington, York, Lincoln, and Stockport, 1899-1923; tutor in Church History at Handsworth College, 1923-43; Principal, 1940-43; President of Methodist Conference, 1940. *Publications:* The Watch Night, 1911; The Hymns of Methodism, 1912; The Spiritual Maxims of Angelus Silesius (trans. from the German), 1914; Nursery Rhymes and Tales, 1924; The Games of Children, 1929; Studies in Religion, 1929; Studies in Literature, 1929; Johannes Scotus Erigena, 1925; Nicholas of Cusa, 1932; Joachim of Flora, 1931; Some Secrets of Style, 1932; Wanderings Among Words, 1936; The Spirit of Methodism, 1937; The Reality of the Religious Life, 1949; English Legends, 1950; English Myths and Traditions, 1952, etc. *Recreation:* walking. *Address:* 13 Wye Cliff Road, Handsworth, Birmingham, 20. [*Died* 1 *April* 1953.

BETTMANN, Siegfried, F.R.S.A.; J.P., Warwickshire; *b.* 18 April 1863; *s.* of Meyer Bettmann and Sophie Weil; *m.* 1895, Annie Meyrick (*d.* 1941), Shifnal, Salop. *Educ.*: Nuremberg. Founded Triumph Cycle Company, Limited, Coventry, in 1885; Managing Director until 1933, when he assumed the Vice-Chairmanship of Company; retired from Board in 1934; at the age of 73, in 1936, acquired from Triumph Co. Ltd. their Cycle and Gear Departments, assumed the chairmanship of manufacturing companies; retired finally from commercial activities in 1939; pioneer of British motor-cycle industry; ex-President of the Coventry Chamber of Commerce; ex-President of British Cycle and Motor-cycle Manufacturers' Union; Mayor of Coventry, 1913-14; ex-Member Advisory Council of Commercial and Industrial Section, Birmingham University; established in 1919 Annie Bettmann Foundation for the Support of Young People Starting in Business. *Publications:* In the Land of the Pharoes; South African Journeyings; A Glance at India; South Africa Revisited; On the Sacred Road; Origins and Causes of the War; translated Dostojevski's novel Downtrodden and Oppressed. *Recreations:* travelling, writing, reading. *Address:* Elm Bank, Stoke Park. Coventry. *T.:* Coventry 63333. *Clubs:* Savage; Drapers' (Coventry). [*Died* 23 *Sept.* 1951.

BETTS, Mrs. E. M.; *see* Hayes, Gertrude.

BETTS, Captain Ernest Edward Alexander, C.B.E. 1919; R.N. retd.; *b.* 12 Aug. 1877; *m.* 1902, Grace Emily Fowler (*d.* 1937); four *s.* Served European War, 1914-19 (despatches, C.B.E.). *Address:* 7 Court Road, Redlands, Weymouth, Dorset. [*Died* 15 *Feb.* 1951.

BETTS, Sir Ernest S.; *see* Beoku-Betts.

BEVAN, Rt. Hon. Aneurin, P.C. 1945; M.P. (Lab.) Ebbw Vale Division of Monmouthshire since 1929; Treasurer, Labour Party, since 1956; County Councillor, Monmouthshire, since 1928; *b.* Tredegar, Mon., Nov. 1897; *s.* of David and Phœbe Bevan; *m.* 1934, Jenny Lee, M.P. *Educ.*: Serhowy Elementary School; Central Labour College. Son of a coal-miner; followed in same occupation after leaving school at age of 13; prominent in the councils of the South Wales Miners' Federation; elected to local Urban District Council after his return from Labour College; miners disputes agent, 1926. Minister of Health, 1945-51; Minister of Labour and National Service, 1951, resigned, 1951. *Publication:* In Place of Fear, 1952. *Recreations:* billiards, tennis. *Address:* Asheridge Farm, Chesham, Bucks. [*Died* 6 *July* 1960.

BEVERIDGE, Lady; (Janet), O.B.E. 1918; *b.* 26 Nov. 1876; *d.* of William Philip and Anne Abbot; *m.* 1st, 1897, David Beveridge Mair; one *s.* three *d.*; 2nd, 1942, Sir William Beveridge, K.C.B. (later 1st Baron Beveridge). *Educ.*: Dundee High School; St. Andrews University (M.A.). Temporary Civil Servant, Ministry of Munitions, 1915-1917; Ministry of Food, Director of Bacon Distribution and Prices, 1917-19; Secretary and Acting Dean, London School of Economics and Political Science, 1919-38. Sunday Times weekly correspondent on London University, *circa* 15 years—1938. Ehrenzeichen of Republic of Austria for services in helping to organize Summer School in Vienna, 1920-. *Publications:* On and Off the Platform, 1949, and Antipodes Notebook, 1949, with Lord Beveridge. Introduction to Housework Without Tears by Priscilla Novy, 1945; Beveridge and His Plan, 1954; An Epic of Clare Market, 1959. *Recreation:* grandchildren. *Address:* Staverton House, 104 Woodstock Road, Oxford. *T.:* Oxford 56060. [*Died* 25 *April* 1959.

BEVERIDGE, Alexander William Morton, J.P.; F.R.S.E.; *s.* of William Beveridge, F.E.I.S., and Christina Morton; *m.* 1909,

Esther, *d.* of Rev. John Pitt, B.D., Dunfermline Abbey; one *s.* Entered service of Bank of Scotland at Dunfermline; Head Office Staff; Manager at Glasgow; Treasurer (General Manager) Bank of Scotland, 1934-39. *Address:* 44 Inverleith Place, Edinburgh. *T.:* Granton (Edinburgh) 83713. *Clubs:* New (Edinburgh); New (Glasgow).
[*Died* 23 *Dec.* 1959.

BEVERIDGE, Major-General Arthur Joseph, C.B. 1953; O.B.E. 1933; M.C. 1917; retd. (Regular Army); Late Assistant Medical Officer of Health, Lincolnshire County Council; *b.* 21 March 1893; *s.* of John Beveridge, B.L., Arborfield, Grosvenor Road, Dublin, and Jane Healy Manus, Clare, Ireland; *m.* 1928, Sheila, *d.* of Lt.-Col. William MacNamara, Retd. R.A.M.C., Dublin; three *s.* two *d.* (and one *s.* one *d.* decd.). *Educ.:* Belvedere College, Dublin; University College, Dublin. M.B., B.C.H., B.A.O., N.U.I., 1915 (1st place 1st Cl. Hons.); M.Sc., N.U.I., 1919; D.P.H., Q.U.B., 1927. Entered R.A.M.C., 1915; specialist in Pathology, Examiner in Pathology, King George V College of Medicine, Singapore, 1935-38; A.D.M.S., Norway, 1940; A.D.M.S., U.K., E. Africa, W. Africa, Palestine, 1941-47; D.D.M.S. Palestine, 1947-48; Scottish Command, 1949-50; D.M.S., M.E.L.F., 1950-53. War Cross of Norway (with Sword), 1942. *Publications:* several scientific articles in Journal of Royal Army Medical Corps, 1935-49. *Recreations:* swimming, stamp collecting. *Address:* 33 Belgrave Sq., Rathmines, Dublin. *T.:* Dublin 92623.
[*Died* 25 *Sept.* 1959.

BEVERLEY, Rt. Rev. Alton Ray; *b.* 1884; *s.* of late Rev. Adelbert Beverley; *m.* 1911, Wynne Longard, *d.* of late C. W. Outhit, Halifax, N.S.; three *s.* one *d.* *Educ.:* Toronto University; Wycliffe College, Toronto. Ordained Deacon, 1907; Priest, 1908. Curate, St. Paul's, Halifax, N.S., 1907-10; Rector, Trinity Ch., Quebec, 1910-19; Vicar, Trinity Ch., Barrie, 1919-35; Suffragan Bishop of Toronto, 1934-47; Bishop of Toronto, 1947-55. *Recreation:* golf. *Address:* 114 Montclair Ave., Toronto 12, Ont. *T.:* Empire 3-9145.
[*Died* 31 *Jan.* 1956.

BEVIN, Rt. Hon. Ernest, P.C. 1940; Lord Privy Seal since 1951; M.P. (Lab.) Central Wandsworth 1940-50, East Woolwich since 1950; *b.* 9 March 1881; *m.* Florence Townley; one *d.* Member of MacMillan Commission on banking; member of Economic Advisory Council, and of a number of other commissions and enquiries; National Organiser of the Dockers' Union, 1910-1921; General Secretary of the Transport and General Workers' Union, 1921-40; member of General Council of Trades Union Congress, 1925-40; Minister of Labour and National Service, 1940-45; Secretary of State for Foreign Affairs, 1945-51; member of the Executive Cttee. of Internat. Transport Workers; Chairman Trades Union Congress, 1937; Hon. Fellow of Magdalen College, Oxford, 1946; Hon. LL.D. Cambridge and Bristol Universities. *Publication:* The Job to be done, 1942 (speeches and broadcast addresses). *Address:* 1 Carlton Gardens, S.W.1. *Club:* Athenæum.
[*Died* 14 *April* 1951.

BEYFUS, Gilbert Hugh, Q.C.; *b.* 19 July 1885; *s.* of Alfred Beyfus and Emma, *d.* of Robert Plumstead; *m.* 1st, 1929, Margaret Malone; one *s.*; 2nd, 1949, Joan Grant; 3rd, 1953, Eileen Louisa Hill. *Educ.:* Harrow; Trinity College, Oxford. Called to Bar, 1908; Bencher, Inner Temple, 1940; K.C. 1933. Contested (L.) Cirencester Div. of Gloucestershire, December 1910; commission, 2nd Lieut. Duke of Wellington's Regiment (3rd Bn.), August 1914; served with 2nd Batt. in Flanders, 1915 (wounded, Ypres, April 1915, taken prisoner at Ypres, May 1915); prisoner of war, May 1915-Dec. 1918 (despatches); retired as Capt., 1919; contested Kingswinford Division of Staffordshire as Coalition candidate, 1922. *Recreations:* fishing, and lawn tennis. *Address:* Derreen, Bell Vale, Haslemere, Surrey. *Clubs:* Brooks's, East India and Sports, Pratt's, Savage.
[*Died* 30 *Oct.* 1960.

BEYNON, Major Godfrey E. S. P.; *see* Protheroe-Beynon.

BEYNON, Maj.-Gen. Sir William George Lawrence, K.C.I.E. *cr.* 1917 (C.I.E. 1916); C.B. 1915; D.S.O. 1895; *b.* 5 Nov. 1866; *s.* of Gen. W. Howell Beynon, and Charlotte, *d.* of Lt.-Gen. Sir G. St. Patrick Lawrence, K.C.S.I., C.B.; *m.* 1899, Edith Norah, *y. d.* of George Petrie of 1 De Vere Gardens; three *d.* *Educ.:* Marlborough; R.M.C., Sandhurst. Joined 2nd Batt. Royal Sussex Regt.; 2nd Lieut. 1887; joined Indian Staff Corps; Lieut. 1889; Capt. 1898; Brevet Major, 1898; Brevet Lieutenant-Colonel, 1904; Major, 1905; Brevet Colonel, 1910; Colonel, 1911; war services: Black Mountain, 1888 (medal and clasp); Chitral Expedition; staff officer to Colonel Kelly (despatches, medal and clasp, D.S.O.); Samana, 1897; Punjab Frontier, 1897 (2 clasps); Tirah, 1897-98 (clasp, Brevet Majority, despatches); Somaliland Expedition, 1901 (despatches, Brevet of Lieut.-Col. on attaining substantive majority, medal and clasp); Tibet, 1904 (despatches, medal and clasp, Brevet Lieut.-Col.); Abor, 1911-12 (medal and clasp); European War, 1915-18 (K.C.I.E., C.I.E., C.B., 3 medals, despatches); Afghan War, 1919 (clasp to medal, despatches); Colonel, 3rd (Queen Alexandra's Own) Gurkha Rifles, 1926-1945; Royal Observer Corps, 1943. *Publication:* With Kelly to Chitral. *Recreations:* fishing, shooting, etc. *Address:* c/o Lloyds Bank, 6 Pall Mall, S.W.1. *Club:* Army and Navy.
[*Died* 19 *Feb.* 1955.

BHALJA, Govardhan Shankerlal, C.I.E. 1943; B.A. (Bom.), B.A. (Cantab.); I.C.S.; Additional Secretary, War Dept., Govt. of India, New Delhi, since Nov. 1944; *b.* Umreth, Bombay Presidency, 8 Aug. 1895; *s.* of late Shankerlal Motichand Bhalja; *m.* 1929, Ushadevi, *d.* of Sir Harilal Gosalia; one *s.* *Educ.:* Jubilee High School, Umreth; Gujarat College, Ahmedabad; Fergusson College, Poona; Gonville and Caius College, Cambridge. Joined I.C.S., 1920, and posted to C.P. and Berar. Director of Industries and Registrar of Co-operative Societies, 1933-37; Member, C.P. Legislative Council, 1933-37; Sec. to Govt., Local Self-Govt., Medical and Public Health Depts., 1937; Financial Sec. and Secretary P.W.D. in addition, 1939-44; Commissioner, Berar Division, Oct. 1944. *Recreation:* bridge. *Address:* 8A Ratendon Road, New Delhi. *T.:* Residence 2064, Office 2480.
[*Died* 30 *Dec.* 1948.
[*But death not notified in time for inclusion in Who Was Who 1941–1950, first edn.*

BHANDARKAR, Devadatta Ramkrishna, M.A., Ph.D. (Hon.), F.R.A.S.B.; *b.* 19 Nov. 1875; *y. s.* of late Sir Ramkrishna Gopal Bhandarkar, K.C.I.E. *Educ.:* High School and Deccan College, Poona. Bhugwandass Purshotumdass Sanskrit Scholar, 1900 and Pandit Bhagwanlal Indraji Lecturer, Bombay University, 1903 and 1917; Sir William Meyer Lecturer, University of Madras, 1938-39; Carmichael Professor of Ancient Indian History and Culture, Calcutta University, 1917-36; Manindra Chandra Nandy Lecturer, Benares Hindu University, 1925; Superintendent, Archæological Survey, Western Circle, 1911-1917; Officer-in-charge, Archæological Section, Indian Museum, Calcutta, 1917-20; Honorary Correspondent of the Archæological Department of the Government of India; Corresponding Member of the Indian Historical Records Commission; Sir James

Campbell Gold Medallist (Bombay Asiatic Society), 1911; Vice-Chairman (1925-27) and Member of Board of Trustees, Indian Museum, since 1917; Fellow since 1918 and Philological Secretary (1920-25) of Royal Asiatic Society, Bengal; joint Editor of the Indian Antiquary, 1911-20, and 1928-33; Editor of Indian Culture, since 1934. *Publications:* Reports of Archæo. Survey, Western Circle; Carmichael Lectures, 1918 and 1921; Asoka, Some Aspects of Ancient Hindu Polity, Origin of the Saka Era, Gurjaras, Lakulisa Guhilots, Foreign Elements in the Hindu Population, and numerous other contribs. on Indian history and archæology.; edited Pt. II. of Vol. CXLV on India of the Annals of the Amer. Acad. Pol. Science, Philadelphia, 1929. *Recreation:* music. *Address:* 2/1 Lovelock St., Calcutta.

[*Died* 30 *May* 1950.

[*But death not notified in time for inclusion in Who Was Who 1941–1950, first edn.*

BHATNAGAR, Sir Shanti Swarupa, Kt., *cr.* 1941; O.B.E. 1936; F.R.S. 1943; D.Sc. (London); F.Inst.P.; Hon. D.Sc. (Patna, Benares, Allahabad, Agra, Lucknow, Delhi and Saugor); Hon. D.Sc. (Oxon); Fellow University College, London; Director of Scientific and Industrial Research, Govt. of India since 1940 and Sec. to Govt. of India Ministry of Natural Resources and Scientific Research, since 1951, and Education, 1952; *b.* Feb. 1895; *s.* of Lala Parmeshwari Sahai and Shrimati Parvati Devi; *m.* 1915, Shrimati Lajwanti; two *s.* two *d.* *Educ.:* Lahore; London; Berlin. Research Scholar, Privy Council's Dept. of Scientific and Industrial Research, London, at Sir William Ramsay Laboratories, Univ. College, London, 1919-21; Univ. Prof. of Chemistry, Benares Hindu Univ., 1921-24; Univ. Prof. of Chemistry and Director, Univ. Chemical Laboratories, Univ. of the Punjab, Lahore, 1924-40; F.C.S., London; F.R.Inst.C.; F.Inst.Physics, Great Britain and Member, Advisory Board of Inst. in India; Hon. Fellow and Vice-Pres. of Soc. of Chem. Industry, London; Fell. Punjab and Benares Hindu Univs.; Past Pres. Indian Chem. Soc.; Reddy Prize in Chemistry, 1947; Sir P. C. Ray Memorial Medal, 1953; Durga Prasad Khaitan Memorial Gold Medal, 1953; Hon. Univ. Prof. of Chemistry, Benares Hindu Univ., Delhi Univ. and Punjab Univ.; Member, Dyal Singh College Trust Society, Lahore. Founder of Lahore Research Scheme under Steel Bros. and Co. Ltd., London, for work on petroleum and allied subjects; Sectional President, Indian Science Congress, 1928 and 1938; General President, Indian Science Congress 1944; Pres. Nat. Institute of Sciences of India, 1947 and 1948; Delegate to the Empire Universities Congress at Edinburgh and at the Centenary Celebrations of Michael Faraday and of the British Association, 1931 and 1936; Delegate to 10th International Chemical Congress, Rome, 1938. Member of the Indian Scientific Mission to U.K. and U.S.A. 1944; Leader of the Official delegation to the Empire Scientific Conference, 1946; officiated as Sec., Education Min., Govt. of India for four months in 1947-48. *Publications:* Principles and Application of Magneto-chemistry; numerous papers on the subject of colloids, magnetism and photochemistry; Ilum-ul-Barq, a treatise on electricity in Urdu and a number of scientific papers in various scientific jls. *Recreation:* mountaineering (Member of the Compton Expedition for Cosmic Rays in Kashmir). *Address:* 23 Tughlak Road, New Delhi, India. [*Died* 1 *Jan.* 1955.

BHOPAL, Air Vice-Marshal H. H. Nawab Sir Hamidullah Khan, Sikander Saulat, Iftikhar-ul-Mulk, Bahadur, Ruler of; G.C.S.I., *cr.* 1932 (C.S.I. 1921); G.C.I.E., *cr.* 1929; C.V.O. 1922; LL.D. (Alig.); Commander-in-Chief, Bhopal State Forces; Hon. Maj.-General in British Army (I.A.); Hon. Air Vice-Marshal, R.A.F. (Indian Air Force); *b.* 9 Sept. 1894; *o. surv. s.* of H. H. Nawab Begum of Bhopal (*d.* 1930); *S.* mother, 1926; *m.* Princess Maimoona Sultan Shah Bano Begam Sahiba; three *d.*; eldest Colonel Nawab Surayya Jah Gauhari Taj Princess Abida Sultan Begam Sahiba. *Educ.:* Mohamedan Anglo-Oriental College (now Muslim University), Aligarh. President Board of Municipality, Bhopal, 1915-16; Trustee M.A.O. College (now Muslim University), Aligarh, 1916; Chief Secretary to Her Highness' Government, 1916-22; Member for law and justice and finance departments to Her Highness' Government, 1922-26. Chancellor, Muslim University, Aligarh, 1930-35; Chancellor of Chamber of Indian Princes, 1931-32 and 1944-47. State is over 7000 square miles in extent, and has a population of 785,322. *Recreations:* yachting, tennis, cycle-polo, of which he is the founder and organiser in India, cricket, fishing, polo; has vast game preserves in his private jagir, notably in Chiklod, Lawakhari, Jaitpur and Kheri. *Address:* Bhopal, Central India.

[*Died* 4 *Feb.* 1960.

BHORE, Sir Joseph William, K.C.S.I., *cr.* 1933; K.C.I.E. *cr.* 1930 (C.I.E. 1923); C.B.E. 1920; represented India at the Silver Jubilee Celebrations in London, May 1935; *b.* Nassik, India, 6 April 1878; *s.* of Rao Saheb R. G. Bhore; *m.* 1911, Margaret W. Stott (*d.* 1945), M.B., Ch.B., O.B.E. 1944, Kaisar-i-Hind Gold Medal; two *s.* *Educ.:* Bishop's High School Poona; Deccan College, Poona; Univ. College, London. Entered Indian Civil Service 1902; Under-Secy. to the Government of Madras, 1910; Dewan (Prime Minister) of the State of Cochin, 1914-19; Deputy Director of Civil Supplies, Madras, 1919; Secretary to High Commissioner for India, 1920; Acting High Commissioner for India in United Kingdom, 1922-23; Secretary to Government of India in Department of Agriculture and Lands, 1924-28; Secretary Indian Statutory Commission, 1928; acting Member of Governor-General's Executive Council, 1926-27; Member of Governor-General's Executive Council, Department of Industries and Labour, 1930-32, Commerce and Railway Dept. 1932-35. *Recreation:* tennis. *Address:* c/o National Bank of India, 26 Bishopsgate, E.C.2; La Maisonette de St. Hélène, St. Andrews, Guernsey, C.I.

[*Died* 15 *Aug.* 1960.

BIBESCO, Prince Antoine; *b.* Paris, 1878; *m.* 1919, Lady Elizabeth Asquith (author plays, poems, short stories, novels; *d.* 1945), *d.* of 1st Earl of Oxford and Asquith; one *d.* *Educ.:* France. Grandson of late reigning Prince of Roumania (*d.* Paris, 1873); Councillor, Roumanian Legation in London, acting as Chargé d'Affaires to 1912; transferred to Petrograd, 1912; Roumanian Minister at Washington, 1920-26; at Madrid, 1926-31; Commander of the Legion of Honour. *Publications:* Plays: le Jaloux, Laquelle?, Quatuor, Mon Héritier, Anne; Collected Letters of Marcel Proust. *Address:* 45 Quai Bourbon, Paris IVe. *T.:* Odéon 14-77. *Clubs:* Garrick, St. James'.

[*Died* 2 *Sept.* 1951.

BICESTER, 1st Baron, *cr.* 1938, of Tusmore; **Vivian Hugh Smith;** Chairman of Morgan Grenfell & Co. Ltd.; Governor of the Royal Exchange Assurance Corporation, 1914-55, Director, 1894-55, Hon. Life Governor, 1955; formerly Director of Associated Electrical Industries, Ltd.; Lord Lieut. of County of Oxford, 1934-54; Hon. Freedom of Oxford, 1955; *b.* 9 Dec. 1867; *s.* of late Hugh Colin Smith and Constance, *d.* of Henry J. Adeane, M.P., of Babraham, Cambridge, and *g. d.* of 1st Baron Stanley of Alderley; *m.* 1897, Lady Sybil Mary McDonnell, *o. d.* of 6th Earl of Antrim; three *s.* four *d.* *Educ.:* Eton; Trinity

Hall Cambridge. *Heir:* s. Hon. Randal Hugh Vivian Smith. *Address:* Tusmore Park, Bicester, Oxon. *T.:* Fritwell 230. *Clubs:* Brooks's, White's, Turf.
[*Died* 17 *Feb.* 1956.

BICKFORD, Colonel William Wilfrid, C.I.E. 1913; late 106th Hazara Pioneers; *b.* 22 Sept. 1871; *s.* of late Staff-Surg. T. L. Bickford, R.N.; *m.* 1903, Ethel Julia Armstrong (*d.* 1944), *d.* of Capt. C. W. Ford, late East India Co. Service; two *s.* *Educ.:* Kelly Coll.; Sandhurst. Joined The Queen's R.W. Surrey Regt., 1891; Indian Army, 1896; served with Ogaden Expeditionary Force, East Africa, 1898 (medal with clasp); 2nd in command and Comdt. Zhob Militia, 1906-12; severely wounded in an affray with raiders in Zhob, 1912; India Despatches, 1916; Waziristan, 1917 (despatches, Bt. Lt.-Col.); Afghanistan, 1919 (despatches); Subst. Col., 1921; retired, 1923. *Address:* Huntly, Bishopsteignton, S. Devon.
[*Died* 24 *Jan.* 1951.

BIDDER, George Parker, Sc.D., F.L.S., F.Z.S., F.R.M.S.; Biologist; President of the Marine Biological Association of the U.K.; *b.* 21 May 1863; *e. s.* of George Parker Bidder, Q.C., J.P., F.R.A.S., and Anna, *d.* of J. R. McClean, M.P., F.R.S., and sister of Frank McClean, F.R.S.; *m.* 1899, Marion (*d.* 1932), *d.* of George Greenwood, Hull and Oxenhope, Yorks; two *d.* *Educ.:* Harrow (Prize Poem, 1881); Trinity College, Cambridge, (Exhibitioner in Mathematics and Science). Natural Sciences Tripos, 1884, 1st Class; 1886, 2nd Class. University Table at Naples Zoological Station, 1886 and 1888; researches on sponges at Naples, Plymouth, and Cambridge, 1886-1939; lectured on sponges at University of Cambridge, 1894 and 1920-27; Naples Jahresbericht (Sponges), 1892-94; Council Marine Biological Association of U.K. since 1899; owner, 1902-9, of steam-trawler Huxley (ex Khedive), British research vessel on International Exploration of North Sea; inventor of bottom trailers, 1904, for determining bottom currents of N. Sea; conducted researches with them, since continued by Ministry of Agriculture and Fisheries; attached to H.M.S. Vernon for research, 1915; Sc.D., 1916; Chairman of Meeting of British Zoologists, 1927, 1928; President of Zoological Section, British Association, 1927; of Devonshire Association, 1929; Vice-President Linnean Society, 1924 and 1931, Zoological Secretary, 1928-31; Proprietor Parker's Hotel, Naples, 1889-1922; Managing Director Cannock Chase Colliery Co., 1897-1908, Chairman, 1915-19; other directorships; Promoter, Secretary, 1925-28, and Director of the Company of Biologists Ltd.; owner of the Quarterly Journal of Microscopical Science. *Publications:* Investigations on sponges, ocean-currents, senescence, death, etc., in Proc. Roy. Soc., Q.J.M.S., Journ. and Proc. Linnean Soc., British Medical Journal, and other scientific journals; article Sponges in Enc. Brit., 1929; edited Vosmaer's posthumous Bibliography of Sponges, 1928: Arcus (Horace C. iii, 26) in Journ. of Philology, 1919; (verse) By Southern Shore, 1899; Merlin's Youth, 1899. *Address:* Cavendish Corner, Cambridge. *T.:* Cambridge 87502. *Clubs:* Savile, National Liberal; Royal South-Western Yacht; Cambridge University Cruising.
[*Died* 31 *Dec.* 1953.

BIDDULPH, Brig.-Gen. Harry, C.B. 1927; C.M.G. 1919; D.S.O. 1917; late R.E.; 3rd *s.* of late General Sir Robert Biddulph, G.C.B., G.C.M.G.; *b.* 1872; *m.* 1904, Constance Emily, *y. d.* of Rowland Smith of Duffield Hall, Derbyshire; two *s.* one *d.* Served Tirah Expedition, 1897 (medal two clasps): Waziristan Expedition, 1902; European War, 1914-19 (despatches, Bt. Lt.-Col. and Col., C.M.G., D.S.O.); Chief Engineer, Southern Command, 1927-28; Director of Works and Buildings, Air Ministry, 1928-31; retired pay, 1929. *Address:* Peters Finger, Salisbury.
[*Died* 21 *April* 1952.

BIGELOW, Poultney, M.A., F.R.G.S.; *b.* New York, 10 Sep. 1855; *y. s.* of late John Bigelow, American Ambassador to France. *Educ.:* Graduated Norwich (Conn.) Academy, 1873, and Yale, 1879; Columbia University Law School; admitted to practice at Supreme Court Bar, New York, 1882. Voyage round the world in sailing ship, 1875-76; wrecked on Japan coast: travelled China, South, West, and East Coast Africa, East and West Indies, Demerara, Australia, New Guinea, N. Borneo, India, Burmah, Java, etc.; canoe voyages on principal waters of the world; first to take canoe through the Iron Gates of the Danube; founder and first Editor of Outing as a monthly magazine of amateur sport; late Lecturer on Colonial Administration and History, etc., University of Boston, U.S.; U.S. Delegate to Berlin Geographical Congress, 1900, etc.; Correspondent London Times and New York Herald Spanish-American War, 1898, in which year he also visited the Philippines; has lectured extensively of late years before different Universities, including those of Japan, on Colonization and International relations; Chevalier Légion d'Honneur; Chairman Ends of the Earth Club, New York; Life Member of many learned Societies. *Publications:* The German Emperor and his Eastern Neighbours, 1891 (translations into German and French); Paddles and Politics down the Danube, 1892 (German translation); The Borderland of Czar and Kaiser, 1893 (German translation); History of the German Struggle for Liberty (4 vols.) 1895, period 1806-48; White Man's Africa, 1897 (French edit.); Children of the Nations, 1901 (German translation); Prussian Memories (1864-1914) (French translation), 1915; Genseric, King of the Vandals and First Prussian Kaiser, 1918; Prussianism and Pacifism, 1919; Japan and her Colonies, 1923; Memoirs: Seventy Summers, 2 volumes, 1925. *Recreations:* yachting, wood chopping. *Address:* Bigelow Homestead, Malden on Hudson, New York. *Clubs:* Athenæum, Authors', Royal Corinthian Yacht; Century (New York).
[*Died* 28 *May* 1954.

BIGGE, Sir Amherst S.; *see* Selby-Bigge, Sir L. A.

BIGGE, Colonel Thomas Arthur Hastings, C.B. 1916; C.M.G. 1919; Royal Engineers; *b.* 8 Dec. 1866; *e. s.* of Major-General T. S. C. Bigge, C.B.; *m.* 1889, Lucy Katherine (*d.* 1946), *d.* of late W. H. Bourne, Burren, Co. Cork; three *d.* *Educ.:* Oxford Military College; Royal Military Academy, Woolwich. Entered Royal Engineers, 1885; served in various parts of the world; European War (despatches, C.B., for service in the field, C.M.G., Commander of the Crown of Belgium); Assistant Adjutant-General for Royal Engineers at War Office, 1917-19; honorary rank of Brigadier-General. *Address:* c/o Lloyds Bank, 6 Pall Mall, S.W.1. *Club:* M.C.C.
[*Died* 29 *Dec.* 1955.

BIGGER, Joseph Warwick, M.A., M.D., Sc.D., F.R.C.P.I.; F.R.C.P. (Lond.); D.P.H.; Hon. F.T.C.D.; M.R.I.A.; Professor of Bacteriology and Preventive Medicine, Dublin University, 1924-50 and Dean of School of Physic, Trinity College, Dublin, 1936-50; *b.* Belfast, 11 Sept. 1891; *s.* of late Sir Edward Coey Bigger and Maude Coulter Warwick; *m.* 1916, Patricia Mai Curtin; one *s.* one *d.* *Educ.:* St. Andrew's Coll., Dublin; Trinity College, Dublin. Junior Exhibitioner, Medical Scholarship, Begley Studentship and Purser Medal; M.B., 1916; Demonstrator in Pathology and Bacteriology, University of Sheffield, 1916-1919; Pathologist and Medical Inspector, Local Government Board, Ireland, 1919-22; Professor Preventive Medicine and Forensic Medicine, Royal College of Surgeons, Ireland, 1920-22. War of 1939-45: Lt.-Col. R.A.M.C. and Assistant Director of Pathology, Northern Command, 1940-44. *Publications:* Hand-

book of Bacteriology (6th Edition, 1949); (Spanish Edition, 1935); Handbook of Hygiene (2nd Edition, 1941); Man Against Microbe, 1939; many scientific papers in Journal of Pathology and Bacteriology, Journal of Hygiene, Lancet, Irish Journal of Medical Science, etc. *Address:* c/o University Club, St. Stephen's Green, Dublin. *Clubs:* Athenæum; University (Dublin); Royal Irish Yacht (Kingstown).
[*Died* 17 *Aug.* 1951.

BIGHAM, Hon. Sir (Frank) Trevor R., K.B.E., *cr.* 1929; C.B. 1919; barrister-at-law; *b.* 1876; 2nd *s.* of 1st Viscount Mersey; *m.* 1st, 1901, Frances Leonora (*d.* 1927), 2nd *d.* of late John L. Tomlin, Richmond, Yorks; two *d.*; 2nd 1931, Edith Ellen, *d.* of Lt.-Col. David Drysdale. *Educ.:* Eton; Magdalen College, Oxford. Called to Bar, Middle Temple, 1901; Chief Constable, Metropolitan Police, 1909; Assistant Commissioner, 1914-31; Deputy Commissioner, 1931-34. *Address:* 3 Durham Place, S.W.3. *T.:* Flaxman 3897. *Club:* Oxford and Cambridge.
[*Died* 23 *Nov.* 1954.

BILLIMORIA, Sir Shapoorjee, Kt., *cr.* 1928; M.B.E. 1919; Sheriff of Bombay, 1935; President Parsee Panchayat Funds; Trustee, Sir Jamshedjee Jeejeebhoy Charity Funds and over a dozen other charity trusts and institutions; Member All India Accountancy Board (Chairman Bombay Local Committee); Chairman of Advisory Panel of Accountants; Pres. The Rotary Club of Bombay, 1936; Director, Rotary International, 1943 (Governor, 1939-40) (2nd Vice-Pres.); Grand Supt. of the Dist. Grand Royal Arch Chapter of India under Scotland; Grand Master of All Scottish Freemasonry in India, Pakistan and Ceylon; Fiscal Agent, for Rotary Internat., India, since 1948; *b.* Bombay, 27 July 1877; *m.* Jerbai, *d.* of Bhickaji N. Dalal; three *s.* *Educ.:* St. Xavier's College, Bombay. Founder Society of Professional Accountants, Bombay; Member City of Bombay Improvement Trust; President Indian Merchants' Chamber, 1928; President Indian Chamber of Commerce in Great Britain, 1928-29, 1929-30; Member, Government of India Back Bay Inquiry Committee; Member Auditors' Council nominated by the Governor of Bombay; Nominee of Bombay Govt. on Board of the Institute of Science, Bangalore and Sir Jamshedjee Jeejeebhoy Benevolent Institution, Bombay; J.P. and Honorary Presidency Magistrate, Bombay; Silver Jubilee Medal, 1935; Coronation Medal, 1937. *Publications:* Balance Sheet and Statutory Requirements under the Indian Companies' Act. *Address:* 21 Cuffe Parade, Colaba, Bombay, India. *T.A.:* Methodical, Bombay. *T.:* 2539 and 64-65. *Clubs:* National Liberal; Willingdon Sports, Orient (Bombay).
[*Died* 27 *Aug.* 1958.

BILLINGHAM, Col. John Alfred Lawrence, C.B.E. 1931; *b.* 1868; *s.* of Alfred Billingham; *m.* Florence (*d.* 1947), *d.* of James Barter, J.P.; one *s.* two *d.* *Educ.:* Bedford Modern School. Entered Staff for Royal Engineer Services 1890; Chief Inspector of Works, War Office, 1928-33; retired 1933; Fellow of the Royal Institution of Chartered Surveyors, London. *Recreations:* horticulture, photography. *Address:* 11 Woodlands Road, Surbiton, Surrey. *T.:* Elmbridge 2737.
[*Died* 21 *March* 1955.

BILLINTON, Lt.-Col. Lawson, C.B.E. 1919; M.I.M.E.; M.I.S.I.; retired; *b.* 1882; *s.* of Robert John Billinton, engineer; *m.* Edith Sarah, *d.* of Frederick Hilton. *Educ.:* Tonbridge School. Served European War, 1914-19 (despatches, C.B.E., Order of Crown of Roumania with Swords). *Address:* The Green Hill, Somers Road, Lyme Regis, Dorset. *T.:* Lyme Regis 110.
[*Died* 19 *Nov.* 1954.

BILTON, Lieut.-Col. Lewis Leonard, C.M.G. 1918; J.P. Edinburgh; *m.* 1911, Helen Rachel, *e. d.* of Neil Robson, of Dixons', Ltd., Glasgow; four *s.* *Educ.:* Edinburgh Academy and University. Passed W.S. 1904; firm L. and L. L. Bilton, W.S.; when the War began, raised a Company of the A.S.C. and served as Captain till the 17th Royal Scots (Rosebery) Regiment was raised, of which he was appointed Major; in France was given command of the 2/8th Worcestershire Regiment and gazetted Lt.-Col. (despatches twice, C.M.G., Croix de Guerre); Vice-President of the Boys Brigade, Edinburgh Battalion. *Recreations:* shooting, golfing, etc. *Address:* 17 Rutland Street, Edinburgh. *T.:* Edinburgh Fountainbridge 5441. *Club:* Caledonian United Service.
[*Died* 2 *Dec.* 1954.

BINGHAM, Colonel Charles Henry Marion, C.M.G. 1919; D.S.O. 1916; *b.* 27 Dec. 1873; *s.* of late Col. C. T. Bingham, Indian Army; *m.* 1905, Rose, *d.* of late Col. A. S. Cameron, V.C., C.B., Seaforth Highlanders and K.O.S.B.; two *s.* one *d.* *Educ.:* Sandhurst. Joined Loyal N. Lanc. Regt. 1893; served with the regt. in S. African War (twice severely wounded, losing the left arm; despatches); joined A.S.C. 1902; passed Staff College, 1908-9; served on the Staff in France, 1915-16 (despatches, D.S.O.), and in Italy, Nov. 17 to end of war (despatches twice, C.M.G.); Ireland, 1922; retired pay, 1926. *Address:* 7 Baldernock Road, Milngavie, Dunbartonshire.
[*Died* 23 *April* 1957.

BINNEY, Admiral Sir (Thomas) Hugh, K.C.B., *cr.* 1940 (C.B. 1936); K.C.M.G., *cr.* 1951; D.S.O. 1919; *b.* 9 Dec. 1883; *e. s.* of T. G. Binney, late of Guisnes Court, Tolleshunt D'Arcy, Essex; *m.* 1942, Elizabeth Bride, C.St.J., *e. d.* of late Lt.-Col. H. F. Blair-Imrie, C.M.G., O.B.E. *Educ.:* H.M.S. Britannia. Gunnery Officer H.M.S. Queen Elizabeth, 1914-18; Staff of C.-in-C., Grand Fleet, 1918; Capt. 1922; H.M.S. Cardiff, 1923-25; Dep. Director of Plans Div., Admiralty, 1925-27; Flag Captain, H.M.S. Nelson, 1928-30; Director Tactical School, 1931-32; commanded H.M.S. Hood, 1932-1933; Chief of Staff to C.-in-C., Plymouth, 1933-35; A.D.C. to King George V., 1934; Rear-Admiral, 1934; Rear-Admiral, First Battle Squadron, 1936-38; Vice-Adm., 1938; Commandant Imperial Defence College, 1939; Adm. Commanding Orkneys and Shetlands, 1939-42; Adm., 1942; retired list, 1943; Flag Officer, Cardiff, 1944. Governor of Tasmania, 1945-51. K.G.St.J., 1946. *Address:* Scrips, Coggeshall, Essex. *T.:* Coggeshall 200. *Clubs:* United Service; (Hon. Member) Royal Yacht Squadron (Cowes).
[*Died* 8 *Jan.* 1953.

BINNIE, Thomas Inglis, C.M.G. 1916; F.R.E.S.; *b.* 17 June 1874; *s.* of Thomas Binnie and Mary Taylor; *m.* 1904, Janie Alexander; one *d.* (one *s.* decd.). *Educ.:* Abbotsford School, Glasgow. Articled to Messrs. Johnston & Rankine, Glasgow, 1891-1896; joined railway survey party in Nyasaland (then British Central Africa), 1896; Supervisor of Roads, British Central Africa Protectorate, 1897; Surveyor to Anglo-Portuguese Provisional Boundary Delimitation, 1899-1900; Chief Surveyor, 1900; Director of Public Works, Nyasaland, 1904. *Address:* 88 Fourth St., Umtali, S. Rhodesia.
[*Died* 18 *July* 1954.

BINNS, Arthur, C.B.E. 1920; late Deputy Chief Inspector of Taxes, Inland Revenue Dept.; *b.* Bradford, 25 Sep. 1861; *m.* Edith Jane (*d.* 1946), *d.* of William Byles, proprietor of the Yorkshire Observer; two *s.* two *d.* *Educ.:* Bradford Gram. Sch. *Recreations:* gardening, and giving voluntary service to religious and philanthropic societies. *Address:* 60 Oxgate Gardens,

N.W.2. *T.:* Gladstone 3101. *Club:* National Liberal. [*Died* 14 *March* 1952.

BINNS, Sir Bernard (Ottwell), K.B.E., *cr.* 1948 (O.B.E. 1941); Expert in Land Tenure, Administration and Settlement, Food and Agricultural Organisation of the United Nations; *b.* 16 July 1898; *s.* of late Ottwell Binns and Rosetta Annie Foote; *m.* 1928, Dorothy Mary Ambrose; one *d.* *Educ.:* Bury Grammar School, Lancs.; Brasenose College, Oxford (Open Scholarship in Classics). Served European War, 1914–18, 2nd Lt., Gen. List, British Army, 1917; Indian Army R. of O., 1917–19, attached 2nd/9th Delhi Inf. and 37th Dogra Regt., I.A. Oxford, 1919–23, B.A. (Lit. Hum.) 1922, M.A. 1949. I.C.S., competitive examination, 1922; appointed I.C.S. 1922; served in Burma, 1923–47, mainly in Finance and Revenue Departments, including: Dep. Secretary, Finance Department, 1935–36, Commissioner of Settlements and Land Records, 1936–41, Governor's Secretary, 1941–42, Comr. Sagaing Div., 1942, Joint Sec. Reconstruction Dept., 1942–45; Financial Comr., 1945–47; leave preparatory to retirement, 1947; retired from I.C.S., 1949. Attended various internat. confs. on agrarian and agricultural matters, including Hot Springs, Va., 1943, Singapore, 1946, Trivandrum, 1947. F.R.S.A. 1950; F.R.G.S. 1951. Recognised as Govt. of Burma's expert on agrarian problems, land taxation, administration and on rice production, and has made considerable studies of agrarian problems in tropical countries especially related to Burma. *Publications:* Revenue Settlement Report, Amherst District, 1930–33, Pegu District, 1932–34; Agricultural Economy in Burma, 1943 (all official publications of Govt. of Burma); Consolidation of Fragmented Agricultural Holdings, 1950, Land Settlement for Agriculture, 1951, Agricultural Credit for Small Farmers, 1951; Cadastral Surveys and Registration of Rights in Land, 1953: Large Centrally Operated Agricultural Estates, 1953 (all official publications of F.A.O.). *Recreation:* field botany. *Address:* Lloyds Bank, Ltd., Eastern Dept., 34 Threadneedle St., E.C.2; (private) Via Guerrieri 5, Rome; (office) F.A.O., Viale delle Terme di Caracalla, Rome. *Club:* East India and Sports. [*Died* 8 *Dec.* 1953.

BINNS, Sir Frank, Kt., *cr.* 1946; Chairman, Managing Director or Director of a number of Companies in the Woollen and Worsted Textile Industry and of Agricultural Estates in Yorkshire; *b.* 3 April 1898; 2nd *s.* of late Asa and of Alice Maud Binns of Allerton, and of Braes Castle, Harden, Yorkshire; *m.* 1927, Edith Mary, 2nd *d.* of Wilfrid Naylor, Riddlesden, Yorkshire; two *s.* *Educ.:* Allerton, Carlton High School; privately. Adviser Ministry of Labour and National Service, 1941–46. Special Mission (Govt.) to advise Economic Mission to Greece, 1946. Other important advisory positions. *Recreations:* shooting, golf, and fishing. *Address:* Swinden Hall, Hellifield, Yorks; Park Grange, Bingley, Yorks. *T.:* Hellifield 238, Bingley 415. [*Died* 23 *Oct.* 1954.

BIRCH, Albert Edward Henry, B.A.; J.P. Norfolk; *b.* 1868; *s.* of late Rev. Canon H. M. Birch and Hariet Julia, *d.* of Thomas Drinkwater of Irwell House, Lancashire; *m.* 1921, Alice Marian (*d.* 1922), *d.* of Geoffrey Hollway; no *c.* *Educ.:* Eton; Trinity Hall, Cambridge. *Recreations:* hunting and shooting. *Address:* Watlington Hall, King's Lynn, Norfolk. *T.A.:* Watlington, Norfolk. *Club:* Junior Carlton. [*Died* 31 *Jan.* 1954.

BIRCH, Francis Lyall, C.M.G. 1945; O.B.E.(1919); M.A.; F.R.Hist.S.; attached to a Dept. of Foreign Office since 1939; Lt.-Cmdr. R.N.V.R.; author, producer, and actor; *b.* 5 Dec. 1889; 3rd *s.* of John Arden Birch and the late Viscountess Barrington; *m.* 1919, Vera Benedicta Gage, *sister* of 6th Visc. Gage, K.C.V.O. *Educ.:* Eton; King's Coll., Cambridge. Exhibitioner in Modern Languages, 1909; Foundation Scholar in History, 1911; 1st class Part I. of the Historical Tripos, 1911; 1st class Part II., 1912; Winchester Reading Prize, 1912. Served with the Navy, 1914–16, Channel, Atlantic, and Dardanelles; Naval Intelligence Division, 1916–19; Fellow of King's College, Cambridge, 1915–34; Lecturer in History at Cambridge University, 1921–28. *Publications:* Mountebanks, a play in 3 acts; Life's a Dream, a translation from Calderon (with J. B. Trend); This Freedom of Ours, 1937. *Recreation:* sailing. *Address:* 11 Montpelier Walk, Knightsbridge, S.W.7. *T.:* Kensington 0561. [*Died* 14 *Feb.* 1956.

BIRCH, S. J. Lamorna, R.A. 1934 (A.R.A. 1926); R.W.S. 1914; R.B.C.; R.W.A.; *b.* Egremont, Cheshire, 7 June 1869; *m.* 1902, Emily Houghton (*d.* 1944); two *d.* Represented in Oil and Water Colour in Public Galleries in Great Britain, Manchester, Liverpool, Preston, Oldham, Bury, Brighton, Newcastle, Glasgow, Belfast, Birmingham, etc., Toronto, New Zealand, Providence, Rhode Island, etc.; visited New Zealand and Australia, 1937; pictures bought for galleries at Wellington, Auckland, Dunedin, Adelaide, Sydney. *Recreations:* trout and salmon fishing. *Address:* Flagstaff Cottage, Lamorna, near Penzance. *T.:* Mousehole 28. *Clubs:* Arts, Chelsea Arts. [*Died* 7 *Jan.* 1955.

BIRCHENOUGH, Very Rev. Godwin, M.A.; Dean Emeritus of Ripon since 1951; *b.* 27 Oct. 1880; *s.* of Walter Edwin Birchenough and Emily Gertrude Godwin; *m.* 1912, Edith Gladys, *e. d.* of Ernest Charles Keay, Edgbaston, Birmingham; no *c.* *Educ.:* Rugby School; Oriel College, Oxford; Leeds Clergy School. Curate of St. Michael's, Wakefield, 1905–08; St. Augustine's, Edgbaston, 1908–13; Vicar of Moor Allerton, 1913–21; Rural Dean of Wanstead and Woodford, 1928–34; Hon. Canon of Chelmsford Cathedral, 1933; Rector of Wanstead, 1921–40; Dean of Ripon, 1941–51, resigned; Vice-Chairman of Additional Curates Society, 1934–44; Master of the Hospital of St. John and St. Mary Magdalen, Ripon, 1941. *Publication:* Human Relationships. *Recreation:* motoring. *Address:* Moore's Orchard, Cobham, Surrey. [*Died* 3 *March* 1953.

BIRD, Rt. Rev. Cyril Henry; *see* Golding-Bird.

BIRD, Sir Robert Bland, 2nd Bt., *cr.* 1922; K.B.E., *cr.* 1954; Former Chairman Alfred Bird & Sons, Ltd., Birmingham; Member of Royal Institution; Liveryman of Barbers' Company; *b.* 20 Sept. 1876; *s.* of 1st Bt. and Eleanor Frances (*d.* 1943), *e. d.* of Robert Lloyd Evans; *S.* father, 1922; *m.* 1904, Edith Wilmshurst, O.B.E. 1957, *y. d.* of Stephen William Challen; one *d.* *Educ.:* King Edward VI School, Birmingham. M.P. (C.), Wolverhampton (West), 1922–29 and 1931–45. Formerly: Trustee of The Royal Orphanage, Wolverhampton; Chairman of Trustees of Manor House, Solihull; Pres. of Midland Union of Conservative Associations; Chm. of Franco Brittanique Inter-Parliamentary Cttee., House of Commons; Vice-Pres. Soc. of Model Aeronautical Engineers. Chevalier de la Légion d'Honneur; Officier de l'Ordre de Léopold. *Recreations:* photography and cinematography in natural colours, particularly portraits; tennis, golf, cycling, motoring, and construction and flight of experimental model aeroplanes; similarly model speed boats operating with miniature explosion engines. *Heir:* *nephew* Donald Geoffrey [*b.* 1906; *m.* 1930, Anne Rowena Chapman; two *s.* one *d.*]. *Address:* The White House, Solihull, Warwickshire.

T.: **Solihull 0080; 25 Chapel St., S.W.1.** *T.:* Belgravia 5677. *Clubs:* Carlton, Royal **Automobile.** [*Died* 20 *Nov.* 1960.

BIRDWOOD, 1st Baron, *cr.* 1938, of Anzac and of Totnes; **Field-Marshal William Riddell Birdwood,** 1st Bt., *cr.* 1919; G.C.B., *cr.* 1923 (K.C.B., *cr.* 1917; C.B. 1911); G.C.S.I., *cr.* 1930 (K.C.S.I., *cr.* 1915); G.C.M.G., *cr.* 1919 (K.C.M.G., *cr.* 1914); G.C.V.O., *cr.* 1937; C.I.E. 1908; D.S.O. 1908; M.A. Cambridge, 1931, Hon. LL.D. Cambridge. 1919, Melbourne (Vict.) and Sydney (N.S.W.), 1920, Bristol, 1935; Hon. D.C.L. Durham, 1931; Hon. Litt.D. Reading, 1938; President, Clifton College, 1935; Captain Deal Castle, 1935; Hon. Fellow Peterhouse, Cambridge, 1920; Knight of Grace, Order of St. John of Jerusalem; Fellow of the Royal Empire Society and of Royal Society of St. George; Freeman of the Borough of Totnes, Devon; Vice-Pres. of the Overseas League and Devonian Association; Trustee unpaid, War Museum; General, Commonwealth of Australia Military Forces, 1920. and Field-Marshal, 1925; Colonel Royal Horse Guards, 1933; 12th Lancers, 1920; 75th A. A. Regiment, R.A., 1938; King Edward's Own Probyns' Horse (XI. Bengal Lancers), 1924, and 6th Gurkha Rifles, 1925; Col. Commandant, 13th Frontier Force Rifles, 1930; Colonel-in-Chief, 1st New Zealand Mounted Rifles, Canterbury Yeomanry Cavalry, 1925; Colonel 3rd Australian Infantry and 16th Australian Light Horse. Hunter River Lancers, 1930; *b.* 13 Sept. 1865; *e. surv. s.* of late H. M. Birdwood, C.S.I., J.P., LL.D., M.A. (Cantab.) I.C.S.; *m.* 1894, Jeannette Hope Gonville (*d.* 1947), Order of the Crown of India, 1930, *e. d.* of Colonel Sir B. P. Bromhead, C.B., 4th Bart., of Thurlby Hall, Lincoln; one *s.* two *d.* *Educ.:* Clifton College; R.M.C., Sandhurst. Lieut. 4th Batt. Royal Scots Fusiliers, 1883; 12th Lancers, 1885; 11th Bengal Lancers, 1887; Capt., 1896; Major, 1900; Lt.-Col., 1902; Col., 1905; Brig.-Gen., 1909; Maj.-Gen., 1911; Lt.-Gen., 1915; Gen., 1917; Field-Marshal, 1925; Adjt. 11th Bengal Lancers, 1889; Adjt. Viceroy's Bodyguard, 1893; Brig.-Major, S. Africa, 1899; D.A.A.G., S. Africa, 1900; Military Secretary to Com.-in-Chief, South Africa (General Lord Kitchener), 1902; A.M.S. and Interpreter to Com.-in-Chief, India, 1902; A.A.G., Headquarters, India, 1904; Military Secretary to Com.-in-Chief, General Viscount Kitchener, India, 1905; Brigade Commander Kóhat Brigade, N.W.F.P., India, 1909; Quartermaster-General in India, 1912; Secretary to the Government of India in the Army Department and Member of the Governor-General's Legislative Council, 1912-14; G.O.C. Australian and N.Z. Army Corps, 1914-18, and Australian Imperial Force, 1915-20; General Officer Commanding-in-Chief, Northern Army in India, 1920-24; Comm.-in-Chief of the Army in India, 1925-30; Mem. of the Executive Council of the Gov.-Gen., and Mem. of the Council of State of India, 1925; Master of Peterhouse, Cambridge, 1931-38; A.D.C. to the King, 1906-11; A.D.C. General to the King, 1917-22; Acting C.-in-C., Member Viceroy's Executive Council and Council of State, India, 1924; served Hazara, 1891 (medal with clasp); Isazai, 1892; N.W. Frontier, India, 1897-98 (medal, two clasps); Tirah, 1897-98 (despatches, clasp); S. Africa, 1899-1902 (severely wounded, despatches five times, brevets of Major and Lieut.-Col., Queen's medal 6 clasps, King's medal 2 clasps); Chief Staff Officer Mohmand Expedition, 1908 (despatches, medal and clasp, D.S.O.); served in command of detached landing of Australian and New Zealand Army Corps above Gaba Tepe (wounded); Com.-in-Chief, Mediterranean Expeditionary Force, and commanded Dardanelles Army, 1915-16, for Evacuation of Gallipoli Peninsula; Aust. and N.Z. Army Corps, and Australian Forces, France, 1916-18; commanded 5th Army, France, 1918-19 (despatches many times—promoted Lieut.-Gen.); Grand Cross of the Legion of Honour, Croix de Guerre, France; Grand Officer of the Crown, and Croix de Guerre, Belgium; Grand Cordon of the Tower and Sword, Grand Officer of the Military Order of Aviz and Grand Cross of the Order of Christ of Portugal; Order of the Rising Sun, 1st Class, of Japan; Order of the Nile, 2nd Class; 1st Class Order of Timsa, Persia; Grand Cross Star of Nepal; American Dis. Ser. Medal. *Publications:* Khaki and Gown, 1941; In My Time, 1946. *Heir: s.* Lt.-Col. Hon. Christopher Bromhead Birdwood, M.V.O. *Address:* Deal Castle, Kent; Hampton Court Palace. *Clubs:* Cavalry, Army and Navy, Guards', Union, Overseas, Naval and Military, United University.
[*Died* 17 *May* 1951.

BIRKBECK, Geoffrey, J.P.; water-colour painter; *b.* Stoke Holy Cross, Norwich, 12 Oct. 1875; *s.* of late Henry Birkbeck and Etheldreda, *sister* of Sir William Ffolkes, 3rd Bt.; *m.*, 1st, 1904, Dora (*d.* 1925), *d.* of late James Christopher Wilson of Lownook, Westmorland; one *s.*; 2nd, 1930, Lady Maud Gundreda (*d.* 1940), *d.* of late Earl of Cavan, and *widow* of Henry J. Barrett; 3rd, 1943, Daisy Muriel Ritchie. *Educ.:* Eton. Convert to Catholic Church, 1901. Works include: Blickling Hall, Storm at Salthouse, Wheatfield at Stoke, the Green Chandelier. *Publication:* Old Norfolk Houses. *Recreations:* travelling, gardening, etc. *Address:* Poringland, Norwich. *Club:* Arts.
[*Died* 25 *April* 1954.

BIRKBECK, Major Henry Anthony, M.C.; J.P.; D.L.; Director of Barclays Bank, Ltd.; *b.* 1885; *e. s.* of late Henry Birkbeck; *m.* 1912, Sybil (*d.* 1948), 2nd *d.* of Robert W. D. and Hon. Mrs. Harley of Brampton Bryan, Herefordshire; two *s.* three *d.* (and one *s.* decd.). *Educ.:* Eton; Trinity College, Cambridge. Served European War, 1914-18, in Gallipoli, Egypt, Palestine, France; Major, Norfolk Yeomanry; patron of two livings. *Recreations:* hunting, shooting, fishing. *Address:* West-acre High House, Castleacre. King's Lynn, Kinloch Hourn, Invergarry. *Clubs:* Brooks's, Boodle's. [*Died* 16 *Aug.* 1956.

BIRKBECK, Col. Oliver; landowner; M.F.H., West Norfolk, 1929-37; *b.* 2 May 1893; *s.* of Edward Lewis Birkbeck and Emily, *d.* of late Vice-Admiral George Henry Seymour, C.B.; *m.* 1928, Lady Joan FitzClarence, sister of 5th Earl of Munster; two *s.* one *d.* *Educ.:* Eton. Served through European War. *Address:* Little Massingham House, Norfolk. *T.A.:* Great Massingham, Norfolk. *T.:* Great Massingham 2. *Clubs:* Buck's, White's.
[*Died* 13 *May* 1952.

BIRKETT, Sir Thomas William, Kt. *cr.* 1918; of Beldorney, Aberdeenshire; *b.* 11 March 1871; *m.* 1910, Dorothy Nina Forbes. *Educ.:* Cheltenham College. Chairman Bombay Chamber of Commerce, 1915-16; Additional Member Bombay Governor's Council, 1914; Additional Member Viceroy's Council, 1915-16; Sheriff of Bombay, 1917. *Recreations:* fishing, shooting. *Address:* 39 Cheyne Walk, S.W.3; Beldorney Castle, Aberdeenshire.
[*Died* 15 *Aug.* 1957.

BIRKS, Falconer Moffat, C.B.E. 1945 (O.B.E. 1918); M.Inst.C.E.; M.Inst.Mech.E., *b.* Ruardene, Gloucester, 13 Apr. 1885; *s.* of H. and F. E. Birks; *m.* 1915, Monica Katharine Lushington (*d.* 1957), *d.* of Rev. W. J. Mellor; one *s.* one *d.* *Educ.:* Crypt School, Gloucester. Asst. Engineer, Swansea Harbour Trust, 1908. Served European War, 1914-18 (O.B.E., despatches). Gas Light & Coke Co., Mechanical Engineer, 1921; Dep. Chief Engineer, 1935; Chief Engineer, 1941;

Managing Director. 1945; Dep. Governor, 1946-49; Deputy Chairman North Thames Gas Board, 1949-56. *Address:* 6 Vine Place, Brighton 1. *T.:* 29312. *Club:* Royal Thames Yacht. [*Died* 13 *April* 1960.

BIRLEY, Leonard, C.S.I. 1926; C.I.E. 1914; *b.* 30 May 1875; *s.* of late Arthur Birley; *m.* 1st, 1902, Grace Dalgleish (*d.* 1906), *d.* of late Maxwell Smith; one *s.* one *d.*; 2nd, 1908, Jessie Craig, *d.* of late Maxwell Smith, Hursingpur, Tirhoot, India. *Educ.:* Uppingham; New College, Oxford. Entered I.C.S. 1897; Joint Magistrate and Deputy Collector, 1907; Magistrate and Collector, 1911; Revenue Secretary to Government of Bengal, 1915-18; Magistrate and Collector of Chittagong, 1922; Chief Secretary to Government of Bengal, 1922-26; Member of Bengal Executive Council, temporarily, 1926; retired from I.C.S. *Address:* 8 Cavendish Road, Bournemouth. *T.:* Bournemouth 3668. [*Died* 18 *Dec.* 1951.

BIRLEY, Captain Sir Oswald Hornby Joseph, Kt. *cr.* 1949; M.C. 1917; R.O.I., painter; *b.* Auckland, New Zealand, 31 March 1880; *s.* of Hugh Francis and Elizabeth Birley, The Mount, St. Asaph, N. Wales; *m.* 1921, Rhoda Vava Mary, *d.* of Robert Lecky Pike, D.L., Kilnock, Tullow, Co. Carlow; one *s.* one *d.* *Educ.:* Harrow; Trinity College, Cambridge. Studied in Dresden, Florence, and Paris (Académie Julian under Marcel Baschet); Hors Concours, Paris Salon; Vice-President Royal Portrait Society; Portraits of first Earl of Birkenhead and Glyn Philpot, R.A. in National Portrait Gallery; Portrait of King George V. and Queen Mary for Windsor Castle; Portraits of King George VI. for Royal Agricultural Society, Royal Naval College, Greenwich, and for the Royal Collection; Portrait of H.M. Queen Elizabeth for R.M.S. Queen Elizabeth; Portraits of Marquess of Reading, Lord Irwin, Marquess of Willingdon and Marquess of Linlithgow in Viceroy's House, New Delhi; series of portraits in National Museum of Wales, Cardiff, of Presidents of the Museum, including portrait of King George V.; Collection of portraits of Admirals of War of 1939-45 for Royal Naval College, Greenwich; Mirror Portrait bought for Edmund Davis Collection, Musée de Luxembourg, 1915; Mamie Cartier acquired for the same Museum, 1930; Represented in National Art Gallery, New Zealand, Birmingham, Liverpool; Painting travels in America, Mexico, Siam, and India; enlisted in 10th Bn. Royal Fusiliers, Sep. 1914; served with Bn. until June 1915; Captain, 1916; in France with Intelligence Corps, 1916-1919 (M.C.). Sussex Home Guard, June 1940-43. *Address:* 62 Wellington Road, N.W.8. *T.:* Primrose 3471; Charleston Manor, West Dean, Seaford, Sussex. *T.:* Alfriston 267. *Clubs:* Turf, Buck's. [*Died* 6 *May* 1952.

BIRLEY, Mrs. Percy Langton, C.B.E. 1938; J.P.; *b.* 7 Aug. 1875; *d.* of late Henry Addison Hassall; *m.* 1902; twin *s.* one *d.* *Educ.:* privately. Chief Commissioner Girl Guides for 10 years; County Pres. Girl Guides for N.W. Lancs.; President Blackburn Diocesan Mothers' Union; elected to House of Laity, 1945, as one of Blackburn representatives. *Address:* Wrea Green, Preston, Lancs. *T.A.:* Wrea Green. *T.:* Kirkham 3229. *Club:* Lady Golfers. [*Died* 30 *Aug.* 1956.

BIRNAGE, Arthur; Editor of Public Opinion, 1925-50; *b.* 1874; *e. s.* of J. W. Birnage, Bournemouth; *m.* 1896, Emily (*d.* 1950), *d.* of B. Bullivant, Dulwich and Plymouth; three *s.* two *d.* *Educ.:* St. Peter's Collegiate School, Peterborough. Assistant Editor, Temperance Chronicle, 1892-95; Amalgamated Press, 1895-1912; served as Director last five years; Editor, Sunday Companion and Allied Journals, and first Editor Woman's Weekly; Editor Court Journal, 1914-25. *Recreation:* walking. *Address:* Finedon, Shirley Drive, Hove. *T.:* Preston Brighton 53289. *Club:* National Liberal. [*Died* 25 *Oct.* 1953.

BIRNAM, Hon. Lord; Sir (Thomas) David King Murray, Kt., *cr.* 1941; K.C. 1933; LL.D. (Glasgow), 1952; M.A., B.Sc., LL.B., F.R.S.E.; Senator of the College of Justice in Scotland and Lord of Session since 1945; *b.* 1884; *s.* of late James Murray, Greenknowe, Bothwell; *m.* 1946, Edith Lilian Archer. *Educ.:* Hamilton Academy; Glasgow High School; Glasgow University. Called to Scots Bar, 1910; served European War as Lieutenant R.N.V.R.; Junior Counsel to the Treasury in Scotland, 1927-28; Sheriff-Substitute of Lanarkshire at Airdrie, 1928-33. Senior Advocate-Depute, 1936-38; Chairman Scottish Land Court (with judicial title of Lord Murray), 1938-41; Chairman Scottish Coalfields Committee, 1942-44; Solicitor-General for Scotland, 1941-45; M.P. (C.) North Midlothian, 1943-45. *Recreations:* golf, travel. *Address:* 36 Colinton Road, Edinburgh. *Clubs:* Constitutional; New (Edinburgh). [*Died* 5 *June* 1955.

BISCHOFF, Thomas Hume, M.C.; Solicitor; Partner in firm of Bischoff & Co., 4 Great Winchester Street, E.C.2, since 1914; *b.* 9 Jan. 1886; *s.* of late Thomas William Bischoff, Solicitor, Ditton Hill, Surrey, and late Menella Frances Dodgson; unmarried. *Educ.:* Rugby; Trinity College, Oxford (M.A.). Solicitor, 1910; served European War, Royal Field Artillery (despatches twice, M.C.); Staff Captain R.F.A., 41st Divisional Artillery; Member of Council of Law Society, 1923-37; Chairman of Legal Education Committee of Law Society, 1928-37; served on Lord Chancellor's Committee on Legal Education under Chairmanship of Lord Atkin; Member of Board of Management of Hospital for Sick Children, Great Ormond Street, Vice-Chairman, 1943, Acting Chairman, 1946; Chairman, 1947 and since 1948. Chairman Institute of Child Health; Member Board of Management, Hospital of St. John and St. Elizabeth. Gentiluomo to the Archbishop of Westminster, 1944. *Recreation:* golf. *Address:* Bell Mount, Watchbell St., Rye. *Clubs:* United University, Canning; Dormy House (Rye). [*Died* 27 *July* 1951.

BISCOE, Brig.-Gen. J. D. T. T.; *see* Tyndale-Biscoe.

BISHOP, Laurence Arthur, C.S.I. 1947; O.B.E. 1941; *b.* 3 Feb. 1895; *s.* of Dr. Arthur Wright Bishop, Ph.D., sometime Director of Public Instruction, Travancore State, S. India, and Constance Eleanor (*née* Hoskyns-Abrahall); *m.* 1932, Dorothy, *d.* of Col. E. W. Slayter, C.M.G., D.S.O., A.M.S. (retd.); one *s.* *Educ.:* Uppingham; Brighton College; R.M.C., Sandhurst. Prize cadetship R.M.C., 1912; joined Indian Police, Madras Presidency, 1914; attached 73rd and 80th Carnatic Inf., 1916-18; Superintendent of Police, 1923; Commr. of Police, Travancore State, 1928-32; Dep. Insp. Gen. of Police, 1939; in charge Madras Presidency C.I.D., Special Branch and Railway Police, 1942; Inspector-General of Police, 1944; retiring Sept. 1949. King's Police Medal, 1944. *Address:* 5 Sweetwaters Road, Pietermaritzburg, Natal, S. Africa. [*Died* 15 *Jan.* 1954.

BISHOP, Walter Frederick, C.B.E. 1944; Director of: W. T. Henley's Telegraph Works Co. Ltd., Henley's Tyre & Rubber Co. Ltd., Henley's (South Africa) Telegraph Works Co. Ltd., Connolly's (Blackley) Ltd., and other companies; *b.* 2 May 1879; *s.* of Emily Elizabeth and George Thomas Bishop; *m.* 1903; one *d.* *Educ.:* Grocers' Company School; City and Guilds, London. Entered W. T. Henley's Telegraph

Works Co. Ltd., 1895; Asst. Gen. Manager, 1925; Gen. Manager, 1932; Director, 1933; sometime Chairman, Cable Makers' Assoc.; Freeman of City of London. *Recreations:* golf, reading, gardening (Past Master of Worshipful Company of Gardeners). *Address:* Ashridge, The Ridgeway, Enfield Chase, Middlesex. *T.:* Enfield 0247. *Clubs:* City Livery, Royal Automobile, Crews Hill Golf. [*Died* 27 *April* 1955.

BISHOP, Air Marshal William Avery, V.C. 1917; C.B. 1944; D.S.O. and Bar, 1917; M.C. 1917; D.F.C. 1918; E.D. 1944; LL.D. (Toronto), 1941; Director, Consolidated Quebec Gold Mining & Metals Corporation; Chairman National Advisory Board, Canadian Salvation Army; *b.* Owen Sound, Canada, 8 February 1894; *s.* of William Avery Bishop and Margaret Louise Greene, Owen Sound, Ont.; *m.* 1917, Margaret Eaton, *d.* of C. E. Burden, 494 Avenue Road, Toronto; one *s.* one *d.* *Educ.:* Owen Sound Collegiate; Royal Military College, Kingston, Canada. Went overseas with 7th C.M.R. as Lt.; transferred to Royal Flying Corps, 1915; Capt. R.F.C., 1917; Major, 1917; Lieut.Col., 1918; officially credited with bringing down 72 enemy aircraft (despatches, M.C., D.S.O. and bar, V.C., D.F.C., Legion of Honour, Croix de Guerre with Palm); Air Vice-Marshal, 1936; Air Marshal, 1938; Chm. Hon. Air Advisory Cttee. to Minister of Nat. Defence, 1938-39; Director Royal Canadian Air Force, 1939-45. Special War Medal of Aero Club of America, Special Medallion Imperial Air Fleet Committee of Great Britain, Gold Medal Aero Club of France; covered principal cities of U.S., lecturing on Aerial Warfare, 1919-20. Church of England. *Publications:* Winged Warfare, 1918; The Flying Squad: Hunting the Huns in the Air; Winged Peace, 1944; contributions to the Press on Aviation matters in Great Britain, Canada and U.S.A. *Recreations:* polo, golf, squash, hunting. *Address:* 1151 Closse St., Montreal, Quebec, Canada. *Clubs:* Buck's; The Brook (New York); Mount Royal (Montreal); York (Toronto); Motor Yacht de la Côte d'Azur (Cannes). [*Died* 11 *Sept.* 1956.

BISPHAM, James Webb, O.B.E.; M.A., B.Sc.; Administrative Staff, Institution of Mechanical Engineers. Formerly Deputy Education Officer, London County Council; *s.* of late Thomas Bispham, B.A., Dulwich; *m.* Ethel Annie, *d.* of late J. Baker, Elstead, Surrey; one *d.* *Educ.:* Emmanuel College, Cambridge. Inspector of Schools, 1909-19; Principal of Borough Polytechnic, 1922-33; Senior Assistant Education Officer, then Deputy Education Officer, L.C.C., 1933-48. Served European War, 1914-18, as Meteorological Officer, 3rd Army (despatches twice). *Address:* High Pines, Warren Lane, Oxshott, Surrey. [*Died* 29 *April* 1956.

BISSET, Vice-Adm. Arthur William La Touche, C.B. 1945; C.B.E. 1944; *b.* 1892; *m.* Margaret, *d.* of late MacCallum Grant, Lt.-Gov. of Nova Scotia; four *d.* Served European War, 1914-18; Capt. 1932; Rear-Adm. 1942; Vice-Admiral 1946; Invalided 1945. Rear-Adm. Naval Air Station, Indian Ocean, 1942; Rear-Adm. Force H., 1943; Rear-Adm. Escort Carriers, 1944. *Address:* Kingsmead, Fulmer Road, Gerrards Cross, Bucks. *T.:* Fulmer 147. *Clubs:* United Service, M.C.C. [*Died* 23 *June* 1956.

BJOERLING, Jussi; Swedish tenor; *b.* Stora Tuna Dalarna, Sweden, 2 Feb. 1911; *s.* of David Bjoerling; *m.* 1935, Anna Lisa Berg; two *s.* one *d.* Graduated Roy. Opera School, Stockholm, 1929; studied with John Forsell and Tullio Voghera. Sang in Bjoerling Quartet (with father and 2 brothers) as boy tenor, U.S.A., 1920-21; made debut as Ottavio in Don Giovanni, Royal Opera, Stockholm, 1929; has sung at: Chicago City Opera, U.S.A., 1937; Metropolitan Opera, N.Y. (Rudolphe in La Bohème), 1938; has sung many leading tenor rôles in all important opera houses. Joint concert tour with wife, U.S.A., 1950-51. Has made many recordings; frequently broadcasts on radio and television. Knight, Order of Leopold II (Belgium). *Address:* Konsertbolaget, Stockholm, Sweden; c/o Coppicus & Shang Inc., Columbia Artists Management Inc., 113 W. 57th St., N.Y.C. 19, U.S.A. [*Died* 9 *Sept.* 1960.

BLACK, Maj. George Cumine Strahan, C.I.E. 1924; M.V.O. 1922; O.B.E. 1919; Deputy Chairman, Grosvenor House (Park Lane) Ltd.; *b.* 3 Jan. 1882; *s.* of late Rev. John Black, M.A., LL.D., Prof. of Humanity, Aberdeen University. *Educ.:* Robert Gordon's College, Aberdeen; Aberdeen University; Royal Military College, Sandhurst. Passed in first, R.M.C. Sandhurst, 1901. Joined Indian Army, 1902; served on the staff of several Governors in India, 1908-24; on active service in Mesopotamia and Persia, 1914-19; many Staff appointments; retired, 1924. *Address:* Sturbridge, Haddenham, Bucks. *Clubs:* Garrick, Oriental, etc. [*Died* 21 *Aug.* 1951.

BLACK, George Norman, Q.C. 1955; M.A., LL.B.; Recorder of Huddersfield since 1950; *b.* 26 Oct. 1907; 2nd *s.* of G. Barnard Black, Scarborough; *m.* 1st, 1935, Margaret Dorothy Wood (*d.* 1936); one *s.*; 2nd, 1948, Elizabeth Jane Yellowlees. *Educ.:* Bootham School, York; King's College, Cambridge. Called to Bar, Middle Temple, 1929. Practised London and North-Eastern Circuit. Served in Royal Artillery, 1939-45. Recorder of Pontefract, 1946-48, of Doncaster, 1948-50. *Publications:* edited various legal works. *Recreations:* fencing, golf, travel. *Address:* 2 Harcourt Buildings, Temple, E.C.4. *T.:* Central 2548. *Clubs:* Leeds (Leeds); County (Durham). [*Died* 7 *July* 1955.

BLACK, Henry, C.B.E. 1935; apartment blocks owner and manager; *b.* 14 Feb., 1875; *s.* of William John and Elizabeth Johnston Black; *m.* 1910, Jennie Lenore Barker (*d.* 1950): four *s.* one *d.* *Educ.:* Public Sch., Grenville Co., Ont.; Business Coll., Brockville, Ont. Alderman of Regina, 1915-17, 1923-24; Mayor, 1918-19; Member General Hospital Board, 1918-1923 and 1924; Member of the Library Board, 1917 and 1918; Chairman of the Saskatchewan Relief Commission, 1931-32 and 1933; Member of the Secondary School Board, 1930-38. *Address:* 2370 Lorne St., Regina, Sask., Canada. *T.:* Lakeside 2-3169. [*Died* 30 *July* 1960.

BLACK, Rev. Hugh, M.A. (Glasgow); D.D. (Yale, 1908; Princeton, 1911; Glasgow, 1911); D.Litt., University of Pittsburgh, 1917; Professor of Practical Theology, Union Theological Seminary, New York, since 1906; *b.* Rothesay, 26 March 1868; *m.* Edith Margaret (*d.* 1949), *y. d.* of Robert Kerr, Paisley; two *s.* two *d.* *Educ.:* Rothesay Academy; Glasgow University; Free Church College, Glasgow. Ordained, 1891; First Minister of Sherwood Church, Paisley, 1891-96; Minister of St. George's United Free Church, Edinburgh, 1896-1906; West Memorial Lecturer, Stanford University, California, 1927; Chairman Montclair Committee of British War Relief Inc., 1941. *Publications:* Friendship, 10th ed.; Culture and Restraint, 4th ed. 1901; Work, 2nd ed. 1903; The Practice of Self-Culture, 1904; Edinburgh Sermons, 1906; Christ's Service of Love, 1907; University Sermons, 1908; Comfort, 1910; Happiness, 1911; Three Dreams, 1912; According to my Gospel, 1913; The Open Door, 1915; The New World, 1916; The Cleavage of the World,

1920; The Adventure of Being Man, 1929; Christ or Caesar, 1938. *Address:* Upper Montclair, N.J., U.S.A. *Club:* Century (New York). [*Died* 6 *April* 1953.

BLACK, John Wycliffe, J.P., LL.D.; retired manufacturer; Alderman of Leicester County Council; M.P. (L.) Harborough, 1923-24; *b.* 1862; *s.* of R. Black; *m.* Eunice, *d.* of J. Marsden, Wigan; one *s.* one *d.* *Educ.:* Bishop Stortford. *Address:* The Rowans, 88 Holmfield Road, Leicester. *T.:* Leicester 25564. *Club:* County (Leicester). [*Died* 18 *June* 1951.

BLACK, Kenneth, F.R.C.S. (Eng.); Hon. L.M.S. Singapore; late Professor of Surgery, College of Medicine, and Surgeon and Ophthalmic Surgeon, General Hospital, Singapore; *b.* London, 12 August 1879; unmarried. *Educ.:* St. Paul's School; Guy's and St. Thomas's Hospitals. Formerly House Surgeon, Guy's Hospital; Casualty Officer, St. Thomas's Hospital; Resident Surgical Officer, Manchester Royal Infirmary; Resident Surgeon Nottingham General Hospital; Consulting Surgeon, Skegness Hospital; served both European Wars, Major, R.A.M.C.: Squadron Leader, R.A.F. *Publications:* many surgical papers; Specialists' German Vocabularies (Pitman's). *Recreation:* travel. *Club:* East India and Sports. [*Died* 27 *Jan.* 1959.

BLACKBURN, Brig. Arthur Seaforth, V.C. 1916; C.M.G. 1955; C.B.E. 1946; Barrister, Adelaide, S. Australia; Commonwealth Conciliation Commissioner; late City Coroner for City of Adelaide; *b.* 25 Nov. 1892; *y. s.* of late Rev. Canon Blackburn of Woodville, S. Australia; *m.* Rose Ada, *d.* of J. H. Kelly Gilberton, South Australia; two *s.* two *d.* *Educ.:* St. Peter's Collegiate School, Adelaide; Adelaide University. Called to Bar, 1913; enlisted as a private in Australian Imperial Force, Aug. 1914; landed at Gallipoli, 25 Apr. 1915; 2nd Lt. at Gallipoli, Aug. 1915; V.C. on Somme, 20 July 1916; represented Sturt in South Australia House of Assembly, 1918-21; served War of 1939-45 (prisoner); Lt.-Col. and C.O. 2/3rd Machine Gun Bn. (2nd A.I.F.), 1940; G.O.C., A.I.F. in Java, 1941-42. *Recreations:* tennis, golf. *Address:* 45 Flinders Street, Adelaide, S. Australia. *Club:* Adelaide (Adelaide). [*Died* 24 *Nov.* 1960.

BLACKBURN, William Ernest, C.B.E. 1920; *b.* 1873; *s.* of Henry Blackburn *m.* 1908, Madeleine M'Kevitt; four *s.* one *d.* A Director in U.S.A., and afterwards Chairman of Ministry of Food during European War. *Address:* Littlecote, Merry Hill Road, Bushey, Herts. *T.:* Bushey Heath 1993. [*Died* 28 *March* 1951.

BLACKBURNE, Gertrude Mary Ireland; *b.* 13 May 1861; *d.* of late John Ireland Blackburne, Chester, and Mary (*née* Buchanan). Chairman Writers' Club, 1916-1917 and 1930; Joint Hon. Sec. Women Writers' Dinner, 1894-1914; Governor Grey Coat Hospital, 1895-1949; on committees for promoting the interests of women and others; Hon. Librarian Vacation Term for Biblical Study, 1912-49; holds Archbishop of Canterbury's Diploma and Licence in Theology. *Publications:* various; has contributed to leading journals and magazines; co-editor of The Churchwoman, 1897-1905; asst. editor of The Sign, 1905-50. [*Died* 28 *Nov.* 1951.

BLACKBURNE, Very Rev. Lionel Edward, M.A.; Dean Emeritus of Ely since 1950; sub-chaplain of the Order of St. John of Jerusalem; *b.* 2 November 1874; *s.* of late Charles Edward Blackburne, Oldham; *m.* 1904, Eleanor, 2nd *d.* of W. Warren, J.P., of Newton Park, Leeds; two *s.* one *d.* (and one *s.* killed in action, 1943). *Educ.:* Lancing College; Clare College, Cambridge; Leeds Clergy School. Curate Leamington Parish Church, 1899-1902; Potternewton, Leeds, 1902-04; Vicar S. Wilfrid's, Bradford, 1904-09; Vicar of S. Mark's, 1909-23, and Rural Dean, 1919-23, of Portsmouth; Rector of Puttenham, Surrey, 1926-27; Hon. Canon of Winchester, 1921; Archdeacon of Surrey, 1922-36; Canon Residentiary of Winchester, 1922-30; Canon Residentiary of Guildford, 1930-36; Dean of Ely, 1936-50. *Publication:* Charles (Lieutenant-Colonel C. H. Blackburne, D.S.O.), 1919—a memoir. *Recreation:* golf (played for Cambridge *v.* Oxford, 1898).' *Address:* Nowton Court, Bury St. Edmunds, Suffolk. [*Died* 4 *Aug.* 1951.

BLACKETT, Adm. Henry, C.B.E. 1919; *b.* 1867; *m.* 1906, Hon. Pamela Mary (*d.* 1949), *y. d.* of 1st Baron Fisher; one *d.* Served European War, 1914-19 (despatches, C.B.E.); a Lieut. of the City of London. *Clubs:* Army and Navy; (Hon.) Royal Yacht Squadron (Cowes). [*Died* 1 *Dec.* 1952.

BLACKETT, Sir Hugh Douglas, 8th Bt., *cr.* 1673; late Captain Northumberland (Hussars) Imperial Yeomanry; *b.* 24 Mar. 1878; *s.* of 7th Bt. and Hon. Julia Frances Somerville *y. d.* of 17th Baron Somerville; *S.* father, 1909; *m.* 1903, Helen Katherine (*d.* 1943) *sis.* of Sir C. B. Lowther, 4th Bt.; four *s.* *Heir:* *s.* Charles Douglas, D.L. *Address:* Matfen Hall, Newcastle upon Tyne. *Club:* Cavalry. [*Died* 13 *Nov.* 1960.

BLACKHAM, Maj.-Gen. Robert James, C.B. 1919; C.M.G. 1918; C.I.E. 1913; D.S.O. 1917; M.D., M.R.C.P.E.; Barrister-at-law; Clerk and Hon. Assistant of Worshipful Company of Glaziers and Glass Painters; a Governor of St. Bartholomew's Hospital and of Saint Bride's Foundation, Fleet Street; late Under Sheriff, City of London; Member of the Court of Common Council, Corporation of London; Trustee C.I.V. Fund; late Deputy Governor the Honourable the Irish Society. Served Tirah Field Force, 1897-98; with the Khyber Brigade, 1898-99; European War, 1914-19 (despatches five times, C.B., C.M.G., promoted Colonel, D.S.O., 1914-15 Star, General Service and Victory medals, Croix de Guerre, with palm and star, 1918, Chevalier of Legion of Honour, 1920); War of 1939-1945, re-employed as Major 1940, Colonel on the Staff 1940, and Major-General 1941 (Defence Medal and War Medal); Army Representative on Government Medical Personnel (Priority) Committee, 1941-45. On plague duty in the Punjab, 1901-2; Member of the Order of Mercy (Medal and Bar); Knight, Member of the Chapter General, Service Medal and three Bars, Order of St. John of Jerusalem; Kaiser-i-Hind medal for public services in India, 1911; Coronation Durbar medal and King George's Police medal, 1911; Special Member of Red Cross of Japan (decoration); on special duty under Government of India, 1914; received thanks of Secretary of State and Government of India for services to Viceroy at Delhi outrage, 1912; Assistant Commissioner, St. John Ambulance Brigade; President, League of Mercy, Wanderers' Branch; Liveryman of the Apothecaries, Glaziers, and Needlemakers' Companies; Freeman of the City of London; on the Staff of the Viceroy of India, 1912-14. *Publications:* Scalpel, Sword and Stretcher—Forty Years of Work and Play, 1931; White Cross of St. John (3rd edition); London's Livery Companies; The Soul of the City; Wig and Gown—the Story of the Temple, Gray's and Lincoln's Inn, 1932; London for Ever! The Sovereign City; Incomparable India, 1933; The Crown and the Kingdom: England's Royal Family, 1933; Apron Men: The Romance of Freemasonry, 1934; Sir Ernest Wild, K.C., 1935; Woman: in Honour and Dishonour, 1936. *Recreation:* farming. *Address:* 1 Garden Court,

BLACK, William Charles, C.B.E. See page xxvii.

Temple, E.C.4; Shortridge Farm, Etchingham, Sussex. *Club:* Army and Navy. [*Died* 23 *Jan.* 1951.

BLACKIE, Walter Wilfrid, B.Sc.; *b.* Glasgow, 1860; 3rd *s.* of late Walter Graham Blackie, Ph.D., LL.D.; *m.* 1889, Anna Christina, *yr. d.* of late George Younger, Glasgow; one *s.* four *d.* *Educ.:* Glasgow Academy; Real Gymnasium, Elberfeld; Glasgow University. Served for about a year in the family business, then went abroad for some three and a half years, in Canada and the United States; returned in 1884, and from then was actively engaged in publishing; Chairman of Blackie and Son, Ltd., Publishers, 1918-37; retired, 1937. *Recreations:* walking, chiefly in his garden, reading. *Address:* The Hill House, Helensburgh. *T.:* Helensburgh 100. *Clubs:* Caledonian; Western, Royal Northern Yacht (Glasgow). [*Died* 14 *Feb.* 1953.

BLACKING, (William Henry) Randoll, F.S.A.; F.R.I.B.A.; Architect; *b.* 3 Jan. 1889; *s.* of Alfred Blacking; *m.* 1927, Josephine Margaret Newcome Waymouth; one *s.* two *d.* *Educ.:* King's College School, Wimbledon. Articled to Sir John Ninian Comper; served European War, 1914-18, and War of 1939-45; commenced practice in Guildford, 1919; Salisbury 1932; First new church, Litton, Derbyshire, 1927; most recent, S. Alban's Northampton. Decorative works and furniture in: S. Alban's Abbey (Font, Chapels); Brighton, S. Peter's and The Good Shepherd; Hove, S. Andrews and S. Thomas's; S. George's, Windsor; Porlock; Basingstoke Parish Ch.; Toddington, Beds., etc. Also works in Worcester (Consulting Archt.), Chichester, Salisbury, Bristol, Gloucester, Sheffield and other Cathedrals and in numerous parish churches. Member of Central Council for the Care of Churches. Is a student of liturgiology and serves on Committee of the Alcuin Club, etc. *Recreations:* music, reading. *Address:* 21 The Close, Salisbury. *T.:* Salisbury 3814. [*Died* 24 *Jan.* 1958.

BLACKLOCK, Donald Breadalbane, C.M.G. 1942; M.D., D.P.H., D.T.M.; formerly Prof. of Tropical Hygiene, Univ. of Liverpool and Liverpool School of Tropical Medicine; *b.* Oban, Argyllshire, 1879; *s.* of late Rev. John Blacklock; *m.* 1922, Mary Georgina, C.B.E. 1945, *d.* of George Matthew Thompson, M.D., D.L., Bellaghy, Co. Derry. *Educ.:* Fettes College; Edinburgh Univ. Director Runcorn Research Laboratory, 1913-14; Member Expedition of Liverpool School of Tropical Medicine to Sierra Leone, 1914-15; Director Sir Alfred Lewis Jones Research Laboratory, Sierra Leone, 1921-29; Mary Kingsley Medallist, Liverpool Sch. Trop. Med., 1949. *Publications:* A Guide to Human Parasitology (with Dr. T. Southwell); An Empire Problem: The House and Village in the Tropics. *Recreations:* various. *Address:* c/o Glyn, Mills & Co., Kirkland House, Whitehall, S.W.1. *Club:* Royal Empire Society. [*Died* 10 *June* 1955.

BLACKMAN, Aylward Manley, M.A. D.Litt.; F.B.A.; Egyptologist; Emeritus Professor of Egyptology, Liverpool University; Brunner Prof. of Egyptology, Liverpool Univ., 1934-48; Special Lecturer in Egyptology, Univ. of Manchester, 1936-48; *b.* Dawlish, S. Devon, 30 Jan. 1883; *e. s.* of late Rev. James Henry Blackman, Vicar of St. Paul's, Norwich, and Anne Mary, *y. d.* of late Rev. G. A. Jacob, D.D. (Oxon), Headmaster of Christ's Hosp.; unmarried; one *d.* (adopted). *Educ.:* Privately until 16 years old; St. Paul's School; The Queen's Coll., Oxford (Sch.). First Class in the Final Honour School of Oriental Studies (Egyptian, Coptic and Arabic), 1906; engaged in excavating and other research work in Egypt and Lower Nubia, 1906-14, and 1920-21; directed the Egypt Exploration Society's excavations at Sesebi, Northern Province, Anglo-Egyptian Sudan, 1936-37; directed the same Society's expedition to Meir, Assyût Province, 1949-50, to complete the recording of the decorated and inscribed tombs in that necropolis; Joint editor with Prof. J. P. Droop of Annals of Archæology and Anthropology, 1935-47; superintended the education of H.I.H. the Crown Prince of Ethiopia, 1937-39; had his house, library, and all his other possessions completely destroyed by enemy action in May 1941; Oxford University Nubian research scholar, 1910; Laycock Student of Egyptology at Worcester College, 1912-18; Pres. Egyptian Soc. of East Anglia from its formation March 1915 till its dissolution during War of 1939-45; engaged off and on in intelligence and office work, European War, 1914-18; Member of Council of the Royal Asiatic Society, 1922-1926, 1927-31, 1932-35 *Publications:* The Temple of Dendûr, 1911; The Temple of Derr, 1913; The Temple of Bîgeh, 1915; The Rock Tombs of Meir, Pt. I., 1914; Pt. II., 1915; Pt. III., 1915; Pt. IV., 1924; Pt. V., 1953; Pt. VI., 1953; Luxor and its Temples, 1923 (translated into German, 1926); Middle-Egyptian Stories, Pt. i (in the series Bibliotheca Aegyptiaca), 1932; The Value of Egyptology in the Modern World, 1935; The Herakleopolitan Period and the Middle Kingdom (with late Professor Peet), in The Art of Egypt through the Ages, 1931; The Psalms in the Light of Egyptian Research, in The Psalmists, 1926; Egyptian Myth and Ritual, in the Myth and Ritual of the Old Testament and the Culture Patterns of the Ancient East, 1932; translations from the German of Erman and Spiegelberg; contributions to Hastings' Encyclopedia of Religion and Ethics, and other works and numerous articles and reviews in archæological and anthropological journals. *Recreations:* music, travelling, walking, and lecturing. *Address:* c/o National Provincial Bank, Abergele, N. Wales. [*Died* 9 *March* 1956.

BLACKSHAW, Rev. William; late Co-Warden and Director of Studies of Mansfield House University Settlement, Fairbairn Hall, E.13; *b.* London, 7 May 1866; 2nd *s.* of Charles and Hannah Blackshaw; *m.* 1st, 1899, Amelia Jane (*d.* 1934), *d.* of late Alderman Thomas Bantock, J.P., Wolverhampton; two *s.*; 2nd, 1945, Laura Ellen, *d.* of late Frederick Stocks. *Educ.:* City of London School; Hackney and Mansfield Colleges; Marburg and Berlin Universities; Oxford. M.A. National University of Ireland; B.Sc. Oxford University; B.D. St. Andrews University. After a brief business career, entered Congregational ministry as Minister of Red Lion Street Congregational Church, Boston; later Assistant to Dr. Rowland at Park Chapel, Crouch End; Minister of Queen Street Chapel, Sheffield, and Founder of Croft House Settlement; late Inspector of Religious Instruction for the Borough of Hornsey; Governor of the Tollington Schools, Muswell Hill; London University Extension Lecturer; after a period of research in Germany suddenly terminated by the war, appointed Minister of Highgate Congregational Church, 1915-26; lectured considerably to the troops during the war (General Service Medal), abroad and at home; served as stretcher-bearer in R.A.M.C.V.; Bevan Lecturer in Adelaide and Livingstone Lecturer in Sydney, 1939. *Publications:* The Community and Social Service, 1939; Science and Society, 1939; has written on German subjects for the Contemporary. *Recreations:* golf, gardening. *Address:* Sneads Green House, Elmley Lovett, Droitwich. *T.:* Cutnal Green 248. [*Died* 24 *July* 1953.

BLACKWELL, Francis Samuel; *b.* 13 Aug. 1869; 2nd *s.* of late S. J. Blackwell, The Manor House, Chipperfield; *m.* 1st, 1897; one *s.*; 2nd, 1921, Alice Maud, *d.* of John Bevan, and *widow* of John William Hand; one *d.* *Educ.:* Rugby. *Address:* White

Cottage, Brookshill Drive, Harrow Weald. *T.:* Grimsdyke 446. [*Died* 27 *April* 1951.

BLACKWOOD, Algernon (Henry), C.B.E. 1949: *b.* 1869; 2nd *s.* of late Sir Arthur Blackwood, K.C.B., and Sydney, Duchess of Manchester (*widow* of 6th Duke). *Educ.:* Moravian School, Black Forest; Wellington College; Edinburgh University; abroad. Farmed in Canada; went Rainy River goldfields; ran a hotel, etc.; joined staff of New York Sun, and later New York Times; dried milk business; began writing books, 1906; lives abroad. Television Society Silver Medal for outstanding artistic achievement, 1948. *Publications:* The Empty House, 1906; The Listener, 1907; John Silence, 1908; The Education of Uncle Paul, 1909; Jimbo, 1909; The Human Chord, 1910; The Lost Valley, 1910; The Centaur, 1911; Pan's Garden, 1912; A Prisoner in Fairyland; Ten Minute Stories, 1913; Incredible Adventures, 1914; The Extra Day, 1915; The Starlight Express (stage version of A Prisoner in Fairyland, with Violet Pearn, music by Sir Edward Elgar, O.M.), 1916; Julius Le Vallon, 1916; The Wave, 1916; Day and Night Stories, 1917; The Promise of Air, 1918; The Garden of Survival; Karma: a Reincarnation Play, 1918; The Crossing, with Bertram Forsyth, 1920; Through the Crack, Children's Play, with Violet Pearn, 1921; The Wolves of God, vol. short stories, with W. Wilson, 1921; The Bright Messenger, 1921; Through the Crack (revised), 1922; Episodes before Thirty, 1923; Tongues of Fire, 1924; Full Circle, Woburn Series, 1929; Dudley and Gilderoy, 1929; The Fruit-Stoners, 1934; Shocks, 1935; The Tales of Algernon Blackwood, 1938; John Silence (new issue), 1942; The Doll and One Other (U.S.A.), 1946; Tales of the Uncanny and Supernatural, 1949; Episodes before Thirty (new issue), 1950; Six television stories filmed by Rayant Pictures, 1950. *Club:* Savile. [*Died* 10 *Dec.* 1951.

BLACKWOOD, James H.; Editor of Blackwood's Magazine, 1942-48, and a Director of William Blackwood & Sons, Ltd., publishers; President of the Publishers' Association of Great Britain and Ireland, 1913-14; *b.* 6 Aug. 1878; *y. s.* of late Major George F. Blackwood, R.H.A. (killed at Maiwand), and *g.-g.s.* of William Blackwood, founder of the publishing firm and of Blackwood's Magazine; *m.* 1906, Sybil Mary, 2nd *d.* of late Admiral Sir G. Digby Morant, K.C.B.; two *s.* two *d.* *Educ.:* Wellington Coll.; Cambridge. *Recreation:* reading. *Address:* Green Hedges, Rye; 45 George Street, Edinburgh. *T.:* Rye 2185. *Club:* United University. [*Died* 29 *March* 1951.

BLACKWOOD, William, C.B.E. 1937; F.S.A.Scot.; Journalist and Publicist; *b.* Alloa, Clackmannan, 21 Dec. 1878; *m.* 1905, Helen Fraser (*d.* 1956); one *s.* one *d.* *Educ.:* Robert Gordon's Coll., Aberdeen; Univ. College, Dundee. Started journalistic career on Dundee Advertiser and afterwards held posts in Glasgow, Belfast, and London; for twelve years a Literary Director of Amalgamated Press, London. *Address:* 17 Gerard Road, Harrow. *T.:* Wordsworth 0612. [*Died Oct.* 1958.

BLADES, Hon. Lord; Daniel Patterson Blades; Senator of College of Justice in Scotland, and Lord of Session, since 1947; *b.* 25 Aug. 1888; *s.* of late Rev. Charles Blades, Minister of Allanton, and Sarah, *d.* of Provost Pow, Armadale; *m.* 1918, Gertrude Thomson Legge; three *s.* one *d.* *Educ.:* Berwickshire High School; Edinburgh Univ., M.A., LL.B. Admitted Advocate, 1915; H.M. Forces, Cameron Hdrs., 1915-18; Advocate-Depute, 1929-32; K.C. 1932; Sheriff of Forfar, 1932-34; Sheriff of Perth and Angus, 1934-45; Solicitor-General for Scotland, 1945-47. F.R.S.E. *Recreations:* angling, motoring, photography. *Address:* 34 India Street, Edinburgh. *T.:* Caledonian 8127. *Clubs:* New, Caledonian United Service and Northern (Edinburgh). [*Died* 6 *Feb.* 1959.

BLAGDEN, Rt. Rev. Claude Martin; *b.* 18 April 1874; 6th *s.* of Rev. H. C. Blagden; *m.* 1st, 1905, Edith Daisy (*d.* 1918), *y. d.* of Henry A. Hassall of Bebington, Cheshire; one *s.* two *d.*; 2nd, 1922, Evelyn Hester, *yr. d.* of late William Dewar and Mrs. Dewar, Horton House, Rugby; one *d.* *Educ.:* Bradfield; Corpus Christi College, Oxford (Scholar). 1st Class Classical Mods., 1894; 2nd Class Lit. Hum., 1896; B.A. 1896; M.A., 1899; D.D. 1927; Lecturer of Christ Church, Oxford, 1896; Student, 1898-1912; Censor, 1900-1905; Lecturer and Assist. Chaplain of Corpus Christi College, Oxford, 1907-12; Deacon, 1898; Priest 1899; Examining Chaplain to the Bishop of Oxford, 1901-12; Select Preacher to the University of Oxford, 1905-07, 1933-1935; Examiner in Honour School of Theology, 1911-12-13; Proctor in Convocation, Worcester, 1918; Coventry, 1919; Canon of Coventry, 1918-20; Archdeacon of Warwick, 1920-23; of Coventry, 1923-27; Bishop of Peterborough, 1927-49; resigned, 1949; Hon. Fellow of Corpus Christi College, Oxford, 1942. *Publications:* The Epistles of Peter, John, and Jude, 1910. *Address:* The Wray, Grasmere, Westmorland. [*Died* 7 *Sept.* 1952.

BLAIKIE, Leonard; *b.* 30 Nov. 1873; *s.* of late John Blaikie, F.L.S., and Elizabeth Simms Bull; *m.* 1912, Edith (*d.* 1931), *d.* of J. C. O'Farrell, Galway; one *s.* two *d.* *Educ.:* Newcastle-under-Lyme; Trinity College, Cambridge (Scholar). 1st Class Natural Sciences Tripos, Part I. 1894, Part II. 1896; Secretary, Lord Rayleigh's National Physical Laboratory Committee, 1897; Assistant Master, Marlborough College, 1899; Junior Examiner, Civil Service Commission, 1900; Assistant Commissioner and Director of Examinations, Civil Service Commission, 1933-39; Godalming Food Office, voluntary worker, 1940-45. *Address:* Galway, The Avenue, Godalming, Surrey. *T.:* Godalming 1390. [*Died* 1 *May* 1951.

BLAINE, Brig. Charles Herbert, C.B.E. 1945; E.D.; *b.* Maseru, Basutoland, 16 Jan. 1883; *s.* of late Major Alfred Blaine, Cape Mounted Riflemen, and *g.s.* of late Rev. William Shaw; *m.* 1930, Jessica Moodie. *Educ.:* St. Andrew's College, Grahamstown, S. Africa; Dover College. Began civil career, 1902 at Christiana, Transvaal, after 18 months service in South African War; Public Prosecutor, Johannesburg, 1905-8; Assistant Magistrate, Germiston, 1909; Krugersdorp, 1910, Barberton, 1911; Senior Public Prosecutor, Johannesburg, 1919; Addtl. Magistrate, Roodepoort, Transvaal, 1920, Durban, Natal, 1924, Johannesburg, 1925; Magistrate and Native Commissioner, Marico District, at Zeerust, Tvl., 1929, Zoutpansberg District, at Louis Trichardt, Tvl., 1931; Under-Secretary for Justice at Pretoria, 1933; Sec. for Justice at Pretoria, 1936; Secretary for Defence, 1939, and O.C. Essential Services Protection Corps in Union Defence Forces, 1939; retired from Public Service and Defence Force, 1945. Served Boer War; European War, 1914-19; S.A. Heavy Artillery (despatches); War of 1939-45 (C.B.E., E.D.). Member National Parks Bd. of Trustees, 1942-50. King's Jubilee Medal, 1935; Coronation Medal, 1937. *Publications:* Consolidated Index to Statute Law of the Union of South Africa, 1924; Dog Law in South Africa, 1928; Native Courts Practice, 1931; New Consolidated Index to the Statute Law of S.A., 1937. *Recreations:* golf, bowls, wild-life protection. *Address:* Barberton, E. Transvaal. *Clubs:* Pretoria (Pretoria); Barberton (Barberton, Tvl.). [*Died* 3 *June* 1958.

BLAIR, Hon. Sir Archibald William, Kt., *cr.* 1946; Judge of the Supreme Court of New Zealand, 1928; Senior Puisne Judge, 1943; retired; *b.* 25 Oct. 1875; *s.* of William Newsham Blair, M.Inst.C.E., late Engineer in Chief of N.Z., and Mary Kennedy; *m.* 1903, Rose (*d.* 1938), *d.* of Samuel Jackson, late of Auckland, N.Z., Barrister and solicitor; three *d.*; *m.* 1942, Ada, *d.* of Robert Reay, late of Christchurch. *Educ.:* Wellington College, Wellington; Canterbury College, Christchurch. Admitted, 1899; practised in Auckland and Wellington; partner of the firm Chapman, Tripp, Blair, Cooke & Watson. *Clubs:* Wellington (Wellington); Hawkes Bay (Napier); Northern (Auckland). [*Died* 11 *April* 1952.

BLAIR, James Richard, C.I.E. 1937; *b.* 20 Aug. 1890; *s.* of late James Blair: *m.* 1921, Alice Jane Hood (*d.* 1956), *d.* of late W. L. Carrie; (one *s.* died of wounds, 1944). *Educ.:* Stewart's College, and University, Edinburgh; Brasenose College, Oxford. Entered I.C.S. 1914; Commissioner, Dacca Division, 1940; Chief Secretary, Govt. of Bengal, 1942; retired 1946. *Address:* 3A Inverleith Place, Edinburgh 4. *T.:* Granton 84850. [*Died* 10 *Jan.* 1958.

BLAIR, Kenneth Gloyne, D.Sc., F.R.E.S.; *b.* Nottingham, 1882; *s.* of William Nisbet Blair; *m.* 1919, Lois Celia, *e. d.* of Edwin J. Lambert, Hampstead; two *d.* *Educ.:* Highgate School; London University, Birkbeck College. Entered Museum, 1910; Deputy-Keeper, Dept. of Entomology, Natural History Museum, 1932-43. *Publications:* numerous papers on Coleoptera, and on general British Entomology. *Address:* Pentwyn, Freshwater Bay, I.W. [*Died* 11 *Dec.* 1952.

BLAKE; *see* Jex-Blake.

BLAKE, Edwin Holmes, C.B.E. 1920; F.R.S.I., F.I.S.E., etc.; Secretary to the Auctioneers' and Estate Agents' Institute of the United Kingdom, 1919-38; *b.* 1873; *s.* of Thomas Holmes Blake, Reading; *m.* 1897, Rosa (*d.* 1951), *y. d.* of A. W. Parry, A.M.I.C.E., F.S.I., Reading. *Educ.:* Reading. Member of original Staff of University College, Reading (now Reading University); for many years member of firm of Parry, Blake & Parry, civil engineers and surveyors, Westminster; Examiner to various Professional Institutions; Deputy Chief Live Stock Commissioner, Ministry of Food, 1917-20. *Publications:* Works on sanitation; a number of papers on professional subjects to Proceedings of Chartered Surveyors' Institution, Auctioneers' and Estate Agents' Institute, etc. *Address:* 14 Shirley Avenue, Cheam, Surrey. [*Died* 28 *May* 1956.

BLAKE, Francis Gilman, A.B., M.A., M.D., Sc.D., F.A.C.P.; Sterling Professor of Medicine, Yale University, since 1927; Physician-in-Chief, New Haven Hospital, New Haven, Conn., U.S.A., since 1921; *b.* Mansfield Valley, Pa., 22 Feb. 1887; *s.* of Francis Clark Blake and Winifred Ballard; *m.* 1916, Dorothy Dewey, Springfield, Mass.; three *s.* *Educ.:* A.B. Dartmouth College, 1908; M.D. Harvard University, 1913. Hon. M.A. Yale, 1921, Sc.D. Dartmouth, 1936; Medical House Officer, Peter Bent Brigham Hospital, Boston, Mass., 1913-14, Asst. Resident Physician, 1914-15, Resident Physician, 1915-16; Moseley Travelling Fellow, Harvard University, 1916-17; Asst. Professor of Medicine, Univ. of Minnesota, 1917-19; Captain Med. Corps, U.S. Army, 1918-19; Assoc. Member, Hospital of Rockefeller Institute for Medical Research, New York, 1919-21; John Slade Ely Professor of Medicine, Yale University, 1921-27; Acting Dean, Yale University School of Medicine, 1940-41; Dean, 1941-47; President, Board for the Investigation of Epidemic Diseases, U.S. Army, 1941-46; Director Field Commission on Scrub Typhus, U.S. Army, New Guinea, 1943. Member Board of Scientific Directors, Rockefeller Institute for Medical Research, New York, 1924-35; Chairman, Division of Medical Sciences, National Research Council, 1933-36; Medical Fellowship Board, Nat. Res. Council, 1927-46, Chairman, 1936-46; President, Amer. Soc. Clinical Investigation, 1931; President, Amer. Assoc. Immunologists, 1935; Chairman, Section on Practice of Medicine, Amer. Med. Assoc., 1938; Regent, Amer. College of Physicians, 1939-47 (Vice-Pres. 1947-48); Pres. Assoc. Amer. Physicians, 1949; Chm. Advisory Council, Life Ins. Medical Research Fund, 1946-50; Chm. Com. on Medical Sciences, Research and Development Bd., Nat. Mil. Establishment. U.S.A., 1948-51; Member Nat. Acad. Sciences; Amer. Philosoph. Soc.; Fellow Amer. Acad. Arts and Sciences; Charles V. Chapin Orator, Providence, R.I., 1945; U.S.A. Typhus Medal, 1945; Presidential Medal for Merit, U.S.A., 1946. *Publications:* Epidemic Respiratory Disease (with Opie, Small and Rivers), 1921; numerous scientific papers on pneumonia, influenza, measles, scarlet fever, chemotherapy, scrub typhus, etc. *Recreations:* philately, gardening. *Address:* 85 Laurel Road, New Haven, Connecticut. *T.A.:* New Haven Hospital, New Haven, Connecticut. *T.:* New Haven, Conn., 8-0049. *Clubs:* New Haven Lawn, Graduate, Harvard (Boston). [*Died* 1 *Feb.* 1952.

BLAKE, Sir John (Lucian), Kt., *cr.* 1952; Comptroller-Gen. of Patents, Designs, and Trade-Marks since 1949; *b.* Watford, Herts, 28 Jan. 1898; *s.* of Samuel John Blake and Anne Eleanor Merrifield; *m.* 1924, Stella Mary Cochie, London; no *c.* *Educ.:* Watford Grammar School; University College, London (Goldsmid Entrance Scholar, Mayer de Rothschild Scholar, Ellen Watson Memorial Scholar and Jessel Student), B.Sc. (1st Class Hons.), 1920, M.Sc., 1922; called to Bar, Gray's Inn, 1944. Served European War, 1914-18, in R.N. and R.N.A.S., 1916-1919. On Examining Staff, Patent Office, 1920-41; Commonwealth Fund Fellow, 1937-38; Principal, Ministry of War Transport, 1941-43; Superintending Examiner, Patent Office. 1944-46; Assistant Comptroller, Patent Office, 1946-49. Fellow of University College, London, 1953. *Publications:* contributor to Encyc. Britannica and Nature. *Recreations:* gardening and walking. *Address:* Trevena, 12 Bournehall Avenue, Bushey, Herts. *T.:* Bushey Heath 1059. *Club:* Royal Empire Society. [*Died* 18 *May* 1954.

BLAKE, Brig.-Gen. William Alan, C.B. 1930; C.M.G. 1918; D.S.O. 1915; late Wilts Regt.; *b.* 8 Oct. 1878; *m.* 1919, Beryl, *e. d.* of late John Harrison Packard, of Ensenada, Mexico; one *s.* two *d.* *Educ.:* Charterhouse. Entered Army, King's Regt., 1899; Wilts Regt. 1899; Captain, 1905; Staff Capt., 1914; Brig. Major, 1915; served European War, 1914-18 (despatches, D.S.O., Bt. Lt.-Col., Bt. Colonel, C.M.G., Legion of Honour, Order of the Redeemer, Grand Officer Order of the Crown of Roumania); commanded 2nd Batt. The King's Regiment, 1922-26; commanded 13th Infantry Brigade, 1926-30; A.D.C. 1930; retired pay, 1935. *Address:* Mill House, Overstrand, Cromer. [*Died* 21 *Dec.* 1959.

BLAKEMORE, Professor Frederick; Professor of Veterinary Medicine and Director of Veterinary Studies, Bristol University, since 1948; *b.* Billinghay, Lincolnshire, 27 July 1906; *m.* 1935, Rachel Helen Duncan Rennie; three *s.* *Educ.:* Hyde Grammar School; Universities of Liverpool and Manchester. M.R.C.V.S., Liverpool, 1927; D.V.S.M., Manchester, 1929. Asst. in general veterinary practice until 1930.

Veterinary Officer, Glamorgan C.C., 1930-31; Veterinary Investigation Officer, School of Agriculture, Cambridge Univ., responsible for teaching Animal Hygiene in Univ., 1931-1946; Supt. Veterinary Investigation Officer, England and Wales, Min. of Agriculture, 1946-1948. Dalrymple-Champneys Medal for research, Nat. Vet. Med. Assoc., 1948. Examiner in Patho'ogy, R.C.V.S. 1939-49, Member of Council, 1949. Hon. D.V.Sc., Liverpool Univ., 1950. *Publications:* Publications in Journal Comparative Pathology, Journal Pathology and Bacteriology, Proc. R. Soc. Med., etc. *Recreations:* mainly gardening. *Address:* Langford House, Langford, Nr. Bristol. [*Died* 8 Aug. 1955.

BLAKENEY, Edward Henry, M.A.; four *s.* one *d.* *Educ.:* Westminster School; Trin. Coll. Cam. English Oration Prizeman, Trinity Coll. (1891); Classical Tripos; B.A. 1891; M.A. 1895. Headmaster of Sandwich Grammar School, 1895-1901; of Borlase's School, Marlow, 1901-04; of the King's School, Ely, 1904-18; Master at Winchester College, 1918-30; Lecturer in English Literature, Southampton University, 1929-31. *Publications:* Several books of verse, and editions of Horace; Plato; Milton's Paradise Regained; The Mosella of Ausonius; The Hero and Leander of Musæus; the Book of Wisdom; the Axiochus of pseudo-Plato; Epistle to Diognetus, 1943; The Speech of Pericles, 1948; Lactantius' Epitome, 1950; Collected Hymns, etc. *Recreations:* mountain-climbing, foreign travel, amateur printing. *Address:* 17 Edgar Road, Winchester. *T.:* 3582. [*Died* 1 *Aug.* 1955.

BLAKENEY, Brig.-Gen. Robert Byron Drury, C.M.G. 1918; D.S.O. 1898; *b.* 18 April 1872; *s.* of late William Blakeney, R.N., of Hillsborough, Westward Ho!; *m.* 1st, 1903, Dorothy (*d.* 1920), *d.* of late Major Nelson Ellis, 101st Munster Fusiliers; one *s.* (and one *s.* killed in action and two *d.* decd.); 2nd, 1921, Clara Isabel Henderson, of Merfield House, Rode, Somerset. Entered Army, 1891; Lt. 1894; served Dongola Expeditionary Force, 1896 (despatches, 4th class Medjidie, British medal, Khedive's medal with clasp); also in operations, 1897 (clasp); expedition, 1898, including battle of Khartoum (despatches, D.S.O., clasp); South African War, 1900-1, commanding 3rd Balloon Section, and Assistant Director of Railways, Lourenço Marquez (medal, 4 clasps); Deputy General Manager, Egyptian State Railways, 1906-19; operations on Suez Canal, 1915; Assistant Director of Railways, Mediterranean Expeditionary Force, Dardanelles, 1915 (1915 Star); Deputy Director Railway Traffic, Egyptian Expeditionary Force, 1916 (despatches four times, King's and Victory medals, Officer Légion d'Honneur; 2nd Class Order of Nile, C.M.G.); Medjidie 3rd class, 1903; Osmanieh 3rd class, 1905; Medjidie 2nd class, 1912; Commander of the Order of the Crown of Belgium, 1923; Director Railway Traffic E.E.F., 8 Apr. 1919, with rank of Brigadier General; retired pay, 1921; General Manager Egyptian State Railways, 1919-23. Home Guard, 1940; in A.R.P. and N.F.S. (Medal), 1941-45. *Address:* Newcote, Mont au Pretre, St. Helier, Jersey, C.I. [*Died* 13 *Feb.* 1952.

BLAKER, Harry Rowsell; Solicitor; *b.* London, 31 Oct. 1872; *s.* of Harry Campbell Blaker, Solicitor, and Edith, *d.* of Canon T. J. Rowsell of Westminster; *m.* 1901, Leila Beatrice, *d.* of Col. Arthur Ford, R.A., C.B.; one *s.* one *d.* *Educ.:* Westminster School. President The Law Society, 1934-35. *Recreation:* golf. *Address:* 50 New Street, Henley on Thames. *T.:* Henley 38. *Club:* M.C.C. [*Died* 30 *March* 1953.

BLAKISTON, Wilfrid Robert Louis, C.B.E. 1943; formerly Ministry of Labour and National Service; *b.* 13 Oct. 1876; 2nd *s.* of Rev. C. D. Blakiston, late of Exwick and Sidbury, Devon; *m.* Mary Gilmore, *d.* of late F. G. Barnett; (one *s.* killed on active service, 1944) two *d.* *Educ.:* Malvern; Exeter School; Keble College, Oxford (Scholar). Secretary, Children's Country Holidays Fund, 1900-11; Board of Trade from 1912, Ministry of Labour from 1916. *Recreation:* gardening. *Address:* Rosemount, Windmill Lane, Henfield, Sussex. *T.:* Henfield 140. [*Died* 16 *Feb.* 1955.

BLAKISTON-HOUSTON, Major-General John, C.B. 1936; D.S.O. 1916; 3rd Bn. Royal Irish Rifles; 11th Hussars and 12th Royal Lancers; *b.* 18 April 1881; 5th *s.* of late John Blakiston-Houston; *m.* 1910, Louisa Henriette (*d.* 1952), *d.* of late M. Le Comte of Port St. Ouen, France; *m.* 1954, Emma Millicent, *d.* of late George Coles. *Educ.:* Cheltenham College. Served South Africa, 1901-2 (Queen's medal, 5 clasps); West African Frontier Force, 1905-8; Adjutant Sussex Yeomanry, 1910-15; European War, 1914-18 (wounded, despatches, D.S.O.); Bde. Major, 1st Cavalry Brigade, 1920-23; commanded XII Lancers, 1923-27; commanded 2nd Cavalry Brigade, 1927-31; Brigadier i/c Administration Northern Command, York, 1931-34; Commandant, Equitation School, Weedon, and Inspector of Cavalry, 1934-38; retired pay, 1938; re-employed 1939, commanding 59th Div.: commanded Central Midland Area, 1940-41; reverted to retired pay, 1941. *Address:* Mullinanogle, Alkerton, Banbury, Oxon. *T.:* Edge Hill 25. [*Died* 14 *Dec.* 1959.

BLAMEY, Field Marshal Sir Thomas Albert, G.B.E., *cr.* 1943; K.C.B., *cr.* 1942 (C.B. 1919); Kt., *cr.* 1935; C.M.G. 1918; D.S.O. 1917; *b.* Wagga, N.S.W., 24 Jan. 1884; *s.* of R. H. Blamey, Sydney; *m.* 1st, 1908, Minnie (*d.* 1935), *d.* of Edwin Millard; one *s.*; 2nd, 1939, Olga, *d.* of late Henry Farnsworth. Commonwealth Military Forces, Deputy Chief of General Staff, Australia; Chief of Staff, Australian Corps, 1918, and of Australian Imperial Force, 1919; served European War, 1914-18 (despatches seven times, D.S.O., C.M.G., C.B.); Australian Defence representative in London attached to the War Office, 1922; Second Chief of General Staff, Commonwealth Military Forces, 1923-25; commanded 3rd Australian Division, 1931-37; Chief Commissioner of Police Victoria, 1925-37; Controller-General of Recruiting Secretariat, Commonwealth of Australia, 1938-39; Chairman of Australian Man Power Committee, 1939-40; G.O.C. 6th Div. A.I.F., 1939-40; G.O.C. 1st Australian Corps, A.I.F., 1940-41; G.O.C. of A.I.F. in Middle East, 1941; Deputy C.-in-C. Middle East, 1941; C.-in-C. allied land forces, South-West Pacific Area, 1942-45. Field-Marshal, 1950. Cross of St. John, Grand Cross Order of Orange-Nassau, 1917, French Croix de Guerre, 1st Class Military Cross of Greece, American D.S.C. *Recreations:* hunting, golf, tennis, shooting, fishing, swimming. *Address:* Punt Road, South Yarra, Melbourne, S.E.1, Victoria, Australia. *Clubs:* Athenæum, Melbourne, Navy, Army and Air Force, (Committeeman) Victoria Racing (Melbourne). [*Died* 27 *May* 1951.

BLAND, E. Beatrice; *b.* Coleby Hall, Lincoln, 1868. Student Slade School; Member New English Art Club: Exhibitor R.A. and numerous other Exhibitions; Pictures bought, Chantrey, Luxembourg, Liverpool, Manchester, Bradford, Capetown and other public Galleries, etc., also Contemporary Art Society. *Address:* 6 Milton Chambers, 128 Cheyne Walk, S.W.3. [*Died* 20 *Jan.* 1951.

BLEDISLOE, 1st Viscount, *cr.* 1935, of Lydney, **Charles Bathurst,** P.C. 1926; G.C.M.G., *cr.* 1930; K.B.E., *cr.* 1917; 1st

BLANKENBERG, Sir Reginald Andrew, K.B.E. See page xxviii.

Baron, *cr.* 1918; F.S.A.; Knight of Justice of the Order of St. John of Jerusalem; County Alderman Gloucestershire County Council; *b.* 21 Sept. 1867; *s.* of Charles Bathurst of Lydney Park, Gloucestershire, and Mary Elizabeth, *o. d.* of late Lieutenant-Colonel Thomas Pasley Hay; *m.* 1st, Hon. Bertha Susan Lopes (*d.* 1926), *d.* of 1st Lord Ludlow; two *s.* one *d*; 2nd, Hon. Mrs. Alina Kate Elaine Cooper-Smith (*d.* 1956), D.G.St.J., Officer Order of Orange Nassau (Netherlands), 2nd *d.* of 1st and last Baron Glantawe. *Educ.:* Sherborne; Eton; University Coll., Oxford; Royal Agric. Coll., Cirencester (Gold Medallist and late Chairman of Governors); ex-Pro-Chancellor and Hon. D.Sc. Bristol; Hon. D.C.L. Oxford; and Hon. LL.D. Edinburgh; Hon. Fellow of University College, Oxford. Chancery Barrister and Conveyancer, 1894-1910; M.P. (C.) South Wilts (Wilton) Division, 1910-18; Parliamentary Secretary to Ministry of Food, 1916-17; Chairman of Federation of County War Agricultural Executive Committees, 1916-18. Chairman of the Royal Commission on the Sugar Supply and Director of Sugar Distribution, 1917-19; Parliamentary Secretary, Ministry of Agriculture, Nov. 1924 to Feb. 1928; Governor-General and Commander-in-Chief of New Zealand, 1930-35; President of Empire Day Movement, 1937-45 (now a Vice-President); Chairman of the Royal Commission on the Land Drainage of England and Wales, 1927; Chairman of Royal Commission on closer union of Southern Rhodesia, Northern Rhodesia, and Nyasaland, 1938; President of the Imperial Agricultural Research Conference, 1927; Pres. Central Chamber of Agriculture in Jubilee year, 1915; Pres. British Dairy Farmers Association, 1919-21; President Bath and West of England Agricultural Society, 1920-21; Pres. Three Counties Agricultural Soc., 1948; Pres. Country Landowners Association, 1921-22 (and its sole surviving founder); President Agricultural Section of British Association, 1922; Chairman of the Farmers' Club, 1923-1924 (and Life Vice-Pres.); late Chairman Cttee. of Lawes Agric. Trust (Rothamsted) and of Agric. Research Cttee., Bristol University; Goodwill Missionary for R.A.S.E. to Australasia, 1947, and to S. Africa and Southern Rhodesia, 1948. Captain Royal Monmouthshire Royal Engineers (S.R.); formerly Captain R.M.R.E.; late Assistant Military Secretary Salisbury Training Centre and Southern Command; Senior Verderer of the Forest of Dean; Director P. & O. Shipping Co. and Australian Mutual Provident Society (London Board); President of the National Council of Social Service, 1935-38; and Chairman of its South-Western Regional Committee, 1940-46; Pres. Museums Assoc. 1939 (Jubilee Year); Pres. Royal Agricultural Soc. of England (of which Silver Medallist and Life Member by Examination), 1946 (Hon. Gold Medallist 1947); Pres. 2nd Internat. Congress of Crop Protection, London, 1949; Chm. Empire Canners' Council, 1940-50; late Pres. C.P.R.E. (Glos. Branch); Pres. Forest of Dean Development Assoc.; late Pres. St. John Ambulance Brigade (Glos.) Knight Grand Cross, Order of Orange Nassau (Netherlands). *Publications:* several papers and pamphlets on Agricultural and Educational questions. *Recreations:* agriculture, cattle-breeding, shooting and fishing. *Heir:* *s.* Hon. Benjamin Ludlow Bathurst, Q.C. *Address:* Redhill, Lydney Park, Gloucestershire. *T.A.:* Bledisloe, Lydney. *T.:* Lydney 37. *Clubs:* Carlton, Oxford and Cambridge, Farmers'. [*Died* 3 *July* 1958.

BLENKINSOP, Edward Robert Kaye, C.I.E. 1911; *b.* 15 May **1871**; *s.* of Col. Blenkinsop; *m.* Florence Edith, *d.* of late Sir Stanley Ismay, K.C.S.I.; two *s.* *Educ.*: St. Paul's School; Christ's College, Cambridge. Entered I.C.S., 1890; Settlement Officer, 1897; Deputy Commissioner, 1902; Kaisar-i-hind medal, 1903; Commissioner of Excise, 1906; Commissioner of Settlements and Director of Land Records, Central Provinces, 1909; Chief Secretary to Chief Commissioner, 1912-13; Settlement Commissioner, Jaipur, 1923; retired, 1926. *Address:* c/o Grindlay's Bank, 54 Parliament Street, S.W.1. [*Died* 19 *Feb.* 1954.

BLENNERHASSETT, William Lewis Rowland Paul Sebastian, D.S.O. 1919; O.B.E. 1920; member of the London Stock Exchange; *b.* 6 Oct. 1882; *m.* 1910, Olivia Frances (*d.* 1953), *d.* of Sir T. F. Grove, 1st Bt.; one *s.* Served European War (Special Intelligence Corps), 1914-15 (despatches). *Publications:* novels: Red Shadow, Dreamer: numerous articles Cornhill and National Review, etc. [*Died* 24 *May* 1958.

BLOCH, Ernest; Composer; Professor Emeritus of Music, University of California, Berkeley, Calif.; *b.* 24 July 1880; *s.* of Maurice and Sophie Bloch, Brunschwig; *m.* 1904, Marguerite Schneider; one *s.* two *d.* *Educ.:* Geneva; Brussels; Frankfurt-am-Main; Munich. Conducted Symph. Concerts, Lausanne, Neuchatel, 1909-10; Lecturer, Teacher, Conservatory of Geneva, 1911-15; came to U.S.A., 1916; Founder Cleveland Institute of Music, Director, 1920-25; Dir. San Francisco Conservatory, 1925-30; conducted own works in America, Italy, London, Paris, and Amsterdam; Hon. Member Accademia di Sta. Cecilia, Rome, 1929; Member American Academy of Arts and Letters, 1943 (Gold Medal, 1942); Hon. Doctor of Hebrew Letters, 1943, Doctor of Humane Letters, 1948. *Compositions:* Operas: Macbeth performed at Opéra Comique, Paris, 1910-11; San Carlo performed in Naples, 1938, Rome, Trieste, 1953. Orchestral and Vocal: Symphony in C sharp minor, 1901-2; Hiver-Printemps (symphonic poem), 1904-1905; Poèmes d'Automne (for voice and orchestra), 1906; Trois Poèmes Juifs, 1913; Two Psalms and a Prelude, 1912-14; Psalm 22, 1914; Schelomo, 1915-16; Israël, 1912-1916; Quartet, 1916; Suite for Viola and Orchestra, 1919; Sonata for Violin and Piano, 1920-21; Quintet, 1923; Poème mystique for violin and piano, 1924; Concerto Grosso for String Orchestra and Piano, 1925; Four Episodes (for Chamber orchestra), 1926; America (symphony), 1926; Helvetia (for orchestra), 1928; Sacred Service, 1930-1933; Sonata for Piano, 1935; Voice in the Wilderness for cello and orchestra), 1936; Evocations (for orchestra), 1937; Concerto for Violin and Orchestra, 1937-1938; Suite Symphonique, 1944; 2nd String Quartet, 1945; Concerto Symphonique for Piano and Orchestra, 1947; Scherzo Fantasque for Piano and Orchestra, 1948; 6 Preludes, 4 Marches, for Organ, 1949; Concertino for Flute, Viola (for Clarinet) and piano, or String Orchestra, 1950; Suite Hébraïque for Viola for Violin) and Orchestra 1961; String Quartet No. 3, 1952; Concerto Grosso 2, 1952; Sinfonia Breve, 1952; String Quartet No. 4, 1953; Symphony for Trombone Solo and Orchestra, 1954; Symphony in E flat, 1954-55; Proclamation for Trumpet Solo and Orchestra, 1955; String Quartet No. 5, 1955-56; Three Suites for Violoncello Solo, 1956; Suite Modale for flute and piano, or string orchestra, 1957; Quintet No. 2, 1957; Suite for Violin Solo, 1958. *Recreations:* reading, hiking, photography. *Address:* Agate Beach, Oregon, U.S.A. [*Died* 15 *July* 1959.

BLOM, Eric Walter, C.B.E. 1955; Editor of 5th edition of Grove's Dictionary of Music and Musicians; *b.* 20 Aug. 1888; *s.* of Frederick Walter Blom; *m.* 1923, Marjory Spencer (*d.* 1952); one *s.* one *d.* *Educ.:* mainly privately. Wrote programme notes for New Queen's Hall Orchestra, in association with Mrs. Rosa Newmarch, 1919-27;

London Music Critic of Manchester Guardian, 1923-31; Music Critic of Birmingham Post, 1931-46; Editor of Music & Letters, 1937-50 and 1954-; Music Critic of Observer, 1949-; Chairman Central Music Library; Member of Council, Royal Musical Association; Editor of Dent's Master Musicians Series. D.Litt. (*h.c.*) Birmingham Univ. 1955; Hon. R.A.M., 1957. *Publications:* Stepchildren of Music, 1923; The Limitations of Music, 1928; The Romance of the Piano, 1928; Tchaikovsky's Orchestral Works (Musical Pilgrim Series), 1927; Strauss's Rose Cavalier (Musical Pilgrim Series), 1930; Mozart (Master Musicians Series), 1935; The Music Lover's Miscellany, 1935; Beethoven's Pianoforte Sonatas Discussed, 1938; A Musical Postbag, 1941; Music in England (Pelican Series), 1943; Some Great Composers, 1944; Everyman's Dictionary of Music, 1947, rev. 1954; Classics: Major and Minor, 1958. *Translations:*—Books: Johannes Brahms, by Richard Specht, 1930; Schubert Documents and Commentary, ed. by O. E. Deutsch, 1947. Opera: Mozart's Impresario (Cambridge, 1937). *Address:* 10 Alma Terrace, Allen Street, W.8. *T.:* Western 7175. *Club:* Garrick.
[*Died* 11 *April* 1959.

BLOOD, Lancelot Ivan Neptune Lloyd-, M.C.; K.C. 1938; Puisne Judge Tanganyika Territory, 1940-50; *b.* 9 Feb. 1896; *s.* of late Adam Lloyd-Blood, solicitor, Wenonah, Winton Road, Dublin, and Helena d'Elsa, *née* Geoghegan; *m.* 1920, Constance Elizabeth, *d.* of late John Ouseley Byrne, barr.-at-law, Ireland; two *s.* *Educ.:* St. Stephen's Green School, Dublin; Tonbridge; Trinity College, Dublin, B.A. Inns of Court O.T.C. T.F., 1915; 2nd Lieut. 5th Royal Dublin Fus., 1916, served in France, 1916-17 and 1918-19 (M.C., despatches); Capt. Regular Army Reserve of Officers; called to Irish Bar, Kings Inns, Dublin, 1920; entered Colonial Service, 1920; Registrar Supreme Court of Kenya, 1920-24; Assistant Attorney-General, Nyasaland, 1924-32; Solicitor-General, Palestine, 1932-36; Attorney-General, Cyprus, 1936-1940. *Recreations:* shooting and fishing. *Club:* Royal Empire Society.
[*Died* 6 *Nov.* 1951.

BLORE, Lt.-Col. Herbert Richard, C.B.E. 1919; D.S.O. 1918; late K.R.R.C.; *b.* 15 May 1871. Entered Army, 1890; Lt.-Col. 1916; served Chitral, 1895 (medal and clasp); S. Africa, 1899-1902 (despatches thrice, Bt. Major, Queen's medal with five clasps, King's medal with two clasps); European War, 1914-19 (despatches, D.S.O., C.B.E.); retired pay, 1919. *Address:* 20 St. Stephen's Rd., Canterbury, Kent. [*Died* 16 *Nov.* 1955.

BLOSSE, Sir Robert Cyril Lynch-, 13th Bt., *cr.* 1622; *b.* 17 Jan. 1887; *s.* of late Rev. Robert Charles Lynch-Blosse; *S.* c., 1942; *m.* 1st, 1911, Dorothy Mary (*d.* 1926), *d.* of late Edward Cunliffe-Owen, C.M.G.; one *s.* one *d.*; 2nd, 1932, Frances Dorothy, *e. d.* of Charles Edward Banks; one *d.* *Educ.:* Twyford School, Winchester; Haileybury. Formerly Capt. (Hon. Major) 3rd Bn. Royal Welch Fusiliers. Served European War, 1914-18, France and Belgium; recalled, 1940-45. *Heir:* *s.* Robert Geoffrey, Lieut.-Comdr. R.N., *b.* 1 April 1915. *Address:* 23 Elm Grove, West Worthing, Sussex.
[*Died* 4 *July* 1951.

BLOUNT, Austin Ernest, C.M.G. 1918; *b.* 30 May 1870; *m.* 1st 1894, Alice Dalpé (*d.* 1919); one *s.*; 2nd, 1922, Louise Rankin Thomson, Glasgow. Private Secretary to Rt. Hon. Sir Charles Tupper, 1896-1901; to Rt. Hon. Sir Robert L. Borden, Prime Minister of Canada, 1901-17. Clerk of the Senate, and Clerk of the Parliaments, Dominion of Canada, 1917-38. *Address:* c/o The Senate, Ottawa, Canada. [*Died* 27 *March* 1954.

BLOUNT, Sir Walter Aston, 10th Bt., *cr.* 1642; *b.* 9 Oct. 1876; *e. s.* of Sir Walter de Sodington Blount, 9th Bt. and Elizabeth Annie Mould, *d.* of James Z. Williams; *S.* father, 1915; *m.* 1929, Margaret, *d.* of Charles Augustus Adames. *Educ.:* Oratory School. *Heir:* *b.* Edward Robert [*b.* 2 Dec. 1884; *m.* 1914, Violet Ellen, *d.* of A. Grant Fowler, M.I.C.E.; one *s.* one *d.*]. *Address:* Mawley Hall, Cleobury Mortimer, Kidderminster, Worcs. *T.:* Cleobury Mortimer 388.
[*Died* 13 *June* 1958.

BLOW, Very Rev. Norman John, M.A.; Dean of Newcastle, N.S.W., since 1949; *b.* 1915; *s.* of F. J. Blow, Stevenage. *Educ.:* Queens' College, Cambridge; Westcott House, Cambridge. B.A. 1935; M.A. 1939; deacon, 1939; priest, 1940; Curate of St. Martin, Epsom, 1939-42; Priest Vicar of Wells Cathedral and Assistant Organising Secretary, Society for the Propagation of the Gospel, South-Western Area, 1942-44; then Candidates Secretary for S.P.G., 1944-45; Permission to Officiate, Diocese of Rochester, 1944; Vicar of St. Saviour's, Oxton, 1945-49; Dean of Christ Church Cathedral, Newcastle, N.S.W., 1949-50. *Address:* The Deanery, Newcastle, N.S.W., Australia.
[*Died* 26 *June* 1950.
[*But death not notified in time for inclusion in Who Was Who 1941–1950, first edn.*

BLOWERS, Arthur R.; Order of the Founder; Commissioner of The Salvation Army; for a number of years was Secretary at the International Headquarters in London for Salvation Army affairs in Europe, Asia, Africa, America (North and South), West Indies and Australasia, now retired; *b.* London, 18 July 1868; *m.* Mary Tomlinson (*d.* 1953), Salvation Army Officer; one *s.* one *d.* Entered Salvation Army as an officer, 1886, in England; served in India for thirty-seven years, his appointments including direction of Salvation Army operations in Madras Presidency, Western India, and Travancore, and Sec. for all Salvation Army Work in India and Ceylon; awarded Kaisar-i-Hind Gold Medal. *Address.* 13 Beckenham Grove, Shortlands, Kent.
[*Died* 24 *March* 1954.

BLUNDSTONE, Ferdinand V., F.R.B.S.; sculptor; *b.* 1882; *s.* of C. Blundstone of Whaley Bridge, Cheshire; *m.* A. M. Gifford, Cambridge; one *d.* *Educ.:* privately. Entered Royal Academy Schools, 1904; gained Landseer Scholarship and awarded Gold Medal and Travelling Scholarship for Sculpture; studied in Paris and Italy; designed and executed the following works: the Prudential Assurance Company War Memorial London, also public works at Folkestone, Stalybridge, Palmerston, North, New Zealand, St. John's, Newfoundland, and in Belgium; Samuel Plimsoll Memorial, Embankment, London; Statue of Sir Solomon D. Bandaranaike, Ceylon; Panels round the Lewis Carroll Memorial Ward, St. Mary's Hospital, London; exhibited at the Royal Academy and other exhibitions for a number of years; awarded Silver Medal for garden-sculpture, Paris Exhibition, 1925. *Recreations:* fishing and philately. *Address:* The Gables, 20 Warwick Road, West Drayton, Middx. *T.:* West Drayton 2486.
[*Died* 5 *Jan.* 1951.

BLUNT, Rt. Rev. Alfred Walter Frank, Hon. D.D., M.A., (Oxon); Bishop of Bradford, 1931-55; *b.* 24 Sept. 1879; *s.* of Capt. F. T. Blunt, Chief Civil Commissioner for the Seychelles; *m.* 1909, Margaret Catharine, *d.* of Lt.-Col. J. Duke, I.M.S.; one *s.* two *d.* *Educ.:* Marlborough (House Scholar); Exeter Coll., Oxford (Scholar); First-class Classical Moderations; First-class Literae Humaniores Assistant Master, Wellington College, 1902; Fellow and Classical Lecturer, Exeter College, Oxford, 1902-07; Assistant Curate of Carrington, Nottingham, 1907-09; Vicar of

Carrington, Nottingham, 1909-17; Vicar of St. Werburgh, Derby, 1917, 1931; Rural Dean of Derby, 1920-31; Hon. Canon of Southwell, and later of Derby; Examining Chaplain to Bishop of Southwell and later of Derby. *Publications:* Studies in Apostolic Christianity, 1909; Apologies of Justin Martyr, 1911; Faith and the New Testament, 1912; The Faith of the Catholic Church, 1916 and 1936; Acts of the Apostles (Clarendon Bible), 1923; Israel before Christ (World's Manuals), 1924; Galatians (Clarendon Bible), 1925; The Teaching of the Old Testament, 1926; Israel in World History (World Manuals), 1927; The Ancient World, 1928; St. Mark (Clarendon Bible), 1929; The Prophets of Israel, 1929; C. of E., what does it stand for?, 1934; Grace and Morals, 1935; The Gospels and the Critic, 1936; Our Need for God, 1937; God and Man, 1937; The Teaching of the New Testament, 1939; For Beginners in Prayer, 1941; The Goodly Fellowship, 1942; What the Church Teaches (Penguin), 1943; Trials of Sickness; The Spirit of Life, 1947, etc. *Recreation:* golf. *Address:* The Horseshoe, Dringhouses, York. [*Died* 2 *June* 1957.

BOAS, Frederick S., O.B.E. 1953; M.A. (Oxon); Hon. LL.D. (St. Andrews); Hon. Lit.D. (Belfast); Pres. of English Assoc., 1944; F.R.S.L. (Vice-Pres.); *b.* 24 July 1862; *e. s.* of Hermann Boas; *m.* Henrietta O'Brien (*d.* 1953), *d.* of Sidney J. Owen, Reader in Indian History, Oxford; one *s.* *Educ.:* Clifton College; Balliol College, Oxford (Exhibitioner). First Classes Classical Moderations, Literæ Humaniores, and Modern History. Lecturer to the Oxford University Extension Delegacy, 1887-1901; Fellow of Royal University of Ireland, 1901; Clark Lecturer in English Literature at Trinity College, Cambridge, 1904; Professor of History and English Literature, 1901-5, and Librarian, 1903-5, Queen's College, Belfast; Inspector L.C.C., Educ. Dept., 1905-27; Member Departmental Committee on English, 1919-21; Editor of the Year's Work in English Studies, 1922-1955. Visiting Professor of English Literature, Columbia Univ., New York, 1934-35; R.S.L. Silver Medal, 1952. *Publications:* Shakespeare and his Predecessors, 1896 (7th reprint, enlarged, 1940); University Drama in the Tudor Age, 1914; Songs of Ulster and Balliol, 1917; Shakespeare and the Universities, 1922; An Introduction to the Reading of Shakespeare, 1927; Richardson to Pinero, 1936; An Introduction to Tudor Drama, 1933; Christopher Marlowe: A Biographical and Critical Study, 1940; British Academy Shakespeare Lecture, 1943; An Introduction to Stuart Drama, 1946; Queen Elizabeth in Drama, 1949; Thomas Heywood, 1950; Introduction to Eighteenth-Century Drama, 1952; Sir Philip Sidney, 1955. Edited Thomas Kyd's Works, 1901 and 1955; The Poems of Giles and Phineas Fletcher, 1908; Fulgens and Lucres, 1926; Turbervile's translation of Ovid's Heroides, 1928; Sir Sidney Lee's Essays, 1930; Marlowe's Dr. Faustus, 1932, 2nd ed. 1949; The Diary of Thomas Crosfield, 1935; Songs and Lyrics from the English Playbooks, 1945; Songs and Lyrics from Masques and Light Operas, 1949; Hon. Edward Howard's The Change of Crownes, 1949; contributions to Vols. V. and VI. of the Cambridge History of English Literature, 1910; The Shakespeare Book of Homage, 1916; The Encyclopædia Britannica (14th edition); New Chambers's Encyclopædia, 1950. *Recreation:* croquet. *Address:* 73 Murray Road, S.W.19. *T.:* Wimbledon 1407. *Club:* Athenæum. [*Died* 1 *Sept.* 1957.

BODDIS, Alfred Charles, C.M.G. 1943; *b.* 28 Sept. 1895; *s.* of Alfred and Edith Boddis. *Educ.:* Merchant Taylors' School. Entered Royal Ordnance Factories, Woolwich, Feb. 1915, as Intermediate Grade Civil Servant. Lt. R.F.A., 1916-19; Royal Ordnance Factories, Woolwich, 1919-22; Air Ministry, 1922-40; Ministry of Aircraft Production, 1940-46. Sec., British Air Mission to Canada, July-Sept. 1938; Adviser on Contracts, British Air Mission to Australia and New Zealand, Jan.-Apr. 1939; Contracts Member, British Supply Board, N. America, Oct. 1939-Sept. 1940; Director of Contracts, British Air Commission, 1940-41; Lend-Lease Liaison, Washington, D.C., 1941-42; Controller of Supply Services, British Air Commission, 1942-44; Director of Contracts, Min. of Aircraft Production, 1945-46; Director of Contracts (Air), Ministry of Supply, 1946; Secretary of Iron and Steel Board, 1946-49; Under-Secretary, Ministry of Supply, 1949-50; retired 1950. *Recreation:* golf. *Address:* 17 High Rd., Chiswick, W.4. [*Died* 9 *Feb.* 1958.

BODINNAR, Sir John (Francis), Kt., *cr.* 1941; J.P. Wilts., Calne Bench; Chairman and Director of companies; *m.* Mabel Frost Latham (*d.* 1948); (*s.* killed on active service, 1941) one *d.*; *m.* 1949, Glenys Lloyd-Roberts. *Educ.:* privately. Took Honours in Accountancy profession; Chairman or Deputy Chairman or Managing Director of groups of companies; assisted Food Ministry during European War, 1914-1918, and in Food (Defence) Plans, 1937; Chairman: Brit. Bacon Curers' Fedn.; Bacon Marketing Board; Member of Bacon Development Board, 1932-57. Director of Bacon and Ham and Director of Bacon Production in Min. of Food, 1939-41; Commercial Sec. and Head of Supply Dept. (unpaid), Min. of Food, 1941-45; Commercial Adviser to Minister of Food, 1946; Pres. Food Manufacturers Federation, 1947-49; Chairman, Food Industries Council; Pres., Institute of Certificated Grocers (Educational), 1932-57; President Royal Warrant Holders Assoc., 1952-53 (now Hon. Treas.). *Recreations:* reading, music, walking. *Address:* Calne, Wilts. [*Died* 17 *Aug.* 1958.

BODKIN, Sir Archibald Henry, K.C.B., *cr.* 1924; Kt., *cr.* 1917; J.P.; *b.* 1 Apr. 1862; 5th *s.* of late W. P. Bodkin, D.L., J.P.; *m.* 1891, Maud Beatrice, *d.* of late Rev. R. Wheler Bush, M.A., Rector of St. Alphage, London Wall. *Educ.:* Cholmeley School, Highgate. Called to Bar, Inner Temple, 1885; Junior Counsel Treasury at Central Criminal Court, 1892; Senior, 1908; Bencher, Inner Temple, 1915; Recorder of Dover, 1901-20 and 1931-47; Director of Public Prosecutions, 1920-30; retired, 1930. Chairman Devon Quarter Sessions, 1931-47. *Address:* Beecher's Croft, Rogate, Petersfield, Hants. *T.:* Rogate 15. *Club:* Garrick. [*Died* 31 *Dec.* 1957.

BODKIN, Gilbert Edwin, C.B.E. 1942; Registrar Co-operative Socs., Mauritius, 1947; retd. 1951; *b.* 1886; *s.* of Frederick Edwin and Louise Jane Bodkin; *m.* 1924, Dorothy Bernton-Benjamin; one *d.* *Educ.:* Repton; Jesus Coll., Cambridge (B.A. 1908); Cambridge University (Diploma of Agriculture, 1910). Engaged at Cambridge University on a soil survey of Huntingdonshire, 1910-11; Govt. Economic Biologist, B. Guiana, 1911; Carnegie Scholar in Economic Entomology, 1912-13; represented B. Guiana at the 3rd Congress of Tropical Agriculture held in London, 1914, and at the Imperial Entomological Conference in London, 1920; Assistant Director, Department of Agriculture, British Guiana, 1919; Government Entomologist, Palestine, 1922; Director of Agriculture, Mauritius, 1932. *Publications:* various articles on Economic Entomology and on British Guiana; Editor, Journal of the Board of Agriculture, B. Guiana, 1913-22. *Recreations:* fishing, photography. *Address:* c/o Barclays Bank, Simmonds St., Johannesburg, S. Africa. [*Died* 23 *Dec.* 1955.

BOGART, Humphrey de Forest; Actor; *b.* 25 Dec. 1899; *s.* of Belmont Bogart and Maude Humphrey; *m.* 1945, Lauren Bacall; one *s.* one *d.* *Educ.:* Trinity School, New York, N.Y.; Phillips-Andover, Andover, Mass. *Plays include:* Cradle Snatchers, Saturday's Children, It's a Wise Child, Petrified Forest. *Films include:* Petrified Forest, Dead End, Angels with Dirty Faces, Dark Victory, Roaring Twenties, They Drive by Night, High Sierra, Maltese Falcon, Casablanca, Sahara, To Have and Have Not, Big Sleep, Dead Reckoning, Dark Passage, The Treasure of the Sierra Madre, Knock On Any Door, Tokyo Joe, Chain Lightning, In a Lonely Place, Sirocco, Murder Inc., The African Queen, Deadline, Battle Circus, The Caine Mutiny, Sabrina Fair, The Barefoot Contessa, We're No Angels, Desperate Hours, The Harder They Fall, etc. *Recreations:* golf, yachting. *Address:* (business) A. Morgan Maree Jr. and Associates, 6363 Wilshire Blvd., Suite 500, Los Angeles, California. *Clubs:* Coffee House, Players (New York); Newport Harbor Yacht (Newport, Calif.); Lakeside Golf (North Hollywood, Calif.). [*Died* 14 *Jan.* 1957.

BOGLE, Very Rev. Andrew Nisbet, D.D., Edinburgh; Ex-Secretary and Deputy of Church of Scotland; Ex-Moderator of Church of Scotland; *s.* of Rev. Andrew Bogle, Callander, Perthshire; *m.* 1896, Helen Milne, (*d.* 1954), *d.* of Michael McCulloch, Montreal; four *s.* one *d.* *Educ.:* Royal High School, Edinburgh; Edinburgh University; New College, Edinburgh. Minister of Free Church, Larbert, Stirlingshire, 1896-1903; North Leith (Ferry Road) United Free Church, 1903-16. *Recreations:* golf and angling. *Address:* 4 Cluny Avenue, Edinburgh. *T.:* 54155. [*Died* 5 *Aug.* 1957.

BOILEAU, Hugh Evan Ridley, Q.C. 1952; Chairman of East and West Suffolk Quarter Sessions since 1950; *b.* 10 Sept. 1906; *s.* of late Lt.-Col. F. R. F. Boileau, R.E., and of Mary Aurora (she *m.* 2nd, 1923, Sir Drummond Spencer-Smith, *q.v.*); *m.* 1941, Angela Violet Jelf; one *s.* one *d.* *Educ.:* Cheltenham College; Trinity College, Oxford (B.A.). Called to the Bar, 1929; practised in London and S.E. Circuit. Joined Devon Yeomanry, 1939; served War of 1939-45 in N. Africa and Italy; later instructor at the Staff College. Returned to the Bar, 1945; Deputy Chairman of Isle of Ely Quarter Sessions, 1948. *Address:* Wynne House, Boxford, nr. Colchester. *T.:* Boxford (Suffolk) 201. *Clubs:* United University; Norfolk County (Norwich). [*Died* 17 *July* 1952.

BOISSIER, Arthur Paul; *b.* 1882; *s.* of Rev. F. S. Boissier, Bloxham, nr. Banbury; *m.* 1st, 1909, Dorothy Leslie Smith (*d.* 1948); one *s.* one *d.*; 2nd, 1950, Kathleen Hardy-Smith. *Educ.:* St. John's, Leatherhead; Balliol College, Oxford. Senior Master, R.N. College, Osborne, 1905-1919; on staff of Harrow School, 1919-42, Headmaster, 1940-42; Director of Public Relations, Ministry of Fuel and Power, 1943-45; Director of Welfare, Stewarts & Lloyds, 1946-49. *Address:* Mains of Haddo, Tarves, Aberdeenshire. [*Died* 2 *Oct.* 1953.

BOJER, Johan; *b.* Trondjhem, 6 Mar. 1872; *s.* of Hans Bojer, merchant, and Johanne Elgaaen; *m.* Ellen Lous Lange; one *s.* two *d.* *Educ.:* The Military School, Trondjhem; Paris, Italy, Berlin, London. *Publications:* A Mother, play; Helga, novel; A Procession, novel; A Pilgrimage, novel; The Power of a Lie, novel; Brutus, play; White Birds, short stories; Our Kingdom, novel; Life, novel; The Eyes of Love, play; Sigürd Braa, play; The Great Hunger, novel; The Face of the World, novel; Dyrendal, novel; The Last Viking, novel; The Prisoner Who Sang, 1924; The Emigrants, 1926; The New Temple, novel, 1928; Folk by the Sea, novel, 1929; The House and the Sea, novel; By Day and by Night, novel; The King's Men, novel. *Address:* Hvalstad, Pr. Oslo, Norway. [*Died* 3 *July* 1959.

BOLAM, Rev. Canon Cecil Edward, F.R.Hist.S.; Chief Chaplain of the National Institute for the Blind, 1929-51; *b.* Durley House, Savernake, 7 March 1875; *s.* of C. G. Bolam; *m.* 1st, 1902, Beatrice Helen Rhodes; one *d.*; 2nd, 1924, Hester Wright; one *s.* *Educ.:* College for the Blind Worcester; private tuition. Ordained, 1898, Rector, Lusby-with-Asgarby, Lincolnshire, 1900; St. Mary Magdalene's, City of Lincoln, 1907; South Willingham, Lincolnshire, 1926; Rector of Greatford-with-Wilsthorpe, 1928-31; Rector of Willoughby Alford, Lincs., 1931-45; Prebendary of Lincoln, 1925-51, Canon Emeritus, 1951-; Actg. C.F., 1918; Officiating Clergyman to R.F.C. and R.A.F., 1916; C.F., 1921. *Publications:* John Bunyan; A Little Child, etc. *Address:* 37 Lucerne Rd., Remuera, Auckland, S.E.2, N.Z. [*Died* 2 *July* 1960.

BOLAND, John Pius; General Secretary, Catholic Truth Society, 1926-47; *b.* 1870; *s.* of late Patrick Boland of Dublin; *m.* 1902, Eileen (*d.* 1937), *d.* of late Dr. Patrick Moloney, of Melbourne, Australia; one *s.* five *d.* *Educ.:* Edgbaston Oratory; Christ Church, Oxford, M.A. 1901; Bonn University. Graduated at London University, B.A. 1892; called to Bar, 1897. Member of the Dublin Commission for setting up the National University of Ireland, 1908 (LL.D., N.U.I., 1950); member of Departmental Committee on Food Production in Ireland, 1915; a Junior Whip of the Irish Party, 1906-18; a keen advocate for the inclusion of the Irish language as an essential subject in the Matriculation Examination of the National University; M.P. (N.) South Kerry, 1900-18; a Knight of Order of St. Gregory the Great; Winner of Singles and Doubles in Lawn Tennis, Olympic Games, Athens, 1896. *Publications:* Irishman's Day: A Day in the Life of an Irish M.P., 1944; Killarney and the Leprechauns (illustrated by Patric O'Keeffe), 1950. *Address:* 40 St. George's Square, S.W.1. *T.:* Victoria 2046. [*Died* 17 *March* 1958.

BOLES, Lt.-Col. Dennis Coleridge; *b.* 4 June 1885; *s.* of late F. J. Coleridge Boles, J.P., and C. A. Jones, Redcliff, Exmouth; *m.* 1921, Monica Reid Walker; two *s.* one *d.* *Educ.:* Private; Eton; R.M.C. Sandhurst. Gazetted 17th Lancers, 1906; served in European War throughout in France; Captain, 1914; Maj. 1925; Bt. Lt.-Col. Royal Horse Guards, 1929; Lt.-Col. 1930. M.P. (C.) Wells Divn. of Somerset, 1939-51. C.C. Somerset, 1952. Church Assembly and House of Laity, 1955. *Recreations:* polo (played for Br. Army *v.* American Army, 1925), cricket (Eton *v.* Harrow, holds record score for match). *Address:* Barrow Court-Galhampton, Yeovil. *T.A.:* Galhampton N. Cadbury. *T.:* N. Cadbury 266; Forsinard, Sutherland. *Clubs:* Cavalry, Hurlingham. [*Died* 25 *April* 1958.

BOLSTER, Captain Thomas Charles Carpenter, D.S.O. 1917; R.N., retired; at present on active service; *m.* 1914, Marguerita Maud Elizabeth, (*d.* 1949), *d.* of late John Edward Arthur Dick-Lauder; two *s.* Served European War, 1914-18 (despatches, D.S.O.); retired list, 1931. *Address:* Crouchers, Apuldram, Chichester. [*Died* 19 *Aug.* 1955.

BOLTON, Louis Hamilton; Shipowner; Member of Lloyd's; *b.* 1884; *s.* of late Sir Frederic Bolton; *m.* 1918, Beryl, *d.* of Bernard Dyer; one *s.* three *d.* *Educ.:* Rugby School. Member of Committee of London General Shipowners, Lloyd's Register of Shipping, Pilotage Committee of Trinity

House, the Board of the Port of London Authority (Vice-Chairman, 1941-46). *Address:* 34 Montpelier Sq., S.W.7; Hinton House, Woodford Halse, nr. Rugby. *Clubs:* Reform, City of London. [*Died* 2 *Sept.* 1953.

BOMPAS, Cecil Henry, C.S.I. 1918; Indian Civil Service (retired); *s.* of late Judge Bompas, K.C.; *b.* 1868; *m.* 1st, 1897, Geraldine (*d.* 1908), *d.* of James Barton; 2nd, 1912, Nita Frances, *d.* of William Goode; three *s.* three *d.* *Educ.:* Westminster; Trinity College, Cambridge. Entered I.C.S., 1887. *Address:* c/o Grindlay's Bank, 54 Parliament Street, S.W.1. [*Died* 22 *Jan.* 1956.

BOND, Brigadier-General Charles Earbery, C.M.G. 1916; D.S.O. 1902; late Royal Sussex Regiment; *b.* 14 Oct. 1877. *Educ.:* Wellington College. Entered Army, 1898; Captain, 1907; Major, 1915; Temp. Lieut.-Colonel, 1915; Temp. Brig.-General, 1917-18; Lt.-Col. 1924; served South Africa, 1899-1902 (despatches twice, Queen's medal with 4 clasps, King's medal 2 clasps, D.S.O.); European War, 1914-18 (despatches five times, Mons medal; C.M.G., Bt. Lt.-Col.); commanded 8th Border Regiment, 1915-17; commanded 51st Infantry Brigade, 1918-19; commanded Thames and Medway Brigade; retired with hon. rank of Brig.-General; retired pay, 1929. [*Died* 31 *Dec.* 1953.

BOND, Maj.-Gen. John Arthur Mallock, C.B. 1946; C.B.E. 1943; *b.* 1891; *e. s.* of late Major A. T. M. Bond. Director, St. James's Advertising and Publishing Company Ltd. Commander Legion of Merit (U.S.A.); Grand Officer, Order of Orange Nassau, with Swords. *Address:* Pitt Manor, Nr. Winchester, Hants. *Clubs:* Naval and Military, Hurlingham. [*Died* 20 *July* 1959.

BOND, Surgeon Vice-Admiral Sir Reginald (St. George Smallridge), K.C.B., *cr.* 1933 (C.B. 1926); M.B. (Edin.); F.R.C.P. (Lond.); F.R.C.S. (Edin.); D.P.H. (Lond.); Certif. Med. Psych. Association; of Gray's Inn, Barrister-at-law; *b.* Ogbourne St. George, Wilts., 1872; *yr. s.* of late Rev. Alfred Bond of Powick, Worcester, and Frances Elizabeth, *d.* of late Charles Smallridge, Clerk of Peace for Gloucester; *m.* 1900, Blanche Alexandra (*d.* 1955), *o. c.* of late Capt. John D'Arcy-Irvine, J.P., R.N., and of Carra Leena, Rathmullan, Co. Donegal; no *c.* *Educ.:* private; University of Edinburgh; University College, London. Mackenzie Bursar in Anatomy; late House Surgeon, Edinburgh Royal Infirmary; Assistant Physician, Royal Morningside Mental Hospital, and Assistant M.O. Caterham Mental Hospital; entered R.N. Medical Service as Surgeon, 1898; Surgeon Commander, 1914; Surgeon Captain, 1922; Surgeon Rear-Admiral, 1926; served European War in Grand Fleet, as a S.M.O., R.N. Hospital, Plymouth, as Naval Health Officer on the staff of the C.-in-C., Plymouth, and as Assistant for Hygiene to the M.D.G. Admiralty; Director of Medical Studies and Professor of Hygiene, R.N. Medical School, Greenwich, 1921-23; Deputy Medical Director-General, Admiralty, 1923-26; Surgeon Rear-Admiral in charge Royal Naval Hospital, Plymouth, 1926-30; Medical Director-General of the Navy, 1931-34; Hon. Physician to the King, 1931-34; retired list, 1934; Gilbert Blane Gold Medal (Roy. Navy); received their Lordships' appreciation of valuable services in connection with the designing and perfecting of an air-purifying apparatus for submarines; Co-Editor of the Journal of the Royal Naval Medical Service, 1920-26. *Address:* 30 Apsley House, N.W.8. *T.:* Primrose 0567. [*Died* 27 *July* 1955.

BOND, Rev. Robert, D.D.; *b.* Willington, Co. Durham; *s.* of Edgar and Harriet Bond; *m.* 1898, Charlotte Wright; two *d.* *Educ.:* British School, Willington; Methodist College, Didsbury, Manchester. Entered Wesleyan Methodist Ministry, 1894; Secretary of the Wesleyan Conference, 1928; Secretary of Methodist Conference at the Union of the Wesleyan Methodist, Primitive Methodist and United Methodist Churches, 1932; President of the Methodist Conference, 1937-38; Moderator of the Federal Council of the Free Churches of England, 1938-39. *Publications:* Articles in British, American and Colonial Magazines and Papers. *Recreation:* gardening. *Address:* 74 Coleridge Avenue, Penarth, Glam. [*Died* 24 *Oct.* 1952.

BOND, William Ralph Garneys; Sudan Political Service (retired); *b.* 12 Dec. 1880; *s.* of William H. Bond and Mary C. Meysey Thompson, sister of late Lord Knaresborough; *m.* 1920, Evelyn I., *d.* of Col. A. M. Blake, C.B., Danesbury, Herts; one *s.* one *d.* *Educ:* Eton; New College, Oxford. In Sudan Political Service; late Governor of Dongola and Fung Provinces. High Sheriff of Dorset, 1945-46. *Address:* Moigne Combe, Dorchester, Dorset. [*Died* 10 *Feb.* 1952.

BONDFIELD, Rt. Hon. Margaret Grace, P.C. 1929; C.H. 1948; J.P.; Vice-President National Council of Social Service; *b.* Somerset, 1873. Trade Unionist and Labour Leader; Assistant Secretary of Shop Assistants Union, 1898-1908; National Officer National Union of General and Municipal Workers; retired, 1938; Lecturer and writer for Socialist and Labour Movement; on General Council of Trades Union Congress, 1918-24 and 1926-29; was delegate to Berne International Conference, 1918; French Trades Union Congress, Paris, 1918; Congress of American Federation of Labour, Atlantic City; delegate for British T.U.C. to Russia, 1920; Labour Adviser to International Labour Conference at Washington, 1919, and Geneva, 1921, 1922, 1923, 1926, 1927, under League of Nations; Government Representative, 1924; Member of Central Committee on Women's Training and Employment; Chairman General Council of Trade Union Congress, 1923. M.P. (Lab.) Northampton, 1923-24; Wallsend, 1926-31; Parliamentary Secretary to Ministry of Labour, 1924; Minister of Labour, 1929-31. Member Oversea Settlement Committee, 1925-29; Chairman of Women's Group on Public Welfare, 1939-49. Lecture tours through Canada, U.S.A., and Mexico, 1938; through U.S.A., 1941-43; received Freedom of Chard, July 1930; LL.D., University of Bristol, 1930. *Publication:* A Life's Work, 1949. *Club:* Y.W.C.A. Central. [*Died* 16 *June* 1953.

BONE, Sir David William, Kt., *cr.* 1946; C.B.E. 1943; LL.D. (Glasgow) 1947; Master Mariner, Commodore of the Anchor Line (retd.); author, writing principally on seafaring life; *b.* Glasgow, 1874; *s.* of David Drummond Bone, journalist, Glasgow; *m.* 1902, Mary Helen Bell (*d.* 1952), *d.* of Archibald Cameron, Edinburgh; one *s.* one *d.* *Educ.:* Glasgow. Merchant Service, 1890; served seven years in sail; joined Anchor Line, 1899; promoted to command, 1915. *Publications:* The Brassbounder, 1910; Broken Stowage, 1915; Merchantmen-at-Arms, 1919, revised edition, 1929; The Lookoutman, 1923; Capstan Bars, 1931; Merchantman Rearmed, 1949; The Queerfella, 1952; Landfall at Sunset, 1955; contributed articles on seafaring life to many journals since 1900. *Recreation:* country life. *Address:* Abbots Holt, Tilford, Surrey. [*Died* 17 *May* 1959.

BONE, Eng.-Rear-Adm. Howard, C.B. 1917; late Manager Engineering Dept. Portsmouth Dockyard; *b.* 1869; *s.* of S. S. Bone; *m.* 1905, Annie Stewart (*d.* 1955), *d.* of Francis Wyatt; one *s.* two *d.* *Educ.:* Battersea Grammar School. Naval Engineer Student, 1883; entered Royal Navy as Assistant Engineer, 1888; served in

China, Channel, Mediterranean, Atlantic, and Home Fleets; Engineer Commander, 1905; Chief Engineer Haulbowline Dockyard, 1912; on staff of Admiral Sir John Jellicoe, G.C.B., O.M., 1914-16; on staff of Rear-Admiral Sir Wm. Pakenham, K.C.B., 1917; retired list, 1922; received Order of St. Anne, 2nd Class, for distinguished service in the Battle of Jutland. *Recreations:* formerly motoring, mountaineering. *Address:* 32 Nettlecombe Avenue, Southsea. *T.:* Portsmouth 31374. [*Died* 9 *Dec.* 1955.

BONE, Sir Muirhead, Kt., *cr.* 1937; LL.D. (St. Andrews, Liverpool, Glasgow); D.Litt. (Oxford); Hon. A.R.I.B.A.; Hon. R.W.S.; Hon. R.E.; Hon. R.S.A.; Trustee Imperial War Museum; *b.* Glasgow, 23 March 1876; *s.* of David Drummond Bone, journalist, Glasgow; *m.* 1903, Gertrude Helena, *d.* of Rev. Benjamin Dodd; one *s.* Etcher, draughtsman, and painter; studied at Glasgow School of Art Evening School; removed to London, 1901; member New English Art Club; Official Artist, Western Front, and with the Fleet, 1916-18; Official Artist, Admiralty, 1940-43; exhibitions of drawings of Spain, Colnaghi Gallery 1930 and 1931. Trustee National Gallery, 1941-48; formerly Trustee, Tate Gallery. *Publications:* Glasgow in 1901 (part author, and the illustrator); Drawings of Glasgow; The Western Front (text by C. E. Montague); Old Spain; Days in Old Spain (illustr.; text by G. Bone); Came to Oxford (illustr.; text by G. Bone). *Address:* Grayflete, Ferry Hinksey, Oxford. *T.:* Oxford 2988. [*Died* 21 *Oct.* 1953.

BONE, Stephen; landscape and portrait painter; writer; *b.* London, 1904; *s.* of Sir Muirhead Bone, *q.v.*, and of Gertrude Bone; *m.* 1929, Mary Adshead; two *s.* one *d.* *Educ.:* Bedales School; Slade School of Art (under Professor Henry Tonks). Paintings in permanent collections at Tate Gallery, Dundee, Dublin, Glasgow and Manchester. Decorative paintings for Underground Railway and Department of Overseas Trade; Médaille d'or Exposition des Arts Decoratifs, Paris, 1926; Member New English Art Club; Camouflage Establishment, 1939-43; Official Naval Artist, 1943-45; Manchester Guardian's London art critic, 1948. Broadcasts. *Publications:* (with Mary Adshead) The Little Boy and His House, 1936; The Silly Snail, 1943; The Little Boys and Their Boats, 1954; Guidebook to the West Coast of Scotland, 1938 (revised 1952); Albion: an Artist's Britain, 1939, republished 1949 as Landscapes of Britain; The British Weather, 1946; England and the English, 1951; Oil-Painting, 1956. Wood-cut and other illustrations to various books by Gertrude Bone, W. H. Davies, and George Bourne. *Recreation:* geography. *Address:* 140 Haverstock Hill, N.W.3. [*Died* 15 *Sept.* 1958.

BONHAM-CARTER, General Sir Charles, G.C.B. *cr.* 1941 (K.C.B. *cr.* 1935; C.B. 1926); C.M.G. 1919; D.S.O. 1917; Hon. LL.D., Royal Malta University; 9th *s.* of late Henry Bonham-Carter and Sibella Charlotte, *e. d.* of late George Warde Norman; *b.* 25 Feb. 1876; *m.* 1st, 1902, Gladys Beryl, *d.* of Lt.-Col. Arthur Blayney Coddington, R.E.; two *s.*; 2nd, 1911, Gabrielle Madge Jeanette, *d.* of Capt. Ernest Fisher, Frithwald, Chertsey; one *s.* *Educ.:* Clifton College; R.M.C., Sandhurst; Staff College. Served South African War, 1900-1 (Queen's medal 4 clasps); European War, 1914-18 (D.S.O., C.M.G., Bt. Col., Officier Légion d'honneur, American Distinguished Service Medal); Maj.-Gen. 1926; Director of Staff Duties, War Office, 1927-31; Commander 4th Division 1931-33; Lt.-Gen., 1933; Director-General of Territorial Army. 1933-36; Governor and Commander-in-Chief of Malta, 1936-40; General, 1937; A.D.C. General to the King, 1938-41; retired pay, 1940. *Address:* Durford Height, Petersfield, Hants. *Club:* United Service. [*Died* 21 *Oct.* 1955.

BONHAM-CARTER, Sir Edgar, K.C.M.G., *cr.* 1920 (C.M.G. 1909); C.I.E. 1919; *b.* 2 April 1870; *s.* of Henry Bonham-Carter (*d.* 1921) and Sibella (*d.* 1916), *d.* of G. Warde Norman; *m.* 1926, Charlotte Helen, *d.* of late Col. William Lewis Kinloch Ogilvy, C.B., 60th Rifles, and Mrs. Lucy Ogilvy, formerly Wickham of Binsted Wyck. *Educ.:* Clifton Coll.; New Coll., Oxford. Called to Bar, Lincoln's Inn, 1895; Legal Sec. to Sudan Government, 1899-1917; Official Member of Council of Governor-General of Sudan, 1910-17; Senior Judicial Officer, Baghdad, 1917; Judicial Adviser, Mesopotamia, 1919-21; L.C.C. (N.E. Bethnal Green), 1922-25; Chairman of First Garden City, Ltd., Letchworth, 1929-39; Chairman British School of Archaeology in Iraq, 1932-1950; Chm. National Housing and Town Planning Council, 1940-42; President, N.E. Hampshire Agricultural Assoc., 1953; holds 1st Class Order of the Nile. *Recreations:* Oxford University Rugby Football XV, 1890-91; English Rugby Football XV, 1891. *Address:* 17 Radnor Place, W.2. *T.:* Paddington 4980; Binsted Wyck, Alton, Hants. *T.:* Alton 3210. *Club:* Athenæum. [*Died* 24 *April* 1956.

BONHAM-CARTER, Ian Malcolm, C.B. 1923; O.B.E. 1919; Air Commodore, late R.A.F.; *b.* 1882; 2nd *s.* of Lieut.-Col. Hugh Bonham-Carter, Coldstream Guards, and Jane MacDonald; *m.* 1911, Ruth Mary, *d.* of Richard Ward, 50 Cadogan Place; one *d.* *Educ.:* Haileybury College. Joined 5th Bn. Northumberland Fusiliers, 1900; 1st Bn. 5th Fusiliers, 1901; seconded Royal Flying Corps, 1914; Royal Air Force, 1918; served South Africa, 1901-2; Indian N.W. Frontier, 1908 (despatches); European War, 1914-18 (despatches) and 1940-42 (despatches); Legion of Honour, 1914; retired list, 1931, 1942. *Address:* Winton House, Priory Road, Sunningdale, Berks. [*Died* 31 *Dec.* 1953.

BONHAM CARTER, Sir Maurice, K.C.B., 1916; K.C.V.O., 1917; retired as Director of Blackburn and General Aircraft Ltd., also as Chm. Local Employment and Disablement Advisory Committees for Paddington and Marylebone; *b.* 11 Oct. 1880; *y. s.* of late Henry Bonham-Carter; *m.* 1915, Lady (Helen) Violet Asquith (Lady Violet Bonham Carter, D.B.E.), *e. d.* of 1st Earl of Oxford and Asquith; two *s.* two *d.* *Educ.:* Winchester; Balliol Coll., Oxford. Called to Bar, Lincoln's Inn, 1909; Private Secretary to Mr. Asquith, 1910-16; Assist. Sec., Ministry of Reconstruction, 1917; Air Ministry, 1918. *Recreations:* cricket (Oxford Univ. XI., 1902), golf, fishing. *Address:* 21 Hyde Park Square, W.2. *T.:* Paddington 1881. *Club:* Brooks's. [*Died* 7 *June* 1960.

BONNAR, John Calderwood; Sheriff Substitute of Renfrew and Argyll at Greenock, 1945-55; *b.* 3 April 1888; 2nd *s.* of William Bonnar and Mary Strachan Baird Calderwood; *m.* 1925, Enid Josephine, *d.* of late Charles Gilbertson, Solicitor, London; two *d.* *Educ.:* George Watson's College, Edinburgh; Edinburgh University. Called to Scottish Bar, 1914; served with Royal Dublin Fusiliers 1914-19, Capt.; called to Bar of Supreme Court of Nigeria, 1920; Member of London Stock Exchange, 1922-42. *Recreations:* golf, fishing, walking. *Address:* Sheriff's Chambers, County Buildings, Greenock. *T.:* Greenock 822. *Club:* Greenock (Greenock). [*Died* 20 *July* 1956.

BONNER, Charles George, V.C. 1917; D.S.C.; *b.* Staffordshire, 1884; *s.* of Samuel Bonner, J.P., Aldridge, nr. Walsall; *m.* Alice Mabel, *d.* of late Thomas Partridge, Walsall. *Educ.:* Sutton Coldfield and Coleshill Grammar Schools; H.M.S. Conway. A Master Mariner since 1907; served European War, decorated for services in action with enemy submarines. *Recreations:* shooting, riding. *Address:* 12 Netherby Road, Edinburgh. [*Died* 8 *Feb.* 1951.

BONNER, Sir George Albert, Kt., *cr.* 1927; Senior Master of the Supreme Court, 1905-1937; and King's Remembrancer, 1927-37; *b.* 9 March 1862; *s.* of Charles Foster Bonner of Spalding, Lincolnshire, and Elizabeth, *d.* of Edward Swaine, Gomersall, Yorks; *m.* 1896, Eveleen (*d.* 1939), M.B.E., Order of Queen Elizabeth of Belgium, *d.* of F. T. Lewis of Whitehall Court, London; two *d.* *Educ.:* New College, Oxford. M.A. Called to Bar, Inner Temple, 1885; A Master of the Bench, 1931; Certificate of Royal Humane Society for saving life in the Thames off the Embankment, 1918. *Publications:* The Law of Motor Cars and Hackney and other Carriages on the Highways, 1st edition, 1898; 2nd edition, 1905; articles on Actions and Interpleader and Practice, 2nd edition, The Laws of England (Lord Halsbury); The Office of the King's Remembrancer in England, 1930. *Recreation:* golf. *Address:* Oakley Hall, Cirencester, Glos. *Clubs:* Oxford and Cambridge; Woking Golf (Woking); Rye Golf (Rye). [*Died* 27 *April* 1952.

BONNEY, Victor, M.S., M.D., B.Sc. (Lond.), F.R.C.S. (Eng.), M.R.C.P. (Lond.); F.R.A.C.S. (Hon.); F.R.C.O.G. (Hon.); Hon. Fellow Assoc. of Surgeons; Consulting Gynæcological Surgeon Middlesex Hospital and late Surgeon to its military branch at Clacton-on-Sea, Eastern Command, 1914-18; Consulting Surgeon to the Chelsea Hospital for Women; late Hon. Consultant in Obstetrics and Gynæcology to the Army; late visiting Gynæcologist, British Post-graduate Medical School; late Gynæcological Surgeon to the Royal Masonic Hospital, the Miller Hospital, and to Queen Alexandra's Military Hospital; late Surgeon County of London and Masonic War Hospitals and Member of Central Midwives Board; Hon. Fellow: American Gynæcological Society; Assoc. of Surgeons of Gt. Britain and Ireland; *s.* of late Dr. W. A. Bonney, 100 Elm Park Gardens, S.W.; *m.* 1905, Annie, *d.* of late Dr. James Appleyard, J.P., Longford, Tasmania. *Educ.:* private school; St. Bartholomew's Hospital; Middlesex Hospital; Qualified, 1896; Resident Officership at the Middlesex Hospital; Chelsea Hospital for Women and Queen Charlotte's Lying-in Hospital, 1897-1901; Obstetric Tutor to Middlesex Hospital, 1903; late Emden Research Scholar and Mercers Prizeman at the Middlesex Hospital Cancer Research Institution; Hunterian Orator, Hunterian Professor and Bradshaw Lecturer, Royal College of Surgeons of England; and Examiner to the Conjoint Board of England, etc.; late Member of Council and Vice-Pres. of the Royal College of Surgeons of England. *Publications:* A Text-book of Gynæcological Surgery; Difficulties and Emergencies of Obstetric Practice; The Technical Minutiae of Extended Myomectomy and Ovarian Cystectomy, etc. *Address:* 149 Harley Street, W.1. *T.:* Welbeck 4444; Seabournes, Fawley, Hereford. *T.:* Carey 17. [*Died* 4 *July* 1953.

BONSAL, Stephen; author and newspaper correspondent; *b.* Baltimore, 29 March 1865; *s.* of Stephen Bonsal and Frances Leigh; *m.* 1900, Henrietta Fairfax Morris. *Educ.:* St. Paul's School, Concord; Heidelberg; Bonn; Vienna. Special Correspondent of New York Herald in various wars, from 1885. Entered Diplomatic Service of U.S.A., 1893. Has travelled in many countries either as correspondent or on special missions. *Publications:* Morocco as It Is, 1892; The Real Condition of Cuba, 1897; The Fight for Santiago, 1899; The Golden Horse Shoe, 1900; The American Mediterranean, 1912; Heyday in a Vanished World, 1937; Unfinished Business, Paris-Versailles, 1919 (awarded Pulitzer Prize), 1944; When the French were Here, 1945; also contributions to magazines. *Address:* 3142 P St. N.W., Washington, D.C., U.S.A. [*Died* 8 *June* 1951.

BONSOR, Major Sir Reginald, 2nd Bt., *cr.* 1925; late Surrey Yeomanry; Chairman John Dickinson & Co., Ltd.; *b.* 9 Aug. 1879; *s.* of 1st Bt. and Emily (*d.* 1882), *d.* of James Fellowes, Dorset; *S.* father, 1929; *m.* 1914, Nancy Frances, *d.* of late Arthur Melville Hood Walrond; two *s.* one *d.* *Educ.* Eton. Served S. Africa, 1900; European War, 1914-19; Sheriff of Buckinghamshire, 1940. *Recreations:* sports. *Heir:* *s.* Capt. Bryan Cosmo Bonsor, M.C., Buckinghamshire Yeomanry [*b.* 27 Sept. 1916; *m.* 1942, Elizabeth, *d.* of late Capt. A. V. Hambro; two *s.*]. *Address:* Liscombe Park, Leighton Buzzard. *T.A.:* Liscombe Park, Soulbury. *T.:* Soulbury 18. *Clubs:* Turf, St. James', Beefsteak. [*Died* 4 *April* 1959.

BONYTHON, Sir (John) Lavington, Kt., *cr.* 1935; Vice-Chairman Board of Directors of Adelaide Advertiser; *b.* 10 Sep. 1875; *s.* of late Hon. Sir Langdon Bonython, K.C.M.G.; *m.* 1st, 1904, Blanche Ada (*d.* 1908), *d.* of Sir John Bray, K.C.M.G.; 2nd, 1912, Constance Jean, *d.* of Charles H. Warren; three *s.* three *d.* *Educ.:* Prince Alfred College, Adelaide. Editor of the Saturday Express, Adelaide, 1912-30; Councillor for the City of Adelaide, 1901-7; Alderman, 1907-11 and 1935-59; Acting Mayor, 1911; Mayor, 1912-13; Lord Mayor, 1928, 1929, 1930; Chairman of Finance Committee of City Council, 1910; of Adelaide School Board, 1907-10; of Metropolitan Abattoirs Board, 1911-12-13, 1928-29-30; of Municipal Association, 1912-13, 1928-29-30; was Mem. Adelaide Hospital Board, Licensing Bench, Municipal Tramways Trust; Chairman Botanic Gardens Board; Pres. of Australian Natives' Assoc., 1901; Member of Metropolitan Fire Brigades Board, 1905-6; Pres. of Chamber of Commerce; Chairman Industrial Stability Committee, Metropolitan Infectious Diseases Hospital, Youth Occupational Committee; Pres. Minda Home for Weak-minded Children; Pres. S.A. Instn. for the Blind and Deaf and Dumb, Inc.; Chm. of Directors of Executor Trustee and Agency Co. of South Australia and other companies; Pres. Royal Society St. George; President of Royal Empire Society; Member of Housing Trust of South Australia; President Taxpayers Assoc. of S.A.; Vice-Pres. Devon and Cornwall Record Society. In 1940 he and his family donated £25,000 to Commonwealth Govt. to defray the cost of building a "pilot" tank for the Australian Army. *Address:* St. Corantyn, Adelaide, and Eurilla, Mount Lofty, South Australia. *Clubs:* Adelaide, Naval and Military (Adelaide). [*Died* 6 *Nov.* 1960.

BOOTH, Mrs. Bramwell, (Florence Eleanor); *b.* Blaina, 1861; *d.* of late Dr. Soper, Plymouth; *m.* 1882, W. Bramwell Booth, C.H. (*d.* 1929); two *s.* five *d.* Commenced Salvation Army work, 1880; began the Women's Social work, 1883, and has continued public work ever since; Director, Mother's Hospital, Hackney; appointed one of Gen. Booth's commissioners, 1888; conducted congresses and other public meetings in Switzerland, Germany, Denmark, Holland, Belgium, Sweden, Norway, Finland, France, Canada and U.S.A.; mem., Women's Advisory Committee, Central Control Board (Liquor Traffic), 1916; member Birth Rate Commission, 1915-18; J.P. London District; a Visiting Magistrate of Holloway Prison; Vice-President League of National Life and British and Foreign Bible Society. *Publications:* Mothers and the Empire; Powers of Salvation Army Officers; Friendship with Jesus; Likeness to God; Wanted an Elite. *Address:* North Court, Finchhampstead, Berks. [*Died* 10 *June* 1957.

BOOTH, James William, R.C.A.; Artist. Exhibited at Royal Cambrian Academy, 1945 and 1946. *Address:* Stoneleigh Lodge, Scalby, near Scarborough. [*Died* 18 *Aug.* 1953.

BOOTH, Sir Philip, 2nd Bt., *cr.* 1916; Director of television films with Cambria Studio, Los Angeles, since 1958; *b.* 8 Feb. 1907; *s.* of Sir Alfred Booth, 1st Bt., Liverpool, and Mary Blake (*d.* 1924), *d.* of Edmund Dwight, of New York City; *S.* father 1948; *m.* 1948, Ethel Greenfield; two *s.* *Educ.:* Malvern College; King's College, Cambridge (B.A.); Yale University Graduate School, New Haven, Connecticut, U.S.A. With Booth Steamship Co., N.Y. City, 1931-1935; Yale Dept. of Drama, New Haven, 1935-36; Asst. Editor London Films, 1937-1938; Commentator during Munich crisis for Nat. Broadcasting Co. of N.Y., 1938; Dir. with Columbia Broadcasting System Television in N.Y., 1939-47; Producer and Dir. Westchester Playhouse, N.Y. State, 1947; Program Director, Paramount Television, 1947-49; Senior television director and producer, American Broadcasting Co., 1949-52; director and producer for various television films, 1952; Director of Production, Allan Hancock Foundation Television, 1953-54; Director and Producer, television films, with Young and Rubicam Inc., 1955; Producer of television films for Ford Foundation Television Programs of America, and other agencies, 1956-57. Served War of 1939-45 as Captain with R.C.A.F., R. Fusiliers and Pioneer Corps. *Heir:* *s.* Douglas Allen, *b.* 2 Dec. 1949. *Address:* 4244 Empress Avenue, Encino, California, U.S.A. [*Died* 7 *Jan.* 1960.

BOOTH, Col. (Hon. Brig.-Gen.) Hon. W. D. S.; *see* Sclater-Booth.

BOOTHBY, Sir Seymour William Brooke, 14th Bt., *cr.* 1660; Land Agent; *b.* 6 Feb. 1866; *s.* of Sir Brooke William Robert Boothby, 10th Bt., and Martha Serena, *d.* of Rev. Charles Boothby, Vicar of Sutterton, Lincs; *S.* brother, 1935; *m.* 1906, Clara Margaret, *d.* of late Robert Valpy; one *s.* one *d.* *Educ.:* H.M.S. Britannia; abroad. *Recreation:* hunting. *Heir:* *s.* Hugo Robert Brooke, [*b.* 10 Aug. 1907; *m.* 1938, Evelyn Ann, *o. d.* of H. C. R. Homfray; one *s.* two *d.*] *Address:* Fonmon Castle, Cardiff. *T.:* Rhoose 6. [*Died* 17 *March* 1951.

BOOTHMAN, Air Chief Marshal Sir John Nelson, K.C.B., *cr.* 1954 (C.B. 1944); K.B.E., *cr.* 1951; D.F.C. 1944; A.F.C. 1931; retired; *b.* Feb. 1901; *s.* of late T. J. Boothman, Co. Wicklow; *m.* 1922, Gertrude, *d.* of late H. Andrews, Paris. Won Schneider Trophy, 1931. Commander of Legion of Merit (U.S.A.); D.F.C. (U.S.A.); Croix de Guerre (France), War Cross (Czechoslovakia). Assistant Chief of the Air Staff (T.R.), 1945-1948; Air Officer Commanding Air H.Q., Iraq, 1948-50; Controller of Supplies (Air), Ministry of Supply, 1950-53; A.O.C.-in-C., Coastal Command, 1953-56; retired 1956. *Address:* 7 Hill House, Stanmore Hill, Stanmore, Middlesex. [*Died* 29 *Dec.* 1957.

BORG, Sir George, Kt., *cr.* 1942; M.B.E. 1920; LL.D.; *b.* Valletta, 23 April 1887; *m.* Beatrice Farrugia (*d.* 1950); one *s.* two *d.* *Educ.:* Malta and Catania Univs., LL.D. Solicitor, 1907; Barrister-at-Law, 1916; Editor Daily Malta Herald; Senator, 1932; elected Member Council, 1938; Leader Constitutional Party, 1940; nominated Executive Council, 1939; Chief Justice, Malta, 1940-52; retired, 1952; Chairman Criminal Code Revision Commission. *Publications:* Draft Constitution for Malta; Draft Commercial Code; Short Essays on Roman Law. *Recreation:* walking. *Address:* Valletta, Malta. *Club:* Casino Maltese (Valletta). [*Died* 28 *June* 1954.

BORRETT, Admiral George Holmes, C.B. 1918. Lieut. of H.M.S. Centurion, China, 1900 (despatches); Transport Officer (Commander), 1901 (despatches); served European War, including Battle of Jutland, 1914-18 (despatches, C.B.); Commanded 5th Light Cruiser Squadron, China, 1919-20; Senior Naval Officer in Yangtse River, China, 1920-21; retired list, 1925; holds 2nd Class Sacred Treasure of Japan. *Address:* Southwood, Weybridge, Surrey. [*Died* 10 *June* 1952.

BORTHWICK, Capt. Alfred Edward, of Burnhouse, Stow, Midlothian; R.S.A. 1938 (A.R.S.A. 1928); A.R.E., P.P.R.S.W.; *b.* Scarborough, 22 April 1871; 2nd *s.* of W. H. Borthwick, of Crookston and Borthwick Castle; *m.* Mary S. Violet, *y. d.* of Captain Pringle, R.N., of Torwoodlee, Selkirkshire; three *d.* Studied at Royal Scottish Academy Life School and in Paris under William Bouguereau and Tony Robert Flury: continued studying in Antwerp. Past Pres. Soc. of Scottish Artists; P.R.S.W., 1931-49; member of various councils and cttees. Has painted large number of portraits; pictures in public collections include: Sir George Washington-Browne (Nat. Portrait Gallery of Scotland); Grizel and her pet, and Marjorie (Roy. Scottish Academy). Served South African War with Scottish Sharpshooters; served European War, 1914-19 (despatches): Remount and Transport till 1915, release from Colours, Min. of Munitions. Hon. LL.D. St. Andrews, 1952. *Address:* 8 Merchiston Crescent, Edinburgh, 10. *T.:* Fountainbridge 6963. *Clubs:* Chelsea Arts; (Hon.) Scottish Artists' (Edinburgh); (Hon.) Glasgow Arts. [*Died* 7 *Dec.* 1955.

BORWICK, Lt.-Col. Malcolm, D.S.O. 1918; D.L.; J.P.Northants; *b.* 1882; *m.* 1909, Violet, *d.* of late Capt. W. G. Middleton; two *s.* one *d.* *Educ.:* Harrow. Joined Scots Greys, 1902; served South Africa (medal): European War, 1914-19 (despatches, D.S.O., Bt. Major); M.F.H., Middleton, 1921-31; D.L. Northants. *Address:* Haselbeach Hill, Northampton. *T.:* Maidwell 208. [*Died* 10 *Dec.* 1957.

BOSANQUET, Captain Henry Theodore Augustus, C.V.O. 1934; R.N. (retired); F.S.A.; Vice-President: Marine Society and Society for Nautical Research; *b.* 3 Aug. 1870; *s.* of Theodore Bosanquet, Bombay Civil Service, and Merelina L. M., *d.* of James W. Bosanquet, Claysmore; *m.* 1899, Lilian Powys (*d.* 1947), 4th *d.* of J. E. Campbell-Colquhoun of Killermont and Garscadden, Dunbartonshire; one *d.* *Educ.:* Summerfield, Oxford; H.M.S. Britannia. Entered Royal Navy 1883; Sub-Lieut. 1890; Lieut. 1892; Secretary, Marine Society, 1898-1917; Commander (retd.), 1916; served European War, 1914-1919; Admiralty War Staff (Trade Division), 1914-15; attached R.N.A.S. and R.A.F., 1915-18; Senior Naval Officer, Dakar, 1918-1919; Captain (retd.), 1918; Secretary, King George's Fund for Sailors, 1921-38; Admiralty War Staff, 1939-45; Member of Committee Marine Society, 1917-48; Member of Council A.R.N.O., 1925-48; Hon. Co Auditor Society for Nautical Research, 1911-1947. *Publications:* The Royal Navy, 1897; The Naval Officer's Sword, 1955; articles on Sea Training for Boys, naval subjects, and history of the Marine Society. *Address:* Woodcote Grove, Epsom. *T.:* Epsom 4584. *Club:* United Service. [*Died* 17 *Jan.* 1959.

BOSANQUET, His Honour Sir (Samuel) Ronald Courthope, Kt., *cr.* 1942; Q.C. 1924; Chancellor of the Diocese of Hereford,

1928; *b.* 6 Sept. 1868; *e. s.* of late S. Courthope Bosanquet of Dingestow Court, Monmouth; *m.* 1911, Mary Acland, *e. d.* of late F. H. Anson, 72 St. George's Square, S.W.; (one *s.* killed on active service, 1944) three *d.* *Educ.:* Eton; Trinity College, Cambridge. President of Cambridge Union, 1891; called to Bar, Inner Temple, 1893; Bencher, 1930; Unionist candidate for Stafford, 1906; Recorder of Ludlow, 1919-28; of Walsall, 1928-31; an Official Referee of the Supreme Court, 1931-43; J.P., Monmouthshire; Chairman of Quarter Sessions, 1935-50. *Recreations:* cricket and shooting. *Publications:* A Magistrate's Handbook; A Manual of Rating; The Oxford Circuit. *Address:* 38 Kensington Park Road, W.11; Dingestow Court, Monmouth. *Club:* Athenæum. [*Died* 5 *Nov.* 1952.

BOSTOCK, Henry John, C.B.E. 1953; J.P.; Director and Chairman Emeritus, Lotus Ltd.; etc.; *b.* 6 Jan. 1870; *s.* of Henry Bostock and Alice Susannah Marson; *m.* 1900, Eleanora Handley; three *s.* one *d.* *Educ.:* King's School, Chester. Joined firm of Edwin Bostock, 1887; elected to Stafford Town Council, 1902; Mayor of Stafford, 1914; Alderman, 1918-55; Freeman of the Borough, 1942; Staffordshire County Council, 1919-22, 1925-28, 1934-46. High Sheriff of Staffordshire, 1948-49. President: Incorp. Fed. Assocs. of Boot and Shoe Manufacturers, 1922-25; British Boot, Shoe and Allied Trades Research Assoc.; Fellow National Institution of Boot and Shoe Industry. *Recreations:* gardening, crosswords. *Address:* Shawms, Radford Rise, Stafford. *T.:* Stafford 140. [*Died* 27 *Dec.* 1956.

BOSTON, 7th Baron (*cr.* 1761), **Greville Northey Irby,** Bt. 1704; *b.* 24 Aug. 1889; *s.* of Hon. Cecil Irby, 2nd *s.* of 5th Baron; *S.* uncle, 1941; *m.* 1st, 1913, Constance Beryl, *d.* of late William Lester of Alderley, Llandudno; three *d.*; 2nd, 1954, Irene Frances, *widow* of Harry Mills and *o. c.* of late Francis Holt, Ewell, Surrey. *Educ.:* Eton; Balliol College, Oxford. Formerly a Principal in the Colonial Office. *Heir:* *b.* Hon. Cecil Eustace Irby, M.C., Major (retd.) Grenadier Guards [*b.* 14 July 1897. *Educ.:* Eton. Served European War, 1916-18 (M.C.)]. *Address:* 155 Oakwood Court, Kensington, W.14. [*Died* 16 *Sept.* 1958.

BOSWALL; *see* Houston-Boswall.

BOSWELL, Percy George Hamnall, F.R.S., 1931; D.Sc., A.R.C.S.; Professor of Geology in the University of London, Imperial College of Science and Technology, and Head of Departments of Geology, Oil Technology and Mining Geology, 1930-38, Emeritus Professor since 1939; *e. s.* of G. J. Boswell, Ipswich; *b.* Woodbridge, Suffolk, 1886; *m.* 1939, Hope, *y. d.* of late William Blount Dobell. *Educ.:* Ipswich; Royal College of Science; Royal School of Mines; Demonstrator in Geology, Royal College of Science, 1914-17; George Herdman Prof. of Geology in the Univ. of Liverpool, 1917-30; Scientific Adviser (Geological) to Ministry of Munitions of War, 1915-19; East African Archæological Expedition, 1934-35; Geological Adviser to Metropolitan Water Board, 1934-54; Gen. Secretary, British Association, 1931-35, General Treasurer, 1935-43; President, Section C, 1932 (York), President, Conference of Delegates, 1935 (Norwich); President, Prehistoric Society, 1936; Secretary, Geological Society of London, 1932-34, Vice-President, 1934-36, President, 1940-41; Hon. Member, Geologists' Association; Hon. Member Geol. Soc. India; Hon. Corresponding Member, Geol. Soc. Amer. and Soc. Géol. Belg.; founder member and Hon. Fellow Soc. Glass Technology; medals and awards from learned societies. *Publications:* Books on Sedimentary Rocks, Sands for Glassmaking; Sands, etc., for Refractory Purposes; American Foundry Practice; Silurian Rocks of North Wales; Resources and Consumption of Water in the Greater London Area; The Muddy Sediments; Memoirs of the Geological Survey; Geological and other papers in proceedings of learned societies. *Recreations:* letter-writing and raising professors. *Address:* Imperial College of Science and Technology, S.W.7. [*Died* 22 *Dec.* 1960.

BOTHE, Professor Walther, Dr.phil.; ordentlicher Professor, University of Heidelberg, since 1932; Director Physics Institute in Max-Planck-Institute for Medical Research, since 1934; *b.* 8 Jan. 1891; *s.* of Friedrich and Charlotte Bothe; *m.* 1920, Barbara Below (*d.* 1951); two *d.* *Educ.:* University of Berlin (Dr.phil.). Assistant, 1913, Member, 1920, Physikal-techn. Reichsanstalt, Berlin; Lecturer, 1925, Asst. Prof., 1929, Univ. of Berlin; ord. Prof., Univ. of Giessen, 1930. Member Academies of Heidelberg, Goettingen, Berlin, Leipzig. Knight of the order Pour le Mérite, peace class, 1952; Planck Medal, 1953; Nobel Prize for Physics (with Max Born), 1954; Grosses Verdienstkreuz der Bundesrepublik Deutschland, 1954. *Publications:* Geiger-Scheel's Handbook of Physics (in collaboration), 1933; Atlas of Typical Cloud Chamber Photographs (with W. Gentner and H. Maier-Leibnitz), 2nd edn., 1954; about 200 scientific papers, mostly in German journals. *Recreations:* music, painting. *Address:* Im Bäckerfeld 6, (17a) Heidelberg, Germany (West). *T.:* 20739. [*Died* 8 *Feb.* 1957.

BOTT, Alan John, M.C.; publisher and author; Chairman, The Book Society Ltd.; Founder and Chairman of The Reprint Society, Ltd., Avalon Press Ltd. and Pan Books Ltd.; R.F.C. France and Palestine, 1915-18; Special Correspondent and Dramatic Critic of various journals, 1920-26; Editor of The Graphic, 1926-32. *Publications:* An Airman's Outings, 1917; Eastern Flights, 1920; Our Fathers, 1931; Our Mothers (with Irene Clephane), 1932; The Londoner's England, 1947. *Address:* 26 Hans Court, S.W.1. *Club:* Garrick. [*Died* 17 *Sept.* 1952.

BOTTERELL, Percy Dumville, C.B.E. 1920 (O.B.E. 1918); member of firm of Botterell and Roche, 24 St. Mary Axe, E.C.3; *b.* 1880; *s.* of John James Dumville Botterell; *m.* 1905, May, *d.* of Isaac Pearson. *Educ.:* Harrow; Trinity College, Oxford. Called to Bar, 1903; admitted a solicitor, 1906; Assistant Commercial Attaché at the Hague, 1916-18. *Address:* Highcroft, Burley, New Forest. *Club:* Garrick. [*Died* 23 *Jan.* 1952.

BOTTOMLEY, Sir (William) Cecil, K.C.M.G., *cr.* 1930 (C.M.G. 1921); C.B. 1926; O.B.E. 1918; *b.* 19 Mar. 1878; *m.* Alice Thistle, *d.* of late Sir Richard Robinson; one *s.* two *d.* *Educ.:* Tettenhall College; Owens College, Manchester; Trinity College, Cambridge; An Assistant Under-Secretary of State in the Colonial Office, 1927-38; Senior Crown Agent for the Colonies, 1938-43. *Address:* 50 Lensfield Road, Cambridge. [*Died* 1 *April* 1954.

BOUCHER, Maj.-Gen. Sir Charles Hamilton, K.B.E., *cr.* 1949 (C.B.E. 1943); C.B. 1945; D.S.O. 1936 and Bar, 1944; Colonel 3rd Q.A.O. Gurkha Rifles, Indian Army, 1946; *b.* 1898; *e. s.* of late Lieutenant-Colonel B. H. Boucher, D.S.O., The Hampshire Regiment; *m.* 1926, Edith Margaret, 2nd *d.* of M. F. Ramsay, Lee Priory, near Canterbury; one *s.* one *d.* *Educ.:* Wellington College. Commissioned 2nd K.E.O. Gurkha Rifles, 1916; 3rd Queen Alexandra's Own Gurkha Rifles. 1918; served European War, Marri Field Force,

BOTTOMLEY, John Mellor, C.I.E. See page xxviii.

1918; E.E.F., 1918-19; Waziristan Campaigns, 1919-20 and 1921-23 (despatches); Mohmand operations, 1935 (despatches, D.S.O.); p.s.c., Camberley, 1932; Major, 1934; Lt.-Col. 1942; Col. 1946; Maj.-Gen. 1947. Instructor (G.S.O. 2) Staff Coll., Quetta, India, 1938-40; served War of 1939-45: Iraq, Chief of Staff, 1941 (C.B.E.); Comd. 10th Indian Inf. Bde., 5th Ind. Div., 8th Army, Libya, 1942; prisoner 1942, escaped from Italy Nov. 1943; Comd. 17th Ind. Inf. Bde., 8th Ind. Div., Italy, 1944 (despatches, Bar to D.S.O.); Greece, 1945. Comd. 4th Ind. Div. (despatches, C.B.); Comd. 2nd Indian Airborne Div. at Karachi, 1946-47; qualified parachutist; G.O.C. Malaya District, Kuala Lumpur, and Major-Gen. Bde. of Gurkhas, 1948-50 (despatches, K.B.E.); retired, 1951. *Recreations:* fishing, shooting, golf. *Address:* River Court, Chartham, nr. Canterbury. *T.:* Chartham 219; Lloyds Bank, 6 Pall Mall, S.W.1. *Clubs:* Royal Automobile, Lansdowne. [*Died* 15 *Nov.* 1951.

BOUGHEY, Sir George Menteth, 9th Bt., *cr.* 1798; C.B.E. 1928; late I.C.S.; *b.* 1879; *s.* of late Col. G. F. O. Boughey, C.S.I., and Harriet Rose Amy, *d.* of Lt.-Col. W. Stuart Menteth; *S.* cousin, 1927; *m.* 1913, Noel Evelyn, *d.* of late J. G. H. Glass, C.I.E.; one *s.* three *d.* *Educ.:* Wellington; Trinity Coll., Cambridge. Entered I.C.S. 1902; retired, 1916. *Heir: s.* Richard James [*b.* 1925; *m.* 1950, Davina Julia, 2nd *d.* of FitzHerbert Wright, Grantham; one *d.*]. *Address:* Glynde Combe, Glynde, nr. Lewes. [*Died* 28 *June* 1959.

BOUGHTON, Rutland; musical composer; *b.* 1878; *s.* of William Rutland Boughton, Aylesbury, and Grace Martha Bishop. *Educ.:* Aylesbury Endowed School; Royal College of Music. Founded the Glastonbury Festival School of Music Drama, 1914. *Works:* The Birth of Arthur; Snow-White, opera ballet; The Round-Table, music-drama; The Ever Young, choral drama; Deirdre, ballet; The Lily Maid, Galahad, Avalon, music dramas; Three Symphonies; Trumpet Concerto; Reunion Variations for Orchestra; Three Games for String Orchestra. *Publications:* The Immortal Hour, music drama; Bethlehem, music-drama; Alkestis, music-drama; The Moon-Maiden, choral ballet; Sonata for pianoforte and violin; Sonata for pf. and v'cello; Trio for pf., violin and v'cello; Agincourt, dramatic scene for male voices; The Queen of Cornwall, music-drama; May-Day, ballet; one Concerto for flute and two for oboe with strings; Bach, in Masters of Music Series; The Reality of Music; many songs, chamber works, orchestral and choral pieces. *Address:* Kilcote, Newent, Glos. [*Died* 25 *Jan.* 1960.

BOULTON, Major-Gen. Harold, C.B. 1928; C.B.E. 1920; I.M.S. (retired); *b.* Horncastle, 7 Sept. 1872; *s.* of Dr. A. E. Boulton; *m.* 1912, Maude M. Garton; two *d.* *Educ.:* Epsom College; Clare College, Camb. (Scholar); St. Bartholomew's Hospital (Epsom Scholar); B.A. Camb.; 1st Cl. Nat. Sci. Tripos, 1894; M.R.C.S., L.R.C.P. Eng. 1897; M.B., B.C. Camb. 1905; D.P.H. London, 1911. Entered Indian Medical Service, 1898; retired, 1932; served in Somaliland, 1901 (despatches); D.A.D.M.S. Meerut Division in France, 1914-1915 (despatches twice, promoted Brevet Lt.-Colonel); Mesopotamia, 1916 (despatches); A.D.M.S. Line of Communications, East Persia, 1918-20 (despatches twice); Afghan Campaign, 1919 (C.B.E.); D.D.M.S. Northern Command (India), 1928-32. *Address:* Laxfield, Fleet, Hants. [*Died* 30 *Nov.* 1955.

BOULTON, William Savage, D.Sc., M.Sc.; A.R.C.S., F.G.S., M.Inst. Min.E., P.Assoc. Inst. W.E.; *b.* Old Swinford, near Stourbridge, 8 Aug. 1867; *m.* 1898, M. K., *d.* of H. T. Munns; one *s.* *Educ.:* King Edward's Middle School and Mason College, Birmingham; Royal College of Science (Scholar). Demonstrator and Asst. Lecturer in Geology, Mason Coll., Birmingham, 1890-1897; Lecturer in Geology and Geography, Univ. College, Cardiff, 1897; Professor of Geology, 1904; Professor of Geology and Dean of Science Faculty in University of Birmingham, 1913-1932, Emeritus Professor since 1933; President of the Geological section of the British Association, 1916; Pres. South Staffordshire and Warwickshire Institute of Mining Engineers, 1922-23; Vice-Pres. Geological Society, London, 1934-35; Member of Safety in Mines Research Board, 1922-28; Member of Govt. Inland Water Survey Committee. *Publications:* Editor of and part contributor to Practical Coal Mining, 6 vols., 1907; numerous papers on Geology, Water-Supply, etc. *Recreation:* golf. *Address:* 37 Canterbury Avenue, Sheffield, 10. *T.:* Sheffield 32085. [*Died* 14 *Sept.* 1954.

BOURGEOIS, Jeanne; *see* Mistinguett.

BOURKE, Lt.-Comdr. Roland, V.C.; D.S.O. 1918; late R.N.V.R.; Extended Defence Officer, Esquimalt, B.C.; *b.* London, 28 Nov. 1885; *s.* of Dr. I. McWilliam Bourke of Curaghlugh, Co. Mayo; *m.* 1919, Rosalind Barnet of Sydney, N.S.W. Served European War, 1914-18 (despatches, D.S.O., V.C., Legion of Honour). Joined R.C.N.V.R. as Lt.-Comdr. Sept. 1939. *Address:* 1253 Lyall St., Esquimalt, B.C., Canada. [*Died* 29 *Aug.* 1958.

BOUSFIELD, Edward George Paul; Physician, specialist in nervous diseases; *b.* 1880; *s.* of late W. R. Bousfield, K.C., F.R.S., and F. M. E. Kelly; *m.* R. Wenger; no *c.* *Educ.:* Bedford and Dulwich; Bristol Univ.; Central Technical Coll.; St. Bartholomew's Hosp. Manager Experimental Works of Henry Simon, Ltd., Manchester, 1902; Managing Director Saxon Iron and Steel Works, Stoke-on-Trent, 1904; Managing Director Metal Finishers, Ltd., London, 1910; Surgical Receiving Officer, St. Bartholomew's Hospital, and Casualty Officer, Queen's Hospital for Children, 1916; Resident Medical Officer, American Women's Hospital for Officers, 1917; Demonstrator in Morbid Anatomy and Assistant Curator of Museum, St. George's Hospital, 1918; Physician to the London Neurological Clinic (Ministry of Pensions), 1919; Editor of St. Bartholomew's Hospital Journal, 1914-18. *Publications:* Sex and Civilisation; The Omnipotent Self; Elements of Practical Psycho-Analysis; Pleasure and Pain; Functional Nervous Diseases; and other works. *Recreations:* sailing, fishing. *Address:* Creek Lodge, St. Just in Roseland, nr. Truro, Cornwall. *T.A.:* St. Mawes. *T.:* St. Mawes 301. [*Died* 21 *Nov.* 1957.

BOUSFIELD, Col. Hugh Delabere, C.M.G. 1918; D.S.O. 1916 (Belgian Croix de Guerre, French Croix de Guerre); D.L. West Riding; Hon. LL.D. (Leeds); J.P.; late West Yorks. Regt.; *b.* 3 Aug. 1872; *s.* of Charles Edward and Jesse Maria Bousfield; *m.* 1902, Mary Ethel (*d.* 1945), *d.* of Henry Spenceley Close, Hillam Hall, Yorks; no *c.*; *m.* 1949, Vena, *widow* of H. Caldecutt, Knutsford, Cheshire. *Educ.:* Leeds Grammar School; Queen's College, Oxford; B.A. Articled to Solicitors in Leeds, 1895; served South African War with Volunteer Service Company attached to 2nd West Yorkshire Regt., 1900-1 (Queen's medal 4 clasps); a partner in Dibb, Lupton & Co., 6 Butts Court, Leeds, Solicitors; went to France with 49th Division, April 1915, and remained until wounded, 9 Oct. 1917; returned to France, 6 Feb. 1918; commanded 1/5th West Yorks Regt. 2 July 1916 to 9 Oct. 1917; taken prisoner, 25 April 1918, with the French on Kemmel Hill. Member of Court, Leeds University. *Recreations:* fishing, golf. *Address:* 6 Butts Court, Leeds. *T.:* Leeds 32151. *Clubs:* Union; Leeds (Leeds). [*Died* 5 *July* 1951.

BOWDEN, Sir Harold, 2nd Bt., *cr.* 1915; G.B.E., *cr.* 1929; President of Raleigh Industries Ltd.; Vice-President of Federation of British Industries; *b.* 9 July 1880; *s.* of 1st Bt. and Amelia Frances (*d.* 1937), *d.* of late Colonel Alexander Houston of San Francisco; *S.* father, 1921; *m.* 1st, 1908, Vera, *d.* of Joseph Whitaker, J.P., Rainworth, Notts; one *s.* one *d.*; 2nd, 1920, Muriel (*d.* 1952), *d.* of late William Ker-Douglas of Dalry, Ayrshire; 3rd, 1952, June (*d.* 1953), *d.* of late Christopher Mackay, Birmingham; 4th, 1957, Valérie Came-Porter, *d.* of late Richard Raymont-Came, F.R.G.S. *Educ.:* Clifton College; Lausanne; Clare Coll., Cambridge. Chairman British Olympic Assoc., 1931-35; Pres. British Cycle and Motor Cycle Manufacturers' Union, 1921-23 and 1936-38; Pres. Motor and Cycle Trades Benevolent Fund, 1924; High Sheriff of Nottinghamshire, 1933. F.R.S.A. 1948. Grand Cross of the Order of the Phoenix (Greece), 1932. *Recreations:* shooting, fishing, and yachting. *Heir:* *s.* Frank, Lieut. R.N.V.R. [*b.* 10 Aug. 1909; *m.* 1st, 1934, Marie-José Stiénon de Messey (marriage dissolved, 1936), *o. d.* of Charles Stiénon, Paris; one *s.*; 2nd, 1937, Lydia Evelyn, *d.* of Jean Manolovici, Bucharest; three *s.*]. *Address:* The Old Farm House, Stockbridge, Hants; 8 Hays Mews, Berkeley Square, W.1. *Clubs:* White's, Leander. [*Died* 24 *Aug.* 1960.

BOWDLER, Lieut.-Colonel Basil Wilfred Bowdler, C.M.G. 1919; D.S.O. 1916; late R.E.; *b.* 30 March 1873; *s.* of late Colonel C. W. B. Bowdler, C.B.; *m.* 1911, Helen Dalrymple (*d.* 1932), *d.* of late Captain R. E. W. Copland-Crawford, 60th Rifles; two *s.* *Educ.:* Bedford Grammar School. Joined R.E., 1892; Capt. 1903; Major, 1912; Lt.-Col. 1920; Student at Staff College, 1907-8; General Staff Officer at War Office, 1910-14; served European War, 1914-1919 (despatches five times, Order of St. Stanislas, D.S.O., Bt. Lt.-Col., Officer Legion of Honour, Officer of the Order of the Couronne, C.M.G., American Distinguished Service Medal); retired pay, 1922; Esquire of the Order of St. John of Jerusalem. *Recreations:* yachting, skating, ski-ing. *Club:* Army and Navy. [*Died* 4 *Jan.* 1960.

BOWEN; *see* Webb-Bowen.

BOWEN, Sir John (Poland), Kt., *cr.* 1952; C.B.E. 1945; B.Sc. (Hons.); *b.* High Wycombe; *s.* of late John Bowen, Civil Engineer, Reading; *m.* Constance, *d.* of late H. G. Willett, C.B.E., Secretary Trinity House; one *s.* one *d.* *Educ.:* Westminster. Municipal Engineering; Admiralty; War Service. Editor British Lighthouses, for British Council. Engineer-in-Chief, Corporation of Trinity House, retd. 1951. *Address:* Pantiles, Queens Promenade, Portsmouth Road, Kingston-on-Thames. *T.:* Kingston 1724. [*Died* 4 *March* 1955.

BOWEN, Marjorie; *see* Long, Margaret Gabriel.

BOWEN, Norman Levi, M.A., B.Sc., Ph.D.; *b.* Kingston, Ont., Canada, 21 June 1887; *s.* of William Alfred and Elizabeth McCormick Bowen; *m.* 1911, Mary Lamont, M.D.; one *d.* *Educ.:* Queen's University, Canada; Massachusetts Institute of Technology. M.A. 1907; B.Sc. 1909; Ph.D. 1912; Sc.D. (hon.), Harvard, 1936, Yale, 1951; LL.D. (hon.) 1941. Field Geologist: Ontario Bureau of Mines, 1907-1910; Geological Survey of Canada, 1910-1912; Petrologist, Geophysical Lab., Washington, D.C., 1912-52 (except 2 interludes: Prof. of Mineralogy, Queen's Univ., Canada, 1919-20, Prof. of Petrology, Univ. of Chicago, 1937-47); retired, 1952. Bigsby Medal Geol. Soc. of London, 1931; Penrose Medal Geol. Soc. of America, 1941; Miller Medal Royal Society Canada, 1943; Wollaston Medal, Geol. Soc. of London, 1950; Roebling Medal, Mineralogical Soc. of Amer., 1950, Pres. 1937; Pres. Geol. Soc. of America, 1946; Foreign Member Royal Society, 1949; Hayden Medal, Philadelphia Acad. of Nat. Sciences, 1953; Bakhius Roozeboom Medal, Roy. Netherlands Acad., 1954. *Publications:* The Evolution of the Igneous Rocks, 1928; about 100 papers in scientific journals. *Address:* Geophysical Laboratory, 2801 Upton St. N.W., Washington, 8, D.C., U.S.A. *Clubs:* Cosmos (Washington); Kingston Yacht (Kingston, Canada). [*Died* 11 *Sept.* 1956.

BOWEN-ROWLANDS, Ernest (Brown), Barrister-at-Law; *b.* 1866; *s.* of late Judge William Bowen Rowlands, K.C., D.L. *Educ.:* Llandovery; Shrewsbury. Entered Inns of Court, 1885; Arden Scholar, 1889; Studentship, 1889; called to Bar, 1889; practised in London and on South Wales Circuit until 1931, when retired from practice; sometime one of the Arbitrators to Ministry of Labour; elected to London County Council, 1892; founded Welsh Review, 1891, in which wrote as Member for Treorky, under which pseudonym has since written many political tracts; engaged at Ministry of Labour in codifying Instructions and Rules, 1917-18; also in that period assisted Ministry of Pensions in drafting their Regulations. *Publications:* Bowen-Rowlands on Criminal Proceedings on Indictment and Information; Liberty of the Subject; Life in the Law of Sir Henry Hawkins; The Betrayal of Wales; How I became a Judge; Judgment of Death, 1923; Seventy-two Years at the Bar, 1924; In Court and out of Court, 1925; In the Light of the Law, 1931; History of Administration of Justice in London, 1936; The Contest of the Shades, 1947; articles in Quarterly Review, Fortnightly Review, The Times, etc. *Recreations:* formerly many kinds of outdoor sport, now reading and walking. *Club:* Savage. [*Died* 31 *Jan.* 1951.

BOWERBANK, Sir Fred Thompson, K.B.E., *cr.* 1946 (O.B.E. 1917); E.D.; K.St.J. 1946; Grand Officer, Order of Orange-Nassau, 1946; M.D.; F.R.C.P. (Edin.); F.R.A.C.P.; Hon. Physician to the King, 1940-47; Hon. Physician to Governor-Gen., 1935-40; Maj.-Gen., retired; Cardiologist; Consulting Cardiologist to Wellington Hospital; *b.* Penrith, 1880; *s.* of Joseph Bowerbank; *m.* 1907, Maud Pick. *Educ.:* Edinburgh University. Served European War in N.Z.E.F., 1914-19 (despatches thrice, mentioned Sec. of State twice, O.B.E.); Director-General Medical Service (Army and Air) in War of 1939-45; Pres. Mil. Section Australasian Medical Congress, Adelaide, 1937; Vice-Pres. R.A.C.P., 1944-46; Dominion President Toc H Wellington Club. *Publication:* Autobiography: A Doctor's Story. *Address:* 1 Cheviot Rd., Lowry Bay, Wellington, N.Z. [*Died* 25 *Aug.* 1960.

BOWERLEY, Walter, C.B.E. 1931; *b.* Sevenoaks, Kent, 17 Aug. 1876; *m.* Dorothy Evelyn, *d.* of late J. E. Barton, M.D. *Educ.:* St. John's College, Cambridge, B.A. H.M. Colonial Civil Service, British West Africa, 1902-32; Colonial Auditor of the Gold Coast, 1909-32; retired, 1932. *Address:* 41 Queen's Gate Gardens, S.W.7. [*Died* 19 *Feb.* 1952.

BOWES, Frederick, C.M.G. 1915; *b.* 1867; *m.* 1939, Evelyn Mary Ollivant (*d.* 1956), *d.* of late W. G. Thackeray. *Educ.:* Dover College; Wadham College, Oxford (Exhibitioner). Entered Ceylon Civil Service, 1891; Chairman Colombo Port Commission and Principal Collector of Customs of Ceylon, 1912; retired, 1923. *Address:* 2 Boyne House, Tunbridge Wells. *T.:* Tunbridge Wells 20637. *Club:* Oxford and Cambridge. [*Died* 28 *Sept.* 1958.

BOWES, Col. Hugh, C.B. 1930; T.D., D.L., J.P. County Durham; Secretary; Territorial Army and Air Force Association, County Durham, 1908-36; 4th *s.* of George Bowes, Darlington. Commanded 1st V.B. Durham L.I., 1904-8; served South African War, 1900-1 (Queen's medal, 5 clasps); European War, 1914-19; first in command 18th S. Bn. Durham L.I., Egypt and France, and later a Bn. K.O.Y.L.I. (despatches, Chevalier of Legion of Honour, 1914-15 star, two medals); Hon. Col. 50th Northumbrian Div. Signals, 1936-48. *Address:* County Club, Old Elvet, Durham. [*Died* 17 *Jan.* 1952.

BOWES, Robert Kenneth, M.D., M.S., F.R.C.S.; F.R.C.O.G., M.C.P.S. (Man.); Surgeon, Obstetric and Gynæcological Dept., St. Thomas's Hospital and to Grosvenor Hospital for Women; Consultant Gynæcologist, S.W. Metropolitan Regional Hospital Board; External Examiner University of Glasgow; sometime Examiner to the University of London and Examining Board in England; *b.* 1904; *s.* of Joseph E. Bowes, M.B., Grange-in-Borrowdale, Cumberland; *m.* 1933, Phyllis, *d.* of late Ernest W. Miller, Fort Qu'Appelle, Saskatchewan, Canada; one *s.* *Educ.:* Queen Elizabeth's Grammar School, Blackburn; University of Liverpool. Gold Medallist in Obstetrics and Gynaecology; after graduation held surgical and gynaecological appointments at Royal Infirmary, Liverpool, and St. Thomas's Hospital, London; Surgeon E.M.S., 1939-45; Arris and Gale Lecturer, College of Surgeons, 1949. *Publications:* books; papers on medical subjects in various journals. *Address:* 40 Harley Street, W.1. *T.:* Langham 1011. [*Died* 1 *Feb.* 1958.

BOWES-LYON, Captain Geoffrey Francis; late 1st Bn. The Black Watch (Royal Highlanders); *b.* 30 Sept. 1886; *e. surv. s.* of late Hon. Francis Bowes-Lyon, J.P., D.L., ; *m.* 1914, Edith Katharine, *d.* of Sir L. A. Selby-Bigge, 1st Bart., ; one *s.* two *d.* *Educ.:* Eton. Served European War, 1914-18 (wounded). *Address:* Sennicott House, Chichester. [*Died* 30 *Aug.* 1951.

BOWES-LYON, Hon. Michael (Claude Hamilton); Vice-Lieut. of the County of Bedford since 1945; *b.* 1893; 3rd *s.* of 14th Earl of Strathmore, K.G., K.T., G.C.V.O.; *heir-pres.* to 16th Earl of Strathmore and Kinghorne; *m.* 1928, Elizabeth Margaret, M.B.E. 1945, *o. d.* of late John Cator, D.L., J.P.; two *s.* twin *d.* Served European War, 1914-17 (prisoner). *Address:* Gastlings, Southill, Bedfordshire. [*Died* 1 *May* 1953.

BOWES LYON, Captain Ronald George, M.V.O. 1925; *b.* 1893; *y. s.* of late Hon. Francis Bowes-Lyon, J.P., D.L., and Lady Anne Lindsay, *d.* of 25th Earl of Crawford and Balcarres; *m.* 1st, 1925, Mary Claire Russell (marriage dissolved); no *c.*; 2nd, 1947, Mrs. Cecilia French. *Educ.:* Summerfields, Oxford; R.N. Colleges, Osborne and Dartmouth. Entered Royal Navy, 1906; Commander, 1929; Captain, 1936; retired, 1947. Equerry to Prince George, 1923-25. Served European War, 1914-19 (despatches); War of 1939-45 (despatches). *Address* 55 Hanover Gate Mansions, N.W.1. *Club:* Naval and Military. [*Died* 17 *April* 1960.

BOWHILL, Air Chief Marshal Sir Frederick William, G.B.E., *cr.* 1941; K.C.B., *cr.* 1936 (C.B. 1935); C.M.G. 1919; D.S.O. 1918; *b.* 1 Sept. 1880; *s.* of late Col. Bowhill, 1st Wilts; *m.* 1932, Dorothy, M.B.E. 1945, *widow* of Wing-Comdr. A. B. Gaskell, R.A.F. *Educ.:* Blackheath; H.M.S. Worcester. Officer in Merchant Service, 1896-1912; held commission in Royal Naval Reserve; commenced flying in 1912; Lieut. Royal Navy, 1913; in R.F.C. (Naval Wing), R.N.A.S. and R.A.F. (C.M.G., D.S.O. and bar, despatches six times); Director of Organisation and Staff Duties, Air Ministry, 1929-31; Air Officer Commanding Fighting Area, R.A.F., Uxbridge, 1931-33; Air Member for Personel on Air Council, 1933-37; Air Officer Commanding-in-Chief, Coastal Command, 1937-41; Commanded Ferry Command, 1941-43; Air Officer Commanding Transport Command, 1943-45; retired, 1945; United Kingdom Member on Council of Provisional International Civil Aviation Organization, 1945-46; Chief Aeronautical Adviser to Ministry of Civil Aviation, 1946-57, retired. Member, Master Mariners' Company, 1957; F.R.G.S.; Commander Legion of Merit (U.S.A.); Grand Cross Order of Orange Nassau (Holland); Grand Cross Order of St. Olaf (Norway); Grand Cross Order of Polonia Restituta. *Club:* Royal Air Force. [*Died* 12 *March* 1960.

BOWLES, George Frederic Stewart; *b.* 17 Nov. 1877; *e. s.* of late T. Gibson Bowles; *m.* 1st, 1902, Marion Joan (who divorced him, 1921), *y. d.* of late John Penn, M.P. for Lewisham; two *c.*; 2nd, 1922, Madeleine Mary, *d.* of late E. J. Tobin; one *s.* one *d.* *Educ.:* Royal Navy; Trinity College, Cambridge. Entered Royal Navy, 1891; resigned Commission, 1898; entered Trinity College, Cambridge, 1898; M.A. 1905; Barrister, Inner Temple, 1901; M.P. (C.) Norwood Division of Lambeth, 1906-1910. *Address:* Olives, Boxted, Colchester, Essex. *T.:* Boxted 248. *Club:* Carlton. [*Died* 1 *Jan.* 1955.

BOWLEY, Sir Arthur Lyon, Kt., *cr.* 1950; C.B.E. 1937; Sc.D., D.Sc. (Manchester), D.Litt. (Oxon); Acting Director of University of Oxford Institute of Statistics, 1940-44; Professor of Statistics in the Univ. of London, 1919-36; Emeritus Professor since 1936; Lecturer at London School of Economics and Political Science from 1895; Mathematical Lecturer at University College, Reading, 1900-07; Professor of Mathematics and Economics, 1907-13; Lecturer in Economics, 1913-19; *b.* 6 Nov. 1869; *s.* of late Rev. J. W. L. Bowley, Vicar of SS. Philip and Jacob, Bristol; *m.* 1904; three *d.* *Educ.:* Christ's Hospital; Trinity College, Cambridge. 10th Wrangler (bracketed), 1891; Cobden Prize, 1892; Adam Smith Prize, 1894; Sc.D. 1913; Guy Gold Medal, Royal Statistical Society, 1935; Member of Council of Royal Statistical Society, 1898 and subsequent dates; Vice-President, 1907-9 and 1912-14, President, 1938-40; Vice-President, Royal Economic Society; Member, Internat. Institute of Statisticians, 1903, Hon. Treas., 1929, Hon. Pres. 1949; Pres. Econometric Soc., 1938; British Association, Section F, secretary, 1899-1901, recorder, 1902-5, pres., 1906, member of council, 1906-11; asst. master St. John's Sch., Leatherhead, 1893-1899; Newmarch Lecturer at Univ. College, London, 1897-98 and 1927-28. *Publications:* England's Foreign Trade in the 19th Century, 1893, 3rd ed. 1922; Wages in the United Kingdom in the 19th Century, 1900; Elements of Statistics, 1901, 6th ed. 1937; National Progress in Wealth and Trade, 1904; An Elementary Manual of Statistics, 1910, 7th ed. 1951; A General Course of Pure Mathematics, 1913; Measurement of Social Phenomena, 1915; War and External Trade, 1915; The Division of the Product of Industry, 1919; Change in Distribution of Income, 1920; Official Statistics, 1921; The Course of Prices and Wages during the War, 1921; The Mathematical Groundwork of Economics, 1924; Some Economic Consequences of the Great War, 1930; Wages and Income in the United Kingdom since 1860, 1937; joint author of Livelihood and Poverty, 1915; Has Poverty Diminished?, 1925; The Third Winter of Unemployment, 1922; Is Unemployment Inevitable?, 1926; National Income in 1924; Family Expendi-

ture, 1935; Studies in National Income, 1924-1938, 1942; articles in the Economic and Statistical Journals. *Address:* Marley Hill, Haslemere. *T.:* Haslemere 744.
[*Died* 21 *Jan.* 1957.

BOWLY, Colonel William Arthur Travell, C.V.O. 1935; C.B.E. 1919; M.C.; D.L.; *b.* 18 April 1880; *s.* of Capt. J. E. Bowly, R.N. (retired), and E. M. Waters; *m.* 1905, Florence Winifred Astley, *d.* of Major L. L. Astley Cooper; two *d.* (one *s.* killed in action, 1944). *Educ.:* Winchester; Oxford. Joined R. Warwick Regt. from Militia, S. Africa, 1902; Lieut., 1905; Capt. Dorset Regt., 1912; Bt. Major, 1916; Major Royal Warwickshire Regt., 1917; Bt.-Lt.-Col., 1928; Lt.-Col., 1930; Col., 1933; A.D.C. to G.O.C. in C. Southern Command, 1913-14; A.D.C. II. Corps and 2nd Army, France, 1914-15; G.S.O. 3rd Grade IV. Corps, France, 1915-16; G.S.O. 2nd Grade IV. Corps and 37th Division, France, 1916-18; G.S.O. 1st Grade 37th Div. and G.H.Q., France, 1918; Personal Military Secretary to S. of S. for War, 1918-19; G.S.O. 1, 68th Div. and War Office, 1919-20; Brigade-Major 1st W.R. Inf. Brigade, 1921-22; G.S.O. 2 War Office, 1923-26; commanded 2nd Batt. Royal Warwickshire Regiment, 1930-33; A.A.G. Aldershot Command, 1933-36; retired pay, 1937; Commandant Duke of York's Royal Military School, 1937-45; D.L. Gloucestershire, 1953. *Address:* Orchard House, South Cerney, Glos. *Club:* Army and Navy.
[*Died* 24 *Oct.* 1957.

BOWMAN, Rev. Sir Paget Mervyn, 3rd Bt., *cr.* 1884; Rector of Shere, 1919, resigned, 1950; *b.* 1 Sept. 1873; *s.* of 2nd Bt. and Emily, *d.* of late Capt. W. Swabey; *S.* father, 1917; *m.* 1st, 1901, Rachel Katherine (*d.* 1936), *d.* of late James Hanning of Kilcrone, Co. Cork; one *s.* one *d.*; 2nd, 1946, Evelyn Florence, *widow* of Sir John Ewart. Ordained 1897; Curate at Eton Mission, Hackney Wick, 1897-1900 and 1904-07; Vicar of Newington, 1907-11; Woodside, S. Norwood, 1911-19. Rural Dean of Cranleigh, 1928-48. *Heir:* *s.* John Paget [b. 12 Feb. 1904; *m.* 1931, Countess Cajetana Hoyos, *d.* of Count Edgar Hoyos, Schloss Soss, Lower Austria; one *s.* one *d.*; *m.* 1948, Frances Edith Marian, *d.* of late Sir Beethom Whitehead, K.C.M.G., Efford Park, Lymington]. *Address:* Joldwynds, Colehill, Wimborne, Dorset. [*Died* 2 *Dec.* 1955.

BOWRING, Admiral Humphrey Wykeham, C.B. 1927; D.S.O. 1916; D.L. Suffolk; *b.* 1874; 4th *s.* of late John Charles Bowring, of Forest Farm, Berks; *m.* 1924, Rose (*d.* 1948), *widow* of Captain Charles N. Tindal-Carill-Worsley, R.N., and *d.* of late Sir William Dalby. Entered R.N. 1887; Lieut. 1895; Commander, 1906; Captain, 1914; Rear-Adm., 1924; Vice-Adm., 1929; Adm., retd., 1933; served with Vitu Expedition, 1890 (medal with clasp); S. African War, 1899-1901 (medal); European War, 1914-18 (despatches twice, D.S.O., Legion of Honour, Order of Leopold of Belgium); Rear-Adm. and Commanding Officer Coast of Scotland, 1926-28; retired list, 1929. *Address:* Lowood, Hasketon, Woodbridge, Suffolk. *Club:* Army and Navy.
[*Died* 21 *Feb.* 1952.

BOX, Charles Richard, M.D., B.S., B.Sc. (Lond.), F.R.C.P. (Lond.), F.R.C.S. (Eng.); F.R.S.M.; Hon. Member British Paediatric Assoc.; Member of the Court of Assistants of the Society of Apothecaries, London; Consulting Physician, St. Thomas's Hospital; late Consulting Physician to the London Fever Hospital; Physician Royal Masonic Hospital; Councillor, Censor, and Lumleian Lecturer, Royal College of Physicians, London; *m.* 1905, Marian Jane, *d.* of George Thyer, Bridgewater, Somerset. *Educ.:* University of London; St. Thomas's Hospital; Dulwich College. Late Examiner in Medicine, University of London, Univ. of Birmingham, Conjoint Board, R.C.P. and S., and Society of Apothecaries, London; Medical Registrar, Resident Assist. Physician, Medical Tutor, Lecturer in Medicine and in Applied Anatomy, and Sub-Dean St. Thomas's Hospital; Bt. Major R.A.M.C., (T.F.) retired; J.G.D. United Grand Lodge of Freemasons; Honoursman in Medicine, Obstetric Medicine and Physiology, University of London. *Publications:* St. Thomas's Hospital Medical Reports, 1893-4-5-6; (with W. M'Adam Eccles) Clinical Applied Anatomy, 1906; Manual of Morbid Anatomy and Post-Mortem Technique, 1910; Articles on Fevers, Price's Text Book of the Practice of Medicine, Oxford Medical Publications, 1926, and subs. eds.; various papers in medical journals. *Address:* 1 Harley House, Regent's Park, N.W.1. *T.:* Welbeck 4320.
[*Died* 3 *April* 1951.

BOXWELL, Lt.-Col. Ambrose, C.I.E. 1916; *b.* 9 Nov. 1876; *s.* of John Boxwell, I.C.S., of Butlerstown, Co. Wexford; *m.* 1920, Hilda, *d.* of Col. Robert Caulfeild, of Camolin House, Co. Wexford. *Educ.:* Shrewsbury; Trinity College, Dublin. Entered Royal Warwicks. Regt. 1899; Capt. 1908; Lt.-Col. 1922; Indian Army, 1909; served S. Africa, 1901-2 (Queen's medal and clasp); European War, Mesopotamia, 1914-17 (despatches twice, C.I.E.); Palestine, 1917-18; retired from Indian Army, May 1927. *Address:* Camolin, Carrickmines, Co. Dublin. *Club:* Army and Navy.
[*Died Jan.* 1959.

BOYCE, Sir (Harold) Leslie, 1st Bt., *cr.* 1952; K.B.E., *cr.* 1944; M.A.; J.P.; Barrister-at-Law; Chairman and Managing Director of the Gloucester Railway Carriage and Wagon Co. Ltd.; Chairman: Wm. Gardner & Sons (Gloucester) Ltd.; Wagon Repairs, Ltd.; Philblack Ltd.; Hatherley Works, Ltd.; Gloucester Foundry, Ltd., and other Companies; *b.* Taree, New South Wales, 9 July 1895; *s.* of late Charles Macleay Boyce, Sydney; *m.* 1926, Maybery, D.St.J., *d.* of late Edward Philip Bevan, Melbourne; three *s.* *Educ.:* Sydney Grammar School; Balliol College, Oxford. Called to Bar, Inner Temple, 1922; served European War with A.I.F., Egypt, Gallipoli and Western Front; Technical Adviser to Australian Rep. before Permanent Mandates Commn. at Geneva, 1922; Substitute Deleg. and Legal Adviser at third Assembly League of Nations, 1922; M.P. (C.) Gloucester, 1929-45; Member of Empire Parliamentary Delegation to Northern Rhodesia in 1930; High Sheriff of Gloucester, 1941-42; Leader of U.K. Trade Mission to China, 1946; Alderman of City of London, 1942-54 (Sheriff, 1947-48); Lord Mayor of London, 1951-52; Past Grand Warden in Grand Lodge of English Freemasons; Chm. Exec. Cttees., King George VI Memorial Fund, King George VI Foundation; Master of the Worshipful Company of Loriners, 1951. K.J.St.J. *Recreation:* golf. *Heir:* *s.* Richard Leslie [*b.* 5 July 1929. *Educ.:* Cheltenham College]. *Address:* Constitutional Club, Northumberland Avenue, W.C.2. *T.:* Whitehall 3801; Badgeworth Hall, nr. Cheltenham, Glos. *T.:* Churchdown 2244. *Clubs:* Carlton, Constitutional, Royal Automobile, Australia, City Livery.
[*Died* 30 *May* 1955.

BOYCE, Brigadier-General Harry Augustus, C.M.G. 1919; D.S.O. 1917; R.A. (retd. 1920); *b.* 30 Nov. 1870; *s.* of late Lieut. H. A. Boyce, R.A. and Indian Staff Corps; *m.* 1900, Minnie Gabrielle, *d.* of late G. R. C. Williams, I.C.S.; three *s.* two *d.* *Educ.:* Clifton College; R.M.A., Woolwich. Royal Artillery, 1890; Staff College, Camberley, 1906-7; served South Africa, 1902 (medal, 2 clasps); European War, 1914-19 (despatches 4 times, D.S.O., C.M.G., Order of the Nile 3rd class). *Address:*

Bell House, Havant Road, Emsworth, Hants. *T.:* Emsworth 433. [*Died* 15 *Feb.* 1954.

BOYCE, Sir Leslie, Bt.; *see* Boyce, Sir H. L.

BOYD, Sir Alexander W. K.; *see* Keown-Boyd.

BOYD, Sir Archibald (John), Kt., *cr.* 1950; Chairman Metropolitan-Cammell Carriage and Wagon Co. Ltd.; Director: Cammell Laird & Co. Ltd.; Associated Electrical Industries Ltd.; Monks Investment Trust Ltd.; General Accident Fire & Life Assurance Corporation Ltd.; The Patent Shaft & Axletree Co. Ltd.; *b.* 27 Dec. 1888; *e. s.* of Archibald Henry Boyd, Westward Ho, N. Devon; *m.* 1916, Mary Leng, *g.d.* of late Sir William Leng, founder and proprietor of Sheffield Daily Telegraph; one *s.* (and one *s.* killed on active service, 1943). *Educ.:* Harrow; Trinity College, Oxford. Joined Cammell Laird & Co., Sheffield, 1912. Served European War, 1914-18; 4th (Hallamshire) Bn. York and Lancs Regt.; Asst. Gen. Manager National Ordnance Factory, Nottingham, 1916; London Manager Cammell Laird & Co., 1921; Director of Midland Railway Carriage & Wagon Co., Ltd., Leeds Forge Co., Ltd., and Newlay Wheel Co., 1925; Managing Director of Metropolitan-Cammell Carriage and Wagon Co. Ltd., 1934-53; Director-General of Tank Production in the Ministry of Supply, Oct. 1942-Dec. 1943. A Member of Overseas Trade Development Council, formed by Pres. of Board of Trade, 1945. *Recreations:* golf, shooting, and fishing. *Address:* Little Marsh, Thorns Beach, Beaulieu, Hampshire. *T.:* East End (Lymington) 222. *Club:* White's. [*Died* 9 *May* 1959.

BOYD, David Runciman, Ph.D. (Heidelberg); D.Sc. (Glasgow); F.R.I.C.; Barrister-at-law of the Inner Temple; Emeritus Professor of Chemistry, University College, Southampton; *b.* Mains, Forfarshire, 1872; 2nd *s.* of Rev. William Boyd, M.A., and Janet, *d.* of Rev. David Runciman, D.D.; *m.* 1909, Marion (*d.* 1955), *d.* of Col. Edward Persse. *Educ.:* John Watson's Institution, Edinburgh; Universities of Glasgow and Heidelberg. *Publications:* contrib. Trans. of the Chemical Society. *Address:* Marchlands, Station Rd., Fordingbridge, Hants. [*Died* 28 *Dec.* 1955.

BOYD, Sir Donald James, K.C.I.E., *cr.* 1936 (C.I.E. 1930); *b.* 1877; *s.* of James Fitzgerald Boyd; *m.* 1st, Laura Caroline (*d.* 1931), *d.* of late Hon. Louis Hope; two *s.*; 2nd, 1932, Winifred (*d.* 1950), *widow* of Lieut.-Col. Meredith Magniac, D.S.O. *Educ.:* George Watson's Coll., Edinburgh; Edinburgh and Oxford Univs. Asst. Commissioner, Punjab, 1900; Under-Secretary to Punjab Government, 1907; Settlement Officer, 1911; Director of Land Records, Inspector-General of Registration, Registrar-General of Births, Deaths and Marriages, 1916; Additional Secretary to the Punjab Government, 1917; Deputy Commissioner, 1918; rendered service in India in connection with the war (Govt. of India Gazette, 1919); Revenue Sec. to Punjab Govt., 1921; Home Sec., 1922; Commr. Rawalpindi Div., 1927; Chief Sec., 1930; Financial Commr., 1932; Finance Member Punjab Govt., 1934-37; retired from I.C.S., 1937. *Address:* 11 Plewlands Avenue, Edinburgh 10. *Club:* East India and Sports. [*Died* 12 *Dec.* 1953.

BOYD, Rev. Halbert Johnston, M.A.; *b.* 1872; *y. s.* of Sir John Boyd of Maxpoffle, Roxburghshire, and Isabella, *d.* of late John Lawson, 14th Laird of Cairnmuir and Netherurd, Co. Peebles; *m.* 1901, Jessie (*d.* 1942), *d.* of Malcolm Mackinnon, of Koladbro, South Australia; two *s.* one *d.* *Educ.:* Edinburgh Academy; Emmanuel College, Cambridge. Formerly Curate of Henfield and Lower Beeding; Vicar of Southwater, Sussex, 1906-14; Rector of St. Pauls, St. Leonards-on-sea, 1914-1927; Rector of St. John's, Cranstonhill, Glasgow, 1927-29; Chaplain of Taiping, 1929-1930; Chaplain to Forces. President of the Berwickshire Naturalists' Club, 1950-51. *Publications:* Verses and Ballads of North and South; Men and Marvels; The Hearts of Prayer; The Phantom (a play produced 1924): Shreds and Patches; Reprieve; Strange Tales of the Wester Isles; Under the Beacon Lights; Kinmont Willie; The Magic of Tamlane (play produced, 1935); Honour is All, novel 1947; Strange Tales of the Borders, 1948. *Address:* c/o Mrs. Curtis, Hurst Court, Ore, Hastings. [*Died* 16 *March* 1957.

BOYD, Robert, C.M.G. 1946; *b.* 26 June 1890; *s.* of late Rev. Robert Boyd and of late Mrs. Boyd, Knock, Belfast, Northern Ireland; unmarried. *Educ.:* Campbell College, Belfast; Trinity College, Dublin. Joined Malayan Civil Service, 1913; served European War 1915-18 ending as Captain, Royal Dublin Fusiliers; returned to Malaya, 1919; Assistant Controller of Labour, 1919-23; Joined Co-operative Societies Dept., 1923; Director of Co-operation F.M.S. and S.S., 1933; Reconstruction Adviser, Department of Co-operation, Malayan Union and Singapore, 1946-48; retired 1948. Secretary, Malayan Planting Industries Employers' Association, 1949-52. *Recreations:* golf and reading. *Address:* c/o The Chartered Bank, Penang, Malaya. *Club:* East India and Sports. [*Died* 15 *June* 1959.

BOYD, Rt. Rev. Robert McNeil, M.C. 1917; D.D. 1943; Bishop of Derry and Raphoe since 1915; *b.* 12 Feb. 1890; 2nd *s.* of Robert Boyd, J.P., Marathon, Kilkeel, Co. Down; *m.* 1st, 1920, Juliet Rachael White (*d.* 1955); two *s.*; 2nd, 1957, Mary Elizabeth, *d.* of late Lt.-Col. J. B. Buchanan, Omagh. *Educ.:* St. Andrew's College; Dublin University Honour and Prizeman in Philosophy and History; B.A. and Divinity Testimonium (2nd Cl.), 1912; Curate of Fiddown, 1912-15; C.F. 1915-19; S.C.F. 1917-19 (despatches); M.A. 1919; B.D. 1929; Rector of Ballingarry, 1920-25; of Shinrone, 1925-32; Canon of St. Patrick's Cathedral, 1931-36; Rector of Killaloe and Treasurer of St. Flannan's Cathedral, 1932-1936; Dean of Killaloe and Diocesan Secretary, 1936-43; Bishop of Killaloe, Kilfenora, Clonfert and Kilmacduagh, 1943-45. Select Preacher, Oxford University, 1945-46. Hon. Chaplain, R.N.V.R. 1953. *Publication:* Membership in the Church of Ireland, 1942. *Recreations:* fishing, gardening, chess. *Address:* Bishop's Lodge, Londonderry. [*Died* 1 *July* 1958.

BOYES, Rear-Adm. Hector, C.M.G. 1918; C.I.E. 1931; *b.* 1881; *s.* of late Admiral Sir George Boyes; *m.* 1919, Eleanora, *d.* of Consul-General Falsen, Oslo; one *s.* Served Boxer Campaign, 1900; European War, 1914-19 (despatches, C.M.G., 2nd Class Order of Aviz of Portugal); lent to Australian Government as Capt. of Flinders Naval Depôt, 1924-26; Senior Naval Officer in the Persian Gulf, 1927-30; Captain-in-charge, Simonstown, 1931-33; Chief of Staff and Maintenance Captain to C.-in-C. The Nore, 1933-34; Rear-Adm. and retired list, 1934; Naval Attaché: Oslo and Stockholm, 1939-40; Tokyo, 1941-42; Venezuela, Colombia, Ecuador, San Domingo, Haiti, 1942-46. *Address:* Flat 1, Grays, Aldwick Avenue, Bognor Regis, Sussex. *Club:* United Service. [*Died* 23 *Oct.* 1960.

BOYES, John Henry, C.M.G. 1946; Public Service Commissioner, New Zealand, 1941, retd. 1946; *b.* 1886; one *s.* two *d.* *Educ.:* Prince Albert College, Auckland, N.Z. Entered N.Z. Public Service, 1903; Asst. Commissioner of Pensions, 1919; Commissioner of Pensions, 1929; Joint Public Service Commissioner, 1936; Chairman,

Social Security Commission, 1938. *Address:* 9 Maxwell Ave., Papatoetoe, N.Z. [*Died* 1 *July* 1958.

BOYLE, Captain Harry Lumsden, C.B.E. 1919; late R.N.; *s.* of late Rear-Admiral R. H. Boyle; *m.* 1908, Lilian (*d.* 1945), *d.* of late Maj.-Gen. Sir J. K. Trotter, K.C.B., C.M.G.; four *s.* one *d.* *Educ.:* H.M.S. Britannia. Retired with rank of Captain 1925. *Address:* Tigh-na-Greine, Comrie, Perthshire. [*Died* 7 *Feb.* 1955.

BOYLE, Robert William, M.Sc., M.A., Ph.D., LL.D., F.R.S.C.; Director of Division of Physics and Electrical Engineering, National Research Laboratories, Ottawa, 1929-48, retd., 1948; *b.* 2 Oct. 1883; *s.* of Dr. Albert D. and Sophie Boyle, Carbonear, Newfoundland. *Educ.:* St. John's, Newfoundland (Diamond Jubilee Scholarship, 1900); McGill Univ. (Scott prize, General Electric Scholarship, British Assoc. medal and prize); and University of Manchester. At McGill University, B.Sc. 1905; M.Sc. 1906; Ph.D., 1909; 1851 Exhibition Science Research Scholarship, Research under Rutherford on Radioactivity, University of Manchester, 1909-11; Lecturer in Physics, McGill University, 1911; Assistant Professor, 1912; Professor of Physics, University of Alberta, 1912. War Research in charge of Asdics for Admiralty Board of Inventions and Research, and Anti-Submarine Division, 1916-19; resumed professorship, Oct. 1919; Dean of Faculty of Applied Science, University of Alberta, 1921; Member Alberta Council of Scientific and Industrial Research, 1923-29; Past-President Section III. Royal Society of Canada (1924-25); Past-President Association of Professional Engineers of Alberta, 1925-26; Chairman, Ottawa Branch, Eng. Inst. Can., 1935-36; Council Eng. Inst. Can., 1937-39; Advisory Board, Royal Miltary Col. Canada, 1927-29, 1935-38; Chairman, 1935-38; Flavelle Medal for Science, Royal Soc. Can., 1940. *Publications:* papers on Properties of Matter, Radioactivity, and Ultra-sonics. *Recreations:* international affairs, fishing, golf, travel. *Address:* Rideau Club, Ottawa, Ontario, Canada. *T.:* 3-7787. *Clubs:* Rideau, Country (Ottawa); McGill Faculty (Montreal). [*Died* 18 *April* 1955.

BOYLE, Vincent, C.M.G. 1949; M.R.C.V.S.; Superintending Veterinary Officer, Animal Health Division, Ministry of Agriculture and Fisheries; *b.* Wick, 26 March 1891; 2nd *s.* of late Thomas J. Boyle, Donamon, Co. Roscommon, Ireland, and Helen Lucy Wright, Henley-in-Arden, Warwickshire; unmarried. *Educ.:* Sligo, Ireland; R.V.C., London. Entered Ministry of Agriculture, Aug. 1913. Served European War, Egyptian Expeditionary Force. Detached for service in South America (Argentina, Brazil, Chile, Paraguay, Uruguay), 1936, with headquarters in Buenos Aires; Attaché, British Embassy, Buenos Aires, 1953. *Address:* Ministry of Agriculture and Fisheries, Whitehall, S.W.1. *Clubs:* Canning, Farmers'; English (Buenos Aires). [*Died* 5 *May* 1956.

BOYS, Sir Francis Theodore, K.B.E., *cr.* 1919; *b.* Baraich, Oudh, India, 12 Feb. 1870; *s.* of Henry Scott Boys, Indian Civil Service, and Ethel Rigaud Boys, *d.* of Capt. Henry Strong; *m.* Christina Josephine De Smidt, New Zealand; one *s.* *Educ.:* Harrow. Seven years on sheep stations in N. Zealand; sixteen years in business; eight years managing N.Z. Refrigerating Company, London; Principal Director of Meat Supplies, Ministry of Food, 1917-19; Director and Vice-Chairman N.Z. Refrigerating Co., Ltd., 1923-33; Commissioner on Waimakariri River Trust, 1927-33; President N.Z. Aero Club, 1930-31; Farmers delegate to Ottawa Imperial Conference, 1932; Chairman, Technical Committee on Abbatoir Design, Ministry of Agriculture, 1933-34; Vice-Chairman: Cattle Committee, Ministry of Agriculture, 1934-35; Bacon Development Board, 1935-38; Director of Meat and Livestock, Min. of Food, 1939. *Recreations:* shooting and golf. [*Died* 4 *July* 1952.

BOYS, Henry Ward, C.B.E. 1919; *b.* Naini Tal, India, 25 July 1874; *s.* of Henry Scott Boys, Bengal Civil Service and Ethel Rigaud, *d.* of Capt. Henry Strong; *m.* Jean Arabella (*d.* 1949), *widow* of Arthur Laing (*née* Scott Moncrieff). *Educ.:* Wellington Coll.; New Coll., Oxford. Called to Bar, Inner Temple, 1901; Licencié en Droit, Paris, 1901; Ministry of Justice, Egypt, 1902; Enemy Trading Office, 1914-19; War Trade and Licensing Officer, 1918-19; Order of the Nile 2nd Class, 1918; Counsel to the King of Egypt, 1919-24; retired, 1924. *Address:* 39 Beaufort Gardens, S.W.3. *T.:* Kensington 9189. [*Died* 17 *Feb.* 1955.

BRACE, Sir Ivor (Llewellyn), Kt., *cr.* 1952; Chief Justice of Sarawak, North Borneo and Brunei since 1951 (of N. Borneo, 1946-51); *b.* 13 May 1898; *s.* of late Right Hon. William Brace, P.C., and Ellen Humphries; *m.* 1931, Dorothy Constance Allen-Evans; one *s.* *Educ.:* Wycliffe; Cardiff University. Barrister-at-Law, Gray's Inn, 1921; Judge, Protectorate Court, Nigeria, 1937; Puisne Judge, Sierra Leone, 1942. *Recreations:* fishing, golf. *Address:* Kuching, Sarawak; Grosmont, nr. Hereford. [*Died* 24 *Oct.* 1952.

BRACEWELL, Rev. Canon William; *b.* 1872; *s.* of late William Metcalfe Bracewell, cotton manufacturer, Barnoldswick; *m.* 1st, Hannah (*decd.*), *d.* of late John Forrest, cotton manufacturer, Blackburn; one *s.* two *d.*; 2nd, Violet Rosa, *widow* of Norwood F. Greaves and *d.* of John Edward Spafford. *Educ.:* Strathmore House School, Southport; Manchester Grammar School; Corpus Christi College and Ridley Hall, Cambridge. Curate of Sheffield Parish Church (now the Cathedral), 1895-1902; Vicar of St. Luke's (Dyers Hill, Sale Memorial Church, Sheffield), 1902-15; Vicar of St. James', Doncaster, 1915-29; Rural Dean of Doncaster, 1926-29; Vicar of St. Mary's, Sheffield, 1929-39; Rural Dean of Sheffield, 1931-39; Hon. Canon of Sheffield, 1928; Residentiary Canon, 1936-39; Canon Emeritus, Sheffield, 1939; Vicar of Barnoldswick and Bracewell, 1939-46. *Recreation:* bowls. *Address:* 6 Snaithing Lane, Ranmoor, Sheffield 10. *T.:* 32023. [*Died* 18 *Aug.* 1954.

BRACKEN, 1st Viscount, *cr.* 1952, of Christchurch; **Brendan Bracken,** P.C. 1940; Chairman of Union Corporation and of Financial Times; Trustee of the National Gallery since 1955; *b.* 1901; *s.* of late J. K. A. Bracken, Ardvullen House, Kilmallock. *Educ.:* Sydney; Sedbergh. M.P. (U.) North Paddington, 1929-45; M.P. (C.) Bournemouth, Nov. 1945-Feb. 1950, East Bournemouth and Christchurch, 1950-51. Parliamentary Private Secretary to the Prime Minister, 1940-41; Minister of Information, 1941-45; First Lord of the Admiralty, 1945. Director of Eyre and Spottiswoode Ltd.; Chairman of Financial News; Managing Director of Economist; Director of Associated Electrical Industries. Hon. LL.D. Univ. of New Brunswick. *Heir:* none. *Address:* 8 Lord North Street, S.W.1. *T.:* Abbey 3212. *Clubs:* White's, Buck's. [*Died* 8 *Aug.* 1958 (*ext.*).

BRACKEN, Sir Geoffrey Thomas Hirst, K.C.I.E., *cr.* 1936 (C.I.E. 1930); C.S.I. 1934; Indian Civil Service (retired); Joint Editor of Economic Digest; *b.* nr. Leeds, 11 April 1879; *m.*; one *s.* two *d.* *Educ.:* Malvern College; Oriel College, Oxon. Served European War, temporary commission, Royal Artillery, Mesopotamia, 1916-18. *Address:* Larchfield, Churt, Surrey. *T.:* Headley Down 3101. *Club:* East India and Sports. [*Died* 25 *May* 1951.

BRACKENBURY, Sir Cecil Fabian, K.C.I.E., *cr.* 1938; C.S.I. 1936; Indian Civil Service, retired; *b.* 13 March 1881; *m.* 1915, Ethel Selina, *d.* of late Captain T. S. Boileau, Indian Army; two *s.* (and one *s.* killed in War of 1939-45). *Educ.:* Uppingham; Selwyn College, Cambridge. Entered I.C.S., 1905; Member Board of Revenue, Madras, 1932-34; Chief Secretary to Government, Madras, 1935; Temporary Member of Governor's Executive Council, Madras, 1936; retired, 1940. *Address:* 97 Cambridge Road, Ely, Cambs. *T.:* Ely 2141. [*Died* 29 *Sept.* 1958.

BRADDON, Hon. Sir Henry Yule, K.B.E., *cr.* 1920; *b.* India, 27 April 1863; *s.* of Sir E. N. C. Braddon, K.C.M.G.; *m.* 1st, 1891, Bertha Mary Russell (*d.* 1942), of Invercargill, New Zealand; one *s.* one *d.* (and two *s.* decd.); 2nd, 1944, Violet May Inglis, *d.* of late J. M. Wheelihan, Blandford, N.S.W. *Educ.:* Germany; France; Dulwich College; Church of England Grammar School, Launceston, Tasmania. Entered Commercial Bank of Tasmania, 1879; Bank of Australasia, Invercargill, 1881; Dalgety & Co., Ltd., N.S. Wales, 1884; Lecturer Sydney University, Business Principles, etc., 1907-19; Member Senate of University, 1920-1930; M.L.C., 1917-40; Commissioner for Australia to the U.S.A., by special permission of Dalgety's, 1918-19; President Sydney Chamber of Commerce, 1912-14; Associated Chambers of Australia, 1914-15 and 1920-21; Member, Commonwealth Notes Issue Board, 1922-24; President Employers' Federation, 1905-7; Superintendent for Australia for Dalgety & Co., Ltd., 1914-28; retired, 1928. *Publications:* Business Principles and Practice (Australia); American Impressions; Essays and Addresses; The Making of a Constitution. *Recreations:* golf; captained N.S.W. Rugby Representative XV., 1892; represented New Zealand (Rugby), 1884; captained Inter-State Rowing Eight N.S.W., 1892. *Address:* Rohini, 388 Edgecliff Road, Woollahra, Sydney, N.S.W. *Club:* Australian (Sydney). [*Died* 7 *Sept.* 1955.

BRADFIELD, Rt. Rev. Harold William, D.D. (Lambeth) 1946; B.D. (London) 1922; Bishop of Bath and Wells since 1946; *b.* 20 Sept. 1898; *s.* of William and Mary Edith Bradfield, Dulwich; *m.* 1st, 1922, Marjorie Fisher (*d.* 1953), *d.* of George Parker, Liverpool; two *s.* two *d.*; 2nd, 1958, Pleasaunce Elizabeth Hope, *d.* of Henry Burroughs Napier, and *widow* of Canon Duncan Armytage. *Educ.:* Alleyn's School, Dulwich; London University (King's College). City of London Yeomanry and Army Cyclist Corps, 1917-19; on active service, France, 1918-19; Deacon, 1922; Priest, 1923; Curate St. Mary, Prestwich, 1922-28; Vicar St. Mark, Heyside, Lancs, 1928-34; Secretary, Canterbury Diocesan Board of Finance, 1934-44; Hon. Canon of Canterbury, 1938-46; F.K.C. London, 1943; Archdeacon of Croydon, 1942-46; Life Governor King's College, London, 1947; Chairman Central Advisory Council of Training for the Ministry, 1950; Hon. Air Commodore, 3507 (County of Somerset) Fighter Control Unit, R.A.A.F., 1954; Pres. Somerset County Cricket Club, 1954. *Publication:* The Church's Property, 1943. *Address:* The Palace, Wells, Somerset. *T.:* Wells 2341. *Clubs:* Athenæum; Bath and County (Bath). [*Died* 1 *May* 1960.

BRADFORD, 5th Earl of (*cr.* 1815), **Orlando Bridgeman,** J.P., D.L.; Bt. 1660; Baron Bradford, 1794; Viscount Newport, 1815; late Lt.-Col., 3rd Bn. Royal Scots; *b.* 6 Oct. 1873; *e. s.* of 4th Earl and Lady Ida Anabella Frances Lumley (*d.* 1936), 2nd *d.* of 9th Earl of Scarbrough; *S.* father, 1915; *m.* 1904, Hon. Margaret Cecilia Bruce (*d.* 1949), *e. d.* of 2nd Baron Aberdare; one *s.* two *d.* (and two *d.* decd.). *Educ.:* Harrow; Trinity College, Camb. (M.A.). Assist. Priv. Sec. to Lord Salisbury, 1899-1900; served S. Africa, 1900-1902; European War, 1914-18; Private Sec. to Rt. Hon. A. J. Balfour, Prime Minister, 1902-5; a Lord-in-Waiting to the King, 1919-24. Owns about 20,000 acres. *Heir: s.* Viscount Newport, T.D. *Address:* Weston Park, Shifnal, Shropshire. *T.:* Weston-under-Lizard 202. *Club:* Shropshire (Shrewsbury). [*Died* 21 *March* 1957.

BRADFORD, Major Sir Edward Montagu Andrew, 3rd Bt., *cr.* 1902; Cameronians (Scottish Rifles); *b.* 30 Nov. 1910; *s.* of 2nd Bt. and Elsie Clifton, *d.* of Colonel Clifton Brown; *S.* father (killed in action), 1914; *m.* 1937, Alison (marriage dissolved, 1947), *er. d.* of John Lawson; one *s.* one *d.*; *m.* 1950, Mrs. Marjorie Chapman. *Educ.:* Eton; Sandhurst. Served War of 1939-45 (wounded, despatches). *Heir: s.* John Ridley Evelyn (*see under* Sir John Bradford, 4th Bt.). [*Died* 1 *April* 1952.

BRADFORD, Sir John Ridley Evelyn, 4th Bt., *cr.* 1902; *b.* 14 Sept. 1941; *er. s.* of Major Sir Edward Bradford, 3rd Bt. and Alison, *er. d.* of John Lawson; *S.* father 1952. *Heir: half b.* Edward Alexander Slade, *b.* 18 June 1952. *Address:* Marylands, Chislehampton, Oxford. [*Died* 23 *Dec.* 1954.

BRADLEY, Colonel Sir (Augustus) Montague, Kt., *cr.* 1910; solicitor (retired); *b.* 23 April 1865; *s.* of John Lade Bradley, Dover; *m.* 1894, Hilda Payn (*d.* 1945); two *s.* *Educ.:* Dover College (Freshfield Exhibitioner). Obtained 1st Division London Matriculation, 1881; Articled as Solicitor, 1881; Solicitors' Final with Honours, 1886; commenced to practise in Dover, 1887; President of Dover Incorporated Chamber of Commerce, 1909; member of Kent Territorial Force Association; held Commission in Volunteer and Territorial Force for 22 years; late Colonel commanding 3rd Home Counties (C.P.) Brigade R.F.A.; formerly the 1st Cinque Ports R.G.A. (Vols.), 1902. *Address:* 34 Alcock Rd., Walmer, Port Elizabeth, S. Africa. [*Died* 9 *June* 1953.

BRADLEY, Rev. Charles Lister, M.A., Mus. Doc.; *b.* 1880; *s.* of E. S. Bradley, Ashbourne, Derbyshire; *m.* 1904, Ethel Mildred Tateson; three *s.* five *d.* *Educ.:* Waterloo High School; Exeter College, Oxford. Held post of Organist at Snelstone, Derbyshire; St. George's Tombland, Norwich, 1901; St. John Baptist, Harlow, 1902; Curate at St. John's, Harlow, 1903; St. Edward's, Barnsley, 1905; Precentor of Peterborough Cathedral, 1906-9; Precentor of Newcastle Cathedral, N.S.W., 1809-10; Rector Pioneer Parish, Queensland, 1910-11; Chaplain of Magdalen College and New College, Oxford, 1917-30; Rector of Tubney, 1920-22; Vicar of Chesterton with Wendlebury, 1924; Rector of Winterbourne Bassett with Berwick Bassett, Wilts, 1929-50; Rector of Frettenham, 1950-1956. President, Oxford Branch of League for Prevention of Cruel Sports. *Publications:* Service in A; *Anthems*—In God's Word; What Reward shall I Give? Suite for Military Band: Izaak Walton; several songs. *Address:* 8 Tennis Road, Hove, Sussex. [*Died* 19 *Dec.* 1957.

BRADLEY, Rear-Admiral Frederic Cyril (retired); *b.* 20 Sept. 1888; *s.* of Frederick Livingstone and Florence Bradley, Cardiff; *m.* 1912, Phyllis Ethel, *d.* of W. Wood, Highgate; no *c.* *Educ.:* Private; Littlejohns. Naval cadet, H.M.S. Britannia, 1904; Destroyer service, 1914-18; Commander, 1923; Captain, 1930; commanded H.M.A.S. Australia and Canberra, 1931-34; Naval Attaché, U.S.A., 1935-38; commanded H.M.S. Edinburgh, 1939; Rear-Admiral (and retired), 1941; Chief Staff Officer to Flag-Officer-in-Charge, Greenock,

1942; Naval Attaché, Lisbon, 1944-46. *Address:* 30 Bath Hill Court, Bournemouth, Hants. *T.:* Bournemouth 5095; c/o National Provincial Bank Ltd., 208/9 Piccadilly, W.1. *Club:* United Service.
[*Died* 9 *April* 1957.

BRADLEY, Col. Sir Montague; *see* Bradley, Col. Sir A. M.

BRADNEY, George Preston, C.M.G. 1946; C.B.E. 1936; B.A. Cantab.; Colonial Service (retired); *b.* 3 Nov. 1877: 4th *s.* of late John Bradney, J.P., Bayford Lodge, Wincanton, Somerset, and Maud Barbara Disney; *m.* 1904, Elizabeth Worthington; one *s.* *Educ.:* Oratory School; Trinity Hall, Cambridge. Exchequer and Audit Department, 1901; Assistant Auditor British Central Africa, 1902; British East Africa, 1904; Uganda, 1907; Local Auditor Fiji and Western Pacific, 1909; Director of External Audit Straits Settlements and Federated Malay States, 1914; Auditor General Federated Malay States, 1921; Acting Treasurer and Financial Adviser, and Member of Federal Council, 1930; Auditor Straits Settlements and Federated Malay States, 1932; retired 1936; Comptroller and Auditor General, Newfoundland, 1940-1946. *Recreation:* golf. *Address:* 21 Motcombe Court, Bexhill on Sea, Sussex.
[*Died* 26 *April* 1959.

BRADSHAW, Evelyn; late Principal and Manager, Royal School of Needlework; *b.* 1862; 4th *d.* of late Thomas Bradshaw, Judge of the County Courts of Northumberland, and Emily, *o. d.* of late Colonel Frederick Halkett, Coldstream Guards. Lady-in-Waiting to Princess Pauline, *d.* of King of Wurttemberg, 1893-94; has lived much abroad, and spent some years in Canada. *Recreations:* music and travelling. *Address:* 4 Empire House, Thurloe Place, S.W.7. *T.:* Kensington 8856.
[*Died* 22 *June* 1952.

BRADSHAW, George Fagan, D.S.O. 1917; marine artist; Commander, retired; *b.* 6 Dec. 1887; 2nd *s.* of late Robert Macnevin Bradshaw and late Agnes Margaret Bradshaw, Dublin; *m.* Kathleen Marion, *e. d.* of late Captain A. Slatter, B.S.A.P., Salisbury, Rhodesia; one *s.* one *d.* *Educ.:* Privately; H.M.S. Britannia. Entered R.N., 1903. *Address:* The Ship Studio, St. Ives, Cornwall; c/o Westminster Bank, 26 Haymarket, S.W.1. [*Died* 27 *Oct.* 1960.

BRADSHAW, Sir William, Kt., *cr.* 1937; J.P.; *b.* Riddings, Derbyshire; *s.* of James and Mary Bradshaw; *m.* 1902, Lilian Mabel, *d.* of late George Bowler, Pentrich, Derbys.; two *s.* *Educ.:* Riddings. Commenced at 13 years of age at the Ripley Co-operative Society; became shop manager and later General Manager of Wirksworth Co-operative Society and afterwards General Manager and Secretary of Grantham Co-operative Society; Director, 1921-36 and Chairman of the Co-operative Wholesale Society, 1936-45. Commander of Dannebrog. *Address:* Pentrich, Harrowby Road, Grantham. *T.A.:* Bradshaw, Grantham 108. *T.:* Grantham 108.
[*Died* 28 *Aug.* 1955.

BRAHAM, Dudley Disraeli; *b.* Birmingham, 23 Jan. 1875; 3rd *s.* of Frederick Braham; *m.* 1902, Julie Swift (Stella), 5th *d.* of H. J. Whiteside of Liverpool and the Isle of Man; one *s.* (and one killed in action). *Educ.:* The Liverpool Institute; New College, Oxford. Joined Berlin office of The Times, 1897; correspondent in St. Petersburg, 1901; correspondent in Constantinople, 1903; at end of 1907 called to London to assist Sir Valentine Chirol, at that time head of Imperial and Foreign Department, whom he succeeded in 1912; was elected same year a Director of The Times Publishing Company; travelled for The Times in Europe, Asia Minor, the Far East and America; left the service of The Times, 1914; Editor of the Daily Telegraph, Sydney, N.S.W., 1914-22; founded and became first Editor of the Forum (Australia), 1922; Editor of the West Australian, Perth, W.A., 1924-30; returned to London, 1930, to rejoin The Times; retired, 1945. *Address:* Hanson Mount, Ashbourne, Derbyshire. *Club:* Athenæum.
[*Died* 25 *March* 1951.

BRAILSFORD, Henry Noel, M.A. and LL.D. (Glasgow); *b.* Mirfield, Yorks, 1873; *s.* of Rev. E. J. Brailsford; *m.* Evamaria Jarvis. *Educ.:* Glasgow University. Assistant to Professor of Logic (Glasgow), and Lecturer in Queen Margaret College, 1895; Leader-writer successively to Manchester Guardian, Tribune, Daily News, and Nation; Volunteer in Greek Foreign Legion, 1897; Relief Agent in Macedonia, 1903; joined I.L.P. 1907; Hon. Secretary to Conciliation Committee for Women's Suffrage, 1910-12; Member of Carnegie International Commission in Balkans, 1913; contested (Labour) Montrose Burghs, 1918; Editor, The New Leader, 1922-26. *Publications:* The Broom of the War-God (novel); Macedonia, 1906; Adventures in Prose (essays); Shelley Godwin, and their Circle (Home University Library); The War of Steel and Gold, 1914; A League of Nations, 1917; Socialism for To-day, 1925; How the Soviet Works, 1927; Olives of Endless Age, 1927; Rebel India, 1932; Property or Peace? 1934; Voltaire, 1935; America our Ally, 1940; Subject India, 1943; Our Settlement with Germany, 1944; (joint) Mahatma Gandhi, 1949. *Address:* 37 Belsize Park Gardens, N.W.3.
[*Died* 23 *March* 1958.

BRAIN, Dennis, F.R.A.M.; Soloist and Principal Horn, Philharmonia Orchestra, since 1946; *b.* 17 May 1921; *s.* of Aubrey H. Brain and Marion Beeley; *m.* 1946, Yvonne Coles; one *s.* one *d.* *Educ.:* St. Paul's School; Royal Acad. of Music. Début, Queen's Hall, with Busch Chamber Players, 1938. Has played with Griller, Lener, Busch, Amadeus Quartets, etc. and recorded with several Quartets. Works written for him: Serenade of Benjamin Britten, with Peter Pears; Concertos of Hindemith, Gordon Jacob, Gordon Bryan, Malcolm Arnold. Has played Concertos, etc., in Switzerland, France, Germany, Holland, Italy and U.S.A. Cobbett Medal of Worshipful Company of Musicians. *Recreations:* motoring, etc. *Address:* Craigmore, 37 Frognal, Hampstead, N.W.3. *T.:* Hampstead 7294. *Club:* I.M.A.
[*Died* 1 *Sept.* 1957.

BRAITHWAITE, Major Sir Albert Newby, Kt., *cr.* 1945; D.S.O. 1918; M.C.; M.P. (C.) Harrow West, since April 1951; *b.* 2 Sept. 1893; *s.* of Albert Braithwaite; *m.* Anne Anderson (*d.* 1950), Augusta, Georgia, U.S.A.; three *s.* one *d.*; *m.* 1950, Mrs. Joan Weiner. *Educ.:* Woodhouse Grove School; Leeds Grammar School; Leeds University. Enlisted as private soldier, August 1914; commissioned Yorkshire Hussars, Jan. 1915; served overseas two and a half years; appointed on British Military Mission to America. M.P. (U.) Buckrose, E. Yorkshire, 1926-45. *Recreations:* golf, tennis, shooting, fishing, motoring. *Address:* Coxland, Ewhurst, Surrey. *Club:* Carlton.
[*Died* 20 *Oct.* 1959.

BRAITHWAITE, Air Vice-Marshal Francis Joseph St. George, C.B.E. 1945 (O.B.E. 1942); Chief of Staff, Far East Air Force, since 1956; *b.* 16 Oct. 1907; *e. s.* of late Major F. J. Braithwaite, The Loyal Regiment; *m.* 1933, Rosemary, *d.* of late G. Grinling Harris, Clifford's Inn, E.C.4; two *d.* *Educ.:* Bradfield College; Corpus Christi College, Cambridge. Commissioned, 1929; R.A.F. Staff College, 1938. Served War of 1939-45 (despatches twice): successively commanded No. 22

Squadron and R.A.F. Stations Abbotsinch and Limavady, 1940-43; Dep. Dir. Ops. (anti ship), 1943-44; comd. R.A.F. Station, North Coates, 1944-45; Dep. S.A.S.O., Transp. Comd., 1945-46. Air Adviser to Foreign Secretary during meetings of Council of Foreign Ministers (peace treaty negotiations), Apr. 1946-July 1947. Sen. Officer, Admin., Air H.Q., Malta, 1947-49; i.d.c., 1950; R.A.F. rep. on Western Union Air Advisory Cttee. and later N.A.T.O. Mil. Standardisation Agency, 1951; Director of Plans, Air Ministry, 1952-54; Air Officer Commanding No. 61 (Eastern) Group, R.A.F., 1954-56. *Recreation:* sailing. *Address:* 5 Fairy Point, R.A.F., Changi, Singapore 17; 14 Park Lane, Southwold, Suffolk. *T.:* Southwold 3322; (official residence) Court Lees, Upper Warlingham, Surrey. *T.:* Upper Warlingham 2207. *Club:* Royal Air Force. [*Died* 21 *Dec.* 1956.

BRAITHWAITE, Col. Francis Powell, C.B.E. 1919; D.S.O. 1918; M.C.; retired; *b.* 2 Nov. 1875; *s.* of late Rev. J. M. Braithwaite, Vicar of Croydon; *m.* 1920, Victoria Alexandrina, *d.* of 1st Marquess of Dufferin and Ava, and *widow* of 5th Baron Plunket; no *c.* *Educ.:* Clifton; R.M.C., Sandhurst. Entered Army, Northumberland Fusiliers, 1894; served South African War, 1899-1900; European War, 1914-19 (despatches four times, M.C., D.S.O., Belgian Croix de Guerre, C.B.E., Order of Leopold of Belgium). *Address:* 49 Lowndes Square, S.W.1. *Club:* White's. [*Died* 23 *Dec.* 1952.

BRAITHWAITE, Sir Joseph Gurney, 1st Bt., *cr.* 1954: Lieutenant-Comdr. R.N.V.R. retired; Member London Stock Exchange; *b.* Burnham-on-Sea, Somerset, 24 May 1895; *s.* of late Joseph Bevan Braithwaite and late Anna Sophia Gillett; *m.* 1st, 1919, Emma Jeanne Louise Teissère; no *c.*; annulled 1932; 2nd, 1932, Emily Victoria, *y. d.* of late A. M. Lomax, Edinburgh. *Educ.:* Bootham School, York. Entered for King's College, Cambridge; on outbreak of European War, served as Sub-Lieut., R.N.V.R. in Gallipoli, 1915, taking part in Suvla Bay landing; served Suez Canal, 1916; took part in Palestine operations during advance from Gaza to Jerusalem, 1917 (promoted Lieut.); Assistant Port Convoy Officer, Suez, 1918; Resident Naval Officer, Port Said, 1919; employed on Stock Exchange since demobilisation, became Member of Stock Exchange, 1926; contested Rotherhithe, 1929; M.P. (U.) Hillsborough Division of Sheffield, 1931-35, Holderness division of E. Yorkshire, 1939-50, Bristol, North-West, Feb. 1950-55; Parliamentary Secretary, Ministry of Transport and Civil Aviation, 1951-53. Lieutenant R.N.V.R. Sept. 1939; Lt.-Comdr. 1940. *Recreations:* cricket, golf, walking. *Heir:* none. *Address:* 97 Hampstead Way, N.W.11. *T.:* Speedwell 5241. *Clubs:* R.N.V.R. M.C.C. [*Died* 25 *June* 1958.

BRAKE, Sir Francis, Kt. 1946; M.I.E.E.; M.I.Prod.E.; F.R.S.A.; Chairman, Creed & Co. Ltd., Telegraph House, Croydon; Vice-President International Standard Electric Corporation; Director: Standard Telephones & Cables Ltd.; Standard Telecommunications Laboratories Ltd.; The Commercial Cable Co. Ltd.; B.O.A.C. Associated Cos. Ltd.; E.P.S. (Development and Research) Ltd.; Milton Abbey School Ltd.; *b.* 10 Dec. 1889; *s.* of late Timothy Francis Brake; *m.* 1914, Ethel Primrose, *d.* of late Frederick Charles Badrick, B.A.; no. *c.* *Educ.:* Mountjoy School, Dublin; Colet Court. Controller, Construction and Regional Services, M.A.P. (War Period). Freeman of City of London; Member of Worshipful Co. of Gold and Silver Wyre Drawers; Life Governor of Haileybury and Imperial Service College; Member of Council Milton Abbey School. *Address:* The Berkeley Hotel, W.1. *T.:* Hyde Park 8282; Telegraph House, Croydon, Surrey. *T.:* Municipal 2424. *Clubs:* City Livery, Bath, Royal Automobile. [*Died* 13 *June* 1960.

BRAKENRIDGE, Col. Francis John, C.M.G. 1916; late Royal Army Medical Corps; *b.* 26 June 1871; 4th *s.* of Wm. Brakenridge, late of Liddlebank, Canobie, N.B.; *m.* 1910, Margery, *d.* of R. Brassey, Bulkeley Grange, Cheshire; four *d.* *Educ.:* Wakefield Grammar School; St. Thomas' Hospital. M.R.C.S. Eng., L.R.C.P. Lond., 1895; and D.P.H. Cambridge, 1896; commissioned R.A.M.C., 1899; Lieut.-Col. 1915; Col. 1924; attached Egyptian Army, 1900-10; served European War, 1914-19 (despatches thrice, C.M.G., Officer of Legion d'Honneur, Order of St. Sava (Serbian)); retired pay, 1928. *Recreations:* outdoor. *Address:* The Orchard, Chew Magna, Bristol. [*Died* 14 *April* 1955.

BRAME, Prof. John Samuel Strafford, C.B.E. 1930; *b.* 1871. *Educ.:* Sir Thomas Rich's School, Gloucester; Royal College of Science, South Kensington. Demonstrator, Royal Naval College, Greenwich, 1897; Instructor, 1910; Professor of Chemistry, 1914-32; President, Institution of Petroleum Technologists, 1921-23 and Chairman of Standardisation Committee. *Publications:* Contributions to Chemical Society, Society of Chemical Industry, and Institution of Petroleum Technologists Journals; Cantor and Howard Lectures, Royal Society of Arts; Treatise on Fuel-Solid, Liquid and Gaseous; Service Chemistry (5th Edn.). *Address:* 3 Vanbrugh Fields, Blackheath, S.E.3. *T.:* Greenwich 2891. [*Died* 10 *Dec.* 1952.

BRAMWELL, Edwin, M.D. (Edinburgh); Hon. M.D. (Melbourne); Hon. LL.D. (Edin.); F.R.C.P. (Edin.); F.R.C.P. (Lond.); F.R.S.E.; Consulting Physician Royal Infirmary, Edinburgh; Consultant Medical Officer, Scottish Union and National Insurance Co.; Hon. Member (Ex-President) Association of British Neurologists; Fellow Royal Soc. of Medicine (Ex-Pres. Neurol. Sect.); President Neurological Section, British Medical Association, Edinburgh Meeting, 1927; President Royal College of Physicians of Edinburgh 1934-1935; Hon. Member Royal Medical Society; Foreign Corresponding Member Philadelphia Neurological Society; Corr. Member Society de Neurol. de Paris; *b.* 11 Jan. 1873; *e. s.* of late Sir Byrom Bramwell, M.D., LL.D., D.C.L.; *m.* Elizabeth Cumming, *e. d.* of late Professor D. J. Cunningham, D.C.L., LL.D., F.R.S.; one *s.* four *d.* *Educ.:* Cheltenham College; Universities of Edinburgh, Freiburg, Heidelberg and Paris. Graduated University of Edinburgh, 1896; President Royal Medical Society, 1896-97; Assistant Physician, 1907, and Physician, 1919, to the Royal Infirmary, Edinburgh; Capt. (ret.) R.A.M.C.T.; Morison Lecturer Royal Coll. of Physicians, Edinburgh, 1917 and 1918; Moncrieff-Arnott Prof. of Clinical Med., Edin. University, 1922-34; Bradshaw Lecturer, 1925 and Croonian Lecturer, 1937, Royal College of Physicians, London; Halford Oration, Canberra, 1935. *Publications:* chapters on Diseases of the Nervous System in Allbutt's System of Medicine, Osler's Modern Medicine, Oxford Medicine, the Encyclopædia Medica, etc., and numerous papers. *Recreation:* fly fishing. *Address:* 29 Ormidale Terrace, Murrayfield, Edinburgh 12. *T.:* 63235. [*Died* 21 *March* 1952.

BRAND, (Charles) Neville; *b.* 5 Jan. 1895; *s.* of late Charles James Brand, J.P., and late Alice Hutchings; *m.* 1918, Nora Joyce, *d.* of late Victor Vaughan; no *c.* *Educ.:* Belsize School, Hampstead; Westminster School. Entered the service of the Bank of England, 1914; served European War as a seaplane pilot R.N.A.S. and also Lieutenant R.N.V.R., engaged in mine-sweeping with the Auxiliary Patrol; has experimented with many forms of literature, from verse to novels, short stories, and plays, which latter have been produced by various amateur societies; A Freeman of the City of London. *Publications:* The House of Time and other Poems, 1918; Perspective Poems, 1921; Novels—Narrow Seas, 1923; The Courtyard, 1925; The Sleeping Queen, 1926; Cloudburst, 1927; Black River, 1927; Honours Even, 1928; The Shadow Dance, 1928; The Winning Trick, 1931; Death in the Forest, 1933; One More Chance, 1933; Death, of a Designer, 1938 (published under own name); Air Liner, 1934; Henrietta, 1935; Nocturne in Sunlight, 1937 (published in U.S.A. as Mexican Masquerade); Flat to Let, 1938 (published under pseudonym of Charles Lorne); Winter Landscape, 1949; The Dark Lady, 1950; has contributed short stories to many magazines and periodicals; Play — Words without Music, produced at the Arts Theatre, 1931. *Recreations:* fishing, sketching, walking, stimulating conversation, yachting. *Address:* 162 Grand Avenue, Berrylands, Surbiton, Surrey. *Club:* Royal Thames Yacht. [*Died* 2 *Sept.* 1951.

BRAND, Sir Harry F., Kt., *cr.* 1942; Governing Director of Charles Brand & Son, Ltd., Civil Engineering Contractors; *b.* 2 Oct. 1873; 3rd *s.* of late James Brand, K.C.S.G., J.P., Glasgow; *m.* 1904, Mercedes, *d.* of late Frank Harwood Lescher; two *s.* three *d.* *Educ.:* Stonyhurst; Glasgow Univ. President British Employers' Confederation, 1940-44. President Federation of Civil Engineering Contractors, 1936-40; President Stonyhurst Association, 1923-24; J.P. for County of the City of Glasgow, 1910-30. *Address:* Harecomb, Crowborough, Sussex. *T.:* Crowborough 203. *Club:* Union. [*Died* 5 *July* 1951.

BRAND, Admiral Hon. Sir Hubert (George), G.C.B., *cr.* 1932 (K.C.B., *cr.* 1927; C.B. 1918); K.C.M.G., *cr.* 1919; K.C.V.O., *cr.* 1922 (C.V.O. 1917; M.V.O. 1903); *b.* 20 May 1870; 2nd *s.* of 2nd Viscount Hampden; *m.* 1914, Norah (*d.* 1924), *d.* of late Rt. Hon. Sir C. Greene G.C.M.G.; one *d.* Entered Navy, 1883; Lieut. 1892; Commander, 1902; Captain, 1907; Naval Attaché at Tokyo, 1912-14; Naval Assistant to 2nd Sea-Lord Admiralty, 1915-16; Chief of Staff to Sir David Beatty, commanding Battle Cruiser Fleet, 1916; Captain of the Fleet and Commodore 1st Class, 1916-19; Rear-Adm. 1919; Commanded His Majesty's Yachts, 1919-1922; Comdg. First Light Cruiser Squadron, 1922-24; Extra Equerry to the Queen, 1952 (to King George VI, 1922-52); Vice-Admiral, 1924; Naval Secretary to First Lord of the Admiralty, 1925; Second Sea Lord, 1925-1927; Commander-in-Chief, Atlantic Fleet, 1927-29; Admiral, 1928; Commander-in-Chief, Plymouth, 1929-32; First and Principal Naval A.D.C. to H.M., 1931-32; retired list, 1932. Rear-Admiral of the United Kingdom and of the Admiralty, 1939-45. *Address:* Park House, Park Road, Winchester, Hants. *Club:* United Service. [*Died* 14 *Dec.* 1955.

BRAND, Engineer-Captain James John Cantley, C.B.E. 1929; R.A.N. (retd.); *b.* Silverton, Devon, 29 June 1880; *e. s.* of Capt. Alex. Brand, Aberdeen; *m.* 1907; no *c.* *Educ.:* St. Joseph's Coll., Rockhampton, Queensland. Consulting Engineer, Sydney, 1907-11; Royal Australian Navy, 1911-29; inventor of Brand System of Powdered Coal Burning and originator of the modern short flame burner; M.I.M.E., M.I.N.A., M.I.Mar.E. *Publications:* extensive contributor to the technical press. *Address:* 7 Beaufort Court, 200 Forbes Street, Darlinghurst, Sydney, Australia. [*Died* 12 *Sept.* 1952.

BRAND, Neville; *see* Brand, C. N.

BRANDER, William Browne, C.I.E. 1927; C.B.E. 1918; *b.* Edinburgh, 1 Aug. 1880; *s.* of W. J. Brander, Edinburgh; *m.* 1909, Matilda Baird, *d.* of Dr. J. A. D. Thompson; one *s.* *Educ.:* George Watson's College, Edinburgh; Edinburgh and Oxford Universities. Joined Indian Civil Service, 1904; appointments held — Under-Secretary to Government of Burma; Registrar Chief Court, Lower Burma; Deputy Commissioner; Excise Commissioner; Secretary to Government; Commissioner; Additional Secretary to Government; Chief Secretary to Government of Burma; Chairman Development Trust, Rangoon; retired I.C.S., 1931; Secretary, Universities Bureau, British Empire, until 1946. *Address:* 5 Coastguards, Kingsdown, nr. Deal, Kent. [*Died* 9 *Jan.* 1951.

BRANGWYN, Sir Frank, Kt., *cr.* 1941; R.A., R.P.E.; Hon. R.S.A.; LL.D. Univ. of Wales; Officer and Cross of Legion of Honour, France; Commander and Cross of the Order of St. Maurice and St. Lazarus, Italy; member of the Institut de France; member of the Reale Accademia di S. Luca, Rome; Hon. Citizen of City of Bruges; Grand Officer Order of Leopold II; Vice-Pres. Poetry Society; *b.* Bruges, of Welsh extraction, 13 May 1867; *s.* of William Curtis and Elenore Griffiths; *m.* Lucy Ray (*decd.*). Mem. many European art societies; Vice-Pres. Imperial Arts League; Vice-Pres. Royal West of England Academy; Hon. Member Royal Soc. of Miniature Painters; Member B.B.C.; Commander and Cross of the Order of Leopold, Belgium; President Senefelder Club; Member of Pulchri Studio, The Hague; Pres. Graphic Arts Society; Hon. member Society of Architects, London; Commander and Cross of the Order of Orange Nassau, Holland; Vice-President Association of Architects and Surveyors; Albert Medal, Royal Society of Arts, 1932. *Publications:* Belgium, 1916; The Way of the Cross, 1935. *Address:* The Jointure, Ditchling, Sussex. [*Died* 11 *June* 1956.

BRANSON, Rt. Hon. Sir George Arthur Harwin, P.C. 1940; Kt., *cr.* 1921; *b.* Great Yarmouth, 11 July 1871; *e. s.* of James H. A. Branson, Barrister-at-law; *m.* 1915, Mona Joyce, *y. d.* of George James Bailey of Invergloy, Inverness-shire, *widow* of F. L. Addison; one *s.* one *d.* *Educ.:* Bedford School (Foundation Scholar); Trinity College, Cambridge (Exhibitioner); Honours degree in Classics. Bow of Cambridge University Boat, 1893; articled to Markby, Stewart & Co., Solicitors, 1894; called to Bar, Inner Temple, 1899; joined the Northern Circuit; Junior Counsel to the Treasury, 1912-21; Judge High Court of Justice, King's Bench Division, 1921-39. *Publication:* joint author of Schwabe and Branson on the Law of the Stock Exchange. *Address:* Bullswater House, Pirbright, Surrey. *T.:* Worplesdon 31. *Clubs:* Leander, Lansdowne; West Suffolk County (Bury St. Edmunds). [*Died* 23 *April* 1951.

BRASH, James Couper, M.C.; M.A., M.B., Ch.B. (Edin.); M.D. (Birm.); Hon. D.Sc. (Leeds); LL.D. (St. Andrews); F.R.S.E.; F.R.C.S. (Edin.); Professor of Anatomy, University of Edinburgh 1931-54; *b.* 1886; *s.* of late James Brash, J.P.; *m.* 1912, Margaret, *d.* of late William Henderson, Leslie, Fife; one *s.* one *d.* *Educ.:* George Watson's College and University of Edinburgh. Demonstrator of Anatomy, Universities of Edinburgh and Leeds; Professor of Anatomy and Dean, Faculty of Medicine, Univ. of Birmingham; Major, R.A.M.C. (S.R.); Struthers Lecturer, Royal College of Surgeons, Edinburgh. Hon. Member, British Dental Association, British Society for Study of Orthodontics (Northcroft Lecturer), and European Orthodontic Society; President, Anatomical Society of

Great Britain and Ireland. *Publications:* The Growth of the Jaws and Palate (Dental Board of the U.K.), 1924; The Aetiology of Irregularity and Malocclusion of the Teeth (Dental Board of the U.K.), 1929; (with Prof. J. Glaister), Medico-Legal Aspects of the Ruxton Case, 1937; Neuro-vascular Hila of Limb Muscles, 1955. Contributons to scientific journals; Editor, Cunningham's Manual of Practical Anatomy and Cunningham's Text-Book of Anatomy. *Recreations:* golf and angling. *Address:* 199 Braid Road, Edinburgh, 10. *T.:* Edinburgh 54305. [*Died* 19 *Jan.* 1958.

BRASH, William Bardsley, M.A., B.D., B.Litt.; *b.* 23 Dec. 1877; *s.* of Rev. J. Denholm and Mary J. Brash; *m.* Florence M. Wall; two *d.* *Educ.:* Kingswood School, Bath; Handsworth College; New College, Oxford. Professor of English and the English Bible at Didsbury College, Manchester, 1928-1945; Principal of Didsbury College, 1939-1945; Principal of Didsbury College, Bristol (associated with Univ. of Bristol), 1945-49; retired, 1949. *Publications:* Love and Life; The Pilgrim Way; Methodism (in Faiths Series); Happy Warrior; The Story of the Colleges, etc.; reviews and articles for magazines. *Recreations:* golf and walking. *Address:* 60 Sandfield Road, Headington, Oxford. *T.:* Oxford 6405. [*Died* 28 *April* 1952.

BRASS, Sir Leslie Stuart, Kt., *cr.* 1950; C.B.E. 1942; Legal Adviser, Home Office, 1947-56; *b.* 1891; *s.* of Lot and Elizabeth Brass, Chelsea Square, Chelsea; *m.* 1955, Jessie, *widow* of John T. West, M.B., Hon. Cons. Surgeon Glasgow Royal Samaritan Hospital for Women, and *d.* of Neil Buchanan. *Educ.:* St. Paul's School; Christ Church, Oxford. Barrister, Inner Temple, 1921. United Kingdom delegate to Internat. Conf. on Suppression of Counterfeiting Currency, 1929, and on Repression of Terrorism, 1937. Member of United Nations Committee on Statelessness, 1951. *Address:* 93 Embassy Court, King's Road, Brighton 1, Sussex. *T.:* Hove 70526. *Club:* Athenæum. [*Died* 17 *Nov.* 1958.

BRASSEY of Apethorpe, 1st Baron, *cr.* 1938, **Henry Leonard Campbell Brassey,** 1st Bt., *cr.* 1922; *b.* 7 March 1870; 2nd *s.* of late Henry Arthur Brassey, *b.* of 1st Earl Brassey; *m.* 1894, Lady Violet Mary Gordon Lennox (*d.* 1946), 2nd *d.* of 7th Duke of Richmond and Gordon, K.G., G.C.V.O., C.B.; two *s.* (and four *s.* decd.). Late Major West Kent Yeomanry Cavalry; Major Northamptonshire Yeomanry, Sept. 1914; M.P. (U.) N. Northants, 1910-1918; Peterborough Division, Northants, 1918-1929; owns about 3000 acres; member of Jockey Club since 1898 (Senior Steward, 1902, 1908 and 1937). *Heir:* *s.* Lt.-Col. Hon. Bernard Thomas Brassey, M.C., T.D., D.L. [*b.* 15 Feb. 1905; *m.* 1931, Crystal Gloria, *d.* of late Lt.-Col. Francis William George Gore; two *s.*]. *Address:* 18 Grosvenor Square, W.1. *Clubs:* Turf, Carlton. [*Died* 22 *Oct.* 1958.

BRAUDE, Professor Ernest Alexander Rudolph; Professor of Organic Chemistry, Imperial College of Science and Technology, since 1955; *b.* 8 June1922; *o. s.* of late R. Braude and of Mrs. E. Braude; *m.* 1946, Catherine Renate Zander. *Educ.:* The Grammar School, Farnham; Birkbeck College; Imperial College of Science and Technology (B.Sc., A.R.C.S.). Frank Hatton Prize, 1942. Rockefeller Research Asst. in Organic Chemistry, Imperial Coll., 1942-45; Ph.D., D.I.C., 1945; Asst. Lectr., 1946; Lecturer, 1947; D.Sc. (London), F.R.I.C., 1950; Reader in Organic Chemistry in the University of London, Imperial Coll., 1952; Member of Council, Chemical Society, 1954; Tilden Lecturer, 1956. Meldola Medal of Society of Maccabaeans and Royal Institute of Chemistry, 1950. *Publications:* The Determination of Organic Structures by Physical Methods, New York, 1955. Scientific papers, mainly in Journal of Chemical Society. *Recreations:* walking, riding, theatre-going. *Address:* 37 Gloucester Court, Kew Gardens, Surrey. *T.:* Richmond 1004. [*Died* 23 *July* 1956.

BRAY, Sir Denys de Saumarez, K.C.S.I., *cr.* 1930 (C.S.I. 1922); K.C.I.E., *cr.* 1925 (C.I.E. 1917); C.B.E. 1919; I.C.S. (retired); B.A.; *b.* 29 Nov. 1875; *s.* of late Rev. T. W. Bray; *m.* Celestina *d.* of late Lt.-Col. H. P. P. Leigh, C.I.E.; one *d.* *Educ.:* Realgymnasium, Stuttgart; Blundell's School, Tiverton; Balliol College, Oxford; Taylorian (German) Scholar. Entered I.C.S. 1898; served in Punjab, N.W. Frontier, Baluchistan, and Government of India; conducted first complete census of Baluchistan, 1911; Deputy Foreign Secretary, 1916; acting Private Secretary to the Viceroy, 1918; Joint Foreign Secretary, 1919; Foreign Secretary, 1920-30; Member of India Council 1930-37; Adviser to Secretary of State for India, 1937; Member of the Imperial Legislative Council, 1918; Council of State, 1921; Legislative Assembly, 1922-29; retired, 1930; Indian Delegation to the League of Nations, 1930-31-32-33-34-35-36-37; Vice-Chairman 6th (Political) Committee, 1933; represented India at International Broadcasting Conference, 1936; and Diplomatic Conference on Terrorism, 1937; League of Nations Mission to Spain on Refugee Relief, 1938; Chairman Winchester and District War Savings Committee, 1940-44; Gold Kaisar-i-Hind medal, 1911; Order of the Rising Sun, Japan, 2nd class; Order of Leopold II., Belgium Grand Officer. *Publications:* Brahui Grammar, 1909; The Brahui Problem, and Etymological Vocabulary, 1933; Life-History of a Brahui, 1913; Baluchistan Census Report, 1913; Ethnographical Survey of Baluchistan, vols. i. and ii.; Statistical Analysis of the Tribes of Baluchistan; The Original Order of Shakespeare's Sonnets, 1925; Shakespeare's Sonnet-Sequence, 1938. *Address:* West Dene, Winchester. *T.:* Winchester 3430. [*Died* 19 *Nov.* 1951.

BRAY, Rt. Rev. Patrick Albert, C.J.M. (Eudist); Bishop of Saint John, N.B., (R.C.), since 1936; *b.* Upper Springfield, Antigonish Co., N.S., 1883; *s.* of John Bray, farmer, and Margaret Floyd. *Educ.:* St. Francis Xavier University, Antigonish, N.S.; Sacred Heart College, Caraquet, N.B.; Holy Heart Seminary, Halifax, N.S.; Gregorian University, Rome. Ordained 1912; Professor of English and Philosophy, Sacred Heart College, Bathurst, N.B.; Director of Eudist Scholasticate, Bathurst, N.B.; Professor of Philosophy, Holy Heart Seminary, Halifax, N.S., 1922-30; Rector of Holy Heart Seminary, 1930-36. *Address:* St. John, New Brunswick, Canada. [*Died* 17 *June* 1953.

BRAYE, 6th Baron (*cr.* 1529), **Adrian Verney-Cave;** J.P.; *b.* 11 Oct. 1874; *e. s.* of 5th Baron and Cecilia (*d.* 1935), *d.* of William Gerard Walmesley of Westwood House, Wigan; *S.* father, 1928; *m.* 1900, Ethel Mary, *d.* of Capt. Edward Bouverie Pusey, R.N.; two *s.* one *d.* Joined R.N.V.R. 1908; Lt.-Commander, 1916. *Heir:* *s.* Hon. Thomas Adrian Verney-Cave. *Address:* Stanford Hall, Rugby. *T.A.:* Yelvertoft. *Clubs:* Bath, Boodle's. [*Died* 12 *Feb.* 1952.

BRAYE, Philip George, C.S.I. 1947; C.I.E. 1944; E.D. 1945; *b.* 1 Dec. 1894; *y. s.* of late Mr. Brée, Jersey, C.I.; *m.* 1921, Olivia Mercy, *y. d.* of late Maj.-Gen. C. W. Wauchope, Crieff, Perthshire; one *s.* one *d.* *Educ.:* Victoria College, Jersey; Exeter College, Oxford. Served European War, 1914-18. Entered I.C.S. 1923; retired, 1947. Surname changed from Brée to Braye, the latter being the original spelling. *Address:* 378 Woodstock Road, Oxford. *Club:* Overseas League. [*Died* 26 *May* 1956.

BRAYNE, Frank Lugard, C.S.I. 1941; C.I.E. 1937; M.C. 1918; V.D.; fruit farmer; *b.* 6 Jan. 1882; *s.* of late Rev. R. T. W. Brayne; *m.* 1920, Iris Goodeve Goble; four *s.* two *d.* *Educ.:* Monkton Combe School; Pembroke Coll., Cambridge (Scholar). I.C.S. 1905; Military Service, 1915; 18th K.G.O. Lancers, 1916-19; Political Service, Aleppo and North Syria, 1918-19; retired from I.C.S. 1941; Military Service, 1941-46, Welfare Branch (Brig.); late Financial Commissioner Development, Punjab. Chm. Christian Literature Council of the Conf. of Missionary Socs. in Great Britain and Ireland. Order of St. Sava (Serbian), 1916; Order of the Nile, 1919. *Publications:* Village Uplift in India; Remaking of Village India; Socrates in an Indian Village; Socrates Persists in India; Socrates at School; Better Villages; The Boy Scout in the Village; In Him was Light; The Villager's ABC, etc. *Address:* The Glebe, Ashill, Thetford, Norfolk. *T.:* Holme Hale 246. *Club:* East India and Sports. [*Died* 3 *April* 1952.

BRAYSHAY, Sir Maurice William, Kt., *cr.* 1934; M.Sc.; A.M.I.C.E.; J.P.; formerly Dir. W. of India Portuguese Rly.; *b.* 7 March 1883; *s.* of W. Brayshay, solicitor; unmarried. *Educ.:* Ripon School; Leeds Univ. Appointed to Indian State Railways (late P.W.D.), 1905; Member Railway Board, 1929; Agent, Bombay, Baroda and Central India Railway, 1932-38; acted as Chief Commissioner of Railways in 1933 and 1935. *Recreations:* tennis and golf. *Address:* High Common, Ripon, Yorks. *T.:* Ripon 58. *Clubs:* East India and Sports, Oriental. [*Died* 2 *Aug.* 1959.

BRAZEL, Claude Hamilton, C.M.G. 1948; M.C. 1918; M.I.E.E.; M.I.Mech.E.; retired 1953; *b.* 1894; *s.* of William Brazel, Swansea; *m.* 1921, Ethel Elizabeth, *d.* of S. J. Cocks, Swansea; two *s.* *Educ.:* Technical College, Swansea. Served European War, 1914-19, with Royal Engineers, Major, 1917 (despatches, M.C., Belgian Croix de Guerre). Director of Electrical Department, Bahamas, 1926-34: Chief Engineer and Manager, Govt. Electrical Undertakings, Ceylon, 1934-1948. *Address:* 6 Glynderwen Close, Ashleigh Road, Swansea, Glam. [*Died* 26 *April* 1959.

BREADALBANE AND HOLLAND, 9th Earl of (*cr.* 1677), **Charles William Campbell,** M.C., D.L., J.P.; Viscount of Tay and Paintland; Lord Glenorchy, Benederaloch, Ormelie, and Weik, 1677; Baronet of Glenorchy; Baronet of Nova Scotia (*cr.* 1625); Lt.-Col. Reserve of Officers, 1926; Scottish Representative Peer since 1924; Member of H.M.'s Bodyguard (Hon. Corps of Gentlemen-at-Arms), since 1935; Member of Royal Company of Archers, H.M.'s Bodyguard for Scotland, since 1937; *b.* 11 June 1889; *s.* of late Major-General Charles William Campbell of Boreland and Mrs. Walter Williams; *S.* kinsman, 1923; *m.* 1918, Armorer, *d.* of late Romer Williams, D.L., J.P., Newnham Hall, Daventry, and *widow* of Capt. Eric Nicholson, 14th (King's) Hussars; one *s.* *Educ.:* Shrewsbury School; Royal Military Academy, Woolwich. Proceeded to France with 2nd Division, Aug. 1914; commanded C/93 Battery and A/311 Battery in European War (wounded, M.C., 1914 Star); Actions—Mons, Basses Maroilles, Villers Cotteret, Marne, Aisne, Loos, Beaumont-Hamel, Vimy Ridge, Messines; sometime A.D.C. to F.M. Commanding-in-Chief, Rhine Army of Occupation; Gunnery Staff Course; Adjutant 94th Dorset and Somerset Yeomanry Bde.; sometime Lt.-Col. Comdg. 8th Bn. Argyll and Sutherland Highlanders; memb., Argyll Territorial Army Association; Pres., Scottish Salmon Angling Federation; Memb. of Departmental Committee on Valuation of Sheep Stocks in Scotland, 1933-34; Member Perthshire County Council, 1941-45; J.P. Perthshire and Argyllshire; D.L. Perthshire, 1937; owns Kilchurn Castle, Argyll, and Finlarig Castle, Perthshire; owned 365,000 acres. *Recreations:* hunting, shooting, golf. *Heir:* *s.* Lord Glenorchy. *Address:* Invereil House, Dirleton, East Lothian. *T.:* North Berwick 194. *Club:* New (Edinburgh). [*Died* 5 *May* 1959.

BREADNER, Air Chief Marshal Lloyd Samuel, C.B. 1943; D.S.C. 1917; late R.C.A.F.; *b.* 14 July 1894; *s.* of Samuel Breadner and Caroline Alberta Watkins; *m.* 1917, Mary Evelyn, *d.* of Thos. Story; three *d.* *Educ.:* Public School, Ottawa; Collegiate Institute, Ottawa. Served European War, 1915-19; at R.A.F. Staff College, 1927; Imperial Defence College, 1935; Chief of the Air Staff, 1940-43; A.O.C.-in-C., R.C.A.F., Oversea, 1943-45; retired, 1945. *Address:* Larrimac Links, Kirks Ferry, Quebec. [*Died* 14 *March* 1952.

BREBNER, John Bartlet, M.A., B.Litt; Ph.D. (Columbia); F.R.Hist.S; Professor of History, Columbia University, New York, since 1942, Gouverneur Morris Professor since 1954; *b.* 1895; *s.* of James Brebner and Frances Elizabeth Bartlet; *m.* Adele Mary Rumpf; one *s.* *Educ.:* University College, Toronto (Edward Blake Scholar); St. John's College, Oxford (Exhibitioner); Columbia University, New York. Military service, 1915-18; Lecturer in Modern History, University of Toronto, 1921-25; instructor in History, Columbia University, 1925-27; Assistant Professor of History, Columbia Univ., 1927-35; Associate Professor of History, Columbia Univ., 1935-42; William A. Dunning Fellow, 1932-33 (Columbia Univ.); Assistant to Director of Division of Economics and History, Carnegie Endowment for International Peace, in its investigation of, and publications concerning Canadian-American relations, 1932-44, Pres. Canadian Historical Assoc., 1939-40; Hon. Life Member, Nova Scotia Historical Soc.; Hon. Member The New Brunswick Museum. Pitt Prof., and Fell. St. John's Coll., Cambridge, 1954-55. Litt.D. (hon.) Brown University, 1944; LL.D. (hon.) McGill, 1954; Litt.D. (Hon.) Univ. of Toronto, 1957. Tyrrell Medal, Royal Society of Canada, 1950. *Publications:* New England's Outpost, 1927; The Explorers of North America, 1933, new edn., 1955 (Die Erforscher von Nordamerika, an abridged translation, Leipzig, 1936); The Neutral Yankees of Nova Scotia, 1937; The Making of Modern Britain, 1943 (Grossbritannien Von Heute: wie es entstand, Düsseldorf, 1946); North Atlantic Triangle: the Interplay of Canada, the United States, and Great Britain, 1945; Scholarship for Canada: the Function of Graduate Studies, 1945; editorial work: completed late M. L. Hansen's The Mingling of the Canadian and American Peoples, I., Historical, 1940; chapters and articles in a number of books and encyclopædias, and in political and historical periodicals. *Address:* Columbia University, New York. *Clubs:* Athenæum; Century Association (New York). [*Died* 10 *Nov.* 1957.

BREITHAUPT, Hon. Louis Orville, LL.D.; Chancellor, Victoria University, Toronto, since 1959; Lieutenant-Governor, Province of Ontario, 1952-57; retired; *b.* 28 October 1890; *s.* of late Louis Jacob Breithaupt (Canadian) and Emma A. Devitt (Canadian); *m.* 1919, Sara C. Caskey; two *s.* two *d.* *Educ.:* Kitchener, Ont.; Naperville, Ill., U.S.A.; Toronto University. Hon. LL.D. from various Universities. Joined tanneries of Breithaupt

Leather Co. Ltd.; 47 yrs. in various depts. of business: eventually President of Company. President Whitehall Apartments Ltd.; Director: Economical Mutual Insurance Co.; Equitable Life Insurance Co. of Canada; Missisquoi and Rouville Ins. Co.; Corporate Investors Ltd.; Canada Trust; Huron and Erie. Alderman, Kitchener, 1919-23; Mayor of Kitchener, 1923, 1924; M.P. for N. Waterloo, 1940-52 (Chm. of Standing Cttee. on Rlys., Canals and Telegraph Lines; member of Parl. Committee on External Affairs and Banking and Commerce). Hon. Governor of McMaster Univ.; Hon. Director: Kitchener-Waterloo Y.M.C.A.; Life Member: Toronto Board of Trade; Kitchener Chamber of Commerce (Pres. 1938 and 1939); Past Pres. Kitchener-Waterloo Sales and Advertising Club; former Dir. Canadian Chamber of Commerce; Past Pres. Tanners Section, Toronto Bd. of Trade and Tanners Assoc. of Canada; Hon. Patron Ont. Div. of Red Cross; Hon. Member Toronto and Kitchener-Waterloo Rotary Club. *Recreations:* golf, swimming, boating, ski-ing, curling. *Address:* 152 Forest Hill Rd., Toronto, Ont., Canada. *T.:* Hu 5-4086. *Clubs:* Royal Canadian Yacht, Granite, National (Toronto); Rideau, Royal Ottawa Golf (Ottawa); Seigniory, Governor (Montebello, P.Q.); Granite (Kitchener, Ont.). [*Died* 6 *Dec.* 1960.

BRENAN, Sir John (Fitzgerald), K.C.M.G., *cr.* 1932 (C.M.G. 1927); *b.* 29 July 1883; *s.* of late E. V. Brenan, Chinese Maritime Customs; *m.* Kathleen, *d.* of late W. Kemble, I.C.S.; no *c.* *Educ.:* Denstone College; Switzerland. Student Interpreter in Siam, 1903; transferred to China, 1905; 2nd class assistant, 1910; called to Bar, Middle Temple, 1913; acting Vice-Consul and Pro-Consul at Tientsin, 1913 and 1914; Pro-Consul at Foochow, 1914-16; Peking; 1st class assistant, 1917; served with Chinese Labour Corps in France, 1917; resumed work in China, 1918; acting Consul at Nanking, 1919-20; one of H.M. Vice-Consuls in China, 1920; acting Commercial Secretary at Peking 1922; acting Consul at Shanghai, 1922-26; acting Consul-General, Canton, China, 1926-29; Consul General, Shanghai, China, 1929-37; Adviser on Chinese Affairs F.O., 1937-43; retired, 1943. *Address:* Manor Cottage, Wadhurst, Sussex. [*Died* 11 *Jan.* 1953.

BRENCHLEY, Winifred Elsie, O.B.E. 1948; D.Sc. (Lond.), F.L.S., F.R.E.S.; Head of Botanical Department, Rothamsted Experimental Station, 1907-48; *b.* 10 Aug. 1883. *Educ.:* James Allen's School, Dulwich; Swanley Horticultural College; University College, London. B.Sc. 1905; D.Sc. 1911; Gilchrist Studentship for University Women, 1906-7; Fellow of University College, London. *Publications:* Inorganic Plant Poisons and Stimulants, 2nd edition, 1927; Weeds of Farm Land, 1921; Manuring of Grassland for Hay, 1924; (with H. C. Long) Suppression of Weeds by Fertilisers and Chemicals, 3rd edn., 1949; various scientific papers, chiefly on weeds, ecology, plant physiology and nutrition, published in the Phil. Trans., Annals Botany, Annals Applied Biology, Journal Ecology, New Phytologist, Journal Linnæan Society, Journal Institute of Brewing, Journal Agricultural Science, etc. *Recreations:* philately, gardening. *Address:* Rothamsted Experimental Station, and 10 Clarence Road, Harpenden. [*Died* 27 *Oct.* 1953.

BRENTFORD, 2nd Viscount, *cr.* 1929, **Richard Cecil Joynson-Hicks,** Bart., *cr.* 1919; *b.* 15 Nov. 1896; *er. s.* of 1st Viscount and Grace Lynn (*d.* 1952), *o. d.* of late Richard Hampson Joynson, J.P., of Chasefield, Bowdon; *S.* father, 1932; *m.* 1st, 1920, Evelyn Mary Rothery (*d.* 1954), *o. d.* of late J. F. McNellan, Dollar, Scotland; 2nd, 1955, Mrs. Grace McNellan, Rustenburg, Transvaal, South Africa. *Educ.:* Harrow; Sandhurst. Served European War, 1914-18, 1st Bn. The Queen's Royal Regt. (wounded); A.D.C. Governor-General, Jamaica, 1916; A.D.C. to G.O.C. 17th Div. B.E.F., 1916-17; attached R.F.C. and R.A.F. 1917-19; Reserve of Officers, 1920; 1939-44 served as Staff Officer in England. *Recreations:* travel, fishing, golf. *Heir:* *b.* Hon. Sir Lancelot William Joynson-Hicks, Bt. *Clubs:* Royal Aero, Carlton. [*Died* 27 *June* 1958.

BRERETON, Brevet Lieut.-Col. Frederick Sadleir, C.B.E. 1919; J.P.; late R.A.M.C., late attached Scots Guards; M.R.C.S., L.R.C.P., M.D. Brux.; *b.* 5 Aug. 1872; *s.* of Franc Sadleir Brereton, late 2nd Bn. 60th Rifles, and Isabella Beeston; *m.* 1898, Ethel Mary Lamb (*d.* 1948), of Eskdale, Birkdale; one *s.* one *d.*; *m.* 1953, Isobel Jessie Murdoch. *Educ.:* Cranleigh; Guy's Hospital. Gazetted Surg.-Lieut. Army Medical Staff, 1896, obtaining first place in competitive entrance examination, and Martin Gold Medal for Medicine and Parke's Medal for Hygiene at Netley; gazetted attached Surgeon to 2nd Scots Guards, 1898, served with Guards until retd., 1902; served S. African War; Capt. 1898; rejoined, 1914; Bt. Lt.-Col. 1919; Commander Crown of Italy; Commander Order of Avis (Portugal). *Publications:* The Great War and the R.A.M.C.; With Shield and Assegai, Zulu War; With Rifle and Bayonet, Boer War, 1900; A Gallant Grenadier, Crimea; The Dragon of Pekin, Boxer revolt; In the King's Service, Cromwell in Ireland; One of the Fighting Scouts, Boer War, 1901; In the Grip of the Mullah, Somaliland; Foes of the Red Cockade, French Revolution; A Hero of Lucknow, Indian Mutiny; With the Dyaks of Borneo; Under the Spangled Banner, Spanish-American War; A Knight of St. John, a tale of the Siege of Malta; A Soldier of Japan; With French at the Front; On the Field of Waterloo; Hemel Hempstead through the Ages, etc. *Recreations:* genealogy, motoring, carpentering, etc. *Address:* Heath Barn, Hemel Hempstead, Herts. *Club:* Authors'. [*Died* 12 *Aug.* 1957.

BRESSEY, Sir Charles Herbert, Kt., *cr.* 1935; C.B. 1930; C.B.E. 1924; D.Sc. (Eng.); D.L.; late Bn. Commander Essex Home Guard; Army Welfare Officer; past President Chartered Surveyors' Institution, and of Junior Institution of Engineers, (Inc.); Past Chm., Road Engineering Industry Committee, British Standards Institution; Hon. Member Institution of Royal Engineers, of Town-planning Institute, of Institution of Municipal and County Engineers and of Institute of Highway Engineers; Member of Permanent International Commission of Road Congresses; *b.* 3 Jan. 1874; *s.* of John T. Bressey, Wanstead, Essex; *m.* 1902, L. Margaret F. Hill; two *s.* *Educ.:* Bremen; Rouen; Forest School, Walthamstow. Served European War, France, Flanders (Lt.-Col. R.E.) (O.B.E., Chevalier Légion d'Honneur); Member Inter-Allied Commission, Rhine Province Communications; Divisional Road Engineer (London), Ministry of Transport, 1919; Chief Engineer, 1921-28; Principal Technical Officer, 1928-35; prepared for Minister of Transport, Highway Development Survey of Greater London, 1935-1938, report published 1938. *Address:* 3 Fernbank, Church Rd., Buckhurst Hill, Essex. *T.:* Buckhurst 2553. [*Died* 14 *April* 1951.

BRETT, Cyril Templeton, C.I.E. 1931; *b.* 23 July 1885; *s.* of late D. J. Brett, Mysore, India; *m.* 1917, Phyllis Mary, *d.* of late Henry John Bell, Dacca, India; three *s.* Deputy Inspector-General of Police, Bihar and Orissa, 1930-38, Inspector-General of Police, 1938-40; retired. *Address:* Sandygate, Elphinstone Road, Highcliffe, Hants. [*Died* 27 *Aug.* 1960.

BRETT, Lieut.-Col. John Aloysius, C.I.E. 1925; *b.* 20 June 1879; *s.* of late

John Henry Brett; *m.* 1910, Alice Fitz-gerald, *d.* of late R. J. Taaffe, M.D.; one *s.* two *d.* *Educ.:* Mount St. Mary's College; Trinity College, Dublin, B.A. Assistant Commissioner, Mardan, 1917; Deputy Commissioner, Hazara, 1918; Political Officer, Dir, Swat, and Chitral, Joint Deputy Commissioner, Peshawar, and Deputy Commissioner, Kohat, 1919; Anglo-Afghan Trade Commission, 1922; Political Agent, Khyber, 1923; Political Agent, Quetta, 1927; Political Agent in Kalat and Political Agent in charge of Bolan Pass, 1929-31; Revenue and Judicial Commissioner, Baluchistan, 1931-33; Retired, 1934; Vice-President Regency Council Cooch Behar, 1934-1936. *Club:* Naval and Military.

[*Died* 7 *Jan.* 1955.

BRETT YOUNG, Francis; *see* Young, F. B.

BREWIS, Captain Charles Richard Wynn, C.B.E. 1920; R.N., retired; *b.* Ibstone House, Stokenchurch, Bucks, 7 Oct. 1874; *s.* of Samuel Richard Brewis and Frances Caroline Williams Wynn; *m.* 1900, Corry Jeannette (*d.* 1946), *d.* of Hon. Wm. Crosby, Hobart, Tasmania; one *s.* four *d.* *Educ.:* Stubbington House. H.M.S. Britannia, 1888; Commander, 1908; Captain R.N., retired 1918; employed by Australian Government to report upon the Lighting of Australian Coast, 1911-13; Principal Naval Transport Officer, Australia; Commanded 2nd Australian Convoy, 1914-15; Captain, R.A.N., 1914-20; District Naval Officer, Victoria, Australia, 1920-23. *Publications:* Reports upon the Coastal Lighting of Australia, 1912-1913. *Recreation:* boat sailing. *Address:* Tuffs Hard, Bosham-Hoe, Sussex. *T.:* Bosham 2140. [*Died* 31 *Jan.* 1953.

BRIANT, His Honour Judge Bruce Edgar Dutton, Q.C. 1953; Judge of County Courts, Circuit No. 50 (Sussex), since 1954; Deputy-Chairman West Sussex Quarter Sessions since 1953; *b.* 31 July 1895; 7th *s.* of Frederick Arthur Dutton Briant, Brighton; unmarried. *Educ.:* Brighton Grammar School. Served European War, 1914-18: Inns of Court O.T.C.; Machine Gun Corps, Lt., France and Mesopotamia. Called to Bar, Middle Temple, 1925; S.E. Circuit. F.C.I.I. 1922. *Address:* The Wood, Spotted Cow Lane, Buxted, Sussex. *T.:* Buxted 3141; 1 Crown Office Row, Temple, E.C.4. *Club:* National Liberal.

[*Died* 15 *Aug.* 1959.

BRICE, Rev. Edward Henry; Canon Emeritus of Gloucester Cathedral since 1948. Vicar of Coleford, 1902-27; Rural Dean of South Forest, 1909-27; Vicar of Barnwood, Gloucester, 1927-35; Hon. Canon of Gloucester, 1916-35, Residentiary, 1935-48. *Address:* The Old House, 30 Barnwood Road, Gloucester. [*Died* 23 *Sept.* 1952.

BRIDGE, Joseph James Rabnett, C.B.E. 1920; *b.* 8 June 1875; *s.* of Joseph Bridge, artist, of Shrewsbury, and Marian Rabnett, of Birmingham; *m.* 1905, Kathleen, *e. d.* of late Thomas O'Shaughnessy of Bruff, Co. Limerick; one *d.* *Educ.:* Shrewsbury School (scholar); Gonville and Caius College, Cambridge (scholar). Powis Medal, 1896; scholarship at Trinity College, Dublin, 1896; First Class Classical Tripos, Cambridge, 1897; Senior Classical Master, Stonyhurst College, 1897-1900; Professor of English Literature, Calcutta University, 1900-1; Junior Inspector Board of Education, 1901; H.M. Inspector (Elementary), 1903; (Secondary), 1905; Survey of Secondary Education in Ceylon, 1911; Secretary War Office Appeals Committee, 1915-19; Civil Adviser to the War Office on Educational Training, 1921-22; H.M. Inspector (Divisional) of Schools; retired 1936; Jt. Hon. Sec. Classical Assoc. 1938-48, Vice-Pres., 1948. *Address:* Mutcombe, 34 Fairfield Park Rd., Bath. *T.:* Bath 2374. [*Died* 6 *Nov.* 1959.

BRIDGES, Colonel Arthur Holroyd, C.B. 1924; C.I.E. 1921; D.S.O. 1917; *b.* 21 April 1871; *s.* of H. W. Bridges of Birch, Essex, and of Frances Matilda, *d.* of Gen. J. Griffith, R.A.; *m.* 1910, Dorothea, *d.* of late W. H. Seth-Smith, Reigate; two *s.* two *d.* *Educ.:* Blundell's School, Tiverton; R.M.C., Sandhurst. Appointed 68th (Durham) Light Infantry, 1891; transferred to Indian Staff Corps, 1892; served in 9th Bombay Infantry and from 1896 in 16th Bombay Infantry; attached 68th (Durham) Light Infantry Jan. to Dec. 1900 in South Africa, Relief of Ladysmith and Operations in Natal and Transvaal (Queen's medal and four clasps, Brevet Majority); Jubaland (East Africa) Expedition, 1901 (medal); Staff College Camberley, 1903-4; Staff at Army Headquarters, Aden and Burma, 1905-11; on deputation to Australia, General Staff and Director of Military Art, R.M.C. Duntroon, 1913-15; Australian Imperial Force, G.S.O. (1), 1st and 2nd Australian Division in Egypt and France, 1915-17; commanded 116th Mahrattas, Mesopotamia, 1918-20; commanded 53rd Infantry Brigade during Arab Revolution, 1920-21; G.S.O.(1) Rawalpindi District, 1921-25 (Belgian Croix de Guerre, Bt. Lt.-Col., D.S.O., C.I.E., despatches six times); retired, 1925. *Address:* 15 Dunsford Place, Bath. *T.:* Bath 3542.

[*Died* 7 *May* 1953.

BRIDGES, Sir Ernest Arthur, Kt., *cr.* 1945; retired Commodore Capt., Royal Mail Lines Ltd.; relieving Capt. Royal Mail Lines Ltd., London; *b.* 17 Aug. 1880; *s.* of Frederic Bridges and Annie Maria Turner; *m.* 1910, Agnes Ida Conyers; three *s.* *Educ.:* Surrey House School, Margate; King's Coll. School, Strand, London. Served as a Cadet in Shaw Saville & Albion's ship Zelandia, 1898-1902; joined Royal Mail Lines, 1902; served in R.N.R. 1915-18, Commander 1917-1918; rejoined Royal Mail 1919 in Command. Trooping, 1939-43. Retired Commodore Master Royal Mail Lines, 1943. *Address:* 47 St. Michael's Road, Bedford. *T.:* Bedford 2185. *Clubs:* Seven Seas, Bedfordshire Golf, Bedford County Cricket (Bedford).

[*Died* 22 *Feb.* 1953.

BRIDGES, Colonel Francis Doveton, C.M.G. 1918; late R.M.L.I.; *b.* 1871; *m.* 1896, Alice (*d.* 1951), *d.* of William de Smidt, Stowel Lodge, Rondebosch, S. Africa. *Educ.:* All Saints' School, Bloxham. Served Benin Expedition, 1897 (medal and clasp); European War, 1914-18 (C.M.G.); retired, 1921. *Address:* The Outspan, Kommetje Road, Fish Hoek, Cape, S. Africa.

[*Died* 11 *Jan.* 1954.

BRIDGES, Rear-Admiral Henry Dalrymple, of Fedderate, Aberdeenshire, C.V.O. 1925; D.S.O. 1916; D.L.; *b.* 1881; 2nd *s.* of late John H. Bridges, of Ewell Court and Langshott, Horley, Surrey, and of Fedderate, Aberdeenshire; *m.* 1927, Aileen Mary, 2nd *d.* of late Charles Innes, Victoria, British Columbia; two *s.* Entered R.N. 1897; Lieut. 1902; Comdr. 1915; Capt. 1921; Rear-Adm. 1933; served in China Campaign Boxer insurrection, 1900; European War, 1914-18 (despatches, D.S.O.); commanded H.M.S. Curlew during tour of Prince of Wales in South America, 1925; retired list, 1933; an A.D.C. to H.M., 1933; Commodore of Convoys, 1939-40. D.L. Aberdeenshire. *Address:* Bonnykelly Lodge, New Pitsligo, Aberdeenshire. *Clubs:* United Service, Royal Northern (Aberdeen).

[*Died* 1 *Feb.* 1955.

BRIDGES, Roy; novelist, historian and journalist; *b.* Hobart, Tasmania, 23 March 1885; *s.* of S. Bridges, Hobart, and L. J. Wood, of Sorell, Tasmania; unmarried. *Educ.:* Queen's College, Hobart; University, Tasmania; B.A. Member of Literary Staff of The Age, Melbourne, 1909-25. Australian Commonwealth Literary Fellowship, 1944-45. *Novels:* The Barb of an Arrow, 1909; By His Excellency's Command, 1910; Mr.

Barrington, 1911; On His Majesty's Service 1914; The Fugitive, 1914; The Fires of Hate, 1915; The Bubble Moon, 1915; Dead Men's Gold, 1916; Merchandise, 1918; The Black House, 1920; The Fenceless Ranges, 1920; The Vats of Tyre, 1921; Rogues' Haven, 1922; The Cards of Fortune, 1922; Green Butterflies, 1923; Rats' Castle, By Mountain Tracks, 1924; Gates of Birth, 1926; A Mirror of Silver, 1927; Through Another Gate, 1927; Legion: For We Are Many, 1928; And All That Beauty, 1929; Negrohead, 1930; Trinity, 1931; Cloud, 1932; Soul from the Sword, 1933; These Were Thy Merchants, 1935; The House of Fendon, 1936; Sullivan's Bay, 1937; The Alden Case, 1937; This House is Haunted, 1939; Old Admiral Death, 1940; The Owl is Abroad, 1941; The Case for Mrs. Heydon, 1944; The League of the Lord, 1950; Youth Triumphant, 1951. *Short Stories:* The Immortal Dawn, 1917. *History:* From Silver to Steel, The Romance of the Broken Hill Proprietary, 1920; One Hundred Years: The Romance of the Victorian People, 1934; "That Yesterday was Home": the Romance of a Tasmanian Farm, 1948. *Recreation:* walking. *Address:* Wood's Farm, Sorell, Tasmania.

[*Died* 14 *March* 1952.

BRIDGFORD, Brig.-General Robert James, C.B. 1918; C.M.G. 1915; D.S.O. 1900; J.P., D.L. Co. Hereford; late King's Shropshire Light Infantry; *b.* 10 Mar. 1869; *s.* of late Sir Robert Bridgford, K.C.B., J.P., D.L., of Upper Newton, Kinnersley, Herefordshire; *m.* 1898, Mary Constance, *d.* of Ven. Frederic Charles Hamilton; (one *d.* decd.). *Educ.:* Charterhouse. Joined Army, 1889; Capt., 1898; served S. Africa, 1899-1900, including defence of Ladysmith (despatches, D.S.O.); European War, 1914-18; temp. Major-General, commanded 31st Division, March 1918; transferred to command 32nd Division, April 1918 (despatches seven times, wounded, C.M.G., prom. Colonel, C.B.); retired pay, 1922. *Address:* Stansbach, Staunton-on-Arrow, Leominster, Herefordshire.

[*Died* 22 *April* 1954.

BRIDIE, James, (O. H. Mavor), C.B.E. 1946; playwright; *b.* Glasgow, 3 Jan. 1888; *s.* of H. A. Mavor and Janet Osborne; *m.* Rona Bremner; two *s.* *Educ.:* Glasgow Academy; University of Glasgow. Served with R.A.M.C., 1914-19 and 1939-42; Hon. Consulting Physician, Victoria Infirmary, Glasgow; for a time professor of medicine in the Anderson Coll., Glasgow; LL.D. (Glasgow, 1939); M.D., F.R.F.P.S.; F.R.S.L.; Member of Council, League of Dramatists; Chm., Glasgow Citizens' Theatre Ltd., etc. First London play, The Anatomist, 1931; followed by Tobias and the Angel, 1931; Jonah and the Whale, 1932; A Sleeping Clergyman, 1933; Marriage is no Joke, 1934; Mary Read, 1934; The Black Eye, 1935; Storm in a Teacup (with Bruno Frank), 1936; Susannah and the Elders, 1938; King of Nowhere, 1938; The Last Trump, 1938; What Say They ?, 1939; The Golden Legend of Shults, 1939; Holy Isle, 1942; Mr. Bolfry, 1943; It Depends What You Mean, 1944; The Forrigan Reel, 1944; Lancelot, 1946; John Knox, 1947; Dr. Angelus, 1947; Daphne Laureola, 1949; Gog and Magog, 1949; Mr. Gillie, 1950; The Queen's Comedy, 1950. *Publications:* Some Talk of Alexander; Sir Bingo Walker; Mr. Bridie's Alphabet for Little Glasgow Highbrows, 1934; One Way of Living, 1939; Tedious and Brief, 1945; (with Moray Maclaren) A Small Stir, 1949; and 10 books of Plays. *Address:* Rockbank, Helensburgh, Dunbartonshire. *Clubs:* Athenæum; Garrick, Savage; Western, Art (Glasgow); University (Edinburgh).

[*Died* 29 *Jan.* 1951.

BRIERLY, James Leslie, C.B.E. 1946 (O.B.E. 1919); J.P.; D.C.L.; Dr. Juris (hon. causa), Oslo University; hon. LL.D. Chicago and Manchester Universities; *b.* 9 Sept. 1881; *e. s.* of Sydney Herbert Brierly and Emily Sykes, of Huddersfield; *m.* 1920, Ada, *e. d.* of J. C. Foreman; one *s.* *Educ.:* Charterhouse; Brasenose College, Oxford (Scholar). Fellow of All Souls Coll., 1906-13 and 1922-47, and of Trinity Coll., 1913-20; Barrister-at-Law, Lincoln's Inn, 1907; Prof. of Law, Manchester Univ., 1920-23, of International Law, Oxford Univ., 1922-47, and of International Relations, Edinburgh Univ., 1948-51. Second Lieut., Wiltshire Regiment, 1914; on staff of Adjutant-General, War Office; D.A.A.G., Army of the Black Sea; Brevet Major, 1919; Member of Hebdomadal Council, 1929-35; Curator of University Chest, 1932-35; Delegate of Univ. Press, 1923-50; formerly Chm., several Wages and Joint Industrial Councils and of U.N. International Law Commission, and a frequent broadcaster on international subjects; member of Institut de droit international. *Publications:* books and articles on legal subjects, chiefly on International Law. *Address:* 6 Brookside, Headington, Oxford.

[*Died* 20 *Dec.* 1955.

BRIFFA, Colonel Alfred, C.M.G. 1918; late Malta Civil Service; *b.* 1868; *s.* of late Henry Briffa, M.D. *Educ.:* St. Ignatius' College, Malta. Served in the King's Own Malta Regiment of Militia, 1889-1919; commanded a Batt. of the same regiment, 1910-19; C.M.G. for valuable services during European War. *Address:* 42 Victoria Avenue, Sliema, Malta. *Clubs:* Casino Maltese, Garrison Library (Malta).

[*Died* 28 *July* 1952.

BRIGGS, Admiral Sir Charles John, K.C.B., *cr.* 1913; *b.* 15 July 1858; *m.* 1901, Frances, *e. d.* of Vice.-Adm. W. Wilson, of Clyffe-Pypard, Wilts; two *s.* three *d.* Entered Navy, 1872; Commander 1892; Captain, 1897; Rr.-Adm. 1907; Rear-Admiral in 1st Division of the Home Fleet, 1909; a Lord of the Admiralty and Controller of the Navy, 1910-12; Vice-Admiral commanding 4th Squadron Home Fleet, 1912-1914; Admiral, 1916; retired, 1917. *Address:* Biddestone, Chippenham, Wilts. *T.:* Corsham 2233.

[*Died* 16 *July* 1951.

BRIGGS, Rev. Canon George Wallace; Canon Emeritus of Worcester Cathedral since 1956 (Canon of Worcester, 1934-56; Vice-Dean, 1944-55), *b.* 1875; *s.* of George Briggs; *m.* 1909, Constance, *d.* of B. B. Barrow; two *s.* three *d.* *Educ.:* Emmanuel College, Cambridge. 1st Class Classical Tripos. Chaplain, Royal Navy (six years); Classical and Theological Tutor, London College of Divinity; Vicar of St. Andrew's, Norwich, 1909-18; Rector of Loughborough, 1918-34; Canon of Leicester, 1927-34; Select Preacher, Cambridge, 1920 and 1943; Proctor in Convocation, 1925-35. *Publications:* Editor (with Percy Dearmer, Ralph Vaughan Williams, and Martin Shaw) of Prayers and Hymns for use in Schools; Prayers and Hymns for Junior Schools; Prayers and Hymns for Little Children; The Daily Service; The Children's Church: Daily Prayer, etc. (with Eric Milner-White); The Daily Reading; The Shorter Oxford Bible (with G. B. Caird and Nathaniel Micklem). *Address:* The Moorings, Hindhead, Surrey.

[*Died* 30 *Dec.* 1959.

BRIGGS, Lieut.-General Sir Harold Rawdon, K.C.I.E., *cr.* 1947; K.B.E., *cr.* 1952 (C.B.E. 1945); C.B. 1946; D.S.O. 1941; I.A. retd.; *b.* 14 July 1894; *s.* of late Henry E. Briggs; *m.* 1940, Irene Mona Wood, Broadstone, Dorset; one *s.* one *d.* by first marriage. *Educ.:* Bedford School; Royal Military College, Sandhurst. Gazetted I.A. 1914; attached 4th Bn. King's Regt. and joined 31st Punjab Regt. 1915; European War, 1914-18, France, Mesopotamia, and Palestine; joined Baluch

Regt. 1923; Waziristan 1930 campaign; commanded 2nd Bn. Baluch Regt. 1937-40; commanded 7th Indian Infantry Brigade in Eritrea and Western Desert, 1940-42 (despatches, D.S.O. and bar); commanded 5th Indian Division in Western Desert, Iraq and Burma, 1942-44 (despatches, 2nd bar to D.S.O., C.B.E.); G.O.C.-in-C., Burma Command, 1946-Jan. 1948; Director of Operations, Federation of Malaya, 1950-51. *Address:* Limassol, Cyprus. [*Died* 27 *Oct.* 1952.

BRIGGS, Colonel Norman, C.I.E. 1946; Indian Medical Service (retired); *b.* 12 Nov. 1891; *s.* of Henry Hunter Briggs, Kingston-upon-Hull; *m.* 1925, Olive Margaret, *d.* of H. Irving Bell, Eastbourne. *Educ.:* Hymer's College, Hull; University of Leeds; University College Hospital, London. Served European War, 1914-18, with R.A.M.C. and I.M.S.; entered I.M.S., 1917; Director of Health Services and Inspector-General of Prisons, Sind, India, 1936-41; Inspector-General Civil Hospitals, United Provinces, India, 1943-47; retired, 1947. K.H.S. 1946; C.St.J. 1947. *Address:* Woodlands, Sandy Cross, Heathfield, Sx. *T.:* Heathfield 145. [*Died* 3 *March* 1960.

BRIGGS, Brigadier Rawdon, C.B.E. 1945; D.S.O. 1918; M.C. 1916; Deputy Lieutenant of Cambridgeshire; Member of Cambridgeshire County Council; *b.* 21 April 1892; *s.* of H. E. Briggs, Birstwith Hall, Yorks, and Georgeina, *d.* of C. T. Tunnard, Frampton House, Lincs.; *m.* 1923, Esther, 2nd *d.* of J. T. Keily, Carrickmines; two *d.* *Educ.:* Bedford School. Served European War, 1914-18 (despatches, M.C., D.S.O.); War of 1939-45 (C.B.E., Officer Legion of Honour, Croix de Guerre with palms; U.S. Legion of Merit, U.S.S.R. Order of the Red Banner); retired Dec. 1945. *Recreation:* fishing. *Address:* The Mill House, Shepreth, Cambs. [*Died* 3 *Sept.* 1960.

BRIGGS, Waldo Raven, O.B.E. 1919; M.A., LL.B.; Stipendiary Magistrate for Huddersfield since 1931; *b.* 7 Aug. 1883; *yr. s.* of late George Briggs (Alderman of City of London, 1917-24) and Mary, *d.* of late Alexander McMorran. *Educ.:* Private School (London); Germany, France; Christ's College, Cambridge. Called to Bar, Middle Temple, 1906; Prosecuting Counsel to Post Office on South-Eastern Circuit, 1923-31. Served European War, Inns of Court O.T.C. (company sergeant-major), France, 1916-19, Staff, Third Army H.Q. as Courts Martial Officer and Staff Captain (despatches twice, O.B.E.). *Address:* 9 Imperial Road, Huddersfield; 2 Garden Court, Temple, E.C.4. *Clubs:* United University; Huddersfield (Huddersfield). [*Died* 7 *Jan.* 1956.

BRIGGS, Colonel William Hilton; Chairman Benskin's Watford Brewery Ltd.; *b.* 13 June 1871; 3rd *s.* of late Col. Charles James Briggs, J.P., D.L., of Hylton Castle, Co. Durham; *m.* 1904, Doris Kathleen, *d.* of late Thomas Benskin, 78 Mount Street, W.1.; one *s.* (*er. s.*, Commander R.N., died on active service Jan. 1943) two *d.* *Educ.:* Rugby. Served S. African War, 1899-1902, with D.L.I. and Mounted Infantry (despatches); European War, 1914-19, commanding 4th Special Reserve Durham Light Infantry (despatches); Bt. Col. 1918; also employed Headquarters Eastern and Irish Commands; Group Commander Herts Home Guard, 1940-1941; D.L. Herts; High Sheriff Herts, 1943. *Address:* Brickendon Grange, near Hertford. *T.:* Bayford 228. *Club:* Carlton. [*Died* 12 *Aug.* 1951.

BRIGHOUSE, Harold; Writer of Plays and Fiction; *b.* Eccles, Lancs, 26 July 1882. *War Service,* R.A.F., attached Intelligence Staff, Air Ministry; literary staff, (retd.), Manchester Guardian; Chairman Dramatic Committee, Authors' Society, 1930-31. *Publications: plays:* Dealing in Futures, 1909; Graft, 1911; The Odd Man Out, 1912; The Game, 1913; Garside's Career, 1914; The Road to Raebury, and (with Stanley Houghton), The Hillarys, 1915; Hobson's Choice, and The Clock Goes Round, 1916; Other Times; a volume of Three Lancashire Plays (The Game, The Northerners, Zack), 1920; Mary's John, 1924; What's Bred in the Bone, 1927; Safe amongst the Pigs, 1929; in America, 1936, adapted Ferenc Molnar's Somebody; *one-act plays:* The Doorway and The Price of Coal, 1909; Lonesome-Like, The Oak Settle, Spring in Bloomsbury, 1911; Little Red Shoes, 1912; Followers, Converts, 1915; Maid of France, 1917; Plays for the Meadow and the Lawn, 1921; Once a Hero, 1922; The Happy Hangman, 1922; The Apple-Tree, 1923; A Marrying Man, 1924; Open-air Plays containing the Laughing Mind, The Oracles of Apollo, The Rational Princess, The Ghosts of Windsor Park, How the Weather is Made, 1926; The Night of Mr. H.; When did they Meet Again? 1927; The Little Liberty; The Witch's Daughter, 1928; The Stoker, 1930; Four Fantasies, 1931; The Wish-Shop, Smoke Screens, 1932; A Bit of War, Exhibit C, 1933; The Dye-Hard, 1934; The Great Dark; New Leisure; Back to Adam, 1935; Albert Gates, 1937; The Funk-Hole, 1938; Under the Pylon, British Passport, 1939; The Man who ignored the War, London Front, 1940; The Girl in the Tube, 1941; Hallowed Ground, 1942; Sporting Rights and The Inner Man, 1944; *novels:* Fossie for Short, and (with Charles Forrest) Hobson's, 1917; The Silver Lining, 1918; The Marbeck Inn, 1920; Hepplestalls, 1922; The Wrong Shadow, 1923; Captain Shapely, 1923; (from Stanley Houghton's play) Hindle Wakes, 1927; *autobiography:* What I Have Had, 1953; *films:* Hobson's Choice; The Game, 1920. *Recreations:* fell-walking and play-going. *Address:* 67 Parliament Hill, N.W.3. [*Died* 25 *July* 1958.

BRIGSTOCKE, Charles Reginald, C.B. 1920; *b.* 1876; *s.* of late T. E. Brigstocke, J.P., Carmarthen; *m.* Dora Constance, *d.* of late Dr. W. Bowen-Davies, Llandrindod Wells; one *s.* two *d.* *Educ.:* Llandovery School. Called to Bar, Middle Temple, 1901; entered Civil Service, 1894; passed Class I. Examination, 1902; Admiralty, 1903-18; Resident Clerk, 1905-13; Private Secretary to Fourth Sea Lord (Admirals Sir A. K. Winsloe and Sir C. Madden) and Civil Lord, 1908-13; Acting Principal Clerk, 1916; transferred to Air Ministry, 1918; Assistant Secretary, 1919; Director of Contracts, 1921-32; Principal Assistant Secretary, 1932-36; attached to Air Delegation, Versailles Peace Conference, 1919; Mission to Berne to negotiate Anglo-Swiss Flying Agreement, 1919; retired 1936. *Address:* Rozel, Church Stretton, Salop. *Club:* Union. [*Died* 7 *April* 1951.

BRINCKMAN, Major Sir Theodore Ernest Warren, 4th Bt., *cr.* 1831; *b.* 21 May 1898; *e. s.* of Col. Sir Theodore Brinckman, 3rd Bt. and late Mary Frances, *d.* of Countess of Aylesford and late Captain J. H. Linton, of Hemingford, Hunts; *S.* father 1937; *m.* 1st, 1921, Gretta, *d.* of Frances, Marchioness Conyngham, of Castle Park, Slane, Co. Meath; 2nd, 1926, Anne Margrethe, Countess Knuth, *d.* of E. T. A. Wennerwald; 3rd, 1939, Ethel Jean Peters, *d.* of Wilson Mills Southam, Rockcliffe, Ottawa. *Educ.:* Eton; Sandhurst. Capt. Household Cavalry; Major, 1945 (reserve). *Heir:* *b.* Col. Roderick Napoleon Brinckman, D.S.O., M.C. *Address:* Nairnside House, Inverness; Estanza Moeriki Cachari, Buenos Aires, S. America. *Clubs:* Naval and Military, Buck's; Travellers' (Paris). [*Died* 26 *July* 1954.

BRIND, General Sir John Edward Spencer, K.C.B., *cr.* 1936 (C.B. 1923);

K.B.E., *cr.* 1935; C.M.G. 1918; D.S.O. 1915; *b.* 9 Feb. 1878; *e. s.* of late Col. E. A. Brind, late Connaught Rangers; *g.s.* of General Sir James Brind, G.C.B.; *m.* 1907, Dorothy M. S. (*d.* 1924), *er. d.* of late Col. W. H. J. Frodsham, late E. Surrey Regt.; two *s.* one *d.* *Educ.:* Wellington College; R.M.A., Woolwich; Staff College, Camberley, 1913-14. Entered Army, 1897; Captain, 1902; Adj., 1903-6; Major, 1914; Bt. Lt.-Col., 1916; Bt. Col., 1919; Col., 1920; Maj.-Gen., 1930; Lt.-Gen., 1935; General, 1939; D.A.Q.M.G., 1914; G.S.O. (2), 1915; G.S.O.(1), 1916; Brigadier-Gen. G.S., 1917; Col. on Staff, General Staff, G.H.Q., Ireland, 1919-1923; Deputy Director at War Office, 1923-25; Col. Comdt. R.A., Aldershot Command, 1925-1927; Brigadier, General Staff, Aldershot Command, 1927-30; A.D.C. to the King, 1928-30; Major-General, Royal Artillery, India, 1930-1931; Deputy Chief of General Staff, Army Headquarters, India, 1931-33; Commander 4th Division, 1933-35; Commander-in-Chief, International Force in the Saar, 1934-35; Lieutenant of Tower of London, 1935-36; Adjutant-General in India, 1936-37; G.O.C.in-C. Southern Command, India, 1937-41; retired pay, 1941; Deputy Regional Commissioner, North Eastern Region, 1941-44. Served S. Africa, 1899-1900 (Queen's medal 2 clasps); European War, 1914-18 (despatches, D.S.O., Bt. Lieut.-Col., C.M.G., Bt. Col.). Col. Comdt. R.A., 1936-47. Legion of Honour, Croix de Guerre, France, Order of St. Maurice and St. Lazarus, Italy, Order of Aviz, Portugal. *Club:* United Service. [*Died* 14 *Oct.* 1954.

BRINTON, Lieutenant-Colonel John Chaytor, C.V.O. 1923 (M.V.O. 1905); D.S.O. 1900; formerly Gentleman Usher-in-Ordinary to H.M.; *b.* 5 April 1867; *m.* 1st, 1913, Evelyn Elizabeth (*d.* 1929), C.B.E. 1922, *e. d.* of Sir Charles Forbes, 4th Bart. of Newe, and *widow* of William D. James, of West Dean, Sussex; 2nd, 1927, Olive Mary, *o. d.* of late Arthur Eisdell. Joined 2nd Life Guards, 1891; Captain, 1899; served Soudan, 1898, including Khartoum (severely wounded, despatches, British medal, Khedive's medal with clasp); South Africa, 1899-1900, on staff of Lieut.-Gen. Sir J. D. P. French (despatches, medal with six clasps D.S.O.); Major, 1906; retired, 1911; rejoined, 1914; served European War, 1914-16 (despatches twice, Bt.Lt.-Col., Chevalier Legion of Honour). *Address:* Uplands Cross, near Ryde, Isle of Wight. *Clubs:* Turf, Royal Yacht Squadron (Cowes). [*Died* 6 *April* 1956.

BRISCO, Sir Aubrey Hylton, 6th Bt., *cr.* 1782; *b.* 11 Dec. 1873; *s.* of late Fleming Brisco, 4th *s.* of 3rd Bt., and Fanny Aubrey, *d.* of Rev. Bulkeley O. Jones, Chancellor of St. Asaph; *m.* 1904, Anna Victoria (*d.* 1929), 2nd *d.* of James Doyle, San Francisco, *niece* of late John Redmond; *S.* cousin, 1922. [Death of 5th Bt. presumed in or since 1929.] Owns about 1000 acres. *Heir:* *b.* Musgrave Wynne Brisco, *b.* 14 Feb. 1886. *Address:* Bayside, Refugio, Texas. [*Died* 16 *June* 1957.

BRISCOE, Sir Charlton; *see* Briscoe, Sir J. C.

BRISCOE, Hugh Kynaston, C.S.I. 1931; C.I.E. 1921; *b.* 1879; *b.* of Sir Charlton Briscoe, *q.v.*; *m.* 1919, Noel, *d.* of John E. Worrall; one *s.* three *d.* *Educ.:* Bedford School; Pembroke College, Oxford, M.A. Entered I.C.S., 1903; Chief Secretary, Bihar and Orissa, 1927; Acting Member, Executive Council, 1930; retired, 1933. *Address:* Ryecroft, Mayfield Road, Weybridge, Surrey. *T.:* Weybridge 4397. [*Died* 6 *July* 1956.

BRISCOE, Sir (John) Charlton, 3rd Bt., *cr.* 1910; M.D., F.R.C.P.; Fellow King's College, London, 1925; Consulting Physician to King's College Hospital; Consulting Physician to the Evelina Hospital for Sick Children; Consulting Physician to St. John and Elizabeth Hospital; Emeritus Lecturer on Medicine, King's College Hospital; *b.* Apr. 1874; 2nd *s.* of Sir J. J. Briscoe, 1st Bt., and Ellen (*d.* 1910), *o. d.* of A. Charlton, Oak House, Altrincham; *S.* brother, 1921; *m.* 1909, Grace Maud, M.B., B.S., J.P., F.S.A., *d.* of late Rev. S. Stagg; two *s.* *Educ.:* Harrow; King's College and Hospital; Göttingen. Entrance Scholarship, King's Coll., 1892; first year Scholarship, 1893; Anatomy and Physiology prizes, 1894; Leathes prize, 1894; Warneford Scholarship, 1895; Prosector to Royal College of Surgeons, 1896; M.R.C.S., L.R.C.P., 1898; Assistant House Physician, and House Physician to King's College Hospital, 1898-99; Medical Registrar, King's College Hospital, 1900-2; M.B. Lond., honours in medicine, and M.R.C.P. 1902; Medical tutor, King's College Hospital, 1903-8; Physician to out-patients, Evelina Hospital, 1903; Censor Royal College of Physicians, 1930-32 and 1933-34; M.D. London, 1903; F.R.C.P. London, 1910; Lieutenant University London, O.T.C. Med. Section, 1909-12; Major R.A.M.C. 1917; Vice-Pres. Special Medical Board for Shell-Shock, etc., Ministry of Pensions, 1918; Examiner in Medicine Royal Society Apothecaries, 1912, and Royal College of Physicians; Fellow and late Hon. Sec., President Medical Section, Royal Society of Medicine; Medical member Committee of Management, King's College Hospital, 1910; Dean of Medical School, King's College Hospital, 1910-11; Arris and Gale Lecturer, Royal College of Surgeons, 1919. *Publications:* Origin of the Complement in the Peritoneal Cavity, 1903; Rheumatoid Arthritis, 1910; Treatment of Bronchitis, 1910; Treatment of Bronchopneumonia, Latham and English Textbook of Treatment, 1912; Post-operative Massive Collapse of the Lungs, Pract. Encycl. Medicine and Surgery; Lumleian Lecturer R.C.P., 1927, The Muscular Mechanism of Respiration and its Disorders; papers in medical journals. *Recreations:* golf, shooting. *Heir:* *s.* John Leigh Charlton [*b.* 1911; *m.* 1948, Teresa Mary Violet, *d.* of late Brig.-Gen. Sir Archibald Fraser Home, K.C.V.O., C.B., C.M.G., D.S.O.; two *s.* one *d.*]. *Address:* Lakenheath Hall, Suffolk. *T.:* Lakenheath 242. [*Died* 28 *Feb.* 1960.

BRISCOE, Percy Charles; *b.* Cawnpore, India; 2nd *s.* of late Major E. J. Briscoe, Lancs. Fusl., of Ross, King's County, Ireland, and late Emma Sophia, *d.* of Rev. R. Biron, Lympne, Kent; *m.* 1911, Lucy Margaret (Anne), *o. d.* of Owen Fleming and late Lucy Pease, 3rd *d.* of John Fowler, Leeds; one *s.* one *d.* *Educ.:* Hurstpierpoint College. Planting in Ceylon 25 years, retired as Managing Director, Rahatungoda Tea Co. Served 1915-19 4th Bn. Suffolk Regt., Asst. Bde. Musketry Officer Halton Camp, 1916; Musketry Adj., Brightlingsea School of Instruction, Australians, 1917; ret. rank of Capt., 1919. High Sheriff, County of Norfolk, 1944-45. *Recreations:* shooting, fishing, edging and weeding garden paths. *Address:* Dudwick Hall, Buxton, Norfolk. *T.:* Buxton-Norwich 206. *Club:* Carlton. [*Died* 5 *Nov.* 1951.

BRISCOE, Captain Richard George; Lord Lieutenant of Cambridgeshire since 1943; *b.* 15 Aug. 1893; *s.* of late William Arthur Briscoe, Longstowe Hall, Cambridgeshire. *Educ.:* Eton; Magdalen College, Oxford. Served European War, 1914-18 (M.C.); Grenadier Guards, 1940-43; M.P. (U.) Cambridgeshire, 1923-45. *Address:* Longstowe Hall, Cambridgeshire. *Club:* Turf. [*Died* 11 *Dec.* 1957.

BRISTOL, 4th Marquis of (*cr.* 1826), **Frederick William Fane Hervey,** M.V.O. 1907; Baron Hervey, 1703; Earl of Bristol, 1714; Earl Jermyn, 1826; *b.* Dresden, 8

Nov. 1863; *e. surv. s.* of late Lord Augustus Hervey and Marianna, *d.* of W. P. Hodnett; *S.* uncle, 1907; *m.* 1896, Alice Frances Theodora, *d.* of George Wythes of Copped Hall, Epping; two *d.* *Educ.:* Tonbridge School, Eastman's R.N. Academy, and H.M.S. Britannia. Joined the Navy, 1877; midshipman, 1878; sub-lieutenant, 1882; obtained the Beaufort Testimonial at the Royal Naval College, Greenwich, 1883; specially promoted to lieutenant for meritorious examination, 1883; was lieutenant of Turquoise during operations at Suakin, 1884-85 (Egyptian medal, Khedive's bronze star); passed for gunnery lieutenant at Greenwich, 1886, receiving a special letter of commendation from the Admiralty for making a record number of marks, and obtained the £80 gun prize; promoted Commander, 1895; Captain, 1901; retired as Rear-Admiral, 1911; served at the Admiralty, 1894-97; M.P. (U.) Bury St. Edmunds, 1906-07; Chairman West Suffolk County Council, 1915-34; President of Institute of Naval Architects, 1911-16. Owns about 32,000 acres. Possesses a few good pictures, Italian, Spanish, and English Schools. *Heir: b.* Lord Herbert Hervey (*see under* 5th Marquess of Bristol). *Recreations:* shooting, cycling. *Address:* Ickworth, Bury St. Edmunds. *Club:* Carlton. [*Died* 24 *Oct.* 1951.

BRISTOL, 5th Marquess of (*cr.* 1826), **Herbert Arthur Robert Hervey;** Baron Hervey, 1703; Earl of Bristol, 1714; Earl Jermyn, 1826; *b.* 10 October 1870; *y. s.* of late Lord Augustus Hervey, M.P. and Marianna, *d.* of W. P. Hodnett; *S.* brother 1951; *m.* 1st, 1914, Lady Jean Cochrane (marriage dissolved, 1933), *d.* of 12th Earl of Dundonald; one *s.*; *m.* 2nd, 1952, Señora Dora Frances Emblim de Zulueta (*d.* 1953). *Educ.:* Clifton College. Entered Consular Service, 1892. Commercial Attaché in the Diplomatic Service, 1913; First Secretary, 1917; Minister in Colombia, 1919; in Peru and Ecuador, 1923-29; Special Ambassador for Centenary Celebration in Peru, Dec. 1924; retd., 1929; Gr. Cross of Order of Sun of Peru. Coronation Medal, 1953. *Heir: s.* Earl Jermyn. *Address:* 5 Washington House, Basil Street, S.W.3. *Clubs:* St. James', Lansdowne. [*Died* 5 *April* 1960.

BRISTOWE, Ethel Susan Graham; *b.* 13 Oct. 1866; *d.* of William Paterson, Shetland and Singapore; *m.* 1885, Sydney C., *s.* of T. Lynn Bristowe, first M.P. for Norwood; three *s.* two *d.* *Educ.:* Home. Studied painting in water colours under Claude Hayes, R.I.; Exhibited in Paris, Salon des Beaux Arts and Salons des Indépendants, also in Berlin, Rome and Stockholm; her water colours were shown in the Modern Gallery, Bond Street, 1907; gave up her painting for research work, 1914; gave two lectures on the subject she was studying at the Lyceum Club, Piccadilly, and wrote five books and four pamphlets; resumed her painting (this time with oils as her medium), 1929; held an exhibition of flowers and still life in Walker's Galleries, New Bond Street, 1934; presented small Art Gallery to Castle Douglas, 1938. *Publications:* A Marvellous Work and a Wonder, 1918; Despise not Prophecies, 1920; The Oldest Letters in the World, 1923; Sargon the Magnificent, 1927; The Man who built the Great Pyramid, 1932; Naphuria, 1936; Cain—An Argument, 1950. *Recreations:* gardening, reading, chess. *Address:* Craig, Balmaclellan, Scotland. [*Died* 2 *March* 1952.

BRITTON, Brigadier Edwin John James, C.B.E. 1937; D.S.O. 1918; retired; *b.* 28 Jan. 1880; *e. s.* of late John Britton, London; *m.* 1910, Mary (*d.* 1953), *o. d.* of late Frederick Charles Erwin, Twickenham; one *d.* (one *s.* killed on active service). *Educ.:* Royal College of Science; Dublin University. Commissioned in R.A.O.C. 1900; served European War in France and Belgium, 1915-19 (despatches thrice, D.S.O., Legion of Honour, promoted Lt.-Colonel); Waziristan, India (Indian G.S. medal); held post of Chief Inspector of Ordnance Machinery of 4th Army in France and later of Army in India; Chief Ordnance Mechanical Engineer Aldershot Command, and later Principal Ordnance Mechanical Engineer at War Office. Served throughout War of 1939-45 and finally retired Dec. 1945. *Address:* c/o Glyn, Mills & Co., Whitehall, S.W.1. [*Died* 12 *Jan.* 1955.

BRITTON, Hubert Thomas Stanley, D.Sc. (London), 1926; D.Sc. (Bristol), 1934; D.I.C., F.R.I.C.; Professor of Chemistry and Director of the Washington Singer Laboratories), University of Exeter, 1935-57, retired; Emeritus Professor, 1957; Leverhulme Research Fellow, 1957-59; *b.* 22 April 1892; *s.* of late Thomas Ernest and Clara Britton, Kingswood, Bristol; *m.* 1916, Edith Greenslade (*d.* 1959), *d.* of R. Greenslade, Bristol; one *s.* one *d.* *Educ.:* St. George Grammar School, Bristol; Merchant Venturers' School, Bristol; Bristol Univ.; King's College, University of London; Imperial College, Royal College of Science, South Kensington. Chemist in Aeronautical Inspection Directorate (Air Ministry), 1916-1920; Assistant Lecturer, University of London, King's College, 1920-23; Lecturer, Norwood Technical College, 1927-28; Lecturer, University College, Exeter, 1928-35; Fellow of Chemical Society; Member of Society for Analytical Chemistry, Soc. of Chem. Industry. *Publications:* Hydrogen Ions, their Determination and Importance in Pure and Industrial Chemistry, 1st Edn. 1929, 4th Edn. 1955; Conductometric Analysis, 1934; Chemistry, Life and Civilisation, 1930, 1940; numerous papers in Chemical Journals on Physical and Inorganic Chemistry. *Address:* 82 Gales Drive, Three Bridges, Sussex. [*Died* 30 *Dec.* 1960.

BROAD, Francis Alfred, J.P.; *b.* 1874; *s.* of William John Broad, Shepherd's Bush; *m.* 1900, Eliza, *d.* of Thomas Macer, Wormley, Herts.; three *s.* *Educ.:* Board School. Contested Edmonton, 1918. M.P. (Lab.) Edmonton, 1922-31 and 1935-45. J.P. Middlesex, 1933; Freeman of Edmonton, 1946. *Address:* 32 Hertford Road, Great Amwell, Ware, Herts. [*Died* 3 *Jan.* 1956.

BROADBENT, Walter, M.A., M.D. Cantab.; F.R.C.P. Lond.; Consulting Physican to Royal Sussex County Hospital and to Royal Alexandra Hospital for Children; Hon. Consulting Physician to Lady Chichester Hospital; Major R.A.M.C. (T.F.); *s.* of late Sir William Broadbent, 1st Bt., K.C.V.O.; and *heir-pres.* to 3rd Bt.; *m.* Edith (O.B.E. 1928), *d.* of late Rt. Hon. John Monroe, P.C., Judge of the High Court of Ireland; two *s.* two *d.* *Educ.:* Harrow; Trinity Coll. Camb.; St. Mary's Hospital. Member of the Swiss Commission, and served in Italy during World War; Treasurer, Ex-President, of the Brighton and Sussex Medico-Chirurgical Society; Past President of Sussex Division and Chairman of the Brighton Branch of the British Medical Association. *Publications:* Editor of The Writings of Sir William Broadbent; writer of several papers on Heart Disease, on Phthisis, and on Pneumonia. *Recreations:* travel, winter sports. *Address:* Field House, Henfield, Sussex. *T.:* 171. *Clubs:* Leander Rowing, Royal Skating. [*Died* 17 *Oct.* 1951.

BROADBRIDGE, 1st Baron, *cr.* 1945, of Brighton; **George Thomas Broadbridge,** 1st Bt., *cr.* 1937; K.C.V.O., *cr.* 1937; Kt., *cr.* 1929; F.C.I.S.; H.M. Lieut. for City of London; *b.* 13 Feb. 1869; *s.* of late Henry Broadridge, Brighton; *m.* 1st,

1895, Fanny Kathleen (*d.* 1928), *d.* of late Richard Brigden; five *s.*; 2nd, Clara Maud (*d.* 1949), *d.* of late John Swansbourne, Bognor, Sussex. *Educ.:* Brighton. Alderman and J.P. for City of London; Sheriff, 1933-34; Lord Mayor of London (Coronation), 1936-37; M.P. (U.) City of London, 1938-45; Member of Council of King Edward Hospital Fund; late President of Purley Hospital; late Chairman Far Eastern Relief Committee; Site and Statue Committee for King George V Memorial; Managing Committee, City of London Mental Hospital; Knight of Grace of St. John of Jerusalem. *Recreations:* golf, tennis. *Heir:* *s.* Hon. Eric Wilberforce Broadbridge [*b.* 22 Dec. 1895; *m.* 1924, Mabel Daisy, *d.* of Arthur Edward Clarke, Carshalton, Surrey; one *s.*] *Address:* 27 Old Bond Street, W.1. *T.:* Regent 1208. *Club:* Carlton. [*Died* 16 *April* 1952.

BROADHURST, George H.; Dramatist; *b.* Walsall, Staffordshire, 3 June 1866; *m.* Lillian Trimble Bradley, playwright. Went to America when sixteen. Made home there for forty-four years; first job, clerk on Board of Trade, Chicago; then journalist, press agent, and business manager of various theatres; finally became lessee and manager of the Broadhurst Theatre, New York; left America twelve years ago and has written no plays since then; has however written numerous short stories which have been published in the Saturday Evening Post and Cosmopolitan in America, and in Nash's, Grand, Storyteller, etc. in England. *Plays:* Bought and Paid for; What Happened to Jones; Why Smith Left Home; The Wrong Mr. Wright; A Fool and His Money; The Duke of Duluth; The Man of the Hour; The Mills of the Gods; To-Day; Innocent; The Law of the Land. *Club:* Lotos (New York.). [*Died* 31 *Jan.* 1952.

BROCK, Henry Matthew, R.I. 1906; Illustrator and Water-Colour Artist; *b.* 11 July 1875; *y. s.* of Edmund Brock of Cambridge; *m.* Doris Joan Pegram; one *s.* two *d.* *Educ.:* Higher Grade School, Camb. Art education received at Cambridge School of Art; first exhibited at R.A. and R.I., 1901; first illustrations published, 1893. *Publications:* Illustrations to Thackeray's Ballads, Macmillan's Standard Novels, Whyte Melville's Novels, Breakfast Table Series (Holmes), Leigh Hunt's Essays, Jerrold's Essays, Sir Roger de Coverley, etc., etc.; drawings in Punch, Graphic, Sketch, etc., and in many magazines. *Address:* 35 Madingley Road, Cambridge. [*Died* 21 *July* 1960.

BROCKBANK, A. E.; member of the Liverpool Academy of Arts, Royal Cambrian Academy (placed on hon. retired list, 1953), and Liver Sketching Club; *b.* 1862. *Educ.:* Liverpool. Studied art at Liverpool, School of Art, London, and Juliens in Paris; was a member of the Royal British Artists for some years; pictures bought for the Liverpool, Preston, and Victoria, Australia, permanent collections; exhibited landscapes and portraits at the Royal Academy. *Recreation:* gardening. *Address:* 34 Hilberry Ave., Liverpool 13; c/o Liver Sketching Club, 11 Dale Street, Liverpool. *Club:* Artists' (Liverpool). [*Died* 29 *Jan.* 1958.

BROCKINGTON, Sir William Allport, Kt., *cr.* 1946; C.B.E. 1928 (O.B.E. 1917); Médaille du roi Albert avec rayure, 1920; M.A.; Director of Education for Leicestershire, 1903-47; *b.* 18 June 1871; *s.* of Thomas Alfred Brockington, Birmingham; *m.* 1898, Jessie (*d.* 1951), *d.* of Alexander MacGeoch; one *s.* *Educ.:* King Edward's Grammar School, Aston; Mason Univ. Coll. Birmingham. Exhibitioner and Prizeman in English and first on list at M.A. (Modern Language Group) in 1893, University of London; Lecturer on English Language and Literature, Mason University College, 1891-98; Principal, Victoria Institute, Worcester, 1898-1903; Member of the Burnham Committees, 1919-47, and Hon. Secretary of the Authorities' Panels, 1944-47; Mem. of Consultative Cttee., Bd. of Education, 1926-44; Member: Polish Education Cttee. and Chm. of Polish University College, 1946-53; Prime Minister's Cttee. on Charitable Trusts, 1950-52; Ex-Pres. and formerly Hon. Treas. to Assoc. of Directors and Secretaries for Education; Commanded 2nd V.B. Leicestershire Regt., 1916-19; Chairman Y.M.C.A. Divisional Council (Leics. and Rutland), 1919-52. *Publications:* Elements of English Prose; Elements of Military Education; A Secondary School Entrance Test; General Editor of the Little Bible; edited Shakespeare's Sonnets, Goldsmith's Citizen of the World, etc.; numerous educational pamphlets and articles. *Recreation:* golf. *Address:* Kay Cottage, Mobberley, Cheshire. [*Died* 14 *Feb.* 1959.

BROCKLEBANK, Captain Henry Cyril Royds, C.B.E. 1919; J.P., D.L.; R.N., retd.; *b.* 1874; *s.* of late Thomas Brocklebank, J.P., D.L., Wateringbury Place, Maidstone; *m.* 1900, Honoria Caroline, *d.* of Capt. W. H. Lewin, R.N., Down House, Frant, Sussex; one *s.* four *d.* Served European War, 1914-19 (despatches, C.B.E., Chevalier Legion of Honour). *Address:* Charlton House, Shaftesbury, Dorset. *T.:* Donhead 208. *Clubs:* United Service; Royal Dorset Yacht (Weymouth). [*Died* 30 *June* 1957.

BROCKLEBANK, Sir Thomas Aubrey Lawies, 4th Bt., *cr.* 1885; Director Thomas and John Brocklebank, Ltd., Liverpool, Crosfields Oil and Cake Co., Ltd., The Midland Bank, Ltd., Royal Insurance Co. Ltd.; *b.* 23 Oct. 1899; *s.* of 3rd Bt. and Hon. Grace Mary Jackson, *y. d.* of 1st Baron Allerton; *S.* father, 1929. *Educ.:* Eton; Trinity College, Cambridge. *Heir:* *b.* John Montague, *b.* 3 Sept. 1915. *Address:* Bathafarn Hall, Ruthin, North Wales. *Clubs:* White's, St. James'. [*Died* 15 *Sept.* 1953.

BROCKMAN; *see* Drake-Brockman.

BROCKMAN, Engineer Rear-Admiral Henry Stafford, C.B. 1939; *b.* 30 Jan. 1884; *s.* of Lieutenant W. Brockman, Royal Navy; m. 1908, Edith Mary Sheppard; two *s.* two *d.* *Educ.:* Plymouth Corporation Grammar School. Joined Royal Naval Engineering College, Keyham, Devonport, 1899; Engineer Captain, 1931; Engineer Rear-Admiral, 1937; Manager Engineering Dept. H.M. Dockyards, Devonport, 1934-41, Portsmouth, 1942-45. Governor, Plymouth College; Life Member, Devon Rugby Referees Society. *Recreation:* Devon Rugby Football Union (Pres. 1948-50). *Address:* Redcot, Fitzroy Rd., Stoke, Plymouth. *T.:* Plymouth 52091. [*Died* 8 *Oct.* 1958.

BROCKWELL, Maurice Walter; art-writer and art-lecturer; Curator, Cook Collection, Richmond, 1920-39; *b.* 24 May 1869; *e. s.* of late Canon J. C. Brockwell. *Educ.:* St. Paul's Cathedral Choir School and Hurstpierpoint; many years abroad. For four years assisted Sir Charles Holroyd, Director of the National Gallery, in rewriting the official catalogues of the National Gallery; Librarian and Secretary in Florence to Mr. B. Berenson, 1910-11; Assistant Secretary of Exhibition of Old Masters at Grafton Galleries, 1911; Hon. Secretary for Great Britain and Ireland of Van Eyck Memorial Fund, Ghent, 1913; Secretary of Exhibition of Spanish Old Masters at Grafton Galleries, 1913; Secretary of Flemish Exhibition, Burlington House, 1927; English correspondent to the Gazette des Beaux Arts; University Extension Lecturer (Cambridge). *Publications:* Leonardo da Vinci, 1909; The National Gallery: Lewis Bequest, 1909; The Adoration of the Magi by Jan Mabuse, 1911; Erasmus: Humanist and Painter, 1918; Catalogue of the Henry E. Huntington Art Gallery,

San Marino, Calif., 1925; Official Catalogues of Flemish Exhibitions, Burlington, House, 1927 and 1953; George Jamesone, 1939; The Pseudo-Arnolfini Portrait, 1953; The Van Eyck Problem, 1954; (joint), The National Gallery: 100 plates in colour, 1909; The National Loan Exhibition Catalogue, 1909; The Louvre: 50 plates in colour, 1910, the Van Eycks and their Art, 1912; Frans Hals: His Life and Work, 1914; The Catalogue of the Cook Collection, Richmond, 1915; Catalogues of several English private collections, etc., and many in U.S.A. and Canada, 1917-20; contributor to Morning Post, Times, Athenæum, Connoisseur, Gazette des Beaux Arts, Art in America, The Library, etc.; copious contributor to Allgemeines Lexikon der bildenden Künstler, Leipsic, 1908-14. *Recreations:* the quest of efficiency, research work and foreign travel. *Club:* Athenæum. [*Died* 7 *Dec.* 1958.

BRODETSKY, Selig, M.A. (Cantab.), B.Sc. (Lond.), Ph.D. (Leipzig); Emeritus Professor of Applied Mathematics since 1949, University of Leeds; Reader, 1920-24; Professor, 1924-48; President of the Hebrew University of Jerusalem and Chairman of its Exec. Council, 1949-51; Mem. Board of Governors of the Hebrew University; formerly Member of Executive, Zionist World Organisation and Jewish Agency for Palestine; Hon. President Zionist Federation of Great Britain and Ireland; Hon. Pres. World Maccabi Union; Immediate Past Pres., Bd. of Deputies of British Jews; *b.* at Olviopol, Russia, 10 Feb. 1888; 2nd *s.* of Akiva and Ada Brodetsky; *m.* Mania, *d.* of P. Berenblum, of Bialystok and Antwerp; one *s.* one *d.* *Educ.:* Jews' Free School, London; Central Foundation School, London; Trinity College, Cambridge; Leipzig University. Bracketed Senior Wrangler, Math. Tripos, 1908; Isaac Newton Research Student, 1910-1913; Lecturer in Applied Mathematics, University of Bristol, 1914-19; F.R.A.S., F.R.Ae.S., F.Inst.P. *Publications:* A First Course in Nomography; the Mechanical Principles of the Aeroplane; Sir Isaac Newton, a Brief Account of his Life and Work; The Meaning of Mathematics; papers on mathematical and physical subjects, including aeronautics; articles on Jewish science and Zionism. *Recreations:* reading, writing. *Address:* 8 Brompton Lodge, Cromwell Rd., S.W.7. *T.:* Kensington 9455. [*Died* 18 *May* 1954.

BRODIE, Harry Cunningham; partner in firm of Findlay, Durham & Brodie, colonial merchants; a director of Ohlsson's Cape Breweries Ltd., and of Ocean Marine Insurance Co. Ltd., Chairman Delagoa Bay Agency Co. Ltd.; Chairman East Africa Engineering & Trading Co. Ltd.; *b.* 1875; *e. s.* of late John Brodie, Hamsell Manor, Sx.; *m.* 1909, Mabel Milburne (*d.* 1951), *d.* of Sir Robert Hart, 1st Bt., G.C.M.G.; two *s.* *Educ.:* Winchester; abroad. Major Middlesex Yeomanry (Duke of Cambridge's Hussars), retired; Member of Eighty Club; M.P. (L.) Reigate Division, Surrey, 1906-10; served in Egypt, 1915-16; France. 1917. On Council of London Chamber of Commerce, Chairman South African Section, 1943-50. *Address:* Russell Hotel, Russell Square, W.C.1; 6 Bloomsbury Square, W.C.1. *Clubs:* Reform, Cavalry, City of London, Hurlingham, Royal Automobile. [*Died* 27 *Feb.* 1956.

BROGLIE, Duc de, (Maurice), D.Sc. (Hon.), Oxford and Leeds; Grand Officer, Legion of Honour; member French Academy since 1934; physicist (X-rays, radiations, atomic physics); member of Académie des Sciences, 1924; Foreign Member (1940) and Hughes gold medal of Royal Society; *b.* Paris, 27 April 1875; *s.* of Victor, Duc de Broglie and Pauline d'Armaillé; eldest brother of Prince Louis de Broglie; *m.* 1904, Camille de Rochetaillée; no *c.* *Educ.:* Collège Stanislas; École Navale (first place on entering and leaving). *Publications:* nombreux memoirs scientifiques sur l'électricité, la radio-activité, les rayons X, la physique du noyau des atomes (nuclear physics). *Address:* Rue de Chateaubriand 27, Paris. VIIIe. *Club:* (pres.) Union (Paris). [*Died* 14 *July* 1960.

BROMAGE, Lieut.-Col. John Aldhelm Raikes, C.I.E. 1941; R.M.retd.; Engineering Inspector, Ministry of Health, since 1948; *b.* Frome, Somerset, 7 May 1891; *s.* of Richard Raikes Bromage; *m.* 1944, Muriel Alice, *widow* of Clifford Light. *Educ.:* City of London School; City and Guilds Engineering College. Served European War, 1914-18, Middlesex Regt. Joined Public Works Dept., India, 1920; Superintending Engineer Health Services with Govt. of India, Delhi; retired from R.M., 1943; Works Adviser to Ministry of Works, 1944; attached H.Q., U.S. Army, London, 1945. M.Inst.C.E., F.R.G.S. *Address:* The Holt, Wadhurst, Sussex. *T.:* Wadhurst 208. *Club:* East India and Sports. [*Died* 6 *Jan.* 1955.

BROMFIELD, Louis; Author; *b.* Mansfield, Ohio, U.S.A., 27 Dec. 1896; *s.* of Charles and Annette Bromfield; *m.* 1921, Mary A. Wood (*d.* 1952); three *d.* *Educ.:* Columbia and Cornell Univs. Journalist, essayist, novelist, playwright, music critic, agriculturalist; attaché 34th and 168th French Divs. Mangin Army, 1916-18 (Croix de Guerre, Legion of Honor); LL.D. Marshall Coll.; Litt.D. Ohio Northern Univ.; LL.D. Parsons Coll.; Lit.D.: Lafayette Univ.; Tri-State Coll. *Publications: novels:* The Green Bay Tree; Possession; Early Autumn; A Good Woman; The Strange Case of Miss Annie Spragg; Twenty-Four Hours; A Modern Hero; The Farm; The Rains Came, 1938; Night in Bombay, 1940; Wild is the River, 1941; Until the Day Break, 1942; Mrs. Parkington, 1943; What became of Anna Bolton, 1944; *stories:* Awake and Rehearse (collection); Tabloid News (special limited edition); Here To-day and Gone To-morrow, 1934; The Man Who Had Everything; It Had to Happen, 1936; It Takes All Kinds, 1939; The World we live in; Pleasant Valley, 1945; A Few Brass Tacks, 1946; Malabar Farm, 1948; The Wild Country, 1948; Out of the Earth, 1950; A New Pattern for a Tired World, 1954; From my Experience, 1956; *plays:* The House of Women, De Luxe; Times Have Changed, 1935; West of the Moon, 1946; Helen in Memphis, 1950. *Recreations:* ski-ing, swimming, painting, gardening. *Address:* Malabar Farm, Lucas, Ohio, U.S.A. *Clubs:* Coffee House, Century, Brook, Nassau Authors' (New York). [*Died* 19 *March* 1956.

BROMILOW, Maj.-Gen. (David) George, C.B.E. 1945; D.S.O. 1917; retired; *b.* 8 Feb. 1884; *s.* of Henry John Bromilow, Rainhill, Lancashire; *m.* 1935, Beatrice Anne Jackson; no *c.* *Educ.:* Eastbourne College; R.M.C., Sandhurst. 1st commission, 1903, 14th Jat Lancers, Indian Army, till 1921; European War, N.W. Frontier and Mesopotamia and Kurdistan, 1914-19 (D.S.O. and bar); Inspector of Cavalry, Iraq Army, 1921-1927; 20th Lancers I.A. 1927-34; retired, 1934; rejoined to raise Senussi Force in Egypt, Sept. 1939-July 1941; Inspector-General, Iraq Army, Aug. 1941; retired, 1944. *Recreations:* polo, pigsticking, shooting, fishing, and trees. *Club:* Cavalry. [*Died* 12 *Jan.* 1959.

BROMLEY-DAVENPORT, Mrs. Muriel Coomber, C.B.E. 1918; Secretary Distressed Gentlefolks Aid Association, 74 Brook Green, W.6; Hon. Secretary Invalid Comforts Section for Prisoners of War (Red Cross and St. John War Organisation), 1939-45; *b.* 1879; *d.* of late John Head; *m.* 1906, Hugh Richard Bromley-Davenport (*d.* 1954); one *s.* one *d.* Vice-Pres. Hove Hospital

Supply Depots during European War; Hon. Secretary Invalid Comforts Fund for Prisoners of War (British Red Cross), 1916-18; Vice-Chairman Emergency Help Committee, Joint Council British Red Cross Society and St. John of Jerusalem, 1921-34; C.St.J., 1947; Joint Secretary, Friends of the Poor, 1927-33. *Address:* 23 Malvern Court. S.W.7. [*Died* 10 *Nov.* 1956.

BROMLEY-DERRY, Henry, M.V.O. 1944; Mus.Doc., F.R.C.O.: F.S.A.; Organist and Master of the Music, The Queen's Chapel of the Savoy, since 1913; *b.* Stratford-on-Avon, 1885. *Educ.:* King Edward VI. Grammar School, Stratford-on-Avon. Entered Royal College of Music, 1906; studying under Sir Walter Parratt and Sir Frederick Bridge; awarded Council Exhibition for organ playing, 1908; F.R.C.O. 1907; graduated Bachelor of Music at Durham University, 1912; at Oxford University, 1913; Bachelor and Doctor of Music at Trinity College, Dublin, 1916; held organ posts at St. Mary's, Lambeth, 1906; All Saints, Ealing, 1908; St. Luke's, Redcliffe Square, 1912; Conductor of the Choral Society at St. Anne's, Soho, 1912; Deputy Instructor in Music, Harrow School, 1915; Member of the Board of Examiners, 1919, Member of the Corporation, and Hon. Fellow, 1937, Director of Studies, 1940, Director and Chairman of the Council and Corporation, 1944, London College of Music; Hon. Fellow, 1944, Tonic-Solfa Coll. of Music; Member (Music) Education Committee Surrey County Council, 1945; Hon. Member Royal Soc. of Musicians, 1945; Member of the Council, Union of Graduates in Music, 1921-23; re-elected, 1943-47-51; Member of Cttee., London Musical Festivals, 1922-3-4; Member of Council, London Society of Organists, 1923; re-elected 1936; Hon. Musical Adviser to Appointments Board for ex-officers (Ministry of Labour), 1919; Registrar, The Queen's Chapel of the Savoy, 1933; Grand Organist (G.L. of Eng.), 1938; Bandmaster 2/7 (D.C.O.) Middlesex Regiment, 1916; served in France with 1st Batt. The King's Own (Royal Lancaster) Regt. *Publications:* History of The Queen's Chapel of the Savoy, 1933; church music, songs. *Address:* 19 North Side, Clapham Common, S.W.4. [*Died* 4 *April* 1954.

BROMLEY-WILSON, Sir Maurice, 7th Bt., *cr.* 1757; D.L., J.P.; *b.* 27 June 1875; *s.* of 5th Bart. and Adela, *o. c.* of Westley Richards, Ashwell, Oakham; *m.* 1st, 1916, Elizabeth Ann (*d.* 1936), *d.* of late W. Turner, Over Hall, Wrinsford, Cheshire, and *widow* of Godfrey Armitage, of Nabwood, Windermere; 2nd, 1942, Violet (*d.* 1953), *widow* of Lt.-Col. Oswald Ames. Assumed by Royal licence in 1897 additional name of Wilson. *S.* brother, 1906. High Sheriff, Westmorland, 1901; Major Nottinghamshire Yeomanry Cavalry. *Heir:* *b.* Rear-Adm. Sir Arthur Bromley, K.C.M.G. *Address:* Dallam Tower, Milnthorpe, Westmorland. [*Died* 7 *Nov.* 1957.

BROOK, Barnaby; *see* Brooks, W. C.

BROOK, Lt.-Col. Sir Frank, Kt., *cr.* 1942; D.S.O. 1918; M.C.; D.L.; *b.* Dewsbury, Yorks, 1883; *m.* Jessie M. Waddell, Cathcart, Glasgow; three *d.* (one *s.* decd.). *Educ.:* Batley Grammar School. Civil Service Inland Revenue. Served European War (three medals): commissioned in King's Own Yorkshire Light Infantry; commanded 2/5th Duke of Wellington's Regt. and 2/4th Hampshire Regiment (despatches, D.S.O. and bar, M.C., French Croix de Guerre, Brevet); served War of 1939-44 (three medals); Adviser to War Office, Civil Affairs, Public Safety; Chief Constable, Southport, Nottingham and Yorkshire West Riding; H.M. Inspector of Constabulary, 1935-53; King's Police Medal, 1933; Jubilee Medal, 1935; Coronation Medals, 1937 and 1953. D.L. Yorkshire West Riding, 1954. K.St.J. *Address:* The Manor House, Pool-in-Wharfedale, Yorks. [*Died* 16 *Feb.* 1960.

BROOK, Air Vice-Marshal William Arthur Darville, C.B. 1951; C.B.E. 1944; p.s.a.; A.O.C., No. 3 Group, Bomber Command, 1951-53; apptd. Vice-Chief of Air Staff Aug. 1953, with actg. rank of Air Marshal; *b.* 5 Feb. 1901; *s.* of W. F. Brook, F.R.C.S., J.P.; *m.* 1932, Jean, *d.* of Sir Allan Grant, *q.v.*; three *s.* *Educ.:* Rugby School; R.A.F. College, Cranwell. Regular Officer, R.A.F. Served in India, Iraq, and Middle and Far East in Flying and Staff appointments; Staff Coll., Andover, 1933. *Recreations:* golf, shooting. *Address:* Shire Combe, Pennard, Glam. *Club:* United Service. [*Died* 17 *Aug.* 1953.

BROOKE, Lieut.-Col. Edward William Saurin, C.M.G. 1918; D.S.O. 1917; late R.F.A.; *b.* 1873; *er. s.* of late Colonel W. Saurin Brooke, I.A.; *m.* 1917, Evelyn Elizabeth (*d.* 1953), *d.* of late H. B. MacMaster; no *c.* Served European War, 1914-18 (despatches, Bt. Lt.-Col., D.S.O., C.M.G.); retired pay, 1921. *Address:* Ellerslie, Salcombe, S. Devon. [*Died* 17 *Oct.* 1954.

BROOKE, Sir Francis (Hugh), 2nd Bt., *cr.* 1903; Capt. late South Irish Horse and 60th K.R. Rifles; *b.* 10 Nov. 1882; *s.* of 1st Bt. and Emily Alma (*d.* 1910), *d.* of Augustine H. Barton; *S.* father, 1926; *m.* 1915, Mabel, *y. d.* of late Sir John Arnott, 1st Bt., and Lady FitzGerald Arnott; one *s.* one *d.* *Educ.:* Winchester. *Heir:* *s.* George Cecil Francis, Major 17/21st Lancers [*b.* 30 March 1916]. *Address:* Pickering Forest, Celbridge, Co. Kildare. *T.:* Celbridge 5. *Club:* Kildare Street (Dublin). [*Died* 4 *Nov.* 1954.

BROOKE, Group-Captain Kennedy Gerard, C.M.G. 1919; late R.A.F.; *b.* 1882, *s.* of late Capt. Gerard Marmaduke Brooke; R.N.; *m* 1913, Dorothy, *d.* of Rev. F. G. M. Powell, Bournemouth. Served European War, 1914-19 (despatches, C.M.G.); retired list, 1929. *Address:* c/o Lloyds Bank Ltd., Brighton, Sussex. [*Died* 11 *May* 1959.

BROOKE-POPHAM, Air Chief Marshal Sir Robert; *see* Popham, Air Chief Marshal Sir H. R. M. B.-.

BROOKS, Collin; *see* Brooks, W. C.

BROOKS, Eric St. John; *see* Brooks, W. E. St. J.

BROOKS, Ernest Walter, F.B.A. 1938; *b.* Hambledon, Hants, 30 Aug. 1863; *o. c.* of Rev. Walter Brooks; *m.* 1927, Ellen Amy, *d.* of Major-General G. B. Mellersh. *Educ.:* Eton College; King's College, Cambridge (Eton Scholar); 1st class in pt. I Classical Tripos (1886) and pt. II (1887); B.A. 1886; M.A. 1890; Hon. Doctor of Philosophy and Letters Univ. of Louvain 1927. After leaving Cambridge devoted himself to study of later Roman and early medieval (mostly Byzantine) history to about A.D. 900; for historical purposes took up study of Syriac; has now ceased to do any regular work. *Publications:* edited and translated many Syriac texts; wrote chapters in Cambridge Medieval History vols. I, II, and IV, and articles and reviews in English and foreign periodicals. *Address:* Dunolly, Pless Road, Milford-on-Sea, Lymington, Hants. *T.:* Milford 279. [*Died* 26 *March* 1955.

BROOKS, Frederick Tom, C.B.E. 1947; F.R.S. 1930; M.A.; Hon. LL.D. St. Andrews; Emeritus Professor of Botany, Cambridge Univ., since 1948; Fellow of Emmanuel College; *b.* Wells, Somerset, 17 Dec. 1882; *s.* of Edward Brooks; *m.* 1907, Emily Broderick. *Educ.:* Sexey's School, Bruton; Emmanuel Coll., Cambridge. Government Mycologist, F.M.S., 1914; formerly Reader in Mycology and Prof. of Botany, Cambridge

Univ.; Pres. Botanical Section, British Association, 1935, and Gen. Sec. 1935-46; Pres. British Mycological Society, 1922; Member of Agricultural Research Council, 1941-46 and since 1949. Pres., Cambridge Philosophical Society, 1945-47; Hon. Fellow Botanical Society of Edinburgh; Hon. F.R.S.E.; Hon. Member British Mycological Society. *Publications:* Plant Diseases; Flowering Plants and Flowerless Plants (with D. H. Scott), and papers in scientific journals. *Address:* 31 Tenison Avenue, Cambridge. *T.:* 4802; Botany School, Cambridge. *T.:* 58304. *Club:* Athenæum. [*Died* 11 *March* 1952.

BROOKS, Thomas Judson, M.B.E. 1931; J.P. West Riding of Yorks; *b.* Eastfield Farm, Thurgoland, near Sheffield, 7 July 1880; *s.* of a farmer; *m.* 1906; one *d.* *Educ.:* Thurgoland Church School. Miner: also Secretary, 1911-42, of Glass Houghton Branch of Yorkshire Mine Workers' Association; Member of Castleford U.D.C., 1914-42; member of West Riding County Council, 1925-42, Alderman, 1940; Chairman of Wakefield and Pontefract War Pension Committee since 1924; Chairman of Trustees, Castleford, Normanton and District Hospital; M.P. (Lab.) Rothwell Division of Yorkshire, 1942-50, Normanton Division of the West Riding of Yorkshire, 1950-51. *Recreations:* Interests, social and educational life of Castleford and his constituency (Rothwell). *Address:* 22 Leake Street, Castleford, Yorks. *T.:* Castleford 2005. [*Died* 15 *Feb.* 1958.

BROOKS, (William) Collin, (Barnaby Brook), M.C.; author and journalist; Chairman The Statist Publishing Company; sometime Honorary Press Director, National Savings Committee, and Editor, City Editor and Feature Writer Sunday Dispatch; *b.* 22 Dec. 1893; *s.* of late W. E. Brooks; *m.* 1916, Lilian Susanna, *e. d.* of late Ernest Marsden, J.P., Wigan and Southport; two *s.* two *d.* *Educ.:* privately; Christ Church Hall, Southport. Pupil James Platt & Son, chartered accountants; in business and Member Manchester Produce Exchange to 1915; founded and conducted Manchester Press Agency, 1913-15; served 16th Bn. King's (Liverpool) Regiment; commissioned M.G.C. 23rd Division; on demobilisation joined Benn Brothers (Ways and Means and Hardware Trade Journal); literary editor and chief leader writer Liverpool Courier, 1920-23; leader writer, chief reviewer, and assistant editor, Yorkshire Post, 1923-28; assistant editor, Financial News, 1928-33; City Editor, The Week-end Review (Capulet), 1933-34; London Correspondent, The Business Week (New York) and Journal of Commerce (New York), 1928-38; Chief Leader Writer The Statist since 1942; Chairman and Editor of Truth, 1940-53; toured America, Europe and Africa with the late Lord Rothermere on unofficial and official re-armament missions, 1936-40. *Publications:* Poems, 1914; The Theory and Practice of Finance, 1928, 3rd edition, 1931; How the Stock Market really Works, 1930; Something in the City, 1931; The Tariff Question, 1931; The Royal Mail Case, 1932; Our Present Discontents (The Economics of Human Happiness), 1933; A Dictionary of Finance, 1934; Echoes and Evasions (collected verse), 1934; Profits from Short Term Investment, 1935; Can 1931 Come Again, 1938; Can Chamberlain Save Britain? 1938; Company Finance, 1938; Devil's Decade, 1947; The First Hundred Years, 1947; Tavern Talk, 1950; More Tavern Talk, 1952; Johnson and Phillips, 1951; The First £100,000, 1954; An Educational Adventure, 1955; Graysons—of Liverpool, 1956. *Fiction:* Mr. X, 1927; The Bodysnatchers, 1927; The Ghost Hunters, 1928; The Catspaws, 1929; Seven Hells, 1929; Found Dead, 1930; Account Paid, 1930; Three Yards of Cord, 1931; Mad-doctor Merciful, 1932; Mr. Daddy, Detective, 1933; They Ride Again, 1934; Frame-up, 1934; The Swimming Frog, 1951; As Barnaby Brook: Wife to John, 1928; Prosperity Street, 1930; Mock Turtle, 1931; Gay go Up, 1933; Ten-Minute Tales, 1938; The Jug, 1946; Harriet Walk, 1948; Young Mrs. Rawley, 1949; For Hellidor, 1949. *Recreation:* broadcasting. *Address:* 27 St. George's Court, Gloucester Road, S.W.7. *T.:* Knightsbridge 9282. *Club:* Royal Thames Yacht, Savage, City Livery, Beefsteak. [*Died* 6 *April* 1959.

BROOKS, (William) Eric St. John, M.A., Litt.D.; Editor, historical works, Irish Manuscripts Commission, since 1949; *b.* Dublin, 6 April 1883; 2nd *s.* of Prof. Henry St. John Brooks, University Anatomist, Dublin University, and Marion, *d.* of Aubrey Ohren, Dublin; *m.* 1st, 1920, Moira Mary, M.B. (*d.* 1937), *d.* of Joseph Brown, M.A., J.P., Foxrock, Co. Dublin; one *s.*; 2nd, 1939, Phyllis Rosalind, *d.* of Alfred C. Chalker, M.B.E., Upper Norwood; one *d.* *Educ.:* Erasmus Smith's School; Trinity College, Dublin. Mathematical sizar, 1902; B.A. (Sen. Mod. and Gold Medallist in Nat. Sci.), 1906; M.A., 1911; Litt.D., 1935. Entered Civil Service, 1900 (Nat. Educ. Office and Dublin Metrop. Police Office, Dublin Castle); Asst. Keeper of Botany, Brit. Mus., 1907-08; joined staff of The Times, 1911; Asst. Editor Times Literary Supplement, 1922-45; Leverhulme Research Grant for work on slave trade, 1946; M.R.I.A. 1950. *Publications:* Register of the Hospital of St. John the Baptist, Dublin, 1936; Sir Christopher Hatton, 1946; Knights' Fees in counties Wexford, Carlow and Kilkenny, 1950; The Irish Cartularies of Llanthony Prima and Secunda, 1954; Sir Hans Sloane, 1954; (as Eric St. John) A Stranger Here, 1945; contrib. to Proc. R.I.A., Roy. Soc. of Antiquaries of Ireland, Hermathena, the Library, The Saturday Book and literary reviews. *Recreations:* history, genealogy, mathematics, botany. *Address:* 42 Elgin Road, Dublin. *T.:* Dublin 64697. *Club:* University (Dublin). [*Died* 29 *Sept.* 1955.

BROOM, Robert, F.R.S. 1920; Hon. F.R.S.E. 1947; M.D., C.M., D.Sc. (Glas.); Hon. D.Sc. (S. Af., Capetown, Witwatersrand, Columbia, Stellenbosch); Hon. LL.D. (Glas.); C.M.Z.S.; Keeper of Vertebrate Palæontology and Anthropology, Transvaal Museum; late Prof. Geology and Zoology, Victoria Coll., Stellenbosch, S.A.; *b.* Paisley, Scotland, 30 Nov. 1866; 2nd *s.* of John Broom; *m.* 1893, Mary Baird Baillie. Temp. Lieut. R.A.M.C., 1915-16; Croonian Lect. R.S. 1913; Corresponding Member, Linnean Soc. N.S.W., Palæontol. Soc. Am., Geol. Soc. China, Am. Mus. N.Y.; Royal Medal of Royal Society, 1928; Wollaston Medal of Geol. Soc., 1949; President South African Association Advancement of Science, 1933. *Publications:* Origin of Human Skeleton, 1930; Mammal-like Reptiles of South Africa, 1932; The Coming of Man: was it accident or design? 1933; Fossil Ape-Men of South Africa (with G. W. H. Schepers), 1946; Finding the Missing Link, 1950; Sterkfontein Ape-man (with J. T. Robinson), 1950. Comparative Anatomy Mammalian Organ of Jacobson (Tr. R.S. Ed. 1897); Develop. and Morph. Marsup. Shoulder Girdle (Tr. R.S. Ed. 1899); Origin of Mammals (Phil. Trans. 1915); and about 430 other papers on Comparative Anatomy and Vertebrate Palæontology in P.Z.S., Ann. S. Africa Mus., Ann. Transvaal Mus., P. Linn. Soc. N.S.W., etc. *Recreations:* fossil hunting and art. *Address:* Transvaal Museum, Pretoria, South Africa. [*Died* 6 *April* 1951.

BROOMAN-WHITE, Major Charles James, C.B.E. 1918; *b.* 8 Nov. 1883; *e. s.* of late R. Brooman-White of Arddarroch, Dunbartonshire; *m.* Ida Lea Hartings, *d.* of late William Hearne of Hearne, Texas, U.S.A.; one *s.* *Educ.:* Eton; Trinity Hall, Cambridge. Served South Africa, 1902; European War, 1914-19; attached Military Mission, U.S.A. 1917-19 (despatches, C.B.E). *Recreations:* golf, racquets, motoring, travelling. *Address:* Arddarroch, Garelochhead, Dunbartonshire; 11 Cambridge Square, Hyde Park, W.2. *T.:* Paddington 2165. *Clubs:* White's, Bath, M.C.C.

[*Died* 20 *March* 1954.

BROOME, Harold Holkar, C.I.E. 1929; M.B., Ch.B.; F.R.C.S.; Lt.-Col. I.M.S., retd.; *b.* 6 Mar. 1875; *s.* of Edward Broome, Southport; *m.* 1902, Clara Alice, *d.* of Rev. W. H. Finney; two *s.* *Educ.:* Privately and Edinburgh University. Junior and later Senior Demonstrator of Anatomy, Owens College, Manchester; entered I.M.S., 1903; Professor of Anatomy, King Edward Medical College, Lahore, 1908; during the war served in campaigns on N.W.F. of India, in Mesopotamia and German East Africa; Professor of Surgery, K.E. Medical College, Lahore, 1922-30; Principal of K.E. Medical College, 1923-30; Fellow of the Punjab University and Dean of the Faculty of Medicine; retired, 1930; war-time employment: Medical Supt. and Surgeon, Alverstoke Emergency Hospital, Gosport, Hants. *Publications:* An Abnormality of the Left Innominate Artery; Extraperitoneal Rupture of the Bladder; The Treatment of Oriental Sores by Co_2 Snow. *Recreations:* shooting, golf, fishing. *Address:* c/o National Bank of India, 26 Bishopsgate, E.C.

[*Died* 31 *Oct.* 1958.

BROOMFIELD, Sir Robert Stonehouse, Kt., *cr.* 1941; Barrister-at-Law; *e. s.* of R. W. Broomfield, Bar.-at-Law, Middle Temple; *m.* Mabel Louisa (*d.* 1955), *d.* of Rev. C. R. Linton, M.A. (Cantab.), Inverkip, Scotland; two *d.* *Educ.:* City of London School; Christ's College, Cambridge. Joined the Indian Civil Service; posted to Bombay Presidency, 1905; Judge of High Court of Judicature, Bombay, 1929-42. *Address:* 53 St. Alban's Avenue, Bournemouth. *T.:* Winton 2246.

[*Died* 29 *June* 1957.

BROTCHIE, James Rayner, D.A. (Edin.), F.R.S.A., F.M.A.; Keeper of Prints and Drawings, National Gallery of Scotland, since 1946; *b.* 7 June 1909; *s.* of T. C. F. Brotchie, author, artist and director of Glasgow Art Galleries, 1919-29; *m.* 1940, Joan Mary Hughes; two *s.* one *d.* *Educ.:* Paisley Grammar School; Shawland Academy. Studied, Glasgow School of Art, 1928-32 (Hart Bursar, 1929; Directors Prizeman, 1931, 1932); France, Holland and Italy. Paintings exhibited at Royal Scottish Academy, Society of Scottish Artists, Glasgow Institute. Assistant Curator, Glasgow Art Gallery, 1932-36; Assistant Keeper, National Gallery of Scotland, 1936-42; military service, Egypt, Tunisia, Italy, 1942-46. F.R.S.A. 1940; F.M.A. 1951. *Publications:* articles in Scottish Art Review, Scots Review, Art Bulletin, Scotsman, Glasgow Herald, etc. *Recreations:* painting, walking, swimming. *Address:* 31 Craiglockhart Crescent, Edinburgh. *T.:* Craiglockhart 1975. [*Died* 20 *Aug.* 1956.

BROUGH, Maj.-Gen. Alan, C.B. 1932; C.M.G. 1918; C.B.E. 1919; D.S.O. 1915; late R.E.; *b.* 20 March 1876. *Educ.:* Cheltenham. Entered Army, 1895; Capt. 1904; Major, 1914; Lt.-Col. 1921; Col. 1925; Maj.-Gen. 1931; served European War, 1914-18 (D.S.O., Bt. Lt.-Col., C.M.G.); South Russia, 1919-20 (C.B.E.); Assistant Director, Engineering, War Office, 1927-31; Director of Mechanization, War Office, 1932-36; retired 1936; Col. Commandant R.E. 1939-46. *Club:* United Service.

[*Died* 24 *Aug.* 1956.

BROUGHALL, Rt. Rev. Lewis Wilmot Bovell; *b.* 27 March 1876; *s.* of Abraham James Broughall and Georgina Harriet Hurd; *m.* 1908, Sophia Margaret Hagarty; one *s.* two *d.* *Educ.:* Trinity College School, Port Hope; Trinity University, Toronto; B.A. 1897; M.A. 1898. Deacon, 1899; Priest. 1900; Clergy House, Minden; Incumbent, Hagersville; Asst. Curate, All Saints, Wimbledon, England; St. James' Cathedral, Toronto; Rector, Oakville, Ontario; Rector, St. George's, St. Catharine's; Rector, Christ's Church Cathedral, Hamilton, and Dean of Niagara, 1925; D.D. Trinity University, Toronto (jure dign.); D.D. (Hon.), Wycliffe College, Toronto, 1933; LL.D. (Hon.) McMaster Univ., Hamilton, 1949; Prolocutor, Provincial Synod of Ontario, 1926-33; Bishop of Niagara, 1933-1949; retired, 1949: Secretary Anglican National Commission, 1927; Member Corporation Trinity University. *Address:* Mountain View Apartments, 325 James Street, S., Hamilton, Canada.

[*Died* 26 *Aug.* 1958.

BROUGHSHANE, 1st Baron (U.K.), *cr.* 1945, of Kensington; **William Henry Davison,** K.B.E., *cr.* 1918; D.L., J.P. County of London; M.A., F.S.A.; *o. s.* of late Richard Davison, of Beechfield, Ballymena, Co. Antrim, and Annie, *d.* of John Patrick, J.P. of Dunminning, Co. Antrim; *m.* 1st, 1898, Beatrice Mary (marriage dissolved, 1929), *d.* of Sir Owen Roberts, D.C.L., LL.D., of Henley Park, Guildford, Surrey, and Plas Dinas, Carnarvon; two *s.* two *d.*; 2nd, 1929, Constance, *d.* of late Major Charles F. Marriott, 6th Dragoon Guards. *Educ.:* Shrewsbury; Oxford (M.A.). Barrister-at-law, Inner Temple; Chairman: Income-Tax Payers' Society; Improved Industrial Dwellings Co., Ltd., East Surrey Water Co.; Vice-President Royal Society of Arts; Governor Foundling Hospital; Freeman City of London; Member of Court of Assistants Worshipful Company of Clothworkers, Master 1941-42; concerned in the administration of a number of Educational Foundations; Mayor of the Royal Borough of Kensington, 1913-19; at beginning of Great War raised men for two Territorial Battalions, and one Service Battalion of the New Army, the 22nd Battalion Royal Fusiliers (Kensington); in connection with the latter he undertook the personal responsibility of housing, clothing, and equipping the men, and selecting the officers, for which he received the special thanks of the Army Council, and was created K.B.E.; M.P. (U.) Kensington South Division, 1918-1945; Hon. Commandant of Kensington Volunteer Battalion; Chairman Kensington Military Service Tribunal; President Kensington Chamber of Commerce; Hon. A.R.I.B.A., 1926; Chairman, Metropolitan Division of National Union of Conservative Associations, 1928-30. *Heir:* *s.* Hon. Patrick Owen Alexander Davison [*b.* 18 June 1903; *m.* 1929, Bettine, *d.* of Sir Arthur Russell, Bt.; one *s.*]. *Address:* 14 Kensington Park Gardens, W. 11. *T.:* Park 6213. *Clubs:* Carlton, Athenæum, Oxford and Cambridge.

[*Died* 19 *Jan.* 1953.

BROWETT, Sir Leonard, K.C.B., *cr.* 1938 (C.B. 1933); C.B.E. 1920; Director: Industrial and Commercial Finance Corporation since 1953; Telephone Rentals Ltd.; Super Oil Seals and Gaskets Ltd.; *b.* 27 Dec. 1884; *s.* of late Charles J. Browett, Birmingham; *m.* 1912, Wymond, *d.* of late Thomas Letcher, Redruth, Cornwall. *Educ.:* King Edward's School, Birmingham. Entered Inland Revenue Department, 1904; Assistant Surveyor and Surveyor of Taxes, 1904-10; Secretaries' Office Inland Revenue, 1910-17; Deputy Director, and later Director, of Ship Requisitioning, Ministry of Shipping, 1917-1919, and British Representative and Chairman of Tonnage Committee, Allied Maritime

Transport Council; Assistant Secretary, Inland Revenue, 1919-30; Principal Assistant Secretary, Board of Trade, 1932-35; Deputy to Chief Industrial Adviser to H.M. Government, 1935-37; Second Secretary to Board of Trade, 1937; Secretary to Ministry of Transport, 1937-41; Secretary-General to British Army Staff—British Ministry of Supply Mission, Washington, D.C. 1942-44; Director National Union of Manufacturers, 1945-53. Chevalier of the Legion of Honour; Chevalier of the Order of the Crown of Belgium; Officer of the Order of the Crown of Italy. *Address:* Burlington Hotel, Eastbourne. *T.:* Eastbourne 2724. *Club:* Union. [*Died* 7 *May* 1959.

BROWN, Alfred R. R.; *see* Radcliffe-Brown.

BROWN, Sir Alfred W., Kt., *cr.* 1941; LL.D. (London); Legal Adviser to the British Military Governor (later High Commissioner) in Germany, 1949-51; *b.* 12 October 1883; 2nd *s.* of John Brown and Kate Davis Allen, Northampton; *m.* 1910, Kate, 2nd *d.* of Frederick Plessen, Neubrandenburg; two *d.* *Educ.:* Northampton County School; London Univ. 1st class honours Law Society's Prize at Solicitors' Final and admitted Solicitor, 1940; LL.B. with 1st class honours, qual. Univ. Schol. 1903; LL.D. 1905; served with 1st V. Bn. Northants Regiment, afterwards 4th Battn. Northants T.F., 1900-09, retiring as Lieut.; entered Dept. of H.M. Procurator General and Treasury Solicitor, 1905; Asst. Treasury Solicitor, 1924; Principal Asst. Treasury Solicitor, 1936; Solicitor H.M. Customs and Excise, 1941-44; Control Commission for Germany, 1944; Legal Adviser to Foreign office (German Section), 1947; Director, Legal Division, Allied Commission for Austria (British Element), 1948; Member of British Deleg. to International Conference for the Codification of International Law, at The Hague, 1930; also to the 3rd and 4th International Conferences on Aviation Law, at Rome, 1933, and at Brussels, 1938; Member of British Delegation to Comité International d'Experts Juridiques Aériens, 1931-45; Delegate to Austrian Treaty Commission, 1947-48. *Address:* 41 Brunswick Square, Hove, 2. *T.:* Hove 70173. [*Died* 5 *Jan.* 1955.

BROWN, Sir Algernon; *see* Brown, Sir T. A.

BROWN, Sir Arnesby; *see* Brown, Sir J. A. A.

BROWN, Rev. Arthur Ernest, C.I.E. 1926; M.A., B.Sc.; formerly Principal Wesleyan College, Bankura, Bengal; *b.* 17 May 1882; *s.* of Rev. J. Milton Brown; *m.* E. Gertrude, *d.* of T. L. Parsons, of Four Oaks, Warwickshire; four *s.* one *d.* *Educ.:* Kingswood School, Bath; Trinity Hall, Cambridge (Scholar). Mathematical Tripos (27th Wrangler); 1904; B.Sc. (London), 1904. Entered Wesleyan Ministry, 1904, and sent to Bengal; awarded the Kaisar-i-Hind Gold Medal, 1917; Fellow of the Calcutta University, 1921-36. *Publication:* Translated from Bengali The Cage of Gold, by Sita Devi. *Address:* The Manor House, Churchdown, Glos. [*Died* 15 *July* 1952.

BROWN, Ashley Geikie; Author, *s.* of Archibald Geikie Brown and Edith Constance, *d.* of Ashley W. Barrett; *m.* 1924, Mary Helen, *e. d.* of William McKay, Overbury, Watford. Admiralty; Special Grants Cttee., Min. of Pensions, 1914-18. One of the founders of the Railway Reform League, 1931; Member of the Council and Committee of the British Railway Stockholders Union, 1932-43, and General Sec. of that organisation, 1933-38; attached to General Manager's Department, G.W.R., 1943-1947. *Publications:* Greece Old and New, 1927; Sicily Present and Past, 1928; two works on railway matters: The Future of the Railways, 1928; The Railway Problem, 1932. *Recreations:* travel, chess. *Address:* St. Brighid, Ballycullen, Ashford, Wicklow, Eire. [*Died* 13 *Sept.* 1957.

BROWN, Air Vice-Marshal Cecil Leonard Morley, C.B. 1955; O.B.E. 1945; M.A.; Director of Educational Services, Air Ministry, since 1952; *b.* 16 July 1895; *s.* of Rev. N. A. Brown and Blanche Harriet Brown (*née* Morley), Melton Mowbray, Leicestershire; *m.* 1924, Edith Marian Norden, *d.* of Rev. H. L. Norden; one *s.* *Educ.:* Worksop College; St. Catharine's College, Cambridge (Open Schol.). Served European War, R.N.V.R. Contributor to Punch (" C.L.M.") etc. R.A.F. Education Service, 1922-. A.D.C. to King George VI and to the Queen, 1950-53. *Publications:* Rhymes of the R.A.F., 1925; The Conquest of the Air, 1926. *Recreations:* literary and country; formerly cricket (Leicestershire). *Address:* Woodpeckers, Lower Wokingham Rd., Crowthorne, Berks. *T.:* Crowthorne 2762. *Club:* East India and Sports. [*Died* 6 *Dec.* 1955.

BROWN, Dame Edith Mary, D.B.E., *cr.* 1932; F.R.C.S. Ed., M.A., M.D. Brux., M.R.C.O.G.; L.R.C.P. & S. Edin.; Principal Emeritus, Christian Medical College, Ludhiana, Punjab. *Educ.:* Girton College, Cambridge, Honours Tripos in Natural Science. Member of International College of Surgeons. *Publication:* Urdu Handbook for Midwives. *Address:* c/o Christian Medical College, Ludhiana, Punjab, India; c/o Ludhiana British Fellowship, 12 Queen Anne's Gate, S.W.1. [*Died* 6 *Dec.* 1956.

BROWN, (Everard) Kenneth, M.B.E. 1918; Solicitor, Senior Partner in and one of the Founders of firm of Kenneth Brown, Baker, Baker; *b.* 19 Aug. 1879; *y. c.* of Rev. John Brown, D.D., Bedford, the biographer of Bunyan; unmarried. *Educ.:* Bedford School. Solicitor, 1903; Law Society First (Clement's Inn and Daniel Reardon) Prizeman 1902; Intelligence Officer, Headquarters, Northern Command, 1917-19; President of Railway Club since 1928. *Publications:* numerous articles on railway subjects. *Recreation:* researches into the history of British railways. *Address:* 10 Upper Park Road, N.W.3. *T.A.:* Sunrising, Estrand, London. *T.:* Primrose 2934. *Clubs:* Devonshire, Royal Thames Yacht. [*Died* 1 *June* 1958.

BROWN, Sir Frank (Herbert), Kt., *cr.* 1937; C.I.E. 1921; F.J.I. 1911; *b.* 13 March 1868; *y. s.* of Rev. J. Brown, Upwell, Wisbech; *m.* Louisa Clara (*d.* 1935), *d.* of Hy. Pinchbeck; one *s.* one *d.* For five years leader writer and asst. editor, Bombay Gazette; two years ed., Indian Daily Telegraph, Lucknow; later London Correspondent of The Times of India; entered Office of The Times 1902, and served on Ed. Staff until 1954 since when a contributor. Hon. Sec. East India Assoc. (India, Pakistan, Burma), 1927-54; Hon. Treas., Royal India, Pakistan and Ceylon Soc., from 1932; Council, Roy. Soc. of Arts, 1941-56; a Vice-Pres., British and Foreign Bible Society, Coronation Medal, 1953. *Publications:* part author, Political India, 1932 and of British Commonwealth — a Family of Nations, 1952; contrib. to Encyclopaedia Britannica, 12th and subsequent eds.; Annual Reg. (India and Burma chapters), 1927-46; India and Burma Chapters in Hutchinson's Quarterly Record of Second World War; numerous articles in Dictionary of Nat. Biog. and contrib. to leading reviews; ed. Sir George Birdwood's Sva, 1915. *Address:* Dilkusha, 9 Westbourne Drive, Forest

Hill, S.E.23. *T.:* Forest Hill 1746. *Clubs:* East India and Sports, Royal Commonwealth Society. [*Died* 14 *Feb.* 1959.

BROWN, Frank James, C.B. 1922; C.B.E. 1920; formerly Assistant Secretary, General Post Office (in charge of the Telegraph Branch); and later Director International Telegraph Companies' Association; *b.* Skelton, near York, 5 Feb. 1865; *s.* of late William Brown; *m.* Lucy (*d.* 1931), *d.* of late Richard Shaw, of Brompton, Yorkshire; one *s.* *Educ.:* privately; B.Sc. (Lond.) 1887; M.A. (Lond.), 1888. Entered Secretary's Office, G.P.O., 1886; Representative of Post Office on Imperial Communications Committee; Technical Adviser on Cable questions at Peace Conference, Paris, 1919; Member of Imperial Wireless Telegraphy Committees, 1920 and 1924; Senior British delegate at Conference on Electrical Communications, Washington, 1920; Technical Adviser on Communications at Arms Conference, Washington, 1921-22; Knight Commander of the Dannebrog, 1921; Member of Broadcasting Committee, 1923, and of Broadcasting Board, 1923-25. *Publications:* Cable and Wireless Communications of the World, 1930; various articles (mainly on technical subjects). *Address:* 12 Heathcroft, Hampstead Way, N.W.11. *T.:* Speedwell 2000. [*Died* 22 *Oct.* 1958.

B R O W N, Frank Percival, A.R.C.A. (Lond.); Fellow of Ancient Monuments Society; Member of Council, Artists' Annuity Fund; *b.* Stoke-on-Trent, 24 Nov. 1877; *s.* of late Nicholas and Elizabeth Brown, Trenton Villa, Stoke-on-Trent; *m.* 1906, Hannah Sherman (author of The Child She Bare, written under pseudomyn of A Foundling; exhibited, R.A., 1930); one *d.* *Educ.:* Middle-Class School, Stoke-on-Trent. Worked for ten years in the factories as a designer's draughtsman, the latter part of the time with Josiah Wedgwood & Sons, Ltd.; in 1902 was awarded a Government Free Studentship at Royal College of Art, South Kensington; awarded Junior Art Scholarship, 1904, and Royal College of Art Scholarship, 1905-7; Full Diploma of Associateship, 1907; Head of Art Department, L.C.C. Norwood Technical Institute, 1907-10; Headmaster, Richmond (Surrey), School of Art, 1910-16; resigned latter appointment to work as machine hand, Shell Factory 3, Royal Arsenal, Woolwich; Art Master, Merchant Taylors' School, 1911-39; Highgate School, 1919-39; Davenant Foundation School, 1920-40; has delivered many special lectures to teachers. *Publications:* South Kensington and its Art Training, with foreword by late Walter Crane, 1912; The Training of Public Taste, 1921; English Art Series: Vol. I London Buildings, Vol. II London Paintings (with illustrations by Hannah Brown), Vol. III London Sculpture (with illustrations by Hannah Brown), 1933-34. *Recreation:* reading. *Address:* Cresta, Lenham Road East, Rottingdean, Sussex. *T.:* Rottingdean 2412. [*Died* 19 *Dec.* 1958.

BROWN, Major Henry Coddington, C.I.E. 1918; B.A., M.B., B.Ch., D.T.M. and H. Cantab.; I.M.S.; retired, 1919; *b.* 1876; 3rd *s.* of F. Latham Brown, P.W.D. India; *m.* 1911, Gladys Mary, *er. d.* of W. Furniss Potter, M.Inst.C.E., Ilkley, Yorkshire; one *s.* one *d.* *Address:* Firlands, Camberley, Surrey. [*Died* 18 *March* 1958.

BROWN, Brigadier James Sutherland, C.M.G. 1918; D.S.O. 1916; A.D.C. to Lieutenant-Governor of B.C. since 1935; *b.* 1881; *m.* 1916, Clare Temple, *d.* of late Thomas Corsan, Toronto; three *s.* *Educ.:* Grammar School, Simcoe, Ont.; Toronto Univ. Served European War, 1914-18 (despatches, D.S.O., C.M.G.); late Canadian Permanent Staff, formerly R. Canadian Regt.; District Officer commanding Military District No. XI., with Headquarters at Victoria, B.C., 1929-33; retired, 1933. *Address:* Bowker Place, in Bowker Place, Oak Bay, Victoria, B.C., Canada. *Club:* Pacific (Victoria, B.C.). [*Died* 13 *April* 1951.

BROWN, Lt.-Gen. Sir John, K.C.B., *cr.* 1934; (C.B. 1920); C.B.E. 1923; D.S.O. 1918; T.D.; J.P.; D.L.; F.R.I.B.A.; F.R.I.C.S.; *b.* 10 Feb. 1880; *er. s.* of late Alderman John Brown of Abington, Northampton, and Kate Davis Allen; *m.* 1904, Annie Maria, 3rd *d.* of late Alderman Francis Tonsley, J.P., of Northampton; two *s.* *Educ.:* Magdalen College School, Brackley. Joined 1st V.B. Northamptonshire Regiment, 1901 (afterwards 4th (T.A.) Bn. Northamptonshire Regiment); served in Suvla landing Aug. 1915, Anzac and Palestine campaigns; Commanded 162nd (East Midland) Infantry Brigade (T.A.), 1924-28; Deputy Director-Gen. of Territorial Army, 1937-39; Deputy Adjutant-General, War Office, 1939-40. Director General T.A. and Inspector General of Welfare and Education, War Office, 1940-41; retired, 1941. Chairman of the British Legion, 1930-34; Chairman British Empire Service League, 1946-53; Hon. Freeman of County Borough of Northampton, 1934; Master of the Worshipful Company of Pattenmakers, 1942-44 and 1950-1951. *Address:* 30A Billing Rd., Northampton. *Clubs:* Royal Automobile; Northampton (Northampton). [*Died* 4 *April* 1958.

BROWN, Sir (John Alfred) Arnesby, Kt., *cr.* 1938; R.A. 1915 (A.R.A. 1903); *b.* Nottingham, 1866; *s.* of late J. H. Brown, Ruddington, Notts; *m.* 1896, Mia (*d.* 1931), *e. d.* of Rev. Charles Smallwood Edwards, formerly vicar of Llanddewi Rhyderch, Abergavenny. *Educ.:* Nottingham High School, under Dr. Dixon. Commenced Art Study with the late Andrew M'Callum; later went to the Herkomer School, Bushey; first exhibited at R.A. 1890; pictures in the following public galleries: Tate Gallery, (Chantrey collection), The Guildhall permanent collection, Manchester, Auckland (N. Zealand), Birmingham, Manchester, Nottingham, Preston, and Worcester; Walker Art Gallery, Liverpool; National Gallery, Canada; National Gallery, Brisbane; City Art Gallery, Aberdeen. *Recreation:* fishing. *Address:* The White House, Haddiscoe, Norwich. *Club:* Athenæum. [*Died* 16 *Nov.* 1955.

BROWN, Kenneth; *see* Brown, Everard K.

BROWN, Lilian Kate Rowland- ("Rowland Grey"); novelist and journalist; *b.* London, 1863; *d.* of late H. Rowland-Brown, Barrister-at-law. *Educ.:* Cambridge; Fontainebleau. *Publications:* In Sunny Switzerland; By Virtue of his Office; Jacob's Letter; The Story of Chris; The Power of the Dog; The Craftsman; The Unexpected; Myself when Young; Green Cliffs; Surrender; La Belle Alliance; The Life and Letters of W. S. Gilbert (with Mr. Sidney Dark); Contributor to Nineteenth Century, Fortnightly, Dublin Review, Cornhill Magazine, Times Literary Supplement, Green Quarterly Review, Church Times, Theology, etc. *Recreations:* reading and music. *Address:* St. Mary's Retreat, Heathfield, Sussex. [*Died* 7 *Sept.* 1959.

BROWN, Percy, M.B.E. 1941; A.R.C.A. 1898; *b.* Birmingham, 1872; *m.* 1st, 1908, Muriel (*d.* 1943), *d.* of Lieut.-Colonel Sir Adelbert Talbot, K.C.I.E.; one *d.*; 2nd, 1948, Genevieve Le Play, rue de Passy, Paris. *Educ.:* Edward VI. Grammar School and School of Art, Birmingham. First Royal Exhibitioner, Royal College of Art, S. Kensington, 1892; National Silver Medallist, 1894; excavating in Upper Egypt for Egypt Exploration Fund, 1894-96; Indian Educational Service, 1899; Principal, Mayo School of Art and Curator

Museum, Lahore, 1899-1909; Principal, Govt. School of Art, Calcutta, 1909-27; retired 1927; Secretary and Curator, Victoria Memorial Hall, Calcutta, retired 1947; on deputation, Assistant Director Art Exhibition Delhi Durbar, 1902-3; Captain Punjab Light Horse, 1905; Newcomen gold medal and challenge cup, 1908; officer in charge, Art Section and Trustee Indian Museum, 1910; designed and executed Indian coinage reverse, 1911. F.R.A.S.B., Vice-Pres., 1936. *Publications:* Picturesque Nepal, 1912; Tours in Sikkim, 1917; Indian Painting, 1918; Indian Painting under the Mughals, 1924; Monuments of the Mughal Period, in the Cambridge History of India, 1937; collaborated with M. Naville in vols. ii., iii., Temple of Deir-el-Bahari, 1896; collaborated with Sir George Watt, Indian Art at Delhi, 1903; Indian Architecture, 1942; Book I, Buddhist and Hindu, Book II Islamic; articles on Indian Art to Nineteenth Century and Empire Review. *Recreations:* travelling and fishing. [*Died* 22 *March* 1955.

BROWN, Captain Percy George, C.B.E. 1919; R.N. (retired); *b.* Dec. 1874: 2nd *s.* of Capt. Robert Brown, 53rd Regt., and Elizabeth Dewar; *m.* 1914, Mary (*d.* 1935), *d.* of S. N. Hutchins, Ardnagashel, Bantry, Co. Cork; no *c.* *Educ.:* Cargilfield, Edinburgh; H.M.S. Britannia. Lieut. 1896; Comm. 1908; retired, 1919; served European War (Croix de Guerre with palms, Chevalier, Legion of Honour, C.B.E.); Major Home Guard, 1941-42; acquired estate of Weens by purchase from Geo. Tancred; sold it and gifted Mansion House to Hawick Eventide Homes; J.P. Roxburgh. *Recreations:* formerly hunting and shooting. *Address:* 18 Belgrave Crescent, Edinburgh 4. *Clubs:* United Service; New (Edinburgh). [*Died* 24 *May* 1954.

BROWN, Brigadier-General Percy Wilson, C.M.G. 1919; D.S.O. 1916; late Gordon Highlanders; Member Queen's Body-guard for Scotland (Royal Company of Archers); *s.* of late Thomas Brown of Dalnair, Stirlingshire; *b.* 12 Oct. 1876; *m.* 1923, Janet, *d.* of late Charles Galbraith of The Barony, Dumfries; three *s.* *Educ.:* Uppingham; Sandhurst. Entered Army, Gordon Highlanders, 1896; Capt. 1901; Maj. 1914; Lieut.-Col. 1920; retired 1922 with rank of Brig.-Gen.; served S. African campaign, 1899-1902 (despatches, Queen's medal 4 clasps, King's medal 2 clasps); European War, 1914-18; Commanded 1st, 2nd, and 6th Battalions Gordon Highlanders, 2nd Batt. Argyll and Sutherland Highlanders, and 71st Infantry Brigade, France (despatches, C.M.G., D.S.O., Bt. Lt.-Col., Croix de Guerre, France, C. Star, Roumania). *Address:* Walton Park, Castle Douglas, Kirkcudbrightshire. *Club:* New (Edinburgh). [*Died* 2 *Jan.* 1954.

BROWN, R. N. R.; *see* Rudmose-Brown.

BROWN, Robert Sidney, C.B.E. 1949 (O.B.E. 1945); Secretary, Services Dept., Commonwealth Relations Office, since 1948; *b.* 10 Feb. 1889; *s.* of John Watt Brown, late Military Works Services, India; *m.* 1919, Hannah (*d.* 1943), *d.* of Samuel Bowyer, H.M. Customs and Excise; one *s.* one *d.* Civil Servant, General Post Office, 1908; Board of Trade, 1909; India Office, 1911; Commonwealth Relations Office, 1947; Secretary to Indian Delegation to Conf. on the Operation of Dominion Legislation, 1929. *Address:* 2 Siward Road, Bromley, Kent. *T.:* Ravensbourne 2011. *Club:* Surrey County Cricket. [*Died* 22 *Aug.* 1959.

BROWN, Sir Stuart Kelson, K.C.I.E., *cr.* 1939; C.B. 1932; C.V.O. 1925; late Deputy Under Secretary of State, India Office; *b.* 1885; *m.* 1920, Dorothy Ierne, O.B.E., *y. d.* of late Sir Evelyn Freeth; one *s.* one *d.* *Educ.:* Dulwich College; King's College Cambridge (Porson Prize, 1906). Appointed to India Office, 1909; retired, 1942; served in R.G.A., 1915-18 (despatches). *Address:* 84 Northway, N.W.11. *T.:* Meadway 2446. [*Died* 27 *Jan.* 1952.

BROWN, Sir (Thomas) Algernon, Kt., *cr.* 1956; **Hon. Mr. Justice Brown;** Chief Justice, Northern Region of Nigeria, since 1955; *b.* 22 May 1900; *s.* of late James Algernon Brown and of Margaret Brown, Windmills, Wheatley, nr. Oxford; *m.* 1941, Mary (Mollie) (*née* Wynne-Savory); two *s.* one *d.* *Educ.:* Marlborough Coll.; Oriel Coll., Oxford (M.A.). Commissioned 16th Cavalry, Indian Army, 1920; active service Waziristan Field Force, 1920-22 (despatches). Called to the Bar, Inner Temple, 1926; Midland Circuit; in practice in England until 1933; Crown Counsel, Gold Coast, 1933; Solicitor-General, Kenya, 1940; Puisne Judge, Singapore, 1946. *Recreations:* polo, shooting and riding. *Address:* Vigers Hall, Tavistock, Devon. *T.:* Tavistock 2616; Chief Justice's Chambers, High Court, Kaduna, Northern Region, Nigeria. *T.:* Kaduna 240. *Club:* Junior Carlton. [*Died* 5 *Oct.* 1960.

BROWN, Walter, M.A., B.Sc., F.R.S.E., A.M.I.E.E.; *b.* Glasgow, 29 April 1886; *s.* of Hugh A. Brown; unmarried. *Educ.:* Glasgow Univ. Assistant Master, Allan Glen's School, Glasgow, 1911-14; Lecturer in Engineering, Hong Kong University, 1914-1918; Professor of Mathematics (Pure and Applied), The University, Hong Kong, 1918-46, Emeritus Professor, 1951. Dean, Faculty of Arts, 1921-22, 1924, and 1938-1939; Dean, Faculty of Engineering, 1923; First Dean, Faculty of Science, 1939; Member of Senate, Council and Court of the University; Assoc. Member, Instit. of Electrical Engineers, 1919; Fellow, Royal Society of Edinburgh, 1923; Adviser on Secondary and Technical Education to the Lester Trust, Shanghai, 1930-31; for various periods, President Hong Kong Philharmonic Soc., Pres. H.K. Univ. Engineering Soc., President H.K.U. Arts Association and Vice-Pres. H.K.U. Education Soc.; Foundation Member, Hong Kong English Assoc., and Sino-British Assoc. First President, Hong Kong Univ. Science Society, 1939; Hon. Vice-Pres., Hong Kong Inst. of Engineers and Shipbuilders, 1939. Non-official J.P.; Life Member, Overseas League; Fellow and Life Mem. Roy. Empire Soc.; Prisoner-of-War, Hong Kong, Dec. 1941-Sept. 1945 (R.N.V.R.). Lecturer, Dept of Civil and Mechanical Engineering, Roy. Tech. College, Glasgow, 1946-47; Lecturer, Department of Mathematics, Glasgow University, 1947-48. Has travelled extensively in Europe, Asia, North and South America, Africa and Australasia. *Recreations:* golf, music, travel. *Club:* Royal Scottish Automobile (Glasgow). [*Died* 14 *April* 1957.

BROWN, William, M.A., D.M. (Oxon), D.Sc. (Lond.), F.R.C.P. (Lond.); Psychologist and Psychiatrist; President British Psychological Society, 1951-52; Wilde Reader in Mental Philosophy, Univ. of Oxford, 1921-46; Director Institute of Experimental Psychology, Univ. of Oxford, 1936-45; *b.* Slinfold, Sx., 5 Dec. 1881; 2nd *s.* of William Brown, Wingates House, Wingates, Morpeth; *m.* 1st, May Leslie Rayment English (*d.* 1916); one *s.*; 2nd, Dorothea Mary Stone; one *s.* one *d.* *Educ.:* Collyer's School, Horsham; Christ Church, Oxford (Scholar); Germany; King's College Hospital. Mathematical Moderations, Oxford, 1902; Natural Science Final Honours (Physiology), 1904; Literæ Humaniores, 1905; John Locke Scholar in Mental Philosophy, 1906; D.M. 1918; D.Sc. Lond. (Carpenter Medallist), 1910 (studied the mathematical theory of probability under Prof. Karl Pearson);

M.R.C.P. Lond. 1921; F.R.C.P. 1930; Reader in Psychology, University of London (King's College), 1914-21; Psychotherapist, King's College Hospital, 1925-31; Fellow R.S.M. and of British Psychological Soc.; Member of Mind Assoc., Royal Medico-Psychological Assoc., Royal Institute of Philosophy (Member of Council), and R.I.I.A. President Section J (Psychology) of the British Association for the Advancement of Science, 1927; Terry Lecturer at Yale University, 1928; Past Chairman of Medical Section, British Psychological Society; Pres. Soc. for Study of Addiction, 1935-37; Associate Foreign Member, Société Française de Psychologie; military service, 1914-19 (despatches); late officer commanding Craiglockhart War Hospital for Neurasthenic Officers, Edinburgh; resident medical officer, Maudsley Hospital for nerve shock cases. Neurologist to the Fourth Army, B.E.F., France; Major, Royal Army Medical Corps. *Publications:* The Essentials of Mental Measurement, 1st ed. 1911 (later editions with Prof. Sir Godfrey H. Thomson, *q.v.*), 4th ed. 1940; Psychology and Psychotherapy, 5th edition, 1944; Suggestion and Mental Analysis, 3rd edition, 1923; Talks on Psychotherapy, 1923; Psychology and the Sciences (Editor). 1925; Mind and Personality, 1926; Science and Personality, 1929; Body and Mind, 1930 (article in Encyclopædia Britannica); Mind, Medicine and Metaphysics, 1936; Psychological Methods of Healing, 1938; War and the Psychological Conditions of Peace, 2nd edition, 1942; Personality and Religion, 1946; Oxford Essays on Psychology, 1948; contributions to scientific and medical journals, from An Objective Study of Mathematical Intelligence (Biometrika, 1910) and Correlation of Mental Abilities (Brit. Journ. Psychol., 1910), to The Inferiority Complex and the Paranoid Tendency: with a Brief Reference to Nazi Psychology (Nature, 1945). *Address:* 22 Upland Park Road, Oxford; 88 Harley Street, W.1. *T.:* Langham 3297. *Club:* Athenæum. [*Died* 17 *May* 1952.

BROWN, Rt. Rev. William F., V.G.; Titular Bishop of Pella; Rector of St. Anne's Catholic Church, Vauxhall, S.E.; Vicar-General of the Diocese of Southwark since 1904; *b.* Dundee, 3 May 1862; 3rd *s.* of late Andrew Brown, of Lochton, Perthshire, and Fanny Mary, *d.* of late Major James Wemyss, Scots Greys. *Educ.:* Dundee High School; Trinity Coll., Glenalmond; University College School and St. Thomas's Seminary, Hammersmith. Priest, 1886; Assistant Priest, Sacred Heart Church, Camberwell; Rector St. Anne's Mission, Vauxhall, 1892, where schools and church have been erected and freed from debt; Protonotary Apostolic ad instar, 1907; Provost of Southwark Cathedral Chapter; consecrated Bishop of Pella, 1924; member of London School Board, 1897-1904; member of Commission on the Decline of the Birth Rate and Cinema Enquiry Commission. *Publications:* Through Windows of Memory, 1946; numerous articles in general, and special papers on Education and Social questions. *Address:* Catholic Church, Vauxhall, S.E.11. *T.:* Reliance 1862. *Club:* Pontifical Court. [*Died* 16 *Dec.* 1951.

BROWN, William John; Trade Union Advisor, Journalist and Author; *s.* of Joseph Morris Brown, Sanitary Inspector, and Rose Spicer; *m.* 1917, Mabel, *d.* of H. Prickett, Penge; two *s.* one *d.* *Educ.:* Salmestone Elementary School, Margate; Sir Roger Manwood's Grammar School, Sandwich. Boy Clerk, Civil Service (P.O. Savings Bank), 1910; Assistant Clerk (H.M. Office of Works), 1912; General Secretary Civil Service Clerical Association, 1919-1942, Parliamentary General Secretary, 1942-1949; M.P. (Lab.) West Wolverhampton, 1929-31; M.P. (Ind.) Rugby, 1942-50. *Publications:* Reactions, and Rhyme and Reason (verse); A History of the Civil Service Clerical Association; The Civil Service Compendium; Whitleyism on its Trial; Three Months in Russia; Very Free Speech; What Have I to Lose; I Meet America; So Far . . .; Everybody's Guide to Parliament; Jamaican Journey; The Land of Look-Behind; Success—Your Birthright; Brown Studies; Contrib. to Time and Tide, under *pseudonym* Diogenes. *Recreations:* books, walking. *Address:* 26 Isokon, Lawn Road, Belsize Park, N.W.3. *T.:* Primrose 1497. [*Died* 3 *Oct.* 1960.

BROWN, W. L. L.; *see* Lowe-Brown.

BROWNE, Rt. Rev. Arthur Heber, D.D., LL.D.; *b.* 1864; *m.* Louisa Bick-Stockton (*d.* 1936). *Educ.:* St. Edmund Hall, Oxford. Rector of St. John, Newfoundland, 1894-98; Vicar of Kempsford, 1898-1904; Missioner in the Diocese of Exeter, 1904-14; Rector of Clyst St. George, 1911-1914; Vicar of St. Michael's, Paddington, 1914-25; Bishop of Bermuda, 1925-48. *Address:* Hamilton, Bermuda. [*Died* 10 *June* 1951.

BROWNE, Sir Charles Ernest Christopher, Kt., *cr.* 1946; Parliamentary Agent to H.M. Government (Sessional appointment) since 1934; *b.* 28 Nov. 1871; *s.* of late George Forrest Browne, former Bishop of Bristol and previously Suffragan Bishop of Stepney, and Mary Louisa, *d.* of Sir John Stewart-Richardson, 13th Bart.; *m.* 1st, 1899, Florence Amelia Woolfrey Bridge (*d.* 1940); two *d.*; 2nd, 1940, Francisse Willy Jeslein. *Educ.:* Shrewsbury; Selwyn College, Cambridge (B.A. 1893). Admitted Solicitor, 1902; partner in firm of Dyson and Co. (now Dyson, Bell and Co.), Parliamentary Agents, since 1902. Twice President of Society of Parliamentary Agents. *Recreation:* golf. *Address:* 21 Bryanston Court, W.1. *T.:* Paddington 2669. *Club:* Oxford and Cambridge. [*Died* 8 *Feb.* 1953.

BROWNE, Lieut.-Colonel Cuthbert Garrard, C.M.G. 1919; D.S.O. 1915; late R.A.M.C.; *y. s.* of late Walter P. Browne and Mrs. Browne, of Bidston, Gipsy Hill; *b.* 3 March 1883; *m.* 1921, Florence (Pat), *e. d.* of late Brig.-Gen. J. W. V. Carroll, C.M.G., D.S.O.; one *s.* one *d.* *Educ.:* Dulwich College; Westminster Hospital. Served European War, 1914-1918 (D.S.O., C.M.G., Bt. Lt.-Col.); War of 1939-45; retired pay, 1926. *Address:* Lakers Farm, West Chiltington, Sussex; Waltham, Grenada, B.W.I. [*Died* 27 *Feb.* 1951.

BROWNE, Brig.-Gen. D. J. E. B.; *see* Beale-Browne.

BROWNE, Maj.-Gen. Edward George, C.B. 1916; C.M.G. 1918; *b.* 28 Mar. 1863; *s.* of late William Browne, Killymaddy, Castle Caulfield, Co. Tyrone; *m.* Mabel (*d.* 1931), *d.* of Major-General Hamilton Robert Hathway, The Croft, Hereford. Served Chitral, 1895 (medal with clasp); European War, 1914-18 (despatches five times, C.B., C.M.G., officer Légion d'Honneur); retired pay, 1922. *Address:* The Lindens, Farnborough Park, Hants. *T.:* Farnborough 67. *Club:* Junior United Service. [*Died* 17 *Jan.* 1952.

BROWNE, Major-General Herbert Jose Pierson, C.B. 1920; retired I.A., 1924; *b.* 21 Jan. 1872; *s.* of late Major-General Sir James Browne, K.C.S.I., C.B., R.E.; *m.* Violet Gertrude Barton, *d.* of late Barton Smith, M.D., Charles Street, W.; no *c.* *Educ.:* Marlborough; Sandhurst. Entered Army, 2nd Lt. King's Own Scottish Borderers, 1891; joined 5th Gurkha Rifles Punjab Frontier Force, 1894; served Mahsud Wazir Expedition, 1894 (medal and clasp); Tochi Valley Expedition, 1897;

Tirah Expedition (Gurkha Scouts), 1897-98 (medal 3 clasps, despatches); Mohmand Expedition, 1907 (medal and clasp); European War, Mesopotamia, 1915-17 (2 medals, star, despatches, brevet Lt.-Col. and Col., temporary Brig.-Gen., C.B.; Order White Eagle Serbia, 2nd class); Commanded 2nd Bn. 5th Gurkha Rifles; Staff appointments: D.A.Q.M.G., D.A.A.G., G.S.O.A.H.Q., Brigade Major Dehra Dun and Garhwal Brigades; passed Staff College, G.S.O. Bombay District; Brigade Major, G.S.O.I. and B.G.G.S. Mesopotamia; B.G.G.S. Southern Command, India; commanded Abbottabad, Dardoni, Ferozepore and Ambala Brigades. *Recreations:* shooting, climbing, fishing, drawing, world travel. *Address:* c/o Lloyds Bank, Montpellier, Cheltenham, Glos. *Club:* United Service.

[*Died* 29 *June* 1953.

BROWNE, Brigadier James Clendinning, C.B. 1935; C.M.G. 1919; D.S.O. 1916; *b.* 1878; *s.* of Major James Browne, Devon Regt.; *m.* 1910, Zaidee, *d.* of James Butler, Johannesburg, S.A.; one *s.* one *d.* Entered Army Service Corps, 1902; Major, 1914; Bt. Lt.-Col. 1918; Lt.-Col. 1921; Col. 1923; Col. Comdt. 1927; served S. African War, 1900-2 (Queen's medal, three clasps, King's medal, two clasps); European War, 1914-18 (despatches five times, C.M.G., D.S.O., Bt. Lt.-Col.); Assistant Director of Supplies and Transport, Aldershot Command, 1927-31; A.D.C. to the King, 1926-35; Brigadier in charge of Administration, Egypt, 1931-35; retired pay, 1935. *Address:* Goodworth Cottage, Goodworth Clatford, Andover, Hants. *T.:* Andover 2511. *Club:* Army and Navy.

[*Died* 22 *Dec.* 1953.

BROWNE, Leonard Foster; Honorary Consulting Psychiatrist to Tavistock Clinic, Beaumont St., W.1; Lt.-Col., 1943; Major R.A.M.C. 1940; Member L.C.C. (N. Kensington) 1946, Alderman 1949, reappointed 1955; J.P. County of London; *b.* Sunderland, 22 May 1887; *y. s.* of John Laing Browne and Elizabeth Foster, niece of Birket Foster, R.W.S.; *m.* 1923, Violet, 4th *d.* of late Rev. Richard Bott, Vicar of Newlands, Keswick; one *s.* two *d.* *Educ.:* Sedbergh; University of Durham College of Medicine, Newcastle upon Tyne. M.B., B.S. (Durham), 1909, M.D. (gold medal), 1913; F.B.Ps.S.; F.R.S.M.; R.I.I.A.; Assistant Surgeon, C.M.S. Hospital, Cairo, 1912; served as an officer in R.A.M.C. in France and Flanders, 1914-17 (1914 Star); Hon. Sec. to Archbishop of Canterbury's Cttee. on Social Service, 1918-19; Medical Officer and Tutor at the Ordination Test School, Knutsford, 1919-21; Deacon, 1920-43; First Treasurer of Talbot House, Poperinghe, 1916-17, and closely connected with the Toc H. Movement since then, Trustee 1947; Command Psychiatrist Eastern Command and London District, 1940-45. Contested (Lab.) Penrith and Cockermouth Div., 1945; Alderman St. Pancras Borough Council, 1945-49; Vice-Chairman, London County Council, 1957-58. *Publications:* chapter The Innkeeper, in Tales of Talbot House (by Rev. P. B. Clayton), 1919; essay (with J. A. Hadfield), The Psychology of Spiritual Healing, in Psychology and the Church, 1925; chapter (with D. G. M. Munro), Psycho-therapy in the treatment of Tuberculosis in The Psycho-pathology of Tuberculosis, 1926; Everyday Relationships, 1938; articles in The Spectator, and in various medical journals. *Recreations:* reading, walking, mountaineering. *Address:* 3 St. Katharine's Precinct, Regent's Park, N.W.1. *T.:* Welbeck 9385; The Warren, Grange, Keswick, Cumberland. *T.:* Borrowdale 250.

[*Died* 15 *May* 1960.

BROWNE, Maurice; actor-manager and dramatist; *b.* Reading, 12 Feb. 1881; *e. s.* of late Rev. F. H. Browne, for many years headmaster of Queen Elizabeth's School, Ipswich, and late Frances Anna Neligan Browne, formerly Principal of Clovelly-Kepplestone, Eastbourne. *Educ.:* Temple Grove; Winchester; Eastbourne; Peterhouse, Cambridge. Co-founder with late Harold Monro of Samurai Press, England, 1906-8, from which the Poetry Bookshop originated and, in part, the Georgian Poets; founder and director, with Ellen Van Volkenburg, of the Chicago Little Theatre, 1912-18, parent theatre of American Little Theatres; director of the Ellen Van Volkenburg-Maurice Browne Repertory Company, New York and the Pacific Coast, U.S.A., 1918-26; Managing Director of Maurice Browne Ltd., London, 1928-37; Director of Maurice Browne Inc., New York, 1929-33. Artist in Residence, Univ. of California, Los Angeles, 1949. Presented Journey's End at the Savoy Theatre, 1929, and then throughout the English-speaking world; has presented many plays in Great Britain and the U.S.A. *Publications:* Proposals for a Voluntary Nobility (with late Harold Monro); Recollections of Rupert Brooke; Wings over Europe (with late Robert Nichols); In Time of War: The Atom and the Way; Road from Delavan; (posthumous) Too Late to Lament. *Address:* Quarrenden, Totnes, Devon.

[*Died* 21 *Jan.* 1955.

BROWNE, Ven. Walter Marshall, M.A.; Archdeacon Emeritus; Canon Residentiary of Rochester, 1933-51, retired; *b.* 1885; *s.* of late T. G. C. Browne; *m.* 1914, Jessie Margaret Vickers; one *s.* two *d.* *Educ.:* Tonbridge School; Christ's College, Cambridge, 2nd Class Hist. Tripos Pts. 1 and 2, 1st Class Theo. Tripos, Pt. 2; Curate St. Anne's, Nottingham, 1909-12; Domestic Chaplain to Dr. Percival, Bishop of Hereford, 1913-16; Vicar of Attenborough-cum-Bramcote, Notts, 1916-23; Vicar of Erith, Kent, 1923-32; Examining Chaplain to the Bishop of Rochester, 1933-51. Select Preacher Cambridge Univ., 1941. *Address:* Albury, 43 Queens Rd., Tunbridge Wells.

[*Died* 6 *Feb.* 1959.

BROWNFIELD, Surgeon Rear-Admiral Owen Deane, C.B. 1948; O.B.E. 1918; M.B., B.S., M.R.C.S., L.R.C.P.; *b.* 22 Feb. 1891; *s.* of Dr. H. M. Brownfield, The Old College, Petersfield, Hants.; *m.* 1916, Mary Agnes Sutherland Mackenzie-Hughes. *Educ.:* Epsom College; St. Thomas's Hospital, S.E.1. Commission Royal Navy, 1914. Medical Officer in charge: Cadets' Sick Quarters, R.N. College, Dartmouth, 1937; H.M.H.S. Vita, 1940; Combined Services Hospital, Trincomalee, Ceylon, 1945; Medical Officer in charge of R.N. Hosp., Malta, 1947-50; Surg. Rear-Adm., 1947; formerly K.H.P.; retd. list, 1950. *Recreations:* tennis, hockey, golf. *Address:* Little Deane, Sussex Road, Petersfield, Hants. *Club:* Naval and Military.

[*Died* 30 *March* 1955.

BROWNING, Lieut.-Colonel Herbert Arrott; *b.* 8 Feb. 1861; 2nd *s.* of late Colin A. R. Browning, C.I.E.; *m.* 1893, Mai, *y. d.* of late Thomas Davis, Banbury, Oxon. *Educ.:* Marlborough; Sandhurst. Entered Army, 1881; joined 30th (East Lancashire) Regiment; entered Indian Staff Corps, 1884; joined 2nd Punjab Infantry, 1884; transferred 2nd Punjab Cavalry, 1885; Captain, 1892; Major, 1901; Lt.-Colonel, 1907; entered Burmah Commission, 1886; served Burmah Expedition, 1886-88 (medal with 2 clasps), and throughout the operations in connection with the pacification of Upper Burmah; received the thanks of the Government of India and of the Burmah Government (twice); Deputy-Commissioner, Burmah, 1896; Officiating Commissioner, Burmah, 1905; Chief Commissioner, Andaman and Nicobar Islands, 1906-13; Commissioner, Burmah, 1914; retired, 1915; re-employed under the War Office, Nov. 1914.

[*Died* 21 *Jan.* 1951.

BRUCE, Hon. Alice Moore, M.A.; Hon. Fellow of Somerville College, Oxford; Vice-President of G.P.D.S.T.; Member of Council of University College of South Wales and Monmouthshire, retired; President of Council of Aberdare Hall, Cardiff, retired; *b.* 1867; *y. d.* of 1st Baron Aberdare. *Address:* White Gables, Headington, Oxford. *T.:* Oxford 6929. [*Died* 4 *Nov.* 1951.

BRUCE, Rev. Douglas William, C.B.E. 1937; M.A.; D.D.; Minister of St. Andrew's (Church of Scotland) Buenos Aires, 1926-53; *b.* 1 June 1885; *s.* of Rev. William Straton Bruce, V.D., D.D., F.R.S.E., Banff Parish Church, and of Anna Maria Duncan; *m.* 1st, 1915, Cicely Mary, M.B., Ch.B. (Edin.) (*d.* 1942), *d.* of Rev. J. T. Kerby, M.A., Vicar of Goosnargh, Lancs.; three *s.* one *d.*; 2nd, 1949, Alice Bevan Chantrill, *widow* of Percy William Bell, Estancia Grande, City Bell, Argentina. *Educ.:* Banff Academy; Aberdeen University (M.A. 1907); Edinburgh Univ. (Divinity). D.D. 1939; Asst. Minister: St. Andrew's, Buenos Aires, 1910-12; St. Cuthbert's, Edin., 1912-14; Minister: Cadzow Parish, Hamilton, 1915-19; St. Stephen's Parish, Broughty Ferry, 1919-26; served European War, Lieutenant (temp. capt.) 1/4th Gordon Highlanders, 51st (Highland) Division, B.E.F., France, 1916-18 (wounded); Member of various public British committees in the Argentine; Chairman of St. Andrew's Society of the River Plate, 1933; chairman Toc H, Argentina, 1936. *Publications:* To Scots in Argentina; various pamphlets. *Recreations:* golf and fishing. *Address:* Perú 352, Buenos Aires. *Clubs:* Overseas, Hurlingham (Hon.). [*Died* 27 *May* 1953.

BRUCE, Rev. Dr. Francis Rosslyn Courtenay, F.L.S.; Rector of Herstmonceux, Sussex, since 1923; Chaplain of The Royal Horse Artillery; Chaplain Nat. Fire Brigade, Southern District; *b.* 14 Aug. 1871; *s.* of Canon Lloyd Bruce of York; *b.* of Rt. Hon. Sir Hervey Bruce, 3rd Bart.; *m.* Rachel, *e. d.* of Richard Gurney, J.P., D.L., Northrepps Hall, Norfolk; two *s.* three *d.* *Educ.:* St. Edward's, Oxford; Edinburgh University; Worcester College, Oxford (M.A. and D.D.). Five years' business training; did work in London slums; sometime senior curate St. Anne's, Soho; eight years rector of Clifton, Notts; ten years Vicar Edgbaston, Birmingham; has been District Councillor since 1907 (Nottingham and Sussex); President of Athletics, and Secretary of the Union at Oxford; lectures at home and abroad on literary and social subjects; President and Trustee of Birmingham R.S.P.C.A. *Publications:* Oxford Verses; Bach's Christmas Oratorio; Men and Women of Soho; The Common Hope; Dr. Gore and Education; The Clifton Book; Letters from Turkey; God and the Allies; Prayers for Daily Use; Studies in Heredity; Sussex Sacred Song; contributes to The Times, and Punch. *Recreations:* freemasonry (Grand Lodge), Rotary (Vice-Chairman, Dist. 12), cricket, horses and dogs. *Address:* Herstmonceux Rectory, Sussex. *T.:* Herstmonceux 3124. *Clubs:* Bath, Kennel (Member of Cttee.); Devonshire (Eastbourne) [*Died* 19 *Jan.* 1956.

BRUCE, Colonel Sir Gerald Trevor, K.C.B., *cr.* 1941 (C.B. 1936); C.M.G. 1919; D.S.O. 1918; T.D.; formerly Lord-Lieutenant, Glamorgan; Chairman of Wales and Mon. Industrial Estates Ltd.; Chairman S. Wales and Mon. Industries Assoc.; *b.* 1872; *m.* 1896, Lilian, *d.* of late Thomas William Booker, of Velindra, Glam. Served European War, 1914-18 (despatches, D.S.O., C.M.G.); Senior Regional Commissioner for Welsh Civil Defence Region, 1939-45. *Address:* The Grange, St. Hilary, Glamorgan. [*Died* 7 *July* 1953.

BRUCE, Henry James, C.M.G. 1917; M.V.O. 1907; *y. s.* of Sir H. Bruce, 4th Bt.; *b.* 1 Nov. 1880; *m.* 1915, Tamara Karsavina; one *s.* *Educ.:* Eton. Entered Foreign Office, 1904; Vienna, 1905; 3rd Secretary, 1906; transferred to Berlin, 1908; 2nd Secretary, 1911; Petrograd, 1913; 1st Secretary, 1918; retired 1920; Secretary General British Delegation, Interallied Commission for Bulgaria, 1921; British Delegate, 1924-26; Adviser, National Bank of Hungary, 1931-39. Treasurer, Peabody Donation Fund, 1949. *Publications:* Silken Dalliance, 1947; Thirty Dozen Moons, 1949. *Clubs:* St. James', M.C.C. [*Died* 10 *Sept.* 1951.

BRUCE, Marcus James Henry, C.B.E. 1942; M.I.Mech.E.; *b.* 10 October 1890; *m.* 1935, Phyllis Irene Smith; no *c.* *Educ.:* Winchester; Royal Military Academy, Woolwich. B.Sc. (Engineering) London University. Joined Royal Army Service Corps, 1911; Q.M.G.'s Dept. War Office, 1915 (despatches, Brevet Major); Deputy Controller, Disposals Board, 1919-20; various civil managerial appointments, 1920-27; Production Engineer, London General Omnibus Company, 1928-32; Works Engineer and a Principal Officer of London Passenger Transport Board, 1933-40; Member of Committee on Air Force Administration, 1939, and of Committee on Repairs of Mechanical Equipment in the Field, 1940; Mechanical Engineering Adviser to Quartermaster-General, War Office, 1940; Director of Mechanical Maintenance, War Office, with rank of Maj.-Gen., 1940-42; Director of Fighting Vehicle Inspection, Ministry of Supply, 1942-44; Director, J. & P. Bruce, Ltd. *Recreations:* golf, tennis, winter sports, scientific and engineering subjects. *Address:* c/o Barclays Bank, 52 Regent Street, W.1. [*Died* 21 *Nov.* 1956.

BRUCE, Sir Michael (William Selby), 11th Bt., *cr.* 1629; late Sqdn. Ldr. R.A.F. Regt.; invalided 1945 with rank, Wing/Commander and returned to R.A.F. as Adjutant, Plymouth Wing, A.T.C., 1951; Director of Public Services, CKNW Radio Station, Vancouver, B.C.; Military Correspondent and Columnist, The Vancouver Herald, 1954; *b.* Ensenada, Lower California, 27 March 1894; *s.* of Sir William Waller Bruce, 10th Bart., and Angelica Mary, *d.* of late General George Selby, Royal Artillery; *S.* father, 1912; *m.* 1925, Doreen Dalziel Greenwell (from whom he obtained a divorce, 1928); one *s.*; *m.* 1933, Constance Elizabeth (*d.* 1943), *d.* of late Frank Plummer, Toronto, Canada; one *d.*; *m.* 1946, Margaret Helen, *d.* of Sir Arthur Binns; one *s.* *Educ.:* The Grange, Stevenage; Roysses School, Abingdon. Lieut. 8th Middlesex Regiment, 1912; seconded to B.S.A. Police Force; served against natives in Portuguese East Africa, 1913-14; against rebels in Transvaal, 1914 (wounded); Major New Zealand Artillery at Dardanelles, 1915-16 (wounded); France, 1916-17 (wounded); German East Africa, 1918; until 1941 was Director of Public Relations for Odeon Theatres; served 1939-40 as Flying Officer 901 (County of London) Squadron A.A.F. but was recalled by Ministry of Information for production of propaganda films; returned to Royal Air Force, Oct. 1941; served France, Mediterranian, Normandy, Germany (wounded). *Publications:* Songs from the Saddle; Hunters' Yarns; Sails and Saddles, 1929; The Royal House of Bruce; Charles, Our Prince; Life of William Wallace; Hundred Years of Headlines; Tramp Royal; wrote and produced the film Territorial Cavalcade. *Heir:* *s.* Michael Ian [*b.* 3 Apr. 1926; *m.* 1947, Barbara Stevens, *d.* of F. J. Lynch, U.S.A.; two *s.* Served European War, 1943-1945, U.S. Marines]. *Recreations:* riding, historical research. *Address:* 2465 West 5th Ave., Vancouver, B.C., Canada; The Vancouver Herald, Georgia St., Vancouver. [*Died* 26 *May* 1957.

BRUCE, Sir Robert, Kt., *cr.* 1918; Hon. LL.D., Universities of Glasgow, Toronto, and St. Andrews; F.R.S.E.; F.J.I.; D.L., J.P.; *b.* Alloa, Clackmannanshire, 26 Oct. 1871; *s.* of late William Bruce; *m.* 1905, Mary, *d.* of late James McNicol, Alva; two *s.* one *d.* Assistant Editor Glasgow Herald, 1914-17; Editor-in-Chief, 1917-36; previously for 20 years London and Parliamentary Correspondent; Lord Dean of Guild of Glasgow, 1941-42; Pres. R. Philosophical Society of Glasgow, 1944-47; Mem. of Scottish Cttee. of L.M. & S. Railway, 1936-1948. Mem. of Admin. Cttee. of Empire Exhibition, Scotland, 1938; Member of Alness Committee on Grants to Universities of Scotland, 1937-38; Acting Chairman of Ministry of Labour Committee on Distressed Areas under Act of 1937; President of Institute of Journalists, 1926; President of Burns' Federation, 1923-27. *Publications:* Greystones; The House of Memories; numerous articles. *Address:* Brisbane House, 9 Rowan Road, Glasgow, S.1. [*Died* 27 *March* 1955.

BRUCE, Major Hon. Robert, C.B.E. 1956; D.L.; J.P.; Major, Special Res., 11th Hussars; Member: Advisory Panel on Highlands and Islands; Scottish Council of Industry for Highlands; Chairman, Highlands and Islands Film Guild; *b.* 18 Nov. 1882; *b.* of 10th Earl of Elgin, K.T., C.M.G., T.D., C.D.; *m.* 1910, Mary Katherine, *o. c.* of late Maj.-Gen. Hon. John E. Lindley; two *d.* (and one *s.* killed in action). Brevet Major, 1917. D.L. Moray, 1949. O.St.J. 1958. *Address:* Glenerney, Dunphail, Morayshire. *Clubs:* Cavalry; New (Edinburgh). [*Died* 31 *Oct.* 1959.

BRUCE, Rev. Dr. Rosslyn; *see* Bruce, Rev. Dr. F. Rosslyn C.

BRUCE, Hon. Victoria Alexandrina Katherine; Governor H.M. Prison, Duke Street, Glasgow, since 1946; *b.* 13 Sept. 1898; 3rd *d.* of 6th Baron Balfour of Burleigh; unmarried. Probation Officer London Juvenile Courts, 1931-37; Deputy Governor Borstal Institution, Aylesbury, 1937-40; Deputy Governor H.M. Prison, Manchester, 1940-43; Governor H.M. Borstal Institution for Girls, Aylesbury, 1943-46. *Recreations:* gardening and cat breeding. *Address:* 6 Cathedral Square, Glasgow, C.4; Red Yetts, Clackmannan, Scotland. [*Died* 25 *Nov.* 1951.

BRUCE, Captain Wilfrid Montagu, C.B.E. 1919; R.D., R.N.R. (retired); *b.* 26 Oct. 1874; 4th *s.* of Rev. Canon Lloyd Stewart Bruce; *m.* 1913, Hon. Dorothy Florence Boot, *d.* of 1st Baron Trent; three *d.* *Educ.:* Edinburgh Academy; H.M.S. Worcester. Served for three years in a large sailing ship; from there joined the P. & O. Service, remaining attached until 1913; during this time served eighteen months in the Navy; joined his brother-in-law Captain Scott, on his last Antarctic Expedition, and was promoted to Commander in the Royal Naval Reserve for his services; when war broke out, appointed to H.M.S. Halcyon, and was working the Lowestoft minesweepers throughout the War; during the latter months, was senior naval officer of Lowestoft and Yarmouth (despatches, promoted to Captain, R.N.R., C.B.E.). *Recreation:* fly-fishing. *Address:* The Elms, Thornbury, Bristol. [*Died* 21 *Sept.* 1953.

BRUCE-GARDNER, Sir Charles, 1st Bt., *cr.* 1945; Kt., *cr.* 1938; M.I.Mech.E.; Chairman, British Iron and Steel Corporation, since 1953; Dir. other industrial cos.; *b.* 6 Nov. 1887; 2nd *s.* of late Henry Gardner; *m.* 1911, Gertrude Amy, *d.* of late C. Rivington Shill; two *s.* one *d.* *Educ.:* St. Dunstan's College; Battersea Technical College, Mechanical Engineering Course. Director of John Summers and Sons, 1913-30, and other Industrial Companies; Member of Sheet Trade Board, 1914-30; Member of Sheetmakers Conference, 1915-30; Member of Central Council of Mining Association, 1920-1930; Chairman of Flintshire Coal Owners Assn.; Chairman of Galvanizing Conciliation Board, 1920-30; Chairman of Iron and Steel Industrial Research Council, 1929-30; Member of Advisory Committee of Department of Overseas Trade, 1929-30; Industrial Adviser to Governors of Bank of England, 1930-38; Managing Director of Securities Management Trust and Bankers Industrial Development Company, 1930-38; Chairman of The London Iron and Steel Exchange, 1936 and 1937. Member: Civil Aviation Planning Committee, 1939; Secretary of State for Air's Industrial Advisory Panel, 1938-39; Air Council Committee on Supply, 1938-39; Air Supply Board, 1939-41; National Production Advisory Council, 1942-43; Chairman, The Society of British Aircraft Constructors, Ltd., 1938-43; Controller of Labour Allocation and Supply, Ministry of Aircraft Production, 1943-44; Chief Executive for Industrial Reconversion, Board of Trade, 1944-46; an Industrial Adviser Board of Trade, 1947. President, Iron and Steel Institute, 1955-56; Pres. Brit. Iron and Steel Research Assoc. Hon. Life Member: Amer. Inst. of Mining and Metallurgical Engineers; Amer. Soc. for Metals. *Recreation:* golf. *Heir:* *s.* Douglas Bruce Bruce-Gardner, *b.* 27 Jan. 1917. *Address:* Kinloss, Woodside, nr. Abingdon, Berks. *Clubs:* Junior Carlton, City of London. [*Died* 1 *Oct.* 1960.

BRUEN, Admiral Edward Francis, C.B. 1918; J.P. Suffolk; *b.* 7 Nov. 1866; 2nd *s.* of late Rt. Hon. Henry Bruen of Oak Park, Carlow, Ireland; *m.* 1912, Constance Dora, *d.* of late Admiral E. C. Drummond of Eskhill, Angus; one *s.* one *d.* *Educ.:* Stubbington, H.M.S. Britannia. Went to sea, 1882; Captain, 1906; Rear-Adm. 1917; Vice-Adm. 1922; served throughout European War in the Grand Fleet, commanding H.M.S. Bellerophon, 1913-16, H.M.S. Resolution, 1916-17, and 2nd Cruiser Squadron, 1918; present at Battle of Jutland (despatches); Director of Naval Equipment, Admiralty, 1920-22; retired list, 1924; Officer of Légion d'Honneur, Companion of Order of St. Anne of Russia; Order of Sacred Treasure of Japan, 2nd Class. *Address:* The Croft, Great Bealings, East Suffolk. *T.:* Grundisburgh 200. *Club:* Naval and Military. [*Died* 22 *Nov.* 1952.

BRUNDRIT, Reginald Grange, R.A. 1938 (A.R.A. 1931); *b.* Liverpool, 13 May 1883; *s.* of Joseph Brundrit; *m.* Lena Florence, *d.* of late W. Worthington, F.I.A. *Educ.:* Skipton Grammar School; Bradford Grammar School. Studied Bradford School of Art, Slade School; several years a pupil of late John M. Swan, R.A.; exhibitor at the Royal Academy, Paris Salon, Royal Institute of Oil Painters, British Provincial Galleries, Carnegie Institute, Pittsburgh, Toronto, Sydney; International Exhibition at Rome and Venice; *Official purchasers:* The Tate Gallery (Fresh Air Stubbs, and Nutwith Common, Masham; Chantrey purchases); The Govt. of New South Wales for the National Gallery in Sydney (A Northern Winter); City of Auckland (A Link with the North); Bradford Corporation Gallery (The River); Blackpool Corporation (Ribblesdale); Southampton Corporation (Autumn by the River); Burnley Corporation (The Wooded Dale). *Other principal works:* The Grip of Winter; The Last of the Snow; The Clay Pit; Nightfall; The North Sea; The Blind Lady. *Recreation:* walking. *Address:* The Old Vicarage, Masham, nr. Ripon, Yorkshire. *T.:* Masham 249. *Clubs:* Arts, Chelsea Arts. [*Died* 27 *Nov.* 1960.

BRUNEL, Adrian Hope, F.R.P.S., F.R.G.S.; Hon. member British Film Academy; Film director and playwright; *b.* 4 Sept. 1892; *s.* of R. N. Brunel-Norman and Mme. Adey Brunel; *m. d.* of Ralph Raphael; one *s.* *Educ.:* Harrow. In charge of film scenarios and production, Ministry of Information, 1917-18; Scenario Editor, British Actors Film Co., 1919; Producer and Founder (with Leslie Howard) Minerva Films, 1920; Director and Co-Founder, Film Society, 1925; Vice-President, British Association of Film Directors, 1938-39; Production Consultant to Leslie Howard, 1940-42; directed films in England, Germany, Austria, Italy, Spain and Morocco, amongst the best known being While Parents Sleep, The Constant Nymph, Blighty, Variety, The City of Beautiful Nonsense, The Crooked Billet, The Vortex, The Man Without Desire and Badger's Green. *Publications:* Filmcraft, 1933; Film Production, 1936; Only Yesterday, 1937; Bad Manners, 1939; Film Script, 1948; Nice Work (reminiscences), 1949; Waifs that Stray, 1944; Broadsheets, 1953; (with H. Zimmerman) Eve Had No Father, 1938. *Recreations:* collecting books relating to Thomas Paine, Morocco and the late Spanish War. *Address:* First House, Bulstrode Way, Gerrards Cross. *T.:* Gerrards Cross 2885. *Club:* Savile. [*Died* 18 *Feb.* 1958.

BRUNKER, Edward George; Director of Free Trade Union (its General Secretary, 1914-45); Editor of Free Trader; Secretary to King George and Queen Mary's Club for the Oversea Forces (Peel House), 1916-19; *b.* Youghal, Co. Cork, 20 Jan. 1871; *s.* of late James E. Brunker, M.A.; *m.* Louie E., *d.* of late Clement More of Metfield Hall, Suffolk; one *s.* two *d.* *Educ.:* High School of Erasmus Smith, and Trinity College, Dublin. *Publications:* numerous pamphlets on the Free Trade question. *Address:* 29 Glebe Road, Barnes, S.W.13. *T.:* Prospect 2702. [*Died* 29 *April* 1951.

BRUNSKILL, Hubert Fawcett, J.P.; *e. s.* of William Fawcett Brunskill and Annie (who *m.* 2nd, 1878, Edward Irwin), *d.* of Samuel Eliot, Mount Galpine, Devon; *b.* 1873; *m.* 1896, Hilda (*d.* 1940), 2nd *d.* of William Barrow Turner, of Ponsonby Hall, Cumberland. *Educ.:* Clifton; Exeter College, Oxford. *Address:* David's Moor, Ivybridge, S. Devon. [*Died* 17 *May* 1951.

BRUNTON, Frederick William, C.B.E. 1934; *b.* 16 Feb. 1879; *s.* of Frederick Septimus Brunton and Mary Plank; *m.* 1912, Mabel Farmer; one *d.* *Educ.:* Private School. Assistant Surveyor General British Honduras, 1903; Surveyor General, 1920-35. *Address:* Broad Hayes, Belstone, Devon. [*Died* 1 *Oct.* 1953.

BRUNTON-ANGLESS, Violet, R.M.S. 1924; *b.* 28 Oct. 1878; *d.* of Arthur D. Brunton, artist, and Annie Brunton, artist; *m.* 1930, W. H. Angless (*d.* 1943), Teacher of Music. *Educ.:* Southport; Liverpool; South Kensington. Studied at Southport and Liverpool Schools of Art; gained County Palatine scholarship and held it at Royal College of Art, South Kensington; specialised in sculpture at both latter places; studied various forms of art, finally specialising in miniature painting and book illustration. *Publications:* Ecclesiasticus; Silver Fairy Book; Green Fairy Book; Miniatures exhibited at R.A., Liverpool, Manchester, etc. *Recreations:* music, wood carving. *Address:* The Bungalow, Chorleywood Lodge, Chorleywood, Herts. [*Died* 18 *Sept.* 1951.

BRUNYATE, Sir James Bennett, K.C.S.I., *cr.* 1918 (C.S.I. 1915); C.I.E. 1910; Indian Civil Service, retired; Director, East Indian Railway Company; *b.* 22 March 1871; *s.* of late Reverend W. Brunyate, of Lansdown, Bath; *m.* 1897, Annie Purvis (*d.* 1941), *d.* of late W. Tombleson, S. Ferriby Hall, Lincs; three *s.* one *d.* *Educ.:* St. Paul's School; Trinity Coll., Cambridge. Entered I.C.S. 1889; Deputy-Commissioner, 1904; Member of International Opium Commission at Shanghai, 1909; of Governor-General's Legislative Council, 1910-1917; Secretary to the Government of India Finance Department, 1913-17; and Member of Council of India, 1917-24; attached to Staff of Lord Reading, Ambassador in U.S.A., 1918, in connection with passage of Pitman Act; Member, Indian Constitutional Relations Committee, 1919; Member, Committee on Indian Exchange and Currency, 1919; Member, Temporary Mixed Commission on Reduction of Armaments, League of Nations, 1921-24; Member, Irish Grants Committee, 1926-30; Chairman, Irish Sailors and Soldiers Land Trust, 1927-46. *Address:* Little Ferriby, Goring, Oxon. *T.:* Goring 81. [*Died* 20 *Oct.* 1951.

BRUTON, Rear-Admiral Charles William, C.M.G. 1917; late R.N.; *b.* 1875; *s.* of Rev. Walter Meddon, of South Yeo, nr. Bideford, N. Devon; *m.* Ava Maude Vidal (*d.* 1947), *d.* of Comdr. James Evans, R.N.; one *s.* one *d.* *Educ.:* Preparatory Sch., Brighton. Served European War, 1914-18 (despatches thrice, C.M.G., Croix de Guerre, Legion of Honour, Order of Leopold of Belgium); retired list, 1922. *Address:* c/o National Provincial and Union Bank, 138 High Street, W.8. *Club:* United Service. [*Died* 1 *March* 1952.

BRYAN, Charles Walter Gordon, M.C.; F.R.C.S.; Hon. Lieut.-Col. R.A.M.C.; Consulting Surgeon: St. Mary's Hospital, Paddington Green Children's Hospital, St. Luke's Hospital and King Edward Memorial Hospital; Fellow of Assoc. of Surgeons of Great Britain and Ireland; *b.* 5 Dec. 1883; *s.* of late F. C. Bryan, M.D., Littlehampton; *m.* 1917, Helen Christine Pirie; two *d.*; *m.* 1941, Molly Kestell, *d.* of John Carmichael Sinclair. *Educ.:* Westminster School; St. Mary's Hospital Medical School. Middlemore Prizeman British Medical Association, 1911; Surgical Specialist (Acting Consulting Surgeon 3rd Army) British Expeditionary Force, France and Belgium, 1914-19 (despatches); Officer i/c Surgical Division, R.A.M.C., 1941-1945 (Acting Consulting Surgeon Southern Command); late Examiner in Surgery University of London; Lecturer in Operative Surgery St. Mary's Med. School; Hunterian Professor Royal College of Surgeons; member of Council (ex-Hon. Treasurer and Hon. Secretary) Royal Society of Medicine; Surgeon to Out-patients, Hampstead General Hospital; Hon. Surgeon Royal Masonic Institution for Girls; Surgeon London Fever Hospital; Surgeon to Orthopædic Dept. and Demonstrator of Anatomy, St. Mary's Hospital; Demonstrator of Bacteriology, Oxford University; House Surgeon Hospital for Sick Children Great Ormond Street; Clinical Assistant St. Peter's Hospital for Urinary Diseases; Vice-President and Hon. Secretary Harveian Society of London. *Publications:* Various contributions to Surgical Journals. *Address:* The Little House, Croughton, Brackley, Northants. *T.:* Croughton 215. *Club:* Junior Carlton. [*Died* 28 *Nov.* 1954.

BRYAN, Rev. J. Ingram, M.A., M.Litt., B.D., Ph.D.; *b.* in Canada, 12 May 1868, of Irish parents; *m.* Lucy Silver (*d.* 1945), *d.* of W. Silver Hall, Whit. Sch., Nuneaton; four *s.* three *d.* *Educ.:* Prince of Wales College; University of Toronto; University of King's College, Halifax; University of California; University of Pennsylvania. Rector of various parishes in Canada and United States, including Church of Advent, Philadelphia; Professor at the Rikkyo University and the Naval College, Tokyo; Lecturer on English Composition and

Rhetoric in the Tokyo Imperial University, Japan; Cambridge University Extension Lecturer in English Literature, and Japanese History and Civilisation; ten years Japan correspondent of the Morning Post, and frequent contributor to leading periodicals; Vicar of Milton Ernest, 1935-45. *Publications:* Films of Blue (poems); The Feeling for Nature in English Pastoral Poetry; The Philosophy of English Literature; The Interpretation of Nature in English Poetry; Japan from Within; The Civilisation of Japan; The Literature of Japan; A History of Japan; Japanese All (Humorous Essays). *Address:* College of St. Barnabas, Dormans, Surrey. [*Died* 31 *Aug.* 1953.

BRYANT, Colonel Frederick Carkeet, C.M.G. 1915; C.B.E. 1919; D.S.O. 1917; late R.H. and R.F.A.; *b.* 10 Dec. 1879; 2nd *s.* of late Theodore H. Bryant of Juniper Hill, Mickleham; *m.* 1915, Rosamund (*d.* 1953), 2nd *d.* of Philip Beresford Hope. *Educ.:* Harrow; R.M.A., Woolwich. Entered Army, 1898; Captain, 1907; Adjutant, R.H.A., 1909-10; Major, 1914; employed with West African Frontier Force, 1910-15; commanded Togoland Field Force, 1914; B.E.F. France, 1915-18 (despatches, C.M.G., C.B.E., D.S.O., Bt. Lt.-Col.); Officer Legion of Honour, Dep. Provost Marshal Northern Command, 1939; Provost Marshal M.E.F., 1940-45 (despatches). *Address:* Hastings House, Churchill, Oxon. *Club:* Bath. [*Died* 27 *March* 1956.

BRYANT, Lt.-Col. George Herbert, O.B.E. 1917; M.C. 1916; D.L., J.P.; Chairman, Warwickshire County Council since 1949; Chairman, Stratford-on-Avon County Bench since 1944; Dep. Chm., Warwickshire Standing Joint Committee since 1948; *b.* 14 July 1883; *s.* of Arthur Charles Bryant, Partner in Bryant & May Ltd.; *m.* Mrs. T. Westray, *d.* of Charles Seton Guthrie. *Educ.:* Repton; Oxford University. Served in European War, 1914-1919, with R.A., retired as Major. Lt.-Col. commanding 4th Warwickshire Bn. Home Guard, 1943. *Recreations:* hunting and shooting. *Address:* Goldicote House, Nr. Stratford-on-Avon. *T.:* 2417 Stratford-on-Avon. *Club:* Cavalry. [*Died* 4 *Aug.* 1952.

BRYCE, William Kirk; *b.* Deanston, Doune, Perthshire, 19 Feb. 1867; *s.* of David and Christine Bryce; *m.* 1899, Annie L., *d.* of late John Ritchie; one *s.* one *d.* (and one *s.* decd.). *Educ.:* Pastor's Coll., London (Spurgeon's). Examined by C. H. Spurgeon and accepted by him as a student. Pastor at West Park Street Baptist Church, Chatteris, Cambs, 1894-97; Nottingham Tabernacle, 1897-1905; Fourth Baptist Church, Chicago, 1905-6; First Baptist Church, South Bend, Indiana, 1906-9; Centenary Baptist Church, March, 1909-13; Pastor of: Park Rd. Baptist Church, Bromley, 1913-26, St. Albans Tabernacle, 1926-35; Pastor at Wymondham, 1935-41; Pastor Emeritus, 1950; has lectured at some of the large Bible confs. in the U.S.. including Winona and at Moody's Northfield; lectured at Culver Academy, Indiana, U.S.A.; a Fellow of Linnean Soc., 1928-38. *Publications:* two volumes of Sermons (Extracts incorporated in Hasting's Great Texts; Biblical Illustrator, and Speaker's Bible); Appeals to the Soul, 1900; Life's Greatest Forces, 1922; has contributed to Christian World Pulpit and Baptist Quarterly. *Recreations:* reading, biography and Biblical Archæology. *Address:* Market Street, Wymondham, Norfolk. [*Died* 26 *Oct.* 1954.

BRYDON, James Herbert, C.B.E. 1918; retd. solicitor; *b.* Manchester, 19 March 1881; 2nd *s.* of Jas. Lockhart and Anne Twyford Brydon; unmarried. *Educ.:* Rossall; Pembroke College, Cambridge (scholar). J.P., Cheshire. *Address:* Ladybrook House, Bramhall Park, Cheadle Hulme, Cheshire. *T.A.:* Cheadle Hulme. *T.:* Hulme Hall 27. [*Died* 12 *Jan.* 1960.

BUCHAN, 15th Earl of (*cr.* 1469), **Ronald Douglas Stuart Mar Erskine;** Lord Auchterhouse, 1469; Baron Cardross, 1606; *b.* 6 April 1878; *e. s.* of 14th Earl and Rosalie Louisa (*d.* 1943), *y. d.* of Capt. Jules Sartoris, Hopsford Hall, Coventry; *S.* father, 1934. *Educ.:* Harrow. Formerly Lieut. Scots Guards, formerly Princess Louise's (Argyll and Sutherland Highlanders); served S. Africa, 1899-1902 (King's medal 2 clasps, Queen's medal 3 clasps); European War, Egypt, Salonika, and Palestine with London Mounted Brigade and Camel Transport Corps; formerly landowner in British East Africa. *Recreations:* horticulture, sylviculture. *Heir:* *Kinsman* 7th Baron Erskine. *Address:* World's End Farm, Chobham, Surrey. [*Died* 18 *Dec.* 1960.

BUCHAN, Lt.-Colonel Charles Forbes, C.B.E. 1919; retired; *b.* 1869; *s.* of late Charles Forbes Buchan, M.D. (formerly R.N.); *m.* 1898, Margaret (*d.* 1928), *d.* of late Captain Walter Hume (75th Regiment), Rock Lodge, Lynton, North Devon. Served European War, 1914-19 (despatches, C.B.E.); Staff, War Office; for many years Hon. Treasurer of The Navy League, also Hon Sec. and Treas. of Training Ship Stork, Hammersmith; Officer, Order of St. John, 1939. *Address:* Collingwood, Chudleigh, South Devon. *Clubs:* Royal Thames Yacht; Devon and Exeter (Exeter). [*Died* 30 *April* 1954.

BUCHAN, Capt. James Ivory, D.S.O. 1915; late The Black Watch; *b.* 4 Sept. 1885; *m.* 1928, Mary, *y. d.* of late John Jack; one *s.* Served European War, 1914-19 (wounded twice, despatches, D.S.O., Croix de Guerre); retired pay, 1927. Scottish Prison Service, 1928-50; retired, 1950. *Address:* 8 Colinton Grove, Edinburgh 11. *T.:* Craiglockhart 1173. [*Died* 8 *May* 1958.

BUCHANAN, Captain Angus, M.C.; F.R.S.G.S.; explorer; *b.* Kirkwall, 5 May 1886; *s.* of late Angus Buchanan and Jean Sanderson; *m.* 1919, Olga May Cherry; one *s.* two *d.* Zoological Expedition to the Barren Grounds, 1914; enlisted in Legion of Frontiersmen (25th Royal Fusiliers), as a private, 1915; after 3 years' service in E. Africa, was invalided home with rank of Capt.; wounded at Beho-Beho, 1917; made expedition to Aïr in the Central Sahara on behalf of Lord Rothschild, 1919-20; in March 1922 again set out to cross the Sahara from South to North, reaching Algiers in June 1923; valuable zoological and scientific data brought home from these regions; served War of 1939-45, Ethiopian Army, Abyssinian campaign, 1940-43; retired (totally disabled). *Publications:* Three Years of War in East Africa; Wild Life in Canada; Out of the World North of Nigeria; Sahara, 1926; The City of the Seven Palms: a Novel, 1927; Gain, novel, 1932. *Recreations:* shooting and fishing. *Address:* 40 Corstorphine Hill Gardens, Edinburgh. [*Died* 5 *Feb.* 1954.

BUCHANAN, Right Hon. George, P.C. 1948; Member of National Assistance Board since 1953 (Chairman, 1948-53); *b.* Gorbals, 30 Nov. 1890; *s.* of George Buchanan, Kilberry, Argyllshire; *m.* 1924, Annie McNee. *Educ.:* Camden Street Public School, Glasgow. Town Councillor, 1918-23; M.P. (Lab.) Gorbals Div. of Glasgow, 1922-48; Chairman of United Pattern Makers' Association of Great Britain, 1932-48; Member of Executive of Patternmakers' Association until 1948; late Member of I.L.P.; Joint Parl. Under-Sec. of State, 1945-47; Minister of Pensions, 1947-48. *Address:* 19 Chiltern Court, Baker St., N.W.1. *T.:* Welbeck 5544. [*Died* 28 *June* 1955.

BUCHANAN, Jack; Actor Manager, Film Producer and Director; *b.* Scotland; *m.* 1949, Susan Bassett, New York. English Stage Appearances: A to Z, Battling Butler, Toni, Sunny, That's a Good Girl, Stand up and Sing, Mr. Whittington, This'll Make You Whistle, Top Hat and Tails; The Last of Mrs. Cheyney, Fine Feathers, Canaries Sometimes Sing, Don't Listen, Ladies!, Castle in the Air, King's Rhapsody, As Long As They're Happy. First pantomime appearance, Christmas, 1940, Buttons in Cinderella. Productions include: The Women, The Body was Well Nourished, Waltz Without End, It's Time to Dance, A Murder for a Valentine, Treble Trouble, The Lady Asks for Help. American Stage Appearances: Andre Charlot's Revues, Cochran's Wake Up and Dream, Pardon My English, Between the Devil, Harvey, 1948. Hollywood Films: Paris, The Show of Shows, Monte Carlo, Band Waggon. English Films: Yes Mr. Brown, Good Night Vienna, That's a Good Girl, Brewster's Millions, Come out of the Pantry, When Knights Were Bold, This'll Make You Whistle, Smash and Grab, The Sky's the Limit, Break the News, The Gang's all here, The Middle Watch, Bulldog sees it through, As Long As They're Happy, Josephine and Men. French Film: The Diary of Major Thompson (bilingual). Now directs most of his own pictures and controls Garrick Theatre, London. Television in U.S.A.: The Max Liebman Show; The Ed Sullivan Show. *Recreations:* golf, tennis, swimming. *Address:* Garrick Theatre, W.C.2.
[*Died* 20 *Oct.* 1957.

BUCHANAN, Rev. Louis George, M.A.; retired; *b.* 5 March 1871; *s.* of Robert Buchanan, J.P., of Fintona, Co. Tyrone; *m.* Violet Theodora, *d.* of late Major Loftus Corbet Singleton, Gordon Highlanders, and Mrs. Singleton of Merville, Wimbledon, S.W. *Educ.:* Foyle College, Londonderry; Trinity College, Dublin. Curate of Christ Church, Leeson Park, Dublin; subsequently Curate, Monkstown and St. Paul's, Portman Square, W.; Vicar of St. Luke's, Wimbledon Park, S.W., 1908-14; Canon of York, 1920; Rural Dean of Hull, 1917; Vicar and Lecturer, Holy Trinity Parish Church, Hull, 1914-23; Vicar of St. Luke's, Redcliffe Square, S.W.10, 1923-28; Hon. Canon of Leicester, 1932-34; Residentiary Canon of Leicester, 1934-37; Vicar of Frensham, 1937-38; Residentiary Canon Emeritus of Leicester and Hon. Chaplain to the Bishop. *Publication:* After the War. *Recreations:* gardening, golf, travel. *Address:* Clifton House, Guildford. *T.:* Guildford 3994. *Club:* County (Guildford).
[*Died* 17 *Dec.* 1952.

BUCHANAN, Milton Alexander, B.A., Ph.D., F.R.S.C.; Emeritus Prof. of Italian and Spanish, University of Toronto; *b.* Zurich, Ontario, 17 July 1878; *s.* of George Buchanan, M.D. and Emma Zeller; *m.* 1913, Marie Avery, Galena, Ill. *Educ.:* Universities of Toronto, Chicago, Paris, Madrid. Fellow, University of Chicago, 1901-2; on the staff of the Romance Department, 1904-6; editor of Spanish Literature in Vollmöller's Kritischer Jahresbericht über die Fortschritte der romanischen Philologie, 1908-14; Chairman of the Canadian Committee on Modern Languages, 1924-28; President of the Modern Language Association of America, 1932. *Publications:* A Graded Spanish Word Book, 1927; (with E. D. MacPhee), An Annotated Bibliography of Modern Language Methodology, 1928; Spanish texts (Calderon's La Vida es Sueño, 1908, etc.); Early Canadian History (trans. Roy. Soc. Can., 1948); studies and reviews in modern language journals. *Address:* 75 Heathdale Road, Toronto. *Club:* Faculty (Toronto).
[*Died* 7 *May* 1952.

BUCHANAN, Hon. William A.; *b.* Fraserville, Ontario, 2 July 1876; *s.* of late Rev. W. and late Mary Pendrie Buchanan; *m.* 1903, Alma Maude, *d.* of E. B. Freeman, Burlington, Ontario; two *s.* *Educ.:* High Schools, Brighton and Norwood, Ontario. Entered newspaper work Peterboro', Ontario, 1893; News Editor, Toronto Telegram, 1898, 1903; Managing Director, St. Thomas, Ontario, Daily Journal, 1903-5; Publisher Lethbridge Herald Daily and Weekly since 1905; elected first Member City of Lethbridge, Alberta Legislature, 1909; Minister without portfolio, Alberta Government, 1909; resigned, 1911; M.P. Medicine Hat, 1911-17; Lethbridge, 1917-21; Member of Special Committee Old Age Pensions, 1912; Member Special Redistribution Committee, 1914; Member Special Committee on Titles of Honour, 1919; appointed to the Senate of Canada, 1925; Liberal; Past Pres. Alberta Liberal Association; Past President Alberta Press Association and Alberta Amateur Athletic Association; Past Pres. Canadian Press; Delegate to Imperial Press Conference, London, 1930, Ottawa, 1950; Vice-Pres. Canadian Geographical Society; O.St.J.; Hon. LL.D., Alberta University. *Address:* Lethbridge, Alberta. *T.:* 3508. *Clubs:* Country (Ottawa); Chinook Flying and Country (Lethbridge).
[*Died* 11 *July* 1954.

BUCK, Sir Peter Henry, K.C.M.G., *cr.* 1946; D.S.O. 1917; M.D., Ch.B., D.Sc. (N.Z.); M.A. (Yale); D.Sc. (University of Rochester), D.Litt. (Univ. of Hawaii); F.R.S., N.Z.; F.R.A.I.; Prof. Emeritus of Anthropology, Yale Univ.; Dir., Bernice P. Bishop Museum, Honolulu, T. H.; *s.* of William H. Buck, Galway, and Ngarongo-ki-tua, Ngati-Mutunga, Maori tribe, Taranaki, N.Z.: *m.* Margaret Wilson, M.B.E., Milton, N.Z.; no *c.* *Educ.:* Te, Aute College; Otago Medical School; Univ. of New Zealand. House Surgeon Dunedin Hospital, N.Z. 1904: Medical Officer of Health to Maoris, N.Z. 1905-8; Member of Parliament, Northern Maori Constituency, N.Z., Member of Cabinet, Representing Maori Race, etc., 1909-14; European War, Captain in N.Z. Medical Corps, Medical Officer, 1st. Maori Contingent, Egypt, Malta, and Gallipoli; Major, Second in Command, N.Z., Pioneer Battalion, Egypt, France, and Belgium; Medical Staff, No. 3. N.Z. General Hospital, 1914-19 (D.S.O., 1914-15 star, General Service and Victory Medals, despatches twice); Director of Maori Hygiene, Depart. of Health, N.Z., 1919; Bishop Museum Visiting Professor in Anthropology, Yale Univ., U.S.A., 1932-34, 1936 and 1939. Royal Orde of the North Star (Sweden), 1949. *Publications:* The Evolution of Maori Clothing; The Material Culture of the Cook Islands (Aitutaki) Samoan Material Culture; The Ethnology of Tongareva; The Ethnology of Manihiki and Rakahanga; Mangaian Society; The Ethnology of Mangareva; Vikings of the Sunrise; Anthropology and Religion; Arts and Crafts of the Cook Islands; An Introduction to Polynesian Anthropology, 1945; The Coming of the Maori, 1949; Arts and Crafts of Kapingamarangi, 1950; various papers in journal of Polynesian Society and Transactions of New Zealand Institute. *Recreations:* Athletic Champion, TeAute College, 1897, 1898; N.Z. University Long Jump Champion, 1902, 1903, 1904; N.Z. Amateur Long Jump Champion, 1900, 1904. *Address:* Bishop Museum, Honolulu 17, T.H.; 144 Judd St., Honolulu.
[*Died* 1 *Dec.* 1951.

BUCKLAND, Sir Henry, Kt., *cr.* 1931; late General Manager of the Crystal Palace; *b.* 13 Aug. 1870; *s.* of William Buckland; *m.* 1908, Maud Irene, *yr. d.* of W. Pearce Jones, Manor House, Church End, Finchley, N. (founder of Messrs. Jones Bros., Holloway Rd., N.); one *s.* two *d.* (and one *s.* decd.). Buyer and Manager of various departments at Jones Brothers (Holloway), Ltd., 1893-1905; General Manager of the Spa Establishments at Harrogate, Yorks, 1905-14; took over on behalf of the Nation the General Management of the Crystal Palace, London, 1914-52, acting as Managing Director throughout the period; served on Committee of South Eastern Hospital for Children, 1915-31; Member of Council of Corporation of the Church House, Dean's Yard, Westminster, S.W.1; member of House of Laity, 1934-1955. *Address:* Chalcedony, Garden Road, Bromley, Kent. *T.:* Ravensbourne 5140. *Club:* Royal Automobile.

[*Died* 16 *Dec.* 1957.

BUCKLAND, Sir Philip Lindsay, Kt., *cr.* 1926; *b.* 12 Sep. 1874; *e. s.* of late Charles Edward Buckland, C.I.E.; *m.* 1901, Mary (*d.* 1942), *d.* of Livingstone Barclay. *Educ.:* Eton; New College, Oxford. Barrister, Inner Temple, 1896; Oxford Circuit; Advocate, High Court, Calcutta, 1898; Vice-President, 1910-21, and Pres., 1921-34, of the Hon. Committee of Management of the Zoological Gardens, Calcutta; Trustee of the Victoria Memorial, Calcutta, 1917-43; Judge of the High Court, Calcutta, 1919-34; officiated as Chief Justice of Bengal, Feb. to July 1934; retired 1934; J.P. West Sussex. *Clubs:* Oxford and Cambridge, Oriental.

[*Died* 10 *May* 1952.

BUCKLE, Major-General Christopher Reginald, C.B. 1918; C.M.G. 1916; D.S.O. 1902; *b.* 18 Oct. 1862; *s.* of late C. Richard Buckle of Norton House, Chichester; *m.* 1886. Elisabeth B. Turner (*d.* 1949); four *d.* (one *s.* killed in action). *Educ.:* Sherborne School; Royal Military Academy, Woolwich. Entered Royal Artillery, 1883; Capt. 1892; Major, 1901; Lt.-Col. 1911; Col. 1916; Maj.-Gen. 1919; served at home and India; was Adjutant Midlothian Artillery (Vol.), and subsequently Adjutant R.A., Isle of Wight; embarked for S. Africa, Jan. 1900, for service as Adjutant of Brigade Div. of heavy guns; appointed to Staff, Aug. 1900, and served continuously on Staff until after cessation of hostilities (despatches, D.S.O.); European War, 1914-18 (despatches, C.B., C.M.G.); A.M.S. to Sir H. E. Wood, 1902-5; Brigade Major (for R.A.), 1908-11; Lt.-Col. commanding Harwich Defences, 1913; Brig.-Gen. commanding Harwich Fortress, Aug. 1914; reverted to Lt.-Colonel to command Howitzer Brigade, B.E.F., May 1915; Brig.-Gen. Commanding Corps Heavy Artillery, Feb. 1916; G.O.C., R.A., 17th Corps, July 1916; G.O.C. R.A., 2nd Army, July 1917; Major-General, R.A., Army of the Rhine, April 1919; retired Feb. 1920. *Address:* The Old Cottage, Warcop, Westmorland.

[*Died* 1 *Dec.* 1952.

BUCKLER, Georgina Grenfell (Mrs. William Buckler), C.B.E. 1918; M.A. (Camb.); D.Phil. (Oxon); *d.* of late Theodore Walrond, C.B., and Charlotte Grenfell; *m.* 1892, late William Hepburn Buckler; two *d.* *Educ.:* Notting Hill High School; Girton College, Cambridge. Classical Tripos, 1891; Social work in Baltimore, U.S.A., 1892-1907; Enquiry Dept. for Wounded and Missing, Red Cross and Order of St. John, 1914-20; on the Council of the Girls' Public Day School Trust, 1912-1937. *Publications:* National Sentiment and Patriotism in the New Testament, 1917; Anna Comnena, 1929; various articles in journals. *Address:* One, Bardwell Road, Oxford. *Club:* University Women's.

[*Died* 28 *April* 1953.

BUCKLER, William Hepburn, M.A. (Camb. and Oxon), LL.B. (Camb.), LL.D. (Aberd.), D.Litt. (Oxon), LL.D. (Johns Hopkins), F.S.A.; F.B.A.; *b.* 1 Feb. 1867; *s.* of Thomas Hepburn Buckler, M.D., Baltimore, Maryland; *m.* 1892, Georgina Grenfell, *q.v.*, *d.* of Theodore Walrond, C.B.; two *d.* *Educ.:* Trinity College, Cambridge; University of Maryland. Member Maryland Bar, 1894-1902; Secretary U.S. Legation, Madrid, 1907-09; member American Expedition to Sardis, 1910-14; special agent at U.S. Embassy, London, 1914-19; attached American Commission to negotiate peace, 1919; Trustee Johns Hopkins University, Baltimore, 1904-12; Vice-President Societies for Hellenic and Roman Studies. *Publications:* History of Contract in Roman Law, 1895; Lydian Inscriptions, 1924; joint-editor Sardis Inscriptions, 1932, Monumenta A. M. antiqua iv and vi; contributions to various books and journals. *Address:* One, Bardwell Road, Oxford.

[*Died* 2 *March* 1952.

BUCKLEY, Brigadier-General Basil (Thorold), C.B. 1919; C.M.G. 1918; C.V.O. 1949; one of H.M.'s Body Guard, Hon. Corps of Gentlemen-at-Arms, 1922-25, Standard Bearer, 1946-49; late Northumberland Fusiliers; *b.* 1874; *m.* 1904, Emmeline Louise, *d.* of late Nathaniel Edwards; one *s.* *Educ.:* Winchester; R.M.C., Sandhurst. Served Nile Expedition, 1898 (medal); South African War, 1899-1902 (despatches, Queen's medal seven clasps, King's medal two clasps, Bt. Maj.); European War, 1914-18 (C.B., C.M.G.). *Address:* Cedar Grove, Richmond Green, Surrey.

[*Died* 16 *May* 1954.

BUCKLEY, Charles William, M.D. (Lond.); F.R.C.P.; formerly Consulting Physician to the Devonshire Hospital for Rheumatic Diseases, and to the Buxton District Hospital; Lecturer on Chronic Arthritis and Rheumatic Diseases to British post-graduate Medical School; *b.* 10 Oct. 1874; *s.* of late Henry Buckley, Derby, and Mary, *d.* of late William Haslam, Derby; *m.* Lilian, *d.* of late Hugh Hughes, Manchester; one *s.* three *d.* *Educ.:* privately; St. Mary's Hospital Medical School (Entrance Scholar and Kerslake Scholar in Pathology and Bacteriology), London University. Hon. Major Canadian A.M.C., attached special hospital for rheumatic diseases, 1916-17; Mayor of Buxton, 1924-25, and Hon. Freeman of the Borough, 1947; F.R.S.M.; past president of Section of Balneology and Climatology; Member of the Science Committee of the Empire Rheumatism Council; Editor of Annals of the Rheumatic Diseases; Honorary Member American Rheumatism Assoc. *Publications:* Arthritis, Fibrositis and Gout: a handbook for the general practitioner; contributions to Proceedings of Royal Society of Medicine, and to Medical Journals on Rheumatic Diseases, Climatology, etc.; articles in The British Encyclopædia of Medical Practice and Hutchison's Index of Treatment. *Recreations:* fly-fishing, golf, archæology. *Address:* Bentley Corner, Ashbourne, Derbyshire. *T.:* Thorpe Cloud 255. *Club:* Union (Buxton).

[*Died* 28 *May* 1955.

BUCKLEY, Rear-Admiral Frederic Arthur, C.B. 1941; Commodore R.N.; Commanding H.M.S. Royal Arthur; *b.* 4 Sept. 1887; *s.* of J. W. Buckley, M.I.C.E., Civil Engineer; *m.* 1913, Eva Godskesen of Copenhagen; one *s.* three *d.* *Educ.:* Stubbington House; H.M.S. Britannia. Served as Gunnery Officer European War, in H.M.S. Venerable, Belgian Coast and Dardanelles: H.M.S. Emperor of India, Grand Fleet and Black Sea; Commander of Warspite, Fleet Flagship, Mediterranean, 1926-27; A.D.N.O. Admiralty, 1928-30; Commanded H.M.S. Shropshire, 1931-33; Director of Training on Staff Division, Admiralty, 1934-36; Commanded H.M.S. Malaya, 1936-39; Retired Rear-Admiral, 1939; re-appointed Commodore R.N. 1939. *Recreations:* shooting, golf. *Address:* Southwick, nr. Fareham, Hants. *T.A.:* Southwick, Hants. *T.:* Cosham 76140. [*Died* 31 *May* 1952.

BUCKLEY, Lieut.-Col. Percy Neville, C.B.E. 1924; late Royal Australian Engineers; *b.* 1867; *s.* of late Mars Buckley; *m.* 1898, Lillian Murray (*d.* 1951), *d.* of late Col. Sir Henry Edward McCallum, G.C.M.G.; one *s.* one *d.* Served S. Africa, 1901 (Queen's medal with clasp); Military Adviser to High Commissioner in London for Commonwealth of Australia, 1910-22. *Address:* Strood Park, Horsham, Sussex. *T.:* Broadbridge Heath 67. *Club:* United Service. [*Died* 19 *Nov.* 1953.

BUCKMASTER, Martin A., A.R.C.A.; Hon. A.R.I.B.A.; F.R.S.A.; *b.* 2 August 1862; *s.* of John C. Buckmaster, J.P. (Science and Art Department, South Kensington); *m.* Dorothy Mary, *d.* of late William Dyer; one *d.* *Educ.:* Aldenham School; Royal College of Art (Medallist and Travelling Scholar in Architecture). Late Assistant Master at Tonbridge School. *Publications:* Elementary Classic and Gothic Architecture; Handbook of Classic and Gothic Architecture; Principal Examiner to the Board of Education, 1885-1910, Oxford, Cambridge, and London Universities; Exhibitor at the Royal Academy, Institute of Painters in Water Colours, etc. *Recreations:* travelling, racquets, tennis, etc. *Address:* 9 Coleherne Mansions, S.W.5. *T.:* Frobisher 1725. *Club:* Arts. [*Died* 14 *Aug.* 1960.

BUDDEN, Rev. Charles William, M.A., M.D., Ch.B.; licensed to officiate in Diocese of Winchester, 1950; Holder of Bishop's Licence under Seal (Diocese of Winchester), 1949; *b.* 30 Mar. 1878; *s.* of late William and Elizabeth Budden, Litherland; *m.* 1903, Jean Effie, M.D., 3rd *d.* of William Prowse. *Educ.:* Merchant Taylors' School, Great Crosby; Univ. Coll. Liverpool (Victoria Univ.). Silver Medal, Therapeutics, 1900; Hon. Anaesthetist, Hospital for Women, Liverpool, 1912-16; Assistant County Director, Cheshire, British Red Cross Society, 1914; M.B., Ch.B. (Vict.), 1901, M.D. (L'pool), 1907, M.A. with Distinction (L'pool), 1925; Capt. R.A.M.C. (T.C.) and Medical Officer i.c. Dysentery Section, Salonika B.E.F. 1916-19; Deacon, 1927; Priest, 1928; Licensed to Liverpool Cathedral, 1927; Bishop's Messenger, the Cathedral, Liverpool, 1927-31; Vicar of St. Mildred, Croydon, 1931-41; Vicar of Alkham with Capel-le-Ferne, near Dover, 1941-45; Vicar of East Meon (Hants), 1945-49; Editor The Liverpool Review, 1927-1931; Secretary and Treasurer, Liverpool Cathedral School of Divinity, 1927, and Liverpool Joint Board of Divinity, 1929; Chaplain, Liverpool Diocesan Lay Readers' Association, 1928; Special Lecturer in Ecclesiology, University of Liverpool, 1929; Secretary, Liverpool Diocesan Board of Lay Service, 1929; Secretary Liverpool Diocesan Fabrics Advisory Committee, 1929. Officiating Chaplain to H.M. Forces, 1942-45. *Publications:* Model Making for the Sunday School, 1914; The Way of Health, 1919; The Beauty and Interest of Wirral, 1921; English Gothic Churches, 1922; English Church Architecture, 1927; Ancient Churches of the Liverpool Diocese, 1929; The Local Colour of the Bible (3 vols.) 1925 (with Rev. Edward Hastings); One Hundred Popular Medical Fallacies, 1932; The Story of St. Mildred, 1937 (with R. R. Hutchinson); How the Bible came to us, 1939; The Life of S. Paul and the Early Church, 1940; Bible Portraits, 1943; numerous contributions to religious and educational papers. *Recreations:* photography, music, painting, illuminating. *Address:* Laneside, Greywell, Hants. [*Died* 4 *July* 1952.

BUDDEN, Lieut.-Colonel F. H., M.C.; *b.* 4 Mar. 1887; *s.* of late H. O. Budden, I.E.S.; *m.* 1913, Mary Ethel Liepmann; one *s.* *Educ.:* Westminster; R.M.A., Woolwich; S.M.E. Chatham. 2nd Lieut. R.E., 1907; M.W.S. India, 1910; Indian State Railways, 1912; served European War, France and Salonika (despatches twice, M.C., Bt. Major); Afghan War, 1919; Divisional Superintendent, East Indian Railway, 1926; Chief Publicity Officer, Indian State Railways, 1928; Institution of Civil Engineers, 1935-52; R. and E. Dept., Ministry of Home Security, 1939-43; Jt.-Sec. New Towns Committee, 1945. *Publication:* Railway Statistics and the Operating Officer, 1925. *Recreations:* market gardening. Hon. Sec. Army Hockey Assoc., 1909-1910. Played hockey, Kent and Hampshire. *Address:* Honeypots, Westfield, Woking, Surrey. *T.:* Woking 21. [*Died* 16 *Oct.* 1953.

BUDDEN, Lionel Bailey, M.A.; F.R.I.B.A.; Professor Emeritus, University of Liverpool; *b.* 1887; *s.* of late William Budden and Elizabeth Adams; *m.* 1921, Dora Magdalene, *e. d.* of late Rev. Norman Fraser; one *s.* one *d.* *Educ.:* Merchant Taylors' School, Crosby; University of Liverpool. University Travelling Scholar in Architecture, 1909; Holt Travelling Scholar in Architecture, 1909; Student, British School at Athens, 1909-10; Essay Medallist of R.I.B.A., 1923; Roscoe Professor of Architecture, University of Liverpool, 1933-52; Member Faculty of Architecture, British School at Rome. *Architectural Work:* War Memorial, Birkenhead; Memorial Tower, Blackpool; Cenotaph, Liverpool and (with C. H. Reilly and J. E. Marshall) Veterinary Hospital, School of Architecture, and extensions to Students' Union, University of Liverpool. *Publications:* contributions to professional journals on architectural theory, history, and education. *Address:* Highfield, The Mount, Heswall, Cheshire. *T.:* Heswall 1780. *Club:* Sandon (Liverpool). [*Died* 21 *July* 1956.

BUDGETT, Hubert Maitland; *b.* 1882; *s.* of Richard S. Budgett, Stoke Park, Guildford; *m.* 1912, Hazel Reaveley, 2nd *d.* of late Arthur Glover; two *s.* *Educ.:* Eton; Cambridge. Master Bicester and Warden Hill Hounds, 1925-31. *Publication:* Hunting By Scent, 1933. *Address:* Kirtlington Park, Oxon. *T.:* Bletchington 36. [*Died* 25 *Feb.* 1951.

BUIST, Colonel Herbert John Martin, C.B. 1920; C.M.G. 1918; D.S.O. 1900; *b.* 5 May 1868; *s.* of late Maj.-Gen. D. S. Buist; *m.* 1912, Gertrude M. K. Logan, *d.* of late J. D. Logan, J.P., Matjesfontein, Cape Province, S.A.; one *s.* Entered R.A.M.C. 1891; served N.W. Frontier, India, 1897, including Malakand Field Force, 3rd Brigade, and Tirah Expeditionary Force (despatches, medal with 2 clasps); S. Africa, 1899-1902; present at actions—Relief of Kimberley, Paardeberg, Driefontein, Johannesburg, Diamond Hill, and Belfast Queen's medal with six clasps, King's medal with two clasps, despatches, D.S.O.); Staff Officer to principal Medical Officer, South Africa, 1903-6; Deputy Assistant Director-General, War Office, 1906-10; served European War, G.S.W.A. Campaign (despatches, C.M.G.), Oct. 1914-Oct. 1915; Salonika, June 1916-July 1919 (despatches, Croix de Guerre, Order of St. Sava, 2nd class Legion of Honour (Officier), C.B.); A.D.M.S., Salonika, June-Dec. 1917; D.D.M.S., Base and L. of C., Jan. 1918-July 1919; D.D.M.S. Scottish Command, Feb. 1920; retired pay, 1921. J.P. resigned, 1948. *Recreations:* cricket, lawn tennis. *Address:* Tweedside, P.O., Matjesfontein, Cape Province, South Africa. [*Died* 24 *July* 1956.

BULKELEY, John Pierson, C.I.E., 1932, M.A.; Director of Public Instruction, Burma, retired; *s.* of Canon H. J. Bulkeley; *m.* 1912, Sybil, *d.* of His Honour Judge Fosset Lock; one *s.* one *d.* *Educ.:* King William's College, Isle of Man. Keble College, Oxford; Sorbonne, Paris. Served as a Schoolmaster in English Public Schools and in Natal, 1903-7; Indian Educational Service, Burma, 1907-33; Oxford Blue for High Jumping. *Publications:* Poems by a Father and Son (Joint Author); Short History of British Empire; Adult Education, A Furlough Study. *Recreations:* riding, fishing, walking. *Address:* Coombe Cottage, Exebridge, Dulverton, Som. [*Died* 18 *Nov.* 1958.

BULKELEY-EVANS, William, C.B.E. 1925 (O.B.E. 1920); LL.D. (Hon. McGill), M.A.; Barrister-at-law; *b.* 1870. *Educ.:* Jesus College, Oxford. Secretary to the Headmasters' Conference, 1904-35; Chairman of the Employment Branch (ex-Officers) of the Officers' Association of the British Legion; Member of the Councils of the Royal Colonial Institute, Overseas League (Chairman during war time), and of the Enham Village Centre for Disabled Men (Hon. Treasurer); Honorary Secretary to the Empire Migration Committee of the Royal Empire Society; Member of the Executive Council of the 1820 Memorial Settlers' Association of South Africa; co-Editor of the Public Schools' Year Book; Director of Exports Branch of Ministry of Food, 1917-18; Chevalier of the Order of the Crown of Belgium, 1919; Coronation Medal, 1937; Chairman of the National Appointments Committee (Ministry of Labour and Officers' Association) for ex-Officers; connected with various war activities. *e.g.* the Public Schools' Hospital of the British Red Cross Society. *Address:* Lee House, 12 Dyke Road, Brighton, Sussex. [*Died* 14 *May* 1952.

BULLEID, Prof. C. H., O.B.E. 1918; M.A.; Assoc. M. Inst. C.E., M.I.Mech.E.; Emeritus Prof. of Engineering, Nottingham University, since 1949; *b.* Hatherleigh, Devonshire, 10 Jan. 1883; *s.* of S. J. Bulleid; *m.* 1912, Dorothy, *d.* of Neville Cox, Derby; two *s.* *Educ.:* Exeter School; Trinity College, Cambridge; 14th Wrangler, Mathematical Tripos, 1904; 1st Class Mechanical Sciences Tripos, 1905; Demonstrator Engineering Laboratory, Cambridge, 1905-7; pupil, Midland Railway, Derby, 1908-10; Assistant to Technical Manager Parsons Marine Steam Turbine Co., 1911-12; Professor of Engineering, University College, Nottingham, 1912-49; during European war, 1914-18, General Manager Nottingham National Shell Factory, and subsequently Chief Engineer Admiralty School of Mines, Portsmouth. *Address:* 3 Lanark Close, Wollaton Park, Nottingham. *T.:* Nottingham 75785. [*Died* 29 *June* 1956.

BULLEN, Percy Sutherland, F.J.I.; American Correspondent London Daily Telegraph, 1902-34; Lecturer on Anglo-American topics; *b.* Hastings, Sussex, 1867; 3rd *s.* of late Capt. Bullen, R.N.; *m.* Bertha, *d.* of late Richard Clark, London; four *s.* one *d.* Has travelled largely in Europe and Morocco; has represented leading American papers in Paris, Berlin, Rome; special correspondent Daily Telegraph in Boer War, 1900; is Corresponding Secretary in America of the Institute of Journalists, London; President of the Association of Foreign Press Correspondents in the United States, 1921-22; Organiser and Hon. Sec. of the American Shakespeare Foundation co-operating with British Committee to rebuild and endow the Shakespeare Memorial Theatre at Stratford upon Avon; Joint Founder with late Joseph Adams, Baron of the Cinque Ports, of the Namesake Towns Association to develop Anglo-American Friendship; Awarded first gold medal conferred upon a foreign correspondent by the University of Missouri (Department of Journalism), 1930; Officer of Public Instruction, France; Officer of Order of Redeemer, Greece; Chevalier Order of Leopold II.; Cavaliere of the Crown of Italy; Boer War, King's Medal; Verdun Medal, given for service to France. Freeman of City of London. *Address:* 14a Alexandra Road, Clifton, Bristol 8. [*Died* 13 *Jan.* 1958.

BULLER, Dame (Audrey Charlotte) Georgiana, D.B.E., *cr.* 1920; R.R.C.; J.P.; Chairman St. Loyes College for Training and Rehabilitation of the Disabled; Vice-Chairman Queen Elizabeth's Training College for the Disabled, Leatherhead; Vice-Chairman, British Council for Rehabilitation; *b.* Downes, Crediton, 1883; *o. c.* of late Rt. Hon. General Sir Redvers Buller, V.C., G.C.B., G.C.M.G., of Downes, Crediton, Devon, and late Lady Audrey Buller, *y. d.* of 4th Marquess Townshend. *Educ.:* home. Appointed head of the Exeter Division Voluntary Aid Organisation (British Red Cross Society), Devonshire Branch, 1910; Deputy County Director of the County Branch 1913; established and administered Exeter V.A. Hospital, 1914; Hospital (1500 beds) taken over by the War Office, and converted into a Central Military Hospital, under the name of Exeter War Hospital, with forty-eight affiliated auxiliary hospitals, 1916; appointed Administrator by the War Office (being the only woman to hold such a post), and retained as such until demobilisation in 1920. O.St.J. *Recreations:* literature and gardening. *Address:* Bellair House, Exeter. *T.:* Exeter 2438. *Club:* Ladies' Empire. [*Died* 22 *June* 1953.

BULLER, Admiral Sir Henry (Tritton), G.C.V.O., *cr.* 1930 (K.C.V.O. *cr.* 1925; C.V.O. 1921; M.V.O. 1911); C.B. 1919; Extra Equerry to the Queen since 1952; *b.* 30 Oct. 1873; *e. surv. s.* of late Admiral Sir Alexander Buller, G.C.B., of Erle Hall, Devon, and Belmore House, West Cowes, and Emily Mary, *e. d.* of late Henry Tritton of Beddington, Surrey; *m.* 1919, Lady Hermione Stuart, *o. d.* of 17th Earl of Moray; one *d.* (two *s.* decd., one of whom having been killed on active service, 1940). Served European War, 1914 (C.B.); Commander Royal Naval College, Dartmouth, 1908-1911; Captain, 1911; Rear-Admiral, 1921; Vice-Admiral, 1926; commanded H.M. Yachts, 1922-1931; Admiral, 1931; retired list, 1931; Groom in Waiting to King George V, 1931-36; Extra Equerry to King George V, King Edward VIII, and King George VI. Grand Croix de l'Ordre de la Couronne (Belgian), 1934. *Address:* Netherwood, Southwater, Horsham, Sussex. *T.:* Southwater 216. *Club:* United Service. [*Died* 29 *Aug.* 1960.

BULLER, Lt.-Col. Sir M. E.; *see* Manningham-Buller.

BULLETT, Gerald (William); M.A. (Cantab.); author; *b.* London, 30 Dec. 1893; *s.* of Robert Bullett, of Weedon, Northants; *m.* 1921, Rosalind Gould; one *d.* *Educ.:* Jesus College, Cambridge. Wrote first-published novel in 1914; served in the 1914 war; author of numerous contributions to literary journals and the following works of fiction, criticism, etc.: The Street of the Eye, 1923; The Innocence of G. K. Chesterton, 1923; Mr. Godly Beside Himself, 1924 (dramatised by the author and produced for The Three Hundred Club by Nigel Playfair on 28 Feb. 1926); The Baker's Cart, 1925; The Panther, 1926; Modern English Fiction, 1926; The Spanish Caravel (for children), 1927; The World in Bud, 1928; Dreaming, 1928; The History of Egg Pandervil, 1928; Nicky, Son of Egg, 1929; Marden Fee, 1931; Remember Mrs Munch, 1931; Helen's Lovers, 1932; The Testament of Light (an anthology), 1932; The Quick and the Dead, 1933; The English Galaxy of Shorter Poems, 1933; Eden River, 1934; The Pattern of Courtesy, 1934; The Bubble, 1934; The Jury, 1935; The Happy Mariners, 1935; The Snare of the Fowler, 1936; Poems in Pencil, 1937; The Bending Sickle, 1938; Problems of Religion, 1938; Twenty-Four Tales, 1938; The Jackdaw's Nest, 1939; A Man of Forty, 1940; The Pandervils (revised), 1943; Winter Solstice (a poem), 1943; Achievement in Feeding Britain, 1944; "Everyman" edition of Keats's Poems, 1944; The Elderbrook Brothers, 1945; Readings in English Literature, 1945; The Golden Year of Fan Cheng-Ta (Chinese Poems), 1946; Judgment in Suspense, 1946; Silver Poets of the Sixteenth Century (Everyman's Library), 1947; George Eliot, her Life and

Books, 1947; Men at High Table and The House of Strangers, 1948; Cricket in Heaven, 1949; Poems, 1949; The English Mystics, 1950; Sydney Smith, a Biography and a Selection, 1951; The Trouble at Number Seven, 1952; News from the Village (poems), 1952; The Alderman's Son, 1954; Windows on a Vanished Time, 1955: The Daughters of Mrs. Peacock, 1957; The Peacock Brides, 1958; Ten Minute Tales and some Others (posthumous), 1959. *Address:* c/o A. D. Peters, 10 Buckingham Street, W.C.2. *Club:* Savile. [*Died* 3 *Jan.* 1958.

BULLOCK, Charles, C.M.G. 1941; late Secretary for Native Affairs, Chief Native Commissioner and Director of Native Development, Southern Rhodesia. *Publications:* Mashona Laws and Customs, 1911; The Mashona, 1927. *Address:* 6 Fairbridge Avenue, Salisbury, Southern Rhodesia. [*Died* 1 *Sept.* 1952.

BULLOCK, Ernest Henry; Town Clerk, Kingston upon Hull, since 1945; Clerk of the Peace, 1952; *b.* 5 March 1911; *m.* 1936, Emily Boodie; one *s.* one *d.* *Educ.:* Hull Technical College; Hull University. Articled with Sir J. R. Howard Roberts; Asst. Solicitor, Hull Corporation, 1936-39; Senior Asst. Solicitor, 1939-41; Deputy Town Clerk, 1941-45. *Publication:* Planning Tomorrow's Britain, 1945. *Recreations:* golf, swimming, sailing. *Address:* Guildhall, Hull. *T.:* 36880. [*Died* 6 *March* 1957.

BULLOCK, Guy Henry, M.A.; *b.* Peking, 23 July 1887; *s.* of Professor T. L. Bullock, Oxford, and Florence, *d.* of S. L. Horton, Shifnal; *m.* 1916, Laura Alice, *d.* of F. M. P. McGloin, Knight of St. Gregory, Judge of the Louisiana Court of Appeal. *Educ.:* Winchester; New College, Oxford. Entered Consular Service, 1913; Vice-Consul at New Orleans, 1913; at Luanda and Fernando Po, 1914; at Marseilles, 1916; at Lima, 1917; in charge of Legation there, 1919; Consul at Havre, 1922; at Addis Ababa, 1924; in charge of Legation there 1924 and 1925; Consul at Zagreb, 1926; Consul-General at Luanda, 1931; Consul at Lyons, 1934-37; Minister Resident in Quito, 1937-41; employed in Prisoners of War Department of Foreign Office; Consul-Gen. at Brazzaville, 1944-47; retired, 1947. Took part in first expedition to Mount Everest, 1921. *Recreations:* mountaineering, golf, etc. *Address:* Loch Oich, 19 Coombe Lane, Kingston, Surrey. *T:* Malden 7887. *Club:* Alpine. [*Died* 12 *April* 1956.

BULLOCK, Brig. Humphry, C.I.E. 1947; O.B.E. 1943; *b.* 9 Jan. 1899; *s.* of late Dr. A. E. Bullock, M.C.; *m.* 1930, Doreen Margaret, *d.* of late W. H. H. Money; one *s.* one *d.* *Educ.:* Dover College; R.M.C., Sandhurst. Served European War, 1914-18, Indian Army, Mesopotamia and Salonika; 2nd Lieut. 1916; Waziristan, 1923 (despatches); Lieut.-Colonel, 1937; War of 1939-45; Colonel, 1940; Brigadier, 1944. Judge Advocate General, India, 1944-47; Judge Advocate Gen. to Supreme Comdr. in India and Pakistan, 1947; retired from army, 1948; First Sec. to the United Kingdom High Commissioner, New Delhi, 1947-51. Member of Council, Society for Army Historical Research, 1953. *Publications:* Indian Cavalry Standards, 1930; Indian Infantry Colours, 1931; Historic Delhi, 1951; History of (Indian) Army Service Corps, Vol. I, 1952, etc. *Recreation:* historical research. *Address:* 43 Dollar Street, Cirencester, Glos.; c/o Lloyds Bank, 6 Pall Mall, S.W.1. [*Died* 19 *Nov.* 1959.

BULTEEL, Major Sir John Crocker, K.C.V.O., *cr.* 1955; D.S.O. 1917; M.C. 1916; Secretary to the Ascot Authority; *b.* 16 Aug. 1890; *s.* of John George Bulteel, Pamflete, S. Devon; *m.* 1919, Doris (*d.* 1953), *d.* of Sir William Petersen, Eigg, Inverness-shire; two *d.* (and one *d.* decd.). *Educ.:* Eton. *Address:* Leighon, Manaton, S. Devon. *Club:* Turf. [*Died* 18 *Feb.* 1956.

BUNBURY, Sir Mervyn William Richardson-, 4th Bt., *cr.* 1787; *b.* June 1874; *s.* of late Mervyn Matthew Richardson-Bunbury, *s.* of 3rd Bt., and Eliza Mary (*d.* 1936), *d.* of William Thorn, M.D.; *S.* grandfather, 1909. *Heir: cousin,* Richard [*b.* 23 May 1899; *m.* 1925, Florence Margaret Gordon, *d.* of Col. Roger Gordon Thomson, two *s.* one *d.*]. *Address:* Windermere, Dunmow, Essex. [*Died* 21 *Oct.* 1952.

BUNIN, Ivan; *b.* Voronezh, 1870. Hon. Academician, Russian Academy of Science, 1909; Nobel Prize for Literature for 1933. *Publications:* The Village, 1911 (in English, 1923); The Brothers; The Gentleman from San Francisco; An Evening in the Spring; The Rose of Jericho; The Well of Days, 1933; Grammar of Love, 1935; She, 1936; Tolstoi's Liberation, 1937; Dark Avenues (and other Stories), 1949; Memories and Portraits, 1951, etc. *Address:* 1 Rue Jacques Offenbach, Paris 16, France. [*Died* 7 *Nov.* 1953.

BURCHARDT, Frank A.; Director of Oxford University Institute of Statistics, since 1949; Fellow of Magdalen College, Oxford, since 1948; Reader in Economic and Social Statistics since 1950; Faculty Fellow of Nuffield College, Oxford, since 1954; *b.* 5 Jan. 1902; *m.* 1932, Arne Herren; one *s.* two *d.* *Educ.:* Kiel and Heidelberg. D.Phil., Kiel. Economic research and lecturing, Universities of Kiel and Frankfurt; economic adviser to joint stock bank, financial editor, 1926-35; research grant, All Souls College, 1936-1944; Special Adviser to Economic Commission for Europe, Geneva, 1956-57. *Publications:* (co-author) Public Investment and the Trade Cycle, 1940; (co-author) The Economics of Full Employment, 1944. *Address:* 71 Rose Hill, Oxford. [*Died* 21 *Dec.* 1958.

BURDEN, Colonel Henry, C.I.E. 1911; F.R.C.S., I.M.S. (retired); late Residency Surgeon, Nepal, India; *b.* 26 April 1867; *s.* of Henry Burden, M.D., Co. Down, Ireland; *m.* 1924, Ellen Muriel Darby. *Educ.:* home. Entered St. Thomas's Hospital London, 1886; House Surgeon, St. Thomas's Hospital, London; Royal Free Hospital, London; Stockwell Fever Hospital, London; passed out second from Netley, and entered Indian Medical Service, 1894; served Relie of Chitral (medal and clasp); North-West Frontier, 1897-98 (two clasps); European War in Egypt, Persia, and India, 1914-19; retired, 1921. *Recreations:* shooting, golfing, sailing. *Address:* Flat E1, Pine Grange, Bath Road, Bournemouth. [*Died* 18 *Jan.* 1953.

BURDETT, Sir Francis, 8th Bt., *cr.* 1618; D.L. Derbyshire; J.P. Derbyshire and Wiltshire; *b.* 5 July 1869; *s.* of 7th Bt. and Mary Dorothy, *y. d.* of John Smyth of Cleatham, Co. Durham; *S.* father, 1892; *m.* 1908, Frances (*d.* 1948), *d.* of Thompson Boyd. *Educ.:* Eton; Trinity College, Cambridge. Late 17th Lancers; served South Africa, 1900 (wounded, medal and 4 clasps); European War; late A.D.C. to Governor of Ceylon; High Sheriff for Derbyshire, 1908. Owns about 7500 acres. *Address:* Ramsbury Manor, Wilts. *Clubs:* Army and Navy, Carlton, Cavalry. [*Died* 13 *April* 1951 (*dormant*).

BURDON, Sir Ernest, K.C.I.E., *cr.* 1934 (C.I.E. 1921); Kt., *cr.* 1931; C.S.I. 1926; B.A.(Oxon); Hon. LL.D. (St. Andrews); I.C.S. retired; Hon. Treasurer and Chairman Finance Department, Joint Committee St.

John and British Red Cross, 1945-Oct. 1956; *b.* 1881; *s.* of late Rev. J. A. Burdon, The Manse, Lasswade, Midlothian; *m.* 1st; one *s.*; 2nd, 1922, Mary Isabella (*d.* 1934), *d.* of Rev. W. Fairweather, D.D., Dunnikier Manse, Kirkcaldy, Fife. *Educ.:* Edinburgh Academy; University College, Oxford (scholar). Entered Indian Civil Service, 1905; Financial Under-Secretary Punjab Govt., 1911; Govt. of India, 1914; Financial Adviser Mesopotamian Expeditionary Force, 1918-19; Financial Adviser, Military Finance, Govt. of India; Member of Indian Munitions Board, and of Imperial Legislative Council, India, 1919; Secretary to Govt. of India Army Department and Member Legislative Assembly, India, 1922-26; Secretary to the Government of India, Finance Department, and Member of the Council of State, India, 1927-29; Auditor-General of India, 1929-40; retd. 1940; was Hon. Sec. and Treasurer Indian People's Famine Trust, 1929-1940; Chairman Indian Red Cross Society, 1936-38; Chairman St. John Ambulance Association Indian Council and Chief Commissioner, St. John Ambulance Brigade in India, 1936-40; Chairman Joint War Committee Indian Red Cross and St. John, 1939; Chairman, Countess of Dufferin Fund, 1936-40; Chairman, V.A.D. Council, U.K., 1941-43; Chairman Finance Committee and Deputy Chm. Executive Committee, War Organisation, British Red Cross Soc. and Order of St. John, 1941-47; Receiver-General of Order of St. John, 1947-55; G.C.St.J., 1952. Order of the Brilliant Star of China, 1949. *Address:* Kingsmead Cottage, Ruislip, Middlesex. [*Died* 12 *Aug.* 1957.

BURGESS, Arthur James Wetherall; R.I., R.O.I., R.B.C.; Naval Artist; Art Editor, Brassey's Naval and Shipping Annual, 1922-1930; acted as Official Naval Artist to the Commonwealth of Australia; *b.* Bombala, N.S. Wales, 6 Jan. 1879; *s.* of late J. O. Burgess (Lieut. R.N.), Sydney; *m.* 1911, Muriel, *d.* of late Major R. H. Coldwell, Shrewsbury; one *d.* *Educ.:* Hutchins, Hobart and Armidale, N.S.W. Settled in England in 1901; studied Naval Subjects in Royal Dockyards; Exhibitor at Royal Academy regularly since 1904; Paris Salon, etc.; contributor to the London Illustrated Papers and Magazines. Pictures: The Brotherhood of Seamen, Nat. Maritime Museum, Greenwich, 1954; The First Australian Fleet, painted for the National Art Gallery of N.S.W. *Publications:* Australian War Records, Canberra. *Recreation:* fishing. *Address:* 8 Primrose Gardens, Hampstead, N.W.3. *T.:* Primrose 0534. *Clubs:* Arts, Langham Sketching. [*Died* 16 *April* 1957.

BURGESS, (Frank) Gelett; author and illustrator; *b.* Boston, Massachusetts, U.S.A., 30 Jan. 1866; *m.* 1914, Estelle Loomis. *Educ.:* Massachusetts Inst. of Technology (B.S., 1887). Civil engineer on railway in California, 1887-1890; instructor in Topographical Drawing in University of California, 1891-94; designer till 1896, when he took up literary work as a profession, illustrating most of his writings; editor of The Lark, 1895-1897; contributor to various American and English periodicals; lived thirteen years in Paris. *Publications:* Vivette, 1897; The Lively City o' Ligg, 1899; Goops, and How to Be Them, 1900; A Gage of Youth, and The Burgess Nonsense Book, 1901; The Romance of the Commonplace, 1902; More Goops, 1903; The Reign of Queen Isyl (with Will Irwin), 1903; The Picaroons (with same), 1904; The Rubaiyat of Omar Cayenne, 1904; Goop Tales, 1904; A Little Sister of Destiny, 1905; Are You a Bromide? 1906; The White Cat, The Heart Line, The Maxims of Methuselah, 1907; The Cave Man (play); Blue Goops and Red, Lady Méchante, 1909; Find the Woman, 1911; The Master of Mysteries, 1912; The Goop Directory, The Maxims of Noah, Love in a Hurry, 1913; Burgess Unabridged, 1914; The Goop Encyclopedia, War, the Creator, 1915; Mrs. Hope's Husband, 1917; Have You an Educated Heart? Ain't Angie Awful! 1923; The Purple Cow (Musical Comedy), 1925; Why Men Hate Women, 1927; The Bromide, 1933; Two O'Clock Courage, 1934; Too Good Looking, 1936; Look Eleven Years Younger, 1937; Short Words are Words of Might, 1938; Ladies in Boxes, 1942. *Address:* Carmel, Calif., U.S.A. *Club:* Bohemian (San Francisco). [*Died* 17 *Sept.* 1951.

BURGESS, Frederick George; lecturer, writer, cartoonist; Member L.C.C., 1937-49. M.P. (Lab.), York, 1929-31; Trustee N.U.R. *Address:* Railway Review, 205 Euston Road, N.W.1. [*Died* 31 *March* 1951.

BURGESS, Gelett; *see* Burgess, Frank G.

BURGESS, Professor William Leslie, C.B.E. 1943; Professor of Public Health and Social Medicine, St. Andrews University, since 1951; *b.* 11 April 1886; *m.* 1929, Helen Duncanson; one *s.* *Educ.:* George Heriot's School, Edinburgh; Edinburgh University. Formerly: medical officer of Health, City of Dundee; Reader in Public Health, St. Andrews University. *Recreation:* fishing. *Address:* 454 Perth Road, Dundee. *T.:* 671,77. [*Died* 22 *April* 1954.

BURGH, 8th Baron, *cr.* 1529 (called out of abeyance, 1916), **Alexander Leigh Henry Leith;** late Lieut. The Black Watch; *b.* 16 May 1906; *s.* of 7th Baron and Phyllis, *y. d.* of Col. Mark Goldie, C.R.E.; *S.* father, 1926; *m.* 1st, 1934, Elizabeth Rose (from whom he obtained a divorce, 1943), *d.* of late Arthur R. Vincent, C.B.E.; one *s.*; 2nd, 1947, Joyce Watts, 2nd *d.* of W. Wilson Wilson, 10 Curzon Road, Hoylake, Cheshire; two *s.* *Educ.:* Wellington College; R.M.C., Sandhurst. *Heir:* *s.* Hon. Alexander Peter Willoughby Leith [*b.* 20 March 1935; *m.* 1957, Anita Lorna, *d.* of Frederick C. Eldridge, Gillingham, Kent]. *Address:* West Close, Middlecombe, Minehead, Somerset. [*Died* 26 *May* 1959.

[*By some reckonings he was 6th Baron and appeared as such in Who's Who Obituary.*

BURKE, Capt. Sir Gerald (Howe), 7th Bt., *cr.* 1797; late Irish Guards; *b.* 17 Nov. 1893; *s.* of 6th Bt. and Catharine Mary Caroline, *d.* of Maj.-Gen. J. H. Burke, R.E.; *S.* father, 1913; *m.* 1st, 1914, Elizabeth Mary (*d.* 1918), *o. d.* of late Patrick Mathews, Mt. Hanover, Drogheda; one *s.*; 2nd, 1920, Merrial, *o. d.* of Edward Christie, 84 Sloane Street, S.W.; two *d.* Served European War, 1914-18 (wounded); retired pay, 1922. Owns 28,000 acres. *Heir:* *s.* Thomas Stanley, *b.* 20 July 1916. *Clubs:* Guards; Kildare Street (Dublin) [*Died* 30 *Dec.* 1954.

BURKE, Lieut.-Colonel Gerald Tyler, C.I.E. 1938; M.D., F.R.C.P.; Indian Medical Service (Retired); *b.* 31 May 1882; *s.* of late Lt.-Col. William Henry Burke, Army Pay Dept.; *m.* 1st, 1909, Edith Beryl Peacock (*d.* 1937); one *d.*; 2nd, 1939, Kathleen, 2nd *d.* of Edward Sharwood-Smith, *q.v.* *Educ.:* St. Bartholomew's Hosp.; London Univ. M.D. Lond. 1922; M.B., B.S. (Hons.) 1907; F.R.C.P. Lond. 1933; entered I.M.S. 1909; served in European War, 1914-18; Lt.-Col. 1929; Professor of Medicine, Lucknow Univ., 1924-35; Secretary Medical Council of India, 1935-37; retired, 1937. *Address:* Greenthwaite, Collington Lane, Bexhill-on-Sea. [*Died* 13 *Nov.* 1952.

BURKE, Kathleen, C.B.E. 1918; Chevalier Legion of Honour, France; Knight of St. Sava, Serbia; Officier de l'Instruction Publique, France, etc.; *b.* London, England, 24 Oct. 1887; *d.* of Thomas Francis Burke of London and North Western Railway and Georgina Connolly; both British; *m.* 1st, 1920, Frederick Forrest Peabody (*d.* 1927), Santa Barbara, California; 2nd, 1929, John Reginald McLean (*d.* 1929); 3rd, 1931, Girard van B.

Hale (*d.* 1958). *Educ.:* London; Paris (Univ.). Formerly Hon. Secretary, London Committee Scottish Women's Hospitals. First woman sent by the British Government to visit the British Front; returned to France in spring of 1940; working with relief units of American Friends of France; Freeman of the cities of San Francisco and Fresno, California, and of Flint, Michigan; Hon. Col. of 138th Field Artillery U.S. Army; the first British woman to be made Colonel of an American regiment; member of the Boilermakers' Union and Sheet Metal Workers' Union of America. *Publications:* The White Road to Verdun; Little Heroes of France; Young Heroes of Britain and Belgium. *Recreations:* shooting and fishing. *Address:* Solana, Santa Barbara, California; Eagle Ranch, Atascadero, California. [*Died Nov.* 1958.

BURKE, Lieut.-Colonel Sir Richard John Charles, Kt., *cr.* 1933; *b.* Cork, 5 May 1878; *y. s.* of late Charles Toler Burke, P.W.D., Bombay; *m.* 1903, Norah Mary (*d.* 1933), *e. d.* of Lt.-Col. Hyde Cates, I.A.; two *d.* *Educ.:* Malvern College; Sandhurst. Indian Political Service; First Commission, 1898; in military employ till 1900, when he joined the Political Service; Administrator, Sangli State, 1905-10; special duty in connection with visit of His late Majesty King George, when Prince of Wales, 1905, and the Amir, 1907; Adviser to the Maharajah of Dewas, Oct. 1911-July, 1914; reverted to military employ March 1915, and was employed as Assistant Secretary, Army Dept., Govt. of India, March-August 1915, and thereafter, till April 1919, attached to the General Staff, A.H.Q., India (despatches, medal); Vice-President, Council of Administration, Bhavnagar, for the next six years; Resident at Baroda, 1927-29; Resident in Mysore and Chief Commissioner of Coorg, 1930-1933; retired 1933; War of 1939-45, Sergeant, Gloucestershire Special Constabulary; Defence Medal. *Address:* c/o Lloyds Bank, Guildford, Surrey. [*Died* 31 *Aug.* 1960.

BURKE, Sir (Ulick) Roland, K.C.V.O., *cr.* 1939; late Chief Agent to the Duke of Devonshire and Chatsworth Estate Co.; *b.* 1872; *s.* of late Ulick John Burke, Newton Valence Manor, Alton, Hants; *m.* 1905, Henrietta May Bell; one *d.* *Educ.:* Eton. Vice-President and Fellow of Land Agents Society; Trustee, Past President, and late Hon. Director of Royal Agricultural Society of England; Member E. Suffolk County Council. *Address:* Melton Mead, Woodbridge, Suffolk. *T.:* Woodbridge 203. *Clubs:* Boodle's; County (Ipswich). [*Died* 3 *Dec.* 1958.

BURKITT, Francis Holy, C.I.E. 1931; O.B.E. 1917; late Chief Engineer and Secretary to Government N.W.F. Province, India; *b.* 5 July 1880; *s.* of Rev. T. H. Burkitt and E. E. Parsons; *m.* 1905, Anna, *d.* of Canon Trotter; three *d.* *Educ.:* Portora; Trinity College, Dublin; Coopers Hill. Entered P.W.D., India, 1903; served Indian Frontier (despatches, O.B.E.). *Publications:* various articles on Hydraulic Engineering. *Address:* 3 Stockton House, Fleet. [*Died* 3 *Oct.* 1952.

BURMESTER, Admiral Sir Rudolf Miles, K.B.E. *cr.* 1934; C.B. 1919; C.M.G. 1916; *b.* 11 Nov. 1875; 3rd *s.* of F. G. Burmester, M.A.; *m.* 1907, Margery Gladys (*d.* 1952), *d.* of Admiral Rodney Lloyd, C.B.; one *s.* one *d.* Lieutenant 1897; Commander 1907; Captain 1914; Rear-Admiral 1924; Vice-Admiral 1929; Admiral 1933; served H.M.S. Highflyer, 1902-3 (medal and Somaliland clasp); War Staff Officer, 1913; H.M.S. Euryalus, Dardanelles, 1915-16 (C.M.G.); Chief of Staff, Mediterranean, 1917-19 (C.B.); Director of Naval Signals, Admiralty, 1919; Chief of Staff, Portsmouth Command, 1920-22; H.M.S. Warspite, 1923; A.D.C. to the King, 1923-24; Director of Mobilisation Department, Admiralty, 1926-28; Commander-in-Chief, Africa Station, 1928-31; retired list, 1933; recalled to active service, 1940; Flag Officer in charge, Cardiff, 1942-44. *Address:* 24 Eaton Mansions, Cliveden Place, S.W.1. *T.:* Sloane 3560. *Club:* Army and Navy. [*Died* 27 *Dec.* 1956.

BURN, Sir Clive; *see* Burn, Sir R. C. W.

BURN, Dugald Stuart, C.I.E. 1932; *b.* 21 July 1877; *s.* of late Robert Burn. In service of Great Northern and North Eastern Railways; joined staff of Great Indian Peninsula Rly. 1901; General Traffic Manager 1921; Agent (General Manager) 1928; retired 1932; President Indian Railway Conference Association and Caledonian Society of Bombay in 1931; Member of Institute of Transport; a Director of the Nizam's State Railway, 1932-37. *Club:* Constitutional. [*Died* 9 *Sept.* 1951.

BURN, Brig.-Gen. Henry Pelham, C.M.G. 1918; D.S.O. 1915; *b.* 1 May 1882; *e. surv. s.* of late C. M. Pelham Burn; *m.* 1928, Katherine Eileen Staveley Staveley-Hill; one *s.* one *d.* Entered Army, 1901; Capt., 1910; Major, 1916 Lt.-Col. 1923; Col. 1927; served South Africa, 1901-2 (Queen's medal 5 clasps); European War, 1914-18; Commanded 152nd Infantry Brigade, 51st Highland Division, 1916-18 (despatches five times, D.S.O., Bt. Lt.-Col., C.M.G.); retired. *Address:* Craigellachie Lodge, Craigellachie, Banffshire. [*Died* 10 *July* 1958.

BURN, Sir (Roland) Clive (Wallace), K.C.V.O., *cr.* 1948 (C.V.O. 1942); Secretary and Keeper of the Records of the Duchy of Cornwall, 1936-54, and Solicitor to Duchy of Cornwall, 1940-54; *b.* 24 Oct. 1882; *o. s.* of late Matthew James Burn, Yarm Court, Leatherhead; *m.* 1912, Phyllis Marjorie, *d.* of late Alan H. P. Stoneham; two *s.* one *d.* (and one *d.* decd.). *Educ.:* Winchester Coll.; Oriel Coll., Oxford. Oxford Univ. Cricket XI, 1902, 1903, 1904, and 1905; Member of Cricket Teams to West Indies and to America in 1905; Solicitor since 1908; retired from firm of Burn and Berridge of 31 Great Queen Street, Kingsway, 1939; served with Sussex Yeomanry and Machine Gun Corps Cavalry, 1914-19. *Address:* 10 Buckingham Gate, S.W.1. *T.:* Victoria 7346. *Club:* Bath. [*Died* 8 *May* 1955.

BURN-MURDOCH, Hector, LL.D.; Major, late Queen's Own Cameron Highlanders; *s.* of late Archibald Burn-Murdoch, W.S., and *g.s.* of late John Burn-Murdoch, D.L., of Gartincaber, Perthshire; *b.* 30 March 1881; *m.* 1921, Katharine Mary, *d.* of late W. P. Bruce, Braeburn, Currie, Midlothian, and Dungallan, Oban; one *s.* four *d.* *Educ.:* Trinity College, Cambridge. B.A., LL.B., 1903; LL.D. Cantab., 1934; LL.B. Edin., 1905; Advocate at Scottish Bar, 1905; Barrister-at-law, Inner Temple, 1907 (Special Prizeman and certificate of honour); Lecturer in English Law at University of Edinburgh, 1912-14 and 1919-22; served European War, 1914-18; Advocate-Depute in Sheriff Court, 1923; Extra-Advocate-Depute, 1924; Advocate-Depute, 1926; Sheriff-Substitute of Berwickshire, 1927; Sheriff-Substitute of Stirling, Dumbarton and Clackmannan at Stirling, 1940-47; retired, 1947. Lay Reader, Edinburgh Diocese, 1931; Chancellor, diocese of Brechin, 1938. *Publications:* Notes on English Law as differing from Scots Law, 1924; Interdict in the Law of Scotland, 1933; Presbytery and Apostolic Succession, 1939; Church, Continuity and Unity, 1945; The Development of the Papacy, 1954. *Recreations:* formerly golf, fishing; now reading and writing. *Address:* 17 Barnshot Road, Colinton, Edinburgh 13. *T.:* Colinton 88305. [*Died* 20 *April* 1958.

BURNE, Lieut.-Col. Alfred Higgins, D.S.O. 1914, Bar 1918; F.R.Hist.S.; R.A.

(retd.); late Assistant Editor of The Fighting Forces; Editor of The Gunner, 1938-57; Military editor of Chambers's Encyclopædia; *b.* 26 Sept. 1886; 5th *s.* of late Col. S. T. H. Burne, V.D., J.P., Loynton Hall, and late Julia Susanna, *d.* of Valentine Vickers, Offley Grove, Staffs. *Educ.:* Winchester College; R.M.A., Woolwich. Commissioned in R.A., 1906; retired pay, 1935; served European War, 1914-18 (D.S.O. and Bar, despatches 6 times); Commandant, 121st O.C.T.U., R.A., 1939-42; Services lectr.; Lees Knowles lectr., 1946. *Publications:* Talks on Leadership, 1921; Some Pages from the History of "Q" Battery R.H.A., 1922; The Royal Artillery Mess, Woolwich, 1934; The Liaoyang Campaign, 1936; Mesopotamia: the Last Phase, 1937; Lee, Grant and Sherman, 1938; The Art of War on Land, 1944; Campaign in Sicily and Italy, 1946; Strategy as exemplified by World War II, 1946; The Noble Duke of York, 1949; Battlefields of England, 1949; More Battlefields of England, 1953; The Crecy War, 1954; The Agincourt War, 1956; The Woolwich Mess, 1955; The Great Civil War (with Colonel P. Young), 1959. *Club:* United Service.

[*Died* 2 *June* 1959.

BURNE, Colonel Newdigate Halford Marriot, C.M.G. 1919; D.S.O. 1916; *b.* 21 July 1872; *y. s.* of late Felix Neeld Burne, of Gritelton, Wilts; *m.* 1905, Hillian Ross Blakeway. Joined Cape Mounted Riflemen, 1890; served with that regiment until its amalgamation with the Permanent Forces, Union of South Africa, on staff of which held various appointments; Imperial Service Commissions in 11th S.A.I.; 60th Rifles (K.R.R.C.); commanded 7th Batt. K.S.L.I. in France and with Army of Occupation, Germany; served Matabele Campaign, 1893-94; Langeberg Campaign, 1896-97; South Africa, 1899-1902; European War, 1914-19 (despatches thrice, D.S.O., French Croix de Guerre, C.M.G.); commanded 1st Special Service (Reserve) Bn. S. African (Union) Forces, 1939-40; S.A. Staff Corps (V.) 1940-42, when retired under age limit. *Address:* c/o Barclays (D. C. & O.) Bank, Umkomaas, S. Coast, Natal.

[*Died* 5 *July* 1950.

[*But death not notified in time for inclusion in Who Was Who 1941–1950, first edn.*

BURNE, Richard Higgins, F.R.S. 1927; M.A.; *b* London, 5 April 1868; *y. s.* of Richard H. Burne, solicitor; *m.* Louisa Joan (*d.* 1945), *d.* of Rev. I. B. Burne; one *s.* one *d.* *Educ.:* Winchester; Oriel College, Oxford; Royal College of Science, London. Anatomical Assistant Royal College of Surgeons, 1892; Assistant Conservator, 1908; Secretary, Malacological Society, 1901-5; Physiological Curator, Royal College of Surgeons Museum, 1912-34; awarded Hon. Gold Medal Royal College of Surgeons, 1925; Hunterian Trustee, 1937. *Publications:* various papers on comparative anatomy, principally on molluscs, fishes, and mammals. *Address:* c/o Westminster Bank. 329 High Holborn, W.C.1.

[*Died* 9 *Oct.* 1953.

BURNETT, Major Sir Alexander Edwin, 14th Bt., *cr.* 1626 of Leys, Kincardineshire; O.B.E. 1919; *b.* 26 April 1881; 2nd *s.* of Sir Thomas Burnett, 12th Bt., of Leys (*d.* 1926; Lord Lieutenant and Convener for County of Kincardine, J.P. and D.L. County of Aberdeen, President of Kincardine T.A.A., Colonel late Royal Horse Artillery) and Mary Elizabeth (*d.* 1928), *e. d.* of James Cumine, of Rattray, Aberdeenshire; *S.* brother (Maj.-Gen. Sir James Lauderdale Gilbert Burnett, 13th Bt., *q.v.*), 1953; unmarried. *Educ.:* Wellington Coll., Berkshire; Trinity Coll., Cambridge. Gazetted the King's Own Scottish Borderers, 1901. Served European War, 1914-19 (severely wounded, O.B.E.); Major, King's Own Scottish Borderers, 1916; retired, 1920. J.P. Kincardineshire, 1925-58. *Heir: kinsman* Sir Alexander Burnett Ramsay, 6th Bt., of Balmain (who was *heir-pres.* to Btcy. Burnett of Leys but did not claim). *Address:* c/o Lloyds Bank, 6 Pall Mall, S.W.1.

[*Died* 9 *May* 1959 *(dormant).*

BURNETT, Sir Digby Vere, Kt., *cr.* 1945; Consulting Mining Engineer, P.O. Box 1861, Salisbury, S. Rhodesia; Director of Cam and Motor Gold Mining Co. (1919) Ltd.; Premier Portland Cement Co. Ltd. and many other companies. *Educ.:* Marlborough College. Went to South Africa, 1892; Resident Director, 1934-50, and General Manager, 1920-50, London and Rhodesia Mining and Land Co. Ltd. *Address:* Sherwood House, 33 Baines Avenue, Salisbury, Southern Rhodesia.

[*Died* 3 *Nov.* 1958.

BURNETT, Maj.-Gen. Sir James Lauderdale Gilbert, of Leys, 13th Bt., *cr.* 1626; C.B., 1932; C.M.G., 1919; D.S.O. 1915; Brigadier, Queen's Bodyguard for Scotland; *b.* 1 April 1880; *e. s.* of Sir Thomas Burnett, 12th Bart., and Mary Elizabeth, *e. d.* of J. Cumine of Rattray, Aberdeenshire; *S.* father, 1926; *m.* 1913, Sybil Aird, *y. d.* of late William Crozier Smith of Whitehill, St. Boswells, N.B.; one *d.* (one *s.* decd. and one *s.* killed in action 1945). *Educ.:* Wellington; R.M.C., Sandhurst. Entered Army, 1899; Captain, 1906; Major, 1915; Bt. Col. 1919; Lt.-Col. 1922; Col. 1927; Maj.-Gen. 1931; served S. African War, 1899-1902 (despatches, Queen's medal 2 clasps, King's medal 2 clasps); European War, 1914-18 (despatches, D.S.O., severely wounded); commanded company of G. Cadets, R.M.C., Sandhurst, 1915-16; Lt.-Colonel, 1st Gordon Highlanders, 1917 (despatches, D.S.O. and bar, C.M.G., Officier Legion d'Honneur, C.M.G., Bt. Col.); Brig.-General 186th Infantry Brigade, 1917-19; Instructor, Senior Officers' School, 1919-22; commanded 2nd Batt. the Gordon Highlanders, 1923-26; commanded 14th Infantry Brigade, Shanghai Defence Force 1927-28; 153rd (Black Watch and Gordon), Infantry Brigade T.A., 1928-30; Commander 8th Infantry Brigade, 1930-31; Comm. 51st (Highland) Div., T.A. 1931-35; retired pay, 1935; Vice-Lieut. since 1944 and J.P. Kincardineshire; owns about 13,400 acres. *Recreations:* shooting, fishing. *Heir: b.* Alexander Edwin (*see* Maj. Sir Alexander Burnett, 14th Bt.). *Address:* Crathes Castle, Aberdeen. *Club:* Army and Navy.

[*Died* 13 *Aug.* 1953.

BURNETT, Colonel Sir Leslie Trew, 2nd Bt., *cr.* 1913; C.B.E. 1944 (O.B.E. 1919); T.D.; one of H.M.'s Lieutenants for the City of London; D.L. Surrey; Dir. Denny, Mott & Dickson Ltd.; Proprietors of Hays Wharf Ltd.; *b.* 22 Sept. 1884; *s.* of Sir David Burnett, 1st Bt., and Emily (*d.* 1917), *e. d.* of late Thomas Sleap; *S.* father, 1930; *m.* 1917, Joan, *d.* of late Sir John Humphery; two *s.* three *d.* Served European War, commanded 4th Bn. London Regiment, 1915-1916 (despatches); Hon. Col. 460 H.A.A. Regt. R.A., T.A., 1936-51. Master, Worshipful Company of Coopers, 1947. *Heir: s.* David Humphery, M.B.E., T.D., M.A., Major R.A., T.A., *b.* 27 Jan. 1918. *Address:* Stratton, Godstone, Surrey; 9-10 Fenchurch Street, E.C.3.

[*Died* 17 *July* 1955.

BURNETT, Admiral Sir Robert Lindsay, G.B.E., *cr.* 1950 (K.B.E., *cr.* 1944; O.B.E. 1923); K.C.B., *cr.* 1945 (C.B. 1942); D.S.O. 1943; LL.D. (Aberdeen Univ.), 1944; C.St.J. 1945; *b.* 22 July 1887; 4th *s.* of J. A. Burnett of Kemnay, Aberdeenshire; *m.* 1915, Ethel Constance, *d.* of R. H. Shaw. *Educ.:* Bedford School; Eastmans, Southsea. Entered R.N. 1902; specialised in Physical Training, 1911; commanded Destroyers in Grand Fleet, 1914-18; Director of Physical Training and Sports, Royal Navy, 1933; Commodore, Chatham, 1939; A.D.C. to the King, 1940; Actg. Rear-Adm. 1940; Rear-Adm., 1941; Rear-Admiral Comdg. Home Fleet Destroyer

Flotillas, 1942; 10th Cruiser Squadron, 1943; Vice-Adm. 1943; C.-in-C., South Atlantic, 1944-46; Adm. 1946; Commander-in-Chief, Plymouth, 1947-50; retired list, 1950. Chairman, White Fish Authority, 1950-54. Order of Souverov (Russia), 1943; Knight Comdr. of the Order of George I (Greece), 1949; Knight Grand Cross of the Order of Orange Nassau (Netherlands), 1950. *Recreations:* fencing, boxing, football, cricket. *Club:* United Service. [*Died* 2 *July* 1959.

BURNETT-STUART, of Dens and Crichie, **General Sir John (Theodosius),** G.C.B., *cr.* 1937 (K.C.B., *cr.* 1932; C.B. 1917); K.B.E., *cr.* 1923; C.M.G. 1916; D.S.O. 1900; *b.* 14 March 1875; *m.* 1904, Nina, *d.* of Major Nelson, late 5th Dragoon Guards; two *d.* (one *s.* decd.). *Educ.:* Repton; Sandhurst. Joined Rifle Brigade, 1895; Lieut. 1897; Capt. 1901; Brevet Major, 1911; served North-West Frontier expedition, 1897-98 (medal with clasp); South African War, 1899-1902 (despatches, Queen's medal 4 clasps, King's medal 2 clasps, D.S.O.); Director of Organisation N.Z. Military Forces, 1910-12; G.S.O. 2 Staff College, 1912-13; European War, 1914-18 (despatches, C.B., C.M.G., prom. Col. 1916, Maj.-Gen. 1919); Malabar, 1921-22 (K.B.E., medal with clasp); G.O.C. Madras District, 1920-22; Director of Military Operations and Intelligence, War Office, 1922-26; commander 3rd Division, 1926-30; Lieut.-General, 1930; G.O.C. British Troops in Egypt, 1931-34; General, 1934; General Officer Commanding-in-Chief, Southern Command, 1934-38; A.D.C. General to the King, 1935-38; retired pay, 1938; Colonel Commandant 1st Bn. The Rifle Brigade, 1936-45; Home Guard, 1940-44 (Defence Medal); Officier Légion d'Honneur, Commandeur Crown of Belgium; French and Belgian Croix de Guerre; D.L. and J.P. Aberdeenshire. *Address:* Avington Park, Nr. Winchester, Hants. Crichie House, Stuartfield, Aberdeenshire. *Club:* Naval and Military. [*Died* 6 *Oct.* 1958.

BURNEY, Sydney Bernard, C.B.E. 1918. Served European War, 1914-18, Captain (C.B.E.); Assistant Director-General of Voluntary Organisations; subsequently became an art dealer. *Address:* 26 Conduit St., W.1. [*Died* 3 *Jan.* 1951.

BURNS, Robert, J.P.; *b.* Exeter, England, 1859; *m.* 1st, 1883, Letitia Graham (*d.* 1919), Islington, London; 2nd, 1920, Sarah King Tonkin, Henley, S. Australia; two *s.* three *d.* *Educ.:* Mint School, Exeter. Served apprenticeship at Flying Post, that city; worked as Reporter North Wales Guardian, Wrexham, and Glasgow News, Greenock branch office; emigrated to Adelaide, 1884; immediately joined literary staff Register, Observer, and Evening Journal; Associate Editor and Chief Leader Writer, 1910; Editor of the South Australian Register, Adelaide, 1922-28, since when, on staff of Advertiser, Adelaide; retired as active journalist, 1947. President, Churches of Christ Conference and Home Missions, 1908. *Recreations:* walking, church activities. *Address:* Wonford, Unley Park, South Australia. [*Died* 3 *Sept.* 1951.

BURR, Alfred, F.R.I.B.A., F.R.San.I., M.Inst.R.A., F.I.Arb.; Sanitary Expert; practising as architect, surveyor, and arbitrator; Surveyor to Licensing Justices of St. Pancras Division; *b.* 1855; *s.* of Thomas Alfred Burr, civil engineer; *m.* Amelia Edith (*d.* 1945); one *s.* *Educ.:* University College School, London; Amersham Hall, Reading; Architectural Assoc. London; Matriculated, London Univ. Commenced practice, London, 1878. *Works:* British Columbia House, Regent St., London; Victoria (Australia) Building, Strand, London; Additions to Club House, Polo Pavilion and Stables at Ranelagh Club; Turkish Baths and alterations, Princes Club, Knightsbridge; Restoration of Dr. Johnson's House and new dwelling for Janitor, Gough Square, E.C.; alterations and renovations to College of Arms, Queen Victoria Street, E.C.; Cemetery Church, Offices and Residence at Greenford; clubs, hotels, shops, flats, offices, warehouses, factories, breweries, licensed premises, etc.; country and West End residences; golf club houses and squash racket courts; sanitation at the Ritz Hotel, Carlton Hotel, London clubs, schools, London and country houses. *Address:* 85 Gower Street, W.C.1. *T.:* Museum 2201-2. [*Died* 10 *April* 1952.

BURR, Malcolm, D.Sc.; Writer and translator; late Editor Journal of British Chamber of Commerce in Turkey; late Professor of English, School of Economics, Istanbul; *b.* Blackheath, 6 July 1878; *s.* of Arthur Burr, Dover and Folkestone; *m.* Clara Millicent, *d.* of late William Goode, Tudor House, Hampstead; four *d.* *Educ.:* Radley; New College, Oxford (M.A., D.Sc.); Royal School of Mines, London (A.R.S.M.). Took active part in pioneering Kent Coalfield; Geological Adviser to Kent Coal Concessions Ltd., 1908-14. Fellow Royal Entomological Society (Council, 1903-4, 1910-11; Vice-Pres. 1912); Co-founder International Entomological Congress and Hon. Secretary Permanent Ex. Committee till 1920; Captain (Special List), Salonica Army, 1915-19; recruited and commanded 1st Serbian Sentry Bn. (despatches, White Eagle Serbia, Redeemer Greece). Served Foreign Office and Ministry of Information Yugoslavia and Turkey, 1939-45. *Publications:* British Orthoptera, 1897; Essai sur les Eumastacides, 1899; Dermaptera in Fauna of B. India Series, 1910; Dermaptera in Wytmsan's Genera Insectorum, 1911; over 100 papers on Orthoptera and Dermaptera in scient. pubns. in several languages; In Bolshevik Siberia, 1931; A Fossicker in Angola, 1933; Slouch Hat, 1935; British Grasshoppers, 1936; The Insect Legion, 1939; numerous articles in Blackwood's, Quarterly Review, Cornhill, Nineteenth Century, Army Quarterly, English Review, etc.; translations from Russian, Serbian, French and Turkish, especially The Code of Stephan Dushan, Hunted through C. Asia, and Moved On! from Russian MS. of P. S. Nazaroff, 1932; Marfa, 1933; Out for a Million, by Krymov, 1935; He's got a Million, by Krymov, 1936; The End of the Imp, by Krymov, 1937; Dersu the Trapper by Arseniev, 1939; Fienka, by Krymov, 1947; Tourist's Guide to Istanbul. *Recreations:* travel, hunting (Master, West St. Harriers, 1911-14), cricket, natural history. *Address:* Izzet Pasa sokagi 43/5, Bomoti, Istanbul, Turkey. *Club:* United University. [*Died* 13 *July* 1954.

BURRAGE, Alfred McLelland; author; *s.* of late Alfred Sherrington Burrage; *b.* Hillingdon, Middlesex, 1 July 1889; *m.* Helene Aletta, *er. d.* of late Rev. Claude Field, M.A., Brighton; one *s.* *Educ.:* St. Augustine's, Ramsgate; Douai School. Took to writing as a means of livelihood when aged seventeen; Artists Rifles (attached R.N.D.) in France, and invalided home April 1918; contributed stories, articles and poems, but mostly stories, to upwards of 150 publications, including Strand, Nash's, Windsor, Pearson's, London, Munsey's, Chambers's; work also included in many British and American anthologies, and broadcast from London, Philadelphia, Berlin, Melbourne, New York, Copenhagen and Ottawa. *Publications:* Poor Dear Esme, 1925; The Smokes of Spring, 1926; Courtland's Crime; and other novels under a pseudonym, 1927; Some Ghost Stories, 1927; War is War, 1930; Someone in the Room, 1931 (under pseudonym, Ex-Private X.); Seeker to the Dead, 1943; Don't break the Seal, 1944; The Waxwork (stage and television play, U.S.A.), 1951; Playmates (Revue Productions Inc., U.S.A.), 1952. *Recreations:* fishing, bridge. *Address:* c/o Stephen Aske, 5 Granville House, Arundel Street, W.C.2. *T.:* Temple Bar 4022. [*Died* 18 *Dec.* 1956.

BURRELL, Sir Merrik (Raymond), 7th Bt., *cr.* 1774; C.B.E. 1919; late Lieut. 1st Royal Dragoons; J.P. West Sussex; Alderman West Sussex; Temp. Major and Assistant-Inspector, Remount Department, May 1915; Temp. Lt.-Col. and Inspector, Jan. 1918; *b.* 14 May 1877; *s.* of 6th Bart. and Etheldreda Mary, *d.* of Sir R. Loder, 1st Bt.; *S.* father, 1899; *m.* 1902, Wilhemina Louisa [whom he *div.* 1907], *d.* of late Walter Winans; two *s.* one *d.*; 2nd, 1908, Coralie Adelaide Mervyn (who obtained a divorce, 1926), *d.* of late J. P. Porter, of Belle Isle, Co. Fermanagh; one *d.* *Educ.:* Eton. Served in South Africa, 1900; High Sheriff for Sussex, 1918; President Royal Agricultural Society of England, 1936; Chairman Royal Veterinary College, 1928-47, Animal Diseases Cttee. of Agricultural Res. Council, 1935-42, Agricultural Committee of County Councils Association, Agricultural Council of England, 1935; Jubilee Medal, 1935; Gold Medal of Roy. Agricultural Society of England. *Heir: s.* Walter Raymond Burrell, C.B.E. *Address:* Floodgates, Horsham, Sussex. *T.A.:* Floodgates, West Grinstead. *T.:* Partridge Green 381. *Club:* Boodle's. [*Died* 22 *Dec.* 1957.

BURRELL, Percy Saville, C.I.E. 1926; M.A. (Oxon); Indian Educational Service (retd.); *b.* 11 Dec. 1871; 5th *s.* of late Benjamin Burrell and Mary Jane, *d.* of late Geo. Depledge, Leeds; *m.* Ethel Marion (*d.* 1945), *d.* of Lewis Bilton, W.S., Edinburgh; two *s.* *Educ.:* Leeds Grammar School (Scholar); Queen's College, Oxford (Hastings Exhibitioner and Honorary Scholar); 1st class classical Moderations, 2nd class Lit. Hum. Assistant Master at S. Peter's School, York, and other schools, 1895-1904; joined Indian Educational Service, 1904; Headmaster, Queen's Collegiate School, Benares; Inspector of Schools, Moradabad, Meerut and Lucknow divisions; Assistant Director of Public Instruction; Principal, Queen's College, Benares; Professor of Philosophy and Head of Department of Philosophy and Dean of Faculty of Arts, University of Allahabad; retired 1926. *Publications:* Articles in various journals. *Address:* 42 St.Michael's Road, Leeds, 6. [*Died* 29 *April* 1958.

BURRELL, Sir William, Kt., *cr.* 1927; J.P. Co. Berwickshire; *b.* 9 July 1861; *s.* of William Burrell, shipowner; *m.* 1901, Constance Mary Lockhart, *d.* of James L. Mitchell. *Address:* Hutton Castle, Hutton, Berwickshire. *Club:* Royal Thames Yacht. [*Died* 29 *March* 1958.

BURRIDGE, Captain Robert Archibald Morison, C.B. 1924; Royal Navy, retired; *s.* of late Robert Burridge, Inspector of Machinery, R.N. Thirty-four years' service in the Royal Navy; Paymaster Commander of the Naval Base at Constantinople during Allied Occupation, 1919-23; retired, 1924. Attached to British Embassy, Lisbon, as Secretary Accountant with British Observers in Portugal under Scheme for Non-intervention in Spain, 1937-39; Assistant Secretary, King George's Fund for Sailors, 1940-45. *Address:* Hill Park, Otterhampton, Bridgwater, Somerset. *Club:* Royal Empire Society. [*Died* 26 *Jan.* 1957.

BURROWS, Alfred John, F.R.I.C.S.; Alderman Kent County Council; Freeman of the City of London; Liveryman of the Haberdashers' Company; *s.* of late Alfred J. Burrows, F.S.I., F.R.G.S., F.L.S.; *m.* 1894, Annie (*d.* 1955), *d.* of George Bensted; three *d.* *Educ.:* privately. Formerly land agent, surveyor and auctioneer practising at Ashford, Kent; late senior partner in firm of Knight, Frank & Rutley; Past Pres. Chartered Auctioneers and Estate Agents Institute of United Kingdom; President, College of Estate Management, 1940-1943. *Recreation:* farming. *Address:* Kennington, Ashford, Kent. *T.:* Kennington-Kent 312. *Club:* Farmers'. [*Died* 14 *Nov.* 1957.

BURROWS, Christine Mary Elizabeth, M.A.; *b.* 4 Jan. 1872; *d.* of late Esther Elizabeth Burrows, first Principal of St. Hilda's Hall, and Henry Parker Burrows. *Educ.:* Ladies' College, Cheltenham; Lady Margaret Hall and St. Hilda's Hall, Oxford; Principal of St. Hilda's Hall (now College), Oxford, 1910-19; Principal of the Oxford Society of Home-Students, (now St. Anne's College) 1921-29; Hon. Fellow of St. Hilda's and St. Anne's Colleges, Oxford; retired. *Address:* Fairfield, 115 Banbury Road, Oxford. *T.:* 58413. *Clubs:* University Women's; English-Speaking Union (Vice-Pres. Oxford branch). [*Died* 10 *Sept.* 1959.

BURROWS, Harold, C.B.E. 1919; Ph.D.; F.R.C.S.; Colonel T.A.R., retired; late Consulting Surgeon, Portsmouth; *b.* 1875; *s.* of late Surg.-Major E. P. Burrows, Bombay Army; *m.* 1st, Lucy Mary Elizabeth, *d* of late Henry Wheeler; two *s.*; 2nd, 1927, Gwendoline Mary, 2nd *d.* of Eng. Rear-Adm. O. R. Paul, C.B.E.; (one *s.* decd.). *Educ.:* Marlborough Coll.; St. Bartholomew's Hospital. Late Assistant-Surgeon, Seamen's Hospital, Greenwich, and Bolingbroke Hospital, Wandsworth Common; Consulting Surgeon, H.M. Forces, 1918-19; Consulting Surgeon, Welsh Orthopædic Hospital, Netley; Gosport War Memorial Hospital; Hunterian Professor, Royal College of Surgeons, 1922, 1933 and 1935; Jacksonian Prize, R.C.S., 1920. *Publications:* Pitfalls of Surgery, 1925; Some Factors in the Localisation of Diseases in the Body, 1932; Biological Actions of Sex Hormones, 2nd Ed., 1949; (with Dr. E. S. Horning) Oestrogens and Neoplasia, 1952; and articles on various surgical and physiological subjects. *Address:* Westridge, Manton Down Road, Marlborough. *T.:* 288. [*Died* 29 *Sept.* 1955.

BURROWS, Brig. Hollis Martin, C.I.E. 1937; *b.* Blackheath, 15 Sept. 1884; *s.* of late Rev. F. R. Burrows, Ancaster House, Bexhill-on-Sea; *m.* Olive Crichton Pocock (awarded Kaisar-i-Hind, 2nd class, 1931), *d.* of late Major F. C. Waller, Groombridge, Salisbury, Southern Rhodesia; two *s.* *Educ.:* Westward Ho!; R.M.C., Sandhurst. Commissioned, 1904; attached The Queens Royal Regt.; Adjutant 28th Punjabis, 1911-14; 51st Sikhs F.F., 1914; Bt. Lt.-Col. 1927; Commandant 1st P.W.O. Bn. 12th F.F. Regt. 1929-33; Commander, Ferozepore Brigade Area, 1934-37; Brigadier, 1934; retired, 1937; Assistant Censor, 1939-41; Indian Army, Liaison Officer, 1942-1943; Deputy Hon. Secretary Indian Comforts Fund, 1944-45; Representative for the Indian Prince's magazine, Indian India, 1946-47. Served N.W.F. India, 1908 (medal and clasp); European War, 1914-1918, Egypt, Aden, Gallipoli, France, Palestine (1914-15 Star, British War Medal, Victory Medal, Serbian Order of White Eagle); G.S. Medal (Kurdistan, 1919); Delhi Durbar Medal, 1911; Jubilee Medal, 1935; Coronation Medal, 1937. *Address:* 122 Chatsworth Court, Kensington, W.8. *T.:* Western 8251-122. *Club:* Army and Navy. [*Died* 6 *April* 1952.

BURROWS, Sir Roland, Kt., *cr.* 1946; Q.C. 1932; M.A., LL.M. (Camb.); LL.D. (London); Barrister-at-law, Bencher Inner Temple; Recorder of Cambridge since 1928; Hon. Fellow of Trinity Hall, Cambridge, 1950; Chairman, West Sussex Quarter Sessions; Reader in Evidence Civil Procedure and Criminal Law (Inns of Court); Deputy Chairman Boundary Commission

for England; *b.* Maidstone, 12 Feb. 1882; 3rd *s.* of late John Henry Burrows, of Solbys, Hadleigh, Essex; *m.* 1908, Dorothy, *e. d.* of late Henry Thomas Cox of Southend, Essex; one *s.* two *d. Educ.:* St. John's College, Southend; London University; Trinity Hall, Cambridge (Scholar). LL.B. Lond., 1901 (Univ. Law Scholar). Studentship at Bar Final Examination and Barstow Scholar, 1903; LL.D. London, 1903 (Gold Medal); Joint Senior Whewell Scholar in International Law, 1903 (Camb.): called to Bar, 1904; George Long Prizeman (Camb.), 1905; Chancellor's Medallist in English Law (Camb.), 1906; Private Secretary to Sir Frederick Smith as Solicitor-General and Attorney-General, 1915-19; Assistant Private Secretary to Lord Chancellor, 1919-22; Recorder of Chichester, 1926-28, and 1951 (for last sitting of City Quarter Sessions); one of the Counsel to the Food Controller, 1916-19; Counsel in Bankruptcy to the Board of Trade, 1927-32; Chairman London Regional Alien Advisory Committee, 1940-45; held Newcastle City Tribunal of Inquiry, 1944; President, Medico-Legal Society, 1942-45; Member Disciplinary Board Metropolitan Special Constabulary, 1926-46; Chairman London Licensing Planning Committee, 1945-49. *Publications:* Interpretation of Documents, 2nd Ed. 1946; edited Judgments of Lord Chancellor Birkenhead, 1919-22; 7th, 8th and 9th editions Phipson on Evidence; Managing Editor, Halsbury's Laws of England; Chief Editor, Halsbury's Statutes; Words and Phrases; Consulting Editor, All England Law Reports. *Address:* 15 Hornton Court, W.8; 1 Brick Court, Temple, E.C.4; Broad Place, Rustington, Sussex.
[*Died* 13 *June* 1952.

BURSTON, Major-General Sir Samuel (Roy), K.B.E., *cr.* 1952 (C.B.E. 1919); C.B. 1942; D.S.O. 1918; V.D.; F.R.C.P. (Lond.); F.R.C.P. (Ed.); F.R.A.C.P.; R.A.A.M.C. Retired; Hon. Medical Adviser, National H.Q. Australian Red Cross Society since 1952; Consulting Physician Royal Adelaide Hospital, 1947; Receiver-General, Priory of St. John in Australian Commonwealth; Pres. Senior Golfers' Association of Victoria, 1952; Chairman of Moonee Valley Racing Club, Victoria, 1952; *b.* 21 March 1888; *s.* of late Major-General James Burston; *m.* 1913, Helen Elizabeth (*d.* 1958), *d.* of late William Culross, Barrister, Adelaide; two *s.* one *d. Educ.:* Melbourne Grammar School; Melbourne Univ. Served European War, 1915-18 (despatches, D.S.O., C.B.E.); Deputy Director of Medical Services, 4th Australian District Base, 1921-39, A.D.M.S. 6 Australian Division, A.I.F., 1939, D.D.M.S. 1st Aust. Corps A.I.F., July 1940; Director of Medical Services A.I.F. H.Q. Middle East, Nov. 1940; D.G.M.S., Allied Land H.Q., Australia, 1942-45; Hon. Physician to Governor-General of Australia, 1939-45; D.G.M.S. Australian Military Forces, 1945-48; Hon. Col. R.A.A.M.C., 1952; Lecturer in Clinical Medicine, Adelaide University, 1932-47; Maj.-Gen. 1941; served War of 1939-45, Middle East, Greece, Burma, S.W. Pacific; Bronze Medal Royal Humane Society (Aust.), 1927; K.G.St.J. 1943; K.H.P. 1945-48. Member, Australian Advisory Cttee. to Nuffield Foundation; Member Board of Directors: Gt. Western Consolidated Gold Mines; Kalgoorlie Southern Gold Mines; Western Mining Corpn.; David Syme & Co. Ltd. *Recreations:* golf, racing. *Address:* 285 Walsh St., S. Yarra, Melbourne, S.E.1. *Clubs:* Adelaide (Adelaide); Melbourne (Melb.); Navy, Army and Air Force (Vic.); Victoria Racing; Victoria Amateur Turf.
[*Died* 21 *Aug.* 1960.

BURT, Joseph Barnes, M.D. Lond., M.R.C.S. Eng., L.R.C.P. Eng.; Consulting Physician, Devonshire Hospital, Buxton; Physician Royal Mineral Water Hospital, Bath; Past President, Section Physical Medicine, Royal Society of Medicine; Past Chairman Int. Society Medical Hydrology; *b.* Kendal; *s.* of J. K. Burt, M.D.; *m.* Dorothy, *d.* of E. Armitage, J.P.; two *s.* one *d. Educ.:* Epsom Coll.; University Coll. Hospital. M.B. 1902; M.D. 1904; Research Scholar Special Diseases, Cambridge; House Surgeon, Univ. Coll. Hospital; Governor, Whitworth Art Gallery; temporary Captain, R.A.M.C.; served in Mesopotamia, 1917-19. *Publications:* Medical Papers on Gout, Neuritis and Rheumatism. *Recreations:* golf, print collecting, etching. *Address:* 10 Circus, Bath. *T.:* 3476. *Club:* University of London.
[*Died* 18 *March* 1953.

BURTON, Claud Peter Primrose, M.A., Mus.B. (Oxon.); F.R.C.O. (CHM); Organist and Master of the Choristers, St. Albans Cathedral, since 1950; *b.* 19 April 1916; *e. s.* of R. C. Burton, M.A., F.R.G.S., late of Eastbourne College. *Educ.:* St. John's College, Oxford (Paddy Organ Exhibitioner). Organist, St. Paul's, King Cross, Halifax, 1939-40; war service, 1940-46. Organist, The Collegiate Church of St. Mary, Warwick, and Director of Music, Warwick School, 1946-1950. *Address:* 36 Holywell Hill, St. Albans, Herts.
[*Died* 6 *July* 1957.

BURTON, Captain Sir Geoffrey Duke, Kt., *cr.* 1942; late R.E.; Chairman: Dennis Bros. Ltd.; Blaw Knox Ltd., and Director of Companies; *b.* 2 Feb. 1893; 5th *s.* of late Rev. Canon A. D. Burton, Casterton; *m.* 1926, Viola Irene, *o. d.* of late Tom E. Donne; two *s.* one *d. Educ.:* Trinity College, Glenalmond (Scholar); Queens' College, Cambridge (Exhibitioner), 1914-18, Commissioned in Royal Engineers and served in Gallipoli, Egypt and Palestine, final rank Captain (despatches twice). General Manager, Metropolitan Carriage Co., Ltd., 1927-30; Managing Director, Round Oak Steel Works, Ltd., 1930-34; Managing Director, Birmingham Small Arms Co., Ltd., 1934-44; Director-General of Mechanical Equipment, Ministry of Supply, 1940-45. U.S.A. Medal of Freedom with Silver Palm, 1947. *Recreations:* yachting and fishing. *Address:* Wickhurst Manor, Sevenoaks, Kent. *T.:* Weald 226. *Clubs:* Carlton, Garrick; Royal Yacht Squadron (Cowes).
[*Died* 2 *July* 1954.

BURTON, Henry, Q.C.; *b.* 18 July 1907; *s.* of Simon and Hettie Burton, Manchester; *m.* 1932, Hilda Shaffer, Manchester; one *s.* one *d. Educ.:* Manchester Grammar School; Merton College, Oxford. Called to the Bar, 1930; K.C. 1951; Q.C. 1952. *Recreations:* golf, cricket. *Address:* 88 Kensington Court, W.8.
[*Died* 8 *Oct.* 1952.

BURTON, Canon Humphrey Phillipps Walcot; Rector of Louth, 1928-52; Rural Dean of Louthesk West, 1929-52; Prebendary of Louth in Lincoln Cathedral, 1934-52, Canon Emeritus since 1952; *b.* 12 May 1888; *s.* of late Preb. John R. Burton and Mary Henrietta Anne Dashwood Walcot; *m.* 1913, Hilda Kathleen (*d.* 1950), *d.* of Isidore Marchand, J.P., M.B.E.; three *d.*; *m.* 1950, Mrs. Jane Western Loft, J.P. *Educ.:* Hereford School; St. John's College, Cambridge (Somerset Exhib., open History Exhib., Naden Divinity Student). 2nd Class Honours, 1st and 2nd Parts of Historical Tripos, President of Cambridge Union, Lent Term, 1911; Organising Secretary of Stepney Council of Public Welfare, 1911-12; deacon, 1912; priest, 1913; Temporary Chaplain to Forces, 1915-19; saw service in Macedonia and France, Hon. C. F., 1919; first Vicar of Crosby Scunthorpe, 1921-28; Scout Commissioner; Chairman of Scunthorpe Employment Committee; Select Preacher, University of Cambridge, 1939; Proctor in Convocation and member of Church Assembly, 1929-50; Co-Secretary of Lincs Ironstone Area Church

BURT, Rev. Henry Chadwick. See page xxviii.

Extension Scheme, 1920-28; Governor of Louth Grammar Schools; Warden, 1946-49; Governor of Modern School; Manager of Primary Schools. *Publications:* Story of Louth Parish Church; Weaver of Webs, 1954. *Address:* Camden Lodge, Cheltenham, Glos. [*Died* 15 *Dec.* 1957.

BURTON, Sir Montague, Kt., *cr.* 1931; LL.D.; J.P.; Chairman, Montague Burton, Ltd., Hudson Road Mills, Leeds; *b.* 15 Aug. 1885; *m.* 1909; three *s.* one *d.* *Publications:* Globe Girdling, Vol. 1, 1936, Vol. 2, 1938; The Middle Path (Collection of Speeches), 1943. *Address:* Foxwood, Harrogate, Yorks. [*Died* 21 *Sept.* 1952.

BURTON, Brigadier-General Reginald George, retired Indian Army; *b.* 8 July 1864; *s.* of General E. F. Burton, of Charlton Kings; *m.* 1901, Elsie, *d.* of W. W. Lumb, of Whitehaven; one *s.* Entered Army (1st West India Regt.), 1884; served on General Staff, A.H.Q. India; in World War, Dardanelles, 1915 (despatches); G.O.C. Madras, 1918-19; interpreter in Russian; big-game hunter and naturalist; corresponding member Bombay Natural History Society; contributor to leading Reviews on these subjects, and on history and the art of war. *Publications:* Tropics and Snows; History of the Hyderabad Contingent; Wellington's Campaigns in India; Revolt in Central India; Napoleon's Campaigns in Italy; From Boulogne to Austerlitz; Napoleon's Invasion of Russia; Sport and Wild Life in the Deccan, 1928; A Book of Maneaters, 1931; The Book of the Tiger, 1933; The Tiger Hunters, 1936, etc. *Address:* Bafford Grange, Charlton Kings, Gloucestershire. [*Died* 2 *Feb.* 1951.

BURTON, William; *s.* of late William Burton, Beckenham, Kent; *m.* Mary Scott, *d.* of late Dr. J. Wills, Southwark, S.E.; one *s.* two *d.* *Educ.:* St. Olave's, Southwark; Christ's College, Cambridge; Gray's Inn. Entered Malaya Civil Service, 1907; held various legal appointments in F.M.S.; Puisne Judge Straits Settlements, 1929-36. *Publications:* Joint Editor of F.M.S. Law Reports, vols. 1-5. *Recreations:* walking, tennis. *Address:* 1 Court Lane Gardens, Dulwich. [*Died* 12 *Oct.* 1954.

BURTON-CHADWICK, Sir Robert, 1st Bt. *cr.* 1925; Kt., *cr.* 1920; Head of firm of Chadwick and Askew, London; Hon. Capt., R.N.R.; *b.* Birkenhead, 20 June 1869; *e. s.* of late Joseph Chadwick and Lucy, *d.* of Rev. T. Wilson, Brailsford; *m.* 1st, 1903, Catherine Barbara (*d.* 1935), *d.* of late Thomas Williams; one *s.* one *d.* (and *er. s.* killed in air ops., 1941); 2nd, 1936, Norah Irene, 2nd *d.* of late Alfred John Gibbs. Spent ten years of early life at sea; has travelled extensively in the East, North and South America, and South Seas; Royal Humane Society's Certificate for saving life; served in Duke of Lancaster's Yeomanry through South African War 1914-15, Founder and Hon. Treasurer of Liverpool Merchants Mobile Hospital, France; during European War, 1915-19, on Staff of the Ministry of Munitions as Director of Munitions Overseas Transport and Director-General Stores and Transport; M.P. (U.) Barrow-in-Furness, Dec. 1918-22, Wallasey, 1922-31; Parliamentary Secretary, Board of Trade, 1924-28; Representative in Argentina, Uruguay, and Chile of British Ministry of War Transport; Counsellor of British Embassy, Buenos Aires, 1939-46; founder 1926, Deputy-Master until 1937, and Master until 1940 of the Hon. Company of Master Mariners. *Heir:* *s.* Robert Burton, *b.* 1911. *Address:* 31 St. Mary Axe, E.C.3. *Clubs:* Carlton, Royal Thames Yacht, City of London; Royal Yacht Squadron (Cowes). [*Died* 21 *May* 1951.

BURY, Sir George, Kt., *cr.* 1917; *b.* Montreal, 6 March 1866; *s.* of George Bury and Catherine Brock; *m.* 1888, May, *d.* of John Aylen, K.C. *Educ.:* Montreal College. Clerk, C.P.R., 1883; General Manager, Western Lines, 1907; Vice-President Canadian Pacific Railway, 1911; visited Russia in 1917 to help in the organisation of shipping. Retired, 1918. *Address:* 1189 Matthews Avenue, Vancouver, B.C. *Club:* Vancouver (Vancouver). [*Died* 20 *July* 1958.

BURY, Lindsay Edward, C.B.E. 1919; J.P.; Order of Nile, 3rd class; Medjidieh, 4th class; Birmingham Regional Hospital Board; Chm. Robert Jones and Agnes Hunt Orthopædic Hosp.; Chm. Ludlow Division Conservative Assoc.; Salop County Council, 1932, Alderman, 1949; Chm. Ludlow Rural District Council, 1933; Chairman Salop Agricultural Wages Board; *b.* 11 June 1882; *s.* of F. G. Bury, C.B.E.; *m.* 1st, 1909, Frances (*d.* 1932), *d.* of Capt. H. G. Beckwith of Millichope Park, Craven Arms; (one *s.* killed in action) one *d.*; 2nd, 1936, Gertrude Worsley Worswick, *d.* of F. E. Harding. *Educ.:* Eton; Trinity College, Cambridge. *Address:* Millichope Cottage, Munslow, Craven Arms, Salop. *T.:* Munslow 33. *Club:* Travellers'. [*Died* 30 *Jan.* 1952.

BURY, Ralph Frederic, Q.C. 1938: D.L., J.P., Essex; Landowner and Barrister at Law; *b.* 1876; *o. surv. s.* of late Chas. Jas. Bury, St. Leonards House, Nazeing, D.L., J.P., C.A., and Anna, 2nd *d.* of Nicholas Loftus Tottenham, Glenfarn Hall, Co. Leitrim; *m.* 1920, Esmé Violet (from whom he obtained a divorce, 1926), *o. c.* of late H. Cumberland Bentley, Nithsdale House, Market Harborough; one *d.* *Educ.:* Trinity College, Cambridge (B.A.). Barrister, Lincoln's Inn, 1901; High Sheriff of Essex, 1910-11; served in Volunteers and Territorial Force, 1900-10; served European war, 1914-1918; Capt. 9th Service Bn., Essex Regt. 1914-16; D.A.A.G., 1916-18 (despatches, wounded, Croix de Guerre, 41 months in France) Hon. Major in Army. Pres. Epping Division Conservative Assoc. Gold Staff Officer, Coronation, 1911. *Recreations:* motoring and farming. *Address:* St. Leonards House, Nazeing, Waltham Abbey, Essex. *T.A.:* Nazeing. *T.:* Nazeing 3100. *Club:* Carlton. [*Died* 15 *Jan.* 1954.

BUSCH, Dr. Adolf; violinist and composer; *b.* Siegen in Westfalia, 8 Aug. 1891; *m.* 1913, Frieda Grüters (*d.* 1946); one *d.*; *m.* 1947, Hedwig Vischer; two *s.* *Educ.:* Cologne. With concert for the first time when 3; Conservatorium, Cologne, under Fritz Steinbach when 11; pupil of Bram Eldering and Willi Hess, with Steinbach concerts in London, then Berlin; first concert-master Vienna Concertverein Orch. when 21, succeeded Joseph Joachim and Henry Marteau at the Hochschule of Music in Berlin when 26, gave up this position 1921; Darmstadt, 1927; many concerts throughout world at Basle since 1927; became Swiss, 1935; toured with Toscanini in U.S.A., 1931; also much earlier with Max Reger Sonata Rec., later with Rudolf Serkin his son-in-law since 1935; Mus. Doc. Edinburgh (Hon. Causa), 1935. *Publications:* Edition of Solo Sonatas of Bach; Composer of Symphonies, Violin Concert, Piano Concert, Concert for Orchestra, Orchestra Variations, Songs, Sonatas, Trios, Quartettes, Quintets, Divertimento for Clarinet, Violin, Viola, Vcl. Clarinet Sonata, Bagatelles for Clarinet and strings, flute and strings; Requiem for Mignon, 1935; 3 Études for big Orchestra, 1939; Sonata Piano and Violin, 1941; Vater unser, for Choir and Orchestra; Organ works; Sonatine, Violin, Piano, G maj. op. 64; Scherzo for Solo Violin, Solo Violoncello, Solo Piano and Small Orchestra op. 65; Variations for Orchestra on a theme by Frieda Busch, op. 66; Sixth Psalm for Choir and Orchestra, op. 70. *Address:* Apt. 14D, 49 E. 96th Street, New York City, SA2. [*Died* 9 *June* 1952.

BUSCH, Fritz, Dr. h.c. University Edinburgh; conductor Statsradiofonie, Copenhagen, Konsertföreningen, Stockholm; chief-conductor Glyndebourne Opera, Sussex; *b.* 13 March 1890; *e. s.* of Wilhelm Busch and Henriette Schmidt; *m.* 1911, Grete Boettcher; one *s.* two *d. Educ.:* Gymnasium Siegburg (Rheinland); Conservatorium der Musik, Köln. Conductor: Stadttheater, Riga (Russia), 1909; concerts, Bad Pyrmont, 1910-12; Aachen, 1912-18 (1914 in the War from August till October, wounded, return to the frontier impossible; Offizier, E.K.); Generalmusikdirektor, Landestheater, Stuttgart, 1918-22; Dresden Staatsoper, 1922-33; Teatro Colon, Buenos-Aires, Copenhagen (s.a.), Stockholm, Glyndebourne and various international invitations, 1933-36. *Address:* Statsradiofonie, Copenhagen. [*Died* 14 *Sept.* 1951.

BUSH, Harry, R.O.I. 1930; *b.* Brighton, 20 Dec. 1883; *s.* of Thomas Bush, Jobmaster; *m.* 1910, Noel L. Nisbet (*d.* 1956); two *d. Educ.:* York Place, Brighton. Studied Art at Regent Street Polytechnic and West Lambeth. Exhibited at R.A., R.S.A., R.O.I., R.W.S., Liverpool, Paris Salon, etc. Works illustrated: Holly Leaves, 1933; Gardens of England; Studio; Strand. Official purchases: The Ash Tree (Nat. Gallery of N.S.W.), 1928; The Christmas Tree (presented to Blackpool Art Gall.), 1933. *Recreation:* model ship building. *Address:* 19 Queensland Avenue, Merton, S.W.19. [*Died* 8 *Oct.* 1957.

BUSH, Reginald Edgar James, R.E., R.W.A., A.R.C.A. London; Principal, Bristol Municipal School of Art, 1895-1934, retired; *b.* Cardiff, 2 June 1869; *s.* of James Bush, B.Sc. Lond.; Headmaster of Cardiff School of Science and Art; *m.* Flora Hyland (*d.* 1940); two *s.* one *d.* (and one *d.* decd.). *Educ.:* privately; The National Art Training School, South Kensington (Studentship in Training); gained the British Institute Scholarship for Engraving, and a Travelling Scholarship of the National Art Training School, 1893; an exhibitor at Paris Salon, Royal Academy, and chief Art Galleries, and several International Exhibitions. Member of the Society of Printmakers of California. *Publications:* Illustrated—The Bristol Avon, The Salisbury Avon, Shakespeare Avon, by S. Wall. *Address:* National Provincial Bank, 115 Whiteladies Road, Bristol. *Club:* Bristol Savages. [*Died* 27 *Aug.* 1956.

BUSHE, Brigadier-General Thomas Francis, C.M.G. 1900; J.P. Co. Donegal; *b.* 25 July 1858; *s.* of late Rev. T. F. Bushe, M.A. *Educ.:* Cheltenham; Woolwich; Lefroy Gold Medallist. Member of the Classical Association and Hellenic Society; has held various technical appointments in the Royal Artillery. *Decorated* for services in South Africa. *Recreation:* burning begging letters. *Address:* Drumalla, Rathmullan, County Donegal. *Club:* Army and Navy. [*Died* 1 *Feb.* 1951.

BUSHE-FOX, Joscelyn Plunket, C.B.E. 1945; M.A., F.S.A. 1915; *b.* 7 July 1880; *s.* of Major Luke Loftus Bushe-Fox, Cordara, Co. Longford, Ireland, and Mary Anne Browne; *m.* 1939, Cicely Catherine Agnes, *d.* of late H. Arthur Pratt, Highfield, Sedlescombe, Sussex. *Educ.:* St. Paul's School. Excavations in Egypt and at Corbridge on the Roman Wall in Northumberland, 1909-11; supervised excavations for the Society of Antiquaries at Hengistbury Head, Hampshire and Wroxeter, Shropshire, 1912-14; at Swalling, Kent and Richborough, Kent, 1920-1939; Inspector of Ancient Monuments for England, 1920-33; Chief Inspector of Ancient Monuments Ministry of Works, 1933-45. Served European War, 1914-18, France, Italy and Germany (despatches twice); granted rank of Major on demobilisation; Hon. M.A. Manchester, 1929. *Publications:* Reports on the excavations at Wroxeter, Hengistbury Head, Swalling and Richborough; various papers on Archæological subjects. *Recreation:* shooting. *Address:* Jasper House, South End Road, Hampstead, N.W.3. [*Died* 15 *Oct.* 1954.

BUSSÉ, John, C.B.E. 1948; Q.C. 1952; B.A., LL.B.; Barrister-at-Law; Recorder of Gloucester, 1956 (of Burton-on-Trent, 1947-1956); *b.* 12 Jan. 1903; *s.* of William and Lena Bussé, St. John's Wood, London; *m.* 1936, Helen, *e. d.* of Col. J. F. N. Baxendale, C.B., T.D.; one *s. Educ.:* Corpus Christi Coll., Camb. (Exhibitioner). History and Law Tripos; B.A., LL.B.; called to Bar, Inner Temple, 1925 (Oxford Circuit). Vice-Chm. Central Price Regulation Committee, 1945-53. Governor, Univ. Coll. of North Staffs. *Publication:* Mrs. Montagu, 1928. *Recreations:* shooting, swimming. *Address:* 1 Brick Court, Temple, E.C.4. *T.:* Central 8845; 901 Hawkins House, Dolphin Square, S.W.1. *T.:* Victoria 3800. *Club:* Oxford and Cambridge. [*Died* 27 *Sept.* 1956.

BUSSEY, Ernest William, C.B.E. 1946; *b.* 9 December 1891; *m.* 1915, Ellen Bessie Baker; one *s. Educ.:* West Ham Technical Institute. Trained as Electrical Engineer; served with West Ham Corporation Electricity Supply, London County Council Tramways and London Transport; General Pres. Electrical Trades Union, 1931-41; Gen. Sec., 1941-48; Member General Council British T.U.C., 1941-47; Member British Electricity Authority, 1947-52; Chairman Negotiating Machineries, Employers' Side, 1952-56. *Address:* 30 Freston Gardens, Cockfosters, Barnet, Herts. *T.:* Barnet 1137. [*Died* 16 *July* 1958.

BUSSEY, Harry Youngman; retired journalist; *b.* Norwich, Nov. 1858; *s.* of Harry Findlater (*d.* 1919) and Ellen Chapman Bussey; *m.* 1883, Elizabeth (*d.* 1935), *d.* of Edward Marwood, Blackburn; two *d. Educ.:* St. John's Middle-class School, North Brixton. After serving on provincial newspapers, entered Parliamentary Press Gallery, 1881; joined Morning Post staff, 1884; Chief of Staff and Parliamentary Sketch Writer, 1904-19; for some years Morning Post Lobby Correspondent; served for over 53 years on staff of Morning Post, retiring at end of 1937 after amalgamation of that journal with Daily Telegraph; has been Hon. Secretary and Chairman of Press Gallery and Chairman of Lobby Journalists' Committee; Fellow of Institute of Journalists. *Recreation:* gardening. *Address:* The Forge House, East Malling, Kent. [*Died* 26 *July* 1951.

BUTE, 5th Marquess of (*cr.* 1796), **John Crichton-Stuart;** Viscount Ayr, 1622; Bt. 1627; Earl of Dumfries, Lord Crichton of Sanquhar and Cumnock, 1633; Earl of Bute, Viscount Kingarth, Lord Mountstuart, Cumrae, and Inchmarnock, 1703; Baron Mountstuart, 1761; Baron Cardiff, 1776; Earl of Windsor; Viscount Mountjoy; Hereditary Sheriff of Bute, M.B.O.U., F.Z.S., F.S.A. (Scot.), F.B.S.A.; V.L. for County of Bute; J.P. Buteshire; Chairman: Mountjoy Ltd., Glenburn Hotel Co. Ltd., Isle of Bute Industries Ltd., Bute Ferry Co. Ltd.; *b.* 4 Aug. 1907; *er. s.* of 4th Marquess of Bute, K.T., and Augusta Mary Monica (*d.* 1947), D.B.E., *d.* of Sir H. Bellingham, 4th Bt.; *S.* father, 1947; *m.* 1932, Lady Eileen Forbes, *yr. d.* of 8th Earl of Granard, K.P., P.C., G.C.V.O.; three *s.* one *d. Educ.:* Downside; Christ Church, Oxford; Edinburgh University. Member of the Queen's Body Guard for Scotland (Royal Company of Archers); Convener of County Council of Buteshire; Member Town Council of Royal Burgh of Rothesay; Pres. Zoological Society of Glasgow and West of Scotland; Member Royal Caledonian Hunt;

Member of Wild Birds Advisory Committee (Scotland). War Service R.A. Territorial and Regular, L.D.V., H.G., and R.N.V.R.; Commander (Brother) of Order of St. John. Owns about 117,000 acres. *Recreations:* shooting and ornithology. *Heir:* s. Earl of Dumfries. *Address:* Mount Stuart, Rothesay; Dumfries House, Ayrshire; 6 Charlotte Square, Edinburgh. *Clubs:* St. James', Farmers'; New (Edinburgh).
[*Died* 14 *Aug.* 1956.

BUTLER, Eliza Marian; *b.* Bardsea, Lancs, 29 Dec. 1885; 3rd *d.* of Theobold Fitzwalter Butler and Catherine Elizabeth Barraclough. *Educ.:* Hanover; Paris; Cheltenham; Cambridge, B.A. 1911. S. Felix School, 1912; Bonn University, 1913-14; Asst. Lecturer Newnham College, Cambridge, 1914-17; Scottish Women's Hospitals, Russia and Macedonia, 1917-18; Avery Hill Training College, 1919-20; Asst. Lecturer, Research Fellow, Director of Studies in Modern Languages, College Lecturer at Newnham College, Cambridge, 1920-36; Associate of Newnham College, 1922; Univ. Lecturer, 1929-36; India, 1934-35; Henry Simon Professor of German Language and Literature, Victoria University of Manchester, 1936-45; Schröder Prof. of German, Univ. of Cambridge, 1945-51; retired, 1951; Professor Emeritus, 1951, Ceylon and Burma, 1953-54, Ceylon, 1957-58. Hon. D.Lit. London University, 1957; Hon. D.Litt. Oxon., 1959. *Publications:* The Saint-Simonian Religion, 1926; the Tempestuous Prince, 1929; Sheridan, a Ghost Story, 1931; The Tyranny of Greece over Germany, 1935; Rainer Maria Rilke 1940; The Myth of the Magus, 1947; Ritual Magic, 1949; Daylight in a Dream, 1951; Fortunes of Faust, 1952; Silver Wings, 1952; Heinrich Heine, 1956; Byron and Goethe, 1956; Paper Boats: an Autobiography, 1959. *Recreations:* travelling, writing. *Address:* 30 Dawson Place, W.2. *T.:* Bayswater 1037.
[*Died* 13 *Nov.* 1959.

BUTLER, Maj.-Gen. Ernest Reuben Charles, C.B. 1918; C.M.G. 1915; F.R.C.V.S.; late Army Veterinary Service; *b.* 8 July 1864. Major, 1902; Lt.-Col. 1908; Col. 1914; Assist. Professor Army Veterinary School, 1892-97; Professor, 1902-5; Inspector Veterinary Office, India, 1911-13; Deputy Director of Veterinary Services, 1914; served Burma, 1885-7 (medal with clasp); European War, 1914-18 (despatches, C.M.G., C.B.); retired pay, 1921. *Address:* Kokstad, East Griqualand, South Africa.
[*Died* 15 *June* 1959.

BUTLER, Sir Harold Beresford, K.C.M.G., *cr.* 1946; C.B. 1919; Hon. LL.D. Manchester, Edinburgh, Toronto and Columbia; Dr. Sc. Econ. Geneva; Hon. Member of Faculty of Law, Univ. of Santiago de Chile; *b.* 6 Oct. 1883; *e. s.* of late A. J. Butler, D.Litt.; *m.* 1910, Olive, *y. d.* of S. A. W. Waters, Woodview, Stillorgan, Co. Dublin; two *s.* one *d.* *Educ.:* Eton Coll.; Balliol Coll., Oxford; Brackenbury Scholar and Jenkyns Exhibitioner: 1st class Lit. Hum., 1905; Fellow of All Souls College, 1905-12. Entered Civil Service (Local Government Board), 1907; transferred to Home Office, 1908; Secretary to British Delegation, International Conference on Aerial Navigation, Paris, 1910; Acting Assistant Secretary, 1914; Secretary, Foreign Trade Department of the Foreign Office, 1916; Ministry of Labour, 1917-19; Assistant General Secretary Labour Commission, Peace Conference, 1919; Secretary-General International Labour Conference, Washington, 1919; Deputy Director, International Labour Office, 1920-32; Director, 1932-38; Warden of Nuffield College, Oxford, 1939-43; Commissioner for Civil Defence, Southern Region, 1939-41; Minister at H.M. Embassy, Washington, 1942-46. *Publications:* Industrial Relations in the United States, 1927; Unemployment-Problems in the United States, 1931; Problems of Industry in the East, 1938; The Lost Peace, 1941; Peace or Power, 1947; Confident Morning, 1950. *Recreations:* lawn tennis, motoring. *Address:* Little Court, Sonning, Berks. *Clubs:* Travellers', Pilgrims.
[*Died* 26 *March* 1951.

BUTLER, Harold Edgeworth; *b.* 8 May 1878; *s.* of Rev. A. G. Butler, first Headmaster of Haileybury, and Fellow of Oriel Coll., Oxford; *m.* 1917, Margaret, *d.* of late Prof. A. F. Pollard; two *s.* two *d.* *Educ.:* Rugby School; New College, Oxford (Scholar). Prox. Acc. Hertford Scholarship, 1898; Newdigate prize poem, 1899; Lecturer New College, Oxford, 1901; Fellow, 1902-11; Professor of Latin, London University, 1911-43; Public Orator, London Univ., 1932-47; Capt. R.F.A. (T.), 1915. *Publications:* Propertii opera omnia; Apologia of Apuleius translated; Golden Ass of Apuleius translated; Post-Augustan Poetry; Propertius translated; Apulei Apologia (text and commentary) (with A. S. Owen); Virgil, Sixth Aeneid; Quintilian translated; Cicero, De Provinciis Consularibus (with M. Cary); Suetonius, Divus Julius (with M. Cary); edited (with Harriet J. Butler) The Black Book of Edgeworthstown; Propertius (with E. A. Barber); The Autobiography of Giraldus Cambrensis; The Chronicle of Jocelin of Brakelonde; (Ed.) Tour in Connemara by Maria Edgeworth. *Recreation:* walking. *Address:* Dunraven, St. John's Avenue, Leatherhead.
[*Died* 5 *June* 1951.

BUTLER, Lt.-Col. Humphrey, C.V.O. 1942 (M.V.O. 1934); M.C. 1915, Bar 1917; late Equerry to Duke of Kent; *b.* 7 Feb. 1894; *s.* of Col. Lewis Butler and Adelaide Bulteel; *m.* 1927, Gwendolyn Van Raalte. *Educ.:* Malvern College. Army 1913-20 and since 1939. *Recreations:* riding, motoring, flying. *Address:* 42 Connaught Square, W.2. *T.:* Ambassador 2277. *Club:* Turf.
[*Died* 26 *Feb.* 1953.

BUTLER, Brig.-Gen. Hon. Lesley James Probyn, C.M.G. 1917; D.S.O. 1916; late Irish Guards; *b.* 22 April 1876; *s.* of 26th Baron Dunboyne; *m.* 1907, Mary Christal (*d.* 1951), *y. d.* of Sir J. Heathcoat Amory, 1st Bt.; one *s.* two *d.* Served S. Africa, 1899-1900 (Queen's medal with four clasps); European War, 1914-18 (D.S.O., despatches six times, Bt. Lt.-Col., C.M.G.); retired, 1922; D.L. Devon. *Address:* Calverleigh Cottage, Tiverton, Devon. *T.:* Tiverton 2724.
[*Died* 31 *Dec.* 1955.

BUTLER, Sir Montagu Sherard Dawes, K.C.S.I., *cr.* 1924; Kt., *cr.* 1924; C.B. 1916; C.I.E. 1909; C.V.O. 1911; C.B.E. 1919; M.A.; *b.* 19 May 1873; 3rd *s.* of late Spencer Perceval Butler; *m.* 1901, Ann (Kaisar-i-Hind Medal, 1st Class, 1929), *y. d.* of late Dr. George Smith, C.I.E.; one *s.* two *d.* *Educ.:* Haileybury; Pembroke College, Cambridge (Scholar, First Class Classical Tripos, Parts I. and II., with special distinction in Part II., Univ. Bhaunagar Medallist, Fellow of Pembroke, 1895-1901; Pres. of the Union, 1895; Hon. Fellow of Pembroke, 1925); Chancellor Nagpur University, 1925-33. Entered I.C.S. 1896; Settlement Officer, Kotah State, 1904-9; Deputy Commissioner, Lahore, 1909-11; Joint Secretary, Royal Commission on the Public Services in India, 1912-15; Deputy Commissioner Attock District, Punjab, 1915-19; President of the Punjab Legislative Council, 1921-22; Secretary to the Govt. of India, Education Dept., 1922-1924; President of Council of State, 1924; Governor of the Central Provinces, 1925-33; Lieut.-Governor, Isle of Man, 1933-37; Master of Pembroke Coll., Cambridge, 1937-48. Member of Council of the Senate, Cambridge Univ., 1938-46; Councillor Borough (now City) of Cambridge, 1940; Mayor, 1941-43; Alderman, 1944; Chairman Savings Cttee., Cambridge, 1944-49; Chairman Fuel Efficiency Cttee.

(Eastern Region), 1948-51. *Address:* 17 Grange Court, Pinehurst, Cambridge. *T.:* 4763. *Club:* Bath. [*Died* 7 *Nov.* 1952.

BUTLER, Sir Paul Dalrymple, K.C.M.G., *cr.* 1944 (C.M.G. 1938); *b.* 2 March 1886; 3rd *s.* of late Rev. George Hew Butler, Hambledon, Hants; *m.* 1913, Helen Maxima, *d.* of Dr. William Scranton; one *s.* two *d.* *Educ.:* Bedford School; on the Continent. Entered Consular Service, 1908; served at Tokio, Seoul, Manila, Tamsui, Yokohama, Mukden; Consul-General at San Francisco, 1938-41; Director-General of Far Eastern Bureau of Ministry of Information at New Delhi, 1942-43; Adviser in the Foreign Office, 1944; British Representative on the Far Eastern Regional Committee of U.N.R.R.A. with rank of Minister in H.M. Foreign Service, Dec. 1944; retired from H.M. Foreign Service, 1946; Far Eastern Research Secretary at Royal Institute of International Affairs, 1946-48. Jubilee Medal, 1935; Coronation Medal, 1937. *Recreations:* riding, tennis, gardening. *Address:* Honeywick, Castle Cary, Somerset. *T.:* Castle Cary 323. [*Died* 2 *Feb.* 1955.

BUTLER, Pierce E. O' B.; *see* O'Brien-Butler.

BUTLER, Commander Sir (Reginald) Thomas, 2nd Bart., *cr.* 1922; late R.N.; *b.* 27 April 1901; *s.* of Sir Reginald Butler, 1st Bt., and Rose Rich (*d.* 1945); *S.* father 1933; *m.* 1st, 1927, Marjorie (marriage dissolved, 1949), *e. d.* of Sidney Woods, K.C., Stirlingswood, Edmonton, Alberta; two *s.* one *d.*; 2nd, 1950, Mrs. Diane Berry, Walton Street, S.W.3. *Educ.:* Clifton; R.N. Colleges, Osborne and Dartmouth. *Heir:* *s.* Reginald Michael Thomas, *b.* 22 April 1928. *Address:* Hazelbridge House, Chiddingfold, Surrey. *T.:* 125. *Club:* Army and Navy. [*Died* 22 *March* 1959.

BUTLER, Col. Richard Barry, C.I.E. 1936; C.B.E. 1930 (O.B.E. 1926); M.C.; p.s.c.; *s.* of late John Philip Butler, J.P., Clonard, Co. Wicklow; *m.* 1st, 1921, Marjorie Stewart (died as result of enemy action, 1941, while serving with the American Ambulance Corps, Great Britain), *y. d.* of late Albert Evans Pullar, J.P. of Durn, Perth (one *s.* Flying Officer L. M. S. Butler, R.A.F.V.R., killed Air Operations, Italy, 1944); 2nd, 1945, Madge, *widow* of John Mein-Austin, Flint Hill, West Haddon, Northants. Joined 5th Bn. Rifle Brigade, 1904; 30th Lancers, Indian Army, 1907; served European War, 1914-19 (despatches 3 times, Bt.-Major, Bt. Lt.-Col., M.C.); Staff College, Camberley, 1919; H.Q. Gen. Staff, 51st Highland Div., 1919-21; A.A.G. Army Headquarters, India, 1922-25; transferred to Royal Deccan Horse, 1926; commanded 16th Light Cavalry, 1931-32; Military Secretary to the following Governors of Bengal: Sir Stanley Jackson, 1927-30, Sir John Anderson (now Viscount Waverley), 1932-37, and to Lord Brabourne, 1937-38; retired, 1938; served war of 1939-45, commanded Havre Garrison and Pioneer Corps Group, B.E.F., 1940 (despatches); D.D.L., H.Q. Western Command, 1941; A.A.G. 5 Corps, 1942; served Home Forces, 1943 to end of hostilities, 1945. High Sheriff of Cumberland, 1954. Order of Crown of Italy; Order of White Eagle of Serbia. *Address:* Garth Marr, Castle Carrock, Cumberland. *T.:* Hayton 206. *Clubs:* Cavalry, White's, Boodle's, Oriental; County (Carlisle). [*Died* 2 *April* 1957.

BUTLER, Sir Richard Pierce, 11th Bt., *cr.* 1628; O.B.E. 1919; D.L.; *b.* 28 Sept. 1872; *s.* of 10th Bt. and Hester Elizabeth, *e. d.* of Sir Alan E. Bellingham, 3rd Bt.; *S.* father, 1909; *m.* 1906, Alice, *d.* of late Very Rev. Hon. James Wentworth Leigh; one *s.* two *d.* *Educ.:* Harrow; Downton Agricultural College. High Sheriff, Co. Carlow, 1905. Served S. Africa, 1901-2 (medal 5 clasps); Hon. Lt.-Col.; served with Remount Dept. Feb. 1915-Apr. 1919 in British, Italian and Egyptian Exped. Forces (despatches twice, O.B.E., 1914-1915 Star, British medal, and Allies' Victory medal). *Heir:* *s.* Lt.-Col. Thomas Pierce Butler, D.S.O., O.B.E. *Address:* 4 Rutland Court, S.W.7. *T.:* Kensington 6922; Ballin Temple, Tullow, Co. Carlow. *T.A.:* Tullow. [*Died* 25 *March* 1955.

BUTLER, Maj.-Gen. St. John D. A.; *see* Arcedeckne-Butler.

BUTLER, Comdr. Sir Thomas; *see* Butler, Comdr. Sir R. T.

BUTLER, Rear-Admiral Vernon Saumarez, D.S.O. 1918; R.N., retired; *b.* 1885; *s.* of late S. E. Butler, J.P., Somerset; *m.* 1915, Helen Montgomerie, *d.* of late Admiral Sir Hugh Tothill, K.C.B.; (two sons killed in action, 1940, 1944). Served European War, 1914-18 (despatches, D.S.O., promoted); Senior Naval Officer, Persian Gulf, 1935-37; Rear-Adm., 1937; retired list, 1937. *Address:* Midway House, Ston Easton, nr. Bath. *Club:* Army and Navy. [*Died* 25 *June* 1954.

BUTLER-HENDERSON, Hon. Eric Brand; *b.* Sept. 1884; sixth *s.* of 1st Baron Faringdon; *m.* Hon. Sophia Isabelle Butler Massey, *d.* of 5th Baron Clarina; four *s.* two *d.* *Educ.:* Eton. *Address:* Faccombe Manor, Andover, Hants. *T.:* Linkenholt 246. *Clubs:* St. James', Bath. [*Died* 18 *Dec.* 1953.

BUTTENSHAW, Hon. Ernest Albert; Managing Director, Farmer's and Graziers' Co-operative Wool and Grain Company; *b.* Young, N.S.W., 23 May 1876; *m.* 1st, 1903; three *s.* four *d.*; 2nd, 1928, Clare Sugars, Roseville, N.S.W. *Educ.:* Young Superior Public School. Went into Post Office for about twelve months on leaving school, then took up farming and grazing; cultivated up to 2000 acres of wheat during European War; President of Farmers' and Settlers' Association of N.S.W. for two years; President of the Bland Shire for five years; Chairman of Voluntary Wheat Pool for four years; entered Parliament, 1917; leader of the Country Party, 1926-32; joined the Bavin Administration in 1927, and Acting Premier during Mr. Bavin's absence in England; Minister for Works and Railways and Deputy Premier, 1927-30; Minister for Lands, N.S.W., 1932-38; Member of Legislative Assembly, N.S.W.; Deputy Leader of Country Party; 1942, a member of Central Wool Committee to carry out British Wool Purchase Agreement. Councillor of Royal Agricultural Society. Trustee of Sydney Cricket Ground. *Recreations:* has played 1st grade cricket and tennis, all-round athlete. *Address:* Strathfield, Sydney, Australia. *Club:* Royal Automobile. [*Died* 26 *June* 1950.

BUTTERWORTH, Reginald, C.B.E. 1920; *b.* 21 July 1879; *s.* of late Reginald Butterworth; *g.s.* of late John Butterworth of Manchester; *m.* 1904, Cornelia Gertrud, *o. d.* of late Victor August Wellenstein of London and Batavia, Java; (*er. s.* died on active service 1941; *yr. s.* killed in action 1940) one *d.* *Educ.:* Denstone. Went to Java, 1900; retired, 1920; when temporarily in England, 1916-19, served with Ministry of Food, 1917-18, and Board of Trade, 1918 (Chairman North-eastern Divisional Road Transport Board). *Address:* 37 Tavistock Square, W.C.1. [*Died* 31 *July* 1951.

BUTTERWORTH, Colonel Reginald Francis Amherst, C.M.G. 1919; D.S.O.

1916; *b.* 4 Jan. 1876; *s.* of late R. W. Butterworth of Rockwell near Bristol; *m.* Margaret Elaine (*d.* 1958), 3rd *d.* of late J. W. Morison of Portclew, Pembroke; (one *s.* died of wounds, 1944) one *d.* *Educ.:* Eton. Entered Army, 1895; was successively at Chatham, Portsmouth, Landguard Fort, and Singapore, on harbour defences; Staff Officer, Royal Engineers, Malta, 1911; returned to England, 1914, and formed a Field Company R.E. for service in the new Army; afterwards C.R.E. 16th Div. and on staff at G.H.Q.; proceeded to France in command, July 1915 (despatches five times, C.M.G., D.S.O. and bar, Bt. Lt.-Col.); Iraq Operations, 1920 (despatches), C.R.E. Hong Kong, 1922-24; C.R.E. 3rd Division Salisbury Plain, 1925; Assistant Director of Fortifications and Works, War Office, 1926-30; Chief Engineer, Malaya Command, Singapore, 1930-31; Commander, 28th Air Defence Brigade, T.A., 1931-32; retired pay, 1933; Director of British Legion Poppy Factory, 1938-; Royal Observer Corps, 1939-41; employed under Ministry of Information, 1943-45. *Recreations:* cricket, shooting, fishing. *Address:* 16 High St., Fareham, Hants. [*Died* 16 *June* 1960.

BUXTON, Countess, G.B.E., *cr.* 1919; J.P.; Mildred; *e. d.* of Hugh Colin Smith; *m.* 1896, as 2nd wife, 1st Earl Buxton (*d.* 1934); one *d.* *Address:* Newtimber Place, Hassocks, Sussex. *T.:* Hurstpierpoint 4. [*Died* 7 *Dec.* 1955.

BUXTON, Alfred Fowell; *b.* 28 March 1854; 4th *s.* of late Thomas Fowell Buxton of Easneye, Herts; *m.* 1885, Violet, O.B.E. 1920 (*d.* 1936), *d.* of late Very Rev. T. W. Jex-Blake, D.D., Headmaster of Rugby, afterwards Dean of Wells; two *s.* (one *d.* decd.). *Educ.:* Rugby; Trinity Coll., Cambridge (M.A.). Was a partner in London Banking Firm of Prescott, Cave & Co.; represented City on L.C.C., 1892-95; Alderman, 1904-22; Chairman Finance Committee, 1907 and 1920; Chairman London County Council, 1916-17; Governor of Rugby School, 1906-36; Member of Port of London Authority, 1916-19; late Member House of Laity; formerly Member Church of England Pensions Board; formerly Director, Alliance Assurance; Director (Extraordinary) of National Provincial Bank. *Publication:* editor of Two-Version Bible. *Address:* Fairhill, Tonbridge. *T.:* Hildenborough 2213. *Club:* Athenæum. [*Died* 5 *May* 1952.

BUXTON, James Basil, M.A., F.R.C.V.S.; D.V.H.; Principal and Dean of Royal Veterinary College since 1936. *Educ.:* Highgate School; Royal Veterinary College, London; Liverpool University. Lecturer in Veterinary Hygiene, Royal (Dick) Veterinary College, 1911-12; Veterinary Superintendent, Wellcome Physiological Research Laboratories, 1912-22; Director, Farm Laboratories, Medical Research Council, 1922-23; Professor of Animal Pathology, Cambridge University, 1923-36; Director, Institute of Animal Pathology; Fellow of Queens' College; President, Royal College of Veterinary Surgeons, 1932-33; Central Veterinary Society, 1920; National Veterinary Medical Association of Great Britain and Ireland, 1925; Veterinary Research Club, 1926; Royal Counties Veterinary Medical Society, 1927; Eastern Counties Veterinary Medical Society, 1929; Membre Correspondant étranger, Académie Vétérinaire de France, 1936; Member of Council, Royal College of Veterinary Surgeons since 1920; John Henry Steel Gold Medal, 1934. *Address:* Royal Veterinary College, Streatley, Berks; Childe Court, Streatley, Berks. *T.:* Goring 45. *Club:* Athenæum. [*Died* 25 *May* 1954.

BUXTON, Colonel John Lawrence, C.M.G. 1919; D.S.O. 1916; Rifle Brigade, retired; *b.* 1 Dec. 1877; *s.* of Francis William Buxton and Hon. Mrs. F. W. Buxton; *m.* 1916, Evelyne, *d.* of late Rev. J. W. Rynd, of Brasted, Kent. *Educ.:* Eton; University College, Oxford; joined Rifle Brigade, 1899; served S. African War (despatches three times, severely wounded); Private Secretary to Governor of Victoria (Australia), 1905-6; served European War, 1914-18 (D.S.O., C.M.G., Bt. Lt.-Col.); Assistant Adjutant-General, Aldershot Command, 1927-30; A.A. and Q.M.G. i/c Administration, Gibraltar, 1930-31; Commander 144th (Gloucestershire and Worcestershire), Infantry Brigade T.A., 1931-34; A.D.C. to the King, 1933-34; retired pay, 1934; Equerry to the Duke of Connaught, 1939-40. *Recreations:* hunting, shooting, fishing. *Address:* Widford Manor, Burford, Oxon. *T.:* Burford 2152. *Club:* Brooks's. [*Died* 16 *Jan.* 1951.

BUXTON, Patrick Alfred, C.M.G. 1947; F.R.S. 1943; Director, Dept. of Entomology, London School of Hygiene and Tropical Medicine since 1925; Prof. of Med. Entomology, Univ. of London, since 1933; *b.* 24 March 1892; *e. s.* of late Alfred Fowell Buxton and late Violet Jex-Blake; *m.* Muryell Gladys, 4th *d.* of late Rev. Hon. W. Talbot Rice; one *s.* four *d.* (and one *s.* decd.). *Educ.:* Rugby; Trinity College, Cambridge (Fellow, 1916-21). Served in Mesopotamia and N.W. Persia; Entomologist to Government of Palestine, 1921-23; leader of Expedition to Samoa, 1923-25; made many journeys in Africa, investigating tsetse flies, etc.: Member Medical Research Council, 1946-49. Linnean gold medal, 1953. *Publications:* Animal Life in Deserts; The Louse; The Natural History of Tsetse Flies; a number of technical publications. *Recreations:* natural history; gardening. *Address:* Grit Howe, Gerrards Cross, Bucks. *T.:* Gerrards Cross 2581. *Club:* Athenæum. [*Died* 13 *Dec.* 1955.

BUXTON, Richard; *see* Shanks, Edward.

BUXTON, Robert Vere, D.S.O. 1917; M.A.; Director Martin's Bank, Ltd. (Chairman of the London Board, U.S. Debenture Corp., Ltd., and London Scottish American Trust Co., Ltd.; Chairman of the British Bank of the Middle East; *b.* 1883; 3rd *s.* of late Francis W. Buxton and Hon. Mrs. Francis Buxton; *m.* 1916, Irene Marguerite, Lady Levinge, *widow* of Sir Richard Levinge, Bart. *Educ.:* Eton; Trinity College, Oxford (M.A. Honours School of History). Sudan Civil Service, 1907-11; served European War, 1914-18; Capt. West Kent Yeomanry and Lt.-Col. Imperial Camel Corps (despatches twice, Crown of Italy, D.S.O., Order of the Nile). *Recreations:* hunting, Joint Master Bicester and Warden Hill Hounds, 1939-46, shooting. *Address:* Thatchways, Priors-Hardwick, Rugby; 32 Orchard Court, Portman Square, W.1. *Club:* Brooks's. [*Died* 1 *Oct.* 1953.

BYASS, Col. Harry Nicholl, C.M.G. 1916; *b.* 2 Dec. 1863; *m.* Served S. Africa, 1900-2 (despatches, Bt. Lt.-Col., Queen's medal 5 clasps); commanded 2nd Battalion York and Lancaster Regiment, 1908-12; 7th Battalion, 1914-16. Served European War, 1914-18 (despatches twice, C.M.G.). *Address:* Winton House, Leamington Spa. [*Died* 12 *May* 1956.

BYRD, Rear-Adm. Richard E., U.S.N. (retd.); apptd. Officer in charge, U.S. Antarctic Programs, 1955 and in charge U.S. Antarctic Expedition, 1955-, in support of International Geophysical Year; trustee National Geographic Society; Hon. chairman International Rescue Committee; member various organizations to do with national and international unity; *b.* Winchester, Virginia, 25 Oct. 1888; *s.* of Richard Evelyn Byrd and E. Bolling Flood; *m.* 1915, Marie D. Ames; one *s.* three *d.* *Educ.:* Virginia Military Institute; Shenandoah Valley Military Academy; University of Virginia; U.S. Naval Academy. In charge navigational preparation first successful flight Navy trans-Atlantic Expedition, 1919; one of navigation officers ZR-2 for proposed T.A. flight. In charge of Navy Unit of Navy MacMillan Arctic Expedition, 1925; made first flight to North Pole, 9 May 1926; flew Fokker Tri-Motor New York to Coast of France, 29 June-1 July 1927; Antarctic Expedition, 1928-30; Discovery of Edsel Ford Mountains and Marie Byrd Land in the Antarctic on the First Byrd Antarctic Expedition, 1928-30; made first flight to South Pole, 29 Nov. 1929; Second Byrd Antarctic Expedition took place in 1933-35; spent 5 months of winter night alone in shadow of South Pole on scientific work; Comdr. U.S. Antarctic Service, an expedition sent to Antarctic by Govt., 1939-40; during War of 1939-45 served as Confidential Asst. to Adm. King as C.-in-C.; had overseas duty 3 times in Pacific War Zone, and once in Belgium and Germany in connection with aviation; decorated 4 times; in charge of U.S. Naval Antarctic Expedition, 1946-47. Patron's Medal, R.G.S., 1931; Congressional Medal of Honor; and three Special Congressional Medals; Congressional Life Saving Medal of Honor; Navy Distinguished Service Medal; Navy Flying Cross; Navy Cross; Commander Legion of Honor of France; Commander Military Order of Avis of Portugal; Elisha Kent Kane medal of Philadelphia Geog. Soc.; Langley medal of Smithsonian Inst.; David Livingstone Centenary medal; Grand Lodge medal for Distinguished Achievement; Loczy Medal of Hungarian Geog. Soc.; Vega Medal of Swedish Geog. Soc.; many other awards and medals; Roosevelt Medal, Gold Star (to be attached to D.S.M.), presented by President Roosevelt, Sept. 1940, in recognition of services as commanding officer of U.S. Antarctic Service, etc. In 1944 received a Citation from the Secretary of the Navy and in 1945 was presented with the Legion of Merit by President Roosevelt for aviation work in the Pacific during War of 1939-45. Later awarded gold star in lieu of second Legion of Merit for War work and two other citations. Numerous hon. degrees; Hon. Member of about 200 societies. *Publications:* Skyward, 1928; Little America, 1930; Discovery, 1935; Exploring with Byrd; Alone, 1938; Reports of three expeditions mentioned above published in National Geographic Magazine; articles on expedition matters in Saturday Evening Post and World's Work. *Address:* 9 Brimmer Street, Boston, Mass., U.S.A. *Clubs:* Explorers', Lions, Kiwanis, Circumnavigators, Century (New York); American Legion (Winchester, Va.); Racquet, American Philosophical Soc. (Philadelphia); Chevy Chase (Washington); Tavern, Somerset, Engineers, University (Boston); Kappa Alpha Soc.; Phi Beta Kappa Soc. [*Died* 11 *March* 1957.

BYRNE, Alderman Alfred; formerly Lord Mayor of Dublin; *b.* 1882; *m.* 1910; four *s.* three *d.* M.P. Harbour Div. Dublin, 1914-18; Mem. (Ind.) Dail Eireann (T.D.) for Dublin City (North), 1923-28 and since 1932; Senator, Irish Free State, 1928-31; Member of Greater Dublin Commission, 1925-26; Lord Mayor of Dublin, 1930-39 and 1954-55; First Lord Mayor of Greater Dublin; Trustee, Royal Liver Friendly Society, 1928-; LL.D. (*h.c.*) Dublin University. Knight of the Grand Cross of Saint Sylvester. *Address:* Mansion House, Dublin. *T.:* 61845; 207 Upper Rathmines Road, Dublin. *T.:* 91425. [*Died* 13 *March* 1956.

BYROM, Charles Reginald, C.V.O. 1938; O.B.E. 1918; Lt.-Col. (retd.) Engineer and Rly. Staff Corps (R.E.) (T.A.); *b.* 7 Nov. 1878; *s.* of late Rev. J.W. Unwin, B.A.; name changed to Byrom by Deed Poll 1907; *m.* 1900, Blanche (*d.* 1944), *y. d.* of late Nicholas Martindale, Liverpool; one *s.* one *d.* *Educ.:* Shrewsbury School. Entered service of L. and N.W. Rly. Co. 1896; passed through various sections in the Traffic Operating Department; Assistant Supt. of the Line of that Railway, 1918; on amalgamation of Railways in 1923 appointed General Supt. (Passenger Commercial) of L.M.S.; Asst. Chief General Supt. 1924; Chief General Supt. 1927; Chief Operating Manager, 1932-38. *Recreations:* fishing, music, golf. *Address:* Stonesfield, Oxon. *T.:* Stonesfield 46. [*Died* 26 *Feb.* 1952.

BYROM, Thomas Emmett, C.B.E. 1920; *b.* 12 Feb. 1871; *s.* of John Byrom, Stockport; *m.* Helen Constance Olga (*d.* 1953). *Educ.:* Stockport. In 1915 he was engaged in Glasgow for several months in active recruiting campaign, raising men for Voluntary Army; from 1917 onwards worked in Home Counties, raising money for War Bond Campaigns (Tank and War Weapons Weeks, etc.). *Recreations:* motoring and golf. *Address:* 145 St. James's Court, S.W.1. *T.:* Victoria 2360. *Clubs:* National Liberal, Royal Automobile; Wimbledon Park Golf. [*Died* 13 *May* 1956.

C

CABELL, James Branch; Author; *b.* Richmond, Virginia, 14 April 1879; *s.* of Robert Gamble Cabell, M.D.; *m.* 1st, 1913, Priscilla (Bradley) Shepherd (*d.* 1949); one *s.*; *m.* 2nd, 1950, Margaret Waller Freeman. *Educ.:* Private School; College of William and Mary, A. B., 1898. Instructor French and Greek, William and Mary, 1896-97; worked in press-room, Richmond (Va.) Times, 1898; on staff, New York Herald, 1899-1901; and of Richmond (Va.) News, 1901; engaged in coal-mining in West Virginia, 1911-13; Genealogist Va. Society of Colonial Wars, 1916-28, and of Va. Sons of the American Revolution, 1917-24, and of Va. Sons of the Revolution, 1919-20; Pres. Va. Writers, 1918-21; Editor The Reviewer, 1921; Editor Va. War History Commission, 1919-26; Editor The American Spectator, 1932-35; Member, Society of the Cincinnati; Hon. Member First Families of Virginia; Kappa Alpha (South.); Phi Beta Kappa; Episcopalian. *Publications:* The Eagle's Shadow, 1904; The Line of Love, 1905; Gallantry, 1907; Branchiana, 1907; The Cords of Vanity, 1909; Chivalry, 1909; Branch of Abingdon, 1911; The Soul of Melicent (republished as Domnei), 1913; The Rivet in Grandfather's Neck, 1915; The Majors and Their Marriages, 1915; The Certain Hour, 1916; From the Hidden Way, 1916; The Cream of the Jest, 1917; Beyond Life, 1919; Jurgen, 1919; The Judging of Jurgen, 1920; Taboo, 1921; Figures of Earth, 1921; Joseph Hergesheimer, 1921; The Jewel Merchants, 1921; The Lineage of Lichfield, 1922; The High Place, 1923; Straws and Prayer-Books, 1924; The Silver Stallion, 1926; The Music from Behind the Moon, 1926; Something about Eve, 1927; Ballades from the Hidden Way, 1928; The White Robe, 1928; The Way of Ecben, 1929; Sonnets from Antan, 1929; Townsend of Lichfield, 1930; Some of Us, 1930; Between Dawn and Sunrise (with John Macy), 1930; These Restless Heads, 1932; Special Delivery, 1933; Smirt, 1934; Ladies and Gentlemen, 1934; Smith, 1935; Preface to the Past, 1936; Smire, 1937; The Nightmare Has Triplets, 1937; Of Ellen Glasgow, An Inscribed Portrait (with Ellen Glasgow), 1938; The King was in His Counting-House, 1938; Hamlet Had an Uncle, 1940; The First Gentleman of America, 1942; The St. Johns (with A. J. Hanna), 1943; There were Two Pirates, 1946; Let Me Lie, 1947; The Witch-Woman, 1948; The Devil's Own Dear Son, 1949; Quiet, Please, 1952; As I Remember It, 1955; introd. to a Bibliography, vol. i (by Frances J. Brewer), 1958. *Address:* 3201 Monument Avenue, Richmond, Virginia, U.S.A.; Poynton Lodge, Ophelia, Virginia. [*Died* 5 *May* 1958.

CADBURY, Barrow, J.P., Birmingham; *b.* 1862; *e. s.* of late Richard Cadbury, J.P., Birmingham; *m.* 1891, Geraldine, (D.B.E. *cr.* 1937, author of Young Offenders Yesterday and To-day, 1939; she died 1941), *d.* of late Alfred Southall, J.P., Birmingham; one *s.* two *d.* Chairman of Cadbury Brothers Ltd., 1922-32; Chm. of British Cocoa and Chocolate Co. Ltd., 1918-32; Freedom City of Birmingham, 1932. *Address:* 73 Wellington Road, Birmingham 15. *T.:* Calthorpe 2558. [*Died* 9 *March* 1958.

CADBURY, Dame Elizabeth Mary, (Mrs. George Cadbury), D.B.E., *cr.* 1934 (O.B.E. 1918); Hon. M.A. Birmingham; J.P., Birmingham; *b.* London, 24 June 1858; *d.* of late John Taylor and Mary Jane Cash; *m.* 1888, G. Cadbury (*d.* 1922); three *s.* three *d. Educ.:* private tuition; Germany; France. Past President National Council of Women; Hon. President of Birmingham Y.W.C.A.; Chairman of the Bournville Village Trust since 1922; President, Birmingham United Hospital, 1941-48; Member of Birmingham City Council, 1919-25, also of Education Committee, and Chairman of its School Medical Service Sub-Committee, 1911-30; Vice-Pres. National Liberal Assoc. and Vice-Pres. County of Birmingham Girl Guides' Assoc.; Pres. of Midland Adult School Union, 1931; Chairman of Woodlands Cripples Hospital, 1920-48; Past Pres. National Council of Evangelical Free Churches, 1925; Pres. of National Union of Educational Institutions, 1935; Convener of Peace and Arbitration Standing Committee of International Council of Women, 1911-36, now Hon. Vice-President; Order of Queen Elizabeth of the Belgians; Belgian Officier de Couronne; Serbian Red Cross; Order of St. Sava of Yugo-Slavia; Officer of the Order of the Hospital of St. John of Jerusalem. *Publications:* papers on education, peace, housing, and social questions. *Recreations:* music, motoring. *Address:* Manor House, Northfield, Birmingham. [*Died* 4 *Dec.* 1951.

CADBURY, Henry Tylor, M.A.; Director: Newspaper Properties, Ltd.; John Bellows Ltd., Gloucester; Vice-Chairman of Bournville Village Trust; *b.* 1882; 3rd *s.* of late George Cadbury, founder of Bournville; *m.* Lucy, *d.* of late John Bellows, Gloucester; two *s.* three *d. Educ.:* Leighton Park School, Reading; Clare College, Cambridge. *Address:* Westholme, Oak Tree Lane, Birmingham 30. [*Died* 25 *Sept.* 1952.

CADELL, Lieutenant-General Charles Alexander Elliott, C.B.E. 1942; M.C.; *b.* 30 May 1888; *s.* of C. R. S. Cadell; *m.* 1920, Magda Jhana Cantacuzine. *Educ.:* Cheltenham College. Entered Army, 1908; Lt.-Col., 1936; Col., 1938; Acting Maj.-General, 1940; Maj.-Gen. 1940; Acting Lt.-General, 1942; formerly instructor at School of Artillery in India; served War of 1939-45, commanding an A.A. Division and subsequently, an A.A. Corps; Served in India, Egypt, Malaya, France, 1915-17 (M.C.). Retired pay, 1944. *Recreations:* shooting, fishing. *Club:* Army and Navy. [*Died* 2 *Feb.* 1951.

CAHILL, Sir (Joseph) Robert, Kt., *cr.* 1932; C.M.G. 1927; Commandeur Legion of Honour; *b.* 12 January 1879; 3rd *s.* of late Mark Cahill of Sandford Court, Co. Kilkenny, and Harcourt Street, Dublin; *m.* 1908, Alice Lilian, *d.* of William Bradley, Cours de Verdun, Bordeaux and Kendal, Westmorland; one *d.* (two *s.* decd.) *Educ.:* Clongowes Wood Coll.; University Coll., Dublin; Balliol Coll., Oxford (B.A. 1904); various universities abroad. Engaged on official economic missions in France, Belgium, U.S.A., Germany, Holland, Austria, and U.K., for Board of Trade, Ministry of Agriculture, Local Government Board, National Service Department, and Ministry of Labour, 1907-18; Acting Commercial Counsellor, British Embassy, Paris, 1918-19; Commercial Secretary, Berne, 1919-21: Commercial Counsellor, British Embassy, Paris, 1921-39. Employed in France and in Portugal, 1939-40, by Ministry of Supply. Interned by German forces of occupation in France at St. Denis and Vittel camps (July 1940-July 1944), and repatriated 10 Aug. 1944 through Lisbon, under exchange agreement. *Publications:* various official reports on France, Germany, Switzerland, Belgium, U.S.A., U.K. *Address:* 3 rue de Constantine, Paris, viime. *T.:* Invalides 08-64; Domaine de Fonteneau, Floirac, Gironde. *T.:* 61 Floirac. *Clubs:* United University; Union Interalliée, Automobile de France (Paris). [*Died* 10 *May* 1953.

CAINES, Clement Guy, C.B. 1944; O.B.E. 1934; *b.* 1882; *m.* 1919, Kathleen Milverton, *d.* of Richard Milverton Drake; two *d.* (one *s.* killed on active service, 1944). Entered Air Ministry, 1919; late Principal Assistant Secretary; Assistant Under-Secretary of State, Air Ministry; retired 1948. *Address:* The Barn, Wargrave, Berks. *T.:* Wargrave 270. [*Died* 23 *Feb.* 1952.

CAIRD, Sir Andrew, K.B.E., *cr.* 1918; *b.* Montrose, 1870; *m.* 1896, Anne (*d.* 1933), *d.* of William Davidson, Montrose; two *s.* two *d. Educ.:* Montrose Academy; University College, Dundee. Administrator of New York Headquarters British War Mission to the United States, 1917-18; Managing Director of The Daily Mail, 1922-26; Chm. and Man. Dir., The Statesman, Calcutta, 1927-28; contested (C.) St. Ives Division of Cornwall, March 1928 and 1929; received freedom of Montrose, 1935. *Address:* 187 Queen's Gate, S.W.7. [*Died* 15 *Dec.* 1956.

CAIRD, Sir James, 1st Bt., *cr.* 1928; Shipowner; formerly Director William Cory & Son, Ltd.; Extraord. Dir. Union Bank of Scotland, Ltd., etc.; *b.* 2 Jan. 1864; *m.* 1894, Henrietta (*d.* 1953), *d.* of William Stephens, Holywood, Co. Down; one *d. Heir:* none. *Address:* The Well House, Arthur Road, Wimbledon Common. *T.:* Wimbledon 0782. [*Died* 27 *Sept.* 1954 (*ext.*).

CAIRNS, Sir Hugh William Bell, K.B.E., *cr.* 1946; M.A., D.M. (Oxon); M.D. (ad eundem gradum), B.S. (Adelaide); Hon. D.Sc. (Northwestern Univ., Chicago); F.R.C.S. England; Hon. F.R.A.C.S.; Nuffield Professor of Surgery, Oxford; Surgeon to the Radcliffe Infirmary, Oxford; Consulting Neuro-surgeon to London Hospital; Hon. Consulting Neurosurgeon to the Army; *b.* 26 June 1896; *o. s.* of William Cairns, South Australia; *m.* 1921, Barbara Forster, *y. d.* of late Arthur Lionel Smith, Master of Balliol; two *s.* two *d. Educ.:* Adelaide High School; Adelaide University (Exhibitioner, Davies-Thomas Scholar and Everard Scholar); Balliol College, Oxford (Rhodes Scholar); London Hospital. Served European war as private and Captain in Australian Army Medical Corps, 1915-18; Member of Oxford University Crew, 1920; House appointments at Radcliffe Infirmary and London Hospital, 1921-25; Hunterian Professor, Royal College of Surgeons, 1925; Rockefeller Travelling Fellow in United States, 1926-27; Hon. Surgeon to Hospital for Paralysis and Epilepsy, Maida Vale, 1931-34; to National Hospital for Diseases of the Nervous System, Queen Square, 1934-37; Triennial Gold Medallist West London Medico-Chirurgical Society, 1935; Lister lecturer, Adelaide, 1948; Victor Horsley lecturer, 1949; Honorary Member Harvey Cushing Society, Society of Neurological Surgeons, U.S.A., Australasian Soc. of Neurological Surgeons; Corresp. Mem. Academia des Ciencias, Lisboa; Foreign Corresp. Member, Académie de Chirurgie, Société de Neurologie de Paris,

Nederlandsche Vereeniging voor Psychiatrie en Neurologie; Fellow of Balliol, 1937; Consultant Adviser on Head Injuries to the Minister of Health, 1939; Pres. Neurological Section R.S.M., 1944; Sims Commonwealth Professor, 1947-48; Pres. Soc. of Brit. Neurological Surgeons, 1946-48; Pres. Assoc. of Surgeons of Gt. Britain and Ire., 1947; Pres. Sect. Neurol., B.M.A., 1950; Member Council R.C.S., 1942-50. *Publications:* Articles on the surgery of the nervous system in medical books and journals. *Address:* 29 Charlbury Road, Oxford. [*Died* 18 *July* 1952.

CALDECOT, Ivone K.; *see* Kirkpatrick-Caldecot.

CALDECOTT, Sir Andrew, G.C.M.G., *cr.* 1941 (K.C.M.G., *cr.* 1937; C.M.G. 1932); Kt., *cr.* 1935; C.B.E. 1926; M.A. Oxon, LL.D. Ceylon; *b.* 26 Oct. 1884; *s.* of late Rev. Andrew Caldecott; *m.* 1918, Olive Mary (*d.* 1943), *d.* of late J. R. Innes, C.M.G.,; one *s.* one *d.*; *m.* 1946, Evelyn May, *widow* of Dr. J. Robertson, and *d.* of late Canon H. Palmer. *Educ.:* Uppingham; Exeter Coll., Oxford (Hon. Fellow, 1948). Between 1907 and 1935 held various appointments in Malayan Civil Service, including acting Controller of Labour; Under-Secretary, Straits Settlements; Commissioner of Lands, F.M.S.; Secretary for Postal Affairs; Acting British Resident, Negri Sembilan; Acting British Resident, Perak; British Resident, Selangor; Chief Secretary to Government, Federated Malay States, 1931-33; Colonial Sec., Straits Settlements, 1933-35; Officer Administering the Government of the Straits Settlements and High Commissioner for the Malay States, 1934; Governor, Hong Kong, 1935-37; Governor, Ceylon, 1937-44; Knight of Grace of St. John of Jerusalem, 1936; was Malayan Commissioner at British Empire Exhibition, 1924-25. Fellow: Roy. Asiatic Soc.; Roy. Soc. of Arts. *Publications:* History of Jelebu; Not Exactly Ghosts; Fires Burn Blue. *Recreations:* music (Fellow R. Philharmonic S., 1947), writing, and painting. *Address:* Pier Point, Itchenor, nr. Chichester, Sussex. *Clubs:* United University, Royal Empire Society, Overseas League; Itchenor Sailing (Itchenor). [*Died* 14 *July* 1951.

CALDER, Hon. James Alexander, P.C. (Can.); B.A., LL.D., Toronto; Member of Senate from 1921; *s.* of James Calder and Johanna M'Kay; *b.* near Ingersoll, Oxford Co., Ontario, 17 Sept. 1868; *m.* 1910, Eva. M. Leslie, St. Mary's, Ontario; one *s.* *Educ.:* Winnipeg Collegiate and Manitoba University. Public and High School teacher, 1887-1904; School Inspector in Alberta and Saskatchewan, 1894-1900; Deputy Minister of Education, Saskatchewan and Alberta, 1901-1905; called to Bar, 1905; first Elected Saskatchewan Legislative Assembly, 1905; Member for Moosejaw, 1917-21; Provincial Treasurer and Minister of Education, 1905-12; later Minister of Railways and Highways; Minister of Immigration and Colonisation, 1917-20; President of the Privy Council and Minister of Health, 1920-21; Conservative; Presbyterian; Member of Imperial War Conference, 1918. *Address:* c/o The Senate, Ottawa, Canada. *Clubs:* Rideau (Ottawa); Assiniboia (Regina). [*Died* 20 *July* 1956.

CALDER, Sir William Moir, Kt., *cr.* 1955; M.A. (Oxon.); M.A. (Manc.); M.A., Hon. LL.D. (Aberd.); Hon. D.Phil. (Athens); Fell. of the British Academy; Corresp. Mitgl. des Oest. Arch. Instit.; Ord. Mitglied des Deutschen Arch. Inst.; *b.* 2 July 1881; *s.* of George M. Calder, Edinkillie, Forres, Scotland, and Isabella Moir, Montrose, Scotland; *m.* 1910, Isabel Watt, *e. d.* of F. R. Murray, Aberdeen; three *s.*; *m.* 1959, Mrs. Renate Strauss. *Educ.:* Universities of Aberdeen, Oxford, Edinburgh, Paris, Rome, Berlin. First Franco-Scottish Bursary in French, Ferguson Scholarship in Classics; Hon. Scholar of Christ Church, Oxford; Gaisford (Prose) Prizeman, 1904; Craven Scholar, 1905; Craven Fellow, 1907; Hulme Research Student in Brasenose College, 1908-12; Hulme Professor of Greek, Manchester Univ., 1913-30; Professor of Greek in Edinburgh University, 1930-51; Wilson Travelling Fellow (Aber.). Has travelled widely in Inner Asia Minor. President: Soc. of Antiquaries of Scotland, 1950; Classical Assoc., 1951; British Institute of Archæology at Ankara, 1956. Hon. Fellow of Brasenose College, 1956. *Publications:* Anatolian Studies pres. to Ramsay, 1923; Anatolian Studies pres. to Buckler, 1939; Monumenta Asiæ Minoris Antiqua, vols. i., iv., vi., vii., 1928-56; Memoirs of Prince Max of Baden vol. i. (trans.), 1928; many articles on the antiquities of Asia Minor in British and Foreign Journals; Editor the Classical Review, 1923-35; Messenger Lecturer in Cornell University, 1936. *Address:* Presley Cottage, Dunphail, Moray. *Club:* New (Edinburgh). [*Died* 17 *Aug.* 1960.

CALDER-MARSHALL, Sir Robert, K.B.E., *cr.* 1938 (C.B.E. 1933); Managing Director, Calder Marshall Co. Ltd., Shanghai Merchants; Chairman, British Chamber of Commerce, Shanghai, 1928-45; Vice-Chairman Board of Trustees for Administration of Indemnity Funds, Nanking remitted by the British Government; *b.* 19 Dec. 1877; *s.* of Henry Calder-Marshall and Johanna Grotjan Cambridge; *m.* 1904, Adelaide Siddall (*d.* 1947); one *d.* *Educ.:* St. Paul's School. Order of Brilliant Jade (Chinese), 1936. *Address:* 620 Hamilton House, Kiangse Road, Shanghai, China. *T.A.:* Redlac, Shanghai, China. *Clubs:* Junior Carlton; Shanghai, Country (Shanghai); Hong Kong (Hong Kong). [*Died* 18 *Dec.* 1955.

CALHOUN, Eleanor; *see* Lazarovich-Hrebelianovich, H.H. Princess.

CALL, Frank Oliver; Professor Emeritus of Modern Languages, University of Bishop's College, Lennoxville, Quebec, Canada; *b.* West Brome, Quebec, 11 April 1878; *s.* of Lorenzo Call and Sarah Hungerford; unmarried. *Educ.:* Stanstead College; University of Bishop's College; M.A., D.C.L.; Marburg; Paris. Chevalier de l'Ordre latin, 1940. *Publications:* poems in various magazines and periodicals and anthologies; Collected Poems, published in Books of Georgian Verse Series, 1916; Acanthus and Wild Grape, Poems, 1919; Blue Homespun, Sonnets, 1924; The Spell of French Canada, 1926; The Spell of Acadia, 1930; Life of Marguerite Bourgeoys; Sonnets for Youth, 1944. *Recreations:* gardening, painting. *Address:* Bishop's College, Lennoxville, Quebec. *Clubs:* P.E.N.; Arts (Montreal). [*Died Aug.* 1956.

CALLAHAN, James Morton, A.M., Ph.D.; *b.* Bedford, Indiana, 4 Nov. 1864; *e. s.* of Martin I. Callahan and Sophia O. Tannehill; *m.* 1907, Maud Louise Fulcher; one *s.* two *d.* *Educ.:* Normal and Commercial schools; Univ. of Indiana, A.B., 1894; A.M., 1895; Univ. of Chicago; Johns Hopkins Univ., Ph.D., 1897. Teacher in Indiana public schools, 1883-90, and normal college, 1890-92; Assistant and Fellow, Johns Hopkins Univ., 1895-97; Acting Prof. of American History and Constitutional Law at Hamilton College, 1897-98; Lecturer on American Diplomatic History and Archives at Johns Hopkins University, 1898-1902; Director of Bureau of Historical Research, 1900-2; Head of Department of History and Politics, W. Va. University, 1902-29 (Dean, 1916-29); Research Professor, 1929-40 (Emeritus since 1940); Lecturer for American Association for International Conciliation, 1915-18; has conducted extensive researches in Manuscript Diplomatic Archives

at Washington, London, Ottawa, and Paris; and has won distinction by his studies in international politics and diplomacy, several of which are published by the Johns Hopkins University; Member of Phi Beta Kappa, and several learned societies; Lake Mohonk Conference on International Arbitration, Pan-American Institute of Geography and History and Conference on Canadian-American Affairs; Pres. Ohio Valley Historical Association 1913-14. *Publications:* Neutrality of the AmericanLakes; Cuba and International Relations; American Relations in the Pacific and the Far East; Diplomatic History of the Southern Confederacy; Seward's Mexican Policy; The American Expansion Policy; The Monroe Doctrine and Inter-American Relations; American Foreign Policy in Mexican Relations; American Foreign Policy in Canadian Relations; Early American Continental Policy; Foundations of American Northern Frontier Development; History of West Virginia; various historical monographs and reviews; and articles on History, Government, and Jurisprudence for magazines and encyclopedias; Editor of W. Va. Univ. Studies in American History. *Recreations:* golfing, walking, and motoring. *Address:* West Virginia Univ., or 632 Spruce St., Morgantown, W. Va. *T.:* 9633. *Clubs:* Cosmos (Washington); Faculty Country (Morgantown).
[*Died* 16 *March* 1956.

CALLAN, John Bartholomew; Hon. Mr. Justice Callan; Judge of Supreme Court of New Zealand since 1935; *b.* 15 Aug. 1882; *s.* of Hon. J. B. Callan, M.L.C. and Ellen Mary Brophy; *m.* 1913, Margaret Elizabeth Mowat; one *s.* *Educ.:* Christian Brothers School, Dunedin; Otago University, Dunedin. Partner in Callan and Gallaway, Barristers and Solicitors, Dunedin, 1906-34; K.C. 1934; practised as Barrister, Wellington, 1934-35. President Otago District Law Society; Member of Council N.Z. Law Society; For 20 years a Law Lecturer Otago University; For 10 years Dean of Law Faculty there; Member of N.Z. Council of Legal Education; ex-Member of Senate of University of N.Z.; 3rd. Bn. N.Z. Rifle Brigade, N.Z.E.F., Captain, 1917-19. Chairman during War of 1939-45 of Aliens Appeal Tribunal, and Commission of Enquiry into Shipping Losses in the Pacific. *Address:* Judge's Chambers, Auckland, N.Z. [*Died* 12 *Feb.* 1951.

CALLANDER, Sir James, Kt., *cr.* 1941; M.I.Mech.E.; M.I.N.A.; *b.* 1877; *s.* of William Callender, Newton Stewart, Wigtownshire; *m.* Alice Rose, *d.* of William Smith, Liverpool; one *d.* Joined Vickers-Armstrongs, Ltd., 1900; Director of Vickers Armstrongs Ltd., 1936-45; Director of Vickers, Ltd., 1945-47. Asst. Mechanical Supt., Mersey Docks and Harbour Bd. Member Technical Cttee., Lloyd's Register of Shipping. *Address:* Leven Hill, Newby Bridge, Ulverston, Lancs. *T.:* Newby Bridge 342. [*Died* 23 *March* 1952.

CALLANDER, Professor Thomas, M.A. (Aberd., Oxon.); Emeritus Professor of Greek, Queen's University, Canada; *b.* 18 May, 1877; 3rd *s.* of William Callander and Elizabeth A. Graham; *m.* 1915, Beatrice, *d.* of Henry Oliver Scott-Thomson, Stoke Cliff, Stapleton, Glos. *Educ.:* Gordon's College and King's College, Aberdeen; Trinity College, Oxford (1st Cl. Hons., Classics and Greats, Aberdeen and Oxford). Travelled as Carnegie Research Student in Asia Minor, 1904; as Wilson Fellow of Aberdeen University, 1906, 1907, 1913; Chancellor's Lectr., Queen's, 1915, 1916; Special Lectr., McGill, 1917; Exchange Professor, Michigan Univ., 1922. *Publications:* Contributions to Jl. of Hellenic Studies, Aberdeen Quater-Centenary Studies, Hibbert Jl., North American Review and Queen's Quarterly Review. *Recreations:* golf and travel. *Address:* Côte de Vauxlaurens, Cambridge Park, Guernsey. *T.:* Guernsey 6240. *Club:* Authors'.
[*Died May* 1959.

CALLENDER, Lt.-Col. David Aubrey, C.M.G. 1915; late Royal Scots; *b.* 11 Nov. 1868; *m.* 1900, Violet (*d.* 1953), *d.* of J. P. Wright, 6 Grosvenor Cres. Edinburgh; two *s.* two *d.* Entered Army, 1887, Captain, 1896; Major, 1904; Lt.-Col., 1912; Adjutant, Volunteers, 1898-1903; served Zululand, 1888; European War, 1914-1918 (C.M.G.); J.P., Perthshire. *Address:* 40 Hay St., Perth. *T.:* 1070
[*Died* 7 *Oct.* 1953.

CALLENDER, Eustace Maude, C.B.E. 1919; T.D.; M.D.; L.R.C.P.; M.R.C.S.; retired; Fellow (President, 1924-25), Medical Society of London; Order of Mercy, 1932; Member (Vice-President 1927 and 1928) Harveian Society of London; *b.* Oakfield, Whalley Range, Manchester, 31 Oct. 1864; *s.* of Samuel Pope Callender; *m.* 1897, Adelaide Frances Jane (*d.* 1942), *d.* of John Beeching Stephens, Maidstone; one *d.* *Educ.:* Rugby School; St. Mary's Hospital, London. Late House Physician, House Surgeon and Resident Obstetric Officer, St. Mary's Hospital; late Physician Medical Aid Society for Necessitous Gentlewomen and St. Agatha's Home, St. John's Wood; member of Artists' Rifle Corps, 1882-85; Surgeon Civil Service Rifle Corps, 1894-1908; Major and Lt.-Col. R.A.M.C. Territorial Force, 1908-21; commanded 2nd London General Hospital, 1912-21; on active service, 5 Aug. 1914-15 April 1919; two years overseas (France) in command of No. 53 General Hospital (despatches thrice, British War medal, Victory medal with Oak Leaf emblem, C.B.E., Territorial War medal); King George's Coronation medal. *Recreations:* shooting (Rugby School Rifle 8, Wimbledon 1881), fishing, deer-stalking, and golf. *Address:* Tentercroft, Cuckfield, Sussex. *T.:* Cuckfield 83. *Club:* Caledonian.
[*Died* 3 *April* 1952.

CALLOW, Graham, D.S.O., M.C.; J.P.; *b.* 13 March 1894; *e. s.* of late J. M. Callow; *m.* 1926, Doris Elisabeth, *e. d.* of W. Rose, Derby. *Educ.:* Derby School. Served European War, 1914-19; Egypt, 2nd Batt. The Foresters, 1919-20; Nigeria, 3rd Batt. Nigeria Regt., 1921-22; Commissioner, Nigeria Police, 1922-34; Magistrate, Protectorate Court, Nigeria, 1934-37; Crown Law Officer, Sierra Leone, 1937-42. Mobilized Sept. 1939; Judge of Supreme Court of Nigeria, 1943-47; Judge of Supreme Court of Malaya, 1947-50, retired 1950. J.P. Wilts. *Address:* The Pen, Milton Lilbourne, Pewsey, Wilts. *Club:* United Service.
[*Died* 4 *Jan.* 1960.

CALMAN, William Thomas, C.B. 1935; F.R.S. 1921; F.L.S., Hon. F.R.S.E.; D.Sc.; Hon. LL.D., St. Andrews; *b.* Dundee, 1871; *m.* 1906, Alice Jean, *d.* of James Donaldson, Tayport, Fife; one *s.* one *d.* *Educ.:* Dundee High School and University College, Dundee (St. Andrews University); B.Sc. 1895, D.Sc. 1900. Assistant Lecturer and Demonstrator in Zoology, University College, Dundee, 1895-1903; Assistant in Zoological Department of British Museum (Natural History), 1904-21; Deputy Keeper of Zoology, 1921-27; Keeper of Zoology, British Museum, 1927-36; Temp. Lecturer in Zoology, Univ. St. Andrews, 1940-1946; Pres. of Section D, British Assoc., Bristol, 1930; Pres. Linnean Society, 1934-1937; Linnean Gold Medallist, 1949; Secretary of the Ray Society, 1919-46. *Publications:* Crustacea, in Treatise on Zoology, edited by Sir Ray Lankester, 1909; The Life of Crustacea, 1911; The Classification of Animals, 1949; articles on Crustacea, etc., in Encyclopædia Britannica (11th edition); papers chiefly on Crustacea in various scientific periodicals. *Address:* Woodcote Grove House, Woodcote Park, Coulsdon, Sy. [*Died* 29 *Sept.* 1952.

CALRY, 6th Count de, Count Magawly de Calry; Count Cerati in Bavaria; Count Magawly de Calry in Italy; Count of the Holy Roman Empire; Grandee of Spain; Irish family; *b.* Dublin, 19 Jan. 1854; *S.* father, 1860; *m.* 1880, Ellen Falkenburg (*d.* 1929), *d.* of Redman Abbott, Philadelphia; one *s.* one *d.* *Educ.:* Stonyhurst Coll. *Heir: s.* Robert Louis [*b.* 11 July 1898. *Educ.:* Eton; Trinity College, Cambridge; M.A. *Club:* St. James']. *Clubs:* (President) British and American (Lausanne); Unione, Florence (Florence); Unione (Parma). [*Died* 27 *April* 1950.

[*But death not notified in time for inclusion in Who Was Who 1941–1950, first edn.*

CALTHORPE, Sir F. H.; *see* Anstruther-Gough-Calthorpe.

CALVERLEY, 1st Baron, *cr.* 1945; **George Muff;** J.P.; D.L.; Army Welfare Officer since 1940; textile worker; *b.* Bradford, Yorkshire, 10 February 1877; *s.* of George Muff, miner, and Sarah J. Muff, weaver; *m.* Ellen, *e. d.* of Chas. and Mary Orford, late of Bath; one *s.* *Educ.:* Ryan Street Elementary, Bradford. Doffer Spinning Mill at ten; been working ever since; a founder of the National Young Liberal Movement, 1905; Chairman of the Yorkshire Young Liberals Union until 1919, then joined the Labour Party; contested (Independent Radical) South Bradford, 1918; (Lab.) Chester, 1922-23; Hull East, 1924; M.P. (Lab.) Hull East, 1929-31 and 1935-45; Member of Bradford City Council, 1922; Prison Magistrate, 1933-54; Pres. W. Riding Magistrates Assoc., 1954; J.P. 1932; D.L. Yorks, W. Riding, 1944. *Recreations:* welfare work amongst young men; studying Bradshaw and football form. *Heir: s.* Hon. George Raymond Orford Muff [*b.* 1 May 1914; *m.* 1940, Mary, *d.* of Arthur Farrar, Halifax; two *s.*]. *Address:* Woodhall, Stanningley, Leeds. [*Died* 20 *Sept.* 1955.

CALVERLEY, Joseph Ernest Goodfellow, C.M.G. 1900; M.D., B.S.; Surgeon and Surgeon-in-Charge, Ear, Throat and Nose Department, Royal Victoria Hospital, Folkestone; Senior Surgeon, Bevan Military Hospital; Surgeon Specialist, Shorncliffe, Military Area; *b.* 16 Mar. 1872; *m.* 1901, Evelyn, *d.* of Edward Brookes Douėt; two *s.* *Educ.:* Dulwich. Served with Portland Hospital in South Africa. *Recreation:* golf. *Address:* Prince's Hotel, Folkestone. [*Died* 11 *July* 1953.

CALVERT, Albert Spencer, C.B.E. 1953 (O.B.E. 1938); Consul-General at Tunis since 1950; *b.* 1 April 1897; *s.* of Albert Ellis Calvert, J.P., and Annie Spencer; *m.* 1938, Martha Adeline, *d.* of Judge Thomas H. Calvert; no *c.* *Educ.:* Widnes; University of Liverpool; Pembroke College, Cambridge. Served European War, 1914-1918, in King's Liverpool Regt. Entered Levant Consular Service, 1920; served in Persia, 1921-28; Alexandria, Egypt, 1928-1933; Jedda, Saudi Arabia, 1933-37; H.M. Chargé d'Affaires each year, 1933-36; Boston Mass., 1939-41; Washington, 1941; Persia, 1941-44; transferred from Kermanshah, 1944, to U.S.A.; Consul-General, New Orleans, 1945-49. Was attached to Representative of Saudi Arabia at Coronation of King George VI, 1937. *Recreations:* sailing, swimming, fishing. *Address:* c/o Personnel Dept., Foreign Office, S.W.1. *Club:* United University. [*Died* 5 *Sept.* 1953.

CAMBRIDGE; *see* Pickard-Cambridge.

CAMERON of Lochiel, Col. Sir Donald Walter, K.T. 1934; C.M.G. 1916; Lord-Lieutenant since 1939 and Convener of Inverness-shire; Deputy Governor of National Bank of Scotland; *b.* 4 Nov. 1876; *s.* of Donald Cameron of Lochiel and Lady Margaret Elizabeth Scott, *d.* of 5th Duke of Buccleuch; *m.* 1906, Lady Hermione Emily Graham, 2nd *d.* of 5th Duke of Montrose; three *s.* two *d.*; *S.* to title and estate, 1905. *Educ.:* Harrow; Royal Military College, Sandhurst. Capt. Grenadier Guards; retired, 1906; served S. Africa, 1899 and 1901-2; raised and commanded 5th (Ser.) Batt. Cameron Highlanders, Aug. 1914-May 1916; served European War, 1914-18 (C.M.G.); Commandant North of Scotland Military Area, 1916-17; commanded Lovat Scouts Sharpshooters, 1917-18; in command 3rd Batt. Cameron Highlanders, 1912-14, and 1918-19; Col. (Mil.) 1919. A.D.C. to Governor of Madras, 1900; A.D.C. 1920-43; contested (U.) Sutherlandshire, 1910. Hon. LL.D. (Glasgow), 1948. *Heir: s.* Donald Hamish [*b.* 12 Sep. 1910; *m.* 1939, Margaret, *o. d.* of Lt.-Col. Hon. Nigel Gathorne-Hardy, D.S.O.; one *s.* two *d.*]. *Address:* Achnacarry, Spean Bridge, Inverness-shire. *Clubs:* Carlton; New (Edinburgh). [*Died* 11 *Oct.* 1951.

CAMERON of Lundavra, Col. Ewen Allan, C.M.G. 1919; D.S.O. 1918; Bar 1919; *b.* 15 Mar. 1877; *s.* of Allan Cameron of Lundavra, Hereditary Chieftain of the Clan Cameron; late Assistant Inspector General, Royal Irish Constabulary (1902); *m.* Edith Pollock (*d.* 1957), *y. d.* of William Pollock-Hill; three *s.* *Educ.:* All Hallows, Honiton; Sandhurst. Served in Royal Warwickshire Regt. and Queen's Own Cameron Highlanders; S. African War (dangerously wounded, Queen's and King's medal 8 clasps); West Africa (wounded, medal); European War, commanded E. Surreys and Loyal North Lancs and 72nd Infantry Bde. (wounded three times, C.M.G., D.S.O. and bar, despatches thrice). Served in battle area with R.N.R.A.U. as Director for Displaced Persons. Liveryman of the Worshipful Company of Tinplate Workers; Freeman of the City of London; Officer of the Venerable Order of St. John of Jerusalem in England; Order of Rising Sun. *Address:* The Grange, St. Anne's Hill, Chertsey, Surrey. [*Died* 14 *Dec.* 1958.

CAMERON, Finlay James, F.F.A.; F.I.A.; F.R.S.E.; retired; *b.* 13 Dec. 1880; *s.* of late Duncan Cameron, Artist, Edinburgh; *m.* 1909, Margaret, *d.* of late J. Corbet Fletcher, M.D., London; one *s.* one *d.* *Educ.:* George Watson's Coll., Edinburgh. Friends' Provident and Century Life Office, Assistant Actuary, 1919-27; Joint Actuary, 1927-28; General Manager and Actuary of Caledonian Insurance Company, 1928-45; President of Insurance Society of Edinburgh, 1930-31; Chairman of Associated Scottish Life Offices, 1938-39; President of Faculty of Actuaries, 1942-44; served in R.N.V.R., European War, 1916-19. *Publication:* Elements of Life Department Practice. *Recreation:* golf. *Address:* Hillcrest, Whitehouse Road, Barnton, Midlothian. *Club:* Royal Scots (Edinburgh). [*Died* 9 *April* 1954.

CAMERON, Hector Charles, M.A., Hon. LL.D. (Glasgow), M.A., M.D. (Cambridge). F.R.C.P. (Lond.); Consulting Physician to Department for Diseases of Children, Guy's Hospital; Fellow of the Royal Society of Medicine; *b.* Glasgow, 17 July 1878; *s.* of late Sir Hector Clare Cameron; *m.* Dorothy, *d.* of late W. E. Hill, Blackheath; two *d.* *Educ.:* Clifton College; University of Glasgow; St. John's College, Cambridge (Foundation Scholar in Science); Guy's Hospital (University Scholar); Berlin. Formerly Demonstrator of Physiology and Dean of the Medical School, Guy's Hospital, London. Lumleian Lecturer R.C.P. (Lond.), 1925; Past President British Paediatric Association and the Sections for Diseases of Children, Royal Society of Medicine and B.M.A. *Publications:* The Nervous Child, 5th Edn., 1948; Joseph Lister, The Friend of Man, 1949; Sir Joseph Banks, K.B., P.R.S., 1953; The History of Mr. Guy's Hospital,

CAMERON, Lieut.-Col. Sir Donald Charles, K.C.M.G., D.S.O. See page xxviii.

1954; books and papers upon medical subjects. *Address:* Enton Rough, nr. Godalming. *T.:* Godalming 277. *Club:* Athenæum. [*Died* 1 *April* 1958.

CAMERON, James Nield, C.B.E. 1936; Sudan Civil Servant (retired); *b.* 14 June 1884; *s.* of James Spottiswoode Cameron, M.D., late of Leeds and Ruth Nield Cameron; *m.* 1918, Doris, *d.* of Herbert James Denby, Garforth, Yorks; three *s.* *Educ.:* Merchiston Castle School, Edinburgh; Leeds University (School of Agriculture). B.Sc. 1907; Spent two years in Egypt in agricultural and engineering work and entered Department of Agriculture and Forests, Sudan, 1912; Chief Inspector, 1924; Asst. Director, 1927; Director, 1931; retired, 1935; Mentioned in despatches, 1917-18 for services in Sudan in connection with the war; Officier Order of the Nile, 1922; Commandeur, 1929; King's Silver Jubilee Medal, 1935. *Recreations:* shooting, fishing, hunting. Joint Hon. Sec. Bramham Moor Hunt, 1952-. *Address:* The Old Vicarage, Wetherby, Yorks. *T.A.:* and *T.:* Wetherby 2120. [*Died* 28 *Oct.* 1960.

CAMERON, John, M.D. (Edin.), D.Sc. (St. And.), F.R.S.E., F.R.S.C., M.R.C.S. (Eng.); Member, New York Academy of Science , 1957; *b.* Laurencekirk, Scotland, 16 Sept. 1873; *s.* of late Major David Cameron, 7th Bn. Gordon Highlanders; *m.* 1925, Elsie (*d.* 1948), *d.* of Provost James Moffat, O.B.E. *Educ.:* Montrose Academy; Universities of Edinburgh [M.B., Ch.B. Edinburgh in 1898 with Honours, and M.D. in 1904 (Thesis Gold Medallist)]; St. Andrews and Leipzig. Demonstrator of Anatomy, University of St. Andrews, 1899-1905; Senior Demonstrator of Anatomy, University of Manchester, 1905-8; Lecturer in Anatomy, University of London (Middlesex Hospital), 1908-15; Professor of Anatomy, Dalhousie University, 1915-30; Formerly Examiner in Anatomy to the Universities of St. Andrews and London, and the Royal College of Surgeons of England; Research Fellow of St. Andrews University, 1902-5; Carnegie Research Fellow, 1903-6; late Captain in the Canadian Army Medical Corps. *Publications:* The Superior Commissure in Vertebrates (D.Sc. Thesis), Journal of Anatomy, 1904; The Development of the Retina (M.D. thesis), ibid., 1905; The Development of the Auditory Nerve, ibid., 1910; and the Development of the Olfactory Nerves (with Sir Wm. Milligan), Transactions International Medical Congress, 1913; The Evolution of the Human Skull, Trans. Royal Soc. Canada, 1918; Text-book of Regional Anatomy, 3rd Edition, 1931; Text-book of Osteology and Arthrology, 1921; Vol. XII. (Osteology) of the Report of the Canadian Arctic Expedition, 1913-18, 1923; Researches in Craniometry, vol. i. 1928, vol. ii., 1931; The Skeleton of British Neolithic Man, 1934. *Recreation:* music. *Address:* Balmashanner, Grove Road, Bournemouth. *T.:* 1621. [*Died* 27 *Nov.* 1960.

CAMERON, John Forbes, M.A. (Cantab.); Hon. LL.D. (Edinburgh and Cambridge); Master of Gonville and Caius College, Cambridge, 1928-48; *b.* 23 July 1873; *s.* of James Cameron, Stanley, Perthshire; *m.* Elfrida, *d.* of John Edmund Sturge, Montserrat; one *s.* one *d.* (and one *s.* died as P.O.W., 1941). *Educ.:* Perth Academy; Edinburgh University; Gonville and Caius College, Cambridge. 2nd Wrangler, 1898; Smith's Prizeman, 1900; Fellow of Caius College, 1899; Lecturer, 1900; Tutor, 1909; Senior Tutor, 1919; Bursar, 1921; Member of Council of the Senate, 1924-44; Ministry of Munitions, 1915-17; Vice-Chairman, Arbitration Tribunal (Ministry of Labour), 1917-18; Chairman of University Press, 1929-48; Vice-Chancellor, Cambridge University, 1933-35. *Address:* 12 Wilberforce Road, Cambridge. *T.:* Cambridge 5186. [*Died* 21 *March* 1952.

CAMERON, Matthew Brown, C.I.E. 1930; M.A. (Glasg.); B.Sc. (Lond.); D.Litt. (Lucknow); *b.* 22 Sep. 1867; 2nd *s.* of Robert Cameron, Paisley; *m.* Margaret, 2nd *d.* of John Croall, Kelso; one *s.* *Educ.:* Glasgow and London Universities. Professor, Canning College, Lucknow, 1895-1921; Principal, 1911-1926; Professor of Philosophy, Lucknow University, 1921-26; Dean of Faculty of Arts, Lucknow University, 1921-26; Vice-Chancellor, Lucknow University, 1926-30. *Address:* St. Leonard's, Juniper Green, Edinburgh. [*Died* 26 *June* 1952.

CAMERON, Major-General Neville John Gordon, C.B. 1918; C.M.G. 1916; A.D.C. to the King, 1920; Colonel of the Queen's Own Cameron Highlanders, 1929-43; Hon. Colonel, 16th Battalion (Cameron Highlanders of Western Australia), 1938-45; *b.* 9 Oct. 1873; *s.* of late General Sir William Gordon Cameron, G.C.B.; *m.* 1915, Joan, *d.* of Colonel P. C. E. Newbigging, late R.A.; three *d.* (one *s.* killed in action, 1944). *Educ.:* Wellington College. Served Nile Expedition, 1898 (despatches, two medals two clasps); S. Africa, 1900-2 (despatches, Queen's medal four clasps, King's medal two clasps, Bt. Major); European War, 1914-18 (despatches, C.M.G., C.B., Bt. Col.); Maj.-Gen., 1925; commanded 49th (West Riding) Division Territorial Army, 1926-30; retired pay, 1931. D.L., Bedfordshire, 1940. *Address;* Dalchonzie, Comrie, Perthshire. *Clubs:* United Service; New (Edinburgh). [*Died* 5 *Dec.* 1955.

CAMERON, Brigadier Orford Somerville, D.S.O. 1917; *s.* of late Colonel A. S. Cameron, V.C., C.B.; *b.* 1878; *m.* Hester Nina (*d.* 1952), *d.* of late Peter Hordern, Bury House, Alverstoke; one *s.* one *d.* (and one *s.* decd.). *Educ.:* R.M.A., Woolwich. Entered Royal Artillery 1897; served in Mauritius as private secretary and A.D.C. to Sir Charles Bruce, Governor; S. African War, including Ladysmith, Battle of Elandslaaghte and operations in Transvaal and Free State (wounded); European War—France, 1914-1916, 1st Battle of Ypres, Festubert, Loos, Salonica, 1916-19, including occupation of Caucasus (D.S.O., despatches five times, Greek Military Cross); Brigadier, R.A., Southern Command, 1930-34; retired, 1934; Hon. Colonel 57th (Wessex) A.A. Brigade, R.A. (T.), 1933-39. *Recreations:* any field sports. *Address:* Forest Lodge, Bells Yew Green, Tunbridge Wells. [*Died* 27 *Dec.* 1958.

CAMERON, Samuel J., LL.D., M.B., F.R.C.O.G., F.R.F.P.S.; Emeritus Professor of Midwifery, Univ. of Glasgow; *b.* 7 Jan. 1878; *s.* of Murdoch Cameron, M.D., and Agnes, Wallace; *m.* 1908; one *s.* three *d.* *Educ.:* Mill Hill School; University of Glasgow. Corresponding Fellow New York Academy of Medicine; Gynæcologist, Western Infirmary, Glasgow; Consulting Obstetric Surgeon, Royal Maternity Hospital, Glasgow, and to the County of Lanark special hospitals; Consulting Obstetric Surgeon and Gynaecologist to the Royal Infirmary, Perth; late Gynaecologist to the Dumfries and Galloway Infirmary, Dumfries; late President, Obstetrical Society of Glasgow. *Publications:* several text books of obstetrics and gynaecology. *Recreations:* out-door sports, especially shooting; collecting antiques and prints. *Address:* Stobieside, Strathaven, Lanarkshire. *T.:* Drumclog 212. *Clubs:* Old Millhillians; Royal Scottish Automobile (Glasgow). [*Died* 29 *Oct.* 1959.

CAMERON, William, B.Sc. (Lond.); A.R.C.S. (Lond.); *m.*; one *s.* one *d.* *Educ.:* Allan Glen's School, Glasgow; Royal College of Science, London. Headmaster (retired) of N. Kelvinside Secondary School, Glasgow; Captain R.A.M.C. (attached); X-ray Specialist 8th (Lucknow) Division, Indian Army; Professor of Physics, St. Mungo's College, Glasgow. *Publications:* Elementary Physics,

Parts 1 and 2. *Recreations:* gardening, music. *Address:* Oakley, Bishopbriggs, Lanarkshire. *T.:* Bishopbriggs 1976. *Club:* Royal Scottish Automobile (Glasgow). [*Died* 17 *May* 1954.

CAMERON-HEAD, Francis Somerville Cameron, of Inverailort; *b.* 17 Nov. 1896; *o. s.* of late James Cameron-Head of Inverailort Castle, Inverness-shire, and Christian, *d.* and *heiress* of Duncan Cameron of Inverailort, D.L., Inverness-shire; *m.* 1942, Lucretia Pauline Rebecca Ann, *er. d.* of Charles Farrell, Druimbeag, Acharacle, Argyll. *Educ.:* Wellington College; Balliol College, Oxford; M.A. Called to Bar, Inner Temple, 1923; Member Royal Company of Archers (The Queen's Body Guard for Scotland); Maj., 2nd Inverness-shire; (West) Bn., Home Guard, 1954; J.P. Inverness-shire; Knight, of Order of St. John of Jerusalem; F.Z.S.; Royal Scottish Pipers Society. *Recreations:* shooting, fishing. *Address:* Inverailort Castle, Lochailort, Inverness-shire. *T.:* Lochailort 204. *Clubs:* Carlton; Highland (Inverness). [*Died* 14 *May* 1957.

CAMERON-SWAN, Capt. Donald; late Royal Air Force; F.R.A.S.; F.S.A. Scot.; *b.* 22 April 1863; *e. s.* of late Sir Joseph Swan, F.R.S., and 1st wife, Frances White (*d.* 1868); assumed additional surname of Cameron by Deed Poll in 1900, being maiden name of Sir Joseph's mother; *m.* 1900, Grace (*d.* 1947), *d.* of Deputy W. H. Williamson, Lieut. for City of London; two *s.* one *d.* *Educ.:* Mr. Lake's School, Caterham; New College, Eastbourne; University College, Bristol. Trained as a mechanical and electrical engineer; one of the founders of the Swan Electric Engraving Co., 1885, in which he took a leading interest for 32 years, as Partner, Proprietor, and Managing Director; served 1st Volunteer Battalion Queen's Royal West Surrey Regiment, 1915-17; Lieutenant R.N.V.R. (attached R.N.A.S.) 1917; Captain R.A.F., 1918; inventor and patentee of several improvements in photo-engraving; Medallist of Royal Photographic Society and Royal Society of Arts; awarded Grand Prix at Franco-British Exhibition, 1908; Chieftain of Clan Cameron Assoc.; Member: British Astronomical Assoc.; Scottish History Soc.; Cape Town Caledonian Society; President, Unitarian Literary Society, Cape Town; President, Astronomical Society of South Africa, 1930-31. *Publications:* Photo-engraving; Observations on Photographing Paintings and Drawings; Pioneers of Photogravure; Highland Chiefs of To-day; A Pageant of the Sun; contributions to magazines and newspapers; lectures and articles on Tristan da Cunha, which he visited, Jan. 1932, in H.M.S. Carlisle. *Recreations:* water-colour sketching, photography, astronomy, and Highland lore. *Address:* The Gables, Ravensberg Av., Newlands, Cape Town. [*Died* 19 *Aug.* 1951.

CAMMAERTS, Emile, Hon. C.B.E. 1927; Hon. LL.D. (Glasgow); Officier de l'Ordre de Léopold; Corresponding Member of the Royal Society of Literature; Professor Emeritus of Belgian Studies and Institutions in the University of London; since Oct. 1947 (Professor, 1931-47); part-time work after 1947; visiting lecturer at other Universities; *b.* Brussels; Belgian subject; *m.* Tita Brand; five *c.* (and one *s.* killed in R.A.F.). In Belgium until 1908; settled in England since that date. *Publications:* Four volumes of translations from J. Ruskin and one of G. K. Chesterton (into French); Les Bellini—An essay in art criticism; The Childhood of Christ as seen by the Primitive Masters, 1922; Les Deux Bossus, La Veillée de Noël (plays); Belgian Poems, 1915; New Belgian Poems, 1917; Messines and other Poems, 1918; Belgium, From the Roman Invasion to the Present Day, 1920; Poèmes Intimes, 1922; The Treasure House of Belgium, 1924; The Poetry of Nonsense, 1925; Discoveries in England, 1930; Rubens, Painter and Diplomat, 1931; Albert of Belgium, 1935; The Laughing Prophet; The Seven Virtues and G. K. Chesterton, 1937; The Child of Divorce, 1938; The Keystone of Europe, 1939; The Prisoner at Laeken: King Leopold, Legends and Facts, 1941; Upon This Rock, 1942; The Flower of Grass, 1944; The Peace That Was Left, 1945; Flemish Painting, 1945; (with Mrs. J. Lindley) Principalities and Powers, 1947; The Devil Takes the Chair, 1949; For Better, For Worse, 1950, The Cloud and the Silver Lining, 1952. *Address:* The Eyrie, 3 Hillside Road, Radlett. Herts. *T.:* Radlett 6764. *Club:* Athenæum, [*Died* 2 *Nov.* 1953.

CAMPAGNAC, Professor E. T., M.A.; *m.*; one *s.* *Educ.:* University College, Oxford (Classical Scholar). Was Warden of Manchester University Settlement; Assistant Lecturer in Classics at Cardiff and one of H.M.'s Inspectors of Schools; Professor of Education, University of Liverpool till Sept. 1938. *Publications:* The Cambridge Platonists; Poetry and Teaching; The Teaching of Composition; Lancashire Legends; Hoole's Art of Teaching; A Theory of Education; Practical Problems in Education; Converging Paths; Sadoleto on Education (with K. Forbes); Brinsley's Ludus Literarius; Elements of Religion and Religious Teaching; Society and Solitude; Mulcaster's Elementarie; Education; Comenius: Way of Light; Reports and Papers on Educational Subjects. *Address:* Little Close, Campden, Glos. [*Died* 10 *June* 1952.

CAMPBELL, Alexander McCulloch, C.M.G. 1944; *b.* 15 July 1879; *s.* of late John Campbell, Luing and Greenock; *m.* 1915, Helen Murdoch, *d.* of Wm. Murray, Glasgow and London: one *s.* *Educ.:* Greenock. Commenced with Jas. Gardiner & Co., Shipowners, in their Greenock office; joined Union-Castle Line in Cape Town, 1904; Head of Freight, Durban, 1921; Asst. Agent, 1925; Agent at Mombasa, 1927; Joint Chief Agent, Cape Town, 1934; Chief Agent for South and East Africa, 1938-49; Director, 1943-1949; Representative of Ministry of Shipping, afterwards Ministry of War Transport, 1939-43. *Recreation:* golf. *Address:* Argyll, Harfield Road, Kenilworth, Cape, South Africa. *T.A.:* Campbell, Unicastle, Capetown. *T.:* Cape Town 74650 *Clubs:* City, Civil Service (Cape Town). [*Died* 20 *Feb.* 1955.

CAMPBELL, Admiral Alexander Victor, C.B. 1924; D.S.O. 1917; M.V.O. 1910; *b.* 1874; *s.* of late L. A. Campbell; *m.* 1932, Elsie Kathleen, *widow* of Major Harry Gordon and *d.* of late F. G. Kennedy. Entered Navy, 1887; Lieut. 1894; Commander, 1905; Captain, 1913; Rear-Admiral, 1923; Vice-Admiral, 1928; Rear-Admiral in charge and Admiral Supt., Malta Dockyard, 1926-28; served Dardanelles, 1915 (despatches, D.S.O.); retd. list, 1928; Adm., retd., 1932. *Address:* 29 Bramham Gdns., S.W.5. *T.:* Frobisher 5421. [*Died* 2 *June* 1957.

CAMPBELL, Archibald Y., M.A.; classical scholar; *b.* 18 April 1885; *e. s.* of late George Campbell, Clydesdale Bank, Blantyre; *m.* 1912, Olwen, *y. d.* of late Professor James Ward, Sc.D.; one *s.* two *d.* *Educ.:* Hamilton Academy; Fettes College, Edinburgh; St. John's College, Cambridge; 1st division, 1st class, Classical Tripos, 1907. Assistant-Lecturer, Liverpool, 1908-9; Lecturer, University College, Reading, 1909-11; Fellowship, St. John's College, Cambridge, 1910; and Lectureship, 1911-22; Gladstone Professor of Greek at the University of Liverpool, 1922-50; taught (part-time) at University of Bristol, 1954. *Publications:* Horace: A New Interpretation, 1924; Poems, 1926; Horati Carmina XX, 1934; The Agamemnon of Aeschylus, edition, 1936; verse translation, 1940; edition of Horace's Odes and Epodes, with Latin notes, 1945; larger edition with

CAMMIDGE, Percy John, M.D. See page xxviii.

English notes, 1953; edition of Euripides' Helena, 1950; many contributions to classical periodicals. *Recreations:* folk-dancing, swimming; but now mainly walking, and picture galleries. *Address:* 7 Bulstrode Gardens, Cambridge. *Club:* University (Liverpool). [*Died* 19 *Feb.* 1958.

CAMPBELL, Sir Archibald Young Gipps, K.C.I.E., *cr.* 1932 (C.I.E. 1911); C.S.I. 1927; C.B.E. 1920; Knight of Grace, Order of St. John of Jerusalem, 1916; V.D.; M.A.; F.R.A.S.; I.C.S. (retired); *b.* 18 May 1872; *s.* of late Archibald S. Campbell; *m.* 1910, Frances Irene, *d.* of late Rev. H. Savill Young of Mallards Court, Stokenchurch, Bucks; three *s.* *Educ.:* Westminster; Trinity College, Cambridge (Scholar, 9th Wrangler, Tyson Medallist, Smith's Prizeman). Entered Indian Civil Service, 1895; served in Madras Presidency as Assistant and Head Assistant Collector, 1896-1902; Under-Secretary to Govt., 1902-6; Private Secretary to Governor of Madras, 1906-12; Collector, 1912-1913, 1917-18; President, Corporation of Madras, 1913; Member, Weights and Measures Committee, India, 1913-14; Secretary to Madras Govt., 1918-19, 1923; Director of Industries, 1919-21; Retrenchment Officer, Coorg, 1922; Member of Board of Revenue, Madras, 1922-1924; Retrenchment Officer, Rajputana, Central India, etc., 1923; Chief Secretary to Madras Govt., 1925-30; Temporary Member of Council, Madras, 1926, 1927, 1928, and 1929; Member of Executive Council, Madras, 1930-35; formerly Major, Southern Provinces Mounted Rifles (India); General Secretary to British Red Cross in France 1915-16 (despatches); founded and organised British Red Cross Central Prisoners of War Organisation, 1916. *Address:* 49 Campden Hill Court, Kensington, W.8. *T.:* Western 6833. [*Died* 30 *Oct.* 1957.

CAMPBELL, Mrs. Bruce; *see* Wilson, Grace Margaret.

CAMPBELL, Brigadier Sir Bruce Atta, K.C.B., *cr.* 1948 (C.B. 1938); C.B.E. 1942; T.D.; Lord Lieutenant of Argyllshire since 1949; *b.* 1888; *m.* 1913, Margaret Helen (*d.* 1954), *d.* of Lieut.-Col. J. Macrae-Gilstrap, of Eilean Donan; two *s.* one *d.* *Educ.:* Glenalmond; Eton; Trinity Hall, Cambridge. Joined Scottish Horse, 1908, commanding, 1928-33; served European War, 1914-19; Bt.-Col. 1932; commanded 8th (Argyllshire) Bn. Argyll and Sutherland Highlanders, 1933-38, Hon. Col. 1940-53; Col. T.A. 1939. Served, 1939-46; Acting Brig. Comd. Inf. Bde., 1939-40; Hon. Brig. 1946. D.L. 1932, J.P. 1924, Argyllshire; Chairman Territorial Army Association of the County of Argyll, 1930-48. *Address:* Arduaine, Argyll. *Club:* New (Edinburgh). [*Died* 28 *Aug.* 1954.

CAMPBELL, Lieut.-Col. Hon. Sir Cecil James Henry, K.B.E., *cr.* 1947; C.M.G. 1930; late Intelligence Corps; Companies Director, Egypt; Managing Director Marconi Radio Telegraph Coy., Egypt, 1933, retd. 1947; *b.* 1891; 2nd *s.* of 1st Baron Glenavy; *m.* 1934, Mrs. Martha Evelyn Audrey Courtney (from whom he obtained a divorce, 1942). *Educ.:* Shrewsbury School; Oxford Univ. Rep. Oxford Univ., British Isles, Irish Free State, and Egypt at lawn tennis; Called to Bar, Gray's Inn, 1917; Legal Secy. to Financial Adviser to Egyptian Govt., 1922-1930; Legal Counsellor to Residency, Egypt, 1930-32. Pres. Brit. Chamber of Commerce of Egypt, 1945-. *Address:* 9A Rue Ahmad Hishmat Pasha, Zamalek, Gezira, Egypt. *Clubs:* Constitutional, All England Lawn Tennis, International Lawn Tennis, Anglo-Egyptian Society; Union, Royal Yacht (Alexandria); Mohamed Aly, Turf (Cairo); Gezira Sporting. [*Died* 11 *May* 1952.

CAMPBELL, Sir (Charles) Duncan Macnair, 2nd Bt., *cr.* 1939; M.A., A.C.A.; *b.* Samarang, Java, Dutch E.I., 12 Sept. 1906; *s.* of Sir Edward Taswell Campbell, 1st Bt., and Edith Jane Warren (*d.* 1951); *S.* father, 1945; *m.* 1941, Gwendolen Olive Mary Gladstone, *d.* of James Martin; no *c.* *Educ.:* Dulwich Coll.; Pembroke College, Cambridge. Chartered Accountant, 1931; spent two years with Cash Stone & Co. (Chartered Accountants), 48 Copthall Avenue, London; next two years on specialised accountancy with Arthur Collins, in Westminster; joined staff of United Kingdom Gas Corporation Ltd., 1936; Manager and Secretary for their subsidiary the Caledonian Gas Corporation, Edinburgh, 1937-44; Ministry of Food, 1944. Joined Honourable Artillery Company, 1928; 2nd Lt. 1932; R. of O. since 1935. *Recreations:* golf, cricket, tennis, rifle shooting. *Address:* Flat 2, 15 Lindfield Gardens, N.W.3. *Club:* M.C.C. [*Died* 16 *Jan.* 1954 (*ext.*).

CAMPBELL, Colin Algernon; company director; former Director of Westminster Bank Ltd.; *b.* 1874; *e. s.* of William Middleton Campbell, Colgrain, Dunbartonshire; *m.* 1911, Mary C. G., *er. d.* of J. B. Barrington, Ashroe, Co. Limerick; four *s.* one *d.* *Educ.:* Eton. *Address:* Underriver House, nr. Sevenoaks, Kent. *T.:* Hildenborough 2123. [*Died* 3 *Jan.* 1957.

CAMPBELL, Colin George Pelham, J.P., D.L.; *b.* 31 May 1872; *e. s.* of John Campbell (*d.* 1887) and Adela Harriet, 2nd *d.* of Lord Chas. Pelham-Clinton; *m.* 1893, Lady Ileene Frances Cairns (*d.* 1946), 2nd *d.* of 13th Earl of Huntingdon; two *s.* Late Lt. Scots Guards. Owns 35,186 acres. *Address:* Stonefield, Tarbert, Loch Fyne. [*Died* 8 *Feb.* 1955.

CAMPBELL, Douglas Colin, C.I.E. 1946; retired; *b.* 28 May 1891; *s.* of late J. Colin Campbell, Edinburgh; *m.* 1920, Mabel Patricia, *d.* of late Sam. Gilliland, Belfast; two *d.* *Educ.:* Trinity College, Glenalmond. Served European War, 1914-18, with Royal Scots and Black Watch; demobilised 1919, with rank of Major. Chartered Accountant, 1919. Director of Commercial Audit, Govt. of India, 1925-32; Chief Accounts Officer, Indian State Railways, 1932-39; Controller of Railway Accounts, Govt. of India, 1939-1946; Director, Railway Board, Delhi, 1942-1946; Principal Control Officer, Control Commission, Germany, 1946-48. *Address:* 8 Church Way, West Tarring, Worthing, Sussex. *T.:* 6241. [*Died* 30 *June* 1957.

CAMPBELL, Lt.-Col. Duncan, of Inverneill, J.P. Co. of Argyll; *b.* 15 Jan. 1880; *e. s.* of Colonel Duncan Campbell of Inverneill, O.B.E., D.L., J.P. (*d.* 1922), and Isabel (*d.* 1911), *d.* of J. A. Tobin of Eastham House, Cheshire; *m.* 1st, 1905, Ethel, *e. d.* of John I. Waterbury of Morristown, New Jersey, U.S.A. (marriage dissolved, 1934); three *s.*; 2nd, 1940, Ada Brookman. *Educ.:* Cargilfield, Edinburgh; Rugby School; Pembroke College, Oxford. Employed in a shipbuilding firm, 1902-06; Secretary to the Western Electric Co., 1910-13. Raised and commanded Reserve Battalion, 8th Argyll & Sutherland Highlanders, 1915-16; served European War with B.E.F., 1916-17. *Recreations:* fishing, shooting, golf. *Heir:* *e. s.* John Lorne Campbell [*b.* 1 Oct. 1906; *m.* 1935, Margaret Fay, *y.d.* of late Henry Clay Shaw, Glen Shaw, Pennsylvania]. *Address:* Inverneill, Ardrishaig, Argyll. [*Died* 19 *Aug.* 1954.

CAMPBELL, Sir Duncan M.; *see* Campbell, Sir C. D. M.

CAMPBELL, Rev. Edward Fitzhardinge, D.S.O. 1918; Vicar of Great Glen with Great Stretton, Leicestershire, 1933-52, retired; *b.* 17 Jan. 1880; *e. s.* of Rev. Ed. Fitzhardinge Campbell, M.A., and *g.s.* of Very Rev. Theo. F. Campbell, D.D.,

Dean of Dromore; *m.* 1917, Edith Mary, *d.* of late Edward Dunk, Gravesend; two *d.* *Educ.:* Trinity College, Dublin; B.A. with honours. Curate of St. Mary's, Dublin, 1904; Chaplain to Forces, 4th class, 1906 served in England three years and S. Africa for five years; embarked with B.E.F. for France in Aug. 1914; Chaplain 3rd class, 1916, and Deputy Assist. Chaplain General, temp. rank 2nd class Chaplain, 1917 (despatches twice, D.S.O.); Chaplain, 2nd class, Jan. 1921; 1st class, 1926; Assistant Chaplain-General, Malta, 1927; Egypt, 1929; Western Command, Chester, 1931; retired pay, 1932; Chaplain to High Sheriff of Leicestershire, 1937, 1938 and 1948; C. C. Leicestershire, 1938. *Recreations:* Irish International Rugby footballer, playing for his school XV. and the International team same year, 1899. *Address:* The Red House, Staverton, Daventry, Northamptonshire. [*Died* 13 *Dec.* 1957.

CAMPBELL, Vice-Adm. Gordon, V.C. 1917; D.S.O. 1916; Younger Brother of Trinity House; *b.* 1886; *s.* of Col. Frederick Campbell, C.B.; *m.* 1911, Mary Jeanne, *d.* of H. V. S. Davids, Hillier House, Guildford; one *s.* one *d.* Served European War, 1914-17 (despatches, V.C., D.S.O. and two bars, Croix de Guerre, Officier Légion d'Honneur); commanded battle-cruiser Tiger, 1925-27; served as Naval A.D.C. to the King, Jan.-April 1928; Rear-Admiral, 1928; retired list, 1928; War of 1939-45; M.P. (Nat.) Burnley, 1931-35; Vice-Admiral, retired, 1932. *Publications:* My Mystery Ships, 1928; Number Thirteen, 1932; Sailormen All, 1933; Brave Men All, 1935; Captain James Cook, 1936; A Son of the Sea, 1936; Witch of the Wave, 1937; Abandon Ship; Two Cadets; The Great Bluff; Dog-Nelson, A.B., 1938; The Book of Flags, 1950. *Club:* Bath. [*Died* 3 *Oct.* 1953.

CAMPBELL, Sir Gordon (Huntly), K.B.E., *cr.* 1920; *b.* 1864; 3rd *s.* of late Hon. Alexander Campbell, M.L.C., Sydney, N.S.W.; *m.* 1902, Ada, *d.* of late Robert Landale; two *d.* Chairman of Headquarters Collection Committee of the British Red Cross Society and the Order of St. John, 1917-19; Chairman of W. Weddel & Co. Ltd.; Director Employers' Liability Assurance Corporation, Ltd., and of the Clerical, Medical, and General Life Assurance Society. *Address:* 6 The Manor, Davies Street, W.1. *T.:* Mayfair 2413. *Club:* Bath. [*Died* 27 *Feb.* 1953.

CAMPBELL, Major Sir Guy Colin, 4th Bt., *cr.* 1815; late King's Royal Rifle Corps (60th Rifles); *b.* 31 Jan. 1885; *e. s.* of Sir Guy Theophilus Campbell, 3rd Bt., and Nina, *d.* of late Frederick Lehmann and Nina, *d.* of Robert Chambers, author of Vestiges of Creation; *S.* father, 1931; *m.* 1909, Mary (*d.* 1948), *o. d.* of late Halswell Kemeys-Tynte, of Halswell Park, Somerset, and Cefn Mably, Glamorgan; twin *s.*; *m.* 1955, Mrs. Lilian Allan, *o. c.* of Aug. Peeters van Nieuwenrode, Pachthof, Nieuwenrode, Belgium. *Educ.:* St. Aubyns, Rottingdean; Eton; St. Andrews Univ. Served European War, 1914-18, with K.R.R.C. and on staff of 36th Ulster Division, battles Messines, Paschendael, Cambrai, March 1918, Ypres 1918, and on Staff Meerut Division, India, 1918-19; War of 1939-45 with 1st Motor Training Battalion K.R.R.C. Editorial Staff The Times, 1920-40. *Publications:* Golf for Beginners, 1922; contributions to Country Life, Chambers's Journal, Sunday Express, Golf Illustrated, Golf Monthly, Weekly Sketch. *Recreations:* (former) cricket, Eton XI 1902, 3, 4, Capt. 1904, I.Z., M.C.C.; golf (semi-finalist Amateur Championship, St. Andrews, 1907; International for Scotland, 1909, 10, 11), interested in golf course construction, reconstruction, maintenance and landscaping; sports grounds; country clubs. *Heir:* *s.* Guy Theophilus Halswell Campbell, M.C., Major K.R.R.C. (60th Rifles), seconded (El Kaimakam Bey) Sudan Defence Force, *b.* 18 Jan. 1909. *Address:* 49 Hill St., W.1; c/o Lloyds Bank (Cox's and King's Branch), 6 Pall Mall, S.W.1. *Clubs:* M.C.C.; New (Edinburgh); Royal and Ancient (St. Andrews). [*Died* 2 *Oct.* 1960.

CAMPBELL, Sir Harold (Alfred Maurice), Kt. 1957; C.M.G. 1953; Editor of The Age, Melbourne, since 1939; Trustee of Victorian Public Library; Director: David Syme & Co. Ltd.; General Television Corporation; Australian Associated Press; *b.* 25 Sept. 1892; *s.* of Frederick J. and Elizabeth Campbell; *m.* 1921, Queenie May (*d.* 1949), *d.* of Charles Davy, Wiluna; two *s.* one *d.* *Educ.:* Bunbury, W.A. Entered journalism through provincial press, W. Australia. Served with A.I.F. in France (M.M.). Political writer on Melbourne Herald; leader writer, Melbourne Age, 1926-38. Member of Australian Delegation to San Francisco Conference, 1945. *Address:* Cliveden Mansions, East Melbourne, Australia. *Clubs:* Melbourne, Savage (Melbourne). [*Died* 31 *July* 1959.

CAMPBELL of Airds, Bt. Col. and Hon. Col. Ian Maxwell, C.B.E. 1927; T.D. 1925; late 8th (Argyllshire) Bn., Argyll & Sutherland Highlanders, T.A.; Commander, 1922-29; *b.* 1870; 2nd *s.* of late Col. Fred Campbell, C.B., of Airds, Argyll; *m.* 1901, Hilda Mary, *d.* of C. F. Wade, Barrister; three *s.* *Educ.:* Dulwich College. London Scottish R.V. 1894-99; Lieut. Argyll and Bute R.G.A. (Vol.) 1899-1907; Capt. 8th A. & S. H. 1914; served European War, 1914-18 (wounded); Brevet Major, King's Birthday Honours, 1919; Major, 1920; Lt.-Col. 1922; Brevet Col., 1926; retired, 1929; Hon. Col. 1929-35; Chairman Board of Governors St. Dunstan's College, Catford, 1924-50; Chevalier de la Légion d'Honneur, 1931. Chairman Wine and Spirit Assoc., 1921-22 and 1941-45. *Publications:* Wayward Tendrils of the Vine, 1947; Reminiscences of a Vintner, 1950. *Recreations:* reading, writing, etc. In youth all games, especially cricket. *Address:* Ridge House, Quill Hall Lane, Amersham, Bucks. *Clubs:* M.C.C., I Zingari. [*Died* 6 *March* 1954.

CAMPBELL, Ignatius Roy Dunnachie; *b.* Durban, S. Africa, 2 Oct. 1901; *s.* of Dr. Samuel George Campbell and Margaret Dunnachie; *m.* 1922, Mary Margaret Garman; two *d.* *Educ.:* Durban High School. Saved the Carmelite Archives of Toledo during the siege (mentioned three times during Spanish War by General Quiepo de Llano). Won the steer-throwing of Provence, 1932 and 1933. Jousted for Martigues, 1928-1931. Hon. Pres. Sociedade Tauromaquica of Mocambique and ex-Rejoneader of bulls. Awarded Silver picador's jacket, Madrid. Volunteered as a ranker and served in the Imperial Army in E. and N. Africa till disabled and discharged in 1944 with the rank of sergeant. Served on Literary Advisory Board of B.B.C., 1945-49. Has made extensive lecture tours; F.R.S.L. 1947; Foyle Prize, London, 1951; elected Soci of Provençal Poets, 1954, and Mem. of Felibrige, Avignon; D.Litt. (*h.c.*) Natal, 1954. *Publications:* The Flaming Terrapin; The Wayzgoose; Adamastor; Flowering Reeds; Mithraic Emblems; The Georgiad; Taurine Provence; Broken Record; Flowering Rifle; Talking Bronco; Collected Poems; Poems of St. John of the Cross; Light on a Dark Horse (Autobiography); Federico Garcia Lorca (a study); Portugal, 1957 (posthumous); translations: Cousin Bazilio (Portuguese); Helge Krog's Plays (Norwegian); Baudelaire's Poems (French); The Mamba's Precipice; Tendencias de la literatura inglesa moderna (Spanish). *Recreations:* reading, writing poetry and prose, painting. *Address:* Linhó, Sintra, Portugal.

Clubs: La Joyeuse Lance Martegale; Tauromaquico (Lourenço Marques); Peña Villalta (Toledo, Spain). [*Died* 22 *April* 1957.

CAMPBELL, James; General Secretary, National Union of Railwaymen, since 1953; *b.* 17 April 1895; Scottish. *Educ.:* elementary schools, Carlisle and Glasgow. Served European War, 1914-18. Glasgow & South Western Railway Co., 1917-21, L.M.S.R., 1921-38; N.U.R.: Branch Secretary; Executive Committee Member; Organiser, 1938; Chief Organiser, Ireland; Assistant General Secretary, 1948. Member of T.U.C. General Council. *Recreation:* reading. *Address:* Unity House, Euston Road, N.W.1. *T.:* Euston 4771. [*Died* 6 *Nov.* 1957.

CAMPBELL, Rear-Admiral James Douglas, M.V.O. 1920; O.B.E. 1919; R.N., retired; *b.* 1882; *m.* 1911, Lilian Alice, *o. d.* of late Sir Joseph Outerbridge; one *s.* one *d.* Lieut. 1903; Lt.-Comdr. 1911; Comdr., 1915; Capt. 1920; Rear-Adm. 1933; Director of Navigation, Admiralty, 1932-33; retired list, 1933. *Address:* 1 Hughenden Drive, Glasgow, W.2. [*Died* 23 *April* 1954.

CAMPBELL, Dame Janet Mary, D.B.E., *cr.* 1924; M.D., M.S. (Lond.); Hon. D.Hy. (Durham); J.P. Glos.; *m.* 1934, Michael Heseltine (*d.* 1952). *Educ.:* London School of Medicine for Women. Late House Surgeon and House Physician, Royal Free Hospital; Senior R.M.O. Belgrave Hospital for Children; Assistant Medical Inspector under London County Council; Senior Medical Officer Board of Education; Senior Medical Officer for Maternity and Child Welfare, Ministry of Health, and Chief Woman Medical Adviser, Board of Education, 1919-1934; retired 1934; Member of Women's Committee, Liquor Control Board, 1915; Medical Sub-committee Health of Munition Workers' Committee; Medical Member of War Cabinet Committee on Women in Industry, 1918; Member of the Committee on the Training of Midwives, 1928; and of the Committee on Maternal Mortality, 1928; Member of Departmental Committee on Hospital Construction, 1933; late Member of Health Committee, League of Nations. *Publications:* Report to Carnegie U.K. Trust on the Physical Welfare of Mothers and Children, 1917; Official Reports on the Arrangements for Teaching Obstetrics and Gynæcology in the Medical Schools, 1923; The Training of Midwives, 1923; Maternal Mortality, 1924; Protection of Motherhood, 1927; Infant Mortality, 1929; Maternity Services, 1935. *Address:* 50 Paultons Square, Chelsea, S.W.3. *T.:* Flaxman 9195. [*Died* 27 *Sept.* 1954.

CAMPBELL, Sir John Alexander Coldstream, 7th Bt. of Aberuchill and Kilbryde, Dunblane, Perthshire, *cr.* 1667; Capt., late 1/3 Scottish Horse; *s.* of 6th Bt. and Edith Arabella Jauncey (*d.* 1884); *b.* 27 June 1877; *S.* father, 1914; *m.* 1921, Janet Thomson Hood, *o. d.* of James Moffat, Well Hall, Hamilton, Lanark.; two *s.* *Heir:* *s.* Colin Moffat [*b.* 4 Aug. 1925; *m.* 1952, Mary Anne Chichester, *er. d.* of Brig. G. A. Bain, Sandy Lodge, Chagford, Devon]. *Address:* Castlenau, Charing, Kent. [*Died* 21 *Jan.* 1960.

CAMPBELL, Sir John Home-Purves-Hume-, 8th Bt., *cr.* 1665; late Royal Naval Division; *b.* 9 Aug. 1879; *S.* *cousin,* 1894; assumed additional surnames of Hume-Campbell, *m.* 1901, Emily Jane (whom he divorced, 1919; she died 1929), *o. d.* of late Rev. R. Digby Ram; two *d.* *Educ.:* Eton. Entered army, 2nd Life Guards, 1899; Lieut. 1900; served South Africa, 1902; retired, 1903; served European War, Dardanelles, 1914-15 (wounded). *Heir:* none. [*Died* 25 *Feb.* 1960 (*ext.*).

CAMPBELL, Captain Leveson (Granville Byron Alexander), D.S.O. 1916; late R.N.; *b.* 1881; *m.* 1906, Norah, *d.* of Rev. Robert Hereford; one *s.* two *d.* Entered Navy, 1897; Commander, 1915; served European War, 1914-18 (despatches, D.S.O.); retired list, 1923; Capt. retired, 1926; Secretary to St. Enodoc Golf Club, Cornwall, 1925-35. Called up as Capt., R.N., Aug. 1939; served in Basra and Hong Kong till 25 Dec. 1941, when taken (on fall of Hong Kong) by Japanese; P.O.W. till Aug. 1945; retired again (invalided out), 1946. *Address:* Fern Cottage, Chilham, E. Kent. [*Died* 20 *Oct.* 1951.

CAMPBELL, Peter, M.B.(Edin.), L.R.C.S., L.R.C.P. 1877; retired; Consulting Surgeon for Diseases of the Throat and Ear, Dundee Royal Infirmary; late Surgeon and Agent for the Admiralty; Medical Referee for the Board of Trade; *b.* near Crieff, Perthshire, 1856; *m.* 1904, Lucy Elizabeth, M.A. (Lond.) (*d.* 1935), fifth *d.* of late Christopher Worsfold of Dover; two *s.* one *d.* *Educ.:* Perthshire; Edinburgh. *Recreations:* golf, curling. *Address:* Balmerino, Fife. [*Died* 3 *Jan.* 1951.

CAMPBELL, Rev. Reginald John, D.D. Oxon 1919; Canon Emeritus of Chichester since 1946; *b.* London, 1867; *s.* and *g.s.* of Nonconformist Ministers, Ulster Protestants of Scottish extraction; *m.* 1st, Mary Elizabeth (*d.* 1924); 2nd, 1927, Ethel Gertrude Smith (*d.* 1943). *Educ.:* privately; University College, Nottingham; Christ Church, Oxford. Graduate in Honours in School of Modern History and Political Science, Oxon. Entered Congregational Ministry, 1895; Minister of City Temple, London, 1903-15; ordained into ministry of Church of England, 1916, and attached to staff of Birmingham Cathedral; Hon. Chaplain to Bishop of Birmingham, 1916; Vicar of Christchurch, Westminster, 1917-21; Incumbent of Holy Trinity, Brighton, 1924-30; Prebendary of Heathfield and Canon-Teacher in Diocese of Chichester, 1929; Residentiary Canon of Chichester, 1930-36; Chancellor of Chichester Cathedral, 1930-46; Chaplain and theological lecturer of Bishop Otter College, Chichester, 1933-36. *Publications:* The Restored Innocence, 1898; The Making of an Apostle, 1899; The Keys of the Kingdom, 1899; A Faith for To-day, 1900; City Temple Sermons, 1903; Sermons to Individuals, 1904; The Song of Ages, 1905; The New Theology, 1907; Christianity and the Social Order, 1908; Thursday Mornings at the City Temple, 1908; The Ladder of Christ, 1912; With our Troops in France, 1916; The War and the Soul, 1916; A Spiritual Pilgrimage, 1916; Words of Comfort, 1917; Problems of Life, 1919; Life of Christ, 1921; Life of Thomas Arnold, 1927; Vision and Life, 1928; Biography of Livingstone, 1929; Christian Faith in Modern Light, 1932; The Call of Christ, 1933; Grace Abounding, 1934; The Story of Christmas, 1935; The Peace of God, 1936; The Life of the World to Come, 1948; many published articles, sermons, and addresses. *Address:* Heatherdene, Fairwarp, Uckfield, Sussex. *T.:* Nutley 34. [*Died* 1 *March* 1956.

CAMPBELL, Rt. Hon. Sir Ronald Hugh, P.C. 1939; G.C.M.G., *cr.* 1940 (K.C.M.G., *cr.* 1936; C.M.G. 1917); *b.* 27 Sept. 1883; *e. s.* of Sir F. A. Campbell, K.C.M.G., C.B., Assistant Under-Secretary of State for Foreign Affairs, 1906-11, and Dora Edith Hammersley; *m.* 1908, Helen Graham (*d.* 1949); one *s.* Entered the Foreign Office, 1907; Private Secretary to Lord Carnock, 1913-16, to Lord Hardinge of Penshurst, 1916-19, and to Marquess Curzon of Kedleston, 1919-20; Counsellor of Embassy, 1928; H.M. Minister at Paris, 1929-35; at Belgrade, 1935-39; Ambassador to France, 1939-40, and to Portugal, 1940-45; retired, 1945. *Address:* Stanswood Cottage, Fawley, Hants. *Club:* Turf. [*Died* 15 *Nov.* 1953.

CAMPBELL, Sidney George, M.A. Edin. and Cantab.; Fellow since 1902, Bursar, 1913-37, Lecturer since 1906, Christ's College, Cambridge; *b.* 30 July 1875; *y. s.* of late Thomas Callender Campbell, J.P. and late Agnes Callender; *m.* 1909, Kathleen Mabel, *d.* of late Rev. C. F. Moss; one *d.* *Educ.:* Londonderry Academy; Universities of Edinburgh (Gray Scholar, Classics, Vans Dunlop Scholar, Sanskrit), Cambridge and Göttingen. Lecturer Epigraphy and Dialects, University of Cambridge, 1906-39. *Publications:* edition of Livy XXVII, revised edition Sandys, Latin Epigraphy. *Address:* Eskaheen, 64 Storey's Way, Cambridge. [*Died* 24 *July* 1956.

CAMPBELL, Walter Stanley (Pen-name, **Stanley Vestal**), Research Professor, The State University of Oklahoma; *b.* Severy, Kansas, 15 Aug. 1887; *s.* of Walter Mallory Vestal and Isabella Louise Wood; *m.* 1917, Isabel Jones; two *d.* *Educ.:* Southwestern State College, Weatherford, Oklahoma; Rhodes Scholar, Merton College, Oxford, Honour School of English Language and Literature, B.A., M.A. Teacher and writer (chiefly upon Western American Life); Public Schools (Male High Schools) Louisville, Ky. 1911-14; Research among Red Indians in Oklahoma, 1914-15; Instructor in English, University of Oklahoma, 1915-17; First R.O.T.C. summer 1917; Commissioned Captain, Field Artillery, 15 Aug. 1917; C.O. Battery F and Battery A, 335th F.A. 87th Div. A.E.F.; Acting Battalion C.O. in France; discharged March 1919; Fellowship to Yaddo, summer 1927; Guggenheim Memorial Fellow, 1930-31; Phi Beta Kappa (Hon.) 1937; Oklahoma Hall of Fame, 1942; Fellow, Society of American Historians, 1948; Fellow, Rockefeller Foundation, 1945. *Publications:* Books; Fandango; Ballads of the Old West, 1927; Happy Hunting Grounds, 1928; Kit Carson, The Happy Warrior of the Old West, a biography, 1928; 'Dobe Walls, a Story of Kit Carson's Southwest, 1929; Sitting Bull, Champion of the Sioux, a biography, 1932; Warpath, The True Story of the Fighting Sioux Told in a Biography of Chief White Bull, 1933; New Sources of Indian History, 1934; The Wine Room Murder, 1935; Mountain Men, 1937; Revolt on the Border, 1936; Professional Writing, 1938; The Old Santa Fe Trail, 1939; Writing Magazine Fiction, 1940; King of the Fur Traders, 1940; Short Grass Country, 1941; Bigfoot Wallace, a biography, 1942; Writing Non-Fiction, 1944; The Missouri, 1945; Jim Bridger, Mountain Man, a biography, 1946; Warpath and Council Fire, 1948; Writing: Advice and Devices, 1950; Queen of Cowtowns: Dodge City 1952; Joe Meek, the Merry Mountain Man, 1952; The Book Lover's Southwest: A Guide to Good Reading, 1955; also books edited. Contributor to Adventure, the American Anthropologist, The Saturday Review of Literature, etc. *Recreations:* riding, polo, motoring, hunting. *Address:* The University of Oklahoma, Norman, Oklahoma, U.S.A. [*Died* 25 *Dec.* 1957.

CAMPBELL, William, F.R.S.(S.Af.); M.B., Ch.B., B.Sc. (Pub. Health); late M.O. to Mandated Territories of Ovamboland and the Kaokoveld for the Administration of S.W. Africa; late Wernher-Beit Prof. of Bacteriology, University of Cape Town; Hon. Bacteriologist, Groote-Schuur Hospital, Cape Town; Consulting Bacteriologist, Rondebosch and Mowbray Hospital and Woodstock Hospital; *b.* Leith, 9 June 1889; *s.* of Rev. J. Kennedy Campbell, M.A., and Anne, *d.* of late James Tait of Inkstack; *m.* Gladys Frankland, *d.* of C. C. Dodgshun, Headingley, Leeds; two *s.* *Educ.:* Daniel Stewart's College, Edinburgh; Universities of Edinburgh, London, and Paris. John Aitken Carlyle Scholar (Anatomy and Chemistry), 1907; University Medallist in Botany, Zoology, Chemistry, Physics, and Physiology, 1906-8; M.B., Ch. B. (with first class honours), 1911; B.Sc. (Public Health), 1913; Pathologist, Royal Hospital for Sick Children, Edinburgh; Assistant to Professor of Public Health in connection with the Bacteriological work of the City of Edinburgh, 1912-14; Assistant to Professor of Pathology, University of Edinburgh, 1914-19; Cholera Officer and Officer in charge of British Bacteriological Laboratory, Cape Helles, Dardanelles, 1915-16; Officer in Charge Quarantine Laboratory, Suez, 1916; Officer in Charge Bacteriological Laboratory No. 19, General Hospital, Alexandria, and O/C Egyptian centre for the collection and preservation of specimens for the War Office (No. 21, General Hospital, Alexandria), 1916-19; pathologist to the Pellagra Commission, 1918; consulting pathologist, Alex. Dist. E.E.F. 1916-19; pathologist to City of Bradford, 1919-24; bacteriologist, St. Luke's Hospital, Bradford, 1919-24; control-bacteriologist, Government Wool (Anthrax) Disinfecting Station (Home Office), Liverpool, 1920-24; Lecturer in Industrial Pathology and Medicine Technical College, Bradford, 1922-24; Extern. Examiner, Government School of Medicine, Cairo, 1918-19; University of the Witwatersrand, 1924-41; Despatches, 1916 and 1919; Member of the South African National Committee of the International Union of Biological Sciences, 1927-32; conducted special investigation into the causes of Morbidity and Mortality at Tsumeb and Abenab, South-West Africa, 1930; Member Health Commission appointed to investigate the health conditions of South-West Africa, 1945-46; Pres. Cape Western Branch, Medical Association of South Africa (B.M.A.), 1933; Member of Council of the Royal Society of South Africa, 1931; Member of Cape Hospital Board, 1933-34; President University Club, Cape Town, 1934; Member of Federal Council of Medical Association of South Africa, 1935-41. *Publications:* papers in medical journals; in Official (Crown) Publications, etc. *Recreations:* golf, swimming. *Address:* Groenberg, Hout Bay, C.P. *T.:* 9-4146. [*Died* 18 *March* 1953.

CAMPBELL, Major William Charles, D.S.O. 1917; M.C.; late R.A.F.; Deputy-Chairman, Crosse & Blackwell (Holdings), Ltd.; Chairman: British Vinegars, Ltd., Champion & Slee, Ltd., Sarsons, Ltd., Plaistowe & Co., Ltd.; Chairman: Brighton & Hove Stadium Ltd., Brighton & Hove Albion Football Club, Ltd. Sometime Chief Instructor, School of Military Aeronautics (European War), 1914-18 (despatches, M.C., D.S.O.). *Address:* 78 Furze Croft, Hove 2, Sussex. [*Died* 26 *Feb.* 1958.

CAMPION, 1st Baron, *cr.* 1950, of Bowes; **Gilbert Francis Montriou Campion,** G.C.B., *cr.* 1948 (K.C.B., *cr.* 1938; C.B. 1932); *b.* Simla, 1882; *s.* of late John Montriou Campion; *m.* Hilda Mary, *d.* of late W. A. Spafford. *Educ.:* Bedford School; Hertford Coll., Oxford. 1st Cl. Mods., 1st. Cl. Lit. Hum.; Hon. Fell., 1946; Hon. D.C.L. (Oxf.), 1950. House of Commons Offices, 1906; 2nd Clerk Assistant, 1921; Clerk Assistant, 1930; Clerk, 1937-48. Clerk of Consultative Assembly of Council of Europe, 1949. *Publication:* Introduction to Procedure of House of Commons, 1929 and 1947; (jointly) European Parliamentary Procedure, 1953. Contributor to Halsbury's Laws of England (2nd ed.); Editor of May's Parliamentary Practice (14th and 15th edns.). *Address:* Little Bowes, Abinger Hammer, nr. Dorking. *T.:* Abinger 162. [*Died* 6 *April* 1958 (*ext.*).

CAMPION, Bernard, Q.C. 1923; LL.B.; *e. s.* of S. S. Campion, J.P., D.L., of Northampton; *m.* 1896, Rose, 2nd *d.* of John Lees, of Nottingham; three *s.* *Educ.:* Taunton School. Called Gray's Inn, 1899; Bencher, 1920; Treasurer, 1935; Recorder of Northampton, 1927-28; a Metropolitan Magistrate, 1928-43;

Gilbart Lecturer on Banking, King's College, 1924 to 1927. *Club:* Reform. [*Died* 10 *March* 1952.

CAMPION, Colonel Sir William Robert, K.C.M.G., *cr.* 1924, D.S.O. 1917; J.P.; *e. s.* of late Col. W. H. Campion, C.B.; *b.* 3 July 1870; *m.* 1894, Katharine Mary, 3rd *d.* of Rev. Hon. Wm. Byron; two *s.* two *d.* *Educ.:* Eton; New College, Oxford. Stock Exchange; contested North Worcester, 1906 and 1910; M.P. (C.) Mid-Sussex now Lewes, Division, 1910-24; Governor of the State of Western Australia, 1924-31; Colonel late 4th Battalion Royal Sussex Regiment. Served European War, 1914-18 (D.S.O., despatches thrice); T.D., D.L. for Sussex; Knight of Grace, Order of Hospital of St. John of Jerusalem. *Address:* The Ham, Hassocks, Sussex. *T.:* Hassocks 195. *Club:* Marlborough-Windham. [*Died* 2 *Jan.* 1951.

CAMROSE, 1st Viscount, *cr.* 1941, of Hackwood Park; 1st Baron, *cr.* 1929, of Long Cross; **William Ewert Berry,** Bart., *cr.* 1921; Hon. LL.D. (Bristol); Editor-in-Chief of the Daily Telegraph since 1928; *b.* 23 June 1879; 2nd *s.* of late Alderman John Mathias Berry, J.P., Gwaelodygarth, Merthyr Tydfil; *m.* Mary Agnes, *e. d.* of late Thomas Corns, Bolton Street, W.; four *s.* four *d.* *Educ.:* privately. Founded Advertising World, 1901; owned and edited various other journals; Chairman of the Daily Telegraph; Chm., Amalgamated Press, Ltd.; Editor-in-Chief of the Sunday Times, 1915-36; Prin. Adviser to Ministry of Information, 1939; D.L. (1941) Southampton. *Publication:* British Newspapers and their Controllers. *Heir:* s. Maj. Hon. John Seymour Berry, T.D. *Address:* Hackwood Park, Basingstoke. *T.:* Basingstoke 630; 24 Carlton House Terrace, S.W.1. *T.:* Whitehall 1805. *Clubs:* Carlton, Athenæum, Turf; (Vice-Cdre.) Royal Yacht Squadron. [*Died* 15 *June* 1954.

CAMSELL, Charles, C.M.G. 1935; B.A., LL.D., F.R.S.C., F.G.S.A., Hon. F.R.G.S., M.E.I.C.; Member, Federal District Commission, Ottawa, 1946; President Royal Society of Canada, 1930 President Engineering Institute of Canada, 1932; Vice-President Geological Society of America, 1937; Director Amer. Inst. Mining and Metallurgical Engineers, 1939-45, Hon. Member 1946; Pres. and Hon. Member Can. Inst. Mining and Metallurgy; *b.* Fort Liard, North-West Territory, Canada, 8 Feb. 1876; *s.* of Capt. Julian S. Camsell, Chief Factor, Hudson Bay Co., and Sarah Foulds; *m.* 1905, Isabel Doucie, *d.* of W. Thomas, Swansea; one *s.* two *d.* *Educ.:* St. John's College and Manitoba University, Winnipeg; Queen's University, Kingston; Harvard University; Mass. Institute of Technology. Explorations in North-Western Canada, 1894-1900; geologist Algoma Central Railway, 1901; geologist Canadian Northern Railway, 1902-3; geologist Geological Survey of Canada, 1904; geological investigations and explorations in British Columbia and Northern Canada, 1904-1920; and responsible for the original exploration and mapping of some of the larger rivers of North-western Canada; in charge of B.C. and Yukon Branch of the Geological Survey, 1918; Deputy Minister of Mines and Resources for Canada, retired 1946; Commissioner and Member of Council of North-West Territories, retired 1946; Charter Member and Fellow Harvard Travellers' Club, 1903; Murchison Grant, R.G.S., for explorations in Northern Canada, 1922; Founder's Medal, R.G.S. 1945; gold medal of Institution of Mining and Metallurgy, 1931; first President Canadian Geographical Society, 1930-41; LL.D. by Queen's University, Kingston, Canada, for explorations in Northern Canada, 1922; LL.D. University of Alberta, 1929, LL.D. University of Manitoba, 1936; Hon. Fellow, St. Johns College, Winnipeg, 1938. *Publications:* Son of the North (autobiography); numerous memoirs and papers on the geology and geography of British Columbia and Northern Canada. *Address:* 240 Mariposa Road, Rockcliffe Park, Ottawa. *Clubs:* Rideau, Royal Ottawa Golf (Ottawa). [*Died* 19 *Dec.* 1958.

CAMUS, Albert; French Author; *b.* 1913. *Educ.:* University of Algiers. Director of theatrical company L'Équipe, 1935-38; Associate Founder and former Editor of Combat. Now a Director of Librairie Gallimard. Nobel Prize for Literature, 1957. *Publications:* L'Étranger, 1942 (New York as The Stranger, and London, as The Outsider, 1946); La Peste, 1947 (New York and London, as The Plague, 1948); La Chute, 1956 (New York and London, as The Fall, 1957); *nouvelles:* L'Exil et Le Royaume, 1957 (New York and London, as Exile and The Kingdom, 1958); *essays:* L'Envers et L'Endroit, 1937; Noces, 1938; Le Mythe de Sisyphe (New York, as The Myth of Sisyphus and Other Essays, 1954); Lettres à un Ami Allemand, 1948 (New York, included in Resistance, Rebellion and Death, 1961); Actuelles (Chroniques, 1944-1948), 1950; Le Minotaure ou La Halte D'Oran (written in 1939), 1950; L'Homme Révolte, 1951 (New York and London, as The Rebel, 1954); Actuelles II (Chroniques, 1948-1953), 1953 (New York, as The Myth of Sisyphus and Other Essays, 1955); L'Été, 1954 (New York, included in The Myth of Sisyphus and Other Essays, 1955); La Peine Capitale, 1957 (in collaboration); Actuelles III (Chroniques algériennes, 1939-1958), 1958 (London 1961); *plays:* La Révolte dans Les Asturies, 1936; Caligula (written in 1938), 1944 (New York and London, 1958); Le Malentendu, 1944 (London, as Cross Purposes, 1948, and New York, as The Misunderstanding, 1958); L'État de Siège, 1948 (New York, as The State of Siege, 1958); Les Justes, 1950 (New York, as The Just Assassins, 1950); also several adaptations including Dostoievski's Les Possédés (New York and London, as The Possessed, 1960). *Relevant Publications:* (by Philip Thody) Albert Camus: A Study of his Work; (by John Cruickshank) Albert Camus and the Literature of Revolt. *Address:* 29 Rue Madame, Paris 6e. [*Died* 4 *Jan.* 1960.

CANDY, Rear-Adm. Algernon Henry Chester, C.B.E. 1919; late R.N.; *b.* 19 May 1877; *o. s.* of William Marshall and Constance Mary Candy; *m.* 1914, Isabel, *y. d.* of Henry Abraham, Southampton; one *d.* *Educ.:* Pinewood, Farnborough, Hants; H.M.S. Britannia, Dartmouth. Entered Royal Navy, 1892; Post Captain, 1916; served in submarine service, 1904-11 and 1913-16; Rear-Admiral (retd.), 1927; recalled, 1939, Commodore of Ocean Convoys (despatches). *Recreations:* out-door sports. *Address:* 5 Solent Gate, Craneswater Park, Southsea. [*Died* 29 *April* 1959.

CANE, Sir Cyril (Hubert), K.B.E., *cr.* 1950 (C.B.E. 1943; M.B.E. 1929); *b.* 6 July 1891; *s.* of Dr. Howard Cane and Alice Barrell; *m.* 1922, Gertrude Lois, *née* Sancton; one *s.* two *d.* *Educ.:* Blackheath Proprietary School; Epsom Coll.; privately. Employed in Consulate-General, Antwerp, 1908-14; in army, 1915-19; Lt. Royal West Kent Regt., 1916-19, Mesopotamia; served H.M. Foreign Service, 1919-51; Vice-Consul at Addis Ababa, 1919-22; San Francisco, 1922-29; in Dept. of Overseas Trade, 1929; Consul at San Francisco with special Commercial duties, 1929-33 and 1933-39; acting Commerical Secretary, British Embassy, Washington, D.C.. 1933; Consul at Detroit, 1939-1943; Consul-General, Detroit, 1943-45, San Francisco, 1945-47; H.B.M. Consul-General, Rabat, Morocco, 1948-51; retired 1951. *Recreations:* walking, riding, music. *Ad-*

dress: 1814 Broadway, San Francisco 9, California, U.S.A.; c/o Lloyd's Bank Ltd., 6 Pall Mall, S.W.1. *Club:* Royal Societies. [*Died* 31 *Dec.* 1959.

CANFIELD, Dorothy (Dorothea Frances Canfield Fisher); author; late President American Adult Education Assoc.; *b.* Lawrence, Kan., 17 Feb. 1879; *d.* of late James Hulme Canfield and Flavia Camp; *m.* 1907, John Redwood Fisher, New York; one *s.* one *d.* Ph.B. Ohio State University, 1899; Ph.D. Columbia, 1904; Litt. D. Columbia University, Dartmouth College, University of Vermont, Middlebury College; Ohio State University; Northwestern University; Swarthmore College, 1935; Mount Holyoke College, 1937; Williams College, 1935; Sec. Horace Mann School, 1902-5. Studied and travelled extensively in Europe, acquired several languages in childhood; three years in France doing war work. Member for two years of Vermont State Board of Education; Member Committee of Selection of the Book-of-the-Month Club organization, 1926-50. *Publications:* Corneille and Racine in England, 1904; English Rhetoric and Composition (with G. R. Carpenter), 1906; What Shall we do Now? 1906; Gunhild, 1907; The Squirrel-Cage, 1912; The Montessori Mother, 1913; Mothers and Children, 1914; Hillsboro People, 1915; The Bent Twig, 1915; The Real Motive, 1916; Fellow-Captains, 1916; Understood Betsy, 1917; Home-Fires in France, 1918; The Day of Glory, 1919; The Brimming Cup, 1921; Rough Hewn, 1923; Life of Christ by Papini, translated from Italian, 1923; The Home-Maker, 1924; Raw Material, 1924; Made-to-Order Stories, 1925; Her Son's Wife, 1926; Why Stop Learning? 1927; The Deepening Stream, 1930; A History of Work, translated from Italian, 1930; Basque People 1931; Bonfire, 1933; Fables for Parents, 1937; Seasoned Timber, 1939; Nothing Ever Happens (with Sarah N. Cleghorn), 1940; The Knothole (a novella), 1942; Our Young Folks, 1943; American Portraits, 1946; Four Square, 1949; Something Old, Something New; 1949; Paul Revere and the Minute Men, 1950; Our Independence and the Constitution, 1950; A Fair World for All, 1952; Vermont Tradition, 1953; A Harvest of Stories, 1956; Memories of Arlington, Vermont, 1957; short stories to magazines. *Recreations:* walking, gardening. *Address:* Arlington, Vermont, U.S.A. [*Died* 9 *Nov.* 1958.

CANNAN, Gilbert; novelist and dramatist; 2nd *s.* of Henry Cannan of Manchester; *b.* 1884. *Educ.:* Manchester; King's College, Cambridge. Called to Bar, 1908; dramatic critic on Star, 1909-10. *Publications:* Peter Homunculus, 1909; John Christopher (translation), 1910; John Christopher, vols. ii. and iii., Devious Ways, 1911; Little Brother, 1912; Round the Corner, John Christopher, vol. iv.; Four Plays, The Joy of the Theatre, The Yoke of Pity, (translation), 1913; Old Mole, 1914; Young Earnest, Samuel Butler, Windmills (Poems), 1915; Three Pretty Men, Mendel, 1916; Everybody's Husband, 1917; Mummery, 1918; The Stucco House, 1918; The Anatomy of Society, 1919; Pink Roses, 1919; Time and Eternity, 1920; Pugs and Peacocks, 1921; Sembal, 1922; Old Maid's Love, 1922; Annette and Bennett, 1922; Noel, 1922; Seven Plays, 1923; Letters from a Distance, 1923; The House of Prophecy, 1924; A. O. Barnabooth: His Diary (translation), 1924. *Plays:* Miles Dixon, 1910; James and John, 1911; Mary's Wedding, 1912; Wedding Presents, 1912; The Perfect Widow, 1912; The Arbour of Refuge, 1913; The Release of the Soul, 1920. *Recreations:* travelling and journalism. [*Died* 30 *June* 1955.

CANNING, Colonel Albert, C.M.G. 1916; J.P. Wilts, Cricklade Division; retired; *b.* 3 Oct. 1861; *s.* of Robert and Amelia Canning; *m.* 1st, Mabel Parry (*d.* 1933), *y. d.* of late J. R. Cobb, F.S.A., of Nythfa, Brecon and Caldicot Castle; 2nd, 1941, Margaret Frances, *d.* of James Whicher, M.D., Deputy Inspector-General R.N. *Educ.:* Clifton Coll. Served in ranks 19th Hussars, 1882-88; South Wales Borderers, 1888-95; Leinster Regiment 1895-1911; retired from Regular Army, 1911; served in Special Reserve Bn. 3rd Leinster Regt. 1912-18; served Egypt, 1882-86 (medal, bronze star); Soudan, 1884, Battles of El Teb and Tamaai (2 clasps); Soudan, 1885, Suakin (clasp); European War, 1914-18; Commanded 3rd Leinster Regt.; Commanded 1/7 Bn. Manchester Regt. T.F., Dardanelles and Egypt (despatches, C.M.G.), Bt. Col. and Col. 1918; served on Staff in France 1918-19; Volunteer, Local Defence Volunteers, 1940, and promoted to Command of Purton Co.; Major 1941; retired 1942, Hon. Sec. S.S. & A.F.A., Cricklade Div. 1920-45. *Address:* Restrop House, Purton, Swindon, Wilts. [*Died* 20 *Nov.* 1960.

CANNING, Rev. Clifford Brooke, M.A. (Oxon); Vice-Chairman Dorset Association of Boys' Clubs; *b.* 5 June 1882; *o. s.* of late Charles Brooke Canning of Glascote House, Glascote, Staffs.; *m.* 1922, Enid, *e. d.* of late Sir Cyril Norwood; three *d.* *Educ.:* Clifton College; Oriel College, Oxford (Classical Exhibitioner). Classical Honours, 1905; Assistant Master, Marlborough, 1906; Housemaster, 1910-27; Priest, 1924; Headmaster of Canford School, Wimborne, 1928-1947. *Address:* Hanford, Child Okeford, Dorset. *T.:* Child Okeford 219. [*Died* 17 *Aug.* 1957.

CANNY, Sir Gerald Bain, K.C.B., *cr.* 1939 (C.B. 1924); K.B.E., *cr.* 1937; *b.* 5 March 1881; *s.* of late John Macnamara Canny; *m.* Mary, *d.* of late George Elliott, K.C.; one *s.* *Educ.:* Malvern College; Queens' College, Cambridge. Entered Civil Service, 1904; Chairman, Board of Inland Revenue, 1938-42; Chairman, Tithe Redemption Commission, 1944; Controller of Matches, 1945; Chairman, London and South-Eastern Regional Board for Industry, 1945-47; Director of London Necropolis Co. Ltd. and of Aero-Research Ltd.; Vice-Chm. Royal Commission on Lotteries and Betting, 1949; Chairman, Malvern College Council, 1950. *Address:* Valley End Cottage, Chobham, Surrey. *T.:* Chobham 300. *Club:* United University. [*Died* 16 *Feb.* 1954.

CANTELLI, Guido; Maestro; Accademic of S. Cecilia, Rome; Permanent Conductor of La Scala Orchestra, Milan; *b.* 27 April 1920; *s.* of Antonio and Riccardone Angela; *m.* 1945, Iris Bilucaglia; one *s.* *Educ.:* Conservatorio G. Verdi, Milan. 1945-, many tours with La Scala Orchestra, Europe and Africa; 1948-, every season, has conducted in America, N.B.C. Orchestra, N.Y. Philharmonic, Boston Symphony, etc.; has conducted Philharmonia Orchestra at Festival Hall, London, annually, 1951-. *Address:* La Scala, Milan, Italy. [*Died* 24 *Nov.* 1956.

CAPE, (Herbert) Jonathan; Chairman and founder, Jonathan Cape, Ltd., publishers; *b.* 1879; *s.* of Jonathan Cape, Ireby, Cumberland, and Caroline Page; *m.* 1st, Edith Louisa Creak (*d.* 1919); two *d.*; 2nd, Olive Vida James (*d.* 1931), one *s.* one *d.*; 3rd, 1941, Kathleen Mary Webb; (*d.* 1953); one *s.* *Educ.:* privately. *Recreations:* reading, walking. *Address:* 30 Bedford Square, W.C.1. *T.A.:* Capajon London. *T.:* Museum 5764. [*Died* 10 *Feb.* 1960.

CAPELL, Colonel Algernon Essex, C.B.E. 1924; D.S.O. 1900; attached to Head Quarter Staff Defence Force, S. Rhodesia; *b.* Tenenhall, near Wolverhampton, 1 Nov. 1869; *m.* 1903, Lois Ethel, *d.* of W. Slatter of Stratton, Cirencester; two *s.* one *d.* *Educ.:* Felsted School. Joined Cape Mounted Rifles, 1889-99, as trooper; served through Pondoland at annexation; joined Bethune's Mounted Infantry, 1899, as Lieut.; Capt. 1900, for "gallantry in the field," at Scheeper's Nek; joined S.A.C. 1900; Major,

1902; served Boer War, 1899-1902 (despatches thrice); ejected from S.A. Constabulary by the Boer Government of 1908; Assistant District Commissioner, Dagoretti, British East Africa; Chief of Police, Grenada; joined British S. Africa Police as Assistant Commissioner, 1913; Commissioner of B.S.A. Police, South Rhodesia, and Commandant Southern Rhodesian Forces, 1923-26; retired, 1926; served British East Africa in command of 2nd Rhodesian Regiment with rank of Lt.-Col., 1915 (despatches); Croix de Guerre. *Publication:* The 2nd Rhodesian Regiment in East Africa. *Recreations:* devoted most of life to big-game and other shooting when on leave. *Address:* Easton Lodge, 2 Princess Drive, Highlands, Salisbury, S. Rhodesia. [*Died* 23 *Feb.* 1952.

CAPELL, Richard, O.B.E. 1946; M.M. 1916; music critic, Daily Telegraph, since 1933; *b.* Northampton, 1885; *e. s.* of Richard Lovat and Charlotte Capell. *Educ.:* Bedford Modern School. Violoncellist (pupil of E. van der Straeten, London, and G. Penant, Lille). Music critic of the Daily Mail, 1911-33. Served European War, 1914-18 (M.M. Vimy Ridge). Daily Telegraph war correspondent in France, 1939-40, Western Desert, 1941-43, Greece, 1944-45. Editor, The Monthly Musical Record, 1928-33; Proprietor (since 1936) and editor (since 1950) of Music & Letters. Member of Arts Council. *Publications:* Schubert's Songs, 1928; Opera, 1930 and 1948; Simiómata: a Greek Note-Book, 1944-45, 1946. Translated: Strauss's Friedenstag, 1938; 200 Schubert songs for Augener's edition. Contributor to Grove's Dictionary of Music and Musicians. *Address:* 3 Abbots Court, W.8. *T.:* Western 8762. *Club:* Savile. [*Died* 21 *June* 1954.

CAPEWELL, Arthur, Q.C. 1945; Chairman Somerset Quarter Sessions since 1957; *b.* 15 December 1902; *er.* and *o. surv. s.* of late Arthur Thomas and Gertrude Capewell; *m.* 1st, V. R. Naylor (marriage dissolved); one *s.* one *d.*; 2nd, Anne Noel, *yr. d.* of late Sydney Martineau and of Edith Martineau, Bolney House, Ennismore Gardens, S.W.7; two *s.* two *d.* *Educ.:* Shrewsbury; Gonville and Caius College, Cambridge (LL.B., B.A.). Called to Bar, Gray's Inn, 1926. Councillor Kensington Borough Council, 1932-38. Served War of 1939-45 until invalided home 1943, D.A.Q.M.G. West Lancs Area; G.S.O.2 Administrative Staff School; G.S.O.2 Junior Staff School (p.s.c. 1942); D.A.Q.M.G. 44 Div.; Assistant Sec. (Legislation) Ministry of Town and Country Planning, 1943-44; Counsel to Lord Chairman of Committees, House of Lords, 1944-46; Counsel to Ecclesiastical Committee of Parliament, 1944-46. Dep.-Chm. Mdx. Q.S., 1945-54; Dep. Chairman Somerset Q.S., 1950-57. Chairman, Royal Commission appointed by Southern Rhodesian Govt. to report on Planning, Incremental Values, etc., 1949. *Address:* Thorncombe House, Crowcombe, Somerset; 20 Lennox Gardens, S.W.1. *Club:* Carlton. [*Died* 18 *Oct.* 1957.

CAPORN, His Honour Judge Arthur Cecil; County Court Judge on Circuit No. 18 (Nottinghamshire, etc.) since 1944, Circuit No. 25 (Wolverhampton, etc.), 1939-44; *b.* Radcliffe on Trent, Notts, 16 April 1884; *s.* of late Arthur L. Caporn, Nottingham, South Africa and London; *m.* 1912, Dorothy Francis, *e. d.* of late Richard Marriott, The Grange, Cropwell Butler, Notts; two *s.* *Educ.:* South African College School; Trinity Hall, Cambridge. Called to Bar, Middle Temple, 1907; Army, 1914-20; M.P. (U.) West Nottingham, 1931-35. *Address:* Newstead Abbey, Linby, Notts. *T.:* East Kirkby 2383. [*Died* 25 *Nov.* 1953.

CAPPER, Maj.-Gen. Sir John Edward, K.C.B., *cr.* 1917 (C.B. 1902); K.C.V.O., *cr.* 1921; *b.* 7 Dec. 1861; 2nd *s.* of late William C. Capper, Bengal Civil Service; *m.* 1895, Edith Mary (*d.* 1942), *e. d.* of Joseph Beausire of Noctorum, Birkenhead; one *d.* *Educ.:* Wellington College. Lt. Royal Engineers, 1880; Capt. 1889; Major, 1899; Bt. Lt.-Col. 1900; Lt.-Col. 1905; Bt. Col. 1906; Col. 1910; Brig.-Gen. 1914; Maj.-Gen. 1915; employed military and public works in India and Burma, 1883-99; served Tirah, 1898 (medal and clasp); South Africa, 1899-1902 (despatches twice, Queen's medal three clasps, King's medal two clasps, Bt. Lt.-Col., C.B.)., European War, 1914-19 (despatches six times, war medals and 1914 Star, prom. Maj.-Gen., K.C.B., Commander Legion of Honour); Commandant Balloon School, 1903-10; Commandant School of Military Engineering, 1911-14; Deputy Inspector-General L. of C., 1914; Chief Engineer, 1915; G.O.C., 24th Division, 1915-17; Director-General of the Tank Corps, 1917; Lieut.-Governor and commanding troops in Guernsey, 1920-25; retired pay, 1925; Col. Commandant, Royal Tank Corps, 1923-34; Governor Wellington College, 1928-46. *Address:* Bourne Side, The Goffs, Eastbourne. *T.:* Eastbourne 241. [*Died* 24 *May* 1955.

CAPRON, Frederick Hugh, B.A.; *b.* 12 Dec. 1857; *s.* of Rev. G. H. Capron, J.P. of Southwick Hall, Oundle, Northamptonshire, and Anna Henrietta, *d.* of John Smith of Oundle, Northamptonshire; *m.* 1883, Enid Alice (*d.* 1940), *d.* of Sir S. B. Boulton, 1st Bt.; (one *s.* decd. one *d.* decd.). *Educ.:* Wellington College; University College, Oxford. Honours (Law), 1880; won the 'Varsity Gymnastic Medal, 1877; rowed for Leander Club at Henley, winning Grand Challenge Cup, 1880; Master of the Plaisterers' Company, 1903. *Publications:* The Antiquity of Man from the Point of View of Religion, 1892; The Conflict of Truth, 1902 (10th edition, 1934); The Anatomy of Truth, 1913 (6th edition, 1946); The Highway to Heaven and a Byway to Nowhere, An Answer to Spiritualism, 1937; contributions to various periodicals. *Recreations:* astronomy, reading, writing, music, and bicycling. *Address:* Rosedale, Mortimer, nr. Reading, Berks. *T.:* Mortimer 61. *Club:* Leander. [*Died* 28 *Feb.* 1955.

CAPRONI, Gianni; Count of Taliedo; *b.* Massone Trentino, Italy, 3 July 1886; *s.* of Joseph Caproni and Paolina Maini. *Educ.:* Rovereto; Polytechnikum, Munich; Electro-techn., Liège. Builder of the Caproni Aeroplanes, the most important Italian building industry of airplanes, founded by him in 1908. Legion of Honour; Cav. Gr. Crown of Italy; Cavaliere del Lavaro; Cav. SS. Maurizio e Lazzaro. *Recreations:* gardening, motoring, shooting. *Address:* Roma, Via Azuni 13, Italy. *Clubs:* Aero of Italy; Automobile d'Italia; Scacchi (Rome). [*Died* 27 *Oct.* 1957.

CARDEW, Claud Ambrose, C.M.G., 1919; *b.* 9 Aug. 1870; *s.* of late Col. Sir Frederic Cardew, K.C.M.G.; unmarried. *Educ.:* United Services College, Westward Ho! Assistant Agent Chinde, British Central Africa Protectorate, 1893; Collector, South Nyasa district, 1894; judicial officer, 1895; 2nd Class Assistant, 1902; district magistrate, Upper Shire, 1902; district resident, 1st class, 1906; Mashonaland medal, 1890; Africa General Service medal (Nyasaland) clasp for services in native rising; employed, in addition to ordinary duties, in supplying transport carriers and food-stuffs for military operations against the Germans in East Africa, 1916-19 (C.M.G.).; retired, 1921. *Address:* Ncheu, Nyasaland. [*Died Sept.* 1959.

CARDEW, Lady (Evelyn Roberta), C.B.E. 1919; *d.* of late Edward John Firth; *m.* 1886, Sir Alexander Gordon Cardew, K.C.S.I. (*d.* 1937); two *s.* two *d.* Vice-President of the Madras Ladies' Committee for the relief of the sick and wounded in the war; mentioned in the Gazette of India for services in India during the war, and received the Souvenir War Badge. *Address:* 35 Coper's Cope Road, Beckenham, Kent. [*Died* 29 *Nov.* 1953.

CARDINALL, Sir Allan Wolsey, K.B.E., *cr.* 1943; C.M.G. 1937; *b.* 21 March 1887; 3rd *s.* of Durrant Edward Cardinall of Tendring, Essex. *Educ.:* Winchester; Melle; Heidelberg. At various times assistant master in prep. schools in Vancouver and Victoria, B.C., and in England; some time on the staff of the Vancouver Daily News Advertiser; appointed to the West African Administrative Service, 1914; retired 1932; accredited representative for Gt. Britain at League of Nations (Togoland Mandate), 1932 and 1933; Commissioner and Judge of Grand Court, Cayman Islands, 1934–40; Colonial Secretary, Falkland Islands, 1940–41; Gov. and Commander-in-Chief, Falkland Islands, 1941–46. *Publications:* Natives of the N. Territories of the Gold Coast, 1920; A Gold Coast Library, 1924; In Ashanti and Beyond, 1927; Tales told in Togoland, 1931; A Bibliography of the Gold Coast, 1933; The Gold Coast, 1931, 1933. *Recreations:* cricket, big-game hunting, big-game fishing. *Address:* c/o Bank of British West Africa, 37 Gracechurch Street, E.C.3. [*Died* 26 *Jan.* 1956.

CAREW-GIBSON, Harry Frederick, M.Inst.C.E.; Captain, S.R.E.S.; late Secretary, Temple Golf Club, Berks; *b.* Sandgate, Sullington, Sussex, 23 Nov. 1869; 4th *s.* of G. C. Carew-Gibson; *m.* 1916, Olive Maria Butler Rees; one *d.* *Educ.:* private schools; University College, Liverpool. Civil engineer, engaged upon public works in Ireland, Wales, Egypt (Assouan Dam), Greece, Sarawak. *Recreation:* field sports. *Address:* Woodlands Cottage, Burchetts Green, Berks. *T.:* Littlewick Green 62. [*Died* 16 *June* 1953.

CAREW HUNT, Captain Roland Cecil, C.M.G. 1919; R.N. retired; *b.* Aug. 1880; *s.* of R. P. Carew Hunt; *m.* 1916, Thelma Reay, *d.* of James Scott of Balnakille, Sutherlandshire; one *s.* (and one killed in action, 1940). Joined Navy, 1896; retired list, 1926; served in R.N.A.S. 1915; R.A.F. 1918 (despatches, C.M.G.). *Address:* Coombe Corner, Highweek, Newton Abbot, Devon. *T.:* Newton Abbot 484. *Club:* United Service. [*Died* 5 *Dec.* 1959.

CAREY, Sir Victor Gosselin, Kt., *cr.* 1945; Honorary Doctor of Law, University of Caen, 1938; Knight of Grace, Order of St. John of Jerusalem; Bailiff of Guernsey, 1935–46; *b.* 2 July 1871; *s.* of late Major-General de Vic F. Carey of Le Vallon, Guernsey, and Harriet Mary, *d.* of late Thomas William Gosselin of Springfield, Guernsey; *m.* 1899, Adelaide Eleanor (*d.* 1936), *d.* of late Julius Jeffreys, F.R.S., of Richmond, Surrey; two *s.* *Educ.:* Elisabeth College, Guernsey; Marlborough; University of Caen. Called to the Guernsey Bar, 1898; Receiver-General for the Island of Guernsey, 1912–35. *Address:* Le Vallon, Guernsey. *Clubs:* Savile; Royal Channel Islands Yacht (Guernsey). [*Died* 28 *June* 1957.

CAREY, Rt. Rev. Walter Julius, D.D.; *b.* Owston Rectory, Leicestershire, 12 July 1875, twelfth *c.* of Rev. A. H. Carey; *m.* 1917, Fanny Emma Parfitt; one *s.* *Educ.:* Bedford School (Head of the School); Hertford Coll., Oxford (Exhibitioner); 2nd Class Mods. 1896, and 2nd Class Greats, 1898; Curate of the Ascension, Lavender Hill, 1899–1908; Librarian Pusey House, Oxford, 1908–14; Chaplain Royal Navy, 1914–19; present at Jutland in H.M.S. Warspite; Warden Lincoln Theological College, 1919–21; Bishop of Bloemfontein, 1921–33; Chief Messenger of Society for Propagation of the Gospel, 1934–35; Chaplain to Eastbourne College, 1936–48; Co-Warden, Village Evangelists, 1948–; Missionary in Kenya (P.O. Kitale), 1950–. *Publications:* The Life in Grace, 1913; My Priesthood, 1915; Prayer, 1915; Have you Understood Christianity? 1916; Sacrifice, 1917, etc.; The Church of England Revisited, 1925; Sin, Suffering, and Sorrow, 1928; The Secret of Christ, 1938; The Search for God, 1939; The Love of God, 1939; As Man to Man, 1940; The Church of England Vindicated, 1946; The Church of England's Hour, 1946; Good-bye to my Generation, 1951. *Recreations:* golf, fishing, tennis, violin; Rugby Football Blue at Oxford; Member English Rugby football team to South Africa, 1896. *Address:* P.R. Kitale, Kenya; c/o Westminster Bank, Clapham Junction, S.W.11. *Club:* Vincent's (Oxford). [*Died* 17 *Feb.* 1955.

CAREY, Brigadier Walter Louis John, C.I.E. 1919; late R.A.; retired pay; *b.* 1872; *m.* 1st, 1904, Maria Grace (*d.* 1946), *d.* of late Capt. E. A. Campbell, Inverawe; two *d.*; 2nd, 1947, Dorothy Lucy, *d.* of late E. G. Mears, East Mersea. *Educ.:* Elizabeth College, Guernsey; R.M.A., Woolwich. 2nd Lieut. R.A., 1892; joined Indian Ordnance Department, 1898; served in India till retirement, 1928; Director of Equipment and Ordnance Stores, 1924–28; served European War, 1914–18, India and Mesopotamia; War of 1939–45, Civil Defence Services—(Hon.) A.R.P. Officer and Sub-controller. [*Died* 27 *Nov.* 1953.

CARGILL, Featherston, C.M.G. 1906; M.B.; *b.* 1870; *s.* of late J. Cargill of Dunedin. *Educ.:* Fettes College, Edinburgh; Edinburgh University. Retired 1st Class Resident, Nigeria. *Address:* c/o National and Grindlay's Bank Ltd., 54 Parliament Street, S.W.1. [*Died* 5 *Dec.* 1959.

CARGILL, Sir John Traill, 1st Bt., *cr.* 1920; LL.D., Rangoon and Glasgow Universities; D.L., J.P., County of the City of Glasgow; late Chairman, Burmah Oil Co., Ltd.; Assam Oil Co., Ltd., Scottish Oils, Ltd.; late Director of the Anglo-Iranian Oil Co. Ltd., and other public companies; *b.* 10 Jan. 1867; 2nd *s.* of David Sime Cargill, East India Merchant, Glasgow, and Margaret, *d.* of John Traill, F.R.C.S. Edin., of Arbroath; *m.* 1895, Mary Hope (*d.* 1929), *d.* of George Moncrieff Grierson, Merchant, Glasgow; one *d.* *Educ.:* Glasgow Academy; went to Burma, 1890; returned, 1893; has taken an active part in the development of the oil industry in Burma and Persia. *Recreations:* all outdoor sports. *Address:* c/o Miller Thompson Henderson & Co., 190 St. Vincent Street, Glasgow, C.2. *Clubs:* Carlton, Royal Automobile; Western (Glasgow). [*Died* 24 *Jan.* 1954 (*ext.*).

CARGILL, Lionel Vernon, F.R.C.S. (Eng.), L.R.C.P. (Lond.), L.S.A.; Fellow of King's College, London; Consulting Ophthalmic Surgeon, King's Coll. Hospital; Consulting Surg., Royal Eye Hospital; Emeritus Lecturer in Ophthalmology, King's Coll. Hospital Med. School; Consulting Ophthalmic Surgeon, Dreadnought, Seamen's Hospital, Greenwich; late Chm., Royal Eye Hospital; Past Master, Society Apothecaries, Lond.; Vice-Pres. and Treasurer Board of Registration of Med. Auxiliaries; late Examiner in Ophthalmology, Oxford University; Consulting Ophthalmic Surgeon, Maternity Charity, Plaistow; Member Cttee. of Management, Chelsea Physic Garden; *m.* 1897, Emma (*d.* 1951), *o. d.* of William Sherwood; three *d.* *Educ.:* King's College School, and King's College, London (Medallist and Exhibitioner). Late House Surgeon to Lord Lister, O.M., and Surgical Registrar, King's College Hospital and Royal Eye Hospital; late Honorary Consultant for Diseases of the Eye to Military Hospitals in London (Red

Cross war medal, 1914-18); late Lecturer in Ophthalmology, London School of Clinical Medicine and Polyclinic; Ophthalmic Surgeon, Imperial Yeomanry Hospitals, South African War (medal and 3 clasps); Fellow Royal Society of Medicine, Medical Society of London, and Ophthalmological Society; F.Z.S. Formerly Chm. of Governors, King's College School. *Publications:* contributions on ophthalmic subjects to various medical publications. *Address:* 63 Highlands Heath, S.W.15. *T.:* Putney 4340. [*Died* 13 *Dec.* 1955.

CARISBROOKE, Marquess of, *cr.* 1917, **Alexander Albert Mountbatten,** G.C.B., *cr.* 1927; G.C.V.O., *cr.* 1911; Earl of Berkhampsted; Viscount Launceston (Cornwall); granted title, attributes of Highness by Royal Warrant, 1886 (discontinued by Royal Warrant, 1917 at H.M.'s request; assumed surname of Mountbatten); *b.* 23 Nov. 1886; *s.* of Prince Henry Maurice of Battenberg, K.G., P.C. (*d.* 1896) and Princess Beatrice (*d.* 1944), 5th *d.* of Queen Victoria; *m.* 1917, Lady Irene Frances Adza Denison, G.B.E., *cr.* 1938, D.St.J. (*d.* 1956), *o. d.* of 2nd Earl of Londesborough; one *d.* *Educ.:* Wellington Coll. Was in R.N. 1902-8; formerly Captain Grenadier Guards; now Hon. Col. Isle of Wight Vols.; served European War, 1914-19, with regt.; subsequently on the Staff; retired, 1919; War of 1939-45, Pilot Officer, R.A.F.V.R. 1941, Flt.-Lt. 1942; resigned 1945. Hon. Col. 1st (C) Battalion The London Rifle Brigade (The Rifle Brigade), 1949; Hon. Group Captain, R.A.F.V.R., 1953. Director Eagle Star Insurance Co. Ltd. and The Australian Estates Co. Ltd. Bailiff Grand Cross, St. John of Jerusalem; Grand Cross: Order of Charles III (Spain); Order of Alexander Nevsky (Russia); Order of Leopold with Swords (Belgium); Order of Crown (Roumania); Order of St. Vladimir with Swords (Russia); Order of Nile (Egypt); Croix de Guerre avec Palme (France). *Heir:* none. *Address:* Kensington Palace, W.8. *Club:* Royal Air Force. [*Died* 23 *Feb.* 1960 (*ext.*).

CARLILL, Harold Flamank; *b.* Hull, 24 June 1875; *m.* Beatrice Newton (*d.* 1924), 2nd *d.* of late John Hope; one *s.* two *d.* *Educ.:* Dulwich College; Trinity College, Cambridge. First Class Classical Tripos, Part I. 1896, Part II. 1897; distinguished, Chancellor's medals, 1898. Entered Board of Trade, 1898; Secretary to Coal Mines Dept., 1917; Assistant Secretary Power Transport and Economic Dept., 1919; Inspector General in Bankruptcy, 1921-28; Asst. Secretary, General Department, 1928-40; delegate to Washington Wheat Meeting, 1941-42. *Publications:* Theaetetus and Philebus of Plato (translation and commentary), 1905; Socrates, or the Emancipation of Mankind, 1926. *Address:* The Red House, Caterham, Surrey. *T.:* Caterham 3309. [*Died* 7 *Dec.* 1959.

CARLING, Sir Ernest Rock, Kt. 1944; M.B. (Lond.), B.S., F.R.C.S. (Eng.), F.R.C.P.; Hon. F.F.R.; Hon. LL.D. Queen's Univ., Belfast; Consultant Adviser Atomic Energy Authority, Home Office and Ministry of Health; Chm. Advisory Cttee. Medical Nomenclature, Somerset House; President: Medical Protection Soc., Institute of Almoners; Member: Cancer and Radiotherapy Cttee. (Central Health Services Council); Cttee. on Protection against Ionising Radiations, Med. Research Council; Radioactive Substances Advisory Cttee.; Health Cttee., Atomic Energy Authority; Advisory Panel Radioactive Substances, Min. of Labour; Council Westminster Hosp. Medical School; Expert Adviser, W.H.O.; *b.* 1877; 3rd *s.* of late F. R. Carling, J.P., Guildford; *m.* Petra (*d.* 1959), *d.* of late Rev. E. D. Rock, Creeting St. Peter, Suffolk; two *s.* Major (retired) R.A.M.C. (T.F.). Consulting Surgeon Westminster Hospital, Seamen's Hospital, Greenwich and other Hospitals; late Chairman: International Commission on Radiological Protection and Examiner in Surgery, Univs. of London, Edinburgh and Sheffield, and Faculty of Radiologists; Trustee, Nuffield Provincial Hospitals Trust; Chm. Court of Examiners, R.C.S. (Eng.); Member: Medical Research Council; Radium Commission; Central Health Services Council and Chm. its Medical Advisory Cttee.; Hon. Mem. Canadian Assoc. of Radiologists; Radioactive Wastes Panel, Min. Housing and Local Govt.; Hon. Mem. Brit. Inst. of Radiology; Hon. Consultant, King Edward VII Convalescent Home for Officers, Osborne; Dean, Westminster Med. School; served in S.A. campaign with Imperial Yeomanry Field Hospital, 1900; in France and Flanders, 1917. *Publications:* Editor, Course of Instruction in Radium Practice, 1929; Editor (with Sir James Paterson Ross) British Surgical Practice; Editor (jointly) British Practice in Radiotherapy, 1954; articles in various journals and text-books. *Address:* 49 Hallam Street, W.1. *Club:* Athenæum. [*Died* 15 *July* 1960.

CARLOW, Charles Augustus; *s.* of Charles Carlow, and *g.s.* of ex-Provost William Lindsay of Leith. *Educ.:* Heriot-Watt College, University of Edinburgh. Lifelong identification with The Fife Coal Company, Limited; Managing Director, The Fife Coal Co. Ltd., Leven, Fife, 1917-39; Chairman and Managing Director, 1939-52; Chairman, The Shotts Iron Co. Ltd., 1939-52; Director, Royal Bank of Scotland, 1941-54; Fellow, the Institute of Fuel; Member Institution of Civil Engineers; Hon. Member, American Institute of Mining and Metallurgical Engineers; Past President of the Mining Institute of Scotland; Past President Association of Mining Electrical Engineers; Past President and Hon. Member of The Instn. of Mining Engineers; D.L., Fife; Hon. LL.D. St. Andrews, 1952; F.R.S.E.; Hon. Col. 586 L.A.A. S.L. Regt., R.A. (H.) T.A.; J.P. *Address:* Kincaple, St. Andrews, Fife. *T.:* Leuchars 217. *Clubs:* Athenæum, Carlton; Edinburgh University, New (Edinburgh); New (Glasgow); Royal and Ancient (St. Andrews). [*Died* 13 *Aug.* 1954.

CARLTON, C. Hope, M.C.; T.D.; M.A., M.Ch. (Oxon.); F.R.C.S. (Eng.); consulting Surgeon; Consultant Surgeon to N.W. Metropolitan Regional Hospital Board (Paddington Group) and to S.E. Metropolitan Regional Hospital Board (Bromley Group); late Surgeon, Seamen's Hospital (Royal Albert Dock); Surgeon, National Temperance Hospital; Senior Surgeon, South Eastern Hospital for Children; Curator of the Museum, National Temperance Hosp.; Consulting Surgeon Bexley Cottage Hosp.; Fellow R.Soc. Med.; Member Assoc. Surgeons; Assoc. Member British Orthopædic Assoc.; Member T. and A.F.A. of County of London; *b.* Nov. 1889; *o. surv. s.* of William Carlton and Mary Elizabeth Rollinson, Grantham; *m.* 1938, Valmai Myfanwy, *y. d.* of late Inspector Lewis Davies, Porth, Glamorgan; two *s.* one *d.* *Educ.:* Doncaster Grammar School; St. John's College, Oxford (Open-Exhibitioner); St. Mary's Hospital, W. (University Scholar); Universities of Harvard, Minnesota, and Toronto. 2nd Class Honour School Physiology, Oxford; served European War, France and West Africa, mainly as Regimental Medical Officer, The London Regt. and 2nd Life Guards, Acting D.A.D.M.S. 47th Division (wounded, M.C., and 1914 star); War of 1939-45, A.D.M.S. 1st A.A. Div. and C.O. 7th and 3rd Gen. Hosps. and 34th W.A. Gen. Hosp. (African and European Stars). House Surgeon Surgical Unit and Demonstrator of Anatomy, St. Mary's Hospital, W.; many clinical appointments in London and abroad; special student on The Mayo Foundation, Rochester, Minn., U.S.A. Late Commanding Officer of No. 3 General Hospital, Middle East Force; late Colonel Army Medical Service, T.A.; commanding Medical Unit, University of London O.T.C.; Warden of Connaught Hall, University of London; Examiner General Nursing Council (Surgery and Preliminary Exams.); Member Military Education Committee Univ. of London. *Publications:* papers in the medical journals. *Address:* 86 Brook Street, W.1. *T.:* Mayfair 5001, Hillside 3467. [*Died* 3 *Oct.* 1951.

CARLYLE, Edward Irving, Fellow Royal Historical Society; *b.* 15 Sept. 1871; *o. s.* of Gavin Carlyle, Presbyterian Minister; *m.* 1913, Susan Mary Catherine, *d.* of late John Williams Hockin of S. Travancore and Launceston, Cornwall; one *s.* two *d.* Exhibitioner and Casberd Scholar, St. John's College, Oxford, B.A. 1894; M.A. 1901; Assistant Editor of Dictionary of National Biography, 1895-1901; Fellow of Merton College, Oxford, 1901-8; Fellow of Lincoln Coll., 1907-44; Bursar, 1920-38. Junior Proctor, 1911-12. *Publications:* William Cobbett: a Study of his Life as shown in his Writings, 1904; articles on the English Privy Council in the English Historical Review (Oct. 1906, April 1912), the Political History of Herefordshire in the Victoria County History, 1908, the History of British South Africa, British East Africa, and British West Africa in the British Empire, ed. Professor Pollard. *Address:* 26 Bardwell Road Oxford. [*Died* 9 *Feb.* 1952.

CARMICHAEL, Captain Hon. Ambrose Campbell, M.C.; J.P., F.I.I.A.; *b.* 1872. M.L.A. for Leichardt, N.S.W., 1907-20; Minister of Public Instruction and Colonial Treasurer, N.S.W., 1912-15; recruited Rifleman's Batt. (Carmichael Thousand), Dec. 1915; went to France with them, 1916 (wounded at Armentieres and Passchendaele, 1917; M.C.); invalided to Australia; recruited second thousand and served in France till declaration of peace. *Address:* Beaufort Court, Forbes Street, Sydney, N.S.W. [*Died* 15 *Jan.* 1953.

CARMICHAEL, Norman Scott, M.B., Ch.B., F.R.C.P.E.; Surgeon Apothecary to the Palace of Holyroodhouse; member of the Royal Company of Archers', King's Bodyguard for Scotland; Consulting Physician to Royal Hospital for Sick Children, Edinburgh; *b.* 1883; *y. s.* of late James Carmichael, M.D., F.R.C.P.E., and late Elizabeth L. Chatfield; *m.* Clare Mary, *y. d.* of late Rev. William Wallis Dodsworth, B.A., Oxford. *Educ.:* Edinburgh Academy; Edinburgh University. Fellow of the Royal College of Physicians, Edinburgh, 1913; Ex-President, Royal Medical Society; late lecturer in Edinburgh University on Diseases of Children; former Superintendent, Leith Hospital; Physician to Chalmers' Hospital, Edinburgh; Superintendent and Medical Specialist of E.M.S. Base and Auxiliary Hospitals; served in R.A.M.C., European War, 1916-19, rank of Major; member of the Order of St. Sava (Serbia). *Recreations:* golf, motoring, travelling. *Address:* 43 Moray Place, Edinburgh 3. *T.:* Edinburgh Central 5225. [*Died* 16 Nov. 1951.

CARNOCK, 2nd Baron, *cr.* 1916, of Carnock; **Frederick Archibald Nicolson,** 12th Bt. of Nova Scotia, *cr.* 1637; M.C.; late 15th The King's Hussars; *b.* 9 Jan. 1883; *e. s.* of 1st Baron and Mary Katherine (*d.* 1951), *d.* of Capt. Arch. Rowan Hamilton, Killyleagh, Co. Down; *S.* father, 1928. *Educ.:* Wellington; R.M.C. Joined 15th The King's Hussars, 1903; served in India and South Africa; A.D.C. to the Viceroy of India, 1911-13; served European War, 1914-19 (Mons star and clasp); G.S.O., 2nd Grade, 1918; Major, 15th Hussars, 1919; retired pay, 1922. Barrister, Inner Temple, 1924; Chevalier Légion d'Honneur. *Publications:* The History of the 15th The King's Hussars, 1932; Cavalry in the Corunna Campaign, 1936. *Heir: b.* Capt. Hon. Erskine Arthur Nicolson. *Address:* 36 Tedworth Square, S.W.3. *T.:* Flaxman 0423. [*Died* 31 *May* 1952.

CARNWATH, Thomas, D.S.O. 1918; Hon. D.Sc. (Belfast); M.B., D.P.H.; *b.* 7 April 1878; *s.* of late J. Carnwath, Tyrone; *m.* 1908, Margaret Ethel, *o. c.* of late Andrew M'Kee, Belfast; two *s.* *Educ.:* Foyle College, Londonderry; Queen's University, Belfast; University of Berlin. Member of Senate, Queen's University. Was Capt. R.A.M.C. (T.F.); Member Hon. Artillery Co.; served European War, 1914-18 (despatches, D.S.O.); Demonstrator of Anatomy, Queen's College, Belfast; Assistant Hygienic Institute, Hamburg; Assistant Reichsgesundheitsamt, Berlin; Deputy M.O.H. Manchester; Lecturer on Public Health, St. Thomas's Hospital; Medical Inspector, Local Government Board; Deputy Chief Medical Officer Ministry of Health, 1935-40; Examiner in Public Health, Universities of London, Manchester, Birmingham and Belfast; Member Army Hygiene Advisory Committee; Member Managing Committee Bureau of Hygiene and Tropical Diseases, Colonial Office; Member Board of Studies in Hygiene and Public Health, University of London; Member National Radium Commission. *Publications:* Official Reports; Über intermittierende Filtration; Zur Aetiologie der Hühner-Diphtherie u. Geflügel-Pocken; Public Health Organisation in U.S.A. *Address:* Cragside, Whitehead, Co. Antrim. *Clubs:* Athenæum; Ulster (Belfast). [*Died* 2 *April* 1954.

CARPENDALE, Major Frederic Maxwell-, C.I.E. 1919; Indian Army, retd.; *b.* 9 July 1887; *s.* of late Col. and Mrs. M. M. Carpendale, Shankill House, Co. Dublin; *m.* 1928, Ivy, *o. d.* of late Col. A. O. B. Wroughton, D.S.O.; three *s.* *Educ.:* Malvern Coll.; R.M.C. Sandhurst. Served European War, 1914-19 (despatches thrice, Bt.-Maj., C.I.E.); Assist. Military Secretary, General Headquarters, Mesopotamia, 1919-20; retired 1931. Served in War of 1939-45, D.A.A.G. Aldershot Command, 1939-41, D.A.A.G Aldershot Area, Feb.-Dec. 1941. *Address:* c/o National Overseas and Grindlay's Bank Ltd., 54 Parliament Street, S.W.1. [*Died* 6 *Dec.* 1958.

CARPENTER, Vice-Admiral Alfred Francis Blakeney, V.C.; *b.* 17 Sep. 1881; *s.* of late Captain Alfred Carpenter, D.S.O; *m.* 1st, 1903, Maud (*d.* 1923), *d.* of Rev. Stafford Tordiffe; one *d.*; 2nd, 1927, Hilda Margaret Alison, *d.* of late W. Chearnley Smith, M.B., C.M. *Educ.:* private school. Joined Royal Navy, 1896; Sub-Lieut. 1901; Lieut. 1903; Lieut.-Cmdr. 1911; Cmdr. 1915; Capt. 1918; Rear-Adm. 1929: service in Crete during massacres, 1898, and in China, Boxer Rebellion, 1900 (Medal); specialised in Navigation 1903 and in War Staff 1913; received thanks of Admiralty for several inventions; Humane Society Medal for saving life at sea, 1913; served European War—Admiral Jellicoe's Staff, July 1914-Nov. 1915; Navigating Commander H.M.S. Emperor of India, Nov. 1915-Nov. 1917; Admiralty War Staff, 1917 and 1918; commanded H.M.S. Vindictive at Zeebrugge during attack on 23 April 1918 (special promotion and awarded Victoria Cross, Officer of Legion of Honour, Croix de Guerre avec palme); lecturing tour through U.S.A. and Canada, 1918-19; in command of War Course for naval officers at Cambridge University, 1919-20; Command of H.M.S. Carysfort in Atlantic Fleet, 1921-23; Captain of Chatham Dockyard, 1924-26; Command of Benbow 1926, Marlborough, 1927-28; retired list, 1929; Vice-Adm., retired, 1934; Home Guard, 1940-44, O.C. 17th Glos. (Wye Valley) Bn.; Shipping Director 1945. *Publication:* The Blocking of Zeebrugge, 1921. *Recreations:* garden and billiards. *Address:*

Chantersluer, St. Briavels, Glos. *T.:* St. Briavels 234. *Clubs:* Authors', English-Speaking Union. [*Died* 27 *Dec.* 1955.

CARPENTER, Geoffrey Douglas Hale, M.B.E.; D.M. (Oxon); M.R.C.S., L.R.C.P.; *b.* Eton College, 26 Oct. 1882; 3rd *s.* of late P. Herbert Carpenter, D.Sc., F.R.S., Assistant Master, and Caroline Emma, *d.* of late Rev. E. Hale, Assistant Master; *m.* 1919, Amy Frances, *y.d.* of late John Franklen Thomas-Peter, Treviles, Cornwall; no *c. Educ.:* Oxford Preparatory School (Lynam's); Bradfield; St. Catherine's, Oxford (2nd Class in Honour School Natl. Science); St. George's Hospital (University Entrance Scholarship). House Surgeon and House Physician; entered Colonial Medical Service, 1910; certificate with distinction, London School of Tropical Medicine, 1910; appointed by Royal Society to Sleeping Sickness Commission in Uganda, 1910-14; active service, East African Campaign, 1914-18; Specialist Officer for control of Sleeping Sickness in Uganda, 1920-30, when retired from Colonial Service; 1930-31 undertook special investigation into Tse-tse fly in Ngamiland at request of Secretary of State; Hope Professor of Zoology (Entomology) University of Oxford, 1933-48, now Professor Emeritus; Vice-Pres. Linnean Society of London, 1935-36; Pres. South Eastern Union of Scientific Societies, 1936-37; Pres. Royal Entomological Society of London, 1945-46. Head Warden, A.R.P., 1940-45. *Publications:* Reports on Tse-tse fly in the Reports of the Sleeping Sickness Commission of the Royal Society since 1913; A Naturalist on Lake Victoria, 1920; A Naturalist in E. Africa, 1925; numerous technical contributions to the publications of the Entomological Society of London, etc; Mimicry, 1933 (Biological Monographs). *Recreations:* gardening, boating. *Address:* Penguelle, Hid's Copse Road, Cumnor Hill, Oxford. *T.A.:* Carpenter, Cumnor Hill, Oxford. *T.:* Cumnor 43. [*Died* 30 *Jan.* 1953.

CARPENTER, Lieut.-General George, O.B.E. 1923; *b.* 29 Nov. 1877; *e. s.* of Major G. Carpenter (late 60th Rifles); *m.* 1910, Violet (*d.* 1943), *e. d.* of W. J. Upton, Rochester. *Educ.:* private school. Joined Royal Marines, 1897; Captain, 1903; Major, 1915; Bt. Lieut.-Colonel, 1918; Instructor of Musketry Hong-Kong, 1905; Commandant H.M. Island Ascension, 1910; served European War, 1914-16 (Distinguished Service Cross); Brigade-Major, Depot Royal Marines, 1916; 8th R.M. Bn. Ireland, 1920-21; Lt.-Col. 1923; commanded 12th R.M. Bn., Shanghai Defence Force, 1927; Commandant Plymouth Div. Royal Marines, 1929; Major-General, 1931; Lt.-Gen., 1933; retired list, 1934. *Address:* The Cottage, Ormond Rd., Richmond, Surrey. [*Died* 11 *Dec.* 1952.

CARPENTER, Rev. James Nelson; *b.* Maffra Maffra, Australia; *m.* Edith Marion Bateman, London. *Educ.:* M.A. Cambridge; D.D. London. Missionary under the C.M.S. to India, 1890-1911; Principal of Emmanuel Coll.; Saskatoon, Canada, 1916; returned to India, 1918; Sec. of U.P. Mission C.M.S., 1919-23; Missionary and Chaplain, Meerut, 1923-27; Anglican Representative of North India United Theological Coll., Saharanpur, N. India, 1929-33; retired. *Address:* C.M.S., Salisbury Square, E.C.4. [*Died* 4 *March* 1949.
[*But death not notified in time for inclusion in Who Was Who 1941–1950, first edn.*

CARPENTER, Rev. Spencer Cecil, M.A., D.D.: *b.* London, 3 Nov. 1877; *s.* of late Robert Spencer Carpenter, M.A.; *m.* 1st, 1908, Sylvia Gertrude (*d.* 1941), *d.* of Rev. Duncan Llewyllyn Davies Jones; one *d.*; 2nd, 1943, C. E. Phyllis Gabriel. *Educ.:* Univ. Coll. School, London; Gonville and Caius Coll., Cambridge. Asst. Curate, St. Paul's, Walworth S.E.; Vice-Principal Westcott House, Cambridge; Warden, Gonville and Caius College Mission, Battersea; Fellow and Tutor, Selwyn College, Cambridge; Vicar and Rural Dean of Bolton, Lancs., 1922-30; Master of the Temple, 1930-35; Chaplain to the King, 1929-35; Professor of Theology, Queen's College, Harley Street, 1930-34; Hon. Canon of Manchester, 1927-1930; Dean of Exeter, 1935-50. Proctor in Convocation, 1929-30 and 1932-50. *Publications:* A Parson's Defence, 1912; Christianity according to St. Luke, 1919; A Large Room, 1923; The Anglican Tradition, 1928; Democracy in Search of a Religion, 1929; Politics and Society in the Old Testament, 1931; Supernatural Religion in Relation to Democracy, 1932; Church and People, 1789-1889, 1933; The Church and Politics, 1934; The Bible View of Life, 1937; The Way of Belief, 1939; Faith in Time of War, 1940; Exeter Cathedral, 1942, 1943; The Household of Faith, 1945; Life of Bishop Winnington-Ingram, 1949; Christianity (Pelican Series), 1953; The Church in England, 597-1688, 1954; Duncan-Jones of Chichester; A Paraphrase of the Epistle to the Ephesians, 1956; Eighteenth Century Church and People, 1959. *Recreation:* gardening. *Address:* Ford House, Broadclyst, Exeter. *T.:* Broadclyst 317. [*Died* 19 *Aug.* 1959.

CARPENTER, Sir Walter Randolph, Kt., *cr.* 1936; Chairman Directors, W. R. Carpenter and Co. Ltd. and several others; *b.* 31 Oct. 1877; *s.* of John Bolton and Emma Frances Carpenter; *m.* 1899, Edith Anderson; two *s.* three *d. Educ.:* Forrest Lodge. Commenced business at Thursday Island and founded J. B. Carpenter and Sons, 1899; Founded W. R. Carpenter and Co. Ltd., 1914; Mayor of Thursday Island 2 years. *Recreations:* tennis, golf. *Address:* c/o W. R. Carpenter (Canada) Ltd., Foot Dunlevy Avenue, Vancouver, B.C., Canada. *Clubs:* Australian Golf (New South Wales); National, Royal Automobile, Tattersalls, Millions (Sydney). [*Died* 1 *Feb.* 1954.

CARR, Rev. Frederick Robert, M.A., T.C.D.; Assistant Curate, St. Mary's, Penzance, since 1948; Canon Emer. of Truro; *b.* 22 Aug. 1869; *s.* of Rev. Canon Carr, Dublin; *m.* Ricarda Mary Kennedy, Limerick; two *s. Educ.:* S. Columba Coll., Co. Dublin; Trinity Coll., Dublin. Assist. Curate, S. Michael's, Limerick, 1893-1900; Eltham, Kent, 1900-2; S. Austell, Cornwall, 1902-6; Curate-in-Charge, Redruth, 1906-1908; Vicar of Kea, 1908-9; S. Gluvias, 1909-15; Rector of N. Tidworth, 1915-21, and Acting C.F.; Vicar of S. Mary the Virgin, Penzance, 1921-36; Dean Rural of Penwith, 1928-36; Asst. Curate St. Agnes, 1936-48; Dean Rural of Powder, 1943-48. *Recreations:* 1 mile steeplechase and 4 miles champion of Ireland, 1892; all sports, especially tennis. *Address:* Regent Hotel, Penzance, Cornwall. [*Died* 8 *Jan.* 1952.

CARR, Gilbert Harry, C.B.E. 1947; Managing Director, Producers International Sales Association Ltd., since 1930; *b.* 13 Feb. 1884; *s.* of Francis Edward Carr and Hattie Grenoble; *m.* 1st, 1906, Mary Curran (*d.* 1930); two *s.* two *d.*; 2nd, 1931, Rose Honour Annison. *Educ.:* Public Schools, New York. 2nd Imperial Light Horse, South African War, 1900-2 (Queen's Medal 3 clasps). Served European War, Captain U.S. Army A.E.F., 1917-19; Director-General, American Ambulance, Great Britain, 1940-45; Dep. Chm., London Cttee. British War Relief Soc. of America, 1940-45, Chm. 1949-; Chm., The American Soc. in London, 1937 and 1938, Hon. Sec., 1939-47; Hon. Treas., 1947-; Vice-Pres., American Chamber of Commerce in London, 1942, 1951, Pres. 1951-52; Comdr., London Post American Legion, 1937-43; Dir., American Relief Soc., 1935-; Exec. Cttee. the English-Speaking Union, 1946-52; Exec. Cttee. The Pilgrims of

Great Britain, 1948; Governor, The American Club, 1938-; National Chairman, The Incorporated Sales Managers Assoc., Great Britain, 1936-38. *Recreation:* social welfare work. *Address:* 53 Fitzjames Avenue, Croydon, Surrey. *T.:* Addiscombe 4038. *Clubs:* English-Speaking Union, American, Allies, Swedish. [*Died* 24 *April* 1954.

CARR, Lieut.-Col. Henry Arbuthnot, D.S.O. 1915; late Worcestershire Regt.; *b.* 2 Sept. 1872; *e. s.* of Col. R. E. Carr, 36th Regt.; *m.* 1913, Elsie Pearson, *d.* of late Sir Thomas Putnam; one *s.* one *d.* *Educ.:* Haileybury; Sandhurst. Entered army, 1893; served S. African War, 1900-1902 (despatches, King's medal 2 clasps, Queen's medal 3 clasps); European War, 1915-17 (wounded, despatches thrice, D.S.O., Bt. Lt.-Col.); retired pay, 1921. *Address:* Woodhill, Otterburn, Northumberland. *Club:* Army and Navy.
[*Died* 22 *Jan.* 1951.

CARR, Howard; composer and operatic conductor; Member of Council, Composers' Guild; one of the founders of The Musical Conductors' Association, and first Hon. Secretary, 1916-23; *b.* Manchester, 26 Dec. 1880; *s.* of late Edward Carr and Lillie Munkittrick; *m.* Beatrix (*d.* 1929), *y. d.* of late R. N. D. Tracy, Government Statist of Victoria, Australia; one *s.* *Educ.:* St. Paul's School (Scholar); City and Guilds of London Inst. Abandoned study of civil engineering at nineteen to undertake theatrical conductorship; since then has conducted numerous productions of light opera; has composed a great deal of theatrical music, including In the Jungle and Master Wayfarer; and part-composer of The Lilac Domino, Shanghai, The Girl for the Boy, and The Blue Kitten; his symphonic works, which he conducted at Queen's Hall Promenade Concerts, include The Jolly Roger, Three Heroes, and The Jovial Huntsmen; Musical Director to the Harrogate Corporation, 1923 and 1924; revisited Australia, 1928-38; conducted Royal Sydney Philharmonic Society; professor of harmony and counterpoint, State Conservatorium; Music Editor to Australian Broadcasting Commission. Choral work, Ode to the Deity, first performed by London Orpheus Choir, 1950. *Publications:* Collection of Sea Songs and Chanties; four vols. edition of classical and original music for the kinema theatre (Carr's Cine-music); numerous songs and orchestral compositions; articles on music to Australian periodicals. *Recreations:* literature, travel. *Address:* 5 Gloucester Walk, W.8. *T.:* Western 1476.
[*Died* 16 *Nov.* 1960.

CARR, Sir Hubert Winch, K.C.I.E., *cr.* 1936; Kt., *cr.* 1925; late Managing Director, Balmer, Lawrie & Co., Ltd., Calcutta; *b.* 1877; *s.* of Ambrose Patient Carr, Beckenham, Kent; *m.* 1923, Evelyn Margaret Bruce, *er. d.* of late Herbert Johnston, W.S., Edinburgh. *Educ.:* The Abbey, Beckenham. President, European Association, India, 1922-25; Member, Indian Round Table Conferences, 1930-33; Director of Tea and Coffee, Ministry of Food, 1939-44; President of India Burma Association, 1945-47 *Address:* 137 Cranmer Court, S.W.3. *T.:* Kensington 6248. *Club:* Oriental.
[*Died* 24 *May* 1955.

CARR, Lieutenant-General Laurence, C.B. 1939; D.S.O. 1917; O.B.E. 1919; Gordon Highlanders; *b.* 1886; *m.* 1916, Elizabeth Montgomery Freer. *Educ.:* Uppingham; Royal Military College, Sandhurst. Served European War, 1914-18 (despatches, D.S.O., O.B.E.); General Staff Officer, 1st Grade, War Office, 1931-34; Directing Staff, Imperial Defence Coll., 1934-36; Comdr. 2nd Infantry Brigade, 1936-1938; Director of Staff Duties, War Office, 1938-39; Assistant Chief of the Imperial General Staff, 1939-40; General Officer Commanding 1st Corps, 1940-41; Gen. Officer Commanding-in-Chief, Eastern Command, 1941-42; Senior Military Assistant Ministry of Supply; retired pay, 1944. *Recreations:* polo, golf, and cricket. *Address:* Park Gate House, Ham Common, Surrey. *T.:* Kingston 6256. *Clubs:* White's, Naval and Military, Roehampton, M.C.C. [*Died* 15 *April* 1954.

CARR, Colonel William Moncrieff, C.B.E. 1950 (O.B.E. 1934); T.D. 1930; Chairman: United Kingdom Construction & Engineering Co. Ltd.; Lincolnshire Chemical Co. Ltd.; Normanby Park Tar Supply Co. Ltd.; Director, National Benzole Co. Ltd., etc.; *b.* 17 August 1886; *e. s.* of Isaac and Mary Carr, Birchfield, Farnworth, nr. Widnes, Lancs.; *m.* 1916, Vera Frances, 4th *d.* of Samuel Richard Dew, Solicitor, Bangor, N. Wales. *Educ.:* Owen's Coll., Manchester; Manchester Univ. Gas and Water Consulting Engineering Practice, Partner with late Isaac Carr, M.Inst.C.E., 1907. Pres.: Manchester Dist. Instn. of Gas Engineers, 1930; The Instn. of Gas Engineers, 1935; developed the U.K. Gas Corp. Ltd., Man. Dir., 1935, Chm., 1947; developed Yorkshire High Pressure Gas Grid, 1938-39; Chm., N. Western Gas Bd., 1949, resigned 1950. Commissioned 55th West Lancs. Div. R.E. (T.A.), 1913; served European War, 1914-19, France and N. Russia; comd. Regt., 1926-34; Bt. Col., 1930; Hon. Col. 55th Divnl. R.E. (now 107 Corps Engineer Regt., T.A.), 1934-. *Publications:* technical contribs. to Roy. Soc. Arts, Instn. of Gas Engineers, Inst. of Civil Engineers, etc. *Recreations:* hunting (Jt. M.F.H. North Cheshire Hounds, 1944-46); gardening. *Address:* Oldfield Brow, Dunham Massey, Cheshire. *T.:* Altrincham 1280. *Clubs:* Bath; Clarendon (Manchester).
[*Died* 1 *Dec.* 1956.

CARRICK, 8th Earl of (*cr.* 1748), **Theobald Walter Somerset Henry Butler;** Baron Butler (U.K.) of Mt. Juliet and Kilkenny, 1912; Baron Butler, 1607; Viscount Ikerrin, 1629; *b.* 23 May 1903; *e. s.* of 7th Earl and Ellen Rosamond Mary (*d.* 1946), *d.* of Lieutenant-Colonel H. G. Lindsay; *S.* father, 1931; *m.* 1st, 1930, Marion Caher (Edwards) (who obtained a divorce, 1938), *er. d.* of Daniel C. Donoghue, Philadelphia, U.S.A.; one *s.*; 2nd, 1938, Margaret Power Drum (*d.* 1954), *e. d.* of Charles B. Power, Helena, Montana, U.S.A.; 3rd, Ruth, *d.* of Francis T. M. McEnery, Cambridge, New York, U.S.A. *Educ.:* Repton. Served as temp. Commander R.N.V.R. *Heir:* *s.* Viscount Ikerrin. *Address:* Kenspur, Pinehurst, North Carolina, U.S.A. [*Died* 31 *July* 1957.

CARRIGAN, William, K.C. Called to Irish Bar, 1897; Inner Bar, 1909; Bencher, King's Inn, 1918; called to English Bar, Gray's Inn, 1923. *Address:* Ballinguile, Eglinton Road, Dublin. [*Died* 25 *Jan.* 1951.

CARROLL, Francis Patrick; *b.* 29 Jan. 1887; *s.* of Michael Carroll and Catherine Fleming; *m.* 1911, Annie Margaret Williams; two *d.* *Educ.:* St. Joseph's, Denmark Hill. Five years Civil Service (Charity Commission); Thirty years, Voluntary Hospital service; Fellow of Institute of Hospital Administrators. *Publications:* Press contributions. *Address:* 58 Tennyson Road, Harpenden, Herts. *T.:* Harpenden 4447.
[*Died* 29 *Nov.* 1955.

CARROLL, Sydney Wentworth, O.B.E. 1918; Editorial Consultant to Viscount Kemsley; Literary Editor The Daily Sketch; from Sept. 1938 to Sept. 1942, Managing Editor of the Daily Sketch; also The Sunday Graphic; Adviser on staff of Allied Publications, Ltd.; Theatrical Manager, Film Critic, and Journalist; *b.* Melbourne, Victoria, Australia, 16 Feb. 1877. *Educ.:* Creswick Grammar School. Formerly an actor, then a publisher of books, periodicals, and prints—also a printer; during the war from 1914-18 served in the Supply Department of the War Office (O.B.E.); Dramatic Critic Sunday Times, 1918-23; Theatrical Manager since 1931; has produced plays at the Ambassadors, Criterion, New, Little, His Majesty's, Wyndham's, Cambridge, and Shaftesbury; established the Open Air Theatre, Regent's Park, 1933; President of Critics' Circle, 1931-32; Commendatore of the Crown of Italy, 1933; ex-Member of National Theatre Appeal Committee Executive. *Publications:* Some Dramatic Opinions; Acting for the Stage. *Recreations:* fishing, walking, boating, archæology. *Address:* Poynings, Victoria Drive, Bognor Regis, Sussex. *Club:* Savage. [*Died* 24 *Aug.* 1958.

CARRUTHERS, Mrs.; *see* Markham, Violet R.

CARSLAW, Horatio Scott, D.Sc. (Glasgow), Sc.D. (Cambridge), D.Sc. (Hon. Adelaide), LL.D. (Hon.) (Glasgow), F.R.S.E.; Emeritus Professor of Mathematics in the University of Sydney; formerly Fellow of Emmanuel College, Cambridge; *b.* 12 Feb. 1870; *s.* of Rev. Dr. Carslaw, Helensburgh; *m.* 1907, Ethel Maude (*d.* 1907), 2nd *d.* of Sir Wm. J. Clarke, 1st Bt., of Rupertswood, Victoria. *Educ.:* Glasgow, Cambridge, Rome, Palermo, and Göttingen Universities. Formerly Lecturer in Mathematics in the University of Glasgow. *Publications:* mathematical works and papers in scientific journals. *Address:* The University, Sydney, N.S.W. [*Died* 10 *Nov.* 1954.

CARSON, Colonel Charles John Lloyd, C.B.E. 1919; D.L., J.P.; *b.* Simla, India, 16 Oct. 1866; *e. s.* of John Lloyd Carson of Egryn Abbey, Merioneth; *m.* Elizabeth Furnival (*d.* 1925), *e. d.* of Robert Wilson of Oak Lodge, Bitterne, Hants, and Sandbach, Cheshire; one *s.* two *d.* *Educ.:* King William's College, Isle of Man. Commanded 3rd Bn. East Lancashire Regt.; served South Africa, 1899-1902 with 1st Bn. East Lancashire Regt. and on Staff; European War, 1914-1918 (C.B.E.). *Address:* Hengwm, Tal-y-bont, Merioneth. *T.:* Dyffryn 210. [*Died* 26 *Nov.* 1953.

CARSON, Brig. Sir Frederick, Kt., *cr.* 1941; C.B.E. 1943; M.C.; retired; *b.* 10 Feb. 1886; *s.* of late Robert James Carson, Kingston, Ontario; *m.* 1913, Dorothy A. C., *d.* of late Frederick Brownfield, Bank of British North America; three *s.* one *d.* *Educ.:* Kingston (Ont.) Collegiate Institute; Queen's Univ. and Royal Military College, Kingston, Ont. Commissioned in R.E., 1908; proceeded India, 1911; served on State Railways, India, 1913-14 and 1919-40; General Manager, North-Western Railway, 1936-40; retired (from Railways and Army), 1941; served in France, European War, 1915-18; commanded 78th Fld. Co. R.E. and 3rd Fld. Sqdn. R.E., 3rd Cav. Div. (despatches twice, M.C. and Bar); War of 1939-45 (C.B.E.). *Recreations:* sailing; outdoor games, excelling at none. *Club:* United Service. [*Died* 3 *May* 1960.

CARTAN, Elie Joseph, F.R.S. 1947; Membre du Bureau des Longitudes; *b.* Dolomieu, Isère, France, 9 avril 1869; *m.* 1903, Marie Louise Bianconi; one *s.* one *d.* *Educ.:* Collège de Vienne; lycée de Grenoble; lycée Janson; École Normale Supérieure. Maître de conférences, Université de Montpellier, 1894-96, Lyon, 1896-1903; professeur, Université de Nancy, 1903-9; maître de conférences, Université de Paris, 1909-12; professeur: Université de Paris, 1912-40, École Physique et Chimie, Paris, 1910-41; professeur honoraire, Université de Paris, 1940; member Académie des Sciences de Paris, 1931; associé étranger de l'Académie des Sciences et des Lettres de Cracovie, 1921, de l'Académie norvégienne des Sciences d'Oslo, 1926, de l'Académie nationale des Lincei à Rome, 1927; membre honoraire de l'Académie Roumaine, 1931; associé étranger de l'Académie royale des Sciences d'Amsterdam, 1937, et de l'Académie royale de Belgique, 1937; Docteur honoris causa de l'Université de Liége, 1934, de l'Univ. Harvard, 1936, de l'Univ. libre de Bruxelles, 1947; de l'Univ. de Bucarest, 1948, de l'Univ. Catholique de Louvain, 1947, de l'Univ. de Pise, 1948. *Publications:* Thèse sur la structure des groupes de transformations finis et continus, 1894; Leçons sur les invariants intégraux, 1922; Leçons sur la géométrie des espaces de Riemann, 1e éd. 1928, 2e éd. 1946; Leçons sur la géométrie projective complexe, 1921; Sur les espaces de Finsler, 1933; Les espaces métriques fondés sur la notion d'aire, 1933; La topologie des groupes de Lie, 1936; Leçons sur la théorie des espaces à connexion projective, 1937; La théorie des groupes finis et continus et la géométrie différentielle, 1937; Leçons sur la théorie des spineurs, Vol. I, II, 1938; Selecta, 1939; Les systèmes différentiels extérieurs et leurs applications géométriques, 1945. *Address:* 95 Boulevard Jourdan, Paris XIV, France. *T.:* Gobelins 93.00. [*Died* 6 *May* 1951.

CARTER, Albert Charles Robinson; Editor of The Year's Art, 1894-1952; Member Council, National Art-Collections Fund; *b.* Bradford, 23 Jan. 1864; *s.* of James Carter, woolstapler; *m.* 1904, Amelia Cooper; one *d.* *Educ.:* Bradford Grammar School. Asst. editor The Year's Art, 1887; writer on miscellaneous art and literary matters for Daily Telegraph, 1901-52; editor of the Year's Music, 1898; contributor to the Art Journal from 1889; formerly art critic Manchester Courier and The Outlook; art critic for Pall Mall Gazette during illness of the late R. A. M. Stevenson; succeeded the late Gleeson White on Photograms of the Year, 1899; writer of the Art Annual, 1900 on War Artists; Four vols.: Christie's, 1928-31; Let me Tell You, 1940; Let Me Add, 1949; An Outburst, 1941; contributor to the Encyclopædia Britannica, The Burlington Magazine, Apollo, and The Studio. *Address:* Orchard House, East Molesey, Surrey. *T.:* Molesey 61. *Clubs:* Knights of the Round Table (King Arthur's Champion); Old Bradfordians (Founder). [*Died* 7 *Nov.* 1957.

CARTER, Sir Archibald; *see* Carter, Sir R. H. A.

CARTER, Captain (S) Bernard, C.B.E. 1942; R.N. (retired); *b.* 22 June 1885; *s.* of Charles and Mary Ann Carter; *m.* 1915, Gladys Mary Bowyer-Smijth; one *s.* two *d.* *Educ.:* Christ's Hospital. Joined Royal Navy, 1902; retired, 1935; called up, 1939; Base Accountant Officer, Alexandria, Egypt, 1939-45. *Address:* The Cottage, Charmouth, Dorset. *T.:* Charmouth 107. [*Died* 28 *March* 1954.

CARTER, Sir Edgar B.; *see* Bonham-Carter.

CARTER, Edward Henry, O.B.E. 1919; M.A.; *b.* Scarning, Norfolk, 1876; *s.* of William Carter and Sophia Wilkinson; *m.* 1903, Margaret, *er. d.* of late Arthur Ruston; one *s.* two *d.* *Educ.:* Jesus College (Scholar), Cambridge; Kiel; Paris. H.M. Inspector of Schools and Training Colleges, and Chief Examiner in History, Board of Education (retired, 1936); late Director of Hollis & Carter Ltd., Publishers. *Publications:* Norwich Subscription Books (1637-1800); (with Sir Henry Marten) Histories; (with H. G. Wells) Short History of Mankind; (with R. A. F. Mears) History of Britain; (with C. K. Ogden) General History (in Basic English); Contributor to

Norfolk Archæological Journal; Russian Cavalcade, 1943; The Search for Peace, 1949; (with Phyllis Wragge) Two Paths to Freedom (Britain and U.S.A.), 1951. *Recreations:* walking, gardening. *Address:* Arley House, Fillongley, Coventry. *T.A.:* Carter, Fillongley. *T.:* Fillongley 204. *Club:* Athenæum. [*Died* 3 *Feb.* 1953.

CARTER, Frederick William, F.R.S. 1932; M.A., Sc.D., M.Inst.C.E., M.I.E.E., etc.; British Thomson Houston Co., Ltd., 1903-1945, retired; *b.* Aston, Birmingham, 16 Dec. 1870; *s.* of J. Carter, Die-sinker and Medallist; *m.* 1908, Edith Mildred Cramp, Coventry; three *s.* *Educ.:* Birmingham and Midland Institute; St. John's College, Cambridge. Lecturer in Electrical Engineering, City and Guilds Engineering College, South Kensington, 1896-1900; with General Electric Co., Schenectady, N.Y., U.S.A., 1900-3. *Publications:* Railway Electric Traction; papers on magnetic fields in air gaps of dynamo electric machines, and air-gap coefficients; on design of transformers; on the repulsion motor; on electric railway engineering in various aspects; on stability of running of locomotives, etc. *Address:* Beechcroft, Long Itchington, Rugby. [*Died* 29 *May* 1952.

CARTER, Sir Gerald Francis, Kt. *cr.* 1943; O.B.E. 1919; late Principal Assist. Treasury Solicitor; *b.* 28 Sept. 1881; *s.* of William Carter; *m.* 1917, Constance Elizabeth Childs; one *s.* *Educ.:* St. Paul's School; Oriel College, Oxford. Barrister-at-law (Gray's Inn), 1906; served in Army throughout European War, 1914-19; D.J.A.G. (France and Flanders) with rank of Lt.-Col., 1919. *Recreations:* photography and yachting. *Address:* Little Wood, Salcombe, S. Devon. *T.:* Salcombe 65. [*Died* 21 *Jan.* 1959.

CARTER, Rev. Henry, C.B.E. 1934; Chairman: World Council of Churches Standing Conference on Refugees; of Christian Council for Refugees; Chairman of Executive of Temperance Council of the Christian Churches of England and Wales; Chairman of National Peace Council; Chairman of Executive of Council of Christians and Jews; *b.* Plymouth, 3 Nov. 1874; *s.* of late George Henry Richards Carter, Plymouth; *m.* 1905, Sarah Elizabeth, *d.* of late James Rumbelow, Cardiff; one *d.* *Educ.:* Private school; Plymouth Public School; Handsworth College, Birmingham. Wesleyan Minister in Bristol, Harrow and Birmingham, 1901-11; General Secretary of Social Welfare Department of Methodist Church, 1911-42; Member of Government Central Control Board (Liquor Traffic), 1916-21; Member of Royal Commission on Licensing (England and Wales), 1929-30. *Publications:* The Church and the New Age, 1911; Destitution, can we end it? 1912; The Control of the Drink Trade (the record of the work of the Central Control Board, Liquor Traffic), 1919; The Nation Surveys the Drink Problem; The English Temperance Movement: a Study in Objectives (Beckly Lecture), 1933; The Methodist: a Study in Discipleship; Liberty and Authority in the Modern World (Merttens Lecture), 1939; Towards World Recovery, 1945; The Refugee Problem in Europe and the Middle East, 1950; The Methodist Heritage, 1951; Editor of Journal of Wesleyan Union for Social Service, 1906-17; numerous pamphlets on the relation of the Christian faith to social questions. *Recreation:* fishing. *Address:* 14 Sumner Place, S.W.7. *Club:* National Liberal. [*Died* 19 *June* 1951.

CARTER, Rev. Henry Child, M.A.; Congregational Minister; *b.* Clapton, 21 June 1875; *y. s.* of Edwin J. and Esther Carter; *m.* 1901, Mabel Lilian Phillips (*d.* 1931); one *s.* two *d.* *Educ.:* Priory House School; Mill Hill School; Oriel College, Oxford and Mansfield College, Oxford, M.A. Oxford, 1901, M.A. Cambridge (by incorporation), 1910. Minister of Queen Street Congregational Church, Wolverhampton, 1901-10; and of Emmanuel Church, Cambridge, 1910-44; Chairman of the Congregational Union of England and Wales, 1932-33. *Publications:* Auto-suggestion and Religion, 1922; Our Father, 1923; Human Relations in the Light of Christ, 1924. *Address:* The Water House, Water Lane, Bishop's Stortford. *T.:* Bishop's Stortford 749. [*Died* 1 *Aug.* 1954.

CARTER, I. M. B.; *see* Bonham-Carter.

CARTER, Sir Morris; *see* Carter, Sir W. M.

CARTER, Sir (Richard Henry) Archibald, G.C.M.G., *cr.* 1949; K.C.B., *cr.* 1938 (C.B. 1930); K.C.I.E., *cr.* 1935; *b.* 1887; *e. s.* of late Col. A. H. Carter, C.M.G.; *m.* 1923, *o.d.* of late W. E. Painter; no *c.* *Educ.:* Eton; Trinity College, Cambridge. Private Sec. to Sec. of State for India, 1924-27; Asst. Sec., Indian Statutory Commission, 1927-30; Sec. General of Round Table Conference, 1930-1931; Assistant Under-Secretary of State for India, 1936; Permanent Secretary of Admiralty, 1936-40; Chairman, Eastern Group Supply Council, Delhi, 1941-42; Chairman of Board of Customs and Excise, 1942-47; Permanent Under-Secretary of State for India, 1947; Joint Permanent Under-Secretary of State for Commonwealth Relations, 1948; Chairman, Monopolies and Restrictive Practices Commission, 1949-53. *Club:* United University. [*Died* 10 *Nov.* 1958.

CARTER, Vivian; organiser, lecturer, journalist; *b.* 1878; *e. s.* of late John Carter, Ringmore, Teignmouth; *m.* 1907, Violet, *e. d.* of late Leslie Antill, solicitor, London; one *s.* two *d.* Adopted journalism, 1901, as member of literary staff, C. Arthur Pearson, Ltd.; Pearson's Magazine; Daily Express, and kindred publications; travelled in all parts of Europe and in America as special correspondent; Manchester Dispatch, 1905; Editor of The Bystander, 1908-16; 2nd Lieut. R.A.S.C., B.E.F., 1917-18; H.M. Foreign Office Press Bureau, Paris, 1918-19; Ministry of Labour Publicity Officer, 1919; British Delegate to International Rotary Conventions in America, 1922 and 1924; General Secretary of the Rotary Clubs of Great Britain and Ireland, 1921-28; Editor and Manager The Rotarian (Chicago); Special Commissioner Rotary International, 1928-31; International Missionary Council, London, 1934-36; Lecturer: New Commonwealth Society, 1936-48; Ministry of Information, S. and S.E. Regions, 1940-45; Free Trade Union since 1946; United Europe Movement, 1950. *Publications:* editorials, essays, and numerous short stories in magazines; literary and musical criticisms in various weekly Reviews. *Address:* 136 Ardingly Drive, Goring-by-Sea, Sussex. *Club:* National Liberal. [*Died* 22 *Feb.* 1956.

CARTER, Sir (William) Morris, Kt., *cr.* 1919; C.B.E. 1918; B.A., B.C.L.; Commander of the Order of the Crown of Belgium, 1921; *b.* 9 Dec. 1873; *s.* of late Sidney James Carter, Canterbury, and Winifred A., *d.* of late William Morris of Petworth; *m.* 1928, Lavinia Florence (*d.* 1943), *d.* of late Arthur Richard Brown; one *d.* *Educ.:* King's School, Canterbury; Brasenose College, Oxford. Certificate of Honour, Bar Examination, and Prize of Council of Legal Education in Constitutional Law and Legal History. Called to Bar, Lincoln's Inn, 1899; Registrar East Africa Protectorate, 1902; Magistrate, Mombasa, 1902; Judge of H.M. High Court of Uganda, and H.B.M. Court of Appeal for Eastern Africa, 1903; Chief Justice, Uganda Protectorate, 1912-20; Temp. Capt. and O. i/c Supplies, Uganda, 1914; Temp. Lt.-Col. Uganda Transport Corps, and A.D.T., Uganda, 1916 (despatches); organised Local Shortages Section Ministry of Food, London, 1917-18; Acting Governor, Uganda, Dec. 1919-July 1920; Chief Justice Tanganyika Territory; 1920-24; Pres., Court of Appeal for Eastern Africa, 1921-24; Chairman, Land Commission, Southern Rhodesia. 1925; Cotton Enquiry Commission, Uganda, 1929; Kenya Land Commission, 1932-1933; Member, Palestine Royal Commission, 1936-37; Colonial Law Research Group, 1943. *Publications:* Joint compiler of The Laws of the Uganda Protectorate, 1910; contributor to Law Quarterly Review. *Address:* Eastlands, Kerves Lane, Horsham. Sx. *T.:* Horsham, 4648. [*Died* 22 *Sept.* 1960.

CARTHEW, Lieut.-Col. Thomas Walter Colby, D.S.O. 1915; Q.C. 1936; late R.F.C. and Bedfords Regt.; *b.* 1 July 1880; *m.* 1st, 1920, Eileen (who obtained a divorce, 1921), *d.* of late Rt. Hon. E. Shortt; 2nd, 1921, Sylvia Cadell (*d.* 1929), *o. c.* of late R. Gordon Shaw; 3rd, 1932, Dorothy Annette, *d.* of late Sir Francis Towle, C.B.E. Entered Army, Northumberland Fusiliers, 1900; retired, 1909; served South Africa, 1899-1902 (Queen's medal 3 clasps, King's medal 2 clasps); European War, 1914-1918 (D.S.O.); contested (U.) S.W. Ham, 1910, 1918; called to Bar, 1909; Recorder of Maidstone, 1936-51; Regional Commandant, Eastern Region, A.T.C., 1941. *Address:* 4 Paper Buildings, Temple, E.C.4. *T.:* Central 3366. [*Died* 18 *April* 1955.

CARTMEL-ROBINSON, Sir Harold (Francis), Kt., *cr.* 1948; C.M.G. 1942; O.B.E. 1933; *b.* 28 Mar. 1889; *s.* of late Rev. J. Cartmel-Robinson; *m.* 1917, Beatrix Elizabeth Whittle; two *d.* *Educ.:* St. Paul's School; Merton Coll., Oxford. Entered Administration, N. Rhodesia, 1912; resigned to proceed active service, 1916; commissioned R.F.A., 1917, Western Front; re-entered N. Rhodesia Administration, 1919, Native Commissioner; Prov. Commr. Northern Prov. 1934, Southern Prov. 1936, Western Prov. 1937; Sec. for Native Affairs, N. Rhodesia, 1944; Chief Sec., N. Rhodesia, 1945-47; retired. 1947; Acting Governor, May 1946. Director of various companies. *Address:* Robinwood, Borrowdale Sub-Post Office, Salisbury, S. Rhodesia. *Clubs:* Salisbury, New (S. Rhodesia). [*Died* 18 *Nov.* 1957.

CARTON, Ronald Lewis; author and journalist; *b.* London, 1888; *m.* 1927, Jane, *y. d.* of late David C. Lamb, C.M.G.; one *s.* one *d.* Editorial staff of The Times, 1910-37; Managing Editor, Country Life Publications, 1937-40; jointly correspondent of The Times in Japan and editor of the Japan Advertiser, Tokyo, 1923-24; was present at and described the great earthquake in Japan, Sept. 1923; returned to London as a special writer and subsequently Editor of The Times Special Numbers; served European War, 1915-18 with Inns of Court O.T.C. and Duke of Cornwall's Light Infantry; Govt. service, 1940-45; has travelled extensively. *Publications:* Steel and Flowers (verse); The English Scene; England; The Gentle Adventure; This Our London. *Address:* 2 Canonbury Place, N.1. *T.:* Canonbury 1871. *Club:* Reform. [*Died* 9 *July* 1960.

CARTON DE WIART, Comte Henry; Member of Belgian House of Representatives for Brussels since 1896; Pres. Supreme Econ. Council of Belgium and Luxembourg; Minister without Portfolio, 1949; *b.* Brussels, 31 Jan. 1869; *s.* of Constant Carton de Wiart, Brussels; *m.* 1897, Juliette, *d.* of George Verhaegen; two *s.* four *d.* *Educ.:* Brussels; Paris. Minister of State and Member of the Government. Envoyé Extraordinaire et Ministre Plénipotentiaire of the King of the Belgians; Minister of Justice, 1911-18; Prime Minister and Minister of Interior, Belgium, 1920 and 1921; Ministre de la Prévoyance Sociale et de l'Hygiène, 1932-34; Doctor of Law; President of Federation des Avocats Belges; President of the Union Interparlementaire; Associate Member of Institut de France; Great Cross of Belgian Order, Great Cross St. Michel et St. Georges, Légion d'Honneur, Sts. Maurice et Lazare, etc. *Publications:* The Way of Honour, 1918; La Belgique, 1928; several books of Essays on International Law and Colonial and Social Economy; five historical novels on Belgian History. *Address:* 137 chaussée de Charleroi, Brussels; Hastière-par-delà (Province de Namur). [*Died* 6 *May* 1951.

CARTWRIGHT, Albert; Editor, West Africa, 1916-47 (when retd.), one of four officially nominated trustees of Aggrey House, London (now replaced by the Colonial Centre); *b.* Lancs.; 25 Dec. 1868; two *d.* (one *s.* decd.). Asst. Editor Johannesburg Star, 1892-96; Editor Diamond Fields Advertiser, 1896-98; Editor South African News, 1899-1905; London Editor Rand Daily Mail, 1905-1907; Responsible Editor Transvaal Leader, 1907-11. *Address:* 38 Amherst Road, Bexhill-on-Sea, Sussex. [*Died* 29 *Feb.* 1956.

CARTWRIGHT, Sir Charles Henry, Kt., *cr.* 1939; Alderman and J.P. County Borough, Bournemouth; *b.* 1865; *s.* of late Henry Cartwright; *m.* 1889, Lucy Emmeline Hendren (deceased); one *s.* three *d.* *Educ.:* Bath (privately). Chairman, Canford Securities, Ltd.; Director, Offer and Co. Ltd. *Address:* 12 St. Anthonys Road, Bournemouth. *T.:* Bournemouth 1556. [*Died* 3 *July* 1959.

CARTWRIGHT, Lieut.-Colonel Francis Lennox, C.B.E. 1919; D.S.O. 1900; late Lord Strathcona's Corps; late Inspector, N.W. Mounted Police, Canada; *b.* 27 March 1874; 5th *s.* of late Rt. Hon. Sir R. J. Cartwright, G.C.M.G.; *m.* 1901, Ada Marion Carlos, (*d.* 1954), *e. d.* of Augustus F. Perkins of Oak Dene, Holmwood, Surrey. *Educ.:* Bishop Ridley Coll.; St. Catherine's, Canada; Queen's University, Kingston, Canada. Capt. 14th Batt. Princess of Wales' Own Rifles, Canadian Militia, 1896; joined North-West Mounted Police, 1897, served in Yukon and North-West Territories; was seconded to serve in Strathcona's Horse, 1900; served in S. Africa with that corps till its return to Canada (D.S.O.); returned to N.W.M.P. 1901; retired, 1904; Capt. 5th Field Battery C.A. 1906; Captain, Strathcona's Horse (Royal Canadians), 1910; served European War, 1914 to the end of the war; retired 1920 from the Canadian permanent force. *Recreations:* shooting, riding, yachting, swimming, football, hockey. *Address:* Bethwines, Black Boy Lane, Fishbourne, Sussex. *Club:* Junior Army and Navy. [*Died* 5 *Dec.* 1957.

CARTWRIGHT, Brig.-General George Strachan, C.B. 1916; C.M.G. 1918; late Chief Engineer; *b.* 29 Aug. 1866; *s.* of late Rev. Conway Cartwright, Vancouver, Canada; *m.* 1898, Kate Mary (*d.* 1943), *o. d.* of late Robert A. Stevenson, M.D., Toronto, Canada; (*s.* killed in action, Nov. 1942; one *d.* decd.). *Educ.:* private school; R.M.C., Canada. Received Commission Royal Engineers, R.M.C., Canada, 1885; served in United Kingdom, India, and Canada; retired pay, 1920; served Isazai Expedition, Indian Frontier, 1892; European War, 1914-18 (despatches, C.B., C.M.G., Officer Legion of Honour). *Address:* c/o Bank of Montreal, 500 Granville St., Vancouver, B.C., Canada. [*Died* 15 *Jan.* 1959.

CARTWRIGHT, Colonel Henry Antrobus, C.M.G. 1945; M.C.; *b.* 23 Mar. 1887; *s.* of Rev. Arthur Rogers Cartwright; *m.* 1918, Cicely Comer Wakefield (*d.* 1955); one *s.* one *d.*; *m.* 1956, Lady Betty Trafford, *widow* of Major S. W. Trafford and *d.* of 7th Earl of Abingdon. *Educ.:* Malvern College; Royal Military

College, Sandhurst. Middlesex Regt. 1906; served European War (prisoner, escaped, M.C., Legion of Honour, Czechoslovak Croix de Guerre); Military Mission, Prague, 1919-1920; H.M. Consul, Bratislava, 1920-22; retired, 1922; Immigration Officer for Palestine, Trieste 1923, Warsaw 1924-25; Observer, Sudetenland, 1938; Military Attaché, Berne, 1939-45, Local Brigadier (C.M.G.). *Publication:* (Part Author) Within Four Walls, 1930. *Address:* c/o Standard Bank of S. Africa, George, Cape Province, S. Africa. *Club:* Army and Navy.
[*Died* 30 *July* 1957.

CARTWRIGHT, Sir William Bramwell, Kt., *cr.* 1942; J.P.; D.L. West Riding of Yorks and City of York; *b.* 7 April 1876; *s.* of William and Alice Cartwright, Leeds; *m.* 1st, 1901, Annie (*d.* 1917), *d.* of Henry Tomlinson, Leeds; one *s.* three *d.*; 2nd, 1927, Doris Mary, *d.* of James Bean, Leeds. *Educ.:* Leeds Boys' Modern School. Left school at 15 years of age. Founder of W. B. Cartwright Ltd., Manufacturing Chemists, Rawdon; Chairman and Managing Director Crestona Ltd. Food Products, Leeds; commenced Local Government career as a member of Rawdon U.D.C.; elected to West Riding C.C., 1919; Chairman, 1939-46; Alderman, 1925. Member of Fabian Society and of Labour Party. *Address:* West Park Drive (East), Leeds 8. *T.:* 662198. *Club:* Moortown Golf (Leeds).
[*Died* 26 *Feb.* 1958.

CARUANA, Colonel Alfred Joseph, C.I.E. 1918; *b.* 1865; *m.*; one *s.* two *d.* Late Indian Army and Judge Advocate-General, India; served N.W. Frontier of India, 1891 (medal with clasp); N.W. Frontier of India, 1897-98 (medal with three clasps); retired 1920. *Address:* 10 Albany Villas, Hove.
[*Died* 8 *Feb.* 1953.

CARY (Arthur) Joyce (Lunel); Hon. LL.D. (Edin.) 1953; Author; *b.* 7 Dec. 1888; *e. s.* of late Arthur P. C. Cary, Wadeford, Som., and Charlotte Joyce; *m.* 1916, Gertrude Margaret Ogilvie (*d.* 1949); four *s.* *Educ.:* Clifton; Trinity College, Oxford; studied art at Edinburgh. Balkan War, 1912-13, Montenegrin Battalion and British Red Cross; 1913, Irish co-operative organisation under Sir Horace Plunkett. Joined Nigerian Political Service, 1913; resigned on ill-health, 1920; Cameroons Campaign, 1915-16, with Nigeria Regt. *Publications: novels:* Aissa Saved, 1932; American Visitor, 1933; The African Witch, 1936; Castle Corner, 1938; Mister Johnson, 1939; Charley is my Darling, 1940; The House of Children, 1941; Herself Surprised, 1941; To be a Pilgrim, 1942; The Horse's Mouth, 1944; The Moonlight, 1946; A Fearful Joy, 1949; Prisoner of Grace, 1952; Except the Lord, 1953; Not Honour More, 1955; (posthumous) The Captive and the Free, 1959; (posthumous) *short stories:* Spring Song, 1960; *political philosophy:* Power in Men, 1939; The Case for African Freedom, 1941; The Process of Real Freedom, 1943; *poetry:* Marching Soldier, 1945; The Drunken Sailor, 1947. *Relevant Publication:* Joyce Cary: a Preface to his Novels, by Andrew Wright. *Address:* 12 Parks Road, Oxford.
[*Died* 29 *March* 1957.

CARY, Max, D.Litt. (Oxon); Emeritus Professor of Ancient History, London University; *b.* Liverpool, 6 Aug. 1881; *m.* Mary Goodrick, *d.* of J. Spencer Swann, Edgbaston, Birmingham; one *d.* *Educ.:* Liverpool College; C.C.C. Oxon (Scholar). *Publications:* books, including A History of the Greek World from 323 to 146 B.C., 1932; A History of Rome, 1935; The Geographic Background of Greek and Roman History, 1949; and articles in various periodicals. *Address:* 7 Bancroft Avenue, N.2.
[*Died* 2 *Jan.* 1958.

CASEMENT, Admiral John Moore, C.B. 1928; *b.* 1877; *s.* of Julius Casement, J.P., Cronroe, Co. Wicklow; *m.* 1905, Annie M., *d.* of F. T. Gervers. Commanded 3rd Battle Sqdn., Atlantic Fleet, 1928-29; Vice-Adm. and retd. list, 1931; Adm. retd., 1936. *Address:* Iron Gate, Wootton, New Milton, Hants.
[*Died* 25 *Jan.* 1952.

CASEY, William Francis, LL.D.*h.c.* (Dublin); *b.* 2 May 1884; *s.* of late Patrick Joseph Casey; *m.* 1914, Amy Gertrude Pearson-Gee, *d.* of late Henry Willmott. *Educ.:* Castleknock College; Trinity College, Dublin. Called to Irish Bar, 1909. Joined Staff of The Times, 1913; served in Washington and Paris; special corresp. at Geneva and in Spain; Dep. Ed. of The Times, 1941-48; Editor of The Times, Mar. 1948-Sept. 1952. Commander Order of St. Olaf. *Publications: plays:* The Man Who Missed the Tide, Abbey Theatre, Dublin, 1908; The Suburban Groove, Abbey Theatre, 1909; More Respectable (One-act), Court, 1913, and others; *novel:* Private Life of a Successful Man, 1935. *Address:* 73 Dorset House, N.W.1. *Clubs:* Athenæum, Beefsteak, Garrick, Savile.
[*Died* 20 *April* 1957.

CASH, Colonel Sir Reginald John, K.B.E. 1958 (C.B.E. 1940); C.B. 1954; M.C.; T.D.; D.L. and J.P. County of Warwick; Chairman, J. & J. Cash Ltd., Coventry; *b.* 14 June 1892; *e. s.* of late Sidney Cash, Coventry; unmarried. *Educ.:* Marlborough; Trinity College, Oxford (B.A.). Served European War, 1914-18; Adjutant 8th Loyal N. Lancs Regt., Brigade Major, 101st Inf. Brigade (M.C., despatches, French Croix de Guerre, with Palm); commanded 7th Royal Warwickshire Regt. (T.A.), 1934-1938; Col. (T.A.), 1938; commanded 182nd Inf. Brigade, 1939; Zone Commander, Home Guard, Warwickshire, 1940-44; Hon. Col., 7th Royal Warwickshire Regt. (T.A.); Chairman Territorial and Auxiliary Forces Assoc., Warwickshire, 1950-57. High Sheriff of Warwickshire, 1950-51. *Address:* Walcote, Blackdown, Leamington, Warwickshire.
[*Died* 11 *March* 1959.

CASH, Rt. Rev. William Wilson, D.S.O. 1917; O.B.E. 1919; D.D.; D.D. Toronto (Wycliffe College); Bishop of Worcester since 1941; *b.* 12 June 1880; *s.* of James Cash, Manchester; *m.* 1906, Alice Maude Ladkin (*d.* 1953), one *s.* two *d.* *Educ.:* Cambridge School, Sale. To Egypt as Missionary under the Egypt General Mission, 1902; joined C.M.S. Egypt Mission, located to Menouf, Egypt, 1909; Deacon, 1910; Priest, 1911; Army Chaplain, Egypt and Palestine, 1915-20; Senior Chaplain, The Delta, Egypt, 1916; S.C.F. Eastern Command, 1917 (promoted to 2nd class Chaplain (Lt.-Col.), D.S.O.); Assistant Principal Chaplain E.E.F., 1918 (O.B.E.); demobilised and gazetted Hon. C.F. (2nd class), 1920; C.M.S. Secretary for Egypt, Palestine, and N. Sudan Mission, 1920; Home Secretary, C.M.S., 1923-25; General Secretary Church Missionary Society, 1926-41; Prebendary of St. Paul's, 1933-41; Chaplain to the King, 1939-41. Select Preacher, Oxford University, 1943-45. *Publications:* The Expansion of Islam; The Moslem World in Revolution; Persia Old and New; The Changing Sudan; Helps to the Study of Ephesians; Helps for the Quiet Hour; Helps to the Study of Philippians; Helps to the Study of Colossians; Christendom and Islam; The Missionary Church; Jeremiah—A Prophet to the Nations; Helps to the Study of I Peter; In the Power of the Spirit. *Address:* 149 Malvern Road, Worcester.
[*Died* 18 *July* 1955.

CASPERSZ, Charles P.; retired; *b.* 1855; *m.* 1885, Alice Margaret (*d.* 1941), *e. d.* of

Rev. Ashton Dibb; one *d.* (and one *d.* decd.). *Educ.:* Harrow; King's College and London University. Barrister-at-law; I.C.S., 1878-1912; Judge, High Court, Calcutta, 1905-12; Lecturer in Bengali at University College, London, 1912-15; War Office, 1915-19; Committee, I.C.S. Pensioners, 1922-36. *Address:* Walnut House, Chelston, Torquay. [*Died* 18 *Sept.* 1951.

CASSAR DE SAIN, 10th Marquess, **James Cassar De Sain;** *b.* 29 May 1907; *s.* of 9th Marquess and Mary Alexandra, *d.* of late James Turnbull; *S.* father, 1927; *m.* 1928, Evelyn, *d.* of late Paul Cassar Torreggiani; two *s.* five *d.* Hereditary Knight of the Holy Roman Empire. Peerage conferred by Philip V of Spain, but officially registered in English form, 1883. *Heir: s.* Anthony, *b.* 19 Sept. 1938. *Address:* 137 Strada Forni, Valetta, Malta. [*Died* 1958.

CASSEL, Rt. Hon. Sir Felix, P.C. 1937; 1st Bt., *cr.* 1920; Q.C. 1906; *b.* 1869; *m.* 1908, Lady Helen Grimston (*d.* 1947), *d.* of 3rd Earl of Verulam; two *s.* two *d.* *Educ.:* Harrow; Corpus Christi College, Oxford. 1st Class Hons. Classical Mods. and Law Final; called to Bar, Lincoln's Inn, 1894; Bencher of Lincoln's Inn, 1912, Treasurer, 1935; contested (C.) Central Hackney, 1910; Member London County Council West St. Pancras, 1907-10; Lieutenant and Captain 19th Batt. London Regt. (T.F.), 1914-16; Judge Advocate General 1916-34; High Sheriff of Hertfordshire, 1942-43; J.P. Herts.; Hon. Fellow Corpus Christi College, Oxford; Member of Council of Legal Education, 1943; Chairman Departmental Committee on Compulsory Insurance, 1936-37; Member of Departmental Committee on Courts Martial, 1938; Master of Company of Musicians, 1939-44; Chairman, Management Committee of Cassel Hospital for Functional Nervous Disorders, Ham Common, Richmond, Surrey; Chairman, Cassel Educational Trust; Member of Council of King Edward VII Sanatorium, Midhurst. *Recreation:* shooting. *Heir: s.* Francis Edward, *b.* 27 May 1912. *Address:* Putteridge Bury, Luton, Beds. *T.:* Luton 353. *Club:* Carlton. [*Died* 22 *Feb.* 1953.

CASSELS, Brig.-Gen. Gilbert Robert, C.B. 1925; D.S.O. 1919; *b.* 1870; *y. s.* of late John Cassels of Bassendean, Bournemouth, and late Mary Gilmour, *e. d.* of late William Ritchie of Middleton House, Midlothian; *m.* 1912, Laura Mary Elizabeth, *d.* of late James Barton of Farndreg, Dundalk, Co. Louth; one *d.* *Educ.:* Elizabeth College, Guernsey; R.M.C., Sandhurst. Entered 2nd Battalion the Worcestershire Regt., 1889; joined 35th Sikhs, Indian Army, 1892; Brigade Major, Presidency Brigade, Calcutta, 1907-8; D.A.A.G. Presidency Brigade, 1908; D.A.A.G., A.H.Q., India, 1908-11; Staff College, Quetta, 1911; G.S.O.2, 9th Secunderabad Division, 1912-13; G.S.O.1, 9th Secunderabad Division, 1914-15; G.S.O.2, A.H.Q., India, 1915; G.S.O.1, A.H.Q. India, 1916; Commandant 1/123rd Outram's Rifles, 1917-20; Commanded 31st Infantry Brigade, Egypt (temp. Brigadier-General), 1920; Colonel Commandant, 20th Indian Infantry Brigade, 1921-25; served Soudan, Dongola expedition, 1896; N.W. Frontier of India, 1897 (severely wounded); N.W.F. of India, Waziristan, 1901-2 (wounded); N.W.F. of India operations against Darwesh Khelwaziris (Staff), 1902; European War, 1914-18; Mesopotamia, G.S.O.1, 1915; Egyptian Expeditionary Force, 1917-18 (Egypt and Palestine) (D.S.O., Order of the Nile, 3rd class, Croix de Guerre (France), Companion of the Order of the Crown of Roumania, despatches (twice); retired, 1927. *Recreations:* shooting, fishing, golf, lawn tennis. *Address:* Flixton Grange, Bungay, Suffolk. *T.A.* and *T.:* Bungay 331. [*Died* 14 *Oct.* 1951.

CASSELS, General Sir Robert Archibald, G.C.B. *cr.* 1933 (K.C.B., *cr.* 1927; C.B. 1918); G.C.S.I., *cr.* 1940 (C.S.I. 1920); D.S.O. 1918; I.A. retd.; *b.* 1876; *m.* 1904, Florence Emily, *d.* of Lt.-Col. H. Jackson; one *s.* Served European War, including Mesopotamia (C.B., D.S.O.); Maj.-Gen. 1919; Lt. Gen. 1928; General, 1929; commanded Peshawar District, 1923-28; Adjutant-General in India, 1928-30; G.O.C.-in-C. Northern Command, India, 1930-1934; A.D.C. General to the King, 1929-33; C.-in-C. of Army in India, 1935-41; Member of Executive Council of Governor-General of India, 1935-41; retired, 1941. *Address:* Green World, Copthorne, Sussex. [*Died* 23 *Dec.* 1959.

CASSON, Elizabeth, O.B.E. 1951; M.D.; Founder and Medical Director since 1930, Dorset House School of Occupational Therapy, Churchill Hospital, Oxford; *b.* 14 April 1881; *d.* of Thomas Casson, J.P., Denbigh, N. Wales. *Educ.:* High Schools; St. Mary's College, Paddington; University of Bristol. Housing Management and Secretary of Red Cross Hall, Southwark, on Octavia Hill's Staff, 1908-13. Qualified M.B., Ch.B., 1919, D.P.M. 1922, M.D. 1926, Gaskell Prize and Medal, 1927. Founded Dorset House Residential Clinic, Bristol, 1929. President, Soroptimist Club, Bristol, 1939. *Publications:* Potted Pestology, 1923; Forty Cases treated at Allendale Curative Workshop, Lancet, 1941; various articles on psychiatry and occupational therapy. *Recreations:* motoring, painting and needlework. *Address:* St. Margaret's, Walton, Clevedon, Som. *T.:* Clevedon 2627. *Clubs:* English-Speaking Union, Federation of University Women, Crosby Hall. [*Died* 17 *Dec.* 1954.

CASSON, Herbert Alexander, C.S.I. 1911; late I.C.S.; *b.* 1867; *s.* of late Rev. George Casson of Oldecourt, Torquay, and late Fellow of Brasenose College, Oxford; *m.* 1897, Gertrude, *d.* of Capt. A. Hamilton Russell, Heath House, Petersfield; one *d.* *Educ.:* Marlborough College; Hertford College, Oxford. Entered Indian Civil Service, 1888; Political Officer Bannu Column, Waziristan Field Force, 1894; Political Officer Tochi Valley, 1895-96; wounded by fanatic, 1896; Judicial and General Secretary to Punjab Government, 1900-1; Commissioner, Lahore, 1912-17; Ambala, 1917-20; Member Legislative Council, Govt. of India, 1920; President Legislative Council, Punjab, 1922-25; retired, 1925. *Address:* Tyn-y-coed, Arthog, Merioneth, N. Wales. [*Died* 10 *May* 1952.

CASSON, Brig.-General Hugh Gilbert, C.B. 1918; C.M.G. 1915; the South Wales Borderers; *b.* 11 Jan. 1866; *s.* of Rev. George Casson. Entered Army, 1886; Captain, 1892; Major, 1904; Lt.-Col. 1911; Col. 1915. Served South African War, 1899-1901 (despatches, Queen's medal 4 clasps); European War, 1914-1918 (despatches, C.M.G., C.B.); retired, 1919. *Address:* c/o Glyn Mills & Co., Kirkland House, Whitehall, S.W.1. [*Died* 5 *Feb.* 1951.

CASSON, Rev. Canon John, M.A.; Canon Emeritus of Leicester Cathedral, 1945; General Licence Diocese of Carlisle, 1945; *b.* 23 Feb. 1869; *s.* of Isaac and Eleanor Casson, Ulpha, Cumberland; *m.* Mary (*d.* 1940), *d.* of James Chapman, Arches Hall, Standon, Herts; three *s.* one *d.* (and two *s.* decd.). *Educ.:* Ulpha School; Durham University. Theological Scholar, Theological Prize, 1896; B.A. 1897; University Hebrew Scholar, 1897; M.A. 1900; Deacon, 1897; Priest, 1898; Curate of St. Mary's, Leicester, 1897-1905; Vicar of St. Augustine's, Leicester, 1905-23; Rector of Croft, Leicester, 1923-45; Priest Canon of St. Martin's Collegiate Church, Leicester, 1922-27; Hon. Canon of Leicester, 1927-34; Canon Theologian of Leicester Cathedral, 1934-41; Canon Residentiary and Canon Treasurer of Leicester Cathedral, 1938-45; Rural Dean of Sparkenhoe II, 1923-41; Warden of Central

Society of Sacred Study, Diocese of Leicester, 1928-41; Member Central Board of Finance of the Church of England, 1934-45, and of Leicester Diocesan Board of Finance, 1927-1945; Hon. Secretary Benefices and Clerical Income Committee, 1927-37; Proctor in Convocation, 1934-45. *Publications:* articles in Peterborough Diocesan Magazine. *Recreations:* fishing, wood cutting, gardening. *Address:* Havelock Cottage, Seathwaite, Broughton-in-Furness. [*Died* 7 *May* 1955.

CASTLE, Lieut.-Col. Reginald Wingfield, C.M.G. 1919; D.S.O. 1917; *b.* 14 July 1874; *e. surv. s.* of late Edward James Castle, K.C., Bencher Inner Temple; unmarried. *Educ.:* Westminster School. Royal Military Academy, Woolwich; 2nd Lieut. R.A. 1894; Capt. 1900; Major, 1914; temp. Lt.-Col. 1916; Lt.-Col. 1921; retired pay, 1922; served European War (despatches five times, D.S.O., C.M.G.). *Recreations:* all games and sports. [*Died* 14 *Jan.* 1952.

CASTLEMAINE, 6th Baron (*cr.* 1812); **Robert Arthur Handcock;** *b.* 19 April 1864; *s.* of 4th Baron and Louisa, *d.* of 2nd Lord Harris; *S.* brother, 1937; *m.* 1894, Ethel Violet (*d.* 1934), *d.* of late Sir Edmond Bainbridge, K.C.B.; one *d.* (and one *s.* decd.). *Educ.:* Harrow. Served European War in France as Lieut. R.A.S.C. *Heir: kinsman* John Michael Schomberg Staveley Handcock [*b.* 10 March 1904; *m.* 1930, Rebecca Ellen, *o. d.* of William T. Soady; one *s.* two *d.*]. *Address:* Garnafailagh, Athlone. [*Died* 31 *May* 1954.

CATER, Sir (Alexander) Norman (Ley), K.C.I.E., *cr.* 1934 (C.I.E. 1930); *b.* 15 June 1880; *s.* of late Charles A. Cater; unmarried. *Educ.:* Wellington College; Christ's College, Cambridge. Entered I.C.S. 1903; served in Punjab, Baluchistan, Hyderabad, and Mysore; Deputy Secretary to Government of India, 1919; Resident at Jaipur, 1925; acting A.G.G. Rajputana, 1929; Agent to Governor-General, Madras States; Agent to Governor-General and Chief Commissioner, Baluchistan, 1931-36; retired, 1936. *Clubs:* Bath, Royal Automobile, M.C.C. [*Died* 21 *Oct.* 1957.

CATHCART, Professor Edward Provan, C.B.E. 1924; F.R.S.; F.R.S.E.; M.D., D.Sc.; Hon. LL.D.(St. Andrews) 1928; LL.D. (Glasgow) 1948; Hon. Lt.-Col. R.A.M.C.; Regius Prof. of Physiology, Glasgow Univ., 1928-47, now Emeritus; Hon. Fellow, Royal Faculty of Physicians and Surgeons, Glasgow; late Mem. War Cabinet Scientific Committee on Food Policy; late Member Adv. Council on Education in Scotland; late Member Medical Advisory Committee (Scotland); late Member Agricultural Research Council (Privy Council); late Member Medical Research Council (Privy Council); late Member Army Hygiene Advisory Committee; late Member General Medical Council; late Chairman Industrial Health Research Board; late Member Advisory Committee on Agricultural Science, Development Commission; late Chairman Scottish Health Services Committee; Member Advisory Committee on Nutrition, Ministry of Health; late Member Committee on Nutrition in the Colonial Empire (Economic Advisory Council); late Member National Advisory Council on Physical Training (Scotland); *b.* Ayr, 1877; *e. s.* of late Edward Moore Cathcart, merchant, Ayr; *m.* Gertrude Dorman, M.B., B.Sc., *d.* of late Henry Bostock, Stafford; three *d.* *Educ.:* Ayr Academy; Glasgow University. M.B., Ch.B. 1900; M.D. 1904; D.Sc. 1906; studied abroad in the Universities of Munich, Berlin, and Leningrad; Research Scholar Lister Institute, London, 1902-4; Assistant, 1904-5; Grieve Lecturer in Chemical Physiology, University of Glasgow, 1905-15; Professor of Physiology, London Hospital Medical School, 1915-19; Gardiner Professor of Chemical Physiology, University of Glasgow, 1919-28; Honorary Research Associateship of the Carnegie Institution of Washington, U.S.A., 1911. *Publications:* The Physiology of Protein Metabolism; The Human Factor in Industry; numerous papers in scientific periodicals both home and foreign. *Recreations:* formerly walking, travelling. *Address:* 80 Oakfield Avenue, Glasgow, W.2. [*Died* 18 *Feb.* 1954.

CATHCART, George Clark, M.A., M.D. Edin.; Consulting Surgeon to the Throat Hospital, Golden Square; Hon. Laryngologist Royal Academy of Music; late Member of the Special Aural Board, Ministry of Pensions; Aurist, Laryngologist, Rhinologist; *b.* Edinburgh; *y. s.* of late James Cathcart; unmarried. *Educ.:* Edinburgh Academy; Loretto; Universities of Edinburgh, Naples, Leipzig, Vienna. Surgeon Captain, retired, 14th Batt. London Scottish (4th London Infantry Brigade). *Publications:* Treatment of Chronic Deafness, 2nd ed., 1931; On Voice Production, Stammering, and Deafness, in various English and American medical journals; Edited Hunter Tod's Diseases of the Ear, 2nd Edition 1926. *Recreations:* golf, music. *Address:* 11 Upper Wimpole Street, W.1. *T.:* Welbeck 1124. [*Died* 4 *Jan.* 1951.

CATTLEY, M. H., M.A., Lady Margaret Hall, Oxford. Headmistress of the Perse School for Girls, Cambridge, 1926-47. *Address:* 95 Barton Road, Cambridge. *T.:* 2889. [*Died* 20 *Sept.* 1958.

CATTO, 1st Baron, *cr.* 1936, of Cairncatto; **Thomas Sivewright Catto,** 1st Bt., *cr.* 1921; P.C. 1947; C.B.E. 1918; Commander Order Leopold II of Belgium, 1919; *b.* 15 March 1879; *y. s.* of William Catto and Isabella Yule Catto of Peterhead, Aberdeenshire; *m.* 1910, Gladys, *d.* of Stephen Gordon, Elgin; one *s.* three *d.* *Educ.:* Academy, Peterhead; Heaton School (Rutherford College), Newcastle on Tyne. Began business career at 16 in shipping office, Newcastle on Tyne; went to Russian Caucasus and to Near and Middle East, 1898-1904; transferred to London as Manager, MacAndrews & Forbes, 1904. Returned to Near and Middle East as Assistant General Manager there of MacAndrews & Forbes, 1906-09; to New York as Vice-Pres. of that Company's American business, 1909-19; since 1919, Chm. and Managing Dir. of Andrew Yule & Co. Ltd., Calcutta; and a Director of the London firm of Yule, Catto & Co. Ltd.; a Director of Bank of England, Morgan Grenfell & Co. Ltd., Royal Bank of Scotland, Mercantile Bank of India Ltd., Royal Exchange Assurance, Union Castle Mail S.S. Co. Ltd., etc.; Director-General of Equipment and Stores and Member of Supply Council, Ministry of Supply, March-June 1940; resigned from all business and directorships in May 1940 at request of Chancellor of Exchequer (Sir Kingsley Wood) on acceptance of specially created war position (unpaid) in the Treasury, of Financial Adviser to the Chancellor of the Exchequer, 1940-44; Governor of Bank of England, 1944-1949. British Admiralty Representative on Russian Commission in U.S.A., 1915-17; Chairman British and Allied Provisions Commission and British Ministry of Food in U.S.A. and Canada, 1918; Member: Indian Govt. Retrenchment (Inchcape) Commn. 1922-23; Coal Sales Commn., 1927-28; Chm. Cttee. on Scottish Financial and Trade Statistics, 1950-52. *Heir: s.* Hon. Stephen Gordon Catto [*b.* 14 Jan. 1923; *m.* 1948, Josephine Innes, *er. d.* of Herbert Packer, Alexandria, Egypt; two *s.* one *d.*]. *Address:* 23 Great Winchester Street, E.C.2. *T.:* London Wall 4545. *Clubs:* Oriental, Reform, Athenæum; Bengal (Calcutta). [*Died* 23 *Aug.* 1959.

CAULLERY, Maurice; Professeur honoraire (Faculté des Sciences) since 1909; Membre de l'Académie des Sciences, 1928;

For. Mem. Roy. Soc.; *b.* Bergues (Nord), 5 Sept. 1868; *m.* Sabine Hubert; one *s.* three *d.* *Educ.:* Lycée de Douai. L'École Normale Supérieure, Paris (Agrégé préparateur); Maître de Conférences de Zoologie à l'Université de Lyon, 1896-1900; Professeur de Zoologie à l'Université de Marseille, 1900-1903; Maître de Conférences de Zoologie à l'Université de Paris, 1903-9. *Publications:* Nombreux articles et mémoires de zoologie principalement sur les invertébrés marins, de philosophie biologique, de pédagogie, de géographie générale, etc. (Revue du Mois, Revue Scientifique, Revue de Métaphysique, etc.); Les Problèmes de la sexualité; Les Universités et la vie scientifique aux États-Unis; Le Parasitisme et la symbiose; Histoire des sciences biologiques; Le Problème de l'évolution; Linnæan Gold Medal, 1947. *Address:* 6 rue Mizon, Paris (15e); laboratoire d'Évolution, 105 Boulevard Raspail, Paris (6e). [*Died* 13 *July* 1958.

CAUSER, William Sidney, R.I.; Trustee Chelsea Arts Club; Member of Council Artists General Benevolent Institution; Member of Royal Birmingham Society of Artists and of National Society; Member Society of Marine Artists; *m.* (wife *d.* 1952); one *d.* *Educ.:* Wolverhampton School. Studied Art, Wolverhampton, London and Italy; Regular Exhibitor, Royal Academy, New English Art Club, Paris Salon, etc.; one man shows, Leger Galleries "England", Fine Art Society, "Spain"; Pictures purchased for permanent collections of Liverpool, Birmingham, Wolverhampton, Bradford, Newcastle on Tyne, Napier Gallery, New Zealand, etc. *Publications:* articles in various magazines. *Address:* 92 Cornwall Gardens, S.W.7. *T.:* Western 0755. *Clubs:* Chelsea Arts, Arts. [*Died* 18 *Dec.* 1958.

CAUTY, Sir Arthur Belcher, Kt., *cr.* 1947; *b.* 26 July 1870; *s.* of Dr. Henry Evans Cauty, Liverpool; *m.* 1894, Alma Emily, *d.* of W. J. Hurst, London; one *d.* *Educ.:* Cambridge House School, Waterloo. Served apprenticeship with Messrs. Richardson, Spence & Co., managing agents in Liverpool of Inman Line of steamers which were acquired by American interests and became the American Line; joined White Star Line in 1899 and in due course became a Director and General Manager. Chairman: Liverpool Steam Ship Owners' Assoc., 1924; National Maritime Board (Owners' side), 1934-46. *Clubs:* Royal Automobile; Exchange (Liverpool). [*Died* 31 *July* 1954.

CAVANAGH, Captain John Duncan Macaulay, C.M.G. 1919; R.N., retired; *b.* 1881; *s.* of Rev. J. Cavanagh; *m.* 1915, Gladys, *d.* of Capt. F. T. Barr; one *s.* one *d.* Served European War, 1914-19 (despatches, C.M.G.); retired list, 1931. *Address:* Glenhurst, Granville Road, Walmer. *T.:* Deal 1141. [*Died* 12 *Aug.* 1957.

CAVE, Rev. Sydney, Hon. M.A. (Cantab.), D.D. (Lond.); Hon. D.D. (Glasgow); Principal of New College (Divinity School, University of London) since 1933; Professor of Theology in London University, Emeritus since 1949; *b.* 18 Nov. 1883; *s.* of late William Cave, *nephew* of late Rev. Alfred Cave, D.D., Principal of Hackney Coll.; *m.* 1909, Elizabeth Jane Baxter (*d.* 1950), Aberdeen; two *s.* one *d.* *Educ.:* City of London School; Hackney College, London. B.A. London, 1905; B.D. 1906; Dr. Williams Scholar, 1906; B.D. Hons. 1st Class Honours in Biblical and Historical Theology, 1907; D.D. 1917; Hon. M.A. (Cantab.) Emmanuel, 1925; Hon. D.D. Glasgow, 1934. In Travancore, South India, under the London Missionary Society, 1908-16, during which time Acting Principal, Scott Christian College, 1909-11 and 1915-16; Principal, Duthie Divinity School, 1911-15; Minister, Henleaze Congregational Church, Bristol, 1918-20; President of Cheshunt College, Cambridge, 1920-33. *Publications:* Redemption: Hindu and Christian, 1919 (Religious Quest of India Series); An Introduction to the Study of Some Living Religions of the East, 1921 (Studies in Theology Series); The Doctrine of the Person of Christ, 1925; The Gospel of St. Paul, 1928; Christianity and some Living Religions of the East, 1929 (Studies in Theology Series); The Doctrines of the Christian Faith, 1931; What shall we say of Christ?, 1932; The Doctrine of the Work of Christ, 1937; Hinduism or Christianity?, 1939; The Christian Estimate of Man (Studies in Theology Series), 1944; The Christian Way, 1949. *Address:* New College, 527 Finchley Rd., N.W.3. [*Died* 8 *Sept.* 1953.

CAVENDISH-BENTINCK, Lt.-Col. Lord Charles, D.S.O. 1916; late 9th (Queen's Roy.) Lancers; *half-b.* of 6th Duke of Portland, K.G., G.C.V.O., and *heir-pres.* to 7th Duke of Portland; *b.* 1868; *m.* 1897, Cicely Mary (*d.* 1936), *d.* of late C. S. Grenfell, of Elibank, Taplow; two *d.* *Educ.:* Eton. Served South Africa, 1899-1901 (wounded, despatches, Brevet Major); European War, 1914-19 (wounded, despatches, D.S.O.). *Publication:* Lord Henry Bentinck's Foxhounds, 1930. *Club:* Turf. [*Died* 19 *June* 1956.

CAVILL, William Victor, M.C.; M.A.; Headmaster Hymers College, Hull, 1927-51. *Educ.:* King Edward's School, Southampton; Oriel College, Oxford. B.A. London University; M.A. Oxford University; Oxford University Travelling Scholarship in French; Oxford University Blue for Association football; Devon County Cap for Rugby football; Assistant Master Ardingly College, 8 years Assistant Master Haileybury College, 4 years; during European War, 1914-18, Staff Captain 18th Infantry Brigade. *Address:* 78B Observatory Street, Oxford. [*Died* 24 *Sept.* 1959.

CAWLEY, 2nd Baron of Prestwich, *cr.* 1918; **Robert Hugh Cawley,** 2nd Bt., *cr.* 1906; J.P. Lancashire; lately Director Heaton Mills Bleaching Co., Middleton; *e. s.* of 1st Baron and Elizabeth (*d.* 1930), *d.* of John Smith, Kynsal Lodge, Audlem; *b.* 16 May 1877; *S.* father 1937; *m.* 1912, Vivienne, *d.* of Harold Lee, of Broughton Park, Manchester; two *s.* (and one killed in action, 1943). Served as Lieutenant 77th Co. Imperial Yeomanry, South African War, 1900-1 (Queen's medal, 4 clasps); Member of Manchester Boards of Guardians, 1910-30. *Heir:* *s.* Capt. Hon. Frederick Lee Cawley, R.A. [*b.* 27 July 1913; *m.* 1944, Rosemary Joan, *y. d.* of R. E. Marsden; four *s.* one *d.*]. *Address:* Berrington Hall, Leominster, Herefordshire. [*Died* 24 *Sept.* 1954.

CAWOOD, Herbert Harry; sculptor; *b.* Sheffield, 21 July 1890; *s.* of late Horace Cawood. *Educ.:* Tideswell Grammar School; Royal Academy Schools. Exhibitor Royal Academy. *Recreation:* golf. *Address:* The Hollies, Lansdowne Road, Angmering, Sussex. [*Died* 27 *Oct.* 1957.

CAY, Armistead; Technical Editor and Correspondent; *b.* Kew, 1872; *m.* 1907, Edith Mary, *o. d.* of S. Pennington Cochrane, Bath. *Educ.:* privately. After a brief period at the Phonetic Institute, under Isaac Pitman, 1889, joined editorial staff of the Bath Herald, 1890, and was connected with that journal until 1896; co-editor New Catalogue of British Literature, 1898; published proposals for an entirely new system of shorthand based on accent, 1899, and is completing for publication; editor Page's Engineering Weekly, 1903-13; acting editor Hardware Trade Journal, 1914-21; editor Export World, 1913-26; connected with Institute of Journalists since 1889; Fellow, 1932; City Volunteer 1st (subsequently 4th) Battalion National Guard (C.L.N.G.V.), 1915-1918; Senior Warden, A.R.P., 1939-42. *Recrea-*

tions: photography, etc. *Address:* Derwent House, Weston, Bath. *T.:* Bath 7131.
[*Died* 3 *March* 1957.

CAYLEY, Hon. Major-General (retired pay) **Douglas Edward,** C.B. 1919; C.M.G. 1915; *b.* 15 July 1870; *s.* of late Deputy Surgeon-General H. Cayley, C.M.G., Indian Medical Service, and late Letitia Mary, *d.* of Rev. Nicholas Walters; *m.* 1906, Jessie, *d.* of late Sir W. D. Gibbon; (one *s.*, lost on active service Royal Navy). *Educ.:* Clifton College. Entered army, 1890; Captain, 1899; Major, 1904; Lt.-Col. Commanding 4th Worcestershire Regt., 1914; served S. African War, 1900-2 (Queen's medal 3 clasps, King's medal 2 clasps); European War, 1914-18; all through Gallipoli campaign, including first landing and evacuation of Suvla and Helles (wounded three times, despatches ten times, C.M.G., C.B., Bt. Col.); commanded the 29th Infantry Division, March 1918; Order of White Eagle, Serbia, 3rd class; Belgian Order Couronne (Commandeur), Belgian Croix de Guerre; French Croix de Guerre avec Palmes. *Address:* Heatherside, Yateley, Hants.
[*Died* 19 *Dec.* 1951.

CAYLEY, Captain Harry Francis, D.S.O. 1919; Royal Navy, retired; *b.* 1873; *s.* of late Digby Cayley of Malton, Yorks, 2nd *s.* of Sir Digby Cayley, 7th Bt.; *m.* 1900, Margery (*d.* 1901), *d.* of Sir Thomas Freake, 2nd Bt.; one *d.* Entered Royal Navy, 1886; served European War, 1914-19 (despatches twice, D.S.O. and bar); retired Captain, Royal Navy. *Recreations:* hunting, shooting, fishing, golf. *Address:* Bix Hill Cottage, nr. Henley-on-Thames. *Club:* Naval and Military. [*Died* 31 *March* 1954.

CAYLEY, Major-General Sir Walter de Sausmarez, K.C.M.G., *cr.* 1917 (C.M.G. 1916); C.B. 1916; *b.* 8 Aug. 1863; *s.* of late Surg.-Gen. Henry Cayley, C.M.G., and Lætitia Mary, *d.* of Rev. Nicholas Walters; *m.* 1896, Constance, *d.* of Rev. R. P. Blakeney, D.D., LL.D., late Rector Bridlington, Canon of York. *Educ.:* Marlborough; Sandhurst. Joined West Yorks Rgt. 1883; Capt. 1890; Major, 1901; Lt.-Col. 1910; Brig.-Gen. Commanded 39th Infantry Brigade, 1914-16; Major-General, July 1916, Commanded 13th Division, Mesopotamia; served Ashanti, 1895-1896 (Star); S. Africa, 1901-2 (Queen's medal, 3 clasps); N.W. Frontier, India, 1908 (medal with clasp); European War (Gallipoli, Mesopotamia), 1915-18 (C.B., C.M.G.); Serbian Decoration—the Order of Karageorge with cross swords; retired pay, 1920. *Address:* Fulford Lodge, Crowthorne. *T.:* Crowthorne 164. *Club:* Junior United Service. [*Died* 17 July 1952.

CECIL of Chelwood, 1st Viscount, *cr.* 1923, of East Grinstead; **Edgar Algernon Robert Cecil,** P.C. 1915; C.H. 1956; Q.C.; M.A.; D.C.L. Oxford; LL.D. Cambridge, Edinburgh, Manchester, Liverpool, St. Andrews, Aberdeen, Princeton, Columbia and Athens; Chancellor of Birmingham University, 1918-1944; Visitor St. Hugh's College, Oxon; President League of Nations Union, 1923-45; Hon. Life President, United Nations Association; *b.* 14 Sept. 1864; 3rd *s.* of 3rd Marquess of Salisbury; *m.* 1889, Lady Eleanor Lambton, *d.* of 2nd Earl of Durham. *Educ.:* Eton; University College, Oxford. Private secretary to his father, 1886-88; called to Bar (Inner Temple), 1887; Q.C., 1889; K.C. 1901; Q.C., 1952. Chancellor and Vicar-Gen. of York, 1915; M.P. (C.) East Marylebone, 1906-10, (Ind. C.) Hitchin Div. Herts, 1911-23; contested Blackburn and North Cambridgeshire, 1910; Parliamentary Under-Secretary for Foreign Affairs, 1915-16; Assistant Secretary of State for Foreign Affairs, 1918; Minister of Blockade, 1916-18; Lord Privy Seal, 1923-24; Chancellor of the Duchy of Lancaster, Nov. 1924-Aug. 1927; Bencher of the Inner Temple, 1910; Chairman Herts Quarter Sessions, 1911-20; Rector of the University of Aberdeen, 1924-27; President National Association of Building Societies, 1928-36; Nobel Peace Prize for 1937. *Publications:* (joint) Principles of Commercial Law; Our National Church; The Way of Peace, 1928; A Great Experiment: An Autobiography, 1941; A Real Peace, 1941; An Emergency Policy, 1948; All the Way, 1949. *Heir:* none. *Address:* Chelwood Gate, Haywards Heath. *T.:* Chelwood Gate 8; 16 South Eaton Place, S.W.1. *T.:* Sloane 7011.
[*Died* 24 *Nov.* 1958 (*ext.*).

CECIL, Algernon; *b.* 31 Jan. 1879; *s.* of Lord Eustace Cecil (3rd *s.* of 2nd Marquess of Salisbury) and Lady Gertrude Scott (*d.* of 2nd Earl of Eldon); *m.* 1923, Lady Guendolen Fanny Godolphin-Osborne (*d.* 1933); no *c.* *Educ.:* Eton; New College, Oxford (M.A.); 1st Class Modern History; Pres. of the Oxford Union Soc., 1901. Barrister-at-law, Inner Temple; F.R. Hist. Society; attached during European War to the Intelligence Division of the Admiralty and subsequently to the Historical Section of the Foreign Office; Knight of Justice of the S.M. Order of Malta. *Publications:* Six Oxford Thinkers, 1909; Essays in Imitation, 1910; A Life of Robert Cecil, First Earl of Salisbury, 1915; A Dreamer in Christendom, 1925; The World we live in, 1925; British Foreign Secretaries, 1927; Metternich, 1933; A Portrait of Thomas More, 1937; Facing the Facts in Foreign Policy, 1941; A House in Bryanston Square, 1944; Queen Victoria and her Prime Ministers, 1952; articles in the D.N.B. on Robert, 3rd Marquess of Salisbury, 1st Earl of Balfour, and Sir George Prothero, and in the Quarterly, Contemporary, Dublin and New English Reviews. *Recreation:* formerly golf. *Address:* 9 Sion Hill Place, Bath. *Club:* Travellers'.
[*Died* 13 *April* 1953.

CHADBURN, Maud Mary, C.B.E. 1934; M.D., B.S. London; *d.* of late Rev. J. Chadburn and Grace Tetley. *Educ.:* University College; London School of Medicine for Women, Royal Free Hospital. Graduated 1893; late Chm. Cancer Research Cttee. and late Surgeon, Marie Curie Hosp.; late President of the London Assoc., Medical Women's Federation; late Senior Surgeon, South London Hosp. for Women; Surgeon Elizabeth Garrett Anderson Hospital; Surgeon Women's Settlement Hospital, Canning Town; Assistant Anæsthetist, Curator of Museum, and Surgical Registrar at the Royal Free Hospital; House Surgeon to Clapham Maternity Hospital; House Surgeon, Clinical Assistant, Senior Obstetrician, Elizabeth Garrett Anderson Hospital. *Address:* Turville Park Cottage, Nr. Henley-on-Thames, Oxon. *T.:* Turville Heath 393; 7 Devonshire Street, Portland Place, W.1. *T.:* Langham 6451. [*Died* 24 *April* 1957.

CHADWICK, Rev. Charles Egerton, M.C., M.A.; Q.H.C.; Rector of Chagford, Devon, 1939-48, retired 1948; *b.* 1880; *s.* of Edward and Elizabeth Chadwick, Bromley, Kent; *m.* 1917, Dorothy Elwin, *o. d.* of Herbert Elwin Harris, F.R.C.S., Clifton, Bristol; three *d.* *Educ.:* Private; Monkton Combe School; Corpus Christi College, Cambridge. Travelled extensively; deacon 1911; priest 1912; Curate Emmanuel, Clifton, Bristol; Chaplain to the Forces, 1913; served European War, 1914-19 (despatches, M.C.); Senior Chaplain 13th Army Corps, 1916; Preston, 1919; Malta, 1922; Gibraltar, 1923; Portsmouth, 1926; Chaplain Brigade of Guards, 1929; Asst. Chap.-Gen., Western Mediterranean, 1931; Southern Command, 1936; Hon. Chaplain to Bishop of Sarum, 1936; Hon. Chaplain to King George VI, 1938; Chaplain to High Sheriff of Devon, 1943-44; Vice-Pres. Old Contemptibles Association. *Recreations:* travel, riding, golf. *Address:* Willow Cottage, Heather Drive, Sunningdale, Berks. *T.:* Ascot 914. *Club:* Junior Army and Navy.
[*Died* 30 *April* 1958.

CHADWICK, Sir David Thomas, K.C.M.G., *cr.* 1937; Kt., *cr.* 1927; C.S.I. 1925; C.I.E.; *b.* 1876; *s.* of late Robert Chadwick, York; *m.* 1912, Jane, 2nd *d.* of L. T. Penman, J.P., Broadwood Park, Lanchester, Durham; one *d.* *Educ.:* Sidney Sussex College. Cambridge (Hon. Fellow, 1937). Indian Civil Service, 1899; joined at Madras, 1900; Settlement Officer, 1904; Director of Agriculture, Madras, 1912; special duty in Russia, France, and Italy, 1916; Government of India Trade Commissioner, London, 1917-22; Secretary to Government of India, Commerce Department, 1922-27; Secretary of the Imperial Economic Committee, 1927-46; Secretary of the Imperial Agricultural Bureaux, 1928-46; Temporary Member Governor-General's Council, 1923. *Address:* South Park Lodge, Sevenoaks, Kent. *T.:* Sevenoaks 4221. *Club:* Athenæum. [*Died* 26 *April* 1954.

CHADWICK, Sir Robert; *see* Burton-Chadwick.

CHADWYCK-HEALEY, Sir Gerald Edward, 2nd Bt., *cr.* 1919; C.B.E. 1919; D.L.; Commander of the Order of the Crown of Italy, 1919; *b.* 16 May 1873; *e. s.* of Sir Charles E. H. Chadwyck-Healey, 1st Bt., K.C.B., K.C., D.L., Hon. Captain R.N.R., of Wyphurst, Cranley and New Place, Porlock, Somerset; *m.* 1897, Mary Verena, *o. c.* of George Arthur Watson of East Court, Finchampstead, Berks; two *s.* one *d.* *Educ.:* Eton; Trinity College, Oxford. Lieut., R.N.V.R., 1915; Assistant to Controller of the Navy, 1917; Director of Materials and Priority, Admiralty, 1918; was a Member of the Admiralty Transport Arbitration Board, and of the Royal Commission on Awards to Inventors. *Heir:* *s.* Edward Randal [Reserve of Officers, now Major R.A., M.C. and Bar, Croix de Guerre; *b.* 1898; *m.* 1924, Rachel, *d.* of L. C. Whitehead Phillips, Unsted Park, Godalming]. *Address:* Balbeg, Straiton, Ayrshire. *Clubs:* United University, Boodle's, Royal Automobile, Leander; County (Ayr). [*Died* 2 *Feb.* 1955.

CHADWYCK-HEALEY, Oliver Nowell, M.A.; Director (formerly Chairman), Morgan Bros. (Publishers) Ltd.; *b.* 19 Dec. 1886; 2nd *s.* of Sir Charles E H. Chadwyck-Healey, 1st Bt., K.C.B., K.C., D.L., Hon. Capt. R.N.R., Wyphurst Cranleigh, Surrey, and New Place, Porlock, Somerset; *m.* 1916, Gwendoline Mary, *d.* of Major Hugh Spencer Charrington, Dove Cliff, Burton-on-Trent; one *s.* one *d.* *Educ.:* Eton; Trinity College, Oxford. Called to Bar, Lincoln's Inn, 1911; served European War, 1914-19, 5th Bn. Royal Berkshire Regt. (despatches) and Staff; Board of Management, Hospital for Sick Children, Great Ormond Street, 1925-47, Vice-Chairman, 1929-34 and 1946-47; Council of British Hospitals Assoc., 1932-41, Vice-Chairman, 1932-36, a Vice-Pres. 1942-48; Voluntary Hospitals Committee for London, 1929-48, Chairman, 1934-41; Council of King Edward's Hospital Fund for London since 1936, member of Management Cttee., 1938-41 and since 1949, member of Distribution Committee, 1942-48, and 1956-59; member of Parliamentary Cttee., 1934-42, member of Emergency Bed Service Cttee. since 1938; mem. of Convalescent Homes Cttee., 1947-56. *Address:* New Place, Porlock, Minehead, Somerset. *T.:* Porlock 17. *Clubs:* Athenæum, United University, Leander. [*Died* 24 *Feb.* 1960.

CHALKLEY, Alfred Philip, B.Sc.; Editor of The Motor Ship; *b.* 1886; *s.* of Alfred Chalkley, Exeter; *m.* Arna Heni (*d.* 1951), Oslo; one *d.* *Educ.:* Tiffins School and King's College, London. *Publication:* Diesel Engines for Land and Marine Work, 1912. *Address:* 4 Campden House Terr., W.8. *T.:* Park 5789; Friars Gate, Withyham, Sussex. *T.:* Crowborough 507. [*Died* 19 *April* 1959.

CHALKLEY, Sir (Harry) Owen, K.C.M.G., *cr.* 1938 (C.M.G., 1931); C.B.E., 1922; *b.* 1882; *m.* 1920, Marjorie Lilian Glover; three *s.* British Vice-Consul, Marseilles, New York; British Consul, Colon; British Chargé d'Affaires, Panama, Buenos Aires; Commercial Counsellor, Buenos Aires, 1916-31; Washington, 1931-42; retired 1942. *Publications:* Financial, Commercial and Economic Conditions of the Argentine Republic; Economic and Trade Conditions in the United States. *Address:* Anderida, Cooden, Bexhill-on-Sea. *Club:* Royal Societies. [*Died* 22 *Oct.* 1958.

CHALLACOMBE, Rev. William Allen; Rector of Farnborough, 1920-48, and Surrogate, retired 1948; Hon. Canon in Southwark Cathedral, 1918-35, Canon Emeritus since 1935; *m.* Jessie (*d.* 1925), *d.* of Christopher Kilvinton Worsfold; one *s.* *Educ.:* Worcester College, Oxford. Ordained, 1888; Curate of Christ Church, Dover, 1888-92; Vicar of New Malden and Combe, 1893-1920. *Address:* at The Lindens, Farnborough Park, Farnborough, Hants. *T.:* Farnborough, Hants 67. [*Died* 16 *Feb.* 1951.

CHALLEN, Charles, M.A., LL.B.; Barrister-at-law; *b.* 1894; *s.* of late Charles Hollis Challen; unmarried. *Educ.:* Merchant Taylors' School; Jesus College, Cambridge. Served European War, 1914-19. Lieut. R.F.A., France and Egypt; called to Bar, Gray's Inn, 1922; Arden Prizeman, 1922; Member of Hampstead Borough Council, 1931-45; Chairman of its General Purposes Committee, 1937-41; Chairman of its General Emergency Committee from outbreak of war until Nov., 1940; from then served in War, Flight Lieut. R.A.F., until Dec. 1945; Chairman Hampstead Conservative and Unionist Association, 1937-42; M.P. (C.) Hampstead, 1941-50; a Liveryman of the Merchant Taylors Company. *Address:* Hall Place, Lyndhurst Terrace, Hampstead, N.W.3. *Club:* Oxford and Cambridge. [*Died* 20 *June* 1960.

CHALLIS, John Humphrey Thornton, F.F.A.R.C.S., D.A.; Senior Anaesthetist London Hospital since 1948, King George V (Ilford) since 1938; Southend Hospital since 1935, etc.; *b.* 8 Nov. 1896; *o. s.* of Dr. H. T. Challis, V.D.; *m.* 1931, Margaret Llewelyn Jones; three *d.* *Educ.:* City of London School; London Hospital. Medical student, 1913; Lieut. R.F.A., T.A., 1914, Regular Army, 1917; Capt. R.F.A., 1918; Capt. R.A. reserve, 1922. Medical student, 1922; M.R.C.S.(Eng.), L.R.C.P.(Lond.), 1925; Clinical Asst., Children's Dept., 1926, Emergency Officer, 1927, Resident Anaesthetist, 1928, London Hosp.; Asst. Consultant Anaesthetist, London Hosp. and other hosps., 1930; D.A., R.C.S.Eng., 1938. Member of Council, Assoc. of Anaesthetists Gt. Britain and Northern Ireland, 1938-39; Founder member of Council of Faculty of Anaesthetists, R.C.S.Eng., 1948; Pres. Anaesthetic Section, Roy. Soc. Med., 1948. *Publications:* Chapter on Spinal Anaesthesia in index of treatment; Chapter on Anaesthesia in Souttar's Surgery; Chapter on Intratracheal Anaesthesia for General Practitioners. *Recreations:* sport and horses. *Address:* Whitehall Lodge, Whitehall Road, Woodford Green, Essex. *T.:* Buckhurst 2770. [*Died* 21 *Jan.* 1958.

CHALMER, Colonel (hon. Brigadier) Francis George, D.S.O. 1919; M.C.; *b.* 28 Nov. 1884; *s.* of Col. G. Chalmer, Gordon Highlanders; *m.* Cecil Mary Key, *d.* of Major William Key Matterson Langford Manor, Fivehead, Taunton; one *d.* *Educ.:* Eton. Served European War, 1914-19 (wounded twice, despatches four times, Bt. Major, D.S.O., M.C.); commanded 2nd Bn. Black Watch, 1933-36; commanded 156th (West Scottish) Infantry Brigade T.A., 1936-40; retired 1939; commanded North Highland Area, 1940-41; commanded 2nd Bn. (Fife) Home Guard, 1942 until disbandment; Fife T. and A.F.A. (Vice-Chm., 1947-49, Chm. 1950). Member, Royal Company of Archers, The King's Bodyguard for Scotland. *Recreation:* shooting. *Clubs:* United Service, Caledonian; New (Edinburgh). [*Died* 21 *May* 1951.

CHAMBERLAIN, Fernley John, C.B.E. 1918; *b.* Plymouth, 19 July 1879; *m.* Gertrude Holloway, Burslem, Staffs.; one *s.* one *d.* *Educ.:* Plymouth Public School; Plymouth Science and Art School. Assistant Secretary Plymouth Y.M.C.A., 1896 - 1900; General Secretary Hanley Y.M.C.A., 1900-06; Nottingham, 1906-08; Divisional Secretary North Midlands, 1908-1910; General Secretary Sheffield Y.M.C.A., 1910-13; Assistant National Secretary of Y.M.C.A., 1913; Associate National Secretary, Y.M.C.A., 1919-30; National Secretary, Y.M.C.A., 1930-38. *Address:* Cliff Top, Babbacombe, South Devon. *T.:* Torquay 88322. [*Died* 25 *Jan.* 1958.

CHAMBERS, Sir Edmund Kerchever, K.B.E., *cr.* 1925; C.B. 1912; F.B.A.; Hon. Litt.D. (Oxford and Durham); late Second Secretary, Board of Education; *b.* Berkshire, 16 March 1866; *e. s.* of late Rev. William Chambers, Fellow and Tutor of Worcester College, Oxford, and Anna Heathcote, *d.* of Rev. Thomas Kerchever Arnold, late Fellow of Trinity Coll., Cambridge; *m.* Eleanor Christabel (Nora), *d.* of John Davison Bowman, late of Exchequer and Audit Office, 1893. *Educ.:* Marlborough; Corpus Christi College, Oxford. Chancellor's English Essayist, 1891; entered Education Department, 1892. *Publications:* The Mediæval Stage, 1903; The Elizabethan Stage, 1923; Shakespeare: A Survey, 1925; Arthur of Britain, 1927; William Shakespeare, 1930; The English Folk-Play, 1933; Sir Henry Lee, 1936; Samuel Taylor Coleridge, 1938; A Sheaf of Studies, 1942; Shakespearean Gleanings, 1944; English Literature at the Close of the Middle Ages, 1945; Sources for a Biography of Shakespeare, 1946; Matthew Arnold: A Study, 1947. Editor of English Pastorals, 1895; Donne's Poems, 1896; Vaughan's Poems, 1896; Red Letter Shakespeare, 1904-8; Early English Lyrics (with F. Sidgwick), 1907; Aurelian Townshend's Poems, 1911; The Oxford Book of Sixteenth Century Verse, 1932, etc. *Address:* Bovey Combe, Beer, Devon. *Club:* Athenæum. [*Died* 21 *Jan.* 1954.

CHAMBERS, Major John Reginald; F.I.D.; Director, Horizon Pictures (G.B.) Ltd. *b.* 1882. *Educ.:* Dulwich; King's College. Royal Engineers, 1914-20, Egypt, Salonica, France; D.A.Q.M.G., General Headquarters, B.E.F. (despatches twice); Disposal of Surplus War Material; H.M. Treasury, 1921-1928; assisted in Allied Debt negotiations; secretarial duties in connection with Enquiry into Government Printing, Royal Commission on Cross River Traffic in London, Royal Commission on National Museums and Galleries; Emergency Compensation Commission, War Compensation Court, Admiralty Transport Arbitration Board; Racecourse Betting Control Board; Deputy Director of Clothing and Textiles, Ministry of Supply, 1939-43. *Publications:* Points on Banking Law and Practice; History of the Adminstrative Services, B.E.F.; miscellaneous writings on economic and commercial subjects. *Recreations:* tennis, boxing (Vice-President of the Civil Service Boxing Club.). *Address:* 16 Second Avenue, Hove, Sussex. *T.:* Hove 30352. *Club:* Royal Automobile. [*Died* 8 *Sept.* 1953.

CHAMBERS, Sir Theodore (Gervase), K.B.E., *cr.* 1918; J.P.; Chairman, Peacock and Nilambe Tea and Rubber Estates Ltd.; *b.* 31 Jan. 1871; *s.* of Charles Harcourt Chambers, Barrister-at-law, and Lucebella Hare; *m.* 1896, Georgina Maria, *d.* of Theophilus Sandeman; two *s.* *Educ.:* Tonbridge; St. Paul's. Secretary and Controller, National Savings Committee, 1916-19; Vice-Chairman, 1919-43; Vice-Pres. 1943; Member of Treasury Committee on Housing Finance, 1919; of Dep. Committee on Old Age Pensions, 1919; of Departmental Committee on Increase of Rent and Mortgage Interest (Restrictions) Act 1920, 1920; Chairman Departmental Committee on Agricultural Credit, 1922; Member of Committee of Enquiry into Savings Certificates and Local Loans, 1923; of Inter-Departmental Committee on Building Prices, 1923; of Dep. Committee on Garden Cities and Satellite Towns, 1925; Chairman of Ministry of Health Rents Tribunal, 1922-27. Formerly Chairman of Uganda Co. Ltd. and Welwyn Garden City Ltd. *Address:* Lochletter, Balnain, Inverness. *T.:* Glen Urquhart 8. *Club:* Athenæum. [*Died* 20 *Nov.* 1957.

CHAMPION, Captain John Pelham, C.B.E. 1944; D.S.O. 1916; R.N. (retd.); *b.* 26 March 1883; *s.* of Rev. Francis Beresford Champion. Retired from Navy, 1922. Naval Control Service Officer, Thames and Medway, 1939-45; retired, 1945. *Address:* Short Hoo, Hasketon, Woodbridge, Suffolk. *T.A.:* Short Hoo, Grundisburgh. *T.:* Grundisburgh 289. [*Died* 13 *Feb.* 1955.

CHAMPION-de CRESPIGNY, Col. Sir (Constantine) Trent, Kt., *cr.* 1941; D.S.O. 1917; V.D.; M.D. (Melb.); F.R.C.P. Lond.; Foundation Fellow (Pres. 1942-44) Royal Australasian College of Physicians; F.R.S.M.; Physician; Consulting Physician, Royal Adelaide Hospital and Adelaide Children's Hospital; *b.* Queenscliff, Vic., Australia, 5 March 1882; 2nd *s.* of late Philip Champion-de Crespigny, Brighton, Victoria, and Annie Frances Chauncy; *m.* 1st, 1906, Beatrix (*d.* 1943), *d.* of late E. W. Hughes, Melbourne; two *s.* two *d.*; 2nd, 1945, Mary Birks, *d.* of W. C. Jolley, Wentworth, N.S.W.; one *d.* *Educ.:* Brighton Grammar School, Victoria; Trinity Coll., Univ. of Melbourne; M.B., Ch.B., M.D. Practised in Adelaide since 1909; on staff of Royal Adelaide Hospital for many years; Lecturer in Univ. of Adelaide in Pathology, 1912-19, and in Principles and Practice of Medicine, 1920-38; Dean of Faculty of Medicine, Univ. of Adelaide, 1928-48. Served, 1915-1919, in Gallipoli Campaign, Egypt, France, and Belgium in command of Australian Gen. Hosps. (despatches twice, D.S.O.); Col. (A.I.F.), 1917; Col. A.A.M.C., retired; C.O. 101st General Hospital, 1942-44; Pres. S.A. Branch B.M.A., 1925-26; Pres. Section of Medicine, Australasian Medical Congress (B.M.A.), Sydney, 1929; Examiner for degree of M.D. in Universities of Sydney, Melbourne and Adelaide. *Publications:* Rennie Memorial Lecture, before the R.A.C.P., Sydney, 1944, and other contributions to medical and scientific journals. *Recreation:* gardening. *Address:* 219 North Terrace, Adelaide; 132 Strangways Terrace, North Adelaide, S. Australia. *T.:* W 2274, M 9731. *Club:* Adelaide (Adelaide). [*Died* 27 *Oct.* 1952.

CHAMPION de CRESPIGNY, Sir Vivian Tyrell, 8th Bt., *cr.* 1805; O.B.E. 1946; *b.* 25 April 1907; *s.* of late Brig.-Gen. Tyrell O. W. Champion de Crespigny (3rd *s.* of 3rd Bt.); *S.* cousin, Comdr. Sir Frederick Philip Champion de Crespigny, 1947; *m.* 1st, 1930, Barbara Helen Gallop (who obt. a divorce, 1940), *d.* of Robert Dobb, Lockend, Shiplake-on-Thames; one *d.*; 2nd, 1943, Monica D. (marriage dissolved, 1947), *d.* of Brig. G. Fleming, O.B.E., M.C., Norton Beauchamp, Kewstoke, Som.; remarried 1st wife, Barbara Helen Gallop (Whitehead), 1947 (from whom he obtained a divorce, 1951). *Educ.:* Sherborne. Served War of 1939-45, N.W. Europe, W. Africa, India, Burma, Malaya (despatches, O.B.E.). Entered Malayan Civil Service, 1946; retired, medically unfit, 1948. Major and Hon. Col. R.A.S.C. *Heir:* none. *Address:* c/o Lloyds Bank, Henley-on-Thames. [*Died* 3 *March* 1952 (*ext.*).

CHAMPNESS, Major Sir William Henry, Kt., *cr.* 1938; one of H.M. Lieutenants of City since 1917; Alderman's Deputy since 1931; *b.* 25 March 1873; *s.* of late William John Champness; *m.* 1896, Elizabeth (*d.* 1939), *d.* of John Butler, King's Langley; one *s.*; 1946, Ethel Harding, widow of Sydney Grave Morris and *d.* of late Charles Henry Taylor, M.V.O. Solicitor (1st class honoursman and prizeman), 1903; Past Master Spectaclemakers' Company and Plumbers' Company; Past President and Hon. Solicitor City Livery Club; Vice-President, Royal Drawing Society; Governor Bridewell and Bethlem Hospitals, City and Guilds Institute; Trustee John Land's Trust; Past President International Optical League; Past Chairman of City Corporation Committees and of Income Tax Commissioners for City; Past Alderman of Acton; Sheriff of City of London, 1937-38; Member, Guildhall and Law Society. Commander Crown of Belgium and Crown of Italy. *Publications:* History of Spectaclemakers' Company; History of Plumbers' Company. *Recreations:* painting, antiquarian research. *Address:* Knole Way, Sevenoaks. *T.:* Sevenoaks 2427. *Club:* City Livery. [*Died* 29 *Oct.* 1956.

CHANCE, Sir Robert Christopher, Kt. *cr.* 1946; J.P., B.A.; Chairman Ferguson Bros. Ltd., Carlisle; *b.* 28 Nov. 1883; *s.* of Sir F. W. Chance, K.B.E.; *m.* 1918, Marjorie Winnifred Bradshaw; two *s.* two *d.* *Educ.:* Malvern College; Trinity College, Cambridge. Mayor of Carlisle, 1929-30; Army Service, 1918-19; County Commandant for Army Cadet Force, 1942-1945; Textile Manufacturer; High Sheriff of Cumberland, 1938; Lord Lieutenant, Cumberland, 1949-58. D.L. Cumberland, 1944. Hon. Freeman, City of Carlisle. Hon. LL.D. Dickinson Coll., Carlisle, Pa., U.S.A., 1952. *Address:* Morton, Carlisle. *T.:* Carlisle 25027. [*Died* 10 *Dec.* 1960.

CHANCE, Thomas Williams, M.A., B.D.; Principal Emeritus South Wales Baptist College, Cardiff; *b.* 23 Aug. 1872; *s.* of Thomas Chance and Mary Williams; *m.* 1900, Mary Maria Morgan; one *s.* *Educ.:* Hampton Grammar School; Cardiff Univ.; South Wales Baptist College, Cardiff. Pastor of High Street Baptist Church, Merthyr Tydfil, 1899-1908; Part-time Prof. of the S.W.B. College, 1904-8, Prof. and Financial Sec., 1908-36, Principal, 1936-44; President E. Glam. E.B. Association, 1934-1935; President Welsh N.C.E. Union, 1906-7 and 1923-4; President British C.E. Union, 1924-25; Dean of the Faculty of Theology, University of Wales, 1929-32. *Publications:* Outline History of the Church (Early Period), 1926; Editor of Dr. William Edwards' Biography, 1934. *Recreations:* bowls, gardening. *Address:* Bryneithin, Erwood, Builth Wells, Breconshire. [*Died* 22 *Dec.* 1954.

CHANCELLOR, Alexander Richard, C.B.E. 1923; retd. civil servant; *e. s.* of Edward Chancellor, Edinburgh; *b.* Edinburgh, 3 June 1869; *m.* 1901, Margaret Pasea (*d.* 1945). *Educ.:* Edinburgh Collegiate School; Blairlodge School, Stirlingshire. Captain in 4th Battalion Highland Light Infantry; entered Colonial Service, 1895; Barbados Police and Adjutant Barbados Volunteers; Straits Settlements Police, 1902; Inspector-General, 1913; Official Member of Legislative Council of the Straits Settlements, 1917-22; on mission for Colonial Office to British Guiana, 1924. *Recreation:* golf. *Address:* 7 Cavendish Place, Bournemouth. *T.:* Bournemouth 6324. *Club:* Caledonian. [*Died* 21 *April* 1959.

CHANCELLOR, Lieut.-Col. Sir John Robert, G.C.M.G., *cr.* 1922 (K.C.M.G., *cr.* 1913; C.M.G. 1909); G.C.V.O., *cr.* 1925; G.B.E., *cr.* 1947; D.S.O. 1898; Knight of Grace of the Order of St. John of Jerusalem, 1928; late R.E.; *b.* Edinburgh, 20 Oct. 1870; 2nd *s.* of late E. Chancellor, Woodhall House, Juniper Green, Midlothian; *m.* 1903, Elsie, 3rd *d.* of G. Rodie Thompson, J.P., D.L., Lynwood, Ascot; two *s.* one *d.* *Educ.:* R.M. Academy Woolwich. Joined Royal Engineers, 1890; served in Dongola Expedition, 1896, with Indian contingent (Khedive's medal and English medal); Tirah Expedition, 1897-98; in charge of Sirmur Imperial Service Sappers; present at capture Dargai Heights, capture of Sampagha Pass and capture of Arhanga Pass, and operations in Bara Valley, 1897 (despatches, medal and three clasps, D.S.O.); passed Staff College, 1902; Staff Captain Intelligence Dept. War Office, 1903; Assistant Secretary (Military) to Committee of Imperial Defence, 1904; Secretary to the Colonial Defence Committee, 1906; Governor and Commander-in-Chief, Mauritius, 1911-16; Trinidad and Tobago, 1916-21; Governor and Commander-in-Chief of Southern Rhodesia, 1923-28; High Commissioner and Commander-in-Chief, Palestine, 1928-31; Chairman of the Agricultural Marketing Facilities Committee; Chairman of Permanent Joint Hops Committee; Chairman of International Conference on Locusts, 1934; President of Trustee Savings Banks Association, since 1951 (Chairman, 1935-1938); Chairman of the Live-stock Commission; Vice-Chairman of the British Council, 1940-41, and Member of Executive Committee; Member of the Colonial Empire Marketing Board; Mem. of Colonial Development Advisory Committee; Member of Council and Foreign Secretary of the Royal Geographical Society; Vice-President of the Royal Empire Society, and Member of Council of the Royal African Society; Member of International Colonial Institute; Director of Imperial Continental Gas Association, British South Africa Co., of the Tilbury Contracting and Dredging Company (ex-chm.). *Address:* 63 Royal Hospital Road, Chelsea, S.W.3. *T.:* Flaxman 1839; Shieldhill, Biggar, Lanarkshire, *T.:* 35. *Clubs:* Army and Navy, Travellers'. [*Died* 31 *July* 1952.

CHANDAVARKAR, Sir Vithal Narayan, Kt., *cr.* 1941; M.A. (Cantab.); Barrister-at-law; Managing Director, N. Sirur & Co. Ltd., Cotton Mill Agents, Bombay; Deputy Chairman, Millowners' Association, Bombay, 1935, 1942, 1951-53, and Chairman, 1936, 1940-41, 1943-45, 1948-50, and 1954; *b.* 26 Nov. 1887; *e. s.* of late Sir Narayan Ganesh Chandavarkar; *m.* Vatsalabai, 3rd *d.* of Rao Saheb M. V. Kaikini of Karwar (N. Kanara); two *s.* two *d.* *Educ.:* Aryan E. S. High School; Elphinstone High School; Elphinstone College, Bombay; King's College, Cambridge. Maths. Trip. Pt. I (1909); Nat. Sc. Trip. Pt. I (1911); Hist. Trip. Pt. II (1912); called to Bar, Lincoln's Inn, 1913; Advocate, Bombay High Court, 1913-20; Acting Professor of History, Elphinstone College, Bombay, July to October 1915; joined firm of N. Sirur & Co., 1920; Member Bombay Municipal Corporation, 1926-39; Mayor of Bombay, 1932-33; Vice-Chancellor, Bombay University, 1933-39; Chairman, Council of Indian Institute of Science, Bangalore; Member Bombay Legislative Council, 1933; Member Indian Legislative Assembly, 1941-45; Pres. Local Board (Bombay) State Bank of India. *Address:* 41 Pedder Road, Cumballa Hill, Bombay, India. *Clubs:* Willingdon Sports, Cricket Club of India (Bombay). [*Died* 24 *Jan.* 1959.

CHANDLER, Raymond Thornton; Free lance writer since 1933; *b.* Chicago, Ill.; U.S. citizen; *m.* 1924, Pearl Cecily Hurlburt (*d.* 1954); no *c.* *Educ.:* Dulwich College; privately in France and Germany. Early contributor of verses, essays and other literary oddments to English publications. Served European War, 1914-18, in 1st Canadian Division and R.A.F. Business career as accountant and oil executive in U.S.A., 1919-32. Wrote for pulp magazines, then mystery novels, film plays,

occasional magazine articles, 1933-. *Publications:* The Big Sleep, 1939; Farewell My Lovely, 1940; The High Window, 1942; The Lady in the Lake, 1943; The Little Sister, 1949; Trouble is My Business (Penguin), 1950; The Simple Art of Murder, 1950; The Long Goodbye, 1953; Playback, 1958. *Address:* 116 Eaton Square, S.W.1. *T.:* Sloane 3691; Box 58, La Jolla, California, U.S.A.; Rushwater, Old Chatham, New York. *Club:* Garrick.
[*Died* 26 *March* 1959.

CHANNON, Sir Henry, Kt. 1957; M.P. (C.) Southend-on-Sea (West) since 1950. M.P. (C.) Southend-on-Sea, 1935-50); Writer; *b.* 7 Mar. 1897; *s.* of Harry Channon and Vesta Westover; *m.* 1933, Lady Honor Guinness (from whom he obtained a divorce, 1945), *e. d.* of 2nd Earl of Iveagh, K.G.; one *s.* *Educ.:* privately; Christ Church, Oxford (M.A.). Parliamentary Private Secretary to Under-Secretary of State for Foreign Affairs, 1938-1941. *Publications:* Joan Kennedy, 1929; Paradise City, 1930; The Ludwigs of Bavaria, 1933. *Address:* Kelvedon Hall, near Brentwood, Essex. *T.:* Ongar 180; 5 Belgrave Square, S.W.1. *T.:* Belgravia 5675. *Clubs:* Carlton, Buck's, Pratt's, Royal Automobile. [*Died* 7 *Oct.* 1958.

CHANT, Clarence Augustus, M.A., Ph.D., LL.D., F.R.A.S., F.R.A.S.C., F.R.S.C.; Emeritus Professor of Astrophysics, and Director of the David Dunlap Observatory, University of Toronto, since 1935; *b.* near Toronto, Ontario, 31 May 1865; father from England (Somerset), mother English descent; *m.* 1894; two *d.* *Educ.:* Markham High School; St. Catharines Collegiate Institute; University of Toronto. B.A., University of Toronto, 1890; M.A., 1900; attended University of Leipzig, 1898; Harvard University, 1900-1901; Ph.D., 1901; Tutorial Fellow, University of Toronto, 1891; Lecturer, 1892; Associate-Professor, 1907; Professor, 1918; and Director of the David Dunlap Observatory, 1933; President, Royal Astronomical Society of Canada, 1904-7; Member International Astronomical Union; Fellow, American Physical Society; American Astronomical Society; Mem. Perpét. Soc. Ast. de France; Editor of Journal of Royal Astronomical Society of Canada from its inception, 1907; organised and led expedition to Australia to observe the solar eclipse to test the Einstein theory, 1922; in his honour the Chant Medal was established in 1940 by R.A.S. of Canada to be awarded for distinction in amateur astronomy. *Publications:* Papers in scientific journals; (with F. W. Merchant) Ontario High School Physics, and Laboratory Manual in Physics, 1911, 3rd ed. as Elements of Physics, 1937; Mechanics for the Upper School, 1919 (3rd edition as Upper School Physics, 1945); Our Wonderful Universe, 1928, new ed. 1940 (trans. into German, Czech, Polish, Spanish, French); Text Book of College Physics (with E. F. Burton), 1933; The Teaching of Astronomy in the University of Toronto, 1954. *Address:* Observatory House, David Dunlap Observatory, Richmond Hill P.O., Ontario, Canada. [*Died* 18 *Nov.* 1956.

CHAPLIN, Brigadier-General James Graham, C.B.E. 1922; D.S.O. 1915; Cameronians; *b.* 1 July 1873; *m.* 1914, Lily Dora, *d.* of late Thomas Alexander of Brentham Park, Stirling; one *s.* two *d.* Entered Scottish Rifles, 1894; Adjutant, 1898-1902; Captain, 1900; Major, 1913; Brig.-Gen. 1917; Col., 1923; Adjutant Special Reserve, 1909-12; served N.W. Frontier, India, 1897-8 (medal 2 clasps); European War, 1914-18 (D.S.O., Bt. Lt.-Col.); Brevet Colonel, 1919; Brigade Commander Military Forces in Iraq, 1925-27; retired pay, 1927. *Club:* Army and Navy.
[*Died* 15 *Jan.* 1956.

CHAPLIN, Rev. W. Knight; editor of the Christian Endeavour Times for 23 years; Hon. Secretary British National C.E. Union for 28 years, President Designate of the Union, 1930-1932; President, 1932-33; *b.* Leamington, 17 June 1863; *m.* Mary, *d.* of Phillip Stranger of Guernsey, 1889; four *s.* one *d.* *Educ.:* New College, London, etc. Pastor of churches at Poplar, Stratford, Wanstead Park, Grantham and Walthamstow; visited America, 1895, and took part in Convention attended by 56,000 delegates; became Hon. Secretary of the Christian Endeavour Union, 1893, at which time the Union embraced only 500 societies; the societies later affiliated numbered 10,000; was organising secretary of the C.E. World's Convention held at Alexandra Park, July 1900; and of the Jubilee Convention held in the Royal Albert Hall at Whitsuntide, 1931; frequent preacher and speaker at gatherings of young people in all parts of the land. *Publications:* The Life of Dr. Clark; Origin and Progress of the Christian Endeavour Movement; Sixty-five Years of Christian Endeavour—a Record and Forecast, etc.; many sermons and magazine articles. *Recreations:* reading and motoring. *Address:* Williston, 1 Bushwood, Leytonstone, E.11. *T.:* Wanstead 5677. [*Died* 14 *Jan.* 1951.

CHAPMAN, David Leonard, F.R.S. 1912; Hon. Fellow of Jesus College, Oxford; *b.* 6 Dec. 1869; *e. s.* of David and Maria Chapman of Wells, Norfolk; *m.* Muriel Catharine Canning, *e. d.* of Samuel Holmes, M.A., late Rector of Braunston, North Hants; one *d.* *Educ.:* Manchester Grammar School; Christ Church, Oxford. Lecturer and Demonstrator in Chemistry in the University of Manchester, 1897-1907; Fellow of Jesus College, Oxford, 1908-44; Vice-Principal, 1935-44. *Publications:* Articles relating to Chemistry and Chemical Physics in scientific journals. *Recreation:* golf. *Address:* 253 Cowley Rd., Oxford.
[*Died* 17 *Jan.* 1958.

CHAPMAN, Capt. Ernest John Collis, M.C.; Gen. Secretary to British Empire Cancer Campaign from its inception in 1923 until 1946 when elected Member of Grand Council of the Campaign; *b.* 14 Sept. 1876; *s.* of John Chapman, formerly of Ealing; *m.* Violet Mabel (*d.* 1957), *d.* of William Frederick Clayton, Wimbledon. *Educ:* Emmanuel Coll., Camb. Lieut., Cambridge University Rifles Volunteers, 1898-99; transferred to 8th Middlesex Regiment until 1908; Railway Transportation Staff in France, 1915-18; commanded section of Railways on Arras Front (mentioned in letter of thanks from Army Commander 3rd Army for special services, 1916; special routine order by Commander Reserve Army for act of courage, 1916, despatches twice, M.C.); Controller, Ministry of Labour (Board of Demobilisation), 1918; Assistant Controller-General, Ministry of Labour (Board of Demobilisation), 1919; Secretary to the Prime Minister's Railway Strike Committee, 1919-20; Deputy Director General, London County Council Housing Bonds Campaign, 1921; Deputy Director General of Combined Appeal for the Hospitals of London, organised by King Edward's Hospital Fund for London, 1921-22; Secretary to the International Conference on Cancer, 1928; former Vice-Pres. Royal West Sussex Hospital, Chichester; a Founder and former Member Exec. Cttee. of Empire Rheumatism Council; Member of Enham Village Centres Council for Disabled Men; Member of Council, Management Cttee. Appeals Cttee. and Finance Cttee., The Victory Ex-Services Club formerly Veterans' Assoc. *Recreations:* horticulture and sailing, handicapper (formerly Chm.) of Federated Sailing Clubs of Chichester Harbour. *Address:* Waterside Cottage, Old Bosham, Chichester. *T.:* Bosham 3140. *Club:* University Union Society (Cambridge). [*Died* 20 *June* 1958.

CHAPMAN, Rev. Percy Hugh, M.A., LL.D.; Vicar of Holy Trinity, Malvern, 1921-1944; Rural Dean of Powyke, 1924; Surrogate in the Diocese of Worcester, 1925; Hon. Canon of Worcester 1929-44, Canon Emeritus 1944; *b.* 13 April 1866; *s.* of late Capt. W. D. Chapman, Madras Staff Corps; *m.* 1898, Katharine Margaret, *d.* of late Hon. Justice Sir George Knox, Puisne Judge, High Court, Allahabad; three *d.* *Educ.:* Felsted School, Essex; King William's College, Isle of Man; Corpus Christi College, Cambridge, B.A. and M.A.; Trinity College, Dublin, M.A., LL.B., LL.D. Deacon, 1889; Priest, 1890; Curate of All Saints', Shooter's Hill, Woolwich; Chaplain to H.M. Indian Government, 1893; Diocese of Lucknow, at various stations. Diocesan Inspector of Schools, 1908; Canon of Lucknow, 1910; Bishop of Lucknow's Commissary, 1914; Archdeacon of Lucknow, and Chaplain to H.M. Indian Government at Naini Tal, U.P., India, 1912. *Address:* The Old Mill House, Diss, Norfolk. [*Died* 1 *Jan.* 1953.

CHAPMAN, Colonel Philip Francis, C.I.E. 1919; I.M.S. retired; *b.* 11 Feb. 1870; *s.* of Charles Edward Chapman, Indian Civil Service; *m.* 1st, 1902, Christina Jeanette (*d.* 1926), *d.* of J. Kirsopp; 2nd, 1933, Margaret Gertrude Campbell, *d.* of late James Currie, LL.D., of Inverawe and Fanans, Argyllshire and Larkfield, Edinburgh. *Educ.:* Repton; Edinburgh University (M.B., C.M., 1894). Civil Surgeon, Jubalpur and Nagpur; Inspector-General of Civil Hospitals, Central Provinces, India; commanded 35 Combined Field Ambulance, 8 Indian General Hospital and 20 I. General Hospital in Mesopotamia, 1917-20 (despatches, C.I.E.). *Address:* Fanans, Taynuilt, Argyllshire. [*Died* 14 *Sept.* 1956.

CHAPMAN, Robert Hall, C.M.G. 1950; M.E., M.I.E. (Aust.); Railways Commissioner, State of South Australia, since 1947; *b.* 5 Jan. 1890; *s.* of late Sir Robert Chapman, Adelaide; *m.* 1923, Maysie W., *d.* of Robert Knox; one *s.* one *d.* *Educ.:* Collegiate School of St. Peter, Adelaide; University of Adelaide. Served European War, Royal Engineers, 1915-19 (wounded, despatches). Formerly Chief Engineer, South Australian Railways. Member of the Council of the University of Adelaide; Member of the Council of Australian Standards Association; formerly Chairman, South Australian Division, Institute of Engineers, Australia. Colonel Railways Staff Corps. *Publications:* papers in engineering journals. *Address:* c/o South Australian Railways, Adelaide, South Australia; 41 West Terrace, Kensington Gardens, Adelaide, South Australia. *Club:* Adelaide (Adelaide). [*Died* 10 *May* 1953.

CHAPMAN, Robert William, C.B.E. 1955; Hon. D.Litt. Oxon; Hon. LL.D. St. And.; F.B.A., 1949; *b.* 1881; *m.* 1913, Katharine, *e. d. of* late Arthur Wharton Metcalfe; three *s.* one *d.* *Educ.:* Univ. of St. Andrews (1st Class Classical Honours); Oriel College, Oxford (1st Class Mods. and Lit. Hum.). Served in the Royal Garrison Artillery (Temp. 2nd Lt.), 1915-19 (Temp. Capt.); Salonica, 1915-18; Member Council, Friends of Bodleian, and Oxford Bibliographical Society; Secretary to the Delegates of the Oxford Univ. Press, 1920-42; Fellow of Magdalen College, Oxford, 1931-47; Clark Lecturer, Trinity College, Cambridge, 1948; Lamont Lecturer, Yale University, 1950. *Publications:* Selections from Boswell, 1919; The Portrait of a Scholar, 1920; Selections from Johnson, 1923; Edition of Jane Austen's Novels, 1923, and Letters, 1932, 1952; Johnson's and Boswell's Tour to the Hebrides, 1924; Sanditon, 1925; Volume the First, 1933; Volume the Third, 1951; Cancels, 1930; Society for Pure English, tracts on Oxford English, 1932, Names a Designations, 1936, Adjectives from Proper Names, 1939, Retrospect, 1948; Review of English Studies, articles on the text of Trollope, 1941-42; Jane Austen: Facts and Problems (The Clark Lectures, Trinity College, Cambridge), 1948; ed. Johnson's Letters, 1952; Johnsonian and Other Essays, 1953; Jane Austen, a Critical Bibliography, 1953; Selections from Samuel Johnson, 1955. Times Literary Supplement, Notes and Queries, etc. *Address:* 19 Barton Lane, Old Headington, Oxford. *T.:* Oxford 62946. [*Died* 20 *April* 1960.

CHAPMAN, Sir Sydney (John), K.C.B., *cr.* 1920 (C.B. 1919); C.B.E. 1917; Litt.D. (Manchester); *b.* Wells, Norfolk, 20 April 1871; 2nd *s.* of David Chapman; *m.* 1903, Mabel Gwendoline, *o. d.* of late T. H. Mordey, J.P., Newport, Mon.; two *s.* one *d.* *Educ.:* Manchester Grammar School; Owens College, Manchester; Trinity College, Cambridge (Major Scholar). 1st class, Moral Sciences Tripos, part i. and part ii.; Univ. prizeman (Cobden, Adam Smith); Guy Silver Medallist Royal Statistical Society; Lecturer in Economic and Political Science, Univ. Coll., Cardiff, 1899-1901; Professor of Political Economy, Owens Coll. Manchester, 1901-17; Dean of the Faculty of Commerce and Administration, Univ. of Manchester, 1904-17; Assistant Secretary of Board of Trade, 1918-19; Permanent Secretary, 1920-27; Chief Economic Adviser to Government 1927-32; President of Section F.(Economics and Statistics) of the British Association, 1909; Vice-President Royal Statistical Society, 1916; Chairman of the Economic (Labour) Commission of the Union of South Africa, 1913; during European War, 1914-18, Director of Industrial (War Inquiries) Branch of the Board of Trade, and mem. of various official Committees; Member of Imperial Shipping Committee 1927-32; Member and Chairman of Imperial Economic Committee, 1931-32; Member Import Duties Advisory Committee, 1932-39; Member of Economic Committee of League of Nations, 1927-32, and President, 1930; Member of Economic Consultative Committee, League of Nations, 1928-32; United Kingdom delegate to International Conferences on Communications and Transit, Import and Export Restrictions, Copyright, Statistics, Treatment of Foreigners, Tariffs, etc.; Member of Central Price Regulation Committee; Chairman of British Arc Lamp Carbon (War Emergency) Pool and Controller of Matches, 1939-44. *Publications:* vols. in continuation of Lord Brassey's Work and Wages, etc. (in collaboration with Lord Brassey); The Lancashire Cotton Industry, 1904; The Cotton Industry and Trade, 1905; Outlines of Political Economy, 1st ed. 1911, etc. *Recreation:* golf. *Address:* The Manor House, Ware, Herts. *T.:* Ware 123. [*Died* 29 *Aug.* 1951.

CHAPMAN-HUSTON, Major Desmond (Wellesley William Desmond Mountjoy); Literary Adviser to Quarterly Review; *o. s.* of Richard Newland Huston of Annagh More and Drumbo Lodge, Co. Leitrim, and Katharine Anna Mountjoy, *d.* of William Chapman of Ashgrove, Co. Monaghan; unmarried. Totally uneducated. Conservative Parliamentary Candidate for Borough of Northampton, 1913-18; Vice-Pres. Conservative Labour Party; Pres. George Eliot Fellowship, 1935-1938; Hon. Col. 6th (C.) Bn. Essex Regt.; served European War, 1914-19 (despatches twice, British and Allied War Medals). *Publications:* The Hills of Hell and Other Verses; A Creel of Peat and Other Essays; The Melody of God: Essays and Biographical Studies; Sir James Reckitt: a Memoir; The Lost Historian: A Memoir of Sir Sidney Low; Lawrence of Ireland and Arabia: an intimate study; (posthumous) Bavarian Fantasy: The Story of Ludwig II; *autobiography:* The Lamp of Memory: Autobiographical Digressions, 1949; The Winged Chalice: More Autobiographical Digressions, 1952; in collab.: Life of General Sir John Cowans, G.C.B., Quarter-master-General of the First World War (with Major Owen Rutter); Bavaria the Incomparable and Don Alfonso XIII (with Princess Pilar of Bavaria); Memoirs of Prince Blücher (with Evelyn Princess Blücher); Through Four Revolutions (with Prince Adalbert of Bavaria); By the Clock of St. James's, with Percy Armytage; Daisy, Princess of Pless, From My Private Diary and What I left Unsaid (with Daisy Princess of Pless); Behind the Scenes at the Prussian Court (with Princess Friedrich Leopold of Prussia); Through a City of London Archway: The Story of Allen & Hanbury's (with Ernest C. Cripps). Editor of Subjects of the Day by the Marquess Curzon of Kedleston; contrib. to D.N.B., Cornhill, Quarterly Review, The New Criterion, National Review, etc.; *plays:* Say it with Flowers: a three Act Comedy; George Eliot's Love Story: A Play in three Acts; Eugénie and Napoleon: a romantic play in three acts and an epilogue. *Recreations:* lecturing, travelling, walking, conversation. *Address:* Carn Brea Castle, Carn Brea, Cornwall. *Club:* Carlton.

[*Died* 15 *Sept.* 1952.

CHARBONNEAU, Most Rev. Joseph, D.D., Ph.D. Ordained for Archdiocese of Ottawa, 1916. Formerly Superior of Grand Seminary, Ottawa; Principal of Normal School, Hull, Province of Quebec. Vicar-General, 1928; Protonotary Apostolic, 1930; first Bishop of Hearst, 1939; Archbishop of Amorio and Archbishop Coadjutor of Montreal, 1940-50, resigned, 1950; translated to titular Archbishop of Bosphorus, 1950. *Address:* St. Joseph Hospital, Victoria, B.C., Canada. [*Died* 19 *Nov.* 1959.

CHARLES, Lieutenant-General Sir (James) Ronald (Edmondston), K.C.B., *cr.* 1932 (C.B. 1918); C.M.G. 1919; D.S.O. 1901; *b.* 26 June 1875; *s.* of late T. Edmondston Charles, M.D., Hon. Physician to H.M.; *m.* 1940, Margaret Lilias, *e. d.* of late Major L. H. Prioleau, Manchester Regt. *Educ.:* Winchester; R.M.A., Woolwich. Entered Army, Royal Engineers, 1894; served S. Africa, 1899-1900, (despatches twice, Queen's medal four clasps, D.S.O.); Bazar Valley Field Force, 1908 (despatches); Mohmand Field Force, 1908 (despatches, Bt. of Maj., medal and clasp); European War, 1914-18; Commanded 25th Div. Aug. 1918-March 1919 (despatches five times, Bt. Lt.-Col., Bt. Col., C.B., C.M.G.); Officer, Legion of Honour; Commanded Waziristan Force, India, May to Oct. 1923 (despatches and clasp to 1908 medal); Commandant of Royal Military Academy, Woolwich, 1924-26; Director of Military Operations and Intelligence, War Office, 1926-31; Master General of Ordnance, War Office, 1931-34; retired, 1934; Col. Comdt. R.E., 1931-46; Colonel Bengal Sappers and Miners, 1940-45; Chief Royal Engineer, 1940-46. *Address:* The Hermitage, Ilminster, Somerset. *Club:* United Service.

[*Died* 24 *Dec.* 1955.

CHARLES, Robert Henry, C.B.E. 1938; *b.* 16 Oct. 1882; *s.* of Robert Fletcher Charles and Frances Dorothea Davenport; *m.* Ursula, *d.* of Lonsdale Holden; one *s.* three *d.* *Educ.:* Aysgarth School, Yorkshire; King's School, Canterbury; Christ Church, Oxford (Open Classical Scholar). Junior Inspector of Schools, 1906; H.M. Inspector, 1910; H.M. Chief Inspector of Schools, 1933-46; Secretary, Institute of Education, University College of South West, Exeter, 1948-51. *Recreation:* fishing. *Address:* 6 Marine Parade, Budleigh Salterton, Devon. *Club:* Athenæum. [*Died* 17 *Sept.* 1951.

CHARLES, Lt.-Gen. Sir Ronald; *see* Charles, Sir J. R. E.

CHARLESWORTH, His Honour Judge John; County Court Judge since 1953; Chancellor of the County Palatine of Durham since 1950; Chairman, Durham Quarter Sessions, since 1953; Deputy Chairman Northumberland Quarter Sessions since 1955; *b.* 19 October 1893; *e. s.* of Arthur Heywood Charlesworth and Lillie Stephens; *m.* 1924, Lilian Ada, *e. d.* of J. B. Waggott; two *s.* two *d.* *Educ.:* Giggleswick School. Served European War, 1914-19, overseas Gallipoli, France and Italy; Lieutenant 5th Manchester Regiment (despatches); called to Bar, Lincoln's Inn, 1921; practiced on North-Eastern Circuit; LL.D. (London), 1922. Recorder of: Pontefract, 1935; Scarborough 1946; Middlesbrough, 1950; Legal Adviser to the Regional Commissioner, Northern Region, 1940-45. *Publications:* Liability for Dangerous Things, 1922; Principles of Mercantile Law, 1929 (8th edn., 1955); Principles of Company Law, 1932 (6th edn., 1954); Law of Negligence, 1938 (3rd edn., 1956); Town Planning Law, 1946 (2nd edn., 1948); Part Editor, Clerk & Lindsell on Torts (9th, 10th and 11th edns., 1954); Chitty on Contracts (20th edn., 1948); editor 9th edn. Brooke's Office of a Notary, 1939; editor 41st edn., Palmer's Private Companies, 1949. *Recreations:* walking, golf. *Address:* Kirkstyle, South Park, Hexham. *T.:* Hexham 601.

[*Died* 13 *Dec.* 1957.

CHARLETON, Henry Charles, J.P.; *b.* 1 March 1870; *s.* of Henry Charleton, sometime engine-driver, Midland Railway; *m.* Louisa Jane, *d.* of Charles Alcock, Kentish Town; one *s.* *Educ.:* Holmes Road Board School, Kentish Town; attended classes at Working Men's College, St. Pancras, and Oxford Summer School. Left school 12 years of age, worked as smith's assistant till 1888; entered service of Midland Railway as engine-cleaner, promoted in due course to fireman and driver; worked express passenger trains from 1907 onward till elected to Parliament; M.P. (Lab.) South Leeds, 1922-31 and 1935-45; Chairman of Select Committee on Estimates, 1930; Parliamentary Private Sec. to the Under Sec. of State for Dominion Affairs, 1929-31; a Junior Lord of the Treasury, 1931; served on the Executive Committee of the National Union of Railwaymen; Member of men's side of Locomotive Conciliation Board of the Midland Railway since inception in 1907; Governor of Queen Mary's (Roehampton) Hospital (Chairman of Governors, 1929-); Alderman, London County Council, 1934-35; Labour Opposition Whip, 1935. *Publication:* compiled Locomotive Men's Conditions of Service after the Negotiations in 1919 at the request of the General Secretary of the N.U.R. *Recreations:* music, gardening, reading. *Address:* 15 St. Andrews Drive, Stanmore, Middlesex.

[*Died* 8 Oct. 1959.

CHARLEY, Colonel Harold Richard, C.B.E. 1920; D.L. Co. Antrim, 1946; late Royal Ulster Rifles; City Commandant U.S.C., Belfast, 1927-51; *b.* 4 April 1875; *s.* of late William Charley, J.P., D.L., of Seymour Hill, Dunmurry, Co. Antrim, Ulster; *m.* 1923, Phyllis, *d.* of late R. S. Hunter, Ma Vie, Cooden; one *s.* (one *d.* decd.) *Educ.:* Cheltenham College, 2nd Lt. Roy. Irish Rifles, 1895; Captain, 1902; Major, 1913; Lt.-Col., 1919; Col. 1923; commanded 1st Royal Ulster Rifles, 1919-23; served with 1st R.I.R. in Natal and India; Adjutant, 1st R.I.R., 1903-6; 5th R.I.R., 1910-13; left Tidworth for France with 2nd R.I. Rifles, 13 Aug. 1914; in actions of Mons and Le Cateau; seriously wounded and taken prisoner at Caudry, 26 Aug. 1914; prisoner of war until interned in Switzerland, 11 Aug. 1916; started workshops for British interned in Mürren, 1916; and after repatriation, Sept. 1917, returned to Switzerland as Officer i/c Technical Instruction for British Interned; Acting Commissioner for B.R.C., and then Commissioner B.R.C. in Switzerland, 1918; Manager B.R.C., Berlin, March-August 1919, when closed down B.R.C. and came to U.K. to take over command of 1st Royal Ulster Rifles; retired pay, 1924. *Address:* Three Trees, Helen's Bay, Co. Down. *T.:* Helen's Bay 3145.

[*Died* 13 *April* 1956.

CHARLOT, André Eugene Maurice; Theatrical Manager and Producer; *b.* Paris, 26 July 1882 (Naturalised British in 1922); *s.* of late Maurice Charlot and late Sargine Battu; *m.* Florence Gladman; one *s.* one *d.* *Educ.:* Lycée Condorcet, Paris. Gained his earlier experience in Paris, where he was engaged as press manager, business manager, or manager of various Parisian theatres and music halls, including the Chatelet, Palais-Royal, Femina, Folies-Bergères, etc. Joint Manager of the Alhambra, 1912; Managing Director until 1916; made a speciality of the production of revues: Kill that Fly, 1912; Eightpence a Mile, Keep Smiling, 1913; Not Likely, 1914; 5064 Gerrard, Now's the Time, Samples, 1915; Some, This and That, Pierrot's Christmas, Poached Eggs and Pearls, See-Saw, Three Cheers, 1916; Cheep, Bubbly, 1917; Flora, Tabs, Very Good Eddie, Tails Up, The Live Wire, Officers' Mess, Buzz-Buzz, 1918; Three Wise Fools, Bran Pie, Wild Geese, 1919; Jumble Sale, 1920; Puss-Puss, Now and Then, A to Z, Pot Luck, 1921; Snap, Dede, Midnight Follies (at the Hotel Metropole), 1922; Rats, London Calling, Yes, 1923; Charlot's Revues, 1924-25; The Charlot Show of 1926; The Enemy. Charlot, Clara Gibbings, 1928; Cabaret Shows at Hotel Splendide and Grosvenor House, 1929; Charlot's Masquerade, Wonder Bar, 1930; Faces, Men About the House, 1932; How d'You Do, Please, 1933; Hi Diddle-Diddle, 1934; Charlot's Char-a-bang, Dancing City, Shall we Reverse, 1935; Stop-Go, Sleeping Beauty, or What a Witch, The Town Talks, 1936. Went to Hollywood, 1937, where he became a screen actor; has appeared in 50 pictures. Has done fifty broadcasts entitled Charlot's Hour. *Address:* c/o The Screen Actors' Guild, 7046 Hollywood Blvd., Hollywood, California. *T:* Hollywood 5-6247.
[*Died* 20 *May* 1956.

CHARLTON, Archibald Campbell, C.M.G. 1935; *b.* 5 Nov. 1877; 2nd *s.* of William Oswald Charlton, Hesleyside, Northumberland; *m.* 1921, Margery, *d.* of late Sir William Haggard, K.C.M.G., C.B. *Educ.:* Oratory School, Edgbaston. Entered Consular Service, 1905; Vice-Consul at Baltimore, 1905; Havana, 1907; Toulon, 1908; Berlin, 1910; Bergen, 1914; Consul, 1916; Consul-General, Berlin, 1920-25; Milan, 1925-31; San Francisco, 1931-1938. *Address:* Frinstead, Sittingbourne, Kent. [*Died* 13 *May* 1952.

CHARLTON, Air Commodore Lionel Evelyn Oswald, C.B. 1919; C.M.G. 1916; D.S.O. 1900; late R.A.F.; *b.* 7 July 1879; *s.* of late William O. Charlton of Hesleyside, Northumberland. *Educ.:* Brighton Coll. Served South Africa, 1899-1902 (twice wounded, despatches, Queen's medal 5 clasps, King's medal 2 clasps, D.S.O.); served W.A.F.F., 1902-7; European War, 1914-17 (wounded); Air Attaché, British Embassy, Washington, 1919-22; Chief Staff Officer, Iraq Command, 1923-24; retired list, 1928; Officer Legion of Honour. *Publications:* A Hausa Reading Book; Charlton; War from the Air; War over England, 1936; The Mystery of Cowsole Wood, 1948; (Ed), The Recollections of a Northumbrian Lady, 1815-1866, 1949; and other works. *Address:* Charlton House, Tarset, Hexham, Northumberland. [*Died* 18 *April* 1958.

CHARNWOOD, 2nd Baron, *cr.* 1911, **John Roby Benson,** T.D. 1944; Consulting Optician; Lay Fellow Roy. Soc. Med.; F.Phys.Soc.; F.R.M.S.; F.Amer. Acad. Opt.; F.S.M.C.; F.B.O.A.; *b.* 31 Aug. 1901; *e. s.* of 1st Baron and Dorothea (*d.* 1942), *d.* of Roby Thorpe, Nottingham; *S.* father, 1945; *m.* 1933, Beryl Joan, *e. d.* of Percy Cuthbert Quilter. *Educ.:* Eton; Balliol College, Oxford. Commissioned in Bedfordshire Yeomanry, 1929; served War of 1939-45, Royal Artillery. *Publications:* various papers on Vision. *Recreations:* motoring and sailing. *Address:* Court Lodge Farm, East Brabourne, Kent; 108 Eccleston Mews, S.W.1. *T.:* Sloane 6603. *Club:* Brooks's. [*Died* 1 *Feb.* 1955 (*ext.*).

CHARPENTIER, Gustave; Compositeur de Musique, Membre de l'Institut de France; Grande Croix de la Légion d'Honneur; Directeur du Conservatoire de Mimi-Pinson; Président d'honneur de la Fédération internationale des Artistes Musiciens et du Syndicat des Musiciens de Paris; *b.* Dieuze, Alsace-Lorraine, 24 juin 1860. *Educ.:* Conservatoire de Paris, classe de M. Massenet. Prix de Rome en 1887. *Publications:* Poèmes chantés, Les Fleurs du mal, Impressions fausses, mélodies avec piano ou orchestre; Didon, scène lyrique; Impressions d'Italie, suite d'orchestre en 5 parties; La Vie du poète, drame lyrique en 4 actes; Le Couronnement de la Muse du Peuple, grande fête populaire, danse, chant, pantomime et chœurs, représentée dans la plupart des grandes villes françaises; Louise, roman musical, en 4 actes et 5 tableaux; Chant d'apothéose pour le centenaire de Victor Hugo; Julien, drame lyrique en un prologue et quatre actes (8 tableaux). *Address:* 66 Bd. Rochechouart, Paris. [*Died* 18 *Feb.* 1956.

CHARRINGTON, Lieut.-Colonel Sydney Herbert, C.M.G., 1918; D.S.O. 1917; F.R.G.S.; 3rd *s.* of late J. D. Charrington, Ashburton House, Roehampton; *b.* 1 Dec. 1878; unmarried. *Educ.:* Eton. 2nd Lt. 15th (The King's) Hussars, 1899; Captain and Adjutant, 1906-10; resigned Commission, 1912; Lt.-Col. R. of O., 15th Hussars, 1919; settled in Kenya, 1912-31; served European War; Signalling Officer, East Africa, 1914; G.S.O. (3), 2nd Mtd. Div., Suvla Bay, 1915; G.S.O. (2), Southern Force, Egypt, 1916; Major, 6th (S.) Batt., Northampton Regt., France, May-Oct. 1916; Lt.-Col. 17 Oct. 1916-3 Feb. 1917; commanding 3rd Tank Battalion, 1917-18; Brig.-Gen. commanding 5th Tank Brigade, 2 Nov. 1918-10 Jan. 1919 (C.M.G., D.S.O., Croix de Guerre with palm); reverted to unemployment, 1919; Member of Legislative Council, Kenya, 1920-21. *Address:* Old Mill House, Rockfield, Monmouth. *T.:* Monmouth 142. *Clubs:* Cavalry, Buck's.
[*Died* 1 *Oct.* 1954.

CHASE, Beatrice; *see* Parr, O. K.

CHATER, Daniel; *b.* 1870, M.P. (Lab.) South Hammersmith, 1929-31, N.E. Bethnal Green, 1935-50. *Address:* 17 Levett Gardens, Seven Kings, Essex.
[*Died* 25 *May* 1959.

CHATTERJEE, Sir Atul Chandra, G.C.I.E., *cr.* 1933 (K.C.I.E., *cr.* 1925; C.I.E. 1919); K.C.S.I., *cr.* 1930; LL.D. (Hon.) Edinburgh; *b.* 24 Nov. 1874; *s.* of Rai Sahib Hem Chandra Chatterjee and Srimati Nistarini Devi; *m.* 1st, Vina Mookerjee (*decd.*); one *d.*; 2nd, 1924, Gladys Mary Broughton, O.B.E., M.A., D.Sc., Barrister-at-Law, Lincoln's Inn, formerly of the Indian Educational Service and Labour Adviser to Indian Government. *Educ.:* Presidency Coll., Calcutta; King's Coll., Cambridge (Government of India Scholar); B.A. Honours. Passed first in the I.C.S. open competition, 1896; Bhownugger Medallist (Cambridge University) 1897; served as Assistant-Magistrate, Joint Magistrate, Magistrate, and Collector in the United Provinces, 1897-1906; special inquiry into industries in the United Provinces, 1907-8; Registrar Co-operative Societies, U.P., 1912-16; Revenue Sec. to U.P. Government, 1917-18; Chief Secretary to U.P. Government, 1919; member Board of Industries and Munitions, Government of India, 1920; Indian Government Representative at International Labour Conference, Washington, 1919, and Geneva, 1921, 1924-33; President of International Labour Conference, 1927; League of Nations Assembly, 1925 and 1946, Member of Board of Liquidation, League of Nations, 1946-47; Member of the Governing Body I.L.O., 1926-31, Vice-President, 1932, and President, 1933; Member of Imperial Economic Committee, 1925-1931; Vice-President Consultative Economic Committee of the League of Nations; Chairman of Permanent Central Opium Board of League of Nations, 1938-46; Member of Allocations Committee of League of Nations; Indian Delegate to London Naval Conference, 1930; Leader of Indian delegation to Ottawa Imperial Conference, 1932; Leader I.L.O. delegation to World Economic Conference, 1933; Fellow of the Univ. of Allahabad, 1908-20; Secretary to the Government of India in the Department of Industries, 1921; member of Indian Legislative Assembly, 1921-24; Industries member of the Viceroy's Executive Council, India, 1923-24; High Commissioner for India in the United Kingdom, 1925-31; Member of Council of India, 1931-36; Adviser to Secretary of State for India, 1942-47; Chairman of Council of Royal Society of Arts, 1940 and 1941; Vice-Pres. Royal Asiatic Society and Royal India Society; Vice-Chairman of Council of East India Association; Member of I.L.O. Committee of Experts. *Publications:* Notes on the Industries of the United Provinces, 1908; New India, 1947: (Jointly) Short History of India, 3rd edn., 1953; various contributions to journals and reviews. *Recreation:* travel. *Address:* 26 York House, Kensington Church St., W.8. *T.:* Western 6190. *Clubs:* Athenæum; Calcutta (Calcutta). [*Died* 8 *Sept.* 1955.

CHATTERJEE, Dr. Gopal Chunder, M.B., Hon. F.R.I. (Lond.); Rai Bahadur; Hon. Lecturer of Protozoology, Calcutta University; Founder Hon. Secretary The Central Co-opt. Anti-Malaria Society, Ltd.; Vice-President and Hon. Treasurer, Central Co-operative Anti-Malaria Society and Public Health Society Ltd., 1952; Founder President Bengal Co-operative Home Crofter Association, Ltd.; *b.* 1873; 2nd *s.* of Dr. Nilmadhab Chatterjee, M.B., Calcutta; *m.*; two *s.* two *d.* *Educ.:* Calcutta University. House Physician to First Physician, Medical College Hospitals, Calcutta, for three years; served as Assistant Bacteriologist to the Govt. of Bengal and Assistant Professor of Pathology and Bacteriology, Medical College, Calcutta, for twenty-two years; Rai Bahadur, 1917; retired from Govt. service, 1922; Commissioner of Panihaty Municipality, 24 Pergs, Bengal, for twenty-one years; has specialised for many years in Bengal on tuberculosis, anti-malaria and public health. *Publications:* many papers on Tuberculosis in medical jls. Editor Sonar Bangha, a monthly jl. *Recreations:* Propaganda for rousing the sanitary conscience of the people in the matters of public health, modern scientific agriculture and co-operative marketing, dairying, home crofting, co-operative water supply, cottage industries, research in intestinal flagellate protozoa and fermentative bacteria. *Address:* 1/2A Prem Chand Bural Street, Calcutta 12, India. *T.A.:* Antimalaria, Calcutta. *T.:* 3070 Avenue. [*Died* 16 *Oct.* 1953.

CHATTAWAY, Edward; *b.* Leamington, 1873; *s.* of W. C. Chattaway; *m.* 1910, Edith May (*d.* 1930) *d.* of Henry Elwell de Hane. *Educ.:* Warwick School. Served articles Warwick Advertiser; King's Lynn News, Birmingham Argus (now Birmingham Evening Dispatch); Joined Star, 1899 and became Chief Reporter, News Editor and Assistant Editor; Editor, The Star, 1930-36; Editorial Director of The Star and News Chronicle, 1936-46; Director of News Chronicle and Star newspapers, 1932-46; Member Newspaper Proprietors Assoc. *Recreations:* motoring, golf, bridge. *Address:* 157 Clarence Gate Gardens, Regent's Park, N.W.1. *T.:* Paddington 6228; Icknield, Watlington, Oxon. *Club:* Devonshire. [*Died* 2 *May* 1956.

CHATTERTON, Sir Alfred, Kt., *cr.* 1919; C.I.E. 1912; K.-i-H. Gold Medal, 1900; B.Sc., F.C.G.I., A.M.I.C.E., M.I.M.E.; Fellow of the Imperial College; *b.* 10 Oct. 1866; *s.* of J. H. Chatterton; *m.* 1st, 1895, Helen Scott (*d.* 1897), *d.* of Henry Borthistle; 2nd, 1901, Alice Gertrude, M.B.E., *d.* of W. H. Wilson; two *s.* one *d.* *Educ.:* Finsbury Technical College; Central Institution, South Kensington. Indian Educational Service, 1888; Professor of Engineering, Madras, 1888-1900; Director of Industries, Madras, 1908; Director of Industries and Commerce in Mysore, 1912; Member of the Indian Industrial Commission, 1916-18; Controller Indian Munitions Board, 1917; Industrial Adviser to the Mysore Durbar, 1918; also Industrial Adviser to the Tata Industrial Bank, Bombay; Consulting Engineer. *Publications:* Agricultural and Industrial Problems in India; Lift Irrigation; Tanning in Madras; Industrial Evolution in India; numerous technical papers in various journals. *Address:* The Store House, Rye, Sussex. *T.:* Rye 2278. [*Died* 26 *July* 1958.

CHAUMEIX, André, membre de l'Académie Française; Directeur de la Revue des deux Mondes; *b.* le 7 Juin 1874; *m.* Mlle. Marcellin-Pellet. *Educ.:* Lycée Henri IV.; École Normale Supérieure. Membre de l'École Française de Rome, 1898; Journal des débats, 1900-40; Directeur de la Revue de Paris, 1920-26; Conseiller d'Ambassade à Berne. 1917-18; Rédacteur politique de Figaro, 1926-30; Président du Comité France-Amerique, 1942; Commandeur de la Légion d'Honneur. *Address:* 85 Avenue Henri Martin, Paris XVIe. [*Died* 23 *Feb.* 1955.

CHAVE, Captain Sir Benjamin, K.B.E., *cr.* 1920; retired; *b.* Southampton, 25 Sept. 1870; *s.* of Benjamin Chave, London, and Agnes Scarff, Essex; *m.* 1908, Rachel Agnes, *d.* of Rev. Thos. Morgan, M.A.; one *s.* (and one, Flight-Lieut. R.A.F.V.R., missing 14/15 Feb. 1943, now officially presumed to have lost his life). *Educ.:* King Edward VI. School, Southampton. *Publications:* Distances and Courses on Routes of U.C. Steamers; articles to Nautical Magazine. *Address:* 10 Glebe Court, Southampton. *T.:* Southampton 54109. *Club:* Southampton Master Mariners. [*Died* 4 *July* 1954.

CHAVE, Elmer Hargreaves, C.I.E. 1944; retired as Chief Engineer, P.W.D., Madras, 1946; *b.* 10 Oct. 1891; *s.* of W. J. Chave; *m.* 1928, Frances Mary Tanner; one *d.* *Educ.:* McGill University. Appointed Indian Service of Engineers, 1919; Chief Engineer, Public Works Dept., Madras, 1940-46. Member Indus Commission, 1941-42. *Address:* 6728 Marine Crescent, Vancouver, B.C., Canada. [*Died* 27 *Nov* 1957.

CHAYTOR, Colonel D'Arcy, C.M.G. 1918; C.B.E. 1919; V.D.; J.P.; Col. (retired) N.Z. Military Forces, and formerly Lieut.-Colonel Royal Marines; *b.* 1873; *m.* 1908, Avis Anne (*d.* 1954), *d.* of Comdr. R. A. Edwin, late R.N., Wellington, N.Z. *Educ.:* Clare College, Cambridge. Served South African War, 1899-1901 (medal and 4 clasps); European War, 1914-19 (despatches, 3 times, C.M.G., C.B.E., Order of the Nile, 3 medals). Maj. H.G., 1940-42. *Address:* Pooley Hall, Polesworth, Warwickshire. [*Died* 9 *Oct.* 1960.

CHAYTOR, Rev. Henry John, M.A.; Litt.D.; *b.* 10 Feb. 1871; *s.* of H. J. Chaytor, M.A., Jesus College, Camb., of Kidderminster; *m.* Mary Rashleigh, 3rd *d.* of Rev. E. Pinwill of Ermington, Ivybridge, South Devon; two *s.* one *d.* *Educ.:* Durham School; All Souls College, Oxford. Classical and Modern Language Master at Stratford-on-Avon, 1896-99; Merchant Taylors' School, Crosby, Liverpool, 1900-5; Second Master at King Edward VII. School, Sheffield, 1905-8; Headmaster of Plymouth College, 1908-19; Fellow, Senior Tutor and Lecturer in Modern Languages, St. Catharine's College, Cambridge, 1919-33; Master of St. Catharine's College, Cambridge, 1933-46. *Publications:* The Troubadours of Dante: Les Poésies

de Perdigon, in Les Annales du Midi; The Troubadours and England; Six Vaudois Poems; A History of Aragon and Catalonia, 1933; Savaric de Mauléon, 1939; From Script to Print, 1945; several school editions of French and German texts; translator of William Pitt, by Ruville; of Ferrero's Greatness and Decline of Rome, and other works from French and German; writer of articles on educational topics, etc. *Address:* 3 St. Paul's Road, Cambridge.
[*Died* 19 *Nov.* 1954.

CHEAPE, Brig.-Gen. (George) Ronald (Hamilton), C.M.G. 1919; D.S.O. 1918; M.C.; *b.* 1881; 2nd *s.* of late Lt.-Col. George Clerk Cheape; *m.* 1912, Margaret Bruce, *d.* of late J. Bruce Ismay; four *s.* *Educ.:* Glenalmond College; Britannia. Four years a midshipman; served in S. Africa, 1900-1902; European War, 1914-19 (despatches six times, M.C., D.S.O., C.M.G.); commanded an Infantry Brigade in France; retired from Army, 1 April 1919; D.L. County Fife. *Address:* Tiroran, Isle of Mull. *Clubs:* Cavalry; New (Edinburgh).
[*Died* 29 *April* 1957.

CHEATLE, Sir (George) Lenthal, K.C.B., *cr.* 1918 (C.B. 1901); C.V.O. 1912; Cav. Uff. Grand Cross of Italy; Associate Order of St. John of Jerusalem; F.R.C.S.; Hon. F.A.C.S.; F.K.C.; Officer of the Grand Cross of Italy, 1910; Chevalier Legion of Honour, France; Surgeon to Nightingale Hospital for Gentlewomen; Consulting Surgeon and Emeritus Lecturer on Surgery, King's College Hospital; Surgeon to Hospital for Paralysis and Epilepsy, Regent's Park; Consulting Surgeon to Sevenoaks Hospital; late Member of Consultative Board and Examiner in Surgery, Member Admiralty Departmental Committee, Naval Medical Service; *b.* 13 June 1865; *m.* 1902, Clara Denman (*d.* 1942), *d.* of Col. Keith Jopp, R.E.; three *s.* one *d.* Late Surgical Registrar, House Surgeon, Assistant House Physician, House Physician, Surgeon to and Lecturer on Surgery at King's Coll. Hospital; Demonstrator of Surgery and Asst. Demonstrator of Anatomy, King's Coll.; late Consulting Surgeon to H.M. Forces in South Africa (despatches, medal four clasps, C.B.); late Surgeon-Rear-Adm.; European War, 1914-19 (K.C.B.); Walker Prizeman, 1926-30, Royal College of Surgeons of England; Prizeman in Surgery, King's Coll. *Publications:* Tumours of the Breast (with Dr. Max Cutler), etc. *Address:* Lismore, Bushey Heath, Herts. *Club:* Athenæum.
[*Died* 2 *Jan.* 1951.

CHEKE, Sir Marcus (John), K.C.V.O. 1957 (C.V.O. 1951); C.M.G. 1955; H.M. Minister to the Holy See since 1957; Extra Gentleman Usher to the Queen since 1957; *b.* 1906; *s.* of late Lieut.-Colonel E. G. Cheke, R.A.; *m.* 1939, Hon. Constance Elizabeth Lopes, *d.* of 1st Baron Roborough; no *c.* *Educ.:* Trinity College, Oxford. Contested (L.) New Forest and Christchurch, 1929; Hon. Attaché, H.M. Embassy, Lisbon, 1931-34; Hon. Attaché, Brussels, 1934-37; Press Attaché, Lisbon, 1938-42; attached to the staff of H.M. Embassy, Lisbon, with local rank of First Secretary, 1942-45; H.M. Vice-Marshal of the Diplomatic Corps, 1946-57. *Publication:* The Cardinal de Bernis, 1958. *Address:* British Legation to the Holy See, Rome. *Clubs:* Brooks's, St. James'.
[*Died* 22 *June* 1960.

CHELMSFORD, Dowager Viscountess; G.B.E., *cr.* 1917; C.I.; **Frances Charlotte;** *b.* 1869; *d.* of 1st Baron Wimborne; *m.* 1894, 1st Viscount Chelmsford (*d.* 1933); one *s.* (and one killed in action, 1917), four *d.* *Address:* 23 Warwick Square, S.W.1. *T.:* Victoria 3543.
[*Died* 24 *Sept.* 1957.

CHENEVIX-TRENCH, Colonel Lawrence, C.M.G. 1919; D.S.O. 1918; R.E.; *s.* of Charles Chenevix-Trench; *b.* 1883; *m.* 1908, Winifred Ross, *d.* of Edward H. Tootal, 25 Upper Phillimore Gardens, W.; two *d.* *Educ.:* Wellington College; Royal Military Academy, Woolwich. Served European War, 1914-18 (wounded, despatches, C.M.G., D.S.O., Legion of Honour); A.Q.M.G., Northern Command, India, 1933-37; retired pay, 1937. A.A. and Q.M.G. France, 1940. *Address:* 26 Lowndes St., S.W.1. *Club:* United Service.
[*Died* 11 *Nov.* 1958.

CHENEVIX-TRENCH, Lieut.-Colonel Sir Richard Henry, Kt., *cr.* 1930; C.I.E. 1923; O.B.E. 1919; *b.* 1876; *m.* 1913, Evelyn May, *d.* of late Capt. Harry Evelyn Stracy Pocklington, 15th Hussars; one *s.* one *d.* *Educ.:* Winchester; R.M.C., Sandhurst. Entered Indian Army, 1896; retired 1931; served China, 1900 (medal with clasp); joined Political Department, 1901 and served in Baluchistan, Kashmir, Rajputana, and Government of India in various capacities; member of the Nizam's Executive Council, 1927-35. *Club:* United Service.
[*Died* 3 *Sept.* 1954.

CHERRY-GARRARD, Apsley (George Benet); explorer, author; *b.* 2 Jan. 1886; *m.* 1939, Angela, *d.* of late Kenneth Turner, Fairfields, Ipswich. *Educ.:* Winchester; Christ Church, Oxford. Member British Antarctic Expedition (Scott), 1910-1913, and took part in the following sledge journeys: Depôt, Winter, Polar, Dog Journey to One Ton, Search; medical expedition on schistosomiasis, China, 1914; commanded squadron of armoured cars, 1914; invalided, 1916; stopped killing of penguins on Macquarie Island, which was declared a bird and seal sanctuary by Tasmanian Government, 1916; obtained certain reforms in treatment of invalided men, 1917. *Publications:* edited South Polar Times, Antarctic, 1911 and 1912; The Worst Journey in the World, 1922; introductory chapter to Wilson of the Antarctic, 1933; Study in T. E. Lawrence by his Friends, 1937; Introductory chapter to Life of Bowers, 1938; Postscript to The Worst Journey in the World, 1951. *Recreations:* rowing; Grand Challenge Cup, Henley, 1908; shooting, painting and book-collecting. *Address:* 23 Dorset House, Gloucester Place, N.W.1. *T.:* Welbeck 5522. *Clubs:* Athenæum, Leander, Antarctic.
[*Died* 18 *May* 1959.

CHERWELL, 1st Viscount, *cr.* 1956, of Oxford; 1st Baron, *cr.* 1941; **Frederick Alexander Lindemann,** P.C. 1943; C.H. 1953; F.R.S.; Hon. Fellow, Wadham College, Oxford, 1956; Emeritus Student of the House, Christ Church, Oxford, 1956; Professor of Experimental Philosophy, Oxford, Fellow of Wadham College, 1919 and again Professor, 1953-56; Student of Christ Church, 1921; *s.* of late A. P. Lindemann, Sidholme, Sidmouth. *Educ.:* Blairlodge; Darmstadt; Berlin University (Ph.D.); Paris. Served European War, 1914-18; Experimental Pilot, Director of Physical Laboratory of R.A.F., Farnborough. Personal assistant to Prime Minister, 1940; Paymaster-General, 1942-45, and 1951-53. *Publications:* The Physical Significance of the Quantum Theory; papers on physical, chemical, and astrophysical subjects in Proc. Roy. Soc., Philosophical Magazine, etc. *Recreations:* lawn tennis, golf. *Address:* Christ Church, Oxford. *Club:* Athenæum.
[*Died* 3 *July* 1957 (*ext.*).

CHESHAM, 4th Baron (*cr.* 1858), **John Compton Cavendish,** M.C.; J.P., Capt. late 10th (Prince of Wales's Own) Royal Hussars; Squadron Leader late R.A.F.V.R.; *b.* 13 June 1894; *s.* of 3rd Baron and Lady Beatrice Constance Grosvenor, 2nd *d.* of 1st Duke of Westminster [she *m.* 2nd, 1910, J. A. Moncreiffe); *S.* father, 1907; *m.* 1st, 1915, Margot (who obtained a divorce, 1937), *d.* of late J. Layton Mills, Tansor Court, Oundle; one *s.*; 2nd, 1938, Countess of Carrick. *Educ.:* Eton; R.M.C. Sandhurst. Served European War, 1914-18 (wounded). Chairman Tanganyika, Southern Highlands, Estates Ltd. *Heir:* *s.* Capt. Hon. John

Charles Compton Cavendish [*b.* 18 June 1916; *m.* 1937, Mary Edmunds, 4th *d.* of late David G. Marshall, White Hill, Cambridge; one *s.* two *d.*] *Recreations:* golf, shooting, travel. *Address:* Southern Highlands Club, Sao Hill, Tanganyika. *Club:* Carlton. [*Died* 26 *April* 1952.

CHESTERFIELD, 12th Earl of (*cr.* 1628), **Edward Henry Scudamore Stanhope,** Baron Stanhope, 1616; Bt. 1807; *b.* 9 Feb. 1889; *s.* of late Capt. Hon. Evelyn Theodore Scudamore Stanhope, *s.* of 9th Earl and Julia Dasha, *d.* of John Gerald Potter; *S.* uncle 1935; *m.* 1st, 1915, Lorna Marie, *d.* of Henry Lever, Wellington, N.Z.; one *d.*; 2nd, 1931, Angela Domatilla (*d.* 1952), *d.* of F. P. Hopkins. *Educ.:* Wellington College. *Heir:* *kinsman*, Earl Stanhope. *Address:* Breinton House, Hereford. [*Died* 2 *Aug.* 1952.

CHESTON, Charles Sidney, R.W.S. 1933; painter and etcher; Member of New English Art Club. *Educ.:* Malvern College; Slade School. Represented in Tate Gallery, British Museum, National Galleries, Cape Town, Queensland; Whitworth Institute, Manchester, Leeds, Huddersfield, Newcastle, Sheffield, and other provincial galleries. *Publication:* Evelyn Cheston, 1931. *Address:* Hillside Studio, Polstead, Colchester. *Club:* Chelsea Arts. [*Died* 2 *Oct.* 1960.

CHETHAM-STRODE, Edward David, C.B.E. 1920 (O.B.E. 1918); *b.* 1871; *s.* of late Capt. Augustus Chetham-Strode, C.B., R.N. *Educ.:* Charterhouse; Trinity College, Cambridge, B.A. Called to Bar, Lincoln's Inn, 1899; Legal Assistant Ministry of Munitions, 1915-19; Legal Adviser to Clearing Office (Enemy Debts). *Address:* 26 Ashworth Road, W.9. *T.:* Cunningham 3235. *Club:* Lansdowne. [*Died* 13 *Feb.* 1958.

CHETTIAR, Sir Ramanatha A.; *see* Alagappa Chettiar.

CHETTLE, Major Henry Francis, C.M.G. 1932; O.B.E. 1918; *b.* Liverpool, 23 Dec. 1882; *er. s.* of Henry Chettle, Hornsey; *m.* Louisa (*d.* 1952), *d.* of William and Ellen Sanders. *Educ.:* City of London School; Corpus Christi College, Oxford; Gray's Inn. Clerk in Charity Commission, 1911-14; served European War 1914-19 (R.A.S.C., France; D.G.R. and E, France and War Office); appointed to staff of Imperial War Graves Commission, 1919; late Assistant Secretary (Records) Imperial War Graves Commission; retired 1947; Recommissioned and promoted Lt.-Col., General List, Sept. 1939; retired as Major, 1949. Officier de l'Ordre de la Couronne (Belgium). *Address:* Fonthill Gifford, Tisbury, Wilts. [*Died* 5 *Feb.* 1958.

CHETTY, Sir Shanmukham, K.C.I.E., *cr.* 1933; Minister for Finance, India, 1947-1948; President of Indian Tariff Board, 1945; Vice Chancellor Annamalai University, 1951, *b.* 17 Oct. 1892; *s.* of Kandaswami Chetty; *m.*: three *d.* *Educ.:* Madras Christian College; Madras Law College. Vice-Chairman of the Municipal Council, Coimbatore, 1919; Member of the Madras Legislative Council, 1921-23; a Member of the Indian Legislative Assembly, 1924-34; Deputy President, 1931; President, 1933-34; Diwan Cochin State, 1935-1941; Head of Govt. of India Supply Mission in United States, 1941-42; represented the Indian employers at the International Labour Conferences at Geneva, 1928, 1929 and 1932; one of the Govt. of India delegates at the Imperial Economic Conference at Ottawa, 1932; visited Australia as the Indian delegate on the Empire Parliamentary Delegation, 1926; Indian delegate to the Assembly of the League of Nations, 1938; Indian Delegate at the Monetary Conference held at Bretton Woods (U.S.A.), 1944; Adviser to the Chamber of Princes, 1945. *Recreation:* tennis. *Address:* Hawarden, Coimbatore, South India. *Clubs:* National Liberal; Cosmopolitan (Madras). [*Died* 5 *May* 1953.

CHETWODE, Admiral Sir George Knightley, K.C.B., *cr.* 1935 (C.B. 1919); C.B.E. 1919; *s.* of Lt.-Col. Sir George Chetwode, 6th Bart.; *b.* 1877; *m.* 1st, 1908, Alice (*d.* 1937), *d.* of late Major V. H. Vaughan-Lee, M.P., of Dillington Park, Ilminster, Somerset; one *s.* (and one killed in action, May 1941); 2nd, 1939, Elizabeth, *d.* of late Frederick Taylor, Jericho, Queensland. Lieutenant 1899; Commander 1912; Captain 1917; Rear-Admiral 1928; Vice-Admiral 1933; Admiral 1936; holds Humane Society's Bronze Medal; served China, 1900 (medal); European War, 1914-18; present at Battle of Jutland, 1916 (despatches, Order of St. Stanislas of Russia with Swords); command of Destroyers, Mediterranean, 1917-19 (despatches twice, C.B.E.); 1918 (despatches, C.B., Italian despatches, and silver For Valour Medal, Legion of Honour); Deputy Director of Naval Intelligence, 1923-1925; commanded H.M.S. Queen Elizabeth and H.M.S. Warspite, 1925-1927; Naval Secretary to First Lord of the Admiralty, 1929-32; commanded First Cruiser Squadron, Mediterranean Fleet, 1932-33; Admiral commanding Reserves, 1933-36; A.D.C. to the King, 1927-28; retired list, 1936. *Address:* (until June 1957) Palais Ausonia, Mentone, A.M., France. *Club:* English-Speaking Union. [*Died* 11 *March* 1957.

CHETWYND-STAPYLTON, Colonel Bryan Henry, C.B.E. 1923; 2nd *s.* of late Lt.-Gen. G. Chetwynd Stapylton and Lady Barbara Chetwynd Stapylton: *m.* 1905, Dorothy Constance (*d.* 1942), *d.* of Chambré Brabazon Ponsonby of Kilcooley Abbey; one *s.* one *d.* *Educ.:* Charterhouse; R.M.C., Sandhurst. Served South African War with 1st Batt. Mounted Infantry, 1899-1902 (despatches, Queen's medal 5 clasps, King's medal 2 clasps); Staff-Capt., War Office, 1910-12; D.A.A.G., War Office, 1912-14; European War (Mons Star and 2 medals); A.A.G., War Office, 1919-20; commanded 1st Bn. Cheshire Regt. 1919-23; Instructor Senior Officers School, 1924-27; Officer in charge of Shrewsbury Record and Pay Office, 1927-30; retired pay, 1930. *Address:* Middleton Hall, nr. Darlington. *Club:* Army and Navy. [*Died* 29 *May* 1958.

CHEVRILLON, André, member of the French Academy; Officier de la Légion d'Honneur; Fellow of Royal Society of Literature; foreign member of American Academy of Arts and Letters; *b.* Ruelle, Charente, 1864; *e. s.* of Major J. Chevrillon, French Naval Artillery, and Sophie Taine; *m.* 1901, Clarisse Porgès; one *s.* two *d.* *Educ.:* University College School, London; École Alsacienne, Paris. Agrégé de l'Université, Docteur ès lettres, Paris; Chargé de Cours à l'Université de Lille, 1889-94; travelled India, Burmah, Egypt, Syria, America, French N. Africa. *Publications:* Dans l'Inde, 1891; English Translation, Romantic India; Sydney Smith et la Renaissance des idées liberales en Angleterre, 1894; Terres mortes, 1898; Etudes anglaises, 1901; Sanctuaires et paysages d'Asie, 1903; Un Crépuscule d'Islam, 1906; La Pensée de Ruskin, 1908; Nouvelles Études anglaises, 1910; L'Angleterre et la Guerre, 1916 (translated into English under the title Britain and the War); Près des Combattants, 1918; Marrakech dans les Palmes, 1919; Les Américains à Brest, 1920; Trois Études Anglaises (English translation, Three Studies in English Literature); L'Enchantement Breton, 1925; Derniers Reflets à l'occident, 1925; Les Puritains du Désert, 1928; Taine, formation de sa pensées, 1932; Visions du Maroc, 1932; La Menace Allemande, 1934; Rudyard Kipling, 1936; contributions to Revue des Deux Mondes and Revue de Paris. *Address:* c/o Plon, 8 rue Garancière, Paris, VI; Roc'h Bleiz, Port Blanc, Penvénan, C. du Nord, France. [*Died* 10 *July* 1957.

CHEYNE, Col. Sir Joseph Lister, 2nd Bt., *cr.* 1908; M.C.; *b.* 12 Jan. 1888; *er. s.* of Sir W. Watson Cheyne, 1st Bt., K.C.M.G., F.R.S., and Mary Emma (*d.* 1894), *d.* of William Servanté, Plumstead; *S.* father, 1932; *m.* 1912, Nelita Manfield, *e.d.* of Andrew Pringle, late of Borgue, Kirkcudbright and Basing House, Banstead; three *s.* *Educ.:* Fonthill, East Grinstead; Uppingham; Sandhurst. Joined 16th Lancers, 1907; served European War in France, 1914-19 (despatches, Military Cross, 1916, Bar to Cross, 1918); commanded 16th/5th Lancers, 1929-33; Major, 1921; Lieut.-Colonel, 1929; Colonel, 1933; retired pay, 1937. Served also 1939-40, France, 1940. *Recreations:* fishing, shooting. *Heir: s.* Joseph Lister Watson [*b.* 10 Oct. 1914; *m.* 1st, 1938, Mary Mort (marr. diss. 1955), *er. d.* of Vice-Admiral J. D. Allen, *q.v.*; one *s.* one *d.*; 2nd, 1955, Cicely, *d.* of Thomas Metcalfe; one *s.*]. *Address:* Leagarth, Fetlar, Shetland. [*Died* 20 *Sept.* 1957.

CHEYNEY, Peter (Major Reginald Evelyn Peter Southouse-Cheyney); O.St.J.; author; controls The Cheyney Organisation, embracing all international activities in writing (both as author and journalist), investigation and research; *b.* 22 Feb. 1896; *s.* of Arthur William Thomas Cheyney, County Clare, Ireland and Katharine Mary Southouse; *m.* 1948, Loretta Theressa, *d.* of William Frederick and Adelaide Groves, Westchester County, N.Y. *Educ.:* Hounslow Coll.; The Mercers School; Univ. of London. Has been law clerk, actor, and soldier; has written professionally since 1910. Served European War, 1914-18; gazetted from Inns of Court O.T.C. to 3rd Bn. The Royal Warwickshire Regt., 1915; 1st Bn. 1916 (severely wounded, 1916). Special Appointment, 1917; resigned Commission, 1919. Formed and directed Editorial and Literary Services (London), 1926; Editor St. John Ambulance Gazette, 1928-1943; News Editor, Sunday Graphic, 1933-1934; formed and directed Cheyney Research and Investigations, 1932. *Publications:* Poems of Love and War, 1916; To Corona and other Poems, 1917; lyrics, monologues and production numbers in conjunction with Messrs. Boosey, Reynolds, etc., 1920-26; Le Rayon Qui Tue and La Dernière Enquète de l'Inspecteur Ralston, 1920-26; This Man Is Dangerous, 1936; Poison Ivy, Dames Don't Care, Can Ladies Kill?, 1937; The Urgent Hangman, Don't Get Me Wrong, 1938; Dangerous Curves, The Peter Cheyney Omnibus, Knave Takes Queen, Another Little Drink, 1939; You'd Be Surprised, You Can't Keep The Change, You Can't Hit A Woman, 1940; Mister Caution—Mister Callaghan, Your Deal My Lovely, It Couldn't Matter Less, Never A Dull Moment, 1941; Dark Duet, Sorry You've Been Troubled, 1942; You Can Always Duck, The Stars Are Dark, 1943; Making Crime Pay, They Never Say When, The Dark Street, 1944; Sinister Errand, I'll Say She Does, 1945; Dark Hero, Uneasy Terms, 1946; Dark Interlude, 1947; Dance Without Music, 1947; No Ordinary Cheyney, 1948; Try Anything Twice, 1948; Dark Wanton, 1948; You Can Call It A Day, 1949; One Of Those Things, 1949; Lady Behave, 1950; Dark Bahama, 1950; Ladies Won't Wait, 1951; (posthumous) Velvet Johnnie, 1952 (stories, with introd. by Viola Garvin). *Recreations:* criminology, fencing, golf, reading, travel. *Address:* 19-21 Chesham Street, S.W.1. *Clubs:* Public Schools, Devonshire; Devonshire (Eastbourne), etc. [*Died* 26 *June* 1951.

CHHAJJU RAM CHOWDHRY, Sir, Kt., *cr.* 1931; C.I.E. 1927; Landowner and jute merchant; *b.* 1865 of humble Jat parentage; *m.* 1898; three *s.* one *d.* *Educ.:* Rewari High School, Gingaov. Started career as a clerk in Hoare, Miller & Co. when in teens; became a hessian broker in the gunny market; later became an independent dealer and exporter of jute goods; purchased the Zemindary of Sheikhpur in the Punjab; was member of the Punjab Legislative Council. [*Deceased.*

CHICHELE PLOWDEN, Lt.-Col. C. T.; *see* Plowden.

CHICK, Herbert George, C.I.E. 1915; C.B.E. 1934; *b.* 19 Nov. 1882; *s.* of Alfred Y. Chick; unmarried. *Educ.:* Tonbridge School. Caius College, Cambridge (Exhibitioner); Russian Scholar, 1904; Student Interpreter in the Levant, 1903; Acting Vice-Consul, Bushire, 1906-9; Commercial Adviser to the Political Resident in the Persian Gulf, 1910-19; Vice-Consul at Bushire, 1909; Acting Vice-Consul, Saffi, Morocco, 1919-20; Tetuan, 1920; H.M. Consul, Cairo, 1920; Shiraz, 1921-30; Consul-General (at Salonica) for Macedonia, Thrace, Thessaly, 1930-33; retired, 1933; holds Delhi Durbar medal. *Address:* Whetley-Powerstock, nr. Bridport, Dorest. *Club:* United University. [*Died* 21 *May* 1951.

CHIENE, George Lyall, M.B., C.M., F.R.C.S. Ed., Consulting Surgeon, Edinburgh Royal Infirmary; *b.* 24 Jan. 1873; *s.* of late Emeritus Professor John Chiene and Elizabeth M. Lyall; *m.* 1902, Elaine S. Turcan; two *s.* *Educ.:* Edinburgh Academy; Christ's College, Cambridge; Edinburgh University. Graduated, 1897; formerly Additional Examiner in Surgery, Aberdeen University; Assistant Surgeon to Edinburgh and East of Scotland S. African Hospital, 1899; Assistant Surgeon, Royal Hospital for Sick Children, Edinburgh, 1901; temp. Major, B.E.F., France; Ex-President, Medico-Chirurgical of Edinburgh, Edinburgh University Union and Royal Medical Society. *Publications:* Surgical Section (conjointly with Mr. Wallace) of Edinburgh and East of Scotland S. African Hospital Reports; papers in the medical journals. *Address:* 11 Magdala Crescent, Edinburgh. *T.:* Edinburgh 61627. [*Died* 19 *Nov.* 1951.

CHIFLEY, Rt. Hon. Joseph Benedict, P.C. 1945; Leader of the Opposition, Commonwealth of Australia, since Dec. 1949; *b.* 22 Sept. 1885; *s.* of late Patrick and Mary Anne Chifley; *m.* 1914, Elizabeth Mackenzie. *Educ.:* Patrician Brothers High School, Bathurst, N.S.W. Joined N.S.W. Railways Dept. as shop-boy, becoming engine-driver; appeared for Locomen's Assn. in State Arbitration Court and for Austn. Federation of Locomotive Enginemen's Union in Federal and State Courts. M.H.R., Macquarie, N.S.W., 1928, 1929, 1940, 1943, 1946, 1949; defeated same seat, 1925, 1931, 1934. Minister for Defence, 1931-1932; Member of Royal Comm. on Monetary and Banking Systems, 1935-36. Minister for Post-War Reconstruction, 1942-45; acting Prime Minister, 30 April-2 July 1945; Prime Minister, 1945-49, and Treasurer, 1941-49, of Commonwealth of Australia. *Recreations:* gardening, reading. *Address:* 10 Busby Street, Bathurst, N.S.W.; Parliament House, Canberra, A.C.T. [*Died* 13 *June* 1951.

CHILD, Brig.-General Sir (Smith) Hill, 2nd Bt., *cr.* 1868; G.C.V.O., *cr.* 1941 (K.C.V.O., *cr.* 1937; C.V.O. 1934; M.V.O. 1902); C.B. 1919; C.M.G. 1918; D.S.O. 1916; D.L., J.P., Staffs.; Extra Equerry to the Queen since 1952 (to King George VI, 1937-52); *b.* 19 Sept. 1880; *e. s.* of John George Child, 2nd *s.* of 1st Bt. and Helen, *d.* of Rev. George Mather, Huntley Hall, Staffordshire, Prebendary of Lichfield; *S.* grandfather, 1896; *m.* 1925, Barbara, *d.* of late Ernest Villiers and Hon. Mrs. Villiers, Hambrook House, Chichester; two *d.* *Educ.:* Eton; Christ Church, Oxford. Served in S. Africa, 1900; European War, 1914-18 (D.S.O., C.M.G., C.B., Croix de Guerre, France); M.P. (Co. U.) Stone Division of Staffordshire, 1918-22; Gentleman Usher in Ordinary to the King, 1927; Deputy Master of the Household, 1929; Master of H.M.'s Household, 1936-41. *Heir:* none. *Address:* Whitton Hall, Shrewsbury, Shropshire. *T.:* Halfway House 270. *Club:* Turf. [*Died* 11 *Nov.* 1958 (*ext.*).

CHILDE, Prof. (emeritus) V. Gordon, D.Litt.; D.Sc.; F.B.A.; F.R.A.I.; F.S.A. Scot.; University Professor of Prehistoric European Archæology and Director of Institute of Archæology, London, 1946-56; Hon. Member Archäol. Institut des deutschen Reichs, Istituto di palentologia italiana, Esthonian Learned Soc., Société Suisse de Préhistoire, R. Irish Academy, Soc. des Antiquaires du Nord, K. Nederlandsche Akademïe van Wetenschappen Det Norske Videnskaps—Akademi; *b.* 14 April 1892; *s.* of Rev. S. H. Childe, Rector of St. Thomas', North Sydney, N.S.W. *Educ.:* Church of England Grammar School and Univ., Sydney; Queen's Coll., Oxford. Left Australia with Graduate Scholarship in Classics, 1914; B.Litt. 1916; first class honours in Literæ Humaniores, 1917; Private Sec. to the Premier of N.S.W., 1919-21; travelled in Greece, Balkans, and Central Europe; Librarian to Royal Anthropological Institute, 1925-27; Professor of Prehistoric Archæology, Edinburgh, 1927-46. Hon. LL.D. Edinburgh, 1957. *Publications:* How Labour Governs, 1923; The Dawn of European Civilisation, new enlarged ed. 1950; The Aryans, 1926; The Most Ancient East, 1928; The Danube in Prehistory, 1929; The Bronze Age, 1931; Skara Brae, 1931; New Light on the Most Ancient East, 1934; The Prehistory of Scotland, 1935; Man Makes Himself, 1936; Prehistoric Communities of the British Isles, 1947; Progress and Archæology, 1944; Piecing Together the Past, 1956; A Short Introduction to Archæology, 1956; Society and Knowledge, 1956; The Prehistory of European Society (posthumous), 1958. *Recreations:* bridge, walking, motoring. *Club:* Athenæum. [*Died* 19 *Oct.* 1957.

CHILDE, Wilfred Rowland Mary, B.A. (Oxon); Lecturer in English Literature at Leeds University since 1922; Dean of the Faculty of Arts, 1943-45; *b.* 1890; *e. s.* of late Henry Slade Childe, J.P., and Kate, *d.* of late Henry France of Thornes, Yorkshire, *Educ.:* Harrow School; Magdalen College, Oxford. Received into the Catholic Church, 1914. *Publications: Verse*—The Little City, 1911; The Escaped Princess, 1916; The Hills of Morning, 1920; The Gothic Rose, 1922; The Garland of Armor, 1923; The Ballad of Jak and Anne, 1924; Ivory Palaces, 1925; The Country of Sweet Bells, 1927; The Happy Garden, 1928; The Golden Thurible, 1931; Fountains and Forests, 1935; Selected Poems, 1936; Thrift and Sea Campion, 1948; The Blessèd Pastures, 1950; Ode for Installation of H.R.H. the Princess Royal as Chancellor of Leeds Univ., 1951; contributions to Edwardian Poetry, 1936, and Neo-Georgian Poetry, 1937; Leeds University Verse, 1950 and 1951; The Jongleur, Bradford. *Prose:* Dream English, a Fantastical Romance, 1917; Blue Distance, 1930; Henry Vaughan (a lecture), 1946; The Poetry of the Brontës (in The Enduring Brontës). *Address:* The Royd, 40 Duchy Road, Harrogate. [*Died* 9 *Nov.* 1952.

CHILTON, Sir Henry Getty, G.C.M.G., *cr.* 1934 (K.C.M.G., *cr.* 1930; C.M.G. 1921); *b.* 15 Oct. 1877; *s.* of late Capt. A. R. T. Chilton, Royal Artillery, Merrow Croft, Guildford, Surrey; *m.* 1906, Katharine, *d.* of Thomas J. O'Brien (U.S. Ambassador to Japan, 1907-1911, and to Rome, 1911-13); two *d.* *Educ.:* Wellington College. Entered Diplomatic Service as attaché, 1902; appointed Vienna, 1903; 3rd Secretary, 1904; transferred Copenhagen, 1905; to the Hague, 1907; to Brussels, 1907; 2nd Secretary, 1908; transferred to Berlin, 1910; to the Hague, 1913: 1st Secretary, 1915; transferred to Washington, 1918; Counsellor of Embassy at Rio de Janeiro, 1920; Counsellor of Embassy at Washington, 1921; Envoy Extraordinary and Minister Plenipotentiary at Washington, 1924-28; Minister to the Holy See, 1928-30; British Ambassador to Chile, 1930-33; Argentine Republic, 1933-35; British Ambassador to Spain, 1935-38; employed in Ministry of Economic Warfare, 1939-40, and in Ministry of Information, 1940. Was a member of Lord Willingdon's mission to South America, 1940-41. *Address:* 31 Brompton Square, S.W.3. *T.:* Kensington 8790. *Clubs:* Travellers', Royal Automobile, M.C.C. [*Died* 20 *Nov.* 1954.

CHILTON, Lieutenant-General Sir Maurice (Somerville), K.B.E., *cr.* 1954 (C.B.E. 1944); C.B. 1945; Quarter-Master General to the Forces since 1955; Colonel Commandant R.A. since 1952; *b.* 11 Jan. 1898; *s.* of late Thomas Christopher Chilton, Liverpool, and Bertha Mothersill; *m.* 1926, Margaret, *d.* of Archdeacon Sinclair, Cirencester; one *s.* two *d.* *Educ.:* Rugby; R.M.A., Woolwich. Commissioned, 1915; served in France, European War, 1916-19; Staff College, 1930-31; War of 1939-45 B.E.F. France and Belgium, Sept. 1939-June 1940; B.L.A. June 1944-Feb. 1946 as Chief of Staff Second Army and D.A.G. 21 Army Group; Director of Air, War Office, 1946-48; Commander, East Anglian District, 1948-50; Vice Quarter-Master General, 1950-53; G.O.C.-in-C. Anti-Aircraft Command, 1953-1955. *Address:* The Grange, Slindon, Sussex. *Club:* Army and Navy. [*Died* 21 *Aug.* 1956.

CHINOY, Sir Rahimtoola Meherally, Kt., *cr.* 1936; Chairman of F. M. Chinoy & Co. Ltd., Bombay; *b.* Bombay, 11 Feb. 1882; *m.* 1909, Sakina; three *s.* four *d.* *Educ.:* Bharda New High School, Bombay. Served on several important Committees formed by Govt. War Purposes Board during European War, 1914-18 and War of 1939-45; Member, Municipal Corporation, 1915-29; Chairman of its Standing Finance Committee, 1923-24, and Mayor, 1926-27; Elected Member, Legislative Assembly, 1931; President, Indian Merchants Chamber, 1936; Non-official adviser to Government of India in connection with the Indo-Japanese Trade Negotiations; Member, Stock Exchange Enquiry Committee, 1936-37; President, Federation of Indian Chambers of Commerce and Industry, 1937-38; Director of many companies; is connected with several benevolent and philanthropic institutions in City; Mem. Council of State, 1936-47. *Publications:* articles in social, political, and financial matters in important papers. *Recreation:* racing. *Address:* Meher Buildings, Chowpatty, Bombay 7. *T.A.:* Friendship Bombay. *T.:* (Residence) 41740. *Clubs:* Royal Western India Turf, Orient, Willingdon Sports; Cricket Club of India, Ltd. (Bombay). [*Died* 27 *Nov.* 1957.

CHISHOLM, Dame Alice, D.B.E., *cr.* 1920; *b.* 3 July 1856; 2nd *d.* of Maj. R. J. Morphy; *m.* 1878, W. A. Chisholm; two *s.* one *d.* (and one *s.* one *d.* decd.). During European War, 1914-18, Organiser and

Superintendent, Soldiers' Club and Rest Camp, Kantara Railway Station. *Address:* New Line Road, West Pennant Hills, N.S.W. [*Died* 31 *May* 1954.

CHISHOLM, Catherine, C.B.E. 1935; B.A., M.D.; late Hon. Consulting Physician for Children, Manchester Northern Hospital; Hon. Physician, Duchess of York Hospital for Babies, Manchester; Consulting Specialist for Children Hope Hospital; Lecture in Vaccination and Clinical Lecturer in Children's Diseases Manchester University; *b.* 2 Jan. 1878; *d.* of Kenneth Mackenzie Chisholm, J.P., M.D., and Mary Thornley. *Educ.:* Private school; Manchester University. B.A. Vict. Univ., Manchester 1898, M.B., Ch.B. 1904; M.D. 1912; F.R.C.P. Lond. 1949. Pres. Med. Women's Fed. 1928-29; Member B.M.A., Medical Women's Federation, Manchester Medical Soc., Manchester Pathological Soc. *Publications:* Medical Inspection of Girls in Secondary Schools; Articles: Defective Girls in Secondary Schools; Menstrual Molimina in Girls, 1913; Breast-milk Feeding, 1924; The Incidence of Rickets in Manchester, 1933. *Recreations:* walking and motoring. *Address:* 30 St. Ann Street, Manchester; 34 Broadway, Withington, Manchester *T.:* Didsbury, Manchester 3926, Blackfriars Manchester 5791. [*Died* 21 *July* 1952.

CHITTY, Sir (Thomas) Henry Willes, 2nd Bt., *cr.* 1924; *b.* 30 July 1891; *s.* of late Sir Thomas Willes Chitty, 1st Bt., and Emily Eliza, sister of Sir Henry Newbolt; *S.* father, 1930; *m.* 1922, Ethel Constance, *d.* of S. H. Gladstone, Darley Ash, Bovingdon, Herts; three *s.* *Educ.:* Winchester; University College, Oxford. Called to Bar, Inner Temple, 1914; served with Territorial Forces, European War, 1914-17; a Headmaster of the Hall Preparatory School, Hampstead; Headmaster of Rosslyn House Preparatory School, 1922-39. *Recreation:* cricket. *Heir:* *s.* Thomas Willes Chitty [*b.* 2 March, 1926; *m.* 1951, Susan Elspeth Russel Glossop, *d.* of Mrs. E. A. Hopkinson; one *s.*]. *Address:* Dalwood, Lower Bourne, Farnham, Surrey. *T.:* Farnham 5327. [*Died* 26 *Feb.* 1955.

CHOLMONDELEY, Lord George Hugo, O.B.E. 1919; M.C.; *b.* 17 Oct. 1887; 2nd *s.* of 4th Marquess of Cholmondeley; *m.* 1st, 1911, Clara Elizabeth (marriage dissolved, 1921; she *d.* 1925), *d.* of Charles Henry Taylor, Washington, and formerly wife of Major John Alexander Stirling, D.S.O., M.C.; one *d.*; 2nd, 1921, Ina Marjorie, O.B.E. 1934 (marriage dissolved, 1948), *d.* of late Canon R. Pelly; 3rd, 1948, Mrs. Diana Charlesworth, *widow* of A. K. Charlesworth and *d.* of late Hon. Rupert Beckett. *Educ.:* Eton Coll. Notts R.H.A. T.F. 1909-17; D.A.A.G. 1918. Served European War (M.C., despatches thrice, O.B.E.); War of 1939-45, Northern Command, W.O.S.B., U.K. and Egypt; retired with rank of Lt.-Col. *Address:* Barrow Lodge, Bury St. Edmund's. *T.:* Barrow 354. *Club:* Turf. [*Died* 26 *Aug.* 1958.

CHOPPING, Col. Arthur, C.B. 1919; C.M.G. 1916; late R.A.M.C.; *b.* 3 Aug. 1871; *s.* of E. Chopping, Colchester; *m.* 1914, Edith, *d.* of J. F. Newlands, Glasgow; one *d.* Lieutenant, 1899; Captain, 1902; Major, 1911; Lt.-Col. 1915; Col. 1926; served S. Africa, 1899-1902 (Queen's medal 4 clasps, King's medal 2 clasps); N.W. Frontier India, 1908 (medal with clasp); European War, 1914-19 (despatches 7 times, C.M.G., Bt. Col., C.B., Order of St. John of Jerusalem, Officier Order of the Crown of Belgium, and Belgian Croix de Guerre, Officier Order of the Crown of Italy); Afghan War, 1919; retired pay, 1928. O.C. Officers Convalescent Hospital, Kildonan House, South Ayrshire, 1940-45. *Address:* Braiswick, Hillcrest Road, Hythe, Kent. [*Died* 9 *Aug.* 1951.

CHOTZNER, Alfred James; *b.* 1873; *s.* of Dr. J. Chotzner; *m.* 1st, Ethel Kathleen Lan Davis (*d.* 1924); one *s.*; 2nd, 1930, Beatrice Violet, *widow* of Benjamin Schofield, J.P. *Educ.:* Harrow School; St. John's College, Cambridge; B.A. 1895. Passed Indian Civil Service Examination, 1895; proceeded to India, 1896: served in Bengal, Behar, and Assam; officiating Judge, High Court, 1921; Judge, High Court, Calcutta, 1924-28; M.P. (U.) Upton Division, West Ham, 1931-34. *Recreation:* music. *Address:* 2 Adelaide Crescent, Hove, Sussex. *Club:* Carlton. [*Died* 12 *Feb.* 1958.

CHOW, Sir Shou-Son, Kt., *cr.* 1926; *b.* 13 Mar. 1861; *s.* of Chow Kum Shu, Hong-Kong. Korean Customs Service, 1882-94; Chinese Consular Service in Korea, 1894-96; Managing Director, China Merchants Steam Navigation Co., Tientsin, China, 1897-1903; Managing Director, Imperial Chinese Railways of North China, Peking-Mukden Line, 1903-7; Customs Superintendent of Trade, Commissioner for Foreign Affairs, Taotai of New-chwang, N. China, 1907-10; Councillor, Foreign Office, Peking, 1910; J.P. Hong-Kong, 1917; Chinese Unofficial Mem. of Legislative Council, Hong-Kong, 1921, and Unofficial Member of Executive Council, since 1926; has Japanese Order of Rising Sun (4th Class) and Chinese Orders of Chia Ho and Pao Kwong Chia Ho. *Address:* Bank of East Asia, Ltd., Hong-Kong. [*Died* 23 *Jan.* 1959.

CHRISTIAN, Bertram; Barrister-at-law; publisher; Director, Nisbet & Co., Ltd.; proprietor of Christophers; *b.* Rossory, Co. Fermanagh; *o. s.* of Robert Culbertson Christian; *m.* Henrietta (*d.* 1948), *d.* of Edmund Clutterbuck, Hardenhuish Park, Wilts; one *s.* two *d.* *Educ.:* Christ's Hospital; Lincoln College, Oxford (Scholar); B.A. Oxon. Special Correspondent The Times, Greco-Turkish War; Literary Editor, Daily News, retiring 1913; Chairman, Macedonian Relief Fund; Chairman, Serbian Relief Fund, 1914-16; President, Publishers' Association, 1931-33; member Lord Chancellor's Committee on Defamation, 1939; Hon. Treasurer, Balkan Committee; J.P. Kent, retd.; Order of St. Sava. *Publications:* Some Hawarden Letters (with Lisle March Phillipps). *Address:* 22 Berners Street, W.1. *T.:* Museum 4333. *Club:* Brooks's. [*Died* 4 *Nov.* 1953.

CHRISTIAN, Dr. Henry A.; Physician-in-Chief, Peter Bent Brigham Hospital, Boston, Mass., 1910-39, Emeritus since 1939; Clinical Professor of Medicine, Tufts College Medical School, Boston, 1942-46; Visiting Physician, Beth Israel Hospital, Boston, 1942-47, Consulting Physician, 1947-; *b.* Lynchburg, Virginia, 17 Feb. 1876; lineal descendant of Thomas Christian who patented land in Virginia, 1657; *s.* of Camillus Christian and Mary E. Davis; *m.* 1921, Elizabeth Sears Seabury, Boston. *Educ.:* Randolph Macon College, Virginia, A.B. and A.M. 1895; Johns Hopkins University, M.D. 1900; Harvard University, A.M. 1903. Hon. Sc.D., Jefferson Med. Coll., 1928; LL.D., Randolph Macom College, 1923; LL.D., Western Reserve U., 1931; Hon. F.R.C.P., Canada, 1936; LL.D., Univ. of Western Ontario (Can.) 1938; Hon. Sc.D., Univ. of Michigan, 1938; Distinguished Service Medal of Am. Medical Assoc., 1947. Asst. Pathologist, 1900-2, Asst. visiting Pathologist, 1902-5, Boston City Hospital; Asst. visiting Pathologist Children's Hospital, 1903-5; Instructor Pathology, 1903-5, theory and practice of physic, 1905-7, asst. professor, 1907-8, Hersey Professor of Theory and Practice of Physic, 1908-39, Professor Emeritus since 1939, Dean Faculty of Medicine and of Medical School, 1908-1912, Harvard; returned 1942-46 to active teaching; asst. visiting Physician Long Island Hosp., 1905; Physician-in-chief Carney Hosp., 1907-12; commissioned Maj. Med. Corps, U.S.A., 1918, not called to service; Resident Chair,

Washington, D.C., Div. Medical Sciences, National Research Council, 1919-20; Fellow American Academy of Arts and Sciences, Master Am. Coll. of Physicians; mem. Assn. Am. Physicians (Pres. 1935), Am. Assn. Pathologists and Bacteriologists, A.M.A., Am. Soc. for Clinical Investigation (Pres. 1919), Am. Soc. for Exp. Pathology, A.A.A.S., Interstate Postgrad. Med. Assoc. (Pres. 1931), Phi Beta Kappa Associates, Sigma Chi, Alpha Omega Alpha, Sigma Xi fraternities, etc.; corr. member Wien Gesellsch. für inner. Med. und Kinderheilkunde 1923, Medico-Chirurgical Soc. Edinburgh, 1937, and Sociedad de Medicima Interna de Buenos Aires, 1944; hon. member Am. Clinical and Climatological Assoc., 1946. *Publications:* Principles and Practice of Medicine; Diagnosis and Treatment of Heart Disease, Bright's Disease; Non-valvular Heart Disease, Purpura and Purpuric States; papers and books on Pathological and Clinical Medicine subjects; Editor of Oxford Medicine and Oxford Monographs on Diagnosis and Treatment. *Address:* 20 Chapel Street, Brookline, Mass., U.S.A. *Clubs:* Somerset, St. Botolph, Thursday Evening, Examiner, Harvard (Boston); Country (Brookline); Century (New York). [*Died* 24 *Aug.* 1951.

CHRISTIAN, Lt.-Col. William Francis, D.S.O. 1918; late Royal Artillery; *b.* 4 Sept. 1879; *s.* of late Major G. A. Christian, Cheshire Regt.; *m.* 1900, Marguerite Annie Hornby; two *s.* two *d.* Served European War, at the siege of Tsing-Tau, and in France and Belgium (D.S.O., Chevalier Order of Leopold, Croix de Guerre, despatches thrice); retired pay, 1931. *Publication:* Unflinching: A Diary of Tragic Adventure, 1937. *Recreations:* shooting and fishing. *Address:* Cypress Close, Guildford Road, Fleet, Hants. *T.:* Fleet 52. [*Died* 14 *Aug.* 1954.

CHRISTIE, Alexander Wishart, C.B.E. 1939; J.P.; Hon. Sheriff Substitute of Aberdeenshire; *b.* Aberdeen, 1871; *s.* of John Christie; unmarried. *Educ.:* Aberdeen Grammar School. Provost of Huntly, 1920-35; engaged in business; for many years member and Convener of various committees, Aberdeen County Council. *Recreation:* golf. *Address:* Torrisoule, Huntly, Aberdeenshire. *T.:* 136. [*Died* 14 *Sept.* 1955.

CHRISTIE, Harold Alfred Hunter, Q.C. 1934; T.D.; *b.* 1 Oct. 1884; *s.* of Sir William Henry Mahoney Christie, K.C.B., F.R.S. and Violette Mary Hickman; *m.* 1921, Nora Agnes Brooks; three *s. Educ.:* Marlborough; Trinity Hall, Cambridge. Called to Bar, Inner Temple, 1913; Lieut. West Kent Yeomanry, 1911; Captain, 1916; Major, 1931; retired, 1934; served European War, 1914-18, Gallipoli, Salonika, Palestine, and France (wounded); War of 1939-45, R.A.F. Squadron Leader, 1940-43. Master of the Clockmakers' Company, 1939. Bencher, 1940, Treasurer, 1960, Lincoln's Inn; Vice-Chairman, General Council of the Bar, 1949-53. *Recreations:* shooting, fishing, golf. *Address:* 13 Old Square, Lincolns Inn; 6 Stone Buildings, Lincolns Inn. *Club:* Athenæum. [*Died* 23 *Oct.* 1960.

CHRISTIE, James Archibald, J.P.; M.P. (C.) South Norfolk, 1924-45; *b.* 1873; *s.* of J. H. Brooke Christie, of Framingham Manor, Norfolk; *m.* 1909, Mabel (*d.* 1939), *e. d.* of late Rev. Canon Gordon Sedgewick; one *s.* three *d. Educ.:* Charterhouse; Magdalen Coll. Oxford. *Address:* Framingham Manor, nr. Norwich. [*Died* 16 *Oct.* 1958.

CHRISTOPHER, Eleanor Caroline; Hon. M.A. Durham; *b.* 16 March 1873; 2nd *d.* of late Henry Seton Christopher, J.P. *Educ.:* Neuwied am Rhein; Paris; Oxford (2nd class Honours, Modern Languages, 1897). Assistant Mistress East Liverpool High School, G.P.D.S.T., 1897; Head Mistress Leamington Municipal High School, 1905; Principal of St. Hild's College, Durham, 1910-33. *Address:* 1 Airlie Road, Winchester. *T.:* Winchester 2929. [*Died* 18 *Feb.* 1959.

CHRISTOPHERSON, John Brian, C.B.E. 1919; M.A., M.D. (Cantab.); F.R.C.P. (Lond.); F.R.C.S. (Eng.); Order of the Nile (3rd Class); Order of St. Sava (Serbia); Consulting Physician, London Chest Hospital, Victoria Park, E.2; (retired); *b.* Batley, Yorks, 1868; *s.* of Canon Brian Christopherson, Rector of Falmouth; *m.* 1912, Joyce Eleanor, *d.* of late J. A. Ormerod, M.D. *Educ.:* Clifton College; Caius College, Cambridge; St. Bartholomew's Hospital, London; Vienna. House Surgeon, House Physician, Demonstrator of Anatomy, St. Bartholomew's Hospital, 1893-1902; late Physician for Tropical Diseases, Royal Masonic Hospital, Ravenscourt Park; late Medical Adviser Universities Mission to Central Africa; late President Tropical Diseases Section Royal Society of Medicine; Surgeon, Seamen's Hospital Society, Albert Dock Hospital, 1896-1902; Surgeon, Imperial Yeomanry Hospital, Deelfontein, South African War, 1900; Physician to the Governor-General, Sudan, 1902-9; Director of the Sudan Med. Dept., Sudan Government, 1904-9; Director of Civil Hospitals, Khartoum and Omdurman; Surgeon, James Berry Red Cross Unit, Vrynatska Banja, prisoner of war, Serbia, 1915-16; Secretary, War Office Commission on Medical Establishments, B.E.F. France, 1917; discovered the cure for Egyptian Bilharzia Disease by intravenous antimony injections, 1917; Special Bilharzia Clinic, Ministry of Pensions, London, 1920-24; Hunterian Orator (Hunterian Society), 1932; Examiner in Tropical Diseases (R.C.P. Lond.), and for the M.D. (Trop.) University of London. *Publications:* Sudan Government Reports (Medical Administration) Blue Books, 1904-9; Bilharzia, Encyclopædia Britannica, 1926; many papers in medical journals, etc. *Address:* Heavensgate, Lydney-on-Severn, Glos. *T.:* Whitecroft 230. *Club:* Athenæum. [*Died* 21 *July* 1955.

CHRYSTALL, Brig. John Inglis, C.B.E. 1939; M.C.; late 13/18 Hussars; *b.* 9 May 1887; *e. s.* of late William Chrystall and Annie Eames, *d.* of John Inglis Ythan, Christchurch, N.Z.; *m.* 1927, Rosita Norah (*d.* 1949), *o. d.* of late Charles Harris and late Lorna Stratton, Codford St. Mary, Wiltshire, Eng.; two *d. Educ.:* Christ's Coll., Christchurch, N.Z.; Lincoln Agricultural Coll., Canterbury, N.Z. (diploma). First Commission, N.Z. Forces, 1912, Wellington East Coast Regt.; in ranks of 7th Q.O. Hussars, 1912-14; 2nd Lt. 13th Hussars, 1914; seconded to Machine Gun Corps, 1916-20; commanded 16th Machine Gun Squadron, 1917-20; G.S.O. 3 Operations G.H.Q. Mesopotamian Exp. Force and staff officer cavalry officiating, 1920-22; Egyptian Army and Sudan Defence Force, 1922-29; Major 13/18 Hussars, 1930; Local Lt.-Col. 1936; commanded Transjordan Frontier Force, 1936-40; Bt. Lt.-Col. 1938; Colonel, 1938; commanded 6th Cavalry Brigade, 1940-41; President of Commission of Control to carry out Terms of Convention which ended hostilities between British and Free French Forces (the Allies) and French Vichy Forces in Syria and the Lebanon, 1941, acting Maj.-Gen.; commanded Cairo Area, 1941-44; retired pay, 1945; served European War, 1914-18, France and Mesopotamia; Iraq Rebellion, 1920-21; M.C., despatches 8 times, 1914 Medal, British War Medal, Allies War Medal, Middle East Medal (Iraq, 1920-1921), General Service Medal (Palestine, 1936-39), General Service Medal, Middle East Medal, Defence Medal; U.S.A. Legion of Merit, Degree of Officer, 1946. *Recreations:* polo, shooting, fishing. *Address:* Kingfisher House, Ampfield, Hants. *Club:* Cavalry. [*Died* 29 *June* 1960.

CHRISTIE, James, C.M.G., LL.M. See page xxviii.

CHUBB, Harry Emory, C.B.E. 1945 (O.B.E. 1919); M.I.Mech.E.; Consultant, Chubb & Son's Lock & Safe Co. Ltd.; Director, Chubb's Australian Co. Ltd., Sydney; Director, Chubb & Sons, S.A. (Pty.) Ltd.; Local Director, Eagle Star Insurance Co. Ltd.; *b.* 13 May 1880; *s.* of Harry Withers Chubb, Chislehurst, Kent; *m.* 1906, Dorothy Frances, *d.* of Charles Cater, Harrow-on-the-Hill; one *s.* three *d.* *Educ.:* Wellington Coll., Berks; France Major, R.A.S.C., M.E.F., 1914-17; Q.M.G. Staff, War Office, 1917-19; Hon. War Department Fleet Adviser, 1940-45. Herts Special Constabulary, 1936-45, Deputy Supt. 1942. *Recreation:* gardening. *Address:* 27 Silverdale Road, Eastbourne. *T.:* Eastbourne 4309. *Clubs:* Carlton, Constitutional, Savage, Alpine; Royal South Western Yacht (Plymouth). [*Died* 8 *Jan.* 1960.

CHUBB, Sir John Corbin, 2nd Bt. of Stonehenge, *cr.* 1919; *b.* 23 Feb. 1904; *o. s.* of Sir Cecil Herbert Edward Chubb, 1st Bt., and Mary Bella Alice Fern; *S.* father 1934. *Heir:* none. [*Died* 9 *May* 1957 (*ext.*).

CHULAPARAMBIL, Rt. Rev. Alexander, D.D.; Bishop of Kottayam, (R.C.), since 1923; *b.* 14 Oct. 1877. *Educ.:* The Papal Seminary, Kandy. Bishop Vicar Apostolic, 1914. Twice travelled all over Europe and Great Britain in 1911 and 1922; went to Australia, Tasmania, and New Zealand in 1928 in connection with the Sydney Eucharistic Congress; attended Eucharistic Congress in Ireland in 1932. *Address:* Catholic Bishop's House, Kottayam, Travancore, S. India. *T.A.:* Catholic Bishop, Kottayam. [*Died* 8 *Jan.* 1951.

CHURCH, Major Archibald George, D.S.O. 1920; M.C. 1918; Chairman Churwick Manufacturing Co. Ltd.; Editor, News Letter; *b.* E. London, 1886; *m.* 1st, 1912, Gladys, *d.* of Albert Hunter; one *s.* one *d.*; 2nd, 1945 Katherine Mary Strange, *d.* of late Captain T. S. Wickham, D.S.O. *Educ.:* University College, London (B.Sc.). Schoolmaster, 1909-1914; President, East London Teachers' Association, 1914; served in Royal Artillery, Royal Air Force in Flanders, France, N. Russia, 1915-20 (despatches, Order of St. Vladimir); contested Spelthorne Division (Middlesex). 1922; M.P. (Lab.) Leyton (East), 1923-24; Central Wandsworth, 1929-31; visited East Africa as Member of East Africa Parliamentary Commission of Inquiry, 1924; Member of Medical Research Council, 1923-24, 1929-1931; Parliamentary Private Secretary to President of Board of Trade in the first Labour Government; to Secretary of State for War, 1929-31; Sec. Trade Union side Co-ordinating Committee for Joint Industrial Councils for Government Establishments, 1921-31; Member Advisory Committee on Education in the Colonies, 1925-42; a member of the Colonial Appointments Committee, 1929, Member of Senate, University of London 1930-35; Member of Royal Commission on Durham University, 1934; General Secretary, Association of Scientific Workers, 1920-31. Secretary, British Science Guild, 1931-33 Member, Advisory Council, Ministry of Information, 1939-40; Asst. Director, Fighting Vehicle Production, Ministry of Supply, 1941-1945. Director, Baird Television Ltd., 1931-39; Founding director of Manchester Oil Refinery, 1935; Chairman, Raven Oil Co., 1937-1951; Founder and Editor of The Realist in 1929. *Publications:* East Africa, a new Dominion, 1927; The Christian Trade Union Movement in Germany; contributor to general press and scientific and technical press. *Recreations:* swimming and foreign travel. *Address:* 17 Wellington Sq., Chelsea, S.W.3. *T.:* Sloane 4433. *Club:* St. James'. [*Died* 23 *Aug.* 1954.

CHURCH, Col. Arthur John Bromley, C.M.G. 1918; *b.* 1869; *s.* of Rev. Canon Church, Wells, Somerset; *m.* 1897, Margaret Frances, *d.* of C. M'Caskie, M.D.; two *s.* two *d.* *Educ.:* Sherborne; R.M.C., Sandhurst. Joined Connaught Rangers, 1889; Army Pay Department, 1898; retired pay, 1929. *Address:* The Rectory Flat, Sampford Peverell, Tiverton, Devon. [*Died* 23 *July* 1954.

CHURCHER, Colonel Sir Arthur, Kt., *cr.* 1937; *b.* 1871; *s.* of late Henry Churcher, Crediton, Devon; *m.* 1902, Edith (*d.* 1950), *d.* of William Kingdon Wyatt, Newton St. Cyres, Devon; one *s.* (one *d.* decd.). Served South African War, 1899-1902; Munshi and other Expeditions, Nigeria, 1905-14; served European War, Cameroons, 1914-15, France, 1915-18; Ireland, 1919-20; Civil Commissioner, Pretoria, 1901; Cantonment Magistrate, Nigeria, 1908; District Commissioner, Nigeria, 1909-15; Chm. Ex-Service Men, Windsor, 1930-35; Vice-Chm. British Legion, Windsor, 1925-30; Secretary King Edward VII Hospital, Windsor, 1924-1939; Member of Windsor Town Council since 1924, Alderman, 1940; Mayor of Windsor, 1935, 1936, 1937. Chairman A.R.P., Windsor, 1939-45. *Recreations:* shooting (Big Game), cricket, tennis, riding. *Address:* Ashstead House, Windsor. *T.:* Windsor 532. *T.A.:* Churcher Windsor. [*Died* 15 *Feb.* 1951.

CHURCHILL, Lord Ivor (Charles Spencer); *yr. s.* of 9th Duke of Marlborough; *b.* 1898; *m.* 1947, Betty, *er. d.* of J. C. Cunningham, 27 Culross Street, W.1; one *s.* *Educ.:* Eton; Magdalen College, Oxford. Served European War, 1917-18, Lt. R.A.S.C. Officer Legion of Honour. *Address:* Little Langleys, Steep, Petersfield, Hants. *T.:* Petersfield 698. *Clubs:* Turf, White's, St. James'. [*Died* 17 *Sept.* 1956.

CHURCHILL, Stella, M.R.C.S., L.R.C.P., D.P.H.; Medical Psychologist; Psycho-Therapist, West End Hospital, since 1946; *y. d.* of George Myers; *m.* 1908, late S. J. A. Churchill, M.V.O., British Consul-General, Naples; one *s.* one *d.* *Educ.:* Edgbaston High School; Girton College, Cambridge; London (R.F.H.) School of Medicine for Women. Qualified 1917; House Physician, Tite St. Hospital for Children; House Surgeon, Italian Hospital, London; Anæsthetist, British Red Cross Hospital, Netley; Clinical Assistant, Gt. Ormond Street, 1919; Assistant Medical Officer of Health for Maternity and Child Welfare, Bermondsey, 1920; Assistant and Deputy M.O.H., St. Pancras, 1922-24; Psychotherapist Tavistock Clinic, 1936-46. Represented S.E. Southwark on London County Council, 1925-32; contested (Labour) for Parliament N. Hackney and Chiswick, 1924 and 1929; Fellow Royal Society of Medicine; Member Society Medical Officers of Health (ex-Pres. Maternity and Child Welfare Group). *Publications:* Nursing in the Home, 1924; Health Services and the Public, 1928; On being a Mother, 1936; The Adolescent and the Family, 1949; various papers on Maternity and Child Welfare. *Recreations:* music, swimming, grandchildren. *Address:* 14 Park Village East, N.W.1. *T.:* Euston 1314. [*Died* 16 *Sept.* 1954.

CHUTE, Ven. Anthony William, O.B.E., M.A.; Vicar of Basingstoke since 1936; Hon. Canon of Winchester, 1944; Archdeacon of Basingstoke since 1948; *b.* 17 Dec. 1884; 3rd *s.* of late Chaloner William Chute, J.P., D.L., of The Vyne, Basingstoke, and Eleanor Jane, *d.* of late Sir Wyndham S. Portal, Bart., of Malshanger, Hants. *Educ.:* Winchester; Magdalen Coll., Oxford. B.A. 1907; M.A. 1910; ordained, 1911; Winchester Coll. Mission, Portsmouth, 1911-19; C.F., France, Belgium, Italy, 1916-19; Vicar of S. Oswald's, West Hartlepool, 1919-25; Fellow and Dean of Divinity of Magdalen Coll., Oxford. 1925-29; Vicar of Highfield, Southampton, 1929-36. *Address:* The Vicarage, Basingstoke. [*Died* 2 *April* 1958.

CHUTE, Sir Charles (Lennard), 1st Bt., *cr.* 1952; M.C.; Barrister-at-law, Inner Temple; *b.* 1879; *e. s.* of late Chaloner William Chute, J.P., D.L., and Eleanor Jane, *d.* of Sir Wyndham Portal, Bt., J.P., D.L., of Malshanger, Hants; *m.* 1912, Laura Joan, *d.* of late Rev. R. Lowbridge Baker of Ramsden, Oxfordshire. *Educ.:* Eton; Magdalen College, Oxford; M.A. 1906. Patron of one living; served in France, Staff Capt. and Bde.-Maj. (M.C.); Chm. Hants. C.C., 1938-1945; Chm. Quarter Sessions, 1938-51; D.L. 1939-; J.P. 1921-. *Heir:* none. *Address:* The Vyne, Basingstoke. *T.:* Bramley Green 227. [*Died* 29 *Sept.* 1956 (*ext.*).

CILCENNIN, 1st Viscount, *cr.* 1955, of Hereford; **James Purdon Lewes Thomas,** P.C. 1951; Lord Lieutenant of Herefordshire since 1957; *b.* 13 Oct. 1903; *s.* of late J. Lewes Thomas, J.P., Caeglas, Llandilo, Carms., and Anne Louisa, *e. d.* of Comdr. George Purdon, R.N., Tinerana, Co. Clare. *Educ.:* Rugby; Oriel College, Oxford. Contested Llanelly Division of Carmarthenshire, General Election, 1929; M.P. (C.) Hereford Division, 1931-55; Assistant Private Secretary to Rt. Hon. Stanley Baldwin, Lord President of the Council, 1931; Parliamentary Private Secretary to the Secretary of State for the Dominions, 1932-35; and Secretary of State for Colonies, 1935-36; Parliamentary Private Secretary to Secretary of State for Foreign Affairs, 1937-38; Chairman of Governing Body of Rugby School, 1958; Parliamentary Private Secretary to Secretary of State for War, 1940; Lord Commissioner of the Treasury, 1940-43; Financial Secretary to the Admiralty, 1943-45; Vice-Chairman of Conservative and Unionist Party, 1945-51; First Lord of the Admiralty, 1951-56. K.St.J. 1958. *Publication:* (posthumous) Admiralty House, Whitehall, 1960. *Address:* The Bush Farm, Colwall, Herefordshire. *Clubs:* White's, Buck's, Pratt's. [*Died* 13 *July* 1960 (*ext.*).

CLAGUE, Sir John, Kt., *cr.* 1942; C.M.G. 1938; C.I.E. 1930; Indian Civil Service, retd., 1937; *b.* 29 Jan. 1882; *m.* 1921, Winifred F. A. (*d.* 1950), *d.* of F. H. Dawkins; one *s.* one *d.* *Educ.:* King William's College, Isle of Man; Peterhouse, Cambridge. Adviser to Secretary of State for Burma, 1937-1942. *Address:* c/o Chartered Bank, 38 Bishopsgate, E.C.2. [*Died* 16 *Sept.* 1958.

CLAMPETT, Ven. Albert Wyndham, M.A.; Archdeacon of Strathalbyn, 1915-39, Archdeacon Emeritus, 1939; General Licence for diocese of Adelaide since 1939; *b.* Waterford, Ireland, 1860; 5th *s.* of late Alderman Clampett of that city; *m.* 1889, Alice, *o. d.* of Robert Patten of Brixton S.W.; two *s.* one *d.* *Educ.:* Waterford; Trinity College, Dublin (B.A. and M.A.); ordained Deacon and Priest and served a curacy of five years in the parish of S. Saviour's, Herne Hill Road, London, S.E.; worked with Bishop Kennion in S. Australia, 1889-91; incumbent of Laura, 1891-93; Rector of Mitcham (and with Hawthorn, 1898-1920), South Australia, 1893-1939; Archdeacon of Mount Gambier and Hon. Canon, St. Peter's Cathedral, Adelaide, 1911-15; Military Chaplain 4th class in Australian Military Forces, 1916-19; Rural Dean of the Eastern suburbs, 1908-11; Canon St. Peter's Cathedral, Adelaide, 1916-1939. *Address:* 7 Ailsa Street, Fullarton, S. Australia. [*Died* 1 *Feb.* 1953.

CLANMORRIS, 6th Baron (Ireland), *cr.* 1800; **Arthur Maurice Robert Bingham;** *b.* 22 June 1879; *e. s.* of 5th Baron Clanmorris, and Matilda (*d.* 1941), *o. c.* and *heiress* of late Robert Edward Ward, Bangor Castle, Co. Down; *S.* father, 1916; *m.* 1907, Leila, *d.* of Gordon Cloete, J.P., Cape Town; one *s.* *Educ.:* Eton. Entered 5th Lancers, 1899; Capt. 1905; A.D.C. to Lord Plunket, Gov.-Gen. of New Zealand, 1904-7; was Page of Honour to Lord Lieutenant of Ireland; served South Africa, 1899-1902 (Queen's medal five clasps, King's medal two clasps); European War, 1915-19. *Heir:* *s.* Hon. John Michael Ward Bingham. *Address:* c/o Lloyds Bank Ltd., 6 Pall Mall, S.W.1. *Club:* Cavalry. [*Died* 24 *June* 1960.

CLANWILLIAM, 5th Earl of, *cr.* 1776; **Arthur Vesey Meade;** Bt. 1703; Viscount Clanwilliam, Baron Gillford, 1766; Baron Clanwilliam (U.K.), 1828; late Captain, Royal Horse Guards; *b.* 14 Jan. 1873; *e. surv. s.* of 4th Earl of Clanwilliam and Elizabeth, *d.* of Sir A. E. Kennedy, G.C.M.G., Governor of Queensland; *S.* father, 1907; *m.* 1909, Muriel, (*d.* 1952,) M.B.E., *d.* of late Russell Stephenson and *widow* of Hon. Oliver Howard; one *s.* two *d.* Served South Africa, 1900-2. *Heir:* *s.* Lord Gilford. *Address:* Montalto, Ballynahinch, Co. Down. [*Died* 23 *Jan.* 1953.

CLAPP, Sir Harold Winthrop, K.B.E., *cr.* 1941; M.Inst.E.E.; Commonwealth Director-General of Transport; *b.* Melbourne, 7 May 1875; *m.* 1906, Vivian, *d.* of Arthur Noel; two *s.* one *d.* *Educ.:* Brighton Grammar School; Melbourne Church of England Grammar School. Chairman of Railway Commissioners, Victoria, 1920-39; Chairman Aircraft Production Commission, Commonwealth of Australia, 1939-42. *Address:* St. George's Court, 11 St. George's Road, Toorak, Melbourne, Australia. [*Died* 20 *Oct.* 1952.

CLARENDON, 6th Earl of, 2nd *cr.* 1776; **George Herbert Hyde Villiers,** K.G. 1937; P.C. 1931; G.C.M.G., *cr.* 1930; G.C.V.O., *cr.* 1939; Royal Victorian Chain, 1952; Bailiff Grand Cross Order of St. John of Jerusalem; Hon. LL.D. Witwatersrand Univ., Johannesburg; D.L., J.P. Herts; Hon. Lt.-Col. in the Army; Permanent Lord-in-Waiting to the Queen since 1952; Chancellor of Order of St. Michael and St. George since 1942; a Director of General Electric Co.; *b.* 7 June 1877; *s.* of 5th Earl and Lady Caroline Elizabeth Agar (*d.* 1894), *e. d.* of 3rd Earl of Normanton; *S.* father, 1914; *m.* 1905, Adeline Verena Ishbel, J.P., Dame of Grace Order of St. John of Jerusalem, Hon. LL.D. Witwatersrand University, Johannesburg, *d.* of late Herbert Haldane Somers Cocks, and sister of 6th Baron Somers, K.C.M.G., D.S.O., M.C.; one *s.* one *d.* *Educ.:* Eton. Captain of the Gentlemen-at-Arms, 1922-25; Parliamentary Under-Secretary of State for Dominion Affairs, and Chairman of Overseas Settlement Committee, 1925-27; Chief Government Whip, House of Lords, 1922-25; Chairman of British Broadcasting Corporation, 1927-30; Governor-General and Commander-in-Chief of Union of South Africa 1931-37; Lord Chamberlain of H.M.'s Household, 1938-52. An extra A.D.C. to Lord-Lieutenant of Ireland (Earl of Dudley), 1902-05. Chancellor of Primrose League, 1919-21. Formerly a director of Barclay's Bank, Dominion Colonial and Overseas. *Heir:* *g.s.* Lord Hyde. *Address:* 8 Chelsea Square, S.W.3. *Club:* Turf. [*Died* 13 *Dec.* 1955.

CLARINA, 6th Baron, *cr.* 1800; **Eyre Nathaniel Massey,** late Captain Scots Guards; *b.* 8 Feb. 1880; *o. s.* of 5th Baron Clarina and Elizabeth Ellen, *d.* of Alex. Bannatyne, Woodstown, Co. Limerick; *S.* father, 1922; *m.* 1906, Alice, 4th *d.* of Wilton Allhusen of Lyme Regis; one *d.* Served with Scots Guards in South African War, 1900-2 (Queen's medal 3 clasps, King's medal 2 clasps); European War (1914 Star, Allied, and British Victory medals). *Heir:* none. *Address:* Vigo Cottage, Corofin, Co. Clare, Ireland. *Club:* Flyfishers'. [*Died* 4 *Nov.* 1952 (*ext.*).

CLARK, His Honour Judge Alfred Alexander G.; *see* Gordon Clark.

CLARK, Dr. Arthur L.; Emeritus Prof. of Physics, Emeritus Dean, Faculty of Applied Science, Queen's University, Kingston; *b.* Worcester, Mass., U.S.A., 19 Feb. 1873; *s.* of Lewis C. Clark and Ellen L. Moses; *m.* 1899, Mary Imogene Whitney, Worcester; one *s.* two *d.* *Educ.:* Worcester Polytechnic Institute, Worcester; Clark University, Worcester. Teacher of Math. and Physics, Bridgton Academy, Maine; Worcester Academy; Ph.D. Clark University, 1905; Professor of Physics, Bates College, Lewiston, Maine; F.R.S. Can.; Hon. Member Engineering Institute of Canada. LL.D. Queen's University, Kingston, Ontario, 1943. *Publication:* papers on various physical topics. *Address:* 200 Albert Street, Kingston, Ontario, Canada. [*Died* 20 *Sept.* 1956.

CLARK, Brigadier Cecil Horace, D.S.O. 1916; late R.A. (retired 1936); *b.* 24 Oct. 1880; *s.* of late W. S. Clark; *m.* 1918, Ivy Murray (*d.* 1946); one *s.* *Educ.:* Harrow. Joined R.A. 1899; S.A. War (despatches); European War (D.S.O., Bt. Lt.-Col., despatches four times). *Address:* c/o Lloyds Bank, 6 Pall Mall, S.W.1. [*Died* 12 *Feb.* 1958.

CLARK, Edmund Graham, C.B.E. 1948; M.C., M.Sc., M.I.C.E.; Secretary of The Institution of Civil Engineers since 1937; *b.* 15 May 1889; *s.* of late Charles A. Clark, Bordeaux, France; *m.* 1919, Vera, *d.* of late Charles M. Henzell, Newcastle on Tyne; two *d.* *Educ.:* Felsted School; Durham University; B.Sc. 1910; Hon. M.Sc. 1953. Civil Engineering pupil, and later Assistant of J. Mitchell Moncrieff, C.B.E., M.I.C.E., Consulting Engineer; served throughout European War as commissioned officer with the 50th (Northumbrian) Division, T.F.; subsequently appointed Chief Technical Assistant, Institution of Civil Engineers, acting as Secretary to a number of technical Committees. *Address:* 57 Cheyne Court, S.W.3. *Club:* Athenæum. [*Died* 23 *April* 1954.

CLARK, Sir Ernest, G.C.M.G., *cr.* 1943 (K.C.M.G., *cr.* 1938); K.C.B., *cr.* 1924; Kt., *cr.* 1920; C.B.E. 1918; *b.* 13 April 1864; *s.* of S. H. Clark; *m.* 1st, 1899, Mary (*d.* 1944), *d.* of J. T. C. Winkfield, D.L.; no *c.*; 2nd, 1947, Constance, *er. d.* of late A. E. McLennan, Melbourne, Australia. *Educ.:* privately; King's College, London. Called to Bar, Middle Temple, 1894; lent to Cape Government, 1904-5; Assistant Secretary, Inland Revenue, 1919; Secretary Royal Commission on Income Tax, 1919-20; Asst. Under-Secretary, Ireland, 1920-21; Sec., Treasury of Northern Ireland, 1921-25; Member Australian Economic Mission, 1928-29; Member of Joint Exchequer Board Great Britain and N. Ireland, 1930, etc.; Director of Underground group, Martins Bank, Harland and Wolff. etc. 1925-33; Governor of Tasmania, 1933-45. *Address:* Tasmania, Seaton, Devon. *Club:* Brooks's. [*Died* 26 *Aug.* 1951.

CLARK, Rt. Rev. (Frederick) Patrick; Bishop of Kootenay since 1948; *b.* Toronto, Ont., 17 March 1908; *s.* of Frederick Daniel Clark and Marion Frances Howe; *m.* 1936, Marion Alice Sherrick Hastings; two *s.* one *d.* *Educ.:* Hughes Public School and Oakwood Collegiate, Toronto; University of Bishop's College, Lennoxville, P.Q. B.A. 1932; M.A. 1942; D.D. (Vancouver) 1948. Deacon, 1932; Priest, 1933; Curate of Church of Advent, Westmount, 1932-34; St. Peter, Regina, 1934-35; Sub-Warden St. Chad's Theological College, Regina, 1935-38 and 1939-40, Warden, 1938-39; Rector of: Pense, 1936-38; St. Matthew, Regina, 1938-1941; Holy Trinity, Vancouver, 1941-45; Dean of Kootenay and Rector of St. Saviour Cathedral, Nelson, 1945-48; Examining Chaplain to: Bishop of Qu' Appelle, 1935-48; Bishop of New Westminster, 1944-48. Grand Chaplain, Grand Lodge of B.C., A.F. & A. M., 1953-54. D.C.L. Bishop's Univ., Lennoxville, P.Q., 1954. *Recreation:* model railroading. *Address:* 1115 Ward St., Nelson, B.C. *T.:* 904. *Club:* Rotary (Nelson). [*Died* 16 *Dec.* 1954.

CLARK, Harold Frederick, C.I.E. 1943; Director, Sephinjuri Bheel Tea Co. Labour Adviser to the Indian Tea Association, 1946-1952. *Address:* Copper Beeches, Prey Heath, Worplesdon. *Clubs:* Oriental; Bengal (Calcutta). [*Died* 24 *Aug.* 1957.

CLARK, Henry H. G.; *see* Gordon Clark.

CLARK, James Oscar Max; thread manufacturer; Director: Clark & Co. Ltd.; Reinsurance Corporation; Scottish Boiler and General Insurance Co. Ltd.; Ex-Dir. Scottish National Trust Co.; Extraordinary director Union Bank of Scotland; *b.* 26 Sept. 1877; *s.* of Robert M. Clark, Paisley; *m.* 1902, Winifred, *d.* of James Halsall, Liverpool; one *d.* *Educ.:* Uppingham; King's Coll., Cambridge. Served with Scots Guards in European War; Member of Prime Minister's Panel of Industrialists, 1938-39. *Publication:* A History of Tennis (jointly with E. B. Noel). *Recreations:* real tennis, shooting, golf. *Address:* Anchor Thread Mills, Paisley; 6 West Eaton Place, S.W.1. *Club:* Carlton. [*Died* 2 *Jan.* 1958.

CLARK, Sir (Reginald) Marcus, K.B.E., *cr.* 1939; Chairman and Managing Director: Marcus Clark and Co. Ltd.; Bon Marché Ltd., Sydney; Hobsons Ltd., Sydney; Chairman Hipsleys Ltd., Sydney; Adviser to Commonwealth Government on Price Control, 1918-19 and 1939-48; Vice-Chairman Commonwealth Requisitioned Cargoes Committee, 1942-48; Member Commonwealth Export Advisory Committee; Chairman Miller Anderson Ltd., Adelaide; and of local board London and Lancashire Insurance Co. Ltd.; President Associated Chambers of Commerce of Australia, 1939-41 and 1943-45 (Hon. Treas., 1949-51); Councillor (Pres. 1934-36) Sydney Chamber of Commerce; Councillor (Pres. 1916-18) Retail Traders Assoc. of N.S.W.; Vice-Chairman and Life Governor (Hon. Treas. 1925-34) Royal Prince Alfred Hospital; Vice-Pres. Citizens Reform Assoc., N.S.W.; Trustee National Art Gallery N.S.W.; *b.* 9 Nov. 1883; *s.* of Henry Marcus Clark and Pattie Day; *m.* 1909, Frances Hanks Rogers; (son died on active service) one *d.* *Educ.:* Sydney Grammar School. Chairman of Contract and Supply Board, 2nd Military District, 1919-20; Member of N.S.W. Government Board of Health, 1934-36, National Relief Board of N.S.W., 1934-36, 150th Anniversary Council of N.S.W., 1937-38; F.R. Empire Society; F.R.S.A., 1951. *Recreations:* art, collector of paintings, numismatics (Pres. Austr. Numismatic Soc. 1949, Vice-Pres. 1951). *Address:* Central Square, Sydney. *T.A.:* Marclark. *T.:* M 4101. *Clubs:* New South Wales, National, Millions (Sydney); Savage (Melbourne). [*Died* 13 *July* 1953.

CLARK, William Clifford, C.M.G. 1935; M.A.; LL.D.; F.R.S.C.; Deputy Minister of Finance, Canada, since 1932; *b.* 1889; *s.* of George Ellis Clark and Catherine Urquhart; *m.* 1916, Margaret Hilda Smith, B.A.; two *s.* two *d.* *Educ.:* Williamstown High School; Queen's University, Kingston,; Harvard University. Was Professor of Economics Queen's University, Kingston, 1915-23; engaged in investment banking, Chicago and New York, 1923-31; Professor of Commerce and Director of Courses in Commerce and Administration, Queen's University, Kingston, 1931-32; author of numerous articles on economic and financial subjects; Financial Adviser, Imperial Economic Conference, Ottawa, 1932; and World Monetary and Economic Conference, London, 1933. Member: Board of Directors and Executive Committee, Bank of Canada and Industrial Development Bank; Canadian Farm Loan Board; Export Credits Insurance Corp.;

Director and member, Executive Committee, Central Mortgage and Housing Corp. *Address:* Department of Finance, Ottawa, Canada. *Clubs:* Rideau, Country (Ottawa).
[*Died* 27 *Dec.* 1952.

CLARK, Sir William (Henry), G.C.M.G., *cr.* 1937 (K.C.M.G., *cr.* 1930; C.M.G. 1903); K.C.S.I., *cr.* 1915 (C.S.I. 1911); Knight of Grace of the Order of St. John of Jerusalem; M.A.; D.C.L. Queen's University, Bishop's University and Western University, Canada; formerly Chairman of Council of Royal Empire Society; *b.* 1 Jan. 1876; *s.* of late J. W. Clark, Scroope House, Cambridge; *m.* 1909, Anne Elizabeth (*d.* 1946), *y. d.* of W. J. Monsell, and *widow* of W. Bennett Pike; one *s.* two *d.* *Educ.:* Eton; Trinity College, Cambridge. Clerk, Board of Trade, 1899; Secretary to Special Mission to Shanghai to negotiate a Commercial Treaty with China, 1901; acting 2nd secretary in Diplomatic Service, 1902; secretary to Royal Commission on Supply of Food, etc., in Time of War, 1903-5; private secretary at Board of Trade to Rt. Hon. D. Lloyd George, M.P., 1906, and to Rt. Hon. W. S. Churchill, M.P., 1908; and to Rt. Hon. D. Lloyd George, M.P., as Chancellor of Exchequer, 1908-10; Member for Commerce and Industry of the Council of the Viceroy of India, 1910-16; Comptroller-General, Commercial Intelligence Department of Board of Trade, 1916-17; Comptroller-General of Department of Overseas Trade, 1917-28; High Commissioner in Canada for H.M. Government in United Kingdom, 1928-34; H.M. High Commissioner for Basutoland, Bechuanaland Protectorate and Swaziland, and High Commissioner in Union of South Africa for H.M. Government in U.K., 1934-39; retired, 1940. *Address:* Binnbrook, Cambridge. *T.:* Cambridge 3872.
[*Died* 22 *Nov.* 1952.

CLARKE, Edward de Courcy, M.A.; Emeritus Professor University of Western Australia, 1949; *b.* 10 Nov. 1880; *s.* of Marsden Clarke and Frances Emily Stuart; *m.* 1915; three *s.* *Educ.:* High School, Napier, N.Z.; University College, Auckland, N.Z. Science master, Auckland Grammar School, N.Z., 1901-5; Field Geologist, Geological Survey of N.Z., 1905-10; Demonstrator in Geology and Biology, University College, Auckland, N.Z., 1910-12; Field Geologist, Geological Survey of Western Australia, 1912-20; Lecturer in charge of geology, University of Western Australia. 1920; Professor of Geology, University of Western Australia, 1930-48. *Publications:* part or sole author of about eight bulletins of the Geological Surveys of N.Z. and Western Australia, of papers on geological subjects; Middle and West Australia in Regionale Geologie der Erde; and elementary text-books of physiography and geology from the Western Australian standpoint. Kelvin Medal, Roy. Soc., W.A., 1941; Clarke Medal, Roy. Soc., N.S.W., 1954. *Address:* c/o Walter Scott, Te Awamutu, N.Z.
[*Died* 2 *Nov.* 1958.

CLARKE, Sir Ernest Michael, Kt., *cr.* 1917; *b.* 7 Jan. 1868; *s.* of late T. Wilson Clarke, Hessle, Yorks; *m.* 1898, Madeline, *d.* of late E. B. Gardiner, Carse Grange, Errol; two *s.* two *d.* *Educ.:* Kensington School. Knight of Grace, Order of St. John; Chevalier of the Legion of Honour. *Address:* Long Acre, Oxted, Surrey. *Club:* Royal Automobile.
[*Died* 27 *Feb.* 1956.

CLARKE, Hon. Sir Francis Grenville, K.B.E., *cr.* 1926; M.L.C., J.P.; President of Legislative Council, Victoria, 1923-43; *b.* 1879; 5th *s.* of late Sir William John Clarke, Bart., of Victoria; *m.* Nina Ellis Cotton (*d.* 1948); two *s.* three *d.* *Educ.:* Melbourne; Exeter College, Oxford. Minister of Lands, Victoria, 1917-19; Minister of Water Supply, 1917-21; Commissioner of Public Works, 1919-23; ex-Vice-Chairman the National Bank of Australasia, Ltd.; Director of Goldsbrough Mort & Co.; Member of the Felton Bequests' Committee; President Melbourne Club, 1929. *Address:* Marne St., South Yarra, Melbourne, S.E.1, Australia. *Club:* Melbourne (Melbourne).
[*Died* 13 *Feb.* 1955.

CLARKE, Sir Fred, Kt., *cr.* 1943; M.A. (Oxon); Litt.D.; Educational Adviser to National Union of Teachers; *b.* 2 Aug. 1880; *s.* of William Clarke, High Cogges, Witney, Oxon; *m.* 1907, Edith Annie Gillams; five *d.* *Educ.:* privately; St. Catherine's, Oxford. Senior Master of Method, Diocesan Training Coll., York, 1903-6; Professor of Education, Hartley University College, Southampton, 1906-11; South African College and Univ. of Cape Town, 1911-29; McGill University, Montreal, 1929-34; Adviser to Overseas Students, Institute of Education, 1935-36; Professor of Education and Director of Institute of Education, University of London, 1936-45. *Publications:* A School History of Hampshire; Essays in the Politics of Education; Foundations of History Teaching; Education and Social Change; various contributions to Year-Books and Official Publications, articles, etc. *Address:* 33 Tavistock Square, W.C.1. *T.:* Euston 4210. *Club:* Athenæum. [*Died* 6 *Jan.* 1952.

CLARKE, Isabel Constance; *d.* of late Colonel Francis Coningsby Hannam Clarke, C.M.G., Royal Artillery. *Educ.:* Privately. Has travelled in Ceylon, North Africa, Italy, France, Greece, Jamaica, U.S. Resident in Italy for many years. *Publications:* Prisoners' Years, 1912; By the Blue River; The Secret Citadel, 1913; Fine Clay; Only Anne, 1914; Whose Name is Legion, 1915; The Potter's House; Lamp of Destiny, 1916; The Deep Heart; Young Cymbeline, 1917; Children of Eve, 1918; The Elstones, 1919; Julian; Lady Trent's Daughter, 1920; Ursula Finch; Tressider's Sister, 1921; The Light on the Lagoon; Average Cabins, 1922; Carina; Viola Hudson, 1923; Anna Nugent; Children of the Shadow, 1924; The Villa by the Sea; It Happened in Rome, 1925; The Story of Selma, 1926; The Castle of San Salvo; A Case of Conscience, 1927; Strangers of Rome, 1928; We that are Left, 1929; Stepsisters; Italian Adventure, 1930; As the Gentle Rain, 1931; Altar of Sacrifice, 1931; Sea Air, 1932; Decree Nisi, 1932; That Which was Lost, 1933; Feet upon the Mountains, 1933; Laughing Prelude, 1934; Roman Year, 1935; Family Symphony; Silence is Golden, 1936; In an Alpine Valley; Mirella, 1937; Mischief in the Wind, 1938; Cloudy Summits, 1939; The Custody of the Children, 1940; Welcome, 1943; Where the Apple Reddens, 1944; Subject to Authority, 1945; Portrait of Celandine, 1947; Lost Heritage, 1948; Quiet Village, 1949; Euphemia, 1950; books of verse—A Window in Whitechapel; and Nomad Songs in the Vigo Cabinet Series; The Pathway of Dreams; Biography—Haworth Parsonage, 1928; Elizabeth Barrett Browning, 1929; Shelley and Byron, 1934; Six Portraits, 1935; Maria Edgeworth, 1949. *Recreations:* sketching, reading, bridge.
[*Died* 13 *April* 1951.

CLARKE, Col. J. de W. L.; *see* Lardner-Clarke.

CLARKE, John Smith; Member of Glasgow Corporation, 1926-56; J.P. for County and City of Glasgow; Member Clyde Navigation Trust, Government Board Glasgow School of Art; lecturer and journalist; Member of Royal Commission of Fine Arts, Scotland, since 1930; Vice-Pres., Zoological Society of Glasgow; *b.* 1885. M.P. (Lab.) Maryhill Division of Glasgow, 1929-31; Member of Ullswater Conference on Electoral Reform, 1930; Trustee of National Portrait Gallery, 1930-33. *Publications:* Satires, Lyrics, and Poems; Pen Pictures of Russia under the Red Terror; Marxism and History; An Epic of Municipalisation; Robert Burns and his

Politics; A Scottish Encyclopedia; Circus Parade. *Address:* 2 Walmer Crescent, Ibrox, Glasgow. [*Died* 30 *Jan.* 1959.

CLARKE, Loftus Otway, C.I.E.; Indian Civil Service (retired); J.P.; 2nd *s.* of Marshal Neville Clarke of Graiguenoe Park, Tipperary; *b.* 1871; *m.* Evelyn Francis, *d.* of Col. Carden, D.L., of Fishmoyne, Co. Tipperary; one *s.* *Educ.:* Charterhouse; Christ Church, Oxford. Entered Indian Civil Service, 1894; served in Behar, Eastern Bengal, and Assam; Political Agent in Manipur, 1920-24; retired, 1925; High Sheriff of Radnorshire, 1939. *Address:* Boultibrooke, Presteigne, Radnorshire. *T.:* Presteigne 234. *Club:* East India and Sports. [*Died* 11 *Jan.* 1954.

CLARKE, Louis Colville Gray, F.S.A.; Fellow of Trinity Hall; *b.* 2 May 1881; 10th and *y. s.* of Stephenson Clarke and Agnes Maria Bridger; unmarried. *Educ.:* Trinity Hall, Cambridge. Curator of the Univ. Museum of Archæology and of Ethnology, Cambridge, 1922-37; Director of Fitzwilliam Museum, Cambridge, 1937-46; Travelled in Central and South America; to Abyssinia twice and other parts of Africa; excavated in New Mexico, U.S.A. in 1923 and on several occasions in Hungary: President of Cambridge Antiquarian Society, 1927-29 and 1938-45; Order of Merit of Hungary; Hon. Fellow of Soc. of Archæological and Historical Arts of Hungary; Hon. LL.D. Cambridge, 1959. *Publications:* articles in journals. *Recreations:* interest in all forms of art. *Address:* Leckhampton House, Cambridge. *T.:* 5153. *Club:* Bath. [*Died* 13 *Dec.* 1960.

CLARKE, Admiral Sir Marshal Llewelyn, K.B.E., *cr.* 1946; C.B. 1942; D.S.O. 1916; *b.* 9 May 1887; *s.* of late Sir Marshal James Clarke, K.C.M.G.; *m.* 1922, Ina Leonora (whom he divorced, 1940), *d.* of J. G. Edwards; two *s.* *Educ.:* Cordwalles, Maidenhead; H.M.S. Britannia. Joined R.N., 1902; served European War, 1914-18. Commodore Malaya, 1936-38; Admiral Supt. Portsmouth, 1940-45; retired, 1945. *Club:* United Service. [*Died* 8 *April* 1959.

CLARKE, Lt.-Col. Matthew John, C.I.E. 1932; late I.A. and Commissioner, Burma; *b.* 19 July 1895; *m.* 1929, Rhona Elizabeth, *d.* of Thomas Lyons, Lyndhurst, Hobart, Tasmania; two *s.* one *d.* Served European War, 1914-19 (despatches); War of 1939-45, Burma, Assam; retired, 1948. *Address:* 1 Battery Square, Hobart, Tasmania. [*Died* 7 *Oct.* 1954.

CLARKE, Sir Reginald, Kt., *cr.* 1922; C.I.E. 1919; *b.* 16 Mar. 1876; *s.* of George Richard Clarke, indigo planter, Bengal; *m.* 1906, Edith Johns (*d.* 1948), *d.* of Andrew Johns of Glencoe, Shortlands, Kent; one *d.* *Educ.:* in Ireland and abroad. Joined Indian Police, 1900; Asst. Inspector-General, Bengal, 1910-Deputy Commissioner, Calcutta, 1912; Commissioner of Police, Calcutta, 1915-22. *Address:* Titlark's Cottage, Sunningdale, Berks. *Club:* Oriental. [*Died* 31 *July* 1956.

CLARKE, Col. Reginald Graham, C.M.G. 1919; D.S.O. 1918; M.B.E. 1958; *b.* 1879; *s.* of William Clarke, The Warren, Ewhurst, Surrey; *m.* 1911, Dorothy Mary (*d.* 1950), *d.* of Henry Seymour Hoare, Bramhope, Torquay; (*s.* killed in action Sept. 1942) two *d.* *Educ.:* Harrow. Served S. Africa, 1899-1902 (despatches, Queen's medal with five clasps, King's medal with two clasps); European War, 1914-18 (despatches four times, Bt. Lt.-Col., D.S.O., C.M.G., Legion of Honour, French Croix de Guerre); retired, 1928. *Address:* c/o Barclays Bank, Folkestone. [*Died* 27 *Oct.* 1959.

CLARKE, Tom; author, journalist; F.J.I.; Chairman, Near and Far East News Ltd. (London) and subsidiaries; Freeman and Liveryman City of London (Stationers and Newspaper Makers); *b.* Bolton, 6 June 1884; *m.* 1st, Elizabeth, *d.* of Richard Waddington; 2nd, Sheila, *d.* of Harry Green. *Educ.:* Bolton School; Ruskin Hall, Oxford. Reporter, Lewisham Journal, 1902, South China Morning Post, Hong-Kong, 1903; Special Correspondent London Daily Mail and Chicago Tribune in French Indo-China during cruise of Baltic Fleet in Russo-Japanese War; visited China, Japan, Korea, Siberia, and Russia, 1903-6; Manchester (Evening Chronicle), 1907; London News Editor Daily Sketch, 1909; foreign staff Daily Mail, 1911; appointed News Editor by late Lord Northcliffe on return from Army, 1919; planned and organised Melba's first wireless concert, June 1920; sent to U.S.A. and Canada by Lord Northcliffe to study newspaper methods, 1920; Assistant Editor, The Herald, Melbourne, Australia, 1923-1926; Managing Editor, Daily News, London, 1926, and then Editor and Director, News Chronicle, till 1933; Adviser to Berlingske Tidende, Copenhagen, 1934; with Australian Test Team (for Daily Mail), 1934; Director of Practical Journalism, London University, 1935-46; Reynolds News columnist, 1936-42; revisited Australia for Sydney Sun, 1936; Deputy Director, News Division, Ministry of Information, 1939-40; special representative of Hulton Press in South America, 1941-42; Broadcast Weekly Letter from London on B.B.C. Latin-American service, 1942-48. *Publications:* My Northcliffe Diary, 1931; Marriage at 6 A.M. (an Australian retrospect), 1934; Brian (the story of a happy lad), 1935; Round the World with Tom Clarke, 1937; My Lloyd George Diary, 1939; The Word of An Englishman (South America), 1943; The Devonshire Club (history), 1944; Journalism, 1946; Northcliffe in History, 1949; Living Happily with A "Heart," 1954. *Address:* Mill Cottage, Great Bardfield, Essex. *T.:* 366. *Clubs:* Savage, Devonshire. [*Died* 18 *June* 1957.

CLARKE, William John, C.B.E. 1920; *b.* 13 March 1857; *s.* of John Clarke of Haddenham, Bucks, and Plymouth, and Eliza Heybourn; *m.* Annie Georgina, *d.* of late Joseph Godfrey of Plymouth; three *s.* *Educ.:* Privately; Clewer House School, Windsor; served articles. Entered Civil Service (department of the Director of Architectural and Engineering Works, Admiralty), 1882; served at Devonport, Portsmouth, Gosport, and Bermuda; Superintending Civil Engineer of H.M. Naval Establishments at Malta, 1894; and afterwards at Chatham, The Admiralty, and Devonport, until 1912; an Assistant Director of Works at the Admiralty, 1912, and later a Deputy Director of Works; retired, 1919; formerly M.Inst.C.E. *Recreations:* country pursuits. *Address:* Wayside, Brockenhurst, Hants. *T.:* 3395. [*Died* 24 *Oct.* 1951.

CLARKE, Hon. William Lionel Russell, M.A.; J.P.; *b.* 31 Mar. 1876; *s.* of Sir William John Clarke, Bt., and Janet Marion Clarke; *m.* 1908, Florence Douglas, 3rd *d.* of Col. Henry Douglas Mackenzie; two *s.* one *d.* *Educ.:* Melbourne Grammar School; Trinity College, Melbourne; New College, Oxford. Served European War as Lieutenant in Field Artillery of Australian Imperial Forces, 1915-1919; a representative of Southern Province in Legislative Council of Victoria, 1910-1937. *Recreations:* tennis, golf. *Address:* 249 Domain Road, South Yarra, S.E.1, Melbourne, Victoria, Australia. *Clubs:* Oriental, Royal Automobile; Melbourne, Royal Automobile, Royal Melbourne Golf (Melbourne); Moonee Valley Racing. [*Died* 15 *May* 1954.

CLARKSON, Lt.-Col. Bertie St. John, C.M.G. 1916; D.S.O 1917; late 2nd Batt. Dorsetshire Regt.; *b.* 9 Nov. 1868; *s.* of late Col. T. H. Clarkson; *m.* 1898, Constance Mary, *e. d.* of late Rt. Hon. Sir J. E. Gorst and *widow* of Lt. E. C. A. Paston-Cooper, R.N.; one *d.* Entered Army, 1889; Capt. 1897; Major, 1907; Lt.-Col.

1914; Assist. Instructor and Comdt. Mtd. Infantry School, India, 1901-5; D.A.A.G. India, 1912-14; served Tirah, 1897-98 (despatches, medal 2 clasps); European War, 1914-18 (C.M.G., D.S.O.). *Club:* Army and Navy. [*Died* 24 *Jan.* 1954.

CLAUDEL, Paul; *b.* Villeneuve-sur-Fère, 6 Aug. 1868; *m.* Reine Saint-Marie Perrin; two *s.* three *d.* *Educ.:* Lycée Louis-le-Grand. Entered Diplomatic Service, 1890; Vice-Consul, New York, 1893; Consul at Fou-Tchéou, 1899; First Secretary, Pekin, 1906; Consul at Prague, 1909; Consul-General at Frankfurt, 1911; Hamburg, 1913; Minister at Rio-de-Janeiro, 1916; Copenhagen, 1919; Ambassador at Tokio, 1921-26; at Washington, 1927-33; to Belgium, 1933-35. *Publications:* Agamemnon, trad. 1906; Connaissance de l'Est, 1900; L'Arbre, 1900-1; L'Otage; Cette Heure qui est entre le printemps et l'été; Art poétique; L'Echange (play, The Exchange, prod. Little Theatre, London, 1915); Partage de Midi; Tête d'or; Le Répos du septième jour; La jeune fille Violaine; La Ville; Cinq grandes Odes; Le Pain dur; Le Père humilié; La Nuit de Noel, 1914; Corona benignitatis; Vers Exil; L'Annonce faite à Marie; Poèmes d'été; Poèmes de guerre; L'Ours et la lune; Feuilles de Saints; Les Euménides d'Eschylle; Un Poète regarde la Croix; L'Epée et le Miroir; Le Soulier de satin; Seigneur, apprenez-nous à prier, Christophe Colombe, etc. *Address:* Chateau de Brangues Morestel (Isère), France; 11 boulevard Lannes, Paris XVIIe. [*Died* 23 *Feb.* 1955.

CLAXTON, Hon. Brooke, P.C. (Can.); D.C.M. 1919; Q.C. (Can.) 1939; LL.D. (*hon. causa*), B.C.L.; Vice-President and General Manager for Canada, Metropolitan Life Insurance Company, Ottawa, since 1954; Chairman, Canada Council, since 1957; Director, The Montreal Trust, and The Employers' Liability Assurance Corporation Ltd. of London; *b.* 23 Aug. 1898; *s.* of late Albert George Brooke Claxton, K.C., and Helen Blanche Simpson; *m.* 1925, Helen Galt Savage; one *s.* one *d.* (and one *s.* decd.). *Educ.:* Lower Canada Coll.; McGill Univ., Montreal. Practised law in Montreal and was part-time prof. of commercial law at McGill Univ., 1921-44. Elected to House of Commons as Liberal Member for St. Lawrence-St. George, Montreal, 1940, re-elected 1945, 1949, and 1953; Parliamentary Assistant to Prime Minister, 1943; Minister of National Health and Welfare, 1944; Minister of Nat. Defence, Canada, 1946-54. Canadian delegate to numerous internat. confs. including: 1st and 2nd session of council of U.N.R.R.A. in Atlantic City, 1943, and Montreal, 1944; Economic and Social Council of U.N., 1946; Paris Conf. on Peace Treaties, 1946; British Commonwealth Conf. on Japan, Australia, 1947; with Prime Minister, signed terms of union with Newfoundland on behalf of Canada, 1949; attended meetings of Defence Cttee. or Council of North Atlantic Treaty, Washington, 1948, Paris, 1949, the Hague, Washington and Brussels, 1950, Washington, Ottawa and Rome, 1951, Lisbon and Paris, 1952, Paris, 1953. Member, Board of Governors, Carleton University. Hon. LL.D., McGill Univ., 1951, Queen's University, and University of British Columbia, 1958, Universities of Saskatchewan and Manitoba, 1959, Royal Military College, 1960; Canadian Conference of the Arts, 1960 Honour Award. Special Commemoratory Award (France), 1947; Greek Red Cross, 1946; Western Hemisphere Award, Amer. Arbitration Assoc., 1950; Médaille de l'Aéronautique awarded by Gov. of France, 1954. *Publications:* Notes on Military Law and Discipline for Canadian Soldiers, 1939; History of 10th Canadian Siege Battery; contrib. to various journals on insurance, internat. questions, constitutional law, etc. *Address:* 112 Acacia, Rockcliffe, Ottawa, Canada. *Clubs:* Mount Royal, University, Reform (Montreal); Rideau, Country, Canadian (Ottawa); Toronto (Toronto); Lotus (New York). [*Died* 13 *June* 1960.

CLAXTON, Thomas Folkes, F.R.A.S.; *b.* London, 29 Apr. 1874; *s.* of J. D. Claxton, of Newmarket and London, and Ellen Folkes; *m.* 1899, Dora Curwen Westray. *Educ.:* Colfe Grammar School. Joined Royal Observatory, Greenwich, 1890; Assistant Director, Royal Alfred Observatory, Mauritius, 1895; Director 1896; Director, Royal Observatory, Hong-Kong, 1912-32; Hon. Sec. Mauritius Meteorological Society, 1896-1911; Member and Hon. Sec. Board of Directors, Mauritius Institute and Museum, 1903-11; Member of Committee of Primary Instruction, 1908-11; J.P. 1913-32; Assistant Cable Censor, 1914; Deputy, 1917; Acting, 1918; Member of International Commissions for the Exploration of the Upper Air, Maritime Meteorology, Terrestrial Magnetism till 1932; President, Conference of Directors of Far Eastern Weather Services, Hong Kong, 1930. *Publications:* Annual Mag. and Met. Observations, Mauritius, 1896-1910; Seismological Observations, 1898-1910; Magnetic Survey, Pamplemousses, Proc. R.S. London, vol. 76, 1905; Climate of Pamplemousses, 8th International Geographic Congress; The Climate of Hong-Kong; The Winds of Hong-Kong; Isotyphs for the Far East, 1932; several papers on Cyclones in the S. Indian Ocean, etc. *Address:* Queen's Hotel, Ramsey, I.O.Man. *Club:* East India and Sports. [*Died* 12 *July* 1952.

CLAY, Lt.-Col. Ernest Charles, C.B.E. 1919 (O.B.E. 1918); 3rd *s.* of late C. J. Clay of Holly Bush Hall, Staffs.; *b.* 1872; *m.* 1902, Dorothy Mary, *d.* of late J. L. Press of Reymerston Hall, Norfolk, and Clifton, Bristol; one *d.* *Educ.:* Marlborough; New College, Oxford, B.A. Called to Bar, Lincoln's Inn, 1899; practised as a Barrister at the Chancery Bar till 1915, when he received a temporary commission (relinquished 1923) in the army; D.A.A.G. and A.A.G. War Office, 1916-23 (despatches, O.B.E., C.B.E.); Lt.-Col. Regular Army Reserve of Officers, 1923-33; Secretary, Gardner's Trust for the Blind, 1924-39. *Recreations:* shooting, fishing, golf, etc. *Address:* Berry Hall, Great Walsingham, Norfolk. *T.:* Walsingham 267. *Club:* Royal Automobile. [*Died* 1 *May* 1955.

CLAY, Sir Henry, Kt., *cr.* 1946; M.A.; M.Com.; Hon. D.Sc. Cape Town; Hon. LL.D. Manchester; *b.* 1883; *s.* of James Henry Clay of Bradford and Elizabeth Bulmer; *m.* 1st, Gladys, *d.* of Arthur Priestman, J.P.; three *s.* one *d.*; 2nd, 1951, Rosalind, *widow* of E. Murray Wrong, and *d.* of Arthur Lionel Smith, Master of Balliol Coll. *Educ.:* Bradford Grammar School; University Coll. Oxford. Lectr. for Workers' Educational Tutorial Classes under the Universities of Leeds, London, and Oxford, 1909-17; Ministry of Labour, 1917-1919; Fellow of New College, Oxford, 1919-1921; Stanley Jevons Professor of Political Economy, Manchester, 1922-27; Professor of Social Economics in the University of Manchester, 1927-30; Economic Adviser to Bank of England, 1930-44; Warden of Nuffield Coll., Oxford, 1944-49. Member of Economic and Wage Commission, S. Africa, 1925; Member of Royal Commission on Unemployment Insurance, 1931. *Publications:* Economics, an Introduction for the General Reader, 1916; The Problem of Industrial Relations, 1929; Post-War Unemployment Problem, 1929; Lord Norman, 1957 (posthumous). *Address:* 29 Charlbury Road, Oxford. *T.:* Oxford 58136. *Clubs:* Reform, Royal Cruising. [*Died* 30 *July* 1954.

CLAY, Reginald S., B.A., D.Sc.; F.Inst.P.; Research Physicist at United Kingdom Optical Co., Mill Hill; *m.* Theodora, *d.* of Eustace Tilly, C.E.; one *s.* three *d.* *Educ.:* Tollington Park College; St. John's

College, Cambridge, 21st Wrangler, 1892; B.Sc. London, 1889; D.Sc London, 1901. Master at Mill Hill School, 1893-95; Head of Physics Dept., Birkbeck College, 1897-1900; Principal, Wandsworth Technical Institute, 1900-2; Principal, Northern Polytechnic, Holloway, N., 1902-31; Secretary, Association of Technical Institutions, 1907-11; President of the Royal Microscopical Society, 1937-38. *Publications:* Practical Exercises in Light, Treatise on Practical Light; (with T. H. Court) History of the Microscope. *Address:* Eskdale, Fortis Green, N.2. *T.:* Tudor 5070.
[*Died* 10 *April* 1954.

CLAYE, Rev. Canon Arthur Needham; *b.* 1863; 2nd *s.* of William Claye, Stockport; *m.* 1894, Ada Augusta (*d.* 1937), *e. d.* of Capt. Moynihan, V.C.; one *s.* one *d.* *Educ.:* Lancing College; Pembroke Coll., Oxford (Scholar). 2nd Class Mods.; 2nd Class Lit. Hum.; B.A., 1885; M.A., 1887; B.D. and D.D., 1907; Priest, 1887; Curate of St. James', Grimsby, 1886; Vicar and Lecturer of Glandford Bridge, commonly called Brigg, 1893-1918; Rural Dean of Yarborough No. 1, 1896-1910; Yarborough, South, 1910-18; Rector of Hagworthingham, 1918-22; Rector of St. Thomas, Stockport, 1922-37; retired, 1937; Proctor in Convocation, 1932-36; Prebendary of Carlton-cum-Dalby in Lincoln Cathedral, 1911-39, Canon Emeritus. *Publications:* Brigg Church and Town, Historical Notes, 1904; A Chapter in the History of Hagworthingham Town, 1922; Reading Aloud in Church, Some Hints, 1939. *Recreation:* botany. *Address:* 19 Beechfield Road, Davenport, Stockport, Cheshire.
[*Died* 22 *April* 1956.

CLAYTON, Col. Edward Robert, C.M.G. 1919; D.S.O. 1916; J.P., D.L. Somerset; County Council, 1931, Vice-Chm. 1943, Chm. 1947; *b.* 1877; *s.* of Rev. Preb. Clayton of Ludlow and Hon. Mrs. Clayton; *m.* 1925, Elsie Margaret, *er. d.* of Colonel W. H. Ames, Bourton, Shrivenham; one *s.* one *d.* *Educ.:* Eton; Sandhurst. Served in Oxfordshire Light Infantry, 1897-1924; commanding 2nd Battalion, 1920-24; retired pay, 1930; served on N.W. Frontier of India, 1897-98, and European War. *Address;* Northmoor, Dulverton, Somerset. *Clubs;* Travellers', Army and Navy. [*Died* 16 *Sept.* 1957.

CLAYTON, Sir Francis (Hare), Kt., *cr.* 1954; O.B.E. 1937; Solicitor; Senior Partner, Clayton Leach Sims & Co., 18 Bedford Square, London; *b.* 24 April 1869; *s.* of Charles Hoghton Clayton, Long Ditton, and Lydia Mary, *d.* of Thomas Hare; *m.* 1906, Gertrude Adelaide, *d.* of Rev. Sir Edmund Armstrong, 2nd Bt. (*d.* 1899), of Gallen; no *c.* *Educ.:* Haileybury and Wiesbaden. Solicitor, 1892; joined Committee Shaftesbury Homes and Arethusa Training Ship, 1894 (Dep. Chm., 1918; Chm. and Treas., 1926-51). *Publication:* The Claytons, 1955. *Address:* Homeclose, Grayswood, Haslemere, Surrey. *T.:* Haslemere 553. *Club:* Carlton.
[*Died* 18 *Oct.* 1956.

CLAYTON, Most Rev. Geoffrey Hare, Hon. D.D. (Camb.) 1948; Archbishop of Cape Town since 1948; *b.* 12 Dec. 1884; *s.* of late Rt. Rev. Lewis Clayton, Bishop of Leicester; unmarried. *Educ.:* Rugby School; Pembroke College, Cambridge; Cuddesdon Theological College. 1st Class Classical Tripos, Part I, 1906; 1st Class Theological Tripos, Part II, 1907; George Williams Prize, 1907; Deacon, 1908; Priest, 1909; Fellow of Peterhouse, Cambridge, 1908-24; Dean, 1910-14 and 1919-20; Hon. Fellow, 1946-; Hon. Fellow of Pembroke Coll., Cambridge, 1953-. Temporary Chaplain to the Forces, 1914-19 (despatches); Vicar of St. Mary's the Less, Cambridge, 1918-24; Vicar of Chesterfield, 1924-34, Rural Dean, 1925-28, Archdeacon, 1928-34; Bishop of Johannesburg, 1934-48. Sub-Prelate of Order of St. John of Jerusalem, 1950-. *Address:* Bishopscourt, Claremont, C.P., S.A. [*Died* 7 *March* 1957.

CLAYTON, Sir Harold Dudley, 10th Bt. of Marden, *cr.* 1732; *b.* 28 Jan 1877; *s.* of late Col. Sir FitzRoy Clayton, K.C.V.O., late Grenadier Guards, and Lady Isabel Taylour, *d.* of 3rd Marquis of Headfort; *S.* kinsman, Sir Robert Clayton-East-Clayton, 1932; *m.* 1903, Leila Cecilia, *d.* of Francis Clayton; two *s.* one *d.* *Educ.:* Eton. Formerly Lieut. Severn Division Submarine Miners R.E. (Vol.); served European War in the R.N.V.R.; is an Associate of Institute of Naval Architects. *Recreations:* yachting, shooting, gardening, photography. *Heir:* *s.* Arthur Harold [*b.* 1903; *m.* 1st, 1927, Muriel Edith (*d.* 1929), *d.* of late Arthur John Clayton; 2nd, Alexandra, *o. c.* of late Lieut. Sergei Andreeovsky]. *Address:* Coombe Bank, Brixham, S. Devon: Harleyford, Marlow, Bucks. *Club:* Royal Thames Yacht.
[*Died* 19 *Oct.* 1951.

CLAYTON, Brig. Sir Iltyd Nicholl, K.B.E., *cr.* 1949 (C.B.E. 1941; O.B.E. 1927); Brig. retd., late R.A.; *b.* 15 Sept. 1886; *s.* of Lt.-Col. W. L. N. Clayton, Sandown, I.W.; *m.* 1917, Marjorie Clemence, *d.* of late Sir (Frederick) William Duke, G.C.S.I., G.C.I.E.; one *s.* two *d.* *Educ.:* Lancing College; R.M.A., Woolwich. Served European War, 1914-19 with R.A. (despatches twice). Operations in Iraq, 1920; attached Iraq Army, 1921-28. War of 1939-1945, Middle East. Temp. Brig. (M.I.) Cairo, 1940-43 (despatches twice, C.B.E.). Adviser on Arab affairs, Minister of State, 1943-45; afterwards to Head of British Middle East Office till 1948; attached British Embassy, Cairo, 1947-48, as Minister. *Address:* c/o Lloyds Bank, Cox's & King's Branch, 6 Pall Mall, S.W.1.
[*Died* 30 *June* 1955.

CLAYTON, Rear-Admiral John Wittewronge, C.B.E. 1942; retired; *b.* 21 April 1888; *s.* of Lt.-Col. W. L. N. Clayton, Sandown, I. of W.; *m.* 1922, Florence Caroline Schuster; one *s.* one *d* *Educ.:* Isle of Wight College. Joined H.M.S. Britannia, 1903; Lieut. 1908; Comdr. 1921; Capt. 1928; Navigating Officer of H.M.S. Amphion, Cornwallis, and Neptune in European war, 1914-1918; commanded H.M.S. Emerald and Furious; Rear-Admiral and Retired List, 1940. *Address:* Quillet, Wrangaton, S. Devon.
[*Died* 15 *May* 1952.

CLAYTON, Lt.-Col. (Bt. Col.) Muirhead Collins, D.S.O. 1917; O.B.E. 1944; T.D. 1949; D.L. (Cambs.); Fruit Grower; Director, The Murphy Chemical Co. Ltd., since 1931; *b.* 24 July 1892; *e. s.* of late Collins Clayton, J.P.; *m.* 1917, Alice, *e. d.* of late Alfred Coates; one *s.* *Educ.:* Gresham's School, Holt. 2nd Lieut. 1st Camb. Regt. T.A., 1910; Lt.-Col., 1918; Bt. Col. 1924; served European War, 1914-1918 (severely wounded, D.S.O., despatches four times); commanded 1st Camb. Reg., 1918-24; H.G. Bn., 1940-45 and 1951-53, and Cadet Bn. for two years. Hon. Col. The Cambridgeshire Regt., 1947-. Director, Wisbech Produce Canners (Smedleys), 1937-1946. Member: County T.A. Assoc.; District Council; Drainage Board; Income Tax Commissioner; Chairman, King's Lynn Divisional Conservative Assoc., 1952-56, Pres., 1956. *Publication:* (with Brig.-Gen. Sir E. Riddell) The Cambridgeshires, 1914-1919. *Address:* West Walton, Wisbech, Cambs. [*Died* 3 *Nov.* 1957.

CLEAVER, (Thomas) Reginald; late Graphic Staff; contributor to Punch; Artist in Black and White. *Address:* c/o Westminster Bank Ltd., 214 High Holborn, W.C.1.
[*Died* 15 *Dec.* 1954.

CLEGG, Sir (Alfred) Rowland, Kt., *cr.* 1939; *b.* 22 Dec. 1872; *e. s.* of Harry Clegg, D.L., J.P., Plas Llanfair, Anglesey; *m.* 1899,

Henrietta Madge, *e. d.* of Joseph Donnell, J.P., Disley, Cheshire; one *s.* two *d.* *Educ.:* Harrow and Abroad. J.P. Cheshire, 1900; J.P. Salop, 1922; High Sheriff, Shropshire, 1923; Anglesey, 1943; County Councillor and Alderman, Salop, 1920-37; Chairman, County Educ. Committee, 1921-37; Chairman Ludlow Division Conservative Association, 1919-38. *Recreations:* shooting, yachting, golf, etc. *Address:* Tres-yr-Afon, Beaumaris, Anglesey. *T.A.:* and *T.:* Beaumaris 35. *Clubs:* Royal Anglesey Yacht (Beaumaris); Royal Welsh Yacht (Caernarvon). [*Died* 6 *March* 1957.

CLEMENS, Benjamin, R.B.S.; sculptor. *Educ.:* Royal College of Art; Assistant to Professor Lanteri, Royal College of Art; Exhibitor Royal Academy and other Galleries; with the British Expeditionary Force, France, 1915-18; Hon. Member International Mark Twain Society, U.S.A. *Address:* 3 Clarence Gardens, Clarence Road, Clapton, E.5. [*Died* 27 *Dec.* 1957.

CLEMENT, Sir Thomas, K.B.E., *cr.* 1919; Chairman of A. Clement & Sons, Ltd., produce importers, London, Manchester, Glasgow and also in Canada, Australia, and New Zealand. Largely interested in agriculture, and farms extensively in Berwickshire, Kirkcudbrightshire, and Renfrewshire; has served on several Commissions and Committees on Commercial and Agricultural questions. *Address:* Barcaple, Newton Mearns, Renfrewshire. [*Died* 15 *Dec.* 1956.

CLEMESHA, Lieut.-Col. William Wesley, C.I.E. 1918; M.D. 1902, D.P.H. 1899 (Victoria); I.M.S. (retd.); late Director, Malaria Control Scheme, Ceylon; *b.* 1871; *m.*; one *d.* *Educ.:* Owens College, Manchester. *Address:* Victoria Road East, Birkdale, Auckland, N.5. N.Z. [*Died* 29 *May* 1958.

CLERK, Rt. Hon. Sir George Russell, P.C. 1926; G.C.M.G., *cr.* 1929 (K.C.M.G., *cr.* 1917; C.M.G. 1908); C.B. 1914; *b.* 29 Nov. 1874; *s.* of General Sir Godfrey Clerk, K.C.V.O., C.B. (*d.* 1908); *m.* 1908, Muriel, *d.* of E. R. Whitwell. *Educ.:* Eton; New College, Oxford. Clerk in Foreign Office, 1899; Acting 3rd Sec. and Sec. to Special Mission to courts of Europe to announce accession of King Edward, 1901; Assistant in H.M. Agency, Addis Ababa, 1903; Acting Agent and Consul-General, 1903-4; Chargé d'Affaires at H.M. Legation in Abyssinia, 1906-7; Assistant Clerk in Foreign Office, 1907; 1st Secretary, H.M. Embassy, Constantinople, 1910; Senior Clerk, 1913; Acting Counsellor of Embassy, 1917; Private Secretary to Acting Secretary of State for Foreign Affairs, 1919; Special Delegate of Supreme Council of Peace Conference on Missions to Bucharest and Budapest, 1919; First Minister Czecho-Slovak Republic, 1919-26, also Consul-General, 1921-26; British Ambassador in Turkey, 1926-33; at Brussels, 1933-34; at Paris, 1934-37; retired 1937; Hon. Fellow, New College; Vice-President, Royal Geographical Society; Grand Cross, St. Stanislaus, Russia; Grand Cross, Légion d'Honneur; Grand Cross, White Lion of Bohemia; Commander SS. Maurice and Lazare, Italy. *Address:* 5 Egerton Place, S.W.3. *Clubs:* Athenæum, Turf, Beefsteak. [*Died* 18 *June* 1951.

CLEVELAND-STEVENS, William, C.M.G. 1953; Q.C. 1930; Director Council of Legal Education, 1939; Chancellor Diocese of Birmingham since 1937, of Truro since 1940, of Gloucester since 1946 (to be addressed as the Worshipful Chancellor); Deputy Chairman Enemy Exports Committee, 1939, Contraband Committee, 1940; *b.* 1881; *s.* of late William Stevens, D.L., J.P., of Winchet Hall, Goudhurst, Kent; *m.* 1914, Ann Felicia (*d.* 1953), Order of Mercy, *d.* of late A. H. Strauss; two *s.* *Educ.:* Westminster (King's Scholar); Christ Church, Oxford (Scholar); 1st Class Hon. Mods., M.A., B.C.L. Called to Bar, Lincoln's Inn, 1907; served as signal officer in H.M.S. New Zealand (Jutland despatches); assistant to Director Signal Division Admiralty; J.P. Essex, 1933; Bencher of Lincoln's Inn, 1935, Treasurer, Lincoln's Inn, 1955. *Address:* Winchet Hall, Goudhurst, Kent. [*Died* 10 *June* 1957

CLEWES, Winston (David Armstrong); Author; Organisation and Methods Controller, Crosse & Blackwell Ltd.; *b.* 20 March 1906; *s.* of James L. and Clara A. Clewes; *m.* 1932, Dorothy Parkin (novelist and writer of children's stories, under name of Dorothy Clewes), Nottingham. *Educ.:* Foyle College, Londonderry; Merchant Taylors' School. With Crosse & Blackwell continuously since 1923. *Publications:* Violent Friends (London and U.S.A.), 1944; Sweet River In The Morning (London and U.S.A.), 1946; Journey Into Spring (London and U.S.A.), 1948; Troy and the Maypole (London and U.S.A.), 1949; Men at Work, 1951; Peacocks on the Lawn (London and U.S.A.), 1952; The Merry Month, 1953; The Tilting Town, 1956; Clementine, 1957; numerous short stories for B.B.C. and magazines; *play:* The Solitary Lover, 1948, and others; several television and radio plays. *Recreations:* writing, reading. *Address:* 25 Southend Road, Beckenham, Kent. *T.:* Beckenham 5352. [*Died* 26 *July* 1957.

CLIFFORD, Ethel; *d.* of late W. K. Clifford, F.R.S.; *m.* 1905, Sir F. W. Dilke, Bt. (*d.* 1944); two *s.* (and one *s.* decd. 1944). *Educ.:* at home; Queen's College, Harley Street. *Publications:* Songs of Dreams, 1903; Love's Journey, 1905; has contributed poems to Fortnightly Review, Blackwood's Mag., etc. *Address:* Lepe Point, Exbury, Southampton. [*Died* 14 *Dec.* 1959.

CLIFT, Col. Sir Sidney William, Kt., *cr.* 1947; Solicitor and Director of Companies; Chairman and Managing Director of Clifton Cinemas and Associated Companies; *b.* 26 Aug. 1885; *s.* of late Thomas and Louisa Clift, Birmingham; *m.* 1910, Gertrude, *d.* of late William and Elizabeth Astley, Birmingham; two *d.* *Educ.:* King Edward's High School, Birmingham. Admitted as Solicitor, 1912; served European War, in R.A., R.F.C. and R.A.F., 1915-20 (twice mentioned for valuable services). Hon. Colonel 4th Bn. Royal Warwickshire Regt., Army Cadet Force, 1948-. Became interested in Cinemas, 1914; Pres. Cinematograph Exhibitors Assoc. of Great Britain and Ireland, 1944; Chm. Birmingham Agricultural Exhibition Society. *Recreations:* salmon and trout fishing, shooting. *Address:* Woodnorton, 2 Moor Green Lane, Moseley, Birmingham. [*Died* 18 *Oct.* 1951.

CLINTON, 21st Baron (Eng.), *cr.* 1299; **Charles John Robert Hepburn-Stuart Forbes-Trefusis,** P.C. 1926; G.C.V.O., *cr.* 1933; D.L., J.P.; Forestry Commissioner from 1919; *b.* 18 Jan. 1863; *s.* of 20th Baron and Harriet Williamina, *d.* of Sir John S. Forbes, 8th Bt. of Pitsligo; *S.* father, 1904; *m.* 1886, Lady Jane Grey M'Donnell (*d.* 1953), *d.* of 4th Earl of Antrim; two *d.* Lieut.-Col. N. Devon Yeo. (Hussars); Privy Seal to the Prince of Wales; Convener of Kincardine, 1899-1904; contested Kincardine (C.), 1895; Joint Parliamentary Secretary, Board of Agriculture, 1918; Lord Warden of the Stannaries, 1921-33; Chairman of the Forestry Commissioners, 1927-32. *Co-heiresses:* two daughters, Harriet (Hon. Mrs. H. N. Fane) and Fenell (Hon. Mrs. John Bowes Lyon). *Address* Heanton, Satchville, Okehampton, N. Devon; Fettercairn House, Fettercairn, Kincardineshire, N.B. *Clubs:* Carlton; New (Edinburgh). [*Died* 5 *July* 1957 (*abeyant*).

CLINTON, Rev. H. J. F.; *see* Fynes-Clinton.

CLIVE, Lieut.-Gen. Sir (George) Sidney, G.C.V.O., *cr.* 1937; K.C.B., *cr.* 1933 (C.B. 1918); C.M.G. 1919; D.S.O. 1915; late Grenadier Guards; Extra Equerry to the Queen since 1952; Marshal of the Diplomatic Corps, 1934-45; *b.* 16 July 1874; *e. s.* of late General Edward Henry Clive and Isabel, *d.* of Daniel Hale Webb; *m.* 1901, Madeline (*d.* 1957), 2nd *d.* of late F. W. Buxton, M.P.; two *s.* two *d.* *Educ.:* Harrow; Sandhurst. Entered Army, 1893; Captain, 1900; Major, 1909; Maj.-Gen., 1924; Lt.-Gen. 1932; passed Staff College, 1903-4; General Staff War Office and London District, 1905-14; served Nile Expedition, 1898 (two medals, clasp); South Africa, 1899-1902 (Queen's medal 5 clasps); European War, 1914-18 (D.S.O., Bt.-Col., C.B., C.M.G.); Military Governor at Cologne, 1919; Commanding 1st Infantry Brigade, Aldershot, 1920; British Military Representative, League of Nations, Geneva, 1920-22; Military Attaché to Paris, 1924-27; Director of Personal Services, War Office, 1928-1930; Military Secy. to Secretary of State for War, 1930-34; retired pay 1934; a Director of the Royal Academy of Music; President Union Jack Club and Hostel, 1944-55. Hon. F.R.A.M., 1939; Order of St. Stanislaus, 1st class (Russia); Grand Croix Legion of Honour; Order of the Crown Commander; Croix de Guerre, French and Belgian; J.P., D.L., Herefordshire, High Sheriff County of Hereford, 1939. *Address:* Perrystone Court, Ross, Herefords. *Clubs:* Guards, Brooks's.
[*Died* 7 *Oct.* 1959.

CLOGG, Rev. (Frank) Bertram, M.A., B.D. (Cantab.); B.D. (Lond.); Principal of Richmond College since 1951; Professor of New Testament Language and Literature in University of London, 1937-49, Emeritus Professor since 1949; *b.* 16 May 1884; 5th *s.* of late Rev. W. H. Clogg; *m.* 1912, Jessie Winifred, *d.* of late H. A. Stinson; one *s.* one *d.* *Educ.:* St. Olave's Grammar School; Emmanuel College, Cambridge. Dr. Williams Scholar, 1907-09; studied in Berlin and Heidelberg Universities, 1908-09; Assistant Tutor in Richmond College, 1909-12; Wesleyan Minister at Hartley Wintney and Luton, 1912-20; Tutor in New Testament Language and Literature in Richmond College since 1920; Reader in New Testament Language and Literature in University of London, 1931; Examiner in Matriculation and General School Examinations in Higher Schools, and in B.D., M.Th., Ph.D., D.D., University of London; Examiner in B.D., University of Wales; Governor of Leys School, Cambridge; Governor of St. Olave's and St. Saviour's Grammar School; Chairman Board of Studies in Theology in University of London, 1944. *Publications:* Commentary on Revelation in the Abingdon Bible Commentary, 1925; An Introduction to the New Testament, 1937; The Christian Character in the Early Church, 1944; Articles and Reviews in Expository Times, London Quarterly Review, etc. *Recreation:* gardening. *Address:* The Principal's House, Richmond College, Richmond, Surrey. *T.:* Richmond 1040.
[*Died* 4 *June* 1955.

CLOSE, Col. Sir C. F. A.; *see* Arden-Close.

CLOTHIER, Henry Williamson, C.B.E. 1938; *b.* 13 Sep. 1878; *s.* of late William Charles Clothier, Liverpool; *m.* 1903, Emily Margaret (*d.* 1949), *d.* of Richard Preston Brunton, Bombay; one *d.* *Educ.:* privately. Entered Admiralty, Asst. Expense Accounts Officer, 1896; called to Bar, Grays Inn, 1914; transferred to Air Ministry as Assistant Principal Clerk, 1918; Principal, 1920; Deputy Director of Accounts, 1924; Director of Accounts, 1934-42; retired, 1942. *Address:* Lordswood House Hotel, Southampton.
[*Died* 19 *Sept.* 1958.

CLOUGH, Blanche Athena; *b.* Aug. 1861; *d.* of Arthur Hugh Clough. *Educ.:* Newnham College, Cambridge. Tutor, Newnham College, 1896-1920; Vice-Principal, 1917-20; Principal, 1920-23; Member of Royal Commission on Oxford and Cambridge Universities, 1919. *Publication:* Memoir of Anne Jemima Clough, 1897. *Address:* 95 Howards Lane, Putney, S.W.15.
[*Died* 14 *June* 1960.

CLOUGH, Frederic Horton, C.B.E. 1920; M.I.C.E.; M.I.E.E.; formerly with the British Thomson-Houston Co., Ltd. of Rugby; *b.* 1878; *s.* of C. F. Clough, Melbourne; *m.* 1916, Olive Lisetta, *d.* of D. McG. Alexander, Rathgar, Dublin; one *d.* *Educ.:* Geelong, Australia; London; Berlin. Was Technical Adviser to the Director of Torpedoes and Mining, Admiralty. *Address:* Orchard Hey, Runcton, nr. Chichester. *T.:* Chichester 2884.
[*Died* 25 *Feb.* 1957.

CLOW, Sir Andrew Gourlay, K.C.S.I., *cr.* 1941 (C.S.I. 1935); Kt., *cr.* 1939; C.I.E. 1928; M.A.; *b.* Aberdeen, 29 April 1890; *e. s.* of late Rev. Principal W. M. Clow; *m.* 1925, Ariadne Mavis, *d.* of late Cyril H. Dunderdale, Westquarter, Stirlingshire; one *d.* *Educ.:* Merchiston Castle School, Edinburgh; St. John's College, Cambridge. Indian Civil Service, United Provinces, 1914; represented Indian Government at International Labour Conferences, Geneva, 1921, 1923, 1929, 1931, and 1934; Deputy Secretary to Government of India, 1924-27; Joint Secretary (Industries and Labour), 1931-35; Secretary (Labour) to Govt. of India, 1936-38; Communications Member of Government of India, 1938-42; Governor of Assam, 1942-1947; acting Governor of Bombay, 1946; rep. U.K. on Economic Commission for Asia and Far East (U.N.), 1947-48; Chairman Scottish Gas Board, 1949-56; Member, Restrictive Practices Court, 1957-. Member of Indian Central Legislature 1923, 1925-29, and 1931-1942; Member Royal Commission on Labour in India, 1929-31. *Publications:* The Indian Workmen's Compensation Act, 1924; Indian Factory Legislation: a Historical Survey, 1927; The State and Industry, 1928. *Address:* 5 Dick Place, Edinburgh 9. *Club:* Athenæum.
[*Died* 31 *Dec.* 1957.

CLUNIES-ROSS, Sir Ian, Kt., *cr.* 1954; C.M.G. 1954; Hon. LL.D. Univ. of Melbourne, 1955; Hon. D.Sc. Univs. of Adelaide, New England; F.Aust.Acad.Sci., 1954; A.R.C.V.S., 1956; Chairman, Commonwealth Scientific and Industrial Research Organization; *b.* 22 Feb. 1899; *s.* of late W. J. Clunies-Ross, Sydney, N.S.W.; *m.* 1927, Janet Leslie Carter; three *s.* one *d.* *Educ.:* Newington College, Sydney; University of Sydney. B.V.Sc., 1921; Lecturer in Veterinary Parasitology, University of Sydney, 1923; Parasitologist, Council for Scientific and Industrial Research, 1926; D.V.Sc., University of Sydney, 1928; Post-Graduate work Institute of Infectious Diseases, Tokyo, 1929-30; Delegate Kyoto Conference Institute of Pacific Relations, 1929; Director McMaster Animal Health Laboratory, Council for Scientific and Industrial Research, 1931; carried out Sheep and Wool Survey in North-East Asia, 1935-36; Chairman and Australian Member, International Wool Secretariat, London, 1937-40; Australian Delegation, League of Nations Assembly, 1938; Director of Scientific Man Power, Commonwealth Directorate of Man Power, 1942-45; President Australian Institute of International Affairs, 1941-45, and Prof. of Veterinary Sci., Sydney Univ. Exec. Officer, Council for Scientific and Industrial Research, Melb., 1946-49. Gold Medal, Royal Agric. Soc. of England, 1956; James Cook Medal, Royal Soc. of N.S.W., 1956. *Publications:* Edited and contributed to Australia and the Far East—Diplomatic and Trade Relations, 1935; Internal Parasites of Sheep (with H. McL. Gorden), 1936. *Address:* Kew E.4, Melbourne, Vic., Australia.
[*Died* 20 *June* 1959.

CLUSE, William Sampson; *b.* 20 Dec. 1875; *m.* 1902; one *s.* *Educ.:* Council School. Orphan at five years; half-time in baker's shop at eleven; full-time worker in printer's at thirteen; apprenticed as compositor at fifteen; joined S.D.F. 1900; R.A.M.C. 1916; elected member of Islington Borough Council in 1919 and 1922; M.P. (Lab.) for South Islington, 1923-31 and 1935-1950; Parliamentary Private Sec. to Ministry of Transport, 1941-42; Ministry of Aircraft Production, 1942-43. *Recreations:* walking and gardening. *Address:* 18 Horsenden Lane South, Perivale, Greenford, Middlesex. [*Died* 8 *Sept.* 1955.

CLUTSAM, George H.; Composer and Musical Critic; *b.* Sydney, New South Wales, 1866. *Educ.:* self-taught. Came to London, 1889; accompanist at principal concerts in London and provinces for ten years, and then relinquished piano-playing for composition. *Publications:* some hundred and fifty songs; a cantata; opera, A Summer Night; König Harlekin, dramatic opera in four acts; and various other works; Vice-Chairman Performing Rights Society. *Recreation:* chess. *Address:* c/o Barclays Bank, Wellington Road, St. John's Wood, N.W.8. [*Died* 17 *Nov.* 1951.

CLUTTERBUCK, Sir Peter Henry, Kt., *cr.* 1924; C.I.E. 1918; C.B.E. 1919; V.D. 1912; F.R.G.S., F.Z.S.; Vice-Pres. Empire Forestry Association; Fellow R. Empire Soc.; Hon. Fellow Soc. American Foresters; Hon. Member Soc. Canadian Forest Engineers; Member, Soc. of Foresters of Great Britain, Royal Scottish Forestry Soc., Fauna Preservation Society; Bombay Natural History Society, East India Association; *b.* 1868; *s.* of late Alexander Clutterbuck of Red Hall, Watford; *m.* 1896, Rose Winifred, *d.* of Alfred Barrow Wilson Marriott, formerly District Superintendent of Police, Central Provinces, India; two *s.* *Educ.:* Clifton College; Bloxham; Royal Indian Engineering College, Coopers Hill. Indian Forest Service, Central Provinces, 1889; transferred to the United Provinces, 1896; Deputy Conservator of Forests, 1897; Conservator of Forests, Eastern Circle, U.P., 1913; Chief Conservator of Forests, U.P., 1915; Member of U.P. Legislative Council, 1919-20; Inspector-General of Forests to the Government of India, 1921-26; Timber Adviser to the High Commissioner for India, 1927-29; Chairman Empire Forestry Association, 1927-32; Chief Conservator of Forests, Kashmir, 1933-1941; Development Minister, Kashmir, 1941-1944; Kaisar-i-Hind Medal (silver), 1911; Editor Indian Forester, 1907-11; served in Volunteer forces, 1887-1918; was Hon. A.D.C. to the Lieut.-Governor of the U.P., 1910-18, and Lt.-Col. in command of the 8th (Northern) U.P. Horse of the India Defence Force, 1917-1918; Delegate for India to the Empire Forestry Conference, London, 1920; Australia and New Zealand, 1928; Chairman Forestry Sub-section British Association, Leeds, 1927; Member, Standing Committee Empire Forestry, 1927-32. *Address:* 25/2 Wimborne Road, Bournemouth, Hants. *T.:* Bournemouth 4274. [*Died* 20 *Dec.* 1951.

CLWYD, 1st Baron, *cr.* 1919; **John Herbert Roberts;** 1st Bt., *cr.* 1908; J.P.; *b.* 8 Aug. 1863; *s.* of late J. Roberts, M.P. Flint, 1878-92; *m.* 1893, Hannah (*d.* 1951), *d.* of W. S. Caine, M.P.; three *s.* *Educ.:* Trinity College, Cambridge. M.P. (G.L.) Denbighshire W., 1892-1918. *Heir:* *s.* Hon. John Trevor Roberts [*b.* 28 Nov. 1900; *m.* 1932, Joan de Bois, *er. d.* of late Charles R. Murray, Woodbank, Partickhill, Glasgow]. *Address:* Bryngwenallt, Abergele, North Wales. *Club:* Reform. [*Died* 19 *Dec.* 1955.

CLYDESMUIR, 1st Baron, *cr.* 1947, of Braidwood; **David John Colville,** P.C. 1936; G.C.I.E., *cr.* 1943; T.D.; Lord Lieutenant of Lanarkshire since 1952; Director, Colville's Ltd., Steelmakers, since 1948; Governor B.B.C. since 1950; Scottish National Governor of the B.B.C. since 1953; *b.* 1894; *o. s.* of late John Colville, M.P., of Cleland, Lanarkshire; *m.* 1915, Agnes Anne (C.I. 1947, C. (Sister) St. J., Kaisar-i-Hind Gold Medal), *er. d.* of Sir William Bilsland, Bart., LL.D.; one *s.* two *d.* *Educ.:* Charterhouse; Trinity College, Cambridge. Brigadier Royal Company of Archers (Queen's Bodyguard for Scotland); K.G.St.J.; served European War, 1914-18, with 6th Bn. The Cameronians (wounded). Contested Motherwell and Wishaw Division, 1922, and North Midlothian, January 1929; M.P. (U.) North Midlothian, 1929-43; Secretary Department of Overseas Trade, 1931-35; Parliamentary Under-Secretary of State for Scotland, 1935-36; Financial Secretary to the Treasury, 1936-38; Secretary of State for Scotland, 1938-40; Temp. Colonel, Staff, 1940-42; Hon. Col. 6th Cameronians, 1941-1946; Governor of Bombay, 1943-48; acted as Viceroy and Governor-General of India, in 1945, 1946 and 1947. *Recreation:* shooting. *Heir:* *s.* Lt.-Col. Hon. Ronald Colville, M.B.E., T.D. [*b.* 21 May 1917; *m.* 1946, Joan Marguerita, *d.* of Lt. Col. E. B. Booth, D.S.O., Darvar Castle, Co. Louth; two *s.* one *d.*]. *Address:* Braidwood, Lanarkshire. *Clubs:* Carlton; New (Edinburgh); Western (Glasgow). [*Died* 31 *Oct.* 1954.

COATES, Albert; British musical conductor and composer; *b.* St. Petersburg, Russia, 1882, of English parents; *s.* of Charles Thomas Coates; *m.* 1st, Madelon, *d.* of Alfred Holland; one *d.*; 2nd, Vera Joanna Nettleford. *Educ.:* Liverpool Institute; Leipzig Conservatoire. After a brief attempt at a business career in St. Petersburg, entered Leipzig Conservatoire; studied under Nikisch. Conducted at Leipzig Opera House, 1904; Elberfeld, 1905 and 1906; Dresden, 1907 and 1908; Mannheim, 1909; Chief Conductor, Imperial Opera House, St. Petersburg, from 1910 until the Revolution; and then President of all Opera Houses in Soviet Russia; returned to England, 1919; conducted at Covent Garden; conductor of the London Philharmonic Orchestra, London Symphony Orchestra and Royal Philharmonic Society; went to America as guest-conductor of the New York Symphony Orchestra, 1920 and again in 1921; Director Philharmonic Orchestra at Rochester, N.Y., 1923-25; Director of British Music Drama Opera Season at Covent Garden, 1936; conducted series of concerts at Hollywood Bowl, U.S.A., 1939; returned to England, 1942; conducted many concerts; Johannesburg Symphony Orchestra, 1946; settled in Cape Town. *Films:* directed and arranged the music for Pagliacci; Song of Russia; Two Girls and a Sailor; *Operas:* Samuel Pepys; Mr. Pickwick; Gainsborough's Duchess; The Boy David; Van Hunks and the Devil (Legend of the Table Mountain composed and produced for tercentenary celebrations, Cape Town, 1952); *Compositions:* Pianoforte Concerto; Symphony, The Eagle; Suite Ancienne; Four Old English Dances; Purcell Suite from the Dramatic (arr.); many songs and piano pieces. *Recreations:* reading, swimming. *Address:* c/o Elkin & Co. Ltd., 20 Kingly Street, Regent Street, W.1. *T.:* Regent 3625. [*Died* 11 *Dec.* 1953.

COATES, Eric, F.R.A.M.; Composer-conductor; Director of the Performing Right Society Ltd.; *b.* Hucknall, Notts, 27 Aug. 1886; *s.* of late W. Harrison Coates, surgeon, and Mary Jane Gwyn Blower; *m.* 1913, Phyllis, *d.* of late Francis Black, R.B.A.; one *s.* *Educ.:* privately and at Royal Academy of Music, London. Conducted Broadcast Concerts of his music for the B.B.C. since 1922 and has appeared as

composer-conductor at many English Music Festivals; visited S. Africa, 1908, Stockholm, 1936, Copenhagen, Oslo, Stockholm, and Hilversum, 1938, Paris, 1937-38-39, Copenhagen, New York (Columbia Broadcasting System), 1946, Buenos Aires (Radio del Estado), La Plata (Radio Provincia), 1948; New York (ABC, WOR and WQXR), and Copenhagen (State Radio), 1955; represented British Music at Interim Congress of Internat. Confed. of Composers and Authors, Washington, 1946 and at the 15th Internat. Congress of Composers and Authors, Buenos Aires, 1948. *Works:* for orchestra include: Miniature Suite, 1911; Countryside Suite, 1914; Summer Days Suite, 1919; Joyous Youth Suite and Merrymakers Overture, 1922; Phantasy, The Selfish Giant, 1925; Phantasy, The Three Bears, 1926; Four Ways, Suite, 1927; Phantasy, Cinderella, 1929; Ballet, Snowdrop and the Seven Dwarfs, 1930; Suite, From Meadow to Mayfair, 1931; Concert Valse, Dancing Nights, 1931; Ballet, The Jester at the Wedding, 1932; The London Suite and Two Symphonic Rhapsodies, 1933; London Bridge March, 1934; Suite, The Three Men, 1935; Song of Loyalty, 1935; Suite, London Again, 1936; Saxo-Rhapsody for Alto Saxophone and Orchestra, 1936; Suite, Springtime, 1937; Ballet, The Enchanted Garden, 1938; Concert Valse, Footlights, 1939; Suite, Four Centuries, 1942; Suite, The Three Elizabeths, 1944; Interlude The Unknown Singer, 1952; March, Rhodesia (composed for the Central Africa Rhodes Centenary Exhibition, Bulawayo), 1953; Autobiography, Suite in Four Movements, 1953; Concert Valse, Sweet Seventeen (composed at invitation of B.B.C. for Light Programme Music Festival of 1954); March, The Dam Busters (composed for Associated Brit. Pictures film, The Dam Busters), 1955; Intermezzo, Impression of a Princess (composed at invitation of B.B.C. for Light Programme Music Festival of 1956). Several Orchestral Marches and many songs. *Recreation:* pottering with a camera. *Address:* 2 Mansfield Street, W.1. *T.:* Langham 2416.
[*Died* 21 *Dec.* 1957.

COATES, Mrs. Geo. J.; *see* Meeson, Dora.

COATES, Rev. John Rider, M.A.; *b.* 1879; *s.* of Robert Coates of Prestwich, Lancs, and Ruth Rider; *m.* 1907, Cecilia Mary Crommelin Brown; one *s.* one *d.* (and one *s.* killed 1943). *Educ.:* Bury Grammar School; Peterhouse and Westminster College, Cambridge; University of Göttingen. Minister of St. John's, Northwood, 1905-19; Bible Study Secretary of Student Christian Movement, 1919-23; Presbyterian Minister at Roath Park, Cardiff, 1923-27; Lecturer at Kuling and Mokansan, China, 1926; Professor of Old Testamen' and Comparative Study of Religion at Selly Oak Colleges, Birmingham, 1928-45; Lecturer at Beyrout, 1933; Minister of Weoley Hill Church, Birmingham, 1945-1947; Cambridge Univ. Preacher, 1951. *Publications:* Proverbs in Sm. Camb. Bible for Schools, 1911; The Christ of Revolution, 1920; Men of Destiny, 1926; part of The Gospel of the Cross, 1918; The Coming of the Church, 1929; History as Revelation, in the Study Bible III, 1930; Personal Freedom through Personal Faith, 1934 (Ed.); Isaiah & the N.T., in the Speaker's Bible XXVI, 1935; The Open Bible (Ed.), 1938-39; War—What does the Bible Say?, 1940; Bible Key Words (Trans.): I. Love (Agape); II. The Church (Ecclesia), 1949; III. Sin; IV. Righteousness, 1951; V. Gnosis, 1952; VI. Apostleship, 1952; The Saving History, 1951. *Address:* Nethy, Northleigh, Witney, Oxon. *T.:* Freeland 325.
[*Died* 8 *March* 1956.

COATES, Brig.-Gen. Reginald Carlyon, D.S.O. 1900; late R.F.A.; *b.* 13 Oct. 1869; *s.* of late Rev. G. A. A. Coates, Earls Croome, Worcester; *m.* 1903, Alice Maud (*d.* 1937), *d.* of late Gen. Sir Henry Daly. Entered R.A. 1889; Captain, 1899; Lt.-Col. 1914; served South Africa, 1899-1902 (despatches; Queen's medal 6 clasps, King's medal 2 clasps; D.S.O.); European War, 1914-18 (wounded, despatches thrice, 1914 Star); retired pay. *Address:* c/o Lloyds Bank Ltd., 6 Pall Mall, S.W.1.
[*Died* 27 *Sept.* 1958.

COATES, Major-General Thomas Seymour, C.B. 1937; O.B.E. 1918; M.B.; B.S.; retired; *b.* 30 May 1879; *s.* of late T. Coates, J.P., Waltham, Lancs; *m.* 1908, Nellie Rose Knee; one *d.* *Educ.:* Louth; Durham University. M.B., B.S. Durham, 1901; R.A.M.C. 1903; served India, Egypt, France, 1914-18 (despatches 4 times); Bt. Lt.-Col. 1919; D.D.M.S. Northern Command, 1930-33; D.D.M.S. Aldershot Command, 1934-37. *Address:* 1 Metropole Court, Folkestone. *T.:* 2120. [*Died* 10 April 1954.

COATES, Wells Wintemute, O.B.E. 1944; F.R.I.B.A., M.R.A.I.C.; R.D.I. 1944; B.A., B.Sc., Ph.D.; Chartered Architect (in practice); *b.* Tokio, Japan, 17 Dec. 1895; *s.* of late Rev. Harper Havelock Wells Coates, M.A., Ph.D., D.D., Professor, and Sarah Agnes Wintemute Coates (Canadian); *m.* 1927, Marion Chamier, *d.* of late Frank Grove, consulting engineer; one *d.* *Educ.:* private tutors, Japan; McGill Univ. Lieut. Canadian Infantry, 1915; France and Belgium, 1917, gunner, C.F.A.; fighter pilot, R.N.A.S. and R.A.F., 66 Squadron, Italy, 1918; scholar, University, British Columbia, B.A., B.Sc., 1922; Research Ph.D. (Engineering), Univ. of London, 1924; practice on own account as architect, London, 1929-39; shops, houses, flats London and provinces; B.B.C. studios; EKCO laboratories; industrial designs in many fields; formed M.A.R.S. Group London, 1933, as first delegate International Congress Modern Architecture; Technical Staff Officer, R.A.F. (V.R.), 1939-45 (Wing Commander); resumed practice, 1945, London. Master of Faculty of Royal Designers for Industry, 1951-53. *Recreation:* yachting. *Address:* 18 Yeoman's Row, S.W.3. *T.:* Kensington 9252. *Clubs:* Reform, R.A.F. Yacht.
[*Died* 17 *June* 1958.

COATS, Robert Hamilton, LL.D. (McGill, Dalhousie, Toronto), F.S.S. (Hon.); F.R.S.C.; Dominion Statistician, Canada; *b.* Clinton, Ont., 25 July 1874; *s.* of Robert Coats of Dykehead, East Kilbride, Scotland; *m.* 1942, Maida B. Skelly, Ottawa; no *c.* *Educ.:* Univ. Coll., Toronto (B.A.). On Staff of Toronto Globe, 1898-1901; Associate-Editor of the Labour Gazette, 1902; Chief Statistician, Department of Labour, 1905; Member of Commission on Official Statistics, 1912; Member of Commission on the Cost of Living, 1913; Dominion Statistician and Controller of Census, 1916; organised Dominion Bureau of Statistics, Canada, 1916-18; Member of League of Nations Commission on Statistics, 1920; Member of the International Institute of Statistics, 1924; Hon. Fellow of Hungarian and Mexican Statistical Societies; delegate of Canadian Government to various international congresses; Chairman, Conference of British Commonwealth Statisticians, 1935; Member of League of Nations Com. of Statistical Experts, 1931-39; Pres. Political Science Assoc. of Canada, 1935-36; Chm. Social Science Research Council, 1943-45; President American Statistical Association, 1938; Treasurer, Inter-American Institute of Statistics, 1940-46; Pres., Section II Royal Society of Canada, 1943-44. Visiting Professor, Dept. of Economics, Toronto University, 1942-1946. Consultant to Food and Agriculture Organisation of the U.N.O., 1947-48. *Publications:* The Labour Movement in Canada; (joint) Sir James Douglas; The American-born in Canada, 1942. *Recreations:* motoring, gardening. *Address:* 572 Manor Avenue,

Rockliffe Park, Ottawa, Canada. *T.A.:* Burostat, Ottawa. *T.:* 4-2803. *Club:* Rideau (Ottawa). [*Died 7 Feb.* 1960.

COATS, Rev. Robert Hay, M.A., B.D.; Workers' Educational Association Tutor in English Literature, 1921-50; *b.* 8 Jan. 1873; *s.* of Allan and Isabella Coats, Paisley; *m.* 1901, Margaret Ramsay, *d.* of John McConnachie, Glasgow; one *s.* one *d.* *Educ.*: Paisley; Glasgow University; Mansfield College, Oxford; Kiel and Leipsic Universities, Graduated M.A., B.D., Glas., and B.A. Oxon with second class honours in Semitic languages; won Elmslie Scholarship, 1896, and Pusey and Ellerton Scholarship, 1897; pastor of Hamstead Road Baptist Church, Handsworth, Birmingham, 1899-1921; Birmingham Univ. Lectr., 1921. *Publications:* Types of English Piety, 1912; Travellers' Tales of Scotland, 1913; The Christian Life, 1915; The Realm of Prayer, 1920; The Changing Church and the Unchanging Christ, 1924; articles on Holiness and Sanctification in Hastings' Encyclopædia of Religion and Ethics; John Galsworthy as a Dramatic Artist, 1926; John Bunyan, 1927. *Recreation:* music. *Address:* 32 Radnor Road, Handsworth, Birmingham. [*Died 9 June* 1956.

COATS, Sir Stuart (Auchincloss), 2nd Bt., *cr.* 1905; *s.* of 1st Bt. and Sarah, *d.* of John Auchincloss, New York; *b.* 20 Mar. 1868; *S.* father, 1913; *m.* 1891, Jane Muir (*d.* 1958), *d.* of Thomas Greenlees, Paisley; one *s.* one *d.* (and one *s.* decd.). Private Chamberlain of Sword and Cape to Pius XII. and previously to Popes Pius X., Benedict XV. and Pius XI; Knight Comdr. with Placca of Noble Order of Pius; Knight Comdr. of St. Gregory the Great; Comdr. of the Order of the Crown of Italy; contested (U.) Morpeth, 1906; Deptford, Jan. and Dec. 1910; M.P. (U.) Wimbledon Division of Surrey, April 1916-18; for Eastern Division, Surrey, Dec. 1918-22; former Chairman of the Italian Hospital; formerly partner in J. & P. Coats; was Pres. of the Canada Thread Co., and Vice-Pres. and Director of the Conant Thread Co., and also of the Coats Thread Co. and Spool Cotton Co., New York. *Recreations:* salmon-fishing, golf. *Heir:* *s.* Lt.-Col. James Stuart Coats, M.C. *Address:* c/o Morgan & Cie, 14 Place Vendôme, Paris 1er; c/o Midland Bank Ltd., 3A Carlos Place, Mount St., W.1. *Clubs:* Carlton; Travellers' (Paris). [*Died 15 July* 1959.

COATS, Sir Thomas Coats Glen Glen-, 2nd Bt., *cr.* 1894; *b.* 5 May 1878; *s.* of 1st Bt. and Elise Agnes (*d.* 1910), *d.* of Alexander Walker, Montreal; *S.* father, 1922; *m.* 1935, Louise, *d.* of late E. A. Hugon. *Educ.:* Eton; Merton College, Oxford, B.A. *Recreation:* yachting. *Heir:* none. *Address:* Craigallan, 82 South Beach, Troon, Ayrshire. [*Died 7 March* 1954 (*ext.*).

COBB, Captain Edward Charles, D.S.O. 1916; J.P.; late Northants, Regt.; *b.* Darwin, Falkland Is., 4 Sept. 1891; *s.* of late George A. Cobb and Julia M. A. Cobb, Lively I., Falkland Is.; *m.* 1918, Gladys Ryder, *e. d.* of H. J. King, of Poles, Ware, Herts; one *s.* three *d.* *Educ.:* St. Paul's School; R.M.C., Sandhurst. 2nd Lieut. Northants Regt. 1911; seconded for duty with West African Regt., 1914; joined Cameroons Expeditionary Force, Sept. 1914 (wounded 25 Jan. 1915); Adjutant 26th Northumberland Fusiliers, Sept. 1915 (wounded 1 July 1916, D.S.O.); Lieut. 1912; Capt. 1915; retired pay, 1924. Member L.C.C., 1925-34; Chmn. Education Cttee., 1932-34. M.P. (C.) Preston, 1936-45; Parliamentary Private Secretary to Under Sec. of State for Air, 1938-39; to President Board of Trade, 1939-40; to Sec. of State for War, 1940; to Secretary of State for India and Burma, 1940-41. *Address:* Rother Hill, Stedham, Midhurst. *Club:* Carlton. [*Died 14 May* 1957.

COBB, Major-General Edwyn Harland Wolstenholme, C.B. 1953; C.B.E. 1945; i.d.c.; p.s.c.; Commandant, Royal Military College of Science, Shrivenham, since 1954; *b.* 6 Aug. 1902; *s.* of late W. H. Cobb, I.C.S.; *m.* 1938, Priscilla Joan Margaret, *d.* of late Capt. P. B. Lendon, M.V.O.; one *d.* *Educ.:* Winchester Coll.; R.M.A. Woolwich. Passed Staff Coll., Camberley, 1938; B.G.S. (Plans), G.H.Q. India, 1943-44; B.G.S. IV Corps, Burma, 1945; Comd. 33 Indian Inf. Bde., Malaya, 1946; Student Imp. Defence Coll., London, 1947; Dep. Director, War Office, 1948-49; Asst. Commandant, Staff College, Camberley, 1950-51; Director of Manpower Planning, War Office, 1952-54. *Recreations:* golf, gardening, shooting, fishing, riding. *Address:* Shrivenham House, Nr. Swindon, Wilts. *T.:* Shrivenham, 266; Penwaun, Nevern, Newport, Pembrokeshire. *T.:* Newport, Pem. 43. *Club:* United Service. [*Died 26 March* 1955.

COBB, Ivo Geikie-, M.D., M.R.C.S., L.R.C.P.; F.R.S.L.; 2nd *s.* of late Rev. Dr. W. F. Geikie-Cobb, Rector of St. Ethelburga's, Bishopsgate; *b.* 30 April 1887; *m.* 1913, Audrey, *o. d.* of Edmond de Poix, J.P., Broome Pl., Norfolk; one *s.* two *d.* *Educ.:* St. George's, Ascot; West Downs, Winchester; Loretto; St. Thomas's Hospital, London; Brussels. Formerly Hon. Consulting Physician, Besford Court Hospital; Physician, Norwich Union Insurance Company; late Chairman, Literature and Information Committee, Member of Council and Executive Committee, New Health Society; late Resident House-Surgeon, Great Yarmouth Hospital; late Physician, London neurological clinic, Ministry of Pensions; assistant to outpatient physician, the Middlesex Hospital; temp. Capt. R.A.M.C., neurologist, B.E.F.; neurologist, Brinnington Section, 2nd Western General Hospital; formerly Editor New Health Society Bulletin; Member of Council R.S.L.; Fellow, Member of Executive Committee, Roy. Inst. of Public Health and Hygiene; worked in Overseas Service Dept. of the B.B.C., editing and writing scripts and broadcasting, 1940-1945. *Publications:* A Guide to Medicine; A Manual of Neurasthenia; The Organs of Internal Secretion; Aids to Organotherapy: The Glands of Destiny; (Ed.) Aspects of Modern Science; articles in med. journals on functional nervous disorders and endocrinology. (As Anthony Weymouth) This Century of Change; Going to London; Of London and Londoners; Who'd be a Doctor (Autobiography); Through the Leper-Squint—the Story of Leprosy throughout the Ages; A Psychologist's War-Time Diary; Plague Year; Good News About Yourself (Essays on Health); Germany: Disease and Treatment; A Journal of the Second World War; *novels:* Frozen Death; The Doctors are Doubtful; No! Sir Jeremy; Hard Liver; Tempt me Not; Cornish Crime; Inspector Treadgold Investigates; Surgical Emergency. *Recreations:* reading and writing. *Address:* 30 Harley House, N.W.1. [*Died 15 Aug.* 1953.

COBB, John Rhodes; Joint Managing Director Anning, Chadwick & Kiver. Ltd.; Vice-Chm. Falkland Islands Co. Ltd.; amateur racing motorist; *b.* 2 Dec. 1899; *s.* of Rhodes H. Cobb, Esher, Surrey; *m.* 1st, 1947, Elizabeth Mitchell-Smith (*d.* 1948); 2nd, 1950, Vera Henderson. *Educ.:* Eton; Trinity Hall, Cambridge. In business in the City. Holder of Brooklands Track Lap Record 143.4 m.p.h.; between 1932 and 1939 broke all world's records for time and distance up to 24 hours; established World's Land Speed Record 394.2 m.p.h., 16 Sept. 1947; first man ever to attain a speed of 400 m.p.h. on land. Awarded Seagrave Trophy, 1947. Served War of 1939-45, R.A.F., 1940-42; A.T.A. Ferry Pilot, 1943-45. *Address:* (office) 15 Arthur St., E.C.4; (home) Cullford, Coombe Park, Kingston, Surrey. *T.:* Mansion House 5544. *Clubs:* City University, M.C.C., Royal Automobile. [*Died 29 Sept.* 1952.

COBBETT, Sir Walter (Palmer), Kt., *cr.* 1943; C.B.E. 1931; Hon. M.A. Manchester; Solicitor practising in Manchester; *b.* 6 March 1871; *m.* 1898, Lucy Hervey, *d.* of Neville Clegg, Altrincham, Cheshire; two *d.* *Educ.:* Clifton College. Chairman Manchester and Salford Trustee Savings Bank (now retired); Vice-Pres. Trustee Savings Banks Assoc. *Address:* Groby Place, Altrincham, Cheshire. *T.:* Altrincham 1983. *Club:* Union (Manchester).
[*Died* 2 *Dec.* 1955.

COBHAM, 16th Baron, *cr.* 1312 (called out of abeyance, 1916), **Robert Disney Leith Alexander;** *b.* 23 Apr. 1885; 2nd *s.* of late Dr. Reginald Gervase Alexander, M.D., J.P., and Alicia, *d.* of late John Greenwood, Castle Hall, Mytholmroyd, Yorks; *S.* brother 1933; *m.* 1934, Evelyn Sinclair (*d.* 1937), *o. d.* of late John Turnure and *widow* of Philip Britt. *Educ.:* Aysgarth Sch.; Marlborough Coll. Entered the law and joined legal staff of the Public Trustee; since resigning this appointment has travelled extensively; has written numerous articles on his travels and on breeding of the thoroughbred. *Recreations;* swimming, walking, motoring, golf.
[*Died* 21 *Feb.* 1951 (*barony in abeyance*).

COBHAM, Brig.-General Horace Walter, C.M.G. 1919; D.S.O. 1917; *s.* of late F. A. Cobham; *m.* 1902, Edith A., (*d.* 1952), *d.* of late Colonel A. Locke Nicholson, late 107th Regt.; one *s.* two *d.* Served on Staff—Brig.-Major and D.A.A.G. 1906-10. Retired, 1910; served in Bechuanaland Expedition, 1884-85; N.W. Frontier of India, Tirah, 1897-98 (medal and two clasps); European War—in command of a Batt. and as Brig.-Commander (despatches five times, Bt. Lt.-Col., C.M.G., D.S.O.). *Recreations:* hunting, fishing. *Address:* Courtlands, Exmouth, Devon.
[*Died* 12 *Sept.* 1958.

COBHAM, Ven. John Lawrence, M.A.; Archdeacon emeritus since 1947; Prebendary of Exeter, 1933-53; Prebendary emeritus since 1953; *b.* 12 May 1873; *s.* of John Cobham and Martha Ann Matches; *m.* 1898, Frances Eliza, *d.* of late Sir William Willis (Accountant General, Navy); two *c.* *Educ.:* Merchant Taylors' School, Great Crosby; Corpus Christi College, and Ridley Hall, Cambridge. Deacon, 1896; Priest, 1897; Curate of Gt. Yarmouth, 1896-1900; Christ Church, Gipsy Hill, 1900-04; Vicar of St. John Evangelist, Carl., 1904-12; T.C.F., 1917-18; St. Peter, Tunbridge Wells, 1912-19; Commissary, Uganda, 1912-22; Treasurer of Uganda Diocesan Fund, 1919-22; C.C.C.S. Chaplain at Entebbe, Uganda, 1920-21; Clarens, 1922; Rector of St. Mark's Torwood, Torquay, 1922-38; Rural Dean of Ipplepen, 1928-1933; Archdeacon of Totnes, 1933-47. *Address:* Inniscarra, 11 Southfield Avenue, Paignton, Devon. *T.:* Paignton 82316.
[*Died* 27 *Dec.* 1960.

COCHRAN, Sir Charles Blake, Kt., *cr.* 1948; Chevalier de la Légion d'Honneur (France), 1950; Theatrical manager and producer; *b.* Lindfield, Sussex, 25 Sept. 1872; *s.* of James Elphinstone and Matilda Cochran; *m.* Evelyn Alice Dade; no *c.* *Educ.:* Lewes; Eastbourne; Brighton, Hove and Sussex Grammar School. Went on stage at Niblo's Garden, New York, 1891; played through U.S.A. with various touring companies for three years; played with Richard Mansfield in New York; produced Ibsen's John Gabriel Borkman in New York, 1895; became Mansfield's personal representative; first London production Sporting Simpson, Royalty Theatre, 4 Oct. 1902; promoted and managed entertainments varying from circus to The Miracle at Olympia, London, and elsewhere; produced for first time in England Mozart and Salieri (opera by Rimsky Korsakov) with Chaliapin, Royal Albert Hall; introduced the great wrestler Hackenschmidt to London; introduced roller-skating in France, Germany, and Belgium; promoted many important boxing matches at Olympia; also Wonder Zoo (a copy of Hagenbeck's Animal Park at Hamburg); presented Diaghileff's Russian Ballet; brought the first Rodeo to Wembley, June 1924; manager of Albert Hall, 1926-38; Vice-Pres. (President 1934-40) Actors Benevolent Fund; Governor, Shakespeare Memorial Theatre, Stratford-upon-Avon; had seven plays running simultaneously in London; has produced 128 plays and revues in London and managed many foreign stars, including Sarah Bernhardt, Eleanora Duse, Lucien Guitry, Sacha Guitry, Pitoeffs, Pirandello's Italian Company, Chaliapin, Katina Paxinou, Elisabeth Bergner and Yvonne Printemps; had four plays running together in New York. *Publications:* The Secrets of a Showman, 1925; I Had Almost Forgotten, 1932; Cock-a-doodle-do, 1941; A Showman looks on, 1945; magazine articles. *Address:* 49 Old Bond Street, W.1. *T.:* Regent 0424. *Clubs:* Beefsteak, Queen's.
[*Died* 31 *Jan.* 1951.

COCHRAN-PATRICK, Sir Neil James Kennedy, K.B.E., *cr.* 1934 (M.B.E. 1918); D.L., J.P.; B.A. (Cantab.); LL.B. (Edin.); *b.* 18 Aug. 1866; *s.* of John Kennedy of Underwood, Ayrshire, and Margaret, *d.* of Colin Macrae; *m.* 1895, Eleonora Agnes, *o. surv. c.* of late Robert W. Cochran-Patrick of Woodside and Ladyland, D.L., J.P., M.P., for N. Ayrshire, 1880-85, Under Sec. for Scotland, 1887-92; three *d.* (one *s.* decd.). *Educ.:* Edinburgh Academy; Monkton Combe School; Cambridge and Edinburgh Univs. Called to Scottish Bar, 1890; Member of the King's Body Guard for Scotland (Royal Company of Archers), 1902; Captain 4th Royal Scots Fusiliers (Territorial), 1914-18; Assistant Commissioner Churches (Scot.) Act, 1904; Vice-Chairman Ayrshire Education Authority, 1926-29; Convener of the County and Chairman Ayrshire County Council, 1930-35; Member Police Consolidation (Scot.) Committee, 1933; Chairman North Ayrshire Agricultural Executive Committee, 1939-47; contested Sitrling Burghs Jan. 1910 and Roxburghshire Dec. 1910 and was for 14 years Hon. Secretary of the Scottish Unionist Association; on death of father-in-law assumed the name of Cochran-Patrick in addition to his own. *Address:* Hunterston, West Kilbride, Ayrshire. *T.A.:* West Kilbride, Ayrshire. *T.:* West Kilbride, 3151.
[*Died* 8 *July* 1958.

COCHRANE of Cults, 1st Baron, *cr.* 1919, **Thomas Horatio Arthur Ernest Cochrane,** D.L., J.P.; LL.D.; *b.* 2 Apr. 1857; *s.* of 11th Earl of Dundonald; *m.* Lady Gertrude Boyle, O.B.E., *d.* of 6th Earl of Glasgow; three *s.* one *d.* *Educ.:* Eton. Hon. Lieut.-Col. 4th Batt. Argyll and Sutherland Highlanders, and served in 93rd Highlanders and Scots Guards; served in South Africa, D.A.A.G.; Lieut.-Col. 2/7 Black Watch, 1914-16; Parliamentary Private Secretary to Rt. Hon. Joseph Chamberlain; Under-Secretary of State for the Home Department, 1902-5; M.P. (U.) N. Ayrshire, 1892-1910. *Recreations:* golf, riding, shooting. *Heir:* *s.* Major Hon. T. G. F. Cochrane, D.S.O. *Address:* Crawford Priory, Cupar, Fife. *Clubs:* Guards', Brooks's, Carlton; New (Edinburgh).
[*Died* 17 *Jan.* 1951.

COCHRANE, Rear-Adm. Archibald, C.M.G. 1918; Royal Navy, retd.; *b.* 20 June 1874; *e. s.* of late Vice-Admiral Basil E. Cochrane, Windlesham House, Windlesham, Surrey; *m.* 1904, Maye, *o. d.* of Colonel A. de V. Brooke, R.E.; four *d.* *Educ.:* Woodcote House, Windlesham; Eastmans, Stubbington; and H.M.S. Britannia. Entered Navy, 1888; going to sea, 1890; Sub-Lieut., 1894; Lieut., 1896; as Lieut. of Anson in 1897 landed in Crete in charge of naval gun protecting water supply of Canea; Flag-Lieut. to Vice-Admiral Sir H. Grenfell in Mediterranean Squadron; Commanded

H.M.S. Speedwell, Home Fleet, 1906; Commander, 1908; was commanding H.M.S. Alacrity, China, on outbreak of war in 1914; commanded H.M.S. Empress of Russia, an armed C.P.R. liner, 1914-15; H.M.S. Sentinel to June 1916; H.M.S. Skirmisher till Sep. 1918; both these ships in Ægian Squadron, Eastern Mediterranean (C.M.G., Officer of Redeemer of Greece, Chevalier Légion d'honneur); Captain, 1918; retired list, 1929; Rear-Adm., retired. 1929. *Recreations:* golf, tennis. *Address:* Windlesham House, Windlesham, Surrey. *T.:* Bagshot 32. *Club:* United Service. [*Died* 15 *July* 1952.

COCHRANE, Captain Hon. Sir Archibald Douglas, G.C.M.G., *cr.* 1937; K.C.S.I., *cr.* 1936; D.S.O. 1915; *b.* 8 Jan. 1885; 2nd *s.* of 1st Baron Cochrane of Cults; *m.* 1926, Julia Dorothy, *o. d.* of 1st Baron Cornwallis; one *s.* one *d.* Entered R.N. 1901. Served European War, 1914-18 (despatches thrice, D.S.O. and bar); retired list, 1922; M.P. (U.) East Fife, 1924-29; Dunbartonshire, 1932-36; Governor of Burma, 1936-41; served as Acting Capt. R.N. (retd.), 1941-45; Director Standard Life Assurance Co. *Address:* Inglisfield, Gifford, East Lothian. *Clubs:* Carlton; New (Edinburgh). [*Died* 16 *April* 1958.

COCHRANE, Sir Arthur William Steuart, K.C.V.O., *cr.* 1937 (C.V.O. 1931; M.V.O. 1911); Clarenceux King of Arms since 1928; *b.* 27 April 1872; 3rd *s.* of Rev. David Crawford Cochrane, M.A., Master of Etwall Hospital, Derbyshire; *m.* 1907, Margaret Peregrina (*d.* 1952), 4th *d.* of Sir Courtenay Ilbert, G.C.B.; two *d.* *Educ.:* Repton. Rouge Croix Pursuivant of Arms, 1904-15; Chester Herald, 1915-26; Norroy King of Arms, 1926-28; Registrar, 1919-28. *Address:* Melbury Cottage, Melbury Road, W.14; Heralds' College, E.C.4. *Club:* Boodle's. [*Died* 11 *Jan.* 1954.

COCHRANE, Sir Cecil Algernon, Kt., *cr.* 1933; Hon. D.C.L. Durham; *b.* 1869; 2nd *surv. s.* of late William Cochrane, M.I.M.E., M.I.C.E.; *m.* 1905, Frances Sibyl, (*d.* 1952), *d.* of Col. Addison Potter, C.B., of Heaton Hall, Newcastle upon Tyne. *Educ.:* Sherborne; Christ Church, Oxford (M.A. 1894). Contested Durham City, 1910; M.P. (L.) South Shields, 1916-18. *Address:* Oakfield House, Gosforth, nr. Newcastle upon Tyne. *T.:* Gosforth 51948. *Club:* Royal Automobile. [*Died* 23 *Sept.* 1960.

COCHRANE, Rev. Canon E. L., M.A.; *b.* West Hartlepool, 3 Aug. 1876; *s.* of Robert Cochrane; *m.* 1st, Susan Annie, *d.* of R. W. Vick; 2nd, Elsie, *d.* of G. B. Birch; two *s.* one *d.* *Educ.:* West Hartlepool; Keble College, Oxford. Curate of Cradley, Worcestershire, 1902; St. Ambrose, Edgbaston, 1905; Vicar of Holy Trinity, Smethwick, 1914; Rural Dean of Harborne, 1922; Vicar of Yardley, Birmingham, 1923-47; retired, 1947; Hon. Canon of Birmingham, 1924; Rural Dean of Solihull, 1927-46; Member of Board of Finance; Governor of Queen's College; Governor of the Yardley Charity Estates; Ex-officio Trustee of the Charles Lane Trust. *Address:* 921 Warwick Road, Solihull, Birmingham. [*Died* 2 *Feb.* 1955.

COCHRANE, Captain Sir Ernest Cecil, 2nd Bt., *cr.* 1903; J.P.; late 3rd Batt. Connaught Rangers; Chairman of Cantrell & Cochrane, Dublin, Belfast, New York, 1903-25; Member of English Bar; adopted the profession of Dramatist under the pen name of Ernest Cecil, 1919; plays produced: A Matter of Fact, Comedy Theatre, 1921; Monica, Everyman Theatre, 1924; 3rd *s.* of 1st Bt. and Margaret, *o. d.* of late Richard Gilchrist, Dublin; *b.* 12 Sept. 1873; *S.* father, 1904; *m.* 1st, 1898, Ethel Amy (who obtained a divorce, 1910), *d.* of John Henry Davis, Cressingham House, Carshalton; one *d.*; 2nd, 1911, Elsa (who obtained a divorce, 1933), *y. d.* of Erwin Schumacher, of 24 Prince's Gate, W.; one *s.* one *d.*; 3rd, 1933, Flora (who obtained a divorce, 1948), *d.* of late Fritz Arnold Sandström, Finland; one *d.*; 4th, 1948, Margaret E. Cooper, *y. d.* of late Mrs. S. M. Fowler, Harrogate. *Educ.:* Trinity College, Dublin. Called to Bar, Inner Temple, 1904; Hon. Gentleman-in-Waiting to Lord-Lieut. of Ireland, 1908-09. *Heir:* *s.* Desmond Oriel Alastair George Weston [*b.* 22 Oct. 1918; *m.* 1946, Yvonne, *o. c.* of late A. Sursock; one *s.*] *Address:* Felstead, Woodmancote, Henfield, Sussex. [*Died* 6 *March* 1952.

COCK, Rev. Prof. Albert A., B.A. (Hons.) Lond.; Fellow, King's College, London; *b.* 1883; 3rd *s.* of late Edwin Cock, of the Civil Service; unmarried; one adopted *s.* *Educ.:* Univ. of London, King's College; graduate in First-Class Honours in Philosophy in Univ. of London; First to take Aesthetics in this Examination; Lecturer in Education and Philosophy in King's College, London, 1906-1919; Special Lecturer in St. Mary's College, Hammersmith, 1909-19; Professor of Education and Philosophy in the University College of Southampton (now University of Southampton), 1916-39, and Vice-Principal, 1937-1939; Senior Warden of the Men's Halls of Residence, 1921-39; Visiting Professor of Christian Apologetics in the General Theological Seminary, New York, 1932-33; ordained 1939; Principal, St. John's Diocesan Training Coll., York, 1939-45; Sec. London Soc. for the Study of Religion. *Publications:* Editor of The Modern Educator's Library (9 volumes out); S. Thomas Aquinas, in A History of Christian Thought, 1937, 2nd edn., 1950; Editor of Selections from Francis Thompson and Mrs. Meynell; Editor of A Century of English Literature, 4 vols.; contributor to and Editor of Speculum Religionis, 1929; various philosophical papers, articles in new Encyc. Brit. 1938 and to new Chambers's Encyc.. 1948; A Critical Study of the Religious Philosophy of Baron von Hügel, 1953 (trans. into Spanish, Italian and Latin). *Recreations:* friendship, music, chess, poetry. *Address:* 9 Collingham Road, S.W.5; c/o Señor Professor Jack Rush, Avenida Mitre 947, Tucuman, Argentina. *Club:* Athenæum. [*Died* 9 *Sept.* 1953.

COCKAYNE, Edward Alfred, O.B.E., 1954, D.M. Oxon; F.R.C.P. London; Consulting Physician, Middlesex Hospital; Consulting Physician, Hosp. for Sick Children, Great Ormond Street; Temporary Surgeon, R.N.V.R., 1915-17; R.N. 1917-19; President Royal Entomological Soc. of London, 1943-45; Pres., Section for Study of Diseases of Children, Royal Society of Medicine, 1938; *b.* 1880; *s.* of late E. S. and Mary Florence Cockayne of Sheffield (she *m.* 2nd, 1906, 2nd Marquis of Aberdeen, and *d.* 1937). *Educ.:* Charterhouse; Balliol Coll. Oxford (First Class Honours, Natural Science School), 1903; St. Bartholomew's Hospital (Brackenbury Scholarship in Medicine), 1907. *Publications:* Inherited Abnormalities of the Skin and its Appendages; papers on the Diseases of Children and other medical subjects; Gynandromorphism, etc. *Recreation:* entomology. *Address:* 8 High Street, Tring. *T.:* Tring 2151. [*Died* 28 *Nov.* 1956.

COCKBURN, Major Ernest Radcliffe, C.B.E. 1938 (O.B.E. 1918); *b.* 17 Sept. 1875; *m.* 1899, Jean Henderson Rodger (*d.* 1950). *Educ.:* Harrow. Lieut., 3/Wilts. Regt., 1894, 2/Wilts. Regt., 1897; Capt., Manchester Regt., 1901, Wiltshire Regt., 1907; Adjutant, 3/Wiltshire Regt., 1908-12; Major, 1915; Secretary, Ayrshire Territorial Force Assoc., 1912-19; Chief Constable of Ayrshire, 1919-28; Chief Constable of Hampshire, 1929-42; served S. African War in Mounted Infantry, Wilts. Regt., 1900-2 (Queen's Medal 5 clasps, King's Medal 2 clasps). *Address:* Ivy Lodge, Ightham, Kent. *Club:* Army and Navy. [*Died* 15 *Sept.* 1955.

COCKBURN, Sir William (Robert Marshall), Kt., 1955; Director, The Chartered Bank, since 1955; *b.* 26 April 1891;

s. of late George Hannah Cockburn, F.E.I.S., schoolmaster, and late Isabella Brodie Marshall; *m.* 1925, Minnie Knox; one *d.* *Educ.:* Paisley Grammar School. Entered Union Bank of Scotland Ltd., 1908; entered Chartered Bank of India, Australia and China, 1911; served Indo-China, Malaya, China and Japan, 1913-36; Asst. Gen. Manager, London, 1936; Gen. Manager, 1938; Chief Gen. Manager, 1940; retired to become Director, 1955. Chm. Eastern Exchange Banks Assoc., 1947-55; Chm., British Overseas Banks Assoc., 1949; Vice-Pres., British Bankers Assoc., 1949; Past Pres., Manchester and Dist. Inst. of Bankers. *Recreation:* fishing. *Address:* Elms House, Twyford, Hants. *T.:* Twyford 2169. *Clubs:* City of London, Oriental, Junior Carlton. [*Died* 1 *Sept.* 1957.

COCKE, Sir Hugh, Kt., *cr.* 1929; A.C.A.; Councillor Petersfield R.D.C. since 1946 (Chairman, 1953-54); Liss Parish Council; Liss Parochial Church Council; Chairman of Hants and Isle of Wight Agricultural Wages Committee; Deputy Chairman, Hampshire Local Valuation Panel; *s.* of late Alfred Golding Cocke, Hampstead, and late Mary Louisa, *d.* of Richard Webb; *m.* Winifred Florence, *d.* of late A. E. Cumming. *Educ.:* Merchant Taylors' School, London. Joined A. F. Ferguson & Co., Chartered Accountants, Bombay, 1907; Bombay Corporation, 1919; Legislative Council, 1923-23; Honorary Presidency Magistrate; President, Bombay Chamber of Commerce, 1928 and 1932; Member of Legislative Assembly, 1924-32; Sheriff of Bombay, 1933. *Address:* Brookdean, Liss, Hants. *T.:* Liss 2207. *Club:* Oriental. [*Died* 27 *May* 1958.

COCKERILL, Brig.-Gen. Sir George Kynaston, Kt., *cr.* 1926; C.B. 1916; *b.* Newquay, Cornwall, 1867; 3rd *s.* of late Robert William Cockerill and Clara Sandys, *d.* of late Major-General Charles Pooley; *m.* 1900, Mildred (*d.* 1935), *y. d.* of late Frederick W. Jowers, of Wivelsfield, Sussex. *Educ.:* Cheltenham. Joined 2nd Queen's (R. W. Surrey) Regiment, 1888; Hazara Expedition, 1891 (medal with clasp); Intelligence Branch, Simla, 1892; special duty in Gilgit, Hunza, and Chitral, as Inspecting Officer, Kashmir troops; explored and mapped the eastern Hindu Kush and Western Karakoram 1892-95 and discovered Mt. Dasht-i-gul (25,868 ft.) (thanks of Govt. of India, and awarded the Macgregor Memorial Medal, United Service Institution of India); Intelligence Officer Chitral Relief Force, 1895; present at storming of Malakand Pass, passage of Swat River, and actions at Panjkora River and Mamagai (four times mentioned in Brigade Reports, thanks of C.-in-C., medal with clasp); officiating D.A.Q.M.G., Intelligence Branch, Simla, 1895-1899; Intelligence Officer, Headquarters, Tochi Field Force, 1897 (despatches, clasp); passed Staff Coll., 1899; D.A.A.G., South Africa, 1900-2 (despatches, Queen's medal with clasp, King's medal with two clasps, Bt.-Major); accompanied Royal Commission on Martial Law Sentences, South Africa, 1902; Staff Captain, D.A.Q.M.G., and Major, General Staff, War Office, 1902-7; Gold Medal, United Service Institution of India, 1906; specially promoted Major, Royal Fusiliers, 1907; British Technical Delegate, Hague Conference, 1907; retired, 1910; Lt.-Col. commanding 7th Royal Fusiliers, 1914; served European War, Deputy Director of Military Operations and Military Intelligence, and Director of Special Intelligence, 1915-19 (despatches, C.B., Bt. Colonel); contested Thornbury Division of Gloucestershire as a Unionist, Dec. 1910; M.P. (U.) for Reigate Division of Surrey, 1918-31. Hon. Director International League for the Protection of Horses, 1930-; Hon. Pres. St. Lukes-Woodside Hospital. F.R.G.S.; F.Z.S.; F.R.Hort.S. Commander of the Legion of Honour, Crown of Belgium and Crown of Italy, Star of the Sacred Treasure, Japan, and Grand Cross of St. Stanislas, Russia. *Publications:* Love's Universe, 1931; What Fools We Were, 1944; Late Harvest, 1946; and articles on military and political subjects. *Recreations:* golf, skating (bronze medallist), sculpture. *Address:* 19 Knightsbridge, S.W.1. *T.:* Sloane 4313. *Clubs:* Royal Thames Yacht; Royal Albert Golf (Montrose). [*Died* 19 *April* 1957.

COCKS, Charles Sebastian Somers, C.M.G. 1903; *b.* 20 Jan. 1870; *s.* of Hon. John Somers Cocks, *b.* of 5th Baron Somers. *Educ.:* Oratory School, Birmingham. Clerk in Foreign Office, 1894; Secretary to British Delegates to International Industrial Property Conference, and an Acting 3rd Secretary in Diplomatic Service, 1897; Secretary to Special Mission sent to Shanghai to negotiate a new Commercial Treaty with China, and an Acting 2nd Secretary in Diplomatic Service, 1901; returned to Foreign Office, 1902; Private Secretary to Viscount Cranborne, M.P., 1903, and to Earl Percy, M.P., 1903; Special Assistant Secretary Indian Foreign Department, 1904-6; returned to Foreign Office, 1906; resigned, 1910; an Assistant Censor at the War Office, 1914. Decorated for services in China. *Club:* Travellers'. [*Died* 10 *Feb.* 1951.

COCKS, Frederick Seymour, C.B.E. 1950; M.P. (Lab.) Broxtowe Division of Nottinghamshire since 1929; *b.* 25 Oct. 1882; *s.* of late Frederick Augustus Cocks, Inspector of Machinery, R.N., Plymouth; *m.* 1907, Hilda Catherine, *d.* of late Charles Derry, Plymouth; one *s.* one *d.* *Educ.:* Plymouth College. Contested Maidstone, 1923 and 1924; Member Joint Select Committee on Indian Constitutional Reform, 1933-34; Member Select Committee on Parliamentary Procedure, 1945-46; Leader of all-Party Parl. Deleg. to Greece, 1946; Chm. External Affairs Group of Parliamentary Labour Party, 1945-47; Mem. Parl. Deleg. to Italy, 1949; Mem. British deleg. to Consultative Assembly of Council of Europe at Strasbourg, and of Cultural and Scientific Cttee. of Assembly, 1949-50. *Publications:* The Secret Treaties, 1918; E. D. Morel: His Life and Work, 1920. *Recreations:* history, topography, travel. *Address:* 8 Wykeham Mansions, Rosendale Road, S.E.21. *T.:* Gipsy Hill 4274. [*Died* 29 *May* 1953.

CODDINGTON, Fitzherbert John Osbourne, M.A. (Oxon); LL.D. (Sheff.), *b.* 27 July 1881; *s.* of Edward Fitzherbert Coddington, *s.* of Capt. Joshua Coddington, R.E., Oldbridge, Co. Meath; *m.* 1923, Marjory Laycock; no *c.* *Educ.:* King Henry VIII School, Coventry; St. John's College, Oxford (Scholar); Sheffield University. Hons. Mathematical Mods. and Finals, 1901, 1903; Mathl. Master Willaston School, 1903-5; Mathl. Lecturer, Sheffield University, 1905-7; Mathl. and English Lecturer, Sheffield Training College, 1907-13; Certificate of Honour, Bar Final; First Class Honours, Sheffield University, LL.B. Final, 1912; LL.D. 1935; called, Inner Temple, 1912; Member of N.E. Circuit. Practised at 42 Bank Street, Sheffield, 1913-34; Stipendiary Magistrate of Bradford, 1934-50; Chm. of Convocation, Sheffield Univ., 1934-37; Trustee Bradford Civic Playhouse, 1937-50, Vice-Pres., 1951. Middle-weight Champion Oxford University, Water Polo and Swimming Team, Oxford University, 1902. *Publications:* Young Officer's Guide to Military Law; Young Officer's Guide to Air Force Law; Constable's Guide to the Laws of Evidence; Advice on Advocacy in the Magistrates Court, 1951; Advice on Advocacy in the Lower Courts, 1954; also articles, etc., in Magistrate, Journal of Criminal Science, Justice of the Peace, Aristotelian Soc. Pro., etc. *Recreations:* living and learning. *Address:* 1 Oak Villas, Bradford 8. *T.:* 41445. [*Died* 18 *March* 1956.

CODNER, Maurice Frederick, R.P.; R.O.I.; Portrait painter; Hon. Secretary Royal Society of Portrait Painters; Member Royal Institute of Oil Painters; *b.* 1888; 3rd *s.* of William Squires Codner, Abbots Kerswell, Devon; married; one *s.* *Educ.:* Stationers' Company School. Exhibitor R.A., R.P., R.O.I., R.I., N.E.A.C. and many galleries at home and abroad. Hon. Mention, Salon, Paris, 1938; portrait of Alderman Sir George Broadbridge, Bt., K.C.V.O., in his coronation robes; full-length portrait of King George VI in Field-Marshal's uniform and Garter robes, as Captain General of the H.A.C., for Armoury House, 1951 (last portrait painted of His late Majesty); portrait of Queen Elizabeth, the Queen Mother, 1952, which was awarded Silver Medal of the Salon, Paris, 1954. Served European War, 1914-18, France. Lieut. Royal North Devon Hussars. *Recreations:* riding and painting. *Address:* 26 Temple Fortune Hill, N.W.11. *T.:* Speedwell 4628. *Clubs:* Arts, Garrick.

[*Died* 10 *March* 1958.

CODRINGTON, Engineer-Commander Claude Alexander, R.N. (retired); J.P.; *b.* 1877; *s.* of late Alexander Codrington and *nephew* of late William Wyndham Codrington, Lord of Manor of Wroughton; *m.* 1917, Ethel May, *o. d.* of Charles E. de Wolf of Gayton Hall, Cheshire; (one *s.* died on Active Service Middle East, 1941), twin *d.* *Educ.:* Mannamead School, Plymouth; Central Technical College, S.W.; Earle's Marine Engineering Works, Hull. Served in H.M.S. Royal Arthur (flagship) during the Duke of Cornwall and York's visit to open Australian Commonwealth Parliament, 1901; in H.M.S. Renown during tour of the Prince and Princess of Wales to India, 1905-6; European War in 3rd Battle Squadron (assisted rescue of about half the survivors, about 50, of H.M.S. Formidable); and in 13th Destroyer Flotilla until surrender of German Fleet; Engineer-Commander, 1917. High Sheriff of Wilts., 1948. *Recreations:* fox-hunting, lawn tennis, golf. Joint Master V.W.H. (Cricklade) Foxhounds, 1920-29. *Address:* Wroughton House, near Swindon, Wilts. *T.:* Wroughton 316. *Club:* Junior Army and Navy. [*Died* 14 *Feb.* 1955.

CODY, Rev. Henry John, C.M.G. 1943; M.A., D.D., LL.D., D.C.L.; Archdeacon of York (Canada), 1909-19; Rector of St. Paul's Church, Toronto, 1899-1932; Minister of Education, Ontario, 1918-19; Chairman of Board of Governors of the Univ. of Toronto, 1923-32, Pres. and Vice-Chancellor, 1932-45, Chancellor, 1944-47, re-appointed to Board of Governors, 1950-56; Member of Senate (Chairman, 1932-45); Member of Board of Trustees of Royal Ontario Museum; Vice-President of Boards of Governors of Ridley College, St. Catharines, and Havergal College, Toronto; of British and Foreign Bible Soc., England, since 1938; of C.M.S. London, 1945; of Upper Canada Bible Society; Member of Advisory Board of the Royal Military College, Kingston, Ont., 1925-28, Chairman, 1932-34; of Executive Committee of Missionary Society of Church of England in Canada; of General Synod of Church of England; President 1944 of General Council of Boy Scouts of Canada; of Order of Golden Grain of China; Chairman of Ontario Royal Commission on Radium Treatment of Cancer, 1931; Chevalier of the Legion of Honour, France, 1935; St. Olaf Medal, Norway, 1947; F.R.S.C., 1935; F.R.S.A. London, 1936; Hon. Fellow of Toronto Academy of Medicine, 1937; Fellow Canadian and American Geographical Societies and Polish Institute of Arts and Sciences; *b.* 6 Dec. 1868; *m.* 1st, 1894, Florence L. (*d.* 1932), *d.* of late H. E. Clarke; 2nd, 1933, Barbara, *d.* of T. G. Blackstock, K.C., and *g.d.* of Geo Gooderham. *Educ.:* Galt Collegiate Institute; Toronto University; Wycliffe College. Ordained, 1893; Professor of Old Testament Exegesis and Church History, Wycliffe College, Toronto, 1894-99; Canon, St. Alban's Cathedral, Toronto, 1903, now Canon of St. James' Cathedral, Toronto; Member of University Commission, Ontario, 1905-6; Member of Ontario Commission on Unemployment, 1914-15; Hon. Chaplain of Queen's Own Rifles, Toronto, and Hon. Col. in Canadian Militia, 1913; Hon. Col. of Canadian Officers' Training Corps, University of Toronto; Efficiency Decoration for long service in Canadian Chaplain Service; Member of Provincial Parliament for North-East Toronto, 1918-20; Chairman of Commission on University Finances in Ontario, 1921; President National Conference of Canadian Universities, 1939-42; Hon. LL.D. McGill, 1928, Toronto, Manitoba, Western Ontario and Glasgow, 1934; Alberta, McMaster, Brown, 1935, Univ. of British Columbia, 1945; Rockford, Ill, 1948; Hon. D.C.L. Bishop's, Lennoxville, 1939; Hon. D.D. Queen's, Kingston; Trinity, Wycliffe and Knox Colleges, Toronto; Emmanuel, Saskatoon; King's, Halifax; Josiah Wood Lectures at Mount Allison University, New Brunswick, on Citizenship in Relation to the Empire, the Dominion and the University, 1938. *Address:* 6 Dale Ave., Toronto, Canada. *Club:* (President, 1935-36) York (Toronto).

[*Died* 27 *April* 1951.

COFFIN, Colonel Campbell, C.M.G. 1915; C.I.E. 1920; late R.E.; *b.* 23 Aug. 1867; *s.* of late General Sir I. C. Coffin, K.C.S.I.; *m.* 1895, Ethel, *d.* of late B. T. Ffinch, C.I.E. *Educ.:* Haileybury; R.M.A. Entered Army, 1886; Capt., 1896; Major, 1904; Lt.-Col. 1912; Col. 1916; served European War, 1914-18 (C.M.G.); Mesopotamia, 1916; India 1917-22 (C.I.E.); retired on Indian pension, 1922. *Address:* c/o Child & Co., 1 Fleet Street, E.C.4. [*Died* 1 *Sept.* 1952.

COFFIN, Maj.-Gen. Clifford, V.C. 1917; C.B. 1919; D.S.O. 1917; *y. s.* of late Lt.-Gen. Sir Isaac Campbell Coffin, K.C.S.I.; *b.* 10 Feb. 1870; *m.* 1894, Helen Douglas (*d.* 1949), *e.d.* of late Admiral Sir Thomas Sturges Jackson, K.C.V.O.; two *s.* two *d.* *Educ.:* Haileybury College; R.M. Academy, Woolwich. 2nd Lieut. Royal Engineers, 1888; Lieut.-Col. 1915; Brev.-Col. 1918; A.D.C. to the King, 1920-24; retired with the rank of Major-General, 1924; Col. Commandant, R.E., 1936-40; served South African War, 1899-1902 (despatches, Queen's medal and 4 clasps, King's medal and 2 clasps); European War, 1915-18 (V.C., C.B., D.S.O. and bar, despatches, Bt.-Col.). *Address:* c/o Glyn, Mills & Co., 1 Fleet St., E.C.4.

[*Died* 4 *Feb.* 1959.

COFFIN, Rev. Henry Sloane, D.D.; President Union Theological Seminary, New-York City, 1926-45, President Emeritus since 1945; *b.* New York City, 5 Jan. 1877; *s.* of Edmund Coffin and Euphemia Sloane; *m.* 1906, Dorothy Prentice Eells; one *s.* one *d.* *Educ.:* Yale University, B.A. 1897; M.A. 1900; New College, Edinburgh, 1897-99; University of Marburg, 1899; B.D. at Union Theological Seminary, 1900; Minister of the Bedford Park Presbyterian Church, New York City, 1900-5; Lecturer at Union Theological Seminary, 1904-1909; Associate Prof. of Pastoral Theology, 1909-1926; Minister of the Madison Avenue Presbyterian Church, 1905-26; Fellow of Yale Univ., 1921-45; Moderator of Presbyterian Church in the U.S.A. 1943-44; Lyman Beecher Lecturer, Yale, 1918; Warrack Lecturer, New College, Edinburgh, and the United Free Church Colleges at Glasgow and Aberdeen, 1926; Univ. Preacher, Yale, Princeton, Harvard, Columbia, Chicago, etc.; Joseph Cook Lecturer in China and India, 1946-47; Hon. D.D. New York, 1906; Yale, 1915; Harvard, 1922; Princeton 1925; Glasgow, 1926; Union College, 1928; Episcopal Theological School, 1935; Bowdoin College, 1944; L.L.D. Amherst, 1927; St. Andrews, 1934; Hamilton College, 1938; Litt.D. College of the Ozarks, 1931; Western Reserve, 1937; D.Theol. Marburg, 1930; Faculté libre de théologie Protestante, Paris, 1938; S.T.D., Jewish Theological Seminary, 1937. *Publications:* The Creed of Jesus,

1907; Social Aspects of the Cross, 1911; Editor of Hymns of the Kingdom of God, 1910 and 1924; University Sermons, 1914; Some Christian Convictions, 1915; The Ten Commandments, 1915; In a Day of Social Rebuilding, 1918; A More Christian Industrial Order, 1920; What is there in Religion?, 1922; The Portraits of Christ in the New Testament, 1926; What to Preach, 1926; The Meaning of the Cross, 1931; What Men are Asking, 1933; God's Turn, 1934; Religion Yesterday and To-day, 1940; The Public Worship of God, 1946; God Confronts Man in History; Communion through Preaching, 1952; A Half Century of Union Theological Seminary, 1896-1945, An Informal History, 1954. *Recreations:* walking, gardening. *Address:* Lakeville, Connecticut. *Club:* Century (New York). [*Died* 25 *Nov.* 1954.

COHALAN, Most Rev. Daniel, D.D.; Bishop of Cork (R.C.), since 1916; *b.* Kilmichael, Co. Cork, July 1858. *Educ.:* St. Vincent's Seminary, Cork; Maynooth College. Curate in Kilbrittain, Cork, 1883; Prof. in St. Finbarr's Seminary and Chaplain to Military Prison, 1884; Curate in Tracton, 1884; Professor of Theology in Maynooth, 1886-1914; Bishop of Vaga, and Assistant Bishop of Cork, 1914-16. *Publications:* Trinity College and the Trinity Commission, 1908; popular edition, Trinity College: its Income and its Value to the Nation, 1911; De Deo Uno et Trino, de Deo Creatore, 1909; De Incarnatione, 1910; De Sanctissima Eucharistia, 1913; a frequent contributor to the Irish Ecclesiastical Record, and Catholic Bulletin. *Address:* 32 South Terrace, Cork. [*Died* 24 *Aug.* 1952.

COHEN, Isaac Michael, R.P., R.O.I.; painter; *b.* Ballarat, Australia, 1884; *s.* of Michael Cohen; *m.* 1914, Edith (*d.* 1940), *d.* of Phillip Duke Mighell. *Educ.:* Melbourne. Studied Melbourne and Paris; awarded Travelling Scholarship of Victoria; silver and gold medal Paris Salon; Member of the Royal Society of Portrait Painters; Royal Institute of Oil Painters; Pastel Society; Society of Graphic Art; works in National Gallery of Victoria, Birkenhead Gallery, Orangetown Gallery, S.A., etc. *Address:* Langton House, 35 Palace Gate, W.8. *T.:* Western 5021. *Clubs:* Arts, Chelsea Arts. [*Died* 25 *Nov.* 1951.

COHEN, Reuben; retired from Registrarships, Nov. 1953; Registrar Middlesbrough, Stokesley and Guisborough County Courts, 1932-53, Stockton, 1933-53; West Hartlepool, 1949-53; J.P. County Durham, since 1938; Deputy Chairman, Durham Quarter Sessions, 1940-55; *b.* 1 July 1880; *s.* of Myer and Elizabeth Cohen; *m.* 1904, Maud Fine, Rhymney, Mon.; two *s.* *Educ.:* Stockton-on-Tees Grammar School. Admitted solicitor 1902. *Publication:* Briefs; A Jocular Jurisdictionary, 1903 (illustrated by author). *Recreations:* reading, sketching, alpine gardening. *Address:* Lynwood, 24 Richmond Road, Stockton-on-Tees. *T.:* 6272. *Club:* National Liberal. [*Died* 19 *Feb.* 1958.

COHEN, Sir Robert Waley, K.B.E., *cr.* 1920; Managing Director Shell Transport and Trading Co., Ltd.; Chairman Palestine Corporation, Ltd., and United British Oilfields of Trinidad, Ltd.; Director, English and Scottish Investors, Ltd.; Chairman of Ramsay Memorial Fellowship Trustees; Vice-Chairman of University College, London University; President of the United Synagogue; late Petroleum Adviser to the Army Council; *b.* 8 Sep. 1877; *s.* of late Nathaniel Louis Cohen, L.C.C.; *m.* 1904, Alice (*d.* 1935), *o. d.* of late Henry Edward Beddington; two *s.* one *d.* *Educ.:* Clifton; Emmanuel College Cambridge (Scholar). Connected with the Shell Company and its associates since 1901; Assoc. C.St.J. Order of the Insignia of St. Sava. *Recreation:* music. *Address:* Southampton Lodge, N.6. *T.:* Mountview 2202; Honeymead, Simonsbath, Minehead, Somerset. *T.:* Exford 242. *Clubs:* Athenæum, Reform, Royal Automobile. [*Died* 27 *Nov.* 1952.

COHN, Jefferson Davis; Honorary Captain in the British Army; *b.* London, 1881; *s.* of Herrman and Anita Cohn; *m.* 1st, Florence Grace, *o. d.* of Horatio Bottomley; 2nd, Marcelle Jenny, *o. d.* of George Favrel, Paris; 3rd, Helen Gleason, Metropolitan Opera, New York, *o. d.* of John Gleason, New York. *Educ.:* City of London School. Godson of the late Jefferson Davis, President of the Confederate States of America; mentioned in Commander-in-Chief's Despatches, 1917 and 1918; Mons Star; North Star, Sweden, 1913; Légion d'Honneur, 1917; Knight of Sweden, 1914. *Recreations:* yachting and racing. *Address:* 6 East 79 St., New York, U.S.A. *Clubs:* Royal Dorset Yacht (Weymouth); Royal Ulster Yacht (Bangor, Co. Down), etc. [*Died* 20 *Feb.* 1951.

COKE, Major Hon. Sir John (Spencer), K.C.V.O., *cr.* 1953 (C.V.O. 1946); Scots Guards, retired; Extra Gentleman Usher to the Queen since 1952 (Gentleman Usher in Ordinary, 1937-38, Extra Gentleman Usher, 1938-52, to King George VI); Equerry to Queen Mary, 1938-53; *b.* 30 Sept. 1880; 7th *s.* of 2nd Earl of Leicester; *m.* 1907, Hon. Dorothy Olive Lawson (*d.* 1937), *o. c.* of 1st Viscount Burnham; one *s.* two *d.* Served S. African War; European War, 1914-16. *Clubs:* Turf, Brooks's. [*Died* 23 *Dec.* 1957.

COKE, Commander Hon. Roger, A.F.C.; R.N. (retired); D.L.; J.P.; owner of Bayfield Hall, Holt, Norfolk; *b.* London, 28 Dec. 1886; 3rd *s.* of 3rd Earl of Leicester, G.C.V.O.; unmarried. *Educ.:* H.M.S. Britannia. Went to sea as naval cadet, 1903; served European War in Grand Fleet and Dardanelles till 1916; then transferred to R.N.A.S. and R.A.F. and served as squadron commander till end of war (despatches, A.F.C.); retired, 1919; promoted to Commander on retired list, 1927; A.D.C. to Prince Arthur of Connaught, S. Africa, 1920; served War of 1939-45 as Comdr. R.N. at home and abroad in Egypt, 1939-43. *Address:* Bayfield Hall, Holt, Norfolk. *Clubs:* White's, Bath. [*Died* 14 *Oct.* 1960.

COLAM, Sir Harold Nugent, Kt., *cr.* 1938; M.Inst.C.E.; B.A. (Camb.); *b.* 19 April 1882; *s.* of William Newby Colam; *m.* 1917, Enid Mary Colam; no *c.* *Educ.:* Dulwich College; Edinburgh Academy; Pembroke College, Cambridge. Jodhpur Bikaner Railway, India, 1904; Bombay Baroda and Central India Railway, 1911; R.N.V.R., 1916-19; Madras and Southern Mahratta Railway Co., 1919-38, Agent 1932-38. *Address:* c/o Lloyds Bank, 6 Pall Mall, S.W.1. *Club:* East India and Sports. [*Died* 4 *Oct.* 1956.

COLBAN, Erik, Hon. G.C.V.O. 1946; *b.* 16 October 1876; *s.* of Erik Colban, Captain in the Norwegian Army and Emilie Biermann; *m.* 1911, Karen Holter; one *s.* one *d.* *Educ.:* Univ. of Oslo. Studied law; passed examination, 1899; entered Foreign Service of Norway, 1903; held posts in Paris and Havre, 1905-6; Head of Consular Office in Foreign Ministry, 1907-8; Secretary of Legation at Stockholm, 1908-11; Consul General at Rio de Janeiro, 1911-16; Special Mission for the Foreign Ministry to London, 1917, and to London and Paris, 1918-19; entered the Secretariat of the League of Nations, 1919; Director of Administrative Commissions (Saar and Danzig) and Minorities Section, 1919-27; Director of Disarmament Section, 1928-30; Minister of Norway in Paris, 1930, in Brussels, 1930, and in Luxemburg, 1931; Norwegian Ambassador at the Court of St. James's, 1942-46, previously Minister 1934-46. Delegate of Norway to different sessions of the Assembly and the Council of the League of Nations, and to the Disarmament Conference,

1930-32; Head of Norwegian Deleg. to Preparatory Comn.: for Establishment of U.N. (Chm. one of main cttees.); on Trade and Employment (ctte. chm.); delegate to first Gen. Assembly of U.N. (cttee. chm.); Head of Norwegian Deleg. to Havana Conf. on Trade and Employment (cttee. chm.); Personal Representative of Secretary-General of U.N. with Commission for India and Pakistan, 1948-49; diplomatic adviser to U.N. Representative on Kashmir question, 1950. *Recreations:* travelling, country life. *Address:* c/o Foreign Ministry, Oslo. [*Died* 28 *March* 1956.

COLBY, Col. Cecil J. H. S.; *see* Spence-Colby.

COLBY, Charles W.; President of Northern Securities, Ltd.; *b.* Stanstead, P.Q., 1867; *e. s.* of late Hon. Charles C. Colby; *m.* 1897, Emma Frances, *d.* of late Walter B. Cobb. *Educ.:* Stanstead College; McGill University (B.A. 1887; LL.D. (Hon.) 1921; Harvard University (M.A. 1889, Ph.D. 1890); D.C.L. University of Bishop's College. Kingford Professor of History, McGill University, Montreal, 1895-1920; Chevalier of Legion of Honour; Fellow of Royal Historical Society. *Publications:* Canadian Types of the Old Régime; Champlain; Frontenac; Editor of Selections from the Sources of English History. *Recreations:* gardening, hill-climbing, fishing. *Address:* 1240 Pine Avenue, West Montreal. *Clubs:* Mount Royal, University (Montreal); York (Toronto); Century, Authors (New York). [*Died* 10 *Dec.* 1955.

COLBY, Sir Geoffrey Francis Taylor, K.C.M.G., *cr.* 1949 (C.M.G. 1947); *b.* 25 March 1901; *e. s.* of Francis Edward Albert Colby, F.R.C.S.; *m.* 1931, Lilian Florence Illingworth; two *d.* *Educ.:* Charterhouse; Clare College, Cambridge (Scholar). Administrative Officer, Nigeria, 1925; Principal Asst. Sec. (acting), 1939; Sec. Nigeria Supply Board, 1942; Director of Supplies, 1943; Administrative Secretary, Nigeria, 1945; Acting Chief Sec. to Govt. and Governor's Deputy on various occasions, 1945-47; Governor and C.-in-C., Nyasaland, 1948-56. *Recreations:* golf, fishing. *Address:* Hanlith Hall, Kirkby Malham, Skipton, Yorks. *T.:* Airton 214. *Club:* Royal Societies. [*Died* 22 *Dec.* 1958.

COLCHESTER-WEMYSS, Sir Francis, K.B.E., *cr.* 1920 (C.B.E. 1917) D.L.; *b.* 12 March 1872; *e. s.* of late Maynard W. Colchester-Wemyss; *m.* 1898, Maria Alice (*d.* 1940), 2nd *d.* of late Gen. R. W Disney Leith, C.B., of Glen-Kindie and Westhall, Aberdeenshire; two *s.* *Educ.:* Eton; Sandhurst. Late The Cameronians (Scottish Rifles) 1890-1903; served in England, India, and South Africa; during last war, member of Joint War Committee of the British Red Cross and St. John, and of its Demobilisation Board; Hon. Controller of Food in Auxiliary Hospitals in England and Wales. For many years Chairman and Vice-Chairman of Severn Conservancy Board; resigned, 1929; J.P. Glos., 1906-49; High Sheriff for Gloucestershire, 1919-20; Member of Wine and Food Society; President the Croquet Association; winner silver medal for Fly-dressing at London Fisheries Exhibition, 1905, and of several similar awards more recently; Member of Croquet Teams representing Great Britain sent by the Croquet Association to play against Australia and New Zealand, 1928-29 and 1935-36; collector of water-colours of Early English School; Lord of the Manors of Mitcheldean, Littledean, The Lea, and Basham. *Publications:* The Pleasures of the Table, 1931; many articles on Fishing, Fly-dressing (mostly in The Field), and Cooking and Wine. *Recreations:* formerly fishing, travelling, fly-dressing, good living, hunting, pig-sticking, polo, shooting, and croquet. *Address:* Wendover, Cheltenham. *T.:* Cheltenham 2156. *Clubs:* Saintsbury, Flyfisher's, Royal Automobile, Hurlingham; New (Cheltenham). [*Died* 28 *Feb.* 1954.

COLDSTREAM, Sir John, Kt., *cr.* 1938; *b.* 1877; *y. s.* of William Coldstream, Indian Civil Service, and Fanny, *e. d.* of Major O. St. George Anson, 9th Lancers; *m.* Phyllis Mary Hambly; one *s.* two *d.* *Educ.:* Edinburgh Academy; Worcester College, Oxford. Indian Civil Service, 1900; joined Punjab Commission, 1901; served as Assistant Commissioner in Punjab and Assistant to Political Agent, Patiala; Under-Secretary to Government, Punjab, 1906; Settlement Officer, Kulu, 1910; on Military Duty in France, 1914-16 (despatches); District and Sessions Judge, Punjab, 1916; Delhi, 1919; Legal Remembrancer and Secretary, Legislative Department, Punjab, 1923; Additional Judge, High Court, Lahore, 1926; Judge, High Court, Lahore, 1928-37; retired, 1937; Chief Minister, Kapurthala State, India until 1939. *Address:* 180 Ebury Street, S.W.1. *T.:* Sloane 1347. *Club:* Athenæum. [*Died* 19 *Aug.* 1954.

COLE, Viscount; Michael Galbraith Lowry Cole; Lt. Irish Guards; *b.* 25 Nov. 1921; *s.* of 5th Earl of Enniskillen, C.M.G.; unmarried. *Educ.:* Eton. *Address:* Florence Court, Enniskillen, N. Ireland. [*Died* 26 *Aug.* 1956.

COLE, Francis Joseph, F.R.S.; D.Sc. Oxon; Emeritus Professor of Zoology, University of Reading; *b.* 3 Feb. 1872; *s.* of William and Elizabeth Cole, Clapham, S.W.; *m.* Annie Clow, *d.* of John and Christina Menzies, Aberfeldy, Perthshire; one *s.* *Educ.:* Sir Walter St. John's School, Battersea; Jesus College, Oxford. Lecturer in Zoology, University of Liverpool, 1895-1906; Professor, University College (now University), Reading, 1906-39; Rolleston Prize, Oxford, 1902; Neill Gold Medal, Royal Society of Edinburgh, 1908. *Publications:* Numerous publications in Scientific Journals and Proceedings relating chiefly to Comparative Anatomy and the History of Zoology; an analysis of the Church of St. Mary, Cholsey, 1911; History of Anatomical Injections, 1921; History of Protozoology, 1926; Early Theories of Sexual Generation, 1930; Leeuwenhoek's Zoological Researches, 1937; Observationes Anatomicae Selectiores Amstelodamensium, 1938; Microscopic Science in Holland in the Seventeenth Century, 1938; Bibliographical Reflections of a Biologist, 1939; History of Comparative Anatomy from Aristotle to the Eighteenth Century, 1944, 1949; Dr. William Croone on Generation, 1947; History of Micro-dissection, 1951; The History of Albert Dürer's Rhinoceros in Zoological Literature, 1953; Bell's Law, 1955; Henry Power and the Circulation of the Blood, 1957; Harvey's Animals, 1957; Obiter Dicta Bibliographica, 1958. *Recreations:* mediæval architecture, bibliography. *Address:* Littlodown, Kingwood, Henley-on-Thames. *T.:* Rotherfield Greys 250. [*Died* 27 *Jan.* 1959.

COLE, George Douglas Howard; Chichele Professor of Social and Political Theory, Oxford, 1944-57; Fellow (Research Fellow, 1957) of Nuffield College, Oxford, and Hon. Fell. University College, Oxford, and of Balliol College, Oxford; President of the Fabian Society since 1952 (Chairman 1939-1946 and 1948-50); *s.* of George Cole, Ealing; *b.* 25 Sept. 1889; *m.* 1918, Margaret Isabel, *d.* of late Professor J. P. Postgate; one *s.* two *d.* *Educ.:* St. Paul's School; Balliol College, Oxford. Fellow of Magdalen College, Oxford, 1912-19; Fellow of University College, Oxford, and University Reader in Economics, 1925-44; Fellow of All Souls College, 1944-57; regular contributor to the New Statesman and Nation. *Publications:* The World of Labour, 1913; Self-Government in Industry, 1917; The Payment of Wages, 1918; Labour in the Commonwealth, 1918; Social Theory, 1920; Chaos and Order in Industry, 1920; Guild Socialism Restated,

1920; The Future of Local Government, 1921; Trade Unionism and Munitions, 1923; Workshop Organisation, 1923; Out of Work, 1923; Labour in the Coal-Mining Industry, 1923; Organised Labour, 1924; William Cobbett, 1925; Robert Owen, 1925; A Short History of the British Working-class Movement, 1789-1947 (revised ed. 1948); The Next Ten Years in British Social and Economic Policy, 1929: Literature and Politics, 1929; Gold, Credit and Unemployment, 1930; British Trade and Industry, Past and Future, 1931; Economic Tracts for the Times, 1932; The Intelligent Man's Guide through World Chaos, 1932; The Intelligent Man's Review of Modern Europe (with M. I. Cole), 1933; The Crooked World Versified, 1933; What Marx Really Meant, 1934; Studies in World Economics, 1934; A Guide to Modern Politics (with M. I. Cole), 1934; Some Relations between Political and Economic Theory, 1934; Principles of Economic Planning, 1935; The Simple Case for Socialism, 1935; The Condition of Britain (with M. I. Cole), 1937; The People's Front, 1937; Practical Economics, 1937; Persons and Periods, 1938; British Trade Unionism To-day, 1938; The Common People (with R. W. Postgate), 1938 (revised 1946); Socialism in Evolution, 1938; A Plan for Democratic Britain, 1939; British Working-class Politics, 1832-1914, 1941; Chartist Portraits, 1941; Europe, Russia, and the Future, 1941; Great Britain in the Post-War World, 1942; Fabian Socialism, 1943; The Means to Full Employment, 1943; Money, Present and Future, 1944; The Opinions of William Cobbett (with M. I. Cole), 1944; A Century of Co-operation, 1945; Building and Planning, 1945; Samuel Butler, 1947; The Intelligent Man's Guide to the Post-war World, 1947; Local and Regional Government, 1947; Meaning of Marxism, 1948; A History of the Labour Party from 1914, 1948; British Social Services, 1948; World in Transition (U.S.A. only), 1949; Essays in Social and Political Theory, 1950; Socialist Economics, 1950; The Co-operative Movement in a Socialist Society, 1951; (with A. W. Filson) British Working-Class Movements; Select Documents, 1789-1875, 1951-Introduction to Economic History, 1750-1951, 1952; Socialist Thought: Vol I, The Forerunners, 1789-1850, 1953, Vol. II, Marxism and Anarchism, 1954, Vol. III, The Second International, 1889-1914, 1955; Vol. IV, Communism and Social Democracy, 1958; Attempts at General Union, 1953; An Introduction to Trade Unionism, 1953; The Post-war Condition of Britain, 1956; Studies in Class Structure, 1955; The Case for Industrial Partnership, 1957. Several series of Film-strips dealing with British Industries 100 years ago: The Industrial Revolution, lives of Robert Owen, William Cobbett, and William Morris, 1946-47; and the following stories, etc., with his wife, Margaret Cole: The Brooklyn Murders, 1923; The Death of a Millionaire, 1925; The Blatchington Tangle, 1926; The Murder at Crome House, 1927; The Man from the River, 1928; Superintendent Wilson's Holiday, 1928; Poison in the Garden Suburb, 1929; Burglars in Bucks, 1930; Corpse in Canonicals, 1930; The Great Southern Mystery, 1931; Dead Man's Watch, 1932; The Death of a Star, 1932; A Lesson in Crime, 1933; The Affair at Aliquid, 1933; End of An Ancient Mariner, 1933; Death in the Quarry, 1934; Big Business Murder, 1935; Dr. Tancred Begins, 1935; Scandal at School, 1935; Last Will and Testament, 1936; The Brothers Sackville, 1936; Disgrace to the College, 1937; The Missing Aunt, 1937; Mrs Warrender's Profession, 1938; Off with her Head, 1938; Double Blackmail, 1939; Greek Tragedy, 1939; Wilson and Some Others, 1940; Murder in the Munition Works, 1940; Counterpoint Murder, 1941; Knife in the Dark, 1942; Toper's End, 1942; Death of a Bride, 1945. *Address:* 107 Oakwood Court, Kensington, W.14. *T.:* Western 1251; Nuffield College, Oxford. [*Died* 14 *Jan.* 1959.

COLE, Harold William, C.B. 1936; C.B.E., 1919; *b.* 1884; *e. s.* of late W. J. Cole, New Malden, Surrey; *m.* 1911, Maude, *y. d.* of late Robert Martin of Kingston; three *s.* *Educ.:* Tiffin's School, Kingston; King's College, London. Entered Civil Service, 1903; Secretary Petrol Control Committee, 1916; Chief Executive Officer Road Transport Board, 1918; Assistant Under-Secretary for Mines, 1920-30 and Director of Petroleum Department, Board of Trade, 1929-30; Principal Assistant Secretary and Deputy Under-Secretary for Mines, 1930-40; Director General of House Coal Distribution (Emergency) Scheme, Aug. 1940-July 1953. *Address:* Little Ripley House, Ripley, Surrey. [*Died* 3 *March* 1959.

COLE, Maj.-Gen. Sir Herbert Covington, K.B.E., *cr.* 1947 (C.B.E. 1918); C.B. 1944; *s.* of Thos. Cole, Finchley; *m.* Marjorie Alice, *d.* of L. Stephen Hogben, Barnes, S.W.; one *d.* Land Agent to War Office, 1908; Chief Valuer and Compensation Officer War Office, 1916; temp. Captain, 1914; Major, 1916; Lieut.-Colonel, 1917; Colonel, 1918; Brigadier, 1939; Maj.-Gen., 1940; served during European War, 1914-18, as Deputy Director of Hirings and Requisitions, B.E.F., France; Controller of Huts and Building Materials Section of Surplus Government Property Disposal Board, War Office, 1919; Member of French Section of above Board, 1922; Chief Land Agent and Valuer, War Office, 1925-39; Comptroller of Lands, War Office, 1939; President of Claims Commission and Director of Hirings, B.E.F., France, Sept. 1939-40; President of Claims Commission, War Office, 1940-48; retired, 1948. Member of Land Agents Society; late Pres. of Royal Institution of Chartered Surveyors; late Pres. of International Federation of Surveyors; F.R.G.S. Commander Legion of Merit (U.S.A.); Officer Legion of Honour. *Recreations:* golf, tennis. *Address:* Villa Sicard, St. Jean Cap Ferrat, France (A-M). *Club:* Union. [*Died* 9 *April* 1959.

COLE-HAMILTON, Lt.-Col. C. G.; *see* Hamilton.

COLEBATCH, Hon. Sir Hal Pateshall, Kt., *cr.* 1927; C.M.G. 1923; M.L.C. W. Australia, 1912-23 and since 1940; *b.* Herefordshire, 29 March 1872; *s.* of G. P. Colebatch, late of Goolwa, S.A.; *m.* 1896, Mary Maud (*d.* 1940), *d.* of V. Saunders of Truro, S.A.; two *s.*; *m.* 1944, Marion Frances, *d.* of Hon. Sir Frank Gibson; one *s.* *Educ.:* State School, Goolwa. Came to Australia, 1878; journalist; Mayor of Northam, W.A., 1909-12; late Minister for Education, Minister for Justice, Minister for North-West, ex-Premier of Western Australia; Agent-General for West Australia, 1923-27, and 1933-1939; Member of Commonwealth Constitution Royal Commission, 1927-28; Member of Commonwealth Senate, 1928-33; Member of Council of Imperial Society of Knights Bachelor. *Publications:* Western Australia, 1829-1929. *Recreations:* bowls, chess. *Address:* Perth, Western Australia. *Clubs:* Savage; West Australian, Northam (Perth); New South Wales (Sydney). [*Died* 12 *Feb.* 1953.

COLEGATE, Sir Arthur, Kt., *cr.* 1955; Chairman Wright Saddle Co. Ltd.; Director British Overseas Stores Ltd. and other companies; President Rural District Councils Association; Vice-President Midland Union of Conservative Associations; *yr. s.* of late R. Colegate, Sutton, Surrey; *m.* 1917, Winifred Mary (*d.* 1955), *d.* of Sir William Worsley, 3rd Bt., and *widow* of Capt. Francis P. C. Pemberton, 2nd Life Guards; four *d.* *Educ.:* University College, London. Formerly Civil Servant before becoming a Director of Brunner Mond & Co. till 1927; Pres. Industrial Property Committee of International Chamber of Commerce, 1925-29; a Governor of Harper Adams Agricultural College, 1941-47; contested Sowerby Div. of W. R. Yorks, 1929; M.P. (C.) Wrekin Div. of Shropshire, 1941-1945; prospective Unionist candidate for Burton-on-Trent div. of Staffs., May 1947; M.P. (C.) Burton Division of Staffordshire, 1950-55. *Recreations:* lawn tennis, sailing. *Address:* Hill Grove, Bembridge, Isle of Wight; 12 Carlton Mansions, Holland Park Gardens, W.14. *Clubs:* Carlton; Bembridge Sailing (Bembridge). [*Died* 10 *Sept.* 1956.

COLEMAN, D'Alton Corry, C.M.G. 1946; Hon. LL.D., Manitoba, 1932; Hon. D.C.L., Bishop's Univ., 1937; Chairman and President, Canadian Pacific Railway Co., 1942-47, retired; Director: Canadian Pacific Railway Co., Metropolitan Life Insurance Co., Odeon Theatres of Canada, Canadian Arena Co., Canadian Hockey Club; Member: Canadian Committee, Empire Trust Company; *b.* Carleton Place, Ontario, 9 July 1879; *s.* of James Coleman and Mary Jane Doherty; *m.* 1st, 1906, Anna (*d.* 1920), *d.* of Alexander D. Grant, Calgary; two *s.*; 2nd, 1922, Florence Mary, *d.* of William J. Lynch, I.S.O., Ottawa. Private Secy., Hon. George A. Cox, Toronto, 1897; Editor, Belleville Daily Intelligencer, 1898-99; entered service Canadian Pacific Railway at Fort William, Ont., 1899; subsequently stationed Winnipeg, Cranbrook, B.C., Nelson, B.C., Vancouver, Calgary, and Montreal; K.G.St.J.; Vice-President Champlain Soc. *Recreations:* collector, Canadiana. *Address:* 3940 Côte des Neiges Road, Montreal, Quebec. *Clubs:* Mount Royal, Saint James's (Montreal); Manitoba (Winnipeg); Ranchmen's (Calgary); Vancouver (Vancouver); Century Association (New York). [*Died* 17 *Oct.* 1956.

COLEMAN, Herbert Cecil, C.B.E. 1949; M.C. 1918; *b.* 28 Jan. 1893; *s.* of late John H. Coleman; *m.* 1928, Gladys Nora, *d.* of late Arthur W. Salmon. *Educ.:* Christ's Hospital. Served European War, 1914-18, with 9th Bn. Royal Sussex Regt. (despatches, M.C.). Entered Ministry of Pensions, 1919; Assistant Secretary, 1945; Accountant-General, 1951; Under-Secretary, 1953-56. *Address:* Eastleigh, The Ridgeway, Oxshott, Surrey. *T.:* Oxshott, 2331. *Club:* National Liberal. [*Died* 22 *Oct.* 1956.

COLEMAN, Rt. Rev. John Aloysius; Bishop of Armidale, (R.C.), 1932-48; *b.* Mount Melleray, Ireland, 1887. Went to Australia 1912; coadjutor Bishop of Armidale, N.S.W., 1929. [*Died* 22 *Dec.* 1947.

COLEMAN, Dr. Leslie Charles, C.I.E. 1931; *b.* Ontario, Canada. *Educ.:* University of Toronto; University of Göttingen. Mycologist and Entomologist to Government of Mysore, 1908-13; Director of Agriculture in Mysore, 1913-26 and 1927; Professor, University of Toronto, 1926-27. *Publications:* numerous scientific papers and bulletins dealing with Plant Pathology, Entomology, Agriculture. *Recreations:* tennis, shooting. [*Died* 14 *Sept.* 1954.

COLERIDGE, 3rd Baron (*cr.* 1873); **Geoffrey Duke Coleridge;** *b.* 23 July 1877; *o. s.* of 2nd Baron and Mary, (*d.* 1940), *e. d.* of late John F. Mackarness, D.D., Bishop of Oxford; *S.* father, 1927; *m.* 1904, Jessie, *y. d.* of late Evelyn Mackarness of Lahard, Co. Cavan; three *s.* *Educ.:* Eton; Trinity College, Oxford (B.A.). Captain 4th (Reserve) Batt. Devonshire Regt. *Heir:* *s.* Hon. Richard Duke Coleridge, C.B.E. *Address:* The Chanter's House, Ottery St. Mary. Devon *T.:* Ottery St. Mary 5. [*Died* 27 *March* 1955.

COLERIDGE, Hon. Gilbert James Duke, M.A.; J.P.; Assistant Master Crown Office, Royal Courts of Justice, 1892-1921; *b.* London, 15 Feb. 1859; *y. s.* of late Lord Chief Justice and Jane, *d.* of Rev. George Turner Seymour; *m.* 1st, Marion (*d.* 1917), *d.* of late Duncan Darroch of Gourock and Torridon; one *s.*; 2nd, 1921, Winifred, *o. d.* of Pierpoint Mitchell, Gateways, Beaconsfield. *Educ.:* Eton; Trinity College, Oxford. Chairman, The Royal Skating Club; V.P. Modern Churchmen's Union; V.P., R.B.A. Arts Club; exhibited sculpture in the R.A.; executed plaque portraits of S. T. Coleridge at Jesus College, Cambridge, Nicholas Murray Butler at Columbia University, N.Y., the late Viscount Hanworth at the Record Office, Charles Lamb at Christ's Hospital, Horsham, and the late Dean of Westminster at Charterhouse. *Publications:* An Instinctive Criminal; Eton in the Seventies; Pan's People, 1923; Some and Sundry, 1931; Pygmalion and other poems, 1935; joint-author with Hon. Mrs. Gilbert Coleridge of Jan van Elselo. *Recreations:* skating, sculpture, golf, rowed in Eton VIII., 1878. *Address:* Haverfield House, Kew Green, Surrey. *T.:* Richmond 5155. *Club:* (Hon. Member) Athenæum. [*Died* 6 *Nov.* 1953.

COLERIDGE, General Sir John Francis Stanhope Duke, G.C.B. *cr.* 1940 (K.C.B. *cr.* 1933; C.B. 1921); C.M.G. 1918; D.S.O. 1916; *b.* 25 April 1878; *s.* of late P. D. Coleridge, R.M.L.I.; *m.* 1907, Marjorie Mary Kemball Cook; two *d.* *Educ.:* Wellington; Sandhurst. Indian Army; served Tibet, 1903-4 (medal and clasp); N.E. Frontier of India, 1911-12 (medal and clasp, despatches); European War, 1914-18 (D.S.O. and bar, Bt. Lt.-Col., C.M.G., Bt. Col., despatches); N.W. Frontier of India, 1930-32 (despatches, clasp); N.W. Frontier of India, 1936-37-38-39-40 (despatches, medal and clasp); Comm. Infantry Brigade, 1917-18; on Gen. Staff Army Headquarters, India, 1919-1923; Assistant Commandant, Staff College, Quetta, 1923-25; Maj.-Gen., 1925; Military Secretary Army Headquarters, India, 1926-1930; Commander, Kohat District, 1930; Peshawar District, 1930-33; Secretary Military Department, India Office, 1933-36; A.D.C. General to the King, 1936-40; G.O.C.-in-C., Northern Command, India, 1936-40; Col. 8th Gurkha Rifles, 1925-49; 2/1st Punjab Regt., 1932-47; Hon. Col. 7th Bn. Devonshire Regt., 1941-46; Lt.-Gen. 1932; General, 1936; retd. 1940. *Recreations:* fishing and shooting. *Address:* Sedgecombe House, Farnham, Surrey. *T.:* Farnham 5668. *Club:* United Service. [*Died* 3 *Nov.* 1951.

COLERIDGE, Wilfrid Duke; *b.* 6 Oct. 1889; *s.* of late Hon. Gilbert Coleridge; *m.* 1923, Frances Mary, *d.* of late Thomas Walker; no *c.* *Educ.:* Eton; Trinity College, Oxford. Called to the Bar, 1913. Served European War, 1914-18, last 2 years in France; Captain 7th City of London Regiment. Clerk of Arraigns Central Criminal Court, 1929; Deputy Clerk of the Court, 1941; Clerk of the Central Criminal Court, 1949-55. Clerk of the Peace for the City of London and Borough of Southwark, 1949-55. *Recreations:* skating, Gold Medallist (English style) N.S.A.; golf; rowed Eton Eight 1906, Trial Eights, Oxford, 1910. *Address:* 25 Kensington Court Gardens, W.8. *T.:* Western 2974. *Clubs:* Athenæum; Leander (Henley on Thames); Royal Skating. [*Died* 31 *May* 1956.

COLES, Major William Hewett, D.S.O. 1918; late Asst. Sec., Home Office; retd. 1948; U.K. Representative on Opium Advisory Committee, League of Nations (Vice-President, 1938; President, 1939); U.K. Representative on United Nations Narcotics Commission; Member of Poisons Board; late The Middlesex Regiment; *b.* 19 May 1882; *e. s.* of Thomas Coles; *m.* 1918, Marjorie Hilda, *y. d.* of late H. C. Goff; one *d.* Served European War, 1914-18 (despatches twice, D.S.O.); Jubilee Medal, 1935; Coronation Medal, 1937. *Address:* Ellesmere, Camborne Road, Sutton, Surrey. *T.:* Vigilant 6266. *Club:* Junior Army and Navy. [*Died* 9 *Dec.* 1955.

COLETTE; authoress; Grand-Officer Legion of Honour; President of the Académie Goncourt; *b.* 1873; *m.* 1st, H. Gauthier-

Villars (marriage dissolved); 2nd, 1912, Henry de Jouvenel (marriage dissolved); one *d.*; 3rd, 1935, Maurice Goudeket. *Publications:* Aventures quotidiennes; La Femme cachée; Le Blé en herbe, roman; L'Envers du Music Hall; La Chambre éclairée; Sept dialogues de bêtes (trans.: Creatures Great and Small, 1951); Les Vrilles de la vigne; La Retraite sentimentale, roman; L'Ingénue libertine, roman; La Vagabonde, roman; l'Entrave, roman (suite à La Vagabonde); La Paix chez les bêtes; Les Heures longues; Dans la foule; Mitsou, ou Comment l'esprit vient aux filles, roman; Prrou, Poucette et quelques autres; Chéri, roman (Eng. trans. 1930); Rêverie de Nouvel An; Celle qui en revient; La Maison de Claudine (trans.: My Mother's House, 1953); La Fin de Chéri, roman (Eng. trans. 1933); also Chéri and The Last of Chéri (new trans.), 1951; La Naissance du jour, roman; Le Voyage égoïste, recueil; La Seconde, roman; Sido ou les points cardinaux (Eng. trans. 1953); Ces plaisirs; Prisons et Paradis; La Chatte, roman, 1933 (Eng. trans. 1953); Duo, roman; Mes apprentissages (mémoires); Le Toutounier; Bella Vista; Gigi (Eng. trans. 1953); Le Fanal Bleu: Discours de réception; Chambre d'hôtel (trans.: Chance Acquaintances, 1952); Journal à Rebours; Le Képi; Mes cahiers; Trois-Six-Neuf; Broderie ancienne; Nudité; Paris de ma Fenêtre; Belles Saisons; Pour un herbier; Trait pour trait; Journal Intermittent; Julie de Carneilhan (Eng. trans. 1952); L'Étoile Vesper; En Pays connu. La Jumelle noire, 4 vols. de critique dramatique; (Avec M. Willy): Claudine à l'école; Claudine à Paris; Claudine en ménage; Claudine s'en va. Théâtre (avec Léopold Marchand); La Vagabonde, pièce en quatre actes; Chéri, pièce en quatre actes. *Address:* rue de Beaujolais, Paris (1er). [*Died* 3 *Aug.* 1954.

COLGRAIN, 1st Baron, *cr.* 1946; of Everlands, **Colin Frederick Campbell,** J.P., Kent; *b.* 1866; *e. s.* of G. W. Campbell, who was a younger son of Colin Campbell of Colgrain; *m.* 1890, Lady Angela Mary Alice (*d.* 1939), 2nd *d.* of 4th Earl of Harrowby; two *s.* two *d.* *Educ.:* Eton. Past Governor, The London Assurance; President of British Bankers' Association, 1938-46; Chairman Telegraph Construction & Maintenance Co., Ltd.; Director: of National Provincial Bank, Ltd. (Chairman, 1933-46); The London Assurance. *Heir:* *s.* Hon. Donald Swinton Campbell, M.C. *Address:* Everlands, Sevenoaks. *T.:* 3303. *Club:* Carlton. [*Died* 3 *Nov.* 1954.

COLIVET, Michael Patrick; General Housing Inspector, Local Govt. Dept., 1945; *b.* May 1884; *s.* of Capt. John Colivet, Jersey, Channel Islands, and Ann Kinnerk, Askeaton, Co. Limerick; *m.* 1912, Anna Hartigan (*d.* 1921), Limerick; one *s.* two *d.*; *m.* 1928, Una Garvey, Kilrue, Co. Galway; one *s.* one *d.* *Educ.:* St. Joseph's Seminary, Galway. Member Dail Eireann, Limerick City, Dec. 1918-21; Limerick City and East Limerick, 1921-23; I.R.A. 1914-23; Manager Shannon Foundry, Limerick, 1910-22. Chairman, Irish Housing Board, 1932-45. *Address:* 65 Brighton Square, Rathgar, Dublin. [*Died* 4 *May* 1955.

COLLETT, Charles Benjamin, O.B.E. 1918; *b.* 1871; *m.* 1896, Ethelwyn May (*d.* 1923), *d.* of Rev. Henry Simon. *Educ.:* Merchant Taylors' School. Pupil, Maudslay Sons & Field, Marine Engineers, 1887-93; entered service of Great Western Railway, 1893; Manager Swindon Locomotive Works, 1913-20; Chief Mechanical Engineer, Great Western Railway, 1921-41; retired, 1941; M.I.Mech.E., 1920-41; M.Inst.C.E., 1922-41; J.P., 1921-38. Member Institute of Experimental Metaphysics, Society for Psychical Research, and London Metapsychical Group. *Address:* Melrose, 32 The Downs, Wimbledon. [*Died* 23 *Aug.* 1952.

COLLEY, Robert D.; *see* Davies-Colley.

COLLIER, Constance; Actress; *b.* 1880; *d.* of A. C. Hardie; *m.* Julian L'Estrange. First appeared on stage at age of 4; first London appearance, Criterion, 1893; engaged by Beerbohm Tree, 1902, and remained in all 12 years at His Majesty's Theatre, appearing as Cleopatra, Nancy Sykes, Viola, Juliet, among other parts; had many other London successes; first appearance in America, 1908; returned to America several times, playing Shakespearean and other rôles. Has acted as producer for Camille, Peter Ibbetson, Hay Fever, Happy Families, etc. Film career began, 1915; has appeared in many pictures. *Publication:* Harlequinade: The Story of my Life, 1929; libretto, Peter Ibbetson (opera); also collaborated on 3 plays with Ivor Novello. *Address:* 157 West 57th St., New York City, U.S.A. [*Died* 25 *Apr.* 1955.

COLLIER, William Douglas; Queen's and Lord Treasurer's Remembrancer since 1948; *b.* 1 Feb. 1894; *s.* of William Reid Collier and Anne White of Gosforth, Northumberland; *m.* 1942, Agnes Cowan Black Murray; one *s.* one *d.* *Educ.:* Newcastle on Tyne Royal Grammar School. Entered Civil Service, 1913; served European War, 1914-19, Royal Scots in Gallipoli, Northumberland Fusiliers in France; Captain and Adjutant. Appointed Chief Executive Officer, H.M. Exchequer, Scotland, 1942. *Recreation:* golf. *Address:* 42 Kirkhill Road, Edinburgh 9. *T.:* Edinburgh 42148. *Clubs:* Prestonfield Golf, Gullane Golf, Royal Scots (Edinburgh). [*Died* 24 *Aug.* 1953.

COLLIN, Annie Rosalie, C.B.E. 1928; Founder of Friends of the Poor, 42 Ebury Street (Hon. Secretary 1906-45); *b.* 1852; *d.* of George Franklin Collin, Henham, Essex. *Address:* Parkfield, Kingston Hill, Kingston, Surrey. [*Died* 15 *July* 1957.

COLLINDRIDGE, Frank, C.B.E. 1950; J.P. 1938; M.P. (Lab.) Barnsley, 1938-51; Comptroller of H.M. Household, 1946-51; member of Exec. of Mine-workers' Federation of Great Britain; Parliamentary Private Sec. to Secretary for Mines (D. R. Grenfell, M.P.), 1941-42; Parliamentary Private Sec. to Parliamentary Sec. Mines (T. Smith, M.P.), 1942-43. Delegate Empire Parliamentary Association, Australia-New Zealand, 1944; a Lord Commissioner of the Treasury, 1945-1946. Former Chairman Wombwell Urban District Council. *Address:* House of Commons, S.W.1. [*Died* 16 *Oct.* 1951.

COLLINGWOOD, Arthur, F.R.C.O., F.T.C.L.; late Dean of Faculty of Music, University of Saskatchewan, Saskatoon, Canada; *b.* Halifax, Yorkshire, 1879; *m.* 1900, Margaret Walker, *d.* of Baillie Peter Hill, Bo'ness; two *d.* *Educ.:* privately. Member of Council, Incorporated Society of Musicians; Member of Council of British Federation of Music Festivals; Lecturer in Music, W.E.A., Marischal College, University, Aberdeen, 1923-1930. *Publications:* Church music, songs and part-songs, many articles to Music Journals. *Recreations:* travel and reading. *Address:* 3400 Ridgewood Avenue, Montreal, Canada. *T.:* A.T. 2893. [*Died* 22 *Jan.* 1952.

COLLINGWOOD, Brig.-Gen. Clennell William, C.M.G. 1918; D.S.O. 1916; late R.A.; *b.* 29 April 1873; 2nd *s.* of late Maj.-Gen. Clennell Collingwood, R.A.; *m.* 1906, Nina Phyllis, *o. d.* of Harry Pollock; one *s.* *Educ.:* abroad; Royal Military Academy, Woolwich. 2nd Lieut. R.A. 1892; Lieut. 1895; Capt. 1900; Major, 1914; Lt.-Col. 1917; Temp. Brig.-Gen., 1917; served abroad at Malta, Quetta, and Bermuda; European War, 1915-18 (D.S.O., Bt. Lt.-Col., C.M.G., Bt. Col.); Assistant Director of Artillery, 1920-24; Brigade Commander 1st Air Defence Brigade, 1924-28; retired pay, 1928. *Address:* The Lawn, Brenchley, Kent. [*Died* 5 *April* 1960.

COLLINS, Sir Archibald (John), Kt., *cr.* 1955; D.S.O. 1918; M.C. 1918; Consulting Physician, in private practice, Australia, for many years; *b.* 19 June 1890; *s.* of James Patrick and Annie Maria Collins; *m.* 1920, Clotilde Donnelly; two *s.* *Educ.:* University of Sydney (1st Cl. Hons., M.B., Ch.M.). House Doctor, Roy. Prince Alfred Hosp., Sydney, 1913-15. Served European War, 1915-19: 1st A.I.F., Egypt and France (D.S.O., M.C., despatches). Roy. Prince Alfred Hospital: Med. Supt., 1920-23; Hon. Asst. Physn., Hon. Physn., 1923-50; Hon. Cons. Physn., 1950-; Hon. Physn., R.A.N., 1927-. Foundation Fell., R.A.C.P. Fell. of Senate, Univ. of Sydney, 1935-54. Pres. Federal Council, B.M.A. *Publications:* numerous articles in Med. Jl. of Australia. *Recreations:* golf, bowls, surfing. *Address:* 185 Macquarie St., Sydney, N.S.W.; 65 Springdale Rd., Killara, Sydney, N.S.W. *T.:* BW 8141. *Club:* Australian (Sydney). [*Died* 24 *June* 1955.

COLLINS, Arthur; in practice in Westminster as Financial Adviser to Public Authorities; *b.* Bury, 17 March 1880; *m.* Mary, *d.* of late Robert Fielding, Bispham; one *s.* two *d.* *Educ.:* Bury Grammar School (Kay Scholarship); Owens College (Manchester University). Financial officer with various public bodies since 1900; City Treasurer of Birmingham till 1921; President of Institute of Municipal Treasurers and Accountants, 1922 (First prizeman, Final examination, 1905); Society of Incorporated Accountants (medallist, Final examination, 1904); Fellow of Institute of Public Administration, Fellow of Institute of Arbitrators, and other professional bodies; Financial witness in Private Bill proceedings in Parliamentary Cttee. Rooms; Mem. of various Departmental Cttees. on National and Local Government administrative matters; advised on organisation of civic departments in a number of counties and towns at home and overseas. Travelled on Municipal Administrative research work throughout South Africa, America, and Canada; Representative of British Local Government Finance at international congresses in various centres abroad; in U.S.A. and Canada for Ministry of Information, 1943; Mayor of Bromley, Kent, 1944-45; Alderman; Hon. Freeman; Chm. of Conservators of Hayes Common. Chm. Bromley Group Hospital Management Committee, National Health Service, 1948-52. *Publications:* Organisation and Audit of Local Authorities Accounts; Municipal Finance for Students; Municipal Internal Audits; The Ratepayers' Money, etc. *Recreations:* golf, music. *Address:* 15 Old Queen Street, Westminster, S.W.1. *T.:* Whitehall 7333; The Orchard, 20 Orchard Road, Bromley, Kent; Summerfield, Fourth Avenue, Frinton-on-Sea. *Clubs:* Carlton, National. [*Died* 26 *July* 1952.

COLLINS, Bernard Abdy, C.I.E., 1926; *b.* 17 Feb. 1880; *s.* of H. Abdy Collins, M.R.C.S., L.C.P.; *m.* 1st, 1912, Beryl Lynch; divorced, 1923; one *s.* one *d.*; 2nd, 1929, Bethe Watson; one *s.* two *d.* *Educ.:* Malvern; B.N.C., Oxford. Passed I.C.S. exam., 1903; arrived in India, 1904; Under-Secretary to the Govt. of Bengal, 1909-10; Govt. of Bihar and Orissa, 1912-13; Registrar of Co-operative Societies, 1913-18; India Office, 1916-17; Indian Munitions Board, 1918-19; Director of Industries Bihar and Orissa, 1920-26; Education Secretary Bihar and Orissa, 1922-26; Director-General of Commerce and Industry, Haiderabad state, 1927-33; retired from I.C.S., 1933; Ministry of Home Security, 1941-45. Managing Director Psychic News. *Publication:* Death is not the End, 1939; The Cheltenham Ghost, 1948. *Recreation:* croquet. *Address:* 57 De Parys Avenue, Bedford. *Club:* English-Speaking Union. [*Died* 22 *Oct.* 1951.

COLLINS, Dale; author; *b.* Sydney, Australia, 1897; *s.* of late Michael Joseph Collins, M.D., and late Esther Collins, Melb., Australia; *m.* 1927, Aileen (*d.* 1933), *d.* of late James Edmonstone, Melb., and late Mrs. A. de Gruchy, Kingston-on-Thames; *m.* 1939, Kathleen, *d.* of G. S. Pratt, Northchurch, Herts; two *d.* *Publications:* Seatracks of the Speejacks, the story of the First Motor-Boat Voyage around the World; *Fiction:* Ordeal; The Haven; The Sentimentalists; Vanity Under the Sun; Idolaters; The Fifth Victim; Rich and Strange; Jungle Maid; Lost; Vulnerable; The Mutiny of Madame Yes; Race the Sun; Utility Baby; Far-off Strands; Bright Vista; Ah, Promised Land!; A Sister for Susan; Wings of Chance; The Happy Emigrants; Simple Simon Smith; Victoria's My Home Ground; By The Waters of Galilee. *For Children:* The Voyage of the Landship; Robinson Carew, Castaway; Coral Sea Adventure; Storm over Samoa. *Dramatic Works:* Ordeal, 1924; Romantic Ladies, 1935; Alas, Poor Ghost! *Address:* c/o Commonwealth Bank, Collins St., Melbourne, Australia. *Club:* Savage. [*Died* 4 *March* 1956.

COLLINS, Sir D(aniel) George, Kt., *cr.* 1931; D.L.; *b.* 1869; *o. s.* of Daniel Collins, Pembroke Dock; *m.* 1890, Frances Upton; (one *s.* decd.); *m.* 1904, Elizabeth Margaret Corneille; one *s.* *Educ.:* King's Coll. Civil Service, 1886-89; started as manufacturing silversmith, 1890; Lee Vestry, 1891; Corporation, City of London, 1899-1938; Chm.: Cattle Markets, 1910-14; Bridge House Estates, 1920; City of London Freemans School, 1925; Chm. City Lands and Chief Commoner, 1929; Sheriff of City of London, 1930, Alderman, 1931-38; Freedom of Pembroke, 1931; Officier Légion d'Honneur, 1931; Officier Académie Française, 1904; Order of Nile, 1929; Star of Afghanistan, 1930. *Address:* Chantreys, Downview Rd., Barnham, Sussex. *T.:* Eastergate 224. [*Died* 10 *May* 1959.

COLLINS, Maj.-Gen. (Hon. Lt.-Gen.) Sir Dudley Stuart, K.B.E., *cr.* 1941; C.B. 1937; D.S.O. 1916; *b.* 1881; *s.* of Henry M. Collins, Gracehill, Frankston, Australia; *m.* 1909, Edith, 2nd *d.* of F. A. Collins, Trelawney, Torquay. Served S. Africa, 1901-02; European War, 1914-16 (despatches, D.S.O. with bar, Brevet Lt.-Col.); Chief Engineer, Southern Command, 1931-35; Director of Fortifications and Works, War Office, 1935-39; Deputy Quartermaster-General, 1939-41; retired, 1941; Colonel Commandant R.E., 1940-49. *Address:* 8 Chivelston, Wimbledon Parkside, S.W. 19. [*Died* 12 *June* 1959.

COLLINS, Admiral Sir Frederick E.; *see* Edward-Collins, Adm. Sir G. F. B.

COLLINS, Sir George; *see* Collins, Sir D. G.

COLLINS, Sir Godfrey Ferdinando Stratford, K.C.I.E., *cr.* 1945 (C.I.E. 1931); C.S.I. 1941; O.B.E. 1919; I.C.S. retired; *b.* 3 Nov. 1888; 2nd *s.* of F. S. Collins, Lincoln Hill, Ross, Herefordshire; *m.* 1927, Joyce Edwina Turville (marriage dissolved, 1948), Kaisar-i-Hind Gold Medal, 1939, O.B.E. 1946, *d.* of G. Turville Brown; one *d.*; *m.* 1949, Constance Neilson, 2nd *d.* of late John Batcheler, Cairo and New Milton, Hants. *Educ.:* Charterhouse; Christ Church, Oxford. Entered the Indian Civil Service, 1912; Asst. Collector and Magistrate, 1912-1916; Indian Army Reserve of Officers, 1916-18; Forest Settlement Officer, 1920-22; Collector and District Magistrate, 1923; Registrar of Co-operative Societies, 1926-27; Home Secretary to the Government of Bombay, 1929-31; Private Sec. to Governor of Bombay, 1934-35; Officiating Commissioner in Sind, 1935; Commissioner Northern Division, Bombay, 1936-37; Revenue Commissioner, Sind, 1937-40; Chief Secretary to Government of Bombay, 1940-41; Adviser to Governor of Bombay, 1941-46; Commissioner Jewish Camps in Cyprus, 1947-49.

C.St.J. *Address:* The Spinney, Stoke Poges, Bucks. *T.:* Farnham Common 626. *Club:* Oxford and Cambridge. [*Died* 3 *Aug.* 1952.

COLLINS, John Henry; *b.* Newry, County Down, 3 March 1880; *s.* of late Henry Collins, Newry; *m.* 1919, Mary, *o. d.* of Joseph Burke, Co. Tipperary and Crewe; two *s.* one *d.* *Educ.:* Schools of Christian Brothers, Newry. Awarded First Year Law Scholarship, Queen's University, Belfast, 1909-10; Special Certificate for Distinguished Answering at Solicitors' Final Examination for all Ireland, Oct. 1910; admitted Solicitor, Supreme Court of Judicature in Ireland, 1911; senior partner Collins & Collins; M.P. South Down, Northern Ireland Parliament, 1929-33. *Address:* Laurel Hill, Dublin Road, Newry. *T.A.:* Collins, Solicitor, Newry. *T.:* Newry 77. *Club:* Newry. [*Died* 12 *Jan.* 1952.

COLLINS, John Philip; Journalist; *m.* Amélia Louise, *y. d.* of Alexander Bounevialle; three *s.* one *d.* *Educ.:* SS. Thomas and Edmund's, Erdington, a Benedictine foundation. Once had ambitions as a draughtsman, but fell among newspapers; trained in Birmingham; ten years literary editor of the Pall Mall Gazette, and five years assistant editor of the Pall Mall Magazine; acted as special on various fronts, 1916-19; Delegate at Imperial Press Conference, Ottawa, 1920; ex-Chairman (London District) Institute of Journalists; for 10 years on the Daily Telegraph; for 25 years London correspondent of the Cape Times, and 40 years of the Civil and Military Gazette (Lahore); 15 years of Boston Evening Transcript; edited Harper's Sports and Games Weekly, 1941-46; Ex-President, Elian Society. *Publications:* Those Magic Isles, 1931; Wonderful South Africa, 1936; Edited Travels in London and The Papers of an Oxford Man; contributor, Quarterly, Essays of the Year, Nineteenth Century, etc. *Address:* Michaelmore, The Pine Walk, Carshalton Beeches, Surrey. *T.:* Vigilant 2670. *Club:* Banstead Downs Golf (Sutton). [*Died* 19 *Jan.* 1954.

COLLINS, Brigadier Lionel Peter, C.B. 1934; C.S.I. 1936; D.S.O. 1915; O.B.E. 1920. *b.* 27 Nov. 1878; 7th *s.* of late Henry Collins, Leopold House, Reading; *m.* 1910, Gladys Lysaght (*d.* 1956), *d.* of late H. T. Rutherfoord, M.D., Taunton; one *s.* one *d.* (and one *s.* killed in action, Burma 1945); *m.* 1956, Margaret Davies. *Educ.:* Marlborough College; Keble Coll., Oxford. Entered army (Worcestershire Regt.), 1901; transferred Indian Army, 1902; served European War, 1914-18 (wounded, despatches thrice, Bt. Maj., D.S.O.); Afghanistan, N.W.F., 1919 (despatches, O.B.E.); First Commandant Indian Military Academy, 1932-36; retired from I.A., 1936. *Address:* Woodcote, Fleet, Hants. [*Died* 27 *Sept.* 1957.

COLLINS, Rear-Adm. Ralph, C.B. 1918; late R.N.; *b.* 17 Feb. 1877; 6th *s.* of late Henry Collins, Leopold House, Reading. Entered Royal Navy, 1891; Commander, 1911; Captain, 1917; served in operations against Zeebrugge and Ostend, 22-23 Apr. 1918 (C.B).; retired list, 1922; Rear-Adm. retired, 1929 *Recreation:* angling. *Address:* Restgarth, Streatley, Berks. *Club:* Flyfishers'. [*Died* 29 *March* 1957.

COLLINS, Lt.-Col. Hon. Richard Henn, C.M.G. 1917; D.S.O. 1902; late Royal Berkshire Regiment; *b.* 2 April 1873; *er. s.* of late Lord Collins; *m.* 1909, May Eveline, *y. d.* of late H. G. Bainbridge, of Malvern Hall, Solihull; three *s.* *Educ.:* Winchester College. Entered Army, 1892; Capt. 1902; Major, 1914; served S. Africa, 1899-1902 (despatches, Queen's medal 3 clasps, King's medal 2 clasps, D.S.O.); European War, 1914-1917 (despatches, promoted Brevet Lt.-Col., C.M.G.); Chevalier Order S.S. Maurice and Lazarus, 1917; D.A.A. and Q.M.G. 3rd Division, 1910-12; Adjutant General to New Zealand Forces, 1912-13; A.A. and Q.M.G., 1915-18; A.Q.M.G., 1918-20; retired pay, 1920. *Address:* Oakleigh, 80 Mount Durand, Guernsey. *T.:* Guernsey 327. [*Died* 9 *May* 1952.

COLLINS, Hon. Sir Stephen O. H.; *see* Henn-Collins.

COLLINS, William Wiehe, H.R.I.; *b.* Parish of St. Mary Abbotts, Kensington, 4 August 1862; *s.* of Brig.-Surg. F. Collins, M.D., late Northumberland Fusiliers, Knaresborough, Yorkshire, and Olympe Amélie, *d.* of P. A. Wiehe, Mauritius; *m.* Jennie, *d.* of Louis Blumfeld, Hampstead; two *s.* one *d.* *Educ.:* Epsom College. Studied at Lambeth School of Art and Académie Julian, Paris; served as A.B. in R.N.V.R. and R.N.A.S. at the Dardanelles and R.E. Egypt. *Pictures:* The Manchester Corporation; The Dom, Erfurt; The Victoria National Gallery, Melbourne; Anzac, 25 April 1915. *Publications:* The Cathedral Cities of England, 1905; The Cathedral Cities of Spain, 1909; The Cathedral Cities of Italy, 1911. *Address:* Cossington, Bridgwater, Somerset. [*Died* 16 *Feb.* 1951.

COLLINSON, Joseph; *b.* Wolsingham, 11 Nov. 1871; *m.* 1896, Jessie Humble; three *s.* two *d.* Took a prominent part in the movements which led to the rejection of the Flogging Bill in 1900; the withdrawal of the Youthful Offenders Whipping Bill in the same year, the more recent abolition of birching in the Royal Navy, and the establishment of the Court of Criminal Appeal, etc. *Publications:* What it Costs to be Vaccinated, The Fate of the Fur Seal, The Hunted Otter, Facts about Flogging, The Lashing of Vagrants, Lawlessness on the Bench, Imprisonment for Debt. *Address:* 39 The Crescent, Letchworth, Herts. [*Died Aug.* 1952.

COLLIS, Edgar Leigh, C.B.E. 1937; M.A., M.D. Oxon.; M.R.C.P., M.R.C.S.; retired; *b.* 25 Nov. 1870; *s.* of W. B. Collis, J.P., and Helen F. Collis, Stourbridge; *m.* Barbara Shields, *d.* of Principal Fairbairn, Oxford; no *c.* *Educ.:* Stourbridge Grammar School; Charterhouse; Keble College, Oxford; St. Thomas' Hospital. General practice at Stourbridge, 1897-1908; H.M. Medical Inspector of Factories, Home Office, 1908-17; Director of Welfare and Health, Ministry of Munitions, 1917-19; Talbot Prof. of Preventive Medicine, Welsh National School of Medicine, 1919-33; Milroy Lecturer, Royal College of Physicians, 1915; Harben Lecturer, 1924; Member Miners' Welfare Commission, 1921-50; Lecturer on Industrial Hygiene, Harvard Univ., 1926-27; D.I.H. (*h.c.*) 1953. Emeritus Professor, Univ. of Wales; J.P. (Morayshire); Medical Officer (Lt.-Col.), Home Guard. *Publications:* Various Home Office White Papers on Industrial Diseases, and articles in Encyclopædia Britannica and medical journals; Industrial Pneumonoconioses (Milroy Lectures); co-author of text-book, Health of Industrial Workers. *Recreations:* ran for Oxford *v.* Cambridge, 1892 and 1893; dead-heat for first place in hurdles, 1893; President of Oxford Univ. Swimming Club, 1893; rowed in College Eight, 1891 and 1892; gardening. *Address:* Tower House, Lossiemouth, Scotland. *T.:* 2051. [*Died* 1 *Oct.* 1957.

COLMAN, Cecil, J.P.; Chairman of Norvic Shoe Co. Ltd.; *b.* 30 May 1878; *s.* of Robert Colman; *m.* 1903, Florence Beatrice Laws; four *s.* one *d.* *Educ.:* Christchurch School, Christchurch, Hants. Joined Norvic Shoe Co., 1901. Councillor of Sutton and Cheam, Alderman, and 2nd Mayor of Borough, 1935; J.P. 1933; Chairman of Juvenile Court. President: Sutton and Cheam General Hospital; Elderly Peoples' Home; Chamber of Trade of Sutton; Boot and Shoe Manufacturers' Association. For many years President Epsom Div. Liberal Assoc. *Re-*

creations: golf, bowls. *Address:* Thaxted, 3 Devonshire Avenue, Sutton, Surrey. *Clubs:* National Liberal, Rotary of London. [*Died* 11 *March* 1954.

COLMAN, Col. Percy Edward, C.B.E. 1944; D.S.O. 1919; M.C. 1917; D.L. Middlesex; Lt.-Col. Canadian Forces (retd.); Hon. Col. Home Guard; Director Redland Tiles Co. Ltd.; *b.* 16 June 1875; *s.* of Robert Colman, J.P., Bournemouth, and Sophia Colman; *m.* 1908, Alice Muriel Debenham; one *s.* one *d.* *Educ.:* Amersham Hall School. Lt. and Sub-Inspector, S.A. Constabulary 1901-8, seeing service in S.A. Campaign (Queen's Medal 5 clasps). Entered Canadian Militia 1914, going overseas as Capt, in the C.M.R.; Staff Capt. 7th Cdn. Inf. Brigade; D.A.A.G. 1st Cdn. Div.; D.A.Q.M.G. and subsequently A.A. & Q.M.G. 2nd Cdn. Div. with Army of Occupation in Germany (despatches twice, D.S.O., M.C., 1914-15 Star, British and Victory Medals); retired in 1919 with rank of Lt.-Col. in R. of O. until 1935. Joined the L.D.V. on its formation; Commander of " X " Sector, London Dist. Home Guard, 1941-44 (C.B.E.). *Recreations:* cricket, big-game shooting. Greatly interested in the British Legion and its work. *Address:* Courtfield, Whyteleafe Road, Caterham, Surrey. [*Died* 19 *May* 1951.

COLMAN, Ronald; film actor; *b.* Richmond, Surrey, 9 Feb. 1891; *s.* of Charles Colman and Marjorie Read Fraser; *m.* 1st, 1919, Thelma Ray (marriage dissolved); 2nd, 1938, Benita Hume; one *d.* *Educ.:* Littlehampton. Member of London Scottish from 1909, went with them to France, 1914 (Mons Star with Bar); invalided out, 1916; first appearance professional stage with Lena Ashwell, 1916; on London stage, 1916-19; New York stage, 1920-22; had appeared in films in England in 1917 and 1919; in 1923 chosen to play lead with Lilian Gish in film The White Sister; films include: Romola, The Dark Angel, Stella Dallas, Lady Windermere's Fan, Kiki, Beau Geste, Leatherface, The Winning of Barbara Worth, Bulldog Drummond, Raffles, The Devil to Pay, Cynara, The Masquerader, Arrowsmith, Clive of India, A Tale of Two Cities, Under Two Flags, Lost Horizon, The Prisoner of Zenda, If I were King, The Light that Failed, Lucky Partners, The Talk of the Town, Random Harvest, Kismet, The Late George Apley, A Double Life, Champagne for Caesar. Academy of Motion Picture Arts & Sciences Award for Best Acting performance of 1947; Foreign Correspondents Golden Globe Award, 1947, etc. *Recreations:* sailing, fishing, golf, oil painting. *Address:* Santa Barbara, California. *Club:* Savage. [*Died* 19 *May* 1958.

COLOMB, Admiral Philip Howard; C.B. 1921; *b.* 13 Dec. 1867; 4th *s.* of late Vice-Admiral Philip Howard Colomb of Steeple Court, Botley; *m.* 1908, Kathleen Charlotte (*d.* 1954), *er. d.* of late Col. Edmund Bacon Hutton, Royal Dragoons, and late Lady Katherine Hutton. *Educ.:* Stubbington House; Britannia. Officer Legion of Honour, 1918; A.D.C. to H.M. 1917-18; retired list, 1923. *Recreations:* fishing, shooting. *Address:* Grove House, Coltishall, Norwich. *T.A.:* Coltishall, Norfolk. *T.:* Coltishall 212. [*Died* 18 *April* 1958.

COLOMB, Rupert Palmer, C.B. 1933; *b.* 6 March 1869; *s.* of Rt. Hon. Sir John C. R. Colomb, K.C.M.G.; *m.* 1904, Mabel, *e. d.* of John Murray Mordaunt, D.L. *Educ.:* Eton; New College, Oxford. Clerk in House of Commons, 1893; Principal Clerk, Committee and Private Bill Office, 1930-34; D.L. Co. Kerry; High Sheriff, 1916. *Recreations:* sailing, fishing, shooting. *Address:* Hotel Rembrandt, S.W.7. *Club:* Bath. [*Died* 24 *May* 1955.

COLQUHOUN, Ethel M. (Mrs. Tawse Jollie), O.B.E. 1930; *d.* of S. Cookson, M.D., Stafford; *m.* 1st, 1900, Archibald Colquhoun, writer and explorer (*d.* 1914); 2nd, 1915, John Tawse Jollie, of Rhodesia. Travelled in the Far East, Africa, North and South America with her first husband; member Executive Committee, Women's Unionist Association and British Women's Emigration Association; has spoken for these societies, and for National Service League; organised free buffet for soldiers and sailors (under War Office) at Paddington Station, 1915; on death of first husband edited the journal of Royal Colonial Institute; member Legislative Council, Southern Rhodesia; first woman elected for any Colonial Legislature: organiser Rhodesian Responsible Government Association. *Publications:* Two on their Travels (illustrated by author), 1902; The Whirlpool of Europe (jointly), 1906; The Vocation of Woman, 1913; The Real Rhodesia, 1923; contrib. to Quarterly, Nineteenth Century, National, etc. [*Died* 21 *Sept.* 1950.

COLSON, Percy; *b.* 1873; *m.* Ethel Pelgram, New York; no *c.* *Educ.:* private tutors; Paris. *Compositions:* Pro Patria, London, 1920, a one-act opera (with Mr. Alfred Kalisch, who wrote the libretto), produced Lyceum Theatre, 1920; She Stoops to Conquer, comedy opera in 3 acts, produced Baden-Baden, 1923; songs, violin pieces, etc.; was responsible for education and bringing up of pianist Solomon, C.B.E. *Publications:* Melba, An Unconventional Biography, 1932; I Hope They Won't Mind, 1930; Victorian Portraits, 1932, Authorised Life of the Bishop of London, 1935; The Strange History of Lord George Gordon, 1936; Georgian Portraits, 1939; The Future of Faith, 1942; Murder to Music (with Douglas Hoare), 1945; Close of an Era, 1945; Lord Goschen and his friends (The Goschen Letters), 1946; Those Uneasy Years, 1947; Their Ruling Passions (introduction by James Laver), 1949; (with the Marquess of Queensberry) Oscar Wilde and the Black Douglas, 1949; The Story of Christie's, 1950; "White's" 1693-1950, 1951; articles Apollo Magazine, Connoisseur, Harper's, Radio Times, Evening Standard, World Review, The World, Studio, The Queen, etc. *Recreations:* bridge, motoring. *Address:* St. Cross Hospital, Winchester. [*Died* 6 *Dec.* 1952.

COLT, Sir Henry (Archer), 9th Bt., *cr.* 1694; D.S.O. 1918; M.C.; Lieut.-Commander R.N. (retired); *b.* 16 Sept. 1882; *e. s.* of late Thomas Archer Colt, O.B.E., *yr. s.* of 7th Bt.; *S.* uncle 1931; *m.* Louisa May, *d.* of J. E. Whitaker and *widow* of J. C. Whittam of Bournemouth. Served European War, 1914-18, Temp. Lieut.-Col. 12th Batt. Gloucestershire Regt. (severely wounded, despatches twice, D.S.O., M.C.); War of 1939-1945, Sqdn.-Ldr. (temp.) R.A.F.V.R., 1939-1947. *Heir:* *nephew* Edward William Dutton, *b.* 1936. *Address:* c/o Westminster Bank, 26 Haymarket, S.W.1. [*Died* 10 *Feb.* 1951.

COLTHURST, Sir George Oliver, 7th Bt., *cr.* 1744; *b.* 1882; *s.* of 6th Bt. and Edith Jane Thomasine, *d.* of late Captain (The Royals) J. Morris, Dunkettle, Co. Cork; *S.* father, 1925. *Educ.:* Harrow; Trinity College, Cambridge. Late Capt. South Irish Horse; served European War, 1914-18 (Croix de Guerre). Owns about 31,300 acres. *Heir:* *b.* R. St. J. J. Colthurst. *Recreations:* foxhunting (M.F.H. Muskerry Foxhounds since 1930), cricket. *Address:* Blarney Castle, near Cork. *T.A.:* Blarney. *T.:* Blarney 1. *Clubs:* Travellers', Bath; Kildare Street (Dublin). [*Died* 28 *Feb.* 1951.

COLTHURST, Captain Sir Richard (St. John Jefferyes), 8th Bt., *cr.* 1744; *b.* 19 July 1887; *yr. s.* of Sir George St. John Colthurst, 6th Bart.; *S.* brother 1951; *m.* 1st, 1911, Cecily Charlotte (who obtained a divorce, 1927), *o. c.* of late Brig.-Gen. Hugh Cholmondeley, C.B., C.B.E.; two *d.*; 2nd, 1927, Denys Maida Hanmer, *e. d.* of Augustus William West of Leixlip House, Leixlip, Co. Kildare; two *s.* *Educ.:* Harrow; Trinity College, Cambridge. Served European War,

1914-18, Capt. London Regiment. High Sheriff of County Dublin, 1920-21. *Heir:* s. Richard La Touche [b. 14 Aug. 1928; m. 1953, Janet Georgina, d. of L. A. Wilson-Wright]. *Address:* Glenmervyn, Glanmire, Co. Cork, Eire. *Clubs:* Bath, M.C.C.; Kildare Street (Dublin); County (Cork); Touring Club de France. [*Died* 18 *Feb.* 1955.

COLTMAN-ROGERS, Muriel Augusta Gillian, C.B.E. 1920; d. of Major Frederick Barclay Chapman, 14th Hussars; m. 1888, Charles Coltman Coltman-Rogers (d. 1929); two s. two d. *Address:* Milebrook, Knighton, Radnor. [*Died* 7 *April* 1952.

COLVILLE, Rev. James, M.A.; Hon. D.D. Toronto, 1945; Minister St. Peter's Presbyterian Church, Upper Tooting, since 1922; Moderator of General Assembly of Presbyterian Church of England, 1945-46; Pres. National Free Church Council, 1937-38; s. of James Colville and Sarah Kirkpatrick; m. 1906, Isabella Lambert, Tweedmouth; one s. one d. *Educ.:* Edinburgh Univ; Westminster College, Cambridge; Marburg. Assistant Minister, Sefton Park Presbyterian Church, Liverpool, 1901-4; West Hartlepool Presbyterian Church, 1904; St. George's, Blackburn, 1916-22; Joint Hon. Secretary The United Society for Christian Literature, 1933-39. *Publications:* The Christian Optimist, 1925; The Inner Advent, 1932; The Christian Highway, 1935. *Recreation:* bowls. *Address:* 102 Huron Road, S.W.17. *T.:* Balham 4133. [*Died* 19 *Oct.* 1953.

COLVIN, Admiral Sir Ragnar Musgrave, K.B.E., cr. 1937 (C.B.E. 1919); C.B. 1932; b. 7 May 1882; 3rd s. late C. S. Colvin, C.S.I.; m. 1918, Sibyl, y. d. of late Brig.-Gen. H. F. Kays, C.B.; one s. one d. Entered Navy, 1896; Commander, 1913; Captain, 1917; Rear-Admiral, 1929; Vice-Admiral, 1934; Admiral, 1939: served Grand Fleet (Jutland), 1914-18; Assistant Director, Plans Division, Naval Staff, 1918-19; Mediterranean and Black Sea, 1919-21; Naval Attaché, Tokio, 1922-24; Director, Naval Tactical School, 1927-29; Chief of Staff, Home Fleet, 1930-32; Rear-Adm. 2nd Battle Squadron, 1932-33; President of Royal Naval College, Greenwich, and Vice-Adm. Commanding R.N. War College, 1934-37; First Naval Member of Commonwealth Naval Board, 1937-41; retired list, 1942; Naval Adviser to High Commissioner for Australia, 1942-44. *Address:* Curdridge House, Curdridge, Botley, Hants. *T.:* Botley 76. *Club:* United Service. [*Died* 22 *Feb.* 1954.

COLYER, Sir Frank, K.B.E., cr. 1920; L.R.C.P., F.R.C.S., F.D.S.R.C.S. Eng.; LL.D.; consulting Dental Surgeon Charing Cross Hospital, and Royal Dental Hospital of London; Hon. Cons. Dental Surgeon Min. of Pensions; b. 1866; m. 1895 (wife d. 1950); one s. one d. Formerly Hon. Consulting Dental Surgeon, Croydon War Hosp., The Queen's Hosp., Sidcup. *Publications:* Old Instruments for Extracting Teeth, 1952. Dental Surgery and Pathology; Dental Disease in its relation to General Medicine; John Hunter and Odontology; Chronic General Periodontitis; Variations and Diseases of the Teeth of Animals, etc. *Address:* 39 Palace Road, S.W.2. *T.:* Tulse Hill 3388. [*Died* 30 *March* 1954.

COLYER-FERGUSSON, Sir Thomas Colyer, 3rd Bt., cr. 1866; b. 11 July 1865; e. s. of Sir J. R. Fergusson, 2nd Bt., and Mary Ann Somes (d. 1868), d. of late Thomas Colyer, Wombwell Hall, Northfleet; S. father, 1924; m. 1st, 1890, Beatrice Stanley (d. 1902), d. of late Rt. Hon. Prof. Max Müller; one s. three d. (assumed additional name of Colyer on his marriage); 2nd, 1914, Mary Freda, d. of late Rt. Hon. Arthur Cohen. *Educ.:* Harrow; Christ Church, Oxford (M.A.). High Sheriff of Kent, 1906. *Heir:* g.s. James Herbert Hamilton [b. 10 Jan. 1917, s. of Max Christian Hamilton Colyer-Fergusson (d. 1940) and Edith Jane (d. 1936), d. of late William White Miller, Portage la Prairie, Manitoba]. *Address:* Ightham Mote, nr. Sevenoaks, Kent. [*Died* 7 *April* 1951.

COMBEN, Robert Stone, C.B.E. 1920; J.P. for Dorset and Borough of Weymouth and Melcombe Regis; b. 1868; s. of Robert Stone Comben, Woodford Bridge, Essex; m. 1923, Alice, d. of late Herbert Jeffries, Andover, Hants. Entered Weymouth Borough Council 1909, resigned 1952: Mayor 1915-18; Member Dorset County Council, 1918-50. *Address:* Melville, Holland Road, Weymouth. [*Died* 30 *Dec.* 1957.

COMBER, Norman Mederson, D.Sc. (Lond.), A.R.C.S., F.R.I.C.; formerly Professor of Agricultural Chemistry and Head of Department of Agriculture, University of Leeds; Emeritus Professor, 1953; b. Brighton, 1888; s. of Samuel Comber; m. Nellie, d. of James Finch, Chelmsford; one s. one d. *Educ.:* Secondary School, Brighton; Royal College of Science, London. Assistant Lecturer, East Anglian Institute of Agriculture; Assistant Lecturer, Lecturer, and Professor of Agricultural Chemistry, Dean of the Faculty of Technology, Univ. of Leeds, 1930-32, 1946-48. Commission 8th Bn. Yorkshire Regt., 1914-18. *Publications:* An Introdution to The Scientific Study of the Soil; An Introduction to Agricultural Chemistry; various papers in Journal of Agricultural Science and other journals. *Address:* Kilchattan, Kirkstall Lane, Headingley, Leeds. *T.:* 53065. [*Died* 5 *Dec.* 1953.

COMMINGS, Maj.-Gen. Percy Ryan Conway, C.B. 1934; C.M.G. 1919; D.S.O. 1916; b. 9 July 1880; m. E. M. F. Wilson, Broom Hall, Colchester; one s. two d. 2nd Lieut., 1900; Lieut., 1903; Adjutant, 1907-10; Captain, 1909; Major, 1915; Lieut.-Col., 1925; Colonel, 1927. Served South African War, 1899-1902 (Queen's medal and three clasps, King's medal and two clasps); European War, 1914-18 (D.S.O., despatches four times, Bt. Lt.-Col., C.M.G., Legion of Honour); Comdg. 2nd Bn. South Staffs Regt., 1925-27; Burma, 1930-32 (despatches); A.A.G. Eastern Command, 1927-31; Comm. Rangoon Brigade Area, India, 1931-33; Comm. 56th (1st London) Div., T.A., 1934-35; The London Division, 1935-38; Colonel of South Staffordshire Regt., 1936-46; retired pay, 1938. *Address:* Parkside, Caterham. *T.:* Caterham 3707. *Club:* United Service. [*Died* 21 *Jan.* 1958.

COMMON, Sir (Lawrence) Andrew, Kt., cr. 1945; D.S.O. 1916; Director: Hindustan Steam Shipping Co. Ltd., Northumbrian Shipping Co. Ltd., Samuel Tyzack & Co. Ltd.; b. 31 March 1889; s. of late Francis James Common; m. 1923, Bessie, d. of Gilbert Pollock, Sunderland; one s. two d. Served European War, 1914-18 (D.S.O.). Director Ship Management Div., Min. of War Transport, 1941-46. High Sheriff of Durham, 1953. *Address:* Hunter House, Shotley Bridge, Co. Durham. [*Died* 6 *April* 1953.

COMPER, Sir (John) Ninian, Kt., cr. 1950; Architect (not registered); b. 10 June 1864; s. of John Comper, founder and incumbent of St. Margaret's, Aberdeen, and Ellen, d. of John Taylor, merchant of Hull; m. 1890, Grace Bucknall; two s. one d. (and two s. and one d. decd.). *Educ.:* Glenalmond; Ruskin's School, Oxford; Royal School of Art, South Kensington, and with C. E. Kempe; then articled to G. F. Bodley and T. Garner. Principal works: St. Mary's, Wellingborough, following St. Cyprian's Marylebone and its corollary St. Crispin's, Yerendawna, Poona, India, 1903; Wimborne St. Giles, 1910; St. Mary's, Rochdale, 1911; St. Martin's Chapel, Chailey, 1912; Stanton Memorial, St. Alban's, Holborn, 1918; work at Southwark Cathedral from 1922; Warriors' Chapel, Westminster Abbey, 1927, and Nave Windows from 1908; Welsh National War

Memorial, Cardiff, 1928; Chapel of All Saints Sisters, nr. St. Albans, 1928; the abortive U.S.A. Cathedral for Aberdeen, 1930; St. Philip's, Portsmouth, 1937, and proposed Church of St. Frideswide, Bletchley, for the late Bishop of Oxford, designed 1950; Parliamentary War Memorial Window in Westminster Hall, 1952: Royal Window, Canterbury Cathedral, 1954; East Window, Holy Trinity Church, Coventry, 1955. *Publications:* Of the Atmosphere of a Church, 1947; Of the Christian Altar and the buildings which contain it, 1950; articles in transactions of ecclesiological societies. *Address:* The Priory, 67 Beulah Hill, Norwood, S.E.19. *T.:* Livingstone 1696. [*Died* 22 *Dec.* 1960.

COMPTON, Karl T(aylor), Hon. C.B.E. 1948; Ph.D.; President, Massachusetts Institute of Technology, Cambridge, Mass., 1930-48; Chairman of Corporation, M.I.T., since 1948; *b.* 14 Sept. 1887; *s.* of Elias Compton and Otelia Augspurger; *m.* 1921, Margaret Hutchinson; one *s.* two *d.* *Educ.:* Wooster College (Ph.B. 1908, Sc.M. 1909); Princeton Univ. (Ph.D. 1912). Instructor in Chemistry, Wooster, 1909-10; Instructor in Physics, Reed College, 1913-15; Asst. Prof. of Physics, Princeton, 1915-19; Professor, 1919-30; Research Prof. and Chm. of Dept., 1929-1930. Member, National Defense Research Com. of the Office of Scientific Research and Develop., 1940-46; Member, Baruch Rubber Survey Com., 1942; Chm. Radar *ad hoc* Com. of Joint Com. on New Weapons of Joint Chiefs of Staff, 1942-45; Chm. U.S. Radar Mission to the United Kingdom, 1943; Chief, Office of Field Service of the Office of Scientific Research and Development, 1943-45; Special Representative of Sec. of War in Southwest Pacific Area, 1943-44; Member, Sec. of War's Special Adv. Com. on Atomic Bomb, 1945; Dir., Pacific Branch of Off. Sci. Research and Development and Member of Scientific Intelligence Mission to Japan, 1945; Chm. Joint Chiefs of Staff Evaluation Board on Atomic Bomb Tests, 1946; Chm. President's Adv. Com. on Universal Training, 1946-47; Member, Atomic Energy Commission Personnel Security Review Board, 1947-48; Chm., Research and Development Bd., Nat. Military Establishment, 1948-49; Member, Nat. Security Training Commission, 1951-. Commander of Royal Norwegian Order of St. Olav, 1948; Officer of French Legion of Honour, 1951. *Address:* Massachusetts Institute of Technology, Cambridge 39, Mass. *T.:* University 7-6900. *Clubs:* Algonquin, Tavern, Thursday Evening, Union, University (Boston); University (New York); Cosmos (Washington). [*Died* 22 *June* 1954.

COMPTON MACKENZIE, Faith; *see* Mackenzie, Lady.

COMYN, Michael, Q.C. 1914; Judge of Irish Free State Judiciary since 1936; *b.* Clareville, Ballyvaughan, Co. Clare, 1877; *e. s.* of James Comyn, Clareville, and Ellen, *d.* of Thomas Quin, Fanta Glebe, Kilfenora, Co. Clare; *m.* 1924, Marcella, *y. d.* of late Francis The O'Donnellan Blake Forster of Ballykeal Court, Kilfenora, Co. Clare; two *d.* *Educ.:* Ruan School, University College, Dublin; Trinity and King's Inns, Dublin. Civil Service; Called to Bar, 1898; began practice 1900; Senator, Irish Free State, 1928-36. *Recreations:* Chemical and Geological Research, discovered Irish phosphate deposits, 1924, and Irish tin deposits, 1931. *Address:* Ballykeal, Kilfrenor, Co. Clare; 9 Northbrook Rd., Dublin. *T.:* Rathmines 634. [*Died* 6 *Oct.* 1952.

CONDE, Harold Graydon, C.M.G. 1955; M.I.E.A.; Chairman, Electricity Commission, New South Wales; formerly General Manager, Electric Light and Power Supply Corporation Ltd.; Dep. Regional Controller of Electricity Supply, N.S.W., 1942; Chm., Army Establishments Investigating Cttee., 1945; Director: Parramatta and Granville Elec. Supply Co.; Muswellbrook Coal Co. Ltd. *Address:* 10 Tranmere St., Drummoyne, N.S.W. *Clubs:* Royal Sydney Yacht Squadron, N.S.W. [*Died* 5 *Oct.* 1959.

CONGREVE, Cecil Ralph Townshend, C.B.E. 1941; *b.* 17 Sept. 1876; *s.* of William Congreve; *m.* 1st, 1911, Maud Esme Rowsell; 2nd, 1932, Margaret Louis Wilson Somerville; three *s.* one *d.* *Educ.:* Charterhouse. Started planting, 1896; late General Manager Peria Karamalai Tea & Produce Co. Ltd.; Planting representative Madras Legislature, 1922-25, 1926-29; Chairman United Planters Association of S. India, 1920-21, 1930-32, 1937-38. *Publication:* History of the Anamalais, 1942. *Address:* Hennor, Leominster, Herefordshire. *Club:* Royal Automobile. [*Died* 3 *June* 1952.

CONGREVE, John; J.P., D.L.; *b.* 1872; *e. s.* of late Ambrose Congreve and Hon. Alice Elizabeth Dillon, 6th *d.* of 3rd Lord Clonbrock; *m.* 1904, Lady Helen Blanche Irene Ponsonby, 2nd *d.* of 8th Earl of Bessborough; one *s.* *Educ.:* Eton. Joined Cumberland Militia, 1890; served as Capt. in Border Regt. in South African War, 1899-1901; served as Major in Westmorland and Cumberland Yeomanry, 1915-18. *Address:* Mount Congreve, Waterford, Eire. *Clubs:* Travellers'; Kildare Street (Dublin). [*Died* 25 *Sept.* 1957.

CONINGSBY, Eric Alfred; Organist and Master of the Choristers, Llandaff Cathedral, since 1950; *b.* 2 Jan. 1909; *e. s.* of Alfred Coningsby, Whaddon, nr. Royston, Herts.; *m.* 1944, Phyllis Kate Bavey; no *c.* *Educ.:* Cambridge and County High School; Trinity College, Cambridge. B.A. 1930; M.A. 1936; L.R.A.M. dipl. 1935; Mus.B., 1937; F.R.C.O. dipl. 1945; C.H.M. (choirmaster) dipl., 1947. Music Master Bridlington School and Choirmaster Bridlington Priory Church, 1931-32; Music Master Glasgow Academy, 1932-36; Organist and Choirmaster, St. Matthew's Church, Glasgow, 1933-36; Organist and Choirmaster, St. Barnabas, Cambridge, and Conductor Cambridge Philharmonic Society, 1937-40. Meteorologist with the R.A.F., 1940-44. Temp. asst. music master, Uppingham School, 1945; Organist and Choirmaster, Folkestone Parish Church, 1945-50; Conductor Folkestone Orpheus Choir and Orchestra; Conductor Dover Choral Society. *Address:* White House Cottage, Llandaff, Glamorgan. *T.:* Llandaff 639. [*Died* 22 *Sept.* 1955.

CONKLIN, Edwin Grant, Ph.D., Sc.D., LL.D.; Professor of Biology, Princeton Univ. Emeritus since 1933; Pres. Science Service, Washington, 1936-45; *b.* Waldo, Ohio, 24 Nov. 1863; *s.* of Dr. A. V. Conklin and Maria Hull; *m.* 1889, Belle (*d.* 1940), *d.* of Rev. L. G. Adkinson; one *s.* two *d.* *Educ.:* Ohio Wesleyan Univ.; Johns Hopkins Univ. Professor of Biology, Ohio Wesleyan, 1891-94; Professor of Zoology, North-western University, 1894-96; Professor of Zoology, University of Pennsylvania, 1896-1908; Professor of Biology, Princeton Univ. 1908-33; Trustee Marine Biological Laboratory since 1897; President Bermuda Biological Station, 1926-36; Amer. Soc. Zool. 1899; American Society of Naturalists, 1912; American Assn. for Advancement of Science, 1936-37; Executive Vice-Pres. American Philosophical Society, 1932-42, Pres., 1942-45, 1948-52; Vice-Pres. Acad. Nat. Sci. of Philadelphia, 1901-50; Member Scientific Advisory Board of Wistar Institute since 1905; National Academy Sciences since 1908; Amer. Academy Arts and Sciences; Foreign Member: Royal Society of Edinburgh, Zoological Society of London, Soc. Belge de Biologie, Acad. roy. de Belgique, Königliche Bömische Gesell. der Wissenschaften, Accad. Nationale dei Lincei, Inst. Lombardo. *Publications:* Heredity and Environment, 6 Eds.; Direction of Human Evolution, 2 Eds.; Synopsis of General Morphology; Man—Real

and Ideal, 1943; Revolt against Darwinism (Lowel Lectures); Mechanism of Evolution (Hale Lectures); Problem of Organic Adaptation (Rice Inst. Lectures); Problems of Development (Sedgwick Lecture): Freedom and Responsibility (Milton Acad. Lecture); The Biological Basis of Democracy (Barnwell Address); Science and Ethics (Amer. Assn. Address); What is Man? (Rice Inst. Lectures); more than 200 Contributions on Embryology and Cytology; Co-Editor of Jour. Morph., Jour. Exp. Zool. Biol. Bull., Genetics. *Recreations:* planting, building, motoring. *Address:* Princeton, New Jersey. *T.:* Princeton 1-0286, *Clubs:* Nassau, Franklin Inn (Philadelphia). [*Died* 21 *Nov.* 1952.

CONNARD, Philip, C.V.O. 1950; R.A. 1925 (A.R.A. 1918); R.W.S. 1934 (A.R.W.S. 1932); *b.* Southport, 1875; *s.* of David Connard; *m.* Mary (*d.* 1927), *d.* of Archdeacon Collyer; two *d.*; 2nd, 1933, Georgina Yorke, Twickenham. Keeper of the Royal Academy, 1945-49; Member of the New English Art Club, National Portrait Society, and International Society of Painters; works in Welsh National Gallery, Cardiff; Dublin and Bradford Art Galleries; Luxembourg, Paris; National Gallery British Art (Tate Gallery); Manchester Art Gallery; works purchased by Chantry bequest for nation, also Southport Art Gallery, the Melbourne Gallery, Australia, and the Aberdeen Art Gallery; Mural Paintings in Windsor Castle. *Address:* Cholmondeley Lodge, Richmond, Surrey. *T.:* Richmond 3485. [*Died* 8 *Dec.* 1958.

CONNAUGHT, H.R.H. Princess Arthur of; *see* Fife, The Duchess of (2nd in Line).

CONNER, Lewis Atterbury, M.D.; Professor of Medicine, Emeritus, Cornell University Medical College; *b.* 17 Jan. 1867; *s.* of Charles Horace and Catherine Atterbury Conner; *m.* 1st, 1900, Emma Witt Harris (*d.* 1921); 2nd, 1923, Laila Ann Coston, M.D.; one *s.* four *d.* *Educ.:* Yale Univ., Ph.B. 1887; College of Physicians and Surgeons, Columbia University, M.D. 1890. Professor of Medicine and Head of Department, Cornell University Medical College, 1916-32; Physician to New York Hospital, 1905-32, Consulting Phys. to New York Hospital since 1932; Editor American Heart Journal, 1925-38; Colonel U.S.A. Medical Corps, 1917-19; Brig. General U.S.A. Medical Officer Reserve Corps. *Address:* 25 East 67th St., New York 19, N.Y., U.S.A. *Club:* University (N.Y. City). [*Died* 3 *Dec.* 1950.
[*But death not notified in time for inclusion in Who Was Who 1941–1950, first edn.*

CONNOLLY, T. J.; *see* Doull-Connolly.

CONNOR, Francis Richard; Editor, South Eastern Gazette, 1899–1951; *b.* 24 June, 1870; *y. s.* of late J. W. Connor, Maidstone; *m.* 1913, Ada Dixey, *d.* of T. Dack Harvey, Colchester; one *s.* Fellow of Institute of Journalists (Hon. Vice-Pres. 1945-46); Member of Maidstone Corporation, 1920-45 (Alderman, 1942); Mayor, 1927-28; J.P. Maidstone; Chairman of Ministry of Labour Local Employment Committee, 1922-46; Chairman of Maidstone Savings Association, 1921-44; Governor of Maidstone Grammar Schools; first chm. Div. Educ. Exec., 1945. J.P. since 1932. *Publications:* various pamphlets and stories. *Address:* Grove End, Barming Heath, Maidstone. *T.:* Maidstone 86266. [*Died* 14 *Feb.* 1956.

CONNOR, Maj.-Gen. Sir Frank Powell, Kt., *cr.* 1926; D.S.O. 1917; F.R.C.S., D.T.M. and H., I.M.S.; late Surg.-Gen. with Government of Madras; late Prof. of Surgery and Surgeon to Medical College Hospital, Calcutta; late Fellow Calcutta University and Member of Syndicate; Examiner in Surgery; *s.* of late James Connor, Survey of India; *m.* 1921, Grace Ellen, *d.* of late Reginald O. Lees, Director, Indian Government Telegraphs; one *s.* *Educ.:* St. Bartholomew's Hospital. Entered Indian Medical Service, 1902; served with 16th Rajputs at Shillong and Manipur and with 13th Rajputs at Calcutta; Resident Surgeon, Medical College Hospital, Calcutta, 1907-10; Civil Surgeon, Gaya, Behar and Orissa, 1910-12; left India with Indian Expeditionary Force, Sept. 1914; served in France, England and Mesopotamia with Indian General Hospital, and Consulting Surgeon Mesopotamia Expeditionary Force, 1917-18 (despatches four times, Bt. Lt.-Col., 1914 Star, D.S.O.); Hon. Surgeon to the King, 1934-37; retired 1937. *Publications:* Surgery in the Tropics, 1929; Sections on Tropical Surgery in Rose and Carless Manual of Surgery and Nelson's Loose-leaf Surgery. *Recreations:* cricket, shooting, polo. *Address:* Greys Thatch, Bolts Cross, Henley-on-Thames. *T.:* Rotherfield Greys 254. *Clubs:* United Service; Madras (Madras). [*Died* 8 *Aug.* 1954.

CONOLLY, Major Edward Michael, C.M.G. 1919; retired military officer; *b.* 20 Feb. 1874; *s.* of Thomas Conolly, M.P.; unmarried. *Educ.:* Harrow; R.M.A., Woolwich; Royal Field and Royal Horse Artillery; served S. African War, despatches; European War (C.M.G., despatches); private secretary to H.E. Sir Henry May, Hong-Kong, 1913-14. *Recreations:* hunting, fishing, farming. *Address:* Castletown, Celbridge, Co. Kildare. *Clubs:* Cavalry; Kildare Street (Dublin). [*Died* 22 *Oct.* 1956.

CONRAN-SMITH, Sir Eric Conran, K.C.I.E., *cr.* 1946 (C.I.E. 1924); C.S.I. 1942; late I.C.S.; *b.* 3 Dec. 1890; *s.* of late Herbert Blomfield Smith, M.I.C.E.; *m.* 1922, Gladys, *d.* of H. R. Dunk; one *d.* (one *s.* killed in action). *Educ.:* Dulwich Coll.; Corpus Christi Coll., Oxford. Entered I.C.S. 1915; served with T.F. Battalion Devonshire Regiment in India and Palestine; returned to India, 1919; Private Secretary to Governor of Madras, 1921; Commissioner Corporation of Madras, 1928; Secretary to Government, Local Self Government Department, Madras, 1931; Additional Joint Secretary, Reforms Office, Government of India, 1934; Officiating Private Secretary to Viceroy, 1935; Joint Secretary, Home Dept., Govt. of India, 1938; Joint Sec. to the Governor-General (Public), 1938; Secretary to the Govt. of India, Home Dept., 1939, to War Transport Dept., 1945; Member for War Transport, Railways, Posts and Air, Governor-General's Executive Council, India, 1946. *Address:* Aramby, Park Avenue, Camberley. *Club:* United University. [*Died* 27 *Jan.* 1960.

CONSTANDUROS, Mabel; radio artist, actress, author; *b.* London; *d.* of Richard Stephen Tilling and Sophie Thorn; *m.* A. Constanduros; one *s.* *Educ.:* Sutton High School; Dulwich High School; Mary Datchelor School; Central School of Speech Training. First broadcast 23 March 1925; originated The Buggins Family; wrote and acted in The Buggins Family broadcast sketches for several years; first stage appearance, London Coliseum, 1929; appeared in Derby Day, Lyric, Hammersmith, 1932; Ann of Cleves in The Rose without a Thorn, 1933; in her own play Three for Luck, 1934; Madam Wang in Lady Precious Stream. *Publications:* Bugginses (with Michael Hogan); Three For Luck, 1934; Mrs. Buggins Calls, 1936; Poison Flower, 1937; Down Mangel Street, 1938; A Nice Fire in the Drawing-Room, 1939; And so They were Married, 1940; This Respected Lady (with Howard Agg), 1947; Shreds and Patches (autobiography), 1947; 40 one-act plays. *Plays:* (with Denis Constanduros), Acacia Avenue, prod. 1943, A Pig in a Poke, prod. 1950; 100 broadcast plays. *Films: Dialogue:* Holiday Camp; Three Family Films for Gainsborough (with Denis Constanduros). *Recreations:* travel, gardening, reading history. *Address:* Five Oaks Cottage, West Burton, Pulborough, Sussex. *T.:* Bury 130. [*Died* 8 *Feb.* 1957.

CONSTANTINE, Maj.-Gen. Charles Francis, C.B. 1944; D.S.O. 1917; Director of Cadet Training for Province of Ontario. *s.* of late Major Charles Constantine; *m.*; three *d.* *Educ.:* Upper Canada College, Toronto; Royal Military College, Kingston. Served Royal Canadian Artillery (Field and Horse), Gunnery instructor, mobile artillery, Canada; Gunnery Staff course, 1908; p.s.c. 1922; served European War, 1914-18 (despatches 4 times, D.S.O. and Bar, Legion of Honour); Prof. of Artillery, Royal Military Coll., Kingston, 1919-25; Commandant Royal Military Coll., 1925-30; D.O.C. M.D. 7, 1930-1931; D.O.C. M.D. 6, 1932-33; Adjt.-Gen. of Canada, 1934; District Officer commanding Military District No. 3; District Officer commanding Halifax, 1939; D.O.C. M.D. 2, 1940-43; retired, Aug. 1943. *Address:* 189 King Street West, Kingston, Ontario, Canada. [*Died* 20 *Oct.* 1953.

CONSTANTINIDES, Most Rev. Michael; Greek Orthodox Archbishop of North and South America (Greek Orthodox Church) since 1949; great Archimandrite M.Th.; *s.* of Michael and Filio Constantinides; *b.* Maronia, W. Thrace, 27 May 1892; unmarried. *Educ.:* Theol. Coll. Halki, Constantinople; Theol. Acads., Petrograd; Kiev, Russia. Ordained priest, Greek Orthodox Church, 1919; lecturer, Theol. College, Halki; Vicar of St. Stefano, Constantinople; *loc. tens.* Metropolis of Maronia, 3½ years; Grand Vicar of the Archbishopric of Athens, 4 years; Dean of the Greek Cathedral, London, 1927-1939; Bishop of Corinth, 1939-49. *Publications:* Bolshevism and the Orthodox Church; The Preaching in the Eastern Orthodox Church; The Education in the Greek Schools; 25 sermons in the Greek newspaper Neos Agon, all in Greek; about a hundred articles and treatises in Greek magazines; Life and Work in the Diocese of Athens (English); The Eastern Orthodox Church (English); The Priest, his life and work (Greek); Pastoral activities of the Parish Priests in the Church of England (Greek Magazine Aghiosspyridon); The Greek Orthodox Church in London (Greek-English); The Imitation of Christ (Greek translation); Life of St. Anthony the Great (Greek); Relations between Anglican and Orthodox (Greek); Christ and the social problems (Greek); My life in Christ (Greek translation); Athanasius the Great, life and times (Greek); Guide of an Orthodox Christian (Greek); Guide of a churchgoing Orthodox Christian (Greek); Faith, Hope, Love, Prayer (Greek); A manual for Orthodox Christians (Greek-English), 1950. *Address:* Greek Archdiocese of North and South America, 10 East 79th Street, New York 21, N.Y., U.S.A. [*Died* 13 *July* 1958.

CONWAY, Conway Joseph, Q.C.; J.P. Bucks; Called to Bar, Inner Temple, 1906; K.C. 1927; Q.C. 1952; bencher Inner Temple, 1935; Dep. Chm. Quarter Sessions, 1939-46. *Address:* 6 King's Bench Walk, Temple, E.C.4. *T.:* Central 2268; Turville Court, Henley-on-Thames. *T.:* Turville Heath 3. [*Died* 2 *Nov.* 1953.

CONWY, Rear-Adm. Rafe Grenville Rowley-, C.M.G. 1919; late R.N.; Lord Lieutenant of Flintshire since 1935; *s.* of late Capt. C. G. H. Rowley-Conwy and Marian, *d.* of late Frederick Harford of Down Place, Berks; *b.* 1875. Served European War, 1914-19 (despatches, C.M.G., Distinguish. Service Medal U.S.A.); retired list, 1922; Rear-Adm. 1928. Commodore R.N.R., North Atlantic Convoys, 1941, 1942. D.L., J.P. Flintshire; Lord of Manor of Rhuddlan. *Address:* Bodrhyddan, Rhuddlan, Flintshire. *T.:* Rhuddlan 337. *Club:* United Service. [*Died* 4 *April* 1951.

CONYBEARE, Alfred Edward; Vice-Provost of Eton; Lower Master, 1929-45; *b.* 25 Aug. 1875; *s.* of late Rev. J. W. E. Conybeare; unmarried. *Educ.:* Eton College; King's Coll., Cambridge. Master at Eton since 1897. *Address:* Vice-Provost's House, Eton College, Windsor. *T.A.:* Eton. *T.:* Windsor 217. *Clubs:* Oxford and Cambridge, Leander. [*Died* 18 *April* 1952.

CONYBEARE, Very Rev. William James; Provost emeritus of Southwell; *b.* 19 Dec. 1871; *s.* of Edward and Francis Conybeare; *m.* 1909, Olive, *d.* of H. C. Malkin, Corrybrough, Inverness-shire. *Educ.:* Eton; Trinity, Cambridge. Assistant Master St. George's Chapel Choir School, Windsor Castle, 1895; Private Secretary to Sir Fowell Buxton as Governor of South Australia, 1895; ordained after Leeds Clergy School, 1898; Domestic Chaplain to Archbishops Temple and Davidson, 1901-3; Head of Cambridge House Lay Settlement, Camberwell, 1903-9; Rector of Newington, S.E., 1909-16; Rector of Southwell, 1916-31, Provost, 1931-45; Archdeacon of Nottingham, 1916-36; Fellow Royal Empire Society. *Publication:* Here's a Church—Let's go in, 1947. *Recreations:* motoring, gardening. *Address:* Quaker Lanes, Warborough, Oxon. [*Died* 13 *May* 1955.

CONYNGHAM, Col. Sir G. P. L.; *see* Lenox-Conyngham.

COOK, Sir Albert Ruskin, Kt., *cr.* 1932; C.M.G. 1922, O.B.E. 1918; M.D., B.Sc. London, B.A. Cantab; late Senior Physician, C.M.S. Hospital, Kampala, Uganda; Consulting Physician Government European Hospital, Kampala; Consulting Physician Mengo Hospital; Vice-President C.M.S.; Life Governor B. and F.B.S.; Member and late President Uganda Society; Silver Jubilee Medal; *b.* 1870; *s.* of William Henry Cook, M.D., and Harriet, *sister* of late Bishop Bickersteth of Exeter; *m.* 1900, Katharine Timpson, O.B.E. (*d.* 1938); one *d.* *Educ.:* St. Paul's School (Foundation Scholar, Senior Exhibitioner Science side on leaving); Trinity College, Cambridge (Major Scholar, Natural Science); 1st Class Science Tripos, Part I. 1891, 1st Class, Part II. 1893); St. Bartholomew's Hospital (Shuter Exhibitioner). Late Captain attached U.M.S., E. Africa and Uganda, 1897-98 (medal and 2 clasps); O.C. Mengo-Base Hospital, 1914-1917 (despatches, O.B.E., C.M.G., Chevalier de l'Ordre de Leopold); President Uganda Branch, B.M.A., 1914-18 and 1936-37; Inter-territorial Meeting of E. African Branches of B.M.A., Kampala, 1947. 3 war medals, 1914-18; B.Sc. 1888; B.A. 1893; M.D. 1901; Silver Medal, African Society, 1928; Representative of Uganda at the Coronation, 1937; Jubilee Medal, 1935; Coronation Medal, 1937. *Publications:* Medical Vocabulary and Phrase Book in Luganda; Luganda Proverbs; A Handbook of Midwifery in Luganda (with Lady A. R. Cook); Midwifery for Native Nurses; Uganda Memories, 1946. *Recreation:* tennis. *Address:* Mabindye, Kampala, Uganda. *T.A.:* Testimony, Uganda. *T.:* Kampala 719. [*Died* 23 *April* 1951.

COOK, Arthur Bernard, Litt.D., F.B.A. 1941; Vice-President of Queens' College, Cambridge; Emeritus Professor of Classical Archæology; *b.* 1868; *s.* of William Henry Cook, M.D., and Harriet Bickersteth Cook, of Hampstead; *m.* 1894, Emily (*d.* 1943), *d.* of George Thomas Maddox, Hampstead; one *d.* *Educ.:* St. Paul's School (Foundation Scholar and Exhibitioner); Trinity College, Cambridge. Major Scholar, 1887; Craven Univ. Scholar, 1889; Chancellor's English Medallist, 1889; Chancellor's Senior Medallist for Classics, 1891; Members' Latin Prize, 1892; Classical Tripos, Part i. Class i. Division i. 1889; Part ii. Class i. 1891; Fellow of Trinity College, 1893-99; Examiner in the Classical Tripos, Part i. 1898, 1899, 1900, 1903, 1904; Part ii. (Archæology), 1901, 1902, 1908, 1909; Professor of Greek at Bedford College, London, 1892-1907; Reader in Classical Archæology to the University of Cambridge, 1908-31; Laurence

Professor of Classical Archæology, Cambridge, 1931-34; General Editor of Methuen's Handbooks of Archæology, 1928-49; Member of Societies for the Promotion of Hellenic and Roman Studies, Classical Assoc., Folk-Lore Soc., Cambridge Antiquarian Soc., the Cambridge Philological Soc., American Philosophical Soc., Philadelphia; Ordentlich Mitglieder des Archäologischen Instituts des Deutschen Reiches; Member of the Council of Ridley Hall, Cambridge. *Publications:* The Metaphysical Basis of Plato's Ethics, 1895; Zeus, a Study in Ancient Religion, vol. i. 1914, vol. ii. 1925, vol. iii. 1940; The Rise and Progress of Classical Archæology, 1931; many articles in the Classical Review, Journal of Hellenic Studies, Folklore, L'Anthropologie, etc. *Address:* Queens' College, and 19 Cranmer Road, Cambridge. *T.:* Cambridge 2509. [*Died* 26 *April* 1952.

COOK, Edgar T., C.B.E. 1949; Mus.D., (Cantuar) 1934; Mus.B., Queen's College; Oxford; F.R.C.M., F.R.C.O., L.R.A.M.; Organist and Director of the Music, Southwark Cathedral, since 1908; *b.* Worcester, 18 March 1880; *s.* of Edgar Cook, Worcester; *m.* 1924, Hilda May, *y. d.* of F. J. Bentley, Waltham Abbey; one *d.* *Educ.:* Worcester Royal Grammar School; private. Organist of Newland, Malvern, 1898; Assistant Organist Worcester Cathedral, 1904; President, London Society of Organists, 1914 and 1921; Hon. Treasurer Royal College of Organists; Vice-President Church Music Society; Examiner, Associated Board of Royal Schools of Music. *Publications:* The Use of Plain-song; anthems, services, part-songs, etc. *Recreations:* croquet, gardening. *Address:* Newlands, Chipstead, Surrey. *T.:* Downland 424. *Club:* Athenæum. [*Died* 5 *March* 1953.

COOK, Sir Edward (Mitchener), Kt., *cr.* 1923; C.S.I. 1923; C.I.E. 1919; *b.* Jan. 1881; *s.* of Charles C. Cook; *m.* 1st, 1904, Christine (who obt. a div., 1924; she *d.* 1950), *d.* of A. A. Duke, M.D.; two *s.* two *d.*; 2nd, 1924, Catharine (*d.* 1938), *d.* of Colonel F. C. W. Rideout, I.A.; one *d.*; 3rd, 1940, Frances, *d.* of Stewart Baxter. *Educ.:* Uppingham; Clare Coll., Cambridge; Math. Tripos, 1902; joined I.C.S. in United Provinces, 1904; Under-Secretary to United Provinces Govt. 1909; Under-Secretary to Govt. of India, Home Department, 1911; Finance Department, 1912; Controller of the Currency, 1917; Financial Secretary to the Govt. of India, 1919-23; Secretary to the High Commissioner for India, 1923-24; Financial Adviser to the Govt. of Siam, 1925-1930; Governor, National Bank of Egypt, 1931-40; Grand Cross of the Order of the White Elephant, Siam; Grand Cordon of the Order of the Nile. *Address:* Kyrenia, Cyprus; Grindlay's Bank Ltd., 54 Parliament Street, S.W.1. *Club:* Oriental. [*Died* 6 *Aug.* 1955.

COOK, Elsie, (Mrs. E. Thornton Cook); *b.* Otago; *d.* of late Norman Prentys of New Zealand Government Survey Dept., and of Rosa Frances, *g.d.* of Thomas Nixson, one time partner in Baring Bros.; *m.* John Thornton Cook. *Educ.:* privately. Spent a few of her childish years on the stage in Australia; has done journalism in Australia, New Zealand, the United States, and England. Came to England; European War, 1914-18, Royal Arsenal for munition work; resumed literary work on conclusion of peace, until outbreak of War of 1939-45, when she served in an Intelligence Section. *Publications:* Her Majesty: The Romance of the Queens of England; Their Majesties of Scotland; Royal Elizabeths; Royal Marys; Kings-in-the Making; Sir Walter's Dogs; The Royal Line of France; What Manner of Men?; They Lived: A Brontë Novel; Royal Daughters: English Princesses on Foreign Thrones; To Fortune's Piping: An Australian Novel; Royal Cavalcade: The Coronation Book of George VI. and Queen Elizabeth; Speaking Dust: Thomas and Jane Carlyle; Justly Dear: Charles and Mary Lamb. *Address:* c/o John Murray, 50 Albemarle Street, W.1. *Club:* Royal Commonwealth Society. [*Died* 7 *Nov.* 1960.

COOK, Ernest Benjamin, C.B.E. 1947; Shipbroker; Governing Director of C. H. Rugg & Co. Ltd., London; *b.* 29 Mar. 1879; *s.* of George Blyth Cook, Stoke Newington, and Emma Esther, *d.* of William Webster, London; *m.* 1912, Lilian, *d.* of James Kerry, Highbury; one *s.* one *d.* *Educ.:* privately. Fellow of Institute of Chartered Shipbrokers (Member of Council, 1936-39); Hon. Adviser to Minister of Transport; Liveryman of Company of Shipwrights, Freeman of City of London. *Recreations:* music, gardening. *Address:* Hillsborough, Totteridge, N.20. *T.:* Hillside 2133. [*Died* 31 *Oct.* 1952.

COOK, Gilbert, F.R.S. 1940; D.Sc., M.Inst. C.E., M.I.Mech.E.; Regius Professor of Civil Engineering and Mechanics, Glasgow University, since 1938; F.K.C., London; *b.* 1885; *s.* of William Cook of Garston, Liverpool; *m.* Florence, *d.* of late A. E. Davies, J.P., Liverpool. *Educ.:* Roomfield School, Todmorden; University of Manchester. Graduated with Honours in Engineering, 1905; Assistant Engineer with Lancashire and Yorkshire Railway Co., 1906-10; Vulcan Research Fellow in University of Manchester, 1910; Lieutenant R.G.A., 1914-17; transferred to R.N.V.R. for service in technical branch of Mining, Minesweeping, and Anti-Submarine service, 1917; Senior Lecturer in Engineering, University of Manchester, 1919-1921; Prof. of Mechanical Engineering Univ. of London, King's College, 1921-36; Pres. Institution of Engineers & Shipbuilders in Scotland, 1949-. *Publications:* numerous papers embodying research in various branches of Engineering, chiefly Strength and Elasticity of Materials. *Address:* University (Glasgow). *Club:* Athenæum. [*Died* 28 *Aug.* 1951.

COOK, John Irvine, C.B. 1950; O.B.E. 1936; Second Secretary, Ministry of Finance, Northern Ireland, since 1949; *b.* 1892; 2nd *s.* of late Thomas and Annie Cook, Kirkcaldy; *m.* 1st, 1918, Aileen Annie, 3rd *d.* of late Wm. Hillis; one *s.*; 2nd, 1938, Sarah Jane, 2nd *d.* of late Benjamin Hobson; two *d.* *Educ.:* Kirkcaldy and Edinburgh. Irish Land Commission, 1912. Served European War, France and Belgium, in Naval and Irish Divisions, 1916-18; Accountant, Charitable Donations and Bequests Office, Dublin, 1919; Ministry of Finance, N.I. Govt., 1921; Private Sec. to Minister, 1922; N.I. Delegation to Ottawa Conference, 1932; H.M. Treasury, London, 1939; N. Ireland: Ministry of Commerce, Coal Controller and Member of Electricity Board, 1942; Ministry of Finance, 1945. *Recreations:* music and golf. *Address:* 23 Morningside, Bangor, Co. Down. *T.:* Bangor 1559. [*Died* 20 *May* 1952.

COOK, Stanley Smith, F.R.S. 1928; M.I.N.A.; M.I.M.E.; Director, The Parsons Marine Steam Turbine Co., Wallsend-on-Tyne; *b.* Canterbury, 25 Jan. 1875; *m.* Emilie Clara Lewis; one *s.* one *d.* *Educ.:* King's School, Canterbury; St. John's College, Cambridge, B.A. 7th Wrangler Math. Tripos, 1896; 1st Class Engineering Tripos, 1897. *Address:* Leyburn, Castleton Grove, Newcastle upon Tyne. [*Died* 21 *May* 1952.

COOK, Thomas Fotheringham; M.P. (Lab.) Dundee, 1945-50, East Dundee since 1950; Parliamentary Under-Secretary of State, Colonial Office, 1950-51; *b.* 7 June 1908; *s.* of Charles Cook and Mary Fotheringham; *m.* 1929, Elizabeth Wallace; one *s.* one *d.* *Educ.:* Glasgow; Cardenden. Associate Member of Society of Instrument Technology; Lecturer in Economics, Economic Geography and Industrial History for National Council of Labour Colleges. Parliamentary Private Secretary to Sir Stafford Cripps, 1947, to Rt. Hon. J. H. Wilson, President of the Board of Trade, 1947-50. *Address:* 13 Wardlaw Drive, Rutherglen, Lanarkshire. [*Died* 31 *May* 1952.

COOKE, Michael Joseph; Chairman of the National Bank, Ltd., 1933-55; *b.* 7 Sept. 1881; *e. s.* of Edmond Cooke and Maria Maher; *m.* 1927, May Donaghy, M.B., B.Ch., *e. d.* of J. I. Donaghy, B.A., J.P., Solicitor, Belfast; one *s.* one *d. Educ.:* St. Munchin's Coll., Limerick. Junior Master there, 1899; entered service of the National Bank, Ltd., 1899; Secretary, 1917; General Manager and Director, 1923; Member: Advisory Council Bankers Industrial Development Co. Ltd., 1930; Council of Institute of Bankers (England), 1931-48; Dep. Chm. May-Sept. 1946; elected a Vice-Pres. 1949; Vice-Pres. Institute of Bank of Ireland, 1934; Pres. of Institute of Bankers in Ireland, 1949. Member of Commission of Enquiry into Banking, Currency, and Credit in Ireland, 1934-38; Signatory to Majority Report, 1938. *Recreations:* fishing, golf. *Address:* Thornton, Kingston Hill, Kingston, Surrey. *T.:* Kingston 8204. *Clubs:* Reform; St. Stephen's Green (Dublin).
[*Died* 22 *April* 1960.

COOKE, O. D. P. P.; *see* Paget-Cooke.

COOKE, William Cubitt; water-colour painter and book illustrator; *b.* near London, 9 May 1866; *e. surv. s.* of late Dr. M. C. Cooke; *m.* 1897, Maud Jane Tilney (*decd.*). *Educ.:* Cowper Street Schools, City Road, E.C. Apprenticed at 16 to chromo-lithography; in painting and in drawing mostly self-taught; studied Heatherley's, Cook's, Westminster School of Art; first exhibit, 1890, at R.B.A.; 1st black and white drawing published, 1892; 1st Royal Academy picture, 1893. Books illustrated: Jane Austen's novels (30 drawings), Evelina, Cecilia, Vicar of Wakefield, British Ballads, etc.; has drawn for nearly all magazines in London; book illustrations; exhibitor at the R.A., R.I., and R.B.A. for years; late teacher of life drawing, anatomy, etc., under the Middlesex County Council Board of Education. *Publications:* nothing original except drawings and paintings. *Recreations:* walking and sketching. *Address:* (temp.) Whiteway, nr. Stroud, Glos.
[*Died* 13 *April* 1951.

COOMBE, Sir Thomas Melrose, Kt., *cr.* 1924; President, many charities; Founder of the Coombe Scholarships; *b.* Melrose, S.A., 3 Dec. 1877; *s.* of late Thomas Coombe and Sarah Beddome; *m.* 1901, Allie Senior (decd.); three *s.* three *d. Educ.:* Prince Alfred College, Adelaide, S.A. *Recreations:* cricket, tennis, golf. *Address:* c/o The National Bank of Australia, Adelaide, South Australia. *Club:* Junior Carlton. [*Died* 22 *July* 1959.

COOMBS, Captain Thomas Edward, C.B.E. 1937 (O.B.E. 1919); R.D.; R.N.R., retd.; *b.* 1884; *s.* of John Coombs, Somersetshire; *m.* 1911, Kathleen, *d.* of Rev. H. A. S. Pitt, Devonshire; two *s.* (and one *s.* killed on active service and one *s.* decd.). *Educ.:* Wells Grammar School. Served European War, Second in Command H.M. Auxiliary Cruiser Patia, 1915-17; in Command H.M.S. Gossamer, 1917-19, and H.M.S. Gainsborough, 1919, sweeping mines off coast of Belgium (despatches, O.B.E.); from then commanded ships of R.M. Lines; A.D.C. to the King, 1936-38; retired, 1941; served War of 1939-45, Commodore of Convoys and at Admiralty; Member of Honourable Company of Master Mariners. *Recreations:* reading, golf, gardening. *Address:* Avoca, Rifeway, Felpham, Bognor Regis, Sussex.
[*Died* 27 *June* 1953.

COOP, Hubert, R.B.A. 1897; *b.* Olney, Bucks, 8 Mar. 1872; *s.* of late Thomas Coop, Birmingham. *Educ.:* private school. Started life as a draughtsman at Railway Carriage Works near Birmingham, then to business in Oxfordshire, where he abandoned all idea of a business career and departed for North Wales with a few brushes and colours. *Address:* Goats Hill, Northam, Devon. [*Died* 14 *Jan.* 1953.

COOPER OF CULROSS, 1st Baron, *cr.* 1954, of Dunnet; **Thomas Mackay Cooper;** P.C. 1935; O.B.E. 1919; M.A., LL.B., F.R.S.E.; F.R.A.S.; F.S.A. (Scot.); Hon. LL.D. (Edin.) 1944; Docteur h.c. (Paris), 1950; Hon. LL.D. (Glasg.) 1951; Hon. LL.D. (St. Andrews), 1953; *b.* 24 Sept. 1892; *s.* of John Cooper, C.E., and Margaret Mackay. *Educ.:* George Watson's College (Dux, 1909; University, Edinburgh. M.A. (1st Class Hons. Classics). Scottish Bar, 1915; Junior Legal Assessor to City of Edinburgh, 1922; K.C. 1927. Prospective Candidate (U.) for Banffshire, 1930-31; M.P. (Nat. U.) Edinburgh, W. Div., 1935-41; Solicitor-General for Scotland, 1935; Lord Advocate, 1935-41; Lord Justice Clerk, 1941-46; Lord Justice General of Scotland and Lord President of the Court of Session, 1947-54. Chairman: Cttee. on Hydro-Electric Development in Scotland, 1941; Clyde Estuary Cttee., 1944-45; Cttee. on Grants to Scottish Universities, 1946; Cttee. of Inquiry into St. Andrews Univ., 1949; Scottish Ancient Monuments Board, 1946-49; Trustee National Galleries of Scotland; Vice-Pres. Royal Society of Edinburgh, 1946-48; Pres. Scottish History Society, 1945-49; Hon. Bencher, Middle Temple; Hon. Member Edin. Merchant Co.; Soc. Public Teachers of Law; Inst. of Municipal Engineers. *Publications:* Law of Housing and Town Planning, 1920; Scottish Cases of the 13th Century, 1944; The Register of Brieves, 1946; edition of Regiam Majestatem, 1947; The Scottish Legal Tradition, 1949; Supra Crepidam, 1952; Dark Age of Scottish Legal History, 1952; numerous contributions to legal and historical periodicals. *Address:* 16 Hermitage Drive, Edinburgh. *T.:* Edinburgh 56369. *Clubs:* Constitutional; New (Edinburgh); Royal Scottish Automobile (Glasgow). [*Died* 15 *July* 1955 (*ext.*).

COOPER, Austin Edwin, B.A., M.D.; B.Ch., Trinity College, Dublin; L.M. Rotunda; Consulting Anæsthetist, London Hospital; Anæsthetist, Poplar Hospital; *b.* Dublin, 8 Feb. 1869; *e. s.* of late George William Cooper of Clonskeagh, County Dublin; *m.* 1898, Mary (*d.* 1946), 2nd *d.* of late John E. Hunter of Hollybrook Park, Co. Dublin; two *s.* one *d. Educ.:* Leeson School; Trinity College, Dublin; Adelaide Hospital, Dublin; St. Thomas's Hospital. M.B. B.Ch. 1895; M.D. 1896. Formerly Anæsthetist to London Hospital and to Royal National Orthopædic Hospital, and Assistant Anæsthetist, West London and other hospitals; during War of 1939-45 acted as Anæsthetic Specialist to Ministry of Health, attached to Whipps Cross Hospital, London. *Publications:* communications relating to general and special anæsthesia in medical publications. *Recreation:* fishing. *Clubs:* Royal Automobile; University (Dublin). [*Died* 19 *Jan.* 1954.

COOPER, Sir Daniel; *see* Cooper, Sir W. G. D.

COOPER, Sir Henry Lovick, 5th Bt., *cr.* 1821; *b.* 2 April 1875; *s.* of Rev. William Bickford Astley-Cooper; *S.* cousin, 1941; *m.* May Adams (*d.* 1911); one *d. Educ.:* Agriculture School, Wellingore Hall, Lincs. Fruit-grower, etc. in Florida, U.S.A. *Heir: cousin* Patrick Graham Astley Cooper [*b.* 4 Aug. 1918; *m.* 1942; one *s.* one *d.*]. *Address:* 2 West Hill, St. Leonards-on-Sea, Sx.
[*Died* 25 *Aug.* 1959.

COOPER, Percival Martin, C.M.G. 1943; O.B.E. 1938; M.Inst.C.E.; M.I.Struct.E., M.I.M. and Cy.E.; Director of Public Works, Jamaica, since 1941; *b.* 14 Apr. 1887; *o. s.*

of late Thomas Cooper; *m.* Kathleen Mary, *d.* of late J. T. Rossiter, solicitor, London, England; no *c.* *Educ.:* Jamaica College, Jamaica. A.M.Inst.C.E. 1914. Served European War with B.E.F. and Army of the Rhine, 1915-19; Capt. R.E.; 2nd Class Supt., Public Works, Jamaica, 1915; 1st Class Supt., 1920; Inspecting Engineer, 1922; Executive Engineer, 1927; Asst. Director of Public Works, 1930; Acting Surveyor-General, 1935; seconded as Chairman, Water Commission, 1937; Deputy Director of Public Works, 1938; Chairman, Transport (Defence) Board, 1942; Chairman, Fuel and Power (Defence) Board, 1942; Chairman, Civil Aviation Committee, 1943. *Recreations:* tennis, golf. *Address:* Public Works Dept., Kingston, Jamaica, B.W.I. *T.A.:* Half Way Tree, Jamaica. *T.:* 6641. *Clubs:* Liguanea (Halfway Tree); Jamaica (Kingston). [*Died* 21 *April* 1951.

COOPER, Wilbraham Villiers, O.B.E. 1920; *b.* 1876; *s.* of late Rev. Canon J. H. Cooper and Mary Agneta, *d.* of Rt. Rev. Hon. H. M. Villiers; *m.* 1902, Hon. Rose Ellen Goodhart, O.B.E. 1920 (*d.* 1927), *d.* of 1st and last Baron Rendel. *Educ.:* Cheam; Eton (K.S. 1889); King's College, Cambridge (B.A. Classical Tripos, 1898; M.A. 1904); called to Bar, Inner Temple, 1903. Organising Secretary of the Cheap Cottages Exhibition, 1905; engaged in local work in Surrey, and in journalism; Unionist Free Trader; during the War engaged in Hospital work and attached to the Foreign Office; with the Inter-Allied Rhineland High Commission, 1920, and the Inter-Allied Administrative and Plebiscite Commission in Upper Silesia, 1921-22; Editor of the Guardian, 1936-39; a Diplomatic Adviser to the Press Censorship, 1940-41; C.Q.M.S. London Home Guard, 1943-44. *Publications:* The Consolation of Philosophy (trans. from Boethius), 1902; Fiscal Reform Sixty Years Ago, 1904; A History of Cuckfield, 1912. *Address:* 42 Gloucester Place, W.1; Villa St. Dominique, Valescure, France. *Club:* Brooks's. [*Died* 2 *May* 1955.

COOPER, Sir (William George) Daniel, of Woollahra, 4th Bt., *cr.* 1863; *b.* 14 Dec. 1877; *s.* of 3rd Bt. and Alice Helen (*d.* 1937), 3rd *d.* of George Hill, of Surrey Hills, Sydney, N.S.W.; *S.* father, 1925; *m.* 1904, Lettice Margaret (*d.* 1950), *y. d.* of 1st Visc. Long; two *s.* one *d.* Late Lieut. 7th Hussars. *Heir: s.* Major Charles Eric Daniel, The Royals [*b.* 5 Oct. 1906; *m.* 1931, Estelle, *y. d.* of late William Manifold, Victoria, Australia]. *Address:* The Elms, East Tytherton, Chippenham, Wilts. *T.:* Kellaways 231. *Club:* Boodle's. [*Died* 27 *Dec.* 1954.

COOPER, Lt.-Col. William W. H.; *see* Herring-Cooper.

COPE, Sir Alfred, K.C.B., *cr.* 1922 (C.B. 1920). Second Secretary, Ministry of Pensions, 1919-20; Assistant Under-Secretary for Ireland and Clerk of Privy Council (Ireland), 1920-22; General Secretary, National Liberal Organisation, 1922-24; Managing Director Amalgamated Anthracite Collieries, Ltd., 1925-35; Chairman, W. Abbott & Sons, Ltd. to 1939. *Address:* Seaford, Sussex. [*Died* 13 *May* 1954.

COPELAND, (Richard) Ronald (John), C.B.E. 1948; J.P., D.L.; President and Chairman of Spode-Copeland firm of china manufacturers since 1913; 2nd *s.* of Richard Pirie Copeland, Kibblestone Hall, Stone, Staffs.; *m.* 1915, Ida (*see* Mrs. Ronald Copeland), *o. d.* of Mrs. Leonard Cunliffe and late C. Fenzi; one *s.* (and one *s.* decd.). *Educ.:* Harrow. Served with Red Cross, 1915, with French Third Army behind Verdun; (with late Robert Heath) founded Children's Orthopædic Hospital, Biddulph; Member Council of Art and Industry, 1934-36; Member Committee of Pottery Section, Royal Society of Arts; Chairman Executive Committee Stoke-on-Trent Children's Convalescent Home, Rhyl; Pres. North Staffs Boy Scouts' Association; Freeman of City of London; Prime Warden of Goldsmiths' Company. High Sheriff, Staffs, 1939; President Staffordshire Society, 1951. *Recreations:* scouting, fishing, gardening; collecting antique china and silver. *Address:* Trelissick, Feock, Truro. *Club:* Carlton. [*Died* 22 *Aug.* 1958.

COPELAND, Theodore Benfey, C.I.E. 1928; late Indian Civil Service; *b.* 7 Oct. 1878; *s.* of late Professor Ralph Copeland, Ph.D., Astronomer Royal for Scotland; *m.* 1916, Mabel Harriet (*d.* 1939), widow of Major L. M. R. Deas, D.S.O., I.A.; no *c.* *Educ.:* Watson's College, Edinburgh; Edinburgh University, M.A. Entered I.C.S. 1901; retired, 1929. *Address:* Cheniston, Compton, Winchester. [*Died* 7 *Jan.* 1952.

COPEMAN, Lt.-Col. Hugh Charles, C.M.G. 1918; D.S.O. 1916; *b.* 19 January 1862; 3rd *s.* of George Copeman, barrister, Dunham Lodge, Little Dunham, Norfolk. *Educ.:* Haileybury; Sandhurst. Entered Army (Essex Regt.), 1881; Captain, 1888; Major, 1900; served as Adjt. to 2nd Batt., 1886-91; commanded Burma M.I. and Mobile Column in S. Africa, 1900-1 (two medals with 7 clasps; retired, 1904; rejoined, 1914 (9th Battalion Essex Regt.); served European War, 1914-18, Lieut.-Colonel, and commanded 4th Bn. Suffolk Regiment, 1916-19 (despatches thrice, D.S.O., C.M.G., Order of St. Stanislaus, 3rd class). *Recreation:* garden work. *Address:* Hapton, Norwich. [*Died* 2 *June* 1955.

COPPARD, Alfred Edgar; short story writer and poet; *b.* Folkestone, 4 Jan. 1878; *s.* of George Coppard and Emily Alma Southwell; *m.* Winifred May de Kok of Bloemfontein; one *s.* one *d.* *Educ.:* Lewes Road Board School, Brighton. *Publications:* Adam and Eve and Pinch Me, 1921; Clorinda Walks in Heaven, 1922; Hips and Haws, 1922; The Black Dog, 1923; Fishmonger's Fiddle, 1925; The Field of Mustard, 1926; Pelagea and other Poems, 1926; Selection from Burns' Songs, 1925; Yokohama Garland, 1926; Silver Circus, 1928; Collected Poems, 1928; Count Stefan, 1928; Pink Furniture, 1930; My Hundredth Story, 1931; a Bibliography (with Jacob Schwartz), 1931; Nixey's Harlequin, 1931; Easter Day, 1931; Crotty Shinkwin, 1932; Rummy, 1932; Dunky Fitlow, 1933; Ring the Bells of Heaven, 1934; Emergency Exit, 1934; Polly Oliver, 1935; Cherry Ripe (poems), 1935; Ninepenny Flute, 1937; Tapster's Tapestry, 1938; You Never Know, Do You?, 1939; Ugly Anna, 1944; Selected Tales, 1946; Fearful Pleasures (U.S.A.), 1946; Dark-eyed Lady, 1947; Collected Tales (U.S.A.), 1948; Fearful Pleasures, 1951; Lucy in her pink jacket (tales), 1954; It's Me, O Lord!, 1957 (posthumous). *Recreation:* resting. *Address:* Hillside, Duton Hill, Dunmow, Essex. *T.:* Great Easton 255. [*Died* 13 *Jan.* 1957.

COPPINGER, Major-Gen. Walter Valentine, C.I.E. 1930; D.S.O. 1918; Indian Medical Service, retired; *b.* 1 March 1875; *s.* of V. J. Coppinger, Barrister-at-law, and *g.s.* of late Sir Robert Kane; *m.* 1910, Margaret Mary, *d.* of William O'Kelly, Monkstown Castle, Dublin; one *s.* one *d.* *Educ.:* Trinity College, Dublin; Medical School (M.B., B.Ch., B.A.O. Dublin, M.D. Dublin, F.R.C.S. Ireland). Joined the Indian Medical Service, 1900; served as Civil Surgeon in many districts in Bengal and Assam and on Staffs of General Hospitals of Calcutta and Rangoon, and as Professor of Ophthalmic Surgery, M.C.H., Calcutta; Inspector-General of Civil Hospitals, Central Provinces; Surgeon General, Bengal; retired, 1933; served in European War, 1915-18, on Indian Frontier and Mesopotamia (D.S.O., despatches). *Address:* Highlands, Midgeham Green, Woolhampton, Berks. *Club:* Bengal United Service (Calcutta). [*Died* 9 *April* 1957.

CORBET, Sir Gerald Vincent, 6th Bt., *cr.* 1808; *b.* 29 Oct. 1868; 2nd *s.* of 3rd Bt. and Caroline, *d.* of late Vice-Adm. Hon. C. O. Bridgeman; *S.* nephew 1915; *m.* 1904, Ella Theresa Florence (*d.* 1939), *d.* of Col. James Henry Prendergast, Indian Army; no *c.* *Educ.:* Radley. Owns about 7000 acres. *Heir: kinsman* John Vincent Corbet, M.B.E. [*b.* 27 Feb. 1911; *m.* 1st, 1937, Elfrida Isobel Francis; 2nd, 1948, Doreen Elizabeth Stewart, *d.* of Arthur William Gibbon Ritchie]. *Seat:* Acton Reynold, Shrewsbury. *Address:* The Old Manor, Preston Brockhurst, Shrewsbury.
[*Died* 4 *March* 1955.

CORBETT, Adm. Charles Frederick, C.B. 1916; M.V.O. 1904; late R.N.; *s.* of late Adm. Sir John Corbett; *b.* 1867; *m.* 1920, Marjorie Ellen, *o. d.* of Mrs. Borrett of Cransford Hall, Saxmundham, Suffolk; one *d.* Entered Navy, 1881; Commander, 1902; Captain, 1907; Vice-Adm., 1924; Admiral retired, 1928; Captain of H.M.S. Flora, China Station, 1911-14; served Dardanelles, 1915 (despatches, C.B.); retired list, 1922. *Address:* The Cottage, Ufford, Woodbridge, Suffolk. [*Died* 29 *Jan.* 1955.

CORBETT, (Edward) James (Jim Corbett), C.I.E. 1944; O.B.E. 1939; author; Honorary Officer, Royal National Parks of Kenya; Honorary Assistant Game Warden; *b.* 25 July 1875; unmarried. *Educ.:* Philander Smith College, Naini Tal, India; St. Joseph's College, Naini Tal. Served on Bengal and North Western Railway, 1895-1914; served European War, 1914-18, in France; served in Waziristan, 1919-21; served War of 1939-45, in India and Burma. Volunteer Decoration, 1920; Kaisar-i-Hind (gold), 1928. *Publications:* The Man-eating Leopard of Rudraprayag, 1948; Man-eaters of Kumaon, 1952; My India, 1952; Jungle Lore, 1953; The Temple Tiger and More Man-eaters of Kumaon, 1954; Tree Tops, 1955 (posthumous). *Recreations:* writing, fishing, bird and animal photography. *Address:* Pax Two, Nyeri, Kenya, British East Africa. *Clubs:* Overseas; Shikar.
[*Died* 19 *April* 1955.

CORBETT, Harvey Wiley; architect; F.A.I.A., F.R.I.B.A., N.A.; Société des Architectes Diplômés Française; *b.* California, 1873; *m.* 1905, Gail Sherman; one *s.* one *d.* *Educ.:* University of California; École des Beaux Arts, Paris. Architect of Bush House, London, and many works of public value in America. *Address:* 1270 Avenue of the Americas, New York 20, N.Y. *T.:* Judson 6-5667; Bush House, Aldwych, W.C.2.
[*Died* 20 *April* 1954.

CORBETT, Jim; *see* Corbett, Edward J.

CORBIN, John; *b.* Chicago, 2 May 1870; *s.* of C. R. and Caroline F. Corbin, novelist and publicist; *m.* Miss Amy Foster, of New York, 1899. *Educ.:* Chicago Grammar and High Schools; Harvard. A.B. 1892, A.M. 1893; Balliol College, Oxford, 1894-95. Instructor in English Composition at Harvard, 1895-96; assistant editor, Harper's Magazine, 1896-99; dramatic critic, Harper's Weekly, 1898-99; editorial staff, Encyclopædia Britannica, 1900-1901; Dramatic Critic, New York Times, 1902; Dramatic Critic, New York Sun, 1905-7; Literary Director, the New Theatre, New York, 1908-10; Dramatic Critic, N.Y. Times, 1917-19; Editorial Staff, N.Y. Times, 1919-26. *Publications:* The Elizabethan Hamlet, 1895; Schoolboy Life in England, 1898; An American at Oxford, 1902; A New Portrait of Shakespeare, 1903; The First Loves of Perilla, 1903; The Cave Man (a novel), 1907; Which College for the Boy? 1908; Husband and The Forbidden Guests (two plays), 1910; The Edge (a novel), 1915; The Return of the Middle Class, 1922; The Unknown Washington: Biographic Origins of the Republic, 1930; Two Frontiers of Freedom, 1940; Dramatic Productions: Husband, a Comedy in Three Acts, 1910; Shakespeare's Tempest, with full text in Elizabethan manner, 1916. *Recreations:* golf, tennis, squash. *Address:* Crow Ledge, Cross River, N.Y. U.S.A.
[*Died* 30 *Aug.* 1959.

CORDINER, George Ritchie Mather, C.V.O. 1951; Hon. Radiologist St. George's Hospital; Consulting Radiologist: Oldchurch Hospital, Romford; Victoria Hospital, Barnet; Lecturer in Radiology, London School of Hygiene and Tropical Medicine. *Educ.:* St. Andrews University. M.B., Ch.B. (St. Andrews) 1922; D.M.R.E. (Camb.) 1924; formerly Radiologist: St. Paul's Hospital; Evelina Hospital for Children. *Publications:* articles in medical journals. *Address:* 7 Upper Wimpole Street, W.1. *T.:* Welbeck 4747.
[*Died* 8 *April* 1957.

CORDON, Cecil Gilbert William, C.I.E. 1942; E.D.; Director Western India Portuguese Railway since 1944. Late General Manager, Madras and Southern Mahratta Railway, retired 1944. *Address:* Old Pastures, West Close, Middleton-on-Sea, Sussex. *Club:* East India and Sports.
[*Died* 22 *Dec.* 1952.

CORI, Gerty T.; Professor of Biochemistry, Washington University Medical School, St. Louis, Missouri, since 1947; *b.* 15 Aug. 1896; *d.* of Otto Radnitz and Martha Neustadtl; *m.* 1920, Carl F. Cori; one *s.* *Educ.:* Prague, Czechoslovakia. Graduated from Realgym, 1914; took M.D. at German Univ. at Prague, 1920; Demonstrator med., Prague, 1917-19; Asst. Biochemist, State Institute for the Study of Malignant Diseases, Buffalo, 1922-31; Fellow and Research Associate, Pharmacology and Biochemistry, Washington Univ. School of Med., St. Louis, 1931-47. Member: Amer. Soc. of Biological Chemists; Amer. Acad. of Arts and Sciences; Amer. Chemical Society; Nat. Acad. of Sciences; Am. Philosophical Soc.; Mid-west Award, Am. Chem. Soc., 1946; Squibb Award in Endocrinology, 1947; Garvan Medal, 1948; St. Louis Award, 1948. Hon. degrees in Science: Boston Univ., 1948; Smith College, 1949; Yale, 1951; Columbia, 1954; Rochester, 1955. Shared Nobel Prize in Medicine and Physiology, 1947; Sugar Research prize, 1950. *Publications:* articles in Journal of Biological Chemistry since 1925. *Address:* 1080 N. Berry Road, St. Louis, Missouri. *T.:* Woodland 1-5534.
[*Died* 26 *Oct.* 1957.

CORKHILL, Percy Fullerton, C.B.E. 1920; Officer of the Order of the Crown of Belgium; Officier de l'Instruction Publique, France; Knight Commander of the Order of the Crown of Italy; Solicitor; *s.* of Thomas Corkhill, Kirk Michael, Isle of Man. On Committees administering the Titanic, Empress of Ireland, Lusitania, Connemara, Gresford Disaster and Hulton Colliery Funds; inventor of many games for lawn, table, and ships, viz., castello, holo, torpedo, stepping stones. Lay Reader, Diocese of Liverpool. *Publications and Plays:* First Impressions; All Change; The 5 o'clock Edition; Two in the Running; In Purple Ink; Cupid and his Consul; The Stop Press; The Land of Anywhere; Town Hall Recollections; The Mother Star; The Space in Between; Peter Pan Pageant, 1928; The Pageant of the Seven Lamps; The Flaming Torch; Silver Trumpets; The Land of Everywhere; Drums and Bells. *Recreations:* tennis, riding. *Address:* 78 Huskisson St., Liverpool. *T.:* Royal 4370. [*Died* 24 *Jan.* 1959.

CORLETTE, Major Hubert Christian, O.B.E., F.R.I.B.A.; F.S.A. (retired); Major, retired, 1st King Edward's Horse; The King's Oversea Dominions Regiment (Special Reserve Cavalry) attached R.F.A., 1915-16; employed on Staff Duty, 1916-18; attached

Ministry of Agriculture, 1918-20; *b.* 27 June 1869 at Ashfield, Sydney, N.S.W.; 2nd *s.* of late Rev. Canon James Christian Corlette, D.D. Oxon, and Frances Edith, *e.d.* of Sir W. M. Manning, K.C.M.G.; *m.* 1903, Florence Gwynedd (*d.* 1939), *d.* of the late Arthur V. Davies-Berrington, of Pant-y-Goitre, Monmouthshire; one *s.* three *d.* *Educ.:* Sydney Grammar School; Sydney University; University College, London; Royal Academy of Arts School of Architecture, London; Slade School of Fine Art, University College, London; and by foreign travel. Gold Medallist, Institute of Architects, N.S. Wales; Hon. Fellow Roy. Aust. Inst. of Architects; Donaldson Medallist, University College, London, 1892, for science of Building Construction and Materials, etc.; Pugin Studentship, R.I.B.A., second silver medal, 1894; Owen Jones Studentship, R.I.B.A., 1896; Silver Medallist, R.I.B.A., 1899; Member of Council, R.I.B.A., 1923-29; Mention Honorable, Paris Salon, 1905, and Bronze Medal, 1923; exhibitor at Royal Academy since 1894. In partnership with Sir Charles Nicholson, Bart., 1895-1916. Has executed various buildings in Domestic Architecture, Public Buildings, Churches and Decorative Art, etc. Among these are works at New College, Oxford; Clifton College; Winchester College; and Burton Manor, Cheshire; Kensington War Memorial, and others, New Law Courts, General Post Office, Treasury Buildings, Government House, and Town Planning of Streets and Squares for the Government of Jamaica; Imperial College of Tropical Agriculture, Trinidad, Churches at Ashby, Crosby, and Hayes; University War Memorial, Sydney, N.S.W., and Archibald Memorial, Sydney (in collaboration with M. Sicard, Pres. French Acad.), etc.; Architect to Netley Hill Estate, Hampshire. *Publications:* Chichester Cathedral, a history of the building, etc.; The Use and Value of Colour in Architecture, a Prize Essay illustrated by the author; Education and Tradition in Architecture; The Abbey Church of S. Savin; Albi Cathedral; Italian Masters and other designers; Oxford: A School of Architecture; English Architecture; The King's House: Spanish Town, Jamaica; The Crown in England; Monarchy or Democracy; and other articles, lectures, and reviews. *Recreations:* hunting, shooting. *Address:* 64 Hendon Lane, Finchley, N.3. *T.:* Finchley 6988.
[*Died* 23 *April* 1956.

CORNELIUS, Percival; *b.* 2 Dec. 1874; *s.* of late George T. Cornelius, Ipswich; *m.* 1898, Florence, *d.* of late Richard Glandfield, Plymouth; one *d.* Joined Western Morning News, Editorial Dept., 1894; Parliamentary Representative, 1899-1907; Daily Telegraph, 1907-15; Official Report (Hansard) House of Commons, 1915-43, Asst. Editor, 1935-39, Editor, 1939-43. Chairman, Parliamentary Press Gallery, 1935-36. *Recreations:* gardening and walking. *Address:* Ditton Lodge, Lower Compton Road, Plymouth. *T.:* Plymouth 61733. [*Died* 30 *Jan.* 1960.

CORNEWALL, Sir Geoffrey, 6th Bt., *cr.* 1764; J.P., D.L. Herefordshire; Barrister-at-law of the Inner Temple; *b.* 7 May 1869; *e. s.* of 5th Bt. and Louisa (*d.* 1900), *d.* of Francis Bayley, County Court Judge; *S.* father, 1908. *Educ.:* Eton; Trinity Hall, Camb.; B.A. High Sheriff, Herefordshire, 1913; retired from Herefordshire C.C. 1949, after 51 years' service. *Heir:* *b.* William Francis, barrister-at-law [*b.* 16 Nov. 1871. *Educ.:* Oxford Univ., B.A.]. *Address:* Newcote, Moccas, Hereford.
[*Died* 21 *Jan.* 1951.

CORNEY, Leonard George, C.M.G. 1946; B.A. (Cantab.); *b.* 27 March 1886; *y. s.* of Alfred and Elizabeth Steele Corney; *m.* 1921, Hilda Fletcher; one *s.* one *d.* *Educ.:* St. John's Coll., Cambridge (Open Exhibitioner). Classical Tripos, 1908; Colonial Audit Branch of Exchequer and Audit Dept., 1910; Asst. Auditor, Gold Coast, 1910; Deputy Auditor, Gold Coast, 1920; Asst. Director, Colonial Audit Dept., London, 1930; Deputy Auditor, Straits Settlements and Fed. Malay States, 1932, Auditor, 1936; Acting Financial Secretary, Straits Settlements, 1940. Served European war, Artists' Rifles, 1916, Gold Coast Regt., 1917-18; interned by Japanese in Singapore, 1942-45. Member East African Salaries Commission, Salaries Commissioner Aden and Somaliland, 1947. *Publications:* Financial Orders, Gold Coast Colony, 1919; General Orders, Gold Coast Colony, 1921. *Recreations:* tennis, golf. *Address:* West Ridge, Moorlands Rd., Budleigh Salterton, Devon. [*Died* 13 *Aug.* 1955.

CORNFORD, Frances (Crofts); Poet; *b.* 30 March 1886; *d.* of late Sir Francis Darwin, D.Sc., F.R.S. and his 2nd wife, Ellen Wordsworth Crofts; *m.* 1908, Francis Macdonald Cornford, Litt.D., F.B.A. (*d.* 1943) sometime Fellow of Trinity College, Cambridge and Professor of Ancient Philosophy; *g.d.* of Charles Darwin, F.R.S.; two *s.* two *d.* (and one *s.* decd.). *Educ.:* home. Awarded (jointly) Heinemann Prize for Poetry, Royal Society of Literature, 1948; Queen's Medal for Poetry, 1959. *Publications:* Poems, 1910; Spring Morning, 1915; Autumn Midnight, 1923; Different Days, 1928; Mountains and Molehills, 1934; Poems from the Russian, 1943; Travelling Home, 1948; Collected Poems, 1954; On a Calm Shore, 1960. *Address:* 10 Millington Rd., Cambridge. [*Died* 19 *Aug.* 1960.

CORNISH, George Augustus; Professor emeritus, University of Toronto; *b.* Courtright, Ontario, 10 April 1874; *m.* 1903, Bessie Maude Samson, Chatham, Ontario; two *d.* one *s.* *Educ.:* Chatham Collegiate Institute; University of Toronto. Teacher in public schools of the province, 1891-95; Science Specialist in the Collegiate Institutes at Niagara Falls and Lindsay, 1903-8; Science Master of the Normal School, Peterboro, 1908-10; Lecturer and Professor in the University of Toronto, 1910-44. *Publications:* Manual on the Teaching of Elementary Science, 1908; Text-Book on Laboratory Equipment, 1913; Nature Study Lessons on Birds, 1914; First Course in Zoology (in part), 1914; High School Text-Book of Chemistry and Laboratory Manual, 1917; Canadian School Geography and Canadian School Atlas, 1922; High School Physical Geography, 1923; Canadian Geography for Juniors and Manual on Teaching of Geography, 1926; Commercial Geography for Canadians, 1930; Senior Chemistry, 1934; Senior Manual of Chemical Experiments, 1935; New Canadian School Geography, vol. 1, 1936; vol. 2, 1937; Social Studies, vol. 1, 1938; Social Canada, 1941; Separate Schools in Ontario, 1948; The Hope Report, 1951; Questions and Answers to Hope Report; Separate Schools in British Columbia, 1952; Should Canada Send an Envoy to the Vatican?, 1957. Numerous contributions to educational publications. *Recreations:* gardening, studying natural history. *Address:* 574 Christie Street West, Toronto, Canada. *T.:* LE 2.3866. [*Died* 29 *April* 1960.

CORNWALL, Rt. Hon. Sir Edwin, P.C. 1921; 1st Bt., *cr.* 1918; Kt., *cr.* 1905; Deputy Chairman of Ways and Means, and Deputy-Speaker House of Commons, 1919-22; Controller of the Household, and Minister for National Health Insurance, 1916-19; Officer of the Legion of Honour; D.L. and J.P. Co. of London; M.P. (C.L.) N.E. Bethnal Green, 1906-22; *b.* 1863; 2nd *s.* of Andrew Cornwall of Lapford, Devon; *m.* 1883, Ellen Mary (*d.* 1929), *d.* of John Day of Oxford; one *s.* two *d.* Member of London County Council, 1892-1910 Vice-Chairman of Council, 1903-5; Chairman, 1905-6; was chief whip of Progressive Party for eight years; took prominent part in securing approval of Council to Kingsway and Aldwych scheme; member of Thames Conservancy,

1900-8; Port of London Authority, 1908-18; first Mayor of Fulham, 1900; Hon. Secretary of the Franco-British Inter-Parliamentary Committee; Vice-Chairman Territorial Force Assoc., County of London, 1907-14. *Recreations:* golf and travelling. *Heir: s.* Reginald Edwin [*b.* 31 May 1887; *m.* 1923, Nellie M. E. King, *d.* of late David E. Morley]. *Address:* Chudleigh House, Esher, Surrey. *T.:* Esher 167. [*Died* 27 *Feb.* 1953.

CORNWALLIS, Sir Kinahan, G.C.M.G., *cr.* 1943 (K.C.M.G., *cr.* 1933; C.M.G. 1926); Kt., *cr.* 1929; C.B.E. 1919; D.S.O. 1917; B.A., F.R.G.S.; *b.* 19 Feb. 1883; *s.* of Kinahan Cornwallis; *m.* 1st, 1911, Gertrude Dorothy (marriage dissolved, 1925), *y. d.* of late Sir Albert Bowen, 1st Bt.; one *s.* one *d.* (and *y. s.* killed in action, 1945); 2nd, 1937, Margaret, *o. d.* of Harry Ralph Clark, Lymington, Hants. *Educ.:* Haileybury College; University College, Oxford. President, Oxford University Athletic Club, 1904-6; Sudan Civil Service, 1906-14 (4th Class, Order of the Mejidie); Egyptian Civil Service, 1914-24; seconded by Egyptian Govt. and held temporary Commission, 1915-20 (despatches, 2nd Class Order of the Nahda, 4th Class Order of the Nile); Director, Arab Bureau, Cairo, 1916-20; Assistant Chief Political Officer, Egyptian Expeditionary Force, 1919; Colonel, Special List; seconded for duty in Foreign Office, London, 1920-21; seconded to Iraq Govt., 1921, and accompanied Emir Feisal to Iraq; Adviser to Ministry of Interior, Iraq Govt., 1921-35; retired, 1935; Foreign Office, 1939-1941; Ambassador in Baghdad, 1941-45; Chairman, Middle East (Official) Committee, Foreign Office, 1945-46; Director, British Bank of the Middle East. 1st Class Order of the Rafidain. *Address:* Castle Mill House, North Warnborough, Basingstoke, Hants. *Club:* Athenæum. [*Died* 3 *June* 1959.

CORNWALLIS-WEST, Major George F. M.; J.P.; *b.* 14 Nov. 1874; *o. s.* of late Col. W. Cornwallis-West of Ruthin Castle, Denbigh, and Lord-Lieut. of that county; *m.* 1st, Jennie, C.I., R.R.C. (*d.* 1921) *widow* of Lord Randolph Churchill; 2nd, Beatrice Stella, Mrs. Patrick Campbell (*d.* 1940); no *c.*; 3rd, Mrs. Georgette Hirsch, *widow* of Adolph Hirsch. *Educ.:* Eton. Joined the Scots Guards, 1895; served S.A. War as aide-de-camp to Lord Methuen until invalided home; transferred to Reserve of Officers, 1901; rejoined the Army, Aug. 1914; commanded the Anson Battn. R.N. Div.; was present at the siege of Antwerp; subsequently acting Provost-Marshal to the 57th Div. and later for the counties of Surrey and Middlesex; transferred to Cork as A.P.M. Southern Ireland, 1919; succeeded to the family estates upon the death of his father, 1917. *Publications:* has written several one-act plays which have been produced; notably, Pro Patria, London, 1916; Methods of Margot (three act), 1933; Life and Letters of Admiral Cornwallis, 1927; Two Wives, 1929; Edwardian Hey-Days, 1930; Edwardians Go Fishing, 1932; Fortune's Favourites, 1933; The Woman Who Stopped War, 1935; Us Dogs, 1938. *Recreations:* golf, fishing, shooting. *Address:* Englemere, Ascot, Berks. *Clubs:* Turf, Royal Thames Yacht. [*Died* 1 *April* 1951.

CORY, Lady, C.B.E. 1929; J.P.; **Elizabeth Cansh,** *d.* of Alexander Walker, J.P.; *m.* 1910, as his 2nd wife, Sir Herbert Cory, 1st Bt.; two *d.* *Recreations:* golf and motoring. *Address:* 7 Princes Gate, S.W.7. *T.:* Kensington 1829. *Clubs:* Ladies' Carlton; Ladies' Cardiff and County (Cardiff). [*Died* 23 *Nov.* 1956.

CORY, Lt.-Col. Evan James Trevor, O.B.E. 1919; T.D. 1918; M.D., L.R.C.P., M.R.C.S. Lond., L.S.A. Lond., L.M.S.S.A. Lond.; on the Chelsea and Kensington 'B' Zone Home Guard; Knight and Member of the Chapter General Venerable Order of St. John of Jerusalem; Hospitaller of Bridgend for the Priory of Wales, 1933; *b.* Aberdare, 1863; *s.* of Jones Evan, V.D., J.P., of Ty-mawr, Aberdare, and Hendreforgan, Glam., and Mary E. Greene, Hurstmonceaux, granted the name of Cory by Special Royal Licence, London Gazette, 1911; *m.* 1st, Edith E., *d.* of Captain J. Messum, R.N.; (two *s.* killed in action); 2nd, Hilda Cory (*d.* 1947), *d.* of Richard Cory, J.P., Oscar House, Cardiff; 3rd, Edith Mabel, *d.* of late Walter Gray, Chelmsford. *Educ.:* Charterhouse School; Brussels Univ. St. Thomas's Hospital. Lieut.-Colonel late R.A.M.C.T. (1914-15 Star, British War Medal, Victory Medal); Knight of Grace and Justice of the Order of St. John of Jerusalem; late D.A.D.M.S. 1st London Division; Surgical Specialist E.E.F. and Gallipoli, 1915; in command 3/1st Welsh Field Ambulance, 1916; in command 309th Service Field Ambulance, 1917; Headquarters Staff War Office, A.M.D.I., 1918-20; late Surgeon-Captain, 5th Welsh Regiment, 1908-15; late Surgeon, Lady Bute's Hospital; Examining Surgeon, G. W. R. Engineering Dept.; Medical Examiner, Board of Education, London; Member and Lecturer St. John's Ambulance Associations; F.R.Soc.Med.; High Constable of Aberdare, 1908; late representative for Aberdare on University of Wales at Cardiff; late Member of the Joint War Finance Committee of the Order of St. John's and British Red Cross Society. *Publications:* contributions to Lancet, British Medical Journal, and other medical papers. *Recreations:* shooting, fishing, tennis, and motoring. *Address:* c/o Cox's Branch, Lloyds Bank, 6 Pall Mall, S.W.1. *Clubs:* Junior Army and Navy, Pilgrims, Royal Automobile. [*Died* 5 *May* 1957.

CORY-WRIGHT, Sir Arthur Cory, 2nd Bt., *cr.* 1903; M.A.; J.P., Herts and Middlesex; *b.* 18 Nov. 1869; *s.* of 1st Bt. and Mima, *d.* of late Sir Hugh Owen. *S.* father, 1909; *m.* 1891, Olive (*d.* 1928), *e. d.* of Henry Clothier, M.D.; four *s.* *Educ.:* Harrow; Oxford. High Sheriff for Herts, 1921-22; ex-Member Port of London Authority. *Heir: s.* Captain Geoffrey Cory Wright, late 3rd Batt. The Buffs [*b.* 26 Aug. 1892; *m.* 1915, Felicity, 2nd *d.* of late Sir Herbert Tree; three *s.*]. *Address:* Mackerye End, Harpenden, Herts. *T.:* Harpenden 77. *Clubs:* Junior Carlton, M.C.C. [*Died* 21 *April* 1951.

COSGRAVE, Sir William Alexander, Kt., *cr.* 1938; C.I.E. 1931; I.C.S. (retired); *b.* 1879; *s.* of late H. A. Cosgrave, J.P., Co. Dublin; *m.* 1911, Maude Elizabeth; *d.* of late C. F. Gale, Cheltenham; three *d.* *Educ.:* Shrewsbury; Trinity College, Dublin (classical scholar) Joined I.C.S. in India, 1903; served in various districts in Bengal, Eastern Bengal, and Assam, and in reconstructed Province of Assam after 1912; Political Agent in Manipur State, 1917-20 Chief Secretary to Government of Assam, 1930-31, 1932-33; Commissioner of a division, 1933; as nominated official representative from Assam on the Indian Legislative Assembly, acted in several sessions as Chief Government Whip; officiated as Member Public Service Commission (India), 1934; Chief Commissioner of Andaman and Nicobar Islands, 1935-38. *Address:* The Cross Farm, Ninfield, nr. Battle, Sussex. *Club:* East India and Sports. [*Died* 11 *Sept.* 1952.

COSSIMBAZAR, Maharaja Srischandra Nandy, M.A., M.L.A.; head of a premier Zemindar family of Bengal; Member Bengal Legislative Council (now West Bengal Assembly) since 1924, and Congress Assembly Party, W. Bengal; *b.* 1897; *m.* 1917, Second Rajkumari of Dighapatia. *Educ.:* Calcutta University (M.A.). Ex-Minister, Govt. of Bengal (Irrigation, Communications and Works, 1936-41). Presided over several All-

India Confs.; Pres., All India Music Conf.; Calcutta Univ. Institute (Fine Arts Section); President and Trustee, Bangiya Sahitya Parisad; Trustee, Indian Museum; Life Member, Viswa Bharati, Indian Science News Assoc.; Member: Asiatic Soc. of Bengal, Royal Agri-Horticultural Soc. of India; Pres. Governing Body several educ. Institutions. Patron, Mohan Bagan Club; Pres. Bengal Lawn Tennis Assoc. and Bengal Table Tennis Assoc.; Vice-Pres., Calcutta South Club; Pres. Hindustan Chamber of Commerce; Ex-Pres., British Indian Assoc.; Member Bengal Nat. Chamber of Commerce; Ex-Pres. Automobile Assoc. of Bengal; Pres. Ramkrishna Mission Sisumangal Pratishthan (Calcutta). Chairman: Manindra Mills Ltd., Cossimbazar Coal & Mineral Co. Ltd.; National Health Products Ltd.; Sealdah Cold Storage & Transport Ltd., C. B. Syndicate Ltd.; Director: Bengal Potteries Ltd.; Jogta Coal Co. Ltd.; Bengal Provincial Railway Co. Ltd.; Rajgaon Stone Co. Ltd., etc. Proprietor: Maharaja Cossimbazar China Clay Mines (Singhbhum); Maharaja Cossimbazar Stone Works (Nalhati), etc. *Publications:* Bengal Rivers and Our Economic Welfare, 1948; Bengal's River Problem, 1939; Select Public Speeches, 1936; Flood and Its Remedy, 1938; Rationale of Food Crisis, 1943; Dasyu-Duhita, 1928; Monopathy, 1932; Which Way lies Peace, 1939, etc. *Recreations:* takes keen interest in literature, music and fine arts; is an all-round sportsman taking particular interest in tennis and billiards. *Address:* Sreepur Palace, P.O. Cossimbazar Raj, Murshidabad, India; Cossimbazar House, 302 Upper Circular Road, Calcutta 9. [*Died* 23 *Feb.* 1952.

COSTER, Howard, (Howard Sydney Musgrave Coster); Owner of Photographic Studio; *s.* of John William Coster and Anne Mary Porter; *m.* 1925, Joan Burr. *Educ.:* at Ventnor. Went to S. Africa 1923; farming for 2 years; returned to England and studied photography, technical and portraiture; later returning to S. Africa opening a studio in Bloemfontein; during the war returned to England, joining the photogr phic section of the Royal Air Force; after the war spent 7 years in S. Africa, Bloemfontein and Johannesberg and in 1926 opened Studio in London, specialising in men's portraiture; his collection of negatives of famous people has been acquired by British Council, and is now held by Central Office of Information as a National Collection. F.R.S.A., 1937; F.I.B.P.; Freedom of City of London, 1944. *Recreations:* walking and sketching. *Address;* 41A Grange Road, Sutton, Surrey. *T.:* Vigilant 5103; 9 Sackville Street, Piccadilly, W.1. *T.:* Regent 4561. [*Died* 17 *Nov.* 1959.

COTTERELL, Cecil Bernard, C.S.I. 1933; C.I.E. 1915; I.C.S., retired; *b.* 27 Dec. 1875; *s.* of George Cotterell, York; *m.* 1922, Dorothy, *d.* of P. Sankey; one *s. Educ.:* St. Peter's School, York; Balliol College, Oxford. Entered I.C.S. 1898; served in the Madras Presidency from 1899; Deputy-Commissioner Salt and Abkari Dept. 1905; Private Secretary to the Governor of Madras, 1912-15; Commissioner Agency Div., 1921; Sec. to the Govt. of Madras, 1925; Board of Revenue, Madras, 1930; retired 1933. *Recreations:* most outdoor sports. *Address:* The Manor House, Frimley, Surrey. [*Died* 24 *Jan.* 1957.

COTTESLOE, 3rd Baron (U.K.) (*cr.* 1874), **Thomas Francis Fremantle,** C.B. 1926; M.A., D.L., J.P.; Bt. 1821; Knight of Justice, Order of St. John of Jerusalem; Baron of Austrian Empire, *cr.* 1816; Lord Lieutenant of Bucks, 1923-54; President Bucks Territorial Army Association; late Pres. County Councils Association; Member Small Arms Committee, War Office, 1905-37; Chairman, 1920-37; Associate Member, Ordnance Board; late Chm. National Rifle Association, 1930-39; late Pres. Society for Army Historical Research; Lt.-Col. and late Hon. Col. Bucks Bn. Terr. Army, V.D., T.D.; *b.* 5 Feb. 1862; *s.* of 2nd Baron Cottesloe and Lady Augusta Henrietta Scott (*d.* 1906), 2nd *d.* of 2nd Earl of Eldon; *S.* father, 1918; *m.* 1896, Florence, *d.* of late Thomas Tapling; two *s.* four *d. Educ.:* Eton; Balliol College, Oxford. *Publications:* Notes on the Rifle, 1896; The Book of the Rifle, 1901; The Englishman and the Rifle, 1946; Purbeck and other Poems, 1951. *Heir:* *s.* Hon. John Walgrave Halford Fremantle. *Address:* The Old House, Swanbourne, Bletchley, Bucks. *Club:* Travellers'. [*Died* 19 *July* 1956.

COTTON, Brig.-Gen. Arthur Stedman, C.B. 1930; C.M.G. 1919; C.B.E. 1920; D.S.O. 1915; A.M.; late R.A.; *b.* 18 Aug. 1873; 2nd *s.* of late Major J. W. M. Cotton, J.P., of 2 Chester Terrace, Regent's Park, N.W., late 21st Hussars and 9th Foot; *m.* 1903, Rose, 2nd *d.* of late Robert Bousfield, D.L.; one *d. Educ.:* Merchant Taylors' School; R.M.A., Woolwich; joined Royal Artillery, 1893; Capt., 1900; Major, 1910; Lieut.-Col., 1916; Colonel, 1919; served China, 1900 (medal); European War, with Royal Artillery in 2nd, 5th, 32nd, and 41st Divisions, in the latter as C.R.A.; as Artillery Adviser with British Military Mission to S. Russia; three times wounded, despatches nine times; Bt. Lt.-Col. 1916; Bt. Col. 1919; D.S.O., C.M.G., C.B.E., 1914 Star, and clasp; G.S. medal, Victory medal; Officer St. Maurice and Lazarus, Italy; 3rd Class St. Vladimir, Russia; Croix de Guerre avec Palmes, France; Croix de Guerre, Belgium; C.R.A., 28th Division (Chanak, Turkey), 1922-23; Commanded 28th-Division, 1923; C.R.A. 56th (1st London) Division T.A., 1924-25; C.C.R.A. Southern Command, India, 1926-27; Brigadier R.A. Northern Command, India, 1927-30; retd. pay, 1930; selected for reward for distinguished service, 1933; awarded Albert Medal for gallantry in saving life at Novorossisk, S. Russia, 1920; Defence Medal for duty with Civil Defence, 1939-45. *Address:* 10 Portarlington Road, West Cliff, Bournemouth. *Clubs:* Army and Navy, M.C.C.; Bournemouth (Bournemouth). [*Died* 13 *Sept.* 1952.

COTTON, Admiral R. G. A. W.; *see* Stapleton-Cotton.

COUCHMAN, Brigadier Sir Harold John, Kt., *cr.* 1937; D.S.O. 1918; M.C.; *b.* 29 July 1882; *y. s.* of late Rev. H. Couchman, Haileybury College; *m.* 1925, Evelyn Beatrice, *y. d.* of late Col. W. L. C. Baddeley; no *c. Educ.:* Haileybury; R.M.A. Woolwich. Commissioned Royal Engineers, 1900; Captain, 1910; Major, 1916; Lieut.-Colonel, 1925; Colonel, 1930; Brigadier, 1933; appointed to Survey of India, 1906; European War, France, 1915-19; Security Printing, India, as Deputy Master, 1926-29; Survey of India, 1929; Surveyor-General, 1933-37. *Address:* c/o Lloyds Bank, R. Dept., 6 Pall Mall, S.W.1. [*Died* 30 *Nov.* 1956.

COULSON, Lieut.-Col. Frank Morris, C.B.E. 1919; late Army Pay Dept.; *b.* 1880; *m.* 1905, Beatrice, *d.* of A. W. Anderson. Served S. Africa, 1901-2 (Queen's medal and five clasps, King's medal with two clasps); European War, 1914-19 (despatches, C.B.E.). *Address:* 52 Telford Avenue, S.W.2. [*Died* 14 *Nov.* 1953.

COULTER, Ven. J. W.; Vicar of Calne and Archdeacon of Wilts, 1927-51, Archdeacon Emeritus since 1951; Canon of Salisbury Cathedral since 1920; *b.* 1867; *s.* of John Coulter and Margaret Shaw; *m.* 1st, 1895, Amelia Sinclair (*d.* 1932), *d.* of Very Rev. Charles Hind, Dean of Ferns; 2nd, 1944, Evelyn Delabere, *d.* of late R. D. Prior. *Educ.:* Trinity College, Dublin. Curate, Ferns Cathedral, 1891-96; Swanage, 1896-1900; Rector of Langton Matravers, 1900-16; Rector of Bridport, 1916-27.

Address: 4 Cranborne Road, Swanage, Dorset. *T.:* Swanage 2792. [*Died* 10 *April* 1956.

COUPER, Sir Thomas, Kt., *cr.* 1935; C.S.I. 1931; M.A.; *b.* 15 March 1878; *s.* of John Couper, Dundee. *Educ.:* Fettes College; Worcester College, Oxford. Entered Indian Civil Service, 1901; member Governor's Executive Council, Burma, 1930-35; acting Governor of Burma, 1935; retired, 1937. *Address:* c/o Grindlay's Bank Ltd., 54 Parliament St., S.W.1. [*Died* 16 *Nov.* 1954.

COUPLAND, Sir Reginald, K.C.M.G., *cr.* 1944; C.I.E. 1928; M.A., Hon. D.Litt. (Durham); F.B.A.; Beit Prof. of History of British Empire at Oxford Univ., 1920-48; *b.* 2 Aug. 1884; 2nd *s.* of late Sidney Coupland, M.D. *Educ.:* Winchester; New College, Oxford. 1st class Literæ Humaniores, 1907; Fellow and Lecturer in Ancient History at Trinity College, Oxford, 1907-14; Beit Lecturer in Colonial History, 1913-18; Editor of the Round Table, 1917-19, and 1939-41; Fellow of All Souls College, 1920-48; and 1952-; Fellow of Nuffield College, 1939-50; Trustee of the National Portrait Gallery since 1941; Member of Royal Commission on the Superior Civil Services in India, 1923; Sir George Watson Lecturer, London, 1928; Adviser, Burma Round Table Conference, 1931; Lowell Lecturer, Boston, 1933; Member of Palestine Royal Commission, 1936-37; Member of Sir Stafford Cripps' Mission to India, 1942. *Publications:* The War Speeches of William Pitt the Younger, 1915; Wilberforce, a Narrative, 1923; The Quebec Act, 1925; Raffles, 1926; Kirk on the Zambesi, 1928; The American Revolution and the British Empire, 1930; The British Anti-Slavery Movement, 1933; The Empire in These Days, 1935; East Africa and its Invaders, 1938; The Exploitation of East Africa, 1939; The Cripps Mission, 1942; The Indian Problem, 1833-1935, 1942; Indian Politics, 1936-1942, 1943; The Future of India, 1943; Livingstone's Last Journey, 1945; India, A Re-statement, 1945; Zulu Battle-Piece, 1948; (posthumous) Welsh and Scottish Nationalism, 1955. *Address:* Black Hill Copse, Boar's Hill, Oxford. *T.A:* Boar's Hill, Oxford. *T.:* Oxford 85227. *Club:* Athenæum. [*Died* 6 *Nov.* 1952.

COURAGE, Comdr. Rafe Edward, D.S.O. 1940; D.S.C.; Royal Navy (retired); *b.* 22 June 1902; *s.* of Lt.-Col. M. R. F. Courage, D.S.O.; *m.* 1934, Irene, *d.* of Gen. Sir David Campbell; one *s.*; *m.* 1942, Nancy, *d.* of P. R. Petersen. *Educ.:* R.N. Colleges, Osborne and Dartmouth. Entered R.N. 1916; served European War; Lieut. 1924; Commander, 1940; commanded H.M.S. Havock at Narvik (D.S.O.) and in various operations (D.S.C. and bar, bar to D.S.O.); late Commander in H.M.S. Queen Elizabeth. Commander, Orange Nassau with Swords. *Recreations:* shooting, polo, rowing. *Address:* The Old Rectory, Bradley, Alresford, Hants. *Clubs:* United Service, Royal Automobile. [*Died* 25 *March* 1960.

COURCHESNE, Most Rev. Georges, D.D.; Archbishop of Rimouski, (R.C.), since 1946; *b.* Pierreville, Qué., 13 Sept. 1880; *s.* of Alexandre Courchesne, farmer, and Celina Bazin. *Educ.:* Nicolet Seminary, Rome. Ordained to priesthood, 1904; Professor of Rhetoric in Nicolet till 1908; completed his theological studies in Rome, where he obtained his grade of Doctor after three years, 1908-11; spent six months at the University of Friburg; again Professor in Nicolet at the Seminary, 1911-19; Principal of the Normal School of Nicolet, and Professor of Pedagogy at Laval University of Quebec, 1920-28; Catholic Bishop of Rimouski, 1928-46. *Publication:* Nos Humanités, 1927. *Address:* Rimouski, Qué., Canada. [*Died* 14 *Nov.* 1950.

COURT, Emily, R.O.I.; Land, sea and flower painter; *d.* of Rev. J. C. L. Court. *Educ.:* Slade School. Exhibitor: Royal Academy up to 1954 (inclusive); and Pittsburgh-Carnegie Institute; Winner of International Flower Painters Prize at Pittsburgh (Garden Club Prize); Exhibitor Royal Institute, New English Art Club, Salon (Paris), Toronto, and many other places in England and overseas. Centenary Exhibition Wellington 1939, New Zealand, Cape Town, America, Australia, etc. *Publications:* Reproductions in Colour, Studio, and other papers. *Recreations:* gardening, reading. *Address:* 4 Avenue Studios, Fulham Rd., S.W.3. *T.:* Kensington 0773. [*Died* 24 *April* 1957.

COURTAULD, Augustine; D.L.; J.P.; *b.* 1904; *s.* of late S. A. Courtauld, Halstead, Essex; *m.* 1932, Mollie, *d.* of late F. D. Montgomerie; four *s.* two *d.* *Educ.:* Charterhouse; Trinity College, Cambridge; Served War of 1939-45: Sub-Lieut., R.N.V.R., 1939; Lieut. 1940-45. Chairman, Essex Association of Boys' Clubs; C.C. Essex, 1945-55; D.L., J.P. Essex, 1946; High Sheriff of Essex for 1953. Vice-President R.N.L.I., 1957; President Cruising Association, 1957. Polar Medal awarded by King George V, 1932. *Publication:* (Autobiography) Man the Ropes, 1957; From the Ends of the Earth (Polar Anthology), 1958. *Address:* Spencers, Great Yeldham, Essex. *T.:* 255. *Clubs:* Boodle's, Alpine; Royal Yacht Squadron. [*Died* 3 *March* 1959.

COURTAULD, Samuel Augustine, Hon. LL.D. Lond.; J.P. and D.L. Essex; *b.* 1865; *e. surv. s.* of George Courtauld of Gosfield, Essex; *m.* Edith Anne (*d.* 1951), *o. d.* of W. V. Lister of Eastry, Kent; two *s.* one *d.* *Educ.:* Charterhouse. For many years a Director of Courtaulds, Ltd. (formerly Samuel Courtauld & Co.); High Sheriff, Essex, 1916; was Chm. of Essex Standing Joint Committee for 21 years; Pres. of Essex County Hospital, Colchester; Chm. of Governors of Felsted School, Essex, where he has endowed scholarships and built the Science and Art block; has built and endowed twenty Homes of Rest at Halstead; provided good cottages there, and given Parish Halls and Sports Grounds to neighbouring villages; a Vice-President of Middlesex Hospital, W., where he was Chm. of the Medical School Council, he has endowed the Professorship of Anatomy there and built and endowed the Institute of Bio-chemistry and supplied the Clinical Research Unit. A former President of Huguenot Society of London. *Publications:* The Odes and Epodes of Horace, Metrical translations by various authors, 1st, 2nd, and 3rd editions. *Recreation:* reading. *Address:* The Howe, Halstead, Essex. *T.:* Halstead 32; 8 Palace Green, W.8. *T.:* Western 5046. *Clubs:* Carlton, Garrick. [*Died* 28 *Jan.* 1953.

COURTAULD-THOMSON, 1st Baron, *cr.* 1944, of Dorneywood, Buckinghamshire; **Col. Courtauld Greenwood Courtauld-Thomson,** K.B.E., *cr.* 1918; Kt., *cr.* 1912; C.B. 1916; *b.* 16 Aug. 1865; *s.* of late Robert William Thomson, of Edinburgh and Stonehaven; assumed by Deed Poll, 1944, surname of Courtauld-Thomson. *Educ.:* Eton; Magdalen Coll., Oxford (M.A.). High Sheriff Bucks, 1933; J.P. Bucks; one of H.M. Lieuts. for the City of London, 1950-; holds Hon. Freedom Livery and Membership of Court of Assistants of Paviors Company; Knight of Grace, Order of St. John of Jerusalem (Hospitaller, 1918-33), Bailiff Grand Cross, 1944-; British Red Cross Commissioner, France, 1914-15 and Chief Comr., Malta, Egypt, Italy, Macedonia, and Near East, 1915-19; attached G.H.Q. Staff B.E.F., Egypt, 1916, and Italy, 1918 (despatches five times); Vice Patron, Univ. Coll. Hosp.; Chm. King Edward VII Sanatorium, Midhurst; Vice-Chairman Cassel Hospital for Functional Nervous Disorders; Gov. and Member Finance Cttee., Star and Garter Home; Council, King Edward VII Hosp. Fund for London; Trustee and Member

Governing Body, Whiteley Village; Trustee, Guild of St. George; Dir. Roy. Acad. of Music; Vice-Pres. King Edward VII Hosp., Windsor; Vice-Pres. and Member of Council, Officers' Assoc.; Nation's Fund for Nurses; Chm. Limmer and Trinidad Lake Asphalt Co. Ltd.; Chm. Merchants Marine Insurance Co. Ltd.; formerly Chm. Employers' Liability Assurance Corp.; Director Cable and Wireless (Holding) Ltd. and Ass. Companies; Dep. Chm. Clerical Medical and General Life Assurance Society; Director Holloways Properties Ltd.; Member, Royal Commission on National Museums and Galleries, 1928-30; Chm. Irish Civil Service Commission, 1921-26; Chm. Imperial Communications Advisory Committee, 1929-33; Chm. National Council for Mental Hygiene, 1922-26; Chairman, University College Hospital, 1937-45; Treasurer, Univ. Coll. Hosp., 1937-48; Chairman, Red Cross Sales, Duke of Gloucester's Red Cross and St. John Fund, 1940-45; Chairman, H.R.H. Princess Christian's Nursing Home, Windsor, 1920-46; Trustee, Red Cross Hospital Library, 1916-46. Officer Legion of Honour, Order of the Nile (2nd class), Knight Commander Order of St. Sava of Servia, Order of St. Maurice and S Lazarus of Italy, Grand Officer of Danilo of Montenegro, and Nichan Iftikhar, Italian Military Cross with Bar, Roumanian Cross of Regina Maria; Italian and Serbian Red Cross Gold Medals. Presented Dorneywood, contents and endowment to the Nation, 1942. for use of Prime Minister or, at his nomination, for a Secretary of State. *Heir:* none. *Address:* The Manor, Davies Street, Berkeley Square, W.1. *T.:* Mayfair 1063; Dorneywood, Burnham, Bucks. *T.:* Burnham 54. *Clubs:* Brooks's; Swinley Forest (Ascot); New (Edinburgh).

[*Died* 1 *Nov.* 1954 (*ext.*).

COURTHOPE, 1st Baron, *cr.* 1945, of Whiligh; **George Loyd Courthope,** P.C. 1937; 1st Bt., *cr.* 1925; M.C., T.D.; J.P.; D.L.; Hon. M.A.; Col. T.A., retired; Barrister-at-law, Inner Temple; *b.* 12 June 1877; *s.* of late G. J. Courthope, J.P., D.L., etc., of Whiligh, Sussex, and Elinor Sarah (*d.* 1895), *d.* of late Col. E. Loyd, J.P., D.L., of Lillesden, Hawkhurst; *m.* 1st, 1899, Hilda Gertrude (*d.* 1940), *o. d.* of late Maj.-Gen. Henry Pelham Close, Bombay S.C.; two *d.*; 2nd, 1944, Margaret, *d.* of late Frederick Barry, Westbury. *Educ.:* Eton; Christ Church, Oxford. M.P. (U.) Rye Division of Sussex, 1906-45; Chairman United Club, 1908-9; Chairman Central Chamber of Agriculture, 1909; Chairman of Departmental Committee on Swine Fever, 1910; President British Sugar Beet Council, 1912; President Sussex Herd Book Society, 1916 and 1923; Capt. House of Commons Rifle Team, 1907-14. Served with British Expeditionary Force in Flanders (despatches, M.C., wounded); commanded 5th Battalion (Cinque Ports) Royal Sussex Regiment, 1920-26; and Kent and Sussex Territorial Infantry Brigade; Asst. Controller of Timber Supplies, 1917; Pres. English Forestry Association, 1916-21; Pres. Royal English Arboricultural Society, 1918-1920; Chairman Empire Forestry Association, 1923-24; Delegate to British Empire Forestry Conference, 1923; Chairman Consultative Committee for England under Forestry Acts, 1919-27; President Central Landowners' Assoc., 1929-31; Forestry Commissioner, 1923-48; Church Commissioner, 1948-55; Vice-Pres. National Rifle Assoc.; Hon. Mem. Chartered Surveyors' Institution; Pres. of Royal Agricultural Society, 1944-45; Vice-President Land Agents' Soc. and Smithfield Club; Freeman of City of London, Prime Warden of Goldsmiths' Co., 1943-45; First Master of the Company of Farmers; Member of Royal Commission on Land Drainage; Member Central Board of Finance of Church of England. *Heir:* none. *Recreation:* shooting. *Address:* Whiligh, Sussex. *T.:* Wadhurst 33; 6A Artillery Mansions, Victoria St., S.W.1. *T.:* Abbey 5761. *Clubs:* Carlton, National, Bath, Farmers'.

[*Died* 2 *Sept.* 1955 (*ext.*).

COURTHOPE-MUNROE, Sir Harry, Kt., *cr.* 1919; K.C. 1914; M.A., J.P.; Recorder of Sudbury, 1927-46; *b.* 1860; *s.* of late L. H. Isaacs, M.P., J.P., F.R.I.B.A., and Eliza, *d.* of John Ratley, Henfield, Sussex; (at birth and baptism named Harry Courthope-Munroe); *m.* 1st, 1881, Ellen (*d.* 1930), *d.* of late James Elliot Shirley; three *s.*; 2nd, 1933, Annie May, *yr. d.* of William Storey, Carlisle. *Educ.:* Trinity Hall, Cambridge. Called to Bar, Inner Temple, 1883; joined S.E. Circuit; Hon. Standing Counsel of the Imperial Soc. of Knights Bachelor; Member of Council of the Surveyors' Institution until 1940; Hon. Member of the Auctioneers and Estate Agents Institute of the United Kingdom; Member of the Estate Management Degree Committee of the University of London; Member of the Chairmen's Panel constituted by the Ministry of Labour under the Industrial Courts Act 1919; Chairman of the Board of Trade Committee, 1916, to deal with release of Railwaymen for Military Service; appointed by the Board of Trade and the Ministry of Labour as Arbitrator for the settlement of differences between employers and employed under the Munitions of War Acts during the war; practised at the Parliamentary Bar; appointed under the Railways Act 1921 as Independent Chairman of the Railway Police Force Central Conference; Member of the Tithe Committee of Queen Anne's Bounty; Member of the Reconstitution Committee of the Ecclesiastical Commission and Queen Anne's Bounty; Member of the Rating Appeal Committee for East Suffolk, 1929-39; Chairman of Gen. Commissioners of Income Tax of Plomesgate Div. of Suffolk. *Recreation:* farming. *Address:* The Manor House, Kelsale, Saxmundham, Suffolk. *T.:* Saxmundham 43. *Club:* Junior Carlton.

[*Died* 8 *April* 1951.

COURTNEY, Janet Elizabeth, O.B.E. 1917; J.P.; *b.* Barton-on-Humber, 27 Nov., 1865; *d.* of late Rev. George Hogarth, M.A.; *m.* 1911, W. L. Courtney (*d.* 1928). *Educ.:* Lady Margaret Hall, Oxford (1st Class Philosophy, 1888). In service of Royal Commission on Labour, 1892-94; Bank of England, 1894-1906; Librarian, Times Book Club, 1906-10; editorial staff Encyclopædia Britannica, 1910-14 and again 1920-22; Adviser on Staff Welfare, Ministry of Munitions, 1916-1917; Member of Executive Committee Carnegie United Kingdom Trust since 1913; Acting Editor, Fortnightly Review, Nov. 1928-June 1929. *Publications:* Pillars of Empire (with husband) 1918; Freethinkers of the 19th Century, 1920; Recollected in Tranquillity, 1926; The Making of an Editor, 1930; An Oxford Portrait Gallery, 1931; Countrywomen in Council, 1933; The Adventurous Thirties, 1933; The Women of My Time, 1934; Simple Annals, 1936. *Address:* 107 Cowper Road, W.7.

[*Died* 24 *Sept.* 1954.

COURTOWN, 7th Earl of (*cr.* 1762), **James Richard Neville Stopford;** O.B.E. 1919; Viscount Stopford, 1762; Baron Courtown (Ireland), 1758; Baron Saltersford (Great Britain), 1796; D.L. Co. Wexford; *b.* 16 Sept. 1877; *e. s.* of 6th Earl and Catherine (*d.* 1884), *e. d.* of 4th Baron Braybrooke; *S.* father, 1933; *m.* 1905, Cicely Mary, O.B.E. 1942, *d.* of late J. Arden Birch and late Viscountess Barrington; three *s.* four *d.* *Educ.:* Eton. Served South African War, 1900-1 (medal); European War (despatches); 1939 War, D.A.A.G., War Office; Mayor of Aylesbury, 1927-28. *Heir:* *s.* Viscount Stopford. *Address:* Redberry House, Bierton, Aylesbury, Bucks. *T.:* 126; Marlfield, Gorey, Ireland. *T.:* 64. *Club:* Kildare St. (Dublin).

[*Died* 25 *Jan.* 1957.

COURY, Captain Gabriel George, V.C. 1916; *b.* June 1896; *s.* of late Raphaël and

Marie Coury, Liverpool; *m.* 1918, Mary Katherine, *d.* of late Stuart Lovell, London; three *d.* *Educ.:* Stonyhurst College. Joined the 6th Liverpool Regiment at outbreak of war; obtained Commission in 3rd South Lancashire Regt. April 1915; went to France Aug. 1915 (V.C.); joined R.F.C. Aug. 1916. Joined R.A.S.C. Sept. 1940, went to France June 1944. *Recreations:* bridge, golf, tennis. *Address:* 103 Brunswick Road, Liverpool 6. *T.:* Anfield 2590.
[*Died* 23 *Feb.* 1956.

COUSINS, Clarence W.; late Secretary to the Ministry of Labour (previously Director of Census) for the Union of South Africa; *s.* of late Rev. W. E. Cousins, M.A., of Oxford (late Madagascar); *m.* Ethelwyn, *d.* of late Sir James A. H. Murray, Editor of the Oxford Dictionary; three *s.* one *d.* *Educ.:* Oxford. Entered the service of the Cape Colony Government, 1896; transferred to the service of the Union Government as Chief Immigration Officer at Cape Town, 1910; Secretary for Labour, 1924; retired 1932. *Address:* Monavein, P.O. Tzaneen, Transvaal, South Africa.
[*Died* 25 *March* 1954.

COUSINS, Edmund Richard John Ratcliffe, C.S.I. 1942; C.I.E. 1938; *b.* 22 April 1888; *s.* of John Ratcliffe Cousins, J.P., and Eleanor Fanny Cousins; *m.* 1912, Henrietta Mary Colebrooke Yewdall (*née* Marshall) (*d.* 1955); no *c.* *Educ.:* Westminster; Christ Church, Oxford. Appointed to I.C.S., 1911; Secretary to Board of Revenue, Bihar and Orissa, 1920-22; District Magistrate and Collector, 1925; Commissioner, Chota Nagpur Division, 1937; Adviser to Governor of Bihar, 1939; Assistant Sec., Ministry of Civil Aviation, London, 1947; Special Commissioner of Lands, Kenya, 1949-51. *Recreations:* hockey, golf, and racquets. *Address:* P.O. Box 3428, Nairobi, Kenya Colony.
[*Died* 16 *July* 1955.

COUSSEY, Sir James Henley, K.B.E. 1957; Kt. 1950; **Hon. Mr. Justice Henley Coussey;** President West African Court of Appeal, since 1955; Justice of Appeal, 1952; 2nd *s.* of late C. L. R. P. Coussey, Cape Coast; *m.* 1930, Renée Dorothy, *o. d.* of late James Edward Biney, Barrister, Cape Coast; two *s.* two *d.* *Educ.:* Hampton Grammar School. Called to Bar, Middle Temple, 1913; practised at Bar, Gold Coast; Puisne Judge, Gold Coast, 1944-52; Member of several committees. Member of Executive Council, 1943; Chairman, Committee on Constitutional Reform, Gold Coast, 1949. *Address:* c/o Supreme Court, Accra, Ghana. [*Died* 6 *June* 1958.

COVENTRY, Henry Robert Beauclerk; *s.* of Capt. Henry A. B. Coventry; *b.* 20 Sept. 1871; *m.* 1893, Lady Mary Muriel Sophie Howard (*d.* 1938), *e. d.* of 18th Earl of Suffolk; one *s.* *Educ.:* Eton. *Recreations:* motoring, yachting. *Address:* Monkton Park, Chippenham, Wilts. *T.:* 2080. *Club:* Carlton.
[*Died* 25 *June* 1953.

COVERNTON, James Gargrave, C.I.E. 1914; M.A.; *b.* 1868; *s.* of Alfred H. Covernton, Aberdeen Park, Highbury, N., and Dryden, Simcoe, Canada; *m.* Alexa Agatha (*d.* 1946), *d.* of Waller Paton, R.S.A.; one *s.* two *d.* *Educ.:* Merchant Taylors' School; St. John's College, Oxford (Scholar), First Class Mods., First Class Lit. Hum.; Senior Scholar. Indian Education Service, retired; Professor of English Literature, Elphinstone College, Bombay, 1894; Education Inspector, Sind, 1898; Director of Public Instruction, Burma, 1906-17; Bombay Presidency, 1917-23. *Address:* 27 Seckford St., Woodbridge, Suffolk. [*Died* 20 *July* 1957.

COWAN, Sir Darcy (Rivers Warren), Kt., *cr.* 1955; F.R.A.C.P.; Hon. Consulting Physician, Royal Adelaide Hospital, since 1938; *b.* 8 Aug. 1885; 6th *s.* of late James Cowan, M.P., and late Sarah Ann Cowan; *m.* 1910, Effie Hewitt Cox. *Educ.:* Prince Alfred College; University of Adelaide. M.B., B.S. 1908; F.R.A.C.P. 1938. Hon. Physician, Roy. Adelaide Hosp., 1924-35; Physician in Charge, Chest Clinic, 1938-50; Medical Director, S.A. Tuberculosis Assoc., 1943-55; President S.A. Branch of B.M.A., 1935-36; President Northcote Home, 1943-1955; Chairman Kalyra Sanatorium, 1950-1955; Hon. Sec. Nat. Assoc. for Prevention of Tuberculosis in Australia, 1948-55. Fell. Amer. Coll. of Chest Physicians, 1946. *Recreations:* triple Blue of University of Adelaide in football, lacrosse, lawn tennis. *Address:* 217 Brougham Place, North Adelaide, S. Australia. *T.:* M. 8375. *Club:* Adelaide (Adelaide).
[*Died* 9 *June* 1958.

COWAN, Hon. Sir John, Kt., *cr.* 1944; retired; *b.* 22 Nov. 1866; *s.* of Thomas Cowan, M.P., Pastoralist, and Mary Jane Armstrong; *m.* 1891; two *s.* three *d.* *Educ.:* Whinham College. M.L.C. South Australia for Southern District, 34 years; Minister of Repatriation and Agriculture, Barwell Govt.; Minister of Agriculture, Repatriation, Irrigation and Drainage, Immigration and Afforestation in the Butler Govt., 1927-30; responsible for Timber Mills at Mount Burr, S.E., Drainage of Murray Swamp lands and other important Govt. works. *Recreations:* hunting, bowls, billiards. *Address:* Glen Lossie, Murray Bridge, South Australia. *T.:* 60. [*Died* 8 *March* 1953.

COWAN, Lieut.-Colonel Percy John, M.B.E.; M.Inst.C.E.; M.I.Mech.E.; F.R.S.A. (Vice-President, 1941-44); 3rd *s.* of late Dr. Thomas William Cowan, F.L.S., etc. *Educ.:* Lausanne; Rugby School; University College, London. Great Northern Railway, Locomotive Department; subsequent appointments in works in United Kingdom and U.S.A., Egyptian State Railways, etc.; served with Mesopotamian Expeditionary Force; R.E. (E. and M. Section) and Railway Directorate (despatches); Afghan Campaign, North Western F.F., 1919; County Army Welfare Officer for Surrey, 1943-45; George Stephenson Gold Medal and Telford Premium, Institution of Civil Engineers, 1903; Willans Premium, Institution of Mechanical Engineers, 1918; travelled in North America, Middle and Far East, Europe, etc. *Address:* Upcott, Cranes Park, Surbiton. *Club:* Royal Empire Society.
[*Died* 15 *Nov.* 1954.

COWAN, Admiral Sir Walter Henry, 1st Bt., *cr.* 1921; K.C.B., *cr.* 1919 (C.B. 1916); D.S.O. 1898; M.V.O. 1904; *b.* 1871; *e. s.* of Captain W. F. Cowan, J.P., Alveston, Warwickshire; *m.* 1901, Catherine Eleanor Millicent (*d.* 1934), *d.* of Digby Cayley. Served Brass River and Mwele Expeditions; Benin, 1897 (despatches); Nile, 1898 (despatches D.S.O.); Nile, 1899 (despatches); S. African War, A.D.C. to Lord Kitchener, and Naval A.D.C. to Earl Roberts, 1901 (despatches, promoted); Captain, 1907; Vice-Admiral, 1923; Admiral, 1927; European War, battle of Jutland Bank, 1 June 1916 (despatches, C.B.); Capt. H.M.S. Princess Royal, 1915-17; commanded First Light Cruiser Squadron of the Grand Fleet, 1917-20; Commanded Baltic Force, 1919; Battle Cruiser Squadron, Atlantic Fleet, 1921-22; Commanding Officer, Coast of Scotland, 1925-1926; Com.-in-Chief North America and West Indies Station, 1926-28; First and Principal Naval A. D. C. to the King, 1930-31; retired list, 1931; served War of 1939-45 with Commando Forces (Bar to D.S.O.); Hon. Col. 18th King Edward VII's Own Cavalry. *Heir:* none. *Address:* Kineton, Warwickshire. *Clubs:* Boodle's, Cavalry; Royal Yacht Squadron.
[*Died* 14 *Feb.* 1956 (*ext.*).

COWAN-DOUGLAS, Hugh; Chartered Accountant in Glasgow since 1924; Partner of Brown, Fleming & Murray, C.A., Glasgow;

b. 21 Nov. 1895; *yr. s.* of late Robert William Cowan-Douglas and late Mrs. Cowan-Douglas, Corbet Tower, near Kelso, Roxburghshire; *m.* 1958, Phyllis Adah, *widow* of Brigadier J. B. McCance, O.B.E. *Educ.:* Alton Burn, Nairn; Marlborough Coll.; Gonville and Caius Coll., Cambridge. Partner of Aitken Mackenzie & Clapperton, C.A., Glasgow, from 1924 till amalgamation with Brown, Fleming & Murray, C.A., Glasgow, in 1948. Chairman: Glenfield & Kennedy Holdings Ltd., The United Turkey Red Co. Ltd., Harland Engineering Co. Ltd.; Scottish United Investors, etc. Director: Halifax Building Society, Royal Bank of Scotland, Scottish Union and National Insurance Co., etc. Commissioned in Rifle Brigade (S.R.), 1914, serving with 4th Battalion, 1915-19, in Belgium, France and Macedonia. Served 5th Bn. Highland L.I. (T.A.), 1921-38, latterly in command. Raised 57th (Glasgow) Searchlight Regt. R.A. (T.A.) in 1938 and commanded till 1942. G.S.O. 1 (H.G.) with A.A. Command, 1942-44; Lt.-Col. 1935; Bt.-Colonel 1939; Hon. Colonel 1947. *Recreations:* shooting and golf. *Address:* 66 Kelvin Court, Glasgow, W.2. *T.:* Western 7615. *Clubs:* Caledonian; Western (Glasgow); New (Edinburgh). [*Died* 12 *July* 1960.

COWGILL, John Vincent, C.M.G. 1946; M.C.; *b.* 19 July 1888; *s.* of late Rev. Harry Cowgill; *m.* 1934, Lilian Josephine, *d.* of late John Alkin, Bonehill, Tamworth; no *c. Educ.:* Durham School; All Souls College, Oxford. B.A. Oxon. 1911; Malayan Civil Service, 1911-46 and 1948-49; British Resident, Negri Sembilan, F.M.S., 1940-46 (interned in Singapore, 1942-45). Served in European war, 1914-18 (despatches, M.C.). *Recreations:* golf, fishing. *Address:* 21 Brunswick Drive, Harrogate. *Club:* East India and Sports. [*Died* 16 *Oct.* 1959.

COWLEY, Air Vice-Marshal Arthur Thomas Noel, C.B.E. 1944; *b.* 20 Dec. 1888; *s.* of Rev. Canon A. E. Cowley and Elizabeth Hart-Davies; *m.* 1923, Marion Gladys Service; one *s.* two *d. Educ.:* St. John's College, Winnipeg; McGill University, Montreal (B.Sc.). Flt. Sub-Lieut. and Flt.-Lieut. R.N.A.S. 1915-18; Capt. R.A.F. 1918-19; Flt.-Lieut. C.A.F. 1922-24; Flt.-Lieut. to Air Vice-Marshal, R.C.A.F., 1924 to date. Controller of Civil Aviation, 1924-26; Supt. Air Regulations, 1926-39; Director of Manning, 1939-40; C.O. No. 1 Service Flying Training School, 1940; A.O.C. No. 4 Trg. Command, 1940-42; Air Member for Organisation, 1942-43; A.O.C. No. 1 Training Command, R.C.A.F., 1943-45; retired, 1945. Dir. of Air Services, Dept. of Transport, 1946-54, retd. *Address:* 1515 Despard Ave., Victoria, B.C. [*Died* 7 *July* 1960.

COWLEY, Sir (William) Percy, Kt., *cr.* 1952; C.B.E. 1945; J.P.; H.M. First Deemster and Clerk of the Rolls, I.O.M., since 1947; *b.* 26 July 1886; *s.* of Robert Cowley, Member of the House of Keys, Ramsey, I.O.M.; *m.* 1st, 1914, Emily Alison Martin (*d.* 1927), Galwally, Belfast; two *s.* one *d.*; 2nd, 1929, Ethel Muriel, *d.* of E. T. Kissack, Douglas, I.O.M. *Educ.:* Ramsey Grammar School. Manx Bar, 1909; High Bailiff, Ramsey and Peel, 1925-31; H.M. Second Deemster, 1934-47; J.P. 1931. Served European War as Paymaster-Sub-Lieut. R.N.V.R., on staff of C.-in-C. Mediterranean Fleet, 1918-19; Chm. War Cttee. of Tynwald, 1939-45. Chm. Manx Blind Welfare Soc., Chm. Merchant Navy Soc., Chm. Ramsey Cottage Hosp. Freeman of Douglas, 1956. *Recreations:* yachting and agriculture. *Address:* Ballaughton, Braddan, nr. Douglas, I.O.M. *T.:* Douglas 114. *Clubs:* Ellan Vannin (Douglas); Raven (Ramsey). [*Died* 13 *Jan.* 1958.

COWPER, Frank Cadogan, R.A. 1934; R.W.S.; R.P.; painter; *b.* Wicken Rectory, Northamptonshire, 16 Oct. 1877; *s.* of late Frank Cowper, M.A. (Oxon), of Lisle Court, Wootton, Isle of Wight, and Edith, *d.* of late Rev. Edward Cadogan, M.A. (Oxon), Rector of Wicken, Northamptonshire. *Educ.:* Cranleigh. Studied art at St. John's Wood Art School, 1896; Royal Academy Schools, 1897-1902; six months in studio of late E. A. Abbey, R.A. Exhibited first at Royal Academy, 1899; exhibits regularly at the Academy, and at the Royal Water-colour Society, at principal provincial Galleries, and has exhibited at the Paris Salon, Rome, Venice, etc. Paintings include: The Good Samaritan, 1900; An Aristocrat answering the Summons to Execution, 1901 (Leeds City Art Gallery); Hamlet (Queensland Art Gallery), 1902; St. Agnes (Tate Gallery), 1905; The Devil disguised as a Troubadour singing a Love Song in a Nunnery, 1907; Erasmus and Thos. More visit the children of Henry VII. at Greenwich (mural painting in the Houses of Parliament), 1910; decorative panels in Houses of Parliament, 1912; Lucretia Borgia reigns in the Vatican in the absence of Pope Alexander VI. (Tate Gallery), 1914; Faust's first sight of Margaret (National Gallery of New South Wales, Sydney), 1915; The Cathedral Scene from Faust, 1919; Fair Rosamund and Queen Eleanor, 1920; The Damozel of the Lake, 1924; Paolo and Francesca, 1927; The Fortune-teller (Russell-Cotes Gallery, Bournemouth), 1940; The Featherbed Farmer, 1951; A jealous husband having disguised himself as a priest, hears his own wife's confession, 1952; many portraits. *Address:* 2 Berkeley Road, Cirencester. *T.:* Cirencester 885. [*Died* 17 *Nov.* 1958.

COX, Alfred, O.B.E. 1918; M.B., B.S.; Hon. M.A. (Univ. Durham) 1921; Hon. LL.D. (University of Manitoba), 1930; late Acting Secretary National Eye Service; one of the founders of the Association Professionelle Internationale des Médecins; *b.* Middlesbro', 1866; *e. s.* of T. B. Cox; *m.* Florence A. (*d.* 1927), *d.* of Thomas Cheesman. *Educ.:* Albert Road School, Darlington; University of Durham. Medical Secretary, British Medical Association, 1912-32; Vice-President British Medical Association, 1933; Joint Secretary Central Medical War Committee, 1915-18; has taken prominent part in medical politics and medical organisation, both in writing and speaking, in this country and in Canada and South Africa; ex-President North of England Branch of the British Medical Association, and was a member of both central committees specially appointed to reorganise the Association; late Town Councillor and J.P., Gateshead; in general practice, 1891-1908. *Publications:* Among the doctors, 1950; many articles on medical organisation and politics. *Address:* 17 Trevor Pl., S.W.7. [*Died* 31 *Aug.* 1954.

COX, Arthur Sambell, C.B.E. 1939 (O.B.E. 1932); *b.* Southampton, 18 June 1876; *s.* of Charles Cox; *m.* 1st, 1904, Fanny Marianne, 2nd *d.* of C. W. Phippard; one *s.*; 2nd, 1949, Florence, *d.* of J. Simpson. *Educ.:* University College, Southampton; Royal College of Science, S. Kensington. B.Sc., LL.B. Lond.; Barrister-at-Law, Middle Temple, 1926; entered Nautical Almanac Office of Admiralty, 1900; joined Examining Staff, Patent Office, Board of Trade, 1903, and was Assistant Comptroller, 1932-44. *Recreation:* boat-sailing. *Address:* Lochinver, 103 The Causeway, Petersfield, Hants. *T.:* Petersfield 141. [*Died* 15 *Nov.* 1951.

COX, Lieut.-Col. Sir (Charles) Henry (Fortnom), K.C.M.G., *cr.* 1937 (C.M.G. 1927); D.S.O. 1917; late R.F.A.; *b.* 1880; *o. s.* of late Prof. S. Herbert Cox; *m.* 1919, Edith Fortescue Blair, *y. d.* of late Roland L. N. Michell, C.M.G.; one *s.* one *d. Educ.:* Rugby; Royal Military Academy, Woolwich. Served South African War, 1901-2 (Queen's medal and five clasps); Sudan Govt.,

1913-15; European War, 1915-18 (despatches, D.S.O. and bar, Bt. Lt.-Col.); Palestine Govt., 1919-24; retired pay, 1923; British Resident, Trans-Jordan, 1924-39. *Address:* Little Orchard, Rocombe, Lyme Regis. *T.:* Lyme Regis 525. [*Died* 14 *Aug.* 1953.

COX, Cuthbert Eustace Connop, C.I.E. 1939; *b.* 9 March 1885; *e. s.* of Rev. W. E. Cox, Lynton and Dartington; *m.* 1927, Barbara Ethel, *d.* of Rev. W. H. Nicol; one *s.* *Educ.:* Bradfield College; Coopers Hill; Magdalen College, Oxford (Diploma of Forestry). Entered Indian Forest Service, 1907; Chief Conservator of Forests, Central Provinces, 1937; retired, 1939. Served European War, 1915-16 with 12th Indian Cavalry, and 1940-1946 with Indian Intell. Corps (Lt.-Col.). *Address:* Bison Lodge, Barton-on-Sea, Hants. *T.:* New Milton 1352. *Club:* R.A.C. [*Died* 17 *May* 1958.

COX, E. Albert, R.B.A.; Associated Craftman of West Essex Chapter of Royal Institute British Architects; *b.* Islington, 16 Oct. 1876; *m.*; one *d.* *Educ.:* various schools in London. Student at People's Palace E. and Technical School, Bolt Court, Fleet Street; in business first as a designer for a manufacturing chemist, afterwards assisted Sir Frank Brangwyn, R.A., in most of his important works; executed a panel in Royal Exchange; decorated a board room in Queen's Gate with eight mural panels; decorative panel for Orient Shipping Co., Cockspur Street Office, and a great many poster designs for shipping and railway companies. Mem.: East Kent Art Soc.; Folkestone Art Soc. *Gifts:* 13 drawings to Art Gallery Canterbury; 20 drawings to Art Gallery, Folkestone; 2 pictures (1 Oil, 1 Water-colour) to Art Gallery, Preston. *Publications:* Lays of Ancient Rome; Westward Ho!; vols. 1 and 2, Illustrations for New Tales of Old Testament; also illustrated; Rubaiyat of Omar Khayyam; Thamesside Yesterday; Sayings of Confucius; Sâlâman and Absál; Abelard and Héloise; Wayfaring Folks; Country Days and Country Ways; Aucassin and Nicolette. *Address:* The Little Thatched Cottage, Woolage Green, near Canterbury. [*Died* 20 *April* 1955.

COX, Bt.-Col. Sir (Edward) Geoffrey Hippisley, Kt., *cr.* 1938; C.B.E. 1919; O.St.J.; partner in the firm of Dyson, Bell & Co., Parliamentary Agents; *b.* 29 Aug. 1884; *o. surv. s.* of late Edward Hippisley Cox; *m.* 1914, Ethel Milsted, *d.* of Mountague Edye; two *s.* Late Hon. Col. The Queen's Westminsters (The King's Royal Rifle Corps); late Lt.-Col. commanding Queen's Westminster and Civil Service Rifles; D.L. for County of London; Member of the Statute Law Committee; a Governor of Queen Mary Coll. (Univ. of London); F.S.A.; Pres. Soc. of Parliamentary Agents, 1951, 1952; served European War, 1914-19; Staff Capt. 1915; Deputy Assist. Quartermaster-General, 1916; Deputy Assistant Adjutant-General, 1917; Assist. Adjutant-Gen. London District Command (temp. Lieut.-Col. in Army), 1918 (despatches, Brevet Major in Army, C.B.E.); Brevet Colonel, 1925; served in War, 1939-1945, Deputy Assistant Adjutant General, 1939; Assistant Adjutant General London District Command, 1940-45. *Address:* 15 Great College Street, Westminster, S.W.1. *T.:* Whitehall 7458. *Clubs:* Carlton, Turf. [*Died* 24 *Feb.* 1954.

COX, Lt.-Col. Edwin Charles, C.V.O. 1937 (M.V.O. 1926); C.B.E. 1918; T.D. 1932; *b.* London, 3 Jan. 1868. Superintendent of the Line, S.E. and Chatham Railway, 1911-23; Chief Operating Superintendent Southern Railway, 1923; Traffic Manager, Southern Railway, 1930-36; Lt.-Col. late Engineer and Railway Staff Corps; Officier de l'Ordre de Léopold, 1935; Officier de la Couronne, Roumania, 1924; Chevalier de l'Ordre National de la Légion d'honneur, 1927; Foundation Member Institute of Transport; Hon. Associate of the Order of the Hospital of St. John of Jerusalem in England. *Address:* Knowle Hotel, Sidmouth, Devon. *T.:* Sidmouth 955. [*Died* 9 *Dec.* 1958.

COX, Bt.-Col. Sir Geoffrey H.; *see* Cox, Bt.-Col. Sir E. G. H.

COX, Lt.-Col. Sir Henry; *see* Cox, Lt.-Col. Sir C. H. F.

COX, Lady; Louisa Belle, D.B.E., *cr.* 1923; *d.* of late Surgeon General J. B. Hamilton, R.A.M.C.; *m.* 1889, Sir Percy Z. Cox; G.C.M.G., G.C.I.E., K.C.S.I. (*d.* 1937); no *c.* *Educ.:* privately; in Switzerland. Has travelled extensively in India, Somaliland, Iraq and Persia. *Address:* c/o Grindlay's Bank Ltd., 54 Parliament Street, S.W.1. *Club:* Ladies' Carlton. [*Died* 30 *Aug.* 1956.

COX, William Edward, C.B.E. 1942; Senior Principal Inspector of Taxes, Inland Revenue, Somerset House, 1936-45; *b.* 1880; *s.* of late Jasper Cox, Torquay; *m.* 1907, Elsie Gertrude Wakefield; two *s.* Entered Inland Revenue Dept., 1901; called to Bar, Middle Temple, 1916. *Address:* 28 Gloucester Road, Teddington, Middlesex. *T.:* Molesey 24. [*Died* 29 *Sept.* 1960.

COYAJEE, Sir Jahangir Cooverjee, Kt., *cr.* 1928; *b.* 11 Sept. 1875; *s.* of late Coverjee Coyajee, Rajkot. *Educ.:* Caius Coll., Cambridge. Lately member Royal Commissions on the Indian Tariff and Indian Currency; Professor of Political Economy, Presidency College, Calcutta; Member of the Council of State, 1930; Delegate to Assembly of League of Nations, Geneva, 1930-32; Principal, Presidency College, 1930-31; retired 1931; Correspondent, Royal Economic Society; Member, Indian Coal Mining Committee, 1936-37. *Publications:* The Indian Fiscal Problem, 1923; Indian Currency and Exchange; The Indian Currency System; India and the League of Nations; The Economic Depression; Cults and Legends of Ancient Iran and China; Studies in Shahnameh. *Address:* 29 Ridge Road, Bombay, 6, India. [*Died July* 1943.
[*But death not notified in time for inclusion in Who Was Who 1941–1950, first edn.*

COYLE, William Thomas, Q.C.; B.A.; District Court Judge and Chairman of Quarter Sessions, 1927-39; son of late Patrick and Margaret Coyle, Enniskillen, North Ireland; *m.*; six *c.* *Educ.:* St. Ignatius and Sydney University. Called to the Bar, Inner Temple, 1896; practised as a Barrister in England, 1896-1901; K.C. 1920; returned to Sydney; held many commissions as Acting District Court Judge; Senior Crown Prosecutor, New South Wales, 1920-1927. *Recreations:* golf, shooting, fishing (trout and deep sea), surfing. *Address:* Woodbridge, Holt Street, Double Bay, Sydney, N.S.W. *Clubs:* University, Imperial Service, Royal Sydney Golf. [*Died* 7 *Sept.* 1951.

COZENS-HARDY, 3rd Baron, *cr.* 1914, of Letheringsett; **Edward Herbert Cozens-Hardy;** D.L.(Lancs); Vice-President and Steward of Royal Automobile Club; M.I.Mech.E., M.I.E.E.; *b.* 1873; 2nd *s.* of 1st Baron Cozens-Hardy; *S.* brother, 1924; *m.* 1906, Gladys Lily, *d.* of Arthur Wrigley Cozens-Hardy; one *s.* two *d.* *Educ.:* Rugby School. *Heir:* *s.* Hon. Herbert Arthur Cozens-Hardy, *b.* 8 June 1907. *Address:* Letheringsett Hall, Holt, Norfolk. *T.:* Holt 3222. *Club:* Athenæum. [*Died* 22 *Oct.* 1956.

COZENS-HARDY, Archibald, C.B.E. 1951; Magistrate County of Norfolk; C.A. 1915-55; President of the Newspaper Society, 1915; *b.* 11 Nov. 1869; *e. s.* of late Theobald Cozens-Hardy of Sprowston. *Educ.:* Norwich; Amersham Hall School. Editor of the Eastern Daily Press,

1897-1937. *Address:* Oak Lodge, Sprowston, Norwich. *T.:* Norwich 21603. [*Died* 9 *March* 1957.

CRABBE, Vice-Adm. Lewis Gonne Eyre, C.B. 1935; C.I.E. 1933; C.B.E. 1945; D.S.O. 1919; R.N.; *s.* of late Brig.-Gen. Eyre Macdonald Stuart Crabbe, Grenadier Guards; *b.* 1882. Served European War, 1914-19 (despatches, D.S.O.); King's Harbour Master, Rosyth, 1927-29; Senior Naval Officer in the Persian Gulf, 1930-33; Rear-Adm. and Senior Naval Officer, Yangtze, 1935-38; Flag officer in Charge, Liverpool, 1939; Vice-Adm. 1937; retired list, 1938; Flag Officer, Liverpool, 1939-40; Commodore R.N.R. for Convoy duty, 1941-45 (C.B.E.). *Club:* Naval and Military. [*Died* 2 *July* 1951.

CRABTREE, Harold, C.B.E. 1944; Chairman, Howard Smith Paper Mills, Ltd., since 1946; President, Canada Paper Co. and subsidiary Companies; President and Chairman, Woods Mfg. Co. Ltd.; Chairman: Bd. of Fraser Companies Ltd.; Donnacona Paper Co. Ltd.; Alliance Paper Mills, Ltd.; Director Royal Bank of Canada, Sun Life Insurance and other Companies; *b.* Bury, Lancs., 28 Sept. 1884; *s.* of Edwin Crabtree and Ann Kay; *m.* 1910, Louisa A. Stafford; one *s.* one *d.* *Educ.:* Joliette Public School, Joliette, Que.; Dufferin Grammar School, Brigham, Que.; Sherbrooke High School, Sherbrooke, Que. Junior in office of Alex. McArthur & Co. Ltd., Joliette, 1899; Sec.-Treas. Edwin Crabtree & Sons, Ltd., 1906-17; Sec.-Treas. Howard Smith Paper Mills, Ltd., 1917-25; General Manager, 1925-28; Vice-Pres. and General Manager, 1928-31; Pres., 1931-46; Pres. Canadian Manufacturers Assn., 1940-41 and 1941-42; Pres. Canadian Pulp and Paper Assn., 1930-1933, incl. Chm. Executive Committee (Montreal) of National Board of Directors of Canadian Chamber of Commerce, 1943-44; Governor, Royal Victoria Hospital, Montreal Children's Hospital, Montreal General Hospital, Children's Memorial Hospital; Director of Financial Federation. *Recreations:* fishing, golf. *Address:* 58 Forden Crescent, Westmount, Que., Canada; 1235 McGill College Ave., Montreal, Que., Canada. *T.:* Elwood 5080, University 6-9341. *Clubs:* Mount Royal, St. James's, Montreal, Seigniory, Royal Montreal Curling, Royal Montreal Golf (Montreal); National (Toronto), etc. [*Died* 18 *Feb.* 1956.

CRACROFT-AMCOTTS, Lieutenant-Commander John, D.S.C.; D.L.; R.N. (retd.); 2nd *s.* of late Major F. A. Cracroft-Amcotts, Kettlethorpe; *m.* 1930, May Redfearn, *d.* of late H. Redfearn-Shaw, Malayan Civil Service; two *d.* *Educ.:* Aysgarth; Stubbington; H.M.S. Britannia. Served through European War (D.S.C., despatches); retired, 1919; succeeded to the Estates of Rauceby by Deed of Gift in 1931; High Sheriff of Lincolnshire, 1937; D.L. Lincolnshire 1951; J.P. Parts of Kesteven; Alderman of Kesteven County Council. *Recreations:* shooting, fishing. *Address:* Rauceby Hall, Sleaford. *T.A.* and *T.:* S. Rauceby 233. *Clubs:* Lansdowne, Flyfishers'. [*Died* 30 *May* 1956.

CRADOCK-WATSON, Henry, M.A.; *b.* 1864; *e. s.* of late Rev. H. G. Watson, Vicar of Great Staughton, Hunts; *m.* 1898, Florence Sophie (*d.* 1944), *e.d.* of Col. A. J. Hepper, D.S.O., R.E.; three *s.* (one *d.* decd.). *Educ.:* Merchant Taylors' School, London; St. John's College Oxford (scholar). 1st Class Classical Moderations, 1885; 2nd Class Literæ Humaniores, 1887; formerly House Master at Tonbridge School; Headmaster of Merchant Taylors' School, Crosby, 1903-29; late Member of I.A.H.M., H.M. Conference, Church National Assembly. *Recreation:* reading. *Address:* 17 Queen's Road, Tunbridge Wells. *T.:* 20617. [*Died* 2 *Jan.* 1951.

CRAGG, Major William Gilliat, D.S.O. 1918; Flight Lt. R.A.F.V.R.; late The Loyal North Lancashire Regt.; Liaison Officer (Petroleum Dept. of Mines) to Regional Commissioner N.E. Area, Leeds, Sept. 1939; *b.* 1883; *e. s.* of Capt. William Alfred Cragg, J.P., F.S.A., Threekingham House, Threekingham, Lincs.; *m.* 1st, 1909, Violet Emily (*d.* 1934), *d.* of Leonard Wodehouse Andrews, Tunbridge Wells; two *s.* two *d.*; 2nd, 1935, Beryl Winifred Reynolds, Wellsbridge Cottage, Ascot. *Educ.:* Shrewsbury; R.M.C., Sandhurst. Retired 1st L.N. Lancs Regt. Oct. 1904; enlisted 5 Sept. 1914; Gallipoli, Aug. 1915; Lt.-Col. commanding 6 L.N. Lancs Regt. during part 1917, and for short period 38th Infantry Brigade, Mesopotamia (despatches); commanded London District Discharge Centre July 1919 till its disbandment June 1920; F.R.G.S.; F.R.E.S.; retired from Political Service, Nigeria, 1932; Sheriff of Lincolnshire, 1933-34; C. C. parts of Kesteven, 1932-52; travelled extensively. *Recreations:* hunting, shooting, fishing. *Address:* The White House, Threekingham, Lincs. *Club:* Royal Air Force. [*Died* 24 *April* 1956.

CRAIG, Maj.-Gen. Archibald Maxwell, C.B. 1944; O.B.E. 1919; R. Marines, retired; *b.* 5 Jan. 1895; *s.* of late Surgeon Rear-Adm. William Maxwell Craig, C.B.; *m.* 1917, Diana, *o. d.* of late Edward Charles Daubeny; two *d.* *Educ.:* Marlborough College. Joined Royal Marines, 1912; Capt., 1917; Bt. Major, 1930; Major, 1931; Lt.-Col., 1937; Col., 1942; Brig., 1943; Major-General, 1943. Adjutant Depôt Royal Marines, Deal, 1924-28; qualified Naval staff, 1929; Staff Officer Intelligence on Staff of C.-in-C., North America and West Indies, 1930-32; Brigade-Major Chatham Division R. Marines, 1933-36; Fleet Royal Marine Officer on Staff of C.-in-C., East Indies, 1936-1937; Asst. Director of Naval Intelligence, then Deputy Director of Naval Intelligence (F), 1938-40; Second in Command at Portsmouth and Plymouth Divisions R. Marines, 1941-42; commanded Chatham Division Royal Marines, 1942-44; retired pay, 1944. A Director of the Air Survey Co. Ltd., Aerographic Surveys Ltd. and Air Survey Co. of Rhodesia Ltd., 1948. *Address:* 4 The Gateways, Chelsea, S.W.3. *Club:* Army and Navy. [*Died* 23 *Sept.* 1953.

CRAIG, Barry; *see* Craig, F. B.

CRAIG, Capt. Rt. Hon. Charles Curtis, P.C. Ire. 1922; D.L. Co. Down; *b.* 19 Feb. 1869; *s.* of late James Craig, J.P., of Craigavon, Co. Down; *m.* 1897, Lillian Bowring (*d.* 1954), *d.* of late John Wimble of Long Ditton, Surrey; one *s.* one *d.* *Educ.:* Clifton College. Served European War, 1914-18, in 11th Royal Irish Rifles, Ulster Div. wounded and prisoner, 1916). M.P. (C.) S. Antrim, 1903-1922, Co. Antrim, Nov. 1922-29; Parliamentary Secretary to Ministry of Pensions, 1923-24. Chevalier Légion d'honneur. *Address:* Old Brewery House, Malmesbury, Wilts. *T.:* Malmesbury, 3188. *Club:* Ulster (Belfast). [*Died* 28 *Jan.* 1960.

CRAIG, Frank Barrington (Barry Craig), R.P. 1949; Member N.E.A.C. 1946; Artist and Art-teacher; *b.* 2 March 1902; *s.* of Frank Craig and Elizabeth Katherine (*née* Moser); *m.* 1st, 1926, Winifred, *d.* of Sir John Flett; one *d.*; 2nd, 1944, Dosia, *d.* of James W. Cropper, *q.v.*; one *s.* one *d.* *Educ.:* Rugby; Slade School of Fine Art. Asst. Professor of Fine Art, Michaelis School of Fine Art, Univ. of Capetown, 1926-33; Part-time teacher, St. Martin's L.C.C. School of Art, 1937, and at present; Directorate of Camouflage, Leamington Spa, 1940-43. Regular exhibitor at Royal Society of Portrait Painters, New English Art Club, and at the R.A. since 1934; pictures also at Leicester Galleries, Tooth's, Agnew's, etc. *Address:* Studio House, 92 Carlton Hill, N.W.8. *T.:* Maida Vale 9148. *Club:* Chelsea Arts. [*Died* 4 *Feb.* 1951.

CRAIG, Sir Gilfrid Gordon, Kt., *cr.* 1939; solicitor; D.L., J.P., C.A., Mx.; retired; *b.* 1871; *s.* of late William Simpson Craig, M.D.; *m.* 1903, Juliet Sisley Stilwell; one *d.* *Educ.:* Bedford School. Sheriff of Middlesex, 1940; Chairman, Middlesex County Council, 1940-1943. *Address:* The Grange, Hillingdon, Mx. *T.:* Uxbridge 215. *Clubs:* Carlton, Oriental. [*Died* 5 *April* 1953.

CRAIG, James A., M.B., B.Ch., F.R.C.S. Eng.; M.D.h.c., Q.U.B., 1951; retired; *b.* Ballymoney, County Antrim; *s.* of James Craig, Ballymoney; *m.* 1917, Blanche, *d.* of J. R. Waldron, The Red Cottage, Hythe, Hants; two *s.* *Educ.:* Coleraine; Queen's College, Belfast; University of Vienna. Graduated in the Royal University of Ireland with first place, first class honours, etc.; Demonstrator of Anatomy, Queen's College, Belfast; afterwards studied diseases of the eye and ear at Vienna; Consulting Ophthalmic Surgeon to Royal Victoria Hospital, Belfast; late Lecturer in Ophthalmology and Otology, Queen's Univ. of Belfast; has travelled extensively; member of Editorial Committee of the British Journal of Ophthalmology; Past President Irish Ophthalmological Society, and Ulster Medical Society. *Publications:* has contributed papers on scientific subjects to the various medical journals. *Recreations:* golf (Past Capt. Royal Co. Down Golf Club), ski-ing, skating. *Address:* Mayfield, Cultra, Co. Down. *T.:* Holywood 2263. *Club:* Ulster (Belfast). [*Died* 26 *Nov.* 1958.

CRAIG, James Ireland, C.B.E. 1942; M.A. (Edin.), B.A. Cantab.; F.R.S.E.; F.R.Econ.S.; Member Institut d'Egypte; Economic and Statistical Consultant; *b.* Buckhaven, Scotland, 24 Feb. 1868; *e. s.* of late Capt. T. M. Craig, one of the pioneers of the development of Borneo; *m.* 1897, Isabella (*d.* 1948), 2nd *d.* of late Major John Wilson, Royal Scots Greys; two *s.* one *d.* *Educ.:* Stewart's College, Edinburgh; University, Edinburgh (Watson Fellowship, 1892); Emmanuel College, Cambridge. (Scholar) 15th Wrangler, 1892; Assistant Master, Eton College, 1893; Winchester College, 1895; Ministry of Education, Egypt, 1896-99; Survey Department of Egypt, 1899-1913; Controller, Statistical Department, Egyptian Government, 1913-17; Controller of Supplies, Egypt, Sept. 1917-March 1918; Ministry of Food (London), Apr. 1918-Jan. 1920; Director of Food Control, Upper Silesia Plebiscite Commission, Jan. 1920-22; Controller-General, 1925-28, of the Egyptian Census for 1927; Financial Secretary, Egyptian Ministry of Finance, 1928-34; Govt. Commissioner for Customs, 1934-47; retired on pension, 1947; has travelled in East Africa, Uganda, the Sudan, and Abyssinia in connection with studies of the Nile (3rd cl. Medjidieh, 1906; 2nd cl. Nile, 1937; 2nd cl. Ismailia, 1947); Member, Internat. Statistical Inst.; Hon. Member Royal Hungarian Statistical Inst. *Publications:* General Theory of Map Projections; Meteorological Reports, 1905-12; Nile Flood of 1909-12 (annual); (with Sir William Willcocks, K.C.M.G.) third edition of Egyptian Irrigation; Elements of Analytical Geometry, 1930 (also Arabic Translation); numerous papers. *Recreations:* rifle shooting, cricket, walking, and sailing. *Address:* 88 Sh. Kasr el Eini, Cairo. *T.A.:* Econostat, Cairo. *Clubs:* Turf (Cairo); Union (Alexandria). [*Died* 26 *Jan.* 1952.

CRAIG, Sir John, Kt., *cr.* 1943; C.B.E. 1918; D.L., J.P.; Hon. LL.D. (Glasgow) 1951; Hon. President Colvilles Ltd.; Chairman: Carnlough Lime Co. Ltd., D. & W. Henderson Ltd., Motherwell Machinery & Scrap Co., Scottish Mutual Assurance Soc., Ardrossan Harbour Co., Fullwood Foundry Co. Ltd.; Director: Clyde Alloy Steel Co. Ltd., Colville Constructional Co. Ltd., Smith & McLean Ltd., Lanarkshire Steel Co. Ltd., Steel Company of Scotland Ltd., Harland and Wolff Ltd., Metal-Gas Co. Ltd.; Governor Bank of Scotland; *b.* 1874; Past President of Iron and Steel Institute. *Address:* Cambusnethan Priory, Wishaw, Lanarkshire. *T.:* Wishaw 245. *Clubs:* Royal Automobile; New (Glasgow). [*Died* 1 *Feb.* 1957.

CRAIG, Sir Marshall Millar, Kt., *cr.* 1944; C.B. 1937; Q.C. 1936; Hon. LL.D. (Edin.), 1950; Legal Secretary to Lord Advocate, 1912-49; Parliamentary Draftsman for Scotland, 1925-49; Assistant Legal Secretary and Parliamentary Draftsman (Temporary) since 1949; *b.* 5 April 1880; *yr. s.* of late John Millar Craig, Teacher of Singing, Edinburgh; *m.* 1911, Christina McDonald, *yr. d.* of late Gilchrist Gray Pattison, Edinburgh; one *s.* one *d.* *Educ.:* Daniel Stewart's College, Edinburgh; Edinburgh University. M.A. 1900; LL.B. 1902; admitted to Faculty of Advocates, 1903. *Address:* 5 Wild Hatch, N.W.11. *T.:* Speedwell 2429. *Club:* Reform. [*Died* 19 *Sept.* 1957.

CRAIGAVON, Dowager Viscountess, D.B.E., *cr.* 1941; **Cecil Mary Nowell Dering Craig;** *o. c.* of late Sir Daniel Tupper, M.V.O., Asst. Comptroller Lord Chamberlain's Dept. and Sergeant-at-Arms to H.M. King George V.; *m.* 1905, Rt. Hon. Viscount Craigavon, Baronet, D.L., M.P., 1st Prime Minister of Northern Ireland (*d.* 1940); two *s.* one *d.* President of Ulster Women's Unionist Council, 1923-43; C.St.J. *Address:* The Old Rectory, Mere, Wilts. *T.:* Mere 317. [*Died* 17 *March* 1960.

CRAIGIE, Rt. Hon. Sir Robert (Leslie), P.C. 1937; G.C.M.G., *cr.* 1941 (K.C.M.G., *cr.* 1936; C.M.G. 1929); C.B. 1930; *b.* 6 Dec. 1883; *o. s.* of late Adm. R. W. Craigie; *m.* 1918, Pleasant (*d.* 1956), *d.* of late Hon. Pleasant A. Stovall, Savannah, Georgia, U.S.A., American Minister at Berne; one *s.* Passed a competitive examination and entered Foreign Office, 1907; acting Third Secretary in the Diplomatic Service, 1908; Secretary to the International Conference relating to the New Hebrides, 1914; Second Secretary at Berne, 1916; British Representative on the Inter-Allied Blockade Committee, 1916-18; First Secretary, 1919; Acting High Commissioner at Sofia, 1920; First Secretary at Washington, 1920; Chargé d'Affaires, 1921; transferred to Foreign Office, 1923; Counsellor, 1928; Assistant Under-Secretary of State in the Foreign Office, 1934-37; Ambassador to Japan, 1937-41; U.K. Rep. to U.N. War Crimes Commn., 1945-1948; headed U.K. Deleg.: Geneva Diplomatic Conf. for Protection of War Victims, 1949; Extraordinary Administrative Radio Conf., Geneva, 1951. *Publication:* Behind the Japanese Mask, 1946. *Recreation:* golf. *Address:* 22 Eaton Square, S.W.1. *T.:* Sloane 8373. [*Died* 16 *May* 1959.

CRAIGIE, Sir William A., Kt., *cr.* 1928; Knight Commander Order of Icelandic Falcon, 1930; M.A. (St. Andrews and Oxon), LL.D. (St. Andrews), D.Litt. (Oxford, Cambridge, Calcutta, Michigan, Wisconsin); Hon. D.Phil. (Iceland); F.B.A.; Hon. Fellow of Oriel College; Professor Emeritus of English, University of Chicago; *b.* Dundee, 13 Aug. 1867; *y. s.* of James Craigie and Christina Gow; *m.* 1897, Jessie K. Hutchen (*d.* 1947). *Educ.:* West End Academy, Dundee. Studied at St. Andrews Univ., 1883-88, taking M.A. (with honours in Classics and Philosophy), 1889; gained Guthrie Scholarship at St. Andrews, 1888, and was elected Bible Clerk at Oriel College, 1889; first class in Litt. Hum. (1890 and 1892); studied Scandinavian languages in Copenhagen, 1892-93; Assistant and Lecturer in Humanity at St. Andrews, 1893-97; Lecturer in Scandinavian Languages at Taylor Institution, Oxford, 1905-1916; Fellow of Oriel College, 1917-25; Rawlinson and Bosworth Professor of Anglo-Saxon, 1916-25; engaged on the Oxford English Dictionary from 1897, joint-editor 1901-33. *Publications:* various articles on Scottish, Gaelic, and Scandinavian subjects in the Scottish

Review, Anglia, Arkiv för nordisk Filologi, etc.; also Scandinavian Folklore, A Primer of Burns, 1896; editions of Burns, 1896 and 1898, and Bellenden's Scottish Translation of Livy, 1901-3; Religion of Ancient Scandinavia, 1906; Skotlands Rimur (Icelandic Ballads on the Gowrie Conspiracy), 1908; Icelandic Sagas, 1913; The Pronunciation of English, 1917; The Maitland Folio Manuscript, 1919–27; The Maitland Quarto Manuscript, 1920; A First English Book, 1920; English Reading Made Easy, 1922; The Asloan Manuscript, 1923-25; Easy Readings in Anglo-Saxon, 1923; Specimens of Anglo-Saxon Prose and Poetry, 1923-31; An Advanced English Reader, 1924; Easy Readings in Old Icelandic, 1924; The Poetry of Iceland (in the Oxford Book of Scandinavian Verse), 1925; A First English Reader, 1927; English Spelling, 1927; The Study of American English, 1927; A Dictionary of the Older Scottish Tongue, 1931-; The Northern Element in English Literature, 1933; A Historical Dictionary of American English, 1936-43; S.P.E. Tracts (Nos. 50, 56-59, 63-65), 1937-46; Specimens of Icelandic Rimur (3 vols.), 1952. *Address:* Ridgehurst, Watlington, Oxon. *T.:* Watlington 84. [*Died* 2 *Sept.* 1957.

CRAIK, Sir Henry Duffield, 3rd Bt., *cr.* 1926; G.C.I.E., *cr.* 1941; K.C.S.I., *cr.* 1933 (C.S.I. 1924); *b.* 1876; *s.* of late Rt. Hon. Sir Henry Craik, 1st Bt., K.C.B., M.P.; *S.* brother 1929; *m.* 1901, Emily Henrietta D'O. (*d.* 1931), *d.* of Rev. R. Baker-Carr; two *d. Educ.:* Eton; Pembroke College, Oxford. Joined Indian Civil Service, served in the Punjab as Settlement Officer, Sessions Judge and Secretary to Government; in Home Dept. Govt. of India, 1919-22; Chief Secretary, Punjab, 1922-27; Commissioner, 1927; Member Punjab Executive Council, 1930-1934; Home Member of Governor-General's Executive Council, 1934-38; Governor of the Punjab, 1938-41; Political Adviser to the Viceroy, 1941-43. *Heir:* none. *Address:* 2 Down Street, W.1. *Clubs:* Athenæum, Cavalry. [*Died* 26 *March* 1955 (*ext.*).

CRAMB, Alexander Charles, M.I.E.E., M.I.Mech.E.; *b.* Melton Constable, Norfolk, 1874; *s.* of William Cramb and Sarah Emma Wells; *m.* 1912, Maud Hillier (*d.* 1949); one *s.* one *d.*; 1950, Dorothy, *o. d.* of E. Riley, Barnsley, Yorks. *Educ.:* West Buckland. Served electrical apprenticeship Cardiff; Chief Asst. Engineer to Croydon Corpn. Electricity Dept., 1902-4; Chief Engineer and Manager, Croydon Corporation Electricity Department, 1904-31; Director and Secretary, British Electrical Development Assoc. Inc., 1931-43; Secretary, Electric Vehicle Assoc. of Great Britain, Inc. to 1943; during European War acted as District Engineer for Metropolitan Munitions Board and was responsible for production of munitions; Hon. Secretary Incorporated Municipal Electrical Association, 1919-31; President of Association, 1914-16; Member of Council of Electrical Development Association since formation in 1919; Chairman of the Council, 1928; Associate and Past President of Association of Public Lighting Engineers; served as Chairman of Electricity Commissioners' Committee on Uniformity of Electricity Charges and Tariffs whose report was issued in 1930; former Member: Council of Illuminating Engineering Society; British Standards Instn. *Recreation:* golf. *Address:* Lamorran, Cheyne Walk, Croydon, Surrey. *T.:* Addiscombe 1020. [*Died* 10 *Feb.* 1956.

CRAMP, Karl Reginald, O.B.E., M.A., F.R.A.H.S., Historian; Past Pres. Nat. Trust of Australia (formed in 1947); Founder and First Pres. Assoc. of ex-Inspectors of Schools (founded in 1949); retired; *b.* Redhill, Surrey, 21 Jan. 1878; *m.* Ethel May Neill, Newcastle, N.S.W.; two *s.* two *d. Educ.:* University of Sydney. 1st Cl. Hons., Frazer Scholar and Professor Wood's Prize for Hist.; Hons. in Philosophy, Prox. Acc. Physiography Prize. In Educ. Dept. service, 1895-1943, with record deptl. marks for Cl. II and Cl. I teachers' certs.; Historian Procurement Div. United States Army Services of Supply in Australia, 1943-1945. Senior Lecturer at Teachers' College, Sydney, 1905-12; Examiner and Chief Examiner, Education Dept., N.S.W., 1912-1923; Inspector of Secondary Schools of New South Wales, 1923-43; Pres. Institute of Inspectors of Schools and of Australasian Conference of Inspectors, 1929. Hon. Sec. R. Australian Historical Society, 1915-21, 1922-27, 1930-36, 1943-44; Pres. 1921, 1928-1929, 1937-39 and 1953; Vice-Pres. 1941-42, 1945-52, 1955-56; first Vice-Pres. of Workers' Educational Assoc., Pres. Teachers' Guild, 1937-39, Vice-Pres., 1931-36 and 1940-50; Chairman, Sir Joseph Banks Memorial Fund Trust, 1943-45; President Wattle League, 1936-37 and Hon. Member, 1943-49; Vice-President Australian English Association till 1942; Pres. Hist. Sec., Science Congress, Auckland, N.Z., 1937; Member of Executive and Chm. and Organiser Historical Exhibn. Cttee. for N.S.W. 150th Anniversary Celebrations, 1938; Director, Jubilee Historical Exhibn., Sydney, for Commonwealth Govt. and Roy. Austr. Hist. Soc., 1951. An original Fellow, Australian and New Zealand Association for Advancement of Science, 1937; Dir., 1947-, Vice-Pres., 1950-, N.S.W. Deaf, Dumb and Blind Instn. for children; Mem., 1933-46, Pres., 1946-48 (Retd.), Capt. Cook's Landing Place Trust, Botany Bay; Pres. (Retd.) La Pérouse Monument Trust. *Publications:* State and Federal Constitutions of Australia; A Story of the Australian People; A Story of the English People (joint); Great Englishmen; Historical Section of Bartholomew and Cramp's Atlas; The Australian V.C. Winners; An English Grammar; (joint) History of United Grand Lodge of Masons of New South Wales, 2 vols., author of 3rd vol. (From Jubilee to Golden Jubilee); History, Lodge University of Sydney; The First Century of the Royal Sydney Yacht Squadron; Food—the First Munition of War (Australian-American Co-operation), 3 vols.; The 'Roar' Material of History—School Boy Howlers; *Pamphlets:* Who discovered Payable Gold?; A critical analysis of Evidence; Sir George Reid's Place in the Federal Movement; and many other papers to R. Aust. Hist. Soc. *Address:* 13 Birriga Road, Bellevue Hill, Sydney, N.S.W. *T.:* FY4112. [*Died* 19 *July* 1956.

CRANAGE, Very Rev. David Herbert Somerset, B.D., Litt.D., F.S.A., Hon. A.R.I.B.A.; *b.* 10 Oct. 1866; *y. s.* of late Dr. J. E. Cranage of the Old Hall, Wellington, Salop; *m.* 1923, Dorothy Elizabeth *o. d.* of late William Tyrer of Stockton House, Warwickshire, and afterwards of Bedford. *Educ.:* King's College, Cambridge. Has travelled in Egypt, India, Ceylon, Palestine and America; Curate of Little Wenlock, 1897-98; Much Wenlock, 1898-1902; Secretary of the Cambridge University Local Lectures, 1902-24, and of the Board of Extra-Mural Studies, 1924-28; Dean of Norwich, 1928-45; Select Preacher at Cambridge, 1908, 1910, 1912, 1914, 1918, 1922, 1924, 1928, 1929, 1932; Select Preacher at Oxford, 1932-34; Ex-Chairman of the Faculty Board of Fine Arts in the University of Cambridge; Ex-Vice-President of Society of Antiquaries; Ex-President, Cambridge Antiquarian Soc.; Ex-President Norfolk and Norwich Archæological Society; Chm. Y.M.C.A. Educ. Cttee., 1918-53; Member Consultative Committee, Board of Education, 1920-28; Chairman of the House of Clergy in the Church Assembly, 1932-45; Prolocutor of Lower House of Convocation of Canterbury, 1936-45. Sec. of the Gilchrist Educational Trust, 1923-48; Chm. of the Central Council for the Care of Churches, 1938-53, and of the Cathedrals Advisory Cttee., 1946-55. *Publications:* An Architectural Account of the Churches of Shropshire,

1894-1912; Summer Meeting Sermons, 1914; The Home of the Monk, 1926; Loyalty and Order, 1934; Cathedrals and how they were built, 1948; Not only a Dean, 1952. *Address:* The Beam House, Winkfield Road, Windsor. *T.:* Windsor 872.

[*Died* 22 *Oct.* 1957.

CRANE, Sir Alfred Victor, Kt., *cr.* 1954; LL.B. (Lond.); *b.* 8 February 1892; *s.* of John Frederick and Rebecca Matilda Crane; *m.* 1917, Mildred Eugene (*née* Garratt); five *s.* two *d.* *Educ.:* privately; Univ. of London. LL.B. (Lond.), 1923. Admitted Solicitor, Supreme Court of British Guiana, 1919, upon examination of Law Society of England. Dep. Mayor, City Council, Georgetown, Br. Guiana, 1923-33; Member Br. Guiana Legislature, 1926-33; Sen. Magistrate, Br. Guiana, 1933-46; called to Bar, Inner Temple, 1935; Actg. Solicitor-Gen. of Br. Guiana, 1946; Judge of Supreme Court, Windward and Leeward Is., B.W.I., 1946-50 (actg. Chief Justice, 1950); Chief Justice, British Honduras, 1950-55, retired. *Publications:* The Law of Unlawful Possession, 1921; The Law of Workmen's Compensation, 1937; Workmen's Compensation Practice, 1938; The Law of Compulsory Motor Vehicle Insurance, 1939; A Manual of Rating Law in Georgetown, 1943. *Recreation:* motoring. *Address:* Belize, British Honduras, Central America. *T.:* No. 5 Belize, British Honduras.

[*Died* 20 *Feb.* 1955.

CRANE, Sir Edmund Frank, Kt., *cr.* 1935; *b.* 21 Nov. 1886; *s.* of Edward John and Edith Maud Crane; *m.* 1st, 1911 (marriage dissolved 1938); one *d.*; 2nd, 1938, Kathleen Margaret Wright. *Educ.:* Handsworth Grammar School. *Recreations:* golf and shooting. *Address:* Villa Millbrook, St. Lawrence, Jersey, C.I. [*Died* 18 *Sept.* 1957.

CRANE, Sir William, Kt. 1958; C.B.E. 1949; J.P.; Member Nottingham City Council since 1913; *b.* 6 June 1874; *s.* of James Crane; *m.* 1914, Gladys Ethel, *d.* of Thomas Fish; one *s.* one *d.* *Educ.:* Nottingham High School. Pro-Chancellor of Nottingham University. Hon. M.A., Nottingham Univ. *Address:* 5 Clumber Crescent, The Park, Nottingham.

[*Died* 21 *Oct.* 1959.

CRANFIELD, Arthur Leslie; Editor and Director, The Star, 1941-57 retired, late Director, Daily News Ltd.; *b.* St. Ives, Hunts, 19 June 1892; *s.* of late A. E. Cranfield, solicitor, St. Ives; *m.* 1916, Mary Frances, *d.* of late George Smyth, sculptor, Dublin: one *s.* one *d.* *Educ.:* St. Ives Grammar School. Served European War, Capt. Essex Regiment and Brigade Signalling Officer, East Anglian (Reserve) Brigade; Managing Editor, Evening Standard, 1939-41; Editor, The Daily Mail, Director, Associated Newspapers, 1935-38; Assistant Editor, Daily Mail, 1930-35; Evening News, 1928-30; first Editor-in-chief of Press Association, 1926-28; Chief Sub-Editor, Evening News, 1922-26; previously on staffs of Star, Birmingham Gazette, Sheffield Daily Telegraph and Warwick Advertiser; Member Middle Temple. Mem. Press Council, 1953-57 (Vice-Chm. 1956-57). *Recreation:* golf. *Address:* 12 Chepstow Villas, W.11. *T.:* Bayswater 7165; Squash Cottage, The Green, Rottingdean. *T.:* Rottingdean 2471. *Clubs:* Garrick; East Brighton Golf (Brighton); West Middlesex Golf (Southall).

[*Died* 9 *Oct.* 1957.

CRANSWICK, Rt. Rev. George Harvard, D.D.; now retired; *b.* Sheffield, England, 1882; *e. s.* of late Canon E. G. Cranswick, Sydney, and Edith Harvard; *m.* 1911, Olive Carr, *e. d.* of E. Carr Hordern of Sydney; two *s.* four *d.* *Educ.:* The King's School, Parramatta, N.S.W.; St. Paul's College, University of Sydney (Scholar and Fellow); Wycliffe Hall, Oxford. Deacon, 1907; Priest, 1908; an Assistant Master Geelong College, 190 -5; a House Master, Armidale School, 1905-6; Curate of St. Margaret's, Brighton, 1907-9; A.O. as a clergyman of the Diocese of Sydney, sent forth on foreign service in the Mission Field, 1910-14; Acting Vice-Principal and Professor of English, Noble College, Masulipatam, South India, 1910-11; Headmaster of the C.M.S. High School Bezwada, South India, 1911-13; Superintending Missionary C.M.S. and Chairman of District Church Council, Khammamett, Deccan, 1913-14; Missioner N.S.W. Church Missionary Association, 1914; Hon. Lecturer, Moore Theological College, Sydney, 1914-17; C.I.C. of Conventional District of St. Alban's, Golden Grove, 1914-15; Rector of St. Paul's, Chatswood, 1915-17; Hon. Secretary, Sydney Diocesan Missionary Committee, 1915-17; Rector of St. Paul's, Bendigo, 1917; Bishop's Chaplain for Lay Readers, 1917; Bishop of Gippsland, 1917-42; Nat. Pres. C. of E. Men's Soc. in Australia, 1926-36; acting Metropolitan of Victoria, 1928-29; Chm. Australian Board of Missions, 1942-49; Commr. Australian Council of World Council of Churches, 1949-50; *Publications:* The Call of India; Roman Catholic Evasions; Confirmation and Baptism; The Bible and Education; Evangelism in the Australian Church, Moorhouse Lectures for 1923; A New Deal for Papua. *Recreations:* fishing, motoring, and motor-boating. *Address:* Cherrywood, 27 Deepdene Road, Deepdene E.2, Victoria, Australia. *T.:* WY 2010. *Clubs:* Rotary, Royal Automobile of Victoria, Athenæum, Savage (Melbourne).

[*Died* 25 *Oct.* 1954.

CRASTER, Sir Edmund; *see* Craster, Sir H. H. E.

CRASTER, Col. George, C.B.E. 1921; D.S.O. 1918; I.A., retired; *b.* 27 Dec. 1878; *y. s.* of late Col. W. R. Craster, Royal (Bengal) Artillery, of Beadnell Hall, Northumberland, and Mary, *d.* of T. C. Hincks, Breckenborough Hall, Yorks; *m.* 1923, Christian Desborough, *d.* of late William Douglas Caroe, F.S.A.; one *d.* *Educ.:* Clifton College; R.M.C., Sandhurst. Commission in Indian Army and came to India, 1898; served with 6th King Edward's Own Cavalry till 1923; Commandant 16th Light Cavalry, 1923-27; Bt. Col., 1927; served in France and Belgium, Nov. 1914-May 1918 (despatches, D.S.O.), Palestine, July and Aug. 1919; Afghan War, 1919 (despatches, O.B.E.); Waziristan-Mahsud Campaign, 1919-20 (despatches); Wana Column, 1920-21 (despatches, C.B.E.); North-West Frontier of India, 1930-31 (despatches); G.S.O.1, Peshawar District, 1930; retired from Indian Army, 1931; Chief Staff Officer in Jaipur State, 1931-35. *Address:* Danny, Hurstpierpoint, Sussex. *T.:* 2299. *Club:* Kennel. [*Died* 19 *Nov.* 1958.

CRASTER, Sir (Herbert Henry) Edmund, Kt., *cr.* 1945; M.A., D.Litt. Oxon; Hon. Litt.D. Cambridge; Hon. Litt.D. Leeds; Hon. D.Litt. Durham; F.S.A.; Fellow of All Souls College, Oxford, 1903; and Librarian since 1946; *b.* 5 Nov. 1879; *s.* of Edmund Craster of Beadnell Hall, Northumberland, Indian Civil Service; *m.* 1912, Ida, *d.* of Gilfrid Baker-Creswell, Preston Tower, Northumberland; one *s.* one *d.* *Educ.:* Clifton Coll.; Balliol Coll., Oxford. Editor of History of Northumberland, 1904-14; Sub-Librarian of the Bodleian Library, 1912-31; Keeper of Western MSS., 1927-31; Bodley's Librarian, 1931-45. *Publications:* History of Northumberland, vols. viii-x, 1907-14; Summary Catalogue of Western MSS. of the Bodleian Library, vols. ii and vi, 1922-24, 1937; Speeches on Foreign Policy by Lord Halifax, 1940; History of the Bodleian Library, 1952; historical and archæological articles. *Address:* All Souls College, Oxford. [*Died* 21 *March* 1959.

CRAUFURD, Brig.-Gen. Sir (George) Standish (Gage), 5th Bt., *cr.* 1781; C.B.

1919; C.M.G. 1916; C.I.E. 1913; D.S.O. 1900; late A.D.C. to King George V.; late Gordon Highlanders; *b.* 19 Nov. 1872; *e. s.* of Sir Charles Craufurd, 4th Bart.; *S.* father, 1939. *Educ.:* Wellington College; Sandhurst. Entered Army, 1892; Captain, 1899; Major, 1911; served Chitral, 1895 (medal with clasp); North West Frontier, India, 1897-98. including action of Dargai and operations in the Maidan, Waran, and Baza Valleys (wounded, two clasps); South Africa, 1899-1902; commanded a Regiment of Mounted Infantry (despatches twice, Queen's medal five clasps, King's medal, D.S.O.); Operations S. Nigeria 1905; Operations in Persian Gulf, 1910-12 (Naval G. S. Medal and clasp); European War, 1914-18 (wounded thrice, C.B., C.M.G., Bt. Col.); commanded Poona Brigade Area, 1924-1928; retired pay, 1928. *Heir: b.* Quentin Charles Alexander, Capt., R.N. retd. [*b.* 11 Feb. 1875; *m.* 1899, Ann, *e.d.* of late Thomas Blackwell]. *Address:* Swindridge Muir, Dalry, Ayrshire. *T.:* Dalry 2162. *Club:* United Service. [*Died* 6 *Jan.* 1957.

CRAUFURD, Sir Quentin Charles Alexander, 6th Bt. *cr.* 1781; M.B.E. 1953; Captain R.N., retired; *b.* 11 Feb. 1875; *s.* of Sir Charles William Frederick Craufurd, 4th Bt. and Hon. Isolda Caroline Vereker, *e. d.* of 4th Viscount Gort; *S.* brother 1957; *m.* 1899, Ann (*d.* 1957), *e. d.* of Thomas Blackwell, Dublin. F.R.S.A.; M.I.E.E., F.Inst.P. *Heir: b.* Alexander John Fortescue Craufurd, *b.* 22 March 1876. *Address:* Ness View, Lydd, Kent. [*Died* 8 *May* 1957.

CRAVEN, Major Hon. Rupert Cecil, O.B.E. 1919; retd., Hon. rank Major; *b.* 1? Apr. 1870; 2nd *s.* of 3rd Earl of Craven; *m.* 1st, 1899, Inez Morton, *d.* of George Broom (marriage dissolved, 1908); 2nd, 1925, Mrs. C. W. Banbury, of Wadley Manor, Faringdon, *widow* of Captain C. W. Banbury, Coldstream Guards; one *s.* Midshipman; electrical engineer; commanded a company R.E., South African War (medal and 5 clasps); served European War, in France, Sep. 1914-Nov. 1914, 1st Batt. R. Scots Fusiliers (wounded); 1 Jan. 1915-14 March 1915, 2nd Batt. R. Scots Fusiliers (gassed and invalided); May 1915-March 1916, 1st Batt. Nigeria Regt. in Cameroon Campaign (wounded); March 1916-Aug. 1916, 5th Batt. M.I. Nigeria Regt., Kano Nigeria; Oct. 1916-April 1917, 3rd Batt. R. Scots Fusiliers, draft conducting; May 1917-Jan. 1919, 4th Regt. King's African Rifles in German East Africa, Uganda, B.E. Africa, and Portuguese E. Africa, (Mons 1914 Star, European War Medal, Victory Medal). *Recreations:* (past) big-game shooting, fox hunting, and polo. *Address:* Wadley Manor, Faringdon, Berks. [*Died* 9 *July* 1959.

CRAVEN-ELLIS, William; Director of Companies and Senior Partner, Ellis & Sons, Manchester; *e. s.* of late Thomas Ellis, Manchester; *g.s.* of William Craven, founder of Craven Brothers (Manchester) Ltd., machine tool makers; *m.* 1906, Grace Stanley, Liverpool; two *d.*; assumed additional name of Craven by Deed Poll, 1931. *Educ.:* Manchester Grammar School. Served European War, 1914-19; Lieut., T.F. (Reserve), 1915; Chm. Hale U.D.C., 1915-16; contested Barnsley (Yorks), 1923 and 1929; M.P. (Nat.) Southampton, 1931-45. Chm. Parl. and Monetary Cttee., House of Commons (advocating monetary reform), 1934-1944; Chm. Ellis & Sons Amalgamated Properties Ltd., Ellis & Sons Second Amalgamated Properties Ltd., Ellis & Sons Third Amalgamated Properties Ltd., Ellis & Sons Fourth Amalgamated Properties Ltd., Ellis & Sons Fifth Amalgamated Properties Ltd., Ellis & Sons (Southern) Property Investments Ltd., E. & S. Builders, Ltd., Ellis & Sons Amalgamated Investments Ltd., Piccadilly Building Society. Director Craven Brothers (Manchester) Ltd., and other cos. Freeman City of London. Master of The Worshipful Company of Glovers of London, 1943-1044. *Publications:* The Rebuilding of Britain, 1935; World Economic Problems—Remove the Causes of War, 1936; Financing the Rebuilding of Britain, 1944; The Need for Reforming the Bank of England, 1944. *Address:* Twineham Grange, Bolney, Sussex. *T.:* Bolney 394; 21 Duchess Mews, Portland Place, W.1. *T.:* Langham 3617. *Clubs:* Royal Automobile; Royal Southampton Yacht (Southampton). [*Died* 17 *Dec.* 1959.

CRAWFORD, Archibald, Q.C. 1924; M.A., LL.B.; Member of Scottish Bar; *b.* Glasgow, 2 Apr. 1882; *s.* of Robert Crawford, LL.D., Glasgow, and Sarah Smith, Liverpool; *m.* Barbara Joan Stuart Crawford; one *s.* one *d.* *Educ.:* Warriston Coll., Moffat; Glasgow Univ. Called to Bar, 1906; contested (U.) Peebles and South Midlothian, 1922 and 1923: Consultant on training in Industrial and Commercial Speech Making technique. *Publications:* Public Speaking, 1935; Tartan Shirts, 1936; Guilty as Libelled, 1938; Mind Training for Speech Making, 1939. *Recreations:* diverse. *Address:* 24 Exeter Road, N.W.2. *T.:* Gladstone 4127. [*Died* 29 *June* 1960.

CRAWFORD, Colin Grant; *b.* 3 June 1890; *s.* of late Henry Leighton Crawford, C.M.G., and Alba, *née* Grant Brown; *m.* 1940, Margaret MacIver, Aberdeen; two *d.* *Educ.:* Clifton College; Trinity Hall, Cambridge. Indian Civil Service, 1914-30; attached Indian Army Reserve of Officers, 1915-19; served Mesopotamia, 1916-18; Kangchenjunga Expedition, 1920; Mt. Everest Expeditions, 1922 and 1933. *Recreations:* mountaineering, fishing. *Address:* Tigh-na-Mara, Rosemarkie, Ross-shire, Scotland. *Club:* Alpine. [*Died* 15 *Aug.* 1959.

CRAWFORD, Lieut.-Col. Frederick Hugh, C.B.E. 1921; J.P.; Home Office appointment (retired); *b.* 21 Aug. 1861; *s.* of J. W. Crawford of Cloreen, Belfast, and Madge Mathews of Anna House, Portadown, Ulster; *m.* Helen Wilson, Acre House, Normanby-le-Wold, Lincolnshire; two *s.* three *d.* *Educ.:* University College School, London, etc. Served in S.A. War, 1900 and 1901, in Donegal Artillery as Captain and Adjutant of Brigade Div. Mil. Artly. (Queen's medal 3 clasps, despatches, Royal Humane Society's Bronze Medal for saving life); European War, appointed O.C. R.A.S.C., Northern Ireland; France 1916 for a tour of Instruction. *Recreations:* when younger, travel, yachting, etc. *Address:* Cloreen, Belfast, Ulster. *Club:* Ulster Reform (Belfast). [*Died* 5 *Nov.* 1952.

CRAWFORD, Lieut.-Col. Gilbert Stewart, C.M.G. 1915; M.D.; late R.A.M.C.; *b.* 14 May 1868. Captain R.A.M.C. 1895; Major, 1904; Lt.-Col. 1914; Officer Commanding Hospital and Relief Party sent to Italy from Malta, Messina Earthquake (Knight Commander Crown of Italy, King of Italy Commemorative Medal, Italian Red Cross Medal, Esquire Order of St. John of Jerusalem); served N.W. Frontier, India, 1897-8 (medal, 2 clasps); South Africa, 1900-2 (Queen's medal 4 clasps, King's medal, 2 clasps); European War, 1914-18 (C.M.G.). *Address:* Lindsay, 54 Victoria Road, Exmouth, Devon. [*Died* 2 *Nov.* 1953.

CRAWFORD, James Archibald, Q.C. (Scot.) 1949; *b.* 24 Sept. 1905; *yr. s.* of James Crawford, M.A., F.E.I.S., Hopeman, Morayshire and Helen Crawford (*née* Robb); *m.* 1940, Joan Murray Woodburn; one *s.* one *d.* *Educ.:* Elgin Academy; Fettes College; Edinburgh University. M.A. (Edin.), 1927, LL.B. (Edin.), 1929. Called to Scottish Bar, 1936. *Recreation:* golf. *Address:* 6 Abercromby Place, Edinburgh. *T.:* Edinburgh Central 3942. *Clubs:* Caledonian; Northern (Edinburgh). [*Died* 12 *Jan.* 1953.

CRAWFORD, Lawrence, M.A., D.Sc., LL.D., F.R.S.E., F.R.S.S.Af.; Member of City

Council of Cape Town since 1944; *b.* Glasgow, 1867; *s.* of late John Crawford, Glasgow; *m.* 1903, Annie M., *y. d.* of late Wm. Spilhaus, Cape Town; three *s.* two *d.* *Educ.:* High School, Glasgow; University of Glasgow; King's College, Cambridge (Fellow, 1893-1899), 5th Wrangler, 1890; Lecturer in Mathematics at Mason College, Birmingham, 1893-1898; Professor of Pure Mathematics at the South African College, Cape Town, 1899-1918, at the University of Cape Town, 1918-38, Member of Council of the University, 1939- ; Hon. Treasurer of the Royal Society of South Africa, 1909-35, President, 1936-41; President of the South African Association for the Advancement of Science, 1915-16; Vice-Chancellor and acting Principal of the University of Capetown, June-Dec. 1931. *Publications:* Mathematical papers in Quarterly Journal of Pure and Applied Mathematics, Proceedings of Edinburgh Mathematical Society, Mathematical Gazette, Reports of South African Association for the Advancement of Science. *Recreation:* golf. *Address:* 21 Pillans Road, Rosebank, Cape Town. *Club:* Civil Service (Cape Town). [*Died* 5 *April* 1951.

CRAWFORD, Osbert Guy Stanhope, C.B.E. 1950; Hon. Litt.D. Camb., 1952, Southampton, 1955, Verdienstkreuz, 1956; Founder and editor of Antiquity, a quarterly review of Archæology, 1927; *b.* 1886; *s.* of late C. E. G. Crawford, late I.C.S., and Alice Luscombe Mackenzie; unmarried. *Educ.:* Marlborough; Oxford. Junior Demonstrator, School of Geography, Oxford, 1912; excavated in Sudan under H. S. Wellcome, 1913-1914; London Scottish, Aug. 1914; served in France, 1914-18, London Scottish, 3rd Army Maps, R.F.C. (despatches); Pres. of South Eastern Union of Scientific Societies. 1930; corresponding member of the German Archæological Institute, the Austrian Anthropological Society, and the Vienna Prehistoric Society; hon. corresponding member of American Geographical Society; hon. F.S.A.Scot.; President of Prehistoric Society, 1938; member of Royal Commission on Ancient and Historical Monuments of England, 1939-46; Victoria Medal, R.G.S., 1940; Rhind Lecturer, Edinburgh, 1943; Pres. Hampshire Field Club, 1946-1949; F.B.A. 1947; Archæology Officer of the Ordnance Survey (Southampton), 1920-46. *Publications:* Man and his Past, 1921; The Andover District, 1922; Air Survey and Archæology, 1924; Long Barrows and Stone Circles of the Cotswolds and the Welsh Marches, 1925; Wessex from the Air (with Alexander Keiller), 1928; Air Photography for Archæologists, 1929; Field Archæology, 1932; Topography of Roman Scotland, 1949; (with F. Addison) Abu Geili Excavations Report, 1950; The Fung Kingdom of Sennar, 1951; Archæology in the Field, 1953; Castles and Churches in the Middle Nile Region, 1953; Said and Done (Autobiography), 1955; The Eye Goddess, 1957. *Recreations:* travel and photography. *Address:* Nursling, Southampton. *Club:* Athenæum. [*Died* 29 *Nov.* 1957.

CRAWFORD, Thomas Clark, C.I.E. 1935; retired; *b.* 13 May 1886; *s.* of late A. B. Crawford. *Address:* 28 Cleveden Drive, Glasgow, W.2. [*Died* 28 *Dec.* 1955.

CRAWFORD, Lieut.-Col. William Loftus, C.B.E. 1941; D.S.O. 1918; V.D.; living in retirement; *b.* 13 Nov. 1868; 5th *s.* of late Surgeon James Robert Crawford, of 69th Regt. and Staff, Ayr, and Jane J. Hatton, Wexford; unmarried. *Educ.:* Epsom College. Largely interested in Coffee and Tea Estates in Mysore and South India; Ex-President of Planters Association; for two years a member of Legislative Council and member of Board of Agriculture in Mysore. Served throughout European War, 1914-18, mostly in France and Flanders (despatches thrice, D.S.O., Croix de Guerre (French), 1914-15 Star, General Service and Victory Medals). *Clubs:* Constitutional, Junior Army and Navy. [*Died* 15 *April* 1951.

CRAWFURD, Major Horace Evelyn, A.F.C.; Chairman of Directors: Wellington Trust Ltd.; Executive Travel Ltd.; Director of: Co-partnership Tenants Ltd.; Merstham Park Tenants Ltd.; Stoke-on-Trent Tenants Ltd.; *b.* 13 Jan. 1882; *s.* of John William Crawfurd. *Educ.:* Merchant Taylors' School; St. John's College, Oxford. Served European War, 1914-19 (A.F.C.); Lecturer on Education at Liverpool University, 1904-10; M.P. (L.), West Walthamstow, 1924-29; Member of Royal Commission on Transport, 1928-31. *Publications:* Liberalism—Yesterday and To-day; The Achievements of Liberalism; The Earnings of Industry; Monkeying with your Money; (with Ernest Short) That's the Way the Money Goes, 1951. *Address:* 610 Duncan House, Dolphin Square, S.W.1. *Club:* National Liberal. [*Died* 14 *March* 1958.

CRAWSHAY, Capt. Geoffrey Cartland Hugh; Chairman: Welsh Land Settlement Soc. Ltd.; Usk River Board and Historical Buildings' Council for Wales; President Council of Social Service for Wales and Monmouthshire; *b.* 20 June 1892; *s.* of late Codrington Fraser Crawshay, D.L., J.P., Llanfair Grange, Abergavenny. *Educ.:* Wellington College; Cardiff University. Captain, Welsh Guards; served European War; retired, 1924; District Commissioner for South Wales (Special Areas Act, 1934) to 1939; Controller (Wales) Ministry of Aircraft Production, 1940-44; Chairman, Welsh Board of Health, 1945-52, retired. D.L., J.P., County of Monmouth; High Sheriff of Monmouthshire, 1939. Hon. LL.D. (Wales) 1954. K.St.J. *Address:* Llanfair Court, Abergavenny. *T.A.* and *T.:* Llanfihangel-Gobion 215. [*Died* 8 *Nov.* 1954.

CREAGH, Rear-Adm. James Vandeleur, D.S.O. 1918; *e. s.* of late Charles Vandeleur Creagh, C.M.G. of Cahirbane, Co. Clare; *b.* 1883; *m.* 1908, Adela May, *d.* of late P. C. Cork, C.M.G.; one *s.* one *d.* Served European War, 1914-18 (despatches, D.S.O., Croix de Guerre); Naval Staff, Admiralty, 1921-23; Capt. 1923; commanded First Destroyer Flotilla, 1925-28; on staff of R.N. War College, 1928-30; Flag Captain H.M.S. Egmont, 1931-32; Senior Naval Officer, Persian Gulf, 1933-35; Rear Adm. and retired list, 1935; Officer of Order of St. John of Jerusalem, 1933. *Club:* United Service. [*Died* 14 *Jan.* 1956.

CREALOCK, Major John Mansfield, R.P.; portrait painter; *s.* of late Major-General North Crealock, C.B.; *m.* Mary (*d.* 1937), *d.* of late William Adam Loch; no *c.* *Educ.:* R.M.C., Sandhurst. 1st and 2nd Bn. Sherwood Foresters; served South African War, 1899, as Lieut., with Imperial Yeomanry; studied painting in Paris at the Atelier Julien, and with A. de la Gandara, 1901-4; served European War, 1914-18, as Brigade-Major to 49th Brigade, and at War Office; Brevet-Major, 1917; Member Royal Society Portrait Painters since 1917; Associé Société Nationale des Beaux Arts, Paris, 1925; Sociétaire, 1927; Major the Home Guard, 1940-43. *Club:* Army and Navy. [*Died* 12 *Jan.* 1959.

CREAN, Sir Bernard Arthur, Kt., *cr.* 1938; *b.* 4 July 1881; *s.* of Michael Crean, Belfast; unmarried. *Educ.:* St. Malachy's and Queen's University, Belfast (Law Scholar). Called to the Bar, Kings Inns, 1912; Deputy Recorder of Titles, British East Africa, 1920; Resident Magistrate, Nairobi, Kenya Colony, 1921; acted as Judge of H.M. Supreme Court of Kenya at different times, Oct. 1924-Dec. 1929; Puisne Judge, Cyprus, 1930-34; Chief Justice, British Guiana, 1934-38; Chief Justice of Cyprus, 1938-43. *Club:* Lansdowne. [*Died* 10 *Oct.* 1956.

CREED, Clarence James, C.S.I. 1947; C.I.E. 1946; O.B.E. 1943; M.C., and Bar, 1918; *b.* 19 July 1894; *s.* of Frederick James Creed; *m.* 1921, Irene Rosina Mathews, *d.* of late William Mathews, Bournemouth; no *c.* Served European War, 1914-18, with Army, 1916-19, originally with East Surrey Regt. and from 1917-19 with Royal Engineers (M.C. and Bar); attained rank of Captain. Appointed to Indian Police in 1919 and posted to Bihar; District Officer, 1924; Deputy Inspector General, 1936; assumed charge of the Provincial Police Administration, as Inspector General, 1944, retd. 1949. King's Police Medal, 1933; O.St.J. 1946. *Recreation:* principal interest is in art. *Address:* Walden, Marley Common, Haslemere, Surrey. [*Died* 6 *Sept.* 1955.

CRERAR, Sir James, K.C.S.I., *cr.* 1929 (C.S.I. 1921); C.I.E. 1917; M.A.; *b.* 1877; *s.* of late John Crerar, Maryport, Cumberland; *m.* 1916, Eve (*d.* 1954), 3rd *d.* of late Hon. Charles Brand; one *s.* one *d.* *Educ.:* George Watson's College and Univ., Edinburgh; Balliol College, Oxford. Entered I.C.S. 1900; Assist. Comsr. in Sind, 1907-11; Municipal Comsr., Bombay, 1913; Private Secretary to Governor of Bombay, 1914; Secretary to the Government of Bombay, Political and Judicial Departments, 1918; Home Secretary to the Government of Bombay, 1920-22; Home Secretary to the Government of India, 1922-27; officiating as Home member of the Viceroy's Executive Council, 1926; Home Member, 1927-1932; retired, 1934. *Address:* c/o National and Grindlay's Bank Ltd., 54 Parliament St., S.W.1. [*Died* 29 *Aug.* 1960.

CRESSWELL, Stuart Cornwallis, L.R.C.P., M.R.C.S.; retired. Late Senior Surgeon, Merthyr General Hospital. *Address:* Hillcrest, Lansdown Rd., Abergavenny, Mon., *T.:* Abergavenny 203. [*Died* 2 *Dec.* 1959.

CRESWELL, Harry Bulkeley, F.R.I.B.A. (ret.); Architect and Author; late Consultant to Crown Agents for the Colonies; *b.* 18 May 1869; *e. s.* of Henry Louis Creswell, Secretary to the Post Office in Scotland, and late Margaret Beauchamp, *d.* of Thomas Hart, Reigate; *m.* 1st, 1903, Ethel Frances Celia (*d.* 1931), *d.* of late Gen. Edward Pym, R.M.L.I.; one *d.*; 2nd, 1934, Gertrude Mary (*d.* 1953), *d.* of Edward Yeld, Hampstead. *Educ.:* Bedford Gram. Sch.; Trinity Coll., Dublin. Articled 1890, Sir Aston Webb, R.A.; Student and Exhibitor R.A.; Member Council Architectural Assoc.; 1900, private practice; domestic buildings Warwickshire, Kent, etc.; Churches, Rugby and Coventry; Commercial Bldgs. Rugby and Flint; Law Courts and Law Offices, Sierra Leone, College of Agriculture, Mauritius, etc.; in association with Egerton Swartwout and John Russell Pope of New York, American Memorial Chapel, Brookwood, and New Parthenon Room, British Museum. *Publications: novels:* Thomas, 1918; Thomas Settles Down, 1919; Diary from a Dustbin, 1935; Grig, 1942; Grig in Retirement, 1943; *technical fictions:* The Honeywood File, 1929; The Honeywood Settlement, 1930; Jago v. Swillerton and Toomer, 1931; *children's books:* Marytary, 1928; Johnny and Marytary, 1936; contributor to Black and White, Punch, etc., Architectural Review, Architect's Journal and other technical publications. Pseudonym—Karshish. *Recreations:* golf, fly fishing, music, chess. *Address:* 41 Woodbury Av., Petersfield, Hants. *T.:* Petersfield 617. [*Died* 4 *July* 1960.

CREWE, Maj. J. H. H. D.; *see* Dodds Crewe.

CRICHTON, Colonel Hon. Sir George (Arthur Charles), G.C.V.O., *cr.* 1933 (K.C.V.O., *cr.* 1924; C.V.O. 1920; M.V.O. 1913); late Comptroller of the Lord Chamberlain's Office; Extra Equerry to H. M. since 1935; 2nd *s.* of 4th Earl of Erne and *heir-pres.* to 6th Earl; *b.* 6 Sept. 1874; *m.* 1913, Lady Mary Dawson, *y. d.* of 2nd Earl of Dartrey; three *s.* two *d.* 2nd Lieut. Coldstream Guards, 1894; Capt., 1901; Major, 1910; served S. Africa, 1900-1 (slightly wounded, Queen's medal 4 clasps); European War (Bt. Lieut.-Col.). *Address:* Queen's Acre, Windsor. *Club:* Guards. [*Died* 5 *March* 1952.

CRICHTON, Brig. Henry Coventry Maitland-Makgill-, C.B. 1937; C.M.G. 1919; D.S.O. 1916; *b.* 29 June 1880; *s.* of late Andrew Coventry Maitland-Makgill-Crichton, 17A Great Cumberland Place, W., and Katherine Charlotte Hulse; *m.* 1911, Dorothy Margaret, *d.* of late Sir Walter Thorburn of Glenbreck; one *d.* *Educ.:* Charterhouse. Joined R.S.F. from R.M.C. Camberley, 1899; served South African War, 1900-01 (severely wounded); served at home with 2nd Batt. till early in 1906, when served with 1st Batt. in India till end of 1910; passed Staff College, 1912, 1913; served European War, 1914-18 (severely wounded during 2nd battle of Ypres, despatches eight times, Bt. Maj. and Lt.-Col., C.M.G., D.S.O., Legion of Honour); commanded 1st Batt. Royal Scots Fusiliers, 1928-31; A.A. and Q.M.G. in charge of Administration, Gibraltar, 1931-33; Commanded 14th Infantry Brigade, 1933-37; A.D.C. to the King, 1934-37; retired, 1937; re-employed, Area Commander, 1939-41; Commander, 1939-41. *Recreations:* all sports, particularly shooting with rifle and gun. *Clubs:* Army and Navy, M.C.C. [*Died* 29 *Sept.* 1953.

CRICHTON, Air Commodore Henry Lumsden, C.B. 1945; M.B.E. 1919; R.A.F., retd.; *b.* 8 Dec. 1890; *s.* of late Robert Crichton, M.Inst.C.E.; *m.* 1927, Doris Irene Baines; one *d.* *Educ.:* Friends College, Lancaster. Joined London Scottish Regiment, Aug. 1914; served in France; commissioned R.A.O.D. 1916; transferred to R.F.C. 1917; Temp. Captain, 1917; Squadron Leader R.A.F. 1923; Wing-Comdr. 1930; Group Capt. 1938; Air Commodore (acting), 1940; Air Commodore (temp.), 1941; Air Commodore, 1947. Served Iraq H.Q. Staff, 1921-22; commanded Stores Depôt, Aboukir, Egypt, 1923-25; Air Ministry Staff, 1926-31; S.E.S.O. Aden Command, 1931-33; S.E.S.O. Wessex Bombing Area, 1934-35; S.E.S.O. Bomber Command, 1937-39; Director of Equipment (A), Air Ministry, 1940-43; S.E.S.O., Flying Training Command, 1943-47; retired, 1947. *Recreations:* golf and tennis. *Address:* Chadstone, Rousdon, Devon. *T.:* Seaton 262. [*Died* 2 *Oct.* 1952.

CRICHTON, Capt. Hon. James Archibald, D.S.O. 1918; *b.* 1877; 4th *s.* of 4th Earl of Erne. *Educ.:* Eton, Royal Military College, Sandhurst. Capt. Rifle Brigade, 1902-1904; served S. Africa, 1901-2; European War, 1914-15; E. Africa, 1916-18 (D.S.O., Croix de Guerre). *Address:* Jannaways, Bagnor, Newbury, Berks. *T.:* Newbury 553. [*Died* 3 *Aug.* 1956.

CRICHTON-MILLER, Hugh, M.A., M.D. (Edin.); F.R.C.P. (Lond.); M.D. (Pavia); Founder Tavistock Clinic; retired, Medical Director, Bowden House, Harrow; Vice-Pres., Internat. Cttee. for Mental Hygiene; Vice-Pres. Nat. Assoc. for Mental Health; Trustee, King George V Hospital, Malta; Corr. member Swiss Society of Psychiatrists; Vice-Pres. C. G. Jung-Institute Zürich; *b.* Genoa, 1877; *s.* of Rev. Donald Miller, D.D., and Mary Wotherspoon; *m.* Eleanor Jane Campbell (*d.* 1954), *d.* of Sheriff Lorimer, K.C., Edinburgh; one *surv. s.* four *d.* *Educ.:* Fettes College, Edinburgh; Edinburgh University; Pavia Univ. President, Edin. University Union; House Surgeon and House Physician, Royal Infirmary, Edin.; in general practice, San Remo, Italy, and Aviemore, Inverness-shire, 1901-11; subsequently engaged in psychotherapeutic work; officer in charge functional cases, 21st General Hospital,

Egypt, and Consulting Neurologist, 4th London General Hospital, 1915-17; Vice-Pres. Section of Neurology and Psychological Medicine, B.M.A.; Chairman, Medical Section, British Psychological Society; President, Psychiatry Section, Royal Society of Medicine and International Society for Psychotherapy; Sir Charles Hastings Lecturer, 1938; M.O. i/c Stanboroughs Psychiatric Hospital (E.M.S.), 1939-41. *Publications:* Functional Nerve Disease (Editor), 1920; The New Psychology and the Teacher, 1922; Insomnia: An Outline for the Practitioner, 1930; Marriage, Freedom and Education, 1931; Psycho-analysis and its Derivatives, 1933; papers in medical and educational journals. *Address:* Bowden House, Harrow-on-the-Hill. *T.:* Byron 1011. [*Died* 1 *Jan.* 1959.

CRICHTON-STUART, Lord Colum (Edmund), J.P.; *b.* 3 April 1886; 3rd *s.* of 3rd Marquess of Bute; *m.* 1940, Elizabeth, Marchioness of Lansdowne, *widow* of 6th Marquess of Lansdowne, and *d.* of late Sir Edward Hope, K.C.B.; two step *d.* (and two step *s.* killed in action, 1944). *Educ.:* Oxford University; B.A. Diplomatic Service; Attaché, 1910; appointed to Cairo, 1911; 3rd Sec., 1913; transferred to Foreign Office, 1914; 2nd Sec., 1919; resigned from Diplomatic Service, 1920. M.P. (U.) Northwich div. of Cheshire, 1922-45. Lord Lieut. of Buteshire, 1953. *Address:* Ardencraig, Rothesay, Isle of Bute. *T.:* Rothesay 430; 23 Charles St., W.1. *T.:* Grosvenor 3081. *Clubs:* Travellers', Turf. [*Died* 18 *Aug.* 1957.

CRIDLAND, Frank, C.B.E. 1920; governing director of Frank Cridland Pty. Ltd., a general transport business; *b.* Meroo, N.S.W., 13 March 1873. Was Assistant Commissioner, Hon. Captain, A.I.F., Australian Comforts Fund in England and France, 1917-18. *Publication:* The Story of Port Hacking, Cronulla and Sutherland Shire, 1924. *Address:* Sunnyside House, Caringbah, N.S.W. *Club:* Imperial Service (Sydney). [*Died* 28 *May* 1954.

CRIPPS, Sir Edward Stewart, Kt., *cr.* 1946; *b.* 22 Oct. 1885; 2nd *s.* of late Francis Henry Cripps, J.P.; *m.* 1921, Helena (*d.* 1949), *d.* of late J. T. Nash; no *c.* *Educ.:* Charterhouse; Oriel Coll., Oxford. Senior Government Broker, 1937-50 (retired). Chairman 1930 Pension Fund for District Nurses; Chairman, Board of Governors, The Royal Cancer Hospital; Governor Imperial Cancer Research Fund; Governor Sutton's Hospital in Charterhouse; Director: Thomas Tilling, Ltd.; Cornhill Insurance Co. *Recreations:* racing, golf. *Address:* 74 Fountain House, Park Lane, W.1. *T.:* Mayfair 1733. *Clubs:* White's, Buck's. [*Died* 18 *May* 1955.

CRIPPS, Major Sir Frederick William Beresford, Kt., *cr.* 1933; D.S.O. 1919; J.P., D.L.; *b.* 1873; *s.* of late E. Wm. Cripps of Ampney Park; *m.* Constance Agnes (*d.* 1958), M.B.E., 1945, *d.* of P. J. D. Wykeham of Tythrop, Thame; two *s.* one *d.* (and one *s.* decd.). *Educ.:* Wellington Coll.; R.M.C., Sandhurst. Served in K.R.R.C., Chitral Campaign (medal and clasp); Royal Glos. Hussars, in European War in France (despatches, D.S.O.). *Address:* Ampney Park, Cirencester. *Club:* Naval and Military. [*Died* 6 *May* 1959.

CRIPPS, Major Hon. Leonard Harrison, C.B.E. 1918; 3rd *s.* of 1st Baron Parmoor, P.C., K.C.V.O., K.C.; *m.* Miriam Barbara, *d.* of late Rt. Hon. Sir Matthew I. Joyce; two *s.* *Educ.:* Radley; Sandhurst. Joined 4th Hussars, 1906; served European War (wounded); retired. *Address:* 8 De Walden Court, 85 New Cavendish Street, W.1. [*Died* 1 *Feb.* 1959.

CRIPPS, Rt. Hon. Sir (Richard) Stafford, P.C. 1941; C.H. 1951; Kt., *cr.* 1930; F.R.S. 1948; Q.C. 1927; J.P.; Chancellor of the Exchequer, 1947-50; M.P. (Lab.) East Bristol, 1931-50, Sth.-East Bristol, Feb.-Oct. 1950; *b.* 24 April 1889; *y. s.* of 1st Baron Parmoor, P.C., K.C.V.O., K.C.; *m.* 1911, Isobel (later Dame Isobel Cripps, G.B.E. 1946), 2nd *d.* of late Comdr. Harold Swithinbank; one *s.* three *d.* *Educ.:* Winchester; University Coll., London. Barrister-at-law, Middle Temple, 1913; Bencher, 1930; Red Cross in France, 1914; Assistant Supt., H.M. Factory, Queen's Ferry, 1915; Solicitor-Gen., 1930-31; British Ambassador to Russia, 1940-42; Lord Privy Seal and Leader of House of Commons, 1942; Minister of Aircraft Production, 1942-45; President Board of Trade, 1945; Minister for Economic Affairs, 1947; Fellow, Univ. Coll., London, 1930; Rector of Aberdeen University, 1942-1945. President of the Fabian Society, 1951. *Publications:* Why this Socialism?; Democracy Up-to-date; Towards Christian Democracy; Democracy Alive; God in our Work. *Address:* Frith Hill, nr. Stroud, Glos. *T.* and *T.A.:* Frampton Mansell 66. [*Died* 21 *April* 1952.

CRISPIN, Edward Smyth, C.B.E. 1920; *b.* London, 18 Dec. 1874; 3rd *s.* of late Alfred Trevor Crispin; *m.* 2nd, 1924, Evelyn Violet Cadogan; 3rd, 1938, Joy Gilmore (*d.* 1953). *Educ.:* Bradfield College; King's College Hospital. M.R.C.S. (Eng.), L.R.C.P. (Lond.), 1898; House Surgeon, Royal Free Hospital, 1898-1899; House Surgeon, King's College Hospital, 1899; Civil Surgeon, South African Field Force, 1899-1900 (Queen's medal and 3 clasps); Civil Surgeon and Hon. Bimbashi, Egyptian Army, 1901-4; Sud Cutting Expedition, White Nile, 1901-2; Punitive Expedition, 1902 (medal and clasp); Cholera Epidemic, Egypt, 1902; Medical Inspector Sudan Government, 1904-6; M.O.H. Quarantine Officer Red Sea Province during construction of Port Sudan, 4th Class Order, Osmanieh; Assistant Director Medical Dept. Sudan Government, 1909; Directo Medical Department, 1915-1922; retired; Member Governor-General's Council, 1919; President Central Sanitary Board, 1915; served Hospital Ship, Gallipoli, 1915 (1914-15 star); Lines of Communication Darfur Expedition (medal and clasp); 3rd Class Order of Nile, 1916; Member Commission of Inquiry into Public Health, Egypt, 1917. *Publication:* Prevention and Treatment of Disease in the Tropics. *Recreations:* shooting, tennis, golf. *Address:* Hyde End, Rottingdean, Sussex. *T.:* 3111 Rottingdean. [*Died* 12 *March* 1958.

CROCE, Benedetto; doct. phil. hon. de l'université de Fribourg en Baden, et de Marburg; et honoris causa de l'Université de Oxford; Membre de l'Académie Prussienne, de l'Académie Américaine de lettres et de British Academy; Minister without portfolio, Italy, 1944; *b.* Pescasseroli (province d'Aquila), 25 fév. 1866; *m.* 1914, Adèle Rossi, de Turin, docteur ès lettres; four *d.* *Educ.:* Naples; université de Rome. Dans sa jeunesse il s'est occupé d'études littéraires et historiques. Depuis (surtout après la trentième année) aussi et principalement d'études philosophiques; dans les dernières années beaucoup d'histoire. Sénateur du Royaume d'Italie, 1910; Ministre de l'instruction publique, 1920-21; *Publications:* Filosofia dello spirito: 1. Estetica, 1902 (trad. anglaise). 2. Logica, 1905 (trad. anglaise). 3. Filosofia della pratica, 1908 (trad. angl.). 4. Teoria della storiografia, 1916 (trad. angl.); Essais: Materialismo storico ed economia marxistica, 1900 (trad. angl.); Saggio sullo Hegel, 1906 (trad. angl.); La Filosofia di Giambattista Vico, 1911 (trad. angl.); Problemi di estetica, 1910 (trad. angl.); Nuovi Saggi di estetica, 1920; Frammenti di Etica, 1921 (trad. angl.); Etica e politica, 1931; Ultimi Saggi, 1935; La Poesia, introduzione alla critica e alla storia della poesia e letteratura (1936) (trad. angl.); La Storia come pensiero e come azione, 1938; Il carattere della filosofia moderna, 1941; Discorsi di varia filosofia, 1945; Filosofia e Storiografia, 1949; Storiografia e idealità morale, 1950; Travaux historiques et littéraires: I teatri di Napoli, 1891, 3e éd., 1927; La Rivoluzione napoletana del 1799, 4e éd., 1926; Saggi sulla letteratura italiana del Seicento, 2e éd., 1924; La Spagna nella vita italiana del Rinascimento, 3e éd., 1940; La Letteratura della Nuova Italia, septante essais critiques en six volumes, 1914-40; nouv. éd., 1942-44; Conversazioni critiche, 1e et 2e série, 1918; 3e et 4e série, 1933; 5e, 1939; Goethe, 1919 (trad. angl.) nouv. édition redoubleé, 1939; Una famiglia di patrioti, 1919; Storie e leggende napoletane, 1919; Ariosto Shakespeare, e Corneille, 1920 (trad. angl.); La Poesia di Dante, 1920 (trad. angl.); Storia della storiografia italiana nel secolo XIX, 1921; Poesia e non poesia, note sulla letteratura europea nel secolo XIX, 1923 (trad. angl.); Storia del Regno di Napoli, 1924; Uomini e cose della vecchia Italia, 1926; Storia d'Italia dal 1871 al 1915 (trad. angl., 1929); Storia dell' età barocca in Italia, 1929; Nuovi saggi sulla letteratura del Seicento, 1931; Storia d' Europa nel secolo XIX, 1932 (trad. angl.); Poesia popolare e poesia d'arte, 1933; Poesia antica e moderna: Interpretazioni, 1942; Poeti e scrittori del pieno e del tardo Rinascimento (2 vols.), 1947; La Letteratura italiana del Settecento, 1949; Letture di Poeti, 1950; Aneddoti di varia letteratura, (3 vols.), 1942; La Critica e la Storia delle arti figurative, Questioni di metodo, 1934; Varietà di storia civile e letteraria, 1935, 1949, (2 vols.); Vite di avventure, di fede e di passione, sei biografie, 1935; Il Pentamerone di G. B. Basile, tradotto e illustrato, 1925; Pagine sulla guerra, 1919; Per la nuova vita d'Italia, discorsi e Scritti, 1944; Pagine politiche, 1945; Pagine sparse, trois vol, 1943; Nuovi pagine sparse, deux vol. 1949; dirige depuis 1903 la revue: La Critica rivista di letteratura storia e filosofia; Quaderni della Critica, 1945-; sur lui: Contributo alla critica di me stesso (Autobiographie, 1918, nouvelle éd., avec appendice, 1945; Traduction anglaise, 1927). *Address:* Trinità Maggiore, 12, Napoli, Italy. [*Died* 20 *Nov.* 1952.

CROCKATT, Brig. Norman Richard, C.B.E. 1945; D.S.O. 1919; M.C.; *b.* 12 April 1894; *s.* of late J. R. Crockatt; *m.* 1920, Sidney Alice Rose Tweedy; two *s.* *Educ.:* Rugby; Royal Military College, Sandhurst. Gazetted to Royal Scots, 1913; served European War, 1914-18, in France and Palestine (despatches thrice, D.S.O., M.C., Order of the Nile); retired, 1927; re-joined Army, Sept. 1939 (C.B.E., U.S. Legion of Merit (Officer), French Légion d'honneur (Chevalier) and Croix de Guerre (with palm)). Colonel, The Royal Scots (The Royal Regiment), July 1946-Dec. 1955. Stockbroker, London; Director, Attock Oil Co. Member Queen's Body Guard for Scotland (Royal Company of Archers). *Address:* Ulverscroft, Virginia Water. *T.:* Egham 575. *Clubs:* Army and Navy; New (Edinburgh). [*Died* 9 *Oct.* 1956.

CROCKER, Brig.-Gen. Sydney Francis, C.B. 1916; *b.* 5 Aug. 1864; *s.* of late Surgeon-General Crocker, A.M.S.; *m.* 1st; one *d.*; 2nd, 1923, Flora Mary, *widow* of Henry Webley and *d.* of late Colonel Charles Edward Macdonald, R.M.L.I. *Educ.:* Private School, R.M.C., Sandhurst. Joined Army, 1883; gazetted to the 9th Bengal Lancers (Hodson's Horse), 1888; appointed to command of 14th Murray's Jat Lancers, 1910, and Risalpur Cavalry Brigade, 1914; served Burma, 1886-87 (medal with clasp); Chitral, 1895, Relief of Chitral (medal with clasp); Tirah, 1897-98 (two clasps); commanded the force at Rustam, N.W.F.P., Aug. 1915, against the Bonerwals (thanks of Government of India); commanded the mounted column at Shabkadr, Sept. 1915, against Mohmands; commanded Cavalry Division, Mesopotamia, in advance to Baghdad; retired, 1920. *Club:* United Service. [*Died* 2 *Aug.* 1952.

CROCKER, Rear-Admiral (S) William Ernest, C.B. 1927; retired list, 1929. *Address:* 30 South Parade, Southsea. [*Died* 9 *Feb.* 1951.

CROFT, Sir Hugh Matthew Fiennes, 12th Bart., *cr.* 1671: owner of sheep and farming property; *b.* 10 May 1874; 3rd *s.* of 9th Baronet; *S.* nephew, 1941; *m.* 1900, Lucy Isabel, *e. d.* of Frederick G. Taylor, Terrible Vale, New South Wales; five *s.* one *d.* *Educ.:* Hereford Cathedral School. Managed sheep stations in New South Wales and now has own property; Chairman Armidale Pasture Protection Board over 28 years; Member and President Dumaresq Shire Council for 10 years; President Uralla Agricultural Society over 30 years; Member of Diocesan Council and Chairman of Committees of Armidale Diocesan Synod. *Recreations:* cricket, golf, fishing. *Heir:* *s.* Bernard Hugh Denman [*b.* 24 Aug. 1903; *m.* 1931, Helen Margaret, *d.* of H. Weaver; three *s.* one *d.*]. *Address:* Salisbury Court, Uralla, N.S.W. *T.A.:* Uralla, N.S.W. *T.:* Uralla 24. [*Died* 15 *June* 1954.

CROFT, Major Owen George Scudamore; *b.* 14 May 1880; *s.* of late Sir Herbert Croft of Croft Castle, Co. Hereford, 9th Bt., M.P., and late Georgiana, *e. d.* and *co-heir* of Matthew Marsh, M.P., Ramridge House, Hants; *m.* 1909, Stella Isabel, *e. d.* of late Nicholas Bouwer, Buenos Aires, and late Mrs. A. C. Brown, Ludford Park, Ludlow, Salop. Commissioned Shropshire Yeomanry, 1905; retired with hon. rank of Major, 1921; served European War, 1914-18; J.P. County Hereford, 1909; High Sheriff of Herefordshire, 1943; Life Vice-Pres. Herefordshire General Hospital (President, 1943); Lord of Croft and Lord of the Manor of Bircher. *Recreations:* shooting, fishing, racing, genealogy; genealogy of the thoroughbred horse; farming. *Publication:* The House of Croft of Croft Castle. *Address:* Croft Castle, Leominster, Herefordshire. *T.:* Yarpole 246. *Club:* Junior Carlton. [*Died* 29 *Feb.* 1956.

CROFTON, Sir Morgan George, 6th Bart., *cr.* 1801; D.S.O. 1918; Lt.-Col. 2nd Life Guards; retired; *s.* of late Capt. Edward Hugh Crofton, Rifle Brigade (*b.* of 4th Bart.), and Isabel Julia, *d.* of Col. Miller, 13th Hussars; *b.* 27 Nov. 1879; *S.* brother, 1902; *m.* 1st, 1905, Margaret (whom he *div.*, 1910), *d.* of late Col. Howard Irby; (one *s.* died while serving with H.Q. Eastern Command, India, 1947); 2nd, 1919, Adèle Violet (*d.* 1931), *e. d.* of late Sir George Donaldson; 3rd, 1933, Margaret, 2nd *d.* of late Judge Morris Dallett, Philadelphia; two *s.* *Educ.:* Rugby. Gazetted to 2nd Lieut. 2nd Battalion Lancs. Fusiliers, 1899; served South Africa, 1899-1901 (severely wounded in the relief of Ladysmith); transferred to Irish Guards, 1901; transf. to 2nd Life Guards, 1903; served European War (D.S.O., Legion of Honour, Order of Leopold, despatches twice); Colonel-Commandant on Staff of Military Adviser to Northern Government of Ireland, 1922; High Sheriff for Hampshire, 1925-26; in War of 1939-1945, raised and commanded 28th Bn. Home Guard, Hampshire Regt., 1940-44. Gold Staff Officer at the Coronation of King George VI. J.P. Hants; and Mem. of Hants County Council. Owns about 11,500 acres. *Heir:* *g.s.* Patrick Simon Hugh [*b.* 2 Dec. 1936; *s.* of late Major Morgan George Crofton]. *Address:* Woodbridge, Brockenhurst, Hants. *Clubs:* Garrick, Cavalry, M.C.C. [*Died* 9 *Dec.* 1958.

CROFTON, Sir Richard Marsh, Kt., *cr.* 1945; C.I.E. 1941; late Indian Civil Service; *b.* 6 April 1891; 4th *s.* of late Capt. D. Crofton, R.N., D.L., Lakefield, Mohill, Co. Leitrim, Ireland; *m.* 1921, Olive Amy Stewart Cox (Kaiser-i-Hind Silver Medal, 1940); one *d.* *Educ.:* Kelly College, Tavistock; Trinity College, Dublin (Senior Moderator). B.A. 1913; entered Indian Civil Service, 1914; arrived in India, 1915; on military duty attached 36th Jacob's Horse,

1917-19; Deputy Commissioner, 1926; served at different times as Finance Secretary and Revenue Secretary to Govt., as Settlement officer and nominated member of Indian Legislative Assembly; Excise and Opium Commissioner in Central India, 1931-34; Director-General of Revenue, Hyderabad, 1935-42; Offg. Revenue and Home Member, 1936-37; confirmed as Commissioner in Central Provinces, 1941, while continuing on Foreign Service; Prime Minister Bahawalpur State, Punjab, 1942-47, retired, 1947. *Address:* Compton Meadows, Minstead, Hants. *Club:* East India and Sports.

[*Died* 27 *May* 1955.

CROFTS, Freeman Wills, F.R.S.A., 1938; novelist; *b.* Dublin, June 1879; *s.* of Freeman Wills Crofts, Army Medical; *m.* 1912, Mary Bellas, *d.* of late J. J. C. Canning, Coleraine, Co. Londonderry; no *c.* *Educ.:* Methodist and Campbell College, Belfast. Pupil in Civil Engineering to late Berkeley D. Wise, M.I.C.E., Chief Engineer, Belfast and Northern Counties Rly.; junior assistant engineer on construction of Londonderry and Strabane Railway, 1899; district engineer, Coleraine, B. and N.C. Rly., 1900; chief assistant engineer at Belfast, 1923, on same railway, now L.M.S. Northern Counties Committee; began to write detective novels, 1919; resigned from railway to devote whole time to writing, 1929; employed by Government of Northern Ireland to hold an enquiry relative to compensation claims in connection with the River Bann Drainage Scheme, 1930. *Publications:* Detective novels—The Cask, The Ponson Case, The Pit Prop Syndicate, The Groote Park Murder, Inspector French's Greatest Case, Inspector French and the Cheyne Mystery, The Starvel Tragedy, The Sea Mystery, The Box Office Murders, Sir John Magill's Last Journey, Mystery in the Channel, Sudden Death, Death on the Way, The Hog's Back Mystery; The 10.30 from Croydon, 1934; Mystery on Southampton Water, 1934; Crime at Guildford, 1935; The Loss of the Jane Vosper, 1936; Man Overboard!, 1936; Found Floating, 1937; The End of Andrew Harrison, 1938; Antidote to Venom, 1938; Fatal Venture, 1939; Golden Ashes, 1940; James Tarrant, Adventurer, 1941; The Losing Game, 1941; Fear Comes to Chalfont, 1942; The Affair at Little Wokeham, 1943; Enemy Unseen, 1945; Death of a Train, 1946; Young Robin Brand Detective (Boy's Book), 1947; Murderers Make Mistakes (short stories), 1948; Silence for the Murderer, 1948; The Four Gospels in One Story (religious book), 1949; French Strikes Oil, 1952; Many a Slip (short stories), 1955; The Mystery of the Sleeping Car Express, 1956; short stories to various magazines and newspapers and short plays to B.B.C. *Recreations:* music (organist and conductor), travelling, gardening, carpentering. *Address:* Grenfell, 131 Brighton Road, Worthing, Sussex. *T.:* Worthing 7586.

[*Died* 11 *April* 1957.

CROKER, Engineer Rear-Adm. (Retd.) Edward James O'Brien, C.B.E. 1937; *b.* 3 July 1881; *e. s.* of E. J. O'Brien Croker, Portarlington, Queen's County, Ireland; *m.* 1908, Dorothy (*d.* 1955), *y. d.* of Col. C. P. Newport, Bury Hall, Alverstoke, Hants; one *s.* one *d.* *Educ.:* Privately; Royal Naval Engineering Coll., Devonport. Eng. Sub. Lieut. 1903; Eng. Commander, 1920; Eng. Capt. 1929; Eng. Rear-Admiral, 1935; served H.M.S. Botha, Grand Fleet and Dover Patrol, 1915-18; Superintendent, R.N. Torpedo Factory, Greenock, and R.N. Torpedo Works, Alexandria, Dumbarton, 1932-37; A.D.C. to King George V, 1935-36; retired list, 1937; mobilised for Special Service (North America), 1940-44. *Address:* Moor Court Hotel, Nr. Stroud, Glos.

[*Died* 4 *Jan.* 1960.

CROKER, Capt. Thomas Joseph, C.B. 1928; R.N., retired; *b.* 1876; *m.* 1918, Gertrude Viti, *d.* of late Vice-Adm. Usborne Moore; one *s.* one *d.* Superintendent Torpedo Experiments, 1919-36. *Address:* Avon Lodge, Hillborough Crescent, Southsea.

[*Died* 16 *March* 1956.

CROMBIE, Alan Douglas, C.I.E. 1935; I.C.S. (retired); *b.* 20 Jan. 1894; *s.* of late Major William Crombie, V.D., Southbourne, Bournemouth; *m.* 1937, Iris Mary Sybil, *d.* of late John Frederick Guillaume, solicitor, and of Mrs. Guillaume, 8 Irving Road, Bournemouth; two *s.* *Educ.:* Wolverhampton Grammar School. Served European War, 1914-19; Lieut. R.G.A.; entered Indian Civil Service, 1920; Sub-Collector and Joint Magistrate, 1922; Under-Sec., Revenue Dept., 1925; Agent to Raja of Parlakimedi, 1927; Deputy Sec., Local Self-Govt. Dept., 1929; Private Sec. to Governor of Madras, 1931; Collector and District Magistrate, 1936; Member, Bd. of Revenue, Madras, 1946. *Recreations:* golf, fishing. *Address:* Avon Lodge, Stanpit, Christchurch, Hants. *Club:* East India and Sports.

[*Died* 16 *Nov.* 1958.

CROMBIE, Colonel David Campbell, C.B.E. 1924; retired; *b.* 19 Nov. 1877; *s.* of late David Alexander John Crombie and Mary Forrester Crombie; *m.* 1914, Thérèse Henriette Pankhurst (*d.* 1939); two *s.* two *d.* *Educ.:* Cargilfield, Edinburgh; Clifton College. Indian Army, 1898-1925. Home Guard Bn. Commander, 1940-45. *Publication:* History of the 5th (Bideford) Bn., Devon Home Guard. *Recreation:* tennis. *Address:* c/o Lloyds Bank Ltd., 6 Pall Mall, S.W.1. [*Died* 1 *April* 1952.

CROMER, 2nd Earl of, *cr.* 1901; **Rowland Thomas Baring,** Viscount, *cr.* 1898; Baron, *cr.* 1892; P.C. 1922; G.C.B., *cr.* 1932; G.C.I.E., *cr.* 1922 (K.C.I.E., *cr.* 1921); G.C.V.O., *cr.* 1927 (C.V.O. 1920; M.V.O. 1908); Royal Victorian Chain, 1935; Permanent Lord-in-Waiting to the Queen since 1952 (to King George VI, 1938-52); Extra Equerry in Ordinary to the Queen since 1952 (formerly to King George V and King George VI); Director of National Provincial Bank, Ltd., Lloyds and National Provincial Foreign Bank, Ltd., London and Lancashire Insurance Co., Marine Insurance Co., P. and O. and British Indian Cos.; Vice-Pres., Gordon Memorial Coll., Khartoum; Chm., King George's Pension Fund for Actors and Actresses; a Governor Peabody Trust Fund; late Lieut. Grenadier Guards; *b.* 29 Nov. 1877; *e. s.* of 1st Earl of Cromer and Ethel Stanley (*d.* 1898), *d.* of Sir Rowland Stanley Errington, Bt.; *S.* father, 1917; *m.* 1908, Lady Ruby Elliot, Dame Grand Cross of St. John of Jerusalem (author of Lamuriac, 1927; Unfettered Ways, 1935; Such Were These Years, 1939), 2nd *d.* of 4th Earl of Minto; one *s.* two *d.* *Educ.:* Eton. Entered Diplomatic Service, 1900; served Cairo, Tehran, and Petrograd; 2nd Sec., 1906; transferred to Foreign Office, 1907; Private Secy. to Permanent Under-Secretary of State for Foreign Affairs, 1st to Lord Hardinge of Penshurst, K.G., 2nd to Lord Carnock, G.C.B.; resigned Foreign Office appointment, 1911; Managing Director Baring Bros. & Co. Ltd. 1913-14; 2nd Lieut. Grenadier Guards, 1914 (Special Reserve); A.D.C. to Viceroy of India, 1915-16; Equerry in Ordinary and Assistant Private Sec. to H.M., 1916-20; Chief of the Staff to Duke of Connaught, Indian Mission, 1920-21, and to Prince of Wales' visit to India and Crown Colonies, 1921-22; Lord Chamberlain of H.M.'s Household, 1922-38. British Government Director of Suez Canal Co., 1926-50; Chm., British Red Cross and St. John War Organisation, 1939-40. Chm., E.N.S.A. International Advisory Council during War; Private in 1st Somerset Home Guard, 1940-1942; Medals: G.S. War, Silver Jubilee, 1936, Coronation, 1937; Bailiff Grand Cross, Order of St. John, 1946; Grand Officer of Legion of Honour, and other foreign decorations, etc. *Recreations:* golf, etc. *Heir:* Viscount Errington. *Address:* 24A St. Petersburgh Place, W.2. *T.:* Bayswater 6866. *Clubs:* Brooks's, Beefsteak, M.C.C. (President, 1934-1935). [*Died* 13 *May* 1953.

CROMPTON, Robert, C.B.E. 1918; Q.C., (Fiji); late member of Executive Council, Fiji; *b.* Raotova, Russia, 1869; *s.* of Robert Crompton, Bolton, Lancashire; *m.* 1st, Rosaline (*d.* 1927), *d.* of Charles Allen, Warrington, Lancashire; two *s.* two *d.*; 2nd, 1929, Thelma Kathleen (*d.* 1933), *d.* of Mr. Sutherland, Suva; 3rd, 1934, Vera Alice, M.B.E. 1944, *d.* of Mr. Crawford, Christchurch, N.Z. *Educ.:* Blue Coat Sch., Warrington; privately. Solicitor of Supreme Court, Eng.; settled in Fiji, 1904; K.C., Fiji, 1924. Life Mem. Roy. Commonwealth Soc.; honour conferred for services in raising contingents for the war and funds to support them. *Address:* Tamavua House, Suva, Fiji. *T.A.:* Crompton, Suva. [*Died* 19 *Dec.* 1958.

CROOKE, Admiral Sir (Henry) Ralph, K.B.E., *cr.* 1940; C.B. 1919; retired; *b.* 7 Dec. 1875; *e. s.* of Frederick James Crooke and Louisa Maud Rich; *m.* 1916, Lilian Ethel, *widow* of late Col. E. P. Smith, R.H.A., and *d.* of late Col. C. E. Harman; no *c.* *Educ.:* Fosters, Stubbington House, Hants; H.M.S. Britannia. Served as Midshipman in H.M.S. Camperdown, Raleigh, and Active; Actg. Sub.-Lieut. 1894; Lieut. 1895 (five firsts in examinations); served in H.M.S. Calypso, 1896-97; specialised in Gunnery, 1897-99; Junior Staff-Officer H.M.S. Excellent, 1899-1900; Gunnery Lieut. H.M.S. Repulse, 1900-1903; Experimental Officer, H.M.S. Excellent, 1903-5; Assistant to D.N.O. Admiralty, 1905-7; Commander, 1905; Commander of H.M.S. Good Hope, 1907-9; and of H.M.S. Black Prince, 1910-12; Capt., 1912; Boom Defence Committee and Director Committee during last three months 1912; Assist. Director of Naval Equipment Admiralty, Feb. 1913-Aug. 1914: commissioned H.M.S. Undaunted, Aug. 1914, and then fitted out H.M.S. Caroline, served in her in 1st and 4th Light Cruiser Squadrons until April 1917, and was present at Battle of Jutland (despatches, Order of St. Anne of 2nd class, crossed swords); Captain of H.M.S. Excellent (Gunnery School), April 1917-June 1918; Director of Naval Ordnance, Admiralty, 1918-20; Captain H.M.S. Benbow, March 1921; H.M.S. Emperor of India, April 1921; H.M.S. Ajax, Oct. 1921; H.M.S. Marlborough, March-Sept. 1922; A.D.C. to the King, 1922; Rear-Adm., 1922; Vice-Pres. of the Ordnance Committee Royal Arsenal, Woolwich, 1924-27; Pres. 1927-28; Vice-Adm. 1928; retd. 1928; Adm., retd. 1932; served as Commodore, R.N.R., Sept. 1939-Jan. 1942; and as Capt. R.N., June 1942 until end of 1944 as N.O. i/c Barry. *Recreations:* yachting and boat sailing. *Address:* c/o Lloyds Bank Ltd., Cox's and King's Branch (G.1), 6 Pall Mall, S.W.1. *Clubs:* Army and Navy; Royal Yacht Squadron, Cowes (Naval Hon. Member); R.N. Sailing Association (Portsmouth). [*Died* 11 *Feb.* 1952.

CROOKE, Sir (John) Smedley, Kt., *cr.* 1938; J.P. City of Birmingham; *b.* Smedley's Hydro, Matlock, Derbyshire; *m.* Pattie, *d.* of late Rev. William Edwards of Kilsby, Northamptonshire; two *s.* one *d.* *Educ.:* Shoal Hill College, Cannock, Staffs. M.P. (U.) Deritend Division, Birmingham, 1922-29 and 1931-45. Served as School-manager Alvechurch, 25 years; Member of Worcestershire County Council, 18 years; Member Bromsgrove Board of Guardians and Bromsgrove Rural District Council, 17 years; Fellow Guild of Church Musicians; Fellow Victoria College of Music; served in Warwickshire Volunteers, Worcester Yeomanry; served European War, 1914-18, as Mil. Representative, Feckenham (Worcs.) District; Substitution Officer, Worcester; Tribunal Dept., Stourbridge; Munitions Area Substitution Officer, Birmingham; Hon. Treasurer Birmingham County Council of the British Legion since 1921, now President; Hon. Treasurer, West Midland Area, British Legion, 18 years, now a National Vice-Pres.; Hon. Treasurer British Legion Unity Relief Fund, 1920-21; was Hon. Sec. of House of Commons Branch of British Legion; was Hon. Secretary of Midland Group of Conservative Members of House of Commons. *Recreations:* music and golf. *Address:* Hopwood, Alvechurch, Worcs.; Plas Meirion, Aberdovey, Merioneth. [*Died* 13 *Oct.* 1951.

CROOKE, Adm. Sir Ralph; *see* Crooke, Adm. Sir H. R.

CROOKE, Sir Smedley; *see* Crooke, Sir J. S.

CROOKS, Captain Robert Crawford, C.B.E. 1941; Royal Navy; *b.* 15 June 1894; *e. s.* of James Kirke Crooks, Chester; *m.* 1915, Honor, *yr. d.* of Rev. Henry Stephens, Colchester, Essex; two *d.* *Educ.:* Daltrys, Hoylake; Osborne and Dartmouth. Served European War, 1914-18, mainly in Destroyers (despatches). C.B.E. for evacuating troops from Greece, 1941; Naval Member of Red Sea Commission, 1941; Naval Member of Intendant General's Mission, 1941; Naval Control Service Officer, Clyde, 1942-44; Senior Naval Disarmament Officer, N.W. Germany, 1945. *Recreation:* sailing. *Address:* 36 Brighton Road, Purley, Surrey. *T.:* Uplands 0491. *Club:* English Speaking Union. [*Died* 27 *Jan.* 1951.

CROOKSHANK, Col. Chichester de Windt, D.L., J.P. E. Lothian; F.S.A.; H.M. Bodyguard of the Honourable Corps of Gentlemen at Arms, 1920-44; Member of Queen's Body Guard for Scotland (Royal Company of Archers); 1929; Knight of Grace of St. John of Jerusalem; Vice-Pres. Royal Archæological Inst.; *e. s.* of Colonel A. C. W. Crookshank, C.B. (*d.* 1888), and Mary (*d.* 1931), *d.* of late Rev. J. B. D'Aguilar; *m.* 1910, Mary, Officer (Sister) St. John of Jerusalem, *y. d.* of Andrew Usher, D.L. of Johnstounburn; three *s.* one *d.* *Educ.:* Brackenbury's School, Wimbledon; R.M. Academy, Woolwich. Entered R.E., 1887; Lt.-Col. Reserve of Officers, 1916; Brevet Colonel (retired), 1924; served Miranzai Expedition, 1891; South Africa, 1900-2 (wounded, despatches); Natal Native Rebellion, 1906; European War, 1914-19; C.R.E., 54th (East Anglian) Division Territorial Army, 1920-24; Liaison Officer R.E. Home Guard, H.Q. Edinburgh Area till 1942; M.P. (U.) Berwick and Haddington, 1924-29; M.P. (U.) Bootle, 1931-1953; Haddington District Council, 1940-48; Pres. East Lothian Antiquarian Soc. until 1950. Chesney Gold Medal (R.U.S.I.), 1932. *Publication:* Prints of British Military Operations, 1066-1868. *Address:* Johnstounburn, Humbie, East Lothian. *T.:* Humbie 2. *Club:* New (Edinburgh). [*Died* 23 *Oct.* 1958.

CROOM-JOHNSON, Hon. Sir Reginald Powell, Kt., *cr.* 1938; LL.B. (Lond.); Judge High Court of Justice, King's Bench Division, 1938-54; J.P. Somerset and Deputy Chairman Quarter Sessions; *e. s.* of Oliver Croom-Johnson, Clifton; *m.* 1909, Ruby Ernestine Hobbs, M.A. Cantab.; two *s.* (and one *s.* killed on active service, 1940). *Educ.:* Bristol Cathedral School; London University. Solicitor, 1901; called to Bar, Inner Temple, 1907; Bencher, 1935; K.C. 1927; Recorder of Bath, 1928-38; M.P. (U.) Bridgwater Division of Somerset, 1929-38; during war, 1914-18, assisted in raising Old Boys' Corps; K.O.Y.L.I., Lieut.; subsequently attached Judge Advocate-General's Dept. for special services in connection with Mesopotamia Commission (despatches); Chm. of original committee for foundation of Stowe School; travelled widely in Europe, Canada, and U.S.A. Member of Council Men of the Trees. *Publications:* prolific contributor to Press of essays on general topics to 1914; Postage Stamp Collecting, 1921; Stamps of Solomon Islands, 1928; Income Tax Law, 1932 (part author), and other legal works. The Origin of Stowe School, 1953. *Address:* Hillbrook House, Dipford-by-Trull, near Taunton, Somerset. *T.:* Taunton 2506. *Clubs:* Carlton, Garrick. [*Died* 29 *Dec.* 1957.

CROOME, Honor Renée Minturn; member of editorial staff, The Economist, since 1947; *b.* 6 July 1908; *e. d.* of Arthur Hugh Scott and Mildred Minturn; *m.* 1931, John Lewis Croome, C.M.G.; four *s.* one *d.* (and one *s.* decd.). *Educ.:* abroad; later at Hayes Court School, Bryn Mawr College, U.S.A. and London School of Economics. Hons. degree, Economics, 1930. Research secretary, New Fabian Research Bureau, 1931-32. Assist. London School of Economics, 1936-40, and 1947-48; Hon. Fell. London School of Economics, 1959. *Publications:* The Approach to Economics, 1932; (with R. J. Hammond) An Economic History of Britain, 1936; O Western Wind, 1943; You've Gone Astray, 1944; The Faithless Mirror, 1946; The Candidate's Companion, 1947; (with W. G. King) The Livelihood of Man, 1953; The Mountain and the Molehill, 1955; Introduction to Money, 1956; The Forgotten Place, 1957; articles, reviews and short stories in various periodicals and newspapers. *Recreation:* domesticity. *Address:* Pearmain, Ruxley, Claygate, Surrey. *T.:* Esher 2597. [*Died* 29 *Sept.* 1960.

CROPPER, James Winstanley; J.P., Lord Lieutenant Westmorland since 1945; *b.* 4 Aug. 1879; *o. s.* of Charles James Cropper and Hon. Edith Cropper, *d.* of 1st Viscount Knutsford; *m.* 1910, Marjorie Constance Bagot (*d.* 1951); one *s.* five *d. Educ.:* Eton; Trinity College, Cambridge. Chairman James Cropper and Co. Ltd., Papermakers; C.C. Westmorland; Major (ret.) Westmorland and Cumberland Yeomanry, served France, 1915-1917; High Sheriff of Westmorland, 1928. *Recreations:* shooting, stalking. *Address:* Ellergreen, Kendal, Westmorland. *T.A.* and *T.:* Burneside 12. *Club:* Brooks's. [*Died* 10 *Nov.* 1956.

CROSBY, Sir Josiah, K.C.M.G., *cr.* 1942; K.B.E., *cr.* 1928 (O.B.E. 1918); C.I.E. 1919; *s.* of J. P. Crosby; *b.* Falmouth, 25 May 1880; unmarried. *Educ.:* Royal Grammar School, Newcastle upon Tyne; Gonville and Caius College, Cambridge (Scholar). B.A. modern languages Tripos, 1902, first-class honours; M.A., 1926. A student interpreter in Siam, 1904; Vice-Consul in Siam and Travelling District Judge, 1907; Vice-Consul at Bangkok, 1911; Vice-Consul at Nakawn Lampang, Siam, 1913; Consul at Senggora, Siam, 1916; for French Indo-China at Saigon, 1917-19; acting Consul-General at Bangkok, 1919-20; Consul-General at Saigon, 1920; at Batavia, 1921-31; British Minister in Panama, 1931-1934; in Siam, 1934-41; retired from Diplomatic Service, 1943. *Publications:* Siam: The Crossroads, 1945; Siam (Oxford Pamphlets on Indian Affairs, No. 26), 1945. *Recreations:* reading, travel. *Address:* c/o Hong Kong and Shanghai Banking Corporation, 9 Gracechurch Street, E.C.3. *Clubs:* Junior Carlton, Royal Automobile; Mombasa (Kenya); Seychelles (Mahé, Seychelles). [*Died* 4 *Dec.* 1958.

CROSFIELD, Bertram Fothergill, M.A. Camb.; A.M.Struct.E.; retd. 1951 as Managing Director, Daily News Ltd.; Vice-Chm. and Man. Dir., News Chronicle Ltd., and Star Newspaper Co. Ltd.; Member Council of Newspaper Proprietors Association; Director Friends Trusts Ltd.; Governor Godstowe School, High Wycombe; *b.* 14 Nov. 1882; *e. s.* of late Albert J. Crosfield and Gulielma Crosfield; *m.* 1910, Eleanor, *d.* of late George Cadbury and late Mary Cadbury, Birmingham; four *s.* two *d. Educ.*; Leighton Park School; Trinity College, Cambridge. *Recreations:* golf, tennis. *Address:* Witheridge, Knotty Green, Beaconsfield, Bucks. *T.:* Beaconsfield 8. *Club:* National Liberal. [*Died* 23 *Aug.* 1951.

CROSLAND, Brigadier Walter Hugh, C.B.E. 1944; D.S.O. 1945; T.D.; D.L., J.P.; Chairman: of Argentine Southern Land Co., Ltd.; of Tecka (Argentina) Land Co., Ltd.; of Parson and Crosland, Ltd.; Director of Evans Thornton & Cia, Buenos Aires, River Plate Trust Loan & Agency Co. Ltd., and Moorside Trust Ltd.; *b.* 1894; 2nd *s.* of Walter Crosland, The Grange, Eaton Hastings, Faringdon, Berks; *m.* 1924, Sybil Cicely, *d.* of John Hargreaves, Drinkstone Park, Suffolk; one *s.* two *d. Educ.:* Malvern. Served European War, 1914-19, with Berks Yeo.; Maj. 1917; Lt.-Col. R.A. (Berks Yeo. T.A.), 1938-42; Commander Berks Yeo. 1942; Commander R.A. 76th Inf. Div., 1942-43; Commander 9th Army Group R.A. serving with 21 Army Group, European Campaign. High Sheriff of Hertfordshire, 1949. D.L. Herts. Hon. Col. Berks. Yeo. (T.A.), 1953. C.St.J. *Recreations:* fishing, shooting. *Address:* Danes, Little Berkhamsted, near Hertford. *T.:* Essendon 225. *Clubs:* Cavalry, City of London, Canning. [*Died* 14 *Oct.* 1960.

CROSS, Col. James Albert, C.M.G. 1946; D.S.O. 1917; K.C. 1916; retired; formerly of Cross, Jonah, Hugg & Forbes, barristers and solicitors, Regina, Sask.; *b.* Caledonia Springs, Ont., 11 Dec. 1876; *s.* of George Henry Cross and Miriam Kenny, Aylmer, Quebec; *m.* 1905, Ida Bell (*decd.*), *d.* of John Dawson, Regina; one *s.* one *d.*; *m.* 1945, Mrs. Edna G. Fayle, Toronto, Ontario, *d.* of late David John Leslie. *Educ.:* Collegiate Institute, Vankleek Hill, Ontario. Called to Bar of Saskatchewan, 1905; represented Soldiers Overseas, Saskatchewan Legislature, 1917-21; Saskatchewan Legislature for Regina, 1921; Willowbunch in Saskatchewan Legislature, 1925; Attorney-General in Government of Saskatchewan, 1922-27; Chief Commissioner, Board of Transport Commissioners for Canada, 1940-1948; served with 28th Battn. C.E.F. and 27th City of Winnipeg Bn. C.E.F.; commanded Military District No. 12 (Sask.), 1918-19; commanded 21st Infantry Brigade, Regina, with rank of Colonel (D.S.O., despatches). Politics—Liberal. *Address:* 223 Somerset St. West, Ottawa, Canada. *Clubs:* Rideau (Ottawa); Assiniboia (Regina). [*Died* 1 *March* 1952.

CROSS, Richard Basil, C.B. 1943; O.B.E. 1918; *b.* 1881; *s.* of Thomas Cross, Beckenham, Kent; *m.* Janet Helen, *d.* of Peter Hurst, Beckenham and Eastbourne; no *c. Educ.:* Dulwich Coll.; Corpus Christi Coll., Oxford (Scholar). B.A. (1st Class Classical Moderations, 2nd Class Lit.Hum.); entered Civil Service (Inland Revenue), 1904; transferred to Local Govt. Board, 1909; Private Secretary to successive Presidents of Board, 1917-19; Assistant Secretary, Min. of Health, 1920; Principal Assistant Secretary, 1936; Adviser on Special Services, Ministry of Health, 1945-47; retired. *Address:* The Pines, Blakes Road, Felpham, Sussex. *Club:* United University. [*Died* 18 *Oct.* 1952.

CROSSE, Rev. Canon Ernest Courtenay, D.S.O. 1917; M.C.; Vicar of Glynde with Firle, since 1955; Preb. of Highleigh, Chichester Cathedral, 1944-47, now Canon Emeritus; *b.* 18 March 1887; *s.* of Rev. E. Ilbert Crosse; *m.* 1922, Joyce, *d.* of Rev. Canon Arthur Temple Williams; two *s.* one *d.* (and one *s.* decd.). *Educ.:* Clifton Coll.; Balliol Coll., Oxford. B.A. Oxon 1910; M.A. Oxon 1913; Asst. Master, Marlborough Coll., 1911-14 and 1919-20; deacon, 1912; priest, 1913; Temp. Chaplain to the Forces, 1915-18, attached 8th Devons (D.S.O., despatches thrice, M.C.); Snr. Chaplain, Church of England, 7th Division, 1917; Headmaster of Christ's College, Christchurch, N.Z., 1921-30; Chaplain, Shrewsbury School, 1932; Headmaster Ardingly Coll., 1933-46; Rector of Henley-on-Thames, 1946-1955. *Publications:* The Place and Work of a Chaplain with Fighting Troops, 1917; The

God of Battles, a Soldier's Faith, 1917; The Defeat of Austria, as seen by the 7th Division. *Address:* The Vicarage, Glynde, Nr. Lewes, Sussex. [*Died* 11 *Dec.* 1955.

CROSSLEY, Sir Kenneth (Irwin), 2nd Bt., *cr.* 1909; J.P. Cheshire; High Sheriff, 1919; Chairman of Crossley Bros., Ltd., and Crossley Motors, Ltd.; Director, Williams Deacon's Bank, Ltd.; *b.* 17 Feb. 1877; *s.* of Sir William Crossley, Bart.; *m.* 1901, Florence Josephine (*d.* 1954), *d.* of Joseph Nash Field, Chicago, U.S.A.; three *d.*; *m.* 1954, Elizabeth Joyce, *d.* of late E. Shenton, Boxmoor, Herts. *Educ.:* Eton (Biology and Physiology prize, 1895); Magdalen College, Oxford; rowed bow in Magdalen eight; B.A., 1898; travelled extensively and made shooting expeditions in Ceylon, India, Nepal, and America, and later in S. Africa, Canada, British East Africa, Uganda, and Upper Nile; Air Pilot's A Licence, 1931. *Heir: gt. n.* Christopher John, *b.* 25 Sept. 1931. *Address:* Combermere Abbey, Whitchurch, Salop. *Club:* White's. [*Died* 22 *Nov.* 1957.

CROSSLEY-HOLLAND, Dr. Frank William; *b.* Quinton Manor, Gloucestershire, 8 Feb. 1878; *s.* of Rev. Manoah Holland, F.L.S., and Kezia Crossley; *m.* 1912 Flora Irene, *d.* of Chas. Alexander Dickins, M.I.E.E., Bridlington; two *s.* *Educ.:* Tamworth Edward VI School; University of London; Sorbonne, Paris. Has followed successively Science, Law, and Medicine; Burroughs Medallist and Prizeman, 1911; F.C.S. 1912; Barrister-at-Law of Gray's Inn and Midland Circuit, 1918; L.M.S.S.A. (Lond.), 1929; Pharmacological research in 1929 at St. Bart's Hospital and at University of Nancy (titre de Docteur, Mention Pharmacie). Member of several learned Societies; Chairman of British Pharmaceutical Conference, Belfast, 1935; in Freemasonry is P.S.G.D., P.Gd.Soj., P.M., P.Z., P.P.G.O. (Essex), P.P.G.P.S., P.P.G.C.O. (Bedfordshire) 30° and one of the Founders of Gray's Inn Lodge; sat as Chairman of the Chemical Board, Ministry of Labour, 1919; contested the Hemsworth Parliamentary Division of Yorkshire (Liberal) 1922; now a Conservative; High Sheriff of Bedfordshire, 1939, D.L. Bedfordshire, 1939, J.P. 1936, C.C. 1937; County Emergency and Standing Jt. Cttees.; Member Eastern Regional Council, Cambridge; Member Advisory Panel, War-Zone Courts; Reserve Chairman Appeals Tribunal, Cambridge Area, also for N.W. Norfolk and King's Lynn Area; scientific missions to Russia and Yugo-Slavia in connection with chemical, timber, and mineral interests; numerous contributions—political, legal, scientific, and medical—to various periodicals. *Recreations:* shooting, yachting. *Address:* Overy Staithe, King's Lynn. *Clubs:* Bar Yacht, Pegasus. [*Died* 27 *Aug.* 1956.

CROSTHWAITE, His Honour Judge Arthur Tinley, O.B.E.; B.A.; J.P.; Judge of County Courts, Circuit 5 (Salford, Bolton, etc.), 1928-40; of Circuit 6 (Liverpool, etc.) since 1940; *b.* 6 May 1880; *s.* of late Alderman Arthur Crosthwaite, J.P., Liverpool, and Florence Heap; *m.* 1908, Agnes Gwendoline, *yr. d.* of late Frederick Edwards Cardiff and London; one *s.* two *d.* *Educ.:* Winchester College; New College, Oxford. Honours in Classical Moderations and Literæ Humaniores; called to Bar, Inner Temple, 1906; practised Liverpool and Northern Circuit; Army, 1914-19; Overseas, 1915-19; 47th (2nd London) Divisional Train and various Staff Appointments, finally D.A.A.G., Army of the Rhine; temporary rank of Major (despatches twice, O.B.E.); Deputy Recorder of Liverpool, 1926-28. *Recreations:* gardening, travel. *Address:* Springcroft, Spital, Bebington, Cheshire. *T.:* Bromborough 2184. *Clubs:* United University; Constitutional (Liverpool). [*Died* 28 *Nov.* 1951.

CROSTHWAITE, Lt.-Col. Henry Robert, C.I.E. 1917; C.B.E. 1919; late Chairman, Basutoland Military Pensions Board; late Registrar Co-operative Credit Societies and Director of Industries, Central Provinces; retired, 1923; *b.* 1876; *s.* of late Sir Charles Crosthwaite, K.C.S.I., and Caroline Alison, *d.* of Sir Henry Lushington, 4th Bt.; *m.* 1896, Ada E. Berry; one *d.* *Educ.:* Clifton; Oxford. On staff of Adjutant-General in India, 1917-19. *Publications:* A Primer of Co-operative Credit; A System of Co-operation. *Address:* 515 Rapallo Flats, Beach Road, Sea Point, Capetown, S. Africa. *Club:* Royal Empire Society. [*Died* 21 *May* 1956.

CROSTHWAITE, Sir Hugh Stuart, Kt., *cr.* 1941; C.I.E.; *b.* 20 Oct. 1879; *s.* of late Sir Robert Crosthwaite, K.C.S.I.; *m.* 1908, Dorothy, *d.* of late Col. Joubert de la Ferté; one *d.* *Educ.:* Rugby; New College, Oxford. Entered Indian Civil Service, 1902; retired 1941. *Address:* St. Anne's, Kyrenia, Cyprus. [*Died* 18 *May* 1952.

CROSTHWAITE, Robert; late Headmaster of Manchester Central High School; *b.* 23 May 1868; *s.* of late Rt. Rev. R. J. Crosthwaite; *m.* 1st, Augusta B. E. R. Whatman (*d.* 1925); one *s.* one *d.*; 2nd, Marian E. Jackson; one *s.* *Educ.:* St. Peter's School, York; Pembroke College, Cambridge (Mathematical Scholar); 9th Senior Optime, 1890; 2nd Class Natural Science Tripos, 1891; Honours in Chemistry, Inter Science, London, 1896; Final, B.Sc., London, 1898; Assistant Master, Exeter School, 1891; Giggleswick School, 1892-93; Senior Science Master, Sherborne School, 1893-1901; Headmaster, Kendal Grammar School, 1901-4. *Address:* 16 The Woodlands, Chesham Bois, Bucks. *T.:* Amersham 1263. [*Died* 26 *July* 1953.

CROSTHWAITE, W. M., B.Sc. (Lond.); Head Mistress of Wycombe Abbey School, 1928-47; *d.* of late Rev. S. M. Crosthwaite, Headmaster, Carlisle Grammar School. *Educ.:* Carlisle High School; Royal Holloway College, University of London. Assistant Mistress Girls' High School, Stamford, Lincs, 1905-6; Assistant Mistress Godolphin and Latymer Girls' School, Hammersmith, 1906-13; Head Mistress Colchester County High School, 1913-1927; retired, 1947. *Address:* Shanagarry, Jordans, Beaconsfield, Bucks. [*Died* 17 *Oct.* 1956.

CROTTY, Rt. Rev. Horace, M.A., D.D., Th.D.; Vicar of Hove since 1943; a Prebendary of Chichester Cathedral since 1944; Rural Dean of Hove since 1945; Proctor in Convocation, 1950; Fellow of Lancing since 1946; *b.* Bleasby, near Nottingham, 9 Oct. 1886; *s.* of Rev. Edward Cassian Crotty and Maria Manning; *m.* 1911, Margaret McLean Cameron; one *s.* two *d.* *Educ.:* Melbourne Grammar School; Trinity College, Melbourne University (Scholar and Exhibitioner). University Final Scholar (First Class) in School of Philosophy; Hastie Exhibitioner (First Class) Logic; Deacon, 1909; Priest, 1910; Headmaster of All Saints' Grammar School, Melbourne, 1907-1911; Vicar of Ivanhoe, Melbourne, 1911-13; Rector S. Thomas, N. Sydney, 1913-19; T.C.F. (France), 1917-19; Dean of Newcastle (N.S.W.), 1919-28; Bishop of Bathurst, 1928-36; Vicar of St. Pancras, 1936-43; Fellow of the Australian College of Theology, 1924. *Publications:* The Vision and the Task, 1921; The Church Victorious, 1938. *Address:* The Vicarage, Hove, Sussex. *T.:* Hove 33331. [*Died* 16 *Jan.* 1952.

CROUCH, Henry Arthur, C.I.E. 1925; F.R.I.B.A.; retired; *b.* 1 Dec. 1870; *e. s.* of late Henry Crouch, Beckenham, Kent; *m.* Ida Muriel, 2nd *d.* of late Col. Hummel, Beckenham, Kent; one *s.* *Educ.:* Brisbane Grammar School. Gold medallist Queensland Institute of Architects, 1891; Associate Royal Institute of British Architects, 1893; Tite Prizeman, 1896; Fellow, 1909; Architect for the Malvern Public Library, Worthing Public Library, Museum and Art Gallery and the Hackney Central Public Library, also several private houses; Consulting Architect to Government of Bengal, 1909-35; officiated as Consulting Architect to Government of India, 1911; designed the School of Tropical Medicine and Hospital for Tropical Diseases, Calcutta; besides numerous other hospitals, judges' courts, post offices, colleges, schools, churches, banks and office buildings, etc., erected in India; Consulting Architect to Royal Calcutta Turf Club, 1919-1925; Trustee Indian Museum, 1915-25. *Recreations:* lawn-tennis, golf. *Address:* Hyde, Oaklands Av., Esher. *T.:* Emberbrook 1265. *Clubs:* East India and Sports; Bengal United Service (Calcutta).

[*Died* 18 *June* 1955.

CROUCH, Colonel Hon. Richard Armstrong, V.D.; *b.* Ballarat, Victoria, 19 June 1869; *s.* of George Crouch. *Educ.:* Mount Pleasant School; Melbourne University (Bowen Prizeman, Chief Justice's Law Prize). Life Member Australian Natives Association; Member Executive Victorian Historical Society, Australia; Chairman Melbourne Co-operative Trust; Chairman National Provident Life Assurance Company; Chairman Commonwealth Building Society; Commanded Yarra Borderers, 56th Australian Infantry Regiment; Officer Commanding 22nd Bn. Infantry, 6th Brigade Australian Imperial Forces (active service) at Dardanelles; M.P. Corio, Australian Parliament, 1901-10, for Corangamite 1920-31; Deputy Chairman Committees Federal Parliament; Australian Delegate to International Labour Conference, Oxford, Aug. 1924; and to British Commonwealth Labour Conference, London, Sept. 1924. *Publications:* Australian Finance at the Cross Roads; Australia a Nation; The Labor Party and the War; The World's Crisis and its Remedy, magazine articles. *Recreation:* book and autograph collecting. *Address:* Point Lonsdale, Vic., Australia. [*Died April* 1949.

CROUCH, Robert Fisher; M.P. (C.) North Dorset since 1950; *b.* 7 Feb. 1904; *s.* of late William Fisher and Ada Stone Crouch; *m.* 1939, Kathleen Mary, *o. d.* of late G. W. Bastable and of Mrs. D. M. Bastable; one *s.* two *d.* *Educ.:* Milton Abbas School, Blandford. Chairman Sturminster Newton Branch, N.F.U., 1927 and 1928; Past Member Dorset and Wilts County Exec., N.F.U.; Member Wilts. Machinery Cttee., 1939-45. Introduced mechanised corn-growing to Wiltshire, 1931; Chairman British Land Council. *Recreation:* gardening. *Address:* Shroton Cottage, Nr. Blandford, Dorset. *T.:* Shaftesbury 2423. *Clubs:* Farmers', Constitutional, Grasshoppers. [*Died* 7 *May* 1957.

CROWE, Sir Edward Thomas Frederick, K.C.M.G., *cr.* 1930 (C.M.G. 1911); Kt., *cr.* 1922; Director: Marconi's Wireless Telegraph Co.; Croda Ltd. (Chairman); *b.* 20 August 1877; *y. s.* of late Alfred Louis Crowe, British Vice-Consul, Zante, Ionian Isles; *m.* 1901, Eleanor (*d.* 1947), *y. d.* of late William Hyde Lay, H.B.M. Consul, Chefoo, China; two *s.* one *d.* *Educ.:* Bedford School. Passed a competitive examination, 1897; appointed a student interpreter in Japan, 1897; 2nd assistant, 1899; held local rank of Vice-Consul at Yokohama, 1901-2; 1st asst., 1903; acting Vice-Consul at Kobe, 1903; acting Consul at Tamsui, 1904-6; Commercial Attaché, 1906-1918; Commercial Counsellor to H.B.M.'s Embassy, Tokio, 1918-25; Seconded for Service as Dir. of the Foreign Division in the Dept. of Overseas Trade, 1924-28; Comptroller-General of Department of Overseas Trade, 1928-1937; retired, 1937; Member of Lord Gorell's Committee on Art and Industry, 1931-32; Member of Viscount Goschen's Committee on the Law relating to Trade Marks, 1933; Vice-President Board of Governors, Imperial Institute, 1928-37; Vice-President International Exhibitions Bureau at Paris, 1928-37; President, Royal Society of Arts, 1941-1943; Governor, Harpur Trust, Bedford, 1938-1945; Member of Lord Fleming's Committee on Public Schools, 1942-44; President Old Bedfordian's Club, 1938-46; Pres. Japan Assoc., 1951-52; Pres. British Section Internat. Centre for Art and Costume, Venice. Comdr. 1st class, Order of the Dannebrog, Denmark, 1948; 1st class, Order of Sacred Treasure, Japan, 1955. *Address:* 5 Roland Way, S.W.7. *T.:* Fremantle 2426. *Club:* Athenæum.

[*Died* 8 *March* 1960.

CROWE, Eric Eyre; H.B.M. Consul-General, Frankfurt, since 1951; *b.* 28 April 1905; *s.* of late Sir Eyre Crowe, G.C.B., G.C.M.G., and of Lady Crowe; *m.* 1932, Virginia Bolling Teusler; one *s.* three *d.* (and one *s.* decd.). *Educ.:* Gresham's; Balliol College, Oxford. Entered diplomatic service, 1927; Sofia, 1930; Tokyo, 1931; Foreign Office, 1935; Prague, 1938; Tehran, 1939; Cairo, 1942; Foreign Office, 1942; Political Secretary to the U.K. High Commissioner in S. Africa, 1944; Oslo, 1948. *Recreations:* riding, tennis. *Address:* c/o Foreign Office, Whitehall, S.W.1. *Club:* Travellers'.

[*Died* 21 *April* 1952.

CROWFOOT, John Winter, C.B.E. 1919; Hon. D.Litt., Oxford University, 1958; *b.* 28 July 1873; *s.* of late John Henchman Crowfoot and Mary Elizabeth, *d.* of Robert Bayly; *m.* Grace Mary (*d.* 1957), *d.* of Sinclair Frankland Hood of Nettleham Hall, Lincoln; four *d.* *Educ.:* Marlborough; Brasenose College, Oxford (Senior Hulme Exhibitioner). Travelled in Greece, Asia Minor, Cyprus; Classical Lecturer, Mason University College and University of Birmingham, 1899-1900; Assistant Master, Ministry of Education, Cairo, 1901-1903; Assist. Director of Education, Sudan Govt., 1903-8; Inspector, Ministry of Education, Cairo, 1908-14; Director of Education, Sudan Government, and Principal of Gordon College, Khartoum, 1914-26; Member of Governor-General's Council, Sudan, 1917-26; Director, British School of Archæology at Jerusalem, 1927-35; Schweich Lecturer, British Academy, 1937; Vice-Pres. Soc. of Antiquaries, 1941-45; Chairman, Palestine Exploration Fund, 1945-50; Third Class Medjidieh Order; Third Class Nile Order. *Publications:* Island of Meroe (Egyptian Exploration Fund); Excavations in the Tyropoeon Valley, Jerusalem, 1927-29; Churches at Jerash, 1931; Churches at Bosra and Samaria, 1937; Samaria-Sebaste I, II and III, 1938, 1942 and 1957; Early Churches in Palestine, 1941. *Recreation:* travelling. *Address:* Geldeston, Beccles, Suffolk. *T.:* Kirby Cane 244. *Club:* Athenæum.

[*Died* 6 *Dec.* 1959.

CROWLEY, Ralph Henry; lately Senior Medical Officer, Board of Education; *b.* 11 Feb. 1869; *s.* of late Alfred Crowley, Croydon; *m.* 1902, Muriel, *d.* of H. B. Priestman, Bradford; two *d.* *Educ.:* Brighton Grammar School; Oliver's Mount School, Scarborough; St. Bart's Hospital; Berlin. School medical officer, Bradford Education Authority; Honorary Physician, Bradford Royal Infirmary; Visiting Physician, Bradford Union Hospital; Visiting Physician, Eastby Sanatorium; M.D. (Lond.), 1895; M.R.C.S., 1893; F.R.C.P., 1930; F.R.San.I.; Vice-chm. Joint Mental Deficiency Committee of Board of Education and Board of Control, 1924-29; member Government Sterilisation Committee, 1932. *Publications:* Hygiene of School Life, 1909; numerous papers to B.M.A., British Assoc. and educational conferences on the Health and Education of Children, also articles in periodicals dealing with similar subjects. *Address:* Sewell's Orchard, Tewin, Welwyn, Herts.

[*Died* 25 *Sept.* 1953.

CROXTON, Arthur; Hon. Life Governor of Charing Cross Hospital, London Fever Hospital, National Hospital, Home for Aged Jews and other charities; *s.* of William Col-

clough Croxton, Manchester; *m.* Edith Miriam, *d.* of Captain John Garden; two *s.* one *d.* On staff Manchester Examiner, 1891-1893; wrote for the Manchester Guardian; joined Sir George Newnes; edited the Tatler, 1906-8; with the late Mr. Hugh Spottiswoode founded Printers' Pie and Winters' Pie, of which, from its first issue until 1915, he was Assistant Editor; founded Woodbury Lantern Lecture Bureau; art critic of The London Letter; initiated, with Frank Lascelles, proposals for London Pageant; edited The World's Greatest Pictures; edited guide to the Tate Gallery in Gems from the Galleries; literary secretary of English Church Pageant, 1909; press secretary of Army Pageant, 1910; Berlitz lecturer in Paris on English Humour; Manager for production of 11th edition Encyclopædia Britannica; originator of National Tributes to Mme. Sarah Bernhardt and Vesta Tilley (Lady de Freece); joined Sir Oswald Stoll as manager of London Coliseum, 1912-27; organiser of Shakespeare Down the Ages Exhibition, 1936. *Publications:* Crowded Nights—and Days, 1934; Westminster Fare (Editor), 1935; A Book of Toynbee Hall (Editor), 1938. *Address:* 6 Shawfield Street, S.W.3. *T.:* Flaxman 6862.
[*Died* 9 *Jan.* 1956.

CROXTON SMITH, Arthur; *see* Smith.

CROZIER, Major-General Baptist Barton, C.B. 1934; C.M.G. 1918; D.S.O. 1915; *b.* 17 July 1878; *e. s.* of late Archbishop of Armagh; *m.* Ethel Elizabeth (*d.* 1944), *e. d.* of W. Humphrys, J.P., Ballyhaise House, Co. Cavan; one *s.* one *d.* *Educ.:* St. Columba's Coll., Rathfarnham; T.C.D. 2nd Lt. R.A. 1898; Lt.-Col. and Col. 1921; Maj.-Gen. 1933; Gen. Staff Officer, 1st Grade, 1917; served South African War, 1900-1 (medal, 3 clasps); European War, 1914-18 (despatches, D.S.O., C.M.G., Bt. Lt.-Col.); Officer of the Order of the Crown of Italy, 1917; Chevalier of the Legion of Honour, 1918; G.S.O.1. and Instructor, Staff College, Camberley, 1919-22: G.S.O. 1st Grade, Headquarters 4th Division, 1923-27; Brigadier R.A. Eastern Command, 1929-33; Commander 43rd (Wessex) Division T.A., 1934-38; retired, 1938. *Address:* 136 Chatsworth Court, Pembroke Road, W.8. *T.:* Western 8251. *Club:* Army and Navy. [*Died* 18 *July* 1957.

CRUDDAS, Bt. Col. Bernard, D.S.O. 1918; late Northumberland Fusiliers; M.P. (Nat. C.) Wansbeck Division, Northumberland, 1931-40; Member of Northumberland C.C.; Director, Newcastle and Gateshead Water Co.; *b.* 1882; *m.* 1908, Dorothy, *d.* of George Wilkinson, Newcastle upon Tyne; four *d.* *Educ.:* Winchester; Royal Military College, Sandhurst. Royal Northumberland Fusiliers, 1900-23; served European War, 1914-18 (despatches, D.S.O.); retired pay, 1923; T.A. 1924-32. Sheriff of Northumberland, 1942; D.L., J.P., Northumberland. *Address:* Middleton Hall, Morpeth, Northumberland.
[*Died* 23 *Dec.* 1959.

CRUDDAS, Colonel Hamilton Maxwell, C.M.G. 1916; O.B.E. 1919; late I.M.S.; *b.* 1 Aug. 1874; *s.* of late John Cruddas; *m.* 1911, Helen Madoline, *d.* of late Thomas Lunham; two *s.* one *d.* Served China, 1900 (medal); N.W. Frontier, India, 1902 and 1908 (medal with clasp); European War, 1914-16 (despatches, C.M.G.); Mesopotamia, 1917-18 (despatches, O.B.E.); Afghan War, 1919; retired, 1928. *Address:* Kingsford, Dinorben Avenue, Fleet, Hants. *Club:* East India and Sports.
[*Died* 29 *March* 1955.

CRUICKSHANK, Dame Joanna Margaret, D.B.E., *cr.* 1931 (C.B.E. 1927); R.R.C. 1920; Member of Council and Cttees. of The Nation's Fund for Nurses, and of Edith Cavell Homes for Nurses; 2nd *d.* of late William Cruickshank. Served European War, 1917-1919; Matron-in-Chief of Princess Mary's R.A.F. Nursing Service, 1918-30; retired, 1930; Chairman, Homes Administration Committee, Invalid Children's Aid Association, 1933-47; Vice-President (Herts) British Red Cross, 1932-34; Matron-in-Chief British Red Cross Society, 1938-40; Matron-in-Chief War Organisation of the British Red Cross and the Order of St. John of Jerusalem, 1939-40; Commandant Alien women's internment camp, Isle of Man, 1940-41; S.R.N. Training School, Guy's Hosp., London; Diploma of Incorporated Society of Trained Masseuses and Central Midwives Board; Sister, Lady Minto's Indian Nursing Assoc., 1912-17; Member of Florence Nightingale International Foundation Cttee., 1938-46; Officer (Sister) Order St. John of Jersualem, 1939. *Address:* c/o Barclays Bank, Ltd., Pantiles Branch, Tunbridge Wells, Kent.
[*Died* 16 *Aug.* 1958.

CRUICKSHANK, Professor John Cecil; Professor of Bacteriology as applied to Hygiene, London School of Hygiene and Tropical Medicine, University of London, since 1947; *b.* 14 Oct. 1899; *s.* of John Cruickshank, M.A., and Robina Wight; *m.* 1928, Mabel Margaret Elizabeth Harvey; two *s.* one *d.* *Educ.:* George Watson's College, Edinburgh; Edinburgh University. Served with Gordon Highlanders, European War, 1917-18. M.B., Ch.B. (Edin.), 1921, M.D. (Edin.), 1952 (Gold medallist), D.T.M. (L'pool), 1923, Dip. Bact. (Lond.), 1933. Alan H. Milne Memorial Medal for Tropical Medicine, 1923. Medical Officer on West African Medical Staff, The Gambia, 1923-1930; since 1933, on staff of Department of Bacteriology, London School of Hygiene and Tropical Medicine as Lecturer, Reader, and Professor. On staff of Emergency Public Health Laboratory Service (Medical Research Council) as Director of Laboratories at Horsham and Exeter, 1939-45. Examiner in bacteriology, University of London. *Publications:* numerous papers in scientific journals on bacteriological subjects. *Recreation:* hill walking. *Address:* London School of Hygiene and Tropical Medicine, Keppel St., Gower St., W.C.1. *T.:* Museum 3041.
[*Died* 30 *Oct.* 1956.

CRUIKSHANK, Robert James, C.M.G. 1945; Director: News Chronicle; Daily News Ltd.; *b.* 19 April 1898; *s.* of Robert James Cruikshank, Balleer, Co. Armagh, and Ellen Bachelor; *m.* 1939, Margaret Adele MacKnight, New York; two *d.* American correspondent of News Chronicle, 1928-36; Asst. Editor News Chronicle, 1936; Editor of Star, 1936-41; Director of American Division of Ministry of Information, 1941-45; Deputy Director-General of British Information Services in United States, 1941-42; U.K. delegate, Sub-Commission on Freedom of Information, of the Human Rights Commission of United Nations, 1947; Editor, News Chronicle, 1948-54. Governor of the Old Vic. *Publications:* The Double Quest (an American study), 1936; Roaring Century, 1946; The Liberal Party, 1949; Charles Dickens and Early Victorian England, 1949; The Moods of London, 1951. *Address:* Daily News Ltd., Bouverie Street, E.C.4. *Club:* Garrick. [*Died* 14 *May* 1956.

CRUM, Rev. John Macleod Campbell, M.A.; Canon of Canterbury, 1928-43, Canon Emeritus, 1943; *b.* 1872; *m.* 1st, Edith Frideswide Paget; one *s.*; 2nd, Emily Clare Bale; two *s.* three *d.* *Educ.:* Eton; New College, Oxford. Curate at Darlington; Domestic Chaplain to the Bishop of Oxford; Curate at Windsor, 1907-10; Vicar of Mentmore-with-Ledburn, Bucks, 1910-12; Rector of Farnham, 1913-28. *Publication:* St. Mark's Gospel, Two Stages in its Making. *Address:* Wilmer House, West Street, Farnham, Surrey.
[*Died* 19 *Dec.* 1958.

CRUMP, Sir Louis Charles, Kt., *cr.* 1928; *b.* 2 Jan. 1869; *s.* of C. W. A. Crump, Barrister-at-law and Helen Anne Crane; *m.* 1893, Alice Clare Russell (*d.* 1959); one *s.* *Educ.:* privately; Balliol College, Oxon. Entered Indian Civil Service,

1888; arrived in India, 1890; served in Bombay Presidency; Under Secretary to Bombay Government, Judicial and Political Departments; Registrar High Court; Secretary to Bombay Government Legal Department; Judicial Commissioner in Sind; Temporary Member of the Executive Council of the Governor of Bombay; Puisne Judge, High Court, Bombay, 1919-29; retired, 1929. *Recreations:* billiards, motoring, chess, and field sports generally. *Address:* c/o Lloyds Bank, Cox & King's Branch, 6 Pall Mall, S.W.1. [*Died* 16 *March* 1960.

CUBBON, William, M.A. (Hon.) Liverpool University, 1949; Director, 1932-40, and Librarian, 1922-40, Manx Museum (now consultant); Knight of Order of St. Olav, 1947; *b.* 28 May 1865; *s.* of James Cubbon and Margaret Powell; *m.* 1st, Margaret Jane Quayle (*d.* 1922); 2nd, 1925, Hortense Mylechraine; two *s.* *Educ.:* Boys' School, Rushen, Isle of Man. Manager and editor Isle of Man Examiner; joint proprietor and editor Manx Sun; Borough Librarian, Douglas, 1912; President Manx Society, 1916. In 1933 and in 1939, offered Knighthood First Class of Order of St. Olav of Norway but on account of a rigid Foreign Office rule that Civil Servants could not accept foreign Orders, it had to be declined; 1940, awarded a Leverhulme Research Grant for researches in the maritime commerce of the Isle of Man. *Publications:* Book of Manx Poetry (an anthology), 1913; Manx Christian Names, 1923; A Bibliography of Literature in the Manx Language, 1924; ed. Manorial Roll of Isle of Man, 1511, 1924; Early Schools and Scholarship in Man, 1926, 1933; Excavation of Cronk yn How, an early Christian and Viking site (with J. Ronald Bruce, M.Sc.), 1928; The Treen (Land) Divisions of Man, coloured, based on the 1511-15 Manorial Roll, 1930; Watch and Ward in the Isle of Man, 1930; Excavation of a Bronze Age Cemetery at Knocksharry, 1930; A Bibliographical Account of the Literature of the Isle of Man, Vol. I., 1933, Vol. II, 1939; The Literary Treasures in the Manx Museum, 1938; The Antiquity of Tynwald and the House of Keys, 1945; The Royal and Ancient Order of Bucks of Douglas, 1764-1816, 1945; Island Heritage, 1952. *Recreations:* walking the Manx hills. *Address:* Cairbrie, Albany Road, Douglas, I. of Man. [*Died* 1 *Jan.* 1955.

CUDMORE, Sir Arthur Murray, Kt., *cr.* 1945; C.M.G. 1936; M.B.; F.R.C.S.; President Medical Board; Consulting Surgeon 4th Military District, Australia; Consulting Surgeon Adelaide Hospital, S. Australia; late Member Council University of Adelaide; *b.* 11 June 1870; *s.* of James Francis Cudmore and Margaret Budge; *m.* 1901, Kathleen Mary, *d.* of Hon. Wentworth and Ellen Jane Cavenagh-Mainwaring, Whitmore Hall, Staffs; two *d.* *Educ.:* St. Peter's College, Adelaide University. M.B., B.S., 1894; after being in residence for one year at Adelaide Hospital, proceeded to London for further study; M.R.C.S., L.R.C.P., 1896; F.R.C.S., 1899; House Surgeon St. Mark's Hospital, City Road; Assistant Surgeon to Adelaide Hospital, 1901, Surgeon, 1904; Lecturer in Clinical Surgery Adelaide University; served European war, 1915 with 3rd Australian General Hospital with rank of Lt.-Colonel; contracted typhoid and invalided home in 1916; returned in 1918 for service with A.I.F. in France; late President of Dental Board and Dean of Faculty of Dentistry. *Recreations:* golf, shooting. *Address:* 64 Pennington Terrace, N. Adelaide, Australia. *T.:* C.4506. *Clubs:* British Empire; Adelaide (Adelaide). [*Died* 27 *Feb.* 1951.

CUFFE, Colonel James Aloysius Francis, C.M.G. 1919; D.S.O. 1916; late R. Munster Fusiliers; *b.* 14 Dec. 1876; *s.* of late Laurence Cuffe, J.P., Clonskeagh, Co. Dublin, and Rathnew, Co. Wicklow; *m.* 1919, Gertrude Ella Mary, *d.* of late Sir John Jackson, LL.D., M.P.; (one *s.* Lieut. Irish Guards, killed 2 April 1945, Western Front) two *d.* Entered Royal Marines, 1896; Capt. 1903; specially promoted for War Service; Major Royal Munster Fusiliers, 1915; Bt. Lt.-Col. 1918; Col. 1922; p.s.c. 1919; Lt.-Col. commanding 1st R. Munster Fusiliers, 1919-22; Allied Military Committee of Versailles 1922-23; served Nandi Expedition, 1905-6 (medal and clasp); European War (despatches, Legion of Honour, Ordre de la Couronne, Belgian Croix de Guerre, C.M.G., D.S.O.); retired, 1926; helped to raise and first C.O. of 5th Bn. Hampshire Home Guard, 1940-41; Councillor of City of Winchester, 1934-38; Hampshire County Council, 1946-49. *Address:* New House, Silvermere, Cobham, Surrey. *Club:* United Service. [*Died* 27 *May* 1957.

CULBERTSON, Ely; author; *b.* 22 July 1891, Native American, mother *d.* of a Cossack General; father, one of the founders of Grozny oil-fields in Caucasus, of Scotch descent; *m.* 1924, Mrs. Josephine Dillon; one *s.* one *d.*; *m.* 1947, Dorothy Renata Baehne; one *s.* *Educ.:* Russian schools; privately; Geneva University; L'École Superieure des Sciences Économiques et Politiques, Paris. Speaks eight languages; specialised in social systems and mass psychology. Became world famous as Bridge authority, creator of the Culbertson System since 1930; organised Contract Bridge as a national industry employing more than ten thousand teachers and specialists throughout the world to serve the needs of twenty million Bridge players. Although devoting much time to Bridge, which is his hobby, continued active in peace movements, which is his life work; Creator of the World Federation System and Chairman, Citizens Committee for United Nations Reform, Incorporated. *Publications:* Total Peace, 1943; Must We Fight Russia ?, 1946; The Strange Lives of One Man, an autobiography; Gold Book of Contract Bridge; Culbertson's Own Summary; Culbertson's Self-Teacher, etc., Queen Twice Guarded, a mystery book; Culbertson on Canasta, 1949; Culbertson Point-Count Bidding, 1952; Contract Bridge Complete, 1954; Editor of the Bridge World magazine; contributor of articles on Mass Psychology and International Politics; Writer of daily syndicated articles for over 200 newspapers in America and other countries. *Address:* 171 West 57 Street, New York City. *Club:* The Whist (New York). [*Died* 29 *Dec.* 1955.

CULLEN, Brig.-Gen. Ernest Henry Scott, C.M.G. 1916; D.S.O. 1912; M.V.O. 1911; 32nd Pioneers, India; *b.* 16 Nov. 1869. Entered Army, 1890; Captain Indian Army, 1901; Major, 1908; Lt.-Col. 1915; Col. 1920; served Chitral, 1895 (medal with clasp); N.W. Frontier, 1897-98 (clasp); Tirah, 1897-98 (clasp); Waziristan, 1902 (clasp); Tibet, 1903-1904 (despatches, medal with clasp); Abor Expedition, 1912 (D.S.O., despatches, medal and clasp); European War (France Mesopotamia, Palestine), 1914-18 (wounded, C.M.G., despatches, 3rd Class Order of St. Stanislaus with Swords); retired pay, 1920. *Address:* 2 Millford Avenue, Sidmouth, Devon. [*Died* 3 *Nov.* 1951.

CULLEN, Kenneth Douglas, M.A., LL.B., Advocate; Sheriff Substitute of Perth and Angus at Dundee since Dec. 1945; *b.* 26 June 1889; *er. s.* of late Hon. Lord Cullen; *m.* 1932, Gladys Margaret, *o. d.* of late Dr. H. Douglas-Wilson, Harrogate; one *s.* *Educ.:* Edinburgh Academy; Edinburgh University. City of Edinburgh (Fortress) Royal Engineers, 1914-19; called to Scottish Bar, 1919; Law Reporter, 1927-37; Editor, Faculty of Advocates' Digest of Cases, 1929-1936; Junior Counsel for Post Office in Scotland, 1934; Honorary Sheriff-substitute of Fife and Kinross, 1936; Sheriff-substitute of Roxburgh, Berwick, and Selkirk, and of Peeblesshire, at Selkirk, 1937-41; of Argyll and Bute at Dunoon, 1942-45. *Address:* Sheriff Court House, Dundee. [*Died* 29 *Sept.* 1956.

CULLIS, Winifred Clara, C.B.E. 1929; M.A. (Cantab.), D.Sc. (Lond.); LL.D. (Hon.) Goucher College, U.S.A., Toronto, Canada, Birmingham University; Professor Emeritus of Physiology, University of London, 1941, on retiring from Sophia Jex-Blake Chair of Physiology, London (Royal Free Hospital) School of Medicine for Women; *b.* Gloucester, 2 June 1875; *y. d.* of Frederick John Cullis, F.G.S., of Gloucester, and Louisa, *d.* of John Corbett. *Educ.:* King Edward VI High School for Girls, Birmingham; Newnham College, Cambridge (Professor Sidgwick Scholar); Natural Sciences Tripos, Camb., Parts I. and II. (1899 and 1900). President, International Federation of Univ. Women, 1929-32; Director of Time and Tide; Member of Council of King Edward's Hospital Fund for London; Deputy Chairman English-Speaking Union and Chairman of Universities Section; Member Committee for King George VI and Marshall Awards; Member Council and Executive Committee Royal Acad. of Dancing; Guest of South Australian Government at Centenary Celebrations, 1936; Delegate to Silver Jubilee of Indian Science Assoc. in Calcutta, 1937; sent by Govt. to Far East, 1940, to Middle East, 1944 and 1945, to give information on activities of British Women in the War; Head of Women's Section British Information Services in the United States, 1941-43. *Publications:* The Body and Its Health (with M. Bond), 1935; Your Body and the Way it Works, 1949; papers and articles in scientific journals and other publications. *Recreations:* reading, x-stitch. *Address:* Vincent House, Pembridge Square, W.2. *T.:* Bayswater 1133. *Club:* University Women's. [*Died* 13 *Nov.* 1956.

CULPIN, Millais, M.D., F.R.C.S.; lately Lecturer on Psychoneurosis, London Hosp. Medical Coll., and Prof. of Medical-Industrial Psychology, University of London; *b.* Ware, 1874; *s.* of Millice Culpin, L.R.C.P. and S.; *m.* 1913, Ethel Maude, *d.* of E. Dimery Bennett; one *d.* *Educ.:* Grocers' Company School; London Hospital. Formerly Rec. Room Officer, House Surgeon, Ophthalmic House Surgeon and Surgical Registrar, London Hospital; War service, 1914-19; Surgical Specialist, 1914-17; Neurological Specialist, 1917-19. *Publications:* Spiritualism and the new Psychology; Psychoneuroses of Peace and War; The Nervous Patient; Medicine and the Man; Recent Advances in the Study of the Psychoneuroses; Mental Abnormality: Facts and Theories; various articles. *Address:* 17A Hatfield Road, St. Albans, Herts. *T.:* St. Albans 6010. [*Died* 14 *Sept.* 1952.

CUMBERBATCH, Sir Hugh (Douglas), Kt., *cr.* 1947; retired; *b.* 29 July 1897; *s.* of late Henry Alfred Cumberbatch, C.M.G., H.M.'s Consul-General, and late Hélène Gertrude Cumberbatch (*née* Rees); *m.* 1925, Sheelagh Elphinstone (*née* Bradley); no *c.* *Educ.:* King's School, Canterbury. Served European War, 1914-18, 6th Bn., The Buffs (despatches). Chairman, Andrew Yule & Co. Ltd., Calcutta, 1945-48; Pres. Bengal Chamber of Commerce, Calcutta, 1947-48; Pres. Associated Chambers of Commerce of India, 1947-48. *Address:* Monks Park, Wadhurst, Sussex. *Clubs:* Oriental, Lansdowne; Bengal (Calcutta). [*Died* 26 *Oct.* 1951.

CUMMING, Sir John Ghest, K.C.I.E., *cr.* 1920 (C.I.E. 1911); C.S.I. 1916; *b.* 29 Dec. 1868; *s.* of late Dr. James Simpson Cumming. *Educ.:* High School and University, Glasgow; Balliol Coll., Oxford; Boden Sanskrit Scholar; M.A. (Glasg., Oxon). Indian Civil Service, Bengal and Bihar, 1889-1921; Settlement Officer, 1894; District Magistrate, 1901; Industrial Enquiries, 1908; Chief Secretary, 1913; Member Executive Council, 1917, retired 1920; Member, Cttee. of Management, Royal National Life-Boat Institution, 1921, Vice-Pres., 1931; Vice-Chm., School of Oriental Studies, London, 1926-46, Hon. Fellow, 1950. *Publications:* Murray's Handbook for India, 1924; The Police Journal, 1928-30; Modern India, 1931; Political India, 1932; Bibliography dealing with Crime, 1935; Literature of the Life-Boat, 1936; The Life-Boat in Verse (with C. Vince), 1938; Revealing India's Past, 1939. *Address:* 52 West Heath Drive, N.W.11. *Club:* East India and Sports. [*Died* 9 *March* 1958.

CUMMINGS, Arthur John; Political Editor, News Chronicle, and chief commentator, 1932-55, retired; *s.* of John and Maria Elizabeth Cummings, Barnstaple, N. Devon; *m.* Nora, *d.* of Arthur and Sarah Maria Suddards, Leeds; one *s.* one *d.* Asst. editor, Yorkshire Post, 1919. Served European War, 1914-18, Western Front, R.F.A. officer, 1915-1918. Asst. editor, Daily News, 1920, then deputy editor; political editor, News Chronicle, 1932; travelled extensively on foreign missions for News Chronicle; reported among other notable events trial of British engineers, Moscow, 1933, and Reichstag Fire Trial, Leipzig, 1933. Selfridge Award for journalism and foreign correspondence, 1933. President Institute of Journalists, 1952-53. *Publications:* Introduction to Journal of a Disappointed Man (W. N. P. Barbellion), 1920; The Moscow Trial, 1933; The Press and a Changing Civilisation, 1936; This England, 1944; numerous political and literary essays and serial writings. *Recreations:* golf, politics, reading. *Address:* 11 St. Mary's Avenue, N.3. *T.:* Finchley 2546. [*Died* 4 *July* 1957.

CUMMINS, Maj.-Gen. Harry Ashley Vane, C.B. 1924; C.M.G. 1919; *b.* 1870; *s.* of late Major-General J. T. Cummins, C.B., D.S.O., Indian Army; *m.* 1899, Mabel Kennard, *d.* of late W. B. Greenfield, Haynes Park, Bedford; one *d.* *Educ.:* Royal Military Coll., Sandhurst. 2nd Lt. Royal Welch Fusiliers, 1889; transferred Royal Fusiliers, 1889; joined Indian Staff Corps, 1891; served in China Expeditionary Force, 1900-1; World War, 1914-18; D.A.Q.M.G. and A.Q.M.G. Embarkation Staff, Bombay, Aug. 1914-July 1915; Mesopotamia, Aug. 1915-April 1916; Commanded 24th Punjabis at Ctesiphon, Nov. 1915 (wounded) and in Defence of Kut-el-Amara, 6 Dec. 1915-29 April 1916; prisoner of war, April 1916-Nov. 1918 (despatches twice, Brevet of Colonel and C.M.G.); Brigade-Commander, Army of the Black Sea, 1920; Major-General, 1921; General Officer commanding Bombay District, 1922-26; retired, 1926. *Address:* The Club, Bournemouth. *Clubs:* United Service; Royal Bombay Yacht. [*Died* 1 *April* 1953.

CUMMINS, Walter Herbert; author and journalist; *b.* Hobart, Tasmania, 6 Dec. 1881. Entered journalism on staff Hobart Mercury and Illustrated Tasmanian Mail; became General Manager, 1921-30; General Manager The Telegraph, Brisbane, 1931-40; editor-in-chief, The Telegraph, 1936-40; Editor and Manager of Australian Associated Press Service, New York to Australia, 1941-42. *Address:* Treeways, 27 Junction Road, Wahroonga, N.S.W., Australia. *T.:* JW1076. [*Died* 28 *March* 1953.

CUMPSTON, John Howard Lidgett, C.M.G. 1929; M.D., B.S., D.P.H.; *b.* Melbourne, 19 June 1880; *s.* of George William and Elizabeth Cumpston; *m.* Gladys Maeva, *d.* of G. A. Walpole; three *s.* four *d.* *Educ.:* Wesley College, Melbourne; Queen's College, University of Melbourne. Graduated 1902; Medical Officer, Metropolitan Asylums Board, London; Medical Officer of Health, Western Australia; Director-General of Health, Commonwealth of Australia, 1922-45; Director of Quarantine, 1913-45; Director-Gen. of Emergency Civil Practitioner Service, 1942; Chairman, National Health and Medical Research Council, 1937; retired 1945. *Publications:*

History of Smallpox in Australia; History of Plague in Australia; History of Intestinal Infections in Australia; Public Health in Australia; Life of Charles Sturt. *Recreation:* historical research. *Address:* Nares Crescent, Forrest, Canberra, A.C.T. [*Died* 9 *Oct.* 1954.

CUNINGHAME, Sir (W.) Andrew (Malcolm Martin Oliphant Montgomery-), of Corsehill, Ayrshire, and Kirktonholm, Lanarkshire; 11th Bt., *cr.* 1672; Established Foreign Service Officer since 1958; *b.* Aberdeen, 14 July 1929; *s.* of Col. Sir T. A. A. Montgomery-Cuninghame, 10th Bt., D.S.O., and 2nd wife, Nancy Macaulay (she *m.* 1946, Jan F. C. Killander), *e. d.* of late W. S. Foggo, Aberdeen and Coldstream, British Columbia, Canada; *S.* father 1945; *m.* 1956, Sara, *d.* of late Brig.-Gen. Lord Esmé Gordon Lennox, K.C.V.O., C.M.G., D.S.O., and of Lady Esmé Gordon Lennox. *Educ.:* Fettes College, Edinburgh; Worcester College, Oxford. *Heir: b.* John Christopher Foggo, *b.* 24 July 1935. *Club:* St. James'. [*Died* 18 *Feb.* 1959.

CUNINGHAME, Lt.-Col. William Wallace Smith, Lord of the Barony of Caprington, D.S.O. 1918; J.P. and D.L., Co. Ayr; late Life Guards; *b.* 1889; *e.* and *o. surv. s.* of late Lieutenant-Colonel J. A. S. Cuninghame of Caprington, late 2nd Life Guards, and Violet Mary (*d.* 1917), *e. d.* of Sir Alfred Slade, Bart., of Maunsel; *m.* 1918, Ella (*d.* 1928), *er. d.* and *heiress* of late Captain R. Cutlar-Fergusson of Craigdarroch, late Scots Guards; two *s.*; *m.* 1949, Lady Joan Philipps (*née* Wentworth Fitzwilliam), 2nd *d.* of 7th Earl Fitzwilliam, K.C.V.O., D.S.O. *Educ.:* Eton; R.M.C. Sandhurst. Joined 2nd Life Guards, 1908; Captain, 1912; Major, 1920; Bt. Lt.-Col. 1929; Lt.-Col. R.A.R.O., 1930; served European War as Captain, 2nd Life Guards, 1914-15; Temp. Major, 10th Scottish Rifles, 1916; acting Lt.-Col. 1st Bn. The King's Own Regt., 1917; and 9th Bn. Cheshire Regt. 1918 (twice wounded despatches, D.S.O.); retired pay, 1930; raised and commanded Ayrshire Zone H.G., 1940; re-employed, 1941, as Lt.-Col. commanding troops in H.M. transports. Member of Queen's Body Guard for Scotland (Royal Company of Archers), 1911; Member of H.M. Bodyguard (Hon. Corps of Gentlemen-at-Arms), 1936-59. *Recreations:* hunting, shooting, and fishing. *Address:* Caprington Castle, Kilmarnock. *T.:* Kilmarnock 157; 27 Hays Mews, Mayfair, W.1. *T.:* Grosvenor 3694. *Clubs:* Turf, New (Edinburgh). [*Died* 5 *July* 1959.

CUNLIFFE, Brig.-Gen. Frederick Hugh Gordon, C.B. 1916; C.M.G. 1916; *s.* of Maj.-Gen. G. G. Cunliffe, B.S.C.; *b.* 22 Sept. 1861; *m.* 1895, Ella Sophie (*d.* 1950), *e. d.* of David Gaussen, Broughton Hall, Lechlade; one *d.* *Educ.:* U.S. College, Westward Ho! Enlisted 9th (Q.R.) Lancers, 1883; transferred to 92nd Gordon Highlanders, 1887; 2nd Lieut. Seaforth Highlanders, 1889; Lieut. 1891; Adjutant, 1892-95; Capt. R. Inniskilling Fusiliers, 1897; Major, Middlesex Regt., 1906; Lt.-Col. 1911; Col. 1915; Commandant Nigeria Regt., W.A.F.F., 9 Sept. 1914; served Hazara Expedition, 1891 (medal with clasp); Chitral, 1895 (medal with clasp); S. African War, 1902 (despatches, Queen's medal, 3 clasps); European War, 1914-18 (despatches thrice; Bt. Col., C.M.G., C.B.); Commander Legion of Honour; Officer, Order of St. Marie and Lazarus, Italy. *Address:* c/o Lloyds Bank (Cox's Branch), 6 Pall Mall, S.W.1. [*Died* 13 *June* 1955.

CUNNINGHAM, Alfred G.; Commissioner (retired); Chief of the Staff and Second in Command of the International Salvation Army, 1939-43; Vice-Chairman Salvation Army Trustee Company; Vice-President Salvation Army Assurance Society, Ltd.; Vice-Chairman Salvation Army Fire Insurance Corp. and Reliance Bank; *b.* 1870; *m.* 1st, 1894, Emily M. Holland (decd.); one *s.* one *d.*; 2nd, 1933, Edith Colbourne (*d.* 1951). Entered Salvation Army as an Officer, 1890; served in South Africa, 1891-96; commanded Salvation Army work in the island of St. Helena, 1896-98; transferred to Editorial Department, London, 1898; Principal of International Staff College, 1922; Publicity Secretary, 1929; Editor, The Staff Review (quarterly), and other Publications; International Secretary for Europe and British Dominions, 1931, also for United States and Latin America Territories, 1935; Editor in Chief, Head of Literary Department and Secretary for Parliamentary Affairs, 1936. *Address:* Ridgefield, Pinewood Road, Bromley, Kent. *T.:* Ravensbourne 5943. [*Died* 25 *Aug.* 1951.

CUNNINGHAM, Sir Edward Sheldon, Kt., *cr.* 1936; LL.D. Glasgow; *b.* Hobart, Tasmania, 21 July 1859; 2nd *s.* of Benjamin M. Cunningham; *m.* 1886, Maud Mary (*d.* 1931), 2nd *d.* of Henry Jackson, Bendigo, Victoria, formerly of Manchester, England; no *c.* *Educ.:* private schools. After serving in junior positions on other papers, joined the Argus, Melbourne, as reporter, 1881; visited United States and Mexico as special correspondent for The Argus on Irrigation investigation, 1885; editor, The Argus, Melbourne, 1906-28, when he retired to take a seat on the Council of Management; finally retired, 1937; accompanied Mr. Deakin as special correspondent to first Imperial Conference, 1887; represented The Argus at Queen Victoria Jubilee Celebrations in London, 1897; delegate to first Imperial Press Conference, 1909; one of six delegates selected for honorary LL.D. degree at Glasgow. *Address:* c/o The Argus, Melbourne, Australia. *Club:* Melbourne (Melbourne.) [*Died* 27 *April* 1957.

CUNNINGHAM, Engineer-Rear-Adm. John Edward Greig, M.V.O. 1925; retired; *b.* 17 Dec. 1878; *s.* of Major J. W. Cunningham; *m.* 1907, Caroline Ann Brokenshaw; two *d.* *Educ.:* Royal Naval Engineering College, Devonport. Joined Navy, 1894; served in H.M. Ships—Nile, Ocean, 1899-1903; Argyll, 1906-08; Indus, 1908-10; Suffolk, 1910-13; Leonidas, 1913-16; Anzac, 1916-17; Carlisle, 1917-20; Indus, 1921-22; on Staff of C.-in-C., Plymouth, 1922-24; Repulse, 1924-26 (Prince of Wales tour to West Africa, S. Africa, and S. America); Chevalier Legion of Honour, 1916; Engr.-Capt. 1926; Staff of Rear-Admiral commanding Mediterranean Destroyer Flotillas, 1927-29; on Staff of Commander-in-Chief Atlantic Fleet, 1930-32; Eng. Rear-Adm. 1932; retired list, 1932. *Address:* 3 Gunnersbury Avenue, Ealing, W.5. *T.:* Acorn 1041. *Club:* Royal Fowey Yacht (Fowey). [*Died* 7 *March* 1954.

CUNNINGHAM, John Jeffrey, Q.C. (Scot.) 1949; Editor Session Cases, since 1959; lately Sheriff of Roxburgh and Selkirk; Chairman, Medical Appeal Tribunal (Scotland), since 1951; *b.* 10 June 1907; *s.* of late R. J. Cunningham, W.S., Annan, and Mabel Davidson; unmarried. *Educ.:* Edinburgh Academy; Edinburgh University. Admitted to Scots Bar, 1930; Standing Junior Counsel to the Ministry of Pensions in Scotland, 1946-49; Clerk of Faculty, Faculty of Advocates, 1948-54; Vice-Dean Faculty of Advocates, 1954-56. Defence Medal. *Recreation:* railway photography. *Address:* 11 Forres Street, Edinburgh, 3. *T.:* Edinburgh Caledonian 5000; North West Castle, Stranraer. [*Died* 26 *Dec.* 1959.

CUNNINGHAM, Patrick; Dairy Farmer; retired, 1950; *m.* 1918; seven *s.* five *d.* An Irish Nationalist, representing Fermanagh and Tyrone in the Imperial Parliament, 1935-1950 (Abstentionist). *Address:* Strathroy, Omagh, Co. Tyrone, Northern Ireland. [*Died* 2 *Feb.* 1960.

CUNNINGHAM, Wilfred Bertram, C.M.G. 1939; *b.* 8 June 1882; 3rd *s.* of late

Rev. E. J. Cunningham, formerly Headmaster of the King's School, Peterborough, and later Vicar of St. Paul's Church, Worthing; *m.* 1917, Gertrude Marrison; no *c.* *Educ.:* Reading School. Entered Japan Consular Service, 1906; Consul at Osaka, 1923-28; at Dairen, 1928-30; Japanese Counsellor at H.M. Embassy, Tokyo, 1930-41; retired, 1943. *Address:* 55 Offington Lane, Worthing. *T.:* Swandean 1910. [*Died* 31 *May* 1960.

CUNNINGHAM, Major-General Sir William Henry, K.B.E., *cr.* 1955 (C.B.E. 1935); D.S.O. 1916; Crown Prosecutor, Wellington, New Zealand, since 1936; *b.* 1883; *s.* of William Henry Cunningham, Wellington, N.Z.; *m.* 1919, Grace Winifred, *d.* of late Sir Charles Manley Luke; one *d.* *Educ.:* Wanganui High School; Wanganui Coll. Admitted Solicitor, 1907; called to the Bar, 1912; Partner, Luke, Cunningham and Clere, Wellington. Served European War, 1914-18, 1 New Zealand Expeditionary Force, in Egypt, Gallipoli and France (despatches four times, D.S.O.); War of 1939-1945: in command 8th N.Z. Brigade Group, S.W. Pacific; Brigadier, in comd. Fiji Defence Forces; G.O.C. Fiji Defences (Major-General); invalided, 1942. Member of the Executive Council, Fiji, 1941-42. Hon. A.D.C. to Governor-General of New Zealand, 1930-35. President of New Zealand Law Society, 1950. *Address:* 2 North Terrace, Kelburn, Wellington, W.1, New Zealand. [*Died* 20 *April* 1959.

CUNNINGHAM, William Ross, M.A., LL.D.; University Librarian and Keeper of the Hunterian Books and MSS. Glasgow, 1925-51; *b.* 23 Feb. 1890; 3rd *s.* of late Richard Cunningham, F.E.I.S., Muirkirk, Ayrshire; *m.* 1917, Helen McGregor (*d.* 1948), *e. d.* of late Alexander Muir, M.A., F.E.I.S., Buckie; one *s.* twin *d.* *Educ.:* Muirkirk; Ayr Academy; Glasgow Univ. (second place in the Open Bursary Competition; Forfar Bursar and Clark (Mile End) Scholar in Classics; Cowan, Blackstone and Ramsay Gold Medallist and Second Muirhead prizeman in Latin; Luke (Univer.) prizeman in Ancient History; Coulter (University) Prize Essayist in Greek; prizeman in various classes; M.A. with 1st Class Honours in Classics, 1912); Hon. LL.D. Glasgow, 1934. Entered Public Record Office 1912, after being successful in concurrent examinations for Home (Class 1), Indian and Colonial Services; resigned from staff of Public Record Office in 1925; sailed to France with 1st Bn. London Scottish as private, 1914; awarded Commission in the field, 1915; transferred to Artillery; Lieutenant 47 Siege Battery, France, 1917-18; severely wounded as Captain and Second-in-Command of 260 Siege Battery (1914 star with clasp, Victory and Allies Medals); Major R.A., commanding Clyde Defences Gun Operations Room, Class A, 1939-1941; Captain R.A., commanding same Gun Operations Room, Class B, 1941-42; Trustee of the National Library of Scotland as representative of Glasgow University Senate; member Editorial Advisory Cttee. (Yale Univ.), for the publication of the James Boswell papers; Hon. Pres. Glasgow Univ. Athletic Club, 1947-51; Hon. Pres. Glasgow Univ. Rugby Club; Hon. Sec. of the Publications Cttee. of Glasgow Univ.; Special Adviser of Studies in the Faculty of Arts; has acted as Examiner for the Scottish Education Department and for London University; has assisted in editing and indexing various volumes produced by the Public Record Office and the Historical MSS. Commission; contributes occasional articles and reviews. *Address:* 16 Holyrood Crescent, Glasgow, N.W. *T.:* Glasgow Western 5318. *Club:* College (Glasgow). [*Died* 25 *Oct.* 1953.

CUNNINGHAME, Sir James Fraser, Kt., *cr.* 1936; O.B.E. 1933 (M.B.E. 1918); J.P., Midlothian, 1918-49; Director of William Murray & Co. Ltd., Craigmillar Breweries, Edinburgh; *b.* 14 Oct. 1870; *s.* of William Cunninghame and Margaret Fraser; unmarried. *Educ.:* Bonnington Academy and Edinburgh Institution. Officer of Ministry of National Service; Hon. President of Leith Unionist Association, 1928-45; was chairman of Edinburgh Conservative Working Men's Assoc. for over 20 years; mem. of Eastern Divisional Council of Scottish Unionist Assoc. since 1904; Trustee and Chairman of Scottish Conservative Club, Edinburgh; Senior Elder of St. Cuthbert's Parish Church, Edinburgh; Hon. Treas. Scottish Church Society, 1933-50; Member of Edinburgh Presbytery of Church of Scotland, 1938-50; Mem. Cttee., Edinburgh Branch of English-Speaking Union; Chairman Robert Louis Stevenson Club, 1943-45; President Ninety Burns Club, Edinburgh, 1899 and 1900. *Recreations:* walking, reading. *Address:* Forth View, Lower Largo, Fife. *T.:* Lundin Links 131. *Club:* Scottish Conservative (Edinburgh). [*Died* 5 *May* 1952.

CUNNINGTON, Maud Edith (Mrs. B. Howard Cunnington), C.B.E. 1948; *b.* 1869; *d.* of Dr. C. Pegge, Briton Ferry, S. Wales, and *g. d.* of R. V. Leach, Devizes Castle; *m.* 1889, Capt. B. Howard Cunnington, F.S.A. Scot. (*d.* 1950); (*o. s.* killed European War, 1914-18). *Educ.:* Cheltenham Ladies' Coll. Hon. Life Mem. Cambrian Archæological Assoc. and of Soc. of Antiquaries, Scotland; Ex-Pres. Wilts. Arch. Soc. *Publications:* Woodhenge; All Cannings Cross; The Sanctuary; Casterley Camp; and articles in Wilts Archæological Magazine from 1900 onwards. *Recreations:* archæology, gardening. *Address:* 33 Long Street, Devizes. *T.A.:* Cunnington, Long Street, Devizes. *T.:* Devizes 152. [*Died* 28 *Feb.* 1951.

CUNNISON, Sir Alexander, K.B.E., *cr.* 1942; C.B. 1938; J.P. County of London, 1934-1945; Permanent Sec., Ministry of Pensions, 1941-45; *b.* 1879: *e. s.* of Thomas Cunnison, Edinburgh, and Johanna Keith; *m.* 1908, Evelyn Jane, *d.* of Edmund Spencer Mansell and Hannah Dore; three *d.* *Educ.:* George Watson's Coll.; Edin. Univ. (M.A.); Oriel Coll., Oxford (B.A.). Entered Admiralty as Clerk, Class 1. in Department of Accountant Gen. of Navy, 1904; Priv. Sec. to Acct. Gen., 1906; Secretary to Mr. Herbert Samuel's Committee on Admiralty Expenditure, 1916; Asst. Acct. Gen., 1917; transferred to Ministry of Pensions, 1919; Asst. Sec., 1925; Deputy Secretary, 1935; member of Special Grants Committee, 1926-41; and of War Service Grants Advisory Committee, 1939-41. *Address:* Whitehall Hotel, Eastbourne, Sussex. *T.:* Eastbourne 6141. [*Died* 27 *Oct.* 1959.

CURIE, Professor Jean F. J.; *see* Joliot-Curie.

CURLE, Alexander Ormiston, C.V.O. 1930; LL.D. Glasgow; *b.* 3 May 1866; 3rd *s.* of Alexander Curle of Priorwood, Melrose, and Christian, *o. d.* of Sir James Anderson, Kt., M.P.; *m.* 1st, 1898, Katharine Wray (*d.* 1906), 2nd *d.* of George Tancred of Weens, Hawick; one *s.* one *d.*; 2nd, 1909, Jocelyn Winifred (*d.* 1925), *o. c.* of Henry Butler, Hans Court, London. *Educ.:* Fettes College, Edinburgh; Trinity Hall, Camb. B.A.; Writer to the Signet; F.S.A.; F.S.A.Scot.; Secretary to the Royal Commission on Ancient Monuments of Scotland, 1908-13, thereafter a member of the Commission; Director of the National Museum of Antiquities, Edinburgh, 1913-19; Director of the Royal Scottish Museum, 1916-31; Rhind Lecturer in Archæology, 1918, subject, the Prehistoric Monuments of Scotland. *Publications:* The Treasure of Traprain, a Scottish Hoard of Roman Silver Plate; numerous contributions to Archæological publications. *Recreations:* gardening and archæological research. *Address:* Weirknowe, Weirhill Place, Melrose, Roxburghshire. *T.:* Melrose 283. [*Died* 7 *Jan.* 1955.

CURLEWIS, Mrs. H. R.; *see* Turner, Ethel.

CURLING, Brig.-Gen. Bryan James, D.S.O. 1915; retired pay; *b.* 21 Sep. 1877; *s.* of Rev. J. J. Curling, late R.E.; *m.* 1907, Lilian M., *d.* of late W. S. Wells, J.P., late I.C.S.; one *s.* one *d.* (and one *s.* killed in Crete, 1941). *Educ.:* Eton; Magdalen College, Oxford. Joined K.R.R.C., 1899; served S. African War, 1899-1902; European War, 1914-19 (D.S.O., Officer Legion of Honour); Major, 1915; Bt. Lt.-Col., 1919; Lt.-Col. York and Lancaster Regt., 1924; retired with rank of Brigadier-General, 1927; Commander Portsmouth Home Guard (9 Bn.), 1940-42. *Recreations:* hunting, yachting. *Address:* Lyneham Lodge, Warsash, Nr. Southampton. *T.:* Locks Heath 3366. *Clubs:* Royal Southern Yacht (Hamble); Island Sailing (Cowes). [*Died* 2 *April* 1955.

CURPHEY, Col. Sir Aldington George, Kt. 1958; C.B.E. 1952 (M.B.E. 1944); M.C.; E.D.; President of Legislative Council, Jamaica, since 1952; physician and surgeon; *b.* St. Andrew, 24 Aug. 1880; *s.* of late Thomas John Curphey; *m.* 1930, Winifred May, *d.* of George Augustus Douët; one *d.* *Educ.:* York Castle High School, Jamaica; Queen's Univ., Canada; Edinburgh Univ.; Glasgow University. M.D., C.M., Queen's Univ., Canada, 1907; L.R.C.P., L.R.C.S. Ed., L.R.F.P.S. Glas. 1909; M.C.P.S. Ont. 1926. Formerly Asst. Surgeon, St. Joseph Hosp., Hamilton, Canada. Entered Civil Service, Jamaica, 1912; Govt. Med. Officer, Jamaica, 1913-36; Senior Military Med. Officer, Jamaica, 1939-44; Welfare Officer, Caribbean Area, 1944-49. Served as M.O. i/c Jamaica War Contingent, 1915; Capt. R.A.M.C., 2nd B.W.I. Regt., 1916-19; Major (despatches, M.C.); War of 1939-45, Major, Local Forces, Jamaica. Chm. Jamaica Br. B.M.A., 1937-38; Island Comr. for Boy Scouts, 1939-45; Custos Rotolorum for Parish of St. Ann, 1949-; Hon. Col. Jamaica Regt.; Chm. of Council of Jamaica Legion; British Commonwealth ex-Services League, 1949-; M.L.C. 1945; J.P. Jamaica. F.R.G.S. *Recreation:* bridge. *Address:* The Ramble, Claremont, Jamaica, T.W.I. *Clubs:* West Indian; Jamaica, Liguanea, Kingston, St. Andrew (Jamaica). [*Died* 28 *Nov.* 1958.

CURRE, Lady, (Dame Augusta); M.F.H.; 2nd *d.* of late Crawshay Bailey of Maindiff Court, Abergavenny; *m.* 1888, Sir Edward Curre, 1st and last Bt., C.B.E. (*d.* 1930); no *c.* *Address:* Itton Court, Chepstow. [*Died* 5 *Oct.* 1956.

CURREY, Rear-Admiral Hugh Schomberg, D.S.O. 1916; R.N. (retired) *b.* 11 November 1876; *e. s.* of late Lieutenant-Colonel C. H. Currey, 4th Dragoon Guards *m.* 1918, Cecil, *o. c.* of late Lieut. Reginald Fulford, R.N.; one *d.* Served European War 1914-17, including Jutland Bank (D.S.O., despatches, Order of St. Stanislas of Russia). retired list, 1922; Rear-Admiral, 1928; Captain Superintendent of training ship, Exmouth, 1923-34. C.C. County of Southampton, 1945-1949. *Address:* Broadlands House, Brockenhurst, Hants. [*Died* 12 *Aug.* 1955.

CURRIE, Captain Bertram Francis George; Director of Glyn, Mills & Co.; *b.* 1899; *s.* of Lawrence Currie, M.A., J.P., Minley Manor, Farnborough, Hants; *m.* 1923, Alexandra Rose, *d.* of Alexander Rowland Alston, The Tofte, Sharnbrook, Beds; two *d.* (one *s.* killed in action, 1945). *Educ.:* Eton; Royal Military Coll., Sandhurst. Served in Scots Guards, 1918-22; re-employed, 1939; served War of 1939-45, Capt. 1940. High Sheriff of Northamptonshire, 1954. *Recreations:* shooting, hunting, and yachting. *Address:* Dingley Hall, Market Harborough; Dunbeath Castle, Caithness; 34 Orchard Court, W.1. *Clubs:* Carlton, Guards; Royal Yacht Squadron. [*Died* 29 *March* 1959.

CURRIE, Mark Mainwaring Lee; *b.* 14 April 1882; *s.* of George Mainwaring Currie and Margaret Caroline Lee; *m.* 1926, Eva Flora Mary Burlton-Bennet. *Educ.:* Cheltenham College; Pembroke College, Oxford, M.A. I.C.S. examination, 1904; Assistant Commissioner, Punjab Commission, 1905; Settlement Officer, Ferozepore, 1910-15; Deputy-Commissioner, Sheikhupura and Mianwali, 1919-24; Sessions Judge, 1924; Additional Judge, High Court of Judicature, Lahore, 1930-36; retired, 1938. *Recreations:* shooting, fishing. *Address:* Elm Lodge, Cheltenham. *T.:* Cheltenham 5033. *Club:* New (Cheltenham). [*Died* 21 *Dec.* 1951.

CURRY, Aaron Charlton, D.C.L.(Hon.); J.P.; F.R.S.A.; Member of Newcastle upon Tyne City Council since 1941, Alderman since 1951; Chairman of Northumberland and Tyneside River Board; Fellow Corporation of Accountants; Director of H. Young (Motors) Ltd., Norbrit Products, Ltd. and other Companies; Fellow Corporation of Certified Secretaries; *b.* 1887; *m.* 1913, Jane Cranston (*d.* 1943), *d.* of George Wilson; one *d.* M.P. (L.) Bishop Auckland, 1931-35; Member of Whickham U.D.C., 1931-37. Founder and formerly senior partner in A. C. Curry & Co., chartered accountants. J.P. for County of Durham; J.P. for County Borough of Newcastle upon Tyne; Lord Mayor of City and County of Newcastle upon Tyne, 1949-50 and again 1956-57. Hon. D.C.L. (Dunelm), 1951. *Address:* 121 Osborne Road, Newcastle upon Tyne 2. *T.:* 811977. *Club:* National Liberal. [*Died* 6 *Jan.* 1957.

CURTIS, Colonel George Reginald, C.B. 1955; O.B.E. 1932; T.D.; D.L.; T.A. retired; *b.* 1892; *m.* 1917. *Educ.:* Stubbington, Hampshire. 2nd Lieutenant 6th (D.C.O.) Hampshire Regiment, 1909. Served European War, 1914-18; Major, 1921; Brevet-Colonel, 1928. D.L. Hampshire, 1951. *Address:* Giblet Ore, Hill Head, Stubbington, Fareham, Hants. *T.:* Stubington 26. [*Died* 29 *Sept.* 1958.

CURTIS, Lionel George, C.H. 1949; *b.* 1872; *m.* 1920, G. E. (Pat), *y. d.* of late Prebendary Scott of Tiverton. *Educ.:* Haileybury; New College, Oxford. Called to Bar; served South African War; Town Clerk of Johannesburg; Assistant Colonial Secretary to the Transvaal for Local Government; Member Transvaal Legislative Council; Beit Lecturer, Colonial History, Oxford; Fellow of All Souls College; Secretary to the Irish Conference, 1921; Adviser on Irish Affairs in the Colonial Office, 1921-24. *Publications:* The Problem of the Commonwealth, 1916; The Commonwealth of Nations, 1916; Dyarchy, 1920; The Prevention of War, 1924; The Capital Question of China, 1932; Civitas Dei, Vol. I, 1934, Vols. II and III, 1937 (new and revised edn., in one vol. 1951); The Protectorates of South Africa, 1935; World War, Its Cause and Cure, 1945; War or Peace?, 1946; World Revolution in the Cause of Peace, 1949; The Open Road to Freedom, 1950; With Milner in South Africa, 1951; Windows of Freedom, 1952; Evading a Revolution, 1954. *Address:* Hales Croft, Kidlington, Oxford. *T.:* Kidlington 2215. *Club:* Oxford and Cambridge. [*Died* 24 *Nov.* 1955.

CURTIS, Sir Roger Colin Molyneux, 4th Bart., *cr.* 1794; late of the Board of Education; held Temporary Commission as Capt. in R.A.S.C. during the war; *b.* 12 Sept. 1886; *s.* of late Sir Arthur Colin Curtis, 3rd Bart., and Sarah Jessie, *d.* of Alexander Dalrymple [she *m.* 2nd, Sir R. Maziere Brady, 3rd Bt.]; *S.* father, 1898. *Heir:* none. *Address:* Lloyds Bank, Pall Mall, S.W.1. [*Died* 7 *Jan.* 1954 (*ext.*).

CURTIS-BENNETT, Frederick Henry, (Derek), Q.C. 1943; *b.* 29 Feb. 1904; *o. s.* of late Sir Henry Honywood Curtis-Bennett, K.C., J.P., and of Elsie Eleanor, *d.* of late A. A. Dangar, Baroona, Whittingham, N.S.W., Australia; *g.s.* of late Sir Henry Curtis-Bennett, J.P., Chief Metropolitan Magistrate; *m.* 1928, Margaret Duncan (marriage dissolved, 1949), *o. c.* of late Dr. D. D. Mackintosh, Worthing; one *s.* two *d.*; *m.* 1955, Janet Farquhar (*d.* 1956), *g. d.* of late James Rusk. *Educ.:* Radley College; Trinity College, Cambridge; B.A. 1925. Called to Bar, Middle Temple, 1926; Member of Bar of Northern Rhodesia, 1950; Member of S. Eastern Circuit, Central Criminal Court Bar Mess, North London Sessions and Herts and Essex Sessions; Recorder of Tenterden, 1940-42; Recorder of Guildford, 1942-56; Chairman of Committee, London Police Court Mission, 1947-49. Mem. Court of Assistants, Gold and Silver Wyre Drawers Co., 1951. Chairman Essex Quarter Sessions, 1955-56 (Dep. Chm. 1952-55); Appeal Steward of British Boxing Board of Control, 1953. *Publications:* "Curtis," The Life of Sir Henry Curtis-Bennett, K.C. (with Roland Wild), 1937; The Trial of Mary Court (with Roland Wild), 1939. *Address:* 1 Garden Court, Temple, E.C.4. *T.:* Central 7520 and 2576. *Clubs:* Beefsteak, Travellers'. [*Died July* 1956.

CURTIS-WILLSON, William Thomas, M.B.E. 1933; J.P.; Chairman and Managing Director, Brighton Herald Ltd., 1933; Chairman Brighton and Hove Mutual Property Society Ltd., 1936; Chairman, Citizen's Permanent Building Society, 1953; Chairman Ministry of Labour Disablement Advisory Committee for Brighton and Mid.-Sussex; Chairman Social Service Centre; Member: General Council of the Press; Council Commonwealth Press Union; Council and Executive Committee, Royal National Institute for the Blind; Council, The Empire Society for the Blind; *b.* 7 April 1888; *m.* 1920, Jessie Elizabeth Robertson; two *d.* (one *s.* killed in action, 1945). *Educ.:* Tottenham Grammar School; privately. President of The Newspaper Society, 1950; Pres. International Federation of the Press (Fédération Internationale des Éditeurs de Journaux et Publications), 1953. F.R.S.A. 1952. Wing Commander, R.A.F.V.R. (T.) Blinded Feb. 1916; trained at St. Dunstan's. Chevalier of the Legion of Honour, 1951. *Recreation:* bridge. *Address:* 262 Dyke Road, Brighton 5. *T.:* Brighton 52105. *Clubs:* Press; Sussex Motor Yacht (Brighton). [*Died* 4 *Dec.* 1957.

CURZON of Kedleston, Marchioness, G.B.E., *cr.* 1922; **Grace Elvina;** *d.* of late J. Monroe Hinds, United States Minister in Brazil; *m.* 1st, Alfred Duggan (*decd.*), Buenos Aires; one *s.* one *d.* (and one *s.* decd.); 2nd, 1917, 1st Marquess Curzon of Kedleston (*d.* 1925). *Publication:* Reminiscences, 1955. *Address:* Bodiam Manor, Sussex. [*Died* 29 *June* 1958.

CURZON, Rt. Rev. Charles Edward; *s.* of Edward Curzon, Kensington; *m.* 1903, May, *d.* of Rev. E. O. Vincent; one *s.* one *d.* *Educ.:* The Royal Grammar School, Lancaster; Christ's College, Cambridge (Classical sch.); Tancred Student Divinity, M.A., D.D. (Lambeth); Curate of S. Andrew's, W. Kensington, 1901-4; Organising Secretary, Additional Curates' Society, 1904-7; Vicar of S. Oswald's, Sheffield, 1908; Vicar of Goole, York, 1917; Secretary to the London Diocesan Fund, 1920; Vicar of S. Barnabas, Kensington, 1926; Rector of S. Margaret's, Lothbury, E.C.; Bishop of Stepney, 1928-36; Bishop of Exeter, 1936-48. *Recreations:* walking, photography. *Address:* 1 Nevern Square, S.W.5. *Club:* Oxford and Cambridge. [*Died* 23 *Aug.* 1954.

CUST, Mrs. Henry (Emmeline Mary Elizabeth), (Nina); *d.* of Sir William Welby-Gregory, 4th Bart., and Hon. Victoria Stuart-Wortley (formerly Maid-of-Honour to Queen Victoria); *m.* 1893, Henry John Cokayne Cust (heir to Barony of Brownlow) (*d.* 1917). *Publications:* Gentlemen Errant, 1909; Wanderers, 1928; Echoes of Larger Life, 1929; Other Dimensions, 1931; Dilectissimo, 1932; Not all the Suns, 1944; A Tub of Gold Fishes, 1950. *Address:* Chancellor's House, 17 Hyde Park Gate, S.W.7. *T.:* Western 6433. [*Died* 29 *Sept.* 1955.

CUST, Brig. Richard B. P.; *see* Purey-Cust.

CUSTARD, R. G.; *see* Goss-Custard.

CUTBILL, Colonel Reginald Heaton Locke, C.M.G. 1919; D.S.O. 1917; *b.* April 1878; *s.* of late Col. H. D. Cutbill, late Royal Irish Rifles, and late Mrs. I. M. Cutbill, *d.* of Joseph Rhodes of Napier, New Zealand; *m.* 1st, 1907, Edith (*d.* 1945), *d.* of late Lt.-Col. L. E. Bearne of Kingsteignton, Devon; one *d.*; 2nd, 1948, Irene M. Woolley, The Laurels, Derby. *Educ.:* St. Helen's Coll., Southsea; Fermoy Coll., Co. Cork. Matabeleland Mounted Police, 1896-98; received Commission in the Royal Irish Rifles, 1899; transferred to Army Service Corps; served Matabele War, 1896; South African War, 1890-92; European War, 1914-18: D.A.Q.M.G. 18th Division, 1915, 1916; A.A. and Q.M.G. 1917-18 (Legion of Honour, C.M.G., D.S.O., Bt. Lt.-Col., despatches five times); A.Q.M.G. Southern Command, India; Deputy Director of Transport, A.H.Q., India; commanded the R.A.S.C. on the Rhine; A.D.S.T. (Scottish Command), 1924-29; retired, 1929; Military Knight of Windsor, 1938-46, resigned, 1946; employed as President Interview Board, War Office, 1940-42; Chief Warden, A.R.P. Windsor, 1942-45; has travelled extensively. *Recreations:* shooting and fishing. *Address:* Roskitt Lodge, Co. Fermanagh, Ireland. *Club:* Army and Navy. [*Died* 21 *June* 1956.

CUTFORTH, Sir Arthur Edwin, Kt., *cr.* 1938; C.B.E. 1926; F.C.A.; *b.* 25 Aug. 1881; *s.* of Samuel Cutforth, Ashlyn, Woodford Green, Essex; *m.* 1920, Alizon Margaret Farrer Ecroyd, *d.* of William Farrer of Whitbarrow Lodge, Grange-over-Sands; three *s.* one *d.* *Educ.:* Bancroft's School, Woodford; Trent College, Derbyshire. Member of the firm of Deloitte, Plender, Griffiths & Co., Chartered Accountants, 1912-1938; President of the Institute of Chartered Accountants, 1934-35 and 1935-36; appointed Accountant Assessor to the Royal Commission on the Coal Industry, 1925; Member of Reorganization Commission for Milk, 1932-33; Member of Food Council, 1932-38; Chairman of the Reorganization Commission for Milk for Great Britain, 1935; Member of Oil from Coal Sub. Cttee. of the Cttee. of Imperial Defence, 1937; Member of the Tithe Redemption Commission till 1938; High Sheriff of Hertfordshire, 1937-38. *Publications:* Audits; Foreign Exchange; Methods of Amalgamation. *Address:* 272 St. James' Court Buckingham Gate, S.W.1; High Crag, Sawrey, Ambleside, Westmorland. *Club:* Alpine. [*Died* 7 *April* 1958.

CUTHBERT, David; retired Commissioner of the Salvation Army; Vice-President and Trustee of the Reliance Benefit Society, 1929-1937; *b.* Perth, Scotland, 1866; *m.* Mary Singer, Salvation Army Officer; two *s.* one *d.* Entered the Salvation Army as an

Officer, 1884; for many years General Secretary for Salvation Army Assurance Society, Ltd.; Director to Empire Migration and Settlement Dept., 1912; Governor of the Hadleigh Land and Industrial Colony, 1924; Chairman of the Board and Joint Managing Director of the Salvation Army Assurance Society, Ltd., 1929-39; went on special mission to Australia and New Zealand, 1939. [*Died* 9 *March* 1953.

CUTHBERT, Harold David; Scots Guards; *b.* 11 Sept. 1909; *s.* of Lady Rayleigh and late Capt. James Harold Cuthbert, D.S.O., Scots Guards; *m.* 1st, 1931, Bridget (who divorced him, 1944), *er. d.* of Sir Clive Milnes-Coates, 2nd Bt. one *s.* two *d.*; 2nd, 1946, Diana Daphne, *d.* of H. L. Holman-Hunt. *Educ.:* Eton; Cambridge. *Address:* Beaufront Castle, Hexham, Northumberland.
[*Died* 2 *July* 1959.

CUTHBERT, William Nicolson; J.P.; *s.* of late William Cuthbert, Edinburgh; *m.* 1915, Berenice Gertrude Bungey; two *s.* one *d.* *Educ.:* Watson's College, Edinburgh. Imperial Bank of Persia, Persia, 1910-31; served 1914-19 East Surrey Regt. and R.A.F., retired Capt. Councillor Bexhill Borough since 1935; Alderman from 1936; Mayor, 1936-42; M.P. (C.) Rye, E. Sussex, 1945-50, Arundel and Shoreham Division of West Sussex, 1950-54. Freeman of Borough of Bexhill, 1942; County Councillor E. Sussex since 1940; J.P. *Recreation:* golf.
[*Died* 7 *May* 1960.

CUTTLE, William Linsdell, M.A.; Fellow Emeritus Downing College, Cambridge (Fellow, 1930-56); *b.* 10 June 1896; 2nd *s.* of George Cuttle, India Office, and Mary, *d.* of James Linsdell; unmarried. *Educ.:* Forest School; Emmanuel College, Cambridge (Scholar); British School at Athens. Served European War, 1914-18; Lieut. R.A.S.C., 1915-19. Class I, Classical Tripos, Parts I and II: Craven student, 1923; British School at Athens, 1923-26. Lecturer in Classics, Univ. of Bristol, 1926-30; Sub-Warden of Wills Hall, 1929-30; Tutor and Dean, Downing College, Cambridge, 1931-1947, Senior Tutor, 1947-50, Librarian, 1934-1956. Has taken part in excavations at Sparta, 1924-26, Vardaroftsa, 1925-26, and Thermi (Lesbos), 1931. *Publications:* articles and reviews mainly on archæological subjects. *Address:* Downing College, Cambridge. *T.:* 59491. [*Died* 15 *Nov.* 1958.

D

DADABHOY, Sir Maneckji Byramji, K.C.S.I., *cr.* 1936; K.C.I.E., *cr.* 1925 (C.I.E. 1911); Kt., *cr.* 1921; LL.D.; *b.* Bombay, 30 July 1865; 2nd *s.* of Khan Bahadur Byramji Dadabhoy, J.P., late Registrar of Joint Stock Companies and Assurances in Bombay; *m.* 1884, Bai Jerbanoo, O.B.E., *d.* of Khan Bahadur Dadabhoy Pallonji; two *d.* *Educ.:* Proprietary High School and St. Xavier's College, Bombay. Joined Middle Temple, 1884; called to Bar, 1887; Advocate of the Bombay High Court, 1887; J.P. Bombay, 1888; Advocate of the Central Provinces Judicial Commissioner's Court, 1890; Member of the Nagpur Municipality, 1890-1930; Government Advocate Central Provinces, 1896. President of the Central Provinces and Berar Industrial Conference at Raipur, 1907; nominated by the Central Provinces Government to the Gov.-General's Legislative Council, 1908; elected to the Governor-General's Legislative Council, 1910; elected by the non-official members of the Central Provinces Legislative Council as their first representative to the Governor-General's Legislative Council, 1914; Governor of Imperial Bank of India, 1920-32; elected to the Council of State, 1921; nominated on the Council of State by Government of India, 1926, 1931, and 1937; President of the All India Industrial Conference held at Calcutta, 1911; Member Indian Fiscal Commission; Member Royal Commission on Indian Currency and Exchange; Delegate Second Round Table Conference, 1931; President of the Council of State, 1933-36 and 1937-46; Managing Director of the Nagpur Electric Light and Power Co., Ltd., and Berar Manufacturing Co., Ltd., Badnera; Managing Proprietor of several Collieries, and a Mining Syndicate; and several Gin and Press Factories in all parts of India. *Publications:* Commentaries on the Central Provinces Tenancy Act, 1888; Commentaries on the Central Provinces Tenancy Act, 1898. *Address:* Nagpur, Central Provinces, India; Kingsnympton Hall, Kingston Hill, Surrey. *Clubs:* Royal Societies (Foreign Member), Overseas League, Royal Automobile; Calcutta (Calcutta); Willingdon, Asian (Bombay); Chelmsford (Simla and New Delhi); Imperial Delhi Gymkhana (New Delhi); Rotary (Delhi); Central Provinces (Nagpur).
[*Died* 14 *Dec.* 1953.

D'AETH, Rear-Adm. A. C. S. H.; *see* Hughes D'aeth.

DAGA, Raja Rai Bahadur Sir Seth Bisesardass, K.C.I.E., *cr.* 1934; Kt., *cr.* 1921; Rai Bahadur 1901; Raja 1938; banker, mill owner and mine owner; *b.* 1877; *s.* of late Dewan Bahadur Sir Kasturchand Daga, K.C.I.E.; *m.* Lady Krishnabai; one *s.* *Educ.:* private. Chairman Nagpur Electric Light and Power Co. Ltd.; Director Model Mills, Nagpur, Ltd.; Director Berar Manufacturing Co. Ltd., Badnera; Director Bank of India, Ltd., Nagpur Branch: Life Member, Countess of Dufferin Fund Committee: Holds First Class Tazim of Bikaner State: Member of Legislative Assembly, Bikaner State. *Publication:* Kasturchand Memorial Dufferin Hospital for Women at Nagpur, C.P. *Address:* Nagpur, C.P., India. *T.A.:* Lucky. *Clubs:* Willingdon (Bombay); Gondewana (Nagpur).
[*Died* 18 *Aug.* 1941.
[*But death not notified in time for inclusion in Who Was Who 1941–1950, first edn.*

DAHL, Dr. Knut; Professor Dr. emeritus; *b.* 28 Oct. 1871; *s.* of Eyvind Dahl, estate manager, Hakedal, and Rebekka Frederikke Elisabeth Praetorius; *m.* Marie Astrup; one *s.* one *d.* *Educ.:* Oslo University. Scientific expedition on behalf of Zoological Museum, Oslo University, to South Africa and N.W. Australia, 1893-96; Fellowship at Trondhjem Museum, 1898-1900; Director of Biol. Station, Trondhjem, 1900-3; scientific assistant Director of Fisheries Department, Bergen, 1903-12; Director of Experimental Freshwater Fishery Work, 1912-45; Professor of Pisciculture, Agricultural College by Oslo, 1921-42; Member of the Academy of Science, Oslo; Corresponding Member Salmon and Trout Association, London; Hon. Foreign Member Flyfishers' Club; Chairman of Salmon and Trout Cttee., Internat. Council for the Study of the Sea, Copenhagen. Knight, Order of St. Olaf, 1948. *Publications:* Dyr og Vildmend, 1898; new edition Afrikanske Jagter, 1923, 1944; Blandt Australiens Vilde, 1927, 1942; Salmon and Trout, a Handbook, 1918; The Age and Growth of Salmon and Trout in Norway, 1911; Vildmandsliv og friluftsferder, 1922, new ed. 1943; In Savage Australia, 1926; between fifty and a hundred papers and treatises on fishing subjects, also biological and economical subjects, mainly fishery, biology. *Recreations:* shooting and fishing. *Address:* Zoological Museum, Trondhjemsveien 23, Oslo; Dalset, Smestad, by Oslo. *T.:* Oslo 699526. *Club:* (Hon.) Flyfishers'.
[*Died* 6 *June* 1953.

DAIN, George Rutherford, C.I.E. 1930; M.C.; *b.* 1884; *m.* 1909, Winifred, *d.* of late A. W. Stanfield, Wakefield; one *s.* two *d.* *Educ.:* Tonbridge School; Clare College, Cambridge.

Joined East India Railway Co., 1906; served European War (France and Gallipoli), 1914-18 (M.C.); Principal, Government of India Railway School of Transportation (Railway Staff College), 1925; Manager, Calcutta Tramways, 1926. [*Died* 7 *Aug.* 1954.

DAIN, Sir John Rutherford, Kt., *cr.* 1938; C.I.E. 1929; Indian Civil Service (retired); *b.* 13 Jan. 1883. *Educ.:* Tonbridge; Hertford College, Oxford, B.A. Entered Indian Civil Service, 1907; Secretary to Government of Bihar and Orissa, 1922; Commissioner, 1930; Revenue Commissioner, Orissa, 1937; Member, Federal Public Service Commission, 1939; retired 1942. *Address:* Pepins, Higham Lane, Tonbridge. [*Died* 31 *Jan.* 1957.

DAINES, Percy; M.P. (Lab.-Co-op.) East Ham North since 1945. Served War of 1939-45 with Royal Engineers. *Address:* House of Commons, S.W.1. [*Died* 3 *March* 1957.

DAINTREE, Capt. John Dodson, C.B.E. 1919; *b.* Swavesey, Cambridgeshire, 2 Jan. 1864; *s.* of John Osborn Daintree and Jane Dodson; *m.* 1893, Mary Francis (*d.* 1934), *d.* of Rear-Admiral Edward Kelly; one *s.* one *d.* *Educ.:* Royal Naval Academy, Gosport; H.M.S. Britannia. Entered Royal Navy, 1877; Midshipman, 1879; served in H.M.S. Monarch at Battle of Alexandria and subsequent operations at Alexandria and Port Said, 1882; Lieut. of H.M.S. Griffon in East India during blockade of E. Africa, 1889; Commander, 1899; Superintendent of Wei Hai Wei Dockyard, 1900; retired with rank of Captain, 1908, to take up appointment under Board of Trade as Inspector, Life Saving Apparatus; Senior Inspector, 1910-23; served as D.N.T.O. and P.N.T.O., Newhaven and Liverpool, 1914-19; Inspector-General of Coastguard, 1923-26. *Address:* The Hatch, Beaconsfield, Bucks. [*Died* 21 *Sept.* 1952.

DAKIN, Henry Drysdale, F.R.S. 1917; F.R.I.C., D.Sc. Leeds, B.Sc. Vict., Hon. D.Sc. Yale; Hon. LL.D. Leeds; Hon. Ph.D. Heidelberg; Director of Research Laboratory, Scarborough; Chevalier Legion of Honour, France; *b.* London, 1880; *m.* Susan Dows Herter. *Educ.:* Universities of Leeds, London, and Heidelberg; Lister Institute. Davy Medallist of Royal Society; Conné Medallist of Chemists Club, New York. *Publications:* Oxydations and Reductions in Animal Organisms; Handbook of Antiseptics. *Address:* Edgehill, Scarborough-on-Hudson, N.Y. *Club:* Century (New York). [*Died* 10 *Feb.* 1952.

DAKYNS, Winifred, C.B.E. 1919; Hon. Serving Sister, Order of St. John of Jerusalem; *b.* 1875; 7th *d.* of late John Pattinson, J.P., of Gateshead on Tyne; *m.* 1902, Henry Graham Dakyns (*d.* 1937), *e. s.* of late Henry Graham Dakyns of Clifton College, Bristol. *Educ:* Gateshead High School; Newnham College, Cambridge. Worked in Women's V.A.D. Department (under Joint Council Red Cross Society and Order of St. John), 1914-17; Assistant Director Women's Royal Naval Service, 1917-19. *Address:* Wickham Farmhouse, Hassocks, Sussex. *T.:* Hurstpierpoint 3119. *Club:* University Women's. [*Died* 22 *Jan.* 1960.

DALAL, Sir Ratanji Dinshaw, Kt., *cr.* 1942; C.I.E. 1936; M.R.C.P. (Lond.); D.P.H. (Lond.); Member Indian Central Legislative Assembly, 1930-45; *b.* Broach, Guzerat, 27 July 1868. *Educ.:* Khan Bahadur R.S. Dalal High School, Broach; Gokuldas Tejpal School, Bombay; Elphinstone High School, Bombay; Grant Medical Coll., Bombay; University College, London; St. Bartholomew's Hospital, London. L.M. & S. (Bombay) 1894; M.R.C.S. (Eng.) 1895; L.R.C.P. (Lond.) 1895; D.P.H., R.C.P.S. (Lond.) 1916; M.R.C.P. (Lond.) 1931; R.M.O., Finsbury Dispensary, London, 1896-1897; Secretary of State's Doctor for Plague Duty in India, 1897; Deputy Sanitary Commissioner, Southern Registration District, Bombay, 1913; Assistant Director of Public Health Southern Registration District, 1921; Director, Vaccine Institute, Belgaum, 1923; retired, 1925. Kaisar-i-Hind Silver Medal, 1923; Silver Jubilee Medal, 1935; Coronation Medal, 1937. *Publication:* A Manual of Vaccination, 1930. *Address:* 14 The Fort, Belgaum, M. & S.M. Railway, Bombay Presidency, India. *Clubs:* English, Parsi, Belgaum; Mahableshwar. [*Died* 6 *April* 1957.

DALE, Charles Ernest, C.M.G. 1914; C.B.E. 1920; late Financial Commissioner to Government of Southern Nigeria; *b.* 26 Feb. 1867; *m.* 1892, Ada, *d.* of late Edmund Parr. *Educ.:* King's College, London. Late Fellow Society Accountants and Auditors; late Fellow Royal Statistical Society; Assistant Director-General Customs, Niger Coast Protectorate, 1895; Assistant P.M.G. (additl.), 1896; Treasurer, 1898; seconded for special service to Lagos Colony pending amalgamation, 1904; Financial Commissioner to the combined Administration, 1906, and Member of the Executive and Legislative Councils; retired, 1914; Assistant Passport Officer, F.O., 1914; Colonial Audit Dept., 1915; Deputy Assistant Director (M.R. 3), War Office, 1917-20; reverted to C.A. Dept., 1920; retired, 1937. *Recreation:* golf. *Address:* 51 Templars Crescent, Church End, Finchley, N.3. *T.:* Finchley 0670. [*Died* 23 *June* 1956.

DALE, Harold Edward, C.B. 1919; *b.* 5 December 1875; *o. surv. s.* of late H. J. Dale; *m.* 1911, Isabel Woodrow (*d.* 1950), *e. d.* of S. G. Warner, F.I.A. *Educ.:* St. Paul's School; Balliol College, Oxford (Scholar); Fellow of New Coll., 1898-1905. Entered Civil Service and appointed to Colonial Office, 1898; Sec. to Development Commission, 1910; Assistant Secretary (acting) to the Board of Agriculture and Fisheries, 1917, and appointed permanent, 1919; special commissioner on the Civil Services of Fiji and W. Pacific, 1920; Financial Comr., Jamaica, 1923-24; Principal Asst. Secretary, Ministry of Agriculture and Fisheries, 1927-35; retired 1935; Sidney Ball Lecturer, Oxford, 1943. *Publications:* The Higher Civil Service of Great Britain, 1941; Personnel and Problems of the Higher Civil Service, 1943; chapter on Parliament and the Civil Service, in Parliament, A Survey, 1952; (jt. ed. with D. J. Allan) fourth edn. Jowett's Translation of Plato, 1953. *Address:* Norham End, Norham Road, Oxford. *T.:* Oxford 57919. *Club:* Savile. [*Died* 30 *July* 1954.

DALE, Rev. Harold Montague, M.A.; B.D.; F.R.S.A.; retired; *b.* 9 Nov. 1873; *s.* of Alfred and Clara Elizabeth Dale; *m.* 1st, 1902, Evelyn Beatrice (*d.* 1934), *d.* of Alfred Arnold, Heathcourt, Bournemouth; two *s.*; 2nd, 1939, Dora Winifred, *d.* of John Wright, Bournemouth. *Educ.:* private schools; London College of Divinity; University College, Durham. Deacon, 1898; Priest, 1899; Curate to the late Bishop of Sodor and Man at Southport and Birmingham Parish Church; Vicar of Christ Church, Summerfield, Birmingham, 1908-18; Vicar of Holy Trinity, Tulse Hill, 1919-33; Vicar of St. Michael and All Angels, Bournemouth, 1933-50. Hon. Canon of Southwark Cathedral, 1932; Canon Emeritus, 1943; formerly Hon. Chaplain to Bishop of Birmingham; Chairman of Governors of Secondary Schools, Bournemouth. *Publications:* Religion, its Place and Power; Worship and Communion, 1930; Religion: its basis and development, 1932; Religious Experience and Religious Expression (pamphlet). *Recreation:* motoring. *Address:* 6A Portarlington Road, Bournemouth. *T.:* Westbourne 63514. [*Died* 30 *May* 1951.

DALE, James A.; *b.* 1874; *s.* of J. A. Dale of Birmingham and Elizabeth Holmes of Manchester; *m.* 1904, Margaret, *y. d.* of James Holden Butler of Birmingham; three *s.* *Educ.:*

Tindal Street School, Birmingham; King Edward VI. Grammar School, Camp Hill; Mason College, Birmingham; Merton College, Oxford. Tutor at Borough Road Training College, Isleworth, London, 1902-3; Oxford Univ. Extension Lecturer in Literature and Education, 1902-8; Professor (first) of Education in McGill University, Montreal, Canada, 1908-20; Professor (first) of Social Science, Univ. of Toronto, and Director Department of Social Service, 1920-30 (retired); President of the University Settlement, Montreal, from its foundation to 1914; Member of the Council of Public Instruction for the Province of Quebec, 1911-20; on Educational Service with the Canadian Corps Overseas, 1918-19; President of the Ontario Federation of Home and School Associations, 1921-26. *Publications:* articles in various reviews on literary, social, and educational subjects. *Address:* 175 New St., Burlington, Ontario, Canada. [*Died* 26 *Nov.* 1951.

DALE, Louise; (Lady Mulleneux-Grayson) (Louise Mary); *b.* Newcastle upon Tyne; *d.* of late Richard John De Lancey; *m.* 1st, Ronald Hamilton Earle (*d.* 1919); one *s.*; 2nd, 1927 (as his second wife), Lt.-Col. Sir Henry Mulleneux-Grayson, K.B.E. (*d.* 1951). *Educ.:* England, France, Germany. Studied singing under Mme. Albani, Sir George Henschel and Monsieur Bouhy in Paris. Member of Women's Guild of Empire; C.St.J. *Recreations:* music, reading, travel. *Address:* Ravenspoint, Holyhead. [*Died* 4 *June* 1954.

DALE, Ven. Canon Percy John, O.B.E. 1919; Archdeacon of Sarum, 1936-50, Archdeacon Emeritus since 1951; Master of S. Nicholas Hospital, Salisbury, since 1938; Canon and Prebendary of Bishopstone in Sarum Cathedral since 1925; *b.* 23 May 1876; *s.* of Henry John Dale and Emmeline Nevill; *m.* 1912, Dorothy, 2nd *d.* of Rev. C. S. Churchill; one *s.* one *d.* *Educ.:* Magdalen College, Oxford; Wells Theological College. B.A. 1898; M.A. 1901; Deacon, 1899; Priest, 1900; Curate of Harrow-on-the-Hill, 1899-1907; London Diocesan Home Missioner, S. Peter's Harrow, 1907-11; Rector of Fittleton, Salisbury, 1911-20; Rector of West Dean with East Grimstead, 1920-38; Hon. Secretary, Welfare of Imperial Forces Board, 1912-19; Treasurer and Secretary, Salisbury Diocesan Board of Finance, 1919-33; Hon. Sec., Salisbury Diocesan Conference, 1933-39; Member of Convocation and Church Assembly, 1935-50 (Proctor, 1935-37); Church Commissioner and member of the Board of Governors, 1947-53. *Recreation:* golf. *Address:* Master's Lodgings, S. Nicholas Hospital, Salisbury, Wilts. *T.A.:* Dale, S. Nicholas, Salisbury. *T.:* Salisbury 2967. [*Died* 22 *April* 1957.

DALRYMPLE, Col. Sir F. N.; *see* Elphinstone-Dalrymple.

DALRYMPLE, Sir Hew (Clifford) Hamilton-, 9th Bt.; *cr.* 1697; *b.* 11 Aug. 1888; *s.* of 8th Bt. and Alice, *d.* of Major-General Hon. Sir H. H. Clifford, V.C.; *S.* father, 1920; *m.* 1919, Ann, *y.d.* of late Augustus Thorne, J.P., D.L.; two *s.* one *d.* (and one *d.* decd.). *Educ.:* Beaumont; Christ Church, Oxford. B.A. J.P. for East Lothian; Member of Queen's Bodyguard for Scotland. *Heir:* *s.* Hew Fleetwood, Major Grenadier Guards [*b.* 9 Apr. 1926; *m.* 1954, Lady Anne-Louise Keppel, *d.* of 9th Earl of Albemarle, M.C.; two *s.*]. *Address:* Leuchie, North Berwick, Scotland. *T.:* North Berwick 403. [*Died* 12 *March* 1959.

DALRYMPLE-HAMILTON, Col. Sir North Victor Cecil, K.C.V.O. *cr.* 1952 (C.V.O. 1937); C.B. 1949; V.L.; Chairman Territorial and Auxiliary Forces Association of County of Ayr; *b.* 1883; *e. s.* of late Col. Hon. North de Coigny Dalrymple-Hamilton, M.V.O., J.P., D.L., Scots Guards, and late Marcia Kathleen Anne, *y. d.* of late Hon. Sir Adolphus Frederic Octavius Liddell, K.C.B.; *m.* 1910, Lady Marjorie Alice Coke (*d.* 1946), *e. d.* of 3rd Earl of Leicester. *Educ.:* Eton; Royal Military College, Sandhurst. Formerly Lt. Scots Guards, and temp. Maj. R.M. 1914-1915; Capt. and Brevet Lt.-Col. (temp Maj.) Scots Guards, Special Reserve; Capt. Queen's Bodyguard for Scotland (Royal Company of Archers). *Address:* 11 Mount Street, W.1. *T.:* Grosvenor 2031; Bargany, Dailly, Ayrshire. *Club:* Guards. [*Died* 16 *Feb.* 1953.

DALRYMPLE HAY, Sir Charles John, 5th Bt., *cr.* 1798; C.V.O. 1928 (M.V.O. 1924); *b.* 21 March 1865; *y. s.* of Admiral Right Hon. Sir John Charles Dalrymple Hay, 3rd Bt., G.C.B.; *S. b.* Sir William Dalrymple Hay, Bt., 1929; *m.* 1906, Rose (*d.* 1927), *d.* of Captain W. T. Hickman. *Educ.:* Harrow. Served in Foreign Office, 1887-95, and in Privy Council Office, 1895-1928. *Heir:* *cousin,* James Brian Dalrymple Hay, *b.* 19 Jan. 1928. *Address:* c/o Lloyds Bank Ltd., Belgrave Rd. Branch, S.W.1. [*Died* 22 *March* 1952.

DALRYMPLE-WHITE, Lieut.-Col. Sir Godfrey Dalrymple, 1st Bt., *cr.* 1926; *s.* of late General Sir Henry Dalrymple White, K.C.B., and Alice, *d.* of late Neill Malcolm of Poltalloch; *b.* 6 July 1866; *m.* 1912, Hon. Catherine Mary Cary, *e. d.* of 12th Viscount Falkland; one *s.* one *d.* *Educ.:* Wellington; Sandhurst. Joined Grenadier Guards, 1885; served as A.D.C. to G.O.C. British North America, 1892-93; to G.O.C. Home District, 1899-1900; served for two years in the S. African campaign (despatches, Queen's medal 3 clasps, King's medal 2 clasps); Commanded Reserve Batt. Grenadier Guards, 1914-16; served on Staff, France, 1916-18 (despatches thrice, Brevet Lieut.-Col.); contested (C.) Devizes Division of Wilts. 1906; M.P. (C.) Southport, 1910-1923, and 1924-31; Governor of Wellington College, 1936; F.Z.S. *Recreations:* shooting, fishing, big game. *Heir:* *s.* Henry Arthur Dalrymple, D.F.C. 1941 and Bar 1942, Wing Commander R.A.F.V.R. [*b.* 5 Nov. 1917; *m.* 1948, Mary, *o. d.* of Capt. Robert Thomas; one *s.* (*b.* 26 Nov. 1950)]. *Address:* Dormer Cottage, Charlwood, Surrey. *Club:* Carlton. [*Died* 1 *April* 1954.

DALTON, Capt. C. G.; *see* Grant-Dalton.

DALTON, Sir John Cornelius, Kt., *cr.* 1942; M.I.E.E., F.C.I.S.; Barrister-at-Law; Chairman, Southern United Telephone Co.; Director, W. T. Henley's Telegraph Works Ltd.; *s.* of late James C. Dalton, D.L., and Janet Denehan; *m.* 1st, 1916, Winifred Robertson (*d.* 1956); one *d.* (and one *s.* killed on active service, 1944); 2nd, Dorothy Irene, *d.* of late Frank Foulston Ashdown. Served European War with R.E. (Signals) in France, 1914-18; Captain R.E. 1917; Hon. Colonel Royal Corps of Signals, 1941; Chairman Public Utilities Coal Cttee. and Regional Fuel and Power Controller, London and S.E. England Regions during War of 1939-45. *Publications:* Editor Wills' Electric Lighting and other Text-Books on the Law relating to Electricity Supply; also numerous papers on public utility and economic subjects. *Recreations:* boxing, golf. *Address:* 10 Chester House, Eccleston Place, S.W.1. *T.:* Sloane 1892; Little Brook, Holmwood, Dorking. *T.:* Dorking 73113. *Clubs:* Savage, Bath. [*Died* 14 *May* 1959.

D'ALVAREZ, Madame (Marguerite Alvarez de Rocafuarte); Opera singer; *d.* of Marquis de Rocafuarte and Marie Poupard de Neuflize. *Educ.:* Paris. Sang at Brussels, Rouen, Marseilles, Algiers, Milan (La Scala), Chicago Opera House, Westminster Abbey, Boston, New York, London Opera House, Covent Gdn. *Address:* 26 Groom Pl., S.W.1. [*Died* 18 *Oct.* 1953.

DALWOOD, Lt.-Col. John; *see* Hall-Dalwood.

DALY, Sir Oscar Bedford, Kt., *cr.* 1942; Q.C.; M.B.E. 1919; Hon. LL.D. Univ. of Dublin, 1944; Chief Justice of The Bahamas, 1939-45; *b.* 1880; *s.* of late Robert Bedford Daly; *m.* 1915, Elizabeth, *d.* of late William Lennon, County Inspector, R.I.C. *Educ.:* Lycée de Pau; Königliches Gymnasium, Leipzig; Trinity College, Dublin (Moderator Modern Literature). Called to Irish Bar, 1903; North East Circuit; admitted Bar, Kenya Colony, 1910; commissioned 9th South Wales Borderers, 1915; transferred 15th Welch Regt., 1916; Somme, Ypres, 1916; Divisional Intelligence Officer, 23rd Division, France, Italy, 1917, 1918 (despatches, M.B.E.); returned practise, Kenya Colony, 1919; called to Inner Bar, Northern Ireland, 1938; Past President Law Society of Colony of Kenya; Acted Registrar, Diocese of Mombasa, several occasions; Hon. Member College Historical Society; Life Member Royal Dublin Society. *Recreations:* golf, tennis, walking. *Clubs:* Mombasa; Nairobi; Country (Bahamas). [*Died* 29 *June* 1953.

DALY, Thomas Denis, C.B.E. 1945; M.C.; p.s.c.; Brigadier (Retd.); Deputy Commissioner-in-Chief, St. John Ambulance Brigade; *b.* 3 December 1890; *e. s.* of late James T. Daly, Raford, Leamington; *m.* 1923, Honor Mary Evelyn, *e. d.* of late Hon. Everard Digby Pepys, Old Park Farm, Waltham Cross, Herts. *Educ.:* Rossall; Munich; University College, Oxford (M.A.). Served European war 1914-18, Royal Welch Fusiliers, Gallipoli, Mesopotamia (wounded, despatches); Army of the Black Sea, Caucasus, 1919-20; Civil Employment, Transcaucasia, 1921; General Staff, Constantinople, 1922-23; Staff, Army of the Rhine, 1927-28; Brigade Major, Northern Command, 1929-31; Military Attaché Belgrade, Prague and Bucharest, 1932-36; Military Member British Services Mission to Portugal, 1938; Military Attaché British Embassy, Berlin, 1939; commanded 183 and 137 Infantry Brigade; Commander North Caribbean Area, 1942-44; Bt. Major, 1929; Bt. Lt.-Col. 1932; Col. 1935; Military Adviser, British Embassy, Paris, 1944; Military Attaché, British Embassy, Paris, 1945-46; retd. Sept. 1946; Chief Berlin Mission, Inter-Allied Reparation Agency, 1946-48; Deputy Chief of Mission, International Refugees Organisation, Rome, 1948-49. Governor Rossall School, 1952. Officier de la Légion d'Honneur, 1947; Croix de Guerre avec palme. K.St.J. *Address:* 2 Petyt Place, Chelsea, S.W.3. *T.:* Flaxman 0211. *Clubs:* United Service, Garrick. [*Died* 21 *Nov.* 1956.

DALYELL OF THE BINNS, Lt.-Col. Gordon, C.I.E. 1935; D.L. West Lothian, J.P.; *b.* 16 Jan. 1887; *s.* of late Lt.-Colonel William Loch, C.I.E., and late Edith Mary, *d.* of James Gibbs, C.S.I., C.I.E.; assumption of name and arms of Dalyell of the Binns in place of Loch officially recognised by Lord Lyon, King of Arms, 1938; *m.* 1928, Eleanor Isabel (Nora), who in 1935 succeeded her father, Sir James Bruce Wilkie-Dalyell of the Binns, 9th Baronet, as *o. c.* and *heir* of tailzie; one *s.* *Educ.:* Cheltenham College, R.M.C., Sandhurst. Attached to The North Staffordshire Regt. 1905; joined the 97th Infantry, I.A., 1906; attached to the Political Resident in the Persian Gulf, 1908; Private Secretary to Sir William Willcocks on the Irrigation Survey of Mesopotamia, 1910; attached Army Headquarters, India (General Staff, Intelligence), 1912; appointed to Indian Political Department, 1913; Army Headquarters, India (General Staff, Intelligence), 1914; Persian Gulf under the C.P.O., M.E.F., 1916-18; Under-Secretary to the Government of India, 1919-23; Political Agent, Gilgit, 1924-1927; Mysore, Kathiawar and Rewa States, 1928-31, Persian Gulf, 1932-37; retired 1938; Member of the Queen's Bodyguard for Scotland (The Royal Company of Archers); Unicorn Pursuivant of Arms, 1939; A.A. Liaison Officer, R.A.F., Turnhouse, 1939-42; Home Guard, 1942-45. *Publication:* The Family of Loch, 1934. *Recreations:* shooting, fishing, Scottish history and genealogy. *Address:* The Binns, Linlithgow. *Clubs:* United Service; New (Edinburgh). [*Died* 15 *Sept.* 1953.

DALZELL, Lt.-Col. John Norton; late 7th Rajput Regt., I.A.; *b.* 17 Nov. 1897; *s.* of late James Taylor of Lisnamallard, Co. Tyrone, and Eleanor Louisa, *d.* of late Capt. F. J. Slade-Gully of Trevennen, Cornwall; *m.* 1927, The Lady Muriel Marjorie Dalzell, *o. d.* of 16th Earl of Carnwath, C.B.; one *s.* *Educ.:* Cheltenham College; R.M.C. Sandhurst. Joined Suffolk Regt. 1915; served European war, France, 1916-17, Salonika, 1918; transferred Indian Army, 1918; served in Afghan War, 1919, with 25th Cavalry F.F. and Waziristan 1919-21; 7th Rajputs 1921; Razmak Field Force 1922-23; retd. 1938, R.A.F.V.R. 1938; re-empld. I.A. 1940; raised and commanded 18th Bn. 7th Rajput Regiment, 1941-45; Administrative Comdt., Cawnpore, 1945-46; retired, 1948; assumed by Royal Licence 1927 surname and Arms of Dalzell in lieu of Taylor. *Address:* 16 Shepherd House, Shepherd Street, Mayfair, W.1. *T.:* Grosvenor 1516. *Club:* United Service. [*Died* 12 *April* 1957.

DAMPIER, Sir William Cecil Dampier (formerly Whetham); Kt., *cr.* 1931; F.R.S. 1901; Sc.D.; Fellow of Trinity College, Cambridge, 1891; Lecturer, 1895-1922; Tutor, 1907-1917; Senior Tutor, 1913-17; Fellow of Winchester Coll., 1917-47; a Vice-Pres. Roy. Agric. Soc., 1948 (Gold Medal) 1936; *b.* London, 27 Dec. 1867; *o. s.* of late Charles Langley Whetham and Mary Ann, *y. d.* of Thomas Dampier of Kingston Manor, Yeovil, Somerset; *m.* 1897, Catherine Durning (*d.* 1952), *e. d.* of late Robert Durning Holt of Liverpool, and High Borrans, Westmorland; one *s.* five *d.* *Educ.:* Trinity College, Cambridge. Coutts Trotter Student, 1889; Clerk Maxwell Scholar, 1893. Sec. Agric. Research Council 1931-35, Member 1935-45; a Development Commissioner, 1933-51; sometime Chm. of Home Office Cttee. on Factory Lighting and of the Machinery Cttees. of the Ministry of Agriculture; an appointed Mem. of the Central Agricultural Wages Board, 1925-42. *Publications:* papers in Transactions of the Royal Society and elsewhere on various scientific, agricultural, economic, and sociolgocial subjects; Solution and Electrolysis, 1895; Theory of Solution, 1902; The Recent Development of Physical Science, 1904-24; The Theory of Experimental Electricity, 1905; The Foundations of Science, 1912; Matter and Change, an Introduction to Physical and Chemical Science, 1924; Politics and the Land, 1927; A History of Science and its relations with Philosophy and Religion, 1929-48; A Shorter History of Science, 1944; Cambridge and Elsewhere; (with his wife) Studies in Nature and Country Life, 1903; Life of Colonel Nathaniel Whetham, a Forgotten Soldier of the Civil Wars, 1907; The Family and the Nation, a Study in Natural Inheritance and Social Responsibility, 1909; Back to the Land, a Medley, 1910; Heredity and Society; An Introduction to Eugenics; (with his daughter) Cambridge Readings in the Literature of Science, 1924. *Recreations:* motoring, etc. *Address:* Upwater Lodge, Cambridge. *T.:* Cambridge 5178. *Clubs:* Athenæum; University Pitt, County (Cambridge). [*Died* 11 *Dec.* 1952.

DANA, Robert Washington, O.B.E.; M.A.; M.Inst.C.E.; *b.* 1868; *s.* of late Wm. P. W. Dana, marine painter, member of the American National Academy of Design, formerly of Boston, U.S.A.; *m.* 1900, Anna Kane (*d.* 1956), of New York. *Educ.:* Paris; Clifton Coll.; Pembroke College, Cambridge; M.A. (Honours in Mathematics). Civil engineering pupil and afterwards Assistant to Sir John Wolfe Barry, K.C.B., on construction of Tower Bridge, Barry Docks, etc.; Resident Engineer for reconstruction of Kew Bridge; Secretary of Institution of Naval Architects, London, and Editor of the Transactions, 1901-1935; awarded Order of Crown of Belgium for work at Ministry of Munitions as Assistant Director of Artillery Supply for Allies; subsequently transferred to Staff of Director of Naval Construction at Admiralty; Chevalier de la Légion d'Honneur; Hon. Freeman of Worshipful Company of Shipwrights. *Recreation:* sailing. *Address:* Cockmoyle, Rock, Cornwall. *Club:* Athenæum. [*Died* 3 *Dec.* 1956.

DANBY, The Rev. Dr. Herbert; Regius Professor of Hebrew, Oxford, and Canon of Christ Church since 1936; Treasurer of Christ Church Cathedral since 1943; *b.* 20 Jan. 1889; *y. s.* of late Ezra Danby, Leeds; *m.* 1923, Hilda, *e. d.* of late Canon P. Stacy Waddy; one *s.* three *d.* *Educ.:* Church Middle Class School, Leeds; Keble College, Oxford. Holroyd Musical Scholar; F.R.C.O., 1907; Junior Septuagint Prize; Pusey and Ellerton Scholar; Final Hon. School Theology (Aegrotat); 1st Class Final Hon. School Oriental Languages; Houghton Syriac Prize; Senior Kennicott Scholar; M.A. 1914; D.D. 1923; Hon. D.Litt. Heb. (New York), 1937. Bishop's Coll., Cheshunt, 1912; Deacon, 1913; Priest, 1914; Curate of Waddesdon, Bucks, 1913-14; Subwarden of St. Deiniol's Library, Hawarden, 1914-19; Librarian, St. George's Cathedral, Jerusalem, 1919; Residentiary Canon, St. George's Cathedral Church, Jerusalem, 1921-36; Grinfield Lecturer on the Septuagint, 1939-43; Examining Chaplain to the Bishop of Jerusalem, 1928-36; Dean of the Palestine Board of Higher Studies, 1923-36; The Times Correspondent for Palestine and Transjordan, 1923-36; Pres. Palestine Oriental Society, 1934; Examining Chaplain to the Bishop of Monmouth, 1939-41. *Publications:* Editor: Journal of the Palestine Oriental Society, 1920-36; Tractate Sanhedrin, Mishna and Tosefta, 1919; The Jew and Christianity, 1927; The Sixty-three Tractates of the Mishnah, translated with Introduction, etc., 1933; English (phonetic) and Modern Hebrew Dictionary, 1939; Maimonides' Mishneh Torah, Book Nine, Book of Offerings, 1950; Book Ten, Book of Cleanness, 1953; (translated from the Hebrew), Joseph Klausner's Jesus of Nazareth, 1925; History of Modern Hebrew Literature, 1932; H. N. Bialik's, And it Came to Pass, Biblical Legends, 1938. *Recreations:* golf, music. *Address:* Christ Church, Oxford. *T.:* Oxford 4317. [*Died* 29 *March* 1953.

DANDRIDGE, Cecil Gerald Graham, C.V.O., 1948; M.Inst.T.; Chief Commercial Manager, Eastern Region, British Railways, Liverpool St., 1948-55; retired 1955; *b.* 29 Aug. 1890; *o. s.* of late Dennis Dandridge; *m.* 1924, Princess Olga Galitzine; no *c.* *Educ.:* privately. Served European War, 1914-18, Major R.E., France, N. Russia, S. Russia, Asia Minor (Russian Order of St. Anne). District Traffic Superintendent, Anatolian Rly., Turkey, 1919; Asst. Dist. Traffic Manager, G.C.R., Manchester, 1921; Dist. Passenger Man., L.N.E.R., Manchester, 1923; London Dist. Pass. Man., L.N.E.R., 1926; Advertising Man., L.N.E.R., 1928; Asst. Pass. Man., Southern Area, L.N.E.R., 1942, Pass. Man., 1944; Chm., Rly. Exec. Pass. Cttee., 1946-47; Actg. Goods Manager, S. Area, L.N.E.R. (in addition to Pass. Man.), 1947. *Publications:* contrib. to Proc. Inst. of Transport. *Address:* 2 Dukes Lane, W.8. *Club:* Arts. [*Died* 17 *Nov.* 1960.

DANIEL, Brig. James Alfred, C.I.E. 1943; D.S.O. 1919; M.C.; late The Welch Regt.; *b.* 26 Oct. 1893; *er. s.* of late Rev. A. Daniel; *m.* 1930, Sheila Vivienne, 4th *d.* of Admiral John Nicholas, Alver Cottage, Alverstoke; one *d.* Entered Army, 1912; Capt. 1915; Major, 1933; Lt.-Col. 1939; Col. 1943; served European War, 1914-19 (wounded twice, despatches twice, D.S.O., M.C.); attached to Sudan Defence Force, 1925-27; Assistant Adjutant, Army Technical School (Boys), 1931-33; retired pay, 1946. *Address:* c/o Westminster Bank, Dean Bradley Street, S.W.1. [*Died* 6 *July* 1959.

DANIELL, Very Rev. Edward M.; Canon of Westminster Cathedral since 1931; Chaplain to Convent of the Sacred Heart, and High School, at 212 Hammersmith Road, W.6; *b.* 1864; *s.* of Edward James Daniell; *g. s.* of Captain Edward Maxwell Daniell, East India Company. *Educ.:* Harrow. Received into the Church 1883; Priest, 1897; Assistant Priest at SS. Peter and Paul, Rosoman Street, E.C.1, 1897, and at The Assumption, Warwick Street, 1899; Rector of SS. Anselm's and Cecilia's, Kingsway, 1906-41. *Address:* 212 Hammersmith Road, W.6. *T.:* Riverside 4370. *Club:* Constitutional. [*Died* 6 *Feb.* 1952.

DANIELL, Lt.-Col. (Bt. Colonel), William Augustus Bampfylde, C.B.E. 1942; D.S.O. 1918; T.D.; retired; *b.* 15 Dec. 1875; *s.* of Augustus Warwick Bampfylde Daniell and Blanche Caroline Leith-Hay; *m.* 1902, Grace, *d.* of John Charles Robbins; one *d.* *Educ.:* Newton College, S. Devon. Served South African War, Paget's Horse and Imperial Yeomanry, 1900-1; T.A. since 1908; Essex R.H.A., 1914-15; 1st East Anglian Brigade R.A., 1916-19 (despatches, D.S.O.); comdg. 1st East Anglian Brigade at Norwich, 1919-26. *Recreation:* shooting. *Address:* The Cottage, Yoxford, Suffolk. *T.:* Yoxford 256. [*Died* 15 *May* 1956.

DANIELS, Harold Griffith; Times Correspondent, Geneva; *b.* 1874; *e. s.* of late E. T. Daniels, Bognor, Sussex; *m.* Wanda Elizabeth Spencer, *y. d.* of late James Jeffrey Thomas, Cardiff. *Educ.:* Leer (East Friesland); King's College, Cambridge. Daily Express, 1903; Reuter's, 1903-5; Manchester Guardian, 1906-14; Assistant Military Censor, Press Bureau, 1914-15; News Dept. Foreign Office, 1915-16; Director, British Wireless Service, 1916-18; Admiralty, 1918; joined The Times, 1919; Berlin Correspondent, 1920-27; Paris Correspondent, 1927-36; League of Nations Correspondent, Geneva, 1936-39; Press Dept., British Legation, Berne, 1939-45. *Publications:* The Rise of the German Republic, 1927; The Framework of France, 1937. *Recreation:* walking. *Address:* 47 rue Plantamour, Geneva. *Clubs:* Savile, United University. [*Died* 23 *May* 1952.

DANIELS, Lt.-Col. Harry, V.C. 1915; M.C.; late the Rifle Brigade and Loyal Regt.; now Resident Manager, the Grand Theatre and Opera House, Leeds, since 1943; *b.* 13 Dec. 1884; *m.* 1914, Miss Perry (*d.* 1949). Served in ranks; 2nd Lt. 2nd Rifle Bde., 1915; Lt., 1916; Capt., 1921; Bt. Maj., 1929; Lt.-Col., 1934; served European War, 1914-17 (V.C. for conspicuous bravery in March 1915 at Neuve Chapelle, Military Cross for conspicuous gallantry, Fromelles, March 1916; retired pay, 1930; Chief Recruiting Officer, North Western Div., 1933-42. *Recreations:* fishing, fencing, gymnastics, boxing, and outdoor sports. *Address:* Flat 1, 2 Thornfield Rd., West Park, Leeds 6. [*Died* 13 *Dec.* 1953.

DANIELS, Sir Percy, K.B.E., *cr.* 1919; *b.* 15 Aug. 1875; *s.* of Edward Daniels, London; *m.* 1907, Florence Grace, *e. d.* of late Sir John Pakeman, C.B.E.; two *d.* *Educ.:* Mill Hill School. Chief of Leather Purchasing Commission, U.S.A. 1917-19. *Address:* 9 Hyde Park Street, W.2. [*Died* 16 *Jan.* 1951.

DANIELSEN, Col. Frederick Gustavus, C.B. 1944; D.S.O. 1917; T.D.; D.L.; an export merchant; a Knight of Grace of Order of St. John of Jerusalem in England; *b.* 1874; *s.* of Frederick Nicholas Danielsen, Edgbaston, Birmingham; *m.* 1905, Elizabeth Okell; one *d.* Served European War, 1914-19 (despatches,

D.S.O., Officer of Legion of Honour, of Order of Crown of Belgium, of Mérite Agricole, Order of White Eagle of Serbia); The Order of The Three Stars (Latvia), 1931; an additional A.D.C. to H.M., 1925-38; Chairman of Warwickshire Territorial Army and Air Force Assoc., 1939-46; Senior Military Liaison Officer, No. 9 Midland Region, 1939-41. *Address:* 48 Farquhar Road, Edgbaston, Birmingham. *Club:* Union (Birmingham). [*Died* 3 *April* 1951.

DANN, Alfred Clarence; General Secretary National Union of Agricultural Workers since 1945; Member of T.U.C. General Council since 1945; *b.* 11 March 1893; *m.* 1913, Gertrude Ethel Turner; one *s.* one *d.* *Educ.:* West Square High Grade School, Southwark. Lawyer's Clerk; Head of Legal Dept., National Union of Agricultural Workers, 1919. *Recreation:* walking. *Address:* 91 Elm Drive, North Harrow, Middlesex. *T.:* Terminus 3913. [*Died* 19 *Jan.* 1953.

DANN, Brig.-Gen. William Rowland Harris, D.S.O. 1917; *b.* 27 Oct. 1876; *s.* of Rev. A. G. Dann, M.A., B.E., Clarina, Co. Limerick; *m.* 1908, Margaret Eleanor, *d.* of A. H. Smith, London, Ontario; three *d.* Lieut. Canadian Militia, 1896; 2nd Lt. Manchester Regt. 1900; Lt. 1901; transferred to Bedfordshire Regiment 1908; Capt., 1910; Maj., 1915, Lt.-Col. 1925; Col. 1929; Brig.-Gen., 1933; served S. Africa, 1901-3 (Queen's medal with five clasps, African General Service medal and two clasps) Singapore, 1903-4; India, 1905-6; British East Africa (King's African Rifles), 1906-11; Adjutant, T.F., 5th Loyal North Lancs, 1913-15; commanded following bns. in France, European War: 5th Loyal North Lancs, 5th Durham Light Infantry, 11th Cheshire Regt., 8th Bedfordshire Regt., 2/4 London Regt.; commanded 60th Infantry Brigade, June 1918 to end of war (Bt. Major, Bt. Lt.-Col., despatches five times. D.S.O. and bar, 1915 Star, two medals); served Iraq, 1925-26; commanded 2nd Bedfs. and Herts. Regt., 1925-29; Officer in charge of Infantry Record and Pay Office, Shrewsbury, 1930-33; retired pay, 1933. A.R.P. Shrewsbury, 1938-40; raised and afterwards commanded 1st Shropshire L.D.V. (1st Shropshire Home Guard), 1940-42; Army Welfare Officer Shrewsbury and Dist. 1942-49. *Address:* Elylands, Edenbridge, Kent. *T.:* Cowden 2204. [*Died* 25 *Oct.* 1957.

DANSEY, Colonel Francis Henry, C.M.G. 1918; D.S.O. 1916; *b.* Ludlow, 31 May 1878; *s.* of late R. I. Dansey and Milburgha, *d.* of late Sir R. D. Green-Price, 2nd Bt.; *m.* 1914, Nora Fitzgerald, 2nd *d.* of Capt. J. F. Tuthill, Moyglare House, Maynooth; one *s.* one *d.* *Educ.:* Cheltenham College; R.M.C., Sandhurst. Entered Wiltshire Regt. 1898; Capt. 1904; Major, 1915; Lt.-Col. 1923; Col. 1927; Adjt. 2nd Batt., 1909-12; D.A.A. & Q.M.G. North Midland Division, 1913-15; D.A.A. & Q.M.G. France, 1915; A.A. & Q.M.G. (with temp. rank of Lt.-Col.), 1915-16; A.A.G. 1916-19 (despatches, D.S.O., Bt. Lt.-Col., C.M.G.; Chevalier Legion d'Honneur, 1918; Comendador of the Order of Aviz, Portugal); Commander 164th (North Lancashire) Infantry Brigade T.A., 1928-32; retired pay, 1932. *Recreations:* hunting, fishing cricket; played in Cheltenham College Rugby XV, 1896; Sandhurst Rugby XV, 1896 and 1897. *Address:* Oakdene, Church Stretton, Shropshire [*Died* 7 *Sept.* 1953.

DARELL, Sir Lionel Edward Hamilton Marmaduke, 6th Bt. of Richmond Hill, Surrey; *cr.* 1795; D.S.O. 1917; J.P. D.L.; late Major 1st Life Guards; *b.* 2 Apr. 1876; *s.* of 5th Bt. and Helen Frances (*d.* 1937), *o. c.* of late Edward Marsland, Henbury Park, Cheshire; *S.* father, 1919; *m.* 1903, Eleanor (*d.* 1953), *d.* of Capt. J. H. Edwards-Heathcote, Apedale, Staffs.; two *d.* *Educ.:* Eton; Christ Church, Oxford. Joined 1st Life Guards, 1899; Captain 1905; Major, 1914; A.D.C. to G.O.C., Cape Colony, 1909-12; served European War, 1914-17 (D.S.O., despatches twice); retired pay, 1922; High Sheriff for Gloucestershire, 1924; Hon. Colonel 5th Bn. Gloucester Regt., 1936-48; County Councillor since 1919 (Eastington Division), Alderman County Council, since 1937. *Heir:* *n.* (William) Oswald, *b.* 5 Nov. 1910. *Address:* Saul Lodge, Gloucestershire. *T.:* Saul 208. *Clubs:* Guards, Buck's. [*Died* 27 *May* 1954.

DARELL, Sir Oswald; *see* Darell, Sir W. O., Bt.

DARELL, Brig.-Gen. William Harry Verelst, C.B. 1929; C.M.G. 1918; D.S.O. 1915; late Coldstream Guards; *b.* 23 Jan. 1878; 2nd *s.* of Sir L. E. Darell, 5th Bt., and *b.* and *heir-pres.* to 6th Bt.; *m.* 1907, Jeffie, C.B.E., *d.* of late Emerson M. Bainbridge; one *s.* one *d.* *Educ.:* Eton; Royal Military College, Sandhurst (Sword of Honour). Entered Army, 1897; Captain, 1903; Major, 1913; Lt.-Col. 1919; passed Staff College, 1914; D.A.A.G., Southampton, 1914; D.A.Q.M.G., 7th Division, B.E.F., 1914; A.A. and Q.M.G., 3rd Division, 1915; Guards' Division, 1915; D.A. and Q.M.G., 4th Corps, 1916; Lt.-Col. 1st Coldstream Guards, 1919; Deputy Director of Mobilization and Recruiting, War Office, 1920; A.A.G., War Office, 1921; Lt.-Col. commanding Irish Guards, 1924-28; retired pay, 1929; served S. African War, 1899-1902 (Queen's medal 5 clasps, King's medal 2 clasps); European War, 1914-18 (despatches five times, D.S.O., Bt. Lt.-Col., C.M.G., Bt. Col.). *Recreation:* Won Diamond Sculls at Henley, 1907. *Address:* Heatherside, Sunningdale, Berks. *T.:* Ascot 54. *Clubs:* Guards, Carlton. [*Died* 7 *Feb.* 1954.

DARELL, Sir (William) Oswald, 7th Bt., *cr.* 1795; *b.* 5 Nov. 1910; *s.* of Brig.-Gen. William Harry Verelst Darell, C.B., C.M.G., D.S.O. (*d.* 1954), 2nd *s.* of 5th Bt., and Jeffie, O.B.E., *d.* of late Emerson Muschamp Bainbridge, Auchnashellach, Ross-shire; *S.* uncle 1954. *Educ.:* Eton; R.M.C., Sandhurst. *Heir:* *kinsman,* Major Jeffrey Lionel Darell, M.C., Coldstream Guards [*b.* 2 Oct. 1919; *m.* 1953, Bridget Mary, *d.* of Maj.-Gen. Sir Allen Adair, Bt., C.B.; one *d.*]. *Address:* 58 Queen's Gate, S.W.7. *Club:* St. James'. [*Died* 10 *Feb.* 1959.

DARLEY, Sir Bernard D'Olier, Kt., *cr.* 1928; C.I.E. 1919; M.I.C.E.; *b.* 1880; *s.* of John Henry Darley, Dublin; *m.* 1st. 1908, Frances Amy Heathcote (*d.* 1933), *d.* of William John Arculus; two *s.* two *d.*; 2nd, 1938, Gladys Noel, *widow* of Garth Ross, Westward Ho! *Educ.:* Trinity College, Dublin; Coopers Hill Royal Engineering College. Assistant Engineer U.P., 1903-9; Executive Engineer, 1909-19; surveyed, designed and built the Mirzapur Canal Systems, U.P., India; Chief Engineer, Sarda Canal, 1919-31; Chief Engineer, Bahawalpur State, Punjab, 1932-37; retired 1937; Technical Adviser, Air Raid Precautions Department, Home Office, 1938-39. *Address:* c/o Lloyds Bank, 6 Pall Mall, S.W.1. [*Died* 11 *Aug.* 1953.

DARLEY, Lt.-Col. James Russell, C.I.E. 1918; D.S.O. 1916; *b.* 5 Jan. 1868; *s.* of B. G. Darley, M.D., Cooloch, Co. Dublin; *m.* H. G. Sandford (*d.* 1944); no *c.* *Educ.:* privately; Trinity College, Dublin. 2nd Lieut. Gloucestershire Regt. 1889; entered Indian Army, 1890; served European War, 1914-18 (D.S.O., C.I.E., despatches six times); commanded 119th Infantry, Indian Army. *Publication:* Military History of Mysore. *Recreations:* pig-sticking, big-game shooting, fishing. *Address:* Fortmount, Lisbellaw, Co. Fermanagh. *Club:* Constitutional. [*Died* 19 *Jan.* 1951.

DARLING, Frederick; Bloodstock Breeder; *b.* 15 May 1884; *s.* of Sam and Violetta Darling; *m.* 1911, Gretel Kopp; no *c.* *Educ.:* Weymouth College. Riding and Training, on the Continent and England. *Recreations:* hunting, shooting, and travelling. *Address:* Beckhampton, Marlborough, Wilts. *T.A.:* Fred Darling Avebury. *T.:* Avebury 219. [*Died* 9 *June* 1953.

DARLINGTON, Col. Sir Henry (Clayton), K.C.B., *cr.* 1925 (C.B. 1921); C.M.G. 1916; T.D., D.L., J.P.; *b.* 27 June 1877; *s.* of late Henry Darlington, Wigan, and Edith Blanche, *d.* of late Captain T. Johnes Smith, 56th Regt.; *m.* 1st, 1909, Mabel Anne (*d.* 1916), *e. d.* of T. J. Hirst of Meltham Hall, Huddersfield; one *s.* three *d.*; 2nd, 1918, Daisy Mary Hirst; two *s.* two *d.* *Educ.:* Shrewsbury. Solicitor, Supreme Court, 1904. Commanded 1/5th Batt. Manchester Regt., Sept. 1914-20; 127th Infantry Brigade, 1920-24; served South African War with 1st Batt. Manchester Regt. 1900-1; served European War in Egypt, Gallipoli, and France (despatches thrice, C.M.G., Order of Crown of Italy (Officer)); High Sheriff of County Palatine of Lancaster, 1945-46. *Address:* Tanglewood, Milford-on-Sea, Hants. *T.:* Milford 102. [*Died* 25 *Dec.* 1959.

DARNLEY, 9th Earl of (*cr.* 1725), **Esme Ivo Bligh;** Baron Clifton of Leighton Bromswold, 1608; Baron Clifton of Rathmore, 1721; Viscount Darnley, 1723; Earl of Darnley, 1725; *b.* 11 Oct., 1886; *e. s.* of 8th Earl and Florence Rose, D.B.E. (*d.* 1944), *d.* of John Stephen Morphy of Beechworth, Victoria; *S.* father, 1927; *m.* 1st 1912, Daphne Rachel (who obtained a divorce, 1919), *d.* of late Hon. Alfred Mulholland; one *s.* one *d.*; 2nd, 1923, Nancy (from whom he obtained a divorce, 1936), *d.* of late Capt. Glen Kidston; one *d.*; 3rd, 1940, Rosemary, *d.* of late Basil Potter; one *s.* two *d.* *Educ.:* Eton; King's College, Cambridge. Served European War, 1914-18. *Recreations:* golf, shooting. *Heir: s.* Lord Clifton of Rathmore. *Address:* Cobham Hall, Cobham, Kent. *T.:* Cobham, Kent 8. *Club:* Bath. [*Died* 29 *May* 1955.

DARTMOUTH, 7th Earl of, *cr.* 1711; **William Legge,** G.C.V.O., *cr.* 1934; T.D.; Baron Dartmouth, 1682; Viscount Lewisham, 1711; *b.* 22 Feb. 1881; *e. s.* of 6th Earl and Mary, C.B.E. 1920 (*d.* 1929), 4th *d.* of 2nd Earl of Leicester; *S.* father, 1936; *m.* 1906, Lady Ruperta Carrington, *d.* of 1st Marquess of Lincolnshire; five *d.* *Educ.:* Eton; Christ Church, Oxford. L.C.C. (M.R.) Lewisham, 1907-10; M.P. (C.) West Bromwich, 1910-18; Lord Great Chamberlain of England, 1928-36; President M.C.C., 1932-33; late Hon. Col. Staffordshire Yeomanry; late Hon. Col. 7th Bn. West Riding Regt. *Recreations:* fishing, shooting, golf. *Heir: b.* Comdr. Hon. Humphry Legge, C.V.O., D.S.O. *Address:* Patshull House, Wolverhampton. *Club:* Bath. [*Died* 28 *Feb.* 1958.

DARWALL, Lt.-General Robert Henry; C.B.E. 1921; D.S.O. 1917; *b.* 3 Oct. 1879; *s.* of late R. C. Darwall, Dover; *m.* 1927, Jessie Giana Maxwell, *o. d.* of W. F. Maxwell Williams, North Lodge, Windsor Forest; two *s.* *Educ.:* Stubbington House, Fareham; Dover College. Joined the Royal Marine Light Infantry, 1898; served as Adjutant of the Portsmouth Division, R.M.L.I., 1905-10; seconded for service with the Egyptian Army, 1911; served Sudan, 1920 (C.B.E.); late commanding 14th Sudanese; Colonel, 1930; Colonel Comdt., Chatham Div. R.M., 1932-34; A.D.C. to the King, 1933-34; Maj.-Gen. 1934; Lt.-Gen. 1936; retired list, 1937. Order of the Nile, 3rd Class (Egypt). *Address:* Meadowscroft, Winkfield, Windsor, Berks. [*Died* 2 *April* 1956.

DARWOOD, Sir John William, Kt., *cr.* 1939; *b.* 15 May 1873; *o. s.* of late John W. Darwood; *m.* Winifred Alice Mary, *d.* of late Thomas Richard Taylor. *Educ.:* Beaumont College. Served in Army, 1915-18. *Address:* 16 Holland Park, W.11. [*Died* 8 *March* 1951.

DASGUPTA, Surendra Nath, C.I.E. 1941; M.A., Ph.D. (Cal. et Cantab.); D.Lit. (Rome, Hon.); I.E.S. (retd.); Life Professor of Philosophy, Benares Hindu University; *b.* Oct. 1887; *s.* of late K. P. Dasgupta and N. Dasgupta; *m.* Surama. *Educ.:* Calcutta; Trinity College, Cambridge. Senior Professor of Sanskrit, Chittagong College, 1911-20; Lecturer, Cambridge Univ., 1920-22; Prof. Chittagong Coll., 1920-24; Prof. of European Philosophy in I.E.S. Presidency Coll., Calcutta, 1924-31; Principal, Sanskrit Coll., Calcutta, and Sec. Bengal Sanskrit Assoc., 1931-42; King George V. Prof. of Philosophy, Calcutta Univ., 1942-45; Member of Senate, Calcutta Univ., 1924-45. Rep. Cambridge at Internat. Congress of Philosophy, Paris, 1921; rep. Calcutta Univ. at Internat. Congress of Philosophy, Naples, 1924, and Harvard, U.S.A., 1926; visiting Prof. to Amer. Univs., 1926; Harris Foundation Lectures, Chicago, 1926; Pres. Internat. Congress of Buddhism, Benares, 1931; visiting Prof. to Italian and German Univs., 1935; visiting Prof. to Paris, 1935 and 1936; rep. India at Internat. Congress of Faiths, London, 1936; visiting Prof. to Italy, Zürich and Warsaw, 1939; rep. India at Internat. Congress of Faiths, Paris, 1939; Stephanos Nirmalendu Lectures at Calcutta Univ., 1941. *Publications:* History of Indian Philosophy, vols. I-IV, 1921-48; A Study of Patañjali; The Yoga Philosophy in relation to other Indian systems; Yoga as Philosophy and Religion; Hindu Mysticism; Indian Idealism; Philosophical Essays; History of Sanskrit Literature; Tagore, The Poet and Philosopher; Religion and the Rational Outlook; Recent Development in European Thought; Lectures on Indian Art; A History of Religions; The Mahābhasya of Patañjali (a transl. with annotation); Vanishing Lines (Transl. of poems in English); numerous books in Bengali. *Recreations:* wide reading, travel and chess. *Address:* c/o Grindlay's Bank, Ltd., S.W.1. [*Died* 18 *Dec.* 1952.

DASHWOOD, Sir Henry Thomas Alexander, Kt. *cr.* 1952; M.A.; formerly senior partner in firm of Lee, Bolton & Lee, solicitors; J.P. for Hertfordshire; *b.* 9 July 1878; 2nd *s.* of late G. L. Dashwood, senior partner Messrs. Child & Co., bankers; *m.* 1909, Norah Creina (*d.* 1948), *er. d.* of late H. A. Whately (*d.* 1957 at age of 102) and of late Hon. Mrs. Whately; one *s.* one *d.* *Educ.:* Harrow; Clare College, Cambridge. Chapter Clerk, 1913-50 (Receiver 1919-44) of St. Paul's Cathedral. Registrar Court of Arches and Court of Faculties and of Vicar-General, 1939-48; Principal Registrar of the Province of Canterbury, Registrar of Diocese of London and Gibraltar, 1924-58, Diocese of Canterbury, 1924-50; Legal Secretary: to Archbishops of Canterbury and Bishops of Winchester, 1913-58; to Bishops of London, 1924-50; Ely, 1924-54; Portsmouth and Guildford, 1927-52 and to Bishop of Worcester, 1919-31. *Address:* 4 Bullingham Mansions, Pitt Street, W.8. *T.:* Western 7527; Farthinghoe Lodge, near Brackley, Northants. *Club:* United University. [*Died* 25 *May* 1959.

DATIA, H.H. Maharajah Sir Govind Singh Bahadur, G.C.I.E., *cr.* 1932; K.C.S.I., *cr.* 1918; one of the ruling Princes of India; Hon. Lt.-Col. in Army; *m.*; two *s.* one *d.* Title of Maharajah, recognised as hereditary, 1865; that of Lokendra, 1877; enjoys full civil and criminal powers, and is entitled to a salute of 15 guns; the State has an area of 912 square miles and a population of over 174,072. Has presented Lord Reading's Statue to the Imperial Capital, Delhi; has built several buildings of public utility in his own capital; has shot 211 tigers and one elephant in Mysore, etc.; celebrated his Silver Jubilee in 1933; Vice-President of Indian Red Cross Society; Patron of St. John Ambulance Association (India). *Address:* Datia, Bundelkhand, Central India. *Clubs:* Lokinder (President), Datia; Cricket of India, Jhansi (Jhansi). [*Died* 22 *Dec.* 1951.

DAUGLISH, Rt. Rev. John, M.A.; *b.* 19 Oct. 1879; *s.* of Algernon Dauglish.

Educ.: St. Edward's School, Oxford; St. John's College, Oxford; St. Stephen's House, Oxford. Priest, 1902; Chaplain R.N., 1905-1924; Rector of Lympstone, Devon, 1924-1931; Bishop of Nassau, 1932-42; Secretary of S.P.G. 1942-44; Hon. Canon and Assistant Bishop of St. Albans, 1942-44. *Recreations:* walking, fishing. *Address:* 10 Cloudesley Road, S. Leonards-on-Sea, Sussex. *Club:* Athenæum. [*Died* 1 *Nov.* 1952.

DAUKES, Rt. Rev. Francis Whitfield; an Assistant Bishop in diocese of Exeter, 1950-52; Archdeacon of Plymouth 1928-1950; *b.* 27 March 1877; *s.* of Rev. S. Whitfield Daukes, Vicar of Holy Trinity, Beckenham, Kent; *m.* 1st, Lucy Matilda (*d.* 1933), *d.* of Lewis Annett, Crowthorne, Berks; four *d.*; 2nd, 1939, Lilian, *d.* of late Thomas Charlton, Cowes. *Educ.:* Harrow; Oriel College and Wycliffe Hall, Oxford (M.A.); 2nd Class Honours, Modern History. Deacon, 1901; Priest, 1902; Curate All Saints, S. Lambeth, 1901-5; Vicar S. Saviour, Denmark Park, 1905-14; S. Peter's, Brockley, 1914-24; St. Andrew, Plymouth, 1924-1938; Rural Dean of Greenwich, 1915-24; Proctor Conv. Southwark, 1922-24; Rural Dean of Three Towns, 1927-28; Examining Chaplain to Bishop of Exeter, 1936; Suffragan Bishop of Plymouth, 1934-50. *Address:* Linkincorn, Woodland Walk, Boscombe, Bournemouth. *T.:* Southbourne 46134. [*Died* 30 *July* 1954.

DAVENPORT, Frederic Richard; *b.* 1872; *y. c.* of late Henry Devereux Davenport; *m.* 1902, Alice Marion Bucknall; no *c.* *Educ.:* Haileybury. Chairman of British Electrical and Allied Manufacturers Assoc., 1912-19; J.P. Warwickshire, 1919-38; Warwick County Council, 1919-22; Member of Govt. Committees such as German Reparations, Safeguarding of Industries, Merchandise Marks, Transport Appeal Tribunal, Air Ministry Licensing Authority. *Address:* Budleigh Salterton, Devon. *T.:* 436 Budleigh Salterton. *Club:* Boodle's. [*Died* 29 *Jan.* 1952.

DAVENPORT, Mrs. M. C. B.; *see* Bromley-Davenport.

DAVENPORT-PRICE, Major Hubert; *see* Price.

DAVEY, Major-General Basil Charles, C.B. 1951; C.B.E. 1944; R.E., retd.; *b.* 21 Nov. 1897; *s.* of Charles Edwin Davey, M.A., B.Sc.; *m.* 1926, Enid Sanford, *d.* of Brigadier-General E. T. Tudor; two *s.* two *d.* *Educ.:* Blundell's School; Royal Military Academy; Jesus College, Cambridge. Served France, 1917-18; Tunisia, Sicily, Italy, 1942-43; France and Belgium, 1944; Italy and Austria, 1945. Commandant, School of Military Engineering, Chatham, 1948-51. Major-General, 1951; Commandant, Royal Military College of Science, Shrivenham, Wilts, 1951-1954, retired Sept. 1954. Jurat of the Royal Court of Jersey, 1955. Comdr. Legion of Honor (U.S.), 1945. *Address:* Le Haut des Côtils, Old Beaumont Hill, Jersey. *Club:* United Service. [*Died* 20 *Nov.* 1959.

DAVEY, George; Assistant Secretary, Commonwealth Relations Office, since 1956; *b.* 23 June 1911; *s.* of J. W. Davey and Ruth (*née* Butcher); *m.* 1941, Irene N. Mills; one *s.* two *d.* *Educ.:* Firth Park Secondary School, Sheffield; Sheffield University (B.A.). With L.N.E.R., 1927-41. Served R.N.V.R., 1941-46, Lieutenant. Lectr. in Economics, City of Birmingham Commercial Coll., 1946. Principal, Burma Office, C.R.O., 1946; on Secretariat of Meeting of Commonwealth Foreign Ministers, Colombo, 1950; in Office of U.K. High Commissioner in Australia, 1950-53; Deputy U.K. High Commissioner in East Pakistan, 1955-58. *Recreations:* tennis and cricket. [*Died* 8 *Oct.* 1959.

DAVEY, Rev. Principal J(ames) Ernest; Principal of the Presbyterian College, Belfast, since 1942, and Professor (of Church History 1917, of Biblical Literature 1922, of Hebrew and Old Testament 1930, of New Testament Language, Literature and Theology since 1933); *b.* Ballymena, Co. Antrim, 24 June 1890; *s.* of Rev. Charles Davey, B.A., D.D., and Margaret (*née* Beatty); *m.* 1927, Georgiana Eliza O'Neill; one *s.* two *d.* *Educ.:* Methodist College, and Campbell College, Belfast; King's College, Cambridge; Edinburgh University; Belfast Presbyterian College. Scholar, R.U.I., 1908; Minor Scholar, 1909, Open Foundation Scholar, 1911-16, King's Coll., Camb.; Fellow of King's Coll., Camb., 1916-22; Classical Tripos Part I, 1st Cl., 1912, Theological Tripos Pt. II, 1st Cl., 1913, Camb. Univ.; B.A. (Cantab.) 1912; M.A. 1916; B.D. (Edin.) 1917; D.D. (hon. causa): St. Andrews, 1928; Edin., 1947; Belfast, 1953; Dublin, 1954. Recognised Teacher, Queen's Univ. Belfast, 1927-. Moderator of Irish Presbyterian Church, 1953-54. *Publications:* Charles Davey, D.D., a Memoir, 1921; Our Faith in God, 1922; The Changing Vesture of the Faith, 1923; The Story of a Hundred Years, 1940; The Jesus of St. John, 1958; various articles. *Recreations:* music, golf. *Address:* 3 College Park, Belfast, Northern Ireland. *T.:* Belfast 26791. [*Died* 17 *Dec.* 1960.

DAVID-WEILL, David; Grand Officier de la Légion d'Honneur; senior partner of Lazard frères et Cie, Paris; director of Lazard Brothers and Co. London; Member of the Institut de France; Président du Conseil des Museés Nationaux; Vice-President (fondateur) de la Fondation Nationale de Cité Universitaire; Vice-president des Amis du Louvre, de l'Union Centrale des Arts Décoratifs; *b.* 30 Aug. 1871; *s.* of Alexandre Weill and Julie Cahn; *m.* 1897, Flora Raphael; two *s.* four *d.* *Educ.:* Lycée Condorcet, Paris. Born of French parents at San Francisco (U.S.), left for New York in 1880 where his father established the firm of Lazard Frères; came to Paris in 1884 and has lived there since as a banker and art collector and philanthropist; served European War 1914-1919, first as Lieutenant and afterwards as Captain; Commander or grand officer of the Etoile Polaire (Sweden), Danebrog (Denmark), Savior (Greece), Saint Sava (Yugoslavia), St. Alexander (Bulgaria); Grand Officer of the Order of Saints Maurice and Lazare (Italy); Commander of the Order of Léopold (Belgium). *Address:* 14 rue de Chézy, Neuilly sur Seine. [*Died* 7 *July* 1952.

DAVIDSON, Rev. Alan Munro, C.B.E. 1949; M.C. 1917; M.A. Edin. 1915; D.D. Edin. 1945; *b.* 20 Oct. 1894; *s.* of Rev. Donald Davidson and Lily Munro, Invergowrie, Perthshire; *m.* 1924, Helen Mary, *d.* of Hamilton Coffey, Clobemon Hall, Co. Wexford; one *s.* two *d.* *Educ.:* Dundee High School; Edinburgh University. Served European War, 1914-18, 2nd Lt. R.A., 1915; Lt. R.A., 1916; Capt. 1918; C. F. 4th Class, 1920, 3rd Class, 1926, 2nd Class, 1933; D.A.C.G. 2nd Corps, 1939 (despatches); A.C.G. Lines of Communication, B.E.F. 1940 (despatches); A.C.G. Egypt, 1941; A.C.G. 8th Army 1941-42 (despatches); A.C.G. Scottish Command, 1942-46; Deputy Chaplain-General H.M. Forces, Jan. 1946-May 1950; K.H.C. 1946-50; retd. pay, 1950. Officer of the Military Order of Christ (Portugal), 1957. *Recreations:* swimming, theatre, travel. *Address:* Manse of Scots Church, Rua da Arriaga II, Lisbon, Portugal; Pinewoods, Kingswear, South Devon. *T.:* Kingswear 206. *Clubs:* Royal Dart Yacht (Kingswear); Royal British (Lisbon). [*Died* 4 *Feb.* 1959.

DAVIDSON, Sir Alfred Charles, K.B.E., *cr.* 1938; *b.* South Brisbane, 1 April 1882; *s.* of late James Madgwick Davidson; *m.* 1916, Hilda Dorothea Mary, *e. d.* of late Charles L. Tange, Solicitor, Sydney. *Educ.:* Brisbane Grammar School. Joined Staff of Bank of N.S.W. at Brisbane, 1901; Inspector's

Office, Brisbane, 1907; went to London and toured Europe, 1910-11; Head Office Staff, 1911; Metropolitan Inspectors' Staff, Sydney, 1913; Relieving Staff, N.S.W., 1919; Manager, Gisborne (N.Z.) Branch, 1922; Wellington as Sub-Inspector, 1924; Manager at Perth, with supervision over all branches in W.A., 1925; General Manager of Western Australian Bank, 1926; Inspector for Bank of N.S.W. in W.A. on amalgamation of the W.A. Bank with the Bank of N.S.W., 1927; Chief Inspector, N.S.W., 1928; General Manager, Bank of New South Wales, 1929-45. *Publications:* Central Reserve Banking, 1929; Australia's Share in International Recovery (Joseph Fisher Lecture in Commerce, University of Adelaide), 1932; The Economics of Peace (John Murtagh Macrossan Lecture, University of Queensland), 1941. *Recreations:* gardening, carpentry, reading. *Address:* 9 Manar, 42 Macleay Street, Potts Point, Sidney, N.S.W. *T.:* FL1024. *Clubs:* Union, Australasian Pioneers (Sydney). [*Died* 18 *Nov.* 1952.

DAVIDSON, Lieut.-Colonel Charles George Francis, D.S.O. 1918, M.C.; *b.* 5 Jan. 1884; *s.* of George James Davidson and Frances Ann Hamilton; *m.* 1911, Estelle May Gordon, *d.* of Colonel Edward Barry Bishop, late 3rd Q.A.O. Gurkha Rifles; two *d.* *Educ.:* Allhallows School, Honiton; Bradfield Coll.; R.M. Academy, Woolwich. 2nd Lt. R.G.A., 1903; Lt. 1906; A.D.C. to Governor and C.-in-C., Malta, 1910-1913; Captain, 1914; served European War, France and Flanders, 1914-18; Comdt. 5th Army Artillery School, 1917-18 (Acting Lt.-Col.); Major, 1917; (wounded, despatches four times, D.S.O., M.C.); Staff Capt. Chapperton Down Artillery School, 1919; Brigade Major R.A., Malta, 1919-22; Assistant-Commandant, Military College of Science, 1925-29; India, 1930-32; retired with rank of Lt.-Col. 1933; Inspector of Danger Buildings, Royal Gunpowder Factory, Waltham Abbey, 1935-39; Royal Ordnance Factories, 1940-41; Armaments Inspection Department, 1942-44; Sec. Royal Solent Yacht Club, 1945-52. *Recreations:* various. *Address:* 5 Ollards Grove, Loughton, Essex. *T.:* Loughton 6512. *Clubs:* (Hon. Life Mem.) Royal Solent (Yarmouth) also of Royal Lymington Yacht. [*Died* 11 *Nov.* 1956.

DAVIDSON, Hon. Sir Colin George Watt, Kt. *cr.* 1952; *b.* Mudgee, N.S.W. 18 Nov. 1878; *s.* of George Davidson, Solicitor, and Jessie, *d.* of David Watt, Pine Ridge, Leadville, N.S.W.; *m.* 1928, Phyllis Hinder, *d.* of late Dr. R. T. Jones, Sydney. *Educ.:* State Public School; Mudgee Grammar School; Univ. of Sydney; B.A., LL.B. Called to N.S.W. Bar, 1901; Lecturer in the law of Divorce and in the Practice in Equity in the Faculty of law, Univ. of Sydney; K.C. 1926; Acting Puisne Judge of the Supreme Court, 1926; Puisne Judge of the Supreme Court of New South Wales, 1927-1948; retired, 1948; Chm. of Federal Royal Commission on Coal Mining Industry, 1929; Chm. Royal Commission on Safety and Health in Coal Mines, 1938-39; Chairman, Commonwealth Coal Board, 1941; Chairman Commonwealth Tribunals for Civilian Internees, 1940-45; Chairman Commonwealth Committee for Refresher Rehabilitation lectures for legal men returning from active service, 1945-46; Chairman Commonwealth Board of Inquiry into the Coal Industry, 1945-46. *Publication:* (with J. H. Hammond, K.C.) Law of Landlord and Tenant in N.S.W. *Recreations:* golf, motoring, bowls. *Address:* 16 Wattle Street, Killara, Sydney, N.S.W. *Clubs:* Australian, Union, Killara Golf (Sydney). [*Died* 8 *July* 1954.

DAVIDSON, Brig. Douglas Stewart, C.B.E. 1945; D.S.O. 1915; M.C.; *b.* 12 Nov. 1892; *m.* 1940, Lilias Mary, *y. d.* of late Dr. Steele and of Mrs. Steele, Ardmuir, Hamilton. *Educ.:* Rugby; Sandhurst. Entered Army, 1911; Bt. Major, 1919; Major, 1929; Bt Lt.-Col. 1933; Lt.-Col. 1938; Col. 1939; served European War, France, Gallipoli, and Mesopotamia, 1914-18, and N.W. Frontier Campaign, 1919 (wounded, D.S.O., Croix de Guerre, Military Cross); Deputy Assistant Director Territorial Army, 1930-34; commanded 1st Bn. Royal Scots Fusiliers, 1938-1939; Commander Infantry Bde., T.A. 1939-1940; officiated as D.A. and Q.M.G. XII Corps, Sept.-Nov. 1940; commanded Herts Sub-Area, 1940-43; Deputy Military Secretary (B) War Office, 1943-44; Deputy Military Secretary A.F.H.Q. Nov. 1944-45; retired pay, 1946. *Address:* c/o Lloyds Bank Ltd., 6 Pall Mall, S.W.1. [*Died* 16 *March* 1958.

DAVIDSON, Rt. Rev. Edwin John; Bishop of Gippsland since 1955; *b.* 12 Feb. 1899; *s.* of William Andrew and Edith Amy Davidson; *m.* 1930, Doris Evelyn (*née* Whatmore); two *d.* *Educ.:* Sydney University; Moore College, Sydney. Served European War, 1916-18, with Aust. Imperial Forces in France and Belgium, as Gunner in Artillery (5th Div.); Toc H Staff Padre, Manchester, 1926-28; Area Padre, Toc H (N.S.W.), 1928-30; Canon, All Saints' Bathurst Cathedral, 1930-32; Rector, St. James' Church, Sydney, and Canon of St. Andrew's Cathedral, Sydney, 1938-55. *Recreation:* yachting. *Address:* Bishopscourt, Sale, Victoria, Australia. [*Died* 1 *April* 1958.

DAVIDSON, James, C.B.E. 1926; *b.* 1875; Assistant District Commissioner, Southern Nigeria, 1901; Resident, Nigeria Southern Provinces, 1916; Senior Resident, 1921; Acting Lieut.-Governor, Southern Provinces, May-December 1925; retired, 1926. *Club:* East India and Sports. [*Died* 29 *Jan.* 1959.

DAVIDSON, Jo; Sculptor; *b.* New York, 30 March 1883; *m.* 1909, Yvonne de Kerstrat (*decd.*); two *s.*; *m.* 1941, Florence G. Lucius. London Exhibitions: Baillie Galleries, 1909, Leicester Galleries, 1914, Knoedler Galleries, 1930; Paris: Gallerie des Arts Modernes, 1919; New York: Retrospective Exhibition at National Institute of Arts and Letters, 1947-48. Officier Légion d'Honneur (France) 1946. *Address:* 323 East 58th St., New York City, U.S.A.; 6 Rue Leconte de Lisle, Paris, France. *Clubs:* Century, Coffee House, Lotus (New York); American (Paris). [*Died* 2 *Jan.* 1952.

DAVIDSON, John, C.I.E. 1938; O.B.E.; B.A.; *b.* 31 Aug. 1878; *s.* of late Major-General Alexander Davidson R.E. and Ellin Amelia Hunt; *m.* 1912, Lilian Mary, *d.* of Surgeon Major-General Alfred Malpas Tippetts; no *c.* *Educ.:* Clifton College; Pembroke College, Cambridge. Joined Finance Dept. Govt. of India 1902; Assistant Accountant-General Burma, 1903; Bengal, 1907; United Provinces, 1908; Punjab, 1909; served European war 1914-19; with I.A.S.C. and as Director of the Blockade Mesopotamia Expeditionary Force (despatches thrice); Deputy Comptroller-General, 1919; Financial Adviser Punjab, 1923; Accountant-General Behar and Orissa, 1926; Burma, 1927-1933; retired 1933. *Recreations:* fishing, motoring, bridge. *Address:* Tolpedn, Cranford Avenue, Exmouth. [*Died* 19 *Jan.* 1957.

DAVIDSON, John, C.B.E. 1942; late Regional Director, London Postal Region, G.P.O.; *b.* 6 April 1882; *s.* of David S. Davidson; *m.* 1920, Mary McFedris; two *s.* *Educ.:* Bathgate Academy, Linlithgowshire. Sorting clerk, Post Office, Edinburgh, 1899; clerk, London Postal Service, 1904; Army, 1914-20, left with rank of Major R.E. (S.R.). *Recreations:* golf and gardening. *Address:* Stanhope Cottage, Trinity Church Lane, Cowes, I. of W. [*Died* 14 *May* 1960.

DAVIDSON, Maj.-Gen. Sir John Humphrey, K.C.M.G., *cr.* 1919; C.B. 1917; D.S.O. 1900; *b.* 24 July 1876; *s.* of George Walter Davidson; *m.* 1905, Margaret, *y. d.* of J. P. Grant of Rothiemurchus, Inverness-shire; one *d.* *Educ.:* Harrow; Sandhurst. Col. Comdt. K.R.R.C., 1937-45. Entered

K.R.R.C., 1896; Adjutant 1st Bn., 1902-05; served S.A. 1899-1902 (despatches, Queen's medal 7 clasps, King's medal 2 clasps, D.S.O.); Staff Coll., 1906-07; Bt. Major, 1913; General Staff Aldershot and War Office, 1908-11; Instructor Staff College, 1911-14; European War, 1914-18, Gen. Staff, and subsequently as Dir. of Mil. Ops. in France (despatches eleven times, French despatches twice, Bt. Lt.-Col., Bt. Col., C.B., K.C.M.G., Comdr. of Légion d'Honneur and Belgian Order of the Crown, French and Belgian Croix de Guerre, Amer. D.S.M., 1914 Star); Maj.-Gen. 1918; retd. pay, 1922. M.P. (U.) Fareham Div. of Hants, 1918-31 (Chm. Select Cttee. on Trng. and Employment of Disabled Ex-servicemen, 1922, and of King's Roll Nat. Council). For some years Vice-Pres. Union Jack Club. Chairman: Union Bank of Australia, 1937-49; Dalgety & Co. Ltd., 1939-47; Dep. Chm. Gresham Insurance Socs. Life and Fire; Director: Nat. Bank of Egypt, 1925-49; Vickers Ltd., 1935-49, etc. *Publication:* Haig Master of the Field, 1953. *Address:* Sandwood, Nairn, Scotland. *T.:* Nairn 2129.
[*Died* 11 *Dec.* 1954.

DAVIDSON, Robert, C.B.E. 1950; Member Docks and Inland Waterways Executive since 1947; *b.* 8 Jan. 1888; *s.* of James Davidson; *m.* 1915, Jessie, *d.* of George Cranston. *Educ.:* Bootle and Liverpool. Entered service of Leeds and Liverpool Canal Co., 1903; General Manager and Engineer, 1925, also Manager of Canal Transport Ltd.; Director, 1940; Chairman and later President of Canal Assoc.; Chairman and Member of various Cttees. set up by Min. of War Transport; Member Institute of Transport (former member of the Council). *Recreations:* follower of all sports. *Address:* 36 Leonard Court, Kensington, W.8. *T.:* Western 3817.
[*Died* 17 *May* 1952.

DAVIDSON, Major-General Sisley Richard, C.B. 1921; C.M.G. 1917; *b.* 26 Aug. 1869; *s.* of late Maj.-Gen. A. G. Davidson, Indian Army; *m.* Dorothy Harvey (*d.* 1946), *d.* of late Sir James Westland, K.C.S.I.; no *c.* *Educ.:* Nelson College, New Zealand. 2nd Lieutenant P.A. Som. L.I. 1890; joined Indian Army, 1892; Coy. Commander 47th Sikhs, 1901; Commandant, 1916; Brigade Commander, 1916; served Relief of Chitral, 1895 (medal and clasp; Mohmand Expedition, 1897 (clasp); Tirah Expedition, 1897-98 (clasp); Expeditions under Sir W. Manning and Sir C. Egerton in Somaliland, 1903-4 (despatches, medal and clasp); European War in France, 1914-15 (despatches, wounded, Brevet Lt.-Colonel, 1914 Star, British War Medal and Victory Medal); Mesopotamia, 1916-18 (despatches twice, Brevet of Colonel, Order of St. Anne 2nd class, C.M.G.); Palestine, 1918 (despatches); in command of 7th Indian Infantry Brigade till Nov. 1919; in command of Jhansi Brigade, India, 12 Dec. 1919; Delhi Brigade Area, 1921-22; Substantive Col. 12 Nov. 1919; Maj.-Gen. 1920; retd. 1922. London Comr. Boy Scouts Assoc., 1922-24; J.P. Middlesex, 1922-24; County Director B.R.C.S. (1) Somerset (2) Sutherland; Dep. Lieut. Sutherland (resigned); organised Home Guard, Sutherland and Caithness. *Address:* c/o Lloyds Bank, 6 Pall Mall, S.W.1.
[*Died* 4 *March* 1952.

DAVIDSON-HOUSTON, Lt.-Col. Wilfred Bennett, C.M.G. 1911; *b.* 3 Jan. 1870; 2nd *s.* of late Rev. B. C. Davidson-Houston, M.A., of County Cork and Dublin; *m.* Annie H. (*d.* 1940), *o. d.* of E. Langley Hunt, of County Limerick; two *s.* *Educ.:* Corrig School, Ireland; St. Edward's, Oxford. 2nd Lieut. 5th Royal Dublin Fusiliers, 1887; Lieut., 1889; Captain, 1892; Major, 1902; Lieut.-Colonel, 1906; British South Africa Company Police, and Assistant Commissioner Mashonaland, 1890-92; Assistant Inspector Gold Coast Hausas, 1894; Captain West African Frontier Force, 1898; Attabubu Expedition, 1894; Special Service, Kwahu, 1894-95; Ashanti Expedition, 1895-96. Commanded Advanced Guard (despatches, star); Special Mission to Samory and N.W. Ashanti, 1896; with Hausa Detachment Jubilee Celebrations, 1897 (medal); Operations N.T. Gold Coast, 1897-98 (medal and clasp); Acting Resident Ashanti, 1899-1900; Ashanti Campaign, 1900 (medal and clasp); South African Campaign, 1901-2, Staff Officer (Queen's medal Five Clasps); Staff Officer Colonial Coronation Contingent, 1911 (medal); Commissioner Ashanti, 1902; Acting Chief Commissioner of Ashanti, 1903-4-5; Commissioner of Montserrat, B.W.I., 1906; Delegate to Imperial Education Conference, London, 1911; Canada-West Indies Reciprocity Conference, Ottawa, 1912; International Road Congress, London, 1913; Imperial Motor Transport Conference, London, 1913; Canada-West Indies Conference, Ottawa, 1925; Colonial Office Conferences, London, 1927 and 1930; D.A.Q.M.G. Central Force, 1915; Eastern Command, 1916; Headquarters 1st Army, B.E.F., 1917; Deputy Controller of Labour, France, 1918 (British War and Victory Medals); Administrator of St. Lucia, B.W.I., 1918-27; Acting Governor, Windward Islands, Mar. 1923, Nov. 1923-July 1924, Sept.-Oct. 1925, and June-July 1926; Chief Secretary, Nyasaland, 1927-1930; Acting Governor, Nyasaland, May-Nov. 1929, Mar.-April 1930; retired, 1930. *Address:* The Old Cottage, Chestnut Avenue, Esher, Surrey. *T.:* Emberbrook 1171. *Clubs:* Royal Commonwealth Society; Kildare Street (Dublin).
[*Died* 18 *Sept.* 1960.

DAVIE, Thomas Benjamin, B.A., LL.D., M.D., F.R.C.P., F.R.S.S.Af., F.R.S.A.; Principal and Vice-Chancellor, University of Cape Town, since 1948; *b.* 23 Nov. 1895; *s.* of T. B. Davie and Caroline Halliday; *m.* 1921, Vera C. Roper; no *c.* *Educ.:* Univ. of Stellenbosch, S. Africa; Univ. of Liverpool. B.A. Stellenbosch, 1914; 2nd Lt. R.A.F. 1918; returned to S. Africa, Science Master in several High Schools, last being Parktown Boys' High School, Johannesburg; medical course, Liverpool Univ., 1924-28; Junior Lecturer in Pathology, Liverpool Univ., 1929-31; Pathologist to Corpn. Hospital, Liverpool, 1931-33; Senior Lecturer in Pathology, University of Liverpool, 1933-35; Prof. of Pathology, Univ. of Bristol, 1935-38; George Holt Prof. of Pathology, Univ. of Liverpool, 1938-46; Hon. and Cons. Pathologist to Roy. Liverpool United Hosp. and other voluntary hosps. in Liverpool; full-time Dean of Faculty of Medicine, Liverpool Univ., 1946-47. *Publications:* Textbook of Pathology (with J. H. Dible); various articles in medical journals. *Recreation:* gardening. *Address:* Glenara, Burg Rd., Rondebosch, Cape Town. *T.:* 6-3895.
[*Died* 14 *Dec.* 1955.

DAVIES, Albert Edward; M.P. (Lab.) for Burslem (Stoke on Trent), 1945-50, North Division of Stoke on Trent since 1950; *b.* 30 May 1900; *s.* of Albert and Emma Davies, Smallthorne, Stoke on Trent; *m.* 1944, Margaret Hilda Joan Batty; one *s.* *Educ.:* Smallthorne Council Board School; Stoke on Trent Technical Schools; Workers' Educational Association; Manchester College, Oxford. Railwayman engaged with L.M. & S. Railway; at Euston H.Q. outbreak War, 1939; worked on Merchandise Services Section and on War Emergency Work. Stoke on Trent City Councillor since 1943. *Recreations:* walking, music, gardening. *Address:* 65 Victoria Road, Tunstall, Stoke on Trent.
[*Died* 19 *Jan.* 1953.

DAVIES, Admiral Sir Arthur John, K.B.E., *cr.* 1943; C.B. 1927; *s.* of late Rev. J. B. Davies of Waters Upton, Salop; *m.* 1916, Dorothy, *d.* of late Capt. J. R. Prickett of Browston Hall, Great Yarmouth; one *s.* one *d.* Entered R.N. Britannia, 1892; Captain, 1915; Rear-Admiral, 1926; Vice-Admiral, 1931; served in North Sea, European War, 1914-18; Chief of Staff, Atlantic Fleet, 1924-27; commanded 3rd Cruiser Squadron, 1929-30; retired list, 1931; Adm., retired, 1936; Commodore of Convoys,

1940-44 (despatches). *Address:* Ravenscourt, Rowlands Castle, Hants. *Club:* United Service. [*Died* 13 *Dec.* 1954.

DAVIES, Rev. Arthur Llywelyn; Canon Residentiary of Sheffield Cathedral, 1936-51, Canon Emeritus since 1951; *s.* of David Davies, M.A., Rector of Hirnant, Oswestry, and Sarah Pugh Davies; *m.* Eleanor Kate, *d.* of W. H. Wixon; two *s.* one *d.* *Educ.:* Bradford Grammar School; Queen's College, Oxford (Hastings Exhibitioner and Honorary Scholar). First Class Classical Moderations, 1905; Second Class Literae Humaniores, 1907; First Class, Theology, 1908; Denyer and Johnson University Scholar, 1909; Curate of St. Clement's, Oxford, 1909-13; of All Saints', Highfield, Oxford, 1913-16; Warden of Ruthin and Incumbent of Ruthin and Llanrhydd, Denbighshire, 1916-22; Vicar of Eglwys Rhos (Llanrhos), 1922-35; Cursal Canon of St. Asaph, 1925-36; Vicar of Doncaster, 1935-50, retired. Examining Chaplain to the Bishop of St. Asaph, 1917-20; to the Archbishop of Wales, 1920-34; to Bishop of St. Asaph, 1934-50; to Bishop of Sheffield, 1937-50; Grinfield Lecturer on the Septuagint, Oxford, 1921-23, and 1923-25; Rural Dean of Llanrwst, 1927-35; of Doncaster, 1935-45. Officiating Chaplain, R.A.F., 1939-43. *Publications:* Assistant General Editor of and contributor to Apocrypha and Pseudepigrapha, 1913; contributor to Hastings' Dictionary of the Apostolic Church; contributor to Geiriadur Beiblaidd. *Address:* 1 Summerhill Road, Banbury Road, Oxford. *T.:* 58629. [*Died* 5 *March* 1957.

DAVIES, Ashton, C.V.O. 1939; O.B.E. 1925; M.Inst.T.; J.P.; *b.* 1874; *s.* of Thomas Davies, Failsworth; *m.* 1902, Annie (*d.* 1951), *d.* of Thomas Whitehead, Failsworth; one *d.* Superintendent of the Line, Lancashire & Yorkshire Railway, 1919-21; General Superintendent, Northern Div., London & N. Western Railway, 1922; General Superintendent, Western Division, London Midland & Scottish Railway, 1923; General Superintendent, Freight Services, 1924; General Superintendent, Passenger Commercial, 1924-31; Passenger Manager, 1931-32; Chief Commercial Manager, 1932-38; Vice-Pres. London Midland & Scottish Railway, 1938-44; former Dep.-Chm. Ribble Motor Services, Ltd.; Director, Crosville Motor Services, North Western Road Car Company, Hebble and W. Yorkshire Motor Services, Joseph Nall & Co. Ltd., Blackpool Omnibus Stations Co. Ltd., Carter Paterson & Co. Ltd., Hay's Wharf Cartage Co. Ltd., etc. *Address:* Busk, St. Anne's Road East, Lytham St. Annes, Lancs. [*Died* 1 *Feb.* 1958.

DAVIES, Bernard N. I.; *see* Langdon-Davies.

DAVIES, Sir Charles; *see* Davies, Sir Reginald C.

DAVIES, Brigadier-General Charles Henry, C.B. 1919; C.M.G. 1917; D.S.O. 1903; late 53rd Sikhs; *b.* 20 Nov. 1867; *s.* of late Maj.-Gen. F. J. Davies of Teignmouth; *m.* 1894, Beatrice Mary, 4th *d.* of late Christopher Sparrow of Urmston Lodge, Cheshire, and Bitton, Devonshire; one *s.* *Educ.:* U.S. College, Westward Ho; Kelly College, Tavistock; Newton College, Newton Abbot. Commissioned 1st Bn. Cheshire Regt., 1887; transferred to 3rd Sikh Infantry, Punjab Frontier Force, 1889; served N.-Western Frontier, India, 1897-98 (medal with 2 clasps); Tirah, 1897-98, including Dargai (clasp); China, 1900 (medal); North-Western Frontier, Gumatti, 1902 (wounded, despatches, D.S.O.); Zakka Khel Expedition, 1908; Mohmand Expedition, 1908 (despatches, medal with 2 clasps); European War (Mesopotamia, Palestine and Syria) 1914-18 (wounded, Bt. Col., C.M.G., C.B., despatches eleven times); Brig.-Gen., 1916; retired, 1920; Colonel of 3rd Batt., 12th Frontier Force Regiment, 1934-37. *Address:* Draynes House, nr. St. Cleer, Liskeard, Cornwall. *T.:* Dobwalls 242. [*Died* 2 *Jan.* 1954.

DAVIES, Brig. Charles S. P.; *see* Price-Davies.

DAVIES, Sir David, Kt., *cr.* 1938; J.P. County of London; *b.* 4 Jan. 1870; *s.* of late John Davies, Tyncae, Tregaron, Cardiganshire; *m.* 1897, Mary Ann, *d.* of late Abraham Edwards, Tymawr, Eglwysfach, Cardiganshire; one *s.* two *d.* Member St. Pancras Vestry, 1897-1900; Councillor St. Pancras Council, 1900-6; Alderman, 1906-45; Mayor of St. Pancras, 1911-12; Member L.C.C., 1912-22; Alderman, 1922-28; Chairman St. Pancras Bench, 1929-32; Member Justices Advisory Committee, 1930; Chairman S.E. St. Pancras Conservative Association, 1917-44, then elected President; Member Metropolitan Water Board; Life Governor, Royal Free Hospital; First President London Retail Dairymen's Association. *Address:* 6 Dukes Road, Tavistock Square, W.C.1. *T.:* Euston 1708. *Club:* Constitutional. [*Died* 25 *April* 1958.

DAVIES, David Alban; *b.* 13 April 1873; *s.* of Capt. Jenkin and Ann Davies; *m.* 1899, Rachel Williams; four *s.* one *d.* *Educ.:* Owens School; Oswestry. Governor of Univ. of Wales (Hon. LL.D.); Alderman of Cardiganshire C.C.; High Sheriff of Cardiganshire, 1940. *Recreation:* bowls. *Address* Brynawelon, Llanrhystyd, Cards. *T.:* Llanon 24. [*Died* 2 *Dec.* 1951.

DAVIES, Ernest S.; *see* Salter Davies.

DAVIES, Rev. (Francis Maurice) Russell, M.A.; Q.C. 1930; now working under a general licence from Bishop of Chichester; *b.* 7 Nov. 1871; *s.* of late Rev. S. Russell Davies *m.* 1st, Louisa Boulton; 2nd, Caroline Webb Holt; one *d.* *Educ.:* King's College School, London; Selwyn College, Cambridge, Math. Tripos. Deacon, 1897; Priest, 1898; called to Bar, Middle Temple, 1910; Junior Counsel, Board of Trade, 1919-29; Recorder of Worcester, 1931-37; Mayor of Hastings, 1929-30; Rural Dean of Hastings, 1953-56. *Address:* 126 Marine Court, St. Leonards on Sea. [*Died* 22 *June* 1956.

DAVIES, Gwendoline Elizabeth, C. H. 1937; Member of Council of National Library of Wales; of Court of Governors, University of Wales; and of Court of Governors, National Museum of Wales; *er. d.* of late Edward Davies, Plâs Dinam, Llandinam, Montgomeryshire, and Mary, *e. d.* of late Rev. Evan Jones, Brynhafren, Llandinam, Mont. *Address:* Gregynog, Newtown, Montgomeryshire. [*Died* 3 *July* 1951.

DAVIES, Henry J.; *see* Jones-Davies.

DAVIES, Henry Meirion; *b.* 29 March 1875; *s.* of William and Anne Davies; *m.* 1902, Margaret J., *d.* of Capt. John Lewis, Borth; one *s.* one *d.* *Educ.:* Tynyberth Council School, Corris; Old Bank School, Aberystwyth; U.C.W. Aberystwyth; Didsbury College. Travelled Bagillt Circuit (2 terms) Abergele: Rhyl, Pwllheli, Holyhead, Llanrwst, Barmouth, Coedpoeth, Towyn, Caernarvon, Llanrhaedr (2 terms), Liverpool (Oakfield Road); District Chapel Secretary (1st N. Wales) Overseas Missions; General Secretary of Overseas Missions for Wales; Journal Secretary of Welsh Methodist Assembly; Assistant Secretary; Secretary of Welsh Methodist Assembly 1921-33; President of Welsh Methodist Assembly 1934-35. *Publications:* Articles in Connexional Periodical (Eurgrawn). *Address:* Bronwylfa, Tregeiriog, Wrexham. [*Died* 28 *Jan.* 1950.

[*But death not notified in time for inclusion in Who Was Who 1941–1950, first edn.*

DAVIES, John Cledwyn, M.A.; J.P.; of the Middle Temple, Barrister-at-Law; late Director of Education for Denbighshire; Member of Court of University of Wales; Member of Council of the Welsh University and of its Finance Committee; Member of

Welsh Joint Education Cttee.; Member of Denbighshire C.C. and its Education Committee, also of Governing Bodies of various Schools in Wales; Former Headmaster, Holywell Secondary School, Flintshire; M.P. (N.L.) Denbigh, 1922-23. *Address*: Tyddyn-y-Parc, Denbigh. [*Died* 31 *Dec.* 1952.

DAVIES, John David Griffith, O.B.E. 1947; *b.* 19 Jan. 1899; *s.* of Rev. Thomas and Margaret Davies; *m.* 1st, Doreen (who obtained divorce), *d.* of late Dr. Ludford Freeman, Director of Education, Bristol; one *s.* one *d.*; 2nd, Elizabeth Irving, *d.* of late Irving Chase, Waterbury, Conn., U.S.A. *Educ.*: Monmouth School; Jesus College, Oxford. B.A. Oxon. Honour School of Modern History, 1923; M.A. Oxon. 1926. Served European War, 1916-19; Schoolmaster, 1923-26; Administrative Assistant, City of Leeds Education Dept., 1926-37; late Assistant Secretary, The Royal Society of London. *Publications*: England in the Middle Ages (with F. R. Worts), 1928; English Life to the End of the Middle Ages, 1929; A History for Senior Schools (with F. R. Worts), 1930; A New History of England, 4 vols., 1931-32; The Nation at Work, 1933; Owen Glyn Dwr, 1933; Henry V, 1934; Henry IV, 1935; George the Third, 1936; Honest George Monck, 1936; A Chronicle of Kingship (with R. B. Mowat), 1937; A King in Toils (George II), 1938; Revolt and Reaction (1789-1878), 1939; contributor to various papers and journals. *Recreations*: reading and music. *Address*: Burgh Fields, and Greystones Farm (bailiff), Bourton-on-the-Water, Glos. [*Died* 18 *Dec.* 1953.

DAVIES, John Llewelyn, O.B.E. 1958; Contractor Public Works; *b.* 18 Mar. 1888; *m.* 1927, Edith Llewelyn; one *d.* *Educ.*: Barmouth and Towyn County Sch. Joined firm of Davies Bros., Public Works Contractors. Mem. of Barmouth U.D.C. since 1915, Chm., 1924, 1931, 1937, 1946, and 1954-55. J.P.; High Sheriff, Merionethshire, 1944-45; Chairman Barmouth Bench Magistrates; Member Merionethshire C.C. Captain Royal St. David's Golf Club. *Recreation*: golf. *Address*: Allt Fawr, Barmouth. *T.*: 278. [*Died* 21 *Feb.* 1959.

DAVIES, J(ohn) Prysor; Solicitor to Ministry of Pensions and National Insurance, 1953-58 (Ministry of National Insurance, 1945-53), retired; also Solicitor to National Assistance Board, 1945-58; *b.* 26 Feb. 1900; *e. s.* of late Rev. David Davies, Harlech, Merionethshire. *Educ.*: University of Wales, Aberystwyth (B.A.). Schoolmaster, Marling School, Stroud, Glos., 1920-23; Solicitor, 1926; Board of Customs and Excise: Solicitor's Office, 1927-45; Asst. Solicitor, 1940. *Recreations*: prowling in street markets, antique shops and art galleries. *Address*: 6 Park Village East, Gloucester Gate, N.W.1. *T.*: Euston 4893. [*Died* 15 *June* 1959.

DAVIES, Sir Joseph, K.B.E., *cr.* 1918; J.P.; representative 1914-17 for Wales and Monmouthshire for the Cabinet Committee for Prevention of Unemployment; Secretary Prime Minister's Secretariat, 1916-20; M.P. (C.L.) Crewe Division of Cheshire 1918-22; Member Roy. Commission on Daylight Saving; Member War Cabinet Delegation to U.S.A. 1917; sometime Director Cambrian Railways, Chm. Totton and Fawley Light Railway Co., Chairman Agwi Petroleum Corporation, Director Anglo-Scottish Amalgamated Trust; *b.* 11 Dec. 1866; *m.* 1894, Blanche (*d.* 1951), *d.* of John Heron Wilson, Cardiff. *Educ.*: Bristol Gram. School. *Publications*: Railway Rates and Charges of United Kingdom; South Wales Coal Annual; The Prime Minister's Secretariat, 1916-1920. *Recreations*: golf, lawn tennis. *Address*: The Rise, Dinas Powis, Glam. *T.*: 3196 Dinas Powis. *Club*: Bath. [*Died* 3 *Dec.* 1954.

DAVIES, Joseph Edward, A.B., LL.B., LL.D., Ph.D., D.Litt., D.Sc.; Lawyer. Writer; *b.* Watertown, Wisconsin, 29 Nov. 1876; *s.* of Edward Davies and Rachel Paynter; *m.* 1st, 1902, Emlen Knight; 2nd, 1935, Marjorie Post; three *d.* *Educ.*: University of Wisconsin. State Prosecuting Attorney, Wisconsin, 1902-6; Chairman, Democratic Party, Wisconsin, 1911-16: Western Manager, Campaign for Election of Woodrow Wilson, 1912; U.S. Commissioner of Corporations, 1913-15; Ex-officio Member of War Industries Board, European War, 1914-18; Chairman, U.S. Federal Trade Commission, 1915-16; Economic Adviser to President Wilson at Versailles, 1918; Counsel for the Govts. of Mexico, Holland, Peru, San Domingo, U.S., in various international matters; Counsel for Tax Payers in Ford Stock Valuation Case, 1918-35; Ambassador of U.S. to U.S.S.R., 1936-38; Ambassador of U.S. to Belgium and Minister to Luxembourg, 1938-39: Special Assistant to Secretary of State Hull in charge of War Emergency Problems and Policies, 1939-1941; Chairman, Inaugural Committee for President Roosevelt, 1941-45; Chairman, War Relief Control Board, 1942-46; Special Envoy of President Roosevelt, with rank of Ambassador, to confer with Marshal Stalin, May-June 1943; Special Envoy of President Truman, with rank of Ambassador, to confer with Mr. Churchill, June 1945; Special Adviser to President Truman and Mr. Byrnes, with rank of Ambassador, to the Potsdam Conference, July-Aug. 1945; U.S. Medal for Merit, 1946; highest decorations of Govts. of Greece, Belgium, Yugoslavia, Luxembourg, San Domingo, U.S.S.R., U.S.A., France, Peru, Panama, Chile. *Publications*: Mission to Moscow, 1941; reports on Taxation of Corporations, Conflict of State Laws in the U.S. as to Corporations, Trust Laws, and Unfair Competition; writings for various periodicals, 1913-46. *Recreations*: yachting, golf. *Address*: 815 15th St., N.W., Washington, D.C. *T.A.*: Davjon, Washington, D.C. *T.*: National 4056. *Clubs*: Metropolitan, Chevy Chase, Capital Yacht (Washington, D.C.); Burning Tree Golf (Bethesda, Md.); The River, Metropolitan, New York Yacht (New York); Cedar Creek, Piping Rock (Locust Valley, N.Y.); Everglades, Bath and Tennis, Palm Beach Country (Palm Beach, Fla.); Gulf Stream (Delray, Fla.). [*Died* 9 *May* 1958.

DAVIES, Very Rev. Joseph Gwyn, M.A., LL.D.; Dean of Monmouth and Vicar of St. Woolos, Newport, Mon., since 1946; *b.* 18 Oct. 1890; *s.* of John Davies, St. David's, Pem.; *m.* 1922, Mary, *d.* of Rev. Morgan Richards, Vicar of Llanddeusant, Carms.; one *d.* *Educ.*: St. David's County School; St. David's College, Lampeter; Keble College, Oxford; Trinity College, Dublin. Curate All Saints, Llanelly, 1915-19; St. Michael, Aberystwyth, 1919-22; Vicar of Llanganten, Brecs., 1922-26; Chaplain of St. Paul's, Valparaiso, 1926-29; Vicar of Talgarth, Brecs., and Chaplain Mid-Wales Mental Hospital, 1929-35; Vicar of St. Andrew's, Cardiff, 1935-41; Examining Chaplain to Bishop of Swansea and Brecon, 1931-39, to Bishop of Llandaff, 1939; Vicar of Sketty, Swansea, and Chaplain to Swansea Mental Hospital, 1941-46; Judge of Provincial Court of Church in Wales, 1942: Canon of Brecon Cathedral, 1944-46; Examining Chaplain to Bishop of Monmouth, 1947; Grand Chaplain (Masonic) of United Grand Lodge of England, 1947-48. *Recreations*: masonic activities, historical research. *Address*: The Deanery, Stow Hill, Newport, Mon. *T.*: Newport 3338. [*Died* 17 *March* 1952.

DAVIES, Sir Leonard Twiston, K.B.E., *cr.* 1939 (O.B.E. 1937); D.L., J.P.; F.S.A.; Hon. LL.D. (Wales); Hon. Capt.

in Army; President Monmouthshire Rural Community Council; Council of Management, Welsh Land Settlement Society; Chairman, Wales Council of Social Service; Vice-Chairman Contemporary Art Society for Wales; Chairman of Governing Body of Monmouth School and Monmouth School for Girls; *b.* 16 May 1894; *s.* of W. L. Davies and M. L. Brown; *m.* Dorothy Savile, *d.* of F. Jackson, Broughton Park, Manchester; two *s.* one *d.* *Educ.:* Charterhouse; Liverpool University. With Imperial Tobacco Company for two years; West Lancs Brigade R.G.A. (T.), 1915-18 (invalided 1918); farmed in Herefordshire, 1918-24; moved to Monmouthshire, 1924; Governor, University of Wales; President of National Museum of Wales; Vice-Pres. National Library of Wales; Member Standing Commission on Museums and Galleries, 1949; Asst. Commissioner for Wales, St. John Ambulance Brigade; Pres. of Monmouthshire Chamber of Agriculture, 1932; High Sheriff, Monmouthshire, 1933; M.F.H. The Monmouthshire, 1931-33. Flight Lieut. R.A.F.V.R., 1940-41; K.J.St.J. *Publications:* Men of Monmouthshire; The Rev. Samuel Davies; (with Averyl Edwards) Women of Wales, and Welsh Life in the 18th Century; (with H. Lloyd Johnes) Welsh Furniture. *Recreations:* shooting, writing. *Address:* Gibraltar, Monmouth; Brynamlwg, Llanon, Cardiganshire. [*Died* 8 *Jan.* 1953.

DAVIES, Sir (Reginald) Charles, Kt., *cr.* 1939; J.P.; Solicitor; Chairman City of Leeds Conservative Assoc., 1933-57; Director Leeds Permanent Building Society since 1935; Manager since 1940; *b.* Colwyn Bay, North Wales, 21 Aug. 1886; *m.* 1st, Nora Procter (*d.* 1938), Boston Spa, Yorks; two *d.*; 2nd, 1940, Dorothy Elizabeth Yeadon, O.B.E. *Educ.:* Ellesmere College, Shropshire; Admitted a Solicitor, 1908; Member Leeds City Council, 1923-35; Alderman of Leeds, 1930-35; Hon. Sec. City of Leeds Conservative Assoc., 1928-33; President Incorporated Leeds Law Society, 1933-34, Hon. Sec., 1938-40; Member of Wades Charity since 1934; Patron Leeds Parish Church; Member Board of Management, Leeds Skyrac & Morley Savings Bank since 1935; Hon. Treas. Hope Hospital, Leeds, 1938-40; Chairman, Leeds Savings Committee, 1941-45; Chairman, Building Societies Assoc., 1948-50. *Address:* Manor Close, Wigton Lane, Alwoodley, Leeds. *Clubs:* Leeds, Leeds County Conservative (Leeds). [*Died* 20 *Nov.* 1958.

DAVIES, Professor Rhisiart Morgan, D.Sc. (Wales), Ph.D. (Cantab.); Professor of Physics, University College of Wales, Aberystwyth, since 1946; Vice-Principal, 1954-56; Visiting Professor California Institute of Technology and Reusselaer Polytechnic Institute, 1956-57; *b.* 4 Feb. 1903; *o. s.* of late Rev. Rhys Davies, Corris, Merioneth; *m.* 1928, Elizabeth Florence, *d.* of T. Davies, Aberystwyth; (one *s.* decd.). *Educ.:* Machynlleth and Dolgelley Grammar Schools; University College of Wales, Aberystwyth; Trinity College, Cambridge. University College of Wales, Aberystwyth: Asst. Lectr. in Physics, 1925, Lectr. 1928, Senior Lectr., 1939-46; Leverhulme Research Fell., Cambridge, 1939-41: research in Cavendish and Univ. Engineering Laboratories, Cambridge, for Admlty., Min. of Home Security and Min. of Supply, 1941-45. *Publications:* Joint Editor and Contributor, Surveys in Mechanics, 1956; papers in various scientific journals on stress waves in solids and liquids and detonation waves in gases. *Recreations:* music and sailing. *Address:* Brynceri, Iorwerth Avenue, Aberystwyth. *T.:* Aberystwyth 7373. [*Died* 18 *Feb.* 1958.

DAVIES, Rhys John; ten years Member Manchester City Council; Ex-Secretary, Distributive Workers Approved Society; *s.* of Rhys and Ann Davies; *b.* Llangennech, Carmarthenshire, 15 April 1877; *m.* 1902, Margaret A. Griffiths, Domestic Arts Teacher, Ton Pentre, Glam.; three *s.* *Educ.:* Elementary Schools. Commenced working life as farm servant; few years coal miner in Rhondda Valley; four years Co-operative Society's Cashier; official of the Distributive Workers' Union since 1906; M.P. (Lab.) Westhoughton, Lancs, 1921-51; Under-Secretary for Home Dept., Labour Govt., 1924; Past Pres. of the Manchester and Salford Labour Party and the Manchester and Salford Trades Council. *Publications:* Welsh books and pamphlets; (Joint) The Working Life of Shop Assistants. *Recreations:* travel, gardening, and music. *Address:* Manceinion, Newton, Porthcawl, Glam. *T.:* Porthcawl 285. [*Died* 31 *Oct.* 1954.

DAVIES, Rev. Russell; *see* Davies, Rev. F. M. R.

DAVIES, Timothy; Income Tax Commissioner, 1917; J.P.; *b.* Panty Fedwen, near Carmarthen, 1857. *Educ.:* Llanpumsaint. Apprenticed to the Textile Trade in Liverpool; founder of business in Fulham, 1885; M.P. (L.) Fulham, 1906-10, and Louth Division Lincs, 1910-20; member Fulham Vestry, 1895-1900; member of first Borough Council, later Alderman; Mayor of Fulham, 1901-2; member of L.C.C., 1901 and 1904. *Recreations:* golf, riding. *Address:* 12 Ulleswater, Putney Hill, S.W.15. [*Died* 22 *Aug.* 1951.

DAVIES, Tudor; Principal Tenor, Vic Wells Opera Co., London; 5th *s.* of David and Sarah Davies, Porth, Glamorganshire. *Educ.:* Cardiff Univ.; Royal College of Music. Vocalist and operatic artist; English début made with the British National Opera Company at Bradford, has sung at all the leading festivals in Great Britain and America, also in Paris, and command performances at the Royal Opera House, Covent Garden; also Grand Opera in America. *Recreations:* tennis, motoring and fishing. *Address:* Trefanwy, Riverside, Egham, Surrey. *T.:* Egham 264. [*Died* 2 *April* 1958.

DAVIES, Hon. Brig.-Gen. Walter Percy Lionel, C.M.G. 1919; D.S.O. 1916; late R.A.; *b.* 14 Jan. 1871; 2nd *s.* of Rev. W. P. Davies, Kirton, Ipswich; *m.* 1924, Florence Mary (*d.* 1933), *widow* of Maj. George Loch, Loyal North Lancs. Entered R.A. 1893; Capt. 1900; Major 1910; Brig.-Gen. 1916; Staff College, 1905-6; Staff Employment, India, 1907-10, and 1912-14; served S. Africa, 1900-2 (despatches, Queen's medal 5 clasps, King's medal 2 clasps); European War, with Indian Expeditionary Force, 1914-18 (despatches twice, D.S.O.); in Mesopotamian Expeditionary Force from 1916 (C.M.G., despatches thrice, Bt.-Col. 1917, Croix de Guerre); operations in Mesopotamia, 1920-21 (despatches); retired pay, 1924. *Address:* Brownheath, Droitwich, Worcs. *T.:* Fernhill Heath 69. *Club:* Army and Navy. [*Died* 15 *Nov.* 1952

DAVIES, Colonel Warburton Edward, C.M.G. 1917; C.B.E. 1923; D.S.O. 1919; *b.* 14 July 1879; *s.* of Byam Davies of Corsley House, Warminster; *m.* 1928, Georgina Mary, *widow* of Captain E. N. Fisher, and *d.* of late W. M. Hammick. *Educ.:* Eton; Sandhurst. Joined Rifle Brigade, 1899; served in Crete; S. African War, 1899-1902; defence of Ladysmith; action of Belfast, 26-27 Aug. 1900 (despatches); Egypt; Capt. 1904; Malta; Staff College, Camberley, 1908-9; Brigade-Major, 8 Infantry Brigade, Devonport, 1911-12; General Staff, War Office, 1913-14; European War: operations in France and Flanders, 1914-15; (despatches five times, Legion of Honour, C.M.G., D.S.O., the order of the Crown of Italy; Order of the Sacred Treasure; Order of the Nile; Order of the White Eagle; Major, Dec. 1914; Bt. Lieut.-Col. 1916); General Staff, War Office, 1916; served in Palestine, Feb. 1918-Dec. 1918; commanded 2nd Batt. Rifle Brigade, 1919-22; Colonel, 1920;

retired pay, 1928; employed at G.H.Q. H.F., 1939-42, as Inspector of V.P.'s and Senior Liaison Officer. *Address:* Heatherside House, Camberley, Surrey. *Club:* Army and Navy. [*Died* 3 *Dec.* 1956.

DAVIES, Sir William Llewelyn, Kt., *cr.* 1944; M.A. (Wales); Hon. LL.D. (Wales), F.S.A.; Librarian of the National Library of Wales, Aberystwyth, since 1930; *b.* Plas Gwyn Schoolhouse, near Pwllheli, 11 Oct. 1887; *m.* 1914, Gwen, *d.* of Dewi Llewelyn, Pontypridd; one *d.* *Educ.:* University College of Wales, Aberystwyth. First Assistant Librarian, National Library of Wales, Aberystwyth, 1919; a Historical MSS. Commissioner since 1943; a Vice-President of British Records Association since 1939; Editor of the National Library of Wales Journal, Journal of Merioneth Historical and Records Soc., High Sheriff of Merionethshire, 1952. *Publications:* The National Library of Wales, A Survey of its History, its Contents, and its Activities, 1937; bibliographical, literary, and historical contributions to Welsh periodicals. *Address:* Sherborne House, Aberystwyth. *T.:* Aberystwyth 392, 393 and 577. [*Died* 11 *Nov.* 1952.

DAVIES-COLLEY, Robert, C.M.G. 1918; M.Ch. Cantab., F.R.C.S. England, Hon. Col. A.M.S.; Consulting Surgeon to Guy's Hospital; *s.* of J. N. C. Davies-Colley, M.A., M.C. Cantab.; *m.* 1908, Emily Crosby Jones; two *d.* *Educ.:* Westminster; Emmanuel College, Cambridge; Guy's Hosp. Late Consulting Surgeon, Mesopotamia Expeditionary Force; served European War, 1914-19 in France, India and Mesopotamia (despatches, C.M.G.); F.R.S.M., F.Z.S., etc. *Publications:* various papers to Medical Journals. *Recreations:* golf and shooting. *Address:* 10 Devonshire Place, W.1; Leas Green, Perry St., Chislehurst. *T.:* Welbeck 7694, Foots Cray 1519. *Club:* Athenæum. [*Died* 16 *April* 1955.

DAVIES-GILBERT, Mrs. Grace Catherine Rose, C.B.E. 1919; *d.* of late George King Staunton Massy Dawson of Ballinacourté, Tipperary; *m.* 1881, late Carew Davies-Gilbert, of Trelissick, Truro, and The Manor House, Eastbourne; five *d.* *Address:* The Manor Hall, Eastbourne. *Club:* Ladies' Empire. [*Died* 8 *July* 1951.

DAVIOT, Gordon; novelist and playwright; *d.* of Colin MacKintosh and Josephine Horne; unmarried. *Educ.:* Inverness. Trained in Birmingham as a physical training instructress and worked as such in various parts of England; wrote short stories which appeared in the English Review and similar periodicals; first accepted play was Richard of Bordeaux. Other plays: The Laughing Woman, produced 1934; Queen of Scots, 1934, both at the New Theatre; The Little Dry Thorn, Citizens' Theatre, Glasgow, April 1946 and Lyric Theatre, Hammersmith, Dec. 1947; Valerius, Repertory Players, 1948; The Stars Bow Down, Malvern, 1949. *Publications:* three novels, the best known being Kif; Claverhouse (biography), 1937; The Stars Bow Down (play), 1939; Leith Sands (one-act plays), 1946. Writes detective stories under the name of Josephine Tey, including the Daughter of Time, 1951. *Recreations:* cinema, country, horse-racing. *Club:* Cowdray. [*Died* 13 *Feb.* 1952.

DAVIS, Arthur J., R.A. 1942; A.R.A. 1933; F.R.I.B.A.; senior partner in firm Mewès & Davis, architects; Chevalier de la Légion d'Honneur (France); Palmes Ordre de la Couronne (Belgium); Former Member of Royal Fine Arts Commission; former Vice-President Royal Society of Arts; *b.* 21 May 1878; *m.* 1924, Rona Jean (*d.* 1940), *d.* of Ernest Lee; one *s.* one *d.* *Educ.:* Ecole Beaux Arts, Paris; Atelier Pascal. *Chief Works:* the interior planning and decoration of the Carlton Hotel, the construction and decoration of the Ritz Hotel and Royal Automobile Club, R.A.C. Woodcote Park, Epsom, the Morning Post Building, the Cavalry Club, Armenian Church, the Hudson's Bay House; Morgan, Grenfell Bank; Westminster Banks, Lothbury, Threadneedle Street, Brussels and Antwerp; Cunard House, London; Consulting Architect, Cunard Building, Liverpool; Hon. Architect, Dulwich Gallery; National Bank of Scotland, Edinburgh; warehouses and factories, as well as numerous town and country residences, and the decorations of the s.s. Aquitania, Laconia, and Franconia. *Recreations:* golf and water-colour sketching. *Address:* 35 Hornton Court, W.8. *T.A.:* Echinus-Piccy, London. *Clubs:* Athenæum, Royal Automobile. [*Died* 22 *July* 1951.

DAVIS, Charles H. H.; *see* Hart-Davis.

DAVIS, Air Vice-Marshal Edward Derek, C.B. 1945; O.B.E. 1939; A.F.R.Ae.S.; special appointment, Ministry of Supply, since 1947; *b.* 18 October 1895; *m.* 1921, Lilian Beatrice Allen; no *c.* *Educ.:* Alleyn's School, Dulwich. Joined Civil Service, 1911, resigned Nov. 1914, having been refused permission to enlist. Served European War, 1914-18, joined Roy. Naval Armoured Car Div. as Driver-Machine Gunner, 1914, Gallipoli; Flight Sub-Lieut. (Pilot) R.N.A.S., 1916, engaged on A.A. and Anti-Submarine duties; permanently commissioned, R.A.F., 1919; flying duties, Mediterranean Command and H.M.S. Pegasus, 1919-24; Specialist Armament Course, 1924; Air Armament School and Armament Practice Camps, 1925-1928; Staff College Course, 1929; Iraq Comd. as Trng. and Armament, 1930-31; Air Armament School and 25 Armament Gp., 1932-35; Chief Armament Experimental Officer, Aeroplane and Armament Experimental Establishment, 1935-36; Asst. Dir. Armament Research and Development, Air Ministry, 1936-39; War of 1939-45: Command Armament Officer, Bomber Cmd., 1940-41; Vice-Pres., Ordnance Bd., 1941-42; A.O.C. 25 Armament, Navigation and Signals Group (Trng.), 1942-45; retired 1946. *Address:* 1 Lansdowne Terrace, W.C.1. [*Died* 19 *Sept.* 1955.

DAVIS, Elmer (Holmes); radio news analyst, American Broadcasting Company; *b.* Aurora, Indiana, 13 Jan. 1890; *s.* of Elam Holmes Davis and Louise Severin; *m.* 1917, Florence MacMillan; one *s.* one *d.* *Educ.:* Franklin Coll. (A.B. 1910, A.M. 1911); Queen's College, Oxford (B.A. 1912). Teacher, Franklin (Ind.) High School, 1909-10; editorial staff, Adventure, 1913-14; on staff of New York Times, 1914-1924; News Analyst, Columbia Broadcasting System, 1939-42; Director Office of War Information, U.S. Government, 1942-1945 (Medal for Merit); Member, Council Authors' League of America, 1926-41 (President 1939-41). Dutch Order of Orange-Nassau; Czechoslovak Order of White Lion (Old Republic). *Publications:* But We Were Born Free (essays), 1954; Two Minutes to Midnight, 1955; various books now out of print. *Recreations:* listening to music, looking at cats. *Address:* 1661 Crescent Place, N.W., Washington, D.C. *Clubs:* Century (New York); Cosmos (Washington, D.C.). [*Died* 18 *May* 1958.

DAVIS, Col. Evans Greenwood, C.M.G. 1916; V.D.; M.D.; M.C.P. and S.O.; F.A.C.S.; consulting physician; Past President College of Physicians and Surgeons of Ontario; one time Director Medical Services Soldiers' Civil Re-establishment, Canada, and Commissioner Board of Pension Commissioners; *b.* 1885; *s.* of late Very Rev. Evans Davis; *m.* 1921, Bernice Owen, *d.* of Alfred T. Davis, Calgary; one *d.* *Educ.:* Western University, Canada; New York; England. Served European War, 1914-19 (despatches twice, C.M.G.), and 1939-42 in war of 1939-45. *Recreations:* hunting,

fishing, riding, etc. *Address:* 496 Waterloo Street, London, Ontario, Canada. *Club:* London Hunt and Country (London, Ont.). [*Died* 24 *May* 1951.

DAVIS, Francis Robert Edward, C.B.E. 1936; late Sec., G.W.R. Co., Paddington Station, W.2; retd. 1947; *b.* 21 March 1887; *s.* of Frederick William and Rebecca Davis; *m.* 1908, Kitty Smith; no *c.* *Educ.:* St. Mark's College, Chelsea. F.C.I.S., Past President; Fellow Chartered Surveyors' Institution; passed Bar Final Examination 1919; served European War, 1915-19, Royal Naval Air Service and Royal Air Force (despatches, O.B.E.); Member of Kensington Royal Borough Council. Lt.-Comdr. R.N.V.R. District Officer Admiralty Sea Cadet Corps, Commanding Officer Kensington Unit, 1942. *Recreation:* golf. *Address:* 37 Porchester Gate, W.2. *T.:* Bayswater 4934. *Club:* Roehampton. [*Died* 12 *July* 1960.

DAVIS, Lieut.-Col. Harold James Norman, C.M.G. 1919; D.S.O. 1917; late The King's Own Scottish Borderers; *b.* 15 March 1882; *s.* of late Lt.-Col. J. Norman Davis of Clondarragh, Foxrock, Co. Dublin; *m.* 1915, Margaret Georgiana, *d.* of Capt. S. Hyde-Smith; two *s.* one *d.* (and one *s.* decd.). *Educ.:* King's School, Warwick; R.M.C., Sandhurst; Commissioned The Connaught Rangers, 1900; served South African War, 1901-2 (Queen's medal and four clasps); European War with 1st and 2nd Connaught Rangers, as Bde.-Major 70th Infantry Brigade; in Command 15th Bn. Highland Light Infantry and 47th and 9th Bns. Machine Gun Corps (despatches 5 times; Brevet Major, D.S.O., C.M.G., Belgian Croix de Guerre); graduate Staff College, Camberley; commanded 1st Bn. K.O.S.B., 1928-32. *Address:* Brookfurlongs, Winchcombe, Gloucestershire. *T.:* Winchcombe 97. [*Died* 16 *April* 1960.

DAVIS, Captain Herbert Ludlow, C.I.E. 1944; R.I.N. retd.; Nautical Adviser to Govt. of India from 1940; *b.* 28 Feb. 1887; *s.* of late J. H. Davis, Dunster, Somerset; *m.* 1920, Olga Parkinson, Australian Army Nursing Service, *d.* of Dr. C. Parkinson, Melbourne, Australia; one *d.* *Educ.:* King's College, Taunton, Somerset. Went to sea, Merchant Service (Sail), 1902; Midshipman R.N.R.; joined late Royal Indian Marine as Sub-Lt. 1908; European War, 1914, various H.M. Ships in Red Sea and Persian Gulf; Commander R.I.M.; Capt. R.I.N. 1934; Technical Adviser to Indian Delegate to London Naval Conference, 1930; Seconded for duty with Dept. of Commerce, Govt. of India, 1935. Retired and re-employed, 1942. *Recreations:* golf, reading, photography. *Address:* c/o Commerce Dept., Govt. of India, Simla; c/o Grindlay's Bank Ltd., 54 Parliament Street, S.W.1. *Clubs:* United Service (Simla); Willingdon, Royal Bombay Yacht (Bombay). [*Died* 10 *Oct.* 1951.

DAVIS, James Corbett, C.M.G. 1922; *b.* 1870; *e. s.* of late James Davis of Norwood; *m.* 1st, Edith (*d.* 1939), *d.* of George Wride Strawson of Lee, Kent; 2nd, 1940, Mrs M. E. Sergeant, *d.* of late George Smart, Nottingham. *Educ.:* privately. Engaged in banking in South Africa, 1895-1906; Treasurer, Zanzibar Protectorate, 1906; Financial Member of Council, 1910; Member of Protectorate Council, 1914; acting First Minister at various times; transferred from Foreign Office to Colonial Office Service, 1914; Commissioner of Currency, Zanzibar; President, Zanzibar Harbour Works Board; Acting Chief Secretary to the Government, 1920, until retirement, 1922; British Residents' Deputy on various occasions; represented the East African Group of Dependencies at the British Empire Statistical Conference held in London, 1920; Second-Class Order Alyieh, 1908; Second-Class Order Brilliant Star of Zanzibar, 1919. *Address:* Chuini Cottage, 3rd Avenue, Frinton-on-Sea, Essex. *T.:* Frinton 143. *Club:* Cricket (Frinton). [*Died* 5 *March* 1957.

DAVIS, John Merle, M.A., B.D.; Hon. D.H.L. Oberlin Coll., 1949; Hon. Research Fellow in Economics, University of California (appointment by Univ. Regents), 1950-52, retd.; *b.* 1 Nov. 1875; *s.* of Jerome Dean Davis and Sophia Demond Strong; *m.* 1903, Valborg Wilhelmina Vea; one *s.* three *d.* *Educ.:* Oberlin College; Hartford Theological Seminary; Göttingen, Leipsic, and Munich Universities. Hon. Sec. Y.M.C.A., Nagasaki, 1906-11, and Tokyo, 1913-22; Executive Sec. International Survey of Race Relations on the Pacific Coast of N. America, 1922-24; General Sec. Institute of Pacific Relations, Honolulu H.T. 1925-30; Director, Department of Social and Economic Research and Counsel, Internat. Missionary Council, 1930-46; Org. Dir. Enquiry into African Family and Marriage Customs (auspices Internat. Afr. Inst. and Internat. Missionary Council, London), 1947-48; Director of Survey and Research, Agricultural Missions, Inc., 156 Fifth Avenue, New York, 1948. Director, Commission to Copper Belt, Belgian Congo and Northern Rhodesia, 1931-32; Director, Bantu Educational Cinema Experiment, Tanganyika, E.A., 1935; Member Commission to Indians of the High Andes, 1943. *Publications:* Davis, Soldier Missionary, 1914; Modern Industry and the African, 1933; The Economic and Social Environment of the Younger Churches, 1938; The Economic Basis of the Evangelical Church in Mexico, 1940; The Cuban Church in a Sugar Economy, 1942; The Church in the New Jamaica, 1942; The Church in Puerto Rico's Dilemma, 1942; How the Church grows in Brazil, 1943; The Evangelical Church in the River Plate Republics, 1943; New Buildings on Old Foundations, 1945; (Joint) Indians of the High Andes, 1946. *Recreations:* mountain climbing, yachting, tennis. *Address:* 2063 Byron St., Palo Alto, California, U.S.A. [*Died* 15 *March* 1960.

DAVIS, John William, G.B.E. (Hon.) 1953; *b.* Clarksburg, West Virginia, U.S.A., 13 Apr. 1873; *s.* of John J. Davis and Anna Kennedy; *m.* 1st, 1899, Julia T. M'Donald (*d.* 1900); 2nd, 1912, Ellen G. Bassel (*d.* 1943); one *d.* *Educ.:* Washington and Lee University, Lexington, Virginia, A.B. 1892, LL.B. 1895, LL.D. 1915. Hon. degrees: LL.D. Univ. of West Virginia, 1919; Glasgow Univ., 1919; University of Birmingham, 1919; Union College, 1921; Yale University, 1921; Dartmouth College, 1923; Brown University, 1923; Princeton, 1924; Oberlin, 1947; New York Univ., 1951; Columbia Univ., 1953. Dr. of Civil Law, Oxford, 1950; Hofstra College, 1953. Admitted to Bar, 1895; Member W. Va. House of Delegates, 1899; candidate for Electoral College, 1900; Member Democratic National Convention, 1904-32; Pres. W. Va. Bar Association, 1906; elected to 62nd and 63rd Congresses, 1911-15; Solicitor-General U.S.A., 1913-18; American Ambassador at the Court of St. James', 1918-21; Commissioner to Conference with Germany on Treatment and Exchange of Prisoners of War at Berne, 1918; President American Bar Association, 1922; Democratic nominee for President, 1924; President, Association Bar of City of New York; Hon. Bencher Middle Temple. *Publications:* Party Government in the United States, 1930; occasional addresses. *Recreations:* golf, riding, fishing. *Address:* 15 Broad Street, New York City, U.S.A. [*Died* 24 *March* 1955.

DAVIS, Hon. Thomas C., Q.C. (Can.); Canadian Foreign Service, retired; *b.* Prince Albert, Saskatchewan, 6 September 1889; *s.* of Hon. Thomas Osborne Davis, Liberal M.P. for Prince Albert, 1896-1904, Senator, 1904-17, and Rebecca B. Jennings,

both Irish; *m.* 1925, Grace E., *d.* of Hon. Mr. Justice Elwood, Regina; no *c.* *Educ.:* St. John's College, Winnipeg; Osgoode Hall, Toronto. Barrister; Alderman at Prince Albert, 1916-20; Mayor, Prince Albert, 1921-1924; first elected to Legislature, 1925; Provincial Secretary, Minister of Municipal Affairs and Minister in charge of the Bureau of Labour and Industries, 1926, re-elected 1926, 1929, 1934 and 1938; Attorney-General of Saskatchewan, 1927-29, 1934-39; Judge of Court of Appeal, Sask., 1939; granted leave of absence as Deputy Minister Dept. National War Services, Government of Canada, 1940; Canadian High Commissioner in Australia, 1942-46; Canadian Ambassador to China, 1946-49, to Federal Republic of Germany, 1950-54; to Japan, 1954-57, retired. Resigned from the Bench, Jan. 1949, and entered Canadian Foreign Service as a permanent member. *Recreations:* golf, fishing and hunting. *Address:* 3605 Cadboro Bay Rd., Victoria, B.C., Canada. *Clubs:* Prince Albert (Prince Albert); Assiniboia, (Regina); Vancouver, Vancouver Union (Victoria).
[*Died* 21 *Jan.* 1960.

DAVISON, Charles Stewart, B.A., M.A., LL.B.; Hon. Fellow Magdalene College, Cambridge; *b.* 14 April 1855; unmarried; *s.* of Edward Francis and Charlotte Sewall (White) Davison. *Educ.:* on the Continent with tutor; Fay School, Newport, R.I.; Harvard; Columbia; Cambridge; Inner Temple. Counselor-at-law in New York City since 1877; Specialist in constitutional and commercial law; formerly Chm. Exec. Committee Assoc. of the Bar of the City of New York, etc.; Chevalier Legion of Honor, 1920; devised the Mystery Ships (Q-Boats) for British and French Navies, 1915; Drew the Fisheries Law of the Province of Quebec. *Publications:* Letters to Hiram Freeborn (1915-18); Reprisal in War; Dealers in Money; Maritime and Belligerent Rights; Treason, etc.; Selling the Bear's Hide, 1902; Freedom of the Seas, 1918; The Alien in Our Midst, 1930; also (with Madison Grant) The Passing of the Great Race, 1916 and The Conquest of a Continent, 1933. *Recreations:* Salmon angling, yachting, golf, large game shooting, breeding domestic animals, etc. *Address:* 25 Broad Street, New York City; Green River Farm, South Williamstown, Mass. *T.A.:* Cedilla, New York. *T.:* Hanover 2-1557, Lackawanna 4-0883. *Clubs:* United University; Downtown Asstn., Harvard, Century (New York); Pitt, Amateur Dramatic (Cambridge).
[*Died* 25 *Nov.* 1942.
[*But death not notified in time for inclusion in Who Was Who 1941–1950, first edn.*

DAVISON, Rev. Gilderoy, M.A. (Cantab.); A.L.C.M.; Vicar of S. Peter's, Braintree; *b.* 30 Aug. 1892; *s.* of late Thomas Davison and Minnie G. Davison, O.B.E. *Educ.:* Allens School, Newcastle; S. Catharine's College, Cambridge. Lt. R.A.S.C., 1915-20 (despatches); Curate S. Thomas Douglas; Curate in Charge S. Edmunds Croydon; Croydon Parish Church; has served on National Savings Cttee., Red Cross Cttee., Communal Feeding Cttee., Actors Church Union, British Legion, Old Contemptibles Assoc., A.R.P., U.D.C. 1938-47, Food Control Cttee., Education Cttee., Girls' Training Corps, A.T.C.; Chaplain Boy Scouts and S. Michael's Hospital, Braintree. Formerly member of Rotary Clubs at Croydon, Douglas (I. of M.), and Braintree. *Publications:* Man with the Twisted Face; Prince of Spies; Traitor Unmasked; Devil's Apprentice; Killer at Scotland Yard; Mystery of Red Haired Valet; Twisted Face the Avenger; The Mysterious Mr. Brent; Exit Mr. Brent; Man with Half a Face; Lily Pond Mystery; Murder in a Muffler; Devil's Diamonds; Jewels of Destiny; Twisted Face Strikes Again; Death in A.R.P.; Twisted Face defends his Title; A Dog-fight with Death; Mysterious Air Ace; Robin Hoodwinker, V.C.; Satan's Satellite. *Recreations:* gardening, tennis, badminton, bridge, writing serious novels under a nom-de-plume. *Address:* S. Peter's Vicarage, Braintree, Essex.
[*Died* 9 *May* 1954.

DAVISON, Sir Ronald Conway, Kt., *cr.* 1938; Writer and Lecturer on unemployment and social questions; *b.* London, March 1884; *s.* of George and Louisa Davison; *m.* 1st, 1911, Sheila Grant (*d.* 1923) of Rothiemurchus; 2nd, 1926, Emily Whiteman; two *s.* two *d.* *Educ.:* Charterhouse; Oriel College, Oxford. At Toynbee Hall, 1908-10; Civil Servant, 1912-28, Board of Trade and Ministry of Labour; retired at age 43 to write and lecture in England, United States and Canada. Lecturer to H.M. Forces overseas, 1944 and 1945. *Publications;* The Unemployed: Old Policies and New, 1929; British Unemployment Policy, 1938; Insurance for All and Everything, 1943. *Recreations:* anything in reason. *Address:* The White House, Shiplake-on-Thames, Oxon. *Club:* Reform.
[*Died* 30 *Sept.* 1958.

DAVISON, Rev. Canon William Holmes, M.A.; Rector of the Church of St. John the Evangelist, 1917-51, Rector Emeritus, 1952, and Canon of Christ Church Cathedral, Montreal, since 1929; *b.* 13 Jan. 1884; *s.* of late William Davison and late Agnes Selina McCarthy; *m.* 1932, Marion Frances Wood; one *s.* one *d.* *Educ.:* Keble College, Oxford; Cuddesdon Theological College. Deacon, 1908; Priest, 1909; Assistant Curate of St. Columba's, Sunderland, 1908-13; Rector of Long Island, Bahamas, 1913-16; Member General Synod of Church of England in Canada; Member of Edinburgh World Conference on Faith and Order, 1937. Prolocutor of Lower House of Ecclesiastical Province of Canada, 1949. *Publications:* Contributor to Symposium: The Great Certainty, 1946; The Nature of Marriage, 1946; He Shall Speak Peace, 1952. *Recreation:* walking. *Address:* 3 Martin Avenue, Dorval, P.Q., Canada. *T.:* Melrose 1.3102.
[*Died* 31 *Jan.* 1955.

DAVISSON, Clinton J., Ph.D.; Sc.D.(hon.) Purdue; D.Sc.(hon.) Princeton and Colby; D.(hon.) Lyon, 1939; *b.* Bloomington, Illinois, U.S.A., 22 Oct. 1881; *s.* of Joseph and Mary Calvert Davisson; *m.* 1911, Charlotte S. Richardson, Yorkshire; three *s.* one *d.* *Educ.:* University of Chicago, B.S. 1908; Princeton University, Ph.D. 1911; Instructor in Physics, Carnegie Institute of Technology, Pittsburgh, Pa., 1911-17; Member Technical Staff of the Bell Telephone Laboratories, New York City, 1917-46; Professor of Physics, University of Virginia, 1947-49; Comstock Prize in Physics, 1928; Elliot Cresson Medal, 1931; Hughes Medal of Royal Society, 1935; Member of National Research Council, 1928-31, 1933-36; Nobel Prize for Physics, 1937; Editorial Board of Physical Review, 1929-32; Alumni Medal, University of Chicago, 1941; Vice-President, A.A.A.S.; Chairman, Sec. B., 1933. Member, Natl. Academy of Sciences, Amer. Philosophical Soc., Amer. Acad. Arts and Sciences, (hon. memb.) New York Acad. of Sciences, Phi Beta Kappa, Sigma Xi. *Publications:* Papers and notes on thermionics, radiation, electron diffraction and electron lenses in scientific journals. *Recreation:* reading. *Address:* 2605 Jefferson Park Circle, Charlottesville, Va., U.S.A.
[*Died* 1 *Feb.* 1958.

DAVY, Colonel Cecil William, C.M.G. 1918; late R.E.; *b.* 25 March 1868; 3rd *s.* of late J. W. Davy, J.P. of Ingoldsthorpe Hall, Norfolk; *m.* 1st, 1896, Ivy (*d.* 1897), *d.* of late Major R. Bainbridge, 17th Lancers; one *s.*; 2nd, 1926, Maude Antoinette, *widow* of Capt. C. J. McI. Lomer, 8th Hussars. *Educ.:* Elizabeth College, Guernsey; R.M. Academy, Woolwich. Joined R.E. 1887; served Malta, 1890-95; South African War (Queen's medal 4 clasps); Colonial employment in S.A., 1902-4; Chief Instructor Electricity, S.M.E. Chatham, 1906-9; Ireland, 1909-12; Hong Kong, 1912-14; European War, France 1915-19 (despatches

twice, C.M.G.); retired pay, 1924; J.P.(Norfolk). *Recreations:* shooting, fishing, golf. *Address:* Ingoldisthorpe Hall, King's Lynn, Norfolk. [*Died* 27 *March* 1957.

DAVY, F. H. M. N.; *see* Humphrey-Davy.

DAVY, Lieut.-Col. Philip Claude Tresilian, C.M.G. 1916; gold medal of the Order of S. John of Jerusalem, 1916; M.B. London, M.R.C.S., L.R.C.P.; *b.* 3 Aug. 1877; *s.* of Jas. Tresilian Davy, Ottery St. Mary, Devon; *m.* 1906, Dorothy Clifford (*d.* 1950), *d.* of George Thompson, M.D., Stapleton, Glos.; one *s.* one *d.* *Educ.:* Blundell's School, Tiverton; University College Hospital, London (Fellowes Medallist). Entered R.A.M.C. 1904; Capt. 1908; Major, 1915; Lt.-Col. 1927; retired 1932; served West Africa, India, France and Egypt; recalled to active list, 1939-41; Member of Pension Appeal Tribunal, 1944. *Publications:* In medical journals. *Recreations:* shooting, fishing, golf, music. *Address:* c/o Glyn Mills & Co., Kirkland House, Whitehall, S.W.1. [*Died* 25 *Sept.* 1951.

DAW, Sir John Edward, Kt., *cr.* 1943; J.P.; *b.* 26 Nov. 1866; *s.* of Richard Rendle Miller and Frances Daw. *Educ.:* Exeter School. Solicitor, 1887; Member of Exeter City Council, 1889-1902; Member of Devon County Council, 1925-55; Alderman, 1933; Vice-Chairman, 1933; Chairman, 1937-46; Registrar of the Exeter, Newton Abbot and Torquay County Courts, 1902-27; Chairman of Governors of Exeter School, Exeter. *Address:* 4 Louisa Terrace, Exmouth, Devon. *T.:* Exmouth 2356. [*Died* 6 *Aug.* 1959.

DAWES, Sir (Albert) Cecil, Kt., *cr.* 1951; C.B.E. 1945; Barrister-at-law; Legal Adviser, Ministry of Education, 1940-54, retd.; *b.* 24 Sept. 1890; *s.* of Albert Henry Dawes and Beatrice Dickson; *m.* 1919, Jeanne Marie Louise De Bruyker; three *s.* *Educ.:* Watford Grammar School; London Univ. B.A. (1st hons.), 1910; LL.B. (3rd hons.), 1913; Bar Final (certificate of honour), 1914, Whittuck Scholar and Quain Prizeman International Law, Bar Criminal Law Prize. H.M. Forces, 1914-19; Board of Education, 1919. Secretary to Statutory Commission, Durham University, 1935-37. *Recreations:* sailing, fishing, gardening. *Address:* Springfield, Copse Hill, West Wimbledon, S.W.20. *T.:* Wimbledon 4216. [*Died* 3 *May* 1959.

DAWES, Brig.-Gen. Charles Gates, C.B.; *b.* Marietta, Ohio, 27 Aug. 1865; *s.* of General Rufus R. Dawes and Mary Beman Gates; *m.* 1889, Caro D. Blymyer, Cincinnati. *Educ.:* Marietta College; Cincinnati Law School. Admitted to Bar, 1886; Comptroller of the Currency, 1897-1902; Director of the Budget, 1921-22; Vice-President of United States, 1925-29; American Ambassador at the Court of St. James, 1929-32; President Reconstruction Finance Corporation, 1932; served in France, 1917-19 (D.S.M., Croix de Guerre, Commander Order of Leopold, Belgium, Commander Legion of Honour, Commander Order of St. Maurice and St. Lazarus, Italy); appointed by Reparations Commission to investigate possibilities of German Budget, 1923; Chairman of Financial Commission to Dominican Republic, April 1929; Member American Delegation to the London Naval Conference, 1930. Nobel Peace Prize (jt.) 1925. *Publications:* The Banking System of the U.S., 1892; Essays and Speeches, 1915; A Journal of the Great War, 1921; The First Year of the Budget of the U.S., 1923; Notes as Vice-President, 1935; A Journal of Reparations, 1939; Journal as Ambassador to Great Britain, 1939. *Address:* Evanston, Ill., U.S.A. [*Died* 23 *April* 1951.

DAWES, Lt.-Col. George William Patrick, D.S.O. 1917; M.B.E. 1946; A.F.C.; *b.* 1880; *m.* 1st, 1913, Margaret, *e. d.* of E. G. Money; one *d.*; 2nd, 1930, Olive, *o. d.* of M. D. Harrel; one *s.* Served S. Africa, Royal Berkshire Regt., 1900-2 (Queen's medal with three clasps, King's medal with two clasps). Took up flying privately, 1909; Pilot's Flying Licence, No. 17, July 1910; posted to R.F.C. 1912; European War, served France and commanded R.F.C. in the Balkans, 1916-18 (despatches seven times, D.S.O., Bt. Lt.-Col., Serbian Order of White Eagle, Order of Redeemer of Greece, Croix de Guerre with three Palms, Officer Legion of Honour, A.F.C.). Served with R.A.F., 1939-46, as Wing Commander (M.B.E.). *Address:* The Manor House, 5 Gregory Street, Old Lenton, Nottingham. *T.:* 77336. [*Died* 17 *March* 1960.

DAWKINS, Richard MacGillivray, F.B.A.; M.A. Cantab. and Oxon; D.Litt., Oxon; Bywater and Sotheby Professor of Byzantine and Modern Greek Language and Literature in the University of Oxford, 1920-1939; Fellow of Exeter College, 1922-39; Honorary Fellow, 1939; Hon. Ph.D. University of Athens, 1937; Hon. Ph.D., Univ. of Thessalonica, 1951; D.Litt. Oxford, 1942; *b.* 1871; *s.* of Rear-Adm. Richard Dawkins, R.N.; unmarried. *Educ.:* Marlborough College; Emmanuel College, Cambridge; Fellow, 1904; Hon. Fellow, 1922; Director of the British School of Archæology at Athens, 1906-14; temporary Lieutenant R.N.V.R. 1916. *Publications:* Modern Greek in Asia Minor, 1916; The Cypriot Chronicle of Makhairas, 1932; The Monks of Athos, 1936; Forty-five Stories from the Dodecanese, 1950; Modern Greek Folktales, 1952; Norman Douglas, 1952; papers on Archæological and Philological subjects in various periodicals. *Address:* Plas Dulas, Llanddulas Abergele, Denbighshire. [*Died* 4 *May* 1955.

DAWNAY, Maj.-Gen. Guy Payan, C.B. 1918; C.M.G. 1918; D.S.O. 1902; M.V.O. 1907; Chairman Dawnay, Day & Co. Ltd.; Chairman of the Gordon Hotels, Ltd.; President of Anglo-Norwegian Holdings, Ltd.; Vice-Chairman of Financial Times, Ltd. and of Financial News, Ltd.; Chairman of Liverpool & London & Globe Insurance Company Ltd. (London Board); Chairman of Central Insurance Company Ltd., and Army and Navy Stores, Ltd.; *b.* 23 Mar. 1878; *s.* of Lt.-Col. Hon. L. P. Dawnay; *m.* 1906, Cecil, *y. d.* of late Francis W. Buxton; two *s.* two *d.* *Educ.:* Eton; Oxford. 3rd Bn. Yorkshire Regiment (Militia), 1895-99; Coldstream Guards, 1899-1911; served South Africa, 1899-1902 (despatches, Queen's medal 6 clasps, King's medal 2 clasps, D.S.O.); European War, 1914-18 (despatches, Bt.-Major and Bt.-Lt.-Col., C.M.G., C.B., Legion of Honour, Orders of St. Maurice and St. Lazarus (Italy) and St. Anne (Russia), Croix de Guerre (France) and distinguished service medal (U.S.A.) *Address:* Longparish House, Longparish, Hants. *Clubs:* Brooks's, Bath, M.C.C. [*Died* 19 *Jan.* 1952.

DAWSON, A. J.; Major European War, 1914-19 (M.B.E., Despatches twice, Croix de Guerre avec Palme); author; *b.* London, 1872; 3rd *s.* of Edward and Sara Dawson. Lived and travelled in many countries; First Secretary Central Committee for National Patriotic Organisations; Temp. Lieut. 11th Bn. Border Regiment, 1914; Captain, Feb. 1915; commanding Company until invalided out of trenches in France, 1916; G.S.O.3 (M.I.), War Office; S.O.3 (A.I.), R.A.F. 1918; Major, 1918; Home Guard XXIII (Sussex) Battn., 1940. Editor, The Standard of Empire, 1908-13; Director of Information, Government of Bombay, 1919-21. *Publications:* Middle Greyness; Mere Sentiment; Leeway (by "Howard Kerr"); God's Foundling; African Nights Entertainments; Bismillah; In the Bight of Benin; Daniel Whyte; The Story of Ronald Kestrel; Joseph Khassan, Half-Caste; Hidden Manna; Things Seen in Morocco; The Fortunes of Farthings; The Message; The Genteel A. B.; Finn the Wolfhound; Jan: Son of Finn; Across Canada; The Land of His Fathers; How to Help Lord Kitchener, 1914; A Temporary Gentleman in France; Somme Battle Stories, 1916; Back to Blighty; For France, 1917; Everybody's Dog Book, 1922; Britain's Life-Boats, 1923; Peter of Monks-lease: His Mortal Tenement, 1924; The Emergence of Marie, 1926; Letters to Young Dog Owners, 1927; The Case Books of X 37, 1930. *Address:* 3 Maze Hill Mansion, St. Leonards-on-Sea, Sussex. *T.:* Hastings 1184. [*Died* 3 *Feb.* 1951.

DAWSON, Maj.-Gen. Arthur Peel, C.B.E. 1942 (O.B.E. 1937); *b.* 16 June 1888; *s.* of Frank Talbot Dawson and Agnes A. G. Hulton; *m.* 1917, Violet Impey, Cape Town; no *c.* *Educ.:* Cheltenham College. Joined Royal Marines, 1906; served in Channel Fleet, Gallipoli and East Africa, during European War, 1914-18; Superintendent of Small Arms, R.M., 1926-29; Fleet Royal Marine Officer, Cape Station, 1929-31; Brigade Major, Portsmouth Div. R.M., 1932-35; Fleet Royal Marine Officer, Mediterranean Fleet, 1935-37; Assistant Adjutant-General R.M., 1938-41; A.D.C. to the King, 1941-42; retired, 1943. *Address:* Montrose Avenue, Clovelly, Cape Town. [*Died* 4 *June* 1958.

DAWSON, Coningsby, F.R.G.S.; *b.* High Wycombe, 26 Feb. 1883; *s.* of Dr. William James Dawson; *m.* 1918, Helen Campbell Wright-Clark, *e. d.* of Peter Campbell of Newark, New Jersey, U.S.A.; one *s.* *Educ.:* Merton College, Oxford, B.A.; Second-Class Honours in Modern History. Went to America, 1905; a free-lance contributor to American magazines, 1905-10; literary adviser to the George H. Doran Co., 1910-13; joined the Canadian Expeditionary Forces as a Lieutenant, Field Artillery; served with First Canadian Division until 1917 and the Fourth till 1918; lectured in the States under the British Mission; returned to the Occupied Territories, 1919; undertook a special mission through Central and Eastern Europe in the interests of the American Relief for starving children, 1920-21. *Publications:* The Worker and Other Poems, 1906; The House of the Weeping Woman, 1908; Last Chance River, 1910; The Road to Avalon, 1912; The Garden Without Walls, 1913; The Raft, 1914; Slaves of Freedom, 1916; Khaki Courage, 1917; Out to Win, 1918; The Glory of the Trenches, 1918; Living Bayonets, 1919; The Test of Scarlet, 1919; The Little House, 1920; It Might Have Happened to You; The Kingdom Round the Corner, 1921; The Vanishing Point; Christmas Outside of Eden, 1922; The Coast of Folly, 1924; Old Youth, 1925; When is Always, 1927; Pilgrims of the Impossible, 1928; The Unknown Soldier, 1929; When Father Christmas was Late, 1929; The Test of Scarlet, 1930; Fugitives from Passion, 1930; The Auctioning of Mary Angel, 1930; A Path to Paradise, 1932; The Moon Through Glass, 1934; Inspiration Valley, 1936; Tell Us of the Night (with Barton Browne), 1941. *Recreations:* horses, travelling, art-collecting. *Address:* Dun Rovin Lodge, 60 Latimer Road, Santa Monica, California, U.S.A. *T.:* Santa Monica 50235. [*Died* 10 *Aug.* 1959.

DAWSON, George W., F.R.C.S.I., D.P.H.; Consulting Surgeon, Throat, Nose, and Ear Hospital, Golden Square; Consulting Surgeon for Diseases of Throat, Nose, and Ear, Bethnal Green Military Hospital; *b.* Dublin 1868; *s.* of late Richard Cecil Dawson; *m.* 1907 Amy (*d.* 1949), *d.* of late Rev. G. P. Ward. *Educ.:* Dublin; London; Vienna. Fellow of the Royal Society of Medicine; late President and Chairman of the Irish Medical Schools and Graduates Assoc.; Medallist in Surgery. *Recreation:* golf. *Address:* Deans Lane, Walton-on-Hill, Tadworth, Surrey. *T.:* Tadworth 2050. *Club:* Bath [*Died* 11 *Dec.* 1959.

DAWSON, James Alexander, C.S.I. 1939; C.I.E. 1931; LL.D. (Aber.); I.C.S., retired; *b.* 4 May 1880; *m.* 1908, Elizabeth, *d.* of Donald McLagan, Galashiels; three *d.* (and two *s.* decd.); *m.* 1939, Isabel Mary Akerman. *Educ.:* Gordon's College and University, Aberdeen, M.A.; Christ Church, Oxford. Chief Secretary, Assam, 1933; retired, 1939. *Address:* Dunolly, Bieldside, Aberdeen. [*Died* 25 *Feb.* 1956.

DAWSON, Lucy; portrait painter and etcher; *m.* Cyril J., *s.* of Rev. R. Crosbie Dawson, M.A.; one *s.* *Educ.:* Private Schools. Studied life drawing, etc., at art schools; has latterly devoted considerable attention to the painting and etching of dogs, both sporting and other types; exhibited in London, provinces, and in America; has held several exhibitions in London and has exhibited notably at the Pastel Society Exhibition and at the Royal Institute. *Publications:* Dogs as I see them, 1936; Dogs, Rough and Smooth, 1937; Lucy Dawson's Dog Book, 1939; Neighbours, 1946; numerous Dry Points, poster designs and book illustrations, etc.; also works under the name of Mac; reproductions in American and English Magazines. *Address:* Whitwell, nr. Hitchin, Herts. *T.:* Whitwell 397. [*Died* 7 *June* 1958.

DAWSON, Richard Cecil; trainer of racehorses, breeder of thoroughbred horses, retd.; *b.* 27 Nov. 1865; *s.* of Richard Cuming Dawson and Eleanor Waters; *m.* Grace Davies Gilbert; three *s.* two *d.* *Educ.:* Santry School; Trinity College, Dublin. Trained winners of Grand National Steeplechase, of three Derbys, and of most of the principal races in England and Ireland. *Recreations:* hunting and golf. *Address:* Ball Hill, Newbury, Berks. *T.:* Highclere 358; Cloghran, Co. Dublin, Eire. *Club:* Kildare (Dublin). [*Died* 15 *Sept.* 1955.

DAWSON, Prof. Robert MacGregor, F.R.S. (Can.) 1933; Professor of Political Science, University of Toronto, since 1940; *b.* 1 March 1895; *s.* of Robert and Mary MacGregor Dawson; *m.* 1924, Sarah Ada Foster; two *s.* *Educ.:* Dalhousie University (M.A.); Harvard University (A.M.); University of London (M.Sc. (Econ.), D.Sc. (Econ.)). Taught at: Dalhousie Univ., 1921-23; Carnegie Inst. of Technology, 1923-1926; Rutgers Univ., 1926-28; Univ. of Saskatchewan, 1928-40; Univ. of Toronto, 1940-. Pres., Canadian Political Science Assoc., 1943-44. Editor of Canadian Jl. of Economics and Political Science, 1931-45; Member Social Science Research Council of Canada, 1941, 1951-55; Guggenheim Fellow, 1950-51; Roy. Comr. on Provincial Development (Nova Scotia), 1943-45; Gov.-General's Award for Academic Non-Fiction, 1947, 1949; Editor of Canadian Government Series, 1945-; appointed Official Biographer of late Rt. Hon. W. L. Mackenzie King, 1951. LL.D. (h.c.) Univ. of New Brunswick, 1950. Dalhousie, Univ., 1952. *Publications:* Principle of Official Independence, 1922; The Civil Service of Canada, 1929; Constitutional Issues in Canada, 1933; The Development of Dominion Status, 1937; Canada in World Affairs (Vol. II), 1943; The Govt. of Canada, 1947; Democratic Govt. in Canada, 1949. *Recreations:* lawn tennis, gardening. *Address:* Laurier House, Ottawa, Canada; Pine Hill, Bridgewater, Nova Scotia. [*Died* 16 *July* 1958.

DAWSON, Lieut.-Col. Thomas Henry, C.M.G. 1918; C.B.E. 1919; V.D.; Member of Dawson & Hopkins, Barristers and Solicitors. *b.* 1878; *s.* of F. W. E. Dawson. Served South Africa, 1900-02 (Queen's medal with three clasps, King's medal with two clasps); European War, 1914-19 (despatches twice, C.M.G., C.B.E.); Home Service, N.Z., 1939. *Address:* 42 St. Stephen's Avenue, Auckland, New Zealand. [*Died* 3 *Sept.* 1956.

DAWSON, Sir Vernon, K.C.I.E., *cr.* 1934 (C.I.E. 1920); late Assistant Secretary, India Office; *b.* 1881; *e. s.* of late Charles R. Dawson; *m.* 1906, Mary (*d.* 1943), *o. d.* of Rev. G. Floyd, Frilsham, Berks; one *s.* (*yr. s. d.* 1928); *m.* 1957, Winifred, *d.* of late Harry Cox. *Educ.:* St. Paul's School; Corpus Christi Coll., Oxford. Entered I.C.S. after exam. of 1904, and served in various capacities in E. Bengal and Assam, Bengal and under Govt. of India 1905-17; on deputation at India Office, 1918-21; retired from I.C.S. on medical certificate, March 1921, and thereupon appointed permanently to India Office; retired, 1941. *Address:* Stedham Hall, Midhurst, Sussex. [*Died* 8 *Nov.* 1958.

DAY, Rev. Alfred E. Bloxsome, D.D.; *o. s.* of late Rev. A. Bloxsome Day, M.A.; *b.* 1873; *m.* 1908, Marian Mabel, 6th *d.* of late Rev. J. Price, M.A., Rector of Llanveigan; four *s.* three *d.* *Educ.:* Richmond School; New College, Oxford; Wells Theological College. Scholar of Durham University, 1892; Minor Exhibitioner of New College, Oxford, 1893; B.A. 1897; M.A. 1903; B.D. 1908; D.D. 1913; Curate and Precentor, S. Chrysostom's, Victoria Park, Manchester, 1899-1901; Sen. Curate, St. Thomas', Pendleton, 1901-2; Minor Canon, Llandaff Cathedral, 1902-10; Precentor of Carlisle Cathedral, 1910-16; Vicar of Rosley with Woodside, Carlisle, 1916-49. *Publications:* contributor to various magazines. *Recreation:* photography. *Address:* Low House, Armathwaite, Cumberland. [*Died* 1 *March* 1951.

DAY, Dr. Bernard, M.D., B.Ch. Cantab.; M.R.C.P. Lond.; late temp. Commission in R.A.M.C.; late Consultant Physician to the Colonial Office; *y. s.* of late Frank Day, 89 Harley Street, W.1; *m.* 1910, Lydia Dorothy, *d.* of late Henry L. Cripps; one *s.* (*er. s.* killed, R.A.F., 1940). *Educ.:* Haileybury College; Caius College, Cambridge; St. George's Hospital. House Surgeon and House Physician at St. George's Hospital: Private Practice, Kuala Lumpur, Federated Malay States, 1910-26; thereafter in London. Served with R.A.M.C. in M.E.F. and India, 1941-44, held rank of T/Lt.-Col. at Quetta and Northern Ireland, 1943-44. Chairman: Medical Boards, Min. of Nat. Insurance, 1949-50. *Address:* 39 Hans Place, S.W.1. *T.:* Kensington 2400. *Club:* Oxford and Cambridge. [*Died* 9 *Dec.* 1952.

DAY, Clive, Ph.D.; Professor of Political Economy, Yale University, 1907-36; retired 1936; *b.* 11 Feb. 1871; *s.* of Thomas M. Day and Ellen Pomeroy; *m.* 1904, Elizabeth Dike, *e. d.* of late Charlton T. Lewis; two *d.* *Educ.:* Hartford High School; Yale University; Berlin; Paris. Taught in University of California, 1895-98; Chief of Balkan Division, American Commission to Negotiate Peace, Paris, 1918-19. *Publications:* Dutch in Java, 1904; History of Commerce, 1907; History of Commerce of U.S., 1925; Economic Development in Modern Europe, 1933. *Recreation:* golf. *Address:* 44 Highland Street, New Haven, Conn. [*Died* 27 *July* 1951.

DAY, Edmund Ezra; President Emeritus Cornell University since 1950 (Pres., 1937-49; Chancellor, 1949-50); *b.* Manchester, N.H., 7 Dec. 1883; *s.* of Ezra Alonzo Day and Louise Moulton Nelson; *m.* 1912, Emily Sophia Emerson, Hanover, N.H.; two *s.* two *d.* *Educ.:* S.B. Dartmouth, 1905, A.M., 1906; Ph.D., Harvard, 1909; LL.D., U. of Vermont, 1931, Dartmouth Coll., Harvard U., U. of Pennsylvania, Syracuse U., 1937, New York U., 1942, St. Lawrence U., U. of Cincinnati, 1943, Coll. of William and Mary, 1945, U. of No. Carolina, Union Coll., 1946, U. of Buffalo, 1946, Princeton U., 1947, U. of Michigan, 1949, L.H.D. Hobart Coll., 1947. Instructor in Economics, Dartmouth, 1907-1910; successively instructor, asst. prof. and prof. of Economics, Harvard, 1910-23; professor of Economics and Dean, School of Business Administration, University of Michigan, 1923-28; on leave with Laura Spelman Rockefeller Memorial, 1927-28; director for social sciences, Rockefeller Foundation, 1928-37; director for social sciences and general education, General Education Board, 1930-37; statistician, division of planning and statistics, U.S. Shipping Board, 1918-19, director, 1919; statistician central bureau of planning and statistics, War Industries Board, 1918; U.S. representative on Preparatory Commn. of Experts for World Monetary and Economic Conference, 1932-33; Member Educational Policies Commission, 1937-45; Chairman, American Council on Education, 1943; Class C director Federal Reserve Bank of New York, 1938-42; Director, National Bureau of Economic Research, 1939-44; Councillor, National Industrial Conference Board since 1939; Trustee, Tuskegee Institute since 1939, Vassar College since 1950; Pres., Assoc. of Land-Grant Colls. and Univs., 1942-43; Pres. World Student Service Fund, 1945-46; Vice-Pres. Assoc. of American Colls., 1946-47; Pres. N.Y. State Citizens Council, 1948-49; Consultant on General Education to State Univ. of New York since 1950; Member, American Economic Assoc., American Statistical Assoc. (pres. 1927), Royal Economic Society (British), Phi Beta Kappa, Theta Delta Chi. *Publications:* Index of Physical Production, 1920; Statistical Analysis, 1925; The Growth of Manufactures (with W. Thomas), 1928; The Defense of Freedom, 1941. *Address:* 27 East Avenue, Ithaca, N.Y.; Cornell University, Ithaca, N.Y. [*Died* 23 *March* 1951.

DAY, Harold Benjamin, M.C.; M.D., F.R.C.P.; Emeritus Professor of Clinical Medicine, Cairo University, Egypt; *b.* Feb. 1880; *e.* and *o. surv. s.* of late Rev. B. W. Day of St. Peter's, Sandwich, Kent; *m.* 1st, 1909, Ruth (*d.* 1914), *d.* of H. H. Witty, Kew Gardens; one *d.*; 2nd, 1920, Winifred Blanche West, 2nd *d.* of W. J. Hughes, Strand House, Sandwich; one *s.* *Educ.:* Westminster School; King's College Hospital. Obtained entrance scholarship and five others at King's College, London; qualified in 1902 and held resident posts at King's College Hospital, Royal Free Hospital, and St. George's Infirmary; won the gold medal M.B., B.S. (London) 1904, and qualified for gold medal M.D. 1905; Registrar Egyptian Government School of Medicine, Cairo, 1906; served in the R.A.M.C. (Volunteers) 1897-1901, and European War, 1914-19 (despatches, M.C., Order of the Nile, 3rd class); retired with rank of Major; Professor of Clinical Medicine, Royal School of Medicine, Cairo, Egypt, 1910-24; 1933-36; Physician, Royal Chest Hospital; Lecturer in Tropical Diseases and in Forensic Medicine and Toxicology, King's College Hospital, 1925-33. *Publications:* various articles in Medical Journals. *Recreation:* sketching. *Address:* 40 Albemarle, Wimbledon Park Side, S.W.19. [*Died* 1 *Nov.* 1959.

DAY, Rev. Father Henry, S.J., M.C.; preacher, lecturer, publicist; *b.* 29 May 1865; 7th *s.* of late Rt. Hon. Sir John Charles Day, Judge of the High Court. *Educ.:* Beaumont College, Old Windsor. Entered the Society of Jesus, 1884; ordained, 1894; spent three years at St. John's, Wigan, and three more in missionary work up and down the country; was on the staff of St. Francis Xavier's, Liverpool, 1901-8; on the staff of the Holy Name, Manchester, 1908-14; missionary staff of English Province, S.J., 1921-39; 1940, Chaplain to Beaumont College; in Canada and the U.S.A., preaching and lecturing, 1925-26; served as C.F. during European War (fifth class Serbian White Eagle with swords, 1917, despatches, M.C.). *Publications:* Marriage, Divorce, and Morality, 1912; Catholic Democracy, Individualism, and Socialism, 1914; A Cavalry Chaplain, 1922; The New Morality, 1924; The Love Story of the Little Flower, 1927; Macedonian Memories,

1930; On a Troopship to India, 1937. *Address:* Beaumont College, Old Windsor, Berks. [*Died* 21 *Jan.* 1951.

DAY, Rev. John Duncan; Hon. Canon and Prebendary of Lincoln, 1938; *b.* 17 Mar. 1882; *s.* of J. C. R. Day, Worcester; *m.* May Stinton (*d.* 1950); one *s.* two *d.* *Educ.:* King's School, Worcester; Hertford Coll., Oxford (Sch.). Asst. Master Warwick School, 1904-12; Chaplain, 1907-12; Chaplain Wroxall Abbey, 1909-12; Headmaster, Stamford School, 1913-47; Vicar of St. Martin's, Stamford Baron, 1947-53. *Address:* Thurlestone, King's Road, Ilkley, Yorkshire. *T.:* Ilkley 314. [*Died* 21 *Aug.* 1954.

DAY, Colonel Maurice Fitzmaurice, M.C.; *s.* of late Bishop of Clogher, Rt. Rev. Maurice Day, D.D.; *m.* Eleanora Carroll, *d.* of late Dr. J. Dudley Morgan, Washington, D.C. *Educ.:* Pembroke College, Cambridge. Enlisted in Suffolk Regiment in South African War, 1900; commissioned into King's Own Yorkshire Light Infantry, 1901; commanded 1st Oxford and Bucks Light Infantry, 1927-30; H.M. Military Attaché to the British Embassy, Washington, 1930-34. *Recreations:* shooting, fishing, golf, tennis. *Address:* c/o Lloyds Bank, Cox's Branch, 6 Pall Mall, S.W.1. *Clubs:* United Service, Sports; Chevy Chase Country (Washington, D.C.). [*Died* 25 *Nov.* 1952.

DEACON, Walter, C.B.E. 1941; Hon. M.Sc. Bristol, 1942; J.P. Bridgwater Borough, also County of Somerset; Chairman of Bridgwater Borough Magistrates Court; *s.* of Samuel Deacon, Swindon; *m.* 1908, Hettie Helena Perrett; no *c.* *Educ.:* Swindon. Pharmacist; Mayor of Bridgwater, Somerset, for 3 years; Alderman Bridgwater Town Council; Member of Council of Pharmaceutical Society of Great Britain (President, 1940-42); Chairman of: Bridgwater Council Health Committee; Bridgwater Grammar School for Girls; Hon. Freedom of Bridgwater, 1953. Member of Society of Radiographers. *Address:* 4 King Square, Bridgwater, Somerset. [*Died* 30 *Aug.* 1955.

DEAKIN, Rt. Hon. Arthur, P.C. 1954; C.H. 1949; C.B.E. 1943; J.P.; Member of Institute of Transport; Member of European Recovery Plan Trade Union Advisory Cttee.; General Secretary Transport and General Workers' Union; Past-Pres. Gen. Council of T.U.C. (Chm. 1951-52); Advisory Cttees. of Ministries of Reconstruction and Production; Advisory Panel, Ministry of Materials; Nat. Advisory Council, Ministry of Labour; Director Daily Herald; British Transport Joint Consultative Council; Member of Executive Cttee. for National Memorial to King George VI; *b.* 11 Nov. 1890; *m.*; two *s.* *Address:* 21 Springfield Gardens, N.W.9. *T.:* Colindale 2544. [*Died* 1 *May* 1955.

DEAKIN, Ralph, O.B.E.; Hon. A.R.I.B.A.; News Editor (Imperial and Foreign) The Times; *b.* Lincoln, 4 Nov. 1888; *m.* Nora Winifred, *d.* of late John Hood. Served in France and Belgium, 1916-19; 2nd Lt. 20th London Regt.; Capt. Intelligence Corps, and subsequently General Staff (despatches three times); joined editorial staff, The Times, 1919; special correspondent in various countries; Foreign News Editor since 1922; a Director of Reuter, 1941-45. *Publications:* A Broken Butterfly (novel, 1911); essays and short stories; Southward Ho! (the Prince's 1925 tour). *Recreations:* architectural photography, travel. *Address:* 41 Gordon Mansions, W.C.1. *T.:* Museum 6094. *Club:* Reform. [*Died* 19 *Dec.* 1952.

DEAN, Frederick William, C.B.E. 1954; J.P., D.L., F.I.A.S., F.R.S.H., F.R.S.A.; Corporate Surveyor and Valuer; Director Portman Building Society; *b.* 29 Dec. 1884. Past Pres. Incorp. Assoc. of Architects and Surveyors. J.P. Co. London 1936-, D.L. 1946-; Councillor St. Marylebone Borough Council, 1919, Alderman, 1925; Mayor of St. Marylebone, 1924-25 and 1951-1952, Hon. Freeman, 1953. Mem. L.C.C., 1934-46; Dep Chm., 1945-46. Freeman City of London; Liveryman of Horners Company. *Address:* 109 Clifton Hill, N.W.8. *T.:* Maida Vale 1313. [*Died* 14 *April* 1959.

DEAN, Brigadier-General George Henry, C.B.E. 1932; V.D.; *b.* 29 June 1859; *s.* of William and Esther Dean; *m.* Florence Ida, *d.* of late Sir E. T. Smith; five *s.* one *d.* *Educ.:* St. Peter's College, Adelaide. Lieut. S. A. Military Forces, 1880; served in Commonwealth Military Forces, 1880-1919; commanded 13th Light Horse, Egypt, Gallipoli, A.I.F.; invalided with enteric, 1916; Sea Transport, A.I.F., 1916-18; commanded Australian Rifle Team to Bisley, 1913; Chairman Commonwealth Council of Rifle Associations of Australia, 1908-21; Brigadier 8th Light Horse Brigade; A.M.F., 1912-19; retired list, 1920; Hon. Col. 3rd Light Horse Regt., C.M.F., S.A., 1925. *Recreation:* has devoted most of time to military work and the encouragement of rifle shooting. *Address:* 10 Park Terrace, Gilberton, South Australia. *Clubs:* Adelaide, S.A. Naval and Military (Adelaide). [*Died* 12 *Feb.* 1953.

DEAN, Gordon Evans; investment banker; Member Lehman Bros., investment bankers, New York City, since 1953; Chairman of Board, Nuclear Science and Engineering Corporation; Senior Vice-Pres., Co-ordinator atomic energy General Dynamics Corporation since 1955; Director, Fruehauf Trailer Co.; Member Western States Loyalty Board, since 1949; *b.* Seattle, 28 Dec. 1905; *s.* of John Marvin Dean and Beatrice Alice (*née* Fisken); *m.* 1st, 1930, Adelaide Williamson (divorced); one *s.* one *d.*; 2nd, 1953, Mary Benton Gore; one *s.* one *d.* *Educ.:* Univ. of Redlands, Calif. (A.B.); Univ. of S. Calif. (J.D.); Duke Univ. Law School, Durham, N.C. (LL.M.). LL.D. Redlands, 1950. Law Clerk, Meserve, Mumper, Hughs & Robertson, Los Angeles, 1927-28; admitted to Calif. bar, 1930, N.C. bar, 1931, U.S. Supreme Court, 1935; instr. in law and asst. to Dean of Law Sch., Duke Univ., 1930-34; special attorney, criminal div., U.S. Dept. of Justice, 1934-36; chief, sect. of criminal appeals, 1936-37; special exec. asst. to U.S. Attorney Gen. in charge all public relations, 1937-39 and Jan.-June 1940; special asst. to U.S. Attorney Gen. in anti-trust litigation, 1939; partner McMahon, Dean & Gallagher, Washington, D.C., June 1940-May 1945. Officer U.S.N.R., 1943-45. Asst. to Justice Robert H. Jackson in trial of leading Nazi war criminals, Nuremberg, Germany, May 1945-Feb. 1946. Prof. of Criminal Law, Univ. of S. Calif. Law Sch., 1946-49; apptd. Mem. Atomic Energy Commn., 1949, Chm., 1950-53. Apptd., by U.S. Supreme Court, Mem. Commn. to Draft Rules of Criminal Procedure for U.S. Courts, 1941. Mem. Amer. Bar Association. Medal of Freedom 1946. Democrat. Baptist. *Publications:* Report on the Atom, 1953; contrib. to legal jls. *Address:* (office) 1 William St., New York, U.S.A. *Clubs:* Burning Tree Country, Cosmos (Washington); Downtown Association, University (New York City). [*Died* 15 *Aug.* 1958.

DEANE, Major-General Sir Dennis, K.C.I.E., *cr.* 1935; C.B. 1926; D.S.O. 1918; p.s.c.; *b.* 1874; *s.* of late Colonel T. Deane, C.B.; *m.* 1909, Gladys Dena, *d.* of late Col. A. D. Saportas, Manchester Regiment. *Educ.:* Felsted; R.M.A., Woolwich. Director of Demobilisation, India, 1919-20; Commanding 11/12th Cavalry (Probyn's Horse), 1920-23; A.Q.M.G., India, 1923; Commanded Ambala Brigade Area, 1923-27; Maj.-Gen. 1927; Military Secretary Army Headquarters, India, 1930-32; Commanded Burma Independent District, 1932-36; retired, 1936. *Recreations:* shooting and fishing. *Address:* Longacre, Fitzroy Road, Fleet, Hants. [*Died* 25 *Feb.* 1953.

DEANE, Rt. Rev. Frederic Llewellyn, D.D.hon., Glasgow and Aberdeen; Asst. Bishop to Bishop of Glasgow and Galloway, 1947; *b.* 19 Sept. 1868; *s.* of Francis Hugh Deane, B.D., law Fellow of Magdalen College, Oxford; *m.* 1st, 1897, Caroline (*d.* 1928), *d.* of late Rev. Canon Lindsay of Kettering; 2nd, 1930, Hon. Mrs. Alexander Erskine, *widow* of Rev. Hon. A. P. F. Erskine, and *d.* of late Bishop of Glasgow and Hon. Mrs. Campbell. *Educ.:* Keble College, Oxford (M.A.). Ordained, 1891; Curate of Kettering, 1891-1900; Vicar of St. Andrew, Leicester, 1900-4; Select Preacher in Univ. of Cambridge, 1915 and 1917; Rector of St. Mary the Virgin, Glasgow, 1904-17; Bishop of Aberdeen and Orkney, 1917-43; Provost of St. Mary's Cathedral, Glasgow, 1908. Bishop to Royal Navy in Northern Waters, 1917-20 and 1939-43. *Address:* 18 Mortlake Rd., Kew, Richmond. *T.:* Richmond 3907. [*Died* 12 *Jan.* 1952.

DEANE, Sir George Campbell, Kt., *cr.* 1930; *b.* 7 July 1873; 2nd *s.* of John C. Deane, of Barbados, and Laura Robinson; *m.* 1904, Maude, *d.* of R. A. Swan, formerly 1st Puisne Judge, Trinidad; one *d.* *Educ.:* Harrison College, Barbados; St. John's College, Oxford. Called to Bar, Inner Temple, 1898; practised at the Bar of British Guiana, 1898-1903, and at Trinidad Bar, 1903-10; Magistrate Arima, Trinidad, 1910-13, when appointed Magistrate of Port of Spain, Trinidad; 2nd Puisne Judge, Trinidad, 1920; Chief Justice of the Leeward Islands, 1923-24; Puisne Judge Supreme Court, Straits Settlements, 1924-29; Chief Justice of the Gold Coast, 1929-35, and President of the West African Court of Appeal; served in the Trinidad Light Horse from 1912, and was Adjutant of the regiment, 1914-18; retired 1935. *Recreations:* riding, racing, swimming. [*Died* 31 *Dec.* 1948.
[*But death not notified in time for inclusion in Who Was Who 1941-1950, first edn.*

DEAS, J. A. Charlton, M.A., F.L.A.; Director, Sunderland Public Libraries, Museum and Art Gallery, 1904-39; Hon. Secretary Sunderland Central Office of Information (N. Reg.), since 1940; *b.* 27 July 1874; *s.* of late John Deas, Accountant, Newcastle upon Tyne; *m.* 1st, 1899, Edith A. Tiplady (*d.* 1909); three *s.*; 2nd, 1913, Gertrude Boddy; one *s.* (and one killed in action, 1940). *Educ.:* Cathedral School, Wells, and Newcastle. Assistant, and later, Sub-Librarian, Newcastle Public Libraries; Fellow of the Library Association; pioneered Open-Access Public Libraries in the four northern counties, 1908; Hon. Librarian, W. Hartlepool, 1914-18; Chairman of Northern Regional Libraries Committee 1935-40; originated the showing of Museum and Art Gallery exhibits to the Blind, 1912; instituted local Reading Circles for Blind; Pres. Museums and Art Galleries Association of Gt. Britain, 1926-27; Founder, and first Pres., Northern Counties Fed. of Museums, 1933-35; organised over 200 Art Loan Exhibitions and several War Charities Exhibs.; M.A. (hon.) Univ. of Durham, 1928; Member of Arts Committee, N.E. Coast Exhibition, 1929; inaugurated committee for Sir Joseph Wilson Swan National Memorial, and Electrical Science annual Post-Graduate travelling Scholarship, 1930, Vice-Chairman of the Committee: University representative on Board of Governors, Durham C.C. Grammar Schools; Member of Nat. Savings and other local cttees.; Elected Hon. Member of Nat. Assoc. of Schoolmasters, 1932; lectures on Blind educational work, etc.; King's Jubilee Medal, 1935; Special Constabulary Service Medal, 1938; served in Northumberland Hussars (Yeomanry), 1900-1905; Home Guard, 1940-42. *Publications:* various Museum Association, Library Association, etc., papers; Encyclopædia and occasional special articles and brochures. *Recreations:* walking and cycling. *Address:* Humbledon View, Sunderland. *T.A.:* Charlton Deas, Sunderland. *T.:* 6626 and 57174. [*Died* 31 *Jan.* 1951.

DE'ATH, Lt.-Col. Ian Dudley, D.S.O. 1940; M.B.E. 1945; Captain, Royal Marines; serving 42 Commando; *b.* 7 Oct. 1918; *s.* of Colonel George Dudley De'Ath, O.B.E., M.C., R.E. (Retd.), and Eileen Mabel Clarke-Morris; *m.* 1947, Patric, 2nd *d.* of late Capt. W. King-Smith and Mrs. King-Smith, Buenos Aires and Eastbourne; one *s.* one *d.* *Educ.:* St. Michaels, Uckfield, Sussex; Wellington Coll., Berks. Joined Plymouth Div. R.M. as Probationary 2nd Lieut. 1937; Lieut. 1939; Capt. 1946; served River Plate, 1939 (D.S.O.); Italy, 2 Cdo. Bde. (M.B.E.). *Recreations:* sailing, ski-ing. *Club:* United Service. [*Died* 1 *Feb.* 1960.

DEBENHAM, Sir Ernest Ridley, 1st Bt., *cr.* 1931; *b.* 1865; *e. s.* of Frank Debenham; *m.* 1892, Cecily (*d.* 1950), *d.* of Right Hon. William Kenrick; three *s.* four *d.* *Educ.:* Marlborough; Trinity College, Cambridge. *Heir:* *s.* Piers Kenrick, *b.* 28 July 1904. *Address:* Moor Lane House, Briantspuddle, Dorset. *T.:* Bere Regis 233. *Clubs:* Athenæum, Brooks's. [*Died* 25 *Dec.* 1952.

de BLOGUE, Rev. Oswald William Charles; R.N., Ex-S.C.F.; A.K.C.; B.D. France; F.R.S.A.; F.R.G.S.; F.R.E.S.; F.S.A.; F.Ph.S.; *b.* London, 1874; *s.* of Charles Basil and Alice Blogg; *m.* 1903, Ethel Langley, *d.* of Charles Hancock, Ryde, I.W.; one *d.* *Educ.:* privately; City of London College; King's College, London University; St. Aidan's Theological College. Colonial Markets, City of London; Curate of St. Mary's, Tunstall, 1900-2; Sawbridgeworth, 1902-3; Hythe, 1904-5; Chaplain to Danubian Ports, 1905-7; Domestic Chaplain to Bishop of Gibraltar; Chaplain R.N., H.M.S. Acheron, 1907-9; Téméraire, 1909-10; Invincible, 1910; Triumph, 1911-12; Actæon, 1912; Warden of Navy Home, Chatham, 1912; Hon. Secretary to C.E.M.S., Rochester Diocese; first Archdeacon in Brazil, 1914; Chaplain, Rio de Janeiro; Hon. Chaplain to the Fleet; 1st S.C.F., 1916, to R.N.D., Queenstown, Ireland, 1917; H.M.S. Courageous, 1918; Holland, for R.N.D., 1918; Vicar of Tamerton Foliot, 1919-21; S. Michael's, Devonport, 1921-26; Rector of Monksilver, Taunton, 1926-29; Rector, Bishopstoke, Hants, 1929-40; in charge of Cromford Parish, 1940; Assistant Master Denstone College Prep. School, 1942, charge of Cartmel Priory Church, 1942. Captain of the Comrades of the Great War, Chatham Branch, 1913-14; Member of the Executive Committee, Kent Division; Chairman of the Sub-Committee, Ministry of Labour Employment Department, Chatham; Hon. Senior Chaplain, A.C.U.; Chaplain Territorial Cadets; Acting Chaplain R.A.F. 1937; H.M.S. Raven, 1939, 1947. Hon. (Life) Chaplain Seaford Coll., Lavington Park, Petworth, 1952-. Mem. Magic Circle, London. *Publications:* You have a Creed, What is it?; Because, 1937; Lavistock, 1956; articles for various magazines. *Recreations:* football, tennis, travelling. *Address:* c/o Midland Bank, Eastleigh, Hants. [*Died* 15 *April* 1959.

de BOER, Henry Speldewinde, C.M.G. 1945; M.C.; M.R.C.S. (Eng.), L.R.C.P. (Lond.), D.P.H. (Cantab.), D.T.M. & H. (Lond.); *b.* 10 May 1889, British; *m.* 1920, Frances Ethel Bartholomeusz; two *s.* *Educ.:* London Hospital, London. R.A.M.C. 1915-20; Medical Officer, Kenya Medical Service, 1920-26; Senior Health Officer, East Africa, 1926-31; Deputy Director of Sanitary Services, N. Rhodesia, 1931-32; Deputy Director of Medical Services, N. Rhodesia, 1932-33; Deputy Director of Medical Services, Uganda, 1933-38; Director of Medical Services, Nyasaland, 1938-42; Director of Medical Services, Uganda, 1942-47; Temp. Medical Officer, Ministry of Health, 1947; Airport Medical Officer, Northolt Airport, 1947-54. *Publications:* various on mosquito control, malaria control, public health propaganda in Africa in medical and health journals. *Recreations:* tennis, golf, bridge.

Address: Shirley, Adeyfield Rd., Hemel Hempstead, Herts. *T.:* Boxmoor 576. [*Died* 7 *June* 1957.

de CARTERET, Samuel Laurence, C.M.G. 1943; retired; a director of Canadian International Paper Company; Primco Limited; Primco (Western) Limited; *b.* Auckland, New Zealand, 24 November 1885; *s.* of Samuel John de Carteret, *b.* St. Helier's, Jersey, and Lucy Jane Burns, Otahuhu, New Zealand; *m.* 1912, Margaret Elizabeth (*d.* 1947), *d.* of Alexander Matheson and Margaret Ann Macleod; two *d. Educ.:* Yale Univ., New Haven, Conn. (Ph.B. in Civil Engineering, 1908). Engaged in various phases of pulp and paper industry in Canada since 1908; Deputy Minister of National Defence (Air), Canada, 1941-44. *Recreations:* fishing, shooting, golf, cards. *Address:* 3940 Côte des Neiges Road, Montreal 25, P.Q., Canada. *Clubs:* St. James's, Mount Royal (Montreal). [*Died* 26 *July* 1956.

de CHAIR, Adm. Sir Dudley Rawson Stratford, K.C.B. 1916 (C.B. 1914); K.C.M.G. 1933; M.V.O. 1908; Hon. LL.D. M'Gill, 1917; *b.* 30 Aug. 1864; *e. s.* of Dudley Raikes de Chair; *m.* 1903, Enid, *y. d.* of H. W. Struben of S. Africa; two *s.* one *d. Educ.:* H.M.S. Britannia. Entered R.N., 1878; served Egyptian War; Naval Attaché to United States of N. and S. America, 1902; commanded H.M.S. Bacchante, Cochrane, and Colossus, 1905-12; Admiralty, 1909; Assistant Controller of the Navy, 1910-12; Naval Secretary to First Lord of Admiralty, 1912-14; Naval Adviser to Foreign Office on Blockade Affairs, 1916-17; commanded 10th Cruiser Squadron (Northern Blockade), 1914-1916; 3rd Battle Squadron during the War, 1917-18; Vice-Admiral, 1917; Admiral, 1920; Admiral commanding Coastguard and Reserve, 1918-21; President Interallied Commission Enemy Warships, 1921-23; retired list, 1923; Governor of N.S.W., 1923-30; Naval Adviser Mr. Balfour's War Mission to U.S.A., 1917; H.G., 1940-42; Commander Legion of Honour; D.S.M. (U.S.A.). *Club:* United Service. [*Died* 17 *Aug.* 1958.

DECIE, Brig.-Gen. Cyril Prescott-, D.S.O. 1917; late R.A.; *b.* 1865; 2nd *s.* of late Col. Richard and late Mrs. Prescott-Decie of Bockleton Court, Tenbury; *m.* 1908, Margaret Elizabeth (*d.* 1949), *d.* of late Major F. H. de Vere, R.E., and *widow* of Frank Joyce of Mervue, Co. Galway. *Educ.:* Clifton College; R.M.A., Woolwich. Entered R.A. 1885; Captain, 1895; Major, 1900; Lt.-Col. 1912; served S. African War (Queen's medal, 2 clasps); commanded the Artillery of the 1st Indian Div. at Peshawar, 1915; took part in operations against Frontier tribes, 1915; served European War, 1916-17; commanded Artillery, 4th Division, in France (severely wounded, D.S.O.). *Recreations:* hunting, fishing, shooting, cricket, pig-sticking. *Address:* Cwm House, Presteigne, Radnor. *Club:* Army and Navy. [*Died* 20 *Sept.* 1953.

De COMARMOND, Sir Joseph Henri Maxime, Kt., *cr.* 1956; **Hon. Mr. Justice de Comarmond;** Chief Justice, High Courts of Lagos and the Southern Cameroons, since 1955; *b.* Mauritius, 1899; *m.* 1922, Gladys Davey; one *s.* one *d. Educ.:* Royal College, Mauritius; Inns of Court, Middle Temple. Called to Bar, 1922; District and Stipendiary Magistrate, Mauritius and Rodrigues, 1927; Second Addtl. Substitute Procureur and Advocate General, 1928; Subs. Procureur and Advocate Gen., 1932; Solicitor-General, Trinidad, 1938; Puisne Judge, Palestine, 1945; on Legal Advisory Staff, Colonial Office, 1948-50; Senior Puisne Judge, Nigeria, 1950. *Address:* Lagos, Nigeria. [*Died* 30 *May* 1957.

DE COURVILLE, Albert Pierre, (Albert Peter Hugh); manager and producer; *b.* London, 26 March 1887; *m.* 1st, Shirley Kellogg (who obtained a divorce, 1924); 2nd, 1927, Edith Kelly Gould, formerly wife of Frank Jay Gould. *Educ.:* London; Lausanne. Became a journalist; then assistant to managing director of London Hippodrome, until 1920. Author and producer of many revues, from 1912. In New York produced and staged from 1940: At the Stroke of Eight, 1940; Ten Little Indians, 1944; The Wind is Ninety, The Ryan Girl, Emily, 1945; Hidden Horizon, 1946, etc. Produced Lute Song, Winter Garden, London, 1948. Entered films during the 1930's and was responsible for making 10 in studios in Britain and 3 in Hollywood. Founded (with James White) the Embassy Club, Bond Street. *Publication:* I Tell You, 1928. [*Died* 7 *March* 1960.

de CRESPIGNY; *see* Champion-de Crespigny.

DEEDES, Lt.-Gen. Sir Ralph Bouverie, K.C.B., *cr.* 1945 (C.B. 1942); O.B.E. 1920; M.C.; *b.* 17 Oct. 1890. 2nd Lt. 1910; Indian Army, 1911; Capt. 1915; Major, 1926; Bt. Lt.-Col. 1932; Lt.-Col. 1934; Col. 1937; Maj.-Gen. 1941; Lt.-Gen. 1945; Deputy Military Secretary, India, 1937-39; Bde. Comd. 1939-40; Comd. Waziristan Dist., 1941-42; Military Secretary, 1943, Adj.-Gen., 1944-45, India; retired, 1946. *Address:* Tilehurst, Pilgrims Way, Guildford, Surrey. *Club:* United Service. [*Died* 3 *March* 1954.

DEEDES, Brig.-Gen. Sir Wyndham (Henry), Kt., *cr.* 1921; C.M.G. 1919; D.S.O. 1916; late 60th Rifles; *b.* 10 March 1883; *y. s.* of late Col. Herbert George Deedes of Sandling Park and Saltwood Castle, Kent. Military Attaché Constantinople, 1918-19; Director-General of Public Security in Egypt, 1919-20; Chief Secretary to the Administration, Palestine, 1920. *Address:* 2 Douglas Avenue, Hythe, Kent. [*Died* 2 *Sept.* 1956.

DE FRECE, Lady; *see* Tilley, Vesta.

DE GASPERI, Dr. Alcide; President of C.E.C.A. (Coal and Steel Pool); President of Christian Democratic Party; *b.* 3 April 1881; *s.* of Amedeo De Gasperi; *m.* 1922, Francesca Romani; four *d. Educ.:* Trento; Vienna University. Deputy: for Trento, Viennese Parl., 1911; at Italian Parl., Rome, 1919; Sec. Partito Popolare Italiano until suppression of political parties, 1925-26; Pres. Popular Party; arrested and imprisoned by Fascists, 1926; Minister without portfolio in first democratic govt.; Foreign Minister, Dec. 1945-Oct. 1946 and July 1951-53. Prime Minister of Italy, Dec. 1945-July 1953. Hon. D.C.L. (Oxford) 1953, etc. *Publications:* I tempi e gli uomini che prepararono la Rerum Novarum, 1945; Studi e appelli della lunga vigilia, 1946. *Recreations:* mountaineering, bowls. *Address:* 21 Via Bonifacio VIII°, Rome, Italy. [*Died* 19 *Aug.* 1954.

DE GLANVILLE, Sir Oscar James Lardner, Kt., *cr.* 1931; C.I.E., 1925; O.B.E., 1918; Officer of St. John of Jerusalem; Barrister; member Burma Legislative Council from 1923, President 1932-35; late member of the Senate, Burma Legislature. [*Died* 1942.
[*But death not notified in time for inclusion in Who Was Who 1941–1950, first edn.*

DE GLEHN, Wilfrid Gabriel, R.A. 1932 (A.R.A. 1923); artist; *b.* 9 Oct. 1870; *m.* 1904, Jane Erin Emmet, New York. *Educ.:* Brighton College; South Kensington; École des Beaux Arts, Paris. Sociétaire of the Société Nationale des Beaux Arts; Member of the Royal Portrait Society; Capt. R.G.A. *Address:* Manor House, Stratford Tony, Salisbury, Wilts. *T.A.:* Stratford Tony. *T.:* Coombe Bisset 217. *Clubs:* Chelsea Arts, Royal Automobile. [*Died* 10 *May* 1951.

de GREY, Nigel, C.M.G. 1945; O.B.E. 1918; *b.* 27 Mar. 1886; *s.* of Hon. Rev. Arnald de Grey, *s.* of 5th Lord Walsingham, Rector of Copdock, Suffolk, and Margaret Maria, *d.* of Rt. Hon. Sir Spencer Ponsonby Fane, G.C.B.; *m.* 1910, Florence Emily Frances, *d.* of Spencer W. Gore; two *s.* one *d.* *Educ.:* Eton College. Temporary Translator Board of Trade, 1907; William Heinemann, Publishers, 1907-14; Royal Naval Air Service, 1914-15; Admiralty, Naval Intelligence Division, 1915-16; Lt.-Comdr. R.N.V.R., Head of Naval Intelligence Mission in Rome, 1917-18 (despatches, O.B.E., Cav. Order of St. Maurice and St. Lazarus of Italy); William Collins Sons & Co. Ltd., Publishers, 1919; Director of the Medici Society Ltd., 7 Grafton Street, W.1, since 1921; temporarily employed in Foreign Office since 1939. *Recreations:* shooting, gardening, acting. *Address:* Bartons Farm, Plaxtol, Kent. *T.:* Plaxtol 300. [*Died* 25 *May* 1951.

d'EGVILLE, Major Alan Hervey, F.R.G.S.; F.C.I.; artist and writer; *b.* 21 May 1891; *s.* of late Louis H. d'Egville of Academy of Dramatic Art, and Jane, *d.* of John Dawson Watson, R.W.S. *Educ.:* Berkhamstead, France, Germany and Spain. Studied motoring at Daimler, Paris, 1912; entered offices of Rolls-Royce, 1912; 1913-14 studied for Indian Civil Service; joined Intelligence Department, 1914, serving with 3rd Corps; joined 5th Corps, spring 1915; controlled construction of roads and defences built by Belgians in Ypres section; Air Photographic Dept., 1915; and became expert in German Coast Defences (despatches); Chief Intelligence Officer 4th Corps (despatches), 1917; demobilised, 1918; joined St. John's Wood Art School; began drawing political caricatures in Bystander, theatrical cartoons for Pan, and later, humorous drawings for Sketch, Tatler, etc.; spent two years as cartoonist in New York and Hollywood; travelled extensively and illustrated own travel articles; for two years humorous columnist on Daily Sketch (till war); Security Service, 1939-45. Contributor to Punch; co-founder of Kandahar Ski-racing Club; Cartoonist in New York for Life, etc.; advertisement artist to many firms. *Publications:* 'S'no Fun: a humorous book of winter sport; Darts with the Lid Off (with Geoffrey d'Egville); Modern Ski-ing; Slalom, text-book of Slalom Ski-racing; The Game of Ski-ing; Huntin', Shootin' and Fishin' (with late K. R. G. Browne); Adventures in Safety, an Autobiography, 1935; Brass Tacks for Britain; Calling all Fly-fishers, 1946; Call me Mister (with Dennis Rooke); Calling all Coarse Fishers, 1949; Calling all Sea-fishers, 1949; A Touch of the Sun, a holiday book (with Dennis Rooke); Ski-ing: Basic Technique for Beginners; Money for Jam, or how to be a Magnate; Let's be Broad-minded (a book on the Norfolk Broads) (with Denis Rooke), 1948. *Recreations:* angling, ski-ing (gold medallist and winner of many open events), and photography. *Address:* Priorton Cottage, Crediton, N. Devon. *Club:* Savage. [*Died* 15 *May* 1951.

de HAAS, Dr. Wander Johannes; Professor of Experimental Physics, Leyden, 1924-48, and Director Kamerlingh Onnes Laboratory (Professor emeritus since 1948); *b.* 2 March 1878; *s.* of Albertus de Haas and Maria Efting; *m.* 1910, Dr. Geertruida Luberta, *d.* of H. A. Lorentz; two *s.* two *d.* *Educ.:* Middelburg; Leyden University (Dr.). Asst. at the Physical Laboratory, Leyden; at the Laboratory of du Bois, Berlin; wissensch. Mitarbeiter Phys. Techn. Reichsanstalt, Berlin; teacher at the secondary school, Deventer; conservator at the phys. Laboratory of Teylers stichting, Haarlem; Professor of Physics at the Technical University, Delft; at Univ. of Groningen; with Einstein, Baumgärtner prize, Vienna Acad., 1916; Rumford Medal of Royal Society, 1934. Associé étranger de l'Institut de France; membre honoraire de la soc. de phys. française; F.R.S.A., London, 1951. *Publications:* numerous papers to scientific journals. *Address:* Hobbemaflat B8, Bilthoven, Holland. *T.:* 03402/4581. [*Died* 26 *April* 1960.

DEHLAVI, Sir Ali Mahomed Khan, Kt., *cr.* 1931; J.P.; Barrister-at-Law, 1896; *b.* Bombay, 1871; *s.* of Khan Bahadur Mohommad Khan, J.P., of Bombay Govt. Political Service. *Educ.:* Bombay; London. Practised in Bombay and Gujrat, 1896-1900, and Sind, 1900-08. Started and edited Anglo-Sindhi paper, Al Haq, in Sind, 1902. Gen. Sec. and Chm. Reception Cttees., which launched All India Muslim League, Karachi, 1906-07. Diwan of Mangrel State, 1908-12; Judge Small Causes Court, 1913; Wazir and Chief Justice of Palanpur State, 1914-1922; M.L.C. Bombay, 1923-37; Minister for Agriculture, Excise, Forests, Co-operative and Registration to Bombay Govt., 1923-27; Pres. Bombay Legislative Council, 1927-36; Minister for Public Health and Local Self-Govt. to Bombay Govt., 1936-37; M.L.A. Bombay (Muslim League) and Leader of Opposition, 1937-46; Member Muslim League Working Cttee. and Council for several years, and also Pres. Bombay Provincial Muslim League; retired from public life, 1946. *Publications:* Origin of Polo; Mendicancy in India. *Recreations:* tiger and panther shooting. *Address:* Dehlavi Road, Surat, Bombay, India. [*Died* 14 *April* 1952.

DE HOGHTON, Sir Cuthbert, 12th Bt., *cr.* 1611; J.P. Lancashire; *b.* 27 Aug. 1880; *e. s.* of Sir James de Hoghton, 11th Bt.; *S.* father, 1938; *m.* 1st, 1917, Helen (*d.* 1943), *o. d.* of late Major Duncan Macdonald of Glencoe, late Cameronians (Scottish Rifles); two *s.*; 2nd, 1944, Philomena, *d.* of late H. Simmons, Walton-le-Dale, Lancs; one *s.* *Educ.:* Harrow; Magdalen College, Oxford. 2nd Lieut. Coldstream Guards, 1902-4; served European War, Lieut. R.N.V.R. and R.N.A.S., H.Q., Dunkirk, France, and H.M. Dockyard, Portsmouth. *Recreations:* golf, shooting, motoring, travel. *Heir:* *s.* Henry Philip Anthony, *b.* 19 April 1919. *Address:* Hoghton Tower, Hoghton, Preston, Lancs. *T.A.:* Hoghton. *T.:* Hoghton 286. *Club:* Royal Automobile. [*Died* 5 *Dec.* 1958.

de KERILLIS, Henri; French author; Officer, Légion d'Honneur; Croix de Guerre (France) with 6 palms; *b.* 27 Oct. 1889; *s.* of Adm. Henri de Kerillis and Antoinette d'Elbauve; *m.* 1914, Anne Demaison; one *d.* (one *s.* decd.). Lieut. 16th Dragoons, 1914; entered Air Force; became Capt. of Squadron 66; resigned, 1919. Formerly Editor of l'Écho de Paris; Director of l'Époque; Delegate Chamber of Deputies, for the Seine, 1936-45; Councillor for the Seine, 1936-45. Now living in the United States. Belgian Croix de Guerre; Knight of Royal Crown of Italy; Knight of Royal Crown of Rumania. *Publications:* De l'Algérie au Dahomey, 1925; Du Pacifique à la mer Morte, 1930; Paris-Moscou en avion, 1935; Faisons le point, 1936; Français voici la guerre, 1937; Laisserons-nous démembrer la France?, 1938; Français, voici la vérité, 1942; De Gaulle dictateur, 1945. *Address:* 135 East 54th Street, New York, U.S.A. [*Died* 13 *April* 1958.

DELAFORCE, Brig.-Gen. Edwin Francis, C.B. 1919; C.M.G. 1916; R.A.; retired pay, 1920; *b.* 27 July 1870; *s.* of late G. H. Delaforce, Oporto; *m.* 1st, 1895, Beatrice (*d.* 1912), *d.* of Lt.-Col. F. N. M. Maynard, Indian Army; 2nd, 1917, Alice Elizabeth, *d.* of late Alfred Benn, Clayton, Bradford. 2nd Lieut. 1890; Capt. 1900; Major, 1908; Lt.-Col. 1915; commanded 1st East Lancashire Brigade R.F.A. 1911-13; served N.W. Frontier, India, 1897-98 (medal with clasp); European War, 1914-18 (despatches, C.B., C.M.G., Bt. Col., Officier Légion d'Honneur, Croix de Guerre). c/o Lloyds Bank Ltd., Cox's and King's Branch, 6 Pall Mall, S.W.1. [*Died* 5 *Nov.* 1954.

DELAGE, Hon. Cyrille Fraser, C.M.G. 1935, Litt.D., LL.D., L.B., LL.B.; F.R.S.C. 1919; Superintendent Public Instruction, P.Q., 1916-39; *b.* 1 May 1869; *s.* of Jean Baptiste Delâge, Notary, and Mary E. E. Fraser; *m.* 1894, Alice Brousseau; three *s.* one *d.* *Educ.:* Quebec Seminary; Laval University. Notary Quebec Harbour Commission, 1900-11; Member of the Catholic Committee of Public Instruction since 1905 and President, 1916-1939; Member of the Protestant Committee of Public Instruction, 1916-39; Member of the Board of Notaries for the Province of Quebec, 1903-42, President 1936-39; Member, Quebec County Legislative Assembly, 1901-16; Deputy Speaker, 1909-12; Speaker, 1912-16; Officier d'académie (France) 1911; Officier d'Instruction publique (France), 1918; Docteur en droit, 1908; Docteur ès lettres Université Laval, Quebec, 1919; Doctor in Pedagogy, University of Montreal, 1930; Docteur en Droit, Univ. of Ottawa, 1946; Commandeur de l'Ordre de Pie IX, 1928; Knight of Legion d'Honneur, France, 1935; Silver Jubilee Medal, 1935; Coronation Medal, 1937; Censor of the Provincial Bank of Canada, 1926-39; Director of the Mutual Society, L'Alliance Nationale, Montreal, 1935-48; President Catholic School Commission, Quebec, 1947-54. Liberal; Roman Catholic. *Publication:* Conférences, Discours et Lettres, 1919, 2nd volume, 1927. *Address:* 3 Ste. Julie, Quebec. *T.:* 2-5338. *Clubs:* Garrison (Quebec); Canadien, Cercle Universitaire (Montréal). [*Died* 27 *Nov.* 1957.

DE LA MARE, Walter, O.M. 1953; C.H. 1948; Hon. D.Litt., Oxford, Hon. Litt.D. Cambridge, Hon. LL.D. St. Andrews; Hon. D.Lit. Bristol and London; Hon. Fellow of Keble College, Oxford; *b.* 25 April 1873; *m.* 1899, Constance Elfrida Ingpen (*d.* 1943); two *s.* two *d.* *Publications:* Songs of Childhood, 1902; Henry Brocken, 1904; Poems, 1906; The Three Mulla-Mulgars; The Return, 1910; The Listeners and Other Poems; A Child's Day, 1912; Peacock Pie, 1913; Motley and Other Poems, 1918; Flora, 1919; The Veil and Other Poems; Crossings, a Play; Memoirs of a Midget, 1921; The Riddle, and other Stories; Come Hither, 1923; new edition, 1928; Ding Dong Bell, 1924; Broomsticks and other Tales, 1925; The Connoisseur, and other Stories, 1926; Told Again; Stuff and Nonsense, 1927; Stories from the Bible, 1929; Desert Islands; On the Edge, short stories; Lewis Carroll, 1932; The Fleeting and other Poems, 1933; The Lord Fish, and other Stories, 1933; Early One Morning, 1935; The Wind Blows Over, 1936; This Year, Next Year, 1937; Memory, and other Poems, 1938; Behold, This Dreamer, 1939; Pleasures and Speculations, 1940; Bells and Grass, 1941; Collected Poems, 1942; Love, 1943; Collected Rhymes and Verses, Collected Stories for Children, 1944; The Burning Glass, 1945; The Traveller, 1946; Inward Companion, 1950; Winged Chariot, 1951; Private View, 1953; O Lovely England, 1953; A Beginning and other Stories, 1955. *Address:* 4 South End House, Montpelier Row, Twickenham, Middlesex. *Club:* Athenæum. [*Died* 22 *June* 1956.

DE LA MOTHE, Sir Joseph Terence, Kt., *cr.* 1939; O.B.E. 1934; Member Legislative Council, Grenada; *b.* 1876; *s.* of H. De La Mothe, Grenada, Windward Is. *Educ.:* Bruges; Aspatria, Cumberland. Kt. Comdr. of Order of St. Sylvester. *Address:* St. George's, Grenada, Windward Islands. [*Died* 7 *Sept.* 1953.

DELANO, William Adams; Architect; Advisory Architect to firm of Delano and Aldrich; *b.* New York, N.Y., 21 Jan. 1874; *s.* of Eugene Delano and Susan Magoun Adams; *m.* 1907, Louisa Potter, New York; one *s.* *Educ.:* Lawrenceville School; Yale Univ. (A.B. 1895, B.F.A. 1908, M.A. 1939); École des Beaux Arts, Paris (Diplôme, 1902). Member firm Delano & Aldrich since 1903, retired from active practice, 1949; has designed Knickerbocker, Colony, India House, Brook and Union Club Bldgs. (all in New York City); American Chancellery, Paris; Post Office Dept. Building, Washington; Japanese Embassy, Washington; La Guardia Field Airport for City of New York; numerous private houses in U.S.A. and in Europe; school and university buildings in U.S.A.; building for Carnegie Institution of Washington; Walters Art Gallery, Baltimore; enlargement of U.S. Military Academy West Point, N.Y.; enlargement of Virginia Military Institute, Lexington, Virginia; Architectural Consultant to Commn. on Renovation of The White House. Professor of Design, Columbia University, 1903-10; Member National Commission of Fine Arts, 1924-28; Mem. Nat. Capital Park and Planning Commn., 1929-46; Academician and Fell. Nat. Acad. of Design; Fell. Amer. Institute of Architects; Mem. Soc. of Beaux-Arts Architects; Member, Architectural League of New York (Firm awarded Gold Medal, 1921, Arch. League); Member Nat. Institute of Arts and Letters (Gold Medal for Architecture, 1940); Member American Academy of Arts and Letters; Gold Medal of Amer. Inst. of Architects, 1953 for achievement in design; Hon. Trustee: N.Y. Public Library; N.Y. Orthopaedic Dispensary and Hospital; V.P. Horticultural Society, N.Y.; Ex-Pres., Art Commission of City of New York; Officier Légion d'Honneur; Corr. Member, Académie des Beaux-Arts, Institut de France. *Publication:* Portraits of Ten Country Houses Designed by Delano and Aldrich, 1924. *Address:* 126 East 38th Street, New York, N.Y. *T.:* MU-5-5850. *Clubs:* Century (First Vice-Pres. 1948; Hon. Mem. 1956), Knickerbocker, Coffee House, India House, The Brook (New York); Piping Rock (L.I.). [*Died* 12 *Jan.* 1960.

DELANO-OSBORNE, Major-General Osborne Herbert, C.B. 1929; C.G.M. 1918; Royal Scots Fusiliers; *b.* 1879; *m.* 1st, 1913, Gertrude Alice (*d.* 1938), *d.* of E. W. Last, of Annandale, Farnham, and *widow* of S. A. Gaussen; one *s.* one *d.*; 2nd, 1939, Olive Underhill. *Educ.:* Harrow. Served South African War, 1899-1902 (despatches, Queen's medal and five clasps, King's medal and two clasps); European War, 1914-18 (despatches, C.M.G., Order of White Eagle, Couronne of Belgium, American Distinguished Service Medal, Legion d'Honneur, Croix de Guerre); Colonel on the Staff in charge of Administration, Northern Command, York, 1926-27; commanded 150th (York and Durham) Infantry Brigade T.A., 1927-29; commanded Mhow District, India, 1930-32; Lieut.-Gov. and Secretary of Royal Hospital, Chelsea, 1933-38; retired pay, 1938. *Address:* The Lodge, Blackhouse Hill, Hythe, Kent. *T.:* Hythe 6696. *Club:* Army and Navy. [*Died* 12 *Nov.* 1958.

de LATTRE de TASSIGNY, Général d'Armée Jean Joseph Marie Gabriel; Maréchal de France, 1952 (posthumous); Grand Croix de la Légion d'Honneur, 1945; Croix de la Libération, 1944; Médaille Militaire, 1945; Military Cross, 1916; Haut-Commissaire de France en Indo-Chine et Commandant en Chef en Extrême-Orient; *b.* Mouilleron en Pareds, Vendée, 2 Feb. 1889; *s.* of Roger de Lattre de Tassigny and Anne Henault; *m.* 1927, Simonne Calary de Lamazière; (one *s.* killed in action, 1951). *Educ.:* Collège des Jésuites de Poitiers et de Paris. Engagé volontaire, 1908; Saint-Cyr, 1909-10; S/Lieut. 12e Régt. de Dragons, 1910. Served European War, 1914-18, in France, Lieut.

12e Dragons, Comdt. de Bataillon 93e Régt. d'Inf.; Campaign of Morocco, 1921-25; Chef de Bataillon, 1926; École de Guerre, 1927; posted to État-Major du Vice-Prés. du Conseil Supérieur de la Guerre; Col. comdt. 151e Régt. d'Inf., 1935-37; Chef d'État-Major du Général Gouverneur Militaire de Strasbourg et Comdt. l'Armée d'Alsace, 1938; Général de Bde., 1939; War of 1939-45, Comd. 14e Div. d'Inf., 1940; Général de Div. comdt. supérieur des Troupes de Tunisie, Tunis, 1941; Général de Corps d'Armée comdg. 16e Div. Militaire de Montpellier, 1942; condemned to 10 years' imprisonment, 11 Nov. 1942; escaped 2 Sept. 1943; flown out of France by R.A.F. Pick-up, 1943; joined Free French Forces; Général d'Armée c.-in-c. 1st French Army, 1944-45; France, Germany, Austria, 1944-45; Inspecteur-Général de l'Armée de Terre et Chef d'État-Major Général de l'Armée, 1945; Vice-Président du Conseil Supérieur de la Guerre, 1947; Inspecteur Général des Forces Armées, May 1948. Commandant en Chef des Armées de Terre de l'Europe occidentale, Oct. 1948. Hon. G.C.B. 1952 (Hon. K.C.B. 1946). *Publication:* Histoire de la Première Armée Française (Rhin et Danube), 1949 (Engl. trans. 1953). *Address:* 4 Place Rio de Janeiro, Paris VIIIe. *T.:* Laborde 90.49. *Club:* Cavalry (Hon. Member). [*Died* 11 *Jan.* 1952.

de LAVIS-TRAFFORD, Marcus Antonius Johnston, C.V.O. 1932 (M.V.O. 1931); O.B.E. 1920; M.D., L. ès Sc., B. ès. L. B.Ph., Officer of Order of St. John of Jerusalem, Emeritus Senior Consulting Physician to and Chm. (1931-37) of the Executive Cttee. of Queen Victoria Memorial Hosp., Nice; Hon. Physician to the American Hosp., Paris; Medical Officer (1922) and Physician-in-Ordinary (1927-42) to late Field-Marshal H.R.H. the Duke of Connaught; *s.* of late Prof. H. J. Johnston (de) Lavis; *b.* 1880; *m.* 1918, Muriel Elizabeth, *o. d.* of late Lt.-Col. Hy. Trafford-Rawson, J.P. of Coldham Hall, Suffolk; one *s.* one *d.* *Educ.:* Epsom Coll.; London, Paris and Lyon Universities. Assumed by royal warrant (1919) additional name of Trafford; served European War, 1916-18, Chief British Oral Propaganda (in Italian), Italy, 1918; Chairman Istituto Italo-Britannico, Rome, 1918; F.R.S.M.; F.R.G.S.; War Service, 1940. Cmdt. Mot. Amb. Unit (France). Member of many British, Continental, and American medical and learned societies; Citoyen d'honneur of Bramans (Savoie), of Tende (A-M) and of La Brigue (A-M); Hon. Corporal of the 99th Regt. Alpine Infantry (French): pioneered Winter Sports in French Alps, 1905: Founder and First Pres. Club des Sports d'Hiver de Nice et des Alpes-Maritimes, 1911. Awarded Buttard Prize for History by the Académie de Savoie, 1951; Membre agréé de l'Académie de Savoie, 1954. Président d'Honneur de la Société d'Histoire et d'Archéologie de Maurienne, 1959. *Publications:* The Neolithic Platform of Beaulieu s/m: Olivula; Recherches sur la pathogénie de l'urémie; Carrattere inglese e fascino d' Italia; Église de Saint-Pierre-d'Extravache, contribution à son histoire et étude de sa toponymie; L'Évolution de la cartographie de la région du Mont-Cenis aux XVe et XVIe siècles, 1950; Commentaire sur l'œuvre, relative aux Alpes, des topographes, cartographes et écrivains au cours de la deuxième moitié du XVIe siècle, 1950; L'Identification Topographique du Col Alpin franchi par Hannibal, 1956; and articles on various subjects in English, French and Italian. *Recreations:* archæology, mountaineering, chamois-stalking. *Address:* Villa Lavis, Beaulieu-sur-mer, France; Le Planay, Bramans, Savoie, France. *Clubs:* Carlton, Royal Societies, Royal Automobile. [*Died* 26 *Feb.* 1960.

de LISLE, General Sir Beauvoir, K.C.B., *cr.* 1917 (C.B. 1900); K.C.M.G., *cr.* 1919; D.S.O. 1886; p.s.c.; *b.* 27 July 1864; *s.* of late Richard de Lisle, Guernsey; *m.* 1902, Leila (*d.* 1938), *e. d.* of late Wilberforce Bryant, of Stoke Park, Stoke Poges, Bucks; one *s.* *Educ.:* Sandhurst. Joined 2nd Durham Light Infantry, 1883; Capt., 1891; Maj., 1902; 2nd in C., R. Dragoons, 1903; Lieut.-Col., 1906; Col., 1910; Maj.-Gen., 1915; Lt.-Gen, 1919; General, 1926; employed with Mounted Infantry, Egypt, 1885-86; present at Giniss (D.S.O. for special service connected with the attack by Arabs on fort at Ambigole Wells); Staff College, 1899; served with Mounted Infantry, South Africa, 1899 to end of war (severely wounded, C.B., Bt. Lt.-Col.); commanded 1st Royal Dragoons, 1906-10; General Staff, Aldershot, 1910-11; 2nd Cavalry Brigade, 1911; served European War, France and Flanders, and Gallipoli, 1914-19; commanded 2nd Cavalry Bde., 1st Cavalry Div., 29th Div., XIII. Corps. and XV. Corps. (promoted Major-General and Lt.-General in the field; K.C.B. and K.C.M.G.; Commandeur, Legion of Honour; Grand Officier, Order of Leopold; Grand Cross, Serbian Order of White Eagle); G.O.C. in C. Western Command, 1919-23; retired pay, 1926. *Publications:* Polo in India; Tournament Polo; Reminiscences of Sport and War, 1939. *Recreations:* riding, hunting, polo (captain of Durham L.I. polo team for ten years). *Address:* 34 Hertford Street, W.1. *T.:* Mayfair 2950. *Club:* Cavalry. [*Died* 16 *July* 1955.

DE LISLE, Brig.-Gen. George de Saumarez, C.M.G. 1917; Indian Army, retired; *b.* 1862; *m.* Florence Smith Ainsley (*d.* 1939). Gazetted to the Royal Scots, 1882. Served N.-W. Frontier of India, 1897-98 (medal with clasp); European War, 1914-19 (despatches, C.M.G.). *Address:* 30 Saumarez Street, Port St. Peter, Guernsey. [*Died* 21 *Jan.* 1954.

DELLA TAFLIA, Marchioness, 5th holder of title **(Malta), Ethel Maud,** *o. c.* of late Lieut.-Col. Frederick Sedley, 4th Marquis della Taflia; *S.* father, 1921; *m.* 1916, Captain James Williamson Wearing (*d.* 1937), J.P., Lancashire, late 5th Bn. The King's Own Royal Regt. *Address:* 5 Brittany Road, St. Leonards-on-Sea. *T.:* Hastings 1345. [*Died* 19 *Jan.* 1953.

DELLA TORRE ALTA, Il Marchese Albert Félix Schmitt; *b.* Boston, Mass. 14 June 1873; *s.* of Theodore Schmitt and Sarah Elizabeth Heitz; *m.* 1916, Esther Rhoads Stokes, *d.* of Henry Sparks Cattell, Philadelphia; no *c.* *Educ.:* Massachusetts Normal Art School; Cowles Art School; School of the Museum of Fine Arts, Boston, under Benson, Tarbell and Decamp. In charge of the art dept. of the Bradford (Mass.) Acad., 1903-13; member of Faculty and Instructor of Drawing from life, Rhode Island School of Design, Providence R.I., 1912-18; Grand Chevalier of the Order of the Holy Sepulchre, 1934. Among his works are On the River Bank (awarded Silver Medal, Panama Pacific Exposition, San Francisco, 1915), Museum of Fine Arts, Boston; Symphony in Blue, City Art Museum, St. Louis, Mo.; Red and Gold, Museum Rhode Island School of Design, Providence, R.I.; La Dame au Léopard (decorated with Grand Cross of Legion of Honour, 1937, Congressional Medal of Honor, United States Congress, 1938, etc.), Musée du Louvre, Paris; The Blonde Girl, and Nymphe Dansant, Musée de Pau, France, etc. *Recreations:* walking and mountain climbing. *Heir:* none. *Address:* Les Bergerettes, 58 Avenue Sarasate, Biarritz, France. *Club:* Art (Boston). [*Died* 14 *Oct.* 1954.

DE LOTBINIÈRE-HARWOOD, C. A.; *see* Harwood.

DELVES, Robert Harvey Addington, C.I.E. 1929; *b.* 1873; *m.* Elizabeth E. Penn; two *s.* one *d.* *Educ.:* Cranleigh. Chairman, Bombay Improvement Trust, 1924-26; Chief Officer Improvements Committee, Bombay. *Address:* 33 London Rd., Tunbridge Wells. [*Died* 26 *June* 1952.

DE MAREES-VAN SWINDEREN, R.; *see* Van Swinderen.

de MARGERIE, Emmanuel; Member of French Académie des Sciences since 1939; Hon. Professor, Strasbourg University, 1933; D.Sc. (Hon.) Lausanne, Toronto; *b.* Paris, 11 Nov. 1862; *s.* of Eugène de Margerie and Charlotte Demion; *m.* 1903, Renée Ferrère; one *d.* *Educ.*: Paris, Chairman, French Geological Society, 1899-1919; Hon. President, French Alpine Club; F.R.S. 1931; Lyell Medal, Geological Society, London, 1921; Victoria Medal, Royal Geographical Society, London, 1930; Premio Piò XII; Officer Legion of Honour and of Crown of Belgium; Commander of the Nile; Commandeur de l'Ordre de Léopold II. *Publications:* Reports on Maps and Surveys, and numerous other papers; La dislocation de l'écorce terrestre (with Alb. Heim), 1888; Les formes du terrain (with General de la Noe), 1888; La face de la Terre, traduit de l'allemand d'Éd. Suess, 1897-1918, 3 volumes; Catalogue des Bibliographies géologiques, 1896; L'œuvre de Sven Hedin, 1928; Description tectonique du Jura français, 1936; Critique de Géologie, vol. I, 1943, etc. *Recreations*: travel, mountaineering. *Address*: 110 rue du Bac, Paris VII. *T.*: Littré 32-98. [*Died* 21 *Dec.* 1953.

DEMETRIADI, Sir Stephen, K.B.E., *cr.* 1920; *b.* 6 Mar. 1880; 3rd *s.* of late C. E. Demetriadi, Prestwich, Lancashire; *m.* 1913, Gulielma Norah Mabel (from whom he obtained a divorce, 1947), *er. d.* of R. G. Bates, Lewes, Sussex; one *s.* one *d.* *Educ.*: Marlborough. President of the British Federation of Traders' Associations; Chairman of the Commercial Aviation Committee (of the London Chamber of Commerce, the Association of British Chambers of Commerce and the Federation of British Industries), 1935-1937; Chairman of the East Indian Grain and Oil Seed Shippers' Association, 1921-34; Chairman of the Direct Taxation Committee, 1925-35, and of the East India Section of the London Chamber of Commerce; Member of the Council of the Federation of Chambers of Commerce of the British Empire; War Pensions Committee, 1916-17; Ministry of Pensions, 1917-19; reported on the War Medals Department of the War Office, 1920; Deputy Chairman of the Council of the London Chamber of Commerce, 1924-26; Chairman, 1926-28; Vice-Pres., 1929-34 and 1937-43; Pres., 1934-37; Member Board of Referees, 1926-38; Member of the Council of Foreign Bondholders, 1929-43; Member of Lord Bridgeman's Committee of three to enquire into the Administration of the British Legion, 1930; Sole Arbitrator in the dispute between the Milk Marketing Board and the Central Milk Distributive Committee regarding Milk Prices, 1938 and again in 1939. High Sheriff of Sussex, 1949. Grand Cross of the Latvian Order of the Three Stars; Silver Jubilee Medal, 1935; Coronation Medal, 1937. *Publications*: Inside a Government Office, 1921; A Reform for the Civil Service, 1921. *Recreations*: shooting and golf. *Address*: Middleton Laine, Westmeston, near Lewes, Sussex. *Clubs*: Carlton, Bath, City of London; Bengal, Turf (Calcutta). [*Died* 11 *March* 1952.

deMILLE, Cecil Blount; Producer and Director; Member, Association of Motion Picture Producers (three times President); President DeMille Foundation for Political Freedom; *b.* Ashfield, Mass., 12 Aug. 1881; *s.* of Henry Churchill deMille, playwright, and Beatrice Samuel deMille; *m.* 1902, Constance Adams; two *s.* two *d.* *Educ.*: Pennsylvania Military Academy, Chester, Pa.; American Academy of Dramatic Arts, New York. Author and playwright until 1913; thereafter director and producer of motion pictures. Founder with Samuel Goldwyn and Jesse L. Lasky in 1913 of the Jesse L. Lasky Feature Play Company for which he was Dir.-Gen.; Company merged in 1918 as Players-Lasky, and in 1927 became Paramount Pictures Corp.; established DeMille Pictures Corp., 1924; joined Metro-Goldwyn-Mayer as producer-dir., 1928; returned to Paramount as indep. producer, 1932. *Films include:* The Ten Commandments (1923 and 1956), The King of Kings, The Volga Boatman, The Sign of the Cross, The Crusades, The Plainsman, The Buccaneer, Union Pacific, North West Mounted Police, Reap the Wild Wind, The Story of Dr. Wassell, Unconquered, Samson and Delilah, Greatest Show on Earth. Produced dramatic plays weekly on the Lux Radio Theatre, 1936-45. Organised and was President of Mercury Aviation Co., first commercial air line in U.S.A. to carry passengers on regular scheduled flights, 1917. Is a member of various societies and clubs. Holds several foreign decorations and numerous U.S. and other awards, including honorary degrees. *Recreations:* tree surgery, creating game refuge. *Address:* 2010 deMille Drive, Hollywood, California. [*Died* 21 *Jan.* 1959.

de MONTMORENCY, Sir Angus; *see* de Montmorency, Sir H. A.

DE MONTMORENCY, Sir Geoffrey Fitzhervey, G.C.I.E., *cr.* 1933 (K.C.I.E., *cr.* 1926; C.I.E. 1915); K.C.S.I., *cr.* 1928; K.C.V.O., *cr.* 1922; C.B.E. 1919; Member Price Regulation Committee Eastern Region (Chairman 1939-46); *b.* 23 Aug. 1876; *s.* of late Ven. W. de Montmorency. *Educ.*: Malvern; Pembroke College, Cambridge (Scholar). Entered I.C.S. 1899; Assistant Colonisation Officer, Chenab Colony, 1903; Colonisation Officer, Jhelum Colony, 1905; Chenab Colony, 1906; Deputy Commissioner, Lyalpur, 1907; Settlement Officer, Chenab, 1909; Junior Sec. to Financial Commissioner, 1911; Personal Assistant to the Chief Commissioner, Delhi, 1912-17; Deputy Commissioner, Lyallpur, 1917-1920; Deputy Sec., Govt., India, 1920-21; Chief Sec. to Prince of Wales during his Indian Tour, 1921-22; Private Sec. to the Viceroy of India, 1922-26; Member of Punjab Executive Council, 1926-28; Governor of the Punjab, 1928-33; Knight of Grace of St. John of Jerusalem; Hon. Fellow, Pembroke College. *Recreations:* shooting, riding, polo, hunting, tennis. *Address:* 9 Manor Court, Cambridge. *T.*: Cambridge 3632. *Club:* Royal Empire Society. [*Died* 25 *Feb.* 1955.

de MONTMORENCY, Sir (Hervey) Angus, 16th Bt., *cr.* 1631; O.B.E. 1918; *b.* 27 Sept. 1888; *er. s.* of Hervey Lodge de Montmorency (*d.* 1899), and Elizabeth Nicolls (*d.* 1937), *d.* of Capt. Archibald Douglas William Fletcher, R.N.; *S.* to baronetcy of kinsman, 7th Viscount Mountmorres, 1951; *m.* 1918, Eleanor Katharine, *d.* of late Rev. Edward Richard Jefferys Nicolls, Rector of Saxelby, Leicestershire; no *c.* *Educ.*: Winchester; Brasenose College, Oxford. Served in National Health Insurance Commission, 1912-16; Admiralty, 1916-17; Ministry of Shipping, 1917-19; Ministry of Health, 1919-44 (Principal, 1919, Asst. Secretary, 1933, Principal Asst. Secretary, 1937); Secretary of the University Grants Committee, 1944-51; retired from Civil Service, 1951. Chevalier, Belgian Order of the Crown, 1918. *Heir:* *b.* Miles Fletcher de Montmorency [*b.* 3 March 1893; *m.* 1931, Rachel Marion, *d.* of late Rev. Charles Coverdale Tancock, D.D.]. *Address:* 35 Leinster Avenue, S.W.14. *Club:* United University. [*Died* 14 *Oct.* 1959.

DE MONTMORENCY, Captain John Pratt, C.M.G. 1917; Officier de la Légion d'Honneur, 1917; *s.* of late Ven. W. De Montmorency of Castle Morres, Co. Kilkenny; *b.* 2 Aug. 1873; *m.* 1st 1908, Margaret, Elinor (*d.* 1932), *e. d.* of late Col. Pym, R.A.; 2nd 1934, Norah, *d.* of late Colonel Mervyn de Montmorency, the Hampshire Regt.; two *d.* Lieut. R.N. 1895; Commander, 1905; D.L., J.P. Kilkenny; Sheriff, 1921. *Address:* Burnchurch, Bennettsbridge, Co. Kilkenny, Eire. [*Died* 11 *Nov.* 1960.

DENDY, Brigadier Murray Heathfield, D.S.O. 1918; M.C.; *b.* 1885; *e. s.* of late Charles Dendy, of Youl Grange, Eastbourne; *m.* 1919, Lettice, *y. d.* of late Charles Van Neck and Mrs. Van Neck, 79 Eaton Place, S.W. *Educ.:* Rugby; R.M.A., Woolwich. Served European War, 1914-18 (despatches, D.S.O., M.C., Legion of Honour); Staff College, 1920; Imperial Defence College, 1931; General Staff Officer, 1st Grade, Deccan District 1933-1936; Brigadier, R.A., Northern Command York, 1936-39; A.D.C. to the King, 1938-39; retired, 1939. *Club:* Army and Navy. [*Died* 4 *June* 1951.

DENHAM, Godfrey Charles, C.I.E. 1915; C.B.E. 1919 (O.B.E. 1918); Chairman and Joint Managing Director, Anglo-Indonesian Plantations; *b.* 18 May 1883; *yr. s.* of Charles Denham; *m.* 1st, Bessadore (*d.* 1936), *d.* of C. P. Maze; 2nd, 1937, Edna May Hendy (marriage dissolved); 3rd, 1948, Sheila, *d.* of H. F. Collum, Surbiton. *Educ.:* Brighton College. Joined Indian Police, 1902; Inspector-Gen. of Police, Straits Settlements, 1923-25; Joint Managing Director Anglo-Dutch Plantations of Java, 1933; Chairman, 1952. *Recreations:* Games. *Address:* 166 Dorset House, N.W.1. *T.:* Welbeck 7894. *Clubs:* Garrick, Portland. [*Died* 12 *Oct.* 1956.

DENISON, Captain Edward C., M.V.O. 1931; R.N. (retired); *b.* 6 Sept. 1888; *o. s.* of late Captain Hon. Henry Denison, and *g.s.* of 1st Lord Londesborough; *cousin* and *heir-pres.* to 6th Baron Londesborough; *m.* 1919, Betty, *y. d.* of late Sir Charles Heaton Ellis, C.B.E.; (one *s.* killed in action. 1945) one *d.* *Educ.:* H.M.S. Britannia. Served European War, 1914-18. Commodore (R.N.R.) of Convoys, 1941-44 (despatches). *Address:* 7 Chelsea House, 26 Lowndes Street, S.W.1. *T.:* Belgravia 8104. *Club:* White's. [*Died* 13 *Nov.* 1960.

DENISON, Robert Beckett, D.Sc., Ph.D.; *b.* Huddersfield, 1879; *s.* of Robert Denison; *m.* Ruby Aldridge, *d.* of Francis Newth. *Educ.:* Universities of Leeds, London, Berlin, and Breslau. University Scholar and Research Exhibitioner of Leeds; formerly Assistant Professor at Heriot-Watt College, Edinburgh; Professor of Chemistry, Natal University College, 1910-1938; Principal, Natal University College, Pietermaritzburg, 1938-45. *Publications:* Physico-Chemical, chiefly on motion of ions in solutions. *Recreation:* golf. *Address:* Imperial Hotel, Pietermaritzburg. *Club:* Victoria (Maritzburg). [*Died* 27 *March* 1951.

DENMAN, 3rd Baron (*cr.* 1834), **Thomas Denman,** P.C. 1907; G.C.M.G., *cr.* 1911; K.C.V.O., *cr.* 1909; J.P. Sussex; *b.* 16 Nov. 1874; *s.* of Richard Denman, *g.s.* of 1st Baron, and Helen, *d.* of Gilbert McMicking, Miltonise, Stranraer; *S.* great-uncle, 1894; *m.* 1903, Gertrude Mary (*see* Lady Denman), *o. d.* of 1st Viscount Cowdray; one *s.* one *d.* *Educ.:* R.M.C., Sandhurst. Served S. Africa as Captain comdg. 35th (Middlesex, Squadron of Imp. Yeomanry, 1900 (wounded); Lieut.-Col. commanding 2/1st County of London (Middlesex) Yeomanry, 1914-15; Governor-General of Australia, 1911-14; late Lt. The Royal Scots; Lord-in-Waiting to H.M., 1905-07; Captain Hon. Corps of Gentlemen-at-Arms, 1907-1911; Deputy Speaker of the House of Lords. *Heir:* *s.* Hon. Thomas Denman, *b.* 2 Aug. 1905. *Recreations:* billiards, golf. *Address:* Beaconsfield, Furze Hill, Hove. *Club:* Brooks's. [*Died* 24 *June* 1954.

DENMAN, Lady, (Gertrude Mary), G.B.E., *cr.* 1951 (D.B.E., *cr.* 1933; C.B.E. 1920); Chairman Women's Land Army Benevolent Fund; Chairman Family Planning Association; Life Trustee Carnegie United Kingdom Trust; *b.* 7 Nov. 1884; *o. d.* of 1st Viscount Cowdray; *m.* 1903, 3rd Baron Denman, *q.v.*; one *s.* one *d.* *Educ.:* privately. Member Executive Committee of Woman's National Liberal Federation, 1909-1910; in Australia, 1911-14, when Lord Denman was Governor-General; 1915, Chairman of sub-committee of Agricultural Organisation Society which was responsible for the formation of Women's Institutes. Became Assistant Director Women's Branch of Food Production Department when the Ministry took over the work. Chairman of National Federation of Women's Institutes, 1917-46; President of Ladies' Golf Union, 1932-38; Member Executive Committee of Land Settlement Association, 1934-39; Hon. Director of Women's Land Army, 1939; was responsible for its organisation to the Ministry of Agriculture; resigned 1945, when the Government announced that gratuities and other benefits given to Civil Defence and Service Women would not be given to members of the W.L.A. *Recreations:* golf, bonfires. *Address:* Balcombe Place, Balcombe, Haywards Heath, Sussex. *T.:* Balcombe 302. *Club:* Cowdray. [*Died* 2 *June* 1954.

DENMAN, Hon. Sir Richard Douglas, 1st Bt., *cr.* 1945; *b.* 24 Aug. 1876; *b.* of 3rd Baron Denman, P.C., G.C.M.G., K.C.V.O., and *heir-pres.* to 4th Baron; *m.* 1914, May, *d.* of late James Spencer of Murrah Hall, Greystoke; three *s.* two *d.* *Educ.:* Westminster School; Balliol Coll., Oxford, B.A. Stanhope Prize Essay, 1898; Chancellor's Prize Essay, 1900. Chm. London Juvenile Advisory Cttee., 1910; Private Sec. to Lord Buxton, 1905-14; temp. Sec. Lieut. R.F.A.; 1915; Parliamentary Private Secretary to Lord Ernle and Mr. H. A. L. Fisher, 1917-18; M.P. (L.) Carlisle, 1910-18; M.P. (Lab.) Central Leeds, 1929-31, (Nat. Lab.) 1931-45; Second Church Estates Commissioner, 1931-1943; Treasurer Queen Anne's Bounty, 1939-44. *Publication:* Political Sketches, 1948. *Heir:* *s.* Charles Spencer Denman, M.C., formerly Major D.C.L.T. [*b.* 1916; *m.* 1943, Sheila Anne, *d.* of late Lt.-Col. A. B. A. Stewart, D.S.O.; three *s.* one *d.* Served War of 1939-45, Middle East (M.C.)]. *Address:* Staffield Hall, Kirkoswald, Cumberland. [*Died* 22 *Dec.* 1957.

DENNEHY, Sir Harold George, Kt., *cr.* 1946; C.S.I. 1942; C.I.E. 1937; *b.* 18 Dec. 1890; *s.* of John George Dennehy, Clifton, Bristol; *m.* 1932, Constance Isolda Alexander (*d.* 1956); no *c.* *Educ.:* Clifton; Emmanuel College, Cambridge. Indian Civil Service, 1914; served European War, with I.A.R.O., 1915-19; Deputy Commissioner, 1933; Secretary Transferred Departments, Government of Assam, 1933; Chief Secretary, Assam, 1939-47. *Recreation:* walking. *Address:* 61A Dublin Road, Sutton, Co. Dublin. *T.:* Sutton 322371. *Clubs:* Oxford and Cambridge; University (Dublin). [*Died* 12 *Sept.* 1956.

DENNIS, Surgeon-Rear-Adm. John Jeffreys, C.B. 1916; M.D., M.Ch.; R.N.; *b.* 1858; *e. s.* of Paymaster-in-Chief T. R. Dennis, R.N.; unmarried. *Educ.:* Mannamead School, Plymouth. Educated for the Medical Profession at Cork and Edinburgh; graduated at Queen's University, Dublin, 1880; joined the Royal Navy, 1880; Surg.-Gen. 1913; served Egypt, 1882; E. Soudan, 1884-5; Burmese War, 1885-7; E. Somaliland, 1902-3; retired, 1918; Commandeur de l'Ordre de la Couronne Belge, 1919. *Recreation:* gardening. *Address:* Manaton, Beaconsfield, Bucks. [*Died* 4 *Aug.* 1958.

DENNISON, Major Gilbert, C.B.E. 1952; Major late R.F.C.; Chairman of Denbro Ltd., and Subsidiary Companies; *b.* 9 Sept. 1883; *s.* of Franklin Dennison; *m.*; one *s.* *Educ.:* Bradfield College. Deputy Regional

Commissioner (Region 9), 1941-45. Past Master Worshipful Co. of Clockmakers; Liveryman Worshipful Co. of Goldsmiths; Guardian, Birmingham Assay Office; Chm. Midland Hosp., Birmingham, 1920-48, and Chm. Brit. Homœopathic Assoc.; Past Pres. Brit. Jewellers' Assoc. and Chm. Export Cttee. Mem. Council and Committees of F.B.I. and of Birmingham Chamber of Commerce. *Recreations:* motoring, aviation and tennis. *Address:* 5 Palmer Street, Westminster, S.W.1. *T.:* Abbey 7219. *Clubs:* Royal Aero, Royal Air Force; Union (Birmingham). [*Died* 13 *April* 1957.

DENNISON, Robert, J.P. Herts and Middlesex; late Assistant Sec., Iron and Steel Confederation; retired 1935; *b.* Glasgow, 30 Dec. 1879; *s.* of William and Mary Sandford Dennison; *m.* Frances Jane Jenkinson, Darlington, Durham; three *s.* one *d.* *Educ.:* Board School, Glasgow. Commenced work 10½ years of age; M.P. (Lab.), King's Norton, Birmingham, 1924-29; visited in official capacity most European countries since European War; California, Hollywood, etc., 1937-38; Munitions Factories and War Office Records, War of 1939-45. *Recreations:* bowls, gardening. *Address:* Chippenham, New Barnet, Herts. [*Died* 10 *Nov.* 1951.

DENNISS, Lt.-Col. Cyril E. B.; *see* Bartley-Denniss.

DENNISTOUN, The Hon. Mr. Justice Robert Maxwell, C.B.E. 1918; LL.D. Queen's University; A Judge of the Court of Appeal for Manitoba, 1918-46, retd. 1946; Hon. Col. Prince Albert and North Battleford Volunteers, 1938; *b.* 24 Dec. 1864; *o. s.* of James Frederick Dennistoun, Q.C. of Castleknock, Peterborough, Canada, and Katherine Adele, *d.* of Stafford Kirkpatrick, Judge of Frontenac; *m.* Mildred, *d.* of Rev. J. W. R. Beck, Rector of Peterborough and Canon of St. Alban's Cathedral; two *s.* two *d.* Col. Canadian Expeditionary Force, European War, 1914-19; Deputy Judge Advocate-General; Bencher Law Society of Upper Canada, 1906-7; Bencher Law Society, Manitoba, 1912-18; Long Service Medal and Colonial Auxiliary Officers' Decoration; Governor, Trinity College School, Port Hope; Lecturer, Manitoba Law School; B.A. Queen's University; King's Counsel of Ontario and Manitoba; mentioned for valuable services in connection with the war, March 1918; Commodore Royal Lake of the Woods Yacht Club, 1923-4; President Canadian Club of Winnipeg, 1925. *Publications:* Notes on Military Law; Notes on District Courts Martial. *Address:* 216 Cockburn St., Winnipeg, Canada. *Club:* Manitoba (Winnipeg). [*Died* 11 *Oct.* 1952.

DENNY, Rev. Sir Henry Lyttelton Lyster, 7th Bt. of Tralee Castle, Co. Kerry, *cr.* 1782; M.A.; F.S.G.; Hereditary Freeman of City of Cork; Rector and Vicar of Burwash, Sussex, 1936-52; Founder, Vice-Pres. and Hon. Secretary of the County Kerry Society; Hon. Member and laureate Institut Historique de France; Hon. Director, London Trustee Savings Bank; Life Governor of the Royal Orphanage, Beddington; *b.* 1878; *o. s.* of Rev. Edward Denny, M.A., Vicar of Laracor, Co. Meath, and Marion G., *e. d.* of Lyttelton H. Lyster; *m.* 1924, Joan Lucy Dorothy, *er. d.* of Major William A. C. Denny, O.B.E.; four *s.*; *S.* cousin, 1928. *Educ.:* Arlington School, Portarlington, Ireland; Trinity College, Dublin. Ordained, 1902; Hon. Minor Canon, National Cathedral of St. Patrick, Dublin, 1907-8; Priest-in-Charge, St. Jude, Chelsea, 1912-16; Chaplain, Duke of York's Headquarters, Chelsea, 1914-15; Metropolitan Special Constable 2nd Chelsea Vol. Training Corps, 1915-16; Vicar of Winslow, Bucks, 1916-18; Provincial Grand Chaplain of Bucks, 1918-19; Rector of Horsted Keynes, Sussex, 1918-20; Vicar of St. Mark's, Myddelton Square, E.C., 1920-25; Rector of West Wickham, Kent, 1925-30; Abinger, Surrey, 1930-36; Evacuation Officer, 1939-40; Officiating Chaplain to the Forces, 1940-46, H.G. (19th Sx.), 1940-45; Fellow of Sion Coll., 1920-25; Founder and Fellow, Society of Genealogists; Ed. of The Genealogists' Magazine, 1925-31; Member of the Council of Empire Settlement, 1928-37, and of Chancellor's Advisory Cttee., Diocese of Guildford, 1930-36. *Publications:* Memorials of an Ancient House, 1913; Anglo-Irish Genealogy, 1916; The Church and Parish of St. Laurence, Winslow, 1917; The Manor of Hawkesbury, 1920; Handbook of Co. Kerry Family History, Biography, etc., 1923; A History of Freemasonry in Co. Kerry, 1932; A Kipling Shrine, 1940-46; Some Old-time Friends of St. Andrew Undershaft, 1947; also various theological, antiquarian, and genealogical pamphlets, articles, and reviews. *Heir:* *s.* Anthony Coningham de Waltham, late Flt. Sgt., R.A.F. [*b.* 22 April 1925; *m.* 1949, Anne Catherine, *er. d.* of S. Beverley, F.R.I.B.A. Served War of 1939-45, Middle East, etc., 1943-47]. *Recreations:* antiquarian and genealogical research. *Address:* Tinkers' Hatch, Cross-in-Hand, Heathfield, Sussex. *T.:* Heathfield 37. [*Died* 1 *May* 1953.

DENNY, Commander Herbert Maynard, D.S.O. 1918; R.N., retired; *b.* 9 April 1876; *s.* of Rev. William Henry Denny, M.A., Vicar of St. James, Fulham; *m.* 1903, Frances Jane, *d.* of Capt. G. H. Edwards, Master Mariner; one *s.* *Educ.:* Stubbington House, Fareham; H.M.S. Britannia. Naval Cadet, 1890; Midshipman, 1893; Sub Lt., 1896; Lieut., 1899; Lieut.-Comm., 1907; Acting Comm., 1917; Comm., retired, 1920; in command of Destroyers for many years; served Africa East Coast, 1895, M'Wele; South African War, 1900-1; European War Patrol Flotillas, 1914-15; Command of Monitor M.16, Gallipoli, 1915-16; Command of Destroyers and Convoys on East Coast and North Sea, 1917-19 (despatches, D.S.O.); Captain Superintendent of the Clyde Training Ship Empress, 1920-23; General Secretary of the Navy League, 1925-32; Chief Lecturer, 1932-36; Captain-Superintendent Lancashire and National Sea Training Homes, Sept. 1939-May 1945. *Recreation:* gardening. *Address:* Jove Cottage, Walberswick, Suffolk. [*Died* 19 *Jan.* 1957.

DENNY, Sir Maurice Edward, 2nd Bt., cr. 1913; K.B.E., cr. 1946 (C.B.E. 1918); LL.D., D.L.; B.Sc.; J.P.; President of William Denny & Brothers, Ltd., Shipbuilders and Engineers; Director of: Union Bank of Scotland, Ltd.; Guest, Keen and Nettlefolds, Ltd.; India General Navigation & Railway Co., Ltd.; Lloyd's British Testing Co., Ltd.; President of Institute of Marine Engineers, 1935; *b.* 11 Feb. 1886; *e. s.* of Sir Archibald Denny, 1st Bt.; *S.* father, 1936; *m.* Marjorie, *d.* of late W. R. Lysaght, C.B.E.; two *s.* two *d.* *Educ.:* Tonbridge School; abroad. *Publications:* contributions to sundry technical journals. *Recreations:* golf, ornithology. *Heir:* *s.* Alistair Maurice Archibald [*b.* 11 Sept. 1922; *m.* 1949, Elizabeth, *y. d.* of Major Sir Guy Lloyd; three *s.*]. *Address:* Gateside House, Drymen, Stirlingshire. *T.:* Drymen 376. *Club:* Union. [*Died* 2 *Feb.* 1955.

DENT, Brig.-Gen. Bertie Coore, C.B. 1921; C.M.G. 1919; D.S.O. 1918; *b.* 1872; *e. s.* of late Lt.-Col. H. F. Dent; *m.* 1909, Violet, *e. d.* of G. A. Duff, Folkestone; one *s.* *Educ.:* Charterhouse; Sandhurst. 2nd Lieut. Leicestershire Regt., 1892; Lieut. 1894; Capt. 1900; Major, 1909; Lieut.-Col. (brevet), 1915; (subst.) 1917; Col. 1919; Garr. Adjutant, Natal, 1898-99; Brigade Comdr., France, 1916 and 1918-19; Mespot E Force, 1920-22; Eastern Command, 1923; retired pay, 1927; served Matabeleland Campaign, 1896 (medal and clasp); S. African War, 1899-1902 (Queen's and King's medals and clasps, despatches twice); Somaliland, 1904 (medal and clasp); European War, 1914-18 (1914 Star and clasp, British War Medal, Victory Medal, C.M.G., D.S.O., Legion of Honour, 5th Class, despatches 6 times); operations in Iraq, 1920 (medal and clasp, C.B., despatches). *Address:* The Vinery, Bury St. Edmunds, Suffolk. *T.:* Bury St. Edmunds 371. *Club:* United Service. [*Died* 20 *May* 1960.

DENT, Adm. Douglas Lionel, C.B. 1919; C.M.G. 1916; *b.* 1869; *m.* 1911. Served European War, 1914-18 (despatches, C.M.G.); Captain Superintendent of Torpedo Boat Destroyers building by contract, 1912-1915; Chief of British Submarine Service, 1919-21; Director of Naval Equipment Department, Admiralty, 1922-24; Vice-Adm. 1925; retired list, 1926; Adm. retired, 1929. *Address:* Aylmerton, Norfolk. [*Died* 11 *July* 1959.

DENT, Edward Joseph, F.B.A. 1953; Hon. D.Mus. Oxon, 1932; Hon. Mus.D. Harvard. 1936; Hon. Mus.D. Cantab. 1947; M.A., Mus.B.; Professor of Music, Cambridge University, 1926-41; Fellow of King's College, Cambridge, 1902-8 and since 1926; *b.* 16 July 1876; *s.* of late John Dent Dent, Ribston Hall, Wetherby, Yorks. *Educ.:* Eton; King's Coll., Cambridge (Scholar). One of the founders of the International Society for Contemporary Music, and has been President of it since its inauguration, 1923, Hon. Life President, 1938; President Société Internationale de Musicologie, 1931-49, Hon. Life Pres., 1949. *Publications:* Alessandro Scarlatti, his Life and Works, 1905; Mozart's Operas, a critical study, 1913 (German translation, 1923, revised ed. 1947); Terpander, or Music and the Future, 1926; Foundations of English Opera, 1928; Ferruccio Busoni, 1933; Life of Handel, 1934; Opera, 1940; A Theatre for Everybody, 1945; several translations of operas for Sadler's Wells Theatre. *Address:* 17 Cromwell Place, S.W.7. *Club:* Athenæum. [*Died* 22 *Aug.* 1957.

DENT, Sir Francis Henry, Kt., *cr.* 1916; C.V.O. 1920; *b.* 31 Dec. 1866; *s.* of Admiral C. B. C. Dent; *m.* 1st, 1902, Helen Janet (*d.* 1920), *d.* of Richard Morten; two *s.*; 2nd, 1923, Winifred Grace Culling, *d.* of Mrs. W. A. C. Fremantle. Entered the service on L. and N.W. Rly. 1884; District Traffic Manager, 1901; London and District Goods Traffic Superintendent, 1902; Chief Goods Manager S.E. and Chatham Rly. 1907; General Manager S.E. and Chatham Rly. 1911-20; Chairman of Railway Clearing House General Managers' Conference, 1918. *Address:* Warblington Lodge, nr. Havant, Hants. *Club:* Boodle's. [*Died* 4 *June* 1955.

DENTON, Mrs. H. S., C.B.E. 1928; *d.* of Col. Edwin Henry Thorne, Wolverhampton; *m.* Captain Harry Stephenson Denton; one *d.* *Educ.:* Privately. Hon. Secretary, Merionethshire Women's Unionist Association, 1913-16; later District Agent, South Eastern Area of England, Women's Unionist Organisation; Visiting Agent Women's Unionist Organisation, England and Wales, 1926-35; Organising for Central Council Care of Cripples, Sussex, 1936-38. *Address:* Camellia Corner, Old Town, Bexhill-on-Sea, Sussex. *T.:* Bexhill 614. [*Died* 24 *Aug.* 1953.

DENVILLE, Alfred, J.P.; Founder of Modern Repertory Companies in the Provinces under title of Denville's Premier Players; *b.* Nottingham, 1876; *s.* of Charles Matthew and Lottie Farren Denville; *m.* Kate, *d.* of George and Kate Saville; two *s.* one *d.* *Educ.:* Ushaw College, Durham. First appearance on stage four weeks old, P.O.W. Greenwich; played children's parts with Barry Sullivan; several years toured with circus theatres; producer pantomimes at all principal theatres; principal comedian with Vezin in Shakespeare and classical comedies; started first and only Repertoire in England at that time in Moriston, 1900; since then 159 Repertories in various parts of the country; Star as an actor through the provinces; last lessee of Oxford Theatre, W.; gave Denville Hall, Northwood, Middlesex, as a Haven of Rest for aged Actors and Actresses, 1925; M.P. (C.), Central Division Newcastle upon Tyne, 1931-45. *Publications:* author of the English stage version The Miracle, Annie Laurie, Reported Missing, The Jewess, Hearts are Trumps. *Recreations:* work, sleep. *Address:* Weathertrees, South Hill Avenue, Harrow, Middlesex. *T.:* Byron 2754. *Clubs:* Constitutional, Stage Golfing. [*Died* 23 *March* 1955.

DENYS, Sir (Charles) Peter, 4th Baronet, *cr.* 1813; *b.* 27 May 1899; *s.* of 3rd Baronet and Grace Ellen, *d.* of late Col. A. W. D. Burton, C.B., and *heiress* of Sir Charles W. Cuffe Burton; *S.* father, 1922; *m.*; one *d.* decd. *Educ.:* Harrow. *Heir:* none. *Address:* Pollacton, Carlow, Ireland. [*Died* 3 *Oct.* 1960 (*ext.*).

DERBYSHIRE, Job Nightingale, F.C.A.; Senior Partner of Derbyshire and Co., Chartered Accountants, Nottingham and London; J.P. for City and County of Nottingham; President Nottingham Mechanics Institution; Life Member of Court, University of Nottingham; Chm. of a number of industrial undertakings; *b.* 12 Aug. 1866; *s.* of Job Nightingale Simpson Derbyshire, Ilkeston, Derbyshire; *m.* 1905, Agnes Dora (*d.* 1952), *d.* of George Travell Travell, Nottingham; one *s.* one *d.* Financial Adviser, 1917-18, Director of Contracts (Mechanical Warfare), 1917-18, Liquidator of Contracts (Mechanical Warfare), 1918-19, at Ministry of Munitions (unpaid); President Nottingham Society of Chartered Accountants, 1917-18; President of Nottingham General Hospital, 1939; Alderman of Notts. County Council, 1931-46; Vice-Chairman of Notts. County Council, 1938-40; High Sheriff of Nottinghamshire, 1942-43; Pres. British Chess Federation, 1942-50. *Recreations:* chess, travelling, farming, and country life. *Address:* Rempstone Hall, Loughborough, Leics. *T.:* Wymeswold 237. *Clubs:* National Liberal; Borough (Nottingham). [*Died* 20 *April* 1954.

DERHAM, Major-General Frank Plumley, C.B. 1944; D.S.O. 1916; V.D.; *b.* Melbourne, Australia, 15 May 1885; *s.* of late Thomas P. Derham, barrister, solicitor, and notary public, Melbourne; *m.* 1909, Adeline Matilda, *d.* of John C. Bowden, Melbourne; no *c.* *Educ.:* Camberwell Grammar School, Melbourne; Melbourne University. Practising as Barrister and Solicitor at Melbourne; left Australia 18 Nov. 1915 in Command of 11th Battery, Australian Field Artillery; in action in France (despatches, D.S.O., Croix de Guerre). *Recreation:* golf. *Address:* 394-396 Collins Street, Melbourne, C.1. *T.:* MU7651. *Clubs:* Naval and Military, Australian, Melbourne (Melbourne). [*Died* 22 *Oct.* 1957.

DERING, Sir Anthony Myles Cholmeley, 11th Bt., *cr.* 1626; Emergency Commission as Lieut. in Pioneer Corps; late Lieut. The Argyll and Sutherland Highlanders; *b.* 29 July 1901; *s.* of 10th Bt. and May Astel Rosina (*d.* 1946), *d.* of William Jameson of Montrose, Co. Dublin; *S.* father, 1931; *m.* 1st, 1932, Barbara (who obtained a divorce, 1939), *o. d.* of late Col. T. G. Ewan, C.B.; 2nd, 1946; Mary Sylvia (who obtained a div., 1955), *widow* of Capt. Meilan Carr, R.A., and *d.* of Major Morritt, Rokeby Park, Yorkshire, *Educ.:* Eton; Sandhurst. *Recreations:* rowing and shooting. *Heir:* *cousin*, Lt.-Col. Rupert Anthony Yea Dering, *b.* 17 Oct. 1915. *Address:* c/o Drummond's Bank, 49 Charing Cross, S.W.1; c/o Banco de Londres y America del Sud, B. Mitre 399, Buenos Aires, Argentina. [*Died* 23 *April* 1958.

DE ROS, 26th Baroness, *cr.* 1264; **Una Mary Ross;** *b.* 1879; *e. d.* of third Earl of Dartrey (*d.* 1933) and 25th Baroness de Ros (*d.* 1939); *S.* mother, 1943; *m.* 1904, Arthur John Ross (killed in action, 1917); one *s.* (and one killed in action, 1940). *Co-heiresses:* grand-daughters, Georgiana

Angela Ross and Rosemary Ross. *Address:* Gatehouse, Strangford, Northern Ireland. [*Died* 9 *Oct.* 1956.

DE ROUGEMONT, Brig.-Gen. Cecil Henry, C.B. 1916; C.M.G. 1918; M.V.O. 1904; D.S.O. 1900; D.L.; J.P.; *b.* 17 Dec. 1865; 4th *s.* of late Irving Frederick de Rougemont and Mary, *e. d.* of Sir Arthur Rugge Price, 5th Bt.; *m.* 1914, Muriel Evelyn, *o. d.* of Evelyn Heseltine, The Goldings, Great Warley, Essex; one *s.* (*yr. s.* killed, 1942, in N. African campaign). *Educ.:* Harrow; Royal Military Academy, Woolwich. Entered R.A. 1885; Captain, 1895; Major, 1898; Lt.-Col. 1912; served Dongola Expeditionary Force (despatches, 4th class Medjidie, British medal, Khedive's medal with two clasps); in operations, 1897 (clasp); Atbara (despatches, clasp); Khartoum (wounded, despatches, brevet of Major, British medal, clasp to Khedive's medal); South Africa, 1889-1901 (D.S.O., despatches, medal, 7 clasps); European War, 1914-18 (despatches seven times, C.B., C.M.G., Officier Légion d'Honneur); retd. *Address:* Coombe Lodge, Great Warley, Essex. *Club:* Naval and Military. [*Died* 18 *Aug.* 1951.

DERRICK, Thomas; Artist; Worker in Mural-Painting, Stained Glass and Portraiture, also Journalism; *b.* Bristol; *m.* Margaret Mary (*d.* 1946), *d.* of late Sir George Clausen, R.A.; three *s.* one *d.* *Educ.:* Sidcot; Royal College of Art. Exhibitor at Royal Academy, etc., but attached to no society or group; for five years instructor in decorative painting, Royal College of Art; cartoonist. *Publications:* The Prodigal Son and other Parables shown in pictures; The Nine Nines (with Hilaire Belloc); Everyman (with pictures by T. D.), etc.; miscellaneous contributions to Punch, Time and Tide, and other journals. *Address:* Cold Ash, nr. Newbury, Berks. *T.:* Thatcham 2221. [*Died* 18 *Nov.* 1954.

DERRIG, Thomas; *see* O'Deirg, Tomàs.

DERRY, Henry B.; *see* Bromley-Derry.

DERWENT, William Raymond; *b.* 5 April 1883; *e. s.* of late H. C. Derwent, Bradford; *m.* 1907, Jessie (*d.* 1957), *o. d.* of late C. H. Woodward, Birmingham; two *s.* *Educ.:* King Edward VI Grammar School, Birmingham. Joined Bradford Daily Telegraph, 1906; General Manager, Nottingham Journal and Nottingham Evening News, 1920-27; General Manager, Bradford and District Newspaper Co., Ltd. (Yorkshire Observer; Bradford Telegraph and Argus), 1927-33; Managing Director, 1933-53; Chairman, 1953-56; Managing Director, Westminster Press Provincial Newspapers Ltd., 1933-53; Director, 1953-56; Director, Press Association Ltd., 1936-44 (Chairman, 1942-43); Director, Reuters Ltd., 1936-43. *Address:* 8 The Glade, Welwyn Garden City, Herts. [*Died* 23 *Aug.* 1960.

DESCH, Cecil Henry, F.R.S. 1923; D.Sc., Ph.D.; *b.* 1874; *s.* of late Henry Thomas Desch; *m.* 1909, Elison Ann, *d.* of Professor W. Ivison Macadam, Edinburgh; two *d.* *Educ.:* Birkbeck School, Kingsland; Finsbury Technical College; Würzburg Univ.; University College, London. In Metallurgical Dept., King's College, London, 1902-7; Lecturer in Metallurgical Chemistry, University of Glasgow, 1909-18; Prof. of Metallurgy, Royal Technical College, Glasgow, 1918-20; Professor of Metallurgy, University of Sheffield, 1920-31; Superintendent of Metallurgy Department, National Physical Laboratory, 1932-39; President, Faraday Society, 1926-28; George Fisher Baker Lecturer, Cornell University, Winter, 1931-32; President, Institute of Metals, 1938-40; President, Iron and Steel Institute, 1946-48; Corresp. member, Académie des Sciences; D.Sc. (London); Ph.D. (Würzburg); Hon. LL.D. (Glasgow); Hon. Dr. Mont. (Montanwissenschaft) (Leoben, S. Austria). *Publications:* Metallography; Chemistry of Cement and Concrete; Intermetallic Compounds; Chemistry of Solids; articles on sociology. *Address:* 34 Calonne Road, S.W.19. *T.:* Wimbledon 2002. [*Died* 19 *June* 1958.

des GRAZ, Charles Geoffrey Maurice, C.B.E. 1942; Chairman, Sotheby & Co., Auctioneers; *b.* 9 Jan. 1893; *e. s.* of late Maurice des Graz, D.L., J.P., Crossboyne, Co. Mayo, and of late Hon. Mrs. des Graz, *d.* of 2nd Baron Oranmore and Browne; unmarried. *Educ.:* Eton; Trinity College, Cambridge. Censor of American Mails, War Office, 1915-18; Officer in charge of Widows' and Dependants' Branch, Ministry of Pensions, 1919; Director, British Library of Information in U.S., 1920; Deputy Chief Postal Censor, 1938; Chief Postal Censor, 1940; Assistant Director, Postal and Telegraph Censorship, 1941; Director, Western Area, 1943. *Address:* D5 Albany, W.1; Fairlea, Warwick West, Bermuda. *Clubs:* Carlton, Buck's, United University, Hurlingham, M.C.C. [*Died* 2 *March* 1953.

DE SILVA, Sir Arthur Marcellus, K.C.M.G., *cr.* 1956; Kt., *cr.* 1949; C.B.E. 1939; F.R.C.S. (Eng.); Consulting Surgeon, General Hospital, Colombo; Consulting Surgeon for Diseases of the Ear, Nose and Throat, Victoria Memorial Hospital, Colombo; Member Public Service Commission; *b.* 5 Nov. 1879; *s.* of Mudaliyar William Marcellus and Johanna de Silva; *m.* 1909, Laura Elizabeth Dias; one *d.* *Educ.:* Royal College, Colombo; London Hospital Medical School (Univ. of London). Surgeon, General Hospital, Colombo, 1907-30, Senior Surgeon, 1930-40; Lecturer in Surgery and Clinical Surgery, Ceylon Medical College, 1907-40; Surgeon for Diseases of the Ear, Nose and Throat, Victoria Memorial Hospital, Colombo, 1908-30; Examiner in Surgery, Ceylon Medical College, 1908-40. *Recreation:* orchid culture. *Address:* Manohari, Ward Place, Colombo, Ceylon. *T.:* Colombo 9062. *Clubs:* Orient, Ceylon Turf (Colombo). [*Died* 22 *Sept.* 1957.

DESLANDES, Sir Charles Frederick, Kt., *cr.* 1945; late Chief Inspector, Board of Customs and Excise; *b.* 1884; *s.* of Alfred Deslandes; *m.* 1914, Edith Katherine, *d.* of Edward Mathew. Retired, 1947. *Address:* Verdley Edge, Henley, Fernhurst, Haslemere, Surrey. *T.:* Fernhurst 285. [*Died* 27 *Feb.* 1957.

DESMOND, Shaw, D.Litt., F.R.S.A.; sociologist, novelist, dramatist, poet; *b.* Ireland, 19 Jan. 1877; father Irish, mother English; *m.* 1911, Karen Ewald (*d.* 1954), Danish author; one *d.* (one *s.* decd.) *Educ.:* by Irish monks and life. Left school at 15 to go into business in London; later one year's farming, etc., in Ireland; lectured widely in Danish and English throughout Scandinavia, otherwise throughout U.K. and U.S.A.; Sec. and Director of public companies in London before giving up business for literature and journalism in 1909; contested Battersea (Socialist) against John Burns, 1910; sailed round Cape Horn in windjammer and travelled 7000 miles in Africa, 1930-31; trawled to Arctic, 1939; Founder of the International Institute for Psychical Research, 1934; Director of the Sunday Theatre. Hon. D.Litt. (Université Internationale), 1948. *Publications:* Fru Danmark (in Danish), 1917; The Soul of Denmark, 1918; Democracy, 1919; Passion, 1920; My Country; Gods; Labour: the Giant with the Feet of Clay, 1921; Citizenship, 1922; The Drama of Sinn Fein, 1923; The Isle of Ghosts, 1925; Ragnarok, 1926; Echo; London Nights of Long Ago, 1927 (illustrated); Tales of the Little Sisters of Saint Francis (illustrated), 1929; The Love-Diary of a Boy, 1930; Windjammer: The Book of the Horn, 1932; The Story of a Light Lady, 1933; We do not Die, 1934; African Log, 1935; God—?; London Pride, 1936; World-Birth, 1937; Chaos, 1938; Reincarnation for Everyman; After Sudden Death, 1939; Life and Foster Freeman, 1940; You can speak with your Dead, Incarnate Isis, Spiritualism ?, 1941; How you live when you Die, 1942; Love after Death; Jesus or Paul?, 1945; Paradise Row (novel), 1946; The Story of Adam Verity (novel), 1947; The Edwardian Story, 1950; Personality and Power, Nathaniel (novel). Psychic Pitfalls, 1950; Pilgrim to Paradise, 1951; Love by the Dark Water (novel), 1952; Adam and Eve, 1954; Irish Moon (novel), 1953; Healing: Psychic and Divine, 1956; God's Englishman, 1956; many of which appeared in U.S. and foreign editions. *Recreations:* music, ju-jutsu, dancing, sailing, fishing, gardening, cricket, tennis. *Address:* Leicester House, 5 Montpelier Row, Twickenham, Middlesex. *T.:* Popesgrove 2664. [*Died* 23 *Dec.* 1960.

DETMOLD, Edward J.; *b.* 21 Nov. 1883; *s.* of Edward and Mary Detmold. *Educ.:* private school, Hampstead, and by private tutors. Exhibited first at the Institute of Painters in Water Colours and the Royal Academy, 1897; the International Exhibition 1899; Fine Art Society's Gallery, 1900; the Dutch Gallery, 1903. *Publications:* Pictures from Birdland, Kipling's Jungle Book, Æsop's Fables; The Life of the Bee, M. Maeterlinck; Birds and Beasts, Lemmonier; Hours of Gladness, Maeterlinck; Nature Pictures, 1920; Life, 1921; Fabre's Book of Insects, 1921; Arabian Nights, 1922. *Address:* Bank House, Montgomery, N. Wales. [*Died* 1 *July* 1957.

DE TRAFFORD (Charles) Edmund, J.P., D.L.; *b.* Trafford Park, Lancashire, 2 May 1864; 2nd *s.* of 2nd Bt. and Annette Talbot, *sister* of 17th Earl of Shrewsbury; *m.* 1892, Lady Agnes Mary Pia Feilding (*d.* 1921), 4th *d.* of 8th Earl of Denbigh; one *s.* [Capt. Hubert E. F. de Trafford, late The Royals; *m.* 1927, Cecilia, 2nd *d.* of 1st Baron Strickland, G.C.M.G.; three *s.* three *d.*] two *d.* *Educ.:* Beaumont College, Windsor. High Sheriff of Leicestershire, 1893. *Recreations:* cricket, hunting, shooting, fishing, motoring. *Address:* The Roserie, Sibbertoft, Market Harboro. *Clubs:* Bath, M.C.C. [*Died* 11 *Nov.* 1951.

DEVADOSS, The Hon. Sir David Muthiah, Kt., *cr.* 1932; *b.* Palamedtah, Madras Presidency, 18 Dec. 1868; *e. s.* of E. Muthiah Pillai; *m.* Masilanioney Chellammal, *e. d.* of J. T. Srinivasagen Pillai; one *s.* four *d.* *Educ.:* C.M.S. High School, Palamcottah; Hindu College, Tinnevelly; Presidency College, Madras, B.A., B.L. Enrolled as a Vakil of the Madras High Court in 1892; practised in the Tinnevelly District, 1892-1908; called to Bar, Inner Temple 1909; settled in Madras, 1909; Puisne Judge High Court Judicature at Madras, 1921-28; Secretary of Provincial Conference, 1906; Member of the District Church Council and Executive Council of the C.M.S., Tinnevelly; nominated to the Madras Corporation, 1917; President of the All-India Christian Conference, Dec. 1917; gave evidence before Southborough Committees 1919; Member of Legislative Council, 1919-21; Pres., I.C.A., for 1920-21; Pres., Madras City Co-operative Bank; Member, Council of State 1930; Nominated to Council of State, Delhi, 1931; President, All India Conference of Indian Christians, 1931; President, South Travancore Indian Christians, 1930. *Recreations:* gardening, tennis, and cutting down trees. *Address:* Sylvan Lodge, Mylapore, Madras. *T.:* 1513. *Club:* Cosmopolitan (Madras). [*Died* 11 *July* 1955.

DEVAS, Anthony, A.R.A. 1953; R.P. 1945; Portrait, Figure, Subject Painter; Member New English Art Club; *b.* 8 Jan. 1911; *s.* of Thomas Gronow and Marjorie Cecilia Devas; *m.* 1931, Nicolette Macnamara; two *s.* one *d.* *Educ.:* Repton. Studied at Slade School, 1927-30. Exhibitions held at Agnew's, Wildenstein and Leicester Galleries. Pictures shown in most of the Principal Exhibitions. Works purchased by Chantrey Bequest, C.E.M.A., Contemporary Art Soc., War Artists' Advisory Committee, Municipal Galleries of Carlisle, Aberdeen, Bradford and Preston. *Address:* 12 Carlyle Square, S.W.3. *Club:* Chelsea Arts. [*Died* 21 *Dec.* 1958.

DEVAS, Rev. Francis Charles, S.J.; D.S.O. 1917; O.B.E. 1919; Hon. C.F. (2nd class); *b.* London, 3 Apr. 1877; *e. s.* of Charles Stanton Devas. *Educ.:* Beaumont College, Old Windsor; abroad. Entered the Society of Jesus, 1895; taught in the Jesuit Colleges of Beaumont, Wimbledon, Stamford Hill; Priest, 1909; Commission as C.F. 14 Nov. 1914; accompanied 29th Div. to Gallipoli, serving throughout campaign with 1st Royal Inniskilling Fusiliers; was at Cape Helles and Suvla, subsequently in France (D.S.O.); Deputy Assistant Principal Chaplain 18th Corps; afterwards to 8th Corps; Chaplain (2nd class) 18th Bn. London Regt. (London Irish Rifles), 1923-38. *Publications:* Life of Mother Magdalen Taylor; Our Ladye of Walsingham and other Verses. *Recreations:* main interests—working boys' clubs and general after-care work. *Address:* 114 Mount Street, W.1. [*Died* 9 *July* 1951.

DEVEREUX, Wallace Charles, C.B.E. 1949; F.R.Ae.S.; Managing Director, Almin Limited; Chairman, International Alloys Ltd., Southern Forge Ltd., Renfrew Foundries Ltd., Warwick Production Co. Ltd., and Structural and Mechanical Development Engineers Ltd.; Chairman, Fulmer Research Institute; Chairman, Modern Electrolytic Patents and Processes Ltd.; *b.* 9 Mar. 1893; *m.* as 3rd wife, 1930, Dorothy Eleanor Anstey; two *s.* four *d.* *Educ.:* King Edward's Gram. Sch., Aston. After studying and practising engineering and metallurgy, became Supt. Nat. Aircraft Factory No. 1 during European War. Founded High Duty Alloys Ltd., 1927. Did much work on industrial reconstruction on Continent, notably in Rumania and in Poland (Order of Polonia Restituta); Director of Light Alloy Forgings and Stampings, 1939; in 1941, organised for Ministry of Aircraft Production reception and assembly of American aeroplanes and engines, and re-organised repair throughout Great Britain of aircraft engines and aeroplanes. Farms extensively at Kimble, Bucks. Founded the first commercial Artificial Insemination Centre there. President Bucks. County Show, 1950-52. F.R.S.A., M.I.N.A., M.S.A.E. Member: British Association for Advancement of Science, American Society for Testing Materials, American Institute of Mining and Metallurgical Engineers; Hon. Col. 114 (County of London) Army Engineer Regt., R.E. (T.A.). *Publications:* Post-War Reconstruction of Industry in South Wales; An Industrial Plan for West Cumberland; numerous papers for learned societies on industrial research and on the development and application of light metals, particularly in aircraft building and structural engineering. *Recreations:* hunting, shooting, golf. *Address:* Meads, Stoke Park, Bucks. *T.:* Slough 22708. *Clubs:* Junior Carlton, Royal Aero. [*Died* 21 *June* 1952.

DE VESCI, 5th Viscount (*cr.* 1776), **Yvo Richard Vesey,** Bt. 1698; Baron Knapton, 1750; a Representative Peer for Ireland; J.P., D.L.; formerly Captain Irish Guards; Major in S.R., Irish Guards, since Aug. 1914; *b.* 15 Dec. 1881; *S.* uncle, 1903; *s.* of late Capt. Hon. Eustace Vesey (*d.* 1886), 9th Lancers, and Constance (*d.* 1951), *d.* of 2nd Baron Wenlock, who married 2nd, Hon. Edward W. B. Portman (*d.* 1911), *e. s.* of 2nd Viscount Portman; *m.* 1st, 1906, Georgiana Victoria (marriage dissolved 1919, she died 1930), *o. d.* of late Gerald E. Wellesley; 2nd, 1920, Lois, *d.* of Sir Cecil and Lady Beatrice Lister-Kaye, and *widow* of 5th Earl of Rosse. *Educ.:* Eton. *Heir: nephew* John Eustace Vesey [*b.* 25 Feb. 1919; *m.* 1950, Susan Anne, *d.* of Ronald O. L. Armstrong-

Jones; one *s.* two *d.*]. *Address:* Abbey, Leix, Ireland. [*Died* 16 *Aug.* 1958.

de VILLIERS, Sir (H.) Nicolas, K.B.E., *cr.* 1948; a Deputy Secretary, Ministry of Pensions and National Insurance, since Dec. 1951; *b.* 22 Jan. 1902; *s.* of J. N. de Villiers who was born at Stellenbosch; *m.* 1926, Ruth (*d.* 1949), *d.* of late Sir David Evans, Cardiff, Director Welsh Nat. Memorial Assoc.; one *d.*; *m.* 1951, Evangeline, *yr. d.* of late Sir David Evans. *Educ.:* Sherborne; New Coll., Oxford (Gaisford Greek verse Prize). Called to Bar, Gray's Inn. Entered administrative grade of Civil Service, 1925, Min. of Labour; Asst. Sec. to Blanesburgh Cttee. on Unemployment Insurance; Private Sec. to Parl. Sec. and subsequently to Permanent Sec. of Ministry. In charge of Military Recruiting Dept. 1941-, also of arrangements for supply of labour for building and civil engineering programme 1943-, and of Military Demobilisation Dept. in 1944. First head of Manpower Div. of Control Commission for Germany. Deputy Secretary, Ministry of Works, 1945-51. Governor of Sherborne School. *Recreations:* tennis, ski-ing, walking, and reading. *Address:* 20 Walton St., S.W.3. *T.:* Kensington 8673. *Club:* Oxford and Cambridge University. [*Died* 4 *Feb.* 1958.

DEVINE, Sir Hugh Berchmans, Kt., *cr.* 1936; M.S. Melbourne University; Hon. F.R.C.S. Eng.; F.R.A.C.S. (Past Pres.); F.A.C.S.; Hon. Fellow of Assoc. of Surgeons of Great Britain and Ireland; Hon. F.R.S.M.; *m.* 1912, Mary O'Donnell; one *s.* two *d.* *Educ.:* Melbourne Univ. and Queen's Coll. Formerly Examiner in Surgery, Melbourne Univ.; one of the three original founders of the Royal Australasian Coll. of Surgeons; late Senior Surg. and Dean, St. Vincent's Hosp. Clinical School; late Stewart Lecturer in Surgery, Melbourne Univ. *Publications:* Text-books, the Surgery of the Alimentary Tract; (with John Devine) Rectum and Colon; and publications on Gastric, Colon and Rectal Surgery. *Recreations:* golf, shooting. *Address:* 57 Collins Street, Melbourne, C.1, Victoria, Australia. *T.:* M.F. 1465; 82 Mathoura Road, Toorak. *T.:* B.J. 2046. *Clubs:* Melbourne, Royal Melbourne Golf (Melbourne). [*Died* 18 *July* 1959.

DeVOTO, Bernard Augustine; Writer; *b.* 11 Jan. 1897; *s.* of Florian Bernard and Rhoda Dye DeVoto; *m.* 1923, Helen Avis MacVicar; two *s.* *Educ.:* Harvard. Instructor and Asst. Prof. of Literature at Northwestern Univ., 1922-27; Tutor and Lecturer at Harvard Univ., 1929-36; Editor of Harvard Graduates Magazine, 1930-32, of Saturday Review of Literature, 1936-38, of The Easy Chair, in Harper's Magazine, since 1935. 2nd Lt. of Infantry, U.S. Army, 1917-1918. Writer of U.S. history, fiction, literary criticism since 1923; author of mystery novels under the pen-name of John August. *Publications: fiction:* The Crooked Mile, 1924; The Chariot of Fire, 1926; The House of Sun-Goes-Down, 1928; We Accept With Pleasure, 1934; Mountain Time, 1947; many short stories, various years; *history:* The Taming of the Frontier (in collaboration), 1925; The Year of Decision, 1943; Across the Wide Missouri (awarded the Pulitzer Prize and the Bancroft Prize), 1947; The Course of Empire, 1952 (National Book Award); Journals of Lewis and Clark, 1953; Westward the Course of Empire, 1953 (English Edition); *criticism:* Mark Twain's America, 1932; Forays and Rebuttals, 1936; Minority Report, 1940; Mark Twain at Work, 1942; The Literary Fallacy, 1944; The World of Fiction, 1950; The Hour, 1951; The Easy Chair, 1955. *Recreations:* motoring, collecting Western Americana, mountain and desert travel. *Address:* 8 Berkeley Street, Cambridge, Mass. *T.:* Kirkland 7-9332. *Clubs:* Century Association, Harvard (New York). [*Died* 13 *Nov.* 1955.

DEWAR, Douglas, B.A., F.Z.S., Indian Civil Service (retired); Barrister; President of Evolution Protest Movement; Vice-President of International Christian Crusade, Canada; *b.* 1875; *s.* of John Dewar, L.R.C.P. and S. Edinburgh; *m.* 1902, Edith, *d.* of late Alfred Rawles; two *s.* one *d.* *Educ.:* foreign schools; Jesus College, Cambridge. In I.C.S. 1898-1924. *Publications:* Bombay Ducks; Birds of the Plains; Indian Birds; Animals of No Importance; The Indian Crow; Jungle Folk; Glimpses of Indian Birds; Birds of the Indian Hills; A Bird Calendar for Northern India; In the Days of the Company; A Handbook to the Pre-Mutiny Records in the U.P.; Birds of an Indian Village, Bygone Days in India; Beasts of an Indian Village; The Common Birds of India; Himalayan and Kashmiri Birds; The Struggle for Existence of Birds in India; Indian Birds' Nests; Birds at the Nest; Game Birds; Difficulties of the Evolution Theory; A critical examination of the supposed fossil links between Man and the Lower Animals; Man: a Special Creation, 1936; A Challenge to Evolutionists, 1937; More Difficulties of the Evolution Theory, 1938; What the Animal Fossils tell us, 1943; Current Theories of the Origin of Living Organisms; The Earliest Known Animals; The Transformist Illusion, 1953; Recent Theories of the Origin of Man, 1953; sundry papers on ornithology and Indian Finance; (with Mr. Frank Finn) The Making of Species, 1909; (with J. Wolfe) The Law Relating to Estate Duty; (with R. G. Wright) The Ducks of India; (with Mrs. E. Morton) A Voice crying in the Wilderness; (with H. S. Shelton) Is Evolution Proved?; (with L. M. Davies and J. B. S. Haldane) Is Evolution a Myth? *Address:* 5 Bath Road, Camberley. *T.:* Camberley 904. [*Died* 13 *Jan.* 1957.

DEWAR, John Arthur; Director of John Dewar & Sons, Ltd. (Chm.), Buchanan-Dewar, Ltd., Distillers Company, Ltd., British Vinegars Ltd., and The Licenses and General Insurance Co. Ltd.; *b.* 3 Aug. 1891; *e. s.* of Charles Dewar, Gt. Massingham Abbey, King's Lynn, Norfolk; *m.* 1932, Mrs. Kathleen McNeill, *d.* of Charles Beart of Johannesburg. *Educ.:* Aldenham School. *Recreations:* racing, coursing, shooting, golf. *Address:* Dutton Homestall, East Grinstead, Sussex. *Clubs:* White's; Jockey (Newmarket). [*Died* 15 *Aug.* 1954.

DEWAR, Robert, M.A. (Glasgow); Emeritus Professor, University of Reading; *b.* 10 March 1882; *s.* of late Alexander Dewar, Kilmarnock; *m.* 1916, Edith Margaret (*d.* 1956), *d.* of late W. E. Butler, Reading; one *d.* *Educ.:* Irvine Royal Academy; Glasgow University; Balliol College, Oxford. Assistant (later Lecturer) in English, Glasgow University, 1907-12; Professor of English, University of Reading, 1912-49. *Address:* at Dorney Vicarage, Windsor, Berks. [*Died* 21 *Sept.* 1956.

DE WESSELOW, Owen Lambert Vaughan; Consulting Physician, St. Thomas's Hospital; Professor Emeritus, Univ. of London; *b.* 1883; *s.* of Rev. C. H. S. de Wesselow; *m.* Margaret (*d.* 1948), *d.* of Sir Charles Craufurd, 4th Bart.; one *s.* *m.* 1952, Mrs. Barbara Barratt. *Educ.:* Haileybury College; Corpus Christi College, Oxford; St. Thomas's Hospital. B.A., D.M., B.Ch. (Oxon), 1st class Honours in Natural Science; F.R.C.P. London; Physician to the General Lying-in-Hospital; served R.A.M.C. France, 1914-18 (despatches); Sector Hospital Officer, E.M.S., 1939-46. Member of the Departmental Committee on Maternal Mortality; Croonian Lecturer R.C.P., 1934; Member British Pharmacopoeia Commission. *Publications:* The Clinical Chemistry of the Blood; The Toxaemias of Pregnancy (with J. M. Wyatt), numerous contributions to Scientific Journals. *Recreations:* travel and entomology. *Ad-*

dress: Chilcote, Quarry Rd., Winchester, Hants. *Clubs:* Alpine, United University. [*Died* 6 *July* 1959.

DE WET, Rt. Hon. Nicolas Jacobus, P.C. 1939; B.A., LL.B.; *b.* Ailwal North, Cape Province, 1873. *Educ.:* Victoria Coll., Stellenbosch; Cambridge. Admitted Advocate of Supreme Court of Cape Colony and of High Court of South African Republic, 1896; Chief Censor and Assistant State Attorney of South African Republic during early part of Boer War; after occupation of Pretoria, Military Secretary to General Botha till end of War; represented Middleburg-West in Transvaal Legislative Assembly, 1907-10; Legal Adviser to the Transvaal Delegates at South African National Convention, 1908; Minister of Justice, Union of S. Africa, 1913-1924; Senator for Transvaal, 1921-29; Judge of Appellate Div. of Supreme Court of S. Africa, 1937-39 (of the Transvaal Provincial Division, 1932-37); Chief Justice of S.A., 1939-43; Officer administering the Govt. of the Union of South Africa from the death of the Governor-General, Sir Patrick Duncan, on 17th July 1943, until 1st Jan. 1946. K.St.J. *Address:* 1003 Church Street E., Pretoria, S. Africa. [*Died* 16 *March* 1960.

DEWEY, (Alexander) Gordon, M.A., Ph.D.; Associate Professor of Political Science, Brooklyn College, New York; *b.* Montreal, Canada, 1890; *s.* of Rev. F. M. Dewey, M.A., D.D., Montreal; *m.* 1926, Rita Chisholm Frame, M.A., Halifax, Nova Scotia; one *s.* *Educ.:* Montreal High School; McGill University (First in History); Columbia University; Gilder Research Fellow in Political Science, Columbia University; formerly Instructor in Government, Columbia University, Lecturer in Political Science, Amherst College, and Associate Professor of Political Science, Union College; Member Canadian Historical Association, American Political Science Association, Canadian Political Science Association, Academy of Political Science, Foreign Policy Association, National Municipal League; Amer. Acad. of Political and Social Science. *Publications:* The Dominions and Diplomacy, 1929; various articles on History and Political Science. *Address:* Brooklyn College, Brooklyn, N.Y., U.S.A. [*Died* 4 *May* 1953.

DEWEY, John; Professor Emeritus of Philosophy, Columbia University, New York; Correspondant de l'Institut de France; *b.* Burlington, Vt., 20 Oct. 1859; 3rd *s.* of Archibald S. Dewey and Lucina Rich; *m.* 1st, 1886, Alice Chipman (*decd.*); one *s.* three *d.*; 2nd, Roberta L. Grant; two *c.* (adopted). *Educ.:* The Univ. of Vermont, (A.B.); Johns Hopkins Univ. (Ph.D.). Teacher of Philosophy at the Univ. of Michigan, Minnesota, and Chicago; late Director of the School of Education in the Univ. of Chicago. *Publications:* Leibniz: a Critical Exposition, 1888; Outlines of Theory of Ethics, 1891; Study of Ethics, 1893; joint author of Psychology of Number, 1894; of Studies in Logical Theory, 1903; and of Ethics, 1908; How We Think, 1910; Influence of Darwin on Philosophy, 1910; German Philosophy and Politics, 1915; Democracy and Education, 1916; Essays in Experimental Logic, 1916; Reconstruction in Philosophy, 1920; Human Nature and Conduct, 1922; Experience and Nature, 1925; The Public and its Problems, 1927; The Quest for Certainty, 1929; Individualism, Old and New, 1930; Philosophy and Civilization, 1931; Art as Experience, 1935; Liberalism and Social Action, 1936; Logic: The Theory of Inquiry, 1938; Culture and Freedom, 1939; Problems of Men, 1946; Knowing and the Known (with A. F. Bentley), 1949. *Address:* 1158 Fifth Ave., New York 29, U.S.A. *Club:* Century (New York). [*Died* 1 *June* 1952.

DEWHURST, Capt. Gerard Powys, J.P. Denbighshire; Chairman and Managing Director, Geo. & R. Dewhurst Ltd., Manchester; Chairman Vulcan Insurance Company, Manchester; Manchester Royal Exchange; Director London Assurance Corporation; Extraordinary Director Royal Bank of Scotland; late Chairman Williams Deacon's Bank, Manchester; *b.* 14 Feb. 1872; *s.* of George Bakewell and Frances Ada Dewhurst; *m.* 1897, Mary Brougham (*d.* 1956); two *s.* *Educ.;* Repton; Trinity Coll., Cambridge. *Recreations;* cricket, football, hunting, shooting. *Address:* Bodidris, Llandegla, Wrexham, N. Wales. *T.:* Llandegla 225. *Club:* Boodle's. [*Died* 29 *March* 1956.

DEWICK, Rev. E. C., M.A.; D.D.; *b.* London, 13 November 1884; *s.* of Rev. E. S. Dewick; *m.* 1929, Hilda, *d.* of late Frederick Schaeffer, London. *Educ.:* Merchant Taylors' School, London; privately; St. John's College, Cambridge; B.A. 1906; M.A., 1909; B.D. 1938, D.D., 1950; Jeremie (Septuagint), Prize, 1907; Hulsean (Essay) Prize, 1908. Curate of St. Peter's, Norbiton, Kingston-on-Thames, 1908-11; of St. John's, Blackheath, S.E., 1916-17; Tutor and Dean of St. Aidan's Coll., Birkenhead, 1911-15; Vice-Principal, 1915-16; Principal, 1917-19; Teacher of Ecclesiastical History in Liverpool University, 1911-19; Examiner, University of Durham, 1918-19; Examining Chaplain to the Lord Bishop of Peterborough, 1917-19; Acting Principal of St. Paul's Cathedral College (C.M.S.), Calcutta, 1919-1923; Fellow of Calcutta University, 1920-1923; Ceylon Secretary, Student Christian Movement of India, Burma and Ceylon, and Warden of Ceylon University College Christian Hostel, Colombo, 1923-25; Examiner, Literature Secretary, Y.M.C.A. of India, Burma, and Ceylon, 1925-34; Principal, St. Andrew's College (N.M.S.) and Chaplain of Christ Church, Gorakhpur, U.P., 1934-38; Lecturer, Hislop College, Nagpur, C.P., and Warden of Y.M.C.A. Student Hostel, Nagpur, 1939-45; Canon of Nagpur Cathedral, 1943-46. Examiner, Agra University, 1935-38; Head Examiner, Nagpur Univ., 1940 and1943; Examiner, Bristol Univ.,1946-1953 and 1956-57; Examiner, General Ordination Exam., C. of E., 1947-50; External Examiner, Univ. of Oxford, 1953; Hulsean Lecturer, Univ. of Cambridge, 1949; Lecturer, St. Andrew's Coll., Pampisford, 1946-1949; delegate of Univ. of Cambridge to Univ. of Strasbourg, 1951; Select Preacher, Univ. of Cambridge, 1951; Lecturer, Baring Christian College, Batala, E. Punjab, 1953-1954; Spalding Lecturer, Univ. of Hull, 1956-58; in the Univ. Coll. of Leicester, 1956; University Extension Lecturer: Cambridge, 1950; Oxford, 1957, 1958. *Publications:* Primitive Christian Eschatology, 1912; Christ's Message in Times of Crisis, 1916; Eschatology (in Hastings' Dictionary of the Apostolic Church), 1915; The Indwelling God, 1938; The World's Greatest Drama, 1941; The Gospel and other Faiths, 1948; The Christian Attitude to other Religions, 1953; contributor to: The Message of Sat Tal, 1931; Canon Law and the Church of England, 1955. *Address:* The White Cottage, Great Shelford, Cambs. *T.:* Shelford 3260. *Club:* Overseas. [*Died* 14 *June* 1958.

DeWITT, Norman Wentworth, A.B., Ph.D., F.R.S.C.; Professor of Latin Literature, Victoria College, Univ. of Toronto, 1908, Emeritus 1944; *b.* Tweedside, Ontario, 18 Sept. 1876; *s.* of Hiram DeWitt and Margaret Conland; became a permanent resident of the United States, 1954; *m.* 1906, Katherine Ida Johnston; one *s.* *Educ.:* Collegiate Institute, Hamilton (Ont.); Victoria College; University of Chicago; American School of Classical Studies in Rome. Fellow, University of Chicago, 1901-3; Fellow, American School in Rome, 1903-4; Professor of Classics, Lincoln (Illinois) College, 1904-5; Instructor in Latin and Greek, Washington University, St. Louis, Mo., 1905-7; Professor of

Greek, Miami Univ., Oxford, Ohio, 1907-8; Dean, Faculty of Arts, 1923-28; Acting Professor of Classics, Cornell Univ., Ithaca, N.Y., 1928-29; Visiting Prof. of Classics, Univ. of North Carolina, Chapel Hill, N.C., U.S.A., 1947-48; President, Section II., R.S.C., 1936; President, Classical Association of the Middle West and South (U.S. and Canada), 1938-39; Director, American Philological Assoc., 1938-40, Vice-Pres., 1946, Pres. 1947; Member of Managing Committee, American School in Athens, 1939-41. Fellow of Royal Academy of Mantua. *Publications:* The Dido Episode in the Aeneid of Virgil, 1906; Virgil's Biographia Litteraria, 1923; Ancient History, 1927; A Brief World History, 1934; Epicurus and his Philosophy, St. Paul and Epicurus, 1954; articles on classical subjects. *Recreation:* motoring. *Address:* 143 Eleventh St., Lincoln, Illinois, U.S.A. *T.:* 452X. [*Died* 22 *Sept.* 1958.

DEXTER, Walter, R.B.A. 1905; artist, painter, and illustrator; *b.* Wellingboro', 12 June 1876; *e. s.* of Walter S. Dexter and Emily, 2nd *d.* of John Allday; *m.* Helen Mary, *o. d.* of John H. Chadwick. *Educ.:* Croad's School, Lynn; Birmingham Municipal School of Art; Royal Society of Artists, Birmingham. On leaving school, and under influence of Pre-Raphaelites, painted The Workshop, bought by the City of Norwich for the Corporation Art Gallery; after studying in Holland and Belgium returned to Lynn, taking great interest in local reform movements; studio in Kensington, 1904; has painted portraits, landscape and figure subjects, interiors and still life, and book illustrations; now making series of drawings of Old Lynn and Fenland Towns; paintings for Literary and Artistic Associations of East Anglia, 1906; A Wanderer in Paris, 1908; for Edinburgh and the Lothians, and English Cathedrals, 1912; Wartime Art Master, the Bolton School, 1916-1919, and in War of 1939-45, Art Master, King Edward's Grammar School, King's Lynn. *Publications:* papers on Art. *Recreations:* motoring, East Anglian archæology. *Address:* The Valiant Sailor, Nelson St., King's Lynn, Norfolk. *T.:* King's Lynn 2310. [*Died* 12 *Feb.* 1958.

DEY, George Goodair, C.I.E. 1928; late Public Works Dept., India; *b.* 13 Sep. 1876; *s.* of late George Goodair Dey, I.C.S.; *m.* 1912, Ethel May, *d.* of Oliver Davey, Bude; two *s.* one *d.* *Educ.:* Bedford School; Coopers Hill. Joined Indian Service of Engineers, 1899; Executive Engineer, 1908; Superintending Engineer, 1915; Chief Engineer and Secretary to Govt. of Bengal, 1922; retired, 1931. *Address:* Mirik, Milford-on-Sea, Hants. [*Died* 11 *July* 1955.

D'EYNCOURT, Sir Eustace H. W. T.; *see* Tennyson-D'Eyncourt.

DHOLPUR, Maharaj Rana of, H.H. Rais-ud-daula Sipahdar-ul-Mulk Saramad Rajhai Hind Maharajadhiraj Sri Sawai Maharaj Rana Sir Udai Bhan Singh Lokindra Bahadur Diler Jang Jai Deo; G.C.I.E., *cr.* 1931; K.C.S.I., *cr.* 1918; K.C.V.O., *cr.* 1922; Bamrolia Jat by caste; *b.* 12 Feb. 1893; *s.* of Maharai Rana Nehal Singh, C.B.; *m.* 1911, *d.* of Sardar of Badrukhan in Jhind State; one *d.* *Educ.:* Mayo College, Ajmer; Imperial College, Dehra Dun. Went on tour in Europe; invested with full powers, 1913. State covers area of 1200 square miles; population, 230,188. *Recreations:* polo, tennis, billiards. *Address:* Palace, Dholpur, India. [*Died* 22 *Oct.* 1954.

DIBBLEE, George Binney; author; *b.* Trichinopoli, India, 1868, of Canadian parents; *m.* 1904, Laura Sterling Thomson (*d.* 1951); three *d.* *Educ.:* Haileybury Coll.; Balliol Coll., Oxford (Scholar). Manager of the Manchester Guardian, 1892; General Manager of the Field and Queen, 1913-19; Fellow and Bursar of All Souls College, Oxford, 1920-24. *Publications:* The Laws of Supply and Demand; The Newspaper; The Psychological Theory of Value; Instinct and Intuition, 1929. *Address:* All Souls' College, Oxford. [*Died* 27 *Aug.* 1952.

DIBDIN, Aubrey, C.I.E. 1943; M.A.; *b.* 4 March 1892; *y. s.* of Sir Lewis Tonna Dibdin and Marianne Aubrey Pinder; *m.* 1921, Sibyl May Luckham; two *s.* two *d.* *Educ.:* Tonbridge; Christ Church, Oxford. Military Service in India, 1914-19; Junior Clerk India Office, 1920; Principal, 1924; Secretary, Royal Commission on Labour in India, 1929-31; Assistant Secretary India Office, 1936; Burma Office, 1945; C.R.O. 1948; retired, 1948. *Address:* Field House, Corfe Castle, Wareham, Dorset. *T.:* Corfe Castle 231. [*Died* 20 *April* 1958.

DIBLEY, Rear-Admiral Albert Kingsley, C.B. 1945; *b.* 15 December 1890; 2nd *s.* of late Albert and Priscilla Dibley, Wimbledon; *m.* 1927, Penelope, *d.* of late Canon J. P. Frend, late Canon of Peterborough and Rector of Collingtree, Northampton; one *s.* four *d.* *Educ.:* Rokeby School, Wimbledon; Edinburgh House School, Lee-on-Solent; R.N.E. Coll., Devonport; R.N. College, Greenwich. Engineer Cadet, 1906; Engineer Lt. 1912. Served in H.M.S. Princess Royal, 1914-17, present actions Heligoland, Dogger Bank, Jutland; Engineer Lt.-Comdr. 1919; H.M.S. Repulse during Empire Cruise, 1923-24; Engineer Comdr. 1924; Admiralty, 1924-28; H.M.S. Frobisher, 1928-29; H.M. Dockyard, Portsmouth, 1929-32; H.M.S. Hood, 1932-1935; Engineer Capt. 1935; Chief Engineer, H.M. Dockyard, Hong Kong, 1935-39; Assistant Engineer-in-Chief, Admiralty, 1939-1941; Naval A.D.C. to the King, 1941; Engineer Rear-Admiral, 1941; Engineer Manager H.M. Dockyard, Devonport, 1941-1946; retired Oct. 1946. M.I.Mech.E., M.Inst.W. Legion of Merit, Degree of Officer (U.S.A.), 1945. *Recreations:* gardening, music. *Address:* Court Barn, Lee on the Solent Hampshire. *Club:* Army and Navy. [*Died* 26 *July* 1958.

DICK, Mrs. E. A.; *see* Ripley, Gladys.

DICK-LAUDER, Lt.-Col. Sir John N. D.; *see* Lauder.

DICK-READ, Dr. Grantly; *see* Read. Dr. G. D.

DICKEN, Charles Vernon, C.B.E. 1927; *b.* 1881; *e. s.* of late Admiral C. G. Dicken; *m.* 1917, Alice Mary, *e. d.* of William Ogden, Indian Public Works Dept.; (only son Pilot Officer in R.A.A.F. lost his life in 1943) one *d.* *Educ.:* Cheltenham College; Pembroke Coll., Cambridge. Entered Egyptian Civil Service, 1906; Civil Compensation Officer, Eastern Delta and Suez Canal Zone, 1915-17. Controller-Gen. of Administration and Pensions, Ministry of Finance, Cairo, 1923; Commander Order of the Nile; retired Egyptian Service, 1924; Financial Expert at the Four Power International Conference at Paris, 1928, on the Tangier question; Assistant Administrator and Director of Finance of the Tangier Zone, Morocco, from 1924; resigned 1937; Minister of Finance, Patiala State, India, 1937-44; Assistant Director (Controller of Budgets) in the European Regional Administration of U.N.R.R.A. in London; retired 1945; Ex-Vice-Pres. of British Merchants Morocco Association; Hon. "Juge-Adjoint" at The Mixed Courts, Tangier. *Address:* c/o Lloyds Bank, 222 Strand, W.C. [*Died* 28 *Jan.* 1955.

DICKIN, Maria Elisabeth, C.B.E. 1948 (O.B.E.); Founder and Hon. Director of the People's Dispensary for Sick Animals; Editor of The Animals' Magazine and of the Busy Bees News; *b.* 22 Sept. 1870; *d.* of Rev. William George Dickin; *m.* 1899, Arnold Francis Dickin; no *c.* *Publications:* The Cry of the Animal, and other humanitarian works. *Recreations:* music, literary work and philanthropic. *Address:* 4 Lansdowne House, Holland Park, W.11; St. Giles, Nutley Avenue, Saltdean, Sussex. [*Died* 1 *March* 1951.

DICKINSON, Anne Hepple (Anne Hepple); *b.* Widdrington, Northumberland, 1877; *d.* of late George Batty and Jane Dodds, Widdrington and Berwick on Tweed; *m.* 1903, William Bain Dickinson; one *s.* one *d.* *Educ.:* Berwick on Tweed; Cronberg in Taunus. Started literary career by writing poetry for Country Life, Outlook, etc.; went on to Nature studies, spent two years in London, wrote poems and nature studies about the Parks; returned to Northumberland and married in 1903; wrote Historical, and Nature Studies of Berwick on Tweed and District; won short story prize offered by Daily News with Fur, and took to short story writing; wrote Jemima Rides (first novel), 1928; won prize offered by Thomsons (Dundee), with The Untempered Wind; Editor of The Woman's Magazine, 1931-34. *Publications:* Jemima Rides, 1928; The Untempered Wind, 1930; Gay-go-Up, 1931; The Runaway Family, 1932; Scotch Broth, 1933; The Old Woman Speaks, 1933; Ask me no more, 1934; And Then Came Spring, 1935; Sweet Ladies, 1936; Annals of a Little Shop, 1936; Heydays and May Days, 1936; Touch Me Not, 1936; Riders of the Sea, 1937; Susan Takes a Hand, 1938; Evening at the Farm, 1939; The Piper in the Wind, 1939; The Taking Men, 1940; The North Wind Blows, 1941; The Green Road to Wedderlee, 1942; Sigh No More, 1942; Sally Cockenzie, 1944; Can I Go There, 1945; Family Affairs: The House of Gow, 1948; Jane of Gowlands, 1949; The Mettlesome Piece, 1951; Contributor to Country Life, Outlook, Quiver, Time and Tide, Scottish papers and magazines. *Recreations:* bird-watching, walking, especially on the Cheviot Hills and Lammermoors, study of wild life history. *Address:* Fairways, Castle Green, Kendal, Westmorland. *Clubs:* Writers', New Century. [*Died* 10 *Nov.* 1959.

DICKSON, Lieut.-Colonel Harold Richard Patrick, C.I.E. 1917; F.R.G.S.; Chief Local Representative Kuwait Oil Coy. Ltd.; *b.* 4 Feb. 1881; *s.* of late John Dickson, H.B.M.'s Consul-General, Jerusalem; *m.* 1920, Violet Penelope, M.B.E. 1942, 2nd *d.* of Neville Lucas-Calcraft of Gautby, Lincoln; one *s.* one *d.* *Educ.:* St. Edward's School, Oxford; Wadham College, Oxford. Joined 1st Connaught Rangers, 1903; served in Ireland, 1903-4; transferred India, 2nd Batt. Connaught Rangers; joined Indian Army, 29th Lancers, 1908; Special Service Officer, Gilgit Agency (Kashmir), 1911-12; Guardian to the Maharaj Kumar of Bikaner till outbreak European War, 1½ years; then rejoined 29th Lancers; was sent Mesopotamia, 10 Nov. 1914; took part in all actions leading up to capture Basra, Kurna, Nasriyeh, and Amarah (despatches); transferred to Political Dept., Aug. 1915; Asst. Political Officer, Suk Esh Shuyukh, Political Officer, Nasriyeh Division (Muntifik), Mesopotamia, 1917-19; transferred to Bahrain as Political Agent, 1919-20; Adviser to Mutasarrif Hilla Liwa, Iraq, 1921-23; Private Secretary to Maharajah of Bikaner, 1927; Secretary to the Hon. the Political Resident, Persian Gulf, 1928-29; Political Agent, Kuwait, Persian Gulf, 1929-36; acted as Political Agent, Kuwait, during summer of 1941, at request of H.M. Govt. *Publication:* The Arab of the Desert, 1949-50 (2nd Edn. 1952); Kuwait and her Neighbours, 1956. *Recreations:* hawking, shooting. *Address:* c/o Kuwait Oil Co. Ltd., Kuwait, Persian Gulf. *Club:* United Service. [*Died* 14 *June* 1959.

DICKSON, Rear-Admiral Robert Kirk, C.B. 1950; D.S.O. 1942; *b.* 18 February 1898; *s.* of late Dr. W. K. Dickson, LL.D.; *m.* 1933, Evelyn Loetitia (from whom he obtained a divorce, 1946), *d.* of Major Campbell Mucklow, R.A.; one *d.*; *m.* 1950, Joyce Mary, *widow* of Lt.-Col. T. E. Hussey, R.A., *d.* of late Adm. Hon. Sir Assheton Curzon-Howe, G.C.V.O., K.C.B., C.M.G. *Educ.:* Cargilfield School; R.N. Colleges, Osborne and Dartmouth. Midshipman, 1914; served European War, 1914-18; Battles of the Falkland Islands, 1914, Gallipoli, 1915, Jutland, 1916; Sub. Lieut., 1917; Grand Fleet destroyers and South Russia, 1917-18; Emmanuel Coll., Cambridge, 1919. Lieut., 1919; Rhine Flotilla, 1920; specialised in navigation, 1921; Naval Staff College, 1926; various navigating and staff appointments afloat in Home waters, Mediterranean, China, and South Pacific, 1921-32; Commander, 1932; Naval Assistant to First Sea Lord and Plans Division, Naval Staff, 1933-36; Executive Officer, H.M.S. Ramillies, 1936-38; Commander of College, Greenwich, 1939; Captain, 1939; War of 1939-45, Admiralty War Room (Duty Capt.), 1939-40; commanded H.M.S. Manxman (Fast Minelayer), 1940-42; various offensive minelaying operations, Malta convoys, Eastern Fleet, Madagascar, etc.; Dep. Dir. of Plans, Naval Staff, 1943-44; Chief of Naval Information (Actg. Rear-Adm.), 1944-46; commanded H.M.S. Theseus (aircraft carrier), 1946-48; Rear-Admiral, 1949; Head of British Naval Mission to Greece, 1949-51; retired, 1952. Shadwell Testimonial, 1924 and 1929. Younger Brother of Trinity House, 1924. *Publications:* Greenwich Palace, 1939; Naval Broadcasts, 1946. *Recreations:* fishing, music. *Address:* Spring Cottage, Hightown Hill, Ringwood, Hants. *T.:* Ringwood 770. *Clubs:* United Service; (Hon.) Royal Yacht Squadron. [*Died* 17 *Sept.* 1952.

DICKSON, Spencer Stuart, C.M.G. 1936; *b.* British Legation, Teheran, Persia, 28 Nov. 1873; *s.* of late W. J. Dickson, of H.M. Diplomatic Service; *m.* Beatrice (*d.* 1946), *d.* of Arthur M. Beaupré, United States Diplomatic Service; one *s.* *Educ.:* St. John's Coll., Oxford; M.A. Vice-Consul at Bogotá, 1900-6; acted as Chargé d'Affaires, 1902 and 1905-6; Vice-Consul at Brest, 1906-12, and Consul, 1912-13; Acting Vice-Consul at Antwerp, 1909; Consul at Rosario (Argentine Republic), 1913-19, except during part of 1914-15, when he was Consul at Port Madryn (Patagonia); Consul at Rouen, 1919-23; Consul-General at Marseilles, 1923-30; transferred to Diplomatic Service; H.B.M.'s Minister to Colombia, 1930-36; Special Ambassador to represent the King at inauguration of Dr. Olaya Herrera as President of Republic of Colombia, Aug. 1930, and again at that of Dr. Alfonso López, Aug. 1934; since 1936 has been associated with Sir Alexander Gibb & Partners, Consulting and Chartered Civil Engineers; a Vice-Pres. of the Seaman's Hospital Society of Greenwich, 1929; Vice-President of Anglo-Colombian Chamber of Commerce. Chevalier of the Order of Isabella the Catholic of Spain; Grand Officer of the Order of Boyacá of Colombia. *Recreations:* music, fly-fishing. *Address:* 12 York House, Turk's Row, Sloane Square, S.W.3. *T.:* Sloane 5741. *Clubs:* Travellers'; Phyllis Court (Henley). [*Died* 17 *Jan.* 1951.

DICKSON, Brig.-Gen. William Edmund Ritchie, C.M.G. 1919; C.I.E. 1917; R.E.; *b.* 28 Feb. 1871. Entered R.E. 1889; Capt. 1900; Major, 1909; Lt.-Col. 1918; Brigade-Major, India, 1905-8; D.A.A.G., India, 1908-9; Gen. Staff Officer, 2nd grade, India, 1911-16; 1st grade, 1916-17; served Waziristan Expedition, 1894-95; European War, 1914-18 (Bt. Col.); Inspector of Engineers and Pioneers in India, 1917-18; Inspector-General of Communications, East Persia, 1918-19; President Anglo-Persian Military Commission, Tehran, 1919-21; retired, 1921. *Publication:* East Persia: a Backwater of the Great War, 1924. *Address:* 10 Rosebery Crescent, Edinburgh. [*Died* 7 *Feb.* 1957.

DICKSON, W(illiam) E(lliot) Carnegie, M.D., B.Sc., F.R.C.P.E.; Consulting Pathologist and Bacteriologist (retired); Consulting Director Pathological Department, West End Hospital for Nervous Diseases and

Pathologist to Grosvenor Hospital for Women, London; *b.* Edinburgh, 1878; *s.* of late George Dickson, M.D., F.R.C.S.E.; *m.* Frances Edith, *d.* of late William S. Greenfield, M.D., F.R.C.P. (London and Edinburgh), Professor of Pathology and Clinical Medicine, University of Edinburgh, two *s.* two *d.* *Educ.:* Edinburgh Academy; Edinburgh University. Editor, Edinburgh Academy Chronicle, 1894-95 B.Sc. with special distinction in Anatomy and Anthropology, 1898; M.B., Ch.B., First Class Honours, 1901; M.D. with First Class Honours and Thesis Gold Medal, 1905; M.R.C.P. 1904, F.R.C.P. 1908 (Edin.); Baxter Scholar in Natural Science, Edin. and Lond. 1898; Stark Scholar in Clinical Medicine, 1901; Crichton Research Scholar in Pathology, 1902-5; Lecturer on Bacteriology in University of Edinburgh, 1907-14; Assistant Pathologist to Edinburgh Royal Infirmary and Pathologist to Royal Hospital for Sick Children, Edinburgh, 1906-14; Director of Pathological Department, Royal Chest Hospital, London; Captain, R.A.M.C.; Pathologist to Fulham Military Hospital, 1915-18; Fellow (past President) of Royal Medical Society, Edinburgh Member (original) of Pathological Society of Great Britain and Ireland, Association of Clinical Pathologists, and of Assoc. of British Neurologists; Royal Society of Medicine; B.M.A.; Hon. Fellow Institute of Medical Laboratory Technology, London. *Publications:* Editor and joint author of Text-book of Pathology (Beattie and Dickson), 5th ed. 1948; Bacteriology, The People's Book Series, No. 6, 2nd ed. 1919; The Cytology of the Bone-Marrow in Health and Disease, 1908; numerous medical and scientific papers. *Recreations:* photography, fishing, and Freemasonry. *Address:* 11 St. George's Road, St. Margaret's-on-Thames, Twickenham, Middlesex. *T.:* Popesgrove 4606. [*Died* 25 *Nov.* 1954.

DIECKHOFF, Hans Heinrich; *b.* Strassburg, Alsace, 23 Dec. 1884; *m.* 1917, Eva Jenke; one *d.* *Educ.:* studied law at Universities of Lausanne, Oxford, Munich, Berlin and Strassburg. Assessor Exam. 1912; entered Diplomatic Service, 1912; Secretary of Legation at Tangiers, 1914; took part in European War as Lieutenant, 1914-16 (Antwerp, Yser, Ypres, Poland, Warsaw, Mesopotamia, Kut-el-Amara); Secretary of Embassy, Constantinople, 1916-18; Foreign Office, Berlin, 1918-20; Consul-General, Valparaiso, Chile, 1920-21; Counsellor of Legation at Lima, Peru, July and August, 1921; Counsellor of Legation at Prague, Czecho-Slovakia, 1921-22; Counsellor of Embassy, Washington, D.C., 1922-26; Counsellor of Embassy, London, 1927-30; Chief of Anglo-Saxon Department, Foreign Office, Berlin, 1930-35; Chief of Political Department, Foreign Office, Berlin, 1935-36; Acting Under-Secretary of State, Foreign Office, Berlin, 1936-37; German Ambassador to the U.S., 1937-41; to Spain, 1943-45. *Recreations:* reading, walking, golf. [*Died* 21 *March* 1952.

DIELS, Professor Otto, Dr.phil., Dr.med, h.c.; Emeritus Professor of Chemistry, University of Kiel, since 1945; *b.* Hamburg, 23 Jan. 1876; *s.* of Prof. Dr. H. Diels. University of Berlin; *m.* 1909, Paula Geyer, Stuttgart; one *s.* two *d.* (and two *s.* killed in action). *Educ.:* Royal Joachimsthalsches Gymnasium and University, Berlin. Asst. in Chemistry, Univ. Institute, 1899; Professor, 1906; Prof. Univ. of Berlin, 1915; Prof. Univ. of Kiel, 1916. Gold medal of International Exhibition, St. Louis, U.S.A., 1904; A.v. Baeyer-Gedenkmünze, 1931; Dr. med. h.c., 1946; (jointly with Kurt Alder) Nobel Prize for Chemistry, 1950; Grosskreuz d. Verdientstordens d. Bundesrepublik Deutschland, 1952. *Publications:* Einführung in die organische Chemie, 1907 (15 Edns.). Many papers on organic chemistry in Ber. d. d. chem. Gesellschaft, Liebigs Annalen, Journal für Praktische Chemie, etc. *Recreations:* reading, travelling, music; formerly mountaineering. *Address:* Clausewitz Strasse 12I., Kiel 24b, Germany. *T.:* 42189. [*Died* 7 *March* 1954.

DIGBY, Colonel Frederick James Bosworth Digby Wingfield, D.S.O. 1917; J.P.; D.L.; T.D., County Councillor since 1910; Hon. Col. 94th (Queen's Own Dorset Yeo.) F/Brigade, R.A. since 1937; *b.* 22 Aug. 1885; *s.* of late J. K. D. Wingfield Digby, J.P., M.P., and 1st wife, Hon. Georgiana Rosamond, 5th *d.* of 4th Viscount Litford; *m.* 1909, Gwendolen Marjory, *d.* of late G. Hamilton Fletcher; two *s.* two *d.* *Educ.:* Harrow; Trinity College, Cambridge. Served European War (Yeomanry), 1914-18 (D.S.O., despatches thrice). *Recreations:* hunting (M. F. H. Blackmore Vale, 1909-46), shooting, fishing, polo, motoring, yachting. *Address:* Sherborne Castle, Dorset; Coleshill House, Coleshill, Warwickshire; Morsgail Lodge, Stornoway. *Clubs:* Carlton, Bath, Royal Motor Yacht; Royal Yacht Squadron (Cowes); Royal Dorset Yacht (Weymouth). [*Died* 23 *Nov.* 1952.

DIGBY, Kenelm Hutchinson, O.B.E. 1939; F.R.C.S Eng.; M.B., B.S. Lond.; Emeritus Professor of Surgery, University of Hongkong, 1950; engaged in research work, at Royal College of Surgeons of England, since 1949; *b.* Ealing, 4 Aug. 1884; *s.* of late William Digby, C.I.E.; *m.* 1913, Selina Dorothy, *d.* of John S. Law; two *d.* *Educ.:* Quernmore, Kent; Guy's Hospital, where held Michael Harris, Hilton and Beaney Prizes and was House Surgeon and Resident Obstetric Attendant. M.B., B.S., 1907; F.R.C.S., 1910; Surgical Registrar and Anæsthetist to Guy's Hosp., 1909-1911; Principal Medical Officer, Great Central Railway, 1912; Professor of Anatomy, Hong Kong Univ., 1913-23. Professor of Surgery, 1923-45, and Ho Tung Professor of Clinical Surgery, 1915-45, Univ. of Hong Kong; Hon. Consultant in Surgery to Government of Hong Kong, 1915-48; Surgeon, Queen Mary Hospital, 1930-48. Was interned Stanley Camp, Hong Kong. *Publications:* Immunity in Health: The Functions of the Tonsils and the Appendix, 1919; papers in med. jls. *Address:* 38 Avondale Rd., Bromley, Kent. *T.:* Ravensworth 1742. [*Died* 23 *Feb.* 1954.

DIGBY, Hon. Robert Henry; *b.* 1903; *s.* of 10th Baron Digby; *m.* 1929, Diana Mary, *o. d.* of Sir Berkeley Sheffield, 6th Bt.; one *s.* one *d.* *Address:* Lewcombe Manor, Evershot, Dorset. *Club:* White's. [*Died* 4 *April* 1959.

DIGGINES, Sir William Ewart, Kt., *cr.* 1941; *b.* 18 Nov. 1881; *s.* of George Diggines, Exeter; *m.* 1907, Annie B. Tulk, Gravesend, Kent; one *s.* one *d.* *Educ.:* Exeter School; King's College, London. Entered Civil Service, 1899; Inland Revenue Dept., 1902, as Asst. Surveyor of Taxes; Deputy Chief Inspector of Taxes, 1935-38; Chief Inspector of Taxes, 1938-43. *Address:* Carlton Mansions, Sidmouth, Devon. [*Died* 4 *June* 1952.

DIGNAN, Most Rev. John; Bishop of Clonfert (R.C.), since 1924. *Address:* St. Brendan's, Loughrea, Co. Galway. [*Died* 12 *April* 1953.

DIMMITT, Hon. James Albert, J.P.; Agent General for Western Australia in London since 1953; *b.* 21 June 1888; *m.* 1912, Florence A. Goodfellow; three *s.* one *d.* (and one *s.* one *d.* decd.). Member, Legislative Council, W. Australia, 1938-53; Chm. of Cttees., Legislative Council, 1947-53; Pres. Royal Aero Club, 1926-36; Founder and Pres. War Blinded Welfare Cttee., 1943-1949; Pres. Perth Rotary Club, 1946-47; Sqdn. Ldr., A.T.C., 1941-44; mem. Rottnest Island Bd. of Control, 1947-53; Director: Armstrong Dimmitt Ltd., W. A. Match Co. Ltd., Employers Liability Assurance Co., Wrights Ltd. *Address:* Savoy House,

Strand, W.C.2. *Clubs:* Royal Thames Yacht; Royal Freshwater Bay Yacht, Cottesloe Golf (W.A.). [*Died* 29 *Jan.* 1957.

DIMNET, Very Rev. Abbé Ernest; Hon. Canon of Cambray Cathedral, 1920; late Professor at the College Stanislas, Paris; writer and lecturer; *b.* 1866, Trélon. Priest 1893. First wrote for the English magazines, 1898. Lowell Lecturer at Harvard Univ., 1919; French Lecturer at the Williamstown (Mass.) Institute of Politics, 1923. *Publications:* La Pensée catholique dans l'Angleterre contemporaine, 1905; Figures de Moines, couronné par l'Académie Française, 1908; Les Sœurs Brontë, 1910; Paul Bourget, a literary biography, 1913; France Herself Again, 1914; French Grammar made clear, 1923; From a Paris Balcony, 1924; Latine de Romanis, 1924; France and her Problems, 1924; The Art of Thinking, 1928; What We Live By, 1932; My Old World, 1935; My New World, 1938; numerous articles in the leading French, English, and American periodicals. *Address:* 16 rue Chanoinesse, Paris IVe. [*Died* 8 *Dec.* 1954.

DIMOND, Maj.-Gen. William Elliot Randal, C.I.E. 1942; C.B.E. 1945 (O.B.E. 1943); K.H.S. 1945; L.R.C.P.I. & L.M., L.R.C.S.I. & L.M.(Rot.) 1915; D.P.H. 1924; Hon. Fellow State Medical Faculty, Bengal; I.M.S. retd.; Ministry of Health, Whitehall; *b.* 29 Sept. 1893; *m.* 1926, Marjorie, *e. d.* of late Sir Hugh Fraser; one *s.* one *d.* War of 1914-18, France and Palestine (twice wounded, despatches). Captain I.M.S., 1919; Major, 1928; Lt.-Col., 1936; Temp. Brig. 1943; Col. 1944; Maj.-Gen. 1945; Waziristan Operations, 1921-23; Assistant Director of Public Health, North-West Frontier Province, 1925; M.F.H. Peshawar Vale Hunt, 1936-38. War of 1939-45; officiating Inspector-General of Civil Hospitals and Director of Public Health, North-West Frontier Province, 1941; Middle East and Burma, A.D.M.S. 23rd Div., D.D.M.S. 4th Corps., 14th Army, 1945 (despatches); late Surgeon-General with Govt. of Bengal; late Inspector-General of Civil Hospitals and Prisons, Assam; retired 1947. O.St.J. *Recreations:* hunting and shooting. *Address:* Cooldaniel, Greystones, Co. Wicklow. *Club:* Naval and Military. [*Died* 5 *Nov.* 1960.

DIMONT, Rev. Canon Charles Tunnacliff, D.D. Oxford; M.A. (ad eund.) Bristol, 1918; Chancellor of Salisbury Cathedral since 1928 (Canon Residentiary until Dec. 1953); Prior of St. John's Hospital, Burcombe, since 1936; sub-chaplain of Order of St. John of Jerusalem since 1941; Canon (Prebendary) of Salisbury since 1914; Examining Chaplain to Bishop of Salisbury; *b.* Worcester, 8 July 1872; *s.* of Rev. C. H. Dimont, Vicar of St. Paul's, Worcester; *m.* 1906, Nora Frances Haydn, *d.* of Sir Frank Green, 1st Bart.; one *s.* three *d.* *Educ.:* King's School, Worcester; Worcester College, Oxford; Wells Theological College. Deacon (Curacy of Mirfield), 1896; Priest, 1897; Chaplain of Leeds Clergy School and Curate of Leeds, 1898; Vice-Principal, 1900-1905; Vicar of Holy Trinity, Halifax, 1905-1909; Vice-Principal of Wells Theological College, 1909-13; Principal of Salisbury Theological College, 1913-37; Chaplain of St. Nicholas' Hospital, Salisbury, 1917-36; Commissary to Bishop of Ballarat, 1916-17; to Bishop of Algoma, 1927; to Bishop of North China, 1932-40; to Archbishop of Brisbane, 1935-42; to Bishop of Shantung, 1940-51; Proctor in Convocation, 1938-45. *Publications:* (With F. de Witt Batty) St. Clair Donaldson, 1939; contributor to Dr. Hastings' Dictionary of Christ and the Gospels, Dictionary of the Apostolic Church, Encyclopædia of Religion and Ethics, and to the New Commentary. *Address:* 35 The Close, Salisbury, Wilts. *T.:* Salisbury 4664. *Club:* Church Imperial. [*Died* 6 *Nov.* 1953.

DIOGENES; *see* Brown, W. J.

DIOR, Christian (Ernest); French couturier; *b.* Granville, Manche, Normandy, 21 Jan. 1905; *s.* of Maurice Dior and Madeleine Martin. *Educ.:* Lycée Gerson, Paris; École des Sciences Politiques. B. ès L., B. ès Sc. Set up art gallery showing works of contemporary artists; travelled abroad and returned to Paris, 1935; illustrated for Figaro; served in French Army, 1939-40; in S. France, 1940-42; designed for Lucien Lelong, 1942-46; opened own establishment, Paris, 1947. Chevalier de la Légion d'Honneur. *Publications:* Je Suis Couturier; Talking about Fashion (U.K.), 1954; Little Dictionary of Fashion (U.K.), 1954; Christian Dior et Moi (Paris 1956, U.K. 1957). *Address:* 30 Avenue Montaigne, Paris 8e, France. [*Died* 24 *Oct.* 1957.

DIRKSEN, Herbert von, Dr. jur.; retired Ambassador; political writer; *b.* Berlin, 2 April 1882; *e. s.* of late Willibald von Dirksen, landowner, Privy Councillor and Member of the Herrenhaus, and late Ella Schnitzler; *m.* 1910, Hilda, *d.* of Freiherr Alfred von Oelsen and Margarethe von Saldern; no *c.* *Educ.:* Kgl. Wilhelmgymnasium Berlin; Universities of Heidelberg and Berlin, Dr. jur. Entered the services of the State, 1903; trained for Civil Service at Düsseldorf and Frankfurt a. O.; Civil Servant at Bonn; a secretary to the Ministry of Trade in Berlin, 1904; travelled round the world, 1907-1908; studied Colonial Economic Conditions in East and South Africa, 1912: served in European War, Captain 3rd Gardeulanen (war decorations); several diplomatic posts: The Hague, Kiew; 1st Secretary 1919, Chargé d'Affaires in Warsaw, 1920-21; Head of Polish Dept. in Foreign Office in Berlin, 1921-22; Consul General in Danzig, 1923-25; Counsellor and Head of East Dept. in Foreign Office in Berlin, 1925-28: German Ambassador in Moscow, 1928-1933; in Tokyo, 1933-38; German Ambassador at the Court of St. James, 1938-39. *Publication:* Moscow, Tokyo, London, 1951. *Address:* 13b Bergen 1, Eicherhof, Upper Bavaria, Germany. [*Died* 19 *Dec.* 1955.

DISNEY, Councillor Hon. Sir James, Kt., *cr.* 1951; *b.* Soldiers' Hill, Ballarat, Vic., 17 June 1896; *s.* of late Hon. J. H. Disney, M.L.C., Melb.; *m.* 1924, Ruby, *d.* of Gustavus N. H. Chapman, Clunes, Vic. *Educ.:* Melbourne, Victoria. Founder and sole Propr. Disney's Motors, Melb.; M.L.C. for Higinbotham, 1940-46. Served European War, 1914-18; landed at Anzac; Commn. No. 2 Scout Squadron, Australian Flying Corps; held Commercial Pilot's licence. Melbourne City Council, 1935-; Chm. Public Works; Metrop. Bd. of Works, 1937-; Sponsor and Chm. Special Carnival Cttee., 1939; Lord Mayor of Melbourne, 1948-49, 1949-50, 1950-51. Member Australian Assoc. of British Manufacturers. *Recreations:* flying, motor racing, gardening. *Address:* Carn Brae, 5 Harcourt Street, Auburn, Vic., Australia. *T.:* Hawthorn 5271. *Clubs:* Navy, Army and Air Force, Hardware (Melbourne). [*Died* 20 *Jan.* 1952.

DIX, Commander Charles Cabry, C.M.G. 1919; D.S.O. 1916; R.N. (retd.); *b.* Newcastle-on-Tyne, 31 Aug. 1881; *s.* of Charles Marshall Dix and Margaret Cabry; *m.* 1927, Helen Audry Curl, *d.* of Rev. C. H. Branch. *Educ.:* Royal Naval School, Eltham; H.M.S. Britannia. Midshipman, 1897; Commander, 1914; Acting Captain, 1917; retired, 1919; served in Boxer Rebellion, 1900 (despatches); Somaliland, 1903-4 (despatches); on staff of Admiral Sir Lewis Bayly, 1911-15; landing at Anzac, 1915, Beachmaster (twice wounded, despatches, D.S.O.); War Staff Admiralty, 1916-17; Naval attaché, Denmark, 1917-19 (C.M.G.); Colonial Service, 1926; Harbour and Shipping Master, Barbados, 1926-27; Marine Superintendent and Harbourmaster, Kingston, Jamaica, 1927-31; Deputy Master Attendant, Straits Settlements, 1931-36; Master Attendant, Straits Settlements, 1936-1941. *Publication:* The World's Navies in the Boxer Rebellion. *Recreations:* Rugby football (Navy, Kent, Devon), boxing (heavy-weight champion, Navy and Army, 1907), rowing, shooting, fishing. *Address:* c/o Bank of N.S.W., Hobart, Tasmania. *Club:* United Service. [*Died* 27 *Jan.* 1951.

DIX, Rev. Dom Gregory (G. E. A. Dix), D.D. (Oxon); monk of Nashdom Abbey since 1926, Prior since 1948; Proctor in Convocation of Canterbury for Diocese of Oxford; *b.* 4 Oct. 1901; *s.* of late Rev. Dr. G. H. Dix, D.Litt., and Mary Jane Dix. *Educ.:* Westminster School; Merton College, Oxford. Lecturer in Modern History, Keble College, Oxford, 1923-26. Proctor in Convocation. 1945, 1950. *Publications:* The Apostolic Tradition of Hippolytus, 1937; A Detection of Aumbries, 1942; The Question of Anglican Orders, 1943; The Shape of the Liturgy. 1944; (posthumous): Jew and Greek: A Study in the Primitive Church, 1953; The Image and Likeness of God, 1953; contributor to: A History of Christian Thought; The Parish Communion; The Apostolic Ministry; Theology; Jl. of Theol. Studies; Laudate; Church Quarterly Review, etc. *Address:* Nashdom Abbey, Burnham, Bucks. *T.:* Burnham, Bucks, 176. [*Died* 12 *May* 1952.

DIXEY, Arthur Carlyne Niven; *b.* 1889; *e. s.* o late Rev. A. N. Dixey, late of Manchester; *m.* 1st, Helen (*d.* 1945), *o. c.* of late Dr. Loynd Blackburn; two *s.* one *d.*; 2nd, 1949, Valerie, *d.* of late E. C. Cole, Crouch End, N.8. *Educ.:* Manchester Grammar School. M.P. (C.) for Penrith and Cockermouth, Dec. 1923-35. *Recreations:* shooting, hound trailing, tennis, golf, bridge. *Address:* 94 Kensington Church Street, W.8. [*Died* 25 *May* 1954.

DIXON, Arthur Lee, F.R.S.; M.A.; Fellow of Magdalen College; *b.* 27 Nov. 1867; 2nd *s.* of Rev. G. T. Dixon; *m.* Hélène (*d.* 1930), *e. d.* of late M. Léon Rieder, Paris; one *d.* *Educ.* Kingswood School, Bath; Worcester College Oxford. Lately Waynflete Professor of Pure Mathematics; formerly Fellow and Tutor of Merton College, Oxford. *Publications:* Papers in Proceedings Royal Society; London Mathematical Society. *Address:* Magdalen College Oxford. [*Died* 20 *Feb.* 1955.

DIXON, (George) Campbell; critic and playwright; Literary Editor of the Daily Mail, 1925-31; joined the Daily Telegraph 1931; President of the Critics' Circle, 1950 *b.* 10 Dec. 1895; *s.* of W. H. Dixon, J.P. and M.P., of Glenmark, Ouse, Tasmania; *m.* 1st, Alice, *d.* of late Randolph Simpson Sydney; 2nd, Lilian, *d.* of Thomas Duff; two *d.* *Educ.:* Hutchin's School and University of Tasmania (High Distinction in Ancient and Modern History). Travelled in East Indies, China, Manchuria, Korea, Japan, Siberia, Russia, etc., as special correspondent of Australian newspapers; in West Africa and North Africa on behalf of the Daily Mail and in U.S.A. as special correspondent Daily Telegraph, 1941-42. *Publications:* From Melbourne to Moscow, 1925; Madame Flowery Sentiment (from French), 1937; The Daily Telegraph Fourth Miscellany, 1947; Venice, Vicenza and Verona, 1959; short stories and film scenarios. *Plays:* This Way to Paradise (from Point Counter Point, by Aldous Huxley), 1930; Ashenden (from the novel by Somerset Maugham); Caesar's Friend (with Dermot Morrah), 1933. *Recreations:* cricket, golf, travel. *Address:* 67 Flask Walk, Hampstead, N.W.3. *T.:* Swiss Cottage 2727. *Clubs:* Garrick, Screenwriters'. [*Died* 25 *May* 1960.

DIXON, Henry Horatio, F.R.S. 1908; Sc.D.; Professor of Botany, Univ. of Dublin, 1904-50; Professor of Plant Biology, Trinity College, Dublin, 1922; Director of Trinity College Botanic Gardens, 1906-51; Keeper of the Herbarium, Trinity College, Dublin, 1910-51; *b.* 1869; *s.* of George Dixon and Rebecca, *d.* of George Yeates; *b.* Dublin; *m.* 1907, Dorothea Mary, *d.* of late Sir John H. Franks, C.B.; three *s.* *Educ.:* Rathmines School; Trinity College, Dublin; University of Bonn. Classical Scholar, 1891; First Senior Moderator in Natural Science, 1892; Assistant to the Professor of Botany, Dublin University, 1892-1904; Member of the Council of the Royal Dublin Society, 1908; Trustee of the National Library of Ireland, 1914; Managing Committee of the Imperial Bureau of Mycology, 1918; Commissioner of Irish Lights, 1924; Visiting Professor, University of California, 1927; Member of the Council of the International Institute of Agriculture and Chairman Commission on Biochemistry, Rome, 1927; Vice-Pres. Royal Dublin Soc., 1930, Pres. 1945-49; Vice-Pres. of the Physiological Section of the International Botanical Congress, Cambridge, 1930; Hon. Chairman Sixth International Botanical Congress, Amsterdam, 1935; Croonian Lecturer in the Royal Society and Corresponding Member of the American Society of Plant Physiologists, 1937; awarded the Boyle medal of the Royal Dublin Society, 1917. In 1939 received, on occasion of his 70th Birthday, a congratulatory address signed by nearly 800 Botanists, Colleagues and Students. Chas. Reid Barnes Life Membership of Amer. Soc. of Plant Physiologists, 1948. In 1949 appointed Hon. President of International Botanical Congress held in Stockholm, 1950; Hon. Fellow Trinity College, Dublin, 1950. *Publications:* Transpiration and the Ascent of Sap in Plants, 1914; Practical Plant Biology, 1922, 2nd ed. 1943; The Transpiration Stream, 1924; and scientific papers, mostly in Proceedings of Royal Dublin Society and of Royal Society of London. *Recreations:* yachting and travel. *Address:* School of Botany, Trinity College, and Somerset, Temple Road, Dublin; Bien Assis, Glenbeigh, Co. Kerry, Ireland. *T.:* Dublin 91695. [*Died* 20 *Dec.* 1953.

DIXON, Kevin; Judge of High Court, Eire, since 1946; *b.* 22 June 1902; *s.* of Martin Dixon and Ellen Sheridan; *m.* 1931, Ognae O'Flynn; one *s.* *Educ.:* Belvedere College, Dublin; National University, Ireland. B.Sc. 1923 (Chem. and Physics); called to Irish Bar, 1926; to Inner Bar, 1940. Bencher (Hon. Soc., King's Inns), 1942. Attorney General of Eire, 1942-46. *Publication:* Landlord and Tenant Act. 1931. *Address:* Dornden 5, Merrion Rd., Ballsbridge, Dublin. [*Died Oct.* 1959.

DIXON, Lieut.-Col. William, C.M.G. 1919; Royal Marine Artillery; retired; *b.* 1868; *yr. s.* of Arthur Dixon, Barrister, Lincoln's Inn. *Educ.:* privately in England, Belgium, and Germany. Entered R.M. Artillery, 1886; acting Governor of St. Helena, 1917-19; J.P. Sussex. *Address:* Barra, Stoke Fleming, Dartmouth, Devon. *Club:* United Service. [*Died* 1 *June* 1958.

DIXON-SPAIN, John Edward, O.B.E.; F.R.I.B.A.; Architect; 2nd *s.* of late Rev. Thomas Dixon-Spain, Vicar of Long Sutton, Lincs; *m.* Elsie Mary, 2nd *d.* of Joseph Clark; three *d.* *Educ.:* privately. Hon. Lieutenant in the Army, 1902; Hon. Freeman of the City of Lincoln, 1905; received into Catholic Church, 1914; Works (with Charles Nicholas) include City Hall and Public Baths, Newcastle; Rock Hotel, Gibraltar; State Medical School and Fuad-el-Awal Hospital, Cairo; Church of St. Joan of Arc, Farnham; Church of St. Alphage, Hendon; and other ecclesiastical work; Primary and Secondary Modern Schools. Service Regular (Hampshire Regiment); S.R. (Royal Field Artillery); seconded (Major and A./Lt.-Col. Royal Flying Corps and R.A.F.); served South Africa, 1901-2

(Queen's medal five clasps); European War, 1914-18, France and Middle East (despatches, O.B.E.); comd. Nos. 3 and 8 Schools of Aeronautics; served War of 1939-45 (despatches, Legion of Honour), R.A.F.; Fine Arts Officer with First U.S. and Second Brit. Armies from Normandy to the Rhine. *Address:* The Grange, Graveley, Hitchin, Herts. *Clubs:* Royal Air Force, Arts; Turf (Cairo).
[*Died* 7 *May* 1955.

DIXSON, Sir William, Kt., *cr.* 1939; *b.* 18 Apr. 1870; *s.* of late Sir Hugh Dixson. *Educ.:* All Saints' College, Bathurst. *Recreation:* collector of Australiana. *Address:* Merridong, Pacific Highway, Killara, N.S.W.
[*Died* 17 *Aug.* 1952.

DOBBS, Lt.-Col. Richard Conway, C.B.E. 1926; D.S.O. 1917; late Royal Irish Fusiliers; *b.* 21 Nov. 1878; *s.* of late Rev. Arthur Macauly Dobbs, M.A., and late Sarah Katherine Dobbs; *m.* 1912, Hamilton Bowen Powell; two *s.* one *d.* *Educ.:* Armagh Royal School; Trinity College, Dublin. Embodied Militia, 4th Royal Irish Fusiliers, 1899; Regular Commission the Royal Irish Fusiliers, 1900; Capt., 1910; Major, 1915; served S. African War, 1899-1902 (King's and Queen's S.A. Medals, five clasps); European War, 1914-18 (D.S.O. and bar, French War Cross, Brevet Lieut.-Col., 1915 Star, Victory Medal, G.S. Medal, despatches four times); Iraq, 1920 (G.S. Medal and two clasps, despatches); retired pay, 1929. *Recreations:* tennis and shooting. *Address:* Camowen Terrace, Omagh, Co. Tyrone. [*Died* 26 *June* 1957.

DOBELL, Lt.-Gen. Sir Charles Macpherson, K.C.B., *cr.* 1916; C.M.G. 1915; D.S.O. 1900; F.R.G.S.; The Royal Welch Fusiliers; *b.* 22 June 1869; 2nd *s.* of late Hon. Richard R. Dobell, P.C. (Canada), of Beauvoir Manor, Quebec; *m.* 1908, Elizabeth Annie, *widow* of Capt. F. L. Campbell, R.N., and *d.* of late Maj. Mayrick Bankes, Winstanley Hall, Lancs.; one *d.* *Educ.:* Charterhouse; R.M.C., Kingston, Canada. Joined The Royal Welch Fusiliers, 1890; Captain, Brevet Major, 1899; Major, and Bt. Lt.-Col., 1907; Bt. Col., 1910; Lt.-Col. Bedfordshire Regt., 1912; Major-Gen., 1915; Adj., 2nd Batt. The Royal Welch Fusiliers, 1896-1900; employed with West African Frontier Force, 1905-6, in command of a battalion; General Staff Officer, War Office, 1907-11; Inspector-General West African Frontier Force, 1913-14; served Hazara Expedition, 1891 (medal with clasp); Crete, 1897-98 (brevet of Major); South Africa, commanded 2nd Batt. Mounted Infantry, 1899-1900 (despatches, Queen's medal six clasps, D.S.O.); China, 1900 (medal); N. Nigeria, 1906 (despatches twice, Bt. Lt.-Col., medal and clasp); European War, in Chief Command, Allied Forces in the Cameroons, 1914-16 (K.C.B., C.M.G., promoted Maj.-Gen.); Commanded successively Western and Eastern Forces of Egyptian Expeditionary Force, 1916-1917, temp. Lieut.-Gen. (despatches twice); in Command of a Division in India, 1917-19 (despatches) and during Third Afghan War, 1919 (despatches twice, medal); G.O.C. in Chief Northern Army, India, 1920; retired pay, 1923; Colonel The Royal Welch Fusiliers, 1926-39; Commander of the Legion of Honour; a Military Aide-de-Camp to the King, 1910-15. *Recreations:* shooting, fishing, hunting. *Address:* 18 Kingston House, Princes Gate, S.W.7. *Club:* Naval and Military.
[*Died* 17 *Oct.* 1954.

DOBIE, William Jardine, LL.D.; Sheriff Substitute of Lanarkshire at Glasgow since 1946; *b.* 21 March 1892; *er. s.* of John Dobie, S.S.C., Edinburgh; *m.* 1922, Agnes Ferguson Ross (*d.* 1951); no *c.* *Educ.:* George Watson's Coll., Edinburgh; Edinburgh Univ. First Prize and Thow Scholarship, Edinburgh University, Scots Law, 1912, and Conveyancing, 1913; admitted Solicitor, 1920; admitted S.S.C. Society, 1932; practised as solicitor and partner of Inglis, Orr and Bruce, W.S., Edinburgh, 1920-39. Sheriff Substitute at Campbeltown, Argyll, 1939-42, and at Hamilton, 1942-46. *Publications:* Udal Law and Allodial Law, Stair Society, 1936; Manual of the Law of Liferent and Fee in Scotland, 1941; Law and Practice of the Sheriff Courts in Scotland, 1948; Sheriff Court Styles, 1951; various articles in Legal and other periodicals. *Recreations:* fishing, sketching. *Address:* Davaar, Uddingston, Lanarkshire. *T.:* Uddingston 126.
[*Died* 31 *Jan.* 1956.

DOBREE, Claude Hatherley, C.B.E. 1929 (O.B.E. 1924); *s.* of late Rev. J. Bonamy Dobree, M.A., West Tilbury, Essex; *m.* 1925, E. Aileen (*d.* 1948), *d.* of Alexander Fraser, M.B., Caistor, Lincs. *Educ.:* Park House School, Gravesend. Associate of Institute of Chartered Accountants, 1902; Northern Rhodesia Civil Service, 1911-33; held following appointments: Auditor, 1913-21; Treasurer, 1921-33; acted as Chief Secretary, 1927-28, and as Governor, 1930. *Address:* 30 Downview Rd., Worthing, Sussex. [*Died* 13 *Dec.* 1960.

DOBSON, Lieut.-Colonel Joseph Henry, D.S.O. 1916; Chairman and Managing Director of Dowson and Dobson, Ltd., civil, mechanical and electrical engineers, merchants and contractors, Johannesburg, Durban, East London, Port Elizabeth, Cape Town, Bulawayo and Salisbury; Mechanical and Electrical Engineer; *b.* 12 Oct. 1878; *m.* 1915, Kathleen Florence, *d.* of Major W. W. Cherrington, Johannesburg; two *d.* D.Eng. (Liverpool); Hon. D.Sc. (Witwatersrand); M.Sc. (Victoria), Wh. Exh.; M.Inst.C.E.; M.I.Mech.E.; M.I.E.E.; M.I.Chem.E., F.R.S. (S.A.). Engineer, London and North Western Railway, Crewe Works, 1900; Professor of Electrical Engineering, Transvaal University College, Johannesburg, 1905 (now the Witwatersrand University); Town Electrical Engineer of Johannesburg, 1909; General Manager of the Gas and Electric Supplies and Tramways of Johannesburg, 1911-19; Pres. South African Institution of Engineers, 1910 and Gold Medallist, 1915 and 1928; Pres. Association of Municipal Electricity Undertakings of Southern Africa, 1915; President South African Institute of Electrical Engineers, 1918 and Gold Medallist, 1914; Pres. Chemical, Metallurgical and Mining Society of South Africa, 1940; Vice-Pres. Institution of Chemical Engineers, London, 1941-43 and Gold Medallist, 1938; Pres. Associated Scientific and Technical Societies of S.A., 1944-45; Hon. Vice-Chm. S.A. National Velt Trust; Hon. Chairman S.A. National Anti-waste and Conservation Organisation, 1942-47. Served European War, 1915-1917 (despatches, D.S.O.); Lt.-Col. S. African Defence Force (retired). *Publications:* numerous papers before engineering societies, etc. *Address:* Dowson and Dobson, Ltd., Dowson Dobson Building, 29 Webber Street, Selby, Johannesburg. *T.A.:* Downright, Johannesburg. *T.:* 33—5041. *Clubs:* Rand, Country (Johannesburg); Pretoria (Pretoria); City (Capetown).
[*Died* 29 *June* 1954.

DOBSON, Mildred Eaton, M.A., B.Sc., B.D.; 5th *d.* of late Henry Austin Dobson, LL.D. *Educ.:* Princess Helena College, Ealing; St. Andrews University. Warden, University Hall, St. Andrews; retired 1936. *Recreation:* philately. *Address:* 2 Normanhurst, St. John's Road, Eastbourne, Sussex.
[*Died* 29 *May* 1952.

DOBSON, Richard Rhimes, M.A. Christ's College, Cambridge; J.P. Gloucestershire; M.Science (Hon. Bristol); Member Gloucestershire County Council since 1938, County Alderman 1949; *b.* 1877; *o. s.* of late William Dobson of Stourton, Leeds, and late Mrs. Dobson, Cheltenham; *m.* Ruth, *d.* of late J. Prentice of Tweedsyde, Berwick-on-Tweed; no *c.* *Educ.:* Christ's College (Exhibitioner), Cambridge. Late Headmaster, Grammar School, Wotton-under-

Edge, 1912-15; Marling School, Stroud, 1915-19; Headmaster, Cheltenham Grammar School, 1919-37; Chairman: Gloucestershire County Council Education Committee, 1952-58; Primary Education Committee; Higher Education Committee; Standish Hospital Management Committee, 1941-53; Education Finance Cttee. Longford's Approved School for Girls (1st Chm.), etc. Member: County Finance Selection, Staff and Salaries Cttee., etc.; Bristol University Court. *Recreation:* gardening. *Address:* Spring Hill House, Nailsworth, Gloucestershire. *T.:* Nailsworth 59. [*Died* 25 *Nov.* 1960.

DOCKER, Rev. Wilfrid Brougham, M.A.; *b.* 1882; *s.* of Arthur Robert Docker and Florence Lucy Lord; *m.* 1909, Constance Louise Langman (*d.* 1942); two *s.* two *d.* *Educ.:* Sydney Grammar School; University of Sydney; Wells Theological College. Assistant curate at S. James, Norlands, London, 1906; Rector of Beaconsfield, Tasmania, 1910; Priest in charge of Angaston, 1911, and S. Cyprians, Adelaide, 1914; Temporary Warden of S. Barnabas College, Adelaide, 1916; Missioner of S. Peter's College Mission and Rector of S. Mary Magdalene's, Adelaide, 1922; Hon. Canon of S. Peter's Cathedral, Adelaide, 1928; Vicar of Emmanuel Church, Forest Gate, 1934-36; Director of Religious Education, Diocese of Lincoln, 1936-45; Preb. and Canon of Lincoln Cathedral, 1944-45. *Address:* c/o Bank of N.S.W., Adelaide, S. Australia. [*Died* 19 *July* 1956.

DODD, Brig. Arthur Harvey Russell, C.I.E. 1935; Indian Army, retired; *b.* 1883; *e. s.* of late Col. C. A. Dodd, I.S.C.; *m.* 1910, Muriel Penelope Russell (*d.* 1944), *d.* of late Alexander Russell Dodd; *m.* 1945, Madge Ethel, *d.* of late Sir Michael Nethersole. Served European War, 1914-18 (despatches four times, Bt. Lt.-Col.); N.-W. Frontier of India, 1921-23 (despatches); retired 1933. *Address:* St. Josefs, Mahé, Seychelles Islands. *Club:* Royal Empire Society. [*Died* 29 *Nov.* 1955.

DODDS CREWE, Major James Hugh Hamilton, C.M.G. 1921; T.D.; *b.* 27 Aug. 1880; *s.* of late James Dodds, of Alton, Berkhamstead; assumed surname of Dodds Crewe by deed poll, 1945; *m.* 1922, Lady Annabel O'Neill (*d.* 1948), *widow* of Capt. Hon. Arthur O'Neill, M.P., 2nd Life Guards, *e. d.* of 1st Marquess of Crewe, K.G., P.C.; two *s.* *Educ.:* private; Eastbourne Coll. Served S. African War, 1901-2 (Queen's medal and five clasps); Somaliland, 1908-10 (Africa General Service medal and clasp); T.D.; H.B.M.'s Consul, Harrar and Consul and Charge d'Affaires, Adis Ababa, Abyssinia, 1911-24; Tripoli, 1924-28; Consul, Palermo, 1928-36; Consul General, Nice, 1936-40; attached Consulate of U.S.A., Marseilles, 1940-41; retired, 1941. D.L. Staffs. until Dec. 1951. Coronation Medal, 1937; Order of St. John of Jerusalem; Star of Ethiopia. *Address:* Norrises, Newick, Sussex. [*Died* 28 *July* 1956.

DODGE, John Bigelow, D.S.O. 1919; D.S.C. 1915; M.C. 1946; Member of London Stock Exchange; *b.* New York, 15 May 1894; *s.* of late Chas. S. Dodge and Flora Bigelow Dodge (now Hon. Mrs. Lionel Guest); *m.* 1929, Minerva Sherman, *d.* of late John Arrington, Charlotte, North Carolina, U.S.A.; two *s.* *Educ.:* St. Mark's School, U.S.A.; McGill University. Joined Hood Battalion, Royal Naval Division, Sep. 1914, as Sub-Lieutenant, R.N.V.R.; served at Antwerp 1914, and landed at Gallipoli 25 April 1915; France, 1916-19 (twice wounded, D.S.O., D.S.C., despatches twice); commanded 16th Battalion Royal Sussex Regiment as Lt.-Colonel at end of that War; served War of 1939-45 with Middlesex Regiment as Major, attached Kensington Regt. Taken prisoner June 1940 with 51st Division at St. Valéry, released 1945 (escaped five times). Travelled in Mongolia, Siberia, China, Burma, India, Iraq, Persia, the Caucasus, 1920-22; imprisoned by the Tcheka in Batoum, 1921. Chairman Ends of the Earth Club. Contested (U.) Mile End Division of Stepney, 1924 and 1929; Gillingham Division of Kent, 1945. Member of London County Council for Mile End, 1925-31; became a naturalised British subject, June 1915. *Address:* 35 Chester Row, S.W.1. *T.:* Sloane 7714. *Clubs:* Carlton, City of London: Royal Yacht Squadron (Cowes). [*Died* 2 *Nov.* 1960.

DODS, Alexander Waddell, C.I.E. 1921; late member of Burn & Co., Engineers and Shipbuilders, Calcutta; *m.* 1923, Enid Laura, *d.* of Hugh Mounteney Lely, Carlton Scroop, near Grantham. Member: Couchman Committee, 1919, for reorganizing Govt. of India Purchasing Depts.; New Delhi Committee, 1922. *Clubs:* Oriental; Bengal (Calcutta). [*Died* 28 *May* 1952.

DOHERTY, F. C., M.B.E., M.A.; Headmaster of Lancing College, 1935-July 1953. *Educ.:* Westminster (Scholar); Christ Church, Oxford (Scholar). Asst. Master, Radley Coll., 1919-24; Senior Classical Master, King's College School, Wimbledon, 1925-29; Headmaster of Oakham School, 1929-34. *Address:* Ladywell, Lindfield, Sussex. [*Died* 20 *Oct.* 1959.

DOHNÁNYI, Dr. Ernest; pianist, composer, conductor; *b.* Porsony, Hungary, 27 July 1877; *m.* Elza Galafrès; one *s.* *Educ.:* under his father; Porsony, under Herr Forstner; Royal Hungarian Academy of Music, Buda Pest, under Professors Hano, Koessler, and Thoman; under Eugen d'Albert. Made début, 1897; Prof. Royal High School, Berlin, 1905-15; Director, Royal Music Academy, Budapest, 1919; General Musical Director, Hungarian Broadcasting Corporation, 1931, and President and leading Conductor of Budapester Philharmonik Orchester; Director, Royal Hungarian Academy of Musical Art, 1934. Left Hungary, 1948, and became Professor at Florida State University, Miami, U.S.A., 1949. Has written concertos, symphonies, operas (Aunt Simone, Tower of the Woivod, The Tenor), ballets (Pierrette's Veil, Moments Musicaux), chamber music, a Mass, etc. Hon. Dr. Univ. of Kolozsvar. *Address:* c/o R.C.A. Victor, 630 Fifth Avenue, New York 20, N.Y., U.S.A. [*Died* 11 *Feb.* 1960.

DOIDGE, Sir Frederick Widdowson, K.C.M.G., *cr.* 1953; High Commissioner for New Zealand in London since 1951; *b.* 26 February 1884; *s.* of Edwin Doidge, of Bere Ferrers, Devon, and Mary Doidge, London, England; *m.* 1910, Lyle Clark, Auckland, New Zealand; no *c.* *Educ.:* in Australia. Entered journalism; Pres. of N.Z. Journalists Assoc., 1910. Served European War, 1914-18, in France, with New Zealand Division; joined British Ministry of Information (seconded from N.Z. Division), 1918. Entered Fleet St., 1918; assoc. with Daily Express, Sunday Express, Evening Standard; was a Director of London Express Newspaper Co. for many years; retired after 17 years in Fleet St.; returned to N.Z. and became member of N.Z. Parl. in 1938; Minister of External Affairs, New Zealand, 1949-51. *Recreations:* golf, bowls, shooting. *Address:* 415 Strand, W.C.2. *Clubs:* Wellington (Wellington); Auckland (Auckland); Tauranga (Tauranga). [*Died* 26 *May* 1954.

DOIG, Peter; General Secretary, Association of Engineering and Shipbuilding Draughtsmen, 1918-45; *b.* 26 Jan. 1882; *s.* of Peter and Martha Rodger Doig; *m.* 1908, Margaret Paterson Scott; one *d.* *Educ.:* Allen Glen's School, Glasgow. Ship Draughtsman, trained at John Brown and Co., Clydebank; worked in shipbuilding in Scotland, Ireland, United States and China (Shanghai); specialist on screw propeller design; Editor British Astronomical Association Journal, 1930-37 and 1948-. *Publi-*

cations: An Outline of Stellar Astronomy; A Concise History of Astronomy; various papers on marine propulsion and on astronomical subjects during about 40 years. *Address:* 96 St. George's Square, S.W.1. *T.:* Victoria 0747. [*Died* 13 *Oct.* 1952.

DOMINY, Reginald Hugh, C.B.E. 1920; R.N.R.; retired; *s.* of John Dominy, Ordnance Office, Southampton; unmarried. *Educ.:* South Hants College, Southampton. Captain, Pacific Steam Navigation Coy., R.M.S. Orbita. *Recreation:* golf. *Address:* The Cabin, Highbury Avenue, Prestatyn, N. Wales. [*Died* 7 *July* 1953.

DOMVILE, Sir Hugo C. P.; *see* Poë Domvile.

DON, Charles Davidson; *b.* Bridge of Allan, Scotland, 1874; *y. s.* of late Rev. John Davidson Don; *m.* 1910, Lucie Blanche Lilian Paley. *Educ.:* Dale College, Kingwilliamstown; Royal High School, Edinburgh. Joined staff of Cape Mercury, 1893; leader-writer on Cape Argus, 1894; Editor of Times of Natal, 1901-1910; Member of Natal Education Commission, 1908; Acting Editor of Transvaal Leader, 1911; Editor, Rhodesia Herald, 1911-15; Editor, The Star, Johannesburg, 1915, Editor-in Chief, 1937; retired 1939. *Publication:* And Having Writ—Memories and Impressions, 1942. *Recreations:* golf, tennis. *Address:* 4 Chamberlain Street, King William's Town, S.A. *Clubs:* Authors'; Rand (Johannesburg); Victoria (Maritzburg); Salisbury (Rhodesia). [*Died* 7 *March* 1959.

DON-WAUCHOPE, Sir John D.; *see* Wauchope.

DONALD, Charles, O.B.E. 1944; Ch.M., F.R.C.S.(Eng.); Surgeon: London Hospital, since 1933; Hospital for Sick Children, Gt. Ormond St., since 1935; Royal Masonic Hospital, since 1945; Hon. Colonel, Army Medical Service; *b.* 14 Feb. 1896; *s.* of John Donald, Aberdeen; *m.* 1927, Amy Stewart Walker; one *s.* one *d.* *Educ.:* Robert Gordon's College, Aberdeen; University of Aberdeen. Served European War, 1914-18, Lieut. Gordon Highlanders; Flight Commander, R.F.C. and R.A.F. (despatches). M.B., Ch.B., Aberdeen, 1922; F.R.C.S. (Eng.), 1925. War of 1939-45, Lieut.-Col., R.A.M.C., 1940-42; Brigadier, Consulting Surgeon, Middle East and Central Mediterranean Forces, 1942-44; Consulting Surgeon, Southern Command, 1944-45. *Publications:* contributions to surgical journals. *Recreation:* golf. *Address:* 139 Harley St., W.1. *T.:* Welbeck 1201. *Club:* Athenæum. [*Died* 8 *July* 1955.

DONALD, Douglas, C.S.I. 1921 (C.I.E. 1903); C.B.E. 1921; *b.* Hashiarpore, Punjab, 19 Nov. 1865; *s.* of the late A. J. S. Donald, Punjab Provincial Civil Service; *m.* 1895, Miss Johnson. *Educ.:* Bishop Cotton School, Simla. Joined the Punjab Police Force at Ambalia, Punjab, 1888; transferred to Peshawar, 1889; served with Sir William Lockhart in both the Miranzai Expeditions, 1891 (medal and clasp); served with Col. Haughton, 36th Sikhs, during the attack on Samana posts, and subsequently with Sir W. Lockhart in the Tirah Field Force (medal and three clasps); Political Assistant B.M. Police, 1894; Political Officer Khyber, 1898, and re-transferred to Kohat, 1899; Comdt. B.M. Police and Samana Rifles, 1899; Superintendent of Police, 1906; Deputy Inspector General of Police, 1914; on special duty as Political Officer, N.W.F. Provinces, 1919; retired, 1922. *Publication:* Note on Adam Khel Afridis. *Address:* c/o Grindlay & Co., 54 Parliament Street, S.W.1; West Ways, New Road, Durrington, nr. Worthing, Sussex. [*Died* 21 *Oct.* 1953.

DONALD, Sir James, Kt., *cr.* 1927; C.S.I. 1924; C.I.E. 1918; LL.D. (Aberdeen); *b.* 1873; *s.* of John Donald, Aberdeen; *m.* 1st, 1904, Gertrude (*d.* 1912), *d.* of G. J. Perram, C.I.E.; one *d.*; 2nd, 1914, Winifred, *d.* of J. C. Bayldon. *Educ.:* Aberdeen University; St. John's College, Cambridge. Entered I.C.S. 1895; posted to Bengal, 1896; transferred to Assam, 1898; Under-Secretary to Chief Commissioner of Assam, 1901-4; transferred to Bengal, 1904, as Magistrate-Collector; transferred to Eastern Bengal and Assam, 1905, as Magistrate-Collector; Superintendent of Census Operations, 1910; Excise Commissioner and Inspector-General of Registration, 1911; transferred to Bengal as Excise Commissioner, 1912; Additional Member of the Legislative Council of the Governor-General; Secretary to the Government of Bengal, Finance and Commerce Departments, 1915; Chairman Corporation of Calcutta, 1919-1921; Chief Secretary Government of Bengal, 1921; Member of Bengal Executive Council, 1922-27; retired, 1927. *Recreation:* golf. *Address:* 11 Rivermead Court, Hurlingham, S.W.6. *Clubs:* East India and Sports; Bengal United Service (Calcutta). [*Died* 26 *April* 1957.

DONALDSON, Rev. Canon Alexander Edward; Hon. Chaplain Brecon Cathedral and Canon Emeritus since 1953; Precentor and Canon Residentiary of Brecon Cathedral, 1939-53; Assistant Chaplain, 1904-55, Christ College, Brecon; *b.* 18 March 1878; *s.* of Augustus Blair Donaldson, late Canon and Precentor of Truro Cathedral and Joanna Maria Mackie. *Educ.:* Newton College; Exeter College, Oxford (Stapeldon Exhibitioner). 2nd Mods, 1899, 2nd Greats, 1901; Assistant Master Christ College, Brecon, 1902-55. *Recreations:* walking and archæology. *Address:* The Almonry, Cathedral Close, Brecon. [*Died* 8 *Sept.* 1960.

DONALDSON, Rev. Frederic Lewis, M.A. Oxon, 1884; Canon of Westminster, 1924-51, Emeritus since 1951, Sub-Dean, 1944-51, Steward, 1927, Treasurer, 1931, and Receiver-General of the Abbey, 1938; *b.* Ladywood, Birmingham, 10 Sept. 1860; *s.* of F. W. and Elizabeth Donaldson of Edgbaston; *m.* 1885, Louise (*d.* 1950), *d.* of Alderman Eagleston, J.P., Oxford; two *s.* four *d.* *Educ.:* Christ Church Cathedral School, and Merton College, Oxford. Deacon, 1884; Priest, 1885; Assistant Curate of St. Nicholas Cole-Abbey, E. C., 1884-86; St. Peter's, Piccadilly Circus, W., 1886-89; St. John's, Hammersmith, W., 1889-95; Rector of Nailstone, Leicestershire, 1895; Vicar of St. Mark's, Leicester, 1896-1918; Rector of Paston with Walton, etc., Peterborough, 1918-24; Hon. Canon of Peterborough, 1918; Canon Residentiary, 1921-24; for many years a worker, writer, and lecturer in the cause of Social Reform; Editor Goodwill, 1903-6; one of the first members of the Christian Social Union, and Chairman of Leicester Branch, 1896-1906; a convinced Christian Socialist, and one of the founders of the Church Socialist League; Vice-Chairman, 1912; Chairman, 1913-16; one of the leaders and organisers of the march of the Unemployed from Leicester to London and back, 1905; led deputation of Church of England Clergy to Premier upon Women's Suffrage, 1913; President of London Council for Prevention of War, 1927; Select Preacher, Cambridge University, 1916; Member of Archbishop's Committee upon Public Worship, 1918; Council Industrial Christian Fellowship, 1920-44; Chairman of the League of Clergy for Peace, 1931-40; Vice-Pres. of Internat. Arbitration League. *Publications:* sermons, lectures, and pamphlets upon social subjects. *Recreation:* walking. *Address:* 21 Dean's Yard, Westminster Abbey, S.W. [*Died* 7 *Oct.* 1953.

DONALDSON, Admiral Leonard Andrew Boyd, C.B. 1925; C.M.G. 1918; R.N.; Naval A.D.C. to the King, 1925; *b.* 1875; 2nd *s.* of A. B. Donaldson and Agnes E., *d.* of R. Twining of 184 Cromwell Road and 216 Strand; *m.* 1st, 1902, Mary Mitchell (*d.* 1944), *d.* of Professor D'Arcy Thompson, D.Litt., etc.; one *s.*; 2nd, 1945, Nora C.,

DOMVILLE-FIFE, Charles William. See page xxviii.

widow of Louis Beaumont, Fareham. Assistant to Director of Naval Ordnance and Torpedoes, 1912; served South African War, 1899-1900 (medal with clasp); Capt. (S.) II. and X. Sub Flotillas, 1915-18; New Zealand, 1918-19; Temeraire. 1919-21; Director of Torpedoes and Mining, Admiralty, 1922-24; Captain Superintendent, Pembroke Dockyard, 1924-26; Rear-Admiral, 1926; Admiral Superintendent of Portsmouth Dockyard, 1927-31; Vice-Admiral and retired list, 1930; Adm., retired. 1935. Trustee Portsmouth Savings Bank, 1931-, Life Pres. 1954 (ex-Chm. 1954). *Address:* Kintyre House, High St., Fareham, Hants. [*Died* 29 *June* 1956.

DONALDSON, Mary Ethel Muir; authority on all Highland subjects; author; *b.* 1876; *o. d.* of Alexander Donaldson, Kenley, Surrey, and Adelaide. *Educ.:* privately and by self. Sometime Exhibitor, Royal Photographic Exhibitions, and Scottish Salon; mem. National Conservative Council, etc., 1920-27; Canterbury Diocesan Conference, 1919-27; sometime Lay Representative of Diocese of Argyll and the Isles on Repres. Ch. Council and Member of Board of Education and Social Service Board of Scottish Episcopal Church. *Publications:* Where is the Church in Scotland; The Isles of Flame; Wayfarer's Christmas Vision, a Mystery Play; Wanderings in the Western Highlands and Islands (three editions); Islesmen of Bride; Further Wanderings—Mainly in Argyll; Scotland's Suppressed History; Till Scotland melts in Flame; numerous contributions on Highland subjects to many newspapers and magazines. *Recreations:* friendships, bird study. *Address:* 16 Denham Green Place, Edinburgh 5. *T.:* 83056; *Club:* Victoria League House (Edinburgh). [*Died* 17 *Jan.* 1958.

DONALDSON, Norman Patrick, C.B.E. 1920; shipowner; Director Donaldson Line, Ltd.; Joint Manager and Director Donaldson Brothers and Black, Ltd.; *b.* 1878; *s.* of W. F. Donaldson, Shipowner; *m.* Katherine Reid Fraser. *Educ.:* Loretto School, Scotland. Served Boer War, trooper, 1900 (Queen's Medal 3 clasps); Hon. Major, 1946. Vice-Chairman, Clyde Anti-Submarine Cttee., 1914-18. *Address:* Ballindalloch, Balfron, Stirlingshire; 14 St. Vincent Place, Glasgow. *Clubs:* Carlton: Western (Glasgow). [*Died* 27 *March* 1955.

DONAT, (Frederick) Robert; Professional Actor; *b.* Withington, Manchester, 18 March 1905; *y. s.* of late Ernst Emil Donat and Rose Alice Green; *m.* 1st, 1929, Ella Annesley Voysey (marriage dissolved); two *s.* one *d.*; 2nd, Renee Asherson. *Educ.:* Central School, Manchester. Member of Sir Frank Benson's company, 1923-28; Member of Liverpool Repertory, 1928; leading man at Festival Theatre, Cambridge, 1929; first appearance in London at the Ambassadors, 1930, as Cartwright in Knave and Quean; subsequently played Gideon Sarn in Precious Bane; King Yovan in Lady in Waiting; Dunois in St. Joan; appeared at Malvern Festivals, 1931 and 1933, creating the part of Charles Cameron in James Bridie's play A Sleeping Clergyman, Piccadilly Theatre, 1933-34, and of Edward Earle in same author's Mary Read, 1935; actor manager, Red Night, 1935; joined Old Vic Co. (Buxton Theatre Festival and on Tour) Aug.-Dec. 1939 (Romeo; Croaker, in The Good Natured Man); Dick Dudgeon in The Devil's Disciple, on Tour and at Piccadilly Theatre, 1940; William Shakespeare in To Dream Again, 1942; Captain Shotover in Heartbreak House, Cambridge Theatre, 1943; entered management of Westminster Theatre, 1943-45; The Cure for Love, Westminster Theatre, 1945; presented The Glass Slipper at St. James's, 1944 and 1945; Benedick in Much Ado About Nothing, Aldwych Theatre, 1946; revival, A Sleeping Clergyman, Criterion Theatre, 1947; played Becket in T. S. Eliot's Murder In the Cathedral with Old Vic Company, 1953. His best known film characterisations have been in The Private Life of Henry VIII, The Count of Monte Cristo, The Thirty-nine Steps, The Ghost Goes West, Knight Without Armour, The Citadel, 1938, and Good-bye Mr. Chips, 1939; The Young Mr. Pitt, 1941; Adventures of Tartu, 1943; Perfect Strangers, 1945; Captain Boycott, 1947; The Winslow Boy, 1948; The Cure for Love, 1949 (Producer-Director); The Magic Box, 1951; Lease of Life, 1954; The Inn of the Sixth Happiness, 1958. *Publications:* Contributor to Footnotes to the Film by Charles Davy; various articles. *Recreations:* reading, walking. *Address:* c/o Christopher Mann Ltd., 140 Park Lane, W.1. *Club:* Savile. [*Died* 9 *June* 1958.

DONCASTER, Sir Robert, Kt., *cr.* 1933; O.B.E. 1919; J.P.; Dep. Chairman Derbyshire Quarter Sessions; Chairman Ilkeston Petty Sessional Justices; *b.* 1872; *s.* of Joseph Doncaster; *m.* 1896, Gertrude Louisa, *d.* of Martin Barber; two *s.* one *d.* *Address:* The Grange, Sandiacre, Nottingham. *T.:* Sandiacre, 3104. *Club:* County (Derby). [*Died* 5 *July* 1955.

DONERAILE, 7th Viscount (*cr.* 1785), **Hugh St. Leger;** Baron Doneraile, 1776; retired sheep farmer; *b.* 6 Aug. 1869; *s.* of Rev. Edward F. St. Leger and Caroline, *d.* of William R. Bishop; *S.* brother, 1941; *m.* 1920, Mary Isobel, *e. d.* of Frank Morice of Whakapunake, Gisborne, New Zealand. Admitted Solicitor, 1893. *Heir:* *c.* Algernon Edward St. Leger (*see under* 8th Viscount Doneraile). *Address:* Doneraile Court, Doneraile, Co. Cork, Eire. [*Died* 18 *Dec.* 1956.

DONERAILE, 8th Viscount *cr.* 1785; **Algernon Edward St. Leger;** Baron Doneraile, 1776; *b.* 10 June 1878; *s.* of Richard William St. Leger (*d.* 1925) (*g.g.s.* of 1st Viscount) and Matilda Emma (*d.* 1901), *d.* of Samuel Higgins Burroughs; *S.* cousin 1956; *m.* 1919, Sylvia Stephen Mitchell, *d.* of Alexander Mitchell, Jarrow-on-Tyne; one *s.* *Educ.:* Erasmus High School; Trinity College, Dublin. *Heir:* *s.* Hon. Richard St. John St. Leger [*b.* 29 Oct. 1923; *m.* 1945, Melva Jean Clifton; two *s.* one *d.*]. *Address:* Doneraile Court, Doneraile, Co. Cork, Eire; 3961 Huron Street, Culver City, California, U.S.A. [*Died* 24 *Nov.* 1957.

DONKIN, Sydney Bryan, M.Inst. C.E., M.I.Mech.E., M.I.E.E., M.Cons.E.; Senior Partner in Kennedy and Donkin, Consulting Engineers; *b.* 24 June 1871; *s.* of Bryan Donkin, M.Inst.C.E., V.P.I.Mech.E., and Georgina, *d.* of Frank Dillon, R.I.; *m.* 1902, Phoebe Smiles (*d.* 1952), *g. n.* of Samuel Smiles; three *s.* one *d.* *Educ.:* Private Schools; Univ. Coll., London. Joined staff of Sir A. B. W. Kennedy, F.R.S., LL.D., Consulting Engineer, in 1897, as assistant; partner, 1908; Firm became Kennedy and Donkin, 1913; Consulting Engineer with partners to British Electricity Authority, to North Scotland H.E. Board, and to several other Electricity supply authorities at home and abroad; Member Egyptian Hydro-Electric Power Commission; sometime Member of Committees of Department of Scientific and Industrial Research; Member of General Board of National Physical Laboratory, 1922-27; President Institute of Civil Engineers, 1937-38; Chairman of Association of Consulting Engineers, 1927 and 1943-1944; President Association of Supervisory Electrical Engineers, 1928-31; Pres. Climbers Club, 1936-39; Fellow of University College, London, 1946. *Recreation:* mountaineering. *Address:* 12 Caxton Street, S.W.1; Winterfold, Albury, Surrey. *T.A.:* Kinematic, Phone, London. *T.:* Abbey 4343, Ewhurst 26. *Clubs:* Athenæum, Alpine. [*Died* 12 *Nov.* 1952.

DONNAN, Prof. Frederick George, C.B.E. 1920; F.R.S.; M.A., Ph.D., D.Sc.; LL.D., F.R.I.C.; *y. s.* of William Donnan, of Holywood, Co. Down, Ireland; *b.* 6 Sept. 1870; unmarried. *Educ.:* Queen's University, Belfast; Universities of Leipzig, Berlin, and London. Hon. Graduate of the Universities of St. Andrews, Belfast, Liverpool, Edinburgh, Durham, Baltimore, Princeton, Coimbra, Athens, Oberlin, and of the National Univ. of Ireland. Junior Fellow and Examiner of the Royal University of Ireland, 1898-1901; Assistant Professor at University College, London, 1902; Lecturer in Chemistry, Royal College of Science, Dublin, 1903-4; Professor of Physical Chemistry and Director of the Muspratt Laboratory of Physical and Electro-Chemistry, University of Liverpool, 1904-13; Prof. of Chemistry, 1913-37 and Director of the Chemical Laboratories, 1928-37, Univ. College, London; studied chemistry under Professors Sir William Ramsay, Ostwald, van't Hoff, and Letts; Longstaff Medallist, Chemical Society of London, 1924; Davy Medal of Royal Society, 1928; Fellow of University College, London; Foreign Member Royal Academy of Sciences, Amsterdam, Royal Society of Sciences, Upsala, and Royal Physiographical Society, Lund; Hon. Fellow, Royal Society, Edinburgh, National Institute of Sciences, India, Indian Academy of Sciences, Bangalore, Hon. Member American Chemical Soc., Dutch Chemical Soc., German Bunsen Soc., Roumanian Chemical Soc., Institution of Chemical Engineers, Austrian Chemical Society, Soc. Chim. industrielle, and Soc. Philomathique, Paris. *Publications:* Scientific Papers. *Address:* Roseneath, Hartlip, nr. Sittingbourne, Kent. *T.:* Newington 225. *Club:* Athenæum. [*Died* 16 *Dec.* 1956.

DONNELLY, Alex. E.; Solicitor; *b.* Omagh, Co. Tyrone; unmarried. *Educ.:* Christian Brothers School, Omagh; Graduate of old Royal University, now merged in National University of Ireland. Practising as solicitor and notary public in Omagh since 1905; Member of Tyrone County Council 1914-51, and Chairman, 1920-24. M.P. (N.) West Tyrone, Northern Ireland, 1925-1949. *Address:* Omagh, County Tyrone, Northern Ireland. *T.:* Omagh 93. [*Died* 9 *May* 1958.

DONNELLY, Sir Arthur (Telford), K.B.E., *cr.* 1949; C.M.G. 1939; Barrister; Crown Solicitor, Christchurch, New Zealand, since 1920; *b.* 6 June 1890; *s.* of Michael Donnelly, Barrister. *Educ.:* Boys' High School, Christchurch; Canterbury University College. LL.B., New Zealand University; admitted Barrister and Solicitor, 1911; Crown Solicitor, Christchurch, 1920; Otago Regiment N.Z. Expeditionary Force, 1916-19; Chairman of directors, Bank of New Zealand, since 1937; Director of N.Z. Newspapers Ltd., and of N.Z. Breweries Ltd.; Beath & Co. Ltd., Christchurch (Chairman 1938); Canterbury Director N.Z. Insurance Co. Ltd., Trustee Dept.; Life member N.Z. Cricket Council (Chairman Committee 1928-38; President, 1946-1948); Steward Canterbury Jockey Club. *Recreations:* cricket, golf, tennis, racing. *Address:* 51 Hagley Street, Christchurch, N.Z. *T.:* Christchurch 32864. *Club:* Canterbury (Christchurch). [*Died* 1 *Feb.* 1954.

DONNER, Ossian; diplomat, retired; *b.* Helsingfors, 24 March 1866; *s.* of Senator Otto Donner, Minister of Education in Finland; *m.* Violet Marion (*d.* 1944), *d.* of G. B. McHutchen, banker, Edinburgh; one *s.* one *d.* *Educ.:* Helsingfors, Svenska Normallyseet, Polytekniska Institutet. Member of Board and Chairman of some of most important industrial undertakings in Finland; Member of Helsingfors Town Council; Chairman, Economic Society, Helsingfors; Chairman, Finnish Finance Committee, Stockholm, during Finnish War of Independence, 1918; Delegate of the Finnish Government in London, Feb. 1919; Chargé d'Affaires, July-Oct. 1919; first Finnish Minister to the Court of St. James, 1919; Representative to the League of Nations on the Aaland Islands Question, 1920 and 1921; retired, 1926. Grand Cross White Rose of Finland, 1926. *Publications:* Atta Ar, Erfarenheter Och Minnen; Min Tid; papers and articles on economic subjects. *Recreation:* yachting. *Address:* Hurstbourne Park, Whitchurch, Hants. *T.:* Whitchurch 143. *Clubs:* Nylandska, Jaktklubben (Helsingfors). [*Died* 2 *Aug.* 1957.

DONOVAN, Maj-Gen. William J.; Lawyer; U.S. Ambassador to Thailand since 1953; *b.* 1 Jan. 1883; parents born in U.S. of Irish origin; *m.* 1914, Ruth Rumsey; one *s.* (one *d.* decd.). *Educ.:* Columbia Univ., A.B. 1905; Columbia Univ. Law School, LL.B. 1907. Capt., Troop I, 1st Cav. N.G.N.Y., 1912; Asst. Chief of Staff, 27th Div. A.E.F.; Lt.-Col. and Col. 165th Inf.; awarded Congressional Medal of Honor, D.S.C., D.S.M. in European War, 1914-18; U.S. District Attorney, Western District of New York; Asst.-Attorney-General of U.S., 1924; Asst. to Attorney-General of U.S., 1924-29; Chairman, Rio Grande Compact Commission; Chm. Boulder Dam Canyon Project Commission; Council for New York Bar Associations investigating bankruptcy proceedings; Council to State Committees investigating bankruptcy proceedings; Council to State Cttees. revising public service commission laws; special mission to England, 1940, to Yugoslavia, Greece and Middle East, 1940-41; Coordinator of Information, 1941-42; Director of Strategic Services, U.S., 1942-45; Brigadier-General 1943; Major-General 1944; resumed law practice, 1946. Oak Leaf Cluster to D.S.M. (U.S.). Hon. K.B.E. and many other foreign decorations. *Address:* U.S. Embassy, Bangkok, Thailand; Chapel Hill Farm, Berryville, Va., U.S.A. [*Died* 8 *Feb.* 1959.

DORAN, Brig. John Crampton Morton, C.B.E. 1919; D.S.O. 1916; late R.A.S.C.; *b.* 23 Aug. 1880; *o. s.* of late Rev. John Wilberforce Doran, M.A., Rector of Soulderne, Oxon; *m.* 1917, Hester Maude, *y. d.* of Edward Field of Blackdown Hill, Leamington; one *s.* one *d.* *Educ.:* St. Edward's School, Oxford. Commissioned 3 Oxf. L.I. (Embodied Militia), 1900; General Duty with Embodied Militia, South Africa (Queen's Medal); commissioned A.S.C., 1902; Somaliland, 1909 (African Gen. Service Medal); D.A.Q.M.G. Base Staff, France, 1914-15 (despatches twice); A.D.S. War Office; A.D.S. & T. Western Command, 1933-37; retired, 1937; re-employed D.D.S. & T. Western Command (Brigadier), 1939-40; Comdt. Mobilisation Centre, 1940-41 (retired); A.D.C. to the King, 1935-37. Asst. Divl. Food Officer, Ministry of Food, Tunbridge Wells, Dec. 1941-June, 1949. *Recreation:* golf. *Address:* Oldgarth, South Newington, Banbury, Oxon. [*Died* 19 *Jan.* 1957.

DORE, Group Captain Alan (Sydney Whitehorn), C.B. 1949; D.S.O. 1918; T.D.; M.A.; D.L. Co. of Mx.; *b.* 16 Sept. 1882; *s.* of late S. L. Dore, Pinner Hill, Pinner; *m.* 1918, Mièle, *d.* of E. A. Maund; two *s.* two *d.* *Educ.:* Mill Hill School; Jesus Coll., Cambridge. 1st Class Honours, Natural Science Tripos; commissioned Worcester Territorials, 1905; proceeded to France, Mar. 1915 (wounded, April 1915, despatches twice, D.S.O.); late commanding 604 (Fighter) Squadron County of Middlesex Auxiliary Air Force, 1930-35; Assistant Air Attaché, Norway, 1940; High Sheriff of Middlesex, 1944-45; Chm. County of Middlesex T. and A.F.A., 1945-51. Commander Order of St. Olav (Norway); Norwegian War Medal, 1941; Air Efficiency Award, 1942; 1939-45 Star. Vice-Lieutenant, Middlesex, 1949. *Recreations:* flying, travelling. *Address:* Eastcote Point, Pluner,

Middlesex. *T.:* Pinner 26. *Clubs:* Oxford and Cambridge, Allied Circle. [*Died* 9 *Aug.* 1953.

DORÉ, Victor, C.M.G. 1944; Hon. D.C.S. University of Montreal; Canadian Ambassador to Belgium and Minister to Luxembourg since 1946; late Superintendent of Education for Province of Quebec; *b.* Montreal, 27 July 1880; *s.* of Hubert Olivier Doré and Sarah Jane Anderson; *m.* 1903, Anna, *d.* of Joseph Aumond; two *d.* *Address:* Canadian Embassy, Brussels. [*Died* 27 *May* 1954.

DORMAN, Sir Bedford Lockwood, 2nd Bt., *cr.* 1923; C.B.E. 1948 (O.B.E. 1918); B.A.; *e. surv. s.* of Sir Arthur Dorman, 1st Bt., and late Clara Share, *d.* of late George Lockwood, Stockton-on-Tees; *S.* father, 1931; *m.* Constance Phelps Webster (*d.* 1946), *d.* of late Alexander S. Hay, Sacombe Park, Ware; one *s.* *Educ.:* Rugby; Trinity College, Cambridge. Called to Bar, Inner Temple, 1902; served European War (O.B.E.); Member of North Riding County Council, 1925. *Recreations:* shooting, golf. *Heir:* *s.* Major Charles Geoffrey Dorman, M.C., 13th/18th Hussars [*b.* 18 Sept. 1920; *m.* 1954, Elizabeth Ann, *o. d.* of George G. Gilmour-White, O.B.E., North Cerney, Cirencester, Glos.] *Address:* Enterpen, Hutton Rudby, Yorks. [*Died* 5 *Sept.* 1956.

DORRIEN, Lady (Olive) Smith; *see* Smith-Dorrien.

DORWARD, Alan James, M.A.; Professor of Philosophy in the University of Liverpool, 1928-54; *b.* Melrose, 19 April 1889; *e. s.* of late Jas. Dorward, Galashiels, J.P., County of Selkirk, and Ella Stewart; *m.* 1932, Cécile Marguerite Gabrielle, *d.* of G. A. M. Smith. *Educ.:* Gala High School; Galashiels Academy; Edinburgh University (Ferguson Scholar in Mental Philosophy, 1910); Trinity College, Cambridge (Scholar, 1912). Assistant to Professor of Logic, St. Andrews University, 1914-15; employed in War Office (Allies' Commission Section), 1915-17; Lecturer in Moral Philosophy and History of Philosophy in the Queen's University of Belfast, 1919-26; Lecturer in Moral Science, University of Cambridge, 1926-28. *Publications:* contributions to various philosophical journals. *Address:* 28 Percy Street, Liverpool 8. [*Died* 17 *Dec.* 1956.

DOUBLEDAY, Rt. Rev. Arthur, B.A.; *b.* 1865. *Educ.:* St. Mary's, Woolhampton; St. Edmund's, Ware; St. Thomas', Hammersmith. Priest, 1888; at Walworth, 1893-1900; Rector of Southwark Dioc. Sem. 1907-20; Domestic Prelate to H.H., 1909; Canon (Supernum.) of Southwark, 1916; Bishop of Brentwood, (R.C.), from 1920. *Address:* Bishop's House, Brentwood. [*Died* 23 *Jan.* 1951.

DOUGHERTY, His Eminence Cardinal Denis J.; Archbishop of Philadelphia (R.C.), since 1918. *Educ.:* St. Charles' Seminary, Overbrook, Pa. First American Bishop of Nueva Segovia, Philippine Islands, 1903; Bishop of Jaro, Philippine Islands, 1908; of Buffalo, 1915; Cardinal, 1921. *Address:* 1723 Race Street, Philadelphia, Pa., U.S.A. [*Died* 31 *May* 1951.

DOUGHTY, Sir Charles, Kt., *cr.* 1941; Q.C. 1925; B.A., B.C.L.; Recorder of Brighton, 1939-55; Bencher and lately Treasurer of the Hon. Society of the Inner Temple; Chairman of Wholesale Food Joint Industrial Council; late Chairman: War Service Grants Advisory Committee, Special Grants Committee of Ministry of Pensions; Sugar Confectionery, and Preserved Food Trade Council; Milk Distributive Trade Council; Conciliation Board for the Trawling Industry of Hull; Furniture Trades Jt. Industrial Council; Retail Food Trade Industrial Council; Agricultural Wages Board; *b.* 27 July 1878; *s.* of Charles Doughty, J.P., of Lincoln; *m.* 1st, 1901, Alice (*d.* 1931), *d.* of late Judge Addison, K.C.; three *s.* one *d.*; 2nd, 1945, Sylvia Ryland. *Educ.:* Oatlands, Harrogate; Rugby; Corpus Christi College, Oxford. Called to Bar, 1902; acted as arbitrator and conciliator in industrial disputes for the Board of Trade and Minister of Labour, 1915-19; Recorder of Canterbury, 1929-1937; of Guildford, 1937-39; late Chm. of General Council of the Bar, Cotton Trade Conciliation Committee, and Hurlingham Club. *Recreations:* shooting, lawn tennis, skating, squash racquets, motoring. *Address:* 33 Lincoln House, Basil St., Knightsbridge; 2 Paper Buildings, Temple, E.C.4. *T.:* Kensington 7686; Central 7768. *Clubs:* Royal Automobile, Hurlingham, Pilgrims, Pegasus. [*Died* 2 *May* 1956.

DOUGLAS, Col. Archibald Philip, C.M.G. 1916; C.B.E. 1920; late R.A.; *b.* 7 June 1867; *e. s.* of late Sir Robert Douglas; *m.* 1st, 1895, Helen (*d.* 1914), *d.* of Col. K. Dunsterville; one *s.* (and one *s.* decd.); 2nd, 1922, Lilian Barton, M.B.E., 2nd *d.* of late Rev. J. L. Wyatt. Entered army, 1887; Capt. 1897; Major, 1906; Lt.-Col. 1914; Deputy Director Ordnance Stores, India, 1911-13; Assist. Director, 1914-15; Col. 1918; served European War, Mesopotamia, 1916-18 (despatches, C.M.G.); Afghan War, 1919 (C.B.E.); retired on Indian pension, 1921. *Address:* 2 Haines Hill Terrace, Taunton, Somerset. [*Died* 24 *Jan.* 1953.

DOUGLAS, Clifford Hugh; Consulting Engineer and Economist; *b.* 20 Jan. 1879; *y. s.* of Hugh Douglas and Louisa Arderne Hordern; *m.* 1st, Constance Mary, *y. d.* of Edward Phillips, younger of Royston House, Herts.; 2nd, Edith Mary, *y. d.* of George Desborough Dale, I.C.S.; one *d.* *Educ.:* Pembroke College, Cambridge. Chief Engineer and Manager in India, British Westinghouse Co., Ltd.; Assistant Chief El. Engineer, B.A. and Pacific Ry.; Assistant Superintendent Royal Aircraft Factory; witness, Canadian Banking Enquiry, 1923; MacMillan Committee, 1930, etc.; Chief Reconstruction Adviser, Government of Alberta, 1935; late Major R.F.C. and R.A.F. *Publications:* Economic Democracy; Credit Power and Democracy; Social Credit; The Monopoly of Credit; The Alberta Experiment. *Recreations:* yachting, fishing. *Address:* Fearnan, Perthshire. *Clubs:* Junior Carlton; Royal Bombay Yacht (Bombay); Solent Yacht (Yarmouth, I.W.). [*Died* 29 *Sept.* 1952.

DOUGLAS, Hugh C.; *see* Cowan-Douglas.

DOUGLAS, James G.; Member of Senate of Eire, 1922-36, 1938-43 and since 1944; *b.* 11 July 1887; *e. s.* of John Douglas, Dublin; *m.* 1911, Ena, *d.* of John Culley, Lurgan; two *s.* *Educ.:* Friends School, Lisburn. Vice-Chairman of the Senate from its inception until 1925, and Chairman of the Joint Committee of both Houses of Parliament on Standing Orders (Private Business), 1922-25; member of the committee which drafted first Constitution of Eire in 1921; Chairman of the Irish Postal Commission, 1922; Hon. Treasurer and Trustee of the Irish White Cross, which distributed relief in Ireland prior to the Treaty; a member of the Religious Society of Friends, and has been prominently identified with its work in Ireland; Pres. of the League of Nations Soc. of Ireland from its formation until 1928; Pres. Linen and Cotton Textile Manufacturers Assoc. of Eire; Member of Council Federated Union of Employers; a Director of several Irish companies. *Recreations:* golf and photography. *Address:* 18 Wexford St., Dublin; 4 Herbert Park, Donnybrook, Dublin. *T.:* (business) Dublin 51925. *Clubs:* Royal Irish Automobile, Hibernian United Service (Dublin). [*Died* 16 *Sept.* 1954.

DOUGLAS, Rev. Canon John Albert, D.D. (Lambeth) 1939; Ph.D., B.D., B.A.; Rector of St. Michael Paternoster Royal 1933-53; Hon. General Secretary, Church of England Council on Foreign Relations, 1933-

1945 (Vice-Chm. 1954); Principal, Society of the Faith, since 1906; Hon. Canon St. Saviour, Southwark, 1924; Member of the Senate (1907), University Extension Board (1907), Theological Board (1909), Deputy Vice-Chancellor (1931), Chairman of Convocation and Member of the Court (1939), of the University of London; *s.* of John Douglas, of Cowes, and Elizabeth Arthur. *Educ.*: Chatham House; Dulwich College. Ordained to Newark, 1894; served at Penge and St. Stephen's, Lewisham; Chaplain, H.B.M. Embassy, Constantinople, 1903-4; served at St. Stephen's, Marylebone, and St. Benet's, Kentish Town, 1900-6; Chairman and Lecturer of Christian Evidence Soc., 1906-1914; Vicar of St. Luke, Camberwell, 1909-1933; Assistant Curate, 1933-34; Proctor in Convocation, Diocese of London, 1936-45; Chaplain of First Surrey Rifles, T.F., 1914-1923; Camberwell National Reserve, Camberwell Volunteers, 1912 and 1915 respectively; served as lecturer in France and received War Medal (general service); active in Scout Movement S.M., 1908; Chaplain Camberwell House Mental Hospital, 1924-32; Chaplain Innholders Company, 1939; received Protopresbyter's Cross of Russian Synod from Patriarch Tikhon, 1923; Second Class St. Sava (Serbian Order), 1922, 1st Class 1945; Third Class Osmanlieh (Turkish), 1905; Third Class Medjidieh, 1912; Grand Officer, Knights of the Holy Sepulchre, 1925; special cross and grammata from Russian Synod of Karlowicz, 1926; Chaplain St. John of Jerusalem, 1932; 2nd Class Crown of Yugo-Slavia; 2nd Class Star of Rumania; Patriarchal Cross of Rumania, 1936; Grand Cross, Polonia Restituta, 1945; 2nd Class Order of the Phoenix, Greece, 1949; helped to found the Society of the Faith in 1905, helped to found Anglican and Eastern Churches Association and Society of St. Willibrord, 1906; original member of Archbishop of Canterbury's Eastern Churches Committee, 1920; Librarian, 1925; Member of Stockholm (1925), Lausanne (1927), and of Oxford and Edinburgh (1937) Oecumenical Conferences. *Publications*: The Young Christian's Progress, and several children's books; St. Sophia, 1918; Anglican Relations with the Orthodox, 1922; Jerusalem Patriarchate, 1925; Validity of Anglican Ordinations by Archbishop of Athens (translated and prefaced), 1931; Teaching of the Abyssinian Church, 1936. Editor of Christian East, 1920-39; Symbol since 1917. *Recreations*: gardening, walking. *Address*: 19 Kensington Court Gardens, W.8. *T.*: Western 0694. *Clubs*: Athenæum, Greek House. [*Died* 3 *July* 1956.

DOUGLAS, Sir Kenneth, 4th Bt., *cr.* 1831; *b.* 29 May 1868; *S. u.* 1884; *m.* 1940, Eleanor Maude, *d.* of late Samuel Pascoe, Remuera, Auckland, N.Z. *Heir*: *cousin*, Sholto Courtenay Mackenzie, M.C. [late Lieut. Seaforth Highlanders; *b.* 27 June 1890; *s.* of late Donald Sholto Mackenzie Douglas and Edith Elizabeth Anne, *y. d.* of George Robinson, Bagatelle, Mauritius; *m.* 1929, Lorna Tichborne, *d.* of Capt. Hugh Nangle, 22 Onslow Square, S.W.; two *d.* Served European War, 1914-18 (M.C.)]. *Address*: P.O. Box 409, Wellington, C.1, New Zealand. [*Died* 28 *Oct.* 1954.

DOUGLAS, Lloyd C.; Novelist; *b.* Indiana, U.S.A., 27 Aug. 1877; *s.* of Alex. J. Douglas and Sarah Jane Cassel; *m.* 1904, Besse Io Porch (*d.* 1944); two *d.* *Educ.*: Wittenberg College; Hamma Divinity School, Springfield, Ohio. Entered ministry, 1903; ordained Lutheran; later Congregationalist; served pastorates in Indiana, Ohio, Washington, D.C., Michigan, California and Montreal, P.Q.; retired from pulpit, 1933, to engage in writing and lecturing. *Publications*: These Sayings of Mine, 1920; Those Disturbing Miracles, 1926; Magnificent Obsession, 1929; Forgive Us Our Trespasses, 1932; Green Light, 1935; White Banners, 1937; Home for Christmas, 1937; Disputed Passage, 1939; Dr. Hudson's Journal, 1940; Invitation to Live, 1940; The Robe, 1942; The Big Fisherman, 1948. *Recreation*: rheumatoid arthritis. *Address*: 721 East Charleston Boulevard, Las Vegas, Nevada. *Clubs*: St. Botolph (Boston); Authors' (Hollywood); Jonathan (Los Angeles). [*Died* 14 *Feb.* 1951.

DOUGLAS, Lt.-Col. Montagu William, C.S.I. 1919; C.I.E. 1903; *b.* 23 Nov. 1863; *o. s.* of late Edward Douglas, Assist. Col. Sec., Mauritius; *m.* 1891, Helen Mary Isabel (*d.* 1943), *d.* of Ven. Archdeacon Downer; two *s.* one *d.* Entered North Staffordshire Regt. 1884; Indian Army, 1887; Captain, 1895; Major, 1902; Assistant Commissioner, 1890; Deputy Commissioner, 1899; Member Executive Committee, Coronation Durbar, Delhi, 1903; Deputy Commissioner of Lyalpur District, Punjab, 1910-13; Chief Commissioner Andaman and Nicobar Islands, 1913-20. President Shakespeare Fellowship, resigned 1944. *Publications*: The Case for the Earl of Oxford as Shakespeare, 1932; Lord Oxford was Shakespeare, a summing up, 1934; Lord Oxford and the Shakespeare Group, 3rd edn., 1952. *Recreations*: art (exhibitor of water-colours and etchings in principal London galleries); formerly mountain climbing (Alps and India). *Address*: 85 Coleherne Court, S.W.5. [*Died* 24 *Feb.* 1957.

DOUGLAS, Norman; *b.* 1868. *Publications*: Unprofessional Tales, 1901; Siren Land, 1911; South Wind, 1917; They Went, 1921; Together, 1923; Fountain in the Sand, 1923; Experiments, 1925; Old Calabria, 1928; Birds and Beasts of the Greek Anthology, 1929; One Day, 1929; Three of Them, 1930; Goodbye to Western Culture, 1930; London Street Games, 1931; Paneros, 1931; Summer Islands, 1931; Experiments, 1932; Looking Back, 2 vols., 1932; An Almanac (anthology by Enid Mason), 1945; Late Harvest, 1946; Footnote on Capri, 1952; (posthumous): Selections (2 different vols.). [*Died* 9 *Feb.* 1952.

DOUGLAS, Capt. Robert Langton, M.A.; art expert; *b.* 1864; *s.* of Rev. Robert Douglas; *m.* 1st, Margaret Jane, *d.* of Percival Cannon; one *s.*; 2nd, Gwendolen Mary, *d.* of T. Henchman; one *s.* two *d.*; 3rd, Jean, *d.* of John Stewart; one *s.* one *d* *Educ.*: New College, Oxford; honours in Modern History. Was a lecturer on University Extension Scheme; formerly in Holy Orders in Church of England; executed deed of relinquishment under the provisions of the Clergy Disabilities Act; Professor of Modern History in the University of Adelaide, 1900-2; Dean of the Faculty of Arts, 1901; lectured on artistic subjects at the Royal Institution and the Society of Arts; lecturer at Harvard, Princeton, and New York Universities, 1940, Yale University, 1941, and at Metropolitan and Boston Museums, 1940; enlisted as a private in Infantry, 1914; Staff Capt., War Office, 1915-17; granted hon. rank of Captain in the Army, 1917; Director, National Gallery, Ireland, 1916-23. *Publications*: Fenton's Certaine Tragicall Discourses, Tudor Translation Series, 1898; Fra Angelico, 2nd ed. 1902; History of Siena; Le Maioliche di Siena, 1904; a new edition of Crowe and Cavalcaselle's History of Italian Painting, vols. i. and ii. 1903, vols. iii. and iv. 1909; Illustrated Catalogue of Pictures of Siena and Objects of Art, Burlington Fine Arts Club, 1904; Histoire de Sienne, 2 vols., 1914; Storia d'Arte Senese, Siena, 1933; Leonardo da Vinci, his San Donato of Arezzo, and the Tax Collector, 1933; Leonardo da Vinci, 1944; Piero di Cosimo, 1946; and other books; articles in Architectural Review, Art in America, L'Arte, Les Arts, The Art Quarterly, The Bookman, The Art Bulletin, Bullettino Senese di Storia Patria, Nineteenth Century; Saturday Review, etc. *Address*: San Girolamo, Fiesole, Italy. *Club*: Bath. [*Died* 14 *Aug.* 1951.

DOUGLAS, Rev. Robert Noel, M.A. Cantab.; *b.* 9 Nov. 1868; 2nd *s.* of late Sir Robert K. Douglas of the British Museum and King's College, London; *m.* 1904, Lina (*d.* 1923), *d.* of Paul David of Uppingham; one *s.* one *d.* *Educ.:* Dulwich College; Selwyn College, Cambridge. Assistant Master at Dulwich College Preparatory School, 1888-89; Assistant Master at Uppingham School, 1892-1910; House-Master, 1904-10; Headmaster of Giggleswick School, 1910-31; Deacon, 1931; Priest, 1932; Curate of Northleigh with Southleigh and Farway; Rector of Farway with Northleigh and Southleigh, 1936-47. *Recreations:* cricket (Cambridge and Middlesex XI.), football, rugby (Cambridge XV.), tennis, golf. *Address:* The Nook, Colyton, Devon. [*Died* 27 *Feb.* 1957.

DOUGLAS, Captain Sholto Grant, C.B.E. 1919; R.N., retired; *b.* 1867; *e. s.* of late Admiral Sholto Douglas, C.B., Southsea, Hants; *m.* 1896, Bessie (*d.* 1938), *y. d.* of late J. Foran, St. John's, Newfoundland; one *s.* (two *d.* decd.). *Educ.:* Royal Naval School, New Cross; Eastman's Royal Naval Academy, Southsea. Entered Royal Navy, 1882; Midshipman of H.M.S. Achilles in Egyptian Campaign, 1882 (Egyptian medal, Khedive's bronze star); King Edward Coronation medal; retired Commander, 1912; Transport Officer, Southampton, Aug. 1914; Liverpool, Feb. 1916; Middlesbro' (in charge), Nov. 1916; Divisional Naval Transport Officer at Glasgow, Feb. 1917; reverting to Retired List, Dec. 1919 (C.B.E., promoted to rank of Captain); General Service Medal, 1914-18. District Officer Board of Trade Coastguard, 1923; Inspector H.M. Coastguard N. Ireland, 1926-29. *Address:* c/o Barclay's Bank, Petersfield, Hants. [*Died* 7 *Feb.* 1956.

DOUGLAS, Major Sholto William, C.B.E. 1928; D.S.O. 1901; Chief Constable The Lothians and Peebleshire, 1914-50; *b.* 11 Oct. 1870; *s.* of late Major G. M. Douglas, 33rd Regt.; *m.* 1901, Grace Catherine (*d.* 1942), *d.* of Lt.-Gen. Sir James Wolfe Murray, K.C.B. Entered R.A. 1890; Capt., 1900; served S. Africa, 1899-1900 (despatches twice, Queen's medal two clasps); Major, 1908; retired, 1911; Chief Constable Metropolitan Police, 1910. *Address:* 20 George Square, Edinburgh 8. *Club:* Brooks's. [*Died* 12 *April* 1959.

DOUGLAS, Sir William Scott, G.C.B., *cr.* 1950 (K.C.B., *cr.* 1943; C.B. 1938); K.B.E., *cr.* 1941; American Medal of Freedom with gold palm, 1947; Company Director, Chairman of Council, Wycombe Abbey School; Chairman, The Hospital for Sick Children, Great Ormond Street; *b.* Edinburgh, 20 Aug. 1890; *s.* of Daniel Douglas, Solicitor; *m.* 1919, Vera Paterson Duffes; two *d.* *Educ.:* George Heriot's School, Edinburgh; Edinburgh University. Entered Customs and Excise Dept., 1914; Financial Adviser Allenstein Plebiscite Commission, 1920; Private Secretary to Lord Bradbury, Reparation Commission, Paris, 1921-26; Ministry of Labour, 1929-37; Divisional Controller, Midlands, 1931-33; Divisional Controller, Scotland, 1933-35; Assistant Secretary, 1935-37; Secretary, Department of Health for Scotland, 1937-39; Under-Secretary, Treasury, 1939-42; Permanent Sec., Ministry of Supply, 1942-45; Permanent Sec., Ministry of Health, 1945-51; retired, 1951. *Recreation:* golf. *Address:* Glebe House, Great Hallingbury, Bishop's Stortford, Herts. *Clubs:* Union, Oriental. [*Died* 17 *Feb.* 1953.

DOUGLAS-JONES, Sir Crawford Douglas, Kt., *cr.* 1934; C.M.G. 1920; *b.* 4 Nov. 1874; *e. surv. s.* of late Col. Douglas Forde Douglas-Jones, R.A., *m.* 1905, Maud Mary, *d.* of Dr. F. W. Johnson, Wattlington, Norfolk; one *s.* one *d.* *Educ.:* Harrow School. Private Secretary to Resident Commissioner, Southern Rhodesia, 1898; Secretary to Resident Commissioner, 1911; Acting Resident Commissioner, Southern and Northern Rhodesia, April 1918; Resident Commissioner, Southern and Northern Rhodesia, July 1918-23; Northern Rhodesia, 1924; Colonial Secretary, British Honduras, Aug. 1924; Administered Government, Sept. 1924-April 1925 and May to July 1926; represented colony at Trade Conference between Canada and West Indian group of Colonies, Ottawa, July 1925; Colonial Secy., British Guiana, 1926-35; Chairman British Guiana Constitution Commission, 1927; Administered Govt. Oct. 1927-March 1928, Aug.-Nov., 1928, July 1929-June 1930, May 1934-April 1935; retired from Colonial Service, May 1935; Member of Commission sent to British Guiana to investigate the possibilities of refugee settlement, 1939; Ministry of Supply, 1941-43. *Recreation:* croquet. *Address:* Ladymead, Hurstpierpoint, Sussex. [*Died* 2 *March* 1956.

DOUIE, Charles Oswald Gaskell; *b.* 1896; *y. s.* of late Sir James McC. Douie; *m.* 1931, Margaret Louise, *y. d.* of late W. M. Cuthbert and of Lady Seymour-Lloyd; one *s.* two *d.* *Educ.:* Rugby (Scholar); The Queen's College, Oxford (Scholar). Served European War in Dorset Regt. and R. Munster Fusiliers in Belgium, France and Italy; Home Civil Service (Board of Education) 1919-27; Secretary Adult Education Committee, Public Libraries Committee, Juvenile Organisations Committee (Board of Education), Prisoners Education Committee (Home Office); Educational Adviser Wormwood Scrubs Prison; Secretary of University College, London, 1927-1938; Secretary Ramsay Memorial Fellowship Trust, 1927-45; visited Universities of British Dominions at invitation of Carnegie Corporation of New York to report on Adult Education, 1932-33; Ministry of Information, 1939. *Publications:* The Weary Road, 1929; Beyond the Sunset, 1935; Night of Stars, 1937; Lost Heritage, 1939; Peace Treaty, 1945; So Long to Learn, 1951; Raynard, 1952; 300 contributions to journals. *Address:* The Red House, Bosham, Sussex. *T.:* Bosham 2139. [*Died* 22 *July* 1953.

DOUTHWAITE, James Lungley; late Librarian to the Corporation of London; late Curator of Guildhall Museum; Director of Guildhall Art Gallery, 1929-43; *b.* 25 March 1877; *yr. s.* of William Ralph Douthwaite, Librarian to the Hon. Society of Gray's Inn; *m.* Laura, *e. d.* of Thomas William Jacobs; three *d.* *Educ.:* City of London School. Joined staff of Guildhall Library as Jun. Assistant, 1893; served ranks of 15th Bn. Essex Regt., European War (despatches). *Address:* 16 Burdon Lane, Cheam, Surrey. *T.:* Vigilant 8913. [*Died* 7 *Nov.* 1960.

DOWDALL, His Honour Harold Chaloner, Q.C., M.A., B.C.L., of the Inner Temple and Northern Circuit; *b.* 1868; *y. s.* of late Thomas Dowdall, Liverpool; *m.* 1897, Hon. Mary Frances Harriet (*d.* 1939), *d.* of 16th Lord Borthwick; one *s.* three *d.* *Educ.:* Rugby; Trinity College, Oxford. Liverpool Local Bar, 1893-1917; Lord Mayor of Liverpool, 1908-9; First Chairman Liverpool Council of Social Service, 1909-17; Chancellor of the Diocese of Liverpool, 1913-48, and of Bristol, 1919-48; K.C. 1920; Judge of the County Court of Lancashire (Circuit No. 6), 1921-40; First Chairman of the Legal Board of the National Assembly of the Church of England, 1923-28; Draftsman of York-Antwerp Rules, 1924. President of the Society of Public Teachers of Law, 1929, and Hon. Member since 1947. *Publications:* Local Development, Law, 1919; Estatification, 1930; various articles in Edinburgh Review, Law Quarterly Review, etc. *Address:* Melfort Cottage, Boars Hill, Oxford. *T.:* 85312. *Clubs:* St. James', Leander. [*Died* 8 *April* 1955.

DOWNEY, Most Rev. Richard, D.D., Ph.D., Hon. LL.D. N.U.I. and Toronto; Hon. F.R.I.B.A.; Archbishop of Liverpool (R.C.), and Metropolitan of Northern Province with Suffragan Sees, Hexham, Lancaster, Leeds, Middlesbrough and Salford, since 1928; *b.* Kilkenny, 1881. *Educ.:* St. Edward's College, Liverpool; London University. Priest, 1907; D.D. Gregorian University, Rome; Extern. Examiner in Philosophy to National Univ. of Ireland, 1915-18, 1925-28; Chairman of the Literary Committee Catholic Truth Soc. (London), 1921; preached and lectured in America on philosophical subjects, 1922 and 1925; Professor of Philosophy for Oblates, Oratorians, and Carmelites at Bayswater Novitiate, 1918-26; Professor of Dogmatic Theology and Dean of the Departments of Theology and Philosophy at Upholland, 1926-28; Vice-Rector, 1927: acting Rector, 1928; Fellow Philosophical Soc. of Eng.; Cofounder and first Ed. of Catholic Gazette; Ed. of Universe, 1917. Freeman of Kilkenny, 1930, Sligo, 1931, Wexford and Limerick, 1932, Clonmel, 1934. *Publications:* Some Errors of H. G. Wells; Personal Immortality; Divine Providence; The Blessed Trinity; Pulpit and Platform Addresses; Critical and Constructive Essays; contributor to Cambridge Summer School vols.: The Religion of the Scriptures, The Papacy, The Incarnation, Aquinas, The Church; Chairman, editorial board of Clergy Review, 1931. Editor Present Problems series. *Address:* Archbishop's House, Woolton, Liverpool. *T.:* Gateacre 1233. [*Died* 16 *June* 1953.

DOWSETT, Colonel Ernest Blair, D.S.O. 1917; T.D., M.R.C.S., L.R.C.P., F.D.S.R.C.S.; Consulting Dental Surgeon to Guy's Hospital: External Expert in Dentistry to London University; President of British Dental Association, 1951-52, late Hon. Treas.; *s.* of late G. H. Dowsett, Lee; *m.* 1904, Ethel Webb, *d.* of late Percy H. Webb, Walton-on-Thames; one *d.* (one *s.* decd.). Late Chairman of Dentists Provident Society; V.M.S.C. and R.A.M.C. (T.), 1900-30; served European War, A.D.M.S. 60th Division, and D.D.M.S. 20th Corps (despatches 4 times). Fellow of Royal Society of Medicine (President Odonto. Section, 1931-32); President of Metro. Branch of B.D.A., 1921-22; late Examiner in Dental Surgery to Royal College of Surgeons, Eng., and to London, Liverpool, Birmingham and Sheffield Universities; Late Lecturer on Dental Surgery, etc., to Guy's Hospital. *Publications:* Dental Surgery and Pathology Notes, 8 editions, 1909-46. *Address:* 12 Gloucester Pl., Portman Sq., W.1. *T.:* Welbeck 4904; Richmond Hill Court, Surrey. *T.:* Richmond 4625. [*Died* 13 *Nov.* 1951.

DOYNE, Philip Geoffry, B.A. (Oxon), M.B., F.R.C.S. (Eng.); Consulting Ophthalmic Surgeon to St. Thomas's Hospital, Moorfields Eye Hospital; Consulting Ophthalmic Surgeon Hospital for Sick Children, Great Ormond Street; *b.* 1886; *s.* of R. W. Doyne, F.R.C.S., founder of the Oxford Eye Hospital; *m.* 1915, Ida, *y. d.* of Harcourt Griffin, Langfield, Bude; one *d.* *Educ.:* Winchester; Trinity College, Oxford. *Publications:* several articles in the Transactions of the Ophthalmological Society and in the British Journal of Ophthalmology. *Recreation:* fencing (Amateur Foil Champion, 1912 and 1920). *Address:* Bix Hill, Assendon, Henley-on-Thames. [*Died* 22 *Jan.* 1959.

DRAGE, Sir Benjamin, Kt., *cr.* 1932. Formerly Technical Adviser and a Director. Drage's Ltd., House Furnishers, Oxford St., London, W.1. *Address:* Grosvenor House. Park Lane, W.1; Weir Courtney, Lingfield, Surrey. [*Died* 14 *Nov.* 1952.

DRAGE, Geoffrey; *b.* 1860; *o. surviving s* of Charles Drage, M.D.; *m.* 1896, Ethel Sealby (*d.* 1952), *d.* of T. H. Ismay, D.L., Dawpool; one *s.* (and one *s.* decd.). *Educ.:* Eton; Christ Church, Oxford; Berlin, Moscow, and other foreign univs. B.A. and M.A. Oxford; Barr. Lincoln's Inn, and Middle Temple, but has never practised. Secretary of Royal Commission on Labour, 1891-94; Vice-President of International Congress on Accidents, Milan, 1894; Member of the M.A.B. 1898-1930; Chairman, Training Ship, Exmouth, 1901, 1903-6, 1909-14, 1919-22; Pres. of the Central Poor Law Conference, 1906; Member Departmental Committees National Register, 1915; Sea Training, 1918; Vice-President Royal Statistical Society, 1916-18; Chairman Denison House Committee on Public Assistance, 1917; Chairman Official Statistics Committee, 1919; President of National Conference on Sea Training, 1910-14; Chairman of National Committee on Sea Training from 1910; Chairman Executive Committee King Edward VII. British-German Foundation, 1911-40; member Anglo-Russian deputation, 1912; Special Constable, Aug. 1914; Sub-Lieut. R.N.V.R. Oct. 1914; attached War Office, Military Intelligence Section, 1916; Director of Investigations Board of Agriculture, 1917; Chairman Finance Committee, O.M.S., 1925-26; Examiner for Degree of Ph.D., London University (Russian Agriculture), 1929; Director Royal Insurance Company (London Board), 1898-1939; Alderman, L.C.C., 1910-19; M.P. (Conservative) Derby, 1895-1900. *Publications:* Criminal Code of German Empire, with Prolegomena and Commentary, 1885; Cyril, a novel, 1st ed. 1889, 8th ed. 1899; Eton and the Empire, 1890; Foreign Reports of Royal Commission on Labour; Eton and the Labour Question, 1894; The Unemployed, 1894; The Aged Poor, 1895; The Labour Problem, 1896; Russian Affairs, 1904; Trade Unions, 1905; Austria-Hungary, 1909; Cambridge Modern History, vol. xi., sections on Russia, 1909; The Imperial Organisation of Trade, 1911; The State and the Poor, 1914; Ephemera, 1915; Pre-war Statistics of Poland and Lithuania, 1918; Report to the Board of Agriculture on Wages and Conditions of Labour in Agriculture, 1919; The Riddle of Japan, 1925; Public Assistance, 1930; Sea Power, 1931. *Recreations:* formerly golf, shooting, fishing, real tennis. *Address:* 39 Hyde Park Gate, S.W.7. *T.:* Western 4265. *Clubs:* United University, Carlton. [*Died* 7 *March* 1955.

DRAKE, Brig.-Gen. Bernard Francis, C.B. 1918; *e. s.* of late Rev. Francis Charles Drake, of Grazeley Court, Berkshire, and Sarah Catherine (*d.* 1895), *d.* of late Captain Joseph Giles; *b.* 1862; *m.* 1st, 1885, Helen Lavinia (*d.* 1926), *d.* of F. M. Wolhuter, Pietermaritzburg; one *d.*; 2nd, 1927, Marion (*d.* 1944), *d.* of W. James Smith, Gattertop, Herefordshire. *Educ.:* Eton; Royal Military Academy, Woolwich; First Commission in the Royal Artillery, 1881; commanded the R.A., Welsh Div., Territorial Force, 1912, and was Staff Officer for R.H.A. and R.F.A., Aldershot Command, 1912-14; Inspector of Royal Artillery (including Anti-Aircraft Defences), with the temporary rank of Brig.-General, 1915; retired pay, 1919. *Address:* Grazeley Lodge, South Farnborough, Hants. *T.:* Farnborough, Hants. 244. *Club:* Army and Navy. [*Died* 24 *Oct.* 1954.

DRAKE, John Alexander, M.D. (Lond.); F.R.C.P., D.P.H., M.R.C.S.; Consulting Physician for Diseases of the Skin, King's College Hospital, London; late Dean, King's College Hospital Medical School; *b.* 1878; *s.* of Alfred Drake, Clifton, Bristol; *m.* 1908, Lorna, *d.* of Charles James Stewart; no *c.* *Educ.:* Malvern College; King's College Hospital. M.R.C.S., L.R.C.P., 1902; M.B. (Lond.), 1903; Practised at Tenby, Pembrokeshire, 1907-15; Physician i/c Medical Division 4th London General Hospital R.A.M.C.(T.) during European War; D.P.H., R.C.P. and S., 1919; M.R.C.P., 1920; M.D.(Lond.), 1920; F.R.C.P., 1926; Physician for Diseases of Skin at King's College Hospital, 1920; Lecturer on

Diseases of the Skin, King's College Hospital, now Emeritus Lecturer; Consulting Dermatologist L.C.C.; Examiner in Medicine, Conjoint Board. *Publications:* Various contributions to Dermatological and Medical Journals. *Recreation:* walking. *Address:* Easton Court, Smith Street, Chelsea, S.W.3. *Club:* Union. [*Died* 29 *Oct.* 1952.

DRAKE, Colonel William Hacche, C.M.G. 1916; R.A.; *b.* 1873; *y. s.* of late Maj.-Gen. John Mervyn Cutcliffe Drake, C.B., R.E.; *m.* 1919, Gladys Henrietta, *y. d.* of late Maj.-Gen. E. D. Newbolt. *Educ.:* R.M. Academy, Woolwich. Joined R.G.A., 1893; R.F.A., 1896; Garrison Adjutant, Egypt; Egyptian Army, 1903; held appointment of Staff Officer, Khartoum Dist.; D.A.A.G. and A.A.G. on H.Q. Staff; rejoined R.F.A., 1913; appointed to command 147th Battery R.F.A.; Egyptian Army 1913, in command of Khartoum District; Adjutant General Egyptian Army, 1913-16; (temp. Col.) rejoined R.F.A., served with B.E.F., France and Flanders (despatches); A.A. and Q.M.G., Thames and Medway Garrison; Officer in charge R.A. Records 1921-25; retired pay, 1925. *Recreations:* various. *Address:* Kintbury, Newbury, Berks *T.:* Inkpen 208. [*Died* 15 *March* 1956.

DRAKE-BROCKMAN, Brig.-Gen. David Henry, C.M.G. 1915; late Royal Garhwal Rifles; 4th *s.* of late Wm. Drake Drake-Brockman, P.W.D., India; *b.* 2 Apr. 1868; *m.* 1910, Agnes Lilian, *y. d.* of late Rev. George Lamont Cole of Wellisford Manor, Wellington, Somerset; one *s.* *Educ.:* Elizabeth College, Guernsey. Entered Royal Marines, L.I., 1887, and joined Plymouth Div., H.M.S. Black Prince, 1889, for Naval manœuvres; H.M.S. Indus, 1889-90; Plymouth Div., 1890-91; transferred Indian Staff Corps, 1891; Captain, Indian army, 1898; Major, 1905; Lt.-Col. Comdt. 2nd Bn. 39th Garhwal Rifles, 1912-17; after battle of Neuve Chapelle, 1915, commanded combined Bns. (2) under title of The Garwhal Rifles; Col., 1918; Brig.-Gen., Inspector Depots, Meerut Div., 1918-19; G.O.C. Delhi Independent Bde., 1919-20; in command at Delhi during riots of 1919, and received thanks of the Chief Comr. Delhi Province, through Govt. of India; served N.W. Frontier, India, Mohmand, 1897-98 (medal with clasp); Tirah, 1897-98 (clasp); China Expedition, 1900-1 (medal); Tibet, 1903-4 (medal); European War, 1914-18; served in France, Egypt, and Mesopotamia (C.M.G., despatches twice, 1914 Star, with clasp, medal, Victory medal); retired, Sept. 1920; Member Military Order of the Dragon, U.S.A., 1909; Grand Officer of the Crown of Roumania, 1922; County Hon. Sec. Soldiers, Sailors, and Airmen's Families Assoc., East Sussex, 1939-44; compiled Vol. II Elizabeth College Register, 1874-1911. *Publications:* With the Royal Garhwal Rifles in the Great War; Record of the Brockman and Drake-Brockman family. *Address:* 50 Holland Road, Hove 2, Sussex. [*Died* 1 *Jan.* 1960.

DRAKE-BROCKMAN, Sir Digby Livingstone, Kt., *cr.* 1937; C.S.I. 1933; C.I.E. 1927; late I.C.S.; *b.* 21 December 1877; 8th *s.* of late W. Drake-Brockman, Supt. Engr. P.W.D. India (U.P.); *m.* Gladys Kate, *d.* of late Major-General S. M. Renny, C.S.I. C.I.E., R.A.; one *s.* one *d.* *Educ.:* Dulwich College; Christ Church, Oxford (Senior Scholar); Litt.Hum. 1st Class, 1900. I.C.S., 1900; arrived India, 1901; Assistant Magistrate and Collector, Muttra, Gorakhpur, Etawah, Agra; Assistant Settlement Officer, Banda, 1905-8; Secretariat, 1908-9; Joint Magistrate and Collector, Jhansi, 1910-12; Settlement Officer, Allahabad, 1912-15; Joint Registrar Co-op. Soc., 1916-17; Settlement Officer, Saharanpur, 1917-20; Revenue Member Regency Council, Jodhpur State, 1920-23; State Council, 1923-29; Commr. Fyzabad Divn., 1929-32; Bareilly, 1932-33; Member, Board of Revenue U.P., 1933-36; retired, 1936. Chm. U.P. Public Services Commission, 1937-42. *Publications:* District Gazetteers of Muttra, Etawah, Azamgarh, Mirzapur, Jhansi, Banda, Hamirpur, Jalaun; Final Settlement Reports Allahabad and Saharanpur. *Recreations:* golf, etc. *Address:* 10 Moorfield Road, Woodbridge, Suffolk. *T.:* 437 Woodbridge. [*Died* 13 *March* 1959.

DRAKE-BROCKMAN, Lieut.-Col. Ralph Evelyn, D.S.O. 1918; Med. Referee, Home Office; Physician, late Specialist (Tropical Diseases) Ministry of Pensions; *b.* 1 Oct. 1875; 7th *s.* of late William D. Drake-Brockman, Bournemouth; *m.* 1917, Helen Maud, 2nd *d.* of late Major Sir Henry Pilkington, K.C.B.; one *s.* one *d.* *Educ.:* Dulwich College; St. George's Hospital. M.R.C.S.Eng., L.R.C.P.Lond., Jan. 1899; M.D. Durham, 1924; served S. African War, 1899-1900 (Queen's medal 2 clasps); Medical Officer, Foreign Office, Uganda and British East Africa Protectorates, 1900-3; Nandi and Suk-Turkana Expeditions (G.A.S. medal and clasp, despatches); Medical Officer, Colonial Office, 1904-15; Somaliland Protectorate Expeditions against Mullah, 1908-10 and 1914-15 (2 clasps to G.A.S. medal); Medical Officer, Anglo-Abyssinian Boundary Commission, 1908-9; Capt. R.A.M.C., 1916; Lt.-Col., 1917; O.C. 150th and 95th Field Ambulances, European War (despatches twice, D.S.O.); retired with rank of Lieut.-Colonel, March 1919; Home Guard, 1940-42. F.Z.S. *Publications:* Mammals of Somaliland; British Somaliland, numerous papers to scientific journals. *Recreation:* gardening. *Address:* Eldama, Salvington, Worthing, Sussex. *T.:* Swandean 17. *Club:* Royal Empire Society. [*Died* 15 *Nov.* 1952.

DRAPER, Charles; *b.* Odcombe, Somerset, 1869; *s.* of Samuel Draper, 'cello player; *m.*; four *s.* one *d.* *Educ.:* Penarth; Royal College of Music (free scholarship). Principal Clarionet at the Crystal Palace, 1895; became a member of Her Majesty's Private Band two years before the death of Queen Victoria; in that capacity attended at Westminster Abbey the Coronations of both King Edward VII. and George V.; Formerly Prof. Guildhall School of Music, and Trinity College of Music. Musician-in-Ordinary to the King; F.G.S.M. *Recreations:* gardening, golf, walking. *Address:* c/o W. B. Draper, 205 Kimbolton Rd., Bedford. [*Died* 21 *Oct.* 1952.

DRAPER, Brig.-Gen. Denis Colbarn, C.M.G. 1919; D.S.O. 1916; Chief Constable, Toronto; *b.* 1873. Served European War, 1915-1918 (wounded, despatches, D.S.O. and bar, C.M.G., Croix de Guerre). [*Died* 8 *Nov.* 1951.

DRAPER, Ruth, Hon. C.B.E. 1951; character actress; *b.* 2 Dec. 1884; *d.* of Dr. W. H. Draper and Ruth Dana. *Educ.:* privately. Hon. M.A. Hamilton Coll., 1926; Dr. Fine Arts, Univ. of Maine, 1941; Dr. of Humane Letters, Smith College, 1947; LL.D. Edinburgh, 1951; Hon. LL.D. Cambridge, 1954. Has toured extensively throughout U.S.A., Canada, England, S. Africa, India, Australia, New Zealand. *Publication:* Translation of Icaro by Lauro de Bosis, 1933; *Relevant Publication:* The Art of Ruth Draper, by Morton Dauwen Label, 1960. *Address:* 66 E. 79 Street, New York, N.Y., U.S.A.; Dark Harbor, Maine, U.S.A. [*Died* 30 *Dec.* 1956.

DRESSER, Horatio Willis, A.B.; A.M.; Ph.D.; Consultant in Psychology; Author; *b.* Yarmouth, Maine, 15 Jan. 1866, parents and grandparents on both sides of English descent; *m.* 1898, Alice Mae Reed; one *s.* one *d.* *Educ.:* Harvard University. Newspaper and magazine writer, teacher of philosophy, and author of books on psychology, ethics, and philosophy; Assistant in Philosophy, Harvard University; Professor of Philosophy, Ursinus College. *Publications:* Thirty-two books on various branches of

philosophy and applied psychology, including The Power of Silence, 1895; Living by the Spirit, 1900; Psychology in Theory and Application, 1925; Outlines of the Psychology of Religion, 1929; Knowing and Helping People, 1933. *Recreations:* gardening and forestry in Maine woods, and mountain-climbing. *Address:* Flower Lane, Marshfield, Mass, U.S.A.
[*Died* 30 *March* 1954.

DREW, Maj.-Gen. Sir James Syme, K.B.E., *cr.* 1944; C.B. 1939; D.S.O. 1917; M.C.; D.L.; *b.* 1 Sept. 1883; *s.* of T. A. Drew; *g.s.* of Alexander Drew of Creggandarroch and James Syme, Edinburgh; *m.* 1918, Victoria, *y. d.* of late W. Herries Maxwell, Munches; one *s.* three *d.* *Educ.:* Harrow. Entered Army, 1902; Capt. 1914; Bt. Lt.-Col. 1923; Lt.-Col., 1927; Col., 1929; Maj.-Gen. 1938; served European War, 1914-18 (despatches, D.S.O., Brevet, M.C.); commanding 2nd Batt. Cameron Highlanders, 1927-29; Assist. Comdt. and Chief Instructor, Netheravon Wing Small Arms School, 1929-32; Assist. Director of T. A., War Office, 1932-35; Brigadier, General Staff, Southern Command, 1936-38; A.D.C. to the King, 1936-38; Commander, 52nd (Lowland) Division T.A., 1938; War of 1939-45 (despatches); Maj-Gen. Training Combined Operations, 1941; Director-General Home Guard and Territorial Army, 1944; retired Dec. 1945. D.L. Perthshire, 1947. late Col., The Queen's Own Cameron Highlanders, 1943-51. *Address:* Balavoulin, Glenfincastle, Pitlochry, Perthshire. *Clubs:* Naval and Military; New (Edinburgh).
[*Died* 27 *June* 1955.

DREW, Vice-Adm. Thomas Bernard, C.B. 1944; C.V.O. 1955; O.B.E. 1919; Royal Navy, retired; Private Secretary to the Lord Mayor of London at the Mansion House, 1946-56; *m.* 1938, Mabel M. Ward. Rear-Admiral, Malaya, and in charge of Naval Establishments at Singapore, 1938; Rear-Admiral, 1939; Vice-Admiral, 1943. *Club:* United Service. [*Died* 27 *April* 1960.

DREW-WILKINSON, Clennell Frank Massy, J.P.; *e. s.* of late Col. Francis Massy Drew of Drews-court, Co. Limerick, J.P.; *b.* 1877; *m.* 1907, Gladys, *y. d.* of late Major H. C. Wilkinson of Oswald House, Co. Durham; two *s.* *Educ.:* Wellington. J.P. Co. Limerick, 1899, Northumberland, 1930; Sheriff of Co. Limerick, 1903, Northumberland, 1934. *Address:* Merriethought, Fordingbridge, Hants. *T.:* 2251. *Clubs:* Junior Carlton, Lansdowne. [*Died* 10 *April* 1956.

DREYER, Admiral Sir Frederic Charles, G.B.E. *cr.* 1937 (C.B.E. 1919); K.C.B. *cr.* 1932 (C.B. (Civil) 1914; C.B. (Mil.) 1916); *b.* Parsonstown, King's County, 8 Jan. 1878; 2nd *s.* of late J. L. E. Dreyer, Ph.D., D.Sc., President of Royal Astronomical Society, 1923-25, and *g.s.* of late John Tuthill of Kilmore, Co. Limerick and Rapla, Co. Tipperary; *m.* 1901, Una Maria, *d.* of Rev. J. T. Hallett; three *s.* two *d.* *Educ.:* Royal School, Armagh. Entered Navy (H.M.S. Britannia), 1891; Lieut. 1898; First with Honours advanced course for Gunnery and Torpedo Lieutenants, 1901; Gunnery Lieutenant, H.M.S. Exmouth, 1904-7; on Special Service in H.M.S. Dreadnought for Experimental Cruise, 1907; Assistant to Director of Naval Ordnance, 1907-9; Commander, 1907; Commander H.M.S. Vanguard, 1909-10; Flag Commander to Vice-Admiral Sir John Jellicoe, 1910-12: appointed to War Staff, 1912; Captain, 1913; commanded H.M. Ships Amphion, 1913; Orion, 1913-10; and the Fleet Flagship of the Grand Fleet, H.M.S. Iron Duke as Flag Captain to Admiral Sir John Jellicoe (Jutland Battle), 1915-16; Assist. Director, Anti-Submarine Division, Admiralty Naval Staff, 1916-17; Director of Naval Ordnance, 1917-18; Director of Naval Artillery and Torpedo Admiralty Naval Staff, 1918-19; Commodore and Chief of the staff to Admiral of the Fleet Viscount Jellicoe, on Naval Mission to India and the Dominions in H.M.S. New Zealand, Feb. 1919-20; Director, Gunnery Division, Admiralty Naval Staff, 1920-22; Commanded Battle Cruiser Repulse, 1922-23; A.D.C. to the King, 1922-23; Rear-Admiral, 1923; War Course, 1924; a Lord Commissioner of the Admiralty and Assistant Chief of the Naval Staff, 1924-27; Tactical Course, 1927; commanded the Battle Cruiser Squadron, 1927-29; Vice-Admiral, 1929; War Course, 1930; a Lord Commissioner of the Admiralty and Deputy Chief of Naval Staff, 1930-33; Commander-in-Chief, China Station, 1933-36; Admiral, 1932; retired list, 1939; served European War, Battle of Jutland, 1916 (despatches, Mil. C.B., Order of St. Anne, 2nd Class, with swords); Order of St. Stanislaus, 2nd Class, with Star; officer of the Legion of Honour: United States Naval Distinguished Service Medal; re-employed war of 1939-45. Commodore of Convoys, 1939-40; on Staff of G.O.C.-in-C. Home Forces, 1940; Inspector of Merchant Navy Gunnery, 1941-42; Chief of Naval Air Services, 1942-43. *Publications:* How to get a First Class in Seamanship, 1900; The Sea Heritage, 1955. *Recreations:* shooting, golf, and reading. *Address:* Freelands, Winchester, Hants. *T.:* 4780. *Clubs:* United Service; Royal Yacht Squadron (Cowes). [*Died* 11 *Dec.* 1956.

DREYER, Maj.-Gen. John Tuthill, C.B. 1922; D.S.O. 1916; *b.* Parsonstown, 24 Dec. 1876; *e. s.* of late J. L. E. Dreyer, *y. s.* of late General J. F. C. Dreyer; *m.* 1914, Penelope Aylmer, *d.* of A. R. Holme, *y. s.* of Bryan Holme Holme of Paul Holme, Yorkshire; two *s.* one *d.* *Educ.:* Royal School, Armagh; Royal Military Academy, Woolwich. Entered R.A. 1897; Instructor in Gunnery, 1st Class, School of Gunnery, 1907-9; Assistant Superintendent of Experiments, Shoeburyness, 1910-13; Staff-Captain War Office, 1913-14; Deputy Assistant-Director of Military Aeronautics, War Office, 1914-15; D.A.Q.M.G., R.F.C. Gen. Headquarters, France, Feb.-Mar. 1915; Special Appointment (graded D.A.A.G.), General Headquarters, France, April-Dec. 1915; Member of the Ordnance Committee, Dec. 1915-Feb. 1918; Assistant Director of Artillery, General Headquarters, France, Feb. 1918-Mar. 1919: Substantive Colonel, 1920; Assistant Director of Artillery, War Office, 1920-23; Director of Artillery, War Office, 1923-24; C.R.A. Portsmouth, 1926-30; Maj.-Gen., 1930; retired pay, 1930; served South African War, 1901-2; operations in the Transvaal, Orange River Colony and Cape Colony (Queen's medal with five clasps); European War, 1914-18 (despatches, D.S.O.); Bt. Lieut.-Col. 1917; Bt. Col. 1919; Chevalier of the Legion of Honour, Officier of the Order of Leopold and Belgian Croix de Guerre); the Lefroy Gold medal of the Royal Artillery Institution, 1914. *Address:* Southside, Instow, N. Devon. [*Died* 23 *May* 1959.

DROGHEDA, 10th Earl of (*cr.* 1661), **Henry Charles Ponsonby Moore,** P.C. 1951; K.C.M.G., *cr.* 1945 (C.M.G. 1919); Baron Moore of Mellifont, 1616; Viscount Moore, 1621; Baron Moore, of Cobham (U.K.), 1954; Chairman of Committees and a Deputy Speaker in the House of Lords; Chairman, Advisory Council on the Treatment of Offenders, 1954; *b.* 21 April 1884; *s.* of 9th Earl and Anne, *d.* of G. Moir, LL.D.; *S.* father, 1908; *m.* 1st, 1909, Kathleen, C.B.E. (who obtained a divorce, 1922; she *m.*, 2nd, Guillermo de Landa y Escandon), *d.* of late Charles Maitland Pelham-Burn, Prestonfield, Midlothian; one *s.*; 2nd, 1922, Lady Victor Paget (Olive Mary Meatyard) (*d.* 1947). *Educ.:* Eton; Trinity Coll., Cambridge. Foreign Office, 1907-18; joint director, Ministry of Economic Warfare, 1940-42, Dir.-Gen., 1942-45. Served in Irish Guards, 1918-19; H.M. Lieut. for Co. Kildare, 1918-21; called to Bar (Inner Temple), 1935. Chairman: Cinematograph Films Council, 1944-54; Films Selection Board, 1946-54. *Heir:* *s.* Viscount Moore, O.B.E. *Recreation:* gardening. *Address:* Leigh Hill House, Cobham, Surrey. *Clubs:* St. James,' Turf. [*Died* 22 *Nov.* 1957.

DROWER, Sir Edwin Mortimer, K.B.E., *cr.* 1941 (C.B.E. 1923); *b.* 1880; *s.* of late John Edmund Drower, C.B.E.; *m.* 1910, Ethel Stefana, *d.* of late Rev. S. W. Stevens, LL.M.; two *s.* one *d.* Solicitor, Cairo, 1904; Advocate, Khartoum, 1906; Barrister, Gray's Inn, 1924; served European War, 1914-1918; Assistant Judicial Adviser, Iraq, 1921; Judicial Adviser, 1922-46. *Address:* 48 Hurlingham Court, S.W.6. *Club:* East India and Sports. [*Died* 23 *Nov.* 1951.

DRUMMOND, Arthur; painter; *b.* Bristol, 1871; *s.* of late John Drummond, painter of marine subjects; *m.* Etheline (*d.* 1941), *d.* of Herbert Sims. *Educ.:* privately. Studied under Sir L. Alma-Tadema, and in Paris under M. Benjamin Constant and M. Jean Paul Laurens; first exhibited at R.A. at the age of 19. *Paintings:* Last Days of Pompeii; The God of the Ancients; His Majesty the Baby; The Queen's Birthday; The King's Courtship; A Royal Gift; Bobs and the Baby; and other works. *Recreations:* engineering, patentee of the Drummond improvements in lathe-beds. [*Died* 1 *Jan.* 1951.

DRUMMOND, Arthur W. H.; *see* Hay-Drummond.

DRUMMOND, Hon. Mrs. Geraldine Margaret; 6th *d.* of 1st Lord Amherst of Hackney; *m* 1890, Malcolm Drummond (*d.* 1924); one *s.* three *d.* *Publication:* Orynthia and Flowers, 2nd edition. *Address:* 202 Fleet Road, Fleet, Hampshire. [*Died* 24 *Aug.* 1956.

DRUMMOND, Sir Jack Cecil, Kt., *cr.* 1944; F.R.S. 1944; D.Sc. (Lond.); F.R.I.C.; Docteur (hon. causa), Univ. de Paris; Comdr. Order of Orange Nassau; U.S. Medal of Freedom with silver palms; Director of Research and Director of Boots Pure Drug Co. Ltd. since 1946; *b.* 12 Jan. 1891; *s.* of late Major J. Drummond; *m.* 1940, Anne, *d.* of Roger Wilbraham, London; one *d.* *Educ.:* Strand School, King's College; Queen Mary's College and King's College, University of London. Research Assistant, King's College, London, 1913; Research Assistant Bio-chemical Dept., Cancer Hospital, Research Institute, London, 1914; Director of Bio-chemical Research, Cancer Hospital, London, 1918; Reader in Physiological Chemistry, University College, London, 1919; Professor of Bio-chemistry, University of London, University College, 1922-45; Scientific Adviser to Ministry of Food, 1939-46; Adviser on Nutrition, Allied Post-War Requirements Bureau and S.H.A.E.F., 1944-45; Adviser on Nutrition, Control Commissions for Germany and Austria (British Element), 1945-46; Hon. Member New York Acad. of Science, 1946. Lane Lecturer, Stanford Univ., California, 1933; Harvey Lecturer, New York, 1933; Fullerian Professor of Physiology, Royal Institution, 1942-44. *Publications:* The Englishman's Food (with Anne Wilbraham); numerous in scientific periodicals. *Address:* Spencer House, Nuthall, Nottingham. *T.:* Kimberley 3154. *Club:* Savage. [*Died* 4 *Aug.* 1952.

DRUMMOND, Col. Hon. Sir Maurice Charles Andrew, K.B.E., *cr.* 1939; C.M.G. 1919; D.S.O. 1916; *b.* 30 Nov. 1877; 3rd *s.* of 10th Viscount Strathallan and Margaret Smythe; *m.* Ida Mary, 3rd *d.* of late George Drummond of Swaylands, Penshurst, Kent, and Drummond's Bank; one *s.* two *d.* *Educ.:* Eton (rowed in the Eight, 1896). Page of Honour to H.M. Queen Victoria, 1890-94; Joined 3rd Batt. The Black Watch, 1897; 2nd Batt. 1899; served South African War (severely wounded at Magersfontein, despatches); Adjutant 2nd Batt. The Black Watch, 1904-07; Staff Captain No. 1 District Scottish Command, 1908-12; A.D.C. to G.O.C. in Chief Scottish Command, 1913-14; served with 1st Batt. The Black Watch in European War, 1914 (severely wounded, battle of the Marne, despatches); Staff Captain, G.H.Q., 3rd Echelon, B.E.F., 1916 (despatches, D.S.O.); D.A.A.G. General Headquarters, 3rd Echelon, B.E.F., 1915-16; D.A.A. and Q.M.G., 9th Corps, June 1916-April 1917; D.A.A.G. 9th Corps, April 1917; A.A.G. Fifth Army, April 1917; D.A.A. and Q.M.G. 9th Corps, 1917 (despatches); Chevalier Legion of Honour (France); A.A.G. Fifth Army, 1918 (despatches, Bt. Lt.-Col.); A.A.G. War Office, 1918 (despatches); Assist. Director War Office, 1919 (C.M.G.); A.A.G. War Office, 1920-23; Deputy Director of Staff Duties, Air Ministry, 1923-27; A.Q.M.G. Eastern Command, 1927-31; Personal Assistant to Commissioner of Metropolitan Police 1931-32; Chief Constable Metropolitan Police, 1932-33; Deputy Assistant Commissioner, 1933-35; Assistant Commissioner, 1935; Deputy Commissioner, 1935-1946. *Address:* Craigbeithe, Dunkeld, Perthshire. *T.:* 349. *Club:* United Service. [*Died* 21 *Feb.* 1957.

DRUMMOND, Rev. Robert J., M.A., B.D., D.D.; Chaplain to the King in Scotland since 1929; Senior Minister of Lothian Road United Free Church, Edinburgh, now Church of Scotland, since 1890; Moderator of Assembly of United Free Church, 1918; *b.* Leith, 1 June 1858; *s.* of Rev. Robert S. Drummond, D.D., of Belhaven Church, Glasgow, and Jeanie, *d.* of Rev. John French, D.D., of College St. Church, Edinburgh; *m.* Rhoda Constance (*d.* 1933), *d.* of John Whitehorn, jeweller, London; one *s.* *Educ.:* Glasgow Academy; University College School, London. Took Arts course at Glasgow University and Theology at the United Presbyterian College in Edinburgh; also attended the Universities of Erlangen and Leipzig; after a visit to India was settled as minister of Princes Street Church, Kilmarnock; has acted as Convener of Assembly's Home Mission Committee, and also of its Social Problems Committee; was Joint Convener of its Committee on Conference with the Church of Scotland. *Publications:* The Joan Kerr Lecture for 1900 on the Relation of the Apostolic Teaching to the Teaching of Christ; Faith's Perplexities; Faith's Certainties; The Christian as Protestant; Outcasts from Rome; The Christian Knight; Forgotten Scotland; All Around Scotland; Lest we forget, Reminiscences of a Nonagenarian. *Address:* 3 East Castle Road, Edinburgh. *T.:* 53415. *Clubs:* Scottish Liberal, Bruntsfield Golf (Edinburgh). [*Died* 20 *July* 1951.

DRUMMOND, Col. William, C.B.E. 1944; M.C. 1917; D.L. Edinburgh; Town Councillor, Edinburgh, since 1950; *b.* 3 May 1880; *m.* 1910, Alice Andersen Duncan; three *s.* one *d.* Joined ranks Gordon Highlanders, 1898; served with above throughout South African War, 1899-1902 (King's and Queen's Medal seven clasps); European War, 1914-18, Commissioned 1914; Staff Captain 152 Brigade, 1917 (despatches thrice, M.C., two medals and Victory star); retired from Army, 1919; joined City of Edinburgh Home Guard, 1940, Zone Commander with rank of Col. 1941-44 (C.B.E.). Member Edinburgh Town Council, 1950, Bailie 1955. *Recreations:* golf and curling. *Address:* 10 Oxford Terrace, Edinburgh. *Club:* Scottish Conservative (Edinburgh). [*Died* 12 *Jan.* 1960.

DRURY, Lady (Amy Gertrude), C.B.E., J.P.; *d.* of late John Middleton, 3 Porchester Gate, W.2; *m.* 1907, Admiral Sir Charles C. Drury, G.C.B., G.C.V.O., K.C.S.I. (*d.* 1914); no *c.* *Educ.:* Home. *Address:* Hayes Farm Hotel, Northiam, Sussex. [*Died* 27 *Dec.* 1953.

DRURY, Lieutenant-Colonel Richard Frederick, C.B.E. 1919 (O.B.E. 1918); late Chief Superintendent, The Land Registry; Hon. Lt.-Col. Royal Air Force; *b.* Aug. 1866; *s.* of Capt. J. D. Drury, R.M.L.I., and J. Price. *Educ.:* Private schools. Joined Colonial Civil Service, Public Works Dept., 1887; Superintendent of Crown Lands, Senior Assistant Engineer and Executive Engineer, Hong Kong; Deputy Assistant Director Air Organisation, War Office, 1917; Assistant Director, 1917; retired from Service, 1931. *Recreations:* fishing, shooting, fencing. *Address:* Brock House, Dawlish, Devon. [*Died* 16 *April* 1956.

DRURY, Rev. Thomas William Ernest, M.A.; *e. s.* of late Thomas C. Drury, M.A., LL.B., K.C., formerly Metropolitan Magistrate, Dublin, and Susan Anna, *d.* of William Symes, M.B., Skerries, Co. Dublin; *m.* 1906, Janet, 4th *d.* of William Brodie of Eastbourne; two *d.* (one *s.* decd.). *Educ.:* Rathmines Sch.; Trinity Coll., Dublin, B.A., and Divinity Testimonium, 1896; M.A. 1901. Curate parish of Belfast, 1896; Minor Canon Belfast Cathedral, 1899; Curate Kilbroney (Rostrevor), 1901; Vicar Kilbroney (Rostrevor), 1904-18; Rector of Raheny, Co. Dublin, 1918-49; Prof. of Pastoral Theology, T.C.D., 1921-26; Treas. of St. Patrick's Cathedral, 1924-35; Precentor, St. Patrick's Cathedral, 1935-49; retd., 1949. *Publication:* Unforgotten (19th Century reminiscences). *Address:* 10 Brighton Vale, Monkstown, Co. Dublin. [*Died* 6 *Feb.* 1960.

DRYERRE, Henry, M.R.C.S., L.R.C.P. (Lond.); Ph.D. (Edin.); F.R.S.E.; Emeritus Prof. of Physiology, Royal (Dick) Veterinary College, Edin.; Examiner in Physiology for the Royal Coll. of Surgeons, Edin.; formerly Lectr. in Physiology, Edin. Univ.; *b.* Blairgowrie, Perthshire, 1881; *s.* of late Henry Dryerre, poet, musician, journalist; *m.* 1st, 1905, Mary (*d.* 1940), 2nd *d.* of late Peter McLaren, Bridge of Allan; one *s.* decd.; 2nd, 1941, Agnes Richardson. *Educ.:* Blairgowrie Public School; Stirling High School; School of Medicine Royal Colleges, and University, Edinburgh. *Publications:* papers in scientific journals; Aids to Physiology. *Recreations:* motoring, cine-photography. *Address:* Kenmore, Lasswade, Midlothian. *T.A.:* Dryerre, Lasswade. *T.:* 2357. [*Died* 5 *Feb.* 1959.

D'SOUZA, Frank, C.I.E. 1939; *b.* 6 Dec. 1883; *s.* of Joseph J. D'Souza, Sukkur, Sind; *m.* 1907, Mary Viegas; two *s.* three *d.* *Educ.:* St. Patrick's, Karachi. Joined North Western Railway, India, 1902; Asst. Traffic Supdt. (officiating) 1918, confirmed, 1922; officiating District Traffic Supdt., 1923; Superior Revenue Establishment of State Railways, 1927; Officer on Special Duty, Railway Board, 1928; Deputy Director, Traffic and Statistics, 1929-34 (twice acting Director); Director of Traffic, Railway Board, 1934-38; member, Railway Board, Government of India, 1938-39; Officer on Special Duty, Railway Board, 1940; General Manager, Bikaner State Railway, 1941-46; Officer on Special Duty, Ministry of Communications (Railway Div.), Pakistan, 1952-53. *Address:* The Emblem, West Avenue, Santa Cruz, Bombay 23. [*Died* 25 *May* 1960.

DU BOULAY, George Cornibert, C.B.E. 1930; *b.* 22 April 1883; *s.* of George Du Boulay and Josephine Gaillard de Laubenque; *m.* 1923, J. Imossi; one *s.* *Educ.:* St. Mary's College, St. Lucia, British West Indies; Colonial Civil Service, St. Lucia, 1902-12; Seychelles, 1912-19; Gibraltar, 1919-22; Sierra Leone, 1922-26; Gold Coast, 1926-38. *Address:* 24 Rua dos Ilheus, Funchal, Madeira. [*Died* 4 *Feb.* 1951.

DUCIE, 5th Earl of (*cr.* 1837), **Capel Henry Berkeley Moreton,** Baron Ducie, 1763; Baron Moreton, 1837; *b.* 16 May 1875; *e. s.* of 4th Earl and Emily Eleanor Kent (*d.* 1921); *S.* father, 1924; *m.* 1903, Maria Emma, *d.* of Frederick Bryant, Maryborough, Queensland. Owns about 5000 acres. *Heir:* *nephew* Basil Howard Moreton, *b.* 15 Nov. 1917. *Address:* Tortworth, Pialba, Queensland. [*Died* 17 *June* 1952.

DUCKETT, Lieutenant-Colonel John Steuart, D.S.O. 1917; retired; British Council 1951; *b.* 1876; *o. s.* of late Steuart James Charles Duckett, D.L., late 13th Hussars, of Russelstown Park, Carlow, and *g.s.* of late Sir John Dick-Lauder, 8th Bt., and late Lady Anne Dick-Lauder, *d.* of 9th Earl of Stair; *m.* 1903, Penrose, *d.* of late Col. Charles Hayter, C.B.; no *c.* *Educ.:* Eton. Lt.-Col. late 9th Lancers; served S. Africa, 1899-1901 (Queen's medal with nine clasps); European War, 1914-18 (despatches thrice, D.S.O., Croix de Guerre, King Albert Medal, Belgium); Deputy Provost-Marshal, 1918, with rank of Lt.-Col.; Recruiting Officer, Sept. 1939-42. Minister of Food, 1942-50. *Address:* 15 York Road, Edgbaston, Birmingham 16. [*Died* 9 *Dec.* 1952.

DUCKWORTH, William Rostron, J.P., F.R.G.S.; *b.* 24 Nov. 1879; *s.* of Wm. Duckworth and Elizabeth Rostron Horrocks; *m.* 1937, Lady (Catherine) Reynolds, Lansdowne, Knowle, Warwickshire. *Educ.:* Farnworth and Bury Grammar Schools. Chartered Accountant Demerara, 1902-9: Captain, Command Cashiers Office, Northern Command, York, 1916-19; Member of Blackpool Town Council, 1921-39; Alderman, 1938; Chairman Library and Art Gallery Committee, 1928-30, and of Education Committee, 1930-37; Deputy Mayor, 1933-34, 1935-36; Mayor, 1938-39; Chairman Blackpool National Service Committee, 1939, and Blackpool National Savings Cttee., 1939; Trustee of Preston Savings Bank, 1939-; Member of Executive of Assn. of Education Committees of Eng., Wales and N. Ireland, 1932-39; Member of Executive Lancs. and N.W. Counties Fisheries Board, since 1933; Member Court of Governors, Manchester University, 1936; Member of Administrative Council of Empire Cotton Growing Corporation, since 1938; M.P. (U.) Moss Side Division of Manchester, 1935-45; introduced the Education (Deaf Children) Bill, which became law in 1937, and the Cotton Industry Act, 1938; Vice-Pres. Nat. Federation of Property Owners, since 1943; Pres. Nat. Soc. of Conservative and Unionist Agents (Lancs. Cheshire and Westmoreland Branch), 1945-46. Chairman, Waller and Hartley Ltd., White Hudson and Co. Ltd., etc. *Recreation:* travelling (100,000 miles by air). *Address:* Ravenshaw Hall, Solihull, Warwickshire. *Club:* Constitutional. [*Died* 14 *July* 1952.

DUCKWORTH, Wynfrid Laurence Henry, M.D., Sc.D., M.A; *b.* Liverpool, 5 June 1870; *s.* of Henry Duckworth, J.P., F.R.G.S., and Mary, *d.* of late Thos. F. Bennett; *m.* 1902, Eva Alice (*d.* 1955), *widow* of late Charles Cheyne, Lieut. Indian Staff Corps, and *d.* of late Frederick Wheeler. *Educ.:* Birkenhead School, Cheshire; L'École libre des Cordéliers, Dinan, Brittany, France; Jesus College, Cambridge (Scholar); First Class in Natural Sciences Tripos, Part I., 1892; First Class in Part II., 1893; M.D. 1905; Sc.D. 1905; Horton-Smith Prize, 1905; Fellow of Jesus College, 1893; University Lecturer in Physical Anthropology, 1898-1920; Reader in Human Anatomy, 1920-1940; Master of Jesus College, Cambridge, 1940-45; University Representative on the General Medical Council, 1923-26. Huxley Lecturer (and Medal), Royal Anthropological Institute, 1947; Linacre Lecturer (St. John's College, Cambridge), 1948. *Publications:* Morphology and Anthropology; Studies from the Anthropological Laboratory; contributions to periodicals dealing with anatomical and anthropological sciences; Report to the British Association upon the ancient and modern inhabitants of Greece and of Crete. *Address:* Jesus College, Cambridge. [*Died* 14 *Feb.* 1956.

DUCKWORTH-KING, Sir George (Henry James), 6th Bt., *cr.* 1792; late Major Grenadier Guards; *b.* 8 June 1891; *s.* of 5th Bt. and Eva Mary, *d.* of Maj.-Gen. Ralph Gore; *S.* father, 1909; *m.* 1915, Barbara, *e. d.* of late Hugh Scott Makdougall of Makerstoun; two *d.* *Educ.:* Eton; Oxford. Served in European War, 1914, and War of 1939-45. *Heir:* *b.* John Richard, *b.* 11 June 1899. *Address:* 18 Culford Mansions, Culford Gardens, S.W.3. *T.:* Kensington 1516; Garstons, Heytesbury, Wiltshire. *Clubs:* Guards, Marlborough-Windham. [*Died* 21 *Feb.* 1952.

DU CROS, Sir Arthur Philip, 1st Bt., *cr.* 1916; *b.* 1871; *m.* 1st, 1895, Maude (*decd.*), *d.* of late William Gooding, Coventry; two *s.* two *d.*; 2nd, 1928, Florence May Walton (*d.* 1951), *d.* of late James Walton King, Walton, Bucks; 3rd, 1951, Mary Louise Joan Beaumont. M.P. (U.) Hastings, 1908-18, Clapham, 1918-22; Hon. Col. (retd.) 8th Bn. Royal Warwickshire Regiment; J.P. retired; Associate of National Gallery of British Art; a Founder, with his father, of the Pneumatic Tyre Industry; the Founder and sometime President of the Dunlop Rubber Co.; a Founder of the Junior Imperial League and first Chairman of its Committee; formed Aerial Defence Committee in House of Commons in 1909 to secure the inclusion of aeronautics in the Naval and Army estimates; initiated Motor Ambulance Movement during European War, 1914-18. *Publication:* Wheels of Fortune: A Salute to Pioneers. *Heir:* *s.* (Harvey) Philip [*b.* 19 June 1898; *m.* 1st, 1922, Dita (marriage dissolved, 1949), *d.* of late Sir Claude Mallet, C.M.G.; one *s.* two *d.*; 2nd, 1950, Rosemary Theresa, *d.* of Sir John Rees, 1st Bt.]. *Address:* Nancy Downs House, Oxhey, Herts. *T.:* Watford 7987; Little Craigweil, Craigweil-on-Sea, Sussex; Florida del Mare, St. Jean, Cap Ferrat, A.M. *Club:* Carlton. [*Died* 28 *Oct.* 1955.

DUDDEN, Rev. Frederick Homes, D.D.; Master of Pembroke College, Oxford, since 1918; Chaplain to King George V and VI, 1929-52; Hon. Fellow of Lincoln College, Oxford, since 1930; Hon. D.Litt. Durham, 1942; *b.* 28 Dec. 1874; *m.* 1910, Muriel Bertha, *d.* of Rev. John Letts. *Educ.:* Bath College; Pembroke College, Oxford (Scholar). 1st Class Lit. Hum. 1897; Liddon Student, 1897; Ellerton Prize Essay, 1898; Denyer and Johnson Scholarship, 1899; Fellow R. Hist. Soc., 1905-37; Examiner in Theology School, Oxford, 1909-11, B.D. Examination, London, 1911-13; Fellow, Lecturer in Theology and Chaplain of Lincoln College, Oxford, 1898-1914; Vicar of St. John's, Notting Hill, W., 1914-16; Rector of Holy Trinity, Sloane Street, 1916-18; Canon of Gloucester, 1918-37; Select Preacher (Oxford), 1924-26; Select Preacher (Cambridge), 1920 and 1930; Member of Hebdomadal Council, 1924-45; Pro-Vice-Chancellor, 1925-1929 and 1932-49; Vice-Chancellor, 1929-32; Member of Royal Commission on the University of Durham, 1934-35; Chairman of Statutory Commission on the University of Durham, 1935-37. *Publications:* Henry Fielding: His Life, Works, and Times (2 vols.), 1953; Gregory the Great, his Place in History and Thought (2 vols.); The Life and Times of St. Ambrose (2 vols.); Christ and Christ's Religion; In Christ's Name; The Future Life; The Problem of Human Suffering and the War; The Heroic Dead and other Sermons; The Delayed Victory; The Dead and the Living, and other Sermons, etc. *Address:* The Master's Lodging, Pembroke College, Oxford. [*Died* 21 *June* 1955.

DUDDING, Surgeon Rear-Admiral John Scarbrough, C.B. 1935; O.B.E. 1924; *b.* 30 July 1877; *s.* of Thomas Dudding, Garthorpe, Lincs. and Emily Mary Scarbrough. *Educ.:* Oundle; London Hospital (Buxton Scholar). Joined Royal Navy as Surgeon, 1900; present at Messina Earthquake 1908 for rescue work at which received the Italian order of Officer of St. Maurice and Lazarus and medal, also expression of appreciation of services by the Lords Commissioners of the Admiralty; served European War in R.N. Hospital, Haslar and the Grand Fleet; Squadron Medical Officer of Special Service Squadron in cruise round the world, 1923; Fleet Medical Officer of Atlantic Fleet, 1924-26; Director of Medical Studies and Professor of Hygiene at R.N. College, Greenwich, 1931; Surgeon Rear-Admiral in charge of R.N. Hospital, Plymouth, 1933-36; Hon. Physician to the King, 1935; retired list, 1936. *Recreations:* outdoor sports. *Address:* Winteringham, Scunthorpe, Lincolnshire. [*Died* 12 *May* 1951.

DUDLEY, Rev. Owen Francis; former Superior of Catholic Missionary Society, Lecturer in philosophy and theology throughout the British Empire and U.S.A.; *b.* May, 1882; *s.* of Rev. Francis Dudley and Alice Isabella Frost; unmarried. *Educ.:* Lichfield Theological Coll.; Collegio Beda, Rome. Licentiate Theol., Durham Univ. Ordained (Anglican), 1911; received into the Catholic Church, 1915; priest, 1917; served as a Catholic chaplain (wounded); joined the Catholic Missionary Soc., 1919. Hon. mem. of Internat. Mark Twain Soc. (U.S.A.), 1949. *Publications:* Will Men be like Gods; The Shadow on the Earth; The Masterful Monk; Deathless Army—Advance; The Abomination in our Midst; The Church Unconquerable; Pageant of Life; The Coming of the Monster; Human Happiness and H. G. Wells; A Punch at Everybody—Daily Mirror Articles; The Tremaynes and the Masterful Monk; Michael; You, and thousands like you; a frequent contributor to the Catholic and secular press. *Recreations:* swimming, tennis, walking. *Address:* The Stables, Woodcock Hill, Berkhamsted, Herts. [*Died* 8 *Dec.* 1952.

DUDLEY, Surgeon Vice-Adm. (Ret.) Sir Sheldon Francis, K.C.B., *cr.* 1942 (C.B. 1940); O.B.E. 1919; F.R.S. 1941; Commander Order of Merit U.S.A., 1947; Commander French Legion of Honour, 1948; M.D., F.R.C.P. (Lond.), F.R.C.S. (Ed.), D.P.H., LL.D. (Edin.) 1953; D.T.M.; *b.* R.N. Sick Quarters, Lisbon, 16 Aug. 1884; *s.* of late Surgeon Captain John Dudley, R.N.; *m.* 1913, Ethel E. Franklyn; one *c.* *Educ.:* Merchant Taylors' School; St. Thomas's Hosp. Joined R.N., 1906; served in Mediterranean and China Stations; took up bacteriology as speciality; served in war at R.N. Hospital, Chatham; R.N. Air Force, Dunkerque; and H.M. Hospital Ship Agadir; Prof. of Pathology to R.N. Medical School, Greenwich and Director of Medical Studies to Royal Navy; earned several medals and distinctions for research work on the spread of infectious diseases, including Chadwick Gold Medal for the officer who had done most to promote the health of the Royal Navy; Principal Medical Officer, H.M. Hospital Ship Maine; Surg. Capt., 1930; Deputy Medical Director General, R.N., 1935-38; Medical Officer in Charge R.N. Hospital, Chatham, 1938-41; Medical Director-General of the Navy, 1941-45; K.H.P., 1939-46; Pres. Epidemiological Section, Royal Society of Medicine, 1935, and 1936-37. *Publications:* The Four Pillars of Wisdom, 1950; Our National Ill-Health Service, 1953; and numerous technical papers and reports, including Arsenuretted Hydrogen Gas Poisoning in Submarines, Medical Research Council special reports on Diphtheria, and the Schick Test and Spread of Droplet Infection. *Recreations:* lawn tennis and golf. *Address:* 109 Kinross Rd., Lillington, Leamington Spa. [*Died* 6 *May* 1956.

DUFF, Bt. Lt.-Col. A. A. S.; *see* Scott-Duff.

DUFF, Admiral Sir Arthur Allan Morison, K.C.B., *cr.* 1929 (C.B. 1917); J.P., D.L.; *b.* 1874; *s.* of General A. G. Duff; *m.* Margaret Grace Rawson; two *s.* two *d.* Commanded Scout Adventure; attached First Destroyer Flotilla, 1907-9; Flag-Capt. in First Battle Cruiser Squadron, 1911-13; commanded H.M.S. Birmingham, 1914-16, which ship was the first to sink a German submarine in the War, and was present at the

actions in Heligoland Bight, Dogger Bank, and Jutland; appointed to command of H.M.S. Inflexible, 1916; commanded H.M.S. Tiger, Aug. 1917-May 1919; 2nd Light Cruiser Squadron, 1919-21; Rear-Adm. 1st Battle Squadron, 1922-23; Director of Naval Equipment, Admiralty, 1924-1926; Vice-Admiral, 1926; Admiral commanding Reserves, 1927-29; Admiral, 1930; retired list, 1930. J.P., D.L. (Dorset). *Address:* Var Trees, Moreton, Dorset. *T.:* Warmwell 366. *Club:* United Service.
[*Died* 5 *April* 1952.

DUFF, David, C.M.G. 1935; M.D., D.P.H.; *b.* 11 April 1883; *s.* of John Duff and Annie Maud Ekins. *Educ.:* Portora; Enniskillen; Trinity College, Dublin. Entered Medical Service, Gold Coast, 1910; Senior Medical Officer, 1925; A.D.M.S., 1927; D.D.M.S., 1931; Director of Medical Services, Gold Coast, 1932-39; Bar, Gray's Inn, 1927. *Recreations:* gardening, chess. *Address:* Ballinagroun, Annascaul, Co. Kerry, Eire. *Club:* Royal Societies. [*Died* 27 *Sept.* 1959.

DUFF, Lt.-Col. Sir Garden Beauchamp, 1st Bt. *cr.* 1952; D.S.O. 1916; late Cameron Highlanders; Vice-Lieutenant, Aberdeenshire, 1934; *b.* 6 Dec. 1879; *e. s.* of late Garden A. Duff and Annie I. (*d.* 1910), *d.* of B. C. Urquhart of Meldrum; *m.* 1913, Doris, *d.* of Lindsay Eric Smith. Joined Cameron Highlanders, 1899; served European War, 1915-19 (despatches thrice, D.S.O., Bt. Lt.-Col.). *Address:* Hatton Castle, Turriff, Aberdeen. *Club:* United Service.
[*Died* 6 *Sept.* 1952 (*ext.*).

DUFF, Sir Hector (Livingston), K.B.E., *cr.* 1918; C.M.G. 1915; formerly Chief Secretary to Government, Nyasaland, with seat on Executive and Legislative Councils; *b.* 10 Jan. 1872; 2nd *s.* of late J. P. Duff, and late Alice, Lady Russell. Assistant Resident, Nyasaland, 1897; Resident, 1909; has frequently acted as Deputy-Governor of the Protectorate; served with Nyasaland Field Force, German East Africa, 1914-15 (despatches); took part in suppression of native rebellion in Shiré Highlands, 1915 (medal and clasp); Chief Political Officer with General Northey's Forces, G. E. Africa, 1916-17 (despatches, 1914-15 Star); administered military government of occupied enemy territory, 1917-18; Acting Governor and Commander-in-Chief of Nyasaland, 1918; called to Bar of Inner Temple, 1919. *Publications:* Nyasaland under the Foreign Office; A History of Nyasaland in the Native Dialect; The Ivory Graves; African Small Chop, 1932; This Small World of Mine, 1936, etc. *Recreations:* shooting and fishing. *Address:* 16 Lansdown Place East, Bath. *Club:* Junior Carlton.
[*Died* 10 *Feb.* 1954.

DUFF, Rt. Hon. Sir Lyman Poore, P.C. 1919; G.C.M.G., *cr.* 1934; *s.* of Rev. Chas. Duff, M.A., and Isabella, *d.* of James Johnson; *b.* 7 Jan. 1865; *m.* 1898, Elizabeth Eleanor (*d.* 1926), *d.* of Henry Bird, Barrie, Ont. *Educ.:* Toronto University. B.A. 1887; LL.B. 1889; LL.D. (Hon.): Toronto, Columbia, Pennsylvania, McGill, Queens, Laval, Montreal, British Columbia, Dalhousie. Pres. of Toronto Univ. Literary and Scientific Society, 1891; called to Bar, Ontario, 1893; British Columbia, 1895; Queen's Counsel, 1899: Counsel for B.C. Legislature in Coal Lands Investigation, 1902; Junior Counsel for Great Britain in Alaska Boundary Arbitration, 1903; Judge of Supreme Court of British Columbia, 1904; Judge of the Supreme Court of Canada, 1906-33; Chief Justice of Canada, 1933-44; Royal Commissioner of Investigation of Contracts of Shell Committee, 1916; Central Appeal Judge under Military Service Acts, October 1917-18; Hon. Bencher, Gray's Inn, 1924; Governor of University of Toronto, 1926; Administrator, Government of Canada, 1931; Chairman of Transportation Commission investigating Railways in Canada, 1932. *Address:* 259 Clemow Avenue, Ottawa, Ont., Canada. *T.:* 3-5504. *Clubs:* Rideau, Country, Royal Ottawa Golf (Ottawa); Union (Victoria); Vancouver (Vancouver). [*Died* 26 *April* 1955.

DUFF-GORDON, Sir Henry William, 6th Bt., *cr.* 1813; D.L.; *b.* 12 Jan. 1866; 2nd *s.* of Cosmo Lewis Duff-Gordon, 2nd *s.* of 2nd Bt., and Anna, *y. d.* of Sir Edmund Antrobus, Bt.; *S.* brother, 1931; *m.* 1891, Maud Emily (*d.* 1951), *d.* of late Hugh Hammersley; one *s.* one *d.* (and one *s.* killed in war, 1916). *Educ.:* Radley. *Heir:* *s.* Douglas Frederick [late Scots Guards, *b.* 12 Sept. 1892; *m.* 1932, Gladys Rosemary (*d.* 1933), *e. d.* of late Col. Vivian Henry, and of Mrs. R. Akroyd, Sutton Court, Ledbury; one *s.* (*b.* 17 Oct. 1933)]. *Address:* Harpton Court, Walton, Radnorshire. *T.A.:* Harpton Court, New Radnor. *T.:* New Radnor 6. *Clubs:* Royal Automobile; Hereford County (Hereford). [*Died* 9 *Jan.* 1953.

DUFFUS, Col. Francis Ferguson, C.M.G. 1917; *b.* 8 Oct. 1870; *m.* 1906, Agnes Evans Whelen (*d.* 1933); one *s.* *Educ.:* Merchiston Castle School, Edinburgh; R. Military College, Canada. Entered Cheshire Regt. 1892; Capt. A.S.C. 1900; Major, 1908; Lt.-Col. 1915; Col. 1919; Embarkation Staff Officer, S. Africa, 1899-1900; Assist. Director of Supplies, 1915; Deputy Director Supplies, 1916; served S. Africa, 1899-1902 (Queen's medal 3 clasps, King's medal 2 clasps); European War, 1914-18 (despatches thrice, C.M.G.); retired pay, 1920. *Address:* Headley, Bordon, Hants. *T.:* Headley Down 3108. *Club:* Army and Navy. [*Died* 1 *Dec.* 1953.

DUFFY, Hon. Mr. Justice; George Gavan Duffy; President, High Court of Ireland, since 1946; Judge since 1936; *s.* of late Sir Charles Gavan Duffy, K.C.M.G.; *b.* 21 Oct. 1882; *m.* 1908, Margaret, *d.* of late A. M. Sullivan, M.P. *Educ.:* France; Stonyhurst. M.P. (S. Fein) S. Dublin, Dec. 1918-23. Irish Envoy Extraordinary to Paris, 1919; Rome, 1920; Member of Irish Peace Delegation to London, 1921; Minister of Foreign Affairs in Irish Government, 1922. *Address:* 81 Bushy Park Road, Dublin.
[*Died* 10 *June* 1951.

DUFY, Raoul; Commander of the Legion of Honour; painter-etcher and engraver; *b.* 3 June 1877; *m.* 1911, Emilienne Bresson. *Educ.:* Le Havre; Collège St. Joseph. Commercial apprenticeship, 1893 (import of Brazilian coffee); military service, 1890-1900; École des Beaux Arts, Paris, 1900-04; designing for fabrics, 1911-23. *Publications:* book illustrations. (Details of 53 of his works are included in "Raoul Dufy", by Pierre Courthion, Geneva, 1951.) *Recreation:* painting. *Address:* 5 Impasse de Guelma, Montmartre, Paris 18e, France.
[*Died* 23 *March* 1953.

DUGAN OF VICTORIA, and of Lurgan in the Co. of Armagh, 1st Baron, *cr.* 1949; **Winston Dugan;** Maj.-Gen.; G.C.M.G., *cr.* 1944 (K.C.M.G., *cr.* 1934; C.M.G. 1918); C.B. 1929; D.S.O. 1915; Worcestershire Regt.; *b.* 8 May 1877; *s.* of late C. Winston Dugan, M.A., of Oxmantown, Birr, Ireland; *m.* 1912, Ruby Lilian, D.G.St.J., *d.* of late Charles Abbott of Abbott Abbey, County Cork, and late Mrs. Applewhaite-Abbott. *Educ.:* Lurgan College, Wimbledon. 2nd Lieut. Lincolns. Regiment, 1900; Adjutant, 1901-1904; Captain Worcesters. Regt. 1904; Adjutant, 1907-9; Garrison Adjutant, Irish Command, 1910-14; D.A.A. and Q.M.G. East Anglian Div., 1914; Assist. Provost Marshal, 1914; Commanded 2nd Royal Irish Regt., France, 1915-16; (wounded); Assist. Inspector-General Training, B.E.F., 1918; served South Africa, 1899-1902 (Queen's medal 3 clasps, King's medal 2 clasps); European War, 1914-18 (D.S.O., C.M.G., despatches six times, Bt. Lt.-Col.); Bde. Comdr. (Temp. Brig.-General), 1916-18; Commander 10th Infantry Brigade, 1919-23; A.A.G. Southern Command, 1926-30; A.D.C.

to the King, 1928-30; Commander 56th (1st London) Division T.A., 1931-34; retired pay, 1934; Governor of South Australia, 1934-39; Governor of Victoria, Australia, 1939-49. *Heir:* none. *Club:* United Service. [*Died* 17 *Aug.* 1951 (*ext.*).

DUGDALE, Thomas Cantrell, R.A. 1943 (A.R.A. 1936); R.P.; Member Internat. Soc.; *b.* Blackburn, 2 June 1880; 3rd *s.* of late Alfred Dugdale, Manchester; *m.* 1916, Amy Katherine Browning, R.P., R.O.I. *Educ.:* Manchester Grammar School. Served in Yeomanry, in Egypt, Dardanelles, Balkans, Palestine, Syria, 1914-19 (1915 Star, despatches); Home Guard from L.D.V. 1st Day 1940; studied Art at Manchester, South Kensington, Paris; British Institute Painting Scholarship; exhibited Royal Academy; New English Art Club; Salon; silver medal Salon des Artistes français, 1921; Carnegie Institute, Pittsburgh, and most galleries at home and abroad; pictures in public collections, Cape Town; Manchester; Rochdale; Imperial War Museum; Leicester; Liverpool; Thorburn-Ross Bequest for Scotland; Tate Gallery; Bournemouth; Glasgow; New Zealand; one-man-show, Leicester Galleries, 1919. *Recreation:* not painting. *Address:* Benhall, Saxmundham; 58 Glebe Place, S.W.3. *T.:* Saxmundham 224, Flaxman 9969. *Clubs:* Chelsea Arts, Arts, Garrick. [*Died* 13 *Nov.* 1952.

DUGDALE, Major William Marshall, C.B. 1946; D.S.O. 1918; D.L., J.P. Montgomeryshire; *b.* 1881; *s.* of late John Marshall Dugdale, Llwyn, Mont.; *m.* 1912, Ruth Edith, 2nd *d.* of late Rt. Hon. Sir John Eldon Bankes, P.C., G.C.B.; one *s.* four *d.* Served South Africa, 1901-2 (Queen's medal with five clasps); European War, 1914-18 (despatches, D.S.O.); High Sheriff of Montgomeryshire, 1927; Chairman Territorial Army Assoc. of the County of Montgomery. *Address:* Glanyrafon Hall, Llanyblodwel, Oswestry, Salop. [*Died* 13 *Nov.* 1952.

DUGGAN, Rear-Adm. Eyre Sturdy, C.B. 1947; O.B.E. 1919; R.N. retd.; *b.* 28 Sept. 1891; *s.* of late George Duggan, 5 College St., Dublin and Ferney, Greystones, Co. Wicklow; *m.* 1925, Doris Hebe, *d.* of late Minton Goode, 6 Netherhall Gardens, N.W.3; no *c. Educ.:* High School, Dublin. Entered Accountant Branch, R.N., 1909; served European War, 1914-18; present at Battle of Jutland in H.M.S. Marlborough. Paymaster Comdr., 1930; Paymaster Capt. and Capt. (S), 1939-44; Actg. Rear-Adm. (S), 1945-47; retired with rank of Rear-Admiral (S), 1947; served at various periods as Squadron, Fleet and Air Command Accountant and Supply Officer, also as Nore Command Supply Officer; served War of 1939-45; Administrative Officer, Treasury, 1947-50. *Address:* Ronder, Heath Road, Oxshott, Surrey. *T.:* Oxshott 187. *Club:* United Service. [*Died* 5 *Dec.* 1956.

DUGGAN, Col. Sir Jamshedji, K.B.E., *cr.* 1945 (O.B.E. 1929); Kt., *cr.* 1935; C.I.E. 1933; D.O. (Oxon), F.C.P.S., L.M. and S.; I.A.M.C.; O.C. Indian Military Hospital, Cumballa Hill, Bombay; J.P.; Superintendent, Tata Memorial Hospital for Cancer, Bombay; Consulting Ophthalmic Surgeon, Sir C. J. Ophthalmic Hospital and Ex-Professor of Ophthalmology, Grant Medical College, and ex-Superintendent, Sir C. J. Ophthalmic Hospital, Bombay; *b.* 8 April 1884; *s.* of Nusserwanji and Jarbai Duggan; *m.* 1914; two *s. Educ.:* Bombay; Oxford; London; Vienna. Was Tutor in Ophthalmology, Grant Medical College, Consulting Ophthalmic Surgeon to War Hospitals and Ophthalmic Surgeon Parsi General Hospital, Bombay; has been private Ophthalmic Practitioner; C.O. Indian Military Hosp., Bombay, 1940-45. Fellow of the Bombay University and Honorary Presidency Magistrate, Bombay; Sheriff of Bombay, 1942. Chairman of Red Cross Society, and St. John Ambulance Association and Commissioner of St. John Brigade no. 3, Bombay; during War of 1939-1945 acted as chairman of Bombay Red Cross and Amenities for Troops Fund and of Bombay Provincial Joint War Committee of Indian Red Cross and St. John War Organisation. Invented an apparatus known as Duggan's Visual Acuity Test for Malingerers. *Publications:* many papers in medical journals. *Address:* Lawnside, Harkness Road, Malabar Hill, Bombay. *T.:* 40715 (Residence), 20373 (Consulting Rooms). *Clubs:* Willingdon Sports, Rotary, Western India Turf (Bombay). [*Died* 15 *Jan.* 1957.

DUGMORE, Arthur Radclyffe; *b.* Wales, 25 Dec. 1870; 2nd *s.* of Capt. F. S. Dugmore and Hon. Evelyn, *d.* of 2nd Baron Brougham and Vaux: *m.* 1901, Henrietta Louise Watkins, *d.* of John B. and Henrietta Pattison of South Orange, New Jersey, U.S.A.; one *s.* one *d. Educ.:* Elizabeth College, Guernsey; Turrells', Smyrna. Studied painting Naples and Rome, 1887-88; went to America, 1889, studied ornithology under W. E. D. Scott; took up photography in 1898 as method for illustrating wild life; travelled extensively through Southern Europe, Asia Minor, Central America, United States, Canada, and British East Africa; life member of New York Zoological Society and American Museum of Natural History; gave 16 exhibitions of his landscape, marine, wild animal and bird paintings, and dry point etchings, in London and many American cities, 1914-1947; did war correspondence and photography in Belgium in Aug. and Sept. 1914; taken prisoner by Germans in Aug., released later; wounded at Alost; enlisted in Inns of Court O.T.C., Dec. 1914; 1st Lieut. 10th K.O.Y.L.I. March 1915; served in France, 1916; gassed in battle of Somme, July 1916; temp. Captain, May 1917; Major, 1917; to U.S. America on special duty, lecturing, June 1917; lectured U.S. and Gt. Britain; enlisted in Home Guard, 1941. *Publications:* Bird Homes, Nesting Habits of Land Birds of Eastern United States, 1900; Nature and the Camera, 1902; Camera Adventures in the African Wilds, 1910; Wild Life and the Camera, 1912; The Romance of the Newfoundland Caribou, 1913; The Romance of the Beaver, 1914; Adventures in Beaver Stream Camp, 1918; When the Somme Ran Red, 1918; Two Boys in Beaver Land, 1920; The Vast Sudan, 1924; The Wonderland of Big Game, 1926; African Jungle Life, 1928; Corsica the Beautiful, 1928; Autobiography of a Wanderer; In the Heart of the Northern Forests, 1930; The Workers in the Wilds, 1934; Through the Sudan, 1938. Produced Film, The Wonderland of Big Game, in connection with W. P. Harries, 1923, and the Vast Sudan Film, 1924, and lectured with it at Polytechnic Hall, Regent Street. *Recreations:* fishing, painting, photography, natural history, boating, camping. *Address:* c/o Lloyds Bank Ltd., Christchurch, Hants; 8 Western Drive, Gervis Rd., Bournemouth. *Clubs:* Shikar; Players' (New York). [*Died* 21 *Mar.* 1955.

DUKES, Ashley; author and dramatist; *b.* 29 May 1885; *s.* of late Rev. E. J. Dukes and Edith Mary Dukes; *m.* 1918, M. Rambert, C.B.E.; two *d. Educ.:* Silcoates School; Universities of Manchester and Munich. Dramatic Critic of various journals, 1909-14 and 1919-25; author and translator of many plays; on active service, 1914-18, with the Machine Gun Corps; at his theatre, the Mercury, has presented Murder in the Cathedral, 1935-36; The Ascent of F.6, 1937, etc. Adviser for cultural affairs in British zone in Germany, 1945-49. *Publications:* Modern Dramatists, 1911; The Youngest Drama, 1923; The Man with a Load of Mischief, 1924-25; The Song of Drums (a heroic comedy), and Drama (essays), 1926; One More River (play), 1927; The World to Play With (essays), and The Fountain-Head (play), 1928; Jew Süss (play), 1929; The Dumb Wife of Cheapside (a comedy after Rabelais), 1929; Matchmaker's Arms (play), 1930; Five Plays of Other Times, 1931; Elizabeth of England (from the German), 1932; The Mask of Virtue, 1935; House of Assignation, 1937; Mandragola (from Machiavelli), 1939; The Scene is Changed, 1942; Parisienne (from Becque), 1943; Celestina, 1950; A Glass of Water (from the French), 1951; The Trap (from the German), 1952; Return to Danes Hill, 1957; The Broken Jug, 1958. *Recreation:* sleep. *Address:* 19 Campden Hill Gardens, W.8. *T.:* Park 5946. *Clubs:* Garrick, Dramatists'. [*Died* 4 *May* 1959.

DULAC, Edmund; Artist; *b.* Toulouse, 22 Oct. 1882; naturalised 1912. *Educ.:* Toulouse University (Litt.Ph.B.); read Law unwillingly; Toulouse Art School (three years); Académie Julian, Paris (three weeks). Exhibited portraits, Paris Salon, 1904-5; private shows in London at the Leicester Galleries yearly, 1907-18; portraits, caricatures, costumes and stage settings; decorations (Empress of Britain's smoking room); modelled King's Poetry Prize medal; designed Coronation Stamp (1937); King's cameo portrait of current issues, complete designs all values above 6d.; Free French colonial stamps and banknotes; first French Metropolitan "Marianne of London"; Olympic Games (1/-); Festival of Britain (2½d). *Publications:* Illustrated books: The Arabian Nights, 1907; The Tempest, 1908; The Rubaiyat of Omar Khayyam, 1909; The Sleeping Beauty and other tales, 1910; Edgar A. Poe's Bells and other poems, 1911; Hans Andersen's Snow Queen and other tales, 1912; Princess Badoura, 1913; Sindbad the Sailor, 1914; Edmund Dulac's Book for the French Red Cross, 1915; Edmund Dulac's Fairy Book, 1916; Tanglewood Tales, 1918; weekly cartoons in the Outlook, 1919; The Kingdom of the Pearl, 1920; Treasure Island, 1927; The Fairy Garland, 1928; Gods and Mortals in Love, 1936; The Golden Cockerel, 1950; The Marriage of Cupid and Psyche, 1951; contributor American Weekly, New York. *Recreations:* music (outside North-West Europe), making bamboo flutes, furniture, etc., Art psychology. *Address:* 64 Marlborough Place, N.W.8. *T.:* Maida Vale 4433. [*Died* 25 *May* 1953.

DULANTY, John Whelan, C.B. 1920; C.B.E. 1918; Hon. LL.D., Leeds; Hon. LL.D. (N.U.I.), Dublin; a Director of the National Bank Ltd. since 1950; *m.* Ann (*d.* 1952), *yr. d.* of George Hutton; two *s.* one *d.* *Educ.:* St. Mary's, Failsworth; University of Manchester. Secretary, Faculty of Technology, University of Manchester, 1908; Educational Adviser to Indian Students in Northern Universities of England, 1910; Honorary Director, under John Redmond, of the United Irish League of Great Britain; Examiner (First Division) in Board of Education, London, 1913; Principal Asst. Secretary, Ministry of Munitions, London, 1917; Asst. Secretary, Treasury, Whitehall, 1920; left Civil Service to become Deputy Chairman and Managing Director of Peter Jones, Ltd., 1921; Commissioner for Trade in Britain, at request of Irish Government, 1926; Irish Delegate to London Naval Conf., 1936; Ambassador for the Republic of Ireland in London July-Sept. 1950 (High Commissioner, 1930-50); retired, 1950. *Address:* 50 Pattison Road, Hampstead, N.W.2. *T.:* Hampstead 8998. *Clubs:* Athenæum, Travellers', Savage; National University of Ireland (Dublin). [*Died* 11 *Feb.* 1955.

DULLES, John Foster; Secretary of State, United States, Jan. 1953-Apr. 1959; Special Consultant to the President, 23rd Apr.-24th May 1959; *b.* Washington, D.C., U.S.A., 25 February 1888; *s.* of Allen Macy Dulles and Edith Foster; *m.* 1912, Janet Pomeroy Avery; two *s.* one *d.* *Educ.:* Princeton, B.A. 1908; Sorbonne, Paris. George Washington University, 1911; LL.D., Tufts, 1939, Princeton, 1946, Wagner, Northwestern, 1947, Union College, 1948, University of Pennsylvania, 1949, Amherst, Seoul (Korea), 1950, Arizona, 1951, St. Lawrence (Canton, N.Y.), Johns Hopkins, Fordham, Harvard, Lafayette, St. Joseph's Coll., 1952, Columbia, Georgetown, 1954, Univ. of South Carolina, Univ. of Indiana, 1955, Iowa, 1956. Began practice law, N.Y. City, 1911, with Sullivan & Cromwell. Secretary at Hague Peace Conference, 1907; Member 2nd Pan-American Scientific Congress: Special Agent Department of State in Central America, 1917; Captain and Major, United States Army, 1917-1918; Assistant to Chairman War Trade Board, 1918; Counsel to American Commission to Negotiate Peace, 1918-19; Member Reparations Commission and Supreme Economic Council, 1919; Legal Adviser Polish plan of financial stabilisation, 1927; American representative to Berlin debt conferences, 1933; Member U.S. Delegation to San Francisco Conference on World Organisation, 1945; U.S. deleg. to U.N. General Assembly, 1946, 1947, 1948, 1950; Actg. Chm. of U.S. Deleg., U.N. General Assembly, Paris, 1948; Adviser to Sec. of State at Council of Foreign Ministers, London 1945, Moscow 1947, London 1947, Paris 1949; United States Senator from N.Y., 1949; consultant to Sec. of State, 1950; special representative of President, with rank of Ambassador, 1950-51, negotiated and signed for U.S. Japanese Peace Treaty and Australian, N.Z., Philippine and Japanese Security Treaties. Former Chairman, Board of Trustees, Rockefeller Foundation, Carnegie Endowment for International Peace, General Education Boards; ex-mem. N.Y. State Banking Board; ex-trustee, Union Theological Seminary, New York Public Library; ex-mem. Association of Bar of City of New York. Presbyterian. Writer and speaker on international affairs. *Publications:* War, Peace and Change, 1939; War or Peace, 1950. *Address:* Department of State, Washington 25, D.C. *Clubs:* Cold Spring Harbor Beach, University, Piping Rock, Down Town Association, Century (New York); Metropolitan, Alibi, Capital Hill, Alfalfa, 1925 F Street (Washington). [*Died* 24 *May* 1959.

DULVERTON, 1st Baron, *cr.* 1929, of Batsford; **Gilbert Alan Hamilton Wills,** Bt., *cr.* 1897; O.B.E. 1919; M.A. Oxon; J.P. Somerset and Gloucestershire; President of the Imperial Tobacco Co. (of Great Britain and Ireland), Ltd.; Lt.-Col., late Royal North Devon Hussars; *b.* 28 Mar. 1880; *s.* of Sir Frederick Wills, 1st Bt., and Anne, *e. d.* of late Rev. James Hamilton; *S.* father, 1909; *m.* 1914, Victoria May (O.B.E. 1951), 3rd *d.* of late Rear-Adm. Sir E. Chichester, 9th Bt.; three *s.* *Educ.:* privately; Magdalen College, Oxford. Extra A.D.C. to Lord-Lieut. of Ireland, 1908-12; M.P. (U.) Taunton, 1912-18; Weston-super-Mare, 1918-22; served European War, Gallipoli, 1915; France, 1917-18 (despatches). Owns about 5000 acres. *Heir:* *s.* Hon. Frederick Anthony Hamilton Wills, Major Lovat Scouts [*b.* 19 Dec. 1915; *m.* 1939, Judith Betty, *e. d.* of Hon. Ian Leslie Melville, T.D.; two *s.* two *d.*] *Address:* Batsford Park, Moreton-in-Marsh, Glos.; 26 Wilton Crescent, S.W.1. *Clubs:* Carlton, Boodle's. [*Died* 1 *Dec.* 1956.

DUNBABIN, Thomas James, D.S.O. 1942; Reader in Classical Archæology, University of Oxford, since 1945. Fellow of All Souls College since 1937, and Domestic Bursar since 1950; *b.* 1911; *o. s.* of Thomas Dunbabin, M.A.; *m.* 1937, Adelaide Doreen Delacour, *d.* of late Bishop P. F. D. de Labilliere; one *s.* one *d.* *Educ.:* Sydney Church of England Grammar School; Corpus Christi College, Oxford; Derby Scholar, 1933. Assistant Director, British School of Archæology at Athens, 1936-45; served War of 1939-45, England, Middle East and Mediterranean, 1940-45 (Lieut.-Col., Intelligence Corps). Leverhulme Research Fellow, 1952.

Order of the Phoenix, 1947. *Publications:* ed. Perachora, I, by H. Payne and others, 1940; The Western Greeks, 1948; articles in learned journals. *Recreation:* travel. *Address:* All Souls College, and 44 Chalfont Road, Oxford. [*Died* 31 *March* 1955.

DUNBAR, Sir Alexander, Kt., *cr.* 1943; Chairman Coupe Bros. (Sheffield) Ltd.; Director of numerous companies; *b.* Glasgow, 21 Sept. 1888; *s.* of Alex. Dunbar and Anne Gilmour; *m.* 1914, Edith, 2nd *d.* of Walter Soulby, Barrow-in-Furness; two *d.* *Educ.:* Barrow Grammar School. Joined Vickers, Ltd., 1904, and served in all parts of Vickers Group; Director English Steel Corporation, 1933; Director Vickers-Armstrongs, 1937; Director in Charge of Vickers-Armstrongs' Aviation Interests, 1938 - 42; Controller General Ministry of Aircraft Production, 1942-43. *Recreations:* golf and fishing. *Address:* Ran Farm, Ranmoor Crescent, Sheffield 10. *Clubs:* Junior Carlton; Sheffield (Sheffield). [*Died* 14 *Oct.* 1955.

DUNBAR, Sir Charles D. H.; *see* Hope-Dunbar.

DUNBAR, Evelyn Mary, A.R.C.A.; Artist; visitor at Ruskin School of Drawing, Oxford, 1950; *d.* of late Wm. Dunbar, Morayshire, and Florence Murgatroyd, Yorkshire; *m.* 1942, Roger Folley, agricultural economist, Oxford. *Educ.:* Rochester School of Art, Royal Drawing Society, London, and Royal College of Art, London, 1929-33. Painted murals in Brockley School, S.E., 1933-36; Official War Artist, 1940-45; Society of Mural Painters; Member New English Art Club, 1945-48; Tate Gallery; Flight, Winter Garden, The Bail Bull; also represented in Imperial War Museum and other public collections. *Publications:* Gardener's Choice (with Cyril Mahoney), 1937; Book of Farm-craft (with Michael Greenhill), 1942. *Address:* Elms, Hinxhill, nr. Ashford, Kent. *T.:* Willesborough 435. [*Died* 12 *May* 1960.

DUNBAR, Sir James George Hawker Rowland, 10th Bt. of Mochrum, *cr.* 1694; *b.* 6 Sept. 1862; *s.* of late George Van Reede Dunbar, *b.* of 7th Bt.; *S. cousin,* 1931; unmarried. *Heir: kinsman* Richard Sutherland Dunbar (*see under* Sir Richard Sutherland Dunbar, 11th Bt.). *Address:* Mochrum Park, Kirkcowan, Wigtownshire; Homelands, 17 Ivydale Rd., Bognor Regis, Sussex. [*Died* 23 *Jan.* 1953.

DUNBAR, Major John Telfer, C.B. 1941; D.L. Midlothian; Chairman City of Edinburgh Territorial Army and Air Force Association. Served European War, 1914-1918, in Italy, 1917-18 (despatches, two medals); Major (retd.) R.A.S.C. (T.A.). *Address:* St. Oswalds, Oswald Road, Edinburgh. [*Died* 31 *May* 1957.

DUNBAR, Sir Richard Sutherland, 11th Bt. of Mochrum, *cr.* 1694; *b.* 7 June 1873; *s.* of Richard Taylor Dunbar (*d.* 1940) and 1st wife, Ellen (*d.* 1910), *d.* of Joseph Maas; *S.* kinsman, 23 Jan. 1953; *m.* 1911, Daisy, *d.* of late John Kinman, Anerley, London, S.E.; two *d.* *Heir: kinsman* Adrian Ivor Dunbar, *b.* 1893. *Address:* (seat) Mochrum Park, Kirkowan, Wigtownshire. [*Died* 25 *Jan.* 1953.

DUNCAN, Rt. Hon. Sir Andrew Rae, P.C. 1940; G.B.E., *cr.* 1938; Kt., *cr.* 1921; M.A., LL.B. Glasgow University; Hon. LL.D. Dalhousie (Canada) and Glasgow; *b.* 1884; *m.* 1916, Annie, *d.* of late Andrew Jordan; one *s.* (and one killed in action). Barrister; Chairman of Executive Committee of British Iron & Steel Federation, 1935-40 and from 1945; Director: Imperial Chemical Industries, Ltd.; Royal Exchange Assurance; North British Locomotive Co. Ltd.; Dunlop Rubber Co. Ltd.: a Bencher of Gray's Inn. M.P. (Nat.), City of London, 1940-50; President of Board of Trade, 1940 and 1941; Minister of Supply, 1940-41 and 1942-45; Hon. M.I.E.E.; Hon. Mem. Am. Iron and Steel Institute; Hon. Fellow Society of Engineers; Chairman of Central Electricity Board, 1927-35 (Member, 1936-40); Director of Bank of England, 1929-40; High Sheriff, County of London, 1939-40; one of H.M. Lieutenants for City of London; Vice-President, Shipbuilding Employers' Federation, 1920-27; Coal Controller, 1919-20; Chairman of Advisory Committee of Coal Mines Department, 1920-29; Chairman of Royal Commissions to inquire into Coal Industry in Nova Scotia, 1925 and 1932; Chairman of Royal Commission to inquire into grievances of Eastern Maritime Provinces of Canada, 1926; Chairman of Sea-Fish Commission for the U.K., 1933-35. *Address:* Dunure, Foxgrove Rd., Beckenham, Kent. *T.:* Beckenham 2316. *Club:* Reform. [*Died* 30 *March* 1952.

DUNCAN, Maj.-Gen. Francis John, C.B. 1919; C.M.G. 1915; D.S.O. 1900; late the Royal Scots; *m.* 1905, Lili, *d.* of late Moritz Linder of Vienna; two *s.* two *d.* *Educ.:* Shrewsbury, Switzerland, Germany. Joined the Royal Scots, 1889; Captain, 1896; Bt. Major, 1902; served S. Africa, in commmand of Mounted Infantry, 1900-2 (despatches twice, Bt. Major, Queen's medal two clasps, King's medal two clasps); European War; commanded the Royal Scots, 165th Infantry Brigade, 60th Infantry Brigade, General Staff, and later commanded 61st Division (once wounded, despatches eight times, C.B., C.M.G., Bt.-Col., Officier Légion d'Honneur, Croix de Guerre avec Palme, Officer Order of Crown of Roumania); Military Attaché Bucharest, 1919-24; retired pay, 1924. Under-Secretary, Secretary to Chairman, and in charge Staff, Imperial Chemical Industries; Organizing Secretary of Empire Society (British National Union); A.R.P. City of London, 1939-45; Freedom of City of London. *Club:* United Service. [*Died* 14 *Jan.* 1960.

DUNCAN, James Lindsay; Sheriff-Substitute of the Lothians and Peebles at Edinburgh since 1951; *b.* 20 November 1905; *s.* of late George Duncan, C.B.E.; *m.* 1938, Irene Winter, Duns; two *s.* one *d.* *Educ.:* Aberdeen Grammar School; Aberdeen University. M.A. (Aberd.) 1927; LL.B. (Aberdeen) 1929; Ph.D. (Edinburgh) 1931; called to Scottish Bar, 1931; Sheriff-Substitute of Ross, Cromarty, and Sutherland at Stornoway, 1940-42, of Ayrshire at Kilmarnock, 1942-51. *Publications:* Editor of Third Edition, 1939, of Law of Reparation in Scotland, by late A. T. Glegg, Advocate, Fourth Edition, 1955. *Recreations:* walking and climbing. *Address:* 6 Corrennie Drive, Edinburgh 10. [*Died* 25 *Dec.* 1954.

DUNCAN, Sir Thomas Andrew, Kt., *cr.* 1951; J.P.; farmer; *b.* Wanganui, 6 June 1873; *s.* of John Duncan; *m.* 1896, Jeannie, *d.* of John McKelvie; four *s.* three *d.* Formerly: Chairman of the Meat Board; Member of Rangitikei City Council. *Address:* Otairi, Hunterville, New Zealand. [*Died* 5 *March* 1960.

DUNCAN, Prof. William Jolly, C.B.E. 1953; F.R.S. 1947, D.Sc., M.I.Mech.E., Hon. F.R.Ae.S.; Mechan Professor of Aeronautics and Fluid Mechanics in the University of Glasgow since 1950; *b.* 26 April 1894; *s.* of late Robert Duncan, M.P., senior partner of Ross & Duncan, Engineers, Glasgow, and Mary, *d.* of William Jolly, H.M.I.; *m.* 1936, Enid Meyler, *d.* of G. S. Baker, O.B.E., D.Sc.; four *d.* *Educ.:* Allan Glen's School, Glasgow; Dulwich Coll.; University Coll., London. War service, 1915-19, R.A.S.C. France, Flanders and in Aeronautical Inspection Dept. Member firm Ross & Duncan, Marine Engineers, 1919-26; scientific staff Aerodynamics Dept., National Physical Laboratory, 1926-34; first Head of Dept. of Aeronautics, Univ. Coll., Hull, 1934; Wakefield Professor of Aeronautics, 1938; war service, 1939-45, in Royal Aircraft Establishment included work on armaments and aerodynamics and headship of Air Defence Research Dept., Exeter; Chief Scientist under Ministry of Aircraft Production at Luftfahrtforschungsanstalt Hermann Göring, Völkenrode, Brunswick, 1945; Professor of Aerodynamics, The College of Aeronautics, Cranfield, 1945. Assessor at Comet Accident Inquiries, 1954. Fellow of University College, London. Chairman, Aeronautical Research Council. *Publications:* The Principles of the Control and Stability of Aircraft, 1952; Physical Similarity and Dimensional Analysis, 1953. (Joint) Elementary Matrices, 1938; (joint) An Elementary Treatise on the Mechanics of Fluids, 1960. Monographs and Reports and Memoranda of Aeronautical Research Council; scientific papers in Proc. Roy. Soc., Phil. Mag., etc. *Address:* The University, Glasgow. *Clubs:* Athenæum; Royal Scottish Automobile (Glasgow). [*Died* 9 *Dec.* 1960.

DUNCAN-JONES, Very Rev. Arthur Stuart, B.D.; Dean of Chichester since 1929; *b.* Oldham, 25 April 1879; *s.* of Rev. D. L. D. Jones; *m.* 1907, Caroline, *d.* of Rev. E. S. Roberts, Master of Gonville and Caius College, Cambridge; six *s.* two *d.* *Educ.:* Pocklington; Caius College, Cambridge (Fellow and Dean). Rector of Blofield, 1912; Rector of Louth, Lincs, 1915; Vicar of S. Mary's, Primrose Hill, 1916; S. Paul's, Knightsbridge, 1928-29; Assistant Editor of the Guardian, 1923; Hon. Secretary Alcuin Club, 1916-23; Vice-Pres., 1923; Chm. 1935; Hulsean Lecturer, 1916; Editor S. Paul's Review, 1929; Chm.,Church Music Soc.,1946, Pres., 1952; Chm. Central Council of Anglo-Polish Socs.; Vice-Chm. British League for European Freedom. Warburton Lecturer, Lincoln's Inn, 1947. *Publications:* Ordered Liberty, 1917; Church Music, 1920; Archbishop Laud, 1927; A Good Friday Service, 1928; Story of Chichester Cathedral, 1933; The Struggle for Religious Freedom in Germany, 1938; From U-Boat to Concentration Camp (with Martin Niemöller), 1938; The Soul of Czechoslovakia, 1941; What is Peace, 1952; also contributor to The Necessity of Art, 1924; Liturgy and Worship, 1932; Northern Catholicism, 1933; Anglican Liturgies, 1939; Walter Howard Frere, 1940; contributed to People Matter, 1945; Christian Witness in the Post-War World, 1946; The Chichester Customary, 1948. *Recreation:* gardening. *Address:* The Deanery, Chichester. *T.:* Chichester 2481. *Club:* Travellers'. [*Died* 19 *Jan.* 1955.

DUNDAS OF DUNDAS, Adam Duncan; Major, R.A.; *b.* 28 July 1903; *e. s.* of late Admiral Sir Charles Dundas of Dundas, K.C.M.G., R.N. (28th Chief of Dundas); *m.* 1928, Effie Isobel, *o. d.* of T. G. Nind; three *d.* *Educ.:* Tonbridge School. *S.* his father as 29th Chief of Dundas, 1924; Served War of 1939-45, commanded H.A.A. Battery, 1939-45; served overseas, 1941-42-1943. Staff appointment, 1945-47. *Recreations:* cricket, amateur film productions. *Address:* St. Mawes, Cornwall. *Club:* New (Edinburgh). [*Died* 7 *May* 1951.

DUNDAS, Hon. Sir Charles Cecil Farquharson, K.C.M.G., *cr.* 1938 (C.M.G. 1934); O.B.E. 1923; 5th *s.* of 6th Viscount Melville; *b.* 6 June 1884; *m.* 1920, Anne, *y. d.* of late Rev. S. Cox Hay, D.D., New York. *Educ.:* Continent. Assistant District Commissioner British East Africa Protectorate, 1908-14; District Commissioner, Kenya Colony, 1914; served as Political Officer in G.E.A. in World War; Senior Commissioner, Tanganyika Territory, 1920; Assistant Chief Secretary, 1924; Secretary for Native Affairs, 1926, and Acting Chief Secretary, Feb.-Sept. 1926; Colonial Secretary, Bahamas, 1929-34; acting Governor, Bahamas, various times since 1929; Chief Secretary, Northern Rhodesia, 1934-37; Governor and C.-in-C. of the Bahamas, 1937-1940; Governor and Commander-in-Chief of Uganda Protectorate, 1940-44; retired, 1945. K.St.J. *Publications:* Kilimanjaro and its People, 1924; African Crossroads, 1955. *Address:* Grasmere, Westmorland. [*Died* 10 *Feb.* 1956.

DUNDAS, Vice-Admiral John George Lawrence, C.B. 1945; C.B.E. 1942; R.N.; *b.* 3 Nov. 1893; *s.* of late Hon. Thomas Dundas and Lady Cordeaux; *m.* 1928, Ruth Coleman; one *s.* four *d.* *Educ.:* Dartmouth Naval College. Assistant Chief of Naval Staff, 1944-45; Vice-Adm. retired list, 1948. Legion of Honour and Croix de Guerre; American Legion of Merit, Officer. *Address:* c/o Lloyds Bank Ltd., 16 St. James's Street, S.W.1. *Club:* United Service. [*Died* 26 *March* 1952.

DUNDAS, Sir Philip, 4th Bt., *cr.* 1898; late Lieut. Black Watch; *b.* 8 Nov. 1899; *s.* of 3rd Bt. and Lady Beatrix Douglas-Home, 2nd *d.* of 12th Earl of Home; *S.* father, 1930; *m.* 1936, Jean Marian, 3rd *d.* of James A. Hood, Midfield, Lasswade, Midlothian; one *s.* three *d.* Member of Royal Company of Archers (King's Bodyguard for Scotland). *Heir:* *s.* Henry Mathew, *b.* 17 May 1937. *Address:* Fairnington, Craigs, Kelso, Roxburghshire. *Club:* New (Edinburgh). [*Died* 23 *Feb.* 1952.

DUNDAS, Robert Hamilton; Emeritus Student of Christ Church, Oxford (1910-57); *b.* 30 Aug. 1884; *s.* of George Smythe Dundas, Sheriff-Substitute of Berwickshire, and Georgina Lockhart, *d.* of Prof. George Lockhart Ross, Edinburgh. *Educ.:* Summer Fields, Oxford; Eton; New College, Oxford. King's Scholar, Eton, 1897-1903; New Coll. Oxford (Schol.) 1903-7; First Classes Hon. Mods., 1905; Lit. Hum., 1907; Lecturer, Liverpool Univ., 1908-9; Lecturer in Greek History, Christ Church, 1909; Censor, 1914, 1919-24, and 1944-45; Examiner Lit.Hum., 1928-29. Joined Black Watch (3rd attd. 2nd Bn.) Jan. 1915; France, 1915; Mesopotamia, 1916; A.H.Q. (Dep. Chief Censor's Office) Delhi, Simla, Rangoon, 1916-19; Captain (wounded, despatches twice). *Recreations:* travel, music. *Address:* Christ Church, Oxford. *T.:* Oxford 44361; Laurel Hill, Stirling. *T.:* Stirling 32. *Clubs:* Savile; New (Edinburgh). [*Died* 1 *Oct.* 1960.

DUNDON, John, M.B., B.Ch.; F.R.C.S. Eng. and F.R.C.S.I.; Professor of Surgery, University College, Cork; Surgeon, Mercy Hospital, Cork; Surgeon, North City and County Cork Infirmary; Member of Free State Medical Council; *y. s.* of Edmond Dundon, of Araglen Mills, Co. Cork; *m.* 1910, May, *y. d.* of John M'Donnell, Chorlemont Terrace, Cork. *Educ.:* Queen's College, Cork. *Publication:* The Diagnosis of Injuries around the Shoulder-Joint. *Recreations:* golf, motoring. *Address:* 16 St. Patrick's Place, Cork. *T.A.:* Dundon, Cork. *T.:* 669. *Clubs:* County, Muskerry Golf (Cork). [*Died* 24 *Feb.* 1952.

DUNDONALD, 13th Earl of (*cr.* 1669), **Thomas Hesketh Douglas Blair Cochrane;** Baron Cochrane, 1647; Bt.; Capt. late Scots Guards; *b.* 21 Feb. 1886; *e. s.* of 12th Earl and Winifred (*d.* 1924), *d.* of Robert Bamford Hesketh, late 2nd Life Guards, Gwrych Castle, Abergele; *S.* father, 1935. *Educ.:* Eton. Entered Army, 1908; served European War, France; also G.S.O.3 Egyptian Expeditionary Force. A Representative Peer for Scotland, 1941-55. Grand Officer of the Order Al Merito per Servicios Distinguidos of Peru; Member of the Order of Merit of Chile. Chairman Anglo-Chilean Society. *Heir:* *nephew,* Major Ian Cochrane, Black Watch [*b.* Dec. 1918; *e. s.* of late Hon. Douglas Robert Hesketh Roger Cochrane and Enid Marion, 3rd *d.* of late Miles Leonard Davis]. *Address:* Auchans, Dundonald, Ayrshire. *T.:* Drybridge 248. *Clubs:* Turf, Carlton, Royal Yacht Squadron (Cowes). [*Died* 23 *May* 1958.

DUNHILL, Alfred; late Chairman of Alfred Dunhill, Ltd.; *b.* Hornsey, 30 Sept. 1872; *s.* of late Henry Dunhill; *m.* 1895, Alice Mary Stapleton, Bedford; two *s.* one *d.* *Educ.:* Private School, Hampstead; tutors. Founded Dunhills, Ltd. (Dunhill's Motorities); severed connection with this firm soon after it became a Ltd. Co., and started in the tobacco business; his collection of rare and historic pipes is next to that of the British Museum, the finest in the world; F.R.S.A. *Publication:* The Pipe Book. *Recreations:* yachting, motoring, music, and cinematography. *Address:* Lynsters, Fourth Avenue, Charmandean, Worthing, Sussex. *Club:* Royal Corinthian Yacht (Burnham-on-Crouch). [*Died* 2 *Jan.* 1959.

DUNHILL, Sir Thomas Peel, G.C.V.O., *cr.* 1949 (K.C.V.O., *cr.* 1933); C.M.G. 1919; M.D.; F.R.C.S. (Hon.); F.R.A.C.S.; Extra Surgeon to the Queen (formerly Sergeant Surgeon to King George VI and Surgeon to King George V); Cons. Surgeon St. Bartholomew's Hospital; *b.* 1876; *s.* of late John Webster Dunhill: *m.* 1914, Edith Florence McKellar (*d.* 1942). Served European War, 1914-19 (despatches thrice, C.M.G.); Cons. Surgeon to A.I.F., 1939-45 (Brigadier). *Address:* Tragowel, North End Avenue, N.W.3. *T.:* Meadway 1616. *Clubs:* Oriental; Melbourne (Melbourne). [*Died* 22 *Dec.* 1957.

DUNLEATH, 3rd Baron (*cr.* 1892), **Charles Henry George Mulholland,** C.B.E. 1921 (O.B.E. 1919); D.S.O. 1915; late Captain, 11th (Prince Albert's Own) Hussars; *b.* 19 Aug. 1886; *e. surv. s.* of 2nd Baron and Norah (*d.* 1935), *o. d.* of Hon. Somerset R. H. Ward, *g.d.* of 3rd Viscount Bangor; *S.* father, 1931; *m.* 1st, 1920, Sylvia Henrietta (*d.* 1921), *e. d.* of late Sir Douglas and late Lady Brooke of Colebrooke, Brookeborough, Co. Fermanagh; 2nd, 1932, Henrietta Grace, *d.* of late Most Rev. C. F. d'Arcy, Archbishop of Armagh; one *s.* *Educ.:* Eton; Sandhurst. Entered Army, 1906; Captain, 1914; served European War, 1914-18 (despatches twice, wounded, D.S.O., O.B.E.); disability pension, 1921; Military Secretary to Lord-Lieutenant of Ireland (Viscount French), 1919-21; Military Secretary to Governor-General of Australia (Lord Forster), 1923-25. K.J.St.J. 1950. *Heir:* *s.* Hon. Charles Edward Henry John Mulholland, *b.* 23 June 1933. *Address:* Ballywalter Park Co. Down. *Clubs:* Carlton, Cavalry; Ulster (Belfast). [*Died* 20 *July* 1956.

DUNLOP, Hugh Alexander, M.D., M.Sc.; F.R.C.P.; Consultant Physician, Charing Cross Hospital; Medical Tutor, Charing Cross Medical School; *b.* 31 Aug. 1903; *y. s.* of David and Marion Dunlop, Ayrshire; *m.* 1926, Kathleen Mary, *d.* of W. Edney and Caroline Mary Hibberd; three *s.* *Educ.:* Midhurst Grammar School; King's College, University of London; Westminster and Charing Cross Hospitals. M.R.C.S. Eng., L.R.C.P. Lond. 1924; M.B., B.S. 1927; M.R.C.P. 1930, F.R.C.P. Lond. 1938; M.D. 1932; M.Sc. Lond. 1934. Consultant Physician with special interest in endocrinology and metabolism in relation to psychosomatic problems. F.K.C. 1948. *Publications:* papers in Jl. Anatomy, Jl. of Physiology, B.M.J., Lancet, Clinical Jl., Medical Press and Circular. *Recreations:* literature, shooting. *Address:* 16 Hocroft Rd., N.W.2. *T.:* Hampstead 3476. *Club:* Junior Carlton. [*Died* 2 *July* 1954.

DUNLOP, Louis Vandalle, J.P.; Director, Harland & Wolff Ltd., Belfast, Shipbuilders and Engineers; *b.* 7 March 1878; *s.* of John Dunlop, Writer and Jean Murray Vandalle; *m.* 1917, Helen Ross; no *c.* *Educ.:* Greenock Academy. Shipbuilding with Caird & Co., Greenock; Harland & Wolff Ltd. at Glasgow; President Shipbuilding Employers Federation, 1942-43; M.I.N.A. Liveryman, Worshipful Company of Shipwrights; J.P., County of City of Glasgow. *Address:* 1 Beaconsfield Road, Glasgow, W.2. *T.:* Glasgow Western 5503. *Club:* Royal Scottish Automobile (Glasgow). [*Died* 16 *Feb.* 1954.

DUNLOP, Bt. Col. Sir Thomas Charles, Kt., *cr.* 1955; T.D., D.L.; *b.* 4 Feb. 1878; *s* of late W. H. Dunlop, Doonside, Ayr; *m.* 1905, Elfrida Louise Grant Watson (*d.* 1946); two *s.* two *d.* *Educ.:* Eton. Served with Ayrshire Yeo. in Gallipoli and Palestine (despatches, Croix de Guerre); A.D.C. (Additional) to the King, 1931-41. M.F.H. Eglinton Hunt, 1923-27. D.L., County of Ayr. *Address:* Doonside, Ayr. *T.:* Alloway 313. *Clubs:* M.C.C., Caledonian: County (Ayr). [*Died* 13 *Aug.* 1960.

DUNN, Lieutenant-Colonel Cuthbert Lindsay, C.I.E. 1928; Indian Medical Service, retired; now Medical Officer, Ministry of Health; *b.* 15 May 1875; *s.* of late Chas. James Dunn of Dunnfield, Co. Londonderry; *m.* 1901, Janet Logan Dalgleish (*d.* 1941), Edinburgh; two *d.*; *m.* 1950, Kathleen Ellen, *o.d.* of A. D. Knott, Bickley, Kent. *Educ.:* Dollar Academy; Edinburgh Univ. Served S. African War, 1900-2 (Queen's medal and four clasps): entered Indian Medical Service, 1902; Director of Public Health, United Provinces, India, 1919-32; retired, 1932; served Tibet Campaign, 1904 (medal and clasp); European War, 1914-19 (1915 Star and two medals, 4th class Serbian Order of St. Sava); Officer of the Order of St. John of Jerusalem, 1938. *Publications:* Dunn and Pandya, Indian Hygiene and Public Health, and The Chemistry and Bacteriology of Public Health; Malaria in Ceylon, 1936; History of the Second World War, U.K. Medical Series, The Emergency Medical Services, Vols. I and II, 1952. *Address:* Ministry of Health, Savile Row, W.1. [*Died* 10 *Oct.* 1956.

DUNN, Most Rev. Edward Arthur, M.A., D.D. Camb., 1919; D.D. Bishop's Univ., Lennoxville, Canada, 1917: *b.* 8 Aug. 1870; *s.* of Rt. Rev. Andrew Hunter Dunn, late Bishop of Quebec, Canada, and Alice, *d.* of late William Hunter, Purley Lodge, Surrey; *m.* 1907, Ellinor (*d.* 1941), *d.* of late Arthur Hunter of Bury St. Edmunds; no *c.* *Educ.:* Marlborough College; Royal Grammar School, Lancaster: Pembroke College, Cambridge, Bell University Scholar, B.A. 1892, (30th Wrangler), 3rd Class Theological Honours, 1894. Deacon, 1894; Priest, 1895; Curate of St. Paul's, Quebec, 1894; Rector, 1895-1901; Professor of Pastoral Theology at Bishop's College, Lennoxville, 1901-07; Professor of Mathematics, 1905-07; Rector of New Carlisle, Rural Dean of Gaspe, 1907-12; Rector of St. Michael's, Bergerville, Quebec, 1912-17: Bishop of British Honduras, 1917-43; Archbishop of the West Indies, 1936-1943. *Address:* Bergerville, Placencia, British Honduras. [*Died* 11 Jan. 1955.

DUNN, Col. Henry Nason, C.M.G. 1918; D.S.O. 1917; retired, 1921; B.A., M.B., B.Ch., B.A.O. Dub.; *b.* 7 Sep. 1864; *s.* of Dr. G. N. Dunn, Kinsale; *m.* Maud, 3rd *d.* of late W. Grosvenor-Jennings, Beamhurst Hall, Uttoxeter; one *s.* one *d.* *Educ.:* Trinity College, Dublin. Seconded Egyptian Army, 1896; served Dongola, 1896 (despatches, medal with clasp); Nile, 1897-98 and 1899 (despatches twice, 4 clasps, medal, 3rd Class Medjidie, 4th Class Osmanieh); served with Abyssinian Expeditionary Force Somaliland, 1903-4 (medal with clasp); N.W. Frontier, India, 1908 (medal with clasp); European War, 1914-18 (despatches four times, D.S.O., C.M.G.); served with 8th, 12th, and 25th Divisions, Xth and XIIIth Corps, France (severely wounded). *Address:* 16 Lansdown Crescent, Bath. *Club:* Bath and County (Bath). [*Died* 21 *Oct.* 1952.

DUNN, Sir James (Hamet), 1st Bt., *cr.* 1921; Chairman and President, Algoma Steel Corporation, Limited, Sault Ste. Marie, Ontario, Canada; *b.* Bathurst, New Brunswick, Canada, 29 Oct. 1875; *s.* of late Robert H. Dunn and Elizabeth Joudray; *m.* 1st, 1901; one *s.* three *d.*; 2nd, 1926; one *d.*

3rd, 1942. *Educ.:* public school, Bathurst; Dalhousie University (LL.B. 1898). Hon. Degrees: New Brunswick University, LL.D. 1942; Dalhousie University, LL.D. 1948; Bishops University, D.C.L., 1950; Queen's University, LL.D., 1951; Laval University, Doctor in Sciences; Honorary President Dalhousie Alumni, 1948. Called to Bars of Nova Scotia and North-west Territories, 1898 and of Quebec in 1901; K.C. (Can.) 1949; practised before Parliamentary Bars at Ottawa and Quebec; Member Montreal Stock Exchange, founded banking firm of Dunn, Fisher & Co., London, England, 1907. *Heir: s.* Major Philip Gordon Dunn [*b.* Montreal, 26 Oct. 1905; *m.* 1933, Lady Mary Sybil St. Clair-Erskine, *d.* of 5th Earl of Rosslyn; two *d.*]. *Address:* Day Spring, St. Andrews, N.B., Canada; Dunn's Camp, Bathurst, N.B. [*Died* 1 *Jan.* 1956.

DUNN, John Freeman; partner, David A. Bevan Simpson & Co., stockbrokers, 37 Threadneedle Street, E.C., and Stock Exchange; Director British American Trading Co., Ltd. (Merchant Banking and Investment Company); *b.* Basingstoke, 12 April 1874; *s.* of George Freeman Dunn; *m.* 1914, Constance, *d.* of David Marr Henderson, Victory House, Hove; one *s.* one *d.* *Educ:* Queen Mary's School, Basingstoke. Fifteen years Manager of the Brighton and Hove Branches of the Midland Bank, Ltd.; Associate of the Institute of Bankers (Gilbert Prizeman); Barrister-at-law (Gray's Inn); M.P. (L.) Hemel Hempstead, 1923-24. *Recreation:* fly-fishing. *Address:* Hazards, Enton, Godalming. *T.:* 373 Godalming. *Clubs:* Reform, Eighty. [*Died* 7 *Dec.* 1954.

DUNN, Piers Duncan Williams, C.B. 1954; C.B.E. 1945; D.S.O. 1918; M.C. 1918; Commandant The Police College, Ryton on Dunsmore, Coventry, since 1948; *b.* 3 Oct. 1896; *s.* of late Lt.-Col. T. D. W. Dunn, Rowdeford, Rowde; *m.* 1934, Honor, *d.* of late Lord Justice Luxmoore; three *s.* *Educ.:* Uppingham; R.M.C., Sandhurst. Served European War, 1914-18; commissioned Lancashire Fusiliers, 1914; transferred Border Regt., 1922; War of 1939-45, Colonel 1940; retd. as Brig., 1948. *Recreations:* fishing, shooting. *Address:* Police College, Ryton on Dunsmore, Coventry. *Club:* Army and Navy. [*Died* 17 *Jan.* 1957.

DUNNE, Lt.-Col. James Stuart, D.S.O. 1914; F.R.C.S.I., L.R.C.P.I., L.M.; late R.A.M.C.; Gold Medallist Operative Surgery, Silver Medallist Theoretical Surgery, Silver Medallist Midwifery; *b.* 2 Nov. 1877; *s.* of late Wm. Dunne of Edenderry, King's County; *m.* 1920, L. Catharine, M.B.E., *d.* of late Adm. Sir W. H. Henderson, K.B.E. Entered Army, 1905; Capt., 1909; Major, 1917; Lt.-Col., 1930; served European War, 1914-18 (despatches, D.S.O.); retired, 1932. *Address:* The Cottage-in-the-Hop-Garden, Whitchurch, Hants. [*Died* 4 *March* 1955.

DUNNELL, Sir (Robert) Francis, 1st Bart., *cr.* 1921; K.C.B., *cr.* 1919; 3rd *s.* of Robert Dunnell, Bury St. Edmunds; *b.* 26 July 1868; *m.* 1897, Ruby C. Garrett (*d.* 1901); no *c.* *Educ.:* Rossall School. Admitted a Solicitor and joined the staff of the Solicitors' Department of the North-Eastern Railway Company, 1891; Assistant Solicitor to the Company, 1900; Secretary, 1905; Solicitor to the Company and Secretary, 1906; lent to the Government as temporary Assistant Secretary, Admiralty, 1917-1918; Secretary to Naval Mission to America, Oct. 1918; Secretary of the Demobilisation Section of the War Cabinet, 1919; lent to the Ministry of Transport as Secretary and Solicitor, 1919-21; late Chief Legal Adviser of the London and North-Eastern Railway Company; retired, 1928; a Railway and Canal Commissioner, 1930-47; J.P. for Suffolk and North Riding of Yorkshire; Chairman of West Suffolk Quarter Sessions, 1932-47; Chairman of North Riding of Yorkshire Quarter Sessions, 1934-45. *Address:* Mitubiri, Kenya Colony. *Club:* Nairobi. [*Died* 16 *July* 1960 (*ext.*).

DUNNETT, Sir James Macdonald, K.C.I.E., *cr.* 1934 (C.I.E. 1922); Kt., *cr.* 1932; an Assistant Secretary, Department of Health for Scotland, since 1940; *b.* 11 Apr. 1877; *m.* 1906, Annie (*d.* 1951), *y. d.* of William Sangster; three *s.* one *d.* *Educ.:* Kilmarnock Academy; Edinburgh University, M.A.; Christ Church, Oxford. Entered Indian Civil Service, 1900; Deputy Commissioner, 1917; Secretary to Government of Punjab, Home Department, 1924; Officiating Chief Secretary, 1926; Joint Secretary, Home Department, Government of India, 1926; Additional Secretary, 1929; Reforms Commissioner, Government of India, 1930-1936; British Delegation Staff, Indian Round Table Conference, 1932; retired, 1936; League of Nations Committee on Alexandretta, 1937; Scottish National Fitness Council, 1938; Chairman, Commission on Refugee Settlement, Northern Rhodesia, 1939. *Address:* Glenegedale, 7 South Inverleith Avenue, Edinburgh. [*Died* 8 *Aug.* 1953.

DUNNICLIFF, Horace Barratt, C.I.E. 1939; M.A., Sc.D., F.R.I.C.; Emeritus Professor of Chemistry, Punjab University; *s.* of Henry Buxton Dunnicliff, London; *m.* 1926, Freda Gladys Burgoyne (A.R.C.M., Kaisar-i-Hind Gold Medal, 1935), *e. d.* of Frederick William Burgoyne Burgoyne-Wallace. *Educ.:* Wilson's Grammar School; Downing College, Cambridge (Foundation Schol.); London and Dublin Universities. Professor of Chemistry, M.A.O. College, Aligarh, U.P., 1908-14; Indian Educational Service, 1914-40; Vice-Principal Khalsa Coll., Amritsar, 1914-17; Research Chemist to the Indian Munitions Board, 1917-18; Prof. of Chemistry, Govt. Coll., Lahore, 1917-39; Cordite Factory, Aravankadu, S. India, 1918-21 and 1923; Professor of Inorganic Chemistry, 1924-44; Fellow (1924-43), Syndic (1930-39) and Dean, Science Faculty (1935-39) Punjab Univ.; Principal, Government College, Lahore, 1936-1939; Special Chemical Adviser, Central Board of Revenue, Finance Dept., Govt. of India, 1928-37; Chief Chemist, Central Revenues Chemical Service, 1937-43; Chief Technical Adviser War Transport Dept., Govt. of India, 1943-46; Specialist Officer, Ministry of Defence, U.K., 1947-54. Member: Drugs Act, Technical Advisory Board, 1940-1943; Drugs Supply Cttee. 1940-45; Delegate Imperial Education Conf., 1927; President, Chemistry Section, Indian Science Congress, 1934; Vice-President, Indian Chemical Society, 1941-43; Foundation Fellow, National Institute of Sciences, India. *Publications:* three books and original papers in scientific literature. *Address:* 97 Ridgmount Gardens, W.C.1. *T.:* Museum 4446. *Club:* Savage. [*Died* 8 *Oct.* 1958.

DUNNICO, Rev. Sir Herbert, Kt., *cr.* 1938; LL.D.; J.P.; Hon. Warden of Browning Settlement, Southwark, since 1932; Secretary International Peace Society since 1916; *b.* Cefn Bedd, North Wales, 1876; *s.* of James Dunnico, Middlewich, Cheshire, and Mary Annie Owen, Newtown, Wales; *m.* 1903, Harriet Emma (*d.* 1952), 2nd *d.* of Robert Rathbone, Manchester; one *s.* *Educ.:* Elementary School; Nottingham University; Rawdon Theological College, Leeds; Midland Baptist College, Nottingham. Worked in factory at age of 10; in coal mine at 12; entered business house age of 13, and after eight years' business training awarded University Scholarship, and subsequently entered Baptist Ministry; settled at Warrington, 1902, and at Kensington Chapel, Liverpool, 1906; M.P. (Lab.) Consett Division of Durham, 1922-31; Deputy Chairman of Ways and Means, 1929-31, and Deputy Speaker, House of Commons, 1929-1931; ex-President of Liverpool Free

Church Council, Liverpool Labour Party, Liverpool Fabian Soc.; Chief Magistrate and Returning Officer for Parliamentary Borough of Ilford, 1925-26; formerly Chm. Magistrates Court House, Stratford, London; Member of International Law Assoc.; is Hon. Director and Vice-Pres. of Bureau International de la Paix, Geneva; formerly Chairman Essex County Licensing Justices; Pres. of the Council of the Counties and other Football Associations; President Essex County Football Assoc.; Vice-President of the Billiards Control Board; late Vice-Pres. of E.N.S.A.; late Chairman E.N.S.A. Broadcasting Council; late Chm. E.N.S.A. Regional Cttee. (Eastern Command); Dir., Radio Luxemburg Ltd.; Life Governor, King George's Hosp., Ilford; Hon. Chaplain to A.T.C., West Essex Wing; President Ilford Girls' Choir; Vice-President The Corporation of Certified Secretaries. *Publications:* The Church and Social Problems; Some Signs of the Times; Handbook for County Councillors; Mother of Parliaments, 1951; frequent and regular contributor to British and foreign magazines and periodicals on religious, international and social subjects. *Recreation:* bowling enthusiast. *Address:* Hendel House, Bathurst Road, Ilford, Essex; 1 Browning Street, S.E.17. *T.A.:* Peasiety (Sedist) London. *T.:* Valentine 1065, Rodney 2806, Rodney 3683. *Club:* National Liberal. [*Died* 2 *Oct.* 1953.

DUNNING, Hon. Charles Avery, P.C. Canada 1926; Hon. LL.D. McGill, 1939, Queen's 1940; Univ. of Montreal, 1944, Univ. of Saskatchewan, 1945; Chancellor Queen's Univ. since 1940; Chairman Ogilvie Flour Mills Co. Ltd.; M.P. Queen's County, Prince Edward Island, 1935-39; Minister of Finance, Canada, 1935-39; *b.* Croft, Leicestershire, England, 31 July 1885; *s.* of Samuel Dunning and Katherine Hall; *m.* 1913, Ada, *d.* of late John Rowlatt, Nassington, Northants; one *s.* one *d.* Came to Canada, 1903; Director, Saskatchewan Grain Growers' Association, 1910, Vice-Pres., 1911-14; organised Sask. Co-operative Elevator Company, Ltd., 1911; General Manager, 1911-16; appointed Royal Commissioner by Sask. Provincial Government to investigate the question of agricultural credit and grain marketing in Europe, 1913; Member Canadian Council of Agriculture, 1911-16; Chairman Sask. Committee Victory Loan, 1917-19; Member Canada Food Board as Director of Food Production for Canada 1918; elected by acclamation Kinistino bye-election, 1916; elected for Moose Jaw County in general election, 1917, 1921, and 1925; M.P. for Regina, 1926-30; Provincial Treasurer for Saskatchewan, 1916, and in addition Minister of Railways, 1917; Minister of Telephones, 1918, and Minister of Agriculture, 1919; Premier of Saskatchewan, 1922-26; entered Federal politics as Minister of Railways, Canada, 1926-29; Minister of Finance, 1929-30; Canadian delegate to League of Nations, 1928. *Address:* 3940 Cote des Neiges Road, Montreal, Canada. *T.:* W1-5734. *Clubs:* Rideau (Ottawa); Mount Royal, St. James's, Mount Bruno Country (Montreal); Seigniory (Montebello); Assiniboia (Regina). [*Died* 2 *Oct.* 1958.

DUNRAVEN and MOUNT-EARL, 5th Earl of, *cr.* 1822; **Col. Windham Henry Wyndham-Quin,** C.B. 1903; D.S.O. 1900; Baron Adare, 1800; Viscount Mountearl, 1816; Viscount Adare, 1822; raised and commanded Glamorgan Imperial Yeomanry; *b.* 7 Feb. 1857; *s.* of late Captain Hon. W. H. Wyndham-Quin; *S.* cousin, 1926; *m.* 1885, Lady Eva Constance Aline Bourke (*d.* 1940), *d.* of 6th Earl of Mayo; two *s.* one *d.* Maj. 16th Lancers; served Boer War, 1881; South Africa, 1900 (despatches, Queen's medal 3 clasps, D.S.O.); M.P. (C.) South Glamorganshire, 1895-1906; High Sheriff, Co. Kilkenny, 1914; Commandant L. of C., 1915. *Publications:* Sir Charles Tyler, G.C.B., Admiral of the White, 1912; The Yeomanry Cavalry of Gloucester and Monmouth, 1897; The Foxhound in County Limerick. *Heir:* *s.* Viscount Adare, C.B., C.B.E., M.C. *Address:* Adare Manor, Limerick. *Clubs:* Carlton; Kildare Street (Dublin). [*Died* 23 *Oct.* 1952.

DUNSANY, 18th Baron (*cr.* 1439), **Edward John Moreton Drax Plunkett,** D.L., Litt.D.; late Captain Royal Inniskilling Fusiliers (wounded 25 Apr. 1916), late 2nd Lieut. 1st Bn. Coldstream Guards; Byron Professor of English Literature, Athens Univ., 1940, until April 1941; *b.* 24 July 1878; *s.* of 17th Baron and Ernle, *o. c.* of Col. Francis A. P. Burton, Coldstream Guards; *heir* to Barony of Killeen of 12th Earl of Fingall, M.C.; *S.* father, 1899; *m.* 1904, Lady Beatrice Villiers, *y. d.* of 7th Earl of Jersey; one *s.* *Educ.:* Eton. Contested (C.) W. Wilts, 1906; took part in South African and European Wars. Owns property in Kent; F.R.S.L., F.R.G.S.; Member of Irish Academy of Letters; President of the Kent County Chess Association; Hon. Member Institute Historique et Héraldique de France. *Publications:* The Gods of Pegana; Time and the Gods; The Sword of Welleran; A Dreamer's Tales; The Book of Wonder; Five Plays; Fifty-one Tales; Tales of Wonder; Plays of Gods and Men; Tales of War; Plays of Near and Far; Unhappy Far-off Things; Tales of Three Hemispheres; The Chronicles of Rodriguez; The King of Elfland's Daughter; The Charwoman's Shadow; Alexander and Three Small Plays; The Blessing of Pan; Seven Modern Comedies; Fifty Poems; The Travel Tales of Mr. Joseph Jorkens; The Curse of the Wise Woman (Harmsworth Literary Award); The Pronouncements of the Grand Macaroni (If I were Dictator); Mr. Jorkens Remembers Africa; Up in the Hills; Rory & Bran; My Talks with Dean Spanley; My Ireland; Plays for Earth and Air; Patches of Sunlight; Mirage Water; The Story of Mona Sheehy; Jorkens Has a Large Whiskey (26 Stories); War Poems; Wandering Songs; The Donnellan Lectures; Guerrilla; A Journey; While the Sirens Slept; The Sirens Wake; The Year: A Glimpse From a Watch Tower; The Fourth Book of Jorkens; The Man Who Ate The Phoenix; To Awaken Pegasus; The Strange Journeys of Colonel Polders; The Last Revolution; His Fellow Men; The Little Tales of Smethers; Jorkens Borrows Another Whiskey; *plays:* The Glittering Gate; King Argimenes; The Gods of the Mountain; The Golden Doom; The Lost Silk Hat; The Tents of the Arabs; A Night at an Inn; The Queen's Enemies; The Laughter of the Gods; Fame and the Poet; The Compromise of the King of the Golden Isles; Mr. Faithful; A Good Bargain; If Shakespear Lived To-day; If; Cheezo; Lord Adrian; Alexander; The Strange Lover, etc.; and for the Radio, The Use of Man, The Bureau de Change, Golden Dragon City, Time's Joke, Atmospherics, The Aurora Borealis. *Recreations:* fox hunting, big-game hunting, shooting, cricket. *Heir:* *s.* Lt.-Colonel Hon. R. A. H. Plunkett. *Address:* Dunsany Castle, Co. Meath; Dunstall Priory, Shoreham, Kent. *Clubs:* Carlton, Beefsteak, Garrick, Athenæum, Authors'; Kildare Street (Dublin). [*Died* 25 *Oct.* 1957.

DUNSTAFFNAGE, The Captain of; Angus John Campbell of Dunstaffnage, 20th hereditary Captain; Chief of Clan Aonghas an Duine; Hereditary Keeper of Royal Forest of Dalness; Steward of Upper Lochow; Knight of the Order of Malta; Member Royal Bodyguard of Scotland; Privy Chamberlain of the Sword and Cape to the Pope; Vice-Lieutenant of the County of Argyll; J.P. and Hon. Sheriff-Substitute, Argyll; *b.* 22 Nov. 1888; *e. s.* of 19th Captain and Jane, *y. d.* and *co-heiress* of Alexander Campbell of Monzie; *S.* father, 1908; unmarried. *Educ.:* privately at home and abroad. *Recreations:* travel; various. *Address:* Dunstaffnage Castle, Connel, Argyll. *T.A.:*

Dunstaffnage, Connel. *T.:* Connel 269. *Clubs:* Carlton, Royal Automobile; New (Edinburgh). [*Died* 16 *Jan.* 1958.

DUNSTAN, William, V.C.; Director, The Herald and Weekly Times, Ltd., Newspaper Proprietors, Melbourne, Victoria; Australian Newsprint Mills Ltd., Tasmania; Amalgamated Wireless (Australasia) Ltd., Sydney, N.S.W.; Perpetual Executors and Trustees Association Ltd., Melbourne, Vic., South African Fire and Accident Insurance Co. Ltd., Melbourne, Vic.; *b.* Ballarat, 8 March 1895; *s.* of William John and Henrietta Dunstan; *m.* 1918, Marjorie L. S., *d.* of H. J. Carnell, of Ballarat; two *s.* one *d.* *Educ.:* State School, Ballarat. With Australian Forces, 1914-18; served Egypt and Gallipoli (despatches twice, V.C., Lone Pine, Gallipoli, 9 Aug. 1915). *Recreation:* racing. *Address:* 20 Wallace Avenue, Toorak, Melbourne, Victoria, Australia. *T.:* BJ. 1600. *Clubs:* Naval and Military, Athenæum, Melbourne, Australian (Melbourne); New South Wales (Sydney); Royal Melbourne Golf, Metropolitan Golf, Moonee Valley Racing, Victoria Racing, Victoria Amateur Turf, Melbourne Racing, etc. [*Died* 2 *March* 1957.

DUNSTERVILLE, Brigadier Knightley Fletcher, D.S.O. 1919; M.I.E.I. 1939; *b.* 24 June 1883; *s.* of late Col. K. S. Dunsterville, C.B.; *m.* 1919, Mary Isaline, *d.* of late J. H. Philpot, M.B.E., M.D.; one *d.* *Educ.:* Cheltenham Coll.; R.M.A., Woolwich. 2nd Lieut. R.G.A. 1902; Lt. 1905; Gunnery Staff Course, 1906-7; Instructor in Gunnery, 1908-1912; Staff Captain to Inspector of R.G.A. 1914; Capt., Nov. 1914; Major, 1917; Lt.-Col. 1931; Bt. Col. 1933; Col. 1935; Brig. 1938; served European War, France, Italy, Egypt, Salonika, Turkey (D.S.O., 1914-15 Star, G.S. medal, Victory medal, despatches thrice; Cav. Crown of Italy); Advanced Class, 1919-22; Assistant Inspector, Inspection Staff, 1922-23; Expl. Officer, Optical Research Dept. Admiralty, 1923-26; Singapore, 1927; Inspector, Inspection Staff, 1928-31; commanded Br. Heavy Batteries, Hong-Kong, 1931-33; Chief Instructor Artillery Equipments; Military College of Science, Woolwich, 1933-36; Chief Inspector of Armaments, 1936-40; retd. 1940; U.K. Technical Mission (Canada), 1940; Inspection Board U.K. and Canada, 1941-45; reverted to retired pay, 1945 (Defence Medal, War Medal, 1939-45). Jubilee Medal, 1935; Coronation Medal, 1937. *Publication:* article on Range-finders in Encyclopedia Britannica. *Recreation:* archivist. *Address:* Hill Crest, Aldeburgh, Suffolk. *Club:* Royal Artillery Yacht. [*Died* 6 *Sept.* 1958.

DU-PLAT-TAYLOR, Francis Maurice Gustavus, M.I.C.E.; J.P. Surrey; Chairman: Surrey Quarter Sessions Rating Appeals Cttee., 1942; Mortlake (Surrey) Petty Sessions; Arbitrator; *b.* 1878; *s.* of late Col. J. L. Du-Plat-Taylor, C.B.; *m.* 1909, Violet, *d.* of late J. F. Clerk, Barrister-at-Law; one *s.* (and one *s.* killed in action) one *d.* *Educ.:* Farnborough School; Winchester College; London University. A pupil of late Anthony George Lyster, Past Pres. Inst. Civil Engineers; on Engineering staff of Mersey Docks and Harbour Board, 1900-04; Engineer, East and West India Docks, London, 1904-09 and Tilbury Docks, 1909-24, in Port of London and executed large dock extensions at Tilbury, 1912. Served in France in R.A., 1914-18, Major 1917. Consulting Engineer, 1924-52. Past Pres. British Section, Société des Ingénieurs Civils de France, 1931-33; Officier d'Académie, 1934. *Publications:* Handbook for Volunteer Field Artillery, 1902; Handbook for Territorial Field Howitzer Batteries, 1908; The Design, Construction and Maintenance of Docks, Wharves and Piers, 1928 and 1949; Cottage Hospitals (with John Coleridge, F.R.I.B.A., and Dr. J. J. Abraham, D.S.O., M.D., F.R.C.S.), 1930; The Reclamation of Land from the Sea, 1931; numerous engineering papers. *Recreations:* joinery and golf. *Address:* 6 Branstone Road, Kew, Surrey. *T.:* Richmond 0900. *Clubs:* Athenæum, Roehampton. [*Died* 22 *May* 1954.

du PONT, Lammot; Retired; *b.* 12 Oct. 1880; *s.* of Lammot du Pont and Mary Belin; *m.* 1903; three *s.* five *d.*; *m.* 1933, Margaret A. Flett; two *s.* *Educ.:* Massachusetts Institute of Technology. B.S. Civil Eng. 1901; employed by E. I. du Pont de Nemours & Co. from 1902 in various positions from Supervisor to President and Chairman of the Board; retd. Jan. 1948. *Address:* Pennsylvania Ave. and Rising Sun Lane, Wilmington, Delaware. *T.:* 2-3144. *Clubs:* Metropolitan (New York); Union League (Philadelphia); Wilmington, Wilmington Country (Wilmington). [*Died* 24 *July* 1952.

DUPREE, Col. Sir William, 2nd Bt., *cr.* 1921; Chairman, The Portsmouth and Brighton United Breweries, Ltd.; *b.* 5 March 1882; *s.* of Sir William Thomas Dupree, 1st Bt., and Mary (*d.* 1907), *d.* of late George Groves of Selsey; *S.* father 1933; *m.* 1908, Edith Mary, *d.* of late Arthur Mutimer, M.A., Edgbaston. *Educ.:* Portsmouth Grammar School; Birmingham University. Served European War, 1914-19. *Heir:* *b.* Vernon, *b.* 23 Dec. 1884. *Address:* Bohunt, Liphook, Hants. *Clubs:* Junior Carlton; Royal Albert Yacht (Southsea). [*Died* 30 *Jan.* 1953.

DURAND, Major Sir Edward Percy Marion, 2nd Bt., *cr.* 1892; Indian Army, retired; *b.* 11 July 1884; *s.* of 1st Bt. and Maude Ellen, *d.* of late A. Heber-Percy; *S.* father, 1920; *m.* 1913, Vera Helen, *d.* of Sir R. L. Lucas-Tooth, 1st Bt. *Educ.:* Wellington College. Served Mesopotamia, 1915-16, on Staff; Mesopotamia, 1916-17; N.W. Frontier, 1919-20; retired, 1922. *Heir:* *b.* Brigadier Alan Algernon Marion Durand, M.C. *Publications:* Ponies' Progress, 1934; Wanderings with a Fly-rod, 1938. *Address:* c/o Lloyds Bank Ltd., 6 Pall Mall, S.W.1. [*Died* 4 *March* 1955.

DURANLEAU, Hon. Alfred, P.C., K.C., LL.D.; Judge, Superior Court, Quebec, from 1935; *b.* West Farnham, Que., 1 Nov. 1871; *s.* of Napoléon Duranleau and Adelaide Patenaude; *m.* 1898, Laure Monty; four *s.* two *d.* *Educ.:* Ste. Marie de Monnoir College; Laval, B.A. Called to Quebec Bar, 1897; first elected (C) to Quebec Parliament for Laurier Division of Montreal, 1923; elected to Federal House of Commons for Chambly-Verchères Constituency, 1930; Minister of Marine, 1930-35; Ex-Member of the Council of Quebec Bar; Batonnier of the Bar Association of the Province of Quebec, 1931; Ex-Member Board of Examiners of Quebec Bar; Governor of Notre-Dame Hospital; Member of Chambre de Commerce. *Recreations:* golf and reading. *Address:* 101 St. Joseph Boulevard West, Montreal, Que., Canada. *Clubs:* Beloeil Golf (Beloeil); Laval sur le Lac Golf; Canadian, L'Alliance Française, Montreal, (Life Member) Universitaire (Montreal). [*Died* 14 *March* 1951.

DURANTY, Walter; Foreign correspondent and author. Foreign correspondent of the New York Times, 1913-39. *Educ.:* Cambridge University. *Publications:* I Write as I Please, 1935; One Life, One Kopek, 1937; The Gold Train, 1938; The Kremlin and the People, 1942; U.S.S.R., 1944; Stalin and Co., 1949. *Club:* Coffee House (New York). [*Died* 3 *Oct.* 1957.

DURRANT, Sir William Henry Estridge, 6th Bt., *cr.* 1783; *b.* 23 Dec. 1872; *s.* of 5th Bt. and Emily Grace, *d.* of John Street, London; *m.* 1900, Ethel May, *d.* of Henry Robert Jeffress of Sydney; two *s.* one *d.* *S.* father, 1912. *Heir:* *s.* William Henry Estridge, *b.* 1 Apr. 1901. *Address:* Scottow, White Street, Balgowlah, N.S.W., Australia. [*Died* 22 *July* 1953.

DURSTON, Air Marshal Sir Albert, K.B.E. 1946; C.B. 1942; A.F.C.; retired; *b.* 1894. Served European War, 1914-18 (despatches twice, A.F.C.). Director of Operations (Naval Co-operation), 1938; Air Commodore, 1941; Air Vice-Marshal (temp.), 1942; Air Vice-Marshal, 1945; A.O.C. No. 18 Group Coastal Command, 1942; Senior Air Staff Officer, Hdqs. Coastal Comd., 1943; A.O.C. 222 group S.E. Asia Air Command, 1944-45; Deputy Chief of Air Staff, 1945-46; retired 1946, with rank of Air Marshal. *Address:* Albany, Durford Wood, Petersfield, Hants. *Club:* R.A.F. [*Died* 24 *Jan.* 1959.

DWELLY, Very Rev. Frederick William, M.A., D.D.; Hon. A.R.I.B.A.; Hon. LL.D.; Dean of Liverpool, 1931-55; Dean Emeritus since 1955; *b.* 1881; *s.* of Robert and Caroline Dwelly; *m.* Mary Bradshaw (*d.* 1950), *d.* of Major Darwin, M.D., Didsbury; no *c.* *Educ.:* Chard School; Queens' Coll., Camb. Deacon, 1906; Priest, 1907; Curate of St. Mary, Windermere, 1906-11; Cheltenham Parish Church, 1911-16; Chaplain of 9th Glosters, 1914-15; Vicar of Emmanuel, Southport, 1916-25; Canon Residentiary of Liverpool Cathedral, 1925; Vice-Dean, 1920: Select Preacher, Cambridge, 1937; Hulsean Preacher, 1947-48; Hon. LL.D. Liverpool, 1954. Chaplain, Order of St. John of Jerusalem. *Publications:* contributor to The Future of the Church of England, a volume of essays. *Address:* 6 Grove Park, Liverpool 8. *T.:* Sefton Park 1055. *Club:* Oxford and Cambridge University. [*Died* 9 *May* 1957.

DWYER, Lt.-Col. Ernest, C.B.E. 1919; M.C., late R.A.S.C.; Hon. Consul of Netherlands at Baghdad; *b.* 20 Aug. 1880. Served European War, 1914-19 (despatches twice, M.C., C.B.E.); Iraq, 1919-20 (medal and clasp); Kurdistan, 1923 (despatches, clasp); Chevalier Order of Orange Nassau. *Address:* Dwyer & Co. (Iraq) Ltd., P.O. Box 22, Baghdad, Iraq. [*Died* 7 *Jan.* 1957.

DWYER, Sir Walter, Kt., *cr.* 1949; Retired Judge; *b.* 27 Aug. 1875; *s.* of Walter and Mary Dwyer; *m.* 1912, Maude Mary, *e. d.* of Charles Smith, Murchison, W.A.; two *d.* *Educ.:* Christian Brothers' School; London University. LL.B. (London Univ. (External)), 1906; admitted to Bar (W.A.), 1907; Member of Legislative Assembly, W.A., Perth Constituency, 1911-1914; President, Court of Arbitration, 1926-1945. *Recreations:* gardening, walking. *Address:* 28 Almondbury Road, Mount Lawley, Western Australia. *T.:* U. 2040. *Clubs:* Celtic (Perth, W.A.); W.A. Turf. [*Died* 23 *March* 1950.

DYE, Sidney; M.P. (Lab.) S.W. Division of Norfolk, 1945-51 and since 1955; J.P.; C.C. (Norfolk); farmer; Alderman Norfolk County Council, Swaffham Rural District Council; *b.* Wells, Norfolk, 1900; *m.* 1932; one *s.* one *d.* *Address:* Redcroft, Norwich Road, Swaffham, Norfolk. *T.:* Swaffham 331. *Club:* Farmers'. [*Died* 9 *Dec.* 1958.

DYER, Arthur Reginald; *b.* 11 May 1877; *s.* of late J. Herbert Dyer, Alton, Hants; *m.* Dudley Beatrice, *e. d.* of F. Edwards, M.D., Sawston, Cambridge; two *d.* *Educ.:* Privately; St. John's College, Hurstpierpoint; King's College, London. Technical Training (Merryweathers, London); Engineering Staff British Westinghouse Electric and Manufacturing Co., England and Pittsburg, U.S.A.; Assistant Divisional Officer London Fire Brigade, 1904; Divisional Officer, 1909; Chief Officer, 1919-33; Royal Humane Society's Medal, 1913; King's medal, 1917. *Publication:* Motor Fire Appliances in London. *Recreation:* fishing. *Address:* Wynchmore, Filsham Road, St. Leonards-on-Sea. *T.:* Hastings 1499. *Club:* East Sussex (St. Leonards-on-Sea). [*Died* 4 *May* 1951.

DYER, Colonel George Nowers, C.B.E. 1935; D.S.O. 1919; late The Queen's Royal Regiment; 3rd *s.* of Frederick Dyer, J.P., The Pentlands, Croydon; *m.* 1913, Dorothy Graham, 4th *d.* of Charles Dyer, 8 Craven Hill Gardens, W.2; two *d.* *Educ.:* Rugby; R.M.C., Sandhurst. 2nd Lieut. The Queen's Royal Regt. 1900; Lieut. 1903; Captain, 1911; Major, 1915; Lt.-Col. 1927; Col. 1931; in India, 1900-10; Adjutant 1st Bn. Queen's Royal Regt., 1912-13; served European War, 1914-19; Staff Capt. 3rd Infantry Brigade, 1914; Brigade Major, 1915; G.S.O. 3, 1916; G.S.O. 2, 1916 (despatches twice, Croix de Guerre, D.S.O.); Commandant Army School of Physical Training, 1927-31; Inspector of Physical Training, 1932-35; retired pay, 1936; Commandant, Army Physical Training Corps and Army School of Physical Training, 1940-41; retired pay, 1941; Company Comdr. Home Guard, 1941-44. Vice-Chairman, Royal tournament, 1947-54. *Recreation:* gardening. *Address:* Corner House, Worplesdon, Surrey. *T.:* Worplesdon 50. *Club:* United Service. [*Died* 31 *Aug.* 1955.

DYKES, Frederick James; Fellow of Trinity College, Cambridge; Director and Technical Adviser, Trojan Ltd.; Director, Armstrong, Stevens and Son, Ltd.; Member of Institution of Mechanical Engineers; *b.* 2 June 1880; 3rd *s.* of late Alfred Dykes, 7 Longfield Road, Ealing, W.; *m.* Winifred, *e. d.* of late Capt. W. S. de Kantzow, R.N., Warblington, Hants; two *s.* *Educ.:* City of London School; Trinity College, Cambridge (Scholar). M.A.; Professor, H.M. Gunnery and Torpedo Schools, Portsmouth, 1903-6; Lecturer at Cambridge, 1906-37; Technical Manager, Newall National Gauge Factory, Walthamstow, 1918; Tutor of Trinity College, Cambridge, 1919-33; Proctor, Cambridge University, 1912-15, 1927-32. Director and Vice-Chairman Cambridge Gas Co., 1923-49; Master of Coopers' Company, London, 1948-49. *Address:* Trinity Coll., Cambridge; The Loke House, 21 West Road, Cambridge. *T.:* 4078. [*Died* 22 *July* 1957.

DYNEVOR, 7th Baron (*cr.* 1780) **Walter Fitz-Uryan Rhys;** *b.* 17 Aug. 1873; *s.* of 6th Baron and Selina, 3rd *d.* of Hon. Arthur Lascelles; *m.* 1898, Lady Margaret Child-Villiers, *e. d.* of 7th Earl of Jersey; three *s.* one *d.*; *S.* father, 1911. *Educ.:* Eton; Christ Church, Oxford. Capt. (retd.) Carmarthens Artillery; D.L. and J.P. Carmarthenshire; Lord Lieutenant of Carmarthenshire, 1928-48, resigned. Assistant Private Secretary to Lord George Hamilton, Secretary of State for India, 1899-1903, and to the Earl of Selborne, 1st Lord of the Admiralty, 1903-5; assisted in the Ministry of Munitions, 1916-18; M.P. (U.) Brighton, 1910-11; Carmarthenshire County Councillor, 1919-35; Chairman of The Land Union, 1920-37. *Heir:* *s.* Captain Hon. Charles Arthur Uryan Rhys, M.C. *Address:* Dynevor Castle, Llandilo, Carmarthenshire. *T.:* Llandilo 2100. *Club:* Carlton. [*Died* 8 *June* 1956.

E

EAKIN, Rev. Thomas, M.A., Ph.D., D.D.; Principal of Knox College, Toronto, and Professor of Old Testament Literature and Exegesis 1925-44; retd., 1944; *b.* 1871; *s.* of Robert Eakin and Mary MacLernon; *m.* 1900, Ethel Elizabeth Kinnear; one *d.* *Educ.:* Univ. of Toronto; Knox College, Toronto; Osgoode Hall Law School, Toronto. Minister of St. Andrew's Church, Guelph, Ontario, 1899-1905; Lecturer and subsequently Professor of Semitic Languages, University College, Toronto, 1905-1913; Minister of St. Andrew's Church, Toronto, 1915-20; Professor of Practical Theology in the Presbyterian College, Montreal, 1920-25; Barrister-at-Law, but never practised. *Publications:* The Text of Habakkuk; numerous magazine articles. *Recreations:* mainly golf.

Address: 116 Madison Avenue, Toronto, Canada. *Clubs:* Authors'; York Downs Golf, Victoria Bowling (Toronto).
[*Died* 11 *Dec.* 1958.

EAMES, Major-General William L'Estrange, C.B. 1900; C.B.E. 1920; V.D. 1911; M.B., B.Ch. Dublin; M.B. Sydney; Colonel and Hon. Major-General (retired), A.A.M.C.; *b.* 18 July 1863; *e. s.* of late Rev. W. L. Eames, Dublin, Army Chaplain; *m.* 1888, Elizabeth Jane (Lily), *o. d.* of late Wm. Kerr Lochhead; two *d. Educ.:* Oswestry Grammar School; Caius College, Cambridge; Trin. Coll., Dublin. Went to Australia, 1887; joined N.S.W.A.M.C. 1891; served as Major commanding No. 2 Bearer Co. N.S.W. in South African campaign; present at the capture of Johannesburg and Pretoria, battles of Diamond Hill and Riet Vlei, and capture of Middelburg and Kaapsche Hoop (despatches, C.B.); European War, 1914-18 (despatches, Bt. Col., C.B.E., Commander of Order of Aviz, Portugal); formerly P.M.O. Military District, N.S.W. *Address:* 30 Mona Road, Darling Point, Sydney, N.S.W. *Clubs:* Australian, University, Royal Sydney Golf (Sydney). [*Died* 26 *Oct.* 1956.

EARL, Sir Austin, Kt., *cr.* 1946; C.B. 1936; C.B.E. 1919; *b.* 1888; *s.* of late Alfred Earl, M.A., Barrister-at-Law, late of Ferox Hall, Tonbridge; *m.* Sylvia Emily Frances, *d.* of late S. C. Bristowe, J.P., Craig, Balmaclellan, Kirkcudbrightshire; no *c. Educ.:* Eton; University College, Oxford (Scholar), B.A., 1st Class Classical Moderations; 1st Class Litt. Hum. Appointed a Higher Division Clerk, War Office, 1912; Private Secretary to the Master General of the Ordnance, 1913-15; Civil Assistant to the Q.M.G. 1919-21; Principal, 1920; Private Secretary to the Secretary of State, 1924-26; an Assistant Secretary, War Office, 1926-34; Assistant Under Secretary of State, 1934; Prin. Assistant Under-Secretary of State, War Office, 1943; additional Civil Service Commissioner, 1948-49; retired 1949; Sec. to Lord Bridgeman's Cttee. on the Post Office, 1932; served European War, 1915-19, R.G.A. France (wounded); subsequently on Staff. *Recreation:* golf. *Address:* 3 Cadogan Court Gardens, S.W.1. *Club:* Athenæum.
[*Died* 24 *April* 1958.

EARLE, Professor Edward Mead; Professor, School of Historical Studies, Institute for Advanced Study, Princeton, N.J., since 1934; *b.* New York, 20 May 1894; *s.* of Stephen King Earle and Helen Martha (*née* Hart); *m.* 1919, Beatrice Lowndes; one *d. Educ.:* Columbia University, City of New York. B.S. 1917; Ph.D. 1923. Hon. L.H.D., Union College, 1941; Colgate University, 1947; Columbia University, 1954; Hon. LL.D., Princeton Univ., 1947. Served European War, Lieut. Air Service, U.S. Army, 1917-19; administrative post with National City Bank of New York, 1919-1920; lecturer, asst. prof., assoc. prof. of history, Columbia Univ., 1920-34. Member, Board of Analysts, Office of Strategic Services, 1941-42; Special Consultant to Comdg. Gen., Army Air Forces, 1942-45 (attached for a time to 8th and 9th Air Forces in Britain); Combined (R.A.F.-U.S.A.A.F.) Ops. Planning Cttee., 1944; special asst. to Supreme Comdr., Allied Powers in Europe (Gen. Eisenhower), May-July 1951. Fellow of Library of Congress, 1943-; Chichele Lectr., and assoc. mem. All Souls Coll., Oxford, 1950; occasional lectr. at Imperial Defence Coll., Joint Services Staff Coll., R.N. War Coll., 1948-; Member Board of Visitors, the Air University, U.S.A.F., 1952-1953. Presidential Medal for Merit (U.S.A.) for War Service, 1941-45; Chevalier, Legion of Honour (French); Medal for Distinguished Public Service, Columbia Univ., 1946. *Publications:* Turkey, the Great Powers and the Bagdad Railway, 1923; (editor and co-author) Makers of Modern Strategy, 1943; Nationalism and Internationalism, 1950; Modern France: Problems of the Third and Fourth Republics, 1951. (With General Carl Spaatz) American Views of Air Power, 1947. *Address:* Institute for Advanced Study, Princeton, New Jersey, U.S.A. *T.:* Princeton 1-0552; (Office) Princeton 1-4400. *Clubs:* Century Association (New York); Army and Navy (Washington).
[*Died* 24 *June* 1954.

EARLE, Col. Maxwell, C.B. 1919; C.M.G. 1918; D.S.O. 1900; Hon. M.A. Oxford, 1912; Cambridge, 1923; *b.* 6 April 1871; *m.* 1900, Hon. Edith Loch (*d.* 1947), *d.* of 1st Baron Loch; one *s.* one *d. Educ.:* Marlborough; Sandhurst; Staff College. Entered Grenadier Guards, 1891; Captain, 1899; Major, 1907; Lt.-Col. 1914; Col. 1918; Col. on the Staff, General Staff, Deputy Director of Staff Duties, War Office, 1921; Lees Knowles Lecturer, Trinity College, Cambridge, 1921-23. Served Matabele War, 1893; South African War, 1899-1900; European War, 1914; retired pay, 1923; Order of Red Eagle of Prussia, Legion of Honour, and silver medal of Society for Saving Life from Fire. *Address:* Shapley Hill, Hartley Wintney, Hants. [*Died* 15 *Feb.* 1953.

EARLE, Colonel Robert Gilmour, C.M.G. 1919; D.S.O. 1915; R.E.; *b.* 1 July 1874; *m.* 1912, Rose Mary Steele; one *s.* one *d.* Entered Army, 1894; Captain, 1904; Major, 1914; Lieut.-Col., 1921; Col., 1922; served South Africa, 1899-1902 (despatches, Queen's medal 4 clasps, King's medal 2 clasps); European War, 1914-18 (D.S.O., C.M.G., Bt. Lt.-Col.); Afghan War, 1919; Colonel, 1922; G.S.O. 1, War Office, 1929-31; A.D.C. to the King, 1923-31; retired, 1931. *Address:* Bodenham, Salisbury, Wilts. [*Died* 22 *March* 1957.

EARLY, Stephen T., D.S.M. (U.S.); Vice-President of Pullman Incorporated, 1945; *b.* Crozet, Virginia, 27 Aug. 1889; *s.* of Thomas Joseph Early and Ida Virginia Wood; *m.* 1921, Helen Wrenn; two *s.* one *d. Educ.* High schools, Washington, D.C.; private tutorage, Virginia. Mem. Washington Staff United Press, 1908-13, Assoc. Press, 1913-17 and 1920-27; advance rep. for Franklin D. Roosevelt, campaign of 1920; Publicity Dir. for Bd. Dirs. Chamber of Commerce of U.S., 1920-21; Washington Rep. Paramount-Publix Corp. and Paramount News, 1927-33; Asst. Sec. to Pres. Roosevelt, 1933-37; Sec., 1937-45; Sec. and Spec. Asst. to Pres. Truman, Apr.-June 1945; Under-Secretary of Defence, U.S., 1949-50; European War, 1917-18, served as Capt. Inf. U.S. Army (Silver Star citation); D.S.M., 1945; Democrat. Baptist. *Publications:* magazine articles in Saturday Evening Post. *Recreations:* golf, hunting, fishing, bridge. *Address:* 7704 Morningside Drive, N.W., Washington, D.C.; Pulstand—1025 Connecticut Ave. N.W., Washington, D.C. *T.:* Republic 8050. *Clubs:* National Press (Washington, D.C.); Columbia Country (Chevy Chase, Md.); Burning Tree (Bethesda, Md.).
[*Died* 11 *Aug.* 1951.

EARP, Frank Russell, M.A.; Emeritus Professor of Classics, and Fellow of Queen Mary College, University of London; *b.* East Molesey, 1871; *s.* of Russell Earp, late of East Molesey; *m.* 1906, Edith Mary (*d.* 1945), *d.* of late Joseph Edgerley Purser, Dublin; one *d.* (and one *s.* killed on actve service). *Educ.:* Uppingham School; King's College, Cambridge (Scholar and Fellow). Travelled in Persia, 1902-1903; Lecturer, Classics at East London College, 1905; Professor of Classics in University of London, 1930-36. *Publications:* Translation of Herodotus into Vernacular Syriac, published at Urmi in Persia, 1904; The Way of the Greeks, 1929; The Style of Sophocles, 1944; The Style of Aeschylus, 1948. *Address:* Hill Crest, Goring Rd., Steyning, Sx. *Club:* Authors'.
[*Died* 14 *Jan.* 1955.

EARP, Thomas Wade; Writer; *b.* 1892; *s.* of Thomas Earp, J.P., M.P.; *m.* Beatrice May Russell. *Educ.:* Magnus

Grammar School, Newark; Exeter College, Oxford (Charles Oldham Scholar). Has carried out much social and antiquarian research in London and Paris. *Publications:* Contacts, 1916; The Gate of Bronze, 1918; Still Life and Flower Painting, 1930; Augustus John, 1934; Van Gogh, 1934; The Modern Movement in Painting, 1935; French Painting, 1945; Translations of Stendhal. *Recreation:* silence. *Address:* Crossways, Selborne, Hants. [*Died* 8 *May* 1958.

EAST, Hubert Frazer, C.M.G. 1937; Chairman of McDonnell and East, Ltd., Brisbane; *b.* Brisbane, 2 June 1893; *m.* 1930, Enid Jennette, *d.* of late W. E. Howes; one *s.* two *d.* Served European War, 1915-19 with A.I.F. in France and Flanders; President, 1923-1930, Queensland Branch of Returned Sailors', Soldiers', and Airmen's Imperial League of Australia, Vice-President, 1933-34. *Address:* Eskmount, Aston Street, Toowong, Brisbane, Queensland. [*Died* 20 *Nov.* 1959.

EAST, Sir (William) Norwood, Kt., *cr.* 1947; M.D. (Lond.); F.R.C.P. (Lond.); Lecturer on Forensic Psychiatry, Maudsley Hosp. (London University); Corresponding foreign member Société de Médicine Légale de France; *b.* 24 Dec. 1872; *s.* of W. Quartermaine East, D.L.; *m.* 1900, Selina, *o. c.* of Alfred Triggs; one *d.* *Educ.:* King's College School; King's College, London; Guy's Hospital. Formerly Senior Medical Officer, H.M. Prison Service; Medical Inspector, H.M. Prisons, England and Wales; Inspector under Inebriate Acts, 1879-1900; H.M. Commissioner of Prisons and Director of Convict-Prisons; Special Consultant to Royal Navy; Vice-Pres. 23 Congrès de Médecine Légale, Paris, 1946. Member of Departmental Committees on the Persistent Offender and on Prison Diets; President of Society for the Study of Inebriety and Drug Addiction, 1940-45; Pres. Psychiatric Section R.S.M., 1943; President Medico-Legal Society, 1945-47. *Publications:* Forensic Psychiatry, 1927; The Medical Aspects of Crime, 1936; The Psychological Treatment of Crime (jointly), 1939; The Adolescent Criminal, 1942; Society and the Criminal, 1949; numerous papers to scientific journals. *Recreations:* fishing, reading, and gardening. *Address:* Rhododendrons, Crowthorne, Berks. *T.:* Crowthorne 354. [*Died* 30 *Oct.* 1953.

EASTON, Lieut.-Col. Philip George, C.B.E. 1919; D.S.O. 1916; J.P., Surrey, 1938; late R.A.M.C.; *b.* 15 Dec. 1878; *y. s.* of late John Easton, M.D.; *m.* 1913, Winifred (*d.* 1959), *y. d.* of late Philip Witham, Sutton Place, near Guildford; two *d.* *Educ.:* Lancing. St. Mary's Hospital, 1895-1901; Indian Medical Service, 1902-8; Royal Army Medical Corps 1908; Major, 1914; Bt. Lt.-Col., 1923; Lt.-Col., 1924; served European War, 1914-18 (despatches thrice, D.S.O.); retired pay, 1927. *Address:* The White Barn, Sutton-Green, nr. Guildford. *T.:* Guildford 61455. *Club:* United Service. [*Died* 21 *Nov.* 1960.

EASTWOOD, Harold Edmund, C.M.G. 1936; *b.* 7 Jan. 1889; *s.* of late John Edmund Eastwood; *m.* 1913, Sibyl Renée Julia, *d.* of Charles Cunningham Church. *Educ.:* Eton; Trinity College, Cambridge. Head of Communications Dept., Foreign Office, 1925-40; Senior King's Foreign Service Messenger, March 1940; retired, 1945. *Address:* 11 Park Square West, N.W.1. *T.:* Welbeck 5291; Dungate House, Balsham, Cambs. *Club:* Travellers'. [*Died* 13 *Jan.* 1960.

EASTWOOD, John Francis, O.B.E.; K.C. 1937; Metropolitan Police Magistrate since 1940; *b.* 1887; *e. s.* of late John E. Eastwood, Gosden House, Bramley, Surrey; *m.* 1st, Alice Leonora Zacyntha (*d.* 1933); 2nd *d.* of late Colonel L. R. C. Boyle, C.M.G., M.V.O.; two *d.*; 2nd, 1934, Dorothea Constance Cecil, *er. d.* of Rupert Butler; one *s.* *Educ.:* Eton; Trinity College, Cambridge. Called to Bar, 1911; lived four years in Western Canada; served European War with Grenadier Guards, Major Reserve of Officers; Courts Martial Officer, London, 1918-20; Legal Officer, Ireland, 1920-22; M.P. (U.) Kettering, 1931-1940; Recorder of Tenterden, 1935-40. *Recreations:* shooting, fishing. *Address:* 5 Sloane Court, S.W.3. *T.:* Sloane 0953. *Club:* Flyfishers'. [*Died* 30 *Jan.* 1952.

EASTWOOD, Lt.-Gen. Sir T. Ralph, K.C.B., *cr.* 1943 (C.B. 1941); D.S.O. 1919; M.C.; Col. Comdt. 1st Bn. Rifle Brigade, 1945-51; *b.* 10 May 1890; 2nd *s.* of late Col. H. de C. Eastwood, D.S.O.; *m.* 1921, Mabel Vivian Prideaux, *d.* of late Joseph Temperley; one *s.* *Educ.:* Eton; Sandhurst. Joined Rifle Brigade, 1910; served with 1st Battalion till 1912; New Zealand as A.D.C. to the Governor-General (Earl of Liverpool) till the outbreak of war, 4 August 1914; European War, Samoa, Egypt, Gallipoli, and France; North Russia on Lord Rawlinson's staff, Aug. 1919; Brigade Major at Aldershot and in Ireland (Cork), 1919-21; Staff College, 1921-22 (D.S.O., M.C., despatches 7 times, Brevet Majority and Bt. Lieut.-Colonel); War Office, 1923-27; G.S.O.2 Staff College, Camberley, 1928-31; commanded Depôt The Rifle Brigade, 1931-34 and 2nd Bn. K.R.R.C., 1934-36; G.S.O.1. 2nd Division, 1936-38; Commandant, Royal Military College, 1938-39; Divisional Commander, 1940; Director-General Home Guard, 1940-41; G.O.C.-in-C. Northern Command, 1941-44; Governor and Commander-in-Chief of Gibraltar, 1944-47; retired, 1947. J.P. (Wilts.), 1951. K.St.J. Grand Cross of St. Adolfe of Nassau, Luxembourg, 1944. *Address:* Irongate House, Rodmarton, Gloucestershire. *T.:* Rodmarton 233. *Club:* Naval and Military. [*Died* 15 *Feb.* 1959.

EATON, (Walter) Cecil, C.B. 1933; Hon. A.R.I.B.A. 1936; M.A.; *b.* 5 Nov. 1875; *yr. s.* of late Rev. Canon J. R. T. Eaton, Hon. Canon of Worcester, and Julia Mary Sargent; *m.* 1905, Gladys Mary, *er. d.* of late John Alexander. *Educ.:* Winchester College (Scholar); New College, Oxford. Entered Board of Education, 1901; Principal Assistant Secretary, Board of Education, 1929-36; retired, 1936. *Address:* c/o Westminster Bank, 154 Harley Street, W.1. *Club:* Overseas. [*Died* 20 *April* 1958.

EBBISHAM, 1st Baron, *cr.* 1928, of Cobham; **George Rowland Blades,** G.B.E., *cr.* 1927, 1st Bt., *cr.* 1922; Kt., *cr.* 1918; F.S.A.; D.L. Surrey; Chairman, Blades, East and Blades, Limited; Treasurer Dr. Barnardo's Homes; *b.* 15 Apr. 1868; *o. s.* of Rowland Hill Blades, Sydenham, Kent; *m.* 1907, Margaret, M.B.E. 1943 (Officer Legion of Honour, Order St. John), *d.* of late Arthur Reiner, Sutton, Surrey; one *s.* three *d.* Alderman for Ward of Bassishaw, 1920-48; Senior Sheriff City of London, 1917-18; Lord Mayor, 1926-27; one of H.M.'s Lieutenants for the City of London; President Federation of British Industries, 1928-29; Past Master of the Haberdashers' and Stationers' Companies; Vice Grand Master, Primrose League; M.P. (U.) Epsom Division of Surrey, 1918-28; J.P. County of London and Surrey; Treas. Conservative Party organisation, 1931-33; President, National Union, 1936; Vice-Pres. City of London Savings Committee; Almoner, Christ's Hospital; Member Committee of Enquiry into Government Printing Establishments, 1923, of Royal Police Commission, 1928, and of Channel Tunnel Committee, 1929; Trustee Surrey County Cricket Club; Grand Officer, Legion of Honour; Grand Officer, Crown of Italy; Grand Officer de l'Ordre de la Couronne, Belgium; Officer of the Order of the Nile (Egypt). *Recreations:* cricket, golf. *Heir:* *s.* Hon. Rowland Roberts Blades. *Address:* 41 Upper Brook Street, W.1. *T.:* Mayfair 7977; The Rookery, Seaview, Isle of Wight. *T.:* Seaview 3139; 17 & 23 Abchurch Lane, E.C.4. *T.A.:* Identical, Cannon, London. *T.:* Mansion

House 4366. *Clubs:* Bath, Carlton, Royal Thames Yacht; Royal Yacht Squadron. [*Died* 24 *May* 1953.

EBBS, Commissioner William Alexander; Salvation Army Officer since 1908; Secretary for Trade and Managing Director, Salvationist Publishing & Supplies Ltd., since 1956; *b.* 20 September 1890; *e. s.* of F. Major W. Alfred Ebbs; *m.* 1913, Louisa Lowe, *e. d.* of Charles Moore, Arbroath; one *d. Educ.:* Board and Church Schools. Various appointments in Gt. Britain until 1919, when transferred to France. Divl. Comdr. Paris-Nord Div., 1919-1922; Second-in-Command, Belgium, 1922-1924; Comdr. for Italy, 1924-29; U.S.A., 1929-40 (Comdr. Metropolitan (New York), Hudson River, W. Pennsylvania Divs.). Chief and Field Sec., N.Z., 1940-43; Chief Sec.-in-Charge, Australia, E. Territory (N.S.W. and Queensland), 1943, 1946; Dir. British Red Shield Services, 1946-47; Territorial Comdr., Union of S. Africa and Portuguese E. Africa, 1947-50; Literary Sec. and Editor-in-Chief Internat. H.Q., London, 1950. Sec. for Internat. Public Relations Dept. and Parliamentary Affairs: Director, Migration, Overseas Settlement and Travel Department, 1952-56. Dir. S.A. Assurance Soc., Ltd. Salvation Army Order of Long Service. Member London Rotary Club. *Recreation:* reading. *Address:* 29 Treewall Gardens, Bromley, Kent. *T.:* Kipling 6829. [*Died* 22 *Aug.* 1960.

EBRAHIM, Sir (Huseinali) Currimbhoy, 3rd Bt., *cr.* 1913; merchant; *b.* 13 Apr. 1903; *o. s.* of Sir Mahomedbhoy Currimbhoy Ebrahim, 2nd Bt., and Bai Sakinabai, *d.* of Jairazhbhoy Pirbhoy; *S.* father, 1928; *m.* 1st, 1921, Zainub (divorced 1924), *d.* of late M. Dawoodbhoy Fazulbhoy; two *d.*; 2nd, 1926, Amina Khanum (divorced 1944), *d.* of Alhaj Cassumali Jairajbhoy, Gulshanabad, Pedder Road, Bombay; one *s.*; 3rd, 1946, Khurshidbanoo (formerly Kathleen Mary Mackenzie) (divorced 1949), *o. d.* of Martin Thomas Smith; 4th, 1949, *remarried* Amina Khanum. *Heir: s.* Mahomed, *b.* 24 June 1935. *Address:* Bait-ul-Aman, 33 Mirza Khalig Bey Road, Jamshed Quarters, Karachi, Pakistan. [*Died* 4 *March* 1952.

EBURY, 5th Baron *cr.* 1857, **Robert Egerton Grosvenor,** D.S.O. 1944; Major, Berks. Yeomanry; *b.* 8 Feb. 1914; *er. s.* of 4th Baron and Mary Adela Glasson; *S.* father, 1932; *heir pres.* to 7th Earl of Wilton; *m.* 1st, 1933, Anne (who obtained a divorce, 1941) *o. d.* of Herbert Walter Acland-Troyte; two *s.*; 2nd, 1941, Hon. Denise Margaret Yarde-Buller (who obtained a divorce, 1954), *d.* of 3rd Baron Churston; two *s.* two *d.*; 3rd, 1954, Mrs. Sheila Anker. *Educ.:* Harrow. Lord-in-Waiting, 1939-40. *Heir: s.* Hon. Francis Egerton Grosvenor, *b.* 8 Feb. 1934. *Address:* Days House, East Hanney, Berks. *Clubs:* Bath, Pratt's; Royal Yacht Squadron. [*Died* 5 *May* 1957.

ECCLES, James Ronald, M.A.; *b.* 9 Jan. 1874; *s.* of Richard Eccles, The Elms, Lower Darwen, Lancashire; unmarried. *Educ.:* Clifton College; King's College, Cambridge (exhibitioner). 1st Class Nat. Sci. Tripos, Part I., 1st Class Nat. Sci. Tripos, Part II.; Assistant Master at Gresham's School, Holt, 1900; Second Master, 1907-19; Headmaster, Gresham's School, Holt, 1919-35. *Publications:* Lecture Notes on Light; Advanced Lecture Notes on Light; Advanced Lecture Notes on Heat. *Address:* The Elms, Lower Darwen, Lancashire. [*Died* 31 *Aug.* 1956.

ECCLES, Launcelot William Gregory, C.M.G. 1944; M.C.; *b.* 1890; *s.* of W. G. Eccles, Hilton Rd., Natal; *m.* 1921, Viva Margot Bagnell; two *s.* two *d. Educ.:* Michaelhouse, Natal; Worcester Coll., Oxford. Asst. Surveyor, N. Rhodesia, 1912; European War, 1914-20, E. Africa, France, N. Russia, Capt. Coldstream Guards (M.C., despatches). Commissioner Lands, Mines and Local Govt., 1933; Comr. Lands and Mines, 1935; Chm. Lands Commission, 1942; Chairman African Housing Commission, 1944; Commissioner for Local Government and African Housing, N. Rhodesia, 1946-49; retired, 1949. Chairman Land Tenure Committee, 1943. *Recreations:* all forms of athletics and fishing. *Address:* Bronte, Baines Av., Salisbury, S. Rhodesia. [*Died* 16 *June* 1955.

ECKENER, Dr. Hugo, Dr.Ing.e.h.; *b.* Flensburg, 10 Aug. 1868; *m.* 1898; one *s.* one *d. Educ.:* Flensburg; Univs. of München, Berlin, and Leipzig. First pilot of the Zeppelin Works since 1906; during European War, 1914-18, trainer of airship pilots with the German Navy; Commander of the Graf Zeppelin on the first transatlantic flights, on the round the world trip, the Arctic trip, and several long distance flights. Chairman of the Luftschiffbau Zeppelin G.M.B.H., the Deutsche Zeppelin-Reederei, Frankfurt, the Maybach Motorenwerke and the Zahnradfabrik Friedrichshafen A.G. Gold Medal of Royal Aeronautical Society, 1936. *Publications:* Graf Zeppelin, 1938; Im Zeppelin über Länder und Meere, 1949. [*Died* 14 *Aug.* 1954.

ECKERSLEY, Roger Huxley; *b.* 28 Nov. 1885; *e. s.* of William Alfred Eckersley and Rachel, *d.* of Professor T. H. Huxley; *m.* 1913, Nancy Edith Alice Rose; two *s. Educ.:* Hillside, Godalming; Charterhouse. Took up law in 1903; after severe illness became Sec. of Littlehampton and then Stoke Poges golf clubs, 1912-15; Foreign office, temp. 1915-1918; King's Messenger, 1918-20; Farmed, 1920-24; Director of Programmes, B.B.C., 1924-30; Assistant Controller, B.B.C., 1930-1939; Chief Censor, B.B.C., 1939-45; retired, 1945. Appeals organiser, 1948, General Manager, 1949-, Guide Dogs for the Blind Association, Ltd. *Publications:* Songs of various kinds, 1904 and thereafter; The B.B.C. and all that, 1946; Some Nonsense, 1947. *Recreation:* gardening. *Address:* Little Renby, Boarshead, Crowborough, Sussex. *T.:* Crowborough 488. *Club:* Boodle's. [*Died* 19 *Nov.* 1955.

ECKERSLEY, Thomas Lydwell, B.A., B.Sc.; M.I.E.E.; F.R.S. 1938; Research Physicist; retired; Scientific Adviser to Marconi's Wireless Telegraph Co. Ltd., 1919, 1946 (taken over by Air Ministry, A.I.4. during the war), retired 1946; *b.* 27 Dec, 1886; *s.* of W. A. Eckersley, Civil Engineer and Rachel, *d.* of Thomas Henry Huxley; *m.* 1920, Eva, *d.* of Barry Pain; one *s.* two *d. Educ.:* Bedales School; University College, London; Trinity College, Cambridge. National Physical Laboratory, 1910; Inspector, Egyptian Government Survey, 1913-1914; Lt. R.E., mainly in Egypt, 1914-19. Faraday Medal, 1951. *Publications:* mainly Scientific Papers for Institution of Electrical Engineers, Phil. Mag., Terrestrial Magnetism and Atmospheric Electricity, and Royal Society. *Recreation:* reading. *Address:* Weatheroak, Danbury, nr. Chelmsford, Essex. *T.:* Danbury 12. [*Died* 15 *Feb.* 1959.

EDE, Comdr. Lionel James Spencer, D.S.O. 1940; D.S.C. 1943; R.N., retired; *b.* 10 Oct. 1903; *s.* of late James Parks Ede, Colonial Service, and Ellen Spencer; *m.* 1st, 1930, Titanya Elizabeth Petrie; one *s.* five *d.*; 2nd, 1952, Edna Mary Smallman. *Educ.:* The Grammar School, Portsmouth. Entered R.N., 1921, as Cadet; Lt., 1927; Lt.-Cdr. 1935; Comdr., 1940 (despatches twice); retired 1953. Legion of Merit (U.S.A.), 1943. *Recreations:* gardening, stock breeding. *Address:* Merrow Down, Four Marks, Hants. *Club:* Goat. [*Died* 8 *May* 1956.

EDELSTON, Sir Thomas Dugald, Kt., *cr.* 1931. Sheriff of Calcutta, 1931; late Senior Partner of Begg, Dunlop & Co., Ltd., Calcutta; *b.* 13 Aug. 1878; *s.* of late James Edelston,

Preston; *m.* Ethel Mary, *d.* of late Frederick William Hirst. [*Died* 19 *Oct.* 1955.

EDEN, Brig.-General Archibald James Fergusson, C.M.G. 1918; D.S.O. 1916; *b.* 20 Jan. 1872; *s.* of late Lt.-Col. A. D. Eden, The Cameronians; *m.* 1903, Isabella Anne, *d.* of late Rev. E. M. Weir, Rector of Tydavnet, Co. Monaghan; one *d.* *Educ.:* Haileybury College; R.M.C., Sandhurst. Gazetted to Oxfordshire Light Infantry, 1892; Captain, 1900; Brevet Major, 1900; Major, 1911; Brevet Lieut.-Col. 1915; Lt.-Col. 1915; Col. 1919; Brig.-Commander, 1916-24; retired pay, 1924; with W. African Frontier Force, 1898-1901; served Niger Hinterland, 1898 (medal with clasp); Ashanti Expedition, 1900 (despatches, brevet-Major, medal with clasp); S.A. War, 1901-2 (medal with 5 clasps); European War (despatches, brevet Lt.-Col., D.S.O., C.M.G., Croix de Guerre). *Address:* Southdown House, Shawford, Winchester. *Club:* Army and Navy. [*Died* 8 *May* 1956.

EDEN, Guy E. Morton; *s.* of Charles Henry Eden, Royal Navy; *m.* Ethel, *d.* of William Holman; three *s.* one *d.* *Educ.:* Westminster. Barrister-at-law, Inner Temple; member of the Bar of New South Wales; attached to Board of Education, Legal Branch 1903-5 and 1906-14; attached to Directorate of Military Intelligence, War Office, 1914-18. *Publications:* book of one act grand opera, The 'Prentice Pillar, produced at His Majesty's Theatre; book and lyrics of comic opera, The Mountaineers, produced at the Savoy Theatre; book and lyrics of Goldman, Ltd., produced at various London and provincial theatres; part author of book and lyrics of The Love Doctor, produced at various London and provincial theatres; part author of two plays entitled respectively, When the Clock Strikes, and The Gun Runner; author of many lyrics for songs; two novels, The Cry of the Curlew, and He Went Out with the Tide; and a volume of Australian verse entitled Bush Ballads. *Recreations:* cricket, lawn tennis, rowing. *Address:* 7 Abbey Road Mansions, St. John's Wood, N.W.8. *Clubs:* Bath, Savage. [*Died* 5 *Dec.* 1954.

EDEN, Helen Parry; poet and critic; *b.* 1885; *e. d.* of late His Honour Judge Sir Edward Parry; *m.* 1906, Denis Eden, artist (*d.* 1949); one *s.* two *d.* *Educ.:* Roedean School; Manchester Univ. History Scholarship, 1902; Vice-Chancellor's Prize English Verse, 1903; studied painting under Byam Shaw, and Rex Vicat Cole at King's College, 1903-5. *Publications:* Bread and Circuses, 1914; Coal and Candlelight, 1918; The Rhyme of the Servants of Mary, 1919; A String of Sapphires, 1921; Whistles of Silver, 1933; Poems and Verses, 1943; contributions (verse, short stories and criticism) to English and American reviews, etc. *Address:* Brookside, Enstone, Oxon. [*Died* 19 *Dec.* 1960.

EDGAR, Surgeon Rear-Admiral William Harold, C.B. 1943; O.B.E. 1933; M.D.; *b.* 9 Sept. 1885; *s.* of Charles Smith and Mary Jane Edgar, Bishop Auckland; *m.* 1915, Gwendoline Ann Elizabeth Smalley (*decd.*); one *d.* *Educ.:* Durham University; St. Mary's Hospital, London. Joined Royal Navy, 1908; i/c Royal Naval Hospital, Malta, 1939-41; K.H.P., 1942-45; retired, 1945. Naval Representative on Council of Brit. Med. Assoc., 1945-49. *Publications:* contrib. to Medical papers. *Recreations:* golf, bridge, literature. *Address:* 16 Beech Grove, Alverstoke, Hants. [*Died* 20 *Nov.* 1959.

EDGCUMBE, Major-General Oliver Pearce, C.B. 1948; C.B.E. 1942; M.C. 1915; *b.* 1892; *s.* of late Sir Robert Edgcumbe and late Frances, *d.* of Adm. Hon. Fitzgerald Algernon Charles Foley; *m.* 1935, Iris, *d.* of late William Pallet Cox. *Educ.:* Winchester; R.M.C., Sandhurst. Commissioned D.C.L.I., 1911; transferred to Royal Signals, 1920; Staff Coll., Camberley, 1927-28; Director of Organisation, War Office, 1941-42; Commissioner Allied Control Commission, Hungary, 1944-47; retired with hon. rank Major-Gen., 1947. Commander Legion of Merit (U.S.A.), 1945. *Address:* Arncliff House, Radnor Cliff, Folkestone. *Club:* United Service. [*Died* 11 *Dec.* 1956.

EDGE-PARTINGTON, Rev. Canon Ellis Foster, M.C. 1917, Bar 1918; Canon Emeritus since 1954; Vicar of St. John's, Dormansland, 1947-54; Rural Dean of Godstone, 1949-54; Chaplain to the Queen, 1952-1956 (to King George VI, 1941-52); *b.* 28 Aug. 1885; *s.* of James Edge-Partington and Ada Caroline Cunliffe; *m.* 1917, Esther Muriel Seymour; two *s.* two *d.* *Educ.:* Felsted School; Trinity College, Cambridge. Played Hockey for the University, 1905-08, for England, 1909. Cambridge House, Camberwell (Social Settlement), 1907-08; Ridley Hall, Cambridge, 1908-09. Deacon, 1909, joined staff of St. Mary, Portsea; Priest, 1910; C.F., 1915-19; Vicar of St. Mary the Less, Lambeth, S. London, 1919; Priest-in-Charge of St. John, Southend, Lewisham, 1923, and Vicar, 1928-43; Canon of Southwark Cathedral, 1935-36; Hon. Canon of Southwark Cathedral, 1936; Vicar of All Saints, Tooting Graveney, S. London, 1943; Select Preacher, Cambridge University, 1943. *Recreations:* carpentry and gardening. *Address:* St. Agnes Home, Garland Rd., East Grinstead, Sussex. [*Died* 17 *Aug.* 1957.

EDGELL, George Harold; Director of Museum of Fine Arts, Boston, Massachusetts, U.S.A., since 1935; *b.* St. Louis, Missouri, 4 March 1887; *s.* of George Stephen Edgell and Isabella Wallace Corbin; *m.* 1914, Jean Walters Delano; two *s.* *Educ.:* Cutler's School, New York; Harvard Univ., Cambridge, Mass. (A.B. 1909; Ph.D. 1913); Art D. (Hon.) 1948. Fellow American Acad. in Rome, 1910-12; Asst. in Fine Arts, Harvard, 1909-10; Instructor, 1912-14; Asst. Professor, 1914-22; Associate Professor, 1922-25; Professor, 1925-35; Dean of the Faculty of Architecture, Harvard, 1922-35; American representative Interallied Commission for Propaganda, Italian General Staff, 1918; Annual professor American Academy in Rome, 1919-20; Exchange professor University of Paris, 1929; Fellow American Academy of Arts and Sciences, 1932; Overseer of Harvard University, 1936-1942; Chairman, Commonwealth of Massachusetts Art Commission, 1941-51; Chevalier of the Legion of Honour, 1935. *Publications:* A History of Architecture, 1918 (with Fiske Kimball); The American Architecture of To-day, 1928; A History of Sienese Painting, 1932; The Bee Hunter, 1949. *Recreations:* travel, hunting, fishing. *Address:* Museum of Fine Arts, Boston, Mass. *T.A.:* Musart, Boston. *T.:* Kenmore 5866. *Clubs:* Athenæum; Harvard, Tavern (Boston); Harvard, Century (New York). [*Died* 29 *June* 1954.

EDGINTON, May; writer; *m.* 1912, Francis E. Baily; one *s.* *Publications:* many novels and short stories and serials in British and American magazines. Part author of Plays: Secrets, The Prude's Fall, The Ninth Earl, His Lady Friends, adapted for stage as No! No! Nanette! Author of plays: Deadlock, The Fairytale, The Harvest is Mine. Associated with the writing of many films, both in England and America. *Recreations:* dancing, motoring, gardening, travelling. *Clubs:* Sesame; Alexandra (Capetown). [*Died* 17 *June* 1957.

EDGLEY, Sir Norman George Armstrong, Kt., *cr.* 1947; Q.C. 1949; M.A. (Oxon.); F.S.A.; Judge, Supreme Restitution Court, Germany, since 1955; *b.* 19 June 1888; *s.* of George Martin and Mary Gertrude Edgley; *m.* 1st, 1914, Kathleen Blanche Bridget Daley (*d.* 1953); one *d.* (one *s.* killed in action, Burma, 1942); 2nd, 1956, Eleanor Barkell Finlay. *Educ.:* Switzerland; New College, Oxford. Passed into I.C.S. 1910; Assistant Magistrate, Bengal,

1911; Under Sec. Political and Appt. Depts., 1916-18; Registrar Calcutta High Court, Appellate Side, 1918-23; Called to Bar (Inner Temple), 1924; District and Sessions Judge in Bengal and Assam, 1924-32; Kaisar-i-Hind Gold Medal, 1930; Judicial Secretary and Legal Remembrancer to the Govt. of Bengal, 1933; Offg. Judge, High Court, Calcutta, 1934; Addl. Judge, High Court, 1937; Puisne Judge, Calcutta High Court, 1939-48; Chairman, District Valuation Board for Southern England under the Coal Industry Nationalisation Act, 1948-1953; Judge, Allied High Commission for Germany, Supreme Court (British Zone), 1953-55; President, Claims Tribunal (British Zone), 1953-55; Pres., Bengal Election Tribunal, 1937; Pres. Royal Asiatic Society of Bengal, 1946; Trustee of Victoria Memorial, Calcutta, 1946; Member, Central Advisory Board of Archæology for India, 1945; Member, Patents Appeal Board (Allied High Commission), 1954. *Recreations:* archæology, travel. *Clubs:* East India and Sports; Royal Calcutta Turf (Calcutta). [*Died* 4 *Feb.* 1960.

EDMAN, Irwin; Professor of Philosophy since 1935, Executive Officer, Dept. of Philosophy, since 1945, Columbia University; *b.* 28 Nov. 1896; *s.* of Soloman Edman and Ricka Sklower; unmarried. *Educ.:* Columbia University (A.B. 1916; Ph.D. 1920). Lecturer in Philosophy, 1918-20, Instructor, 1920-24, Asst. Prof., 1925-31, Assoc, Prof., 1931-35, Columbia University; Henry Ward Beecher Lecturer, Amherst College, 1935; Summer Lecturer, Univ. of California, 1939; Wm. Mitchell Fellow, Columbia, 1916-17; Member; ed. board, American Scholar; editor, Journal of Philosophy. *Publications:* Human Traits and their Social Significance, 1920; Richard Kane Looks at Life, 1925; Poems, 1925; The World, The Arts and the Artist, 1928; Adam the Baby, and the Man from Mars, 1929; The Contemporary and his Soul, 1931; The Mind of Paul, 1935; Four Ways of Philosophy, 1937; Philosopher's Holiday, 1938; Arts and the Man, 1939; Candle in the Dark, 1939; Philosopher's Quest, 1946. Ed.; Works of Plato, 1930; Philosophy of Santayana, 1936; Philosophy of Schopenhauer, 1928. Co-author; Living Philosophies, 1931; American Philosophy Today and Tomorrow, 1935; Columbia Studies in History of Ideas, 1935; Fountainheads of Freedom; The Growth of Democratic Idea, 1941. *Recreations:* writing light verse, collecting records of classical music, travel. *Address:* 315 West 106th Street, New York, N.Y. [*Died* 4 *Sept.* 1954.

EDMEADES, Major Henry; late York and Lancaster Regt.; *b.* 8 Feb. 1875; *s.* of late Maj.-Gen. H. Edmeades, R.A., and Mary Elizabeth, *d.* of Rev. W. T. Collings; *m.* 1911, Violet, *d.* of T. F. Burnaby-Atkins of Halstead Place, Kent; two *s.* one *d.* *Educ.:* Harrow. Entered army, 1897; Capt. 1902; Major, 1915; served European War. *Address:* Nurstead Court, Meopham, Kent. *T.A.:* Meopham. *Club:* Junior United Service. [*Died* 20 *April* 1952.

EDMOND, Colin Alexander; formerly Envoy and Minister in H.M. Foreign Service; *b.* 23 June 1888; *yr. s.* of John Edmond, of Kingswells, Aberdeenshire, and Eva, *e. d.* of Gen. John Fraser, C.B.; *m.* Effie, *e. d.* of Lt.-Col. F. W. Burr, R. Scots Fus.; one *s.* one *d.* *Educ.:* Malvern; Christ Church, Oxford (M.A.); abroad. F.R.G.S. Served in Portugal and Brazil; Spain, Cuba, Venezuela, Panama and Ecuador; Norway, Switzerland and Baltic; has also travelled in other European and South American countries, West Indies and U.S.A. *Address:* Milford, 13 The Goffs, Eastbourne, Sussex. *T.:* Eastbourne 4324. [*Died* 13 *Dec.* 1956.

EDMONDS, Air Vice-Marshal Charles Humphrey Kingsman, C.B.E. 1943 (O.B.E. 1919); D.S.O. 1915; late R.A.F.; *b.* 20 April 1891; *s.* of Charles Edmonds, Lymington, Hants; *m.* 1917, Lorna Karim Chadwick, *d.* of Col. George Osborn, R.A.; one *s.* one *d.* Served Balkan War, 1911-12; Central Flying School, 1912; Squadron-Commander, 1916; European War, 1914-19; Cuxhaven raid, Dec. 1914 (despatches, D.S.O.); Gallipoli, 1915 (despatches); British Naval Mission to Greece, 1927-29; Deputy Director of Manning, Air Ministry, 1932-35; A.O. i/c Admin. Allied Expeditionary Air Force, 1944; Wing Commander, 1918; Group Capt. 1929; Air Commodore, 1940; Air Vice-Marshal, 1942; retired, 1945. French Croix de Guerre with palm, 1918; Commander of the Order of the Crown of Italy, 1918; Greek Order of Merit, 1929; Commander of Order Polonia Restituta, 1945; Commander of American Legion of Merit, 1945. Passed Staff Colleges, Camberley and Andover. *Publications:* numerous articles on professional subjects in service journals, Encyclopaedia Britannica, etc. *Address:* The Robins, Hillview Road, Woking, Surrey. *Club:* United Service. [*Died* 26 *Sept.* 1954.

EDMONDS, Brigadier-General Sir James Edward, Kt., *cr.* 1928; C.B. 1911; C.M.G. 1916; Officier Légion d'Honneur, 1915; D.Litt. (Oxford); *b.* 25 Dec. 1861; *s.* of J. Edmonds; *m.* 1895, Hilda Margaret Ion (*d.* 1921), *d.* of late Rev. M. Wood; one *d.* *Educ.:* King's College School, London; R.M.A., Woolwich. Entered R.E. 1881; Capt. 1890; Major, 1899; Lieut.-Colonel, 1906; Colonel, 1909; p.s.c., 1897; Instructor Royal Military Academy, 1890-96; D.A.A.G. Headquarters of army, 1899-1901; D.A.Q.M.G., etc., 1904-8; General Staff Officer, 1st Grade, War Office, 1909-10; General Staff Officer 1st Grade, 4th Division, 1911 14; served S. Africa, 1901-2 (Queen's medal 4 clasps); European War, 1914-19; Gen. Staff Officer of 4th Division, August 1914; Deputy Engineer in Chief, B.E.F., 1918, etc. (six times in despatches); Officer in charge of Military Branch, Historical Section, Committee of Imperial Defence, now Cabinet Office, 1919-49; Secretary to British Delegation to Geneva Conference, 1906; British Delegate to Red Cross Conference, 1907; Officer of Bulgarian Order of St. Alexander. *Publications:* A History of the Civil War in the United States, 1861-65; A Handbook of the German Army; Official History of the War: Military Operations in France and Belgium, 1914, vol. i. 1922, vol. ii. 1925; 1951, vol. i. 1927, vol. ii. 1928; 1916, vol. i. 1931; 1917, vol. ii. 1949; 1918, vols. i.-v., 1935-45; A Short History of World War I, 1951; Laws and Usages of War (with Prof. L. Oppenheim), etc. *Address:* Brecon House, Sherborne, Dorset. [*Died* 2 *Aug.* 1956.

EDMONSTONE, Sir Archibald, 5th Bt., *cr.* 1774; C.V.O.; J.P., D.L.; *b.* 30 May 1867; *e. s.* of 4th Bt. and Mary Elizabeth, *d.* of Lt.-Col. Parsons, C.M.G.; *S.* father, 1888; *m.* 1895, Ida, (*d.* 1946) *o. d.* of G. Stewart Forbes; three *s.* (*e. s.* killed in action). *Educ.:* Christ Church, Oxford. Groom-in-Waiting to King Edward VII. *Heir:* *s.* (Archibald) Charles, *q.v.* *Address:* c/o Williams Agency Ltd., 116 Victoria Street, Westminster, S.W.1. [*Died* 1 *April* 1954.

EDMONSTONE, Sir (Archibald) Charles, 6th Bt., *cr.* 1774; J.P.; *b.* 16 June 1898; landed proprietor; *er. surv. s.* of Sir Archibald Edmonstone, 5th Bt., C.V.O., and Ida (*d.* 1946), *o. d.* of G. Stewart Forbes; *S.* father, 1954; *m.* 1923, Gwendolyn Mary, *d.* of late Marshall Field and of Mrs. Maldwin Drummond; one *s.* four *d.* (and one *s.* decd.). *Educ.:* Wellington College; R.M.C., Sandhurst. Late Lieutenant 9th Lancers and A.D.C. to Governor of Madras. Served European War, 1914-18. *Recreations:* hunting, shooting, racing, Joint Master, Fernie Hounds, 1928-34. *Heir:* *s.* Archibald Bruce Charles Edmonstone, [*b.* 3 Aug. 1934; *m.* 1957, Jane, *er. d.* of Maj.-Gen. E. C. Colville,

C.B., D.S.O., two *d.*] *Address:* Duntreath Castle, Blanefield, nr. Glasgow. *T.:* Blanefield 215. *Clubs:* Turf, White's; New (Edinburgh). [*Died* 5 *June* 1954.

EDMUNDS, Rev. Horace Vaughan, M.A., Hon. C.F.; Rector of Birdbrook, 1941-1957, retired; *b.* Leyton, Essex, 21 Feb. 1886; *y. s.* of Rev. Charles Edmunds and Dora Young; *m.* 1937, Ethel Mary Scrivener; two *s.* one *d.* *Educ.:* Tonbridge (Scholar); Jesus College, Cambridge (Scholar); B.A. 1st Class Classical Tripos, 1908; 1st Class Theological Tripos, 1910; Jeremie Prize, 1910; Ridley Hall, Cambridge. Deacon, 1911; Priest, 1912; Curate of St. Luke, Liverpool, 1911-13; Curate, St. Matthew's; Warden, St. Matthew's House, Cambridge, 1913-15; Curate St. Barnabas, Cambridge, 1915-16; Curate, St. Peter's; Warden, St. Peter's Hostel, Belsize Square, Hampstead, 1916-17; Territorial C.F. 1917-20; Principal, Bishop Wilson Theological College; Domestic Chaplain to Lord Bishop of Sodor and Man, 1920-24; Vicar of All Saints', Forest Gate, 1925-41. *Recreations:* intellectual pursuits. *Address:* Highlands, Fingringhoe, Colchester, Essex. [*Died* 7 *Aug.* 1958.

EDMUNDS, Nellie M. Hepburn; Vice-Pres. Royal Society of Miniature Painters since 1912; *d.* of late Henry Chase Edmunds. *Educ.:* Slade School under Prof. Fred Brown; Westminster School of Art under Mouat Loudan. Has exhibited at the Royal Academy regularly for between 45 and 50 years (her work first accepted there while a student at the Slade School), and by special invitation at important International Exhibitions on the Continent; numerous notices in regard to her work, also reproductions; an example of her work is on permanent exhibition at the Victoria and Albert Museum, South Kensington, the only miniature by a living artist. *Address:* 77 Egerton Road, Bexhill, Sussex. [*Died* 14 *Feb.* 1953.

EDMUNDS, Sir Percy James, Kt., *cr.* 1946; C.I.E. 1943; M.A., B.Sc.; *b.* 1 Feb. 1890; *m.* S. E. Scott, Melbourne, Aust.; one *s.* one *d.* *Educ.:* Christ's Hospital; Queen's College, Oxford. Served European War, 1914-18, Captain R.E. Joined Indian Posts and Telegraph Dept., 1919; Director of Wireless, 1926; Chief Engineer, 1941-46; retired, 1946. *Address:* c/o Lloyds Bank, 6 Pall Mall, S.W.1. [*Died* 5 *Sept.* 1959.

EDRIDGE-GREEN, Frederick William, C.B.E. 1920; M.D., F.R.C.S. (Eng.); M.B. (First Class Hon.); M.D. (Gold Medal); late Special Examiner and Adviser of the Ministry of Transport on Vision and Colour-vision; late Ophthalmic Surgeon, London Pensions Boards; late Chairman Ophthalmic Board, Central London Medical Boards National Service; *m.* 1893, Minnie (*d.* 1901), *d.* of Henry Hicks, M.D., F.R.S. *Educ.:* St. Bartholomew's Hospital; Durham University; St. John's College, Cambridge. Member, British Association; late President, Durham Medical Graduates Association; late member, International Code of Signals Committee; late Beit Memorial Research Fellow; late Hunterian Professor and Arris and Gale Lecturer of the Royal College of Surgeons; inventor of colour perception spectrometer and colour perception lantern, the official test of the Navy; and the Railways and other bodies; and Bead Test the official test of the National Service; Président d'honneur de la séance plénière annuelle de la Société d'Ophtalmologie de Paris, 1930; Thomas Gray Memorial Prize for Colour Perception Lantern, 1936. *Publications:* Colour Blindness and Colour Perception, 1909; The Hunterian Lectures on Colour Vision and Colour Blindness, 1911; Memory and its Cultivation, 1897; The Physiology of Vision, 1920; Science and Pseudo-Science, 1933; and Card Test for Colour Blindness; Colour Vision and Colour Blindness, Encyclopædia Britannica, 1922; The Solution of the Problem of Vision, Chemistry Industry 12 Aug. 1939; and numerous papers in English and foreign Scientific Journals. *Recreations:* golf, chess, bridge. *Address:* Stanbrook, Littlehampton Rd., Ferring, Sussex. *Club:* Savage. [*Died* 17 *April* 1953.

EDWARD-COLLINS, Admiral Sir (George) Frederick (Basset), K.C.B., *cr.* 1941 (C.B. 1937); K.C.V.O., *cr.* 1939 (C.V.O. 1937); *b.* 26 Dec. 1883; 2nd *s.* of late E. C. Edward-Collins, Trewardale, Bodmin; unmarried. *Educ.:* H.M.S. Britannia. Midshipman of H.M.S. Goliath during Boxer War in China, 1900-3; Lieut. H.M.S. Thistle, 1906 (Royal Humane Society's Bronze Medal); served in H.M. Ships Superb and Tiger during war of 1914-1918; Admiralty representative Wei-Hai-Wei Rendition Commission, 1922-23; Capt., 1923; commanded H.M. Ships Carysfort, Comus and Renown; Assistant and Deputy-Director of Plans, Admiralty, 1927-30; Naval Assistant to 2nd Sea Lord, 1932-35; A.D.C. to H.M. The King, 1935; Rear-Admiral, 1935; Chief of Staff, Mediterranean Station, 1936-38; commanded Royal Escort to Their Majesties on the occasion of their visit to Canada and the U.S.A., 1939; commanded 2nd Cruiser Squadron, 1938-40 (despatches); Vice-Adm., 1939; Vice-Adm. Commanding Eighteenth Cruiser Squadron and 2nd in Command Home Fleet, 1940; Comdg. the North Atlantic Station, 1941-43; Temporary Governor of Gibraltar, 1942; Admiral, 1943; retired Feb. 1944; Flag Officer in charge Falmouth, 1944-45; D.L. Cornwall, 1945; Order of Polonia Restituta, 2nd Class (Poland), 1943; Commander of Order of Legion of Merit (U.S.A.), 1946. *Recreations:* shooting, fishing. *Address:* Benthams, Lostwithiel, Cornwall. *T.:* Lostwithiel 172. *Clubs:* United Service; Royal Fowey Yacht. [*Died* 17 *Feb.* 1958.

EDWARDES, Arthur Henry Francis; *b.* London, 8 Feb. 1885; *s.* of late Lieut.-Colonel Hon. C. E. Edwardes, 2nd *s.* of 3rd Baron Kensington and late Lady Blanche Edwardes, *d.* of 2nd Marquess of Ormonde; *m.* 1913, Sybil Frances Christina Lilah, 2nd *d.* of Rev. Lord Theobald Butler. *Educ.:* Haileybury College. Entered Chinese Maritime Customs Service of China, 1908; Officiating Inspector-General of Chinese Maritime Customs, 1927; resigned, 1928. *Recreations:* golf, shooting. *Address:* 208 Clive Court, W.9. [*Died* 22 *July* 1951.

EDWARDS, Alfred; *b.* 1888; *s.* of Thomas and Sarah Edwards; *m.* 1917, Anne Raines Hoskison; two *d.* Joined Labour Party 1931, Middlesbrough Town Council, 1932; M.P. (1935-48, Lab.; 1948-49, Ind.; 1949-1950, C.) E. Middlesbrough; joined Conservative Party, 1949; writes and lectures on international politics and economics. *Address:* Hemble Hill, Guisborough, Yorks. *T.:* 111. [*Died* 17 *June* 1958.

EDWARDS, Rt. Hon. Sir Charles, P.C. 1940; Kt., *cr.* 1935; C.B.E., 1931; J.P.; M.P. (Lab.) Bedwelty Division of Monmouthshire, Dec. 1918-50; Miners' Agent; *b.* 19 Feb. 1867; 5th *s.* of John and Catherine Edwards, Gravel, Radnorshire; *m.* M. A., *d.* of William and Jane Davies, Abercarn, Mon.; one *s.* one *d.* *Educ.:* National School, Llangunllo, Radnorshire. Miner, checkweigher; a Lord Commissioner of the Treasury, 1929-31; Chief Labour Whip, 1931-42; Joint Parliamentary Secretary to the Treasury, 1940-42; also served on Urban Council, Risca, and Mon. County Council, Education Authority, etc. *Recreation:* work. *Address:* Stafford House, Gelli Crescent, Risca, Mon. [*Died* 15 *June* 1954.

EDWARDS, Dr. Charles Alfred, F.R.S. 1930; Principal, 1927-47, and Professor of Metallurgy, 1920-47, University College, Swansea; *b.* 1882; *m.* 1908, Florence Edith Roberts; one *s.* Apprentice in foundries of Lanc. and Yorks Railway Works, 1898;

Chemical Laboratory, 1903-5; Assistant in Metallurgical Dept. N. P. Laboratory, Teddington, 1905-7; Lecturer in Metallurgy, Manchester University, 1907-10; Metallurgist, Bolckow, Vaughan & Co. and Dorman, Long & Co., Middlesbrough, 1910-14; Professor of Metallurgy, Manchester University, 1914-20. *Publications:* numerous publications dealing with properties of metals and alloys, in journals of Iron and Steel Institute, Institute of Metals, and Institute of Mechanical Engineers. *Address:* 20 Corrymore Mansions, Swansea, Glam. [*Died* 29 *March* 1960.

EDWARDS, Lieut.-Comdr. Charles Peter, C.M.G. 1946; O.B.E.; R.C.N.V.R.; Deputy Minister, Department of Transport, Ottawa, Canada, since 1941; *b.* Chester, England, 11 Dec. 1885; *s.* of Peter and Sarah Edwards; *m.* 1911, Ethel Maud Dickieson, Ottawa. *Educ.:* Arnold School, Chester, England. Junior Engineer, English Marconi Company, 1903; Engineer, Canadian Marconi Company, 1906; Director of Radio, Dominion Government, 1909; Director of Air Services, Dominion Government, 1936. *Recreations:* golf, fishing. *Address:* 454 Cloverdale Rd., Rockcliffe Park, Ont., Canada. *Clubs:* Rideau, Royal Ottawa Golf (Ottawa). [*Died* 13 *July* 1960.

EDWARDS, Brig.-General Christopher Vaughan, C.M.G. 1919, D.S.O. 1917; late Green Howards; *b.* 15 Jan. 1875; *m.* 1902, Violet, *d.* of Col. R. Charlton; two *d.* *Educ.:* St. Edward's, Oxford; R.M.C., Sandhurst. Joined the Green Howards, 1895; served Tirah, West Africa, S. Africa, Somaliland; European War, 1914-18 (twice wounded; Couronne de Belge, and Croix de Guerre); Officer in charge of Record and Pay Office, York, 1928-32; retired pay, 1933. *Recreation:* fishing. *Address:* Kirkland House, Whitehall, S.W.1. *Club:* Army and Navy. [*Died* 1 *Sept.* 1955.

EDWARDS, Rev. Father Douglas (Allen); Monk of the Community of the Resurrection, Mirfield, since 1941; *b.* 29 Aug. 1893. *Educ.:* Monkton Combe School; Exeter College, Oxford. M.A. (Oxon) 1923, B.D. (Oxon) 1943. Active Service, Royal Fusiliers, European War, 1915-18. Curate, Holy Redeemer, Clerkenwell, 1923-24; Vice-Principal, St. Stephen's House, Oxford, 1924-1929; Priest-in-Charge, St. James' with St. Anne's, Buxton, 1929-34; Vicar, St. Peter's, Stockport, 1934-36; Missionary Priest, Acting Archdeacon of Ziguland (Zanzibar diocese), 1936-38. Principal of the College of the Resurrection, 1947-49. *Publications:* Shining Mystery of Jesus, 1928; The Virgin Birth in History and Faith, 1943; The Defence of the Gospel, 1946; Jesus: the Gospel Portrait, 1948; The Ultimate Choice—Belief or Fantasy, 1949. *Recreations:* walking; study of the Gospels. *Address:* House of the Resurrection, Mirfield, Yorks. [*Died* 16 *Sept.* 1953.

EDWARDS, Evangeline Dora, M.A., D.Lit.; Prof. of Chinese in Univ. of London (School of Oriental and African Studies), 1939-54; Emeritus Professor, 1954; *b.* 13 Aug. 1888; *d.* of late Rev. John Edwards. *Educ.:* University of London. Lecturer in Chinese at School of Oriental Studies, Univ. of London, 1921-31; Reader in Chinese in Univ. of London, 1931-39. Acting-Head of the Percival David Foundation of Chinese Art, 1951-55. *Publications:* Chinese Prose Literature of the T'ang Period, Vol. I, 1937, Vol. II, 1938; The Dragon Book, 1939; Confucius, 1940; Bamboo, Palm and Lotus: An Anthology of South-East Asia, the Far East and the Pacific, 1947; articles in journals. *Club:* Lady Golfers'. [*Died* 29 *Sept.* 1957.

EDWARDS, Sir (George) Tristram, Kt. 1942; Hon. President (late Director), Smith's Dock Co., Ltd. (formerly Chairman and Joint Managing Director); Ex-Director Consett Iron Co., Ltd.; *b.* 1882; *s.* of late George S. F. Edwards, late of Nunthorpe Hall, Nunthorpe, Yorks; *m.* 1915, Aline Mary, *d.* of late Lt.-Col. W. H. Ritson, C.M.G., V.D., Hindley Hall, Stocksfield, Northumberland; two *s.* two *d.* *Educ.:* Uppingham School. Entered Smith's Dock Co., 1902; Director, 1914. Served in France during European War, 1914-18. President, Shipbuilding Employers Federation, 1933; Chairman, Shiprepairers' Central Council, 1940-42; President Shipbuilding Conference, 1944 and 1945. *Address:* The Hill, Broadway, Worcestershire. *T.:* Broadway 3391. [*Died* 10 *April* 1960.

EDWARDS, Air Marshal Harold, C.B. 1943; Air Officer Commanding-in-Chief, Royal Canadian Air Force Overseas; *b.* Chorley, Lancashire, England, 1892; *m.*; one *s.* one *d.* *Educ.:* England, Canada, and Germany. Joined Royal Canadian Navy, 1914; R.N.A.S. 1915; prisoner of war, 1916; joined newly formed Royal Canadian Air Force, 1920; was in command of various units of R.C.A.F. in Canada; commanded R.C.A.F. detachment at Coronation of King George VI, 1937; in charge of R.C.A.F. arrangements for Royal visit to Canada in 1939; in charge of arrangements for visit of Duke of Kent to Canada in 1941; held appointment of Air Member for Personnel on Canadian Air Council prior to taking command of R.C.A.F. Overseas. *Recreations:* fishing and golf. *Club:* Wings (New York). [*Died* 23 *Feb.* 1952.

EDWARDS, Rt. Hon. John; *see* Edwards, Rt. Hon. L. J.

EDWARDS, John, D.S.O. 1918; *b.* Llanbadarn, Aberystwyth, 1882; *s.* of late Rev. James Edwards, and Rachael Jones, Neath; *m.* Gwen, *d.* of late Dr. J. Davies Bryan, Alexandria; two *s.* one *d.* *Educ.:* British and Intermediate Schools, Neath; Univ. College of Wales, Aberystwyth (Scholar); B.A., London University. Barrister (Gray's Inn), 1921; served European War (R.W.F.), 1914-18 (Lieut.-Col., D.S.O., despatches twice); M.P. Aberavon Division of Glamorganshire, Dec. 1918-22; Independent Candidate University of Wales, 1923; High Sheriff of Cardiganshire, 1942; member of Court of University of Wales, Court and Council of University College of Wales; active part in Welsh Drama. *Publications:* The Call of the Sea; Edwards Castellnedd; contributions to English and Empire Law Digest, etc. *Address:* 11 West Road, Kingston, Surrey. *Club:* National Liberal. [*Died* 23 *May* 1960.

EDWARDS, John, C.B.E. 1920 (O.B.E. 1918); Chairman Windermere Diamond Die Co. Ltd., Staveley, nr. Windermere, Westmorland. Late Chm. and Man.Dir.: William Ryder, Ltd., Bolton; British Heating Industries, Ltd., Bolton and London. *Address:* Longtail Cottage, Windermere, Westmorland. [*Died* 22 *June* 1954.

EDWARDS, Vice-Admiral John Douglas, C.B. 1916; retired; *b.* 29 Sep. 1871; *m.* 1897, Mary Caroline Alice Kerr; no *c.* *Educ.:* H.M.S. Britannia. Served H.M.S. Sutlej as Commander (2nd in command) at time of Messina earthquake; commanded H.M.S. Falmouth during European War; present at Heligoland action and Jutland Battle, 1914-17 (despatches, C.B.); Commodore and S.N.O. H.M.S. Kent, Vladivostock, 1918-19; retired, 1920; ship sunk by German submarine, Aug. 1916; officer Legion of Honour; Order of St. Anne, 2nd Class with Swords, Russia; Czechoslovak Croix de Guerre. *Recreation:* golf. *Address:* Pittville Ct., Albert Rd., Cheltenham. [*Died* 30 *March* 1952.

EDWARDS, Rt. Hon. (Lewis) John, P.C. 1953; O.B.E. 1946; M.P. (Lab.) Brighouse and Spenborough since May 1950 (Blackburn, 1945-50); *b.* 27 May 1904; *s.* of late L. J. Edwards and Annie Rickard, Aylesbury; *m.* 1931, Dorothy May

Watson; two *d.* *Educ.:* Aylesbury Grammar School; University of Leeds. B.A. (Leeds), 1928; Staff Tutor University of Leeds, 1932-36; Secretary for Adult Education, University of Liverpool, 1936-1938; contested Leeds North, 1931 - 35; Parliamentary Private Secretary to Sir Stafford Cripps, President, Board of Trade, 1945-47; Parliamentary Secretary, Ministry of Health, 1947-49; Parliamentary Secretary, Board of Trade, 1949-50; Economic Secretary to Treasury, Oct. 1950 - Oct. 1951; Chairman Public Accounts Cttee., 1951-52; Leader, Argentine Trade Mission, 1951. Member: Select Cttee. on Delegated Legislation, 1953; Ecclesiastical Cttee., 1955-; Archbishops' Commission on Redundant Churches, 1959. Consultative Assembly, Council of Europe, 1955- (Vice-President 1957-59, President, 1959-); Assembly of W.E.U., 1955- (Chm. Budget Cttee., 1955-); President Socialist Inter Group (Council of Europe), 1956-59. Chairman: Dunford College (Y.M.C.A.); Board of Christian Frontier Trust; Exec. Chairman P.E.P.; a Vice-Pres. Assoc. of Municipal Corporations; Member Leeds City Council, 1933-36; Executive Member W.E.A. 1931-47; General Secretary P.O. Engineering Union, 1938-47; Member National Whitley Council for Civil Service, 1938 - 45; Vice - Chairman, P.O. Engineering Whitley Council, 1939 - 47; Deputy Commander, P.O. Home Guard, 1940-45. *Address:* 103 Hampstead Way, N.W.11. *T.:* Speedwell 3679. *Club:* Reform. [*Died* 23 *Nov.* 1959.

EDWARDS, Engineer Rear-Admiral Macleod Gamul Arthur, C.B. 1941; O.B.E. 1918; *b.* 3 Nov. 1884; *s.* of Rev. W. G. A. Edwards; *m.* 1st, 1909, Winifred (*d.* 1933), *d.* of Roland Richardson; one *s.*; 2nd, 1933, Cynthia, *d.* of Capt. Basil Piercy, R.N., Fornham House, Suffolk. *Educ.:* Fettes College, Edinburgh; Royal Naval Engineering College, Keyham. Entered Royal Navy, 1901; served Grand Fleet, 1914-17, Dover Patrol, 1917-18 (despatches twice, O.B.E.); Engr. Comdr., 1921; Engr. Capt., 1931; Engr. Rear-Admiral, 1937; Engr. Rear-Adm. on Staff of C.-in-C., Portsmouth, 1939-44; retired list, 1944. *Address:* Ware House, Stebbing, Essex. *Club:* Army and Navy. [*Died* 2 *Jan.* 1957.

EDWARDS, Sir Tristram; *see* Edwards, Sir G. T.

EDWARDS, Wilfred Norman, B.A. (Camb.); F.G.S.; Keeper of Department of Geology, British Museum (Natural History), 1938-55; *b.* 1890; 2nd *s.* of late C. L. Edwards; *m.* 1921, Winifred, *d.* of F. J. How; one *s.* *Educ.:* Cambridge County School; Christ's College, Cambridge (Scholar). Entered British Museum (Natural History), 1913; Deputy-Keeper of Geology, 1931-38; Secretary, Geological Society, 1939-1944 (Lyell Medallist, 1955). *Publications:* Papers, mainly on fossil plants, in scientific journals; guide-books issued by British Museum (Natural History). *Recreations:* reading, travel, folk-dancing. *Address:* The Old Rectory, Ickleford, Hitchin, Herts. *T.:* Hitchin 2697. [*Died* 17 *Dec.* 1956.

EDWARDS-MOSS, Sir Thomas, 3rd Bt., *cr.* 1868; *b.* 17 Jan. 1874; *er. s.* of Sir John Edwards Edwards-Moss, 2nd Bt. and Margaret (*d.* 1942), *d.* of Col. Ireland Blackburne, Hale Hall; *S.* father, 1935; *m.* 1926, Eda, *d.* of Edward Goodison, Bradford. *Educ.:* Eton. *Heir:* *n.* John Herbert Theodore Edwards-Moss [*b.* 24 June, 1913; *m.* 1951, Jane Rebie, *d.* of Carteret John Kempson; one *s.* one *d.*]. *Address:* Ashleigh, Chiddingfold, Surrey. [*Died* 26 *July* 1960.

EELES, Dr. Francis Carolus, O.B.E. 1938; D.Litt.; LL.D.; Secretary, Central Council for Care of Churches, since 1924 (Hon. Sec. of its Central Cttee., 1917-24); *b.* 28 Feb. 1876; *s.* of John and Isabella Caroline Eeles; *m.* 1908, Mary Hall, *d.* of Dr. J. R. Wolfe, Glasgow; no *c.* *Educ.:* privately. Engaged in own ecclesiological and liturgical work, also writing. D.Litt. Lambeth, 1938; LL.D. St. Andrews, 1951. *Publications:* The Holyrood Ordinale, Prayer Book revision and Christian Re-union; Edwardian Inventories of: Bedfordshire, Buckinghamshire; Church bells of: Linlithgowshire, Kincardineshire; short histories of churches; The Anglican Tradition, Ornaments and Fittings, in Post War Church Building; contrib. to: Proc. Soc. of Antiquaries of Scot., Trans. various Archæological and Ecclesiological Socs. *Address:* Earlham, Dunster, Somerset. [*Died* 17 *Aug.* 1954.

EGERTON of Tatton, 4th Baron, *cr.* 1859; **Maurice Egerton,** *b.* 4 Aug. 1874; *s.* of 3rd Baron and Anna Louisa (*d.* 1933), *d.* of S. Watson Taylor of Erlstoke Park, Wilts; *S.* father, 1920. *Heir:* none. *Address:* Tatton Park, Knutsford, Cheshire. [*Died* 30 *Jan.* 1958 (*ext.*).

EGERTON, Sir Alfred (Charles Glyn), Kt., *cr.* 1943; F.R.S. 1926; M.A.; F.R.I.C.; F.Inst.Phys.; D.Sc. London; Hon. D.Sc.: Birmingham, Fuad I University, Cairo, Nancy (France); Hon. D.Tech. (Finland); M.I.Chem.E.; Fellow of University College and Imperial College, London; Emeritus Professor of Chemical Technology, University of London, since 1952; Editor of Fuel; *b.* 1886; 4th *s.* of late Colonel Sir Alfred Mordaunt Egerton, K.C.V.O., and Hon. Mary Georgina, *e. d.* of 2nd Lord Harlech; *m.* 1912, Hon. Ruth Julia Cripps, *o. d.* of 1st Baron Parmoor, P.C., K.C.V.O., K.C. *Educ.:* Eton; University College, London. Reader in Thermodynamics, Oxford University, 1921-36; Prof. of Chemical Technology, Imperial Coll. of Science, 1936-1952; Chairman of Scientific Advisory Council to Minister of Fuel and Power, 1948-1953; late Member of the Advisory Council of the D.S.I.R.; Member Sci. Adv. Comm. (War Cabinet); Secretary of the Royal Society, 1938-48; Chm. Reviewing Cttees., Indian Inst. of Science, 1948; Chm. C.S.I.R., India, 1954. Hon. President Combustion Institute, 1958. Director of the Salters' Institute of Industrial Chemistry, 1949-1959. Rumford Medal of Royal Society, 1946; Coal Science Medal (British Coal Utilisation Research Association), 1952; Melchett Medal (Inst. of Fuel), 1956; U.S. Medal of Freedom with silver palm, 1946. *Publications:* lectures and contribs. in scientific journals chiefly relating to combustion and utilisation of energy. *Recreation:* painting. *Address:* 63E Princes Gate, S.W.7. *Club:* Athenæum. [*Died* 7 *Sept.* 1959.

EGERTON, Major-General Granville (George Algernon), C.B. 1905; *b.* 10 May 1859; *e. s.* of late Col. Hon. A. Egerton, Grenadier Guards, 4th *s.* of 1st Earl of Ellesmere. *Educ.:* Charterhouse; Sandhurst. Entered army, 72nd Highlanders, 1879; served Afghan War, 1879-80, including march to Kandahar (severely wounded, despatches, medal and two clasps and star); Egyptian War, 1882, as Adjutant Seaforth Highlanders, present at the battle of Tel-el-Kebir (medal and clasp, Khedive's Star); International occupation of Crete, 1897; Sudan Campaign, 1898, battles of Atbara and Omdurman (despatches, two medals and two clasps, Bt. Lt.-Col.); commanded 1st Yorkshire Regiment, 1903; Commandant Hythe School of Musketry, 1907-1909; comdg. Infantry Brigade, Malta, 1909-13; Major-General, 1912; Lowland Division, 1914-15; Inspector of Infantry, 1916; retd. pay, 1919; Colonel Highland Light Infantry 1921-29; served European War, Dardanelles (despatches). *Address:* 7 Inverleith Place, Edinburgh. *T.:* Edinburgh 83994. *Club:* New (Edinburgh). [*Died* 3 *May* 1951.

EGERTON, Hon. Thomas (Henry Frederick), 3rd *s.* of 3rd Earl of Ellesmere; *b.* 10 Sept. 1876; *m.* 1902, Lady Bertha Anson, *e. d.* of 3rd Earl of Lichfield; two *d.* Was Assistant Private Secretary to Lord St. Aldwyn when Chancellor of the Exchequer; late partner in firm of Cocks, Biddulph & Co., bankers, of 43 Charing Cross, S.W. *Address:* 16 Whitehall, S.W.1; Clarence Lodge, Englefield Green, Egham, Surrey. *Clubs:* Turf; Jockey (Newmarket). [*Died* 1 *Oct.* 1953.

EGGAR, Sir Arthur, Kt., *cr.* 1938; M.A.; Barrister-at-Law; retired Advocate-General, Burma; *b.* Farnham, Surrey, 22 May 1877; *s.* of late Sir Henry Eggar, M.V.O.; *m.* 1957, Margaret Gibb Cowan, *d.* of James Edward Cowan and *widow* of James D. Cowan, C.A., Glasgow; one step *s.* and one step *d.* *Educ.:* Uppingham; Trinity College, Cambridge. Professor of Law, Rangoon University, 1923-1937; served European War, R.G.A. and R.A.F., Captain (despatches). *Publications:* The Hatanee, 1906; Laws of India; Fairbairn's Rowing Notes; The Flying Dutchman. *Address:* The Dell, Bishopsgate Road, Englefield Green, Surrey. *T.:* Egham 3347. *Clubs:* Leander, East India and Sports. [*Died* 14 *May* 1958.

EGGINTON, Wycliffe, R.I. 1913; R.C.A. 1926; Landscape painter; *b.* Edgbaston, Birmingham, 12 Oct. 1875; *e. s.* of late J. W. Egginton, Birmingham; *m.* 1902, Edith, *e. d.* of late F. L. Calder, New Brighton, Cheshire; three *s.* two *d.* *Educ.:* Birmingham and Wallasey. A follower of the traditions of the old English Water Colour School; works included in the Victoria and Albert Museum, Feeney Art Gallery, Birmingham, Walker Art Gallery, Liverpool, Aberdeen Art Gallery, Corporation Art Gallery, Plymouth; the Municipal Museum and Art Gallery, Bristol; Corporation Art Gallery, Bury, Bournemouth, Museum and Art Gallery, Lincoln, and the Mackelvie Art Gallery, Auckland, N.Z.; exhibits at the Royal Academy, R.I., The Salon, Paris, and the leading provincial galleries; one man shows at The Fine Art Societies Galleries, New Bond Street, W. *Recreations:* caravaning, billiards. *Address:* South View, Teignmouth, South Devon. *T.:* Teignmouth 506. [*Died* 15 *June* 1951.

EGGLESTON, Sir Frederic William, Kt., *cr.* 1941; *b.* Brunswick, Melb., 17 Oct. 1875; *s.* of late J. W. Eggleston; *m.* 1904, Lulu (*d.* 1935), *d.* of F. A. Henriques, Perth, W. Australia; two *s.* one *d.* *Educ.:* Leys School, Cambridge; Melbourne University. Called to Bar, 1897; served European War with Aus. Imp. Force, 1916-18; M.L.A. St. Kilda, Victoria, 1920-27; Attorney-General and Solicitor-General, Victoria, 1924-27; Minister for Railways, 1924-26; Chairman Commonwealth Grants Commission, 1934-41; Minister to China, 1941-44; to U.S., 1944-46, retd. Chm. Cttee. appointed by Commonwealth Govt. to consider amalgamation Papua New Guinea, 1939; Member of Council, Institute of Pacific Relations. *Publications:* Editor of The Australian Mandate for New Guinea, 1928; Public Life of Hon. George Swinburne, 1931; State Socialism in Victoria, 1932; Search for a Social Philosophy, 1941; Reflections of an Australian Liberal, 1953; chapter on Australia and the Empire in Cambridge History of the British Empire. *Address:* 18 Royal Crescent, Camberwell, E.6, Victoria, Australia. [*Died* 12 *Nov.* 1954.

EINSTEIN, Prof. Albert, Ph.D. (Hon.), M.D. (Hon), D.Sc. (Hon.); discoverer and exponent of theory of relativity; Professor of Theoretical Physics; Permanent Member of Institute for Advanced Study, Princeton, N.J., 1933, working there for United States Navy Ordnance Bureau from 1943; *b.* Ulm, Württemberg, 14 March 1879; *s.* of Hermann Einstein and Pauline Koch; became Swiss citizen, 1901; *m.* 1st, 1901, Mileva Maritsch (marriage dissolved); two *s.*; 2nd. Elsa *d.* 1936), *d.* of Rudolf Einstein. *Educ.:* Luitpold Gymnasium, Munich; Aarauer Kantonsschule, Switzerland; Technische Hochschule, Zürich, Switzerland. Technical Asst., Swiss Patent Office, Berne, 1902; Privatdozent, Berne, 1908; Prof. Extraord., Zürich, 1909; Prof. of Theoretical Physics, Prague, 1911; returned to Zürich to corresponding post, 1912; Prof. of Physics, Univ. of Leyden, 1912-28, also Director of Kaiser Wilhelm Institut fur Physik, and Prof. of Physics, Univ. of Berlin, 1914-33. Mem. Prussian Acad. of Sciences. German citizen, 1914 (renounced 1933); went to U.S. 1933; U.S. citizen, 1940; after War, was a leading figure in World Government Movement; was offered, but did not accept, the Presidency of the State of Israel; collaborated with Dr. Chaim Weizmann in establishment of Univ. of Jerusalem. During the 1920's he lectured in Europe (including London), U.S., and the Far East. Rhodes Memorial Lecturer at Oxford, 1931; Research Student, Christ Church, 1931-32; Rouse Ball Lecturer, Cambridge, 1931-32. Nobel Prize for Physics, 1921; Copley Medal of Roy. Soc., 1925; Medal of Franklin Inst., 1935. Hon. degrees from Oxford, Cambridge, Manchester, London, and many other European and American Univs. *Publications:* Special Theory of Relativity, 1905; Relativity (Eng. trans.), 1920 and 1950; General Theory of Relativity, 1915; Investigations on Theory of Brownian Movement, 1926; About Zionism (Eng. trans.), 1930; (with Sigmund Freud) Why War? (Eng. trans.), 1933; My Philosophy, 1934; The World as I see it (Eng. trans.), 1935; (with Leopold Infeld) The Evolution of Physics, 1938; Out of My Later Years, 1950. *Address:* 112 Mercer Street, Princeton, N.J., U.S.A. [*Died* 18 *April* 1955.

EINSTEIN, Alfred, Dr. Phil.; *b.* Munich, Bavaria, 30 Dec. 1880; *s.* of Ludwig Einstein and Johanna Guttenstein; *m.* 1906, Hertha Heumann; one *d.* *Educ.:* Munich University. Private scholar until 1918; Editor of Zeitschrift für Musikwissenschaft, 1918-33; music critic of Berliner Tageblatt, 1927-33; lived London, Italy, 1933-38; came to U.S.A., 1939; Professor of Music, Smith College, Northampton, Mass., 1939-50; visiting Prof. William A. Neilson chair, Smith College, Northampton, Mass., 1939 and 1949; Hon. Member of Royal Music Assoc., London, 1937; Dr. (h.c.) Princeton Univ., Princeton, N.J., 1947. *Publications:* A Short History of Music, (Leipzig) 1917, (London) 1936; Greatness in Music, (New York) 1941; Mozart—His Character His Work, (New York) 1945, (London) 1947; Music in the Romantic Era, (New York) 1947; The Italian Madrigal (3 vols., Princeton), 1949; Schubert, A Musical Portrait (New York and London), 1951; ed.: Riemann's Musiklexicon (9-11th ed., 1919, 1922, 1929); Köchel's Thematic Catalogue of Mozart's Works, (Leipzig) 1937, (Ann Arbor) 1947. Essays on Music (Posthumous). *Address:* 509 Village Drive, El Carrito 8, Calif., U.S.A. [*Died* 13 *Feb.* 1952.

ELCHO, Lord; Iain David Charteris; *b.* 20 June 1945; *s.* of 12th Earl of Wemyss and March. [*Died* 3 *April* 1954.

ELCOCK, William Dennis; Professor of Romance Philology and Medieval French Literature in the University of London since 1947; Head of Department of French at Westfield College since 1947; *b.* 11 Dec. 1910; *s.* of Ernest Edwin Elcock, schoolmaster, and Miriam Evelyn (*née* Thorpe), Osgathorpe, Loughborough, Leics.; *m.* 1938, Hilde-Elisabeth, *o. c.* of late Judge (Kammergerichtsrat) Ernst Goldmann, Zehlendorf, Berlin. *Educ.:* Ashby-de-la-Zouch Grammar School; Manchester University. B.A., 1st Class Hons. French, 1932; Zimmern Travelling Fellow, Faulkner Fellow, and Langton Fellow of Univ. of Manchester; M.A. (Manc.), 1933; L. ès L. (Grenoble), 1934; Doct. de l'Univ. (Toulouse), 1938. Asst. Lecturer in French and Spanish at Univ. of Edinburgh, 1936-37; Lecturer in French at Univ. of Sheffield, 1937-40. Served War of 1939-45,

Royal Navy, 1940-45; Lieut., R.N.V.R. Lecturer in French Philology and Old French Literature at Univ. of Oxford, 1945-47; M.A. Oxon. (Trinity College); Lecturer in French at University College, Oxford, 1947. *Publications:* De quelques affinités phonétiques entre l'Aragonais et le Béarnais (Paris), 1938; Toponimia menor en el Alto Aragón, 1949; The Romance Languages, 1960; articles and reviews in linguistic periodicals. *Address:* 300 Finchley Rd., N.W.3. *T.:* Hampstead 1689. [*Died* 7 *Oct.* 1960.

ELDERTON, Ethel Mary, D.Sc. London; retired; *b.* 31 Dec. 1878; *d.* of late William Alexander Elderton. *Educ.:* Streatham High School; Bedford College. Secretary to Eugenics Record Office, London University, 1906; Galton Scholar; Galton Fellow; Assistant Professor at University College successively between 1906 and 1931; Reader, London University, 1931-35; Fellow of University College, 1921; Weldon Medallist, Oxford University, 1919. *Publications:* Report on English Birth Rate, 1914; Primer of Statistics; Nature and Nurture, etc.; many contributions to scientific journals on statistical, biometric and eugenic subjects. *Address:* c/o Barclay's Bank, 256 Brixton Hill, S.W.2. [*Died* 5 *May* 1954.

ELEY, Sir Frederick, 1st Bt., *cr.* 1921; Chairman, Cope and Timmins (London 1911) Ltd.; *b.* 22 Nov. 1866; *m.* 1894, Victoria Gertrude Patti, *y. d.* of James Ellis, Stourbridge, Worcestershire; one *d. Educ.:* Shrewsbury School. Late Chairman of John Waddington, Limited; retired General Manager and Director of National Provincial Bank Ltd.; Chairman, Bank of British West Africa Ltd., 1942-48. *Heir:* none. *Address:* South View House, Chale, I.W.; 49 Albion Gate, W.2. [*Died* 7 *Feb.* 1951 (*ext.*).

ELFORD, Dr. William Joseph, F.R.S. 1950; Head of Division of Physical Chemistry, National Institute for Medical Research; *b.* 4 Jan. 1900; *e. s.* of Joseph Elford, Malmesbury, Wilts. *Educ.:* Malmesbury County Secondary School; Bristol University. B.Sc. 1st class hons. chemistry, 1923. Pres. Univ. Chemical Soc., 1922-23; Colston Research Fellow, 1923-25; Ph.D. (Bristol), 1925; Colours at cricket, hockey and tennis. Joined scientific staff of Medical Research Council at National Inst. for Medical Research, 1925. Researches on application of physical chemical methods to study of viruses and bacteriophages. *Publications:* The sizes of viruses and bacteriophages and methods for their determination (contrib. to Handbuch der Virusforschung, Vienna, 1938); Cultivable filterable micro-organisms from London sewage, and Studies on purified bacteriophages (Proc. 3rd Int. Congress for Microbiology, New York, 1940). Over 50 papers on viruses, bacteriophages and proteins in learned scientific journals. (Jointly) Chemotherapeutic and other studies of typhus (M.R.C. Special Report Series, No. 255, 1946). *Address:* National Institute for Medical Research, The Ridgeway, Mill Hill, N.W.7. *T.:* Mill Hill 3666, Ext. 23. [*Died* 14 *Feb.* 1952.

ELIAS, David Henry, C.M.G. 1936; M.C.; *b.* London, 7 Dec. 1882; *s.* of David Elias, London; *m.* 1944. Great Western Railway, 1899-1902; South African Railways, 1902-22; Kenya and Uganda Railways, 1922-25; Nigerian Railway, 1925-31; F.M.S. Railway, 1931; General Manager, F.M.S. Railway, Federated Malay States, 1933-37; retired, 1937. *Recreation:* golf. *Address:* Pit Orchard, Sidbury, Sidmouth, Devon. *T.:* Sidbury 219. *Club:* East India and Sports. [*Died* 13 *March* 1953.

ELIBANK, 2nd Viscount, of Elibank (*cr.* 1911), **Gideon Murray;** 11th Bt. of Nova Scotia, 1628; 11th Baron Elibank of Ettrick Forest (*cr.* 1643); D.L. Peeblesshire; *b.* 1877; *e. surv. s.* of 1st Viscount and Blanche (*d.* 1936), *e. d.* of Edward John Scott; *S.* father, 1927; *m.* 1908, Ermine, Dame of Justice of the Order of St. John of Jerusalem, Order of Mercy, J.P. Peeblesshire, *d.* of Henry Robarts Madocks of Glanywern, Denbigh and Llay Hall, Gresford, and Hon. Anne, *d.* of F. M. 1st Baron Napier of Magdala. Private Secretary to Lt.-Governor of British New Guinea, 1898; Resident Magistrate Western Division, 1900-Jan. 1901; British representative on Joint Commission with Resident of Dutch New Guinea to determine perpetrators of devastations by natives in British territory; Acting Commandant Armed Native Constabulary, 1901; Private Secretary to Commissioner for Native Affairs, Transvaal, 1901; Asst. Native Commissioner, Zoutpansberg, 1902-6 (Queen's medal with two clasps), Anglo-Boer War; Assistant Private Secretary to Permanent Under-Secretary State for Colonies, 1907-9; Administrator, St. Vincent, 1909-15; Hon. Member Royal Company Archers, The King's Bodyguard, Scotland; Coronation medal, 1911; King's Jubilee medal, 1935; Coronation medal, 1937; received, 1909, silver medal Royal Society of Arts for paper entitled The Road to South African Union; Administrator of St. Lucia, 1915-17; Acting Governor Windward Islands, 1916; Food Commissioner, Glasgow and Western Counties of Scotland, 1917-18; M.P. (U.) St. Rollox, Glasgow, 1918-22; Lord Lieutenant of Peeblesshire, 1934-45; Hon. Colonel 8th Batt. The Royal Scots, 1939-45; Member of Speaker's Parliamentary Devolution Conference, 1919-20; formerly Chairman Southern Areas Electricity Corporation, Ltd., and Chairman of London and Rhodesian Mining and Land Co. and other companies; President of Federation of Chambers of Commerce of the Empire, 1934-37; President at Empire Chambers of Commerce Congress, New Zealand, 1936; President West India Committee, 1930-36. *Publications:* United West Indies: A Man's Life, 1934. *Heir:* *b.* Lieut.-Colonel Hon. Arthur Murray, C.M.G., D.S.O. *Address:* c/o The Standard Bank of South Africa, Cape Town. *Club:* Carlton. [*Died* 12 *March* 1951.

ELIOT, Lt.-Col. Nevill, C.B.E. 1919; late R.A.; *b.* 25 Oct. 1880; *s.* of late Sir John Eliot, K.C.I.E.; *m.* Margaret Winifred, *d.* of late Adm. C. L. Oxley, The Hall, Ripon; two *s.* one *d. Educ.:* Malvern; Royal Military Academy, Woolwich. Retired pay, 1930. *Address:* Bonporteau, Cavalaire, Var, France; c/o Lloyds Bank, 6 Pall Mall, S.W.1. [*Died* 11 *May* 1957.

ELIOT, Vice-Admiral Ralph, C.B.E. 1919; R.N., retired; *b* 1881. Served European War, 1914-19 (C.B.E., Chevalier Legion of Honour); A.D.C. to the King, 1929; retired list, 1929; Vice-Adm., retired, 1935. *Address:* Tempest, nr. Hawkchurch, Axminster, Devon. [*Died* 20 *Dec.* 1958.

ELIOT, Rev. Samuel Atkins, D.D., LL.D.; Minister Emeritus of the Arlington St. Church, Boston, Mass.; *b.* Cambridge, Mass., 24 Aug. 1862; *s.* of late Dr. C.W. Eliot; *m.* 1889, Frances S. Hopkinson, Cambridge. *Educ.:* Harvard. Minister, Unity Church, Denver, 1889-93; Church of the Saviour, Brooklyn, 1893-1898; Pres. American Unitarian Association, 1898-1927; Pres. Federation of Churches. *Address:* 25 Reservoir St., Cambridge, Mass., U.S.A. *Clubs:* Faculty (Cambridge, Mass.); City, Rotary (Boston); Harvard (New York). [*Died* 11 *Oct.* 1950.

[*But death not notified in time for inclusion in Who Was Who 1941–1950 first edn.*

ELIOTT, Sir Gilbert Alexander Boswell; of Stobs, 10th Bt., *cr.* 1666; Chief of the Clan Eliott; member of the Queen's Body Guard for Scotland (R.C.A.); *b.* 5 May 1885; *s.* of 9th Bt. and Lilla, *d.* of John Burbank; *m.* 1912, Dora Flournoy Adams, *o. d.* of late Alexander Hopkins, Atlanta, U.S.A.; one *s.* two *d.* (and *yr. s.* killed in action, with R.C.A.F., Germany, 1942). *S.* father, 1926. *Heir:* *s.* Arthur Francis Augustus Boswell [*b.* 1915; *m.* 1947, Frances Westmacott, *e. d.* of late Sir Francis McClean;

one *d.*]. *Address:* 42 Eaton Square, S.W.1; Redheugh, Newcastleton, Roxburghshire. *T.:* Liddesdale 213. *Clubs:* Carlton; New (Edinburgh). [*Died* 26 *July* 1958.

ELKAN, Benno, O.B.E. 1957; Sculptor and Medallist; *b.* Dortmund (Westphalia), 2 Dec. 1877; *s.* of S. Elkan and Rosa Oppenheimer; *m.* 1907, Hedwig Einstein (*d.* 1959); one *s.* one *d.* *Educ.:* Gymnasium, Dortmund; Château du Rosey, Rolle, nr. Lausanne; Royal Academy, Munich and Karlsruhe i/B as painter; self-trained as sculptor; studied and worked in Paris, Rome, Alsbach, near Darmstadt, Frankfurt a/Main; London from 1933. *Works:* tombs, busts, medals and monuments; Exhibitor in International Exhibitions in Germany, France, Italy, and England (R.A.); works in many museums in Europe, busts, medals, etc.; first statue in Britain of Sir Walter Raleigh, London; Oran-Utan group, Edinburgh Zoological Gardens; Mowgli's Jungle Friends, plaque in lead on Rudyard Kipling Memorial Building, Windsor; bronze candelabra: with Biblical Figures at King's College Chapel, Cambridge, New College, Oxford, Buckfast Abbey, Devon; Two Great Bronze Candelabra of the Old and New Testament with about 80 figures erected in Westminster Abbey; King David, the Psalmist; tomb for Abbot Anscar Vonier in Buckfast Abbey; Great War Memorial, To the Victims, Symbol of All Mourning Mothers at Frankfort a/M., removed by Nazis in 1933, re-erected 1946; Gold Medal for Children's Hospital, Great Ormond Street; Fighting Cock life size in silver gilt for Arsenal Football Club; seven-branched Candelabra for Parliament in Jerusalem (gift of British parliamentary members and others). Busts include: Lord Beveridge (erected in Balliol College, Oxford), Lord Lee of Fareham, Samuel Courtauld, Prince Edward, John D. Rockefeller, sen., Lord Samuel, Lord Keynes (at King's College, Cambridge and at Internat. Monetary Fund, Washington, U.S.A.), James de Rothschild, M.P.; late Marquess of Salisbury (erected House of Lords); bust from life of Mr. Winston Churchill; Dr. Weizmann, John Spedan Lewis, Yehudi Menuhin, Toscanini (Metropolitan Opera House, New York) and at new concert hall, Tel Aviv). *Publications:* books written and illustrated on Spain (1926), Poland (1918), Children's Book (1921); many articles on art and travelling. *Recreation:* resting mind and body, if possible. *Address:* 26 Exeter Road, Shoot-up-Hill, N.W.2. *T.:* Gladstone 4929. [*Died* 10 *Jan.* 1960.

ELLAND, Percy; Chairman and Managing Director, Evening Standard, since 1959; *b.* 7 October 1908; *s.* of Walter and Annie Elland, Doncaster; *m.* 1935, Winifred Margaret Baines; three *s.* one *d.* *Educ.:* Doncaster Grammar School. Junior Reporter, Doncaster Gazette, 1926; Reporter, Daily Chronicle, Leeds, 1927; Reporter, Daily Express, Manchester, 1929; Sub-editor, North Mail, 1930-32; dep. chief sub-editor, Manchester Evening Chronicle, 1932-1934; Chief sub-editor, Daily Express, Manchester, 1934-38; Editor, Daily Express, Manchester, 1938-47; Deputy Editor, Daily Express, London, 1947-50; Editor, Evening Standard, 1950-59. *Address:* 64 Princes Way, S.W.19. *T.:* Putney 4698. *Clubs:* Press, Reform. [*Died* 3 *March* 1960.

ELLIOT, Sir Duncan; *see* Elliot, Sir J. D.

ELLIOT, Sir George, Kt., *cr.* 1928; O.B.E. 1918; *b.* 1868; *s.* of late William Elliot, Jedburgh, Scotland, and Janet Easton; *m.* 1897, Rachel Winifred, *d.* of late Rev. J. M. McKerrow, B.A., Dunedin, New Zealand; one *s.* (and one *s.* killed, Italy, War of 1939-45). *Educ.:* St. John's School, Jedburgh. President of Auckland Exhibition, 1913-14; Member of Alien Enemy Royal Commission, 1915; Chairman, Samoan Epidemic Royal Commission, 1918; Chairman, Pacific Islands Trade Commission (Royal), 1920; Chairman, Bank of New Zealand, 1922-1931 and 1936-37. *Recreations:* golf and tennis. *Address:* 31/33 Burg Street, Cape Town, South Africa. *Club:* City (Cape Town). [*Died* 23 *June* 1956.

ELLIOT, Sir (James) Duncan, K.B.E., *cr.* 1920; *b.* 1862, *s.* of late Rev Henry Lettsom Elliot; *m* 1896, Dora Marguerite Jeannette, *d.* of James McIntosh; two *s.* *Educ.:* Felstead School; Portsmouth Dockyard; Royal Naval College, Greenwich. Assistant under Sir A. M. Rendel, K.C.I.E., 1887; Assistant to John Carruthers, 1900; partner with John Carruthers (Carruthers & Elliot), 1904-18, Consulting Engineers to the New Zealand Govt., etc.; and Consulting Engineer on own account to the New Zealand Government, etc., 1919-23; Member of Committee on Production, 1917-18; Member of Interim Court of Arbitration, 1918-1919; Member of Industrial Court, 1919-42. *Recreations:* shooting and fishing. *Address:* c/o Lloyds Bank, 86 High Street, Wimbledon, S.W.19. *Club:* St. Stephen's. [*Died* 9 *Aug.* 1956.

ELLIOT, Rt. Hon. Walter Elliot, P.C. 1932; C.H. 1952; M.C.; F.R.S. 1935; F.R.C.P. 1940; M.P. (C.) Kelvingrove Div. of Glasgow since 1950; Colonel, 1941; *b.* 1888; *s.* of William Elliot, Muirglen, Lanark; *m.* 1st, 1919, Helen (*d.* 1919), *d.* of Col. D. L. Hamilton, R.A.M.C.; 2nd, 1934, Katharine, *d.* of Sir Charles Tennant, 1st Bt., and later Baroness Elliot of Harwood, D.B.E.). *Educ.:* Glasgow Acad. and University. B.Sc. 1910; M.B., Ch.B., 1913; D.Sc. 1923; LL.D. (Universities of Aberdeen, 1929, Leeds, 1935, Glasgow, 1937, Edinburgh, 1938, Manchester, 1940, St. Andrews, 1951); D.Sc. University of South Africa, 1929; served European War in France, 1914-18 (M.C. and bar); M.P. (U.) Lanark, Dec. 1918-23; Kelvingrove Division of Glasgow, 1924-45; Scottish Universities, 1946-50; Parliamentary Under-Secretary for Health for Scotland, 1923-24, and Nov. 1924-26; Parliamentary Under-Secretary of State for Scotland, 1926-29; Financial Secretary to the Treasury, 1931-32; Minister of Agriculture and Fisheries, 1932-36; Secretary of State for Scotland, 1936-38; Minister of Health, 1938-40; Director of Public Relations, War Office, 1941-42; Lord High Commissioner to the General Assembly of the Church of Scotland, 1956 and 1957; Rector of Aberdeen Univ., 1933-36; Rector of Glasgow Univ., 1947-50; Freedom of City of Edinburgh, 1938. *Publications:* Toryism and the Twentieth Century, 1927; Long Distance, 1943. *Address:* 17 Lord North Street, Westminster, S.W.1; Harwood, Bonchester Bridge, Hawick, Roxburghshire. *Clubs:* Carlton; New (Edinburgh) [*Died* 8 *Jan.* 1958.

ELLIOTT, Lieut.-Colonel Alfred Charles, C.B.E. 1918; late Commissioner Multan Div., Multan, Punjab; *b.* 20 Sept. 1870; *s.* of late Sir Charles Elliott, K.C.S.I., late Lt.-Governor of Bengal, of Fernwood, Wimbledon Park, S.W.; *m.* Maud (*d.* 1946), *e. d.* of Thomas Beeching; one *s.* one *d.* *Educ.:* Elstree; Harrow; Sandhurst. Gazetted to the 2nd Batt. Royal Sussex Regt., 1890; passed into Indian Army and gazetted to 3rd Sikhs Punjab Frontier Force, 1891; passed into Civil employ in Punjab, 1893; rose from Assistant Commissioner to Commissioner of the Ambala Division, and later of the Multan Division; during two periods was Political Agent and Resident at Patiala; Member of the Council of State for India, 1921-22; retired from the Service, 1923; Chairman of the Governors, St. Mary's Hall, Brighton, 1930-46 (Trustee). *Publication:* The Chronicles of Guj-rat, 1901. *Address:* Stella Maris, Budleigh Salterton, Devon. *Club:* English-Speaking Union. [*Died* 29 *July* 1952.

ELLIOTT, Colonel Charles Hazell, C.M.G. 1918; D.S.O. 1917; V.D.; *b.* Hobart,

19 Aug. 1882; *m.* 1917, Alice Gordon, *d.* of late W. W. King; one *s.* *Educ.:* The Friends' School, Hobart. Entered service of Australian Mutual Provident Society, 1899; retired, 1945; 2nd Lieut. A.M.F., 1907; Hon. Col. 1928; retired list, 1937; A.D.C. to Governor-General of Australia, 1924-27; Commanded 12th Battalion Australian Imperial Force, Gallipoli and France (thrice wounded, D.S.O. and Bar, C.M.G., Croix de Chevalier du Légion d'Honneur). *Recreation:* has been an official of amateur athletic, rowing, and boxing associations. *Address:* Peniston, Bay Road, New Town, Tasmania. *Club:* Naval, Military, and Air Force (Hobart). [*Died* 28 *April* 1956.

ELLIOTT, David L. L.; *see* Lee-Elliott.

ELLIOTT, Sir James Sands, Kt., *cr.* 1936; V.D., M.D., Ch.B. Edin.; Hon. LL.D. Aberd.; F.R.A.C.S.; F.A.C.S.; Past President N.Z. Branch of B.M.A.; Member New Zealand Board of Health; *b.* Randalstown, Northern Ireland, 28 May 1880; *s.* of late Rev. James Kennedy Elliott, B.A., D.D., and Margaret Dickson; *m.* 1905, Ann Allan Forbes, M.B.E. 1946, D.St.J.; three *s.* *Educ.:* Wellington College; University of Edin. R.A M.C. South African War (Queen's medal two clasps); Lt.-Col. N.Z.M.C. European War; formerly A.D.M.S. Central Command, N.Z.; Ex-Pres. N.Z. Branch, British Empire Cancer Campaign; Member various Royal Commissions. Bailiff Grand Cross, Priory of St. John of New Zealand, G.C.St.J. *Publications:* Outlines of Greek and Roman Medicine, 1912; Scalpel and Sword, 1936; The Hundred Years, 1939. *Address:* 43 Kent Terrace, Wellington, C.3, N.Z. [*Died* 26 *Oct.* 1959.

ELLIOTT, John Wilson, C.B.E. 1951; Chairman: Swan, Hunter & Wigham Richardson Ltd.; Wallsend Slipway & Engineering Co. Ltd.; Hopemount Shipping Co. Ltd.; Director of other Companies; *b.* 9 December 1886; *y. c.* of late Robert and Mary Elliott; *m.* 1926, Vera Collingwood, *y. d.* of late Thomas and Mary Alderson; one *d.* *Educ.:* Rutherford Coll., Newcastle upon Tyne. Commander Royal Order of St. Olav (Norway), 1956. *Recreation:* reading. *Address:* Marbury House, Gosforth, Newcastle upon Tyne 3. *T.:* Gosforth 54158. [*Died* 20 *March* 1957.

ELLIOTT, Rev. Canon Wallace Harold; Chaplain to the Queen since 1952 (to King George VI, 1926-52); *s.* of Tom Henry Elliott, Horsham; *m.* 1918, Edith Evelyn Plaistowe, *d.* of Frank Kilburn, Roundhay, Leeds; two *s.* one *d.* *Educ.:* Collyers' School; Brasenose College, Oxford (Colquitt Exhibitioner); Ripon Clergy College. B.A. (2nd class Hons. Theology) 1906; M.A. 1910; Deacon, 1907; Priest, 1908; Curate of Guisborough, 1907-09; Organising Secretary, Northern Province C.E.M.S., 1909-12; Hon. Curate, Leeds Parish Church, 1909-12; Curate, 1913-18; Senior Curate and Clerk in Orders, 1915-18; Vicar of Holy Trinity, Folkestone, 1918-29; Six Preacher of Canterbury Cathedral, 1924-1929; Canon and Precentor of St. Paul's Cathedral, 1929-30; Vicar of S. Michael, Chester Square, S.W., 1930-40. Precentor, Deputy Clerk of the Closet, and Sub-Almoner, 1941. Sub-Dean, 1945-48. H.M. Chapels Royal; retd. as Domestic Chaplain, 1948; Vicar of St. Mary's, Warwick, 1948-49; Hon. Canon of Coventry Cathedral, 1948-49, Emeritus, 1949. Chaplain of Order of St. John of Jerusalem, 1944-. *Publications:* Undiscovered Ends (Autobiography); Rendezvous; The Christian in His Blindness; about 50 other books, including Broadcast Addresses. *Recreation:* photography. [*Died* 5 *March* 1957.

ELLIS, Sir Alan Edward, K.C.B., *cr.* 1948 (C.B. 1941); Q.C. 1951; Counsel to the Speaker since Oct. 1955; *b.* 21 Dec. 1890; *s.* of late Sidney Ellis. *Educ.:* Cheltenham College; Brasenose College, Oxford. Served in 12th Bn. London Regiment, 1914-18; Barrister, Inner Temple, 1920, and Lincoln's Inn; Bencher of Inner Temple, 1953; First Parliamentary Counsel to Treasury, 1947; Chairman, Statute Law Cttee., 1953-55. Church Commissioner, 1953. *Address:* 52 Pont St., S.W.1. *T.:* Kensington 9331. *Clubs:* Athenæum, Oxford and Cambridge, M.C.C., Leander. [*Died* 28 *Aug.* 1960.

ELLIS, Sir Albert Fuller, Kt., *cr.* 1938; C.M.G. 1928; New Zealand Commr. on Board of British Phosphate Commissioners since 1920; *b.* Roma, Queensland, 28 Aug. 1869; *s.* of late George C. Ellis, Auckland; *m.* 1st, 1900, Florence Christina (*d.* 1909); 2nd, 1913, Nellie Isabel, both daughters of late Andrew Stewart, Auckland; one *d.* *Educ.:* Cambridge (N.Z.) District High School. In 1900, when in the employ of the Pacific Islands Co. of London, discovered the Phosphate Deposits on Nauru and Ocean Islands in Central Pacific; subsequently Island Manager for the Pacific Phosphate Co. of London, and afterwards Local Director. *Publications:* Ocean Island and Nauru: Their Story, 1935; Adventuring in Coral Seas, 1937; Mid-Pacific Outposts, 1946. *Recreations:* golf, tennis. *Address:* Motirawa, 9 Argyle Street, Herne Bay, Auckland, N.Z. *Clubs:* Northern, Rotary, (Auckland). [*Died* 11 *July* 1951.

ELLIS, Colonel Alfred Charles Samuel Burdon, C.B.E. 1922; *b.* 9 June 1876; *s.* of Sir Alfred Burdon Ellis, K.C.B., and *g.s.* of Sir Samuel Burdon Ellis, K.C.B.; *m.* 1898, Mabel, *d.* of Captain J. Dwyer; two *d.* (one *s.* decd.). *Educ.:* privately and at Sandhurst. Entered Army, 1896; employed on Plague Duty, India, 1898; Commandant Asergarh Fortress, 1898; Asst. Director Military Farms, 1900; commanded a Pioneer Batt. of the Indian Army; held several appointments on the Staff in India and Burma; (including Gen. Staff Officer 1st Grade Army H.Q., India, and Assistant Adjutant and Q.M.G. Burma); served as D.A. and Q.M.G. in Mesopotamia, 1915 (despatches); Waziristan N.W. Frontier, India, 1921-22 (C.B.E., despatches); conducted special investigation into grievances of Indian Army pensioners, 1923-25, and received the official thanks of Government of India; employed at India Office on work of a secret nature, 1926, and received the "High Appreciation" of the Sec. of State for India; retired from Army, 1930; passed Staff College and London School of Economics. Home Guard, 1939. *Address:* c/o The Standard Bank of South Africa, 63 London Wall, E.C.2; c/o The Standard Bank of South Africa, Adderley St., Cape Town, S. Africa. *Club:* Junior Army and Navy. [*Died* 31 *Oct.* 1955.

ELLIS, Rear-Admiral (E) Clement, C.B. 1949. Served European War, 1914-19. Captain, 1930. Served War of 1939-45; retired list, 1949. *Address:* c/o The Admiralty, Whitehall, S.W.1; Bridge House, Dymchurch, Kent. [*Died* 11 *Sept.* 1953.

ELLIS, Ernest Tetley, F.J.I., F.R.E.S., F.R.H.S.; F.R.S.A.; Author, Editor Lecturer; Horticultural, Botanical, and Agricultural Specialist; *b.* 27 Nov. 1893; *s.* of late Sir William Henry Ellis, G.B.E., and late Lucy Rimington Tetley. *Educ.:* privately; S.E. Agricultural College, Wye, Kent. Began career as writer, 1908. *Publications:* Allotment Gardening for Profit; Insect Pests; Jottings of a Gentleman Gardener; Jottings of an Allotment Gardener (3rd ed.); Paperboard Packet and Cardboard Box Manufacture, a number of pamphlets and leaflets; short stories to various magazines (pseudonym: Eveline T. Everton); Editor of Black's Gardening Dictionary (2nd ed.), Bardswell's The Herb Garden, 2nd ed., Cook's Gardens of England, 2nd ed.; and The Garden for Expert and Amateur, 3rd ed.; Joint Editor of Mr.

Middleton's Garden Book. *Recreations:* reading, philately, travel and walking. *Address:* 35 Hoghton Street, Southport. *T.A.:* and *T.:* Southport 4045. [*Died* 30 *May* 1953.

ELLIS, Sir Geoffrey; *see* Ellis, Sir R. G.

ELLIS, Colonel Herbert Charles, C.B.E. 1919; *b.* 24 Feb. 1874; *s.* of late Col. C. H. Fairfax Ellis, R.A.; *m.* 1912, Monica Helen, *d.* of late Lt.-Col. H. G. Fincham, A.O.D.; one *s.* *Educ.:* Stonyhurst College; R.M. College, Sandhurst. Joined Royal Berkshire Regt. 1894; transferred Army Pay Dept., 1901; seconded R.A.F., April 1918–August 1924; served in France and Belgium with 5th Cavalry Brigade, and 2nd Cavalry Division, 1914-15, and at Base till Aug. 1915 (despatches, C.B.E.); retired pay, 1934. *Club:* Army and Navy. [*Died* 30 *Sept.* 1952.

ELLIS, J(ohn) Hugh, C.M.G. 1955; Principal, Commonwealth Relations Office; Chief Secretary, Sarawak, 1955-58, retired; *b.* 15 Jan. 1909; *o. s.* of Humfrey Edward Ellis; *m.* 1947, Gwendolen Enid Mary Saunders; one *s.* two *d.* *Educ.:* Queen Elizabeth's School, Carmarthen; privately; Jesus College, Oxford. B.A. Hons. Oxon. 1930. Appointed Colonial Service (Nigeria), 1931; Development Secretary, Sarawak, 1948; Deputy Chief Secretary, 1950. *Recreations:* racing, fishing. *Address:* Craiglas House, Talybont-on-Usk. *T.:* 224; 33 Queen's Gate Gardens, S.W.7. *Clubs:* Travellers', East India and Sports; Usk Valley Casting. [*Died* 26 *Aug.* 1959.

ELLIS, Lyle Fullam, D.S.O. 1918; *b.* 5 Sept. 1887; *s.* of Edwin Ellis; *m.* 1916, Dora Sophia Hoey; two *s.* *Educ.:* Liverpool Institute. Entered Martins Bank, 1903; served with King Edward's Horse, 1910-16; with this regiment in France, 1915-16, until gazetted to R.F.A.; served with D/83 Brigade R.A. in France until Armistice (D.S.O., despatches twice); rejoined service of Martins Bank on demobilisation: Manager of their Woolton Branch, Liverpool, 1920; of their Southampton Branch, 1925-35; Manager, Martins Bank, Ltd., Blundellsands, Liverpool, 1935-47; retired, 1947; commissioned in Hampshire Yeomanry Brigade, Territorial Army, 1926; Captain 72nd (County of Lancaster) Crosby Battalion Home Guard, 1941; Major i/c 172 (101) Rocket A.A. Battery R.A., 1943. *Recreations:* golf, motoring. *Address:* The Flat, 11 Glenn Buildings, Moor Lane, Crosby, Liverpool, 23. *T.:* Great Crosby 2312. [*Died* 10 *Sept.* 1951.

ELLIS, Maj.-Gen. P. G. S. G.; *see* Gregson-Ellis.

ELLIS, Sir (Robert) Geoffrey, 1st Bt., *cr.* 1932; D.L., West Riding of Yorkshire; *b.* Shipley, Yorks, 4 Sept. 1874; 3rd *s.* of late Wm. Henry Ellis, J.P., Shipley Hall, Yorks, and Jane, *d.* of late Henry Martin, of Adelaide, S. Australia; unmarried. *Educ.:* Peterhouse, Cambridge (M.A.); Inner Temple (Barrister-at-law). Bar until joined Beckett & Co., Bankers, of Leeds, in 1910; partnership amalgamated with Westminster Bank, Ltd., 1921; President (ex-Chm.), Monotype Corp., Ltd.; Chm. Key Industries Committee, 1935; Member Royal Commission on Mining Subsidence; during the 1914-18 War, Chairman Leeds Munitions Tribunal; Chairman of Court of Referees under Insurance (Unemployment) Act; Labour Adviser to Ministry of National Service (Yorks area); Chairman of Substitution Committee for West Riding (Ministries of Labour and National Service); contested Holmfirth Division of Yorkshire, 1910 and 1912; Wakefield, 1923 and 1929; M.P. (C.) Wakefield City, 1922-23, and 1924-29, Hants (Winchester), 1931-35, Ecclesall (Sheffield), 1935-45. Chm. W. Riding Quarter Sessions, 1938-42. *Publications:* in reviews on Banking and Economics. *Recreation:* travelling. *Heir:* none. *Address:* Moat House, Melbourne via Royston, Herts. *Clubs:* Athenæum, Oxford and Cambridge. [*Died* 28 *July* 1956 (*ext.*).

ELLIS, Valentine Herbert; Consulting Orthopædic Surgeon; Orthopædic Surgeon, St. Mary's Hospital, W.2; Surgeon, Royal National Orthopædic Hospital, W.1, and Paddington Green Hospital for Children; Consulting Surgeon Lord Mayor Treloars Hospital, Alton; *b.* Naini Tal, India; *s.* of Major-General Philip Mackay Ellis, O.B.E., A.M.S.; *m.* 1937, Angela Peart Robinson; one *s.* one *d.* *Educ.:* Wellington; Clare College, Cambridge; St. George's Hospital, London. M.A., B.Ch., Camb. 1926; F.R.C.S. Eng. 1928; L.R.C.P. Lond. 1925; late Surgical Registrar Royal National Orthopædic Hospital; Resident Medical Officer Victoria Hospital for Children, Chelsea; House Surgeon, House Physician and Resident Obstetric Asst. St. George's Hospital; F.R.S.M.; Member British Orthopædic Association. *Publications:* (Joint) Recent Advances in Orthopædic Surgery, 1937; Adolescent Coxa Vara, Lancet, 1935; Notochordal Tumour of cauda equina in a child of 8 years, Brit. Journal of Surgery, 1935; Discussion acute suppurative arthritis of the knee joint, Proc. Roy Soc. Med. 1933. *Recreations:* ski-ing, tennis. *Address:* 14 Wimpole Street, W.1. *T.:* Langham 4202. *Club:* Travellers'. [*Died* 15 *Sept.* 1953.

ELLIS, Walter Devonshire, C.M.G. 1919; *b.* 1871; *s.* of Alexander Ellis, Wychall, King's Norton. *Educ.:* Winchester; New College, Oxford (Scholar). 1st Class Lit. Hum. 1894; B.A. 1894; M.A. 1897; entered Colonial Office, 1895; Principal Clerk, 1909; Assist. Secretary, 1920; retired, 1931. *Address:* 11A Marine Drive, Paignton, Devon. [*Died* 10 *Aug.* 1957.

ELLIS, William C.; *see* Craven-Ellis.

ELLIS, Lieut.-Col. W(illiam) Francis, C.M.G. 1945; O.B.E. 1919; British Vice-President, International Legislative Assembly, Tangier, 1925-40 and since 1945; *b.* 1878; 4th *s.* of late William Henry Ellis, J.P., Shipley Hall, Yorks, and Jane, *d.* of late Henry Martin, Adelaide, S. Australia; *m.* 1st, 1904, Catherine Mary, *d.* of late Edwin Carter; one *s.*; 2nd, 1926, Julia Grace Hawtrey (*d.* 1948); *y. d.* of late Ralph Hawtrey Deane, Eastcote, Middx.; one *d.* *Educ.:* Bradford Grammar School; London Hospital. M.R.C.S., L.R.C.P. Lond. 1901; Lt.-Col. (ret.) R.A.M.C. 1902-24, surgical and ophthalmic specialist. Served S. Africa (Queen's medal with five clasps); European War, 1914-18, France, Dardanelles, Palestine (despatches four times, O.B.E., Bt. Lt.-Col., 1914 star, two medals). Member Tangier Port Commission; Press Attaché, British Consulate-General, 1939-45. *Address:* Tangier, Morocco. *Club:* Army and Navy. [*Died* 11 *July* 1953.

ELLIS, Col. William Montague, C.I.E. 1916; R.E. retired; *b.* 15 Oct. 1862; *s.* of Francis Ellis, Omagh; *m.* 1901, Kate Hannah (*d.* 1940), *widow* of Newton Jennings, A.M.I.C.E.; no *c.* *Educ.:* Cheltenham College; Royal Military Academy, Woolwich. Entered Royal Engineers, 1881; Lieutenant 1881; Capt. 1890; Major, 1899; Lieut.-Col. 1906; Bt. Col. 1909; Col. 1911; served at Chatham, 1881-83; in India since 1884; retired on pension, 1919; in charge of Submarine Mining Defences, Rangoon, 1884-88; in civil employ in the Madras Public Works Department since 1888 in following grades: Assistant-Engineer, 1888; Executive Engineer, 1895; Superintending Engineer, 1909 Chief Engineer for Irrigation and Secretary to Govt. of Madras Public Works Department, 1913-17. *Publication:* Madras College of Engineering Manual Irrigation, 1st Edn., 1920. *Address:* c/o Lloyds Bank, 6 Pall Mall, S.W.1. [*Died* 19 *April* 1952.

ELLIS-FERMOR, Una Mary, D.Lit.Lond., M.A., B.Litt.Oxon; F.R.S.L.;

Writer; Hildred Carlile Professor of English, Univ. of London, Bedford Coll., since 1947; *b.* 20 Dec. 1894; *d.* of Joseph Turnley Ellis-Fermor and Edith Mary Katharine Ellis-Fermor, London. *Educ.:* South Hampstead High School; Somerville College, Oxford. Assistant, Ashburne Hall, Manchester University, 1917-18; Assistant Lecturer, then Lecturer in English Literature, 1918-30, Reader in English Literature, 1930-1947, Bedford College, University of London; Rose Sidgwick Fellow at Yale and Columbia Univs., U.S.A., 1922-23; Fulbright and Smith-Mundt Travel and Research Grant, U.S.A., 1951; Rose Mary Crawshay Prize for Literature, 1930. *Publications:* Christopher Marlowe, 1926; Tamburlaine, Parts 1 and 2 (ed.), 1930; Jacobean Drama, 1936; Fulke Greville: Caelica (ed.), 1937; Some Recent Research in Shakespeare's Imagery, 1937; The Irish Dramatic Movement, 1939 (2nd edition, 1954); Masters of Reality, 1942; Essays and Studies (ed.), 1944; Frontiers of Drama, 1945; Shakespeare the Dramatist (Annual Shakespeare Lecture of the British Academy, 1948); (trans.) Three plays of Ibsen (Penguin Classics), 1950; Four plays of Ibsen (Penguin Classics), 1958. Quarterly dramatic reviews for "English," 1936-43; articles for various periodicals, English and foreign; General Editor of Arden Shakespeare. As Christopher Turnley: Twenty-Two Poems, 1937. *Recreations:* walking, climbing, camping. *Address:* 12 Abbey Road Mansions, St. John's Wood, N.W.8. *T.:* Cunningham 8775.

[*Died* 24 *March* 1958.

ELLISSEN, Lieut.-Col. Sir Herbert, Kt., *cr.* 1923; C.B.E. 1919; Member of the London Stock Exchange; *b.* London, 29 Sep. 1876; *m.* Florence Kathleen, *d.* of late Henry Frederic Lucas, Hamilton, Canada. *Educ.:* Clifton Coll. Barrister-at-law; Member of Committee of London Stock Exchange, 1910-15, and 1929-45, Member of Council, 1945-52; served European War, 1915-18; Controller and Financial Adviser, Imperial War Graves Commission, 1920-27; Member of Lord Chancellor's Committee on Stock Exchange Arrangements in Public Trustee's Office, 1930; Hon. Secretary Imperial War Graves Endowment Fund Trustees, 1928; Adviser on post-war organisation and reconstruction to Imperial War Graves Commission, 1943, Commissioner, 1948. *Address:* The Old Bake House, Horam, Sussex. *T.:* Horam Road 79.

[*Died* 20 *June* 1952.

ELLISTON, Sir George Sampson, Kt., *cr.* 1944; M.C., M.A. (Cantab.); D.L.; J.P.; Member of Corporation of City of London (Chief Commoner 1943); Director of printing and publishing companies; ex-Pres., Natl. Smoke Abatement Society; Hon. Fellow, Soc. of Medical Officers of Health; Vice-Pres. Framlingham College, Suffolk; Vice-Pres. (emeritus) Royal Sanitary Institute; *b.* 1875; 4th *s.* of late W. A. Elliston, M.D., J.P., of Stoke Hall, Ipswich; *m.* 1904, A. Louise, 4th *d.* of late Joseph Causton, D.L., and niece of late Lord Southwark; two *s.* (and one killed in action) one *d.* *Educ.:* Ipswich; Framlingham; St. Catharine's College, Cambridge. Barrister-at-law, Lincoln's Inn; Capt. (T.F.); attached 1917-1918 to 1st Cavalry Division, B.E.F. M.P., (U.) Blackburn, 1931-45. K.St.J. *Address:* 40 Heathcroft, Hampstead Way, N.W.11. *T.:* Speedwell 8870. *Club:* Athenæum.

[*Died* 21 *Feb.* 1954.

ELLISTON, William Rowley, O.B.E., T.D., B.A., LL.B.; Recorder of Great Yarmouth, 1913-51, and a Judge of Court of Survey for Suffolk, 1913-51; Barrister; formerly editor of the Weekly Sun; Major Suffolk Regiment, served B.E.F. France, 1917-19; Long Service Territorial Medal; *b.* Manor House, Ipswich, 1 Feb. 1869; *e. s.* of late W. A. Elliston, M.D.; *m.* 1898, Ethel Mary Walton, *niece* of late Sir Frederick Wilson; one *s.* two *d.* *Educ.:* Ipswich School; Christ's College, Cambridge. Pemberton Scholar, Ipswich School, 1885; elected simultaneously to Open Classical Demyship, Magdalen College, Oxford, 1887, and Open Classical Scholarship, Christ's College, Cambridge; Professor Skeat's Prize for English, 1888 Cambridge; 1st class Classical Tripos, part i. 1890; 1st class Law Tripos, part ii. 1891; Scholarship Law of Real and Personal Property and Equity, Lincoln's Inn, 1892; Barr. Lincoln's Inn, June 1893; Member of the South-Eastern Circuit; contested Woodbridge Division of Suffolk, Dec. 1910, Dec. 1918, Dec. 1923, Oct. 1924, and Colchester, May 1929; Mayor of Ipswich, 1927-28; Member Ipswich Borough Council, 1905-28; Alderman, 1932-38; Governor of Ipswich School; Governor Ipswich Girls' High School; Member of the Canadian Dominion Government Press Party, 1907; Member National Executive Council, British Legion, 1930-42; Chairman Suffolk Preservation Society; Lay Hon. Sec. Diocesan Conference of St. Edmundsbury and Ipswich Diocese, 1930-51; Member Central Committee for Protection of Churches; Chairman Bishop's Advisory Committee for Protection of Suffolk Churches. *Recreations:* walking and nature study. *Address:* 4 Parkside Avenue, Ipswich. *T.A.:* Elliston, Ipswich. *T.:* Ipswich 3427. *Club:* Church House.

[*Died* 12 *Feb.* 1954.

ELLSWORTH, Lincoln; explorer; *b.* Chicago, 12 May 1880; *s.* of James William Ellsworth and Eva Butler; *m.* 1933, Mary Louise Ullmer. *Educ.:* Hill School, Pottstown, Pa.; Columbia University; M.S., Yale; LL.D., Kenyon College. Worked as axman on Grand Trunk Pacific trans-continental route, Canada, 1902-7; resident engineer C.P.R. west of Montreal; gold prospecting, Peace River, 1909; mining engineer, Alaska, 1910; organized Andes geological expedition, 1924; commander and navigator Amundsen-Ellsworth polar air expedition; joint leader Amundsen-Ellsworth-Nobile transpolar flight Spitzbergen-Alaska, 1926; scientific director Wilkins-Ellsworth transarctic submarine expedition, 1931; flew 2300 miles across Antarctic, 1935, claiming 300,000 square miles for U.S. (awarded gold medal by Congress); Grand Cross of St. Olav, Norway, 1926; Great King Humbert medal, Italian Geog. Soc., 1920; David Livingstone centenary medal, American Geog. Soc.; Hubbard medal, Nat. Geog. Soc., 1936; Patron's Gold Medal, Royal Geog. Soc., 1937. *Publications:* The Last Wild Buffalo Hunt, 1915; Our Polar Flight (with Amundsen), 1925; First Crossing of the Polar Sea, 1926; Search, 1932; Beyond the Horizon, 1938. *Address:* c/o Morris and McVeigh, 60 Wall Street, New York. *Clubs:* Union, Century Association, Explorers, Boone and Crockett (New York).

[*Died* 26 *May* 1951.

ELLWOOD, George Montague, S.G.A.; decorative artist and writer; Art Workers Guild, and Society of Graphic Art; *b.* 1875; *s.* of George Ellwood, of Eton; *m.* 1900, Ida Florence, *d.* of Walter Ravaisou; one *d.* *Educ.:* Central Foundation School; South Kensington. As decorative artist has furnished and decorated many residences, and some churches; designed much from posters to pottery; gained gold medal at South Kensington for design, and exhibited Paris Exhibition, 1900 (being awarded medal); Exhibitor R.A.R.I., Liverpool, Paris, Vienna; first editor of Drawing and Design. *Publications:* English Furniture, 1680-1800; Some London Churches; Figure Studies for Artists; The Human Form; Pen Drawing; Art in Advertising; English Domestic Art; Human Sculpture (with Bertram Park). *Address:* 1 Hamilton Road, Boscombe, Hants. *T.:* Boscombe 1174.

[*Died* 19 *Sept.* 1955.

ELMSLEY, Major-Gen. James Harold, C.B. 1918; C.M.G. 1917; D.S.O. 1916; R. Canadian Dragoons; *b.* Toronto, 1878; *s.* of late Remy Elmsley and Nina Bradshaw of Barnstable,

Elmsley Place, Toronto; *m.* 1908, Florence Athol Gordon, *e. d.* of Melfort Boulton, Toronto, one *s.* one *d.* *Educ.:* Oratory School, Edgbaston; Lieut. 1898; Capt. 1905; Major, 1907. Served S. African War, 1899-1902 (dangerously wounded, Queen's medal 5 clasps, King's medal 2 clasps); European War, 1914-18 (C.M.G., C.B., D.S.O., Brig.-Gen., Belgian Croix de Guerre); passed Staff College (Camberley), 1913; Chief of Staff, Military District No. 2, Canada (Toronto), 1913 and 1914; left Canada with 1st Canadian Contingent as 2nd in Command of Royal Canadian Dragoons; Lt.-Col. Staff of 1st Canadian Division, 1915; Command of Canadian Cavalry Corps; Command of 8th Canadian Infantry Brigade, 1916-18; Maj.-Gen. and Command of British Expeditionary Force to Siberia, Sept. 1918; D.O.C. Military District No. 10, 1928-29. [*Died* 3 *Jan.* 1954.

ELMSLIE, Noel, C.M.G. 1934; *b.* 25 Dec. 1876; *s.* of Captain James A. Elmslie, R.N.R., and Cecilia Cheyne; *m.*; no *c.* *Educ.:* Brighton Grammar School. Served European War, 1914-19 in Artists' Rifles; entered Dept. of Overseas Trade, 1919; Trade Commissioner in New Zealand, 1923-25; Senior Trade Commissioner in South Africa, 1925-35; H.M. Senior Trade Commissioner in the Irish Free State, 193-36; retired, 1936. *Recreation:* gardening. *Address:* Osford, Boscastle, North Cornwall. [*Died* 18 *Dec.* 1956.

ELNOR, Rev. William George, M.A.; Vicar of St. Mary's, Dover, 1912-39; Hon. Canon Emeritus of Canterbury (Hon. Canon 1919). *Educ.:* St. Catharine's College, Cambridge. Vicar of Chilham, 1900-12. *Address:* Leyburne House, Dover. *T.:* 70. [*Died* 24 *June* 1956.

ELPHINSTONE, 16th Lord (*cr.* 1509), **Sidney Herbert Elphinstone;** K.T., 1927; LL.D.; Baron Elphinstone (U.K.), 1885; Lord Clerk Register of Scotland and Keeper of the Signet since 1944; Chancellor of Order of the Thistle since 1949; *b.* 27 July 1869; *s.* of 15th Baron and Constance, *d.* of 6th Earl of Dunmore; *S.* father, 1893; *m.* 1910, Lady Mary Bowes Lyon, D.C.V.O., *cr.* 1939, *d.* of 14th Earl of Strathmore, K.G., K.T., G.C.V.O.; two *s.* three *d.* *Educ.:* Marlborough. Lord High Commissioner of the Church of Scotland, 1923-24; Capt. Gen. of Royal Company of Archers, 1935-53. Formerly Governor of the Bank of Scotland. *Heir: s.* Master of Elphinstone. *Address:* Carberry Tower, Musselburgh, Scotland; 9 Thurloe Street, S.W.7. *Clubs:* Carlton, Turf. [*Died* 28 *Nov.* 1955.

ELPHINSTONE, Hon. Mountstuart (William); *b.* 5 March 1871; *b.* of 16th Lord Elphinstone, K. T. Contested (C.) Edinburghshire, 1910; Private Secretary to the Military Secretary, War Office, 1914-19. *Recreation:* portrait photography (F.R.P.S., A.I.B.P.). *Address:* 24 St. George's Court, Gloucester Road, S.W.7. *T.:* Western 7348. *Club:* Turf. [*Died* 7 *April* 1957.

ELPHINSTONE-DALRYMPLE, Colonel Sir Francis Napier, 7th Bt., *cr.* 1828; C.B.E. 1922; D.S.O. 1918; *b.* 17 July 1882; *s.* of 5th Bt. and Flora Loudoun, *d.* of late James William M'Leod (Raasay); *S.* brother, 1913; *m.* 1909, Betty, *o. d.* of late Col. E. H. Le Breton; two *d.* Entered army, 1901; Adjutant T.F., 1910-13; served European War, 1914-18 (despatches, D.S.O., Serbian White Eagle, Crown of Italy); D.A.A.G. at G.H.Q., Egypt, 1917; A.A.G., G.H.Q., Palestine, Aug. 1917-19; Bt. Col. 1919; A.A. and Q.M.G. Curragh Camp, Ireland, 1919-22; Col. 1925; Commandant Royal Military School of Music, 1925-29; retired pay, 1934; served with the Army as A.A. and Q.M.G. 1939; reverted to retired pay 1943. *Heir: c.* Hew Drummond Elphinstone-Dalrymple, *b.* 27 Jan. 1857. *Address:* Bench House, Lyndhurst, Hants. *Club:* Army and Navy. [*Died* 18 *Dec.* 1956 (*dormant*).

ELSE, Joseph, F.R.B.S.; late Principal, Nottingham City College of Art; Sculptor; Exhibitor at Royal Academy; *b.* Nottingham, 8 Feb. 1874; *s.* of William Else; *m.*; one *s.* two *d.* *Educ.:* City of Nottingham School; Royal College of Art, London, S.W.7. Formerly modelling master and lecturer on anatomy at Belfast School of Art. [*Died* 8 *May* 1955.

ELSEE, Rev. Charles, M.A.; Vicar of St. Cuthbert, Hunslet, Leeds, 1916-55; Hon. Canon of Ripon, 1927; Canon Emeritus of Ripon Cathedral, 1955. *Educ.:* Rugby School; St. John's College, Cambridge. 1st class Classical Tripos; 1st class Theological Tripos, 1900; Assistant Curate at St. John's College Mission, Church of Lady Margaret, Walworth, 1901-6; Leeds Parish Church, 1906-9; Diocesan Supernumerary, Argyll and Isles, 1909-11; Kinlochleven, Argyllshire, 1911-16. *Publication:* Neoplatonism in Relation to Christianity, 1908. *Address:* Clynnog, Caernarvon. [*Died* 2 *Nov.* 1960.

ELSMIE, Major-General Alexander Montagu Spears, C.B. 1920; C.M.G. 1915; Indian Army, retired; *b.* 2 Nov. 1869; 2nd *s.* of late George Robert Elsmie, LL.D., C.S.I.; *m.* Annie Todd, fourth *d.* of late James Todd, Banchory; two *s.* two *d.* (and two *s.* who lost their lives in the R.A.F.; one *d.* decd.) *Educ.:* Clifton College (Scholar); Sandhurst. Entered 1st Bn. Border Regt. 1889; 2nd Punjab Infantry (after 56th Punjabi Rifles), 1890; served in all grades up to Commandant, 1913; Colonel 2/13th Frontier Force Rifles, 1920-39; p.s.c. (Camberley) 1902; Brig.-Maj. Jullundur, 1907; General Staff Officer, 2nd Grade, Headquarters, Simla, 1908-9; Professor, Staff College, Quetta, 1909-11; Bt. Lieut.-Col., 1912; Bt. Col. 1916; Maj.-Gen., 1920; served Miranzai Expeditions, 1891 (medal with clasp); Waziristan, 1894-95 (clasp); N.W. Frontier, India, 1897-98 (despatches twice, medal 2 clasps); Tirah, 1897-98 (clasp); European War, 1914-18 (C.B., C.M.G., despatches four times, very severely wounded); Brig.-Gen., Ferozepore, 1918; G.O.C. Bushire Field Force, 1919; G.O.C. Kohat Kurram Force, 1920; retired 1923. *Address:* Beechwood, Chobham, nr. Woking. *T.:* Chobham 387. [*Died* 12 *Nov.* 1958.

ELSNER, Colonel Otto William Alexander, C.B.E. 1919; D.S.O. 1917; late R.A.M.C. (R.P.); *b.* 4 June 1871; *s.* of late Frederick Wm. Elsner, Leopardstown Road, Co. Dublin; *m.* 1902, Agnes Josephine Lamb (*d.* 1938), Grahamstown, Cape Colony; two *s.* one *d.* (and one *s.* serving R.A.F., decd.); 1942, Audrey Jane Cloudsdale Nunn, Darlington, Co. Durham. *Educ.:* The Grammar School, Galway; R.C.S. Ireland. L.R.C.S. and L.R.C.P. (Ireland) and L.M. 1892; D.P.H. 1909; M.O. to Ibadan-Ilorin Railway Survey for Lagos Government Railway, 1897-1898; joined R.A.M.C. 1899; served South Africa, 1899-1902 (Queen's medal 5 clasps, King's medal 2 clasps); served in India, 1902-1905; S. Africa, 1910-14; European War, 1914-18: joined B.E.F., Sep. 1914, 6th Cavalry Field Ambulance, 3rd Cavalry Division; operations in Belgium, first battle of Ypres; Commanded 27th Field Ambulance, 9th (Scottish) Div. 1915-17; and A.D.M.S. 9th (Scottish) Division from 1917 to Armistice, and in the Army of Occupation (despatches five times, D.S.O., Croix de Guerre (Belge), C.B.E.); retired pay, 1926. *Recreations:* riding and tennis. *Address:* Desmesne House, Heighington, Darlington, Co. Durham. [*Died* 12 *Jan.* 1953.

ELTON, Sir Ambrose, 9th Bt., *cr.* 1717; *b.* 1869; *s.* of 8th Bt. and Agnes, *d.* of Sir A. H. Elton, 7th Bt.; *S.* father 1920; *m.* 1901, Dorothy, *o. d.* of Arthur Wiggin of Oddington Estate, Ceylon; two *s.* *Educ.:* Lancing College; Jesus College, Cambridge. B.A.; Barr. 1896; J.P., Somerset. Owns about 3000 acres. *Heir: s.* Arthur Hallam Rice, *b.* 10 Feb. 1906. *Address:* Clevedon Court, Somerset. [*Died* 14 *July* 1951.

ELVIN, Sir Arthur J., Kt., *cr.* 1946; M.B.E. 1945; D.L.; Hon. Freeman of Borough of Wembley, 1945; Chm. since 1947, and Managing Director since 1927, of Wembley Stadium Ltd.; *b.* 5 July 1899; *s.* of John Elvin, Norwich; *m.* 1925, Jean, *d.* of late William Charles Harding and *widow* of William Heathcote Dolphin; no *c.* *Educ.:* Norwich. *Recreation:* golf. *Address:* Norfolk House, 24 Ingram Avenue, Hampstead, N.W.11. *T.:* Speedwell 3180. *Clubs:* Royal Automobile, Buck's. [*Died* 4 *Feb.* 1957.

ELWELL, Frederick William, R.A. 1938 (A.R.A. 1931); R.P. 1931; *b.* 29 June 1870; *m.* 1914, Mary Dawson (*d.* 1952), *e. d.* of John Bishop, Liverpool. *Educ.:* Lincoln School of Art; Royal Academy, Antwerp; Juliens, Paris. Exhibitor at Royal Academy and Paris Salons, etc.; Pictures purchased by Chantrey Bequest for the Tate Gallery and by the Corporations of Liverpool, Glasgow, Hull, Bristol, Preston, Birkenhead, Bournemouth. *Recreation:* gardening. *Address:* The Bar House, Beverley, E. Yorkshire. *Clubs:* Arts, Chelsea Arts. [*Died* 3 *Jan.* 1958.

EMANUEL, Joseph George, M.D., B.S., B.Sc. (Lond.), M.R.C.S. (Eng.), F.R.C.P. (Lond.), Captain R.A.M.C. (T.), M.B., Ch.B. (Birm.); Consulting Physician, Queen Elizabeth Hospital, Birmingham, the Birmingham and Midland Free Hospital for Sick Children, The Dental Hospital, Birmingham and Guest Hosp. and Eye Infirmary, Dudley; *e. s.* of late Rev. G. J. Emanuel, B.A.; *b.* Birmingham, 1871; *m.* Ethel (*d.* 1951), *o. d.* of late Alfred Wolff, M.R.C.S.; one *s.* *Educ.:* King Edward's High School; Mason and Queen's Colleges. After qualifying at the Birmingham Medical School in 1896, came to London and held a number of appointments at various metropolitan hospitals, including that of resident medical officer at the City of London Hospital for Diseases of the Chest; Pathologist to the General Hospital, Birmingham, 1901; Physician to Queen's Hospital, Birmingham, 1903; Physician to Children's Hospital, Birmingham, 1904; Practising as consulting physician since 1903. *Publications:* A Child's Diet; Blood from a Clinical Aspect; Ingleby Lectures, 1925, Auricular Fibrillation. *Recreation:* golf. *Address:* 10 Harborne Road, Edgbaston, Birmingham. *T.:* Edgbaston 2241. *Club:* Union (Birmingham). [*Died* 3 *March* 1958.

EMBERTON, Joseph, F.R.I.B.A.; Architect; *b.* Audley, Staffordshire, 23 Dec. 1889; *s.* of Samuel Emberton; *m.* 1926, Kathleen Marie Chantrey; two *d.* *Educ.:* Royal College of Art; Royal Academy Schools. In partnership with P. J. Westwood, 1922-26; some of works executed during partnership, Austin Reed shop, Regent Street, various Pavilions, British Exhibition Wembley. Executed works include: Royal Corinthian Yacht Club, Burnham (R.I.B.A. Bronze Medal); Empire Hall, Olympia; Universal House, Southwark Bridge; Simpson, Piccadilly; Olympia Garage; Pavilions, Paris Exhibition, 1937; Gramophone Building, Oxford Street; Casino, Blackpool; Easiwork Factory, Gillingham; Stafford Cripps Estate, Finsbury (flats and commercial buildings); Standard Hosps. for Ministry of Health; Extensions to Linton Hosp., Maidstone. During the war was Housing Officer to M.A.P.; Architectural Adviser on Hostels to Ministry of Works; Consultant to Ministry of Supply on design of prefabricated steel house. *Recreations:* sailing, golf. *Address:* 17 Chantrey House, Eccleston Street, S.W.1. *T.:* Sloane 9962; Appledore, Hill Brow, Dyke Road Avenue, Hove. *Clubs:* St. Stephen's, Royal Automobile; Royal Corinthian Yacht. [*Died* 20 *Nov.* 1956.

EMBLING, Air Vice-Marshal John Robert André, C.B.E. 1954; D.S.O. 1943; Air Officer commanding No. 12 Group, Fighter Command, R.A.F., since 1959; *b.* 15 April 1913; *s.* of Jacques L. Embling of Chiswick, later of Stockton-on-Tees, Co. Durham, and Dorothy E. Embling (*née* Burden), Adelaide, S. Australia; *m.* 1945, Esme Nina, *d.* of Harold Gaydon, Hornsea House, Hornsea, E. Yorks.; one *s.* two *d.* *Educ.:* Stockton Grammar School; King's School, Worcester; University College, Oxford (M.A.); R.A.F. College, Cranwell. No. 58 (B) Sqdn., R.A.F., 1936-38; Air Liaison Officer, Basrah, Iraq, 1939-41; O.C. No. 77 (B) Sqdn., 1942. P.O.W. in France, escaped, Dec. 1942-Mar. 1943; R.A.F. Staff College, 1943; Chairman, Mediterranean Estabs. Committee, R.A.F., 1943-44; Gp. Capt. Organisation, H.Q. Transport Command, 1944-46; O.C., Oxford University Air Squadron, 1946-48; Directing Staff, Joint Services Staff College, 1948-51; Gp. Capt. Plans, H.Q. 2nd Tactical Air Force, 1951-54; Chief Instructor, R.A.F. Flying College, 1954-56; Sector Commander, Eastern Sector, Fighter Comd., 1956-57; Imperial Defence College, Student, 1958. Order of Rafidain, Iraq, 1941. *Recreations:* rowing, sailing, gardening. *Address:* (official) Bowthorpe Hall, Norwich. *T.:* Norwich 45251, Ext. 250. *Club:* R.A.F. [*Died* 15 *July* 1959.

EMBURY, Lieut.-Col. P. Robinson, C.M.G. 1917; *b.* Corner Hall, Hemel Hempstead, Herts, 31 March 1865; *m.* 1898, Mary (*d.* 1940), *d.* of J. S. Clayton, of Standfield, Liverpool; two *d.* *Educ.:* Malvern College; Royal Indian Engineering College, Coopers Hill. Passed out R.I.E.C., 1885; Assistant Engineer, New Tay Viaduct; received commission in Royal Engineers, 1886; special mechanical course, Elswick works, 1887-1889; served at Shoeburyness, Gibraltar, and Hong-Kong on R.E. work, 1889-93; Assistant Inspector of Steel, Manchester, 1893-95; Inspector Carriages, Woolwich Arsenal, 1895-1900; Ceylon, 1900-2; retired, 1902; manager, Coventry Ordnance Works, 1902-13; raised and commanded the 4th South Midland Howitzer Brigade, Territorial Field Artillery, 1908, retiring in 1912; Deputy Director of Inspection, U.S.A., 1914-17; Director of Inspection, of Munition Areas, 1917-19. *Recreation:* golf. *Address:* Combe Down House, Combe Florey, Somerset. *T.:* Bishops Lydeard 260. [*Died* 14 *June* 1952.

EMERSON, Major-Gen. Henry Horace Andrews, C.B. 1939; D.S.O. 1917; *b.* 14 Sept. 1881; *s.* of Robert Henry Mulock Emerson and Georgena Rebecca Andrews; *m.* Lillie H. Godfrey (*d.* 1952), Courtrai, Belgium; one *s.* one *d.* *Educ.:* Rathmines Sch., Dublin (Capt. of the School); Trinity College, Dublin (Stewart Scholarship, Physiology and Anatomy). B.A., B.A.O., B.Ch., M.B. 1905; joined R.A.M.C. 1905; served in France, 1915-19 (D.S.O., Croix de Guerre, despatches three times); Bt. Lt.-Col. 1928; Deputy Director Hygiene and Pathology, Army H.Q., India, 1928; Director of Hygiene, War Office, 1935-39; Hon. Surgeon to the King, 1937-39; retired pay, 1939; Lt.-Col. 1929; Col. 1934; Maj.-Gen. 1937. *Recreations:* rowed (Captain of D.U.B.C.), played football, golf. *Address:* Sweetland, Bishopstrow, Warminster, Wilts. *T.:* Warminster 2409. [*Died* 17 *Nov.* 1957.

EMERSON, Thomas, C.S.I. 1926; C.I.E. 1918; I.C.S., retired; *b.* 2 June 1870; *s.* of late Jn. Emerson of Corofin, Co. Clare; *m.* Barbara, *d.* of late John Lees; one *s.* *Educ.:* Clongowes Wood College; Queen's College, Galway; Emmanuel Col., Cambridge. Arrived in India in the Indian Civil Service, 1894; served in Bengal, Assam, and Behar as Assistant Magistrate and Collector, as Deputy Commissioner, and as Collector and Magistrate; Member of the Imperial Legislative Council of India, 1918; Chairman Calcutta Improvement Trust, 1922-24; Commissioner and temporary Member Bengal Executive Council, 1924-25; Member Council of State, 1925-26, retired 1927. *Recreation:*

golf. *Address:* c/o Coutts & Co., 440 Strand, W.C.2. [*Died* 22 *July* 1956.

EMLYN - JONES, John Emlyn, J.P. Cardiff; Joint Managing Director of Emlyn-Jones, Griffin & Co., Ltd., Cardiff; Director of many companies; *b.* 22 Jan. 1889; *m.*; one *s.* one *d.* *Educ.:* Cardiff; France; Spain; Italy. M.P. (L.) North Dorset, 1922-24. *Address:* 4 Dock Chambers, Cardiff. *T.:* 2950 Cardiff. *T.A.:* Emyln, Cardiff. *Clubs:* National Liberal, Royal Automobile. [*Died* 3 *March* 1952.

EMMONY, Alderman Harry Oliver, J.P.; *b.* London, 4 March 1897; *s.* of Edgar and Elizabeth Emmony; *m.* 1920, Violet, 2nd *d.* of Charles and Violetta Steventon; three *s.* *Educ.:* Hampstead School; Gospel Oak. Served European War, R.A.S.C., 1915-1919. Elected to Board of Guardians, 1923, to Nottingham City Council, 1928; Sheriff of Nottingham, 1946-47; Lord Mayor of Nottingham, 1950-51; J.P. Nottingham. *Recreations:* golf, gardening. *Address:* 175 St. Ann's Well Road, Nottingham. *T.:* 40160. *Club:* Constitutional (Nottingham). [*Died* 28 *Aug.* 1956.

EMMOTT, Charles Ernest George Campbell, M.A. Oxon.; *b.* 12 Nov. 1898; *s.* of Charles Emmott, Oldham, and Lady Constance Campbell, *d.* of George, 8th Duke of Argyll. *Educ.:* Lancing; Oxford Univ. Classical Scholar of Lancing (1st Scholarship), and of Christ Church, Oxford; Honours Degree in Lit. Hum., 1921. Served in R.F.A., France, 1917-19 and in R.A.F. during War of 1939-1945; Barrister-at-Law, Middle Temple, 1924; contested Preston, 1929; M.P. (C.) Springburn Division of Glasgow, 1931-35; M.P. (C.) Eastern Division of Surrey, 1935-45; visited South Africa and Rhodesia, 1940, on behalf of Empire Parliamentary Assoc.; Chm., British-Italian Soc., 1945; travelled extensively in Europe, N. America, Near East, Africa, India; delivered courses of lectures on historical and political subjects to academic bodies and general audiences in U.S.A. and Canada. Received into the Catholic Church, 1948. *Publications:* articles in English and American reviews. *Recreations:* gardening, lawn tennis, riding. *Address:* 39 Smith Street, Chelsea, S.W.3. *Club:* Carlton. [*Died* 14 *April* 1953.

ENDICOTT, The Very Rev. James, B.A., D.D., LL.D.; *b.* Chudleigh, Devonshire, 8 May 1865; *s.* of James Endicott and Susan Steer; *m.* 1st, Sarah Diamond (*d.* 1925); two *s.* three *d.*; 2nd, 1930, Marie Matilda Wilson McIrvine (*d.* 1946). *Educ.:* Chudleigh; Wesley Coll., Winnipeg. Missionary to West China, 1893-1910; erected the Publishing House at Chengtu, 1904; first principal of the Chengtu School for study of Chinese Language; Field Secretary, The Missionary Society of the Methodist Church in Canada, 1912; General Secretary, The Missionary Society of the Methodist Church in Canada, 1913-25; Secretary, Board of Foreign Missions, The United Church of Canada 1925-37; First Chairman, The Council of the Canadian School of Missions, Toronto; Chairman of the Foreign Missions Conference of North America, 1923; Member, The International Missionary Council, Jerusalem, 1928; Moderator of the second General Council of The United Church of Canada, 1926-28; made official visitation of the foreign mission fields of the Church in Trinidad, Africa, India, Korea, Japan, and China, 1926-28; Member of Order of Golden Grain of China. *Publications:* Chinese Mandarin Lessons. *Recreations:* boating, tennis. *Address:* 81½ Woodlawn Ave. E., Toronto, Ont., Canada. [*Died* 8 *March* 1954.

ENGELBACH, Mrs. Florence, R.O.I.; Painter; *b.* in Spain; *d.* of Albert and Leonora Neumegen; *m.* 1902, Charles R. F. Engelbach, O.B.E.; two *s.* *Educ.:* privately; Slade School. Started at an early age as Portrait Painter, exhibited R.A. etc.; after a lapse of 20 years re-started painting in 1931; had 1st personal Exhibition in London, Beaux Arts Gallery, Leicester Galleries, 1939, and in other well-known galleries in 1931, 1934 and 1939; sixteen pictures, mostly flowers, in public galleries in England, including Tate Gallery (Rose Picture), Walker Art Gallery and Cartwright Memorial Hall, Bradford. Contemporary Art Society purchased one; Exhibitor Salon, Royal Academy, etc.; Member National Society of Painters, Engravers, Society of Coventry and Warwickshire Artists. *Recreations:* gardening, reading. *Address:* 3 Carlyle Mansions, Cheyne Walk, S.W.3. *T.:* Flaxman 8559. [*Died* 27 *Jan.* 1951.

ENGLAND, Philip Remington, O.B.E.; Senior Partner S. M. Bulley & Son, Liverpool; *b.* 23 May 1879; *s.* of E. B. England, Litt.D., and E. H., *d.* of S. M. Bulley; *m.* 1st, 1922, A. A. Goldring (*d.* 1943); no *c.*; 2nd, 1944, Frances Esther, *y. d.* of late T. Goldring. *Educ.:* Manchester Grammar School; Victoria Univ., Manchester. Served Gallipoli and Salonika, Temp. Major, acting Lt.-Col. R.A.S.C. (despatches twice, O.B.E.); Pres. Liverpool Cotton Association, 1924 - 25. Member of Pilgrims Society. *Recreations:* fishing, chess. *Address:* Pengwern Old Hall, Blaenau Festiniog, Merioneth. *Clubs:* Chess, Old Hall (Liverpool). [*Died* 12 *Sept.* 1959.

ENRIGHT, Adm. (Ret.) Sir Philip King K.B.E., *cr.* 1952 (C.B.E. 1946); C.B. 1949 *b.* 4 Aug. 1894; *s.* of John Enright; unmarried. *Educ.:* Royal Nava School, Greenwich. Comdr. 1931; Capt. 1937; A.D.C. to H.M. 1946; Rear-Adm. 1947; Vice-Adm., 1950; Adm. 1953; retd. 1953. Capt.: H.M.S. Grimsby, 1937-39; H.M.S. Cardiff, 1939-41; Capt. of Fleet, Mediterranean, 1942-44; Capt. H.M.S. Cumberland, 1944-46; Noble Committee on Warrant Officers, 1946-47; Flag Officer, Training Squadron, 1947-48; War Course, 1948-49; Admiral Supt., H.M. Dockyard, Devonport, 1950-53. *Recreations:* golf, fishing. *Address:* Neston, Raddenstile Lane, Exmouth, Devon. [*Died* 29 *Sept.* 1960.

ENSLIN, Brigadier - General Barend Gotfried Leopold, D.S.O.; D.T.D.; retired as farmer, J.P. and Director of various co-operative societies, in 1947, when he left Pietersburg district; also retired after 15 years' service as Director S.A. Iron & Steel Corporation, Pretoria, in 1948; *b.* 6 June 1879; *s.* of Comdt. George F. Enslin, Bloemfontein, O.F.S.; *m.* 1st, S. J., *d.* of D. J. J. Oosthuizen, of Colesberg; one *s.* one *d.*; 2nd, Mona Muriel Van Duyn, domestic science expert, Pretoria; one *s.* three *d.* *Educ.:* Potchefstroom and Grey Coll., Bloemfontein. Took part in Anglo-Boer War as 2nd in Command Theron Scouts, rank Lieut.; seriously wounded and captured at Jagersfontein Road; sent as prisoner of war to Bermuda (D.T.D.); on declaration of peace visited America, England, and Europe; entered business on return to South Africa, and in 1906 proceeded with General Botha to the Imperial Conference of Prime Ministers, England, as Joint Private Secretary; Private Secretary to Minister of Agriculture and chief clerk of Dept. of Agriculture, 1908; Chief of Sheep and Wool Division of the Agricultural Dept., 1912-24; proceeded to German West African Front on outbreak of European War as Chief Staff Officer to the O.C. Southern Force; commanded Enslin's Horse (which he formed), also Botha's Hogeveld Ruiters Regiments, 1914; Wing Commander of the 4th Mounted Brigade, German West, 1915; O.C. 4th Mounted Brigade with rank of Colonel, 1915 (Légion d'Honneur, Croix d'officier); Acting Director of Transport and Remounts for purpose of reorganising department; O.C. 2nd Mounted Brigade, German East Africa, with rank of Brig.-Gen. 1917 (despatches, D.S.O.); Chairman of the Central Wool Purchasing Committee (1917); Director Govt. Wool Purchasing Scheme, 1921-22. During War 1939-45 served as Hon.

Chief Defence Liaison Officer, Northern Transvaal. *Publications:* Departmental Bulletins in connection with Sheep and Wool Questions. *Recreations:* (formerly) tennis, shooting, riding, swimming. *Address:* 241 Athlone Street, Arcadia, Pretoria, Transvaal, S.A. *T.:* 43183. *Club:* Pretoria.
[*Died* 21 *Sept.* 1955.

ENSOR, Sir Robert Charles Kirkwood, Kt., *cr.* 1955; M.A.; Hon. Fellow of Corpus Christi College, and of Balliol College, Oxford; *b.* 16 Oct. 1877; *s.* of late Robert H. Ensor, Milborne Port, and Olivia, *d.* of Charles Curme, Dorchester; *m.* 1906, Helen, *d.* of late W. H. Fisher, Manchester; two *s.* three *d.* *Educ.:* Winchester College; Balliol College, Oxford. 1st Class. Mods, 1898; Latin Verse, 1899; Craven Scholarship, 1899; President of the Union, 1900; 1st Lit. Hum., 1900; leader-writer on Manchester Guardian, 1902-4; called to Bar, Inner Temple, 1905; Member of London County Council, 1910-13; leader-writer on Daily News, 1909-11; Chief Leader-writer on Daily Chronicle, 1912-30; lecturer at London School of Economics, 1931-32; Deputy for Gladstone Prof. of Political Theory and Institutions Oxford, 1933 and 1940-44; Research Fellow of Corpus Christi College, Oxford, 1937-46, Research Lecturer of All Souls College, 1937-46, and Faculty Fellow of Nuffield College, Oxford, 1938-46; Herbert Spencer Lecturer, Oxford, 1946; Ritson Lecturer, Univ. of Aberdeen, 1947; Member Executive Committee of the National Trust; Member Royal Commission on the Population, and of Royal Commission on the Press. *Publications:* Modern Socialism, 1903; Modern Poems, 1904; Belgium, 1915; Odes, 1917; Catherine, a Romantic Poem, 1921; Columbus, A Historical Poem, 1925; Courts and Judges in France, Germany, and England, 1933; England 1870-1914, 1936; Hedge Leaves, 1942; A Miniature History of the War, 1945; three Oxford Pamphlets; a weekly article on foreign affairs to Sunday Times over penname Scrutator, 1940-53; numerous articles in periodicals. *Recreations:* gardening, walking, observing birds. *Address:* The Beacon, Upper Sands, High Wycombe; Corpus Christi College, Oxford. *T.:* High Wycombe 350. *Club:* United University. [*Died* 4 *Dec.* 1958.

ENTHOVEN, Reginald Edward, C.I.E. 1910; Underwriting Member of Lloyd's, 1921; *b.* 23 Nov. 1869; 5th *s.* of James Henry Enthoven, 14 Connaught Place, W.; *m.* 1913, Beatrice, *e. d.* of Thomas Huntington of Norwich, Connecticut; two *d.* *Educ.:* Wellington; New College, Oxford. Entered Indian Civil Service, 1887; First Assistant and Under-Secretary to Government, 1900-2; Superintendent of Revision of Imperial Gazetteer, 1902; Junior Collector, 1905; Senior Collector, 1910; Secretary to the Government of India, 1912-15; Controller of Import Restrictions, Board of Trade, 1916; Comr. of Customs, Salt, and Excise, Bombay, 1920; Comdr. of Leopold II., 1919. *Publications:* Cotton Fabrics of the Bombay Presidency; Folk Lore Notes; Tribes and Castes of Bombay; Folklore of Bombay. *Address:* Vale House, Wootton, Boar's Hill, Oxford. *Club:* East India and Sports. [*Died* 21 *May* 1952.

ENTWISTLE, William James, M.A. (Oxford and Aberdeen), LL.D. (Aberdeen and Glasgow), Litt.D. (Pennsylvania), Doutor em Letras (Coimbra); F.B.A. 1950; King Alphonso XIII Professor of Spanish Studies, Univ. of Oxford since 1932 and Director of Portuguese Studies, 1933; Fellow of Exeter College; *b.* Chen Yang Kwan, China; *s.* of Rev. W. E. Entwistle of the China Inland Mission and Mrs. Entwistle (*née* Buchan); *m.* 1921, Jeanie Drysdale, *d.* of J. Buchanan, Kirkcaldy; one *s.* *Educ.:* China Inland Mission Schools, Chefoo, China; Robert Gordon's College, Aberdeen. Bursar at University of Aberdeen, 1912-16; M.A. 1916; Simpson and Jenkyns Prizeman and Seafield and Town Council Medallist; Fullerton Classical Scholar, 1919; War Service with R.F.A. and Scottish Rifles, 1916-19; Carnegie Research Scholar at University of Madrid and Centre for Historical Studies, Madrid; Lecturer in Hispanic Studies to the Victoria University of Manchester, 1921-25; Stevenson Professor of Spanish in the University of Glasgow, 1925-32; Member of the Hispanic Society of America and American Folklore Society; Member of the Glasgow University Oriental Society; Corresponding Member of the Portuguese Academy of History, Buenas Letras and Centre of Catalan Studies (Barcelona) the Royal Spanish Academy, and of the Norwegian Academy. Delegate to P.E.N. Congresses (Barcelona, 1935, Buenos Aires, 1936), Coimbra Univ. Quatercentenary (1937), Bogotá Quatercentenary (1938), Pennsylvania University Bicentenary (1940): Oxford University delegate to Portugal, 1941. British Council Lecturer in S. America, 1941 and Portugal and Spain, 1945. Temporary Educational Director, 1942-43, and Member of Humanities Committee of British Council, 1945; Visiting Prof. in Univs. of Pennsylvania and California, 1948. *Publications:* The Arthurian Legend in the Literatures of the Spanish Peninsula; The Spanish Language; European Balladry; Cervantes; The Literature of England (with E. Gillett); Russian and the Slavonic Languages (with W. A. Morison); Portugal and Brazil (joint); Aspects of Language; contrib. to Chambers's Encyclopædia, The Modern Language Review and elsewhere. *Recreation:* walking. *Address:* 12 Fyfield Road, Oxford. *T.:* Oxford 3898. *Clubs:* Authors', P.E.N.
[*Died* 13 *June* 1952.

EPHRAIM, Lee; Managing Director Lee Ephraim Co. Ltd. Has produced (in association with other managements) for: Rose-Marie, Drury Lane, 1925; Sunny, London Hippodrome, 1926; The Desert Song, Drury Lane, 1927; Funny Face, Princes, 1928; Gay Divorce, Palace, 1933; On Your Toes, Palace, 1937; Hide and Seek, London Hippodrome, 1937; Under Your Hat, Palace, 1938; Full Swing, Palace, 1942; Claudia, St. Martin's, 1942; Panama Hattie, Piccadilly, 1943; Something in the Air, Palace, 1943; Under the Counter, Phoenix, 1945; Here Come the Boys, Savile, 1946; Carissima, Palace, 1948. *Address:* Magnet House, 21 Denman St., W.1.
[*Died* 26 *Sept.* 1953.

EPPS, Sir George Selby Washington, K.B.E., *cr.* 1942 (C.B.E. 1926); C.B. 1931; B.A., F.I.A.; *b.* 26 Feb. 1885; *s.* of Dr. Washington Epps; *m.* 1915, Leonora, *d.* of Edward Eden Peacock; two *d.* *Educ.:* Highgate School; Emmanuel Coll., Cambridge. Deputy Govt. Actuary, 1926-36; Govt. Actuary, 1936-44; Joint Hon. Secy., 1928 and 1929, Vice-President, 1930 and 1931, Institute of Actuaries. *Address:* High Aisholt Farm, Spaxton, Bridgwater, Somerset.
[*Died* 8 *Feb.* 1951.

EPSTEIN, Sir Jacob, K.B.E., 1954; Hon. LL.D. Aberdeen, 1938; Hon. D.C.L. Oxford, 1953; British Sculptor; *b.* New York, 1880, of Russian-Polish parents; *m.* 1906, Margaret Gilmour Dunlop (*d.* 1947); one *s.* one *d.*; 1955, Mrs. Kathleen Garman. Commissioned to execute eighteen figures to decorate the new building of the Brit. Med. Assoc., Strand and Agar Street, 1907-8; the work when finished was attacked by newspapers, religious bodies, etc., was defended by Times; commissioned to execute the tomb of Oscar Wilde for Père Lachaise Cemetery, Paris, 1909; the tomb was carved by the sculptor out of Derbyshire marble; carving, Venus, exhibited publicly, 1917, over life-size marble figure (white); over life-size figure, Christ, in bronze, 1920 now the property of A. Cherry Garrard, Lamer Park, Wheathampstead; commissioned to execute memorial to W. H. Hudson in Hyde Park;

the monument was carved by the sculptor on a block of Portland stone and unveiled by the Prime Minister, Stanley Baldwin, on 19 May 1925; made life-size figure in bronze called Visitation, 1926, now in Tate Gallery; made The Madonna and Child, over life-size group in bronze, 1927, now in Tate Gallery; Portrait of Admiral Lord Fisher, 1915; Duchess of Hamilton, 1915; The Tin Hat, 1916; The American Soldier, 1917; The Duke and Duchess of Marlborough, 1923; First Portrait of Ramsay MacDonald, Prime Minister, 1926; commissioned to carve two groups in Portland Stone, "Day" and "Night," on Underground Headquarters Building (St. James Park Station), Tothill Street and Broadway, Westminster, S.W.1, Dec. 1928-June 1929; carved marble figure, Genesis, 1931; in Hopton Wood, stone Primeval Gods and Sun God panel carved on both sides, 1933; Exhibition, 50 Paintings of Epping Forest, 1933; twice life-size statue carved in Subiaco stone, Ecce Homo, 1933; exhibited 100 Flower Paintings, 1936; carving in alabaster of recumbent figure (over life-size), Consummatum Est, 1937; 35 Drawings of "Jackie," 1935-39 and 60 drawings for Fleurs Du Mal by Charles Baudelaire; Commissioned by Limited Editions Club for a book of Charles Baudelaire's Poems les Fleurs Du Mal; Adam, over life-size figure in English alabaster, exhibited 1939 in Leicester Galleries and in New York, 1940; Group of two figures in alabaster over life-size, Jacob and the Angel, exhibited Leicester Galleries, 1942. Portraits in Bronze of Cunninghame Graham, 1923; Joseph Conrad, 1924; Professor Samuel Alexander, 1925; C. P. Scott (creator of the Manchester Guardian), 1926; Lord Rothermere, 1928; Doctor William Cramer, Cancer Research Investigator, 1931; Lord Beaverbrook, 1933; Professor Albert Einstein, 1933; Dr. Chaim Weizmann, 1933; Michael Balkin, 1933; Isador Ostrer, 1933; Ramsay MacDonald, Prime Minister, 1934; George Bernard Shaw, 1934; Monsieur Ivan Maisky, 1941; Maj.-Gen. Sir Alan Cunningham, Air Chief Marshal Sir Charles Portal, 1942; Very Rev. Hewlett Johnson, Dean of Canterbury; Denis Nowell Pritt, 1943; Dr George Black, the Oculist, 1944; Robert Sainsbury, 1944; Exhibition 1945 in Leicester Galleries of over life-size winged figure in bronze, Lucifer; Yehudi Menuhin; Lord Wavell; Sir John Anderson; Ernest Bevin; Mrs. D. N. Pritt, 1946. Second exhibition of 100 Flower Paintings in Leicester Galleries, October 1940; The Girl with the Gardenias in exhibition of 21 pieces of Sculpture, Leicester Galleries, 1944; exhibition of portrait bronzes, Leicester Galleries, 1953; bronze group, Virgin and Child, Convent of the Holy Child Jesus, 1953. bronze bust of late Sir Stafford Cripps, 1954; portrait bust of Dr. J. J. Mallon, 1954; statue of Field Marshal Smuts in Parliament Square, 1956; "Christ in Majesty" for Llandaff Cathedral, 1957; William Blake, in Westminster Abbey, 1957; bronze group of St. Michael triumphing over the Devil (for Coventry Cathedral, 1959), unveiled, 1960; portrait bronze of Princess Margaret (on which he was working at the time of his death, for the University College of North Staffordshire), exhibited at R.A. Summer Exhibn., 1960. *Publications:* The Sculptor Speaks, 1931; Autobiography, Let There Be Sculpture, 1940; Epstein: An Autobiography, 1955. *Address:* 18 Hyde Park Gate, S.W.7. *T.:* Western 5723 *Club:* Athenæum. [*Died* 19 *Aug.* 1959.

ERNEST, Maurice, LL.D.; biologist and author; *b.* 21 May 1872; *s.* of late Dr. Louis Ernst. *Educ.:* Paris and Vienna: Studied first Medicine, afterwards Law. London Correspondent of important Austrian, Swedish and American dailies 1897-1909; Hon. Secretary, Foreign Press Association, 1898; assisted the late Sir Arthur Conan Doyle (1900) in countering Anti-British propaganda in Europe, raised during Boer War. Resigned (1909) all Press appointments; has since devoted himself to biological study and research; founded (1928) the Centenarian Club, the aim of which is to investigate the means "whereby health and vigour may be retained beyond the century." *Publications:* Slaves of Love, 1892: Wireless Telegraphy and Telephony, 1903; The New Homoeopathy, 1910; Everyday Chronic Maladies, 1912; The Longer Life, 1938; Lives of 300 years and Continual Rejuvenation, 1942; and many contributions to political and medical journals. *Recreations:* collecting books on longevity, old age and rejuvenation. *Address:* New Court, Esher, Surrey. *T.:* Esher 379. [*Died* 18 *May* 1955

ERRINGTON, Colonel Roger, C.B.E. 1939; M.C. 1915; T.D.; M.D.; *b.* 26 Oct. 1887; *s.* of late Roger Errington, Sunderland; *m.* 1925; one *s.* *Educ.:* Durham University. Served European War, 1914-19 (despatches, M.C. and Bar); Colonel Army Medical Services, B.E.F., 1939-45 (despatches). K.H.P. 1944-49. *Recreations:* golf, fishing. *Address:* 29 West Av., Gosforth, Newcastle upon Tyne, 3. *T.:* Gosforth 51817. *Club:* Northern Conservative. [*Died* 14 *March* 1960.

ERSKINE, 6th Baron (U.K.), *cr.* 1806; **Montagu Erskine;** *s.* of 5th Baron, and Caroline, *d.* of late William Grimble; *b.* 13 April 1865; *S.* father, 1913; *heir-pres.* to 15th Earl of Buchan, *q.v.*; *m.* 1895, Florence (*d.* 1936), *y. d.* of Edgar Flower of The Hill, Stratford-on-Avon, and Middlehill, Broadway, Worcestershire; two *s.* one *d.* Church of England, Conservative. *Heir:* *s.* Lt.-Col. Hon. Donald Cardross Flower Erskine. *Club:* Carlton. [*Died* 9 *Feb.* 1957.

ERSKINE, Lord, G.C.S.I., *cr.* 1940; G.C.I.E., *cr.* 1934; **John Francis Ashley Erskine;** Major late Scots Guards; *b.* 26 April 1895; *e. s.* of 12th Earl of Mar and Kellie, *q.v.*; *m.* 1919, Lady Marjorie Hervey, Commander of the Order of St. John of Jerusalem, Kaisar-i-Hind Gold Medal, 1939, *e. d.* of 4th Marquess of Bristol,; three *s.* *Educ.:* Eton; Christ Church, Oxford. M.P. (U.) Weston-super-Mare Division of Somerset, 1922-23 and 1924-34; Assistant Private Secretary (unpaid) to Rt. Hon. Walter Long (1st Lord of Admiralty), 1920-21; Parliamentary Private Secretary (unpaid) to the Postmaster-General (Sir W. Joynson-Hicks), 1923; Principal Private Secretary (unpaid) to Home Secretary, 1924; Assistant Government Whip in National Government, 1932; Governor of Madras, 1934-40; M.P. (U.) Brighton, 1940-41; Knight of Grace of St. John of Jerusalem, 1936. *Heir:* *s.* Master of Erskine. *Address:* 64 Chelsea Sq., S.W.3; Alloa House, Alloa, Clackmannanshire. *Club:* Carlton. [*Died* 3 *May* 1953.

ERSKINE, Col. Henry Adeane, C.B. 1911; C.M.G. 1915; C.B.E. 1919; V.D.; T.D.; *b.* 1 March 1857; *s.* of Rev. Thomas Erskine; *m.* Florence Eliza Palmer (*d.* 1943), *d.* of Ven. Archdeacon Chapman; three *d.* *Educ.:* Charterhouse. In service of Agra Bank in India, 1879-89; sub-agent, Bank of England, at Newcastle and Manchester, 1889-95; Agent, Bank of England, Newcastle, 1896-1920; commanded 3rd V.B. Northumberland Fusiliers, 1902-8; Northumbrian T. and S. Column, 1908-13; served European War, 1914-19 (despatches thrice, C.B., C.M.G., C.B.E., Order of Leopold); Hon. Colonel Northumbrian Transport and Supply Column, 1908-31. *Address:* Sherwoods, West Green, Hartley Wintney, Hants. *T.:* Hartley Wintney 31. [*Died* 9 *Feb.* 1953.

ERSKINE, John, A.B., A.M., Ph.D., LL.D., Litt.D., L.H.D., Mus.D.; Author; Professor Emeritus of English at Columbia University; *b.* New York, 5 Oct. 1879; *s.* of James Morrison Erskine and Eliza Jane Hollingsworth Erskine; *m.* 1910, Pauline Ives (marriage dissolved), N.Y.; one *s.* one *d.*; *m.* 1945, Helen Warden. *Educ.:* Columbia Grammar School; Columbia Coll., A.B.,

A.M.; Columbia University, Ph.D. Chairman Army Educational Committee of A.E.F., 1918-19; Educational Director A.E.F. University at Beaune, 1919; Chevalier de la Légion d'Honneur, 1919; Officier, 1939; D.S.M., 1919; Honorary Citizen of Beaune, 1919; taught at Amherst College six years; returned to Columbia, 1909 as adjunct professor of English; Chairman Board of Directors, 1946, and Trustee of Juilliard School of Music since 1927; President, 1928-1937; Member Board of Directors, Metropolitan Opera Co., since 1935; Director, French Institut; Member Municipal Art Comm. New York City, 1935-39; Chm., National Comm. for Musical Appreciation, 1940-41; Pres. Poetry Society of America, 1922; Member Executive Committee American Council of Learned Societies; Phi Beta Kappa; David Bispham Opera Medal, 1933; Butler Medal, 1919. *Publications:* The Elizabethan Lyric, 1903; Selections from the Faerie Queene, 1905; Actaeon and other Poems, 1906; Leading American Novelists, 1909; Written English (with Helen Erskine), 1910; The Golden Treasury (edited with W. P. Trent). 1912; Great American Writers (with W. P. Trent), 1912; Selections from the Idylls of the King, 1912; A Pageant in Honor of Roger Bacon, 1914; The Moral Obligation to be Intelligent, 1915; The Shadowed Hour, 1917; Democracy and Ideals, 1920; The Kinds of Poetry, 1920; Collected Poems, 1922; The Literary Discipline, 1923; Sonata and other Poems, 1925; The Private Life of Helen of Troy, 1925; The Enchanted Garden, 1925; Galahad, 1926; Prohibition and Christianity, 1927; Adam and Eve, 1927; The Delight of Great Books, 1928; Penelope's Man, 1929; Sincerity, 1929; Uncle Sam, 1930; Cinderella's Daughter, 1930; Unfinished Business, 1931; Jack and the Beanstalk, opera libretto, 1931; Tristan and Isolde, 1932; Bachelor of Arts, 1934; Helen Retires, opera libretto, 1934; Forget if You Can, 1935; Solomon, My Son!, 1935; Edited Musical Companion, 1935; Influence of Women—And its Cure, 1936; Young Love, 1936; The Brief Hour of François Villon, 1937; The Start of the Road, 1938; Give me Liberty, 1940; Casanova's Women, 1941; Song Without Words, A Life of Mendelssohn, 1941; Mrs. Doratt, 1941; The Complete Life, 1943; History of Philharmonic Symphony Society of N.Y., 1917-1942; The Voyage of Captain Bart, 1943. Co-author, 1943, Ten Commandments; What is Music?, 1944; The Human Life of Jesus, 1946; The Memory of Certain Persons, 1947; My Life as a Teacher, 1948; Venus, the Lonely Goddess, 1949; My Life in Music, 1950; English Titles for French films, Baker's Wife, 1939; Story of a Cheat, 1937; Joint editor of the Cambridge History of American Literature. *Address:* 540 Park Avenue, New York City. *Clubs:* Columbia University, Century (New York).

[*Died* 2 *June* 1951.

ERSKINE of Marr, Hon. Ruaraidh; *b.* Jan. 1869; 2nd *s.* of 5th Baron Erskine; *m.* 1st, Muriel, *d.* of Maj.-Gen. G F. I. Graham; 2nd, Maria Guadalupe de Heaven y Ramirez de Arellano, (*d.* 1956) *o. d.* of the Marquesa de Braceras and late R. J. Heaven of the Forest of Birse, Aberdeenshire, and 24 Grosvenor Square, W. *Educ.:* Uppingham. *Publications:* Changing Scotland; King Edward VII and Some Other Figures, 1936; The Crown of England, 1937; The Stout Adventure of Mary Stewart, 1937; The Great Baltic Bubble, 1940; MacBeth, an historical sketch of that worthy, and (with Professor Eoin MacNeill), The Irish and Scottish Picts.

[*Died* 5 *Jan.* 1960.

ERSKINE, Rt. Hon. Sir William (Augustus Forbes), P.C. 1930; G.C.M.G., *cr.* 1930 (K.C.M.G., *cr.* 1926); M.V.O. 1906; *b.* 30 Oct. 1871; 2nd *s.* of 11th Earl of Mar and Kellie; *m.* 1908, Viola, *d.* of late W. H. Dudley Ward; two *d. Educ.:* Eton; Magdalen College, Oxford. Entered Foreign Office, 1894; Acting Third Secretary, Buenos Ayres, 1897-98; Teheran, 1901-3; Assistant Clerk, Foreign Office, 1906; Acting First Secretary at Rome, 1908; a First Secretary in Diplomatic Service, 1910; Chargé d'Affaires, Stockholm, 1913; Counsellor of Embassy, 1913; First Secretary and British Delegate on International Financial Commission, Athens, 1913-17; Counsellor of Embassy, Rome, 1917-19; H.B.M. Minister to Cuba, 1919-21; Bulgaria, 1921-27; H.B.M. Minister to Poland, 1928, Ambassador 1929-34. *Address:* 53 Campden Hill Road, W.8. *T.:* Western 3487. *Club:* Turf.

[*Died* 17 *July* 1952.

ERTZ, Edward, R.B.A. 1902; Member Society of Arts, 1905; Société des cinquant, Paris; Union des Beaux arts et des lettres, Paris; *b.* Chicago, 1862; *s.* of late John Ertz of the 12th Ill. Cavalry; *m.* 1900, Ethel Margaret Horsfall; one *s.* one *d. Educ.:* Chicago; Paris. Began career in Chicago as an engraver, designer, and illustrator; migrated to New Orleans, and helped to organise the New Orleans Etching Club and the N.O. Artists' Association; went to New York, 1885, and engraved for The Century and Scribner's Magazine; painted at intervals, and went to Paris to study, 1888; exhibited in Salon, 1889, and each year to the present time; professor of water-colour painting and drawing at the Academy Delecluse, 1892-99; came to England, 1890, to paint a picture, which was exhibited at the World's Fair, Chicago, 1893; exhibits at Royal Academy, London, at Berlin, Munich, Glasgow, Paris, Pittsburg, etc.; received five medals and diplomas at International Exhibitions in France; 3 awards Bristol Arts and Crafts; bronze and silver medals American Artists' Society, Philadelphia; represented in permanent collection, Alexandra Palace Galleries, London; Congressional Library, Washington, D.C.; California State Library; N.Y. Public Library; Art Institute, Chicago; Boston Museum of Art; The Green Art Gallery, Rochester, N.Y., etc. President of the Eclectic Art Society, 1934. *Recreation:* travelling. *Address:* Pulborough, Sussex. *T.:* Pulborough 23.

[*Died* 13 *March* 1954.

ESDAILE, Arundell James Kennedy, C.B.E. 1952; M.A.; Hon. Litt.D., Liverpool; *b.* 25 April 1880; *s.* of late James Kennedy Esdaile, J.P., D.L., of Saint Hill and Horsted Keynes, Sussex; *m.* 1907, Katharine Ada (*d.* 1950), *d.* of late Andrew McDowall; two *s.* one *d. Educ.:* Lancing; Magdalene College, Cambridge (scholar). Entered British Museum (Printed Books), 1903; Secretary, 1926-40; Lecturer in Bibliography, London University School of Librarianship, 1919-39; Sandars Reader in Bibliography, Cambridge University, 1926-27; Editor of the Library Association Record, 1924-35; The Year's Work in Librarianship, 1929-39; Sussex Notes and Queries, 1940-48; Prior of the Johnson Club, 1925-26; President of the Library Association, 1939-45; Chairman of Committee of English Assoc., 1944-46. Hon. Fellow of SS. Mary and Nicolas, Lancing, 1948. *Publications:* A List of English Tales and Prose Romances printed before 1740 (Bibliographical Society), 1912; The Lancing Register, 1913; The Sources of English Literature, 1928 (2nd ed., 1929); A Student's Manual of Bibliography, 1931, 2nd ed., 1932, 3rd ed. (revised by Roy Stokes), 1954; National Libraries of the World, 1934; Famous Libraries (joint), 1937; Autolycus' Pack; essays, addresses and verses, 1940; The British Museum Library, 1946; Wise Men from the West (poems), 1949. Ed. Daniel's Delia and Drayton's Idea, 1908; The Journals, Letters and Verses of Marjory Fleming, 1934. *Recreations:* librarianship, writing verse. *Address:* 72 Rosebery Road, Epsom, Surrey.

[*Died* 22 *June* 1956.

ESMOND, Mrs Henry V.; *see* Moore, Eva.

ESMONDE, Capt. Sir John Lymbrick, 14th Bt., *cr.* 1629; Barrister-at-Law (called 1921, Ireland), Senior Bar, 1942; Bencher King's Inn, 1948; *b.* 15 Dec. 1893; *e. s.* of late Dr. John Esmonde, M.P.; *S.* kinsman, 1943; *m.* 1922, Eleanor, *d.* of Laurence Fitzharris, Dublin. *Educ.:* Germany; Belgium, Clongowes. Worked at Harland & Wolffs, Belfast, 1911-14; enlisted Leinster Regt., 1914; Capt. 1915; served European War, 1914-18, Dublin Fusiliers and Intelligence Corps; elected bye-election, 1915. Nat. M.P. N. Tipperary; M.P., 1915-18. Member of Dail Eireann for Wexford, 1937-44 and 1948-51. *Heir: b.* Anthony Charles [*b.* 18 Jan. 1899; *m.* 1927, Eithne, *d.* of Sir Thomas Esmonde; two *s.* two *d.*]. *Address:* 26 The Rise, Mt. Merrion, Dublin; Ballynastragh, Gorey, Co. Wexford. *Club:* Stephen's Green (Dublin). [*Died* 6 *July* 1958.

ESPITALIER, A. N.; *see* Noel-Espitalier.

ESSELL, Colonel Frederick Knight, C.M.G. 1918; *b.* 18 July 1864; *s.* of George Ketchley Essell, Rochester; *m.* Nella Lilian (*d.* 1921), 2nd *d.* of Robert Narcissus Batt of Purdysburn, Co. Down; three *s.* three *d.* Commissioned to the Buffs, 1885; retired, 1902; rejoined for service, 5 Aug. 1914; Temp. Col. 1917; Col. 1919. *Recreations:* all forms of sport. *Address:* Beveré Knoll, near Worcester. *Club:* Naval and Military. [*Died* 16 *March* 1951.

ESSENHIGH, His Honour Judge Reginald Clare, J.P. Sheffield City, Rotherham County Borough and West Riding of Yorkshire; Judge of County Courts Circuit No. 13 (Sheffield) since 1936; member of Lord Chancellor's Standing Committee for framing rules etc. for County Courts; member of Appeals Committee West Riding Quarter Sessions of Yorkshire; Member of the Faculty of Law of Sheffield Univ.; Referee, District Conciliation Scheme, N.C.B. (N.E. Region) and Nat. Union of Mineworkers (coke oven plants, N.E. Region); *b.* Warrington, 7 Sept. 1890; *y. s.* of late Henry Streeter and late Elizabeth Essenhigh, Warrington; *m.* 1924, Helen Hogg, M.B., Ch.B., *d.* of John Hogg, Cambuslang, Glasgow; three *s.* one *d.* *Educ.:* Warrington Secondary School; Manchester School of Art; Royal College of Art (National Book prizeman and studentship); School of Architecture. London University O.T.C., 1914; gazetted to 3rd Bn. the Manchester Regt.; joined 2nd Bn. Manchester Regt., France, Aug. 1915 (1914-15 Star); Captain; severely wounded June 27th 1917, at Nieuport, Flanders, losing leg; retired, 1919 (King's Badge for disabled soldier). Called to the Bar by Gray's Inn, Jan. 1922; Member Northern Circuit; M.P. (U.) Newton Division of Lancashire, 1931-35; contested the Newton Division, 1929 and 1935. *Publications:* (Joint Author) Benas and Essenhigh on Pleadings in Common Law and Chancery. *Recreations:* painting and gardening. *Address:* Brantwood, Kenwood Bank, Sheffield 7. *T.:* Sharrow 50131. *Club:* Sheffield (Sheffield). [*Died* 1 *Nov.* 1955.

ESSERY, William Joseph, C.V.O. 1912; Bachelor of Medicine; retired; *b.* 1860; *s.* of late William Essery of Launceston, Cornwall; *m.* 1919, Blanche Gertrude, *y. d.* of late John Inett Ward, of the Manor House, Abbots Langley, Herts. *Educ.:* Christ's Hospital; King's College; Durham Univ. *Address:* Goose Green Cottage, Yateley, Hants. *T.:* Yateley 3189. [*Died* 13 *July* 1955.

ESSEX, Air Vice-Marshal Bertram Edward, C.B. 1952; C.B.E. 1949; *b.* 13 October 1897; *s.* of late Captain Bertram Edward Essex and late Jean Cameron Essex. *Educ.:* Colchester Royal Grammar School; privately. Served European War, 1914-18; joined Stock Exchange Battalion, Royal Fusiliers, 1914; commissioned Suffolk Regt., 1917; transferred R.A.F. 1918; Air Cdre., 1947; Dir. of Equipment (A), Air Ministry, 1949-53; Air Vice-Marshal, 1953; Senior Air Staff Officer, Maintenance Command, 1953-56, retired. *Address:* 1 Margaret Road, Harrogate, Yorkshire. *T.:* Harrogate 4946. *Club:* R.A.F. [*Died* 5 *June* 1959.

ESTCOURT, Capt. Thomas E. S.; *see* Southern-Estcourt.

ESTEY, Hon. Mr. Justice James Wilfred; Judge, Supreme Court of Canada, since 1944; *b.* 1 Dec. 1889; *s.* of Byron Leslie Estey and Sarah Ann (*née* Kee); *m.* 1916, Muriel Alice Irving Baldwin; three *s.* *Educ.:* Public Schools; University of New Brunswick, Fredericton, N.B.; Harvard University, Cambridge, Mass., U.S.A. Admitted to Bar of Saskatchewan, 1917, and practised at Saskatoon; Lecturer in law, Univ. of Sask., 1915-25; Agent of Attorney-Gen., Judicial Dist. of Saskatoon, Sask., 1921-29; Governor of Univ. of Sask., 1926-1934; K.C. (Can.) 1928; Q.C. (Can.) 1952; elected to Saskatchewan Legislature, 1934; Minister of Education, Sask., 1934-41; Attorney-General, Sask., 1939-44. Hon. LL.D., New Brunswick, 1945; Hon. D.C.L. Saskatchewan, 1953. *Recreations:* golf, curling. *Address:* Judges' Chambers, Supreme Court of Canada, Ottawa, Ont., Canada. *T.:* 9-4725. *Clubs:* Rideau, Rideau Curling (Ottawa); Royal Ottawa Golf (Hull, Que.). [*Died* 22 *Jan.* 1956.

ETHERIDGE, Rt. Rev. Edward Harold, D.D.; *b.* 15 Sept. 1872; *s.* of Ada Frances and Rev. Sanders Etheridge, Rector of Haslemere; unmarried. *Educ.:* Marlborough; Keble Coll., Oxford (History exhibition, 2nd class Modern History, M.A.); Wells Theological College. Ordained, 1895; curate at Slough, 1895-98; afterwards St. John the Divine, Kennington; missionary work in Mashonaland Diocese, 1900; Assistant Priest at Salisbury, Rhodesia; Principal of St. Augustine's, Penhalonga; Canon of Salisbury Cathedral, 1909; Archdeacon of Mashonaland, with the superintendence of Native Missions, 1912-23; Bishop of St. John's, Kaffraria, 1923-43. Canon and Chancellor of Grahamstown Cathedral, 1945-52. *Publications:* has translated Portions of the Book of Common Prayer, the New Testament and other small books into Chiswina the language of Mashonaland. *Address:* 11 Huntly Street, Grahamstown, Cape Province, S. Africa. [*Died* 16 *Sept.* 1954.

ETHERINGTON, Colonel Frederick, C.M.G. 1916; M.D.; F.R.C.S. (C.); LL.D.; *b.* 1878; *m.* 1921, A. M. Richardson. Served European War, 1915-18 (despatches, C.M.G.). *Address:* 118 University Avenue, Kingston, Canada. [*Died* 10 *Nov.* 1955.

EUSTACE, Mrs. M. E.; *see* Robertson-Eustace.

EVANS, Alan Frederick Reginald, M.A.; *s.* of F. G. Evans; *b.* 29 Nov. 1891; *m.* 1st, Edith Evans; 2nd, 1949, Gwenda K. Jackson. *Educ.:* Ipswich School; Pembroke College, Cambridge (Open Scholar); 1st Class Natural Sciences Tripos. Science Master, Malvern Coll., Gresham's School, Holt; Senior Science Master and Housemaster at Stamford School; Headmaster, Dunstable School; retired, 1948. Instructor Lieut. R.N., 1915-19. *Recreation:* fishing. *Address:* Elm Tree House, Ashbrook, Nr. Cirencester, Glos. *T.:* Poulton 316. [*Died* 17 *Sept.* 1960.

EVANS, Colonel Sir Arthur, Kt. 1944; F.R.S.A.; Commander, Southern Cross (Brazil); Director of Public Companies, and Member London Stock Exchange; Past Master, Worshipful Company of Glaziers; Vice-President and Chairman, British Society of Master Glass Painters; Deputy President, Anglo-Brazilian Society; *b.* London, 1898; *s.* of late Arthur S. Evans and late Ina Mary Bolton; *m.* 1920, Mary

Stewart, *y. d.* of late John Claflin, Morristown; (one *s.*, killed in action, North Africa, Dec. 1942). *Educ.:* privately and abroad. Enlisted Westminster Dragoons, 1914 (1914-1915 Star); commissioned T.F., 1915; Captain R.A.R.O. Welsh Guards, 1920; posted B.E.F., France, 1939, subsequently commanded Le Havre Defence Force and Garrison (Rear Headquarters) (despatches, 1939-43 Star); invalided on account of physical disability, Dec. 1941; Lieut.-Col. Regular Army Reserve (retd.); Hon. Col. T.A. (retd.). Contested L.C.C. election, 1921; M.P. (C.) Leicester (East), 1922-1923, Cardiff (South), 1924-29 and 1931-1945; sometime Chairman, Parliamentary Select Committee of Private Bills, Welsh Parliamentary Party, Welsh Conservative Parl. Party, Inter - parliamentary Union (British Group); President (*ad interim*) du Conseil Interparlementaire, 1943-45; sometime Treasurer of Conservative Private Members (1922) Cttee. and Member Speaker's Conference on Electoral Reform; Leader of British Parl. Delegation to Inter-parliamentary Conf., Oslo, 1939; Parliamentary mission to President and U.S.A. Congress, 1943; Secretary of Parl. Delegation to West Indies, 1926. A.D.C. and Personal Asst. to late Admiral of the Fleet Earl Jellicoe, on his Canadian tour, 1931. For 20 years on Board of Governors of Univ. of Wales, Welsh National Library and National Museum of Wales; a Freeman of City of London; Life Member: Interparliamentary Union, Commonwealth Parliamentary Assoc.; Hon. Society of Cymmrodorion; West India Committee, Royal United Services Institution; King Edward VII Hospital for Officers. Lord of the Manor of Norton (Radnorshire) and of Shimpling (Norfolk). *Address:* 39 Egerton Crescent, S.W.3. *T.:* Knightsbridge 2756. *Clubs:* Guards, Carlton, 1900, The Pilgrims, City Livery, West Indian, Clwb y Cymry; Household Brigade Yacht.
[*Died* 25 *Sept.* 1958.

EVANS, Brig. Brian P.; *see* Pennefather-Evans.

EVANS, Cecil Herbert; Headmaster Merchiston Castle School, Edinburgh, since 1936; *b.* 23 April 1898; *e. s.* of late Rev. E. F. Evans, Rector of North Ockendon, Essex; *m.* 1923, Constance Eleanor, *o. d.* of late J. F. Reynolds, Tonbridge. *Educ.:* Tonbridge School; Brasenose College, Oxford. *Address:* Merchiston Castle School, Edinburgh.
[*Died* 15 *Aug.* 1957.

EVANS, Col. Charles Robert, D.S.O. 1915; late R.A.M.C.; *b.* 14 April 1873; *m.*; two *s.* Entered Army, 1899; Captain, 1902; Major, 1911; Lt.-Col., 1915; Col., 1919; served S. African War, 1900 (Queen's medal 2 clasps); European War, 1914-18 (despatches, Brevet Col., D.S.O.); retired pay, 1930. *Address:* Glyn, Mills & Co., Kirkland House, Whitehall, S.W.1.
[*Died* 5 *May* 1956.

EVANS, Sir (David) Rowland, Kt., *cr* 1937; *s.* of late Richard Evans, Caersws, Mont.; *m.* 1918, Helen, *e. d.* of late Alderman C. T. Bateman, Guildford. Principal Private Secretary to Sir John Simon (now Viscount Simon), 1922 - 35; General Secretary of National Liberal Organization and Hon. Treas. of National Liberal Council, 1935-51. *Publications:* Britain and World Peace, 1935; Let it Roll (A Plan for Anglo-American Co-operation), 1941; Prelude to Peace, 1943; Beware of a Twice-Beaten Germany, 1943. Editor of Comments and Criticisms by Sir John Simon, 1930. *Address:* 44 Hurlingham Court, S.W.6. *Club:* National Liberal.
[*Died* 2 *Sept.* 1953.

EVANS, Maj.-Gen. David Sydney Carlyon, C.B.E. 1943; *b.* 27 July 1893; *s.* of Lewis Evans, M.A. *Educ.:* Parkfield; St. Paul's; R.M.A., Woolwich. 2nd Lt. R.G.A., 1913; Capt. 1917; Maj. 1932; Bt. Lt.-Col. 1937; Col. 1939; Acting Maj.-Gen 1942; Temp. Maj.-Gen. 1943. Served in France and Belgium, 1914-16 and 1917-18; Instructor, Artillery College, 1922-26; Asst. Inspector, Inspection Department, 1928-30; Expt. Officer, Admiralty Research Laboratory, 1930-34; Asst. Supt. Design Dept., 1935-39; Lefroy Gold Medal 1937; Secretary, Ordnance Board, 1939; Asst. Director of Artillery, 1939-42; Vice-Pres. and Senior Military Member Ordnance Board, 1942-47; retired pay, 1947. *Recreation:* gardening. *Club:* United Service. [*Died* 6 *Dec.* 1955.

EVANS, Rev. E. Gwyn, B.A.; Minister of the Welsh Presbyterian Church, Charing Cross Road, London, since 1939; *b.* 30 May 1898; *m.* 1927, Enyd Jones; two *s.* *Educ.:* Secondary Schools, Bridgend and Maesteg; Univ. Coll. of Wales, Aberystwyth; Theological Colls., Aberystwyth and Bala. Welsh Presbyterian Minister: Rock Ferry, 1927-31; Cathedral Road, Cardiff, 1931-36; Trinity, Swansea, 1936-38. Moderator of Free Church Federal Council, March 1957-March 1958. *Address:* 14 Raleigh Close, Hendon, N.W.4. *T.:* Hendon 7997. [*Died* 23 *July* 1958.

EVANS, Edward, C.B.E. 1949; Chairman, Advisory Committee for the Health and Welfare of the Handicapped; Chairman National Institute for the Deaf; Vice-President: National College for Teachers of the Deaf; College of Teachers of the Blind; Deaf Children's Society; Governor and Trustee Mary Hare Grammar School for the Deaf; Deputy Secretary National Institute for the Blind, 1943-45; President and Trustee National Deaf-Blind Helpers' League; Patron, Soc. for Higher Education for the Deaf; Vice-Pres. Central Council for Care of Cripples; *b.* 11 Jan. 1883; *s.* of Daniel Thomas Evans and Mary Beynon; *m.* 1915, Victoria Evelyn Muir (*d.* 1953), two *s.* *Educ.:* Llanelly Elementary and Science Schools; St. Paul's College, Cheltenham; London University. Assistant Master Linden Lodge for Blind boys; served European War, H.A.C., 1915-16; Old Kent Road Deaf School (now Manager). Lip-reading classes, Ministry of Pensions; Founder Member, Southern Regional Assoc. for the Blind; Headmaster East Anglian Schools for Blind and Deaf, 1928-43; Member: Great Yarmouth Borough Council and of Education Committee; M.P. (Lab.) Lowestoft Division of East Suffolk, 1945-September 1959. Parliamentary Deleg. Austria, 1946, Iceland, 1953, Denmark, 1955; Survey on Social Services for Blind in Germany, 1946; Conf. on European Union, The Hague, 1948; Inter-Parl. Conf. on European Union, Interlaken, 1948; Consultant Mem., Internat. Congress on Deaf-Blind, N.Y., 1957. Formerly: Chm. All-party Committee on Coast Erosion and Flooding; Vice-Chm. All-party Resorts and Tourists Committee; Chairman Labour Party Fisheries Committee. *Publications:* A Manual Alphabet for the Deaf-Blind; formerly Editor Braille School Magazine; contributed widely to Educational and general Press. *Recreations:* music, theatre. *Address:* 128 Waxwell Lane, Pinner, Middlesex. *T.:* Pinner 1092. *Club:* Savage. [*Died* 30 *March* 1960.

EVANS, Edward Francis Herbert; High Sheriff of Herefordshire, 1948-49; *b.* 12 Sept. 1873; *s.* of Edward Wallace Evans, Alfrick Court, nr. Worcester, and Frances Rhoda, *d.* of A. H. Cocks, C.B., Whitbourne Court; *m.* 1905, Fanny Isherwood, *d.* of Rev. Preb. J. H. Brierley, Rector of Whitbourne; four *s.* three *d.* *Educ.:* Eton; Oriel College, Oxford. 2nd Lt. 3rd Worcs. Regt., 1893; seconded I.Y., S. Africa, 1900-1; resigned commission, 1902. Served European War, 1914-18, Capt. 10th (S) Worcs. Regt., 1914 (wounded). J.P. 1903 (now on supplementary list), C.C. 1925, Herefordshire (Alderman, 1949). Chairman: R.D.C. (resigned 1954, after 21 years); Grammar School, Bromyard. Group Warden, 1939-45; Home

Guard, 1940-42. Chairman Board of Hill, Evans & Co. Ltd. *Recreations:* shooting and fishing; formerly hunting, cricket, lawn tennis, hockey. *Address:* Whitbourne Hall, nr. Worcester. *T.A.:* Whitbourne. *T.:* Knightwick 223. *Club:* Public Schools. [*Died* 14 *April* 1958.

EVANS, Ellen, C.B.E. 1948; M.A. (Wales); Principal of the Glamorgan Training College, Barry, S. Wales, since 1923; *b.* 10 Mar. 1891; *d.* of John Evans and Ellen Evans, Pentre, Rhondda, Glam. *Educ.:* Rhondda Secondary School; University College of Wales, Aberystwyth. Lecturer in Welsh Language and Literature at the Glamorgan Training College, Barry, 1915-1923; member of the Honourable Society of Cymmrodorion; member of the University Court, University of Wales; Council, Univ. College of Wales, Aberystwyth; Executive Coleg, Harlech; Departmental Cttee. on Welsh; has lectured to numerous societies; Adjudicator at National Eisteddfodau. *Publications:* Y Mabinogion i'r Plant (The Children's Mabinogion), four volumes for children; The Teaching of Welsh, 1924; articles to Welsh and English magazines; Llawlyfr i Athrawon (a Teacher's Handbook) and Hwiangerddi Rhiannon (a Collection of Nursery Rhymes, Poems, Games, etc.); Cynllun Cymraeg Ellen Evans (a scheme for the teaching of Welsh), 1927; Y Wen Fro, 1931. *Recreations:* walking, travelling, photography. *Address:* The Training College, Barry, S. Wales. *T.:* Barry 124. [*Died* 26 *Sept.* 1953.

EVANS, Emily, C.B.E. 1920; J.P.; e. d. of Frank J. and Mary N. Batchelor; *m.* John L. T. Evans, M.A. (Oxon), Assistant Head Master, King Edward VI School, Stratford-on-Avon. *Educ.:* Church of England College, Edgbaston, Birmingham; Roedean, Brighton. Worked as a voluntary outside helper with the Women's Settlement, Birmingham, until the war; during the war as a V.A.D. at the 1st Southern General, and in sundry small hospitals; afterwards with the French Red Cross at Vendeuvre sur Barse and Troyes, and finally as worker and afterwards Directrice of the Women's Emergency Canteens in Paris until the close of war; Chairwoman from 1928 of Women's Section British Legion, Stratford-on-Avon, now Patron; Member Executive Council of Shakespeare Memorial Theatre. J.P. 1936. *Recreations:* music, games, and travelling. *Address:* Burnside, Shottery, Stratford-on-Avon. *T.:* Stratford-on-Avon 2112. [*Died* 15 *July* 1958.

EVANS, Sir Evan G. G., Bt.; *see* Gwynne-Evans.

EVANS, Frederick Buisson, C.S.I. 1922; late Indian Civil Service; *b.* Hampstead, 9 Aug., 1874; unmarried. *Educ.:* St. Paul's School; Trinity College, Oxford (Scholar); 1st Class Mods. 2nd Lit. Hum.; M.A. Served in the Madras Presidency from 1898, mainly in the district of Malabar and in the Secretariat; Collector of Malabar, 1915-19; special secretary to Government for reforms, 1920; special civil officer in the Malabar Rebellion, 1921-22; Second Secretary to Govt., 1925; retired, 1928. *Publication:* edited Malabar District Gazetteer, 1908. *Address:* Star House, E. Blatchington, Seaford, Sussex. [*Died* 8 *Sept.* 1952.

EVANS, Geoffrey (A.), M.A., M.D. (Cantab.); F.R.C.P. (London); Consulting Physician to St. Bartholomew's Hospital; formerly: Member Assoc. of Physicians, Great Britain; Pres. Section of Medicine, R.S.M.; Member of Council R.C.P.; *b.* 1886; *o. surv. s.* of late Patrick F. Evans, Recorder, Newcastle-under-Lyme; *m.* 1917, Hon. Ermine Mary Kyffin, *o. c.* of 1st Baron Maenan, *q.v.*; one *s.* three *d.* *Educ.:* Charterhouse; Trinity Coll., Cambridge (Exhibitioner); 1st Class Natural Science Tripos, Parts 1 and 2; St. Bartholomew's Hospital (Senior Entrance Science Scholar, Brackenbury Medical Scholar, Lawrence Research Scholar, Gold Medal); late Hon. Assistant Physician Bürgerspital, Bâle; Horton-Smith Prize, University Cambridge; Goulstonian Lecturer, 1923, Lumleian Lecturer, 1943, R.C.P.; Temp. Surgeon, R.N., 1914-19; late Assist. Physician, Metropolitan Hospital; late Assistant Director medical unit St. Bartholomew's Hospital. *Publications:* Editor, Medical Treatment—Principles and their Application, 1950; Nephritis (Brit. Encyc. of Med. Practice, 2nd Ed.).; numerous publications on medical and scientific subjects. *Address:* 7 Mansfield Street, W.1. *T.:* Langham 1717; Harpley House, Clifton-on-Teme, Worcestershire. [*Died* 30 *Aug.* 1951.

EVANS, Rt. Rev. Henry St. John Tomlinson; Bishop of St. John's (Kaffraria) since 1951; *b.* Swansea, 1905; *s.* of Rev. William Evans and Louisa Helen Jones. *Educ.:* Merchant Taylors' School; St. John's College, Oxford (Scholar, M.A.). Ordained, 1928; Rector of St. Augustine's College, Kumasi, 1931; Archdeacon of Ashanti, 1937-1941; Chaplain to the Forces, 1942-44; Librarian, Pusey House, Oxford, 1944-45; Director of Missions, Diocese of S. Rhodesia, 1948-51. *Publications:* The Church in S. Rhodesia, 1946; contributor to African Idea of God, 1949; articles on anthropological subjects. *Recreations:* cricket, billiards, ornithology. *Address:* Bishopsmead, Umtata, C.P., S. Africa. [*Died* 25 *July* 1956.

EVANS, Herbert Walter Lloyd, C.V.O. 1935; O.B.E. 1918; retired, 1939; late Superintendent, Royal Mint, E.C.3; *b.* 22 August 1877; *s.* of late John Lloyd and Lilian Gertrude Evans; *m.* 1903, Susan Georgina Thatcher; two *s.* one *d.* *Educ.:* City of London School. Engineering training with J. and E. Hall Ltd., Dartford; staff of Royal Mint, 1900. *Address:* 11 Eltham Park Gardens, Eltham, S.E.9. *T.:* Eltham 2196. [*Died* 16 *June* 1956.

EVANS, Ifor Leslie; Principal, University College of Wales, Aberystwyth, since 1934; Chairman, University of Wales Estates Committee and Press Board; *b.* 17 Jan. 1897; *s.* of late W. J. Evans and late M. E. Milligan; *m.* 1938, Ruth Jolles, *d.* of Frau Wolff-Mönckeberg, Hamburg; one *s.* one *d.* *Educ.:* Wycliffe Coll., Stonehouse; France and Germany. Civilian Prisoner of War in Germany, 1914-18; entered St. John's College, Cambridge, 1920; first class in Economics and History; Whewell Scholar in International Law; Fellow of St. John's Coll., Cambridge, 1923-34; and University Lecturer in Economics; Vice-Chancellor, Univ. of Wales, 1937-39 and 1946-48; Hon. D.Litt. Royal Univ. of Malta, 1948. Travelled widely in Central Europe and the Balkans, and in Tropical Africa. *Publications:* The Agrarian Revolution in Roumania; The British in Tropical Africa; Native Policy in Southern Africa; The Agriculture of Wales and Monmouthshire (with Prof. A. W. Ashby). *Address:* University College of Wales, Aberystwyth. *Club:* Athenæum. [*Died* 31 *May* 1952.

EVANS, John Cayo, M.A. (Oxon); late Professor of Mathematics, St. David's College, Lampeter; *b.* 1 March 1879; *s.* of William and Sarah Evans; *m.* 1923, Freda, *d.* of Dr. Cluneglas Davies; two *s.* *Educ.:* St. David's College School, Lampeter; University College, Aberystwyth; Jesus College, Oxford. 1st class Mathematical Moderations, Oxford, 1899; 1st class Final School of Mathematics, 1901; 1st class Final School of Natural Science, 1903; B.A. 1901; M.A. 1927; entered Indian Educational Service, 1905; Officiating Director of Public Instruction, Central Province, 1920-21; retired from Indian Service, 1922; High Sheriff of Cardiganshire, 1941-42. *Recreations:* golf and shooting. *Address:* Glandenys, Lampeter, Cardiganshire. *T.:* Lampeter 60. [*Died* 8 *March* 1958.

EVANS, Meredith Gwynne, F.R.S. 1947; D.Sc.; Professor of Physical Chemistry, University of Manchester, since 1949; Professor of Inorganic and Physical Chemistry, The University of Leeds, 1945-48; *b.* 2 Dec. 1904; *e. s.* of F. G.

Evans, Atherton; *m.* 1931, Millicent Trafford; one *s.* one *d.* *Educ.:* Leigh Grammar School; Manchester University. Asst. Lecturer, Univ. of Manchester, 1929; Rockefeller Foundation Research Fellow, Univ. of Princeton, 1933; Lecturer, Univ. of Manchester, 1936; Prof. of Physical Chemistry, Univ. of Leeds, 1939. *Publications:* papers on Kinetics and Mechanism of chemical reactions in scientific journals. *Address:* The University, Manchester. *T.:* Ardwick 2681; Mayfield, Beaufort Road, Brooklands, Cheshire. *T.:* Sale 1418. [*Died* 25 *Dec.* 1952.

EVANS, Percy William, B.A., B.D. (London); D.D. Edinburgh; Principal Spurgeon's College (Baptist) 1925-50, Emeritus Principal since 1950; *b.* Hereford, 5 Mar. 1882; *s.* of James and Elizabeth Evans, Hereford; *m.* 1913, Dorothy, *o. d.* of Rev. J. W. Padfield; one *s.* two *d.* *Educ.:* Hereford Blue Coat School; Birkbeck College and Spurgeon's (formerly Pastors') College. Baptist minister (1911-25 in pastoral charge); Classical Tutor at Spurgeon's College, 1922-25; President, Baptist Union of Great Britain and Ireland, 1940-41; Moderator, Free Church Federal Council, 1948-1949. Senator, University of London, 1948-. *Publication:* The Cross as a Tree, 1945. *Recreations:* walking, golf. *Address:* 38 Deakin Leas, Tonbridge, Kent. [*Died* 23 *March* 1951.

EVANS, Sir Rowland; *see* Evans, Sir D. R.

EVANS, Sir Walter (Harry), 1st Bt., *cr.* 1920; *b.* 19 May 1872; 2nd *s.* of late Joseph Evans, J.P., County of Stafford; *m.* 1907, Margaret Mary, *y. d.* of late Thomas Adney Dickens; one *s.* two *d.* *Heir: s.* Anthony Adney, *b.* 5 Aug. 1922. *Address:* The Mead House, Shipley, Wolverhampton. *T.:* Pattingham 279. [*Died* 7 *Nov.* 1954.

EVANS, William B.; *see* Bulkeley-Evans.

EVANS, Brigadier William Harry, C.S.I. 1931; C.I.E. 1927; D.S.O. 1918; Royal Engineers, 1896-1931; *b.* Shillong, Assam, 22 July 1876; *s.* of late General Sir H. M. Evans, K.C.B., Indian Army, and *d.* of late Surgeon-General T. Tresidder; *m. d.* of late Arthur Young-Harvey, Adelaide, S.A.; one *s.* *Educ.:* King's School, Canterbury. Served Somaliland, 1903-4 (despatches, medal and clasp); European War, 1914-18 (depatches, D.S.O., Bt. Lieut.-Col.); Chief Engineer, Western Command, Quetta, India, 1927-31; retired, 1931. *Publications:* various publications on lepidoptera. *Recreation:* natural history. *Address:* 12 Harrington Gardens, S.W.7. *T.:* Frobisher 1814. [*Died* 13 *Nov.* 1956.

EVANS, William Percival, C.B.E. 1956; M.A., Ph.D., F.R.S.N.Z., F.I.C.N.Z.; Emeritus Professor of Chemistry; *b.* 22 Nov. 1864; *s.* of William and Louisa Bishop Evans; *m.* 1893, Chrissie Mayo Kebbell; two *d.* *Educ.:* Nelson College; Canterbury College; University of Giessen. Sometime mathematical and science master Christ's College, Christchurch; lecturer and, later, professor of chemistry in the University of New Zealand; retired 1922; Hector medallist of R.S.N.Z., 1931, for research in chemistry; President R.S.N.Z., 1937-38; First Pres. N.Z.I.C., 1931; First Hon. Fellow N.Z.I.C. 1944. *Publications:* Many scientific papers mostly dealing with the use and micro-structure of the lignitic coals of New Zealand (1894-1938). *Recreations:* gardening and tramping. *Address:* Reculver, Rosetta Rd., Raumati South, via Wellington, New Zealand. [*Died* 2 *Sept.* 1959.

EVANS-GORDON, Col. Kenmure Alick Garth, C.I.E. 1939; Indian Army, Indian Political Service, retired; *b.* 20 Aug. 1885; *m.* 1915, Irene Earle, *d.* of late Col. Sir Henry McMahon, G.C.M.G., G.C.V.O., K.C.I.E., C.S.I.; two *s.* one *d.* Resident for Kolhapur and Deccan States, 1937-1940; retired, 1940; re-employed under War Dept., New Delhi, 1941-46; Col. 1943. *Address:* c/o Lloyds Bank, Ltd., 6 Pall Mall, S.W.1. [*Died* 12 *June* 1960.

EVANSON, Maj.-Gen. Arthur Charles Tarver, C.B. 1947; M.C.; *b.* 6 Apr. 1895; *s.* of late A. M. Evanson, J.P., Hougham, Kent; *m.* 1922, Barbara, *d.* of late E. P. Barlow, Kearsney Court, Dover; two *d.* *Educ.:* Haileybury; R.M.C. Sandhurst. Commissioned E. Surrey Regt. 1914; retired 1947. *Address:* Chilverton Elms, nr. Dover, Kent. *Club:* Army and Navy. [*Died* 13 *Feb.* 1957.

EVE, Frank Cecil; Consulting Physician: Royal Infirmary; Children's Hospital, Hull; *b.* Silsoe, Beds.; *s.* of J. R. Eve; *m.* 1911, S. E. Buyers, M.B.; one *s.* *Educ.:* Bedford School; Emmanuel College, Cambridge (Scholar); St. Thomas's Hospital (Scholar). B.A. (1st class nat. science), M.D., F.R.C.P. London; Demonstrator of Physiology, Leeds, 1896. *Publications:* Artificial Respiration explained, 1946 (including the author's Rocking Method); papers in B.M.J. and Lancet on Halometer, etc. *Recreations:* gardening, and natural philosophy. *Address:* 9 Newbegin, Beverley, Yorks. *T.:* Beverley 338. [*Died* 7 *Dec.* 1952.

EVELEGH, Major-General Vyvyan, C.B. 1943; D.S.O. 1944; O.B.E. 1940; *b.* 14 Dec. 1898; *s.* of Maj. C. N. Evelegh; *m.* 1930, Vida Eleanor, *d.* of Frederick Parkin. *Educ.:* Wellington College. 2nd Lt. D.C.L.I. 1917. Served European War, France and Belgium, 1918, Russia, 1919 (wounded); War of 1939-45: comd. 78 Div., 6 Armd. Div. (O.B.E., C.B., D.S.O.); retired pay, 1950; Colonel D.C.L.I., 1953-. *Address:* Warnscombe, Dunsford, nr. Exeter. *T.:* Longdown 343. [*Died* 27 *Aug.* 1958.

EVERARD, E. E. E. W.; *see* Welby-Everard.

EVERETT, Dorothy, M.A. (Oxon. Cantab. Lond.); Reader in English Language, University of Oxford, since 1948; Fellow of Lady Margaret Hall, Oxford, since 1926; *b.* King's Lynn, Norfolk, 1894. *Educ.:* Norwich High School; Girton College, Cambridge, First Class, Mediæval and Modern Languages Tripos, 1916. British Scholar, Bryn Mawr College, Pa., U.S.A., 1916-17; Assistant Lecturer in English, Royal Holloway College (Univ. of London), 1917-21; Tutor in English Literature, St. Hugh's College, Oxford, 1921-23; Tutor in English Language and Literature, Lady Margaret Hall, 1926-48. *Publications:* The Prose Psalter of Richard Rolle of Hampole, Modern Languages Review, 1921; Editor of Annual Bibliography of English Language and Literature (Publ. by Mod. Hum. Research Assoc.), 1925, joint Editor, 1926-27; Middle English Chapter, Year's Work in English Studies, 1925-26-27-28-29, etc.; Another Collation of the Ellesmere Manuscript of the Canterbury Tales, Medium Aevum, 1932; Some Reflections on Chaucer's 'Art Poetical', Gollancz Mem. Lecture, British Academy, 1950, etc. *Recreation:* gardening. *Address:* Lady Margaret Hall, Oxford; 3 Crick Road, Oxford. *T.:* Oxford 2214. [*Died* 22 *June* 1953.

EVERETT, Harry Poore, J.P.; Senior partner in firm of Witherington and Everett, Shipowners, Newcastle upon Tyne; Director, Granta Steamship Co., Ltd.; *b.* 3 Sept. 1862; *s.* of Henry Poore Everett and Elizabeth Goddard; *m.* 1887, Mary Catherine Brown; one *s.* one *d.* *Educ.:* Abroad. Ex-Chairman of Tyne Improvement Commission. *Address:* The Cedars, Sunderland. *T.:* 4767. [*Died* 23 *June* 1955.

EVERETT, Maj.-Gen. Sir Henry Joseph, K.C.M.G., *cr.* 1919 (C.M.G. 1917); C.B. 1915; D.L.; Somerset L.I.; *b.* 5 March 1866; 2nd *s.* of late Col. John Frederick Everett; *m.* 1917, Violet Althea, *e. d.* of Rev. C. N. Wyld. Entered army, 1885; Adjutant, 1890-94; Capt. 1892; Major, 1906; Lt.-Col. 1910; Col. 1913;

retired, 1920; Staff Officer, South Africa, 1900-1902; D.A.Q.M.G. Straits Settlements, 1903-5; D.A.A.G., India, 1908-9; A.A. and Q.M.G., 1914; served South Africa, 1899-1902 (despatches, Bt. Major; Queen's medal 5 clasps, King's medal 2 clasps); European War, 1914-1918 (despatches, C.B., C.M.G., K.C.M.G.); Chm. Wilts Territorial Army Assoc., 1924-45. *Publication:* The History of the Somerset Light Infantry, 1685-1914, 1934. *Address:* Avon Turn, Alderbury, Salisbury. *T.:* Alderbury 203. *Club:* Army and Navy. [*Died* 9 *Oct.* 1951.

EVERETT, Sir Percy Winn, Kt., *cr.* 1930; M.A., F.S.S.; Deputy Chief Scout since 1941; member of Executive Committee of Boy Scouts; Vice-President, Girl Guides Association; a member of Eastman Dental Clinic, and Royal Free Hospital; *b.* Rushmere, Ipswich, 22 April 1870; 2nd *s.* of late R. L. Everett, J.P.; *m.* 1896, Rita, *d.* of late Matthew Cay, S. Shields; one *s.* one *d.* *Educ.:* Queen Elizabeth's School, Ipswich; Trinity College, Cambridge (Foundation Scholar and 15th Wrangler). *Recreations:* bridge, scouting. *Address:* Schopwick, Elstree, Herts. *T.:* Elstree 1008. [*Died* 23 *Feb.* 1952.

EVERIDGE, John, O.B.E.; F.R.C.S.; Consulting Urological Surgeon, King's College Hospital; Consulting Urologist, Queen Alexandra Military Hospital, Millbank; Consulting Urologist to several Ministry of Health Hospitals; Fellow of King's College, London; *s.* of James Walter Everidge and Temperance Bartlett; *m.* Kathleen Isobel Robertson; one *s.* one *d.* *Educ.:* King's College School. Appointed to the Hon. Staff of King's College Hospital, 1919; military service in R.A.M.C. (T.F.), 1914-19; served in France as Surgical Specialist to the Forces (despatches); retired with rank of Major. Late Pres., Section of Urology, Royal Society of Medicine; late Treas., British Assoc. of Urological Surgeons, and Member of Council. *Publications:* mainly upon Urological subjects in surgical text-books and journals. *Recreations:* golf, fishing. *Address:* 7 Wimpole Street, W.1. *T.:* Langham 1707. *Clubs:* Flyfishers'; Royal St. George's Golf (Sandwich). [*Died* 8 *June* 1955.

EVERSHED, John, C.I.E. 1923; F.R.S. 1915, F.R.A.S. 1892; late Director, Kodaikanal and Madras Observatories; *b.* 26 Feb. 1864; 4th *s.* of John and Sophia Evershed, Gomshall, Sy.; *m.* 1906, Mary Acworth Orr (*d.* 1949); *m.* 1950, Margaret G. Randall. *Educ.:* Private schools. Made a series of solar observations at private observatory, 1890-1906; took part in six expeditions to observe total solar eclipses, viz. Norway 1896, India 1898, Algeria 1900, Spain 1905, Australia 1922, and Yorkshire 1927; Assistant Director, Kodaikanal and Madras Observatories, 1906; discovered radial movement in sunspots, 1909; visited New Zealand to select site for the Cawthron Observatory, 1914; undertook astronomical expedition to Kashmir, 1915; built and equipped private Observatory at Ewhurst in 1925, where research work with powerful spectrographs of novel design has been carried out during recent years; gold medal Royal Astronomical Soc., 1918. *Publications:* papers in scientific jls. *Address:* Highbroom, Ewhurst, Sy. *T.:* 72. [*Died* 17 *Nov.* 1956.

EVERY, Sir Edward Oswald, 11th Bt., *cr.* 1641; *b.* 14 Jan. 1886; *o. s.* of Capt. Henry E. Every and Leila Frances Harford (*d.* 1890), *d.* of Rev. H. A. Box; *S.* grandfather, 1893; *m.* 1909, Ivy Linton, *d.* of Major Meller, The Limes, Rushmere; two *s.* one *d.* *Educ.:* Harrow; Trinity College, Cambridge; B.A. 1908; served European War (Bt. Major, 1918). *Heir:* *s.* John Simon [*b.* 24 Apr. 1914; *m.* 1st, 1938, Annette Constance (marriage dissolved, 1942), *o. c.* of late Major F. W. M. Drew; 2nd., 1943, Janet, *d.* of John Page, Blakeney, Norfolk; one *s.* two *d.*]. *Address:* The Cottage, Egginton, Derby. *T.:* Etwall 245. [*Died* 11 *Nov.* 1959.

EVETTS, Sir George, Kt., *cr.* 1946; O.B.E.; M.Inst.C.E.; M.Inst.GasE.; Director of Public Utility Companies at home and overseas; *b.* 18 Dec. 1882; *s.* of William and Ellen Louisa Evetts; *m.* 1909, Helen Lena Roberts; two *s.* *Educ.:* Mason Coll.; Birmingham University. Three years Junior Assistant in the City Engineer's Office, Westminster; 10 years Assistant to late Hy. E. Jones, M.Inst.C.E., M.Inst.Gas E.; 21 years Consulting Gas Engineer, practising in Palace Chambers, Westminster. During European War, 1914-18, Works Manager of Explosives Loading Co.; during 1939-45 War, Gas Adviser to Board of Trade Gas Division and later to Ministry of Fuel and Power; Chairman of Advisory Committee on Benzole Recovery; Assistant Director of Compressed Gases (Air Ministry). Liveryman of Worshipful Company of Wheelwrights; Freeman of City of London. *Publications:* Administration and Finance of Gas Undertakings, 1922; Gas Legislation, 1935; Technical papers read before Junior Institution of Engineers, Institution of Gas Engineers (Jones Medallist), etc., and many contributions to the Technical Press. *Address:* Penlee, Warren Lane, Friston, Nr. Eastbourne, Sussex. [*Died* 12 *June* 1958.

EVILL, Lt.-Col. Charles Ariel, D.S.O. 1915; T.D.; D.L.; Head of a Chepstow firm of Solicitors; *b.* Hewelsfield Court, Gloucester, 14 Oct. 1874; *yr. s.* of Walter Evill; *m.* 1905, Lily, *d.* of late Charles Chapman of Carlecotes Hall, Yorkshire; three *s.* one *d.* *Educ.:* Christ College, Brecon. Served European War, France, 1915-18, and Flanders, Egypt, 1916; O.C. 1st Batt. Monmouthshire Regt. (T.F.), 1915-18; served Royal Observer Corps, 1937-45. Clerk to Chepstow and Lydney magistrates, 1937-49; for 45 years was Clerk to General Commissioners of Inland Revenue. Pres. Chepstow Branch British Legion. *Address:* Brynderwen, Chepstow. *T.:* 213. [*Died* 12 *Feb.* 1954.

EWART, Richard, J.P.; M.P. (Lab.) South Division of Sunderland since 1950, Sunderland, 1945-50; C.C.; Trade Union Official (full time) since 1936; *b.* 15 Sept. 1904; *s.* of Richard Ewart; unmarried. *Educ.:* St. Bedes, South Shields. Member South Shields County Borough Council, 1932-1943; Member North Riding C.C. since 1943; J.P. North Riding Yorks, 1944. Parliamentary Private Secretary to the President of the Board of Trade, 1951. *Address:* House of Commons, S.W.1. [*Died* 8 *March* 1953.

EWART, Sir Talbot, 5th Bt., *cr.* 1887; *b.* 2 Nov. 1878; *s.* of late Richard Hooker Ewart, 3rd *s.* of 1st Bt. and of Fanny Melbourne Talbot, Lowell, Massachusetts; *S.* cousin, 1939; *m.* 1913, Sydney Stuart, *d.* of Louis P. Henop, New York. Graduate of Harvard University and New York Law School. Member of New York Bar. *Heir:* *c.* William Ivan Cecil, *b.* 18 July 1919. *Club:* Union (New York). [*Died* 23 *Oct.* 1959.

EWART, William Herbert Lee, C.B.E. 1920; *b.* 6 Sept. 1881; *s.* of late William Lee Ewart, and *g.s.* of late William Ewart, M.P., of Broadleas, Devizes; *m.* 1911, Katherine Cassandra, *d.* of late Commander Sebastian Gassiot, R.N.; one *s.* two. *d.* *Educ.:* Eton; Trinity College, Cambridge. Late Hon. Attaché H.M.'s Diplomatic Service; Assistant Private Sec. to Secretary of State for Foreign Affairs; Sheriff of Wiltshire, 1942. *Address:* Belmont, Mont Au Prêtre, Jersey, C.I. *Club:* Travellers'. [*Died* 14 *March* 1953.

EWEN, Sir David (Alexander), K.B.E., *cr.* 1952 (O.B.E. 1946; M.B.E. 1918); Chairman of Directors, Sargood Son & Ewen Ltd., 1940; *b.* 12 Feb. 1884; *s.* of J. A. Ewen, J.P., and M. E. Ewen, Potters Bar, Mx.; *m.* 1912, Marian McDowell Nathan; two *s.* one *d.* *Educ.:* Mill Hill School,

Middlesex. Managing Director, Sargood Son & Ewen Ltd., 1913; Director, Reserve Bank of N.Z., 1934-37; Member: N.Z. Supply Council, 1940-45; War Assets Realisation Board, 1945-46. Board of Trustees, Nat. Gallery and Museum, N.Z., 1936-; Pres. N.Z. Academy of Fein Arts; Dominion Pres. Boy Scouts Assoc. N.Z., 1955. *Recreations:* golf, tennis, fishing, shooting. *Address:* Lochaber, Lower Hutt, New Zealand. *T.:* 63-378 Wellington. *Clubs:* Wellington (Wellington, N.Z.); Christchurch (Christchurch, N.Z.); Dunedin (Dunedin, N.Z.); Northern (Auckland, N.Z.). [*Died* 7 *April* 1957.

EWING, Sir Ian L. O.; *see* Orr Ewing.

EWING, Rev. John William, M.A. (Lond.); B.D. (St. Andrews); (Hon.) D.D. (McMaster, Canada); Organiser, Baptist Union Continental Fund, 1937; *b.* Bythorn, Hunts, 31 July 1864; *s.* of Thomas John Ewing, Baptist Minister, and Elizabeth Maria Ewing; *m.* 1889, Annie Elizabeth Hawkins; two *s.* three *d.* *Educ.:* Nonconformist Grammar School, Bishop's Stortford; Spurgeon's College; Birkbeck College. Minister, Baptist Church, East Hill, Wandsworth, 1886-95; Rye Lane, Peckham, 1896-1916; addressed Baptist World Alliance Congresses, Berlin, 1908, Philadelphia, 1911, Stockholm, 1913; President, London Baptist Association, 1906-7 and 1934-35; President, Baptist Union of Great Britain and Ireland, 1912-13; Secretary, London Baptist Association, and Superintendent, for London, of Baptist Union, 1916-34; President, Spurgeon's College Conference, 1920-21; four times President, Baptist Board; Chairman, Baptist Missionary Society Committee, 1936-37; President, General Body of the Protestant Dissenting Ministers of the Three Denominations, 1936-37; President of National Council of the Evangelical Free Churches, 1939-40; Vice-President World's Evangelical Alliance; Governor Bishop's Stortford College, 1904-1946. *Publications:* Talks on Free Church Principles; The Undying Christ; Goodly Fellowship, 1946; Able to Save (Tract, translated into other languages). *Recreations:* reading, walking. *Address:* 40 Grove Park, S.E.5. *T.:* Brixton 3368. [*Died* 1 *May* 1951.

EWING, Brig.-Gen. Sir Norman A. O.; *see* Orr Ewing.

EWING, Robert, C.M.G. 1933; *b.* East Maitland, N.S.W., 31 Aug. 1871; *s.* of late Robert Ewing and Elizabeth Cunningham; *m.* 1909, Maude Olivia, *d.* of late John Church, Sydney, N.S.W.; no *c.* *Educ.:* Sydney High School. Junior reporting staff Sydney Morning Herald; joined Civil Service of N.S.W. in Taxation Dept.; transferred to Customs Dept. 1900; entered the Public Service of the Commonwealth, 1901; joined Commonwealth Taxation Dept. upon its establishment 1910 as Secretary (till 1915); Deputy Commissioner for the State of Victoria till 1916; Acting Commonwealth Commissioner till 1917; Federal Commissioner of Taxation, Commonwealth of Australia, 1917-39. Member Rotary Club of Melbourne. *Publications:* two official handbooks one on War Time Profits Tax and one on Sales Tax; Taxes and their incidence; A Plan of Economic Reconstruction, 1941; Money pitfalls in Labor's Socialism—The Cure, 1947. *Recreations:* philosophy, music, golf. *Address:* 20 The Ridge, Canterbury, E.7, Melbourne, Australia. [*Died* 15 *Nov.* 1957.

EWINS, Arthur James, F.R.S. 1943; D.Sc.; formerly Director of Research, May & Baker Ltd., Dagenham, Essex, retired 1952, now acting as consultant; *b.* 3 Feb. 1882; *s.* of Joseph and Sophia Ewins, Norwood; *m.* 1905, Ada Amelia Webb; one *s.* one *d.* *Educ.:* Alleyn's School, Dulwich; London University (Chelsea Polytechnic). Entered Wellcome Physiological Research Laboratories as Assistant in 1899; B.Sc.(Lond.), 1906, becoming member of the staff; D.Sc. (Lond.), 1914; Member of Scientific Staff of the Central Research Institute of the Medical Research Committee (now the Medical Research Council), 1914-17; Research Chemist to May & Baker Ltd., 1917. *Publications:* numerous in Journal of Chemical Society, Biochemical Journal and other scientific periodicals since 1907; contributor to Thorpe's Dictionary of Applied Chemistry. *Recreations:* motoring, gardening, and reading. *Address:* 32 Berkeley Gardens, Leigh-on-Sea, Essex. *T.:* Hadleigh 58647. [*Died* 24 *Dec.* 1957.

EXETER, 5th Marquess of (*cr.* 1801), **William Thomas Brownlow Cecil;** Baron Burghley, 1571; Earl of Exeter, 1605; K.G. 1937; C.M.G. 1919; T.D.; Knight of Order of St. John of Jerusalem; Hereditary Grand Almoner; Lord Lieut. County of Northampton, 1923-52; Custos Rotulorum of the Soke of Peterborough; J.P., Soke of Peterborough, Kesteven, Rutland, and Northants; Hon. Freeman City of Peterborough; Col. R.F.A. (T.), retired; *b.* 27 Oct. 1876; *o. c.* of 4th Marquess and Isabella, *o. c.* of Sir Thomas Whichcote, 7th Bt.; *S.* father, 1898; *m.* 1901, Hon. Myra Rowena Sibell Orde-Powlett, Comdr. (sister) of Order of St. John of Jerusalem, *o. surv. d.* of 4th Baron Bolton; two *s.* two *d.* *Educ.:* Eton; Magdalene College, Camb. Formerly Capt. 3rd Batt. Northamptonshire Regiment; Chairman Soke of Peterborough C.C., 1910-49, Alderman, 1898-1949; Chairman Stamford Board of Guardians, 1898-1930; Mayor of Stamford, 1909-10; Chairman: Governors Stamford Endowed Schools, 1899-1955; Barnack R.D.C., 1898-1950. A.D.C. to the King, 1920-31. *Heir:* *s.* Lord Burghley, K.C.M.G. *Address:* Burghley House, Stamford. *T.A.:* Stamford. *T.:* 3131. *Clubs:* Carlton, Junior Carlton. [*Died* 6 *Aug.* 1956.

EXMOUTH, 8th Viscount (*cr.* 1816); **Edward Irving Pownoll Pellew;** Bt. 1796; Baron, 1814; O.B.E.; B.A. Cantab.; M.R.C.S. Eng.; L.R.C.P. Lond.; *b.* 3 May 1868; *s.* of late Capt. Pownoll W. Pellew, R.N.; *S.* cousin, 1945; *m.* 1902, Frances, *d.* of Alfred W. Edwards; one *s.* one *d.* *Educ.:* Clifton; Trinity College, Cambridge. Ordre Mérite Agricole. *Heir:* *s.* Hon. Pownoll Irving Edward Pellew [*b.* 1908; *m.* 1938, Maria Luisa (Marquesa de Olias), *d.* of Luis de Urquijo, Marques de Amurrio, Madrid; two *s.* two *d.*]. [*Died* 19 *Aug.* 1951.

EYLES, (Margaret) Leonora; author; *b.* 1 Sep. 1889; *d.* of A. Tennant Pitcairn, Tunstall, Stoke-on-Trent. *m.* 1st, A. W. Eyles, *s.* of Sir A. Eyles, K.C.B., K.B.E.; one *s.* two *d.*; 2nd, D. L. Murray. *Publications:* Margaret Protests, 1919; Captivity, 1922; Hidden Lives, 1922; The Woman in the Little House, 1922; The Hare of Heaven, Family Love, 1923; Women's Problems of To-day, 1926; Shepherd of Israel, 1929; Feeding the Family, 1929; Strength of the Spirit, 1930; Careers for Women, 1930; Commonsense about Sex, 1933 (re-written, 1956); They Wanted Him Dead, 1936; Death of a Dog, 1936; No Second Best, 1939; Eat Well in War-Time, 1940; For My Enemy Daughter, 1941; Is Your Problem Here?, 1947; Unmarried, but Happy, 1947; The Ram Escapes, 1953. *Recreations:* none. *Address:* 32 Eton Avenue, N.W.3. *T.:* Swiss Cottage 4691. [*Died* 27 *July* 1960.

EYTON, A. J. F.-W.; *see* Fairbairn-Wynne-Eyton.

F

FABER, Knud, M.D. LL.D.; *b.* Odense, 29 Aug. 1862; *m.* 1st, Thyra Petersen, 1891; 2nd, 1910, Ellen Becker; two *s.* *Educ.:* University of Copenhagen. Cand. Med. 1885; M.D. Copenhagen, 1890; Professor of Internal

Medicine and Head Physician Royal State Hosp., 1896-1932; retired 1932; Member of the Senate of the Univ., 1902; Rector of the Univ., 1916-17; Vice-Pres. of the National Union against Tuberculosis, 1906; Hon. LL.D. (Edin.); Hon. M.D. (Upsala), 1927; Hon. M.D. (Aarhüs), 1946; Hon. Member of Academies of Medicine in Ireland, Belgium, Bologna, Stockholm, Paris, etc.; Hon. F.R.S.M. and F.R.C.P.E. *Publications:* Tetanus as Infectious Disease, 1890; Pathology of Digestive Organs, 1905; Pernicious Anæmia and Atrophy of Intestines, 1920; Diseases of the Stomach and the Intestines, 1920; Nosography in Modern Internal Medicine, 1923; Tuberculosis in Denmark, 1926; Functional Diseases of the Digestive Organs, 1927; Lectures on Internal Medicine delivered in the United States, 1926; Report on Medical Schools in China, 1931; Gastritis and its Consequences, 1935; Tuberculosis and Nutrition, 1938. *Address:* Kronprinsessegade 6, Copenhagen, Denmark.
[*Died* 2 *May* 1956.

FABER, Oscar, C.B.E. 1951 (O.B.E. 1919); D.C.L.(Hon.); D.Sc.; M.Inst.C.E.; P.P.Inst. Struct.E.; F.C.G.I.; Past President Institution of Heating and Ventilating Engineers; Consulting Engineer; *b.* 5 July 1886; *s.* of Harald Faber, Danish Commissioner of Agriculture in London; *m.* 1913, Helen Joan Mainwaring; one *s.* two *d.* *Educ.:* St. Dunstan's, Catford; City and Guilds Engineering College, S. Kensington. Senior Partner Oscar Faber and Partners. Consulting Engineer for new Bank of England, House of Commons Rebuilding, Church House Westminster, South Africa House, India House, Martins Bank, Glyn Mills Bank, Barclays Bank, and many similar works in China, S. Africa, and throughout the world. Designer of many important war-time and other factories. Consulting Engineer for House of Commons Reconstruction and Air Conditioning. Gold medals of Inst. of Civil Engineers for papers on Plastic Yield of Concrete and Aesthetics of Engineering Structures. *Publications:* Reinforced Concrete Design; Reinforced Concrete Simply Explained; Constructional Steelwork Simply Explained; Heating and Air Conditioning of Buildings. *Recreations:* painting, music and gardening. *Address:* Chatley Dene, Rothamsted Avenue, Harpenden, Herts. *T.:* Harpenden 1084. *Club:* St. Stephen's.
[*Died* 7 *May* 1956.

FAGAN, Major-General Sir Edward (Arthur), K.C.B., *cr.* 1932 (C.B. 1923); C.S.I. 1920; C.M.G. 1918; D.S.O. 1917, and bar 1918; Indian Army, retired; *b* 1871; *s.* of late Major Horace Christopher Fagan, Bengal Staff Corps; *m.* 1906, Mary Dawbney, *d.* of Rev. R. F. Follett. Served Tirah Expedition, 1897-98 (medal and clasp); Tibet, 1903-4 (medal); European War, 1914-18 (wounded, despatches four times, C.M.G., D.S.O., and bar, Bt.-Col.); Afghan War, 1920 (C.S.I.); G.O.C. Kohat District, India, 1927-1930; Commanded Rawalpindi District, 1930-31; retired, 1931. *Club:* Cavalry.
[*Died* 21 *June* 1955.

FAHY, Francis Patrick, B.A.; Barrister-at-law; H. Dip. Ed.; M.P. (S. Fein) South Galway, Dec. 1918-22; Galway (Dail Eireann) since 1921; *b.* Galway 1880; *s.* of John Fahy, N.T. of Kilchreest, Co. Galway; *m.* 1908, Anna, *d.* of D. Barton, Tralee. *Educ.:* Mungret College S.J.; R.U.I. and N.U.I. Was a teacher of Latin and Science at St. Vincent's College, Castleknock. Ceann Comhairle (Speaker) of Dail Eireann, 1932-51. *Address:* Tudor Lodge, Park Drive, Ranelagh, Dublin.
[*Died* 12 *July* 1953.

FAIR, Lt.-Col. Frederick Kendall, C.B. 1916; late R.E.; *b.* 29 May 1868; *e. s.* of late Frederick Fair. Entered R.E. 1886; served S. Africa, 1900-2 (Queen's medal 3 clasps, King's medal 2 clasps); European War, 1914-18 (despatches, C.B.); retired pay, 1923. *Address:* 5 Fourth Avenue, Hove, Sussex. *Club:* United Service.
[*Died* 28 *Dec.* 1953.

FAIRBAIRN, Vice-Admiral Bernard William Murray, C.B.E. 1934 (O.B.E. 1919); *e. s.* of late Rev. W. M. Fairbairn; *b.* 18 April 1880; *m.* 1905, Alice Mary, *d.* of late Wm. Phillipps; two *s.* two *d.* *Educ.:* H.M.S. Britannia. Lieutenant, 1901; Commander, 1914; Captain, 1919; Rear-Admiral, 1931; Vice-President of the Ordnance Committee, 1932-34; President, 1934-36; Vice-Admiral, 1936; retired list, 1936; Commodore of Convoy, 1939-1942; Flag Officer in Charge, Milford Haven, 1942-45. Officer Legion of Merit, U.S.A. *Recreation:* golf. *Address:* Hillcott, Steeple Claydon, Bletchley, Bucks.
[*Died* 5 *April* 1960.

FAIRBAIRN-WYNNE-EYTON, Alan John; *s.* of Rev. A. H. Fairbairn Rector of Fawley, Henley-on-Thames, and Anna Gertrude Fuller-Maitland, and *g.s.* of Sir W. Fairbairn, Bt.; *m.* 1928, Violet Hope Wynne Eyton, J.P., of Leeswood Hall, Flintshire, and assumed by deed poll the additional name of Wynne-Eyton. *Educ.:* Haileybury College; Royal School of Mines. Travelled extensively as a mining engineer; High Sheriff of Flintshire, 1938. *Recreations:* golf and gardening. *Address:* Leeswood Hall, Mold, Flintshire. *T.:* Mold 220.
[*Died* 14 *Nov.* 1960.

FAIREY, Sir (Charles) Richard, Kt., *cr.* 1942, M.B.E.; Hon. F.R.Ae.S.; Hon. F.I.Ae.S.; Commandeur de l'Ordre de la Couronne (Belgium); Medal of Freedom with Silver Palm (U.S.A.); Fellow of the City and Guilds Institute; Chairman and Managing Director of The Fairey Aviation Company Limited; Hon. Vice-President Anglo-Belgian Union; Vice-President Institute of Directors; *b.* 5 May 1887; *m.* 1st (marriage dissolved); one *s.*; 2nd, 1934, Esther Sarah, *y. d.* of Stephen Francis Whitmey, Parkstone, Dorset; one *s.* one *d.* *Educ.:* Merchant Taylors; Finsbury Technical College in engineering and chemistry; 1st Cl. hons. Electrical Engineering City and Guilds. Manager, Blair-Atholl Aeroplane Syndicate, 1912-13; Chief Engineer to Short Bros. 1913-1915; founded The Fairey Aviation Co. Ltd. 1915; Chm., Society of British Aircraft Constructors, Ltd. 1922-24; Member of the Aeronautical Research Committee, 1923-26; Director-General of the British Air Commission, Washington, D.C., 1942-45; Member of the Joint Aircraft Committee, Combined Aluminium/Magnesium Committee, Washington, D.C. 1942-45; President of The Royal Aeronautical Society, 1930-31, and 1932-33; awarded Wakefield Gold Medal by The Royal Aeronautical Society for invention and development of the wing flap. *Publications:* various papers and articles on aviation and sporting subjects. *Recreations:* yacht racing, fishing, shooting. *Address:* Bossington House, Houghton, Stockbridge, Hants. *T.:* Kings Somborne 247; Woodlands Park, Iver Heath, Bucks. *T.:* Uxbridge 2120; Lyndham, Paget, Bermuda. *Clubs:* Bath, Savage, British Sportsmen's, Royal London Yacht, Royal Thames Yacht, Royal Aero, Kongelig Norsk Seilforening (Oslo).
[*Died* 30 *Sept.* 1956.

FAIRGRIEVE, James, M.A. (Oxon), B.A. (Lond.); *b.* 1870; *e. s.* of Rev. George Fairgrieve, West U.P. Church, Saltcoats; *m.* 1898, Emily (B.A., Shipley, Leeds, Aberystwyth; she *d.* 1949), *e. d.* of W. T. Croft, Asst. Town Clerk of Bradford; three *d.* (and one *d.* decd.). *Educ.:* Saltcoats Academy; Ardrossan Academy; High School, Glasgow; University College of Wales, Aberystwyth (Exhibitioner); Jesus College, Oxford (Exhibitioner); London School of Economics. Mathematical Master Kelso High School; Mathematical Master Campbeltown Grammar School; Head of New Southgate High School; Geography Master and Second Master William Ellis Endowed School, 1907-

1912; Reader in Education with special reference to Geography in the University of London Institute of Education, 1931-35 (Lecturer in Geography, 1912-31); Head of Dept. of Colonial Education, 1927-35; retired, 1935. President Geographical Association, 1935, and Chairman of Council, 1948; Pres. of Guild of Institute Geographers; Vice-Pres. Royal Meteor. Soc. 1932-33; Chm. of Films Cttee. of Geographical Assoc.; original member of Commission on Educational and Cultural Films; member of Delegacy of Institute of Education, 1932-35; Moderator for Geography Examinations of University of London, Central Welsh Board; Examiner at various times and different stages from sch. to M.A. for Universities of London, Manchester, and Reading, Central Welsh Board, L.C.C., etc.; visiting lecturer in Chicago University, 1921. *Publications:* Geography and World Power; Geography in School; The Gradient Wind (Meteorological Office); many school text books incl. Real Geographies Books; Chapter in Adam's New Teaching, Chapter in Compass of the World. Editor New Regional Geographies, many papers in the Educational press, the Meteorological Journal and The Meteorological Magazine. *Recreations:* gardening, reading detective stories, films. *Address:* Frocester, 72 Friern Barnet Lane, New Southgate, N.11. *T.:* Enterprise 3317. [*Died* 8 *Oct.* 1953.

FAIRHOLME, Edward George, O.B.E. 1918; *y. s.* of late Captain Charles Fairholme, R.N.; *m.* Eleanor (*d.* 1940), *e. d.* of late W. L. Chew, J.P., Hankelow Court, Audlem, Cheshire; one *s.* two *d.* *Educ.*: privately; Chatham House School, Ramsgate. Entered firm of William Heinemann, publishers, 1896; joined firm of Lawrence & Bullen, Ltd., 1901; Chief Secretary R.S.P.C.A. 1905-33; Capt. R.A.V.C.; Deputy Assistant Director Veterinary Service, B.E.F., 1915-16; secretary of third International Publishers' Congress, London, 1899; English representative fourth Congress, Leipzig, 1901. *Publications:* (with W. Pain) A Century of Work for Animals, 1924; sundry stories, articles, etc., in The Nineteenth Century, The Sketch, The Outlook, The Academy, etc. *Address:* 62 Campden Hill Court, W.8. *T.:* Western 9793. [*Died* 6 *Jan.* 1956.

FAIRHURST, Councillor Frank; M.P. (Lab.) Oldham, 1945-50, East Division of Oldham, 1950-51; *b.* 1892. Late President of Nat. Assoc. of Power Loom Overlookers, and of Wigan Textile Trades Federation; late Member of Wigan Town Council. *Address:* 195 Beech Hill Avenue, Gillow, Wigan, Lancs. [*Died* 30 *Aug.* 1953.

FAIRLIE, Reginald Francis Joseph, R.S.A. 1934; LL.D.; Architect; *b.* 1883; *e. surv. s.* of late J. Ogilvy Fairlie, of Myres, Fife. *Educ.:* Oratory School, Birmingham. Served apprenticeship with Sir Robert Lorimer, A.R.A., and afterwards studied in Italy; commenced practice in Edinburgh 1909, since which time has been occupied with domestic and ecclesiastical work; principal buildings designed—Abbey Church, Fort Augustus; National Library of Scotland; Restoration of Mediæval University Chapel at St. Andrews. Held commission in Royal Engineers (T.F.), 1915-19; saw service in France; a member of the Ancient Monuments Board for Scotland. Member Royal Fine Art Commission for Scotland. *Recreation:* shooting. *Address:* 7 Ainslie Place, Edinburgh. *T.:* Central 4992. *Club:* New (Edinburgh). [*Died* 27 *Oct.* 1952.

FAITHFULL, Lilian Mary, C.B.E. 1926; *b.* Hoddesdon, Herts, 1865; *d.* of late Francis G. Faithfull, M.A., Clerk to the Merchant Taylors' Co. *Educ.:* Somerville College, Oxford, 1883-87. Oxford Honour School of Eng. Literature and Language, Class I. Secretary to the Principal Somerville Coll. 1887-88; Mistress in the Oxford High School, 1888-89; Lecturer in English Literature, Language, and History at the Royal Holloway College, 1889-94; Vice-Principal King's Coll. London, Women's Department, 1894-1907; Principal of the Ladies' Coll., Cheltenham, 1907-22; Fellow of King's Coll., London, 1904; M.A. Dublin, 1905; Hon. M.A. Oxford University, 1925; J.P. Gloucestershire; Member of Council of Malvern Girls' College; W.V.S. Canteen Adviser for Gloucestershire; Member of Gloucestershire Social Service War Council; Founder of Old People's Housing Society, Cheltenham. *Publications:* In the House of My Pilgrimage, 1924; You and I, 1927; The Evening Crowns the Day, 1940. *Recreation:* motoring. *Address:* Four Winds, Birdlip, Glos. *Club:* Forum. [*Died* 2 *May* 1952.

FALCONER, Lt.-Col. Alexander Robertson, C.B.E. 1919; V.D.; B.A., B.Sc., M.B., B.Ch. (N.Z.); D.P.H. (Lond.); Lt.-Col. N.Z.M.C. (ret.); Hon. Cons. Physician Dunedin Hosp. (Otago Medical School), since 1927; Senior K.St.J. and Member N.Z. Priory Chapter in Order of St. John; Member Executive Joint Council Order of St. John and N.Z. Red Cross Society and Member Dominion Executive Great War Funds Administrative Cttee. since 1933; Member Otago Provincial Council N.Z. Patriotic Funds Board since 1939; Hon. Sec., N.Z. Natl. Council for Mental Hygiene and Life Member, 1948, now Life Member of its Council for Mental Health (being a Member-Assoc. of World Federation for Mental Health); *b.* 1874; *s.* of Alexander R. Falconer, Dunedin, N.Z., and Edinburgh, Scotland; *m.* 1909, Agnes, *d.* of William A. Simpson, Christchurch, N.Z., and Banff, Scotland; three *s.* two *d.* A.M.O. Seacliff Mental Hospital, 1898-1901; R.M.O. West London Hospital, 1904; Sen. A.M.O. New Zealand Mental Hospital Department, 1905; R.M.O. 1906-9, and Medical Suptd., Dunedin Hosp., 1910-27; Medical Suptd. Ashburn Hall Psychiatric Institute, near Dunedin 1927-47. Member Organising Cttee., 1924-1930, of the International Cttee. for Mental Hygiene (inaugurated 1930 in New York); represented, 1947, the Organising Cttee. of the International Congress for Mental Health (Lond., Aug. 1948) in initiating the preparatory steps in N.Z. Past Vice-Pres. West London Medico-Chirurgical Soc.; Foundation Dominion Vice-Pres. S. African War Veterans Assoc., 1924; Vice-Pres. Otago Branch British Sailors Soc. (N.Z.), 1940-49. Served S. Africa, 1902 (Queen's medal with two clasps); European War, 1915-19 (despatches, C.B.E.); P.M.O. Otago and Sen., A.D.M.S. N.Z., 1914-19. *Address:* 60 Queen St., Dunedin, N.I., New Zealand. [*Died* 27 *Sept.* 1955.

FALCONER, Arthur Wellesley, C.B.E. 1919; D.S.O. 1918; M.D., F.R.C.P. (Lond.), LL.D. (Aberdeen and Cape Town); Physician. *Educ.:* Aberdeen, London, Berlin, and Vienna. M.B., Ch.B. Aberdeen, 1901; M.D. with honours, 1907; F.R.C.P. (London); Hon. Fellow of Royal Society of Medicine. Late Temp. Lt.-Col. R.A.M.C. and Consulting Physician British Salonika Forces. Late Professor of Medicine, Cape Town University; Principal and Vice-Chancellor, 1938-48; retired, 1948. *Publications:* numerous papers in various medical journals chiefly on diseases of the heart and blood-vessels and malaria. *Address:* St. Andrews, Mains Avenue, Kenilworth, Cape Town, South Africa. [*Died* 26 *Sept.* 1954.

FALCONER, Sir John Ireland, Kt., *cr.* 1946; M.A., LL.B., LL.D.; W.S.; *b.* Fortrose, Ross-shire, 1879; *s.* of Rev. Charles Falconer; *m.* 1913, Catherine Louise Mary (*decd.*), *d.* of John Norman Robinson; two *s.* one *d.* *Educ.:* George Watson's College, Edinburgh; Edinburgh University. Lord Provost of Edinburgh, 1944-47; Mem. B.B.C. Gen. Advisory Council, 1952. Served European War, 1914-18. *Address:* Ardtornish, Colinton, Edinburgh. *Club:* New (Edinburgh). [*Died* 6 *April* 1954.

FALK, Bernard; occupied in matters artistic; *b.* Manchester, 11 Aug. 1882; *m.* 1909, *d.* of Arthur Carter Lamplough; one *s.* *Educ.:* Manchester Grammar School; privately. News-Editor, Evening News, London; helped to start London Evening Times; Editor, Reynolds'; with allied Forces in Siberia, 1918, as special Daily Mail correspondent; editor, Sunday Dispatch, 1918-31; special writer, mainly on literary topics, Daily Mail, 1931-1932; has written largely on literary and art subjects. *Publications:* He Laughed in Fleet Street (an autobiography), 1933; The Naked Lady or Storm over Adah, 1934 (new and revised ed., 1952); Rachel the Immortal, a life of the famous French tragédienne, 1935; Old Q's Daughter: The History of a Strange Family (The story of the founders of the Wallace Collection), 1937; revised edn., 1951; Five Years Dead; A postscript to He Laughed in Fleet Street, 1938; Turner the Painter: His Hidden Life, 1939; The Naughty Seymours: Companions in folly and caprice, 1940; The Bridgewater Millions: A Candid Family History, 1942; The Berkeleys of Berkeley Square: And Some of their Kinsfolk, 1944; The Way of the Montagues, 1947; Thomas Rowlandson: His Life and Art, 1949; The Royal Fitz Roys, 1950; Bouquets for Fleet Street: Memories and Musings over Fifty Years (revised, much amplified one-vol. edn. of his two books on Fleet Street), 1951. *Recreation:* picture-collecting. *Address:* Highcroft, 79 Hove Park Road, Hove 4, Sussex. *T.:* Brighton 52638. [*Died* 9 *Oct.* 1960.

FALKNER, Brigadier Eric Felton, C.M.G. 1919; D.S.O. 1917; p.s.c.; C.St.J. 1933; *b.* 30 March 1880; *e. s.* of Rev. T. Felton Falkner, D.S.O., M.A.; *m.* 1907, Elaine Adelaide, *o. c.* of late Maj.-Gen. Sir Walter G. A. Bedford, K.C.M.G., C.B., D.C.L., of Eynsham; one *d.* Joined The Hampshire Regiment from 3rd D.C.L.I. (Militia), 1900; served South African Campaign, 1900-1 (Queen's medal with 3 clasps); transferred to Army Service Corps, 1901; served European War, 1914-18; D.A.Q.M.G. 1915-17; A.A. and Q.M.G. 1917-19; (1914 Star and clasp, despatches seven times, C.M.G., D.S.O., Bt. Lt.-Col., Officer Order of Crown of Italy; Croce di Guerra, two awards); Associate of the Order of St. John of Jerusalem, 1918; Passed Staff College, Camberley, 1919; D.A.A. and Q.M.G., Inter-allied Military Commission of Control in Austria, 1920; D.A.Q.M.G. and Instructor, School of Military Administration, 1920-24; Instructor, Senior Officers' School, Sheerness, Kent, 1924-25; A.Q.M.G. Western Command, Chester, 1927-31; Brigadier i/c Administration, and sometime commanding the Troops, Malta, and a Member of the Nominated Council of Malta, 1931-35; A.D.C. to King George V., 1934-35; retired with honorary rank of Brigadier, 1935; R.A.R.O. 1935-40; R.A.R.O. (voluntary member over age), 1940; A.A. and Q.M.G. of an Area, 1940; Invalided by Medical Board, 1940. Member Bristol Diocesan Board of Finance, 1940-47; Hon. Sec. Bristol Diocesan Advisory Cttee. for Care of Churches, 1943-47, and a Member, 1941-52. *Address:* Wormscliffe House, near Box, Wiltshire. *T.:* Box (Wilts) 330. [*Died* 6 *March* 1956.

FALL, Capt. Ernest Matson, C.B.E. 1943; D.S.C. 1918; R.D.; R.N.R. retired; late commanding Cunard White Star Liner, Queen Elizabeth; *b.* Oswestry, Salop, 17 Feb. 1883; *s.* of Alfred Fall, York, and Annie Richmond, Harrogate; *m.* 1944, Mrs. Alice Spencer. *Educ.:* Brighton High School. Royal Navy, 1898-1900; Merchant Service, 1900; South African Light Horse, 1900-1 (medal); rejoined Merchant Navy, 1901; officer R.N.R. 1912; served in R.N., 1914-19, present at Battle of Jutland (D.S.C.). Joined Cunard Line, 1911, and commanded seven of their liners including the Queen Mary and the Queen Elizabeth. Commander American Legion of Merit. *Recreations:* music, art, golf. *Address:* c/o Standard Bank of South Africa, East London, South Africa. [*Died* 21 *Sept.* 1955.

FALLIS, Lt.-Col. Rev. George Oliver, C.B.E. 1919; E.D.; B.D.; D.D.; Senior Chaplain Pacific Command; *b.* Sarnia, Ontario, 28 Feb. 1885; *s.* of Rev. J. G. Fallis and Mary Legear; *m.* 1911, Mabel Lavinia, M.A., *d.* of Rev. Arthur Hockin; two *s.* one *d.* *Educ.:* Public and High Schools of Ontario; Wesley College, Winnipeg; Columbian College, B.D.; University of Chicago. Served with 2nd C.M.R.; Lt.-Col. A.D.C.S. in France (despatches twice, C.B.E.); built Canadian Memorial Chapel in memory of all those from Canada who laid down their lives in European War; and served as its minister, 1920-33; Minister of Trinity United Church, Toronto, 1933-45; *Publications:* Leaves from a Chaplain's Diary; The Soldier as he was; The Padre's Corner; Spiritual Values in Rehabilitation; Shields against Despair; Human Nature as I saw it. *Recreations:* tennis, golf, and badminton. *Address:* 3777 Cambie St., Vancouver, B.C., Canada. [*Died* 15 *Feb.* 1952.

FALLOON, C. H.; Director, late General Manager, Atlas Assurance Co. Ltd.; retired 1958; *b.* Chester, 2 Mar. 1875; 2nd *s.* of Rev. Hugh Falloon, *g.s.* of Canon Falloon, Liverpool; *m.* 1907, Mary Constance, *d.* of Capt. Cocker, Chinese Imperial Maritime Customs; one *s.* two *d.* *Educ.:* Blundell's Sch., Tiverton; Queens' Coll., Cambridge. Entire business career with Atlas Assurance Co., Ltd., in London, Hong Kong, Shanghai and Bombay; Pres. London Insurance Institute, 1925-26; Pres. Chartered Insurance Institute, 1931-32; Chm. British Insurance Assoc., 1938-39. *Address:* 35 Batchworth Lane, Northwood, Middlesex. *T.:* Northwood 802. *Clubs:* Royal Bombay Yacht (Bombay); Moor Park (Rickmansworth). [*Died* 9 *April* 1959.

FALWASSER, Arthur Thomas, D.S.O. 1918; M.R.C.S., L.R.C.P.; *b.* 1873; *s.* of late Rev. John Falwasser; *m.* 1901, Charlotte Annie Gilson, O.B.E. 1946, *d.* of late W. T. Sheild, solicitor, Uppingham; one *s.* two *d.* (and one *s.* decd.). *Educ.:* Marlborough. Served European War, 1914-18 (despatches, D.S.O.). *Address:* Rutland House, West Malling, Kent. *T.:* West Malling 3226. [*Died* 11 *July* 1959.

FANE, Col. Cecil, C.M.G. 1917; D.S.O. 1900; late 12th (Prince of Wales's Royal) Lancers; *b.* 15 Sep. 1875; *s.* of F. A. Fane; *m.* 1918, Gladys Macgeorge (who obtained a divorce, 1931), *d.* of Mrs. Stanley Barry; one *s.*; *m.* 1948, Mrs. Florence Ethel Allison (*d.* 1953). *Educ.:* Rugby. Entered Army, 1897; Captain, 1904; Major, 1912; Col. 1921; served S. Africa, 1899-1902 (despatches twice, Queen's medal 6 clasps, King's medal 2 clasps, D.S.O.); European War, 1914-15 (despatches thrice, Brevet Col., wounded twice C.M.G.); retired pay, 1922. *Address:* Union Club, 21 Boulevard Peirera, Monte Carlo. *Club:* Royal Automobile. [*Died* 20 *March* 1960.

FANSHAWE, Lt.-Gen. Sir Edward Arthur, K.C.B., *cr.* 1917 (C.B. 1914); *b.* 4 April 1859; 2nd *s.* of Rev. H. L. Fanshawe, of Chilworth, Oxon.; *m.* 1893, Rose (*d.* 1950), *d.* of Sir James Higginson, K.C.B.; three *s.* *Educ.:* Winchester. Entered Royal Artillery 1878; Capt., 1886; Major, 1896; Lt.-Col., 1903; Col., 1908; Maj.-Gen., 1915; Lt.-Gen., 1919; served Afghan War, 1878-80 (medal); Soudan, 1885 (medal with clasp, bronze star); European War, 1914-18 (despatches, prom. Maj.-Gen., Lt.-Gen., C.B., and K.C.B.); retired pay, 1923; Col. Comdt., R.A. 1923-34; R.H.A., 1930-34. *Address:* Rathmore, Naas, Co. Kildare. *T.:* Naas 66. [*Died* 13 *Nov.* 1952.

FANSHAWE, Lt.-Gen. Sir Hew Dalrymple, K.C.B., *cr.* 1925 (C.B. 1908); K.C.M.G., *cr.* 1919; *b.* 30 Oct. 1860; *s.* of Rev.

Henry Leighton Fanshawe, Chilworth House, Oxon; *m.* 1894, Paulina Mary (*d.* 1929), *e. d.* of late F.-M. Sir Evelyn Wood; two *s.* one *d.* *Educ.:* Winchester. Lieut. 19th Hussars, 1882; Captain, 1884; Major, 1893; Lieut.-Col., 1903; Brev.-Col., 1904; Major-Gen., 1913; Lieut.-Gen. (retd.), 1920; A.D.C. to Major-Gen. Cork District, 1890; to C.O.C. Aldershot, 1890-93; A.M.S. to Lieut.-Gen., India, 1897-98; served Egypt, 1882-84 (medal with clasp, bronze star); Soudan, 1884 (two clasps); Soudan, 1884-85 (two clasps); S. Africa, 1899-1902 (despatches twice, Brevet Lieut.-Col., Queen's medal 5 clasps, King's medal 2 clasps); Commanding The Queen's Bays, 1903-7; 2nd Cavalry Brigade (Canterbury), 1907-10; Presidency Brigade (India), 1910-13; Jubbelpore Brigade, 1913-14; 1st Indian Cavalry Division (France), 1914-15; British Cavalry Corps, 1915; Fifth Army Corps, 1915-16; 58th London Division, 1916-17; 18th Indian Division (Mesopotamia), 1917-19; No. 3 Area, France, 1919; retired, 1920; Colonel of the Queen's Bays, 1921-30; J.P. (Oxon), 1920. *Address:* Cotmore Wells, Thame, Oxfordshire. *T.:* Thame 173. [*Died* 24 *March* 1957.

FARADAY, Wilfred Barnard; Barrister-at-law; Recorder of Barnstaple and Bideford; *b.* 14 March 1874; *s.* of late F. J. Faraday, Commercial Editor, Manchester Guardian, and Lucy Richmond; *m.* 1904, Millie (*d.* 1951), *d.* of late Thos. Briggs, J.P., Manchester; one *s.* three *d.* *Educ.:* Grammar Sch.; Coll. of Technology and University, Manchester (LL.B. 1897). Called to Bar, Gray's Inn, 1900; Lee Prize, 1898; Hon. Secretary Tariff Reform League for Lancashire, 1902; Economic Tutor Anti-Socialist Union, 1909-12; Lieut. 5th Batt. York and Lancaster Regt., 1914-16; Secretary Royal Aeronautical Society, 1917-19; Editor Aeronautical Journal, 1917-19; Member of Civil Aerial Transport Committee, 1917; contested (C.) Combined English Universities, 1922; Attercliffe Division of Sheffield, 1924 and 1929; Standing Counsel to the National Union of Manufacturers. *Publications:* Democracy and Capital, 1921; The Collapse of the Foreign Exchanges, 1922; The Safeguarding of Industries Act, 1921; A Glossary of Aeronautical Terms, 1919; Pendragon, 1930; The Milk in the Cocoanut, 1933; History of the English and Welsh Boroughs, 1950; many pamphlets and review articles on economic subjects. *Recreations:* sketching, walking, fishing, gardening. *Address:* 20 Beauchamp Avenue, Leamington Spa. *T.:* Leamington 1130. [*Died* 15 *June* 1953.

FAREWELL, Captain Michael Warren, C.I.E. 1916; *b.* 30 June 1868; 6th *s.* of Maj.-Gen. W. T. Freke Farewell, Madras Staff Corps; *m.* 1912, Katherine Irene (*d.* 1950), *e. d.* of F. Griffith, P.W.D.; one *s.* four *d.* *Educ.:* Somersetshire College, Bath; The Conway, Liverpool. Went to sea in the sailing-ship Garfield, 1885; Sub-Lieutenant Royal Indian Marine, 1890; at R.N. College, Greenwich, 1893-94; Lieut. 1895; Capt. 1917; second course R.N. College, Greenwich, and Torpedo and Gunnery Courses, H.M.S. Excellent and H.M.S. Vernon, 1903-4; Commander, 1906; commanded Lawrence, Canning, Mayo, Minto, Hardinge, Dalhousie; employed in connection with gun-running operations in command R.I.M.S. Hardinge, 1910; Deputy Conservator, Madras, 1910-13; Principal Marine Transport Officer, Karachi, 1914-18; Captain Supt. and Divisional Naval Transport Officer, Calcutta, 1918-19; retired 1921. [*Died* 3 *Sept.* 1953.

FARFAN, Brigadier Arthur Joseph Thomas, C.B. 1937; D.S.O. 1917; O.B.E. 1921; Royal Artillery; *b.* 1882; *s.* of Dr. Vincent Farfan, Trinidad; *m.* 1940, Elisabeth Hosmer, *d.* of R. S. Dods, Brisbane, Queensland, Australia. *Educ.:* Reading School; R.M.A., Woolwich. Served European War (D.S.O., Bt. Lt.-Col., Croix de Guerre); 3rd Afghan War, 1919; North-West Frontier of India, 1920-22 (O.B.E.); N.W.F. Waziristan operations, 1937-38 (C.B.); commanded 10th Field Brigade R.A. at Deepcut, 1928-31; Colonel-Commandant School of Artillery, India, 1931-34; Brigadier, Royal Artillery, Northern Command, India, 1934-38; retired, 1938. Private Secretary to Governor of Queensland, 1938-39; recalled to Army, 1939; Brig. R.A. Eastern Command, 1940-41; Brig. R.A., N.W. Army, India, 1941-43; Comdt. (G.S.O. 1) Indian Artillery Depot and Records, 1943; reverted to retired pay, 1946. *Address:* c/o Lloyds Bank Ltd., 6 Pall Mall, S.W.1. *Club:* Army and Navy. [*Died* 20 *May* 1953.

FARIE, Rear-Adm. James Uchtred, C.M.G. 1919; retired; *m.* 1st, 1907, Gertrude Mary Stourton (*d.* 1915), *d.* of late Arthur Joseph Langdale; 2nd, 1928, Eila Isabel, *y. d.* of Sir Wilfrid Laurie, 5th Bt. Served European War, 1914-19 (despatches, C.M.G., 2nd Class Order of St. Anne of Russia with swords); was Captain Dockyard, Simonstown. *Address:* Church Lane House, Lymington. [*Died* 17 *Sept.* 1957.

FARIS, Desmond William George, C.B.E. 1946; M.B., B.S., M.R.C.S., L.R.C.P., D.P.H.; Hon. LL.D. 1956; Dean of the Medical Faculty, Univ. of Malaya, Singapore, 1949-56, retd.; *b.* 30 Apr. 1901; *m.* 1930; one *s.* one *d.* *Educ.:* Epsom College; London Hospital Medical School, University of London. Health Officer, Malayan Medical Service; Chief Health Officer, Singapore; Principal, College of Medicine, Singapore, Malaya. *Publication:* The History of King Edward VII College of Medicine, Malayan Med. Jl. *Address:* 55 Hove Park Road, Hove 4, Sussex. [*Died* 20 *March* 1957.

FARJEON, Joseph Jefferson; author and playwright; *b.* 4 June 1883; *s.* of late B. L. Farjeon, author; *m.* 1910, Frances Antoinette Wood; one *d.* *Educ.:* Peterborough Lodge and privately. Editorial work, Amalgamated Press, 1910-20. Plays include: No. 17, After Dark, Enchantment, Highwayman, Philomel. *Publications:* 80 novels, including: Exit John Horton, 1939; Aunt Sunday Sees It Through, 1940; Room No. 6, 1941; The Judge Sums Up, 1942; House of Shadows, 1943; Greenmask, 1944; Rona Runs Away, 1945; Peril in the Pyrenees, 1946; Back to Victoria, 1947; Smith Minor, 1947; Death of a World, 1948; Shadow of Thirteen, 1949; Cause Unknown, 1950; House over the Tunnel, 1951; Ben on the Job, 1952; Number Nineteen, 1952; Money Walks, 1953; The Double Crime, 1953. Contributions to Punch, Evening News, Evening Standard, etc. *Address:* St. David's, Ditchling, Sussex. *T.:* Hassocks 282. [*Died* 6 *June* 1955.

FARLEY, Albert Henry, D.L. 1950; J.P. 1939; Colonel; *b.* 10 Oct. 1887; *y. s.* of William Edwin Farley, St. Olaves, S.E.; *m.* 1913, Ethel Saunders (*née* Dexter), *e. d.* of L. Dexter; no *c.* *Educ.:* Dulwich College. 3rd Vol. Bn. The Queen's Royal West Surrey Regt., 1903-08; 22nd County of London Regt. (T.A.), 1908-09; served European War, 1914-18; Canadian Army Staff (Ministry of Munitions), 1914-16; R.A.O.C., Lieut. 1916, Capt. 1918 (France and Mesopotamia). Reg. Army Res. 1920. Served War of 1939-45 61st A.A., R.A., Major, 1942; O.C. 4/6th (C.) Bn. Middlesex Regt., Lt.-Col., 1943-45; Hon. Col. 1st (C.) Regt., Middlesex Regt., 1950. Managing Director, Phoenix Oil group of companies, 1920-47. Friern Barnet U.D.C. 1931-39 (Chm. 1935-38); Middlesex C.C.; Councillor, 1939, Alderman, 1949, Chm., 1949-51. Chm.: Alexandra Palace Trustees; 1949; London Airport Consultative Cttee., 1949-52; Pentonville Prison Visiting Magistrates Cttee., 1948-52; West Sussex County Council Councillor, 1953; Worthing Borough Council Councillor, 1953. *Publications:* contrib. to oil technical journals; talks on oil and travel, B.B.C. *Recreation:* motoring. *Address:* The Croft, 77 Grand Avenue, Worthing. *T.:* Worthing 5368. [*Died* 15 *March* 1954.

FARLOW, Sir Sydney N.; *see* King-Farlow.

FARMAN, Henry; aeroplane builder, now retired; *b.* May 1874. Started as painter at Beaux-Arts, then became cyclist; was Champion several times, then raced for Panhard cars; won Paris-Vienne and several local races; opened a business in motor cars; owned largest garage in Paris, Palais De L'Automobile; had enough of selling cars; studied the flying which had long been in his mind; first trials were made at Issy les Moulineaux in November 1907, and January 1908; won the Prix Deutsch Archdeacon, 50,000 frs., for the first "kilomètre bouclé", 1908; travelled in Europe with his machine, and was very proud when he flew the height of 20 metres; won all the prizes at that time, including the Grand Prix of Reims, first official meeting; kept on studying new models; made the first flight across country with his machine, Bouy-Reims, alone and with passenger; was the first man to fly in New York; kept on his experiments, and opened important works at Billancourt for the supply of machines to the French Army and also other countries, including England. Supercharger-drives utilising the Farman patents and airscrew reduction gears were largely used on British engines during War of 1939-45. Médaille de l'Aéronautique; Médaille d'Or, d'Arts, Sciences et Lettres, 1955; Commandeur de la Légion d'Honneur. *Address:* 55 Avenue Foch, Paris, XVIe. [*Died* 17 *July* 1958.

FARMAR, Maj.-Gen. George Jasper, C.B. 1918; C.M.G. 1915; late Lancashire Fusiliers and Worcestershire Regt.; *b.* 20 July 1872; *s.* of late Maj.-Gen. W. R. Farmar, Bedford House, Southampton; *m.* 1913, Bertha Frances (*d.* 1951), *d.* of late Maj.-Gen. William Paget; one *s.* one *d.* Entered Army (Lancs Fusiliers) 1892; Worcs Regt. 1908; A.D.C. to F.M. Lord Grenfell, Governor of Malta, 1898-1902; Gen. Staff Officer, 3rd grade, 1908-9; Brigade-Major, 12th Infantry Brigade, 1910-11; D.A.A. and Q.M.G. 3rd Division, 1912; A.Q.M.G. II. Corps, 1914; A.Q.M.G. Second Army, 1915; D.A. and Q.M.G. Canadian Corps, 1916; D.A.G., Staff College, Camberley, 1919-22; Commanding Norfolk and Suffolk Infantry Brigade, 1922; Director of Personal Services, War Office, 1925-28; Lieut.-Governor Royal Hospital, Chelsea, 1928-33; Commissioner of Royal Hospital, Chelsea, 1923-50; a Governor of Corps of Commissionaires; Council, Royal Patriotic Fund Corporation; President Sevenoaks and Holmesdale Hospital; Freeman of the City of London; Kent Territorial Association; Kent Army Cadet Committee; retired pay, 1933; served Nile Expedition, 1898 (Queen's medal with clasp, Khedive's medal); European War, 1914-18 (C.M.G., Bt. Col., C.B., Officer of the Order of St. Maurice and St. Lazarus, Officer of the Ordre de Mérite Agricole, despatches eight times, 1914 Star). Home Guard, 1941-44. *Address:* Millwood Wrotham Heath, Kent. *T.:* Borough Green 42. *Clubs:* Army and Navy, M.C.C. [*Died* 3 *Nov.* 1958.

FARMER, Ernest Harold, F.R.S. 1948; Assistant Director and Senior Organic Chemist, British Rubber Producers' Research Association. B.Sc. (Lond.) 1911, M.Sc. 1921, D.Sc. 1924. Late of Loyal North Lancashire Regiment and of Chemical Warfare Department, Ministry of Munitions. Formerly teacher of Chemistry. Associate of University College, Nottingham. *Address:* British Rubber Producers' Research Association, 48 Tewin Road, Welwyn, Hertfordshire. [*Died* 13 *April* 1952.

FARMER, John Cotton, C.I.E. 1938; Retired Inspector General of Police, Bengal, India; *b.* 18 May 1886; *s.* of late John Edward Farmer, Ludlow, Salop; *m.* 1933, Margaret, *d.* of late Sidney Smith, Warminster, Wilts; one *s.* one *d.* *Educ.:* Ludlow Grammar School. Joined Indian Police Service, 1906; Inspector General, 1935-38; Indian Police Medal in connection with the Chittagong Armoury Attack in 1931. *Recreation:* tennis. *Address:* 46 Filsham Road, St. Leonards-on-Sea, Sussex. *Clubs:* Royal Empire Society; Bengal United Service (Calcutta). [*Died* 29 *Feb.* 1952.

FARNDALE, Joseph, C.B.E. 1924; *b.* Wakefield, 6 April 1865; *s.* of Thomas Farndale; *m.* Emma, *d.* of William Selby, Wakefield; three *d.* *Educ.:* Field House Academy, Aberford. Chief Constable of Margate, York, and Bradford; retired, 1938; Chairman Traffic Commissioners (Yorkshire Area), 1931-38. *Address:* 5 Ripon Road, Harrogate, Yorks. [*Died* 22 *Feb.* 1954.

FARNHAM, 11th Baron, *cr.* 1756; **Arthur Kenlis Maxwell;** Bt. (Calderwood), *cr.* 1627; D.S.O. 1918; Lt.-Col. late North Irish Horse; Irish Representative Peer since 1908; *b.* 2 Oct. 1879; *s.* of 10th Baron and Florence Jane, 5th *d.* of 3rd Marquess of Headfort; *S.* father, 1900; *m.* 1903, Aileen Selina, 2nd *d.* of late Charles Purdon Coote of Bearforest, Mallow; one *d.* *Educ.:* Harrow; Sandhurst. Late Lieut. 10th Hussars; served S. Africa, 1900-2. European War (D.S.O.). Church of Ireland. Conservative. *Recreations:* hunting, golf, cricket, shooting. *Heir:* *g.s.* Barry Owen Somerset Maxwell, *b.* 1931. *Address:* Farnham, Co. Cavan. *T.A.:* Drumconnick. *T.:* Cavan 54. *Club:* Kildare Street (Dublin). [*Died* 5 *Feb.* 1957.

FARNOL, (John) Jeffery; author; *b.* 10 Feb. 1878; *e. s.* of late Henry John and Katherine (*d.* 1921) Farnol; *m.* 1st, Blanche V. W. (marriage dissolved, 1938), *y. d.* of F. Hughson Hawley of New York; one *d.*; 2nd, 1938, Phyllis Clarke (one adopted *d.*). *Educ.:* private school. Began to write at age of 19; published some short stories in magazines, etc.; in 1902 went to New York, and there had a number of stories, etc., published; returned to England, 1910; for 2 years painted scenery at Astor Theatre, New York. *Publications:* My Lady Caprice (in England, The Chronicles of the Imp); The Money Moon; The Broad Highway; The Amateur Gentleman; The Honourable Mr. Tawnish (dramatised, 1924); Beltane the Smith, 1915; The Definite Object, 1917; Some War Impressions, 1918 (in America, Great Britain at War); Our Admirable Betty, 1918; The Geste of Duke Jocelyn, 1919; Black Bartlemy's Treasure, 1920; Martin Conisby's Vengeance, 1921; Peregine's Progress, 1922; Sir John Dering, 1923; The Loring Mystery, 1925; High Adventure, 1926; The Quest of Youth, 1927; Epics of The Fancy, 1928; Gyfford of Weare, 1928; The Shadow, 1929; Another Day, 1929; Over the Hills, 1930; The Jade of Destiny, 1931; Voices from the Dust, 1932; Charmian Lady Vibart, 1932; The Way Beyond, 1933; A Pageant of Victory, 1936; The Crooked Furrow, 1937; The Lonely Road, 1938; The Happy Harvest, 1939; Murder by Nail, 1942; The King Liveth; The Fool Beloved; My Lord of Urybourne; The Ninth Earl, 1950; The Glad Summer, 1951. *Address:* Little Dene, Denton Road, Meads, Eastbourne. [*Died* 9 *Aug.* 1952.

FARQUHAR, Sir Harold (Lister), K.C.M.G., *cr.* 1950 (C.M.G. 1945); M.C.; *b.* 15 April 1894; *s.* of late Ernest Farquhar, Whiteway, Chudleigh, Devon; *m.* 1917, Constance Audrey, *d.* of late Hon. Arthur Capell, J.P.; two *s.* *Educ.:* Eton; Magdalen College, Oxford. Served European war, 1914-18, 2nd Lt. 2nd Life Guards, 1914; Lieut. Coldstream Guards, 1915; Capt. (G.S.O. 3 Army of Occupation) 1918; retired, 1922; entered Diplomatic Service, 1922; 2nd Sec., 1925; 1st Sec., 1934; Counsellor, 1941; served in Warsaw, Madrid, Budapest, Rome, Mexico, Bucharest, Cairo and Tehran. Transferred to Foreign Office, 1939; Consul-General, Barcelona, 1941-45; Minister at Addis Ababa, 1946-48; British Ambassador to Sweden, 1948-51. *Address:* Whiteway,

Chudleigh, Devon. *T.:* Chudleigh 3127. *Clubs:* Carlton, St. James', Guards. [*Died* 31 *Jan.* 1953.

FARQUHARSON, Alexander Charles; *b.* 15 Mar. 1864; *s.* of James and Jane Farquharson, Aberdeen; *m.* 1903, Elizabeth Dodington Blockley, 4th *d.* of Edward Blockley, Isle of Wight; no *c. Educ.:* Peterhead Academy; Glasgow University. Graduate in Science, Medicine, and Surgery of Glasgow University; Diplomate in Public Health, University of Cambridge; Barrister-at-law, Middle Temple; Major R.A.M.C. (T.F.); D.A.D.M.S., Northern Command, 1916-18; twice mentioned for valuable services; one of the founders of Students' University Union and Students' Representative Council, Glasgow University; M.P. (C.L.) North Leeds, 1918-22; Member of Central Council B.M.A. and President of North of England Branch; Governor, Royal Scottish Corporation. *Publications:* Ptomaines and other Animal Alkaloids: Auto Toxæmia; Organic Sulphur Compounds in Nervous Diseases; Medico-Legal Importance of Ptomaines; The Law in relation to Pollution of Rivers. *Address:* 48 St. George's Drive, S.W.1. [*Died* 27 *May* 1951.

FARR, Captain John, J.P. Nottingham; *b.* 28 Feb. 1882; 2nd *s.* of Edward Robinson Farr, Daybrook, Notts; *m.* 1906, Margaret Anne (J.P. Notts), *d.* of Henry Heath, J.P., Bestwood Park, Notts; two *s.* two *d. Educ.:* privately. Won Notts Rifle Championship. South Notts Hussars, Boer War, and European War, Camel Corps, Egypt; invalided out, 1917, with rank of Capt.; Sheriff of Nottingham, 1922-23; Lord Mayor of Nottingham, 1933-34; High Sheriff of Nottinghamshire, 1943-44; Chairman of Home Brewery Co. Ltd. and of J. & S. Farr Ltd.; Chairman Leicester Race Course Company; owner of Worksop Manor Stud; gave Spitfire to Nation, 1940, during Battle of Britain. *Recreations:* shooting, racing, golf. *Address:* Worksop Manor, Notts. *T.:* Worksop 2025. *Club:* Carlton. [*Died* 15 *Feb.* 1951.

FARRANT, His Honour Reginald Douglas, F.S.A.(Scot.); F.R.A.I.; *b.* Ballamoar, Jurby, I.O.M., 19 July 1877; *y. s.* of William Farrant, J.P. of Ballamoar, and Lucy, *d.* of Joseph Kincaid, J.P., Merrion Square, Dublin; *m.* Marion Rose *d.* of J. A. Barthelemy, B.Sc.; one *s. Educ.:* King William's College, I.O.M.; St. Paul's. Admitted to Manx Bar, 1899; Clerk to Justices, 1903; High Bailiff and Stipendiary, 1919; Lieut. R.N.V.R. (Auxiliary Patrol), 1916-1919, Anti-Submarine Service English Channel and North Sea; Section Commander Loyal Manx Association, 1914-16; 2nd Deemster, 1925-1934; First Deemster and Clerk of the Rolls, High Court of Justice, Isle of Man, 1934-47; retired; J.P. and C.P.; Chm. of Trustees of Manx Museum; of War Pensions Board; I.O.M. National Savings; Pres. of National Lifeboat Institution, Douglas, I.O.M., Red Cross (Auxiliary); Pres. British Legion (Douglas); Pres. I.O.M. Sea Cadet Corps; Chairman National Trust (I.O.M.) Cttee.; Pres. Manx Field Club, Celtic Congress, I.O.M.; Chairman I.O.M. Officers' Association; Trustee of House of Industry, Police Court Mission, Douglas Grammar School; Licensed Lay Reader C. of E. *Publications:* The Constitution of the Isle of Man; Land Tenure of the Isle of Man; Origin of Manx Lords Rent; History of the Office of Deemster, etc. *Recreations:* yachting, ski-ing, golfing. *Address:* 4 Albert Terrace, Douglas, Isle of Man. *T.A.:* Farrant, Douglas, Man. *T.:* Douglas 407. *Club:* R.N.V.R. [*Died* 19 *Sept.* 1952.

FARRAR, Hon. Ernest Henry; President of the Legislative Council, N.S.W., 1946; Member since 1912; Chairman of Committees, Legislative Council, 1934-46; *b.* Barnsley, Yorkshire, 1879; *m.*; one *s. Educ.:* Granville and Petersham Public Schools, N.S.W. President: Australian Saddlery Trades Federation, 1907-12; Labour Council, N.S.W., 1910; Political Labour League, 1911-13; 8 Hour Demonstration Committee, 1911; Trades Union Congress of N.S.W., 1910-12; N.S.W. Board of Fire Commissioners, 1915-22; Vice-Pres. National Party of N.S.W., 1917-28; Minister for Labour and Industry, 1922-25, 1927-30; Executive Commissioner for N.S.W. at British Empire Exhibition, London, 1924; Joint Pres. Empire Parliamentary Assoc. (N.S.W. Branch), 1946-; Pres. Ku-ring-gai Chase Nat. Park Trust, 1947; Trustee, Sydney Grammar School; Trustee, Australian Museum. *Address:* 51 Fairlight Street, Manly, N.S.W., Australia. *Clubs:* National (Pres.), Tattersall's, Manly Bowling (Sydney). [*Died* 16 *June* 1952.

FARRELL, Jerome; *see* Farrell, W. J.

FARRELL, Robert Hamilton, C.B. 1952; *b.* Guernsey, 3 Sept. 1895; *s.* of R. H. Farrell, Guernsey; *m.* 1920, Florence Edith Woods; one *s. Educ.:* Elizabeth College, Guernsey; Univ. of London (London Sch. of Economics). Entered Home Civil Service, 1914; first appointment in National Health Insurance Commission (England); transferred to Ministry of Health, 1919; member Beveridge Cttee. on Social Insurance, 1941-42; transferred to Ministry of National Insurance, 1945; Under-Secretary and Dir. of Establishments and Organisation, Ministry of Pensions and National Insurance, 1951-57, retired. *Recreation:* gardening. *Address:* Frensham, Lyme Regis, Dorset. *T.:* Lyme Regis 204. *Club:* National Liberal. [*Died* 26 *June* 1959.

FARRELL, (Wilfrid) Jerome, C.M.G. 1946; O.B.E. 1936; M.C.; Capt. (retired); *b.* 29 Nov. 1882; *s.* of Thomas Farrell, Solicitor, Hull, and Monica, *d.* of J. A. Collingwood, Hull; unmarried. *Educ.:* Ushaw College; Hymers College; Jesus College, Cambridge (Senior Scholar and Fellow). 1st Class Classical Tripos 1904 and 1905; Student, British School of Archæology, Athens, 1906-1910, taught at Rugby and Haileybury, 1911-15; European War, 1914-18; served R.F.A. and Intelligence Corps, France, Egypt, Iraq, Trans-Caucasia (M.C.); Education Service, Iraq Government, 1919-22; Acting Director and Adviser to Minister of Education, 1921-22; Education Service, Palestine, 1923-47; Director of Education, Palestine Govt., 1937-47; reported to Foreign Office on education in Libya, 1949. *Publications:* occasional articles in reviews. *Address:* Tibur, Castle Townshend, Co. Cork, Eire. [*Died* 2 *July* 1960.

FARRER, 4th Baron, *cr.* 1893; Bt., *cr.* 1883; **Oliver Thomas Farrer;** *b.* 5 Oct. 1904; 2nd *s.* of 2nd Baron and Evangeline, *d.* of late Octavius Newry Knox, J.P.; *S.* half-brother 1948; *m.* 1931, Hon. Katharine Runciman, *y. d.* of 1st Viscount Runciman of Doxford, P.C.; no *c. Educ.:* Westminster; Trinity College, Cambridge. B.A. 1925. Served P. & O.S.N. Co. and their agents at home and abroad, 1925-40. Served War of 1939-45, in R.A.F.V.R., 1940-45, 203 Sqdn., H.Q.R.A.F.M.E. and Air Ministry, Wing Comdr. (despatches). C.C. Herts since 1946; Vice-Chairman 1952; D.L. Herts, 1951; J.P. Herts, 1949. Director of Trust Houses and other cos.; Chairman: Herts Playing Fields Assoc.; Dep. Chm. National Playing Fields Assoc. *Recreations:* country sports. *Heir: cousin,* Anthony Thomas Farrer, *b.* 22 Apr. 1910. *Address:* Puddephat's Farm, Markyate, Herts. *T.:* Markyate 317. *Club:* Marlborough-Windham. [*Died* 24 *Jan.* 1954.

FARRER, Augustine John Daniel, B.A.; *b.* South Hampstead, Oct. 1872; *s.* of Rev. Wm. Farrer, B.A., LL.B., for forty-six years Secretary and Librarian of New College, London; *m.* 1899, Evangeline, *d.* of R. Archer of Clerkenwell and S. Hampstead; one *s.* two *d. Educ.:* City of London School; University Coll., London; Regent's Park

College. Matriculation (London), 1890; B.A. (London), 1893; Baptist Minister at Leamington Road Church, Blackburn, 1898-99 and at Jesmond Church, Newcastle on Tyne, 1918-19; Theological Tutor, Regent's Park College, London, 1900-37; Recognised Teacher in Theology at New College, London University, 1930-37; Tutor and Librarian, Baptist College, Oxford, 1937-40. *Publications:* Essays in Periodicals and Translations in various books. *Recreation:* handwork. *Address:* Cherrywood, Croxley Green, Herts. [*Died* 21 *Feb.* 1954.

FARRER, Edmund Hugh, C.M.G. 1922; *b.* 1876; *m.* 1st, 1913, Violet Isabella (*d.* 1918), *d.* of late Col. William Hay Macnaghton, and *widow* of F. Harold Carlyon, M.D.; one *d.*; 2nd, Ada Jane (*d.* 1942); 3rd, 1948, Cecile Hope, *d.* of late William Pickering, D.S.O., Kimberley, and *widow* of Guy Sinclair Scott. Secretary for Finance, Union of South Africa, 1918-31. [*Died* 19 *Feb.* 1955.

FARRER, Roland John, C.M.G. 1930; Malayan Civil Service, retired; *b.* London, 1873; *s.* of Frederick Willis Farrer. *Educ.:* Eton; Balliol College, Oxford. Cadet Straits Settlements, Civil Service, 1896; Province Wellesley, 1897-1900; Singapore Secretariat, 1901-02; Province Wellesley, 1902-07; Land Office, Singapore, 1908-11; Municipality Singapore Assessor, 1911-15; acting British Adviser, Kelantan, 1915-19; President Municipal Commissioners, Singapore, 1919-31. *Recreations:* cricket, football. *Address:* St. John's Island, Singapore. [*Died* 24 *July* 1956.

FARRÈRE, Claude (Frédéric Charles Bargone); French Author; Member of the French Academy, 1935; *b.* Lyons, 27 April 1876; *s.* of Colonel Pierre Dominique Bargone and Isabella Noble; *m.* 1919, Henriette Roger; no *c.* *Educ.:* Lycées of Marseilles and Toulon; École Navale; École d'Application de Cannonage (Baccalauréat ès Lettres. Baccalauréat ès Sciences). Midshipman, 1896; Ensign, 1899; Lieut., 1906; served European War, 1914-18 (Croix de Guerre); Captain, 1917; retired 1919. Chevalier, Legion of Honour, 1911, Officer, 1922, Commander, Legion of Honour, 1930; Grand-croix de la Couronne d'Épine et de l'Ordre du Temple; Grand-Officier de Medjid, du Trésor Sacré, de Léopold Ier, etc. *Publications:* 30 Novels including: Fumées d'opium, 1904; Les Civilisés (Prix Goncourt), 1905; La Bataille, 1909; Thomas d'Agnelet, 1914; Le Dernier Dieu, 1926; Le Chef, 1930; Imaginaires, 1938; L'Onzième Heure, 1940; L'Homme Seul, 1942; Fern-Errol, 1944; La Seconde Porte, 1945; Job siècle XX, 1949; La Sonate à la Mer, 1951; Le Traitre, 1952; various plays, short stories, essays and historical works, etc. *Recreations:* automobile et voyages, air, terre, mer. *Address:* 10 square Henry Paté, Paris, 16e, France. *T.:* Paris Jas. 06-97. *Clubs:* Hoche, Aero (Paris). [*Died* 21 *June* 1957.

FARSON, Negley; Author; *b.* Plainfield, N.J., U.S.A., 14 May 1890; *e. s.* of Enoch and Grace Farson and *g.s.* of Major-Gen. James Negley, Plainfield; *m.* 1920, Eve, *o. d.* of Thomas Stoker, C.S.I.; one *s.* *Educ.:* Andover; Pennsylvania University, U.S.A. Civil Engineer; left College to go into business but shortly came to England and then Czarist Russia, where he had an export business for 3 years; saw Russian Revolution; enlisted in British R.F.C. and sent to Egypt, where as scout pilot he had bad crash which has left him lame ever since; went to live 2 years in forests of British Columbia; went to Chicago and became manager in the Macktruck Co.; left that to take small sail boat across Europe from North to Black Sea; joined staff of Chicago Daily News, special missions India and Egypt, and was their correspondent in most capitals of Europe, including 5 years in London; resigned to become free-lance writer, 1935; President Association American Correspondents, London, 1933. *Publications:* 2 novels published in America; Sailing Across Europe; Seeing Red; The Way of a Transgressor; Transgressor in the Tropics; The Story of a Lake; Behind God's Back; Bomber's Moon; Going Fishing; The Sons of Noah; Last Chance in Africa; Caucasian Journey; A Mirror for Narcissus. *Recreations:* reading and writing. *Address:* The Grey House, nr. Georgeham, N. Devon. *T.:* Croyde 200. [*Died* 12 *Dec.* 1960.

FARTHING, Walter John; *b.* 4 July 1889; *m.* 1913. *Educ.:* Wembdon Elementary School. Member of Labour Party since 1913; Member of Transport and General Workers' Union; Member of its General Executive Council, 1925-45, and many other committees; Member Trade Union Congress General Council, 1935-44; Member Bridgwater Town Council since 1928; Mayor, 1939-40, now Alderman; J.P. County of Somerset; Chairman Regional Committee War Pensions and many other social activities. M.P. (Lab.) Frome Division of Somerset, 1945-50. *Recreation:* bowls. *Address:* 21 Blacklands, Bridgwater. *T.:* Bridgwater 2131. [*Died* 29 *Nov.* 1954.

FAULKNER, John; *b.* 1871; *s.* of John Faulkner, C.C., St. Martin's le Grand, E.C.; *m.* 1895, Agatha Annie Pugh (*d.* 1944); one *d.* *Educ.:* private school: City of London College. Foreign Bankers in City, 1884-89; Cashier and Accountant, N.S.P.C.C, 1889-1910; Associate and Financial Secretary, London Central Y.M.C.A., 1910-14; Headquarters Travelling Secretary, National Council of Y.M.C.A's., 1914-24; Headquarters Travelling Secretary, Dr. Barnardo's Homes, 1924-35; Appeals Secretary, 1935-36; General Secretary, 1936-40. *Publications:* Numerous articles on Nature Study. *Recreations:* botany, ornithology, gardening, meteorology, antiquarian research. *Address:* Witley Cottage, Seafield Road, Rustington, nr. Littlehampton, Sussex. *T.:* Rustington 1188. [*Died* 2 *July* 1958.

FAULKNER, Odin T., C.M.G. 1928; *b.* 1890; *m.* Mildred, M.S., F.R.C.S., *o. d.* of Dr. W. B. Warde, Hook Road, Surbiton; four *s.* *Educ.:* Caius College, Cambridge. Federated Malay States, 1912-14; Indian Agricultural Service, 1914-21; Director of Agriculture, Nigeria, 1921-36; Adviser on Agriculture, Malaya, 1936-1938; Principal, Imperial College of Tropical Agriculture, 1938; retired. *Address:* Woodacre, Beech Road, Wroxham, Norfolk. [*Died* 14 *Feb.* 1958.

FAWCETT, Charles Bungay, D.Sc.; Professor of Geography, University of London, 1928-49, retd.; Prof. Emeritus since 1949; *b.* 25 Aug. 1883; *s.* of John Fawcett and Eva Bungay; *m.* 1917, Nora Loxston; two *d.* *Educ.:* Staindrop School; University College, Nottingham; School of Geography, Oxford. Lecturer in Geography, University Coll., Southampton, 1913-19; Lecturer (1919-20), Reader (1920-28) in Geography, University of Leeds; Visiting Professor at Clark University, Worcester, Mass., 1930-31, 1946-47, and 1949-51 (Hon. Sc.D. 1950); at Univ. of Ceylon, 1951-52; President, Institute of British Geographers, 1933-36, Section III (Human Geography), International Geographical Congress, Warsaw, 1934, Section E (Geography) British Association, 1937, and Association of University Teachers, 1945-46; leader British Delegation to Internat. Geog. Congress, Lisbon, 1949. *Publications:* Frontiers; Provinces of England; A Political Geography of the British Empire; The Bases of a World Commonwealth; A Residential Unit for Town and Country Planning; many articles in geog. periodical press. *Address:* c/o University College, W.C.1. [*Died* 21 *Sept.* 1952.

FAWCETT, Sir Charles Gordon Hill, Kt., *cr.* 1927; I.C.S., retired 1929; *b.* 28 June 1869; *s.* of Lieutenant-Colonel R. H. Fawcett, Duke of Wellington's Regiment; *m.* 1894, Marion Edith, *d.* of Surgeon-Major W.

Fry; one *d.* *Educ.:* Aysgarth; Harrow; Pembroke College, Cambridge. Entered I.C.S. 1890; Judicial Under-Secretary to Govt. of Bombay, 1898; Remembrancer of Legal Affairs, 1899; Judge of Judicial Commissioner's Court, Sind, 1911; a Puisne Judge of Bombay High Court, 1920-29; Chairman of Bombay Strike Enquiry Committee, 1928-29; Fellow of the Royal Historical Society; Editor of the India Office Series: The English Factories in India; Editor of: Hakluyt Soc. work, The Travels of the Abbé Carré in India and the Near East, 1672-1674; Sir Evan Cotton's book, East Indiamen, 1949. *Publication:* The First Century of British Justice in India, 1934. *Address:* 14 Highbury Road, Wimbledon, S.W.19. *Club:* East India and Sports. [*Died* 7 *March* 1952.

FAWCETT, (Edward) Douglas; man of letters; *s.* of E. Boyd Fawcett and Myra Macdougall; *b.* Hove, Brighton, 1866; *m.* 1896, M. B. V. Jackson; *m.* 1947, Mrs. Vera Dick-Cunyngham, *d.* of Mr. Mostyn Pryce, Gunley, Mont. *Educ.:* Newton College, South Devon; Westminster School (Queen's Scholar). Interests divided between study and sport; in philosophy an idealist whose distinctive mark is the discussion of Imagination as the fundamental reality of the Universe; for this Imaginism see Contemporary British Philosophy, vol. ii. 1925. *Publications:* Divine Imagining, 1921; The World as Imagination, 1916; The Zermatt Dialogues, 1931; From Heston to the High Alps, 1936; The Oberland Dialogues (on the Soul), 1939; and a long philosophical poem, Light of the Universe, 1957. In Hartmann the Anarchist, 1893, anticipated the romance of the war aeroplane. *Recreations:* mountaineering, motoring, skating and other winter sports, swiming, flying; made the only recorded ascent to the Mer de Glace, from Chamounix, up the mule-path on a motor-car of ordinary size. *Address:* 98 Walton Street, S.W.3. [*Died* 14 *April* 1960.

FAWCETT, Edward Pinder, C.B.E. 1918; *b.* Sheffield, 1874; *s.* of John Edward Fawcett; *m.* May, *d.* of W. H. Clifford; three *d.* (two *s.* decd.). *Educ.:* Leys School; Caius College, Cambridge (B.A.). Entered the Indian Civil Service, 1898; retired, 1930. *Address:* George, Cape Province, S. Africa. [*Died* 9 *Nov.* 1954.

FAWCETT, Sir Luke, Kt., *cr.* 1948; O.B.E. 1943; Chairman of Southern Regional Board for Industry since 1952; *b.* 8 June 1881; *s.* of Hewson Fawcett, North Thoresby, Lincs; *m.* 1st, 1904, Easter Ellen (*d.* 1949), *d.* of John Plows, Scholes, nr. Leeds, Yorks; two *s.* one *d.*; 2nd, 1958, Phyllis May Tanner, Worthing. *Educ.:* Elementary. Mem. T.U.C. Gen. Council, 1941-52; first full-time Pres., Amalgamated Union of Building Trade Workers, 1934-41; General Secretary, Amalgamated Union of Building Trade Workers of Great Britain and Ireland, 1941-1952; Part-time Member of Atomic Energy Authority, 1954-58; Member of War Damage Commission and Central Land Board, 1948-1959. President of the National Federation of Building Trades Operatives; Member: National Joint Council for Building Industry (Vice-Chairman) and various committees associated therewith; War Works Commission; Director, Building and Civil Engineering Holidays Management Ltd.; Member: Ministry of Works Joint Consultative Cttee.; Ministry of Labour Joint Consultative Cttee. *Publications:* Building Workers and the Work of the Building Industry, 1942; We Can Build All the Houses, 1943; The Struggle for Homes, 1943; The Availability of Building Labour, 1943; The Building Workers Charter, 1943; Achievement, 1945; Building Workers, Forward!, 1946, etc. *Recreation:* propaganda. *Address:* 2 Queensville Road, Clapham Park, S.W.12. *T.:* Tulse Hill 1882. [*Died* 25 *Oct.* 1960.

FAWCUS, George Ernest, C.I.E. 1927; O.B.E. 1923; V.D. 1923; *b.* 12 Mar. 1885; *s.* of Ernest Augustus Fawcus, Liscard, Cheshire; *m.* 1911, Mary Christine, *d.* of late Walter Dawes, J.P., Rye, Sussex. *Educ.:* Winchester College; New College, Oxford. Joined the Indian Educational Service, 1909; Director of Public Instruction, Bihar and Orissa (later Bihar), 1917-37; Chairman of Joint Public Service Commission for Bihar, Central Provinces and Berar, and Orissa, India, 1937-39; Finance Officer, Land Settlement Assoc. Ltd. 1939-43; Treasurer of the Durham Colleges, 1943-51. *Address:* Furzedene, Budleigh Salterton, Devon. *T.:* Budleigh Salterton 107. [*Died* 29 *Dec.* 1958.

FAY, Sir Sam, Kt., *cr.* 1912; J.P., Hants; ex-Director, Buenos Ayres Great Southern and Buenos Ayres Western Railways; A Freeman of City of London; Lt.-Col. Engineer and Railway Staff Corps; *b.* 30 Dec. 1856; *m.* 1883, Frances (*d.* 1946), *d.* of C. H. Farbrother, Kingston-on-Thames; two *s.* three *d.* Member of the Committee on Post Office Wages, 1904; Member of Departmental Committee on Inshore Fisheries, 1913; Pres., Institute of Transport, 1922-23; Chairman of Royal Commission on New South Wales Government Railways and Tramways, 1924; Reported to New Zealand Government on working of New Zealand Railways, 1925. *Educ.:* Blenheim House, Fareham. Entered L. & S.W. Railway service as clerk, 1872; General Manager Midland & South Western Junction Railway, 1892; Superintendent of the Line L. & S.W.R., 1899; General Manager, Great Central Railway Co., 1902-22; Mem. of Railway Executive Committee and of Ports and Transit Executive Com., 1913-21; Director of Movements, War Office, 1 Jan. 1917–1 Mar. 1918; Director-General of Movements and Railways, War Office, and Member of Army Council, 1918-19. *Publications:* The War Office at War, 1937; Alone, and other poems and prose, 1944. *Address:* Awbridge Danes, Romsey, Hants. *Clubs:* Reform, Argentine. [*Died* 30 *May* 1953.

FEA, Allan; Historian and Antiquary; *b.* 25 May 1860; *s.* of William Charles Fea and Marie, *née* Quensell; *m.* Louie, *d.* of Thos. Hallmark, Newport, Salop. *Educ.:* Grove House School, Highgate. Was engaged upon special work in the library of the India Office, Whitehall, under his friend Dr. R. Röst (the librarian), 1877; Private Sec. to Field-Marshal Lord Strathnairn, 1879; entered the service of the Bank of England, 1880, from which institution, retired through ill-health, Dec. 1900. *Publications:* The Flight of the King; Secret Chambers and Hiding Places; King Monmouth; Picturesque Old Houses; After Worcester Fight; Memoirs of the Martyr King; Pictorial Edition of the Memoirs of Count de Gramont; Some Beauties of the Seventeenth Century; Nooks and Corners of Old England; James II. and His Wives; Seymour Lucas, R.A., a Monograph; Old English Houses (a revised edition of Picturesque Old Houses); My Lady Wentworth; The Real Captain Cleveland; Old World Places; Quiet Roads and Sleepy Villages, 1913; Where Traditions Linger, 1923; Recollections of Sixty Years, 1926; The Loyal Wentworths, 1927; Rooms of Mystery and Romance, 1931; The Latest Adventures in Wonderland, 1950, under pseudonyms: (as author) M.A.D. Hatter, (as illustrator) J. Abberwock. Realistic Peeps into the Past (Gentleman's Magazine, 1903); Tom Killigrew: Charles II.'s Jester (Country Life, 23 April 1938); Charles II. in Suffolk (Suffolciensiam Antiquariorum, 1938); Contributor to Blighty, 1939-41; Portraits of Nell Gwyn, Moll Davis and Others (The Connoisseur, March 1943); Portraits of Lucy Walter, Monmouth's Mother (Burlington Magazine, 1945); Stuart Relics, and the Stories they Tell (Everybodys, 1945); The Mystery of a Historical Portrait (Country Life, 1949). *Address:* Rest-a-While, Vale View Road, Whitstable, Kent. [*Died* 9 *June* 1956.

FAWSITT, Charles Edward. See page xxviii.

FEARNLEY-WHITTINGSTALL, William Arthur, T.D.; Q.C. 1949; Recorder of Leicester since 1957; Barrister-at-Law; *b.* 27 May 1903; *s.* of late Rev. H. O. Fearnley-Whittingstall; *m.* 1928, Margaret Nancy, *y. d.* of Alan James Morphew, Style Acre, Wallingford; one *s.* two *d.* *Educ.:* Malvern. Called to Bar, Inner Temple, 1925, practising London and Midland Circuit; Deputy Chairman Bedfordshire Quarter Sessions, 1946-49. Hon. Recorder of High Wycombe, 1949. Recorder of Grantham, 1946-54, of Lincoln, 1954-57. Master of the Bench of the Inner Temple, 1958. Contested Seaham Division (C.), 1929, South Bedfordshire (C.), 1950; Chairman, Special Grants Cttee., Ministry of Pensions and National Insurance, 1958-. 2nd Lieutenant R.A., 1939; Lieut.-Colonel commanding 18 Indian L.A.A. Regt., 1943-45 (despatches). *Address:* 1 Harcourt Buildings, Temple, E.C.4; 90 Campden Hill Court, W.8. *Clubs:* Carlton, Junior Carlton. [*Died* 28 *Oct.* 1959.

FEARON, William Robert, M.A., Sc.D., M.B.; Senior Fellow of Trinity College, Dublin, and Professor of Biochemistry, University of Dublin; Physiologist to the Royal City of Dublin Hospital; Consulting Biochemist to Rotunda Hospital, Dublin; Ex-Mem. Medical Research Council of Ireland; Hon. Prof. of Chemistry, Roy. Hibernian Acad.; Univ. Representative in the Senate of Eire since 1943; *b.* 1892; *o. s.* of late Rev. Wm. Fearon, of Kells, Co. Meath. *Educ.:* Trinity Coll., Dublin (ex-Scholar), 1st Sen. Mod., Sc.D. 1919; Vice-Chancellor's Prizeman in English; Emmanuel Coll., Cambridge (Exhibitioner and Research Student, B.A. 1921). Harvey Research Prize, Royal Coll. of Physicians, Ireland, 1918; Carmichael Prize, Royal Coll. of Surg. Ireland; Research Worker for the Food Ministry and Food Investigation Board, 1917-19; Fellow of the Royal Institute of Chemistry; Member of the Royal Irish Academy, 1923; Fellow of the Royal Academy of Medicine (Ireland); Mackinnon Research Student of the Royal Society, 1919-21; Buckston Browne Prize, Harveian Society, 1935. *Publications:* An Introduction to Biochemistry, 3rd Ed., 1948 (2nd Spanish Edn., 1949); Nutritional Factors in Disease, 1936; Parnell of Avondale, 1937; scientific articles in The Biochemical Journal, Analyst, etc. *Address:* 24 Trinity College, Dublin. *Club:* Dublin University (Dublin). [*Died* 27 *Dec.* 1959.

FEAVEARYEAR, Sir Albert Edgar, K.B.E., *cr.* 1951; C.B. 1947; D.Sc.(Econ.); Deputy Secretary, Ministry of Food, since 1948; *b.* 19 July 1896; *m.* 1931, Ruby Louisa Castleton; one *s.* *Educ.:* Ipswich Municipal Secondary School (now Northgate (School); London University. D.Sc.(Econ.) 1933. *Publication:* The Pound Sterling, 1931. *Address:* Bushley, Willow Grove, Chislehurst, Kent. *T.:* Imperial 3021. [*Died* 24 *April* 1953.

FEDDEN, Walter Fedde, F.R.C.S. Eng.; M.S., Lond.; Consulting Surgeon St. George's Hospital; Consulting Surgeon Victoria Hospital for Children, Chelsea. *Educ.:* St. Paul's School; London Univ. (Honours in Anat. and Surgery); St. George's Hospital (the Treasurer's Prize, the Pollock Prize, the Thompson Medal, Certificate of Honour in Anat.). Late Surgeon, Bolingbroke Hospital, Wandsworth Common; late Lecturer in Surgery, St. George's Hospital; late Examiner in Surgery, London and Cambridge Universities. Editor Surgical part of Gray's Anatomy, 20th edition. *Address:* 5 Glenalmond House, Manor Fields, S.W.15. *T.:* Putney 5815. [*Died* 12 *March* 1952.

FEILDEN, Theodore John Valentine; Empire Journalist and Imperial Trade Propagandist; for many years advocate of British-American Unity; World Traveller; F.R.E.S.; Member of Canada Club; Founder and Director-General of The Empire Unity League; Organising Director Empire Migration Settlement Movement; Original Member of Overseas League; Founder-Member Incorporated Sales Managers' Assoc.; *b.* Birmingham, 14 Mar. 1863; *e. s.* of late Lieut.-Col. M. J. Feilden, M.P.; *m.* 1st, 1887, Julia Anne (*d.* 1943), *e. d.* of Thos. Sampson, Brympton D'Evercy, Somerset; two *s.* (and one died on active service); 2nd, 1945, Jane (*d.* 1952), 3rd *d.* of late Capt. Edmund Albert Phillips, Brixham, Devon. *Educ.:* Mullin's Preparatory School, Croydon; Afton College, Chiswick; Godolphin Sch., Hammersmith. Founder-editor: school magazine, Excelsior Journal; weekly, The Comet, The Cycling Newspaper, The Manufacturer; Managing-editor American-European News Letter, Printing News, Trade and Industry; Founder and original Editor-in-chief of Feilden's Magazine (now The Engineering Review); Founder and late Managing-editor of The Electrical Magazine; Founder-editor, Motor Trade Record; Industrial contributor to Daily Mail and Daily Express, 1898-99; Member of Postal Reform Cttee. and of Tariff Reform Council, 1898-1900; on staff of The Times, 1908-17; originated and was Business Manager of The Times Engineering Supplement and The Times Trade Supplement. Originator and Controller of The Imperial Trade Organisation; Founder and Editor-in-Chief, 1918-45, of The Empire Mail and Imperial Review, Comercio Hispano-Britanico, Comercio Argentino-Britanico; Chairman and Managing Director of the British Commonwealth Trade Press Ltd. and afterwards of Feilden Publications Ltd. Boer War service; promoted and organised National Motor Volunteers, and was Chief Executive Officer (Hon. Col.) (Herts Corps) during European War, 1914-18; commended and thanked by late Lord Kitchener for recruiting services; visited Canada (with Imperial Press Conference Delegation), 1920; temp. War Correspondent in Germany, 1945. *Publications:* The Victorian Era, Sixty Years of Unprecedented Progress, 1887; St. Albans Past and Present; Ten Thousand Miles in Five and a Half Weeks, 1905; Britain's Electrical Industries, 1906; The Story of Canada, 1924 and 1928; Birmingham Tells the World, 1932; The Story of Leicester, 1933; Progressive Luton, 1933; The Romance of Lancashire, 1934; Imperial London, 1934; Yorkshire, Industrial Commercial, Historic, 1936; Sheffield the City of Steel, 1936; Birmingham To-Day, 1938; Britain and America, 1941-43. *Recreations:* gardening, fishing, photography, stamp and curio collecting. *Address:* 3 Chantlers Close, East Grinstead, Sussex. *T.:* East Grinstead 1173. [*Died* 8 *June* 1955.

FELIX, Arthur, F.R.S. 1943; D.Sc. (Vienna); Hon. D.Sc. (Belfast); formerly Director, Central Enteric Reference Laboratory and Bureau, Public Health Laboratory Service (Medical Research Council), London; *b.* Andrychow, Poland, 3 April 1887; *s.* of Theodore and Regina Felix; *m.* 1923, Leah, *d.* of L. Gluckman, Telaviv, Palestine. *Educ.:* Bielsko, Polish Silesia; Vienna. During European War, 1914-18, a bacteriologist in the Austrian Army (work on the Weil-Felix reaction (1916) for the diagnosis of typhus fever); research work at University, Prague, 1919-20; Director of Bacteriological Laboratory, Hadassah Medical Organisation, Telaviv, Palestine, 1921; Chief Bacteriologist, Hadassah Medical Organisation, Jerusalem, 1922-27; Chairman, Health Council, Palestine Zionist Executive, Jerusalem, 1924-27; Member of Scientific Staff, Lister Institute of Preventive Medicine, London, 1927-45; during War of 1939-45 served as Specialist with Emergency Public Health Laboratory Service (Medical Research Council, London); Chm., Internat. Cttee. for Enteric Phage Typing, 1947-; Foreign Corresp. Member, Société de Pathologie Exotique, Paris, 1947; Associate Editor, Jl. of

Hygiene (Cambridge) and Excerpta Medica (Amsterdam). *Publications:* numerous papers on bacteriological and immunological subjects in British and foreign medical journals; (with J. A. Arkwright) chapter on Typhus Fever in A System of Bacteriology, 1930. *Recreations:* walking, travelling. *Address:* 98 Oakwood Court, Kensington, W.14. *T.:* Western 7339. [*Died* 14 *Jan.* 1956.

FELL, Sir Bryan Hugh, K.C.M.G., *cr.* 1935; C.B. 1933; *b.* 23 Nov. 1869; *s.* of John Fell and Jane Black; *m.* 1898, Marion Kennedy, 2nd *d.* of Albert Greg, Escowbeck, Caton, Lancaster; one *s.* three *d.* *Educ.:* Sedbergh School; Queen's College, Oxford (Hastings Exhibitioner). Assistant Clerk, House of Commons, 1893; Principal Clerk, Public Bill Office, House of Commons, 1931-1934; retired, 1934. *Publications:* Guide Book to House of Commons; articles on Empire Parliaments. *Recreation:* gardening. *Address:* Haverthwaite, Ulverston, Lancs. *Club:* Brooks's. [*Died* 12 *Nov.* 1955.

FELL, Sir Godfrey (Butler Hunter), K.C.I.E., *cr.* 1918 (C.I.E. 1909); C.S.I. 1917; O.B.E. 1944; *b.* 22 Apr. 1872; *s.* of Rev. G. H. Fell, D.D., Fellow, Magdalen Coll., Oxf.; *m.* 1904, Janet Camilla (*d.* 1948), *o. d.* of Gen. Sir D. J. S. McLeod, K.C.B., K.C.I.E., D.S.O.; one *d.* *Educ.:* Eton; Magdalen College, Oxford. Entered I.C.S. 1894; Assistant Commissioner Burma, 1895; Under-Secretary to Burma Government, 1899; Private Sec. to Lt.-Gov., 1903; Deputy-Sec. Home Department, Government of India, 1906-9; Financial Adviser, Military Finance Department, Government of India, 1915, and Member Indian Munitions Board, 1916; Member, Army in India Committee, 1919 Secretary Govt. of India, Army Depart., 1921-23 retired, 1924; O.C., B. Coy., 2nd Inverness shire (West) Bn. Home Guard, 1940-45 (O.B.E.) Member of Inverness-shire County Council 1944. *Recreations:* fishing, shooting. *Address* Peinmore, Portree, Isle of Skye. *T.:* Portree 74 *Club:* Oriental. [*Died* 14 *March* 1955.

FELL, Herbert Granville; artist and journalist; Editor of Connoisseur since 193 and regular contributor; Associate Editor 1934-35; *b.* 1872; *m.* Mary, 2nd *d.* of late Sir J. D. Linton, P.R.I.; one *s.* three *d.* *Educ.* King's Coll., Lond.; studied art in London chiefly; also in Paris, Brussels, and in various German cities. Editor of book dept., classics and reprints, and Art Library, George Newnes, Ltd. 1907-8; Art editor of The Ladies' Field, 1907 1919; Art editor Strand Magazine, 1910-12 editor Femina, London edition, 1920-21; editor of the Queen, 1920-24; Art critic of The Queen, 1924-28; Director of Drawing, Painting, and Design, Royal Albert Memorial College, Exeter, for many years; exhibitor at Royal Academy, first in 1891, and several subsequent years. *Publications:* Cézanne; Vermeer of Delft, 1933; illustrator of The Book of Job, The Song of Solomon, Wonder Stories from Herodotus, The Serious Poems of Hood, Aucassin and Nicolette, A Wonder Book, and Tanglewood Tales, by Nathaniel Hawthorne, and several smaller books of fairy tales; various designs in the Pall Mall Magazine, the Studio, Artist, Ladies' Field, King, Country Life, and others; has been contributor to Apollo and principal art journals. *Recreations:* books, music, fencing, and the study of natural history. *Address:* 30 Esmond Gardens, Bedford Park, W.4. *T.:* Chiswick 2029. [*Died* 10 *Sept.* 1951.

FELL, Lt.-Gen. Sir Matthew Henry Gregson, K.C.B., *cr.* 1922 (C.B. 1919); C.M.G. 1917; D.L., J.P.; F.R.C.S.; late R.A.M.C.; *b.* 20 March 1872; *s.* of John Fell, J.P., D.L.; *m.* 1908, Marion Isobel Wallace; two *s.* two *d.* *Educ.:* Sedbergh; St. Bartholomew's Hospital. Served S. African War, 1899-1902 (Queen's medal four clasps, King's medal two clasps, despatches); South African Constabulary, 1902-05; European War (despatches eight times, C.M.G., C.B., two Brevets); Director R.A.F. Medical Service, 1919-21; Director-General A.M.S., 1926-29; Hon. Physician to King George V, 1926-29; retired, 1929. *Address:* Flan How, Ulverston. *Club:* Flyfishers'. [*Died* 28 *Jan.* 1959.

FELLOWES, Rev. Edmund Horace, C.H. 1944; M.V.O. 1931; M.A., Mus. Doc.; Minor Canon of St. George's Chapel, Windsor Castle, since 1900; Director of the Choir and Master of the Choristers, 1924-27; Hon. Fellow of Oriel College, Oxford, 1937; Hon. Freeman of Worshipful Company of Musicians, 1937; Librarian, St. Michael's Coll., Tenbury, 1918-1948; Pres. Royal Musical Assoc. 1942-47; Pres. Church Music Soc., 1946; Pres. Union of Graduates in Music, 1943-48; *b.* London, 11 Nov. 1870; 2nd *s.* of Horace D. Fellowes and Louisa, *d.* of Captain Edmund Packe, Royal Horse Guards; *m.* 1899, Lilian Louisa, *y. d.* of Admiral Sir R. Vesey Hamilton, G.C.B.; three *s.* one *d.* *Educ.:* Winchester; Oriel Coll., Oxford. B.A. 1892, M.A. 1896, Mus. Bac. 1896; Mus. Doc. Hon., Trinity Coll., Dublin, 1917, Oxford, 1939, Camb., 1950. Deacon 1894, Priest 1895, Curate, St. Anne's Wandsworth, 1894; Minor Canon and Precentor of Bristol Cathedral, 1897; James W. Alsop Lecturer in Music, Liverpool Univ., 1932-33; Cramb Lecturer in Music, Glasgow University, 1937-38; several Lecture tours in United States and Canada, 1925-36. *Publications:* William Fellowes of Eggesford, 1910; English Madrigal Verse, 1920; The English Madrigal Composers, 1921; William Byrd, 1923; Orlando Gibbons, 1925; The English Madrigal, 1925; A History of Winchester Cricket, 1930, and Supplement, 1942; A History of the Frederick Family, 1932; Catalogue of the Tenbury Music Manuscripts, 1934; Byrd, a critical study, 1936; Morley's Plaine and Easie Introduction to Practicall Musicke, 1937; Organists and Choir-Masters of St. George's Chapel, 1939; The Knights of the Garter 1348-1939, 1939; English Cathedral Music, 1941; The Military Knights of Windsor, 1944; The Minor Canons of Windsor, 1945; Memoirs of an Amateur Musician, 1946; The English Madrigal School, complete in 36 vols., 1912-24; The English School of Lutenist Song-Writers, in 32 vols., 1920-32; Merbecke's Communion Service, 1949; The Complete Works of William Byrd, in 20 vols., 1950; The Registers of St. George's Chapel, 1951; joint-editor Carnegie Edition of Tudor Church Music (Supplement, 1948); joint author Windsor Castle, St. George's Chapel and Choir, 1927; Westminster Abbey and its Music, 1927; Songs and Lyrics from the Plays of Beaumont and Fletcher, 1928; A Joyous Adventure, 1928; The Tenbury Letters, 1942; contributor to Grove's Dictionary of Music and Musicians; church music; songs, etc. *Recreations:* chamber music (violin), heraldry and genealogy, water-colour drawing. *Address:* The Cloisters, Windsor Castle. *Clubs:* Athenæum, M.C.C. [*Died* 20 *Dec.* 1951.

FELLOWES, Air Commodore Peregrine Forbes Morant, D.S.O. 1918; late R.A.F. and R.N.; *b.* 1883; *s.* of Capt. Peregrine H. T. Fellowes, Chief Constable, Hampshire; *m.* 1914, Eleanor Mary, *d.* of late Colonel C. W. Long, R.A., M.P.; one *s.* *Educ.:* Winton House, Winchester; H.M.S. Britannia. Served European War, 1914-18 (despatches twice, D.S.O. and bar); wounded and prisoner of war, 1918; Director of Airship Development, Air Ministry, 1924-29; Air A.D.C. to King George V, 1924-29; surveyed and opened world's first regular Air Route between Cairo and Baghdad; retired list, 1933; Leader of Mount Everest Air Expedition, 1933. *Publications:* First Over Everest, 1933; Britain's Wonderful Air Force. *Address:* Woodhaven, Pietermaritzburg, Natal, S. Africa. *Club:* Army and Navy. [*Died* 12 *June* 1955.

FELLOWS, Brig.-General Bertram Charles, C.M.G. 1919; retired Royal Air

Force and Indian Army; *b.* 1877; *s.* of late Rev. E. T. Fellows; *m.* 1915, Frances Mary (*d.* 1952), *d.* of late T. Clayhills-Henderson, of Invergowrie; no *c.* *Educ.:* privately; R.M.C., Sandhurst. First Commission, 1897, Unattached List for Indian Army, joined 30th Lancers, I.A. 1898; A.D.C. Political Resident Aden, 1904-6; A.D.C. to Governor of Bombay, 1906-7; retired from Indian Army, 1913; rejoined Army, Aug. 1914; joined Royal Flying Corps, 1915; Director of Air Personal Services; D.A.G. Royal Air Force in the Field; demobilised, March 1919. *Address:* Glenowen, Lansdown Rd., Cheltenham. *Club:* Army and Navy.
[*Died* 26 *Nov.* 1956.

FENBY, Thomas Davis; Vice-Chairman East Riding C.C.; *b.* 1875; *s.* of G. W. Fenby, Bridlington; *m.* 1900, Elizabeth Ann, *d.* of late Henry Adamson Helperthorpe, Yorks; two *d.* *Educ.:* Bridlington School. M.P. (L.) East Bradford, 1924-1929. *Address:* Hawarden, Bridlington, Yorks. *Club:* Yorkshire Yacht.
[*Died* 4 *Aug.* 1956.

FENTON, Sir John Charles, Kt., *cr.* 1945; K.C. 1923; Sheriff of the Lothians and Peebles and Sheriff of Chancery in Scotland since 1942; *b.* 5 May 1880; *s.* of James Fenton, Edinburgh, and Elizabeth Jack; *m.* 1909, Isabella Catherine, *d.* of James Coutts, S.S.C., Edinburgh. *Educ.:* George Watson's College, Edinburgh; Edinburgh University; Sorbonne, Paris. Admitted a member of the Faculty of Advocates, 1904; served European War, 23rd R.F., 1914-16 (wounded); National Service, 1917-18; Solicitor-General for Scotland, 1924; Sheriff of Fife and Kinross, 1926-1937; Sheriff of Stirling, Dumbarton, and Clackmannan, 1937-42. *Address:* 22 Abercromby Place, Edinburgh. *T.:* Edinburgh 25840.
[*Died* 3 *Jan.* 1951.

FENTON, Richard, D.L.; J.P. County of City of Dundee; *b.* 20 May 1899; *s.* of Benjamin Lewis Fenton and Sarah Murray; *m.* 1930, Barbara M. R. Fraser; one *s.* *Educ.:* Dundee. Auctioneer and Fish Salesman. Lord Provost of Dundee, 1949-52; Deputy Lieutenant of the County of the City of Dundee. *Recreation:* fishing. *Address:* Balnaguard, Marchfield Road, Dundee. *T.:* 67567.
[*Died* 21 *Feb.* 1959.

FENTON, William James, M.D., F.R.C.P.; Consulting Physician to the Brompton Hospital; late Dean of the Medical School; late Tuberculosis Officer for the Borough of Chelsea; late Examiner in Tuberculous Diseases for University of Wales; Consulting Medical Referee, Confederation Life Association; Consulting Physician to Charing Cross Hospital; late Dean Charing Cross Hospital Medical School; late Examiner in Medicine, Cambridge Univ. and Conjoint Bd. and Mem. of Court of Examiners Soc. of Apothecaries; *b.* 24 Dec. 1868; *s.* of late William James Fenton, Gorton Lodge, Longdon, Staffs; *m.* Lillian Olive Coxon (*d.* 1930), *o. d.* of Major H. Feguson, 10 Glazbury Road, W.14; one *s.* one *d.* *Educ.:* Cambridge. *Publications:* Diseases of the Chest (with Dr. L. S. T. Burrell), 1930; Diseases of the Chest and Medical subjects generally. *Address:* 44 Auriol Road, W.14. *T.:* Fulham 2972.
[*Died* 24 *Dec.* 1957.

FENWICK, Major-Gen. Charles Philip, C.B. 1946; C.B.E. 1944; M.C. 1917; C.St.J. 1946; E.D. 1940; Chief of Medical Services, Canadian Pacific Railway Company; *b.* 10 July 1891; *s.* of late Rev. Mark Fenwick, D.D., and Margaret Hudson, late of St. John's, Newfoundland; *m.* 1921, Jacqueline, *d.* of late Dr. J. W. S. McCullough, D.P.H., Toronto, Ontario; two *d.* *Educ.:* Methodist College, St. John's, Newfoundland; Univ. of London, Matriculation; University of Toronto (M.B. 1916, M.D. 1925). Capt. 1916, Canadian Expeditionary Force (M.C.); Lt.-Col. 1939; Col. 1940; Brig. 1943; Maj.-Gen. 1945. Fellow Amer. Coll. of Surgeons, 1951; Fellow in Aviation Medicine, Aero Med. Assoc., 1952. *Address:* Canadian Pacific Railway, Windsor Station, Montreal. *T.:* Plateau 2211, Local 2213. *Clubs:* St. James's (Montreal); Canadian Military Institute (Toronto).
[*Died* 20 *March* 1954.

FENWICK, Colonel Percival Clennell, C.M.G. 1916; V.D.; M.D., F.R.C.S.E., F.R.G.S., J.P.; Consulting Surgeon to Christchurch Hospital; Director of Deep-Therapy and Radium Dept., Christchurch Public Hospital, since 1924; Lecturer and Examiner of St. John's Ambulance Association; *b.* 1870; *s.* of Samuel Fenwick, Harley Street; *m.* 1903, Nona Evelyn (*d.* 1938), *d.* of Fortunatus Evelyn Wright, Christchurch, N.Z.; one *s.* one *d.* Served S. Africa, 1900 (Queen's medal 4 clasps); European War, 1914-18 (despatches, C.M.G.); Assistant Director of Medical Services, Southern Command, N.Z., 1922-26; Hon. Surgeon to the Governor General, 1925-30; Hon. Chief Commissioner, New Zealand Boy Scouts Association, 1929-37. *Address:* 5 Head Street, Sumner, Christchurch, N.Z.
[*Died* 6 *July* 1958.

FERGUSON, Alexander Stewart, M.A. (St. Andrews and Oxon); LL.D. (St. Andrews); Regius Professor of Logic in the University of Aberdeen, 1926-53, subsequently emeritus professor; *b.* 28 July 1883; *e. s.* of J. M. Ferguson, I.S.O.; *m.* 1911, Ethelwyn (*d.* 1956), *y. d.* of Henry Bradley, Litt.D., F.B.A., Fellow of Magdalen Coll. *Educ.:* Emanuel School, London; St. Andrews Univ.; Univ. Coll., Oxford; 1st class Classical Hons., Guthrie Scholar, St. Andrews, 1904; Lodge Exhibitioner, University College, 1904; 2nd class Mods. 1906; 1st class Litt. Hum., 1908; Assistant Professor of Philosophy, 1909-11, and Professor of Mental Philosophy, 1911-23, in Queen's University, Kingston, Canada; Professor of Philosophy in Armstrong College (University of Durham), Newcastle upon Tyne, 1924-26; Visiting Professor in Columbia University, New York, 1931-32; Terry Lecturer, in Yale University, 1947. *Publications:* (with W. Scott) Hermetica, vol. iv, 1936; The Platonic Revolution (Terry Lectures), 1950; contributions to Classical Quarterly, etc. *Address:* c/o King's College, Old Aberdeen; 74 Ann St., Old Aberdeen. *T.:* 4354.
[*Died* 18 *March* 1958.

FERGUSON, Allan; lately Asst. Professor of Physics, Queen Mary College, London (retired, 1945); Gen. Sec. British Association, 1936-46; Fellow of Queen Mary College; *b.* Entwistle, near Bolton, 11 May 1880; *e. s.* of Alexander Cameron Ferguson, calico printer, Glasgow, and Alice, *e. d.* of Wm. Matthews, Darwen; *m.* 1919, Nesta, *e. d.* of John Thomas, B.A., late Vice-Principal of the Normal College, Bangor; one *s.* *Educ.:* Harris Institute, Preston; University College, Bangor; M.A. (Wales); D.Sc. (Lond.). Formerly Assistant Lecturer in Physics, University College, Bangor, and Lecturer in Physics, Manchester College of Technology; Editor, The Philosophical Magazine; Advisory Editor, Physics and Engineering Subjects, Chambers's Encyclopædia; President of Section A, British Association, 1936; Secretary, 1928-38, and President, 1938-41, of the Physical Society; Advisory Editor of Nature, 1939-40; Examiner in Natural Philosophy to Univ. of Glasgow, 1940-44. Pres. Hertford Divisional Liberal Assoc., 1929-47. *Publications:* critical articles and reviews in scientific journals. *Recreations:* eighteenth-century literature, church architecture, book-hunting. *Address:* 88 Hadham Road, Bishop's Stortford, Herts. *T.:* Bishop's Stortford 900. *Club:* Athenæum.
[*Died* 9 *Nov.* 1951.

FERGUSON, Charles Edward Hamilton, C.M.G. 1947; M.C.; F.S.A.A., F.C.A. (Aust.); Chartered Accountant (Aust.); *s.* of late John Charles Ferguson, Launceston, Tasmania; *m.* 1919, Winefrid

Hannah, *d.* of Thomas Winstanley Hughes, Liverpool, England; one *d.* *Educ.:* Launceston (Tasmania) High School. State Councillor Australasian Corp. of Public Accountants, 1920; State Councillor Inst. Chartered Accounts (Aust.), 1931 (Vice-Chm. 1933-36); Tas. Rep. Gen. Council, 1933-36; State Chm. 1936-43; Fellow Soc. of Accountants and Auditors, Eng. With Sir Herbert Nicholls, K.C.M.G., C.J., was Royal Comr. on Soldier Settlers, 1926; with Mr. Justice Clark, Royal Comr. on Fruit Industry, 1931. Served European War, 1916-19 (despatches, M.C.). Member State Repat. Bd. 1919-20; Chm. State Repat. Purchase Bd., 1929-52; Member Council Tas. Univ. 1936-38; Member Rhodes Selection Cttee., 1937-51; State Pres. Boy Scouts' Assn., 1936-40; Chm. Tas. Assoc. Public Schools Examination Board, 1939-47; Chm. Third Party Insurance Premium Board, 1941-; Chm. R.A.A.F. Welfare Fund Cttee., 1945-48; Member Board Business Administration, Defence Dept., 1942-46. *Address:* Sunbank, 18 Nutgrove Avenue, Lr. Sandy Bay, Hobart, Tasmania. *T.A.:* Tongkah, Hobart. *T.:* Hobart 9292. *Club:* Tasmanian (Hobart). [*Died* 8 *March* 1958.

FERGUSON, Sir Edward A. J. J.; *see* Johnson-Ferguson.

FERGUSON, Harry George; inventor of Ferguson System of mechanised farming; Chairman: H. F. Holdings Ltd., Harry Ferguson Research Ltd., Coventry, Harry Ferguson (Motors) Ltd., Belfast, etc. (resigned as Chm. of Massey-Harris-Ferguson Ltd., 1954); *b.* Dromore, Co. Down, 4 Nov. 1884; 3rd *s.* of James Ferguson, Dromore; *m.* 1913, Mary Adelaide, *d.* of Adam Watson, Dromore; one *d.* Joint sponsor with late Henry Ford of National Farm Youth Foundation, Dearborn, Michigan. Pioneer in Crusade for a Price Reducing Economy; pioneer in automobile and aeroplane development; designed, built and flew own aeroplane, 1909, being first man to fly heavier-than-air machine in Ireland. Evolved a linkage for attaching implements to a popular make of tractor, 1920; perfected Ferguson system, 1935; partnership with Henry Ford, 1939, until death of latter, 1947. For very many years has been developing revolutionary designs for motor vehicles, involving new chassis principle and advanced automatic transmission. Hon. D.Sc. (Belfast); Hon. M.A.I. (Dublin); Hon. D.Sc. (Louvain); A.F.R.Ae.S.; F.R.S.A. *Recreations:* motor racing and reading. *Address:* Abbotswood, Stow-on-the-Wold, Gloucestershire. *T.:* Stow-on-the-Wold 366. *Clubs:* Royal Automobile, British Racing Drivers. [*Died* 25 *Oct.* 1960.

FERGUSON, Herbert, C.B.E. 1924; *b.* 23 Jan. 1874; 2nd *s.* of late R. C. Ferguson, Ferndale, Perth; *m.* 1st, 1899, Lizzie Sanderson (*d.* 1936), *d.* of late R. A. Hay, J.P., Perth; two *s.* (and one *s.* decd.); 2nd, 1937, Mrs. Ellinor Branks Bell, *d.* of late Andrew Wilson, J.P., Provost of Motherwell, Lanarkshire. *Educ.:* Perth; Stewart Thomson's Prep., Aberdeen. Entered Imperial Inland Revenue Department, 1894; Treasurer, Grenada, and Member, *ex officio*, of Executive and Legislative Councils, 1909; Colonial Secretary, Grenada, 1915; Delegate representing Windward Islands at Canada-West Indies Trade Conference at Ottawa, 1920; administered the Government of Grenada on numerous occasions; acting Governor of the Windward Isles, 1926, 1928, and 1929; retired, 1930. *Recreation:* golf (Hon. life member, Nairn Golf Club). *Address:* 11 Elliot Place, Colinton Road, Edinburgh. *T.:* 88215. *Club:* Scottish Conservative (Edinburgh). [*Died* 12 *Sept.* 1953.

FERGUSON, Joshua, M.A., M.B., C.M., F.R.F.P.S.; Member of Council, St. Leonards and St. Katharines Schools, St. Andrews; late Medical Referee for Renfrewshire under Workmen's Compensation Act; President Royal Medico-Chirurgical Society of Glasgow, 1928-30; late Medical Referee to the Ministry of Pensions; *b.* Dalkeith, Midlothian, 1870; *e. s.* of late Rev. Fergus Ferguson, D.D., Queen's Park, Glasgow; *m.* 1900, Mary, *d.* of late Rev. R. S. Horne, Minister of Slamannan. *Educ.:* High School and University of Glasgow. Prosector in Anatomy, 1892-94; graduated with Honours, 1895; Brunton Memorial Prize, awarded to most distinguished medical graduate of year; Pres. of Glasgow University Union, 1893-95; Resident Clinical Clerk, Royal Asylum, Gartnavel; Senior Resident Assistant, Western Infirmary, Glasgow; Pathologist and Assistant Physician, Royal Alexandra Infirmary, Paisley, 1898; Visiting Physician, 1900-35; President of Paisley Philosophical Institution, 1911-14; Convener of the Coats Observatory; President of the Scottish Photographic Salon, 1913. *Publications:* articles in medical journals. *Address:* 11 Windmill Road, St. Andrews, Fife. *T.:* St. Andrews 873. *Club:* Royal and Ancient (St. Andrews). [*Died* 29 *Dec.* 1951.

FERGUSON, Rachel; *b.* Hampton Wick, 18 Oct. 1893; *yr. d.* of late Robert Norman Ronald Ferguson, Treasury Official, and late Rose Geraldine Cumberbatch; *g.d.* of Doctor Robert Ferguson, Physician Extraordinary to Queen Victoria. *Educ.:* Italy and London. Co-founder of Juvenile branch of W.S.P.U., 1910; first playlet produced and published for W.S.P.U., 1910; took secretarial training at Kensington College, 1910; studied at Academy of Dramatic Art, 1911-13; awarded certificate of honour, 1913; was three years on the stage; entered journalism, 1919; co-dramatic critic of Sunday Chronicle under pen-name Columbine, 1919-20; specialised in parodies; one-act play, The Pridington Touch, produced at all-star matinée at Chelsea Palace before Queen Mary in 1923; first wrote for Punch (Rachel), 1925. President Kensington Kitten and neuter Cat Club; Member Council Kensington Society. *Publications:* False Goddesses (novel), 1923; Sara Skelton: the Autobiography of a famous Actress (parody), 1929; The Brontës went to Woolworth's (novel), 1931; Victorian Bouquet (Memoirs), 1931; Popularity's Wife (novel), 1932; The Stag at Bay (novel), 1932; Nymphs and Satires (parodies), 1932; Charlotte Brontë (play in 3 acts), 1933; A Child in the Theatre (novel), 1933; Celebrated Sequels (Parodies), 1933; A Harp in Lowndes Square (novel), 1936; Alas, Poor Lady (novel), 1937; Passionate Kensington (Memoirs), 1939; A Footman for the Peacock (Novel), 1940; Evenfield (novel), 1942; The Late Widow Twankey (Fantasy), 1943; Memoirs of a Fir-tree (Fantasy), 1946; A Stroll before Sunset (Novel), 1946; Kindness or the Goad of Fear? (pamphlet, published by Performing Animals Defence League), 1924; ed. Autobiography of Edouard Espinosa (And Then he Danced), 1947; Royal Borough (Memoirs), 1950; Sea Front (novel), 1954; We Were Amused (Autobiography), 1958. *Recreations:* drawing caricatures, playing piano, listening to cases in the Law Courts, driving into the country. *Address:* 2 Phillimore Terrace, Kensington, W.8. *T.:* Western 6230. [*Died* 26 *Nov.* 1957.

FERGUSSON, Col. Arthur Charles, C.M.G. 1918; D.S.O. 1917; *b.* 2 July 1871; *s.* of late F. J. Fergusson, Calcutta; *m.* 1907, Madeleine, *d.* of W. A. C. Strettell of Mobberley, Surbiton; one *s.* one *d.* *Educ.:* Haileybury; R.M.A., Woolwich. Royal Artillery, 1891-1922; served Tirah Expeditionary Force, 1897-98 (medal and 2 clasps); N.W. Frontier of India, 1902; European War, 1914-18 (despatches seven times, D.S.O., C.M.G., Order of St. Anne of Russia); 3rd Afghan War, 1919 (medal). *Recreations:* usual sports and games. *Address:* c/o Westminster Bank, 46 Terminus Rd., Eastbourne, Sussex. [*Died* 18 *July* 1958.

FERGUSSON, General Sir Charles, 7th Bt. of Kilkerran, *cr.* 1703; G.C.B., *cr.* 1932

(K.C.B., *cr.* 1915; C.B. 1911); G.C.M.G., *cr.* 1924 (K.C.M.G., *cr.* 1918); M.V.O. 1906; D.S.O. 1898; D.L., J.P., LL.D. Glasgow University, 1924; *b.* Edinburgh, 17 Jan. 1865; *e. s.* of 6th Bt. and Edith (*d.* 1871), *d.* of Marquis of Dalhousie (extinct); *S.* father, 1907; *m.* 1901, Lady Alice Mary Boyle, 2nd *d.* of 7th Earl of Glasgow; three *s.* one *d.* *Educ.:* Sandhurst. Joined Grenadier Guards, 1883; Battalion Adjutant, 1890-94; joined Egyptian Army, 1895; present with 10th Soudanese Batt. throughout campaigns of 1896-97-98, severely wounded Rosaires (medal with eight clasps, brevet of Major, D.S.O., and brevets of Lieut.-Col. and Col., despatches five times); commanded 15th Soudanese, 1899 (2nd class Mejidie); Garrison and District of Omdurman, 1900; Adjutant - General, Egyptian Army, 1901-03; commanded 3rd Battalion Grenadier Guards, 1904-07; Brig.-General, General Staff, Irish Command, 1907-08; Inspector of Infantry, 1909-13; served European War, 1914-18, in command of 5th Division, and subsequently, of 2nd and 17th Army Corps; military Governor of occupied German territory, 1918-19 (despatches seven times, K.C.B., K.C.M.G.); retired pay, 1922; Governor-General and Commander-in-Chief of the Dominion of New Zealand, 1924-30; Chairman West Indies Closer Union Commission, 1932. Lord Lieutenant of Ayrshire, 1937-50; is President Ayr T.F. Association. *Heir:* *s.* James [*b.* 18 Sept. 1904; *m.* 1930, Louise Frances Balfour Stratford, *d.* of Edgar Dugdale; two *s.* two *d.*]. *Address:* Ladyburn, Maybole, Ayrshire.
[*Died* 20 *Feb.* 1951.

FERGUSSON, Sir Thomas C.; *see* Colyer-Fergusson.

FERMI, Professor Enrico; Professor of Physics, Institute for Nuclear Studies University of Chicago, since 1946; *b.* Rome, Italy, 29 Sept. 1901; *s.* of Alberto and Ida de Gattis Fermi; *m.* 1928, Laura Capon; one *s.* one *d.* *Educ.:* University of Pisa; Doctor's degree, 1922. Professor of Theoretical Physics, University of Rome, Italy, 1926-38; Professor of Physics, Columbia University, New York, 1939-42; Physicist, Manhattan Project, Chicago and Los Alamos, 1942-45. Nobel Prize for Physics, 1938. *Publications:* Introduzione alla Fisica Atomica, 1928; Molecole e Cristalli, 1934; Thermodynamics, 1937; Elementary Particles, 1951; articles in Physical Review. *Address:* 5327 University Avenue, Chicago, Illinois, U.S.A. *T.:* Plaza 2-6651.
[*Died* 28 *Nov.* 1954.

FERMOR, Sir Lewis Leigh, Kt., *cr.* 1935; O.B.E. 1919; F.R.S. 1934; D.Sc. (London); A.R.S.M. (Metallurgy); F.G.S.; M.Inst.M.M.; F.A.S.B.; *b.* 18 Sept. 1880; *s.* of Lewis Fermor; *m.* 1st, 1909, Muriel Aileen, *d.* of late Charles Taaffe Ambler, Dharbara, India; one *s.* one *d.*; 2nd, 1933, Frances Mary, *d.* of late Edward Robert Case, Fiddington, Somerset. *Educ.:* Wilson's Grammar School, Camberwell; National Scholar, 1898; Royal College of Science and Royal School of Mines; Murchison Medal and Prize, 1900; Assoc. Roy. School of Mines, 1901. Joined Geological Survey of India, 1902; Supt., 1910; Officiating Director, 1921, 1925, 1928 and 1930-32; Director, 1932-35. Rep. Govt. of India at Internat. Geological Congresses in Sweden, 1910, Canada, 1913, Spain, 1926, and South Africa, 1929; Minerals Adviser to Indian Munitions Board, 1917 and 1918; Pres. Governing Body, Indian School of Mines, 1930-35; Hon. Treas. and Ed. of Transactions, 1916, 1924-25, 1928 and 1930-35, Vice-Pres. 1918; Pres. Mining and Geological Institute of India, 1922; Pres. Geological Section, Indian Science Congress, Bombay, 1919; Pres. Indian Science Congress Assoc., Patna, 1933; Bigsby Medal, Geological Soc. of London, 1921; Vice-Pres., 1931-33 and Pres., 1933-36 Asiatic Soc. of Bengal; Pres. National Institute of Sciences of India, 1935 and 1936; Pres. Bristol Naturalists' Soc., 1945-47; Pres. South-Western Naturalists' Union, 1948, 1949; Vice-Pres. Himalayan Club, 1931 and 1932; Vice-Pres. Soc. of Economic Geologists, 1932; Asst. Editor, Economic Geology, 1923-37; Trustee Indian Museum, 1930-35; Member Governing Body, Government School of Art, Calcutta, 1930-36; and of Indian Research Fund Assoc., Delhi, 1933-1936; P. N. Bose Memorial Medal of Royal Asiatic Society of Bengal, 1944; Hon. Member, Mining, Geological and Metallurgical Institute of India, 1938, and Malayan Chamber of Mines, 1943; Hon. Fellow, Indian Association for the Cultivation of Science, 1943. R.S.A. 1948; Pres., Instn. of Mining and Metallurgy, 1951. *Publications:* numerous papers on geology, petrology, mineralogy, meteorites, ore-deposits and mineral statistics in the publications of the Geological Survey of India and other Journals; Manganese-ore Deposits of India, 1909; Garnets and their Role in Nature, 1938; Report upon the Mining Industry of Malaya, 1939. *Address:* c/o Lloyd's Bank, 6 Pall Mall, S.W.1.; Gondwana, Horsell Park, Horsell, Surrey. *Clubs:* East India and Sports; Bengal United Service (Calcutta).
[*Died* 24 *May* 1954.

FERMOR, Una Mary; *see* Ellis-Fermor.

FERMOY, 4th Baron (*cr.* 1856), **Edmund Maurice Roche**; B.A., Harvard Univ.; Flying Officer (R.A.F.V.R., resigned); *b.* 15 May 1885; *s.* of 3rd Baron and Frances (*d.* 1947), *d.* of F. Work, New York; *S.* father, 1920; *m.* 1931, Ruth Sylvia, O.B.E., 1952, *y. d.* of W. S. Gill, *q.v.*; one *s.* two *d.* M.P. (C.) King's Lynn, 1924-35 and 1943-45; Mayor of King's Lynn, 1931-32. *Heir:* *s.* Hon. Edmund James Burke Roche, *b.* 20 March 1939. *Address:* Park House, Sandringham. [*Died* 8 *July* 1955.

FERNANDO, Sir Ernest (Peter Arnold), Kt., *cr.* 1955; C.B.E. 1954; Governing Director, Bogala Graphite Ltd., Colombo, Ceylon; *b.* 7 Feb. 1904; *s.* of M. A. Fernando and Angela Fernando; *m.* 1927, Gymara Wickremasooriya; no *c.* *Educ.:* St. Joseph's College and Ananda College, Colombo, Ceylon. Director: Bank of Ceylon; Colombo Apothecaries Co. Ltd.; E.P.A. (Bogala) Estates Ltd.; E.P.A. (Bogala) Exports & Imports Ltd.; E.P.A. (Bogala) Motors Ltd. Member Income Tax Board of Review, Ceylon; a Vice-President Arts Council of Ceylon. *Recreations:* golf, billiards and cinematography. *Address:* (home) Udayasiri, 232/3 Havelock Road, Colombo 5. *T.:* 8665; (office) P.O. Box 406, Colombo, Ceylon. *T.:* 91605 and 91606. *Clubs:* Empire Air League, Ceylon Golfing Society (U.K.); Havelock Golf, Royal Colombo Golf, Nuwera Eliya Golf, (Vice-Pres.) Sinhalese Sports, Ceylon Turf (Ceylon), (Founder) Carlton (Moratuwa, Ceylon). [*Died* 3 *Dec.* 1956.

FERRERS, 12th Earl (Gt. Brit.), *cr.* 1711; **Robert Walter Shirley,** Viscount Tamworth, 1711; Bt. 1611; *b.* 7 July 1894; *er. s.* of 11th Earl and Jane (*d.* 1944), *y. d.* of late Robert Moon, 10 Princes Gardens, S.W.; *S.* father 1937; *m.* 1922, Hermione Justice; *e. d.* of late A. Noel Morley of Lychwood, Worplesdon; one *s.* two *d.* *Educ.:* Winchester; New College, Oxford. *Heir:* *s.* Viscount Tamworth. *Address:* Staunton Harold, Ashby-de-la-Zouch. *T.:* Ashby 85.
[*Died* 11 *Oct.* 1954.

FERRIER, Kathleen, C.B.E. 1953; Singer; *b.* 22 April 1912; *d.* of Wm. Ferrier, Headmaster, and Alice Murray Ferrier. *Educ.:* Blackburn, Lancs, High School. Telephone operator, Blackburn Post Office. Pianist and accompanist, 1927-1936; first singing lesson, 1940. C.E.M.A. concerts in factories and towns during War of 1939-45; first London engagement, The Messiah, Westminster Abbey, 1943; Choral Society engagements, 1943-46; début in Opera,

Glyndebourne, title rôle of Benjamin Britten's The Rape of Lucretia, 1946; first appearance on Continent, Amsterdam, 1946; Orfeo by Gluck, Glyndebourne, 1947; Das Lied von der Erde, conducted by Bruno Walter, at first Edinburgh Festival, 1947, and repeated in America, 1948. Has toured in Europe, Cuba, Canada and America, including appearances in Carnegie Hall, New York; La Scala, Milan; and international festivals at Salzburg, Zürich, Vienna and Amsterdam, and has performed at every Edinburgh Festival. Pupil of Dr. J. E. Hutchinson, 1940-42, of Roy Henderson, 1943-50. Gold Medal Royal Philharmonic Soc., 1953. *Recreations:* golf, painting, reading. *Address:* 40 Hamilton Terrace, St. John's Wood, N.W.8. *Club:* Allies.
[*Died* 8 *Oct.* 1953.

FETHERSTONHAUGH, Lt.-Col. Edward Phillips; Professor of Electrical Engineering, University of Manitoba, 1909-49; Dean of the Faculty of Engineering, 1921-49 (now retired); *b.* Montreal, 20 July 1879; *s.* of Edward C. B. Fetherstonhaugh and Janet Cross Phillips; *m.* 1924, Margaret Adele Bain. *Educ.:* McGill Univ., Montreal. B.Sc. in Electrical Engineering, McGill University, 1899; draughtsman, 1899-1900; Manager, Fetherstonhaugh and Co., Patent Solicitors, Ottawa Branch, 1900-4; Lecturer in Electrical Engineering, McGill University, 1905-7; summer of 1906, Testing Dept., Westinghouse Electric and Manufacturing Co., Pittsburg; Engineer, Winnipeg Office, Canadian Westinghouse Co., 1907-9; with Canadian Engineers, 1915-19; in France, Jan. 1916-Feb. 1919 (M.C., rank—Major); Member National Research Council of Canada, 1937-46; Life member: American Institute of Electrical Engineers; Engineering Institute of Canada (Chairman Winnipeg Branch 1921); President Engineering Institute of Canada, 1945. Hon. D.Sc. (McGill), 1945; Hon. LL.D. (Manitoba), 1947. *Address:* 801 Dorchester Avenue, Winnipeg. *Club:* St. Charles Country (Winnipeg).
[*Died* 19 *Oct.* 1959.

FEUCHTWANGER, Dr. Lion; *b.* Munich, 1884; *m.* 1912, Martha Löffler, Munich. *Educ.:* Munich University; Berlin. *Publications:* Jew Süss; Warren Hastings; Vasantasena; The Prisoners of War; Thomas Wendt; The Ugly Duchess; The Oil Islands; Success; Josephus: a Historical Romance, 1932; The Oppermanns, 1933; The Jew of Rome, 1935; The False Nero, 1937; Paris Gazette (novel), 1939; The Devil in France, 1941; The Day Will Come, 1942; Double, Double Toil and Trouble (novel, published in London as The Lautensack Brothers), 1943; Simone (novel), 1944; Proud Destiny (novel), 1947; Odysseus and the Swine (short stories), 1949; This is the Hour (novel about Goya), 1951; 'Tis Folly to be Wise (or Death and Transfiguration of Jean-Jacques Rousseau) (novel), 1953; Raquel the Jewess of Toledo (novel), 1955; Jephthah and His Daughter (novel), 1957. *Address:* P.O. Box 325, Pacific Palisades, California, U.S.A.
[*Died* 21 *Dec.* 1958.

FFINCH, Captain Matthew Benjamin Dipnall, C.B.E. 1918; *s.* of late Matthew S. Ffinch, The Old House, Deptford, Kent; *m.* Crystal, 3rd *d.* of Sir Claude Champion de Crespigny, 4th Bart.; no *c.* *Educ.:* Haileybury College; R.M.C., Sandhurst. Lieut. in the Prince of Wales' North Staffordshire Regt., 1886; Capt. and Adjt. N. Stafford Regt., 1895; badly injured in Somaliland, and invalided out of Army; Assistant Chief Constable of Essex for term of European War. *Recreations:* shooting, cricket. *Address:* 85 Campden Hill Court, Kensington, W.8.
[*Died* 14 *Feb.* 1951.

FFOLKES, Capt. Sir (Edward John) Patrick (Boschetti), 6th Bt., *cr.* 1774; late Indian Army, 1918-22; late Lieut. Suffolk and Norfolk Yeomanry, R.A. (T.); *b.* 16 Jan. 1899; *s.* of Sir Francis ffolkes, 5th Bt., M.V.O.; *S.* father 1938; *m.* 1939, Geraldine, *d.* of late William Roffey; one *s.* one *d.* *Educ.:* Greshams School; R.M.C., Sandhurst. Served War of 1939-45, with East African Forces. *Heir:* *s.* Robert Francis Alexander, *b.* 2 Dec. 1943. *Address:* Uphall, Hillington, King's Lynn, Norfolk.
[*Died* 27 *March* 1960.

FFORDE, Sir Cecil Robert, Kt., *cr.* 1930; Judge President of Special Courts of Bechuanaland and Swaziland, Judicial Commissioner of Basutoland and Legal Adviser to High Commissioner for South Africa since 1934; High Commissioner for above Territories, Dec. 1935 and from May to Oct. 1936; represented the Territories at Coronation 1937; 2nd *s.* of Arthur Brownlow Fforde, formerly of Co. Down, N. Ireland; *m.* Mary Constance, 4th *d.* of late Edward Chetham-Strode, of Southill House, Cranmore, Somerset. Joined King's Inns as student; called to Irish Bar; joined Leinster Circuit; Crown Counsel in Ireland, 1912-21; sometime member of Council of the Bar of Ireland and of the Standing Committee; K.C., 1919; Counsel to the Attorney-General, 1919; Senior Counsel to the Crown, 1920; left Ireland, Dec. 1920; member of Gray's Inn; called to English Bar, 1922; Judge of the High Court of the Punjab, 1922-31. *Address:* Clover, Headley, near Bordon, Hants.
[*Died* 20 *Oct.* 1951.

FFRENCH, 6th Baron (*cr.* 1798), **Charles Austin Thomas Robert John Joseph ffrench,** Bt. 1779; *b.* 20 June 1868; *S.* father, 1893; *m.* 1st, 1892, Mary Margaret (*d.* 1944), *d.* of Matthew James Corbally, D.L., Rathbeale Hall, Co. Dublin; 2nd, 1951, Kathleen Elizabeth, *y. d.* of late Rt. Hon. Sir Christopher Nixon, Bt. *Educ.:* Clongowes Wood College; Trinity College, Dublin. *Heir:* *n.* Peter Martin Joseph Charles John Mary ffrench, *b.* 2 May 1926. *Address:* Castle ffrench, Ballinamore Bridge, County Galway, Ireland. *Club:* Stephen's Green (Dublin).
[*Died* 4 *March* 1955.

FFRENCH-MULLEN, Lt.-Col. John Lawrence William, C.S.I. 1920; C.I.E. 1912; late 18th Duke of Connaught's Lancers (Watson's Horse), I.A.; *b.* 1868; *e. s.* of Col. T. Ffrench-Mullen, I.M.S., of Tuam, Co. Galway; *m.* Madeleine (*d.* 1947), *y. d.* of Christopher Healy; no *c.* *Educ.:* The Oratory School, Edgbaston; R.M.C., Sandhurst. Joined 7th Dragoon Guards, 1887; 2nd Bengal Lancers, 1889; 18th Duke of Connaught's Lancers, 1893; served Kachin Hills, 1893 (wounded, medal and clasp); commanded Military Police Escort to the Burma China Boundary Commission, 1898-1900; commanded Military Police Column which entered Pienma, N.E. Frontier, 1910; Deputy Inspector General, Military Police, Burma, 1914; in charge British Military Police Operations against Chins and Kukis, 1917-18; Staff Officer to the Kuki Punitive Measures Force, N.E. Frontier, India, 1918-19 (C.S.I.); King's Police Medal, 1920; retired, 1920. *Recreation:* golf.
[*Died* 26 *Oct.* 1951.

FIELD, Bradda; Author; *b.* Nanaimo-British Columbia; unmarried; *d.* of late W. G. H. Y. Field, adventurer, and Agnes Herbert, *q.v.*; named after headland owned by grandfather in Isle of Man; brought up in Lancashire home of maternal grandparents; uneducated, but learnt to read and write before falling a victim to successive Lancashire governesses. *Publications:* The Earthen Lot, 1928; Small Town, 1931, (awarded Femina Vie Heureuse prize, 1932-33); Grand Harbour, 1934; Miledi, 1942, published in America as Bride of Glory (Literary Guild choice). *Recreation:* change of work. *Address:* Westminster Bank, Ltd., 26 Haymarket, S.W.1. *T.:* Laburnum 1614.
[*Died* 4 *Feb.* 1957.

FIELD, Lt.-Col. Sir Donald Moyle, Kt., *cr.* 1937; C.I.E. 1935; *b.* 19 Nov. 1881; *s.* of George Moyle Robert Field and Katharine Davies; *m.* 1st, 1910, Gertrude Muriel Hay (marriage dissolved, 1938; she died, 1952); no *c.*; 2nd, 1938, Muriel Wilhelmina Carmen, *d.* of Elena, Lady Forster and late Horace Parodi; one *s.* *Educ.:* Tonbridge School; Sandhurst. Indian Army, 1900-7; Foreign and Political Dept. Govt. of India, 1907. Chief Minister, Jodhpur State, India, 1935-46. *Recreations:* tennis, golf, shooting, riding. *Address:* c/o Lloyds Bank, 6 Pall Mall, S.W.1. *Club:* Army and Navy. [*Died* 11 *Nov.* 1956.

FIELD, Frederick William, C.M.G. 1933; *b.* 4 April 1884; *s.* of Frederick Field and Amelia Parsons; *m.* 2nd, 1931, Maud Alice Whipps (*née* Webb); four *c.* *Educ.:* Tiffin's School, Kingston-on-Thames. Assistant Editor and Editor, The Monetary Times, Toronto, 1906-17; Imperial Trade Correspondent to Commercial Intelligence Branch of Board of Trade, 1908-17; H.M. Trade Commissioner at Toronto, 1918-24; H.M. Senior Trade Commissioner in Canada, 1924-38. *Publications:* Capital Investments in Canada; Resources and Trade Prospects of Northern Ontario. Periodical reports on economic conditions in Canada. *Address:* 29 Russell Green Close, Purley, Surrey. [*Died* 8 *Sept.* 1960.

FIELD, Guy Cromwell, M.A., D.Litt., F.B.A.; Emeritus Professor, and Hon. Fellow, University of Bristol, since 1952; *b.* 15 Jan. 1887; *e. s.* of Henry Cromwell Field and Ruth, *d.* of Rt. Hon. Jesse Collings, M.P.; *m.* 1919, Doris, *e. d.* of Col. F. St. D. Skinner. *Educ.:* Marlborough; Balliol Coll., Oxford. Lecturer, Balliol College, 1910; Assistant Lecturer in Philosophy, University of Birmingham, 1911; Lecturer in Ethics and Politics, University of Manchester, 1912; military service in England and France, prisoner of war in Germany, Intelligence Department, War Office, 1914-19; Lecturer in Philosophy, University of Liverpool, 1919; Dean of Faculty of Arts, 1923-26; Associate Prof., 1925; Professor of Philosophy, Univ. of Bristol, 1926-52; Dean of Faculty of Arts, 1929-33; Pro-Vice-Chancellor, 1944-45 and 1947-52. Member of South-Western Conscientious Objectors Tribunal, 1940-44. *Publications:* Guild Socialism, 1920; Moral Theory, 1921; Plato and His Contemporaries, 1930; Prejudice and Impartiality, 1932; Studies in Philosophy, 1935; Pacifism and Conscientious Objection, 1945; The Philosophy of Plato, 1949; Political Theory, 1955; articles in philosophical journals. *Recreations:* gardening, motor touring. *Address:* 2 Sion Hill, Clifton, Bristol. *T.:* Bristol 33488. *Club:* Athenæum. [*Died* 28 *April* 1955.

FIELD, Marshall; President and Director of Field Enterprises Inc. (which publishes Chicago Sun-Times, World Book Encyc., and Childcraft); Director Parade Publications Inc.; Simon & Schuster Inc. and Pocket Books Inc.; Pres. and Dir., Field Foundation Inc.; Dir. American Houses Inc.; *b.* 28 Sept. 1893; *s.* of Marshall Field II and Albertine Huck; *m.* 1936, Ruth Pruyn; two *d.* One *s.* two *d.* by a previous marriage. *Educ.:* Eton; Cambridge. Pte. 1st Illinois Cavalry, 1917, afterwards 122nd F.A., 33rd Div.; promoted through grades to Capt., arrived in France, March 1918; participated in St. Mihiel and Meuse-Argonne operations; hon. discharged, 1919. Democrat. *Address:* 250 Park Avenue, New York, U.S.A. *T.:* Yukon 6-6318. *Clubs:* Buck's; Knickerbocker, Racquet and Tennis, Brook, Links, Piping Rock, Turf and Field, Creek (New York); Chicago, University (Chicago). [*Died* 8 *Nov.* 1956.

FIELDING, Marjorie; Actress; *b.* 17 Feb. 1892; *d.* of John and Pauline Fielding. *Educ.:* Cheltenham Ladies' College. Toudre in His House in Order and Passers-By, 1913-1915; various short engagements, 1920-24; Bristol's Little Theatre (repertory), 1924-26; Liverpool Repertory, 1926-33; The Shining Hour, New York and London, 1934; Quiet Wedding, 1938; Quiet Weekend, 1941-45; The Chiltern Hundreds, 1947-49; The River Line, Edinburgh Festival, 1952; Aren't We All?, 1953; Small Hotel, 1955; Tabitha, 1956. *Films:* Quiet Wedding, 1940; Demi-Paradise, Yellow Canary, 1942; Quiet Weekend, 1945; Fame is the Spur, 1946; Chiltern Hundreds, 1949; Portrait of Clare, Sanatorium, The Franchise Affair, 1949-1950; The Lavender Hill Mob, 1951; Rob Roy, 1953; Laughing in the Sunshine, 1954. *Address:* 803 Nelson House, Dolphin Square, S.W.1. *T.:* Victoria 3800, ext. Nelson 803. [*Died* 28 *Dec.* 1956.

FIELDING-OULD, Robert, M.A.; M.D. (Oxon); M.R.C.P. (London); Consulting Physician, Mount Vernon Hospital for Diseases of the Chest; Consulting Physician to Ministry of Pensions; Vice-Pres. National Medical Union; Memb. of Council London Psychical Laboratory; *b.* Feb. 1872; *s.* of late Rev. F. Fielding-Ould, M.A., and *d.* of Henry Neuman, J.P., Wincham Hall, Northwich; *m.* 1905, Jane (*d.* 1941), *d.* of William E. Constable, Elm Lodge, Dulwich Hamlet; one *d.* *Educ.:* Canterbury; Keble College, Oxford; London Hospital Medical School. Travelled extensively in West Africa, 1900-2, India, Burmah, and Japan, on Medical Research Missions, chiefly in regard to malaria and leprosy; Lecturer in Liverpool School of Tropical Medicine, 1902; Physician to Out-patients, Victoria Park Hospital for Diseases of Chest; Captain King's Liverpool Regiment, 1902; Captain R.A.M.C. attached 1st Life Guards, 1915, and subsequently in Macedonia during the War; Barrister-at-law, Inner Temple. *Publications:* numerous papers to medical press. *Address:* 69 St. James's St., S.W.1. *Club:* Carlton. [*Died* 18 *Jan.* 1951.

FIENBURGH, Wilfred, M.B.E. 1945; J.P.; M.P. (Lab.) North Islington since 1951; *b.* Ilford, Essex, 4 Nov. 1919; *s.* of Harry Fienburgh, Bradford, Yorks; *m.* 1940, Joan Valerie Hudson, *d.* of Capt. T. McDowell, Belfast; two *s.* two *d.* *Educ.:* elementary and secondary schools, Bradford. Manual worker, office boy and unemployed, 1935-39; served War of 1939-45, Rifleman, Rifle Brigade, 1940; commissioned, 1940; demobilised as Major (General Staff), 1946 (now serving as Major, T.A.). Assistant Secretary, Civil Service Clerical Association, 1946-47; Labour Party Research Dept., 1947-51. Secretary Labour Party Policy Cttee.; Member Economic Sub-Cttee. of General Council of T.U.C., 1950-51. *Publications:* Steel is Power, 1948; International Control of Basic Industries, 1950; 25 Momentous Years, 1955; No Love for Johnnie (novel, posthumous), 1958. *Recreations:* gardening, swimming. *Address:* Little Coxpond Farmhouse, Leverstock Green Road, Hemel Hempstead, Herts. *T.:* Boxmoor 4286. [*Died* 3 *Feb.* 1958.

FIFE, The Duchess of; (H.R.H. Princess Alexandra Victoria Alberta Edwina Louise; Princess Arthur of Connaught), R.R.C., S.R.N.; Dukedom (U.K.) *cr.* 1900; also Countess of Macduff; *b.* 17 May 1891; *d.* of 1st Duke and the late Princess Royal (H.R.H. Princess Louise), *e. d.* of King Edward VII; *S.* father 1912; *m.* 1913, H.R.H. Prince Arthur of Connaught, K.G., P.C., K.T., G.C.M.G., G.C.V.O. (*d.* 1938); (one *s.*, Alastair Arthur, Earl of Macduff, who succeeded his grandfather as 2nd Duke of Connaught and Strathearn, 1942, and died on active service, 1943). Trained: St. Mary's Hospital, Paddington; Queen Charlotte's Hospital and Samaritan Hospital for Women. Nursing Duties, 15 years, University College Hospital. Sister i/c Casualty Clearing Station, outbreak of War of 1939-45; Matron of Fife Nursing Home, 1939-49. Colonel-in-Chief, R.A.P.C., 1939. A Councillor of State during the King's absences abroad, 1939, 1943 and 1944. G.C.St.J. *Heir:* *nephew* Lord Carnegie. *Recreations:* shooting, golf, gros point needlework. *Address:* 64 Avenue Road,

N.W.8; Mar Lodge, Braemar, Aberdeenshire. [*Died* 26 *Feb.* 1959.

FIGGINS, James Hugh Blair; *b.* 8 March 1893; *m.* 1916, Mrs. A. Clark; no *c.* *Educ.:* Public Schools, Largs and Dalry, Ayrshire. N.U.R.: Annual Gen. Meeting Delegate, 1924; Executive Member, 1931-33; District Organiser, 1938; Assistant to General Secretary, 1943; General Secretary, National Union of Railwaymen, 1948-53. *Recreation:* golf. *Address:* 37 Harefield Avenue, Cheam, Surrey. *T.:* Vigilant 6183. [*Died* 27 *Dec.* 1956.

FINCH, Charles Hugh, J.P.; *b.* 1866; *s.* of Peter Finch, J.P., Hurst Grove, Berkshire and Eliza Fetherstonhaugh; *m.* 1900, Mildred Bertha, *d.* of Walter Long, Preshaw, Hants; one *s.* *Educ.:* Hawtrey's, Windsor; Shrewsbury School. High Sheriff of Norfolk, 1935; Sheriff of Norwich, 1919; Norwich Town Council, 1905-32; Alderman, 1921-32; Director of Steward and Pattesons Ltd., The Brewery, Norwich. *Address:* Costessey House, near Norwich. *T.:* Costessey 12. *Clubs:* Constitutional; Norfolk County (Norwich). [*Died* 18 *March* 1954.

FINCH, Sir Ernest (Frederick), Kt., *cr.* 1951; M.D., M.S. (London); F.R.C.S. (Eng.); Consultant Surgeon, Royal Infirmary Sheffield; Hon. Lecturer, History of Medicine, University of Sheffield (late Professor of Surgery); Vice-President, R.C.S. (Eng.); Major R.A.M.C. (T.F.); Member: Association of Surgeons of Great Britain (Pres., 1939-42); Sheffield Medico-Chirurgical Society (President 1931); F.R.Soc. Med. (Pres. of Surgical Section, 1945-47); *b.* 2 Sept. 1884; *s.* of Frederick James Finch; *m.* 1912, Mary Ainsworth; one *s.* *Educ.:* Royal Commercial Travellers' Schools, Hatch End, Mx.; University of Sheffield. Univ. of Sheffield Med. Entrance Schol., 1901; M.B., B.S. (London, Hons. Pathology), 1906; M.D. (Lond.), 1909; M.S. (Lond.), 1913; F.R.C.S. (Eng.), 1911; M.B., Ch.B. (*ad eund.*, Sheffield), 1908; D.Sc. (*Honoris Causa* Sheffield), 1952; Hon. F.R.C.S.I., 1959. Formerly Surgical Registrar, Res. Surgical Officer, Casualty Officer House Surgeon to various depts., 1907-12; Demonstrator of Physiology, Univ. of Sheffield, 1905-07; Prof. of Surgery, 1934-44, Lecturer in Clinical Surgery, Demonstrator in Physiology, Applied Anatomy and Surgical Pathology, Univ. of Sheffield. Member (Sec. 1926-47) and Pres. of Moynihan Surgical Club; Member Sheffield Town Trust, 1946-. Bradshaw Lecturer Vicary Lecturer, Hunterian Orator, R.C.S. 1957. *Publications:* Shock (in Surgery of Modern Warfare), 1940; Lettsomian Lectures, Med. Soc. of Lond., 1947: Contrib. to Lancet, B.M.J., Brit. Jl. of Surgery, Proc. Roy. Soc. Med. *Address:* 344 Glossop Rd., Sheffield, 3. *T.:* 26821; Green Farm, Curbar, via Sheffield. *T.:* Grindleford 363. *Club:* Sheffield (Sheffield). [*Died* 16 *Dec.* 1960.

FINDLAY, Sir Charles Stewart, Kt., *cr.* 1929; I.C.S. M.A., LL.B. (Edin.); *b.* Thurso, 28 Aug. 1874; *s.* of Rev. Charles Stewart Findlay, Thurso; *m.* 1901, Alice (*d.* 1951), *o. d.* of James Brims, Procurator-Fiscal of Caithness; two *s.* one *d.* *Educ.:* Thurso Academy; privately; Aberdeen and Edinburgh Universities; Univ. College, London. Served in Central Provinces since 1898; Divisional and Sessions Judge, 1909; Legal Remembrancer C.P., 1913-19; Judicial Commissioner, C.P., India, 1925-32; retired 1932. Reader in English Law, 1932, and Member of Senatus, Edinburgh Univ., retired 1943. *Recreations:* tennis, golf, fishing. *Clubs:* Caledonian United Service (Edinburgh); Nerbudda (Jubbulpore). [*Died* 22 *July* 1951.

FINDLAY, George William Marshall, C.B.E. 1935; M.D., D.Sc.Edin., F.R.C.P.; Editor, Abstracts of World Medicine and Abstracts of World Surgery, Obstetrics and Gynæcology, B.M.A., London; *b.* 1893; *s.* of George Findlay, M.D., Brailes, Warwickshire; *m.* Margaret, *d.* of Rev. Leonard Williams, Sidmouth, Devon; two *d.* *Educ.:* Dean Close School, Cheltenham; University of Edinburgh. Served European War, 1914-18, Surgeon Lieutenant R.N. (1914 Star, O.B.E., Médaille du roi Albert); Lecturer in Pathology, University of Edinburgh and Assistant Pathologist, Royal Infirmary, Edinburgh, 1920-23; Alice Memorial Fellow and Assistant, Imperial Cancer Research Fund, 1923-28; Member Scientific Staff, Wellcome Research Institution, 1928-46. Brig. and Consulting Physician in Tropical Medicine West African Forces, 1942-46. President, Roy. Microscopical Soc., 1950-51. *Publications:* Recent Advances in Chemotherapy, 3rd edn., 1950; contributions to pathology and bacteriology in English and foreign journals. *Address:* Gillians, Gill's Hill, Radlett, Herts. *Club:* Athenæum. [*Died* 14 *March* 1952.

FINDLAY, Harriet, Lady, D.B.E., *cr.* 1929; **Harriet Jane;** *d.* of Sir Jonathan Backhouse, 1st Bt.; *m.* 1901, Sir John Ritchie Findlay, 1st Bt. (*d.* 1930); three *s.* two *d.* President, Scottish Unionist Association, 1927; late Trustee of National Library of Scotland; J.P. Edin. 1926. *Address:* 13 Moray Place, Edinburgh. [*Died* 24 *July* 1954.

FINDLAY, William; *b.* 22 June 1880; 4th *s.* (2nd *surv. s.*) of late John and Hannah Findlay, Maviscourt, Liverpool; *m.* 1907, Mary Eleanor, *o. d.* of late Richard James Tylden, Milstead Manor, nr. Sittingbourne, Kent. *Educ.:* Eton; Oriel College, Oxford. Eton XI, 1898 and 1899, Captain, 1899; Oxford XI, 1901, 1902, 1903, Captain, 1903; Played for Lancashire 1902-6; Secretary Surrey County Cricket Club, 1907-1919 (except 1915-18, when served in Royal Army Ordnance Corps); Assist. Secretary M.C.C., 1919-26; Secretary M.C.C., 1926-36; Pres. Lancashire County Cricket Club, 1947 and 1948; President, M.C.C., May 1951-Sept. 1952. *Recreation:* cricket. *Address:* Westwell, Tenterden, Kent. *Clubs:* East India and Sports, Lansdowne, Royal Automobile, M.C.C. [*Died* 19 *June* 1953.

FINLAYSON, George Daniel, C.M.G. 1943; B.A.; Superintendent of Insurance, Dominion of Canada, 1914-48, retd.; *b.* Nova Scotia, 31 Dec. 1882; *s.* of Edward Finlayson and Catherine Smith; *m.* 1914, Isabel M., *d.* of A. M. Grant; one *s.* two *d.* *Educ.:* Pictou Academy; Dalhousie Univ. *Address:* 200 Carling Avenue, Ottawa, Canada. [*Died* 12 *April* 1955.

FINLAYSON, Gen. Sir R. G.; *see* Gordon-Finlayson.

FINLOW, Robert Steel, C.I.E.; B. Sc.; F.R.I.C.; *b.* Aug. 1877; *e. s.* of late Robert Finlow of Elton, Sandbach, Cheshire; *m.* 1907, Lucy, *y. d.* of late William O'Meara, Colonial Civil Service; three *s.* *Educ.:* Sandbach School; University College, Bangor. Private assistant to late Sir W. Hartley, F.R.S., and late Sir James Dobbie, F.R.S., 1900; Assistant Chemist Royal Commission on sewage disposal, 1900-3; Indian Agricultural Service, 1904, work on Indigo; Fibre expert to Govt. of Bengal, 1905; Director of Agriculture in Bengal (officiating), 1919; Director of Agriculture in Bengal, 1922-32; retired 1932; Chairman, Bengal Govt. Jute Enquiry Committee, 1933. *Publications:* Extension of Jute Cultivation in India, and various administrative and technical reports on Indian Agriculture. *Address:* Abbeyfields, nr. Sandbach, Cheshire. [*Died* 2 *Jan.* 1953.

FINNY, Maj.-General Charles Morgan, O.B.E. 1928; F.R.C.S.(Eng.); *b.* 9 July 1886; *m.* 1928, Doris Manners Smith; two *d.* *Educ.:* Shrewsbury School; Dublin Univ. Joined R.A.M.C., 1911; Hon. Surgeon to King George VI, 1940-42; retired pay, 1942. *Recreation:* golf. *Address:* Home, King's Ride, Camberley. *T.:* Camberley 529. [*Died* 20 *June* 1955.

FINZI, Gerald, Hon. R.A.M.; *b.* 14 July 1901; *s.* of John and Eliza Emma Finzi; *m.* 1933, Joyce Black; two *s.* *Educ.:* privately. Studied under Sir Edward Bairstow at York, 1918-22; privately with R. O. Morris for a few months, 1925. Professor of Composition at The Royal Academy of Music, 1930-33. *Publications:* orchestral, choral works, chamber music, songs, part-songs, etc. *Address:* Ashmansworth, nr. Newbury, Berks. [*Died* 27 *Sept.* 1956.

FIRTH, Canon John D'Ewes Evelyn, M.A.; Master of the Temple since 1954; *b.* 21 Feb. 1900; *o. s.* of John Benjamin Firth, of the Daily Telegraph, and Helena Gertrude, *d.* of D'Ewes Lynam, Nottingham; *m.* 1939, Josephine Priscilla, *e. d.* of Rt. Rev. E. S. Woods, sometime Bishop of Lichfield. *Educ.:* Winchester College (Scholar); Christ Church, Oxford (Scholar). M.A. Oxon 1928. Assistant Master, Winchester College, 1923-1954; Housemaster, 1939-46; Chaplain, 1931-54. Hon. Canon of Winchester Cathedral, 1952-54; Canon Emeritus, 1955-. Fell. Roy. Philatelic Soc., London. *Publications:* Winchester College, 1949; Rendall of Winchester, 1954. *Address:* The Master's House, Temple, E.C.4. *T.:* Central 9426. *Club:* Brooks's. [*Died* 21 *Sept.* 1957.

FIRTH, Sir William (John), Kt., *cr.* 1932; late Director of Alliance Assurance Company; late President of Royal Metal Trades Benevolent Society; late Vice-Pres. British Iron and Steel Federation; Member of Advisory Committee, Federation of British Industries; late Fuel and Power Controller, North Midland Area; late Chairman and Managing Director of Richard Thomas & Co., Ltd., Steel Sheet and Tinplate Manufacturers, and all their subsidiary Companies; late Chairman of International Tinplate Cartel; and of the Welsh Plate and Sheet Manufacturers' Association; late President Swansea Metal Exchange; late member of International Tin Committee; *b.* 21 July 1881; *s.* of late Richard Firth; *m.* 1909, Helena Adelaide, *e. d.* of late Joseph Garrett; two *s.* Attended Ottawa Conference as the representative of the Welsh sheet and tinplate manufacturers. *Address:* The Chalet, Winston Park, P.O. Box Kloof 163, Natal, South Africa. *Club:* Carlton. [*Died* 11 *Nov.* 1957.

FISCHER, Edwin, Dr.h.c.; pianist; *b.* Basel, 6 Oct. 1886. *Educ.:* Basel. Berlin Stern'sches Conservatorium; teacher at Staatl. Hochschule, Berlin, until 1933. Tournées as pianist through Europe; Conductor at Lübeck and Munich; founder of an orchestra di camera. *Publications:* Schott Söhne: Lieder; Editions of Bach and Mozart Piano Works; Bachbiographie; Transcription of Mozart Works; Reflections on Music. *Recreation:* garden. *Address:* Zürich, Stockerstrasse 54, Switzerland. [*Died* 24 *Jan.* 1960.

FISCHER, Percy Ulrich; retired; *b.* 22 March 1878; *s.* of Abraham Fischer, late Prime Minister, O.F.S., and Ada, *d.* of Dr. Robertson; *m.* 1907, E. Fichardt; four *s.* one *d.* *Educ.:* Grey College, Bloemfontein; S.A. College, Cape Town; Trinity Hall, Cambridge. Called to Bar in London; on return to Bloemfontein practised at Bar, O.F.S. since 1903; a leader of the Bar at Bloemfontein; formerly Judge of Supreme Court of South Africa, Judge-Pres. O.F.S. Provincial Division; has been a Chairman of the Orange Girls' School Committee and a trustee of the Rambler's Club; President of numerous sporting clubs, including the Orange Free State Rugby Football Club. *Recreations:* tennis, farming, gardening. *Address:* 3 Goodale St., Bloemfontein, O.F.S., South Africa. *Club:* Bloemfontein. [*Died* 10 *June* 1957.

FISET, Major-Gen. Hon. Sir Eugene Marie Joseph, Kt., *cr.* 1917; C.M.G. 1913; D.S.O. 1903; V.D.; M.D.; F.R.S.C. (Canada); LL.D.; D.C.L.; Lieutenant-Governor of Province of Quebec, 1939-1950; M.P. County of Rimouski since 1924; *b.* 15 March 1874; *s.* of Hon. J. B. R. Fiset; *m.* 1902, Stella, *d.* of Linière Taschereau; four *d.* *Educ.:* Rimouski Seminary; Laval University, Quebec (B.A., M.D., Hon. LL.D.). Director-General Medical Services, Canada, 1903-6; Surgeon-General, 1915; Deputy Minister of Militia and Defence in Canada, 1906; served in that capacity during European War of 1914-18; retired 1923; Served South Africa with 2nd Bn., Royal Canadian Regt., First Canadian Contingent, 1899-1900 (despatches, D.S.O., Brevet Lt.-Col., medal 4 clasps); K.G.St.J. 1941. Commander of the Legion of Honour, 1917; Commander of the Order of the Crown, Belgium; Order of St. Sava, Serbia; Military Cross of Czecho-Slovakia. A Catholic. *Address:* Spencerwood, Quebec, Canada. [*Died* 8 *June* 1951.

FISHENDEN, Richard Bertie, O.B.E. 1954; M.Sc. (Tech.); C.G.I.A.; Hon. F.R.P.S.; Hon. F.S.I.A.; Print Consultant, Spicers Ltd., since 1943; Editor Penrose Annual since 1935; Technical Editor King Penguin Books since 1942; Hon. Adviser, Min. of Works, since 1953; *b.* 6 Aug. 1880; *s.* of Richard Fishenden; *m.*; one *s.* Works Manager Gee & Watson, Ltd., 1900-02; Lecturer, and later head of Printing, Coll. of Technology, Manchester, 1902-21; London Manager Stephenson Blake & Co., Ltd., 1921-30; Chm. Typography Advisory Committee City and Guilds of London Inst., 1942-. Has acted as occasional Inspector of Printing Schools for Board of Education, as Local Adviser to Indian Govt. scholars and as Secretary of Faculty of Technology, Univ. of Manchester. Took part in forming Manchester Branch of Design and Industries Assoc. (now Vice-Pres.). Research work on printing technology. Member of Council and Chairman Research Cttee., 1955, Printing and Allied Trades Research Assoc.; Member of Technical Committee, British Federation of Master Printers; Liveryman Stationers' Company; Member of Art Workers' Guild. *Publications:* technical and scientific communications; contributions in Times Printing Supplements. *Recreations:* music and books. *Address:* 19 New Bridge Street, E.C.4. *T.:* Fleet Street 4211. *Clubs:* Press, Double Crown (Pres. 1951). [*Died* 7 *Oct.* 1956.

FISHER, 2nd Baron of Kilverstone, *cr.* 1909; **Cecil Vavasseur Fisher;** *b.* 18 July 1868; *o. s.* of 1st Baron Fisher and Frances (*d.* 1918), *d* of Rev. T. Delves Broughton; *m.* 1910, Jane (*d.* 1955), *d.* of Randal Morgan, Philadelphia, U.S.A.; one *s.* three *d.*; *S.* father, 1920. *Educ.:* Charterhouse; Magdalen College, Oxford. Joined the Indian Civil Service, 1890; served in Bengal; retired, 1906. *Recreations:* arboriculture, horticulture, shooting. *Heir:* *s.* Hon. John Fisher, D.S.C., [*b.* 24 July 1921; *m.* 1949, Elizabeth Ann Penelope, *yr. d.* of Herbert P. Holt, M.C.; one *s.* one *d.*] *Address:* Kilverstone Hall, Thetford, Norfolk. *T.:* Thetford 2222. *T.A.:* Kilverstone, Thetford. [*Died* 11 *May* 1955.

FISHER, Rev. Canon Bernard Horatio Parry; *b.* Fulham, 29 April 1875; *e. s.* of the late Rev. Canon F. H. Fisher. *Educ.:* Haileybury; Pembroke College, Cambridge (Scholar); 2nd Class Classical Tripos, 2nd Class Theol. Tripos. Fellow of St. Augustine's College, Canterbury, 1899-1903; S.P.G. Missionary, Cawnpore, 1903-36; Head of S.P.G. Brotherhood, Cawnpore, 1910-36; Canon of Allahabad Cathedral in diocese of Lucknow, 1913-36, Canon Emeritus, 1943; Chairman, United Provinces Christian Council, 1929-31; Tutor, St. Boniface College, Warminster, 1937-41; Acting-Warden, College of The Ascension, Selly Oak, 1942-45; Hon. Fellow, St. Augustine's College, Canterbury, 1938. *Address:* 17 The Abbey, Romsey, Hants. *T.:* Romsey 3142. [*Died* 14 *Feb.* 1953.

FISHER, Dorothea F. C.; *see* Canfield, Dorothy.

FISHER, Francis Marion Bates; *b.* Wellington, 22 Dec. 1877; *s.* of late George Fisher, M.P., F.R.S.S., Consul for Italy in Wellington; *m.* 1947, Sophie Florence Lothrop (*d.* 1952), *d.* of late Algernon Brinsley Sheridan and *widow* of 1st and last Baron Wavertree of Delamere; *m.* 1957, Mireille Boyer, Noumea, New Caledonia. *Educ.:* Wellington Coll., Capt., N.Z. Volunteer Force, 1900; Capt. N.Z. Army, South African War (medal and clasp); M.P. Wellington City, 1905-15; Minister of Trade and Customs, Marine, Pensions, etc., N.Z. 1912-14; elected to Wellington City Council, 1907; Director Imperial Commercial Assoc., London, 1920-25; official visit to West Indies on behalf Imperial Govt., 1924; Director Dunlop Rubber Co. Sports Division, 1925-35; Director Deutsche Dunlop, Germany; represented Canterbury Province New Zealand at Rugby Football and athletics; Chairman, N.Z. L.T.A., 1905; Captain, N.Z. versus Great Britain, 1913; Member first N.Z. Davis Cup Team, 1924; Winner Men's Doubles and Mixed Championships S. Australia, 1910; holder world's covered court championship mixed doubles, 1920-21; winner London championship men's doubles, 1929; winner national doubles, Czecho-Slovakia, 1925; Winner New Zealand doubles 5 times; mixed doubles 4 times; finalist All-England Plate, Wimbledon, 1921; winner national championship, Egypt doubles, 1933; winner of over 50 tournaments in England and abroad since 1918, including many mixed, with Suzanne Lenglen of France. *Address:* Sunset Road, Rotorua, N.Z. *Clubs:* All-England, Royal Automobile; Wentworth (Virginia Water); Coombe Hill (Kingston-on-Thames); Rot-Weiss (Berlin); Cesky (Prague). [*Died* 25 *July* 1960.

FISHER, Mrs. F. M. B.; *see* Wavertree, Lady.

FISHER, Vice-Admiral Frederick Charles; retired; *b.* 16 Dec. 1877; *y. s.* of Richard Fisher, Winterbourne, Newbury, Berks; *m.* 1918, Ella, *d.* of Admiral R. W. Craigie; one *d.* *Educ.:* Stubbington. Entered R.N. 1892; served China Campaign, 1900; Somaliland, 1904; European War, Chief of Staff, China; A.D.C. to the King, Rear-Admiral, 1928; retired, 1928; Vice-Admiral, 1933. *Address:* Oak Bend, Cross-in-Hand, Sussex. [*Died* 23 *Oct.* 1958.

FISHER, Frederick Victor; Editor and Lecturer; *b.* 10 July 1870; *o. s.* of late Dr. Frederick O. S. Fisher and Emma, *d.* of late Samuel Taylor, Cheshunt, Herts; *m.* 1st, Irene San Carolo (*d.* 1942), *d.* of Col. Cecil Le Mesurier, R.A., C.B., D.S.O.; 2nd, 1944, Esther, *e. surv. d.* of late W. Nicholls. *Educ.:* London and Paris. Member Eighty Club, 1898; Colleague with late W. M. Thompson in formation of National Democratic League; Member of Fabian Society, 1899; joined Social Democratic Party, 1908; resigned from British Socialist Party on their pacifist policy, 1914; Founder and Hon. Secretary Socialist National Defence Committee, 1914; Founder and Hon. Secretary British Workers' League, 1915-18; Organised International Socialist Demonstration on behalf of Allies, 1915; Delegate to Allied Socialist Conference, 1916; Founder and first Editor of British Citizen, 1916-18; initiated Nat. Democratic Party as Parliamentary Expression of League, 1918; visited French and Italian fronts; Hon. Dir. of the Society for Study of Religions and Editor of Religions, the Society's official review; Founder and Chm. of the Anglo-French Alliance; contested Stourbridge, 1918; Stratford, 1923; F.R.E S., F.R.Econ S.; Hon. Dir. Empire Workers' Council; Hon. Dir. and Chairman, Friends of France; Chairman, National Organisation of Ratepayers. *Publications:* Paris as It is, 1890; Programme of National and Industrial Reconstruction, 1918; The Shameful Years, 1944; Break up the German Reich, 1944; Britain, France and Security; The Unending Quest; innumerable articles in the periodical press. *Recreations:* reading and arguing. *Address:* 26 Buckland Crescent, N.W.3. *T.:* Primrose 3417. *Club:* Royal Empire Society. [*Died* 30 *Jan.* 1954.

FISHER, Lt.-Col. Julian Lawrence, C.M.G. 1919; D.S.O. 1905; late R. Fusiliers; *b.* 1 May 1877; *s.* of late Walter Fisher, Amington Hall, Tamworth; *m.* 1913, Dora, *y. d.* of late Sir W. Richmond-Brown, 2nd Bt.; one *s.* one *d.* Entered Army, 1897; served Thibet Expedition, 1904 (D.S.O., medal with clasp); European War, 1914-15 (wounded, despatches); retired 1920. *Address:* The Manor House, Kings Sutton, Banbury. *Club:* Army and Navy. [*Died* 1 *May* 1953.

FITCHETT, Rt. Rev. William Alfred Robertson, M.A.; Bishop of Dunedin since 1934; *b.* Christchurch, N.Z., 1872; *s.* of late Very Rev. Alfred Robertson Fitchett, C.M.G.; *m.* 1905, Emily, *d.* of Ratcliffe Taylor, England; three *s.* three *d.* *Educ.:* Otago Boys' High School; Selwyn College, Cambridge. Deacon 1899; priest 1901; priest in charge of St. Thomas, Wellington, N.Z., 1902; Vicar of Dunstan, N.Z., 1902-11; of Roslyn, N.Z. 1911-39; Archdeacon of Dunedin, 1915-34. *Address:* Bishop's House, Roslyn, Dunedin, N.W.1, N.Z. *T.:* 20084. *Club:* University (Dunedin). [*Died* 15 *Aug.* 1952.

FITT, Mary; *see* Freeman, Kathleen.

FITTON, James; Member of Royal Commission on Licensing England and Wales; *b.* Gorton, 28 Aug. 1864; *s.* of Thomas Fitton; *m.* 1887, Janet, *d.* of James Chadwick, Oldham; one *s.* Commenced work at nine years of age in an Oldham Cotton Mill; entered engineering trade at fourteen years of age; J.P., Borough of Oldham, 1909-24; Assistant General Secretary, United Machine Workers Trade Union, 1913-20; National Organiser, Amalgamated Engineering Union, 1920-28; retired on age limit. *Recreation:* gardening. *Address:* 53 Herbert St., Watersheddings, Oldham, Lancs. [*Died* 19 *May* 1952.

FITZE, Sir Kenneth Samuel, K.C.I.E., *cr.* 1941 (C.I.E. 1932); I.C.S. (retired); *b.* 6 Jan. 1887; 2nd *s.* of late Samuel Fitze, Eastbourne; *m.* 1920, Helena, *e. d.* of F. J. Bairsto; one *d.* *Educ.:* Marlborough College; Corpus Christi, Oxford. Entered Indian Civil Service, 1911; employed in the Government of India Political Department, 1915-44, and as an Adviser to Secretary of State for India, 1944-47. *Publication:* Twilight of the Maharajas, 1956. *Address:* 2 Kewhurst Manor, Little Common, Bexhill-on-Sea, Sussex. [*Died* 4 *May* 1960.

FITZGERALD, Major-Gen. Fitzgerald Gabbett, C.B. 1936; D.S.O. 1917; L.R.C.S.I. and L.M., L.R.C.P.I. and L.M.; L.M. Rotunda Hospital, Dublin; late R.A.M.C.; *m.* 1907, Emily, *o. d.* of Lieut.-General Vincent Watson; one *s.* two *d.* *Educ.:* Royal College of Surgeons of Ireland. Served European War, 1914-18; was in Retreat from Mons (despatches five times, Brevet Lt.-Col., Croix de Guerre avec Palme, D.S.O., bar 1918); Assistant Director of Medical Services, India, 1929-32; Deputy Director of Medical Services, Eastern Command, 1933-37; Hon. Surgeon to the King, 1934-37; retired pay, 1937. *Address:* Penharbour, Greystones, Co. Wicklow, Eire. [*Died* 21 *Dec.* 1954.

FITZGERALD, Colonel George Alfred, C.M.G. 1915; D.S.O. 1900; retired pay; *b.* 31 Jan. 1868; *s.* of late Capt. M. G. B. FitzGerald; *m.* 1928, Norah, *widow* of Geoffrey Francis Terry. Entered R.A. 1887; Capt. 1897; Major, 1902; retired, 1908; served South Africa, 1899-1900 (wounded, despatches, Queen's medal 2 clasps, D.S.O.); British Expeditionary Force in France, 1914-18 (despatches, C.M.G.). *Address:*

Hackney Lodge, Melton, Woodbridge, Suffolk. *T.:* Woodbridge 53. *Club:* Cavalry. [*Died* 1 *Sept.* 1959.

FITZGERALD, Major-Gen. Gerald Michael, C.B. 1943; M.C. 1916; *b.* Esquimalt, B.C., 28 Aug. 1889; *s.* of late Inspector-Gen. M. FitzGerald, C.M.G., R.N., Roughan House, Kilnaboy, Co. Clare, Ireland; unmarried. *Educ.:* Cheltenham College; R.M.C., Sandhurst. Attached 1st Bn., South Lancs Regt., 1910; joined 19th Lancers (Fane's Horse), 1911; served with B.E.F. in France, 1914-18, and with Indian I.E.F. in Palestine and Egypt until the Armistice (despatches, M.C.); Brigade Major, 11th Cavalry Bde. and Cairo Cavalry Bde. 1919-1922; Brigade Major, 2nd Cavalry Bde. in India, 1929-31; Commanding 19th K.G.O. Lancers, 1936-38; A.A. and Q.M.G., Eastern Command, India, 1938-39; Commander, Lahore Brigade, 1939-41; Commander Lucknow District, U.P.; retired, 1944. *Recreations:* shooting and fishing. *Clubs:* Naval and Military; County (Cork). [*Died* 5 *Dec.* 1957.

FITZGERALD, Sir John (Peter Gerald Maurice), 3rd Bt., *cr.* 1880; 21st Kt. of Kerry; M.C.; Maj. late R. Horse Guards; *b.* 14 May 1884; 2nd *s.* of 2nd Bt. and Amelia (*d.* 1947), *d.* of late H. L. Bischoffsheim; *S.* father, 1916; *m.* 1919, Lady Mildred Follett, *sis.* of Earl of Dunmore, and *widow* of Brig.-Gen. G. B. S. Follett, D.S.O., M.V.O. *Educ.:* Harrow; R.M.C. Sandhurst. Served European War (M.C.). *Heir: b.* Capt. Arthur H. B. Fitzgerald, *b.* 6 July 1885. *Address:* 32 Upper Brook St., W.1. *T.:* Mayfair 2240. *Club:* Brooks's. [*Died* 19 *Feb.* 1957.

FITZGERALD, Maurice Pembroke, Q.C. 1938; *s.* of Hon. J. D. Fitzgerald, K.C., and Ysolda, *d.* of Sir Thomas Barrett-Lennard, 2nd Bt., of Belhus, Essex; *m.* 1920, Christine, *o. c.* of Maunsell Bradhurst and Evangeline Wood, Rivenhall Place, Essex; four *d. Educ.:* Harrow; Trinity College. Cambridge. Called to Bar, Inner Temple, 1912; served European War, 1914-19, Capt. R.F.A. (wounded, despatches). A Deputy Chairman of Essex Quarter Sessions; Leader of the Parliamentary Bar. Master of Worshipful Company of Skinners, 1941-42 and 1948-49; a Governor of Tonbridge School, and of Felsted School. *Recreations:* shooting, lawn tennis. *Address:* Farrar's Building, Temple, E.C.4; 14 The Boltons, S.W.10; Green Isle, Wargrave Road, Henley-on-Thames; Rivenhall Place, Witham, Essex. *Clubs:* United University, Athenæum, M.C.C. [*Died* 13 *March* 1952.

FITZGERALD, Professor Richard Charles; Professor of English Law in the University of London, at University College, London, since October 1953; Chairman, University of London Board of Studies in Laws, since 1958; *b.* 1 Aug. 1905; *e. s.* of late Richard Aloysius FitzGerald and of Mrs. Hilda Ann FitzGerald. *Educ.:* Birkbeck Coll., and Univ. Coll., London. LL.B. (hons.), 1930; English Law Prize, 1930; Quain Prize in Comparative Law, 1932; Admitted Solicitor of Supreme Court, England, 1937. Lecturer in Constitutional Law, Birkbeck Coll., 1941-45; Brit. Council Lecturer in Constitutional Law to lawyers and senior civil servants of Allied Govts. in London, 1942-44; Reader in English Law, Univ. Coll., London, 1948-53; Dean, Faculty of Laws, University College, London, 1955-57. Chm. Univ. of London Bd. of Examiners for LL.B. degree, 1952-57; University of Khartoum, 1958-; External Examiner in Law, Durham Univ., 1955-58; Review Editor, Jl. of Soc. of Public Teachers of Law, 1947-55. U.K. Editorial Corresp., Canadian Bar Review; Mem. Scientific Cttee., Revista di Diritto Agrario; Mem., Cttee. of Management, Inst. of Advanced Legal Studies; Member: The Law Society; Grotius Society; Member Selden Society; Antiquarian Horological Society; Associate Member Court of Electors, Birkbeck College. Member: Accademia Economico-Agraria dei Georgofili, Florence, 1954; Instituto di Diritto Agrario Internazionale e Comparato, University of Florence; F.R.S.A. *Publications:* Some Aspects of the British Constitution, 1944; numerous articles in Eng., Scot., Canadian and Italian legal periodicals, and Chambers's Encyclopædia. *Recreations:* walking and talking. Affection for old English furniture and clocks. *Address:* University College, London; 110 St. Julian's Farm Road, West Norwood, S.E.27. *T.:* Gipsy Hill 1039. [*Died* 4 *Feb.* 1959.

FITZGERALD, Rt. Rev. Richard Joseph, C.B.E. 1953; Bishop of Gibraltar (R.C.), since 1927; *b.* 12 August 1881; *s.* of late Richard Fitzgerald, Midleton, County Cork. *Educ.:* Christian Brothers' Schools, Midleton; St. Colman's College, Fermoy; Maynooth College, Ireland. Priest, 1905; Student of Dunboyne and Lecturer in Theology, 1905-07; Curate in Edinburgh and Stirling, 1907-09; Professor of Theology, St. Kieran's College, Kilkenny, 1909-12; Vice-Rector and Professor in the College of Irish Nobles, Salamanca, Spain, 1912-25; Curate Macroom, Co. Cork, 1926-27. *Address:* S. Mary's the Crowned, Gibraltar. [*Died* 15 *Feb.* 1956.

FITZGERALD, S. G. V.; *see* Vesey-Fitzgerald.

FITZGERALD, Thomas, C.M.G. 1935; O.B.E. 1927; late Postmaster-General, Amalgamated Service of Kenya, Uganda, and Tanganyika Territory; *b.* 26 Jan. 1879; *s.* of John Fitzgerald and Catherine Slattery; *m.* 1916, Elizabeth Lyons; two *s. Educ.:* Dublin; King's College, London. Entered Home Civil Service, 1900; Federated Malay States, 1908; East Africa, 1920; retired, 1936; late member of Kenya and Tanganyika Legislative Councils; member of Trinidad Commission of Enquiry, 1937, and of Rhodesia Nyasaland Royal Commission, 1938; Ministry of Supply (temp.), 1940-45; East Africa Salaries Commission, 1947. *Address:* 20 Burton Court, Chelsea, S.W.3. *Clubs:* East India and Sports; St. Stephen's Green (Dublin). [*Died* 8 *Oct.* 1959.

FITZGERALD-KENNEY, James C.; Member Dail Eireann for South Mayo since 1927; *b.* 30 April 1878; 2nd *surv. s.* of James Christopher Fitzgerald-Kenney, of Kilclogher, Co. Galway, and Helena, *e. d.* and *co-heiress* of Major P. Crean-Lynch, of Clogher House and Hollybrook, Co. Mayo. *Educ.:* Clongowes Wood College; University College, Dublin, B.A. 1898. Called to Irish Bar, 1899; Inner Bar, 1926; Parliamentary Secretary to Minister for Justice, 1927; Minister for Justice, Irish Free State, 1927-32. *Recreations:* shooting, farming, golf. *Address:* Clogher House, Clogher, Claremorris, Co. Mayo; 4 Waterloo Road, Dublin. *T.:* Ballsbridge 557. *Club:* Stephen's Green (Dublin). [*Died* 21 *Oct.* 1956.

FITZGIBBON, Gibbon, M.D., M.Ch., F.R.C.P.I., F.R.C.O.G.; Retired; *s.* of Henry FitzGibbon, M.D.; *b.* Dublin, 16 Aug. 1877; *m.* Lilian (*d.* 1947), *d.* of William Stoker, F.R.C.S.I.; two *s.* one *d. Educ.:* School, Dublin; Trinity College, Dublin. B.A., M.D., B., B.Ch., B.A.O., 1900. Attached R.A.M.C., South African Field Force, 1900-01; Assistant Master, Rotunda Hospital, 1902-05; Gynæcologist Royal City of Dublin Hospital, 1911-19; Master, Rotunda Hospital, Dublin, 1919-26; Gynæcologist, Mercer's Hospital, Dublin, 1926-50; Past President, Obstetric section, R.A.M.I.; Vice-President, Obstetric section B.M.A., 1927; President VII. British Congress Obstetrics and Gynæcology; Consulting Gynæcologist, Rotunda Hospital. *Publications:* Practical Obstetrics; Contracted Pelvis; Obstetrics, 1937; Chapters on Eclampsia, in Modern

FITZGERALD, Sir John Joseph, 2nd Bt. See page xxviii.

Technique in Treatment and in Modern Methods in Abnormal and Difficult Labour, Lancet; various original articles B.M.J., Jl. Obs. and Gynæc. Bt. Emp., Surg. Gynæc. and Obs., Dublin Jl. of Medicine. *Recreations:* various. *Address:* 9 St. James Terrace, Clonskeagh, Dublin. *T.:* 92582. *Club:* Royal Irish Yacht (Kingstown).
[*Died* 1 *Dec.* 1952.

FITZHERBERT, Ven. Henry Edward; Archdeacon Emeritus of Derby since 1952; *b.* 29 December 1882; 4th *s.* of Rev. Sir Richard FitzHerbert, 5th Bt., Tissington Hall, Ashbourne, and *brother* and *heir-pres.* to Sir William FitzHerbert, 7th Bt.; *m.* 1907, Hon. Margaret Elinor Holmes à'Court (*d.* 1957), *o. c.* of 3rd Baron Heytesbury; three *s.* four *d.* *Educ.:* Charterhouse; Downton Agricultural College; Trinity Hall, Cambridge (M.A.). Land Agent; Deacon, 1912; Priest, 1913; Rural Dean of Higham Ferrers II Deanery, 1919; Repton Deanery, 1932; Hon. Canon Derby Cathedral, 1936, Chaplain to the King, 1940; Archdeacon of Derby, 1943-52; Chaplain to the Queen, 1952-55. *Address:* Old Vicarage, Quarndon, Derby. *T.:* Duffield 2166. *Club:* Derbyshire County (Derby).
[*Died* 3 *April* 1958.

FITZHERBERT, Admiral Sir Herbert, K.C.I.E., *cr.* 1941; C.B. 1937; C.M.G., 1919; Royal Navy; *b.* 10 Aug. 1885; *s.* of late Samuel Wyndham Fitzherbert of Kingswear, Devon; *m.* Rachel, 2nd *d.* of late Colonel L. H. Hanbury, C.M.G.; one *s.* Joined H.M.S. Britannia, 1900; Lt., 1907; Comdr., 1917; Capt., 1924; Rear-Adm., 1936; Vice-Adm., 1939; Adm., 1943; served Battle of Jutland (despatches); Flag-Lieut. to Adm. Commanding-in-Chief, 1914-16; commanded Signal School, Portsmouth, 1932-34; H.M.S. Devonshire, 1934-36; Flag Officer Commanding R.I.N. 1937-43; Chevalier Legion of Honour; Russian Order of St. Anne. *Recreations:* shooting, cricket, tennis. *Club:* United Service.
[*Died* 30 *Oct.* 1958.

FITZMAURICE, Rev. Sir Henry, K.B.E., *cr.* 1939 (M.B.E. 1918); C.M.G. 1934; Vicar of Brenchley, Kent, since 1943; *b.* Lindfield, Sussex, 8 July 1886; *s.* of late Dr. Richard Fitzmaurice and Alexina Lindsay; *m.* 1925, Olga, *o. d.* of late Lt.-Col. C. L. Seton-Browne, D.S.O. Entered Far Eastern Consular Service as Student Interpreter, Siam, 1907; Vice Consul (local rank), Bangkok, 1915; Vice-Consul, Nakawn Lampang, 1916; acted at various Consular posts in Siam, Indo-China, and Netherlands East Indies; Consul at Medan, Sumatra, 1923; Consul-General Batavia, 1931; retired, 1939; ordained deacon, 1940; ordained priest, 1940. *Address:* The Vicarage, Brenchley, Kent. *T.:* Brenchley 140.
[*Died* 29 *Jan.* 1952.

FITZMAURICE, Nicholas, C.I.E. 1934; *b.* 13 Oct. 1887; *s.* of late Dr. Richard Fitzmaurice, Lindfield, Sussex, and Alexina Lindsay; *m.* 1933, Eleanor Joan Margarita, *yr. d.* of late Frederick Malcolm Wharton, Edgbaston, Birmingham; one *s.* one *d.* Student Interpreter in China, 1908; Consul in China, 1930; one of H.M. Consuls-General in China, 1938; retired, 1943. *Address:* Greycourt, Dunmow Hill, Fleet, Hants. *T.:* 317.
[*Died* 7 *July* 1960.

FITZMAURICE, Brig.-Gen. Robert, C.B.E. 1919; D.S.O. 1917; R.A. (retired, 1920); *b.* 7 Jan. 1866; *m.* Violet Beryl, 2nd *d.* of late C. G. Macpherson, C.I.E. *Educ.:* Royal School, Armagh; Trinity College, Dublin. Adjt. R.H.A., 1901-2; Commanded 35th Battn. I.Y., 1902; Commanded E, Z and B batteries R.H.A. and R.H.A. Depot; served European War, 1914-17 (despatches 4 times, D.S.O., C.B.E., Order of Leopold). *Address:* 80 Bouverie Road W., Folkestone, Kent. *Club:* Army and Navy. [*Died* 11 *Nov.* 1952.

FITZROY, Sir Charles Edward, Kt., *cr.* 1934; *b.* 19 Jan. 1876; *s.* of Major-Gen. William FitzRoy, J.P., and Gertrude Mary, *d.* of Capt. S. H. Wentworth, R.E.; *m.* 1915, Sarah Louise, *d.* of late Henry Limmer; no *c.* *Educ.:* Bedford School. Solicitor for H.M. Customs and Excise, 1929-41. *Address:* St. Budeaux, Hannafore, Looe, Cornwall.
[*Died* 4 *April* 1954.

FITZSIMONS, Frederick William; Director, Port Elizabeth Museum, 1906-36; parentage Irish; *b.* 1875; *m.*; two *s.* *Educ.:* Natal; Ireland. Director of the Natal Museum for ten years; Creator of Snake Park in Port Elizabeth; Discoverer of a new treatment for Epilepsy in the form of a combination of detoxicated Snake Venoms. *Publications:* The Snakes of South Africa: their Venom and the Treatment of Snake Bite; The Natural History of South Africa, in 4 vols. (Mammals); The House Fly: A Slayer of Men; Natural History of South Africa, Birds, 2 vols.; The Monkeyfolk of South Africa; Pythons and their Ways; Snakes and Treatment of Snake Bite; Ants and their Ways; Snakes; Opening the Psychic Door; Squire: His Romance; Papers on Various Departments of South African Natural History. *Recreation:* psychic research. *Address:* FitzSimons' Snake Park and Laboratory, Marine Parade, Durban, South Africa.
[*Died* 25 *May* 1951.

FITZWILLIAM, 9th Earl (*cr.* 1716), **Eric Spencer Wentworth-Fitzwilliam;** Baron Fitz-William, 1620; Viscount Milton, 1716; Baron Milton (Great Britain), 1742; Earl FitzWilliam and Viscount Milton, 1746; *b.* 4 Dec. 1883; *s.* of Hon. Sir William Charles Wentworth-Fitzwilliam (*d.* 1925), 4th *s.* of 6th Earl and Constance Anne (*d.* 1941), *d.* of late Henry Brocklehurst; *S.* cousin, 1948; *m.* 1912, Jessica Gertrude (from whom he obtained a divorce, 1917). *Educ.:* Eton. Formerly Lt. Leicestershire Yeomanry; served European War, 1914-18, 1916-17. Order of Rising Sun of Japan. *Heir: kinsman,* William Thomas George Wentworth-Fitzwilliam, D.L., J.P., *b.* 28 May 1904. *Address:* Barnsdale, Oakham, Rutland. *T.:* 71; Wentworth-Woodhouse, Rotherham, Yorkshire; Coollattin, Shillelagh, Co. Wicklow, Ireland. *Club:* St. James', M.C.C.
[*Died* 3 *April* 1952.

FITZWILLIAMS, Duncan Campbell Lloyd, C.M.G. 1919; M.D. (Gold Medal), Ch.M., F.R.C.S. Edin., F.R.C.S. Eng.; late Surgeon to Mount Vernon Hospital and Radium Institute for Cancer; Surgeon to Freemasons' Hospital; Consulting Surgeon to St. Mary's Hospital, Paddington; *b.* 31 Dec. 1878; *s.* of late Charles H. L. Fitzwilliams, J.P., Cilgwyn, Newcastle Emlyn, Cardiganshire; *m.* 1st, Mary Elizabeth (*d.* 1919), *e. d.* of late Oliver Dwight Filley, St. Louis, U.S.A.; two *s.* three *d.*; 2nd 1920, Francesca Christine, M.B.E., *d.* of late Ferdinand Wagner and Mrs. Wagner, Riga. *Educ.:* Edinburgh Univ. (Lechie-Mactier and Goodsir Memorial Fellow), Fellow, late President of Royal Medical Society of Edinburgh and numerous other scientific societies. Served in the R.A.M.C. during S. African War (medal 4 clasps); European War in R.A.M.C. (T.F.), 1st City of London Field Ambulance; was Consulting Surgeon N. Russian Expeditionary Force, 1918 (despatches twice); Comdr. St. John of Jerusalem; Chevalier of the Legion of Honour. *Publications:* numerous surgical. *Recreations:* shooting, fishing, golf. *Address:* La Mésange, Mont Cochon, Jersey, C.I. *T.:* 258 Millbrook. *Club:* Royal Automobile. [*Died* 18 *Nov.* 1954.

FLADGATE, Maj.-Gen. Courtenay William, C.B.E. 1940; *b.* 19 Nov. 1890; *s.* of late Sir Francis Fladgate; *m.* 1922, Evelyn Barbara, *d.* of late G. W. Finch; one *s.* one *d.* *Educ.:* Harrow; R.M.C., Sandhurst, Joined 60th Rifles, 1910; served European War, 1914-18; transferred to R. Corps of Signals, 1922; Chief Signal Officer, Aldershot Command, 1938-39; A.D.C. to the King, 1942-

1946; retired, 1946; Col. Comdt. Royal Signals, 1947-55. *Address:* Inglewood Cottage, Fleet, Hants. *T.:* 1218. *Club:* Army and Navy. [*Died* 15 *June* 1958.

FLAHERTY, Robert Joseph, F.R.G.S., *b.* 16 Feb. 1884; *s.* of Robert Henry Flaherty and Susan Kloeckner; *m.* 1914, Frances J. Hubbard (author of Elephant Dance, 1937); three *d.* *Educ.:* Upper Canada College, Toronto. Led 4 expeditions into subarctic eastern Canada, explored and mapped large island archipelago known as Belcher Islands, Hudson Bay, explored and mapped the unknown barren lands of northern Ungava, making two sea-to-sea crossings of the Peninsula 1910-16; engaged in motion pictures, 1920; produced Nanook of the North, picture of Eskimos of N.E. coast of Hudson Bay 1920-22; made Moana, with natives of the Samoan Islands, South Seas, 1923-25; made experimental film of New York City 1927; Co-produced with F. W. Murnau, the picture, Tabu, made in Tahiti, South Seas 1929-31; made Man of Aran, on Aran Is. off coast of Ireland 1932-34; in India, directing film, Elephant Boy, based on Kipling's Jungle Book story, Toomai of the Elephants, 1935; in U.S. directing pictures for Department of Agriculture, The Land, 1939-41; film sequences for War Dept., 1942; documentary film for Museum of Art, Providence, R.I., 1944; produced documentary film for Botanical Garden, New York, 1946; series for Sugar Research Foundation; produced and directed The Louisiana Story (judged as best documentary film of 1949). *Publications:* (with his wife) My Eskimo Friends, 1924; Samoa, in German, 1932; The Captain's Chair (novel), 1938; White Master, 1939; A Film-Maker's Odyssey, 1939; and various articles. *Recreations:* music, films, exploration. *Address:* Black Mountain Farm, R.F.D.1, Brattleboro, Vermont, U.S.A. *Clubs:* Coffee House, Explorer's, Players (New York). [*Died* 23 *July* 1951.

FLANAGAN, Lt.-Col. Edward Martyn Woulfe, C.M.G. 1919; D.S.O. 1917; late E. Surrey Regt.; *b.* 1870; *y. s.* of Rt. Hon. Stephen Woulfe Flanagan. *Educ.:* Oratory School. Served B.S.A. Police, 1897-1910; South African War (wounded); European War (wounded, despatches four times, D.S.O., C.M.G., Legion of Honour); retired pay, 1920. *Address:* 18 Calverley Park, Tunbridge Wells. *Clubs:* Army and Navy; Kildare Street (Dublin) [*Died* 27 *May* 1954.

FLANDIN, Pierre Etienne; Avocat honoraire à la Cour d'Appel; Conseiller Général de l'Yonne, 1955; *b.* 12 April 1889; *m.* 1912, Mlle. Léon-Barbier; three *c.* (and one *s.* decd.). *Educ.:* Paris Univ. Docteur en Droit, 1913; Diplomé de l'École des Sciences politiques, 1909; Doctor h.c. Université de Montréal, 1934; France Député de l'Yonne, 1914; Dir. du Service Aéronautique Interallié, 1917; Délégué au Traité de paix (Convention Inter. de Navigation Aérienne), 1919; Sous-Sec. d'État à l'Aéronautique, 1920; Ministre du Commerce, 1924 and 1929-1930; Vice-président de la Chambre des Députés, 1928; Ministre des Finances, 1931-1932; Ministre des Travaux Publics, 1934; Prime Minister, 1934-35; Minister of State, 1935-36; Minister for Foreign Affairs, 1936; Minister of Foreign Affairs, Pétain Government, Dec. 1940-Feb. 1941; Délégué de la France à la Société des Nations, 1930-31; Président du Parti républicain démocratique, 1933; Président de l'Alliance Démocratique, 1946; Président du Centre des Hautes Études Américaines, 1954. *Publications:* Paix et liberté, 1939; Politique française, 1919-40, 1947; nombreux articles dans la presse et dans les revues (Revue de Paris, Revue de France, Ecrits de Paris, Revues des Deux-Mondes). *Address:* 139 Boulevard Malesherbes, Paris, 17e. *T.:* Wagram 25.30; St.-Jean-Cap-Ferrat, A.M. *T.:* 252-11; Domecy-sur-Cure, Yonne. *T.:* 2. *Clubs:* Aéro de France (Prés. 1923), Automobile de France (Paris). [*Died* 13 *June* 1958.

FLANNERY, Sir Harold Fortescue, 2nd Bt. *cr.* 1904; M.B.E. 1918; M.I.N.A., A.M.I.C.E., F.C.M.S.; *b.* 13 Dec. 1883; *o. s.* of Sir James Fortescue-Flannery, 1st Bt.; *S.* father 1943; *m.* 1917, Maud, *y. d.* of St. George Boswell, Quebec; (only son killed in action in War of 1939-45) one *d.* *Educ.:* Trinity Hall, Cambridge; B.A. 1910. Capt. Essex R.H.A. *Heir:* none. *Address:* The Old Rectory, Claydon, Suffolk. *Club:* Royal Thames Yacht. [*Died* 19 *April* 1959 (*ext.*).

FLATT, Leslie Neeve, C.I.E. 1943; V.D.; B.Sc.Eng. (Lond.); M.Inst.C.E., M.I.Mech.E., M.I.Loco.E.; Technical Consultant, United Steel Company Ltd.; *b.* 26 March 1889; *s.* of G. N. Flatt, Wanstead, Essex; *m.* 1918, Barbara, *d.* of C. H. Allen, Theydon Bois, Essex; one *s.* one *d.* *Educ.:* Forest School; London University. Premium apprentice with Great Eastern Railway at Stratford, 1906-11, and Material and Running Inspector, 1911-12; joined East Indian Railway, 1913; service with R.E. (Capt.) in Mesopotamia, 1916-18 (despatches); transferred Great Indian Peninsula Railway, 1920; Eastern Bengal Railway, 1927; North Western Railway, 1936; Chief Mechanical Engineer on E.B. and N.W. Railways, 1934-40; Director of Mech. Engineering, and Chief Contr. of Standardisation Railway Board, New Delhi, India, 1940-45; Chairman, Delhi Central Electric Power Authority Ltd., 1940-45. *Address:* 8-10 Grosvenor Gardens, S.W.1. *T.:* Sloane 4533; 15 Walton Terrace, Aylesbury, Bucks. *T.:* 4102. *Clubs:* East India and Sports, Junior Army and Navy; Tollygunge, Royal Bombay Yacht (Bombay), etc. [*Died* 16 *Aug.* 1957.

FLECKER, H. L. O., C.B.E. 1949; M.A.; Principal of Lawrence College, Murree Hills, Pakistan, 1955-58; Headmaster of Christ's Hospital, 1930-July 1955; Member Royal Commission on Marriage and Divorce, 1951; *b.* 1896; *s.* of late Rev. W. H. Flecker; *m.* 1933, Mary Patricia, *d.* of late Brig. Gen. W. F. Hessey, D.S.O.; one *s.* two *d.* *Educ.:* Dean Close School; Brasenose College, Oxford (Classical Scholar), First Class in Hon. Mods. Served European War; Assist. Master, Marlborough, 1921; Headmaster of Berkhamsted, 1927-30. *Address:* c/o Childs Bank, 1 Fleet Street, E.C.4. [*Died* 7 *Oct.* 1958.

FLEISCHMANN, Louis, C.B.E. 1938; Partner in Merchant Banking firm of Seligman Brothers, 18 Austin Friars, E.C.2; *b.* in Germany, 8 Sept. 1868; *m.* 1905, Ruby Irene, *d.* of late John Pollok, D.L., Lismany, Co. Galway, and of late Hon. Mrs. Barry; two *d.* *Educ.:* in Germany. Came to England, 1886; naturalised British subject, 1892; formerly Chairman of Roy. Nat. Orthopædic Hosp. and of the Inst. of Orthopædics. *Recreation:* farming. *Address:* Chetwode Manor, Buckingham. *T.:* Finmere 271. *Club:* Devonshire. [*Died* 31 *Dec.* 1954.

FLEMING, Sir Alexander, Kt., *cr.* 1944; F.R.S. 1943; M.B., B.S. (Lond.); F.R.C.S. (Eng.); F.R.C.P. 1944; Emeritus Professor of Bacteriology, Univ. of London, since 1948 (Professor, St. Mary's Hospital Medical School, 1928-48); William Julius Mickle Fellowship London University 1942; Charles Mickle Fellowship Toronto Univ. 1944; *b.* Darvel, 6 Aug. 1881; *s.* of Hugh Fleming; *m.* 1st, Sarah Marion (*d.* 1949), *d.* of John McElroy, Leigherntain House, Killala, Co. Mayo; one *s.*; 2nd, Dr. Amalia Coutsouris, Athens. *Educ.:* Kilmarnock Acad.; St. Mary's Hospital Medical School (almost all class prizes and scholarships, including senior entrance scholarship in natural science). Honours in Physiology, Pharmacology, Medicine, Pathology, Forensic

Medicine and Hygiene; University Gold Medal, in M.B., B.S. 1908. Dr. *h.c.* of many univs. in Europe and America. Hunterian Professor and Arris and Gale Lecturer, Royal College of Surgeons; John Scott Medal, City Guild of Philadelphia, 1944; Cameron Prize, Univ. of Edinburgh, 1945; Nobel Laureate in Medicine, 1945; Albert Gold Medal, R.S.A.; Medal for Therapeutics, Soc. of Apothecaries, Gold Medal, R.S.M.; Hon. Gold Medal, R.C.S.; Moxon Medal, R.C.P.; Harben Medal, Royal Institute of Public Health; late Pres. London Ayrshire Society and Pathological Comparative Medicine Sections, R.S.M.; and Soc. for General Microbiology; Member Pontifical Acad. of Sciences and Hon. Member of many Academies of Medicine and Science. Rector of Edinburgh University, 1951-54. Hon. Freeman: Boroughs of Paddington, Darvel, Chelsea and the City of Verona; Hon. Freeman and Liveryman, Worshipful Company of Dyers; Hon. Chief Doy-gei-taun of Kiowa tribe. Comdr. Legion of Honour; Medal for Merit, U.S.A.; Grand Cross of Alphonse X The Wise (Spain). Private in London Scottish for 14 years; Capt. R.A.M.C. (despatches). *Publications:* numerous on Bacteriology, Immunology and Chemotherapy—including original descriptions of Lysozyme and Penicillin. *Address:* 20 Danvers Street, S.W.3. *T.:* Flaxman 8909; The Dhoon, Barton Mills, Mildenhall, Suffolk. *T.:* Mildenhall 3155. *Clubs:* Athenæum, Chelsea Arts; Savage, Caledonian (Hon.). [*Died* 11 *March* 1955.

FLEMING, Rt. Rev. Archibald Lang, D.D., F.R.G.S.; *b.* Greenock, 8 Sept. 1883; *s.* of John and Jessie Fleming, Greenock, and Aleppo, Hunter's Quay, Scotland; *m.* 1st, 1913, Helen Grace (*d.* 1941), *d.* of Walter and Laura Gillespie, Toronto, formerly of Edmonston, Biggar, Scotland; no *c.*; 2nd, 1942, Elizabeth Nelson, *d.* of Lewis and Edith C. Lukens, Haverford, Pa., U.S.A. *Educ.:* Greenock Academy; Glasgow University; Wycliffe College, Toronto (D.D. 1933); D.D., Emmanuel College, Saskatoon, 1942. In drawing-office, shipyard John Brown & Co., Clydebank, 1901-6; Scientific Department of the same firm, 1906-8, including special course at Glasgow University in naval architecture and marine engineering, 1905-6; prizeman, Naval Architectural Drawing, 1906; went to Canada to prepare for missionary work at Wycliffe College, 1908; Deacon, 1912; Priest, 1913; Missionary Baffinland until 1916; Locum Tenens, St. John's Church, Port Hope, Ontario, 1916; St. John's Church, St. John, N.B., 1917; served at Military Orthopedic Hospital, Toronto, 1917-18; Chaplain and Financial Secretary, Wycliffe College, Toronto, 1918-1921; Rector, St. John's Church, St. John, N.B., 1921-27; Archdeacon of the Arctic and Executive Officer of the Arctic Mission Fund, 1927-33; Examining Chaplain for the Bishops of Moosonee, Mackenzie River, and Yukon; first Bishop of the Arctic, 1933-49. *Publications:* For Us, a series of devotional addresses on the Seven Last Words, 1923; A Book of Remembrance, a History of St. John's Church, St. John, N.B., 1925; Dwellers in Arctic Night, 1928; The Hunter-Home, 1930; Perils of the Polar Pack, 1932; Flying Beyond the Arctic Circle, 1933. *Recreations:* golf, fishing, motoring, photography, travelling. *Address:* Huron Cliffs, Goderich, Ont., Can. *Club:* Overseas League. [*Died* 17 *May* 1953.

FLEMING, Sir Arthur Percy Morris, Kt., *cr.* 1945; C.B.E. 1920; D.Eng., M.Sc. (Tech.), LL.D.; F.C.G.I.; Hon. M.I.E.E., M.I.MechE., F.Inst.P.; Director, B.S. & W. Whiteley, Ltd., and other companies; *b.* 1881; *s.* of Frank Fleming, Marvel, Newport, Isle of Wight; *m.* Rose Mary (*d.* 1948), *d.* of late William Ash, Newport, Isle of Wight; two *s.* one *d.* *Educ.:* Portland House Academy, Newport; Finsbury Technical College. With London Electric Supply Corp., London, 1899; Elliott Bros. 1900; Westinghouse Electric Co., Pittsburg, Pa., U.S.A., 1900-1902; British Westinghouse, subsequently the Metropolitan Vickers Electrical Co., Manchester, since 1902; engaged with this Company as insulation expert, then transformer designer, and subsequently as Manager of Research and Education; Past Pres., I.E.E., 1938-39; Pres., Section L. British Assoc., 1939; Pres. Section G. British Assoc., 1949; Member Ministry of Labour Advisory Council of Central Register, 1938; Chairman of Electrical Engineering Committee of Central Register of the Ministry of Labour, 1939; Governing Body of Imperial College of Science and Technology; Delegacy of City and Guilds College; War Cabinet Engineering Advisory Committee, 1941; Lord Hankey's Technical Personnel Cttee., 1941; member Technical Personnel Cttee. set up 1951; Bd. of Education Committee on Training of Teachers and Youth Leaders; Member of the National Advisory Council for Further Education; Chairman, Management Cttee., Athlone Fellowships, 1950; Vice-Pres. Brit. Assoc. for Commercial and Industrial Educ.; Thomas Hawksley Medal of I.Mech.E., 1937; Faraday Medal of I.E.E., 1941. *Publications:* Industrial Research in the U.S.A., and many technical papers before technical and scientific socs.; (joint) Engineering as a Profession; Insulation and Design of Electrical Machinery; Principles of Apprentice Training; Research in Industry; Introduction to Study of Industrial Organisation; History of Engineering. *Address:* Luccombe Chine House, Bonchurch, Ventnor, Isle of Wight. *T.:* Shanklin 2037. [*Died* 14 *Sept.* 1960.

FLEMING, Mrs. D. L.; *see* Sayers, Dorothy.

FLEMING, Geoffrey Balmanno, M.B.E., B.A., M.D. (Camb.), LL.D. (Glas.), F.R.C.P. (Lond.), F.R.F.P.S.G.; Emeritus Professor of Paediatrics Glasgow University since 1930; Hon. Consulting Physician Royal Hospital for Sick Children, Glasgow, and Children's Home Hospital, Strathblane; *b.* 20 Feb. 1882; *s.* of William James Fleming, M.D., late Surgeon, Royal Infirmary, Glasgow, and Annie Cole, *d.* of William Walls, Glasgow; unmarried. *Educ.:* Haileybury; King's College, Cambridge; Glasgow University; Vienna. B.A. (Hon.), 1903; M.B. 1908; M.D. 1914, Camb.; Dispensary Physician Western Infirmary and Royal Hospital for Sick Children, Glasgow; Assistant to Professor of Medicine, Anderson's College of Medicine, 1912-14; European War, 1914-19 (despatches); Retired from R.A.M.C. (T.A.), 1921, with rank of Lt.-Col.; Gow Lecturer Medical Diseases of Infancy and Childhood, 1924-30. Late President R.F.P.S.G. *Publications:* numerous contributions to Medical literature. *Recreations:* hunting, shooting, golf. *Address:* 13 Lynedoch Crescent, Glasgow. *T.:* Douglas 4529. *Clubs:* Royal Automobile; Western (Glasgow). [*Died* 16 *April* 1952.

FLEMING, Major-Gen. George, C.B. 1935; C.B.E. 1932; D.S.O. 1916; *b.* London, 3 Nov. 1879; *s.* of late Colonel George Fleming, C.B., LL.D., Principal Veterinary Surgeon, and Susan Fleming; *m.* 1919, Simone, *d.* of late Marie G. P. Gresy, Paris; one *s.* *Educ.:* Epsom College; University College, London. On outbreak of South African War joined 7th Batt. Imperial Yeomanry; Commission in the Prince Albert's (Somerset Light Infantry), 1901; served S. Africa, 1900-01 (Queen's medal with four clasps); served in India, 1901-08; Adjutant, 3rd Batt. 1912-15; served European War, 1915-16, with 1st Batt. in France, including Battle of Pilkem (D.S.O.); in December 1915 joined 13th Division (Madras) accompanying it to Mesopotamia as Staff Captain to the 39th Infantry Brigade; was present at all fighting for relief of Kut (despatches); 3rd Class of the Order of St. Stanislas with swords; in command of the 7th Gloucesters, N. Staffs. and the 9th Service Batt. of Royal Warwickshire Regt. in capture of Kut and Baghdad and operations north of Baghdad, 1916-18 (Bt. Lt.-Col.); afterwards through Transcaspia and the Caucasus, Constantinople, 1919; commanded 1st Batt. the Welch Regiment, 1926-30; Commander Shanghai Area, 1930-33; Maj.-Gen., 1933; Commander Madras District, Southern Command, India, 1934-38; retired pay, 1938. *Recreation:* gardening. *Address:* Lodge Farm, Melton, Woodbridge, Suffolk. [*Died* 27 *Aug.* 1957.

FLEMING-BERNARD, Andrew Milroy, C.M.G. 1898; C.B.E. 1924; Medical Director, Southern Rhodesia, retired, 1931; *b.* Edinburgh, 28 Jan. 1871; *s.* of Rev. John Fleming, Edinburgh; *m.* 1896, Philadelphia Alice (*d.* 1944), *d.* of late William Fisher, B.C.; one *s.* one *d.* *Educ.:* Edinburgh Academy; Durham School; Edinburgh University (M.B., C.M.). F.R.C.S.E., D.P.H. Camb. 1903; member Legislative Council, Southern Rhodesia, 1923. *Address:* Dunsinnan, Balbeggie, Perthshire. *T.:* Kinrossie 202. *Clubs:* Authors'; New (Edinburgh); Salisbury (Salisbury, S. Rhodesia). [*Died* 6 *Nov.* 1953.

FLETCHER, Air Cdre. Albert, C.M.G. 1919; C.B.E. 1918; M.C.; R.A.F., retd.; *s.* of John Richard Fletcher; *m.* 1st, Ethel Mary (*d.* 1934), *d.* of F. S. Futcher, Andover; 2nd, Doris Maud, *er. d.* of Arthur Tomkin Norman; one *s.* *Educ.:* privately. Director of Air Quartermaster's Services, Air Ministry, 1918-1920; Deputy Director of Organisation, Air Ministry, 1928-30; Deputy Director of Personal Services, Air Ministry, 1939-43; Air Officer-in-Charge Administration, Transport Command, R.A.F., 1943-44; Deputy Senior Air Staff Officer on liaison with B.O.A.C., H.Q. Transport Command, 1944; reverted to retired list, 1945. *Recreations:* golf, riding, fencing. *Address:* 22 Goldsmith Avenue, W.3. *T.:* Acorn 0388. [*Died* 29 *Jan.* 1956.

FLETCHER, Sir Angus Somerville, K.C.M.G., *cr.* 1941; C.B.E. 1931; *b.* 13 May 1883; *s.* of Patrick Fletcher, Jura, Argyll; *m.* Helen, *d.* of Archibald Stewart, Achallader, Argyll; three *s.* *Educ.:* South African College, Cape Town. 1st Rhodesian Regiment, 1914-1915; R.F.A., 1915-19; British War Mission to U.S.A., 1918; National Industrial Conference Board (U.S.), 1919-22; Director British Library of Information, New York, 1928-41; British Consultant World-Wide Broadcasting Foundation, 1942-43. Chairman, Headquarters Commission, United Nations, 1946. *Address:* East Hampton, Long Island, N.Y., U.S.A. *Club:* Century (N.Y.). [*Died* 6 *Aug.* 1960.

FLETCHER, Sir (Arthur George) Murchison, K.C.M.G., *cr.* 1930 (C.M.G. 1922); Kt., *cr.* 1929; C.B.E. 1919; *b.* 27 Sept. 1878; *s.* of late Dr. George Fletcher, Highgate; *m.* 1915, Dorothy, *d.* of Lieut.-Colonel Rogers-Harrison, I.M.S.; one *s.* *Educ.:* Cheltenham; Trinity College, Oxford. Cadet, Hong-Kong Civil Service, 1901; Colonial Sec., Ceylon, 1926-29; Administered Govt. of Ceylon, 1927; Governor of Fiji and High Commissioner for Western Pacific, 1929-36; Governor and Commander-in-Chief of Trinidad and Tobago, 1936-38. *Address:* 5 Chartfield Avenue, Putney, S.W.15. *T.:* Putney 0702. [*Died* 9 *April* 1954.

FLETCHER, Sir Banister (Flight), Kt., *cr.* 1919; D.Lit. (Lond.); F.S.A.; Past President R.I.B.A.; F.R.I.C.S.; M.Arch. (Ireland); F.R.S.L.; architect, surveyor, author, lecturer; Barrister-at-law of the Inner Temple; Past Vice-Pres. and Hon. Sec. of Architectural Association; Hon. Member of the British Academy of Arts at Rome; Hon. Member of American Institute of Architects; Hon. Corres. Member of Société Centrale des Architectes Français; Member of Court of Common Council; one of H.M. Lieutenants of the City of London; Chairman of the City Lands Committee (Chief Commoner), 1921; Chairman of City of London School, 1914 and 1915; Chairman of Library Committee, 1917; Senior Sheriff of City of London, 1918-19; Chairman of Greater London Regional Planning Cttee. 1927-33; Master of the Worshipful Company of Carpenters, 1937; *e. s.* of late Professor Banister Fletcher; *m.* 1st, 1914, Alice Maude Mary (*d.* 1932), *d.* of Edward Bretherton and *widow* of Sir J. Bamford-Slack; 2nd, 1933, Mrs. Howard Hazell (*d.* 1949). *Educ.:* Univ. Coll., London; Royal Academy. Architectural Association Medal for Design, 1888; Godwin Bursary and Travelling Studentship, 1893; Tite Medal for Architectural Design, 1895; the R.I.B.A. Essay Medal, 1896; the Arthur Cates Travelling Studentship, 1889; formerly Lecturer and Assistant Professor at King's College, London and Examiner to the City and Guilds of London Institute; University Staff Lecturer on Architecture at London University; partner in firm of Banister Fletcher & Sons; Officier Légion d'Honneur; Commander of the Crown of Roumania, of the Order of the Crown of Italy, of the Order of King George of Greece, of the Order of Leopold II. of Belgium, of the Order of the Rising Sun of Japan; Knight Commander of the Order of Ta Shou Chia Ho (The Excellent Crop) of China; Order of St. Sava of the Kingdom of the Serbs, Croats, and Slovenes; has travelled extensively on sketching expeditions. *Publications:* A History of Architecture on the Comparative Method (15th edition); Andrea Palladio, His Life and Work; Architecture and the Humanities; The Influence of Material on Architecture; The English Home, Architectural Hygiene, and other professional text-books. *Recreations:* golf, motoring, sketching, and travelling. *Address:* 3 King's Bench Walk, E.C.4; 4 Whitehall Court, S.W.1. *T.:* Whitehall 3160. *T.A.:* Banister, London. *Clubs:* Athenæum, Authors', Royal Automobile; Walton Heath Golf; Mid Surrey Golf (Richmond). [*Died* 17 *Aug.* 1953.

FLETCHER, Lieut.-Col. Edward Walter, C.B.E. 1952; *b.* 23 July 1899; *s.* of Col. W. B. Fletcher; unmarried. *Educ.:* Marlborough College; Royal Military Academy Woolwich. Entered Royal Artillery, 1919; transferred to Indian Army, 1928; joined Indian Political Service, 1928. Appointments held: H.B.M. Vice-Consul Khuramshahr; British Trade Agent, Gyantse, Tibet; Secretary, British Legation, Kabul; Political Agent States of Western India; Secretary to Resident, States of Western India; Additional Dep. Sec., External Affairs Dept., Govt. of India; Political Adviser to British Forces in Iran; H.B.M. Consul-General, Ahwaz; H.B.M. Consul-General for the French Establishments in India, 1945; late Deputy Secretary in Ministry of Foreign Affairs and Commonwealth Relations, Government of Pakistan; retired 1950. War of 1939-45 (despatches twice). F.R.G.S. *Recreations:* tennis, fishing, and sailing. *Club:* Travellers'. [*Died* 9 *Feb.* 1958.

FLETCHER, Sir Frank, Kt., *cr.* 1937; M.A. (Oxon), Hon. M.A. (Adelaide); *b.* 3 May 1870; *s.* of late Ralph Fletcher, Atherton, Manchester; *m.* 1902, Dorothy, *d.* of W. Pope of Crediton. *Educ.:* Rossall School; Balliol College, Oxford (1st cl., Classical Moderations, 1891, and in final Classical School, 1893, Craven, Ireland, and Derby Scholarships, Hon. Fellow, 1924). Assistant Master, Rugby School, 1894-1903; Master of Marlborough College, 1903-11; Headmaster of Charterhouse, 1911-35; Chairman Headmasters' Conference, 1913-15, 1919, etc.; President Incorporated Association of Headmasters, 1933. President Classical Association, 1946. *Publications:* Brethren and Companions, 1936; After Many Days, 1937; Virgil, Aeneid VI., 1941; Notes to Agamemnon, 1949. *Address:* Gate House, Eashing, Godalming. *T.:* Godalming 664. *Club:* Alpine. [*Died* 17 *Nov.* 1954.

FLETCHER, Frank; *b.* 13 Oct. 1867; *s.* of John Fletcher, Gloucester; *m.* 1901, O. M. R. (*d.* 1953), *d.* of E. d'Avigdor, and *sister* of Sir Osmond d'Avigdor Goldsmid, 1st Bart.; three *d.* *Educ.:* privately; Balliol Coll., Oxford (Classical Exhibitioner); Gaisford Prizeman (Greek Verse, 1888); B.A. and M.A.; Secretary in literary matters to Prof. Jowett, Master of Balliol College, 1889-93; Teacher in Elementary Schools (six years under the London School Board in Mile End, 1895-1900), and in the Whitechapel Foundation School, 1901; Assistant Lecturer in Education, University College of North Wales, 1901-02, and in the University of Liverpool, 1903-04; Professor of Education in the Hartley University Coll., Southampton, 1904-05; Assistant Lecturer in Education and Philosophy, University College of North Wales, 1907; Sub-Editor on the staff of the Victoria County History, 1907-09; Head of the Department of Classics, University College of the South-West, 1909-33; Professor of Classics, University College of the South-West, Exeter, 1927-33; formerly Member of Council of the University College of the South-West; Member of the Council of the Classical Association, 1925-27, and Secretary (1922-33) and Vice-President of the South-Western Branch; Examiner in the University of London, 1932-34; Governor of the N.W. Polytechnic; Governor of Holloway School and of Avery Hill Training College; Member of Committee of St. John's Hospital; Contributor to the Oxford Latin Dictionary (*Vitruvius*). *Publication:* History of the Schools of Rutland (Victoria County History). *Address:* 114 Streathbourne Road, S.W.17. *T.:* Balham 6390. [*Died* 26 *Feb.* 1956.

FLETCHER, Hanslip; *b.* London, 1874; *s.* of G. Rutter Fletcher. *Educ.:* Merchant Taylors' School. Member of Art Workers' Guild; Committee of Society Protection of Ancient Buildings; drawings and etchings in London and Provinces and illustrated topographical works; four vols. of Changing London, also pictorial contributions to The Sunday Times; Works purchased by Contemporary Art Society, Walker Art Gallery, National Museum of Wales; drawings of London purchased by Guildhall Libraries Committee. Bombed London (a collection of thirty-eight drawings in the second World War, 1939-1945; Four in colour), 1947. *Publications include:* London: Passed and Passing, 1908; Changing London, 1934; Bombed London, 1948. *Recreation:* travel. *Address:* 118A Gloucester Place, Portman Square, W.1. *T.:* Welbeck 9308. [*Died* 21 *Feb.* 1955.

FLETCHER, Henry Prather; *b.* Green Castle, Pennsylvania, 10 Apr. 1873; *s.* of Lewis Henry Clay Fletcher and Martha Ellen Rowe, Scotch-Irish descent; *m.* 1917, Beatrice Bend (*d.* 1941), New York. *Educ.:* Chambersburg Academy; LL.D. University of Chile, Lafayette College, Dickinson College, Juniata College. Called to Bar, 1894; served as private in Roosevelt's Rough Rider Regiment in Cuban Campaign, 1898, and as Battalion Adjutant in 40th U.S.V. Infantry in the Philippines, 1899-1901; entered diplomatic service, 1902; served as Secretary in Cuba, China, and Portugal; Minister and Ambassador to Chile, 1910-16; Ambassador to Mexico, 1916-20; Under-Secretary of State, 1921-22; Ambassador to Belgium, 1922-24; Ambassador to Italy, 1924-29; Member American delegations to Fifth and Sixth Pan-American Conferences; special mission to Haiti, 1930; Chairman United States Tariff Commission, 1930-31; Chairman, Republican National Committee, 1934-36; American Society of International Law; Council on Foreign Relations. *Publications:* magazine articles on foreign affairs. *Recreations:* golf, tennis, travel. *Address:* Newport, Rhode Island, U.S.A. *Clubs:* The Brook, Links (New York); The Links (Long Island); Metropolitan (Washington); Clambake, County, Reading Room, Newport (R.I.). [*Died* 10 *July* 1959.

FLETCHER, John Gould; *b.* Little Rock, Arkansas, 3 Jan. 1886; *o. s.* of John Gould and Adolphine Krause Fletcher; *m.* 1st, Florence Emily Arbuthnot (divorced, 1936); 2nd, 1936, Charlie May Hogue. *Educ.:* Phillips Academy, Andover, Massachusetts; Harvard College; LL.D. University of Arkansas, 1933. Travelled extensively in Europe, 1908-14; in America 1914-16, visiting California, Arizona, and going down Mississippi River in a steamboat; resident in London, 1916; revisited America 1920, 1923, 1926-27, 1929, 1931; resident in America since 1933. *Publications:* Fire and Wine, 1913; The Dominant City, 1913; Irradiations, 1915; Goblins and Pagodas, 1916; The Tree of Life, 1918; Japanese Prints, 1918; Some Contemporary American Poets (pamphlet), 1920; Breakers and Granite, 1921; Paul Gauguin, His Life and Art, 1921; Parables, 1925; Branches of Adam, 1926; The Dance over Fire and Water, translated from the French of Elie Faure, 1926; The Reveries of a Solitary, translated (with introduction) from the French of J. J. Rousseau, 1927; Captain John Smith, 1928; The Black Rock, 1928; Europe's Two Frontiers, 1930; XXIV Elegies, 1935; Life is my Song, 1937; Selected Poems, 1938 (Pulitzer Prize in Poetry, 1939); South Star, 1941; The Burning Mountain, 1946; Arkansas, 1947. *Recreations:* gipsying and gardening. *Address:* Johnswood, Route 5 Box 435, Little Rock, Arkansas, U.S.A. [*Died* 10 *May* 1950.
[*But death not notified in time for inclusion in Who Was Who 1941–1950, first edn.*

FLETCHER, Sir Murchison; *see* Fletcher, Sir A. G. M.

FLETCHER, Sir Walter, Kt., *cr.* 1953; C.B.E. 1947 (O.B.E. 1919); Chairman and Managing Director Hecht, Levis and Kahn (Rubber Merchants), 15-18 St. Dunstans Hill, E.C.3, since 1926; *b.* 18 April 1892; 2nd *s.* of Paul and Cecile Fleischl; *m.* 1928, Esme Mabel Boyd. *Educ.:* Charterhouse; Lausanne Univ. In business in Paris, Budapest and Hamburg up to 1914. Major in R.A.O.C., 1914-18, served in E. Africa (despatches, O.B.E.); in business in E. Africa, 1918-24; travelled extensively in Far East, East Indies, Europe and U.S.A., 1924-1939; several times Chm. of London Rubber Trade Assoc. Contested E. Birkenhead as Conservative candidate and stood down in favour of Liberal Minister in Coalition, 1931; M.P. (C.) Bury, 1945-50, Bury and Radcliffe, 1950-55. Exhibited pictures in Royal Academy, 1937 and 1938; also privately in London, 1947. Special Service in Far East, 1939-46 (C.B.E.). *Recreations:* farming, painting. *Address:* 26 Carlyle Square, S.W.3. *T.:* Flaxman 4344. *Clubs:* Bath, Garrick, Pratt's. [*Died* 6 *April* 1956.

FLETCHER, William Charles, C.B. 1921; M.A.; *b.* 1865; *s.* of George Fletcher, Wesleyan Minister, late Governor Wesleyan Theological College, Richmond; *m.* Kate Edith Penny (*d.* 1923); two *s.* two *d.* *Educ.:* Kingswood School; St. John's College, Cambridge. 2nd Wrangler, 1886; Fellow of St. John's, Camb., 1887; Asst. Master at Bedford Grammar School, 1887-96; Headmaster of Liverpool Institute, 1896-1904; H.M. Chief Inspector of Secondary Schools, 1904-26; Asst. Master at the Grove School, Hindhead, 1926-53. President of the Mathematical Association during War of 1939-45, Hon. Mem., 1958. *Address:* Kelso, Sandheath Road, Hindhead, Surrey. [*Died* 13 *Jan.* 1959.

FLEXNER, Abraham, A.B., A.M., LL.D., Litt.D.; M.D. (Berlin and Brussels hon.); Director of Inst. for Advanced Study, Princeton, N.J., 1930-39, Director Emeritus since 1939; Rhodes Memorial Lecturer, Oxford University, 1928; Taylorian Lecturer, Univ. of Oxford, 1928; Director of Division of Studies and Medical Education of General Education Board, New York, 1925-28; Associate Member All Souls, Oxford, 1928; *b.* Louisville, Kentucky, 13 Nov. 1866; *s.* of Morris Flexner and Esther Abraham; *m.* 1898, Anne Laziere Crawford (*d.* 1955); two *d.* *Educ.:* Johns Hopkins Univ.; Harvard Univ.; Univ. of Berlin. Expert Carnegie Foundation for Advancement of Teaching, New York, 1908-12; Officer of General Education Bd. 1913-28; Comm. of Legion of Honour, 1926. *Publications:* The American College, 1908; Medical Education in U.S. and Canada, 1910; Medical Education in Europe, 1912; Prostitution in Europe, 1914; A Modern School and a Modern College, 1923; Medical Education: A Comparative Study, 1925; Do Americans Really Value Education?, 1927; Universities: American, English, German, 1930; I Remember, an Autobiography, 1940; Henry S. Pritchett, a Biography, 1943; Daniel Colt Gilman: Founder of the American Type of University, 1946; (in collaboration with Esther S. Bailey) Funds and Foundations: Their Policies Past and Present (New York) 1952; also educational papers in periodicals. *Address:* 522 Fifth Av., New York. [*Died* 21 *Sept.* 1959.

FLIGHT, Claude; Painter; interior decorator in partnership with Edith Lawrence; Lino-Cut Colour printer, Writer, Lecturer, etc.; *b.* 16 Feb. 1881; *s.* of late Dr. Walter Flight, F.R.S.; *m.*; two *d.* *Educ.:* various schools. 2 years engineering; 1½ years as a librarian; 7 years farming and bee-keeping in Sussex; started to study art just before the War; served throughout European War, 1914-18, 3½ years in France, shoeing smith to Capt. R.A.S.C. (four medals, chevalier order of Mérite Agricole); since when has studied art; Lino-cut colourprints bought by British and South Kensington Museums, watercolour paintings by V. & A. Museum; pictures exhibited at International Exhibitions, Holland, France, Switzerland, Germany, S. Africa, Australia, China, Japan, Canada, America, and Italy; water colour bought by Birmingham Public Gallery; has organized the first eight yearly exhibitions in London of British Linocuts; has made an educational film of lino cutting and printing, and has developed a style of painting and designing which is entirely his own. Many of his pictures and all his colour blocks were destroyed by enemy action in 1941. *Publications:* Linocuts (2nd Ed.); Tinker, Tailor; Animal, Vegetable, or Mineral; Lino Cutting and Printing; Christmas and other Feasts and Festivals; The Practice of Lino Cutting and Printing in Colours and Black and White; (with Edith Lawrence, in Basic English) A little about Geography, A little about History, A little about Art; late Editor of Arts and Crafts quarterly; various articles on art. *Address:* Wood Cottage, Pigtrough Lane, Donhead St. Andrew, near Shaftesbury, Dorset. [*Died* 10 *Oct.* 1955.

FLINT, Ethelbert Rest; Professor of Surgery, Univ. of Leeds, 1936-40, Emeritus Professor since 1940; Hon. Consulting Surgeon to the General Infirmary at Leeds, etc.; *b.* 1880; *s.* of Frederic Flint and May Lance; *m.* 1918, Alicia Bay Farrer; three *s.* *Educ.:* Leeds University and Medical School. M.B., Ch.B., 1906; M.R.C.S., L.R.C.P. (Lond.), 1905; F.R.C.S. (Eng.), 1912; House Surgeon, Norfolk and Norwich Hospital; General Infirmary at Leeds, 1907; R.C.O., 1911; R.S.O., 1912; Private Assistant to Sir Berkeley Moynihan, 1919-26; Lieutenant and Captain, R.A.M.C., 1915-19; Assistant Surgeon to Leeds General Infirmary, 1922; Surgeon, 1933. *Publications:* papers in medical journals. *Recreations:* formerly cricket, football, hockey, now golf and tennis. *Address:* Myrtle Lodge, Kilbride, Co. Wicklow, Eire. *T.:* Brittas Bridge 29. [*Died* 5 *Jan.* 1956.

FLOOD, Brig.-Gen. Richard E. S.; *see* Solly-Flood.

FLORENCE, Mary S.; *see* Sargant-Florence.

FLOUD, Peter Castle, C.B.E. 1954; Keeper of Circulation Department, Victoria and Albert Museum, since 1947; *b.* 1 June 1911; *e. s.* of Sir Francis Floud, K.C.B., K.C.S.I., K.C.M.G., D.C.L.; *m.* 1938, Jean Esther McDonald; one *s.* two *d.* *Educ.:* Gresham's School, Holt; Wadham Coll., Oxford; London School of Economics. Assistant-Keeper, Victoria and Albert Museum, 1935-39; Principal, London Regional Headquarters, Ministry of Home Security, 1939-44; Service with U.N.R.R.A. Balkan and Middle East Missions in Cairo and Teheran, 1944-46; Chief of U.N.R.R.A. Mission to Albania, 1946-47; Chairman: Children's Section, Internat. Council of Museums, 1950-53; Mem. Court of Governors, Nat. Museum of Wales, 1955. *Address:* 42 Well Walk, N.W.3. *T.:* Hampstead 5883. [*Died* 22 *Jan.* 1960.

FLOWERDEW, Spencer Pelham, C.B.E. 1936; M.Inst.C.E.; *b.* 6 Oct. 1881; *s.* of Arthur John Blomfield Flowerdew and Hannah Symonds; *m.* 1908, Angel Dorothy Knox; three *s.* *Educ.:* Framlingham; Royal Indian Engineering College, Coopers Hill. Appointed Assistant Engineer, Indian State Railways, 1902; Divisional Superintendent, 1925; Chief Engineer, 1927; Director of Civil Engineering, Railway Board, 1929; Retired 1930; appointed Chief Engineer, Construction, Nyasaland Rys. Ld. Nyasaland; built railway from Blantyre to Lake Nyasa; Retired, 1935. *Address:* The Cottage, Rickinghall, Diss, Norfolk. *T.A.* and *T.:* Botesdale 58. [*Died* 21 *March* 1959.

FLUGEL, John Carl, B.A. (Oxon); D.Sc., (Lond.); Hon. F.B.Ps.S.; Hon. Member, Indian Psychological Association; Special Lecturer in Psychology, University College, London, since 1944; *b.* 13 June 1884; *s.* of Carl Flugel and Mary Eccles; *m.* 1913, Sofie Mabel Ingeborg Klingberg; one *d.* *Educ.:* Balliol College, Oxford; University of Würzburg. Demonstrator in Psychology, University College, London, 1909; Assistant, 1910; Senior Lecturer, 1920; Asst. Prof. of Psychology, University College, London, 1929-43. Hon. Sec. British Psychological Soc., 1911-20; Hon. Librarian, 1921-32; Pres. 1932-35; Hon. Sec., Internat. Psychoanalytical Assoc., 1920-22; John Locke Scholar in Mental Philosophy, Univ. of Oxford, 1908; Carpenter Medallist, Univ. of London, 1931; Conway Memorial Lecturer, 1941; Chairman, Programme Cttee. International Congress on Mental Health, 1948; President Section J, British Association, 1950. *Publications:* The Psycho-analytic Study of the Family, 1921; Practice, Fatigue, and Oscillation: a Study of Work at High Pressure, 1928; The Psychology of Clothes, 1930; An Introduction to Psycho-analysis, 1932; A Hundred Years of Psychology, 1933; Men and their Motives, 1934; Man, Morals and Society, 1945; Population, Psychology and Peace, 1947; many articles on psychological subjects in technical journals and contrib. to various books on psychology. *Recreations:* lawn tennis, swimming, cycling. *Address:* 20 Merton Rise, N.W.3. *T.:* Primrose 0559. [*Died* 6 *Aug.* 1955.

FOGARTY, Most Rev. Michael; Bishop of Killaloe (R.C.), since 1904; *b.* Kilcoleman Nenagh, 1859. *Educ.:* Maynooth College. Priest, 1885; Professor of Philosophy and Canon Law, Carlow College, 1886-89; Professor of Dogmatic and Moral Theology, Maynooth College, 1889-1904. Personal title of Archbishop conferred 1954, on his appointment as an Assistant at the Pontifical Throne. *Address:* Bishop's House, Westbourne, Ennis, Co. Clare. [*Died* 25 *Oct.* 1955.

FOLEY, Major Francis Edward, C.M.G. 1941; *b.* Highbridge, Somerset, 24 Nov. 1884; *s.* of Andrew Wood Foley, Burnham on Sea, Somerset, and Isabella Turnbull; *m.* 1921, Katharine Eva, *d.* of William Lee, Dartmouth; one *d.* *Educ.:* France. Served European War, Herts. Regt. and 2/6 North Staffs. Regt. Capt., 1918 (despatches); General Staff (I) G.H.Q. Rhine Army; H.B.M. Passport Control Officer for Germany, 1920-39; H.B.M. Passport Control Officer, Scandinavia, 1939-40; recommissioned, 1940; attached C.-in-C. Norwegian Forces in the Field, 1940; retired, 1949. Knight's Cross of Order of Saint Olaf. *Address:* 32 Eveson Road, Norton, Stourbridge, Worcs. [*Died* 8 *May* 1958.

FOLLETT, Mrs. J. R.; *see* Mann, Cathleen.

FOLLICK, Mont, Dr. Phil.; *b.* Cardiff, 1887; unmarried. *Educ.:* Sorbonne, Paris; Univ. of Halle a/S.(Dr. Phil.); Univ. of Padua. Professor of English at Univ. of Madrid for four years; founder and proprietor of Regent School of Languages (demolished by enemy action), London. An advocate of English spelling reform and Decimal Currency. Contested (Lab.) Ashford (Kent) 1929, East Surrey 1931, West Fulham 1935; M.P. (Lab.) Loughborough, 1945-55. Member Fabian Society, F.R.G.S., F.R.S.A. Inventor and Patentee of the Geodok system of teaching geography. Secretary to the Aga Khan, Sir Robert Philp (Prime Minister of Queensland) and Muley Hafid (Emperor of Morocco). Governor of Uppingham, and of Nottingham University. *Publications:* The Adam's Lottery, 1919; Influence of English, 1934; Facing Facts, 1935; Efforts of Chance, 1938; English Grammar for Foreigners, 11 editions; The Twelve Republics, 1952; etc. *Address:* 18 Regency House, Jersey, C.I. [*Died* 10 *Dec.* 1958.

FOOT, Right Hon. Isaac, P.C. 1937; *b.* 23 Feb. 1880; *s.* of late Isaac Foot, Plymouth; *m.* 1904, Eva (*d.* 1946), *d.* of Angus Mackintosh, M.D.; five *s.* two *d.*; *m.* 1951, Mrs. Catherine Elizabeth Taylor, *d.* of Frederick Dawe, Crow's Nest, Liskeard. Senior partner in Foot and Bowden, solicitors, Plymouth; contested Totnes (Devon), Jan. 1910; S.E. Cornwall or Bodmin Division, Dec. 1910 and Dec. 1918; Plymouth (Sutton), Nov. 1919; St. Ives (Cornwall), June 1937; Tavistock (Devon), 1945. M.P. (L.) Bodmin Division of Cornwall, 1922-24, 1929-35; Deputy Mayor of Plymouth, 1920-21, Lord Mayor, 1945-46; Member of Round Table Conference on India, 1930-31; Secretary for Mines, 1931-32; Member of Joint Select Committee on India; Pres. National Commercial Temperance League; National Pres. Brotherhood Movement, 1936-37; Vice-Pres. Methodist Conference, 1937-38; Pres. National Sunday School Union, 1938-39; Pres. Liberal Party Organisation, 1947; Pres. Cromwell Assoc.; J.P. Cornwall; Dep. Chm. Cornwall Quarter Sessions, 1945-53, Chm. 1953-55. Director United Kingdom Provident Institution. D.Litt. Exeter University 1959. F.R.S.L. *Publications:* Oliver Cromwell and Abraham Lincoln: A Comparison, 1944; Michael Verran and Thomas Carlyle, 1946; contributions on political and literary subjects to newspapers, etc. *Recreations:* reading and book collecting. *Address:* Pencrebar, Callington, Cornwall. *T.:* Callington 204. *Clubs:* National Liberal, Reform, Eighty. [*Died* 13 *Dec.* 1960.

FOOTNER, Colonel Foster Lake, D.S.O. 1919; T.D., D.L.; *b.* 1881. *Educ.:* Marlborough. Served Mesopotamia, 1914-16; present at defence of Kut (despatches, D.S.O.); Mayor of Romsey, 1921-22, 1929-30 and 1930-31. *Address:* Romsey, Hants. [*Died* 18 *April* 1953.

FORBER, Sir Edward Rodolph, K.C.B., *cr.* 1932 (C.B. 1924); C.B.E. 1918; *b.* 20 July 1878; *e. s.* of Thomas Forber, Liverpool; *m.* 1st, 1905, Catherine Mary, *d.* of F. Howell, Liverpool; 2nd, 1929, Janet Elizabeth Lane-Claypon, M.D., D.Sc., J.P., *d.* of W. W. Lane-Claypon, Boston, Lincs. *Educ.:* Liverpool Coll.; Univ. Coll., Liverpool; Trinity Coll., Cambridge. Dep. Secretary Ministry of Health, 1925-30; Chairman of the Board of Customs and Excise, 1930-34; Chairman of the Board of Inland Revenue, 1934-38. *Address:* Flat 1, White House, Claremont Rd., Seaford, Sussex. *Club:* Oxford and Cambridge. [*Died* 8 *July* 1960.

FORBES, 22nd Lord (*cr.* 1442 or before), **Atholl Laurence Cunyngham Forbes;** Major, late Reserve of Officers, Grenadier Guards; late Representative Peer Scotland; *b.* 14 Sept. 1882; *s.* of 21st Baron Forbes and Margaret Alice (*d.* 1943), *d.* of Sir William Hanmer Dick-Cunyngham of Prestonfield, Midlothian, 8th Bart.; *S.* father, 1916; *m.* 1914, Lady Mabel Anson, *d.* of 3rd Earl of Lichfield; one *s.* *Educ.:* Winchester; Christ Church, Oxford. *Heir: s.* Master of Forbes. *Address:* Castle Forbes, Keig, Aberdeen. *T.:* Keig 224. *Clubs:* Guards; New (Edinburgh): Royal Northern (Aberdeen). [*Died* 26 *Nov.* 1953.

FORBES, Lt.-Col. Hon. Bertram Aloysius, Pasha, C.M.G. 1937; O.B.E. 1919; Retired Officer; *b.* 26 May 1882; *yr. s.* of 7th Earl of Granard. *Educ.:* Oratory School, Edgbaston. Joined Royal Ulster Rifles from Militia, 1902; Bt. Lt. Col., 1923; attached Egyptian Army, 1913; was Officer Commanding 12th Sudanese, Eastern Arab Corps and General Staff Officer and Assist. Act. Quarter-Master, General Headquarters, Khartoum; Assistant Inspector General Egyptian Army, 1932-37; at G.H.Q., M.E.F., 1941-42 as Inspector of Prisoner of War Establishments; served European War, Dardanelles, 1915; and Egyptian Expeditionary Force, Sudan, 1917, operations against Lau Nuers (despatches twice, medal and clasp, O.B.E., Order of Nile, 2nd Class). *Recreation:* shooting. *Clubs:* Army and Navy, Turf; Kildare Street (Dublin). [*Died* 5 *Aug.* 1960.

FORBES, Admiral of the Fleet Sir Charles Morton, G.C.B., *cr.* 1940 (K.C.B., *cr.* 1935; C.B. 1929); D.S.O. 1916; *b.* 22 Nov. 1880; 2nd *s.* of late James Forbes of Colombo, Ceylon, and Mount Grace, Potters Bar; *m.* 1st, 1909, Agnes Millicent (*d.* 1915), *y. d.* of late J. A. Ewen, J.P., of Potters Bar; 2nd, 1921, Marie Louise, *d.* of late Axel Berndtson, Stockholm, Sweden; one *d.* *Educ.:* Dollar Academy; Eastman's, Southsea. Entered Royal Navy, 1894; Commander, 1912; Capt. 1917; Rear-Adm. 1928; Vice-Adm. 1933; Adm. 1936; Adm. of the Fleet, 1940; served European War, 1914-18, including Jutland (D.S.O.); Director of Naval Ordnance, 1925-28; Rear Admiral (D) Commanding Destroyer Flotillas Mediterranean Fleet, 1930-31; Third Sea Lord and Controller of the Navy, 1932-34; Vice-Admiral commanding 1st Battle Squadron and Second in Command Mediterranean Fleet, 1934-36; Commander-in-Chief, Home Fleet, 1938-40; Commander-in-Chief, Plymouth, 1941-1943. *Address:* Cawsand Place, Wentworth, Virginia Water. *Club:* United Service. [*Died* 28 *Aug.* 1960.

FORBES, Sir Courtenay; *see* Forbes, Sir V. C. W.

FORBES, Lt.-Col. Frederick William Dempster, C.M.G. 1919; D.S.O. 1917; V.D.; J.P.; *s.* of late Robert A. Forbes; *b.* 24 Feb. 1883; *m.* 1915, Violet Carter. Served European War, 1914-19 (despatches, D.S.O., C.M.G.). *Address:* 33 Carrier Street, Benalla, Victoria, Australia. [*Died* 22 *Sept.* 1957.

FORBES, Sir George Arthur D. Ogilvie-, K.C.M.G., *cr.* 1937 (C.M.G. 1934); D.L. Aberdeenshire; *b.* Dec. 1891; *e. s.* of late J. C. M. Ogilvie-Forbes, J.P., D.L., of Boyndlie, Aberdeenshire, and Christine, *d.* of Captain George Augustus Vaughan; *m.* Clare Mary, *o. d.* of late H. C. V. Hunter, of Abermarlais, Llangadock; one *d.* *Educ.:* Beaumont; New College, Oxford; Univ. of Bonn. Formerly Captain, Scottish Horse

Yeomanry; served European War, Gallipoli, Egypt, Mesopotamia; A.D.C. to Lieut.-General Sir F. S. Maude, C.-in-C., Mesopotamia (wounded, despatches twice); General Staff, War Office, 1918; entered Diplomatic Service, 1919; 3rd Secretary, Foreign Office, 1919; Stockholm, 1919; Copenhagen, Helsingfors, 1920; 2nd Secretary, 1920; Foreign Office, 1923; First Secretary, Belgrade, 1925; Mexico City, 1927-30; Chargé d'Affaires at the Holy See, 1930-32; Acting Counsellor, British Embassy, Baghdad, 1932-35; Counsellor British Embassy, Madrid, 1935-37; Chargé d'Affaires in Madrid and Valencia, 1936 and 1937; Counsellor, British Embassy, Berlin, 1937-1939; Counsellor, British Legation, Oslo, 1939; Minister at Havana, 1940-44; H.M. Ambassador to Venezuela, 1944-48; retired 1949. Member of Council, Catholic Union of Gt. Britain, 1649; Commissioner of 4th Nat. Assembly of Scotland for the Covenant. 1950; Member of Council, Saltire Society, 1950; Member Exec. Cttee. Scottish Council for Industry and Development, 1953. *Recreations:* Highland bagpipes, sailing, rowing, country pursuits. *Address:* Boyndlie, Fraserburgh, Aberdeenshire. *T.:* New Aberdour 27. *Clubs:* Travellers', Royal Automobile; Royal Northern (Aberdeen). [*Died* 10 *July* 1954.

FORBES, Colonel Ian Rose-Innes Joseph, D.S.O. 1920; late Royal Scots Fusiliers; late Captain Gordon Highlanders; Hon. Col. 6th. Bn. Gordon Highlanders, 1945; *b.* Jacobabad, India, 28 Oct. 1875; *e. s.* of late Lieut.-Colonel John Forbes, J.P., D.L. of Rothiemay, and Mary Livesey (*d.* 1929), *o. d.* of Thomas Wardle; *m.* 1st, 1901, Lady Helen (*d.* 1926), *d.* of 3rd Earl of Craven; two *s.* four *d.*; 2nd, 1932, Mary Sibell Agnes, A.R.R.C., (*d.* 1957), *e.d.* of late Walter R. Shaw-Stewart, M.B.E. Entered army, 1894; Captain, 1901; Major, 1914; Lt. Col. 1915; A.D.C. to Viceroy of Ireland (Earl Cadogan), 1901-2; Adjutant 1st Lanark R.V. 1903-8; served South Africa, 1899-1900, including Siege of Ladysmith (Queen's medal 3 clasps, wounded); European War, 1914-18 (wounded, despatches thrice, 1914 star, D.S.O.); late director of the Scottish Australian Coy., and Chairman of the Scottish Australian Mining Coy.; late Crown Mandatory for the District of the River Deveron; J.P. Banffshire; late D.L. and V.L. for County of Banff; Tory; R.C. *Heir: s.* Ian George, M.B.E., M.C., T.D., late Lt. Gren. Guards, now a Benedictine Father [*b.* 1902. Served as Chapl. 1st Guards Brigade, C.M.F.]. *Publications:* essays on military and motoring subjects. *Recreations:* fishing, shooting, motoring, pipe-playing. *Address:* Beckford Lodge, Tisbury, Wilts. *T.:* Tisbury 350. [*Died* 18 *Sept.* 1957.

FORBES, Robert Jaffrey, C.B.E. 1948; Pianist and Conductor; Principal, Royal Manchester College of Music, 1929-53; President Incorporated Society of Musicians, 1938; *b.* Stalybridge, 1878; 2nd *s.* of David Forbes, newspaper proprietor; *m.* 1907, Beatrice Mary, *o. d.* of John Green, J.P., of Lowton, Lancashire; three *d.* *Educ.:* Leigh Grammar School; Royal Manchester College of Music. *Address:* Ballabeg, Winton Road, Bowdon, Cheshire. *T.:* Altrincham 4838. *Club:* Union (Manchester). [*Died* 13 *May* 1958.

FORBES, Sir (Victor) Courtenay (Walter), K.C.M.G., *cr.* 1945 (C.M.G. 1941); Managing Director of the Beauship Trading and Shipping Co. Ltd.; *b.* 29 Jan. 1889; *s.* of Capt. Hon. W. R. D. Forbes and Eveline, *d.* of J. Farwell; *m.* 1916, Luia Juta (marriage dissolved); one *d.*; *m.* 1950, Mary, *widow* of Walter Carter Bizley, and *e. d.* of Francis Olivieri. *Educ.:* Eton; Univ. Coll., Oxford. Clerk in Foreign Office, 1913; 1st Secretary, 1924; Mexcio City, 1930-32; Counsellor of Embassy, Madrid, 1932-34; H.B.M. Envoy Extraordinary and Minister Plenipotentiary in Peru, 1934-44, Ambassador, 1944-45. Retired on pension Dec. 1945. *Recreations:* shooting and fishing. *Address:* Pine Ridge, 9 The Great Quarry, Guildford, Surrey. [*Died* 26 *Jan.* 1958.

FORBES-ROBERTSON, Colonel James, V.C., D.S.O. 1917; M.C.; D.L. Sutherland; *b.* 7 July 1884; *s.* of late F. Forbes-Robertson; *m.* 1927, Hilda, A.R.R.C., *y. d.* of late Sir Ralph Forster, 1st Bart.; one *s.* two *d.* Entered Border Regiment, 1904; Captain 1914; Major, 1921; Lieut.-Col., Gordon Highlanders, 1926; Colonel 1930; served European War, 1914-18 (wounded, despatches thrice, M.C., D.S.O. with bar, V.C., Bt. Lieut.-Col.); commanded 2nd Batt. Gordon Highlanders, 1926-30; Commander 152nd (Seaforth and Cameron) Infantry Brig., T.A., 1932-34; retired pay, 1934. *Address:* Chardwar, Bourton-on-the-Water, Glos. [*Died* 5 *Aug.* 1955.

FORD, Arthur Clow, O.B.E. 1949 (M.B.E. 1919); B.A.; 3rd *s.* of George Ford, late Registrar for Estate Duties for Scotland, and Charlotte Henrietta Clow, Edinburgh; *m.* 1912, Jessie Cecilia Kinvig; one *s.* one *d.* *Educ.:* George Watson's College, Edinburgh; University of Lausanne. Assistant Master in different schools in England, Ireland, and Switzerland, 1905-14; interned in Germany and Holland, 1914-18; administrative staff, University of London, 1919; External and Extension Registrar, 1936-46; Sec. to Universities Council for Adult Education, 1947-1950; Director of Dept. of Extra-Mural Studies, Univ. of London, 1936-48. Hon. Member of Pharmaceutical Society; Hon. Sec. London Regional Committee for Education among H.M. Forces, 1940-50. Chevalier de l'Ordre de la Couronne, 1948; Knight of the Orde Van Oranje-Nassau, 1949. *Publications:* miscellaneous articles in Educational Press. *Recreation:* gardening. *Address* Windrush, Spade Oak Reach, Bourne End, Bucks. *T.:* Bourne End 795. [*Died* 14 *May* 1952.

FORD, Colonel Sir Bertram, Kt., *cr.* 1936; T.D., D.L., LL.D., Birmingham University, 1938; F.C.A.; Managing Director Birmingham Post and Mail Ltd., 1943-47 (General Manager, 1913-43); *b.* 1869; *s.* of late Major William Henry Ford, V.D., Wolverhampton; *m.* 1903, Kate Constance, *d.* of late Henry Richards, Wolverhampton. *Educ.:* Wolverhampton Grammar School. Life Governor, Birmingham Univ.; Pres. of Birmingham Blue Coat School; Chairman, Board of Management, Birmingham Hospitals Contributory Association since 1927; Pres. British Hospitals Contributory Schemes Association since 1932; President, Birmingham Dental Hospital, since 1936; Pres., Sales Managers' Association (Midlands Branch), 1932 and 1934; Vice-Pres., Birmingham and Midland Ear and Throat Hospital; Chairman, Birmingham Joint Committee, British Red Cross Society and St. John Ambulance Brigade; Liveryman, Worshipful Company of Stationers, and Freemen of the City of London; Knight and Member of Chapter General Order of St. John of Jerusalem; Dir.-Gen., St. John Amb. Assoc., 1948-51; Diocesan Reader, Diocese of Lichfield, 23 years; Provost's Warden, Birmingham Cathedral; served in Infantry, R.A.M.C. Volunteers Force, and R.F.A. (T.F.), European War, 1914-18; Commanded 4th Staffordshire Battery and other R.A. Units, 3rd North Midland Brigade, 46th Div.; Col. Commanding 1st Birmingham Batt., C.L.B., 1922-33; County Staff Officer for Cadets (Warwickshire), 1926-30; Member of Governing Body, C.L.B.; Hon. Colonel, Royal Corps of Signals 48th Division, 1933-37; Hon. Col. R.A.M.C. Units 48th (S.M.) Division T.A. since 1937; County Commissioner, St. John Ambulance Brigade (Birmingham County); Life Governor Royal Society of St. George; President, Unit No. 40 Sea Cadet Corps. *Address:* Flat 105, Majestic Hotel, Folkestone, Kent. [*Died* 20 *July* 1955.

FORD, Jeremiah Denis Matthias; Smith Professor Emeritus of the French and Spanish Languages, Harvard University; *b.* Cambridge, Mass., U.S.A., 2 July 1873; *s.* of Jeremiah D. Ford and Mary Agnes Collins; *m.* 1902, Anna Fearns; two *s.* two *d.* *Educ.:* North Monastery, Cork; Harvard University (A.B. 1894, A.M. 1895, Ph.D. 1897); University of Paris. Instr. in French and Italian at Harvard, 1895-97; Harvard Fellow at Univ. of Paris, 1897-98; Instr. in Romance Languages, Harvard, 1898-1902; Asst. Professor, 1902-7; Smith Professor of French and Spanish, 1907-43; Harvard Exchange Prof. at Univ. of Paris, 1922; Director of Am. University Union for Europe, with Bureau at Paris, 1925-26; Hyde Lecturer at French provincial Univs., 1925-26, and also in Spain; on educational mission in South America, visiting seven countries, 1913, Director of Harvard Council on Hispano-Am. studies; Officer, Legion of Honour, France; Commander, Royal Order Isabel the Catholic, Spain; Officer, Royal Order of the Crown, Italy; Knight, Order of Merit, Rumania; Officer, Order of Public Instruction, Portugal. Hon. Docteur-ès-lettres, Univ. of Toulouse, France, 1922; D.Lit., Natl. U. of Ireland, 1932; Litt.D., Trinity Coll., Dublin, 1934; Bowdoin Coll., 1935; Harvard Univ., 1942; L.H.D., Fordham Univ., 1940. Corr. Member Institut de France (Académie des Inscriptions et Belles-lettres) and of Royal Spanish Academy; Fellow (and former Pres.) Am. Academy of Arts and Sciences; Fellow (and former Pres.) Medieval Academy of Am.; Fellow Am. Assn. Advancement of Science; Fellow (V.P.) of Hispanic Soc. of Am.; Member (and former Pres.) Modern Humanities Research Assn.; Member (twice V.P.) of Mod. Language Assn. of Am.; Member (former Pres.) of Am. Catholic Historical Assn.; Delegate to Am. Council of Learned Societies, etc. Laetare Medallist of Univ. of Notre Dame; Medallist of Hispanic Soc. of America; Cervantes Medallist of Hispanic Inst. in Florida, 1951. *Publications:* As author, co-author, editor, co-editor, and editor-in-chief, published more than 60 books and innumerable articles dealing with French, Spanish, Italian, Portuguese and their literatures. Among them are Main Currents of Spanish Literature, 1919; A Spanish Anthology, 1900 and later; Chivalrous Romances in Italian Verse; Selections from Don Quixote; Lusiadas of Camões, 1946; Letters of John III of Portugal, 1930; Letters of Court of John III; Crónica de João de Castro; four Grammars of Spanish; two Grammars of Portuguese. *Recreations:* forestry, gardening. *Address:* 9 Riedesel Avenue, Cambridge, Massachusetts, U.S.A. *T.:* Kirkland 7-9650, Cambridge, Mass. *Clubs:* Harvard, Club of Odd Volumes (Boston); Harvard Faculty (Cambridge, Mass.); Cercle de la Renaissance ou des amis X (Paris). [*Died* 13 *Nov.* 1958.

FORD, Maj.-Gen. Sir Reginald, K.C.M.G., *cr.* 1919 (C.M.G. 1915); C.B. 1917; D.S.O. 1900; *b.* 7 Dec. 1868; *s.* of late Rev. C. H. Ford of Bishopton; *m.* 1st, 1894, Alice Hope (*d.* 1923), *d.* of Major-General Balmain, and *widow* of E. H. Lockley, of The Grange, Chobham, Surrey; 2nd, 1924, Pearl Gertrude (*d.* 1947), *d.* of W. Tuthill Dudley of Ohio, U.S.A. Entered Royal Marines, 1889; transferred A.S.C. 1893; Captain 1896; served S. Africa as A.A.G. (despatches twice, medal five clasps, and D.S.O.); European War, 1914-18 (despatches eight times, C.B., C.M.G., prom. Maj.-General, K.C.M.G.); Colonel Commandant R.A.S.C., 1930-38. *Address:* c/o Midland Bank, 431 Oxford Street, W 1. [*Died* 28 *April* 1951.

FORD, Brigadier Vincent Tennyson Randle, D.S.O. 1918; late York and Lancaster Regiment; Food Officer for North Midland Division, 1946-47; *b.* 24 Nov. 1885; *s.* of late Major C. W. Randle Ford, York and Lancaster Regiment, and Emilia, *d.* of Frederick Tennyson, brother of 1st Lord Tennyson; *m.* 1917, Dorothy, *o. d.* of Lt.-Col. A. C. Richards, O.B.E., late Hampshire Regt.; one *d.* *Educ.:* Wellington College; Royal Military College, Sandhurst. Entered York and Lancaster Regt., 1906; Major, 1921; Lt.-Col. 1923; Col. 1927; Brig., 1937; Commandant Boys Technical School, 1923-27; D.A.A.G. Northern Command, 1928-1932; D.A.A. and Q.M.G West Lancs Area, 1932-36; Commander 127th (Manchester) Infantry Brig. T.A., 1937-39; A.D.C. to the King, 1938-40; retired pay, 1940; served European War, Gallipoli, France, 1914-18; Batt. Comdr., 1916-19 (wounded twice, D.S.O. and bar, Crown of Italy, Brevet-Majority, despatches five times); A.A.Q.M.G., B.E.F., France, 1940 (despatches), Comdr. Chester Sub-Area, 1940; reverted to retired pay, 1945. *Address:* 15 Portman Square, W.1. *T.:* Welbeck 4307. *Club:* United Service. [*Died* 25 *Feb.* 1957.

FORDHAM, Brig. William Marshall, C.B. 1928; C.B.E. 1924; *b.* 9 Aug. 1875; *s.* of late J. W. Fordham, Bedford; *m.* 1915, Anne Lilian, *d.* of late T. W. Jacobs, Thames Ditton; one *s.* (and one killed on active service, 1941). *Educ.:* Bedford; R.M.C., Sandhurst. Served N.W. Frontier of India, 1897-98 (medal with clasp); China, 1900 (medal); European War, 1914-19 (despatches, 3rd class Order of the Nile); Waziristan, 1922-23 (despatches, C.B.E.); A.D.C. to the King, 1930-32; commanded 1st Infantry Brigade, Abbottabad, India, 1928-32; retired, 1932. *Address:* 11 Thornley Road, Felixstowe, Suffolk. *T.:* Felixstowe 1540. [*Died* 9 *Dec.* 1959.

FORMAN, Brig.-Gen. Arthur Baron, C.M.G. 1918; D.S.O. 1914; R.A.; *b.* 26 Sept. 1873. Entered army, 1894; Captain, 1900; Major, 1910; Lt.-Col. 1916; Col. 1920; served S. Africa, 1902 (Queen's medal 3 clasps); European War, 1914-18 (despatches, D.S.O., C.M.G.); Brig.-Gen. 1917-19; retired pay, 1927. *Club:* Army and Navy. [*Died* 27 *April* 1951.

FORRES, 2nd Baron, of Glenogil, *cr.* 1922; **Stephen Kenneth Guthrie Williamson,** Bt., *cr.* 1909; Chairman of Lobitos Oilfields Ltd.; Anglo Ecuadorian Oilfields Ltd.; a Director of Balfour Williamson & Co. Ltd.; and other companies; Member of the Willingdon Mission to S. America; *b.* 20 March 1888; *er. s.* of 1st Baron and Caroline Maria (*d.* 1911), *d.* of late James Charles Hayne; *S.* father 1931; *m.* 1918, Jessie, *er. d.* of late William Alfred Harford, J.P., of Petty France, Badminton, Glos.; two *s.* one *d.* *Educ.:* Eton; Trinity College, Cambridge. Served European War, 1914-18 in France, Egypt, and Gallipoli (despatches). *Recreations:* shooting, fishing. *Heir:* *s.* Hon. John Archibald Harford Williamson [*b.* 30 Oct. 1922; *m.* 1945, Gillian Maclean, *d.* of Maj. J. Maclean Grant; one *s.* two *d.*]. *Address:* Glenogil, Forfar, Angus. *T.:* Fern 224; 20 Marlborough Place, N.W.8. *T.:* Primrose 1740. *Clubs:* Brooks's, City of London. [*Died* 26 *June* 1954.

FORREST, Andrew Bryson, M.M., 1917; *b.* 2 July 1884; *s.* of James Forrest, Ironfounder, and Agnes Brown, *d.* of Andrew Bryson, Farmer; *m.* 1914, Agnes Donaldson Campbell; two *s.* (and one *s.* killed in Burma, 1944). *Educ.:* Dalkeith High School. Stockbroker. Chairman of the Edinburgh Stock Exchange, 1949, 1950; President of the Council of Associated Stock Exchanges, 1949-50. Mason, Provincial Grand Master of Midlothian, 1945-50. *Recreations:* cricket, golf, angling and curling. *Address:* Netherlea, Eskbank, Dalkeith, Midlothian; 8 George Street, Edinburgh. *T.:* (home) Dalkeith 2122; (office) Edinburgh 25006. *Club:* Northern (Edinburgh). [*Died* 11 *Sept.* 1951.

FORREST, Col. John Vincent, C.B. 1919; C.M.G. 1916; M.B.; late A.M.S.; *b.* 21 Mar. 1873; *s.* of late W. Forrest, Woodham Ferrers, Essex; *m.* 1927, Mary Gundreda, *y. d.* of late Sir William Quartus Ewart, Bart., of Glenmachan; one *s.* one *d.* Served S. Africa, 1900-2 (Queen's medal 7 clasps, King's medal 2 clasps); European War, 1914-18 (despatches six times, C.M.G., C.B.); retired pay, 1921, O.St.J. *Address:* Glenmachan, Strandtown, Belfast. *Club:* Ulster (Belfast). [*Died* 10 *Oct.* 1953.

FORREST, Sir John William, Kt., *cr.* 1925; O.B.E.; J.P. Lancashire; late cotton spinner and manufacturer; late member of National Savings Committee; Trustee Savings Banks Inspection Committee; *b.* 1867; *s.* of John Forrest, Blackburn, and Susannah Greaves of Brindle and Balderston; *m.* 1898, Alice (*d.* 1947), *d.* of William Carr, Blackburn; one *d.* *Educ.:* Queen Elizabeth's Grammar School, Blackburn. Town Council, Blackburn, 1913-38; Alderman, 1921-1938; Mayor, 1926-27; Chm. Finance Cttee. 1915-27; Educ. Cttee., 1919-38; War Pensions Com., 1916; Blackburn Conservative and Unionist Association, 1916-24; Leader of Town Council 1916-26; Chairman Blackburn Trustee Savings Bank since 1928. *Recreations:* motoring, swimming. *Address:* Norland, Blackburn. *T.:* Blackburn 5183. [*Died* 6 *May* 1951.

FORROW, Air Commodore Henry Edward, C.B. 1945; O.B.E. 1936; Royal Air Force. Director of Technical Training, Department of the Air Member for Supply and Organisation, Air Ministry, since 1951. *Address:* 117 Kenilworth Court, Lower Richmond Road, S.W.15. [*Died* 2 *Dec.* 1959.

FORSTER, Brigadier David, C.B. 1933; C.M.G. 1919; D.S.O. 1916; late R.E.; *b.* Woolwich, 23 Jan. 1878; *s.* of Lieut.-Colonel W. D. Forster, late R.A.; *m.* 1st, 1903, Isabel Frances (*d.* 1955), *d.* of Lt.-Gen. H. A. Brownlow, late R.E.; one *s.* two *d.*; 2nd, 1958, Noel Ethelreda Poynder. *Educ.:* St. Paul's School; R.M.A. Woolwich (Pollock Medal). Joined R.E., 1896; was at Chatham and Aldershot; served S. Africa with 11th Field Coy. R.E., 1899; present at battles of Belmont, Graspan, Modder River, and Magersfontein; invalided with enteric, 1900 (Queen's medal, 2 clasps); went to India, 1901; was at Jubbulpore, Bangalore, N.W. Frontier, and Burma, mostly with the 2nd Q.V.O. Sappers and Miners; Capt. 1905; passed Staff College, 1912-13; returned to India and was in Dera Ismail Khan District and Waziristan; on outbreak of war became Staff Capt. Garhwal Bde., Meerut Division, and served in France through winter 1914-15; Major, 1914; General Staff, 1915; returned to France, Sept. 1915 (battles of Loos, the Somme, Arras, 3rd Ypres; wounded twice, despatches four times, D.S.O., Bt. Lt.-Col.); General Staff, War Office, 1918-22; British Delegation, Washington Conference, Nov. 1921; official tour in Canada, Jan.-Feb. 1922; C.R.E. Dublin, Aug. 1922; R.N. War College, Mar. 1923; A.C.R.E., Catterick, Nov. 1923; C.R.E. Malaya, 1924-26; Deputy Military Secretary, War Office, 1927-30; Commander 13th Infantry Brigade, 1930-34; retired, 1934; visited Australasia, 1925; Col. 1926; Brigadier (Temp.) 1928; Army Welfare Officer, Chatham Area, Feb. 1940, Home Counties Area, Aug. 1940, S.E. Command, 1941-42; since 1921 has taken an active part in the work of the Oxford Group in different parts of the world. *Publications:* Mind and Method in Modern Minor Tactics, 1919 (with Col. W. H. Franklin); The Signs of the Times, 1918, reprinted as Coming Events, 1919; 5th edition, 1927; The Vital Choice, Endor or Calvary, a reply to Conan Doyle's New Revelation, 1919; Modern Ideas about the Bible, 1927; Bible Study in Switzerland, 1930; The Background War, 1950. *Address:* 4 Hays Mews, W.1. *T.:* Grosvenor 3443. *Club:* United Service. [*Died* 20 *Nov.* 1959.

FORSTER, Rear-Adm. Forster D. A.; *see* Arnold-Forster.

FÖRSTER, Max Theodor Wilhelm, Ph.D., Hon. Litt.D. (Dublin); Member of the Academies of Leipzig, München, Heidelberg, Royal Ac. Dublin, British Academy; Professor Emeritus of English Language and Literature at München University, 1934 and since 1948; *b.* Danzig, 8 March 1869; *s.* of late Dr. Theodor Förster, Surgeon-General. *Educ.:* High School, Münster; Universities of Münster, Bonn, Berlin. Reader and (from 1897) Professor of English Language and Literature, University of Bonn, 1894-98; University of Würzburg, 1898-1909; University of Halle, 1909-10; University of Leipzig, 1910-25; University of München, 1925-34; Visiting Professor at Yale University, New Haven, U.S.A., 1934-36; Vice-President of German Shakespeare Society. *Publications:* Beowulf-Materialien, 1900, 5th ed. 1928; British Classical Authors, 1905, 16th ed. 1947; English Authors, 1911, 11th ed. 1954; Altenglisches Lesebuch, 1913, 5th ed. 1949; English Poems, 1912; English Prose, 1915; Der Vercelli-Codex CXVII, 1913; Il Codice Vercellese con omelie e poesie in lingua Anglo-sassone, 1913; Das elisabethanische Sprichwort, 1918; Die Beowulf-Handschrift, 1919; Keltisches Wortgut im Englischen, 1921; Die Vercelli-Homilien, 1932; The Exeter Book of Old English Poetry (with R. W. Chambers and Robin Flower), 1933; Der Flussname Themse und seine Sippe, 1941; Zur Geschichte des Reliquienkultus in Altengland, 1943; Vom Fortleben antiker Sammellunare im Englischen und in anderen Volkssprachen, 1944; Frühmittel Kymrische und früh-mittelenglische Stücke bei Giraldus Cambrensis, 1953; A New Version of the Apocalypse of Thomas in Old English, 1954. Editor of the Jahrbuch der deutschen Shakespeare-Gesellschaft, 1907-18; of Beiträge zur englischen Philologie (37 vols.), 1919-41, of Englische Bibliothek (6 vols.), 1922-30; of Anglistische Abteilung des Sächsischen Forschungsinstitutes (3 vols.), 1919-24. *Recreation:* music. *Address:* 2 Hochgarten-Weg, Wasserburg a. Inn, Germany. [*Died* 10 *Nov.* 1954.

FORSYTH, Gordon M., R.I., A.R.C.A., F.R.S.A.; Consultant Designer; *b.* Fraserburgh, Aberdeenshire, 1879; *o. s.* of late Kilgour Forsyth; *m.* 1904, Elizabeth Lamont, *e. d.* of late J. L. Aiken, Aberdeen; one *s.* one *d.* *Educ.:* Robert Gordon's College; Gray's School of Art, Aberdeen; Royal Coll. of Art, London (Royal Exhibition, gained Travelling Scholarship in Design); Studying Art in Italy, 1902; Associate of Royal College of Art (design); appointed Art Director, Minton Hollins & Co., Stoke-upon-Trent, Staffordshire, 1902; Art Director, Pilkington Tile and Pottery Co., Clifton Junction, near Manchester, 1906; Royal Air Force, 1916-19; Medallist, Franco-British, Brussels, Turin, Venice, and Paris Exhibitions; Fellow of the British Society of Master Glass Painters; ex-Principal, City of Stoke-on-Trent Schools of Art; Art Adviser British Pottery Manufacturers Federation, *Publications:* Art and Craft of the Potter, 20th Century Ceramics. *Recreation:* golf. *Address:* The Grange, Gravenhunger, Woore, nr. Crewe, Cheshire. [*Died* 19 *Dec.* 1952.

FORSYTH, Thomas Miller, M.A.; D.Phil. (Edin.); *b.* Edinburgh, 7 Mar. 1871; *e. s.* of R. T. Forsyth; *m.* 1908, Elise Kersten. *Educ.:* George Watson's College; Moray House Training College; University of Edinburgh; Halle; Sorbonne. M.A. 1899; D.Phil. 1908; Private Assistant in Logic and Metaphysics, and in Education, Edinburgh; Assistant and Lecturer in Logic and Metaphysics in the University of St. Andrews, 1905-11; Professor of Philosophy in Grey University College, Bloemfontein, 1911-33; Chairman of Senate (Acting-Principal) of Grey University College, 1914-15; Acting Professor of Philosophy in Rhodes University College, Grahamstown,

1941-44. *Publications:* English Philosophy, A Study of its Method and General Development, 1910; God and the World, 1952; Articles in Mind, Philosophy, and South African Journal of Science. *Address:* 23 Stanley Road, Edinburgh 6. [*Died* 12 *Aug.* 1958.

FORT, George Seymour, C.B.E. 1918; Director of Public Companies; *b.* Oct. 1858; *s.* of Rev. R. Fort; *m.* 1906, Aileen Maud, *d.* of late Hubert Martineau; no *c.* *Educ.:* Uppingham; Hertford College, Oxford. Private Secretary to Major-General Sir Peter Scratchley, first High Commissioner for New Guinea, 1885-87; Private Secretary to Lord Loch, as Governor of Victoria, Governor Cape Colony, and High Commissioner S. Africa; visited Rhodesia, 1891; Magistrate and Commissioner for Manicaland, 1895; subsequently resided in Rhodesia as manager for various companies; Capt. King Edward's Horse, 1909. *Publications:* Life of Dr. Jameson; Alfred Beit: A Study of his Life and Work; Chance or Destiny, a Pioneer looks back, 1943; articles in Nineteenth Century, Fortnightly Review, Empire Review, etc. *Recreation:* golf. *Club:* Bath. [*Died* 10 *Jan.* 1951.

FORT, Richard; M.P. (C.) Clitheroe Division of Lancashire since 1950; *b.* 8 Aug. 1907; *s.* of late J. A. Fort, sometime second Master of Winchester College, and late Geraldine Guinness; *m.* 1st (marriage dissolved); 2nd, 1943, Jean *d.* of G. B. Rae; four *s.* one *d.* *Educ.:* Eton; New Coll., Oxford; Vienna. Hons. School of Chemistry and B.Sc. (Oxon.), 1930. Employed I.C.I. 1932; Brit. Supply Mission (New York and Washington) and Ministry of Supply, 1940-1945. Parliamentary Private Secretary to Minister of Education, 1951-54; Lay Member, Medical Research Council, 1955; Governor, Imperial College of Science and Technology, 1957; Chairman, Parliamentary and Scientific Committee, 1957. *Recreations:* lawn tennis, music, gardening. *Address:* Ruscombe House, Twyford, Reading, Berks. *T.:* Twyford 86. *Club:* Brooks's. [*Died* 16 *May* 1959.

FORTESCUE, 5th Earl (*cr.* 1789), **Hugh William Fortescue,** K.G. 1951; P.C. 1952; C.B. 1946; O.B.E. 1942; M.C.; K.St.J.; Baron Fortescue, 1746; Viscount Ebrington, 1789; Col. 96th Brigade, R.F.A., T.A., 1929; late Major Scots Greys; Captain of the Gentlemen at Arms since 1951; Lord Lieutenant of Devon since 1936; Member of Duchy of Cornwall Council since 1933; Chief Government Whip, House of Lords; *b.* 14 June 1888; *e. s.* of 4th Earl and Emily, C.B.E. 1920 (*d.* 1929), *d.* of 2nd Lord Harlech; *S.* father, 1932; *m.* 1917, Hon. Margaret Helen Beaumont (*d.* 1958), British Pres., Y.W.C.A. (C.B.E. 1958), *d.* of 1st Visc. Allendale; two *d.* *Educ.:* Eton, Sandhurst. Entered Army, Royal Scots Greys, 1907; Capt., 1915; Maj., 1919; Army Signalling Service, 1915; Gen. Staff, 1916-19; Instructor Cavalary Sch., 1914 and 1919-20; A.D.C. to Commander-in-Chief in India, 1921-22; retired on retired pay, 1922; Lt.-Col. Royal Devon Yeomanry Field Brigade R.A., 1924-1930; Col. 1930; served European War, 1914-18 (wounded twice, M.C., despatches, Bt. Maj., Legion of Honour); General Staff, 1939-43; Col. Comdt. Hon. Artillery Co., 1935-41; a Lord-in-Waiting, 1937-45; Capt. H.M. Bodyguard of Gentlemen-at-Arms, 1945; Chief Opposition Whip House of Lords, 1945; J.P., D.L. Devon. *Heir:* *b.* Hon. Denzil George Fortescue, M.C., T.D. [*b.* 1893; *m.* 1st, 1920, Marjorie Ellinor Trotter, O.B.E. (who obtained a divorce, 1941); two *s.* one *d.*; 2nd, 1941, Sybil Mary, *d.* of 3rd Viscount Hardinge; one *s.*]. *Address:* 26 Lowndes Street S.W.1. *T.:* Sloane 2679; Castle Hill, Barnstaple. *T.:* Filleigh 227. *Clubs:* Turf, White's. [*Died* 14 *June* 1958.

FORTESCUE, Col. Archer I.; *see* Irvine-Fortescue.

FORTESCUE, Brig.-Gen. Hon. Charles Granville, C.B. 1911; C.M.G. 1899; D.S.O. 1900; retired pay since 1919; *b.* 30 Oct. 1861; 6th *s.* of 3rd Earl Fortescue; *m.* 1906, Mrs. Ernest Campbell, *widow* of Captain Ernest G. Campbell, Rifle Brigade, and *e. d.* of General Sir Charles Mansfield Clarke, 3rd Bt.; two *d.* Formerly private secretary to Secretary of State for War; joined Rifle Brigade, 1881; Major, 1898; served Burmese Expedition, 1888-1889 (medal with clasp); Northern Territories of Gold Coast, including expedition Karaga, 1897-98 (despatches, C.M.G., Brevet of Lieut.-Col., medal with clasp); Brigade Major, Natal Field Force, 1899-1902 (D.S.O., despatches); Brevet Col., 1905; Brig.-Gen., 1912; served European War, 1914-18. *Address:* Annes House, Pitsford, Northampton. [*Died* 1 *Feb.* 1951.

FORTESCUE, Hon. Lady; Winifred; *b.* 7 Feb. 1888; *er. d.* of Rev. Howard Beech, M.A.; *m.* 1914, Hon. Sir John William Fortescue, K.C.V.O., LL.D. Edinburgh, D.Litt. (Oxford), Honorary Fellow Trinity College, Cambridge, Historian of the British Army, Librarian and Archivist Windsor Castle (*d.* 1933); no *c.* *Educ.:* St. Augustine's, Cliftonville; Wentworth Hall, Mill Hill. *Publications:* Perfume from Provence; Sunset House; There's Rosemary . . . There's Rue . . ., 1939; Trampled Lilies, 1941; Mountain Madness, 1943; Beauty for Ashes, 1948. *Address:* Fort Escu, Opio, A. M., France. *T.A.:* Opio, Alpesmaritimes. *T.:* Opio 7. [*Died* 9 *April* 1951.

FORWARD, Ernest Alfred, A.R.C.S., M.I.Mech.E.; *b.* 5 Sept. 1877; *s.* of William Forward; *m.* 1909, Annie (*d.* 1948), *d.* of John Harland Blandford, I.C.S.; three *d.* *Educ.:* East London Technical College; Bow Works, North London Railway; Royal Coll. of Science, A.R.C.S. (Mechanics), 1901; Assistant Science Museum, 1901; Deputy Keeper, Engineering Division, 1930; Keeper, Science Museum, 1935-37; National Physical Laboratory, 1915-18. *Publications:* Various Official Publications of the Science Museum, and contributions to Technical Press. *Recreation:* gardening. *Address:* 16 Bramley Avenue, Coulsdon, Surrey. *T.:* Uplands 4510. [*Died* 14 *Oct.* 1959.

FOSS, Brigadier Charles Calveley, V.C. 1915; C.B. 1937; D.S.O. 1915; *e. s.* of late Rt. Rev. H. J. Foss, D.D., late Bishop of Osaka, Japan; *b.* 9 Mar. 1885; *m.* 1915, Vere Katharine (*d.* 1947), *widow* of Captain Collard, 90th Punjabis, and 3rd *d.* of late J. Lambert Ovans; *m.* 1950, Phyllis Ruth, *widow* of Arthur Howie, Ceylon and 3rd *d.* of late T. W. B. Crowther, Ceylon. *Educ.:* Marlborough Coll.; R.M.C., Sandhurst. Entered Bedfordshire Regt. 1904; Captain, 1912; Major, 1921; Lt.-Col. 1930; Colonel, 1933; served European War, 1914-18 (D.S.O., V.C., Bt. Major, Bt. Lt.-Col., despatches five times); commanded 2nd Batt. The King's Regiment, 1930-33; commanded Rangoon Brigade Area, 1933-37; Area Organiser L.D.V., 1940; Lt.-Col. Home Guard, 1941-42; Colonel Home Guard, 1942-43; A.D.C. to the King, 1935-37; retired pay, 1937; County Cadet Comdt. Bedfordshire Army Cadet Force, 1942-47; D.L., J.P. Bedfordshire. *Address:* 18 St. Michael's Road, Bedford. [*Died* 9 *April* 1953.

FOSS, Hubert James; *b.* 2 May 1899; 13th *c.* of Frederick Foss, J.P., Croydon, Surrey; *m.* 1st, Kate Frances Carter Page; 2nd, Dora Maria Stevens; one *s.* three *d.* *Educ.:* Bradfield College, Berks. 2nd Lieutenant Middlesex Regiment, 1918; Assistant Editor of Land and Water, 1919-20; joined educational staff of Oxford University Press in 1921; 1924 founded Music Department and was Musical Editor and Manager of it till 1941; Music Advisory Council of ENSA, 1942; music critic New Witness, 1922-23; Daily Graphic, 1923; Typographical adviser to Henderson and Spalding since 1924; a frequent broadcaster on music and other subjects. Editor of Music Lover, 1947. F.R.S.A. 1950. *Publications:* Ralph Vaughan Williams—a study; Delius (revised edn. of Heseltine); César Franck (trans. of Léon Vallas); The Concertgoer's Handbook; Music in my Time; edited many volumes on music by late Sir Donald Tovey; numerous articles on varied subjects and on music; music: Seven Poems by Thomas Hardy for baritone solo and male voice chorus; and a number of songs and instrumental pieces. *Recreations:* music, the English scene. *Address:* 60 Corringham Road, N.W.11. *T.:* Speedwell 7776. [*Died* 27 *May* 1953.

FOSTER, Col. Alfred James, C.M.G. 1918; C.B.E. 1919; T.D.; Officier Légion d'Honneur; Officier de l'Ordre de Leopold; J.P., D.L., Northumberland; J.P. Durham and Sussex; Northumberland Fusiliers; Hon. Col. 4th Batt.; *b.* 1864; *o. s.* of James Foster, Hindely Hall, Northumberland; *m.* 1885, Mabel, (*d.* 1940), *d.* of late Col. Sir Charles Reed, K.C.B., of The Cragg, Northumberland, and of Dringthorpe, York; one *s.* two *d.* *Educ.:* Grove House, Tottenham; Rugby. Commanded the Northumberland R.F.A. (Special Reserve); Commanded 4th Batt. N.F. in France in 1915 including 2nd Battle of Ypres (despatches thrice, C.M.G.); later Assistant Controller Ministry of Munitions. *Address:* Hall Place, Seal, Sevenoaks, Kent. *Clubs:* United Service, Hurlingham; Northern Counties (Newcastle upon Tyne). [*Died* 20 *April* 1959.

FOSTER, Captain Alwyn; late 7th Batt. King's Royal Rifle Corps and the Queen's Own Oxfordshire Hussars, I.Y.; *b.* 12 April 1874; 4th *s.* of late John Foster of Coombe Park, Oxfordshire, and Egton in Cleveland, Yorkshire; *m.* 1907, Muriel Wave Frances, 3rd *d.* of late Uvedale Bennett Corbett, J.P., Mollington Hall, Chester; one *d.* *Educ.:* Eton. Served in South Africa, 1900; Remount Department for East Kent, 1914; temp. Lt.-Comdr. R.N.R. 1914; served in France, 1917; joined Surrey Special Constabulary, 1940. *Address:* Felshall House, Hythe, Kent. *T.:* Hythe 67836. *Clubs:* Boodle's, Marylebone Cricket, Royal United Service Institution; Royal Yacht Squadron (Cowes). [*Died* 25 *Aug.* 1953.

FOSTER, Sir Berkeley; *see* Foster, Sir H. W. B.

FOSTER, Capt. Sir Edward, Kt., *cr.* 1950; C.B.E. 1942 (O.B.E. 1919); Farmer; Chairman Shropshire Agricultural Executive Committee since 1939; Liaison Officer to Minister of Agriculture; *b.* 1881; *s.* of late Henry Foster, J.P., Ludlow; *m.* 1919, Kathleen, *d.* of Charles James Exley; two *s.* one *d.* *Educ.:* Lucton School. Alderman of Salop C.C. 1941; J.P. Salop. Served European War, 1914-19, Capt. R.A.S.C. (despatches thrice, O.B.E.). *Address:* Newton House, Bridgnorth, Shropshire. *T.:* Worfield 206. *Clubs:* Farmers'; Shropshire (Shrewsbury). [*Died* 14 *March* 1958.

FOSTER, Lt.-Col. Harold William Alexander, D.S.O. 1917; M.C. 1916; Q.C. 1928; *o. s.* of late W. A. Foster, Q.C., and late Jane Margaret Bowes; *m.* 1915, Anna H. G., *e. d.* of late John A. Strathy of Barrie, Ontario; two *s.* (and one *s.* killed in action, Dieppe, 1942). *Educ.:* Dulwich College; Osgoode Hall Law School. Call to Bar, 1909; LL.B., Toronto Univ., 1909; Bencher, Law Society of Upper Canada; firm, Denison and Foster, barristers, 24 King Street West, Toronto; served European War, 1914-19 (M.C. and bar, wounded three times, D.S.O., despatches twice); 1939-45, O.C. Osgoode Hall C.O.T.C. *Recreation:* golf. *Address:* 100 Bedford Road, Toronto, Canada. *Clubs:* Toronto, Toronto Golf. [*Died Jan.* 1960.

FOSTER, Maj.-Gen. Henry Nedham, C.M.G. 1918; C.B.E. 1919; late R.A.S.C.; *b.* 1878; *s.* of J. R. Foster, of Co. Tyrone; *m.* 1904, Norah (*d.* 1949), *d.* of late T. Hayward, Killarney, Co. Kerry, *widow* of E. M. Howden; one *s.* *Educ.:* St. Paul's School. Served South African War, 1900-2 (despatches, Queen's medal and five clasps, King's medal and two clasps); European War, 1914-19; Deputy Director (Temp. Col.) War Office, 1917-19; Chief Inspector M.T., 1924-26; Assistant Director of Supplies and Transport, Southern Command, Salisbury, 1927-31; Maj.-Gen., 1931; retired pay, 1933; re-employed Headquarters Eastern Command, 1939-41; Officer Legion of Honour. *Address:* The Vicarage, Colnbrook, Bucks. [*Died* 1 *Oct.* 1951.

FOSTER, Sir (Henry William) Berkeley, 4th Bt., *cr.* 1838; M.C. 1917; formerly Chief Valuator to Diamond Corp. and Manager of the Company's Office, White Waltham, Berks, retired 1952; *b.* 3 April 1892; *o. surv. s.* of Col. Sir William Foster, 3rd Bt., C.B.E., R.A., and Aileen Ethel (*d.* 1948), *d.* of late Col. Augustus Portman; *S.* father 1948; *m.* 1927, Janet Elizabeth, *d.* of late Charles Bullen-Smith; one *s.* one *d.* *Educ.:* Wellington Coll.; Sandhurst. Served European War, 1914-18 (M.C.); Major, Northumberland Fusiliers, 10th (S) Bn. Member of Diamond Corp. of London and South Africa. *Heir:* none. *Address:* 84 Church Rd., Bracknell, Berks. *T.:* Bracknell 84. [*Died* 2 *Jan.* 1960 (*ext.*).

FOSTER, Sir Hugh Matheson, Kt., *cr.* 1946; T.D.; Solicitor, retd.; *b.* 25 Jan. 1886; *s.* of Sir William Edward Foster, Lindum House, Aldershot; *m.* 1928, Moira, *d.* of late Very Rev. Dean G. S. Mayers; one *s.* *Educ.:* Wellington College, Berkshire. Solicitor, 1907; Notary Public, 1907. Major 4th Hampshire Regt. T.F., Mesopotamia, 1915-16; D.A.A.G. 4th (Indian) Division. President Hampshire Law Society, 1921-22; President Law Society, 1945-46. Mayor of Aldershot, 1927-29; formerly Senior Partner in firm of Foster, Wells & Coggins, Aldershot; formerly Coroner Aldershot Division of Hampshire. *Address:* Ashe Grange, Aldershot. *T.:* Ash Vale 2243. *Clubs:* Carlton, Lansdowne. [*Died* 10 *Feb.* 1955.

FOSTER, Ivor (Ivor Llewellyn Foster), Hon. A.R.C.M.; retired baritone and teacher of singing; *b.* Pontypridd, Glam., 1 March 1870; *s.* of Ebenezer and Sarah Foster of Penygraig, Rhondda Valley; *m.* 1897, Mary, *d.* of Thomas and Sarah Jones, Tonypandy, Rhondda; one *s.* one *d.* *Educ.:* locally; after a successful career as an Eisteddfod competitor, came to London 1896, and studied singing at the Royal College of Music, under late Henry Blower, and opera under Sir Charles Stanford; won the Henry Leslie Prize and Charlotte Holmes Exhibition, and played the title-rôles in Mozart's Don Giovanni and Wagner's The Flying Dutchman, student performances at the Lyceum Theatre; created the part of Don Pedro in Stanford's Much Ado About Nothing, Covent Garden, 1901; apart from appearing in the Promenade concerts, Royal Choral Society's concerts, and all the principal London concerts, sang in The Boosey London Ballad concerts, at the Royal Albert Hall, for twenty-seven consecutive seasons; has also sung in every town of importance throughout the British Isles, and at three of the Cardiff Festivals; created several of the best-known and popular ballads of the present time. *Address:* Waun-y-mer, Porthcawl, Glamorgan. [*Died* 29 *March* 1959.

FOSTER, Sidney; *b.* 15 Dec. 1885; *s.* of Albert and Sarah Foster; *m.* 1912, Elsie Marie, *d.* of George Cobbett Harding, Cobham; three *c.* *Educ.:* Holy Trinity School, Sittingbourne. Accountancy; Sec., General Manager, London Cooperative Socy. Ltd.; General Manager, Milk Marketing Board, 1933-48. *Address:* Silverwood, Fairmile Lane, Cobham, Surrey. [*Died* 1 *April* 1958.

FOSTER, Sir Thomas Saxby Gregory, 2nd Bt., *cr.* 1930; Secretary to The Country

Club, Johannesburg, since 1945 (Assistant Secretary, 1932-45); *b.* 1 Feb. 1899; *er. s.* of Sir (T.) Gregory Foster, 1st Bt., and Fanny Maude Sledge (*d.* 1928); *S.* father 1931; *m.* 1925, Beryl, *d.* of late Dr. Alfred Ireland, Cradock, Cape Province; one *s.* one *d.* *Educ.:* Marlborough. Served European War, 1917-1919; served with South African Artillery, 1940-45, last rank, Lt.-Col. *Heir: s.* John Gregory, *b.* 28 Feb. 1927. *Address:* The Country Club Cottage, Auckland Park, Johannesburg, South Africa.
[*Died* 17 *May* 1957.

FOSTER, Major Wilfrid Lionel, C.B.E. 1919; D.S.O. 1903; late R.A.; *b.* 2 Dec. 1874: *s.* of late Rev. Henry Foster; *m.* 1909, Evelyn Mary (*d.* 1955), *d.* of Bernard Cammell; one *s.* two *d.* (and one *s.* decd.). Entered army, 1894; Captain, 1901; served South Africa, 1899-1902 (despatches, Queen's medal with 4 clasps, King's medal with 2 clasps); Somaliland, 1902-03 (despatches, medal and clasp, D.S.O.). *Address:* Ryton, near Shifnal, Shropshire.
[*Died* 22 *March* 1958.

FOSTER, Sir William, Kt., *cr.* 1925; C.I.E. 1913; Registrar and Superintendent of Records, India Office, 1907-23; Historiographer, 1923-27; *b.* 19 Nov. 1863; *s.* of William Foster, late Inland Revenue Department; *m.* 1911, Jessie Winifred, *d.* of late Rev. H. W. Holland. *Educ.:* Coopers' Grammar School; London University. Joined India Office, 1882; Hon. Secretary of the Hakluyt Society, 1893-1902; President, 1928-45. *Publications:* A Catalogue of the India Office Pictures; The English Factories in India, 1618-1669 (13 vols.); The Embassy of Sir Thomas Roe to the Court of the Great Mogul, 1615-19 (2nd edition, 1926); The Journal of John Jourdain, 1608-17; Early Travels in India, 1583-1619; four volumes of Letters Received by the East India Company, 1615-17; The East India House; John Company; Downing's History of the Indian Wars; Herbert's Travels in Persia, 1627-1629; Hamilton's New Account of the East Indies; Sanderson's Travels in the Levant; British Artists in India, 1760-1820; England's Quest of Eastern Trade; The Voyage of Capt. Best to the East Indies; The Voyages of Sir James Lancaster; The Voyage of Sir Henry Middleton; The Red Sea in 1700 with Sir George Birdwood, The First Letter-book of the East India Company, 1600-19, and Relics of the East India Company. *Address:* 179 West Heath Road, N.W. 3. *T.:* Speedwell 1508. [*Died* 11 *May* 1951.

FOSTER, Maj.-Gen. William Wasbrough, C.M.G. 1944; D.S.O. 1916; V.D.; Power Commissioner, B.C.; *b.* England; *s.* of William Foster, Vancouver, B.C.; *m.* Olive, *d.* of G. A. Stewart, C.E., Peterboro', Ont.; three *s.* two *d.* *Educ.:* Wycliffe College, Stonehouse. Deputy Minister Public Works, British Columbia, 1910-14; enlisted for service Aug. 1914; overseas as Captain 2nd Canadian Mounted Rifles; Major, 1916; Lt.-Col. 52nd Inf. Batt., 1917; Commander 9th Inf. Bde., 1918 (D.S.O. and two bars, Belgian and French Croix de Guerre, despatches 5 times); Pres. Pacific Engineers Ltd. until 1935; by request of City of Vancouver, undertook reorganisation of Police Force, 1935; Pres., Pacific Coast, Internat. Assoc. of Law Enforcement Officials, 1946; between the Wars commanded D.C.O.R. and Inf. Bde., Vancouver; Hon. Col. 15th Artillery Bde.; Hon. A.D.C. to Gov.-Gen.; Director of auxiliary services, 1939; overseas with 1st Cdn. Div.; Officer Commanding District 12, Saskatchewan, 1941; District 6, Nova Scotia and P.E.I., 1942; Chm.-in-Chief, Cdn. Officers' Selection Bd.; Special Commissioner for Defence Projects in N.W. Canada, 1943. Made first ascent of Mount Robson in B.C. and in 1925 rep. Can. Alpine Club as member of U.S.-Canadian expedition in the Yukon and Alaska, with an Internat. Party making first ascent of Mount Logan, Canada's highest peak, 19,850 ft.; Past President Alpine Club of Canada (life member) and First Pres. (later Hon. Pres.) Canadian National Parks Association; associated in formation of Canadian Legion B.E.S.L. (Provincial Pres. for B.C. and Pres. of Dominion Comd.); Director Canadian Geographical Society; F.R.G.S., Commander U.S.A. Legion of Merit, 1945. *Recreations:* mountaineering, riding. *Address:* P.O. Box 550, Victoria, B.C., Canada. *Clubs:* Alpine; Union (Victoria); Vancouver (Vancouver).
[*Died* 2 *Dec.* 1954.

FOTHERGILL, (Charles) Philip; Merchant; *b.* Earlsheaton, Dewsbury, 23 Feb. 1906; *o. s.* of late Edward Richardson Fothergill and of Edith Mary Leaf; unmarried. *Educ.:* Wheelwright School, Dewsbury; Bootham School, York. Chm. and Man. Dir. of C. P. Fothergill & Co. Limited, Dewsbury; Director, Joseph Rowntree Social Service Trust, Director, Dewsbury Reporter; President, United Kingdom Alliance, 1952-; Trustee, Civil Defence Welfare Fund. Member of Council, Central Council of Physical Recreation; Dep. Transport Commissioner for Scotland, 1943-1945; Joint Treasurer, Liberal Party, 1954-; Chairman, Executive Liberal Party Organisation, 1946-49, and 1952-54; President, 1950-1952; Vice-President, 1952-55; contested (L.) Forfarshire, General Election, 1945, Middlesborough West, 1950, Oldham West, 1951. *Address:* 70 Alexandra Crescent, Dewsbury. *T.:* Dewsbury 493. *Clubs:* Reform, National Liberal, Penn, Eighty; New (Edinburgh). [*Died* 31 *Jan.* 1959.

FOTHERGILL, John Rowland; author; *b.* 27 Feb. 1876; *s.* of late George Fothergill, Allan Bank, Grasmere, Westmorland, and Binswood House, Leamington, and Isabel, *d.* of Francis Crawshay, Bradbourne Hall, Sevenoaks; *m.* 1st. Doris Gillian Herring; 2nd, Kate Headley Kirby; two *s.* *Educ.:* Bath College; St. John's College, Oxford; Leipzig University; Slade School of Art. Collaborated with E. P. Warren in forming the Boston Museum Fine Arts Collection of Classical Antiquities; Pioneer Amateur Innkeeper from 1922 at the Spreadeagle, Thame, Royal Ascot Hotel, 1932, Three Swans, Market Harboro', 1934-52. *Publications:* The Rendering of Nature in early Greek Art, transl. from the German of E. Löwy; Innkeeper's Diary; Gardener's Colour Book; Fothergill Omnibus; Confessions of an Innkeeper; John Fothergill's Cookery Book; The Art of James Dickson Innes; My Three Inns; Contrib. to Encyc. Brit., 1911; Ed. The Slade. *Recreations:* none. *Address:* 32 Lancaster Road, Rugby.
[*Died* 26 *Aug.* 1957.

FOTHERGILL, Philip; *see* Fothergill, C. P.

FOULDS, Linton Harry, C.B.E. 1946; *b.* 25 March 1897; *s.* of late Edwin Foulds, Clayton, Yorkshire; *m.* 1925, Catherine Mary, *d.* of late Joseph Robinson, Clayton, Yorkshire; one *d.* *Educ.:* Grange High School, Bradford; Trinity College, Cambridge. Student Interpreter, Japan Consular Service, 1921; Vice-Consul, Yokohama 1924, Manila 1925, Kobe 1927, Manila 1929; Consul, Grade II Manila, 1935; Consul, Grade I Dairen, 1936; Foreign Office, 1941; Consul-General, Foreign Office, 1945; H.M. Envoy Extraordinary and Minister Plenipotentiary to Republic of the Philippines, 1946-51; designated H.M. Ambassador to the Republic of Ecuador, 1951, but did not proceed owing to ill-health; retired on pension, 1951. *Recreations:* shooting, walking. *Address:* 77 Oakleigh Road, Clayton, Bradford. *Clubs:* Royal Automobile; Manila (Manila). [*Died* 30 *Sept.* 1952.

FOULSHAM, Sir Charles (Sidney), Kt., *cr.* 1949; *b.* 22 April 1892; *e. s.* of late Sidney S. Foulsham, Sidmouth, Devon; *m.* 1926, Mary Hilda, *d.* of late Robert Rodger, Bangor, Co. Down; one *s.* one *d.* *Educ.:* St. Paul's

School. Entered Inland Revenue, 1910. Served European War, 1914-18, in Artists' Rifles and Suffolk Regiment, 1914-19. Dep. Chief Inspector of Taxes, 1943-47; Chief Inspector of Taxes, 1947-52. *Address:* Shandon, Boxgrove Ave., Guildford. *T.:* Guildford 2783. [*Died* 25 *June* 1955.

FOUNTAIN, Sir Henry, K.C.M.G., *cr.* 1929 (C.M.G. 1912); C.B. 1917; *b.* 31 October 1870; *s.* of late Edward Fountain of Hillingdon; *m.* 1900, Agnes Maud Laughton (*d.* 1954), *e. d.* of late James Matthew Leishman of Rangoon; two *s.* *Educ.:* Winchester; King's College, Cambridge. Entered Civil Service, 1899; Principal Asst. Sec., Board of Trade, 1923-32; Second Secretary, Board of Trade, 1932-35; retired from Civil Service, 1935; has been British delegate on the Permanent International Sugar Commission (Brussels) and a Member of the Royal Commission on the Sugar Supply; Member of the Economic Delegation at the Peace Conference (Paris, 1919), of the Economic Commission for the Treaty of Peace with Turkey (London and San Remo, 1920), and of the British Delegation for the conclusion of the Treaty of Lausanne, 1922-23; Chairman of the Imperial Customs Conference, 1921; Member of the United Kingdom Delegation at various Economic Conferences, including the Ottawa Imperial Conference, 1932, and Monetary and Economic Conference, 1933. Chairman of International Beef Conference and Empire Meat Council up to the outbreak of the War in 1939. *Address:* Little Mote, Eynsford, Kent. *T.:* Farningham 2197. [*Died* 17 *March* 1957.

FOWLE, Colonel Sir (Henry) Walter Hamilton, K.B.E., *cr.* 1919 (C.B.E. 1919); *b.* 1871; *s.* of late T. E. Fowle, D.L., of Chute Lodge, Hants, and Durrington Manor, Wilts; *m.* 1931, Elizabeth C., *o. d.* of late J.W. Connolly, Westbourne, Reading; one *s.* *Educ.:* Shrewsbury; Clare College, Cambridge. Served S. African War, 1899-1902 (two medals and six clasps); Commissioner of Enemy Subjects in So. Africa, 1915-16; Custodian of Enemy Property, 1916-21. *Address:* Rosehaugh, Transvaal, South Africa. [*Died* 17 *May* 1954.

FOWLER, Lieut.-Colonel Edward Gardiner, C.B.E. 1921; late Royal Artillery; *b.* 2 Dec. 1879; *s.* of late Edward Willoughby Fowler of Cleaghmore, Ballinasloe, Co. Galway; unmarried. *Educ.:* Cheltenham College; Royal Military Academy, Woolwich. Entered Army, 1899; served with Mountain Artillery on N.W. Frontier, India; Adjutant, R.G.A., Sheerness, 1907-10; Qualified Entrance Exam. Quetta Staff College, 1914; served European War, 1914-18; O.C. No. 9 Mountain Battery, India; Instructor Staff School, India, G.S.O.2; O.C. 479 Siege Battery, France; O.C. 2nd Siege Brigade, France (despatches); 3rd Afghan War, 1919, O.C. No. 6 Mountain Battery; Waziristan, Mahsud Expedition, 1919-20; Brigade Major, R.A., Waziristan Force; O.C. 11th Mountain Artillery Brigade, C.R.A. Waziristan Force and C.R.A. Wana Column, 1920-21 (C.B.E., despatches); O.C. 15th Field Brigade, R.A. 1925-29; retired pay, 1929. *Recreations:* shooting, motoring. *Address:* Leyrath, Kilkenny. [*Died* 19 *March* 1953.

FOWLER, Professor Harold North, Ph.D.; Hon. Litt.D.; Hon. Consultant in Classical Literature, Library of Congress, 1929; Professor of Greek, College for Women of Western Reserve University, 1893; Professor Emeritus, 1929; *b.* Westfield, Massachusetts, 25 Feb. 1859; *s.* of Samuel Fowler and Maria Jones; *m.* 1st, 1890, Helen (*d.* 1909), *d.* of Hon. Charles H. Cell, of Exeter, New Hampshire; no *c.*; 2nd, 1925, Mary Zay, *d.* of Frank P. Blackford, of Findlay, Ohio. *Educ.:* Westfield and Stockbridge, Mass.; Dresden; Harvard Univ. (A.B.); American School at Athens; Berlin; Bonn (Ph.D.). Instructor, Harvard, 1885-88; Professor, Phillips Exeter Academy, 1888-92; University of Texas, 1892-93; American School of Classical Studies at Athens, 1903-04, 1924-25; Associate Editor American Journal of Archæology, 1897-1906; Editor-in-Chief, 1906-16; Vice-President Archæological Institute of America, 1916-36; corresponding member Deutsches Archæologisches Institut; President American Philological Association, 1913. *Publications:* editor—Panaetii et Hecatonis Librorum Fragmenta, 1885; Thucydides, Book V., 1888; Plautus, Menaechmi, 1889; Quintus Curtius, Books III. and IV., 1890; Allen and Greenough's Ovid, 1891; joint author—Tuell and Fowler's First Book in Latin, 1893; Tuell and Fowler's Beginner's Book in Latin, 1900; Fowler and Wheeler's Handbook of Greek Archæology, 1909; The Erechtheum, 1927; The Picture Book of Sculpture, 1929 (with Mary B. Fowler); Corinth, results of excavations conducted by the American School of Classical Studies at Athens, Vol. I., 1932; author—History of Ancient Greek Literature, 1902, 2nd ed. 1923; History of Roman Literature, 1903, 2nd ed. 1923; History of Sculpture, 1916; translator—Plato, Vol. I., in the Loeb Classical Library, 1914; Vol. II., 1921; Vol. III., 1925; Vol. VI., 1926; Plutarch's Moralia, Vol. X., 1936. *Address:* 936 South Main St., Findlay, O., U.S.A. [*Died* 29 *Sept.* 1955.

FOX, Sir Cyril Sankey, Kt., *cr.* 1943; D.Sc.; M.I.Min.E.; F.G.S.; *b.* 24 Feb. 1886. Served European War, 1914-18, Bde. Sig. Officer, R.E., 15th (Scottish) Div., 1915 (despatches). Asst. Supt. Geological Survey of India, 1911; Supt. 1930; Director, 1939-1943; retired, 1 Jan. 1944. Chairman Fuel Research and Heavy Chemical Committees for Council, Scientific and Industrial Research in India, 1942-44; Consulting Mining Geologist. Experience: in Abyssinia, Arabia, Afganistan, Nepal, U.S.S.R., India, Burma and Egypt (1950-51). Special contributions on the subject of Coal, Bauxite and all problems of Engineering Geology, water-supply, and radio-active minerals exploration. *Address:* Tudor House, 19 Queensmere Road, Wimbledon, S.W.19. [*Died* 28 *Dec.* 1951.

FOX, Dame Evelyn Emily Marion, D.B.E., *cr.* 1947 (C.B.E. 1937); Vice-Pres. National Assoc. for Mental Health; *b.* 1874; *d.* of Richard Fox, Fox Hall, Edgeworthstown, Co. Longford, Eire, and of Emily Godley. *Educ.:* Home; High School, Morges, Switzerland; Somerville College, Oxford (Hons. History); Women's University Settlement. Co-opted Member, London County Council Mental Hospitals Committee, 1914-24; first Hon. Secretary Child Guidance Council; Member of Joint Committee on Mental Deficiency (Wood Committee); British Representative International Congress on Mental Hygiene, Washington, etc.; Hon. Secretary, Central Association for Mental Welfare Inc., 1913; late Hon. Sec. Provisional Nat. Council Mental Health. *Publications:* papers and articles on Mental Welfare and kindred subjects in various journals. *Recreations:* country life, dogs, motoring. *Address:* The Nook, Laughton, nr. Lewes, Sussex. *T.:* Ripe 239. [*Died* 1 *June* 1955.

FOX, Sir Frank, Kt., *cr.* 1926; O.B.E.; journalist, author; *b.* Adelaide, S.A., 12 Aug. 1874; *s.* of Charles James Fox; *m.* Helen Clint (*d.* 1958); one *s.* two *d.* *Educ.:* Christ's College, Hobart. Edited Australian Workman, 1892; edited National Advocate, 1895, and championed the cause of Australian Federation; later joined Bulletin staff and was for a time acting editor; founded and was first editor The Lone Hand; came to London 1909, and on the platform and in the press urged preparation against the menace of European War; joined Morning Post staff; their war correspondent during Balkan war, with Bulgarian army; and with Belgian army during the first phase of the Great War. Served with the Royal Field Artillery from Dec. 1914 (wounded twice in Battle of Somme); subsequently on Quarter-master-General's Staff, France, and on General Staff, War Office, with rank of Major (de-

spatches, O.B.E., Order of the Crown of Belgium); after the armistice was engaged again in journalistic work, business organisation, and advocacy of Imperial causes; as Secretary, organised the Fellowship of the British Empire Exhibition, which established itself in every part of the Empire; organised the British Empire Cancer Campaign in the North West and Northern Counties, 1927-1929; organised Empire Rheumatism Council, 1936-46. *Publications:* Australia; Oceania; The British Empire; Mastery of the Pacific; Our English Land Muddle; Bulgaria; G.H.Q. (under pseudonym G.S.O.); History of The Royal Inniskilling Fusiliers in the two World Wars; The King's Pilgrimage; Beneath an Ardent Sun; The English; Finland To-day; Italy To-day, etc. *Address:* Courtyard, West Wittering, Sussex. *Club:* Savage.
[*Died* 4 *March* 1960.

FOX, Sir Gifford (Wheaton Grey), 2nd Bt., *cr.* 1924; *b.* 2 Feb. 1903; *s.* of Sir Gilbert Fox, 1st Bart., and May (*d.* 1954), *e. d.* of Edward William Jones, Hoylake, Cheshire; *S.* father, 1925; *m.* 1st, 1927, Hon. Myra Newton (marriage dissolved, 1952), *o. c.* of 1st Baron Eltisley, K.B.E.; one *d.*; 2nd, 1954, Mrs. Maryoth Trotter, *d.* of late Lord Edward Hay. *Educ.:* Eton; Magdalen College, Oxford. Barrister-at-law, Middle Temple, 1926. M.P. (U.) Henley Div. of Oxfordshire, 1932-50; Sqdn. Ldr. R.A.F.V.R., Asst. Provost Marshal, 1940-46. *Heir:* none. *Address:* Towersey Manor, Thame, Oxfordshire. *T.:* Thame 77; 41 Eaton Mews North, S.W.1. *T.:* Sloane 9338. *Clubs:* Carlton, Leander.
[*Died* 11 *Feb.* 1959 (*ext.*).

FOX, Joscelyn P. B.; *see* Bushe-Fox.

FOX, John Howard, J.P.; Alderman County Council, Somerset; Director of: Fox Bros. & Co. Ltd., and Candy & Co. Ltd.; *b.* 1864; *s.* of Thomas Fox, The Court, Wellington, Somerset; *m.* 1892, Marion Elizabeth (*d.* 1942), *d.* of Henry Pease, Pierremont, Darlington; two *s.* *Educ.:* Clifton College. Partner in Fox, Fowler & Co., Bankers; Amalgamated with Lloyds Bank, Ltd., 1921. *Recreations:* golf, lawn-tennis, etc. *Address:* Robin's Close, Wellington, Somerset. *T.:* 32. [*Died* 13 *March* 1951.

FOXLEY, Barbara, M.A.; Professor Emeritus, University College, Cardiff. *Educ.:* Newnham College, Cambridge. Head Mistress, Queen Mary's High School, Walsall; Mistress of Method, Victoria University, Manchester.
[*Died* 26 *Aug.* 1958.

FOY, Ernest Rudolph, C.I.E. 1926; M.I.C.E.; late Indian Service of Engineers; *widower.* Chief Engineer and Secretary to Government, Punjab (P.W.D.), 1921; retired, 1926. *Address:* Prime Farm, Whitchurch Canonicorum, Bridport, Dorset. *T.:* Chideock 332. [*Died* 27 *Oct.* 1951.

FRANCIS, Arthur Gordon, O.B.E. 1941; D.Sc. (Lond.); F.R.I.C.; retired as Acting Head of the Government Chemist's Department, 1944; *b.* 1880; 3rd *s.* of late Edward and Mary Francis; *m.* 1913, Mabel, 3rd *d.* of late William and Eleanor Davies, Swansea; one *d.* *Educ.:* Nottingham High School; Royal College of Science, South Kensington. Entered the Government Laboratory, 1901; Superintending Chemist, 1929; Research Assistant to Sir Edward Thorpe, 1906-9; Researches and investigations on strontium, radium, helium, Dead Sea waters and salts; Director of Research to the Ethyl Petrol Committee; Deputy Government Chemist, 1937; Member of Council of Chemical Society, 1938-41; of Institute of Chemistry, 1926-29, 1931-34, 1937-40. *Publications:* Papers on chemical subjects in scientific and technical journals. *Recreations:* Association football, fives, lawn tennis, swimming, gardening. *Address:* Uplands, Tootswood Road, Bromley, Kent. *T.:* Ravensbourne 1228. [*Died* 10 *Feb.* 1958.

FRANCIS, Lieut.-Col. Charles John Henry Watson, C.B.E. 1919; R.E.; *o. s.* of H. B. Francis, Kenilworth; *b.* 12 Feb. 1879; *m.* 1911; two *d.* *Educ.:* Clifton; King's College, London. Pupil of F. W. Webb, L.N.W.R., Crewe; Inspecting Engineer, Egyptian Govt.; served European War, Royal Engineers (despatches twice, C.B.E.); Controller under Disposals Board, 1920; Stores Supt. L.S.W.R. and at Amalgamation, 1923, Stores Supt. Southern Railway; retired 1945. *Recreations:* hunting, shooting, cricket, Rugby football, tennis, golf, etc. *Address:* Château Beaurivage, Trinity Place, Eastbourne. *T.:* Eastbourne 1360. *Club:* Public Schools.
[*Died* 3 *June* 1959.

FRANCIS, Major John, D.S.O. 1918; T.D.; D.L.; R.E., F.S.I., F.A.I.; Member of firm of John Francis & Son, Estate Agents, Carmarthen; Sec. Carmarthenshire Hunt; *b.* 16 Nov. 1879; *e. s.* of late John and Louisa Francis, Myrtle Hill, Carmarthen; *m.* 1920, Marguerite (*d.* 1944), *o. c.* of late T. E. Thomas, J.P., and Edith Thomas, J.P., Trehale, Pembrokeshire; two *s.* one *d.* *Educ.:* Cheltenham College. Served articles with and then became partner in firm, and has continued (except for War period) to date; estate agency of 40,000 acres and deals with agricultural valuations, arbitrations and sales and development; Member of County Agricultural Committee; Sec. Shire Horse Society; Pres. United Counties Agricultural Society, 1954; Vice-Chairman Royal Welsh Agric. Soc.; President Carmarthenshire Chamber of Agriculture; Member of the Governing Body of the Church in Wales; Chm. Carmarthenshire Territorial Assoc.; served European War, 1915-18, in Gallipoli and Palestine (despatches, D.S.O.); T.A. Reserve; Vice-President of Carmarthen T.A. Assoc. *Recreations:* fox-hunting, shooting. *Address:* Myrtle Hill, Carmarthen. *T.A.:* John Francis, Carmarthen. *T.:* Carmarthen 465 & 466. *Clubs:* Junior Army and Navy; County (Carmarthen). [*Died* 9 *April* 1960.

FRANCIS, Brig.-Gen. Sidney Goodall, D.S.O. 1900; J.P.; late Royal Berks Regt.; *b.* 24 Dec. 1874; *s.* of late Charles Francis, Melbourne; *m.* 1916, Catherine Gwendoline, *y. d.* of W. B. Lowry, Lee-on-the-Solent; three *d.* (two *s.* killed in action, Burma). 2nd Lt. West York Regt. 1895; Captain, 1904; Major, 1915; General Staff Officer, 3rd Grade, 1915; temp. Lt.-Col. commanding 7th Irish Rifles, 1916-17; temp. Brig.-Gen. 1917; to command 1st R. Berks Regt. 1920; served S. Africa, 1899-1902 (despatches twice, Queen's medal 5 clasps, King's medal 2 clasps, D.S.O.); North-West Frontier, Mohmand Expedition, 1908 (medal and clasp); European War, 1914-18 (despatches, Bt. Lt.-Col. 1917, Bar to D.S.O. 1918, Bt.-Col. 1919, Chevalier Legion of Honour; 1914 Star, British War Medal and Victory Medal); retired pay, 1925. *Address:* Kingsdown, Sway, Hants. *T.:* 318.
[*Died* 29 *March* 1955.

FRANCKENSTEIN, Sir George, G.C.V.O., *cr.* 1937; Kt., *cr.* 1938; a Director of artistic and of commercial companies; *b.* 1878; *s.* of Baron Karl Franckenstein, Austrian Envoy Extraordinary and Minister Plenipotentiary, and Elma, *née* Countess Schoenborn; naturalized British subject, 1938; *m.* 1939, Editha, *d.* of late Capt. Nigel Keppel King, R.N.; one *s.* *Educ.:* Vienna. Attaché to Austro-Hungarian Embassy in Washington; Secretary of Embassy at Petersburg and Rome; Private Secretary to the Austro-Hungarian Foreign Minister, Count Aehrenthal; Chargé d'Affaires in Tokio; sent on special mission to India; Counsellor and Commercial Director to the Austro-Hungarian Embassy in London; Representative of the Austro-Hungarian Govt. in Belgium, and later on in the Caucasus; Austrian Envoy Extraordinary and Minister Plenipotentiary in London, 1920-38; Member of the Peace Delegation at St. Germain-en-Laye;

Head of the Loan Commission entrusted with negotiations for the League of Nations Loan for the reconstruction of Austria, in Great Britain and the financial centres of the Continent, 1922; Initiator of the scheme of holding an Exhibition of British Art in Vienna in the autumn of 1927; Member of Austrian Delegation to World Economic Conference, 1933. Hon. D.C.L. (Oxford), 1935; Hon. Freeman Worshipful Company of Musicians, 1949. Grand Cross of the Austrian Order of Merit; Austrian Order of Merit (First Class) for Art and Science, 1938. *Publication:* Facts and Features of My Life, 1939. *Recreations:* golf, lawn-tennis, hunting, collector of oriental works of art. *Clubs:* St. James', International Sportmen's.
[*Died* 14 *Oct.* 1953.

FRANK, Sir (Thomas) Peirson, Kt., *cr.* 1942; T.D.; M.I.C.E., F.R.I.C.S.; Partner in firm of Coode, Vaughan-Lee, Frank, and Gwyther, Consulting Engineers; *b.* 23 July 1881; *e. s.* of late Thomas Peirson Frank and Jane Shepherd; *m.* 1914, Irene Augusta, *y. d.* of late H. M. Thirlway, J.P.; one *s.* four *d.* Formerly Borough Engineer and Surveyor, Stockton-on-Tees; served European War, 1915-18, with Royal Engineers; Borough Engineer and Surveyor, Plymouth; City Engineer, Architect and Surveyor, Cardiff; City Engineer, Liverpool; Hon. Surveyor to East Glamorgan Regional Planning Committee, 1923-26; Honorary Surveyor, 1926-30, to S.W. Lancs. Regional Town Planning Committee; Chief Engineer and County Surveyor, London County Council, 1930-46; Co-ordinating Officer, Road Repairs and Public Utility Services, London Civil Defence Region, 1939-45; Past President Institution of Civil Engineers; Past President Town Planning Institute; member of Departmental Committee of Ministry of Health on Garden Cities and Satellite Towns, 1932-34; member since 1930 of Ministry of Transport's Committee on Experimental Roads; member of Highways Research Board of Dept. of Scientific and Industrial Research, 1935-40; member of the Ministry of Works National Consultative Council of the Building and Civil Engineering Industries, 1942-44. *Address:* 8 Chartfield Avenue, Putney Hill, S.W.15. *Clubs:* Devonshire, Royal Automobile.
[*Died* 12 *Nov.* 1951.

FRANKAU, Capt. Gilbert; Author; *b.* 21 April 1884; *e. s.* of late Arthur Frankau and late Julia Frankau (Frank Danby); *m.* 1st, 1905, Dorothea Drummond Black (marriage dissolved; she died 1945); two *d.*; 2nd, 1922, Aimée de Burgh (marriage dissolved; she died 1946), 3rd, 1932, Susan Lorna, *o. d.* of late Walter Harris and Mrs. Harris (*née* Hollingsworth). *Educ.:* Eton. Entered his father's business, 1904; commenced writing, 1910; left England and travelled round the world, 1912-14; first commission 9th E. Surrey Regt. Oct. 1914; transferred to R.F.A. March 1915; appointed Adjt. to 107th Brigade, and proceeded overseas in that capacity; fought at Loos, Ypres, the Somme; promoted Staff Captain for special duty in Italy, Oct. 1916; invalided from the Service and granted rank of Captain, Feb. 1918; Re-Commissioned R.A.F. (Volunteer Reserve) August 1939; promoted Squadron Leader, April 1940; invalided from the Service, Feb. 1941. Awarded permanent disability retired pay, 1944. *Publications:* One of Us, 1912; Tid'apa, 1914; The Guns, 1916; The City of Fear, 1917; The Woman of the Horizon, 1917; The Judgement of Valhalla, 1918; One of Them, 1919; Peter Jackson, Cigar Merchant, 1919; The Heart of a Child (Dramatic version of Frank Danby's novel), in collaboration with Aimée de Burgh Frankau, 1920; The Seeds of Enchantment, 1921; The Love-Story of Aliette Brunton, 1922; Men, Maids, and Mustard-Pot, 1923; Gerald Cranston's Lady, 1924; Life—and Erica, 1925; Masterson, and My Unsentimental Journey, 1926; Twelve Tales, 1927; So Much Good, 1928; Dance, Little Gentleman, 1929; Martin Make Believe, 1930; Concerning Peter Jackson and Others, 1931; Christopher Strong, 1932; Wine, Women, and Waiters, 1932; The Lonely Man, 1932; Everywoman, 1933; Secret Services, 1934; Three Englishmen, 1935; Farewell Romance, 1936; Experiments in Crime, 1937; More of Us (A Novel in Verse), 1937; The Dangerous Years, 1937; Royal Regiment, 1938; Self-Portrait, 1939; Winter of Discontent (U.S.A. title: Air Ministry, Room 28), 1941; Escape to Yesterday, 1942; World Without End, 1943; Selected Verses, 1943; Michael's Wife, 1948; Mesmer, a monograph, 1948; Son of the Morning, 1949; Oliver Trenton, K.C., 1951; (posthumous novel) Unborn Tomorrow, 1953. *Address:* 4A King's Gardens, Hove, Sussex. *T.:* Hove 32131. *Club:* Cavalry.
[*Died* 4 *Nov.* 1952.

FRANKFORT, Henri, M.A. (Lond.), Ph.D. (Leiden), F.BA.; F.S.A.; Director, Warburg Institute, London, and Professor of the History of Pre-Classical Antiquity in the University of London since 1949; *b.* Amsterdam, 24 Feb. 1897; *s.* of Benjamin Philippe and Mathilde Frankfort; *m.* 1923, Henriette Antonia Groenewegen (marriage dissolved, 1952); one *s.*; *m.* 1952, Enriqueta Harris. *Educ.:* Univ. of Amsterdam; Univ. Coll., London; University of Leiden; British School of Archæology at Athens. M.A. (Lond.), 1924; Ph.D. (Leiden), 1927. Dir. of excavations for Egypt Exploration Soc. at Abydos, Tell El Amarna, and Erment, 1925-1929; field dir. of Iraq Expedition (Tell Asmar and Khorsabad) of Oriental Inst. of Univ. of Chicago, 1929-37; Extraordinary Prof. of History and Archæology of Ancient Near East, Univ. of Amsterdam, 1932-38; Research Prof. of Oriental Archæology, Oriental Inst. of Univ. of Chicago, 1932-49. Served in European War, 1914-18, in Netherlands Army, 1915-17. Foreign Member of the Royal Netherlands Academy of Sciences. Fellow of University College, London. *Publications:* Studies in Early Pottery of the Near East, I, 1924, II, 1927; (jointly) The Mural Painting of El-Amarneh, 1929; Archæology and the Sumerian Problem, 1932; The Cenotaph of Seti I at Abydos, 1933; Cylinder Seals, a Documentary Essay on the Art and Religion of the Ancient Near East, 1939; Sculpture of the Third Millennium B.C. from Tell Asmar and Khafajah, 1939; More Sculpture from the Diyala Region, 1943; (jointly) The Intellectual Adventure of Ancient Man, 1947; Kingship and the Gods, An Essay on Ancient Near Eastern Religion as the Integration of Society and Nature, 1947; Egyptian Religion, an Interpretation, 1948; The birth of civilization in The Near East, 1951. *Address:* 61 Kenway Rd., S.W.5. *T.:* Frobisher 1406. [*Died* 16 *July* 1954.

FRANKLAND, Edward Percy, Ph.D., M.Sc., B.A. Trinity College, Cambridge; *b.* London, 5 Jan. 1884; *s.* of late Professor Percy Frankland, C.B.E., F.R.S.; *m.* 1915, Maud, 2nd *d.* of late Anthony Metcalfe-Gibson, J.P. of Coldbeck, Ravenstonedale, Westmorland; two *s.* one *d.* Studied Chemistry, Universities of Birmingham, Cambridge, Würzburg; Major Scholar, Trinity College, Cambridge; Lecturer on Chemistry, Birmingham University, research work published in Journal of Chemical Society, resigned owing to ill-health; Commenced writing, 1922. Owns over 1300 acres in Westmorland and Yorkshire. *Publications:* Swarthmoor Tragedy, 1922; Retreat, 1926; Power, 1927; Reform, 1928; Mystery at Grimsdale, 1929; The Nymph at Bay, Sour Park, 1930; Huge as Sin, 1932; The Path of Glory, 1935; The Bear of Britain, 1944; England Growing, 1946; The Half Brothers, 1947; The Foster Brothers, 1954; The Murders at Crossby, 1955; The Invaders, 1958. *Recreations:*

afforestation, painting, archæology. *Address:* Needlehouse, Ravenstonedale, Kirkby Stephen, Westmorland. *T.:* Sedbergh 254. [*Died* 22 *Oct.* 1958.

FRANKLAND-PAYNE-GALLWEY, Sir John; *see* Gallwey, Sir John F.-P.-.

FRANKLIN, Philip, F.R.C.S. Eng., Hon. F.A.C.S.; Major, late R.A.M.C.; Surgeon, Chest Hospital, Margaret Street, W.1; Consulting Adviser Deaf Baby Clinic, Westminster Children's Hosp.; *b.* San Francisco; *er. s.* of J. Lewis Franklin; *m.* 1903, Ethel (*d.* 1935), *y. d.* of late Lewis White, London; two *s.* one *d.* *Educ.:* University of California; University of Heidelberg; King's College, London. Surgeon Specialist R.A.F. Voluntary Hospitals, 1914-18 (despatches). Late Surgeon Infants, Italian Metropolitan, Princess Elizabeth of York, and Italian Hospitals; Pathologist London Throat Hospital; Salters' Company Cancer Scholar, Middlesex Hospital; Hon. Secretary and Treasurer Onodi Collection of Anatomy Fund; gave evidence before Royal Commission on Post-Graduate Education in London. *Publications:* papers in medical journals. *Recreation:* music. *Address:* 11 Wimpole Street, W.1. *T.:* Langham 4781. [*Died* 7 *Jan.* 1951.

FRANKLIN, Sir Reginald (Hector), K.B.E., *cr.* 1950 (C.B.E. 1941); C.B. 1947; formerly Deputy Secretary, Ministry of Agriculture and Fisheries, retired 1954; *b.* 8 Feb. 1893; *s.* of late Hector G. Franklin; *m.* 1918, Evelyn, *o. d.* of late Henry Huntington, Northwood, Middlesex; one *s.* two *d.* *Educ.:* Christ's Hospital, Horsham. Served European War, 1914-18, B.E.F. (despatches); entered Ministry of Agriculture and Fisheries, 1919; Private Secretary to successive Ministers of Agriculture, 1922-30 and 1936-37. *Address:* Lower Ricks, Balcombe, Sussex. *T.:* 279. *Club:* Union. [*Died* 6 *May* 1957.

FRANKS, Major-General Sir George McKenzie, K.C.B., *cr.* 1927 (C.B. 1917); R.A.; *b.* 16 Oct. 1868; *s.* of late T. J. Franks, Ballyscaddane, Co. Limerick; *m.* 1901, Paula, *d.* of Manuel Garcia; one *s.* two *d.* *Educ.:* Marlborough. Entered R.A. 1887; Captain, 1898; Major, 1906; Lieutenant-Colonel, 1915; Professor Staff College, India, 1909-12; served Waziristan, 1894-95 (medal with clasp); N.W. Frontier, India, 1897-98 (medal and clasp); Nile Expeditions, 1898 and 1899 (despatches twice, medal, Egyptian medal 4 clasps, 4th class Medjidie, and 4th class Osmanie); European War, 1914-18 (despatches six times, Bt. Col., C.B., promoted Maj.-Gen.); Inspector-General of Artillery, Great Britain, 1918-20; President Allied Sub-Commission of Organisation in Turkey, 1920-22; commanded Kohat District, 1924-25; G.O.C. Meerut District, India, 1925-28; retired pay, 1928; Colonel Commandant R.A., 1931-38. Commander of the Crown of Belgium; Croix de Guerre of Belgium. *Address:* Ryecroft, Bray, Co. Wicklow. [*Died* 12 *Oct.* 1958.

FRASER, Major-General Alexander Donald, D.S.O. 1917; M.C., M.B.; *b.* 9 June 1884; 2nd *s.* of Rev. Hugh Fraser, M.A., Alvah, Banff; *m.* 1942, Dilys E. C. M. Jones; three *d.* *Educ.:* Aberdeen Grammar School; Aberdeen University. M.B., Ch.B. 1906; entered R.A.M.C. 1907; seconded to Colonial Office and employed on Sleeping Sickness Investigations in Uganda, 1908-11; served in France, 1914-18 (D.S.O. with bar, M.C., French Croix de Guerre); North Russia, 1919; Mesopotamia, 1920-21; also served in Palestine, Sierra Leone, India and Egypt; D.D.M.S. Southern Cmd., India, 1937-41; K.H.S. 1938-41; retired pay, 1941. *Address:* c/o Glyn, Mills and Co., Kirkland House, Whitehall, S.W.1. [*Died* 8 *Jan.* 1960.

FRASER, Lieut.-Col. Cecil, C.M.G. 1919; O.B.E. 1919; M.C.; late North Staffordshire Regiment; *b.* 25 July 1885; *s.* of late General A. Fraser, C.B.; *m.* 1918, Volta Kathleen, *yr. d.* of Beaufoi Moore, Barrister-at-law, Middle Temple; no *c.* *Educ.:* Bradfield College, Sandhurst. 2nd Lieut. 1st Bn. N. Staffordshire Regt., 1906; Lieut., 1908; Adjutant, 1914; to France 7 Sep. 1914 with 1st Bn.; Captain, 1914; Major, 1923; Adjt. 6th Wing R.F.C., Dover, 1915; Adjt. 5th Wing R.F.C., Egypt, 1916; Brigade-Major, Middle East Brigade R.F.C., 1916; A.A.Q.M.G. (Temp. Lt.-Col.), 1917, Middle East Division R.F.C.; Wing-Commander R.A.F. 1918-25; served in England, France and Egypt throughout the European War, 1914-18 (C.M.G., O.B.E., M.C., Order of St. Sauveur of Greece, despatches thrice); retired, 1925; Director of Public Relations Navy, Army and Air Force Institutes, 1941-42. *Address:* Westfield, 18 Spencer Road, E. Molesey, Surrey. *T.:* Molesey 2922. *Club:* Naval and Military. [*Died* 15 *May* 1951.

FRASER, Lt.-Col. Sir Denholm (de Montalt Stuart), K.C.V.O. 1948; C.S.I. 1944; C.I.E. 1938; *b.* 5 Oct. 1889; *s.* of Sir Stuart Fraser, K.C.S.I.; *m.* 1925, Sheila St. George Molesworth Battye; three *s.* *Educ.:* Rugby; Sandhurst. Joined 39th K.G.O. Central India Horse, 1910; European War, Mesopotamia, and Assistant Political Officer Bushire Field Force, 1918; Political Dept. Govt. of India, 1919; Secretary, Political Resident, Persian Gulf; Under-Secretary and Secretary A.G.G., Central India, 1921-1924; Asst. Commissioner, Kohat, 1925; Deputy Commissioner, Dera Ismail Khan, 1926; Political Agent, Eastern Kathiawar States; Political Agent, Southern States, C.I. and Malwa; Foreign Service in Tonk State, Rajputana, 1930-34; Political Agent, Malwa, C.I.; officiating Resident in Central India, 1938; resident in Kashmir, 1938-41; Resident in Mysore, 1941; retired, 1944; Political A.D.C. to the Secretary of State for India, 1945-48. *Recreations:* shooting, fishing, tennis, golf, etc. *Address:* Reswallie House, Forfar, Angus, Scotland. *T.:* Letham (Angus) 305. *Club:* Overseas. [*Died* 19 *Oct.* 1956.

FRASER, Eric Malcolm, C.B.E. 1946; retired from I.C.I. Ltd., 1958; *b.* 17 November 1896; *y. s.* of late Sir Thomas R. Fraser, M.D., F.R.S., LL.D., Acharacle, Argyllshire, and of Susannah Fraser, *e. d.* of Rev. John Duncan; *m.* 1929, Joy, *er. d.* of late Ernest Pease, Ledge House, Bembridge, Isle of Wight; no *c.* *Educ.:* Edinburgh Academy; Oriel College, Oxford. Commissioned Seaforth Highlanders, 1915 (despatches); joined Brunner, Mond & Co. Ltd. (now I.C.I.), 1919. Assistant Director-General of Progress and Statistics, War Office, 1939; Director of Investigation and Statistics, War Office, 1940; Director-General of Equipment Production, Ministry of Aircraft Production, 1942; Director-General of Aircraft Production, Ministry of Aircraft Production, 1943. Member Television Advisory Cttee., Oct. 1952-Dec. 1953; Member Council and of Exec. Cttee., Brit. Inst. of Management, 1952-56; Sales Controller, I.C.I. Ltd., 1946-58; Chm. Plant Protection Ltd., 1954-58; Director of Pan Britannica Industries Ltd., 1954-58. *Recreations:* fishing, horticulture. *Address:* Radnor House, New Street, Henley-on-Thames, Oxon. *T.:* Henley-on-Thames 146. *Clubs:* Union; Phyllis Court (Henley). [*Died* 9 *Dec.* 1960.

FRASER, Capt. Gordon Colquhoun, C.B.E. 1919; retired; *b.* Stafford, 19 Sep. 1866; 2nd *s.* of late Rev. S. J. G. Fraser, H.M. Inspector of Schools; *g.s.* of Simon Fraser, Commissioner of Delhi, killed there during Indian Mutiny, 1857; *m.* 1st, 1898, Anne Madeline (*d.* 1915), *d.* of late Sir Walter Mytton Colvin; 2nd, 1925, Claire Gertrude, *d.* of late Rev. Robert Grierson; no *c.* *Educ.:* private school (Fonthill Gifford, near Tisbury); obtained Winchester scholarship, 1879; entered Royal Navy, 1879; Midshipman of H.M.S. Monarch at bombardment of Alexandria, 1882; specialised in torpedo duties; invalided from Navy, 1907; rendered service as Captain in charge Defensive (Controlled) Mining during European War (C.B.E.). *Recreations:* various. *Address:* Rosebank, Causey Lane, Pinhoe, Exeter, Devon. [*Died* 13 *Oct.* 1952.

FRASER, Henry Lumsden Forbes, LL.B.; *b.* Gallebodde, Ceylon, 13 Oct. 1877; *e. s.* of John Fraser, Planter; *m.* 1914, Agnes, *y. d.* of Robert Stewart, Glasgow; three *d. Educ.:* Robert Gordon's College, Aberdeen: Aberdeen Univ. (M.A.); Edinburgh Univ. (LL.B.). Law Agent, Edinburgh, 1903-8; Legal and Parliamentary Assist., Lanark County Council, 1908-12; Assistant Secretary and Legal Adviser, Scottish Insurance Commissioners, 1912; Principal Assist. Secretary, Scottish Board of Health, 1919; Assistant Secretary, Department of Health, Scotland, 1929-31; County Clerk and Treasurer, and A.R.P. Controller, County Council of Aberdeen, 1931-44; Member of Radium Commission, 1929-31, 1939-43; Member Dental Board of the United Kingdom, 1929-34; Chairman East of Scotland Civil Service Nursing Association, 1925-31; Member Cancer Advisory Committee, Scotland, 1939-44; Food Executive Officer, Aberdeenshire, 1939-43; Member Scottish Committee of National Corporation for Care of Old People, 1948. *Publications:* articles and official publications. *Recreations:* golf, fishing, music. *Address:* Myrtle Cottage, 10 Northfield, Liberton, Edinburgh 9. *T.:* 79770. *Clubs:* Northern (Edinburgh); University (Aberdeen). [*Died* 16 *April* 1951.

FRASER, Kate, C.B.E. 1945; M.D., D.P.H., B.Sc.; Commissioner of the General Board of Control for Scotland, 1935-47; Deputy Commissioner, 1913-35; Chairman of the Scottish Association for Mental Health since 1947; *b.* Paisley, 10 Aug. 1877; *d.* of Donald Fraser, M.D., and Margaret Coats. B.Sc. Glas., special distinction in Physiology, 1900; M.B., Ch.B., 1903; assistant physician in Consumptive Sanatorium, Bridge of Weir, Crichton Royal Institution and Southern Counties Asylum Dumfries; five years in general practice in Glasgow; Extra Hon. Physician Royal Hospital for Sick Children; one of the Medical Officers of Govan Parish School Board, 1908; took Diploma of Public Health, 1912; M.D., Glasgow University, with high commendation, 1913. *Publications:* The Examination of Mentally Defective Children; The Rôle of Syphilis in Mental Deficiency and Epilepsy; University thesis on An Inquiry into Mental Deficiency in School Children, with special reference to Syphilis as a causative factor as determined by the Wassermann reaction. *Address:* 20 Greenlaw Avenue, Paisley, Renfrewshire. *Club:* Royal Scottish Automobile (Glasgow). [*Died* 20 *March* 1957.

FRASER, Major-General Sir Theodore, K.C.B., *cr.* 1921 (C.B. 1916); C.S.I. 1918; C.M.G. 1916; late R.E.; *b.* Inverness, 15 June 1865; *s.* of Rev. Donald Fraser, D.D., of Inverness and Marylebone, and 4th *d.* of Maj.-Gen. Alex. Gordon, R.E.; *m.* 1903, Constance Ruth (*d.* 1918), *y. d.* of late Nathaniel Stevenson of Wimpole Street, W., two *s.* one *d. Educ.:* University College School, London; Clare Coll., Cambridge. Direct Commission in Royal Engineers, 1886; Brevet Major, 1900; Lt.-Col. 1912; Substantive Col. 1916; Brevet Colonel, 1917; Maj.-Gen. 1919; served Chin-Lushai Expedition, 1889-90 (medal with clasp); Hazara, 1891 (clasp); Tirah, 1897-98 (medal 2 clasps); South Africa, 1900 (despatches, Bt. Major, Queen's medal 2 clasps); European War, 1914-19 (despatches 7 times, Bt. Col., promoted Major-General, C.B., C.S.I., C.M.G., Serbian White Eagle, 1914-15 Star, British War Medal, Victory Medal); Operations in Kurdistan and Iraq, 1919-20 (despatches twice, G.S. Medal 2 clasps, K.C.B.); commanded British Forces in Iraq, 1922; commanded the Troops in Malaya, 1924-27; passed Staff College, 1901-2; Naval War College, 1913; has held many commands and staff appointments; retired on Indian pension, 1927. *Address:* c/o Lloyds Bank, 6 Pall Mall, S.W.1. [*Died* 22 *May* 1953.

FRASER, Colonel Thomas, C.B.E. 1919; D.S.O. 1918; T.D.; D.L.; Consulting Physician, Aberdeen Royal Infirmary; *b.* 1872; *m.* Maria Theresia Kayser, Hanover; two *s. Educ.:* Robert Gordon's College, Aberdeen; Aberdeen University. M.A.; M.B., Ch.B.; D.P.H.; LL.D. (Hon.). Formerly Lecturer in Clinical Medicine, University of Aberdeen. Served European War, 1914-18, Gallipoli and France (despatches five times, D.S.O., C.B.E.); Lt.-Col. 1914, comdg. 89th (1st Highland) Field Ambulance, 29th Div.; Col. 1918. Assistant Director of Medical Services, 47th (London) Div. Pres. B.M.A., 1939-42, Member of Council, 1926-43; Member of General Medical Council, 1941-46. *Publication:* Relations of the Islands of Langerhans to Diabetes, Jl. Chem. Physiol., 1907. *Address:* 16 Albyn Place, Aberdeen. *Club:* Royal Northern (Aberdeen). [*Died* 2 *Jan.* 1951.

FRASER, William Stuart, C.I.E. 1931; O.B.E.; V.D.; M.I.L.E., Colonel, A.F. (India); *b.* 15 Oct. 1876; *s.* of William Murray Fraser; unmarried. *Educ.:* Privately; Hulme Grammar School; Victoria University. Pupil of Sir John Aspinall; Lancashire and Yorkshire Railway Co. at Horwich, 1895-1900; Loco. Foreman, L. and Y. Rly., Liverpool and Blackpool, 1900-2; Assistant Loco. Supt., District Loco. Supt. B.B. and C.I. Rly. Co., 1902-11; Loco. Supt. 1911-31; retired Feb. 1931. *Recreations:* golf, bowls, shooting. *Address:* Bere Regis, Northcourt, Abingdon-on-Thames, Berks. *T.:* Abingdon 208. [*Died* 10 *March* 1954.

FRAZER, Col. George Stanley, C.M.G. 1916; late 110th Mahratta Light Infantry; *b.* 9 Feb. 1865; *s.* of Col. W. M. Frazer, Indian Police; *m.* Geraldine, *y. d.* of W. F. Parsons, Risley Hall, Derbyshire. *Educ.:* Wellington. Entered East Yorks. Regt. 1885; Capt. Indian Army, 1896; Major, 1903; Lieut.-Col. 1910; Col. 1916; served Burma, 1887-88 (medal, two clasps); European War, Mesopotamia, 1914-17 (C.M.G.); retired, 1919. *Address:* Heathfield, Ootacamund, South India. [*Died* 15 *Dec.* 1950.
[*But death not notified in time for inclusion in Who Was Who 1941–1950, first edn.*

FRAZER, Robert Alexander, F.R.S. 1946; D.Sc. (Lond.); B.A. (Cantab.); F.R.Ae.S.; F.I.Ae.S.; *b.* 5 Feb. 1891; *s.* of Robert Watson and Hannah Frazer; *m.* 1923, Alice May Gwendoline Goldie; one *s.* two *d. Educ.:* City of London School; Pembroke College, Cambridge (Wrangler and Rayleigh Prizeman). Formerly Dep. Chief Scientific Officer, Aerodynamics Div., Nat. Physical Laboratory, retd. Nov. 1954. Mem. Oscillation Sub-Committee of Aeronautical Research Council. *Publications:* numerous papers on flutter and allied subjects in Reports and Memoranda of Aeronautical Research Council and in technical journals. *Address:* Bachelors, Ockham, Woking, Surrey. [*Died* 10 *Dec.* 1959.

FRAZER, Prof. William Mowll, O.B.E. 1939; M.D., M.Sc., D.P.H.; Barrister-at-law; Professor of Public Health, University of Liverpool, 1933-53, Prof. Emeritus, 1953; *b.* 7 March 1888; *s.* of Frederick William Frazer and Lydia Frazer; *m.* 1917, Gladys Mary Gubbins; one *s.* one *d. Educ.:* Oakes Institute, Liverpool; Universities of Liverpool and London; Gray's Inn. Late Assistant Medical Officer of Health, Blackburn, Medical Officer of Health, Dewsbury; Medical Officer of Health City and Port of Hull; Medical Officer of Health, City and Port of Liverpool; Newsholme Lecturer, Univ. of London, 1954; Fellow of the Royal Sanitary Institute and the Royal Institute of Public Health; Hon. Fellow American Public

Health Assoc. *Publications:* Text-book of Public Health, 13th edn.; Duncan of Liverpool; A History of English Public Health; numerous articles in scientific and medical journals on Public Health and Housing. *Address:* 2 Chantry Walk, Heswall, Cheshire. *T.:* Heswall 3442. [*Died* 8 *Sept.* 1958.

FREAKE, Sir Charles Arland Maitland, 4th Bt., *cr.* 1882; *b.* 13 Oct. 1904; *s.* of 3rd Bt. and Alison (*d.* 1935), *d.* of late Christopher Ussher of Eastwell, Co. Galway; *S.* father, 1950; *m.* 1929, Claire M., *d.* of H. T. S. Green, Hewlett, Long Island, U.S.A.; one *d.* *Heir:* none. *Address:* Cantorist House, Childrey, Berks.; Todenham House, Moreton-in-Marsh, Glos. [*Died* 14 *Nov.* 1951 (*ext.*).

FREDERICK, Lieut.-Col. Sir Edward Boscawen, 9th Bart., *cr.* 1723; C.V.O. 1944; *b.* 1880; *s.* of Sir Charles Frederick, 7th Bart., late of Shawford House, Hampshire; *S.* brother 1938; *m.* 1913, Kathleen, *d.* of late Col. W. H. Mulloy, R.E., late of Hughestown, Roscommon, Hereditary Standard Bearer to the Crown in Ireland; one *s.* (and one killed, North Africa, April 1943) one *d.* *Educ.:* Eton; R.M.C., Sandhurst. Served in the Royal Fusiliers, 1899-1919; South African War, 1899-1902; European War, 1914-18 (wounded severely); Instructor at the Royal Military College, Sandhurst, 1912-14; Home Guard, 1940; Coy. Commander, 1941; Bn. Commander, 1941-45; played much cricket, principally for I Zingari, Free Foresters, and Hampshire on occasions. Exon, of the King's Body Guard of the Yeomen of the Guard, 1925-37, Ensign, 1937-1950, retired. *Recreation:* fishing. *Heir:* *s.* Charles Boscawen, Major, late Grenadier Guards [*b.* 11 April 1919; *m.* 1949, Rosemary, *er. d.* of late Lt.-Col. R. J. H. Baddeley, White Cottage, Middle Combe, Shaftesbury; one *s.* two *d.*]. *Address:* 7 St. John's Wood Court, N.W.8. *Clubs:* Army and Navy, M.C.C. [*Died* 26 *Oct.* 1956.

FREDERICK, Capt. George Charles, C.B.E. 1918; R.N. (retired); *b.* 2 Aug. 1855; *e. s.* of late George Septimus Frederick, Comptroller Audit and Exchequer Department of the Treasury; *m.* 1881, Nellie (*d.* 1942), *d.* of George Peter Martin, C.B., R.N., Emsworth, Hants; no *c.* Entered the Royal Navy, 1869; when a Sub-Lieutenant specialised in the Surveying Service, and was employed on many important surveys in various parts of the world, his last appointment being in command of a surveying vessel on the Australian station, 1888-92; employed at Admiralty as assistant to the Hydrographer, 1893-1900; Naval Adviser to the Board of Trade, 1900-10; Captain (retired), 1908; a Member of the Anglo-French Pilotage Commission, 1909-1910; Member of the Royal Commission on Coast Erosion and Afforestation, 1906-11; British Representative on the International Commission on the Port of Tangier, 1914; on the outbreak of war 1914 on Admiralty War Staff at Liverpool, subsequently Shipping Intelligence Officer at that port until 1 May 1919. *Club:* United Service. [*Died* 5 *Jan.* 1951.

FREEDMAN, Barnett, C.B.E. 1946; R.D.I.; Artist; *b.* London, 19 May 1901; *s.* of Lewis and Rachel Freedman; *m.* Beatrice Claudia Guercio, Palermo; one *s.* *Educ.:* L.C.C. Board School. Bedridden for years as a boy; started work at 15; Architectural draughtsman; Scholarship to Royal College of Art, 1922; left R.C.A. in 1925; starved; paintings and drawings subsequently acquired by Tate Gallery, Contemporary Art Society, British Museum, Duveen Fund, Victoria and Albert Museum, Fitzwilliam, Cambridge, Ashmolean, Oxford. Municipal Galleries of Leeds, Birmingham, Nottingham, Carlisle, Salford, and Manchester, Graves Gallery, Sheffield, Fine Arts Museum, Helsingfors; Illustrator and Lithographer, etc.; Commissions executed for London Passenger Transport Board, Shell Mex and B.P. Ltd., British Broadcasting Corporation, Genera Post Office, Ministry of Information, etc.; designed King George V Jubilee Stamp, First Silver Jubilee Stamp designed for Great Britain; illustrated Siegfried Sassoon's Memoirs of an Infantry Officer, George Borrow's Lavengro, Tolstoy's War and Peace and Anna Karenina, Dickens' Oliver Twist, Brontë's Wuthering Heights, Jane Eyre, Shakespeare, and Walter de la Mare's Love Anthology for Limited Editions Club, New York, U.S.A., and Faber's, London; Official War Artist to B.E.F., 1940, and Admiralty, 1941-46. *Recreations:* none. *Address:* 11 Canning Place, Palace Gate, W.8; (studio) 59 Cornwall Gdns., S.W.7. *T.:* Western 2449. *Club:* Athenæum. [*Died* 4 *Jan.* 1958.

FREEMAN, Harry, C.M.G. 1954; retired; *b.* 4 Jan. 1888; *s.* of Louis Freeman; m. 1914, Ida, *y. d.* of Joshua Jacobs; one *s.* two *d.* *Educ.:* Owen's School, Islington; Christ's College, Cambridge. B.A. 1909; M.A. 1913. Entered Civil Service, 1919; Principal Actuary, Government Actuary's Dept., 1947-54. Fellow, Institute of Actuaries, 1922. *Publications:* An Elementary Treatise on Actuarial Mathematics, 1931; Mathematics for Actuarial Students, 1939; articles on mathematics and actuarial subjects for various journals. *Address:* 17 Kings Close, Hendon, N.W.4. *T.:* Sunnyhill 1343. *Club:* National Liberal. [*Died* 5 *Aug.* 1959.

FREEMAN, Kathleen; *b.* 22 June 1897; *o. c.* of late Charles Henry Freeman, Birkenhead, and late Catharine (*née* Mawdesley), Southport. *Educ.:* University College of South Wales and Monmouthshire. B.A., 1918, M.A., 1922, D.Litt., 1940, Wales. Lecturer in Greek, Univ. Coll. of S. Wales and Monmouthshire, Cardiff, 1919-46; resigned, 1946, to devote herself to writing and research. During War of 1939-45, lecturer to Ministry of Information and in National Scheme of Education for H.M. Forces in South Wales and Monmouthshire on Greece, etc. Research on Greek subjects, especially Greek Philosophy and Law. Writer of detective novels, 1936-. *Publications:* The Work and Life of Solon, 1926; Voices of Freedom, 1943; What They Said at the Time, 1945; Companion and Ancilla to the pre-Socratic Philosophers, 1946 and 1948; The Murder of Herodes and other trials from the Athenian law courts, 1946; The Greek Way: an Anthology, 1947; Greek City-States, 1950; God, Man and State: Greek Concepts, 1951; The Sophists (trans. from Italian I Sofisti by M. Untersteiner), 1954; T'other Miss Austen, 1956; *detective novels* (as Mary Fitt): Death and Mary Dazill, 1941; Clues to Christabel, 1944; Pity for Pamela, 1950; Death and the Shortest Day, 1952; The Nightwatchman's Friend, 1953: Love from Elizabeth, 1954; Sweet Poison, 1956, The Late Uncle Max, 1957, Case for the Defence, 1958, etc.; *Children's books:* adventure-stories for children, 1954-. *Recreation:* foreign travel. *Address:* Larks' Rise, St. Mellons, Monmouthshire. *T.:* Cardiff 77136. *Clubs:* University Women's, Detection. [*Died* 21 *Feb.* 1959.

FREEMAN, Percy Tom, M.B.E.; B.Sc., Ph.D., F.R.I.C., F.Z.S., J.P.; Headmaster, Peter Symonds' School, Winchester, since 1926; *b.* 26 Feb. 1891; *s.* of late Tom Freeman, R.N.; *m.* 1914, Daisy Gertrude, *e. d.* of late Benjamin J. Hill; one *s.* one *d.* *Educ.:* Queen Elizabeth's Grammar School, Wimborne Minster; University College, Southampton; St. Edmund Hall, Oxford. Assistant Master, Portsmouth Secondary School; King Edward VI School, Southampton; Head Master, Purbrook Park County High School; Captain, Royal Engineers; Member of Council, University of Southampton; Past-President, Winchester Rotary Club; Cadet-Lieut.-Colonel, Commanding 1st Cadet Battalion, The Hampshire Regiment; J.P.

City of Winchester; President, Incorporated Association of Head Masters, 1948. *Publications:* Christianity and Boys, etc. *Recreations:* outdoor games, biology. *Address:* Peter Symonds' School, Winchester. [*Died* 15 *Aug.* 1956.

FREEMAN, Peter; M.P. (Lab.) Newport since 1945; *b.* 19 Oct. 1888; *s.* of George James Freeman, London, and Edith Marion Freeman, London; *m.* Ella Drummond, *d.* of Late Sir Andrew Torrance, M.P.; one *s.* one *d.* *Educ.:* Haberdashers' School, Hampstead. Director and Manager J. R. Freeman & Son, Ltd., London and Cardiff, 1908-29; M.P. (Lab.) Brecon and Radnor 1929-31; Guardian of the Poor, Hoxton, London, 1910-12; Councillor, Penarth Urban District Council, 1924-26; Councillor, Cardiff City Council, 1928-30; County Coun. Glamorgan C.C., 1927-31; Welsh Lawn Tennis Champion, 1919-21; Gen. Sec. of The Theosophical Soc. in Wales, 1922-44; Pres. of The Vegetarian Society, 1937-42; Chairman, Council for Ethiopia, 1945-55. *Publications:* The Druids and Theosophy; Brotherhood; Our Younger Brothers, the Animals; Our Duty to India; World Peace and Vegetarianism; The Government of the World. *Address:* Penarth, Wales. *T.:* Penarth 423. [*Died* 19 *May* 1956.

FREEMAN, Sterry Baines, C.B.E. 1920; M.Eng.; *b.* 9 Nov. 1875; *s.* of Thomas W. Freeman of Great Crosby, Lancs; *m.* Edith Gertrude, *d.* of Peter Ashcroft, Liverpool. *Educ.:* Merchant Taylors' School, Great Crosby; Gymnasium, Lüneburg, Hanover. M.I.Mech.E., M.I.N.A., M.I.Mar.E., F.C.M.S.; Past President Soc. Consulting Marine Engineers and Ships Surveyors; Vice-President Institute Naval Architects, and Institute Marine Engineers; sometime representative of the Director of the Board of Invention Research on the Engineer-in-Chief's Committee at the Admiralty. *Publications:* contributions to technical institutions and press. *Address:* Meland Dee, Heswall, Cheshire. *T.:* Heswall 2716. [*Died* 6 *March* 1953.

FREEMAN, Air Chief Marshal Sir Wilfrid Rhodes, 1st Bt., *cr.* 1945; G.C.B., *cr.* 1942 (K.C.B., *cr.* 1937; C.B. 1932); D.S.O. 1916; M.C.; F.R.Ae.S.; *b.* 1888; 3rd *s.* of W. R. Freeman; *m.* 1st, 1915, Gladys, *d.* of J. Mews; one *s.* one *d.*; 2nd, 1935, Elizabeth, *yr. d.* of E. T. Richmond; two *d.* *Educ.:* Rugby; R.M.C. Served European War, 1914-18 (despatches, D.S.O., M.C., Legion of Honour); Deputy Director of Operations and Intelligence, Air Ministry, 1927-28; Chief Staff Officer Inland Area, 1930; Air Officer Commanding Palestine and Transjordan, 1930-33; Commandant Royal Air Force Staff College, 1933-36; Member of Air Council for Research Development and Production, 1936-1940; Air Chief Marshal, 1940; Vice-Chief of Air Staff, 1940; Chief Executive, Ministry of Aircraft Production, 1942-45. *Heir:* *s.* John Keith Noel [*b.* 28 July 1923; *m.* 1946, Patricia, *yr. d.* of late C. W. Thomas, Sandown, I.W.]. *Address:* 8 Victoria Road, W.8. *Club:* Travellers'. [*Died* 15 *May* 1953.

FREEMAN, William Marshall; Recorder of Stamford, 1925-51; *b.* 1868; *e. s.* of late John Freeman, Birmingham; *m.* 1897, Janie, *e. d.* of late Frederick Crisp, Handsworth; one *s.* two *d.* *Educ.:* King Edward's, Birmingham; London Univ. Began in business; called to Bar, Middle Temple, 1904; contested (C.) four times Ilkeston Division of Derbyshire; Civil Liabilities Commissioner, 1916-20; Counsel to Ministry of Food (Midland Circuit), 1920; Chairman Wholesale Profiteering Tribunal, and various other Board of Trade Committees, also several Ministry of Labour Committees during European War; Member of Church Assembly, 1920-1945; Hon. Treasurer Christian Evidence Soc.; Hon. Counsel Pedestrians' Assoc.; Member of Council, British Archæological Assoc. *Publications:* legal text-books on: Compensation for public Land Acquisition, Rights of Way, Planning Development and other Local Government subjects; also specialises in Ecclesiastical Law; Contributor to Encyclopædia Britannica, Halsbury's Statutes of England, The Encyclopædia of English Law, and to legal journals. *Recreations:* walking and natural history (ornithology). *Address:* 3 Essex Court, Temple, E.C.4. *T.:* London Central 3808; 14 Avenue Rd., N.W.8. [*Died* 23 *Sept.* 1953.

FREESTON, Sir (Leslie) Brian, K.C.M.G., *cr.* 1945 (C.M.G. 1941); O.B.E. 1930; *b.* 11 Aug. 1892; *s.* of late C. L. Freeston, F.J.I.; *m.* 1923, Mabel, *d.* of late H. W. Cassels; three *d.* *Educ.:* Willaston School; New College, Oxford. On Military Service, Sept. 1914-March 1919; joined Colonial Office, 1919; visited Ceylon (1921), W. Indies and B. Honduras (1927); Secretary, Colonial Development Advisory Committee, 1929-31; Secretary, East African Governors' Conference, Nairobi, 1936; reverted to Colonial Office as Assist. Sec. 1938; Chief Sec. Tanganyika, 1939-43; Governor Leeward Islands, 1944-48; Governor, Fiji, and High Commissioner, Western Pacific, 1948-52; Secretary-General South Pacific Commission, 1951-54. *Address:* Walnut Tree Cottage, Knockholt, Kent. *T.:* Knockholt 3240. [*Died* 16 *July* 1958.

FREMANTLE, Charles Albert, D.S.O. 1918; Member of Lloyd's, 1922; *b.* 1878; 4th *s.* of late Hon. Sir Charles Fremantle, K.C.B.; *m.* 1906, Margaret Griselda (*d.* 1918), *d.* of Sir William Wedderburn, 4th Bt.; one *d.* Served Royal Navy, 1894-1921; European War, 1914-19 (D.S.O., Legion of Honour); served in Navy in war of 1939-45; Russian Orders of St. Stanislaus and St. Anne. *Club:* Travellers'. [*Died* 19 *June* 1952.

FREMANTLE, Admiral Sir Sydney Robert, G.C.B., *cr.* 1929 (K.C.B., *cr.* 1919; C.B. 1917); M.V.O. 1909; *e. s.* of late Admiral Hon. Sir E. R. Fremantle, G.C.B., G.C.V.O.; *b.* 16 Nov. 1867; *m.* 1st, 1896, Leila Hope (*d.* 1930), *d.* of late Lieut. David Delvin Fremantle, R.N.; two *s.* two *d.*; 2nd, 1931, Geraldine, *widow* of Lt.-Col. J. S. Fitz-Gerald and *d.* of Col. Cooke-Collis, C.M.G., D.L. Entered R.N. 1881; Lieut. 1887; Comdr. 1899; Capt. 1903; Rear-Adm. 1913; Vice-Adm. 1919; Adm. 1922; served Dardanelles, 1915 (despatches); Commanded 9th Cruiser Squadron, 1916; 2nd Cruiser Squadron, 1917; Ægean Squadron, 1917-18; Deputy Chief of Naval Staff, 1918-19; Vice-Admiral commanding First Battle Squadron, 1919-21; Commander-in-Chief, Portsmouth Station, 1923-26; retired list, 1928; is a Commander of Legion of Honour, Commander of the Order of the Redeemer of Greece, a Commander of the Order of St. Maurice and St. Lazarus of Italy, and has the 2nd Class of the Order of the Rising Sun of Japan, and the U.S. of America Distinguished Service Medal; awarded Beaufort Testimonial, 1888; Goodenough Gold Medal, 1888. *Publications:* My Naval Career, 1880-1928, 1949; part author Nautical Terms and Phrases in French and English; article on Naval Ordnance in Ency. Brit.; Magazine and Press articles on Naval subjects. *Recreations:* golf, dowsing. *Address:* 30 Bullingham Mansions, Church Street, Kensington, W.8. *T.:* Western 2071. *Club:* Naval and Military. [*Died* 29 *April* 1958.

FRENCH, Brig. Charles Newenham, C.M.G. 1917; C.B.E. 1922; Officer Legion of Honour (France), St. Michael and Lazarus (Italy), Crown of Belgium, Commander St. Stanislaus (Russia); *b.* 1875; *e. surv. s.* of late S. French, D.L., of Cuskinny, Queenstown, Co. Cork; unmarried. *Educ.:* Clifton College; Royal Military College, Sandhurst. Joined 2nd Hampshire Regt. 1895; passed Staff College; held many staff appts.; retired pay, 1924. Asst. Director Empire Cotton Growing Corp., 1924-29; Secretary, St. Luke's Hosp., 1944-48. *Publications:* A Countryman's Day Book, 1929; The Story of St. Luke's Hospital, 1951.

Address: Daira More, Moor Park, Farnham, Surrey. *T.:* Runfold 426. [*Died* 14 *Feb.* 1959.

FRENCH, Herbert (Stanley), C.V.O. 1930; C.B.E. 1919; M.A., M.D. (Oxon), F.R.C.P. (Lond.); Consulting Physician to Guy's Hospital, London; Hon. Lieut.-Colonel R.A.M.C.; *b.* Newcastle, 11 November 1875; *s.* of late H. Hutchins French, Sutton, Surrey, and Mary Craig Dixon, Hamilton, Lanarkshire; *m.* Amy (*d.* 1946), *d.* of late Sir James Sawyer; one *s.* one *d.*; *m.* 1948, Mrs. Nora McDonald, Cobham, Surrey. *Educ.:* Dulwich Coll.; Christ Church, Oxford; Guy's Hospital, London; Radcliffe Travelling Fellow of Oxford University; Goulstonian Lecturer to Royal College of Physicians. *Publications:* Medical Laboratory Methods and Tests; The Differential Diagnosis of Main Symptoms; contributions to various medical periodicals. *Recreations:* fruit farming, yachting, shooting. *Address:* Cudworth Manor, Newdigate, Surrey. *T.:* Newdigate 251. *Clubs:* Authors', Royal Automobile, Cruising Association; Royal Motor Yacht; Royal Galway Yacht; Irish Cruising. [*Died* 1 *Jan.* 1951.

FRENCH, Sir James (Weir), Kt., *cr.* 1941; D.Sc.; Ex-Chairman, Barr and Stroud, Ltd., Engineers and Instrument Makers and Optical Glass Manufacturers; *b.* April 1876; *s.* of Andrew Gordon French, Metallurgical Specialist; *m.* Jasmine Wallace, Commander Royal Order of the Phoenix, *d.* of John Wallace Johnstone, J.P., Mumbles, S. Wales; two *s.* *Educ.:* Bearsden Academy; Glasgow University; Glasgow Technical Coll.; Berlin. Ex-Chairman Glasgow Royal Tech. Coll.; Past Lay Pres. Glasgow Art Club; Past Pres. Glasgow Royal Phil. Soc.; Membre Protecteur Fondation Egyptologique, Reine Elisabeth, of Brussels; was attached after war of 1914-18 as Expert to the Inter-Allied Commission of Control in Germany; has extensive technical experience abroad; F. Inst. P.; F. Phys. Soc.; F.S.A.; F. Soc. Glass Tech.; holds several hundred patents in the field of Range and Height Finders, Submarine Periscopes, Inclinometers, Gunnery Fire Control, both Surface and Anti-aircraft, Aeroplane and other sights and Radar Equipment. *Publications:* Several technical books on General Engineering, Machine Tools, Optical Computation and Science; many technical papers on Physiological Optics, Practical Optics, Geology, Optical Glass History and Manufacture, Science, Engineering, Industrial Economics and Industrial Politics. *Recreations:* Specialist interest in Egyptian and other ancient glass and in Porcelain. *Address:* Carlston, 998 Great Western Road, Glasgow. *T.:* Glasgow Western 2980; Balfron, Marytwill Lane, Mumbles, S. Wales. *Clubs:* Art, Scottish Automobile (Glasgow). [*Died* 14 *Jan.* 1953.

FRENCH, John Gay, M.B., M.S. Lond.; F.R.C.S. England; Surgeon, Ear, Nose, and Throat Department, Royal Masonic Hospital, London; late Senior Surgeon, Ear, Nose, and Throat Department, Royal Northern Hospital; late Consulting Specialist to War Office; Consulting Surgeon to Ear, Nose, and Throat Department, Royal Free Hospital (London School of Medicine for Women); Consultant Emeritus Hornsey Central Hospital; late Examiner, Laryngology and Otology, Royal College of Physicians and Surgeons; *b.* Mymensing, Bengal, India; *y. s.* of late Lt.-Col. J. Gay French, M.D., M.Ch., F.R.C.S. (Eng.); I.M.S.; *m.* Elinor May, *y. d.* of late Francis Stafford Pipe-Wolferstan of Statfold, Staffordshire; (three *s.* decd.). *Educ.:* Trinity Coll., Dublin; University of London. Obtained open entrance science scholarship at St. Mary's Hospital; held resident surgical posts there; also was at St. Bartholomew's Hospital, and at Great Ormond Street Hospital for Children, and Golden Square Hospital for Diseases of Throat and Ear; was Assistant Surgeon (formerly Registrar) at Central London Throat and Ear Hospital, Gray's Inn Road. *Publications:* An Investigation into the Action and Uses of Fibrolysin in Middle-Ear Deafness, Lancet, 1909; Chronic Middle-Ear Suppuration: its Sequelæ and Treatment, Trans. Harveian Society, 1910; Diseases of Larynx and Pharynx, Dictionary of Practical Medicine, 1923; many other publications on Diseases of Throat, Nose, and Ear. *Recreations:* golf, gardening, billiards. *Address:* 33 Harley House, Marylebone Road, N.W.1. *T.:* Welbeck 4359. [*Died* 13 *April* 1951.

FRENCH, Brig. John Linnaeus, C.B. 1951; C.B.E. 1943; T.D., D.L. Essex; Director W. & C. French Ltd.; *b.* 18 Nov. 1896; *s.* of William French, North Farm, Loughton. *Educ.:* Bancrofts School; Worcester College, Oxford. Served, 1914-18, Essex Regt., Gallipoli, Egypt, Palestine (despatches); 55th (Cokes) Rifles I.A., East Africa, Baluchistan, Afghan War, 1919; passed into I.C.S. 1921, subsequently resigned; comd. 4th Bn. Essex Regt. T.A., 1928-36; Col. 1932. War of 1939-45 Col. X Force, B.E.F. (despatches); comd. Colchester Garrison, Brig., Chief Engineer, Persia; retired 1944. Liveryman, Drapers' Company. *Recreations:* reading and riding. *Address:* North Farm, Loughton, Essex. *T.:* Loughton 92. *Clubs:* United University; Royal Burnham Yacht. [*Died* 12 *March* 1953.

FRENCH, Admiral Sir Wilfred Frankland, K.C.B., *cr.* 1936 (C.B. 1932); C.M.G. 1919; *b.* 1880; *s.* of late Savage French; *m.* 1927, Marianne Nora, *e. d.* of late Brig.-Gen. W. G. Hamilton, C.B., C.S.I., D.S.O.; one *d.* *Educ.:* Stubbington. Rear-Admiral 2nd Battle Squadron, 1931-32; Vice-Admiral in Charge, Malta, 1934-37; Member of Executive Council of Malta, 1936-37; retired list, 1938; Admiral, retired, 1939; British Administrative and Maintenance Representative, Washington, 1941-44. *Address:* Paiges Cottage, Crawley, Hants. *Club:* United Service. [*Died* 6 *Dec.* 1958.

FRERE, Sir Bartle Henry Temple, Kt., *cr.* 1918; Q.C.; J.P.; *s.* of late Rev. Henry Temple Frere, Rector of Burston, Norfolk, and Sarah Maria Heath, *e. d.* of W. H. Jary, Burlingham House, Norfolk; *b.* 26 Aug. 1862; *m.* 1896, Gwendolen (*d.* 1950), *y. d.* of John Tudor Frere, Roydon, Norfolk; one *s.* one *d.* *Educ.:* Charterhouse; Trinity Coll., Cambridge. Called to Bar, Lincoln's Inn, 1887; President of District Court, Cyprus, 1897-1902; Police Magistrate and Coroner, Gibraltar, 1902-11; Attorney-General, 1911-14; Judge of Prize Court, 1914-21; Chief Justice of Gibraltar, 1914-22; Chairman of Quarter Sessions; Norfolk County Council, 1923-1951; High Sheriff of Norfolk, 1930; County Controller A.R.P., 1938-41. *Publications:* Guide to the Flora of Gibraltar; The Laws of Gibraltar; Amy Robsart. *Address:* Mangreen Hall, nr. Norwich. *Club:* Norfolk (Norwich). [*Died* 20 *Feb.* 1953.

FRERE, Noel Gray, C.M.G. 1934; *b.* 5 Dec. 1885; *s.* of late Rev. Hugh Corrie Frere and Florence, *d.* of Rt. Rev. Bishop Gray, South Africa; *m.* 1912, Agnes Barbara, *d.* of J. W. Sunderland, R.N.; two *s.* *Educ.:* Wanganui Collegiate School, N.Z.; Cranleigh School. Employed in Egypt, 1904-8; Assistant District Commissioner, Sierra Leone, 1909; District Commissioner, 1915; Provincial Commissioner, Sierra Leone, W.A., 1929-38. *Recreations:* shooting, golf. *Address:* 8 Blenheim Gardens, Sanderstead, Surrey. *Club:* Royal Empire Society. [*Died* 14 *Oct.* 1955.

FRIEDLANDER, Max J., Dr.phil., Geheimer Regierungsrat; Director of the picture gallery at Berlin, retired; *b.* 5 June 1867; *s.* of Leopold and Helene Friedländer. *Educ.:* Leipzig; München; Florenz. Assistant and Director at the State museums in Berlin, printroom and picture gallery, to 1933. *Publications:* Die Altniederländische Malerei, 14 vols.;

On Art and Connoisseurship, 1942; Landscape, Portrait, Still-Life, 1949; ed. Sijthoff, Leiden and other books on German and Flemish painting. *Address:* 38 Beethovenstraat, Amsterdam Z. Holland. [*Died Oct.* 1958.

FRIGON, Augustin, C.M.G. 1946; D.Sc. (Paris); Director of Planning, Canadian Broadcasting Corp. since 1951; President, Corp. of École Polytechnique of Montreal, since 1935; *b.* Montreal, 6 March 1888; *m.* 1913, Elsie Owen; one *s.* one *d.* *Educ.:* École Polytechnique of Montreal (C.E. 1909); Post-Graduate course in Electrical Engineering at Massachusetts Institute of Technology, Boston, 1909-10; degree of Electrical Engineer of École Supérieure d'électricité de Paris, 1921; D.Sc. Université de Paris (Sorbonne), 1922. Professor, École Polytechnique of Montreal, 1910-28; Dean, École Polytechnique of Montreal, 1923-35; Member National Research Council, 1923-39. Director-General, Technical Education of the Province of Quebec, 1924-35. Secretary, La Revue Trimestrielle Canadienne, 1915-35; Director of the review Technique, 1924-35; Dir., Institut Scientifique Franco-Canadien since 1926; Director Canadian Information Service, 1940-45; Consulting Engineer to Quebec Public Service Commission, 1910-17. Junior partner of firm Surveyor & Frigon, consulting engineers, 1912-17; Manager and Engineer, Canadian Seigwart Beam Co., 1915-17. Chairman, Electrical Commission of the City of Montreal, 1924-35; Member, Royal Commission on Radio Broadcasting, 1928-29; Member, Electricity Commission, Province of Quebec, 1934-35. President, Quebec Electricity Commission, 1935-36. Assistant General Manager, Canadian Broadcasting Corporation, 1936-44; General Manager, 1944-51. Julian C. Smith Medal, Engineering Institute of Canada, 1941. *Address:* 125 Pagnuelo Avenue, Montreal, Canada. *Clubs:* Cercle Universitaire, University, Canadian (Montreal); Rideau (Ottawa); Winchester. [*Died* 9 *July* 1952.

FRITH, Brig.-Gen. Gilbert Robertson, C.B. 1922; C.M.G. 1918; D.S.O. 1916; R.E.; *b.* Halifax, Canada, 15 Sept. 1873; *m.* 1916, Olive, *d.* of R. Arklay Fergusson, Ethiebeaton, Forfarshire; one *d.* *Educ.:* Upper Canada College; Royal Military College, Canada. Served S. African War, 1899-1902 (despatches, Queen's medal four clasps, King's medal two clasps); Kano-Sokoto Campaign, 1903 (medal and clasp); European War, 1914-18 (despatches, Bt. Major, Bt. Lieutenant-Colonel, Bt. Colonel, C.M.G., D.S.O.; Officier Légion d'Honneur, France, Croix de Guerre, France; Commandeur, Mérite d'Agricole, France); Col. on Staff in charge of Administration, Irak, 1920-22; retired pay, 1923. *Address:* Lloyds Bank, Ltd (Cox & Co.), 6 Pall Mall, S.W.1. *Club:* United Service. [*Died* 6 *Oct.* 1958.

FRITSCH, Felix Eugen, F.R.S. 1932; D.Sc. (Lond.). Ph.D. (Munich); (Hon.) LL.D. (Lond.); Emeritus Professor of Botany in the University of London; Head of Department of Botany, Queen Mary Coll. (Univ. of London), 1911-48; *b.* Hampstead, 26 April 1879; *o. s.* of H. Fritsch, Hampstead; *m.* 1905, Hedwig, *d.* of M. Lasker; one *s.* *Educ.:* Warwick House School, Hampstead; University of London and of Munich. Assistant, Botanical Department, University of Munich, 1899-1901; assistant, botanical department, University College, London, 1902-6; Assistant Professor, University College, London, 1906-11; lecturer, Birkbeck College, 1905-6; lecturer, East London College, 1907-11; President of Botanical Section, British Association, 1927; Hon. Mem. Ind. Bot. Soc.; Hon. Mem. Soc. Roy. Bot. Belgique; Hon. Mem. Zool.—Bot. Ges. Wien; Corresp. Mem. Bot. Soc. America; Hon. Mem. K. Natuur. Genootsch. Dodonaea, Gent; Corr. Philadelphia Acad. Sci.; For. Mem. K. Fysiogr. Sällsk. Lund, Sweden; For. Mem. Norwegian Acad. Sci. and Letters, Oslo; For. Mem. Reg. Soc. Scient., Uppsala; Fellow of Queen Mary College (University of London); Chairman of Council of Freshwater Biological Association of the British Empire. President of Linnean Society, 1949-52; President of Institute of Biology, 1953-. *Publications:* Plant Form and Function; An Introduction to the Study of Plants; British Fresh-water Algæ; The Structure and Reproduction of the Algæ; numerous papers on Algæ, including special reports on Antarctic Algæ, articles in Chambers's Ency.; translations, etc. *Recreation:* music. *Address:* 34 Causewayside, Cambridge. *T.:* Cambridge 54845. [*Died* 23 *May* 1954.

FRIZELL, Brig.-General Charles William, D.S.O. 1917; M.C.; *b.* Jan. 1888; *s.* of late W. H. Frizell, Castle Kevon, Co. Wicklow; *m.* 1915, Nancy Tulloch, *d.* of late Colonel John McCausland Denny, C.B., Shipbuilder, Dumbarton; one *d.* *Educ.:* Stubbington House; Rossall; R.M.A., Woolwich. Entered Army, Royal Berkshire Regiment, 1907; served European War, 1914-18 (twice wounded, despatches six times, D.S.O. and bar, M.C., Brevets Major and Lieut.-Col.); promoted to Major in the South Staffordshire Regt., 1921; Lt.-Col., 1929, commanded 1st Batt. South Staffordshire Regt., 1929-32; Col. 1932; Instructor Senior Officers' School, Sheerness, 1932-34; Commander 3rd (Jhelum) Infantry Brigade, 1934-36; operations, N.W. Frontier of India, 1935; retired pay, 1936. *Address:* Garmoyle, St. Brelade, Jersey, C.I. *Club:* Junior United Service. [*Died* 2 *Dec.* 1951.

FROST, Mark Edwin Pescott, O.B.E. 1918; I.S.O. 1916; *b.* Southsea, 2 Oct. 1859; *s.* of Mark Edwin Frost; *m.* 1888, Alice Charlotte Mercy (*d.* 1946), *d.* of Francis Pineo, formerly of War Office and Admiralty; one *s.* two *d.* *Educ.:* privately. Joined the Admiralty service 1877; served in several Departments at home and abroad; Secretary to Admiral Superintendent, Portsmouth Dockyard, on return from Hong Kong, 1899; retired, 1921; founded the Naval Museum, Portsmouth Dockyard, 1906; awarded Coronation medals of King Edward VII. and King George V. *Publications:* Descriptive Museum Catalogue, including historical sketch of Portsmouth Dockyard, also Press Articles. *Recreations:* gardening and historical research. *Address:* The Old Vicarage, Purbrook, near Portsmouth, Hants. *T.:* Cosham 76102. *T.A.:* Frost, Purbrook, Hants. [*Died* 6 *March* 1953.

FROST, Captain Meadows, M.C.; late Cheshire Regiment; late Resident Councillor, Penang; *b.* 18 April 1875; *s.* of late Meadows Frost and Rosalie Croshaw Elizabeth Russell; *m.* 1911, Catherine Fulton Carver; two *s.* one *d.* *Educ.:* Charterhouse; Brasenose College, Oxford. Entered Civil Service of Federated Malay States, 1898; served European War (M.C.). *Address:* Dial House, Seend, Wiltshire. *T.A.:* Seend. *T.:* Seend 229. [*Died* 28 *Aug.* 1954.

FRY, Col. Arthur Brownfield, C.B. 1930; C.I.E. 1919; D.S.O. 1917; I.M.S. (retired); *b.* 1873; *s.* of late J. W. Fry, M.R.C.S., etc. of Wateringbury, Kent; unmarried. *Educ.:* Eastbourne College; London Hospital; London University. M.R.C.S. Eng.; L.R.C.P. Lond.; M.D. London Univ.; D.P.H., D.T.M. and Hy; late Professor of Hygiene, Calcutta School of Tropical Medicine; served N.W. Frontier, Waziristan, 1900-2; Thibet Mission, 1904; Great War, France and Mesopotamia, 1914-19 (despatches thrice, D.S.O., C.I.E.); A.D.M.S. Presidency District, India, 1925-30. *Publication:* First and Second Reports on Malaria in Bengal. *Recreations:* golf, shooting, fishing. *Address:* Oatlands Park Hotel, Weybridge, Surrey. [*Died* 1 *Sept.* 1954.

FRY, Cecil Roderick; Chairman J. S. Fry & Sons Ltd.; *b.* 1890; *s.* of late Roderick J. Fry, Abbots Leigh, Bristol; *m.* Olave Kate (*d.* 1949), *d.* of W. C. Anderson, Keston, Kent; two *s.* one *d.* *Educ.:* Harrow; Trinity Coll., Camb. *Recreations:* shooting, yachting. *Address* c/o National Provincial Bank, Ltd., Dartmouth. *Club:* Royal Thames Yacht. [*Died* 8 *July* 1952.

FRY, Charles Burgess, M.A., F.R.G.S.; Hon. Captain, R.N.R.; *b.* 25 April 1872; *e. s.* of Lewis Fry, formerly of Rotherfield, Sussex; *m.* Beatrice Holme-Sumner (*d.* 1946); one *s.* two *d.* *Educ.:* Repton; Wadham College, Oxford (senior scholar). First Class Mods.; Hons. in Literæ Humaniores; Captain Oxford University Association Football, 1893; President Oxford Univ. Athletic Club, 1893; Capt. Oxford Univ. Cricket Club, 1893; formerly holder of world's record for long jump; played for England at Cricket and Association Football; contested (L.) Brighton, 1921; Banbury Division of Oxfordshire, 1923; Oxford City, 1924. Hon. Director T. S. Mercury, 1908–1950. Member of the Horatian Soc. *Publications:* A Mother's Son, 1907 (with Beatrice Fry); Life Worth Living, 1939; Key Book of the League of Nations; edited The Book of Cricket, 1899; Cricket, 1912; contributor of prose and verse to various magazines and journals. *Recreations:* cricket, Rugby and Association football, running, hunting, fishing, shooting, motoring, etc. *Address:* 8 Moreland Court, N.W.2. *T.:* Hampstead 2636. *Clubs:* Oxford and Cambridge, Authors', Savage, Savile, Royal Automobile, M.C.C.; English-Speaking Union. [*Died* 7 *Sept.* 1956.

FRY, Sir Geoffrey Storrs, 1st Bt., *cr.* 1929; K.C.B., *cr.* 1937 (C.B. 1923); C.V.O. 1929; *b.* 1888; *s.* of late Francis James Fry, of Cricket St. Thomas, Chard; *m.* 1915, Hon. Alathea Gardner, 2nd *d.* of late Lord Burghclere; one *d.* *Educ.:* Harrow; King's College, Cambridge. Called to the Bar, 1913; Home Office, 1915-17; Treasury, 1917-19; Private Secretary (unpaid) to Rt. Hon. A. Bonar Law, M.P., 1919-21, 1922-23, and to Earl Baldwin of Bewdley, 1923-39. *Heir:* none. *Address:* Oare House, Marlborough. *T.A.:* Fry, Oare. *T.:* Pewsey 2128. *Club:* Travellers'. [*Died* 13 *Oct.* 1960 (*ext.*).

FRY, Sir John Pease, 2nd Bt., *cr.* 1894 J.P., M.A., F.S.A.; formerly Chairman or Director of 4 Colliery Cos. and other Cos.; *b.* 26 Feb. 1864; *s.* of Sir Theodore Fry, M.P., D.L., F.S.A., 1st Bt., and Sophia, *d.* of John Pease, East Mount, Darlington, and Cleveland Lodge, Great Ayton; *S.* father, 1912; *m.* 1891 Margaret Theodora (*d.* 1941). *d.* of Francis Edward Fox, J.P., of Uplands, Tamerton Foliot, Plymouth; three *s.* three *d.* *Educ.:* Clifton; Trinity College, Cambridge. *Recreation:* fishing. *Heir:* *s.* Theodore Penrose Fry. *Address:* Cleveland Lodge, Great Ayton, Middlesbrough. *T.A.:* Fry, Great Ayton. *T.:* Great Ayton 215. [*Died* 25 *Jan.* 1957.

FRY, (Sara) Margery, J.P., M.A.; *b.* 1874; *d.* of late Rt. Hon. Sir Edward Fry, G.C.B.; unmarried. *Educ.:* Home: Miss Lawrence's School, Brighton (afterwards Roedean); Somerville College, Oxford. Librarian Somerville College, 1898-1904; Warden of University House, Birmingham, 1904-14; Work with Quakers' War Victims Relief Mission in France, 1915-17; Principal of Somerville College, Oxford, 1926-31; Hon. Fellow, 1932; Hon. Secretary, Howard League for Penal Reform, 1919-26; Governor of British Broadcasting Corporation, 1937-39; Member of the Treasury Univ. Grants Cttee., 1919-48. Hon. LL.D., Manchester, LL.D., Birmingham. *Publications:* Arms of the Law, 1951; various pamphlets. *Address:* 48 Clarendon Road, W.11. [*Died* 21 *April* 1958.

FRY, Mrs. T. Penrose; *see* Kaye-Smith, Sheila.

FRY, Thomas; *b.* 14 Jan. 1889; *s.* of Thomas William Fry; *m.* 1915, Margaret, *d.* of George William Davis, M.D.; three *s.* two *d.* *Educ.:* Blackheath School; City of London School; Trinity College, Cambridge (Scholar). Civil Service, Admiralty, Secretary's Department, 1911; Private Secretary to successive First Lords, 1922-32; Assistant Secretary, 1932; Principal Assistant Secretary, 1936; Director of Greenwich Hospital, 1939; Under-Secretary, 1944-50. President, Bath Natural History Soc., 1947-52. *Recreation:* bird-watching. *Address:* 8 Richmond Hill, Bath. [*Died* 27 *Dec.* 1958.

FRYER, Herbert; Pianist and Composer; F.R.A.M. and F.R.C.M.; *b.* Hampstead, 21 May 1877; *s.* of George Henry Fryer and Clara S., *y. d.* of Charles Roberts; unmarried. *Educ.:* Merchant Taylors' School; Royal Academy of Music; Royal College of Music. Prof. of Pianoforte at the Royal College of Music, retired 1947. Adjudicator of Pianoforte in most of the important Musical Competition Festivals, and has toured Canada for the same purpose; Examiner to the Associated Board of the Royal Schools of Music. Commenced London Recitals, 1898; since when he has given Recitals in most of the Continental Capitals, played at the Royal Philharmonic Society's Concerts, regularly at the Queen's Hall Promenade Concerts, and in most provincial towns; made many Recital tours in Europe, in Canada and the United States; made extensive tours in Australia, Ceylon, South Africa, and Canada; recently toured for the second time through all the principal cities of India, holding examinations and giving pianoforte recitals. *Publications:* Suite for Pianoforte, Op. 11; various pianoforte pieces including transcriptions of Bach and of old English Songs (Op. 1-24); Hints on Pianoforte Practice; many songs. *Recreations:* golf, gardening, and philately. *Address:* Friar's Elm, Dorking. *T.:* Westcott 94. *Clubs:* Arts; Effingham Golf. [*Died* 7 *Feb.* 1957.

FUCHS, Carl; violoncellist; *b.* Offenbach am Main, 3 June 1865; *s.* of Henry Fuchs and Mina Arnold; *m.* 1893, Nellie Jordan; one *s.* (and one *s.* decd.). *Educ.:* Offenbach. Studied violoncello under Cossmann, Frankfort, and under Davidoff, St. Petersburg; for many years Prof. (violoncello) Royal Manchester Coll. of Music and Matthay School, Liverpool; principal violoncellist of the Hallé Orchestra, Manchester, the Liverpool Philharmonic Orchestra, and Member of the Brodsky-Quartet, Manchester. *Publications:* Violoncello Method, in three vols.; various editions of standard works for violoncello; short pieces for the study of positions; Musical and Other Recollections of Carl Fuchs, 'Cellist, 1937. *Recreations:* walking, climbing. *Address:* 32 Oak Road, Withington, Manchester, 20. *T.:* Didsbury 4203. [*Died* 9 *June* 1951.

FULFORD, Dame Catherine, D.B.E., *cr.* 1953 (M.B.E. 1918); Alderman London County Council, 1931-34, then member for Chelsea, and again Alderman L.C.C., 1952-58; unmarried. *Educ.:* private. Concerned in Local Government in London, 1921-; Board of Guardians (9 yrs.); Chelsea Borough Council (11 yrs.); Fulham Borough Council (6 yrs.); J.P. Kensington (15 yrs.). *Recreations:* gardening, mountains. *Address:* Bowlhead Green, Godalming, Surrey. *Club:* English-Speaking Union. [*Died* 17 *Jan.* 1960.

FULLER, Rev. Arthur Rose, C.V.O. 1942 (M.V.O. 1935); M.A.; *b.* 2 Jan. 1874; *s.* of Rose Fuller and Sarah Elizabeth Cookson; *m.* 1905, Evelyn Maud Charter, *d.* of late Lieut.-Comdr. W. Boileau Charter, R.N. *Educ.:* Eton; Magdalen Coll., Oxford; Wells Theological College. Curate, Eton Mission, Hackney Wick, 1897-1903; Holy Trinity, Sloane Street, 1903-7; Rector of Filleigh, 1907-14; Chaplain Territorial Army, 1912-23; Vicar of Paignton, 1914-20; Rector of Shalstone, 1921-24; Rector of Sandringham and Domestic Chaplain to the King, 1926-42; Rural Dean of Rising, 1933-42; retired,

1942. *Address:* Meldon Cottage, The Road to Tilford, Hindhead, Surrey. [*Died* 3 *June* 1959.

FULLER, Sir Benjamin John, Kt., *cr.* 1921; Pres. Chm. Australian United Nations Assembly; Pres. Australian Branch Internat. Migration Service; Pres. Australian Art and Education Guild, Melbourne; Vice-Patron Arts Council of Australia, N.S.W. Div.; Governing Director Fullers' Theatres Ltd., etc.; *b.* London, 20 March 1875; *s.* of John and Harriett Fuller; *m.* 1900, Elizabeth Mary, *d.* of Henry Thomson, Auckland, N.Z.; one *s.* two *d.* *Educ.:* Board School and Birkbeck College. *Recreations:* billiards, walking, reading. *Address:* 233 Castlereagh St., Sydney, N.S.W. *T.A.:* Fullers, Sydney. *T.:* FM 2446. [*Died* 10 *March* 1952.

FULLER, Major-General Cuthbert Graham, C.B. 1926; C.M.G. 1919; D.S.O. 1917; p.s.c.; Colonel Commandant R.E., 1937-44; *b.* 1874; *s.* of late George Fuller, M.I.C.E., D.Sc.; *m.* 1912, Princess Sophia, *d.* of late Prince Vladimir Shahoffsky; one *d.* *Educ.:* St. Paul's; Beaumont Coll.; R.M.A., Woolwich; 2nd Lieut. R.E. 1893. Served in South African War, 1899-1902 (despatches); European War, 1914-18, in Gallipoli, Egypt and France (despatches, Bt. Lieut.-Col. and Col., D.S.O., C.M.G. Commander Legion of Honour); commanding 130 (T.A.) Brigade, 1923-25; commanding Canal Brigade, Egypt, 1925-28; Maj.-Gen. in charge of Administration, Eastern Command, 1929-31; Commander 48th (South Midland) Division T.A., 1931-35; retired pay, 1935. *Address:* Longmead, Mayfield, Sussex. *T.:* 2193. [*Died* 15 *March* 1960.

FULTON, Eustace Cecil; *b.* 1880; *s.* of late Sir Forrest Fulton, K.C.; *m.* 1913; one *d.* *Educ.:* Malvern; Cambridge. Called to Bar, Middle Temple, 1904; Recorder of Rye, 1931-37; Senior Prosecuting Counsel to the Crown at the Central Criminal Court, 1932-36; Chairman of County of London Sessions, 1936-49. [*Died* 26 *Sept.* 1954.

FULTON, John Farquhar, Sterling Professor, History of Medicine, Yale University, since 1951; M.D., F.R.C.P. (Lond.); Hon: D.Litt. Oxon., 1957, LL.D. Birm., 1948, M.D. Oslo Louvain, 1951, Uppsala, 1956; O.B.E. (Hon.); Officier Légion d'Honneur, 1949; Comdr. Ord. Leopold II (Belg.), 1951; *b.* 1 Nov. 1899; *s.* of John Farquhar Fulton, M.D., and Edith Stanley Wheaton Fulton; *m.* 1923, Lucia Pickering Wheatland; no *c.* *Educ.:* Harvard Univ. (B.S., M.D.); Oxford (B.A., M.A., D.Phil., D.Sc.). Demonstrator (Physiol.), Oxford, 1923-25; Assoc. Neurol. Surg., Peter Bent Brigham Hosp., Boston, 1928; Fellow, Magdalen Coll., Oxf., 1928-; Prof of Physiology, 1929-1931, Sterling Prof., 1931-51, Yale University. Member, Amer. Philos. Soc., 1949-; Trustee, Inst. Advanced Study, 1942-. Curator, Osler Library, McGill Univ., 1950-. Lecturer: Heath Clark, London, 1947; Withering, Birmingham, 1948; Ludwig Mond, Manchester, 1949; Sherrington, Liverpool, 1951; Francqui, Louvain, 1951. George Sarton Medal, Hist. Sci. Soc., 1958. *Publications:* Muscular Contraction, 1926; Physiology of the Nervous System, 3rd Edn., 1949; Bibliog. Robert Boyle, 2nd Edn., 1959; Harvey Cushing. 1946; biographies, bibliographies, lectures. *Recreations:* book collecting, writing, travel. *Address:* Magdalen College, Oxford, England; 100 Deepwood Drive, New Haven 17, Conn., U.S.A. *T.:* New Haven, Locust 2-0597. *Clubs:* Century, Yale (New York); Odd Volumes (Boston). [*Died* 29 *May* 1960.

FULTON, Rev. William, D.D., LL.D., B.Sc.; Principal of Trinity College, Glasgow, since 1938; *b.* Glasgow, 18 Dec. 1876; *e. s.* of David Fulton, F.E.I.S., formerly Headmaster of Golf-hill School, Glasgow; *m.* 1913, Annie Ida Sutherland Strachan; two *s.* three *d.* *Educ.:* Glasgow High School; Universities of Glasgow, Marburg, and Berlin. M.A., 1st Cl. Hons. in Classics, 1898; B.Sc., Special Distinction Mathematics and Astronomy, 1900; B.D. 1902; D.D. (Glas.) 1920; LL.D. (Edin.) 1946; LL.D. (Glas.) 1948; Cowan Medallist and Muirhead Prizeman in Humanity; Jeffrey Medallist in Greek; Muir Bursar and Cunningham Medallist in Mathematics; Cleland and Rae Wilson Medallist in Divinity, and in Biblical Criticism; Black Theological Fellow, 1902-3; Minister of Wigtown Parish, 1906-9; Collegiate Minister of Paisley Abbey, 1909-15; Officiating Chaplain to the Troops at Paisley, 1910-15; Professor of Systematic Theology in the University of Aberdeen, 1915-27; Prof. of Divinity in the Univ. of Glasgow, 1928-47; Examiner in Philosophy of Religion and Christian Ethics, Queen's Univ., Belfast, 1929-31, 1935-37, 1945-47; Examiner in Systematic Theology, Univ. of Edinburgh, 1942-46; Baird Lecturer, 1939-40. *Publications:* edited the late Professor Hastie's Theology of the Reformed Church; articles, Teleology, Theodicy, etc., in the Encyclopædia of Religion and Ethics, vol. xii.; Nature and God (Alexander Robertson Lectures, 1926); articles and reviews in religious and theological magazines. *Recreation:* golf. *Address:* 53 Hillhead St., Glasgow. *Clubs:* College, Western (Glasgow). [*Died* 13 *Aug.* 1952.

FURLEY, John Talfourd, C.M.G. 1922; O.B.E. 1918; *b.* 31 March 1878; *o. surv. s.* of late Henry Furley, Rector of Kingsnorth, Kent; unmarried. *Educ.:* Tonbridge School. Cadet, Gold Coast Civil Service, 1902; District Commissioner, 1904; Provincial Commissioner, 1911; Secretary for Native Affairs, 1917; Colonial Secretary, Sierra Leone, 1923; retired, 1924. *Club:* Athenæum. [*Died* 11 *May* 1956.

FURNESS, Reginald Albert, C.M.G. 1947; Member, British Food Mission, Washington, U.S.A. *Address:* U.K. Treasury and Supply Delegation, Bradford Building, 1800 K. Street N.W., Washington, D.C., U.S.A. [*Died* 19 *Oct.* 1951.

FURNESS, Sir Robert Allason, K.B.E., *cr.* 1951 (C.B.E. 1926); C.M.G. 1944; *b.* 1883; 3rd *s.* of Rev. John Monteith Furness; *m.* 1945, Joyce Lucy Sophie Marc; one *d.* *Educ.:* Rugby School; King's College, Cambridge (M.A.). Entered Egyptian Civil Service, 1906; seconded to staff of High Commissioner for Egypt, 1919; retired from Egyptian Civil Service, 1923; Oriental Secretary to High Commissioner, 1923-26; Deputy Director-General, Egyptian State Broadcasting, 1933-1934; Press Officer, Government of Palestine, 1934-36; Professor of English, Fuad I University, Cairo, 1936-44; and Deputy Chief Censor of Publications, Anglo-Egyptian Censorship, 1939-44; Representative in Egypt of British Council, 1945-50. Grand Officer Order of the Nile. *Publications:* Translations from the Greek Anthology, 1931; Poems of Callimachus, 1931; contributions to The Oxford Book of Greek Verse in Translation, 1938. *Address:* South Lodge, Little Shelford, Cambs. *T.:* Shelford 3169. [*Died* 4 *Dec.* 1954.

FURNESS, Sir Robert Howard, Kt., *cr.* 1929; *b.* 10 Feb. 1880; 2nd *s.* of late R. P. Furness, Preston; *m.* 1917, Helen, *e. d.* of late Major Arthur Smyth, R.M.L.I.; one *d.* *Educ.:* King William's College, Isle of Man. Solicitor (Hons.), 1902; Bar, Lincoln's Inn, 1919; held legal appointments in British Honduras, Tanganyika Territory, Trinidad; Chief Justice of Barbados and a Judge of the West Indian Court of Appeal, 1926; Chief Justice of Jamaica, 1936-44. A.D.C. to Governor of British Honduras, 1913-15; served European War with British West Indies Regt., 1915-19. *Address:* Glenbrae, Mandeville, Jamaica. [*Died* 28 *Feb.* 1959.

FURNISS, John Mawdsley, C.B.E. 1944; J.P.; Director Martins Bank Limited since 1939; *b.* 6 Aug. 1877; *s.* of Charles Strong Furniss and Elizabeth Jane Mawdsley; *m.* 1905, Edith Tait (*d.* 1945). *Educ.*: Birkenhead Institute. Entered Bank of Liverpool Ltd., 1894; held various managerial positions in that Bank and its successor Martins Bank Limited; Assistant General Manager, 1926; General Manager, 1933; Director and General Manager, 1939; Director and Chief General Manager, 1942; retired, as Chief General Manager, 1945. *Address*: Thornton House, Thornton Hough, Cheshire; 18 Fursecroft, Brown St., W.1. *T.*: Thornton Hough 315, Paddington 0449. [*Died* 3 *Jan.* 1956.

FURSE, Dame Katharine, G.B.E., *cr.* 1917; R.R.C.; Lady of Grace Order of St. John; *b.* 23 Nov. 1875; *d.* of John Addington Symonds and Janet Catherine North; *m.* Charles W. Furse, Painter; two *s.* *Educ.*: at home. Wood Carver; Commandant-in-Chief, V.A.D.; proceeded to France, Sep. 1914, and started V.A.D. work there; came home Jan. 1915 and started the V.A.D. Dept. under Red Cross; resigned, 1917; Director Women's Royal Naval Service, 1917-1919; Director World Bureau Girl Guides and Girl Scouts, 1928-38. *Publications*: Ski-running, 1924; Hearts and Pomegranates, 1940. *Address*: 34 Sloane Court, S.W.3. *Clubs*: Allies', Portsmouth, Service Women's. [*Died* 25 *Nov.* 1952.

FURSE, Rt. Rev. Michael Bolton, K.C.M.G., *cr.* 1947; D.D.; Prelate of Order of St. Michael and St. George, 1936-51; 4th *s.* of late Charles Wellington Furse, Archdeacon and Canon of Westminster, Halsdon, Dolton, N. Devon; *b.* 1870; *m.* 1903, Frances Josephine (*d.* 1947), *d.* of Capt. James Redfield, U.S. Army. *Educ.*: Eton (King's Scholar); Trinity College, Oxford. B.A. 1893; M.A. 1896; D.D. (Hon.) 1911; Deacon, 1896; Priest, 1897, by Bishop of Oxford; Fellow and Dean of Trinity College, Oxford, 1895-1903; Archdeacon of Johannesburg, 1903-09; Bishop of Pretoria, 1909-1920; Bishop of St. Albans, 1920-44; Member of the House of Lords, 1923-44; Hon. Fellow of Trinity College, Oxford, 1921; *Publications*: A School of Prayer; God's Plan; Stand Therefore! *Recreations*: golf, fishing. *Address*: Framland, Wantage, Berks. [*Died* 18 *June* 1955.

FURSE, Lieut.-General Sir William T., K.C.B., *cr.* 1917 (C.B. 1915); K.C.M.G., *cr.* 1935; D.S.O. 1900; R.A.; *b.* 21 Apr. 1865; *s.* of late Ven. the Archdeacon of Westminster; *m.* 1899, Jean Adelaide, 2nd *d.* of late H. Evans-Gordon; two *s.* one *d.* *Educ.*: Eton. Entered army, 1884; Captain, 1893; Major, 1900; Colonel, 1911; A.D.C. to Lord Roberts when Comm.-in-Chief in India, 1890-93; graduated at Staff College, 1897; Army Headquarters, 1897-1902; D.A.Q.M.G. 2nd Army Corps, 1902-4; Army Headquarters, 1905-7; G.S.O. 2nd Grade, Staff College, 1908-11; O.C. 12th Brigade, R.F.A., 1911-13; G.S.O. 1st Grade, 6th Division, 1913-14; B.G.G.S., II. Corps, France, 1915; G.O.C. 9th (Scottish) Division, 1915-16: served S. Africa, 1899-1900 (despatches, Queen's medal 5 clasps, D.S.O.); European War, 1914-18 (despatches, K.C.B.; prom. Maj.-Gen. and Lt.-Gen.); Master-General of Ordnance, 1916; member of Army Council; retired, 1920; Director of the Imperial Institute, 1926-34. *Address*: 43 Worminghall, Aylesbury, Bucks. [*Died* 31 *May* 1953.

FURTWANGLER, Wilhelm, Ph.D. (Hon.); Guest Conductor, England, European centres and Argentina since 1935; Permanent Guest Conductor, Vienna Philharmonic Orchestra and Vienna State Opera; Regular Conductor Festivals of Salzburg and Lucerne; Composer and music writer; *b.* Berlin-Schoeneberg, 25 January 1886; *s.* of Adolf Furtwängler, Prof. of Archaeology in Munich, and Adelheid Wendt; *m.* 1923, Zitla Lund, of Kopenhagen; *m.* 1943, Elisabeth Albert, Wiesbaden. *Educ.*: Munich. Conductor at the operas of Breslau, Zürich, Munich, Strassburg; Conductor of the Opera and Symphony Concerts at Lübeck, 1911-15; first Conductor of the Mannheim Opera, 1915-20; Conductor of the Berlin State-Opera Concerts of the Museum Concerts in Frankfurt-a.-M.; Conductor of the Tonkünstler Orchestra in Vienna, 1920-22; Director: Gewandhaus, Leipzig, 1922-28; Berliner Philharmonischen Konzerte, 1922-1934, Berlin State Opera, 1933-34; New York Philharmonic Orchestra, 1927-29; Wiener Philharmonische Konzerte, 1927-30 and 1948-; Wiener Gesellschaft der Musikfreunde, 1922-29, 1948 and 1949. Conductor, Bayreuth Festival, 1931, 1936, 1937; after War of 1939-45, regularly conducting in Berlin, Vienna, Milano (Scala), London. *Publication*: Concerning Music, 1953. *Address*: Villa l'Empereur, Clarens, Vaud, Switzerland. [*Died* 30 *Nov.* 1954.

FYERS, Major Hubert Alcock Nepean, M.V.O. 1901; late Rifle Brigade; *e. s.* of late Lieut.-Gen. Sir William Fyers, K.C.B., and Mary Stuart Fyers; *b.* 2 Sept. 1862; *m.* 1897, Evangeline Blanche, *e. d.* of late Captain Hon. Francis Chichester and the Lady Emily Chichester; one *s.* two *d.* *Educ.*: Eton; Royal Military College, Sandhurst. Entered Army, 1884; joined Rifle Brigade; served in India; retired from Army, 1899; rejoined Royal Rifle Reserve, 1900, during Boer War; on Lord Northcote's Staff as A.D.C. in Australia, 1907-8; on outbreak of War rejoined the army on promotion to Major in 5th Batt. Rifle Brigade, 1914; Commandant on Lines of Communication, served in France, Egypt and Salonika, 1915-18; demobilised, 1919; became Equerry to H.R.H. Duke of Connaught on outbreak of War, Sept. 1939. *Recreations*: shooting, fishing, yachting. *Club*: Naval and Military. [*Died* 1 *Aug.* 1951.

FYFE, Sir Cleveland, Kt., *cr.* 1943; C.B.E. 1935; Fellow, Guild of Agricultural Journalists, 1950, Vice-President, 1951 and Chairman, 1953; Organising Secretary, Animal Health Trust, 1947-51; *b.* 8 Jan. 1888; *s.* of late William T. Fyfe, M.A.; *m.* May, *y. d.* of late James Church, New Southgate; one *s.* *Educ.*: George Watson's Coll., and Univ., Edinburgh. Served in Infantry during European War and granted rank of Captain on demobilisation in 1919; served for a short period as Asst. Commissioner under Ministry of Labour in connection with resettlement of ex-soldiers; Parliamentary Secretary to National Farmers' Union, 1919, Joint General Secretary, 1923; General Secretary, 1932-44; Member of Treasury Committee on Malting Barley Duty, 1923; served on National Milk Publicity Council (Chairman, 1936-37); acted as Secretary *pro tem.* to Milk Marketing Board on its inception, 1933; King's Silver Jubilee Medal, 1935; Coronation Medal, 1937; Delegate to first British Empire Producers' Conference, Sydney, N.S.W., 1938, in connection with Australia's 150th Anniversary Celebrations; Member of Advisory Committee on Publicity to Ministry of Agriculture, 1939-44; Member of Red Cross Agriculture Fund Committee, 1940-46 (Deputy Chairman, 1942-46); Hon. Pres. Finchley Division, St. John Ambulance Brigade, 1946-52; Chairman, Finchley Div. Conservative Assoc., 1945-46; Captain, Finchley Golf Club, 1949-50, and President, 1950-55 (Hon. Life Mem., 1955); Founder-member and Liveryman, Worshipful Co. of Farmers; Master, 1956-57. *Publications*: Editor of N.F.U. publications, 1919-1944, and was responsible for inception, in 1920, of the Union's News Service, official monthly journal and Year Book. *Recreation*. golf. *Address*: 7 Wentworth Park, N.3. *T.*: Finchley 4197. *Clubs*: Farmers'; Finchley Golf (Finchley). [*Died* 1 *March* 1959.

FYFE, H. Hamilton; author and journalist; *b.* London, Sept. 1869; *e. s.* of late J. Hamilton Fyfe, barrister-at-law; *m.* 1907, Eleanor, *d.* of late William Kelly of the War Office. *Educ.*: Fettes College, Edinburgh. Joined staff of The Times,

1889; was in turn reporter, sub-editor, editorial secretary, reviewer, dramatic critic, etc.; Editor of Morning Advertiser, 1902-3; Editor of Daily Mirror, 1903-7; circulation raised from 40,000 to 400,000; dramatic critic, The World, 1905-10; special correspondent of Daily Mail, 1907-18; served as war correspondent with French, Russian, Roumanian, Italian, and British armies, 1914-18; lecturing tour in Spain and Portugal on the War and Russian Revolution, 1917; Hon. Attaché, British War Mission to U.S. 1917; in charge of British propaganda in Germany and among the German armies, July-Nov. 1918; lectured all over Great Britain, 1918-22; Editor Daily Herald at invitation of Trade Union Congress and Labour Party, 1922-26, raised circulation from 130,000 to 450,000; followed Philip Snowden as political writer for Reynolds News, 1930-1942. Labour Candidate, Sevenoaks Division, 1929; Yeovil Div., 1931; Pres., League Against Cruel Sports, 1934-46. *Publications:* books on Canada, South Africa, Egypt, Mexico, Switzerland; several novels; A Modern Aspasia (Play), produced London, 1909, Prague, 1910, Petrograd, 1916; The Pool, wordless play (Alhambra), 1912; The Borstal Boy, play (Coliseum), 1913; The Meaning of the World-Revolution, 1919; The Kingdom, the Power and the Glory (Play), 1920, Twells Brex, 1920; The Making of an Optimist, 1921; Behind the Scenes of the Great Strike, 1926; The Religion of an Optimist, 1927; The British Liberal Party, 1928; Pinero's Plays and Players, 1930; Revolt of Women, 1933; Life of T. P. O'Connor, 1934; My Seven Selves, 1936; Press Parade, 1936; What Communism Means To-day, 1937; The Illusion of National Character, 1940, republished in Thinker's Library, 1946; But for Britain . . ., 1943; Britain's War-time Revolution, 1944; The Most Civilized People in Europe: How the Swiss do it, 1948; A History of the Next Hundred Years — Unless, 1948 Sixty Years of Fleet Street, 1949; Poems in Praise of Cats (Anthology), 1949. *Address* 8 Downs View Close, East Dean, nr. Eastbourne, Sussex. *T.:* East Dean 3101. *Club:* Savage. [*Died* 15 *June* 1951.

FYLEMAN, Rose, Writer and Lecturer; *b.* Nottingham; Jewish parentage. *Educ.:* Private School; Univ. College, Nottingham. Studied singing with Sir Henry Wood, also in Berlin and Paris, and at the Royal College of Music, London, where took A.R.C.M. diploma; first public appearance in London, Queen's Hall, 1903; since then engaged in public singing, teaching, and lecturing; regular contributor to Punch for many years (R.F.); also writes for various London papers; and translates from French, German and Italian. Lecture Tours in America, 1929-30 and 1931-32. *Publications:* Fairies and Chimneys, 1918; The Fairy Green, 1919; The Fairy Flute, 1921 The Rainbow Cat, 1922; A Small Cruse, 1922; Forty Good-night Tales, 1923; Eight Little Plays for Children, 1924; Fairies and Friends, 1925; Letty, 1926; Forty Good Morning Tales, 1926; A Princess comes to our Town, 1927; Seven little plays for Children and Some old-fashioned Girls, 1928; Gay go Up; Twenty Tea Time Tales, 1929; Fifty New Nursery Rhymes; The Adventures of Captain Marwhopple; Hey-ding-a-ding, 1931; The Easter Hare; Rose Fyleman Birthday Book, 1932; The Princess Dances, 1933; Jeremy Quince. 1933; Nine Small Plays, 1934; Bears, 1934; Widdy-Widdy-Wurky, 1934; Six Short Plays, 1935; Monkeys; Six Longer Plays for Children; Billy Monkey, 1936; The Magic Pencil eight plays, 1938; Calendar of Saints, 1939; Folk-tales from many lands, 1939; Runabout Rhymes, 1941; Timothy's Conjuror, 1942; Hob and Bob, 1943; The Timothy Toy Trust, 1944; Adventures with Benghazi, 1946; Rhymebook for Adam, 1949; Over the Tree Tops, 1949; Daphne and Dick, 1951; White Flower, 1953. Christmas Play performed at Old Vic., Dec. 1926: Children's Opera (with Thomas Dunhill) performed at Guildford, Nov. 1933; Puppet play performed in Hampstead, 1948; Nursery Tales—Stories and Play, Televised, 1949; Play-games for children (music by Ruth Dyson), 1955. *Recreation:* travelling. *Address:* c/o Mrs. Williams, 10 Porchester Terrace, W.2. [*Died* 1 *Aug.* 1957.

FYNES-CLINTON, Rev. Henry Joy, M.A.; Rector of St. Magnus the Martyr's with St. Margaret's, New Fish Street, and St. Michael's, Crooked Lane, City of London; Hon. Chaplain and Past-Master of Worshipful Co. of Plumbers; Chaplain of Roy. Soc. of St. George (City Branch); Fellow of Coll. of Guardians of Walsingham; Fellow of Sion College; Chm. of Governors: St. Michael's Sch., Otford; Quainton Hall Sch., Harrow; Dir. of Catholic League; *b.* 6 May 1875; *s.* of Rev. Charles Henry Fynes-Clinton, Rector of Blandford Forum, and Thomasina Gordon Shaw, Ballyoran, Co. Down. *Educ.:* King's School, Canterbury; Trinity College, Oxford; Ely Theological College. Assistant Curate, St. John's, Upper Norwood, 1901-4; St. Martin's, Brighton, 1904-6; Chaplain of All Saints's and Asst. Curate, St. Stephen's, Lewisham, 1906-14; Founder of Anglican and Eastern Churches Assoc., and Gen. Secy., 1906-20; General Secretary of Archbishop of Canterbury's Eastern Churches Committee, 1920-23; Serbian Order of St. Sava, 1st Class, conferred 1918; Greek Order of St. George, 3rd Class, 1918; Archpriest's Cross and Cincture of Serbian Church, 1922; Hon. Secretary, Russian Church Aid Fund, 1927-34; Russian Archpriest's Cross, 1930. *Address:* 176 St. James' Court, Westminster, S.W.1. *T.:* Victoria 2360, Mansion House 4481. *Club:* Royal Commonwealth Society. [*Died* 4 *Dec.* 1959.

FYNNE, Robert John, M.A. (Dublin and London); Professor of Education and Registrar of the School of Education, Dublin University, 1922-50; External Examiner in Education, Glasgow University; Examiner in Psychology, Royal College of Surgeons, Ireland; Member of Royal Society of Teachers; Fellow, Royal Society of Arts; Member Royal Institute of Philosophy; *e. s.* of late John Fynne of Summerville, Millisle, County Down; *m.* Sarannie (*d.* 1944), *e. d.* of late David S. McAuley, Dromara, Co. Down; *m.* 1949, Dr. Margaret Sutcliffe. *Educ.:* Athenry School for Boys, and privately; Marlboro' Training College; Trinity College, Dublin; King's College, London. Teaching and lecturing experience in many types of schools and colleges; research in history and theory of education; University Higher and Honours Diplomas in Education. *Publications:* Montessori and her Inspirers, 1924; Modern Teaching: A First Book (editor and contributor), 1937-38; papers, essays, articles on educational subjects; reviews; notes on historical and literary subjects. *Recreations:* history and literature, golf, angling. *Address:* 1 High View Road, Sidcup, Kent. *T.:* Footscray 1041. *Club:* University of London. [*Died* 1 *Jan.* 1953.

G

GABBATT, John Percy, M.A. (Cantab.), D.Sc. (Liv.); *b.* Preston, 3 Feb. 1880; *m.* 1913, Clara Lister, 5th *d.* of Sir William P. Hartley. *Educ.:* University College, Liverpool (Scholar); Peterhouse, Cambridge (Exhibitioner and Scholar). Mathematical Lecturer, University College, Nottingham, 1904-8; Professor of Mathematics, Canterbury College, Christchurch, New Zealand, 1908-22. *Publications:* Geometrical papers in scientific journals. *Address:* Durford Edge, Petersfield. *T.:* Liss 3118. [*Died* 30 *June* 1956.

GABLE, Clark; Actor; *s.* of William H. Gable; *m.* 1st, Josephine Dillon (divorced);

2nd, Rhea Langham (divorced); 3rd, Mrs. William Powell (Carole Lombard; she died 1942); 4th, 1949, Sylvia, Lady Stanley of Alderley; 5th, 1955, Mrs. Kay Spreckels; one *s.* (posthumous). *Educ.:* Akron University. Played extra parts in stock company; appeared on New York stage; played The Last Mile in Los Angeles; was placed under contract by Metro-Goldwyn-Mayer Studios; has appeared in The Secret Six, A Free Soul, Night Flight, It Happened One Night, Men in White, China Seas, Mutiny on the Bounty, San Francisco, Parnell, Saratoga, Test Pilot, Too Hot To Handle, Honky Tonk, They Met in Bombay, Comrade X, The Hucksters, Gone with the Wind, Somewhere I'll Find You, Adventure, Homecoming, Any Number Can Play, To Please A Lady, The Wide Missouri, Lone Star, Never Let Me Go, Mogambo, Betrayed, Soldier of Fortune, The Tall Men, The King and Four Queens, Band of Angels, Teacher's Pet, Run Silent Run Deep, It Started in Naples, The Misfits. *Recreation:* riding. *Address:* c/o Metro-Goldwyn-Mayer Studios, Culver City, California. [*Died* 16 *Nov.* 1960.

GADDUM, Capt. Walter Frederick (Jim), D.L.; *b.* 1888; *s.* of late W. Gaddum, Brockhole, Windermere; *m.* Benita Violet, *d.* of late C. E. Fisher, Distington, Cumberland; no *c.* *Educ.:* Eton; Trinity College Cambridge. Joined Westmorland and Cumberland Yeomanry, 1914; served in France, European War, 1914-18, with Regt., and afterwards with Border Regt.; Major, Home Guard, 1942; High Sheriff of Westmorland, 1943; formerly Mem. Cumberland and Westmorland Territorial Army Assoc.; Master, Windermere Harriers, since 1923. *Recreations:* field sports. *Address:* Braban House, Burneside, Kendal. *T.A.:* Burneside, Westmorland. *T.:* Burneside 20. *Clubs:* Junior Carlton; Cumberland County (Carlisle); Royal Windermere Yacht. [*Died* 9 *Oct.* 1956.

GADSDEN, Cecil Holroyd, C.I.E. 1938; *b.* 18 Aug. 1887; *s.* of Edward Holroyd Gadsden, I.S.O., Latrobe, Tasmania; *m.* 1924, Frances Winifred, *d.* of Richard Haden. *Educ.:* St. Paul's School, London. Joined Indian Police, 1907; Deputy Inspector-General of Police, Madras, 1930-39; retired, 1939; Asst. Provost Marshal, R.A.F. Police, 1940-47. *Address:* 2 Windsor Avenue, Margate, Kent. [*Died* 13 *Oct.* 1957.

GAGE, Brig.-Gen. Moreton Foley, D.S.O. 1916; D.L. Northamptonshire; *b.* 1873; *y. s.* of late Lt.-Gen. Hon. Edward Thomas Gage, C.B., and 2nd wife, Ella Henrietta, *d.* of late James Maxse; *m.* 1st, 1902, Anne Massie, *d.* of William Everard Strong, New York; two *s.*; 2nd, 1916, Frances, *d.* of Senator H. F. Lippitt, Providence, Rhode Island; one *s.* one *d.* *Educ.:* Sandhurst and Staff College, Camberley. 5th Dragoon Guards; served Uganda, 1898-99 (despatches, medal with clasp); South Africa, 1900-2 (despatches, medals with seven clasps); European War, 1914-18 (despatches twice, D.S.O., Bt. Lt.-Col.); was Military Attaché at Washington. *Club:* Carlton. [*Died* 6 *July* 1953.

GAIR, Walter Burgh; *b.* 1854; *e.* and *o. surv. s.* of late Thomas Gair, Liverpool; *m.* 1880, Elizabeth (*d.* 1921), 2nd *d.* of late Henry Jevons, Liverpool; one *d.* (only son killed, 1918, European War). *Educ.:* Rugby School. Formerly a partner and a Managing Director of Barings (retired, 1920); Deputy Chairman of the Great Central Railway Co.; a Commissioner of Land Tax and Income Tax for the City of London, resigned 1923; a Trustee; 1917-41, and member of the Governing Body, 1921-41, of Rugby School; Director Colne Valley Water Co., 1922-45. *Recreations:* fishing, gardening. *Address:* temp.: Hotel Rembrandt, S.W.7. *Club:* Oriental. [*Died* 12 *June* 1951.

GAISFORD, Hugh William; *b.* 1874; *s.* of Thomas Gaisford of Offington and Lady Alice Kerr, *d.* of 7th Marquess of Lothian; *m.* Virginia, *d.* of J. P. Bryce of Bystock. Attaché, 1897; 1st Secretary, 1910; H.M. Minister in C. America, 1920-22; British Consul-General at Munich, 1925-32. *Address:* c/o Martins Bank, 36 Curzon Street, W.1. *Club:* Bath. [*Died* 31 *Aug.* 1954.

GALE, Anthony Eugene Myddelton; *b.* 8 July 1901; *yr. s.* of Ernest Sewell Gale and Charlotte Sarah Goddard; *m.* 1st, 1922, Jean Mary (marriage dissolved, 1950), *e. d.* of Sir Percy Graham MacKinnon,; three *s.* (and *e. s.* killed in action, 1944); 2nd, 1950, Joyce, *o. d.* of John Goodenday. *Educ.:* Magdalen College School, Oxford. Entered Lloyd's, 1920; Under-writing Member, 1922; served Committee of Lloyd's, 1940, 1951-54 and 1956-. Member of Committee of Lloyd's Register of Shipping, 1949-. Joined Coldstream Guards, 1940; served U.K., 1940-43; Military Operations Directorate, War Office, 1943-45, G.S.O. 2 and G.S.O. 1; Deputy Chairman and Treasurer, Lloyd's Register of Shipping, 1949-54. *Recreations:* music, golf. *Address:* The Hermitage, 108 Bayswater Road, W.2. *Clubs:* Brooks's, City of London; Pratt's; Royal St. George's Golf. [*Died* 16 *June* 1959.

GALLACHER, William, C.B.E. 1943; J.P.; Member of Council, Scottish Industrial Estates Ltd.; Member, Executive Council, State Medical Service, Lanarkshire; Lanarkshire Rents Tribunal, 1943, etc.; *b.* 2 April 1876; *s.* of James Gallacher and Bridget Gilluley; *m.* 1900, Mary Anne Fairley; two *s.* five d. *Educ.:* St. Mary's Roman Catholic School, Larkhall, Lanarkshire. Began work in coal-mine, aged twelve; Miners' Union Official, 1901-12; Director Scottish Co-operative Wholesale Society, 1912-43; Member Lanarkshire Education Authority, 1919-31; Licensing Court, 1930, Chairman of Court, 1942; on Consumers Council, Ministry of Food, 1917-19; on Committee on Trusts, 1919-22; on Government Commission, Wholesale and Retail Prices, 1930; Board of Trade Advisory Council, 1924-27, 1933-36; visited many European countries, India, Ceylon, U.S.A. and Canada on business of S.C.W.S. *Publications:* political pamphlets; six one-act plays; several short stories. *Recreations:* reading, writing and the drama; outdoor athletics, golf and bowling. *Address:* 24 Machan Road, Larkhall, Lanarkshire. *T.A.:* Maryville, Machan Road, Larkhall. *T.:* Larkhall 57. *Club:* Scottish P.E.N. (Glasgow). [*Died* 1 *Aug.* 1951.

GALLANNAUGH, Bertram William Leonard, F.R.I.B.A.; Principal of Ellis, Clarke & Gallannaugh, Chartered Architects; *b.* 25 May 1900; *m.* 1st, 1923 (marriage dissolved); one *s.* one *d.*; *m.* 1951, Althea Joyce Bradley, Croydon, Surrey. *Educ.:* privately; Central School of Art, London; Royal Academy, Piccadilly. Architect of the Franklin Roosevelt Memorial erected by the British people in Grosvenor Square, 1948; has also been responsible for many commercial City buildings and principal newspaper offices in London and the Provinces, also abroad. *Recreation:* fishing. *Address:* Clay Slope, 7 Fountain Drive, College Road, S.E.19; (office) 37 Soho Square, W.1. *T.:* Gerrard 1857. *Club:* Arts. [*Died* 26 *Aug.* 1957.

GALLIENNE, Wilfred Hansford, C.B.E. 1931; British Ambassador to Cuba since 1954; *b.* Guernsey, 20 May 1897; *s.* of Peter Gallienne, Guernsey; *m.* 1921, Rose Estick. Enlisted in R.F.A. 1914; to France with 9th Division, April 1915; commissioned in R.F.A. 1915; with 39th Brigade, 1st Division, 1916; seriously wounded, 1917; seconded R.E. for service at War Office, 1918; placed on Reserve, 1919; entered Consular Service and appointed Vice-Consul at Marseilles, 1919; acting Consul-General there during 1920, 1921, and 1922; transferred to Algiers, 1922, and acting Consul-General there during 1923 and 1924; transferred to Chicago, 1925, and acting Consul-General there during 1927 and 1928; H.M. Chargé d'Affaires and Consul at Santo Domingo, 1929-30; Special Envoy there for inauguration of President, 30 Aug. 1930; transferred to Los Angeles, 1931, and to Detroit, 1932; H.M. Chargé d'Affaires at Tegucigalpa, Honduras, 1933-1935; attached to Estonian Delegation to the Coronation, 1937; Chargé d'Affaires and Consul at Tallinn, 1935-40, Envoy Extraordinary and Minister Plenipotentiary there, 1940; one of H.M. Consuls at New York, 1941-42; Consul-General, Chicago, 1942-47; Minister to Guatemala, 1947-54. *Address:* British Embassy, Havana, Cuba; Longfield, Amherst, Guernsey, C.I. *Club:* St. James'. [*Died* 17 *July* 1956.

GALLWEY, Sir John Frankland-Payne-, 4th Bt., *cr.* 1812; J.P. North Riding, Yorks; A.M.I.M.E.; M.I.Min.Mech.E. (N.); F.R.G.S.; F.Z.S.; at present acting Major R.E.; *s.* of late Capt. Edwin John Payne-Gallwey, R.N., 2nd *s.* of 2nd Bt. and Susan Isabel, *y. d.* of Major Francis Gresley; *b.* 23 Dec. 1889; *S.* uncle, 1916; *m.* 1915, Evelyn Florence, *d.* of James Lee. *Educ.:* Winchester; Durham University (Armstrong College). Served European War, 1914-18, retired, 1918 (Bt. Lt.-Col., R.E.); War of 1939-45, retired (Bt. Lt.-Col.). *Heir:* *c.* Reginald Frankland Payne-Gallwey, *b.* 1889. *Address:* 11 St. James's Road, Hampton Hill, Middlesex. [*Died* 13 *Feb.* 1955.

GALTON, Frank Wallis; Secretary of the Fabian Society, 1920-39; *b.* London, 1867; *m.* 1899, Jessie, *d.* of J. J. Cottridge of Tottenham; two *d.* *Educ.:* Medburn St. Board School; Working Men's College, Gt. Ormond Street. Apprentice to silversmith and engraver City of London and Freeman of the City by servitude; turned to journalism and politics in youth and became Private Secretary to Mr. and Mrs. Sidney Webb, 1892-98: Secretary of the London Reform Union, 1899-1918; and of the City of London Liberal Association, 1903-5; during the war an Assistant Secretary to the Central Association of Volunteer Regiments and Editor of the Weekly Organ The Volunteer Gazette; Editor of the Municipal Journal, 1918-20; Member of the Royal Commission on Transport, 1929-30. *Publications:* The Tailoring Trade, published by the London School of Economics; Workers on their Industries in the Social Science Series, and many articles, pamphlets, leaflets, etc. *Recreation:* walking. *Address:* Bleak House, Bassingbourn, Royston, Herts. *T.:* Steeple Morden 254. [*Died* 9 *April* 1952.

GAMBLE, Victor Felix, C.I.E. 1923; C.B.E. 1926; *b.* Dec. 1886; 2nd *s.* of late David Gamble, Talardy, St. Asaph; *m.* 1st, 1911, Myrta Vivienne (from whom he obtained a divorce, 1932), *d.* of late Frederick Stubbs, Liverpool; one *s.*; 2nd, 1936, Kathleen Anne Brewer, *d.* of Alfred Button, Knowle, Warwickshire. *Educ.:* Uppingham. Royal Artillery, 1914; 26th K.G.O. Light Cavalry, 1918-22; Private Secretary to the Governor, United Provinces, India, 1918-23; Private Secretary to the Governor of Burma, 1923-26. *Recreation:* fishing. *Address:* Cove Cottage, Portloe, Cornwall. [*Died* 3 *March* 1952.

GAMELIN, Général Maurice, Grand Croix Légion d'Honneur; Médaille Militaire Française; Grand Croix de l'Ordre du Bain, 1939; Grand Croix de Victoria, 1938; Compagnon St. Michel et St. George, 1915; *b.* 20 Sept. 1872. Entra à l'École Spéciale Militaire de Saint-Cyr en 1891; Sorti 1er et nommé en 1893 Sous-lieutenant au 3ème régiment de Tirailleurs algériens; Lieutenant, 1895; à l'École de Guerre, 1899-1901; Capitaine, 1901; Affecté en 1904 au 15eme Btn. de Chasseurs à pied; Officier d'Ordonnance du Général Joffre, 1906; l'État-Major du 2eme C. A. lorsque le Général Joffre en prend le Commandement; Chef de Cabinet du Général Joffre, 1911; Chef de Bataillon, 1911; Lieut.-Col. 1914; Général de Brigade et Commandant d'une Division, 1916; Chef de la Mission militaire au Brésil, 1919; Commandant Supérieur des Troupes du Levant, 1925; Général de Division, 1925; Commandant de Corps d'Armée, 1927; Commandant du 20ème Corps d'Armée (Nancy) 1929; 1er Sous-Chef de l'État-Major de l'Armée, 1930, et Chef d'État-Major Général de l'Armée et Membre du Conseil Supérieur de la Guerre, 1931; Vice-Président du Conseil Supérieur de la Guerre et Chef d'État-Major Général, 1935; Chef d'État-Major Général de la Défense Nationale, 1938; Commandant en Chef des Forces Terrestres jusqu'à 1940. *Publications:* Œuvres Militaires. *Address:* 55 Av. Foch, Paris 16e. *T.:* Kle. 8897. [*Died* 18 *April* 1958.

GAMLEN, John Charles Blagdon, M.C., M.A.; *b.* 1885; *o. s.* of William Blagdon Gamlen, Oxford. *Educ.:* Rugby; Balliol College, Oxford (exhibitioner). Second Class Modern History, 1906. Partner in firm of Morrell Peel and Gamlen, Solicitors, Oxford, 1914-46; late Solicitor to University of Oxford and Registrar of Archdeaconry of Oxford; Extraordinary Member of Council of Law Society, 1939-45. *Recreations:* reading, travel. *Address:* 82 Banbury Road, Oxford. *Club:* Athenæum. [*Died* 25 *June* 1952.

GAMMANS, Sir (Leonard) David, 1st Bt., *cr.* 1955; M.P. (U.) Hornsey, Middlesex, since 1941; *b.* 10 Nov. 1895; *er. s.* of David Gammans, East Court, East Cosham, Hants.; *m.* 1917, Muriel, *er. d.* of Frank Pau, Warblington, Hants.; no *c.* *Educ.:* Portsmouth Grammar School; London Univ. Royal Field Artillery, B.E.F., France, 1914-1918; Royal Military College of Canada, 1918-20; Colonial Service in Malaya, 1920-1934; British Empire Exhibition, Wembley, 1925; attached to British Embassy, Tokyo, 1926-28; 1930, undertook extensive tour in India, Europe, and America studying the organisation of agriculture; retired from Colonial Service; lectured in U.S.A. and Canada, 1934; Director and Secretary of Land Settlement Association, 1934-1939; Ministry of Information, 1939-41; Assistant Postmaster-General, 1951-55. Mem. of British Delegation to Conf. of Institute of Pacific Relations, Canada, 1942 and U.S.A., 1945; of Parliamentary Delegation to West Indies, 1944, Sarawak 1946 and Ceylon 1949. *Heir:* none. *Address:* 19 Buckingham Palace Mansions, S.W.1. *T.:* Sloane 4463; Canhouse Farm, Milland, Nr. Liphook, Hants. *T.:* Milland 281. *Clubs:* Royal Automobile, Royal Empire, St. Stephen's. [*Died* 8 *Feb.* 1957 (*ext.*).

GAMON, His Honour Hugh Reece Percival; Judge of County Courts on Circuit No. 15 (York, etc.) 1936-37, Circuit No. 2 since 1937; *b.* 9 Jan. 1880; *s.* of John Gamon, Solicitor, Chester and 2nd wife Mary Ellen Gamon; *m.* 1914, Eleanor Margaret, *d.* of E. W. M. Lloyd, Hartford House, Hartley Wintney, Hants.; one *s.* three *d.* *Educ.:* Hartford House, Hartley Wintney; Harrow School; Exeter College, Oxon. 1st Class Hon. Mods., 1st Class Lt. Hum.; Called to Bar, Middle Temple, 1906; joined Northern Circuit; Practised in Liverpool at the Chancery Bar of the County Palatine of Lancaster. *Publication:* The London Police Court To-day and To-morrow, 1907. *Address:* The Lodge, 21 Front Street, Acomb, York. *T.:* York 78304. *Club:* County (Durham). [*Died* 26 *Jan.* 1953.

GANDY, Eric Worsley, O.B.E., V.D., M.A.Cantab.; M.R.C.S., L.R.C.P.; Chevalier Légion D'Honneur; Consulting Anæsthetist to Westminster Hospital, and to Chelsea Hospital for Women; *s.* of William Gandy, medical practitioner, The Hilltop, Norwood, and Julia Matilda Worsley; *b.* 6 July, 1879; *m.* 1st, Edith Margaret (*d.* 1951), *d.* of John Kenyon, Rawtenstall, Lancashire; one *s.* three *d*; *m.* 2nd, Elsie, *d.* of Mrs. Nash Burrett, Pangbourne. *Educ.:* Private school in Sussex; Emmanuel College, Cambridge; Westminster Hospital. During war acted as King's Messenger for Naval Service and afterwards as Admiralty Despatch Service, carrying despatches to Embassies in Europe and to all fleets; travelled in Spain, West Indies, Canada, S. America, and all over Europe. *Publication:* Administration of Anæsthetics for Cæsarean section, Journal of Obstetrics, 1921. *Recreations:* book collector, golf. *Address:* The Hill Top, Gipsy Hill, Norwood, S.E.19. *T.A.:* Gandy, Norwood. *T.:* Gipsy Hill 0243. *Clubs:* Travellers'; Addington Golf (Croydon). [*Died* 21 *July* 1958.

GANGULEE, Nagendra Nath, C.I.E. 1929; B.Sc.; Ph.D., agricultural scientist-author; formerly Professor of Agriculture and Rural Economics University of Calcutta; ex-Member, Royal Agricultural Commission of India; Imperial Advisory Council of Agricultural Research, New Delhi; Leverhulme Research Scholar; *b.* 1889; *s.* of late Bamon Chandra Ganguleo, Brahmo Samaj; *m. y. d.* of late Sir Rabindra Nath Tagore; one *d.* *Educ.:* University of Calcutta; University of Illinois; University of London. Returned to India and started farming; joined a commercial firm in Calcutta; organised a rural welfare centre in Bengal; carried on research in Soil-Biology at the Rothamsted Experiment Station; while in England drew the attention of the Imperial Government to the necessity of a Royal Commission on Indian Agriculture; visited Denmark, Sweden, Belgium, Holland, Germany, France, Italy, Ireland and Egypt, to study agricultural organisations. *Publications:* Problems of Indian Agriculture (vernacular) 1917; War and Agriculture, 1919; Researches on Leguminous Plants, 1925-26; Problems of Indian Rural Life, 1928; Notes on Indian Constitutional Reform, 1930; India, What Now?, 1933; Christ Triumphant, 1934; The Indian Peasant and his Environment, 1935; The Making of Federal India, 1936; Problems of Health and Nutrition in India, 1938; The Testament of Immortality, 1940; The Red Tortoise and other Tales, 1940; What to Eat and Why, 1942; The Mind and Face of Nazi Germany, 1942; Constituent Assembly for India, 1942; The Battle of the Land, 1943; The Russian Horizon, 1943; Mazzini, 1945; The Teachings of Sun Yat-Sen, 1945; Indians in the Empire Overseas, 1947; Sher Shah—the Bengal Tiger, 1946; Thomas Paine, 1948; Thoughts for Meditation, 1951; There shall be Peace, 1953; and several vernacular books for juvenile readers. *Clubs:* Royal Empire Society, P.E.N. [*Died* 1 *Feb.* 1954.

GANNON, Rev. Patrick Joseph, S.J.; B.A.; Professor of Dogmatic Theology, Milltown Park, Dublin; *b.* 7 Jan. 1879; *s.* of late John Gannon, J.P., Cavan. *Educ.:* St. Patrick's College, Cavan; Clongowes Wood College, Co. Kildare. Classical Scholar R.U.I., 1900; Honours Degree, 1903; studied Philosophy at Valkenburg, Holland, 1903-5; taught Classics and English at Mungret College, Limerick, 1905-7; Clongowes Wood College, 1907-10; studied Theology at Milltown Park, 1910-14, and Ore Place, Hastings, 1915-17; Professor of Theology from 1918. *Publications:* Holy Matrimony; The Catholic Rule of Faith; The Old Law and the New Morality: articles in Irish Theological Quarterly, Studies, Irish Ecclesiastical Record, Irish Monthly, etc.; lectures and sermons on various occasions. *Address:* Milltown Park, Dublin, S.4. [*Died* 12 *Dec.* 1953.

GARBE, Louis Richard, R.A. 1936 (A.R.A. 1929); Hon. F.R.B.S.; Hon. A.R.C.A.; late Professor of sculpture, Royal College of Art, S. Kensington; retired 1946. *Works:* Group representing the modern and medieval periods of culture in the National Museum of Wales, Cardiff; Represented by 3 works at the Tate Gallery, Millbank; also at Glasgow, Stoke-on-Trent, Preston, Chicago; Ivory Group Autumn R.A. 1930 (Silver medal from R.S.B.S.). *Address:* Milton Way, Westcott, nr Dorking, Surrey. *T.:* Westcott 86. [*Died* 28 *July* 1957.

GARBETT, Most Rev. and Rt. Hon. Cyril Forster, P.C. 1942; G.C.V.O. 1955; D.D.; M.A.; Archbishop of York since 1942; *b.* 6 Feb. 1875; *s.* of Charles Garbett, Vicar of Tongham. *Educ.:* Portsmouth Grammar School; Keble College (2nd Class History Honours); Cuddesdon College, Oxford. B.A. 1898, M.A. 1903, D.D. 1921, Oxford. Hon. D.D.: Leeds, 1943; Berkeley Divinity School, U.S.A., 1944; T.C.D., 1946; Cambridge, 1948; King's College, Halifax; Vancouver; Occidental College, U.S., 1949; Hon. LL.D.: Manch. 1944; Columbia, U.S., 1944; Sheffield, 1951; Liverpool, 1953. Pres. Oxford Union, 1898; Asst. Curate, Portsea, 1900-09; Vicar, 1909-19; Bishop of Southwark, 1919-32; Bishop of Winchester, 1932-1942; Hon. Canon of Winchester, 1915; Rural Dean of Portsmouth, 1915; Proctor for Clergy in the Lower House of Canterbury Convocation, 1918; Clerk of the Closet to the King, 1937-42. *Publications:* The Church and Modern Problems; The Challenge of the King; The Work of a Great Parish; After the War; Secularism and Christian Unity; In the Heart of South London; A Call to Christians, 1935; The Church and Social Problems, 1939; What is Man?, 1940; We would see Jesus, 1941; Physician, heal Thyself, 1945; The Burge Memorial Lecture, 1945; Watchman, What of the Night?, 1948. Trilogy: Vol. I, The Claims of the Church of England, 1947; Vol. II, Church and State, 1950; Vol. III, In an Age of Revolution, 1952; The Church of England Today, 1953; World Problems of To-day, 1955. *Address:* Bishopthorpe, York. [*Died* 31 *Dec.* 1955.

GARDINER, Sir Chittampalam Abraham, Kt., *cr.* 1951; *b.* 6 Jan. 1899; *m.* 1923, Angelina Mary Casi-Chetty (*d.* 1949); *m.* 1951, Letitia Abeyesundre; no *c.* *Educ.:* St. Joseph's, Colombo, Ceylon. Senator of Ceylon, 1948-53. Chairman and Managing Director, Ceylon Theatres, Ltd.; Chairman of United Theatres Ltd.; Chairman or Director of many other companies in Ceylon. Kt. of St. Sylvester, 1947; Kt. of St. Gregory the Great, 1950. *Recreations:* big game hunting, horse racing, swimming. *Address:* 61 Gregory's Road, Colombo, Ceylon. *T.:* 9727, 3615. *Clubs:* Turf, Orient (Colombo). [*Died* 10 *Dec.* 1960.

GARDINER, Brigadier Richard, C.B. 1928; D.S.O. 1918; Indian Army, retired; *b.* 1874; *s.* of Lt.-Col. R. Gardiner, R.E.; *m.* 1908, Amelia Mary, *d.* of Maj.-Gen. C. J. Tyler, R.A. three *s.* one *d.* *Educ.:* R.M.C., Sandhurst. Commission, 1895; served with 2nd Batt. South Lancashire Regt. 1895-98; joined Indian Army, 1898; served with Royal 3/12 Frontier Force Regt. 1899-1920; Staff College, 1905-7; attached General Staff, Canada, 1912-13; European War, 1914-19, in Mesopotamia and Palestine (despatches twice, D.S.O., C.B.); A.A.G. Headquarters Northern Command, India, 1921-24; Colonel, 1922; Commanding 3rd Infantry Bde., 1926-30; retired, 1931; Vice-Pres. Dorset County British Legion; Vice-Pres. Dorset Archeological and Natural History Society. *Address:* The Manor, Upwey, Weymouth, Dorset. *T.:* Upwey 311. [*Died* 13 *Dec.* 1957.

GARDNER, Benjamin, O.B.E. 1951; Gen. Sec. Amalgamated Engineering Union since 1943; *b.* 24 Oct. 1896; *s.* of William Ernest

Gardner, dock foreman, and Lilly Gardner; *m.* 1928, Mabel Evelyn Perkins; two *d.* *Educ.:* Trafford Road Council School, Salford 5. Apprentice Instrument maker and engineer, Metropolitan Vickers Elec. Co., Manchester, 1910-12; Salford Electrical Instruments Ltd., 1912; Sir W. H. Bailey & Co. Ltd., 1912-14; Metropolitan Vickers Electrical Co. 1914-17; served European War, 1914-18; R.F.C. and R.A.F. 1917-19; toolmaker, Metropolitan Vickers Elec. Co. 1919-34; Asst. Gen. Sec., A.E.U., 1934-43. Joined Scientific Instrument Makers Trade Society (amalgamated with A.E.U. in 1920), 1915; Branch Sec. A.E.U. 1919-34; shop steward and member of Works Cttee., Metropolitan Vickers Elec. Co., 1919-34; Sec. Works Cttee. 1922-34. Director Cooperative Printing Society. *Publications:* Monthly Journal, Woman s Angle, and Unions reports. *Address:* 110 Peckham Road, S.E.15. *T.A.:* Edifying. Peck London. *T.:* Rodney 4231 (office), Rodney 4557 (home). [*Died* 6 *April* 1956.

GARDNER, Sir Charles; *see* Bruce-Gardner.

GARDNER, Edmund, J.P. Bootle; Director of: Joseph Gardner & Sons, Ltd., J. L. and F. Wilkinson, Ltd.; Walter Holme & Sons Ltd.; *b.* 5 December 1874; *s.* of late Joseph Gardner, J.P., Blundellsands, Lancs; *m.* 1898, Dora. 4th *d.* of late Thomas Goffey, Blundellsands; no *c.* *Educ.:* Merchant Taylors' School, Great Crosby. Hardwood Merchant; Chairman of Bootle Licensing Bench, 1929-49; Member of Bootle Town Council, 1920-36, 1937-52; Mayor, 1927-28, 1928-29; Member of the Mersey Docks and Harbour Board, 1928-58 (Chairman, 1949-50); Chairman of Liverpool Board of Commercial Union Assurance Company, Limited; Member of Court of Liverpool University. *Recreations:* travelling golf, yachting, lawn tennis. *Address:* Storrsthwaite, Storrs Park, Windermere. *T.:* Windermere 184. *Clubs:* Royal Automobile; Exchange (Liverpool); Royal Windermere Yacht (Windermere). [*Died* 6 *Sept.* 1960.

GARFORTH, Capt. Francis Edmund Musgrave, C.B.E. 1919; R.N., retired; *b.* 1874; *s.* of late Rear-Adm. Edmund St. John Garforth, C.B. Served China, 1901 (medal); European War, 1914-19 (Italian medal for valour, 1914-15 Star, C.B.E.). Called up for active service, 1940. Queen Victoria's Silver Jubilee Medal. *Address:* 15 Norland Square, W.11. *T.:* Park 8124; Westons, Walberswick, Suffolk. *Clubs:* United Service; Royal Yacht Squadron (Cowes). [*Died* 11 *Aug.* 1953.

GARLAND, Charles Samuel; *b.* 23 June 1887; *s.* of Charles Garland of Stourbridge, Worcester, and Annie Mayo; *m.* 1912, Constance Marion Avis, *d.* of Alfred Rye; one *d.* (one *s.* decd.). *Educ.:* Camberwell Grammar School; Royal College of Science. B.Sc. (Hons.) London; A.R.C.S.; F.R.I.C.; M.I.Chem.E.; M.P. (U.) S. Islington, 1922-23; Vice-Pres. and Hon. Treas. 1925-51, Pres. 1956-58, Nat. Union of Manufacturers; Vice-Pres. Soc. of Chemical Industry; Vice-President of Institution of Chemical Engineers, 1928, President 1941-42; President British Association of Chemists, 1925-26, Hon. Treas. Parliamentary Scientific Committee, 1943-46; a Crown Governor and Fellow of the Imperial College of Science and Technology, and of City and Guilds Engineering College. 1923-; Member: National Production Advisory Cttee., 1952-60; Clean Air Council, 1957-60; Central Transport Consultative Cttee., 1958. *Recreation:* golf. *Address:* By-the-Links, Sundridge Park, Bromley, Kent. *T.:* Ravensbourne 4365. *Clubs:* Carlton. Chemical. [*Died* 6 *Dec.* 1960.

GARNAR, Sir James Wilson, Kt., *cr.* 1933; Leather Manufacturer; Past Master of Worshipful Company of Leathersellers; Past Pres. of British Leather Federation; *b.* 11 May 1871; *e. s.* of late James Garnar, of Bermondsey and Blackheath; *m.* 1895, *e. d.* of late Walter William Tyler; one *d.* *Educ.:* Margate College; Hampton Grammar School. Interested in public work. *Address:* The Grange, Bermondsey, S.E.1. *T.:* Bermondsey 1181. *Club:* City Livery. [*Died* 10 *Oct.* 1957.

GARNER, William, C.M.G. 1917; T.D.; D.L., Middlesex; *b.* 18 July 1870; *m.* 1st, 1898, Margaret Fanny Merriman (*d.* 1948); one *s.*; 2nd, 1949, Adine Barbara Duncan Campbell. *Educ.:* Stoke House. Lately Hon. Colonel, 8th Battn., Middlesex Regt.; served European War, 1914-17 (despatches, C.M.G.). *Address:* Ingleby, Budleigh Salterton, Devon. *T.:* 188. *Club:* Junior Army and Navy. [*Died* 16 *Jan.* 1953.

GARNER, William Edward, C.B.E. 1946; F.R.S. 1937; D.Sc. (Birm.); Leverhulme Professor of Physical Chemistry, University of Bristol, 1927-54, Pro-Vice-Chancellor, 1952-54; Dir. of Chemical Laboratories, 1936; retired; *b.* 1889; *s.* of William Garner, Wymeswold, Loughborough; unmarried. *Educ.:* Universities of Birmingham and Göttingen; Univ. College, London. Lecturer in Chemistry, Univ. of Birmingham, 1919; Lecturer at Univ. College, London, 1919-25; Reader in Physical Chemistry at Univ. Coll, Lond., 1925-27; Fell. of Univ. Coll., Lond., 1930; Corresp. Councillor, Patronato "Alfonso el Sabio," 1959. *Publications:* Scientific papers on flame, adsorption, long chain organic compounds, solid decomposition, and detonation of solids Chemistry of Solid State (Ed.), 1955; Chemisorption (Ed.), 1957. *Recreation:* fishing. *Address:* Oakwood, 168 Westbury Road, Bristol. *T.:* Bristol 62-7257. [*Died* 4 *March* 1960.

GARNETT, Sir George, Kt., *cr.* 1954; J.P.; F.T.I.; Vice-President of the Federation of British Industries; Chairman and Joint Managing Director of G. Garnett & Sons Ltd.; *b.* 2 Nov. 1871; *e. s.* of Joshua F. Garnett, Wool Cloth Manufacturer, Apperley Bridge; *m.* Edith, *d.* of W. B. Woodhead, Civil Engineer, Wrose, Shipley; one *s.* one *d.* (and one *s.* killed on active service, 1939). *Educ.:* Salts Schools, Shipley, Yorks. Commenced training 1889 for a director in manufacture of woollen and worsted cloth; elected liveryman of Worshipful Co. of Dyers, 1917; visited S. Africa in interests of Empire Chambers of Commerce, 1928. Chairman local board, London and Lancashire Insurance Co. Ltd.; Past Pres. Textile Institute, Inc.; Foundation Member and Member of Executive, Wool Industries Research Assoc. Life Governor Yorkshire United Independent Coll.; J.P. City of Bradford, 1924; Pres. City of Bradford Conservative and Nat. Liberal Assoc. *Recreations:* motoring and walking. *Address:* Parkfield, Eccleshill, Bradford 2, Yorks. *T.:* Bradford 37104. *Clubs:* National Liberal; Bradford Liberal (Bradford). [*Died* 22 *Jan.* 1955.

GARNETT, Rear-Adm. Herbert Neville, C.M.G. 1918; R.N., retired; late Captain-Superintendent of the Dockyard, Sheerness; *b.* 1875; *m.* 1900, Ethel Mildred, (*d.* 1957), *d.* of T. T. B. Hooke, of Norton Hall, Worcester; one *d.* *Address:* Crofton, Stubbington. Hants. [*Died* 23 *March* 1960.

GARNETT, (James Clerk) Maxwell, C.B.E. 1919; M.A.; Sc.D.; Barrister-at-law; *b.* Cambridge, 13 Oct. 1880; *s.* of late William Garnett, M.A., D.C.L.; *m.* 1910, Margaret Lucy, 2nd *d.* of late Prof. Sir Edward Poulton, F.R.S.; three *s.* three *d.* *Educ.:* St. Paul's School; Trinity College, Cambridge. Major scholar and Fellow of Trinity; Sheepshanks Astronomical Exhibitioner; 1st Class, 1st Division, Pt. ii. of the Mathematical Tripos; Smith's Prizeman; rowed in University trial eight; lecturer on Applied Mathematics in University College, London, 1903; examiner, Board of Education, 1904-12; Principal of the College of Technology, Manchester, and Dean of the Faculty of Technology in the University of Manchester, 1912-20; Sec. of the League of Nations Union, 1920-38 Chairman of British Association's Committee on Post-War University Education, 1941-44 *Publications:* Education and World Citizenship, 1921; World Loyalty, 1928; (with Nowell Smith) The Dawn of World Order, 1932; Organising Peace, 1936; Knowledge and Character, 1939; A Lasting Peace, 1940; The World We Mean To Make, 1943: papers on mathematical and physical subjects, published in the Philosophical Transactions of the Royal Society; papers on psychology, published in the Proceedings of the Royal Society, in the British Journal of Psychology, and in other philosophical journals; and papers on education. *Recreations:* walking, sailing. *Address:* Horestone, Sea View, Isle of Wight. *T.:* Seaview 3220. *Clubs:* Athenæum, Leander. [*Died* 19 *March* 1958.

GARNETT, Walter James, C.M.G. 1950; O.B.E. 1941; retired; *b.* 3 July 1889; *e. s.* of late James Garnett; *m.* 1st, Lily Covins (*d.* 1921), *d.* of late Henry Philpot Wright; one *d.*; 2nd, Mary (*d.* 1948), *d.* of Walter Giddings; one *s.* *Educ.:* Wilson's Grammar School; London University. Colonial Office, 1907-19; Oversea Settlement Dept., 1919-30; Asst. Br. Govt. Rep., Australia, 1931-34; Asst. Sec. U.K. High Comr.'s Office, Canberra, 1935-37; Official Sec. U.K. High Comr.'s Office, Wellington, 1941; Official Sec. U.K. High Comr.'s Office, Canberra, 1944-48; Asst. Under Sec. of State, Commonwealth Relations Office, 1949; Deputy High Commissioner for U.K. in Australia, 1949-52; retd. 1952. *Recreation:* golf. *Address:* c/o Midland Bank, 22 Victoria St., S.W.1. [*Died* 6 *July* 1958.

GARRAN, Sir Robert Randolph, G.C.M.G., *cr.* 1937 (K.C.M.G., *cr.* 1920; C.M.G. 1901); Kt., *cr.* 1917; Q.C.; barrister; *b.* Sydney, 10 Feb. 1867; *s.* of late Hon. Andrew Garran; M.A. (Lond.), LL.D. (Syd.), M.L.C. (N.S.W.); *m.* 1902, Hilda (*d.* 1936), 3rd *d.* of late John Shield Robson, of Monkwearmouth, Durham; four *s.* *Educ.:* Grammar School and University Sydney. Captain, Sydney Grammar School, 1884; Scholarships for Classics, Mathematics, and General Proficiency, University of Sydney, 1885-87; B.A. 1888; M.A. with 1st class honours and University Medal in School of Mental, Moral, and Political Philosophy, 1899. Barrister-at-law, N.S.W., 1890; K.C. 1932; Secretary to Representative of N.S.W. Govt. in Legislative Council, 1896-98 and 1899-1901; Secretary, Attorney-General's Dept., 1901-32, and Solicitor-General, 1917-32, Commonwealth of Australia; Sec. to Drafting Committee of Australian Federal Convention, 1897-98; Chairman of Council of Canberra Univ. College, 1930-53; Chairman of Indian Military Expenditure Tribunal (London), 1932-33; Chairman of Commonwealth Book Censorship Committee, 1933-37, Appeal Censor since 1937; Chancellor, Diocese of Goulburn since 1939. *Publications:* The Coming Commonwealth, 1897; Heine's Book of Songs, translated, 1924; Schubert and Schumann, Songs and Translations, 1946; joint-author, with Sir John Quick, of Quick and Garran's Annotated Constitution of the Australian Commonwealth, 1901; articles in learned jls. *Address:* Roanoke, Red Hill, Canberra, A.C.T., Australia. *Clubs:* Melbourne; Australian (Sydney); Commonwealth (Canberra). [*Died* 11 *Jan.* 1957.

GARRARD, Apsley G. B. C.; *see* Cherry-Garrard.

GARRETT, Lieut.-Col. Sir Frank, K.C.B., *cr.* 1946 (C.B. 1938); C.B.E. 1918; T.D.; D.L., J.P. Suffolk; A.M.I.C.E., A.M.I.M.E.; *b.* 9 December 1869; *s.* of Frank Garrett, Aldringham, Leiston, Suffolk; m. Evelyn Rosa (*d.* 1951), *d.* of Henry Brooks, Hersham Lodge, Walton-on-Thames; five *d.* *Educ.:* Rugby. Served in France during European War, 1914-15, commanding 4th Suffolk Regt.; late Hon. Col. 4th Suffolk Regt.; late Chairman Suffolk County Territorial Force Association and of Suffolk Army Cadet Committee; Past-Pres. Suffolk County Rifle Assoc.; Past-Pres. Agricultural Engineers Assoc.; Past-Pres. Framlingham College, Corp., Suffolk. Formerly Chm. of late Richard Garrett & Sons Ltd. and Dir. of late Agricultural and General Engineers Ltd. *Address:* Minsmere, Leiston, Suffolk. *T.:* Leiston 6. [*Died* 19 *March* 1952.

GARROD, Heathcote William, C.B.E. 1918; M.A.; Hon. LL.D. (Edin.); F.B.A.; 1931; F.R.L.S.; Hon. D.Litt. (Durham); Hon. Fellow of Merton Coll., Oxford; *b.* 21 Jan. 1878; *s.* of late Charles William Garrod, Wells, Somerset. *Educ.:* self-educated. Craven and Hertford Univ. Scholarships, 1899; Gaisford Prize, 1900; Newdigate Poem, 1901; Fellow of Merton, 1901; Tutor of Corpus, 1902-04; Tutor of Merton, 1904-25; Ministry of Munitions, 1915-18 (1917, Deputy Assistant Secretary, Labour Dept.); visited U.S.A. 1917, with C. W. Bowerman and J. H. Thomas, as member of special Labour Mission; Assistant Secretary, Ministry of Reconstruction, 1918; Professor of Poetry, Oxford, 1923-28; Norton Professor of Poetry at Harvard Univ., 1929. *Publications:* Religion of All Good Men, 1905, 1906; Text of Statius, 1906; Oxford Book of Latin Verse, 1912; Manilius II., Translation and Commentary, 1911; Oxford Poems, 1912; A Book of Latin Verse, 1915; Einhard's Life of Charlemagne (with R. B. Mowat) 1915; new edition of Wickham's Text of Horace, 1912; Essay on Vergil in English Literature and the Classics; Worms and Epitaphs, 1919; Wordsworth; Lectures and Essays, 1923, 1927; The Profession of Poetry, 1923; Byron, 1923; Coleridge, Prose and Poetry, 1924; Introduction to Goldsmith (Nelson's Poets), 1924; Keats, 1926; Merton Muniments (with P. S. Allen), 1927; William Collins, 1928; Poems from the French, 1928; The Profession of Poetry and other Lectures, 1929; Poetry and Life, 1930; Tolstoi's Theory of Art, 1935; The Study of Poetry, 1936; Letters of Erasmus (Oxford edn.), vols. ix, x, xi (with Mrs. Allen), 1938-1947; Poetical works of John Keats, 1939; Donne Prose and Poetry, 1946; Scholarship: its meaning and Value, 1946; Epigrams, 1946; Genius Loci, 1950. Ed., Essays and Studies (English Association), 1928; numerous papers in classical and other journals; formerly editor of Journal of Philology. *Recreations:* none. *Address:* Merton College, Oxford. *T.:* Oxford 2259. [*Died* 25 *Dec.* 1960.

GARSTANG, John, C.B.E. 1949; M.A., D.Sc., B.Litt. (Oxon); Hon. LL.D. (Aberdeen); F.S.A.; Professor Emeritus, University of Liverpool, since 1942; Corresp., Institut de France, 1947; Chairman Cttee. 1947-52; Hon. Dir., 1947-48 and President, 1949-, British Institute of Archæology at Ankara; *b.* 1876; *y. s.* of late Dr. Walter Garstang, M.R.C.P., of Blackburn; *m.* 1907, Marie L. Bergès (*d.* 1949), Toulouse; one *s.* one *d.* *Educ.:* Blackburn Gram. Sch.; Jesus Coll., Oxford (Mathematical Schol.), 1895-99; Hon. Fellow, 1956. Hon. Reader in Egyptian Archæology, Univ. of Liverpool, 1902; Professor of the Methods and Practice of Archæology, 1907-1941, Engaged in Archæological Research since 1897; conducted excavations on Roman Sites in Britain at Ribchester, Melandra Castle, Richborough, Brough; in Egypt, Nubia, Asia Minor and North Syria, 1900-1908; in the Sudan at Meroë, 1909-14; in Palestine at Askalon, 1920-21, and Jericho, 1930-36 and in Turkey at Mersin, 1937-47; on voluntary service in France as Red Cross Delegate, 1915-19; Chevalier de la Légion d'Honneur, and Reconnaissance Française, 1920. Director, British School of Archæology in Jerusalem, 1919-26; Hon. Adviser on Antiquities to Military Administration of Palestine, 1919-20; Director, Department of

Antiquities, Government of Palestine, 1920-1926; Director of the Neilson Expedition to the Near East, 1936-52; Order of St. John of Jerusalem, 1926; King's Silver Jubilee Medal, 1935. *Publications:* Roman Ribchester; El Arâbeh; Mahâsna and Bèt Khallâf; The 3rd Egyptian Dynasty; Burial Customs of Ancient Egypt, 1907; The Land of the Hittites, 1910; Meroë, 1911; The Hittite Empire, 1929; The Foundations of Bible History, Joshua, Judges, 1931; The Heritage of Solomon, 1934; Prehistoric Mersîn, 1953. Reports on the Excavation of Abydos, Meroë, Jericho, and at Mersîn in Liverpool Annals of Archæology, 1908-40. *Recreations:* trout fishing, travel, carpentry. *Address:* c/o Bayworth Corner, Boars Hill, Oxford. *Club:* Royal Societies. [*Died* 12 *Sept.* 1956.

GARTHWAITE, Sir William, 1st Bt., *cr.* 1919; underwriter and shipowner; *b.* 11 July 1874; *s.* of William Garthwaite of Staindrop, Co. Durham, and Sarah da Costa Andrade, London; *m.* 1st, Francesca Margherita, *d.* of James Parfett; one *s.*; 2nd, Janet (*d.* 1938), *d.* of late José Carlos Rodrigues, LL.B., Rio de Janeiro; one *s.* one *d.*; 3rd, Mrs. Gladys Galie; one *s.* *Educ.:* private. Brazil, construction of railways, ports, shipping, land; France and Canada, shipping, railway equipment; U.K. was interested in development Q ships; Presented H.M.S. Prize to Admiralty for duration of War and H.M.S. Adventuress; During war of 1939-45 again rendered special service to Admiralty; officially appointed to contract for Fleet of Special Service steamers in Rio de Janeiro and received official thanks for service on voluntary basis. Insurance (underwriter at Lloyd's), Shipping; owner of s.v. Garthpool, last square-rigged ocean-going ship under British flag; Chairman and Founder Sea Lions Soc. for providing Sail Trng. Ship for the Nation; Mauritius, sugar planting. Shipwrights Company, Freeman of City of London. *Recreations:* horse riding, fencing, tennis, skating, swimming, yachting. *Heir:* *s.* Lt.-Cdr. William Francis Cuthbert Garthwaite, D.S.C. and Bar [*b.* 3 Jan. 1906; *m.* 1st, 1931, Dorothy, *o. d.* of 1st Baron Duveen; 2nd, 1945, Patricia, *widow* of Cdr. Barry Leonard, R.N.; one *s.*]. *Address:* Nassau, Bahamas. *Clubs:* Royal Thames Yacht, Bath; Nassau Yacht. [*Died* 20 *June* 1956.

GARVAGH, 4th Baron (*cr.* 1818), **Leopold Ernest Stratford George Canning,** D.L., J.P.; *s.* of 3rd Baron and Alice, *d.* of Baron Joseph de Bretton, Copenhagen; *b.* 21 July 1878; *S.* father, 1915; *m.* 1919, Gladys Dora May Bayley Dimmer, *widow* of late Lt.-Col. Dimmer, V.C., M.C., and *d.* of William Bayley Parker; one *s.* two *d.* (and one *s.* killed in War of 1939-45). *Educ.:* Eton. Formerly Lieut. 4th Batt. H.L.I. and Lieut. Royal Flying Corps. *Heir:* *s.* Hon. (Alexander Leopold Ivor) George Canning [*b.* 6 Oct. 1920; *m.* 1947, Christine, *yr. d.* of Jack Cooper, Little Bridley, Worplesdon; one *s.* two *d.*]. *Recreations:* motoring and travelling. *Address:* The Grange, Keswick, Cumberland. *Club:* Royal Automobile. [*Died* 16 *July* 1956.

GARWOOD, Lieut.-Col. Henry Percy, D.S.O. 1918; *b.* 13 April 1882; *s.* of late Col. J. F. Garwood, R.E., and Margaret Scott. *Educ.:* Marlborough; Woolwich. Commissioned Royal Artillery, 1900; Captain, 1913; Major, 1915; served Malta, Ceylon, Hong Kong; Adjutant, Sheerness, 1910-12; Adjutant, S. China, 1912-14; Staff Officer, R.A., Salonika Army, 1916-18 (despatches twice, D.S.O., Order of the Redeemer and Greek Medal of Military Merit, French Medal of Honour, Brevet Lt.-Col.); A.Q.M.G., Constantinople, 1919; special duty, G.H.Q., Dublin, 1920; commanded R.A. Survey Company, Chanak, 1922-23; retired, 1928. *Address:* 2 Sussex House, Raymond Road, S.W.19. *T.:* Wimbledon 5813. *Club:* United Service. [*Died* 29 *Jan.* 1956.

GASCOIGNE, Hubert Claude Victor, A.R.A.M.; Professor of Pianoforte and Examiner at Royal Academy of Music and Ipswich Conservatoire of Music; Examiner for the Associated Board of the Royal Academy of Music and the Royal College of Music; *b.* Leyton, Essex; *s.* of Channing Kiddell Gascoigne of H.M. Customs, and *g.s.* of Rev. Michael Castle Gascoigne; *m.* 1910, Lillian Flower, *d.* of late Frederick Church. Thorington Lodge, Essex. *Educ.:* privately; Royal Academy of Music. Commenced musical studies at Guildhall School of Music, later becoming a private pupil of Signor Carlo Ducci; entered the Royal Academy of Music, 1898, where he studied pianoforte with Mr. Tobias Matthay, F.R.A.M., and Harmony and Composition with Mr. Frederick Corder, F.R.A.M.; while at R.A.M. gained many awards, including the Macfarren Gold Medal (1904), Heathcote Long Prize (1904), and the Erard Centenary Scholarship (1901) on leaving in 1904 was unanimously elected an Associate; has given many recitals and concerts in London and provinces; served in the London Rifle Brigade during the War, and was stationed at the Headquarters, Le Havre, where he organised and played at a great many concerts for the troops. *Publications:* various articles on musical subjects. *Recreations:* walking, tennis, billiards. *Address:* 10 Nelson Road Whitstable, Kent. *Clubs:* R.A.M., London Musicians. [*Died* 27 *Sept.* 1959.

GASK, George Ernest, C.M.G. 1919; D.S.O. 1917; M.A.Oxon; F.R.C.S.; J.P.; Officer of the Legion of Honour, 1937; Emeritus Prof. of Surgery in the University of London; Consulting Surgeon St. Bartholomew's Hospital; ex-Chairman Medical Advisory Cttee. Oxford Regional Hospital Board; late Regional Adviser in Surgery E.M.S.; late Member of Medical Research Council; late Vice-President Royal College of Surgeons, England; late Member of Governing Body of British Postgraduate School; late President of Medical Society of London; Hon. Fellow of American College of Surgeons; Corresponding Member of Academy of Medicine of Rome; Hon. member Académie de Chirurgie de France; Membre d'Honneur Société Chirurgicale de Lyons; Late Surgeon and Director of Surgical Unit to St. Bartholomew's Hospital; Late Examiner in Surgery to Universities of London, Oxford, Cambridge, Bristol; *b.* 1 Aug. 1875; 4th *s.* of late Henry Gask; *m.* 1913, Ada A., *d.* of Lieut.-Colonel Alexander Crombie, C.B., M.D., I.M.S.; one *s.* *Educ.:* Dulwich College Freiburg-i-Baden; St. Bartholomew's Hospital; late temporary Colonel A.M.S. Consulting Surgeon, British Expeditionary Force, France (despatches). *Publications;* Surgery of the Sympathetic Nervous System (Gask and Ross), 1934; Spencer and Gask Theory and Practice of Surgery; Surgery —Gask and Wilson; Surgical Reports, St. Bartholomew's Hospital. *Recreation:* mountaineering. *Address:* Hatchman's, Hambleden, Henley-on-Thames. *T.:* Hambleden 3. *Clubs:* Athenæum, Alpine. [*Died* 16 *Jan.* 1951.

GASKELL, Surg. Vice-Admiral Sir Arthur, K.C.B., *cr.* 1930 (C.B. 1916); O.B.E. 1919; F.R.C.S. (Eng.), L.R.C.P. (Lond.), D.P.H. (Lond.); Hon. Surgeon to the King; Fellow of University College, London; Fellow of the Royal Sanitary Institute; *b.* 6 July 1871; *s.* of late Hunter Gaskell, J.P.; *m.* 1911, Sophie, *d.* of late Hon. Sir Lewis Michell, C.V.O.; one *s.* one *d.* Joined Royal Navy, 1893; Staff-Surgeon, 1902; Fleet-Surgeon, 1906; Surg.-Capt. 1920; Surg. Rear-Admiral, 1923; Surg. Vice-Admiral, 1927; Medical-Director-General of the Navy, 1927-31; retired list, 1931. *Publications:* various papers connected with the Royal Naval Medical Service. *Recreation:* out-door sports. *Address:* Greenwood, Fareham, Hants. *T.:* Fareham 2195. *Club:* Army and Navy. [*Died* 12 *Jan.* 1952.

GASKELL, Henry Melville, J.P.; *o. s.* of late Henry Brooks Gaskell and Helen

Mary, C.B.E. 1917, *o. d.* of Rev. David Melville, D.D., Canon of Worcester; *b.* 1879; *m.* 1905, Dorothy, *e. d.* of late Lt.-Col. Josceline FitzRoy Bagot, of Levens Hall, Westmorland; two *s.* one *d.* *Educ.:* Eton. Is Lord of the Manor of Kiddington. *Address:* Kiddington Hall, Woodstock, Oxfordshire. [*Died* 21 *Oct.* 1954.

GASKELL, Major-General Herbert Stuart, C.B. 1937; D.S.O. 1916; *b.* 24 April 1882; *s.* of late Lieutenant-Colonel Thomas Gaskell, R.A., and Katherine Anne Walker; *m.* 1906, Sybil, *d.* of Charles Edward Mogridge Hudson, Wick, Worcestershire; two *s.* one *d.* *Educ.:* Westminster School; R.M.A., Woolwich. 2nd Lieut., R.E., 1900; Col. 1928; Temp. Brigadier, 1932; Major-Gen., 1935; served European War, France, Belgium, and Mesopotamia (despatches twice, D.S.O. and brevet of Lieut.-Colonel); Persia, 1918-20 (despatches, Persian Order of the Lion and Sun); Arab Rebellion, 1920 (despatches, bar to D.S.O.); Chief Engineer, Northern Command, India, 1932-35; Engineer-in-Chief, A.H.Q., India, 1936-39; retired 1939; Col. Comdt. R.E., 1940-50. *Address:* The Lookout, Lyme Regis. *T.:* Lyme Regis 325. [*Died* 24 *Dec.* 1957.

GASKELL, Sir Holbrook, Kt., *cr.* 1942; O.B.E. 1917; *b.* 1878; *s.* of Holbrook Gaskell, Frodsham, Cheshire; *m.* 1906, Mary, *d.* of T. J. Ridgway, Lymm, Cheshire; no *c.* *Educ.:* Rugby: Trinity College, Cambridge. Mechanical Science Tripos, Cambridge, 1900; joined United Alkali Co. Ltd. as Assistant Engineer, 1901; Chief Engineer, 1914; Director, 1922; Managing Director, 1926; on formation of Imperial Chemical Industries (of which United Alkali Co. was one of constituent companies) became Chairman of Delegate Boards of General Chemical and Lime Groups; Director of Imperial Chemical Industries Ltd. 1934-46. *Address:* 52 Orchard Court, Portman Square, W.1. *T.:* Welbeck 2382. *Clubs:* Royal Thames Yacht, Royal Automobile. [*Died* 31 *March* 1951.

GASKELL, Colonel Joseph Gerald, C.B. 1952; T.D.; D.L.; Chairman, William Hancock & Company Limited, The Brewery, Cardiff, since 1935; Local Director, General Accident, Fire & Life Assurance Corp. Ltd.; *b.* 17 May 1885; *s.* of Colonel J. Gaskell, C.B.E., T.D., D.L., J.P.; *m.* 1910, Eleanor Vaughan Carey-Thomas; one *s.* three *d.* *Educ.:* Malvern; Cambridge. Volunteer and Militia, 1902; Territorial, 1908, R.A.; served European War, 1914-19; retired, 1921; Managing Director, 1921; Glamorgan County T.A. and A.F. Association, 1923; Cardiff City Council, 1925-31: Home Guard, 1940; Colonel Commanding Gardiff Sector Glamorgan Home Guard, 1941-44; High Sheriff, Glamorgan, 1941; Chairman of The Territorial and Auxiliary Forces Association of the County of Glamorgan, 1949-53. *Address:* Beverley, Llanishen, Cardiff. *T.:* Cardiff 53054. *Clubs:* Cardiff and County (Cardiff); Royal Porthcawl Golf (Porthcawl). [*Died* 9 *Jan.* 1959.

GASKELL, William, C.I.E. 1925; Indian Civil Service, retired; *b.* 14 Jan. 1874. *Educ.:* Loughborough Grammar School; St. John's College, Cambridge, M.A. Entered I.C.S. 1897; Deputy Commissioner and Joint Secretary Board of Revenue, 1912; Magistrate and Collector, 1918; Commissioner of Income Tax, United Provinces, 1920; Opium Agent, Ghazipur, 1924; officiating Member Central Board of Revenue, 1928; retired 1932. *Address:* Hilliers, St. Mary Bourne, Andover, Hants. [*Died* 30 *Sept.* 1954.

GASKOIN, Charles Jacinth Bellairs, M.A.; 2nd *s.* of late Herman John Richard Gaskoin, a Principal in the War Office, and Catherine Anna, *d.* of Rev. G. Maclear, A.M. *Educ.:* Fitzwilliam Hall and Jesus College, Cambridge. First Class Historical Tripos, 1898; Senior, Law Tripos Part I., 1899; Hulsean Prizeman, 1899; Proxime accessit, Members' Prize (English Essay), 1901; Lecturer for the Historical Tripos and other Examinations, 1901-39; Lecturer in History at Wren's, 1907-16, in charge of a Code Department in the Postal Censorship, 1916-19, and again 1939-45; Professor of History and Economics at Queen's College, London, 1919-26; Director of Civil Service Studies and Lecturer in Indian History, Cambridge, 1924-40; etc. *Publications:* Alcuin: his Life and his Work, 1904; The Hanoverians, 1914; Britain in the Modern World, 1923; (part Editor) Cambridge Marriage Registers, Phillimore's Series. *Recreation:* acting. *Club:* Athenæum. [*Died* 24 *March* 1955.

GASTRELL, Lieut.-Colonel Everard Huddleston, O.B.E. 1937; I.A. (retd.); late Indian Political Service; *b.* 30 Apr. 1898; *o. c.* of late Col. E. T. Gastrell, I.A., and Mabel (*née* Huddleston); *m.* 1927, Delicia Crampton; one *s.* one *d.* *Educ.:* Clifton and Cheltenham Colleges. Commissioned, 1916; joined Indian Political Service, 1922; served Persia, Punjab, N.-W.F.P., Kolhapur, Persian Gulf; Consul-General, Meshed, 1934; Quetta Earthquake Claims Comr., 1935; Political Agent, Quetta, 1936, Kalat State and Bolan Pass, 1937; Census Supt., Baluchistan, 1939; Consul-General, Pondicherry, 1941; Additional Counsellor, Tehran, 1944; Consul-General, Meshed, 1947-49. *Recreation:* walking. *Address:* 82 Ridgway, Wimbledon, S.W.19. *T.:* Wimbledon 1422. *Club:* Royal Over-Seas League. [*Died* 21 *Sept.* 1960.

GATENBY, James Brontë, M.A. (Dubl.), B.A., B.Sc., D.Phil. (Oxon.); Ph.D. (Dubl.); D.Sc. (Lond.); Professor of Cytology Trinity College, Dublin, since 1959; (Professor of Zoology and Comparative Anatomy, 1921-1959), Resident Research Associate Emeritus, Argonne National Laboratory, Lemont, Ill., U.S.A. 1958; *b.* New Zealand, 1892; *y. s.* of R. Mackenzie Gatenby and Catherine Jane Brontë Gatenby; *m.* 1922, Enid Kathleen Mary (Molly) Meade (*d.* 1950); two *s.* two *d.*; *m.* 1951, Constance Harris. *Educ.:* Wanganui Collegiate Sch.; St. Patrick's College, Wellington, N.Z.; Jesus College Oxford (Exhibitioner). Lecturer in Human Histology School of Medicine; Demonstrator in Forest Zoology and Human Embryology, Oxford, 1916-19; Senior Demy, Magdalen College, Oxford, 1917; Senior Assistant in Zoology and Comparative Anatomy, University College London, 1919; Lecturer in Cytology, University of London, 1920; Biological sub-Editor of Science Progress, 1919-27; Theresa Seessel Fellow, Yale Univ., 1930-31; Fondation Universitaire Lecturer at Universities of Louvain, Ghent, and Brussels, 1933; Medal of St. Michael, Brussels Univ., 1933; Hon. Member R. Soc. of N.Z., 1934; Hon. F.R.M.S. (Lond.), 1954; Hon. Fell. Acad. of Zoology (India), 1955; Visiting Prof. of Zoology, King Farouk University, Alexandria, 1951-52; Hon. Mem. of Internat. Soc. for Cell Biology, 1957; Research Cytologist at Victoria Univ. and Dominion Physical Laboratory, Lower Hutt, N.Z. and at Sydney University, 1959; O.E.E.C. Senior Visiting Fellow, Paris Univ., 1960. *Publications:* Editor and Reviser of the 1950 edition of Bolles Lee's Microtomist's Vade-Mecum; Biological Technique, 1937; numerous papers in Scientific Journals; contributor to Encyclopædia Britannica and Chambers's Encyclopædia. *Recreations:* motoring, fishing, travelling. *Address:* University Zool. Dept., Trinity College, Dublin. *Club:* Royal Irish Yacht. [*Died* 20 *July* 1960.

GAULT, Brig. A(ndrew) Hamilton, D.S.O. 1915; Hon. Col. Princess Patricia's Canadian Light Infantry; *b.* England, 18 Aug. 1882; *o. s.* of late A. F. Gault, Montreal, and Louisa S. Harman; *m.* 1st, 1904, Marguerite, *d.* of Hon. G. W. Stephens; no *c.*; 2nd, 1922, Dorothy Blanche, *yr. d.* of late C. J. Shuckburgh. *Educ.:* Bishop's College School, Lennoxville; McGill University. Served as subaltern Boer War 2nd Canadian Mounted Rifles

(Queen's medal 3 clasps); raised and equipped Princess Patricia's Canadian Light Infantry for active service, European War, 1914-18 (despatches four times, wounded thrice, D.S.O., 3rd class Order of St. Anne with crossed swords, Order of the Crown of Belgium); War of 1939; recalled to Active List (Canada) from R.O., 1940; Col. 1940; Brig. 1942; Consul-General for Sweden in Canada, 1909-11; Member Council Montreal Board of Trade, 1911-13; M.P. (U.) Taunton 1924-35. Presented with the Freedom of the Borough of Taunton, 1932; Conservative; Anglican. *Recreations:* hunting, fishing, aviation. *Address:* St. Hilaire, Quebec. *Clubs:* Carlton, Bath; Mount Royal (Montreal); Rideau (Ottawa). [*Died* 28 *Nov.* 1958.

GAUNT, Adm. Sir Guy (Reginald Archer), K.C.M.G., *cr.* 1918 (C.M.G. 1916); C.B. 1918; A.D.C. 1918; is a Master Mariner and Younger Brother of Trinity House; 3rd *s.* of late William Henry Gaunt, formerly of Leek, Staffordshire, Governor of the Gold Fields, and Judge in Victoria, Australia; *b.* 1870; *m.* 2nd, 1932, Sybil, *d.* of A. Grant-White, Worthing, and *widow* of W. Joseph; two *d.* *Educ.:* Melbourne Grammar School; The Worcester. Lieutenant of the Swift during operations in the Philippines, 1897; commanded British Consulate, Apia, Samoa, 1899, during the rebel attack on the town; raised and commanded Gaunt's Brigade during the following operations (despatches, promoted Commander); Commander of the Vengeance, China Station, during the Russian-Japanese War; Captain, 1907; Commanded Andromeda, Niobe, Challenger, Majestic, Thunderer 1913; Naval Attaché to H.B.M. Embassy in Washington, U.S.A., 1914-1918; Liaison Officer for United States of America, with rank of Commodore, first class, March 1917; served European War, 1914-18 (despatches, C.B.); employed on convoy service with broad pendant in Leviathan, 1918; Naval Intelligence, Admiralty; Rear-Admiral, 1918; retired 1918; Vice-Adm., retired 1924; Adm., retired 1928. M.P. (C.) Buckrose Division of Yorkshire, 1922-26; *Publication:* The Yield of the Years, 1940. *Clubs:* United Service, Garrick, Royal Automobile, Royal Thames Yacht; Royal Yacht Squadron (Cowes); Union (Malta); Victoria Racing (Melbourne); Royal Hong Kong Yacht. [*Died* 18 *May* 1953.

GAUNT, Walter Henry, C.B.E. 1938; J.P.; F.L.A.S.; M.Inst.T.; M.I.Mech.E.; Director J. Lyons & Co. Ltd.; *b.* Bradford, Yorks, 13 Jan. 1874; *s.* of William Gaunt; *m.* 1900, Kate (*d.* 1941), *er. d.* of Alfred Brooks Kearsley; no *c.* *Educ.:* Manchester Grammar School. Concerned with Trafford Park Estates Ltd. development, and that of the First Garden City, Letchworth; distribution supt. for Board of Trade (Coal Mines Dept.) during European War; Member of Salter Conference, 1932; Member Transport Advisory Council; Transport Adviser to Ministry of Food, 1940; Member Lord Reith's Committee on New Towns, 1946; Member Town Planning Institute Council; Chm. Thames Barrage Association; Chairman Thames Waterside Manufacturers' Assoc.; pres. Mansion House Assoc. on Transport; exec. cttee. of A.A.; ex-pres. National Housing and Town Planning Council. *Recreations:* sailing and travelling. *Address:* Ladybarn, Letchworth, Herts. *Club:* Royal Automobile. [*Died* 31 *Oct.* 1951.

GAUSSEN, Brigadier-General James Robert, C.M.G. 1916; C.I.E. 1919; D.S.O. 1900; late 3rd Skinner's Horse; *b.* 20 March 1871; *s.* of David Gaussen of Broughton Hall, Lechlade; *m.* 1894, Hilda (*d.* 1940), 3rd *d.* of late Col. Hennessy, I.S.C.; one *s.* two *d.*; 2nd, 1942, Mrs. Molly Beddow (*d.* 1947). *Educ.:* Uppingham. Joined Hants Regiment, 1892; Bengal Cavalry, 1894; served China, 1900, including relief of Pekin (wounded, British and American despatches); European War, commanded 11th S.W.B. and raised 40th Cavalry; France and Indian Frontier (wounded, despatches thrice); Afghan War, Commanding Cavalry Force, 1919; Commanded Forces in E. Persia, 1919-20; retired, 1921. *Address:* 6 Pall Mall, S.W.1. [*Died* 3 *July* 1959.

GAYE, Sir Arthur Stretton, Kt., *cr.* 1941; C.B. 1928; O.B.E. 1919; *b.* 22 May 1881; *y. s.* of late Arthur Gaye; *m.* 1st, Dulcibella Chester (*d.* 1921), *d.* of late Col. W. B. Wilson, Indian Army; one *s.* (and one *s.* killed in action); two *d.*; 2nd, 1938, Mary Baird, *d.* of late Sir David Wilson, 1st Bt., of Carbeth. *Educ.:* Westminster (Queen's Scholar); Trinity College, Cambridge (Scholar); M.A. 1st Class, Classical Tripos. Tancred Student in Common Law, Lincoln's Inn; Barrister-at-law, 1906; entered Civil Service (Board of Education), 1909; Private Secretary to Presidents of Board of Agriculture and Fisheries (Mr. Runciman and Lord Lucas), 1912-15; served in Army, 1915-19 (despatches twice); Secretary, Office of Woods and Forests, 1921; Commissioner of Woods and Forests (title changed to Commissioner of Crown Lands, 1925), 1924-34; U.K. representative on Phosphate Commission, 1934-46. *Publication:* Bacon's Essays. *Recreations:* fishing, gardening. *Address:* Grattans, Bow, Crediton, Devon. *Clubs:* Athenæum, United University. [*Died* 22 *Sept.* 1960.

GAYER, Arthur David, B.A., M.A., D.Phil. (Oxon.); Associate Professor of Economics, Queen's College, New York; *b.* 19 March 1903; *s.* of Jack A. Gayer and Marie Milionchick. *Educ.:* St. Paul's School (Senior Scholar, History Scholar, etc.), Hammersmith; Lincoln College, Oxford (Senior Classical Scholar). First Class Hons., Modern Greats Senior Medley Research Scholar in Economics, Oxford, 1925-27; Fellow of the Rockefeller Foundation, New York, 1927-30; Research Associate, National Bureau of Economic Research, New York, 1930-31; Lecturer in Economics, Columbia University, New York, 1931-1937, Assistant Professor, 1937-40; Executive Secretary, Commission on Economic Reconstruction, 1932-34; Research Economist, Federal Public Works Administration and Consultant, National Planning Board, Washington, 1933-34; Chairman, Commission on Puerto Rican sugar industry, 1936-38; Senior Economist, Board of Governors of the Federal Reserve System, Washington, 1936-37, Economic Consultant since 1937; Economic Consultant, National Resources Committee, Washington, 1939; Sec. The Political Economy Club, New York since 1934; Member, Economists' National Committee on Monetary Policy since 1935; Governor, Society for Stability in Money and Banking since 1936. *Publications:* Planning and Control of Public Works, New York, 1931 (in part); Economic Reconstruction, Report of the Columbia University Commission, New York, 1934 (in part); Monetary Policy and Economic Stabilisation, London and New York, 1935, 2nd ed, 1937; Report on Public Works and Economic Planning to U.S. National Planning Board, 1934; Public Works in Prosperity and Depression, New York, 1935; Unemployment Relief and Public Works in the United States, New York, 1936; The Lessons of Monetary Experience, New York and London, 1937 (editor); The Sugar Economy of Puerto Rico, Report of the Puerto Rican Economic Commission, New York, 1938; American Economic Foreign Policy, New York, 1939; How Money Works, New York, 1940; contributions to British, Continental and American economic and statistical journals, etc. *Recreations:* travel and civilised loafing. *Address:* 14 Edith Road, Kensington, W.14. *T.:* Fulham 4498; Queen's College, New York. *T.:* Independence 3-4700. *Club:* Columbia Faculty, N.Y. [*Died* 17 *Nov.* 1951.

GAYER-ANDERSON, Colonel Thomas Gayer, C.M.G. 1919; D.S.O. 1917; late R.A.; *b.* 29 July 1881; *s.* of Henry Gayer-Anderson, The Lodge, Old Marston,

Oxon. *Educ.:* Tonbridge School; Royal Military Academy, Woolwich. 2nd Lieut. Royal Field Artillery, 1899; Captain, 1908; Major, 1914; Lieut.-Colonel, 1921; Col., 1925; served South African War, 1900-2 (medal, five clasps, despatches), Mandal Sabai Expedition (Soudan), 1913 (medal, clasp, Egyptian despatches, Star of the Nile); European War, 1914-18, Brigade Major 29th Infantry Brigade, G.S.O. 2, 12th Corps, G S.O. 1, 22nd Division (three medals, D.S.O., Brevet Lieut.-Colonel, C.M.G. despatches five times, Serbian White Eagle, Greek Military Cross); Instructor at the Royal Military Academy, 1905-10; Adjutant 20th Brigade R.F.A., 1910-11; Egyptian Army, 1911-14; G.S.O. 1 Operations at G.H.Q. Constantinople, 1918-20; passed Staff College, Camberley, 1921; commanded 2nd Training Brigade, R.F.A., 1922; commanded 10th Field Brigade, Royal Artillery, 1923-24; G.S.O. 1, 4th Deccan Division, India, 1926-29; retired pay, 1929; Chief Liaison Officer to the I.G. Home Guards, 1940; Commanding the Cambridge Sub-area, 1940; Administrative Officer to the Commissioner of the Eastern Region, 1941. *Club:* Army and Navy. [*Died* 10 *June* 1960.

GAZE, Alfred Harold, C.B.E. 1933; General Manager for the British Phosphate Commissioners since 1920; *b.* 22 Oct. 1885; *s.* of late Alfred Henry Gaze and Winifred Wilson; *m.* 1912, Ethel Elizabeth Victoria, *d.* of late S. Summons, Senior Inspector of State Schools, Melbourne; four *s.* one *d.* *Educ.:* London: Bedford. In service of the Pacific Phosphate Co. Ltd. of London in Sydney and Melbourne until 1920; representative in Australia for that Co. when as from 1 July 1920 their phosphate undertaking at Nauru and Ocean Islands was bought out by the British, Australian and New Zealand Governments and vested in the Board of the British Phosphate Commissioners. Chairman and joint representative of Australian and New Zealand Governments on the Christmas Island Phosphate Commission from its inception in Feb. 1952. *Recreation:* golf. *Address:* 38 Canterbury Rd., Camberwell, Melbourne, E.6, Australia. *Club:* Australian (Melbourne) [*Died* 25 *March* 1954.

GEARY, Lieut.-Col. Hon. George Reginald, O.B.E., M.C., Q.C., P.C.; retired; *b.* 12 Aug. 1874; *s.* of Thecphilus Jones Geary and Mary Goodson; *m.* 1927, Beatrice (*d.* 1935), *d.* of late Lt.-Col. Frank Caverhill; one *s.* one *d.* *Educ.:* Upper Canada College; Osgoode Hall; University of Toronto. Mayor of Toronto, 1910-11-12: M.P. for Toronto South, 1925-35; Minister of Justice and Attorney-General of Canada, 1935; European War 1915-19, Subaltern 58th Bn. C.E.F.; Major at end of war (O.B.E., M.C., Légion d'Honneur, despatches); O.C. Royal Grenadiers, Toronto 1923-26. *Recreations:* garden, golf. *Address:* Caverhill, Toronto, 5. *T.:* MI6206. *Clubs:* York, University, Toronto Golf, Toronto Cricket (Toronto). [*Died* 30 *April* 1954.

GEDDES, 1st Baron, *cr.* 1942; **Auckland Campbell Geddes,** P.C. 1917; G.C.M.G., *cr.* 1922; K.C.B., *cr.* 1917 (C.B. 1917); *b.* 21 June 1879; *s.* of Auckland Campbell Geddes, Edinburgh; *m.* 1906, Isabella Gamble. 3rd *d.* of W. A. Ross, New York; four *s.* one *d.* *Educ.:* George Watson's College, Edinburgh; Edinburgh University; London Hospital; Freiburg. Formerly Demonstrator and Assistant Professor of Anatomy, Edinburgh University; Professor of Anatomy, Royal College of Surgeons, Dublin; formerly Professor of Anatomy, McGill University, and Principal of McGill University, Montreal, Canada, 1919-20. Served S. African War, Lieut. 3rd H.L.I.; European War, 1914-16; Director of Recruiting, War Office, 1916-17; Minister of National Service, 1917, 1918, and 1919; President of the Local Government Board, 1918; and Minister of Reconstruction, 1919; President of the Board of Trade, 1919-20; British Ambassador to the U.S.A., 1920-24; Hon. Brig.-Gen., Unattached List, T.F.; M.P. (U.) Basingstoke and Andover Division of Hants. 1917-20; late Regional Commissioner for S.-E. and N.-W. Regions, 1939-42; M.D., LL.D. *Publication:* The Forging of a Family, 1952. *Heir:* *s.* Hon. Ross Campbell Geddes [*b.* 20 July 1907; *m.* 1931, Enid Mary, *d.* of Clarance H. Butler, Tenterden, Kent and late of Shanghai; one *s.* one *d.* *Educ.:* Rugby; Caius College, Cambridge]. *Address:* c/o Bulcraig and Davis, Amberley House, Norfolk St., W.C.2. [*Died* 8 *Jan.* 1954.

GEDDES, Norman Bel, M.A., LL.D.; B.F.A.; American designer, city planner, theatrical producer and author; *b.* Adrian, Michigan, 27 April 1893; *e. s.* of Clifton Terry Geddes and Luella Yingling; *m.* 1st, 1916, Helen Belle Sneider, Toledo, Ohio (*decd.*): two *d.*; 2nd, 1933, Frances Resor Waite, New York (*decd.*); 3rd, 1944, Ann Howe, Philadelphia, Pa. *Educ.:* in general self-educated; public schools of Michigan, Ohio, Pennsylvania, Illinois, and Indiana; Cleveland School of Art for three months; Chicago Art Institute for seven weeks. First public recognition as portrait painter; started as stage designer at Los Angeles Little Theatre, 1916; pioneer of American Stage Design movement; designed over 200 theatrical productions; first New York production Shanewis (Metropolitan Opera Co., 1918); subsequently Ziegfeld Follies (1925), Lysistrata (1930), Hamlet (1931) all New York; Dead End, 1935. Spectacles for Max Reinhardt The Miracle, 1924, and The Eternal Road, 1935. Associate to Architectural Commission of Chicago World's Fair, 1929; Ukranian State Theatre, Kharkov, 1930 (U.S.S.R. prize); Industrial design since 1927 includes first streamlined ocean liner, 1932, interiors for Pan American Clipper Ships, 1934, General Motors "Futurama" Exhibit and building, New York World's Fair, 1939-40; automobiles, refrigerators, vacuum cleaners. radios, service stations, office equipment, internat. business machines and furniture for many well-known firms. Originated technique of model photography for Navy Ordnance, Navy Intelligence, 1941; Navy ship and plane identification, 1942. Training films for Navy, 1942; Army Air Corps, 1943. Official record Battle of Midway, 1946; Consultant Q.M.G., U.S.A.; Member: U.S.A. Inventors' Council; Authors League of America; Nat. Acad. of Science; Nat. Research Council; and of many other societies and assocs. Toledo Tomorrow, master city plan for Toledo, 1945. Paintings, models, and drawings exhibited in New York, Chicago, Vienna, Amsterdam, Milan, London, San Francisco, Seattle, Los Angeles, Cairo, Moscow, Paris. Member Authors League of America. *Publications:* A Project for a Theatrical Presentation of the Divine Comedy of Dante Alighieri, 1923; Horizons, 1932; Magic Motorways, 1940; contributor Encyclopaedia Britannica, 1926; Model Photography stories for Life Magazine, 1943-46; and Encyclopædia Britannica, 1943-46; Master Plan of Boca Raton, 1948, Los Angeles Ambassador Hotel, 1948, Copa City, 1949; numerous magazine articles. *Recreations:* sailing, naval and military strategy and tactics; experimental motion picture photography. *Clubs:* Players, Coffee House, North American Yacht, Racing Union (New York). [*Died* 9 *May* 1958.

GEDGE, Montagu Lathom, Q.C. 1949; *b.* 24 June 1899; *yr. s.* of late Leslie Lathom Gedge and Edith Wallace Russell. *Educ.:* Königliches Kaiserliches Gymnasium, Bonn; Merchant Taylors' School. Served European War, 1917-19. Called to Bar, Inner Temple, 1922. Member of Company Law Amendment Committee, 1943. Chairman, Cttee. on Shares of No Par Value, 1952. *Address:* Conholt Park, Andover, Hants. *Club:* Reform. [*Died* 24 *Nov.* 1958.

GEE, Col. Ernest Edward, C.B.E. 1946; D.S.O. 1917; M.C. 1916; *b.* 17 Nov. 1888; *s.* of late Lionel Edgar Gee; *m.* 1914, Winifred May Veale (*d.* 1941); one *s.*; *m.* 1942,

Jean Marjorie Souter. Served in ranks R.G.A. from 1904; Bermuda, 1907-11; Commissioned 1915; B.E.F. France, 2nd Lt. 50th Siege Bty. R.G.A. Sept. 1915; Acting Capt. 192 Siege Bty., May 1917; Acting Major 270 Siege Bty. Aug. 1917 (M.C., D.S.O.). Instructor in Gunnery, Lydd, 1919-20 and Western Command, 1920-24; Adjt. 61st Med. Bde. R.A. (T.A.), 1924-28; Mauritius, 1928-31; Retired Pay, 1933. Secretary, Anglesey and Caernarvonshire T.A. Assoc, 1933-39 and 1945-48; School of Artillery, Larkhill, 1939-45; Chief Instructor in Equipment, 1941-45. Officer, American Legion of Merit, 1946. *Address:* Eighty-one, Forest Road, Worthing, Sussex. [*Died* 2 *April* 1959.

GEE, Hubert George, C.M.G. 1947; Under-Secretary, Employment Policy Department, Ministry of Labour and National Service, since 1954; *b.* 29 Nov. 1909; *m.* 1937, Dora Eleanor Burge; two *s.* one *d.* *Educ.:* Hackney Downs Secondary School; University College, London. Andrews Scholar, Univ. Coll., 1928-31; graduated, 1931, B.A. hons. first class (history). Entered Ministry of Labour, 1932; Commonwealth Fellow (New York), 1938-39; Principal Private Secretary to Minister, 1940-43; Asst. Secretary, Overseas Branch Ministry of Labour and National Service, 1945-47; seconded to Foreign Office, 1947; Adviser, International Labour Relations, Foreign Office, 1947-51; Assistant Secretary, Industrial Relations Department, Ministry of Labour and National Service, 1951-52; Chief Industrial Commissioner, 1952-54. *Address:* 17 The Glade, West Wickham, Kent. *T.:* Springpark 4281. [*Died* 14 *April* 1959.

GEE, Capt. Robert, V.C., M.C.; *b.* 1876; *m.* 1902, Elizabeth, *d.* of Peter Dixon, Huntingdon, and *g.-n.* of John Jones, Talysarn; two *d.* Was twenty-two years in the ranks of the Royal Fusiliers; served European War (despatches four times, commissioned May 1915, V.C., M.C.); two years on staff of 29th Division (wounded thrice). Contested Consett and Bishop Auckland Divisions of Durham and Newcastle East; M.P. (U.) East Woolwich, 1921-22; Bosworth Division of Leicester, 1924-27. Commissioner of Declarations, Western Australia, 1953-. *Address:* Dunmuvin, Orange Road, Darlington, Western Australia. [*Died* 2 *Aug.* 1960.

GEIKIE-COBB, Ivor; *see* Cobb.

GEMMELL, Sir Arthur (Alexander), Kt., 1955; M.C. 1918; T.D. 1927; retired 1957; Obstetrician and Gynæcologist, United Liverpool Hospitals, 1924-57; Lecturer in Obstetrics and Gynæcology, University of Liverpool, 1931-57; *b.* 2 Nov. 1892; *e. s.* of late John Edward Gemmell, M.B., F.R.S.E.; *m.* 1919, Gladys Freda (*d.* 1957), *d.* of late William Alfred Reading; one *s.* two *d.* *Educ.:* Uppingham; King's College, Cambridge (M.A., M.D.); Liverpool University. F.R.C.S.E., F.R.C.O.G.; Hon. M.M.S.A. 1955. Served European War, 1914-18; Liverpool Scottish and Q.O. Cameron Highlanders (despatches); comd. Liverpool Scottish, 1923-27 (Bt.-Col.); Liverpool Medical Institution: Council, 1930-33; Treasurer, 1936-38; Vice-Pres., 1940-41; Trustee, 1933-; Pres. N. Eng. Obst. and Gyn. Soc., 1945; Pres. Section of Obstetrics and Gynæcology of Roy. Soc. Med., 1957-58; Roy. Coll. Obst. and Gyn.: Council, 1943-46; Hon. Treasurer, 1946-52; President, 1952-55; William Meredith Fletcher Shaw Memorial Lecturer, 1959; Member: Cent. Health Services Council, 1952-55; Liverpool Reg. Hospital Board, 1948-; Board of Governors United Liverpool Hosps., 1948-52; Merseyside Blood Transfusion Service, 1930-39; Liverpool Cancer Control Org., 1945-; Cancer Co-ordinating Cttee. for Liverpool Area, N. Wales and I.O.M., 1949-; Arthur Wilson Memorial Lecturer (Melbourne), 1954; Blackham Memorial Lecturer, 1954. Hon. Fell. Edin. Obst. Soc.; Amer. Gynæcological Society; Hon. Member: New Orleans Gyn. and Obst. Society, Amer. Gyn. Club. Greek Military Cross, 1918. *Publications:* articles in med. jls. *Recreations:* fishing, military history. *Address:* 46 Salisbury Road, Cressington Park, Liverpool 19. *T.:* Cressington Park 2248. *Clubs:* Oriental; University (President, 1939-41) (Liverpool). [*Died* 24 *Sept.* 1960.

GENN, Captain Otto H. H.; *see* Hawke-Genn.

GENNINGS, John Frederick, C.I.E. 1939; C.B.E. 1933; Commissioner of Labour, Government of Bombay (retired); *b.* 21 Sept. 1885; *m.* 1911, Edith, *d.* of late T. J. Wallis, Croydon; one *s.* *Educ.:* Aske's Hatcham (Haberdashers); Dulwich College. Journalist on staffs of Morning Leader, Daily Mail, Daily Telegraph; Barrister-at-Law, Middle Temple, 1911; Army, 1916-19; Director of Information, Government of Bombay, 1920; Director of Labour Office, 1925; Commissioner of Workmen's Compensation, 1928; Indian Government Delegate, International Labour Conference, 1933. *Address:* 8 Northampton Road, Croydon. *Clubs:* Constitutional, Press; Royal Bombay. [*Died* 22 *March* 1955.

GEOGHEGAN, The Hon. James; Commissioner of Charitable Donations; *m.* 1928, Eileen, *yr. d.* of late James Murphy, Clyde Road, Dublin, *g. d.* of late John Baldwin Murphy, K.C.; two *s.* Called to Irish Bar, 1915; called to English Bar, 1923; Inner Bar (Ireland) 1925; Minister for Justice, 1932-33; Attorney General, 1936; Judge of the Supreme Court, Ireland, 1936-50; retired, 1950. *Address:* Carne Lodge, Cowper Gardens, Rathmines, Dublin. [*Died* 27 *March* 1951.

GEORGE, Senator Walter Franklin, B.S., B.L., LL.D. (Mercer); U.S. Senator, 1922-57; President Eisenhower's personal representative (designate) to North Atlantic Treaty Organisation from 1957; *b.* Preston, Georgia, 29 January 1878; *s.* of Robert Theodric George and Sarah Stapleton; *m.* 1903, Lucy Heard; one *s.* (and one *s.* killed in action, 1944). *Educ.:* Mercer University, Georgia (B.S., B.L.). Practised law, Vienna, Georgia, 1901; Solicitor General, Cordele Judiciary Circuit, Georgia, 1907-12; Judge of the Superior Court, Cordele Judiciary Circuit, 1912-17; Judge, Court of Appeals of Georgia, Jan.-Oct. 1917, resigned; Associate Justice, Supreme Court of Georgia, 1917-22, resigned. Chairman Senate Finance Committee until 1953; ex-Chm. Senate Foreign Relations Committee. Democrat. *Address:* Vienna, Georgia, U.S.A.; c/o North Atlantic Treaty Organisation, Palais de Chaillot, Paris, France. [*Died* 4 *Aug.* 1957.

GEPP, Sir Herbert William, Kt., *cr.* 1933; Director Kelvinator (Australia) Ltd.; *b.* Adelaide, South Australia, 28 Sept. 1877; *s.* of William John Gepp and Marion Rogers, both of Adelaide; *m.* 1904, Jessie Powell, 2nd *d.* of James Walker Hilliard, Melbourne; one *s.* four *d.* *Educ.:* State and Secondary Schools, Adelaide; Melbourne Univ. Junior Chemist, Australian Explosives and Chemical Co., Victoria, 1894; Manager, 1902; joined Zinc Corporation at Broken Hill, N.S.W., and built and operated their sulphuric acid plant, 1904; General Manager Amalgamated Zinc (De Bavay's) Ltd., 1909; Australian Government Representative to U.S.A., on metals and munitions, 1914-16; General Manager of Electrolytic Zinc Co. of Australia, Ltd., 1916; with Mr. Gilbert Rigg was awarded the gold medal of Inst.M.M., 1924; Federal Commissioner of Australia, Empire Exhibition Commission; President Inst.M.M. of Australia, 1924; Chairman Development and Migration Commission, 1926-30; Consultant on Development to the Govt. of the Commonwealth of Australia, 1930-33; Chairman of Commonwealth Royal Commission on the Wheat

Flour and Bread Industries, 1934 and 1935; Managing Director Australian Paper Manufacturers, Ltd., 1936-48; Chairman Commonwealth Central Cargo Control, 1942-1944; Lt. Field Engineers, Military Reserve Forces of Australia. Federal Pres. Royal Australian Chemical Inst., 1949-50; Pres. Soc. of Chemical Industry of Victoria (first secy., 1900). *Publications:* When Peace Comes, 1943; Democracy's Dangers, 1939; Vice-President's Address, Dec. 1923, for Inst. M.M., Hobart; The Defence of Australia and the Relation of Primary and Secondary Industries thereto; Developing a White Continent; Development and Migration Commission—Its Task. *Recreations:* farming, golf. *Address:* Clivedon Mansions, 192 Wellington Parade, East Melbourne, Australia. *Club:* Australian (Melbourne).

[*Died* 14 *April* 1954.

GERARD, 3rd Baron (*cr.* 1876), **Frederic John Gerard,** Bt. 1611; M.C.; late Captain R. Horse Guards; *b.* 10 Nov. 1883; *o. s.* of 2nd Baron and Mary, *d.* of Henry B. Milner, W. Retford; *S.* father, 1902; *m.* 1906, May, *d.* of late Sir Martin Gosselin, and Hon. Lady Gosselin, of Blakesware, Herts; one *s.* three *d.* *Educ.:* Ratcliffe. Entered army, 1907; Captain, 1909; served European War, 1914-17 (severely wounded, M.C.). *Heir: s.* Hon. Robert William Frederick Alwyn Gerard, *b.* 23 May 1918. *Address:* Garswood, Newton-le-Willows, Lancashire; Eastwell Park, Ashford.

[*Died* 12 *Feb.* 1953.

GERARD, Hon. James Watson, G.C.B. (Hon.) 1917; lawyer; *b.* New York, 25 Aug. 1867; *s.* of James Watson Gerard and Jennie Angel; *m.* 1901, Mary Daly; no *c.* *Educ.:* Columbia University. Elected Supreme Court Judge, State of New York, 1907; U.S. Ambassador to Germany, 1913-17; Returned to Law, 1917; Representative of the President as Special Ambassador at the Coronation of King George VI. *Publications:* My Four Years in Germany, 1917; Face to Face with Kaiserism, 1918; My First Eighty-three Years in America, 1951. *Address:* Union Club, Park Avenue and 69th Street, New York City. [*Died* 6 *Sept.* 1951.

GERE, Charles March, R.A. 1939 (A.R.A. 1934); R.W.S.; *b.* Gloucester, 1869; *s.* of late Edward W. Gere, Leamington Spa; unmarried. *Educ.:* Birmingham; Italy. Was connected for many years as student and teacher with the Birmingham School of Art; as book illustrator worked with William Morris for the Kelmscott Press; later, for the Ashendene Press; at present painter of portraits, and landscapes; Pictures in the National Gallery, Millbank, and in the Chief provincial Galleries. *Address:* Painswick, Gloucestershire. *T.:* Painswick 3268. [*Died* 3 *Aug.* 1957.

GERMAN, Major Sir James, K.B.E., *cr.* 1920 (O.B.E. 1918); J.P.; *b.* 3 April 1879; *s.* of late Alfred John German; *m.* 1902, Gwladys Rose, *d.* of Thomas Eynon of Penarth; one *s.* three *d.* *Educ.:* Exeter. Chairman of several companies. *Address:* Crossways, Penarth, Glam.

[*Died* 5 *June* 1958.

GERMANOS, Strenopoulos, D.D., D.Phil., Hon. K.C.V.O. 1934; G.C.A.O (R), G.C.S.O. (Y), G.C.P.O. (S), K.C.S.O. (G); G.C.S.O. (L); Lambeth Cross, 1942; Archbishop of Thyateira and Metropolitan since 1922; Exarch of Western and Central Europe and Apokrisiaros of the Oecumenical Patriarch to the Archbishop of Canterbury with see in London since 1922; *b.* Delliones (Dist. Sylembria Eastern Thrace) 15 Sept. 1872 (o. s.); *s.* of Pantoleon Strenopoulos and Helena K. Kyropoulos. *Educ.:* Theological College, Halki (Const.); Halle; Leipzig; Strasburg; Lausanne. Headmaster and preacher, Rodosto and Metras, 1897-1900; after returning from Germany, Prof. of Divinity at the above College, 1904, Principal, 1907; Metropolitan of Selefkia 1912) and remained Principal and Prof. until 1922, then called as 1st Archbishop of the newly founded Metropolis of Thyateira, having under his pastoral care all Greek Orthodox Communities in Western and Central Europe; has represented the Oecumen. Patriarchate in Russia, U.S., Finland, Latvia, Stockholm, Geneva, Lausanne, Oxford, Edinburgh and Amsterdam; one of six presidents of World Council of Churches and Vice-Chm. Cttee. of Faith and Order; took part in Theological meetings of Orthodox and Anglican Reps. at Lambeth, 1930-31, and represents the Church of Constantinople for the Old Catholics of Europe and for the Lutheran Church of Sweden. *Publications:* Hippolyt's philosophische Anschauungen, 1904; The Preliminary Conference on Faith and Order, 1921 (Gr.); The Revision of the Anglican Prayer Book, 1928 (Gr.); The Oxford Movement, 1933 (Gr.); many articles in the Greek magazines; and English reviews. *Address:* 8 Dawson Place, Bayswater, W.2. *T.:* Bayswater 2947. *Club:* Athenæum.

[*Died* 23 *Jan.* 1951.

GERTY, Paymaster Captain Francis Hamilton, C.M.G. 1917; R.N. (retired); late Secretary of King George's Sanatorium for Sailors, Liphook, Hants; *b.* 2 Feb. 1876; *s.* of late Rev. H. L. Gerty, D.D.; *m.* 1906, Ethel, *d.* of late Charles Wiltshire, J.P.; no *c.* *Educ.:* Christ's Hospital. Entered R.N. 1893; Paymaster H.M.S. Renown when Prince and Princess of Wales visited India in her, 1905-6; served on River Niger, 1895 (medal and clasp); Mombasa, 1895; Benin City, 1897 (despatches, clasp); specially promoted Paymaster in recognition of war services in Africa, 1904; retired, 1910; served European War, France, 1914-16 (C.M.G.); specially promoted for war services, 1918. *Address:* Yennadon Lodge, Dousland, Yelverton, S. Devon. [*Died* 11 *Dec.* 1955.

GETTINS, Lt.-Col. Joseph Holmes, D.S.O. 1918; O.B.E. 1933; B.A. (Lond.); late Army Educational Corps; *b.* 19 Nov. 1873; *y. s.* of John and Mary Gettins, Hay Mills, Birmingham; *m.* 1st, Katherine, *y. d.* of Rev. E. P. Legge, M.A., Litton Cheney, Dorset; two *s.*; 2nd, 1934, Kathleen Winifred, *widow* of Major Francis E. A. Campbell, O. B. E. *Educ.:* Isleworth Training College; University of London. Lecturer and Professor of Education, University College, Reading, 1899-1907; Principal, University Training College, Liverpool, 1907-1920; War Service, 1914-19; Chief Education Officer, Royal Military College, Sandhurst, 1921-27; Command Education Officer, Eastern Command, 1927-31; Comdt. Army School of Education, Shorncliffe, 1931-33; retired pay, 1933. *Publications:* Some Chapters on Writing English; Edited: Some Military Conversations and Correspondence in French. *Address:* 7 Wolsey Road, East Molesey, Surrey. [*Died* 6 *June* 1954.

GHORMLEY, Vice-Adm. Robert Lee; U.S. Navy, retd.; *b.* Portland, Ore., 15 Oct. 1883; *s.* of David Owen Ghormley and Alice Irwin; *m.* 1911, Lucile Elizabeth Lyon; two *s.* one *d.* *Educ.:* Univ. of Idaho (B.A. 1903); U.S. Naval Academy (B.S. 1906); Naval War College. Hon. LL.D. Univ. of Idaho, 1946. Ensign U.S. Navy, 1906; during European War, 1914-18, served as Flag Lt. to Vice-Admiral Grant, Commander Battleship Force One, U.S. Atlantic Fleet; Asst. Director Naval Overseas Transportation Service, 1918; Capt. 1929; Rear-Adm. 1938; Vice-Adm. 1941. Commanded U.S. Battleship Nevada, 1935; Fleet Operations Officer, U.S. Fleet, 1936; Director of War Plans, Navy Dept., 1938; Asst. Chief of Naval Ops., Navy Dept., 1939; Special Naval Observer, London, Eng., 1940; Commander, South Pacific Forces and South Pacific Area, 1942; Commander Hawaiian Sea Frontier and Commandant 14th Naval District, 1943-44; Commander U.S. Naval Forces in Germany, 1944-45; Chairman General Board Navy Dept., Washington,

D.C., 1946; retired, 1946. *Address:* 3305 Macomb Street, N.W., Washington 8, D.C., U.S.A. *Club:* Army and Navy (Washington, D.C.). [*Died* 21 *June* 1958.

GHOSH, Sir Jnan Chandra, Kt., *cr.* 1943; D.Sc.; F.N.I.; Member in charge of Education, Health and Scientific Research, Planning Commission, Government of India, since 1955; *b.* 14 Sept. 1894; *s.* of late Ram Chandra Ghosh; *m.* 1922, Nilima Palit; three *s.* two *d.* *Educ.:* Giridhi School; Presidency Coll., Calcutta; University Coll., London. Palit Scholar and Prem Chand Roy Chand Student, 1918; in Europe, 1918-21; Lecturer in Chemistry, Calcutta University, 1915-21; Professor and Head of Dept. of Chemistry, Dacca University, 1921-39; Dean of Faculty of Science, Dacca University, 1924-28; Provost, Dacca Hall, 1926-39; Director, Indian Institute of Science, Bangalore, 1939-47; Director, Indian Institute of Technology (East) Hijli Kharagpur, Bengal, 1950-54; Vice-Chancellor, University of Calcutta, 1954-55. Member, Council and Board of Scientific and Industrial Research since 1940; Pres. Indian Chemical Soc., 1935-1937; National Institute of Sciences, 1943; General Pres. Indian Science Congress, Lahore, 1939; Member Indian Scientific Mission to U.K. and U.S.A., 1944-45; lately Director General of Industries and Supplies, Govt. of India. Member of Delegation to: Empire Scientific Conf., U.K., 1946; 4th Gen. Assembly of Unesco, Paris, and U.N. Conf. on Conservation and Utilization of Resources, Lake Success, 1949; Pres. of Indian Assoc. for Cultivation of Science, 1951-. *Publications:* in various journals in Europe and India. *Address:* Planning Commission, New Delhi, India. [*Died* 21 *Jan.* 1959.

GHULAM MOHAMMED, (Kt., *cr.* 1946; C.I.E. 1941); M.A., LL.B.; *b.* 29 August 1895. *Educ.:* M.A.O. College, Aligarh, India (M.A., LL.B.). Member Exec. Council of Muslim Univ., Aligarh, and Member Court of Muslim Univ., Aligarh, and Delhi Univ. Passed examination and joined Indian Audit Dept., 1920; Comr. of Development to Bhopal State, 1932-34; Dep. Dir. of Finance, Posts and Telegraphs, and Financial Adviser, Communications, Govt. of India, 1934-39; Controller-Gen. of Purchases, Govt. of India, 1940; Additional Sec., Govt. of India, Dept. of Supply, 1941; Finance Minister to Nizam's Govt., Hyderabad-Deccan, 1942-45; Director of Tatas, Ltd., 1945-47; Minister of Finance and Economic Affairs, Pakistan, 1947; Pres. Internat. Islamic Economic Organisation; Governor for Pakistan of Internat. Bank for Reconstruction and Development and Internat. Monetary Fund, 1950. Governor-General of Pakistan, 1951-55, retired. Hon. LL.D., Punjab, 1949. *Address:* Karachi, Pakistan. [*Died* 29 *Aug.* 1956.

GIBB, Sir Alexander, G.B.E., *cr.* 1920 (K.B.E., *cr.* 1918); C.B. 1918; F.R.S. 1936; Comdr. Order of Crown of Belgium; Dist. Service Medal (American naval); Grand Officer Order of Boyaca, Colombia; Grand Cross Order of the Three Stars (1st class) Latvia; King's Silver Jubilee Medal, 1935; Brig.-Gen., R.M., retd. 1919; Hon. Associate of the College of Technology, Manchester; LL.D. (Edin.), F.R.S. (Edin.), M.Inst.C.E., M.I.Mech.E., M.Cons.E., Hon. M.E.I.C. (Canada), M.Am.Soc.C.E., M.Soc.C.E. (France), M.I.Chem.E., M.J.Inst.E., M.Inst.T., A.Inst. N.A., F.Inst.F., F.Inst.W., F.G.S., F.R.G.S.; F.S.A. Scot.; Founder of the firm of Sir Alex. Gibb & Partners, Consulting Civil Engineers; *b.* Broughty Ferry, 12 Feb. 1872; *e. s.* of late Alex. Easton Gibb; *m.* 1900, Norah Isobel Monteith (*d.* 1940), *y. d.* of late Fleet-Surgeon Lowry John Monteith, R.N.; two *s.* (and one *s.* decd.). *Educ.:* Rugby; University College, London; pupil of late Sir John Wolfe Barry and H. M. Brunel. Past Member Royal Fine Art Commn.; Past President Inst.C.E., London Chamber of Commerce, Inst. of Transport and Inst. of Welding; Vice-Pres. of Kipling Soc.; Member British Nat. Cttee. on Large Dams World Power Conference; Consultative Cttee. on Engineering, Educ. Cttee. of L.C.C.; Past President: Instn. of Chemical Engineers; Instn. of Engineers-in-Charge; Junior Instn. of Engineers; Past Chm. of Assoc. of Consulting Engineers; Member of Royal Instn. of Gt. Britain; Fellow of Univ. Coll., London; Technical Adviser to H.M. Treasury under the Trades Facilities Act; Past Mem. Bd. of Referees apptd. under Finance Act; late Chm. of Easton Gibb & Son, Ltd., Contractors for construction of H.M. Dockyard, Rosyth, and other public works; Consulting Engineer to the Admiralty for the Singapore Naval Base; Consulting Engineer to Government of Republic of Colombia and Technical Member of Colombian National Council of Ways of Communication; Consulting Engineer for public works and industrial development to the Republic of Turkey; Consulting Engineer for certain work in Persia for the Persian Government. Joint Consulting Engineer to Dean and Chapter of St. Paul's Cathedral; advised Govt. of Canada on administration and development of all Canadian National Ports; Joint Consulting Engineer to Mersey Docks and Harbour Board; Consulting Engineer for new Dock at Sydney, Australia, 1941-45; Hon. Pres. of College Hall, London; Mem. Council and Exec. Cttee. of Princess Helena College; Past Chief of London Ross and Cromarty and Sutherland Assoc.; Past Pres. Old Rugbeian Soc.; Past Pres. Burns Federation; Past Pres. London Fife Assoc.; Member of the Queen's Bodyguard for Scotland (Royal Company of Archers); was Chief Engineer Ports Construction to British Armies in France and Belgium, 1916-18; Deputy Director of Docks (O), B.E.F., France, 1917-1918; Civil Engineer-in-Chief, Admiralty, 1918-19; Director-Gen. of Civil Engineering, Ministry of Transport, 1919-21; Chairman of Technical Committee on London Traffic, 1920-21; Chm. of Light Railways Investigation Committee, 1920-21; Consulting Civil Engineer, Ministry of Transport, 1921; Member of Electrification of Railways Advisory Committee. *Publication:* The Story of Telford—The Rise of Civil Engineering, 1935. *Recreations:* shooting, fishing, and hunting. *Address:* Queen Anne's Lodge, Westminster, S.W.1. *T.A.:* Gibbosorum, Parl, London. *T.:* Whitehall 9700; The Anchorage, Hartley Wintney, Hants. *Clubs:* Athenæum, Carlton, Travellers', Reform, Caledonian, Royal Automobile, Flyfishers'; New (Edinburgh); Royal Clyde Yacht. [*Died* 21 *Jan.* 1958.

GIBB, Alistair Monteith, T.D.; Consulting Engineer; Senior Partner, Sir Alexander Gibb & Partners, Consulting Civil Engineers, Westminster, since 1949; *b.* 2 April 1901; *e. s.* of Sir Alexander Gibb, *q.v.*; *m.* 1st, 1927, Lady Diana King, *y. d.* of 3rd Earl of Lovelace (marriage dissolved 1940); 2nd, 1944, Hon. Yoskyl, *widow* of Hon. R. B. Gurdon, and *e. d.* of 2nd Viscount Cowdray; one *d.* *Educ.:* Eton; Pembroke College, Cambridge. Pupil Mott, Hay & Anderson, Consulting Civil Engineers, Westminster. Served War, 1939-44: Roy. Wilts. Yeomanry, Middle East and Italy; Lt.-Col. Comdg., 1942-44; Hon. Col. Roy. Wilts. Yeomanry since 1951. Partner, 1944, of Sir Alexander Gibb & Partners. Member, Exec. Council, Jt. East & Central African Bd.; Chm. Council, College Hall (Univ. of London); Vice-Chm., Roy. Central Asian Soc.; Bd. of Governors, Princess Helena Coll.; Dep. Chm., Conservative Commonwealth Council, Lond., 1953 (Chm. E. & Central Africa Group, 1953); contested (C.) Swindon Div. of Wilts., 1945. Mem. H.M. Govt. Good-Will Trade Mission to Iraq, Syria, Lebanon and Cyprus, 1946.

Recreations: hunting, shooting, fishing. *Address:* Cotswold Park, Cirencester, Glos.; Gruinard, Laide, Ross-shire; Ol'Kalou, Kenya Colony. *Clubs:* Turf, Cavalry, United University, Bath.
[*Died* 29 *July* 1955.

GIBB, Sir Claude Dixon, K.B.E., *cr.* 1956 (C.B.E. 1942); Kt., *cr.* 1945; F.R.S. 1946; D.Sc., M.E.; Chairman and Managing Director C. A. Parsons & Co. Ltd., Newcastle upon Tyne, since 1945; Chairman: A. Reyrolle & Co. Ltd., Hebburn-on-Tyne (until Oct. 1958, remaining a Director); The Nuclear Power Plant Co., Ltd., Newcastle upon Tyne; Anglo Great Lakes Corp. Ltd., Newburn-Haugh; Board of Governors Rutherford College; Vice-Pres. Royal Society, 1957; *b.* Adelaide, S. Australia, 29 June 1898; *s.* of John Gilbert and Caroline Gibb; *m.* 1925, Margaret Bate Harris. *Educ.:* South Australian School of Mines, University of Adelaide, S. Australia. Pilot Australian Flying Corps, 1917-19; Senior Research Assistant Engineering Laboratory, University of Adelaide, 1920-23; C. A. Parsons & Co. Ltd., Newcastle on Tyne, 1924-40, Chief Engineer and Director, 1929, General Manager and Director, 1937; Joint Managing Director 1943; Engineering Assistant to the Director-General, Munitions Production, 1940, then Deputy to D.G.M.P.; Director-General Weapons and Instrument Production, 1941; Director-General Fighting Vehicles (Research and Development), 1943; Director-General Armoured Fighting Vehicles, 1943, and Chairman of Tank Board, 1944, Ministry of Supply. James Watt Internat. Medal of Instn. of Mechanical Engineers (awarded posthumously). *Publications:* various to Institution of Mech. Engineers, etc. *Address:* 15 Moor Court, Gosforth, Northumberland. *T.:* Gosforth 51498. *Clubs:* Athenæum, Royal Automobile.
[*Died* 15 *Jan.* 1959.

GIBBARD, George, O.B.E. 1948; J.P.; Farmer; Member of Council National Farmers Union since 1930; *b.* 7 September 1886; *o. c.* of Daniel and Mary Ellen Gibbard; *m.* 1910, Rosa Mary Bliss; two *s.* *Educ.:* Banbury Academy. Represented Board of Agriculture before Oxfordshire County Appeal Tribunal during European War, 1914-18; Chairman Oxfordshire Farmers Union, 1930-32; helped to found Oxfordshire Farmers, Ltd. (Farmers' Co-op.), 1920 (President 1934 and 1935); Director Midland Marts, Ltd. Banbury, since its formation, 1924; Chairman Labour Committee, N.F.U., 1934-35; represented Agriculture at International Labour Office at Geneva, 1935; President N.F.U. 1938; Chairman: Livestock and Wool Cttee. N.F.U., 1939-51; N.F.U. Legal Cttee., 1952; British Wool Marketing Board, 1950; formerly Member of Agricult. Wages Board. *Address:* 84 Oxford Road, Banbury, Oxon. *T.:* Banbury 3207.
[*Died* 3 *April* 1960.

GIBBARD, Maj.-Gen. Thos. Wykes, C.B. 1918; C.B.E. 1919; M.B. Durham; M.R.C.S. Eng.; late Hon. Surgeon to H.M.; Associate King's Coll., London; *b.* 26 March 1865; *m.* 1895, Lilian Beatrice, *d.* of late B. Lewis Rice, C.I.E.; one *d.* *Educ.:* King's College, London; Durham Univ. Entered R.A.M.C., 1891; Brevet Lt.-Col., 1912; Lt.-Col., 1913; Brevet Col., 1914; Colonel, 1917; Major-General, 1922; served S. African War, 1901 (medal, 4 clasps); European War, Dardanelles, Egypt, and France (despatches 3 times, C.B., C.B.E.); Afghan War, 1919 (despatches, medal); retired pay, 1925; lately a Commissioner of Roy. Hosp. Chelsea. *Address:* Mardale, Angmering-on-Sea, Sussex.
[*Died* 11 *Aug.* 1957.

GIBBINGS, Robert John, M.A. (Hon.); F.R.S.L.; A.R.H.A., F.R.G.S.; F.Z.S.; Artist and author; *b.* Cork, 23 Mar. 1889; *s.* of Rev. Edward Gibbings, canon of Cork Cathedral, and Caroline Rouvière, *d.* of Robert Day, F.S.A., M.R.I.A., Cork; *m.* 1st, Mary Pennefather; three *s.* one *d.*; 2nd, Elisabeth Empson; one *s.* two *d.* *Educ.:* Univ. Coll., Cork; Slade School; Central School of Arts, London. Served European War, Royal Munster Fusiliers, 1914-18 (Gallipoli, 1915). Director of Golden Cockerel Press, 1924-33; lecturer in book production, Univ. of Reading, 1936-42. Representative collection of engravings in British Museum, Victoria and Albert Museum, and other public collections at home and abroad. Founder-member Society of Wood-engravers. *Publications:* author and illustrator of: Iorana, A Tahitian Journal; A True Tale of Love in Tonga; Coconut Island; John Graham, Convict; Blue Angels and Whales; Sweet Thames run softly; Coming down the Wye; Lovely is the Lee; Over the Reefs; Sweet Cork, of Thee; Coming down the Seine; Trumpets from Montparnasse; Till I End My Song; and others. *Recreation:* travel. *Address:* Footbridge Cottage, Long Wittenham, Abingdon, Berks. *T.:* Clifton Hampden 298.
[*Died* 19 *Jan.* 1958.

GIBBINS, Theodore, J.P.; *b.* Neath, 1876; 4th *s.* of F. J. Gibbins, J.P.; *m.* 1905, Eleanora E., 2nd *d.* of late Alex. Baird, J.P., The Willows, Wickhambreaux, Canterbury, Kent; one *d.* *Educ.:* Leighton Park. Sheriff, Glamorgan, 1928-29. *Recreations:* farming, shooting. *Address:* Glynfelin, Neath, S. Wales. *T.:* 115.
[*Died* 22 *Feb.* 1952.

GIBBON, Sir Douglas Stuart, Kt., *cr.* 1946; M.C.; Chief Master Supreme Court of Judicature Taxing Office, 1932-54; *b.* 2 July 1882; *s.* of Rev. James Morgan Gibbon, Stamford Hill. *Educ.:* University College School, Wadham College, Oxford (B.A.). Solicitor, 1908. Capt. Royal Welch Fusiliers, 1914-18 (M.C.). Master of Supreme Court Taxing Office, 1921. Lord Chancellor's Cttee. on Cost of Litigation. *Recreations:* golf, shooting, gardening. *Address:* Glanavon, Woodford Rd., S. Woodford, E.18. *T.:* Wanstead 3268. *Clubs:* Oxford and Cambridge, Royal Automobile.
[*Died* 13 *Sept.* 1960.

GIBBON, Brigadier John Houghton, D.S.O. 1916; late R.A.; *b.* 22 July 1878; *e. s.* of late Rev. John Houghton Gibbon, Rector of Willersey, Glos.; *m.* 1916, Jessie Willoughby, 2nd *d.* of Brabazon Campbell, The Northgate, Warwick; two *s.* two *d.* *Educ.:* Eton; Trinity College, Camb. (M.A.). Entered R.A. 1900; Capt. 1909; Maj. 1914; Lt.-Col. 1925; Col. 1923; served West Africa (Aro Expedition), 1901-2 (medal with clasp); S. Nigeria, 1904-5, and N Nigeria, 1905-6 and 1907-8; European War (France, Dardanelles, Egypt), 1914-19 (despatches thrice, D.S.O., Bt. Lt.-Col.); Commander R.A. 42nd (East Lancs) Division Territorial Army, 1931-32; Commander R.A. 53rd (Welsh) Division, T.A., May-July 1932; Garrison Comm. and Comdt. Royal Artillery Depôt, Woolwich, 1932-35; retired pay, 1935; re-employed as Lieut.-Colonel Commanding 4th Field Training Regt., R.A., 1940-46. *Recreations:* rowing, riding, shooting, fishing, ski-ing. *Address:* Hen Bersondy, Llanover, Abergavenny, Mon. *T.:* Gobion 339. The Manor House, Little Stretton, Shropshire. *T.:* Church Stretton 53. *Clubs:* Naval and Military, Flyfishers', Leander.
[*Died* 13 *Aug.* 1960.

GIBBON, Lieutenant-Colonel William Duff, C.B.E. 1945; D.S.O. 1917; M.C.; T.D.; LL.D. (hon.) Queen's University, Belfast; Headmaster of Campbell College, Belfast, 1922-43; *b.* 1880; *s.* of late Sir W. D. Gibbon and Katherine (*d.* 1916), *d.* of Andrew Murray of Allathan, Aberdeen. *Educ.:* Dulwich College, Trinity College, Oxford, M.A. Served S. Africa, 1900-1; European War, Gallipoli, 1915; Mesopotamia, 1916-17 (D.S.O.); Persia, 1918; Trans-Caucasia. Col. Comdt. A.C.F. in Northern Ireland, 1943-46; Chairman City of Belfast T. & A.F.A., 1947-50. *Publication:* First Steps to Rugby Football, 1923. *Address:* Dunmow House, Dunmow Hill, Fleet, Hants.
[*Died* 16 *Feb.* 1955.

GIBBONS, Major Sir Alexander Doran, 7th Bt., *cr.* 1752; *b.* 14 Dec. 1873; *s.* of 6th Bt. and Lydia, *d.* of Maj. J. Doran, Ely House, Wexford; *S.* father, 1909; *m.* 1899, Gladys Constance (*d.* 1945), *d.* of late Rev. Charles Watkins; one *s.* four *d.* Served as Captain in 6th Bn. Middlesex Regt. (Militia) S. Africa, 1900-2; as Captain 1/5 Hants Battery, R.F.A. (Territorial), Mesopotamia, Feb. 1915, and afterwards with 6″ and 9·2″ Howitzer Batteries in France; Major, 1917. *Heir:* *s.* John Edward, Hon. Capt. Dorset Regt. [*b.* 14 Nov 1914; *m.* 1937, Mersa Wentworth (marriage dissolved, 1951), *yr. d.* of late Major Edward Baynton Grove Foster; one *s.* two *d.* *Educ.:* Charterhouse; Peterhouse, Cambridge. Asst. Regional Dir., Arts Council of Great Britain, 1946-50]. *Address:* Greenham House, Crewkerne, Somerset. [*Died* 30 *Sept.* 1956.

GIBBONS, Cdre. George, C.B.E. 1942; R.D.; R.N.R.; retired; *s.* of late Henry Gibbons, High Street, Wallingford, Berks; unmarried. *Educ.:* Wallingford Grammar School. At sea from 1894: Apprentice, 3rd Mate, 2nd Mate, and Mate of the Four Masted Barque Buckingham, 1894-1901; an Officer in S.S. Indra, 1901-4, T. B. Royden and Co.; joined Cunard S.S. Co. Ltd., 1904; in command, 1919-42, of several ships of that company, including Alaunia, Franconia, Mauretania, Berengaria, and Aquitania; served in H.M. Service during European war, 1914-19, as Lieut. to Commander R.N.R., Dardanelles, Aegean, Corfu, in command H.M.S. Valhalla II, H.M.S. Osiris II; Royal Naval Reserve A.D.C. to the King, 1932-34. *Address:* The Maypole, Chieveley, Nr. Newbury, Berks. *T.:* Chieveley 286. [*Died* 13 *Nov.* 1959.

GIBBONS, James Francis, M.A., F.R.G.S.; Headmaster, Oswestry High School for Boys, 1931-56; *b.* 18 Feb. 1890; *er. s.* of late Arthur Gibbons, Brierley Hill; *m.* 1920, Essyllt, *d.* of late Dr. W. Bowen-Davies, Llandrindod Wells; two *s.* *Educ.:* King Edward VI School, Stourbridge; Queen's College, Oxford. Final School of English Language and Literature, 1911; Barrister-at-Law, Inner Temple, 1922; Assistant Master at Alcester Grammar School, 1912-19; Queen Elizabeth's Grammar School, Crediton, 1919; King Edward VI School, Southampton, 1919-26; Headmaster, The Kelsick Grammar School, Ambleside, 1926-31; War Service, Artists Rifles, 1915-19. *Publications:* Two school text books of Geography. *Recreations:* golf, tennis, badminton. *Address:* Glan Severn, The Mount, Shrewsbury. *T.:* Shrewsbury 2938. [*Died* 29 *Nov.* 1957.

GIBBONS, Sir William Kenrick, Kt., *cr.* 1943; C.B. 1938; late Principal Clerk of the Public Bill Office and Clerk of the Fees, House of Commons; *b.* 1876; *s.* of late Sir William Gibbons, K.C.B.; *m.* 1915, Aileen Margaret Dale, *d.* of Captain George Trotter, Staindrop, Co. Durham; three *d.* *Educ.:* Charterhouse; New College, Oxford. Junior Clerk, House of Commons, 1900; Assistant Clerk, 1911; Senior Clerk, 1920; Principal Clerk, 1934. *Recreations:* fishing, gardening. *Address:* Harefield, Sandridge, St. Albans. *T.:* St. Albans 51853. [*Died* 26 *March* 1957.

GIBBS, Cecil Armstrong, B.A., Mus.D (Cantab.); Hon. A.R.C.M.; Composer; Professor of Harmony and Composition, Royal College of Music, London, 1920-39; *b.* Great Baddow, Essex, 10 Aug. 1889; *s.* of D. Cecil Gibbs, soap manufacturer, of The Vineyards, Great Baddow, Essex; *m.* 1918, Honor Mary (*d.* 1958), *d.* of John Mitchell Mitchell; one *d.* *Educ.:* Winchester; Trinity College, Cambridge. Several years a schoolmaster; after the war took up music altogether and studied with Chas. Wood and Vaughan Williams; Vice-Chairman British Federation of Festivals, 1937-52; Council Composers' Guild of Great Britain, 1954; Cobbett Gold Medallist of Musicians Company, 1934. *Publications:* 2 operas, 3 string 4tet. (several in MS.); The Highwayman, Songs of Enchantment, La belle dame sans merci, the Ballad of Gil Morrice, Deborah and Barak, The High Adventure, Behold the Man for Chorus and Orchestra, Before Daybreak, A Saviour Born, Women's Choir and Orchestra, The Gift (Choral Mime (Women's Voices), The Turning Year (Chorus and Orchestra); over 100 songs; several orchestral works in MS. including 2 Symphonies; Choral Symphony, Odysseus; part songs, incidental music to plays, etc. *Recreations:* bowls, fishing. *Address:* The Cottage in the Bush, Danbury, Chelmsford, Essex. *T.:* Danbury 346. [*Died* 12 *May* 1960.

GIBBS, Captain George Louis Downall, D.S.O. 1916; late R.N.; *b.* 30 July 1882; *s.* of Rev. W. Gibbs, Temple Hill, East Budleigh; *m.* 1926, Susan Fayth Harding Newman (*d.* 1942); two *d.* Served European War in command of Crusader in bombardment of German Army left wing from coast, 1915 (despatches); patrol work, 1916 (D.S.O.); 1917 and 1918 (despatches), serving in H.M.S. Thruster, Harwich Force; commander Royal Naval College, Dartmouth, 1919; retired list, 1923; Special Service under Foreign Office, 1939; served War of 1939-46 (despatches, Bar to D.S.O.); H.M.S. Queen Emma, 1942-44; H.M.S. Ganges, 1944-46; retd. May 1946. *Address:* Malthouse, Standish, Gloucestershire. [*Died* 31 *Oct.* 1956.

GIBLIN, Major Lyndhurst Falkiner, D.S.O. 1918; M.C.; retired; engaged in history of central banking in Australia; *b.* 1872; *s.* of late Hon. William Robert Giblin, sometime Premier and Puisne Judge of Tasmania; *m.* 1918, Eilean Mary, *d.* of Edward P. and Ada M. Burton, of Homefield, East Molesey, Surrey. *Educ.:* Hutchins School, Hobart; University College, London; King's College, Cambridge. Served European War, 1915-18 (wounded, despatches, D.S.O.); miner, boatman, teamster, sailor, cook, lumberman, schoolmaster, fruit-grower, labour agitator, soldier, Member of Parliament; Government Statistician, Tasmania and Deputy Commonwealth Statistician, 1920-29; acting Commonwealth Statistician, 1931-32; Ritchie Professor of Economics in Melbourne Univ., 1929-40; Commonwealth Grants Commission, 1933-36; Director of Commonwealth Bank, 1935-42; Supernumerary Fellow of King's College, Cambridge, 1938; Chairman, Advisory Committee on Financial and Economic Policy, 1939-47. *Publication:* The Australian Tariff: an economic enquiry (with others); Australia, 1930; The Growth of a Central Bank, 1950. *Recreation:* the garden. *Address:* 12 Lynton Lane, Hobart, Tasmania. [*Died* 2 *March* 1951.

GIBLIN, Colonel Wilfrid Wanostrocht, C.B. 1916; V.D.; M.R.C.S. Eng., F.R.A.C.S.; *b.* 12 May 1872; *s.* of Thomas Giblin, Hobart; *m.* 1899, Muriel Gertrude, *d.* of C. M. Maxwell, Hobart; two *s.* two *d.* Principal Medical Officer, Tasmania, 1903-14; Officer Commanding 1st Australian Clearing Hospital, Egypt, 1914; Gallipoli, 1914-15; Deputy Director Medical Service Australian Imperial Force, England, 1915-17; served European War, 1914-17 (despatches, C.B.). *Address:* 142 Macquarie Street, Hobart, Tasmania. *Club:* Tasmanian (Hobart). [*Died* 10 *Oct.* 1951.

GIBSON, Arnold Hartley, D.Sc., LL.D. (St. Andrews and Manchester); Mem.Inst. C.E.; Mem.Inst.Mech.E.; Emeritus Professor Engineering, University of Manchester; *b.* 26 July 1878; *s.* of W. H. Gibson, The Hollins, Sowerby Bridge, Yorks; *m.* 1905, Amy, *d.* of James Quarmby of Meltham; three *s.* *Educ.:* Rishworth Grammar School; Manchester University (B.Sc. 1903, D.Sc. 1909). Head of Mathematical Department, Salford Technical Institute, 1903-4; Assistant Lecturer in Engineering and Hydraulics, Manchester University, 1904-9;

Prof. of Engineering, University of St. Andrews, 1909-20; President Section G (Engineering) of British Association, 1921; Member of Board of Trade Committee on Water Power of British Isles; Member of Air Ministry Engine Research Committee; Member of Severn Barrage Committee; Ewing Medal, Institute Civil Engineers, 1939. *Publications:* Hydraulics; Water Hammer in Hydraulic Pipe Lines; Natural Sources of Energy; A Study of the Circular-Arc Bow Girder; Hydro-Electric Engineering; several papers before the Royal Society and the Institutes of Civil and Mechanical Engineers, etc. *Address:* Beech House, Elm Grove, Alderley Edge, Cheshire; The University, Manchester. *T.:* Alderley Edge 2358. [*Died* 16 *Feb.* 1959.

GIBSON, Arnold Mackenzie; *s.* of late William Yates Gibson, Manchester; *m.* Isabel, *d.* of late Alderman J. B. Martin, J.P., Helston; three *s.* one *d.* *Educ.:* Manchester Grammar School; Gonville and Caius College, Cambridge (Foundation Scholar); Prizeman in Modern Languages and Musical Composition; Modern Language Tripos Pt. I. 1919, Pt. II. 1921; M.A., 1922; Hon. Secretary Cambridge University Musical Club; Lieut. R.G.A. and Intelligence Corps; Liaison Officer with Italian Army Staffs; Intelligence Officer, G.H.Q., Italy, and XIV Corps (Croce di Guerra); Professorial Staff, Royal Naval College, Dartmouth, 1919-20; Sixth Form Master and Head of Modern Language Department, Repton School, 1920-29; Headmaster of Liverpool Collegiate School, 1930-42; individual witness before Consultative Committee of Board of Education; formerly Member of Headmasters' Conference, of Council of Incorporated Association of Headmasters, of Committee of Liverpool Philharmonic Concerts Society, etc. *Publications:* Critical Edition of Bismarck's Memoirs, 1940; The Modern Humanities in Education (Harrow Lectures on Education, 1930); General Editor of George Bell and Sons Modern Language Texts (1920-30); other educational and musical publications. *Recreations:* music, walking, gardening. *Address:* Bryn Aethwy, Menai Bridge, Anglesey. *T.:* Menai Bridge 133. [*Died* 25 *April* 1956.

GIBSON, George, C.H. 1946; LL.D.; *b.* 3 April 1885. General Council, T.U.C., 1928-1948; Chairman, 1940-41; Member Overseas Settlement Board, 1936-39; Vice-Chairman National Savings Cttee., 1943-49; Chairman, Children's Overseas Committee, 1944-; h.c. LL.D. Manchester Univ. 1945; General Sec. Confederation of Health Service Employees; Chairman N.W. Regional Board for Industry, 1945-48; Chairman North-West Industrial Estates Ltd., 1946-49; Director of Bank of England, 1946-48; Chairman N.-West Area Power Board, 1948-1949; Member Lancashire Industrial Development Council, retired. *Address:* 2 Demesne Road, Manchester, 16. *T.:* Mosside 3519. [*Died* 4 *Feb.* 1953.

GIBSON, Harold Charles Lehrs, C.M.G., 1947; retired; *b.* 1897; *e. s.* of late Charles J. Gibson; *m.* 1st, 1921, Juliet Rachel Kalmanoviecz (*d.* 1947); one *d.*; 2nd, 1948, Ekaterina Alfimova; one *s.* one *d.* *Educ.:* on the Continent; Tonbridge School. Served 1914-18 and 1939-45 wars (M.E.F.; Lt.-Col.). H.M. Foreign Service, 1923-58; First Secretary, British Embassy, Rome, 1955-58, retired 1958, and resident in Rome. Secretary, Commonwealth Club of Rome; Representative in Rome of British Chamber of Commerce for Italy; Member Royal Institute of International Affairs, London. Holds Orders of Saint Vladimir and Stanislaw (Russia); Polonia Restituta (Poland); Legion of Merit (U.S.). *Recreations:* tennis, fishing. *Address:* 25 Via Antonio Bosio, Rome, Italy. *Club:* Royal Automobile. [*Died* 24 *Aug.* 1960.

GIBSON, Harry F. C.; *see* Carew-Gibson.

GIBSON, Herbert Mellor, J.P. Manchester; Director Colonial Development Corporation since 1948; Director Co-operative Wholesale Society, Ltd.; Chm. English and Scottish Joint Co-operative Wholesale Society, Ltd.; Director Marcom Ltd.; Director Manchester Ship Canal Co.; Member of Joint Industrial Council of the Soap, Candle, and Edible Fats Industries; *b.* Manchester, 22 Feb. 1896. M.P. (Lab.) Mossley Division of Lancs, 1929-31; Member of Council for Development of Over-Seas Trade, 1930-31; Member Special Departmental Committee Ministry of Health on Recruitment of Staff, etc., in Local Government Service, 1931; member Central Cttee. Internat. Cooperative Alliance. *Address:* Sherwood, Lyme Road, Disley, Cheshire. [*Died* 27 *March* 1954.

GIBSON, Rt. Rev. James Byers, D.D.; Bishop of Caledonia since 1945; *b.* 31 Jan. 1881; Irish; *s.* of J. O. Gibson and I. A. Mould; *m.* 1929, Alice Francis Du Vernet; one *s.* two *d.* *Educ.:* Emmanuel College, Saskatoon. Deacon, 1910; priest, 1912; Incumbent St. Cuthberts Perdue, Sask., 1910-12; Rector, St. Johns Lloydminster, Sask., 1912-20; Incumbent: Christ Church, Anyox, B.C., 1920-24; St. James Church Smithers, B.C., 1924-28; Dean and Rector, St. Andrews Cath., Prince Rupert, B.C., 1928-45. *Address:* Bishop's Lodge, Prince Rupert, B.C. *Club:* Rotary (Prince Rupert). [*Died* 25 *July* 1952.

GIBSON, Sir Leslie (Bertram), Kt., *cr.* 1948; Q.C., LL.B.; Assistant Legal Adviser, Colonial Office and Commonwealth Relations Office since 1951; *b.* 14 Apr. 1896; *s.* of late George F. Gibson, Coventry; *m.* 1930, Irene Sylvia Alan North, Godalming. *Educ.:* King Henry VIII School, Coventry. Malayan Civil Service, 1920-37; Colonial Legal Service, 1937-. Attorney-General, Trinidad, 1940-44; Attorney-General, Palestine, 1944-48; Chief Justice, Hong Kong, 1948-50; Legal Adviser in London to the Foreign Office Administration of African Territories, 1950-51. *Address:* Weywards, Godalming. *T.:* Godalming 502. *Club:* East India and Sports. [*Died* 21 *Sept.* 1952.

GIBSON, Michael Joseph, M.D., M.A., F.R.C.O.G.; Consulting Gynæcologist to the Richmond Hospital, Dublin; Consulting Surgeon to the Coombe Hospital, Dublin; *b.* 3 June 1876; *er. s.* of Thomas Gibson, Dublin; *m.* 1912, Mary Vandeleur (*d.* 1941), *y. d.* of Dawson Westropp, Kildimo, Co. Limerick; four *d.* *Educ.:* Trinity College, Dublin; Berlin, Dresden, Tübingen (postgraduate). B.A. 1900; M.B., B.Ch. 1901; M.A. 1904; M.D. 1904; late Master of the Coombe Hospital, Dublin; late Surgeon and Gynæcologist to Jervis Street Hospital, Dublin; late Gynæcologist to the Richmond Hospital, Dublin; late University Examiner in Midwifery and Gynæcology, University of Dublin; late President of the Obstetrical Section of the Royal Academy of Medicine in Ireland; retired, 1935. *Address:* Cartref, Terrick, Aylesbury, Bucks. *T.:* Stoke Mandeville 2151. [*Died* 13 *Sept.* 1953.

GIBSON, Robert Clarence, C.M.G. 1957; *b.* 13 Dec. 1892; *s.* of late Frank S. and late Maria C. Gibson; *m.* 1926, Esther, *d.* of Joseph Gardner; one *s.* one *d.* *Educ.:* Young Superior Public School, N.S.W. Served European War, 1914-18; farmer, auctioneer, saw-miller, company director, 1919-39; War of 1939-45, Area Officer (Capt.); Adviser Aust. Delegation, F.A.O. Conf., Quebec, 1945; Leader Aust. Delegation London Internat. Federation of Agric. Producers, 1946. President, Primary Producers Council, 1943-48; Gen. Pres., Primary Producers Union, 1943-57; Vice-Pres. Aust. Dairy Farmers Fed., 1943-58; Vice-Pres. Nat. Farmers Union of Aust., 1950-58. *Address:* 2 Spring Street, Sydney, N.S.W., Australia. *T.:* BU 1751; 65 Wyong Road,

Cremorne, N.S.W. *T.:* XY 5260. *Club:* Lismore (Lismore, N.S.W.). [*Died* 28 *May* 1959.

GIBSON, Strickland, M.A. Oxford; *b.* 27 Jan. 1877; *s.* of S. H. Gibson, Oxford; *m.* 1908, Margaret Alice Clinkard; one *s.* one *d.* *Educ.:* New College School; St. Catherine's Society, Oxford. Assistant, Bodleian Library, 1895-1912; Brassey Research Student, 1904; Secretary to Bodley's Librarian, 1912-31; Keeper of the University Archives, 1927-45; Sub-Librarian, Bodleian Library, 1931-45; Lecturer in Bibliography (Fac. of English), 1923-45; Hon. Secretary and General Editor, Oxford Bibliographical Society, 1922-45; Gold Medallist, (London) Bibliographical Soc., 1947. *Publications:* Some notable Bodleian bindings, 1901-4; Early Oxford Bindings, 1903; Some Oxford Libraries, 1914; ed. of Statuta antiqua Univ. Oxon, 1931; Oxford Univ. Ceremonies (with L. H. D. Buxton), 1935; Print and Privilege at Oxford to 1700 (with John Johnson), 1946; A bibliography of Francis Kirkman, 1949; The University of Oxford (Victoria County Hist.), 1954; various historical and bibliographical articles. *Address:* 34 Hill Top Road, Oxford. [*Died* 18 *Feb.* 1958.

GIBSON, Rt. Rev. Theodore Sumner, M.A.; *b.* 21 Sept. 1885; *y. s.* of late Rt. Rev. E. C. S. Gibson, Bishop of Gloucester; *m.* 1919, Ruth Barnabine, *y. d.* of late Rev. Canon W. Durst; three *d.* *Educ.:* Marlborough College; Keble College, Oxford; Wells Theological College. Deacon, 1909; priest, 1910; curate, All Saints', Wokingham, 1909-13; St. Albans Cathedral, Pretoria, 1913-16; St. Matthews, Brixton, 1916-19; Chaplain to De Beers' Compounds and Convict Stations, Kimberley, 1920; Archdeacon of Kimberley, 1922-28; Bishop of Kimberley and Kuruman, 1928-43; Bishop of St. John's, Kaffraria, 1943-51; Priest-in-charge, Madehurst, Sussex, 1951-. *Address:* The Vicarage, Madehurst, Arundel, Sussex. [*Died* 29 *Aug.* 1953.

GIBSON, William Pettigrew; Keeper, National Gallery, since 1939; *b.* 3 Jan. 1902, *e. s.* of Edwin Arthur Gibson, M.D., and Ellen Shaw Pettigrew; *m.* 1940, Christina, *d.* of Francis Ogilvy and Dorothy Fairfield. *Educ.:* Westminster School; Christ Church, Oxford. B.A. Hon. (Physiology) 1924; Assistant Keeper, Wallace Collection, 1927-36; Reader in History of Art, London University; Deputy Director, Courtauld Institute of Art, 1936-38. *Publications:* contributions to Vasari Society Publication, Old Masters Drawings, Apollo, London Mercury, Sunday Times. *Address:* National Gallery, Trafalgar Sq., W.C.2. *T.:* Whitehall 7618; Wyddiall Hall, Buntingford, Herts. *Club:* St. James'. [*Died* 22 *April* 1960.

GIBSON, William Victor Halliday; *b.* 13 Jan. 1884; *s.* of Matthew and Annie Gibson; *m.* 1908, Lily Emma Hogdon. *Educ.:* privately. Joined staff of Motor Union, 1905, and came to A.A. on amalgamation of the two bodies in 1910. Served European War, 1914-18, in Sherwood Foresters. On returning to the A.A. devoted himself to Legal and Parliamentary activities; later appointed Parl. Sec., and then Asst. Secretary, 1937; Jt. Sec. of Standing Jt. Cttee. of R.A.C., A.A., and R.S.A.C. since its formation in 1944; Secretary, Automobile Association, 1948-53. Played a prominent part in campaign (including organisation of national Petition to Parliament) for the restoration of an unrestricted petrol ration for private motoring, 1947; member of the Petrol Rationing Advisory Committee to Minister of Fuel and Power, 1948. Member of the Worshipful Company of Coachmakers and Freeman of the City of London. *Recreations:* gardening, golf, fishing, cricket. *Address:* 28 Dulwich Wood Avenue, S.E.19. *T.:* Gipsy Hill 0743. *Clubs:* Devonshire, Royal Automobile, Green Room; Royal Scottish Automobile (Glasgow); Royal Irish Automobile (Dublin). [*Died* 11 *Sept.* 1954.

GIBSONE, Major-Gen. William Waring Primrose, C.M.G. 1918; D.S.O. 1917; O.B.E. 1919; retired; *b.* 1872; *m.* 1st, 1915, Marie Caroline Delima, *d.* of Couillard de Beaumont; 2nd, 1945, Alice Gregoire. Served European War, 1914-19 (despatches, D.S.O., C.M.G., O.B.E., Croix de Guerre). *Address:* 410 Sherbrooke St. W., Montreal, P.Q., Canada. [*Died* 3 *Nov.* 1957.

GIDDY, Harry Douglas; Partner of Wilson, Danby and Giddy, Chartered Accountants (Australia), 105 King Street, Melbourne; *b.* 4 Jan. 1887; *s.* of William Henry Giddy, Bolton Percy, Yorkshire, and Mary Ann Sellars Radcliffe; *m.* 1st, 1916, Jessie Edith Milford (*d.* 1932); one *d.*; 2nd, 1935, Florence Cederholm, M.Sc. (Melb.); one *s.* one *d.* *Educ.:* St. Paul's Cathedral Choir School, Melbourne. Chartered Accountant (Aust.). Chm. of Dirs.: Nat. Bank of Australasia Ltd.; The Herald & Weekly Times Ltd.; Australian Newsprint Mills Ltd.; Rowntree & Co. (Aust.) Pty. Ltd.; Kayser Pty. Ltd.; Tweedside Manufacturing Co. Ltd.; Mem. of Cttee. of Management of Royal Melbourne Hosp.; Hon. Treas. and Mem. of Bd. of Management of Walter and Eliza Hall Institute of Medical Research. *Recreations:* mechanics, fishing. *Address:* (private) 57 St. George's Road, Toorak, S.E.2, Victoria, Australia. *T.:* BJ4660. *T.A.:* (business) Mathematic, Melbourne. *Clubs:* Melbourne, Australian, Savage (Melbourne); Adelaide (Adelaide); Tasmanian (Hobart). [*Died* 12 *Dec.* 1959.

GIDE, André Paul Guillaume; Author; M.R.A.; *b.* Paris, 21 Nov. 1869; *s.* of Paul and Juliette Gide; *m.* 1892 (wife died 1939). *Educ.:* Paris (École Alascienne et Lycée Henri IV). Nobel Prize for Literature, 1947. *Publications:* Cahiers d'André Walter, 1891; Le Traité du Narcisse, Les Poésies d'André Walter, 1892; Le Voyage d'Urien, La Tentative amoureuse, 1893; Paludes, 1895 (Eng. trans. posthumous, as Marshlands, 1953); Les Nourritures terrestres, 1897; Philoctète, Le Prométhée mal enchaîné, 1899 (Eng. trans. posthumous, as Prometheus Misbound, 1953); Le Roi Candaule (Drama), 1901; L'Immoraliste, 1902 (Eng. trans. posthumous, as The Immoralist, 1953); Saül (Drama), Pretextes, (Essays), 1903; Amyntas, 1906; Le Retour de l'enfant prodigue, 1907; La Porte étroite, 1909; Oscar Wilde, 1910 and 1951; Isabelle, Nouveaux Prétextes, 1911; Bethsabé (Drama), 1912; Souvenirs de la cour d'Assises; Les Caves au Vatican, 1914 (Eng. trans. posthumous, as Vatican Cellars, 1953); La Symphonie Pastorale, 1919; Corydon, Si le grain ne meurt, 1920; Dostoiewsky, 1923; Incidences, 1924; Les Faux-Monnayeurs; Le journal des Faux-Monnayeurs, 1926; Voyage au Congo, 1927; Le Retour du Tchad (following Voyage au Congo), 1928; L'École des femmes, Montaigne, 1929; Œdipe (Drama), 1931; Perséphone, 1934; Geneviève, 1935; Les Nouvelles Nourritures, 1935; Le Retour de l'U.R.S.S., 1936; Retouches à mon Retour de l'U.R.S.S., 1937; Interviews Imaginaires, 1945; Thésée, 1946; The Journals of André Gide, Vol. I, 1947, Vol. II, 1948, Vol. III, 1949, Vol. IV, 1951. Translations—Rabindranath Tagore: L'Offrande Lyrique (Gitanjali), 1913; Joseph Conrad: Typhon; Walt Whitman: Œuvres choisies, 1918; William Blake: Le Mariage du ciel et de l'enfer, 1923; Rabindranath Tagore: Amal et la Lettre du Roi (The Post-Office), 1924; Shakespeare: Antoine et Cléopâtre, 1926; A. Pouchkine: Nouvelles, 1928; Shakespeare: Hamlet, 1946. *Address:* 1 bis, Rue Vaneau, Paris VII. [*Died* 19 *Feb.* 1951.

GIDEON, Col. James Henry, C.B. 1917; retired pay; *b.* 5 Feb. 1862; *m.* Agnes

Elliot (*d.* 1929), 2nd *d.* of John Elliot Christie of Forth Bank, Stirlingshire; *m.* 1952, Dorothy Ileene, *d.* of late Thomas John Hutchins, Neath, S. Wales. Entered Army, 1881; Capt. 1890; Lt.-Col. 1905; Bt. Col. 1908; Col. 1915; retired, 1909; late Lancs Fusiliers; Adjutant, 1st Royal Jersey Militia, 1897; commanded 1st Lancashire Fusiliers, 1905-09; commanded reinforcements in France, 1914-18 (despatches thrice). *Address:* 8 Pine Avenue, Southbourne, Bournemouth. [*Died* 17 *Feb.* 1958.

GIELGUD, Lieut-Col. Lewis Evelyn, M.B.E.; Head of Bureau of Personnel and Management, U.N.E.S.C.O., since 1951; *b.* 11 June 1894; *e. s.* of late Frank Gielgud and Kate Terry Lewis; *m.* 1937, Zita Gordon (marriage dissolved, 1951); one *d.* *Educ.:* Eton (King's Scholar); Magdalen College, Oxford (Exhibitioner 1912, Classical Demy 1913). B.A. 1916; M.A. 1924. 2nd Lieut. 6th K.S.L.I. Sept. 1914; Lieut. 1915; wounded in France, 1915; War Office, 1916-1917; British Military Mission, Paris, 1917-1919; Captain, 1918. Joined staff of International League of Red Cross Societies, 1919; Under-Secretary General, 1927; travelled on Red Cross business throughout Europe, and four times round the world (lecturing, broadcasting, and organising international Red Cross Conferences); resigned Sept. 1939. Recommissioned 1940; War Office, 1940-41; Major (Intelligence Corps), 1941; Lt.-Col. 1942. Released, Dec. 1944. British Red Cross Sub-Commissioner in Paris, 1945; Co-ordinating Officer Inter-Allied Reparation Agency, Brussels, 1946-49; Counsellor, O.E.E.C., 1949-51. Legion of Honour, 5th Class; Crown of Roumania, 4th Class; White Eagle of Yugo-Slavia, 5th Class; Rising Sun of Japan, 4th Class. *Publications: novels:* Red Soil, The Wise Child; *travel:* About It and About; *plays:* (with Naomi Mitchison): The Price of Freedom, As It Was in the Beginning; Full Fathom Five. Radio plays (with Zita Gordon). Translations from French, Latin, and Polish. *Recreations:* travel, reading, writing. *Address:* 7 rue de l'Alboni, Paris XVI[e]. [*Died* 25 *Feb.* 1953.

GIESEKING, Walter Wilhelm; Concert Pianist; *b.* Lyons, France, 5 Nov. 1895; *s.* of Wilhelm Gieseking, M.D., Entomologist, Westphalia, and Martha Bethke, Berlin; *m.* 1925, Annie Haake, Hanover (*d.* 1955); two *d.* *Educ.:* Privately. Began to play piano at 4½ years; no regular musical training until 1911; studied with Karl Leimer at the Hanover Municipal Conservatory, 1911-15; First Concerts, 1913-14; Army Service, 1916-18; Concert tours over Europe since 1920, and including North America since 1926; First appeared in England in 1923. Chevalier of Legion of Honour (France); Officer of Order of Leopold (Belgium). *Publications:* A few piano pieces; A Quintet for Piano, Oboe, Clarinet, French Horn and Bassoon; Sonatina for Flute and Piano, 1937; Variations (for Flute or Violin and Piano) on a theme by Grieg, 1938; Serenade for String Quartet, 1939; Little Music for 3 Violins, Concert-Sonatina for Cello and Piano; Spiel um ein Kinderlied (variations) for Piano (4 hands). *Recreations:* Entomology, combined with mountain climbing. *Address:* Kohlweg 12, Saarbruecken/Saar. [*Died* 26 *Oct.* 1956.

GIGLI, Commendatore Beniamino; late Tenor, Metropolitan Opera House, New York; *b.* Recanati, Italy, 20 March 1890; *m.* Costanza Cerroni-Gigli; one *s.* one *d.* *Educ.:* Recanati. Musical studies under Professor Enrico Rosati in the Rome Conservatory (Liceo Musicale S. Cecilia); debut at Rovigo near Venice, 1914, as Enzo in La Gioconda; afterwards in the chief Italian cities; Torino, Palermo, Genova, Bologna, Firenze, Napoli, Roma, and finally in the Scala of Milan; engaged for the theatres of Rio Janeiro and S. Paul (Brazil), Coliseo and Colon of Buenos Aires (Argentina), Urquiza of Montevideo (Uruguay); created the tenor rôle in Mascagni's Lodoletta, Piccolo Marat; in Puccini's Rondine in Italy and South America; in Lalo's Le Roi d'Ys at the Metropolitan of New York; sings also: Mefistofele, Tosca, Bohème, Cavalleria Rusticana, Lucia, Fedora, Lucrezia Borgia, Loreley, Madame Butterfly, Andrea Chenier, Manon Massenet, Manon Puccini, Traviata, Lohengrin, Favorita, Rigoletto, Adriana di Lecouvreur, Amore dei tre Re, Francesca da Rimini, Gioconda, Romeo e Giulietta in French, etc. Recordings by the Victor Co. Concerts in principal cities of U.S.A.; sang in opera and concerts Budapest, Vienna, Hamburg, Berlin, Munich, Zürich, etc. *Publication:* The Gigli Memoirs, 1957. *Recreations:* hunting, swimming, horseback and other sports. *Club:* Lambs (New York). [*Died* 30 *Nov.* 1957.

GILBERT, Sir Bernard William, G.C.B., *cr.* 1950 (K.C.B., *cr.* 1946; C.B. 1937); K.B.E., *cr.* 1943; Member, Restrictive Practices Court since 1957; *b.* 1891; *s.* of late Harry Gilbert, Nottingham; *m.* 1925, Janet Maud, *d.* of late Alfred H. Fison, D.Sc.; one *s.* three *d.* *Educ.:* Nottingham High School; St. John's College, Cambridge. Hon. Fellow, St. John's College, 1952. Entered Treasury, 1914; served European War, R.H.A. and R.G.A., 1917-18; Joint Second Secretary, H.M. Treasury, 1944-56, retired. *Address:* Cherry Tree Corner, Chesham Bois, Bucks. *T.:* Amersham 305. *Club:* United University. [*Died* 7 *Nov.* 1957.

GILBERT, Mrs. G. C. R. D.; *see* Davies-Gilbert.

GILCHRIST, Alexander Fitzmaurice, C.B.E. 1946; *b.* Blaenavon, Monmouthshire, 10 Sept. 1878; *o. s.* of late Percy Carlyle Gilchrist, F.R.S., and Norah, 2nd *d.* of late Captain L. R. Fitzmaurice, R.N.; *m.* 1909, Beatrice (*d.* 1949), 3rd *d.* of Frederick William Osborne; one *s.* *Educ.:* Repton. Solicitor, 1903; Treasury Solicitor's Department, 1903-32; Official Solicitor to Supreme Court of Judicature, 1932-50. Served European War (Queen's Westminster Rifles), 1914-19, Major T.F., retired. J.P. Norfolk. *Recreation:* gardening. *Address:* Dennington, Suffolk. [*Died* 9 *March* 1956.

GILCHRIST, Philip Thomson, R.B.A. 1906; Member of Imperial Arts League; *b.* Castle View, Stanwix, near Carlisle, 22 Oct. 1865; *s.* of Geo. Gilchrist, retired Manchester Bank Manager, and Jane Helen, *d.* of Philip Thomson, one of the seven founders of Anti-Corn Law League; *m.* 1910, Katharine Gray, *e. d.* of Rev. James Mellis, M.A. *Educ.:* Queenwood College, Hampshire. After some years a partner in calico-printing business, studied under Tom Mostyn; for many years a member of Manchester Athenæum Graphic Club, becoming Vice-President in 1896 and retiring from the club in 1903; elected to membership of Manchester Academy of Fine Arts and of Liverpool Academy of Arts, retiring 1927; first exhibited in R.A. 1900; pictures in permanent collections of Manchester and Liverpool Corporations, provincial galleries and National Gallery of South Africa. *Address:* The Dolphin House, Sunderland Point, Morecambe, Lancs. *T.:* Overton 237. [*Died* 31 *March* 1956.

GILCHRIST, William James; *b.* British Guiana, 18 March 1879; 2nd *s.* of late Alexander Mennie Gilchrist and Mary Gray Gilchrist (*d.* 1916), both of Aberdeenshire; *m.* 1921, Dora, *d.* of Henri D. Seedorff, Georgetown, British Guiana; no *c.* *Educ.:* Brunswick House Private School, British Guiana. Barrister, Gray's Inn, 1914; passed Inns of Court Exam. Roman Dutch Law (additional to Bar Final), 1913; entered H.M. Customs, British Guiana, 1899; Copyist Registrar's Office, 1900; acting 4th class clerk Central Board of Health (now Local Government Board), 1901-2; 6th class clerk there, 1902; 5th class clerk H.M. Customs, 1903; Assistant Commissary, 1905;

Clerk to Attorney-General, 1906; Stipendiary Magistrate, a J.P., Coroner, and Commissioner of Oaths, 1910; Chairman Rose Hall Village Partition of Lands Commission, 1911; acting Assistant Colonial Secretary, 1914; Censor (War) under Defence Scheme, 1914-20 (received thanks of Secretary of State); Commissioner to inquire into disturbance and management of H.M. Penal Settlement, British Guiana, 1922; acting Puisne Judge, 1923; acting Attorney-General, 1923-24, 1924-25, and again acting Puisne Judge, 1925-26 and 1927; Puisne Judge, British Guiana, 1927; First Puisne Judge, Trinidad and Tobago, 1931; Acting Chief Justice, Trinidad and Tobago, 1932-33, 1935, 1937, 1939; retired, 1941. *Address:* 46 Main Street, Georgetown, British Guiana. *Club:* Georgetown (British Guiana). [*Died* 24 *June* 1955.

GILES, Lionel, C.B.E. 1951; M.A., D.Litt.; late Keeper of Oriental Printed Books and Manuscripts, British Museum; Examiner in Chinese to the University of London; *b.* Sutton, Surrey, 29 Dec. 1875; 4th *s.* of late Herbert Allen Giles; *m.* 1903, Phyllis Isabel, *d.* of late James B. Coughtrie, Hongkong; one *s.* one *d.* *Educ.:* Collège St. Servais, Liège; Feldkirch, Austrian Tyrol; University of Aberdeen; Wadham College, Oxford. 1st Class Classical Mods., 1897; 2nd Class Lit. Hum., 1899; M.A. 1902, D. Litt., 1913; entered British Museum, 1900; retired, 1940. Chinese Order of the Brilliant Star, 1947. *Publications:* The Sayings of Lao Tzŭ, 1904; Musings of a Chinese Mystic, 1906; The sayings of Confucius, 1907; Sun Tzŭ on the Art of War, 1910; The Chinese Language (with Professor H. A. Giles) for Encyclopaedia Britannica, 1910; An Alphabetical Index to the Chinese Encyclopaedia Ch'in Ting Ku Chin T'u Shu Chi Ch'êng (printed by order of the Trustees of the British Museum), 1911; Taoist Teachings, 1912; An Ethical System based on the Laws of Nature (translated from the French), 1917; The Lament of the Lady of Ch'in, 1926; Chinese Inscriptions: Appendix to Stein's Innermost Asia, 1928; The Analects of Confucius (Limited Editions Club, New York), 1933; Dated Chinese MSS. in the Stein Collection, 1935-43; The Book of Mencius, 1942; Brief Glossary of Chinese Topographical Terms, 1943; Six Centuries at Tunhuang, 1944; A Gallery of Chinese Immortals, 1947. *Address:* The Knoll, Abbots Road, Abbots Langley, Herts. [*Died* 22 *Jan.* 1958.

GILKES, Christopher Herman; Master of Dulwich College since 1941; *b.* 1898; *s.* of Rev. Arthur Herman Gilkes; *m.* 1939, Kathleen Josephine, *d.* of Beverley Murray, Trinidad; two *s.* one *d.* *Educ.:* Dulwich College; Trinity College, Oxford. Assistant Master Uppingham School, 1922-28; Headmaster, The Grammar School, Stockport, 1929-41. *Address:* Dulwich College, S.E.21; Elm Lawn, Dulwich Common, S.E.21. *T.:* Gipsy Hill 1202. [*Died* 2 *Sept.* 1953.

GILL, Ernest Walter Brudenell, O.B.E., B.Sc., M.A., Fellow and Domestic Bursar, Merton College, Oxford; *b.* 12 Aug. 1883; *s.* of Canon Ernest Compton Gill; *m.* 1921, Mary Beatrice Harriss; three *s.* one *d.* *Educ.:* Bristol Grammar School; Christ Church, Oxford (Exhibitioner and Hon. Scholar). Demonstrator Electrical Laboratory, Oxford, 1907; Fellow Merton College, Oxford, 1908-14 and 1919; Private 9th Hants, 1914; Lt. R.G.A. 1915; Capt. and Major R.E. Wireless Intelligence), 1915-19, Egypt and Salonika: Member Hebdomadal Council, Oxford Univ., 1928-33; Univ. Alderman on Oxford City Council; rejoined army, Dec. 1939. Major R. Sigs., M.I.8., Operational Research and S.H.A.E.F. *Publications:* War, Wireless and Wangles; various scientific papers in Philosophical Magazine. *Recreations:* rebuking sin, and research. *Address:* Larkfield, Boars Hill, Oxford. *T.:* Oxford 75368. [*Died* 20 *Dec.* 1959.

GILL, Sir Harry; *see* Gill, Sir Thomas H.

GILL, Hubert Alexander, C.M.G. 1951; M.A.Cantab.; Fellow of the Chartered Institute of Patent Agents; *b.* 1881; *s.* of Joseph John Gill and Lucy Cheal; *m.* 1909, Marjorie, *d.* of Arthur Priestman, J.P.; one *s.* three *d.* *Educ.:* Friends' School, Ackworth; Yorkshire College, Leeds; Queens' College, Cambridge. Past President of the Chartered Institute of Patent Agents; Member of the British Delegation to the Industrial Property Conference at The Hague, 1925; Member of the Dating of Patents Committee appointed by the Board of Trade, 1927; Member of the Patents Committees appointed by the Board of Trade in 1929 and 1944. *Recreation:* lawn tennis. *Address:* 51 Chancery Lane, W.C.2; Houw Hoek, Upper Selsdon Road, Sanderstead, Surrey. *T.:* Holborn 7764, Sanderstead 1012. *Club:* Athenæum. [*Died* 3 *Nov.* 1954.

GILL, Major James Herbert Wainwright, C.B.E. 1919; Consulting Engineer; A.M.I.C.E.; M.I.M.E.; *b.* 1876; *s.* of James Gill, Blundellsands, Lancs; *m.* 1913, Louisa Ethel, *d.* of C. W. Neville Rolfe, Heacham, Norfolk; one *s.* one *d.* *Educ.:* Liverpool College; Liverpool Nautical College. Engineer Ceylon Government Service, 1904-10; served European War, 1914-19 (despatches, C.B.E.); Superintendent, Admiralty Experimental Station, 1918-20. *Address:* 2 Queensberry Mews West, S.W.7. *T.:* Kensington 2181. [*Died* 27 *Nov.* 1951.

GILL, Sir (Thomas) Harry, Kt., *cr.* 1950; President International Co-operative Alliance, 1948; *b.* 5 Dec. 1885; *e. s.* of W. Gill, York; *m.* 1st; one *d.*; 2nd, 1930, Leile Gladys, *o. d.* of Charles A. Elliott, Blackpool; one *d.* *Educ.:* Driffield Grammar School. M.P. (Lab.) Blackburn, 1929-31. Late Board (ex-Pres.), Co-operative Wholesale Society, Manchester; retd. 1951. *Address:* Carlton Villa, Carlin Gate, Blackpool. [*Died* 20 *May* 1955.

GILL, Col. William Smith, C.B. 1919; D.L. Aberdeen City; *b.* 1865; *e. s.* of late A. O. Gill, D.L. Aberdeen City; *m.* 1898, Ruth, *y. d.* of late David Littlejohn, LL.D., D.L. Aberdeen County; two *s.* three *d.* *Educ.:* Merchiston Castle School, Edinburgh; Aberdeen University; Royal School of Mines, London Lieut. 1st A.R.E. (V), 1884; Colonel commanding, 1904-8; Colonel commanding R.E. Highland Division (T.), 1908-10; Chairman, Aberdeen City Territorial Army Association, 1913-22; Hon. Col. Royal Engineers 51st (The Highland) Division, 1922-27; Queen Victoria Diamond Jubilee medal, 1897; V.D., 1908. *Address:* Dalhebity, Bieldside, Aberdeenshire. *T.A.:* Dalhebity, Cults. *T.:* Aberdeen 47804. *Club:* Royal Northern (Aberdeen). [*Died* 25 *Dec.* 1957.

GILLESPIE, Charles Melville, M.A. (Oxon); *b.* 12 Oct. 1866; *s.* of late James Donaldson Gillespie, M.D., of 10 Walker Street, Edinburgh; *m.* 1921, Christabel Ann, *d.* of late Alfred Fowler, Hitchin; one *s.* *Educ.:* Edin. Academy and University (Vans Dunlop Scholar in Classics); Trinity College Oxford (Scholar); 1st class Hon. Moderations, 1887; 1st class Lit. Hum., Oxford, 1889: B.A., 1889; M.A., 1892; Assistant Lecturer, Yorkshire College, Leeds, 1891; Lecturer in Philosophy, 1893; Professor of Philosophy, University of Leeds, 1912-32; Chairman of the Northern Universities Joint Matriculation Board, 1929-32; Emeritus Professor since 1932. *Publications:* Papers in Mind, Classical Quarterly, Journal of Philology, Archiv für Geschichte der Philosophie. *Address:* 5 Moor Park Avenue, Leeds 6. *T.:* Leeds 52054. [*Died* 7 *June* 1955.

GILLESPIE, Col. Rollo St. John, C.I.E. 1918; O.B.E. 1920; R.E., retired; *b.* 28 Sept. 1872; *s.* of late Maj.-Gen. W. J. Gillespie; *m.* 1898, Florence (*d.* 1947), *d.* of Captain H. H. Grenfell, R.N.; no *c.* Commission R.E. 1892; served Tibet Expedition, 1904; France 1914-16 (despatches, C.I.E.); Afghan War (despatches,

O.B.E.); most of service spent in India including native state of Chamba, 1909-11. *Address:* Pato House, Wilcove, Torpoint, Cornwall. *T.:* Torpoint 99. *Club:* United Service. [*Died* 18 *Nov.* 1952.

GILLETT, Col. Sir Alan; *see* Gillett, Col. Sir W. A.

GILLETT, Canon Charles Scott, M.A.; Canon Emeritus of Chichester since 1954; *b.* Woolsthorpe-by-Belvoir, 12 Dec. 1880; *s.* of Rev. E. A. Gillett and Katharine Ellerton Scott. *Educ.:* St. Edward's School, Oxford; Queen's College, Oxford (Classical Scholar), Hon. Mods. Lit. Hum. Assistant Master, St. Edward's School, 1905-10; Assistant Curate, Halesowen, 1913-1914; Chaplain, Liddon House, S. Audley Street, 1914-21; Vice-Principal, Westcott House, 1921-22; Fellow of Peterhouse, Cambridge, 1922-32 (Dean, Chaplain, Junior Bursar), Fellow Emeritus, 1943; Junior Proctor, 1926; Principal of Chichester Theological College, 1933-46; Acting Principal Scottish Theological College, Edinburgh, 1943-46; Select Preacher, Oxford, 1927-28; Select Preacher, Cambridge, 1923, 1932, 1936, 1942. Examining Chaplain to Bishop of Southwell, 1924-27; to Bishop of Derby, 1927-36; to Bishop of Brechin since 1936; Proctor in Convocation for Chichester Diocese, 1943-50. *Address:* 4 Newnham Terrace, Cambridge. *Club:* Oxford and Cambridge. [*Died* 18 *Oct.* 1957.

GILLETT, Lieut.-Col. Edward Scott, C.I.E. 1917; late Deputy Director of Remounts, India; *b.* 15 Sep. 1877; 3rd *s.* of late Rev. E. A. Gillett, Islip; *m.* 1906, Katherine Seale, 2nd *d.* of late Rr.-Adm. A. Gillett. *Educ.:* Lancing. Capt. A.V.C. 1906; Major, 1915; Lt.-Col. 1918; served S. Africa, 1900-2 (Queen's medal 3 clasps, King's medal 2 clasps); Afghanistan, 1919 (despatches). *Address:* Redlynch, Bruton, Som. *Club:* Naval and Military. [*Died* 4 *March* 1952.

GILLETT, Col. Sir (William) Alan, Kt., *cr.* 1949; T.D., D.L.; Member of legal firm of Baileys Shaw & Gillett, 5 Berners Street; *b.* 18 Jan. 1879; *s.* of William Edward Gillett, Streatham, S.W.; *m.* 1911, Ella Mabel, J.P., *d.* of late Granville Chetwynd-Stapylton; three *s.* two *d.* (and two *s.* decd.). *Educ.:* Marlborough. Admitted Solicitor, 1902. Served European War, 1914-19; late Hon. Col. 5th Bn. East Surrey Regt. D.L. Surrey. Pres. of Law Society, 1948-49. *Recreations:* mountaineering and music. *Address:* Glebe House, Leatherhead, *T.:* Leatherhead 2142. *Club:* Alpine. [*Died* 18 *Feb.* 1959.

GILLIATT, Sir William, K.C.V.O., *cr.* 1949 (C.V.O. 1936); Kt., *cr.* 1948; M.D.; M.S. London; F.R.C.P.; F.R.C.S.; F.R.C.O.G.; Surgeon - Gynaecologist to The Queen; ex-President, Royal Society of Medicine; ex - Pres. Royal College of Obstetricians and Gynaecologists; Consulting Surgeon King's College Hospital; Consulting Surgeon Samaritan Free Hospital for Women; *b.* Boston, Lincs, 1884; *s.* of late William Gilliatt; *m.* Anne Louise, *d.* of late John Kann, Lyne, Surrey; one *s.* one *d.* *Address:* 100 Harley Street, W.1. *T.:* Welbeck 8474. [*Died* 27 *Sept.* 1956.

GILLICK, Ernest George, A.R.A. 1935; F.R.B.S. 1938; Sculptor; *s.* of Cornelius Gillick; *m.* Mary, *d.* of Thomas Tutin. *Educ.:* The Royal College of Art (Travelling Scholar). Served on the Faculty of Sculpture, British School at Rome, and on Council of Imperial Arts League; Master of the Art Workers' Guild, 1935; awarded Royal Society of British Sculptors Medal, 1935. Principal works include memorials at Emmanuel College and Trinity College, Cambridge; Winchester College; Frampton Memorial, St. Paul's Cathedral; Harrison and Chemical Society's Memorial, Burlington House, London; Ouida Memorial, Bury St. Edmunds; War Memorial, Forest Row. Statues at Cardiff (City Hall); Foord Almshouses, Rochester; Bikaner and Cochin in India, and at Christchurch, New Zealand; Sculpture of the War Memorial at Glasgow and of Memorial to the Missing at Vis-en-Artois, France. Medals for the Royal Mint, Royal Academy, Inner Temple, Kosciuszko Medal (with Mary Gillick), and the Lord Mayor's Seal for the City of London. *Address:* Moravian Close, 381 King's Road, Chelsea, S.W.10. *T.:* Flaxman 6454. *Club:* Athenæum. [*Died* 25 *Sept.* 1951.

GILLIES, Arthur Hunter Denholm, B.A. (Oxon), LL.B.; Advocate; Sheriff-Substitute (retd.); *b.* 8 July 1890; *s.* of late William Gillies, LL.D., and late Margaret Mitchell Gilchrist Gillies (*née* Finlay); *m.* 1st, 1918; one *d.*; 2nd, 1932, Mrs. Helena Kathleen Shepstone, *d.* of late William Baird Grainger Grieve. *Educ.:* St. Ninian's, Moffat; Fettes Coll., Edinburgh; Christ Church, Oxford; Edinburgh Univ. Served European War, 1914-19 (wounded); called to Scots Bar, 1919; Interim Sheriff-Substitute, Ayr, 1927; Perth, 1929; Airdrie, 1929; Glasgow, 1930; Aberdeen, 1931; Dingwall, 1932; Sheriff-Substitute of Caithness, Orkney, and Zetland, at Kirkwall, Jan. to March 1933; of Ross, Cromarty, and Sutherland, at Dingwall, 1933-37; of Lanarkshire, at Airdrie, 1937-43; of Lanarkshire, at Glasgow, 1943-48; retired Sept. 1948. *Recreations:* curling, shooting, fishing, golf. *Address:* 97A Whitehall Court, Westminster, S.W.1. *T.:* Whitehall 3160. *Club:* Oxford and Cambridge. [*Died* 4 *Nov.* 1953.

GILLIES, Brigadier Frederick George, C.B. 1934; O.B.E.; Indian Army, retired; *b.* 28 Jan. 1881; *s.* of late Colonel G. J. Gillies, R.A.; *m.* 1911, Ivy M. L., *d.* of late R. Thom; two *d.* *Educ.:* Tonbridge School; Royal Military College, Sandhurst. 2nd Lieut. 1900; Col., 1923; commanded Ambala Brigade, 1932-34; retired 1934. *Address:* c/o National Provincial Bank, Ltd., Exeter, Devon. [*Died* 17 *Nov.* 1955.

GILLIES, Sir Harold Delf, Kt., *cr.* 1930; C.B.E. 1920; Commander: Order of the Dannebrog, 1924; Order of St. Olav, 1948; F.R.C.S. England; B.A. Cantab.; M.D. Hon. (Ljubljana); Civil Consultant (Plastic Surgery) Admiralty; Hon. Consultant (Plastic Surgery) Ministry of Pensions, R.A.F. and Army at Home; Hon. Fellow Royal Society of Medicine; Hon. Fellow American College of Surgeons; Hon. Mem. American Dental Association; Hon. Mem. Soc. Vaudoise de Med. Lausanne; *b.* Dunedin, New Zealand, 17 June 1882; *s.* of Robert Gillies, M.H.R. of N.Z., and Emily Street; *m.* 1st, Kathleen Margaret Jackson (*d.* 1957); two *s.* two *d.*; 2nd, 1957, Marjorie E. Clayton. *Educ.:* Wanganui College, N.Z.; Cambridge; St. Bartholomew's. Late Plastic Surgeon to St. Bartholomew's Hosp., to St. Andrew's Hospital, Dollis Hill, N., to North Staffordshire Royal Infirmary; late Plastic Surgeon, Queen's Hospital for Facial Injuries, Sidcup, Kent; late Consultant Adviser, Ministry of Health and Department of Health for Scotland. *Publications:* Plastic Surgery of the Face, 1920; The Principles and Art of Plastic Surgery, 2 vols., 1957. *Recreations:* School Captain of Cricket XI; rowed for Cambridge, 1904; played golf for Cambridge, 1903, 1904, 1905; played golf for England *v.* Scotland, 1908, 1925, and 1926; won St. George's Grand Challenge Cup, 1913; fly-fishing, landscape painting; one-man show at Foyle's Galleries, 1947, 1959. *Address:* 149 Harley Street, W.1. *T.:* Welbeck 4444. *Clubs:* Garrick; Junior Carlton; Rye Golf (Rye). [*Died* 10 Sept. 1960.

GILLIES, William King, LL.D., M.A. (Glas.), B.A. (Oxon), F.E.I.S.; *b.* 20 March 1875; *e. s.* of William Gillies, Gateside, Beith, Ayrshire; *m.* 1st, 1900, Jean Menzies (*d.* 1937), *e. d.* of John Carnie, J.P., Manufacturer, Kilmarnock; two *s.* three *d.*; 2nd, 1939, Annie Scott Gow, M.A.,

Girls' High School, Glasgow. *Educ.:* Spier's School, Beith; Glasgow University (First Class Honours in Classics and in Philosophy, Logan Memorial Medallist and Snell Exhibitioner); Balliol College, Oxford (Hons. in Mods. and Greats). Adopted Teaching Profession; taught Classics in Greenock, Campbeltown, Perth; became Senior Classical Master in the High School of Glasgow, 1904; Rector of Hutcheson's Grammar School, Glasgow, 1913; Rector, Royal High School, Edinburgh, 1919-40; Grand Sec., Grand Lodge of Scotland, 1941-48. *Publications:* A Latin Reader, Latin of the Empire, and A Latin Grammar for Schools and Colleges (in collaboration). *Recreation:* golf. *Address:* Davaar, 12 Suffolk Road, Edinburgh. *T.:* 42468. *Clubs:* Scottish Conservative, Royal Scots (Edinburgh). [*Died* 15 *Nov.* 1952.

GILLIGAN, Frank William; Headmaster, Wanganui Collegiate School, N.Z., 1936-54; Lay Canon of Cathedral Church Wellington; *b.* 20 Sept. 1893; *s.* of late Willie Austin Gilligan and Alice Eliza Kimpton; *m.* 1921, Clara Elizabeth Brindle; one *s.* two *d.* *Educ.:* Dulwich Coll.; Worcester Coll., Oxford (Exhibitioner). Hons. Degree English Literature, 1920; served European War Essex Regt., 1914-19, Captain (despatches); held commission in R.N.Z.A.F. with rank of Flight Lieutenant while commanding Wanganui A.T.C. Town Squadron, 1941-50; Assistant Master Uppingham School, 1920-35; House Master, 1925, 1935. *Recreations:* Cricket, Oxford University XI, 1919-20 (Capt. 1920), Essex County XI, 1919-30; Rugby Football; Hockey, Oxford University Occasionals. *Address:* 5 Parkes Avenue, St. John's Hill, Wanganui, N.Z. *Club:* Wanganui (Wanganui). [*Died* 3 *May* 1960.

GILLINGHAM, Rev. Canon Frank Hay, B.A.; Rector of St. Stephen, Walbrook with St. Benet Sherehog since 1940 (also officiating Curate-in-charge, St. Michael's, Chester Square, 1942-52); Hon. Canon of Southwark since 1935; Chaplain to the Queen's Household since 1952 (to the Household of King George VI, 1939-52); *b.* Japan, 1875; 2nd *s.* of J. and S. Gillingham; *m.* 1st, Mary Ryder (d. 1949), 2nd *d.* of Rev. E. W. Matthews; two *s.* one *d.*; 2nd, 1950, Mrs. Pamela Field Simmons, *d.* of Sir Kenneth Crossley, *q.v.* *Educ.:* Dulwich Coll.; Univ. Coll., Durham. Ordained, 1899; Curate at Parish Church, Leyton, 1899-1905; Army Chaplain, 1905-7; Curate, Bethnal Green, 1907-10; Vicar, Holy Trinity, Bordesley, Birmingham, 1910-14; Rector of Parish Church, Bermondsey, 1914-23; Rector of St. Margaret, Lee, 1923-40; in France Aug. 1914 as A.C.F.; Rural Dean of Bermondsey, 1919-1921; Rural Dean of Lewisham, 1932-40. *Recreations:* cricket, etc., first played County Cricket for Essex, 1903; Gentlemen *v.* Players, 1908, 1919, 1920. *Address:* 37 Melton Court, S.W.7. *T.:* Kensington 6808, Mansion House 9000. [*Died* 1 *April* 1953.

GILLON, Stair Agnew, of Wallhouse; B.A. Oxon; LL.B. Edin.; *b.* 8 Sept. 1877; *y. s.* of Andrew Gillon of Wallhouse, late H.E.I.C.S., Vice-Lt. of Co. of Linlithgow, and Isabella Agnew, *d.* of Stair H. Stewart of Physgill and Glasserton, Wigtownshire; *m.* 1919, Nina Johnstone Douglas, O.B.E.; two *d.* *Educ.:* Haileybury; New Coll., Oxford; Edinburgh University. Advocate, 1903; Legal Secretary to the Lord Advocate, 1909; Advocate Depute, 1912; served European War, 1914-18, K.O.S.B. (Captain); 87th Brigade; Intelligence service; private secretary to Director of Information (Col. John Buchan), 1917; attached Neutral Press Section, Ministry of Information, 1918; Solicitor in Scotland to Board of Inland Revenue, 1919; retired from Civil Service, 1942; Sheriff-Substitute of the Western Division of Dumfries and Galloway, 1942-48. *Publications:* The Story of the 29th Division, 1925; The K.O.S.B. in the Great War, 1929; (for Stair Society) Selected Justiciary Cases, 1624-50, Vol. I, 1953. *Recreations:* were golf and mountaineering; now reading, music, walking and travel when possible. *Address:* Abbey Saint Bathans, Berwickshire. *T.:* Abbey Saint Bathans 202. *Clubs:* Brooks's, New (Edinburgh); Hon. Company of Edinburgh Golfers (Capt. 1925-26) (Gullane). [*Died* 11 *Aug.* 1954.

GILMAN, Edward Wilmot Francis, C.B.E. 1929; Member House of Laity Church Assembly; Member Oxford Diocesan Board of Finance, Board of Patronage and Diocesan Council of Education; Chairman of Governors Gosford Hill County Secondary School; Vice-Pres. and Dep. Chm. Oxfordshire Branch C.P.R.E.; *b.* Shanghai, China, 16 Aug. 1876; 2nd *s.* of late Francis Gilman, Solicitor, Southampton; *m.* 1904, Bessie Violet, *d.* of late C. M. Bagot, Adelaide, S. Australia; two *s.* one *d.* *Educ.:* Bradfield; Brasenose College, Oxford (Scholar), 2nd Class Mods. 1896; 2nd Class Lit. Hum. 1898; B.A. 1898; M.A. 1936. Entered Malayan Civil Service, 1899; held various appointments in Straits Settlements and F.M.S.; Controller of Labour, Malaya, 1922; acting British Resident, Selangor, 1929; Resident Councillor, Penang, 1930; retired, 1931. Hon. Sec. C.P.R.E., Oxfordshire Branch, 1934-47; Member Oxfordshire County Regional Planning Cttee., 1939-47; Chief Warden A.R.P., 1939-45. *Publications:* (Poems) The Wheat with the Chaff, 1944; Not without Flowers, 1948. *Address:* The Cottage, Islip, Oxon. *T.A.:* Islip. *T.:* Kidlington 3172. *Club:* Royal Empire Society. [*Died* 13 *March* 1955.

GILMER, Dame Elizabeth May, D.B.E. 1951 (O.B.E. 1946); *b.* Kumara, N.Z., 1880; *d.* of Rt. Hon. Richard John Seddon, sometime Premier of New Zealand; *m.* 1907, Knox, *s.* of Hamilton Gilmer; two *d.* *Educ.:* Kumara School; Wellington Girls' Coll. Member: Wellington Post-primary Schools Council; Wellington Hosp. Bd., 1938-53; Wellington City Council, 1941-53; Wellington Coll. Bd. of Governors; Pres. Social Club for the Blind; Bd. of Y.W.C.A. N.Z. Rep. at Internat. Council of Women, 1949. Vice-Pres. English-Speaking Union; life member Victoria League. F.R.Hort.S. (Eng.); Associate N.Z. Roy. Inst. Hort. Jubilee Medal, 1935; Coronation Medal, 1953; Greek Red Cross Medal. *Recreations:* music, gardening. *Address:* 3 Eccleston Hill, Wellington, N.1, N.Z.; Te Marua, Upper Hutt, N.Z. [*Died* 28 *Feb.* 1960.

GILPIN, Archibald, M.D.; F.R.C.P.; Physician to King's College Hospital; *b.* 30 Aug. 1906; *s.* of Archibald Gilpin, O.B.E.; *m.* 1936, Margaret Alison Anderson; two *s.* one *d.* *Educ.:* Alleyns Coll.; London Univ.; King's Coll. Hosp.; Freiburg University. Medical Tutor, Morbid Anatomist, Physician, King's College Hospital, S.E.5; University of London Post-Graduate Travelling Fellowship, 1933-34. Hons. degree London University. Examiner in Medicine in Conjoint Board, London University and Society of Apothecaries; late Harveian Librarian, Royal Coll. of Physicians, London. *Publications:* Various on blood diseases and endocrine diseases in English and German journals. *Recreation:* scientific progress. *Address:* 105 Dulwich Village, S.E.21. *T.:* Gipsy Hill 0440; 152 Harley Street, W.1. *T.:* Welbeck 0444. [*Died* 29 *Nov.* 1959.

GILZEAN, Andrew, O.B.E., 1945; D.L., J.P.; *b.* 3 Dec. 1877; *m.* 1904, Annie Thomson; three *d.* *Educ.:* St. Leonard's School, Edinburgh. Member of Edinburgh Town Council, 1924-45. Curator of Patronage, University of Edinburgh, 1934-45. M.P. (Lab.) Central Edinburgh, 1945-51. Served with R.A., 1916-19. *Recreation:* reading. *Address:* 4 Bernard Terrace, Edinburgh 8. *T.:* Edinburgh 43771. [*Died* 6 *July* 1957.

GIMBLETT, Charles Leonard, F.R.C.S. (Eng.); Senior Surgeon, Moorfields, Westminster and Central Eye Hospital since 1947; War and Victory Medals (World War I); *b.* 19 June 1890; *o. s.* of Robert Wheddon Gimblett and Emmeline Ella (*née* Rawle), Somerset; *m.* 1935, Audreen Isobel McKenzie, *d.* of Duncan McNicol; two *s.* *Educ.:* Clifton College; Gonville and Caius College, Cambridge; St. Thomas's Hospital. M.A., M.D. Camb., M.R.C.P. Lond. 1919; F.R.C.S. Eng. 1922. European War, 1914-18: Temp. Surgeon, R.N., in med. charge of H.M.S. A.M.C. Morea; Ophthalmic Surgeon R.N. Hosps., Portland and Chatham. Ophthalmic Surgeon Schools, East Ham Co. Boro', 1919-1927; Hon. Asst. Surgeon, Roy. Westminster Ophth. Hosp., 1923; Hon. Ophth. Surgeon: Roy. Northern Hosp., 1923-27; Assoc. Retired Naval Officers, 1929; Hon. Surgeon, Roy. Westminster Ophth. Hosp., 1927; Hon. Ophth. Surgeon: Lord Mayor Treloar's Hosp., Cripples' Hosp., Alton, Hampshire, 1937; War of 1939-45: E.M.S. Hosp. Haymeads, Bishop's Stortford. Ophth. Surgeon, Gen. Hosp. Bishop's Stortford, 1940; Ophth. Consultant, Nat. Health Service, 1946. Certified teacher in Ophthalmology, London Univ. *Publications:* Report on Myopia in School Children in the County Borough of East Ham, 1920-26; Chapter on Eye Disease in Romanis' and Mitchiner's Textbook of Surgery. *Recreations:* literary (medieval art); sailing. *Address:* Grogport House, Argyllshire; 12 Devonshire Place, Wimpole Street, W.1. *T.:* Welbeck 1763. *Club:* Royal Automobile. [*Died* 21 *Jan.* 1957.

GINNER, Charles, C.B.E. 1950; A.R.A. 1942; R.O.I.; R.W.S. 1945 (A.R.W.S. 1938); *s.* of I. B. Ginner, Ore, Hastings; *b.* Cannes, Alpes Maritimes, 4 March 1878. *Educ.:* College Stanislas, Cannes. Studied painting in Paris; settled in London, 1910; works in Tate Gallery, Manchester Art Gallery, Victoria and Albert Museum, Leeds City Art Gallery, Birmingham Art Gallery, Pietermaritsburg, South Africa, and Belfast Art Gallery; member of London Group. *Address:* 66 Claverton Street, Pimlico, S.W.1. [*Died* 6 *Jan.* 1952.

GIRDWOOD, Brig. Gen. Austin Claude, C.B. 1927; C.M.G. 1919; D.S.O. 1900 (Bar 1917); late Northumberland Fusiliers; *b.* 24 April 1875; *er. s.* of late John Girdwood, J.P., Binstead, Isle of Wight; *m.* 1903, Constance Elizabeth, 2nd *d.* of late S. Adshead of Prestbury, Cheshire. *Educ.:* privately. 4th Bn. Cheshire Regt. (Militia) 1894; entered Army, 1896; Captain 1900; p.s.c.; served Soudan, 1898, present at battle of Khartoum (British medal, Khedive's medal with clasp); South Africa, 1899-1902, including the battles of Belmont, Graspan, Modder River; operations in Orange Free State, 1900; operations in Transvaal, 1900-1902 (severely wounded, despatches twice, D.S.O., Queen's medal with 4 clasps, King's medal and clasps); North West Frontier, 1908 (Mohmand Expedition, medal and clasp); European War, 1914-18 (bar to D.S.O., Bt. Lt.-Col., Bt. Col., Croix de Guerre and C.M.G., despatches 6 times); G.S.O. 48th and 32nd Division; Commanded 11th Border Regt. 1916-17; 96th Infantry Brig., 1917-19; Assist. Comdt. Royal Military Coll., 1919-23; commanded 158th (Royal Welch) Infantry Brigade, 1924-27; O.C. Troops, Ceylon, 1927-31; retired, 1931. *Recreations:* golf, shooting, and fishing. *Address:* 30 Albert Court, Kensington Gore, S.W.7. *Club:* Bath. [*Died* 13 *March* 1951.

GIRLING, William Henry, O.B.E. 1948; *b.* Islington, 2 Apr. 1872; *m.* 1893, Henrietta Walker, O.B.E., J.P.; four *s.* six *d.* Has spent over 50 active years in Labour Movement and in public work; member Shoreditch Borough Council for 45 years; 4 times Mayor of Shoreditch; first Freeman of Shoreditch, 1948; Hon. Sec., Shoreditch Trades Council for 44 years; Clerk to Trustees of United Charities of St. Leonard, Shoreditch 1940-. Appointed Metropolitan Water Board, 1920; Vice-Chairman, 1946; Chairman, 1948-53. *Address:* 15 Newton Grove, N.1. [*Died* 1 *Oct.* 1958.

GIRTIN, Thomas, M.A.; D.Litt. (Hon); retired metallurgist; *b.* 27 Dec. 1874; *s.* of George Wyndham Girtin; *m.* 1910, Sabina Cooper (*d.* 1959); one *s.* *Educ.:* Highgate Sch.; Pembroke Coll., Cambridge. M.A. 1896. Director: Johnson Matthey & Co. Ltd., 1920-54; Johnson & Sons, Smelting Works Ltd., 1930-55 (Chm.). Fell. Inst. Metallurgists. Master Worshipful Co. of Clothworkers, 1940; a Governor of Girton Coll., Cambridge, 1941-53. Member: Council and Exec. Cttee., City and Guilds Institute, 1941; Education Cttee., Roy. Soc. of Arts, 1943; Court, Univ. of Leeds, 1944; Council, Walpole Soc., 1918. Hon. D.Litt. Univ. of Leeds, 1953. *Publications:* (with C. F. Bell) John Robert Cozens, 1935 (Walpole Society); (with D. Loshak) The Art of Thomas Girtin, 1953. Various contributions to artistic publications. *Recreation:* study and research into English water-colour drawings. *Club:* Oxford and Cambridge University. [*Died* 7 *March* 1960.

GISBORNE, Henry Paterson, J.P. London; Solicitor (Senior Partner of Lewis & Lewis and Gisborne & Co., 10, 11, and 12 Ely Place, E.C.1); *b.* 11 Dec. 1888; *m.* 1st, Katherine Helen (*d.* 1925), *d.* of Sir William Noble; 2nd, 1928, Dorothy Mary, *d.* of late Henry Pratt, Chesford Grange, Kenilworth, Warwickshire; two *d.* Solicitor, 1912; served European War, 1916-18, Lieut. Duke of Wellington's (West Riding) Regt.; contested Scarborough and Whitby Division, 1929. *Address:* 5 Abingdon Court, Kensington, W.8. *T.:* Western 3336. *T.A.:* Justipeace, London; Henfield Place, Henfield, Sussex. *T.:* Henfield 26. *Clubs:* Garrick, Royal Thames Yacht, City Livery. [*Died* 8 *Aug.* 1953.

GISBOROUGH 2nd Baron, *cr.* 1917; **Thomas Weston Peel Long Chaloner;** B.A., J.P., T.D.; *b.* 6 May 1889; *o. surv. s.* of 1st Baron Gisborough, who was 2nd *s.* of late Richard Penruddocke Long, M.P., of Rood Ashton and Wraxall, Wilts, and assumed by Royal licence, 1888, the surname of Chaloner, in lieu of his patronymic (under the will of his maternal granduncle, Admiral Thomas Chaloner, C.B.); *S.* father, 1938; *m.* 1923, Esther Isabella Madeleine, *yr. d.* of late Charles O. Hall, Eddlethorpe; one *s.* one *d.* *Educ.:* Eton; Radley; Trinity College, Cambridge. Served R.F.C., European War, 1914-18, and War of 1939-45 in R.A.F.V.R. *Heir:* *s.* Hon. Thomas Richard John Long Chaloner, Lt. 16th Lancers [*b.* 1 July 1927. *Educ.:* Eton. Late Welsh Guards]. *Address:* Gisborough Hall, Cleveland, Yorks. *T.:* Guisborough, 2; Bowbrook House, Peopleton, Pershore, Worcestershire. [*Died* 11 *Feb.* 1951.

GIVEN, Brig. Thomas Frederick, D.S.O. 1940; O.B.E. 1950; M.C.; late East Yorkshire Regiment; *b.* 25 Jan. 1894; *s.* of Rev. Precentor H. W. S. Given; *m.* 1935, Kathleen Gwendoline Shaw; one *d.* *Educ.:* St. Columba's College, Rathfarnham; Trinity College, Dublin. Temp. 2nd Lt. Royal Irish Fusiliers, Sept. 1914; Temp. Capt., 1916; Lt. Royal Munster Fusiliers, 1920; transferred East Yorkshire Regt., 1922; Capt., 1923; Major, 1936; Acting Lt.-Col., 1940; Temp. Lt.-Col., 1940; served European War, France and Flanders, 1915-17 (wounded, despatches, M.C., 1914-1915 Star, General Service and Victory Medals); war of 1939-41, France and Belgium (D.S.O.); retired pay, 1946. Late Political Secretary, British Administration, Somalia. *Club:* Army and Navy. [*Died* 1 *Nov.* 1952.

GLANCY, Sir Bertrand James, G.C.I.E., *cr.* 1946 (K.C.I.E., *cr.* 1935; C.I.E. 1924); K.C.S.I., *cr.* 1940 (C.S.I. 1933); *b.* 31 Dec. 1882; *s.* of Colonel T. Glancy, R.E.; *m.* 1914, Grace Steele, C.St.J.; one *s.* *Educ.:* Clifton; Monmouth; Exeter College, Oxford. Indian Civil Service; Political Adviser to the Crown Representative, 1938-41; Governor of the Punjab, 1941-1946; Foreign and Political Department, Government of India. K.St.J. *Club:* East India and Sports. [*Died* 17 *March* 1953.

GLANVILLE, Mrs. Edythe Mary, C.B.E. 1926; LL.B.; *b.* 1876; *d.* of late Robert Kane; *m.* 1903, Frank Henry Glanville (*d.* 1938); one *s.* *Educ.:* Alexandra Coll., Dublin; Royal University of Ireland (B.A., Hons., 1896; LL.B., Hons. 1900). First Woman Vice-Chairman of Metropolitan Division of National Unionist Association, 1919-24; member of Executive Committee of National Union of Conservative and Unionist Associations, 1920-28. *Publications:* The Pinnacle, many short stories. *Recreations:* travelling and gardening. *Club:* Royal Commonwealth Society. [*Died* 13 *June* 1959.

GLANVILLE, James Edward; *b.* 1891. President of a miners' lodge for 25 years; member of executive of Durham Miners' Association. M.P. (Lab.) Consett Division of Durham, 1943-55 (returned unopposed, by-election). *Address:* 22 Gray's Terrace, Oxhill, Stanley, Co. Durham; Celtic Hotel, 62 Guilford Street, W.C.1. [*Died* 18 *Sept.* 1958.

GLANVILLE, Stephen Ranulph Kingdon, M.B.E.; M.A.; F.B.A.; F.S.A.; Provost of King's College, Cambridge, since 1954; Herbert Thompson Professor of Egyptology, University of Cambridge, since 1946; Honorary Fellow of Lincoln College, Oxford; *b.* Westminster, 26 Apr. 1900; *e. s.* of Stephen James Glanville and Elizabeth, *d.* of Francis Kingdon; *m.* 1925, Ethel Mary, *e. d.* of J. B. Chubb; two *d.* *Educ.:* Marlborough College; Lincoln College, Oxford (Modern History Scholar); Lit. Hum. and B.A., 1922; M.A., 1926. Assistant Master, Egyptian Government Service, 1922; member of Egypt Exploration Society's Expedition to Tell-el-Amarneh, 1923; Assistant in Department of Egyptian and Assyrian Antiquities, British Museum, 1924; Assistant Keeper, First Class, 1930; Reader in (1933-35), and Edwards Prof. of, Egyptology in the Univ. of London (University College), 1935-46; Fellow of King's College, Cambridge, 1946-54; excavated at el-Amarneh, 1925, and Armant, 1928, for Egypt Exploration Society; Hon. Secretary, Egypt Exploration Society, 1928-1931 and 1933-36, Chairman of Committee since 1951; Laycock Student of Egyptology at Worcester Coll., Oxford, 1929-35; delivered Royal Institution's Christmas Lectures for Children, 1929; Guest-lecturer of the National Council of Education, Canada, 1932. Served R.A.F. (Air Staff), War of 1939-45 (M.B.E.; Czechoslovak Order of the White Lion, Fourth Class, and War Cross; Order of Orange Nassau, with Swords, Fourth Class; Yugo-slav Order of the Crown, Fifth Class). *Publications:* The Mural Painting of El-Amarneh (with N. de G. Davies, H. Frankfort, and T. Whittemore), 1929; a chapter in Great Ones of Ancient Egypt (Portraits by Winifred Brunton), 1929; Daily Life in Ancient Egypt, 1930; Bible Illustrations (with H. R. Hall and Sidney Smith) in Helps to Study of the Bible, 1931; edited Studies Presented to F. Ll. Griffith, 1932; The Egyptians, 1933; Catalogue of Demotic Papyri in the British Museum I; A Theban Archive of the Reign of Ptolemy, vol. I. Soter, 1939; edited Legacy of Egypt, 1942; The Growth and Nature of Egyptology, 1947; Notes on a demotic papyrus from Thebes (B.M. 10026) in Essays and Studies presented to Stanley Arthur Cook, 1950; Catalogue of Demotic Papyri in the British Museum, vol. II; The Instructions of 'Onchsheshougy, Part 1, 1955; papers and articles. *Address:* King's College, Cambridge. *T.:* Cambridge 4411. *Clubs:* Athenæum, Sette of Odd Volumes. [*Died* 26 *April* 1956.

GLASGOW, Edwin; Keeper and Secretary, National Gallery, 1933-35; *b.* 5 Dec. 1874; *s.* of Robert James Glasgow; *m.* Eva Cecilia (*d.* 1940), *d.* of Rev. R. Postance, Liverpool; one *s.* two. *d.* *Educ.:* University College, Liverpool; Wadham College, Oxford. Sixth Form Master, Forest School; H.M.I., Northumberland, Warwickshire; seconded for educational work in Gibraltar; exhibitor R.A., R.I., Salon, etc.; works in Public Galleries, Newcastle on Tyne, Cheltenham, and abroad. *Publications:* Sketches of Wadham and Magdalen Colleges, Oxford; Report on Educational System of Gibraltar; The Painter's Eye, 1936. *Address:* Charlbury, Oxford. *T.:* Charlbury 49. [*Died* 6 *May* 1955.

GLASGOW, George, B.A.; author of the Foreign Affairs section of the Contemporary Review, 1923-55; regular contributor to Catholic Times since 1942; former contributor to the Queen's Quarterly, Canada, and Fortnightly Review, London; *b.* Bolton, 18 Aug. 1891; *s.* of Thomas Glasgow; *m.* 1937, Una Geraldine, *d.* of late Dr. C. J. Ridgeway, Bishop of Chichester. *Educ.:* Bolton School; Hulme Hall, Victoria University, Manchester (Seaton Scholar, Oliver Heywood Scholar). Sub-editor of Dr. R. W. Seton-Watson's The New Europe, 1916-20; diplomatic correspondent to the Observer, 1920-42; special correspondent in foreign affairs to the Manchester Guardian, 1920-1928; correspondent to l'Europe Nouvelle, Paris, 1920-26; correspondent to the Prager Presse, 1921-38; received with his wife into Roman Catholic Church, 1939. *Publications:* Archæology: The Minoans, 1923; Biography: Ronald Burrows, 1924; International Diplomacy and Politics: MacDonald as Diplomatist, 1924; From Dawes to Locarno, 1925 (New York, 1926); General Strikes and Road Transport, 1926, Continental Statesmen, 1930; Peace with Gangsters?, 1939; Diplomacy and God, 1941; Child of Terror, 1958; International Finance: The Dupe as Hero (under pen-name Logistes), 1930; edited, with introduction, The End of Reparations by Hjalmar Schacht, 1931; Pure Finance: The English Investment Trust Companies, 1930 (New York, 1931); The Scottish Investment Trust Companies, 1932; Glasgow's Guide to Investment Trust Companies, 1935; contributions to European and American journals, Ency. Brit., etc. *Address:* 54 Broadstairs Road, Broadstairs, Kent. *T.:* Thanet 61279. [*Died* 12 *July* 1958.

GLASGOW, Maj.-Gen. Hon. Sir (Thomas) William, K.C.B., *cr.* 1919 (C.B. 1918); C.M.G. 1916; D.S.O. 1900; V.D.; Hon. LL.D. Univ. of Manitoba, 1942; former High Commissioner for Commonwealth of Australia in Canada; *b.* Tiaro, Qld., 6 June 1876; *s.* of late Samuel Glasgow, Gympie; *m.* 1904, Annie Isabel, *e. d.* of Jacob Strumm. *Educ.:* Maryborough Grammar School. Served S. Africa, Queensland Mounted Infantry, 1899-1900 (despatches, Queen's Medal, 5 clasps, D.S.O.); European War, A.I.F. 1914-19 (C.M.G., C.B., Legion of Honour, Croix de Guerre avec palme). Senator for Queensland, 1920-32; Minister for Home and Territories, 1926-27; Minister for Defence, 1927-29. *Address:* Neulans Rd., Indooroopilly, Qld. [*Died* 4 *July* 1955.

GLAZEBROOK, William Rimington; *b.* West Derby, Liverpool, 18 July 1864; *s.* of Dr N. S. Glazebrook; *m. d.* of late S. Field, Liverpool; four *s.* *Educ.:* Mostyn House, Parkgate, Cheshire. Retired Cotton Merchant; President of Liverpool Cotton Association, 1916; late Dir. Royal Insurance, Ltd.; Liverpool and London and Globe Insurance Co.; Martins Bank, Ltd.; Sheriff of Denbighshire, 1940. *Address:* Manley Hall, Erbistock, Ruabon, Denbighshire: The Lydiate, Willaston, Wirral, Cheshire. *T.:* Willaston 118. [*Died* 28 *June* 1954.

GLEESON, Most Rev. Edmund, D.D., C.SS.R.; Bishop of Maitland (R.C.), since 1932; *b.* near Cashel, Co. Tipperary, 1869. *Educ.:* Rockwell College; St. Patrick's, Thurles. Ordained, 1893; secular priest of the diocese of Maitland (N.S.W.) till 1904, when he entered the Redemptorist Noviciate, Dundalk; Redemptorist in Australia since 1912; Coadjutor to the Bishop of Maitland and consecrated titular Bishop of Vatarba, 1929; Editor of "Emmaus" (Clerical Quarterly); Assistant at Papal Throne, 1943. *Publication:* Eucharistic Hours. *Address:* Bishop's House, Maitland, N.S.W., Australia. [*Died* 4 *March* 1956.

GLEN-COATS, Sir Thomas C. G.; *see* Coats.

GLENDAY, Roy Gonçalves, M.C. 1916; M.A., LL.B.; *b.* 13 July 1889; *s.* of Alexander and Marie Glenday; *m.* 1924, Pamela Isabel Frances Rogers; one *d.* *Educ.:* Brighton College; Emmanuel College, Cambridge. 1st and 2nd Part Natural Science Tripos, Part II Law Tripos, M.A., LL.B.; Chief Research Chemist Magadi Soda Company, Kenya Colony, 1913-15; European War, 1914-18, Lt. 3rd King's African Rifles (despatches, M.C.); called to Bar, Middle Temple, 1918; joined Staff Federation of British Industries, 1918. Retired as Economic Director Federation of British Industries. *Publications:* Passing of Free Trade, 1930; Economic Consequences of Progress, 1933; The Future of Economic Society, 1944; papers and articles on Business Forecasting and Allied economic subjects. *Recreations:* ski-ing, cooking and golf. *Address:* Flat 8, 69 Onslow Square, S.W.7. *T.:* Kensington 0714. *Clubs:* United University, Athenæum. [*Died* 24 *Aug.* 1957.

GLOVER, Sir (Edward) Otho, Kt., *cr.* 1951; Chairman Cheshire County Council since 1948; Chairman, Group XIV, Liverpool Regional Hosp. Board; *b.* 28 Oct. 1876; 2nd *s.* of Walter Twiss Glover and Margaret Glover; *m.* 1906, Minnie Mary Heyder; one *s.* three *d.* (and *e. s.* and 2nd *s.* killed on active service, 1939 and 1941). *Educ.:* Shrewsbury; Liverpool University. Technical staff Castner Kellner Alkali Co. Ltd., 1897-1926; I.C.I. Ltd., 1926-39, as delegate director of General Chemical Group. A.M.I.E.E., 1915; C.C., 1928; C.A., 1940; Chairman Liverpool Consumption Hospital Bd. until 1948; a Governor of The Police College; member of The Northwich Salt Compensation Board. *Recreation:* golf (Capt. Roy. Liverpool Golf Club, Hoylake, 1939-45). *Address:* The Bent, Frodsham, Cheshire. *T.:* 3257 Frodsham. *Club:* Royal Liverpool Golf (Hoylake). [*Died* 21 *Nov.* 1956.

GLOVER, Colonel William Reid, C.M.G. 1919; D.S.O. 1917; T.D.; J.P.; late London Regt.; Hon. Colonel 8th Bn. Royal Fusiliers (City of London Regiment) since 1947; *b.* 1882; *e. s.* of late Richard Thomas Glover; *m.* 1936, May, *d.* of late John Waghorn, and *widow* of Lt.-Comdr. Hardinge Shephard, R.N. *Educ.:* Uppingham. Formerly Lt.-Col. 1st Bn. London Regt. (Roy. Fusiliers); late Col. T.A. R. of O. Served European War, 1914-17 (despatches thrice, D.S.O., C.M.G., 1914-15 star, two medals). Master of Haberdashers' Company, 1949-50. *Address:* 42 Montpelier Street, Knightsbridge, S.W.7. *T.:* Kensington 1639; Soal Farm, Petersfield, Hants. [*Died* 25 *Aug.* 1959.

GLUCKSTEIN, Major Montague, O.B.E. 1917; President of J. Lyons & Co. Ltd. (Chairman, 1950-56); Director, Strand Hotels, Ltd.; *b.* 13 Oct. 1886; *m.* 1910, Hannah Joseph; one *s.* one *d.* *Educ.:* City of London. Hon. Catering Adviser to Ministry of Food, 1939-48. Director, Alliance Assurance Co. Ltd., 1950-58. *Address:* Woodsmill House, Henfield, Sussex. *T.:* Henfield 186. *Club:* Royal Automobile. [*Died* 25 *Dec.* 1958.

GLUCKSTEIN, Sir Samuel, Kt., *cr.* 1933; partner in firm of Bartlett & Gluckstein, Solicitors; *b.* 28 Sept. 1880; *s.* of Isidore Gluckstein and Rose Cohen; *m.* 1909, Julia (*d.* 1956), *d.* of Samuel Joseph; no *c.* *Educ.:* City of London School; privately. Hon. LL.D. (Lond.). Member Westminster City Council since 1906; Alderman since 1924; Mayor, 1920-21; Hon. Freeman City of Westminster, 1953. Member of the Metropolitan Boroughs Standing Joint Committee, 1924-32; Chairman, 1931; Vice-Chairman Abbey Division of Westminster Constitutional Association, 1923-27, and Chairman, 1927-54; Member of London County Council for Abbey Division, 1929-49, Chairman of Finance Committee 1932-34, Deputy Chairman, 1939-40; Past Chairman Court of the Univ. of London, Deputy Chairman, 1939; contested Devonport, 1924 and 1929; North Hammersmith, 1926. Commander of the Order of Leopold; Coronation Medal. *Address:* 24 Abbey Lodge, Regent's Park, N.W.8. *T.:* Ambassador 0654. *Club:* Athenæum. [*Died* 19 *Aug.* 1958.

GLYN, 1st Baron, *cr.* 1953, of Farnborough, Berks; **Ralph George Campbell Glyn,** Bt., *cr.* 1934; M.C.; late Rifle Brigade; High Steward of Wallingford since 1933; Vice-Lieutenant, Berkshire, since 1957; *s.* of late Rt. Reverend Hon. Edward Carr Glyn and Lady Mary, *d.* of 8th Duke of Argyll; *b.* 3 March 1885; *m.* 1921, Sibell (*d.* 1958), *widow* of Brig.-Gen. Walter Long, C.M.G., and *d.* of 2nd Lord Derwent. *Educ.:* Wixenford; Harrow; Royal Military College, Sandhurst. Joined the Rifle Brigade, 1904; contested Moray and Nairn, S. Edinburgh (by-election), and College Division of Glasgow during 1910; M.P. (Co. U.) Clackmannan and East Stirlingshire, 1918-22, (U.) Abingdon Division of Berks., 1924-53; Parliamentary Private Secretary to Prime Minister, 1931-35, and Lord Pres. of the Council, 1935-37. Served European War in France, Dardanelles, Balkans (Legion of Honour, White Eagle, and St. Anne); formerly Director, L.M.S. Railway; British Match Corporation; Director J. Samuel White & Co., Ltd. *Recreations:* shooting and fishing. *Address:* 120 Wigmore Street, W.1. *T.:* Welbeck 9090; Coombe Lodge, Farnborough, Wantage, Berkshire. *T.:* Chaddleworth 341. *Clubs:* Carlton, Beefsteak. [*Died* 1 *May* 1960 (*ext.*).

GLYN, Sir Richard Fitzgerald, 4th Bt., *cr.* 1800, and 8th Bt., *cr.* 1759; D.S.O. 1916; *b.* 13 May 1875; *s.* of 3rd Bt. and Frances, *d.* of Major Fitzgerald, Maperton House, Somerset; *S.* father, 1918 and kinsman, 1942; *m.* 1906, Edith Hilda, (*d.* 1957), *e. d.* of D. G. Hamilton-Gordon; two *s.* two *d.* Served S. Africa, Royal Dragoons, 1899-1902; European War, 1914-18 (despatches twice); Chevalier, Legion of Honour. *Heir: s.* Col. Richard Hamilton Glyn, O.B.E. *Address:* Crab House, Colehill, Wimborne, Dorset. *T.:* Wimborne 234. [*Died* 23 *March* 1960.

GLYNN, Sir Joseph (Aloysius), Kt., *cr.* 1915; K.C.S.G. 1943; *b.* 12 April 1869; *s.* of John M'Mahon Glynn of Gort, Co. Galway; *m.* 1st, 1894, Bride (*d.* 1921), *d.* of John O'Neil Donnellon, Riverview, Ballinrobe, Co. Mayo; four *s.*; 2nd, 1923, Kate, *y. d.* of said John O'Neil Donnellon. *Educ.:* Blackrock Coll., Co. Dublin. Royal Univ. of Ireland (B.A. and Gold Medallist). Solicitor, 1891; LL.D. (hon.) National University, Ireland, 1929; Member Galway Co. Council, 1899-1912; Chairman, 1902-12; Chairman Irish

Insurance Commissioners, 1911-33. *Publications:* Life of Matt Talbot; has written several historical and other pamphlets for Irish Catholic Truth Society. *Address:* St. Jarlaths, Ailesbury Road, Dublin. *T.:* 63073. [*Died* 7 *March* 1951.

GNIEN IS-SULTAN, Paul Nicholas Apap-Pace-Bologna, 5th Marquis of, an Hereditary Knight of the Roman Empire and a Roman Patrician; a Knight of Malta; *b.* 1880; *e. s.* of 4th Marquis of Gnien Is-Sultan and of the Noble Maria Carmela de Conti Manduca; *m.* 1st, 1899, the Noble Teresa de Piro d'Amico Inguanez, four *s.* one *d.*; 2nd, 1922, The Noble Giuseppina Caruana Gatto, *d.* of 3rd Count of Beberrua; one *d.* *Educ.:* St. Ignatius' Coll., Malta; Gozo Seminary; private tuition. A member of and Honorary Secretary to Committee of Privileges of Maltese Nobility, 1902-7; President Cttee. of Privileges, 1908-09, 1919-27, and since 1948. Vice-President of the Malta Senate, and Representative of the Maltese Nobility, recognised by the Crown, 1921-27; Hon. President of the M.S.A.M. and C.; President of the Conservartorio V. Bugeja; President of the branch of the Society St. Vincent de Paul for Attard, Balzen and Lia, Malta. Elected several times Pres. Malta Agrarian Soc. (formerly Società Economica Agraria), re-elected, 1950, 1952. *Heir:* *g.s.* John Anthony, Marchesino of Gnien Is-Sultan (who has now succeeded as 6th Marquis), *b.* 1935. *Address:* Villa Apap-Bologna, Malta. *Club:* Maltese (Valetta, Malta). [*Died* 9 *Oct.* 1955.

GOAD, Harold Elsdale, O.B.E.; *b.* 1878; *o. s.* of Capt. F. T. Goad (Seaforths, killed in action, Afghanistan, 1878), and of Catherine Elsdale. *Educ.:* Harrow; Trinity College, Oxford. B.A. 2nd Class Hon. History, 1900; M.A. 1904; travelled in Italy and Eastern Europe; literature, occasional journalism and social work; founded industrial schools in Assisi, Italy, 1902; rejected for Army, 1914, 1915; lectured in U.S.A. for French Hospitals and founded American Fund for French Wounded; enlisted, 1915 (passed for Home Service only); Interpreter for Modern Greek; Salonika, 1916; British liaison officer with Italian Army in the Balkans, Turkey and Albania, 1916-20 (Capt. and G.S.O. 3, despatches twice, Italian War Cross and Silver Medal for Military Valour, O.B.E., Commander Crown of Italy); Reader in Italian, London University, 1920-22; Hon. Director, British Institute of Florence, 1922-39; started institute in Milan 1937, in Rome 1938. *Publications:* The Blind Prophet (verse), 1903; The Kingdom (novel), 1913; Franciscan Italy, 1926; The Making of the Corporate State, 1932; Greyfriars, 1947; many articles in reviews, Fortnightly, Contemporary, etc. *Address:* Mirabello, Fiesole, Florence. *Clubs:* Athenæum, Royal Inst. International Affairs; Leonardo da Vinci (Florence). [*Died* 26 *May* 1956.

GOADBY, Sir Kenneth (Weldon), K.B.E., *cr.* 1918; Hon. Vice-President, late President, Scientific Film Association; late Medical Referee for Industrial Poisoning, County of London (1913); Member Medical Advisory Committee, Ministry of Mines; late Lecturer on Bacteriology, National Dental Hospital, from 1904; late Lecturer on Oral Hygiene, London School of Tropical Medicine; *b.* Gravesend, 7 March 1873; *s.* of Rev. J. J. Goadby; *m.* 1898, Constance Eva, *d.* of G. Olding; one *s.* *Educ.:* Grammar School, Henley-on-Thames; University Extension College, Reading; Guy's Hospital. Studied Bacteriology and Bacteriological Research, Guy's Hospital, 1899-1902; investigated Operation of Phosphorus Rules for Match Factories for H.M.'s Home Office; investigated Causes and Pathology of Lead Poisoning (Departmental Committee Home Office); since engaged in Bacteriological and Pathological Research, Investigation of Lead Poisoning in Industrial Processes, and Pathology and Bacteriology of Diseases of the Mouth and Upper Air-Passages; and Rheumatoid Arthritis; Erasmus Wilson Lecturer R.C. Surgeons, 1907, and Hunterian Professor in 1911; Hon. Bacteriological Specialist for Vaccine Therapy, Royal Herbert Hospital, Woolwich (during War); Member of War Office Committee for the Study of Tetanus; Represented Medical Science on Advisory Committee to Secretary of State for Mines (Metalliferous Mines). *Publications:* Mycology of the Mouth, a text-book of Oral Bacteria; The Vaccine Treatment of Pyorrhœa Alveolaris; The Relation of Diseases of the Mouth to Rheumatism; Report to the Home Office on the Working of Special Rules in Force in Match Factories; Lead Absorption and Lead Poisoning; Manual of Industrial Lead Poisoning (with T. M. Legge); Text-Book on Diseases of Mouth and Oral Mucous Membrane, third edition, 1927; papers to scientific journals. *Recreations:* golf, motoring. *Address:* 148 Harley Street, W.1. *Club:* Athenæum. [*Died* 10 *Aug.* 1958.

GODBOUT, Hon. Joseph Adélard, B.A., B.A.S., D.A.Sc., D.L.; *b.* St. Eloi, Temiscouata County, 24 Sept. 1892; *s.* of Eugène Godbout, farmer, ex-Member for Temiscouata, Quebec Parliament, and of Marie-Louise Duret; *m.* 1923, Marie-Dorilda Fortin, L'Islet; two *s.* three *d.* *Educ.:* Rimouski Seminary, Quebec (B.A. 1913); Ste. Anne de la Pocatière Agricultural College (B.A.S. 1918); Massachusetts State College, Amherst, Mass. D.A.Sc. Laval University, Quebec, 1930; Hon. LL.D. Bishop University, Lennoxville, 1941, McGill Univ., Montreal, 1940, Massachusetts State College, Amherst, Mass., 1943; Hon. D. en Méd. Vét., Montreal Univ., 1940; Professor at Ste. Anne Agricultural College, 1918-29; Agronomist for county of L'Islet, 1922-25; M.L.A. Quebec, 1929-36 and since 1939; Minister of Agriculture, Quebec, 1930-36; Prime Minister, Minister of Agriculture and Minister of Colonisation, Quebec, 1936; Prime Minister of Province of Quebec, 1939-44; Leader of Liberal Opposition, 1944-48; appointed to Senate of Canada, 1949; Member of Knights of Columbus; President of Canadian Society of Technical Agriculturists, 1933; Member Canadian General Council of Boy Scouts' Association; Hon. President Canadian Ayrshire Breeders' Association; Hon. President League of Nations (Quebec Div.); Patron Navy League of Canada; Hon. Prof. at Agricultural Faculty, Laval Univ., 1940; Commander of L'Ordre du Mérite Agricole of Province of Quebec: Commander of L'Ordre du Mérite Agricole de France. *Recreation:* owns a model farm at Frelighsburg, Missisquoi County. *Address:* The Senate, Ottawa, Canada; Frelighsburg, Missisquoi County, Canada. *Clubs:* University, Reform, Press, Garrison (Quebec); Mount Stephen (Montreal). [*Died* 18 *Sept.* 1956.

GODBY, Col. (Brig.-Gen.) Charles, C.B. 1918; C.M.G. 1917; D.S.O. 1917; Surrey County Councillor, since 1934; Chief Engineer, 1915-1919; *b.* 31 Oct. 1863; *m.* 1895, Emmeline Hawtrey Sara Hamilton-Jones (*d.* 1926) of Moneyglass, Co. Antrim; one *s.* four *d.* Lieut. R.E. 1882; Colonel 1911; served Sudan, 1885 (medal 2 clasps, bronze star); Sudan, 1889 (clasp, 4th Class Mejidieh); European War, France (C.B., C.M.G., D.S.O.). *Address:* Rowledge, Farnham, Surrey. [*Died* 31 *Jan.* 1956.

GODDARD, Alexander, C.B.E. 1918; Secretary to Chartered Surveyors' Institution, Westminster, 1905-32; *b.* 1867; 2nd *s.* of late J. Goddard, J.P., the Manor House, Newton Harcourt, Leicester; *m.* 1901, Ellen Henrietta (*d.* 1946), *d.* of late S. E. Illingworth, J.P., Borough Court, Hampshire; two *d.* *Educ.:* Haileybury College; Royal Agricultural Coll., Cirencester (Ducie Gold Medal and Diploma). Inspector Board of Agriculture, 1893; Private Secretary to President R. W. Hanbury, 1901-2, and Earl of Onslow, 1902-5; Hon. Secretary Agricultural Consultative Committee, 1914-15, Agricultural

Policy Committee, 1916-17, Professional Classes War Relief Council, 1914-21; Secretary, Royal Commission on Agriculture, 1919; member of National Agricultural Council for England since 1921; Governor Royal Agricultural College, Cirencester, and College of Estate Management, Lincoln's Inn Fields; Member Diocesan Board of Finance; High Bailiff, Northleach Court Leet. *Publications:* Reports and Papers on Agricultural and Cognate Subjects. *Address:* Norfolk Court Hotel, Belsize Grove, N.W.3. [*Died* 12 *Dec.* 1956.

GODDARD, Brig.-Gen. Henry Arthur, C.M.G. 1919; D.S.O 1918; V.D., J.P.; retired list, Commonwealth Military Forces; *b.* 13 Dec. 1871; *m.* 1897, Maud, *d.* of late E. Morrow; one *s.* one *d.* Served European War, 1915-18 (despatches, D.S.O., Croix de Guerre); commanded: 17th Bn. A.I.F., Egypt, Gallipoli, 1915-16; 35th Bn., France, 1916-18; commanding 9th Australian Infantry Brig., 1918; commanded 14th Infantry Brigade, Hon. Colonel 17th and 35th Battalion Australian Infantry. *Clubs:* Imperial Service (Sydney); Brisbane (Brisbane). [*Died* 24 *Oct.* 1955.

GODDARD, Sir (Joseph) Holland, Kt., *cr.* 1949; President, Wadkin Ltd., Green Lane Works, North Evington, Leicester. Past-Pres. Machine Tool Trades Association. *Address:* Highgrove, Stoughton Drive South, Leicester. [*Died* 30 *Jan.* 1958.

GODFREY, Ernest Henry, F.S.S.; *b.* Northampton, 17 July 1862; *s.* of Valentine and Charlotte Godfrey, Glaston, Rutland; *m.* 1894, Emmeline Stuart (*d.* 1945), *d.* of Frederick Lindesay, D.L., J.P., Loughry, Co. Tyrone; two *s.* one *d.* *Educ.:* Northampton Grammar Sch., Committee Clerk, Royal Agricultural Society of England, 1887-98; Secretary Central and Associated Chambers of Agriculture, 1898-1901; Assistant Editor Royal Agricultural Society of England, and Secretary National Agricultural Examination Board, 1901-07; Editor Society's Journal, 1905-6; Editor Census and Statistics Office, Canada, 1907-20; Editor Canada Year Book, 1912-19; Chief, Agricultural Branch, Dominion Bureau of Statistics, Canada, 1920-1928; Assistant Secretary Agricultural Sub-Committee, Royal Commission for Paris Exhibition, 1900; Member International Statistical Inst., 1910, and Delegate of Canadian Government to 14th Session, Vienna, 1913; attended 19th Session of Inst., Tokyo, 1930, travelling round the world, and Jubilee Session, London, 1934; Member Comm. on Official Statistics of Canada, 1912; Delegate of Canada to Br. Empire Statistical Conf., 1920. *Publications:* The Lindesays of Loughry, County Tyrone: A Genealogical History, 1949. Contributions to agricultural and economic literature. *Recreations:* gardening, chess. *Address:* St. Peter's Vicarage, Bishopsford Road, Morden, Surrey. *T.:* Mitcham 3792. [*Died* 22 *Sept.* 1952.

GODFREY, Robert Samuel, C.B.E. 1933; M.A.; F.S.A.; F.F.A.S.; Registered Architect; Surveyor and Clerk of the Works to the Dean and Chapter, Lincoln Cathedral; *b.* 23 Aug. 1876; *s.* of Samuel Godfrey and Elizabeth Key; *m.* 1st, 1872; one *d.*; 2nd, 1904, Mildred Eleanor, *d.* of Thomas Price. *Educ.:* Public School; Univ. College. Inaugurated the method of drilling of Ancient Buildings by compressed air and the improved method of grouting same under air pressure; first adopted for the special repairs of Lincoln Cathedral, 1922-32; advised on the repairs of many ancient and mediæval buildings at home and abroad. Hon. M.A. (Lambeth) 1952. *Publications:* a paper on the early history and the various disasters and restorations in the past of Lincoln Cathedral, 1929; Half-an-Hour at Lincoln Cathedral and the Special Repairs, 1931; The Romance of Lincoln Cathedral. *Address:* Priory Gate, Minster Yard, Lincoln. *T.:* 237. [*Died* 30 *March* 1953.

GODFREY, General Sir William Wellington, K.C.B., *cr.* 1939 (C.B. 1932); C.M.G. 1916; *b.* 2 April 1880; *s.* of George Godfrey, Newry, Co. Tyrone; *m.* 1904, Laura Beatrice, *er. d.* of Colonel S. M. Salaman, I.M.S.; one *s.* one *d.* *Educ.:* Dulwich College. 2nd Lieut. 1898; Lieut. 1899; Capt. 1907; Major 1916; Bt. Lieut.-Col. 1917; Lieut.-Col. 1927; Bt.-Col. 1930; Col. 1931; Col.-Comdt. 1933; Maj.-Gen. 1935; Lieut.-Gen. 1937; General, 1939; Adjt., 1906-9; served European War (Dardanelles), 1914-18 (despatches twice, C.M.G.); A.A.G., R.M. 1930-33; Col. Comdt. Portsmouth Division R.M. 1933-35; Adjutant-General R.M. 1936-39 and again in 1940; retired list, 1939; A.D.C. to the King, 1934-35; Hon. Col. Comdt. Plymouth Division R.M. 1940-49; Chevalier Legion of Honour, France; Order of Redeemer, Greece; Rising Sun, Japan. *Address:* Tavistock, Devon. *T.:* Tavistock 454. [*Died* 18 *May* 1952.

GODLEY, General Sir Alexander John, G.C.B., *cr.* 1928 (K.C.B., *cr.* 1916; C.B., 1910); K.C.M.G. *cr.* 1914; Grand Officier Légion d'Honneur, Grand Officer Crown of Belgium, Grand Officer White Eagle of Serbia; Gran Cruz Merito Militar of Spain; Grand Croix Ouissam Alaouîte and Gran Encomienda Mehdania of Morocco; French and Belgian Croix de Guerre; Colonel, Otago Mounted Rifles, and North Auckland Regiment of New Zealand and 13th (West Maitland) Regiment of Australia; *b.* 4 Feb. 1867; *e. s.* of late Col. W. A. Godley, 56th Regiment; *m.* 1898, Louisa Marion (*d.* 1939), *e. d.* of Robert Fowler, D.L., Rahinston, Co. Meath. *Educ.:* Royal Naval School; Haileybury; United Services College; Royal Military College, Sandhurst. Joined Royal Dublin Fusiliers, 1886; Adjt. R.D.F.; Adjt. Mounted Infantry, Aldershot; Adjt. Special Service battalion M.I., S. Africa, 1896 (despatches, medal, brevet of major); Staff College, 1898; Special Service S. Africa; 1899-1901; Adjt. Protectorate Regt. commanded Western Defences, Siege of Mafeking; Staff Officer to Gens. Baden-Powell and Plumer; commanded Rhodesian Brigade (despatches, medal with 3 clasps, brevet of lieut.-colonel); transferred to Irish Guards, 1900; Staff, Aldershot, 1901; commanding M.I. Aldershot till 1903; Commandant M.I. Longmoor, 1903-6; brevet of Colonel, 1905; Col. General Staff 2nd Division, 1906-10; Major-Gen. Imperial General Staff, and G.O.C., New Zealand Forces, 1910-14 (K.C.M.G.); commanded Division and Army Corps, Dardanelles and Egypt, 1914-16; Army Corps in France, Belgium, and Germany, 1916-19, and the New Zealand Expeditionary Force throughout the War (despatches repeatedly, promotion to Lieut.-Gen., K.C.B.); Military Secretary to the Secretary of State for War, 1920-22; Commander-in-Chief, British Army of the Rhine, 1922-24; General Officer Commanding-in-Chief, Southern Command, 1924-28; A.D.C. General to the King, 1925-1929; Governor and Commander-in-Chief, Gibraltar, 1928-33; Colonel Royal Ulster Rifles, 1922-37; retired pay 1933. Master Staff College and Wolmer Hounds, and captained the R.D.F., M.I., and Irish Guards' polo teams. Late Chairman Royal Empire Soc.; Governor Haileybury and Imperial Service College. Commanded a platoon Home Guard, War of 1939-45. *Publications:* Life of an Irish Soldier, 1939; British Military History in S. America, 1942. *Address:* Boxford Mill House, Newbury. *T.:* Boxford 248. *Club:* Guards. [*Died* 6 *March* 1957.

GODLEY, Hon. Eveline Charlotte, F.R.Hist.S.; Fellow Royal Agricultural Society; 2nd *d.* of 1st Lord Kilbracken. *Educ.:* home. V.A.D. Sussex 72, 1914-18. *Publications:* The Great Condé, 1915; Charles XII. of Sweden, 1928; The Trial of Count Königsmarck, 1930; contributor to Dictionary of National Biography, Longman's Magazine and the National Review.

Address: Durrants Court, High Halden, Kent. *T.:* High Halden 210. [*Died* 16 *May* 1951.

GODMAN, Air Commodore Arthur Lowthian, C.M.G. 1919; D.S.O. 1918; J.P., D.L., late R.A.F.; *b.* 1877; *e. s.* of late Col. A. F. Godman, C.B.; *m.* 1908, Ivy Mary, *d.* of late Brig.-Gen. R. Bayard; D.S.O.; one *d.* (one *s.* killed in action, 1940). *Educ.:* Rugby. Joined the Green Howards, 1898; served with M.I. in Somaliland Expedition, 1904-5; European War as Staff Capt. 21st Infantry Brigade, and later on staff of R.F.C. and R.A.F. (C.M.G., D.S.O., despatches thrice); retired list, 1931; Commandant, Northern Area, Observer Corps, 1938-43. *Address*: Smeaton Manor, Northallerton, Yorkshire. *Clubs:* Army and Navy; Yorkshire (York). [*Died* 26 *July* 1956.

GODWIN, Lt.-Gen. Sir Charles Alexander Campbell, K.C.B. *cr.* 1930 (C.B. 1925); C.M.G. 1919; D.S.O. and bar, 1918; *b.* 28 Oct. 1873; *s.* of Colonel C. H. Y. Godwin and Grace Matilda Campbell; *m.* Catherine, O.B.E. 1935 (*d.* 1939), *e. d.* of Colonel V. Milward, M.P., D.L., and High Sheriff of Worcester; two *d. Educ.:* U.S. College, Westward Ho; Sandhurst. Entered Army, 1895, attached Suffolk and Welsh Regiments in Secunderabad, 1895; joined Madras Lancers. 1896; transferred to 3rd Punjab Cavalry) P.F.F., 1898; 1st Adjutant of and assisted to raise North Waziristan Militia, 1900; Mahsud Blockade, 1902 (medal and clasp); Adjutant 23rd Cavalry, 1902-07; Staff College, Quetta, 1908-09; Brigade Major, Cavalry Brigade, Meerut and G.S.O. II Mhow up to 1914; France, 1914-17 on Cavalry Brigade and Divisional Staff; commanded 6th Yeomanry Brigade; Dorset, Berks. and Bucks. Yeomanry in advance on Jerusalem, including actions of Elmughar, Abu-Shuseh; Brigadier-General, General Staff, Desert Mounted Troops in advance on Damascus and Aleppo, and after to North Force, Syria; returned to War Office, 1920 as G.S.O.1; commanded 5th Indian Cavalry Brigade and Secunderabad Garrison, 1921-23; Major-Gen. Cavalry A.H.Q., G.S. Branch, 1923-1927; Commandant, Staff College, Quetta, 1927; G.O.C. Peshawar District, 1927-30; retired 1932; Order of Nile, 3rd Class, El Nadha, 2nd Class; Croix de Guerre. *Recreations:* outdoor games and sports. *Address:* Lloyd's Bank, Cox and King's Branch, 6 Pall Mall, S.W.1. [*Died* 18 *July* 1951.

GOEHR, Walter; conductor and composer; *b.* 28 May 1903; *m.*; one *s. Educ.:* Berlin Acad. of Fine Arts (Scholar). Composer (pupil of Arnold Schönberg) of symphonic and chamber-music; musical director at many continental theatres; musical director of Columbia and His Master's Voice (gramophone companies); late Director of B.B.C. Theatre Orchestra; composer of many well-known films and conductor of symphonic concerts; has conducted in all European countries and in S. and Latin Amer.; has made many long-playing records of large symphonic works and operas (Grand Prix du Disques, 1954, for recording of own edn. of Monteverdi's opera, L'Incoronazione di Poppea); conducts normal symphonic repertoire; is a specialist in contemporary and 17th and 18th century music. *Publications:* own compositions of all types; editions of Monteverdi: Vespers of 1610, 1956; Purcell: Fantasias, 1955; Moussorgsky: Choral Scenes from Boris Godounov, 1956; contribs. to books and jls. on music (English and German). [*Died* 4 *Dec.* 1960.

GOGARTY, Col. Henry Edward, C.M.G. 1919; D.S.O. 1917; late Royal Scots Fusiliers, and Worcestershire Regt., retired pay, 1920; *b.* 1868; *m.* 1903, Grace (*d.* 1953), *d.* of late Lt.-Gen. J. Sargent, C.B. Served South African War, 1899-1901 (Queen's medal and six clasps; King's medal and two clasps, Bt. Major); European War, 1914-17 (despatches, D.S.O., C.M.G.). *Address:* c/o Lloyds Bank, Falmouth, Cornwall. [*Died* 13 *Oct.* 1955.

GOGARTY, Oliver St. John, M.D., F.R.C.S.I.; *b.* 17 Aug. 1878; *m.* 1906, Martha, *d.* of Bernard Duane, Ross Dhu, Co. Galway; two *s.* one *d. Educ.:* Stonyhurst; Trinity College, Dublin; Oxford. Senator, Irish Free State, 1922-36. *Publications:* An Offering of Swans, 1924; Poems and Plays, 1920; Hyperthuliana; Wild Apples, 1930; As I was going down Sackville Street, 1937; I Follow St. Patrick, 1938; Others to Adorn; Tumbling in the Hay, 1939; Going Native, 1941; Mr. Petunia, 1946; Intimations; Rolling down the Lea, 1950; Mourning became Mrs. Spendlove; Collected Poems, 1952; It Isn't This Time of Year at All!, 1954; Start from Somewhere Else. *Recreations:* archery and aviation. *Club:* St. James'. [*Died* 22 *Sept.* 1957.

GOLD, Sir Harcourt (Gilbey), Kt., *cr.* 1949; O.B.E. 1918; B.A.; President Henley Royal Regatta; *b.* 3 May 1876; *y. s.* of Henry Gold, J.P., D.L., and Charlotte Anne, *sister* of Sir Walter Gilbey, 1st Bt.; *m.* 1902, Helen Beatrice, *o. d.* of T. J. Maclagan, M.D.; one *s.* one *d.* (and one *d.* decd.). *Educ.:* Eton; Magdalen College, Oxford. Captain of Boats at Eton, 1895; President O.U.B.C. 1899. In the seven years, 1893-99, rowing as stroke won three Ladies Plates for Eton, three Varsity Boat Races, three Grand Challenge Cups and two Stewards Cups at Henley. Coached Oxford, Magdalen and Leander Crews—and winning Olympic Eights at Henley, 1908, and Stockholm, 1912. R.F.C. and R.A.F. 1915-19, Lt.-Col. Member London Stock Exchange. *Recreations:* shooting, golf. *Address:* 32 Sussex Square, W.2. *Clubs:* Bath, Sports, Leander. [*Died* 27 *July* 1952.

GOLDING, Louis, M.A. Oxon, F.R.S.L.; novelist, essayist, traveller, lecturer; *b.* Manchester, Nov. 1895; 3rd *s.* of Philip and Yetta Golding; *m.* 1956, Annie Wintrobe. *Educ.:* The Manchester Grammar School; Queen's Coll., Oxford. Has broadcast frequently and collaborated in original stories and scripts for films (Freedom Radio, Mr. Emmanuel, Theirs is the Glory, etc.). *Publications: fiction:* Forward from Babylon; Seacoast of Bohemia; Day of Atonement; Give up Your Lovers; Store of Ladies; The Miracle Boy; The Prince or Somebody; Magnolia Street (dramatised); Five Silver Daughters; The Camberwell Beauty; The Pursuer; The Dance Goes on; Mr. Emmanuel (filmed); Who's There Within?; No News from Helen; The Glory of Elsie Silver; Three Jolly Gentlemen; Honey for the Ghost; The Dangerous Places; The Loving Brothers; To the Quayside; Mr. Hurricane; The Little Old Admiral; *short stories:* The Doomington Wanderer; Paris Calling; Pale Blue Nightgown; Mario on the Beach; *verse:* Sorrow of War; Shepherd Singing Ragtime; Prophet and Fool; The Song of Songs, rendered as a Masque; Poems Drunk and Drowsy; *travel:* Sunward; Sicilian Noon; Those Ancient Lands, a Journey to Palestine; In the Steps of Moses the Law-giver; In the Steps of Moses the Conqueror; Louis Golding Goes Travelling; Goodbye to Ithaca; *belles-lettres:* Adventures in Living Dangerously; A Letter to Adolf Hitler; We Shall Eat and Drink Again (with André Simon); James Joyce; The Jewish Problem; Hitler Through the Ages; The World I Knew; *sport:* Louis Golding's Boxing Tales; My Sporting Days and Nights; The Bare-Knuckle Breed; *translations:* from various tongues. Has also contributed to many English, Continental and American periodicals. *Recreations:* wandering, reading, talking, listening. *Address:* 16 Hamilton Terrace, N.W.8. *Club:* Savage. [*Died* 9 *Aug.* 1958.

GOLDING-BIRD, Rt. Rev. Cyril Henry, M.A., D.D. Oxon; Hon. D.D., T.C.D. 1924; Hon. D.D. Ontario; Hon. S.C.F.; Sub-Prelate of the Order of St. John; Assistant Bishop of Guildford since 1930; Chairman Advisory Committee for the Care of Churches; *b.* 18 Sept. 1876; *s.* of late Rev. Robert J. Golding-Bird, D.D. *Educ.:* Merchant Taylors' School; Lincoln College, Oxford. Assistant Curate, All Saints, Margaret St., W., 1898-1902; C.F.S. Africa, 1900-01; Vicar of St. Barnabas', Dover, 1902-1907; Dean of Falkland Islands, 1907-08; J.P. 1907; Dean of Newcastle, N.S.W., and Vicar-General of the Diocese, 1909-14; Chaplain Australian Expeditionary Force, European War, 1914-15; Senior Chaplain Commonwealth Military Forces, 1915-19; Bishop of Kalgoorlie, 1914-19; Bishop of Mauritius, 1919-30; Archdeacon of Dorking, 1930-36; Archdeacon of Surrey, 1936-49. *Address:* Tiltmead, Cobham, Surrey. [*Died* 9 *April.* 1955.

GOLDMAN, Charles Sydney; *b.* Cape Colony, 1868; *m.* 1899, Hon. Agnes Mary Peel, 2nd *d.* of 1st Viscount Peel; two *s.* Interested in East Africa and S. African mining, he has chiefly resided in the Transvaal; during Boer War served as Special War Correspondent with Sir Redvers Buller's relief force as far as Ladysmith, after which he joined the cavalry in the same capacity on the western side in their advance north; M.P. (U.) Penryn and Falmouth, 1910-18. Major, Cornwall R.G.A., Territorial Force. *Publications:* With General French and the Cavalry in So. Africa, 1902; The Empire and the Century 1905; Cavalry in Future Wars, 1906; Proprietor of the Outlook weekly newspaper; several text-books on South African Mining and its Development; compiled several survey maps of the Witwatersrand. *Clubs:* Carlton, Junior Carlton. [*Died* 7 *April* 1958.

GOLDNEY, Col. George Francis Bennett, C.M.G. 1919; D.S.O. 1915; late R.E. *b.* 12 April 1879; *s.* of late George Goldney, Chippenham House, Exmouth; *m.* 1914, Hilda Margaret (*d.* 1953), *y. d.* of late Maj.-Gen. H. Edmeades, Nurstead Court, Meopham, Kent; two *d.* Entered army, 1898; Capt., 1907; Lt.-Col. 1924; Col. 1928; Adjutant, 1911-14; Staff Captain, War Office, 1909-11; served South Africa, 1899-1901 (Queen's medal three clasps); European War, 1914-18 (despatches four times, C.M.G., D.S.O.; Chevalier Legion of Honour, Bt. Lt.-Col. 1918); Asst. Director of Works, War Office, 1929-31; President Royal Engineer Board, 1931-35; retired pay, 1935. *Address:* The Cedars, Farnborough, Hants. *T.:* Farnborough, Hants, 47. [*Died* 9 *June* 1953.

GOLDRING, Douglas; writer; *b.* Greenwich, 7 January 1887; *m.* 1st, Beatrix Duncan; one *s.* (and one *s.* died of wounds, 1942); 2nd, Malin Nordström. *Educ.:* Felsted. After a year at Oxford, joined the staff of Country Life; sub-editor, 1908; sub-editor of the English Review under Ford Madox Hueffer, 1909; Editor, The Tramp, 1910; as literary adviser to Max Goschen, Ltd. (1912-14), was responsible for the publication of The Golden Journey to Samarkand and other works by James Elroy Flecker; Lecturer in English at the University Coll. of Commerce, Gothenburg, Sweden, 1925-27; Founder and Hon. Sec., Georgian Group, 1937. *Publications:* Ways of Escape; Dream Cities; Streets; James Elroy Flecker; The Loire; Margot's Progress; Polly; The Fortune; The Black Curtain; Nobody Knows; Miss Linn; Cuckoo; The Merchant of Souls; Gone Abroad; Northern Lights and Southern Shade; Reputations; The Façade; The French Riviera (Kit-bag Travel Books); Sardinia: The Island of the Nuraghi; Impacts; The Coast of Illusion; To Portugal; Odd Man Out; Pot Luck in England; A Tour in Northumbria; Facing the Odds; South Lodge: Reminiscences of Violet Hunt, Ford Madox Ford and the English Review Circle; The Nineteen-Twenties: Home Ground; Journeys in the Sun; Marching with the Times; The Last Pre-Raphaelite; Life Interests; Foreign Parts; Regency Portrait Painter: The Life of Sir Thomas Lawrence, P.R.A.; Three Romantic Countries; The South of France; Privileged Persons, etc. *Address:* Stonar House, Deal, Kent. *T.:* Deal 825. *Club:* National Liberal. [*Died* 9 *April* 1960.

GOLDSMITH, Edward, C.B.E. 1929; Commandant Metropolitan Special Constabulary Reserve since 1919; *b.* 24 Nov. 1868; *s.* of Adolphus Goldsmith, London; *m.* Georgina (*d.* 1950), *d.* of Arthur Kennedy, Cultra, Ireland. *Educ.:* St. Leonards. Assistant Commander C Div. Metropolitan Special Constabulary, 1914; Commander, 1914; M.B.E. 1917; O.B.E. 1919. *Address:* The Brown House, Worplesdon Hill, Woking, Surrey; Aston Lodge, Aboyne, Aberdeenshire. *Clubs:* Marlborough-Windham, St. James'. [*Died* 24 *Aug.* 1951.

GOLDSMITH, Colonel Harry Dundas, C.B.E. 1941; D.S.O. 1916; *b.* 6 May 1878; *e. s.* of H. St. B. Goldsmith, of Halfway House, near Guildford; *m.* 1906, Grace Apperley, *y. d.* of late Rev. F. C. Kinglake, West Monkton, Somerset; one *s.* *Educ.:* Felsted School. Joined 1st Batt. Duke of Cornwall's Light Infantry, 1897; served with Tirah Expedition, 1897-98 (medal and two clasps); Egyptian Army, 1904-6; Staff College, 1911-12; served European War on General Staff, 1914-18 (despatches, Brevet Major, D.S.O.); G.S.O. 1st Grade; Bt. Lt.-Col., 1917; Lt.-Col. 1923; Col., 1927; Commander 130th (Devon and Cornwall) Infantry Brig. T.A. 1931-35; A.D.C. to the King, 1932-35; retd. pay, 1935. D.L. Devon, 1936-53. *Address:* c/o Lloyds Bank, 6 Pall Mall, S.W.1. *Club:* Army and Navy. [*Died* 29 *Sept.* 1955.

GOLDSMITH, Vice-Admiral Sir Malcolm Lennon, K.B.E., *cr.* 1943; D.S.O. 1917; R.N., retired; Commodore 2nd Class R.N.R. since Sept. 1939; *b.* Lexden, Plymouth, 22 Aug. 1880; *e. s.* of J. P. Goldsmith and Elizabeth Mills; *m.* Ellen Mary, *d.* of F. A. Gray, M.R.C.S., Ottery St. Mary, Devon; four *d.* *Educ.:* Pencarwick House, Exmouth. Entered Navy, 1894; Heligoland, special promotion to Commander and D.S.O. while commanding Laertes; Dogger Bank; Lowestoft (put out of action); Jutland in command of Lydiard (despatches); Crimea (Bar to D.S.O.); promoted Captain, 1919; King's Harbourmaster and Captain of Dockyard, Malta; in command H.M.S. Harebell, as Captain of Fishery and Minesweeping Flotillas, 1929-30; Naval A.D.C. to the King, 1931; Rear-Adm. and retired list, 1931; Vice-Adm., retired 1936; Order of Sword of Sweden (Chevalier); Orders of Stanislas and St. Vladimir of Russia. *Recreation:* yachting. Won Royal Cruising Club Challenge Cup, 1926 and 1928. *Address:* Deadly Nightshade, King Saltern Road, Lymington, Hants. *Clubs:* Royal Cruising (Commodore), Little Ship; Royal South Western (Plymouth). [*Died* 4 *Oct.* 1955.

GOLDSMITH, Col. Perry Gladstone, C.B.E. 1919; V.D.; late Canadian Army Medical Corps; *b.* 1874; *s.* of P. D. Goldsmith, M.R.C.P. Served European War, 1915-19 (despatches, C.B.E.). *Address:* 500 Medical Arts Building, Toronto 5, Canada. [*Died* 21 *Jan.* 1951.

GOLDSTONE, Sir Frank (Walter), Kt., *cr.* 1931; *b.* Sunderland, 7 Dec. 1870; *s.* of late Thos. F. Goldstone, stained glass artist; *m.* Elizabeth Alice (*d.* 1942), *d.* of late Luke Henderson, of Whittingham, Northumberland; one *s.* one *d.* *Educ.:* Diamond Hall Council School, Sunderland; Borough Road College, Isleworth. Schoolmaster at Sheffield; M.P. (Lab.) Sunderland, 1910-18; General Secretary of the National Union of Teachers, 1924-31; was a member of the Consultative Committee of Ministry of

Education and of the Departmental Committees on Scholarships and Free Places in Secondary School, and the partial exemption of Scholars; was a member of the Speaker's Conference on the Franchise, and a member of the Royal Commission on the Civil Service, 1929-31. *Publications:* contrib. Educational Press. *Address:* 12 Temple Road, Ipswich. [*Died* 25 *Dec.* 1955.

GOLIGHER, Hugh Garvin, C.B.E. 1918; Assist. Administrator and Director of Finance of the Tangier Zone, Morocco, from Sept. 1937 till Dec. 1940, when the Spanish Military Authorities took control of the International Zone; reinstated as Financial Adviser to the Committee of Control under the new International regime, Tangier, 1946-49; late Asst. Secretary and Comptroller of Lands, War Office; retired, 1933; *y. s.* of late John Goligher, J.P., Londonderry; *b.* 1873; *m.* 1907, Lilian Mary Stacey, O.B.E. 1947 (*d.* 1958); one *s.* *Educ.:* Foyle Coll., Londonderry; Trinity Coll., Dublin (Classical Scholarship, Stewart Scholarship in Modern Literature. Univ. Studentship with 1st Senior Moderatorship in Classics and 1st Senior Moderatorship in Modern Literature; B.A. 1895, M.A. 1898; Hon. LL.D. 1918). European War; Acting Director of Finance. War Department, and Financial Adviser to the Commander-in-Chief, British Armies in France, 1915-19 (with grading as Brigadier-General) (despatches; Croix d'Officier, Légion d'Honneur, 1917; C.B.E., 1st Class Order of Aviz (Portugal), 1918; American Distinguished Service Medal, 1919); Member of British Delegation, Reparation Commission, Paris, Dec. 1919–April 1925; British Member of Commission of Interpretation in connection with services rendered by Germany to the Armies of Occupation, 1925-29; attended Hague Conference, Aug. 1929, as an expert in connection with the financial conditions of the evacuation of Germany. *Recreations:* reading, bridge. *Address:* c/o Lloyd's Bank, Ltd., 6 Pall Mall, S.W.1. [*Died* 13 *Dec.* 1958.

GOMME, Prof. Arnold Wycombe, M.A., LL.D.; F.B.A. 1947; Emeritus Professor of Greek, University of Glasgow, 1957, Professor of Greek, 1946-57; *b.* London, 16 November 1886; 5th *s.* of late Sir Laurence Gomme; *m.* 1917, Phyllis Emmerson; one *s.* *Educ.:* Merchant Taylors' School; Trinity College, Cambridge. Asst. Lecturer in Classics, Liverpool Univ., 1910-1911; Asst. Lecturer, later Lecturer, in Greek and Greek History, Univ. of Glasgow, 1911-45, Reader in Ancient History, 1945-46; Sather Professor, Univ. of California, 1951-1952; Editor, Hellenic Journal, 1951-; Visiting Fell. Brit. School at Athens, 1955; Pres. Hellenic Soc., 1956-; Pres. Scottish Classical Assoc., 1956-57. Served European War, Intelligence and A.S.C., 1914-19. Temp. Principal Officer, H.M. Treasury, 1941-45. Hon. Dr., University of Thessalonike, 1950; Hon. LL.D., Glasgow, 1958. *Publications:* Population of Ancient Athens, 1933; Sections on Greece and Roman Republic in Eyre's European Civilization, 1935; Essays in Greek History and Literature, 1937; Historical Commentary on Thucydides, vol. i, 1945, Vol. ii-iii, 1956; Greece 1945; The Greek Attitude to Poetry and History, 1954; contributions to British and foreign classical journals. *Address:* Long Crendon, Aylesbury, Bucks. *T.:* Long Crendon 235. [*Died* 18 *Jan.* 1959.

GOMPERTZ, Brigadier Martin Louis Alan; *b.* 1886; *e. s.* of Major A. C. M. Gompertz, Hants Regt.; *m.* 1912, Beryl Constance, *d.* of W. Fitch; one *s.* one *d.* *Educ.:* St. Edmund's College, Ware. 3rd Batt. Hants Regt. (Militia) 1903; 1st Batt. Yorks Regt., 1904; Indian Army, 1906; Capt., 1913; Major, 1919; served European War, 1914-18 (Brev. of Maj.); Mahsud Waziristan campaign, 1919-20 (wounded); N.W. Frontier India, 1930; Burmese Rebellion, 1931-32 (despatches); Staff College Quetta, 1922 (p.s.c.); Brig. Major, Delhi Brigade, 1919; D.A.A.G., and D.A.Q.M.G., Northern Command, India, 1923-26; Brevet of Lieut.-Colonel, 1929; Lt.-Col. 1930; Col. 1932; A.A. and Q.M.G., Kohat District, 1934-1936; D.A. and Q.M.G., Western Command, India, 1935-38; Commander Thal Brigade, India, 1938; retired, 1939. *Publications:* (under pseudonym Ganpat) Harilek; Road to Lamaland; High Snow; Magic Ladakh; Roads of Peace; Fairy Silver; (under own name), The Sleepy Duke, 1938, etc.; various articles in magazines. *Recreation:* fishing. *Club:* Authors'. [*Died* 29 *Sept.* 1951.

GOOCH, Sir Henry Cubitt, Kt., *cr.* 1928; J.P.; *b.* 7 Dec. 1871; *s.* of the late C. C. Gooch; *m.* 1897, Maud Mary (*d.* 1951), *d.* of Rev. J. H. Hudleston, Cayton Hall, S. Stainley, Harrogate; two *s.* one *d.* *Educ.:* Eton; Trinity College, Cambridge (Honours in Classics and Law Tripos). B.A., LL.B.; called to Bar, 1894; studied abroad, 1895-96; Member of the School Board for London, 1897-1904; M.P. (U.) Peckham, 1908-10; Member of Committee to inquire into the position of modern languages in the educational system of Great Britain, 1916-18; Member of original Secondary and Technical Burnham Committees; Master of Merchant Taylors' Co., 1929; Military Manœuvres Commissioner, 1909; L.C.C., 1907-10 and 1914-34; Alderman of L.C.C. 1914-19, Chairman or Vice-Chairman of L.C.C. Education Sub-Committees for many years; Chairman L.C.C. Education Committee, 1921-22; Vice-Chairman L.C.C. 1922-23; Chairman, 1923-24; Member of General Nursing Council; Member of London County Justices' Advisory Committee, and of first Cambridge University Women's Appointments Board and first London Voluntary Hospitals Cttee.; Pres. of Cambridge House, Camberwell; Vice-Pres., King's College Hospital, London. Co-founder of All Saints, Peckham, London. *Club:* Athenæum. [*Died* 15 *Jan.* 1959.

GOOCH, Henry Martyn, O.B.E. 1949 (M.B.E. 1920); General Secretary of the World's Evangelical Alliance (British Organisation), 1904-49; *b.* Falmouth 8 Sept. 1874; *s.* of late Rev. W. Fuller Gooch; *m.* 1921, Adrienne May, *e. d.* of late James Alden Punnett. *Educ.:* Privately; Stanley House, Cliftonville. Travelling Sec., Children's Special Service Mission, 1898-1904, for which travelled round world visiting Schools and Col., etc.; London Diocesan Reader, 1916; Southwark Diocesan Reader, 1921; Archbishop's Messenger, National Mission Repentance and Hope, 1916; organised the Queen's Hall, W. and Mansion House War United Prayer Meetings, 1915-18; has travelled extensively in Europe in interests of Christian Union and Religious Liberty, etc.; Member of the British Section Swiss Alpine Club. *Publications:* Editor of Evangelical Christendom, 1904-49; Editor The Universal Standard Stamp Catalogue; Assistant-Editor The London Philatelist, 1892-98; contributed serial articles to The Captain, 1899-1900, and other magazines. *Publication:* William Fuller Gooch: A Tribute and Testimony, 1929. *Recreations:* alpine climbing and walking, gardening and horticulture. *Address:* Green Wood, 9 Offington Avenue, Broadwater, Worthing, Sussex. *T.:* Swandean 787. [*Died* 13 *June* 1957.

GOOD, Alan Paul; Deputy Chairman and Director (ex-Managing Dir.) The Brush Electrical Engineering Co. Ltd. (parent company of Brush Aboe Group); *b.* 9 April 1906; *er. s.* of William Ireland and Ethel Beatrice Good; *m.* 1st, 1931, Doreen Priscilla Cory; two *d.* (and one *d.* decd.); 2nd, 1945, Mrs. Mary Brough; no *c.* *Educ.:* Marlborough; Hertford College, Oxford (M.A.). Solicitor, Pennington & Sons, 1930-39; Chairman: Lagonda Motors Ltd., 1936; Heenan and Froude Ltd., 1936; Petters Ltd., 1937; Associated British Engineering, 1937; Darwins Ltd., 1939; Fielding & Platt, 1935; Mirrlees Bickerton & Day Ltd., 1938; Director: Brush Electrical Engineering Co. Ltd., 1938 (Dep. Chm. and Man. Dir., 1941-45 and 1946-); Guardian Assurance Co. Ltd.,

1937-51 (Vice-Chm. 1951-); Vivian Diesels & Munitions Ltd., 1951; Vivian Engine Works Ltd., 1951. *Recreations:* shooting, farming and gardening. *Address:* Glympton Park, nr. Woodstock, Oxon. *T.:* Woodstock 300. *Club:* Oxford and Cambridge.
[*Died* 10 *Feb.* 1953.

GOODACRE, Hugh George; J.P. Leicestershire, High Sheriff, 1917-18; Lord of the Manor of Ashby Parva, Leicestershire; *b.* 1 July 1865; *e. s.* of Rev. F. B. Goodacre, M.D., Wilby, Norfolk; *m.* 1898, Mabel Paton (*d.* 1941), 2nd *d.* of S. Mackenzie; one *s.* *Educ.:* Marlborough College. Taken a leading part in the Boy Scout Movement in Leicestershire, for which county he was Commissioner, 1909-35. *Publications:* The Bronze Coinage of the Late Roman Empire; Handbook of the Coinage of the Byzantine Empire; Parson Paul and other poems; Justice Byrd, a historic novel; Sausages for Supper, poems; Land of the Ridge and Furrow, and other poems; editor of Dyson's History of Lutterworth. *Recreation:* numismatics. *Address:* Rectory Close, Ashby Parva, nr. Rugby. *T.A.:* Ullesthorpe. *T.:* Leire 255. [*Died* 1 *Feb.* 1952.

GOODCHILD, George Frederick, M.A. (Cambridge), B.A. and B.Sc. (London); External Registrar, University of London, 1915-1936; *b.* Hartley, Westmorland, 1871; *e. s.* of late J. G. Goodchild, H.M. Geological Survey; *m.* 1901, Edith Mary, *d.* of late J. S. Stephens. *Educ.:* private school; Sidney Sussex College, Cambridge (Exhibitioner and Scholar). 1st Class Natural Science Tripos, 1897; 1st Class Mechanical Sciences (Engineering) Tripos, 1898; Lecturer, Winchester Diocesan Training College; Senior Science Master, Wyggeston and Queen Elizabeth's Grammar School, Leicester; Principal, Wandsworth Technical Institute, 1902-15. *Publications:* Editor various scientific and technical works. *Recreations:* travel, mountaineering, scientific and mechanical work. *Address:* Rose Lawn, Sycamore Grove, New Malden. *Club:* Athenæum.
[*Died* 26 *Sept.* 1956.

GOODDEN, Colonel John Bernhard Harbin; T.D., D.L. Dorset; J.P. Dorset and Somerset; Hon. Lieut. in Army, 1900; C.C. Dorset (County Alderman, 1944); Governor of Sherborne School; *b.* 18 Nov. 1876; *e. s.* of Col. J. R. P. Goodden; *m.* 1908, Joyce Marianne Poyntelle Crane; three *s.* *Educ.:* Harrow; Trinity College, Oxford, B.A. 1898. Formerly Lieut.-Col. Dorset Q.O. Yeomanry; served S. African War, 1900 (medal); European War, 1914-19, Gallipoli and Egypt (1914-15 star, 2 medals, T.D.); joined Stuckeys Bank, 1899 (later Westminster Bank, of which one time Local Director); retired, 1936; High Sheriff of Dorset, 1937. *Recreations:* fishing, shooting, gardening. *Address:* Compton Hawy, Sherborne, Dorset. *T.A.* and *T.:* Yeovil 12. *Club:* Royal Dorset Yacht (Weymouth).
[*Died* 18 *July* 1951.

GOODE, Sir Richard Allmond Jeffrey, Kt., *cr.* 1928; C.M.G. 1924; C.B.E. 1918; *b.* Channel, Newfoundland, 30 April 1873; *e. s.* of late Rev. T. A. Goode; *m.* 1904, Agnes, *d.* of Thomas Codrington, M.I.C.E.; three *s.* *Educ.:* Fettes College. Sec. to the Administration, N.E. Rhodesia, 1900; Sec. to the Administration and Member of the Administrator's Court, N.-W. Rhodesia, 1908; Sec. to the Administration, N. Rhodesia, 1911; Deputy Administrator, 1920; Chief Sec. to the Government, 1924; acted as Governor in 1926 and 1927; Railway Commissioner for Northern Rhodesia, 1927-36; Vice-Pres. South African Red Cross Soc., 1939. *Publications:* occasional papers. *Recreations:* golf and fishing. *Address:* Civil Service Club, Capetown. *Clubs:* Union, West Indian; Civil Service (Capetown).
[*Died* 25 *May* 1953.

GOODEN, Stephen, C.B.E. 1942; R.A. 1946 (A.R.A. 1937); R.E.; *b.* 1892; *m.* 1925, Mona, *d.* of Dr. George Price, Bray, Co. Wicklow. *Educ.:* Rugby; Slade School. Pte. in 19th Hussars and Sapper in Royal Engineers in B.E.F., France, 1915-18; began engraving, 1923; has illustrated books for Nonesuch Press, Heinemann, Harrap, etc.; works to be seen at British Museum, Victoria and Albert, Fitzwilliam, etc. *Address:* End House, Chiltern Road, Chesham Bois, Bucks. *Club:* Athenæum.
[*Died* 21 *Sept.* 1955.

GOODENOUGH, Rear-Admiral Michael Grant, C.B.E. 1946; D.S.O. 1940; Assistant Chief of Naval Staff since 1954; *b.* 18 June 1904; *s.* of late F. C. Goodenough, D.C.L., Filkins, Oxon., Chairman of Barclays Bank, and Maive, *d.* of C. N. Macnamara; *m.* 1934, Nancy, *d.* of late Sir Ramford Slater, G.C.M.G.; two *s.* one *d.* *Educ.:* St. Aubyns (Rottingdean); Osborne; Dartmouth. War of 1939-45: Comdr., Plans Div., Admiralty, 1939-41; H.M.S. Prince of Wales, 1941; Home Fleet, 1942-43; Dir. Plans, S.E.A.C., 1943-46. Mediterranean, Capt. Frigate Sqdn., H.M.S. Pelican, 1946-1947; Gunnery Div., Admiralty, 1947-49; Asst. Chief of Supplies and Transport, Admiralty, 1949-52; E. Indies, 1952-54. Comdr., Order of Orange Nassau, 1940; Amer. Bronze Star, 1946. *Recreations:* fishing, hunting, shooting, gardening. *Address:* Lower Woodlands, Shiplake, Henley-on-Thames. *T.:* Wargrave 198. *Clubs:* United Service; Naval (Portsmouth).
[*Died* 31 *Dec.* 1955.

GOODENOUGH, Sir William Macnamara, 1st Bt., *cr.* 1943; Hon. LL.D. (Manchester); D.L., J.P., Chairman, Barclays Bank Ltd., 1947-51 (Director, 1929-51); Chairman of Trustees of Nuffield Trust for the University Medical School, Oxford, the Nuffield Foundation, Nuffield College, Oxford, Nuffield Dominions Trust, Oxford, Nuffield Trust for the Forces of the Crown, Nuffield Provincial Hospitals Trust and Imperial Relations Trust; Deputy Steward, Oxford University; Hon. Student, Christ Church, Oxford, 1947; Director of Mercantile and General Reinsurance Co. Ltd., Westminster Chambers Assoc. Ltd. and Foundling Estates Ltd.; Member of Council of Foreign Bondholders; Governor, Wellington College; Chairman of Governors of Dominion Students' Hall Trust; *b.* 10 March 1899; *e. s.* of late Frederick Craufurd Goodenough and Maive, *d.* of late N.C. Macnamara, F.R.C.S.; *m.* 1924, Dorothea Louisa, *d.* of late Hon. and Ven. Archdeacon Kenneth Gibbs, D.D.; three *s.* one *d.* *Educ.:* Wellington College; Christ Church, Oxford (History Scholar). Served European War with the 2nd Battn. Coldstream Guards. Chairman, Oxfordshire County Council, 1934-37. *Recreations:* hunting and shooting; Chairman and Joint Master V. W. H. Cricklade Hunt. *Heir:* *s.* Richard Edmund, *b.* 9 June 1925. *Address:* 54 Lombard Street, E.C.3; Filkins Hall, Lechlade, Glos. *Club:* Brooks's. [*Died* 23 *May* 1951.

GOODEY, Tom, O.B.E. 1950; F.R.S. 1947; formerly Head of Nematology Department, Rothamsted Experimental Station, Harpenden, Herts; *b.* 28 July 1885, *y. s.* of Thomas and Hannah Goodey, Wellingborough, Northants; *m.* Constance, 2nd *d.* of William Henry and Lucy Anne Lewis, West Bromwich, Staffs.; one *s.* three *d.* (and one *d.* decd.). *Educ.:* Victoria Board School, Wellingborough; County School, Northampton; Univ. of Birmingham. B.Sc., 1908 (hons. in Zoology and Botany); M.Sc., 1909; D.Sc., 1915; Mackinnon Student of Royal Society of London, 1910-11. Protozoologist, Rothamsted Exp. Sta., 1912-1913, and in Laboratory of Agricultural Zoology, Univ. of Birmingham, 1913-19; Plant Helminthologist, Rothamsted Exp. Sta., 1920; on research staff of Dept. of Helminthology, London School of Tropical Medicine, and later Institute of Agricultural Parasitology, Winches Farm, St. Albans,

1926-47. *Publications:* various early papers on the jelly fish, *Aurelia aurita*, the frilled shark, *Chlamydoselachus anguineus* and on the protozoa of the soil, 1908-16; numerous papers on nematode parasites of animals, insects and plants as well as on free-living soil nematodes, 1922-, largely in Jour. Helminthology; Plant Parasitic Nematodes and the Diseases they Cause, 1933; Soil and Freshwater Nematodes, 1951. *Recreations:* gardening and singing. *Address:* 45 Meadow Walk, Harpenden, Herts. *T.:* Harpenden 918. [*Died* 7 *July* 1953.

GOODHART-RENDEL, Harry Stuart, C.B.E. 1955; Mus. Bac. Cant.; M.A. Oxon.; F.S.A.; P.-P.R.I.B.A.; *o. s.* of Harry Chester Goodhart (*d.* 1895) and Hon. Rose Ellen (*d.* 1927), *e. d.* of Lord Rendel of Hatchlands; *b.* 1887; assumed by royal licence additional name of Rendel, 1902. *Educ.:* Eton; Trinity College, Cambridge. Studied music at Cambridge and with late Sir Donald Tovey; has practised as an architect in England since 1910, and for a time in the South of France as well; Slade Professor of Fine Art, Oxford Univ., 1933-1936; Governor of Sadler's Wells, 1934-; Director of Architectural Association School of Architecture, 1936-38; President of the Architectural Association, 1924-25; President of Royal Institute of British Architects, 1937-39; Pres. Guild of Catholic Artists and Craftsmen, 1946-52; President, Design and Industries Assoc., 1948-50; Vice-Pres. Royal Academy of Music, 1953-; Pres. Franco-British Union of Architects, 1954-55. Mem. Advisory Cttee. on Buildings of special Architectural or Historic Interest, Min. of Housing and Local Govt., 1945-; served in Grenadier Guards, 1915-20, 1940-45. Hon. F.R.A.M., 1958. *Publications:* Monograph on Nicholas Hawksmoor in the Masters of Architecture series, 1924; Vitruvian Nights, 1932; Fine Art, 1934; The Squad Drill Primer, 1944; How Architecture is Made, 1947; English Architecture since The Regency, 1953. *Address:* 114 Eaton Square, S.W.1.; The Old Parsonage, East Clandon, Guildford; Villa St. Maximin, Valescure St. Raphael, France (Var.). *Clubs:* Garrick, Guards, Travellers', Turf. [*Died* 21 *June* 1959.

GOODLAND, Colonel Herbert Tom, C.B. 1928; D.S.O. 1918; *b.* Taunton, 6 Nov. 1874; 3rd *s.* of late C. J. Goodland, J.P.; *m.* 1st, 1900, Ethel Haill (*d.* 1930), *d.* of W. J. Hawkins, Oxfordshire; no *c.*; 2nd, 1931, Marjorie Kathleen, *d.* of Rev. S. Ryall, M.A., Victoria, B.C. Canada; one *d.* *Educ.:* Taunton School. Emigrated to Canada, 1891; engaged in farming in Manitoba; later entered business various parts of Canada, principally British Columbia; held many public positions in Western Canada; Captain, Canadian Militia; was in England on business at outbreak of European War; absorbed at once in Imperial Forces; appointed to Staff 10th (Irish) Division; served in Gallipoli, Serbia, Macedonia; transferred to 16th (Irish) Division in France, 1916; commanded 1st Batt. R. Munster Fusiliers; in 1918 commanded 5th R. Berkshire Regt. (White Eagle of Serbia, D.S.O. in the field, despatches thrice; médaille de reconnaissance française; Gold Medal, Souvenir Français); Deputy Controller Imperial War Graves Commission (France and Flanders), 1919; responsible for construction British War Cemeteries and Memorials; retired, 1928 (C.B.). *Recreations:* motoring, golf; identified with Canadian Legion activities. *Address:* Westways, Uplands, Victoria, British Columbia, Canada. [*Died* 13 *Aug.* 1956.

GOODMAN, Rev. Arthur Worthington; Hon. Canon, 1924, Emeritus, 1950, and Librarian 1925-46, of Winchester Cathedral; F.S.A.; F.R.Hist.S.; *b.* 26 Oct. 1871; *s.* of Thomas Davenport Goodman of Chapel-en-le-Frith and Emily Jane, *d.* of Andrew Jukes Worthington, Leek, Staffs; *m.* 1903, Florence Remington (*d.* 1939), *d.* of Rev. J. H. Merriott, sometime Assistant Master at Eton College; no *c.* *Educ.:* Newcastle, Staffs.; Christ's College, Cambridge (Scholar). B.A. 1st Class Classical Tripos, 1893; 1st Class Theol. Trip. 1895; M.A. 1897; B.D. 1922; Classical Lecturer at Diocesan College, Rondebosch, 1895; Assistant Master at Aysgarth School, Yorks., 1897; at Sedbergh School, 1898-1909; Rector of St. Botolph's, Cambridge, 1910-22; Visiting Chaplain 1st Eastern General Hospital, 1916-1919; Examiner to Oxford and Cambridge Schools Exam. Board, 1910-39; to Cambridge Local Exams., 1922-40; Hon. Assistant Librarian of Winchester Cathedral, 1923. *Publications:* Six Lectures on St. John's Gospel, 1907; A Little History of St. Botolph's, Cambridge, 1922; The Manor of Goodbegot, 1923; Winchester Cathedral Statutes (with Dr. Hutton), 1925; Winchester Cathedral Chartulary, 1927; Register of Bishop Woodlock (Cant. & York Society), 1945. *Recreation:* Oxford and Cambridge Athletic Sports, 1894, Mile (3rd string). *Address:* Dormy Cottage, S. Cross Road, Winchester. *T.A.* and *T.:* Winchester 4187. *Club:* Hampshire (Winchester). [*Died* 8 *March* 1951.

GOODMAN, Brig.-Gen. Sir Godfrey Davenport, K.C.B. *cr.* 1935 (C.B. 1924); C.M.G. 1916; D.S.O. 1918; V.D.; T.D.; *b.* 14 Oct. 1868; *e. s.* of Thomas Davenport Goodman and Emily Jane, *d.* of Andrew Jukes Worthington of Leek; *m.* 1901, Elizabeth Jane Cleland (*d.* 1932), *e. d.* of late Major Herbert Buchanan of Arden, Dunbartonshire; two *s.* one *d.* *Educ.:* Manchester Grammar School. served S. African War, 1901; European War, 1915-19; Commanding 6th Battalion Sherwood Foresters, 1914-16, 52nd and 21st Infantry Brigades, 1916-19, and 139th Sherwood Foresters Brigade, 1920-24; A.D.C. to the King, 1925-35; District Registrar, High Court, 1926-43; Chairman, Territorial Army Assoc., 1933-43; Devonshire Royal Hospital, Buxton, 1935-48; Hon. Freeman of Buxton, 1939; D.L., J.P. Co. Derby. *Address:* Eccles House, near Chinley, Derbyshire. [*Died* 24 *May* 1957.

GOODSHIP, Harold Edwin, C.B.E. 1930; *b.* 1877; 2nd *s.* of late W. Goodship; *m.* Violet Mary, 3rd *d.* of late Rev. E. Greensill, M.A., Accrington; one *s.* one *d.* *Educ.:* privately. In service of G.N.R., England, 1895-1903; Assistant Accountant, Sierra Leone Government Railway, 1904-8; Assistant Chief Accountant, Uganda Railway, 1908-15; Chief Accountant, Kenya and Uganda Railways and Harbours, 1915; Deputy General Manager and Chief Accountant, Kenya and Uganda Railways and Harbours,1928-31; retired 1931. *Recreations:* golf, bridge, music. [*Died* 3 *Dec.* 1951.

GOODSON, Katharine; F.R.A.M., pianist; *m.* Arthur Hinton, composer, (*d.* 1941). *Educ.:* Royal Academy of Music; Vienna, under Leschetizky; soloist with all the most famous orchestral organizations throughout the world; has toured as a virtuosa in Great Britain, Belgium, Holland, France, Scandinavia, Germany, and Austria; has made seven tours in the United States; has also given many concerts in Canada, Australia, and Honolulu, and a series of 30 recitals in Dutch E. Indies; Two Television engagements, Alexandra Palace, 1947. *Address:* 2 Ormonde Gate, Chelsea, S.W.3. *T.:* Flaxman 9658. [*Died* 17 *April* 1958.

GOODWIN, Lt.-Gen. Sir (Thomas Herbert) John (Chapman), K.C.B., *cr.* 1919 (C.B. 1918); K.C.M.G., *cr.* 1932 (C.M.G. 1915); D.S.O. 1898; J.P. Co. Hertford; late Hon. Surgeon to the King; Knight of Grace, Order of St. John of Jerusalem; F.R.C.S. England; Hon. F.R.C.S. Edinburgh; Hon. Fellow American College of Surgeons; Hon. Fellow Royal College of Surgeons, Australia; Hon. D.Sc. Oxford; Fellow Royal Society of

Medicine; M.A. University of Michigan; *b.* Kandy, Ceylon, 24 May 1871; *e. s.* of Surgeon-Major J. Goodwin, Army Medical Staff, and Marion Agnes Power; *m.* 1897, Lilian Isabel, *y. d.* of late James Torrence Ronaldson. *Educ.:* Newton College, Devon; St. Mary's Hospital, London. Commissioned Army Med. Service, 1893; Battle of Shabkadar, 1897 (D.S.O.); staff surgeon in Mohmand Field Force, N.W. Frontier, 1897 (despatches, medal and clasp); European War, 1914-18 (despatches three times, C.B., C.M.G., Mons Star 1914, Allied and Victory Medals); A.D.M.S. with Mr. Balfour's Mission to the United States, 1917; Dir.-Gen. Army Medical Service, 1918-23; retired pay, 1923; Governor of Queensland, 1927-32; Col. Comdt. R.A.M.C., 1932-38; Commander; Legion of Honour, Belgian Order of Leopold, Crown of Italy; Belgian Croix de Guerre; American Distinguished Service Medal. *Publications:* Field Service Notes for R.A.M.C.; Notes for Medical Officers on Field Service in India; Notes for Army Medical Officers; Prevention of Disease on Active Service; Making a Shoot, 1935. *Recreations:* hunting, shooting, fishing. *Address:* Ivy House Hotel, Marlborough, Wilts.
[*Died* 29 *Sept.* 1960.

GOODWIN, William, M.Sc., Ph.D.; formerly Advisory and Research Chemist, South-Eastern Agricultural College, Wye; formerly Principal, Midland Agricultural and Dairy College, Sutton Bonington and Kingston-on-Soar; Official Agricultural Analyst of Notts and Lindsey (Lincs) County Councils; late Secy. Notts War Agricultural Committee; *b.* Macclesfield, 1873; *s.* of George James Goodwin; *m.* 1908, Helene Käthe Elizabeth Zyska; two *d.* *Educ.:* King Edward VI. Grammar School, Macclesfield; Owens College, Manchester; Glasgow University; Glasgow Agricultural College; University of Göttingen; Laboratory for Vegetable Physiology, Paris; Queen's Coll., Galway (1851 Exhibition scholar). Demonstrator and Assistant Lecturer, Queen's College, Galway; Lecturer in Agricultural Chemistry, Harper-Adams Agricultural College; Lecturer in Agricultural Chemistry and Head of Chemistry Department, South-Eastern Agricultural College, Wye; Examiner London University, University College Reading, etc. *Publications:* Contributions to the Journals of the Chemical Societies of London, Paris, and Berlin; articles in Journal of Ministry of Agriculture, etc.; Scientific Feeding of Animals; Methods used in the Examination of Milk and Dairy Products. *Address:* Brougham House, Wye, Ashford, Kent. *T.:* Wye 144.
[*Died* 30 *Dec.* 1953.

GOODWIN, Colonel William Richard Power, D.S.O. 1917; late R.A.M.C.; *b.* 26 May 1875; 3rd *s.* of Surg.-Major J. Goodwin, late Army Medical Staff, and Marion Agnes Goodwin; *m.* 1907, Myrtle, *y. d.* of late Elton Forrest, Indian Forest Service, and Mrs. Elton Forrest; three *s.* *Educ.:* Newton College, Devon; St. Mary's Hospital, London. Entered the Royal Army Medical Corps, 1900, after obtaining M.R.C.S. England qualification; served in Ireland, India, and England; while in India served as personal assistant to the principal medical officer, Punjab Command, for two years; served for three years as Medical Officer at the Royal Arsenal, Woolwich; served European War (D.S.O., Bt. Col.); Medical Officer, Royal Military College, Sandhurst, 1919-23; in charge Military Hospital, Gibraltar; Assistant Director-General at War Office, 1926-29; Assistant Director of Medical Services, E. Anglian Area, 1929-32; Hon. Physician to the King, 1928-32; retired pay, 1932; O.C., Red Cross and St John Officers' Convalescent Hospital, Somerley, Ringwood, 1940-45; Medical Officer, Eastbourne College, 1933-40 and 1945-47. *Address:* c/o Glyn, Mills & Co., Whitehall, S.W.1.
[*Died* 30 *Jan.* 1958.

GORDON, Alec Knyvett, M.A., M.B., B.Ch., Cantab.; Retired Consulting Pathologist, G.W.R. Medical Fund and Victoria Hospital, Swindon; *b.* 1870; *s.* of Col. E. S. Gordon, R.A.: *m.* Gertrude Mildred, *d.* of Maj. Lewis Archer; one *s.* one *d.* *Educ.:* Clifton Coll.; King's Coll., Cambridge (Exhibitioner and Glyn Prizeman); University scholar, St. Mary's Hospital; Senior Assistant Officer, M.A.B.; Demonstrator Pathology St. Mary's Hospital, London; Medical Superintendent Manchester City Fever Hospital; Vice-President, W. London Medical Society; Fellow, Royal Society of Medicine; Fellow, Member Council Medico-legal Society. *Publications:* Health in the Home; Hæmatology in General Practice; Systemic Infections; Lectures on Clinical Pathology; numerous papers on pathological matters. *Recreations:* music and painting. *Address:* King's College, Cambridge.
[*Died* 11 *Aug.* 1951.

GORDON, Douglas John, C.B. 1955; Clerk Assistant, House of Commons, since 1954 (second Clerk Assistant, 1948-54); *b.* 14 Sept. 1900; *e. s.* of Hon. Huntly D. Gordon, Advocate, Sheriff-Substitute, Ross and Cromarty, and Violet, *d.* of John Gaspard Fanshawe, Parsloes. *Educ.:* Edinburgh Academy (Exhibitioner); Balliol College, Oxford (Warner Exhibitioner); B.A. Clerk in the House of Commons, 1924. *Address:* 6 Culford Mansions, Culford Gardens, S.W.3; Kilvannie, Strathpeffer, Ross-shire. *T.:* Kensington 8597, Strathpeffer 269. *Clubs:* Athenæum, Travellers', Oxford and Cambridge. [*Died* 30 *Aug.* 1959.

GORDON, Lieut.-Col. Edward Hyde Hamilton-, C.M.G. 1918; D.S.O. 1916; *s.* of Colonel G. H. Gordon, R.E.; *m.* 1897, Hilda Winifred D'Arcy (who obtained a divorce, 1920; she married, 1921, Vice-Adm. Alfred Charles Sykes, C.M.G.), *d.* of John Timothy D'Arcy Hutton, of Marske, Richmond, and Aldburgh Hall, Masham, Yorkshire. *Educ.:* Wellington College. Formerly Lieut.-Col. Gordon Highlanders; served European War, 1914-18 (despatches, D.S.O.). *Address:* 66 Forest Drive, Pinelands, Cape Town, South Africa.
[*Died* 11 *July* 1955.

GORDON, Hampden Charles, C.B. 1937; *s.* of late John Percy Gordon, Croughly, Banffshire; *m.* 1st, 1920, Barbara Mary Scott, *d.* of late Leonard Stokes; one *s.*; 2nd, 1932, Mary Eileen, *d.* of late Llewelyn James Llewelyn, Codnor Park. *Educ.:* Haileybury College; Hertford College, Oxford. 1st Class Lit. Hum., 1908; War Office, 1908; Private Sec. to Col. Sir Edward Ward and to Sir Reginald Brade; Assistant Secretary, 1924; Director of Army Contracts, 1936-39; Under Secretary for Finance, Ministry of Supply, 1943; retired, 1947. Chevalier of the Légion d'Honneur. *Publications:* The War Office (Whitehall Series); Old English Furniture, 1948; A Key to Old Houses, 1955, etc. *Recreations:* writing, antiques. *Address:* 4 Motcomb Street, Belgrave Square, S.W.1. *T.:* Belgravia 2526. *Club:* Royal Thames Yacht. [*Died* 25 *Sept.* 1960.

GORDON, Brig.-Gen. Herbert, C.B. 1919; C.M.G. 1917; D.S.O. 1915; *b.* 30 June 1869. Entered army, 1889; Captain, 1898; Major, 1907; Lt.-Col. 1914; Bt. Col. 1915; served Sudan, 1900-2 (medal with clasp); Sudan, 1905 (clasp); European War, 1914-18 (despatches, D.S.O., C.M.G., Bt. Col.); retired pay, 1924. *Address:* 29 Stoneygate Court, Leicester. *Club:* United Service.
[*Died* 11 *June* 1951.

GORDON, Sir Home Seton Charles Montagu, 12th Bt. of Embo, *cr.* 1631-J.P.; *b.* Brighton, 30 Sep. 1871; *o. s.* of 11th Bt. of Embo, and Mabel (*d.* 1940), *o. c.* of Montagu David Scott, M.P.; *S.* father, 1906; *m.* 1st, 1897, Edith Susan (*d.* 1945), *d.* of Richard John Leeson-Marshall, Callinafercy House, Co. Kerry; 2nd, 1953, Katharine, *y. d.* of late J.E. Hornsby, Rottingdean. *Educ.:* Eton. Retired Chairman of

publishing firm of Williams and Norgate Ltd.; Director Electric Supply Corporation until Nationalisation; formerly an Underwriting Member of Lloyd's; Controller of Staff, National Service Ministry, 1917; Air Ministry, 1918; President, London Club Cricketers Conference, 1917-19; Chairman, Sports Conference, 1919; Committee of National Alliance of Employers and Employed, 1918-19; Committee of Sunday Games Association, 1919; Captain Rye Golf Club, 1937; Staff Captain, Brighton Home Guard, 1940; Hon. Match Sec., 1943, Hon. Sec., 1944, Pres., 1948, Sussex County Cricket Club. *Publications:* Cricket Form at a Glance, 1902; Reminiscences of an Irish Land Agent, 1904; A Man's Road, 1915; Leaders of Men, 1915; Memorial Biography of W. G. Grace, 1919; That Test Match, 1921; Cricket Form at a Glance in this Century, 1924; Eton *v.* Harrow at Lords, 1926; Sussex Cricket Handbook, 1929; Lancashire Cricket, 1930; Notts Cricket Annual, 1932; Kent Cricket Annual, 1933; Essex Cricket Annual, 1935; Cricket Form at a Glance for Sixty Years, 1938; Background to Cricket, 1939; Facts and Figures about Essex Cricket, 1948; Sussex Cricket Annual, 1949; History of Sussex County Cricket, 1950. Has translated several works from French; has written articles in Encyclopædia Britannica, Quarterly Review, Fortnightly, National Review, English Review, Empire Review, etc. *Recreations:* music, cricket, golf. *Address:* St. Edmunds, Rottingdean, Sussex. *T.:* Rottingdean 2746. *Clubs:* Carlton, M.C.C.; Union (Brighton).
[*Died* 9 *Sept.* 1956.

GORDON, Lieut.-Col. John de la Hay, C.S.I. 1941; C.I.E. 1937; O.B.E. 1918; M.C.; *b.* 30 March 1887; 3rd *s.* of A. H. Gordon, D.L., Delamont, Killyleagh, Co. Down; *m.* 1920, Esme Violet, *d.* of C. Bevan; two *s.* one *d.* *Educ.:* Rossall; R.M.C., Sandhurst. Joined 18th Royal Irish Regt., 1906; transferred Indian Army, 1908, and Indian Political Dept., 1911; retired from I.A. 1942; served European War, 1914-18 (M.C., O.B.E.); Military Governor, Basra, 1916-17; Deputy Military Governor, Bagdad, 1917-18; Officiating Agent to the Governor General, Western India States, 1936; Resident, Mysore, 1937. *Address:* c/o Lloyds Bank, Ltd., 6 Pall Mall, S.W.1. [*Died* 22 *Dec.* 1959.

GORDON, Brig.-Gen. John Lewis Randolph, C.B. 1916; C.S.I. 1921; late 15th Sikhs, Indian Army; *b.* 17 Nov. 1867; 3rd *s.* of John Lewis Gordon, West Park, Elgin; *m.* 1901, Gwendoline, *d.* of Rev. Hugh Pearson, Roden House, Cheltenham; four *d.* *Educ.:* Glenalmond. Entered army (Worcesters Regt.), 1888; transferred 15th Sikhs, 1891; commanded escort to Mission to Chitral, 1893 (thanks of Govt.). Served Chitral, 1895 (medal with clasp); N.W. Frontier, India, 1897-98 (two clasps); Tirah, 1897-98 (despatches, clasp); European War, 1914-15 (wounded); Senussi Expedition, 1915-16 (despatches, C.B., 1914 Star, British War Medal, 1914-19, Victory Medal); Waziristan Campaign, 1917 (Inspector Gen. Communications); Afghan Campaign, 1919 (Brigade Commdr., despatches, medal with clasp); Waziristan Campaign, 1919-1920 (Brigade Commander, despatches, C.S.I.); retired, 1920; Colonel of the 2nd Royal Battalion 11th Sikh Regiment, 1935-37. *Address:* Newlandside, Sandy Lane Road, Charlton Kings, Glos. *T.:* Cheltenham 2622.
[*Died* 17 *April* 1953.

GORDON, Col. Kenmure A. G. E.; *see* Evans-Gordon.

GORDON, Kenneth, C.B.E. 1944; M.C. 1917; Director-General of Ordnance Factories, Ministry of Supply, since 1952; *b.* 18 Apr. 1897; *s.* of Frederic Shirley Gordon, Civil Servant, St. Leonards, and Edith Mary Lidwell; *m.* 1925, Winifred Henning, Norton-on-Tees; one *s.* *Educ.:* Merchant Taylors' School, London; St. John's College, Oxford. 1st Class Hons. Nat. Sci. 1921, Univ. Lectr. 1922. Served European War, 1915-19, East Surrey Regt. and Machine-Gun Corps, France (wounded). 1923-48; Synthetic Ammonia and Nitrates, later Billingham Div. I.C.I.; Research Manager, 1927; Director, 1931; Jt. Man. Dir., 1936. Responsible for Coal Hydrogenation plant, 1933, Aviation Petrol plant, Heysham, 1940. Vice-Chm., diffusion Cttee., Tube Alloys (Atomic Energy), 1942-43; Design of petroleum chemical plant, Wilton and Billingham, 1946-1947. Joined Trinidad Leaseholds Ltd., as Technical Director, 1948; Managing Director, 1949. Member Fuel Research Board, 1948-51; Melchett Medallist, Inst. of Fuel, 1947. Dep. Man. Dir., Head Wrightson Processes Ltd., 1951-52. Comd. 174 (H) A.A. Battery, R.A. (T.A.), 1937-39. *Publications:* several papers on coal and oil hydrogenation and allied subjects. *Recreations:* shooting, yachting. *Address:* St. Peter's Well, Lodsworth, nr. Petworth, Sussex. *T.:* Lodsworth 302. *Clubs:* Constitutional, Roya Thames Yacht. [*Died* 29 *Nov.* 1955.

GORDON, Mervyn Henry, C.M.G. 1917; C.B.E. 1919; M.D. Oxon.; M.A., B.Sc., F.R.S.; Hon. Lt.-Col. R.A.M.C.; Hon. LL.D. (Edin.) 1936; Hon. F.R.S.M. 1940; Consulting Bacteriologist to St. Bartholomew's Hospital; member of Army Pathology Advisory Committee; *b.* 22 June 1872; *s.* of late Canon H. D. Gordon, M.A., Rector and Vicar of Harting, Sussex, and E. O., *d.* of late Dean Buckland; *m.* 1916, Mildred Olive (*d.* 1953), *d.* of late Sir William Power, K.C.B., F.R.S. *Educ.:* Marlborough; Oxford. Continuously occupied since 1898 at medical research in connection with problems of infection and immunity; appointed by Army Council Consulting Bacteriologist for Cerebro-spinal Fever, 1915-19. *Publications:* numerous papers in Medical and Scientific Periodicals, and Official Reports to the Local Government Board, Office of Works, and Medical Research Council. *Recreation:* archæology. *Address;* Holly Lodge, East Molesey, Surrey. *T.:* Molesey 111.
[*Died* 26 *July* 1953.

GORDON, Air Commodore Robert, C.B. 1920; C.M.G. 1919; D.S.O. 1915; late R.A.F.; Deputy Area Commandant, Scottish Area, Edinburgh, Observer Corps, since 1939; *b.* Burmah, 1882; *e. s.* of Robert Gordon, M.I.C.E., and Gertrude Mary Gordon; *m.*; one *d.* *Educ.:* Fettes College, Edinburgh. Joined Royal Marines, 1900; commenced flying, 1911; joined Naval Air Service, 1911; active service—Seaplane Patrol, North Sea, East Africa (Königsberg operations in Rufigi River) (D.S.O.); Mesopotamia with Gen. Townshend's Force, and after with force attempting to relieve Kut; Ægean Sea during 1917 and 1918; South Russia (Caspian Sea), 1918 and 1919; commanded Somaliland operations, R.A.F., 1920 (C.B.); retired list, 1925. *Recreations:* golf, fishing.
[*Died* 25 *Sept.* 1954.

GORDON, Robert Abercromby, Q.C. 1924; J.P. Eastbourne; Recorder of Margate, 1936-44; *m.* 1934, Hilda Speid, *d.* of late Herbert Michell, J.P., Eastbourne. *Educ.:* St. Paul's School; Peterhouse, Cambridge, M.A., LL.M. Called to Bar, 1904; Bencher of Inner Temple, 1931; Member of S.E. Circuit; has been twice to South America on Legal Commissions; Lecturer to the Law Society on Commercial Law, 1921-23; during war (1914-19) employed abroad by Military Intelligence Department of the War Office, subsequently a Military Service (C.L.) Commissioner; Member of Church Assembly for Diocese of Chichester, 1934-41. *Publications:* Compulsory Acquisition of Land and Compensation, 1929; 2nd Edit. 1936; sole editor of 7th Edition of Cripps on Compensation, 1931, 8th edition, 1938; with late Lord Hanworth, Master of the Rolls, contributed the articles on Damages to Hailsham's Laws of

England, 1933. *Address:* 4 St. John's Mansions, Eastbourne. *T.:* Eastbourne 465. [*Died* 5 *Nov.* 1954.

GORDON, Roland Graham, C.I.E. 1932; *b.* 30 October 1880; *s.* of late Rev. A. Gordon; *m.* 1907, H. C. Z., *d.* of Rev. R. Z. Walker; (*s.* died on active service) one *d.* *Educ.:* Marlborough; Selwyn Coll., Cambridge. Entered Indian Civil Service, 1903; Collector of Kolaba, 1920-23; of Bijapur, 1924-26; of Nasik, 1927-31; Member of Indian Legislative Assembly, 1926; retired 1932; Alderman of the City Council of Salisbury City; Mayor of Salisbury, 1947-49. *Publication:* R.G.G. His Verses, 1917. *Address:* 1 The Crescent, Hill View Road, Salisbury, Wiltshire. *T.:* Salisbury 3357. [*Died* 1 *April* 1958.

GORDON, Walter Maxwell, M.A.; *m.* Gladys. *Educ.:* Rossall School (Scholar); Christ's College, Camb. (Scholar). Assistant Master, Tonbridge School; Upper VI Form Master and Housemaster, 1900-23; Headmaster of Wrekin College, Wellington, Shropshire, 1923-44. *Address:* Parlor's Hall, Bridgnorth, Shropshire. [*Died* 30 *June* 1951.

GORDON CLARK, His Honour Judge Alfred Alexander; Judge of County Courts since 1950; *b.* 4 Sept. 1900; 3rd *s.* of late Henry Herbert Gordon Clark; *m.* 1933, Mary Barbara, *e. d.* of Sir William Lawrence, 3rd Bt., and of late Lady Lawrence; one *s.* two *d.* *Educ.:* Rugby; New College, Oxford. Called to the Bar, Inner Temple, 1924. Temporary Officer, Ministry of Economic Warfare, 1940. Temporary Legal Assistant, Director of Public Prosecutions Department, 1940-45. *Publications:* (ed.) Roscoe's Criminal Evidence, 16th edn., 1952; under *pseudonym* of Cyril Hare: Tenant for Death, 1937; Death is No Sportsman, 1938; Suicide Excepted, 1939; Tragedy at Law, 1942; With a Bare Bodkin, 1946; The Magic Bottle, 1946; When the Wind Blows, 1949; An English Murder, 1951; That Yew Tree's Shade, 1954; He Should Have Died Hereafter, 1958; short stories, etc., in various publications. *Address:* Berry's Croft, Westhumble, Dorking, Surrey. *T.:* Dorking 3169. *Club:* Reform. [*Died* 25 *Aug.* 1958.

GORDON CLARK, Henry Herbert, M.A., D.L., F.R.G.S., *b.* 24 March, 1861; *s.* of Gordon Wyatt Clark and Anna Maria Welch; *m.* 1895, Helen, 4th *d.* of Nathaniel Tertius Lawrence; three *s.* one *d.* *Educ.:* Winchester; Exeter College, Oxford. Entered his family's House, Matthew Clark and Sons, Foreign wine and spirit importers, London 1883; Member of Surrey County Council, 1895-1908; High Sheriff Surrey, 1920-21; 2nd Lieutenant Hampshire Carabiniers Yeomanry Cavalry, 1900; transferred to Surrey (Princess of Wales's) Imperial Yeomanry, 1901; raised and commanded 'C' Squadron; Major, 1902; raised and commanded 10th Bn. Surrey Volunteer Regt. 1916 which in 1917 became 4th (V.B.) The Queen's (Royal West Surrey) Regt. of which he was 2nd in command, and is Hon. Major; joined the Direction of the London Life Association, 1913, resigned, 1950; Chm., 1931, Pres. 1934-45, Reigate Division of Surrey Conservative and Unionist Assoc.; Chm. of Council of St. John's Foundation School, Leatherhead, Surrey, 1930-34. *Recreations:* all field sports, and bird watching. *Address:* Mill Way, Westcott, Dorking, Surrey. *T.:* Westcott 57. *Club:* City of London. [*Died* 9 *July* 1951.

GORDON-FINLAYSON, General Sir Robert, K.C.B., *cr.* 1937 (C.B. 1937); C.M.G. 1918; D.S.O. 1915; D.L. Suffolk; *b.* 15 April 1881; *s.* of late David Finlayson, 27 The Grove, Boltons, S.W.; *m.* 1912, Mary Leslie, *d.* of late James Richmond of Kincairney, Perthshire; two *s.* one *d.* Entered Army, from Suffolk Artillery Militia, 1900; Capt. 1908; Maj. 1914; Maj.-Gen. 1930; Lt.-Gen. 1936; Gen. 1937; served European War, 1914-18 (despatches eight times, Bt. Lt.-Col., Bt. Col., D.S.O., C.M.G.); North Russia, 1918-19; Mil. Asst. to C.I.G.S., 1921; A.D.C. to the King, 1929-30; G.S.O. 1 War Office, 1922-25; G.S.O. 1 Staff Coll., 1925-1927; C.R.A., 3rd Division, 1927-30; Commanded Rawalpindi District, 1931-34; Commander 3rd Division, 1934-36; Commander-in-Chief British Troops in Egypt, 1938-39; Adjutant-General to the Forces, 1939-40, and Member of Army Council; General Officer Commanding-in-Chief, Western Command, 1940-41; A.D.C. General to the King, 1940-1941; retired pay, 1941; Special Commissioner Imperial War Graves Commission, 1942; Special Commissioner Duke of York's R. Mil. School, 1942; Colonel Commandant R.A., 1936-46; Colonel Commandant R.H.A. 1937-47. Member of W. Suffolk C.C., 1949. *Address:* Wickerstreet House, Kersey, Hadleigh, Suffolk. *T.:* Boxford (Sfk.) 210. *Clubs:* United Service; West Suffolk County (Bury St. Edmunds). [*Died* 23 *May* 1956.

GORDON-LUHRS, Lt.-Col. Henry; *see* Luhrs.

GORDON-SMITH, Sir Allan Gordon, K.B.E., *cr.* 1941; Kt. *cr.* 1939; D.L. Middlesex; Chairman S. Smith & Sons (England) Ltd.; *b.* 1881; *s.* of late Samuel Smith; *m.* 1904, Hilda Beatrice, *d.* of late Edward Jarvis Cave; one *s.* three *d.* *Address:* Molecomb, Goodwood, Chichester, Sussex. *T.:* Halnaker 236. [*Died* 12 *Feb.* 1951.

GORDON-TAYLOR, Sir Gordon, K.B.E., *cr.* 1946 (O.B.E. 1919); C.B. 1942; Hon. LL.D. (Toronto), 1941; (Melb.) 1947; Hon. M.D. (Athens) 1948; (Lille) 1960; Hon. Sc.D. (Camb.), 1952; M.A. Aberd., M.S., B.Sc. Lond.; F.R.C.S.; F.R.A.C.S. (Hon.); F.A.C.S. (Hon.); F.R.C.S. (Can.) (Hon.); F.R.C.S. Ed. (Hon.); F.R.C.S.I. (Hon.); F.F.A.R.C.S. (Hon.); Commander Legion of Merit, U.S.A., 1946; Temp. Surgeon Rear-Admiral. Consulting Surgeon to R.N., to Middlesex Hospital, to Alfred and St. Vincent's Hosp., Melbourne; late Surgeon to Out-Patients, Royal Northern Hosp.; Surgeon to Roy. Scottish Hosp. and Corp.; Member of the Council (1932-48) and Vice-Pres. (1941-43) R.C.S. of England, Hunterian Professor of Surgery (1929, 1942 and 1944), Examiner in Anatomy, R.C.S.; late Lecturer on Surgery and Hon. Demonstrator of Anatomy, Middlesex Hospital; late Examiner in Surgery, Univs. of Cambridge, London, Belfast, Leeds, Durham, Edinburgh; Moseley Prof. of Surgery, Peter Bent-Brigham Hosp., Harvard Univ., pro tem., 1941 and 1946; Post-Graduate Prof. of Surgery, Univ. Cairo, 1947. Donald Balfour Lecture in Surgery, Univ. of Toronto, 1938; Orator, Medical Society of London, 1940; First Moynihan Memorial Lecture, Univ. Leeds, 1940; Pres. Med. Soc. of London, 1941-42; Pres. R. Soc. of Medicine, 1944-46; Pres. Assoc. of Surgeons, Great Britain and Ireland, 1944-45; Bradshaw Lecture, R.C.S., 1942; Thomas Vicary Lecture, R.C.S., 1944-45 and 1954; Lettsomian Lectures, Med. Soc. Lond., 1944-1945; Syme Oration, R.A.C.S., 1947; Sheen Memorial Lecture, Univ. of Wales, 1949; Harveian Lecture, Harveian Soc., 1949; Centenary Rutherford Morison Lecture, 1953; Hunterian Oration, Hunterian Soc., 1954; Diamond Jubilee R.A.M.C. Oration, 1958; Hon. Mem. Soc. of Medical Consultants to the Armed Forces, 1955; Triennial Gold Medal, Roy. Soc. Med., 1956; John Fraser Memorial Lecture, Edin. Univ., 1957; Cavendish Lecture, 1958; Mitchell Banks Lecture, 1958; Huxley Lecture, 1960; Fleming Lecture, Royal F.P.S. Glasgow, 1960; Chairman Horatian Society. Hon. Fellow: Royal Society Medicine; Hunterian Soc., 1949; Assoc. of Surgeons of Gt. Britain and Ireland, 1955; Amer. Surgical Assoc.; Membre d'Honneur International Soc. of Surg. (Vice-President Congress, 1949); Member hon étranger Académie Royale de Médecine de Belgique, 1948; Membre (Hon.) Académie de Chirurgie de

Paris, 1952, Société Belge de Chirurgie and other Belgian, also Greek, Surgical Socs.: membre, Assoc. Française de Chirurgie, Soc. Chir. de Lyon; Corr. Mem. Deutsche Gesellschaft für Chir.; Member, Norwegian Med. Assoc.; *m.* 1920, Florence Mary, F.R.S.A. (*d.* 1949), *e. d.* of late John Pegrume, Ex. *Educ.:* Gordon's Coll., Aberdeen; Aberdeen Univ.; Middlesex Hosp. Demstr. of Anatomy at King's College; served European War, 1915-1919; and War of 1939-46; sometime Acting Consulting Surgeon, 4th Army, B.E.F., 1918. *Publications:* books and contributions to medical jls. on anatomy and on abdominal, cancer, military surgery, and biography. *Address:* 102 Harley St., W.1. *T.A.:* Anastomose, Wesdo, London. *T.:* Welbeck 8000. *Clubs:* Oriental, M.C.C. [*Died* 3 *Sept.* 1960.

GORE, Lt.-Col. Frederic Lawrence, C.I.E. 1921; D.S.O. 1932; O.B.E. 1918; *b.* 18 Jan. 1884; *s.* of John Lawrence Gore; *m.* 1914, Rhoda Plaistowe; no *c.* *Educ.:* Malvern College; Sandhurst. 2nd Lieut. The Green Howards (Alexandra, Princess of Wales's Own Yorkshire Regiment), 1904; Co. Officer, 1/113th Infantry, Indian Army; Captain, 1913; Major, 1919; Lt.-Col. 1929; Co. Comn. 5/2 Punjab Regt., 1922; 2nd-in-command 5/2 Punjab Regiment 1928; seconded to the Ministry of Defence, Baghdad; D.A.Q.M.G. Iraq Army, 1921-27; commanded 5/2 Punjab Regt. 1929-33; retired, 1933; served East Africa (Somaliland), 1908-10 (medal with clasp); European War, 1914-19; Mesopotamia, 1917-18 (despatches twice, O.B.E.); Iraq, 1920-21 (despatches, C.I.E.); N.W. Frontier of India, 1930-31 (despatches D.S.O.). Served war of 1939-45, Royal Observer Corps, 1940-45, Observer Commandant 26th Group. *Address:* Bryn Mynach, Abbey Road, Llangollen, Denbighshire. *T.:* Llangollen 3200. *Club:* East India and Sports. [*Died* 21 *April* 1952.

GORING, Capt. Sir Forster Gurney, 12th Bt., *cr.* 1627; late Lieut. 1st Royal Sussex Regt.; Captain of Invalids Royal Hospital, Chelsea; *b.* 19 June 1876; *s.* of 11th Bart. and Sarah Anne (*d.* 1904) *d.* of late John Hickin, Lichfield; *S.* father, 1911; *m.* 1st, 1917, Lenore Consuelo Marguerite (*d.* 1941), *o. d.* of Sir W. L. R. Currie, 4th Bart; 2nd, 1943, Hilda Macmillan, *d.* of late Major R. M. Dunlop, J.P., Holehird, Windermere. Served S. Africa, 1900-2 (Queen's medal 2 clasps, King's medal 2 clasps). *Heir:* *nephew* William Burton Nigel, 2nd. Lieut., 1st. Bn. Royal Sussex Regt., *b.* 21 June 1933. *Address:* Hyden, Broadwater Green, Worthing, Sx. *T.:* 1155; The Royal Hospital, Chelsea, S.W.3. [*Died* 1 *May* 1956.

GORMAN, Albert; Chairman, Metropolitan Water Board, since 1953; *b.* 30 Dec. 1883; *m.* 1905, Ethel Jane Wrangle; three *s.* two *d.* Member, Woolwich Borough Council for 30 years (Mayor 1940-41); Member, L.C.C. Welfare Cttee. for 20 years; Vice-Chairman, Metropolitan Water Board, 1948-53. *Address;* 61 Woolwich New Road, S.E.18. *T.:* Woolwich 0440. [*Died* 27 *May* 1959.

GORRINGE, Rev. Reginald Ernest Pennington; Custos of St. John's Hospital, Heytesbury, Wilts, since 1937; Canon of Alton Borealis in Salisbury Cathedral; *b.* 7 Sept. 1871; *s.* of Peter Rollins and Fanny Eliza Gorringe; *m.* 1907, Rachel Emilia Louisa Morrell (*d.* 1951). *Educ.:* Blundell's School; B.N.C. Oxford; Wells Theological College. Curate of Higham Ferrers cum Chelveston, Northants, 1897-99; S. Mark, Peterborough, 1899-1906; Vicar of Maxey cum Deeping Gate, Northants, 1906-10; Rector of Manston, Dorset, 1910-28; Vicar of S. Thomas', Salisbury, 1928-37; Rural Dean of Wilton, 1930-37; Rural Dean of Heytesbury, 1944-46; C.F., 1916-17; Hon. C.F., 1919-. *Address:* St. John's Hospital, Heytesbury, Wilts. *T.:* Sutton Veney 217. [*Died* 23 *Aug.* 1959.

GORTON, Rt. Rev. Neville Vincent, D.D., M.A.; Bishop of Coventry since 1943; *b.* 1888; *s.* of Rev. C. V. Gorton, Hon. Canon of Manchester; *m.* 1926, Ethel Ingledew Daggett; two *s.* one *d.* *Educ.:* Marlborough; Balliol College, Oxford (Exhibitioner and Aubrey Moore Student). Deacon, 1914; priest, 1916; Assistant chaplain at Sedbergh School, 1914-34; Headmaster Blundell's School, Tiverton, 1934-43. *Address:* The Bishop's House, Coventry. *T.:* Coventry 2167. *Club:* National Liberal. [*Died* 30 *Nov.* 1955.

GORVIN, John Henry, C.B.E. 1920; Assistant Secretary (retired) in Ministry of Agriculture and Fisheries; Officer of Crown of Belgium; Chevalier of Crown of Italy; St. Sava of Serbia; Mérite Agricole of France; *b.* Sept. 1886; *s.* of John Hall Gorvin and Clara Hinks, Bideford, Devon; *m.* 1914, Winifred, *d.* of James Seldon; three *d.* *Educ.:* Strand School; King's College, London. Ministry of Agriculture and Fisheries, 1906-14, and 1926-38; 1914-25 Royal Commission on Wheat Supplies; Allied Food Council and Official Food and Relief Organisations in Europe; Member of Jamaica Banana Commission, 1935-36; Special Commissioner to Turks and Caicos Islands, 1936; Commissioner of Government, Newfoundland, 1939-41; Inter-Allied Committee on Post-War Requirements, 1941-44; U.N.R.R.A., 1944-47; Chairman Mauritius Economic Commission, 1947-48. *Address:* Beacon Road, Seaford, Sussex. [*Died* 20 *Jan.* 1960.

GOSCHEN, 2nd Viscount (*cr.* 1900); **George Joachim Goschen** of Hawkhurst; P.C. 1930; G.C.S.I., *cr.* 1929; G.C.I.E., *cr.* 1924; C.B.E. 1918; Commandant Sussex Special Constabulary; late Lt.-Col. 2nd Vol. Batt. East Kent Regiment; *b.* 1866; *e. s.* of 1st Viscount Goschen and Lucy, *d.* of John Dalley; *S.* father, 1907; *m.* 1893, Lady Evelyn Gathorne-Hardy, C.I. 1930 (*d.* 1943), 5th *d.* of 1st Earl of Cranbrook; two *d.* *Educ.:* Rugby; Balliol College, Oxford. Was Private Secretary to Governor of N.S. Wales, and (unpaid) to his father at Admiralty; Joint Parliamentary Secretary, Board of Agriculture, 1918; M.P. (C.) E. Grinstead, Sussex, 1895-1906; Governor of Madras, 1924-29; Viceroy and Acting Governor-General, India, June-Nov. 1929; A.D.C. to Lord Roberts, Commander-in-Chief; late Hon. Col. 4th Buffs East Kent Regiment. *Heir:* *nephew,* John Alexander, *b.* 1906. *Address:* The Cottage, Flimwell, Hawkhurst, Kent. *T.:* Flimwell 54. *Club:* Carlton. [*Died* 24 *July* 1952.

GOSFORD, 5th Earl of (*cr.* 1806); **Archibald Charles Montagu Brabazon Acheson,** M.C.; Bt. of Nova Scotia, 1628; Baron Gosford, 1776; Viscount Gosford, 1785; Baron Worlingham (U. K.), 1835; Baron Acheson (U.K.), 1847; D.L. Co. Armagh; Lt.-Colonel, retired; Director, British American Tobacco Co. (China), Ltd.; *b.* 26 May 1877; *e. s.* of 4th Earl and Lady Louisa Augusta Beatrice Montagu, D.B.E. (*d.* 1944), 2nd *d.* of 7th Duke of Manchester; *S.* father, 1922; *m.* 1st, 1910, Mildred (who obtained a divorce, 1928), *d.* of late John Ridgely Carter; two *s.* two *d.*; 2nd, 1928, Mrs. Beatrice Breese. *Educ.:* Harrow. Late Lt. Coldstream Guards; served S.A., 1899-1901 (wounded Modder River); European War, 1914-18 (wounded, despatches, M.C., Croix de Guerre, Brevet Major and Lt.-Col.); a Knight of Grace, Order of St. John of Jerusalem in England. *Heir:* *s.* Viscount Acheson. *Address:* Gosford Castle, Markethill, Co. Armagh, N. Ireland. [*Died* 20 *March* 1954.

GOSLING, Reginald George, C.B.E. 1955; Director, Co-operative Wholesale Society, since 1942; Chairman: Welwyn Garden City Development Corporation (New Town) since 1948; Hatfield Development Corporation since 1948; *b.* 18 Feb. 1899; *s.* of Isaac Gosling and Mary (*née* Quye); *m.* 1925, Mary Law; one *s.* one *d.* Director London Co-operative Society, 1929-34 (Pres. 1934-

1942). *Address:* 6 Hall Grove, Welwyn Garden City, Herts. *T.:* Welwyn Garden 787. [*Died* 17 *July* 1958.

GOSS, John; baritone vocalist; *b.* 10 May 1894; *s.* of Charles Joseph and Nellie Goss, London; *m.* Mabel, 2nd *d.* of Edward Gill, Lewisham; one *d.* *Educ.:* various Council Schools; Woodbrooke Settlement, Birmingham; Ruskin College, Oxford. Errand boy, golf-caddy, page-boy; labourer in Lancashire cotton factory; fitter's mate; clerk, etc.; first engagement as vocalist with a touring concert party, The Buskins; definitely adopted singing profession, 1920; pupil of Victor Beigel and Reinhold von Warlich; has toured much in U.S.A., Canada and the Orient in recent years. Settled in Canada as teacher of singing, in 1940. *Publications:* Cockroaches and Diamonds (novel), 1937; The Oxford Song Anthology; Ballads of Britain, 1938; The Daily Express Community Song Book; Musical Editor of The Week-End Book. *Recreations:* gardening and motoring. *Address:* 4114 West 14th Avenue, Vancouver, British Columbia, Canada. [*Died* 13 *Feb.* 1953.

GOSS-CUSTARD, Reginald, F.R.C.O.; Organist, Alexandra Palace, since 1930; Organist and Choirmaster, St. Michael's, Chester Square, W.1, 1923-48; *b.* 29 March 1877; *s.* of Walter Goss-Custard; *m.* Lilian (*d.* 1944), *d.* of Stephen C. Jones; one *d.* *Educ.:* privately. Organist, Battle Abbey Church, 1894-1900; Assistant St. Margaret's, Westminster, 1900-2; then Organist and Choirmaster, 1902-13; Organist Bishopsgate Institute, E.C., 1914-39; American Tour, 1916; Hon. Fellow, R.C.O. *Publications:* Systematic Organ Pedalling and General Interpretation; over thirty Original Organ Compositions; many arrangements of Wagner, Tschaikowsky, etc.; articles in musical periodicals relating to Modern Organs and Organ Playing. *Recreation:* motoring. *Address:* Ingleside, 8 Deepdene Vale, Dorking, Surrey. [*Died* 13 *June* 1956.

GOSSE, Alfred Hope, T.D., M.D., F.R.C.P.; retired from medical practice; Consulting Physician: Brompton Hospital; St. Mary's Hospital; King Edward VII Sanatorium, Midhurst; *b.* Wallaroo, S. Australia, 1882; *s.* of John Gosse, M.R.C.S., L.R.C.P.; unmarried. *Educ.:* St. Peter's College, Adelaide, S. Australia; Gonville and Caius College, Cambridge. M.A Cantab., 1910; M.D. Cantab., 1914; F.R.C.P. Lond., 1923; served European War, 1914-19; O.C. Officers Hospital, Beit Naama, Mesopotamia, 1917-19 (despatches thrice, Bt. Major); Pres. Harveian Med. Soc., 1933-34; Pres., 1942 1943, and Hon. Treasurer Med. Soc., London. *Publications:* Short articles in medical journals, dealing with diseases of the heart and lungs. *Address:* 129 Chiltern Court, Baker St., N.W.1. *Club:* United University. [*Died* 23 *June* 1956.

GOSSE, Sir James Hay, Kt., *cr.* 1947; President R. Zoological Soc. of S.A., 1923-1947, on Council since 1919; Chairman Fauna and Flora Board of S.A. (Flinders Chase) since 1939; Member Board of S.A. Museum since 1939; President Boy Scouts Assoc., 1926-29; *b.* 1876; *s.* of William Christie Gosse; *m.* 1908, Joanna Lang, M.B.E., *d.* of T. E. Barr Smith; four *s.* one *d.* Chairman: George Wills & Co. Ltd.; Executor Trustee and Agency Co. of S.A., Ltd.; Wills Gilchrist & Sanderson, Pty. Ltd., Brisbane; Bank of Adelaide, S. Australia; Director: Adelaide Steamship Co. Ltd.; S. Aust. Portland Cement Co. Ltd.; Royal Insurance Co. Ltd. (S.A. Local Board); Gilchrist Watt & Sanderson Pty. Ltd., Sydney; J. A. Brown & Albermain Seaham Collieries, Ltd.; Consul for Denmark at Adelaide; Pres. Adelaide Chamber of Commerce, 1936-37; Rep. Australian Chambers of Commerce at Internat. Business Conf., New York, 1944. O.St.J., 1946; Kt. of Dannebrog, 1934. *Recreations:* gardening, walking. *Address:* Wairoa, Aldgate, S. Australia. *Club:* Adelaide (Adelaide). [*Died* 14 *Aug.* 1952.

GOSSE, Philip, M.D., M.R.C.S., L.R.C.P.; Fellow of Royal Society of Literature; Author; Chairman of the Golden Head Press; late Fellow Commoner, Trinity College, Cambridge; *b.* 13 Aug 1879; *o. s.* of late Sir Edmund Gosse, C.B.; *m.* 1st; one *d.*; 2nd; one *d.*; 3rd, 1943, Anna Gordon Keown (*d.* 1957). *Educ.:* Haileybury; St. Bartholomew's Hospital. Late Medical Superintendent, The Radium Institute, London; accompanied the FitzGerald Expedition to the Andes as Naturalist, 1896-97; joined the Army, 1914; served in France with 23rd Division until autumn 1917, and then in India till close of the War; Member of the Friends of the National Libraries, Society for Nautical Research; Corr. Mem. Jamaica Institute; Member of St. Helena branch of Ancient Order of Foresters; Member Anglo-Danish Society. *Publications:* Notes on the Natural History of the Aconcagua Valleys, 1899; The Pirates' Who's Who, 1924; Birds of the Balearic Islands; Mammals of Flanders; My Pirate Library, 1926; Tuberculous Adenitis treated by Radium, 1926; Bibliography of Capt. Ch. Johnson; Gathered Together (with H. Gosse); Rest Billets; Life of Sir John Hawkins, 1930; The History of Piracy, 1932; Memoirs of a Camp Follower, 1934; Go to the Country, 1935; Traveller's Rest, 1937; St. Helena, 1938; The Squire of Walton Hall, 1940; A Naturalist Goes to War (Penguin); An Apple a Day, 1948; Dr. Viper, 1952. *Recreation:* wrestling. *Address:* 15 Grantchester Street, Cambridge. *Clubs:* Savile, Fountain, Sette of Odd Volumes. [*Died* 3 *Oct.* 1959.

GOSSIP, Alex.; General Secretary, National Amalgamated Furnishing Trades Association, 1906-41; cabinetmaker; *b.* 11 Sept. 1862; Scottish parentage; *m.* 1884; three *c.* *Educ.:* Madras Academy, Cupar, Fife. Member of Trade Union from 1881; filled all Trade Union Branch positions; District Secretary for Glasgow for many years; General Secretary for Scottish Cabinetmakers Union until amalgamation with the English Union 1902, when removed to London; joined I.L.P. at beginning of that organisation and has been a member ever since; connected with the Socialist Sunday School Movement since its inception and had a large school in Glasgow; opened some twenty Socialist Sunday Schools since coming to London; opened Fulham Socialist Sunday School on 4 Sept. 1904, and has been Superintendent ever since; a supporter of the Left Wing, Industrial and Political sides of Labour Movement; made a Freeman of Fulham Borough, 1935. *Recreations:* reading and Socialist Sunday School movement. *Address:* 2 Pellant Road, Fulham, S.W.6; 219 Golders Green Road, N.W.11. *T.:* Speedwell 8273. [*Died* 14 *May* 1952.

GOSSIP, Rev. Arthur John, M.A.; D.D. (Edin.); LL.D. (Glas.); *b.* 1873; *y. s.* of late Robert Gossip, newspaper editor in Glasgow and Edinburgh, and Margaret Grieve, *d.* of David Mundell, Inverlaul, Loch Broom, Ross-shire; *m.* 1900, Nina (*d.* 1927), *d.* of Rev. W. H. Carslaw, D.D., Helensburgh; three *s.* two *d.* *Educ.:* George Watson's Coll., Edinburgh; Edinburgh Univ.; New College, Edinburgh. Licensed to Ministry of Free Church of Scotland, 1898; Minister at St. Columba's, Liverpool, 1899; West United Free Church, Forfar, 1901; St. Matthew's, Glasgow, 1910; Chaplain at Front, 1917-18; Minister of Beechgrove Church, Aberdeen, 1921-28; Professor of Christian Ethics and Practical Theology, Trinity College, Glasgow, 1928, and in Glasgow University, 1939; retired, Sept. 1945; Warrack Lecturer, 1925; McNeil-Frazer Lecturer, 1932-35. *Publications:* From the Edge of the Crowd (Scholar as Preacher Series), 1924; In Christ's Stead, 1925; The Galilean Accent, 1926, The

Hero in Thy Soul, 1928, Experience Worketh Hope, 1945 (all three in Scholar as Preacher Series); In the Secret Place of the Most High, 1947; John's Gospel in the Interpreters Bible, etc *Address:* Inverton, Kingussie, Inverness-shire. *T.:* Kingussie 326.
[*Died* 26 *May* 1954.

GOTTO, Basil; sculptor; *b.* 10 Aug. 1866, *s.* of late Henry J. Gotto, of New House Park, St. Albans; *m.* 1913, Sibyl, *e. d.* of late Sir Ellis Ashmead Bartlett, M.P.; two *s.* *Educ.:* Harrow (Drawing Prize, 1888). Studied Art in Paris; entered Royal Academy Schools, 1887; Landseer Scholar, 1890; War Correspondent for Daily Express, South Africa, 1899; first exhibited Sculpture, R.A. 1892; regular exhibitor since 1899; award at Salon, 1909; Staff-Officer for Musketry, 1917-19. Principal works: Bacchus; Beggar Man; Nausicaa; Memorial to Middlesex Yeomanry, St. Paul's Cathedral; The Fighting Newfoundlander and the Caribou (Newfoundland Battle Memorial); Army and Navy Club War Memorial. *Recreations:* shooting, sailing, bridge. *Address:* The Bridge House, Twyford, Winchester. *T.:* Twyford 23. *Clubs:* Arts; Hants County.
[*Died* 19 *Oct.* 1954.

GOTTO, Brig. Christopher Hugh, D.S.O. 1919; M.C.; *b.* 29 Dec. 1888; *s.* of Christopher Gotto; unmarried. *Educ.:* Harrow. 2nd Lieut. in Lancashire Field Artillery, 1907; Regular Commission Devon Regt., 1911; served European War, 1914-19 (despatches, D.S.O., M.C.), retired pay, 1945. Order of the Crown of Italy; Belgian Croix de Guerre. *Recreations:* cricket, golf, shooting and fishing. *Address:* Yeolmbridge House, nr. Launceston, Cornwall. *Club:* United Service. [*Died* 16 *Nov.* 1959.

GOUDEKET, Mdme. Maurice; *see* Colette.

GOUDGE, James Alfred, C.B.E. 1920; F.C.I.S.; *b.* 28 Dec. 1862, *s.* of late James Valentine Goudge of London; *m.* 1896, Cecil Amelia (*d.* 1933), *d.* of late John Barfield, Thatcham, Berks; one *s.* two *d.* *Educ.:* Thanet School, Margate. Manager, Buenos Aires and Pacific Railway in Buenos Aires, 1900-13; Member, Buenos Aires Port Commission and other National Commissions in Argentine; travelled extensively and reported on railways in South and Central America, Canada, and Asia Minor; Member War Cabinet Commission on Utilization of Ports, 1917. *Address:* Rannoch Lodge, Reigate. *T.:* 3238. [*Died* 18 *Feb.* 1955.

GOUGH, 4th Viscount (of Goojerat, Punjab, and Limerick), *cr.* 1849; **Hugh William Gough,** M.C.; Lt.-Col.; *b.* 22 Feb. 1892; *e. s.* of 3rd Viscount Gough and Lady Georgiana Frances Henrietta Pakenham (*d.* 1943), *e. d.* of 4th Earl of Longford; *S.* father, 1919; *m.* 1935, Margaretta Elizabeth, *o. d.* of Sir Spencer Maryon-Wilson, 11th Bt.; one *s.* *Educ.:* Eton; New College, Oxford (B.A.). Served European War, 1914-18 (severely wounded, despatches twice, M.C., brevet majority); Lt.-Col. 1st Regiment of Iraq Levy Cavalry in Kurdistan, 1922; commanded 1st Batt. Irish Guards, 1930-34; Training Batt. Irish Guards, 1939-42; Inverness Burgh Batt. Home Guard, 1942-1944. J.P., D.L. and C.C. for Inverness-shire. *Heir:* *s.* Hon. Shane Hugh Maryon Gough, *b.* 26 Aug. 1941. *Address:* Inshes House, Inverness. *T.:* Inverness 959. *Clubs:* White's; Highland (Inverness).
[*Died* 4 *Dec.* 1951.

GOUGH, Lt.-Col. Henry Worsley Worsley-, C.M.G. 1915; *b.* 17 Oct. 1874; *o. s.* of George Gough, Fairfield, Lymington, and Caroline, *d.* of late Francis Worsley of Billingham Manor, Isle of Wight; *m.* 1902, Lilias Duff (*d.* 1943), *y. d.* of late Walter Seymour of Ballymore Castle, Co. Galway; two *d.* Entered army, 2nd Batt. Connaught Rangers, 1894; served with Tirah Expeditionary Force, 1897-98 (medal 2 clasps); European War with 3rd Batt. Monmouthshire Regt. 1914-16 (despatches, C.M.G.); Barrister-at-law of the Inner Temple. *Address:* Wicks Close, Binfield, Berks. *T.:* Bracknell 426. *Clubs:* Army and Navy, Travellers'.
[*Died* 17 *Oct.* 1957.

GOULD, Sir Basil John, Kt., *cr.* 1941; C.M.G. 1929; C.I.E. 1921; Indian Civil Service, 1907-47; *b.* 1883; *y. s.* of late Charles Gould, K.C., J.P. of Inner Temple and of Farnham, Surrey; *m.* 1st, 1921, Lorraine Macdonald (*d.* 1935), *e. d.* of Cecil Kebbell, of Te Hoe, Alfredton, N.Z.; one *s.* (and one *s.* died on active service, 1944); 2nd, 1948, Cecily Brent-Good, Yarmouth, I.O.W.; one *s.* *Educ.:* Winchester; New College, Oxford. Appointed to Indian Civil Service (Punjab), 1907, and to Political Department, Government of India, 1909; Under-Secretary to Government of India, Foreign Department, 1910-12; Assistant Private Secretary to Viceroy, 1917; Consul, Sistan, Persia, 1918-25; Counsellor, British Legation, Kabul, 1926-29; various posts in N.W.F.P. and Baluchistan, 1929-35; Political Officer in Sikkim, and for Bhutan and Tibet, 1935-45. *Publications:* (with H. E. Richardson) Tibetan Word Book; and other books on Tibetan Language. *Recreations:* sailing, fishing. *Address:* Westways, Yarmouth, Isle of Wight. *Clubs:* Flyfishers'; Royal Solent Yacht (Yarmouth, I.W.).
[*Died* 27 *Dec.* 1956.

GOULD, Herbert Ross, C.I.E. 1931; *b.* 17 April 1887; *s.* of late A. P. Gould; *m.* 1921, Florence Mary Butler; one *s.* *Educ.:* Clifton College; B.N.C., Oxford. Indian Civil Service, Bombay, 1911; Indian Army Reserve of Officers, 1916-19; Deputy Commissioner, Upper Sind Frontier, 1920-23; Collector, Sholapur, 1924-28; Collector, Poona, 1929-31; Private Secretary to the Governor of Bombay, 1931-34. *Recreations:* golf, lawn tennis, riding, shooting. *Address:* Chestnut Lodge, Horsham, Sussex. *Clubs:* East India and Sports; Phyllis Court (Henley)
[*Died* 20 *Dec.* 1954.

GOULD, Howard Gould; *b.* New York, 1871; *s.* of late Jay Gould and Helen Miller; *m.* 1st, 1898, Viola Kathrine Clemmons; 2nd 1937, Margarete, *d.* of Dr. Marcus Mosheim, Berlin. Member of New York Stock Exchange since 1898; won Lord Dunraven's challenge cup with yacht Niagara. *Address:* No. 1 East 44th Street, New York City, 17, U.S.A.
[*Died* 9 *Sept* 1959.

GOULDEN, Charles Bernard, O.B.E. 1919; M.A., M.D., M.Chir. (Cambridge); F.R.C.S. (England); retired; *b.* 20 Aug. 1879; *e. s.* of late H. J. Goulden of Canterbury and late Isabel Goulden (*née* Wind), of Ashford, Kent; *m.* 1911, Norah, *y. d.* of late J. H. O'Brien, Dublin. *Educ.:* S. Edmund's College, Old Hall; Downing College, Cambridge; Middlesex Hospital. Freeman Scholarship and Leopold Hudson Exhibition, 1903; House-Surgeon Middlesex Hospital, 1903-4, and Royal London Ophthalmic Hospital, 1904-7; Demonstrator of Anatomy University College, Bristol, 1907-1908; Ophthalmic Surgeon Oldham Royal Infirmary, 1909-19. Served European War, Captain R.A.M.C., 1916-19; Ophthalmic Surgeon-in-Charge of Centre at Rouen (despatches). Ophthalmic Surgeon Victoria Hospital for Children, Tite Street, 1919-22; Surgeon-Oculist to Household of H.M. Queen Mary, 1936-49; Cons. Ophth. Surgeon to Queen Alexandra Military Hosp., Millbank, 1933-49; Ophthal. Surgeon to, and Lecturer in Ophthalmology at Medical School of London Hosp., 1919-47; Surgeon to, and Dean of Medical School at, Royal London Ophthalmic (Moorfields) Hosp., 1919-39; Consultant in Ophthalmology, Min. of Pensions and Appeal Board, War Office, and Pensions Appeal Tribunal. Montgomery Lecturer R.C.S. in Ireland, 1926 and 1932; Ophthalmic Surgeon, S. Vincent's Orthopædic Hospital, Eastcote, and the Hostel of S. Luke; Cons. Ophthalmic Surgeon to Kent County Ophth. and Aural Hosp.,

Maidstone; Examiner: D.O.M.S. Conjoint Bd.; Part III M.S., Univ. of London; Vice-Pres. Ophthalmological Soc. of U.K., Pres. 1944-46, Sec., 1924-27; F.R.S.M., Pres. Ophthalmological Branch, 1948-49; F.R.I.P.H.H., Member: Council and Exec. Cttee.; Board of Advanced Medical Studies, Univ. of London, 1926-39; Member of Council of Faculty of Ophthalmologists; Member Cttee. of Applied Optics, Imperial Coll. of Science; Consultant Adviser in Ophthalmology to the E.M.S., Ministry of Health. *Publications:* The Refraction of the Eye, 1924, 2nd Edition, 1938; Translated with Clare Harris, Koby's Slit Lamp Microscopy of the Living Eye, 1925, 2nd Edition, 1930; Contributions to: Encyc. Brit.; Trans. Ophthalmological Soc. of U.K.; Roy. Soc. Med.; British Journ. of Ophthalmology; Bristol Medico-Chirurgical Journ.; Official Hist. of the War. *Address:* Mill House, Shepreth, Camb. *T.:* Melbourn 305. *Club:* Athenæum. [*Died* 20 *Sept.* 1953.

GOVETT, John Romaine, M.C. 1918; Chairman of Consolidated Zinc Corporation and its principal subsidiary companies since 1941; *b.* 16 March 1897; *e. s.* of late Francis A. Govett; *m.* 1929, Angela Mary Mostyn Pritchard; two *s.* one *d.* *Educ.:* Harrow. Served European War, 1914-18, in Army. Partner in Govett, Sons & Co., Stockbrokers, 1919-41. *Recreations:* fishing and shooting. *Address:* Manor House, Newton Stacey, Stockbridge, Hants. *T.:* Chilbolton 260. *Club:* Boodle's. [*Died* 28 *Nov.* 1956.

GOVINDAN NAIR, Diwan Bahadur Chettur, C.I.E. 1939; Endowments Commissioner (on leave) and Secretary to Orissa Legislative Assembly; *b.* 23 Dec. 1881; *s.* of U. Raman Menon and C. Narayani Amma; *m.* 1911, K. Lakshmi; two *s.* four *d.* *Educ.:* Madras Christian College. B.A. and B.L. Madras Univ. and Barrister-at-Law (Cert. of Hons.) Gray's Inn; Advocate, Madras High Court for some years; joined Madras Judicial Service and rose to position of District and Sessions Judge; was Asst. Sec., Under Sec., and Joint Sec. in Law Dept. of Madras Secretariat; attached Officer and Deputy Sec. in Legislative Dept. of Govt. of India; Joint Sec. in Reforms Dept. of Govt. of Bihar and Orissa and Judicial Sec. and Legal Remembrancer to Govt. of Orissa; was nominated Member of Madras Legislative Council and Council of State and Central Assembly in New Delhi; was Sec. to Council of State and Sec. to Advisory Council and Legislative Assembly of Orissa; was a member of Senate of Madras Univ. and Examiner of Master of Law Examination of that Univ. and for Govt. Examinations of Madras and Orissa. *Publication:* A Commentary on the Malabar Tenancy Act. *Recreation:* tennis. *Address:* Cuttack, Orissa, India. [*Died Nov.* 1945.
[*But death not notified in time for inclusion in Who Was Who 1941–1950, first edn.*

GOW, Alexander, M.A., B.Sc.; *b.* Wolverton, 15 May 1869; 5th *s.* of late J. Gow, engineer; *m.* 1904, Lillie Mary (*d.* 1955) *o. d.* of Robert Beaty, Manchester. *Educ.:* Borough Rd. Trg. Coll.; Caius College, Cambridge. Director of Education, Blackburn; Principal, Technical School and Adviser in Higher Education, Blackburn; Principal, Municipal Technical and Secondary School, Warrington; Science Master, County High School, Isleworth; Science Lecturer, Borough Road Training College, Isleworth; Secretary, Imperial College of Science and Technology, London, 1908-34; Hon. Fellow Imperial College, 1946. *Recreation:* golf. *Address:* c/o National Provincial Bank, 18 Cromwell Place, S.W.7. [*Died* 13 *Oct.* 1955.

GOW, Alexander Edward, M.D., B.S. (Lond.); F.R.C.P.; Physician to Household of Duchess of Kent; consulting Physician to St. Bartholomew's Hospital, London; Chief M.O. to Phoenix Assurance Co. and to Equity and Law Life Assurance Soc.; Consulting Physician to London Division of Royal Marines Old Comrades Assoc.; *b.* 9 March 1884; *m.* 1929, Helen Gordon Rannie; two *s.* one *d.* *Educ.:* King Edward VI's, Stratford-on-Avon; St. Bartholomew's Hospital Medical College. Temporary Surgeon Lieutenant R.N., served with R.N.D. throughout Gallipoli Campaign. *Publications:* various Medical. *Address:* 149 Harley St., W.1. *T.:* Welbeck 4444; Robinwood Cottage, Kingston Vale, S.W.15. *T.:* Kingston 2556. [*Died* 19 *Sept.* 1952.

GOWANS, Surgeon Rear-Admiral Francis Jollie, C.B. 1939; M.D., B.S.; *b.* 1880; *s.* of late William Gowans, M.D., F.R.C.S.(Ed.) J.P., of Westoe, South Shields; *m.* 1911, Sara, *d.* of late Robert Lewis. *Educ.:* University of Durham. Joined R.N. 1903; Commanded Royal Naval Hospital, Plymouth, 1936-39; Hon. Surgeon to the King, 1937; retired, 1939; recalled 1939; Commanded Royal Naval Auxiliary Hospital, Newton Abbot, 1939; reverted to retired list, 1942. Russian Order of St. Anne (with Swords), 1916, for services in Battle of Jutland. *Address:* Eversley, Highwick, Newton Abbot, Devon. *T.:* Newton Abbot, 947. [*Died* 16 *April* 1952.

GOWER; *see* Leveson Gower.

GOWER, Ivon Llewellyn Owen; Colonial Civil Servant, retired; *b.* 1874; *s.* of late Samuel John Gower, of California and Hong Kong; *m.* 1911, Ursula Margaret, *e. d.* of late Dr. J. G. Clark, London; two *s.* (and one killed in Normandy D-Day). Barrister, Lincoln's Inn, 1904; Conveyance, Land Dept., East Africa Protectorate (now Kenya Colony and Protectorate), 1908-14; Legal Assistant, Land Dept., 1914-17; served European War, 1914-18; Solicitor-General, 1917-26; sometime acting Attorney General; a Judge of the High Court, Tanganyika Territory, sometime acting Chief Justice, 1926-32. *Recreations:* football, cricket, tennis, golf. *Address:* Hawthorns, The Midway, Nevill Court, Tunbridge Wells, Kent. [*Died* 28 *July* 1955.

GOWER, Sir Robert (Vaughan), K.C.V.O., *cr.* 1935; Kt., *cr.* 1919; O.B.E. 1919 (M.B.E. 1918); Knight of Grace, Order of St. John of Jerusalem; J.P. Kent; Chairman Tunbridge Wells Bench since 1932; Hon. D.C.L. (Budapest); Hon. LL.D. (Szeged); F.S.A.; F.S.G.; late Hon. Col. 88th (City of London) A.A. Regt. (T.A.) R.A. (retired 1947 with permission to retain rank); Pres. 129th Squadron A.T.C. (late Hon. Air Commodore); *e. s.* of late J. R. Gower, of Tunbridge Wells, and Kate, *d.* of late John Fagge, of Tonbridge; *b.* 10 Nov. 1880; *m.* 1st, 1907, Dorothy Susie Eleanor (*d.* 1936), O.St.J., *o. d.* of late H. McClellan Wills, M.A., Exeter; one *d.* (and one *d.* decd); 2nd, 1944, Vera, *d.* of late Dr. C. H. Thomas, and *widow* of R. A. Daniel, M.D., F.R.C.S., Fort View, Co. Wexford. *Educ.:* privately. Law Society Final and Honours, 1903; M.P. (C.) Central Hackney, 1924-29; M.P. (C.) Gillingham Div. of Rochester, 1929-45; Member of Royal Tunbridge Wells Corporation, 1909-34; Alderman, 1914-34; Deputy Mayor, 1910-11-1912-13-20-21; Mayor, 1917-18, 1918-19; Hon. Freeman of Borough, 1925; Freeman of City of London; County Councillor for Kent, 1910-25; Commissioner Land Tax (Kent); Appeal Military Representative Kent Tribunals, 1916-17; Member Ministry of Health Departmental Committee on Superannuation of Municipal and other Local Government Officials, 1925-6-7; Chairman Naval Dockyards Members Committee, House of Commons, 1930-45; Chairman. House of Commons Committee of Members representing Evacuation Areas, 1940-45; Chairman Solicitor Members Group, House of Commons, 1940-45; Chm. Animal Welfare Cttee. in House of Commons, 1929-45; Press R.S.P.C.A. since 1951 (Chm., 1928-51); awarded Society's Silver Medal, 1932, and presented by President of French Republic with Sèvres Vase in recognition of animal welfare work in France, 1931; presented with grande médaille of Ligue Française pour le protection du cheval, 1949; Chairman and Hon. Treasurer National Canine Defence League since 1920; Hon. Member of a number of Overseas Animal Protection Societies; President Pit Ponies Protection Society; Chairman R.S.P.C.A. War Animals (Allies) Fund and Aid for Russian Horses Fund, 1940-45; introduced and piloted through all stages in House of Commons Protection of Animals (Cruelty to Dogs) Act, 1933, Protection of Animals Act, 1934; Cinematograph Films (Animals) Act, 1937, and Dogs Act, 1938; has introduced Dogs Protection Bill, Pit Ponies Protection Bill; Protection of Animals Bill, 1939; President Property Owners' Protection Association since 1931; Chm. Order of St. John Council for County of Kent; F.R.G.S.; Hon. F.F.A.S.; Pres. Kent Law Society, 1939-41; Member International Law Society; Member several Friendly and Benevolent Societies. Master of Turners' Company, 1936-37: Master Pattenmakers' Company, 1935-36; 1936-37; Master Needlemakers' Company, 1929-30; Acting Chairman Canning Town Women's Settlement, 1939-47; Chevalier, Legion of Honour (France); Officer Order of Crown of Belgium; Grand Officer Order of the Nile; Commander Order of Crown of Italy; 2nd Class (with Star) Order of Merit (Hungary); King George Coronation Medal; Special Constabulary Medal. *Publications:* Treaty Revision and the Hungarian Frontiers, 1936; The Succession States and the Hungarian Minorities, 1937; frequent articles in political and genealogical reviews. *Recreations:* genealogy, archæology, and psychical research. *Address:* Sandown Court, Tunbridge Wells. *T.:* Tunbridge Wells 593. *Clubs:* Carlton, Junior Carlton, City Livery; Tunbridge Wells and Counties (Tunbridge Wells). [*Died* 6 *March* 1953.

GOWERS, Sir William Frederick, K.C.M.G., *cr.* 1926 (C.M.G. 1919); M.A.; Barrister (Inner Temple); *b.* 1875; *s.* of late Sir William Gowers, M.D., F.R.S.; *m.* Winifred Bruce, *y. d.* of late William Paul, North Lynn. *Educ.:* Rugby; Trinity Coll., Cambridge; 1st Class Classical Tripos. In service of British South Africa Co. (Southern Rhodesia), 1899-1902; entered Colonial Civil Service, Northern Nigeria, 1902; served with Cameroons Expeditionary Force, 1915-16; Lieut.-Gov., Nigeria, 1921; Governor and Commander-in-Chief, Uganda Protectorate, 1925-32; Senior Crown Agent for the Colonies, 1932-38; Deputy Chm., Cereals Control Board, 1939-40; Civil Defence Liaison Officer, S. Command, 1940-42. Member Governing Body of School of Oriental and African Studies (London University), 1933-. Vice-Pres., Fauna Preservation Society. Legion of Honour, 1917; Grand Officier Order of Leopold. *Recreations:* various. *Address:* 39 Queen's Grove, St. John's Wood, N.W.8. *Clubs:* Bath, Brooks's, M.C.C. [*Died* 7 *Oct.* 1954.

GOWING, Ven. Ellis Norman, M.A.; Vicar of Prittlewell since 1917; *b.* Sydney, 24 April 1883; 3rd *s.* of F. L. Gowing, Sydney; *m.* 1917, Dorothy Mary, *d.* of late Dr. Watts-Ditchfield, 1st Bishop of Chelmsford; two *s.* *Educ.:* University of Sydney. Ordained to Curacy of Picton and the Oaks, 1907-09; Armidale Cathedral, 1910-11; St. James the Less, Bethnal Green, 1911-14; Domestic Chaplain to the Bishop of Chelmsford, 1914-17; Hon. Canon of Chelmsford, 1921-38; Rural Dean of Canewdon and Southend, 1918-49; Archdeacon of Southend, 1938-53; Archdeacon (Emeritus), 1953; Freedom of County Borough of Southend-on-Sea, 1953. *Publication:* John Edwin Watts-Ditchfield, First Bishop of Chelmsford; The Story of Prittlewell Church. *Address:* The Vicarage, Prittlewell, Southend-on-Sea, Essex. *T.:* Southend-on-Sea 43470. [*Died* 2 *March* 1960.

GOWRIE, 1st Earl of, *cr.* 1945; 1st Baron *cr.* 1935, of Canberra and of Dirleton; Viscount Ruthven of Canberra and of Dirleton, *cr.* 1944; **Brig.-Gen. Alexander Gore Arkwright Hore-Ruthven,** V.C. 1899; P.C. 1937; G.C.M.G., *cr.* 1935 (K.C.M.G., *cr.* 1928; C.M.G. 1918); C.B. 1919; D.S.O. 1916, Bar 1918; *b.* Windsor, 6 July 1872; 2nd *s.* of 8th Baron Ruthven; *m.* 1908, Zara, *d.* of John Pollok and Hon. Mrs. Barry of Lismany, Co. Galway, and Ronachan, Argyllshire (*er. s.* killed in action; *yr. s.* died in infancy). *Educ.:* Eton. Joined 3rd Batt. Highland Light Infantry, 1891; attached to Egyptian Army, Soudan, 1898; commanded Camel Corps Detachment at Battle of Gedaref, and subsequent operations (V.C., 4th Class Osmanieh; English and Egyptian medals with clasp; thrice despatches); White Nile, 1899 (despatches); gazetted to Cameron Highlanders, 1899; Special Service Officer, Somaliland, 1903-04; Military Secretary, Viceroy of Ireland, 1905-08; Military Secretary Governor-General of Commonwealth Australia, 1908; served European War, 1914-15 and 1916-18, France and Gallipoli (severely wounded, D.S.O. and bar, C.B., C.M.G., despatches five times); temp. Brig.-Gen. 1917-18; commanded the Welsh Guards, 1920-24; commanded 1st Infantry Brigade (Guards), Aldershot, 1924-1928; Governor of South Australia, 1928-34; Governor of New South Wales, 1935; Governor-General of Commonwealth of Australia, 1936-44; Colonel 1st King's Dragoon Guards, 1940-45; Deputy Constable and Lieutenant-Governor of Windsor Castle, 1945-53; Colonel, Welsh Guards; K.G.St.J.; D.C.L. Oxford, 1945; LL.D. Edin., 1938. Pres. M.C.C., 1948. *Heir:* *g.s.* Viscount Ruthven of Canberra. *Clubs:* Cavalry, Guards; Jockey, Newmarket. [*Died* 2 *May* 1955.

GRABHAM, George Walter, O.B.E.; M.A., F.R.S.E., F.G.S.; *b.* Funchal, Madeira, 1882; *y. s.* of late M. C. Grabham, M.D. *Educ.:* University College School; St. John's College, Cambridge. Formerly Geologist, Geological Survey of Great Britain; subsequently Govt. Geologist also Acting Conservator of Antiquities, Anglo-Egyptian Sudan; retired, 1939, 4th Class Order Mejidie, 3rd Nile. *Publications:* few Government Reports, papers in science journals. *Recreation:* wandering. *Address:* Quinta do Val, Funchal, Madeira. *Clubs:* Athenæum, Union; English Rooms (Funchal). [*Died* 29 *Jan.* 1955.

GRACEY, Captain George Frederick Handel, D.S.O. 1919; *b.* Belfast, Sept. 1878; *s.* of John Gracey, Belfast, and Anna Wood, Dundonald; *m.* 1909, Amelia Turnley Coulter, Belfast; two *s.* two *d.* *Educ.:* Professor O'Neil's Military Law and Training College, Belfast. Missionary, Urfa, Turkey, 1904; Member of American Relief Expedition to the Caucasus to assist the 200,000 Armenians who fled from Turkey to Russia for safety, 1915; piloted the evacuation of 25,000 Armenians from Van to Igdir single-handed, 1916; Intelligence Staff Officer attached to British Military Mission, Tiflis, 1917; raised large numbers of Armenians, Russians and Georgians to hold positions being evacuated by the Russian troops who had turned Bolshevik; captured later by Bolsheviks and imprisoned in Valadikavkaz and Moscow for nine months, 1918; exchanged by British Government and returned to England, 1919; sent out to the Caucasus as British representative to the Armenian Republic at Erivan, Sept. 1919; returned home after the Bolsheviks had overthrown the Trans-Caucasian Republics, 1920. Fellow of The Royal Institute of International Affairs, 1921-. Russian Order of St. Anne, 2nd Class, with Cross Swords; Order of St. Gregory Illuminator, 1st Class; despatches; Overseas Delegate, The Save the Children Fund, 1929; General Secretary,

1937; retired, 1948. *Publications:* magazine articles. *Recreation:* riding. *Address:* 116 Powys Lane, N.13. *T.:* Palmers Green 4248. *Club:* Royal Automobile. [*Died* 17 *March* 1958.

GRÆME, Patrick Neale Sutherland, C.B.E. 1921; D.L.; J.P.; Lord Lieutenant of Orkney since 1948; Vice-Convener and Hon. Sheriff-Substitute, County of Orkney; Barrister-at-law, Lincoln's Inn; S.-E. Circuit; Sec. to Rt. Hon. Viscount Alverstone, Lord Chief Justice of England, 1902-13; Legal Assistant to Judge-Advocate-Gen., 1914-18; Deputy Judge-Advocate, 1918; Deputy Judge-Advocate-General, 1932-38; *b.* 7 Mar. 1877; *s.* of Alexander Malcolm Sutherland Græme and Margaret Isabel, *d.* of Rev. John Mason Neale, D.D., Warden of Sackville College, East Grinstead; *m.* 1903, Bethea Hamilton (*d.* 1943), *d.* of Alexander Maclean, Edinburgh; three *d.* *Educ.:* Malvern College; Pembroke College, Cambridge. B.A., Classical Tripos, 1898; called to Bar, 1903. *Recreations:* shooting, fishing, cricket, golf. *Address:* Græmeshall, Orkney. *Clubs:* M.C.C., Public Schools. [*Died* 26 *Sept.* 1958.

GRAFFTEY-SMITH, Sir Anthony (Paul), Kt. 1960; C.B.E. 1945 (O.B.E. 1944); T.D.; Governor of Bank of Rhodesia and Nyasaland since 1956; *b.* 24 May 1903; *s.* of late Rev. Arthur Grafftey-Smith and late Mabel Barton; *m.* 1938, Marie Eugenie, *d.* of Leopold Leblique, Newcastle upon Tyne; no *c.* *Educ.:* King's School, Ely; privately abroad. Dep. Chief Cashier, alternate Exec. Dir. for U.K. in Internat. Monetary Fund, Washington, 1946, with Bank of England; U.K. Rep. on: Four-Power Commn. of Enquiry into Free Territory of Trieste, 1947; Trieste Commn. at Council of Foreign Ministers, Moscow, 1947; Financial Adviser to: Govt. of S. Rhodesia, 1952-54; Govt. of Fed. of Rhodesia and Nyasaland, 1954-56; Chairman: Kariba Gorge Cttee., 1952-54; Central Africa Currency Bd., 1954-56; Federal Apportionment Commn., 1953-54; Roy. Commonwealth Soc., Salisbury, 1952-; Governor of Rhodesian Coll. of Music, 1954-; Chm. Economic Advisory Council, 1957-; Pres. Inst. of Bankers in S. Africa, 1958-59. Served War of 1939-45 (despatches, O.B.E., C.B.E.); second in Comd. 3rd County of London Yeomanry attached 4/7 Dragoon Guards, France and Belgium; C.O. 1941; Controller of Finance, A.M.G.O.T., 1943; Chief Financial Officer, Allied Commn. for Italy, 1944; demobilised as Brig. 1946. Officer, American Legion of Merit, 1945. *Recreations:* golf, cinemaphotography, motoring in Europe. *Address:* Threadneedle House, Chancellor Avenue, Salisbury, N.12, S. Rhodesia. *T.:* Salisbury 20940. *Clubs:* Bath, M.C.C.; Salisbury, Ruwa Country (S. Rhodesia). [*Died* 14 *Oct.* 1960.

GRAHAM, Brigadier-General Cuthbert Aubrey Lionel, D.S.O. 1915; O.B.E. 1942; D.L. Oxon.; late R.A.; p.s.c.; Director, Joseph Terry and Sons; *b.* 1 Apr. 1882; *s.* of late Eng.-Capt. J.E.D. Graham, R.N.; *m.* 1911, Josephine Margaret, *d.* of late Sir Joseph Terry. Joined R.A., 1900; Bt. Lieut.-Col., 1919; Col. 1923; retired with rank of Brig.-Gen., 1931; served European War, France, 1914-16, North Russia, 1918-19 (despatches six times); B.E.F. and N.W.E.F., 1940 (despatches); County Councillor, 1945-1952; Order of Vladimir, Order of St. Olav, Croix de Guerre (France). *Address:* Denton House, Cuddesdon, Oxon. *Club:* Army and Navy. [*Died* 25 *Aug.* 1957.

GRAHAM, Maj.-Gen. Sir Edward Ritchie Coryton, K.C.B., *cr.* 1915 (C.B. 1900); K.C.M.G., *cr.* 1918; Cheshire Regiment; *b.* 7 Nov. 1858; *s.* of J. Graham, K.C.; *m.* 1884, Ada Douglas (*d.* 1943), *d.* of W. Crace. *Educ.:* Eton; R.M.C., Sandhurst. Served South Africa on staff and in command of 2nd Batt. 1900-2 (despatches, Queen's medal 3 clasps, King's medal 2 clasps, C.B.); European War, 1914-18 (despatches eight times, K.C.B., K.C.M.G.); Brigade Commander, 8th Infantry Brigade, 1908-12; Commander S. Midland Division 1914; D.A.G. Aug. 1914; retired pay, 1920; Commander, Legion of Honour; Star of Roumania. *Recreations:* rowing and shooting. *Address:* Manor Cottage, Thornbury, Holsworthy, Devon. *Club:* Army and Navy. [*Died* 29 *Jan.* 1951.

GRAHAM, Gilbert Maxwell Adair, C.B.E. 1919 (O.B.E. 1918); *b.* 1883; *s.* of late James N. Graham, D.L., J.P., Lanarkshire; *m.* 1913, Phyllis, *d.* of F de Mierre Turner, Oporto. *Educ.:* Eton; New College, Oxford. *Recreations:* shooting, etc.; rowed in Eton VIII., 1902, and for Oxford *v.* Cambridge, 1906. Comendador of Military Order of Christ, 1934, and grande oficial of Order of Merit, 1950 (Portugal). *Address:* Quinta da Povoa, Oporto, Portugal. *T.:* Maxgraham Oporto. *Clubs:* Union, Bath; New (Edinburgh). [*Died* 25 *May* 1960.

GRAHAM, Right Rev. Henry Grey, M.A.; Titular Bishop of Tipasa and Rector of Holy Cross, Crosshill, Glasgow, since 1930; *b.* 8 Mar. 1874; *s.* of Rev. M. H. Graham, minister of Maxton, Roxburghshire. *Educ.:* Kelso High School; St. Andrews University; Scots College, Rome. Parish minister of Avondale, Lanarkshire, 1901-3; received into Catholic Church at Benedictine Abbey, Fort-Augustus 1903; Priest, 1906; Curate, Motherwell, 1907; Parish Priest, Longriggend, 1916; Auxiliary to Archbishop of St. Andrews and Edinburgh, 1917-29. *Publications:* Where we got the Bible; Prosperity, Catholic and Protestant; Hindrances to Conversion to Catholic Church; What Faith Really Means; Cardinal Beaton, Purgatory, From the Kirk to the Catholic Church, The Church in Scotland, pamphlets in Catholic Truth Society; contributions to various journals. *Address:* 113 Dixon Avenue, Glasgow, S.2. *T.:* Queen's Park 105. [*Died* 5 *Dec.* 1959.

GRAHAM, Maj.-Gen. Sir James Drummond, Kt., *cr.* 1934; C.B. 1931; C.I.E. 1919; M.B., D.T.M.; I.M.S., retired; late Public Health Commissioner with Govt. of India; late Officiating Director General Indian Medical Service; Fellow of Royal Soc. of Tropical Medicine and Hygiene; late Delegate for British India on the Office Internationale d'Hygiène Publique, Paris; Member of the Health Committee of the League of Nations and Member and late Chairman of Advisory Council of the Eastern Bureau of League of Nations, Singapore; late Adviser to Ministry of Public Health, Irak; Director of Health Services, Mesopotamia, and Civil, U.P., India; *b.* 1875; *e. s.* of late James Drummond Graham, M.A., F.E.I.S., of Ayr, Scotland, and Agnes Nisbet; *m.* 1912, Violet Augusta, 2nd *d.* of Colonel C. Seymour, A.M.S.; one *s.* *Educ.:* Ayr Academy; Glasgow University, M.B., C.M. (High Commendn.), 1895; Edinburgh and Liverpool Universities, D.T.M., 1907. I.M.S. Entrance Exam. (1st), January-June 1900; Military duty, India, 1900-1907; Campaign North-West Frontier, Waziristan, 1901-2 (Medal with Clasp); Civil, United Provinces, India, 1908-14; served Egypt Expeditionary Force on Staff of 11th Indian Division, Canal Defences, and 9th (British) Army Corps; Mesopotamia Expeditionary Force on Staff of Tigris Corps and G.H.Q. and A.D.M.S. (San.) G.H.Q. Mesopotamia (C.I.E., Bt. Lt.-Col., despatches 4 times); K.H.S., 1931-34; retired 1934. *Publications:* Numerous reports published by Government of United Provinces and Government of India. *Address:* Le Mas de Jylloue, St. Martin, Mougins, A.M., France; c/o National Bank of India, 26 Bishopsgate, E.C.2. *Club:* East India and Sports. [*Died* 4 *April* 1958.

GRAHAM, John, M.B., Ch.B., B.Sc., F.R.F.P.S.G.; *b.* Glasgow, 12 May 1879; *e. s.* of late Daniel Graham, Glasgow; *m.* 1916, Isabella Milligan, 2nd *d.* of late William Fraser, J.P.; one *d.* *Educ.:* Glasgow University; Berlin; London. B.Sc. 1902, M.B., Ch.B. 1904, Glasgow University. House Surgeon, Victoria Infirmary, 1905; Post Graduate Study of Anatomy and Surgery in Berlin and London for 18 months; late Assistant Surgeon Royal Samaritan Hospital for Women, Glasgow; Professor of Anatomy, The Anderson College of Medicine, Glasgow, 1919-46; late Examiner in Anatomy to the Royal Faculty of Physicians and Surgeons of Glasgow; retired, 1946; mobilised, 1914; served as M.O. with various units; Major R.A.M.C. (T.) and second in command 94th F. Ambulance, France (Despatches); retired with rank of Major, 1921; Fellow of the Royal Faculty of Physicians and Surgeons of Glasgow, 1919; President Glasgow Southern Medical Society, 1922-23. *Recreations:* golf, reading. *Address:* 87 Hyndland Road, Glasgow, W.2. *T.:* Western 8660. [*Died* 15 *Dec.* 1958.

GRAHAM, Sir Lancelot, K.C.S.I., *cr.* 1936; K.C.I.E., *cr.* 1930 (C.I.E. 1924); M.A. Oxon; Barrister-at-law; I.C.S. (retd.); *b.* 1880; *s.* of late William Edgar Graham; *m.* 1910, Olive, Kaisar-i-Hind Gold Medal, 1941, *d.* of late Major-Gen. Sir J. F. Maurice, K.C.B.; one *s.* one *d.* *Educ.:* St. Paul's School; Balliol College, Oxford. Entered I.C.S. 1904; retired, 1941; Governor of Sind, 1936-41. *Address:* 35 Lansdowne Road, W.11. *T.:* Park 6392. *Club:* Athenæum. [*Died* 7 *Feb.* 1958.

GRAHAM, Richard Brockbank, M.A.; Headmaster, Bradford Grammar School, 1939-53; *b.* 29 Oct. 1893; *s.* of John William Graham and Margaret Brockbank; *m.* 1925, Gertrude, *d.* of G. E. Anson; one *s.* two *d.* *Educ.:* Sidcot School, Somerset; Bootham School, York; Manchester Grammar School; Magdalen College, Oxford. Assistant Master, Bishop's Stortford College and Leighton Park School, Reading; Headmaster, King Edward VII School, Sheffield, 1928-38. Member Hobhouse Cttee. on National Parks, 1945-47. *Recreations:* mountaineering, bee-keeping, interests in education and agriculture. *Address:* Helsington Lodge, Brigsteer, Kendal, Westmorland. *Clubs:* Alpine, Fell and Rock. [*Died* 12 *Feb.* 1957.

GRAHAM, Robert Henry; a Justice of the Supreme Court of Nova Scotia, 1925-49, retired; *b.* 30 Nov. 1870; *s.* of John George Graham and Jane Marshall; *m.* 1901, Maude M. Johnston; two *d.* *Educ.:* Dalhousie University. Legislature of Nova Scotia, 1916-25; Mayor of New Glasgow, N.S., 1898-1900. *Publication:* Notes on Nova Scotia Decisions, 1940. *Address:* 150 Coburg Road, Halifax, N.S. *Club:* Scotia (New Glasgow, N.S.). [*Died* 28 *May* 1956.

GRAHAM, William, C.B.E. 1942; General Secretary and Treasurer of National Farmers Union of Scotland (President, 1940-1943) since 1943; *b.* 25 Nov. 1896; *er. s.* of late Robert Graham, Kaimflat, Kelso; *m.* 1921, Norah, *o. d.* of late Andrew Hogarth, Caverton, Hillhead, Kelso; two *s.* Served 4th K.O.S.B., rank Captain. *Address:* 5 Wilton Road, Edinburgh, 9. *T.A.:* Agrarian Edinburgh. *T.:* Edinburgh 41381. [*Died* 2 *March* 1955.

GRAHAM, William Murray, C.M.G. 1950; C.B.E. 1946; Legal Counsellor, British Embassy, Cairo, since 1949; *b.* 20 Dec. 1884; *s.* of late William John Graham and late Mary Josephine Graham of Treveor, Avenue Road, Malvern; *m.* 1919, Edyth Frederica, *d.* of late Dr. Frederic J. A. Davidson, Toronto, Ontario, Canada; three *s.* one *d.* *Educ.:* Newton College, South Devon; Corpus Christi College, Oxford. M.A., B.C.L. (Oxon), 1910. Barrister-at-law, Lincoln's Inn, 1907; Advocate and Solicitor of Straits Settlements and Federated Malay States, 1910-14; served European War, 1914-18; Pilot in French Aviation Corps, 1915-17; R.F.C. and R.A.F., 1917-19, rank of Lieutenant (Pilot). Legal Adviser in Egyptian Government Service, 1919-29; Judge in Mixed Courts of Egypt, 1929-49; Judge of Mixed Court of Appeal, Alexandria, 1934-49. Croix de Guerre (French). *Recreations:* golf and sailing. *Address:* c/o British Embassy, Cairo; 2 Hussein Said, Pyramid's Road, Giza, Cairo. *T.:* 897304. *Clubs:* Junior Carlton; Royal Fowey Yacht; Turf, Gezira Sporting, Cairo Yacht (Cairo); Union, Yacht Club of Egypt, British Boat, New Sports (Alexandria). [*Died* 21 *Nov.* 1956.

GRAHAM-HODGSON, Sir Harold K.; *see* Hodgson.

GRAHAM-MOON, Sir Wilfred; *see* Moon, Sir A. W. G.

GRAHAME, Lieut.-Colonel John Crum, D.S.O. 1902; late Highland Light Infantry; *b.* 2 Feb. 1870; *o. surv. s.* of James Grahame; *m.* 1905, Alice Clara, *d.* of John Purvis of Kinaldy, Fife. *Educ.:* Harrow. Entered army, 1892; Capt. 1900; Maj. 1908; Lt.-Col. 1916; served North-West Frontier, India, 1897-98 (medal with clasp); with the Ashanti Field Force, 1900 (despatches, medal with clasp); with Aro Expedition in Southern Nigeria, 1901-2 (slightly wounded, despatches, D.S.O., medal with clasp); private secretary and extra A.D.C. to Lieut.-Governor of Ceylon, 1899; attached Egyptian Army, 1903; Sudan Civil Administration, 1904-7; Officiating D.A.Q.M.G. Headquarters, India, 1908-9; appointed to command the 10th (Service) Battalion Highland Light Infantry, 1914; commanded in the field, 1915; severely gassed at battle of Loos, 1915 (despatches); commanded in the field 10/11th H.L.I., 12th H.L.I., and 9th H.L.I. (Glasgow Highlanders), promoted to command of the 2nd H.L.I. (very severely wounded at Oppy, 1917, 1914-15 Star, Great War Medal, Victory Medal); King's Bodyguard for Scotland (Royal Company of Archers), 1921; late commanding 2nd Batt. Highland Light Infantry; retired pay on account of wounds received in action, 1921; in Home Guard, 1940-44 (Defence Medal). Coronation Medal, 1911; Silver Jubilee Medal, 1935; Coronation Medal, 1937. *Address:* Lingo, Largoward, Fife. *T.A.* and *T.:* Arncroach 223. *Clubs:* Army and Navy; New (Edinburgh). [*Died* 19 *Aug.* 1952.

GRAHAME-WHITE, Claude; aviator and aeronautical engineer; 2nd *s.* and *y.* of family of three; *b.* 21 Aug. 1879; *m.* 1st, 1912, Dorothy, *o. d.* of Bertrand Le Roy Taylor, New York; 2nd, 1916, Ethel (Grace) Levey (who obtained a divorce, 1939); 3rd, 1939, Phoebe Lee. *Educ.:* Crondall House College; Bedford Grammar School. Owned one of the first petrol-driven cars in England; toured South Africa; established motor engineering business in Albemarle Street; became interested in aeronautics 1909, the first Englishman granted a certificate of proficiency as an aviator; started a school of aviation at Pau, 1909—the first British flying school; contested for the London-Manchester £10,000 prize with Paulhan in April 1910; in the same year won many flying prizes in this country; also toured America and won Gordon Bennett trophy; on returning, formed the Grahame-White Aviation Company, which became proprietors of the London Aerodrome, Hendon, and is now known as the Grahame-White Company; Flight Commander, 1914; resigned to superintend the carrying out of Government contracts for building aeroplanes; the London Aerodrome, Hendon, and the whole of the companies' factories and assets were acquired by H.M.'s Government Dec. 1925; owner of Lady Vagrant, 485 tons, and several fast racing motor boats. *Publications:* The Story of the Aeroplane; The Aeroplane, Past, Present, and Future, 1911; The Aeroplane in War; Aviation, 1912; Learning to Fly, 1914; Aircraft in the Great War, 1915; Air Power, 1917; Our First

Airways, their Organisation, Equipment, and Finance, 1918; Books for Boys; Heroes of the Air; With the Airmen; The Air King's Treasure; The Invisible War-Plane; Heroes of the Flying Corps; Flying, an Epitome and a Forecast, 1930; many contributions to the daily papers, reviews, and monthly magazines dealing with the subject of aeronautics in its military and commercial aspects. *Recreations:* shooting, yachting, motoring, cricket, and flying, principally attention to his business. *Address:* Belair, Sunset Boulevard, Beverly Hills, California, U.S.A. *Clubs:* Naval and Military; Royal Automobile, Royal Motor Yacht, Authors', Overseas; Royal Mersey Yacht; Aero of America. [*Died* 19 *Aug.* 1959.

GRANE, Rev. William Leighton; Prebendary of Chichester; *b.* London, 4 Aug. 1855; *s.* of William James Grane, solicitor, and Harriet, *d.* of James Dallaway, M.A., M.B., F.S.A., author and antiquarian; *m.* 1881, Amy Caroline, *d.* of Sidney Locock, Envoy in H.M. Diplomatic Service. *Educ.:* Repton School; Caius College, Camb., B.A. 1878, M.A. 1881. Ordained deacon, 1879; priest, 1880; curate of Tunbridge Wells, 1879-81; Steyning, Sussex, 1881-83; rector of St. Thomas, Lewes, 1883-89; Bexhill-on-Sea, 1889-1900; Vicar of Cobham, Surrey, 1903-23; Canon of Chichester in Prebend. of Sutton, 1898; morning preacher, Berkeley Chapel, Mayfair, 1901; lecturer to Dante Society, 1901; select preacher, Cambridge, 1904-5; Hulsean Lecturer, 1913-14. *Publications:* The Word and the Way, 1894; Hard Sayings of Jesus Christ, 1899 (2nd ed. 1901); The Passing of War, 1st and 2nd eds. 1912, 4th ed. 1914; Church Divisions and Christianity, 1916 (2nd ed. 1917); War: its Curse and Cure, 1935. *Address:* Westering, Bishop's Down, Tunbridge Wells. *T.:* 21218. [*Died* 28 *Aug.* 1952.

GRANGER, Sir (Hugh) Rupert, Kt. *cr.* 1955; Director: Duke's Grain Warehousing Co. Ltd. (Chm.); Dee Oil Co. Ltd. (Chm.); J. Heap & Sons Ltd.; Member of London Board: Royal Insurance Co. Ltd.; Liverpool & London & Globe Insurance Co. Ltd.; Browns of Chester Ltd.; *b.* 9 October 1890; *s.* of F. M. Granger, M.R.C.S., F.R.C.P., Fron Haul, Bodfari, N. Wales, and Chester; *m.* 1915, Judith, *d.* of H. M. Mayhew, J.P., D.L., Broughton Hall, Chester; two *s.* *Educ.:* The Leas School, Hoylake; Uppingham. Commenced business, 1908; Director, 1924. Pres. Liverpool Corn Trade Assoc., 1939; Chm. Nat. Federation Corn Trade Assocs., 1936-39; apptd. Mem. Food Defence Cttee., 1940; liaison officer between Min. of Food and grain trade of U.K., 1942-. Served H.M. Forces, 1914-19. High Sheriff of Cheshire, 1955. *Recreation:* golf. *Address:* Littleton Hall, Chester. *T.:* Chester 35234. *Club:* Palatine (Liverpool). [*Died* 15 *March* 1959.

GRANNUM, Sir Edward Allan, Kt., *cr.* 1926; C.M.G. 1915; *b.* 11 Dec. 1869; 2nd *s.* of late Edward Thomas Grannum, C.M.G.; *m.* 1914, Marjorie Adie, 2nd *d.* of late Sir Francis Watts, K.C.M.G.; one *d.* *Educ.:* privately. Entered West India Civil Service, 1886; Assistant Auditor Sierra Leone and Gambia, 1897-1900; Gold Coast and Lagos, Jan. to Mar. 1900; then Auditor; Cyprus, 1902; Auditor-General, Mauritius, 1909; Receiver-General, 1912; Colonial Secretary, Mauritius, and Member *ex officio* Executive and Legislative Councils, 1923-32, during which period administered the Govt. on many occasions. *Address:* Phœnix, Mauritius. [*Died* 16 *April* 1956.

GRANT, Sir Allan John, Kt., *cr.* 1941; retired, 1954, as Director, John Brown & Co. Ltd.; Managing Director, Thos. Firth and John Brown, Ltd., Atlas Works, Sheffield, 1929-44; Chairman and/or Director Firth Vickers Stainless Steel Ltd., 1934-1944; *b.* 8 Sept. 1875; *s.* of late Alexander Allan Grant and late Maria Jane Tidd; *m.* 1909, Isa Florence Hillyers; four *d.* *Educ.:* Cheltenham College. Pupil at Laird Bros., Birkenhead, Marine Engineers and Shipbuilders, and Walker Engineering Laboratories; Liverpool University, Whitworth Exhibitioner, 1896; joined staff of John Brown Co., Ltd., Sheffield, 1911; Director, 1919; President, British Iron and Steel Federation, 1932; Chairman Steel Delegation to Ottawa for Imperial Economic Conference, 1932; Member of Council, Institution of Mechanical Engineers, 1939-45; M.I.N.A.; Master Cutler, Company of Cutlers in Hallamshire, 1938-39; President, Sheffield Chamber of Commerce, 1937-1938; Member Board of Trade Advisory Council, 1933-36; Chairman, Ministry of Production East and West Ridings Regional Board, 1940-42; Vice-Chairman, 1942-45; Member National Production Advisory Council, 1942-45; Chairman North East Derbyshire Conservative and Unionist Association, 1934-45; Hon. Colonel, 13th Light Anti-Aircraft Regt. R.A. (T.A.); Member Sheffield University Council, 1939-45; Council, Cheltenham College; Sheffield Church Burgesses Trust, 1940-45. *Recreations:* shooting, fishing, sailing. *Address:* Coldharbour Cottage, Hurst Green, Sussex. *Club:* Royal Thames Yacht. [*Died* 19 *July* 1955.

GRANT, Engineer Rear-Adm. Arthur Robert, C.B.E. 1919; retired; *b.* Devonport, 25 Dec. 1870; *e. s.* of Richard Samuel Grant, Devonport; *m.* 1905, Margaret Emilie (*d.* 1949), *d.* of John Bird, Brampton, Huntingdon; one *s.* two *d.* (and one *d.* decd.). *Educ.:* High School, Devonport; Royal Naval Engineering Coll., Devonport. Newman Memorial Prize, 1890; passed special course of training at the Royal Naval College, Greenwich, 1890-1893; served at the Admiralty, Devonport, Portsmouth, Sheerness, and Hong-Kong Dockyards, and in various ships afloat; East African (Somaliland) medal, 1903; on the outbreak of war was employed at Portsmouth Dockyards on refits of Invincible, Kent, etc.; Chief Engineer of Pembroke Dockyard in charge of engine work in the building of Light Cruisers and Submarines and refits of Torpedo Boat Destroyers, 1915-17; transferred to H.M.S. Barham as Engineer Captain on Staff of Vice-Admiral commanding the 5th Battle Squadron (afterwards the 2nd Battle Squadron); Engineer Manager of Devonport Dockyard, 1919-22. *Address:* Denali, Hill Head, Fareham, Hants. *T.:* Stubbington 49. [*Died* 22 *Aug.* 1952.

GRANT, Commander Duncan, C.B.E. 1920; R.N. (retired); *b.* 1882; 3rd *s.* of late Major Seafield Grant, Oxfordshire Light Infantry; *m.* 1923, Beatrice Edith, *o. d.* of C. D. Moggridge, Wykeham, Burgess Hill; two *s.* Entered Royal Navy as Cadet, 1896; Lieutenant, 1903; Commander for Services rendered during European War, 1918; Captain of Royal Australian Naval College, 1917-19; Private Sec. to Adm. Sir Dudley de Chair, Governor of N.S.W., 1923-25. *Recreations:* tennis, golf, cricket. *Address:* Middle Farm, Haywards Heath, Sussex. *Club:* United Service. [*Died* 5 *Feb.* 1955.

GRANT, Admiral Sir (Edmund) Percy (Fenwick George), K.C.V.O., *cr.* 1920; C.B. 1916; R.N., retired; D.L. for Anglesey; Officer (Brother) St. John of Jerusalem; *y. s.* of late John Glasgow Grant, C.M.G., and Mary Elizabeth, *d.* of John Walter; *b.* 1867; *m.* 1926, Gwendoline (*d.* 1950), *widow* of Rear-Adm. Henry Montagu Doughty, C.B., C.M.G., *e. d.* of late Lt.-Col. Gaitskell-Burr. *Educ.:* Britannia; R.N. College, Greenwich. Served in Egyptian War, 1882 (Egyptian medal, Khedive's bronze star); Lieut. of Racer during Brazilian Revolution, 1893; commanded Halcyon, Arrogant, Gibraltar, Falmouth, King Edward VII., Marlborough, Ramillies. Received thanks of Australian Government for services rendered, 1910, and in 1921; special mission to Somaliland in command of H.M.S. Gibraltar; Flag-Captain to Vice-Adm. Sir Lewis Bayly in King Edward VII. and Marlborough; Flag-Capt., and afterwards Chief of Staff in Marlborough to Admiral Sir Cecil Burney, 2nd in command of the Grand Fleet; present at Battle of Jutland (despatches, C.B.); Commodore, 2nd class, 1916; Rear-Admiral, 1919; A.D.C. to H.M., 1918; 1st Naval Member and Chief of Australian Naval Staff, 1919-21; Commander-in-Chief of Australia Station, 1921-22; one of the three C.-in-C. who investigated the possibilities of Singapore as a base; had a seat on The Empire Conference, London, 1921, as adviser on Defence to Rt. Hon. Morris Hughes, Prime Minister of Australia; Admiral Superintendent, Portsmouth Dockyard, 1922-25; Vice-Adm. 1924; Adm. retired, 1928; retired list, 1928. Captain of the Port Holyhead for duration of the War; retired 1945. President of Board for entry of Naval Cadets into Dartmouth, 1927, and of Board for entry of Cadets into the Navy, Army and Air Force, 1927; holds Russian order Vladimir, 4th class with swords. *Recreations:* fishing, shooting, golf. *Address:* 8 Palmeira Court, Hove, Sussex. *Clubs:* United Service, M.C.C.; (hon.) Royal Yacht Squadron (Cowes). [*Died* 8 *Sept.* 1952.

GRANT, Sir Francis James, K.C.V.O., *cr.* 1935 (C.V.O. 1931); LL.D. (Aberdeen); Albany Herald since 1945; *b.* 4 Aug. 1863; 2nd *s.* of John Grant, Marchmont Herald, and nephew of James Grant, novelist; *m.* 1st, 1899, Anne Irvine Cruickshank (*d.* 1918), *e. d.* of late David Charles Edmondston of Buness, Shetland; two *d.*; 2nd, 1935, Violet Madeline Bourne, *er. d.* of late Rev. Joseph B. C. Murphy, Chaplain to the Forces. *Educ.:* Royal High School, Edinburgh; University of Edinburgh. Writer to H.M. Signet from 1887; Carrick Pursuivant of Arms, 1886-98; Rothesay Herald; Lyon Clerk and Keeper of the Records in the Court of Lord Lyon, 1898-1929; Lord Lyon King of Arms in Scotland and Secretary to the Order of the Thistle, 1929-45; Convener of the Benefice Register and Church Records Committee, and a General Trustee of the Church of Scotland; Chief of The Gaelic Society of Inverness, 1937. *Publications:* Zetland County Families, 1893; Catalogue of Heraldic Exhibition, Edinburgh, 1891; Grants of Corrimony, 1895; Zetland Family Histories, 1907; The Manual of Heraldry, 1914, 2nd ed. 1924, 3rd ed. 1930; co-author of History of Society of Writers to the Signet, 1890; Alexander Nisbet's Heraldic Plates, 1892; contributor to The Scots Peerage, 1904-1910; joint editor of new edition of Fasti Ecclesiae Scoticanae; edited for Scottish Record Society, Indexes to Commissariat Registers of Edinburgh, Glasgow, St. Andrews, and seventeen others, 1897-1904; Edinburgh Apprentice Register, The Faculty of Advocates in Scotland, 1532-1943, Court of the Lord Lyon, 1318-1945, and eleven others, and numerous contributions to magazines and newspapers. *Address:* 18 George Square, Edinburgh, 8. *T.:* 44224. [*Died* 17 *Feb.* 1953.

GRANT, Frederick, Q.C. 1943; M.C. 1918; Independent Chairman, Executive Cttee., British Iron and Steel Federation, since 1953; *b.* 25 April 1890; *s.* of John Grant, Craigmills, Dundee; *m.* 1916, Grace Winifred, *d.* of Henry McLaren, LL.D., Leeds; one *s.* one *d.* *Educ.:* Fettes College; Oriel College, Oxford. M.A. 1st Class Classical Mods. 1911; 1st Class Litt. Hum. 1914. Served European War, 1914-18; Staff Captain Tay Defences, 1915; Adjutant 45th Heavy Artillery Group, 1916; cmdg. 94th Siege Battery, 1917 (M.C.); called to Bar, 1925, Bencher, Inner Temple, 1951. Member of Monopolies and Restrictive Practices Commission, 1949-52; Chm. Purchase Tax (Valuation) Committee, 1952-53. *Recreation:* golf. *Address:* 46 Ladbroke Grove, W.11. *T.:* Park 7696; 6 King's Bench Walk, Temple, E.C.4. *T.:* Central 4606. *Clubs:* Oxford and Cambridge, Caledonian; Royal Mid-Surrey Golf. [*Died* 19 *Sept.* 1954.

GRANT, Sir George M.; *see* Macpherson-Grant.

GRANT, Maj.-General Ian Cameron, C.B. 1945; C.B.E. 1940; D.S.O. 1916; D.L.; *b.* 28 May 1891; *o. s.* of late John Cameron Grant, Albert Lodge, Albert Place, W.; *m.* 1918, Pamela Molony, *y. d.* of late Roderick O'Connor of Cragganowen Castle, Co. Clare; two *d.* *Educ.:* St. Neots; Eversley; Cheltenham Coll; R.M.C., Sandhurst. 2nd Lt., Cameron Highlanders, 1910; Lieut., 1914; Capt., 1915; Brevet-Maj., 1919; Maj., 1925; Lt.-Col., 1931; Colonel, 1935; acting Maj.-Gen., 1941; temp. Maj.-Gen., 1942; served European War as Regimental Officer and as G.S.O.3, 29th Division; Brigade-Major, 86th Brigade, and D.A.A.G. War Office (twice wounded; Brevet-Majority D.S.O., despatches three times, home service once, Chevalier, Order of the Crown of Belgium); D.A.Q.M.G. 52nd Lowland Division, T.A., 1924-28; commanded 1st Batt. Q.O. Cameron Highlanders, 1931-35; Commander 160th (South Wales) Infantry Brigade T.A., 1935-38; Commander Cairo Infantry Brigade, Egypt, 1938-39; A.D.C. to the King, 1944; invalided, 1944; during 1917, while suffering from wounds, was for three months Assistant Private Secretary (unpaid) to Rt. Hon. John Hodge, P.C., M.P., Minister of Labour; Hon. Treas., Committee of Social Investigation and Reform, 1919-21; Town Councillor, Royal Burgh of Inverness, 1949; Bailie, Royal Burgh Inverness, 1952; D.L. County of Inverness, 1950. Director: R. S. Macdonald Ltd., Inverness; Moray Firth Foods Ltd., Inverness. *Recreations:* fishing, stamp collecting. *Address:* Culcabock House, Inverness. *T.:* 707. *Clubs:* Royal Automobile; New (Edinburgh); Highland (Inverness). [*Died* 26 *Aug.* 1955.

GRANT, Rt. Rev. Kenneth; Bishop of Argyll and the Isles (R.C.), since 1946; *b.* 18 March 1900. *Educ.:* St. Mary's College, Blairs, Aberdeen; St. Peter's, Bearsden, Glasgow. Chaplain to the Forces; Prisoner of War, June 1940-May 1945. *Address:* Bishop's House, Oban, Argyll. [*Died* 7 *Sept.* 1959.

GRANT, Adm. Sir Percy; *see* Grant, Adm. Sir E. P. F. G.

GRANT, Sir Robert W. L.; *see* Lyall Grant.

GRANT, Brig.-Gen. Ronald Chas., D.S.O. 1900; O.B.E. 1918; late Cape Mounted Riflemen and S.A. Mounted Riflemen; *b.* 22 Nov. 1864; *e. s.* of Lt.-Col. James Murray Grant, late 85th Light Infantry and C.M.R.; *m.* 1898, Mina (*d.* 1941), *e. d.* of Rev. James Stewart, M.D., D.D., of Lovedale, S. Africa; one *s.* two *d.* Joined C.M.R. 1880; served Basutoland Campaign, 1880-81 (medal and clasp); Anglo-Boer War, 1899-1902 (S.A. medal and 4 clasps, King's medal 2 clasps, D.S.O., despatches); European War, 1914-18, severely wounded 1914 (O.B.E., despatches); retired Jan. 1922. *Address:* Low Gill, St. Patricks Rd., Newlands, Cape, S. Africa. [*Died* 29 *Jan.* 1951.

GRANT, Lady Sybil; poet, writer, designer, and artist; *e. d.* of 5th Earl of Rosebery; *m.* General Sir Charles Grant, K.C.B., K.C.V.O., D.S.O. (*d.* 1950). Editor (and Staff) of first weekly War newspaper, The Home Letter, for No. 2 Co. 1st Batt. Coldstream Guards, Aug. 1914 to Dec. 1918; official photographer to R.N.A.S. Admiralty, 1915; film operator of all airship official films until Armistice; first Special Airship Correspondent (Glasgow Herald), 1919; organised and ran Scottish Command Canteen, 1939-40; Editor (and Staff) of The Home Letter Newspaper for Scottish Regiments, and Serve Scotland League until Dunkirk. After return to Pitchford representative for all war work in that area; Founder and Pres. of Pitchford Circle. At present managing a private firm for production of own work. *Publications:* Samphire: Collected Essays, 1912; Chequer-Board; Collected Short Stories, 1912; Founded on Fiction, 1913; Dream Songs, a volume of poems, 1914; The End of the Day, volume of poems, 1922; second edition, 1923; Riding Light (novel), 1926; two Impressions under the name of Neil Scot; contributor of articles on airships to Observer and other newspapers, 1919-21; since then much unsigned journalism, mostly humorous, also songs. *Recreations:* work and play. *Address:* Pitchford Hall, Shrewsbury; The Durdans, Epsom; Bearnoch, Glen Urquhart. [*Died* 25 *Feb.* 1955.

GRANT-DALTON, Captain Charles; *b.* 10 Dec. 1884; *e. s.* of Horace Grant-Dalton and Constance Thellusson; *m.* 1916, Sylvia Joan Cecil West; one *d.* *Educ.:* Repton. Served European War, France, 1915-18; High Sheriff of Yorkshire, 1942-43. *Address:* Brodsworth Hall, Doncaster. *T.:* Adwick-le-Street 2198; Quinish, Isle of Mull. *T.:* Dervaig 23. *Clubs:* Royal Yacht Squadron (Cowes); Western Isles Yacht (Tobermory). [*Died* 3 *Feb.* 1952.

GRANT-WILSON, Sir Wemyss, Kt., *cr.* 1920; a Director of Haydock Collieries, Lancashire and allied concerns; *b.* 21 Feb. 1870; *yr. s.* of late George Grant-Wilson, formerly of Hawick, Scotland, and Redroofs, Streatham Common. *Educ.:* Westminster; Trinity College, Cambridge. M.A., LL.M.; Barrister-at-law, Inner Temple; J.P. County of London; was Director of the Borstal Association, 1903-35, and of the Hollington Club for boys, Camberwell, 1893-1935. *Address:* 55 Woodbourne Avenue, Streatham. [*Died* 21 *Jan.* 1953.

GRANTLEY, 6th Baron, *cr.* 1782; **Richard Henry Brinsley Norton,** Baron of Markenfield, 1782; Captain (Special Reserve) Scots Guards; Manager European Merchant Banking Co. Ltd., bankers, 1922-31; entered film business with United Artists Co., 1931; now Director of British and Dominions Film Corporation Ltd.; Director Pinewood Studios Ltd.; Executive Director D. & P. Studios Ltd.; Chairman British Film Production Association, 1939; Member of the Board of Trade Films Council, 1938-40; *b.* 2 April 1892; *o. s.* of 5th Baron; *S.* father 1943; *m.* 1919, Jean (*d.* 1945), *e. d.* of Sir D. Kinloch, 11th Bt.; one *s.* one *d.* *Educ.:* Wellington; Oxford. Served Expeditionary Force, 1914, Headquarter Staff, 1915. *Recreations:* golf, motoring, gardening. *Heir:* *s.* Hon. John Richard Brinsley Norton, *b.* 1923. *Address:* Markenfield Hall, Ripon; 44 Springfield Rd., N.W.8. *Clubs:* White's, Buck's. [*Died* 16 *July* 1954.

GRANVILLE, 4th Earl (*cr.* 1833); **Vice-Admiral William Spencer Leveson Gower,** K.C.V.O., *cr.* 1945; C.B. 1932; D.S.O.; LL.D. (Hon.) The Queen's University, Belfast; R.N., retd.; Viscount Granville, 1815; Baron Leveson, 1833; Governor of N. Ireland 1945-Dec. 1952; Hon. Col. 15th Light A.A. Regt.; Chm. of the Lilleshall Co.; *b.* 11 July 1880; *S.* brother 1939; *m.* 1916, Lady Rose Bowes-Lyon, D.C.V.O., *cr.* 1945, *d.* of 14th Earl of Strathmore, K.G., K.T., G.C.V.O.; one *s.* one *d.* Served in suppression of slave trade and piracy in the Red Sea in 1902 and 1903; made a journey through the Yemen; served European War, 1914-19 (Captain, despatches, D.S.O.); Naval A.D.C. to the King, 1929; Rear-Admiral, 1929; Rear-Admiral and Commanding Officer Coast of Scotland, 1931-33; Vice-Admiral and retired list, 1935; Lieut.-Governor of Isle of Man, 1937-45; Order of St. Anne, Russia; Order of the Redeemer, Greece; K.St.J. *Recreations:* shooting, fishing, fencing, golf. *Heir:* *s.* Major the Lord Leveson, M.C. *Address:* Pearsie, Kirriemuir, Angus. *Club:* United Service. [*Died* 25 *June* 1953.

GRAS, Norman | Scott Brien, M.A., Ph.D., LL.D. (*hon. causa*) Professor of Business History, Harvard School of Business, 1927-50; *b.* Toronto, 18 July 1884; *m.* 1915, Ethel Culbert; three *s.* one *d.* *Educ.:* University of Western Ontario; Harvard University. Assistant Professor of History, Clark University, 1912-18; Professor of Economic History, University of Minnesota, 1918-27; Member of the Council, Economic History Society, London, 1926-38; Vice-President since 1939; Managing Editor, Journal of Economic and Business History, Boston, 1928-31, Editor 1931-32; Editor, Harvard Studies in Business History, 1931-50; President Business History Foundation, Inc., 1947-52. *Publications:* Evolution of the English Corn Market, 1915; The Early English Customs System, 1918; An Introduction to Economic History, 1922; A History of Agriculture in Europe and America, 1925, 1940; The Economic and Social History of an English Village (Crawley, Hampshire), 1909-1928 (with wife), 1929; Industrial Evolution, 1930; The Massachusetts-First National Bank of Boston, 1784-1934, 1937; Business and Capitalism: an Introduction to Business History, 1939, 1946; Casebook in American Business History (with H. M. Larson), 1939; Harvard Co-operative Society, Past and Present, 1882-1942, 1942; Are You Writing a Business History?, 1944, 1947; Shifts in Public Relations, 1945, 1947; Behavior of Business Men in a Changing World, 1949; posthumous, in progress, ed. by Ethel C. Gras, a 3-volume work on the Business History of the United States. *Recreation:* walking. *Address:* 20 Craigie Street, Cambridge, Mass., U.S.A. [*Died* 9 *Oct.* 1956.

GRATTAN, Colonel Henry William, C.B.E. 1919; D.S.O. 1918; M.R.C.S. Eng.; L.R.C.P., R.C.P.S., Lond.; D.P.H.; Chairman, Bedford Medical Board, Armed Forces Acts, 1939-45; retired; late M.O.H., Biggleswade Urban and Rural District, Welwyn Rural and Welwyn Garden City Urban Districts and Hatfield Rural District; *b.* 11 April 1872; *s.* of Dr. M. H. Grattan, Ongar House, Ongar, Essex; *m.* Mabel Mary Austin, *e. d.* of Lewis Rice, C.I.E., Director of Archæology, Mysore Government; one *d.* *Educ.:* St. Laurence College, Ramsgate. Entered Army Medical Service, 1895; Assistant to Sir William Leishman, with charge of the Army Antityphoid Vaccine Dept., 1906-10. In charge Enteric Depot and Bacteriological Laboratory, Northern Army, India, 1912-14; served in France Nov. 1914 to date of Armistice, and afterwards in Germany to 1919; Chief Administrative Medical Officer to a division (A.D.M.S.) for 18 months; at the time of the Armistice was Chief Administrative Medical Officer (D.D.M.S.) of the IX. Army Corps; Kaisar-i-Hind Gold Medallist; late Hon. Surgeon to the Viceroy; late Deputy Director of Hygiene, War Office. *Publications:* articles in R.A.M.C. Journal, etc. *Recreations:* motoring, fishing. *Address:* Half Acre, Sollershott West, Letchworth, Herts. [*Died* 30 *April* 1952.

GRATTAN, John Henry Grafton, B.A. (Lond.); Fellow of University College, London; Professor Emeritus; Baines Prof. of English Language and Philology, Univ. of Liverpool, 1930-43; *b.* Croydon, 15 Sept. 1878; *e. s.* of late Grafton John Grattan, Addiscombe, Croydon, and Emma Ann Whenmouth; unmarried. *Educ.:* Whitgift Grammar School; University College, London; University of Berlin. English Lector in the Seminar für Orientalische Sprachen of the University of Berlin and in the University of Halle, 1901-1904; Quain Student, University College, London, 1904-9; Lecturer in English Language, Birkbeck College, London, 1909-19; Assistant Lecturer in English Language and Literature, University College, London, 1912-21; Senior Lecturer, 1921-28; Reader in English and Germanic Philology in the University of London, 1928-30. *Publications:* Our Living Language (with P. Gurrey); The Owl and The Nightingale (ed.); contributions to Mod. Lang. Review, Studies in Philology, Rev. of Eng. Studies and Essays and Studies by members of the Eng. Assoc. *Recreation:* walking. *Address:* 40 Danehurst Rd., Wallasey, Cheshire, *Club:* University (Liverpool. [*Died* 22 *Oct.* 1951.

GRAVES, Captain Sir Cecil George, K.C.M.G., *cr.* 1939; M.C.; Member: Scottish Committee of Arts Council; Broadcasting Council for Scotland; *b.* 4 March 1892; *s.* of late Charles L. Graves and Alice Grey (*e. sister* of late Viscount Grey of Fallodon); *m.* 1921, Irene Helen, *y. d.* of late H. W. J. Bagnell, I.C.S.; one *s.* (and one *s.* decd.). *Educ.:* Gresham's School, Holt; R.M.C., Sandhurst. Joined the Royal Scots, 1911; with B.E.F. to France, August 1914; taken prisoner 26 August 1914; served on General Staff, War Office (Intelligence Branch), 1919-25; retired 1925; joined B.B.C., 1926; Assistant Director of Programmes, 1929-32; Empire Service Director, 1932-35; Controller of Programmes, 1935-38; Deputy Director-General, 1938-42; Joint Director-General, 1942-43. Grand Officer of Order of Orange Nassau (Netherlands). *Address:* Fernbank, West Cults, Aberdeenshire. *T.:* Aberdeen 47361. *Clubs:* Brooks's, M.C.C.
[*Died* 12 *Jan.* 1957.

GRAVES, Philip Perceval; *b.* Bowdon, Cheshire, 25 Feb. 1876; *s.* of late Alfred Perceval Graves; *m.* 1st, 1912, Leila Millicent Knox (*d.* 1935), *d.* of Gavin Gilchrist of Kadikeui, Constantinople; one *d.*; 2nd, 1937, Mrs. Katherine Eleanor Dewar, *d.* of late W. H. E. H. Palmer. *Educ.:* Newton College; Haileybury; Oriel College, Oxford. M.R.I.A. Journalist (retired) and author; Times Correspondent at Constantinople, 1908-14; served in the Army, 1915-19, as a Temporary Officer in Egypt, Palestine, Arabia, and Turkey (despatches); with The Times until retirement, 1946; contributed to the exposure of the Protocols of the Elders of Zion; has travelled extensively in the Near East; Chevalier Legion of Honour; Crown of Italy. *Publications:* The Land of Three Faiths; The Pursuit; The Question of the Straits, 1931; Hutchinson's Quarterly Record of the War, the Third Quarter to the Twenty-fourth Quarter, 1940-1947; Briton and Turk, 1941; The Life of Sir Percy Cox, 1941; Edited memoirs of King Abdullah of Transjordan, 1950; and several scientific and historical papers. *Recreations:* natural history, Celtic antiquities, fishing. *Address:* Ballylickey House, Bantry, Co. Cork, Eire. *T.:* Bantry 71. *Club:* Kildare Street (Dublin). [*Died* 3 *June* 1953.

GRAVES, Richard Massie, C.B.E. 1932; *b.* 14 Sept. 1880; *s.* of late Alfred Perceval Graves and Janey, *d.* of James Cooper of Cooper Hill, Limerick; *m.* 1912, Eva (*d.*1960), *d.* of Maj. H. C. Wilkinson, 82nd Regt., Oswald House, Durham; one *d.* *Educ.:* Haileybury; Magdalen Coll., Oxford; King's Coll., Cambridge. Entered Levant Consular Service, 1903; Assistant, Constantinople, 1905; Acting Vice-Consul, Salonica, 1906; Uskub, 1906; Diarbekir, 1907; Vice-Consul, Alexandria, 1908; Cairo, 1909; entered Egyptian Civil Service, 1910; Inspector of Interior, 1910-22; Assistant Director General European Department, Ministry of Interior, 1924; Director, Labour Dept., Egyptian Ministry of Commerce and Industry, 1930-39; Major, Intelligence Service, 1939-40; Labour Adviser to Palestine Govt., 1940-42; Director, Dept. of Labour, Palestine Govt., 1942-1946; Chairman Municipal Commission, Jerusalem, 1947-48; Adviser on Social Affairs, Internat. Administration, Tangier, 1949-51. Order of Ismail, 1926; Commander Order of the Nile, 1937. *Publications:* Experiment in Anarchy; Singing for Amateurs; numerous translations. *Clubs:* Savile, Curzon House. [*Died* 14 *Aug.* 1960.

GRAY, A(rthur) Herbert, M.A. (Edin.); D.D. (Glas.); Presbyterian minister, retd.; *b.* 9 Sept. 1868; *s.* of Alexander Gray, Edinburgh; *m.* 1897, Mary Christian, *d.* of Principal Marcus Dods, D.D.; two *s.* three *d.* *Educ.:* Leys School, Camb.; Edinburgh Univ.; New College Divinity Hall, Edinburgh. Minister of Grosvenor Square Presbyterian Church, Manchester, 1887-1909; College and Kelvingrove Church, Glasgow, 1909-13; White Memorial Church, Glasgow, 1913-21; Army Chaplain during European war; on staff of Student Christian Movement (three years); Minister of Crouch Hill Presbyterian Church, London, 1924-32; retired, 1932; 1942-45, served as Minister in St. John's Wood Presbyterian Church. *Publications:* Aspects of Protestantism; What's the Good of Religion; As Tommy sees Us; Men, Women and God; The Christian Adventure; With Christ as Guide; Jesus and the Art of Living; Finding God; About People, 1934; The Difficulty and the Art of Living, 1936; Love the One Solution; Successful Marriage, 1941; The Secret of Inward Peace. *Address:* 56 Kingsley Way, N.2. *T.:* Speedwell 7408.
[*Died* 9 *March* 1956.

GRAY, Douglas S., R.P. 1933; portrait painter; *b.* 4 June 1890; *s.* of Robert Stannus Gray and Emily Susanne, *d.* of Alfred Galer; *m.* Kathleen Mary Chambers; one *d.* *Educ.:* Croydon; Royal Academy Schools. Served with 2nd and 3rd Battalions London Regt., 1914-18; picture entitled Rosalind purchased by the Trustees, Chantrey Bequest, 1926; Royal Society of Portrait Painters and Society of Sussex Painters; sometime member of R.O.I. and London Portrait Society. *Address:* The Hall, The Green, Southwick, Sussex. *Club:* Brighton Arts. [*Died* 2 *Nov.* 1959.

GRAY, Edward Francis; *b.* 15 Jan. 1871; *s.* of late Rev. Edward Gray of Wembley Park, Middlesex, and Donnington Hall, Ledbury; *m.* 1906, Diana Norah (*d.* 1953), *d.* of Capt. W. J. Smyth, Rifle Brigade, of Heath Hall, Yorks; two *d.* (one *s.* decd.). *Educ.:* Haileybury; Oriel College, Oxford; Scoones. Pro-Consul, Christiania, 1896; Vice-Consul, 1900; to Caracas, 1906; to Bergen, 1907; Consul at Christiania, 1910; H.B.M. Consul-General for the States of Massachusetts, Vermont, New Hampshire, Maine, and Rhode Island, 1922-31; retired on pension, 1931. For some time Member of Worcestershire C.C. *Publications:* Leif Eriksson, Discoverer of America, 1930; and in Trans. of Worcs. Archæological Soc. *Recreations:* archæology, garden. *Address:* Ripple Hall, Tewkesbury. *T.:* Upton-on-Severn 86.
[*Died* 21 *June* 1960.

GRAY, Sir Harold William Stannus, K.B.E., *cr.* 1938; landowner; County Councillor, Cambridgeshire; thoroughbred stock-breeder; *b.* Graymount, Co. Antrim, 1867; *s.* of Major George Gray, D.L., Graymount, Co. Antrim; *m.* 1894, Rowena, *d.* of T. R. Stannus, J.P. of Maghraleave, Co. Antrim; one *s.* *Educ.:* Eton; Magdalene College, Cambridge. M.P. (C.) Cambs. Nov. 1922-23; High Sheriff of Co. Antrim, 1895, also of Cambridgeshire and Huntingdonshire, 1939. Travelled considerably; runs horses of his own breeding in England, and Ireland; during European War, 1914-18, drove his motor ambulance for the French Red Cross, and both he and Mrs. Gray worked continually in France in the hospitals at the care of the wounded. *Recreations:* yachting, shooting, racing. *Address:* Gogmagog Hills, Cambridge. *Clubs:* Carlton; Irish Turf, Kildare Street (Dublin); St. George's Yacht.
[*Died* 23 *May* 1951.

GRAY, James Neville, D.S.O. 1917; Q.C. 1938; Barrister-at-law; Chancellor of County Palatine of Durham, 1958; Chancellor of Dioceses of Southwell since 1936, Worcester since 1943, and Wakefield since 1944, and Commissary-General of Diocese of Canterbury since 1944; Dep. Chm. Herts Quarter Sessions; *yr. s.* of late James Gray, 53 Montagu Square, W.1; *m.* 1919, Hildegard Mary, *er. d.* of late R. Marcus Gunn, F.R.C.S.; two *d.* *Educ.:* Rugby; University College, Oxford. Called to Bar, Lincoln's Inn, 1909; Major in Inns of Court O.T.C.; service in France, Aug. 1914-Aug. 1919, attached to Gen. Staff (D.S.O.). Grand

Registrar, Grand Lodge of England, 1950. Vice-Chairman of Bar Council, 1953-55. *Recreation:* gardening. *Address:* Fair Green House, Sawbridgeworth, Herts. *Club:* Athenæum. [*Died* 20 *April* 1959.

GRAY, Robert W. W.; *see* Whytlaw-Gray.

GRAY, Ronald, R.W.S. 1942 (A.R.W.S. 1934); *b.* 1868; *s.* of James and Elizabeth Gray. *Educ.:* private school. Studied art under Prof. Frederick Brown and at Julien's in Paris; pictures in Tate Gallery, British Museum, Victoria and Albert Museum and War Museum; member of New English Art Club; silver medal Salon, Paris. *Club:* Chelsea Arts. [*Died* 16 *Nov.* 1951.

GRAY, Ven. William James; Archdeacon of Tonbridge, 1940-53, Archdeacon Emeritus since 1953; *b.* 1874; 2nd *s.* of Samuel Gray; *m.* Florence Jessie (*d.* 1935), *e. d.* of Capt. J. E. A. Dolby; no *c.* *Educ.:* privately; London, College of Divinity. Curate of St. Saviour's, Brixton, 1905-08; Christ Church, Beckenham, 1908-11; Vicar of Ide Hill, and Chaplain to Sevenoaks Workhouse and Infirmary, 1911-15; Vicar of St. Nicholas with St. Clements, Rochester, 1915-42; Vicar of Kippington, 1942-52; Hon. Chaplain to Missions to Seamen, River Medway, 1920-42; 15 times Chaplain to Mayors of Rochester; Rural Dean of Rochester, 1925-40; Hon. Canon Rochester Cathedral, 1931-40; Proctor in Convocation, 1924-35. *Recreations:* golf and shooting. *Address:* 20A Hillside Avenue, Frindsbury, Rochester. *T.:* Strood 7763. [*Died* 17 *Sept.* 1960.

GRAYSON, Sir Denys Henry Harrington, 2nd Bt. of Ravens Point, *cr.* 1922; late Lt. Irish Guards; Member Standing Council of Baronetage; *b.* 10 July 1892; *e. s.* of Lt.-Col. Sir Henry M. Grayson, 1st Bt.; *S.* father 1951; *m.* 1st, 1916; one *s.*; 2nd, 1927, Sylvia, *y. d.* of late Richard Keown-Boyd of Ballydugan, Co. Down; 3rd, 1951, Jeanette, *d.* of late John Evan Glen. *Educ.:* Harrow; Pembroke Coll., Camb. Chm. Grayson, Rollo and Clover Docks Ltd. Served European War, 1914-18 (War and Victory Medals). As a hobby, studied composition under Frank Bridge and Maude Valerie White; composed the incidental music to Sir Arthur Conan Doyle's play, The Speckled Band, 1921, and the incidental music to Haddon Chambers' drama, The Card Players, 1922; has composed a number of songs; also music for Sir Gerald du Maurier's production of Alfred Sutro's play, The Choice, 1919, and Denis Eadie's production of Summertime, 1920; has a number of orchestral works regularly broadcast, notably The King's Way (concert march), 1935, Nocturne for orchestra, 1936, and In Linden Time (strings only), 1936; Five Preludes for Harp Quintet, 1938; Three Sketches for Strings and Piano, 1938; Valse Caprice, 1939; Winter Reverie, 1940; Serenade for small orchestra, 1942; Prelude to An Eastern Play, 1943. *Heir:* *s.* Ronald Henry Rudyard [*b.* 15 Nov. 1916; *m.* 1st, 1936, Babette Vivienne (marriage dissolved), *d.* of Count Vivien Hollender; 2nd, 1946, Dorothy Vera Hoare, *d.* of Charles Serrel]. *Address:* Kim's Wood, Wadhurst, Sussex. *T.:* 291. *Clubs:* Devonshire, M.C.C. [*Died* 22 *Feb.* 1955.

GRAYSON, Lieut.-Col. Sir Henry Mulleneux, 1st Bt. of Ravens Point, *cr.* 1922; K.B.E., *cr.* 1920 (C.B.E. 1920); M.P. (C.U.) Birkenhead West Division, Dec. 1918-22; Executive Committee Standing Council of the Baronetage; Chairman Anglesey Joint War Organisation and North Wales Regional Council; Commissioner for Anglesey St. John Ambulance Brigade, 1934-45; Member of Joint War Committee of Order of St. John and British Red Cross Society; President, Association of Lancastrians, 1922; Life Governor Princess Beatrice Hospital; Liveryman of Worshipful Company of Shipwrights; Member of Institution of Naval Architects, 1896. Freeman of the City of Liverpool by Birthright; *b.* 26 June 1865; *s.* of Henry Holdrege Grayson, J.P.; *m.* 1st, 1891, Dora Beatrice (marriage dissolved, 1927; she *d.* 1946), *d.* of Frederick Harrington; six *s.* six *d.*; 2nd, 1927, Louise Mary, *widow* of Capt. R. H. Earle and *d.* of R. J. Delaney. *Educ.:* Winchester College. Director of several shipping and shipbuilding companies; High Sheriff of Anglesey, 1917-18; Member of Shipbuilders' Advisory Committee to the Admiralty, 1914-18; Director of Ship Repairs (Hon.) Admiralty, 1916-19; Lieut. Col. Royal Marines, 1918 (Hon.); General Staff Officer; Commendatore of the Order of the Crown of Italy, 1918; Officier Légion d'Honneur, 1919; Commander of the Order of Leopold II. 1918; K.St.J.; General Service and Victory Medals, 1914-18 Defence Medal, 1939-45. *Heir:* *s.* Denys Henry Harrington, *b.* 10 July 1892. *Address:* 47 Orchard Court, Portman Square, W.1. *Clubs:* Carlton, Royal Thames Yacht. [*Died* 27 *Oct.* 1951.

GRAZEBROOK, William, C.B.E. 1947; M.C. 1917; Brilliant Star of Zanzibar; Chairman and Managing Director Nyanza Salt Mines (Tanganyika) Ltd.; *s.* of late Michael Grazebrook; unmarried. *Educ.:* Cranleigh School and Brussels. Was Member Zanzibar Legislature and has served on a number of East African Government Committees. Served European War, 1914-19 (despatches, M.C.); War of 1939-45, temp. Govt. Servant, 1939-49 (C.B.E.). *Address:* P.O. Box 1159, Nairobi, Kenya Colony. *Clubs:* Carlton, White's; Muthaiga (Nairobi). [*Died* 24 *July* 1955.

GREAVES, Rt. Rev. Arthur Ivan, D.D.; Assistant Bishop of Lincoln since 1958; Canon and Prebendary Lincoln Cathedral, since 1959; *b.* 11 January 1873; *e. s.* of late James Henry Greaves, C.E.; *m.* 1905, Blanche A. M. (*d.* 1945), *d.* of J. Meadows, Crossfintan, Carne, Wexford; one *s.* three *d.* *Educ.:* Hurstpierpoint; Keble College, Oxford; Cuddesdon Coll.; B.A. 1895; M.A. 1898; D.D. (Lambeth) 1947. Asst. Curate of Kettering, 1897-1903; Vicar of St. Mary's, Northampton, 1903-06; St. Peter's, Leicester, 1906-11; Vicar of Finedon, Northants, 1911-1928; Residentiary Canon of Peterborough, 1926-34; Archdeacon of Oakham, 1924-34; Sub-Dean of Lincoln Cathedral, 1934-37; Bishop of Grantham, 1935-37; Bishop of Grimsby, 1937-58; Residentiary Canon of Lincoln Cathedral, 1934-59; Precentor of Lincoln Cathedral, 1937-59. Archdeacon of Stow, 1937-51; Surrogate of Diocese of Peterborough, 1906; C.F. France, 1917-18; Hon. C.F., 1919; Warden of Peterborough Lay Readers' Association, 1911-19 and 1924-34; Hon. Canon of Peterborough, 1920; Rural Dean of Higham Ferrers I., 1923; Member of the Mission of Help to India, 1922-23. *Recreations:* rowing, golf. *Address:* Precentory, Lincoln. *T.:* 23608. [*Died* 29 *Nov.* 1959.

GREAVES, Sir (William) Ewart, Kt., *cr.* 1924; *b.* 11 Aug. 1869; *e. s.* of late William Greaves. *Educ.:* Harrow; Keble College, Oxford. Assistant Master at Evelyns, nr. Uxbridge, 1894-99; called to Bar, Lincoln's Inn, 1900; Judge of the Calcutta High Court 1914-27; Vice-Chancellor Calcutta University, 1924-26; Delegate on Indian Delegation to the Assembly of the League of Nations, Sept. 1929 and 1930; Delegate on Indian Delegation to the Hague Conference on the codification of International Law, 1930; Pres. of Nat. Council of Y.M.C. Assocs. since 1947. *Address:* Totehill, Slinfold, Horsham, Sussex. *T.:* Slinfold 264. *Clubs:* United University, M.C.C. [*Died* 14 *March* 1956.

GREAVES, Prof. William Michael Herbert, M.A. (Cantab.); F.R.S., 1943; Astronomer Royal for Scotland and Professor of Astronomy in the University of Edinburgh since 1938; *b.* Barbados, B.W.I., 10 Sept. 1897; *s.* of Dr. E. C. Greaves, M.B., C.M. (Edinburgh); *m.* 1926, Caroline Grace, *d.* of H. D. Kitto, Melrose, Whiteshill, Gloucestershire; one *s.* *Educ.:* Lodge School and Codrington Coll., Barbados, B.W.I.; St. John's College, Cambridge. Wrangler (with star in Schedule B.) Mathematical Tripos Part 2, 1919, and Tyson Medallist in Astronomy; Smith's Prizeman, 1921, Isaac Newton Student in the University of Cambridge, 1921-23; Fellow of St. John's College, Cambridge, 1922-25; Chief Assistant, Royal Observatory, Greenwich, 1924-38; served as Pres. to Royal Astronomical Soc. (former Sec.), as Vice-Pres. to Roy. Soc. of Edinburgh (former Sec. to ordinary meetings), as Secretary and Recorder to Section A of British Association for the Advancement of Science. *Publications:* papers in Monthly Notices of Roy. Astronomical Soc.; and Publications of Roy. Observatary, Edin.; also some papers in Proc. Roy. Soc., Proc. Cambridge Philosophical Soc., and Philosophical Magazine. *Recreations:* walking, motoring, etc. *Address:* Royal Observatory, Edinburgh 9. *Club:* Scottish Arts. [*Died* 24 *Dec.* 1955.

GREEN, Sir Alan Michael, Kt., *cr.* 1935; C.I.E. 1933; M.A.; I.C.S.; retired; *b.* 11 April 1885; *s.* of Michael A. Green and Netta Halford; *m.* 1919, Joan Frances, *o. c.* of F. D. Elkin; one *s.* one *d.* *Educ.:* St. Paul's School; Lincoln College, Oxford. Appointed to Indian Civil Service, 1908; District Officer, Bombay Presidency, 1909-13; Secretariat Officer, Bombay and Assistant Censor, 1913-15; Bombay Customs Dept., 1915-18; throughout war served with Coast Defence Artillery, temp. Captain (Civil despatches twice); Under Secretary, Govt. of India, Commerce and Industries Dept., 1918; Collector of Customs and Port Trustee, Karachi, 1919-21; Madras, 1921-22; Bombay and member of Bombay Board of Film Censors, 1921-28; Member of Indian Cinematograph Committee (Govt. of India), 1927-28; Indian Trade Commissioner, London, 1929; Deputy High Commissioner for India in the United Kingdom, 1930-34; Assistant Secretary, Imperial Economic Committee and Executive Council, Imperial Agricultural Bureaux, 1935; seconded to Ministry of Supply, 1939, and retired as Principal Priority Officer, 1946; Member, Herts C.C., 1952-58. *Publications:* occasional articles and official reports only. *Recreations:* chamber music, bridge, gardening. *Address:* Meads, Frithesden Copse, Berkhamsted, Herts. *T.:* Berkhamsted 503. *Clubs:* English-Speaking Union; Royal Bombay Yacht, Willingdon Sports (Bombay). [*Died* 3 *Aug.* 1958.

GREEN, Colonel Ernest Edward, C.B. 1949; T.D., D.L.; Solicitor; *b.* 1878; *s.* of late Edward Green, Frome, Somerset; *m.* 1902, Margaret, *d.* of Thomas Williams, Llanelly; one *d.* *Educ.:* Endowed School, Frome. Formerly commanded 6th and 7th Bns. Welch Regt. (T.A.); served European War, 1914-19 (despatches); Chairman, Glamorgan T. & A.F.A., 1945-49; D.L. Glamorgan. *Address:* The Hermitage, Fairwater Road, Llandaff, Cardiff. *T.:* Llandaff 863. *Club:* Cardiff and County (Cardiff). [*Died* 25 *Sept.* 1956.

GREEN, Sir Francis Haydn, 2nd Bt., *cr.* 1901; *b.* 7 May 1871; *s.* of 1st Bt. and Kate, *d.* of Joseph Haydn; *m.* 1904, Viola Evelyn, *d.* of late H. B. Wheatley; one *d.*; *S.* father, 1902. *Educ.:* University College School. Member of the Common Council, City of London. *Heir:* *b.* Leonard, *b.* 14 Aug. 1879. *Address:* 1 Inglewood House, West End Lane, N.W. [*Died* 23 *Feb.* 1956.

GREEN, Frederick Lawrence; novelist; *b.* Portsmouth, Hants, 1902; 2nd *s.* of George Edward Green and Elizabeth Jermy; *m.* 1929, Margaret Edwards. *Educ.:* Salesian Coll., Farnborough. *Publications:* Julius Penton, 1934; On the Night of the Fire, 1939; The Sound of Winter, 1940; Give us the World, 1941; Music in the Park, 1942; A Song for the Angels, 1943; On the Edge of the Sea, 1944; Odd Man Out, 1945; A Flask for the Journey, 1946; A Fragment of Glass, 1947; Mist on the Waters, 1948; Clouds in the Wind, 1950; The Magician, 1951; Ambush For The Hunter, 1952; (with Carol Reed) Script of Film, Odd Man Out. *Recreations:* conversation, music. *Address:* c/o Pearn, Pollinger & Higham, Ltd., 39-40 Bedford Street, Strand, W.C.2. [*Died* 14 *April* 1953.

GREEN, Rev. Frederick Wastie, B.D., M.A.; Canon Emeritus of Norwich Cathedral since 1951; *b.* 27 Oct. 1884; *y. s.* of late James Wastie Green, Rector of March, Cambs, and Mary Frances Walton, *d.* of Edward Thornton Codd, Vicar of Tachbrooke, Warwickshire; *m.* Marjorie, *d.* of E. H. Gosling, Highwood, Paget, Bermuda; two *s.* two *d.* *Educ.:* Norwich School; Brasenose College, Oxford. Curacies at S. Anne, Limehouse, E., 1909-15, and S. Paul's, Knightsbridge, 1915-18, T.C.R.N. 1918-19; Fellow, and Tutor, Merton College, Oxford, 1919-32; Junior Proctor in University of Oxford, 1922; Univ. Lecturer in Patristic Studies, 1930-31; Select Preacher, Oxford, 1929-31, Cambridge, 1938; Canon Residentiary of Norwich Cathedral, 1931-50; Treasurer, 1934-37; Vice-Dean, 1936-50. *Publications:* St. Matthew, Clarendon Bible, 1936; Oecumenical Documents of the Faith (new edn.), 1950, contributed to Essays on the Trinity and the Incarnation, 1928; Apostolic Ministry, 1946. *Address:* Further Ford End, Clavering, Saffron Walden, Essex. *T.:* Brent Pelham 273. [*Died* 14 *Jan.* 1953.

GREEN, Frederick William E.; *see* Edridge-Green.

GREEN, Sir George Arthur Haydn, 4th Bt. *cr.* 1901; *b.* 29 July 1884; 4th *s.* of Alderman Sir Frank Green, 1st Bt. (Lord Mayor of London, 1900-01); *S.* brother, Rev. Sir Leonard Henry Haydn Green, 3rd Bt., 1958; *m.* 1905, Ethel, 2nd *d.* of late Edward Dodington, Toronto. *Educ.:* Merchant Taylors' School. *Heir:* none. *Address:* 194 Collier Street, Barrie, Ontario, Canada. [*Died* 7 *May* 1959 (*ext.*).

GREEN, George Henry, B.Sc., Ph.D. (Lond)., M.A. (Wales), B.Litt. (Exeter College, Oxford); F.R.A.I.; formerly Professor, Egyptian Inst. of Education, Alexandria; *b.* 2 July 1881; *e. s.* of Henry Green, Portsmouth; *m.* Lena Sophia Beatrice (*d.* 1945), *yr. d.* of James Pritchard, Bristol and London; no *c.* *Educ.:* University College of Southampton; Exeter College, Oxford. Formerly Senior Lecturer, Dept. of Education, Univ. Coll. of Wales, Aberystwyth. *Publications:* Psychoanalysis in the Classroom; The Daydream; The Mind in Action; The Terror Dream; The Child's Religion (translation of Bovet's Le Sentiment Religieux); Healthway Books, etc.; (in collab.) textbooks of Education in Arabic. *Address:* 4 South Marine Terrace, Aberystwyth, Cards. *Clubs:* Royal Empire Society; St. Davids (Aberystwyth). [*Died* 25 *June* 1956.

GREEN, Sir John (Little), Kt., *cr.* 1919; O.B.E. 1918; *b.* 6 Sept. 1862; *yr. s.* of late George Green; *m.* 1890, Dorothy Ann (*d.* 1947), *d.* of late William Henry Bagnall; two *s.* For over thirty years Sec. of the Rural League, and Editor of its organ, The Rural World; subsequently Director of Rural Industries, Ministry of Agriculture; then for ten years Secretary of Conservative and Unionist Parliamentary Agricultural Committee, and at the same time Director of Agricultural Department of Conservative Party Organisation; now retired; a voluntary worker during European War, 1914-18, receiving the thanks of the Army Council, the Food Production Dept., and the then Board of Agriculture for suggesting and creating movement for establishment of Pig Clubs amongst the cottager and artisan population; and also for advice and assistance given to Ministry of Agriculture in connection with the campaign for re-starting the Pig Club movement during War of 1939-45; has also given much evidence to Government Committees, resulting in legislation for providing allotments, small-holdings and setting up of rural industries. *Publications:* The Rural Industries of England; English Country Cottages; Allotments and Small-holdings; Village Industries; Life of the Right Hon. Jesse Collings; etc. *Address:* 1 Sidbury Rd., Chorlton-cum-Hardy, Manchester. *Club:* Farmers'. [*Died* 15 *Jan.* 1953.

GREEN, Rev. Sir Leonard (Henry Haydn), 3rd Bt., *cr.* 1901; retired; *b.* 14 Aug. 1879; 2nd *s.* of Sir Frank Green, 1st Bt. and Kate (*d.* 1900), *d.* of Joseph Haydn; *S.* brother 1956; *m.* 1935, Miriam Annie, *d.* of late Charles Roberts, Stamford Hill, N.15; no *c.* *Educ.:* University College School, London; Trinity College, Toronto; Lichfield Theological College. L.Th. 1911, Trin. Coll., Toronto. Deacon, 1913; Curate of Brasted, Sevenoaks, 1913-15; Priest, 1914; Curate of St. John's, Stamford Hill, 1915-25; Permission to officiate at St. Jude's, Gray's Inn Road, 1925-30, Curate, 1930-34; Vicar of Badby-cum-Newnham, Northants, 1934-1951. *Heir:* *b.* George Arthur Haydn Green [*S.* 1958; *Died,* 1959; Btcy. Ext.; *see* Addenda]. *Address:* Trader's Cottage, Trader's Passage, Rye, Sussex. [*Died* 1 *Sept.* 1958.

GREEN, Vincent, M.D., Edin.; retired; *s.* of H. C. Green, J.P., Ealing; *m.* 1st, *d.* of S. Kemp Welch, of Godstone and St. George's Square, S.W.; two *d.*; 2nd, 1929, Muriel Eleanor, *yr. d.* of W. C. Holmes, Canterbury. *Educ.:* St. Paul's; Edinburgh University. Held house appointments London Homœopathic Hospital, Liverpool Homœopathic Hosp.; consulting surgeon Nose and Throat London Homœopathic Hosp., 1912; Medical Officer Hahnemann Convalescent Home; Member of Hunterian Society. *Publications:* Adenoids, Cause and Treatment; Nasal Suppuration. *Address:* Beechleys, Winkton Common, Christchurch, Hants. [*Died* 21 *Dec.* 1958.

GREEN, Walter Henry, C.B.E. 1949; J.P.; formerly Alderman of Deptford Borough Council, retd., 1956; J.P., County of London, since 1920; *b.* 8 Mar. 1878; *s.* of Thomas William and Sarah Amelia Green; *m.* 1904, Grace Edith Puddefoot; one *s.* one *d.* *Educ.:* Stanley Street L.C.C. Elementary School. Apprenticed to Engineering; Councillor Deptford Borough Council since 1909, 12 years of this period as Alderman; Mayor of Deptford, 1921 and 1922; Chairman of Parliamentary Committee L.C.C., 1934-37; M.P. (Lab.) Deptford, 1935-45; member of National Executive of Labour Party, 1935; Chairman of Labour Party, 1941-42; Member of Executive of London Labour Party, 1923-43; Governor of Stanhope Secondary School, retd., 1955; Mem. Metropolitan Water Board, 1946-Oct. 1953, retd. Governor of S.E. London Technical Coll. 1949-55; formerly Alderman of L.C.C. Freedom of Borough of Deptford, 1944. *Address:* 64 Southwood Road, New Eltham, S.E.9. *T.:* Eltham 1612. [*Died* 13 *April* 1958.

GREEN, William, Hon. C.B.E. 1946; Award of Merit (U.S.), 1947; Hon. Doctor of Laws, Kenyon Coll., 1949; President American Federation of Labor since 1925; Editor of American Federationist; *b.* Coshocton, Ohio, 3 Mar. 1873; *s.* of an English miner; *m.* 1894, Jennie Mobley; one *s.* five *d.* Worked in the coal mines at an early age; Secretary-Treasurer of United Mine Workers of America, 1912-24. Served two terms in Ohio Senate and introduced and secured passage of Ohio Workmen's Compensation Law. Elected to Executive Council of American Federation of Labor, 1913; chosen President on death of Samuel Gompers; re-elected unanimously each succeeding convention. Has served on many committees and boards. Awarded Gold Medal of Honor, 1930, by Roosevelt Memorial Association, for distinguished service in promotion of industrial peace. *Publication:* Labor and Democracy, 1939. *Address:* American Federation of Labor Building, Washington 1, D.C., U.S.A.; Coshocton, Ohio, U.S.A. [*Died* 21 *Nov.* 1952.

GREEN, William Curtis, R.A. 1933 (A.R.A. 1923); F.R.I.B.A.; Retired; Officier d'Académie Française; Royal Gold Medallist, 1942; *b.* 16 July 1875; *s.* of Frederic Green, M.A., Barrister-at-law; *m.* 1st, Cicely Dillworth Lloyd (*d.* 1934); one *s.* four *d.*; 2nd, 1935, Laura Gwenllian, Lady Northbourne (*d.* 1952). *Principal Works:* Barclays Bank, Piccadilly; R.I.B.A. Medal, 1922; Westminster Bank, Piccadilly; London Life Assoc., King William St.; Stratton House, Piccadilly; Offices in Duke St. for Clerical Medical & General Life Assurance Soc.; Lloyds Bank, Branches: Spitalfields and Regent St.; Stanmore Housing Estate, Winchester; Chepstow Housing Estate; Village Club, Painswick; Mary Datchelor School, Camberwell; Church of the Good Shepherd, Dockenfield, Frensham; Adult School Hall, Croydon; (with Christopher Green, M.A., and W. A. S. Lloyd, M.A.), The Dorchester Hotel, Park Lane; Queens Hotel, Leeds; Whitehall Development Scheme, extension of Scotland Yard; The Scottish Widows' Fund and Life Assurance Soc. Office Cornhill; Stockgrove Park, Leighton Buzzard; Cambridge Univ. Press, Euston Rd.; Barclays Bank: Branches in Bournemouth, New Bond Street, Plymouth; Churches at Waddon, Cove, and Rough Close; Diocesan Training Coll., The Close, Salisbury. *Address:* 16 Pall Mall, S.W.1. *T.:* Whitehall 3840. *Club:* Athenæum. [*Died* 26 *March* 1960.

GREENAWAY, Sir Percy Walter, 1st Bt., *cr.* 1933; Kt., *cr.* 1932; Chairman of: Daniel Greenaway & Sons Ltd., printers and stationers; Bowles & Sons (Printers) Ltd.; Frederick Steel & Co. Ltd., all of 69 Old Broad Street, E.C.2; a Lieut. and J.P. for City of London; *b.* 11 June 1874; *e. s.* of late Daniel Greenaway, Deputy of the City of London; *m.* 1907, Lydie Amy, *e. d.* of late James Burdick; two *s.* two *d.* *Educ.:* Privately. A Member of Court of Common Council of City of London, 1917-; since chairman of several committees; Alderman, 1923-; Senior Sheriff, 1931-32; Lord Mayor, 1932-33; elected Master of Stationers' and Newspaper Makers' Co., 1932 (re-elected 1933); Treasurer, 1951; Gov. Hon. Irish Soc., 1945. *Recreations:* fly fishing, shooting, golf. *Heir:* *s.* Derek Burdick [*b.* 27 May 1910; *m.* 1937, Sheila Beatrice, *o. d.* of late R. Cyril Lockett, 58 Cadogan Place, S.W.1; one *s.* one *d.*]. *Address:* Eastcott, Kingston Hill, Surrey. *Clubs:* Carlton, Constitutional, Royal Automobile. [*Died* 25 *Nov.* 1956.

GREENE, 1st Baron, *cr.* 1941, of Holmbury St. Mary; **Wilfrid Arthur Greene,** P.C. 1935; Kt., *cr.* 1935; O.B.E. 1919; M.C.; F.S.A.; Hon. F.R.I.B.A. 1941; Trustee Pilgrim Trust since 1941; British Museum since 1937; Chantrey Trust, 1941-50; Commander of the Order of St. Olav (Norway); *b.* 1883; *s.* of late Arthur Weguelin Greene; *m.* 1909, Nancy, *d.* of late Francis Wright, Allerton, Yorks. *Educ.:* Westminster School; Christ Church, Oxford (M.A.); Craven, Hertford, and Vinerian scholar, Chancellor's Latin Verse Prize; Fellow of All Souls College, 1907. Hon. Student of Christ Church (Oxford) 1935; Hon. D.C.L. (Oxford) 1935; Hon. LL.D. Birmingham 1936, Sheffield 1946, Wesleyan Univ., U.S.A., 1941, St. Andrews 1948; Hon. Mem. N.Y. City Bar Assoc., 1941; called to Bar, Inner Temple, 1908; K.C. 1922; Bencher Inner Temple, 1925; Standing Counsel to Oxford University, 1926-35; Lord Justice of Appeal, 1935-37; Master of the Rolls, 1937-49; a Lord of Appeal in Ordinary, 1949-50, resigned. Principal of Working Men's College, Crowndale Road, N.W.1, 1936-44; Chairman of Council of National Buildings Record, 1941-

1945. Joined 2/1st Bucks Battalion O. and B.L.I. (T.F.) as 2nd Lieut. Nov. 1914; served in France, Flanders, and Italy; G.S.O. 3 on staff of Fifth Army 1917, afterwards G.S.O. 2 on G.H.Q. staff, Italy, and G.S.O. 2 British Section Supreme War Council, 1918, rank of Major (O.B.E., M.C., Croix de Guerre (French), Cavaliere Order of the Crown of Italy). *Address:* The Wilderness, Holmbury St. Mary, Surrey. *T.:* Forest Green 324. *Club:* Brooks's.
[*Died* 16 *April* 1952 (*ext.*).

GREENE, Jerome Davis, LL.D.; *b.* Yokohama, Japan, 12 Oct. 1874; *s.* of Daniel Crosby Greene and Mary Jane Forbes; *m.* 1900, May Tevis, Haverford, Pa.; one *s.* *m.* 1942, Dorothea Dusser de Barenne; one *s.* *Educ.:* Harvard University, A.B.; University of Geneva; Harvard Law School; Hon. A.M. Harvard and Rutgers; Hon. LL.D., Harvard and Norwich (U.S.A.). Secretary to the President, Harvard University, 1901-1905; Secretary to the Corporation, Harvard University, 1905-10 and 1934-43; Hon. Keeper of Corporation Records, Harvard University, 1943-; Manager of the Rockefeller Institute for Medical Research, New York, 1910-12; Trustee, 1912-32; Secretary of the Rockefeller Foundation, 1913-17; Trustee, 1913-17 and 1928-39; Member of the General Education Board, 1912-39; Wilson Professor of International Politics, University of Wales, Aberystwyth, 1932-34; Executive Secretary of the American Section, Allied Maritime Transport Council, 1918; Joint Secretary of the Reparations Committee, Peace Conference, Paris, 1919; Member of the Board of Overseers of Harvard Univ., 1911-13, 1917-23, 1944-50; Trustee Brookings Institution of Washington, 1928-1945; Trustee American Academy in Rome, 1920-39; Chairman American Council Institute of Pacific Relations, 1929-32; Internat. Chairman, 1929-33; Trustee: New England Conservatory of Music since 1937; Boston Symphony Orchestra, 1938-49, Pres., 1942-45; President, American Asiatic Assoc. 1929-32; Treasurer and Trustee Isabella Stewart Gardner Museum, Boston, since 1936; Trustee Mt. Auburn Hospital, Cambridge, Mass., 1935-57; Pres., Cambridge Club, 1946-47; Fellow: Am. Acad. of Arts and Sciences; Pres. East Asiatic Soc., 1950-; Mem. of Mediaeval Acad. of America; Chm., Distribution Cttee., Camb. Foundation, 1950-57. Grand Officer Order of St. Sava; Officier Légion d'Honneur; Officer Order of Orange-Nassau. *Address:* 54A Garden Street, Cambridge, Mass. *Clubs:* Harvard, Century (New York); Harvard, Tavern (Boston); American (Tokyo); Faculty (Cambridge, Mass.). [*Died* 29 *March* 1959.

GREENE, Brigadier-General John, D.S.O. 1917; late Queen's Royal Lancers; *b.* 26 May 1878; *o. s.* of John Greene, Stelling Hall, Stocksfield, Northumberland; *m.* 1931, Iris Marguerite, *e. d.* of Lt.-Col. D. L. Selby-Bigge, The Crescent, Ripon, Yorkshire; one *s.* three *d.* *Educ.:* Marlborough College. Joined 7th Dragoon Guards, 1900; served in South African War (King's and Queen's medals); West African Frontier Force, 1908-12; European War, 1914-18, commanded 13th Batt. Middlesex Regt. and 10th Infantry Brigade (D.S.O. and bar, Croix de Guerre, 1914 Star, British War Medal, Allies War Medal); Mesopotamia, 1919-21 (Middle East Medal); posted to 9th Lancers, 1922; retired pay, 1928. *Recreations:* all sports. *Address:* The Lodge, Greenlaw, Berwickshire. [*Died* 20 *Sept.* 1956.

GREENE, Maurice Cherry, B.A.; LL.D.; *b.* 4 Nov. 1881; *y. s.* of Rev. Thomas and Kathleen Dalton Greene; *m.* 1925, Maud Quiney (*d.* 1953); two *d.* *Educ.:* Strangways Sch., Dublin; Trinity Coll., Dublin. Asst. Resident, Nigeria, 1912; Station Magistrate, Nigeria, 1914; served European War, West African Frontier Force, 1914-16; Police Magistrate, Lagos, Nigeria, 1920-27; Pres. District Court, Cyprus, 1928; Acting Puisne Judge, Cyprus, various occasions; Puisne Judge, Palestine, 1937; Chairman, Waqf Commission, Palestine, 1938-39; Chief Justice, Gibraltar, 1941-42; Chairman Claims Tribunal, Gibraltar, 1942; Member of the Colonial Research Committee for Research on Law and Legal Systems in the Colonies, 1943; Proper Officer of the Crown Prize Court, Bermuda, 1945-49; retired, 1949. *Recreations:* motoring, golf, chess. *Address:* 12 Frant Road, Tunbridge Wells, Kent. *T.:* Tunbridge Wells 647. *Club:* Tunbridge Wells and Counties (Tunbridge Wells).
[*Died* 6 *Dec.* 1959.

GREENE, Hon. Sir Walter M.; *see* Massy-Greene.

GREENE, William Pomeroy Crawford, J.P.; M.A.; *b.* New South Wales, 28 June 1884; *s.* of Hon. George Greene, M.L.C. (N.S.W.), and Ellen Elizabeth, *d.* of Lieut.-Colonel Andrew Crawford, I.S.C. *Educ.:* Haileybury; Trinity College, Cambridge. A landowner in Australia; was President of Grenfell Landowners' Association, and Member of Young Landowners' Association and Grenfell Farmers' and Settlers' Association; has travelled extensively in Europe, North Africa, the Near East, India, and the Antipodes; served in Cambridge University Mounted Infantry and King Edward's Horse; later raised and commanded a half squadron in 11th Australian Light Horse; in 1908 brought about affiliation of all Australian Light Horse Regts. with King Edward's Horse in England; held Captain's Commission in 13th Hussars (S.R.), with which served in France and Mesopotamia, 1915-19. M.P. (C.) for City of Worcester, 1923-45. *Address:* 5 West Eaton Place, S.W.1. *T.:* Sloane 5056. *Clubs:* Cavalry, Carlton; Union (Worcester). [*Died* 10 *May* 1959.

GREENFIELD, Herbert; *b.* Winchester, 1869; *m.* 1st, 1900, Elizabeth Harris (*d.* 1922), Strathroy, Ontario; two *s.*; 2nd, 1926, Marjorie Greenwood, *widow* of Shibley Cormack, Edmonton, Alberta. *Educ.:* Wesleyan School, Dalston, England. Migrated to Ontario, Canada, 1892; farmed there; moved west to Alberta, 1905; active in municipal work; President Alberta Association of Municipalities several years; active in Farmers' Movement; served on Canadian Council of Agriculture; Vice-President, United Farmers of Alberta, 1919-21; Premier of Alberta, 1921-25; Commissioner of Colonisation, Alberta, 1926; Agent-General for Alberta, 1927-31. *Address:* Toronto General Trust Building, Calgary, Alberta.
[*Died* 23 *Aug.* 1949.
[*But death not notified in time for inclusion in Who Was Who 1941–1950, first edn.*

GREENFIELD, Stanley Samuel, C.V.O. 1936; *b.* 21 July 1873; *s.* of Samuel Challen and Rosa Greenfield; *m.* 1st, 1900, Nan Murray Aitken; two *d.*; 2nd, 1940, Dorothy Margery, *widow* of S. Roberts. *Educ.:* Aske's School; Lycée de Caen. Secretary to Coutts and Co., Bankers; retired, 1938. Order (2nd Class) of St. Sava, Yugo-Slavia. *Recreations:* gardening, reading. *Address:* Green Farm, Elmswell, Suffolk. *T.:* 340 Elmswell.
[*Died* 23 *April* 1956.

GREENHALGH, Mrs. Stobart; *see* Stobart, Mrs. St. Clair.

GREENHOUGH, Col. Frederick Harry, D.S.O. 1918; R.E. retired; Order of Leopold; Legion of Honour; M.Inst.C.E.; late Deputy General Manager and Chief Engineer, Nigerian Railways and Collieries (retd.); Principal Engineering Work, Port Talbot Docks, Vera Cruz Harbour, Mexican Govt., Admiralty Harbours Dover and Malta; Arapuni Hydro Electric development, New Zealand Govt., and various railways; Grimsby New Fish Dock Harbours at St. Helier's, Jersey, and Famagusta, Cyprus; *b.* 1871; *s.* of Frank Greenhough, Bradford, Yorks; *m.* 1900, Agnes Lucy, *d.* of late Captain R. B. Cay, R. N., Dover; one *s.* Served European War, 1914-18 (despatches,

D.S.O.); Technical representative of the British Army in France on the Interallied Commission for Navigable Waterways and Defensive Inundations, 1917-19. *Address:* The Homestead, Grouville, Jersey, C.I. [*Died* 2 *Jan.* 1953.

GREENLAND, Rev. William Kingscote; Formerly Editor of Good Lines, Commercial Travellers Magazine, until 1950; Correspondent to Methodist Recorder, etc.; *b.* Brierley Hill, Staffs, 1868; *o. s.* of James Greenland (Wesleyan minister) and Louisa Kingscote; *m.* 1st, Florence Lock, King's Lynn; one *d.*; 2nd, 1920, Evelyn, 2nd *d.* of late William Mutch, Highgate. *Educ.:* King Edward's Grammar School, Coventry; Kingswood School, Bath; Handsworth College, Birmingham. After leaving school was a schoolmaster; entered Wesleyan ministry, 1890; held pastorates in Wisbech, Bury St. Edmunds, Westminster (London), Shanklin, Hanley, Chingford; resigned the Ministry, 1919; Assistant Editor of Methodist Times and Leader for 15 years; late Editor of The Young Man; lectured much on literary and social subjects—Gospel of Robert Louis Stevenson, etc. (*nom de plume*, W. Scott King) League of Nations in Paris and all over Europe. *Publications:* Heavens of Brass, 1899; Behind the Granite Gateway, 1901; The Seekers, 1903; The Master of Dunholme; The Price of Victory; God's Englishman; Hearts Triumphant; Cameos from Camps; The Victorious Child. *Recreations:* tramping thro' Lake District, Highlands, Switzerland, France, Holland, Germany, Italy, Ireland, Russia. *Address:* c/o Mrs. Hayes, Dibley's, Blewbury, Berks. *Club:* National Liberal. [*Died* 12 *Dec.* 1957.

GREENLEES, James Robertson Campbell, D.S.O. 1915; M.A., M.B.; B.C. Cantab.; Chairman S.E. Regional Hospital Board, 1947; Physician; Headmaster of Loretto School, Musselburgh, 1926-45; Surgeon, King's Body Guard for Scotland, Royal Company of Archers, since 1948; *b.* 14 Dec. 1878; *yr. s.* of Matthew Greenlees, Langdale, Dowanhill, Glasgow; *m.* 1922, Allison Hope, *o. d.* of Sir John T. Cargill, Bt., *q.v.*; one *s.* one *d.* *Educ.:* Loretto; Cambridge and Glasgow Universities. Out-patient Staff, Western Infirmary, Glasgow, 1908-19; Royal Hospital for Sick Children, Glasgow, 1908-25; Lt. R.A.M.C., 12 Aug. 1914; 22nd Field Ambulance, 14 Sept. 1914; Capt. 12 Aug. 1915; Act. Lt.-Col. Commanding 98th Field Ambulance, Aug. 1916; served European War, 1914-18 (D.S.O. and bar, Legion of Honour (Chevalier), despatches four times). Chairman Royal Hospital for Sick Children, Edinburgh, 1945. *Address:* Huntington, Haddington, East Lothian. [*Died* 16 *May* 1951.

GREENLY, Edward, D.Sc. (Hon.) Wales, F.G.S., etc.: *b.* Bristol, 3 Dec. 1861; *s.* of Charles Hickes Greenly and Harriett Dowling; *m.* 1891, Annie Barnard (*d.* 1927), Bristol. *Educ.:* Clifton College; University College, London. Joined H.M. Geological Survey (Scotland), 1889; worked mainly in N.W. Highlands and in N.E. Sutherland; began an (unofficial) re-survey of Anglesey, 1895, working at it for 24 years; the result was published by the Geological Survey in 1919; is now surveying the country between the Menai Strait and the mountains with the aid of Dr. David Williams, F.G.S., but recently disabled by loss of a leg; Lyell Medal, Geological Society, 1920; V.P.G.S., 1927-30; Hon. Member Geological Societies, Edinburgh and Liverpool, and Anglesey Antiquarian Society; Medal of Liverpool Geological Society, 1933. *Publications:* The Geology of Anglesey, Mem. Geol. Surv., 2 vols. 1919; The One Inch Geological Map of Anglesey, 1919; contributions to Scottish Survey maps and memoirs; Methods in Geological Surveying, Greenly and Williams, 1930; The Earth, 1927, 2nd Ed., 1930; Chapter on Geology in The Mountains of Snowdonia, 2nd. Ed. 1948, also similar chapter in the Forestry Commission's Guide 1948; A Hand through Time (partly autobiography, partly the grounds of confidence in Immortality), 1938; Geological Papers, about 80; other essays, about 20. *Recreations:* architecture and cats. *Address:* Aethwy Ridge, Bangor, North Wales. *T.:* Bangor 593. [*Died* 4 *March* 1951.

GREENLY, Major-General Walter Howorth, C.B. 1919; C.M.G. 1915; D.S.O. 1900; D.L., J.P. Co. Hereford; *b.* 2 Jan. 1875; *e. s.* of late Edward Howorth Greenly of Titley Court, Titley, Co. Hereford, J.P. and D.L. *Educ.:* Eton; Sandhurst. Joined 12th Lancers, 1895; served S. Africa, 1899-1902; Lt.-Col., 19th Royal Hussars, 1912-16; Colonel, 1916; Colonel 12th Royal Lancers, 1917-20; European War, 1914-18 (Bt. Col., C.M.G., prom. Maj.-Gen., C.B.); Commanded 2nd Cavalry Division, 1916-1918; Chief of Military Mission Roumania, 1918-20 (Commander of Legion of Honour, Star of Roumania, St. Anne and St. Stanislaus of Russia, White Eagle of Serbia); retired, 1920. *Address:* Titley Court, Kington, Herefordshire. *Club:* Royal Automobile. [*Died* 20 *May* 1955.

GREENUP, Rev. Albert William, Litt.D., D.D., M.R.A.S.; Rector of Great Oakley, Essex, 1925-31; Examining Chaplain to the Bishop of Chelmsford, 1914-46; *b.* 5 June 1866; *s.* of W. T. Greenup, of Mount House, Ryde, I.W.; *m.* Evelyn, *d.* of A. P. Heron of Wigan and Oxford; one *s.* one *d.* *Educ.:* Leys School, Camb.; London School of Economics; St. John's College, Cambridge (Scholar, Hebrew Exhibitioner, Hughes Ecclesiastical History Exhibitioner, and Naden Divinity Student). B.A. (1st class Theo., distinguished in Hebrew and Septuagint), 1890; M.A. 1893; Carus Greek Test., Univ. Hebrew, and Jeremie Septuagint Prizeman; Tyrwhitt Hebrew Scholar; Litt.D., Trinity Coll., Dublin, 1909; D.D. (Ontario) *honoris causa*, 1902; Chaplain to H.E. Earl Cadogan, 1893-1915; Rector of Alburgh, Norfolk, 1897-99; Principal of, 1899-1925, and Macneil Professor of Biblical Exegesis in, 1900-25, the London College of Divinity, Highbury; Public Examiner at Cambridge, 1898-99, 1909-10, 1924; Member of Faculty of Theology, University of London, 1900-25; Examiner in Hebrew and Greek Testament, University of London, 1903-12, 1922-24; in Ecclesiastical History, 1905-6; in Hebrew and Syriac, 1924-46; Member of the Board of Oriental Studies, 1907-25; Limborough Lecturer and Chaplain to the Weavers Company, 1908-12; Dean of the Faculty of Theology, University of London, 1908-12; Examiner in Hellenistic Greek, University of Liverpool, 1915-18; Teacher in Hebrew and Syriac, University of London, 1919-25; Examiner in Theology, University of Durham, 1921-23; Univ. of London, 1922-24; Acting Principal of Missionary College, Clifton, 1932; Professor of Biblical Languages, 1932-47. *Publications:* Commentary of R. Tobia ben Elieser on Echah; Marginal References to the Revised Version (N.T.): Forms of Absolution; Commentary of R. Meyuhas on Genesis; The Yalkut Machiri on Hosea and Zechariah (Editio Princeps); The Poems of Mordecai Dato; The Shekel Ha-Kodesh of Moses de Leon (Editio Princeps); The Yalkut Machiri on Amos-Habakkuk; The Book of the Moon; Essay II. in London University Theological Essays; The Yalkut Machiri on Joel, Zephaniah, Haggai, and Malachi; Notes on the Greek Text of St. Mark; The Iggereth Hamudoth of Eliah Genazzano (Editio Princeps); A Collection of Segulloth (Krakau); The Commentary of R. D. Kimchi on Psalms i.-viii.; The Treatise Taanith of the Jerusalem Talmud, translated into English; Commentary of R. Tobia ben Elieser on Canticles (Editio Princeps); The Mishnah Taanith, translated into English; The Megillath Taanith, translated into English for the first time; A critical edition of the Hebrew text of the Mishnah Sukkah; A newly discovered fragment of the Yalkut Machiri; Translation of the Mishnah and Tosefta of Sukkah; The Story of Jonah in Rabbinic Hebrew; Yalkut Shimeoni on the Book of Nahum; Commentary of R.

Meyuhas on Exodus; The Targum on Lamentations, translated into English; A Cabbalistic Epistle of R. Isaac Hayyim Sephardi; Essay II in Judaism and Christianity (ed. Gillet) 1939. *Recreation:* formerly cricket. *Address:* St. John's Cottage, Baughurst, Basingstoke. [*Died* 9 *Jan.* 1952.

GREENWOOD, Rt. Hon. Arthur, P.C. 1929; C.H. 1945; M.P. (Lab.) Wakefield since 1932; Deputy Leader and Acting Chm. Labour Party, 1942, Treas., 1943, Chm. 1952; *b.* 8 Feb. 1880; *m.* 1904, Catherine Ainsworth Brown; one *s.* one *d.* *Educ.:* Victoria University. Sometime head of the Economics and Law Department, Huddersfield Technical College; late Lecturer in Economics in the University of Leeds; late Chairman of the Yorkshire District of the Workers' Educational Association, and Vice.-Pres. of the National W.E.A.; late Gen. Sec. of the Council for the Study of International Relations; late Secretary Labour Party Research and Information Dept. Asst. Sec. Reconstruction Cttee., 1917; of Ministry of Reconstruction, 1917-19; M.P. (Lab.) Nelson and Colne (Lancs), 1922-31; Parliamentary Secretary to Ministry of Health, 1924; Minister of Health, 1929-31; Deputy Leader of the Labour Party, 1935; Member of the War Cabinet, and Minister without Portfolio, 1940-42; Lord Privy Seal, 1945-47, and Paymaster-General, 1946-47; Joint-Sec. of the Committee on Relations between Employers and Employed (the Whitley Committee) and of the Ministry of Reconstruction Committee on Adult Education; Member of the Central Profiteering Committee and of the Standing Committee on Trusts; Vice-Chairman of the Minister of Health's Consultative Council on General Health Questions; Secretary of the Labour Commission to Ireland; General Secretary of the Labour Party's Advisory Committees, 1920-21; Member of the Departmental Committee on the Stopping-up and Diversion of Highways; Member of Departmental Committee on Local Government Officers Superannuation; Hon. Freeman of City of Leeds, 1930; Hon. LL.D. University of Leeds, 1930. *Publications:* Juvenile Labour Exchanges and After Care; The Health and Physique of School Children (Part) The War and Democracy; (Part) An Introduction to the Study of International Relations; with H. Clay, An Introductory Atlas of International Relations; The Education of the Citizen; Public Ownership of the Liquor Trade; The Labour Outlook, 1929; Why We Fight: Labour's Case, 1940. *Address:* 8 Gainsborough Gardens, Hampstead, N.W.3. [*Died* 9 *June* 1954.

GREENWOOD, George David, C.B.E. 1920 (O.B.E. 1918); Joined Management of the Royal Mail Steam Packet Company, 1921, now Royal Mail Lines, Ltd.; Chairman and Managing Director of Trade and Travel Publications, Ltd.; *b.* November 1881; *s.* of George D. Greenwood; *m.* 1905, Maud, *d.* of G. Gane-Clark, Johannesburg; one *s.* one *d.* *Educ.:* St. Mary's Charterhouse; City of London. Transport Department, Admiralty, 1914; Assistant Accountant General, Ministry of Shipping, 1917-21. *Recreations:* motoring, golf. *Address:* 317 Wimbledon Park Road, S.W.19. *T.:* Putney 3057. [*Died* 4 *Nov.* 1953.

GREENWOOD, John Frederic, R.E. 1939; R.B.A. 1940; *b.* 13 June 1885; *s.* of Robinson and Anne Greenwood; *m.* 1913, Laura Josephine Teale; one *s.* two *d.* *Educ.:* still in progress. Began work at 14 in local industry: Textiles, 1899; Art student Shipley & Bradford, 1904-8; Royal College of Art, 1908-11; Teacher of Art, Batley, 1911-1912; Battersea Polytechnic, 1912-27; Bradford College of Art, 1927-37; late Head of School of Design in Leeds College of Art; personal work, mainly wood-engraving and water colour; exhibitions: R.A., Venice International, Florence, Paris, Brussels, Stockholm, Zürich, Belgrade, Zagreb, Ankara, Madrid, Copenhagen, Oslo, Tokio, Buenos Aires, Chicago International and other cities of U.S.A., Toronto, Quebec, Cairo, Jerusalem, Helsinki, Warsaw, Prague, Buda-Pesth, Reykjavik, and various British Galleries; works in public collections: British Museum, Victoria and Albert Museum, Stockholm, New York Free Library, Moscow, Quebec, Glasgow, Belfast, Bradford, Leeds, Salford, etc.; A.R.C.A. (Lond.). *Publication:* The Dales are Mine, 1952. *Address:* 53 The Grove, Ilkley. *T.:* 1095. [*Died* 28 *April* 1954.

GREER, Brig.-Gen. Frederick Augustus, C.M.G. 1918; D.S.O. 1917; late Irish Fusiliers; *b.* 1871; *m.* 1923, Vera Cecilia, *yr. d.* of Richard A. Willis, Burley. Served South African War, 1902 (Queen's medal and two clasps); European War, 1914-18 (despatches, D.S.O., C.M.G.); retired pay, 1921. *Address:* Yalton Kiln, East Portlemouth, Salcombe, Devon. [*Died* 26 *March* 1958.

GREFFULHE, Comtesse, *née* Princesse de Caraman-Chimay. *Educ.:* Paris; brevet de capacité du 1er degré. Présidente de la Société des Grandes Auditions musicales de France; Présidente de l'œuvre des Convalescents Militaires, dans toutes les régions de la France et du Gouvernement militaire de Paris; Œuvre rattachée au Ministère de la Guerre (800 formations); Présidente de l'Union de France pour la Belgique (Magasins des Aveugles, œuvre des permissionnaires Belges) Propagande de la Veillée des Tombes (en mémoire des 1ers soldats morts au Champ d'Honneur, qui furent des soldats belges) Réfugiés. *Address:* 8 et 10 rue d'Astorg, Paris; *T.A.:* Comtesse Greffulhe, Paris; *T.:* Anjou 08.49; Château de Bois, Boudran, par Nangis, Seine et Marne. [*Died* 21 *Aug.* 1952.

GREG, Lt.-Col. Alexander, C.B.E. 1919; *b.* 1867; 4th *s.* of Edward Hyde Greg, Styall, Cheshire; *m.* 1st, 1906, Mildred (*d.* 1914), *d.* of Thos. Worthington, Alderley Edge, Cheshire; 2nd, Anna, *d.* of F. Jevons, Birkenhead. *Educ.:* Repton. Joined 3rd Batt. Cheshire Regiment (Militia), 1890; served S. African War, 1900-2, having transferred to 3rd S. Lancs Regt. (despatches, Queen's Medal, 3 clasps, King's Medal, 2 clasps); European War, 1914 (2nd in Command 3rd S. Lancs), 1915 (despatches twice, C.B.E.); Commanded 3rd Batt. Cheshire Regt., 1915-25; retired 1925, under age clause; Special Constabulary, 1926-36; Home Guard, 1940-43. J.P. Cheshire, 1903-39, Hants, 1934-39. *Address:* Westmill, Buntingford, Herts. *T.:* Buntingford 178. *Club:* Junior Army and Navy. [*Died* 14 *July* 1952.

GREG, Sir Robert Hyde, K.C.M.G., *cr.* 1929; *b.* 24 Dec. 1876; *s.* of Edward Hyde Greg, J.P., D.L., Norcliffe Hall and Quarry Bank, Styal, Cheshire; *m.* 1914, Julia Schreiner (*d.* 1953), New York; no *c.* *Educ.:* Bilton Grange, nr. Rugby; Repton. A Clerk in the Foreign Office, 1899; Assistant Clerk, 1909; attached to the British Agency at Cairo, 1911-14; 1st Secretary in the Diplomatic Service, Lisbon, 1915; Counsellor of Embassy, 1919; seconded for service under the Egyptian Government, 1917-21, and placed in charge of the Ministry for Foreign Affairs in Cairo; British Minister at Bangkok, 1921-26; Bucharest, 1926-29; British Commissioner on the Egyptian Public Debt, Cairo, 1929-40; retd. 1940; Grand Cordon Egyptian Order of the Nile; Coronation Medal. *Recreations:* travel and archæology. *Address:* Sharia Wisa Wasif, Giza, Cairo, Egypt. *Clubs:* Athenæum, Brooks's. [*Died* 3 *Dec.* 1953.

GREG, Sir Walter Wilson, Kt., *cr.* 1950; Litt.D. (Cantab.), Hon. D.Litt. (Oxon), Hon. LL.D. (Edin.); F.B.A.; Member of American Philosophical Society; Hon. Fellow of Trinity College, Cambridge; Hon. Lecturer in Bibliography at University College, London; President, Malone Society (Gen. Editor, 1906-39); *b.* 1875; *s.* of William Rathbone Greg and Julia, *d.* of Rt. Hon. James Wilson; *m.* 1913, Elizabeth Gaskell, *d.* of Walter Greg of Lee Hall, Cheshire; two *s.* one *d.* *Educ.:* Harrow; Trinity College, Cambridge. Editor of Modern Language Quarterly, 1903-1904; Librarian of Trinity College,Cambridge, 1907-13; Sandars Reader in Bibliography, 1913; Friends' Ambulance Unit, 1915; War Trade Intelligence Department, 1915-19; Fellow of the British Academy, 1928; President of the Bibliographical Society, 1930-32; Clark Lecturer at Trinity College, Cambridge, 1938-1939; James P. R. Lyell Reader in Bibliography, Oxford University, 1954-55. *Publications:* A List of English Plays, 1900; A List of Masques, etc., 1902; Capell's Shakespeariana, 1903; Pastoral Poetry and Pastoral Drama, 1906; Henslowe's Diary (edited), 1904-08; Henslowe Papers (edited), 1907; Eton Shakespeariana, 1909; The Merry Wives of Windsor, 1602 (edited), 1910; Facsimiles of Twelve MSS. in T.C.C., 1913; Bibliographical and Textual Problems of the English Miracle Cycles, 1914; The Assumption of the Virgin (edited), 1915; Two Elizabethan Stage Abridgements (Alcazar and Orlando), 1923: The Theatre of Apollo, by J. Beaumont (edited), 1926; The Calculus of Variants, 1927; Principles of Emendation in Shakespeare, 1928; English Literary Autographs, 1550-1650 (in collaboration), 1925-32; Records of the Court of the Stationers' Company, 1576-1602 (with E. Boswell), 1930; Dramatic Documents from the Elizabethan Playhouses, 1931; The Chester Play of Antichrist (edited), 1935; Chester Play Studies (with F. M. Salter), 1935; A Bibliography of the English Printed Drama to the Restoration vol. I, 1939, vol. II, 1951; The Variants in the First Quarto of King Lear, 1940; The Editorial Problem in Shakespeare (Clark Lectures), 1942, 2nd ed. 1951, 3rd ed. 1954; Marlowe's Doctor Faustus (parallel-texts, 1604-16), (reconstructed text), 1950; Jonson's Masque of Gipsies, 1952; Respublica (re-edited, E. E. T. S.), 1952; The Shakespeare First Folio, its bibliographical and textual history, 1955; Some Aspects and Problems of London Publishing between 1550 and 1650 (Lyell Lectures), 1956. *Address:* Tanners Knap, Petworth, Sussex. *T.:* Lodsworth 242. *Club:* Athenæum. [*Died* 4 *March* 1959.

GREGG, Sir Cornelius Joseph, K.C.B., *cr.* 1944 (C.B. 1932); K.B.E., *cr.* 1941; Hon. LL.D. (N.U.I.); formerly Director of National Bank Ltd.; *s.* of Jas. Gregg, Kilkenny; *m.* Mary Anne, *d.* of Thos. Crotty, Kilkenny; two *s.* three *d.* *Educ.:* Christian Schools, Kilkenny; Blackrock; Univ. Coll., Dublin. Chairman, Board of Inland Revenue, 1942-48. *Address:* 12 Bushy Park Road, Dublin. *Clubs:* Reform; St. Stephen's Green (Dublin). [*Died* 14 *Nov.* 1959.

GREGG, John Frank; Town Clerk, City of Birmingham, since 1949; *b.* 6 Dec. 1912; 2nd *s.* of late H. N. Gregg, Birmingham; *m.* 1938, Winifred Mary Bates; three *s.* one *d.* *Educ.:* King Edward's School, Birmingham; University of Birmingham. Admitted Solicitor, 1935; Asst. Solicitor: Nuneaton Corporation, 1935; Huddersfield Corpn., 1937; Deputy Town Clerk: York, 1939; Bournemouth, 1943; Birmingham, 1946. Pres. Society of Town Clerks, 1959-60; Life Governor of University of Birmingham. Chevalier de la Légion d'Honneur, 1955. *Address:* Council House, Birmingham. *T.:* Central 7000. *Clubs:* National Liberal; Union (Birmingham). [*Died* 23 *Jan.* 1960.

GREGORY, Eric Craven, Hon. LL.D. (Leeds); Hon. A.R.I.B.A.; Chairman: Percy Lund, Humphries & Co. Ltd.; Ganymed Press London Ltd.; Design Research Unit; Director, Burlington Magazine; Member Standing Commission on Museums and Galleries since 1952; *b.* 6 Oct. 1887; *s.* of James and Martha Gregory; unmarried. *Educ.:* Bradford Grammar School. Governor, Chelsea Polytechnic; Governor, St. Martin's School of Art; Governor, Bath Academy of Art, Corsham Court; Mem. Cttee. Contemporary Art Society; Hon. Treas. Inst. of Contemporary Arts; Member Art Panel for Arts Council of Gt. Britain, 1954-56; Mem. Cttee. for Battersea Park Open Air Sculpture Exhibition, 1951. *Recreations:* chess and walking. *Address:* 139 Swan Court, S.W.3. *T.:* Flaxman 0217. [*Died* 10 *Feb.* 1959.

GREGORY, Sir Henry Stanley, K.C.M.G., *cr.* 1948; C.B. 1941; Secretary to Trade Marks, Patents and Designs Federation, since 1957; *b.* 1890; *m.* 1919; one *s.* *Educ.:* Shebbear; London School of Economics (B.Sc. Econ.); Gerstenberg Scholar, University of London. Asst. Sec., Bd. of Customs & Excise, 1932; Controller of the Clearing Offices, 1937-38; Comr. of H.M. Customs & Excise, 1938-46. Director of Establishments, Ministry of Supply, 1939-41; Controller-General, Trading with the Enemy Dept., 1942; Custodian of enemy property for England, 1948-50; administrator of enemy property, 1948-50; Principal Finance Officer and Second Secretary, Board of Trade, 1949-55, retired; Adviser on Copyright to the Board of Trade, 1956. Commander, Order of Orange Nassau (Netherlands). *Address:* 3 Daines Close, Thorpe Bay, Essex. *T.:* Thorpe Bay 8430. *Club:* Reform. [*Died* 29 *March* 1959.

GREGORY, John Duncan, C.B. 1925; C.M.G. 1920; *b.* 26 May 1878; *s.* of late Sir Philip Gregory; *m.* Gwendolen Lind, *d.* of late Raymond Maude; two *d.* *Educ.:* Eton. Entered Foreign Office, 1902; Third Secretary Diplomatic Service, 1903; Second Secretary, 1907; employed at H.M. Embassy, Vienna, 1907-09; acted as Chargé d'Affaires at Bucharest, 1909; First Sec. 1914; Sec. to the British Mission to the Holy See, 1915; Counsellor in H.M. Diplomatic Service, 1919; Assistant Secretary, Foreign Office, 1920-25; Assistant Under-Secretary of State, Foreign Office, 1925-28. *Publication:* On the Edge of Diplomacy, 1929; Dollfuss and His Times, 1935. *Address:* Ireland House, Ashburton, S. Devon. [*Died* 29 *Jan.* 1951.

GREGORY, Sir Richard (Arman), 1st Bt., *cr.* 1931; Kt., *cr.* 1919; F.R.S., 1933; Hon. D.Sc. (Leeds and Bristol); Hon. LL.D. (St. Andrews); F.R.A.S.; F.R.Met.Soc.; F.Inst.P.; Emeritus Prof. of Astronomy, Queen's College, London; *b.* Bristol, 29 Jan. 1864; *s.* of John Gregory; *m.* 1st, 1888, Kate Florence Dugan (*née* Pearn) (*d.* 1926); (one *s.* one *d.* decd.); 2nd, 1931, Dorothy Mary, *d.* of late William Page, D.Litt., F.S.A. *Educ.:* Elementary sch.; evening classes. Laboratory Assistant in Physical Laboratory, Clifton College, 1882-1885; teacher in training at the Royal College of Science, 1886-1887; Science Demonstrator in H.M. Dockyard School, Portsmouth, 1887-88; Computor to Solar Physics Committee, and Asst. to Sir Norman Lockyer, 1889-93; asst. editor of Nature, 1893-1919; editor 1919-39; joint editor of The School World and of the Journal of Education, with which it was incorporated in 1918, 1899-1939; Oxford Univ. Extension Lecturer, 1890-95; Pres. of Educational Science Section of the British Association, 1922; Chairman of Council of the Norman Lockyer Observatory Corporation (now incorporated in the University College of the South-West, Exeter), 1920-48; Pres. Geographical Association, 1923-24; of the South-Eastern Union of Scientific Societies, 1924; of the Science Masters' Association, 1927; Pres. of the R.Met.S., 1928-29; of the Gilbert White Fellowship, 1928-31; of the Education Guild, 1928; of the Conference of Educational Associations, 1931, and of the Association of Special Libraries and Information Bureaux, 1934-35; Pres. British Assoc. for the Advancement of Science, 1940-46; Pres. Ethical Union, 1947-

1950. *Publications:* several textbooks of physical geography, physiography, physics, chemistry, and general experimental science; The Vault of Heaven; Discovery, or the Spirit and Service of Science; Religion in Science and Civilization; British Scientists; Science in Chains; Education in World Ethics and Science; Gods and Men, etc. *Recreations:* gardening and reading. *Heir:* none. *Address:* The Manor House, Middleton-on-Sea, near Bognor Regis. *T.:* Middleton-on-Sea 153. *Clubs:* Athenæum, Royal Societies, Sesame. [*Died* 15 *Sept.* 1952 (*ext.*).

GREGSON-ELLIS, Major-General Philip (George Saxon), C.B. 1945; O.B.E. 1940; D.L.; *b.* 31 Aug. 1898; *s.* of Col. W. S. Gregson-Ellis, Plas Clough, Denbigh, N. Wales, and L. Blair-Oliphant, Ardblair, Blairgowrie; *m.* Joan, *d.* of Sir Marteine Lloyd, 2nd and last Bt., Bronwydd, S. Wales; two *d.* *Educ.:* Eton; R.M.C., Sandhurst. 2nd Lt., Grenadier Guards, 1917; Staff College, 1928-29; Brigade-Major, 5th Infantry Brigade, 1931, 1st Guards Brigade, 1932-34; Instructor, Staff College, 1937-39; G.S.O.1 Operations, G.H.Q., B.E.F., 1939-40; commanded 2nd Bn. Grenadier Guards, 1940; B.G.S. Northern Ireland, 1941; Deputy C.G.S., G.H.Q. Home Forces, 1942. Commanded 30th Armoured Brigade, 1943, 1st Guards Brigade, 1943, 5th Division, 1944; Commandant, Staff College, 1945-46; Commander 5th Division, 1946-47; Commander 44th Division (T.A.), 1947-50; retd., 1950. D.L. Kent, 1954. *Recreations:* shooting, stalking, cricket. *Address:* Calico House, Newnham, near Sittingbourne, Kent. *T.:* Eastling 266. *Club:* Guards. [*Died* 20 *Oct.* 1956.

GREIG, Charles Alexis; Consul-General, retired; *b.* Clifton, Gloster., 8 Sept. 1880; *o. s.* of late Charles Greig, F.R.C.S., Ed., M.R.C.S., and *g.g.s.* of Adm. Sir Samuel Greig, F.R.S., High Admiral of Russia; *m.* 1915, Emily, (*d.* 1932), *d.* of Nicholas Vladica; one *s.* one *d.* *Educ.:* Harrow; New College, Oxford; King's College, Cambridge. Entered Levant Consular Service, 1903; Vice-Consul, 1908; Consul, 1918; Consul-General, 1930; H.M. Consul-General, Smyrna, 1930-41; retired from H.M. Consular Service, 1941. Intelligence Officer in Macedonia, 1916-17 (despatches). Silver Jubilee Medal, 1935; Coronation Medal, 1937. *Club:* Caledonian. [*Died* 4 *May* 1958.

GREIG, Rev. Lt.-Col. John Glennie, C.I.E. 1911; Indian Army, retired; ordained R.C. Priest in Rome, 1935; now in charge of Ringwood Parish, Hampshire; *b.* 24 Oct. 1871; *s.* of late Colonel Piercy Henderson Greig. *Educ.:* Ushaw College; Downside College; Sandhurst. Joined L.N. Lancashire Regiment, 1892; appointed to Indian Army, 1895; served Mohmand Expedition, N.W.F., 1897; Tirah Expedition, N.W.F., 1897-8; Somaliland Expedition, 1903-4; Mahsud Expedition, N.W.F., 1917; on active service, Mesopotamia, 1917, and Palestine, 1918; A.D.C. to Lord Sandhurst, Governor of Bombay, 1898-1900; to Lord Northcote, Governor of Bombay, 1900-2; to Lord Lamington, Governor of Bombay, 1904-6; Military Secretary to Lord Sydenham, Governor of Bombay, 1907-12; Military Secretary to Lord Willingdon, Governor of Bombay, 1913-16; to Sir George Lloyd, Governor of Bombay, 1919-21; Secretary to Hampshire County Cricket, 1922-31; Pres. Hampshire County Cricket Club, 1945. *Address:* Maryland Convent, Milford-on-Sea, Hants. [*Died* 24 *May* 1958.

GREIG, Group Captain Sir Louis, K.B.E., *cr.* 1932; C.V.O. 1917; R.A.F.; Deputy Ranger of Richmond Park since 1932; Extra Gentleman Usher to the Queen since 1952 (Gentleman Usher in Ordinary to King George VI, 1924-36, Extra Gentleman Usher, 1937-52); *b.* 17 Nov. 1880; *s.* of David Greig, of Glasgow and Fife; *m.* Phyllis, *d.* of J. Walter Scrimgeour, Hemsby Hall, Norfolk; one *s.* two *d.* *Educ.:* Merchiston Castle School, Edin.; University, Glasgow. M.B., Ch.B. Joined R.N. as Surgeon-Lieut., 1906; served Hibernia, R.N. Coll., Osborne, Cumberland, R.M. Depôt, Deal; France, R.M. Bde., 1914 (prisoner of war); Surg.-Lieut. Comdr., Attentive, Dover Patrol, and Malaya, Grand Fleet; joined R.A.F. (Major), 1918, Independent Force; Comptroller to the Duke of York, 1920-23; Personal Air Sec. to Sir Archibald Sinclair, 1940-46; D.L. London, 1948; Chevalier of Légion d'Honneur; Beligan Croix de Guerre; Chevalier Order of Couronne, Belgium; Order of Orange-Nassau with Swords; Legion of Merit, U.S.A. Governor Westminster Hosp.; Chm.: Not-Forgotten Assoc.; All England Lawn Tennis Club. *Recreations:* shooting, lawn tennis, hunting; played International Rugby football for Scotland. *Address:* Thatched House Lodge, Richmond Park, Surrey. *T.:* Kingston 2351; Binsness, Forres, Moray, Scotland. *Clubs:* White's, Buck's; Royal Yacht Squadron (Cowes). [*Died* 1 *March* 1953.

GRENTE, His Eminence Cardinal George; Archbishop of Le Mans, Sarthe, since 1918; Cardinal since 1953; Member of the French Academy; Commandeur de la légion d'honneur; *b.* Percy, Manche, 5 May 1872. Professor of Literature in the Smaller Seminary of Mortain; Director of the free Institute of Saint Lo; Superior of the Saint Paul's Institute, Cherbourg. *Publications:* Le poète Jean Bertaut; Quae fuerit in cardinali Davy du Perron vis oratoria; Saint Pie V.; Sainte Marie-Madeleine Postel (trans. publ. London); La Composition et le Style; Semailles et semeurs; Une Mission dans le Levant; Aux Parents; Œuvres oratoires et pastorales: Tomes I à XI; Écrits et paroles; En Amérique; Fléchier; Rayons de France; Pierre de Nolhac; Notre-Dame; Les Pensées de Joubert, L'Éminence grise, La Magnificence des Sacrements (trans., The Power of the Sacraments, publ. New York); Paroles romaines; Notre Père; Vie et passion de Jeanne d'Arc, Saintes de France; Ces Français qui furent des Saints; Notre Seigneur Jésus-Christ; Dictionnaire des lettres françaises (direction). *Address:* Le Mans (Sarthe), France. [*Died* 4 *May* 1959.

GRESTY, Hugh, R.B.A., R.I.; Painter in water-colours and oils of subjects where architecture is the main theme; *b.* Nelson, Lancashire, 14 March 1899; *m.* 1926, Elizabeth, *d.* of James Waters, Nelson, Lancashire. *Educ.:* Goldsmiths' College, University of London. Exhibitor at all principal exhibitions. *Recreation:* gramophone. *Address:* Mincarlo, Carbis Bay, Cornwall. *T.:* St. Ives 434. *Club:* Chelsea Arts. [*Died* 7 *Aug.* 1958.

GRETTON, Brigadier John Cunliffe, C.B. 1936; Indian Army, retired; *b.* 7 May 1880. Joined P.W.O. West Yorkshire Regt. 1899; S. African War (Queen's Medal, 5 clasps, King's Medal, 2 clasps); transferred to Indian Army, The Baluch Regt. 1904. Mesopotamia, 1917-18 (despatches). Commanded Lahore Bde. Area, 1932-35; retired 1935. Served with R.A.F.V.R., 1939-45. *Club:* United Service. [*Died* 13 *Oct.* 1953.

GREVILLE, 3rd Baron, *cr.* 1869; **Captain Charles Beresford Fulke Greville,** O.B.E., late 7th Hussars; *s.* of 2nd Baron and Lady Beatrice Violet Graham, *d.* of 4th Duke of Montrose; *S.* father, 1909; *b.* 3 Mar. 1871; *m.* 1909, Olive Grace, *d.* of late J. W. Grace of Leybourne Grange, Kent, and *widow* of Henry Kerr; one *s.* A.D.C. to Lord Lieutenant of Ireland, 1892-93; to Governor of Bombay, 1900-04; Military Secretary to Governor-General of Australia, 1904; Member L.C.C. (M.R.), W. Marylebone, 1912-16; served in Reserve Cavalry and General Staff, 1914-19; Chairman St. George's Hospital, 1914-44. *Heir:* *s.* Hon. Ronald Charles Greville, *b.* 11 April 1912. *Address:* 7 Cheyne Walk, S.W.3. *T.:* Flaxman 6116. *Club:* Turf. [*Died* 14 *May* 1952.

GREVILLE, Hon. Maynard; 2nd *s.* of 5th Earl of Warwick; *b.* 21 Mar. 1898; *m.* 1918, Dora (*d.* 1957), *d.* of late Edward James Pape, Moor Hall, Battle; one *d.* *Educ.*: Oundle; Cambridge. Joined R.F.C. 1916; served European War, R.F.C. and R.A.F.; joined Daily Express reporting staff, 1919; Morning Post, 1921; Motoring Correspondent, Morning Post, 1927-29; Daily Mail, 1929-31. Motoring Editor Country Life, 1927-39. During War of 1939-45 was in Ministry of Information and A.R.P. Retired from regular journalism after the War and took up former pursuit of arboriculture and forestry; is engaged in making census of every tree of interest and importance in the British Isles. Mem. Royal Forestry Society of England and Wales (Chairman Home Counties Div. of that Society, 1954-56). *Recreation:* tree snooping in car, cycle, or on foot. *Address:* Easton Lodge, Dunmow, Essex. *Clubs:* Bath, Press, Royal Automobile. [*Died* 22 *Feb.* 1960.

GREY, Sir Charles George, 4th Bt. *cr.* 1814; L.S.A.; *b.* 26 June 1880; *s.* of late Capt. Harry George Grey, R.N., *g.s.* of 1st Bt.; *S.* kinsman, Viscount Grey of Fallodon, 1933; *m.* 1910, Jessie Elizabeth, *d.* of Paton Sutherland. Was in West African Medical Service, S. Nigeria: served Cameroons, 1915-16. *Heir:* *b.* Harry Martin, M.R.C.S., L.R.C.P., *b.* 12 March 1882. [*Died* 12 *Dec.* 1957.

GREY, Charles Grey; Chairman of All the World's Aircraft Publishing Co. Ltd.; Writer on Aviation (Service, Civil and Technical); Air Correspondent since 1939 to Edinburgh Evening News, Yorkshire Evening News, Lancashire Daily Post, and other papers, home and overseas; *b.* Regent's Park, London, 13 Nov. 1875; 3rd *s.* of Charles Grey Grey, Dilston Hall, Northumb. and of the Irish Land Commission; *g.s.* of late John Grey of Milfield and Dilston, and *n.* of late Josephine Butler (*née* Grey); *m.* 1st, 1899, Beatrice Thorneloe; no *c.*; 2nd, 1929, Margaret Sumner, *d.* of John Sumner Marriner, Oxford; one *s.* one *d.* *Educ.*: The Erasmus Smith School, Dublin; the Crystal Palace School of Engineering. Trained as an engineer; detailed to watch the development of flying on behalf of The Autocar, 1908; co-editor and founder of The Aero, 1909: Founder, The Aeroplane, June 1911, with E. V. (later Sir Victor) Sassoon, Editor until Sept. 1939. Succeeded the late Fred T. Jane as editor and compiler of All the World's Aircraft, 1916-42; Founder-Member: Royal Aeronautical Society, 1909 (Hon. Companion, 1950); Royal Aero Club, 1909 (Hon. Life Member, 1950). *Publications:* The Why and Wherefore of Flying, 1909; Tales of the Flying Services, 1915; A History of the Air Ministry, 1940; British Fighter-Planes, 1941; How an Aeroplane Flies, 1941; Bombers, 1941; The History of Combat Airplanes (The James Jackson Cabot Memorial Treatise, for Norwich University, Vermont, U.S.A.), 1942; Sea Flyers, 1942; The Luftwaffe, 1943; The Civil Air War, 1944. *Recreations:* reading, writing, motoring. *Address:* Coombe Hill Lodge, New Malden, Sy. *T.:* Malden 0213. *Clubs:* Royal Aero, Roadfarers, Circle of Aviation Writers. [*Died* 9 *Dec.* 1953.

GREY, Sir (Harry) Martin, 5th Bt., *cr.* 1814; retired; *b.* 12 March 1882; 2nd *s.* of late Capt. Harry George Grey, R.N.; *S.* brother (Sir Charles George Grey, Bt.), 1957; *m.* 1920, Gwladys, *y. d.* of late William Maxwell, West Hartlepool; no *c.* *Educ.*: Cleveland House, Weymouth; Fauconberge Sch., Beccles, Suffolk; St. Bartholomew's Hospital, London. M.R.C.S., L.R.C.P., 1908. Served European War, R.A.M.C., 1917-19: Radiologist, Island of Malta, Maj. 1918; War of 1939-45: Radiologist under the Emergency Medical Service. Retired from Medical Profession, 1950. *Heir:* *kinsman* Robin Edward Dysart Grey [*b.* 1886; *s.* of late Edward George Grey; *m.* 1918, Maud Wilson, Queensland; one *s.*]. *Address:* Whitehall Court, Bishops Stortford, Herts. [*Died* 12 *Dec.* 1960.

GREY, Sir John Howarth, Kt., *cr.* 1935; Chairman, John Grey Ltd., Burnley, Cotton Manufacturers; President Cotton Spinners and Manufacturers Association; Chairman Burnley Building Society; Director: Lancashire Cotton Corporation, Ltd.; Manchester Board of North British Mercantile Ins. Co. Ltd.; *b.* 19 July 1875; *s.* of late James Mitchell Grey; *m.* 1901, Emma Harling (*d.* 1958); one *s.* one *d.* *Educ.*: Burnley. Entered Burnley Town Council, 1910; Alderman, 1923, resigned, 1949; J.P. Burnley, 1913. *Address:* Thornleigh, Burnley. *T.A.*: Grey Thornleigh Burnley. *T.*: 4267. *Club:* Reform (Manchester). [*Died* 1 *Jan.* 1960.

GREY, Sir Martin; *see* Grey, Sir H. M.

GREY, Lieut.-Col. William George; Urdu Lecturer, Cambridge University, 1929-1940; M.A. Cantab. (Hon.), 1931; *b.* Wellington, New Zealand, 12 Oct. 1866; *m.* 1909, Mary Evelyn, *d.* of late Aymer Ainslie, J.P., formerly of Hall Garth, Lancs.; (one *s.* decd.). *Educ.*: Westward Ho! North Devon. Joined S. Lancs. Regt. as Lieut. 1886; served with them in Natal, Straits Settlements, and Gibraltar; transferred to Indian Army, 1889; served with 3rd and 23rd Madras Light Infantry; transferred to Political Service as Vice-Consul Bandar Abbas, 1902; subsequently served as Political Agent H.B.M.'s Consul at Maskat, Oman, Arabia, 1904-8; permanently appointed to Political Department, Government of India, 1906; Political Agent Koweit, Persian Gulf, 1914-16; served in Mysore, Calcutta, and Baluchistan; Consul-General for Khorassan, 1916-20; retired 1921. *Address:* Meadowcroft, Trumpington Rd., Cambridge. [*Died* 6 *April* 1953.

GRIBBLE, Colonel (Hon.) Howard Charles, D.S.O. 1919; retd. Bank Manager; *b.* St. Margaret's, Mx., 16 May 1886; *e. s.* of late Edwin Frank Gribble; *m.* 1913, Augusta Grace (*d.* 1935), *o. c.* of late Arthur Wellesley Gosset, Capt. (retired) Queen's Regt., of Town Court, Orpington, Kent, and niece of late Major-General Sir Matthew William Gosset, K.C.B.; two *d.* *Educ.*: Bishop's Stortford School. 2nd Lieut. R.F.A. (T.F.), 1909; Lieut. 1910; Captain, 1916; Major, 1918; served European War in France, 1914-19 (D.S.O., despatches). Major R.G.A., R.A.R. of O., 1922-36; Major Sussex Home Guard, 1940-44; acting Lieut.-Col. Sussex Army Cadet Force, 1944; acting Colonel, County Cadet Commandant, 1945-51. Councillor, Borough of Lewes, 1945-52. Mem. Army Cadet Force Assoc. Exec. Cttee. 1948-. Mem. Lewes Advisory Cttee. S.E. Trustee Savings Bank, 1951-56. County Chief Warden, E. Sussex Division, Civil Defence Corps, 1951-52. *Address:* 2 Knoyle Road Brighton 6, Sussex. *T.*: Brighton 52829. [*Died* 19 *Oct.* 1956.

GRIER, Sir (Edmund) Wyly, Kt., *cr.* 1935; D.C.L., R.C.A.; former President of Royal Canadian Academy; *b.* Melbourne, Aust., 1862; *s.* of late Charles Grier, L.R.C.P., M.R.C.S., and Maria Agnes Monro; *m.* Florence Geale Dickson (*d.* 1954); three *s.* two *d.* *Educ.*: Pridham's, Bristol; Upper Canada College, Toronto. Studied under Alphonse Legros at Slade School, London; Julian Academy, Paris; Scuola Libera Rome. Exhibited R.A. 1886-96; Salon, Paris, 1883 (1890 medal 3rd Class); returned to Canada, 1894, and painted portraits: including Hon. Edward Blake, M.P. (R.A., 1896), Goldwin Smith, Sir Sandford Fleming, Miss Mabel Cawthra (R.A., 1892); painted at St. Ives, Cornwall 1885-91; Corr. Mem. National Academy of Design, U.S.A., 1938. *Publications:* many articles on Art and literature. *Address:* Credit, 1648 Queen St. E., Preston, Ontario, Canada. *Clubs:*

(Hon. Life Member) Arts and Letters (former Hon. Pres.) Progress (Toronto). [*Died* 7 *Dec.* 1957.

GRIERSON, Edgar, J.P.; *b.* 1884; *s.* of William Grierson, Scotby, nr. Carlisle; *m.*; two *s.* one *d.* Mayor of Carlisle, 1941-42; Deputy-Mayor, 1942-43, 1943-44; Member Carlisle City Council; M.P. (Lab.) Carlisle, 1945-50. *Address:* 268 Warwick Road, Carlisle. *T.:* Carlisle 1237. [*Died March* 1959.

GRIERSON, Sir Herbert John Clifford, Kt., *cr.* 1936; M.A. (Aberdeen), M.A. (Oxon), Hon. LL.D. (St. Andrews, Edinburgh and Aberdeen); Hon. Litt.D. Cambridge, Columbia, London, Manchester, Oxford, Princeton and Trinity College, Dublin; Docteur (Hon.) L'Université de Bordeaux; Hon. Litt. et Phil. d., Univ. of Amsterdam: Fellow of the British Academy; *b.* 1866; 2nd *s.* of Andrew J. Grierson, D.L. of Quendale, Shetland Isles; *m.* 1896, Mary Letitia (*d.* 1937), *e. d.* of late Sir Alexander Ogston, K.C.V.O.; five *d.* *Educ.:* King's College, Aberdeen; Christ Church, Oxford. Prof. at Aberdeen, 1894-1915; Prof. of Rhetoric and English Literature, Edinburgh University, 1915-35; Rector of Edinburgh University, 1936-39. *Publications:* The First Half of the Seventeenth Century (Periods of European Literature), 1906; The Poems of John Donne, edited with Introduction and Commentary, 1912; Metaphysical Poets, Donne to Butler, 1921; contributions to Cambridge History of Literature; Blake's Illustrations to Gray's Poems, 1922; The Background of English Literature, and other Collected Essays, 1925; The Poems of John Milton, 1925; Lyrical Poetry from Blake to Hardy, 1928; Cross-Currents in the Literature of the Seventeenth Century, 1929; Letters of Sir Walter Scott, twelve vols. issued 1937; Carlyle and Hitler, 1933; Milton and Wordsworth, Prophets and Poets, 1937; Sir Walter Scott. Bart., 1938; Essays and Addresses, 1940; The English Bible, 1944; Critical History of English Poetry (with J. C. Smith, C.B.E.), 1945; Rhetoric and English Composition, 1945; And the Third Day, 1948; Criticism and Creation (Essays and Addresses) 1950; Swinburne (British Council Pamphlets), 1954. *Address:* 3 Brookfield, Newnham Walk, Cambridge. *Club:* Arts (Edinburgh). [*Died* 19 *Feb.* 1960.

GRIERSON, Sir Robert Gilbert White, 10th Bt., of Rockhall, Dumfriesshire, *cr.* 1685; *b.* 27 Sept. 1883; *s.* of 9th Bt. and Fanny, *d.* of Major G. White, of the Royal Marines; *m.* 1911, Hilda, *d.* of James Stewart, Surbiton, Surrey; one *s.*; *S.* father, 1912. *Educ.:* Uppingham School. Late Royal Scots; served European War with Batt. K.O.S.B., retired with rank of Major. *Heir:* *s.* Richard Douglas, *b.* 25 June 1912. *Address:* 29 Withdean Court Avenue, Brighton; Rockhall, Dumfriesshire. *T.:* Brighton 56124. [*Died* 16 *June* 1957.

GRIEVE, Rev. Alexander James, M.A. (Oxon), B.A., D.D. (Lond.); Principal of Lancs. Independent College, 1922-43; Principal Emeritus, 1943; *b.* Pembroke Dock, 18 March 1874; *e. s.* of John Grieve; *m.* 1897, Evelyne Mary Thomas; four *s.* two *d.* *Educ.:* Univ. Coll., Aberystwyth; Mansfield Coll. Oxford; Univ. of Berlin. First Class Hons. Theology, Oxford, 1897, and London, 1912; Registrar, University of Madras, 1900-1902; Professor of English, Central College, Bangalore, 1902-04; Minister of Congregational Church, Romsey, 1905-09, St. Anne's-on-the-Sea, 1910-11, Salem, Bradford, 1916-1917; Cavendish, Suffolk, 1943-50; on staff of Encyclopædia Biblica, 1898-1900, Encyclopædia Britannica, 1905-11; Professor of New Testament Studies and Church History, Yorkshire United Independent College, Bradford, 1909-17; Principal and Professor of Systematic Theology, Scottish Congregational College, 1917-21; Lecturer in Church History, University of Edinburgh, 1919-21, University of Manchester, 1922-43, and Dean of the Faculty of Theology 1931-32; Examiner in Theology (various dates), Universities of London, Bristol, Wales and Manchester; a governor of John Rylands Library, 1936-43, Chairman of Lancs. Congregational Union, 1934, Suffolk Congregational Union, 1946; Chm. of Congregational Union of England and Wales, 1936-37; Member of Senate of Univ. of London, 1944-48. *Publications:* Assistant Editor of Peake's Commentary; articles in Bible Dictionaries and Encycs. *Address:* 4 Holly Lane, Erdington, Birmingham 24. [*Died* 23 *Sept.* 1952.

GRIEVE, Robert G., C.I.E. 1930; Principal, Teachers' College, Saidapet, 1920; late Director of Public Instruction, Madras; retired, 1934; *b.* 1881; *s.* of late Robert Grieve, Glenholm, Greenock. *Educ.:* Fettes; Hertford College, Oxford (M.A.). *Recreation:* fishing. *Address:* 6 Western Terrace, Edinburgh 12. *T.:* 62786. *Club:* University (Edinburgh). [*Died* 19 *May* 1952.

GRIFFIN, Lieut.-Col. Atholl Edwin, C.B.E. 1919; D.S.O. 1918; *b.* 1877; *s.* of Caleb Nelson Griffin, Wingham, Ont.; *m.* 1905, Jessie Anne, *d.* of John Murray. *Educ.:* Pennsylvania College, Philadelphia. Served European War, 1914-19 (despatches, D.S.O., C.B.E.). *Club:* Vancouver (Vancouver). [*Died* 6 *May* 1956.

GRIFFIN, His Eminence Cardinal Bernard W., D.D., D.C.L.; Archbishop of Westminster since 1943; *b.* Birmingham, 1899. *Educ.:* Cotton College; Oscott; English College, Rome; Beda College, Rome. Ordained priest, 1924; Sec. of Archbishops of Birmingham, 1927-37; Chancellor of Archdioc. of Birmingham, 1929-38; Administrator of Fr. Hudson's Homes, Coleshill, 1937-43; Bishop Auxiliary of Birmingham, 1938-43; Cardinal, 1946. Protector of Sisters of Charity of St. Paul the Apostle (Selly Park), Dec. 1948. Papal Legate to Hierarchy Centenary Congress, Sept. 1950. *Publication:* Seek ye First, 1949. *Address:* Archbishop's House, Westminster, S.W.1. [*Died* 20 *Aug.* 1956.

GRIFFIN, Brig.-Gen. Christopher Joseph, C.M.G. 1918; D.S.O. 1915; late 2nd Batt. the Lancashire Fus.; *b.* 24 Dec. 1874; 5th *s.* of Patrick Griffin, Woodhill Terrace, Tivoli, Cork; *m.* 1919, Ruby (*d.* 1946), *widow* of Capt. A. C. Ward, D.S.O. Entered army, 1895; Capt. 1900; Major, 1913; Col. 1923; served S. African War, 1899-1902 (Queen's medal 6 clasps, King's medal 2 clasps); European War, 1914-18 (wounded, despatches, D.S.O. and bar, Bt. Lt.-Col., C.M.G.); retired pay, 1923 *Club:* Army and Navy. [*Died* 26 *July* 1957.

GRIFFIN, William Vincent, Hon. K.B.E. 1952; Chairman of Board, Brady Security & Realty Corp.; Vice-Chairman and Director of Time, Life and Fortune; Director: Chase-Manhattan Bank, Emigrant Industrial Savings Bank, Continental Oil Co., Dresser Industries Inc., Manati Sugar Co., Purolator Products, Inc., Servel, Inc.; *b.* Middletown, Conn., 1 Jan. 1886; *s.* of John Griffin and Katherine Stack; *m.* 1914, Isabel Shumard Carden (*d.* 1954); one *s.* decd. *Educ.:* Yale University, B.A. 1912. Director of Lend-Lease, British Empire Branch, 1942-1945. Pres., English-Speaking Union, 1947-1957; Presidential Certificate of Merit, 1947; Knight Commander of St. Gregory, 1926; Knight Official of Crown of Italy, 1928; Papal Chamberlain Cape and Sword, 1929; Knight of Malta, 1940; Knight Grand Cross of the Holy Sepulchre, 1953; K.St.J., 1956. *Address:* Peapack, New Jersey, U.S.A.; Alresford House, Alresford, Hampshire, England. *Clubs:* Recess, Grolier, Racquet and Tennis, Union, Yale (New York); Essex Fox Hounds, Somerset Hills (New Jersey); Metropolitan (Washington, D.C.). [*Died* 15 *Jan.* 1958.

GRIEVE, Edward William Lawrence. See page xxix.

GRIFFITH, Hubert Freeling; dramatic critic, journalist, and playwright; *b.* 1896; *s.* of late Nöel Ledbrook Griffith, barrister-at-law, and Nina Freeling; *m.* Kathleen Margaret Grayson; one *d.* *Educ.:* St. Paul's School; Berlin. Private, Royal Fusiliers, 1914-16; 2nd Lieut. Scottish Rifles, 1916; Staff Lieut. (Intelligence), 1917; Flying Officer, Observer, Royal Flying Corps, 1918; entered Slade School, London, 1919; contributor to The Observer, Manchester Guardian, etc. since 1919; dramatic critic: The Evening Standard, 1926-29; Sunday Graphic, 1945-1950; Dramatic Critic New English Review, 1947-50; President Critics' Circle, 1952. London Editor, Britanskii Sóyuznik (The British Ally), British Weekly Illustrated, published, in Russian, by H.M. Embassy in U.S.S.R., 1942. Sqdn.-Leader, R.A.F. *Publications:* Tunnel Trench, 1924; Red Sunday, 1929; Children of the Age, 1932; Youth at the Helm, 1934; Nina (from Bruno Frank's Play), 1935; Return to Yesterday (from Charles Vildrac's play), 1936; Distant Point (from the Russian); *criticism:* Iconoclastes, or The Future of Shakespeare, 1927; *travel:* European Encounters, 1931; Seeing Soviet Russia, 1932; Playtime in Russia, 1935; R.A.F. in Russia, 1943; This is Russia, 1944. *Recreations:* hunting, sailing. *Address:* 37 Paulton's Square, S.W.3; Burnt House Barn, Charing, Kent. *T.:* Flaxman 5066, Charing 221.
[*Died* 2 *March* 1953.

GRIFFITH, William, M.B., Ch.B. Vict.; M.R.C.P. Lond.; Physician to St. John's Hospital for Diseases of the Skin, Leicester Square, W.C., and practising as consulting physician on diseases of the skin; *b.* 1868; *s.* of J. J. Griffith, Sebonig, Dyffryn, North Wales. *Educ.:* Christ College, Brecon; The Owens College, Manchester; University College, and Middlesex Hospitals. Qualified in medicine in 1891 and held resident and other posts at various general hospitals; later became a member of the Royal College of Physicians of London, and was appointed successively Registrar, Assistant Physician and Physician to St. John's Hospital for Diseases of the Skin, Leicester Square, W.C.; Temporary Commission in the Royal Army Medical Corps, 1914, and acted as Specialist for Diseases of the Skin, Aldershot Command, 1914-19. *Recreation:* golf. *Address:* c/o Lloyds Bank Ltd., 18 Wigmore Street, W.1
[*Died* 28 *Dec.* 1953.

GRIFFITHS, Surgeon Rear-Admiral Cyril Verity, C.B. 1941; C.B.E. 1946; D.S.O. 1918; *b.* 1883; *s.* of Richard S. P. Griffiths, R.N., Inspector-General of Hospitals and Fleets; *m.* 1st. 1910, Muriel Joy, *d.* of R. Fletcher Beaumont, Reigate, Surrey; one *s.*; 2nd, 1946, Frances Rosemary, *d.* of Frank Brocklehurst, late of Caldy, Cheshire. *Educ.:* Ludlow Grammar School; King's College Hospital, London; M.R.C.S., L.R.C.P., 1906. Served European War, 1914-19 (despatches, D.S.O.); Deputy to Medical Director General of the Navy, 1933-34; i/c of R.N. Hospital, Portland, 1934-37; Surgeon Rear-Admiral, 1937; Deputy Medical Director-General, Admiralty, 1938-46; Hon. Physician to the King, 1940, 1946. *Address:* Dyke House, Lavant, Chichester, Sussex. *T.:* Chichester 7296.
[*Died* 12 *Sept.* 1959.

GRIFFITHS, Sir David (Edward), Kt., *cr.* 1953; O.B.E. 1946; Vice-Chairman of Executive Committee of Royal Air Force Cinema Corporation; President of Kinematograph Renters' Society; Chairman: Radiant (Colour) Laboratories Ltd.; Malta United Film Corporation Ltd.; Director: Hospital Film Services Ltd., etc. etc. *Address:* Argyll, 54 Gunnersbury Ave., Ealing, W.5.
[*Died* 8 *Oct.* 1957.

GRIFFITHS, Engineer Commander Percy Frederick, C.M.G. 1919; R.N., retired; *b.* 1873; *s.* of late J. H. Griffiths, The Grove, Whitchurch, Glam.; *m.* 1908, Guendolen Isobel (*d.* 1960), *yr. d.* of Sir Percy Oxenden, 10th and last Bt.; two *s.* Entered Royal Navy, 1896; served as Engineer Lieut.-Commander and Engineer Commander in H.M.S. Agincourt, Grand Fleet, Aug. 1914-March 1915; Engineer-Commander, 1914; served as Engineer Commander on staff of Rear-Admiral Commanding Harwich Force, 1915-19 (C.M.G.) Engineer Commander of Emperor of India Flagship of Black Sea Squadron 1919, retired from R.N. 1919; China Medal for Boxer Rebellion; 3 war medals. *Address:* Atworth, Eldorado Road, Cheltenham. *T.:* Cheltenham 2124. *Club:* New (Cheltenham).
[*Died* 1 *April* 1960.

GRIFFITHS, Thomas; *b.* Neath, 1867; *m.* 1891, Mary Elizabeth, *d.* of Dr. Morgan, architect, Neath. *Educ.:* Ruskin College, Oxford. Divisional Officer, Iron and Steel Trades' Confederation, 1916; M.P. (Lab.) Pontypool Division, Monmouthshire, Dec. 1918-35; a Lab. Whip, 1919-25; Treasurer of the King's Household, 1924. *Address:* 71 Lewis Road, Neath.
[*Died* 4 *Feb.* 1955.

GRIFFITHS, Sir William Thomas, Kt., *cr.* 1946; D.Sc.; F.R.I.C., F.Inst.P., F.I.M.; *b.* 19 April 1895; *s.* of late Rev. Caradoc and Elizabeth Griffiths, Cardiff, formerly of Dowlais, Glam.; *m.* 1922, Grace, *d.* of Henry and Amelia Jenkins, Cardiff; two *d.* *Educ.:* Cardiff College, University of Wales. Research Metallurgist, Research Dept., Woolwich, 1921-26; Manager, Research and Development Dept., Mond Nickel Co. Ltd., 1926-45; Chairman and Managing Director of Mond Nickel Company Limited, 1945-50; Vice-President International Nickel Company of Canada, Limited, 1945-50. President, Institute of Metals, 1944-46. Member Advisory Council, D.S.I.R. *Publications:* number of papers on Metallurgical subjects in Scientific and Technical Journals. *Recreations:* golf, photography. *Address:* Highclere, Kenley, Surrey. *T.:* Uplands 2080. *Clubs:* Athenæum, Royal Automobile.
[*Died* 30 *July* 1952.

GRILLE, Sir Frederick Louis, Kt., *cr.* 1937; retd., *b.* 20 Feb. 1889; *s.* of Fredrick Augustus and Pauline Grille; unmarried. *Educ.:* Harrow; Jesus College, Cambridge. Entered Indian Civil Service, 1912; Asst. Commissioner Central Provinces; attached 2/3rd Q.A.O. Gurkha Rifles (I.A.R.O.); Registrar Judicial Commissioners Court; Subordinate Judge; District and Sessions Judge; Legal Secretary to Government and Secretary to Legislative Council; Additional Judicial Commissioner; Judicial Commissioner; Puisne Judge, High Court of Judicature, Nagpur, 1936-43. Chief Justice, 1943. *Recreations:* books, puzzles of all kinds. *Club:* East India and Sports.
[*Died* 6 *Oct.* 1958.

GRIMBLE, Sir Arthur Francis, K.C.M.G., *cr.* 1938 (C.M.G. 1930); M.A.; *b.* Hong Kong, 1888; *s.* of Frank Grimble and Blanche Ann Arthur, Surrey; *m.* 1914, Olivia Mary, *d.* of Lewis Jarvis, The Toft, Sharnbrook, Beds., and Ada Mary Vesey-Dawson, London; four *d.* *Educ.:* Chigwell School; Cambridge; France, Germany. Entered Colonial Service as Cadet, 1914; District Officer, Gilbert and Ellice Islands, 1917; Lands Commissioner, 1922; First District Officer, 1924; Resident Commissioner, 1926-33; Administrator, and Colonial Secretary, St. Vincent, Windward Islands, 1933-36; Governor and Commander-in-Chief of Seychelles, 1936-42; Governor and C.-in-C., Windward Islands, 1942-48. *Publications:* (autobiog.): A Pattern of Islands, 1952; (posthumous) Return to the Islands, 1957. *Club:* Royal Empire Society.
[*Died* 12 *Dec.* 1956.

GRIMLEY, Bertram Griffiths; Pres. Society of Stipendiary Magistrates of England and Wales; (formerly member, now hon. member); *b.* 4 April 1867; *e. s.* of late

John Grimley, Edgbaston, Birmingham; *m.* 1904, May, *d.* of late Joseph Friend Bell, Fulham; no *c.* *Educ.:* Birmingham and Edgbaston Proprietary School; Eastbourne College; Jesus College, Cambridge. B.A., LL.B. 1886; called to Bar, Middle Temple, 1890; J.P. Staffordshire and Wolverhampton, 1923; read with late E. P. Wolstenholme, Conveyancing Counsel to Court, and Hugo Young, K.C., and practised as Conveyancing Counsel in Birmingham until 1923; Stipendiary Magistrate, South Staffs, 1923 - 50. Ex - Speaker Birmingham Parl. Debating Society; ex-Pres. Birmingham and Edgbaston Debating Society; Deputy Stipendiary Magistrate, Birmingham, 1906-1923. *Recreations:* golf, Inter-University Sports, 3 miles, 1886. *Address:* 15 Hermitage Road, Edgbaston, Birmingham. *T.:* Edgbaston 0344. *Club:* Union (Birmingham). [*Died* 22 *Sept.* 1952.

GRIMSHAW, Beatrice; author; 3rd *d.* of late Nicholas Grimshaw, of Cloona, Co. Antrim; *b.* Cloona. *Educ.:* Caen; Victoria Coll., Belfast; Bedford Coll., London. Has travelled alone in many parts of the world, the South Seas, Fiji, the New Hebrides and Solomon Islands, the unknown cannibal country of Papua, New Guinea, Celebes, Borneo, the Moluccas, New Britain, Burma, Straits Settlements, New Caledonia, Java, Dutch New Guinea, mandated territory of New Guinea; especially interested in Tropical Colonisation; first white woman to ascend notorious Sepik River and Fly River. *Publications:* From Fiji to the Cannibal Islands, 1907; In the Strange South Seas, 1907; Vaiti of the Islands, 1907; The New New Guinea, 1910; When the Red Gods Call, 1910; Guinea Gold, 1912; The Sorcerer's Stone, 1914; Red Bob of the Bismarcks, 1915; Nobody's Island, Kris Girl, 1916; White Savage Simon; The Coral Queen, 1919; The Terrible Island, 1920; The Coral Palace, The Little Red Speck, 1921; Conn of the Coral Seas, 1922; The Valley of Never-Come-Back, The Sands of Oro, 1923; The Candles of Katara, 1925; The Wreck of the Redwing, 1926; The Paradise Poachers, 1927; Eyes in the Corner, 1928; My Lady Far-Away, 1929; The Star in the Dust, 1930; Dream Islands, 1930; The Beach of Terror and Other Stories, 1931; The Mystery of Tumbling Reef, 1932; The Long Beaches, 1933; The Victorian Family Robinson, 1934; Pieces of Gold, 1936; Rita Regina, 1939; Lost Child, 1940; South Sea Sarah, 1940; Wild Mint of Moresby. *Address:* Post Office, Oberon, N.S.W., Australia. [*Died* 30 *June* 1953.

GRIMSHAW, Sir William (Josiah), Kt., *cr.* 1953; J.P.; *b.* 29 November 1886; *s.* of William Thomas and Margaret Kettlewell Grimshaw, Leeds; *m.* 1st, Mary Johnston (decd.), *d.* of late James Kellock, Glasgow; 2nd, Jane Issott Briggs, Cleckheaton and Harrogate; one *d.* *Educ.:* Ashville College, Harrogate. Hornsey Borough Council: Councillor, 1927; Alderman, 1940-58; Mayor, 1933-34, 1934-35, 1953-1954; Freeman, 1948. Middlesex County Council: Councillor, 1939; Alderman, 1949-1955; Chairman, 1951-52, 1952-53. Assoc. of Municipal Corporations: Vice-Chm. Gen. Purposes Cttee., 1948-58; Chm. Non-County Boroughs Cttee. of England and Wales, 1947-1958. Gov. Ashville Coll., Harrogate, North London Collegiate Sch., etc. Mem. Council Reading Univ. Served on: Local Govt. Manpower Cttee.; Stevenage Development Corp., 1946-49; Govt. Cttee. for Publicity for Local Govt.; Metropolitan Water Board, 1942-48, etc. J.P. Middlesex, 1944-. Silver Jubilee Medal, 1935; Coronation Medal, 1953. *Publication:* The Municipal Borough, 1951 (booklet). *Address:* Oaklea, 25 Sheldon Avenue, Highgate, N.6. *T.:* Mountview 6714. *Club:* Constitutional. [*Died* 12 *Sept.* 1958.

GRIMWADE, Sir (Wilfrid) Russell, Kt., *cr.* 1950; C.B.E. 1935; *b.* 15 Oct 1879; *s.* of Frederick Sheppard and Jessie Taylor Grimwade; *m.* 1909, Mabel Louise, *o. d.* of George and Agnes Dalziel Kelly; no *c.* *Educ.:* Church of England Grammar School and Melbourne University, B.Sc. Chemical and technical secondary industries; Director of several companies; Victorian Committee of Council of Scientific and Industrial Research; Council of Melbourne University; President Trustees of National Museums of Victoria; Past President Australian Chemical Institute; Chairman Felton Bequest; Complimentary member, B.M.A. (Victorian Branch); Hon. life member, Institute of Foresters of Australia. *Publication:* Anthrography of the Eucalypts. *Recreations:* arboriculture, carpentry, photography. *Address:* 139 Orrong Road, Toorak, Melbourne, S.E.2, Australia. *T.:* B.J. 1351. *Clubs:* Melbourne, Australian, (hon. life member) Royal Automobile of Victoria (Melbourne). [*Died* 2 *Nov.* 1955.

GRINDLE, Bernard Richard Theodore, C.B.E. 1930; *yr. s.* of late Edmund Samuel Grindle; *b.* 1879; *m.* 1925, Edith Ellen (*d.* 1940), 2nd *d.* of late Henry Banks Spencer, M.D. *Educ.:* St. Paul's School; Queen's Coll. Oxford, M.A. Late Assistant Secretary, War Office; Comptroller of Lands, 1933 - 39. *Address:* 277 Woodstock Road, Oxford. [*Died* 9 *July* 1955.

GRINSTED, Harold, C.B.E. 1946; B.Sc., F.R.Ae.S., F.C.G.I.; *b.* 14 March 1889; *s.* of William Grinsted, Slinfold, Sussex and Emily Grinsted; *m.* 1918, Ella Margery White; two *s.* *Educ.:* Colliers School, Horsham; City and Guilds Engineering College, S. Kensington. Royal Aircraft Establishment, 1912-31; Air Ministry, Ministry of Aircraft Production and Ministry of Supply, 1931-50, retired. Hon. Fell. Roy. Aeronautical Soc., 1955. *Address:* Nevern, The Avenue, Claygate, Surrey. [*Died* 21 *May* 1955.

GRIPPER, Col. Hugh Thomas, C.M.G. 1918, V.D.; *b.* 1867; *s.* of Jasper Gripper, Bengeo, Herts; *m.* 1899, Priscilla Matilda Fielder (*d.* 1955), *d.* of Henry Fielder Johnson. Served German South-West Africa, 1914-18 (despatches). *Address:* 59 Frost Street, Queenstown, C.P., S. Africa. [*Died* 23 *July* 1956.

GRISCOM, Sir Lloyd C., K.C.M.G., *cr.* 1919; Newspaper Proprietor and Publisher; *b.* Riverton, New Jersey, U.S.A., 1872; *s.* of Clement A. and Frances C. Griscom; *m.* 1st, 1901, Elizabeth Duer Bronson (*d.* 1914); two *s.*; 2nd, 1929, Audrey M. E. Crosse. *Educ.:* University of Pennsylvania. Secretary American Embassy in London; Chargé d'affaires American Legation Constantinople; Minister to Persia; to Japan; Ambassador to Brazil; to Italy; Lt.-Col. U.S.A. Staff of Gen. John J. Pershing in European War. *Publications:* Tenth Avenue, a melodrama; Diplomatically Speaking, an autobiography. *Recreations:* shooting, tennis, golf. *Address:* Syosset, L.I., New York. *T.:* Walnut 1-0890. *Club:* Knickerbocker (New York). [*Died* 8 *Feb.* 1959.

GRIST, Frederic Edwin, C.I.E. 1938; *b.* 9 Nov. 1883; *m.* 1910, Elfrida Muriel, *d.* of William Moore, Salisbury; one *s.* two *d.* *Educ.:* King's College School. Secretary Financial Dept., India Office, 1931 - 46; retired, 1946. *Address:* 3 Nigella Court, Southside, Weston super Mare. [*Died* 5 *Oct.* 1951.

GROSVENOR, Capt. Robert Arthur, M.C.; late the Queen's Bays; *b.* 25 May 1895; *s.* of late Lord Arthur Grosvenor, 2nd *s.* of 1st Duke of Westminster, and Helen, 2nd *d.* of Sir R. Sheffield, 5th Bt.; *cousin* and *heir-pres.* to 2nd Duke; *m.* 1925, Doris May, *o. d.* of late F. W. Wignall; one *d.* Served European War, 1914-18, in R.A.F. (despatches, M.C. and bar). *Address:* Oak-Ash Farm, Chaddleworth, Berks. *T.:* Chaddleworth 203. *Club:* Turf. [*Died* 12 *June* 1953.

GROTRIAN, Sir Herbert Brent, 1st Bt., *cr.* 1934; K.C. 1925; J.P.; 2nd *s.* of late Fred. Brent Grotrian (M.P. East Hull, 1886-1892) of Ingmanthorpe Hall, Wetherby, and West Hill House, Hessle, near Hull; *m.* 1902, Mary Lilian, *d.* of late Robert Adams, Barrister-at-law, of Hamilton, Ontario; one *s.* (and two killed on active service) two *d.* *Educ.:* Rossall; Trinity College, Oxford; M.A., B.C.L., M.P. (C.) S.W. Hull, 1924-29; High Sheriff of Bedfordshire, 1931-32; is Chairman of Argus Press, Ltd.; Chairman Beds. Quarter Sessions. *Recreations:* shooting, fishing, lawn tennis (played 2 years for Oxford University *v.* Cambridge, and for Yorkshire). *Heir: o. surv. s.* John Appelbe Brent, *b.* 16 Feb. 1904. *Address:* St Fillans, Nassau, Bahamas, B.W.I. *Club:* United University. [*Died* 28 *Oct.* 1951.

GROUSSET, René; Member Académie Française, 1946; Director of the Chinese Museum, Cernuschi, since 1933; *b.* 5 Sept. 1885; *s.* of late Professor Grousset, professor of Græco-Roman Archæology, Grenoble University; *m.* Louise Albouy; two *s.* *Educ.:* University of Montpellier (Licence d'histoire et de géographie, 1905). Attaché à la Direction des Beaux Arts, Paris, 1912; served European War, 1914-18, as Chef de Section Infanterie (Croix de Guerre). *Publications:* Histoire de l'Asie, 1922; Histoire de l'Extrême Orient, 1929; In the Footsteps of the Buddha (English Trans.), 1932; Civilisations of the East (English translation), 1932-34; Les Philosophies indiennes, 1932; Histoire des Croisades, 1935; L'Empire des steppes, 1938; L'Epopée des Croisades, 1939; Histoire de la Chine, 1944; (English translation: The Rise and Splendour of the Chinese Empire, 1952); Bilan de l'histoire, 1946; L'Empire du Levant, 1947; Histoire de l'Arménie, 1948; Figures de proue, 1950; La Chine et son art, 1951. *Address:* 7 Avenue Velasquez, Musée Cernuschi, Paris. *Club:* Autour du Monde (Paris). [*Died* 12 *Sept.* 1952.

GROVES, Brig.-Gen. Percy Robert Clifford, C.B. 1919; C.M.G. 1918; D.S.O. 1916; Order of the White Eagle of Serbia 3rd Class, with swords, 1916; Commander of the Legion of Honour, 1920; *e. s.* of J. Groves, late P.W.D. India; *m.* 1920, Suzanne, *d.* of E. Steen, Oslo; one *s.* *Educ.:* Bedford. Joined Army (K.S.L.I.), 1899; served South African War (Queen's medal 4 clasps, King's medal 2 clasps); employed with West African Regiment, 1903-4; Territorial Adjutant, 1909-12; joined R.F.C. 1914; served with Air Services France, 1914-15; Dardanelles, 1915-16; Middle East, 1916-18; Air Ministry, 1918-19, observer, pilot, G.S.O. 3, G.S.O. 2, G.S.O. 1, Wing Commander; Director of Flying Operations Air Ministry, April 1918; British Air Representative, Peace Conference, Jan. 1919 (despatches thrice); Captain, 1910; Major, 1915; Temp. Lieut.-Colonel, 1916; Temp. Brig.-General, 1918; Substantive Colonel, 1919; transferred to Royal Air Force with rank of Group Captain, 1919; retired with rank of Brig.-Gen., 1922; Associate Fellow Royal Aeronautical Society; Hon. Secretary General Air League of British Empire, and Editor of Air, 1927-29; Group Captain, hon. Air Commodore, R.A.F.V.R. Sept. 1939; Deputy Director Intelligence, Air Ministry, till April 1940, then seconded to Foreign Office; demobilized, 1946. *Publications:* Behind the Smoke Screen, 1934; Our Future in the Air, 1935. *Address:* c/o Standard Bank of South Africa, Cape Town, South Africa. *Club:* United Service. [*Died* 12 *Aug.* 1959.

GROVES, Thomas Edward; County Borough of West Ham: ex-Alderman, J.P.; Member of Finance, Legal and General, and Education Committees; Pres. Amusement Caterers Assoc., 1933-44; *b.* Stratford, 1884; father, G.E. Railway engine-driver; *m.* (he and wife won the Dunmow Flitch for Domestic Felicity, 1923); two *s.* one *d.* Attended West Ham Elementary School, thence Carpenters Company's Technical Institute and Mechanics' Institute, G.E. Rly.; apprenticed G.E. Rly. to coach-building; won scholarship residence at Ruskin College, Oxford, 1907-10; returned to industrial life—employed by L.C.C. Tramways as coach-builder; continued studies and became lecturer upon Economics, Local Government, Logic, Sociology, Astronomy, Constitutional History; M.P. (Lab.) Stratford, 1922-45; Labour Party Whip, 1931; elected to West Ham Council, 1916, 1919, 1922, and 1925; Mayor of West Ham, 1934-35; Chairman of Special Schools and Welfare Committee dealing with feeding of necessitous children and treatment of mental and physical subjects; President National League of the Blind (West Ham Branch); Student for Law at Gray's Inn. *Address:* 34 Hall Farm Rd., South Benfleet, Essex. [*Died* 29 *May* 1958.

GRUER, Harold George, M.A.; Barrister-at-law; late I.C.S.; *b.* 6 May 1886; *e. s.* of William Gruer and Mary Smith, Aberdeenshire; *m.* 1918, Eileen Murphy; one *s.* (and one killed on active service). *Educ.:* Gordon's Coll., Aberdeen; Aberdeen Univ. (M.A., 1st Cl. Hons. in Classics, 1908); Christ Church, Oxford. Called to Bar, Gray's Inn, 1926; entered I.C.S. 1910; Lieut. I.A.R.O. 1917-1918; served in Central Provinces as Asst. Commissioner, Deputy Commissioner, District and Sessions Judge, Additional Judicial Commissioner; Puisne Judge, High Court of Judicature, Nagpur, 1936-43; retired from Indian Civil Service, 1943. *Recreations:* walking, reading, travel. *Address:* 505 El Rio, Main Road, Sea Point, Cape Town, S. Africa. *T.:* Cape Town 4-7970. *Club:* City (Cape Town). [*Died* 2 *Aug.* 1956.

GRUFFYDD, William John, M.A.; Emeritus Prof. of Celtic, University College of South Wales and Monmouthshire, Cardiff; Hon. Docteur ès Lettres (Rennes); Hon. D.Litt. (Wales); *b.* 14 Feb. 1881; *e. s.* of John Gruffydd, Gorffwysfa, Caernarvonshire; *m.* 1909, Gwenda, *e. d.* of Rev. John Evans, Persondy, Abercarn; one *s.* *Educ.:* Caernarvon School; Jesus College, Oxford. Assistant Lecturer in Celtic, University College, Cardiff, 1906; Crown of National Eisteddfod, London, 1909; Sub-Lieut. R.N.V.R., 1915; Lieutenant, 1916-18; served North Sea and Egypt; M.P. (L.) University of Wales, 1943-50; Member of Government's Departmental Committee on Welsh; of Government Committee on Public Schools; President Council of National Eisteddfod of Wales. Member of various Welsh and English Committees and Councils. *Publications:* Trystan ac Essyllt, 1902; Caneuon a Cherddi, 1906; Beddaur Proffwydi, 1902; History of Welsh Literature (1450-1600), 1922; History of Welsh Prose (1540-1660), 1926; Ynys Yr Hud, 1923; and other plays and poems; Math son of Mathonwy (Mabinogion), 1928; Poems (Gregynnog Press), 1932; Flodeugerdd Gymraeg (Anthology of Welsh Verse), 1931; Hen Atgofion (Memoirs), 1936; Life of Sir Owen Edwards, 1937; Tro Olaf (Essays), 1939; Rhiannon, the Origins of the Mabinogion, 1953; etc. Editor of Llenor; Contributor: Encyclopædia Britannica, Nation, Manchester Guardian, Daily Herald, News Chronicle; Medium Aevum, Spectator, etc. *Recreation:* yachting. *Address:* Rhiw, Bangor Road, Caernarvon. [*Died* 29 *Sept.* 1954.

GRUNDY, Francis; Chairman of Woodhouse Hambly & Co. Ltd., Radcliffe, Lancs.; *b.* 25 Feb. 1882; *s.* of late Albert Walker Grundy, Prestwich; *m.* 1914, Edyth Dorothy (*d.* 1918), *d.* of late J. H. Thomson, Montreal. *Educ.:* Shrewsbury. Director: Manchester Royal Exchange; Ingot Mills (Pty.) Ltd., Sydney; Manchester Chamber of Commerce, 1934-(Pres. 1938 and 1939). Member of the Court of Governors, Manchester University. J.P. 1937; High Sheriff, Co. Palatine of Lancaster, 1951. *Address:* Oak Lodge, Prestwich, nr. Manchester. *T.:* Prestwich

2315. *Clubs:* Public Schools; Clarendon (Manchester). [*Died* 17 *Feb.* 1953.

GRUNDY, William Mitchell, J.P. Berkshire; M.A.; Lay Reader since 1913; *s.* of late Rev. W. Grundy, Headmaster of Malvern College. *Educ.:* Malvern College; All Souls College, Oxford. Classical Tutor Boro Road Training College, 1904-5; Diploma in Pedagogy, London University; Classical VI Form Master, Oakham School, 1906-8; Loretto School, 1908-13; Headmaster of Abingdon School, 1913-47; C.C., Berkshire, 1922-31, and 1949-55; Member Abingdon Borough Council, 1947-54. *Recreations:* golf, Oxford *v.* Cambridge, 1903 and 1904; chess, Oxford *v.* Cambridge, 1901-03. *Address:* Heathcot, Faringdon Road, Abingdon, Berks. *T.:* 214. [*Died* 16 *Nov.* 1960.

GSELL, Most Rev. Francis Xavier, O.B.E. 1935; D.D.; R.C. Bishop of Darwin, 1938-49; Titular Bishop of Paros; assistant at the Pontifical throne, Rome, 1951; *b.* Benfeld, Alsace Lorraine, 27 Oct. 1872. *Educ.:* Issoudun, France; Rome. Priest, Missionary of the Sacred Heart; went to Sydney, Australia, 1897; Papua, 1900; Darwin, 1906; Bathurst Island native mission, 1911. Legion of Honour (France), 1952. *Publication:* The Bishop with 150 Wives, 1951. *Address:* Sacred Heart Monastery, Kensington, Sydney, N.S.W., Australia. [*Died* 12 *July* 1960.

GUESS, George A.; *b.* Oct. 1873; *m.* 1st, 1901, Emma Steveash (*d.* 1926); 2nd, 1927, Edna Ashley. *Educ.:* Queen's University, Kingston, Canada. Engineering work has been in connection with copper smelting at Cananéa, Mexico, in 1905; Superintendent, Tennessee Copper Co., 1907-10; Metallurgical Superintendent, Cerro de Pasco, Peru; consulting work in smelting operations, Granby Co., at Anyox, B.C., 1914; Vermont Copper Co., 1916; Professor of Metallurgical Engineering, University of Toronto; retired, Oct. 1943. *Publications:* various articles in technical papers and society transactions. *Address:* Oakville, Ontario, Canada. [*Died* 21 *Oct.* 1954.

GUEST, 1st Baron; *see* Haden-Guest.

GUEST, Lt.-Col. Hon. (Christian) Henry (Charles); *b.* 15 Feb. 1874; 2nd *s.* of 1st Baron Wimborne; *m.* 1911, Hon. Frances Lyttelton (*d.* 1918), *d.* of 8th Viscount Cobham; one *s.* *Educ.:* Eton. Obtained commission in 3rd Batt. Lancs Fusiliers, 1892; 1st Royal Dragoons, 1894; M.P. (L.) East Dorset, 1910; Pembroke Burghs, 1910-18; (N.L.) North Bristol, 1922-23; M.P. (Nat. C.); Drake Division of Plymouth, 1937-45; Parliamentary Secretary to the Right Hon. Charles Hobhouse, M.P., late Postmaster-General; served South Africa, 1899-1902 (despatches, Queen's medal 5 clasps, King's medal 2 clasps); India, 1902-7; Staff College, 1907; Instructor in Cavalry School; served European War, 1914-15 and 1918. *Address:* St. Leonard's Grange, Beaulieu, Hants. *T.:* Bucklers Hard 234. *Clubs:* Carlton, Turf; Royal Yacht Squadron (Cowes). [*Died* 9 *Oct.* 1957.

GUEST, Hon. Oscar (Montague); *b.* 1888; 5th *s.* of 1st Baron Wimborne; *m.* 1924, Kathleen Susan, *o. c.* of late Graham Paterson; two *s.* two *d.* *Educ.:* Trinity College, Cambridge. On the outbreak of war joined the Lothian and Border Horse, and later transferred to the Royal Flying Corps (wounded); later a Staff Officer in the Air Ministry; M.P. (C.L.), Loughborough Division of Leicestershire, Dec. 1918-22; M.P. (U.) N.W. Camberwell, 1935-45. *Address:* Cabalva House, Whitney-on-Wye, Hereford. *T.:* Clifford 232. *Clubs:* Turf, White's, Brooks's. [*Died* 8 *May* 1958.

GUETERBOCK, Col. Sir Paul (Gottlieb Julius), K.C.B., *cr.* 1949 (C.B. 1943); D.S.O. 1919; M.C.; T.D.; D.L.; J.P. Bristol; T.A. General List (retired); Additional A.D.C. to the Queen since 1952 (to King George VI, 1947-52); Past Pres. Institute of Metals; Member of Council Institution of Mining and Metallurgy; Managing Director Capper Pass & Son, Ltd., Bristol, tin and lead smelters; *b.* 13 Sept. 1886; *s.* of Alfred Gueterbock; *m.* 1929, Winsome, *d.* of late E. S. Gange, J.P.; one *s.* one *d.* *Educ.:* Rugby School (Scholar); Trinity College, Cambridge (Scholar). Research in Alloys of Tin and Lead, 1909-14; developed and invented new processes for recovery and refining of Tin since 1919; M.A.; M.I.M.M.; F.I.M. 2nd Lt. Camb. Univ. Rifle Volunteers, 1907; transferred to 4th Bn. Gloucestershire Regt., 1909; served with this battalion and in various staff appointments in France during European War, 1914-19 (despatches, M.C., D.S.O.); commanded 4th Gloucesters, 1924-29; Col. Territorial Army General List, 1929; Chairman Gloucestershire County Rifle Association 1923-34; Chairman Gloucestershire T. and A.F.A., 1938-52; Chairman British Non-Ferrous Smelters Association, 1945-50. *Publications:* Various scientific and technical papers on Tin and Alloys of Tin. *Recreations:* Rifle shooting (Captain, Rugby and Cambridge University Teams), lawn tennis, ski-ing, gardening, music. *Address:* George's Plot, Abbots Leigh, near Bristol. *T.A.:* Abbots Leigh, Bristol. *T.:* Pill 31259. [*Died* 8 *March* 1954.

GUICHARD, Beatrice Catherine; (Beatrice Baskerville); *b.* Chatham, Kent, 1878; *d.* of late John Dunbar and Lucy Maud Baskerville; *m.* 1939, Eugene Guichard, (*d.* 1952), The Old Barn, Sorgues-sur Ouvèze, Vaucluse, France; no *c.* *Educ.:* privately. Russian and Balkan Correspondent of New York World, 1911-14; Rome Correspondent, 1914-31; Rome correspondent of the Daily Telegraph, 1933-40; Rome Correspondent of Yorkshire Post, 1940. *Publications:* The Polish Jew, 1906; Taras Bulba (from the Russian), 1907; Their Yesterday, 1909; When Summer Comes Again, 1915; Baldwin's Kingdom, 1917; Love and Sacrifice, 1918; Passover, 1920; The Enchanted Garden, 1921; What Next, O Duce?, 1937; (with Eliott Monk) By Whose Hand, 1922; The Amethyst Button, 1926; The St. Cloud Affair, 1931. *Recreation:* walking. *Address:* The Old Barn, Sorgues-sur-Ouveze, Vaucluse, France. [*Died* 23 *June* 1955.

GUILLAMORE, 9th Viscount, *cr.* 1831; **Standish Bruce O'Grady,** Baron O'Grady of Rockbarton, *cr.* 1831; *b.* 17 March 1869; *s.* of late James Waller O'Grady and Ada, sister of Sir W. C. Bruce, 9th Bt.; *S.* brother, 1943. *Address:* Rathredagh, Newcastle West, Co. Limerick. [*Died* 15 *Oct.* 1955 (*ext.*).

GUILLEMARD, Sir Laurence Nunns, G.C.M.G., *cr.* 1927 (K.C.M.G., *cr.* 1923); K.C.B., *cr.* 1910 (C.B. 1905); *b.* 7 June 1862; *o. s.* of Rev. William Hy. Guillemard, D.D.; *m.* 1902, Ella (*d.* 1940), *e. d.* of Thomas Spencer Walker. *Educ.:* Charterhouse; Trinity College, Cambridge. Entered Treasury, 1888; Private Secretary to Sir W. V. Harcourt and Sir M. Hicks-Beach, 1892-1902; Governing Body of Charterhouse School, 1906-20, and 1931-45; Deputy Chairman, Board of Inland Revenue, 1902-8; Chairman Board of Customs and Excise, 1909-19; Governor of the Straits Settlements and High Commissioner for Malay States, 1919-1927; First Class of the Order of the Rising Sun, Japan, 1921. *Publication:* Trivial Fond Records, 1937. *Address:* Rodsall Manor, Puttenham, Guildford. *T.:* Puttenham 233. *Clubs:* Athenæum, Brooks's; (Hon.) Royal Yacht Squadron (Cowes). [*Died* 13 *Dec.* 1951.

GUINNESS, Sir Algernon Arthur St. Lawrence Lee, 3rd Bt., *cr.* 1867; Steward of the Royal Automobile Club; Flight-Lt., R.A.F.V.R.; *b.* 11 May 1883; *s.* of late Benjamin Lee Guinness and Lady Henrietta St. Lawrence (*d.* 1935), *d.* of 3rd Earl of

Howth; *S.* uncle, 1st Baron Ardilaun in Baronetcy, 1915; *m.* 1928, Winifred Mounteney, *d.* of Mrs. George Hall, Hamilton, Ontario; one *d.* European War, 1914-18, acting Lieut.-Commander R.N.V.R.; Flight-Lt. R.A.F.V.R. Air Sea Rescue, War of 1939-1945 (despatches). *Heir: nephew,* Kenelm Ernest Lee [*b.* 13 Dec. 1928; *s.* of late Kenelm Edward Lee Guinness]. *Address:* Riverdene, Cookham, Berks. *Club:* Royal Automobile. [*Died* 26 *Oct.* 1954.

GUINNESS, Arthur Eustace Seymour; *b.* 2 Dec. 1867; *s.* of Richard Seymour Guinness; *m.* 1897, Wilhelmine (*d.* 1943), *d.* of H. W. Forester of Somerby, Oakham; one *d.* High Sheriff, Northants, 1921; J.P. County of Northants. *Address:* Green's Norton Hall, Northants. *T.:* Towcester 6. *Club:* Union. [*Died* 4 *Sept.* 1955.

GUINNESS, Sir Arthur Rundell, K.C.M.G., *cr.* 1949; Partner, Guinness Mahon & Co., Merchant Bankers, London; Director, Guinness Mahon Representation Co. Inc., New York, and various Companies; *b.* 26 May 1895; *s.* of late Howard Rundell and Mary Alice Guinness; *m.* 1923, Frances Patience, *d.* of late Edward Fortescue Wright, C.M.G., Chudleigh, Devon, and Jamaica; two *s.* one *d.* *Educ.:* Winchester College. Joined family merchant banking business of Guinness, Mahon & Co. as a partner, 1923; Pres. Internat. Chamber of Commerce, 1947-49; Chairman British National Cttee. Internat. Chamber of Commerce, 1943-47; Hon. Pres. Internat. Chamber, 1949-; Member Overseas Trade Development Council, Dept. of Overseas Trade, 1944-45; Member of Grand Council, F.B.I., Member and Treasurer of Chinese Government Purchasing Commission in London; Member Exec. Cttee. Help Holland Council, 1945-46; Member League of Nations Special Joint Cttee. on Private Foreign Investment, 1945; Member Council English-Speaking Union; Liveryman Goldsmiths' Company. European War, 1914-18, Capt. and Adjutant, Manchester Regt., and on staff (wounded Ypres, 1915); Lt.-Col. commanding 27th Bn. Hampshire Home Guard, 1942-45. *Recreations:* hunting, shooting, yachting. *Address:* 53 Cornhill, E.C.3; Hawley Place, Blackwater, Hants. *T.A.:* Guimaco, London. *T.:* Mansion House 6142, Camberley 328. *Clubs:* Carlton, White's; Royal Yacht Squadron (Cowes); Kildare Street (Dublin); Royal St. George Yacht (Kingstown); Metropolitan (New York). [*Died* 12 *March* 1951.

GUITRY, Sacha; *b.* 21 Fév. 1885; fils de Lucien Guitry (*d.* 1925); *m.* 1st, Charlotte Lysès; 2nd, Yvonne Printemps; 3rd, 1935, Jacqueline Delubac; 4th, 1939, Geneviève de Sèreville; 5th, 1949, Lana Marconi. *Educ.:* Saint-Ange Bautier; lycée Janson-de-Sailly; Saint-Croix de Neuilly; dominicains d'Arcueil; École Cotta; École Cardwell; École Blandin; École Prax; institution Chevalier; institution Mariaux. *Œuvres:* Le Page, opérabouffe, 1901; le Kwrtz, drame, 1904; Nono, comédie 3 actes, 1905; Chez les Zoaques, comédie 3 actes, 1906; Les Nuées d'Aristophane, comédie en 4 actes, 1907; La Clef, comédie en 4 actes, 1907; Le Crin, comédie, 1907; Petite Hollande, 1908; Le Muffle, 1908; Le Veilleur de nuit, 1911; Jean III., 1911; Beau Mariage, 1912; La Pèlerine écossaise, 1914; La Jalousie, 1915; Faisons un rêve, 1916; Jean de la Fontaine, 1916; L'Illusionniste, 1917; Deburau, 1918; Pasteur, 1919; Le Mari, la femme et l'amant, 1919; Mon Père avait raison, 1919; Béranger, 1920; Je t'aime, 1920; Le Grand Duc, 1921; Jacqueline, 1921; Le Comédien, 1920; Une Petite Main qui se place, 1922; Un Sujet de roman, 1923; L'Amour masqué, 1923; Le Lion et la poule, 1923; L'Accroche-Cœur, 1923; On ne joue pas pour s'amuser, 1925; Mozart (play), 1929; Desireé (play), 1932; Florestan, Prince of Monaco, operetta, 1933; Le Nouveau Testament, 1934; Mon Double et ma moitié (play), 1935; If I Remember Right, 1935; Le Mot de Cambronne, 1936; Quadrille, 1938; N'écoutez pas, mesdames, 1943; Ten Words of English, 1946; Toâ, 1949; Tu m'as sauvé la vie, 1950; Une Folie, 1951; Ecoutez Bien, Messieurs, 1953, etc. Has written, directed and played in many films including: Pasteur; Le Roman d'un tricheur (The Cheat); Les Perles de la couronne; Le Mot de Cambronne; Remontons les Champs-Élysées; Ils étaient neuf célibataires; Le Destin fabuleux de Desirée Clary; Talleyrand; le Trésor de Cantenac; La Poison; Si Versailles m'était conté; Napoleon; Si Paris nous était conté; etc. *Recreations:* collectionneur de tableaux, de livres et d'objets d'art. *Address:* Paris VII, 18 av. Elisée-Reclus. [*Died* 24 *July* 1957.

GULBENKIAN, Calouste Sarkis; *b.* Scutari, Istanbul, Turkey, 1869; *m.* London, 1892, Nevarte (*d.* 1952); one *s.* one *d.*; became a British subject, 1902. *Educ.:* Stamboul, Marseilles, London. Fellow of King's College, University of London. Has pursued a commercial and industrial career, chiefly in oil; with a fortune of millions of pounds he caused to be set up, with 3 trustees, the Calouste Gulbenkian Foundation; his famous art collection was to go to the Foundation with headquarters in Lisbon; administration to benefit people of any nationality. *Recreations:* art and gardening. *Address:* 3 rua Latino Coelho, Lisbon, Portugal. [*Died* 20 *July* 1955.

GULL, Capt. Sir Richard Cameron, 3rd Bt., *cr.* 1872; late Rifle Brigade; *b.* 18 Mar. 1894; *s.* of 2nd Bt. and Hon. Annie Clayton Lindley, *d.* of Rt. Hon. Lord Lindley; *S.* father, 1922; *m.* 1917, Dona Eva Swinnerton, *e. d.* of late Sir Thomas Swinnerton Dyer, 11th Bt.; one *s.* one *d.* *Educ.:* Eton; Christ Church, Oxford; Sandhurst. Served European War, 1914-16 (despatches, wounded). *Heir: s.* Michael Swinnerton Cameron, *b.* 24 Jan. 1919. *Address:* Fairways, Hillcrest, Natal, S. Africa. *Club:* Bath. [*Died* 5 *Sept.* 1960.

GULLAN, Marjorie Isabel Morton, M.B.E. 1952; President of The Speech Fellowship, London; *d.* of James Thomas Campbell Gullan and Christiana Jane Voss. *Educ.:* Hutcheson's Girls' Grammar School, Glasgow. For many years head of a school of speech training and dramatic art in Glasgow; Head of School of Speech Training, Polytechnic, London, 1926-1932; Founder and Conductor of Glasgow and London Verse Speaking Choirs; Visiting lecturer University of California, 1933 and Teachers' College, Columbia University, 1935; Joint Founder of the Speech Institute of London, 1932; Lecturer in Speech Training, Univ. of London, Inst. of Education, 1932-38, 1945-49. War Work: Member of W.V.S. *Publications:* Spoken Poetry in the School; Choral Speaking; Speech Training in the School; Poetry Speaking for Children (with Dr. P. Gurrey); The Speech Choir: The Poet Speaks (with Clive Sansom). *Recreations:* travel, music, swimming. *Address:* 19 York Street Chambers, Bryanston Square, W.1. [*Died* 8 *Oct.* 1959.

GUMBLETON, Rt. Rev. M. H. M.; *see* Maxwell-Gumbleton.

GUNESEKERA, Sir Frank (Arnold), Kt. *cr.* 1950; C.B.E. 1948 (O.B.E. 1935); E.D. 1936; Senator, Ceylon, since 1947; *b.* 14 Nov. 1887; *s.* of Francis Gunesekera, J.P. and Bessie Charlotte Gunesekera; *m.* 1915, Mary Margaret Rajepakse; four *s.* two *d.* *Educ.:* Royal College, Colombo; Ceylon Medical College; London Hospital Medical College. L.M.S. (Ceylon) 1910; M.R.C.S. (Eng.), L.R.C.P. (Lond.) 1913. President British Medical Association (Ceylon Branch), 1931; Vice-President Ceylon Medical Council since 1933; Member of Court, Council and Faculty of Medicine,

Univ. of Ceylon, since 1942; President, Independent Medical Practitioners' Assoc. of Ceylon, 1950. Officer Commanding, Ceylon Medical Corps, 1935-39; Colonel, Ceylon Defence Force, since 1939. *Recreations:* tennis, motoring. *Address:* 143 Campbell Place, Colombo, Ceylon. *T.:* 9660 and 9263. *Clubs:* Orient, Sinhalese Sports (Colombo). [*Died* 23 *Jan.* 1952.

GUNN, James Andrew, C.B.E. 1947; M.A., M.D., D.Sc. (Edin.), D.M. (Oxon), F.R.C.P.; Emeritus Professor, University of Oxford; Director of the Nuffield Institute for Medical Research, 1935-46; Prof. of Pharmacology, University of Oxford, 1917-37; Reader, 1912; Professor of Therapeutics, 1937-46; formerly Fellow of Balliol College; *b.* Kirkwall, 26 Jan. 1882; *s.* of John R. Gunn, Kirkwall; *m.* Anne Marie Gunn; two *s.* one *d.* (and *y. s.* killed in action, Salerno, 1943). *Educ.:* Edinburgh University. Graduated with First-Class Honours in Medicine and with Special Distinction in Science; Thesis Gold Medallist; Milner-Fothergill Gold Medallist in Therapeutics; Baxter Scholar; Beit Research Fellow; Past President (Therapeutics) Royal Society of Medicine; Past President (Pharmacology) British Medical Association; Past Pres. Oxford Medical Society; Chairman of the Pharmacopœia Revision Commission, 1939-48; Hon. Member: British Pharmacological Society, British Pharmaceutical Society, Pharmacological Society of Argentine; Dohme Lecturer, Johns Hopkins University, 1935; Oliver-Sharpey Lecturer, Royal College of Physicians, 1939. *Publications:* Papers to the Royal Societies and in Medical Journals; An Introduction to Pharmacology and Therapeutics, 8th edition, 1948; Edited Cushny's Text-book of Pharmacology and Therapeutics, 12th edition, 1940; contributions to Dictionary of National Biography and to Encyclopædias. *Recreations:* fishing, golf. *Address:* Old Cottage, Hermitage, nr. Newbury, Berks. *T.:* Hermitage 339. [*Died* 21 *Oct.* 1958.

GUNSBOURG, Raoul; *b.* Bucarest, 6 Jan. 1859; *s.* of Louis Gunsbourg, Captain Staff of Marshal Canrobert. Served with the Red Cross in Russo-Turkish War; studied medicine in Paris; founded and directed first French operas in Moscow and St. Petersburg; Director of the Monte Carlo Opera from 1892. Officier de la Légion d'Honneur; Commandeur de l'Ordre de Saints Maurice et Lazare (Italie); Commandeur de l'Ordre de Saint Sava (Yougoslavia); Commandeur de l'Ordre de Vasa (Sweden); Commandeur de l'Ordre de Saint Charles (Monaco); Médaille Militaire sur Ruban de St. George (Russia) etc. *Operas:* Ivan le Terrible; Djaileh; La Conteuse du Padischah; Viel Aigle; Lysistrata; La Fille de Don Juan; Venise, etc. *Address:* rue de Vaugirard 20, Paris, VIe. [*Died* 31 *May* 1955.

GUPTA, J. N., C.I.E. 1927; M.B.E.; I.C.S.; Retired as Member Board of Revenue, Bengal; *b.* 1870; *s.* of late Ghanashyama Gupta, retired subordinate Judge under Government; *m.* 1894, 4th *d.* of late Romesh Chandra Dutt, C.I.E., I.C.S.; four *s.* one *d.* *Educ.:* Presidency College, Calcutta; Balliol College, Oxford. Entered the Indian Civil Service, 1892; held successively post of District Magistrate and Commissioner of a division; on special duty on several occasions, notably in 1903, when he was deputed to the Delhi Durbar held under Lord Curzon and was placed in charge of the Indian section of the Press Camp; Secretary of Lord Sinha when the latter went to England, 1918; Represented the Government of India at the Labour Branch of the League of Nations Conference, 1921. *Publications:* Life of Romesh Chandra Dutt, C.I.E., I.C.S., 1910; Foundations of National Progress, with an introduction by the Rt. Hon. Lord Sinha, 1927; Social Drama in Bengali Monisha and Kasti Pathar. *Recreations:* fond of shooting, plays golf, rides, etc. *Clubs:* National Liberal; Darjiling (Darjiling); South (Calcutta). [*Died* 1947. [*But death not notified in time for inclusion in Who Was Who 1941–1950, first edn.*

GUPTA, Satyendra Nath, C.I.E. 1935; B.A. (Cantab.); I.C.S. retd.; *b.* 29 July 1895; *s.* of Lieut.-Col. Kali Pada Gupta, Indian Medical Service, and Muktakeshi Roy; two *s.*; *m.* 1938, Frieda Rogge. *Educ.:* St. Paul's School, London (Foundation Scholar); Trinity Hall, Cambridge (Classical Scholar). Entered Indian Civil Service after examination of 1917; Bengal district work, deputed to Indian Customs for 2½ years; in charge of Bengal district for 4 years as District magistrate and Collector; Deputy Trade Commissioner in London under High Commissioner for India, 1928; Indian Trade Commissioner, Hamburg, 1931-37; Joint Secretary, Commerce Dept., Govt. of India, 1938; Collector of Customs, Karachi and Bombay, 1939; Commissioner of Excise, Bengal, 1942; retd. 1943; economic staff, U.N.R.R.A., London, 1946-47; U.K. and Eire Representative, India Steamship Company Ltd., Calcutta, 1949-55. *Publications:* Official Reports and articles in English and German Press on Indian trade to Europe; U.N.R.R.A. Economic Bulletins on Finland and Byelorussia. *Recreation:* stamp collecting. *Address:* Grindlay's Bank, 54 Parliament Street, S.W.1. *Clubs:* National Liberal; Calcutta (Calcutta); Karachi (Karachi). [*Died* 1 *Oct.* 1956.

GURDON, Maj.-Gen. Edward Temple Leigh, C.B. 1948; C.B.E. 1944; M.C.; retired; *b.* 20 Oct. 1896; *o. s.* of late Francis Gurdon, D.D., Bishop of Hull, and Florence, *d.* of Sir John Hoskyns, 9th Bt.; *m.* 1923, Elizabeth Madeleine, *d.* of late Douglas and Elizabeth Wilson, then of Eltham Court; two *s.* two *d.* *Educ.:* Summer Fields; Rugby; R.M.C., Sandhurst. E. Yorks, 1914; Rifle Brigade, 1915; European War, 1914-1918, Flanders and East Africa (despatches, M.C.); A.D.C. and Private Sec. to Governor, Uganda, 1919-20; Black Watch, 1922; Staff College, 1929-30; Bt. Major, 1935; Instructor Staff College, 1937-40; Bt. Lt.-Col. 1938; commanded 1st Black Watch, 1940; Bde. Comdr. 1941; B.G.S. of a Corps, 1941-42; B.G.S. of an Army, 1942-43; Director of Military Training, India, and Div. Comdr. India, 1943-45; M.G.G.S. Home Forces, 1945; Divisional Comdr., B.A.O.R., 1945-46; District Comdr., Salisbury Plain, 1947-48. Burma-Assam, 1942-43 (C.B.E.); Actg. Lt.-Gen., 1947. *Address:* Burgh House, near Woodbridge, Suffolk. *T.:* Grundisburgh 273. *Clubs:* Army and Navy, M.C.C. [*Died* 15 *Dec.* 1959.

GURNER, Sir (Cyril) Walter, Kt., *cr.* 1946; C.S.I. 1941; *b.* 18 Jan. 1888; *m.* 1918, Phyllis Mills; three *d.* *Educ.:* Merchant Taylors' School; Oriel College, Oxford. Entered Indian Civil Service, 1911; Chairman Calcutta Improvement Trust, 1933; Regional Controller, Ministry of Town and Country Planning, 1947-51. *Address:* 10 Richmond Bridge Mansions, Twickenham, Middlesex. [*Died* 14 *Aug.* 1960.

GURNEY, (Ernest) Russell, LL.B.; Recorder of Rotherham, 1935-55; of Pontefract, 1934-35; *b.* 20 Jan. 1879; *s.* of James Gurney, Cumberland Priory, Headingley, and Mary (*née* Luck), Tring; *m.* 1905, Caroline Clara (*d.* 1951); *d.* of James Wm. Townsend Ward, of Elford, Tamworth, Staffs; one *s.* one *d.* (and two *s.* died through war service). *Educ.:* Yorkshire College, Leeds; London Univ. LL.B., Honours Common Law and Equity; called to Bar, Gray's Inn, 1907; joined North Eastern Circuit; Chm. Court of Referees at Wakefield, 1926-28, and at Leeds, 1928-43; Chairman Pensions Appeal Tribunal, 1943-46; Deputy Chairman Traffic Commissioners for Yorkshire, 1936-56; President Leeds Circle Catenian Assoc., 1929-30; Grand Director Yorkshire Province, 1936-46.

Contribs. to The Times, Manchester Guardian and Yorkshire Post. *Recreations:* swimming, golf. *Address:* 113 West End Avenue, Harrogate. *T.:* 6217; 38 Park Sq., Leeds. *T.:* 23601. *Club:* Conservative (Harrogate). [*Died* 24 *Oct.* 1958.

GURNEY, Sir Henry Lovell Goldsworthy, K.C.M.G., *cr.* 1948 (C.M.G. 1942); Kt., *cr.* 1947; High Commissioner for Federation of Malaya since 1948; *b.* 27 June 1898; *s.* of G. G. H. Gurney, Reeds, Bude, Cornwall, and F. M. L. Chamier; *m.* 1924, I. L. Weir; two *s. Educ.:* Winchester; Univ. Coll., Oxford. Served in 60th Rifles, 1917-19; entered Colonial Service, Kenya, 1921; Assistant Colonial Secretary, Jamaica, 1935; Chief Secretary to Conference of East African Governors, 1938-44; Colonial Secretary, Gold Coast, 1944-46; Chief Sec. to Palestine Government, 1946-48. *Recreation:* golf. *Address:* King's House, Kuala Lumpur; Cotchford Hill, Hartfield, Sussex. [*Died* 6 *Oct.* 1951.

GURNEY, Russell; *see* Gurney, E. R.

GUTHRIE, Charles, F.F.A.; formerly Manager and Actuary of The Scottish Equitable Life Assurance Society, now a Director; *s.* of late William Guthrie, LL.D., Sheriff-Principal of Lanarkshire. *Educ.:* Glasgow Academy; Glasgow University. President of the Faculty of Actuaries in Scotland; Chairman of the Associated Scottish Life Offices, etc. *Address:* Craigour, Gullane, East Lothian. *Club:* Hon. Company of Edinburgh Golfers (Edinburgh). [*Died* 27 *May* 1953.

GUTTERIDGE, Harold Cooke, Q.C. 1930; Bencher of Middle Temple, 1936; Lent Reader, Middle Temple, 1948; LL.D., M.A., Docteur en Droit (Honoris Causa) Lyon, 1927, Grenoble, 1939; Paris, 1945; Hon. LL.D. Salonika, 1948; President of the Society of Comparative Legislation; Emeritus Prof. of Comparative Law in the Univ. of Cambridge; Fellow of Trinity Hall, Cambridge; Member of Council of Senate, 1937-1945, of the Financial Board, 1940-43, of the Press Syndicate, 1940-47, and of Septemviri; formerly Cassel Professor of Law and Dean of the Faculty of Laws in the University of London; Member of the Institute of International Law; David Murray Lecturer, University of Glasgow, 1950; *b.* 16 July 1876; *er. s.* of late Michael and Ada Gutteridge, Ballindune, Haslemere; *m.* 1905, Mary Jackson; one *s.* one *d. Educ.:* Leys School; King's College, Cambridge (Scholar). First Class Historical Tripos, 1898; First Class Law Tripos, Pt. I., 1899. Called to Bar, Middle Temple, 1900; in practice from that date; enlisted in the Territorial Force 10 Aug. 1914; served with the British Salonika Force, 1916-19 (despatches); demobilised with the rank of Captain, March 1919; Senator of the University of London, 1924-1930; Dean of the Faculty of Laws, 1923-27 and 1929-30; President of the Society of Teachers of Law, 1928; LL.D. (London) 1928; LL.D. (Cantab.) 1941; British Delegate to the Hague Conference on Private International Law and the Geneva Conferences on the Unification of the Law of Bills of Exchange and Cheques, 1930 and 1931; Member of the Law Revision Committee 1933, and of the Lord Chancellor's Committees on the Enforcement of Foreign Judgements, 1932, and on Legal Education, 1933 and 1938; Member of the Royal Commission on the Manufacture of and Traffic in Arms, 1935; President League of Nations Committee on Civil Status of Women, 1938; Member Shipping Claims Tribunal, 1939; Mem. Law Advisory Committee of British Council, 1942. *Publications:* Nelson and the Neapolitan Jacobins (Navy Records Series), 1903; Comparative Law, 1946; The Law of Bankers' Commercial Credits, 1932. Jt. Ed. Cambridge Series on International and Comparative Law; various articles and essays on legal and other subjects. *Recreations:* travel, fishing, and photography. *Address:* Trinity Hall, Cambridge; 2 Essex Court, Temple, E.C.; The Rydings, Sylvester Road, Cambridge. *T.:* Central 1984, Cambridge 2626. *Club:* Oxford and Cambridge. [*Died* 30 *Dec.* 1953.

GUY, Commander Basil John Douglas, V.C. 1900; D.S.O. 1917; R.N., retired; *b.* 9 May 1882; *s.* of late Canon D. S. Guy; *m.* 1917, Mary, *d.* of late W. Sayles Arnold, Doncaster and Harrogate; two *d. Educ.:* Llandaff Cathedral School. Served China War, 1900, (V.C., China medal and clasp); European War, 1914-18 (D.S.O.); Commander, 1918; retired, 1923; Recalled for service in War of 1939-45. *Address:* Stanford Farm, Pirbright, Surrey. *T.:* Worplesdon 93. [*Died* 29 *Dec.* 1956.

GUY, Ven. Archdeacon Cuthbert Arnold; Priest in charge of Holcombe, Dawlish; late Rector of St. John's Pro-Cathedral, Buenos Aires, and Archdeacon of the Republics of the Plate; *b.* 26 Aug. 1884; *s.* of late Canon Douglas Sherwood Guy; *m.* 1935, Evelyn Maud Benitz, née Jefferies. *Educ.:* Winchester College; Oriel College, Oxford. Deacon, 1908; Priest, 1909; Curate of St. Paul's, King's Cross, Halifax, Yorkshire, 1908-11; St. Mary's Cathedral, Johannesburg, 1911-14; Vicar of St. Saviour's, Johannesburg; Naval Chaplain, 1915-19; Curate of St. Michael and All Angels, Colombo, Ceylon, 1920-22; Vicar of St. Paul's, Kandy, Ceylon, 1923-31. *Publication:* Scouting and Religion. *Recreations:* golf and tennis. *Address:* St. Georges, Holcombe, Dawlish, Devon. [*Died* 15 *April* 1954.

GUY, Sir Henry (Lewis), Kt., *cr.* 1949; C.B.E. 1943; F.R.S. 1936; D.Sc.; M.I.Mech.E., F.Amer.Soc.M.E.; Whitworth Exhibition; Secretary of Institution of Mechanical Engineers, 1942-51; *b.* 15 June 1887; *s.* of late R. Guy, Penarth; *m.* 1914, Margaret Paton Williams; two *d. Educ.:* University College of South Wales; College of Technology, Manchester. Engineering pupil to T. Hurry Riches, T. V. Railway, Cardiff; joined Technical Staff British Westinghouse, 1910; Chief Engineer Mechanical Department Metropolitan Vickers Co., 1919-42; Member Advisory Council for Research and Development, Min. of Supply, 1939-42 and 1943-; Chm. of Gun Design Cttee.; Chm. Cttee. on Armaments Development, 1942; Chm. Static Detonation Cttee., 1943; Chm. Cttee. on Aircraft Armament Development, M.A.P., 1945; Chm. of Cttee. on Technical Organisation of the Army, 1944; Member of Advisory Council to Cttee. of Privy Council for Scientific and Industrial Research, 1944-; Member Mechanical Engineering Advisory Cttee. Ministry of Labour since 1942; Chm. Armaments Development Board, Ministry of Supply and of Aircraft Production, 1945-47; Trustee of Imperial War Museum, 1946-48; Chairman Cttee. on Essential Requirement of Mechanical Engineering Research, D.S.I.R., 1945-46; Chairman Mechanical Engineering Research Board, D.S.I.R., 1947; Associate Member of Ordnance Board and of Board of Chemical Warfare; Vice-President Institution of Mechanical Engineers, 1938-41; Member of Council Royal Society, 1938-39; Chairman Engineering Sciences Sectional Committee, Royal Society, 1939-40; Hon. D.Sc. Welsh Univ. 1939; Hon. Associate Manchester College of Technology; Hon. Member: Instn. Mech. Engineers; Roy. Artillery Inst.; Belfast Instn. of Engineers; President Whitworth Soc., 1952. Bayless Prize, Institution of Civil Engineers; Thomas Hawkesly Medal Institution of Mechanical Engineers; Charles Parsons Memorial Lecture and Medal, 1939. *Publications:* Various Papers on Technical Subjects read before the Institution of Mechanical Engineers, Institution of Civil Engineers, The Institution of Naval Architects of Japan, etc. *Address:* Enniskerry, Ravine Rd., Canfords Cliffs, Bournemouth. [*Died* 20 *July* 1956.

GUY, Lt.-Col. Philip Langstaffe Ord; *b.* 23 Jan. 1885; Director Archaeological Survey and Excavation in Israel since 1948; *s.* of Robert Guy, Sheriff-Clerk of Lanarkshire, and Lucy, *d.* of John Ord, Great Crosby, Lancashire; *m.* 1925, Yemima, *e. d.* of Eleazer Ben Yehuda, Hebrew Lexicographer; one *d. Educ.:* Charterhouse; Merton College, Oxford; Glasgow University. Solicitor's Office; Motor Works, Paisley and Paris, 1911-14; served European War, Légion Étrangère, M.M.G.S. and M.G.C., 1914-19; Assistant on archaeological excavations at Carchemish, 1919-20, and at El Amarna, 1920-22; Chief Inspector of Antiquities in Palestine, 1922-1927; Director, Megiddo excavations, 1927-1935; Director, British School of Archaeology in Jerusalem and Archaeological Survey of Palestine, 1935-39: Dean, Palestine Board of Higher Studies, 1936-47; Member Palestine Soil Conservation Board, 1939-46; served R.A.S.C., chiefly in Middle East, 1939-46. *Publications:* Archaeological reports. *Address:* P.O. Box 586, Jerusalem, Israel. [*Died* 7 *Dec.* 1952.

GUYOMARD, Rt. Rev. John Alfred, D.D., O.M.I., Titular Bishop of Assava; an Assistant at the Pontifical Throne; Bishop of Jaffna, (R.C.), 1924-50; Oblate of Mary; *b.* St. Brieuc, 14 Oct. 1884; *s.* of John Guyomard and Marie Coupé. *Educ.:* St. Martin, Rennes; Grand Seminaire, St. Brieuc; Scholasticate of Liége; Cambridge University, 1910, B.A. Sent to Ceylon, 1914; Professor of Classics, St. Patrick's College till 1921; Rector, St. Patrick's, 1921-24. [*Died* 27 *Feb.* 1956.

GWENN, Edmund; actor; *b.* London, 26 Sept. 1877; *m.* Minnie Terry. *Educ.:* St. Olave's; King's College, London. Went on the Stage in 1895 and after ten years' hard work made his first London success as the Chauffeur in Bernard Shaw's Man and Superman at the Court Theatre under the Management of Vedrenne & Barker. Stayed there three years in plays by Shaw, Galsworthy, Ibsen, Granville-Barker, Hauptman, Schnitzler, etc. Subsequently appeared at other London Theatres in What Every Woman Knows, Justice, The Twelve-Pound Look, Rosmersholm, The Bear Leaders, etc. Entered into Management with Hilda Trevelyan at the Vaudeville, 1912-14. In the European War joined up as Private, demobilised as Captain, 1919. Reappeared on the London Stage in Three Wise Fools, followed by The Skin Game and Pins and Needles. First New York appearance in The Voice from the Minaret, 1922; returned to London as Old Bill, M.P., at the Lyceum, then in Lilac Time (Lyric), Good Luck (Drury Lane), Bubbly, Charlot's Revue, Sleeping Partners, etc. Played Samuel Pepys in And So to Bed for over a year, 1926-27, and then appeared in The Dance of Death, The Monster, The House of the Arrow, These Pretty Things, Exiled, Here Comes the Bride, The Devil's Disciple, Laburnum Grove, etc. Returned to New York Stage and played in The Wookey, The Three Sisters, Sheppey, Laburnum Grove, You Touched Me, The Ravelled Sleeve of Care, etc. Went to Hollywood and made the following films: Anthony Adverse, The Bishop Misbehaves, Sylvia Scarlett, The Walking Dead, The Earl of Chicago, Pride and Prejudice, Foreign Correspondent, Charley's Aunt, Lassie Come Home, The Keys of The Kingdom, Of Human Bondage, Life With Father, Bob, Son of Battle, The Big Heart, Outward Bound, Green Dolphin Street, Bewitched, Undercurrent, Master of Lassie, A Night in Lisbon, Miracle on 34th Street, Apartment for Peggy, Challenge to Lassie, A Woman of Distinction, Pretty Baby, Louisa, Mister Eight-Eighty, For Heaven's Sake, Random Harvest, All American Chump, Parnell, Them, Thunder in the Valley, The Meanest Man in the World, Scotland Yard, Les Miserables, Cheers for Miss Bishop, The Doctor Takes a Wife, The Devil and Miss Jones, Peking Express, A Dog's Life, The Student Prince, Dangerous Partners, She Went to the Races, Something for the Birds, The Scoutmaster, Bonzo Goes to College, Sally and St. Ann, The Bigamist. His other films include: The Good Companions, I was a Spy, Hindle Wakes, Smithy, A Yank at Oxford, Tell Me To-Night, The Admiral's Secret, Penny Paradise, An Englishman's Home, Laburnum Grove, South Riding, The Trouble with Harry, Calabuig, etc. *Address:* 3 Wardrobe Place, Doctors Commons, E.C.4. *Clubs:* Garrick, Beefsteak, Green Room, Arts. [*Died* 6 *Sept.* 1959.

GWYER, Rt. Rev. Herbert Linford, M.A.; *s.* of late John Edward and Edith Gwyer; *m.* 1915, Margaret, *d.* of late William Cairns. *Educ.:* Uppingham; Magdalene College, Cambridge; Westcott House, Cambridge. Curate of Kirkburton, 1906-11; Missionary to Railway Mission in West Canada, Qu'Appelle, 1911-15; Curate of Mirfield, 1915-16; T.C.F., 1916-19; Vicar of Staincliffe, Yorks, 1919-28; Vicar of St. Johns, Wakefield, 1928-37; Hon. Canon Wakefield Cathedral, 1933; Rural Dean of Wakefield, 1936; Bishop of George, 1937-51; Vicar of Amberley, Sussex, 1952-57; Rural Dean of Storrington, 1952-. *Address:* 21 St. Martin's Square, Chichester. [*Died* 18 *Nov.* 1960.

GWYER, Sir Maurice Linford, G.C.I.E., *cr.* 1947; K.C.B., *cr.* 1928 (C.B. 1921); K.C.S.I., *cr.* 1935; *b.* 25 April 1878; *e. s.* of John Edward Gwyer; *m.* 1906, Alsina, *e. d.* of late Sir Henry C. Burdett, K.C.B., K.C.V.O.; one *s.* two *d. Educ.:* Westminster; Christ Church, Oxford. Fellow of All Souls, 1902-16; Hon. Student of Christ Church, 1937; Hon. D.C.L., 1939; Hon. LL.D. (Travancore), 1943; (Patna), 1944; Hon. D.Litt. (Delhi), 1950; called to Bar, Inner Temple, 1903; Hon. Bencher, 1937; Q.C. 1930; Western Circuit; Lecturer in Private International Law, Oxford, 1912-15; Solicitor to Insurance Commissioners, 1912-16; Legal Adviser, Ministry of Shipping, 1917-19; Solicitor and Legal Adviser to Ministry of Health, 1919-26; H.M. Procurator General and Solicitor to the Treasury, 1926-33; First Parliamentary Counsel to the Treasury, 1934-37; Chief Justice of India and Pres. of the Federal Court, 1937-43; Vice-Chancellor of Delhi Univ., 1938-50; member of Royal Commission on London Squares, 1927-1928; first Brit. Delegate to Hague Conference on Codification of International Law, 1930; Member of Indian States Inquiry Committee, 1932; Member of Governing Body, Westminster School, 1936; Hon. Member of Surveyors' Institution, 1937. *Publications:* Editor of Anson's Law of Contract (12th to 16th Edns.); Vol. I. (Parliament) of Anson's Law and Custom of the Constitution; Pollock and Mulla's Indian Contract Act (7th Edn.). *Address:* 14 Kepplestone, Eastbourne, Sussex. *T.:* 845. *Club:* Marlborough-Windham. [*Died* 12 *Oct.* 1952.

GWYNN, John Tudor, C.I.E. 1921; *b.* 13 Nov. 1881; *s.* of Rev. John Gwynn, D.D.; *m.* 1913, Joan Katharine, *d.* of J. D. Sedding; one *s.* two *d. Educ.:* St. Columba's College, Dublin; Trinity College, Dublin. Indian Civil Service, Madras Presidency, 1905; retired from service, 1922; correspondent Manchester Guardian in India, 1922; in Ireland, 1923, 1926-36; Headmaster Baymount Preparatory School, 1936; retired, 1946. *Publication:* Indian Politics, 1924. *Recreation:* cricket. *Address:* 22 Kensington Park, Bangor, Co. Down. [*Died* 17 *May* 1956.

GWYNNE, Rt. Rev. Llewellyn Henry, D.D.; C.M.G. 1917; C.B.E. 1919; LL.D. Cambridge, 1920; D.D. Glasgow, 1919; *b.* 11 June 1863; *s.* of Richard and Charlotte Gwynne, of Kilvey, near Swansea. *Educ.:* Swansea Grammar School; St. John's Hall, Highbury. Curate of St. Chad's, Derby, 1886-89; St. Andrew's, Nottingham, 1889-1892; Vicar of Emmanuel, Nottingham,

1892-99; went out as missionary to Khartoum after the recovery of the Sudan, 1899; Archdeacon of the Sudan, 1905; Volunteer Chaplain with Expeditionary Force in France, Aug. 1914 to Aug. 1915; Deputy Chaplain-General in France, 1915; Bishop of Khartoum; 1908-20; Bishop of Egypt and the Sudan, 1920-45; Bishop in Egypt, 1945-46. *Address:* The Chequers, Epping Uplands, Epping, Essex. *T.:* 2561 Epping. *Club:* National. [*Died* 3 *Dec.* 1957.

GWYNNE, Nevile Gwyn, C.B.E. 1920; M.A., M.I.N.A., M.I.Mech.E.; Director of Gwynne's Pumps Ltd.; Director of Wm. Foster and Co., Lincoln; *b.* 2 Aug. 1868; *s.* of late J. E. A. Gwynne, Folkington Manor, Sussex; *m.* Isabel Violet, *d.* of late Admiral Charles Wake, R.N.; one *s.* three *d.* *Educ.:* Lancing; Pembroke College, Cambridge (M.A.). *Address:* Deans, Piddinghoe, Sussex. *T.:* Newhaven 48. *Club:* Oxford and Cambridge. [*Died* 9 *July* 1951.

GWYNNE-EVANS, Sir Evan Gwynne, 2nd Bt., *cr.* 1913; *b.* 4 May 1877; *s.* of 1st Bt. and Mary Anna (*d.* 1902), *d.* of Evan Williams; *m.* 1908, Ada, *d.* of late W. S. Andrews, New York; two *s.*; *S.* father, 1927. *Educ.:* Eton; Lincoln Coll., Oxford, B.A. High Sheriff of Gloucestershire, 1943. *Heir:* *s.* Ian William, Lieut. Royal Navy [*b.* 21 Feb. 1909; *m.* 1st, 1935, Elspeth, *o. d.* of late Rt. Hon. Sir Godfrey Collins, K.B.E., C.M.G.; two *d.*; 2nd, 1946, Monica Dalrymple, *d.* of late Douglas Clinch, Durban, Natal]. *Address:* Oaklands Park, Newnham, Co. Gloucester. *T.:* Newnham 230. [*Died* 2 *Feb.* 1959.

GYE, Ernest Frederick, C.M.G. 1925; *b.* 1879; *o. c.* of late Ernest Gye and late Dame Emma Albani. Entered Foreign Office, 1903; 2nd Secretary, 1908; Assistant Clerk, 1918; Senior Clerk, 1921; Counsellor, 1924; Minister, Tangier, 1933-36; Minister Plenipotentiary to Venezuela, 1936-39. Retired from H.M. Diplomatic Service, 1939. *Address:* 5 Holmbush Road, S.W.15. *T.:* Putney 8093. *Club:* Garrick. [*Died* 4 *Aug.* 1955.

GYE, William Ewart, F.R.S. 1938; M.D.; F.R.C.P.; Professor Emeritus (lately Professor of Experimental Pathology), Royal College of Surgeons of England; Director, Imperial Cancer Research Fund, 1936-49; *b.* 11 Aug. 1884; *m.* 1st, Elsa Gye (*d.* 1943); three *s.*; 2nd, Ida Mann, C.B.E. *Educ.:* Risley Latin School; Edinburgh University. *Publications:* Scientific papers in many journals. *Address:* c/o Imperial Cancer Research Fund, Mill Hill, N.W.7. [*Died* 13 *Oct.* 1952.

GYI, Sir Joseph Augustus Maung, Kt., *cr.* 1927; *b.* 1872; *m.* Mary (*d.* 1936). Member Executive Council of Governor of Burma, 1926-31; Acting Governor of Burma, 1930; Forest Minister, Burma, 1933-34; President of the Senate, Burma, 1940. Sometime a Judge of the High Court, Rangoon. *Address:* Rangoon, Burma. [*Died* 9 *March* 1955.

H

HAAS, Paul, D.Sc., Ph.D., F.C.S.; Fellow of and formerly Reader on Plant Chemistry at University College, London; Lecturer on Physics and Chemistry, Royal Gardens, Kew; Lecturer on Chemistry at St. Mary's Hospital Medical School and St. Thomas' Hospital Medical School; *b.* London, 1877; *s.* of Dr. E. Haas, Prof. of Sanscrit, U.C. and Librarian to the Brit Museum and India Office; *m.* 1938, Beryl Grace Wood, Rock Ferry, Cheshire; one *s.* *Educ.:* University College Sch.; Univ. College, Univ. of London; Geneva and Freiburg. *Publications:* Laboratory Notes on Organic Chemistry for medical students; An Introduction to the Chemistry of Plant Products (with T. G. Hill). *Address:* 56 Sandy Lane, Cheam, Surrey. *T.:* Vigilant 7379. [*Died* 6 *April* 1960.

HACKFORTH, Edgar, C.B. 1928; *s.* of late Joseph P. Hackforth; *m.* 1909, Joyce, *y. d.* of late Charles E. Clayton, Henfield, Sussex; three *s.* *Educ.:* Westminster School; Trinity College, Cambridge; B.A. 1900; M.A. 1906; Secretary to Brighton Education Committee, 1906-12; Principal, National Health Insurance Commission, 1912-19; Deputy Controller of Health Insurance, 1919-37; Controller of Health Insurance, Ministry of Health, 1937-41; Officer of the Order of the Crown of Belgium, 1918. *Address:* Green Hedges, Gander Hill, Haywards Heath, Sussex. [*Died* 1 *Dec.* 1952.

HACKFORTH, Reginald, F.B.A. 1946; M.A.; Fellow of Sidney Sussex Coll. since 1912; *b.* 17 Aug. 1887; *y. s.* of late J. P. Hackforth; *m.* 1922, Lily, *d.* of late H. R. Mines, H.M. Inspector of Schools. *Educ.:* Westminster School; Trinity College, Cambridge. Assistant Lecturer, University of Manchester, 1910-12; Classical Lecturer, Sidney Sussex College, Cambridge, 1912-39; University Lecturer in Classics, 1926-39; Laurence Prof. of Ancient Philosophy, Cambridge, 1939-52. *Publications:* The Authorship of the Platonic Epistles, 1913; The Composition of Plato's Apology, 1933; Plato's Examination of Pleasure, 1945; Plato's Phædrus, 1952; Plato's Phædo, 1955. Papers in Classical periodicals. *Address:* 4 Selwyn Gardens, Cambridge. *T.:* 3916. [*Died* 6 *May* 1957.

HADATH, Gunby, M.A.; F.R.S.A.; Member of the Inner Temple; author and song writer; *b.* Owersby Vicarage; *o. s.* of late Rev. E. E. Hadath, M.A., and Charlotte Elizabeth, *e. d.* of Rev. John Mowbray Pearson; *m.* Florence Annie, *y. d.* of late William Webber. *Educ.:* St. Edmund's School, Canterbury; Peterhouse, Cambridge. Capt. 6 V.B. Middlesex Regt., 1916-18; Military Representative 57th R.D.R.A., 1916-18; Citoyen d'honneur, of Commune of St. Gervais-les-bains, 1932. Co-trustee of the Benevolent Fund, of the Performing Right Society. *Publications:* Author of numerous popular works for youth in Great Britain, U.S.A., and (in translation) in France and Scandinavia; six books in Braille and author of film, Fortune Lane. Lyrics (Down the Vale; In my Garden; etc.). *Recreation:* reading history. *Address:* 39 Chichele Road, N.W.2.; *T.:* Gladstone 6998. *Club:* Alpine (Français). [*Died* 17 *Jan.* 1954.

HADEN-GUEST, 1st Baron, *cr.* 1950, of Saling, Essex; **Leslie Haden Haden-Guest,** M.C.; author, journalist, doctor; Assistant Opposition Whip, House of Lords, since 1951; *b.* Oldham, 10 March 1877; *s.* of late Alexander Haden Guest, surgeon and physician of Manchester; *m.* 1st, 1898, Edith (*d.* 1908), *d.* of Max Low, London; two *s.*; 2nd, 1910, Muriel Carmel (*d.* 1943), *d.* of late Col. Albert Goldsmid, M.V.O.; one *s.* one *d.* (and one *s.* decd.); 3rd, 1944, Edith Edgar, *d.* of late George Macqueen. *Educ.:* William Hulme's Gram. Sch.; Owens Coll., Manchester; London Hosp. Served S.African War, European War, 1914-18, and War of 1939-45. Founder of Anglo-French Com. of Red Cross Society and Order of St. John; M.P. (Lab.) North Southwark, 1923-27; M.P. (Lab.) North Islington, 1937-45 and 1945-50; Founder Labour Party Commonwealth Group; L.C.C. Woolwich (East), 1919-22; Member Empire Parliamentary Delegation to Newfoundland and Canada, 1925; travelled extensively, 1919-37; Member of Parliamentary Committee on Evacuation of Civil Population, 1938; Member West Africa Commission to Nigeria, Gold Coast, etc., 1938-39. Vice-Chairman Med. Parliamentary Group; a Lord-in-Waiting to the King, Feb.-Oct. 1951. *Publications:* various. *Recreations:* riding and travelling.

Heir: s. Hon. Stephen Haden Guest, b. 7 June 1902. *Address:* Hitchcocks, Little Saling, Essex; 44 Westminster Palace Gardens, Artillery Row, S.W.1.
[*Died* 20 *Aug.* 1960.

HADLEY, Arthur Edward, C.B.E. 1918; formerly Assistant Controller of Inspection Dept., Ministry of Munitions; b. 1870; s. of Edward Alfred Hadley, M.A.; m. 1914, Clare Louise, d. of William Robert Shuff; one s. *Educ.:* Charterhouse. Chairman of the Victoria Falls and Transvaal Power Company; Chairman of Rhodesia Railways Ltd.; Director of British South Africa Co.; Member of Institution of Electrical Engineers; awarded the Premium of the Institution for the year 1913. *Recreations:* tennis, skating. *Address:* Haworth, Sheringham, Norfolk.
[*Died* 8 *April* 1954.

HADLEY, William Waite. Trained as a journalist on Northampton Mercury; editor of Merthyr Tydfil Times, 1892-93; of Rochdale Observer, 1893-1908; Managing Editor, Northampton Daily Echo and Northampton Mercury, 1908-23; Parliamentary Correspondent and leader writer Daily Chronicle, 1924-30; Editor Sunday Times, 1932-50. *Publication:* Munich: Before and After, 1944. *Address:* Innisfree, Bramshott Chase, Hindhead, Surrey. *T.:* Hindhead 500.
[*Died* 16 *Dec.* 1960.

HADWICK, Sir William, Kt., cr. 1950; Chief General Manager, National Provincial Bank, Ltd., since 1945; Director of Lloyds and National Provincial Foreign Bank Ltd.; Member Export Credits Advisory Council; Member Council Associated British Chambers of Commerce; b. 17 Jan. 1891; s. of Charles and Sarah Anne Hadwick; m. 1915, Nellie, d. of Walter and Edith Rhodes, Bradford; one s. *Educ.:* Hanson School, Bradford. Entered Bradford Commercial Joint Stock Bank, 1908; served War of 1914-18 in Artists' Rifles and Green Howards; General Manager, National Provincial Bank, 1931. *Address:* Hollingbourne, Cobham, Surrey. *T.:* Cobham 115. [*Died* 30 *Oct.* 1951.

HAGAN, Very Rev. Edward J., O.B.E.; D.D.; Minister Emeritus of Warrender, Edinburgh; b. 6 April 1879; s. of Capt. S. Hagan, Belfast; m. 1908, Agnes Pairman, d. of J. Ford Cormack, Writer, Lockerbie, Dumfriesshire; no c. *Educ.:* Royal Acad. Inst., and Queen's University, Belfast; New College, Edinburgh. Minister at Cockenzie, Elgin (High Church), Glasgow (Gilmorehill Church). Chaplain in France, 1915-18 (despatches, O.B.E.). Moderator of General Assembly of Church of Scotland, 1944; President Presbyterian Alliance, 1948-1954. *Publication:* Makers of the Early Church, 1930. *Recreation:* European travel. *Address:* 12 Bruntsfield Gardens, Edinburgh 10. *T.:* Fountainbridge 8266.
[*Died* 11 *Jan.* 1956.

HAGART-SPEIRS, Alexander A.; *see* Speirs.

HAGGARD, Admiral Sir Vernon (Harry Stuart), K.C.B., cr. 1932 (C.B. 1925); C.M.G. 1918; J.P., D.L., Essex; b. Buxar, Bengal, 28 Oct. 1874; s. of late Alfred Hinuber Haggard, Bengal C.S.; m. 1905, Dorothy, d. of Richard Adam Ellis, Stock, Essex; one s. three d. Entered Royal Navy, 1888; Lt. 1896; Comdr. 1906; Capt. 1913; Rear-Adm. 1923; Vice-Adm. 1928; Adm. 1932; served Benin Expedition, 1897; European War, 1914-1918; commanded H.M. ships Boadicea, 1911; Blenheim, 1912; Good Hope, 1913; Vulcan, 1913; Hibernia, 1915; Highflyer, 1917; R.N. Brigade on the Danube, 1919; H.M.S. Ajax, 1920-21; Director of Training and Staff Duties at the Admiralty, 1921-23; Chief of Submarine Service, 1925-27; Fourth Sea Lord and Chief of Supplies and Transport, 1928-30; Commander-in-Chief, America and West Indies Station, 1930-32; retired list, 1932; Croix de Guerre. *Address:* Littlecourt, Stock, Essex. *Club:* United Service. [*Died* 30 *Jan.* 1960.

HAGGITT, Very Rev. Percy Bolton, M.A.; Dean Emeritus of Nelson, N.Z.; b. 19 May 1878; s. of D'Arcy and Caroline Haggitt; m. 1st, 1907, Kathleen Graham; two d. (one s. killed, War of 1939-45); 2nd, 1932, Elsie Dawe. *Educ.:* Otago Boys' High School, Dunedin; Otago University; Selwyn College, Cambridge. Deacon, 1903; Priest, 1904; Curate St. Michael and All Angels, Christchurch, 1903-6; Chiswick Parish, London, 1906-7; Precentor, Christchurch Cathedral, N.Z., 1907-9; Vicar St. Alban's, Christchurch, 1915-33; Vicar of Merivale, 1915-34; Archdeacon of Christchurch, 1918-34; Dean of Nelson and Vicar of Cathedral Parish, 1934, retd.; Commissary in charge of Diocese, 1940 and 1948. *Address:* 32 Chapter St., Christchurch, New Zealand. [*Died* 10 *March* 1957.

HAGUE, Sir Harry, Kt., cr. 1931; o. s. of late Councillor James Hague, Blackpool; m. 1913, Lily, o. d. of Thomas Kenyon, Blackpool; one s. *Educ.:* Bury Grammar School; The Northern College. Chairman Blackfriars Skin Hospital, 1931-45; Chairman Industrial Orthopædic Society, 1932, 1937, 1938; President British Percheron Horse Society, 1945; President Royal Warrant Holders' Association, 1957. *Recreation:* horticulture. *Address:* 42 Upper Grosvenor St., Grosvenor Square, W.1. *T.:* Grosvenor 3931; The Chantry, Elstree, Herts. *T.:* 1155.
[*Died* 19 *Oct.* 1960.

HAIG, Lieut.-Col. Alan Gordon, C.M.G. 1919; D.S.O. 1916; late R.A.; b. 1877; s. of H. A. Haig; m. 1905, Mary Astley (d. 1951), d. of John Bromwich, Southborough, Kent; two s. *Educ.:* Winchester College. Served South African War, 1900-2 (Queen's medal and three clasps, King's medal and two clasps); European War, 1914-19 (despatches, C.M.G., D.S.O., Bt. Lt.-Col.); retired pay, 1922. *Address:* Kingsmere, Shawford, near Winchester. [*Died* 22 *Dec.* 1951.

HAIG, General Sir (Arthur) Brodie, K.C.B., cr. 1942 (C.B. 1937), M.C.; b. 31 Jan. 1886; y. s. of Henry Alexander Haig; m. 1919, Marguerite Theodora Hyde, d. of H. T. Wadley. *Educ.:* Winchester College. 24th Punjabis, I.A., 1906; served European War, Suez Canal and Mesopotamia (prisoner despatches twice, M.C. and Bar); G.S.O. 2, India, 1922; Instructor, Staff College, Quetta, 1923-26; commanded 4/14th Punjab Regt. (late 24th Punjabis), 1930-32; G.S.O. 1, India, 1932-33; commanded 7th Dehra Dun Inf. Bde., 1933-35; D.A. and Q.M.G., Eastern Command, India, 1936-37; Comdt. Staff Coll., Quetta, 1937-40; Quartermaster General in India, 1940-41; Adj.-Gen., India, 1941; G.O.C.-in-C., Southern Command, India, 1941; retired, 1942. *Address:* Baringa, Grouville, Jersey, C.I.
[*Died* 9 *Feb.* 1957.

HAIG, Colonel Claude Henry, C.B.E. 1925; D.S.O. 1917; late Leicesters Regt.; 2nd s. of late Henry Alexander Haig and Agnes Catherine, d. of Matthew Pollock; b. 16 Jan. 1874; m. 1905, Mabel, d. of Sir Horatio Davies. *Educ.:* Winchester College. Served S. Africa, 1899-1902 (Queen's medal 5 clasps, King's medal 2 clasps); European War, 1914-18 (D.S.O., Bt. Lieut.-Col.); retired pay, 1926. *Address:* Mells Lodge, Halesworth, Suffolk.
[*Died* 12 *Nov.* 1955.

HAIG, Sir Harry Graham, K.C.S.I., cr. 1933 (C.S.I. 1930); C.I.E. 1923; b. 13 April 1881; 4th s. of late Henry Alexander Haig; m. 1908, Violet May (K.I.H. Gold Medal, 1936), d. of Joseph Deas, late I.C.S.; three s. *Educ.:* Winchester; New College, Oxford; 1st Class Lit. Hum., 1904. Entered I.C.S., 1905; Under-Secretary to Government, U.P., 1910-12; Indian Army Reserve of Officers, 1915-19; Deputy Secretary to Government of India, Finance Department, 1920; Secretary Indian Fiscal Commission, 1921-22; attached to Royal Commission on Superior Civil Services in India, 1923-34; Private Secretary to the Viceroy, 1925; Secretary to the Government of India, Home Department, 1926-30; Home Member of Executive Council of Governor-General, India, 1932-34; Governor of United Provinces, 1934-39; Regional Commissioner for Civil Defence in the North West Region, 1940-41, in the Southern Region, 1942-45. *Address:* Valelands, Oxted, Surrey. *T.:* Oxted 887. *Club:* Athenæum. [*Died* 14 *June* 1956.

HAIG, Brig.-General Roland Charles, D.S.O. 1915; *b.* 1 Feb. 1873; *o. s.* of Charles Edwin Haig, Pen-Ithon, Radnors.; *m.* 1899, Geraldine Dorothy, *e. d.* of Rev. Beauchamp K. W. Kerr-Pearse, Bats Park, Somerset. Entered 16th Lancers, 1894; Special Reserve R. Brigade, 1907; retired, 1923; S. African War, 1900 (Queen's medal 4 clasps); European War, 1914-18 (despatches 5 times, D.S.O. and two bars, Bt. Lt.-Col.). *Address:* 62 Marine Parade, Hythe, Kent; Pen Ithon, Newtown, Mont., N. Wales. *Club:* Army and Navy. [*Died* 28 *Feb.* 1953.

HAIG, Lieut.-Col. Wolseley de Haga, C.I.E. 1939; D.S.O. 1918; late R.E.; *b.* 1884; *s.* of William Spencer Haig; *m.* 1909, Katherine Chittenden (*d.* 1951), 2nd *d.* of C. A. Murray, Burlington, Vermont; *m.* 1951, Jacqueline, *widow* of Lewis Barber, Tenterden, Kent. Served European War, 1914-18 (despatches four times, D.S.O., Brevet-Majority); Lieut.-Col. 1929; Chief Engineer P.W.D., Lucknow, India; retired, 1939. *Address:* c/o National Provincial Bank, St. Helier, Jersey, C.I. [*Died* 25 *June* 1960.

HAIGH, Sir Fred, Kt., *cr.* 1952; Director John Halliday & Sons Ltd., Textile Cloth Manufacturers, since 1924; *b.* 25 July 1889; *s.* of Charles and Adeline Haigh; *m.* 1915, Julia Gladys (*d.* 1953), *d.* of William Wilde Bland, Bradford, Yorkshire; one *d.* *Educ.:* Carlton Commercial School, Bradford; Bradford Technical College. Joined John Halliday & Sons Ltd., 1904 (Director 1924). President: Bradford and District Manufacturers' Fed., 1939-47, Life member 1952; Woollen and Worsted Trades Fed., 1946-50; Chairman: Wool Textile Delegation, 1947-53; Wool (and Allied) Textile Employers' Council, 1939-54; Nat. Wool Textile Export Corp., 1951-52; Council Wool Textile Research Assoc., 1949-52; Employer Member Wool Working Party; 1945-46; Jt. Rationing Cttee. (Wool Control), and West Riding Rationing Cttee. (Wool Control), 1939-48. Provost's Warden, Bradford Cathedral, 1945-1950. Long service Medal, 1948 (25 years West Riding Special Constabulary). *Recreations:* formerly tennis, golf; also reading. *Address:* 30 Bankfield Drive, Nab Wood, Shipley, Yorkshire. *T.:* Shipley 53918. [*Died* 17 *Dec.* 1954.

HAINE, Paymaster-Commander Alec Ernest, C.M.G. 1919; R.N., retired; *b.* 1885; *s.* of Robert Webb Haine; *m.* 1922, May Morrish. Served European War, 1914-19 (despatches, C.M.G.); African General Service Medal, Somaliland, 1902-4, clasp. *Address:* Crossways, Crewkerne, Somerset. [*Died* 29 *Dec.* 1953.

HAILEY, Hammett Reginald Clode, C.I.E. 1916; C.B.E. 1919; B.A., late I.C.S. *Educ.:* Merchant Taylors' School; St. John's College, Oxford. Entered I.C.S. 1892; Joint Magistrate, 1899; Deputy Commissioner, 1905; Joint-Secretary, Board of Revenue, 1906; Director of Land Records and Agriculture, U.P., 1912; Commissioner, 1920; retired 1924. *Address:* 7 Chadlington Road, Oxford. [*Died* 25 *Dec.* 1960.

HAINES, Air Commodore Harold Alfred, C.B.E. 1943; D.F.C; M.A.; *b.* 22 Nov. 1899; *s.* of A. T. Haines, Coombe Wood, Salcombe Regis, Sidmouth, Devon; *m.* 1925, Phyllis Mary Riches; one *s.* one *d.* *Educ.:* City of London School; Peterhouse, Cambridge. R.N.A.S., 1917-18; R.A.F., 1918; Dir. of Aircraft Safety, 1943; Commandant Royal Air Force Regiment Depot, 1945; retired, 1948. *Recreation:* penmanship. *Club:* Royal Automobile. [*Died* 26 *June* 1955.

HAINING, General Sir Robert Hadden, K.C.B., *cr.* 1940 (C.B. 1936); D.S.O. 1915; late R.A.; Lord Lieutenant of Surrey, 1949-57; *b.* 28 July 1882; *e. s.* of late Dr. Wm. Haining; *m.* Hilda, *d.* of late Towry Piper. *Educ.:* Uppingham (Scholar); R.M.A., Woolwich. Entered Army, 1901; Capt., 1914; Major, 1915; Bt. Lt.-Col., 1918; Col., 1922; Major-Gen., 1934; Lt.-Gen., 1938; General, 1941; served European War, 1914-18 (despatches six times, D.S.O., Bt. Lt.-Col.) p.s.c.; Barrister-at-law, Lincoln's Inn, 1919; Imperial Defence College, 1927; A.A. and Q.M.G. Second Division, Aldershot, 1928-29; G.S.O.1 4th Div. Colchester, 1930-31; M.O.1 War Office, 1931-33; Deputy Director of Military Operations and Intelligence, War Office, 1933-34; Commandant Imperial Defence College, 1935-36; Director of Military Operations and Intelligence, War Office, 1936-38; General Officer Commanding British Forces in Palestine and Trans-Jordan, 1938-39; G.O.C. in C., Western Command, 1939-40; Vice-Chief Imperial General Staff, 1940-41; Intendant-General, Middle East, 1941-42; retired pay, 1942; Col. Comdt. R.A., 1939-50. J.P. Surrey; C.A. Surrey; Chairman Farnham Bench, 1943. *Address:* Chart House, Ash Vale, Surrey. *Clubs:* United Service, Athenæum. [*Died* 15 *Sept.* 1959.

HAIRE, Very Rev. James, M.A. (Royal Univ. of Ireland and Queen's Univ., Belfast), B.D. (Lond.), D.D. (St. Andrews). Professor of Theology, General Assembly's College, Belfast, and a Dean of Residences, Queen's University, Belfast until retirement, 1944. Moderator of the General Assembly of the Presbyterian Church in Ireland, 1939. *Address:* College Park, Belfast. [*Died* 12 *Oct.* 1959.

HAIRE, Norman, Ch.M., M.B.; J.P. State of N.S.W.; Sexologist, Gynæcologist and Obstetrician; President Sex Education Society; F.R.S.M.; Member (late Councillor) British Society for Study of Sex Psychology; Member Harveian Society; Freeman, City of London; *b.* Sydney, Australia, 1892; 11th and *y. c.* of Henryk and Clara Zajac; unmarried. *Educ.:* Fort Street School; Sydney University; Sydney Hospital; Institut fuer Sexualwissenschaft, Berlin. Formerly Resident Medical Officer, Hospital for Sick Children, Brisbane; No. 4 Australian General Hospital; N.S.W. State Mental Hospitals; Chief R.M.O. Royal Hospital for Women, Sydney; Medical Superintendent Newcastle Hospital, N.S.W.; Casualty Physician and Surgeon and House Surgeon, Hampstead General Hospital, London; Clinical Assistant, London Lock Hospital; Hon. Medical Officer, Saffron Hill Maternity Centre London; Hon. Medical Director Cromer Welfare Sunlight and Birth Control Centre; Co-President World League for Sexual Reform; after settling in England in 1919, took an active part in the Birth Control movement; in 1921 was one of the founders and Medical Officer-in-Charge of the Walworth Welfare Centre—the first British Welfare Centre to give contraceptive advice to its patients; English delegate to Birth Control Conference at Amsterdam, 1921; President, Contraceptive Section, 5th International Birth Control Conference, London, 1922; has studied and taught in five continents; English delegate to 6th International Birth Control Conference, New York, 1925; attended the First International Congress for Sexual Research, Berlin, 1926, as official representative of American Birth Control League and International Birth Control League; organised 3rd International Congress of W.L.S.R. London, 1929; Capt. A.A.M.C. 1915-19; formerly Councillor, New Education Fellowship, N.S.W. and Member N.S.W. State Executive, W.E.A. *Publications:* Hygienic Methods

of Family Limitation, 1922; Technique of Contraception, 1923; Birth Control in relation to Infant and Child Welfare, 1924; Recent Developments of Steinach's Work, 1921; Rejuvenation, the work of Steinach, Voronoff and others, 1924; various lectures and articles on Sex; Comparative Value of Current Contraceptive Methods; Marriage; The Truth about Rejuvenation; Hymen: the Future of Marriage, 1927; Some More Medical Views on Birth Control, 1928; How I Run My Birth Control Centre, 1928; Sterilisation, Abortion and Birth Control, 1929; Vorlaeufiger Bericht Uber Das Haire-Pessar und Den Intrauterinen Silberring, 1930; Zehnjaehrige intensive Erfahrungen ueber Praeventivverkehr, 1932; Birth Control Methods, 1936; translator of Rutgers' The Sexual Life, 1923 and Bauer's Woman, 1926; Editor Boelsche's Love-Life in Nature, 1931, Man and Woman in Marriage, 1932, Man into Woman, 1933, Sex Life and Sex Ethics, 1933; Encyclopædia of Sexual Knowledge, 1934; Sex Problems of Today, 1942; Sex Talks, 1946; Everyday Sex Problems, 1949; Editor Journal of Sex Education. Editor, International Library of Psychology and Sexology; Asst. Editor, Sexus; Member Comité de Rédaction, Le Problème Sexuel, and International Board of Editors, Anthropos. Also writes under the pseudonym Wykeham Terriss. *Address:* 127 Harley Street, W.1. *T.:* Welbeck 7840; Nettleden Lodge, Hemel Hempstead, Herts. *T.:* Berkhamsted 688; 193 Macquarie Street, Sydney, Australia. *T.:* BW 9849.
[*Died* 11 *Sept.* 1952.

HAKE, Sir Henry M., *cr.* Kt., 1947; C.B.E. 1933; F.S.A.; F.R.Hist.S.; Director National Portrait Gallery since 1927; *b.* London, 30 Jan. 1892; *s.* of late Henry Wilson Hake, Ph.D., F.I.C., F.C.S.; *m.* 1920, Patricia, *d.* of late Rev. James Robertson. *Educ.:* Westminster School; Trinity College, Cambridge. Assistant in Dept. of Prints and Drawings, British Museum, 1914; served European War, 1915-19 (Croix de Guerre); Hon. Treasurer of the Walpole Society. *Publications:* Catalogue of Engraved British Portraits in the British Museum, Vol. V. (part) and Vol. VI.; various papers. *Recreation:* fishing. *Address:* 11 Cadogan Mansions, Sloane Square, S.W.1. *Club:* Oxford and Cambridge.
[*Died* 4 *April* 1951.

HALCROW, Sir William Thomson, Kt., *cr.* 1944; M.I.C.E.; Consulting Civil Engineer; *b.* 4 July 1883; *o. s.* of late J. A. Halcrow, Redmain, Cumberland. *Educ.:* George Watson's College, Edinburgh; Edinburgh University. Articled to late P. W. and C. S. Meik, MM.I.C.E.; Assistant and Resident Engineer to them on various dock. harbour and water power works at home and abroad; Chief Engineer on King George V graving-dock, Singapore, 1910; submarine defences, Scapa Flow, 1915-18; Johore Causeway, 1919-21; Partner, 1921, late C. S. Meik; principal consultant of firm under style Sir William Halcrow and Partners; professional work widely spread in Europe, Africa, South America, and Far East includes Docks and Harbours, Dams, Tunnels and Hydro-electric Schemes; consulting engineer to Government Departments Dominion and Colonial Governments, London Transport Executive (for tube railways) and to other Public Corporations and Companies; Member of War Cabinet Engineering Advisory Committee; Chairman: Panel of Engineers for design of Mulberry Harbour; Advisory Council of Building and Civil Engineering Industries to Minister of Works; Panel, Advisers on Severn Barrage to Minister of Fuel and Power; on Panel advising Rhodesian Govt. on Kariba and Kafue hydro-electric schemes; on Panel advising Minister of Transport on scheme for subaqueous road crossing of Firth of Forth; Advisory Council of D.S.I.R.; formerly Member Royal Fine Art Commission; Hon. Consulting Engineer to Imperial War Graves Commn.; Member of Advisory Council on Science and Technology, Festival of Britain, 1951; Past-President Institution of Civil Engineers (Telford Gold Medal, 1930); Smeatonian Soc. of Civil Engineers, 1954; Hon. Mem. Institution of Royal Engineers; Past Chairman Assoc. of Consulting Engineers; Past Pres. British Section Société des Ingénieurs Civils de France (Prix Annuel Gold Medal, 1939); Col.-Comdt. Engineer and Railway Staff Corps R.E. (T.A.), 1948-49. Chevalier de la Légion d'Honneur; Officier de l'Ordre d'Étoile Noir. *Publications:* engineering papers. *Recreations:* golf, fishing, music. *Address:* Alliance House, Caxton Street, S.W.1. *Clubs:* Athenæum, Royal Thames Yacht, Hurlingham; Radnor (Folkestone).
[*Died* 31 *Oct.* 1958.

HALDANE, Henry Chicheley, O.B.E.; *b.* 10 May 1872; *s.* of James Haldane and Emily Sophia Grove; *m.* 1908, Norah Bowden; one *d.* *Educ.:* Charterhouse; B.N.C. Oxford. Admitted Solicitor, 1897; Member of the Council of the Law Society, 1932-44; Member of the Lord Chancellor's Law Revision Committee; served in France, 1915-19 (despatches 5 times, O.B.E.). *Address:* 35 Moray Pl., Edinburgh, 3.
[*Died* 18 *May* 1957.

HALDANE, Sir William Stowell, Kt., *cr.* 1912; Writer to the Signet; B.L. Edin.; *b.* Edinburgh, 1864; *y. s.* of Robert Haldane of Cloanden, W.S., and Mary Elizabeth Burdon Sanderson; *m.* 1892, Edith (*d.* 1943), *e. d.* of Thomas Nelson of Achnacloich, publisher; two *s.* one *d.* *Educ.:* Edinburgh Academy and Univ. Admitted to Society of Writers to the Signet, 1888; Crown Agent for Scotland and Prison Commissioner, 1905-17; Commissioner under the Development Fund Act, 1910-39. *Address:* Cloan, Auchterarder, Perthshire. *T.:* Auchterarder 100. *Clubs:* Brooks's; University (Edinburgh).
[*Died* 7 *Nov.* 1951.

HALDIN, Sir Philip Edward, Kt., *cr.* 1939; Chairman of Haldin and Co. Ltd., Shipowners, London; *b.* 24 March 1880; *m.* 1917, Edna, *d.* of late D. Neville-Cohen, Sydney, New South Wales; one *s.* one *d.* *Educ.:* Harrow. President of the Chamber of Shipping of the U.K., 1940-41; Member of Ministry of War Transport Shipping Advisory Council, 1940-45; mem. of General Council of British Shipping; Advisory Cttee. on Merchant Shipbuilding, 1940-44; Mem. of Tramp Shipping Subsidy Cttee. and of Tramp Shipping Administrative Cttee., 1935-37; Member Shipping Defence Advisory Cttee., Admiralty, 1940-51; Member of Executive Councils of Chamber of Shipping of the U.K. and Shipping Federation of Great Britain; Member of Executive Committee of London General Shipowners Society; First hon. member Executive Cttee. of West of England Protection and Indemnity Association (Chairman, 1940-53); Liveryman of Worshipful Company of Skinners. *Recreations:* shooting, golf. *Address:* Lympne Place, Lympne, Kent. *T.:* Hythe 6183; 16 Devonshire Street, W.1. *T.:* Langham 6247. *Clubs:* Reform, Royal Automobile.
[*Died* 7 *Nov.* 1953.

HALE, Mrs. G. van B.; *see* Burke, Kathleen.

HALE, John Howard; R.B.A. 1920; F.R.S.A. 1928; F.S.A.M. 1908; retired, 1929; Instructor and Director of the Blackheath School of Arts and Crafts, 1887-1928; Chairman Eltham Arts and Crafts Society, 1922-25; *b.* 16 June 1863; *o. s.* of late J. Hale, Farnham, Surrey; unmarried. *Educ.:* Farnham Grammar School; privately; Westminster and South Kensington (now R.C.A.) Schools of Art. Commenced the study of Art at a very early age; Fellow of the Society of Art Masters, 1908; paints both portraits and landscapes; has exhibited at Royal Academy, Institute of Painters in Oils, Royal Society of British Artists, Paris Salon; invited to exhibit at the British Section of the

Canadian National Exhibition, Toronto, Canada, 1935, etc. Pictures: The Laughing Gipsy; The Startled Nymph; Dawn, etc.; organised and directed Craft Education for Convalescent Soldiers at the Bermondsey Military Hospital during the World War. Assisted in starting Art Dept. of Goldsmiths' Institute (now Goldsmiths' College), 1891-94; organised Art Section Woolwich Polytechnic, 1892-1904. *Recreations:* sketching, golf. *Address:* The White Cottage, 13 High Park Road, Farnham, Surrey.
[*Died* 15 *April* 1955.

HALES, Ven. John Percy, D.S.O. 1917; O.B.E. 1931; T.D.; *b.* Birstwith, Yorks, 7 Oct. 1870; *y. s.* of George and Anne Hales; *m.* 1898, Augusta Margaret, *e. d.* of Col. and Mrs. Cantrell-Hubbersty; one *s.* four *d.* *Educ.:* Winchester; Jesus College, Cambridge, M.A. Deacon, 1893; Priest, 1895; Rector of Cotgrave, Nottingham, 1897-1924; Rector of Gedling, Notts, 1924-37; Rural Dean of Gedling, 1929-37; Hon. Canon of Southwell Minster, 1931-36; Archdeacon of Newark, 1936-46, emeritus since 1946; Chaplain to 8th Sherwood Foresters, 1913, and to the Sherwood Foresters Territorial Brigade, 1915, on its leaving for service abroad; Div. Chaplain, 1916; Temp. Deputy Assistant Chaplain-General, 12 Feb. 1918; Senior Chaplain 46th North Midland Division, 1922. *Address:* Hill House, Southwell, Notts. *T.:* Southwell 3268.
[*Died* 6 *Sept.* 1952.

HALFORD, Frank Bernard, C.B.E. 1948; Major; Chairman and Technical Director, de Havilland Engine Co. since 1944; Director of de Havilland Aircraft Co.; *b.* 7 March 1894; *s.* of late H. B. Halford and of Ethel Halford, Nottingham; *m.*; one *d.*; *m.* 1939, Marjorie Moore, London. *Educ.:* Felsted School; Nottingham University. Instructor, Bristol School of Flying, 1913; served European War, 1914-18, in R.F.C. and R.A.F., 1914-19. For Wm. Beardmore designed B.H.P. and 160 Beardmore; independent designer of aero engines from 1922. Responsible for design of Cirrus, Aidisco, Napier, Nimbus; Rapier, Dagger, and Sabre; de Havilland Gipsy, Goblin, and Ghost engines. President Royal Aeronautical Society, 1951. *Address:* Monkbarns, Sandy Lane, Northwood, Middx. *T.:* Northwood, 2027. *Clubs:* R.A.F., Royal Aero.
[*Died* 16 *April* 1955.

HALIFAX, 1st Earl of (*cr.* 1944), **Edward Frederick Lindley Wood,** K.G. 1931; P.C. 1922; O.M. 1946; G.C.S.I. 1926; G.C.M.G. 1957; G.C.I.E. 1926; T.D.; Hon. R.A. 1941; 3rd Viscount Halifax, *cr.* 1866; 1st Baron Irwin, *cr.* 1925; Bt. 1784; High Steward of Westminster since 1947; Chancellor of University of Oxford since 1933, of Sheffield, 1948-59; Chancellor of Order of the Garter since 1943; Grand Master of the Order of St. Michael and St. George since 1957; *b.* 16 April 1881; *o. surv. s.* of 2nd Viscount Halifax and Lady Agnes Elizabeth Courtenay (*d.* 1919), *o. d.* of 11th Earl of Devon; *S.* father, 1934; *m.* 1909, Lady Dorothy Evelyn Augusta Onslow, C.I. 1926, D.C.V.O. 1953, D.St.J. (an Extra Lady of the Bedchamber to Queen Elizabeth the Queen Mother since 1946), *yr. d.* of 4th Earl of Onslow; two *s.* (and one killed in action, 1942) one *d.* *Educ.:* Eton; Christ Church, and All Souls, Oxford (M.A., Fellow). Parliamentary Under-Secretary for the Colonies, 1921-22; President of Board of Education, Oct. 1922-Jan. 1924; Minister of Agriculture, Oct. 1924-Nov. 1925; M.P. (U.) Ripon Division, West Riding, Yorks., January 1910-25; Viceroy of India, 1926-1931; President of the Board of Education, 1932-35; Secretary of State for War, 1935; Lord Privy Seal, 1935-37; Leader of the House of Lords, 1935-38 and 1940; Lord President of the Council, 1937-38; Secretary of State for Foreign Affairs, 1938-40; British Ambassador at Washington, 1941-46. Formerly Lieut.-Col. Yorkshire Dragoons Yeo. (Hon. Col. 1935). Hon. Freedom of: Fishmongers' Company, Grocers' Company, Weavers' Company. J.P. East and West Riding of Yorks. Hon. M.I.C.E. Hon. LL.D. Leeds, 1923, Cambridge, St. Andrews, Sheffield, 1931, Toronto, 1932, Dublin, Liverpool, London, 1934, Columbia, Yale, Harvard, 1941, Syracuse, Princeton, 1942, Laval, Quebec, Idaho Puget Sound, Tacoma, Louisville, 1943, Cincinnati, 1944, Manchester, 1948, Athens, 1952; Hull, 1957; Hon. D.C.L. Oxford, 1932, Durham, 1933, Univ. of the South, Sewanee, 1942, Boston, 1944; Hon. Dr., Grenoble, 1939; Hon. Dr. Canon Law, Philadelphia, 1942; Hon. Doctor of Humanities, Wesleyan Univ., Ohio, 1942. K.St.J. *Publications:* John Keble, in Leaders of the Church series; The Great Opportunity (with Lord Lloyd); Indian Problems, 1932; Speeches on Foreign Policy, 1940; Fulness of Days, 1957. *Heir: s.* Lord Irwin, D.L. *Address:* Garrowby, York; 7 Kingston House North, Princes Gate, S.W.7. *T.:* Kensington 4912. *Clubs:* Athenæum, Carlton, Brooks's; Yorkshire (York).
[*Died* 23 *Dec.* 1959.

HALKETT, Brig.-General Hugh Marjoribanks Craigie, C.M.G. 1919, D.S.O. 1917; late Highland Light Infantry; *b.* 1880; *o. surv. s.* of late Colonel C. Craigie Halkett; *m.* 1922, Violet Mary Ella, *e. d.* of late Robert Stuart Dalzell, Glen Ae, Dumfriesshire, and late Mrs. Dalzell, 3 St. Leonard's Road, Exeter; one *s.* three *d.* Served South African War, 1900-2 (Queen's medal and two clasps, King's medal and two clasps); Somaliland, 1904 (medal and clasp); Nandi Expedition, 1905-6 (clasp); Sudan, 1912 (medal and clasp); European War, 1914-18 (despatches, Bt. Lt.-Col. C.M.G., D.S.O., and 2 bars); retired pay, 1928 *Address:* Silver Birches, Bromham Road, Bedford. *T.:* Bedford 2619.
[*Died* 1 *Aug.* 1952.

HALL, Alfred, M.A. (Manchester); B.D. (London); D.D. (Meadville Theological School, U.S.A.); Unitarian Minister, retired; *b.* Boston, Lincs, 27 April 1873; 2nd *s.* of Alfred Hall, mariner, Boston; *m.* 1903, Amy (*d.* 1958), *e. d.* of John Sudbery, London; one *s.* four *d.* (and one *s.* one *d.* decd.). *Educ.:* Boston Grammar School; Unitarian College and Owen's College, Manchester; Manchester College (Tate Scholar), and St. Catherine's, Oxford University; Berlin University, Hibbert Scholar. Minister, Octagon Chapel, Norwich, 1900-8; Church of Divine Unity, Newcastle, 1908-18; Upper Chapel, Sheffield, 1918-39; Lincoln Unitarian Church, 1939-49. President of the General Assembly of Unitarian and Free Christian Churches, 1932-34; Pres. of the International Association for Liberal Christianity and Religious Freedom, 1934-37; President, Manchester College, Oxford, 1945-49. *Publications:* The Story of James Martineau; Fifty Points in Favour of Unitarianism; Jesus and Christianity in the Twentieth Century; Editor and Joint Author of Aspects of Modern Unitarianism; Religious Problems of the Layman; The Beliefs of a Unitarian; Human Forggiveness. *Address:* Dunham Road Parsonage, Altrincham. *T.:* Altrincham 0246.
[*Died* 18 *Dec.* 1958.

HALL, Anmer; *see* Horne, A. B.

HALL, Instructor Rear-Adm. Sir Arthur Edward, K.B.E., *cr.* 1945 (C.B.E. 1935; O.B.E. 1925); C.B. 1939; C.St.J.; A.R C.S.; Fellow Imperial College; Fellow Institute of Navigation; English Association (Treas., 1939-43 and 1950-1951, Vice-Chm., 1944-46, Chm., 1947-49 and since 1951); Chm. Royal School for Naval and Marine Officers' daughters since 1943; Governor, Imperial College of Science and Technology; Hon. Vice-Pres., Institute of Naval Architects, Treasurer since 1945; Treasurer, Navy Records Society, since 1949; Glass Advisory Committee, Sheffield University; Chairman R.N. Scholarship Fund since 1950; R.N. Benevolent Soc. Cttee.; *b.* 1 Feb. 1885; *s.* of Charles Edward Hall, J.P., and Emma Jane Hall; *m.* 1920, Constance Martha Gibbens; one *s.* one *d.* *Educ.:* The College, Swindon; Royal College of Science, London. Lecturer, Sir John Cass Institute, 1907-9; Physics Dept. Imperial College of Science, 1909-15; entered R.N., 1915; H.M.S. Inflexible (Jutland), 1916-18; R.N. College, Dartmouth, 1918-21; H.M.S. Thunderer, 1921-22; R.N. Eng. College, Keyham, 1922-26; H.M.S. Renown, 1926-27; Fleet Education Officer, Atlantic and Mediterranean Fleets, 1927-32; Dep. Inspector of Naval Schools, 1932-36; Director, Education Department, Admiralty, 1936-45; retired, 1945; Director of Studies and Dean of R.N. College, Greenwich, 1946-50; President, Royal College of Science Association, 1936-1938; Chairman, Jun. U.S. Club, 1942-1945; Lord Hankey's Government Cttee. on Further Education and Training, 1943-45; Adm. Harwood's Cttee. on R.N. Coll., Greenwich, 1945-46; Master, Worshipful Company of Glass Sellers, 1947-48. Council, Soc. Nautical Research, 1947-51; President: West Kent Science Society, 1949-51 and 1957 (centenary); Greenwich and Lewisham Antiquarian Soc., 1952-54; The Anchorites, 1950; Chm. British Society for International Understanding, 1949-59. *Publications:* edited various service educational publications. *Recreations:* travel, music. *Address:* 10 Liskeard Gardens, S.E.3. *T.:* Greenwich 2263. *Club:* United Service.

[*Died* 21 *Nov.* 1959.

HALL, Sir Arthur John, Kt., *cr.* 1935; M.A., M.D. Cantab., D.Sc. (Hon.), Sheffield; F.R.C.P. Lond.; late Phys., South Yorks Mental Hosp.; late Visiting Physician, Rampton State Inst.; late Censor R.C.P., Examiner, Universities of Oxford, Cambridge, London, Manchester, Liverpool, Glasgow, Leeds, Birmingham and Bristol; Conjoint Board R.C.P. and R.C.S.; Lumleian Lecturer R.C. of P., 1923; Fellow Royal Society of Medicine; late Member Radium Commission; Chairman of Committee of Medical Research Council on Pulmonary Dust Diseases; late Member Industrial Health Committee Research Board; hon. member of Pathological Society of Manchester; hon. member (Pres. 1904-5) of Sheffield Medico-Chirurgical Society; Emeritus Professor of Medicine, University of Sheffield; consulting Physician, Sheffield Royal Hospital; *b.* 27 July 1866; *s.* of John Hall, surgeon, of Sheffield; *m.* 1900, Hilda Mary (*d.* 1945), *d.* of Charles Vickers, The Manor House, Sheffield; one *s.* one *d.* *Educ.:* Rugby; Caius College, Cambridge (Natural Science Tripos, 1887); St. Bartholomew's Hospital. *Publications:* epidemic encephalitis (encephalitis lethargica) numerous articles in the medical periodicals *Address:* 342 Glossop Road, Sheffield. *T.* 21679.

[*Died* 3 *Jan.* 1951.

HALL, Arthur Lewis, F.R.S., 1935; M.A., Sc.D., Consulting Geologist; *b* Birmingham, Jan. 1872; *m.* 1900, Rosalie Riddick Powell; three *s.* one *d.* *Educ.:* University College, Bristol; Caius College, Cambridge. Senior Science Master, Dulwich College, 1900-2; Field Geologist, Geological Survey of the Transvaal, 1903-15; Assistant Director, Geological Survey, Union of South Africa, 1915-32; Past President of the Geological Society of South Africa (Draper Medal); Fellow of Geological Society of London (Murchison Medal) and of the Royal Society of S.A.; Foreign Correspondent Geological Society of Belgium; General Secretary, International Geological Congress, S Africa, 1929 *Publications:* some eighty papers and memoirs on the Geology of S. Africa *Recreation:* chamber music *Address:* 160 Pine Street, Pretoria, S.A.

[*Died* 13 *Aug.* 1955.

HALL, Sir Basil; *see* Hall, Sir R. W. B.

HALL, Ernest Thomas, C.B.E. 1929; *b.* 1871; *s.* of W. C. Hall, Geelong, Victoria; *m.* 1905, Annie J. Black (*d.* 1949), Molong, N.S.W.; two *s.* (and one son killed in action in Malaya), one *d.* *Educ.:* High School, Victoria. Victorian and Commonwealth Trade and Customs Services; Collector of Customs, South Australia, 1923; Collector of Customs, Victoria, 1925; Chairman of Tariff Board, 1927; Comptroller General of Customs, Commonwealth of Australia, 1927-34; retired, 1934. *Recreations:* golf and motoring. *Address:* 25 Martin Street, Elwood, S 3, Vic., Australia.

[*Died* 11 *March* 1954.

HALL, George, C.M.G. 1916; M.D., B.Sc., F.R.C.P.; Consulting Physician, Royal Victoria Infirmary, Newcastle; late Physician, Ingham Infirmary, South Shields; late Hon. Neurologist, Sanderson Orthopædic Hospital School, Gosforth; Visiting Consulting Physician, Ministry of Pensions Hosp., Dunston Hill; late Examiner in Med., Univ. of London and Royal College of Physicians (London); *b.* 1879; *o. s.* of M. Stokoe Hall, Bishop Auckland; *m.* 1913, Margaret (*d* 1949), *e. d.* of Nicholas Mein, Newcastle; one *s.* one *d.* *Educ.:* Armstrong Coll., Newcastle; University College, London (Fellow); Bucknill and Atkinson Morley Scholar; Gold Medal and Exhibition; Cluff Prizeman. House Surgeon and Physician, University College Hospital; House Physician National Hospital Paralysed and Epileptic London; served European War, 1914-18, as Major, R.A.M.C. (T.F.) (C.M.G.); J.P. Newcastle. *Publications:* medical papers. *Address:* 12 Eslington Terrace, Newcastle upon Tyne 2. *T.:* Jesmond 109.

[*Died* 10 *Jan.* 1955.

HALL, Rt. Rev. Herbert William, D.D.; Bishop of Aberdeen and Orkney since 1943; *b.* 22 December 1889; *s.* of Charles Hall and Barbara Black; *m.* 1919, Helen Maven Aitken; one *s.* one *d.* *Educ.:* St. John's School, New Pitsligo; Aberdeen University (M.A. 1911, D.D. 1944); Berkeley Divinity College, U.S.A. (S.T.D.). Edinburgh Theological College. Teacher, 1904-11, New Pitsligo and Peterhead Academy; Curate St. John's, Greenock, 1913-19; Rector of St. Mary's, Port Glasgow, 1919-28; St. Peter's, Galashiels, 1928-36; Church Army Chaplain (Flanders), 1917; Home Mission Organiser in Scotland, 1934-36; Rector of St. Mark's Scottish Episcopal Church, Portobello, 1936-1943; Canon of St. Mary's Cathedral, Edinburgh, 1939-43; Hon. Chaplain R.N.V.R. 1950; Editor Scottish Chronicle, 1927-31; Editor Scottish Churchman, 1928-32. *Address:* Bishop's House, Aberdeen. *T.:* Aberdeen 33563.

[*Died* 6 *Dec.* 1955.

HALL, I. Walker, M.D.; Emeritus Professor Bristol University; late Director of Preventive Medicine Laboratory and Curator of Canynge Hall, Bristol University; *b.* 16 Sept. 1868; *m.*; one *d.* *Educ.:* Owens College, Manchester. Senior Demonstrator of Physiology, Manchester University, 1900; Lecturer in Pathology, 1901; Professor of Pathology, Bristol University, 1906-33. *Publications:* Purin bodies of Foodstuffs, 1901; Methods of Morbid Histology, 1903; editor, Metabolism and Practical Medicine, 1908; about 50 research papers to various medical papers. *Recreation:* garden. *Address:* Highpath, Grosvenor Road, Godalming. *T.:* 849.

[*Died* 9 *Oct.* 1953.

HALL, Sir John Frederick, Kt., *cr.* 1938; C.S.I. 1937; C.I.E. 1931; O.B.E. 1919; *b* 1882; *s.* of late John Hall of Hull; *m.* 1908, Lucy Elizabeth, *d* of Rev. John Tate, Thessalon, Canada; one *s* one *d.* *Educ.:* Hymers College Hull; Clare College, Cambridge Entered I.C.S. 1905; Collector and District Magistrate; Secretary to Government Revenue Department; Commissioner of Labour; Member of the Board of Revenue Madras; retired from I.C.S., 1940; Chairman, Madras Public Service Commission, 1940-46. *Address:* Norfield House, St. Andrew's Road, Bridport, Dorset. *T.:* Bridport 647. *Club:* Madras (Madras).

[*Died* 1 *March* 1959.

HALL, Brig.-General John Hamilton, C.M.G. 1918; D.S.O. 1916; retired list, 1925; *b.* 23 Feb. 1871; unmarried; *s.* of late Major John Greive Hall, R.E., and Agnes Robertson, Edinburgh. *Educ.:* Fettes College, Edinburgh; Sandhurst. Second Lt. Middlesex Regt. 1891; Lt.-Col. 1916; temp. Brig.-Gen. 1918-19; Col. 1921; Staff Services; Ass. Provost Marshal; Staff Capt., D.A.Q.M.G. and D.A.A.G. South Africa, from 1902 to 1907; Assist. Inspector of Recruiting, Eastern Command, 1913-1914; in charge of Record Office, Lichfield, 1921-25; served South Africa (medal, 4 clasps); European War, 1914-18 (D.S.O., one bar, despatches four times, C.M.G.). *Address:* Otterburn, Broadstone, Dorset. [*Died* 12 *April* 1953.

HALL, John Thomas, J.P. 1939; M.P. (Lab.) West Gateshead since 1950; *b.* 9 Nov. 1896; *m.* 1927, Blanche Bethulia Gardner; one *s.* two *d.* (and two *d.* decd.). *Educ.:* Council School; Ruskin College, Oxford. Colliery worker, 1910; served European War, Trooper 1st Life Guards, 1915-18; railway worker from demobilisation until 1950; Trade Union Branch Secretary, 1921. C.C., Durham, 1934-50; J.P. 1939. District Chm. Northern District Nat. Union of Gen. and Municipal Workers, 1943-; lecturer on Economics and Social History, Labour Colleges. *Recreations:* gardening, reading. *Address:* 14 The Crescent, Shiney Row, Houghton-le-Spring, Co. Durham. [*Died* 11 *Oct.* 1955.

HALL, Captain Leonard Joseph, C.B.E. 1935; R.D., R.N.R. (Retired List); late Director of Marine, Nigeria; *b.* Oct. 25 1879; *s.* of Joseph Hall and Elizabeth, *d.* of Rev. C. B. Holder; *m* 1913, Eveline, *d.* of Rev. E. W. Matthews; one *s.* two *d.* *Educ.:* H.M.S. Worcester. Merchant service, 1896-1904; R.N. 1904-7; extra master's B.O.T. certificate; Marine officer Nigeria, 1908; served Cameroons expeditionary force, 1914-15; mentioned in French despatches and received special appreciation of Secretary of State for services rendered; Admiralty-Transport dept., 1916-17; seconded to Army as Major R.E., 1917; Lieut.-Colonel R.E. and Assistant Director of Inland Water Transport, Mesopotamia, 1919; mentioned in despatches and awarded O.B.E.; resumed duty Nigeria, 1920; promoted deputy director of Marine, 1925; director, 1930; retired from Nigerian Service, 1935; Observing Officer International Commission for Non-Intervention in Spain, 1937-38. *Publication:* The Inland Water Transport in Mesopotamia. *Recreation:* golf. *Address:* Encombe, Sewardstone Bury, Chingford Essex. *T.:* Silverthorn 1174. *Club:* East India and Sports. [*Died* 9 *April* 1953.

HALL, Marie; violinist; *b.* Newcastle upon Tyne, 8 April 1884; *m.* 1911, Edward Baring (*d.* 1951); one *d.*; At age of ten years studied with Edward Elgar for a year, and then under Max Mossel for three years in Birmingham; later studied for twelve months under Prof. Johann Kruse, and then for two years under Sevcik; made her début in Vienna in Jan. 1903; appeared in London Feb. 1903, since when she has toured extensively in England, America, Canada, New Zealand, Australia, S. Africa, India, The Far East, etc.; also numerous broadcasts. *Publications:* many articles in leading newspapers and magazines. *Recreations:* reading, motoring, and walking. *Address:* Inveresk, Cheltenham. [*Died* 11 *Nov.* 1956.

HALL, Sir Martin Julian, of Dunglass, 10th Bt. Nova Scotia, *cr.* 1687; O B.E. 1918; *b.* 23 March 1874; *s.* of Lt.-Gen. Julian Hamilton Hall, Coldstream Guards, *s.* of 5th Bt., and Mina, *d.* of Colonel John Fremantle, C.B.; *S.* brother, 1928; *m.* 1905, Alice Mary (*d.* 1952), 2nd *d.* of William Wyndham Hasler, J.P., of Aldingbourne House, Sussex; one *s.* *Educ.:* Radley. Formerly in Bechuanaland Civil Service; Director of Food Section, Ministry of Munitions, during European War; Chief Reconstruction Officer for Scotland under the Ministry of Labour, 1919. *Heir:* *s.* Julian Henry [*b.* 22 Feb. 1907. *Educ.:* Eton (Captain of the Oppidans); Balliol College, Oxford (Scholar)]. *Address:* Orchard, Cape Province, South Africa. [*Died* 31 *Jan.* 1958.

HALL, Oliver, R.A., 1927; R.W.S.; *b.* 1869; *s.* of John Hall, London; *m.* 1899, Sarah Agnes (*d.* 1946), *d.* of W. Stephenson, Nettleslack, Lancs; three *s.* His Shap Moors was bought under the Chantrey Bequest for the Tate Gallery; many of his pictures have been purchased for Public Galleries both here and abroad, also two large pictures for Government House, Delhi. *Recreation:* golf. *Address:* Bay View, Bardsea, Ulverston, Lancs. [*Died* 5 *Dec.* 1957.

HALL, Percy, M.R.C.S. (Eng.); L.R.C.P. (Lond.); Rheumatologist; Consulting Physician (and Founder) the Hull Municipal Light Clinic; *b.* 1882; *s.* of late Chas. Hall, Man. Director Hull Central Dry Dock and Engineering Co. Ltd.; *m.* Agnes (*d.* 1944), 2nd *d.* of late Dr. W. H. Johnson; two *s.*; *m.* 1945, Elizabeth M. Anderson, M.D. *Educ.:* privately; Hymer's College, Hull; St. Bartholomew's Hospital, London. Engaged in general professional practice, 1909-19; served R.A.M.C. 1915-16, England and France; invalided; further service civilian capacity Northern Command, etc.; Surgeon, Merchant Navy, 1940-42; late Physician, Charterhouse Rheumatism Clinic; late Clinical Assist. the City of London Hospital for Diseases of the Chest, Victoria Park, London; Hon. Surgeon Hull and Sculcoates Dispensary; Hon. Surgeon the Lloyd Hospital, Bridlington; Medical Referee (Workmen's Compensation Act) to the leading Accident Insurance Companies; Hon. Actinotherapist the Hendon Cottage Hospital; late Medical Editor the British Journal of Actinotherapy; late Hon. Actinotherapist Mount Vernon Hospital for Diseases of the Chest; late Consulting Physician the Newspaper Press Fund for Yorkshire, N. and E. Ridings and York. *Publications:* Ultra-Violet Rays in the Treatment and Cure of Disease, 5th reprint (4th edition), 1927; Diathermy in the Treatment of Pulmonary Tuberculosis (The Practitioner), 1922; Asthma and its Treatment, 1930; Bismuth Salts in the Treatment of Arthritis (Lancet and Medical Press and Circular, 1944); numerous other articles. *Address:* 50 Bickenhall Mansions, W.1. *T.:* Welbeck 4760. [*Died* 8 *Nov.* 1955.

HALL, Surgeon Vice-Admiral Sir (Robert William) Basil, K.C.B., *cr.* 1936 (C.B. 1930); O.B.E. 1924; C.St.J.; Order of the Redeemer (Greece); Gilbert Blane Gold Medal; M.R.C.S. Eng.; L.R.C.P. Lond.; R.N., retired; *b.* 1876; *s.* of Robert Hall, R.N.; *m.* 1st, 1906, Gertrude Grace (*d.* 1948), *d.* of Eng. Capt. H. C. Goldsmith, R.N.; 2nd, 1950, Dorothy, *widow* of Rear-Adm. (S) C. W. Capner. *Educ.:* Portsmouth Grammar School; Guy's Hospital. Medical Director-General of the Navy, 1934-37; Hon. Physician to the King, 1934-37; retired list, 1937; Director of Medical Services International Council for Non-Intervention in Spain, 1937-39; Chairman National Service Medical Board, Guildford, 1939-44. *Publication:* Handbook for Medical Officers of the Submarine Service, 1920. *Address:* Appletrees, Derby Road, Haslemere. [*Died* 16 *May* 1951.

HALL, Admiral Sydney Stewart, C.B. 1914; *b.* 16 June 1872; 3rd *s.* of John Selby Hall; *m.* 1906, *o. d.* of late Rev. Frank Mudie, M.A., Arbroath; three *s.* (and two *s.* decd., R.A.F., War of 1939-45). Entered Britannia, 1885; served in West Indies, N. America, Australia, and Home Fleets; Specialist in Torpedo; commanded Submarine Service, 1906-10; H.M.S. Diana, 1910-12; H.M.S. Roxburgh, 1914; Submarine Service, 1915-18; Rear-Adm., 1919; retired, 1919; Vice-Adm. retired, 1925; Adm. retired, 1929. *Address:* St. Kilda, Kilcreggan, Dunbartonshire. *T.:* Kilcreggan 2247. [*Died* 10 *Jan.* 1955.

HALL, T. Walter, Hon.M.A. (Sheffield); F.S.A.; F.R.Hist.S.; solicitor; *b.* 21 Jan. 1862; *e. s.* of John Hall, surgeon, Sheffield; unmarried. Articled to late Francis Patrick Smith of Barnes Hall near Sheffield, 1878; retired from practice, 1910; actively interested in the formation and production of the Triennial Musical Festivals, Sheffield; chairman of the executive committee, 1896-1914; for sixteen years a citizen member of the Libraries and Museums Committee of the Sheffield City Council; since 1910 engaged in collecting, indexing, and publishing historical and topographical material; editor of the first five volumes of the Sheffield Parish Register, 1560 to 1719. *Publications:* Sheffield Pedigrees, vol. i., 1909; Manuscripts at Sheffield Public Library, 1912; Ancient Charters of Sheffield Capital Burgesses, 1913; Jackson Collection at Sheffield (with A. Hermann Thomas), 1914; Sheffield Pedigrees, vol. ii., 1915; Sheffield and Rotherham Charters, 1916; Wheat Collection, Sheffield, 1920; Wincobank Charters, 1921; Brooke-Taylor Collection, 1922; Hawksyard, 1922; Edmunds Collection, 1924; Sheffield Manorial Records, vol. i., 1926; Sheffield Manorial Records, vol. ii., 1928; Thundercliffe and the Hermitage of St. John, 1928; Yorkshire Records, including Bosville and Lindsay Collections, 1930; Waldershelf Manor and the Knights Hospitallers, 1930; South Yorkshire Historical Sketches, 1931; The Aula in Hallam, 1931; The Fairbanks of Sheffield, 1932; Etton, an East Yorkshire Village, 1932; Sheffield Manorial Records, vol. iii., 1934; Ancient Charters relating to the borderland of Sheffield, 1935; Tankersley and Fanshawe Gate, Sheffield, 1937; Incunabula of Sheffield History, 1938; Early Charters relating to Sheffield, 1938: Vills and Burghs of North Derbyshire, 1939. *Recreations:* palæography and search for local history, orchestral and chamber music, Wagner, and many others. *Address:* 6 Gladstone Road, Ranmoor, Sheffield, 10. *T.:* Sheffield 32,096. *Clubs:* Junior Constitutional (Hon. Member); Sheffield (Sheffield). [*Died* 11 *Nov.* 1953.

HALL, The Hon. William Lorimer, Q.C., D.C.L.; Judge of the Supreme Court of Nova Scotia since 1931; *b.* Melvern Square, Nova Scotia, 28 July 1876; *s.* of Rev. William E. Hall and Margaret Barss; *m.* 1907, Edith H. Hamm; one *s.* two *d.* *Educ.:* Acadia University, B.A.; Dalhousie, LL.B. Member of Legislature Nova Scotia for Queen's County, 1910, 1911, 1916, 1925, 1928; Crown Prosecutor for the City and County of Halifax; Attorney-General, Nova Scotia, 1926-31. *Address:* 89 South Park Street, Halifax, N.S. *Clubs:* Halifax, Halifax Golf and Country, Halifax Curling (Halifax). [*Died* 26 *May* 1958.

HALL-DALWOOD, Lt.-Col. John, C.B.E. 1920; barrister. Called to Bar, Middle Temple, 1906; 4 years (acting) D.A.A. and Q.M.G., Thames District, Chatham; Assistant Chief Constable, Kent, 1902; Chief Constable, Leicester, 1908, and Sheffield, 1913; Founder of National Volunteers, 1914 (August). *Publications:* Police Reform, (1917 Merger scheme, etc.); Police Officer's A.B.C.; Law Treatises and Plays; National Police Training (non-collegiate or residential); Pro. Con. Pocket Dictionary. *Address:* The Halt, 27 Hythe Road, Worthing, Sussex. [*Died* 5 *March* 1954.

HALL-THOMPSON, Lt.-Col. Rt. Hon. S. H., P.C. (Northern Ireland), 1944; D.L., J.P.; Chairman of Cairnburn Estates Ltd.; *b.* 1885; *s.* of Rt. Hon. Robert Thompson, P.C., D.L., M.P., Belfast; *m.* Margaret, *o. d.* of late T. T. MacLean, Glenanne, Co. Armagh; two *s.* one *d.* *Educ.:* Dulwich Coll. Served Donegal Artillery, Royal Field Reserve Artillery and 4/R.U.R., Egypt and Palestine, 1915-19; Chief Ordnance Officer, N. Ireland, 1939-42; Minister of Education, Northern Ireland, 1944-50; M.P. (U.) Clifton Division of Belfast, Parliament of Northern Ireland, 1929-53; Deputy Speaker and Chairman of Ways and Means, 1950-53. High Sheriff of Belfast, 1929; Ex-Chairman Ulster Unionist Council, Junior Imperial League, Presbyterian Health Insurance Society; Ex-President Irish Bowling Association; Ex-Master North Down Hunt; Capt. Holywood Golf Club, 1952-54. *Address:* Cairnburn, Belfast. *T.:* Belfast 63113. [*Died* 26 *Oct.* 1954.

HALLAM, (Arthur) Rupert; Hon. Consulting Physician to the Rupert Hallam Dermatological Dept., Royal Infirmary, Sheffield; *b.* 1877; *s.* of late Dr. Arthur Hallam; *m.* Kathleen Edge Shifnal; two *s.* one *d.* *Educ.:* Germany; Edinburgh University. [*Died* 29 *Aug.* 1955.

HALLAM, Rt. Rev. William Thomas Thompson, M.A., D.D., LL.D.; Assistant Bishop of Huron from 1949; *b.* 1878; *s.* of Thomas Hallam, Leicester, and Matilda Thompson, Derby; *m.* 1904, Lillian Gertrude Best, Cornwallis, Nova Scotia; two *s.* one *d.*; *m.* 1943, Kathleen Coggs, Toronto, Ontario. *Educ.:* Dalhousie College, Halifax, Nova Scotia. Professor, Wycliffe College, Toronto, 1908-22; Principal, Emmanuel Coll., Saskatoon, 1922-27; Rector, Church of Ascension, Hamilton, Ont., 1927-31; Bishop of Saskatoon, 1931-49; Chancellor, University of Emmanuel Coll., Saskatoon, 1931-49. *Publications:* Victory of Faith, 1953; editor Canadian Churchman, 1918-22. *Address:* c/o Huron College, London, Ontario, Canada. [*Died* 25 *July* 1956.

HALLETT, Vice-Admiral Sir Theodore John, K.B.E., *cr.* 1944 (C.B.E. 1919); C.B. 1931; *b.* 1878; *s.* of late Rev. J. T. Hallett; *m.* 1908, Helen Blanche, *d.* of late Col F. Dakeyne; one *s.* one *d.* Served European War, 1914-19 (despatches, C.B.E.); Naval Assistant to Second Sea Lord, 1922-24; Commanding Officer, Coast of Scotland, 1929-31; Vice-Admiral, 1933; retired list, 1933. Served War of 1939-45 (despatches). *Address:* Hayfield, Eastergate, Sussex. *T.:* Eastergate 129. *Club:* United Service. [*Died* 1 *June* 1957.

HALLINAN, Major Thomas John C.B.E., 1932 (O.B.E., 1923); M.B., B.S. (Lond.), M.R.C.S., L.R.C.P., D.P.H. Dublin University; Director of Medical Services Jamaica, 1933-46; M.L.C. Jamaica; *b.* 17 Jan. 1886; *s.* of late John Thomas Hallinan, J.P. Mayor of Lewisham, 1929-30) and Ellen Martha O'Neill; *m.* 1910 Agnes May, *d.* of late Dr. James Hanafin, Miltown, Co. Kerry; one *s.* *Educ.:* Archbishop Tenison's School; Charing Cross Hospital (Entrance Scholarship and Pereira Prize). Casualty Officer, East London Hospital for Children, 1908-9; entered Royal Army Medical Corps as subaltern, 1910; served Aldershot, Ireland, 1911-13; India, 1913-14; European War—Egypt, 1914-16, Mesopotamia, 1916-20; Deputy Assistant Director of Medical Services (Sanitary), Amara, 1918; Basrah, 1918-20; (1914 Star, despatches thrice); seconded for service with Iraq Government, 1920; Medical Officer of Health, Basrah, 1920-1922; Inspector General of Health Services, Iraq, 1922-33; retired from R.A.M.C. to Reserve of Officers with rank of Major, 1925. *Recreations:* motoring, bridge, gardening. *Address:* Ropley, Irish Town P.O., Jamaica. *Club:* East India and Sports. [*Died* 28 *May* 1960.

HALLS, Walter; Trades Union Organiser, N.U.R.; *b.* Tugby, 16 June 1871; father was shepherd on farm; *m.* Jane Hanes of Sharnford, Leicestershire, *d.* of postmaster; three *s.* five *d.* *Educ.:* Gaulby Village School, Leicestershire; worked on farm until 18 years of age; joined the Midland Railway service in goods dept. at Leicester at above age, in whose employ continued until 38 years of age; member of the N.U.R. since 1896 and Secretary of the Leicester Branch for nine years, during which time filled various official positions; been member of the Co-operative movement for a similar period and served on Board of Management of the Dublin Society, also the Nottingham Co-operative Society, of which he has now been President for nearly

three years; elected Organiser of the N.U.R. in Dec. 1909, sent to Dublin for 3½ years, during which time travelled Ireland in connection with that work; M.P. (Lab.) Heywood, 1921-22; contested Northampton, 1918. *Address:* 169 Loughboro Road, West Bridgford, Notts.
[*Died* 20 *Oct.* 1953.

HALLSWORTH, H. M., C.B.E. 1931 (O.B.E. 1919); M. Com. (University of Durham); *b.* 11 Dec. 1876; 3rd *s.* of late Harry Hallsworth, Oldham, Lancs; unmarried. *Educ.:* University of Manchester, M.A., B.Sc., Jevons Student. Assistant Lecturer in Economics, University of Manchester; Hunter Lecturer in Economics, Armstrong College. During war, Major, R.E., Deputy Assistant Director of Docks; later, on Staff of Inspector-General of Transportation; David Dale Professor of Economics, King's College, Newcastle on Tyne (in the University of Durham); member Assistance Board (now National Assistance Board), 1934-49. County Commissioner for Huntingdonshire Boy Scouts Assoc., 1945-52. *Publications:* Unemployment in Lancashire (jointly with Professor S. J. Chapman); The Elements of Railway Operating. *Address:* Chesneys, St. Ives, Huntingdonshire.
[*Died* 22 *Aug.* 1953.

HALLWARD, Reverend Lancelot William, M.A.; *b.* 4 July 1867; *s.* of Rev. John Leslie Hallward; unmarried. *Educ.:* Haileybury College; Oriel College, Oxford; Leeds Clergy School. Curacies at Great Yarmouth and Carshalton; Incumbent of Cala, Diocese of St. John's, Kaffraria, 1899; Dean of St. John's, Kaffraria, S. Africa, and Rector of the Cathedral Parish, Umtata, Transkei, 1912-40; Archdeacon of Umtata; on pension. *Address:* The Rectory, Port S. Johns, South Africa. *Club:* Umtata (Umtata).
[*Died* 20 *July* 1951.

HALNON, Frederick James, F.R.B.S. 1906; sculptor; Modelling Master, University of London (Goldsmiths' College), retired; *b.* London, 8 March 1881; *o. s.* of late Frederick James Halnon; *m.* 1912, Amelia Elsie, *d.* of late Stafford Henry Corfield. *Educ.:* Goldsmiths' Institute, commencing Art study at age of 11 years. Pupil of Alfred Drury, R.A.; awarded two National Gold Medals, 1902 and 1903, and three Silver Medals; exhibited at the Royal Academy since 1904 and most of the provincial galleries; work purchased by the Queen; represented in the Royal Albert Memorial Museum Art Gallery, Exeter, and the Birkenhead Art Gallery; chief Exhibition works: Mother and Child, Isabella, Bacchante, Laurels of Youth, The Crown of Victory, Vintage, Beatrice, A Legend of Metallurgy, Spring, etc. *Recreations:* sketching and music. *Address:* 1 Arran Road, Catford, S.E.6.
[*Died* 12 *March* 1958.

HALSALL, Rt. Rev. Joseph Formby, Ph.D., D.C.L., S.T.L.; titular Bishop of Zabi, auxiliary to Archbishop of Liverpool, (R.C.), since 1945; *b.* 15 Feb. 1902; 3rd *s.* of late William Halsall and Ellen Formby, Kiln Farm, Ince Blundell, Lancs. *Educ.:* Upholland College, Lancs; Ven. English College, Rome. Secretary to late Cardinal Hinsley, 1936-38; Professor of Philosophy, St. Edmund's College, Ware, 1938-40; Vice-Rector Pontifical Beda College, Rome, 1940-1945. *Recreation:* granted Scout Wood Badge by Boy Scout Association, 1938. *Address:* 161 Liverpool Road, Great Crosby, Liverpool 23. *T.:* Waterloo 3456.
[*Died* 13 *March* 1958.

HALSEY, Captain Arthur, C.B.E. 1919; Royal Navy (retired); *b.* 31 July 1869; 2nd *s.* of late Rt. Hon. Sir Frederick Halsey, 1st Bt., of Gaddesden; *m.* 1st, 1909, Blanche Helen Kerr (*d.* 1917), *d.* of late Admiral M. R. Pechell; (one *d.* decd.); 2nd, 1922, Dorothy Mary (*d.* 1950), *d.* of Samuel Gurney Leatham, Hemsworth, Yorkshire. Entered H.M.S. Britannia, 1883; Flag Lieut. Nore, 1894-6; commanded H.M.S. Bruizer, blockade of Crete; served in Boer War and landed in charge of guns from H.M.S. Philomel (African medal 5 clasps, despatches and promoted); served on Embarkation Staff, 1914-17, and as Naval Vice-Consul, 1917 to end of the War, controlling Scandinavian food convoys (C.B.E.). *Address:* Cherry Orchard, Wye, Kent. *T.:* Wye 123. *Club:* United Service.
[*Died* 15 *Aug.* 1957.

HALWARD, Rt. Rev. (Nelson) Victor, M.C., M.A.; Assistant Bishop of British Columbia since 1951; *b.* 12 Dec. 1897; *s.* of late William Halward, Canterbury. *Educ.:* King's School, Canterbury; Jesus College and Westcott House, Cambridge. Served European War, 1916-19; Deacon, 1922; Priest, 1923; Curate, St. Saviour's, Croydon, 1922-25; Diocesan Chaplain, Hong Kong and S. China, 1926-35; Missionary in Canton, S. China, 1936-46; Assistant Bishop of Hong Kong and South China, 1946-51. Hong Kong Colony Commissioner for Boy Scouts, 1935-50. *Address:* c/o Diocesan Office, 912 Vancouver St., Victoria, B.C., Canada.
[*Died* 17 *Dec.* 1953.

HAMBER, Col. Hon. Eric W., C.M.G. 1946; B.A.; LL.D.; Knight of Grace of Order of St. John of Jerusalem; Ex-Lieut.-Gov. of Province of British Columbia; *b.* Winnipeg, Manitoba, 21 April 1879; *s.* of Eric Frederick Marsh Hamber and Ada Jefferson; *m.* 1912, Aldyen Irene Hendry. *Educ.:* St. John's College, Winnipeg, Manitoba; B.A. University of Manitoba, 1898. Entered Dominion Bank, Winnipeg, 1899; Director since 1912; Manager of London, England, Branch, 1909-12; Head of Hastings Sawmill Company Limited, formerly British Columbia Mills, Timber and Trading Company Limited, since 1912; also President and General Manager of: London and Canadian Investment Co. Ltd.; also President of several privately owned companies; Director: Toronto-Dominion Bank; Canadian Pacific Rly. Co.; Toronto General Trusts Corporation; Crown Zellerbach Canada Ltd.; Past Commodore (5 years) Royal Vancouver Yacht Club; Chancellor Emeritus of Univ. of British Columbia; Hon. President British Columbia Cancer Foundation; Life Governor Vancouver General Hospital; Hon. Col. 5th (B.C.) Coast Brigade R.C.A. and Seaforth Highlanders of Canada. *Recreations:* polo, golfing and yachting. *Address:* 3838 Cypress Street, Vancouver. *Clubs:* Bath, Union, Royal Victoria Yacht (Victoria); Vancouver, Royal Vancouver Yacht (Vancouver). [*Died* 10 *Jan.* 1960.

HAMBOURG, Mark; pianist, composer; *b.* Bogutchar, South Russia, 30 May 1879; now naturalised Englishman; *e. s.* of late Prof. Michael Hambourg; *m.* 1907, Hon. Dorothea, *d.* of late Lord Muir Mackenzie, G.C.B.; four *d.* *Educ.:* by his father, and subsequently by Prof. Leschetitzky, Vienna, where he obtained the Liszt scholarship, 1894. First public appearances in Moscow, 1888; London, 1890; Vienna, 1895; Australia, 1895-96; Paris, Berlin, 1897; first American tour, 1899-1900; second American tour, 1902-3; third Australian and New Zealand tour, 1903; toured in South Africa, 1905; Holland, 1906; second tour in South Africa, 1907; third American tour, 1907; fourth Australian tour, 1908; made his first Canadian tour, 1910, since which he has toured all over the world continuously. *Publications:* Variations on a Theme by Paganini; Volkslied; Espièglerie; Romance; Impromptu Minuet, and other compositions for Pianoforte; How to become a Pianist, 1922; From Piano to Forte (Autobiography), 1931; The Eighth Octave, 1951. *Recreations:* golf and antique collecting. *Address:* 5 Langford Close, Langford Place, St. John's Wood, N.W.8. *T.:* Maida Vale 5500. *Club:* Savage. [*Died* 26 *Aug.* 1960.

HAMBRO, Captain Angus Valdemar, J.P., D.L. Dorset; *b.* 8 July 1883; 3rd *s.* of late Sir Everard Hambro, K.C.V.O.; *m.* 1st, 1907, Rosamund Maud (*d.* 1914); one *d.*; (one *s.* killed in action, 1943); 2nd, 1916, Vanda, *d.* of John Charlton of Malpas; four *d.*

Educ.: Eton. M.P. (C.) South Dorset, 1910-22; M.P. (Nat.U.) North Dorset divn., 1937-45; P.P.S. to Under Sec. for Air, 1917-18; High Sheriff of Dorset, 1934-35. *Recreations:* golf, cricket. *Address:* Milton Abbas, Blandford, Dorset. *Club:* Carlton. [*Died* 19 *Nov.* 1957.

HAMBRO, Lt.-Col. Harold Everard, C.B.E. 1919; *b.* 1876; *s.* of late Sir Everard Hambro, K.C.V.O., of Milton Abbey, Blandford; *m.* 1st, 1902, Katharine Alethea (*d.* 1938), *d.* of late William Charles Scott, Thorpe House, Chertsey; one *s.*; 2nd, 1941, Dowager Countess Cadogan. *Educ.:* Eton. Joined the Royal Artillery, 1899; Captain Royal Horse Artillery, 1908; left the Service, Reserve of Officers, 1914; called up Aug. 1914; demobilised June 1919 (despatches, Bt. Lieut.-Colonel, C.B.E.); High Sheriff of Suffolk, 1930; D.L., J.P. Suffolk. *Recreations:* hunting (Master of Suffolk Hounds, 1923-38), golf, cricket, and shooting. *Address:* Coldham Hall, Bury St. Edmunds. *T.:* Cockfield 204. *T.A.:* Lawshall. *Club:* Boodle's. [*Died* 5 *Aug.* 1952.

HAMER, Captain Richard Lloyd, D.S.O. 1940; R.N. retired; *b.* 13 Jan. 1884; *e. surv. s.* of late John Parry Hamer, J.P., Glanyrafon, Llanyblodwel, Shropshire; *m.* 1914, Beena, *d.* of late Admiral Sir Richard Peirse, K.C.B., K.B.E., M.V.O.; one *s.* one *d.* *Educ.:* Stubbington House; H.M.S. Britannia. Retired from Royal Navy, 1923; on staff of Royal National Life Boat Institution, 1925; Deputy Chief Inspector, 1930. *Address:* Castellmoch Fawr, Llanrhaiadr Mochnant, Montgomeryshire. *T.:* Llanrhaiadr 254. [*Died* 16 *Dec.* 1951.

HAMERTON, Brevet Col. Albert Ernest, C.M.G. 1918; D.S.O. 1904; late R.A.M.C.; Pathologist, Zoological Society London, 1928-46; *b.* 9 Dec. 1873; *s.* of Rev. T. J. Hamerton; *m.* 1919. Entered army, 1900; Captain, 1903; Major, 1912; served East Africa, action at Jidballi, 1904 (despatches, D.S.O.); member Sleeping Sickness Commission, Uganda, 1908-10; member Sleeping Sickness Commission, Nyasaland, 1911-13; served British Expeditionary Force, France, Aug. 1914-19 (despatches, C.M.G.); Lt.-Col. 1917; Bt. Col. 1926; retired, 1928. *Address:* c/o Glyn, Mills & Co., Holt's Branch, Whitehall, S.W. [*Died* 31 *Jan.* 1955.

HAMILL, John Molyneux, O.B.E.; M.D.; D.Sc.; M.A.; *b.* 30 July 1880; *s.* of Philip Hamill and Annie Molyneux; *m.* 1932, Lesley, (*d.* 1957), *o. d.* of late R. B. N. Findlater, Cults, Aberdeenshire. *Educ.:* St. Paul's School; Trinity College, Cambridge (Scholar); St. Bartholomew's Hospital. University scholar and gold medallist of the University of London; Scholar and Prizeman of St. Bartholomew's Hospital; Sharpey Lecturer in Physiology, University College of London. Entered Local Government Board as Inspector of Foods, 1907; Senior Medical Officer in charge of Foods Division, Ministry of Health, 1934; retired 1940; served on various Departmental and Inter-departmental Committees; Major, R.A.M.C. (T.F.); late Examiner in Hygiene, R. Army Medical College and R.C.P., London; was D.A.D.M.S., General Headquarters, B.E.F.; British Government Delegate to the World's Dairy Congress, Washington, U.S.A., 1923, London, 1928, Copenhagen, 1931, Rome, 1934, and Berlin, 1937; Chairman of Commission to Enquire into Milk Production in Holland and Denmark, 1927; British Govt. Deleg. to League of Nations Nutrition Cttee., 1937. *Publications:* Official Reports to Local Government Board, 1908-14; Diet in Relation to Normal Nutrition, 1921; Notes on the Pasteurisation of Milk, 1924; various contributions to the Journal of Physiology. *Address:* 10 Holland Park Court, W.14. *T.:* Park 7185. *Club:* Savage. [*Died* 29 *Nov.* 1960.

HAMILTON of Dalzell, 2nd Baron, *cr.* 1886; **Gavin George Hamilton,** K.T. 1909; C.V.O., 1908; M.C. 1917; Major (retired) Scots Guards; Lord Lieutenant of Lanarkshire since 1938; Chairman of Royal Fine Art Commission for Scotland since 1932; *b.* 29 June 1872; *s.* of 1st Baron Hamilton of Dalzell and Lady Emily Eleanor Leslie Melville, *d.* of 8th Earl of Leven and Melville; *m.* 1912, Sybil (*d.* 1933), *d.* of late Sir Frederick Marshall, K.C.M.G. *Educ.:* Eton; Royal Military Coll., Sandhurst. Served South Africa with Imperial Yeomanry; and in European War with Scots Guards, and as Assistant Military Secretary, Fourth Army; Lord-in-Waiting to King Edward VII and King George V, 1906-11. Owns about 2500 acres. *Heir:* *n.* John d'Henin Hamilton, M.C. *Address:* Dalzell, Motherwell, Scotland. *T.:* Motherwell 53. *Clubs:* Jockey, Brooks's, Turf. [*Died* 23 *June* 1952.

HAMILTON, Hon. Adam; M.P. for Wallace, N.Z., 1919-22 and 1925-46; Chairman of directors, Southland Farmers Co-op. Assoc. Limited; President: Invercargill Savings Bank; Associated Savings Banks of New Zealand; *b.* 20 Aug. 1880; *s.* of John and Mary Hamilton; *m.* 1913, Mary A McDonald; no *c.* *Educ.:* Forest Hill; Otago University; Knox College. Reared on a farm; practical farmer; in business for years as grain and seed merchant; Minister of Labour and Postmaster-General, 1931-35; also Minister of Unemployment, 1932-35; Leader of National Party, 1936-40; member N.Z. War Cabinet, 1940-45; Minister in charge of War Expenditure, 1942-45. *Recreations:* shooting, fishing, tennis. *Address:* 101 Duke St., Invercargill, N.Z. *T.:* 1204 Invercargill. [*Died* 29 *April* 1952.

HAMILTON, Alexander Michell, Q.C., Scotland, 1920; M.A., LL.B.; *b.* 1872. *Educ.:* Glasgow University. Member of Faculty of Advocates, 1896; Sheriff Substitute at Oban, 1921-23; Sheriff Substitute of Renfrew and Bute at Paisley, 1923-50. *Publication:* A Commentary on the Bills of Exchange Act, 1904. *Address:* 20 Stanley Road, Edinburgh 6. *Clubs:* New (Edinburgh); Western (Glasgow). [*Died* 24 *June* 1959.

HAMILTON, Colonel Andrew Lorne, C.M.G. 1918; *b.* 1871; *s.* of Andrew W. H. Hamilton, M.D., Melbourne, Quebec. Served European War, 1914-18 (despatches thrice, C.M.G.): with Canadian Section, General Headquarters, 3rd Echelon, as Col. and A.A.G. and subsequently as Director of Records, Overseas Military Forces of Canada. *Address:* 100 Madrid Rd., Barnes, S.W.13; Toronto, Canada. [*Died* 6 *April* 1951.

HAMILTON, Charles Gipps, O.B.E.; Barrister; *b.* 27 June 1857; *s.* of Edward William Terrick Hamilton and Ann Thacker; *m.* 1892, Anna Gertrude Montgomerie Lang (*d.* 1937); three *d.* *Educ.:* Eton; Trinity College, Cambridge. Private Secretary to Lord Chancellor Herschell, 1892-95; Director of: Law Union and Rock Ins. Co.; Australian Agricultural Co.; Governor Peabody Donation Fund; Director of London and Lancashire Insce. Co., 1919-52. *Recreation:* golf. *Address:* 36 Sloane Court, S.W.3. *Clubs:* Brooks's; Royal and Ancient Golf (St. Andrews). [*Died* 8 *June* 1955.

HAMILTON, Cicely; writer, speaker, actress; *b.* London, 1872. Started professional career as a journalist; later went on the stage and spent twelve years between acting and free-lance journalism; first play (in one act) produced Brighton, 1906, and later at Wyndham's Theatre; first long play, Diana of Dobson's, 1908; a contributor to various journals and magazines; lectures chiefly on feminist topics. *Publications:* Plays—Diana of Dobson's; Just to get Married; The Sixth Commandment; The Sergeant of Hussars; A Pageant of Great Women; Jack and Jill and a Friend; A Matter of Money; The Homecoming: The Constant Husband; Phyl; The Child in Flanders; Mrs. Armstrong's Admirer; The Brave and the Fair; The Beggar Prince; The Old

Adam, 1925; Lady Noggs (adaptation from Edgar Jepson's story); Caravan (adaptation from Carl Zuckmayer); (with Christopher St. John) How the Vote was Won, and The Pot and the Kettle. Books—Marriage as a Trade; Diana of Dobson's; Just to get Married; A Pageant of Great Women; A Matter of Money; Senlis, 1917; William, an Englishman, 1919; Theodore Savage, 1922; (with Lilian Baylis) The Old Vic, 1926; Lest Ye Die, 1928; Modern Germanics, 1931; Full Stop, 1931; Modern Italy, 1932; Modern France, 1933; Modern Russia, 1934; Modern Austria, 1935; Life Errant, 1935; Modern Ireland, 1936; Modern Scotland, 1937; Modern England, 1938; Modern Sweden, 1939; Lament for Democracy, 1940; Holland To-day, 1950. *Address:* 44 Glebe Place, S.W.3. *T.:* Flaxman 4605. [*Died* 5 *Dec.* 1952.

HAMILTON, Lieut.-Colonel Claud George Cole-, C.M.G. 1917; D.S.O. 1902; J.P., D.L.; Knight of Justice Order of St. John of Jerusalem; Chief Constable of Breconshire, 1912-47; retd. 1947; *b.* 27 Jan. 1869; *s.* of Capt. W. Cole-Hamilton, Ballitore House, Co. Kildare, and Beltrim, Co. Tyrone; *m.* 1893, Lucy (*d.* 1951), *d.* of Reginald H. Thorold. Served S. Africa, 1901-2 (despatches, Queen's medal 5 clasps, D.S.O.); European War, 1914-18 (C.M.G., bar to D.S.O., despatches thrice); in Command of the 8th (Service Batt.) Royal Irish Rifles, B.E.F.; later in command of 15th (Service Batt.); prisoner in Germany 21 Mar. 1918; retired. *Address:* The Old Barn, Eastfield Lane, Ringwood, Hants. [*Died* 6 *Jan.* 1957.

HAMILTON, Colonel Claud Lorn Campbell, C.M.G. 1918; D.S.O. 1916; D.L.; J.P.; Member H.M. Body Guard for Scotland, Royal Company of Archers, since 1932; *b.* 14 Feb. 1874; *s.* of Hugh Hamilton, Ayr, and Clayton, Fairlie, N.Z.; *m.* 1908, Veronica, *d.* of J. I. Boswell of Crawley Grange, Newport Pagnell; one *s.* one *d.* (and one *s.* decd.). *Educ.*: Haileybury; Woolwich. Entered R.A. 1893; Capt. 1900; Adjt., 1905-8; Maj., 1910; Lt.-Colonel, 1915; Colonel, 1919; served South African War, 1902 (Queen's medal three clasps); European War, 1914-18 (despatches, D.S.O., C.M.G.); A.Q.M.G., 1920-23; retd. 1923; Lt.-Col. Comdg. 4/5th Bn. R. Scots Fus. 1924-29; Bt.-Col. (T.A.), 1928; retd. 1929. *Address:* Rozelle, Ayr. *Clubs:* United Service; Ayr County (Ayr). [*Died* 8 *Jan.* 1954.

HAMILTON, Sir Frederic Howard, Kt., *cr.* 1936; *b.* 1865; *s.* of George Hamilton and Mary Purser; *m.* 1st, Helen Mary, *d.* of H. Didcott, Queenstown, South Africa; 2nd, Mary Alice Forster, *d.* of A. L. Smith, late Master of Balliol College. *Educ.:* Mill Hill School; Caius College, Cambridge. Studied for the Bar; went to South Africa, 1889; was Editor Johannesburg Star; sent from Johannesburg to Mr. Rhodes to stop Jameson Raid; subsequently imprisoned in Pretoria as member of Reform Committee; was largely interested in mining in Africa, Australia, and elsewhere; former Chm. of Executive Committee Liberal National Council; Vice-President of Royal Free Hospital. *Recreation:* golf. *Address:* Russet House, Tadworth, Surrey. *T.:* Tadworth 3207. *Clubs:* Brooks's, Reform, City University. [*Died* 29 *Jan.* 1956.

HAMILTON, Rt. Rev. Heber James, D.D.; *b.* Collingwood, Ontario, 1862; *s.* of W. Basil Hamilton; *m.* 1894, Minnie Spence; one *d.* *Educ.:* Toronto University and Wycliffe College, Toronto. Ordained, 1887; Curate of St. John's, Port Hope, Ontario, 1887-1889; Dean of Wycliffe Coll., 1889-92; Missionary at Nagoya, 1892-96 and 1903-12; at Gifu, 1896-1900; Tokyo, 1901-2; Bishop of Mid-Japan, 1912-1934. *Address:* 40 Charles St. East, Toronto, Canada. [*Died* 4 *March* 1952.

HAMILTON, Hugh Brown, C.M.G. 1951; President: Mitchell Cotts & Co. (E.A.) Ltd.; British East Africa Corporation Ltd.; East African Sisal Estates, Ltd., Ruiru, Kenya; *b.* 19 Nov. 1892; widower; three *s.* one *d.* *Educ.:* Glasgow High School. Director: Mitchell Cotts & Co. (Middle East) Ltd.; East African Extract Corporation Ltd., Nairobi; Unga Ltd., Nairobi. *Address:* P.O. Box 822, Nairobi, Kenya Colony. *Clubs:* Royal Commonwealth Society, Junior Carlton; Muthaiga Country (Nairobi). [*Died* 26 *Dec.* 1960.

HAMILTON, Brig. Hugh William Roberts, C.B.E. 1940; D.S.O. 1917; M.C.; late R.E.; *b.* 13 Apr. 1892; *s.* of late Brig.-Gen. W. G. Hamilton, C.B., C.S.I., D.S.O., and May, *d.* of General Sir Hugh Gough, V.C.; *m.* 1927, Mary Olive, *d.* of W. F. Houghton, Foulks Court, Johnstown, Co. Kilkenny; two *s.* *Educ.:* Rugby. First Commission, 1911; Captain, 1917; Major, 1926; Lt.-Col., 1934; Col., 1938; served in France, 1914-15; Mesopotamia, 1916-18; Palestine, 1918 (despatches twice, D.S.O., M.C.); Waziristan, 1922-23 (despatches); France, 1939-40 (C.B.E.); retired pay, 1946. *Publication:* History of the 20th (Fd.) Co., Royal Bombay Sappers and Miners. [*Died* 4 *Nov.* 1959.

HAMILTON, Lt.-Col. James S.; *see* Stevenson-Hamilton.

HAMILTON, Admiral Sir Louis Henry Keppel, K.C.B., *cr.* 1944 (C.B. 1943); D.S.O. 1915; *b.* 1890; *e. s.* of late Adm. Sir F. T. Hamilton, G.C.V.O., K.C.B., and Maria Walpole, *d.* of Adm. of the Fleet Hon. Sir Henry Keppel, G.C.B. *Educ.:* Osborne. Flag Officer-in-Charge, Malta, 1943-45. Served European War (Cameroons), 1915 (despatches, D.S.O.); First Naval Member and Chief of Naval Staff of Commonwealth Naval Board, 1945-48; retired list, 1948. Russian Order of St. Stanislas; 1940 Bar to D.S.O.; Norwegian War Cross, 1942. *Clubs:* United Service, Turf. [*Died* 22 *June* 1957.

HAMILTON, Col. Sir N. V. C. D.; *see* Dalrymple-Hamilton.

HAMILTON, Sir Robert Caradoc, 8th Bt., *cr.* 1647; late Major Royal Warwickshire Regt.; *b.* 22 Mar. 1877; *s.* of 7th Bart. and Mary (*d.* 1918), *d.* of H. Willan; *S.* father, 1919; *m.* 1907, Irene, 2nd *d.* of Sir C. Mordaunt, 10th Bart.; two *s.* one *d.*; Lieut. Norfolk Regt. *Recreation:* shooting, etc. *Heir: s.* (Robert Charles) Richard Caradoc, [*b.* 8 Sept. 1911; *m.* 1952, Elizabeth Vidal, *yr. d.* of late Sir William Barton, K.C.I.E.] *Address:* Collaven Manor, Sourton, Okehampton, Devon. [*Died* 15 *Feb.* 1959.

HAMILTON, Lt.-Col. Roland, O.B.E. 1924; retired regular army officer, R.E.; *b.* 23 Nov. 1886; *s.* of late Major Henry Hamilton, 4th Gurkha Rifles, Indian Army; *m.* 1933, Sarah Elizabeth Mary Stern (*née* Campbell). *Educ.:* Cheltenham College; R.M.A., Woolwich. Commissioned Royal Engineers, 1905. Served European War in Baluchistan, Persia and Mesopotamia, 1916-18 (despatches), and in Kurdistan Expedition, 1923 (O.B.E.); retired 1934 and rejoined army in 1939, serving till 1945 in administrative appointments in Scotland and England. M.P. (Lab.) for Sudbury Division of Suffolk, 1945-50. *Recreations:* walking, preferably on mountains; gardening, travel, swimming and sun bathing. *Address:* Maryfield, Shottermill, Haslemere, Surrey. [*Died* 10 *Feb.* 1953.

HAMILTON, Rev. William (Hamilton), M.A.; D.D.; Minister of Leslie and Waulkmill Parish, Garioch, Aberdeenshire, 1949-56; *b.* Barnhill, by Dundee, 24 March 1886; *s.* of George G. Hamilton, Broughty Ferry; *m.* 1914, Annie, *d.* of John Seivwright, Aberdeen, and Cleveland, Ohio; two *d.* *Educ.:* Collegiate School, Broughty Ferry; High School of Dundee; University of St. Andrews; Trinity College, Glasgow. Minister at Barrhead, Renfrewshire, 1913-19; Logie and Gauldry, 1919-

1923; Greenock, 1923-27; General Sec., Alliance of Presbyterian and Reformed Churches, 1927-49; travelled extensively in Europe and America in interests of international Christianity; organiser of, and delegate to, various Œcumenical Conferences; Editor of Great Heart (Scottish Churches' Magazine for the Young), 1921-28, and developed the Great Heart Order of World-Friendship to promote international friendship among the young people of all nations; W.E.A. Lecturer in English Literature; Moderator, Synod of Aberdeen, 1953-1954; Presbytery of Garioch, 1954-55. *Publications:* College Echoes, 1906-7; Murray's Scarlet Gown, 1909; Gauldry, and other Poems, 1920; John Masefield, a Popular Critical Study, 1922, enlarged edition, 1925; The Desire of the Moth, and other Poems, 1925; Dent's Holyrood Anthology of Modern Scots Poems, 1929; Scott's Lady of the Lake, 1932; Kate Kennedy's Eve, 1933; The Church and Youth, 1934; Children Praising (with Herbert Wiseman), 1936; Student Songs for Camp and College (with A. G. Abbie), 1937; Come, Lasses and Lads (collected lyrics); Report on alleged persecution of religious minorities in Transylvania (with F. J. Paul and J. M. Webster); Queen Madeleine (play); Editor of Presbyterian Alliance Council Proceedings (1929, 1933, 1937, and 1948) and Quarterly Register (1927-48); contributor to many prose and verse anthologies, hymnals, literary and ecclesiastical journals, and to British Students' Song Book; has written unbroken diary of persons, events, books, etc., since 1908, and Prolegomena, 1886-1908. *Recreations:* poetry and literary criticism, music, press correspondence, gardening, travel. *Address:* The Manse of Leslie, by Insch, Aberdeenshire. *T.:* Insch 360. *Club:* University (Aberdeen). [*Died* 25 *Dec.* 1958.

HAMILTON, Maj.-Gen. (local Lt.-Gen.) William Haywood, C.B. 1937; C.I.E. 1919; C.B.E. 1921; D.S.O. 1916; F.R.C.S., D.T.M. & H., D.P.H. (Lond.), 1928; I.M.S., retired; *s.* of late W. R. Hamilton, I.C.S. *Educ.:* Tonbridge School (prize-winner and exhibitioner); St. Bartholomew's Hospital (prize-winner). Held various appointments, including Ophthalmic house surgeon, house physician and extern (midwifery), clinical assistant in Ear, Nose and Throat; Dermatological and Gynæcological departments, also held appointments at North London, Westminster Ophthalmic, Temperance Hospitals, and St. Luke's Hospital for Mental Cases. Entered I.M.S. 1905; Ophthalmic specialist and Surgical specialist appointments; D.A.D.M.S. Lucknow Division, 1911-1915, Abor Expedition (medal and clasp); A.D.M.S. and D.D.M.S., G.H.Q., Mesopotamia during European War, 1915-22 (C.I.E., C.B.E., D.S.O., Chev. Corona d'Italia, Bt. Lt.-Col., Bt. Col. eight mentions, 1915 Medal, Victory Medal, Allied Medal, Post-War Operations Medal); The Kurdistan operations; Operations in Persia; Arab Rebellion, N.W. Frontier, Waziristan; Officiating A.D.M.S. Secunderabad District, Waziristan District, Pindi District, and Bombay District; A.D.M.S. Meerut District; D.D.M.S., Northern Command; D.M.S. in India; Honorary Physician to the King, 1935-41; retired, 1941. *Publications:* Occasional articles, scientific and sporting, written for medical journals, etc. *Recreations:* Rugby—for the school, Bart's., Blackheath, and Middlesex county; cricket—for the school, Bart.'s, Netley, Sirhind Brigade; tennis—open champion of Iraq, 1922, etc.; hockey, boxing, shooting (Bisley), athletics, swimming, etc. *Address:* c/o Grindlay & Co., 54 Parliament Street, S.W.1. [*Died* 18 *Oct.* 1955.

HAMILTON-DALRYMPLE, Sir Hew C.; *see* Dalrymple.

HAMILTON-GORDON, Lt.-Col. Edward H.; *see* Gordon, Lt.-Col. E. H. H.

HAMILTON-SPENCER-SMITH; *see* Spencer-Smith.

HAMMERSTEIN, Oscar, 2nd; librettist; *b.* 12 July 1895; *s.* of William Hammerstein and Alice Nimmo; *m.* 1st, 1917, Myra Finn; one *s.* one *d.*; 2nd, 1929, Dorothy Blanchard; one *s.* *Educ.:* Columbia University (A.B.). Holder of Hon. Doctorates at several American Univs. and Colls. Author of following: *musical plays:* Wildflower, 1923; Rose Marie, 1924; Sunny, 1925; The Desert Song, 1926; Show Boat, 1927; New Moon, 1928; Sweet Adeline, 1929; Music in The Air, 1932; Oklahoma, 1943; Carmen Jones, 1943; Carousel, 1945; Allegro, 1947; South Pacific, 1949 (Pulitzer Prize); The King and I, 1951; Me and Juliet, 1953; Pipe Dream, 1955; Flower Drum Song, 1958; The Sound of Music, 1959; *screen plays:* Show Boat—Swing High Swing Low; High, Wide and Handsome; Story of Irene and Vernon Castle; State Fair. *Co-Producer of:* I remember Mama, 1944; Annie Get Your Gun, 1946; Happy Birthday, 1946; Show Boat (revival), 1946; John Loves Mary, 1947. *Author of lyrics of many songs including:* Ol' Man River, All The Things You are, Lover, Come Back to Me, When I Grow Too Old to Dream, The Last Time I Saw Paris, Only Make Believe, Oh What a Beautiful Mornin' The Surrey With The Fringe On Top, People Will Say We're In Love, It Might As Well be Spring, If I Loved You, Some Enchanted Evening, I whistle a Happy Tune, Hello! Young Lovers, We kiss in a Shadow, Getting to Know You, Shall We Dance?, I Enjoy Being A Girl, Do Re Me, The Sound of Music, My Favorite Things, Climb Ev'ry Mountain. Director, Am. Soc. of Composers, Authors and Publishers; Member National Institute of Arts and Letters. Partner Williamson Music, Inc. *Publications:* Oklahoma, 1943; Carmen Jones, 1944; Carousel, 1945; Allegro, 1947; South Pacific, 1949; The King and I, 1951; Me and Juliet, 1953; Pipe Dream, 1955; Flower Drum Song, 1958; The Sound of Music, 1959. *Recreations:* tennis, chess, bridge. *Address:* Doylestown, Pennsylvania, U.S.A. *Clubs:* Lotos, Columbia University (N.Y.). [*Died* 23 *Aug.* 1960.

HAMMETT, Richard C., C.C.; *b.* 25 Dec. 1880; *m.* 1902, Violet Constance Davies; one *s.* one *d.* *Educ.:* Upper Grade, Putney. Commenced business in London in 1901, being the founder of R. C. Hammett Ltd., Meat Traders and Produce Merchants; established first Technical School in connection with Meat Trade; Member of Board of Governors of National College of Food Technology. Work concentrated on supervision and distribution of Food Supplies, 1914-18 and 1939-45; Member Court of Common Council for Ward of Farringdon Without; Past Pres. Farringdon Ward Club: Member Special Labour Committee, etc., at Guildhall; Past Master Worshipful Company of Butchers; Liveryman Worshipful Company of Poulters; Sheriff of City of London, 1947-48. Member of London Chamber of Commerce; Chm. of many Trade Associations; Member: a Joint Industrial Council; Institute of Food Technology; Institute of Hygiene. Governor St. Bartholomew's Hospital, Chairman of its House Sub-Committee and Member Medical Coll. Council. *Publication:* Handbook on Meat and Text-book for Butchers, 1926. *Recreation:* horse riding. *Address:* 14 West Smithfield, E.C.1. *T.:* City 1212. *Clubs:* City Livery, United Wards of the City of London, Royal Empire Society; Guildhall. [*Died* 19 *Dec.* 1952.

HAMMILL, Capt. John Schomberg, C.B.E. 1944; R.N.; *b.* 5 Oct. 1890; *s.* of late Capt. Tynte Ford Hammill, C.B., R.N., and Anne Schomberg; *m.* 1925, Anna Bertholde Frances Browning; two *d.* *Educ.:* R.N. Colleges, Osborne and Dartmouth. Midshipman, 1908; Lieut. 1912; served in H.M.S. Cornwall at Falkland Isles action, 1914, and in Vanguard, Jutland, 1916; Harwich, 1916-18, and Grand Fleet remainder of war; qualified in gunnery, 1915; Gunnery Officer, H.M.S. New Zealand, Lord Jellicoe's world cruise, 1919-20; Comdr. 1925; Admiralty, 1936. Gunnery Div. Naval Staff; retired, 1946. *Address:* Bere Farm, Wickham, Hants. *Club:* Army and Navy. [*Died* 28 *Sept.* 1959.

HAMMOND, Brig.-Gen. Frederick Dawson, C.B.E. 1919; D.S.O. 1916; *b.* 10 Nov. 1881; *s.* of late Col. Frederick Hammond, C.B., 5th Punjab Cavalry. *Educ.:* Temple Grove; Eton (King's Scholar). 2nd Lieutenant, Royal Engineers, 1900; served South African War, 1901-2; European War (D.S.O., Brevet Lieutenant-Colonel, C.B.E., Légion d'Honneur, despatches seven times); Head of Allied Railway Mission to Poland, Apr. 1919-Jan. 1920; Director of Communications, Upper Silesia, 1920; since then has inspected and reported on railways and communications in Kenya, Uganda, Tanganyika, Greece, Nigeria, Gold Coast, Rhodesia, Jamaica, Sierra Leone, Nyasaland, Mozambique, Iraq, and Ceylon, and has advised the Govt. of India on the Statutory Control of Railways; Special Commissioner to the Chinese Government to inspect and report on the Chinese Railways, 1935; Chm. British Railways in Uruguay from 1939 until their sale to Uruguayan Govt., 1949. *Address:* c/o Westminster Bank, 1 Stratford Place, Oxford St., W.1. *Club:* Brooks's. [*Died* 29 *Nov.* 1952.

HAMMOND, Gertrude Demain, R.I.; water-colour painter and illustrator; *b.* Brixton; 2nd *d.* of Horatio Demain Hammond and Eliza Mary Wood; *m.* 1898, Henry Going M'Murdie. Entered Lambeth Art School, 1879; R.A. Schools, 1885; gained Sketch Club Prizes there, 1886, 1887; prize for decorative design, 1889, the commission for its execution in a public building being also given, the first time to a woman student; exhibited R.I. every year, 1886-1940; elected member, 1896; exhibited R.A. since 1886; exhibited Paris Exhibition, 1900, and awarded bronze medal for a water-colour painting; exhibited at St. Louis, 1904, and at New Zealand International Exhibition, 1907. *Publications:* since 1892 illustrations for books, and Queen, Graphic, etc.; illustrated The Virginians, 1902; Martin Chuzzlewit and Our Mutual Friend, 1903; Illustrations for new American edition of George Eliot, 1907; for Marion Crawford's novel Arethusa, 1907; Illustrations in colour for edition of Shakespeare (America), 1902-3; The Pilgrim's Progress, 1904; Faerie Queene, 1909; Stories from Shakespeare, 1910; Shakespeare's Kings, 1912; David Copperfield, 1920. *Address:* Gracemere, 53 Richmond Road, Worthing, Sussex. [*Died* 21 *July* 1952.

HAMP, Arthur Edward, C.M.G. 1945; C.B.E. 1937; M.Inst.C.E.; M.Inst.T.; *b.* 23 Nov. 1886; *s.* of Rev. A. Hamp, M.A.; *m.* 1923, Mary, *d.* of Rev. E. T. Mateer; one *s.* four *d.* *Educ.:* King Edward VIth School, Bury S. Edmunds; Imperial College of Technology, S. Kensington. Articled pupil and Assistant to Mr. Baldwin Latham, M.Inst.C.E., Westminster; Asst. Engineer P.W.D. Kenya, 1912-14; entered service of Kenya and Uganda Railways and Harbours, 1914; served European War, East Africa Protectorate, 1914-18; Chief Engineer Kenya and Uganda Railways and Harbours, 1928-1942; General Manager Tanganyika Railways and Ports Services, 1943-46; retd. 1946. *Address:* Little Birches, Tilford, Farnham, Surrey. *T.:* Frensham 158. *Club:* East India and Sports. [*Died* 4 *Dec.* 1951.

HAMPDEN, 3rd Viscount, *cr.* 1884; 25th Baron Dacre, *cr.* 1307; **Brig.-Gen. Thomas Walter Brand,** G.C.V.O., *cr.* 1935; K.C.B., *cr.* 1921 (C.B. 1917); C.M.G. 1915; late Major 10th Hussars; Herts Regt. (T.F.); Lord Lieut. Hertfordshire, 1915-52; *b.* 29 Jan. 1869; *e. s.* of 2nd Viscount Hampden and Susan Henrietta, *d.* of Lord George Cavendish, *bro.* of 7th Duke of Devonshire; *S.* father 1906; *m.* 1899, Lady Katharine Mary Montagu-Douglas-Scott (*d.* 1951), *d.* of 6th Duke of Buccleuch; three *s.* four *d.* *Educ.:* Eton; Trinity College, Cambridge. Entered army, 1889; served South Africa, 1899-1901 (despatches, Bt. Major, Queen's medal six clasps); served European War, 1914-18 (despatches seven times, temp. Brig.-Gen., C.B., C.M.G.); a Lord-in-Waiting, 1924-36; Hon. Col. Hertfordshire Regt. T.A., 1930-48; Col. 10th Royal Hussars, 1935-1939. *Heir:* *s.* Hon. Thomas Henry Brand, C.M.G. *Address:* Mill Court, Alton, Hants. *T.:* Bentley 3125. *Club:* Turf. [*Died* 4 *Sept.* 1958.

HAMPSHIRE, Charles Herbert, C.M.G. 1949; M.B., B.S. (Lond.), M.R.C.S., L.R.C.P., B.Sc. (Lond.); F.R.I.C.; pharmaceutical chemist; Secretary, British Pharmacopœia Commission, 1929-50; Editor, Journal of Pharmacy and Pharmacology; Chairman, Expert Committee on the Unification of Pharmacopœias, World Health Organisation; *b.* Ilkley, Yorks, 5 Feb. 1885; *s.* of William Henry Hampshire and Martha Emmott; *m.* 1915, Grace Mary (*d.* 1954), *d.* of C. D. Taylor, Nottingham; one *d.* *Educ.:* Ilkley Grammar School; London University. Jacob Bell Scholar, Pharmaceutical Society, 1905; Society's silver medallist, 1907; Pharmacist and Lecturer, University College Hospital, 1914-29; Examiner to Pharmaceutical Society; Chairman, British Pharmaceutical Conference, 1933 and 1934. *Publications:* papers in Journal of Chemical Society and Year Book of Pharmacy; Manual of Volumetric Analysis. *Address:* Foxcote, Northwood, Mx. *T.:* 289. [*Died* 25 *Jan.* 1955.

HAMPTON, Frederick, C.B.E. 1951; *b.* 17 June 1889; *s.* of Walter and Mary Hampton; *m.* 1910, Mary May Long; three *d.* *Educ.:* Bridge Trust School, Handsworth, Birmingham. Entered Civil Service, 1911, Board of Trade; Staff Officer for Juvenile Employment, Ministry of Labour, Midlands Div., 1919-35; Manager, Employment Exchange, Min. of Labour, Nottingham, 1935-40; Regional Industrial Relations Officer, Min. of Labour and Nat. Service, North Midlands Region, 1940-42; Labour Adviser to Nigerian Govt., West Africa, 1942-44; Deputy Regional Controller, Min. of Labour and Nat. Service, North Midlands Region, 1944-47; Counsellor-Labour Attaché, British Embassy, Athens, 1947-55, retired. *Address:* Darien, Oak Hill Drive, Prestatyn, Flintshire. [*Died* 30 *Aug.* 1958.

HAMSUN, Knut; farmer; *b.* 4 Aug. 1859; *s.* of Peder Pedersen and Tora Olsdatter; *m.* Marie Andersen; two *s.* three *d.* *Educ.:* no education. Clerk in store and in post office; farming; teacher for small children in country school; street car conductor in U.S.; since 1889 mostly writing; the last thirty years also farming; Nobel Prize. *Publications:* Shallow Soil, 1914; Growth of the Soil, 1920; Hunger, 1921; Pan, 1920; Mysteries, 1927; The Women at the Pump, 1928; Chapter the Last, 1929; Vagabonds, 1931; August, 1932; The Road Leads On, 1935, etc. *Address:* Grimstad, Norway. *T.A.:* Grimstad, Norway. [*Died* 19 *Feb.* 1952.

HANBURY, Lt.-Col. and Hon. Col. Lionel Henry, C.M.G. 1916; V.D., J.P. Bucks; Royal Warwick Regt.; late Lt.-Col. 4th Batt. Royal Berks; Lieutenant of City of London; *b.* Dec. 1864; *e. surv. s.* of late George Hanbury of Hitcham House, Bucks; *m.* Maisie (*d.* 1949), *d.* of late Henry Allhusen of Stoke Court, Bucks; two *s.* three *d.* *Educ.:* Eton. Served European War, 1914-17 (despatches, C.M.G.); High Sheriff County of London, 1920; Member of the Royal Commission on Awards to Inventors. *Recreations:* shooting, fishing. *Address:* Hitcham Park Cottage, Burnham, Bucks. *T.A.:* Burnham, Bucks. *T.:* Burnham 6. *Club:* Carlton. [*Died* 8 *Feb.* 1954.

HANCE, Lt.-Gen. Sir (James) Bennett, K.C.M.G., *cr.* 1953; K.C.I.E., *cr.* 1946 (C.I.E. 1939); O.B.E. 1920; M.A., M.D., B.Ch.

(Cantab.), F.R.C.S.E., M.R.C.S., L.R.C.P., late I.M.S.; late K.H.S.; F.R.S.M.; Fellow Roy. Soc. Trop. Med. and Hygiene; Medical Adviser, and President of Medical Board, Commonwealth Relations Office, 1946–; *b.* Liscard, Cheshire, 21 Apr. 1887; *y. s.* of late Edward M. Hance, Bar.-at-Law, and late Mary Amelia Hance, Liverpool; *m.* 1st, 1916, Catherine Herriette Lawson, *o. d.* of late Charles Lester Leonard, A.M., M.D., of Philadelphia, U.S.A.; two *d.*; 2nd, 1938, Frau Richildis von Kaan, *yr. d.* of late Richard von Warton of Vienna and Ehrenhausen, Styria. *Educ.:* Oundle School; Cambridge University; Guy's Hospital. House Surgeon Royal Surrey County Hospital, Guildford; entered I.M.S., 1912; seconded as House Surgeon and Clinical Asst. in Gynaecology to late Prof. W. Blair Bell in Liverpool; sometime Specialist in Midwifery and Gynaecology, 7th Meerut Division; field service: France, 1914-16; South Persia, 1917-19 (despatches twice); Agency Surgeon, Foreign and Polit. Dept. Govt. of India, from 1919; services lent to Jodhpur State as P.M.O. 1925-28; Chief Medical Officer States of Western India, Rajkot, 1928-33; Residency Surgeon in Mysore, Bangalore, 1933-40; Inspector-General Civil Hospitals and Director Public Health, Central Provinces and Berar, 1940-42; Deputy Director-General, I.M.S., 1942-43; Director-General, 1943-46. Services lent to Govt. of Ceylon to survey medical and health services of the Island and advise on their development, 1956. K.St.J. 1946. *Publications:* articles in Guy's Hospital Reports, 1926 and 1928, Indian Medical Gazette, 1929-38. *Recreations:* travel, angling. *Address:* Commonwealth Relations Office, Whitehall, S.W.1; Box Cottage, Donnington, Newbury, Berks. *Club:* Athenæum. [*Died* 5 *Sept.* 1958.

HANCOCK, Anthony Ilbert; Secretary, Committee of London Clearing Bankers; Secretary, Bankers' Clearing House Ltd.; Secretary, British Bankers' Association, since 1951; *b.* 28 June 1906; 2nd *s.* of late William Ilbert Hancock, F.R.C.S.; *m.* 1939, Eileen Mary King; one *s.* *Educ.:* Tonbridge School. Bank of England, 1926-51. *Address:* Post Office Court, 10 Lombard Street, E.C.3. *T.:* Mansion House 3341. [*Died* 28 *March* 1955.

HANCOCK, Sir Henry T., Kt., *cr.* 1939; J.P.; Alderman Lancs. C.C.; Chairman Crosby (Lancs.) Conservative Unionist Assoc. since 1922; Lancashire Education Committee; *b.* 25 April 1877; *m.* 1901; one *s.* one *d.* *Educ.:* Liverpool Institute. Charter Mayor of Crosby, 1937; Officer of the Order of George I, King of the Hellenes, 1937. *Address:* Riverslea, Blundellsands, Lancashire. *T.A.:* Judge Liverpool. *T.:* Liverpool Central 5981, Crosby 1101. *Club:* Constitutional (Liverpool). [*Died* 24 *Oct.* 1957.

HANDFORD, Sir John (James William), Kt., *cr.* 1949; C.B. 1946; O.B.E. 1919; *b.* 5 Dec. 1881; 2nd *s.* of John James Handford; *m.* Gladys Victoria (*d.* 1926), *yr. d.* of late John W. Trist, F.S.A.(Lond.); one *s.* one *d.* *Educ.:* Latymer Upper School. Post Office Savings Bank, 1900; Scottish Office, 1902; Associate Institute of Actuaries, 1910; Board of Agriculture for Scotland, Asst. Accountant, 1913; Asst. Sec. and Accountant, 1918; Department of Agriculture for Scotland, Asst. Sec. in charge of Land Settlement, 1930; Chief Liaison Officer in London, 1940; Principal Assistant Secretary, 1942; late Asst. Under-Sec. of State for Scotland. *Address:* 22 Fountainhall Road, Edinburgh. *Clubs:* Reform; Caledonian United Service (Edinburgh). [*Died* 28 *Oct.* 1959.

HANHAM, Sir John Ludlow, 10th Bt. *cr.* 1667; Apparitor-General to Province and Diocese of Canterbury; *s.* of 9th Bt. and Hon. Cordelia Lucy (*d.* 1945), 2nd *d.* of the 1st Lord Ludlow; *b.* 23 Jan. 1898; *S.* father, 1911. *Educ.:* Winchester College; Magdalen College, Oxford, M.A. Barrister-at-Law, Inner Temple, 1926; served European War (wounded); A.D.C. to Lord Bledisloe, Governor-General of New Zealand, 1930-32; Hon. Corresponding Member of the New Zealand Numismatic Society; County Alderman, J.P., D.L. Dorset. Served (not overseas) War of 1939-45, Grenadier Guards, Captain. *Heir:* *b.* Henry Phelips [*b.* 6 April 1901. Served War of 1939-45]. *Address:* Dean's Court, Wimborne, Dorset. *Club:* Guards. [*Died* 30 *April* 1955.

HANKEY, Brig.-Gen. Edward Barnard, C.B. 1927; D.S.O.; *b.* 1875; *s.* of late John Barnard Hankey of Fetcham Park, Surrey; *m.* 1908, Katharine (*d.* 1946), *d.* of M. J. Dohan, Philadelphia, U.S.A.; one *d.* (and one *d.* decd.). *Educ.:* Eton. Formerly Major and Brevet Colonel, Worcestershire Regt.; served S. Africa, 1899-1902 (wounded, Queen's medal 4 clasps); Sudan, 1904 (medal with clasp); European War, 1914-191, with Worcestershire Regt. and Tank Corps (wounded, despatches, D.S.O., Brevet Colonel, Croix de Guerre); retired pay, 1929. *Recreations:* hunting, shooting, golf. *Address:* Cecily Hill, Cirencester. *Club:* Army and Navy. [*Died* 22 *March* 1959.

HANKEY, W. L.; *see* Lee-Hankey.

HANKINSON, Charles J.; *see* Holland, Clive.

HANLEY, James Alec, Ph.D., University of Munich; an Associate of the Royal College of Science, London; *b.* 26 Nov. 1886; *e. s.* of late Frederick Hanley, Hemsworth, Yorks. *Educ.:* Wakefield Grammar School. Research work, Rothamsted Experimental Station; Board of Agriculture Research Scholar, 1912-14; Lecturer in Agricultural Chemistry and Advisory Chemist in Leeds University; Lecturer in Agricultural Science, Bristol University, 1924-27; Professor of Agriculture and Chief Advisory Officer, Bristol University, 1927-31; Principal of Royal Agricultural College, Cirencester, 1927-31; Professor of Agriculture and Rural Economy, King's College, Newcastle upon Tyne, and scientific Director of Cockle Park Experimental Station, Northumberland, 1931-47. *Publications:* Grass Land (with Prof. Sir R. G. Stapledon); An Agricultural Survey of the Northern Province (4 northern counties) with map; Editor of Progressive Farming, 1949; articles in scientific and agricultural journals and papers, chiefly on liming and grass land. *Address:* Applethwaite, Keswick. [*Died* 10 *April* 1960.

HANNAFORD, Charles E.; Member Royal Society of British Artists, 1916-29; *b.* 1863; *m.* 1st, Helen, *d.* of Richard Lean, Truro; two *s.*; 2nd, Margery, *y. d.* of Frederick Wright, Harpenden. *Educ.:* Paris. Studied Art under Stanhope Forbes, R.A.; works purchased for Royal Collection, 1906 and 1909; one-man show, Walker Gallery, Bond Street, 1910 and 1912, from which exhibition water-colour drawing purchased by King George; exhibitor R.A., R.I., R.B.A., Royal Canadian Academy, Royal Cambrian Academy, Manchester, 1913; works in collection of Queen Alexandra, Earl of Mount Edgcumbe, Earl Morley, Lord Kingsale, etc. *Address:* 7 Boulton Road, Thorpe, Norwich. *T.:* 34040 Norwich. [*Died* 21 *Oct.* 1955.

HANNAY, Alexander Howard; Hon. Secretary Aristotelian Society for Philosophical Studies since 1924; Editor, 1929; *b.* 1889; *s.* of Arnold Hannay and Alys M. Hannay; *m.* 1st, 1912, Winifred Lynton; three *s.*; 2nd, 1932, Leonora Lockhart. *Educ.:* Winchester College; Balliol College, Oxford; art critic the London Mercury, 1920-34; Secretary and Treasurer 7th International Congress of Philosophy, Oxford, 1930. *Publications:* Roger Fry and other Essays; tr. de Ruggiero's Modern Philosophy; articles in the London Mercury and other periodicals, and papers in Proceedings of Aristotelian Society. *Recreations:* gardening, landscape painting. *Address:* 18 Kensington Park Road, W.11. *Club:* United University. [*Died* 4 *Aug.* 1955.

HANNAY, Col. Frederick; *see* Rainsford-Hannay.

HANNAY, Capt. Walter Maxwell; *b.* 3 May 1873; *s.* of Colonel E. A. Hannay, J.P.; *m.* 1918, Kathleen, *d.* of Robert Fleming, Joyce Grove, Oxon; three *s.* *Educ.:* in France. Served in European War, 1915-19 (despatches, French Croix de Guerre); Sheriff, Worcestershire, 1940; J.P. Glos. *Address:* Spring Hill House, Moreton in Marsh, Glos. *T.A.:* Bourton on the Hill. *T.:* Broadway 70. *Club:* Guards. [*Died* 3 *Oct.* 1952.

HANSEN, Brig. Percy Howard, V.C. 1915; D.S.O. 1918; M.C.; *b.* 26 Oct. 1890; *s.* of late V. Hansen; *m.* Marie Rose, *d.* of G. Emsell; one *d.* *Educ.:* Eton; Sandhurst. Served European War, 1914-18; Dardanelles, Egypt, 1915; France, 1916-18 (despatches five times, V.C., M.C., D.S.O., Croix de Guerre (French)); V.C. for bravery at Hill 10, Gallipoli, for rescuing six men from burning scrub under terrific fire; Brevet Major, 1919; p.s.c., 1919; Brigade Major and G.S.O.2 (France), Brigade Major 8 and 12 Inf. Bds., 1920-23; General Staff Officer, 2nd grade, 55 Div., 1924-28, Jamaica, 1931-1934; Bt. Lt.-Col., 1932; D.A.A.G. Western Command, 1934-35; Lt.-Col., 1937; commanding 2nd Bn. Lincolnshire Regiment, 1937-39; Col., 1939; A.A.Q.M.G., 55th Div., 1939; Brigadier, D.A. and Q.M.G. 12 Corps, 1941; Commander Belfast Area, 1942-43; Commander Ashford Sub-District, 1943; S.H.A.E.F. Mission to Norway, 1943-45; Head of Civil Affairs. Retired R.A.R.O. with Hon. Rank of Brig., 1946; Commander Royal Order of St. Olav (Norway); Officer Legion of Merit (U.S.); France and Germany Star; Defence Medal; War Medal. *Recreations:* travelling, lecturing, cinematography. *Address:* 146 Oakwood Court, Kensington, W.14. *T.:* Western 9235. *Club:* United Service. [*Died* 12 *Feb.* 1951.

HANSEN, Sir Sven Wohlford, 1st Bt., *cr.* 1921; M.B.E. 1920; *b.* 1 Apr. 1876; *s.* of Carl Frederick Hansen; *m.* 1st, 1899, Jane, (*d.* 1951), *d.* of Thomas Welsh, Twizil, Durham; (*s.* killed in action) one *d.*; 2nd, Emily Alice, *widow* of R. A. Fulford, Sutton. *Educ.:* privately. *Heir:* none. *Address:* Grand Hotel, Eastbourne, Sussex. [*Died* 9 *Oct.* 1958 (*ext.*).

HANSFORD, Colonel Sir Benjamin, K.C.B. *cr.* 1939 (C.B. 1913); T.D. 1947; Hon. Colonel 54th H.A.A. Regiment (City of London) T.A., 1928-47; one of His Majesty's Lieutenants for the City of London since 1911 and a Member of the Committee for the City of London Lieutenancy; Past Master of the Company of Gardeners of London; Member of the London Stock Exchange since 1900; *b.* 26 April 1863; *m.* 1902, Mary, 3rd *d.* of late Hyman Montagu, F.S.A.; two *d.* Capt. Rifle Brigade (Prince Consort's Own) T.A., and Officer commanding its Administrative Centre, 1915; Organizing Officer of the City of London National Reserve and Chief Staff Officer of the City of London National Guard, 1914-15; Military Representative on the City of London Tribunal (Derby Scheme), 1915; Officer Commanding No. 1 Observer Company Royal Defence Corps, 1916; Commander No. 10 Observer Company, Northern Command, Royal Defence Corps, 1916-17; granted the permanent rank of Colonel, 1947. A Military Member of the City of London Territorial Association, 1920-43; Special Constabulary Long Service Medal; has done much to encourage the shooting and general efficiency of Territorials and Reservists. *Address:* 24 Kingston House, Princes Gate, S.W.7. *T.:* Kensington 3356. *Club:* Junior Carlton. [*Died* 1 *Dec.* 1954.

HANSI, pseudonym of **Jacques Waltz;** caricaturist; native of Alsace-Lorraine; contributor to journal Durchs-Elsass; Commander Legion of Honour; Correspondant de l'Institut; condemned at Leipzig to year's imprisonment for children's book which offended the Germans, but was not caught; served with French army in European War, 1914-18; Membre Correspondant of the Académie des Beaux-Arts. *Publications:* A French History of Alsace-Lorraine for Children; Mon Village; Professor Knatschke, 1917; Le Paradis Tricolone; L'Alsace heureuse, 1920; Le Voyage d'Erika, 1922; L'histoire de Saint Florentin d'Alsace, 1925; L'Alsace, 1929; Les Clochers dans les Vignes, 1930; Au pied de la Montagne Ste. Odile, 1934; L'art héraldique en Alsace, 1937; Le Retable d'Issenheim au Musée de Colmar, 1938; Madame Bissinger, 1950; Le premier Phonographe, 1950 *Address:* Colmar (Haut-Rhin). [*Died* 10 *June* 1951.

HANSON, Major Sir Charles Edwin Bourne, 2nd Bt., *cr.* 1918; M.A., Cantab.; Member of London Stock Exchange; *b.* 17 May 1874; *s.* of 1st Bt. and Martha Sabina, *d.* of late James Appelbe of Trafalgar, Halton, Canada; *S.* father, 1922; *m.* 1908, Violet Sybil, *d.* of John B. Johnstone; one *s.* two *d.* *Educ.:* Leys School, Cambridge; Clare College, Cambridge. Served South African War, 1899-1902 (Queen's medal and clasp, King's medal and two clasps); European War, 1914-18, with Duke of Wellington's Regiment; Lieutenant of City of London, 1910; High Sheriff of Cornwall, 1939. *Recreations:* yachting, golf, shooting. *Heir:* Captain Charles John Hanson, late D.C.L.I. [*b.* 28 Feb. 1919; *m.* 1944, Patricia Helen, W.R.N.S., *o. c.* of Rear-Adm. E. J. P. Brind; one *s.* one *d.*]. *Address:* Fowey Hall, Cornwall; 14 Cranmer Court, S.W.3. *Club:* United University. [*Died* 7 *Sept.* 1958.

HANSON, Daniel, D.Sc.; Professor of Metallurgy and Director of Department of Metallurgy, University of Birmingham; *b.* 1892; *e. s.* of late Daniel Hanson, Preston Brook, Cheshire; *m.* 1920, Hilda, 3rd. *d.* of late Rev. H. J. Fry; two *d.* (one *s.* decd.). *Educ.:* Wallasey Grammar School; Univ. of Liverpool. Joined staff of Research Department, Royal Arsenal, Woolwich, and later National Physical Laboratory, becoming Principal Scientific Officer in the Department of Metallurgy. *Publications:* Numerous scientific papers dealing with original research in metallurgical subjects. *Recreations:* climbing, fishing. *Address:* Haselor, near Alcester, Warwickshire. *T.:* Great Alne 43. [*Died* 12 *June* 1953.

HANSON, Sir Philip, Kt., *cr.* 1920; C.B. 1917; late Chairman of the Board of Works, Ireland; *b.* Bradford, Yorks, 18 Sept. 1871; *e. s.* of late Charles Hanson, journalist; *g.s.* of James Hanson, late chairman of School Board, Bradford; *m.* 1914, Constance Geraldine (Deena), *d.* of late R. Y. Tyrrell; two *s.* *Educ.:* Royal High School and University, Edinburgh; Balliol College, Oxford (Exhibitioner, B.A., 1st class honours, Lit. Hum.; Gaisford Greek prose prize). Joined War Office, 1895; Private Secretary to the Rt. Hon. George Wyndham, M.P., 1898-1903; served in Ministry of Munitions, 1915-19. *Address:* 79 Upper Leeson Street, Dublin. [*Died* 23 *Oct.* 1955.

HANSON, Sir Richard Leslie Reginald, 3rd. Bt., *cr.* 1887; *b.* 21 Nov. 1905; *s.* of Sir Gerald Stanhope Hanson, 2nd Bt., and Sylvia Dutton Cook; *S.* father 1946. *Educ.:* Eastbourne College. Late 10th Hussars Supernumerary Reserve. Served R.A., 1941-45. *Recreations:* hunting, racing. *Heir:* *half b.* Anthony Leslie Oswald, *b.* 27 Nov. 1934. *Address:* Imray, Kingston-Gorse, Sussex. *T.:* Rustington 1387. *Club:* United Hunts. [*Died* 7 *Oct.* 1951.

HARBERTON, 8th Viscount, *cr.* 1791; **Ralph Legge Pomeroy;** Baron Harberton, 1783; *b.* 31 Dec. 1869; *s.* of 6th Viscount Harberton and Florence, *o. d.* of William Wallace Legge, Malone House, Co. Antrim; *S.* brother, 1944; *m.* 1907, Mary

Katherine, *o. d.* of A. W. Leatham J.P.; three *s.* one *d.* *Educ.*: Charterhouse; Balliol College, Oxford (B.A. 1891). Major late 5th Dragoon Guards; served S. Africa (severely wounded, Queen's medal 3 clasps, King's medal 2 clasps); Major 4th Reserve Dragoons, Aug. 1914-Mar. 1919; O.B.E. 1919; J.P. Northampton. *Publication*: Regimental History 5th Dragoon Guards. *Heir*: *s.* Hon. Henry Ralph Martyn Pomeroy, *b.* 1908. *Address*: Highfield House, Husbands Bosworth, Rugby. *Club*: Cavalry. [*Died* 4 *July* 1956.

HARBORD, Brig.-Gen. Cyril Rodney, C.B. 1927; C.M.G. 1919; D.S.O. 1918; Order of the Nile; *b.* 1873; *m.* Kathleen, *d.* of late Capt. J. J. Paterson Fox; three *s.* (and one killed in action) one *d.* Served South Africa, 1900-02 (despatches, King's medal 2 clasps, Queen's medal 3 clasps); Somaliland, 1904 (medal and clasp); European War, 1914-19 (despatches, D.S.O., C.M.G.); retired, 1929. *Address*: 25 Sussex Mansions, Old Brompton Road, S.W.7. *T.*: Kensington 2761. *Club*: Cavalry. [*Died* 28 *Sept.* 1958.

HARBORD, Capt. Eric Walter, D.S.O. 1917; R.N.; *b.* 14 March 1879; *e. s.* of late Hon. Walter Harbord and 1st wife, Lady Eleanor Fitzroy, *o. d.* of 7th Duke of Grafton and *widow* of Herbert Fitzroy Eaton, Stetchworth Park, Cambridge; *m.* 1911, Rose Mary Adeline Dagmar Amelia, *d.* of Lt.-Col. George Charles Keppel Johnstone, late Grenadier Guards. *Decorated* for mine-sweeping; retired list, 1922; re-employed Aug. 1939; served as Mine-sweeping Officer on staff of Commander-in-Chief, Portsmouth; reverted to Retired List, June 1945. *Address*: Pinewood House, Sunninghill, Berks. *T.*: Ascot 468. [*Died* 18 *March* 1952.

HARBORD, Captain Maurice Assheton; 8th *s.* of late Hon. and Rev. John Harbord, 5th *s.* of 3rd Baron Suffield, and Caroline Penelope, 4th *d.* of Anthony Hamond of Westacre, Norfolk; *b.* 24 Oct. 1874; *m.* 1st, 1905, Isabel Jessie Lowth (whom he divorced, 1918), 4th *d.* of Baron Frederic von Wurtzburg-Schade; 2nd, 1929, Ethel Florence, *d.* of G. W. Goldsmith and *widow* of Francis Tugwell-Cowley; two *s.* *Educ.*: Haileybury. Captain R. of O.; served S. Africa, 1899-1902; Inspector Johannesburg Town Police, 1902-8. *Publication*: Froth and Bubble, 1916. *Address*: Morden House, 138 Parker Rd., Hastings. [*Died* 9 *Jan.* 1954.

HARBY, Sir Frank (Neville), Kt., *cr.* 1949; C.B.E. 1946; Chairman, Budget Committee, O.E.E.C., since 1949; *b.* 8 July 1888; *s.* of Charles Edward Harby, Exeter; *m.* 1923, Anna Jeanne Pavie. *Educ.*: Harleigh School, Bodmin. Entered Civil Service, 1906; Examiner Exchequer and Audit Dept., 1908; Deputy Secretary, 1942; Secretary, 1944. *Address*: Royal Madeleine Hotel, 26 Rue Pasquier, Paris. *T.*: Anjou 64-81. *Clubs*: Union; International Centre (Paris). [*Died* 28 *April* 1952.

HARCOURT, Alfred; Special Consultant George S. Armstrong & Co., Industrial and Management Engineers, New York; Founder, and until 1942 President, of Harcourt, Brace and Company, Inc.; *b.* New Paltz, Ulster County, New York, 31 Jan. 1881; *s.* of Charles M. Harcourt and Gertrude M. Elting; *m.* 1st, 1906, Susan Harreus (*d.* 1923), Stapleton, New York; 2nd, 1924, Ellen Knowles Eayrs, New York City; one *s.* *Educ.*: New Paltz State Normal School; A.B., Columbia, 1904. Began with Henry Holt and Co., publishers, New York, 1904, and became director and secretary; resigned 1919, and founded Harcourt, Brace and Co.; founded Blue Ribbon Books, Inc., from which resigned as Vice-President in 1938. *Publication*: Compiler (with Crosby Gaige) Books and Reading, 1908. *Recreations*: fishing, sailing, swimming, golf. *Address*: Riverside, Connecticut; 383 Madison Avenue, New York City. *T.A.*: Harbrace, New York. *T.*: Old Greenwich 7-0458. *Clubs*: Century (N.Y.); Country (Greenwich, Conn.); Valley (Santa Barbara, Calif.). [*Died* 20 *June* 1954.

HARCOURT, Admiral Sir Cecil Halliday Jepson, G.B.E., *cr.* 1953 (C.B.E. 1940); K.C.B., *cr.* 1945 (C.B. 1943); *b.* 11 April 1892; *s.* of late Halliday Harcourt and Grace Lilian, *d.* of Dr. Jepson; *m.* 1st, 1920, Evelyn (*d.* 1950), *widow* of Gerard Gould and *d.* of Brig.-Gen. W. H. Suart, C.M.G.; no *c.*; 2nd, 1953, Stella, *widow* of Air Cdre. David Waghorn. *Educ.*: Fonthill, East Grinstead; Royal Naval Colls., Osborne and Dartmouth. Lieutenant 1913; served European War, 1914-18; Commander 1926; Captain, 1933; lent Royal Australian Navy, 1935-1937, and Commanded H.M.A. Flotilla; Deputy Director of Operations Division, 1938-39; Director of Operations Division, 1939-41; Commanded H.M.S. Duke of York, 1941-42; Rear-Admiral, 1942; Commanded in succession 10th, 12th, and 15th Cruiser Squadrons, 1942-44, taking part in landings in North Africa (U.S. Legion of Merit), operations leading to the capture of Tunisia (C.B.), capture of Pantellaria and Lampedusa, landings in and capture of Sicily, and landing at Salerno (despatches); Naval Secretary to First Lord of the Admiralty, 1944-45; Commanded 11th Aircraft Carrier Squadron, 1945; in commard of Force which re-occupied Hong-Kong 30th Aug. 1945; Commander-in-Chief and Head of Military Administration, Hong-Kong, 1945-1946; Vice-Adm., 1946; Flag Officer (Air) and Second in Command Mediterranean Fleet, 1947-48; Admiral, 1949; Second Sea Lord, 1948-50; Commander-in-Chief, The Nore, 1950-52. Retired, 1953. Chairman: London and Greater London Playing Fields Assoc. Thames Youth Venture Council; Joint Commonwealth Societies Conference; Past Chm. Victoria League. Grand Cordon Order of Cloud and Banner, China, 1946; Knight Commander of Order of St. Olav, Norway, 1951; Grand Cross of Order of Dannebrog, Denmark, 1952. *Address*: 140 Rivermead Court, S.W.6. *Club*: United Service. [*Died* 19 *Dec.* 1959.

HARCOURT WILLIAMS, E. G.; *see* Williams.

HARDCASTLE, Engineer-Capt. Sydney Undercliffe, C.B. 1922; *b.* 1875; *s.* of late Major Richard Hardcastle, R.A., Sunnyholme, Knaresborough; *m.* 1908, Annie (*d.* 1915), *d.* of Dr. James Preston, Mallow, Co. Cork. *Educ.*: N.E. County School, Barnard Castle; College of Science, Newcastle on Tyne. Entered R.N. 1896; Engineer-Com., 1912; Engineer-Capt. (retired), 1925; inventor of Hardcastle torpedo; Inspecting Torpedo Officer at R.N. Torpedo Factory, Greenock, 1912-19; Assistant to Chief Inspector of Naval Ordnance for Torpedo Inspection, 1919-23. *Club*: Junior Army and Navy. [*Died* 28 *July* 1960.

HARDIE, Mrs. George Downie, (Agnes); *d.* of John Pettigrew; *m.* 1909, George Downie Blyth Crookston Hardie (*d.* 1937). M.P. (Lab.) Springburn division of Glasgow, 1937-45. *Address*: 44 Hillside Court, Hampstead, N.W.3. *T.*: Hampstead 4816. [*Died* 24 *March* 1951.

HARDIE, Major-General John Leslie, D.S.O. 1918; O.B.E. 1919; *b.* 1882; *s.* of John Hardie, Melbourne, Australia; *m.*; one *s.* *Educ.*: Hawthorn College and University of Melbourne. Australian Staff Corps; served European War, 1917-18, France and Belgium; was Gen. Staff W. Australia, 1911-13; D.A.A.G., 1915-16; General Staff, 1919; D.A.M.Q.G. 1920; D.A.A.G., 1920-1921, South Australia; A.A. and Q.M.G., 2nd Cavalry Division, 1921-25; District Base Commandant West Australia, 1925-27; A.A. & Q.M.G. 2nd District Base, N.S.W., 1927-30; Commander Field Troops and District Base Commandant 4th Military District (South Australia), 1931-35; Commander 1st Division and Commandant 2nd District Base, N.S.W., 1935-39; Inspector-General, Dept. of Defence Co-ordination, 1939; Inspector of Administration, A.H.Q., 1940; retired 1940; Officer of Order of St. John of Jerusalem. *Address:* Neutral Bay, N.S.W., Australia. *Club:* Royal Sydney Yacht Squadron. [*Died* 23 *July* 1956.

HARDIE, Martin, C.B.E. 1935; R.E. 1920; R.S.W. 1933; Hon. R.W.S. 1943; S.M.A. 1948; Vice-President, Imperial Arts League and E. Kent Art Society; Chairman of Council and Vice-President, Artists' General Benevolent Institution since 1946 (Hon. Sec., 1934-1938, Hon. Treasurer, 1939-45); *b.* London, 15 Dec. 1875; *e. s.* of late James Hardie, M.A., Headmaster of Linton House School; *m.* 1903, A. Madeline, *d.* of late Admiral J. R. E. Pattisson; two *s.* *Educ.:* Linton House School; St. Paul's School; Trinity College, Cambridge (B.A. 1898). Assistant in the Victoria and Albert Museum, S. Kensington, 1898; Assistant Keeper, 1914; Keeper, 1921-35, in charge of the Departments of Paintings and of Engraving, Illustration and Design; studied etching under Sir Frank Short; A.R.E. 1907; Fellow and Member of Council, 1920; Hon. Sec. of the Royal Society of Painter-Etchers and of the Print Collectors Club, 1920-39; R.I., 1924-36, Vice-President, 1934-36; member of Council, Royal College of Art, 1938-48. Has exhibited etchings at the Royal Society of Painter-Etchers, Royal Academy, etc., since 1908, and water-colours at various exhibitions; served in European War, 2nd Lieut. Sept. 1915; Deputy Assistant Field Censor to B.E.F. France (despatches); Head Censor, Base, Italian E.F., Jan. 1918-Feb. 1919; Lieut. Sept. 1916; Captain Jan. 1917; President of the Omar Khayyám Club, 1931-32. *Publications:* English Coloured Books, 1906; Engraving and Etching (translated from the German of Dr. Lippman), 1906; John Pettie, R.A., 1908; Frederick Goulding, Master Printer of Copper Plates, 1911; Boulogne: a Base in France, 1918; Our Italian Front (text by Warner Allen), 1920; War Posters (with A. K. Sabin), 1920; The British School of Etching, 1920; The Etched Work of W. Lee Hankey, R.E., 1921; Etchings and Dry-Points by James McBey, 1925; Samuel Palmer, 1928; Peter de Wint, 1929; J. S. Sargent, 1930; Charles Meryon, 1931; The Etched and Engraved work of Sir Frank Short, 3 vols., 1938-40; English Water-Colours of the XVIII Century, 1949; Editor Norgate's Miniatura, 1919; Pageant of Empire Souvenir Volume, 1924; Catalogue of R.A. Exhibition of Scottish Art, 1939; and of various Official Publications (Victoria and Albert Museum); contributor on art subjects to Dictionary of National Biography, publications of the Old Water-Colour Society's Club, and to numerous papers and magazines. *Recreations:* etching, sketching, motoring. *Address:* Rodbourne, Yardley Park Road, Tonbridge, Kent. *T.:* Tonbridge 3974. *Clubs:* Arts, Art Workers' Guild, Omar Khayyam. [*Died* 20 *Jan.* 1952.

HARDIE NEIL, James, C.B.E. 1947; D.S.O. 1918; F.R.A.C.S.; F.A.C.S.; President New Zealand League for the Hard of Hearing; *b.* 27 Feb. 1875; *s.* of J. F. Neil and M. Anne Hardie; *m.* 1903, Mary Elizabeth Coates; one *s.* four *d.* *Educ.:* Otago University Medical School. Surgeon Capt. 4th N.Z. Mounted Rifles, 1900-01; served European War, 1914-18, Lt.-Col. O.C. No. 3 N.Z. Rifle Bde. Field Ambulance, 1915-1918; Cons. Aural Surgeon Auckland Hosp.; Surgeon, Mater Hospital, Auckland; Regional Dep. in charge Auckland Medical Boards, 1940-46; Past President B.M.A., Auckland Division; Past President Pan Pacific Surgical Association. *Publications:* Field Ambulance Organization and Administration, 1918; Ear, Nose and Throat Nursing, 4th Ed., 1948. *Recreation:* bowling. *Address:* 64 Symonds Street, Auckland. *T.:* 45480. *Club:* Officers' (Auckland). [*Died* 28 *Jan.* 1955.

HARDING, Sir (Alfred) John, K.C.M.G., *cr.* 1935 (C.M.G. 1930); C.B.E. 1927 (O.B.E. 1918); Director of Colonial Audit, 1928-41; *b.* 1878; *s.* of late John Goulding Harding, formerly of Tetbury; *m.* 1922, Constance Emily, *e. d.* of late Vincent Whittenbury Meacham, formerly of Ledbury; two *d.* *Educ.:* Christ College, Brecon; St. John's College, Cambridge (Foundation Scholar), 1st class Nat. Sci. tripos, Part 1, 1900, B.A., 1900; M.A., 1920. 2nd Class Clerk Colonial Office, 1901; Assistant Private Secretary to Lord Crewe, 1909-10, to Mr. Lewis Harcourt, 1910-12; First class clerk, 1914; Asst. Secy., 1920; Member of W. African Currency Board and of Palestine Currency Board, 1926-28. *Publications:* Editor of the Dominions Office and Colonial Office List, 1920-40. *Address:* 2 Wollaston Road, Southbourne, Hants. [*Died* 21 *May* 1953.

HARDING, Edward Archibald Fraser; Assistant Head of Drama Dept., B.B.C., since 1949; *b.* 1 Oct. 1903; *e. s.* of late Colonel E. W. Harding, R.M., and late N. M. Harding; *m.* 1940, Joan Leach; no *c.* *Educ.:* Cheltenham College; Keble College, Oxford. Entered B.B.C. (as Announcer, London Station), 1927; North Regional Programme Director, 1933; Chief Instructor, Staff Training Dept., 1936; Director of Staff Training Dept., 1941; Acting Head, Drama Dept., 1948-49. *Publications:* contributions to B.B.C. Quarterly and other professional radio publications. *Recreations:* gardening and travel. *Address:* Byron Cottage, 17 North Road, Highgate Village, N.6. *T.:* Mountview 0291. [*Died* 25 *Jan.* 1953.

HARDING, Sir Edward John, G.C.M.G., *cr.* 1939 (K.C.M.G., *cr.* 1928; C.M.G. 1917); K.C.B., *cr.* 1935 (C.B. 1926); M.A. 1907; retired; *b.* 1880; *o. s.* of late Rev. John Harding; *m.* 1929, Marjorie (*d.* 1950), *er. d.* of late Henry Huxley, formerly of Wootton Close, Boar's Hill, Oxford. *Educ.:* Dulwich College; Hertford College, Oxford (Scholar and now Hon. Fellow). 1st Class Classical Moderations, 1901; 2nd Class Lit. Hum. 1903; Colonial Office, 1904; called to Bar, Lincoln's Inn, 1912; Sec. Dominions Royal Commission, 1912-17, in which capacity visited N.Z., Australia, S. Africa, Newfoundland and Canada; 2nd Lt. R.G.A., 1915, Lt. 1918; Deputy Sec., Imperial Conferences, 1923 and 1926; Assistant Secretary, Colonial Office, 1921-25; Assistant Under-Secretary of State, Dominions Office and Registrar, Order of St. Michael and St. George, 1925-30; visited Canada, 1927, on staff of Mr. Stanley Baldwin, then Prime Minister, for Diamond Jubilee Celebrations; Permanent Under-Secretary of State Dominions Office, 1930-40; visited, with Lady Harding, Australia and N.Z., 1936-37, as guests of S. Australian Govt. for S. Australian Centenary Celebrations; H.M.'s High Commissioner for Basutoland, the Bechuanaland Protectorate and Swaziland, and High Commissioner for the United Kingdom in the Union of South Africa, 1940-41, retired 1941; Representative in Capetown of High Commissioner for U.K., 1942-44; Lieut. St. John Commandery in S. Africa, 1940-42; Sub-Prior, South African Priory, 1942-45; K.St.J., 1939-49; Governor of Dulwich College, 1932-39; Member of Royal Commission for 1851 Exhibition; Member of Council, Royal College of Music; Vice-President People's Refreshment House Assoc.; Hon. Life Vice-Pres. Merchant Seamen's Welcome Fund, Capetown. *Address:* Greenacre, Peaslake, Surrey. *T.:* Shere 101. *Club:* Owl (Capetown) (Hon. Life Member). [*Died* 4 *Oct.* 1954.

HARDING, Gilbert Charles; broadcaster; *b.* Hereford, 5 June 1907; *s.* of late Gilbert Harding and May (*née* King). *Educ.:* Wolverhampton Royal School; Queens' College, Cambridge. Formerly schoolmaster, lecturer and police constable; also correspondent for The Times in Cyprus. First broadcast, 1940; since then with Outside Broadcasts Department, B.B.C., and the Microphone Wants to Know series; Chairman of Brains Trust; Question Master in the Twenty Questions series, and Quiz Master in Round Britain Quiz. Asst. to B.B.C. Canadian Representative, 1944-47. Has also appeared in many television programmes, including What's My Line?, Harding Finds Out, I Know What I Like and Who Said That?. *Publications:* Treasury of Insult, 1952; Along My Line, 1953; Book of Manners, 1956; Master of None, 1958; A Book of Happiness, 1959. *Recreations:* reading, talking, listening, looking, waiting. *Address:* 6 Weymouth Court, W.1. *Club:* Savile. [*Died* 16 *Nov.* 1960.

HARDING, Sir John; *see* Harding, Sir A. J.

HARDING-NEWMAN, Brig.-Gen. Edward; *see* Newman.

HARDINGE OF PENSHURST, 2nd Baron (*cr.* 1910); **Alexander Henry Louis Hardinge,** P.C. 1936; G.C.B., *cr.* 1943 (K.C.B., *cr.* 1937; C.B. 1934); G.C.V.O. *cr.* 1937 (C.V.O. 1931; M.V.O. 1925); M.C. 1918; late Grenadier Guards; late Indian Army; Extra Equerry to the Queen since 1952 (to King George VI, 1936-52); *b.* 17 May 1894; *o. surv. s.* of 1st Baron Hardinge of Penshurst and Hon. Winifred Sturt (*d.* 1914), *d.* of 1st Baron Alington; *S.* father, 1944; *m.* 1921, Helen Mary, *o. c.* of late Lord Edward Cecil and late Viscountess Milner, Great Wigsell, Bodiam, Sussex; one *s.* two *d.* *Educ.:* Harrow; Trinity College, Cambridge. Served European War, 1915-18 (wounded, M.C.); A.D.C. Personal Staff, British Military Mission, Berlin, 1919; Adjutant, Grenadier Guards, 1919-20; Equerry and Asst. Private Secretary to the King, 1920-1936 and Assistant Keeper of H.M. Privy Purse, 1935-36; Private Secretary to King Edward VIII., 1936; Private Secretary to King George VI. 1936-43. *Heir: s.* Lieut. (S.) Hon. George Edward Charles Hardinge, R.N. [*b.* 1921; *m.* 1944, Janet Christine Goschen, *d.* of Lt.-Col. F. C. C. Balfour, C.I.E.; three *s.*]. *Address:* Clock House, Rutland Gate, S.W.7. *T.:* Kensington 1323; Oakfield, Penshurst, Kent. [*Died* 29 *May* 1960.

HARDWICK, Rev. John Charlton, M.A., B.Sc., Vicar of Partington, Cheshire, since 1923; *b.* 2 Dec. 1885; *s.* of Stewart Hardwick and Kate Charlton; unmarried. *Educ.:* King's School, Grantham; Durham University; Wadham College, Oxford. Schoolmaster, 1908-11; Curate, St. Margaret's Church, Dunham Massey, Cheshire, 1911-21; Chaplain and Tutor, Ripon Hall, Oxford, 1921-23. Jt. Editor of The Modern Churchman, 1952. *Publications:* Religion and Science from Galileo to Bergson, 1920; Institutional Religion, 1929; A Professional Christian, 1932; A Letter to an Archbishop, 1932; Freedom and Authority in Religion, 1932; Lawn Sleeves—a Life of Samuel Wilberforce, 1933; The Light that Failed, 1933; What to Believe, 1935; No Casual Creed, 1937; While I was Musing, 1938; Conquest of Disability, 1942; Meditations on the Parables, 1942. *Recreation:* the open air. *Address:* Partington Vicarage, Manchester. *T.:* Irlam 220. [*Died* 27 *Jan.* 1953.

HARDY; *see* Cozens-Hardy.

HARDY, Major Sir Bertram, 3rd Bt., *cr.* 1876; *b.* 11 Feb. 1877; *e. s.* of Sir R. Hardy, 2nd Bt., and Lucy Marion (*d.* 1921), *d.* of late Capt. Gladstone, R.N., Bowden Park, Wilts.; *S.* father, 1938; *m.* 1899, Violet Agnes Evelyn, *d.* of late Hon. Sir Edward Chandos Leigh, K.C.B., K.C.; two *s.* *Educ.:* Eton; Trinity Hall, Cambridge. Joint Master, Atherstone Hounds, 1922; Joint Master, Meynell Hounds, 1929; High Sheriff of Staffordshire, 1925-26; Staffordshire Yeomanry, 1898-1918. *Recreations:* hunting, shooting, fishing. *Heir: er. s.*, Rupert John Hardy, Lt.-Col. Life Guards (retd.), *b.* 1902. *Address:* Dunstall Hall, Burton-on-Trent. *T.:* Barton-under-Needwood 324. [*Died* 16 *Sept.* 1953.

HARDY, Edward Arthur; Member Salford City Council since 1922; *b.* 1884; *s.* of late George Ernest Hardy; *m.* 1907; one *s.* one *d.* *Educ.:* St. Clement's Church School, West Park Street, Salford. Member Salford Bd. of Guardians, 1919-25; Mayor of Salford, 1933-1934. M.P. (Lab.) East Division of Salford, 1950-55 (Salford South, 1945-50). J.P. 1933. Late Area Secretary of Confederation of Health Service Employees. *Address:* 19 Otranto Avenue, Salford 6. *T.:* Eccles 1768. [*Died* 4 *Feb.* 1960.

HARDY, Henry Harrison, C.B.E. 1943 (M.B.E. 1918); *b.* 2 Jan. 1882; *y. s.* of Canon A. O. Hardy and Blanche Parry; *m.* 1st, Eleanor Mary (*d.* 1916), *d.* of Charles Colbeck; two *d.*; 2nd, Edith Jocelyn, *d.* of Preb. Sydney Dugdale; three *s.* *Educ.:* Rugby; New College, Oxford. 1st class Honour Mods.; 2nd class, Greats; Assistant Master, Rugby School, 1905-14; Headmaster of Cheltenham College, 1919-32; Headmaster of Shrewsbury School, 1932-44; Secretary Old Rugbeian Society, 1908-13, Pres. 1946; 2nd Lieut. 2nd Vol. Batt. R. Warwickshire Regt. 1906; Captain, 1908; commanded Rugby Contingent, O.T.C. 1913-14, and 1919; Captain, 8th Bn. Rifle Brigade, 1914; Major, 1918; General Staff, 1917-19; served in B.E.F with Fifth Army (despatches); R.A.R.O. until 1932; Chm. of Headmasters Conference, 1936-7-8; Member of Sec. of State for War's Committee on Supply of Officers, 1939; Minister of Agriculture's Harvest Camps Committee, 1942-48; employed by Admiralty, 1944-45; Director of Studies, R.M.A. Sandhurst, 1946-48; Admiralty Interview Board, 1950-52. Chairman, R. College for Blind; Chm. of Dean Close School; Chm. of Malvern Girls' Coll., 1950-56; Gov. St. Paul's Training College, William Temple College, and Wycliffe Hall, Oxford; Member of (Church Assembly's) C.A.C.T.M. Chm. Glos. Music Cttee., Chm. Glos. Association of Boys Clubs; Mem. of Council, N.A.B.C. *Publications:* History of Rugby School, 1911; The Shorter Aeneid, 1914; The Shorter Iliad, 1927. *Address:* Old Farm, Bishop's Cleeve, Glos. *T.:* Cleeve Hill 89. *Clubs:* Athenæum, Alpine, M.C.C. [*Died* 24 *Dec.* 1958.

HARDY, Herbert Ronald, F.I.D.; General Commissioner of Income Tax, Pevensey Division; Member East Sussex County Council; *b.* 22 April 1900; *o. s.* of late Guy Charles Hardy, J.P., and Eva Kathleen, *d.* of Sir Spencer Maryon-Wilson, 11th Bt.; *m.* 1923, Beryl, *d.* of late Col. St. J. Loftus, 60th Rifles; two *s.* one *d.* *Educ.:* H.M.S. Conway; Cheltenham College; Trinity College, Oxford. Served as Midshipman R.N.V.R., Rhine Flotilla, 1917-18; Flag Lieut. to Board of Admiralty, 1940-45, in rank of Lieut. Comdr., R.N.V.R. First expedition to Ivory Coast for Natural History Museum, 1921-22. Mid-Sussex Boy Scouts Assoc., 1923-43 (Medal of Merit, 1952); Chm. Haywards Heath Housing Soc. Ltd., 1932-53; Chm. Home Counties Area, Nat. Federation of Housing Societies, 1935-45. High Sheriff of Sussex, 1951; Vice-Chm. Conservators of Ashdown Forest, 1940-53; Life-Member Royal Society of St. George. *Recreations:* farming, shooting, fishing, and brickmaking (re-started ancient brickworks, Danehill, 1923). *Address:* Keysford, Horsted Keynes, Sussex. *T.:* Danehill 272. *Clubs:* R.N.V.R. (life), Lansdowne (Sussex). [*Died* 12 *May* 1954.

HARDY, Major Jocelyn Lee, D.S.O. 1919; M.C.; Connaught Rangers (retired); *b.* 1894; *m.* 1919, Kathleen Isabel, *d.* of Alec Hutton Potts. Served European War, 1914-19 (prisoner, despatches, M.C., and bar, D.S.O.). *Publications:* I Escape!, 1927; Everything is Thunder; The Key, a play with Robert Gore-

Browne; Never in Vain, 1936; Recoil, 1936; The Stroke of Eight, 1938; Pawn in the Game, 1939. *Address:* Chancery Lane, Wells-on-Sea, Norfolk. [*Died* 30 *May* 1958.

HARDY, Lieut.-Col. Leonard Henry, M.C.; *b.* 12 May 1882; 2nd *s.* of Sir R. Hardy, 2nd Bt.; *m.* 1938, Diana O'Carroll Philips, *widow* of Edward M. Philips, Alsop-en-le-Dale Hall, Derbyshire, and *e.d.* of late Jonathan C. Darby, Leap Castle, King's County. *Educ.:* Eton; New College, Oxford. 2nd Lt. 1st Life Guards, 1906; temporary Lieut.-Col. commanding Reserve Household Battalion, 1916-18; M.G. Guards, 1918; temporary Major, Guards, M.G.R., 1918-19; Major (Bt.), 1919; Major (Subst.), 1919; L.G., Major, 1922; Lt.-Colonel (Brev.), 1925; Lieut.-Col. (Sub.), 1929; served France and Belgium, 1914 (wounded, despatches, Brevet of Major, 1914 star and clasp, B.W.M., V.M., M.C.); commanded the Life Guards, 1929-33; retired; Sheriff of Derbyshire, 1936; J.P. Derbys. 1936. *Recreations:* hunting, polo. *Address:* Alsop-en-le-Dale Hall, Ashbourne, Derbyshire. Kyllachy, Tomatin, Inverness-shire. *T.:* 212. *Clubs:* Turf, Guards, Buck's. [*Died* 27 *Oct.* 1954.

HARE, Cyril; *see* Gordon Clark, His Honour Judge Alfred Alexander.

HARE, John Gilbert; late Bacteriologist and Pathologist, Fullbourn Mental Hospital; *b.* 25 March 1869; *s.* of Sir John Hare and Lady Mary Hare; *m.* 1894, Hélène (*d.* 1942), *d.* of Leo Stern, Brighton; one *d.*; *m.* 1947, Frances Emily, *d.* of Dr. W. P. Cockle, Ealing. *Educ.:* Harrow; Jesus Coll., Cambridge; Univ. of Göttingen. For nine years was connected with the theatrical profession, from which he retired, 1904, to resume the career for which he was educated, i.e. science; late Bacteriologist St. John's Hospital for Diseases of the Skin; Bacteriologist, Seamen's Hospital, Greenwich, London Homœopathic Hospital, Fulbourne Mental Hospital, Cambridge; Demonstrator and Lecturer in Bacteriology, King's Coll., University of London; in France, 1914-15, Hospital Bacteriologist; Egypt, 1916, Capt. R.A.S.C. *Publications:* Lancet and British Medical Journal, Journal of Hygiene. *Recreations:* cricket, racquets. *Address:* 43 Warwick Road, Earl's Court, S.W. *T.:* Flaxman 7456; Jesus College, Cambridge. *Clubs:* M.C.C.; University Pitt (Cambridge). [*Died* 21 *May* 1951.

HARE, Brig.-General Robert William, C.M.G. 1919; D.S.O. 1900; D. L. Norfolk; late Norfolk Regiment; *b.* 14 Nov. 1872; *o. s.* of late R. D. Hare of Ballymore House, Queenstown, Co. Cork; *m.* 1908, Helen Mary, *o. d.* of late Lt.-Col. G. N. Atkinson of Cangort, Shinrone; one *s.* two *d.* *Educ.:* Harrow. Served South Africa, 1896 (Mashonaland medal); South Africa, 1899-1902 (despatches twice, Queen's medal four clasps, King's medal two clasps, D.S.O.); European War, 1914-18 (despatches twice, Bt.-Col., C.M.G., Legion of Honour); retired pay, 1923. *Address:* Town Close, Norwich. *T.:* Norwich 24762. *Clubs:* Army and Navy; Norfolk (Norwich). [*Died* 26 *Dec.* 1953.

HARE, Major-Gen. Sir Steuart Welwood, K.C.M.G., *cr.* 1919; C.B. 1917; Col. Comdt. of 2nd Bn. King's Royal Rifle Corps, 1933-37; *b.* 9 Sept. 1867; *s.* of late Lt.-Col. Hare of Calderhall and Blairlogie, K.R. Rifle Corps and 22nd Regt.; *m.* 1896, Mary Nina (*d.* 1949), *d.* of Francis Ruttledge; three *s.* *Educ.:* Eton; Sandhurst. Joined K. R. Rifle Corps, 1886; Col., 1912; Brig. Commander of the Scot. Rifle Brigade, 1912; served Hazara Expedition, 1891 (medal and clasp); Miranzai Expedition, 1891 (clasp); Chitral, 1895 (medal and clasp); commanded the 86th Fusilier Brigade at the landing of the 29th Division on the Gallipoli Peninsula (wounded); was at the evacuation of Suvla Bay; commanding the 54th Division, Egypt and Palestine, 1916-19 (K.C.M.G., Maj.-Gen., 1918); commanding East Anglian Division T.F., 1919-23; retired pay, 1923. *Publications:* Martial Law from a Soldier's Point of View, 1924; The Annals of the King's Royal Rifle Corps, Vol. IV. 1929, Vol. V. 1932. *Club:* Travellers'. [*Died* 25 *Oct.* 1952.

HARE, Tom, M.D., Ch.B., B.V.Sc., M.R.C.V.S.; Pathologist; Member of Council of British Veterinary Association; *b.* 8 Oct. 1895; *s.* of George Edward Hare and Mary Ann Knight Hare; *m.* Joyce Frideswide, *d.* of Rev. Canon Frank J. Powell, M.A. (Oxon.), Liverpool; one *s.* four *d.* *Educ.:* Loughborough Grammar School; University of Liverpool. Late of Lister Institute, London, 1927; Thelwall-Thomas Fellow in Pathology, 1924; Holt Fellow in Pathology, 1925; Department of Pathology, University of Liverpool, 1926; Professor of Pathology, Royal Veterinary College, 1927-33; Director, The Veterinary Research Laboratories, 1934-40; Chairman: St. Albans Div., B.M.A., 1937-38; Medical War Cttee., Mid-Herts, 1938-46; President, Central Vet. Soc. 1941-; (Victory Medal, C.V.S., 1954); Member of Council R.C.V.S., 1944-48. President: Guild of Undergraduates, University of Liverpool, 1921-1922; Harveian Society of London, 1953; Herts. and Beds. Vet. Soc., 1953; Chairman Inter-Varsity Athletic Board of Great Britain and Ireland, 1920; Capt. The Cheshire Regiment, 16th Batt., 1914-19. *Publications:* Contributions to Veterinary and Medical Journals. *Recreations:* tennis, ornithology. *Address:* 70 Holywell Hill, St. Albans. *T.:* 53459. [*Died* 17 *March* 1959.

HARGREAVES, Professor Anthony Dalzell, M.A., LL.B. Cantab.; Barber Professor of Law, University of Birmingham, since 1950; *b.* 30 March 1904; *s.* of late Anthony Hargreaves and Henrietta Elizabeth Hargreaves, Lancaster; unmarried. *Educ.:* Arnold School, Blackpool; St. Catharine's College, Cambridge. Solicitor of Supreme Court, 1929; Lecturer in Law, University of Leeds, 1929-31; Reader in Law, University of Birmingham, 1931-50. *Publications:* section on Property in Stephen's Commentaries on the Laws of England, 21st edn., 1950; Introduction to Land Law, 3rd edn. (revised), 1956; articles and reviews in legal and historical journals. *Recreation:* music. *Address:* 860 Warwick Rd., Solihull, Warwickshire. *T.:* Solihull 1272. [*Died* 5 *Feb.* 1959.

HARGREAVES, Lionel Stanley, C.B.E. 1924; chartered accountant; *b.* 1882; *s.* of Charles Hargreaves, Bolton; *m.* 1920, Kathleen, *d.* of Ernest Victor Eames, M.D., F.R.C.S. *Educ.:* Ellesmere. Entered Egyptian Government Service, 1911; Custodian of Enemy Property in Egypt, 1918-24. *Address:* 49 Southfield Rd., Plumstead, Cape Town, S. Africa. [*Died* 30 *July* 1954.

HARGREAVES, Sir Walter Ernest, K.B.E., *cr.* 1946; Kt., *cr.* 1936; Chairman of the War Risks Insurance Office, Ministry of Transport; *b.* 1865; *s.* of B. C. Hargreaves of Lloyds; two *s.* three *d.* *Educ.:* Merchant Taylors' School. *Address:* Orchards House, East Grinstead, Sussex. [*Died* 3 *Nov.* 1954.

HARKER, Brigadier Arthur William Allen, C.B.E. 1941; *b.* 7 September 1890; *yr. s.* of late Professor J. Allen Harker; *m.* 1919, Mabel Violet, *d.* of late Maj.-Gen. C. G. Jeans, C.B.; no *c.* *Educ.:* Cheltenham College; R.M.A., Woolwich. 2nd Lt. R.A. 1910; Capt. 1916; served European War, 1914-18; R.A.O.C. 1921; Bt. Lt.-Col. 1935; Bt. Col. 1939; Brig. 1939; War of 1939-45; retired 1947. *Recreations:* golf, tennis, shooting, fishing. *Address:* Ivor Lodge, Milton Lilbourne, Wilts. *Clubs:* Army and Navy, Flyfishers'. [*Died* 23 *Jan.* 1960.

HARKNESS, Edward Burns, C.M.G. 1922; retired from Public Service, 1939;

b. Grafton, N.S.W., 25 Nov. 1874; *m.* 1907, Vera Ladell, *d.* of Captain A. W. Jack; two *s.* one *d.* *Educ.:* Grafton Superior Public School and Grafton Grammar School. Entered New South Wales Public Service, 1891; Private Secretary to successive State Premiers, 1900-1914; first Sec. and Permanent Head of the Premier's Dept., 1914; Under-Sec., Departments of Chief Sec. and Public Health, 1916-1939; Chief Electoral Officer, 1916-29; Commissioner for redistribution of State Electoral boundaries, 1919; conducted the first Election (1920) in New South Wales in accordance with the principles of Proportional Representation; directed the succeeding General Elections under that system (1922 and 1925); Chairman the Lord Howe Island Board of Control; Honorary Organiser with late Judge Cohen of Australia Day, 1915; acted as Honorary Organiser of Red Cross Day with Judge Cohen and Mr. A. L. Blythe, 1918. *Recreations:* swimming, horticulture, golf. *Address:* Irlam Farm, Castle Hill, Sydney, N.S.W. [*Died* 28 *April* 1957.

HARLAND, Albert; *b.* 6 Sept. 1869; 2nd *s.* of late Rev. A. A. Harland, Harefield Vicarage, near Uxbridge. *Educ.:* Rugby School; Corpus Christi College, Cambridge. President F. Graucob Ltd.; Nu-Swift Ltd. M.P. (U.) Sheffield (Ecclesall), 1923-29; Member Sheffield City Council, 1902-11, 1923-24, and 1929-36; Alderman, 1932; Town Trustee, 1929-52; Church Burgess; Patron, Sheffield Royal Institution for the Blind. *Address:* 311 Ecclesall Road South, Sheffield. *Club:* Sheffield (Sheffield). [*Died* 25 *Feb.* 1957.

HARLEY, Alexander Hamilton, M.A.; I.E.S. (retired); Reader, School of Oriental and African Studies, London; *b.* Hamilton, 1882; *e.s.* of William Harley, Hamilton and Lochgoilhead, Scotland; *m.* Celia Lucilla, 6th *d.* of Jas. B. Coughtrie, Hong Kong and London; two *s.* two *d.* *Educ.:* Hamilton Academy; Universities of Glasgow, Edinburgh, and Berlin. Graduated from Glasgow University, 1902; read in Scot. Congregational Theological Hall, 1903-5; medallist and prizeman in Semitic Languages, Edinburgh University; Assistant Professor of Semitic Languages, Edin. University, 1905-1910; Dept. of Oriental Printed Books and MSS. (Arab.), British Museum, 1910; Principal, Calcutta Madrasah, in Indian Educational Service, 1910-26; Principal, Islamia College, Calcutta, 1926-37, in Indian Educational Service; Officiating Sec. to Board of Examiners, Government of India, thrice between 1915-21; passed Degree of Honour in Arabic, 1916, in Urdu, 1920; Fellow and Syndic of Calcutta University. *Publications:* Musnad of Umar bin Abdi'l Aziz; A Manual of Sufism; Sad Kalima of Ali bin Abi Talib; Colloquial Hindustani. *Recreations:* collecting Or. MSS. and paintings, early English water-colours, curios; tennis, golf. *Address:* 65 Aldenham Avenue, Radlett, Herts. [*Died* 9 *Jan.* 1951.

HARLEY, Sir Harry, (Herbert Henry), Kt., *cr.* 1950; C.B.E. 1942; Chairman Coventry Gauge & Tool Co. Ltd., since 1915; *b.* 8 March 1877; *s.* of late Wm. Geo. and Elizabeth Harley, Coventry; *m.* 1st, 1902, Lydia Tatlow (*d.* 1946); one *s.*; 2nd, 1948, Mrs. Sarah J. Moy. *Educ.:* privately, and Coventry Technical College. Seven years' apprenticeship, 1892-99, with Alfred Herbert Ltd. In 1913 he formed a new Company, named Coventry Gauge & Small Tool Co. Ltd. (now Coventry Gauge & Tool Co. Ltd.); Director of Coventry Precision Engineering & Repetition Co. Ltd., Gauge Control Products Ltd. Freeman of City of Coventry, 1899; Burgess and Freeman of City and Royal Burgh of Brechin, Angus, 1944. Deputy President Coventry Engineering Soc.; first President of Gauge and Tool Makers' Association, 1942; Member: Inst. of Production Engineers. Member of Coventry City Council, 1949-. Freemason. *Address:* 58 Kenilworth Road, Coventry. *T.:* 68049. *Club:* Coventry Golf. [*Died* 19 *Jan.* 1951.

HARMAN, Brig.-General Alexander Ramsay, C.M.G. 1918; D.S.O. 1916; *b.* 1877; *s.* of late Sir George Byng Harman, K.C.B.; *m.* *Educ.:* Marlborough. Served Nile Expedition, 1898 (medal and clasp, Khedive's Star); South African War, 1899-1901 (despatches, Queen's medal and 3 clasps); European War, 1914-18 (C.M.G., D.S.O.); retired, 1920. *Address:* 20 Wynnstay Gardens, W.8. *T.:* Western 7017. [*Died* 12 *April* 1954.

HARMSWORTH, Sir Harold Cecil Aubrey, Kt., *cr.* 1935; Chairman of West Country Publications Ltd.; The Harmsworth Press Ltd.; The Western Morning News Co. Ltd.; The Western Times Co. Ltd.; *b.* 13 June 1897; 2nd *s.* of late Sir Leicester Harmsworth, 1st Bart. *Educ.:* Westminster; Christ Church, Oxford. Lieut. Royal Marine Artillery, 1915-19. *Recreation:* golf. *Address:* Worstead Hall, North Walsham, Norfolk; 7 Ilchester Place, Kensington, W.14. *Clubs:* Oxford and Cambridge; Royal and Ancient (St. Andrews); Norfolk (Norwich). [*Died* 7 *Sept.* 1952.

HARMSWORTH, Vyvyan George; *b.* 1881; *y.* and *o. surv. b.* of 1st (and last) Viscount Northcliffe and of 1st Viscount Rothermere; *m.* 1906, Constance Gwendolen Mary, *d.* of C. W. Catt; two *s.* (and one *s.* killed in action, with Welsh Guards, N. Africa, 1943) one *d.* *Educ.:* Charterhouse; Trinity Hall, Cambridge. *Recreations:* shooting, fishing. *Address:* Thrumster House, Caithness. *Clubs:* M.C.C., East India and Sports; Royal and Ancient Golf (St. Andrews). [*Died* 14 *July* 1957.

HARNETT, Walter Lidwell, C.I.E. 1933; M.A., M.D. (Cantab.), F.R.C.S. (Eng.); Lt.-Col. I.M.S., retired; Medical Secretary to Clinical Cancer Research Committee of British Empire Cancer Campaign, 1938-51; *b.* 7 June 1879; *s.* of William John Harnett, F.R.C.P. (Ed.), Barnet, Herts; *m.* 1909, Nellie, *d.* of William Bartingale, Chelsea; no *c.* *Educ.:* City of London School; St John's College, Cambridge (Scholar and Exhibitioner); St. Thomas's Hospital (University Scholarship). First Class Natural Science Tripos, Camb., 1899; House Surgeon and Assistant Pathologist, St. Thomas's Hospital; Passed first into Indian Medical Service, 1907; 1st Montefiore Prize for Military Surgery, R.A.M. College, 1907; late Surgeon to the Governor of Bengal; late Superintendent, Campbell Medical School, Calcutta; late Prof. of Surgery, Medical Coll. Calcutta; retired 1934; Additional Member India Office Medical Board, 1941-45; served European War in India, British Salonica Force, Army of the Black Sea (despatches); Chairman, Hammersmith Branch, Invalid Children's Aid Assoc., 1936-46; Chairman, Chelsea and Fulham Div., B.M.A., 1950-; Esquire, Order of St. John. *Publications:* A Survey of Cancer in London (British Empire Cancer Campaign), 1952; articles: (Jt.) Elephantiasis (in Vol. III) and Filariasis (in Vol. IV), in British Surgical Practice, 1948. *Address:* 5 Dorchester Court, Sloane Street, S.W.1. *T.:* Sloane 6430. *Club:* East India and Sports. [*Died* 24 *April* 1957.

HARPER, Harry; Author of books dealing with the past, present, and future of aviation and with space-flight and interplanetary travel; *b.* 1880; *s.* of Henry George Harper; *m.* 1908, Beatrice Mary Tebbutt; no *c.* *Educ.:* private schools. First British Air Correspondent on staff of any great national newspaper; before first aeroplanes flew, was building man-lifting kites and gliders, and making balloon and airship voyages with pioneer aeronauts; has devoted himself to subject of flying for more than 50 years; Air Corresp. Daily Mail during all pioneer days of flying; present at historic flights of Wilbur Wright, Bleriot, and others, 1908-11; Lord Northcliffe's aero-

nautical secretary and consultant during European war, 1914-18; technical secretary of Civil Aerial Transport Committee, 1917; associated with Imperial Airways in development of first long-distance Empire air mails, and of first experimental trans-ocean flying-boat services. Royal Aero Club Medal, 1958. *Publications:* The Aeroplane—Past, Present, and Future, 1910; The Aeroplane in War, 1911; With the Airmen, 1912; Aircraft in the Great War, 1916; Our First Airways, 1919; The Steel Construction of Aeroplanes, 1922; The Romance of the Flying Mail, 1935; Riders of the Sky, 1936; Lords of the Air, 1940; Armies of the Air, 1941; Man's Conquest of the Air, 1942; Greatest Air Stories, 1942; Highways of the Sky, 1943; Winged World: Our Life in the Air Age, 1943; I saw the First Men fly, 1944; Coming Wonders of Spaceship Flight, 1945; Dawn of The Space Age, 1946; Flights into the Future, 1947; Conquerors of the Air, 1947; Wonders of the Spaceship, 1947; The Cavalcade of the Air, 1948; My Fifty Years in Flying, 1949; Winged Memories, 1953; From Kites and Balloons to Jets and Rockets, 1954; I Was There!, 1956; Book of air reminiscence, Flying Witness (in collaboration with Graham Wallace), 1958. *Recreations:* collecting historical books and pictures relating to the conquest of the air. *Address:* Hatherton, Worple Road, Epsom, Surrey. *T.:* Epsom 9453.
[*Died* 6 *June* 1960.

HARPER, Lieut.-Col. Reginald Tristram, O.B.E. 1919; *b.* New Zealand, 11 Feb. 1876; 6th *s.* of late Leonard Harper, Barrister-at-Law, Middle Temple, and Joanna, *g.d.* of Rt. Hon. Sir Thomas Dyke Acland, 10th Bart.; *m.* 1st, 1906, Gwladys (*d.* 1935), *d.* of Robert Wilson, F.R.S.E.; one *s.* one *d.*; 2nd, 1939, Patricia Winifred (*d.* 1956) *widow* of Charles Keen. *Educ.:* Christ's College, Christchurch, New Zealand. Company Director; F.C.A.; F.C.I.S. (Past President). Served in South African War, 1900 (medal and three clasps), awarded R.H.S. Vellum for saving life in Vaal River; served European War, 1914-19, in Egypt, Salonika, and France (1915 Star, General Service and Victory Medals, despatches twice, O.B.E.). Chm. Maida Vale Hosp. for Nervous Diseases, 1930-37. County Director (Surrey), British Red Cross, 1940-45; contested Cheltenham (C.), 1937; High Sheriff of Surrey, 1943; D.L. Surrey 1945. *Address:* Oakfield, The Common, Cranleigh, Surrey. *Clubs:* Carlton, Royal Thames Yacht, City of London. [*Died* 9 *March* 1958.

HARREL, William Vesey, C.B. 1912; C.B.E. 1919; M.V.O. 1903; *b.* 1866; 2nd *s.* of late Rt. Hon. Sir David Harrel, P.C., G.C.B., G.B.E.; unmarried. *Educ.:* Royal School, Armagh; Trinity College, Dublin. Cadet in Royal Irish Constabulary, 1886; served in that Force as District Inspector, 1886-98; H.M. Inspector of Prisons in Ireland, 1898; Assistant Commissioner Dublin Metropolitan Police, 1902-14; a Knight of Grace of the Order of St. John of Jerusalem; received the King's Police Medal, 1911; Temp. Commander Royal Naval Volunteer Reserve, 1915-19. *Address:* 1 Clifton Terrace, Monkstown, Co. Dublin. *Clubs:* Kildare Street (Dublin); Royal St. George Yacht (Kingstown, Co. Dublin).
[*Died* 4 *May* 1956.

HARRIES, Sir Arthur Trevor, Kt., *cr.* 1939; **The Hon. Mr. Justice Harries;** Chief Justice of the High Court, Calcutta, since 1946; *b.* 13 June 1892; *s.* of Rees and Mary J. Harries; unmarried. *Educ.:* University College of Wales, Aberystwyth; Emmanuel College, Cambridge. B.A. (Wales), 1913, B.A., LL.B. (Cantab), 1921, George Long Prizeman Law Tripos Part (I), 1920, Chancellor's Medal Law Tripos Part (II), 1921; Called to Bar, Middle Temple, 1922; practised on South Wales Circuit till May 1934; Judge of High Court of Judicature, Allahabad, 1934-38; Chief Justice, High Court: Patna, 1938-43; Lahore, 1943-46. Served 2nd Royal Welsh Fusiliers, 1915-17; Staff Captain 98th Infantry Brigade, 1918. *Recreations:* tennis, golf.
[*Died* 1 *July* 1959.

HARRINGTON, Thomas Joseph, C.M.G. 1930; *b.* 1 June 1875; *s.* of late T. Harrington, London; *m. d.* of late G. Blundell, Yokohama; one *s.* one *d.* *Educ.:* St. Joseph's College, South London. Student Interpreter, Japan, 1896; 1st Assistant, 1903; acting Commercial Attaché, Japan, 1906-7; Vice-Consul, Yokohama, 1909; Consul for Island of Formosa, 1913; Nagasaki, 1918; British Consul-General, Philippine Islands, 1920-35. *Clubs:* Junior Carlton; Manila (Manila).
[*Died* 23 *Oct.* 1953.

HARRIS, Sir Austin Edward, K.B.E., *cr.* 1920; *b.* 1870; *s.* of late Frederick W. Harris, J.P., D.L.; *m.* Cara Veronica (*d.* 1952), *d.* of late George Batten, I.C.S.; one *s.* two *d.* *Educ.:* Harrow. Chairman of the Board of Contracts and Assistant Surveyor Gen. of Supply at the War Office, 1916-18. *Recreations:* fishing and gardening. *Address:* 10 Catherine Place, Buckingham Gate, S.W.1. *T.:* Victoria 1666; The Old Rectory, Stockbridge, Hants. *Club:* Brooks's.
[*Died* 30 *Sept.* 1958.

HARRIS, Rear-Admiral Charles Frederick, C.B. 1945; *b.* 2 Jan. 1887; *y. s.* of Bernard Francis and Mary Harris; *m.* 1916, Winifred Amy Weekley; two *s.* (and *e. s.* killed in action, 1940). *Educ.:* Junior School, Brighton College; Marlborough; H.M.S. Britannia. Commander 1922; Capt. 1928; Rear-Adm. 1939; retired, 1939; Flag Officer Commanding Reserve Fleet, 1944. Master of Drapers' Company, 1953-54. *Address:* Western House, Micheldever, Hants. *T.:* Micheldever 88.
[*Died* 2 *March* 1957.

HARRIS, David R., M.A. (Cantab.), B.A. (Lond.); Principal Emeritus Normal College (the North Wales Teachers' College), Bangor, since 1935 (Principal, 1905-35); *b.* Merthyr Tydfil, South Wales; *s.* of William Harris, Twynyrodyn, Merthyr; *m.* Evelyn, B.Sc. (*d.* 1945), *d.* of John Kempster, J.P., founder and first editor of the Police Review; two *s.* one *d.* *Educ.:* St. John's College, Cambridge; University College, Aberystwyth. Lecturer on Educational Theory and Master of Method, University College, Aberystwyth, 1898-1902; Vice-Principal London Day Training College, and recognised teacher in Pedagogy, University of London, 1902-5; Member of the Carnarvonshire Education Authority and Secondary Education Committee; Member of the Anglesey Education Authority and of its Intermediate Education Committee; Member of Court of University of Wales; Member of Welsh Nat. Council of Music. *Publications:* numerous articles on educational topics in educational journals; Chm. and Dir. of the Police Review Publishing Co. since 1918. *Recreations:* music, golf, walking. *Address:* Wood Edge, Copthorne Road, Croxley Green, Herts. *T.:* 4496 Rickmansworth. *Club:* National Liberal. [*Died* 18 *March* 1958.

HARRIS, Captain Hon. Frank Ernest, C.M.G. 1941; D.S.O. 1919; Merchant; Minister of Agriculture, S. Rhodesia, 1934-46; also Minister of Co-ordination, 1941-46; *b.* 24 June 1877; *s.* of late John Harris; unmarried. *Educ.:* Ashburton Grammar School. Served European War, 1914-19 (prisoner, despatches, D.S.O.). *Recreations:* shooting and golf. *Address:* P.O. Box 649, Bulawayo, S.A. *T.A.:* Granary. *Club:* Bulawayo. [*Died* 22 *May* 1951.

HARRIS, George Montagu, O.B.E. 1918; M.A.; *b.* 26 Nov. 1868; *s.* of Rev. Prebendary G. C. Harris and Percy, *d.* of Hon. F. Primrose, Q.C.; *m.* 1898, Violet Estelle Martineau (*d.* 1950); one *d.* *Educ.:* Newton Coll., South Devon; Winchester; New Coll., Oxford. Called to Bar, Middle Temple, 1893; contested South St. Pancras,

1895 and 1896, as Liberal; Secretary of New Reform Club, 1901-2; Secretary of County Councils Association, 1902-19; Member of Departmental Cttee. on Educational Endowments, 1910; Member of Local Govt. Sub-Cttee., Ministry of Reconstruction, 1917; Acting Clerk of the Peace and County Council, East Sussex, 1915-19; Head of Foreign Branch of the Intelligence Division, Ministry of Health, 1919-33; President Town Planning Institute, 1927-28; Secretary of Greater London Regional Planning Cttee. 1927-33; Research Lecturer in Public Administration, Univ. of Oxford, 1935-41. Alderman City of Oxford, 1937-45. President of International Union of Local Authorities, 1936-48. *Publications:* The Garden City Movement, 1906; Problems of Local Government, 1911; Local Government in Many Lands, 1925 and 1932; Westward to the East, 1935; Municipal Self-Government in Britain, 1937; Comparative Local Government, 1949; also Editor of Local Government Abroad, Local Govt. Administration, etc. *Recreations:* travel, modern languages. *Address:* Sorel, Meadfoot Road, Torquay. *Club:* English-Speaking Union. [*Died* 25 *Sept.* 1951.

HARRIS, Col. Gerald Noel Anstice, C.B.E. 1919 (O.B.E. 1918); R.M.A., retired; *b.* 1866; unmarried. Served European War, 1914-19 (O.B.E., C.B.E.). *Recreations:* shooting and golf. *Address:* 4 Seaview Terrace, Hayling Island. *T:* Hayling Island 77673. *Club:* United Service; Royal Naval (Portsmouth). [*Died* 4 *March* 1952.

HARRIS, (Henry) Wilson, M.A., F.R.S.L., Hon. LL.D. (St. Andrews); author and journalist; Editor of the Spectator, 1932-53; *b.* Plymouth, 21 Sept. 1883; *s.* of Henry Vigurs Harris; *m.* 1910, Florence, *d.* of A. M. Cash, M.D., Torquay; one *d.* *Educ.:* Plymouth Coll.; St. John's Coll., Cambridge (Foundation Scholar). President of Cambridge Union, 1905; joined in 1908 staff of Daily News, becoming successively News Editor, Leader Writer, and Diplomatic Correspondent; contributor to various English, American, and Continental periodicals. Member of Council, Roy. Inst. of Internat. Affairs; Member of Governing Body, Leys School, Camb. M.P. (Ind.) Cambridge University, 1945-50. *Publications:* President Wilson, His Problems and his Policy, 1917; The Peace in the Making, 1919; What the League of Nations Is, 1925; Human Merchandise, 1928; Arms or Arbitration, 1928; The League of Nations, 1929; Naval Disarmament, 1930; The Future of Europe, 1932; The Daily Press, 1943; Ninety-Nine Gower Street, 1943; Problems of the Peace, 1944; Caroline Fox, 1944; J. A. Spender, 1945; Life So Far, 1954. *Recreation:* motoring. *Address:* 57 Gordon Mansions, Torrington Place, W.C.1. *T.:* Langham 1897; Foxholt, Abinger Common, Dorking. *T.:* Abinger 111. *Club:* Reform. [*Died* 11 *Jan.* 1955.

HARRIS, Leonard Charles; Director of Ellerman and Bucknall Steamship Co. Ltd., 1920-48; President of Chamber of Shipping of U.K., 1935; *b.* 10 Aug. 1873; *s.* of Lewis Philip and Elizabeth Harris; *m.* 1900, Harriett Ellis (*d.* 1953); six *s.* one *d.* *Educ.:* Dartford Grammar School. Joined staff of Bucknall Brothers, 1890, now the Ellerman and Bucknall Steamship Co. Ltd.; has been member of many shipping and associated committees. *Address:* c/o Westminster Bank, 91 High St., Harrow-on-the-Hill. [*Died* 17 *Oct.* 1953.

HARRIS, Leonard Tatham, C.S.I. 1921. *Educ.:* Bath College; New College, Oxford. Entered I.C.S. 1891; District Magistrate and Collector, Bangalore, 1899; Commissioner, Coorg, 1905-12; Ministry of Food, 1917-19; Agency Commissioner and Member, Board of Revenue, Madras, 1919-22; Secretary to the Government of Madras, Revenue Department, 1922-24; retired, 1924. *Address:* Hangersley Height, Ringwood, Hants. [*Died* 21 *Oct.* 1960.

HARRIS, Rt. Hon. Sir Percy Alfred, P.C. 1940; 1st Bt., *cr.* 1932; D.L.; M.A.; L.C.C.; *b.* 1876; 2nd *s.* of Wolf Harris, 197 Queen's Gate; *m.* 1901, Frieda, 2nd *d.* of John Astley Bloxam, R.F.C.S.; two *s.* *Educ.:* Harrow; Trinity Hall, Cambridge. Graduated Honours in History, 1897; called to Bar, Middle Temple, 1899; travelled round the world three times; lived in New Zealand three years; contested Ashford Division, Kent, 1906; Harrow Division of Middlesex, 1910; member L.C.C., S.W. Bethnal Green, 1907-34 and since 1946; chief Progressive Whip, 1912-15; Deputy Chairman London County Council, 1915-16; M.P. (L.) Harborough Division, Leicestershire, 1916-18; M.P. (L.) South-West Bethnal Green, 1922-45; Chief Whip Liberal Parliamentary Party, 1935-45; Deputy Leader, 1940-45; Hon. Sec. Central Association Volunteer Regiments, 1914; Hon. Assist. Direct. Volunteer Services, War Office, 1916; Chairman House of Commons All Party Panel, 1940-45; Vice-Pres. British American Assoc; Treasurer Inter-Parliamentary Union, 1935-45 *Publications:* New Zealand and its Politics; London and its Government; Forty Years in and out of Parliament. *Recreation:* golf. *Heir:* *s.* Jack Wolfred Ashford [*b.* 23 July 1906; *m.* 1933, Patricia, *o. d.* of A. P. Penman, Wahroonga. *Educ.:* Shrewsbury; Trinity Hall, Cambridge]. *Address:* Morton House, Chiswick Mall, W.4. *Clubs:* Reform, Eighty. [*Died* 28 *June* 1952.

HARRIS, Sir Richard Olver, Kt., *cr.* 1954; C.M.G. 1950; *b.* 24 Dec. 1894; *s.* of late Albert Harris, Hobart, Tasmania; *m.* 1923, Lilian Spode, *d.* of late Hon. Ellis Dean, Tasmania; one *s.* *Educ.:* Queen's College, Hobart. Director Y.M.C.A., Hobart, 1934-1938; Warden Hobart Marine Board, 1942-44; Alderman Hobart City Council, 1944-; Deputy Lord Mayor, 1946-48; Lord Mayor of Hobart, 1948-50 and 1952-1954; Member Hutchins School Board of Management, 1941-47; Chairman, 1946-47; Pres. Hobart Rotary Club, 1941-42; Coroner and Territorial Justice of Peace; Pres. Aero Club, S. Tasmania, 1947-49; Pres. Royal Life Saving Soc. (Tasmanian Branch); Consul for Sweden at Hobart. *Recreation:* bowls. *Address:* 11 Quorn St., Sandy Bay, Hobart, Tasmania. *T.:* 9629. *Club:* Athenæum (Hobart). [*Died* 11 *Oct.* 1955.

HARRIS, Thomas Emlyn, C.B. 1951; C.B.E. 1946; M.I.Mech.E., M.I.E.E.; Dep. Dir.-Gen. Ordnance Factories, Min. of Supply; *b.* 31 May 1894; 3rd *s.* of Thomas and Mary Harris, Aberbeeg, Mon.; *m.* 1924, Ann Davies; two *s.* *Educ.:* Univ. Coll. of South Wales and Monmouthshire, Cardiff (County Schol.). Early training in S. Wales coalfield and allied industries; Metropolitan-Vickers, Manchester, special trainee and erection engineer; entered Woolwich Arsenal, 1924; successively Shop Manager, Supt. R.O.F. Blackburn; transferred to Headquarters Staff as Asst. Director of Ordnance Factories; then Deputy Director, Director, and Deputy Director-General. *Recreations:* motoring, gardening, photography. *Address:* 7 Hervey Road, Blackheath, S.E.3. *Club:* National Liberal. [*Died* 18 *July* 1955.

HARRIS, Wilfred John, M.D., Cantab.; F.R.C.P.; late Captain R.A.M.C.(T.); retired Consulting Physician to St. Mary's Hospital and to London Chest Hospital; Physician, Maida Vale Hospital for Nervous Diseases, 1903-45; Specialist in Diseases of the Nerves; 3rd *s.* of late Surg.-Gen. W. H. Harris, I.M.S.; *b.* Madras, 1869; *m.* 1906, Mabel, *e. d.* of late Rear-Admiral Richard Mayne, C.B., M.P.; two *s.* one *d.* *Educ.:* Sherborne School; University College; Caius Coll., Camb. After graduating in

Natural Science Tripos at Camb. in 1891, Entrance Scholarship at St. Mary's Hospital; later Resident two years Queen Square Hosp. for Nervous Diseases; Examiner in Medicine, Royal College of Physicians, 1910-1914; Examiner in Medicine, Durham University, 1912; Cambridge University, 1913; Fellow Roy. Soc. Med., late Pres. Section of Neurology, 1921; Pres. Assoc. of Brit. Neurologists, 1933. *Publications:* Neuritis and Neuralgia; The Facial Neuralgias, 1937; Morphology of the Brachial Plexus, 1939; numerous articles on Sciatica, Headache, and other Nervous Diseases in various Textbooks and Medical Journals. *Recreation:* golf. *Address:* 74 Harley House, N.W.1. *T.:* Welbeck 2708.
[*Died* 28 *Feb.* 1960.

HARRIS, Wilson; *see* Harris, H. W.

HARRISON, Sir Charlton Scott Cholmeley, Kt., *cr.* 1932; C.I.E. 1928; *b.* Hordley, Jamaica, 18 May 1881; *s.* of late Hon. Mr. James Harrison, J.P., Custos of St. Thomas, Jamaica, and Caroline Page; *m.* 1905, Violet Muriel Monamy, 2nd *d.* of late Dr. E. H. Buckell, J.P., Chichester; three *s.* *Educ.:* R.N.A., Northwood Park, Winchester; R.I.E.C., Coopers Hill. Entered the Indian Service of Engineers as Assistant Engineer, Bombay Presidency, and served in Belgaum, 1902-6; Assistant on Construction of Irrigation Works, Nasik District, 1906-9; Executive Engineer Nasik District, 1909-10; Executive Engineer Irrigation Canals Construction, Nasik and Ahmednagar District, 1911-19; arbitrator in irrigation dispute between Jamnagar and Porbandar States, 1916; Superintending Engineer, Special Duty, Sind, 1921-23; Chief Engineer, Sukkur Barrage and Canals Construction, 1923-31; Chief Engineer, P.W. Dept., Bombay Presidency, and Chief Engineer in Sind, 1931-33. *Recreations:* tennis, golf, shooting. *Address:* Prospect, Morant Bay, Jamaica. [*Died* 3 *July* 1951.

HARRISON, Sir Edward Richard, Kt., *cr.* 1923; Vice-President, Kent Archæological Society; *b.* 19 June 1872; *o. surv. s.* of late Benjamin Harrison of Ightham, Kent; *m.* 1909, Elsie, *d.* of late Rev. Ralph Green. Barrister, Middle Temple, 1901; entered Inland Revenue Department, 1894; Clerk to the Special Commissioners of Income Tax, 1914; Assistant Secretary, Board of Inland Revenue, 1919; Director of Establishments, 1919; Chief Inspector of Taxes, 1922-32. Hon. Sec., Kent Archæological Soc., 1935-50. *Publications:* A Digest and Index of the Official Reports of Tax Cases, 1907; Harrison of Ightham, 1928; The History and Records of Ightham Church, 1932; Contributions to Archaeologia Cantiana, etc. *Address:* 53 Brittain's Lane, Sevenoaks, Kent. *T.:* Sevenoaks 51183.
[*Died* 10 *Nov.* 1960.

HARRISON, Fred., M.A., J.P.; *b.* 9 Nov. 1865; *s.* of late Joseph Harrison, of Carleton Grange, Skipton; *m.* 1898, Mabel Mary, *d.* of late Capt. Mitchell, of Barnetby, Lincolnshire; one *s.* one *d.* *Educ.:* Giggleswick School; New Coll., Oxford. (Scholar) 1st Classes in Mathematical Moderations and Final Schools, and in Natural Science (Physics); University Junior Mathematical Scholar; Physics Master at Manchester Grammar School, 1889-92; Head of the Engineering Side and Principal Physics Master at Dulwich College, 1892-1900; Head Master of the High School, Newcastle, Staffs, 1901-25; Mayor of Godalming, 1929-30; Fellow of the Physical Society. *Recreations:* tennis, golf, climbing. *Address:* Overdene, Godalming, Surrey. *T.* Godalming 475. *Club:* Alpine.
[*Died* 1 *May* 1954.

HARRISON, Rev. Frederick; Chancellor Emeritus of York Minster; *b.* 17 July, 1884; *s.* of William Harrison, silk manufacturer; *m.* 1st, 1910, Mabel (*d.* 1912), *d.* of Francis Pritchard; one *s.*; 2nd, 1918, Helen (*d.* 1949), *d.* of T. A. Wilson; 3rd, 1953, Helen May, *d.* of Col. J. C. Gaskell, and *widow* of Capt. Hugo Dillon, R.A. *Educ.:* King's School, Macclesfield; King's College, Cambridge. B.A. 1906, M.A. 1910. Extension Lecturer, Liverpool Univ., 1908-1911; Ripon Clergy School, 1912-14; Curate of Christ Church, Harrogate, 1914-18; Vicar-choral of York Minster, 1919-27; Librarian, 1925-56; Rector of Moor Monkton, 1927-35; Hon. Sec., York Diocesan Board of Finance, 1929-43; Canon of York, 1932; Chancellor, 1935-56. F.S.A. 1923. *Publications:* York Minster, 1926; The Painted Glass of York, 1927; Treasures of Illumination, 1937; English Illuminated MSS. (14th c.); A Book about Books, 1943; Medieval Man and his Notions, 1947; Life in a Medieval College, 1952. *Address:* 5 Precentor's Court, York.
[*Died* 18 *Aug.* 1958.

HARRISON, George Leslie; Director, New York Life Insurance Co., 1941, Chairman of the Board, 1948-53; Director: First Nat. Bk. of City of N.Y.; Radio Corporation of America; National Broadcasting Company, Inc.; RCA Communications, Inc.; Harper & Brothers; *b.* San Francisco, Cal., 26 Jan. 1887; *s.* of Col. George Francis Edward Harrison and Mary Ross Ray; *m.* 1940, Alice Gertrude Gordon Grayson. *Educ.:* Yale University, A.B. 1910, Hon. M.A. 1929; Harvard Law School, LL.B. 1913. Hon. LL.D. Colgate, 1933, Wesleyan, 1934; admitted to Bar, District of Columbia, 1914, and New York, 1937; Legal Secretary to Justice Oliver W. Holmes of the United States Supreme Court, 1913-14; Assistant General Counsel, 1914-18 and General Counsel, 1919-20, Federal Reserve Board; Deputy Governor, Federal Reserve Bank of New York, 1920-28, Governor, 1928-1936, President, 1936-41; served as Special Consultant to Secretary of War, 1943-46. Captain, American Red Cross, Overseas, 1918; Member Board of Incorporators, American Red Cross, 1936-47; Board of Directors New York Chapter, 1937-47; Co-ordinator of Red Cross Emergency Relief in Greater New York, 1942; Vice-Chairman, N.Y. Chapter, Amer. Red Cross, 1947-52; Member New York State Banking Board, 1943; Vice-President, Chamber of Commerce, N.Y., 1947; Director, Life Insurance Assoc. of America, 1949; Pres. 1952; Dir., Inst. of Life Insurance, 1947-53; Life Trustee, Columbia Univ., 1941; Trustee, Foreign Service Educational Foundation Cttee. for Economic Development; Army Relief Soc.; Member, Cttee. for Life Insurance of Dept. of Commerce of City of N.Y.; Advisory Cttee., E.C.A.; Exec. Cttee., Pilgrims of the United States; Citizens' Cttee. on Reorganization of Federal Govt. Director, New York Heart Assoc., Inc.; Incorporator and Director, The Arthritis and Rheumatism Foundation. Comm. with Cross and Stars, Order of Polonia Restituta (Poland), 1928, Medal for Merit, 1946. *Address:* 51 Madison Avenue, New York 10, N.Y., U.S.A.; 200 East 66 St., New York 21, N.Y., U.S.A. *Clubs:* Links, Yale, Century Association, Newcomen Society of England (New York); Turf and Field (Long Island); Metropolitan, Alfalfa (Washington, D.C.); Chevy Chase (Chevy Chase, Md.). [*Died* 5 *March* 1958.

HARRISON, Gerald Joseph Cuthbert; *b.* 1895; *y. s.* of late John Robinson Harrison of Scalesceugh, near Carlisle, and of Croft House, Helensburgh, Dunbartonshire; *m.* Isobel Margaret, *o. c.* of James W. Schmidt, Pooley Bridge, Cumberland; two *s.* one *d.* *Educ.:* Charterhouse; Exeter College, Oxford. Commissioned 2nd Lieut., R.F.A. (T.F.), 1914, 3rd Lowland Brigade, 52nd Lowland Division; with E.E.F. Sinai, Palestine, Syria, 1916-19; demobilised Feb. 1919; retired Capt., R.F.A. (T.F.); M.P. (U.) Bodmin Division of Cornwall, 1924-29; Parliamentary Private Secretary to the First Lord of the Admiralty, 1926-1929. High Sheriff of Cumberland, 1945-46; D.L. Cumberland, 1953; Chm. Cumberland and Westmorland T. and A.F.A. *Recreations:* golf, shooting. *Address:* Wetheral, by Carlisle. *Clubs:* Junior Carlton; County (Carlisle). [*Died* 6 *Dec.* 1954.

HARRISON, Henry, O.B.E. 1918; M.C. 1916; *b.* 17 Dec. 1867; *s.* of Henry Harrison, J.P., D.L., Holywood and Ardkeen, Co. Down, and Letitia Tennent. *Educ.:* Westminster School (Queen's Scholar); Balliol College, Oxford. M.P. (Parnellite Nat.) Mid-Tipperary, 1890-92; 2nd Lt. Royal Irish Regt., 1915; served European War, 1915-1918, Western Front, as Scout Officer (wounded, M.C. and Bar, O.B.E.); invalided out as Lt., 1919; Sec. of Irish Dominion League, 1920-21, in association with Sir Horace Plunkett; Editor-Owner of Irish Truth (Weekly, Dublin), 1924-27; Irish Correspondent of The Economist, 1922-27; with Gen. Sir Hubert Gough, founded Commonwealth Irish Assoc. (a Vice-Pres.), 1942. *Publications:* Parnell Vindicated—The Lifting of the Veil, 1931; Ireland and the British Empire, 1937; Conflict or Collaboration?, 1937; Parnell, Joseph Chamberlain, and Mr. Garvin, 1938; Ulster and the British Empire, 1939; Help or Hindrance?, 1939; The Neutrality of Ireland, 1940; pamphlets on Anglo-Irish economic and constitutional controversies, 1932-39. *Recreations:* formerly squash racquets, golf, billiards, bridge; cricket and football. *Address:* Lloyds Bank, 6 Pall Mall, S.W.1. *Club:* Stephen's Green (Dublin). [*Died* 20 *Feb.* 1954.

HARRISON, James; M.P. (Lab.) Nottingham North since 1955 (East Nottingham, 1945-55); *b.* 30 Aug. 1899; *s.* of George Harrison; *m.* 1924, Mary A. Gladys Earnshaw; one *d.* *Educ.:* London Labour College. Employee of L.M.S. Railway Co.; Executive Member of National Union of Railwaymen; Member National Civil Defence Institute; ex-Member National Pensions Tribunal. *Address:* 270 Breedon Street, Long Eaton, Notts. [*Died* 2 *May* 1959.

HARRISON, Major-General James Murray Robert, C.B. 1936; D.S.O. 1916; *b.* 1880; *s.* of late George Devereux Harrison of Fron Llwyd, Welshpool; *m.* 1924, Stella Mary, *er. d.* of late Dr. V. E. Travers-Smith and Mrs. Travers-Smith, 1 Gloucester Walk, W.8; *m.* 1945, Carina Mary Marcelle, *er. d.* of late Henry Stewart Anderson, Bishopthorpe, York; one *d.* Entered R.A. 1900; Capt. 1910; Maj. 1914; Bt. Lt.-Col., Lt.-Col. 1918; served European War, 1914-18 (despatches, D.S.O., Croix de Guerre, Crown of Italy, Brevet Lieut.-Col.); Commander Royal Artillery, 55th (West Lancashire) Division, T.A., 1930-1932; Commandant School of Artillery, 1932-34; Maj.-Gen. R.A., Army Headquarters, India, 1935-36; Commander 2nd Anti-Aircraft Div., 1936-39; Lt.-Gov. of Jersey, 1939-40. *Club:* Army and Navy. [*Died* 30 *Dec.* 1957.

HARRISON, Sir (John) Wyndham, 3rd Bt., *cr.* 1922; *b.* 13 Jan. 1933; *s.* of Sir John Fowler Harrison, 2nd Bt., and Kathleen, *yr. d.* of late Robert Livingston, The Gables, Eaglescliffe, Co. Durham; *S.* father, 1947. *Heir:* *b.* Robert Colin, *b.* 25 May 1938. *Address:* The Red Cottage, Nunthorpe, Middlesbrough, Yorks. *T.:* Middlesbrough 56225. [*Died* 24 *June* 1955.

HARRISON, Joseph Richard, C.S.I. 1946; C.I.E. 1942; *b.* 25 Feb. 1888; *s.* of late Richard William Harrison. Entered Indian State Railways, 1916; lent to Great Indian Peninsula Railway, 1918; Member of Indian Coal Committee, 1924; Superintendent of State Railway Collieries, 1925; Chief Mining Engineer, Govt. of India, Railway Board, 1934; President Indian Coal Grading Board; Chairman Wagon Supply Committee: Adviser on Overseas Coal Supplies to H.M. Govt. and Royal Indian Navy; Coal Commissioner, Govt. of India, 1946-48; retired 1948. F.G.S.; M.I.M.E. *Address:* 64 Gloria Mansions, 63 Promenade des Anglais, Nice, A.M., France. *Club:* Bengal (Calcutta). [*Died* 19 *Nov.* 1957.

HARRISON, Bt. Col. and Lieut.-Col. Louis Kenneth, C.B.E. 1919; M.A., M.B., B.C. Cantab.; R.A.M.C.T.; O.C. 5th Northern General Hospital; Emergency Officer for Leicestershire and Rutland; Chairman Local Medical War Committee; Advisory Medical Officer to Sub-Area Headquarters, Leicestershire Home Guard; *b.* 19 Dec. 1871; *s.* of late John E. Harrison of Northwood, Buxton; *m.* Edith (*d.* 1937), *d.* of Septimus March; two *s.* *Educ.:* Repton; Caius Coll., Cambridge; St. Bartholomew's Hosp. Served European War, 1914-19 (despatches, C.B.E.); Ex-President Leicester Medical Society. *Address:* Springfield House, Leicester. *T.:* Leicester 77627. [*Died* 28 *March* 1951.

HARRISON, May; violinist; *b.* Roorkee, India. *Educ.:* Royal College of Music under Arbos and Rivarde; later in St. Petersburg under Prof. Auer, after which toured Europe. *Address:* 647 Nell Gwynn House, Sloane Avenue, S.W.3. *T.:* Kensington 6967. [*Died* 8 *June* 1959.

HARRISON, Ross G.; Sterling Professor of Biology, Emeritus, Yale University; Chairman, National Research Council, U.S.A., 1938-46; *b.* 13 Jan. 1870; *s.* of Samuel Harrison and Katherine Diggs; *m.* 1896, Ida Johanna Lange; two *s.* three *d.* *Educ.:* Johns Hopkins University (A.B. 1889; Ph.D. 1894); University of Bonn (M.D. 1899). Lecturer in Morphology, Bryn Mawr College, 1894-95; Instructor in Anatomy, Johns Hopkins Univ., 1896-97; Assoc. in Anatomy, Johns Hopkins Univ., 1897-99; Assoc. Prof. of Anatomy, Johns Hopkins Univ., 1899-1907; Bronson Prof. of Comparative Anatomy, Yale Univ., 1907-27; Sterling Prof. of Biology, Yale Univ., 1927-1938; Chairman, Dept. of Zoology, Yale Univ., 1912-38; Director of Osborn Zoological Laboratory, Yale Univ., 1918-38; Managing Editor, Journal of Experimental Zoology, 1904-46; Hon. Sc.D. Cincinnati, Michigan, Trinity (Dublin), Harvard, Yale, Columbia, Chicago; Hon. Ph.D., Freiburg; Hon. M.D., Budapest; LL.D. Johns Hopkins Lecturer: Harvey Society; Dunham, Harvard; Croonian, Royal Society; Linacre, Cambridge; Silliman, Yale. Member Council, National Academy of Science, 1932-46; Foreign or Corres. Member of several European academies; Royal Society, Zoological Society. *Publications:* numerous scientific papers. *Recreations:* gardening, mountain climbing. *Address:* 142 Hunting-ton Street, New Haven, Connecticut, U.S.A. *T.:* New Haven Main 4-6571. *Club:* Cosmos (Washington, D.C.). [*Died* 30 *Sept.* 1959.

HARRISON, Sir Thomas Dalkin, Kt., *cr.* 1942; *b.* 30 March 1885; *s.* of John Harrison, Middlesbrough; *m.* 1st, 1913, Margaret Blanch Cave, *d.* of late Rev. E. J. F. Johnson, Rector of Sarsden, Oxfordshire; one *s.* one *d.*; 2nd, 1927, Clarice, *d.* of late Charles Lockstone, Bristol. *Educ.:* Shrewsbury; Christ Church, Oxford. Solicitor, 1912; Inns of Court O.T.C., 1914; 9th Bn. Hampshire Regt. (T.A.), 1915–19; Legal Branch, Ministry of Transport, 1919-1923; Treasury Solicitor Dept. (Ministry of Transport Branch), 1923-28; Asst. Solicitor Ministry of Health, 1929-33; Solicitor and Legal Adviser, Ministry of Health, 1934-Dec. 1951; retd. 1951. *Recreation:* golf. *Address:* Fretherne, Downs View Road, Seaford, Sussex. *Club:* United University. [*Died* 11 *March* 1954.

HARRISON, Captain Walter Gordon, C.B.E. 1942; in command Blue Funnel Line; *b.* 5 Jan. 1888; *s.* of Daniel and Mary Harrison; *m.* 1916, Maud Sowerby; (*o. s.* missing since 5 May 1942), one *d.* *Educ.:* Science and Art School, Workington. Apprenticeship with Peter Iredale & Porter;

has Extra Master's ticket (square rigged); since leaving sailing ships has been with Alfred Holt & Co. (Blue Funnel Line). Lloyd's Medal for bravery at sea, 1943. *Address:* 25 Corporation Road, Workington, Cumberland. [*Died* 6 *June* 1951.

HARRISON, Hon. Mr. Justice, William Henry, D.S.O. 1918; Q.C. (Can.) 1923; LL.D.; Hon. D.Cn.L. (Univ. of King's Coll., N.S.); Judge Supreme Court of New Brunswick Appeal and Chancery Divisions since 1935; Past-President New Brunswick Command Canadian Legion B.E.S.L.; Past-President St. George's Society and Canadian Club; Member of Senate, University of New Brunswick; Trustee, Beaverbrook Scholarships; Director N.B. Museum; *b.* Saint John, N.B., 25 Sept. 1880; *s.* of Legh Richmond Harrison and Susan Louise Thorne, both Canadians, descendants of United Empire loyalists; *m.* 1909, Constance Roy, *d.* of Dr. P. R. Inches, Saint John, N.B.; three *d.* *Educ.:* Rothesay Collegiate School; University of New Brunswick; Harvard Law School, B.A. 1900, LL.B. 1903, LL.D. 1936. Reporter of Supreme Court, New Brunswick, 1908-19; served overseas as Lieut.-Colonel commanding 2nd Canadian D.A.C., 1914-19 (D.S.O., despatches three times); commanded 3rd N.B. Medium Brigade Artillery, 1919-22; Member New Brunswick Legislative Assembly, 1925-35; President Executive Council, 1931-33; Attorney-General of New Brunswick, 1933-35; Chairman Board of Referees for Canada under Excess Profits Tax Act, 1940-44; Anglican. A.F. and A.M. Scottish Rite. *Publications:* Reports Supreme Court of New Brunswick, volumes 39 to 46 inclusive. *Recreations:* fishing, golf. *Address:* Provincial Bldg., Saint John, New Brunswick. *Clubs:* Riverside Golf and Country, Union, Cliff (Saint John); Mount Royal (Montreal). [*Died* 18 *July* 1955.

HARRISON, Sir Wyndham; *see* Harrison, Sir J.W.

HARRISSON, Sydney Thirlwall, C.M.G. 1908; O.B.E. 1919; *b.* Apr. 1865; *s.* of late H. L. Harrisson, and Clara Julia de Thirlwall; unmarried. *Educ.:* Blackheath. Assist. Accoun., P.W.D. Gold Coast Colony, 1894; Chief Accountant, 1897-98; Assist. Accountant, W. African Frontier Force, 1898-99; Chief Accountant, 1899; Treasurer, Northern Nigeria, 1900-8; Comptroller of Customs, Barbados, 1908; permanently invalided from West Africa; holds medal and clasp for 1897-98; retired 1925. *Address:* Royal Bank of Canada, Bridgetown, Barbados. [*Died* 8 *March* 1953.

HARROD, Frances M. D.; novelist and student of painting; *b.* 15 Dec. 1866; *y. c.* of John Forbes-Robertson, art critic, and sister of late Sir Johnston Forbes-Robertson; *m.* H. D. Harrod (*d.* 1919), New College, Oxford, *s.* of Henry Harrod, of Aylsham, Norfolk, F.S.A.; one *s.* *Educ.:* France and Italy; studied Art under Brangwyn and at the Slade School. *Publications:* The Potentate; Odd Stories; The Hidden Model; Mother Earth; What we Dream; The Taming of the Brute; The Wanton; The Devil's Pronoun; The Horrible Man; The Triumphant Rider; Lovers; Trespass; Stained Wings; Temperament, etc. *Address:* 51 Campden Hill Square, W.8. [*Died* 23 *May* 1956.

HARROWBY, 5th Earl of (*cr.* 1809), **John Herbert Dudley Ryder,** J.P.; Baron Harrowby, 1776; Viscount Sandon, 1809; partner in Coutts & Company's Bank; Lord Lieutenant of Staffordshire, 1927-48; *b.* 1864; *e. s.* of 4th Earl of Harrowby and Susan, *d.* of late Villiers Dent; *S.* father, 1900; *m.* 1887, Hon. Mabel Danvers Smith, D.B.E. (*d.* 1956), *y. d.* of late Rt. Hon. W. H. Smith, M.P., and 1st Viscountess Hambleden; one *s.* one *d.* *Educ.:* Trinity College, Camb. Held commission in Staffordshire Yeomanry; M.P. (C.) for Gravesend, 1898-1900. *Heir:* *s.* Viscount Sandon (Dudley Ryder). *Address:* Sandon Hall, Stafford; Burnt Norton, Campden, Gloucestershire. *Club:* Carlton. [*Died* 30 *March* 1956.

HARRY, Philip A.; retd.; formerly Cons. Ophthalmic and Aural Surgeon, Rochdale Infirmary; *b.* Kingston, Jamaica; *s.* of Archippus Harry, M.D., Kingston, Jamaica; *m.*; one *s.* one *d.* *Educ.:* Edinburgh; London; Berlin. Diploma in Tropical Medicine; Diploma in Public Health; Fellow Royal Society of Medicine. *Publication:* Eye Diseases in School Children. *Recreation:* badminton. *Address:* Dolebury House, Churchill, Somerset. [*Died* 25 *May* 1953.

HART, Alfred H., F.R.I.B.A. (retired); (Hart and Waterhouse) Architect; *s.* of H. W. Hart; *m.* Ethel Adeline Mills (*d.* 1945); one *s.* two *d.* *Educ.:* privately; Royal Academy Schools. Articled to Jas. Edmeston, and Assistant to late Sir Ernest George, R.A.; awarded Gold Medal in Architecture at Royal Academy in 1891, and other distinctions; has travelled largely and studied architecture in many European countries; past Hon. Sec. and Vice-President Architectural Association; has practised architecture since 1894, and has designed and carried out the following buildings, some in collaboration with late P. L. Waterhouse: Trafalgar House, Charing Cross; Parkside, Albert Gate; Roy. Colonial Institute (remodelling); The Pryors, Hampstead; Clapham Maternity Hospital; School buildings at Brighton, Swanage, etc., and numerous Private Houses in different parts of the country; has designed and carried out additions to Cuddesdon College, Oxford, and designed and erected important Business Premises in London; associated with Sir Herbert Baker and his partner A. T. Scott in the reconstruction of the Royal Empire Society's Building, Northumberland Avenue. *Publications:* many drawings of historical architecture in the Architectural Association Sketch Book; has exhibited designs in architecture and water-colour drawings on many occasions at the Royal Academy. *Recreations:* golf, water-colour drawing. *Address:* Bridge Close, Burton Bradstock, Dorset. *T.:* Burton Bradstock 270. [*Died* 5 *April* 1953.

HART, Sir Ernest Sidney Walter, Kt., *cr.* 1935; M.B.E., F.R.G.S.; J.P.; *b.* 11 July 1870; *s.* of Sidney George Hart and Marion Emily Austin; *m.* 1895, Ella Mary (*d.* 1941), *d.* of Lieut. Charles Prime, M.I.C.E., P.W.D., Ceylon, J.P.; two *s.* Joined the Staff of the Clerk of the Peace and Clerk of the County Council for Middlesex, 1890; Deputy Clerk of the Peace and Deputy Clerk of the County Council, 1909; Clerk of the Peace and Clerk of the County Council of Middlesex, 1919-35; Clerk of the Middlesex Lieutenancy and Lord Lieutenants Advisory Committee, 1919-35; Joint Hon. Secretary Middlesex Military Appeal Tribunal, 1916-18; Chairman and Hon. Secretary of the Society of Clerks of the Peace of Counties, 1925-35; Hon. Secretary Society of Chairmen and Deputy Chairmen of Quarter Sessions, 1919-35; Hon. Secretary North Middlesex Joint Town Planning Committee, 1926-35; Hon. Secretary West Middlesex Joint Town Planning Committee, 1922-35; Hon. Secretary Middlesex and Northern Home Counties Joint Vagrancy Committee, 1934-35; One of the Honorary Managers of the Probation Officers Superannuation Fund set up under the Criminal Justice Act, 1925, since 1926; Member of the Home Office London Probation Committee, 1922-36; Member of the Home Office Advisory Committee on Probation and After Care, 1922-1936; Chairman of the Records Preservation Section of the British Records Association, 1935-38; Chairman Horley Army Cadets Local Committee, 1942-49. *Address:* Corner House, Godstone, Surrey. *T.:* Godstone 255. [*Died* 29 *Jan.* 1957.

HART, Frank; Artist, Writer, and Lecturer; *b.* Brighton, 1 Nov. 1878; *m.* 1st, 1916, Violet E. Oswald (*d.* 1945); 2nd, 1947, Marjorie Anne, *d.* of late Mr. Justice Graham,

I.C.S. Drawings, illustrated verse, and articles to many journals and periodicals; lectured to societies and schools with blackboard sketches and slides from published drawings and travel notes; Exhibitor R.A. and R.I.; Sussex examples in Public Galleries of Brighton and Eastbourne. *Publications:* How the Animals Did Their Bit, 1914-18; Andrew Bogey and Jack; One Long Holiday; Everyhorse; Illustrations to Master Toby's Hunt; Little Lass; Peter and Co. *Recreations:* swimming, walking. *Address:* Shirley Cottage, Cooden Sea Road, Bexhill, Sussex. *T.:* Cooden 741. *Club:* Chelsea Arts. [*Died* 23 *May* 1959.

HART, Rt. Rev. John Stephen, M.A., B.Sc.; *b.* Caulfield, Victoria, 27 Dec. 1866. *Educ.:* Melbourne. Ordained, 1893; Incumbent of Holy Trinity, Benalla; St. Anselm, Middle Park, Melbourne; St. Martin, Hawksburn; Warden of St. John's Theological College, Melbourne, 1914; Dean of Melbourne, 1919; Bishop of Wangaratta, 1927-43; Moorhouse Lectr., 1915 and 1928. *Address:* Maitland St., Glen Iris, Victoria, Australia. [*Died* 29 *May* 1952.

HART, Air Marshal Sir Raymund (George), K.B.E. 1957 (C.B.E. 1944); C.B. 1946; M.C.; A.R.C.S., M.I.E.E.; M.Brit.I.R.E.; retired; Director of the Radio Industry Council since 1959; *b.* 28 Feb. 1899; *s.* of Ernest Joseph Hart and Emily Caroline Simmons; *m.* 1927; one *s.* *Educ.:* Imperial College of Science and Technology; École Supérieure d'Électricité, Paris. Served European War, 1917-18, in No. 15 Squadron R.F.C. (M.C.); served in India, 1930-33. Employed at Radar Research Station, Bawdsey, 1936 until war commenced, then developed operational use and controlled operation of Radar defence system in Great Britain, developed operational use of Radar for Night Fighter Control. Deputy Director of Radar, Air Ministry, 1941; Chief Signals Officer Fighter Command, 1942; Chief Air Signals Officer A.E.A.F., 1943, and subsequently in S.H.A.E.F.; Chief Air Signals Officer, B.A.F.O., 1945; Air Officer Commanding No. 27 Group, R.A.F., 1946; Director of Technical Policy, Air Ministry, 1947; A.O.C. 90 Group, R.A.F., 1949-51; Director-General of Engineering, Air Ministry, 1951-55; Air Officer Commanding No. 41 Group, 1955-56; Controller of Engineering and Equipment, Air Ministry, Oct. 1956-59; Comdr., Legion of Merit (U.S.A.); Chevalier, Légion d'Honneur (France). *Recreation:* horse riding. *Address:* The House on The Green, Aston Rowant, Oxon. *T.:* Kingston Blount 335. *Club:* United Service. [*Died* 16 *July* 1960.

HART, Thomas Wheeler, C.B.E. 1917; D.L., Co. Lancaster; Retired from practice; Deputy President, British Red Cross Society, East Lancs, 1948; *b.* 13 May 1875; *m.* 1st, Edith Heywood; three *s.* one *d.*; 2nd 1948, Ida Maud Fecht. *Educ.:* Manchester Grammar School and University, M.B., Ch.B. Chairman E. Lancashire Tuberculosis Colony. *Address:* 21 Delaunays Road, Sale, Manchester. [*Died* 1 *April* 1958.

HART-DAVIS, Charles Henry, C.M.G. 1931; *b.* 1874; *e. s.* of late Major H. V. Hart-Davis, D.L., J.P.; *m.* 1908, Vyvien, *d.* of late Captain Bishop, Cheshire Regiment; two *s.* one *d.* *Educ.:* Eton; New College, Oxford, B.A. Served South African War, 1900; Assistant Inspector of Schools, Cyprus, 1901-6; Inspector of Schools, Gold Coast, 1906; District Commissioner, 1906-10; on military service, 1915-19; Commissioner in Cyprus, 1922-34; Member Legislative and Executive Council, 1924-34; retired, 1934. *Address:* The Old House, Nether Stowey, near Bridgwater, Somerset. *T.:* Nether Stowey 300. [*Died* 20 *April* 1958.

HARTE, Walter James, M.A.; Emeritus Professor of History at University College of the South West of England, Exeter; *b.* Wells, Somerset, 1866; *s.* of Edward Harte and Eliza Susannah, *d.* of E. Parfitt; *m.* 1899, Clotilda Eliza Christian Bennett (*d.* 1900); one *s.* *Educ.:* Bath Coll.; Worcester Coll., Oxford. Master at Bath Coll., Bancroft's School and Victoria Coll., Jersey; Professor of History at the University Coll. of the South West of England, Exeter, 1901-31; President of the Historical Association, 1932-36; President of the Devonshire Assoc., 1937-38, its Hon. Sec., 1940-49. *Publications:* annotated edition of Hooker's History of Exeter; Drake: Control of Foreign Policy in the British Commonwealth of Nations; Articles in History and in Trans. of Devonshire Assoc. *Address:* Windsor Hotel, Exeter. [*Died* 19 *Nov.* 1954.

HARTER, Major-Gen. James Francis, D.S.O. 1918; M.C.; D.L.; late Royal Fusiliers; owns and manages Langham Fruit Farms, Ltd.; *b.* 1888; *s.* of C. B. Harter; *m.* 1917, Violet Emily, *d.* of Thomas Cheney Garfit, of Kenwick Hall, Louth, Lincs; one *s.* two *d.* Served European War, 1914-18 (despatches five times, D.S.O., M.C., Croix de Guerre); retired pay, 1926; Lt.-Col. commanding 5th Bn. Suffolk Regt. T.A., 1939; Garrison Commander Portsmouth, 1940; commanded Northern Midland District, 1942; Colonel Royal Fusiliers, 1948-54. D.L. Essex, 1949. *Address:* Highfields, Langham, nr. Colchester. *Club:* Army and Navy. [*Died* 1 *Nov.* 1960.

HARTLEY, General Sir Alan Fleming, G.C.I.E., *cr.* 1944; K.C.S.I., *cr.* 1941; C.B. 1936; D.S.O. 1917; i.d.c.; p.s.c.; *b.* 1882; *s.* of late Reginald Hartley, M.D.; *m.* 1914, Philippa, Kaisar-i-Hind Gold Medal, 1943, *d.* of late P. H. Osborne, Currandooly, N.S.W. *Educ.:* Charterhouse; R.M.C., Sandhurst. Joined 68th Durham Light Infantry, 1901; transferred 11th Bengal Lancers (Probyn's Horse), 1905. Served S. Africa, 1901-2 (Queen's medal with three clasps); European War, 1914-18, in France, Belgium, the Balkans, and Iraq (despatches thrice, D.S.O., 1914 star, two medals); N.W. Frontier of India, 1930 (despatches). G.S.O. 2, A.H.Q. India, 1921-23; Instructor, Staff College, Quetta, 1925-26; Commandant, Probyn's Horse, 1927-30; Imperial Defence College, 1931; Commander 4th (Secunderabad) Cavalry Brigade, 1932-33; Director of Military Operations and Intelligence, A.H.Q., India, 1933-36; Major-General, 1936; Commander Waziristan District, 1937-38; Rawalpindi District, 1939-40; Lt.-Gen. 1940; G.O.C.-in-C. Northern Command, India, 1940-42; General, 1941; C.-in-C., India, Jan.-March 1942; Deputy C.-in-C., India, 1942-44; A.D.C. General to the King, 1942-44; retired, 1944. *Address:* 13 Cottesmore Court, Kensington, W.8. *T.:* Western 1527. *Club:* United Service. [*Died* 7 *Sept.* 1954.

HARTLEY, Arthur Clifford, C.B.E. 1944 (O.B.E. 1918); M.I.C.E. (President), Hon. M.I.Mech.E. (President, 1951); Consultant in private practice since retiring from post of Chief Engineer, Anglo-Iranian Oil Co. in 1951; Consultant, Messrs. Rendel, Palmer & Tritton, Consulting Civil Engineers; Director, Messrs. Johnson & Phillips Ltd.; *b.* 7 Jan. 1889; *er. s.* of G. T. Hartley, surgeon, Hull; *m.* 1st, 1920, Dorothy Elizabeth (*d.* 1923), *d.* of late Gavin Wallace, Shanghai; one *s.* (and one *s.* decd.); 2nd, 1927, Florence Nina, *d.* of William Hodgson, Doncaster; two *s.* *Educ.:* Hymers College, Hull; City and Guilds College, Imperial College of Science and Technology, A.C.G.I. B.Sc. (Hons.), London 1910. N.E. Rly., Hull, Docks Office, 1910-1912; Messrs. Rose Downs & Thompson Ltd., Engrs., Hull, 1912-13; Limmer and Trinidad Asphalt Co., 1913-15; R.F.C. and R.A.F., 1916-19, retd. subst. Maj. Partner, Maxted & Knott, Consulting Engrs., 1919-24; Anglo-Iranian Oil Co., 1924-51. On development of aircraft armament equipment, 1940; Tech. Dir., Petroleum Warfare Dept., 1942-1945; responsible for develop. of 'Pluto' oil pipeline and 'Fido' airfield fog clearance system. F.C.G.I. 1936; Hon. Fell., Imperial

College, 1953. Mem. Council and Redwood Medallist, Inst. of Petroleum; Member of Council R.S.A. U.S. Medal of Freedom, 1946. *Publications:* papers and lectures to various Institutions and contrib. to tech. press. *Recreation:* golf. *Address:* Rubers Law, Madeira Road, West Byfleet, Surrey. *T.:* Byfleet 4136. *Clubs:* Athenæum, Royal Air Force; New Zealand Golf; Rye Golf. [*Died* 28 *Jan.* 1960.

HARTLEY, Colonel Bernard Charles, C.B. 1946; O.B.E. 1925; M.A. (Cantab); *b.* 16 March 1879; *s.* of late Charles Rowley Hartley; *m.* 1907, Violet (*d.* 1946), *d.* of late Charles William Richardson; one *d.*; *m.* 1947, Adeline Dorrien, *d.* of late Lawrance Walter Vann; one *s.* one *d.* *Educ.:* Dulwich Coll.; Jesus Coll., Camb. Served European War, 1914-18, with Hertfordshire Regt. Army Sport Control Board, War Office, Secretary, 1918-41, Director, 1941-46; Member Executive Committee of National Playing Fields Association for 21 years from inception until 1946. President Rugby Football Union, 1947 - 48. Represented England, Cambridge, Kent and Blackheath at Rugby football, Cambridge in athletics, Jesus College, Cambridge, at rowing. Capt. Eltham Warren Golf Club, 1911, Hunstanton, 1925. *Address:* Troon, Felpham, Bognor Regis. *T.:* Middleton-on-Sea 2150. *Clubs:* United Service, British Sportsman's, Achilles. [*Died* 24 *April* 1960.

HARTLEY, Sir Percival, Kt., *cr.* 1944; C.B.E. 1936; M.C. 1917; F.R.S. 1937; D.Sc. (Lond.); Hon. D.Sc. (Leeds); *b.* 28 May 1881; *s.* of late W. T. Hartley, Calverley, Yorks; *m.* 1920, Olga (*d.* 1950), *er. d.* of late John Parnell, Walton-on-Thames; two *d.* *Educ.:* Tech. Coll., Bradford; Univ. of Leeds; Grocers Company Research Scholar, The Lister Institute of Preventive Medicine, 1906-8; William Julius Mickle Fellow, University of London, 1927. Member of staff of Imperial Bacteriological Laboratory, Muktesar, U.P., India, 1909-13; Lister Institute of Preventive Medicine, 1913-1919, and 1949-53; Welcome Physiological Research Laboratories, 1919-21; National Institute for Medical Research, 1922-46; Wandsworth Fellow, London School of Hygiene and Tropical Medicine, 1946-48; Sir William Dunn School of Pathology, Oxford, 1948-49; Member British Pharmacopoeia Commn., 1933-48; Member Medical Research Council, 1949-53 (late Director of Biological Standards); served European War, as Captain R.A.M.C. (T.F.), in B.E.F. 1915-19 (M.C.). *Publications:* on Biochemistry, Bacteriology and Immunity, in scientific journals and in publications of Government of India and Health Organisation of League of Nations. *Address:* 12 Bigwood Road, N.W.11. *T.:* Speedwell 5543. *Club:* Athenæum. [*Died* 16 *Feb.* 1957.

HARTLEY, Sir Percival Horton-Smith-, Kt., *cr.* 1921; C.V.O. 1912; Knight of the Order of St. John of Jerusalem; M.A., M.D. (Cantab.); F.R.C.P.; Major R.A.M.C.(T.), 1st London General Hospital (retired); Consulting Physician to St. Bartholomew's Hospital, to Hospital for Consumption and Diseases of Chest, Brompton; *b.* 2 Dec. 1867; *e. s.* of late R. H. Horton-Smith, K.C.; *m.* 1895, Josephine, *o. d.* and *heiress* of late Lieut.-Col. Joseph Hartley, D.L., J.P., LL.D., of The Old Downs, Hartley, Kent, and Hartley Hill, Leeds; one *s.* one *d.* Assumed the additional surname of Hartley, 1904. *Educ.:* Marlborough; St. John's College, Cambridge (late Fellow). Studied Medicine at Cambridge, St. Bartholomew's Hospital (London), Paris, and Vienna; delivered the Goulstonian Lectures before the Roy. Coll. of Physicians, 1900; Member Court of Company of Ironmongers; Master 1942. *Publications:* Diseases of the Lungs and Pleuræ, 5th and 6th Editions, with Sir R. Douglas Powell, Bart., K.C.V.O., M.D.; The Typhoid Bacillus and Typhoid Fever; The After Histories of Patients treated at the Brompton Hospital Sanatorium, Frimley, 1905-14 (jointly); The Expectation of Survival in Pulmonary Tuberculosis (jointly); Johannes de Mirfeld, his Life and Works (with H. R. Aldridge); The Longevity of Oarsmen (with G. F. Llewellyn); articles on Tuberculosis, and on the Climate of the Midland Counties of England; also numerous contributions to Medical Journals. *Address:* Adkins, Ingatestone, Essex; Hartley Hill, Leeds. *T.:* Ingatestone 143. *Club:* Athenæum. [*Died* 30 *June* 1952.

HARTON, Very Rev. Frederic Percy; Dean of Wells since 1951; *b.* 10 June 1889; *s.* of William Henry and Catherine Harton; *m.* 1921, Gladys Mary Sibyl Robin; no *c.* *Educ.:* privately; King's College, London; Bishops' College, Cheshunt. A.K.C. (2nd Cl. Hons.), 1912; B.D. (Lambeth), 1934; F.K.C. 1935. Deacon, 1913; priest, 1914; Curate: S. George, Hornsey, 1913-15; Holy Trinity, Stroud Green, 1916-22; Vicar: Ardeley, 1922-26; S. Paul's, Colombo, Ceylon, 1926-27; Warden, Sisters of Charity, Knowle, Bristol, 1928-35; Vicar of Baulking, 1936-51. Hon. Sec. Archbishops' Advisory Council on Religious Communities, 1935-51; Warden, Society of Holy and Undivided Trinity, South Leigh, Oxon, 1939-51; Commissary for Religious Communities to Bishop of Oxford, 1943-51; Select Preacher Univ. of Cambridge, 1951; Governor, S. Paul's School, 1946-50, and 1954-; Governor, Dauntsey's School, West Lavington, 1946-; Master of Mercers' Co., 1949-50; Fellow Corp. of S.S. Mary and Nicolas (Western Div.), 1952-. *Publications:* The Elements of the Spiritual Life, 1932; Life in Christ, 1937; The Faith That Abides, 1939; The Mystery of the Cross, 1940. Contrib. to: Dictionnaire de Spiritualité, 1934; The Theory and Practice of Penance, 1935; The Union of Christendom, 1938; Training in Prayer, 1939; Theology, The Church Quarterly Review, Chambers's Encyclopædia. *Recreation:* music. *Address:* The Deanery, Wells, Somerset. *T.:* Wells 2224. [*Died* 3 *Nov.* 1958.

HARTREE, Douglas Rayner, F.R.S. 1932; M.I.E.E. 1945; M.A., Ph.D. (Cantab.); Plummer Professor of Mathematical Physics, University of Cambridge, since 1946; *b.* Cambridge, 27 March 1897; *s.* of W. Hartree, Cambridge; *m.* 1923, Elaine, *d.* of Eustace Charlton, Keswick; two *s.* one *d.* *Educ.:* St. Faith's School, Cambridge; Bedales; St. John's College, Cambridge (Entrance Scholar). Anti-Aircraft Experimental Section, Munitions Inventions Dept., 1916-19; Lt. R.N.V.R.; 2nd cl. Nat. Sci. Trip., Pt. II., 1922; Fellow of St. John's College, Cambridge, 1924-27; of Christ's College, Cambridge, 1928-1929; University Demonstrator in Physics, Cambridge, 1928 - 29; Beyer Professor of Applied Mathematics, University of Manchester, 1929-37; Professor of Theoretical Physics, Univ. of Manchester, 1937-45; temporarily attached to scientific staff of Ministry of Supply, 1939-45; Kelvin Lecturer Institution of Electrical Engineers, 1943; Actg. Chief Institute of Numerical Analysis (U.S. Bureau of Standards), July-Sept. 1948; Higgins Visiting Prof., Princeton Univ., 1955. *Publications:* Calculating Instruments and Machines, 1949; Numerical Analysis, 1952; The Calculation of Atomic Structures, 1957. Papers, mainly on atomic structure and related subjects, on propagation of radio waves, and on calculating machines and their applications, in various scientific periodicals. *Recreations:* music, interest in railways, real and model. *Address:* 21 Bentley Road, Cambridge. *T.:* 4807; Cavendish Laboratory. *T.:* 55478 ext. 12; Christ's College, Cambridge. [*Died* 12 *Feb.* 1958.

HARTWELL, Charles Leonard, R.A. 1924; R.B.S.; *b.* 1 Aug. 1873; *m.* 1905, Nellie Mary Woodhams. Bronze group purchased for the nation, 1907, also marble statue, 1914; A.R.A. 1915; awarded R.B.S. silver medal for his Goatherd's Daughter in bronze at R.A., 1929; Liveryman Carpenters Company since 1931. *Principal Work:* colossal bronze group, St. George, at St. John's Wood, N.W., 1937. *Address:* Studio, Boyne Cottage, Aldwick, Sussex. *Club:* Arts. [*Died* 12 *Jan.* 1951.

HARTY, Lady (Agnes Helen), C.B.E. 1923; formerly Agnes Nicholls; *b.* 14 July 1877; *d.* of Albert Chapman Nicholls and Elizabeth Vent; *m.* 1904, Sir Hamilton Harty (*d.* 1941); no *c.* *Educ.:* Bedford High School; Royal College of Music. Soprano professional singer under maiden name of Agnes Nicholls; started career while still at Royal College; sang at all the most important concerts in England, all the English Musical Festivals, Leeds, Norwich, Birmingham, Three Choir Festivals, also in America, Germany, etc.; was for many years engaged by the Covent Garden Syndicate; then toured the world, Australia, South Africa, etc., in opera, playing all the principal rôles; became a Director of the British National Opera Coy.; has sung much for Royalty. *Recreations:* gardening, motoring. *Address:* 37 St. John's Wood Road, N.W.8. *T.:* Cunningham 6270. [*Died* 21 *Sept.* 1959.

HARVEY, Lieut.-Colonel Cecil Walter Lewery, C.I.E. 1945; O.B.E. 1938; M.C. 1919; I.P.S. retd.; *b.* 27 Oct. 1897; *s.* of late Rev. F. N. Harvey, M.A., Winchester Diocese; *m.* 1930, Beryl Betty Hope, *d.* of late Lt.-Col. P. H. Kealy, R.E.; one *s.* (and one *s.* decd.). *Educ.:* Marlborough College. Enlisted Hampshire Regt. 3 Aug. 1914; served European War, 1914-19 (M.C.); Commission, Nov. 1914; transferred Indian Army 1st Gurkha Rifles, 1918; Waziristan, 1920-21 (despatches); Indian Political Service, 1924; Under-Sec. Pol. Dept. (India), 1929-30; President Manipur State Durbar, 1931-32; Political Agent, Western Kathiawar, 1934-36; Prime Minister, Alwar State, 1938-41; Political Agent, Malwa, 1942; Political Agent, Bhopal, 1943-44; Resident at Kolhapur, 1945-46; Resident Eastern States, 1947. *Recreations:* golf, squash, bridge. *Address:* c/o Grindlay's Bank Ltd., 54 Parliament Street, S.W.1. [*Died* 12 *April* 1958.

HARVEY, Sir Charles Robert Lambart Edward, 3rd Bt., *cr.* 1868; *b.* 16 April 1871; *s.* of 2nd Bt. and Jane (*d.* 1891), *d.* of B. Green, Newcastle; *S.* father, 1928; *m.* 1st, 1891, Jessie (*d.* 1913), *d.* of late Ebenezer Turnbull, of Smedley, Manchester; one *d.*; 2nd, 1921, Lydia, *e. d.* of Alexis Konshine, of Petrograd. *Heir:* *half-b.* 1st Baron Harvey, G.C.M.G. *Club:* Bath. [*Died* 15 *Nov.* 1954.

HARVEY, Major-Gen. David, C.B. 1930; C.M.G. 1917; C.B.E. 1919; M.D.; *b.* Glasgow, 9 Dec. 1871; *s.* of William Gourlay Harvey, J.P., Gourock, and Sara Tennant Sloan; *m.* 1902, Fanny (*d.* 1955), *d.* of William Gibson, Cork; three *s.* one *d.* *Educ.:* Greenock Academy; Glasgow Academy. Lorimer Bursar, 1895-98; M.B., B.Ch., Glasgow University, 1898; 2nd Lieut. 1st V.B. Argyll and Sutherland Highlanders, 1893; Lieut., Royal Army Medical Corps, 1899; served S African War, 1900-2; Assist. Prof. of Pathology, R.A.M. Coll., 1903, 1906; Commission of Inquiry Enteric Fever in India, 1906-8; M.D. Glasgow University, High Commendation, 1911; Royal Society Commission Sleeping Sickness, Nyasaland, 1911-13; European War, 1913-18 (C.M.G., C.B.E., despatches), Deputy Director of Pathology, War Office, 1919-22; D.D.M.S., Gibraltar, 1923; Director of Pathology, War Office, 1923-30; retired pay, 1930; Hon. Surgeon to the Viceroy of India, 1909-10; Hon. Surgeon to the King, 1926-30; Lecturer in Tropical Hygiene, Liverpool School of Tropical Medicine, 1930-34; examiner for Diploma of Public Health and Tropical Medicine, Universities of Glasgow, St. Andrews, London and Liverpool, District Warden A.R.P. Bembridge, 1938-45. *Publications:* numerous contributions to Journal of Royal Army Medical Corps; Assistant Editor, 1916-22; Chapter on Enteric Fevers, Byam's Tropical Medicine. *Recreations:* Rugby football; University Team, 1893-98 (Capt. 1897-1898); athletics (Member Scottish Internat. Athletic team against Ireland, 1898); lawn tennis, golf. *Address:* The Mill House, Bembridge, I. of W. [*Died* 11 *June* 1958.

HARVEY, Sir Ernest Musgrave, 1st Bt., *cr.* 1933; K.B.E., *cr.* 1920 (C.B.E. 1917); a Lieutenant for the City of London; *b.* 27 July 1867; 3rd *s.* of late Rev. Prebendary C. M. Harvey, late Vicar of Hillingdon; *m.* 1896, Sophia (*d.* 1952), *y. d.* of late Capt. Catesby Paget; one *s.* two *d.* (and one *d.* decd.). *Educ.:* Marlborough. Entered service of Bank of England, 1885; Comptroller, 1925-1928; Deputy Governor, 1929-36; Chevalier Légion d'Honneur, 1918; Chevalier Order of Leopold, 1919. *Heir:* *s.* Richard Musgrave, Lt.-Comdr. R.N. (retd.) [*b.* 1 Dec. 1898; *m.* 1930, Frances Estelle, *er. d.* of late Lindsay Crompton Lawford, Montreal; one *s.* one *d.*]. *Address:* Pennings, Mildenhall, Marlborough, Wilts. *T.:* Marlborough 477. *Club:* Athenæum. [*Died* 17 *Dec.* 1955.

HARVEY, Lieut.-Col. Francis Henry, C.M.G. 1919; D.S.O. 1917; *b.* 1878; served S. African War, 1899-1902 (Queen's medal with three clasps); European War, 1914-18 (despatches, D.S.O. Brev. Lieut.-Col., Legion of Honour, Order of Crown of Italy); Siberia, 1919 (C.M.G.). *Club:* Naval and Military. [*Died* 9 *June* 1960.

HARVEY, Maj.-Gen. George Alfred Duncan, C.B. 1938; C.M.G. 1917; L.R.C.P. and L.R.C.S. Ireland; *m.* 1916; one *d.* Served European War 1914-19 (despatches, C.M.G., two medals); Asst. Director of Hygiene, War Office, 1926-30; Col. 1933; late Assist. Director of Medical Services for Waziristan District; Maj.-Gen. 1935; Dep. Director of Med. Services, Western Command, India, 1935-38; K.H.P. 1937-39; retired pay, 1939; served war of 1939-45 (prisoner). *Recreations:* shooting and fishing. *Club:* Army and Navy. [*Died* 22 *Sept.* 1957.

HARVEY, Rear-Admiral Harold Lane, C.B. 1941; *b.* 11 July 1884; *o. s.* of H. B. Harvey, Bournemouth; *m.* 1913, Dorothy, *d.* of A. Bartlett, Bath; two *s.* *Educ.:* Queen Elizabeth's School, Wimborne; Royal Naval Engineering Coll., Keyham. Engineer, Sub-Lt., 1905; Engineer Lieutenant, 1907; Engineer Lieut.-Comm., 1915; Engineer Comm., 1922; Engineer Captain, 1931; Engineer Rear-Admiral, 1938; A.D.C. to the King, 1938; Staff of Rear-Admiral, Yangtse, 1922-24; Engineer Officer, H.M.S. Cornwall, in China, 1927-31; Staff of C.-in-C. Mediterranean, 1931-33; in command of Mechanical Training Establishment at Chatham, 1934-38; Staff of Commander-in-chief, Plymouth, 1939-44; retired Oct. 1944; Admiralty Regional Officer (Wales), 1945-48. *Address:* Oak Lodge, 24 Teddington Park, Teddington, Middlesex. *T.:* Teddington Lock 2168. [*Died* 10 *Jan.* 1960.

HARVEY, Herbert Frost; Editor Birmingham Mail, 1907-44; *b.* 7 Aug. 1875; *s.* of Jas. Frost Harvey, Hertford, Herts; *m.* 1905, Adeline, *d.* of late Thomas Hulme of Stretford, Manchester; two *s.* one *d.* *Educ.:* Hertford; was a member of literary staffs of Birmingham Post and Manchester Daily Dispatch. *Recreations:* horticulture, golf, motoring. *Address:* Rednal Road, King's Norton, Birmingham. *Club:* Royal Automobile. [*Died March* 1959.

HARVEY, James Graham, Q.C., 1907; B.A., LL.B.; practising Barrister-at-Law in the City of Winnipeg: Solicitor and Counsel for Greater Winnipeg Water District; *b.* Lanark Co., Ontario, 3 June 1869; *s.* of J. G. Harvey and Catherine Ferguson; *m.* 1897, Ida Mills, Omeemee, Ontario; two *s.* one *d.* *Educ.:* Winnipeg Public Schools; Manitoba University,

B.A. 1887; LL.B. 1890; Barrister and Attorney, 1891; practised law in Winnipeg till 1896; moved to Dauphin, Manitoba, and practised law there until 1913, when returned to Winnipeg; elected to represent the Provincial Constituency of Dauphin in the Manitoba Legislature, 1910; Presbyterian. *Club:* St. Charles Country (Winnipeg). [*Died* 12 *Nov.* 1950.
[*But death not notified in time for inclusion in Who Was Who 1941–1950, first edn.*

HARVEY, Major Sir Samuel Emile, Kt., *cr.* 1935; D.L., J.P. Devon; *b.* 7 Dec. 1885; *s.* of late Sir Robert Harvey of Dundridge, Totnes, Devon; *m.* Elizabeth Sybil, *d.* of late R. R. Lockett, Liverpool; four *d.* *Educ.*: Eton. Joined 1st King's Dragoon Guards from Militia 1905; served with regiment until 1922; M.P. (U.) Totnes, Devon, Nov. 1922–Nov. 1923, and 1924-35; Sheriff of Devon, 1941. *Recreation:* shooting. *Address:* The Bays, Sidmouth, Devon. *T.:* Sidmouth 1768.
[*Died* 9 *Nov.* 1959.

HARVEY, Thomas Edmund, Hon. LL.D. (Leeds); Master of the Guild of St. George, 1934-51; Chairman, National Loan Collection Trust; *b.* Leeds, 4 Jan. 1875; *e. s.* of late Wm. Harvey, Leeds; *m.* 1911, Irene, *y. d.* of late Professor Silvanus Thompson, F.R.S. *Educ.*: Bootham School, York; Yorkshire College, Leeds; Christ Church, Oxford; Universities of Berlin and Paris. B.A. (Vict.) 1893; M.A. (Oxford), 1900; 1st Class Litteræ Humaniores, 1897; studied abroad, 1897-99; Assistant in the British Museum, 1900-4; Resident of Toynbee Hall, 1900; Warden of Toynbee Hall, 1906-11; Member London County Council, 1904-7; Member Central (Unemployed) Body, 1906-10; Member Stepney Borough Council, 1909-11; Member of Standing Committee on Boy Labour in the Post Office, 1910-17; Parliamentary Private Secretary (unpaid) to Mr. Ellis Griffith, K.C., 1912-13, and to Mr. C. F. G. Masterman, 1913-14; M.P. (L.) West Leeds, 1910-18; Dewsbury, 1923-1924; M.P. (Ind. Progressive) Combined English Universities, 1937-45; engaged in relief work in the war zone in France on behalf of the War Victims' Relief Committee of the Society of Friends, 1914-20; Member Pelham Committee, 1916-19; Warden of Swarthmore Settlement, Leeds, 1920-21. *Publications:* The Rise of the Quakers, 1905; Poor Raoul and other Fables, 1905; A Wayfarer's Faith, 1913; The Long Pilgrimage, 1921; Stolen Aureoles, 1922; Silence and Worship, 1923; Along the Road of Prayer, 1929; St. Ælred of Rievaulx, 1932; The Christian Church and the prisoner in English Experience, 1941; Songs in the Night, 1942; Workaday Saints, 1949. *Address:* Rydal House, Grosvenor Road, Leeds 6. *Club:* National Liberal.
[*Died* 3 *May* 1955.

HARWOOD, Charles Auguste de Lotbinière-, Q.C. 1911 (Canada); B.C.L.; Barrister, Solicitor; *b.* Vaudreuil, Canada, 2 Aug. 1869; *s.* of Robert William de Lotbinière-Harwood, M.P., and Charlotte M'Gillis; *m.* 1898, Marie Adelaide, *d.* of Hon. L. F. Roderick Masson, Lieut.-Governor of Quebec, Senator; three *s.* three *d.* *Educ.*: St. Laurent College; Laval and McGill Universities. Syndic of Montreal Bar, 1911-1913; Assistant Solicitor Grand Trunk Railway System at Montreal since 1920; Solicitor Canadian National Railway, Province of Quebec, 1923; Chief Solicitor Canadian National Railways for Quebec, 1937-43; retired, 1943; Commissioner South African Dominions; Member of Antiquarian and Numismatic Society of Montreal; and of Art Gallery of Montreal; Order of Lords of Colonial Manors, New York Section; Conservative; many years on Board of Directors of Conservative Association in Montreal, and on Election Committees; candidate to Quebec Legislature for Vaudreuil, 1912; Provincial (Quebec) Secretary for Naval Recruiting, 1917; R.O. Electoral District St. Lawrence, St. George, Montreal, 1917. Bâtonnier of Bar of Montreal, 1943-44. *Publications:* Fort Garry Convention of 1870; Hon. M. A. E. G. C. de Lothiniere; contributions on historical matters. *Recreation:* golf. *Address:* Alaincour, Les Chenaux, Vaudreuil, P.Q. *Clubs:* Canadian, France-Amérique, Alliance Française (Montreal).
[*Died* 20 *June* 1954.

HARWOOD, Harold Marsh, M.A. Camb., M.B., B.C. Camb.; *s.* of George Harwood, late M.P. for Bolton; *m.* F. Tennyson Jesse (*d.* 1958). *Educ.*: Marlborough; Trin. College, Cambridge; St. Thomas's Hospital. Qualified as doctor; was House Physician at St. Thomas's Hospital; then went into business; was Managing Director and Chairman of Richard Harwood and Sons, Cotton Spinners, of Bolton, Lancs; Chairman of Fine Cotton Spinners and Doublers Association, 1940-50; served in R.A.M.C. as Captain (France and Egypt), 1914-19; went into theatrical management, 1919. *Productions:* as Manager—Sylvia's Lovers; Grain of Mustard Seed; The White Headed Boy (with J. B. Fagan); If; Deburau; The Pelican; Anyhouse; Emperor Jones; Madras House; as Author—The Mask (1 Act), with F. T. Jesse; Honour Thy Father (1 Act), 1912; Interlopers, 1913; Please Help Emily, 1916; Theodore and Co. (with G. Grossmith), 1916; Figaro (Sir T. Beecham's production, libretto), Billeted (with F. T. Jesse), 1917; the Grain of Mustard Seed, 1920; A Social Convenience, 1921; The Pelican (with F. T. Jesse), 1924; The Transit of Venus, 1927; The Golden Calf, 1927; Excelsior, 1928; A Girl's Best Friend; The Man in Possession; Cynara (with R. Gore-Browne), 1930; So Far and No Father, 1932; King, Queen, Knave (with R. Gore-Browne), 1932; The Old Folks at Home, 1933; These Mortals, 1935; The Innocent Party (with Laurence Kirk), 1938; London Front, 1940; While London Burns, 1942, and A Pin to see the Peep-Show, 1951 (with F. T. Jesse); The Thin Line, 1953. *Recreations:* yachting, tennis. *Address:* Pear Tree Cottage, 11 Melina Place, St. John's Wood, N.W.8. *Club:* Garrick.
[*Died* 20 *April* 1959.

HARWOOD, Sir Ralph Endersby, K.C.B. *cr.* 1934 (C.B. 1924); K.C.V.O. *cr.* 1931 (C.V.O. 1921); C.B.E. 1918; has received Orders from the Governments of France, Italy, Roumania, Egypt, Afghan, Abyssinia and Iraq; *b.* 28 March 1883; *s.* of Charles Harwood, Shefford, Beds; *m.* 1903, Kitty (*d.* 1943), *d.* of Wm. Rule Endersby; one *s.* three *d.* *Educ.*: Modern School, Bedford. Telegraphist G.P.O., 1898-1901; Second Class Clerk; India Office, 1901; Second Division Clerk at War Office, Inland Revenue Department and N.H. Insurance Commission, 1901-12; Staff Clerk, 1912; Assistant Accountant, 1912; Junior Clerk, Class I., Private Secretary to Permanent Secretary N.H.I. Commission, 1913; Seconded to War Trade Dept. 1915; Controller War Trade Statistical Dept. and Chairman of Inter-Allied Rationing and Statistical Committee, 1916-18; Principal, Finance Division, Air Ministry, 1918; Principal Establishment Officer, Treasury, 1919; Assist. Secretary, Treasury, 1919-22; Deputy Treasurer to the King 1922-35; Financial Secretary to the King, 1935-37; lately Governor, London School of Economics and Political Science. *Address:* Seckford Hall, nr. Woodbridge, Suffolk. *T.:* Woodbridge 678.
[*Died* 28 *Feb.* 1951.

HASELDEN, William Kerridge; Cartoonist and Caricaturist; *b.* Seville, 1872; 2nd *s.* of Adolphe Henry Haselden, Civil Engineer, and Susan Elizabeth Kerridge. Began drawing professionally, 1903; joined staff of Daily Mirror, 1904, retired, 1940; first contributed to Punch, 1905; contributed at various times to other well-known periodicals. *Address:* Aldeburgh, Suffolk.
[*Died* 25 *Dec.* 1953.

HASKELL, Harold Noad, O.B.E. 1948; M.A.; *b.* London, 1887; *y. s.* of Samuel Haskell and Sarah Noad; *m.* 1918, Minnie Maude, *e. d.* of

S. S. Robinson, M.C.P. of Constant and Newmarket Plantations, Barbados; two *s.* one *d.* *Educ.:* Christ's Hospital (Thompson gold medal Mathematics, Tyson gold medal Mathematics and Astronomy, Leaving Exhibition); Merton College, Oxford (Open Postmastership); 1st Class Mathematical Moderations; 2nd Class Finals (Mathematics); 3rd Class Finals (Physics). Assistant Master, Harrison College, Barbados, 1910-23; Headmaster of Harrison College, Barbados, 1923-48; resigned 1948; Overseas Member of Headmasters' Conference, 1925-48; Member of the Royal Society of Teachers, 1932. *Address:* Rydal, Pine Hill, St. Michael, Barbados. [*Died* 17 *Nov.* 1955.

HASKINS, M. Louise; Author; *b.* 12 May 1875; *d.* of Joseph and Louisa Haskins; unmarried. *Educ.:* Clarendon College, Clifton; London School of Economics, University of London. School work in home village and London; educational work in India; Supervisor of Women's Employment and Industrial Welfare work in controlled factory during the European War; after the war Tutor and Asst. Lecturer in Social Science Dept. of London School of Economics till outbreak of war in 1939; retired, 1939; reappointed London School of Economics, 1940-44. *Publications:* The Desert (verse) privately printed about 1908; Through Beds of Stone, 1928; A Few People, 1932; The Gate of the Year (verse), 1940; Smoking Flax (verse), 1942. *Address:* Brooklands, Crowborough, Sussex. *T.:* Crowborough 299. [*Died* 3 *Feb.* 1957.

HASLAM, John Fearby Campbell, C.M.G. 1941; M.C.; M.D.; D.P.H.; F.R.C.P.E.; formerly Colonial Medical Service; *b.* 13 June 1888; *s.* of late John Bailey Haslam and late Helen Maria Grant; *m.* 1921, Edith Helen Georgiana Mackenzie; no *c.* *Educ.:* Dollar Academy; Edinburgh University. Resident Hospital appointments, 1912-14; served European War, R.A.M.C., 1914-19, Serbia, Salonica, Palestine, France (despatches, M.C.); Asst. to Professor of Medical Jurisprudence, Ed. Univ., 1919-21; M.O.H. in Colonial Med. Service, British Guiana, 1921-25; Asst. Director, Bureau of Hygiene and Tropical Diseases, London, 1925-30; Physician and Bacteriologist, Shell Group of Oil Companies, Venezuela, 1930-32; Chief Medical Officer, Barbados, 1932-35; Director of Medical Services, N. Rhodesia, 1935-47; Chm. Silicosis Medical Bureau, N. Rhodesia, 1947-50; Silicosis Commissioner, N. Rhodesia, 1950-52; retd. 1952. Member, Federal Assembly of Federation of Rhodesia and Nyasaland, and Chairman, Standing Cttee. (African Affairs Bd.) of Assembly, 1953; resigned, ill-health, 1954. *Publications:* Recent Advances in Preventive Medicine, 1930; various papers in scientific journals. *Recreations:* riding, and schooling horses, gardening. *Address:* Kamfinsa Inika, nr. Kitwe, N. Rhodesia; P.O. Box 999, Kitwe. *Club:* Bath. [*Died* 2 *Sept.* 1955.

HASLAM, Robert Heywood; *b.* White Bank, Bolton, 1878; *e. s.* of William Haslam and Mary Heywood; *m.* 1916, Dolores, *y. d.* of late E. D. Lomax. *Educ.:* Sedbergh School; Bedale's School. Articled to C. F. A. Voysey, Architect; member of Art-Workers Guild, Surrey Archæological Society and Hambledon Rural District Council. *Publications:* articles on art, etc. *Recreations:* gardening and fishing. *Address:* Mill House, Wonersh, Surrey. *T.A.:* Haslam-Wonersh. *T.:* Bramley 2034. *Clubs:* Reform, Arts. [*Died* 9 *April* 1954.

HASLEGRAVE, Lt.-Col. Henry John, C.M.G. 1916; T.D.; T.F.; J.P.; *b.* 8 Jan. 1871; *m.* 1908, Martha Kathleen (*d.* 1947), *d.* of W. H. Kingswell, Holmfield, Wakefield; one *s.* two *d.* Served European War, 1914-16 (despatches, C.M.G.). *Address:* Painthorp House, Crigglestone, nr. Wakefield. *T.:* Horbury 275. [*Died* 24 *Feb.* 1956.

HASLETT, Dame Caroline, D.B.E., *cr.* 1947 (C.B.E. 1931); Companion I.E.E., M.R.I.; J.P., Co. London, 1950; Member of Central Electricity Authority, 1947-56; Hon. Adviser Electrical Association for Women, Inc.; Past Pres. The Women's Engineering Society, Inc.; *e. d.* of Robert Haslett, Worth, Sussex. *Educ.:* Haywards Heath High School. 5 years at London and Annan with the Cochran Boiler Company; Member of Court of Governors of London School of Economics and Political Science and of Administrative Staff College; of Council of Queen Elizabeth College; Governor of Bedford Coll. for Women; member: of various Engineering and Electrical Committees; of Council of Industrial Welfare Soc.; Member of Women's Consultative Committee, Ministry of Labour; Pres. of Internat. Federation of Business and Professional Women, 1950-56; Chairman: British Electrical Development Assoc., 1953; mem. Council, British Inst. of Management, 1947-1954; Crawley Development Corporation, 1947-55; Vice-Pres. and mem. Council, R.S.A., 1941-55; Hosiery Working Party set up by President of Board of Trade, 1945-46. *Publications:* papers and articles in Engineering and Industrial Journals; Founder and Editor of The Woman Engineer and The Electrical Age; Editor, The Electrical Handbook for Women, Household Electricity; Problems have no Sex. *Recreations:* golf, motoring, and gardening. *Address:* 25 Fouberts Place, W.1. *Club:* Forum. [*Died* 4 *Jan.* 1957.

HASLETT, Sir William John Handfield, Kt., *cr.* 1938; J.P. for Middlesex; M.R.C.S. Eng.; L.R.C.P.; President of Spelthorne Divn. Conservative and Unionist Assoc.; a Commissioner for Income Tax; *b.* 10 Sept. 1866; *s.* of S. T. Haslett, M.D., Colonial Medical Service; *m.* 1922, Norah, *d.* of William Arthur Macan, J.P., Beds., M.F.H., and niece of Sir Claude Champion de Crespigny, 4th Bt.; one *s.* three *d.* *Educ.:* Trinity College, Dublin; London Hospital. Has specialised in mental and nervous disorders and held various hospital appointments; has been interested in public and political work in the County of Middlesex for many years; as Chairman of the Committee for care of Mental Defectives for Middlesex has been concerned in the provision of Colonies. *Publications:* various medical. *Recreation:* Public work. *Address:* Larchwood, Portmore Park Road, Weybridge, Surrey. *T.:* 723 Weybridge. *Club:* Carlton. [*Died* 17 *Dec.* 1954.

HASSARD-SHORT, Adrian Hugh, O.B.E. 1944; Secretary, Law Society's Poor Persons Committee, 1926-51; *b.* 3 Aug. 1879; *s.* of Frederick Hugh Hassard-Short and Maud Eliza Downes; *m.* 1908, Amelia Eliza Renouf, Jersey, Channel Islands. *Educ.:* H.M.S. Britannia, Dartmouth. Cadet and Midshipman Royal Navy, 1894-99; served in H.M.S. Immortalite on China Station, 1896-99; present at Manila during American-Spanish War; Associate, King's Bench Division, Royal Courts of Justice, 1900-8; Deputy Chief Clerk, Criminal Appeal Office, 1908-14; Secretary London Prescribed Officers (Poor Persons), 1914-26; also served in Artists Rifles (then 20th Middlesex R.V.); Sergeant Metropolitan Special Constabulary, 1914; A.R.P. Warden at Royal Courts of Justice and Paddington Borough Council, 1939-45; re-joined C. D. Corps, 1949. *Publications:* The Practice in Poor Persons Cases, 1916; various articles and pamphlets on Poor Persons Procedure; Legal Aid for the Poor (Jour. of Comparative Legislation and International Law—Feb. 1941); Divorce—The Layman's Guide to procedure and legal aid; also one Article on Gardening about 1904; has written and composed several songs. *Recreations:* golf, stamp collecting. *Address:* 2 Princess Court, Queensway, W 2. *T.:* Bayswater 5589. [*Died* 28 *March* 1956.

HASSARD-SHORT, Rev. Canon Frederick Winning, M.A. Cantab.; Hon. C.F.; Vicar of St. Luke's, Bromley Common, Kent, since 1923; Hon. Canon of Rochester Cathedral since 1934; Rural Dean of Bromley since 1941; Chairman Automobile Association since 1942; *b.* 5 Aug. 1873; *s.* of Frederick Hugh Short and Maud Eliza, *d.* of John Downes. *Educ.:* Blackheath Proprietary School; Christ's College, Cambridge. B.A. 1895, M.A. 1899. Ordained Deacon and Priest, 1897; Curate of St. James, Tunbridge Wells, 1897-1901; St. John Baptist, Cardiff, 1901-06; St. Mary, Chatham, 1906-07; Vicar of St. Alban's, Dartford, 1907-23. C.T.A. 1911-33; Hon. C. F. since 1933. Member: Dartford Bd. of Guardians, 1911-23 (latterly Vice-Chm.); Bromley Bd. of Guardians, 1925-33. Elected Member Motor Union Cttee., 1906; on amalgamation with Automobile Association, 1910, became member cttee. of joint body. F.R.Hort.S., 1931-. *Recreations:* (past and present) rifle shooting, swimming, cycling, motor-cycling, sea-fishing, gardening, photography. *Address:* St. Luke's Vicarage, Southlands Rd., Bickley, Bromley, Kent. *T.:* Ravensbourne 1517. *Clubs:* Royal Automobile; Royal Scottish Automobile (Glasgow).
[*Died* 12 *Feb.* 1953.

HASSÉ, Henry Ronald, M.A. (Cambridge); D.Sc. (Manchester); *b.* 27 July 1884; *s.* of Rev. L. G. Hassé, B.D.; *m.* 1912, Kathleen Norah, *d.* of Rev. S. Kershaw, B.A.; no *c.* *Educ.:* Moravian School, Fulneck, nr. Leeds; Owens College (now Manchester University); St. John's College, Cambridge. Isaac Newton Student, 1907; Fellow of St. John's College, Cambridge; 1911; Assistant Lecturer in Mathematics, Liverpool University, 1908-10; Lecturer in Mathematics, Manchester University, 1910-1919; Professor of Mathematics, University of Bristol, 1919-49; Dean of the Faculty of Science, Bristol University, 1926-30; Pres. of Mathematical Assoc., 1950-51. *Publications:* Papers on Mathematics and Mathematical Physics in Journals of Scientific Societies. *Address:* 64 Coldharbour Road, Bristol 6. *T.:* Bristol 36253. [*Died* 16 *June* 1955.

HASSELKUS, John William, C.B.E. 1944; late Chairman and Managing Director of the Optical Works, Ross Ltd.; resigned Oct. 1948; *b.* 27 Nov. 1874; *s.* of late August Hasselkus; *m.* Louise Henriette, *y. d.* of late Joseph Crémieux, Lyons; no *c.* *Educ.:* on the Continent. *Recreation:* motoring. *Address:* 29 Macaulay Road, S.W.4. *T.:* Macaulay 2558.
[*Died* 10 *Jan.* 1951.

HASTINGS, 21st Baron (*cr.* 1290), **Albert Edward Delaval Astley,** Bt. 1660; *b.* 24 Nov. 1882; *s.* of 20th Baron and Hon. Elizabeth Evelyn Harbord, 3rd *d.* of 5th Lord Suffield; *S.* father, 1904; *m.* 1907, Marguerite Helen, *d.* of 3rd Marquess of Abergavenny; one *s.* three *d.* *Educ.:* Eton; R.M.C. Sandhurst. South Africa, 1902; A.D.C. to Viceroy of Ireland, 1905-6; served European War, 1914-18 (despatches twice); Norfolk County Council, 1909-19; Pres. North Norfolk Conservative Assoc. since 1937; Chairman Independent Peers Assoc., House of Lords, since 1935; Member of Indian States Inquiry Committee, 1932; Pres. Central Landowners' Assoc. since 1939; Member of Council Royal Agricultural Society of England since 1908, Vice-Pres. since 1938; Chairman of Forestry Committee since 1930; Member of Council of Agriculture for England since 1933; Chairman Norfolk Agricultural Station since 1912; Pres. Smithfield Club, 1936; Commissioner for Clergy Discipline, Province of Canterbury; Trustee Friends of Norwich Cathedral; High Steward, Norwich Cathedral; Hereditary Bearer of a Golden Spur at the Coronation; Lieut.-Col. Reserve of Officers 7th Hussars till 1937; Hon. Lieut.-Col. King's Own Royal Regt. Norfolk Yeomanry; Lt.-Col. Norfolk Home Guard since 1940; J.P., D.L., Vice-Lieutenant, Norfolk. *Heir:* *s.* Maj. Hon. Edward Delaval Henry Astley, Coldstream Guards, R.A.R.O. [*b.* 14 April 1912; *m.* 1954, Mrs. Catherine Cecilia Rosaline Ratcliffe Coats, *d.* of late Mr. Ratcliffe-Hinton]. *Address:* Melton Constable, Norfolk. *Clubs:* Carlton; Norfolk County (Norwich). [*Died* 18 *Jan.* 1956.

HASTINGS, Sir Patrick, Kt., *cr.* 1924; Q.C. 1919; Barrister-at-law (retd.); *b.* 1880; *m.* 1906, Mary Ellenore, 3rd *d.* of Col. Grundy, late Warwicks.; one *s.* three *d.* *Educ.:* Charterhouse. Mining Engineer, 1898-9; served South African War, 1900-1; Journalist, 1902-3; called to Bar, Middle Temple, 1904; Bencher Middle Temple, 1924; M.P. (Lab.) Wallsend, 1922-26; Attorney-General, 1924. *Publications:* various; The River (play), 1925; Scotch Mist, 1926; Escort (play), 1942; The Blind Goddess (play), 1947; Autobiography, 1948; Cases in Court, 1949. *Relevant publication:* The Life of Patrick Hastings, by Patricia Hastings, 1959. *Address:* A.10 The Albany, Piccadilly, W.1. *T.:* Regent 5992. *Club:* Garrick.
[*Died* 26 *Feb.* 1952.

HASWELL, Brigadier Chetwynd Henry, C.I.E. 1930; *b.* 1879; *s.* of late Fleet Paymaster William Henry Haswell, Royal Navy; *m.* 1916, Dorothy, *d.* of late Lt.-Col. John B. Berry, Penn, Bucks; two *s.* one *d.* *Educ.:* Mannamead; R.M. Academy, Woolwich. Commissioned in Royal Engineers 1899; served Tibet Expedition, 1903-4 (medal); European War (despatches twice, medal); Bt. Lt.-Col., 1918; Afghan War, 1919 (medal and clasp); Waziristan; 1921-24 (clasp, despatches); Bt. Colonel, 1924; Col. 1927; N.W. Frontier, 1930-31 (clasp); retired 1935. *Address:* Penbury End, Penn, Bucks. *T.:* Penn 2241. *Club:* United Service.
[*Died* 30 *Aug.* 1956.

HAUGHTON, Major-General Henry Lawrence, C.B. 1937; C.I.E. 1927; C.B.E. 1931; *b.* 1 Nov. 1883; *s.* of late Colonel John Haughton; *m.* 1912, May (*d.* 1949), *d.* of J. Shepherd of The Hill, Twyford, Berks; one *s.* *Educ.:* Winchester; Sandhurst, 1st Commission, 1902; Commandant, Prince of Wales's Royal Indian Military College, 1922-27; served European War, 1914-18; N.-W. Frontier of India, 1930 (C.B.E.); Brevet Lieut.-Colonel, 1923; Lieut.-Col. 1927; Col. 1931; Major-General, 1936; Commandant 11th Sikh Regiment, 1927; Deputy Military Secretary, Army Headquarters, India, 1931-33; commanded 1st (Abbotabad) Infantry Brigade, 1933-36; A.D.C. 1935-36; Commander Kohat District, 1936; retired 1940, re-employed, 1940; retired, 1943. *Publication:* Sport and Folklore in the Himalayas. *Recreations:* shooting, fishing, cricket, and rackets. *Address:* c/o Grindlay's Bank Ltd., 54 Parliament St., S.W.1; Manor Cottage, Blewbury, Berks. [*Died* 22 *March* 1955.

HAUGHTON, Colonel Samuel George Steele, C.I.E. 1935; O.B.E. 1931; Gold Kaisar-i-Hind, 1933; Indian Medical Service, retired; *b.* Dublin, 3 Sept. 1883; *s.* of Samuel Haughton, late Ceylon Civil Service, and Helena Sophia, *d.* of Edmond Henry Casey, D.L., J.P., Co. Dublin; *m.* 1919, Marjorie Winifred, *d.* of Everard Porter, Haddenham, Cambs.; one *s.* one *d.* *Educ.:* Blundells; Trinity College, Dublin. B.A. 1904; M.B., B.Ch., B.A.O. 1906; M.D., M.A.O., 1913; Lieut., I.M.S., 1906; Capt. 1909; Major 1918; Lt.-Col. 1926; Colonel, 1935; K.H.S., 1937-39; retired, 1939. *Address:* Red Stack, Horsham Road, Cranleigh, Surrey.
[*Died* 30 *May* 1956.

HAUGHTON, Colonel Samuel Gillmor, E.R.D.; D.L. Co. Antrim; a Managing Director Frazer & Haughton Ltd., Cullybackey, Bleachers, Finishers and Makers-up; Chairman: W. S. Moore Ltd.; John Kelly Ltd., Coal Importers, John Milligen & Co. Ltd., Alexander King Ltd., R. & A. Duncan, Wm. M. Barkley & Sons Ltd., Belfast; T. & J. Connick Ltd., Dundalk; Howdens Ltd.,

Larne; Director: Robert McCowen & Sons Ltd., Tralee; Partner of The Calculating & Statistical Service, Belfast and Dublin; Member London Advisory Board of Friends' Provident and Century Life Office; *b.* 1889; *s.* of late T. W. Haughton, J.P.; *m.* 1912, Dorothy Lyall, *d.* of M. Wilson, Director Belfast Bank, Co. Down; (one *s.* decd.). *Educ.:* Cambridge House School, Birmingham; St. Edward's School, Oxford. Served War of 1939-45, Middle East, with 21st Battery, R.A., 1939-44 (despatches); Chief A.A. Adviser, Egyptian Army, 1942. Past Pres. Belfast Chamber of Commerce; Member: N. Ire. Development Council; Belfast Harbour Commissioners; Irish Lights Commissioners; Chm. N. Ire. Shipowners Assoc.; F.Inst.D. M.P. (U.) County of Antrim, House of Commons, 1945-50; Chm. N.I. Govt. Cttee. to investigate Betting Laws, 1945-47. High Sheriff, Co. Antrim, 1955. *Recreations:* hunting, racing, shooting. *Address:* Red Cottage, Cullybackey, Co. Antrim, Northern Ireland; Broughan, Ballycastle, Co. Antrim; Frazer & Haughton Ltd., Radnor House, 93-97 Regent St., W.1. *T.A.:* Haughton, Cullybackey. *T.:* Cullybackey 209. *Clubs:* Junior Carlton; Ulster, Union (Belfast); Friendly Brothers (Dublin). [*Died* 19 *May* 1959.

HAVARD, Sir Godfrey Thomas, K.C.M.G., *cr.* 1941 (C.M.G. 1925); *b.* 1885; *s.* of late John T. Havard, Monkton House, Penarth; *m.* 1915, Marcelle, *d.* of Madame Michelin, La Rochelle, France; two *s.* one *d.* (and one *d.* decd.). *Educ.:* Leys School, Cambridge; on the Continent; Trinity College, Cambridge. Entered Levant Consular Service, 1907; Constantinople, Sofia, 1909; transferred to Tehran, 1909; H.M. Vice-Consul Tehran, 1912; Acting Oriental Secretary at H.M. Legation, Tehran, 1922: Oriental Secretary, with local rank of 1st Secretary in H.M. Diplomatic Service, to H.M. Legation, Tehran, 1923-31; Department of Overseas Trade, 1932 and 1933; Consul-General at Beirut 1934-41; Asst. Chief Political Officer to G.O.C. Syria and Palestine with Hon. rank of Brig. 1941; attached to office of Minister of State, Cairo, 1942-43; retired, 1944; Member of Scarbrough Commission, 1945-46. *Address:* Thorenciel, Av. Fragonard, Cannes, France. [*Died* 3 *March* 1952.

HAVARD, Rt. Rev. William Thomas, M.C., T.D., D.D., M.A.; Bishop of St. David's since 1950; *b.* 23 Oct. 1889; 3rd *s.* of William and Gwen Havard, Neuadd, Sennybridge, Breconshire; *m.* Florence Aimée, *d.* of late Joseph Holmes, Penyfai, Llanelly, Carmarthenshire; two *s.* two *d.* *Educ.:* University College of Wales; Aberystwyth, B.A. (Hons.); University of Oxford, Jesus College, B.A. (Hons.); St. Michael's Theological College, Llandaff. Late Scholar of University of Wales; Deacon, 1913; Curate of Llanelly, 1913-19; Chaplain to the Forces, 1915-19; Welsh Division and Guards' Brigade, served overseas, France and Belgium (despatches, M.C.); Hon. C.F. 1919; Chaplain, Jesus College, Oxford, 1919-1922; Vicar of Hook, Surbiton, Surrey, 1922-24; Senior Chaplain London Division (T.A.), 1925-29; Vicar of St. Luke, Battersea, 1924-28; Vicar of Swansea, 1928-34; Surrogate; Bishop of St. Asaph, 1934-50; Chaplain to late Bishop of Swansea and Brecon; Canon of East Gower in Brecon Cathedral; Mem. of Governing Body; Mem. of Representative Body of Church in Wales; Mem. of Court of Governors of Univ. Coll. of Aberystwyth; Member of Court of University of Wales; Chaplain and Sub-Prelate, Order of St. John of Jerusalem, 1940; Select Preacher St. Andrews Univ., 1943, Cambridge, 1946-1947, Yale (U.S.A.), 1951. *Address:* The Palace, Abergwili, Carmarthenshire. [*Died* 17 *Aug.* 1956.

HAVELOCK-ALLAN, Sir Henry Spencer Moreton, 2nd Bt., *cr.* 1858; D.L., J.P.; *b.* 30 Jan. 1872; *s.* of 1st Bt. and Lady Alice Moreton, *d.* of 2nd Earl of Ducie; *S.* father, 1897; *m.* 1st, 1903, Edith Mary, O.B.E., J.P. (*d.* 1935), *d.* of Thos. C. J. Sowerby; 2nd, 1936, Mary Isobel (marriage annulled on his petition, 1937), *d.* of H. Sharpe Gordon, Yateley Place, Hants; 3rd, 1937, Doris Pamela, *d.* of Sir Maurice Levy, 1st Bt., J.P., D.L. *Educ.:* Eton; Trinity College, Cambridge. Major 17th Lancashire Fusiliers, 1915-18; served European War, France, 1916-18 (wounded); M.P. (L.) Bishop Auckland Division, Durham, 1910-18; Private Parliamentary Secretary to Hon. E. S. Montagu, Under-Secretary of State for India, 1912-14. *Heir: nephew* (Henry) Ralph Moreton, Lieutenant late Scots Guards [*b.* 31 Aug. 1899; *s.* of late Allan Havelock-Allan, and of Annie Julia, *d.* of Sir William Chaytor, 3rd Bt.]. *Address:* Blackwell Grange, Darlington. *Clubs:* Brooks's; Durham County. [*Died* 28 *Oct.* 1953.

HAVENGA, Hon. Nicolaas Christiaan; Minister of Finance, Union of South Africa, 1924-39 and 1948-54; M.P. for Ladybrand, 1948-54 (for Fauresmith, 1915-41); also farmer and has business interests. Member of the Provincial Council for Fauresmith and Member of Executive Committee for the Orange Free State, 1910-15. *Address:* Memel, Fauresmith, Orange Free State, South Africa. [*Died* 13 *March* 1957.

HAWARD, Sir Harry (Edwin), Kt., *cr.* 1917; *b.* 3 Jan. 1863; *s.* of late Henry Gilbert Haward; *m.* 1st, 1886, Alice, *d.* of late H. W. Bates, F.R.S., Secy. of the Royal Geographical Society; one *d.*; 2nd, 1899, Edith (*d.* 1925), *d.* of late Howel Thomas, Local Government Board; one *s.* two *d.*; 3rd, 1933, Vera Morris, *d.* of late H. Robert Morris-Parker of Clough, Rotherham, Yorkshire, and *widow* of Capt. W. S. (Vavok) Hopper, late 17th Dragoons, Imperial Russian Army. *Educ.:* Univ. College School; graduated in Arts at London University. Comptroller of the London County Council, 1893-1920; Electricity Commissioner, 1920-30; President of the Institute of Municipal Treasurers and Accountants, 1908-9; Treasury representative on Royal Patriotic Fund Corporation, 1915-1936; Councillor Royal Borough of Kensington, 1933-40. *Publication:* The London County Council from Within, 1932. *Address:* Weston Hall Hotel, Bournemouth. *Club:* National. [*Died* 8 *Sept.* 1953.

HAWARD, Lawrence, M.A.; Hon. M.A. (Manchester); *b.* London, 7 Aug. 1878; *e. s* of late J. Warrington Haward; *m.* 1911, Suzanne *o. d.* of Colonel Courvoisier-Guinand of La Chaux-de-fonds, Switzerland; two *s.* one *d.* *Educ.:* Uppingham; King's College, Cambridge; Classical Tripos, 1900. Librarian to the University of London, 1905-6; on musical staff of The Times, 1906-14; Curator of Manchester Corporation Art Galleries, 1914-45; Trustee on National Loan Collection Trust, 1917-45; Royal Society of Arts Medallist, 1922. *Publications:* Bibliography of Walter Headlam, 1910; translation of Arthur Pougin's History of Russian Music, 1915; The Effect of War upon Art and Literature, 1916; The Problems of Provincial Galleries and Art Museums, 1922; Illustrated Guide to the Art Collections in the Manchester Corporation Galleries, 1938; Music in Painting; Bibliography of Edward J. Dent, 1946; On the Verge (trans. of Maurice Sandoz's La Limite), 1950; The Balance (trans. of Maurice Sandoz's La Balance), 1952; The Crystal Salt Cellar (trans. of Maurice Sandoz's La Salière de Cristal), 1954; Edward J. Dent: A Bibliography, 1956; various contributions to Grove's Dictionary of Music, Burlington Magazine, Edinburgh Review, Times Literary Supplement, Manchester Guardian, Gazette de Lausanne, etc. *Address:* Avenue de Sully 9, La Tour de Peilz, Vand, Switzerland. [*Died* 18 *Nov.* 1957.

HAWARD, Sir Walter, Kt., *cr.* 1944; O.B.E. 1938; M.B.; B.S.; *b.* 23 Jan. 1882; *s.* of late Henry Tippell Haward and Annie Elizabeth Bedford; *m.* 1905, Louisa Ayton Mann; one *s.* three *d.* (and one *d.* decd.). *Educ.:* private school; Durham University; St. Thomas's. M.B. (Hons.), B.S. Durham, 1904; M.R.C.S., L.R.C.P. 1904; Asst. House Physician, House Physician and Clinical Asst. Skin Dept., St. Thomas's, 1904-5; private practice, 1905-15. Temp. Major R.A.M.C., European War, 1914-1918; Officer i/c Medical Div. 36th General Hospital (attached to Serbian Army) and 28th General Hospital Salonica Army (despatches. Order of St. Sava 4th class). D.C.M.S. Ministry of Pensions, 1919; Principal Medical Officer, 1925; Director of Medical Services, 1938; Director-General of Medical Services, Ministry of Pensions, 1942-1947; K.H.P. 1947-50. Fellow Medical Society of London. *Recreations:* gardening; formerly hockey, cricket, tennis, golf. *Address:* The Wold, Woldingham, Surrey. *T.:* Woldingham 3117. [*Died* 2 *Sept.* 1959.

HAWARDEN, 7th Viscount, *cr.* 1791; **Eustace Wyndham Maude;** Major, late The Queen's Royal Regiment; *b.* 20 Sept. 1877; *o. s.* of late Ludlow Eustace Maude, *g.s.* of 1st Viscount and Clara Louisa, *d.* of Rev. W. C. Madden; *S.* cousin, 1914; *m.* 1920, Marion Wright of Butterley Hall, Derby; two *s.* one *d.* Joined Honourable Artillery Company, 1896; 3rd Battaliion the Hampshire Regiment 1900; The Queen's, 1901; attached Egyptian Army, 1910; temporarily employed under the Sudan Govt. in the Bahr-el-Ghazal Province since 1912; O.C. Bahr-el-Ghazal District and Governor Bahr el Ghazal Province, 1917-20; J. P. Kent, 1922. *Heir: s.* Hon. Robert Leslie Eustace Maude [*b.* 26 March 1926; *m.* 1957, Susannah Caroline Hyde Gardner]. *Recreations:* shooting, tennis, golf. *Address:* Bossington, Adisham, near Canterbury *T.:* Wingham 240. [*Died* 6 *April* 1958.

HAWKE-GENN, Captain Otto Hermann, C.B.E. 1919; Royal Navy; *b.* Rock Ferry, Cheshire, 1875; *m.* 1909, Annie, *y. d.* of George Wall; one *s.* one *d.* *Educ.:* Eastman's R.A. Academy, Stubbington, Hants. Entered Royal Navy, H.M.S. Britannia, 1889; Captain, 1917; served in Britannia as Commander, 1914-1916; commanded Vindictive in North Russia, 1916-17; Teutonic on Convoy Escort, 1918 (C.B.E.); retired list, 1922. *Recreations:* golf, tennis. *Address:* Endsleigh, Graham Road, West Kirby, Cheshire. *T.:* Hoylake 708. *Club:* Royal Liverpool Golf. [*Died* 21 *Oct.* 1955.

HAWKES, Arthur John, F.S.A., Borough Librarian of Wigan, 1919-50; *b.* Bournemouth, 1885; 4th *s.* of late Charles George and Elizabeth Denman Hawkes; *m.* Annie Elizabeth (*d.* 1951), *e. d.* of late William Thomas Hirst, Leeds; one *s.* *Educ.:* Bournemouth. Commenced library career in the Bournemouth Public Libraries; assistant Leeds City Reference Library, 1909; National Library of Wales, 1912; served in the Air Force in France; Member of the Council of the Library Association, 1924-30, 1933-42; Hon. Educ. Secretary, N. Western Branch, Library Association, 1926-36; President, 1945-1946; Lecturer in Librarianship at the Victoria University, Manchester; Examiner, Library Association Professional Examinations; Chairman Wigan Educ. Soc., 1932-42; Editor (1938-1949) and President (1944-45) of Lancashire and Cheshire Antiquarian Society; Member of Council of Record Society of Lancashire and Cheshire since 1941. *Publications:* Degradation of Womanhood; Suggestions towards a Revision of the Dewey Classification; Bibliography of Robert Owen; Best Books, 1914; Taste and Reason in Art; Lancashire Printed Books, a bibliography to 1800. with historical introduction (sec. edition Vol. xlii, Lancashire and Cheshire Antiq. Soc. 1925); Treasures of the Wigan Library; Birchley Hall Secret Press (c. 1604-1642); Annotated Catalogue of Early Mining Literature with historical introduction; Calendar of Markland Deeds, etc. (with Rev. T. C. Porteus); Wigan's Part in the Civil War, 1639-51; Outline of the History of Wigan; Twelve Epochs of Artificial Lighting; Some Electrical Epoch Makers; Reading and the Use of Books (in Employment of Leisure); Book Classification (in Primer of Librarianship); Find it Yourself; Wigan Grammar School, 1596-1936, The German War, 1939-45: a preliminary book classification (2nd edition, 1943); Sir Roger Bradshaigh, 1st Bart., 1628-1684; The Clockmakers and Watchmakers of Wigan, 1650-1850. Several brochures on Book Classification and Antiquarian topics. *Recreations:* golf, bridge, and bookshop-crawling. *Address:* Hawksnest, 95 Dicconson Street West, Wigan. *T.A.:* Hawksnest, Wigan. *T.:* Wigan 3181. [*Died* 12 *Dec.* 1952.

HAWKES, Charles John; Professor Emeritus, Univ. of Durham; O.B.E. 1939; D.Sc. (Dunelm); Eng. Comdr., R.N., retd.; *b.* 22 April 1880; *s.* of late John Hawkes and late Catherine Preston; *m.* Henrietta Rosina, *d.* of late J. Macfarlane Paramor; two *s.* *Educ.:* Sir J. Williamson's School, Rochester. Eng. Sub. Lieut., R.N. College, Greenwich, 1900-3; H.M.S. Montagu, 1903-4; Assistant to Chief Engineer, H.M. Dockyard, Sheerness, 1904-7; Staff of Director of Dockyards, Admiralty, 1907-8; H.M.S. Black Prince, 1908-10; Eng. Lieut. on staff of E.-in-C., Admiralty, 1910-12; Joint Secretary, Royal Commission on Fuel and Engines, 1912-14; Staff of E.-in-C., Admiralty, 1914-15; Assistant Secretary Board of Invention and Research, 1915-17; First Superintendent, Admiralty Engineering Laboratory, 1917-20; Professor of Engineering, King's College, Newcastle on Tyne, 1920-46; Member of Institution of Naval Architects, Member of Institution of Mechanical Engineers, Hon. Fellow and Past-President of N.E. Coast Institution of Engineers and Shipbuilders. Hon. Member Society of Naval Architects and Marine Engineers (U.S.A.). *Publications:* technical papers. *Address:* 45 King's Drive, Eastbourne. *T.:* Eastbourne 137. [*Died* 30 *Jan.* 1953.

HAWKES, Lieut.-Col. Charles Pascoe; Lt.-Col. (retd.) Special Reserve of Officers, Royal Northumberland Fusiliers; *b.* 3 April 1877; *s.* of late C. S. Hawkes, Rio de Janeiro, Edgbaston, and Beckenham, Kent, and Frances, *d.* of late F. W. Richards; *m.* 1904, Eleanor Victoria, *e. d.* of late Charles Davison Cobb; one *s.* one *d.* *Educ.:* Dulwich College; Trinity College, Cambridge (M.A.). 2nd Lieut., 5th (Mil.) Bn. Northumberland Fusiliers, 1900; Lieut., 1904; Captain Special Reserve of Officers Northumberland Fusiliers, 1908; commanded detachment 3rd Bn. King George V. Coronation, 1911; served European War from Aug. 4, 1914; Major 1915; 2nd-in-command 3rd Bn., 1916 (despatches); Lt.-Col. Commanding, 1918-20; retired 1920. Bar, Inner Temple, 1901; practised on North-Eastern Circuit and Probate Divorce and Admiralty Division; Chairman, Court of Referees (Unemployment Insurance), 1922-25; Registrar in the Supreme Court (Probate, Divorce and Admiralty Division), 1925-50, retd.; wrote and drew for Granta while at Cambridge; political cartoonist Daily Graphic, 1907-08; held exhibition drawings and caricatures Bruton Galleries, 1912; acting member Old Stagers. Hon. Secretary Pegasus Club (Bar Point-to-point races), 1919-25; President, 1934. President Royal Northumberland Fusiliers Old Comrades Association since 1922. *Publications:* The London Comedy, 1925; Mauresques, with some Basque and Spanish Cameos, 1926; Bench and Bar in the Saddle, 1928; Chambers in the Temple, 1930; The Wind in the Bus-Tops, 1931; Heydays, A Salad of Memories and Impressions, 1933; Authors-at-Arms, The Soldiering of Six Great Writers, 1934; Siege Lady, 1938; contributions to Punch, Times, Sunday Times, XIXth Century, Cornhill, and other daily, weekly and monthly periodicals and magazines. *Recreations:* travel and amateur acting. *Address:* 21 Campden Hill Square, W.8. *T.:* Park 4828. [*Died* 22 *July* 1956.

HAWKEY, Sir (Alfred) James, 1st Bt., *cr.* 1945 of Woodford; Kt., *cr.* 1926; Chairman of the Woodford Conservative Association; *b.* 1877; *s.* of Richard Hawkey of Sunny Croft, Woodford Green; *m.* Vera Kathleen (*d.* 1949), *d.* of late F. E. Price; one *s.* one *d.* *Educ.:* Woodford Collegiate School. Chairman Woodford Urban Council eighteen years; chairman of Wanstead & Woodford Urban District Council, 3 years; Charter Mayor of the Borough of Wanstead & Woodford, 1937, and Mayor of the Borough, 1937-38, 1943-45. First Freeman of Borough, 1939. Ex-member Essex County Council. *Heir:* *s.* Roger Pryce, *b.* 25 June 1905. *Address:* Great Coopers, Takeley, Essex. *T.:* 0167 Buckhurst. [*Died* 22 *May* 1952.

HAWKINS, Sir Villiers Geoffry Caesar, 6th Bt., *cr.* 1778; Compound Manager West Driefontein Gold Mine; *b.* 18 Aug. 1890, *o. surv. s.* of late H. C. Hawkins; *S.* cousin 1939; *m.* 1920, Blanche Marjorie Hampden-Smithers; one *s.* one *d.* *Educ.:* Hilton College, Natal. Served European War, 1914-19, as Capt., R.F.A. *Recreation:* golf. *Heir:* *s.* Humphry Villiers Caesar [*b.* 10 Aug. 1923; *m.* 1952, Anita Funkey, Michigan, U.S.A.]. *Address:* Kelston, Carletonville, Transvaal, S. Africa. [*Died* 14 *Feb.* 1955.

HAWKSLEY, Vice-Admiral James Rose Price, C.B. 1917; C.V.O. 1917 (M.V.O. 1907); *m.* 1899, Gertrude Emily Rose (*d.* 1949), *e. d.* of Comdr. G. E. Price. Entered Navy, 1885; Commander, 1905; Capt. 1912; Commodore commanding Grand Fleet flotillas during European War; battle of Jutland Bank, 1916 (despatches, C.V.O., C.B.); Captain in charge Portland, 1920-22; Rear-Adm. 1922; retired list, 1922; Vice-Adm. 1928. *Club:* Naval and Military. [*Died* 7 *April* 1955.

HAWLEY, Arthur; *b.* 13 July 1870; *yr. s.* of late Alfred Hawley, Hampstead, and Mary Sylvia, *e. d.* of late Richard Coombes Soutter, Highbury; unmarried. *Educ.:* Uppingham (Scholar); Christ Church, Oxford. 3rd Class Mod. History B.A., 1892; Barrister, Inner Temple, 1899; High Sheriff of Rutland, 1941; F.R.G.S.; Life Member, Royal Australian Historical Society; A Governor of the Foundation of Oakham and Uppingham Schools; a Trustee of Uppingham School, 1931-39. *Publication:* A Translation of the Foundation Grant of Oakham and Uppingham Schools, 1587, 1929. *Recreations:* fishing and shooting. *Address:* Cranhill, Weston Road, Bath. *Club:* Carlton. [*Died* 17 *March* 1952.

HAWORTH, Lieut.-Colonel Sir Lionel Berkeley Holt, K.B.E., *cr.* 1928; *b.* 30 Sept. 1873, *s.* of J. H. Haworth, Old Falinge, Lancs; *m.* 1st, Lilian Maude (*d.* 1906), *d.* of Col. A. D. Geddes, late commanding Inniskilling Fusiliers: one *s.*; 2nd, Gwendoline Olivia, *d.* of Col. A. D. Geddes; one *d.* *Educ.:* Dulwich College; Elizabeth College, Guernsey. Entered K.O. Yorkshire Light Infantry, 1893; entered Indian Army, 1898; served 2nd Bombay Lancers and 9th Bombay Infantry; entered Foreign and Political Department, Government of India, 1901; held political appointments in India and Persia; served as D.A.Q.M.G. and D.A.A. and Q.M.G. in 60th Division in European War, 1914-16; Intelligence Officer Arabia, 1916-19, while Political Agent Muscat; was Consul-General at Meshed in Khorasan; Political Resident in the Persian Gulf and H.B.M. Consul-General for Fars, Khuzestan, and the Persian Coasts and Islands of the Persian Gulf, 1927-29; retired, 1929. *Address:* c/o Lloyds Bank Ltd., 6 Pall Mall, S.W.1. [*Died* 11 *Sept.* 1951.

HAWORTH, Peter, M.A., Ph.D., B.Litt.; Emeritus Professor of English at Rhodes University, Grahamstown; *b.* 1 May 1891; *s.* of late John Haworth, Manchester; *m.* 1921; one *d.* *Educ.:* Manchester University; Innsbruck; University College, Oxford. Lektor in English, Innsbruck University, 1912-14; Lecturer in English, University of Bristol, 1914-32; Heath Harrison Scholar, University of Oxford, 1926; Chancellor's Prizeman (English Essay), 1926. *Publications:* English Hymns and Ballads; An Elizabethan Story-book; Before Scotland Yard; Rumours and Hoaxes; The Dead Man's Chest; Trollope's South Africa; Humorous Readings from Charles Dickens, etc. *Address:* 19 Edingight, Duke Rd., Rondebosch, Cape, S.A. [*Died* 1 *Nov.* 1956.

HAWORTH, Very Rev. William; Dean of Glasgow and Galloway, 1946-1959; *b.* 30 March 1880; *s.* of Joseph and Elizabeth Haworth. *Educ.:* Leeds Grammar School; Emmanuel College, Cambridge; Cuddesdon College, Oxford. B.A. 1902, M.A. 1912 (Camb.). Curate Tynemouth, 1903; Curate St. Matthew's, Newcastle, 1906; Diocesan Chaplain, Glasgow and Galloway, 1910; Curate of St. Mary's Cathedral, Glasgow, 1911; Precentor, St. Mary's Cathedral, Glasgow, 1919; Rector St. George's, Maryhill, Glasgow, 1920; Acting C.F., 1920; Canon of St. Mary's Cathedral, Glasgow, 1926; Canon of Cumbrae, 1938; Rector of St. Columba's, Largs, 1944; Acting C.F. (R.N.), 1944. *Address:* The Rectory, Largs, Ayrshire. *T.:* Largs 3143. *Club:* R.N.V.R. (Glasgow). [*Died* 13 *Feb.* 1960.

HAWTREY, Air Vice-Marshal John Gosset, C.B.E., 1946; Air Officer Commanding, Iraq, since Aug. 1952; *b.* 1901. Formerly Head of Royal Air Force delegation and Air Officer Commanding R.A.F. in Greece; Senior Air Staff Officer, Far East Air Force, Oct. 1951. *Address:* Air Headquarters, Royal Air Force, British Forces in Iraq, M.E.A.F. 19; Yew Tree Cottage, Woodland St. Mary, Gt. Shefford, Berks. [*Died* 26 *Oct.* 1954.

HAY, Sir Charles J. D.; *see* Dalrymple Hay.

HAY, Sir David Allan, K.B.E., *cr.* 1939 (O.B.E. 1919); Kt., *cr.* 1934; J.P.; Chartered Accountant, Glasgow; *b.* 19 Dec. 1878; *s.* of James Hay, Paisley and Christina Foulis; *m.* 1911, Frances Margaret, *d.* of late Thomas Walker, North Berwick; one *s.* one *d.* *Educ.:* Grammar School, Paisley; Glasgow University. Commissioner for Special Areas in Scotland, 1936-1937; Chairman, Scottish Special Areas Housing Association, 1937-39; President Scottish Unionist Association, 1932-33; Hon. Treasurer Soldiers', Sailors' and Airmen's Families Association (Glasgow Branch), 1914-36; President, Institute of Accountants and Actuaries in Glasgow, 1944-46; Pres. Inst. of Chartered Accountants of Scotland, 1952-53; Lord Dean of Guild, Glasgow, 1950-52. *Address:* 3 Redlands Terrace, Glasgow, W.2. *Clubs:* Western, New, Conservative (Glasgow); Conservative (Edinburgh). [*Died* 6 *May* 1957.

HAY, Ian; *see* Beith, Maj.-Gen. J. H.

HAY, John, M.D., F.R.C.P., M.R.C.S.; D.L.; Hon. F.R.S.M. 1952; retired; late Professor of Medicine, Liverpool University, now Professor Emeritus; Consulting Hon. Physician, Liverpool Royal Infirmary; Regional Adviser in Medicine, Ministry of Health; Gas Expert to Ministry of Health; Honorary member of Cardiac Society of Great Britain and Ireland; late Visiting Physician, City Hospital, Walton; late Senior Medical Officer, Royal Insurance Co.; Ex-Pres. Microscopical Society; Ex-President, Liverpool Medical Institution; Ex-President, Liver Sketching Club; Consulting Physician, Victoria Central Hospital, Wallasey, Liverpool Maternity Hospital, the Children's Convalescent Home, West Kirby, the County Hospital, Kendal; Lieut.-Colonel

R.A.M.C. (T.), Hon. consulting Physician to Ministry of Pensions in Cardiovascular cases in the North-Western region; late Specialist in Cardiac Disorders, Western Command; *s.* of James Murdoch Hay, architect; *b.* 25 Nov. 1873; *m.* 1906, Agnes Margaret (*d.* 1947), *d.* of late William Duncan, M.D., Tyldesley; two *s.* two *d.* *Educ.:* The Liverpool Institute, High School; Liverpool University. Medallist in Medicine, Anatomy, and Physiology; M.D., Victoria, Man., 1901, Mark of Commendation; M.D., Liverpool, 1904; M.B., B.Ch. Honours; Holt Fellow in Anatomy and Surgery, 1895-96; Hon. Physician, Liverpool Stanley Hospital; Hon. Physician, Hospital for Consumption and Diseases of the Chest; Hon. Pathologist, David Lewis Northern Hospital; Senior Assistant Medical Officer, Mill Road Infirmary; Medical Tutor and Registrar, Royal Infirmary, 1900-3; Bradshaw Lecturer; St. Cyres Lecturer, 1933; James Mackenzie Lecturer; T. Strickland Goodall Lecturer, 1936. *Publications:* Heart Disease; Graphic Methods; ex-Editor, Liverpool Medico-Chirurgical Journal; numerous contributions to the Medical Journals. *Recreations:* gardening, painting. *Address:* Underfell, Bowness-on-Windermere. *T.:* Windermere 503. *Club:* University (Liverpool). [*Died* 21 *April* 1959.

HAY, John Arthur Machray, R.P.; Member Royal Society of Portrait Painters, 1928 and London Portrait Society; *b.* Aberdeen, 1887; *e. s.* of late James Hay, Aberdeen. Has exhibited at the Royal Society of Portrait Painters Exhibition and Royal Academy since 1919. *Address:* 30 St. Margaret's Road, Oxford. *T.:* 55041. *Club:* Chelsea Arts. [*Died* 24 *Nov.* 1960.

HAY, Peter Alexander, R.I., R.S.W.; portrait painter; *b.* Edinburgh, 1866; *s.* of late Peter Hay, Edinburgh; *m.* 1911, Mary Beatrice, *o. d.* of James Troup (late H.M. Consul-General, Yokohama, Japan); one *s.* *Educ.:* George Watson's College, Edinburgh. Studied at Royal Scottish Academy, Académie Julian, Paris, and Antwerp; exhibited at Royal Academy since 1892, also Royal Scottish Academy, New Gallery, Royal Institute, Paris Salon; member of Royal Scottish Society of Painters in Water-Colours, member of the Royal British and Colonial Society of Artists. *Club:* Arts. [*Died* 13 *March* 1952.

HAY, Thomas, C.V.O. 1938 (M.V.O. (5th class) 1927); late Superintendent, Royal Central Parks; V.M.H. (Royal Horticultural Society) 1924. O.St.J. 1938. *Address:* Stoatley Cottage, Bunch Lane, Haslemere. [*Died* 22 *Jan.* 1953.

HAY, Lieut.-Colonel Thomas William; Lt.-Col. in Leicestershire Yeomanry, retired; *b.* 25 Aug. 1882; *s.* of late Adm. of the Fleet Lord John Hay, G.C.B.; unmarried. *Educ.:* Clifton College. Served European War in France with Leicestershire Yeomanry and 16th Lancers, 1914-18 (despatches); M.P. (U.) S. Norfolk, 1922-23; Pilot Officer R.A.F.V.R. 1940; Squadron Leader 1941-. *Recreations:* hunting, shooting, fishing, aviation. *Club:* R.A.F. [*Died* 10 *July* 1956.

HAY-DRUMMOND, Arthur William Henry, J.P.; *e. s.* of late Col. Hon. C. R. Hay-Drummond; *b.* 1862; *m.* 1891, Mary (*d.* 1948), *y. d.* of Sir Edward Henry Scott, 5th Bart., of Lytchet Minster, Dorsetshire; one *s.* three *d.* *Educ.:* Eton. Lt.-Col. 3rd Bn. Royal Berkshire Regt., 1880-1901, and Bt. Col. commanding 2/6 Black Watch, 1914-18; lately Ensign Royal Company of Archers, King's Bodyguard for Scotland. *Heir:* *s.* George Vane Hay-Drummond [*m.* 1933, Lady Betty Mary Seton Montgomerie, *y.d.* of 16th Earl of Eglinton and Winton; one *d.*]. *Address:* Cromlix, Dunblane, Perthshire. *Club:* Turf. [*Died* 21 *July* 1953.

HAYCOCK, Rev. T. R.; *see* Hine-Haycock.

HAYDAY, Arthur, J.P.; *b.* Tidal Basin, West Ham, London, E., 24 Oct. 1869; *m.* twice; five *s.* seven *d.* *Educ.:* St. Luke's, National School, Tidal Basin, London, E.; started work on market gardens at 9 years of age; later, kitchen boy at Central Buffet, Albert Docks; worked in chemical and carrying trades, and public works; in Merchant Service as trimmer and stoker; on West Ham Town Council, 1896-09; London representative of the National Union of General Workers, 1898; took charge of the Midland Area, 1909; M.P. (Lab.) West Nottingham, 1918-31 and 1935-45; sent by British Trades Union Congress to American Convention of Labour, Buffalo, Nov. 1917; Member of Governing Body I.L.O., Geneva, 1931-37. *Recreation:* walking. [*Died* 28 *Feb.* 1956.

HAYDEN, John Patrick; editor and proprietor of Westmeath Examiner, Mullingar; *b.* 25 April 1863; 7th *s.* of late Mr. Luke Hayden, Roscommon; *m.* 1912, Henrietta Hill, *d.* of Thomas Scott, Hannaville, Green Island, Antrim; one *s.* *Educ.:* Roscommon. Was four times imprisoned under different Coercion Acts; M.P. (Nationalist) for South Roscommon, 1897-1918; Member Irish Board of Agriculture. *Address:* Mullingar. *T.:* Mullingar 126. [*Died* 3 *July* 1954.

HAYDON, Arthur Lincoln; author and journalist; literary coach; *b.* 1872; *s.* of late Hillyard Haydon of Highgate. *Educ.:* City of London School; Woodhouse Grove School, Yorks. Sub-editor, Cassell and Co., 1890-1900; later, Editor, Boys of Our Empire, The Week's Survey, The Lady's World, Our Home; Assist. Ed., New Health; Nuttall's Standard English Dictionary and the Nuttall Encyclopædia; Editor of The Boy's Own Paper and the Empire Annuals, 1912-24. *Publications:* The Riders of the Plains (history of the Royal North-West Mounted Police of Canada); The Trooper Police of Australia; Canada, Britain's Largest Colony; The Book of the V.C.; The Book of the Lifeboat; Pole for Cock House!; The Book of Robin Hood; and other volumes of stories for boys. *Recreations:* lawn tennis, swimming, natural history. *Address:* 57 Gordon Square, W.C.1. [*Died* 16 *Nov.* 1954.

HAYDON, His Honour Judge Thomas Edmett, Q.C. 1923; M.A. Barrister Inner Temple, 1891; Judge of County Courts, Circuit 20, 1925-35, Circuit No. 45, 1935-40. *Address:* Branksome Tower Hotel, Bournemouth. [*Died* 30 *July* 1952.

HAYES, Major-General Eric Charles, C.B. 1946; *b.* 19 June 1896; *er. s.* of late Charles Frederick Hayes, Digby, Lincs; *m.* 1924, Florence Lilyanne, *d.* of late Henri Sudreau, Paris; two *d.* *Educ.:* Sleaford, Lincs; R.M.C., Sandhurst. Served European War, 1916-19 (despatches); graduate of Staff College, Camberley; during War of 1939-45 commanded: 2nd Bn. Royal Norfolk Regiment in France, Infantry Coy. Commanders' School, 169 Infantry Brigade, Yorkshire County Division and 3rd Division in England; Nigeria Area, West Africa; East Central District in England; G.O.C. British Troops in China and Head of British Military Mission to China; retired pay, 1947. Colonel, Royal Norfolk Regiment, 1951-. *Recreations:* golf, gardening. *Address:* 30 Astell Street, Chelsea, S.W.3. *Club:* Army and Navy. [*Died* 25 *Aug.* 1951.

HAYES, Gerald Ravenscourt, O.B.E. 1950; formerly Head of Welfare and Accommodation, Admiralty; *b.* 18 April 1889; *e. s.* of late Frederick William Hayes, landscape painter; *m.* 1918, Mary Winifred, *d.* of late James Yule, Aberdeen; one *s.* *Educ.:* Cranleigh. Entered Admiralty service by open competition (Hydrographic Dept.), 1911; Principal Civil Hydrographic Officer (then Chief Cartographer), 1934; transferred to Secretary's Dept., 1946-53. Worked with late Arnold Dolmetsch for nearly twenty years in the revival of early instrumental music; one of the founders, and first Hon. Sec. of Dolmetsch Foundation, 1927; Hon. Treasurer of Georgian Historical Society from its inception; Chm.

Galpin Soc., 1952-, and Hon. Editor, 1955-. *Publications:* The Making of an Admiralty Chart, 1924; Anthony Munday's Romances (bibliographical study), 1925; Treatment of Instrumental Music, 1928; The Viols and Other Bowed Instruments, 1930; King's Musick, 1937; (with M. Chriss) Introduction to Charts and their Use, 1944; Charting the Seas in Peace and War, 1947; numerous articles in newspapers and periodicals on music and romances of chivalry; contrib. to Grove's Dictionary of Music; New Oxford History of Music; Oxford Companion to Music. *Recreations:* heraldry, painting, sailing. *Address:* May Cottage, Old Bosham, Sussex. *T.:* Bosham 2245. *Clubs:* Athenæum, Art Workers Guild; Bosham Sailing. [*Died* 13 *Sept.* 1955.

HAYES, Gertrude, (Mrs. E. M. Betts), A.R.E. 1897; Member of Coventry and Warwickshire Society of Artists; *b.* London, 23 Nov. 1872; *d.* of James Harmer Hayes; *m.* 1st, Alfred Kedington Morgan, A.R.C.A., F.S.A. (*d.* 1928), Art Master of Rugby school; 2nd, 1936, Edwin M. Betts, formerly Art Master, Nottingham High School. *Educ.:* Royal College of Art. Royal Exhibitioner three years, 1892; British Institution Scholarship, 1897, two years; Silver and Bronze medallist; Art Master's certificate; Exhibitor at Royal Academy and Royal Scottish Academy; Liverpool, St. Louis, New Zealand, Australia; works in permanent collection of Federal Library, Washington, South Kensington Museum, Liverpool, Los Angeles Museum; Head of L.C.C. Art Centre, 1904-7; Assistant Art Mistress at Rugby School, 1915-19. *Publications:* Etchings; among which are: The Tower of London; Boston Stump; Canterbury; Rugby; Butcher Row, Coventry; Leicester's Hospital, Warwick; The Shambles, York; Tantallon Castle; Dover Castle; Richmond Castle; Guys Cliffe; Warwick. *Recreations:* travelling, motoring, gardening. *Address:* Hillcrest, Shawell, Rugby. [*Died* 1956.

HAYES, Hon. John Blyth, C.M.G. 1921; Senator for Tasmania in Commonwealth Senate, 1923-47; President of Senate, 1938-1941; *b.* 21 Apr. 1868; *m.* 1906, *d.* of late William Blyth. Minister of Lands, Works, and Agriculture, 1916-19; Premier of Tasmania, 1922-23, and Minister of Works and Agriculture, 1919-23; Member House of Assembly, 1913-23. *Address:* Scottsdale, Tasmania. [*Died* 12 *July* 1956.

HAYES, Brig.-General Wade Hampton, O.B.E. 1944; Chairman, Edmundson's Electric Co. Ltd., and Chairman or Director of its associated Companies; Director English Electric Co. Ltd., D. Napier & Son, Ltd., Marconi's Wireless Telegraph Co. Ltd., and associated Cos.; *b.* 12 May 1879; *s.* of William Arnold Hayes and Emma Mathews, North Carolina, U.S.A.; *m.* 1905, Julia Florence (*d.* 1939), *d.* of Frederick A. Yard, Brooklyn, N.Y.; one *d.* *Educ.:* Norfolk Academy, Va.; Columbia University. Sunday Editor New York Tribune, 1908-14. Served in Spanish-American War on staff of Maj.-Gen. Fitzhugh Lee, 1898; European War, 1914-18; served in France, 1917-19; Lt.-Col. 107th U.S. Infantry; on staff of Gen. Pershing; G.H.Q.A.E.F., 1918-19; Col. 107th U.S. Infantry, 1919-31; Brig.-Gen., retired; organised and commanded American Squadron, H.G., 1940-44. Chm. American Soc. in London; Member Council English-Speaking Union, Member Exec. Cttee. of the Pilgrims; formerly Member of Hayes & Lord, investment bankers, Vice-Pres. Chase Securities Corp., and Chm. Greater London and Counties Trust Ltd.; Commander Legion of Honour (France). *Recreations:* golf, riding. *Address:* 30 Gillingham St., S.W.1. *T.:* Victoria 8171; 48 Ennismore Gardens, S.W.7. *T.:* Kensington 9396. *Clubs:* Carlton, American, Turf, Royal Automobile; Salmagundi, Racquet and Tennis, Down Town (New York). [*Died* 4 *Sept.* 1956.

HAYMAN-JOYCE, Maj.-Gen. Hayman John, C.B.E. 1946; D.S.O. 1940; *b.* 2 May 1897; *s.* of John Hayman-Joyce and Eleanor Frances Fletcher; *m.* 1923, Irene May Swann; one *s.* two *d.* *Educ.:* Radley; R.M.C., Sandhurst. Commissioned Border Regt., 1915; served with Border Regt. in France and Belgium, 1916 and 1918; subsequently in India, Sudan, and China; p.s.c.; in General Staff, War Office (G.S.O. III, G.S.O. II and G.S.O. I in succession), 1936-40; commanded 5th Battalion King's Own Royal Regiment in France, April-June 1940, and then in England. Subsequently commanded Infantry Brigade and a Division in England, a Division in the Mediterranean and a District in Egypt: retired pay, 1947. *Address:* Chibbet, Exford, Minehead, Somerset. *Club:* Naval and Military. [*Died* 7 *July* 1958.

HAYS, Arthur Garfield; Member of Firm of Hays, St. John, Abramson & Schulman, 120 Broadway, New York, N.Y.; *b.* Rochester, N.Y., 12 Dec. 1881; *s.* of Isaac M. Hays and Laura Garson; *m.* 1st, 1908, Blanche Marks; one *d.*; 2nd, 1924, Aline Davis; one *d.* *Educ.:* Columbia College (A.B. 1902); Columbia Law School (LL.B. 1905, A.M. 1902). Admitted to practice 1905. Resided in England, representing American shipowners and shippers before British Prize Court, 1915-16. In charge of investigations for Am. Red Cross, 1917. Represented American Civil Liberties Union in Anthracite coal strike in Pennsylvania, 1922, and in W. Va. Associated with Clarence Darrow and Dudley Field Malone in trial in Tennessee of John Thomas Scopes. Retained by National Association for Advancement of Colored People with Darrow, to defend Dr. Ossian H. Sweet and ten other Negroes charged with murder in Detroit. Represented American Mercury and editor H. L. Mencken, Boston, 1926; Vera, Countess of Cathcart, 1927; defence in last days of Sacco-Vanzetti case. Defended John Strachey in deportation case. Member of neutral commission sitting in London to hear facts concerning burning of German Reichstag, attended trial in Berlin and Leipzig two months. Member of Commission of Inquiry of Committee for Fair Trial for Draja Mihailovich, 1946. Chairman of Commission of Inquiry in Civil Rights, Puerto Rico, 1937. *Publications:* Enemy Property in America, 1925; Let Freedom Ring, 1928; rev. ed. 1937; Trial by Prejudice, 1933; Democracy Works, 1938-39; City Lawyer, 1942. *Recreations:* chess, boating, tennis. *Address:* 120 Broadway, New York 5, N.Y.; 24 East 10th Street, New York City; Sands Point, Long Island, N.Y. *T.:* Digby 9-4141, Gramercy 3-8038. *Clubs:* Bankers, P.E.N. [*Died* 14 *Dec.* 1954.

HAYS, Will H., Lawyer; President, Motion Picture Producers and Distributors of America, Inc., 1922-45; *b.* Sullivan, Ind., 5 Nov. 1879; *s.* of John T. Hays and Mary Cain; *m.* 1st, 1902, Helen Louise Thomas; one *s.*; 2nd, 1930, Jessie Herron Stutsman, Indiana. *Educ.:* Wabash College, A.B. 1900; A.M. 1904; LL.D., Lincoln Memorial Univ., 1919, Mount Union Coll. 1926, Wabash Coll. 1940. Admitted to Ind. Bar, 1900; City Attorney, Sullivan, 1910-13; Member, firm Hays & Hays; Director, Continental Baking Company and Chicago and Eastern Illinois R. R.; Vice-President Roosevelt Memorial Assoc.; Member National Council Boy Scouts of America; Trustee, Institute for Crippled and Disabled Men; Trustee Wabash College; elected Republican Precinct Committeeman before age of twenty-one; Chairman, Republican County Committee, Sullivan Co., and Member Republican State Advisory Com. Ind., 1904-8; Chairman, Speakers' Bur. Rep. State Com., 1906-8; District Chairman, Rep. State Com. 2nd Dist. Ind., 1910-14; Chairman, Rep. State Central Com., Ind., 1914-18; Chairman, Ind. State Council of Defence, 1917-18; Chairman, Rep.

Nat. Com., 1918-21; Postmaster-General, U.S.A., 1921-22; Member National Board of Incorporators American Red Cross; Member American Bar Association Ind. State Bar Assn., Phi Delta Theta (St. Pres. for Ind., 6 years, Nat. Pres. 1920 22); Chairman, Co-ordinating Comm. Am. Red Cross and Near East Relief, 1922 Citizens' Committee Salvation Army, America; Col., Officers' Reserve Corps; Chairman Laymen's Committee, Presbyterian Board of Ministerial Relief and Sustentation, 1923; Elder of Presbyterian Church: 33° Mason K.T. and Shrine R; K. of P. Order of Elks; Loyal Order of Moose. *Address:* 630 Fifth Avenue, New York City. *T.:* Columbus 5-4596; (Branch offices Hays & Hays); 300 American National Bldg., Indianapolis, Indiana, U.S.A.; Sullivan, Indiana, U.S.A. *Clubs:* Columbia, Indianapolis Country, Indianapolis Athletic, Terre Haute Country (Indiana); Illinois Athletic, Chicago (Chicago); Metropolitan, National Press, University, (Washington); Cloud, National Republican, Advertising, Hudson River Country, Union League, Bankers, Friar's, Sleepy Hollow Country, Economic, Rockfeller Center Luncheon, Coffee House (New York); Hollywood Athletic, California, Bohemian, Lincoln (California); Chevy Chase (Maryland), etc. [*Died* 7 *March* 1954.

HAYWARD, Evan; Major, 14th Batt. Worcester Regt.; *b.* Wotton under Edge, Gloucester, 2 Apr. 1876; *s.* of Robert and Catharine Hayward, formerly of Wotton-under-Edge, Gloucester; *m.* 1913, Elizabeth M. Bergfeldt, Boston, U.S.A. *Educ.:* Katherine Lady Berkeley's Grammar School, Wotton under Edge, Glos. M.P. (L.), S.E. Durham, 1910-18; Seaham, Co. Durham, 1918-22. Is a solicitor (retired) (honoursman) and special prizeman, Glos. and Wilts. Incorporated Law Society. *Publication:* Guide to Industrial Assurance Act, 1923. *Address:* Westcot, Wotton-under-Edge, Glos. [*Died* 30 *Jan.* 1958.

HAYWARD, Marjorie Olive, F.R.A.M.; Professor at Royal Academy of Music; *b.* Greenwich, 1885; *d.* of late Geo. O. and Eliz. Hayward; *m.* 1916, R. G. K. Lempfert, C.B.E., *q.v.*; one *d.* *Educ.:* Royal Academy of Music; at Prague under Professor O. Sevcik. Solo Violinist; Leader of the Marjorie Hayward Quartet; Violinist of the English Ensemble Piano Quartet; Violinist of Kamaran Piano Trio; Strings Adjudicator at Competition Festivals. *Address:* 35 Fitzjames Avenue, W.14. *T.:* Fulham 6961. [*Died* 10 *Jan.* 1953.

HAZELTINE, Harold Dexter, M.A., Litt.D.; F.B.A.; *b.* Warren, Pennsylvania, 18 Nov. 1871; *s.* of Abram Jones Hazeltine and Harriet Emeline Davis, of Warren, Pennsylvania; *m.* 1911, Hope, *d.* of George Franklin Graves and Belle Woodman of Bellevue, Bennington, Vermont; one *d.* *Educ.:* Brown University, Providence: Harvard Law School; Germany, France, and England. Law Lecturer, Emmanuel Coll., Camb., 1906-19; Lecturer on Law, Univ. of Chicago, 1906; Univ. Reader in English Law at Cambridge, 1907-1919; Professor of Law, University of Wisconsin, 1908; Lecturer, University at London, 1910; Carpentier Lecturer on Jurisprudence, Columbia University, N.Y., 1912 and 1916; Fellow of Emmanuel Coll., Cambridge, 1908-19; Downing Professor of the Laws of England in the University of Cambridge, 1919-42; Dr. Jur. Berlin, 1905; Hon. LL.D., Brown University, 1920; Hon. LL.D., Harvard Univ., 1924; Hon. Fellow Downing Coll., 1942; Barrister, Inner Temple. *Publications:* Geschichte des englischen Pfandrechts, 1907; The Law of the Air, 1911; various articles and essays, mostly upon English legal history, air law, and legal education. *Address:* Downing College, Cambridge; Harvard Law School, Cambridge, Massachusetts. *Club:* United University. [*Died* 23 *Jan.* 1960.

HAZELTON, Maj.-Gen. Percy Orr, C.B. 1918; C.M.G. 1916; *b.* 2 Mar. 1871; *o. s.* of late R. P. Hazelton, F.R.C.S.; *m.* Mabel. *d.* of late Edmond Thomas, Silverlea, Wynberg, one *d.* *Educ.:* Trinity College, Dublin; R M.C., Sandhurst. Served S. Africa, 1900-2 (Queen's medal 5 clasps, King's medal 2 clasps); European War, 1914-18 (despatches five times, C.M.G., Bt.-Col., C.B.); Director of Supplies and Transport, War Office, 1921-25; retired pay, 1925; Commander of the Order of the Crown of Belgium; A.D.C. to the King, 1921-22. *Address:* c/o Westminster Bank, 1 High Street, Kensington, W.8. *Club:* United Service. [*Died* 14 *Dec.* 1952.

HEAD, Lt.-Col. Alfred Searle, C.M.G. 1919; F.R.C.V.S.; J.P.; Veterinary Surgeon at Coinage Hall, Helston, Cornwall; *b.* East Grinstead, Sussex, 24 Oct. 1874; *s.* of George Searle Head; *m.* 1906, Mabel Hoadley; two *s.* one *d.* *Educ.:* Marlborough College. Qualified as veterinary surgeon, 1897; served in Army Veterinary Corps South African War, 1900-2 (despatches); Brevet Major, 1917; Lt.-Col., Reserve of Officers, since War. *Address:* Coinage Hall, Helston, Cornwall. *T.A.:* Head, Helston. *T.:* Helston 16. [*Died* 9 *Jan.* 1952.

HEAD, Lieut.-Col. Charles Octavius, D.S.O. 1917; J.P. Co. Tipperary; *b.* 1869; 3rd *s.* of W. H. Head, D.L., Derrylahan Park, Birr, Ireland; *m.* 1908, Alice Margaret, *d.* of Charles Threlfall, Tarporley, Cheshire; one *s.* two *d.* *Educ.:* Private; R.M.A., Woolwich. In R.A., 1887-1910; in Reserve of Officers actively employed since Aug. 1914; served in England, Ireland, India, China, France, and South Africa (China medal, 1900, Mons Star, War and Victory medals). *Publications:* The Art of Generalship, 1930; A Glance at Gallipoli, 1931; Napoleon and Wellington, 1939; No Great Shakes, 1943. *Address:* Hinton Hall, Shrewsbury. *T.A.:* Hinton, Pontesbury. *Club:* Naval and Military. [*Died* 16 *Oct.* 1952.

HEAD, F. S. C.; *see* Cameron-Head.

HEAD, Robert, Mus. Doc. (Edin.); Mus.Bac. (Dunelm); F.T.C.L.; F.R.C.O.; A.R.C.M.; Organist and Master of the Choristers, St. Mary's Cathedral, Edinburgh, since 1929; Lecturer, Edinburgh Episcopal Theological Coll.; Examiner for Trinity Coll. of Music, London; *b.* Congleton, Cheshire; *e. s.* of Robert Head, the Editor, publisher, and proprietor of the Congleton Chronicle; *m.* 1939, Evelyn, 3rd *d.* of late James Wyse Mackie. *Educ.:* St. Paul's Cathedral Choir School, London (Merchant Taylor Scholar). Organist and Choirmaster St. James' Church, Congleton, Cheshire, 1911-19; Oswestry Parish Church and Grammar School, Salop, 1919-25; St. Matthias Church, Richmond Hill, Surrey, and Professor of Theory of Music and Aural Training, Kneller Hall, The Royal Military School of Music, London, 1925-29. *Address:* St. Mary's Cathedral, Edinburgh. [*Died* 3 *March* 1957.

HEADFORT, 5th Marquess of (*cr.* 1800), **Terence Geoffrey Thomas Taylour;** Bt. 1704; Baron Headfort, 1760; Viscount Headfort, 1762; Earl of Bective, 1766; **Baron Kenlis (U.K.), 1831; Chairman of** Bective Electrical, Ltd.; Captain Warwickshire Yeomanry; T.D.; *b.* 1 May 1902; *er. s.* of 4th Marq. and Rose (*d.* 1958), *d.* of Charles Boote; *S.* father, 1943; *m.* 1928, *d.* of J. Partridge Tucker, Sydney, N.S.W., and *widow* of Sir Rupert Clarke, 2nd Bt. of Rupertswood; one *s.* one *d.* *Educ.:* Harrow; Magdalen College, Oxford. A.D.C. to Sir Malcolm Barclay Harvey, Governor of S. Australia, 1939-40; Staff Capt. att. Australian Military Forces, 1940-42; Staff Capt. (Mil. Sec. branch) War Office, 1943. *Heir:* *s.* Earl of Bective. *Clubs:* Lansdowne; Kildare Street (Dublin). [*Died* 24 *Oct.* 1960.

HEADINGTON, Kenneth George John, C.B.E. 1943; **Imperial Bank of India (retired); *b.* 29 Oct. 1898; *e. s.* of**

George and Clara Headington, Buxton, Derbyshire; *m.* 1944, Rosemary Frances Elizabeth, *d.* of late Capt. Ramsay Shields, Little Island, Co. Cork, Eire. *Educ.:* Newman's, Buxton; New Mills. Served in France, 1914-18, with H.A.C. Entered Imperial Bank of India (late Bank of Bengal), 1920. *Recreation:* motoring. *Address:* Hillcrest, Raglan Road, Reigate, Surrey. *T.:* Reigate 2793.
[*Died* 12 *May* 1960.

HEADLAM, Gerald Erskine, M.A.; *b.* 21 Oct. 1877; *y. s.* of late Morley Headlam, Gilmonby Hall, Yorks., and Whorlton Grange, Co. Durham; unmarried. *Educ.:* Giggleswick and Sherborne Schools; All Souls College and St. Catherine's Society, Oxford. Assistant Master: Ladycross, Bournemouth, 1899-1900; The Oratory School, 1901-23 and 1927-38; Assistant Master and Housemaster, St. Edmund's College, Ware, 1924-27; Headmaster of the Oratory School, Woodcote House, Reading, 1938-42; Captain, T.A. (retired); commanded Oratory School O.T.C., 1914-23 and 1928-34; Commanded St. Edmund's College O.T.C., 1925-27. *Address:* The Oratory School, Woodcote House, Reading.
[*Died* 16 *June* 1954.

HEADLAM, Brig.-Gen. Hugh Roger, C.B. 1930; C.M.G. 1918; D.S.O. 1915; *b.* 15 July 1877; 4th *s.* of late F. J. Headlam. *Educ.:* Wellington College (classical scholar); R.M.C., Sandhurst. Entered Army, York and Lancaster Regt., 1897; Capt. 1903; Major, 1915; Staff Officer, 1901-2; with Egyptian Army, 1903-13; Staff Captain, 1914; Brigade-Major, 1915; p.s.c.; Bt. Lt.-Col. 1917; Bt. Col. 1919; Col. 1924; served S. Africa, 1899-1902 (despatches twice, Queen's medal, 6 clasps, King's medal, 2 clasps); Sudan, 1905 (medal with clasp, despatches, 4th class Medjidieh, 3rd class Osmanieh); European War, 1914-18 (D.S.O., C.M.G., Officier Légion d'Honneur, despatches 7 times, wounded); Waziristan 1919 (medal with 2 clasps); commanded 1/5 West Riding Regt. (T.F.), 1915-16; Brigadier-General in Command 64th Infantry Brigade, June 1916; Inspector of Infantry Home Forces, Aug. 1918; G.S.O.I., A.H.Q., India, Oct. 1919; Col. Commandant Castlebar Brigade, 1921; Col. Commandant 25 Prov. Brigade, 1922; Col. Commandant British Troops in Soudan, 1924-26; in command of 1st Batt. The King's Own Royal Regiment (Lancaster), 1920-24; Brigadier 12th (Secunderabad) Infantry Brigade, 1926-30; retired pay, 1930; Inspector, Staff School, Iraq Army, 1931-34; operations in Kurdestan (with Iraq Army), 1932 (medal with clasp, despatches, Iraqi Army medal); 3rd Class Rafidein, 1934. *Address:* Cobbles, Shillingstone, Dorset.
[*Died* 25 *Oct.* 1955.

HEADLAM, Maurice Francis, C.B. 1923; C.M.G. 1929; M.A. Oxon.; *e. s.* of late Francis John Headlam, Stipendiary Magistrate of Manchester; *b.* 19 Oct. 1873; *m.* 1922, Lady Vera Grimston, *y. d.* of 3rd Earl of Verulam; three *s.* *Educ.:* Eton (K.S.); Corpus Christi College, Oxford (scholar). Clerk, Board of Trade, 1897; Treasury, 1899; Asst. Private Secretary to the Chancellor of the Exchequer (Rt. Hon. Austen Chamberlain), 1903-5; Treasury Remembrancer and Deputy Paymaster for Ireland, 1912-20; an Assistant Secretary to the Treasury, 1920-26; Comptroller-General and Secretary of National Debt Office, 1927-38; a British representative on the Pacific Cable Board, 1923-1942; Acting Chairman, 1927-42; Silver Jubilee Medal, 1935; Coronation Medal, 1937. *Publications:* A Holiday Fisherman, 1934, 2nd edn., 1949; Rod, Horn, and Gun, 1942; Bishop and Friend, 1945; Irish Reminiscences, 1947. *Recreation:* fishing. *Address:* Pré Mill House, St. Albans. *T.:* St. Albans 57586. *Clubs:* Travellers'; St. George's Yacht (Kingstown).
[*Died* 2 *Nov.* 1956.

HEADLAM, Rev. Canon Morley Lewis Caulfield; Vicar of Atcham, Shrewsbury; Surrogate; *b.* 13 Feb. 1868; *s.* of Morley Headlam and Louisa Kate Beamish; *m.* 1908, Olive Muriel Newton; one *s.* two *d.* *Educ.:* Aysgarth and Durham Schools (Kings Scholar); All Souls College, Oxford (Bible Clerk); Leeds Clergy School. Lit. Hum., 1891; M.A. 1896; deacon 1894; priest 1895; Curate St. Saviour's, Leicester, 1894-98; Chaplain, Home Missions, Adelaide, S. Australia, 1898-1902; Warden of Theological College, 1900-2; Curate of St. John's, Middlesbrough, 1902-4; Vicar, 1904-1906; Vicar of St. John's, Keswick, 1906-18; Horsham, 1918-34; Rural Dean, Surrogate, 1919-34; Proctor in Convocation, 1928-29; Prebendary of Chichester, 1931; Canon Emeritus of Chichester, 1934; Rural Dean of Shrewsbury, 1935-39; O.C.F., 1941. *Recreations:* gardening, fishing. *Address:* The Vicarage, Atcham, Shrewsbury, Salop. *T.A.:* Atcham Cross Houses. *T.:* Cross Houses 231.
[*Died* 24 *Nov.* 1953.

HEAL, Sir Ambrose, Kt., *cr.* 1933; F.S.A., R.D.I.; Head of the Business of Heal & Son, Ltd.; designer and maker of furniture; *b.* 3 Sept. 1872; *s.* of late Ambrose Heal; *m.* 1st, 1895, Rose Rippingille; 2nd, 1904, Edith Florence Digby Todhunter (*d.* 1946); two *s.* one *d.* *Educ.:* Marlborough College. Served apprenticeship to cabinet making, 1890-93; entered Heal & Son, 1893; partner, 1898; Managing Director, 1907; Chairman, 1913; Royal Designer for Industry; Mem. Art Workers Guild, etc. Vice-Pres. Design and Industries Assoc. Gold Albert Medal of Royal Society of Arts, 1954. *Publications:* London Tradesmen's Cards of the Eighteenth-Century, 1926; The English Writing Masters and their Copy-Books, 1570-1800, 1931; The London Goldsmiths, 1200-1800, 1935; The Signboards of Old London Shops, 1947; London Furniture Makers from 1660 to 1840, 1953. *Recreations:* collections eighteenth century trade-cards, caligraphic works of early writing masters, modern press books. *Address:* Baylin's Farm, Knotty Green, Beaconsfield, Bucks. *T.:* Beaconsfield 188; 196, etc., Tottenham Court Road, W.1.
[*Died* 15 *Nov.* 1959.

HEALEY; *see* Chadwyck-Healey.

HEALEY, Col. Coryndon William Rutherford, C.M.G. 1916; C.B.E. 1919; late A.M.S.; *b.* 22 May 1864; 2nd *s.* of late Lt.-Col. John Healey, 32nd Foot. Served N.W. Frontier, India, 1897-98 (medal with clasp); S. Africa, 1899-1902 (despatches, Queen's medal 6 clasps King's medal 2 clasps, prom. Major); European War, 1914-18 (despatches, C.M.G., C.B.E.); retired, 1919. *Address:* 205 Rusden St., Armidale, N.S.W., Australia.
[*Died* 2 *March* 1953.

HEANE, Brig.-Gen. James, C.B. 1918; C.M.G. 1917; D.S.O. 1915; V.D; *b.* Sydney, 29 Dec. 1874; *s.* of late James Heane, of Gloucester; *m.* 1923, EdnaDulcie, *d.* of Charles Martyn, Beecroft, N.S.W.; two *d.* *Educ.:* Sydney High School. Served Dardanelles, European War, 1914-18; Commanded 1st Bn. A.I.F., 1916; 2nd Infantry Bde., 1916-19; 1st Corps Divisional demobilization Group, 1919 (despatches 7 times, D.S.O., C.M.G., C.B., Croix de Guerre); Hon. Col. 4th Inf. Bn. C.M.F.; retired list; commanded N.S.W. Volunteer Defence Corps, 1940-42. President N.S.W. Fruit Growers Federation, 1922-41. Jubilee Medal, 1935; Coronation Medal, 1937. *Recreations:* golf and bowls. *Address:* Worcester Avenue, Collaroy, New South Wales, Australia.
[*Died* 20 *Aug.* 1954.

HEARD, Admiral Hugh Lindsay Patrick, C.B. 1923, D.S.O. 1915; *b* 2 Aug. 1869; 3rd *s.* of Samuel Thomas Heard of Rossdohan, Co. Kerry. Midshipman, 1885; Lieut. 1892; Commander, 1903; Captain, 1910; Rear-Adm., 1921; Vice-Adm., 1926; retired list, 1926; Admiral retired 1930; Admiral Superintendent, Devonport Dockyard, 1922-24; served

European War, 1914-18 (D.S.O.). *Address:* 86 Campden Hill Court, W.8. *T.:* Western 8669. *Club:* United Service. [*Died 23 July* 1954.

HEARD, Rev. Richard Grenville, M.B.E. 1946; M.C. 1945; Fellow and Dean of Peterhouse, Cambridge, since 1934; University Lecturer in Divinity; *yr. s.* of Lieut.-Colonel Samuel Ferguson Heard and Florence Roberta Heard; *m.* 1945, Dorothy Helen Robertson, M.R.C.P.; three *d. Educ.:* Shrewsbury; Exeter College, Oxford (Scholar), 1st Class Honour Classical Moderations, 1927; 1st Class Honour School of Theology, 1929; Junior Hall Houghton Septuagint Prize, 1929; Assistant Master at Dulwich, 1929-34; Temporary C.F. 1939-45. *Address:* Peterhouse, Cambridge. [*Died* 24 *Nov.* 1952.

HEARN, Sir Arthur Charles, Kt., *cr.* 1945; *b.* 16 March 1877. Admiralty service at Portsmouth, Jamaica and Admiralty, 1899-1919; Chairman (Hon. Col. R.M.) of Anglo-French Commission to Rumania, 1919-1920; joined Anglo-Iranian Oil Company, 1920; resigned from Board, 1938; Oil Adviser, Admiralty, and Petroleum Division, Ministry of Fuel and Power; Member Executive Committee, Oil Control Board; retired, 1946. Member Governing Board School of Oriental Studies. Legion of Honour, American Naval Cross, Commander, Crown of Rumania. *Recreations:* literature, art, fly-fishing. *Address:* Picketwood, Merstham, Surrey. *T.:* 388. *Club:* Flyfishers'. [*Died* 24 *Nov.* 1952.

HEARN, Colonel Sir Gordon Risley, Kt., *cr.* 1926; C.I.E. 1924; D.S.O. 1917; Assoc. Inst. C.E.; M.Inst. Engrs. (Ind.); R.E. (retired, 1926); *b.* 7 Sept. 1871; *s.* of late Major-General C. S. Hearn, C.I.E.; *m.* 1908, Olive, *d.* of Lieut.-Colonel Hyde Cates; two *s. Educ.:* Temple Grove, East Sheen, Winchester College (Scholar); Woolwich. Commission in the R.E., 1890; Indian State Railways, 1894; was on active service with the Malakand, Mohmand, and Tirah Field Forces, 1897-98 (medal with 2 clasps); Deputy Consulting Engineer for Railways, Madras; construction Agra Delhi Chord Railway; Government Inspector of Railways, Burma; in charge of railway surveys in Burma, 1906, and Central Provinces, 1911, and in Zhob Valley; returned to England and commanded a Field Company, 1914, afterwards becoming C.R.E. of 9th (Scottish) Division (despatches four times, D.S.O., Bt. Lt.-Col.); North-West Frontier Force, 1919 (medal with clasp, Afghanistan); Engineer-in-Chief survey and construction Khyber Railway; Chief Engineer, Indian State Railways; General Manager of Eastern Bengal Railway; Crampton Prize, Inst.C.E., 1926. *Publications:* The Seven Cities of Delhi; The Railway Engineer's Field Book (with the late A. G. Watson); Editor, Murray's Handbook to India, Burma and Ceylon, 1938, 1949; Cole's Permanent Way; and two standard technical works on surveying. *Address:* 52 Woodbourne Avenue, S.W.16. *Club:* Royal Empire Society. [*Died 7 June* 1953.

HEARN, Rt. Rev. Robert Thomas, B.A., LL.D.; Bishop of Cork, Cloyne and Ross, since 1938. *Educ.:* Trinity College, Dublin. Deacon 1898; priest 1899; Archdeacon of Cork, 1934-38. *Address:* The Palace, Cork. [*Died* 14 *July* 1952.

HEARST, William Randolph; Ex-Representative in Congress; editor and proprietor of New York American, New York Evening Journal, Boston American, Boston Advertiser, Chicago Herald and Examiner, Chicago American, San Francisco Examiner, Los Angeles Examiner; *b.* San Francisco, Ca., 1863; *s.* of late Geo. Hearst, U.S. senator; *m.* 1903, Millicent Willson; five *s.* Contested mayoralty New York City, 1905. *Address:* Hearst Ranch, San Simeon, California. [*Died* 14 *Aug.* 1951.

HEARTZ, Hon. Frank Richard, LL.D. Mount Allison University, New Brunswick, 1931; *b.* 7 January 1871, Canadian; *m.* 1895, Bessie Matthew; one *d. Educ.:* West Kent Street School, Charlottetown; Prince of Wales College, Charlottetown; Upper Canada College, Toronto. Associated with father for several years in Banking and Ranching in the Province of Alberta, Canada; Liberal in politics; candidate for local House, 1909; Lieutenant-Governor of the Province of Prince Edward Island, Canada, 1924-30. *Recreations:* shooting and fishing. *Address:* 5 West St., Charlottetown, Prince Edward Island. *T.A.:* Heartz, Charlottetown, Canada. *T.:* 1060. [*Died* 15 *Sept.* 1955.

HEATH, Albert Edward, C.M.G. 1935; J.P.; Chartered Accountant (Aust.); *b.* 9 Nov. 1887; *s.* of late Henry Arthur Heath, Sydney; *m.* 1910, Minnie, *d.* of Wm. Swanton; one *d. Educ.:* Albert School, Maryborough, Queensland. Director and General Manager, A. C. Saxton and Sons Ltd., 1916-1934; Agent-General for N.S.W., 1934-38; Member Unemployment Relief Council, N.S.W., 1930; Vice-Chairman Metropolitan Transport Trust of Sydney, 1931; Chairman Conference of Australian Transport Authorities, 1932; Council Employers' Federation of N.S.W., 1929; Council Sydney Chamber of Commerce, 1929-34, 1938-50, President, 1940-42, 1944-46 and 1947-49; Pres. Associated Chambers of Commerce of Australia, 1949-50; President Sydney and Suburban Timber Merchants' Association, 1928-33; now a Director; Chm. of Directors Babcock & Wilcox of Australia Pty. Ltd.; Associated Plywoods Pty. Ltd.; Director Union Trustee Co. of Australia, Beard Watson & Co., Ltd., and Wright Heaton & Co. Ltd.; Member: Commonwealth Capital Issues Board, 1951-53; Commonwealth Immigration Advisory Council, 1950-53. *Recreations:* motoring, fishing. *Address:* Strathkyle, 19-23 Bligh Street, Sydney, N.S.W. *Clubs:* Union, Australasian Pioneers, New South Wales (Sydney). [*Died* 27 *Dec.* 1956.

HEATH, Admiral Sir Herbert Leopold, K.C.B., *cr.* 1917 (C.B. 1916); M.V.O. 1907; D.L.; *b.* 27 Dec. 1861; 4th *s.* of Adm. Sir Leopold Heath, K.C.B.; *m.* 1891, Elizabeth (*d.* 1951), *d.* of Colin Simson; two *d.* Entered Navy, 1874; Lieutenant, 1884; Commander, 1896; Captain, 1902; Midshipman of Shah during engagement with Huascar; Lieut. wrecked in H.M.S. Victoria, 1893; Naval Attaché, Berlin, 1908-10; served European War; commanded cruiser line, battle of Jutland Bank (despatches); commanding 7th Cruiser Squadron, 2nd Cruiser Squadron, and 3rd Battle Squadron; Admiral Superintendent, Portsmouth Dockyard, 1912-15; 2nd Sea Lord, 1918-19; Commander-in-Chief, Coast of Scotland, 1919-22; retired voluntarily, 1922; King of Arms of Order of British Empire, 1929-1947; Commandeur Légion d'Honneur; Cross of Order of Naval and Military Merit, Spain; Order of Red Eagle, Germany; Order of Redeemer (Greece); Order of Rising Sun (Japan); Distinguished Service medal (American); D.L., J.P. West Sussex. *Address:* Ebernoe House, near Petworth, Sussex. *T.:* North Chapel 213. *Club:* Naval and Military. [*Died 22 Oct.* 1954.

HEATH, Lt.-Gen. Sir Lewis Macclesfield, K.B.E., *cr.* 1941; C.B. 1939; C.I.E., 1921; D.S.O. 1933; M.C.; *b.* 23 Nov. 1885; *s.* of Col. Lewis Forbes Heath, I.S.C.; *m.* 1st, 1915, Marjorie, *d.* of late Brig.-Gen. A. B. H. Drew, C.I.E.; three *s.* two *d.*; 2nd, 1941, Katherine, *d.* of T. Lonergan, Auckland, N.Z.; one *s. Educ.:* Wellington. Entered Indian Army, 1906; Capt., 1914; Major, 1920; Bt. Lt.-Col. and Lt.-Col., 1929; Bt. Col. 1932; Col. 1933; Maj.-Gen. 1939; Lt.-Gen. 1941; served European War, 1914-18 (wounded, despatches, M.C.); Afghanistan, 1919; East Persia, 1919-21 (C.I.E.); N.W.

Frontier of India, 1930 (despatches, Bt. Col.), 1932 (despatches, D.S.O.) and 1937 (despatches); commanded 1st Batt. 11th Sikh Regt. 1929-33; Instructor Senior Officers' School, Belgaum, 1934-36; Commander Wana Brigade, India, 1936-39; Commander Deccan District, 1939; served war of 1939-45 (despatches thrice, K.B.E., prisoner); 7th Indian Div., 1940-41; 3rd Indian Corps, 1941-42; retired, 1946. *Club:* United Service. [*Died* 10 *Jan.* 1954.

HEATHCOTE, Professor Reginald St. Alban; Professor of Pharmacology, University of Wales (Cardiff), since 1933; *b.* 17 June 1888; *yr. s.* of late Rev. G. V. Heathcote, and late Mary H., *d.* of late S. A. Perceval; *m.* 1st, 1913, Viola (*d.* 1947), *y. d.* of late Osbert Salvin, F.R.S.; one *s.*; 2nd, 1948, Amy, *y. d.* of late R. G. Howson. *Educ.:* Winchester; New College, Oxford; University College Hospital. Scholar: Winchester Coll., 1902, New Coll., 1907; Theodore Williams Exhibition, 1910; 1st Class Physiology, 1911; B.M., B.Ch., Oxon. 1914. Served European War, 1914-19. D.M. Oxon. 1920, B.Sc. 1922. Prof. of Pharmacology, Cairo, 1922-33. M.R.C.P. 1932, F.R.C.P. 1937. Order of the Nile, Commander, 1933. *Publications:* numerous articles in scientific journals. *Recreations:* genealogy, travel. *Address:* 35 Palace Road, Llandaff, Cardiff. *T.:* Llandaff 163. *Club:* Authors'. [*Died* 19 *May* 1951.

HEATON, Joseph Rowland, J.P.; late Chairman and Managing Director of Crosses and Heatons Ltd., 99 Lever Street, Bolton, Lancs.; *b.* 1881. *Address:* Ridgewood, Chorley, Lancs. [*Died* 14 *Jan.* 1951.

HEAWOOD, Percy John, O.B.E. 1939; M.A., Hon. D.C.L. (Durham); Emeritus Professor; *b.* Newport, Salop, 8 Sept. 1861; *e. s.* of late Rev. John Richard Heawood; *m.* Christiana (*d.* 1954), *d.* of Rev. H. B. Tristram, Canon of Durham, 1890; one *s.* (one *d.* decd.). *Educ.:* Queen Elizabeth's School, Ipswich; Exeter Coll., Oxford, Scholar; 1st cl. Mathematical Mods.; 1st class Mathematical Finals; 2nd class Lit. Hum.; Junior and Senior University Mathematical Scholar. Professor of Mathematics, Durham University, 1911-39; Lecturer, 1887-1911; Censor of Unattached Students, 1897-1901; Senior Proctor, 1901-1904, 1910-11, 1921-23; Junior Proctor, 1907-10, 1919-21; Vice-Chancellor, 1926-1928; Representative of Diocese of Durham in National Assembly of the Church of England, 1922-45. *Publications:* papers in the Quarterly Mathematical Journal, Proceedings of the London Mathematical Society, Journal of Theological Studies, Jewish Quarterly Review, etc. *Recreations:* walking, botany, architecture, Hebrew. *Address:* 11 South Bailey, Durham. [*Died* 24 *Jan.* 1955.

HEBERT, Godfrey Taunton, M.A., M.D., F.R.C.P.; late Physician in charge of Tuberculosis Department, St. Thomas's Hospital, S.E.1; late Pres., Tuberculosis Association; *s.* of late Rev. S. Hebert, Vicar of Seal, Sevenoaks; *m.* 1919, Constance Tatton; two *d.* *Educ.:* Harrow; Christ Church, Oxford; St. Thomas's. 1st class Honour School Natural Science (Physiology), Oxford. *Publications:* Pulmonary Tuberculosis, 1927; various publications in Lancet, Tubercle, Quarterly Journal of Medicine, etc. *Recreations:* golf, motoring. *Address:* Sheldon, Highfield Road, West Byfleet, Surrey; 18 Harley Street, W.1. *T.:* Langham 3443. [*Died* 4 *Jan.* 1957.

HEDGCOCK, Frank Arthur; Chevalier de la Légion d'Honneur, France; Divisional Inspector of Schools, L.C.C., 1929-39; *b.* 1875; *s.* of Edward Hedgcock, Hoo, Kent; *m.* 1907, Georgette de Mendiri, Paris; two *s.* *Educ.:* Brighton High School; Brighton Grammar School; University of Paris. Licencié ès Lettres (mention Bien), 1909; Docteur ès Lettres (mention Très Honorable), 1911; the only Englishman who has ever won this degree; M.A., Birmingham; Officier d'Académie; Officier de l'Instruction publique; formerly master at Brighton Grammar School and University College School; Lecturer in English Literature, Paris University; Lecturer in French Literature, Birmingham University; District Inspector of Schools, L.C.C., 1919; Chairman Mod. Lang. Assoc., 1934. *Publications:* Thomas Hardy, Penseur et Artiste, 1911; David Garrick et ses Amis français, 1911; David Garrick, 1912; The Progressive French Grammar; Practical French Teaching; The Active French Course; En Riant; Matriculation French Composition and Junior French Composition; The Active French Preparation Book; La Gerbe d'Or, recueil de Poésies Françaises; Légendes et Contes de France; L'Année Française; Le Chemin du Français; Vacances Françaises; Modern Constructive French (in three vols.) etc.; Articles in Paris Journal, Revue de Paris, Revue de Belgique, Nat. and Eng. Review, Times Educ. Supp., Modern Languages, and other educational papers. *Address:* 21 Onslow Court, E. Worthing. *T.:* 8199. [*Died* 5 *Feb.* 1954.

HEDGES, Frederick A. M.; *see* Mitchell-Hedges.

HEDIN, Sven Anders, Hon. K.C.I.E., *cr.* 1909; Geographer, Traveller; President of Royal Swedish Academy of Sciences, 1924-25; *b.* Stockholm, 19 Feb. 1865; *s.* of Ludwig Hedin, Chief Architect of Stockholm, and Anna Berlin; unmarried. *Educ.:* Stockholm, Upsala, Berlin, Halle. Doctor Philosophiæ. Journey through Persia and Mesopotamia, 1885-1886; member of King Oscar's Embassy to the late Shah of Persia, 1890; journey through Khorasan and Turkestan, 1890-1891; journey through Asia from Orenburg to Pekin, viâ Lop-nor and Tibet, 1893-97; journey down the Tarim River to Lop-nor, through the Gobi Desert and Tibet, 1899-1902; journey through Persia to India, through Tibet, and eight crossings of Trans-Himalaya, 1905-8; Sino-Swedish Expedition, 1927-35. Ennobled by the King of Sweden, 1902; Founder's Medal, 1902; Victorian Memorial Medal of the R.G.S.; Grand Cross North Star of Sweden; Grand Cross of German, Austrian, Bulgarian, Persian, Japanese, and Chinese orders; Member of numerous European Academies; one of the 18 in the Swedish Academy; Hon. D.Sc. Oxon, Cambridge, Breslau, Rostock, Heidelberg, Karlsruhe, Upsala, Munich. *Publications:* Journey through Persia and Mesopotamia, 1887; King Oscar's Embassy to the Shah of Persia, 1891; Journey through Khorasan and Turkestan, 1892; and Through Asia, 1898 (published in 9 languages); Die geographischwissenschaftlichen Ergebnisse meiner Reisen in Zentralasien, 1894 bis 1897; Central Asia and Tibet (in 12 languages); Adventures in Tibet, 1904; Scientific Results of a Journey in Central Asia, 1899-1902, six vols. text and two vols. atlas; Trans-Himalaya, 2 vols., 1909; Overland to India, 2 vols., 1910; From Pole to Pole, 1911 (in 14 languages); Ett Varningsord; Trans-Himalaya, vol. iii., 1913; With the German Armies in the West, 1915; The War against Russia, 1915; Bagdad, Babylon, Ninive, 1917; Jerusalem, 1917; Southern Tibet, 9 vols. text, 3 vols. atlas, 1917-22; Eine Routenaufnahme durch Ostpersien, 2 vols., 1918-26; Mount Everest, 1922; The Pilgrimage of Tsangpo Lama, Vols. I. and II., 1922 (fiction); From Peking to Moscow, 1924; My Life as an Explorer, 1925; The Grand Canyon of Arizona, 1925; Adolf Erik Nordenskiöld, 1926; The Gobi Desert, 1928 (English edition, 1931); Jehol, City of Emperors, 1931; Lop-nor, the Wandering Lake, 1937; Riddles of the Gobi Desert, 1933; A Conquest of Tibet, 1935; Big Horse's Flight, 1936; The Silkroad, 1936; Germany and the World Peace, 1937; Chiang Kai-shek, Marshal of China, 1939; Scientific Results of the Sino-Swedish Expedition 1927-35, 35 vols., 1937-49; History of the

Expedition in Asia, 3 vols., 1926-35; Amerika in Kampf der Kontinente, 1942; På svensk mark, 1944; Utan uppdrag i Berlin, 1949; Stormän och Kungar (Celebritie and Kings), Vols. I, II, 1950. *Address:* 66 Norr Mälarstrand, Stockholm, Sweden.
[*Died* 26 *Nov.* 1952.

HEDLEY, John Prescott, M.A., M.B., M.C. (Cantab.), F.R.C.S. (Eng.), F.R.C.P; (Lond.); F.R.C.O.G.; Hon. M.M.S.A. (Lond.); Consulting Obstetric Physician to St. Thomas's Hospital; Consulting Physician to the General Lying-in Hospital; Gynæcologist to Ministry of Pensions; Member of General Medical Council; *b.* Jan. 1876; *s.* of John Hedley, M.D., J.P., of Cleveland Lodge, Middlesbrough; *m.* Kathleen (*d.* 1945), *d.* of James Halliday of Harrow-on-the-Hill; five *s.* one *d.* *Educ.:* Uppingham School; King's College, Cambridge; St. Thomas's Hospital. After taking the M.B. in 1902, held the offices of House Surgeon and Obstetric House Physician at St. Thomas's Hospital, and House Physician at the Brompton Hospital; during 1905 and 1906 was Resident Medical Officer to St. Thomas's Home, and Obstetric Tutor and Registrar, 1907-1910; Examiner to Universities of Cambridge, Edinburgh, the Conjoint Board of England, Society of Apothecaries of London and the Central Midwives Board; Capt. R.A.M.C. (T.), attached 5th London General Hospital. *Publications:* medical articles. *Address:* 16 Pall Mall, S.W.1. *T.:* Whitehall 2947. *Club:* Athenæum.
[*Died* 17 *July* 1957.

HEDLEY, Walter, D.S.O. 1919; K.C. 1928; *b.* 25 Feb. 1879; *s.* of John Hedley, M.D., Cleveland Lodge, Middlesbrough; *m.* Phyllis (*d.* 1951), *d.* of J. Grant Mackenzie; one *s.* one *d.* *Educ.:* Uppingham; King's Coll. Camb. (Schol.). Called to the Bar, 1904; Recorder of Richmond, Yks., 1920-28; Middlesbrough, 1928-29; Newcastle-on-Tyne, 1929-31; Sheffield, 1931-34; Metropolitan Police Magistrate, Clerkenwell, 1934-1941, Marlborough Street, 1941-46; served European War with R.G.A. in France, Salonica, and Palestine, 1914-19 (despatches, D.S.O.). *Address:* 70 Westminster Gardens, S.W.1. *T.:* Victoria 3040. *Clubs:* Reform, Oriental.
[*Died* 9 *Dec.* 1951.

HEDSTROM, Sir (John) Maynard, Kt., *cr.* 1922; J.P.; Chev. North Star (Sweden), 1939; Chm. of Directors Morris Hedstrom Ltd.; Director Pacific Insurance Co. Ltd., Fiji Pastoral Co. Ltd.; *b.* Levuka, 22 Feb. 1872; *e. s.* of Nicholas Samuel Hedstrom and Alice, *d.* of John Wilkinson, S. Australia; *m.* 1st, 1895, Grace (*d.* 1931), 4th *d.* of Alexander Eastgate; two *s.* two *d.*; 2nd, Joyce (*d.* 1950), *y. d.* of Walter Lassetter Beauchamp, Sydney, N.S.W. *Educ.:* Wesley College, Melbourne. European Elected member of Legislative Council of Fiji, 1908-37; member of Executive Council 1917-37; Nominated Member under the new Constitution of both Legislative and Executive Councils, 1937, resigned Dec. 1937; Commissioner for Fiji to British Empire Exhibition, 1924; President Suva Chamber of Commerce, 1925-48. *Recreations:* golf and fishing. *Address:* Tamavua, Suva, Fiji. *T.A.:* Maynard, Suva. *Clubs:* Fiji, Defence, Ovalau (Fiji); Australian (Sydney); Northern (Auckland).
[*Died* 2 *June* 1951.

HEENAN, Sir Joseph William Allan, K.B.E., *cr.* 1949 (C.B.E. 1937); LL.B.; *b.* Greymouth, New Zealand, 17 Jan. 1888; *s.* of late William Joseph Heenan, latterly of Wellington; *m.* 1912, Hilda May, *d.* of James Andrew, Tangitu, N.Z.; three *s.* one *d.* *Educ.:* Wellington College and Victoria University College, Wellington, N.Z. Clerk Colonial Secretary's Office and Dept. Internal Affairs, 1906-20; Asst. Law Draftsman, 1920-30; 1st Asst. Law Draftsman, 1930-35; Under-Secretary for Internal Affairs and Clerk of the Writs, Dominion of New Zealand, 1935-48; during term of office as Under-Secretary, was Deputy Chairman, National Council of Physical Welfare and Recreation and of King George V Memorial Fund Board; Chief Exec. Officer, N.Z. National Centennial Organisation; Govt. Director, N.Z. Centennial Exhibition; Member Local Govt. Loans Board; Town Planning Board; National Patriotic Council; N.Z. Patriotic Fund Board; Board of Trustees National Art Gallery and Dominion Museum, and N.Z. Geographic Board; Member Royal Commission on Gaming and Racing, 1947; Manager-designate Royal Tour of N.Z., 1949 (tour abandoned); now member of N.Z. Centre P.E.N.; N.Z. Literary Fund Advisory Cttee.; Exec. Forest and Bird Protection Soc. of N.Z.; Jubilee 1935 and Coronation 1937 medals; Fellow Royal Numismatic Society of N.Z. *Publications:* newspaper articles on literature, sport, and racing and breeding. *Recreations:* management of various amateur sports, racing, and study of thoroughbred breeding, reading. *Address:* 28 Tuatoru Street, Eastbourne, Wellington, N.Z. *T.:* Eastbourne 38.
[*Died* 11 *Oct.* 1951.

HEILBRON, Professor Sir Ian, Kt., *cr.* 1946; D.S.O. 1918; F.R.S. 1931; D.Sc., Ph.D., Hon. LL.D. (Glasgow, Edinburgh); F.R.I.C.; Member of Advisory Council on Scientific Research and Technical Development, Min. of Supply, since 1958; Prof. Emeritus of Organic Chemistry, University of London; Hon. Fellow, Imperial College of Science and Technology; *b.* Glasgow, 6 Nov. 1886; *y. s.* of late David Heilbron, Glasgow; *m.* Elda Marguerite (*d.* 1954), *d.* of late H. J. Davis, Liverpool; two *s.* *Educ.:* High School, Glasgow; Royal Technical Coll., Glasgow; Univ. of Leipzig (Ph.D.); Glasgow University (D.Sc.). Lecturer in Royal Technical College, Glasgow, 1909-14; Professor of Organic Chemistry, 1919-20; Heath Harrison Professor of Organic Chemistry, Liverpool, 1920-33; Professor of Organic Chemistry, University of Manchester, 1933-35; Sir Samuel Hall Professor of Chemistry and Director of Chemical Laboratories, 1935-38; Professor of Organic Chemistry and Director of the Organic Chemical Laboratories, Univ. of London, Imperial Coll. of Science and Technology, 1938-1949; Director of Research, Brewing Industry Research Foundation, 1949-58, retired. Longstaff Medallist, Chemical Soc., 1939; Hugo Muller Lecturer, Chemical Soc., 1940; Davy Medallist, 1943, Roy. Medallist, 1951, of Royal Soc.; Priestley Medallist of American Chemical Society, 1945; Pedler Lecturer, 1947, Pres., 1948-50, Chemical Society, London; Hon. Member, French Chemical Society; Foreign Member, Royal Netherlands Acad. of Sciences. Scientific Adviser to Director of Scientific Research, Ministry of Supply, 1939-42; Scientific Adviser, Ministry of Production, 1942-45; Chairman: Colonial Insecticides Cttee., Colonial Office, 1947-49; Advisory Council to Committee of Privy Council for Scientific and Industrial Research, 1950-54; Advisory Council of Royal Military College of Science, 1952-55. Lt. R.A.S.C., 1910, 52nd Division, proceeded overseas, 1915; D.A.D.S.T., G.H.Q., Salonika, 1917; Lt.-Col. (Asst. Dir. of Supplies), Gen. Headqtrs., Salonika, 1918 (despatches thrice, D.S.O., Greek Order of the Redeemer, Médaille d'Honneur). American Medal of Freedom, with Bronze Palm, 1947. *Publications:* Editor-in-Chief of Dictionary of Organic Compounds; Chairman, Editorial Board, Thorpe's Dictionary of Applied Chemistry; numerous papers in chemical journals. *Recreations:* golf, music, philately, ceramics. *Address:* 60A Oakwood Court, W.14. *Club:* Athenæum.
[*Died* 14 *Sept.* 1959.

HEISER, Rev. Canon F. B.; Vicar of Collier Street, Kent, since 1950. *Educ.:* Jesus College, Oxford. Curate St. Luke's, Hampstead, 1907; Incumbent Christ Church, Madras, 1914; Principal, Fourah Bay College, Sierra

Leone, 1921; Vice-Principal, St. Aidan's College, 1924; Principal, 1929-50; Hon. Canon of Chester, 1942. *Address:* Collier Street Vicarage, Marden, Kent. *T.:* Collier Street 277. [*Died* 14 *Dec.* 1952.

HEKTOEN, Ludvig, M.D.; President, Chicago Tumor Institute, 1938-51; Director John M'Cormick Inst. for Infectious Diseases, 1902-41; Executive Director National Advisory Cancer Council, U.S. Public Health Service, 1937-45; Prof. of Pathology, Rush Medical Coll., Univ. of Chicago, from 1895, now Emeritus; *b.* 2 July 1863 of Norwegian parents in Wisconsin; *m.* Ellen Strandh (Swede). *Educ.:* Luther College, Decorah, U.S.A.; University of Wisconsin. M.D. Coll. of Physicians and Surgeons, Chicago, 1887; Hon. M.D. Univ. of Christiania; Sc.D. University of Michigan, University of Wisconsin and Univ. of Chicago; LL.D. Univ. of Cincinnati, Western Reserve Univ., Cleveland, Luther College, Decorah; Member of American Medical Association, and other Medical Societies; Chairman, National Research Council, 1936-38; Member of National Academy of Sciences and Norwegian Academy of Science; Chairman of Division of Medical Sciences of National Research Council, 1924-25, 1926-27, 1929-30; Centennial Award of State Medical Society of Wisconsin, 1941, and of D.S.M. of Amer. Medical Assoc. 1942; Gold-headed cane, Assocation of American Pathologists and Bacteriologists, 1944; Howard Taylor Ricketts Award, University of Chicago, 1949. *Publications:* Postmortem Technique, 1894; edited Durck's Pathological Histology; editor and contributor American Text-Book of Pathology, 1901; edited Collected Works of Christian Fenger and Contributions to Medical Science by Howard Taylor Ricketts; contributions to current literature on infectious diseases and immunology; editor, Journal of Infectious Diseases, 1904-40; editor-in-chief, Archives of Pathology, 1926-49. *Address:* 21 West Elm Street, Chicago, 10. *T.A.:* Hektoen, Chicago. *T.:* Dorchester 4833. *Club:* University (Chicago). [*Died* 5 *July* 1951.

HELE, Thomas Shirley, O.B.E. 1919; M.A., M.D. Cambridge; F.R.C.P.; retd.; *b.* 24 Oct. 1881; *yr. s.* of Warwick Hele, Carlisle and Teignmouth, and Catherine Mary, *d.* of John Rigden Mummery; *m.* 1st, 1914, Audrey Muriel Hill; two *d.*; 2nd, 1942, Audrey Louise, *widow* of Frederick Mowbray Davis. *Educ.:* Carlisle Grammar School; Sedbergh; Emmanuel College, Cambridge; St. Bartholomew's Hospital (Shuter Scholar). Natural Sciences Tripos part 1, Class 1, 1903; part 2, Class 1, 1904; British Medical Association Research Student, 1907; Fellow of Emmanuel College, 1911; Capt. R.A.M.C. (T.F.), 1914-19; University Lecturer in Biochemistry, 1921; Tutor, Emmanuel College, 1922; Vice-Chancellor University of Cambridge, 1943-45; Master of Emmanuel College, Cambridge, 1935-51. *Publications:* Papers in scientific journals. *Address:* 8 Lyndewode Road, Cambridge. *T.:* Cambridge 54168. [*Died* 23 *Jan.* 1953.

HELM, Rev. George Francis, M.C.; T.D.; M.A.; Canon Emeritus of Gloucester, since 1951; *b.* 20 September 1882; *s.* of George Frederick Helm, M.D., F.R.C.S. (Eng.) and Catherine Emma Shearme; *m.* 1911, Margaretta Beaufoy (*d.* 1954), *d.* of Temple Cooke, J.P., Recorder of Southampton; one *s.* *Educ.:* Allhallows, Honiton; Bradfield (Foundation Scholar); Exeter Coll., Oxford (Stapledon Scholar, 3rd Class Cl. Mods., 2nd Class Lit. Hum.); Wells Theological College. Ordained, 1906; Curacies Upton St. Leonards, Cirencester, S. Peters, S. Leonards; Vicar of S. Anne's, S. Lambeth, 1917-22; All Saints, Gloucester, 1922-27; Stroud, 1927-34; Berkeley with Sharpness, Wick, Purton, Brookend, Newport, Breadstone, 1934-39; Rector of Dursley, 1944-51; Rural Dean of Dursley, 1934-39 and 1945-51; Assistant Curate, St. Peter's, Bournemouth, 1951-55; Hon. Chaplain to the King, 1938-42; Chaplain T.A. 1911, B.E.F., 1915-17; Sen. Chaplain (T.A.) Southern Command, 1926; Dep. Asst. Chaplain-Gen., 1940-1942; Asst. Curate, S. Catharine's, Gloucester, 1942-44; Asst. Curate, The Abbey Church, Tewkesbury, 1955-56; Assistant Curate, St. Peters, Leckhampton, Cheltenham, 1956-58. Proctor in Convocation, 1932-50. *Recreations:* golf, fishing, and shooting (Oxford Univ. Shooting VIII, Capt.). *Address:* c/o Barclays Bank Ltd., Gloucester. *Clubs:* English-Speaking Union; Gloucester County (Gloucester). [*Died* 20 *Nov.* 1958.

HELPS, Rev. Canon Arthur Leonard, M.A.; Vicar of Puddletown, 1906-56; and Vicar of the U.B. of Puddletown with Athelhampton and Burlston, 1933-56; Prebendary of Highworth and Canon of Salisbury Cathedral since 1927; Surrogate, 1918-56; *b.* 30 March 1872; *s.* of late Rev. C. L. Helps, *s.* of Sir Arthur Helps, K.C.B., D.C.L., Order of the Golden Fleece, and Emily, *y. d.* of James Theobald, J.P., D.L., Hyde Abbey, Hants, Nunny Castle, Somerset, and Grays Thurrock, Essex; *m.* 1919, Kathleen (*d.* 1956), *y. d.* of late Col. D. Belgrave, North Kilworth, Leics.; two *s.* *Educ.:* Marlborough College; Trinity College, Cambridge; Wells Theological College. Attaché to the Court of the King of Saxony, 1893; travelled Asia. Sinaitic Peninsula, Palestine, Syria, (Armenian Massacres), Asia Minor, Greece, Italy, 1894 and 1895; ordained 1896, and curate of Okehampton and R.H.A. Camp, 1896; Private Chaplain to the Bishop (Dr. Gott) of Truro, 1898; acting Chaplain to troops on active service, Anglo-Boer War, S. Africa, 1900-1902 (despatches, medal, five clasps); travelled abroad, Europe and N. Africa, 1902; Curate of Sturminster Newton, Dorset, 1903; Spain, N. Africa, Morocco, 1905; Canada, America, 1908; Rural Dean of Bere Regis, 1912-30; T.C.F. European War, Aug. 1914-1918; served in Flanders and France, most of the time with 18th Queen Mary's Own Hussars, and VIth Cavalry Brigade (despatches, wounded, three medals, clasp and palm). *Publication:* St. Mary's Church, Puddletown. *Recreations:* formerly hunting, shooting, hockey (played for English ice-hockey team in Germany, 1893), tennis; now gardening. *Address:* 51 Queen's Avenue, Dorchester, Dorset. *T.:* Dorchester 129. [*Died* 3 *Aug.* 1960.

HELSHAM, Rev. Edward, S.J.; Instructor of Tertians since 1952; *b.* 5 July 1891; *s.* of Dr. H. P. Helsham, Beccles, Suffolk. *Educ.:* Mount St. Mary's College, Spinkhill, Sheffield; Campion Hall Oxford (M.A.); Gregorian Pontifical University, Rome (Mag. Aggregatus). Professor of Dogmatic Theology, Heythrop College, Chipping Norton, Oxon., 1928-40; Rector, 1929-37, and 1947-1950. Rector of Beaumont College, Old Windsor, Berks, 1941-47; Superior of English Province of the Society of Jesus, 1950-52. *Address:* St. Beuno's College, St. Asaph, Flints., N. Wales. [*Died* 4 *Dec.* 1955.

HELY-HUTCHINSON, Christopher Douglas, M.C. 1919; Director, Westminster Bank Ltd. and Westminster Foreign Bank Ltd.; *b.* 30 Jan. 1885; *s.* of late Hon. Sir Walter Hely-Hutchinson, P.C., G.C.M.G.; *m.* 1914, Gladys, *d.* of William Beachy Head, Johannesburg; one *d.* *Educ.:* Cheam School; Eton College. Served European War with Royal Artillery, 1914-19. *Address:* 3 Cadogan House, 93 Sloane Street, S.W.1. *T.:* Sloane 2341. *Clubs:* Travellers', Beefsteak. [*Died* 7 *Nov.* 1958.

HEMEON, Clarence Reid; Hon. Mr. Justice Hemeon; Chief Justice of High Court of Judicature, Nagpur, C.P., India, since 1950; *b.* 30 Jan. 1897; *s.* of James Lynn and Frances Marion Hemeon, Yarmouth, Nova Scotia, and Cork, Ireland; *m.* 1930, Maidie Frances Lavater; one *s.* one *d.* *Educ.:* Cork Grammar School; University

College, Cork. Served in Indian Army in Mesopotamia and North-West Frontier, 1916-1921; appointed to Indian Civil Service, 1921; posted to Central Provinces; officiated as District and Sessions Judge, 1927; Legal Secretary to Govt. 1932-39, and M.L.C. 1932-1937; Puisne Judge of High Court of Judicature, Nagpur, C.P., 1944; Acting Chief Justice, June 1949. *Publications:* Editor of A Compilation of Important Criminal Trials in the Central Provinces and Berar, 5 vols., 1933-39; Compiler of A Handbook for Honorary Magistrates, 1936. *Recreations:* golf, tennis, fishing, philately, collecting first editions. *Address:* Nagpur, C.P., India. *Clubs:* East India and Sports; Cricket Club of India (Bombay). [*Died* 18 *Nov.* 1953.

HEMMING, Major-General William Edward Gordon, C.B. 1953; C.B.E. 1945; General Officer Commanding the Troops, Malta, since Oct. 1951; *b.* 26 Feb. 1899; *s.* of late Major-Gen. Edward Hughes Hemming, C.M.G.; *m.* 1923, Amy Hyde, *d.* of Dr. H. Rennie Robertson; two *s.* *Educ.:* Tonbridge School; R.M.A., Woolwich. 2nd Lieut. R.A., 1917; served European War, B.E.F., France, 1918; Lieut. 1918; Capt. 1930; Maj. 1938; long gunnery staff course, 1938-39; served War of 1939-45; Temp. Lt.-Col. Counter Battery Officer, 3 Corps, 1940; Comdg. 54 L.A.A. Regt., 9 Armd. Div., 1941, and 6 Regt., R.H.A., 1941; Temp. Brig. C.R.A., 9 Armd. Div., 1943, and 6 Armd. Div., 1944; C.M.F., Italy, 1944; Chief Instructor in Gunnery, School of Artillery, 1945; C.R.A., 56 Armd. Div., T.A., 1947; Comdt. Coast Artillery School, 1948; B.R.A., B.A.O.R., 1950; Maj.-Gen., 1952. *Recreations:* flyfishing, hunting, polo. *Clubs:* United Service, Flyfishers'. [*Died* 17 *Oct.* 1953.

HEMPEL, Frieda; Opera and Concert Singer; *b.* Leipzig; *m.* 1918, William B. Kahn, New York (divorced, 1926). *Educ.:* Leipzig and Stern's Berlin Conservatories. Début 1905 in Merry Wives of Windsor, Berlin Royal Opera; created rôle of Marschallin in Rosenkavalier, Berlin, 1911; Berlin Royal Opera, 1907-12; Metropolitan Opera, New York, 1912-23; chosen to impersonate Jenny Lind at Historical Centennial Concert, Oct. 6, 1920; has since given (300) three times as many Jenny Lind concerts as Jenny herself gave in this country, and twice toured the British Isles in the historic rôle. *Address:* 271 Central Park West, New York. [*Died* 7 *Oct.* 1955.

HEMPHILL, 4th Baron, *cr.* 1906, of Rathkenny and Cashel; **Martyn Charles Andrew Hemphill;** Barrister-at-law, King's Inns, Dublin and Middle Temple; *b.* 17 Feb. 1901; *o. s.* of 3rd Baron and Mary, *o. c.* of Andrew Martyn of Spiddal, County Galway; *S.* father, 1930; *m.* 1927, Emily, daughter of F. Irving Sears, Webster, Massachusetts; one *s.* *Educ.:* Downside; New College, Oxford, B.A.; Freiburg im Breisgau. *Heir:* *s.* Hon. Peter Patrick Fitzroy Martyn Hemphill, [*b.* 5 Sept. 1928; *m.* 1952, Olivia Anne, *er. d.* of Major R. F. Ruttledge, Cloonee, Ballinroke, County Mayo; one *s.* one *d.*]. *Address:* Tulira, Ardrahan, Co. Galway; 28 Fitzwilliam Place, Dublin. *Clubs:* United University. Reform; Stephen's Green (Dublin); County (Galway). [*Died* 19 *March* 1957.

HEMSTED, Capt. John Rustat, C.B. 1939; V.R.D.; R.N.V.R., retired; Director: Courage & Co. Ltd., Brewers; Noakes & Co. Ltd.; C. N. Kidd & Co. Ltd.; *b.* 29 June 1881; *e. s.* of late Arthur Hemsted, M.R.C.S., L.R.C.P. *Educ.:* Merchant Taylors; Hurstpierpoint. Retired list, 1941. *Address:* Place Manor, Streatley, Berks. [*Died* 2 *April* 1953.

HEMSTED, Rupert William, C.M.G. 1935; O.B.E. 1919; retired; *b.* 30 July 1876; 7th *s.* of Dr. H. Hemsted, Whitchurch, Hants; *m.* 1933. Muriel, *widow* of H. Duncan Robson; no *c.* *Educ.:* private; St. Dunstan's College, London. Colonial Administration, 1899-1930, Kenya and Somaliland. Was Member of Kenya Land Commission. *Recreations:* shooting, cricket, golf. *Address:* Ngong, Nairobi, Kenya. *T.:* Ngong 471. *Clubs:* East India and Sports; Nairobi (Nairobi). [*Died* 12 *March* 1952.

HENDERSON, Professor Alexander; Visiting Professor: Carnegie Institute of Technology, Pittsburgh, Pa., since 1951; University of California, Berkeley California, 1950-51; *b.* 28 June 1914; *s.* of John Edward and Eva May Henderson; *m.* 1937, Emilia Lowensöhn; one *d.* *Educ.:* University College School, Hampstead; King's College, Cambridge. Lecturer in Economics, Edinburgh, 1937-46. Served War of 1939-45, Royal Tank Regiment, 1940-1943; Royal Fusiliers, 1943-46; Captain. Manchester University: Lecturer, 1946-49; Professor of Economic Theory, 1949-50. *Publications:* In Economic Journal, Manchester School, etc. *Address:* 266A Great Clowes St., Salford 7. *T.:* Broughton 2410. *Club:* United University. [*Died* 23 *Jan.* 1954.

HENDERSON, Colonel Andrew, C.M.G. 1916; T.D.; Hon. Col. 9th Durham L.I. (T.A.); *b.* 24 July 1867; *e. s.* of late James Henderson of Claremont House, Morpeth; *m.* 1921. *Educ.:* private school. Joined 5th Durham Rifle Volunteers, 1884; first Commission, 1892; Capt. 1898; Major, 1910; Lt.-Col. 1918; Bt. Col. 1922; Col. retired, 1924; command of 1st Line 9th Durham Light Infantry, Sept. 1914 took battalion to France, April 1915; present at second battle of Ypres (despatches twice, C.M.G.); Salonica Force, February 1918 (despatches twice); Fellow of the Institute of Chartered Shipbrokers; Hon. Vice-President, Newcastle and Gateshead Chamber of Commerce; D.L., J.P., Durham. *Recreations:* played in Novocastrian Hockey Team 11 years, Vice-Chairman of Council of Durham County Rifle Association, member of Tyneside Golf Club. *Address:* 5 Regent Tce., Gateshead, Co. Durham. [*Died* 15 *June* 1951.

HENDERSON, Arthur Edward, R.B.A.; F.S.A.; R.I.B.A. retd.; Artist and Architect; *b.* Aberdeen, 17 April 1870; *s.* of John S. Henderson, Advocate, and Emily, *d.* of Rev. J. Newsam; *m.* Susannah Colier Moore; one *s.* *Educ.:* Aberdeen. Articled to T. Heygate Vernon, A.R.I.B.A., of Westminster; obtained the Owen Jones Travelling Studentship, 1896, and settled in Constantinople; practised as Artist, Archæologist, and Architect; appointed Architect to the British Excavations at the Temple of Diana at Ephesus, and on Archæological Survey of Cyzicus; settled in London, 1906; Pictures of Sancta Sophia, Constantinople, in the Victoria and Albert Museum; War Memorials at many churches; many ecclesiastical ornaments, and the large model of the Great Temple of Diana at Ephesus in the British Museum, 1931. Frescoes in Christ Church, Streatham Hill, London, S.W.2. *Publications:* Chapters and the Atlas in British Excavations at Ephesus by the Brit. Museum; Illustrations and assistance to Prof. A. Van Millingen, in Walls of the City Constantinople; Byzantine Churches in Constantinople; Architectural Survey of Conway walls and Castle, Archæologia Cambrensis, June and December 1938; Then and Now series: Abbeys: Tintern, 1935; Glastonbury, 1935; Melrose, 1936; Fountains, 1936; Westminster, 1937; some Yorkshire Abbeys; 1939; Beaulieu Abbey; Cathedrals: St. Paul's, London, 1937; Christ Church, Canterbury, 1938; Christchurch Priory, Hants; Bury St. Edmunds, Suffolk; St. Augustine's Abbey, Canterbury; ⅛ in. scale model of Fountains Abbey in 1539. *Address:* Oakleigh Annexe, Lewes Rd., East Grinstead, Sussex. [*Died* 8 *Nov.* 1956.

HENDERSON, Charles Alexander, C.S.I. 1938; V.D.; Indian Civil Service (retired); *b.* 2 May 1882; *y. s.* of E. Henderson, M.D., of Shanghai; *m.* 1916, Daisy, *e. d.* of A. W. Lushington, C.I.E.; two *s.* two *d.* *Educ.:* Haileybury College; Exeter College, Oxford; I.C.S., 1904; Madras, 1905. *Address:* Kodaikanal, S. India. [*Died* 21 *July* 1956.

HENDERSON, Hon. E. B. B.; *see* Butler-Henderson.

HENDERSON, Very Rev. George David; Regius Professor of Divinity and Church History, Univ. of Aberdeen since 1924; Moderator of the General Assembly of the Church of Scotland, 1955-56; *b.* 26 March 1888; *e. s.* of Rev. Robert Henderson, Minister of Flowerhill Parish, Airdrie; *m.* 1924, Jenny Holmes McCulloch, *d.* of Thomas Smith, Greenock; two *s.* *Educ.:* Universities of Glasgow, Berlin, and Jena; M.A. (Glas.) with First-Class Honours in Philosophy, 1910; B.D. 1914; D.Litt. 1931; D.D. 1935; D.Th. (Paris), 1954; Hon. Professor, Ref. Theol. Academy, Budapest, 1946; Minister of East Parish, Greenock, 1916-22; St. Mary's Parish, Partick, Glasgow, 1922-24; Chaplain to Forces in Mesopotamia, 1918-20; F.S.A. Scot.; F.R.Hist.S.; formerly member educl. and other public boards; Aberdeen University Court, 1940-48; Master of Christ's College, Aberdeen (Church of Scotland), 1947; Convener, Church of Scotland Colonial and Continental Committee, 1951. *Publications:* Mystics of the North-East, 1933; The Scottish Ruling Elder, 1935; Religious Life in 17th Century Scotland, 1937; The Scots Confession, 1560 (Introduction), 1937; The Church of Scotland, a Short History, 1939; Heritage: a Study of the Disruption, 1943; The Founding of Marischal College, 1947; (joint editor) Diary of James Gordon, 1692-1710, 1950; The Claims of the Church of Scotland, 1951; Church and Ministry, 1951; Chevalier Ramsay, 1952; Why we are Presbyterians, 1953; Presbyterianism, 1954; etc. *Address:* 3 The Chanonry, Aberdeen. *T.:* 43800. [*Died* 28 *May* 1957.

HENDERSON, Sir George Henry, K.B.E., *cr.* 1947; C.B. 1943; *b.* 18 May 1889; *s.* of late Walter Henderson, Wooler, Northumberland; *m.* 1919, Isabel Briggs. *Educ.:* Duke's School, Alnwick, Northumberland. Entered Civil Service, 1907; Asst. Secretary, Dept. of Health for Scotland, 1935; Principal Asst. Secretary, 1939; Deputy Secretary, 1941; Secretary, 1943-53; Member Departmental Committee on Scottish Poor Laws, 1935-38; on Scottish Building Costs, 1938-39; Member of Council of Management of Internat. Hosp. Federation, 1951-; Chm. Scottish Cttee., Nuffield Provincial Hosps. Trust; Chairman Edinburgh Royal Infirmary Bd. of Management. *Recreation:* golf. *Address:* 10A Dick Place, Edinburgh. *T.:* Edinburgh 44356. *Clubs:* Caledonian, United Service (Edinburgh). [*Died* 13 *Dec.* 1958.

HENDERSON, Lady; Henrietta Caroline, D.B.E., *cr.* 1919; *d.* of Henry R. Dundas; *m.* 1895, Lt.-Gen. Sir David Henderson, K.C.V.O., K.C.B., D.S.O., (*d.* 1921); one *d.* *Address:* 17 West Eaton Place, S.W.1. [*Died* 14 *April* 1959.

HENDERSON, Sir Hubert Douglas, Kt., *cr.* 1942; Fellow of All Souls College, Oxford, since 1934; *b.* 20 October 1890; *s.* of John Henderson, Glasgow; *m.* 1915, Faith, *d.* of Philip H. Bagenal, O.B.E.; one *s.* two *d.* *Educ.:* Aberdeen Grammar School; Rugby School; Emmanuel College, Cambridge. President Cambridge Union, 1912; Secretary Cotton Control Board, 1917-19; Fellow of Clare Coll., Cambridge and University Lecturer in Economics, 1919-23; Editor of the Nation and Athenæum, 1923-30; Joint Secretary to the Economic Advisory Council, 1930-34; Member of West India Royal Commission, 1938-39; of Royal Commission on Population, 1944 (Chairman, 1946); Economic Adviser, H.M. Treasury, 1939-44; Chairman of Statutory Cttee. on Unemployment Insurance, 1945-48. Professor of Political Economy, Oxford, 1945-1951; appointed Warden of All Souls College, Oxford, 1951, but did not take up appointment. Hon. Fellow of Nuffield College, Oxford, 1952. F.B.A. 1948. *Publications:* Supply and Demand; The Cotton Control Board. *Address:* 5 South Parks Road, Oxford. *T.:* Oxford 2862. *Clubs:* Reform, Royal Automobile. [*Died* 22 *Feb.* 1952.

HENDERSON, R. B., M.A. (Oxon); B.D. (Lambeth), 1934; Lecturer in Historical Theology, University College of North Staffordshire, 1950-54; *b.* 1880; *s.* of late Rev. W. J. Henderson; *m.* Beatrice Elizabeth Mansfield; one *s.* *Educ.:* King Henry VIII School, Coventry; Bristol Grammar School; New College, Oxford. Master at King Edward's School, Birmingham, 1901-1902; Rugby School, 1902-11; Headmaster Strand School, 1911-20; Headmaster Alleyn's School, 1920-40; Chairman of Council of Modern Churchmen's Union, 1937-45; Manchester Reader in Religious Education, Oxford Univ., 1940-45; Headmaster Bristol Grammar School, Sept.-Dec. 1942; commissioned 2nd Lieut. R.G.A. 1915; rose to rank of Lt.-Col. (despatches); Comdt. 2nd Army College, Cologne, 1919. *Publications:* The Scaly Winged; Prayers, Psalms, and Hymns for Schools; Handbook to the Old Testament; Mediterranean Civilization; The Four Witnesses; Belief in God; articles in Blackwood's Magazine, Greece and Rome, Church Quarterly Review, The New Education, The Modern Churchman, Religions and Inquirer, editor and contributor The Modern Meaning of the Bible; The Battle of the Old Testament; editor of The Interpreter Series. *Recreations:* rowing, stroke of New College Torpid (Head of River); mountaineering, music. *Address:* 17 The College, Keele, Staffordshire. *T.:* Keele Park 262. *Club:* Athenæum. [*Died* 20 *Oct.* 1958.

HENDERSON, Hon. Robert Hugh, C.M.G. 1902; Minister without portfolio, Union Cabinet, S. Africa 1938-39; retired from S. African Parliament, 1943; *b.* Armagh, Ireland, 6 March 1862. *Educ.:* Armagh. Emigrated to South Africa. 1884; associated with firm of R. H. Henderson, Ltd.; chief citizen of Kimberley when it was besieged by the Boers; M.P. for Boksburg, 1921, subsequently Hospital Division, Johannesburg. *Decorated* for services rendered during Boer War. *Publication:* An Ulsterman in Africa (3 edns.). *Address:* Armagh House, 12th Avenue, Lower Houghton. Johannesburg, S.A. [*Died* 6 *Oct.* 1956.

HENDERSON, Sir Thomas, Kt., *cr.* 1919; hosiery manufacturer, retired; J.P. Roxburghshire; Hon. Sheriff-Substitute for Roxburghshire; *b.* 15 July 1874; *s.* of James Henderson; J.P., Hawick; *m.* 1900, Helen Scott Thyne; two *s.* one *d.* *Educ.:* Hawick; Blairlodgeg. M.P. (N.L.) Roxburgh and Selkirk, 1922-23; Director of Innes, Henderson and Company, Limited; past President, South of Scotland Chamber of Commerce. *Recreations:* golf and travel. *Address:* 10 Greenhill Park, Edinburgh 10. *T.:* Jubilee 1856. *Club:* Northern (Edinburgh). [*Died* 3 *May* 1951.

HENDERSON, Thomas, C.B.E. 1931; retd. member Board of Management of Glasgow Co-operative Society; *b.* Burntisland, Fife, 1867. *Educ.:* Elementary School. M.P. (Lab. Co-op.) Tradeston Division of Glasgow, 1922-31 and 1935-45. Scottish Labour Whip, 1925-31; Comptroller of H.M. Household, 1929-31; member of Glasgow Town Council, 1919-22. *Address:* 14 Ardshiel Rd., Drummoyne, Govan, Glasgow, S.W.1. [*Died* 28 *Jan.* 1960.

HENDERSON, Thomson, M.D.; Ophthalmic Surgeon (Retired); *b.* Leghorn, Italy; *s.* of

late J. Thomson Henderson, Leghorn; *m.* 1904, Margaret, *d.* of late G. T. Groome, London; two *s.* *Educ.:* George Watson's College, Edinburgh; Edin. Univ.; Vienna; London, etc. De Vincentiis Gold Medallist, XI. International Ophthalmological Congress, Naples, 1909; Doyne Memorial Medallist, Oxford Congress, 1926. *Publications:* Glaucoma; Principles of Ophthalmology, 1950; also numerous contributions to Ophthalmic literature. *Address:* North End House, Hursley, Hants.
[*Died* 28 *May* 1960.

HENDERSON, Brigadier William Alexander, C.M.G. 1919; D.S.O. 1918; V.D.; F.R.I.B.A.; Asst. Chief Architect, State Savings Bank, Melbourne (granted leave during war), retired 1947; *b.* Richmond, Melbourne, 28 Nov. 1882; *s.* of James Alexander Henderson, Sackville Street, Kew, Melbourne; *m.* 1912, Ella Rose Mary, *d.* of Charles F. Oberfuchsuber, Ulmarra, Clarence River, New South Wales; one *s.* one *d.* *Educ.:* Ulmarra Public School. Articled architectural pupil to Mr. John Little, 1899-1903; Verdon Prize, Melbourne Technical College, also Bronze and Silver Medals of the Royal Victorian Institute of Architects; Assistant Instructor Architectural Classes, Melbourne Technical College, 1902; Instructor Building Construction Melbourne Technical College, 1912-33; A.R.V.I.A. 1906; A.R.I.B.A. 1922; F.R.V.I.A. 1924; F.R.I.B.A. 1926, resigned membership, 1947; in partnership with late R. J. Haddon, 1910-1929; enlisted as Sapper in Australian Military Forces, 1906; served European War in Egypt and France with 2nd Division, Engineers, A.I.F., as Major, 1915; Lt.-Col. commanding 1st Pioneer Batt., 1917; transferred to Divisional Staff and commanding 1st Divisional Engineers, 1918 (C.M.G., D.S.O., despatches four times); commanding 4th Divisional Engineers, Australian Military Forces, 1922; Colonel and commanding 4th Infantry Brigade, 3rd Division, Australian Military Forces, 1926-30; Chief Engineer, Southern Command, 1940-42; Chief Engineer, 2nd Aust. Army, 1942; Retired List, 1944. *Recreations:* gardening, politics; Nationalist; Creed, Methodist. *Address:* Harwood, 112 Yarrbat Avenue, Balwyn, Melbourne, E.8, Victoria, Australia.
[*Died* 20 *Sept.* 1949.

HENDERSON, William Craig, Q.C.; D.Sc.; LL.D. (Hon.) Glasg. Univ. 1943; Leader of Parliamentary Bar, 1938 (resigned 1949); Leader of Midland Circuit, 1940 (resigned 1950); *b.* Glasgow, 1873; 2nd *s.* of late Jas. Henderson, M.A., schoolmaster, Glasgow, and Margaret, *d.* of late Jas. Hunter, schoolmaster, Newton Mearns, Renfrewshire; *m.* 1913, Mildred, *d.* of late Geo. H. Steinberg, Solicitor, London, and Bertha, *d.* of late Wm. Tiplady, Wetherby, Yorks; one *s.* two *d.* *Educ.:* Father's school; High School of Glasgow; University of Glasgow; Trinity College, Cambridge (Research Student). At University of Glasgow medallist in Mathematics and Physics; First Prizeman, Natural Philosophy and Astronomy; M.A. (1894) and B.Sc. (1895), both with Highest Honours in Mathematics and Natural Philosophy; D.Sc. for original research in Physical Science, 1902; 1894 gained John Clark Fellowship in Mathematics, and in 1896 the 1851 Exhibition Science Research Scholarship; B.A. (Camb.) for work done in Cavendish Laboratory; was President of Glasgow University Conservative Club and of Students' Union; at Cambridge was President of Cambridge Union Society; for two years before call to Bar was Private Secretary to the late Lord Kelvin; Barrister, Middle Temple, 1900; K.C. 1923; Q.C. 1952; Master of the Bench, Middle Temple, 1929; Treasurer of Middle Temple, 1946; Mem. of Cttee. on Rating of Machinery appointed under Rating Valuation Act, 1925, 1926; Chm. of Cttee. appointed by President of Board of Trade to consider and report on Problems in Retail Trades, 1941. *Address:* 7 Ferncroft Avenue, Hampstead, N.W.3. *Club:* Athenæum.
[*Died* 5 *March* 1959.

HENDERSON, William Walker, C.B.E. 1938; M.R.C.V.S., D.V.S.M.; Director of Veterinary Services, Nigeria, 1927-45; retired 1945; *b.* 5 Nov. 1886; *s.* of George Henderson and Janet Walker; *m.* 1932, Nina Gloria Scott; two *d.* *Educ.:* Glasgow, Edinburgh, and Manchester. M.R.C.V.S., Royal Dick Vet. Coll., Edinburgh, 1908; D.V.S.M., Victoria University, Manchester, 1910; Veterinary Officer, Colonial Veterinary Service, Kenya, 1913-20; Veterinary Officer, Peruvian Government, 1921-23; Veterinary Officer, Colonial Veterinary Service, Nigeria, 1924; served European War, 1914-18, East African Veterinary Corps (despatches twice); Captain, late Royal Army Veterinary Corps. *Publications:* numerous professional. *Recreation:* golf. *Address:* Fairfield, Lymington, Hants. [*Died* 27 *May* 1960.

HENDERSON - HOWAT, Very Rev. Rudolph, L.Div.; Dean of Brechin since 1953; *b.* Vesinet, Paris, 1896; *s.* of late Barclay Henderson-Howat, Edinburgh and Liverpool; *m.* 1927, Agatha Mary Dorothea, *d.* of late Rev. Selwyn Montagu Cooke; two *s.* one *d.* *Educ.:* privately; Bootle Grammar School. L.Div., St. David's Coll., Lampeter, 1922; B.D. (Part 1) Lampeter, 1923. Served European War, 1914-19, The King's Regt. Deacon, 1923, Priest, 1924; Asst. Curate, Wigan Parish Church, 1923-25; Precentor, St. Mary's Cathedral, Edinburgh, 1925-27; Priest-in-Charge, Dennistoun, Glasgow, 1927-30; Rector of: Girvan, 1930-35, Lochee, 1935-47, Invergowrie, 1947-; Canon of St. Paul's Cathedral, Dundee, 1951. Editor of the Scottish Guardian, 1939-48. Member of Dundee Education Committee, 1937-46 and 1950-55. *Address:* The Rectory, Invergowrie, by Dundee. *T.:* Invergowrie 245.
[*Died* 14 *May* 1957.

HENDERSON-SMITH, Mrs.; *see* Klickmann, Flora.

HENDRIKS, Sir Charles; (C. A. C. J. Hendriks), Kt., *cr.* 1950; C.B.E. 1939; M.C.; Principal, H.M. Treasury; Private Secretary to Leader of House of Lords since 1935; *b.* 26 June 1883; *er.* and *o. surv. s.* of late Cecil Morgan Hendriks, M.B., M.R.C.S.(E.), Bicester, Oxon, and Lydia Jane Gunter; *m.* 1923, Evelyn Duckworth, *yr. d.* of late Charles Denham. *Educ.:* Brighton College; Clare College, Cambridge (Scholar and Prizeman), B.A. Classical Tripos, 1905; Historical Tripos, 1906; Served European War, 1914-1919, Capt. and Adj. 9th King's Own Yorkshire L.I. (M.C.). *Address:* 179 Ashley Gardens, S.W.1. *T.:* Victoria 6010.
[*Died* 31 *Jan.* 1960.

HENDRY, Charles, F.C.I.I.; Director London and Lancashire Insurance Co. Ltd.; Director British Fire Insurance Co. Ltd., Law Accident Insurance Society Ltd., and Agar Cross & Co. Ltd.; Chairman British Insurance Association, 1935-36; President, Chartered Insurance Institute, 1934-35, Manchester Insurance Institute, 1914-15, London Insurance Institute, 1927-28; Member of Compulsory Insurance Committee set up by Board of Trade, 1936-37; *b.* 16 July 1870; *s.* of Charles Hendry, Master Mariner, Ardrossan; *m.* Bessie Mabel (*d.* 1947), *d.* of Wm. Righton, Buxton; one *s.* two *d.* *Educ.:* Ardrossan Academy. Joined London and Lancashire, Glasgow, 1892; Head Office, Liverpool, 1894; Local Manager, Glasgow, 1905; Local Manager, Manchester, 1910; London Secretary, 1919; Joint Manager at Chief Administration, 1921; General Manager, 1929-36. *Recreation:* golf. *Address:* Bryanston, Parkside, Wimbledon Common, S.W.19. *T.:* Wimbledon 1975. *Clubs:* Bath, Royal Wimbledon Golf (Wimbledon).
[*Died* 8 *Dec.* 1952.

HENDRY, Brigadier-General Patrick William, C.B. 1918; V.D.; T.D.; D.L. of City of Glasgow; *b.* 1861; *s.* of late George

Thoms Hendry, J.P. Glasgow, and Agnes, *d.* of David Robertson, Glasgow; *m.* 1885, Robertina (*d.* 1942), *d.* of late Thomas Struthers, Blackness, Linlithgowshire; three *d.* *Educ.:* Glasgow Academy; Madras College, St. Andrews; Edinburgh Collegiate. Chairman of Hendry Brothers, Ltd.; 2nd Lt. Glasgow Highlanders, 1883; Capt. Reserve of Officers, 1900; Hon. Capt. in Army, 1902; commanded Glasgow Highlanders, 1905; Brig. Major H.L.I. Brigade, 1906; Col. commanding Brigade, 1911; commanded Service Coy. Highland Light Infantry S.A. War, 1901-2 (Queen's medal and 5 clasps); Temp. Brig.-Gen. Regular Army, Aug. 1914; commanded Brigade European War, Egypt and Gallipoli, 1915; brought to notice of Secretary of State for War for valuable services rendered in connection with the war in 1917 and in 1918. *Recreations:* shooting, fishing, yachting. *Address:* Bendarroch, Garelochhead. *T.:* Garelochhead 275. *Clubs:* Royal Automobile; Western (Glasgow); Royal Northern Yacht, Royal Clyde Yacht (Glasgow). [*Died* 26 *Nov.* 1952.

HENDRY, Robert; *b.* 1876; 3rd *s.* of Andrew Hendry, solicitor, Dundee, and Ann, *d.* of John Mitchell, of Arngask, Glenfarg; *m.* 1901, Mary Lillias Hall (*d.* 1946), *d.* of George Whyte, Pitteadie, Kirkcaldy. *Educ.:* Merchiston Castle School and University, Edinburgh. Advocate, 1901; Counsel to Secretary for Scotland, Private Legislation Procedure (Scotland) Act 1899, 1909-24; Sheriff-Substitute of Renfrew and Bute at Greenock, 1924-36; Sheriff Substitute of Stirling, Dumbarton, and Clackmannan at Falkirk, 1936; retired Nov. 1944; War Service, 9th Royal Scots, retiring with rank of Captain, 1914-19. *Recreations:* shooting and golf. *Address:* Orchard House, Bridge of Allan. *Club:* University (Edinburgh). [*Died* 10 *April* 1951.

HENDY, Arthur, M.I.Ex.; F.I.C.A.; Chairman and Managing Director of Hall's Barton Ropery Co., Ltd., Hull, since 1900; *b.* 20 Sept. 1874; *s.* of John Ede and Anna Hendy; *m.* 1898; three *s.* *Educ.:* Hull Trinity House Navigation School. With Carlill and Burkinshaw, Chartered Accountants, Hull, 1896-1900; Member of Council, Hull Chamber of Commerce. *Publications:* Story of the Hallmark; Wire Ropes: How they are made; various articles Times Trade Supplement. *Recreations:* gardening, boating. *Address:* Belmont, Pearsons Park, Hull. *T.:* Hull 16145. [*Died* 30 *Nov.* 1953.

HENDY, Roy, C.M.G. 1938; F.C.I.S. (Eng.); Town Clerk, Sydney, Australia, 1931-56, retd.; *b.* 4 March 1890; 2nd *s.* of James A. and Louisa M. Hendy; *m.* 1921, Irene L. Le Fanu; two *d.* *Educ.:* Cleveland St. High School, Sydney. Alderman of Randwick, Sydney, 1912-21; Lieut. A.I.F., Egypt and France, 1915-18; Deputy Town Clerk, Sydney, 1923. *Recreation:* golf. *Address:* 5 Wybalena Rd., Hunters Hill, N.S.W., Australia. *Club:* Tattersall's (Sydney). [*Died* 27 *May* 1959.

HENEAGE, 2nd Baron (*cr.* 1896), **George Edward Heneage,** O.B.E. 1919; Lieut.-Col.; D.L., J.P. for Parts of Lindsey; *b.* 3 July 1866; *e. s.* of 1st Baron and Lady Eleanor Cecilia Hare, *d.* of 2nd Earl of Listowel; *S.* father, 1922. *Educ.:* Eton; Trin. Coll. Camb. (B.A.). Alderman Lindsey C.C., Chairman, 1924-46; Chairman Lincolnshire Territorial Army Association, 1920-47; Chairman Southwold Hunt Club; served in 3rd Batt. Lincolnshire Regt., 1890-1913; Lt.-Col. commanding, 1909-13; served S. Africa, 1902; Lt.-Col. commanding 10th (Service) Batt. Lincolnshire Regt. 1914-16; served in France, 1916. *Heir:* *b.* Rev. Hon. Thomas R. Heneage, *b.* 1877. *Address:* Hainton Hall, Lincoln. *Club:* Brooks's. [*Died* 26 *Jan.* 1954.

HENN-COLLINS, Hon. Sir Stephen Ogle, Kt., *cr.* 1937; C.B.E. 1925; *yr. s.* of Baron Collins (Life Peer; *d.* 1911); *m.* 1899, Agnes Julia, D.J.St.J. (*d.* 1955), *d.* of late Frederick Lambert, of Banstead; three *d.* *Educ.:* Winchester; New Coll., Oxf. Called to Bar, Middle Temple, 1899; Bencher, 1924; Junior Common Law Counsel to the Admiralty, 1927; K.C. 1932; Judge of High Court of Justice; Judge of Probate, Divorce and Admiralty Division, 1937-45; Judge of King's Bench Division, 1945-48. *Address:* Eastwick House, Great Bookham, Surrey. [*Died* 16 *Oct.* 1958.

HENNESSY, Lieut.-Col. John, C.B. 1915; C.M.G. 1919; M.B.; late R.A.M.C.; *b.* 5 Feb. 1867; *s.* of late D. Hennessy, of Dromin, Blarney, Co. Cork; *m.* 1893, Mary Teresa, *d.* of late E. O'Flynn, J.P., The Gables, Patrick's Hill, Cork; three *s.* *Educ.:* University College, Cork. Served S. Africa, 1899-1902 (Queen's medal 3 clasps, King's medal 2 clasps); European War, 1914-18 (despatches, C.B., C.M.G.); retired pay, 1921. *Address:* 9 North Mall, Cork. [*Died* 13 *May* 1954.

HENNESSY, Captain Richard; *b.* 1876; *e. s.* of late Richard Hennessy; *er. b.* of 1st Baron Windlesham, *q.v.*; *m.* 1902, Ethel Frederica (*d.* 1930), *o. d.* of Charles Selmes of Playden, Sussex; two *s.* two *d.* *Educ.:* Cadet H.M.S. Worcester; Wellington College. Served in the S.A. War in Gordon Highlanders; Captain in the 8th Batt. Gordon Highlanders, Sept. 1914; went out in the B.E.F., France, with 9th Scottish Division, May 1915; attached General Staff with British Mission, Belgian Headquarters, Feb. 1916; attached as Liaison Officer, French Army in Belgium, till June 1916; attached British Mission, French War Ministry, June 1918; Assistant Military Attaché British Embassy, Paris, Nov. 1918-June 1919. *Publications:* Leaves from the Log of the Mona; Yachting Recollections. *Recreations:* yachting, shooting and outdoor games, painting. *Address:* Denton Lodge, Harleston, Norfolk. *Clubs:* Army and Navy, Royal Thames Yacht, Royal Automobile; Royal Yacht Squadron (Cowes); Highland Brigade Yacht (Commodore); Household Brigade Yacht (Hon. Member). [*Died* 28 *Aug.* 1953.

HENNIKER, 6th Baron (*cr.* 1800), **Charles Henry Chandos Henniker-Major;** Bt. 1765; Baron Hartismere (U.K.) 1866; Lt.-Col. (retired) Rifle Brigade; *b.* 25 Jan. 1872; *s.* of 5th Baron Henniker and Alice, *o. d.* of 3rd Earl of Desart; *S.* father, 1902. *Educ.:* Eton; Sandhurst. Entered army, 1891; served N.W. Frontier of India, 1897-98; European War. D.L., J.P. Suffolk; owns about 5000 acres. *Heir:* *b.* Hon. John Ernest De Grey Henniker-Major. *Address:* Thornham Hall, Eye, Suffolk. [*Died* 4 *Feb.* 1956.

HENNIKER, Lieut.-Colonel Sir Robert John Aldborough, 7th Bt., *cr.* 1813; M.C.; late Duke of Wellington's Regt.; *b.* 26 May 1888; *s.* of late John Granville Henniker (*g.s.* of 1st Bt.); *S.* cousin, 1925; *m.* 1914, Lucy Mabel, *d.* of late Edward Swan Hennessy of Hazelbrook, Roscommon; one *d.* *Educ.:* Clifton College; R.M.C., Sandhurst. Served European War, 1914-18 (M.C., wounded, despatches); retired pay, 1936; served 1940-46 in Royal Engineers, Mata Terrl. Forces. *Heir:* *cousin,* Brig. Mark Chandos Auberon Henniker, C.B.E. *Address:* 9 Salterville, Halifax, Yorks. [*Died* 19 *Feb.* 1958.

HENNIKER-MAJOR, Hon. Gerald Arthur George; *b.* 3 Dec. 1872; 4th *s.* of 5th Baron Henniker, J.P., D.L.; *m.* 1921, Monica (*d.* 1950), *e. d.* of late Hamilton Howard Curtis, Poole, Dorset. *Educ.:* Eton. [*Died* 18 *Jan.* 1955.

HENRY, Hon. George Stewart, B.A., LL.D.; Director, Toronto Mortgage Co., North American Life Assurance Co., Acme-Farmers' Dairy, Dominion Dairies Ltd.; *b.* King Township, Ontario, 16 July 1871; *s.* of William Henry and Louisa Stewart; *m.* 1902, Anna Ketha, *d.* of Rev.

T. W. Pickett; two *s.* two *d.* *Educ.:* Toronto Public Schools; Upper Canada College University of Toronto (B.A., LL.D.); Ontario Agricultural College. Member of York Township Council, 1903-10, Reeve, 1907-10; Warden of York County, 1909; Past Chairman, Toronto and York Roads Commission; Past President, Ontario Good Roads Association; Past President, Canadian Good Roads Association, 1926-27; Past Member, Niagara Parks Commission; Member, Legislative Assembly of Ontario for constituency of East York, 1913-43; Minister of Agriculture for Province of Ontario, 1918-19; Minister of Public Works and Highways, 1923-31; Premier of Ontario, 1930-34; Minister of Education, 1931-34; Provincial Treasurer, 1934; Conservative; Protestant. *Address:* R. R. 1, Todmorden, Ontario, Canada. *Clubs:* Albany, Granite, Canadian (Toronto); Empire Club of Canada. [*Died* 2 *Sept.* 1958.

HENRY, Paul, R.H.A.; *b.* Belfast; *s.* of Rev. R. M. Henry. *Educ.:* Belfast; Paris. Studied in Paris with Jean Paul Laurens, James McNeill Whistler; did book illustrations for John Lane and a large amount of black and white for newspapers and magazines; painted portraits and exhibited R.A. and Paris Salons; has had exhibition of Irish Landscapes in New York, Boston, Melbourne and Toronto; French Government purchased his large landscape, A West Ireland Village, for the Luxembourg 1922; has done some L.M.S. Posters, including Connemara. *Publications:* An Irish Portrait (autobiography), 1951, illustrated in colour and black and white; numerous broadcasts from B.B.C. Fine Art Reproductions: In Connemara, The Blue Lake, The Blue Hills of Ireland, and many others. *Recreations:* walking, fishing and gardening. *Address:* 1 Sidmonton Square, Bray, Co. Wicklow. *T.:* Bray 2258. [*Died* 24 *Aug.* 1958.

HENSON, Leslie Lincoln; Actor; *b.* 3 Aug. 1891; *s.* of Joseph Lincoln Henson and Alice Mary, *d.* of William Squire, Glastonbury, Somerset; *m.* 1919, Madge Saunders (marr. diss.); *m.* 1925, Gladys Gunn (marr. diss.); *m.* 1944, Harriet Martha Day. *Educ.:* Cliftonville College; Emanuel School. Trained for the stage by Ernest D'Auban and Cairns James; obtained engagement in Concert Party, The Tatlers; first London engagement with Grossmith and Laurillard, Gaiety Theatre, in To-night's the Night, 1915; followed by Theodore and Co., Yes Uncle, Winter Garden Theatre, Kissing Time, A Night Out, Sally, Cabaret Girl, Beauty Prize, revival To-night's the Night, Primrose, Tell me More, and Kid Boots; toured Kid Boots; opened in Lady Luck, Carlton Theatre, April 1927; Funny Face, Princes Theatre, 1928; Follow Through, Dominion Theatre, 1929; A Warm Corner, 1930; Films, Alf's Button, and Tons of Money; presented Ralph Lynn in four farces at the Aldwych Theatre with Tom Walls; produced Skin Deep, Criterion, Yellow Mask, His Majestys, So This is Love, Winter Garden for Laddie Cliff, Delysia in Her Past, Shaftesbury Theatre, 1929; A Warm Corner, Princes Theatre, 1929; It's a Boy, 1930-31; It's a Girl, 1931-32; presented Ivor Novello's Party and The Night of the Garter, Strand Theatre, 1932; produced Counsel's Opinion, The Love Pirate, Strand Theatre, 1932-33; Ladies' Night, Indoor Fireworks, Aldwych Theatre, 1933-34; produced and played Nice Goings On, Strand Theatre, 1933-34; Lucky Break, 1934-35; Seeing Stars, Gaiety, 1936; Produced Baby Austin and Aren't Men Beasts, Strand, 1936; Spot of Bother, Strand, 1937. Produced and played in Swing Along, Gaiety, 1936; Going Greek, Gaiety, 1937-38; Running Riot, Gaiety, 1938-39; Toured Swing Along and Going Greek, South Africa, 1939; Toured The Gaieties Concert Party with B.E.F., France, Christmas, 1939-40, under E.N.S.A.; Produced and played in Up and Doing Revue, Saville Theatre, 1940; Robinson Crusoe, Palace Theatre, Manchester, Christmas, 1940-41; reopened Saville Theatre with Up and Doing, May 1941; Fine and Dandy, Saville Theatre, April 1942; toured Middle East for E.N.S.A., May-Aug. 1943; Italy, Sicily, Malta, North Africa, Jan.-April 1944, Holland, Belgium and France, Nov.-Dec. 1944. Produced The Gaieties, Winter Garden Theatre, 1945. Toured India and Burma (E.N.S.A.), Nov. and Dec. 1945. Babes in the Wood, Opera House, Blackpool, Xmas 1945-46. Played The Common Man in 1066 and All That, Season, Shakespeare Memorial Theatre, Stratford-on-Avon, Jan. 1947 and Saville Theatre, April 1947; Produced Bob's Your Uncle, Saville Theatre, 1948; Toured Provinces, Bob's Your Uncle, 1949; Played Elwood P. Dowd in Harvey, Prince of Wales and Piccadilly, 1950; toured Middle East with The Gaieties, for Combined Services Entertainment Unit, 1951; 1066 and All That, Windsor Rep., 1951; Pepys in And So To Bed (set to music), New, Strand, and tour, 1951; Toad of Toad Hall, Brighton, 1952; Face The Music, Brighton, 1953; Relations Are Best Apart, 1954; The Diary of a Nobody, 1955; Alice Through the Looking Glass, 1955; Davy Crockett, Olympia Theatre, Dublin, Dec. 1956; Toured as Albert in Small Hotel. 1956-1957. Appeared in several films, 1930-. Vice-Pres.: Actors' Orphanage; Actors' Benevolent Fund; Counsellor King George V Pension Fund for Actors and Actresses; Pres. Roy. Gen. Theatrical Fund. *Publications:* My Laugh Story; Yours Faithfully. *Recreations:* cinephotography, swimming, golf. *Address:* Harrow Weald House Farm, Middx. *T.:* Grimsdyke 2064. *Clubs:* Green Room, Stage Golfing Society, Garrick. [*Died* 2 *Dec.* 1957.

HEPBURN, Hon. Mitchell F.; late Member of Ontario Legislature for Elgin; *b.* 12 Aug. 1896; *s.* of Wm. Frederick Hepburn and Margaret Fulton; *m.* 1918, Eva, *d.* of John Burton, Fingal, Ont.; one *s.* two *d.* *Educ.:* St. Thomas Collegiate Institute; La Salle Extension University. Three years with Canadian Bank of Commerce; Lieutenant, Canadian Infantry and Royal Air Force; Farmer; House of Commons, Ottawa, 1926 and 1930; Resigned to accept leadership of Ontario Liberal Party and was elected to Ontario Legislature, 1934, re-elected, 1937; Premier of Ontario 1934-42; Provincial Treasurer, Ontario, 1934-43. *Address:* R.R.5, St. Thomas, Ont., Canada. [*Died* 5 *Jan.* 1953.

HEPPLE, Anne; *see* Dickinson, Anne H.

HERBERT, Agnes, O.B.E. 1931; author, critic and journalist; editor, Writers' and Artists' Year-Book, 1922-29; *d.* of late Helena Agnes and James Bateman Thorpe, The Hut, Port Erin, Isle of Man, and Sandywood, Pendlebury, Lancs; *m.* 1st; (one *d.* decd.); 2nd, 1913, Commander A. T. Stewart, O.B.E., R.N. *Educ.:* home. *Publications:* Two Dianas in Somaliland; Two Dianas in Alaska; The Isle of Man; The Life Story of a Lion; Casuals in the Caucasus; The Moose; Her Mighty Youth (under a pseudonym); The Elephant; Northumberland; Korea, in the Peeps Series; short stories, articles, literary ghosting, etc. *Recreations:* writing and reading. *Address:* Westminster Bank Ltd., 26 Haymarket, S.W.1. *T.:* Laburnum 1614. [*Died* 6 *Feb.* 1960.

HERBERT, Sir Alfred, K.B.E., *cr.* 1917; Deputy Director-General and subsequently Controller of Machine Tools, Ministry of Munitions; Chairman and sole Managing Director of Alfred Herbert, Ltd., Coventry; President of Société Anonyme Alfred Herbert, France; President of Societa Anonima Italiana Alfred Herbert, Italy; Ex-President Machine Tool Trades Association; *b.* 5 Sep. 1866; *s.* of William Herbert, Leicester; *m.* 1st, 1889, Ellen Adela, *d.* of Thomas Ryley, Coventry; four *d.*; 2nd, 1913,

Florence (*d.* 1930), *widow* of Lt.-Col. H. F. E. Lucas, Dragoon Guards; 3rd, 1933, Marion Fraser (Nina), of Bryncoedwig, Sevenoaks, *d.* of late Sir A. T. Arundel, K.C.S.I., and *widow* of Lt.-Col. A. J. Pugh. *Educ.:* Stoneygate School, Leicester. Officer Legion of Honour; Order of St. Stanislaus, 2nd Class with star; Officer Order of Leopold (Belgium). *Recreations:* shooting, fishing. *Address:* Dunley Manor, Whitchurch, Hants. *T.A.:* Dunmanor, Whitchurch, Hants. *T.:* Whitchurch, Hants, 70.
[*Died* 26 *May* 1957.

HERBERT, Brigadier-General Otway Charles, C.M.G. 1918; M.C.; retired pay; *b.* 1 July 1877; *y. s.* of late Gustavus Wybrants Herbert, J.P., Co. Cork; *m.* 1913, Hilda Marion (*d.* 1933), *y. d.* of B. W. Jones. Joined Argyll and Sutherland Highlanders, 1898; served Sudan, 1908 (medal, 4th class Mejidieh); Capt. 1909; retired, 1913; European War, 1914-18 (despatches, M.C., C.M.G., Chevalier Légion d'Honneur). *Recreation:* nil. *Address:* Heath Cottage, Hartley-Wintney, Hants. *T.:* Hartley-Wintney 24. *Club:* Army and Navy. [*Died* 12 *Dec.* 1955.

HERDMAN, Hon. Sir Alexander Lawrence, Kt., *cr.* 1929; *b.* Dunedin, 17 July 1869; *e. s.* of late Alexander Herdman, Banker, Dunedin; *m.* 1st, 1896, Eva (*d.* 1918), *d.* of late Edmund Smith, Dunedin; four *s.* three *d.*; 2nd, 1921, Mrs. Alice Elizabeth Brown (*d.* 1938), of Christchurch. *Educ.:* Otago Boys' High School; Oamaru. Joined National Bank; studied law; admitted 1894; practised, Palmerston South, Naseby; Member Naseby Borough Council; Mayor, 1898; Member for Mt. Ida in House of Representatives, 1902-5; practised at Bar, Wellington; Member Wellington North, House of Representatives, 1908-18; Attorney-General, 1912-1918; Minister of Justice, 1912-15; a Judge of Supreme Court, New Zealand, 1918-35; retired 1935. *Recreations:* tennis, swimming. *Clubs:* Northern (Auckland); Christchurch.
[*Died* 14 *June* 1953.

HERDMAN, Sir Ernest, Kt., *cr.* 1934; D.L. Belfast; J.P.; Chairman, Belfast Harbour Commissioners, 1926-45; *b.* 21 March 1856; *s.* of John Herdman, J.P., Belfast, and Elizabeth Finlay; *m.* 1891, Lucy Lambert, *d.* of Henry Matier, J.P., Belfast; two *d.* *Educ.:* privately; Germany and France. J.P. County Down and County Belfast; President of Belfast Linen Merchants Association, 1904; President of Belfast Chamber of Commerce, 1914; President of Dock and Harbour Authorities Assoc., 1931-32; Vice-President National Lifeboat Institution. *Recreations:* golf, fishing, gardening, collecting antiques. *Address:* Rogate, Cross Lane, Findon, Sussex. *Clubs:* Constitutional; Ulster, Royal Belfast Golf, Royal Ulster Yacht (Belfast).
[*Died* 4 *June* 1952.

HERDON, Major-Gen. Hugh Edward, C.B. 1924; C.I.E. 1920; Indian Army, retired; Col. of 1st Bn. (Coke's) 13th F.F. Rifles, 1933-45. Served Tirah Expedition, 1897-98 (medal, two clasps); N.W. Frontier of India, 1901-2 (clasp); European War, 1919 (despatches, C.I.E.); Waziristan, 1922-23 (C.B.); G.O.C. Waziristan District, 1927-31; retired 1931. *Address:* c/o Westminster Bank Ltd., 9 Glasshouse St., Piccadilly Circus, W.1. [*Died* 11 *March* 1958.

HEREFORD, 17th Viscount (*cr.* 1550), **Robert Charles Devereux;** Bt. 1611; Premier Viscount of England; D.L. Co. Brecon; J.P. Co. Hereford; *b.* 11 Aug. 1865; *o. s.* of 16th Viscount and Hon. Mary Anna Morgan (*d.* 1924), *y. d.* of 1st Baron Tredegar; *S.* father, 1930; *m.* 1892, Ethel Mildred (Dame of Justice, Order of St. John of Jerusalem) (*d.* 1945), *d.* of late John Shaw of Welburn Hall, County York; two *d.* *Educ.:* Eton; New College, Oxford (B.A. 1888). Contested Breconshire (C.), 1906 and 1910; Captain 1st (Breconshire) V.B.S.W. Borderers, 1889-95; Alderman Breconshire County Council, 1898-1904; County Councillor, Llyswen Division, 1907-13; Llanigon Division, 1918-25; Chairman Quarter Sessions for Breconshire, 1907-27; Knight of Justice Order of St. John of Jerusalem. *Recreations:* shooting, motoring. *Heir:* *g.s.* Robert Milo Leicester Devereux [*b.* 4 Nov. 1932; *s.* of late Hon. Robert Godfrey de Bohun Devereux and Audrey Maureen Leslie, *d.* of late James Meakin, Westwood Manor, Staffs.]. *Address:* Hampton Court, Leominster. *T.:* Bodenham 35. *Clubs:* Carlton, 1900; Herefordshire (Hereford). [*Died* 16 *April* 1952.

HERFORD, Ethilda B. Meakin, M.B.; B.S. (Lond.); Hon. Physician, British Hospital for the Treatment of Mental Disorders; Hon. Physician, London Clinic of Psychoanalysis; Psychological research, Maudsley Hospital; Psycho-therapist (consultant); *b.* Surrey, 6 Dec. 1872; *d.* of Edward Meakin and S. Ann Budgett; *m.* 1907, O. G. Herford; three *s.* one *d.* *Educ.:* University College, London; Royal Free Hospital; post-graduate work: Berlin, Munich, Vienna, Budapest, etc. *Publications:* A Case of Ectopic Gestation? Ovarian; Ovarian Cysts and their Origin; Sixteen Unselected Cases of Hebosteotomy, 1911; The Infantile Mind and its Relation to Social Problems; Mental Hygiene, 1928. *Recreations:* music, folk-dancing, nature rambles by land and water-travel. *Address:* Ongar House, Ongar, Essex. *T.:* Ongar 11. *Club:* Crosby Hall. [*Died* 26 *Aug.* 1956.

HERGESHEIMER, Joseph; novelist; *b.* Philadelphia, Pennsylvania, U.S.A., 15 Feb. 1880; *s.* of Helen Janet, *d.* of Thomas MacKellar, and Joseph Hergesheimer, U.S.C.G.S.; *m.* 1907, Dorothy Hemphill; no *c.* *Educ.:* Short period at Quaker School and Academies of Art. *Publications:* The Lay Anthony, 1914; Mountain Blood, 1915; The Three Black Pennys, 1917; Gold and Iron, 1918; Java Head, 1919; The Happy End, 1919; Linda Condon, 1919; San Cristóbal de la Habana, 1920; Cytherea, 1922; The Bright Shawl, 1922; The Presbyterian Child, 1923; Balisand, 1924; From an Old House, 1925; Tampico, 1926; Quiet Cities, 1928; Swords and Roses, 1929; The Party Dress, 1930; The Limestone Tree, 1931; Sheridan, 1931; Berlin, 1932; Tropical Winter, 1933; The Foolscap Rose, 1934. *Address:* 84 102nd Street, Stone Harbor, New Jersey, U.S.A.
[*Died* 25 *April* 1954.

HERIOT-MAITLAND, Brig.-General James Dalgleish, C.M.G. 1916; D.S.O. 1900; late Rifle Brigade; *b.* 21 Jan. 1874; *e. s.* of late Sir James Makgill Heriot Maitland, K.C.B.; *m.* 1903, Mary Turner (*d.* 1937), 2nd *d.* of late H. S. Wedderburn of Wedderburn; one *s.* two *d.* Served S. Africa, 1899-1902 (severely wounded, despatches, Queen's medal 4 clasps, King's medal 2 clasps, D.S.O.); European War, 1914-18 (despatches, C.M.G., Bt. Col.); retired, 1922. *Address:* White House of Aros, Isle of Mull. *T.:* Aros 31.
[*Died* 18 *Jan.* 1958.

HERITAGE, James Edgar, C.M.G. 1948; *b.* 17 July 1880; *s.* of George T. Heritage, Hobart, Tasmania; *m.* 1912, Marjorie, *d.* of Frank Yeoland. *Educ.:* St. Ignatius College, Sydney. LL.B. 1901; admitted a Solicitor 1901. *Address:* 114 Frederick Street, Launceston, Tasmania. [*Died* 19 *July* 1957.

HERMON-HODGE, Rear-Admiral Hon. Claude Preston, D.S.C.; *b.* 1888; 5th *s.* of 1st Baron Wyfold; *u.* and *heir-pres.* to 3rd Baron; *m.* 1918, Gwendoline R. (*d.* 1949), *d.* of J. Goulding Davis; (one *s.* killed in action 1942), two *d.* *Educ.:* Summerfields; H.M.S. Britannia. Served European War, 1914-19 (despatches, D.S.C.); Naval Assist. Secretary to Committee of Imperial Defence, 1924-28; Deputy Director of Naval Intelligence, 1936-38; retired, 1940. *Address:* Huntercombe, Henley-on-Thames. *T.:* Nettlebed 207. *Club:* Carlton.
[*Died* 25 *March* 1952.

HERRERA, Senator Luis Alberto de, Hon. G.B.E., *cr.* 1928; *b.* Montevideo, 22 July 1873; *s.* of Juan José de Herrera and Manuela Quevedo; *m.* Margarita Uriarte; one *d.* *Educ.:*

University of Montevideo. Lawyer; Magistrate, 1901; Chargé d'affaires of Uruguay in the United States of America, 1903; Member of Parliament, 1905 and 1915; President of the National Council, 1923; candidate to the Presidency of the Republic, 1923, 1927, and 1942; Special Ambassador to Great Britain, 1928; Special Envoy for Coronation of H.M. King George VI., 1937. *Publications:* Por la Patria; Las Bases de la Paz de Aceguá; Tierra Charrúa; La Revolucion Francesa y Sud America; Desde Washington; Buenos Aires, Urquiza y el Uruguay; Labor Diplomatica; Uno que vió . . .; Accion Parlamentaria; La Diplomacia Oriental en el Paraguay; El Uruguay Internacional; El Drama del 65; La Encuesta Rural; Una Etapa; En la Brecha; Sin Nombre; La Mision Ponsonby; La Paz de 1828; Origenes de la Guerre Grande. *Address:* Larrañaga 3760, Montevideo, Uruguay. *T.:* 2.4183. [*Died* 8 *April* 1959.

HERRING, Brig.-Gen. Sydney Charles Edgar, C.M.G. 1919; D.S.O. 1917; V.D.; *b.* 8 Oct. 1882; *s.* of late G. E. Herring, N.S.W.; *m.* 1910, Florence Elizabeth, *d.* of late T. de M. Murray-Prior, Marroon, Queensland; one *d.* Left Australia, Dec. 1914, as a Capt. in the 13th Battalion A.I.F.; Major in Egypt, Jan. 1915; took part in the landing at Gallipoli, April 1915, and served there continuously until the evacuation, Dec. 1915; temp. Lt.-Col. Nov. 1915; Legion of Honour; served in Egypt, Jan.-May 1916; transferred to 45th Battalion and promoted Lt.-Col. March 1916; landed in France, June 1916, and served there continuously (C.M.G., D.S.O.); Col. June 1918; Brig.-Gen. 30 June 1919; Croix de Guerre, Sept. 1918 Commander of Volunteer Defence Corps of N.S.W., 1944. *Address:* Bracondale, Northcote Avenue, Killara, N.S.W. [*Died* 27 *May* 1951.

HERRING-COOPER, Lieut.-Col. William Weldon, C.B.E. 1919; D.S.O. 1902; late R.A.S.C.; *b.* 19 March 1873; 2nd *s.* of late Herman Herring-Cooper of Shrule Castle, Carlow, Ireland; *m.* 1924, Muriel Stewart, *widow* of W. L. Weldon, LL.M., Barrister, and *d.* of W. Richardson, 11 Harley House, Regent's Park; one *d.* *Educ.:* Corrig School, Ireland. Served South Africa, 1900-2 (King's and Queen's medal, D.S.O.); European War (Bt. Lt.-Col., C.B.E.); retired pay, 1928. *Address:* Manor House, Stockton, Warminster, Wilts. [*Died* 11 *Jan.* 1953.

HERRIOT, Edouard; Permanent Honorary President of the French National Assembly since 1954 (President, 1947-54); President of Socialist-Radical Party, France, 1945; Member of the French Academy since 1947; Chevalier of Legion of Honour, 1917, but returned Cross, 1942; *b.* 5 July 1872; *m.* Miss Rébatel. Minister without portfolio, France, 1934-36; late Prime Minister and Minister of Foreign Affairs, France; Mayor of Lyons; Président de la Chambre des Députés, 1925, 1936 and since 1947. World Council of Peace Prize, 1955; Gold Medal, International Peace Prize, 1955. *Publications:* Philon le Juif, 1897; Madame Récamier et ses Amis, 1904; Précis d'histoire des lettres françaises, 1905; Agir, 1915-16; Créer, 1919; La Russie Nouvelle, 1922; La Forêt Normande, 1925; Sous l'Olivier, 1930; Beethoven, 1932; La Porte Océane, 1932; La France dans le Monde, 1933; Orient, 1934; Esquisses; Impressions d'Amerique; Europe Nouvelle; Pourquoi je suis Radical Socialiste; Normale; Le Problème de Dettes; The Wellsprings of Liberty, 1940. *Address:* 1 Cours d'Herbouville, Lyons, France. [*Died* 26 *March* 1957.

HERRON, Very Rev. David Craig, C.B.E. 1954; M.C.; Chancellor of the University of Otago since 1945; *b.* 17 Sept. 1882; *s.* of Thomas and Ann Jane Herron; *m.* 1919, Edith Stewart Smart, M.A., *d.* of John and Margaret Smart, Pollokshields, Glasgow; three *s.* one *d.* (and one *s.* killed in war of 1939-45). *Educ.:* Otago Univ. (M.A.); United Free Church Coll., Glasgow. Chaplain, 1st N.Z.E.F. Formerly: Minister, St. David's Presbyterian Church, Auckland; Knox Church, Dunedin; Moderator of the General Assembly, 1943-44; Vice-Chancellor Univ. of Otago, 1942-45. Hon. D.D. St. Andrews, 1948. *Address:* University of Otago, Dunedin. [*Died* 1 *July* 1955.

HERTZBERG, Major-General Halfdan Fenton Harbo, C.B. 1945; C.M.G. 1919; D.S.O. 1918, M.C.; *b.* Toronto, 3 Sept. 1884; *s.* of late A. L. Hertzberg, civil engineer, Toronto, *s.* of late Col. P. H. Hertzberg, Norwegian Army, and *d.* of late Captain W. F. McMaster, Toronto Naval Brigade; *m.* 1919, Dorothy Hope, *d.* of late Ernest Judah, Montreal; one *s.* two *d.* *Educ.:* Upper Canada College; St. Andrew's College; University of Toronto. Civil Engineer, Railway Location and Construction, 1903-10; Chief Engineer, Trussed Concrete Steel, Reinforced Concrete Design, 1911-14; Lieut. in 2nd Company Field Canadian Engineers, 1905; served in Belgium and France, 1915 to end of war with Canadian Engineers in 1st and 3rd Canadian Divisions, B.E.F.; Lieut. in Royal Canadian Engineers, 1915; Captain, 1917; Major and Brevet Col., 1920 (despatches four times, C.M.G., D.S.O., M.C.); Col. and Temp. Brig., 1934; Major-Gen., 1938; Quartermaster-General, Canada, 1938-40; Adjutant-General, April-July 1940; Commandant R.M.C., Kingston, Ont., 1940-1944; retired 1944. *Club:* Union (Victoria, B.C.). [*Died* 19 *Dec.* 1959.

HERVEY-BATHURST, Major Sir F. E. W.; *see* Bathurst.

HERZOG, Chief Rabbi Isaac, M.A., D.Litt.; Chief Rabbi of Palestine since 1936; *b.* Lomza, Poland, 1888; *o. s.* of late Rabbi Joel Herzog, Rabbi of the Russian-Polish Jewish Community in Paris, and Liba Cirowitz; *m.* 1917, Sarah, *o. d.* of Rabbi S. I. Hillman, London, Assessor to Chief Rabbi of the British Empire; two *s.* *Educ.:* Univs. Leeds, Paris. Brought over to Leeds, 1897; matriculated in First Division at Univ. of London, 1905; graduated B.A. at London Univ. in Classical and Modern Languages and in Mathematics, 1909; ordained Rabbi, 1910; M.A. in Semitics at London Univ., 1911; Doctor of Literature at London Univ., 1914; Rabbi to the Jewish Community of Belfast, 1915; Chief Rabbi of Jewish Community of Dublin, 1919; Chief Rabbi of the Jewish Community in the Irish Free State, 1925-36. *Publications:* Last two chapters in Samuel ben Hofnis *Kitab Ahkam Shr'a al-Sisith*; Dibrei-Ishak (Talmudic dissertations in Hebrew); The Main Institutions of Jewish Law (in five volumes) Vol. I. 1936; Vol. II. 1938; Torath ha-Ohel, on Maimonides' Code, (Jerusalem) 1948; articles in numerous periodicals; contributed to Maimonides VIIIth Century Memorial Volumes (London, English, Jerusalem, Hebrew). *Address:* Jerusalem, Israel. *T.:* 2361. [*Died* 25 *July* 1959.

HESELTINE, Michael, C.B. 1919; *b.* 1886; *s.* of Rev. Ernest Heseltine. *Educ.:* Winchester; New College, Oxford. Assistant Secretary, Ministry of Health, 1928-33; Registrar, Dental Board, 1933-46; Registrar, General Medical Council, 1933-51. *Address:* 44 Hallam Street, W.1. [*Died* 13 *March* 1952.

HESILRIGE, Arthur George Maynard; Consulting Editor of Debrett since 1935; *b.* 5 Sept. 1863; *s.* of late Arthur Hesilrige, Lieut. 59th Regt., and Mary Augusta, *d.* of George John Nicholls, F.R.C.S., Bourne, Lincolnshire; *m.* 1889, Amy Florence (*d.* 1947), *d.* of M. S. Myers; three *d.* *Educ.:* Wellington Coll. Editor of Debrett's Peerage, Baronetage, Knightage, and Companionage, 1887-1935; also of Paper Makers' Directory of All Nations, 1897-1944; retired, 1945. *Publications:* edited Debrett's House of Commons and the Judicial Bench, 1887-1931; Debrett's Dictionary of the Coronation, 1902; Debrett's Coronation Guide,

1911; Debrett's Heraldry, 1914; Debrett's City of London Book, 1922; Debrett's West End Book, 1923; Debrett's British Empire Book, 1924, etc. *Address:* Grantleigh Hotel, Inverness Terrace, W.2. [*Died* 13 *April* 1953.

HESKETH, 2nd Baron, *cr.* 1935, of Hesketh; **Frederick Fermor-Hesketh,** 9th Bt. *cr.* 1761; Major Scots Guards, retired, 1946; *b.* 8 April 1916; *s.* of 1st Baron Hesketh and Florence Louise, *d.* of late J. W. Breckinridge; *S.* father, 1944; *m.* 1949, Christian Mary, *o. d.* of Capt. Sir John Helias F. McEwen, Bt., of Marchmont, J.P.; three *s.* *Educ.:* Eton. *Heir:* *s.* Hon. Thomas Alexander Fermor-Hesketh, *b.* 28 Oct. 1950. *Address:* Easton Neston, Towcester; 7 Rutland Gate, S.W.7. [*Died* 10 *June* 1955.

HESKETH, Colonel Rawdon John Isherwood, C.B.E. 1919; *b.* Feb. 1872; 2nd *s.* of late Captain William Pemberton Hesketh, 42nd Royal Highlanders and 18th Hussars; *m.* Grace, 2nd *d.* of late H. Holditch Marten of Bishops Down, Tunbridge Wells; two *s.* (and *e.s.* decd. as result of war service). *Educ.:* privately. Joined 6th Batt. Royal Fusiliers, 1900; served South Africa with Mounted Infantry, 1901-2 (Queen's medal and 3 clasps); commanded 7th Batt. Royal Fusiliers, 4 Aug. 1914; took the Batt. to France, 1916 until invalided in 1917; commanded 5th Batt. Jan. 1918 until demobilisation. [*Died* 13 *Aug.* 1959.

HETHERINGTON, Arthur Lonsdale, C.B.E. 1938; *b.* 1881; *s.* of late William Lonsdale Hetherington, Highgate; *m.* 1908, Doris, *d.* of late Edward Perronet Sells; four *s.* two *d.* *Educ.:* Highgate School; Trinity College, Cambridge (M.A.). Principal of Govt. Collegiate School, Rangoon, 1905-7; Asst. Director of Public Instruction, Burma, 1907; Board of Education, Junior Examiner, 1908-14; Secretary of Carnegie United Kingdom Trust, 1914-19; Sec. Univ. Grants Committee, 1912-14 and 1919-21; Asst. Sec., Dept. of Scientific and Industrial Research, 1922-43; Administrative Adviser to British Coal Utilisation Research Assoc. 1943-44; Past Master of Worshipful Company of Turners. *Publications:* Early Ceramic Wares of China; Chinese Ceramic Glazes; (with R. L. Hobson) Art of the Chinese Potter; (with Sir Frank Heath) Industrial Research and Development. *Recreations:* reading and rumination. *Address:* c/o G. G. Hetherington, Southfields, Stone Grove, Edgware, Mddx. [*Died* 14 *Aug.* 1960.

HETHERINGTON, Sir Roger (Gaskell), Kt., *cr.* 1945; C.B. 1932; O.B.E. 1918; M.I.C.E.; *b.* 1876; *s.* of late William Lonsdale Hetherington, Highgate; *m.* 1906, Honoria, *d.* of late Arthur Ranken Ford, Highgate; three *s.* one *d.* *Educ.:* Highgate School; Trinity College, Cambridge, M.A. Engineering Inspector, Local Government Board, 1909; Chief Engineering Inspector, Ministry of Health, 1930-44. President Institution of Civil Engineers, 1947-48. *Address:* 6 Bishopswood Road, Highgate, N.6. *T.:* Mountview 1271. *Club:* Oxford and Cambridge. [*Died* 24 *Feb.* 1952.

HETHERINGTON, Group Captain Thomas Gerard, C.B.E. 1918; late Royal Air Force; late 18th Royal Hussars; *b.* 1886; *s.* of late Thomas Hetherington, J.P., Berechurch Hall, Colchester; *m.* 1921, Clementine Dundas, *d.* of late Thomas Dundas Bartolucci of Cantiano, Italy; one *d.* *Educ.:* Harrow. Served three years in works of Mandslay, Coventry; entered 4th Batt. Essex Regt., afterwards 18th Hussars; represented Great Britain at International Horse Shows, 1910, at Brussels, San Sebastian, New York, and Chicago; took up flying privately, 1911, and took Aviator's Certificate June 1911, No. 105; attached to the Air Battalion, R.E., March 1912; joined Royal Flying Corps on formation, May 1912; obtained Aeronaut's Certificate, No. 25; Airship Pilot's Certificate, No. 11, July 1912; C.B.E. for services in connection with origination of Tanks; Order of Military Merit of Spain; Air Attaché, British Embassy, Washington, 1926-30, Rome, 1931-35; retired list, 1935. *Recreations:* flying, motoring. *Clubs:* Cavalry, Royal Automobile. [*Died* 14 *Oct.* 1951.

HEWETT, Lieut.-Col. Edward Vincent Osborne, C.M.G. 1916; D.S.O. 1917; O.B.E. 1919; late The Queen's Own (Royal West Kent Regt.); *b.* 14 Mar. 1867; *s.* of Lieut.-Gen. E. O. Hewett, C.M.G., R.E.; *m.* 1904, Brenda, 2nd *d.* of Frederick Platt Higgins, J.P., M.P. North Salford; one *d.* Served Sudan, 1885-86 (medal, bronze star), N.W. Frontier of India, 1897-98 (despatches, medal with clasp); Professor Strategy, Tactics, Military History, Reconnaisance, Royal Military Coll., Canada, 1900-6; Acting-Commandant for the last six months; commanded 6th Batt. South Wales Borderers; European War, 1914-1917 (C.M.G., D.S.O., despatches thrice); commanded 3rd Batt. The Queen's Own Royal West Kent, Regt., 1918-19 (O.B.E.). *Address:* c/o Lloyds Bank Ltd., Parkstone, Dorset. [*Died* 22 *Feb.* 1953.

HEWETT, Sir (Frederick) Stanley, K.C.B., *cr.* 1929; K.C.V.O., *cr.* 1921 (M.V.O. 1916); K.B.E., *cr.* 1926; Extra Surgeon Apothecary to the Queen since 1952 (formerly to King George VI and to Queen Mary); *b.* 1880; *s.* of Frederick Hewett, Hythe, nr. Southampton; unmarried. *Educ.:* Haileybury; Caius College, Cambridge. M.R.C.S., L.R.C.P. 1905; M.B., B.C. (Cantab.), 1906; M.D. (Cantab.), 1910; held various appointments at St. Thomas's Hospital and at the West London Hospital; Deputy-Surgeon Apothecary to the King, 1911; Surgeon Apothecary to the late King, to late Queen Alexandra, to the Prince of Wales and his Household, to King George VI and to Queen Mary. *Recreations:* shooting, golf. *Address:* 44 Mount St., W.1. *T.:* Grosvenor 5297. *Club:* Bath. [*Died* 11 *Aug.* 1954.

HEWINS, Harold Preece, C.M.G. 1930; O.B.E.; President, Central Economic Board, and Director, Commercial Intelligence Branch, Sudan Government, retired, 1930; *b.* 15 Dec. 1877; *y.s.* of late S. Hewins; *m.* Margaret Elizabeth, *d.* of late D. G. Britton; one *s.* two *d.* *Educ.:* Wolverhampton; Queen's College, Oxford. Joined North Eastern Railway 1900; entered Sudan Government Service 1904, and appointed to Sudan Agency, Cairo; Secretary, Central Economic Board, Khartoum, 1906; Director, Commercial Intelligence Branch, 1913; during the war was President, Resources Board, responsible for organisation of economic resources of Sudan and provision of supplies for British Forces in Egypt and Palestine; Licensing Officer for Imports and Exports, Executive Officer for food control, Custodian of enemy property, Controller of Enemy Trading and in charge of Commercial Censorship (despatches twice); Member of Governor General's Council, 1920; 2nd Class, Order of the Nile. *Recreations:* golf and tennis. *Address:* Quarry House, Liphook, Hants. [*Died* 20 *Dec.* 1956.

HEWINS, Maurice Gravenor, Q.C. 1952; *b.* 22 June 1897; *o. s.* of late Professor William Albert Samuel Hewins and Margaret Slater, Bescot Hall, Walsall; *m.* 1931, Constance Edith Mary Stephenson (*d.* 1953), Carrick-on-Suir, Co. Tipperary; two *s.* *Educ.:* Westminster School; Christ Church, Oxford. B.A. 1921. Called to the Bar, Lincoln's Inn, 1923. *Address:* 6 Stone Buildings, Lincoln's Inn, W.C.2; 24 Lancaster Road, Wimbledon Common, S.W.19. *T.:* Holborn 1497, Wimbledon 5918. *Club:* Carlton. [*Died* 23 *Oct.* 1953.

HEWISON, Robert, C.B.E. 1929 (O.B.E.); *b.* Holm, Orkney, 4 Aug. 1876; *s.* of late George Hewison, farmer; *m.* Christina Bews, *d.* of J. P. Petrie; two *s.* one *d.* (and *y. s.* killed in Greece, R.A.F., 1941). *Educ.:* private; Agricultural College, Aspatria. Joined Abukir Land Co., Egypt, 1899; Agricultural Dept., Sudan Govt., 1904; Assistant Director of Agriculture, 1910; Director of Agriculture and Forests, Sudan Govt.; Member of Governor General's Council, 1920. *Recreations:* riding, shooting, golf. *Address:* Venn Cottage, Whitchurch, Nr. Pangbourne, Reading. [*Died* 28 *Nov.* 1959.

HEWIT, Forrest, R.B.A.; Vice-President Federation of British Industries; Hon. Life Governor of British Cotton Industry Research Association; Member: International Chamber of Commerce; Joint Committee of Cotton Trade Organisations; Hon. Vice-President Manchester Academy of Fine Arts; J.P. Cheshire; *s.* of late Robert Patterson Hewit; *m.* Edith, *d.* of Richard Dalziel Graham, Edinburgh; one *s.* one *d.* *Educ.* Manchester Grammar School; Tettenhall College. Studied art under T. C. Dugdale and Richard Sickert; Exhibited Royal Academy, Royal Society of Arts, Royal Hibernian Academy of Arts, Dublin, Salon, Salon d'Artistes Français, Salon d'Automne, New English Art Club, Royal Society of British Artists, Royal Institute of Oil Painters, London Group; New York; Ottawa; Australia and many Provincial Exhibitions; pictures in Public collections: Manchester, 1929 and 1939, Rutherford collection, 1929, Rochdale, 1940; has had one-man shows: Grosvenor Gallery, 1937, Goupil Gallery, 1939, Manchester Academy Gallery, 1938, Salford 1943. *Recreations:* golf, walking. *Address:* Overhill, Wilmslow, Cheshire. *T.:* Wilmslow 3338. *Club:* Reform (Manchester). [*Died* 11 *Feb.* 1956.

HEWITT, John Theodore, O.B.E.; F.R.S.; Emeritus Professor of Chemistry and Fellow, Queen Mary College, London; Hon. Fellow of Imperial College of Science and Technology. *Educ.:* Hartley Institute, Southampton; Normal School of Science; A.R.C.S. (Lond.); St. John's College, Cambridge (Scholar Hutchinson Research Student, M.A.); D.Sc. (Lond.); Universities of Berlin and Heidelberg (Ph.D.). M.E.F. 1915; Director of D.E.S. Chiswick Laboratory (Ministry of Munitions) 1916-19; demobilised 1919 (Major, O.B.E.). *Publications:* Papers recording the results of Chemical Researches published in the Transactions of the Chemical Society; Berichte der deutschen chemischen Gesellschaft, etc. *Address:* Lines Road, Hurst, near Reading. [*Died* 9 *July* 1954.

HEWITT, William Graily, O.B.E. 1949; B.A., LL.B.; Artist (Scribe and Illuminator); *b.* 20 July 1864; *o. s.* of William Morse Graily Hewitt, M.D., and Elizabeth Bolton Hollis; *m.* 1908, Lilian Maud (*d.* 1943), 5th *d.* of Robert Davie Peebles and Agnes Georgina Steel; no *c.* *Educ.:* Westminster; Trinity College, Cambridge. Called to Bar, 1889, Lincoln's Inn; took to writing and later to studying Mediaeval MSS.; Teacher at L.C.C. Central School of Arts and Crafts, of the Art of Writing for more than 30 years from 1902; after European war prepared many Memorial Records (in Book Form mostly) for Public Schools, Colleges, Public Companies, Parishes, Inns of Court, various Regiments, House of Lords, The Times, etc., beginning with the late King George V's Scroll sent by H.M. to all relatives of the Fallen; now writes important documents for the Crown Office and Home Office. *Publications:* The Oxford Copy Books, 1913; Lettering, 1930; The Pen and Type Design, and the Treyford Type, 1928; The Treyford Writing Cards, 1932; Handwriting: Everyman's Craft, 1938; Pen to Pantograph, 1944. *Recreations:* golf, chess. *Address:* Steward's, Stodham, Liss, Hants. *T.:* Liss 100. *Clubs:* Double Crown; Royal N. Devon Golf (Bideford). [*Died* 22 *Dec.* 1952.

HEWLETT, Thomas Henry; J.P. for City of Manchester; Chairman of The Anchor Chemical Company Ltd., of Joseph Anderson and Sons, Ltd., and of United Oil and Natural Gas Products Corporation, Ltd., all of Clayton, Manchester; former Director District Bank Ltd.; *b.* 23 Nov. 1882; *s.* of Alderman Thomas Richard Hewlett, J.P., and Mary Elizabeth Hewlett; *m.* 1931, Joan Margaret Allen; two *s.* one *d.* *Educ.:* Manchester. Joined the Anchor Chemical Co. Ltd., 1895, and Joseph Anderson and Sons Ltd., 1909; M.P. (C.) for Exchange Division of Manchester, 1940-1945; Controller of Dyestuffs, Board of Trade, 1941-46. Pres. Windsor Institute (Pendleton Ragged School); Hon. Treasurer of Manchester and Salford Street Children's Mission (Wood Street Mission); Member of Board of Management of Manchester Young Men's Christian Association; Underwriting Member of Lloyd's; Past Master of the Tinplate Workers alias Wire Workers and a Freeman of the City of London; Vice-Pres. of Manchester Conservative and Unionist Assoc.; Vice-Pres. Clayton and District Ex-Service Men's Association (British Legion); President Clayton Conservative Club, Manchester. *Address:* Bramley, Cavendish Road, Bowdon, Cheshire. *Club:* Constitutional. [*Died* 25 *May* 1956.

HEYNER, Herbert; baritone singer; *b.* London, 1881; *s.* of Augustus and Caroline Heyner; *m.* Mary Louise, *o. d.* of Surg.-Gen. Sir Henry Hamilton, K.C.B., I.M.S; two *d.* *Educ.:* Clifton. Studied with Frederick King and Victor Maurel; first concert appearance Queen's Hall, 1907; since appeared as principal baritone at chief London musical events, such as London Festival 1910, Queen's Hall and London Symphony Concerts, Royal Choral Society, etc., and at all the provincial festivals and concerts; much associated with Elgar's works; has extensive repertoire of over 100 operatic and choral works; is also a singer of modern art songs, lieder, etc., in which capacity has appeared on the Continent; favourite rôles Elijah, Jesus in Bach's Passion, and Elgar's Apostles; soon after outbreak of European War was commissioned in Durham Light Infantry; in France, summer of 1915 and through all engagements up to and including Somme, 1916, where serious wounds resulted in over two years in hospital; resumed concert work in winter of 1919; engaged in concerts U.S.A. and Canada, 1928-29 and 1929-30; Germany, 1929-30; American and Continental tour, 1932, and principal broadcasts (recitals, etc.) for B.B.C.; Promenade Concerts. *Publication:* A Singer Looks Back. *Recreations:* literature, ceramics (Lowestoft and early Chinese), gardening and bull terriers. *Address:* Westleton, Saxmundham, Suffolk. *T.:* 257. [*Died* 18 *Jan.* 1954.

HEYWOOD, Rt. Rev. Bernard O. F., D.D.; *b.* 1 March 1871; *s.* of Rev. Canon H. R. Heywood, late Vicar of Swinton; *m.* Marion Maude (*d.* 1957), 2nd *d.* of late Captain Percy Reid Lempriere, R.A.; five *s.* two *d.* *Educ.:* Sunningdale; Harrow; Trinity College, Cambridge; Leeds Clergy School. Curate of Bury, 1894-97; Vicar of St. Paul's, Bury, 1897-1907; Vicar of Swinton, 1907-17; Leeds, 1917-26; Rural Dean, 1917; Chaplain to H.M., 1918; Bishop of Southwell, 1926-28; Assist. Bishop in Diocese of York, 1929-31; Bishop Suffragan of Hull, 1931-34; Bishop of Ely, 1934-40; Canon of St. Albans Cathedral and Assistant Bishop to Bishop of St. Albans, 1942-51; Proctor in Convocation, 1920. *Publications:* Seeking God; The Interpretation of the Old Testament; About the Lambeth Conference; The Bible Day by Day; The Life of the World to Come; This is our Faith. *Address:* 1 The Cottage, Winslow, Bucks. *T.:* Winslow 316. [*Died* 13 *March* 1960.

HEYWOOD, Rt. Rev. Richard Stanley; Hon. Canon of Coventry, 1937; *e. s.* of B. A. Heywood of Banner, Beckenham, and of Messrs. Bridges, Sawtell, Heywood & Co., solicitors; *b.* 27 Oct. 1867; *m.* 1894, Mary Isabel Courtier, *e. d.* of H. J. Whitley, Stuckeys Bank, Bath; three *d.* *Educ.:*

Windlesham House, Brighton; Wellington College (scholar); Trinity College (scholar); Ridley Hall, Cambridge. B.A. 1889; M.A. 1893; D.D. 1920; 27th Wrangler; ordained, 1892; Curate of Walcot, Bath; Prin. of C.M.S. Divinity School, Poona, India, 1894; Sec., C.M.S., Bombay, 1903-1917; late Hon. Canon, Bombay Cathedral, and Examining Chap. to the Bishop of Bombay; Bishop of Mombasa, 1918-36; Asst. Bishop of Coventry, 1937-52. *Address:* Lawnside, 29 Birches Lane, Kenilworth. *T.:* Kenilworth 197. [*Died* 16 *Dec.* 1955.

HIBBERT, Admiral Hugh Thomas, C.B.E. 1919; D.S.O. 1918; R.N., retired; *b.* 5 Aug. 1863; *s.* of late Col. H. R. Hibbert, Royal Fusiliers, D.L., J.P., Birtles Hall, Cheshire; *m.* 1892, Katharine Brownlow, *d.* of N. A. Butterfield, Bermuda; one *s.* *Educ.:* Rev. J. W. Hawtrey, Slough; H.M.S. Britannia, Dartmouth. As a Lieutenant, R.N., captured two dhows, Pemba, Zanzibar, 1888; commanded Coastguard South of Ireland, 1912; served European War, 1914-18. *Address:* Orchards, Longparish, Hants. *T.:* Longparish 212. *Club:* Army and Navy. [*Died* 30 *April* 1951.

HICKIE, Brigadier-General Carlos Joseph, C.M.G. 1919; 3rd *s.* of Lt.-Col. J. F. Hickie, 7th Royal Fusiliers, of Slevyre, Borrisokane, Co. Tipperary; *m.* 1903, Edith (*d.* 1952) *o. d.* of Captain M. H. Thunder, Royal Scots Fusiliers, of Coolnagloose, Co. Wexford; one *s.* one *d.* *Educ.:* Oscott College; Beaumont College. 2nd Lieut. Gloucester Regt. 1893; served South African War, including siege of Ladysmith (wounded at Rietfontein, 24 Oct. 1899, Queen's medal 4 clasps, King's medal 2 clasps); Captain K.O.Y.L.I., 1902; Major Royal Fusiliers, 1912; served European War, Egypt and Gallipoli as Brigade Major 126th Brigade (severely wounded 4 June 1915); commanded 14th Batt. Hants Regt. Jan. 1916, on Western Front until appointed Brigade Commander, Aug. 1916; commanded 115th, 224th, and 7th Infantry Brigade successively (Brevet of Lieut.-Colonel, C.M.G.); Temp. Br.-Gen., Aug. 1916-April 1919; commanded 1st Bn. Royal Fusiliers; retired pay, 1923. *Address:* Slevyre, Terryglass, Nenagh, Co. Tipperary, Eire. [*Died* 6 *Dec.* 1959.

HICKLING, Henry George Albert, F.R.S. 1936; D.Sc., F.G.S., M.I.Min.E. P.A.I.W.E.; J.B. Simpson Professor of Geology, King's College, Newcastle on Tyne, 1920-48, Emeritus Professor since 1948; *b.* Nottingham, 1883; *s.* of Charles Hickling; *m.* 1st, 1910, Gertrude Hermine Geiler (*d.* 1952); one *s.* two *d.*; 2nd, 1954, Grace Watt. Grad. Univ., Manchester, 1905; Lecturer University of Manchester, 1907-20; Murchison Medal, Geol. Soc. Lond. 1934; President Section C. British Association, 1935; Member Geological Survey Board, 1936-40; Fuel Research Board, 1943-48. Greenwell Medal, N. Eng. Inst. Mining Eng., 1950. *Publications:* Various papers on Fossil Botany, on the Old Red Sandstone, Carboniferous and Permo-Triassic rocks, on palæontological subjects, on the Lancashire and North-Eastern Coalfields and on the structure and composition of coal. *Address:* King's College, Newcastle on Tyne. *T.:* Newcastle 52695; 66 The Grove, Gosforth, Newcastle upon Tyne, 3. [*Died* 26 *July* 1954.

HICKMAN, Major-General Henry Temple Devereux, C.B. 1940; O.B.E.; 1932; M.C.; Indian Army, retd.; *b.* 24 Feb. 1888; *s.* of Major D. W. Hickman, Indian Staff Corps; *m.* 1913, Lilian, *d.* of late John Young, New Kilpatrick, Scotland. *Educ.:* Wellington College, Berks; R.M.C., Sandhurst. 2nd Lieut. Indian Army, 1906; Capt., 1915; Bt. Major, 1919; Major, 1921; Bt. Lt.-Col., 1929; Lt.-Col., 1931; Col., 1933; Maj.-Gen., 1940. Served against Mohmands, 1908; France, 1914-15; Mesopotamia, 1916-18; Palestine, 1918; against Kurds in Iraq, 1930; in Waziristan, 1936-37; retired, 1944. *Recreations:* hunting, shooting, fishing, farming. *Address:* Swinford Demesne, P.O. Mweiga, Nyeri, Kenya Colony. *Club:* United Service. [*Died* 22 *May* 1960.

HICKS, (Ernest) George, C.B.E. 1946; Hon. A.R.I.B.A.; *b.* 1879; *m.* 1st, 1897; one *s.* one *d.*; 2nd, 1938, Mrs. Emma Ellen Ellis. *Educ.:* Elementary School and Polytechnic. Commenced work as a general builders' youth at 11 years of age: later decided to become a bricklayer; appointed by turn to all offices in branch of the Operative Bricklayers' Society; National Organiser for the Bricklayers' Society, 1912; elected General Secretary of the Operative Bricklayers' Society and President of the National Federation of Building Trades Operatives, 1919 and 1936-37; the first general Secretary of the Amalgamated Union of Building Trade Workers of Great Britain and Ireland, 1921-40; M.P. (Lab.), East Woolwich, 1931-50; Parliamentary Secretary, Ministry of Works, 1940-45. Elected representative of Building Trade Group of the British Trades Union Congress General Council in 1921, and Pres. of Congress in 1926-27; Chairman, Trades Union Unemployment Insurance Association; a Member of General Council, International Federation of Trade Unions, Executive Council, National Housing and Town Planning Council, Executive Committee National Council of Labour Colleges, Social Democratic Federation; Advisory Committee of the L.C.C. School of Building, of H.M. Government Building Materials Prices Committee, Central Housing Advisory Committee (Housing Act, 1935), Holidays with Pay Committee; Joint Consultative Committee on Building Programme of Government Departments; Lord Privy Seal's Conference on Air Raid Shelters; Committee on Efficient Use of Fuel; National Defence Public Interest Committee; Gen. Committee King George Memorial Fund; Member Anglo-Russian Parliamentary Committee; Empire Parliamentary Association; Vice-Chairman National Joint Council for Building Industry; Building Industries National Council; General Council, Workers' Travel Association; President, Federation of Trade Union, Labour, Socialist and Co-operative Clubs of Great Britain and Ireland; President, Incorporated Ophthalmic Council; Director National Camps Corporation. Freeman City of London; Liveryman Companies of Glaziers and Paviors. *Publications:* various pamphlets on Housing. *Recreation:* propaganda. *Clubs:* Albany, National Trade Union, London Hampshire Society, Surrey County Cricket, South Battersea Labour, Woolwich Labour Institute, Hyndman; Luton Labour. [*Died* 19 *July* 1954.

HICKS, Rt. Rev. George Bruno, M.A., O.S.B.; Abbot of Reading since 1939; *b.* 24 July 1878; *s.* of Hastings Hicks and Edith, *d.* of late George Ellis. *Educ.:* Downside School; Peterhouse, Cambridge (Historical Tripos); S. Anselmo, Rome. Master at Downside School, 1903-14; Bursar of Downside Abbey and School, 1914-33; Abbot of Downside 1933-39; formerly Member of Clutton Board of Guardians, Shepton Mallet Rural District Council and Midsomer Norton Urban District Council; President Downside Wanderers Cricket Club; Vice-President Somerset County Cricket Club, etc. *Publications:* Hugh Edmund Ford (First Abbot of Downside); pamphlets and articles on historical subjects. *Address:* Downside Abbey, nr. Bath, Somerset. [*Died* 18 *Jan.* 1954.

HICKS, Lieut.-Col. Sir Maxwell, Kt., *cr.* 1920; C.B.E. 1919; *b.* 20 March 1878; 4th *s.* of late Henry Hicks of Plaistow Hall, Kent, and Harriet, *d.* of late Thomas Watts; *m.* 1904, Kate (*d.* 1950), *o. d.* of late John Giblett of Woodside Park, Middlesex. *Educ.:* privately. Articled to Jackson Pixley & Co., 1894; admitted Institute of Chartered Accountants, 1900; Honours Interm. and Final; admitted Fellowship, 1908; senior partner of firm of Maxwell, Hicks & Co., Chartered Accountants, until 1948;

European War, 1914-18, commanded M.H.S. Accountants, a technical unit of R.A.S.C. dealing with the financial side of Expeditionary Force Canteens (despatches, C.B.E.); War of 1939-45, Member of Inland Transport War Council. *Recreations:* shooting, golf, fishing. *Address:* The Old Rectory Cottage, Upper Clatford, nr. Andover, Hants. *T.:* Andover 2918. [*Died* 1 *March* 1959.

HICKSON, Lt.-Gen. Sir Gerald Robert Stedall, K.C.V.O. *cr.* 1951; Kt., *cr.* 1946; C.B. 1933; C.B.E. 1919; *b.* Wallington, Sy., 6 Aug. 1879; *s.* of Charles Hickson; *m.* Winifred B. Kloetgen; one *d.* (and one *d.* decd.). *Educ.:* Portsmouth Gram. School. Joined R.M.L.I., 1897; Lieut. 1898; Capt. 1903; Maj., 1915; Lt.-Col. 1925; Col. 1929; Maj.-Gen. 1933; Lt.-Gen. 1934; Director of Naval Recruiting, Admiralty, 1927-30; Brig. commanding Portsmouth Div. Royal Marines, 1931-33; a Royal Marine A.D.C. to the King, 1931-33; retired list, 1935; Hon. Colonel Comdt. Portsmouth Division, R.M., 1942-49; D.L. County of London, 1948; Secretary King George's Fund for Sailors, 1938-50; Member Merchant Navy Welfare Board, 1940-1950. *Address:* 6 Iverna Court, W.8. *Club:* United Service. [*Died* 4 *Aug.* 1957.

HICKSON, Joseph William Andrew; Professor Metaphysics and Logic, McGill University, 1909-24; *e. s.* of late Sir Joseph Hickson; *b.* Montreal; unmarried. *Educ.:* McGill University; Universities of Freiburg, Berlin, and Halle. Member of the Alpine Club and of the American and Swiss Alpine Clubs; Past Pres. of Alpine Club of Canada, now Hon. Pres. *Address:* 3428 Ontario Avenue, Montreal, Canada. *Clubs:* Mount Royal, University, Royal Montreal Curling (Montreal). [*Died* 22 *April* 1956.

HIGGINS, Ellen C., B.A. (Hons.) (London); *b.* London; Scotch parentage and extraction. *Educ.:* Edinburgh Ladies' College; Royal Holloway Coll. Oxford Honours in Mathematics, Class I. in Moderations and Final Schools; on staff of Cheltenham Ladies' Coll., 1895-1907; Principal of Royal Holloway Coll., 1907-35, and Senator of Univ. of London, 1911-35; Member of Councils of: King's College of Household Science; Cheltenham Ladies' Coll., etc. *Recreations:* music, reading, walking. *Address:* 8 Warrender Park Crescent, Edinburgh. *Club:* Ladies' Alpine. [*Died* 13 *Dec.* 1951.

HIGGINS, Major-General Harold John, C.B. 1950; O.B.E. 1946; F.D.S., R.C.S. 1948; K.H.D.S. 1948; Dir., Army Dental Service, since 1948; *b.* 2 Nov. 1894; British; unmarried. *Educ.:* Castleknock College, Dublin; Royal College of Surgeons, Ireland. Lieut., British Army, 1918; Capt., 1919; Major, 1930; Lt.-Col., 1941; Col., 1946; Maj.-Gen., Sept. 1948. *Recreations:* golf, tennis, sailing, etc. *Address:* The War Office (A.M.D.6), S.W.1. *T.:* Grosvenor 8040 Ext. 471. *Club:* Naval and Military. [*Died* 4 *March* 1951.

HIGGINS, John Comyn, C.I.E. 1920; *e. s.* of F. Higgins, J.P., of Alford, Lincolnshire; *b.* 21 May 1882; *m.* 1912, Elsie Isabel, *d.* of J. Elwin, Kuttal, Silchar, Assam; (two *s.* killed in action) one *d.* *Educ.:* Bradfield; Brasenose College, Oxford. Indian Civil Service, 1905; Assistant Magistrate and Collector, Bakarganj, Bengal, 1907-8; Subdivisional Officer, Jorhat, Assam, 1908-9; Madaripur, Bengal, 1909-10; Vice-President and President of the Manipur State Darbar, 1910-17; Political Agent, Manipur State, 1917-33; Political Officer, Kuki Punitive Operations, 1917-19; Deputy Commissioner, Nowgong, Assam, 1920-1923; Commissioner Assam Valley, 1934; Member, Assam Revenue Tribunal, 1939; retired, 1942; Commission in Indian Engineers, 1942; resigned commission, Sept. 1942; Civil Liaison Officer with Army, 1942-44; Chairman, Assam Public Service Commission, 1944-45; retired, 1945. *Recreations:* polo, shooting, golf. *Address:* Alford, Lincs. *Clubs:* East India and Sports; Bengal United Service (Calcutta). [*Died* 8 *Dec.* 1952.

HIGGINS, Air Commodore Thomas Charles Reginald, C.B. 1926; C.M.G. 1919; D.L. Beds., 1931; late R.A.F.; *b.* 21 July 1880; *s.* of W. F. Higgins of Turvey House, Turvey, Beds., and Adela, *d.* of General Wilby, C.B.; *m.* 1915, Doris Anna, *d.* of late Charles Van Neck of Lilley Hill, Bracknell, Berks.; one *d.* *Educ.:* H.M.S. Britannia. Midshipman, Royal Navy, 1897-1900; The King's Own Regt., 1900–1 April 1917; R.A.F. since 1917; Air Commodore, 1922; Director of Training, Air Ministry, 1922-26; Chief Staff Officer, Iraq, 1926-28; served with Mediterranean Fleet; served two years S.A. War with the King's Own Regt.; served N. Nigeria Regiment four years, including operations at Sartiru near Sokoto (King's and Queen's S.A. Medal, African General Service Medal, 1906); served with B.E.F., France, Aug. 1914-17 (1914 Star, C.M.G.); served Iraq, 1926-28 (Southern Desert Iraq Medal); retired list, 1929; re-employed with R.A.F. and R.A.F. Regt., 1939-45. Pilot Aviator's Certificate (Number 88), May 1911. *Address:* Turvey House, Turvey, Bedford. *T.A.:* Turvey. *Club:* Travellers'. [*Died* 22 *Sept.* 1953.

HIGGINS, Rev. Canon Walter Norman, M.A.; Prebendary of Cudworth since 1951; Residentiary Canon in Wells Cathedral, 1947-55; *b.* 27 April 1880; *s.* of Henry Higgins, Willsbridge House, Glos; *m.* 1913, Dora Molyneux Quilter (*d.* 1954); one *s.* one *d.* *Educ.:* King's School, Bruton; Emmanuel Coll., Cambridge; Wells Theological Coll. Deacon, 1905; Priest, 1906; Asst. Curate S. Andrew, Battersea, and S. Paul, Herne Hill; Domestic Chaplain to Bishop of Adelaide; Rector of Maylands, S. Australia, and Hon. Chaplain to Bishop; Chaplain to Australian Imperial Force; Vicar of All Saints, Portsea; Rector of Great Bookham, Surrey; Rector of Mells, Somerset, 1934-44. Archdeacon of Wells, 1940-51. *Address:* c/o Twerton Vicarage, Bath, Somerset. [*Died* 17 *May* 1957.

HIGGINSON, Brigadier-General Cecil Pickford, C.M.G. 1915; D.S.O. 1900; *s.* of late James Pickford Higginson of Fir Vale, Wavertree, near Liverpool; *b.* 9 Apr. 1866; *m.* 1904, Maud, 2nd *d.* of late Lt.-Col. Goslin of Rathvilly, Co. Carlow; two *s.* one *d.* *Educ.:* Repton. Entered army, 1886; Captain, 1895; Major, 1907; Lt.-Col. 1913; served S. Africa, 1899-1902; present at Paardeberg (despatches twice, Queen's medal 4 clasps, King's medal 2 clasps, D.S.O.); European War, 1914-15 (despatches, C.M.G); commanded 1st Batt. King's Shropshire Light Infantry; retired pay, 1919. *Address:* Wendiri, P.O. M'Sonneddi, S. Rhodesia. *Clubs:* Army and Navy; Salisbury S. Rhodesia). [*Died* 17 *Aug.* 1951.

HIGGINSON, Brig. Sir Frank, Kt., *cr.* 1956; C.B. 1952; C.M.G. 1937; A.R.I.B.A.; M.Inst.R.A.; Architect; *b.* 22 April 1890; 3rd *s.* of late H. Higginson, Architect, Carlisle; *m.* 1917, Violet Lindsley, *o. d.* of late William Young, Melton-Mowbray; no *c.* *Educ.:* Carlisle Grammar School; École des Beaux Arts, New York, U.S.A. Joined Royal Montreal Regiment, 1914; served European War, 1914-18 (despatches twice); seconded to Imperial War Graves Commission, Nov. 1918, Chief Administrative Officer of Commission's Central European District, 1928-38; Director of Works and Controller, 1938-47; Secretary, 1947-56. Silver Jubilee Medal, 1935; Coronation Medal, 1937. *Recreations:* golf and tennis. *Address:* Gartree Drive, Melton Mowbray, Leics. [*Died* 20 *Nov.* 1958.

HIGGINSON, Major-General Harold Whitla, C.B. 1919; D.S.O. 1916; *b.* Bannu, India, 10 Nov. 1873; *o. surv. s.* of late Col. Theophilus Higginson, C.B., and *g.s.* of late H. T. Higginson, J.P., of Carnalea House, Co. Down; *m.* 1903, Ivy Letitia (*d.*

1952), 4th *d.* of late James Broun, J.P., of Petit Menage, Jersey, and Orchard, Carluke, Lanark; one *s.* one *d.* *Educ.:* St. Lawrence College, Ramsgate; R.M.C., Sandhurst, 2nd Lieut. Royal Dublin Fusiliers, 1894; Lieut. 1896; Capt. 1899; Major 1913; Temp. Lt.-Col. 1915; Bt. Lt.-Col. 1916; Temp. Brig.-General 1916; Bt. Colonel 1918; temp. Maj.-General 1918; Maj.-Gen. 1927; served W. Africa, 1897-98; (medal with 2 clasps); S. Africa, 1899-1902 (Queen's medal with 4 clasps, King's medal with 2 clasps, despatches); Aden, operations in the interior, 1903; Blue Nile, 1908 (Khedive's medal); European War, 1914-18 (despatches, D.S.O. and bar, Bt. Lt.-Col. and Col. Commander Star of Rumania, C.B., Officier de la Légion d'Honneur); Adjutant 4th Royal Dublin Fusiliers, 1904-7; 2nd Royal Dublin Fusiliers, 1911-13; Brigade-Major, 143rd Infantry Brigade, 1914-15; commanded 2nd Royal Dublin Fusiliers, 1915; 53rd Infantry Brigade, 1916-18; 12th Division, 1918-19; 17th Infantry Brigade, Cork, 1919-22; 2nd Infantry Brigade, Aldershot, 1922-23; O.C. Troops, Ceylon, 1924-27; G.O.C. 55th (West Lancs) Division T.A. 1928-32; A.D.C. to the King, 1923-27; retired list, 1932. *Address:* c/o Lloyds Bank, 16 St. James's St., S.W.1.
[*Died* 30 *Oct.* 1954.

HIGGS, Hon. William Guy; Christian Metaphysician; *b.* Wingham, Manning River, N.S.W., 18 Jan. 1862; *s.* of W. G. Higgs, St. Columb, Cornwall, and E. Gregg, Ballyconnel, County Cavan; *m.* M. A. Knight of Shoalhaven, N.S.W.; two *s.* one *d.* *Educ.:* Public Schools, N.S.W. Compositor, printer, journalist; alderman, Brisbane Municipal Council, 1899-1900; represented Fortitude Valley, Queensland State Parliament, 1899-1900; elected to first Commonwealth Parliament, 1901; member of Royal Commission Commonwealth Tariff, 1905-6; formerly one of the six senators representing the State of Queensland in Australian Commonwealth Parliament; Senate Chairman of Committees, 1904-6; one of the Australian delegates to Coronation of King George V. and Queen Mary, 22 June 1911; Treasurer of the Commonwealth, 1915-16; representative for Capricornia, Queensland, Commonwealth Parliament, 1910; re-elected, 1913, 1914, 1917, 1919; Deputy-Leader Federal Labour Party in House of Representatives, 1916-19; defeated at Federal Elections, Dec. 1922; Chairman, Royal Commission on the Finances of Western Australia as affected by Federation, 1925; Hon. President, Welfare and After-Care Society for Mental Patients, 1929-1946. *Publications:* Plea for Better Treatment of the Mentally Afflicted; Thoughts, and A Prayer, based on Christian Metaphysics. *Address:* 98 Wellington Street, Kew, E.4, Vic., Australia. *T.:* Hawthorn 4795.
[*Died* 11 *June* 1951.

HIGHT, Sir James, K.B.E., *cr.* 1947; C.M.G. 1932; M.A., Litt.D.; LL.D.; Professor of History and Political Science, Univ. of N.Z., Emeritus since retirement, 1949; Dep.-Chm. N.Z. Council of Educational Research; *b.* Christchurch, N.Z., 1870; *m.* 1897, Margaret Frances Green, Christchurch; one *d.* *Educ.:* Malvern District School and Canterbury College, Christchurch. B.A. and Senior Univ. Scholar in English and French, 1893; M.A. and First-Class Honours in Languages and Literature, 1894; awarded Margaret Condliffe Memorial Medal, 1950. Chief Modern Languages Master at Auckland Grammar School, 1896-1901; Lecturer on Constitutional History and Political Economy at Canterbury Univ. Coll., and Editor to the publishing house of Whitcombe & Tombs, Ltd., 1901-5; F.R.Econ.S. 1904; Litt.D., first in N.Z., 1906; Lecturer in History and Economics, 1906-8; Professor of History and Economics and Director of Studies in Commerce, 1909-20; Examiner to the N.Z. Govt. and the N.Z. University; Chairman of Board of Governors of Christchurch Technical College, 1906-10; Fellow of the University of N.Z. since 1911, Chairman of the Academic Board, 1934-48, and Pro-Chancellor of the University, 1938-48; Member of the Royal Commission on Cost of Living in N.Z., 1912, and of Board of Trade investigation into the Coal Industry, 1918; Professor of History, University of Leeds (on exchange with Prof. A. J. Grant), 1927; Rector of Canterbury University Coll., 1928-41; Representative for N.Z. at World Association for Adult Education Conference; Delegate of N.Z. Govt. at International Economic Conference, Geneva, 1927, and Imperial Education Conference, London, 1927; Lectured at various Universities, U.S.A.; Delegate to Congress of the Universities of the Empire, Edinburgh, 1931; Chairman Economics Committee, Govt. of New Zealand, 1932. *Publications:* The Governance of New Zealand: its Origin, Establishment, and Early Development, 1905; general editor of the Makers of Australasia Series; Constitutional History and Law of N.Z., 1914; History of Canterbury College, 1927; Uses of History, 1935; Adviser for N.Z., and contributor to Cambridge History of the British Empire, 1927-33; Articles on British and American Education; contributor to Ency. of the Social Sciences, New York, 1930. Joint Editor Official Centennial History of Canterbury, N.Z., 1950-53. *Recreations:* music, bowling. *Address:* 69 Glandovey Road, Christchurch, N.W 1, N.Z.
[*Died* 17 *May* 1958.

HILDER, Lieut.-Col. Frank, T.D.; D.L.; J.P.; *b.* 3 Oct. 1864; *s.* of late Edward Martin Hilder, Ash, Kent; *m.* 1895, Evelyn Mary, R.R.C. (*d.* 1939), *d.* of late Lt.-Col. G. Wilding Wood, D.L., J.P., Docklands, Ingatestone, Essex; one *s.* two *d.* *Educ.:* Privately. Captain Essex Imperial Yeomanry, 1902-8; Major Essex R.H.A., 1908-14; Major 2nd King Edward's Horse since 1914; Lt.-Col 2/3 S. Mid. R.F.A., 1915; O.C. Reserve Battery, R.F.A., Ripon, Nov. 1916-May 1917; O.C. 21st Corps Ammunition Parks, 1917-18; Egyptian Expeditionary Force; M.P. (C.) S.E. Essex, 1918-23; High Sheriff of Essex, 1935-36. In 1913 formulated and circulated among leading statesmen of the world a definite plan for a League of Nations under the heading, A Senate of Civilisation; President, Essex Federation Junior Imperial League, 1931-34. *Address:* Huskards, Ingatestone, Essex. *Club:* Carlton.
[*Died* 23 *April* 1951.

HILDESLEY, His Honour Alfred, Q.C.; Judge of County Courts, Circuit No. 33 (Essex and Suffolk), 1931-47; Chairman, East Suffolk Quarter Sessions, 1932-47; *b.* Manchester, 5 Sept. 1873; *m.* 1st, 1908, Cicely Ayliffe, *d.* of late Walter Glynn, Willaston, Cheshire; three *s.* one *d.*; 2nd, 1934, Dora Cecilia Heyworth, *d.* of late Richard Stubbs, Birkenhead. *Educ.:* privately; Pembroke College, Oxford. Barrister, Inner Temple, 1898; K.C. 1929; Q.C. 1952. Retired, 1947. *Recreations:* bibliography, fly-fishing. *Address:* 102A Banbury Road, Oxford. *T.:* 59347; 2 Paper Buildings, Temple, E.C. *T.:* Central 0169. *Club:* Oxford and Cambridge.
[*Died* 31 *May* 1958.

HILDYARD, His Honour Gerard Moresby Thoroton, Q.C. 1920; County Court Judge on Circuit No. 18, 1928-43; Bencher of Lincoln's Inn; *b.* 3 June 1874; *s.* of late General Sir H. J. T. Hildyard, G.C.B.; *m.* 1911, Sybil Hamilton, *d.* of H. W. Hamilton Hoare; three *s.* *Educ.:* Eton; University College, Oxford. Called to Bar, Lincoln's Inn, 1899; Master in Lunacy, 1923-1928; Chairman Notts. Quarter Sessions, 1932-1947; D.L. Notts. *Recreations:* rowed for Eton; ran for Oxford. *Address:* Flintham Hall, Newark. *T.:* East Stoke 214.
[*Died* 22 *April* 1956.

HILDYARD, Brigadier-General Harold Charles Thoroton, C.M.G. 1919; D.S.O. 1916; *b.* 16 July 1872; *e. s.* of General Sir Henry Hildyard, G.C.B.; *m.* 1909, Selina Constance, (*d.* 1950), 2nd *d.* of Rev. Savile L'Estrange Malone; one *s.* two *d.* *Educ.:* Marlborough

College; Royal Military Academy, Woolwich. Joined Royal Artillery, 1891; served South African War (despatches twice, Queen's medal 4 clasps, King's medal 2 clasps); retired as Major Royal Horse Artillery to join S.E. and C.R., 1913; called up as Reserve of Officers for European War (C.M.G., D.S.O., despatches five times); Deputy Director General Transportation B.E.F. *Recreations:* hunting, shooting, golf. *Address:* 2 The Close, Seaford, Sussex. *T.:* Seaford 2378.
[*Died* 24 *Feb.* 1956.

HILL, 6th Viscount (*cr.* 1842), **Charles Rowland Clegg-Hill,** Bt. 1726-27; Baron Hill of Almarez and of Hawkstone, Salop, 1814; D.S.O. 1900; J.P. for Salop; late Royal Welch Fusiliers; *b.* 5 May 1876; *s.* of 3rd Viscount and 2nd wife Hon. Isabella Elizabeth Wynn, 5th *d.* of 3rd Baron Newborough; *S.* half-brother, 1924; *m.* 1st, 1903, Mildred (*d.* 1934), *d.* of Thomas Bulteel of Radford, S. Devon; one *s.* (and one *s.* killed in action, 1945); 2nd, 1936, Berthe Maria Emilie, *d.* of Alfonse Immer, Strasbourg. Entered army, 1896; served South Africa, Nov. 1899 to Dec. 1900 with 2nd Batt. Mounted Infantry, Dec. 1900 to termination of war as Adjt. 1st Batt. Royal Welch Fusiliers (wounded twice, despatches); retired, 1912; served European War with 2nd Batt. R. W. Fusiliers, 4 Aug. 1914-Sep. 1915 (wounded Sept. 1915); served on Staff, March 1916 to termination of war (despatches 3 times, Brevet Lt.-Col.). *Heir: s.* Captain Hon. Gerald Rowland Clegg-Hill [Royal Welch Fusiliers, *b.* 31 March 1904; *m.* 1st, 1930, Betty, *yr. d.* of late Brig.-Gen. George N. T. Smyth-Osbourne, C.B., C.M.G., D.S.O.; two *s.*; 2nd, 1942, Catherine Mary (Molly) Lloyd-Williams]. *Address:* Coton Hall, Whitchurch, Shropshire.
[*Died* 3 *May* 1957.

HILL, Alfred Francis, C.M.G. 1960; O.B.E. 1953; retired; *b.* 16 Dec. 1870; *s.* of Charles and Liza Ann Hill; *m.* 1897, Sarah Brownhill Booth, Sydney; one *s.* two *d.*; *m.* 1921, Mirrie Irma Solomon, Sydney. *Educ.:* Leipzig Conservatorium (Helbig Prize). Conductor, Wellington Orchestral Society, 1892-96; wrote Maori cantata Hinemoa, 1896; joined company of virtuoso violinist Ovid Musin and went to Sydney, 1897; conductor, Sydney Liedertafel, 1897-1902; first romantic opera, Lady Dolly, 1900; returned N.Z., 1902; Maori romantic opera, Tapu, 1903; began collecting Maori music; romantic opera, The Moorish Maid, 1905; wrote song, Waiata-Poi, 1905; conducted Christchurch Exhibition Orchestra, 1906-07; returned to Sydney, 1910; formed Opera League with Fritz Hart, 1914; appointed first Professor of Harmony and Composition, N.S.W. Conservatorium, 1915; deputy conductor of N.S.W. State Orchestra; retired from Conservatorium, 1935. Since retirement has written many symphonies, concertos, and much chamber music. *Publication:* Harmony and Melody, 1926. *Recreations:* gardening, reading. *Address:* 37A Raglan Street, Mosman, N.S.W., Australia. *T.:* XM 4347. *Clubs:* Savage (Life member), Musical Association (Life member) (Sydney). [*Died* 30 *Oct.* 1960.

HILL, Lord (Arthur) Francis (Henry); *b.* 28 Aug. 1895; 2nd *s.* of 6th and *b.* and *heir-pres.* to 7th Marquess of Downshire; *m.* 1927, Sheila, *y. d.* of late Col. MacDougall, of Lunga, Argyll; one *s.* (Arthur Robin Iain, *b.* 10 May 1929) two *d.* *Educ.:* Eton; R.M.C. Captain late The Greys; served European War, 1915-19 (despatches); A.D.C. to Gov.-Gen. of South Africa, 1921-24; R.A.R.O.; served War of 1939-1945. *Address:* The White House, Ringmer, Sussex. *T.:* Ringmer 35. *Club:* White's.
[*Died* 25 *Oct.* 1953.

HILL, Major-General Sir Basil Alexander, K.B.E., *cr.* 1941; C.B. 1937; D.S.O. 1917; *b.* 23 April 1880; *s.* of late Michael Hill and Mrs. M. Hill (*née* Don); *m.* 1907, Edith Marian, *d.* of late Alex. Thomson, Edinburgh; no *c.* *Educ.:* Neuenheim College, Heidelberg. Gazetted to Royal Marine Artillery, 1897; joined Army Ordnance Department, 1908; served with the British and Japanese Forces at the siege of Tsingtau, Nov. 1914; with the Mediterranean Expeditionary Force during the Gallipoli operations (despatches); with the Egyptian Expeditionary Force (despatches, D.S.O., Bt. Lt.-Col.); Controller of Ordnance Services War Office, 1939-40; retired pay, 1941. Colonel Commandant R.A.O.C., 1936-47; Colonel Commandant R.E.M.E., 1942-47. President, Rugby Football Union, 1937-38; J.P. Surrey. *Recreations:* English Rugby Football International 1903-7, golf, fishing, shooting. *Club:* United Service. [*Died* 31 *July* 1960.

HILL, Lord Francis; *see* Hill, Lord A. F. H.

HILL, Lieutenant-Col. Francis Robert, C.B.E. 1919; T.D.: retired Ophthalmological Surgeon; *b.* 16 Feb. 1873; *y. s.* of Laurence Hill, C.E., Glasgow; *m.* Jeannette (*d.* 1947), *d.* of late Sir James Watt; one *s.* *Educ.:* Loretto; Glasgow Univ. M.B., C.M., 1895; Resident Surgeon Glasgow Eye Infirmary; Hon. Ophthalmic Surgeon, Carlisle Infirmary, till 1914; Commanded 331 Brigade, R.F.A. (T.), France and Flanders till Aug. 1917 when he was automatically transferred to R.A.M.C.; D.A.D.G., War Office, 1918. *Address:* c/o Messrs. Rainnie and Mack, W.S., 40 Castle Street, Edinburgh. [*Died* 1 *April* 1956.

HILL, Brig.-General Frederic William, C.B. 1919; C.M.G. 1918; D.S.O. 1916; late 1st Canadian Infantry Battalion; retired Canadian Permanent Staff; *b.* 1866; *m.* 1894, Henrietta (*d.* 1937), *d.* of H. T. Johnson; one *d.* Called to Bar, Ontario, 1891; K.C. 1921; served European War, 1914-18, 1st Can. Inf. Bn. and 9th Can. Inf. Bde. (despatches six times, D.S.O., C.M.G., C.B.); Hon. Col. Carleton and York Regt., Canadian Army. *Address:* 24 Waterloo Row, Fredericton, New Brunswick, Canada.
[*Died* 12 *March* 1954.

HILL, Sir George Rowley, 7th Bt., *cr.* 1779; *b.* 28 Apr. 1864; *s.* of late Rt. Rev. Rowley Hill, Bishop of Sodor and Man, 3rd *s.* of 3rd Bt. and Caroline Maud, *d.* of Captain Alfred Chapman, R.N.; *S. cousin,* 1929; *m.* 1890, Alice Estelle Harley (*d.* 1940), *d.* of Edward Bacon, Eywood, Kington, Herefordshire, and *g.-g.d.* of last Earl of Oxford; one *s.* *Educ.:* Haileybury; Gonville and Caius College, Cambridge. For many years an official in the Bank of England; retired, 1915; author of Mull and Iona Poems; very interested in Ex-Service Men and British Legion, for whom he has with help of friends built headquarters for Ross of Mull Branch of British Legion at Bunessan, Mull. *Heir: s.* George Cyril Rowley, *b.* 18 Dec. 1890. *Address:* Watson's Hotel, Watson's Bay, Sydney, N.S.W.
[*Died* 30 *June* 1954.

HILL, Colonel Gerald Victor Wilmot, D.S.O. 1915; retired; *b.* Hounslow, Mddx., 24 Aug. 1887; *s.* of late Brig.-Gen. Augustus West Hill, C.B.; *m.* 1916, Enid Geraldine O'Bryen Callaghan. *Educ.:* United Services College, Westward Ho!; Woolwich. Entered Royal Irish Fusiliers, 1906; Lieut. 1908; Captain, 1913; Bt. Major, 1916; Bt. Lt.-Col. 1918; Major, 1928; Lt.-Col. 1933; Col. 1937; served European War, 1914-19 (despatches six times, D.S.O. and two bars); G.S.O. 3rd grade, 1915; Brigade-Major, 1915; commanded 8th Batt. The Suffolk Regt., 1916-1918, and 7th Batt. The Suffolk Regt., 1918-19; commanded 1st Bn. The Norfolk Regt., 1933-37; Officer i/c Infantry Record and Pay Office, Lichfield, 1937-38, Preston, 1938-41; served War of 1939-45, Sub Area Comdr., 1941; A.D.C.; retd., 1944. *Recreations:* represented Ireland in the International Cross-Country Race at Glasgow in 1907; Shropshire County Hockey Club, 1907-9; Kent County Hockey Club, 1911-14, 1919-24; Army Football team *v.* Dutch Army,

1913-14; Army Hockey team, 1913-14, 1919-20, 1921-22, 1923-24; Combined Services Hockey team, 1921-22, 1923-24; England v. Ireland at Lawn Tennis, Dublin, 1920. *Address:* c/o Lloyds Bank Ltd., 6 Pall Mall, S.W.1. [*Died* 9 *Oct.* 1958.

HILL, Colonel Henry Warburton, C.M.G. 1918; D.S.O. 1917; R.A., retired; *b.* 4 Feb. 1877; *y. s.* of late Pearson Hill, and *g.s.* of Sir Rowland Hill, K.C.B.; *m.* 1919, Ellinor Janet Marcia, *o. d.* of Rowland Percy Walters; one *s.* one *d.* *Educ.:* Bradfield College; R.M.A., Woolwich. On Experimental Staff, Shoeburyness, 1906-9; served South African War (Queen's and King's medals, despatches); European War, went out with 7th Division, Oct. 1914 (wounded at Ypres 1914, despatches thrice, C.M.G., D.S.O., Croix de Guerre); Commandant Anti-Aircraft Defence School, 1925-29; Commander 26th (London) Air Defence Brigade, 1929-33; retired pay 1934; Lefroy Gold Medal. *Publications:* Rowland Hill and the Fight for Penny Post, 1940; articles in the R.A. Journal on artillery and ballistic questions; various inventions for artillery purposes and for anti-aircraft guns. *Recreations:* various. *Address:* Avalon, Oban, Argyll. *Club:* Army and Navy. [*Died* 16 *May* 1951.

HILL, J. Arthur; *b.* 4 Dec. 1872. *Educ.:* Thornton Grammar School, Bradford, preparing for a business career. Manufacturer's manager to 1898; then invalided by heart wrench while cycling; partial recovery, 1918; Hon. Associate of Society for Psychical Research. *Publications:* New Evidences in Psychical Research; Religion and Modern Psychology; Spiritualism and Psychical Research (People's Books series); Psychical Investigations; Man is a Spirit; Spiritualism, its History, Phenomena, and Doctrine; Psychical Miscellanea; Emerson and his Philosophy; From Agnosticism to Belief; Psychical Science and Religious Belief; Letters from Sir Oliver Lodge; Experiences with Mediums; Towards Cheerfulness; articles in Contemporary Review, Nineteenth Century and After, National Review, Hibbert Journal, Spectator, Chambers's Journal, etc. *Address:* Claremont, Thornton, Bradford. *T.:* Thornton 3169. [*Died* 22 *March* 1951.

HILL, James Peter, F.R.S. 1913; D.Sc. (Edin.), Hon. Sc.D. (Dubl., Belf.), F.Z.S.; Professor of Embryology, University of London, University College, 1921-38, Prof. Emeritus since 1938; *b.* Langside, Kennoway, Fifeshire, Scotland, 21 Feb. 1873; *m.* 1900, *e. d.* of late John Steele, C.B., J.P.; two *d.* *Educ.:* Royal High School, Edinburgh; Royal College of Science, London; University of Edinburgh. Demonstrator of Biology, University of Sydney, 1892, and Lecturer on Embryology, 1904; Jodrell Professor of Zoology, University of London, University College, 1906-21; Bell-Baxter Natural Science Scholar, Gunning Prizeman, George Heriot Fellow, Edinburgh University; Mueller Medallist, Australian Association Advancement of Science, 1906; Croonian Lecturer, Royal Society, 1929; Linnean Gold Medallist, 1930; Darwin Medallist, Royal Society, 1940; Hon. Mem. R. Soc., N.S.W.; Linn. Soc., N.S.W.; Soc. Roy. de Bohême; Mem. Corr. Soc. Portug. Sci. Nat.; For. Mem. Holl. Maatsch. Wet. Haarlem; For. Assoc. Nat. Acad. Sci. U.S.A. *Publications:* various papers on Zoological subjects and on the Embryology of the Monotremata, Marsupialia and Eutherian Mammals. *Address:* Kanimbla, 33 Dollis Avenue, Finchley, N.3. *T.:* Finchley 3775. [*Died* 24 *May* 1954.

HILL, Laurence Carr, D.S.O. 1919; M.C.; on staff of Rio Tinto Co. Ltd., 1912-52; Consultant to Rio Tinto Co. Ltd. since 1952; Director, Compania Española de las Minas de Rio Tinto since 1955; *b.* 19 June 1890; *e.* and *o. surv. s.* of late Alexander Hill, M.I.M.M.; *m.* 1920, Nan Brolochan, *e. d.* of late R. Russell Ross, M.B.; three *s.* *Educ.:* St. Lawrence College, Ramsgate; Royal School of Mines, London. A.R.S.M.; B.Sc. (London); M.I.M.M. Served European War, 1914-18 (M.C., D.S.O., despatches thrice); Major, Tunnelling Company R.E.; War of 1939-45, with Tunnelling Engineers in U.K. and Malta; Col. C.E. Malta, 1944. Past Pres. Inst. of Mining and Metallurgy, London; Fellow, Imperial Coll. of Science and Technology. Served on H.M. Mineral Development Cttee. for the investigation of mineral resources (other than coal) in the U.K., 1946-49. [*Died* 4 *May* 1959.

HILL, Sir Leonard Erskine, Kt., *cr.* 1930; F.R.S., M.B.; Fellow of University College, London; Hon. A.R.I.B.A.; LL.D. Aberdeen; late Director of Research, St. John Clinic and Institute of Physical Medicine; late Director Department of Applied Physiology, National Institute of Medical Research, Mount Vernon, Hampstead; late President, Association Sanitary Inspectors; Member of the Navy Medical Advisory Board; late Member of Army Medical Advisory Board; *b.* 2 June 1866; *s.* of late Dr. G. Birkbeck Hill; *m.* 1891, Janet Alexander; four *s.* two *d.* *Educ.:* Haileybury; University College, London; late Member of Senate, London University, and Professor of Physiology, London Hospital. *Publications:* The Physiology and Pathology of the Cerebral Circulation; Manual of Physiology; Physiology for Beginners; Sunshine and Open Air; (with A. Campbell) Health and Environment; (with Mark Clement) Common Colds, 1929; Science of Ventilation and Open Air Treatment: Report to Med. Res. Council, 1919; editor of Recent and Further Advances of Physiology; physiological papers on the circulation of the blood, cerebral anæmia, caisson disease, and divers' palsy, ventilation, action of light, etc., in the Physiological Journal and Trans. and Proc. Royal Society. *Recreations:* landscape, flower and animal painting. *Address:* Field Cottage, Corton, nr. Lowestoft. [*Died* 30 *March* 1952.

HILL, Matthew Davenport; *b.* London, 17 July 1872; 2nd *s.* of late M. Berkeley Hill, M.B., F.R.C.S., *y. s.* of late M. D. Hill, Q.C., Recorder of Birmingham, and Alice Campbell, *y. d.* of late Sir Thomas Howell; grandnephew of late Sir Rowland Hill, K.C.B. *Educ.:* Eton. Scholar of Eton, 1885; Scholar of New College, Oxford, 1890; 1st Class Final Honour School of Natural Science, 1894; Naples Biological Studentship; M.A.; Assistant Lecturer in Zoology, Owens College, Manchester, 1895; Assistant Master, Eton, 1896-1927. *Publications:* Researches on Animal Cytology; Eton Nature Study, Eton and Elsewhere, 1928. *Address:* Uplands Cottage, Ledbury, Herefordshire. *T.:* Ledbury 60. [*Died* 24 *Jan.* 1958.

HILL, (Philip) Maurice, M.A. Oxon; S.M.A., St. Ives Society of Artists; *b.* 18 June 1892; *e. s.* of late Hon. Sir Maurice Hill, Judge of the Probate, Divorce, and Admiralty Div. and of Susan Ellen (Berta) Hadwen; *m.* 1918, Megan (*d.* 1950), *er. d.* of late Ernest Rhys, poet, author and editor of Everyman's Library, and of Grace Rhys, poetess and essayist; three *d.* *Educ.:* King's College School; Balliol College, Oxford; Architectural Association. British Red Cross Society, France, 1915-16; Ministry of Munitions, 1916-19; Solicitor, 1922; Member of Law Society; Assistant General Manager of Chamber of Shipping, 1923; Deputy Gen. Manager, 1938, General Manager, 1941-50; Joint Secretary, General Council of British Shipping, 1941-50; Assistant Secretary, International Shipping Conference, 1921; Secretary-General International Chamber of Shipping, 1947-50; Sec. Advisory Cttee. on New Lighthouse Works, 1923-50; Member of Shipping Mission to Australia, 1929; Member Executive of British National Committee, International Chamber of Commerce, 1926; Rapporteur, Cttee. on Sea Transport of Internat. Chamber of Commerce, 1946-50;

Br. deleg. at Congresses of Internat. Chamber of Commerce; represented Shipping at World Economic Conf., 1927, and numerous Confs. and Cttees. of League of Nations, 1924-1938; Mem. Bureau Permanent Comité Maritime Internat., 1947-50; Mem. Council, Institute of Transport, since 1941; Member Governing Body of City of London Coll., 1943-1951; Member of Council and Hon. Secretary, Soc. of Marine Artists, 1938; Member of St. Ives Society of Artists, 1939; Member of Chelsea Art Soc., 1952; Exhibitor in Royal Academy, Paris Salon, New English Art Club, Royal Scottish Academy, Royal Institute of Oil Painters, Royal Society of British Artists, Loan Exhibitions in Birmingham, Bournemouth, Eastbourne and numerous other provincial art galleries. *Publications:* Euripides and Christianity, 1927; The Martyrs, 1931; Ocean Transport, 1946; Transactions from the Greek of Sappho, 1952. *Recreation:* painting. *Address:* Chimneys, Porthmeor Square, and 4 Piazza Studios, St. Ives, Cornwall. *Club:* Athenæum. [*Died* 5 *Aug.* 1952.

HILL, Vice-Adm. Hon. Sir Richard A. S., K.B.E., *cr.* 1941 (C.B.E. 1930); C.B. 1933; *b.* 2 Apr. 1880; 2nd *s.* of Capt. A. B. G. Sandys Hill, R.B., (*s.* of Lord George Hill), and Helen Emily, 3rd *d.* of Richard Chenevix Trench, D.D., Archbishop of Dublin; raised to rank of Baron's son, 1950; unmarried. *Educ.:* H.M.S. Britannia. Served in Somaliland, 1902-4 (medal); European War, 1914-18; Chevalier Legion of Honour; Captain, 1918; Commodore, 1928; Rear-Admiral, 1930; Rear-Adm. in charge Hong Kong, 1928-30; A.D.C. to the King, 1929; Rear-Admiral and Senior Naval Officer, Yangtze, 1931-33; Vice-Admiral and retired list, 1935. Served in War of 1939-45 as Commodore of Convoys, Sept. 1939-Feb. 1942, and as Flag Officer in Charge, Greenock, Feb. 1942-46. Officer of the Legion of Merit (American), 1946; Croix de Guerre with palm; Commandeur Legion of Honour. *Club:* United Service. [*Died* 5 *July* 1954.

HILL, Sir Roderic Maxwell, Air Chief Marshal (retired), K.C.B., *cr.* 1944 (C.B. 1941); M.C., A.F.C., M.A. (Oxon); LL.D. (Glas.); Fellow of University College, London; F.R.Ae.S.; Rector of Imperial College of Science and Technology since 1948; *b.* 1 March 1894; *s.* of late Prof. M. J. M. Hill, M.A., D.Sc., F.R.S.; *m.* 1917, Helen, *d.* of late Lt.-Col. E. R. Morton, Indian Army; two *d.* (and one *s.* killed in action, 1944). *Educ.:* Bradfield College; University College, London. Private, 18th Royal Fusiliers, Oct. 1914; Commissioned 12th Northumberland Fus., Dec. 1914; (wounded, despatches); transferred, Royal Flying Corps, 1916; served with No. 60 Squadron, France, 1916-17 (M.C., despatches); in charge of Experimental Flying Department, Roy. Aircraft Establishment, 1917-23 (A.F.C. and Bar for experimental flying); Graduated Royal Air Force Staff College, Andover, 1924; Commanded No. 45 (Bomber) Squadron, Iraq, 1924-26; Technical Staff, Middle East Headquarters, Cairo, Egypt, 1926-27; Directing Staff, Royal Air Force, Staff College, Andover, 1927-30; Chief Instructor, Oxford University Air Squadron, 1930-32; Deputy Director of Repair and Maintenance, Air Ministry, 1932-36; Air Officer Commanding, Royal Air Force, Palestine and Trans-Jordan, 1936-38 (despatches twice); Director of Technical Development, Air Ministry, and Ministry of Aircraft Production, 1938-40; Director General of Research and Development, Ministry of Aircraft Production, 1940-1941; Controller of Technical Services, British Air Commission, Washington, D.C., 1941-42; Commandant R.A.F. Staff College, 1942-43; A.O.C. No. 12 (Fighter) Group, 1943; Air Marshal Commanding, Air Defence of Great Britain, 1943-44; Air Officer Commanding-in-Chief, Fighter Command, 1944-1945; Member of Air Council for Training, Air Ministry, 1945-46; for Technical Services, 1946-48; Principal Air A.D.C. to the King, 1946-48; retired, 1948. Vice-Chancellor, Univ. of London, 1953-54. *Publication:* The Baghdad Air Mail. 1929. *Recreation:* art. *Address:* c/o Grindlay's Bank Ltd., 54 Parliament St., S.W.1. *Club:* Athenæum. [*Died* 6 *Oct.* 1954.

HILL, Thomas George, D.Sc., A.R.C.S.; Professor Emeritus of Plant Physiology in the University of London; Major (T.F. Ret.); *b.* London, 13 Feb. 1876; *s.* of Henry William Hill. *Educ.:* St. Olave's; Royal College of Science. Various Lectureships in Biology and Botany in the University of London; Assistant Professor of Botany, University College, London, 1910; Reader, 1912, and Professor, 1929, of Plant Physiology in the University of London; Head of the Department of Botany and Director of the Botanical Laboratories, University College, London, 1929; retired, 1945; President, Botany Section, British Association, Centenary Meeting, 1931. *Publications:* Chemistry of Plant Products, 1913 (with Dr. P. Haas); The Essentials of Illustration, 1915; numerous papers, chiefly on the anatomy, ecology and physiology of plants. *Recreation:* gardening. *Address:* Hambledon, Godalming, Surrey. [*Died* 25 *June* 1954.

HILL, Thomas William; *b.* 28 July 1866. Secretary of the Athenæum till 1936; Secretary to Herbert Spencer's Trustees till 1937 and Editor of final volumes of Descriptive Sociology founded by Herbert Spencer; Vice-President of the Dickens Fellowship; formerly Trustee of the Dickens House; for forty years a Church Organist (retired). *Publication:* Open-air Statues in London, 1910; numerous articles on Dickens' work. *Recreations:* music, archæology, London, annotating Dickens. *Address:* Hillsden, Madeira Avenue, Bromley, Kent. *T.:* Ravensbourne 1614. *Clubs:* Athenæum, Savage. [*Died* 29 *July* 1953.

HILL, Thomson; *see* Hill, W. T.

HILL, William Henry, M.A. Oxon; Licencié en Droit, Paris; *b.* 31 Jan. 1872; *s.* of late Henry Hill, Great Western Railway, Swindon; *m.* Mary Agnes (*d.* 1947), *d.* of Rev. F. W. Quilter, D.D.; one *s.* one *d.* *Educ.:* King's School, Worcester; Lincoln College, Oxford. Ministry of Education, Cairo, Egyptian Government; Lecturer, Khedivial School of Law, Cairo; Director, 1907-12; Chief Inspector of Native Tribunals, Ministry of Justice, 1912-14; Judge, Mixed Tribunal First Instance, Cairo, 1914-17; Judge, Native Court of Appeal, Cairo, 1917-25; Lecturer on Mohammedan and Turkish Law, University College, University of London, 1928; British Judge, Anglo-Turkish Arbitral Tribunal, Constantinople, 1928-32; Medjidieh 3rd Class, Nile 3rd Class. *Recreations:* formerly rowing, cricket, football, lawn tennis. *Address:* Country House Hotel, Crowborough, Sussex. *T.A.:* Crowborough. [*Died* 16 *Jan.* 1957.

HILL, (William) Thomson, F.S.A., F.J.I.; *b.* Peterborough, 1875; 2nd *s.* of Walter Hill, Peterborough, and Mary Jane, *er. d.* of William Cockey, Frome; *m.* 1900, Edith Gertrude (*d.* 1951), *e. d.* of Henry Jackson, Leighton Buzzard; no *c.* *Educ.:* The King's School, Peterborough (a King's Scholar). A Journalist, since 1893; The Times, since 1943; First Editor, Sunday Graphic; Acting Editor, Daily Sketch; Leader Writer, Daily Dispatch; deputy night editor of Morning Leader; editorial staff of Daily News, Daily Mail, Evening Standard, Daily Chronicle, etc.; served H.M. Forces, 1916-19, as private, 2/5 and 2/4 the Buffs, Lieut. R.N.V.R., Captain R.A.F. *Publications:* Edith Cavell, 1916; St. Saviour's, Dartmouth; through the Centuries, 1938; Buried London, 1955; Octavia Hill, 1956; contribs. to Encyclopædia Britannica, 1955, Oxford Junior Encyc., Adventure and Discovery, The Times Literary Supplement, The Fortnightly, Contemporary

Review. (Ed.) The Times Broadsheets, 1948; Old and True, 1946. Numerous articles on antiquarian, classical and historical subjects. *Clubs:* National Liberal, Press. [*Died* 9 *Feb.* 1959.

HILL WATSON, Hon. Lord; Laurence Hill Watson, M.C.; B.A. (Oxon), LL.B. (Glasgow); LL.D. (St. Andrews); one of the Senators of the College of Justice in Scotland since 1952; Judge of Restrictive Practices Court since 1957; *b.* 26 February 1895; *s.* of Thomas Watson, Glasgow; *m.* 1918, Margery Winifred Broadberry; two *d.* *Educ.:* Fettes College, Edinburgh; Oriel College, Oxford; Glasgow University (Law). Served European War, 5 Bn. Highland Light Infantry, 1914-19 (M.C.); called to Scottish Bar, 1921; K.C. (Scot.) 1937; Q.C. (Scot.) 1952. Advocate Depute, 1936-37, 1938-45; Sheriff of Perth and Angus, 1948-52. *Recreation:* golf. *Address:* Barlanark, Arboretum Road, Edinburgh. *T.:* 83388. *Club:* New (Edinburgh). [*Died* 22 *Aug.* 1957.

HILL-WOOD, Capt. Sir Basil Samuel Hill, 2nd Bt., *cr.* 1921; Grenadier Guards; *b.* 5 Feb. 1900; *e. s.* of Major Sir Samuel Hill-Wood, 1st Bt. and Hon. Decima Bateman Hanbury, 6th *d.* of 2nd Lord Bateman; *S.* father 1949; *m.* 1925, Hon. Joan Louisa Brand, *e. d.* of 3rd Viscount Hampden, G.C.V.O., K.C.B.; one *s.* one *d.* *Educ.:* Eton; Trinity Coll., Cambridge. *Heir: s.* David Basil, *b.* 12 Nov. 1926. *Address:* Dacre Farm, Farley Hill, nr. Reading, Berks. *Club:* White's. [*Died* 3 *July* 1954.

HILLARY, Albert Ernest, J.P.; *b.* 20 Jan. 1868; *s.* of John Hillary, Dans Castle, Tow Law, Co. Durham; *m.* 1897, Annie Maud Mary (*d.* 1945), *d.* of William Bartleet, Sparkhill; one *s.* one *d.* Late Managing Director of Carsons, Ltd., chocolate manufacturers, Glasgow. Contested Barnard Castle, 1918; M.P. (L.) Harwich Division of Essex, 1922-24. *Address:* Royston, Frinton-on-Sea. *T.:* Frinton 519. *Club:* National Liberal. [*Died* 10 *Feb.* 1954.

HILLIARD, Harvey, C.B.E. 1922; M.R.C.S. (Eng.), L.R.C.P. and D.P.H. (Lond.); M.D.(Zürich); (retired); Consulting Anæsthetist Royal Dental Hospital, late Lecturer on Anæsthetics at the Medical School; temporary Lieut. R.A.F., Medical Service; Originator of the Empire Hospital for Paying Patients; *e. s.* of late Robert Harvey Hilliard, M.D., F.R.C.S. Ed.; *m.* 1st, 1900, Charlotte Hazell; two *s.*; 2nd, 1925, Margaret Rustat, *d.* of late Dr. A. Hemsted. *Educ.:* Epsom College; Charing Cross Hospital; St George's Hospital. Formerly Demonstrator of Anatomy, Charing Cross Hospital, and Resident Medical Superintendent of St. George's, Hanover Square Provident Dispensary; joined the Colonial Medical Service as Registrar in Charge Ceylon Medical College and Assistant to P.C.M.O.; Lecturer on Public Health, Ceylon Medical College and Surgeon, Ear, Nose and Throat Hospital, Colombo; late Anæsthetist to King George Military Hospital, the French Hospital, and Charing Cross Hospital; formerly: Liveryman of the Worshipful Company of Glass-sellers; a member of the Knights of the Round Table Club; Instructor in Anæsthetics at London Hospital. *Publications:* A Method of prolonging Nitrous Oxide Anæsthesia in Dental Practice; Ethyl Chloride as an Anæsthetic in General Practice; The Administration of Anæsthetics to Children; A Plea for the Infants; Some Meteorological Effects upon Nitrous Oxide Anæsthesia; and (with Mr. F. Coleman) Anæsthetics in Dental Surgery; The Medical Perspective of Multiple Extractions and other Major Dental Operations, 1928. *Address:* 1 Gardens Crescent, Lilliput, Parkstone, Dorset. *T.:* Canford Cliffs 77817. *Club:* Royal Air Force (Hon. Life Member). [*Died* 17 *Feb.* 1956.

HILLIARD, Rt. Rev. William George, Th.D., M.A.; Rector of St. John's, Parramatta, N.S.W., and Coadjutor Bishop of Sydney since 1940. *Educ.:* Sydney University. Bishop of Nelson, N.Z., 1934-40. *Address:* St. John's Rectory, Parramatta, Sydney, N.S.W. [*Died* 1 *Feb.* 1960.

HILLIER, Frank Norton; retired, 1957; *b.* 2 February 1894; 2nd *s.* of late F. J. Hillier, a Director of the Daily News; *m.* 1917, Kathleen, *y. d.* of John Platts Hughes, Berkswell, Warwickshire; one *s.* *Educ.:* Dulwich College. Assistant Paris Correspondent of the Daily News, 1912-1913; on the staff o the Daily Mail, 1913-22; Special Correspondent, France, U.S.A., and other appointments; Assistant New York Correspondent, Daily Mail and Times, 1919-1922; later appointed London Correspondent, New York Sun; joined Westminster Gazette, 1924; Managing Editor of the Westminster Gazette until amalgamation with Daily News and then on staff of Daily News; Paris Correspondent News-Chronicle, 1933-35; Foreign Editor of the Daily Mail, 1935-38; Press and Publicity Officer, Ministry of Home Security, 1938-41; Publicity Controller, B.O.A.C., 1941-48; B.S.A.A., 1948-49; Royal Field Artillery (Special Reserve), 1915-19 (M.C.). Secretary-General of the Air League of the British Empire, and Editor, Air Pictorial, 1950-57. *Publications:* England's Industrial Salvation, 1930; essays and articles on military and civil aviation. *Recreations:* music, growing fruit and keeping chickens. *Address:* 157 The Vale, Southgate, N.14. *Club:* Royal Aero. [*Died* 26 *Jan.* 1959.

HILLINGDON, 3rd Baron, *cr.* 1886; **Arthur Robert Mills,** D.L.; Bt. 1868; partner in Glyn, Mills and Co., Bankers, and a Director of Union Bank of Australia; Chairman Marine Insurance Company; *b.* 19 Oct. 1891; *s.* of 2nd Baron and Hon. Alice Marion Harbord, 2nd *d.* of 5th Baron Suffield; *S.* father, 1919; *m.* 1916, Hon. Edith Mary Winifred Cadogan, D.B.E., *cr.* 1939, *d.* of late Viscount Chelsea; one *s.* three *d.* *Educ.:* Eton, Magdalen College, Oxford. Went with West Kent Yeomanry to Gallipoli, Sept. 1915; recalled on death of brother to stand for Parliament; transferred to Reserve of Officers, May 1916; M.P. (U.) Uxbridge Division of Middlesex, 1915-18. *Heir: s.* Hon. Charles Hedworth Mills, 2nd Lt. Life Guards [*b.* 12 Jan. 1922; *m.* 1947, Lady Sarah Stuart, 2nd *d.* of 18th Earl of Moray; one *s.* one *d.*]. *Address:* The Gote, Hassocks, Sussex. *T.:* Plumpton 328. *Club:* Royal Yacht Squadron (Cowes). [*Died* 5 *Dec.* 1952.

HILLS, Sir Andrew Ashton Waller, 1st Bt., *cr.* 1939; *b.* 29 Oct. 1933; *o. s.* of late Rt. Hon. John Waller Hills (*d.* 1938, before his intended nomination to a Baronetcy) and Mary Grace, *er. d.* of late Leon Dominic Ashton. *Educ.:* Oratory School; Balliol College, Oxford. *Address:* 34 Brunswick Gardens, Kensington W.8. *T.:* Bayswater 6503. [*Died* 4 *Feb.* 1955 (*ext.*).

HILTON, James; Author; *b.* 9 Sept. 1900. *Educ.:* Leys School, Cambridge; Christ's College, Cambridge. *Publications:* Novels: Catherine Herself, 1920; And Now Goodbye, 1931; Contango, 1932; Knight Without Armour, 1933; Lost Horizon (awarded Hawthornden Prize, 1934), 1933; Goodbye, Mr. Chips, 1934 (dramatised 1938); We Are Not Alone, 1937; To You, Mr. Chips, 1938; Random Harvest, 1941; The Story of Dr. Wassell, 1944; So Well Remembered, 1945; Nothing So Strange, 1947; Morning Journey, 1951, Time and Time Again, 1953, etc. *Recreations:* travel, mountain-climbing. *Address:* c/o John Farquharson, 8 Halsey House, Red Lion Square, W.C.1. [*Died* 20 *Dec.* 1954.

HIMBURY, Sir William Henry, Kt., *cr.* 1926; M.A.; Chairman of the British Cotton Growing Association; Member of Council of Empire Cotton Growing Corpora-

tion; Director of the B.C.G.A. (Punjab), Ltd.; Member of the Governing Body of the Imperial College of Tropical Agriculture; Hon. M.A. Manchester University, 1930. *Publications:* numerous connected with cotton growing within the British Empire. *Recreations:* travel, various. *Address:* 333-350 Royal Exchange, Manchester. *Clubs:* East India and Sports; Union (Manchester).
[*Died* 28 *Nov.* 1955.

HIND, Arthur Mayger, O.B.E. 1918; M.A., F.S.A.; Hon. R.E.; Hon. LL.D. (Glasgow); Historian of Engraving; *b.* Burton-on-Trent, 26 Aug. 1880; 2nd *s.* of late Henry Robert Hind, F.C.S.; *m.* 1912, Hon. Dorothy Alice Pakington, 3rd *d.* of 3rd Lord Hampton; three *d.* *Educ.:* City of London School; Emmanuel College, Cambridge. 1st Class Classical Tripos, 1902; entered British Museum, 1903; served European War, France, 1915-19 (despatches); Slade Professor of Fine Art in the University of Oxford, 1921-27; Charles Eliot Norton Prof. of Poetry, Harvard Univ., 1930-31; Leverhulme Research Fellowship, 1945; Keeper of Prints and Drawings, British Museum, 1933-45; invited to lecture by National Gallery, Washington, 1949. *Publications:* Works of Native and Foreign Line-engravers in England from Henry VIII. to the Commonwealth (British Museum, 1905); Short History of Engraving and Etching, 1908 (3rd ed., 1923); Catalogue of Early Italian Engravings in the British Museum, 1910; Great Engravers, 12 vols., 1911-13; Rembrandt's Etchings (2nd ed., 1923); Catalogue of Drawings by Dutch and Flemish Artists in the British Museum, 1915-31; Hollar and his Views of London, 1922; Piranesi and his Views of Rome, 1922; etchings of D. Y. Cameron, 1924; Drawings of Claude Lorrain, 1925; Claude Lorrain and Modern Art (Rede Lecture), 1926; Rembrandt (Norton Lectures), 1932; History of Woodcut, 1935; Nielli in the British Museum, 1936; Early Italian Engraving, 7 vols., 1938, 1948; Engraving in England in the 16th and 17th Centuries, 1952, etc. *Recreations:* music, drawing. *Address:* Saragossa House, Henley-on-Thames. *T.:* Henley 33. *Club:* Athenæum.
[*Died* 22 *May* 1957.

HIND, Rt. Rev. John, M.A., D.D.; *b.* Belfast, 17 Feb. 1879; *e. s.* of John Hind, engineer, and Margaret McVicker; *m.* 1st, 1904, Alice Carpenter (*d.* 1908), Cheltenham; one *s.*; 2nd, 1928, Florence Winifred, M.D., *yr. d.* of George B. Heyworth, Fremont, West Derby, Liverpool. *Educ.:* Coleraine Academical Institution; Trinity College, Dublin. Ordained, 1902; went to China, 1902; Missionary of the Dublin University Fukien Mission, 1902-18; Headmaster of Middle School, Trinity College, Foochow, 1911-18; Bishop in Fukien, 1918-40; C.M.S. organising secretary in Northern Ireland, 1940; retired. *Recreation:* astronomy. *Address:* Nantai, Ballyfinaghy, Belfast.
[*Died* 7 *July* 1958.

HINDE, Rev. Herbert William, M.A., Hon. C.F.; retd.; *b.* 1877; 2nd *s.* of Frank P. Hinde, Norwich; *m.* Kathleen, 4th *d.* of Alderman John Yeomans, Burton-on-Trent; one *d.* (and one *d.* decd.). *Educ.:* private; Pembroke Coll.; Ridley Hall, Camb. Ordained 1900; Curate, St. Andrews the Less, Barnwell, Camb., 1900-5; St. James, Hatcham, S.E., 1905-9; Vicar of St. John the Baptist, Ipswich, 1909-21; Chaplain, St. John's Home, Ipswich, 1909-21; East Suffolk Hospital, 1914-15; Ipswich Workhouse and Infirmary, 1916-21; Vicar of Islington and Rural Dean 1921-32; Hon. Canon, St. Edmundsbury and Ipswich, 1919-21; Chaplain to the Forces, 1918-19; Hon. C.F., 1919; Chaplain London Fever Hospital, 1921-32; Principal Oak Hill Theological College, 1932-1945; Vicar of Fairlight, Hastings, 1945-48. Proctor in Convocation, 1924-50; Prebendary, St. Paul's, 1928-50. *Address:* 11 Gorringe Rd., Eastbourne, Sussex. *T.:* Eastbourne 3361. [*Died* 1 *Oct.* 1955.

HINDLE, Sir Frederick, Kt., *cr.* 1943; *b.* 1877; *s.* of late Frederick George Hindle; *m.* Alys, *d.* of James Lawrence, J.P., of Anderton Hall, Chorley. *Educ.:* Charterhouse; Owens College, Manchester. Admitted solicitor, 1899; 1st Class Honours; Clement's Inn Prizeman and Daniel Reardon Scholar; served World War, 1914-19 (Lieut. Chevalier Légion d'honneur and Croix de Guerre and two palms); Clerk to Darwen Justices; Mayor of Darwen, 1912-13; Alderman Lancashire County Council; contested Darwen Division, 1918 and 1922; M.P. (L.) 1923-24; contested 1924; Deputy Regional Commissioner for Civil Defence, North Western Region, 1941-45; Chm. Hosp. Management Cttee. Blackburn and East Lancs Group; Chm. Lancashire Parish Councils Association. *Address:* Astley House, Whitehall Rd., Darwen, Lancashire.
[*Died* 23 *April* 1953.

HINDS, Benjamin, J.P.; Chairman, Milk Marketing Board, since 1949; *b.* 3 Sept. 1882; *s.* of James and Elizabeth Hinds; *m.* 1910, Bariah Thomas; one *s.* one *d.* *Educ.:* White Mill British School, Carms.; Old College, Carmarthen. Drapery business, 1897-1906; Farming, 1906-39. Member for South Wales Region Milk Marketing Board (England and Wales), 1933; Vice-Chm. Milk Marketing Board, 1934. *Address:* Bron Tywi, Carmarthen. *T.:* Carmarthen 7350. *Club:* National Liberal.
[*Died* 30 *March* 1952.

HINDS HOWELL, Conrad Meredyth; *see* Howell.

HINE-HAYCOCK, Rev. Trevitt Reginald, M.V.O. 1931; M.A.; Vicar of Christ Church, Greyfriars, E.C.1, and Rector of St. Leonard, Foster Lane, since 1912; Hon. Priest to the Queen since 1952 (formerly to King George VI); *b.* 3 Dec. 1861; *s.* of W. Hine-Haycock, The Priory, Shrewsbury and Belmont, Sidmouth; *m.* 1915, Grace Josephine Thornton (*d.* 1945), *d.* of Preb. Joseph Salvin, and *widow* of Walter Thornton. *Educ.:* Woodcote House, Windlesham; Wellington College (Cricket XI., 1878-1880, Capt. 1880); New College, Oxford (Capt. Cricket XI., Oxford University Cricket XI., 1883-84; Hon. Sec. 1884). Called to Bar, 1886; ordained, 1890; Curate successively of Rotherham, St. Giles in the Fields, and St. Michael's, Cornhill; Curate in charge of St. Michael's 1903-1906; Minor Canon of Westminster, 1895-1912; Custodian, 1902-9; Precentor, 1909-12. Priest in Ordinary to the King, 1905-31. *Address:* Hill House, Bedford. *T.:* Bedford 2145.
[*Died* 2 *Nov.* 1953.

HINTON, Mrs Arthur; *see* Goodson, Katharine.

HINWOOD, George Yorke; Director: Lloyds Bank, since 1957; Bank of British West Africa Limited, since 1955; Anglo-Israel Bank Ltd., since 1959; Richard Costain Limited, since 1958; *b.* 20 May 1894; *s.* of late Frederick Louis and Martha Hinwood; *m.* 1941, Kathleen Mary, *o. c.* of Maimie and late Roy Wylie, Bromley, Kent; one *s.* one *d.* *Educ.:* Clevedon College, Somerset. Entered Wilts and Dorset Bank, 1910 (later absorbed by Lloyds Bank). Served European War, Army, 1916-18. Attached to London and River Plate Bank, Argentine, Chile Uruguay and Brazil, 1922-24; India (Lloyds Bank), 1928-33; Joint General Manager, Lloyds Bank, 1951; Chief General Manager, Lloyds Bank, Limited, 1954-57. *Recreations:* gardening and foreign travel. *Address:* Redroofs, Edward Road, Bromley, Kent. *T.:* Ravensbourne 3587. [*Died* 26 *Nov.* 1960.

HIPPISLEY, Richard John Bayntun, C.B.E. 1937 (O.B.E. 1915); J.P.; D.L.; M.I.E.E.; Comdr. R.N.V.R. Ret.; Traffic Commissioner Western Area; County Alderman for Somerset; *s.* of John and Christine Ellen Lydia Hippisley; *m.* 1905, Constance Amy, (*d.* 1955), *d.* of late A. L. Francis, Head Master of Blundell's School, Tiverton; two *s.* one *d.* *Educ.:* Rugby; Faraday House. Served in Naval Intelligence Division, 1914-20. *Address:*

Ston Easton Park, Nr. Bath. *Clubs:* Junior Carlton, Royal Automobile, Royal Aero. [*Died* 27 *March* 1956.

HIRACHAND, Walchand; Chairman of Premier Automobiles Limited; *b.* Sholapur, 1882. *Educ.:* Sholapur, Poona, and Bombay. Took large contracts for construction of railway lines, river bridges, large military barracks, Quetta Reconstruction Works for Military Authorities, etc.; Municipal Water Supply Scheme of Bombay, Bhore Ghat Tunnel Work for G.I.P. Railway, Victoria Terminus Remodelling, Chola Power House and Bridge, works for G.I.P. Railway, and other large public buildings, etc.; President: Indian Merchants' Chamber, Bombay, 1927; Maharashtra Chamber of Commerce, 1927-38; Indian National Cttee. of Internat. Chamber of Commerce, 1931-33; Federation of Indian Chambers of Commerce and Industry, 1932-33; All India Organisation of Industrial Employers, 1933-34; Vice-Pres., International Chamber of Commerce, Paris, 1934-35 and 1936-37; was President Indian National Shipowners' Association; was a member of Governing Body of Imperial Agricultural Research Council of Government of India for five years; Employers Delegate to the International Labour Conference at Geneva, 1932; Leader of the Indian Delegation to Congresses of International Chamber of Commerce at Berlin, 1937, and Copenhagen 1939. *Address:* Construction House, Ballard Estate, Bombay, India. *T.A.:* Hincon, Bombay. *T.:* 26036 (five lines) Office, 41877 Residence. [*Died* 8 *April* 1953.

HIRSCH, Paul Adolf; retired from business; engaged on private research in Music-History and Bibliography; *b.* Frankfurt a/Main, Germany, 24 Feb. 1881; *s.* of late Ferdinand Hirsch; *m.* 1911, Olga A. H., *d.* of Ernst Ladenburg, President of Chamber of Commerce, Frankfurt; two *s.* two *d.* *Educ.:* Städt. Gymnasium (Municipal College), Frankfurt a/Main. After leaving College worked with firms in London and Paris; partner of Hirsch and Co., Frankfurt, Iron Merchants, 1907-36, when firm was sold; Vice-Pres. Frankfurt Chamber of Commerce, and on Board of many commercial and official organisations until 1933; began about 1900 forming a private Library of Music; this was open to the public for research work, 1909-36, when, for political reasons, he left Germany and the Library was removed to England; after being on loan at the University Library, Cambridge, for 10 years, the collection was in 1946 acquired for the nation and is now housed at the British Museum; he was also founder of Frankfurter Bibliophilen-Gesellschaft (Pres. 1922-33), at the same time being a member of many learned societies. *Publications:* Katalog einer Mozart-Bibliothek, 1906; Katalog der Musikbibliothek P.H. Vol. 1-4; Editor of Veröffentlichungen der Musikbibliothek P.H., 12 vols., 1922-45; contributions on musical, typographical, and bibliographical subjects to various periodicals. *Recreations:* music, collecting books. *Address:* 10 Adams Road, Cambridge. *T.:* Cambridge 5288. *Club:* Reform. [*Died* 25 *Nov.* 1951.

HIRST, Sir Amos (Brook), Kt., *cr.* 1954; O.B.E. 1948; retired; Director Huddersfield Building Society; Trustee Huddersfield Savings Bank; *b.* 6 Dec. 1878; *s.* of Benjamin and Hannah Hirst; *m.* 1906, Violet Hilda Woolven; one *d.* (one *s.* decd.). *Educ.:* Huddersfield College. Solicitor in private practice, 1901-27; Registrar of County Courts, and District Registrar of High Courts, Huddersfield, Halifax and Dewsbury, 1927-49, when retired. Chairman Football Assoc. Long Service Medal, Special Constabulary, with 2 Bars. Chevalier de la Légion d'Honneur, 1953. *Recreation:* (later years) golf. *Address:* Brookleigh, 46 New Hey Rd., Huddersfield. *T.:* Huddersfield 1523. *Club:* Huddersfield (Huddersfield). [*Died* 26 *Nov.* 1955.

HIRST, Francis W.; *b.* 1873; *s.* of Alfred Hirst and Mary Wrigley, both of Huddersfield; *m.* 1903, Helena, *d.* of Charles Cobden. *Educ.:* Clifton College; Wadham College, Oxford (Scholar). 1st Cl. Classical Mods.; 1st Cl. Lit. Hum. 1896; Pres. Oxford Union Soc.; Russell Studentship; Cobden Prize. Barr.-at-Law, 1899; editor of The Economist, 1907-16; Lectured on Political Economy in California, 1921, and South Africa, 1923; a Governor of the London School of Economics; Hon. Secretary of Cobden Club. Contested (Ind. L.) South Suffolk and Shipley. Hon. Fellow of Wadham College, Oxford. *Publications:* part author of Essays in Liberalism; Local Government in England (with J. Redlich), 2 vols., 1903; Adam Smith, 1904; Trusts and Cartels, 1905; The Arbiter in Council, 1906; Stock Exchange, 1911; Progress of the Nation, 1912; Political Economy of War, 1915; From Adam Smith to Philip Snowden, 1925; Life of Thomas Jefferson, 1926; Early Life and Letters of John Morley, 1927; Safeguarding and Protection, 1928; Wall Street and Lombard Street, 1931; Gladstone as Financier and Economist, 1931; Gold, Silver and Paper Money, 1933; Consequences of the War to Great Britain, 1934; Liberty and Tyranny and Economic Freedom, 1935; Armaments, 1937; Free Markets or Monopoly, 1942; Problems and Fallacies of Political Economy, 1943; Foreign Policy, Past and Future, 1944; Principles of Prosperity, 1945; Repeal of the Corn Laws, 1946; In the Golden Days, 1948. *Recreations:* angling, chess. *Club:* National Liberal. [*Died* 22 *Feb.* 1953.

HIRST, Reginald John, C.I.E. 1927; *b.* 11 July 1880. *Educ.:* Rossall; Pembroke College, Cambridge (B.A. 1912). Entered Indian Police Service, 1901; Inspector-General of Police, Bihar and Orissa, 1931; retired 1934. *Address:* Kastane, Greville Park Road, Ashtead, Surrey. [*Died* 16 *July* 1959.

HITCH, Frederick Brook, F.R.B.S.; sculptor; *b.* 7 Nov. 1877; *s.* of Sarah Anne and late Nathaniel Hitch, sculptor; *m.* 1911, c. Ivy Emily Hitch; one *s.* one *d.* *Educ.:* Tunbridge Wells (privately); City Guilds Institute; Royal Academy Schools. *Address:* Allestree, Highfield Road, Hertford. *T.:* 3701; *Studio:* Highfield Road, Hertford. *Club:* Chelsea Arts. [*Died* 30 *April* 1957

HITCHCOCK, Sir Eldred (Frederick), Kt. 1955; C.B.E. 1920; F.S.A.; Chevalier Order of Crown of Belgium; St. Stanislas (2nd class); Chairman: Tanganyika Sisal Growers Association; Bird & Co. (Africa), Ltd.; *b.* 1887; *s.* of Eldred and Louie Naomi Hitchcock; *m.* 1915, Patricia (*d.* 1956), *d.* of Adolphus Lorie, New Zealand; one *s.* one *d.* *Educ.:* Economics Diploma, Oxford, 1910. Warden of Toynbee Hall (resigned, 1919); Life Fell. Roy. Statistical Soc.; during European War, 1914-18, Govt. Wool Statistician and Dep.-Dir. of Wool Textiles, War Office; Member of Wool Control Board; War Office Representative on War Trade Department, and Comité International de Ravitaillement; Assistant Director of Raw Materials; Chairman, Standard Clothing Committee. *Publications:* mainly articles on sisal industry, and general economic subjects in The Times, Encyclopædia Britannica, etc. *Address:* Tanga, Tanganyika. *Clubs:* Arts, Chelsea Arts; Tanga, Dar-es-Salaam (Tanganyika); Zanzibar (Zanzibar); Nairobi, Muthaiga (Kenya). [*Died* 6 *April* 1959.

HITCHCOCK, Rev. Francis Ryan Montgomery, D.D. (T.C.D.); Litt.D. (T.C.D.) 1949; Rector of Tolleshunt Knights; *b.* Dublin 1867; *e. s.* of late George R. Hitchcock (Dublin and London) C.E., the *g.-g.s.* of the Chevalier de Johnstone (Memoirs of Scottish Rebellion); *m.* 1st, K., *d.* of late Capt. R. Ingram (D.F.B.); one *s.* (and one *s.* decd.); 2nd, Mrs. A. I. Traill, *d.* of late Capt. R. Gage, Sherwood Foresters, Bellarena,

Derry. *Educ.:* Trinity College, Dublin. Univ. student (Classics); double first at degree (First of First and First); Fellowship Prizeman (three times); Donnellan Lecturer T.C.D. 1912; Rector of Kinnitty, King's Co., 1903-24; Examining Chaplain to the Bishop of Killaloe, 1918-24. *Publications:* The Atonement and Modern Thought (Donnellan Lectures); Irenaeus of Lugdunum; Fresh Study of the Fourth Gospel; Celtic Types of Life and Art; Midland Septs and the Pale; St. Patrick and his Gallic Friends; The Holy Communion in the New Testament; Christ's Answer to Our Questions; The Reformation in England and Ireland; Gospel Miracles; Controversy on Prayer; Harvest Thoughts; Hebrew Types; Christ and His Critics; St. Augustine's City of God (Trans.); The Mystery of the Cross; The Present and the Future Christ; A Translation of Irenaeus; Clement of Alexandria; Transubstantiation, The Roman Dogma examined; frequent contributions to ecclesiastical journals. *Recreations:* swimming, Latin verse, and walking. *Address:* The Rectory, Tolleshunt Knights, Maldon, Essex. *T.A.:* Tiptree. *T.:* Tiptree 12. [*Died* 10 *April* 1951.

HITCHINS, Colonel Charles Faunce, D.S.O. 1919; late 3rd Bn. the Queen's Own Royal West Kent Regt.; 2nd *s.* of late Edward Bulwer Lytton-Hitchins, Exeter; *m.* Anne (*d.* 1956), *e. d.* of late Andrew Moseley, F.R.I.B.A. *Educ.:* Dulwich College. Apprenticed with Maudslay Sons & Field Ltd., Engineers at Lambeth, S.E.; M.I.Mech.E.; M.I.N.A.; of Hitchins, Jervis, and Partners, Consulting Engineers, 40 Broadway, Westminster, S.W.1. Served European War, France, 1914-18 (despatches, D.S.O.). Member: Worshipful Co. of Broderers; The Pilgrims. *Clubs:* United Service, Royal Automobile, British Sportsman's, Savage, Hurlingham; Militia. [*Died* 12 *Sept.* 1959.

HITCHINS, Brigadier Edward Norman Fortescue, C.B.E. 1941; D.S.O. 1919; M.C.; *b.* 16 Jan. 1884; *s.* of late Tom Fortescue Hitchins, Truro; *m.* 1915, Frances Dorothy, *d.* of Alec Warde, Sevenoaks; one *s.* three *d.* *Educ.:* Dulwich College. 2nd Lt., Duke of Wellington's Regt., 1904; served European War. 1914-18 as Regimental Signals and Staff Officer (despatches, D.S.O., M.C., Brevet of Major); transferred Royal Signals, 1920; Brevet of Lt.-Col., 1927; Substantive Lt.-Col., 1928; Colonel, 1932; Chief Signal Officer, Eastern Command, 1933-37; Signal Officer in Chief, India, 1938. *Address:* Border Lodge, North Brewham, Bruton, Somerset. *T.:* Upton Noble 278. *Club:* Army and Navy. [*Died* 16 *April* 1959.

HOARE, Arthur Hervey; Managing Partner C. Hoare & Co., Bankers; *b.* 25 July 1877; 2nd *s.* of Charles Hoare and Katherine P. G., *d.* of Lord Arthur Hervey, Bishop of Bath and Wells; *m.* 1912, Anna Margaret, *d.* of Rear-Admiral Samuel Long. *Educ.:* Eton College; Christ Church, Oxford. Served European War, 1914-18, Lt. Wessex Hants R.G.A. (T.); invalided home 1916; Financial Censorship War Office; Instructor to Heavy Batteries, Larkhill and Colchester. *Recreations:* shooting, trout fishing, yachting. *Address:* East Lane, Ovington, Alresford, Hants. *T.:* Alresford 115. *Clubs:* Travellers'; Royal Yacht Squadron. [*Died* 9 *Dec.* 1953.

HOARE, Maj.-Gen. Francis Richard Gurney, C.B. 1944; C.B.E. 1919; Reserve of Officers, U.D.F.; *b.* 1879; *s.* of late Charles Richard Gurney Hoare; *m.* Melicent, *d.* of R. K. Loveday, M.L.A.; one *d.* *Educ.:* Harrow; Trinity, Cambridge. Served S. Africa, 1899-1900; European War, 1914-19 (despatches, C.B.E.); War of 1939-45 (C.B.). *Address:* 939 Schoeman Street, Pretoria, S. Africa. *Club:* R.A.F. [*Died* 29 *May* 1959.

HOARE, Lieut.-Colonel Geoffrey Lennard, C.B.E. 1918; Retired, R.F.A.; a Managing Partner in Hoare's Bank; Director Messrs. Hoare Trustees; *b.* 10 April 1879; *e. s.* of late William Hoare, of Staplehurst, and Laura, 2nd *d.* of Sir John Lennard, 1st Baronet, of Wickham Court, West Wickham, Kent; *m.* 1922, Lady Alma Stopford, *d.* of 6th Earl of Courtown; one *s.* two *d.* *Educ.:* Eton; Christ Church, Oxford. Secretary, Hoare's Brewery, 1904-9; Director of Agencies, 1909-1914; 2nd Lieut. Eton College Volunteers, 1897; Kent Artillery Militia, 1898; served South Africa, 1901-2 (Queen's medal three clasps); Captain, 1902; resigned commission in Kent R.F.A. Special Reserve, 1908; served in European War as G.S.O. in charge of economic and miscellaneous section of Directorate of Military Intelligence, War Office, 1914-18 (despatches, C.B.E., Bt. Lt.-Col., Croix de Chevalier, Légion d'Honneur). A Master of Christ Church, 1956. *Recreations:* cricket, shooting. *Address:* 37 Fleet Street, E.C.4; Summerhill, Benenden, Cranbrook, Kent. *T.:* Benenden 3113. *Clubs:* Travellers', M.C.C. [*Died* 28 *Feb.* 1960.

HOARE, Henry, J.P., Hampshire; partner in Hoare's Bank; *b.* 25 Dec. 1866; *e. s.* of late H. Hoare of Iden, Staplehurst, and *d.* of Rev. G. B. Paley; m. 1898, Lady Geraldine (*d.* 1955), 2nd *d.* of late Lord Augustus Hervey and Lady Augustus Hervey of Hampton Court Palace; two *s.* one *d.* *Educ.:* Eton; Trinity College, Cambridge. Major Loyal Suffolk Hussars; Dep. Dir. of Milk Supplies, Ministry of Food, 1916-18. Member of Basingstoke R.D.C., 1926-46. *Publications:* Flowering Trees and Shrubs; Spade-work. *Recreations:* golf, gardening, and travel. *Address:* Ellisfield Manor, Basingstoke. *T.:* Herriard 259; White Wings, Angmering-on-Sea; La Lucertola, Lago di Como, Italy; 37 Fleet Street, E.C.4. *Clubs:* Leander; Basingstoke Golf. [*Died* 29 *July* 1956.

HOARE, Oliver Vaughan Gurney; *b.* 18 July 1882; *yr. s.* of Sir Samuel Hoare, 1st Bt., of Sidestrand, Cromer; *b.* (and *heir-pres.* to Baronetcy of) 1st Viscount Templewood, Bt.; *m.* 1906, Phoebe Alice Van Neck; no *c.* *Educ.:* Harrow; New College, Oxford. *Recreations:* shooting and tennis, etc.; played rackets for Harrow, 1900, tennis for Oxford, 1904. *Address:* 1 Swan Walk, S.W.3. *Club:* Carlton. [*Died* 6 *May* 1957.

HOARE, Sir Reginald Hervey, K.C.M.G., *cr.* 1933 (C.M.G. 1926); 4th *s.* of Charles Hoare and Katharine, *d.* of Lord Arthur Hervey, Bishop of Bath and Wells; *m.* Lucy Joan Cavendish Bentinck; one *s.* *Educ.:* Eton College. Passed into Diplomatic Service, 1905; served at Constantinople, Rome, Peking, Petrograd, Foreign Office, Warsaw, and Cairo; British Minister at Teheran, 1931-34; Minister in Bucharest, 1935-41; retired, 1942; remained in Government service until spring of 1944 when he joined the family bank in Fleet Street. *Recreations:* fishing, gardening. *Clubs:* Travellers', M.C.C. [*Died* 12 *Aug.* 1954.

HOBART, Major-General Sir Percy Cleghorn Stanley, K.B.E., *cr.* 1943 (O.B.E. 1919); C.B. 1939; D.S.O. 1916; M.C.; p.s.c.; *b.* 14 June 1885; *s.* of late R. T. Hobart, I.C.S., and Janetta, *d.* of C. Stanley, Roughan Park, Tyrone; *m.* 1928, Dorothea, *d.* of late Col. C. Field, Royal Marines; one *d.* *Educ.:* Temple Grove; Clifton College. Joined Royal Eng., 1904; to India and joined 1st Sappers and Miners, 1906; served Mohmand Expedition, N.W. Frontier, 1908 (medal and clasp); Staff Delhi Durbar, 1911; with 1st S. and M. in France, 1915; present at Neuve Chapelle (M.C.); Festubert, May 1915, and September Offensive, 1915; General Staff, Sept. 1915; Mesopotamia, 1916-18 (D.S.O., Bt. Maj.; wounded, prisoner of war); Palestine, 1918

(O.B.E.) (Despatches six times); Waziristan Force, 1921 (despatches, Bt. Lt.-Col.); Royal Tank Corps, 1923; Bt. Col. 1928; Lt.-Col. 1930; Col. 1933; Inspector Royal Tank Corps, 1933-36; Commander Tank Brigade, 1934-37; Deputy Director of Staff Duties, War Office, 1937; Maj.-Gen., 1937; Director of Military Training, War Office, 1937-38; raised 7th Armoured Division, Egypt, 1938-39; retired pay, 1940: re-employed, 1941. Raised 11th Armoured Division, 1941-42; raised 79th (specialised) Armoured Division, 1942, and commanded it throughout N.W. Europe till 1945 (despatches thrice, K.B.E., Comdr. U.S. Legion of Merit); reverted to retired pay, 1946. Col. Comdt. R.T.R., 1947-51 (Rep. 1948-1951). Lieutenant Governor Royal Hospital, Chelsea, 1948-53. *Address:* Bull Lodge, Trebor Ave., Farnham, Surrey. *T.:* 6471. *Clubs:* United Service, R.T.R. Officers'.
[*Died* 19 *Feb.* 1957.

HOBART, Robert Charles Arthur Stanley, C.I.E. 1937; I.C.S.; *b.* Naini Tal, U.P., India, 27 July 1881; *e. s.* of Robert Thompson Hobart, Bengal Civil Service, and Janetta Stanley, Dungannon, Co. Tyrone, Ireland; *m.* 1915, Elsie, *y. d.* of George Hinds, Goudhurst, Kent; one *s.* one *d.* *Educ.:* Temple Grove; Charterhouse; Trinity College, Oxford. I.C.S., 1905; Assistant Commissioner or Collector, 1905-18; Collector, 1918-31; Divisional Commissioner, 1931-37. *Address:* May Cottage, Mayfield, Sussex. *T.A.:* Mayfield, Sussex. *T.:* Mayfield 2236. *Club:* Royal Empire Society.
[*Died* 20 *Oct.* 1955.

HOBBINS, Thomas Phillips, C.B.E. 1919; Lt.-Col. R.E.; *b.* 1877; *m.* 1899, F. Isabel, *d.* of late B. Ingham; one *s.* one *d.* Served with Army Postal Service, France and Italy, European War, 1914-19 (despatches twice, C.B.E., Officer of Order of Crown of Italy); Regional Director, North-Eastern Region, G.P.O., 1935-39 (retired); late C.S. (12th Middx.) V.R. and R.E.S.R.; Amateur Champion of Fencing, England, Sabres, 1899, 1900, and 1902, foils, 1901. *Recreations:* music and golf. *Address:* c/o Lloyds Bank, Park Row, Leeds 1. [*Died* 13 *Jan.* 1959.

HOBBS, Brig.-Gen. Reginald Francis Arthur, C.B. 1931; C.M.G. 1915; D.S.O. 1902; *b.* 30 Jan. 1878; *s.* of late Captain S. H. Hobbs, 89th Foot; *m.* 1906, Frances Graham, *y. d.* of late Gen. Sir William Stirling; one *s.* (and one killed in action in 1942 and one in 1943). *Educ.:* Wellington College; R.M.A., Woolwich. Entered army 1898; Lieut. 1901; Captain. 1907; Major, 1914; served South Africa under Lord Methuen and Col. Von Donop, 1899-1902 (Queen's medal with 4 clasps, King's medal with 2 clasps; D.S.O.; despatches); Somaliland campaign, 1903-4 (medal and clasp); European War, 1914-18 (despatches five times, C.M.G., Bt. Lt.-Col.); Brevet Colonel, 1919; A.Q.M.G. Southern Command, 1924-27; Brigadier in charge of Administration, Western Command, 1927-31; retired pay, 1931. *Recreation:* shooting. *Address:* Little Newnham, Sutton Veny, Warminster, Wilts. *T.:* Sutton Veny 254.
[*Died* 10 *July* 1953.

HOBMAN, Joseph Burton; *b.* Sheffield, 25 May 1872; *m.* 1st, Margaret H. Linacre (*d.* 1924); 2nd, Daisy L. Adler; three *c.* *Educ.:* Wesley Coll., Sheffield. Asst. Editor Sheffield Independent, 1898-1912; Editor Birmingham Gazette, 1912-21; Editor Westminster Gazette, 1921-28; Editorial Staff, Westminster Press (Provincial), 1928-42; contested Hallam (Sheffield), 1928; N. Bradford, 1929; N.E. Bethnal Green, 1935. *Publications:* David Eder, a Memoir, 1945; ed. Palestine's Economic Future, 1946. *Address:* 66 Tisbury Rd., Hove, Sussex. *T.:* Hove 30614. [*Died* 30 *Sept.* 1953.

HOBSON, Alice Mary; *b.* 27 Jan. 1860; *d.* of late W. S. Hobson, The Fosse, Leicester. *Educ.:* Coedbel, Chislehurst, Kent. Studied under John Fulleylove, R.I., Wilmot Pilsbury, O.W.S., and James Orrock, R.I.; travelled in Switzerland, Germany, Italy, and Egypt; spent two winters in Corsica, and five years in Basutoland; painted in all these countries, but likes British scenery best; retired R.I. *Recreations:* reading, sewing. *Address:* Pengersick House, Praa Sands, Penzance, Cornwall. *Club:* Lyceum.
[*Died* 12 *Feb.* 1954.

HOBSON, Clement; *b.* 1 June 1877. *Educ.:* Lausanne, Switzerland. Breeder of race-horses, having bred many good winners in France including those of the French Guineas and the Grand Prix de Deauville; Racing-motorist, owner-driver; winner of many events at Brooklands; for several years holder of the world's record for speed at Brooklands. *Publications:* French racing correspondent under the nom de plume of Faraway, in Horse and Hound. *Recreations:* racing and breeding. *Address:* Château de Varaville, Par Bavent (Calvados), France. *T.A.:* Hobson, Cabourg. *T.:* 92 Cabourg. *Club:* Automobile de France (Paris).
[*Died* 16 *March* 1952.

HOCKEN, Colonel Charles Augustus Frederick, C.B.E. 1922; Indian Army, retired; *b.* 1870; *m.* 1906, Clara Mary, *d.* of H. A. R. Thomson, Kenfield Hall, nr. Canterbury, Kent; one *d.* Served Chitral Relief Force 1895 (medal with clasp); China 1900 (medal); European War, 1914-19 (despatches). *Address:* Duxhams, Dulverton, Somerset. [*Died* 5 *Aug.* 1958.

HOCKING, William John, C.V.O. 1926; C.B.E. 1918; *b.* 10 Mar. 1864; *o. s.* of W. T. Hocking; *m.* 1st, 1890, Agnes Pavitt; 2nd, 1903, Elizabeth Jane Stokoe; one *s.* *Educ.:* privately. Entered Mint, 1883; Assistant Superintendent, 1899; Superintendent of the Operative Department, Royal Mint, 1919-26. *Publications:* Catalogue of Coins, Dies, Seals, etc., in Mint Museum, 1906-10; numismatic and other papers. *Address:* Bristol House, Danbury, Essex. *T.:* Danbury 108.
[*Died* 10 *April* 1953.

HODDER-WILLIAMS, Robert Percy; retired Publisher; Hodder and Stoughton Limited, 1896-1947 (Chairman, 1927-47); *b.* 23 May 1880; 2nd *s.* of late John and Mary Williams, Bromley Common, Kent; *m.* 1908, Ragnhild Sophie, *d.* of late Sogneprest Herman Lunde, Oslo, Norway. *Educ.:* City of London School. *Address:* Weald Place, Sevenoaks, Kent.
[*Died* 29 *Nov.* 1958.

HODGE, Rear-Adm. Hon. C. P. H.; *see* Hermon-Hodge.

HODGE, Frederick Webb; archæologist, ethnologist; *b.* Plymouth, 28 Oct. 1864; taken to United States when seven years of age; *m.* 1st, Margaret Whitehead Magill (*d.* 1935), of Washington; one *s.* two *d.*; 2nd, Zahrah E. Preble (*d.* 1934); 3rd Gene P. Meany. *Educ.:* public schools of Washington; Arlington Academy; Columbian (now George Washington) University. D.Sc., Pomona College, 1933; LL.D., University of New Mexico, 1934; Lit.D., Univ. of Southern California, 1943; entered United States Geological Survey, 1884; Field Secretary of Hemenway Archæological Expedition in Arizona and New Mexico, 1886-89; served as Librarian, Editor, and Ethnologist, Bureau of American Ethnology of the Smithsonian Institution; conducted various expeditions in Arizona and New Mexico; scaled the Enchanted Mesa in New Mexico, finding evidences of prehistoric occupancy, 1897; Assistant in Charge of Office of the Smithsonian Institution, and Acting Curator of International Exchanges in 1901-5; Ethnologist, Bureau of American Ethnology, 1905-9; Ethnologist-in-charge of same, 1910-18; with Museum of American Indian, New York, 1918-31, for which (1917-23) he conducted archæological excavations at Hawikuh, New Mexico; Director, Southwest Museum, Los

Angeles, California, since 1932; Director emeritus, 1956; Founder, Editor (1902-10, 1912-1914), President (1917), American Anthropological Association; Pres. Anthropological Soc. of Washington, 1911-12; member and Hon. Fellow numerous learned societies; Founder Quivira Society, 1929; Member Managing Committee, School of American Research; Honorary Companion, Order of Indian Wars. *Publications:* Coronado's Route from Culiacan to Quivira, 1899; History of Hawikuh (Vol. I. of Frederick Webb Hodge Anniversary Pub. Fund), 1937; and many others; editor Handbook of American Indians North of Mexico, Part i., 1907; Part ii., 1910; of the American Anthropologist, and of the Memoirs of the American Anthropological Association, 1902-10, 1912; the narrations of Francisco Vasquez Coronado and Alvar Nuñez Cabeza de Vaca, 1907; M'Kenney and Hall's Indian Tribes, 1933-34; Curtis's The North American Indian (20 vols., 1907-30); Falconer's Texan Santa Fé Expedition, 1930; The Masterkey and other publications of Southwest Museum; (with C. F. Lummis) The Memorial of Fray Alonso Benavides, 1630, 1916; also (with G. P. Hammond and Agapito Rey) The Memorial of Fray Alonzo Benavides revised in 1634, 1945. *Address:* P.O. Box 1552, Santa Fé, New Mexico, U.S.A. *Clubs:* Zamorano, Westerners, Death Valley '49ers (Los Angeles). [*Died* 28 *Sept.* 1956.

HODGE, Horace Emerton; (Merton Hodge), M.B.Ch.B., Dramatist; *b.* 13 March 1904; *s.* of Alfred Horace Hodge and Mary Downie-Jones; unmarried. *Educ.:* King's Coll., Auckland, N.Z.; Auckland University; Univ. of Otago; Univ. of Edinburgh. Always interested in the stage, but for six years studied medicine at University of Otago, Dunedin; Qualified 1928; did post-graduate work in Edinburgh and later held a temporary commission with R.A.M.C. for two years, Millbank, London and Ireland; on staff of St. George's Hospital, as anæsthetist until he went to New York for the American production of The Wind and the Rain; also to do the English adaptation of the Pulitzer Prize winning play Men in White; returned to London for the production of this play with Gilbert Miller; specialised in anæsthetics, as well as carrying on his work as a dramatist; in New York during 1939, but with outbreak of war returned to London to join staff of Camberwell House Hospital for Nervous Diseases. 1941-44, granted leave from hospital work to do twenty weeks' tour of The Wind and The Rain, playing Charles Tritton himself. Followed this with six weeks' tour for E.N.S.A., with The Wind and The Rain, at Garrison Theatres and R.A.F. Stations. Since 1948 reverted to medical work, Hornsey, Wood Green, and Knightsbridge. Member British Medical Association. *Plays:* The Wind and the Rain, St. Martin's Theatre, 1933, 1934, 1935; Men in White (anglicised form), Lyric Theatre, 1935; Grief Goes Over, Globe Theatre, 1935; The Orchard Walls, St. James's Theatre, 1937; The Island, Comedy Theatre, 1938; Story of an African Farm, New Theatre (from Olive Schreiner's novel), 1938; To Whom We Belong, Q Theatre, 1939; Once There was Music, Q Theatre, 1942; My Life in the Theatre, series, for Overseas broadcast, for B.B.C. Also instructional films for forces, writing, producing, acting (later with Two Cities Films). *Publications:* The above plays and Novelised version of The Wind and the Rain, 1936. *Recreations:* motoring and going to the theatre. *Address:* c/o Bank of New Zealand Ltd., 1 Queen Victoria Street, E.C.4. *Club:* Dramatists'. [*Died* 9 *Oct.* 1958.

HODGES, Admiral Sir Michael Henry, K.C.B., *cr.* 1925 (C.B. 1919); C.M.G. 1919; M.V.O. 1914; *b.* 29 Sept. 1874; *s.* of Lt.-Col. J. F. Hodges; *m.* 1903, Frederica Octavia, *d.* of late H. F. Tiarks, Foxbury, Chislehurst; four *s.* one *d.* Entered R.N. 1887; Lt. 1895; Commander, 1902; Captain, 1908; Vice-Adm. 1925; Admiral, 1929; served South Africa, defence of Ladysmith, 1899-1900 (despatches); Commanded H.M.S. Doris, Atlantic Fleet, 1910-12; H.M.S. Cornwall (Training Cruiser), 1912-14; Naval Attaché in Paris, 1914; Principal Naval Transport Officer Salonica; Commanded H.M.S. Indomitable and H.M.S. Renown, Grand Fleet, 1916-18; Commodore, First Class, 1919; Chief of Staff to Sir Charles Madden, 1918-20; commanding Destroyer Flotillas, Atlantic Fleet, 1920-22; Naval Secretary to First Lord of the Admiralty, 1923-25; Second-in-Command Mediterranean Fleet, 1925-27; Second Sea Lord at the Admiralty, 1927-30; Commander-in-Chief, Atlantic Fleet, 1930-31; retired list, 1932; R.N.O. Folkstone, 1940; Flag Officer in charge, Trinidad, West Indies, 1941-42; R.N.O. Teignmouth, 1942-43. Officer Legion of Honour. *Address:* 85 Cadogan Gardens, S.W.3. *T.:* Kensington 2025. *Club:* Boodle's. [*Died* 3 *Nov.* 1951.

HODGETTS, Charles Alfred, C.M.G. 1917; V.D.; M.D., C.M., L.R.C.P. Lond., D.P.H.; *b.* 23 Aug. 1859; *s.* of Geo. and Susanah Hodgetts; *m.*; two *s.* three *d.* *Educ.:* Toronto Model School; Toronto School of Medicine. Graduated with honours, Ontario College of Pharmacy, 1878; M.D., C.M., Victoria University, 1886; L.R.C.P. London, 1889; Member College of Physicians and Surgeons, Ontario, 1890; Diploma of Public Health, Queens, 1907; Medical Inspector, Provincial Board of Health, Ontario, 1891-1904; Chief Health Officer and Secretary, Provincial Board of Health, 1904-09; Deputy Registrar-General, Ontario, 1904-09; Medical Adviser on Public Health, Commission of Conservation of Canada, 1909-1920; Director-General, Canadian Branch, St. John Ambulance Association, 1921; retired, 1934; First Hon. Secretary, Canadian Red Cross—also one of founders; was Canadian Red Cross Comr. Overseas, 1914-1918, with rank of Colonel Canadian Army Medical Corps (despatches, C.M.G.); Asst. Commissioner, Ministry of National Services in Ireland, 1918; War Service Medals, Star and two medals; Col. Aux. Forces Officers' Decoration; Coronation Medal, 1937; Commander of Crown of Italy; Officer, Order of Leopold, Belgium; Knight of Grace, Order of St. John of Jerusalem. *Publications:* Editor—Report of Ontario Board of Health, 1904-09, Health Report of Commission of Conservation, Ottawa, 1909-20, and Publication, St. John Ambulance Association (Canada); contributor of many health articles to medical publications. *Recreation:* philatelist. *Address:* 103 Elmwood Avenue, London, Ontario, Canada. [*Died* 3 *April* 1952.

HODGKIN, Jonathan Edward, R.B.A.; F.S.A.; M.I.E.E.; M.I.Min.E.; J.P. for County of Durham; *b.* Darlington, 4 Nov. 1875; *e. s.* of late J. Backhouse Hodgkin, Darlington; *m.* 1902, Elspeth Lilian, 3rd *d.* of late James E. Backhouse, Darlington; four *s.* one *d.* *Educ.:* Bootham School, York; Leighton Park School, Reading. Apprenticeship as electrical engineer with Ernest Scott and Mountain Ltd. of Newcastle on Tyne; subsequent business career includes thirty-five years with Motor Union Insurance Co. Ltd.; now Chm. Darlington Wire Mills, Ltd., and about twenty other public and private companies; Consulting Electrical Engineer; for twelve years Chairman of Friends Central Education Committee; Member of Flounders Trust (formerly Treasurer); formerly Chairman: Committee of Visiting Magistrates Durham Prison; Wolsingham Petty Sessions; Vice-Chairman, Durham County Bench (Darlington) (now on supplementary list); Mem. County of Durham Standing Jt. Cttee.; member of governing body of Ayton School and Vice-Chm. of Leighton Park School; as archaeologist formed

Piercebridge Excavation Committee and personally excavated British Camp at Hamsterley, Co. Durham; N.E. District representative of the Society of Antiquaries and of the National Trust; Chairman and Founder of Darlington Society of Arts; has exhibited water colours in Paris Salon and many British galleries. Founder Member Darlington Rotary Club, President, 1935-36, Vice-Chairman No. 3 District, 1937-38. *Publications:* Little Guide to Durham County; The Hodgkin Apocrypha; Occasional Verse. *Recreations:* travel; artist in water colour and pencil; motoring and shooting. *Address:* Dryderdale, Hamsterley, Bishop Auckland, Co. Durham. *T.:* Witton-le-Wear 44. [*Died* 19 *Dec.* 1953.

HODGKIN, Lucy Violet (Mrs. John Holdsworth); *b.* Benwelldene, Newcastle on Tyne, 1869; *e.d.* of late Thomas Hodgkin, D.C.L., and Lucy Anna Fox; *m.* 1922, John Holdsworth (*d.* 1935) of Swarthmoor, Havelock North, N.Z. *Educ.:* home. *Publications:* Pilgrims in Palestine, 1890; The Happy World, 1902; contributor to The Fellowship of Silence, 1915; A Book of Quaker Saints, 1917; Silent Worship, Swarthmore Lecture, 1919; George Lloyd Hodgkin's Life and Letters, 1921; A Quaker Saint of Cornwall; Loveday Hambly and her Guests, 1927; The Romance of the Inward Light, 1932; Anima, the Pilgrim of the Cross, 1933; A Day Book of Counsel and Comfort from the Epistles of George Fox, 1937; Seas of the Moon, 1940, 1946; The Shoemaker of Dover, 1943; In Quietness: Thoughts on Silent Worship, 1945; Gulielma: Wife of William Penn, 1947. *Address:* Bareppa House, near Falmouth. [*Died* 6 *April* 1954.

HODGKIN, Robert Howard, Hon. Fellow of Queen's College, Oxford, since 1946; *b.* Newcastle on Tyne, 24 April 1877; *s.* of late Thomas Hodgkin, D.C.L., banker and historian, and Lucy Anna Fox; *m.* 1908, Dorothy, *d.* of A. L. Smith, Master of Balliol; two *s.* *Educ.:* Repton; Leighton Park School, Reading; Balliol College, Oxford. Proxime in Stanhope Essay and First Class in Modern History, 1899; Lecturer in Modern History at Queen's College, Oxford, 1900; Fellow, 1904-37; Tutor, 1910-37; University Lecturer in Modern History, 1928-1934; Pro-Provost, Queen's College, 1936-37; Provost, 1937-46. Captain 7th Bn. Northumberland Fusiliers, 1914-19; G. S. Operations, War Office, 1917-19. *Publications:* Elizabeth of Bohemia (in Five Stuart Princesses), 1901; A History of the Anglo-Saxons, 1935; Six Centuries of an Oxford College, 1949. *Address:* Crab Mill, Ilmington, Shipston-on-Stour, Warwickshire. *T.:* Ilmington 33. [*Died* 28 *June* 1951.

HODGSON, Sir Edward Highton, K.B.E., *cr.* 1945 (O.B.E. 1919); Kt., *cr.* 1941; C.B. 1923; *b.* 23 Mar. 1880; *e. s.* of I. Hodgson, Keswick; *m.* 1906, Gertrude, *d.* of late Thomas Adamson, Bolton; three *s.* one *d.* *Educ.:* St. Bees. Entered Customs Service, 1899; Assistant Secretary H.M. Customs and Excise, 1919; seconded to Ministry of Pensions as Director of Establishments, 1920; Principal Assistant Secretary, Board of Trade, 1928; Under Secretary, 1932-41; Second Secretary, 1941-46; Principal Finance Officer, 1946-49; retired, 1949. Member Cohen Cttee. on Company Law Amendment, 1943-45; Chairman, Cttee. on Weights and Measures, 1949-50; Member National Research Development Corporation, 1949-54. *Address:* 4 Rosscourt Mansions, Palace Street, S.W.1. *T.:* Victoria 9776. *Club:* Royal Automobile. [*Died* 17 *Feb.* 1955.

HODGSON, Sir Harold (Kingston) Graham-, K.C.V.O., *cr.* 1950 (C.V.O. 1929); F.R.C.P.; F.F.R.; M.B., B.S., D.M.R.E.; retired; 2nd *s.* of late Dr. G. Graham Hodgson, Eastbourne, and Josephine Iredale; *m.* Winifred Elizabeth, *d.* of George Jenkins, Newcastle upon Tyne; one *s.* one *d.*; *m.* 1943, Rosa Dorothy, *widow* of Frank L. Hallam. *Educ.:* Mulgrave; St. Edward's School, Oxford; Clare Coll., Camb. Served European War in France as a despatch rider, Aug.-Dec. 1914; temp. Lieut. R.A.M.C., 1916-17; Major R.A.M.C., 1918. Late lectr. in Radiology, University of London; Univ. Teacher in Radiology to Middlesex Hospital Medical School; late Physician-in-Charge Dept. of X-Ray Diagnosis, Middlesex Hosp.; Chairman of Medical Committee, 1952-53, and Member of Board of Governors, Middlesex Hospital; Hon. Radiologist to: Central London Throat, Nose and Ear Hosp.; Middlesex Hosp.; Consulting Radiologist to R.N., Brit. Red Cross, and King Edward VIIth Hosp. for Officers; late Hon. Radiologist to King's Coll. Hosp., the Hampstead and N.W. London Hospital; late Radiologist, Ministry of Pensions Hospital, X-Ray Specialist to 2nd Northern General Hospital, Leeds; Senior House Surgeon, House Physician, and Assistant R.M.O., Royal Victoria Infirmary, Newcastle upon Tyne; F.R.S.M. (Past Pres., Section of Radiology); F.F.R.; Hon. Fellow: American College of Radiology; S. African Assoc. of Radiologists. *Publications:* numerous papers. *Recreations:* shooting, fishing, golf, sailing, farming. *Address:* Tidmarsh House, Tidmarsh, Berks. [*Died* 21 *Aug.* 1960.

HODGSON, Sir Robert MacLeod, K.C.M.G., *cr.* 1939 (C.M.G. 1920); K.B.E., *cr.* 1925; *b.* West Bromwich, 25 Feb. 1874; *e. s.* of late Ven. Robert Hodgson, Archdeacon of Lichfield; *m.* Olga, *d.* of Paul Bellavin; one *s.* *Educ.:* Radley; Trinity College, Oxford. M.A. 1898; Vice-Consul at Marseilles 1907; Vladivostok; 1907-11; Consul at Vladivostok, 1911-1919; Acting High Commissioner in Siberia; Commercial Counsellor in Russia, 1919-21; British Agent to the Soviet Government, 1921-24; H.M. Chargé d'Affaires at Moscow, 1924-27; Minister and Consul-General to Albania, 1928-36; retired, 1936; British Agent in Nationalist Spain, 1937-39; Chargé d'Affaires at Burgos, Feb.-April 1939; Chairman of Council of School of Slavonic Studies and Foreign Office Advisor to the Censorship, 1942-44. *Publication:* Spain Resurgent, 1953. *Address:* 56 Redcliffe Square, S.W.10. *T.:* Fremantle 8404. *Club:* Athenæum. [*Died* 18 *Oct.* 1956.

HODGSON, Brig. Walter Thornton, D.S.O. 1919; M.C.; *b.* 1880; *y. s.* of late Barnard Becket Hodgson, of Bolney, Sussex; *m.* 1912, Barbara, *d.* of late Rt. Hon. James Tomkinson, M.P., of Willington Hall, Tarporley, Cheshire; two *s.* *Educ.:* Eton College. Joined 1st Royal Dragoons, 1902; Lt.-Col. 1923; served South Africa, 1900-2 (Queen's medal and six clasps); European War, 1914-19 (despatches, M.C., D.S.O., Belgian Croix de Guerre); Commander 1st Cavalry Brigade, Aldershot, 1928-1932; Officer-in-Charge of the Cavalry Record and Pay Office, Canterbury, 1933-34; retired pay, 1934. *Address:* Wodards Close, Fritwell, Bicester, Oxon. *Club:* Cavalry. [*Died* 16 *Sept.* 1957.

HODGSON, Lieut.-Col. William Roy, C.M.G. 1951; O.B.E.; LL.B.; A.F.I.A.; A.C.A.A.; *b.* Kingston, Victoria, 22 May 1892; *s.* of Robert Hodgson, St. Kilda, Victoria; *m.* 1919, Muriel Bruce (*d.* 1946), *d.* of George McDowell, Mentone, Victoria; one *s.* one *d.* *Educ.:* School of Mines, Ballarat, Vic.; Univ. of Melbourne; Royal Military College, Duntroon, A.C.T. Served European War, A.I.F., 2nd F.A. Brigade, Lieutenant. Gallipoli landing (severely wounded, despatches, Croix de Guerre avec Palme); invalided home to Australia 1917; General Staff, Army H.Q. Melbourne, Training, Operations and Intelligence Sections, specialising in Foreign Affairs and particularly Pacific and Far Eastern questions; Assistant-Secretary, Department of External Affairs Canberra, 1933; Secretary, Department of External Affairs, 1935; Adviser on Foreign Affairs to Australian Delegation at Imperial Conference, 1937; attended Aust.-

N.Z. Aviation Conf., Oct. 1944; Br. Commonwealth Conf. at Montreal, Oct. 1944; International Civil Aviation Conf. at Chicago, 1944; High Commissioner for Australia in Canada, 1945; United Nations Conf. on Internat. Organization at San Francisco, Apr. 1945. Head of Aust. deleg. to U.N. Preparatory Commission held in Lond., 1945; member Aust. delegation to 1st Pt. of 1st Session of U.N. Gen. Assembly, London, 1946; Aust. rep. on Security Council in New York, 1946; member Aust. deleg. to Paris Peace Conf., 1946; Deleg. of Aust. before Council of Dep. Foreign Ministers in London, 1947; then, March 1947, rep. of Australia on Security Council and Head of Australian Mission to U.N. in New York; rep. on Atomic Energy Commission; rep. on Human Rights Commission; rep. on U.N. Commission on the Balkans, April-June 1948; Rep. on Economic and Social Council, U.N., 1948; deleg. U.N. Gen. Assembly, Paris, 1948; Head of Deleg., Diplomatic Conf., Geneva, April 1949; Head of Deleg., F.A.O., Paris, June 1949; Aust. Ambassador to France, 1948-49 (Minister, 1945-48); Head of Australian Mission, Japan, Nov. 1949-June 1952, and British Commonwealth Rep. on Allied Control Council for Japan; High Commissioner for Australia in S. Africa, July 1952-July 1957. *Recreations:* tennis, cricket, bowls, reading. *Address:* c/o Department of External Affairs, Canberra, A.C.T.
[*Died* 24 *Jan.* 1958.

HODSON, James Lansdale, O.B.E. 1947; Author and Journalist; *b.* Hazlehurst, Lancashire, 27 August 1891; *y. s.* of John and Alice Crompton. Joined Daily Mail, 1913; War service, 1914-18; private and N.C.O. 3rd Public Schools Battn., Sub-Lieut. Royal Naval Division; later attached Special Intelligence Branch Ministry of Munitions; News Editor, northern editions Daily Mail, 1924-29; later special writer News Chronicle; also Sunday Times and Allied Newspapers; investigated unemployment 9 European countries, 1932-1933; War Correspondent, 1939-42; worked on official films and publications, 1943-45, including Desert Victory and Tunisian Victory; wrote Merchantmen at War; Assoc. Producer and Literary Ed. of This Modern Age, 1947-1950. *Publications: novels:* Harvest in the North; God's in His Heaven; Grey Dawn—Red Night; North Wind; Mr. Arkwright's Marriage; Carnival at Blackport; Jonathan North, or Life's a Fight; English Family; Morning Star, The Youngest Son; Return to the Wood, etc.; *diary:* Through the Dark Night and Towards the Morning (both 1941); Before Daybreak and War in the Sun (both 1942); Home Front (1944); And yet I like America (1945); The Sea and The Land (1945); The Way Things Are (1947); Thunder in the Heavens (1950); *plays:* Nelson; Harvest in the North; Red Night; Heart and Heritage; The Case of Private Hamp; A Week in July; *plays in one act:* Nathaniel Titlark, Love at the Bus-stop, Midsummer Love, Before Trafalgar; *travel:* Our Two Englands. *Recreations:* painting and golf. *Club:* Savile.
[*Died* 28 *Aug.* 1956.

HODSON, Rt. Rev. Robert Leighton, M.A.; Prebendary of Lichfield Cathedral since 1947; *b.* 30 March 1885; *s.* of John Humphries and Annie Hodson; *m.* 1913, Margery Gertrude Corker; one *s.* two *d.* *Educ.:* Berkhamsted School; S. Edmund Hall, Oxford. Curate, S. Peter's, Wolverhampton; Curate-in-charge, Staverton, with Boddington, Glos.; Vicar of S. Stephens, Cheltenham; Vicar of S. Giles', Willenhall, Staffs; formerly Rector of S. Peter's Collegiate Church, Wolverhampton; Rural Dean of Wolverhampton; Archdeacon of Stafford and Canon of Lichfield Cathedral, 1935-44; Precentor, 1936-44; Rector of Edgmond, 1944-55; Bishop Suffragan of Shrewsbury, 1944-Oct. 1959, retired; Provost of Denstone, 1950-60. Temp. C.F., 1918-19. *Address:* Bronwylfa, Park Drive, Llanfairfechan, N. Wales.
[*Died* 8 *Jan.* 1960.

HODSON, Thomas Callan, M.A.; late I.C.S.; Professor Emeritus; *e. s.* of late Arthur Hodson, R.N.; *m.* Kathleen, 4th *d.* of late Henry Manly, F.I.A.; two *s.* two *d.* *Educ.:* Christ's Hospital. Entered I.C.S. 1894; served Bengal, Khasia Hills, Assam Secretariat, and Manipur; retired, 1901; Registrar, East London College (University of London), 1903-14; Hon. Secretary Royal Anthropological Institute, 1912, to War; served in France, 1914-20 (despatches); 2nd Lieut. 1914; Colonel, 1919; Principal, Hornsey Rise Training College, 1921-23; Lecturer Universities, Oxford, London, Cambridge, Michigan, 1923-24; Reader in Ethnology, Cambridge, 1926-1932; William Wyse Professor of Social Anthropology, Cambridge, 1932-37; Fellow (Professorial) St. Catharine's College, 1933-37; Assistant Editor Encyclopædia Britannica, 1925-26; Associate Editor, 1927-29; Silver medal of Royal Society of Arts, Officier d'Instruction Publique, Hon. Member Sigma XI. *Publications:* The Meitheis, the Naga Tribes of Manipur; Thado Grammar; Primitive Culture of India; Languages, Customs and Religions of India (Oxford Survey of British Empire); Census Ethnography of India. *Address:* The Lodge, Tisbury, Wilts. *T.:* Tisbury 303
[*Died* 25 *Jan.* 1953.

HOFFE, Monckton; dramatic author; *b.* 1881; *m.* Barbara Hoffe (who obtained a divorce, 1923). *Plays:* The Lady who Dwelt in the Dark, 1903; Father Varien, 1907; The Little Damozel, 1909; Improper Peter, subsequently renamed Proper Peter, 1912; Panthea, 1913; Things We'd Like to Know, 1914; Carminetta, 1916; Anthony in Wonderland, 1917; The Faithful Heart, 1921; Pomp and Circumstance, 1922; The Lady Cristilinda in America, 1922; The Crooked Friday, 1925; Cristilinda, 1925; The Unnamed Play, 1926; Many Waters, 1928.
[*Died* 4 *Nov.* 1951.

HOFFMAN, Philip Christopher; *b.* Stratford, Essex, 26 June 1878; *s.* of J. C. Hoffman, silk mercer, City of London; *m.* 1913, Annie Mary Morgan, Treorcky, S. Wales; two *d.* *Educ.:* Coopers' School, Stepney; Warehousemen's, Clerks', and Drapers' School, Purley. Apprenticed to Drapery Trade; was shop assistant until 1904; organiser Shop Assistants' Union in home counties, and then West of England and Wales until 1912; London organiser until 1923; conducted campaigns against Living-in-System, done much to improve conditions of shop life; Ex-Chairman L.C.C. Advisory Committee on Needlework Training; Deputy Chairman L.C.C. Advisory Committee on Distributive Training; represented Union at International Conferences since 1901; M.P. (Lab.) S.E. Essex, 1923-1924; Central Sheffield, 1929-31. *Publications:* regular contributor to New Dawn; Shops and the State; They Also Serve. *Recreation:* gardening. *Address:* 38 Oakwood Road, Hampstead Garden Suburb, N.W.11. *T.:* Speedwell 3194.
[*Died* 20 *April* 1959.

HOFFNUNG, Gerard, F.S.I.A.; Free-lance artist and illustrator; musician; *b.* 22 March 1925; *s.* of Ludwig and Hilde Hoffnung; *m.* 1952, Annetta Perceval Bennett; one *s.* one *d.* *Educ.:* Highgate School; Harrow School of Arts. Art Master, Stamford School, 1945-46; staff artist, Evening News, 1946; Asst. Art Master, Harrow School, 1948; staff artist, Cowles Magazines Inc., New York, 1950. Contributor to British, Continental and American publications and to Punch. One-man exhibitions at Little Gallery, Piccadilly, 1949, Royal Festival Hall, 1951 and 1956. Work featured in Graphis. Broadcasting regularly for B.B.C., 1951-. Hon. Pres. L.S.E. Students' Union, 1958-59. Plays the Bass Tuba; Vice-Pres. Morley Coll. Symphony Orchestra;

creator of Hoffnung Music Festival, 1956, and Hoffnung Interplanetary Music Festival, 1958 and 1959, Royal Festival Hall. *Publications:* (with James Broughton) The Right Playmate, 1952; (with John Symonds) The Isle of Cats, 1955; The Maestro, 1953; The Hoffnung Symphony Orchestra, 1955; The Hoffnung Music Festival, 1956; The Hoffnung Companion to Music, 1957; Hoffnung's Musical Chairs, 1958; Ho Ho Hoffnung, 1959; Hoffnung's Acoustics, 1959. *Recreations:* travelling, reading fairy stories, good food, cinema. *Address:* 5 Thornton Way, N.W.11. [*Died* 28 *Sept.* 1959.

HOFMANN, Josef; Pianist; Director and Dean of Curtis Institute of Music, 1926-38; *b.* Cracow, Poland, 20 Jan. 1876; since 1926 U.S. citizen; *s.* of Casimir Hofmann, Professor, Warsaw Conservatory; *m.* 1st, 1905, Marie C. Eustis; one *d.*; 2nd, Betty Short; three *s.* Studied under Anton Rubinstein (only private pupil). *Compositions:* Symphony; Suite; five Concertos; two Sonatas and other pieces for piano alone. *Publications:* Piano Playing, 1908; Piano Questions Answered, 1909. *Address:* 321 South Occidental Blvd., Los Angeles 5, California, U.S.A. [*Died* 16 *Feb.* 1957.

HOGARTH, Major-General Donald Macdonald, C.M.G. 1918, D.S.O. 1917; *b.* 1879; *m.* Madge, *d.* of H. R. Patterson, Winnipeg; two *s.* one *d.* Canadian Army Service Corps; served European War, 1915-18 (despatches, D.S.O.). *Address:* Glen Edyth Place, Toronto, Ont.; 3100 Bank of Commerce Building, Toronto, Canada. [*Died* 2 *June* 1950.

HOGARTH, Robert George, C.B.E. 1918; F.R.C.S. Eng.; Hon. LL.D. Edin. 1927; J.P.; D.L. 1948; Past Mem. Council R. College of Surgeons of England; Past Pres., British Medical Association; Hon. Consulting Surgeon, General Hospital, Nottingham; Hon. Consulting Surgeon, Children's Hospital, Nottingham, and others; Inspector of British Red Cross and St. John's War Organisation Hospitals 1940-1946; *b.* 15 May 1868; *o. s.* of George Hogarth, Eccles Tofts, Berwickshire; *m.* Mabel Winifred (*d.* 1952), *d.* of D'Ewes Lynam, Nottingham. *Educ.:* Felstead School; St. Bartholomew's Hospital, London (House Surgeon, 1893). Senior Resident Medical Officer, General Hospital, Nottingham, 1894; Consulting Surgeon to the War Hospitals in Nottingham, 1914-18. *Publications:* Various in medical literature. *Recreations:* shooting, fishing, and golf. *Address:* 48 Ropewalk, Nottingham. *T.A.:* Ropewalk, Nottingham. *T.:* 41385. *Club:* Nottinghamshire County (Nottingham). [*Died* 29 *June* 1953.

HOGG, Brig.-Gen. Rudolph Edward Trower, C.M.G. 1919; C.I.E. 1911; Central India Horse; late Brigade-Commander Royal Air Force, resigned commission, 1919; *b.* 19 Jan. 1877; *s.* of Col. T. W. Hogg; *m.* 1922, Mildred Deborah (*d.* 1954), *d.* of Gen. Sir H. Rhodes Green, K.C.S.I., C.B.; one *d.* *Educ.:* R.M.A., Woolwich. Entered R.A., 1896; transferred to Indian Cavalry, 1901; R.H.S. certificate for life-saving, 1907; Assist. Military Secretary to H.I.M. the King Emperor, 1911, and served on staff during Royal Tour in India (Durbar Medal, C.I.E.); served European War (Gallipoli and France), 1914-18 (despatches, Bt. Lt.-Col.). *Address:* Cedar Farm, St. John's, Jersey, C.I. [*Died* 29 *June* 1955.

HOLBECH, Ronald Herbert Acland, O.B.E. 1951; Landowner; *b.* 5 Jan. 1887; *o. surv. s.* of late Lt.-Col. W. H. Holbech and Mrs. Holbech of Farnborough, Banbury; *m.* 1915, Catherine Emma, *y. d.* of Sir Leigh Hoskyns, 11th Bt.; three *s.* (and one *s.* decd.). *Educ.:* privately; Magdalen College, Oxford. J.P. Warwickshire; C.A. Warwickshire County Council. Director, Hunt Edmunds & Co. Ltd., Midland Marts, Ltd., Burgis & Colbourne, and Warwick Newspapers, Ltd. *Address:* Farnborough Hall, Banbury. *T.:* Farnborough 204. [*Died* 2 *Jan.* 1956.

HOLBROOKE, Josef; musician; *b.* Croydon, 5 July 1878; *o. surv. s.* of J. C. Holbrooke, Bristol, musician, and Alice Scotland, Newport, Fife; *m.* 1903, Dorothy, *d.* of T. Hadfield of Morthen; two *s.* three *d.* *Educ.:* privately. Started at 12 years of age as pianist in the Collins and Bedford Music Halls; then in pantomime tours at £1 a week; has played all his piano and Chamber works many times in public and conducted all his works. Examiner 5 years, London College and Trinity College, London. Orchestral works performed: The Raven, The Viking, Ulalume, Queen Mab, Byron, The Bells, Auld Lang Syne, Les Hommages, Wildfowl, Ballet (Markova tours-Aucassin et Nicolette), 3 Blind Mice, Girl I left behind me, 2 National Suites, 8 Concertos: (3 Piano, 1 Violin, 1 'Cello, 1 Saxophone and Bassoon, 1 Clarinet and Bassoon); 1 Quadruple (Fl.C.A.Cl.Bn.); 8 Symphonies; Works conducted by Godfrey, Manns, Pierné, Steinbach, Richter, H. J. Wood, Sokoloff, Rinskoff, Nikisch, Kussevitski, Weingartner, Beecham, Hammond, Raybould, Sargent, etc.; 12 Military and 12 Brass Band Works, 4 String Orchestra works; has given 25 years, in all, of Chamber Concerts in London and Provinces, always including British composers; 6 Ballets; 8 Operas; The Stranger, His Majesty's; The Children of Don (drama), Drury Lane, 1912; Dylan (music drama), 1914, London Opera House; The Enchanter (opera ballet), Chicago; The Sailors Arms (light opera), Guildford; The Snob (comic opera); Bronwen (music drama); (Carl Rosa tour) Tamlane. *Publications:* 125 works; 20 Choral works; The Blake Choral; Musical Adventures; Contemporary British Composers, Memoirs, etc.; has taken British music to many countries. *Recreations:* walking and gardening. *Address:* c/o Modern Music Library, 55 Alexandra Rd., N.W.8. [*Died* 5 *Aug.* 1958.

HOLBROOKE, Major-General Philip Lancelot, C.B. 1925; C.M.G. 1919; D.S.O. 1915; late R.A.; *b.* 25 Nov. 1872; *m.* 1st, 1903, Eleanor Louisa (*d.* 1935), *d.* of late Captain F. J. Slade-Gully, Indian Staff Corps, of Trevennen, Cornwall, 2nd, 1936, Mabel Dixon. Entered army, 1892; Captain, 1900; Major, 1913; Lt.-Col. 1917; Col. 1921; Maj.-Gen. 1929; Instructor, School of Gunnery, 1908-12; Commandant, Shoeburyness, 1920-24; C.R.A. Scottish Command, 1925-29; served South African War, 1900-2; (Queen's medal 6 clasps, King's medal 2 clasps); European War, 1914-18 (despatches, D.S.O., C.M.G., Bt. Lieut.-Col. and Colonel); A.D.C. to The King, 1921; retired pay, 1929; 3rd class St. Stanislas (Russia); Officer Legion of Honour (France). *Address:* Pendennis, Derby Road, Bournemouth. *Club:* United Service. [*Died* 2 *Oct.* 1958.

HOLCROFT, Sir George Harry, 1st Bt. (2nd creation), *cr.* 1921; J.P. Worcestershire and Staffordshire; High Sheriff, Staffordshire, 1913; *b.* 14 Aug. 1856; *s.* of late W. Holcroft, J.P., of Prescott House, Stourbridge; *m.* 1893, Annie Gertrude (*d.* 1929), *d.* of late Rev. J. Coombes; one *s.* (and one killed in action, 1915, and another killed in action, 1941) two *d.* *Educ.:* Radley College; Exeter College, Oxford, M.A. *Heir:* *s.* Reginald Culcheth [Lieutenant in Indian Frontier Cavalry (retired); now Flying Officer in R.A.F.; *b.* 6 April 1899; *m.* 1928, Mary Frances, *yr. d.* of late William Swire, C.B.E.; two *s.* two *d.*]. *Address:* Eaton Mascott Hall, Shrewsbury. [*Died* 19 *April* 1951.

HOLDEN, 3rd Baron of Alston, *cr.* 1908; **Angus William Eden Holden;** Bt., *cr.* 1893; Hon. Ensign, Coldstream Guards; *b.* 1 Aug. 1898; *o. s.* of 2nd Baron and Ethel

Eden (*d.* 1913), *d.* of late Major William Cookson, 80th Foot; *S.* father, 1937. *Educ.:* Eton; Magdalen College, Oxford. Hon. Attaché to H.M. Special Mission to Holy See, 1918; to H.M. Embassy, Madrid, 1922; Berlin, 1925; contested (L.) North Tottenham, 1929; Officers' Emergency Reserve, 1938; Lieut. R.N.V.R. 1944. Joined Labour Party, May 1945; Dep.-Chm. and Speaker, House of Lords, 1947; Parliamentary Under-Sec. of State, Commonwealth Relations Office, Feb.-July, 1950. *Publications:* Uncle Leopold, the Life of the First King of the Belgians; Elegant Modes in the Nineteenth Century; Four Generations of Our Royal Family, 1937; Ceylon, 1939; Purgatory Revisited, 1950. (With Ralph Dutton): English Country Houses open to the Public; French Châteaux open to the Public; The Land of France. *Heir:* (to Baronetcy only), *kinsman*, Isaac Holden, *b.* 1867. *Address:* 6 Wilton Street, S.W.1. *T.:* Sloane 4210. *Clubs:* St. James', R.N.V.R. [*Died* 6 *July* 1951 (*ext. as to barony*).

HOLDEN, Charles, R.D.I. 1943; Hon. Litt.D., Manchester University, 1936; Hon. D.Lit. London University, 1946; F.R.I.B.A.; M.P.T.I.; Senior Partner in the firm of Adams, Holden & Pearson; *b.* 12 May 1875; *s.* of Joseph Holden; *m.* Margaret (*d.* 1954), *d.* of J. C. Macdonald. *Principal works:* Bristol Central Reference Library, Bristol Royal Infirmary; British Hospital, Constantinople; British Medical Association, Strand; Institution of Electrical Engineers; King's College of Household and Social Science (now Queen Elizabeth College), Kensington; Sutton Valence School and Chapel, Kent; Torquay Hospital; Head Offices, Underground Railway, Westminster; Piccadilly Circus Station and other stations, etc. for the Underground Railway; St. Luke's Hospital, Malta; War Memorials, New College, Oxford, Clifton College, etc.; one of the principal architects, Imperial War Graves Commission, 1918-22; R.I.B.A. London Architecture Medal, 1929, for the Head Offices of the Underground Railway, Westminster; sole architect for the New London University Buildings on the Bloomsbury Site, 1931; town planning consultant, City of Canterbury; town planning consultant (with Professor W. G. Holford), City of London, 1944-54; Architectural and planning consultant: to Edinburgh Univ.; to the L.C.C. for the South Bank; to the County Borough of Tynemouth; awarded the Royal Gold Medal of the Royal Institute of British Architects, 1936; Member of Royal Fine Art Commission, 1933-47. *Address:* Harmer Green, Welwyn, Herts. *T.:* Tewin 376. *Club:* Athenæum. [*Died* 1 *May* 1960.

HOLDEN, Major-General William Corson, C.S.I. 1944; C.B.E. 1940; D.S.O. 1919; M.C.; *b.* Nassau, Bahamas, 10 Feb. 1893; *s.* of late F. W. Holden, Imperial Lighthouse Service; *m.* 1st, 1920, Claire Ethel Jessop, Sydney, N.S.W.; one *s.*; 2nd, 1947, Mary Enid, *widow* of Robert Whillis, F.R.C.S. *Educ.:* Nassau Grammar School. Entered R.A. 1913 from Special Reserve; served European War, 1914-18, Belgium, France, Egypt, Palestine, and Macedonia; Gunnery Staff Course, 1920-21; Instructor, School of Artillery, 1922-25; Staff College, Camberley, 1926-27; Brigade Major, R.A., 1928-29; G.S.O. 2, 22 Group R.A.F., 1930-31; G.S.O. 2, War Office, 1932-36; Imperial Defence College, 1937; G.S.O. 1 and B.G.S., War Office, 1938-39; B.G.S. 1 Corps B.E.F. 1940; B.G.S. Home Forces, June-Dec. 1940, for duties in connection with Home Guard; 1941-42, Military Member of the Eastern Group Supply Council (Delhi-Simla), in which capacity visited Australia, N. Zealand, South Africa, Malaya, Burma, Rhodesia, Kenya, Uganda, and Netherlands East Indies; Deputy Chief of General Staff, India, 1943; Deputy Master-General of Ordnance, India, 1944-46; retired pay, 1946. *Recreation:* yachting. *Address:* Parsons Mead, Beaulieu, Hants. *T.:* 271. *Clubs:* United Service; Royal Yacht Squadron, Royal Ocean Racing. [*Died* 15 *March* 1955.

HOLDING, Edgar Thomas, R.W.S. 1929 (A.R.W.S. 1920); Member of Art Workers' Guild and Society of Sussex Painters; Landscape painter in water colours and oils; *b.* Horncastle, Lincs., 1870; *s.* of T. H. Holding; *m.* May (*d.* 1947), *d.* of William Smith, Athlone; one *s.* two *d.* Early years spent in business with painting and sailing as recreations; later abandoned business for painting; principal works in private collections, and at Victoria and Albert Museum, South Kensington, at Leeds, Birkenhead, Eastbourne, Brighton, Bristol, Southport, Hull and Worthing Art Galleries and Whitworth Museum, Manchester. Treasurer R.W.S., 1931-48; President R.W.S. Art Club, 1924-1951. *Recreations:* painting, motoring, ship model making. *Address:* The Croft, Sutton, Pulborough, Sussex. [*Died* 29 *July* 1952.

HOLDSWORTH, Mrs. John; *see* Hodgkin, Lucy V.

HOLLAND, Clive; (Charles James Hankinson); M.B.E. 1920; J.P.; Knight of the Royal Order of Dannebrog (Denmark), 1931; Chevalier de l'Ordre de la Couronne (Belgium), 1932; Médaille du Roi Albert (Belgium) avec rayure; King Christian X's Frihedsmedaille (Liberty Medal), Denmark, 1947; Hon. Member Institute of Journalists (Member of its International Committee); *b.* Bournemouth, 23 April 1866; *s.* of Thomas James Hankinson, J.P. (1st Mayor of Bournemouth), Eastbury, Bournemouth, and of Frances Housden; *m.* 1894, Violet (*d.* 1945), 2nd *d.* of late Wm. Downs, C.E.; three *s.* three *d.* (and one *s.* decd.). *Educ.:* Mill Hill School; privately. Commenced contributing to various boys' papers, 1887; trained for the law; joined staff of several important London papers, 1893; travel Editor The Queen, 1937-39. J.P., Bournemouth, 1908. Has lectured on travel and literary subjects; novels and books translated into German, French, and Swedish. Celebrated 60th Anniversary of publication of his first book, April 1948. Broadcasts in England, Denmark, Hungary, and Norway. *Publications:* The Golden Hawk, 1888; Raymi, 1889; Book of Essays (Anonymous), 1894; My Japanese Wife, 1895; The Lure of Fame, 1896; A Writer of Fiction, 1897; The Use of the Hand Camera; An Egyptian Coquette; The Seed of the Poppy, 1898; Marcelle of the Latin Quarter; Gossipy Guide to Swanage; Gossipy Guide to Bournemouth and District, 1900; Mousmé, a story of West and East, 1901; The Heart of O Hans San, a Japanese Play; Paris, 1903; A Japanese Romance; The Indiscretions of Marcelle: A Play in Four Acts, 1904; How to Use a Camera, 1905; Wessex; Warwickshire; Things Seen in Japan, 1906; Japan Old and New, 1907; The Heart of a Geisha (a Play); From the North Foreland to Penzance, 1908; Without the Pale; Tyrol and its People, 1909; The Belgians at Home; Brown Face and White; Musume, Die Geschichte einer anglo-japanischen Heirat, 1911; In the Vortex, 1912; A Madonna of the Poor; The Lovers of Mademoiselle, 1913; The Hidden Submarine, 1916; The Cinema Star, 1917; Things Seen in Normandy and Brittany, 1924; Belgium, in the Picture Guides, Flanders and Hainault, vol. i. 1925, also in French; Things Seen in Paris; Unknown Hampshire, 1926; Things Seen in Shakespeare's Country; Denmark; The Ardennes, vol. ii. also in French; Denmark, the Land of the Sea Kings, 1928; Things Seen in the Channel Islands, 1929; Things Seen in Belgium; Czechoslovakia: a Modern Guide to the Land and its People, 1931; Belgium, the Land and its People; Thomas Hardy, O.M., The Man, His Works and the Land of Wessex, 1933; In and About the Mediterranean, 1934; Hungary, the Land and Its People, 1935; Thomas Hardy's Wessex

Scene, 1948. Contrib. to a large number of leading British, American, and foreign newspapers, magazines and reviews. *Recreations:* travel, the collection of photos, books and reading. *Address:* 10A Woodville Gardens, Ealing, W.5. *T.:* Perivale 7725. [*Died* 14 *Feb.* 1959.

HOLLAND, Dr. F. W. C.; *see* Crossley-Holland.

HOLLAND, Hetty L.; *see* Lee-Holland.

HOLLAND, Instructor Capt. Horace Herbert, C.B. 1922; B.A.; R.N.; 2nd *s.* of late John Holland, J.P.; *m.* Edith Marian (*d.* 1951), *e. d.* of late Edward Robinson, J.P.; one *d.* *Educ.:* Queen Mary's School, Walsall; Sidney Sussex Coll., Cambridge. Entered Royal Navy, 1891; lent to Turkish Government as Director of Studies at Imperial Ottoman Naval College, Constantinople, 1911-14 (Osmanieh decoration); Deputy Inspector of Naval Schools, 1918-22; Instructor Capt. 1919; retd., 1922. *Address:* 27 Ravine Road, Boscombe, Bournemouth. *T.:* Southbourne 2492. [*Died* 15 *May* 1952.

HOLLAND, Rear-Admiral Hubert Henry, C.B. 1917; R.N., retired list, 1922; *b.* 3 March 1873; 4th *s.* of late Joseph Holland, Cheadle, Cheshire; *m.* 1912, Alice Margaret (*d.* 1918), 2nd *d.* of Theodore Crombie, Culter House, Milltimber, Aberdeenshire; three *d.* *Publications:* Shakespeare through Oxford Glasses, 1923; Shakespeare, Oxford, and Elizabethan Times, 1933. *Address:* Southdown, Crease Lane, Tavistock, S. Devon. [*Died* 19 *Aug.* 1957.

HOLLAND, Major-General John Charles Francis, C.B. 1945; D.F.C.; p.s.c.; retd.; *b.* 21 Nov. 1897; *s.* of late Sir Thomas Holland, K.C.S.I., K.C.I.E.; *m.* 1924, Anne Christabel, *d.* of late Sir James Brunyate, K.C.S.I., C.I.E.; two *s.* one *d.* *Educ.:* Rugby; Royal Military Academy, Woolwich. Served European War, 1916-18 (despatches, D.F.C.). Served War of 1939-45, G.S.O. 1, C.R.E., Deputy Engineer-in-Chief War Office, Maj.-Gen. R.E., Mediterranean Theatre (despatches, C.B.); Chief of Staff, Western Command, 1947-48; specially employed, 1949-50; retd. Dec. 1951. Legion of Merit and Medal of Freedom with Silver Palm (U.S.A.). *Club:* United Service. [*Died* 17 *March* 1956.

HOLLAND, Rev. Preb. William Edward Sladen, M.A.; Prebendary of Rugmere in St. Paul's Cathedral since 1949; Rector of St. Mary Woolnoth with St. Mary Woolchurch Haw since 1933; *b.* 8 July 1873; *e. s.* of late Rev. Canon W. L. Holland; *g.s.* of Canon H. B. Tristram, D.D., LL.D., F.R.S.; *m.* 1st, Muriel Ardill (*d.* 1904), *d.* of Rev. D. A. Maxwell, of Broomholm, Langholm; two *d.*; 2nd, 1924, Cicely Dillworth, *yr. d.* of Arthur E. Thomas, Clifton, Bristol, and *g.d.* of James Inskip; one *s.* one *d.* *Educ.:* Loretto; (King's Scholar) Durham; Magdalen College, Oxford (Exhibitioner); Wycliffe Hall, Oxford. Second Class Classical Mods. and Lit. Hum.; late Fellow of Allahabad and of Calcutta Universities; Travelling Secretary Student Christian Movement, 1895-96; Curate, Parish Church, Birmingham, 1897-99; C.M.S. Missionary, India, 1899-1933; Founder and Warden, Oxford and Cambridge Hostel (now Holland Hall), Allahabad, 1900-13; Hon. Chaplain, Allahabad Cathedral, 1906-13; First Principal, St. Paul's Cathedral College, Calcutta, 1913-18; Secretary, National Missionary Council of India, 1912-14, Treasurer, 1914-18; Leader of the Archbishops' Campaign for Service in the Kingdom of God, 1918-20; in France, Y.M.C.A., 1918-19; Principal, Kottayam College, 1921-24; lecturer, Union Christian College, Alwaye, Travancore, 1924-28; Curate, University Church, Oxford, 1929; Chaplain, Balliol College, Oxford, 1929; Principal, St. John's College, Agra, 1929-1933; Canon of Allahabad Cathedral, 1931-33; Chaplain to Lord Mayor of London, 1933-34, 1938-39, and 1942-43; High Sheriff's Chaplain, 1940-41 and 1944-45; Commissary to the Bishops of Lucknow and Travancore; White's Lecturer (St. Paul's Cathedral), 1934. *Publications:* The Call of the World; The Goal of India; The Indian Outlook. *Address:* Hurstmead, Chislehurst, Kent. *T.:* Imperial 743, Mansion House 9701. [*Died* 27 *March* 1951.

HOLLAND-MARTIN, Christopher John; M.P. (C.) Ludlow Division of Shropshire since 1951; *b.* 16 Nov. 1910; *y. s.* of late R. M. Holland-Martin, C.B., and late Mrs. Holland-Martin, Overbury Court, Tewkesbury; *m.* 1949, Lady Anne Cavendish, M.B.E., J.P. (who *m.* 1st, 1929, Henry Hunloke, from whom she obtained a divorce, 1945), *y. d.* of 9th Duke of Devonshire, K.G., P.C., G.C.M.G., G.C.V.O. *Educ.:* Eton; Balliol College, Oxford. Military Secretary to Gov.-Gen., New Zealand, 1942-44; Secretary to Governor of Kenya, 1945. Director Martin's Bank Ltd. and other companies. Joint Hon. Treas. Conservative and Unionist Party since 1947. *Address:* 28 Kinnerton Street, S.W.1. *T.:* Belgravia 3066; Old Colwall, Malvern, Worcs. *T.:* Colwall 313. *Clubs:* Brooks's, White's, Carlton, Pratt's, Beefsteak. [*Died* 5 *April* 1960.

HOLLAND-PRYOR, Maj.-Gen. Sir Pomeroy; *see* Pryor.

HOLLIDAY, Professor Clifford, M.A.; M.Arch.; F.R.I.B.A.; M.T.P.I.; (First) Professor and Head of Department of Town and Country Planning, University of Manchester, since 1952; *b.* 21 Dec. 1897; *e. s.* of late Robert Holliday; *m.* 1921, Eunice, *y. d.* of late Joshua Blackwell; four *s.* *Educ.:* Bradford Grammar Sch.; University of Liverpool. Graduated at the School of Architecture (B.Arch, with distinction); Diploma in Civic Design; Holt Travelling Scholarship; Lever Prize; R.I.B.A. Distinction in Town Planning; Research Fellow and Jt. Ed. of Town Planning Review, 1920-21; Civic Adviser to the City of Jerusalem, 1922-26; began private practice as Architect and Planner, 1927; Adviser to Palestine Govt., 1927-34; Consultant to Ceylon Govt., 1939-43; to Colonial Govt., Gibraltar, 1944-46; (First) Chief Architect and Planner to Stevenage Development Corp., 1946-52; Technical Expert U.N. Mission, Indonesia, 1953; Lecturer, Istituto Universitario di Architettura, Venice, 1960; late External Examiner, University of London and the Leeds and Birmingham Schools of Planning. Order of the Holy Trinity of Ethiopia; Silver Jubilee Medal. *Works:* St. Andrew's Church, Jerusalem; Khan for the Order of St. John of Jerusalem; three banks for Barclay's (D.C. & O.). Palestine; Haifa Harbour Reclamation Area (with Pearce Hubbard); Ceylon University (with late Prof. Sir Patrick Abercrombie); various schools, churches, offices, industrial buildings and residential areas; conservation of ancient monuments: City Walls and Gates and Church of the Holy Sepulchre, Jerusalem; town plans for: Jerusalem (Geddes Plan), Emek Zebulun, Tiberias, Nathanya, Colombo, Buddhist Sacred City of Anuradhapura, and Gibraltar. *Publications:* papers and articles on architecture and planning. *Recreations:* travel, archaeology and cooking. *Address:* The University, Manchester. *T.:* Ardwick 3333; 8 The Beeches, West Didsbury, Manchester 20. *T.:* Didsbury 6192. *Clubs:* Royal Societies; Lancs. County Cricket. [*Died* 26 *Sept.* 1960.

HOLLINS, Alderman James Henry; M.P. (Lab.) Silvertown Division of West Ham, 1940-45. *Address:* The Rest, Fobbing, Stanford-le-Hope, Essex. [*Died* 22 *Sept.* 1954.

HOLLIS, Rt. Rev. Francis Septimus, L.Th. Durham; Assistant Bishop and Senior Canon of Leicester since 1949; Vicar of Stanford, with Swinford, Leics., since 1948; *b.* 10 November, 1884; *s.* of late George Hollis, of the Inner Temple. *Educ.:* S. George's School, Harpenden; Germany and France. Fellow of Surveyors Institute, 1908; Dorchester Missionary College, 1910; ordained, 1914; Curate of Ashby de la Zouch, 1913-1916; Assistant Priest at S. Thomas Cathedral, Kuching, Sarawak, 1916-23; Priest in charge of Land Dayak Mission, Quop and Tai, 1923-28; Principal of S. Thomas's School, Kuching, Sarawak, 1928-38; Archdeacon of Sarawak, 1934-38; Bishop of Labuan and Sarawak, 1938-48; interned in Kuching by Japanese, 1941-45. *Publications:* Translation of parts of Prayer book and Psalms into Quop Dialect, Land Dayak. *Recreation:* motoring. *Address:* All Saints Vicarage, Swinford, nr. Rugby. *Clubs:* Church Imperial, Overseas League, Corporation of Church House. [*Died* 4 *Feb.* 1955.

HOLLOWAY, Frederick William; *b.* 18 Sept. 1873; *s.* of Arthur Dixon Holloway and Frances Frank; *m.* 1st, 1897, Grace McIlroy (*d.* 1917); two *s.*; 2nd, 1935, Hilda Falkner. *Educ.:* St. Ives; London. F.R.C.O. at the age of 19; Assistant Organist at Crystal Palace at age of 20; Organist, St. Paul's, Herne Hill, 1892-1909; Precentor and Organist, All Saints, Dulwich, 1909-50; Conductor Crystal Palace Choral and Orchestral Society, 1932-49. *Publications:* numerous organ, pianoforte, and vocal compositions. *Address:* 61 Palace Road, S.W.2. *T.:* Tulse Hill 7102. [*Died* 20 *Jan.* 1954.

HOLLOWAY, Sir Henry Thomas, Kt., *cr.* 1945; Chairman and Managing Director of Holloway Bros. (London) Ltd.; also Chairman of Holloways' Properties Ltd.; *b.* 29 March 1876; *s.* of H. Thomas Holloway, West Lavington, Wilts; *m.* 1911, Brucine Mildenhall Pimm; two *s.* Past Pres. of Federation of Civil Engineering Contractors and of Institute of Builders; Chairman of the Uniformity Joint Board in the Building and Civil Engineering Industries, 1943-47, when Board was dissolved; served on Joint Consultative Council of Building and Civil Engineering Industries at Ministry of Works, 1941-46; active interest in Agriculture; breeder of pedigree Dairy Shorthorns and Wessex Saddleback Pigs. *Address:* West Lavington Manor, Wilts; 157 Millbank, S.W.1. *Club:* Devonshire. [*Died* 18 *Sept.* 1951.

HOLMAN, Arthur Treve, O.B.E. 1944; J.P., M.I.Mech.E.; Chairman since 1949, formerly Joint Managing Director, Holman Bros. Ltd.; Chairman Dustuctor Co. Ltd., since 1955; *b.* 1893; *s.* of late John Henry Holman, J.P., and late Mary Elizabeth Carthew Holman, J.P., Tregenna, Camborne, Cornwall; *m.* 1920, Ellen Muriel, *d.* of late W. Gundry Mills, Torfrey, Golant, Cornwall; two *s.* two *d.* *Educ.:* Blundell's School; Birmingham University. Served with B Battery H.A.C., 1914-15; R.F.A. 1916-17; R.A.F. 1918; Chm., Cornwall Technical Coll., 1928-55; Chairman, Cornish Engines Preservation Society, 1944; Member Council, Institution of Mechanical Engineers, 1952-55; Comd. 11th Cornwall Bn. Home Guard, 1941-45. High Sheriff of Cornwall, 1942-43. *Publications:* Papers on methods to prevent silicosis and pneumonoconiosis in jls. of Tech. Socs. *Recreation:* gardening. *Address:* Chyverton, Zelah, Truro, Cornwall. *T.:* Zelah 24. *Club:* Bath. [*Died* 6 *June* 1959.

HOLME, C(harles) Geoffrey, M.B.E.; Cav. Order of the Crown of Italy; *b.* Hampstead, 1887; *s.* of Charles Holme, Founder of The Studio; *m.* Margaret, *d.* of Thomas Bolton of Oakamoor; two *s.* two *d.* *Educ.:* Abbotsholme, and by travel. Served European War, 1914-18, France (M.B.E.). Member Council for Art and Industry. F.R.S.A. Past Editor of The Studio and the Studio Year Book, and most of the Studio Publications up to 1945. Resident abroad. [*Died* 12 *Dec.* 1954.

HOLME, Constance (Mrs. Punchard); author; *y. d.* of late John Holme, J.P., D.L., of Owlet Ash, Milnthorpe, Westmorland; *m.* 1916, Frederick Burt Punchard, (*d.* 1946), J.P., F.S.I., resident agent for Lady Henry Bentinck's Underley Estates, retired 1937. *Publications:* Crump Folk Going Home; The Lonely Plough; The Old Road from Spain; Beautiful End; The Splendid Fairing (awarded the Femina-Vie Heureuse Prize of 1920-21); The Trumpet in the Dust; The Things which Belong; He-Who-Came?; The Wisdom of the Simple; I Want (3 act Play); Four One-Act Plays. *Address:* 13 Orchard Road, Arnside, Carnforth. [*Died* 17 *June* 1955.

HOLME, Ernest Rudolph, O.B.E.; M.A. (Sydney), McCaughey Professor of English Language, University of Sydney, 1921-41, now Professor Emeritus; *s.* of late Rev. Thomas Holme, Rector of Leichhardt, Sydney; unmarried. *Educ.:* The King's School, Parramatta; University of Sydney; Paris and Berlin Universities. First class honours Latin and English, aeq. MacCallum Prize; M.A. Sydney; Assistant Master, Sydney Church of England Grammar School, 1891-94; Lecturer in English Univ. of Sydney, 1894-1908; Assist. Prof., 1908-20; Sec. of University Extension, 1906-11; President of the Union, 1911 and 1912; Member of the Advisory Committee on Disputed Pronunciations, for the New Standard Dictionary; Assistant Censor, 1914-17; Hon. Organiser, Sydney University Company (Australian Imperial Force Reinforcements), 1918; Hon. Captain A.I.F. and Chairman of the Advisory Committee of Australian Universities (A.I.F. Education Service); acted as Communications Censor, Sydney, for Australian Govt., 1939-40. Dean of the Faculty of Acts, Sydney, 1921-25; Director, Sydney University Appeal (for £250,000), 1927-28; Special Editor (Australian terms), Webster's New International Dictionary (Second Edition); Royal Jubilee Medal; Commandeur de l'ordre de Léopold II, 1935; Commander of Order of the Three Stars (Latvia), 1940. *Publications:* Aspects of Commercial Education in Europe; English Narrative Poems (ed. with M. W. MacCallum); First Principles of French Pronunciation (with Em. Saillens); The American University; Shore: The Sydney Church of England Grammar School. *Address:* Roun, 36 Shell Cove Road, Neutral Bay, Sydney, N.S.W. *Club:* University (Sydney). [*Died* 20 *Nov.* 1952.

HOLME, Sir Randle Fynes Wilson, Kt., *cr.* 1941; B.A.Oxon; Solicitor; *b.* 4 July 1864; *s.* of James Wilson Holme and Caroline Fynes Clinton; *m.* 1892, Evelyn Frances d'Egville (*d.* 1934); no *c.* *Educ.:* Sherborne; Corpus Christi College, Oxford. First Class Honours (Law) Oxford, 1887; Exploration in Labrador, 1887, (Royal Geographical Society's Proceedings, April 1888); Senior Member of firm of Godden Holme and Co., 5 Upper Belgrave Street, S.W.1; drafted an Income Tax Consolidation Bill in 1914, and co-operated as representing the Taxpayers with the Inland Revenue on the Bill leading to the Income Tax Act, 1918; Pres. of the Law Soc., 1939-40; Chm. Solicitors' Disciplinary Cttee., 1941-53; F.R.G.S.; Past Master of Wheelwrights Co. *Publications:* English versions of Wagner's Nibelungen Ring and Parsifal under nom de plume of Randle Fynes. *Recreations:* yachting, music. *Address:* 20 Hyde Park Place, W.2; 5 Upper Belgrave Street, S.W.1. *T.A.:* Satisdatio, Knights, London. *T.:* Paddington 6580, Sloane 5215. *Club:* St. Stephen's. [*Died* 23 *Dec.* 1957.

HOLMES, Lady; *see* Rivington, Madame Hill.

HOLMES, Albert Edward, C.B.E. 1937; retired Secretary of Printing and Kindred Trades Federation, and Joint Secretary of Joint Industrial Council of Printing and Allied

Trades of Great Britain and Ireland; *m.*; two *s.* two *d.* *Educ.:* King's Lynn, Norfolk. Life-long association with the Printing Industry. *Recreations:* motoring and golf. *Address:* 275 Battersea Park Road, S.W.11. *T.:* Macaulay 4000. [*Died* 8 *Feb.* 1953.

HOLMES, Sir Arthur William, K.B.E., *cr.* 1921 (C.B.E. 1918); F.Z.S., F.R.Hort.S.; late Member, Court of Common Council, City of London Corp. (Aldgate Ward); *b.* Hampstead, 9 Nov. 1877; *m.* 1905, Lottie, *o. d.* of late Charles Wood, Lewes, Sussex; one *s.* *Educ.:* International College, Hampstead. Late Managing Director of Shipton, Anderson & Co., Ltd., grain importers and merchants; Director of Contracts Royal Commission on Wheat Supplies, 1916; Member of Royal Commission on Wheat Supplies, 1919; Past Chm., National Federation of Corn Trade Associations; Past Director, Baltic Mercantile and Shipping Exchange; Freeman of the City of London; Past Senior Warden of Carmen's Co.; Past Mem. Council The Football Assoc.; Life Vice-Pres. London Football Assoc.; Past Chm. (Life Mem.) Isthmian Football League; Past Pres. London Football League, etc.; Order of the Nile, 1920; Order of the Crown of Italy, 1921; Legion of Honour, 1921. *Recreations:* hunting, football, cricket, motoring, golf. *Address:* Killiecrankie, Summersdale, Chichester, Sussex. *T.A.:* Summersdale, Chichester. *T.:* 7473. *Clubs:* Royal Automobile, East India and Sports, City Livery, M.C.C., etc.; West Sussex County (Chichester); West Somerset County (Minehead). [*Died* 8 *Feb.* 1960.

HOLMES, Burton; Lecturer on Travel, retired 1952; *b.* Chicago, Jan. 1870; *s.* of Ira and Virginia Burton Holmes; *m.* 1914, Margaret Elise Oliver. *Educ.:* Allen Academy; Harvard School, Chicago. First visit to Europe, 1886; First travel lecture, 1893; average five months' foreign travel yearly; first to use motion pictures in travel lectures, 1897; four tours around world; five new lectures with films in colour presented every year. *Publications:* The Burton Holmes Travelogues, 15 Volumes of travel lectures illustrated, 1910, out of print; The Traveler's Russia, 1 Vol., 1934; *autobiography,* The World is Mine, 1953; four volumes B.H. Travel Stories used as school readers. *Recreations:* travel and photography. *Address:* 2020 Grace Ave., Hollywood, California, U.S.A. *T.:* Hollywood 7-6882. *Clubs:* Metropolitan, Players', Lamb's, Explorers (New York). [*Died* 22 *July* 1958.

HOLMES, Daniel Turner; *b.* 23 Feb. 1863; *m.* 1896, Margaret (*d.* 1953), *d.* of Peter Eadie, formerly Provost of Paisley; two *d.* *Educ.:* London University (1st class honours); Universities of Paris and Geneva. Engaged in scholastic work, Greenock Academy and Paisley Grammar School till 1900; since then lecturing and literature; spent two years abroad, studying scholastic systems of France and Switzerland; M.P. (L.) Govan Division of Lanarkshire, 1911-18. *Publications:* French Essays on British Poets; Greek Lyrics; Lectures on Scottish Literature; Outline of French Literature; Literary Tours in the Highlands of Scotland. *Recreations:* reading and walking. *Address:* Midland Bank, Central Hall, Westminster, S.W.1. [*Died* 7 *April* 1955.

HOLMES, Ernest Hamilton, C.M.G. 1928; *b.* 1876; *s.* of Lieut.-Colonel W. P. Holmes of Ballingrawn, King's Co. Ireland; *m.* 1st, 1902, Ina (*d.* 1934), *d.* of William Hudleston Leslie; two *s.* two *d.*; 2nd, Florence Evelyn (*d.* 1956), *d.* of George Findlay Shirras, J.P. *Educ.:* Wellington College. Appointed to H.M. Consular Service in Japan, 1897; Vice-Consul, 1910; Consul, 1914; Consul-General, 1920; Consul-General, Yokohama, Japan, 1920-36 (retired 1936). *Recreations:* fishing. *Address:* Mount Nebo House, Taunton, Somerset. *T.:* 3219. [*Died* 26 *Nov.* 1957.

HOLMES, Haywood Temple, C.V.O. 1930; C.B.E. 1926; I.S.O. 1918; *b.* 18 Sept. 1865; *s.* of Haywood Holmes of Stamford Hill, formerly of Sheerness; *m.* 1891, Annie, *d.* of W S. Hoal of Fowey, Cornwall; one *s.* three *d.* *Educ.:* Tottenham Grammar School. Civil Servant, Board of Trade, 1883; Treasury, 1888; Assistant Accountant, Treasury, 1910; Accountant 1918-30; retired. *Address:* Penhale, Shoreham Lane, Riverhead, Sevenoaks. *T.:* Sevenoaks 2782. [*Died* 21 *Feb.* 1959.

HOLMES, Sir Hugh Oliver, K.B.E., *cr.* 1946; C.M.G. 1941; Q.C. 1920; M.C.; Puisne Judge, Kenya, since 1953; *b.* 12 Jan. 1886; 2nd *s.* of Rt. Hon. Hugh Holmes, Lord Justice of Appeal in Ireland; *m.* 1912, Rose, *d.* of Thomas Falls, D.L., of Lislap, Co. Tyrone; one *s.* four *d.* *Educ.:* Charterhouse; Trinity College, Dublin (Classical Scholar and Gold Medallist), John Brooke Scholar, 1910. Called to Irish Bar, 1910; Commission in R.F.A. 1914; landed at Suvla Bay, Aug. 1915; served in 29th Division in Gallipoli, France, and Egypt (despatches twice, M.C. and bar, Belgian Croix de Guerre); demobilised with rank of Major, 1919; returned to Irish Bar; Counsel to the Crown in Ireland, 1919-20; Judge in Native Court, Cairo, 1920-23; Judge of the Mixed Court, Cairo, 1924-29; Procurator-Gen. Mixed Court of Appeal, Alexandria, Egypt, 1929-49. *Recreation:* golf. *Address:* Supreme Court, Kenya. *Clubs:* Union (Alexandria); Turf (Cairo). [*Died* 1 *Oct.* 1955.

HOLMES, Colonel Robert Heuston, C.M.G. 1916; F.R.C.V.S.; late R. Army Veterinary Corps; *b.* 24 June 1870; *s.* of late Rev. John Holmes, The Manse, Tipperary; *m.* 1905, E. Athol, *y. d.* of late Rev. William Clarke, B.A., ex-Moderator, General Assembly of Ireland; one *s.* two *d.* *Educ.:* The Abbey, Tipperary. Captain, 1903; Major, 1910; served Tirah Expeditionary Force, 1897-98 (medal, two clasps); European War, 1914 (despatches twice, C.M.G.); retired pay, 1923. *Recreations:* polo, hunting, fishing, and shooting. *Address:* Carnone, Tipperary. [*Died* 4 *Oct.* 1952.

HOLMES, Sir Valentine, Kt., *cr.* 1946; Q.C. 1945; *b.* 24 July 1888; *s.* of late Rt. Hon. Hugh Holmes, Lord Justice of Appeal, Ireland; *m.* 1914, Gwendolen Armstrong, Dublin; one *s.* one *d.* *Educ.:* Charterhouse; Trinity College, Dublin. Called to Bar, 1913; Bencher of Inner Temple, 1934; Junior Treasury Counsel, 1935-45; retired, 1949. *Address:* Goldsmith Building, Temple, E.C.4. *T.:* Central 6104. [*Died* 19 *Nov.* 1956.

HOLMES, Rt. Rev. William Hardy; *b.* 25 June 1873; *s.* of William Hardy Holmes, Dublin; *m.* Ruth Williams, *d.* of George J. Scott, Londonderry; one *s.* *Educ.:* Trinity College, Dublin, D.D., LL.D., Curate of Christ Church, Derry, 1896-98; Rector of Lislimnaghan, 1898-1905; Rector of Kilbarron, 1905-16; Canon of St. Patrick's Cathedral, Dublin, 1909-32; Rector of Conwall and Archdeacon of Raphoe, 1916-19; Rector of Tamlaghtfinlagan, 1919-26; Archdeacon of Derry, 1921-32; Rector of Clonleigh, 1926-32; Bishop of Tuam, Killala and Achonry, 1932-38; Bishop of Meath, 1938-1945. *Address:* 17 Temple Villas, Palmerston Road, Rathmines, Dublin. *T.:* Dublin 92263. *Club:* Dublin University (Dublin). [*Died* 26 *May* 1951.

HOLMES à COURT, Col. Rupert Edward, D.S.O. 1917; *b.* 6 Feb. 1882; *s.* of late Col. Hon. E. A. Holmes à Court and Adelaide Sophie, *y. d.* of Hugh Hamersley of Pyrton Manor, Oxfordshire; *m.* 1917, Linda (*d.* 1935), *y. d.* of Rev. Cecil E. Smith; one *d.* *Educ.:* Haileybury; R.M.C., Sandhurst. Served South Africa, 1900-02; European War, 1915-18 (wounded, D.S.O., Bt. Lt.-Col.); commanded 2nd Batt. King's Shropshire Light Infantry, 1929-33; Officer-in-Charge Infantry Record and Pay Office, Shrewsbury, 1933-37; retired pay, 1937;

served War of 1939-45, until 1941; retired pay, 1941. *Address:* Makalanga, Mazoe, Southern Rhodesia. [*Died* 15 *May* 1958.

HOLMYARD, Eric John, M.A. (Cantab.), M.Sc., DLitt. (Bristol), F.R.I.C.; Editor, Pelican Science Series; *b.* 11 July 1891; *s.* of late I. B. Holmyard, Midsomer Norton, Somerset; *m.* 1916, Ethel Elizabeth (*d.* 1941), *er. d.* of late Egbert C. Britten, Midsomer Norton; two *s.* *Educ.:* Sexey's School, Bruton; Sidney Sussex College, Cambridge. Sixth Form Master (Science), Marlborough College, 1917-19; Head of Science Dept., Clifton College, 1920-40; Scientific Editor, J. M. Dent and Sons, Ltd., 1928-44; Chairman Science Masters' Assoc. 1926; Science Editor Everyman's Encyclopædia; Editor of Endeavour, 1941-54. Chairman, Soc. for the Study of Alchemy and Early Chemistry; Membre Correspondant de l'Académie Internationale de l'Histoire des Sciences; Chairman, World List of Scientific Periodicals. *Publications:* (co-editor), A History of Technology (Vol. I, 1954, Vol. II, 1956, Vol. III, 1957, Vols. IV, V, 1958); Alchemy, 1957; many textbooks of chemistry, and several texts of mediæval Arabic works on alchemy. *Recreations:* walking, travel. *Address:* Deefa, Prince's Road, Clevedon, Somerset. *Club:* Clevedon Golf (Clevedon). [*Died* 13 *Oct.* 1959.

HOLROYD, Michael, M.A., F.S.A., F.R.G.S., Fellow, Brasenose College, Oxford; *b.* 21 Sept. 1892; *s.* of late Sir Charles Holroyd and Fannie Fetherstonhaugh Macpherson; *m.* 1932, Winifred Beatrice Colwill. *Educ.:* Westminster; Christ Church, Oxford. Served with Hampshire Regiment (B.E.F. France) 1914-15, subsequently at War Office as Capt. 3rd Hampshire Regt., attached Intelligence; Fellow of Brasenose and Lecturer in Ancient History, 1919; Chairman Oxford Co-operating Committee, International Student Service since 1931. Served on General Staff (as Capt., R.A.R.O.), 1940-45; Chairman of Council (1947-) of the Oxford Playhouse performing co. (Oxford Repertory Players, Ltd.). *Publications:* Chapters on Greek and Roman Art in F. S. Marvin, Art and Civilization, 1928; articles (Roman biographies) in Oxford Classical Dictionary. *Recreation:* gardening. *Address:* Foxwood, Boar's Hill, Oxford. *T.:* Oxford 85295. [*Died* 12 *Oct.* 1953.

HOLT, Lt.-Col. Alwyn Vesey, D.S.O. 1918; O.B.E. 1944; late 1st Black Watch; *b.* 1887; 4th *s.* of late Sir Vesey Holt, K.B.E.; *m.* 1947, M. A. Calthrop, *d.* of F. G. Calthrop, and *widow* of Capt. D. Lumsden. *Educ.:* Eton; Sandhurst. Joined 1st Black Watch, 1907; served with Black Watch in European War, 1914-18 (wounded); attached to Royal Flying Corps, 1915; Wing Commander, 1918 (despatches, D.S.O., Officer Legion of Honour, Officer Croix de Guerre with Palm Leaves, Belgium Order of the Crown). D.L. Perthshire. *Address:* Craigmakerran, Guildtown, Perthshire, *Clubs:* Caledonian; New (Edinburgh). [*Died* 20 *Sept.* 1956.

HOLT, Very Rev. Edward John, M.B.E. 1938; Rector of Holy Trinity and Dean of Trinidad, Port of Spain, 1914-46; resigned on grounds of ill-health, after 57 years' work, 1947; *b.* Grantham, Lincs, 29 Sept. 1867; *e. s.* of late Rev. T. E. Holt, Diocesan Missioner, Winchester; *m.* 1895, Mary Jane, 5th *d.* of D. S. Osment, Colonial Engineer, St. Vincent. *Educ.:* St. Augustine's College, Canterbury. Ordained, 1890; Curate of St. George's Cathedral, Windward Islands, 1890-93; All Saints, Port of Spain, 1893-95; Cathedral, 1895-1914; Chaplain to the Local Forces, 1918. *Recreations:* music (organ), campanology (Member of Soc. College Youths), photography, Freemasonry (P.M., Kt. 30 deg.), wood-carving. *Address:* Long Circular Road, Port of Spain, Trinidad. [*Died* 6 *Nov.* 1948.

[*But death not notified in time for inclusion in Who Was Who 1941–1950, first edn.*

HOLT, Martin Drummond Vesey; late a Managing Director of Glyn, Mills & Co., Bankers and Army and Air Force Agents; *e. s.* of late Sir Vesey Holt, K.B.E., of Mount Mascal, Bexley, Kent; *m.* 1918, Phyllis Hedworth Camilla (now Lady Phyllis Holt), 2nd *d.* of late Colonel E. W. Herbert (60th Rifles) of Orleton, Wellington, Salop; one *s.* *Educ.:* Eton; Trinity College, Cambridge. Amateur Champion, Epée, 1920 and 1923; Member of Olympic Epée team, 1908, 1912, 1920, 1924, 1928. *Recreations:* fencing, shooting, fishing, etc. *Address:* 27 The Fairway, Aldwick Bay Estate, Bognor Regis, Sussex. *T.:* Pagham 2664. *Clubs:* Carlton, Union. [*Died* 2 *Nov.* 1956.

HOLT, Maj.-Gen. Sir Maurice Percy Cue, K.C.B., *cr.* 1919 (C.B. 1915); K.C.M.G., *cr.* 1917; D.S.O. 1902; M.R.C.S., L.S.A.; late A.M.S.; *b.* 8 June 1862; *m.* 1887, Sarah Annie, *d.* of late Thomas M. Busteed of Madras; one *s.* one *d.* *Educ.:* King's College School; King's College Hospital. Joined R.A.M.C. 1887; in medical charge expedition to Sambana's and North Zululand (thanks of Colonial Office), 1895; served South Africa, 1899-1902, including Siege of Ladysmith and Transvaal (despatches, King's and Queen's medals five clasps); European War, 1914-18 (despatches ten times, C.B.); retired pay, 1922; Col. Commandant R.A.M.C. 1928-32; specialist in operative surgery. *Address:* 2 Salisbury Road, Farnborough, Hants. [*Died* 6 *Sept.* 1954.

HOLT, Rev. Raymond Vincent; Minister of Pound Square Chapel, Cullompton: Principal, The Unitarian College, Manchester, 1944-55; *b.* 6 Feb. 1885; *s.* of Peter Holt and Alice Sansome Holt (*née* Farn); *m.* 1916, Isabel Clark Copland; no *c.* *Educ.:* Leigh Grammar School; Lincoln and Manchester Colleges, Oxford (Stanhope Historical Essay Prizeman; B.A. 1906; B.Litt. 1913; M.A. 1933); Marburg University. Minister, St. Mark's Chapel, Edinburgh, 1912-21; Manchester Coll., Oxford: Tutor 1921-44, Librarian and Warden; Lectr., History of Doctrine, Manchester Univ., 1945-55. Pres., General Assembly of Unitarian and Free Christian Churches, 1945-46; Mem. Oxford City Council, 1941-44. *Publications:* The Unitarian Contribution to Social Progress, 1938, 2nd edn. 1952; Progress and Christianity; Religion and History (Essex Hall Lecture, 1943); Protestantism and the Life of To-Day; Religion as an Adventure, 1954. *Recreation:* walking. *Address:* 38 High St., Cullompton, Devon. [*Died* 20 *March* 1957.

HOLT, Vice-Adm. Reginald Vesey, C.B. 1938; D.S.O. 1917; M.V.O. 1923; R.N.; *b.* 1884; 2nd *s.* of late Sir Vesey Holt, K.B.E.; *m.* 1914, Evelyn Constance, *d.* of late Colonel Robert Day and Mrs. Day of Lawford House, Manningtree; two *s.* two *d.* *Educ.:* Eton; H.M.S. Britannia. Capt., 1925; Rear-Adm. 1936; Vice-Adm. 1939; Capt.-in-Charge, Bermuda Dockyard, 1928-30; Chief of Staff to Com.-in-Chief at the Nore, 1931-1933; commanded H.M.S. Shropshire, 1933-34; Capt., Roy. Naval Coll., Dartmouth, 1934-36; Rear-Adm. and Sen. Naval Officer, Yangtse, 1937-1939 (despatches); United States Distinguished Service Medal, 1938; Vice-Adm. 1939; retired May 1940; re-employed as Flag Officer Humber Oct. 1940-42; Commodore L.S.T., 1942-43; Senior British Naval Officer, Azores, 1943-44; Naval Officer-in-Charge Newhaven, April-Oct. 1944; Flag Officer Denmark, 1945 (Knight Commander of the Order of the Dannebrog). *Address:* Little Glebe, Fontwell, Nr. Arundel, Sussex. *T.:* Eastergate 444. *Club:* United Service. [*Died* 9 *Dec.* 1957.

HOLT, Sir Vyvyan, K.B.E., *cr.* 1956; C.M.G. 1939; M.V.O. 1933; *b.* 25 January 1896; *s.* of Arthur Ernest Holt and Theresa Perkins; unmarried. *Educ.:* private tutors, Served with 9th Bn. Middlesex Regiment, Indian Signals and North-West Frontier

Intelligence Corps, 1914-18; Iraq Political Service, 1919; A.D.C. to High Comr., 1922; Private Sec., 1924; Oriental Sec., 1926; Oriental Counsellor, British Embassy, Teheran, 1946; apptd. Minister to Korea, 1949; interned in North Korea, 1950; released, 1953. Minister at San Salvador, 1954-56; retired from Foreign Service, 1956. Attached to suite of late King Feisal during his state visit to London, 1933 (M.V.O., Rafidain Order 3rd Class). *Recreation:* polo. *Address:* 38 Haven Green Court, Ealing, W.5. *Club:* Junior Army and Navy. [*Died* 29 *July* 1960.

HOLYMAN, Sir Ivan (Nello), K.B.E., *cr.* 1956; M.C. 1918; Chairman since 1950 and Managing Director since 1936 of Australian National Airways Pty. Ltd.; Chairman since 1950 and Managing Director since 1940 of Wm. Holyman & Sons Pty. Ltd.; Chairman McIlwraith McEacharn Ltd. since 1956; *b.* 9 July 1896; *s.* of late William Holyman; *m.* 1924, Enid Colville McKinlay; two *s.* one *d.* *Educ.:* Launceston Church of England Grammar School, Tasmania. Joined Wm. Holyman & Sons Pty. Ltd., 1911; enlisted A.I.F., 1914; rejoined Holyman & Sons, 1919; founded Australian National Airways, 1936. *Recreation:* golf. *Address:* 65 Albany Road, Toorak, Victoria. *T.:* UY 2686. *Clubs:* Australia, Athenæum, Savage, Royal Melbourne Golf (Melbourne); Royal Sydney Golf (Sydney); Commonwealth (Canberra); Launceston (Launceston, Tas.). [*Died* 18 *Jan.* 1957.

HOME, 13th Earl of (*cr.* 1604), **Charles Cospatrick Archibald Douglas-Home,** K.T. 1930; Baron Home, 1473; Baron Dunglass, 1604; Baron Douglas (U.K.), 1875; Lord Lieutenant of Berwickshire since 1930; Capt. King's Bodyguard for Scotland, Royal Company of Archers; *b.* 29 Dec. 1873; *o. s.* of 12th Earl of Home and Maria, *o. d.* of Capt. Charles Conrad Grey, R.N.; *S.* father, 1918; *m.* 1902, Lilian, *d.* of 4th Earl of Durham; four *s.* two *d.* (and one *s.* killed in action, 1943.) Lt.-Col. Lanarkshire Yeomanry Cavalry; contested Berwickshire (C.), 1900. *Heir:* *s.* Lord Dunglass. *Address:* The Hirsel, Coldstream, Berwickshire; Castlemains, Douglas, Lanarkshire. *Club:* Carlton. [*Died* 11 *July* 1951.

HOME, Brig.-Gen. Sir Archibald Fraser, K.C.V.O., *cr.* 1936 (C.V.O. 1933); C.B. 1919; C.M.G. 1918; D.S.O. 1915; *b.* 14 Sept. 1874; *e. s.* of late Col. F. J. Home, C.S.I.; *m.* Violet Mary Bertha (*d.* 1944), *d.* of late W. K. D'Arcy; one *s.* two *d.* Entered Army, 1895; Captain, 1904; Major, 1914; Captain attached General Staff, Southern Command, 1905; Brigade-Major, 3rd Cavalry Brigade, Irish Command, 1912-13; General Staff Officer, 2nd Grade, Staff College, 1913; served European War, France and Flanders, 1914-19 (despatches, C.B., C.M.G., D.S.O., Bt. Lt.-Col. and Col.); Commander Legion of Honour; retired, May 1919; J.P. Suffolk, 1925; High Sheriff for Suffolk, 1929; D.L. Suffolk, 1930; Clerk of the Cheque and Adjutant, 1926-35; Lieut., 1938-45, H.M.'s Body Guard of the Honourable Corps of Gentlemen-at-Arms, Standard Bearer, 1935-38; Col. 11th Hussars, 1939-45. *Address:* 9 Montpelier Sq., S.W.7. *T.:* Kensington 5759. *Club:* Cavalry. [*Died* 20 *Jan.* 1953.

HOME, Ethel, M.A.; Lecturer on Musical and other subjects; Member of Board of Musical Studies, London University; *d.* of Sir Anthony Dickson Home, V.C., K.C.B., and Jessey Hallett. *Educ.:* Clapham High School; Newnham College, Cambridge; Headmistress Kensington High School, 1900-31; Member of various Musical and Educational Societies; Founder of Kensington High School Music Training Dept. for Teachers. *Publications:* Music as a Language; Concise Teaching of Sight-singing; Transposition, etc. *Recreations:* travelling, etc. *Address:* 50 Bullingham Mansions, Church Street, Kensington, W.8. [*Died* 9 *Dec.* 1954.

HOME, Lieut.-Colonel George, C.B.E. 1919 (O.B.E. 1918); Lt.-Col. N.Z. Medical Corps (retired list); President N.Z. Branch of British Medical Association, 1932-33; retired from medical practice, 1945; *b.* 1870; *s.* of John Home, Peeblesshire; *m.* 1898, Lily (*d.* 1932), *d.* of Robert Wade, Wallasey, Cheshire; one *d.* *Educ.:* Wanganui Collegiate School; Edinburgh University (M.B., C.M., M.D.); King's College, London. Served European War, 1914-19 (despatches, O.B.E., C.B.E.); Regimental Medical Officer, Gallipoli Campaign; Divisional Surgical Officer, and later Officer Commanding New Zealand General Hospital, Walton on Thames, 1918-1919. *Address:* Haumoana, Glenalmond Road, New Plymouth, New Zealand. [*Died* 7 *Feb.* 1956.

HOMER, Sidney; Composer; *b.* Boston, 9 Dec. 1864; *s.* of George Homer; *m.* Louise Dilworth Beatty (Louise Homer, *d.* 1947); one *s.* four *d.* (and one *d. decd.*). *Educ.:* Phillips Andover; Munich Conservatory of Music. Hon. Doctor of Music, Rollins College, Florida, Curtis Institute, Phila., Pa. *Works:* Prospice; Paupers Drive; How's My Boy; Requiem; Song of the Shirt; Sheep and Lambs; The Bandanna Ballads; Dearest; Chamber Music for private circulation. *Publications:* My Wife and I, Biography, 1939; Over a hundred songs; Organ Sonata; Widow in the Bye Street (three numbers); The Everlasting Mercy; the Lay of The Laborer; Three collections, piano pieces for children. *Address:* 36 Gramercy Park, New York City, N.Y., U.S.A. [*Died* 10 *July* 1953.

HONE, Evie S.; *b.* Ireland, 1894; *d.* of Joseph and Eva Hone. *Educ.:* Dublin. Studied (with Walter Sickert and B. Meninsky), London; also studied in Paris. Exhibits regularly in Irish Exhibition of Living Artists; work also shown in many London exhibitions and in Paris. Stained-glass window commissioned by Irish Government in 1939 for Irish Pavilion; windows, mostly in Ireland: Jesuit Seminary, Tullamore; St. Mary's, Kingscourt, Co. Cavan; in England: Ettington Park, Warwickshire; Lanercost Abbey, Cumberland; Downe, Kent; East window for Eton College Chapel; window of Wellingborough Parish Church, Northants.; engaged on windows for Farm Street Jesuit Church and new Cathedral of Washington, D.C. *Address:* Dower House, Marlay, Rathfarnham, Co. Dublin, Ireland. *T.:* Dublin 95896. [*Died* 13 *March* 1955.

HONE, Frank Sandland, C.M.G. 1941; B.A.; M.B., B.S.; F.R.A.C.P.; Hon. Consulting Physician, Adelaide Hospital; late Hon. Director Radio-Therapy Clinic; Chairman Anti-Cancer Campaign; Member of University Council since 1919. *Educ.:* Adelaide University, B.A., 1889, M.B., B.S., 1894. F.R.A.C.P., 1938. *Address:* 178 North Terrace, Adelaide, South Australia; 16 Thornber Street, Unley Park, Adelaide, South Australia. [*Died* 9 *May* 1951.

HONE, Joseph Maunsell; Writer; *b.* 8 Feb. 1882, Irish; *s.* of William Hone, Killiney, Co. Dublin, and Sarah Cooper, Cooper Hill, Co. Limerick; *m.* 1911, Vera Brewster, New York; two *s.* one *d.* *Educ.:* Cheam School; Wellington College; Jesus College, Cambridge. President of Irish Acad. of Letters, 1957. *Publications:* Bishop Berkeley, 1932, and Swift or the Egoist, 1935 (with Dr. M. M. Rossi); Life of George Moore, 1935; Henry Tonks, 1938; Moores of Moore Hall, 1939; Life of W. B. Yeats, 1943; Letters of John B. Yeats, 1944; Biographical contribution to History of the Bank of Ireland, 1949; Victoria's Ireland. *Recreations:* formerly cricket, now reading Italian and German philosophies. *Address:* 4 Winton Road, Dublin. *Club:* Kildare Street (Dublin). [*Died* 26 *March* 1959.

HONEGGER, Arthur; Composer; *b.* Havre, 10 March 1892. *Educ.:* Zürich Conservatory; Havre, under R. C. Martin; Paris, Gédalge,

Widor, d'Indy. *Works:* Horace Victorieux, pantomime symphony, 1922; Le Roi David, dramatic psalm, 1922; le Chant de Nigamon, 1917; Pastorale d'été, 1920; Chant de Joie, 1923; Pacific 231, 1923; Concertino, piano et orchestre, 1925; Judith, dramatic psalm, 1925; Skating-Rink ballet, 1921; la Tempête, 1923; sonatas, songs, Cantique de Paques, 1918; Pâques à New York 1920; Antigone; Amphion; Le Roi Pausole, 1931; Semiramis; L'Aiglon, 1936; Jeanne d'Arc au bûcher, 1936, etc.; works include 5 symphonies. Wrote scores for films including Mayerling, Pygmalion and Harvest. *Address:* 71 Boul. de Clichy, Paris 9e. [*Died* 27 *Nov.* 1955.

HONEY, William Bowyer, C.B.E. 1951; F.S.A.; Keeper, Department of Ceramics, Victoria and Albert Museum, 1938-50; *b.* 13 Apr. 1889; *m.* 1st, Winifred, *d.* of late Alfred Rich; one *s.*; 2nd, Helen Julie, *d.* of late Dr. Newman Neild, F.R.C.P.; one *s.* *Educ.:* Sir Walter St. John's School, Battersea. *Publications:* Guide to Later Chinese Porcelain (V. and A. Museum Handbook), 1927; Old English Porcelain, 1928, 2nd edn. 1948; English Pottery and Porcelain, 1933; Dresden China, 1934, 3rd edn. 1954; English Pottery, Old and New (V. and A. Museum), 1936; Gardening Heresies and Devotions, 1939; The Sacred Fire, an Anthology of English Poems (now Broadway Book of English Verse), 1939; (under name of William Bowyer) Brought out in Evidence, an autobiography, 1941; The Ceramic Art of China and other Countries of the Far East, 1945; The Art of the Potter, 1945; Science and the Creative Arts, 1945; Glass (V. and A. Museum Handbook), 1946; English Glass ('Britain in Pictures'), 1946; German Porcelain, 1947; Corean Pottery, 1947; Wedgwood Ware, 1948; Nature, God and Man, a pamphlet, 1949; Many Occasions, essays, 1949; European Ceramic Art, Vol. I, Illustrated Historical Survey, 1949; Vol. II, Dictionary, 1952; French Porcelain, 1950; (with J. P. Cushion) A Concise Handbook of English Pottery Marks, 1956; editor Faber Monographs on pottery and porcelain, 1947-54; articles in the Encyclopædia Britannica, Apollo, Burlington Magazine, Connoisseur, Old Furniture, Pantheon, etc. *Address:* The White House, Jordans, Bucks. [*Died* 13 *Sept.* 1956.

HONEYBALL, Mrs. Olympia Lœtitia, R.R.C. 1919; F.R.H.S.; landowner, Kent; *b.* 1876; *y. d.* of Rev. W. Waddon-Martyn, Tonacombe, Morwenstow, Cornwall, and Rector of Lifton, Devon; *m.* 1900, Colonel J. F. Honeyball, V.D., J.P. (*d.* 1923), of Newgardens, Teynham, Kent; two *s.* *Educ.:* Moorfield, Mannamead, Plymouth. Served entire war; Commandant of Auxiliary Military Hospital, Whitehall, Sittingbourne, 1914-20; Gold Order Red Triangle, 1920; Defence Medal, 1946; Champion cherry grower; winner of the Golden Vase for cherries, 1935. F.R.E.S., resigned 1948. *Address:* Newgardens, Teynham, Sittingbourne, Kent. *T.A.:* Honeyball, Teynham. *T.:* Teynham 208. *Club:* Ladies' Carlton. [*Died* 22 *Jan.* 1956.

HONYWOOD, Constance, Lady; Constance Mary; Founder of group of the Honywood Hotels; London Chamber of Commerce; O.St.J., 1951; *d.* of late Rev. Charles Henry Vincent Pixell; *m.* Sir Courtenay John Honywood, 9th Bt. (*d.* 1944). *Address:* 16 Empire House, Thurloe Place, S.W.7. *T.:* Kensington 8623. [*Died* 9 *April* 1956.

HOOD, Sir Hugh (Meggison), K.C.I.E., *cr.* 1942 (C.I.E. 1934); C.S.I. 1939; *b.* 5 June 1885; *s.* of Christopher Hood and Melinda Dix; *m.* 1916, Alice Fenton Millar, M.B.E. 1944; one *s.* *Educ.:* Middlesbrough High School; Jesus College, Cambridge. Joined I.C.S., 1909; War Service, 1916-19; Collector, 1923; Registrar Cooperative Societies, 1923-1924 and 1926-29; Chm. Madras Provincial Banking Enquiry Committee, 1929-30; Financial Secretary to Govt. of Madras, 1931; Collector, 1935; Home Secretary, 1936; Acting Chief Sec., 1938; Adviser to Governor of Madras, 1939-44; Bengal Administration Enquiry Committee, 1944-45; Adviser on Co-operation to Govt. of Bengal, 1945. Principal Sec. Finance Dept., Govt. of India, 1946. *Address:* Kiln House, Crookham, Hants. *Club:* Oriental. [*Died* 2 *Feb.* 1952.

HOOD, Sydney Walter, C.B. 1947; *b.* 4 Apr. 1886; *m.* 1911, Grace Harrisson; one *s.* one *d.* *Educ.:* Woodbridge School, Suffolk; privately. Permanent Civil Servant since 1908 when entered the Service as an Assistant Examiner of Patents. Military service Sept. 1914-May 1919; Board of Trade to March 1938; Food (Defence Plans) Dept. and Ministry of Food (Under-Secretary); retired 1948. Barrister-at-law. *Recreations:* gardening, reading. *Address:* Orchard Cottage, Broad Street, nr. Guildford, Surrey. *T.:* Guildford 62007. [*Died* 29 *May* 1960.

HOOLEY, Lt.-Col. Vernon Vavasour, C.B.E. 1919; *b.* 1862; *e. s.* of W. Hooley of Portswood, Southampton; *m.* 1895, Mary (*d.* 1925), 3rd *d.* of late Col. Thomas Maxwell, Natal. Formerly Lieut.-Col. R.A.S.C.; served European War, 1914-19 (despatches, C.B.E.). *Recreations:* shooting, fishing, motoring. *Address:* Hauteville, Welbeck Avenue, Southampton. *T.:* 74340. [*Died* 28 *Dec.* 1952.

HOOPER, Barrington, C.B.E. 1920; Chairman and Managing Director, Industrial Newspapers, Limited; *b.* 1885; *s.* of Charles Hooper, of Awre, Gloucester; *m.* 1911, Josephine Crook; two *s.* one *d.* *Educ.:* private schools. Journalist and publicist; seven years, staff of Daily Mail; organised War Bond Tank Campaign, 1916, Victory Loan, Food Economy Campaign; political publicity; Controller of Publicity, British Empire Exhibition, 1924 and 1925. *Recreations:* motoring and golf. *Address:* Southward, Mount Park, Harrow, Middx.; John Adam House, John Adam Street, Adelphi, W.C.2. *Clubs:* Constitutional, Thirty, etc. [*Died* 2 *Sept.* 1960.

HOOPER, Charles Arthur, C.M.G. 1944; Puisne Judge, Kenya, since 1954; *b.* 26 Nov. 1889; *er. s.* of late Charles Joseph Hooper and Ellen Dixon; *m.* Therese Leonie, *d.* of late Ernest Pointin; no *c.* *Educ.:* University College, London Univ. (Ouseley and Gilchrist Memorial Scholarships in Turkish, Arabic, and Persian). Called to Bar, Inner Temple, 1924; served European War, 1914-18; held legal posts in service of Govt. of Iraq, 1925-31; Judicial Adviser to Govt. of Trans-Jordan, 1931-36; Procureur and Advocate-General of Mauritius 1936-44; Puisne Judge, Gold Coast, 1944-49. Lately Legal Adviser to Govt. of Cyrenaica. Order of Istiklal, 2nd Cl., Trans-Jordan, 1934. *Publications:* various legal. *Address:* Supreme Court, Nairobi, Kenya. [*Died* 28 *Feb.* 1960.

HOOPER, Cyril Noel, C.B.E. 1945; one of H.M's. Lieutenants for the City of London; *b.* 25 Dec. 1884; *e. s.* of late Miller Hooper, barrister-at-law; *m.* 1914, Winifred Leslie, *e. d.* of late William John Gibson, Loughton, Essex; three *d.* *Educ.:* St. Paul's School. Called to Bar, 1913; served European War, 1915-19, with Inns of Court O.T.C., and King's African Rifles; on staff at Nairobi, 1917-19, as Temp. Capt. Clerk of the Fishmongers' Company, 1922-48; retired 1948. Clerk to Governors of Gresham's School, Holt, 1922-48; Member of Court of Fishmongers' Company; Dep. Chm. and Chm. of Exec. Cttee., Public Schools Appointments Bureau; Hon. Secretary Assoc. of Governing Bodies of Public Schools; Hon. Treasurer Salmon and Trout Assoc.; a Vice-Pres. of River Boards' Assoc., Member Executive Committee of National Assoc. of Fishery Boards, etc. *Address:* 20 Embankment Gardens, Chelsea, S.W.3. *T.:* Flaxman 7545. *Club:* Brooks's. [*Died* 28 *Oct.* 1952.

HOOPER, Ian Mackay; Chairman, The General Steam Navigation Company Ltd., since 1954; Director, P. & O. Steam Navigation Co.; *b.* 5 Jan. 1902; *s.* of Captain Henry Brereton Hooper, R.I.M., and Anna Maria Mackay; *m.* 1st, 1928, Alison Margaret Blair (marriage dissolved); two *s.* one *d.*; 2nd, 1952, Mrs. Ursula Winifred Skerry; one *d.* *Educ.:* R.N. Colleges Osborne and Dartmouth; Trinity Hall, Cambridge. Joined H.M.S. Valiant, 5th Battle Squadron, as Midshipman, 1918; was present at surrender of German High Seas Fleet; served 2 years in H.M.S. Hawkins on China Station; resigned to go to Cambridge. Assistant to Mackinnon, Mackenzie & Co., India, 1923-1934; Director of The General Steam Navigation Co. Ltd., 1934. Commissioned R.N.V.R., 1939; Asst. Naval Attaché, Athens, 1940; served 1941-46 with Ministry of War Transport: Deputy to Sir Ernest Murrant, Alexandria, and later Special Planning Rep. of Director of Sea Transport, Cairo, Algiers, Caserta, Versailles and Delhi. Dep. Chm., King George's Fund for Sailors. Officier de l'Ordre du Mérite Maritime, 1950; Knight Commander in the Order For Merits to the Italian Republic, 1957. *Recreations:* ski-ing, riding. *Address:* Doubleton Farmhouse, Penshurst, Kent. *T.:* Penshurst 373. *Clubs:* Bath; Kandahar. [*Died* 28 *Aug.* 1958.

HOPE, Colonel Adrian Victor Webley, C.I.E. 1919; retired on pension; *b.* 16 Feb. 1873; *s.* of Rear-Admiral Charles Webley Hope; *m.* 1920, Ethel Mary Middleton (*d.* 1938); one *d.* *Educ.;* Kelly College, Tavistock. Indian Army; served in Aden and Mesopotamia, 1914-18 (despatches twice, C.I.E.). *Address:* Elm Corner, Marlow Common, Bucks. *T.:* Marlow 191. [*Died* 20 *Aug.* 1960.

HOPE, Adm. Sir George Price Webley, K.C.B. *cr.* 1923 (C.B. 1916); K.C.M.G., *cr.* 1919; R.N., retired; 2nd *s.* of late Admiral Charles Webley Hope; *b.* St. Andrews, 11 Oct. 1869; *m.* 1899, Arabella Philippa (*d.* 1945), 2nd *d.* of John Sutton Sams; one *s.* one *d.* *Educ.:* Mannamead School, Plymouth; H.M.S. Britannia. Midshipman in Minotaur and Opal; Lieut. 1889; served in Colossus, Excellent, Empress of India, and Magnificent; Admiralty in Dept. of Director of Naval Ordnance, 1900; Commander, 1900; commanded H.M.S. Pioneer in Mediterranean, 1902-4; Staff of War College till July 1905; Captain, 1905; Flag Captain to Rear-Adm. Neville in Good Hope, 1905-7; and Magnificent and Bulwark, 1909-11; at War College, 1908, and Admiralty War Staff, 1911-13, as Assistant Director of Operations Divisions; commanded Superb, 1913-14; King Alfred, Aug. 1914; served during operations at Dardanelles, Feb.-May 1915 (C.B.); in command of H.M.S. Queen Elizabeth; Director of Operations Division, Admiralty War Staff, 1917; Rear-Adm. 1917; Vice-Adm. 1920; Admiral 1925; Deputy First Sea Lord of the Admiralty, 1918-19; was present at negotiations for and signing of the Armistice, near Compiègne, 11 Nov. 1918; Admiralty representative at Peace Conference, 1919; commanded Third Light Cruiser Squadron, Mediterranean, 1919-21; President and Flag Officer commanding the Royal Naval College, Greenwich, 1923-26; retd. list, March 1926; a Trustee of National Maritime Museum. *Recreations:* golf, shooting, fishing. *Address:* Common House, Plaistow, Billingshurst, Sussex. *Club:* United Service. [*Died* 11 *July* 1959.

See also Brig. A. G. Neville.

HOPE, Sir Harry, 1st Bt., *cr.* 1932; Kt., *cr.* 1920; *b.* 24 Sept. 1865; *s.* of late James Hope, Eastbarns, Dunbar; *m.* 1897, Margaret Binnie (*d.* 1948), *d.* of R. K. Holmes Kerr, Largs, Ayrshire; two *s.* one *d.* President of Scottish Chamber of Agriculture, 1908; was a member of the Scottish Agricultural Commission which, on the invitation of the Canadian Government, reported on the agricultural resources of the Dominion, 1908; has served on many local public boards; Vice-Lieutenant and Convener County of Angus since 1937; J.P. Angus; an ex-militia officer, retiring as captain; contested Elgin and Nairn, 1906; M.P. (C.) Buteshire 1910-Dec. 1918, W. Stirlingshire and Clackmannan, Dec. 1918-22; Forfarshire, 1924-31; President County Councils Assoc. of Scotland, 1940-42; Trustee Scottish Unionist Association. *Heir: er. s.* James, *b.* 2 May 1898. *Address:* Kinnettles; Forfar. *Club:* New (Edinburgh). [*Died* 29 *Dec.* 1959.

HOPE, Col. Hon. John Andrew, D.S.O. 1918; K.C. 1929; M.C.;, V.D.; a Justice of Appeal of the Court of Appeal Ontario since 1945; a Governor of University of Toronto, 1945; *b.* Perth, Ontario, 4 May 1890; *s.* of Peter Hope and Jane L. Holmes; *m.* 1919, Hilda, *o. d.* of W. J. Southcombe, Surbiton, Surrey; one *d.* *Educ.:* Perth Collegiate Institute; Toronto University; Law School, Osgoode Hall, Toronto. Barrister-at-law, 1914; read law with and later a partner of the late Hon. J. A. Stewart, P.C., K.C.; Lieutenant 42nd Lanark and Renfrew Regt., 1910; Capt. and Adjutant 59th Batt. Canadian Expeditionary Force; went to France 20 Sept. 1916, joining 46th Batt. Saskatchewan Regiment; served as Company Commander, Adjutant, and 2nd in command battalion; wounded at Passchendaele, 27 Oct. 1917, and at Drocourt Queant, 3 Sep. 1918 (despatches, M.C., D.S.O.); commanded the Lanark and Renfrew Scottish Regiment, which he converted into a Highland Regiment allied with The Black Watch; formerly commanding 8th Canadian Infantry Brigade; President of the Great War Memorial Hospital of Perth District 13 years; Commandant Canadian Bisley Team, 1931; formerly Hon. A.D.C. to Governor-General of Canada, Lord Bessborough; Pres. Canadian Infantry Association, 1934; Chairman, 1933, Conference Defence Associations of Canada; Chief Commissioner of The Board of Review for Ontario under F.C.A. Act, 1935-40. Chairman, Royal Commission on Education for Ontario, 1945; a Justice of Supreme Court, High Court Division, Ontario, 1933-45. *Address:* Glynwood, Riverview Drive, Toronto 12, Canada. *T.:* HU 9-3712 Toronto. *Clubs:* Canadian Military Institute, University (Toronto). [*Died* 31 *Dec.* 1954.

HOPE, Sydney, J.P. 1950; *b.* 1905; *s.* of Thomas Hope, Manchester. *Educ.:* Glossop Grammar School; Ellesmere Coll., Shropshire. Admitted a solicitor, 1930; M.P. (U.) Stalybridge and Hyde Division of Cheshire, 1931-35. *Address:* Knowles House, Handforth, Wilmslow, Cheshire. *T.:* Wilmslow 3864. [*Died* 20 *Dec.* 1959.

HOPE-DUNBAR, Sir Charles Dunbar, 6th Bt., *cr.* 1664 (revived 1916); D.L., J.P.; *b.* 1873; *o. s.* of Capt. John Hope, R.N. (*d.* 1915); *m.* 1906, Edythe Mary (*d.* 1948), *e. d.* of Richard Ramsden, of Siddinghurst, Surrey; one *s.*; *m.* 1948, Marjorie MacRobert. Major, R.F.A., 1900-10; served S. African War, 1900-2 (two medals and clasps); European War, 1914-18. *Heir: s.* Basil Douglas, Capt. The Queen's Own Cameron Highlanders [*b.* 16 Feb. 1907; *m.* 1st, 1932, Evelyn Diana, *er. d.* of late Col. G. I. Fraser; 2nd, 1940, Edith Maude Maclaren, *e. d.* of Mrs. Cross, Earlston, Borgue, and of the late Malcolm Cross; one *s.*]. *Address:* Park House, Kirkcudbright, Scotland. *Club:* Army and Navy. [*Died* 6 *Jan.* 1958.

HOPEWELL, Alan Francis John, M.A.; Headmaster of Hereford Cathedral School since 1945; *b.* 1 March 1892; 2nd *s.* of late E. W. Hopewell (formerly of Hartlebury, Worcs., and of Abbotswood, Guildford); *m.* 1933, Barbara Mary Gibbs; one *d.* *Educ.:* Hereford Cathedral School; Queens' College, Cambridge (Open Classical Exhibitioner). 1st Division of 111rd Cl. Classical Tripos, Part I, 1914; Commission in Duke of

Wellington's Regt., Aug. 1914; wounded at Suvla Bay, Gallipoli, Aug. 1915; invalided out, July 1917; Assistant Master, Lancing College, 1917-19; Inspector, Ministry of Pensions, 1919-20; Assistant Master, Ashdown House, Forest Row, 1922-23 (and again 1928-33); Assistant Master and Housemaster, Cranleigh School, 1924-27; Assistant Master, King Edward VI School, Stafford, 1933-34; Master-in-Charge, Preparatory Dept., Victoria College, Jersey, 1935 - June 1940; Assistant Master, Victoria College, Jersey, at Bedford School, 1940-43; Assistant Master, Elms School, Colwall, 1943. Assistant Master and Housemaster, Hereford Cathedral School, 1944-45. *Recreations:* cricket, Association football, lawn tennis, golf, winter sports, motoring, printing. *Address:* Cathedral School, Hereford. *T.:* Hereford 3757. [*Died* 21 *Jan.* 1957.

HOPKIN, Major Daniel, M.C., M.A., LL.B.; Barrister-at-law; Metropolitan Police Magistrate since 1941; *b.* Llantwit Major, nr. Cardiff, July 1886; *s.* of David Hopkin, farm labourer; *m.* 1919, Edmée Viterbo; one *s.* one *d.* *Educ.:* Elementary School Llantwit Major; Training College, Carmarthen; St. Catharine's College, Cambridge (Exhibitioner). School teacher; served European War, 4 Aug. 1914-18, Suvla Bay, France, Palestine (M.C.); demobilised rank of Major; four years in business in Cairo; M.P. (Lab.) Carmarthen 1929-31 and 1935-41; Barrister-at-law on South Wales Circuit; rejoined Army Dec. 1939, commanded Company Pioneer Corps. *Recreations:* golf, walking. *Address:* Great Marlborough Street Police Court, W.1. [*Died* 30 *Aug.* 1951.

HOPKINS, Charles James William, C.B.E. 1949 (M.B.E. 1918); M.I.N.A. 1917; R.C.N.C. 1910; *b.* 25 November 1887; *e. s.* of Charles and Elizabeth Hopkins; *m.* 1916, Christian Robertson Riddell, Edinburgh; one *d.* *Educ.:* Sir Joseph Williamson's Mathematical School, Rochester; R.N.C., Greenwich. Asst. Constructor in R.C.N.C., 1910; Chatham Dockyard, 1910-11; Admiralty, 1911-12; Sea Service H.M.S. Vanguard, 1912-13; Admiralty, 1913-27; Sea Service H.M.S. Ramillies and Barham, 1927-28; Admiralty, 1928-30; H.M. Dockyard Simonstown, S. Africa, 1930-34; H.M. Dockyard Devonport, 1934-37; Admiralty, 1937-39; Ministry of Supply (Director of Naval Land Equipment, Deputy Director-General, Deputy Controller), 1940-44; Admiralty, Supt. of Contract Work (Landing Craft), 1944; Admiralty, Director of Contract Work (Supplies), 1944; Deputy Director of Naval Construction (Production), 1946-51; N.A.T.O. Shipbuilding, 1950-51; retired from service, 1951. Legion of Honour, 1918. *Recreations:* golf and bridge. *Address:* (Temp.) 48 Roland House, S.W.7. *T.:* Fremantle 4622. [*Died* 29 *Jan.* 1954.

HOPKINS, Harry Sinclair, C.B.E. 1929 (O.B.E. 1920); *b.* 1870; *s.* of William Pratt Hopkins; *m.* 1901. *Address:* Bulawayo, Southern Rhodesia. [*Died* 24 *Aug.* 1953.

HOPKINS, Henry Mayne Reid, C.S.I. 1921; late Senior Member, Board of Revenue, U.P., India; *b.* 1867; *s.* of late David Hopkins, H.B.M. Consul, Fernando Po; *m.* 1890, Jessie (*d.* 1953), (gold Kaisar-i-Hind Medal, 1923), *d.* of late F. W. Dolman; two *s.* two *d.* *Educ.:* Dulwich College; Trinity College, Oxford. Entered I.C.S., 1887; Deputy Commissioner, 1898; Magistrate and Collector, 1900; Opium Agent, 1911; Commissioner, 1915; Member Board of Revenue, 1919; Additional Member Viceroy's Council, 1920; ret. 1922. *Club:* East India and Sports. [*Died* 22 *Nov.* 1956.

HOPKINS, Lionel Charles, I.S.O. 1909; *b.* 20 Mar. 1854; *s.* of late Manley Hopkins. *Educ.:* Winchester. Student Interpreter in China, 1874; 2nd class assistant, 1880; 1st assistant, 1891; Vice-Consul, Shanghai, 1895; Consul, Chefoo, 1897; Consul-General, Tientsin, 1901-8; retired on pension, 1908. *Address:* The Garth, Haslemere, Surrey. [*Died* 11 *March* 1952.

HOPKINS, Rt. Hon. Sir Richard Valentine Nind, P.C. 1945; G.C.B., *cr.* 1941 (K.C.B., *cr.* 1920; C.B. 1919); Chairman, Central Board of Finance of Church Assembly; Member of Imperial War Graves Commission; Member of Court of London University; hon. Fellow of Emmanuel College, Cambridge; *b.* 13 Feb. 1880; *s.* of late Alfred Nind Hopkins, Edgbaston; *m.* 1923, Lucy Davis, M.B., Ch.B., D.P.H., 3rd *d.* of late Francis Cripps; one *s.* *Educ.:* King Edward's School, Birmingham; Emmanuel College, Cambridge. Member of Board of Inland Revenue, 1916; Chairman of Board, 1922; Controller of Finance and Supply Services, H.M. Treasury, 1927-32; Second Secretary H.M. Treasury, 1932-42; Permanent Secretary to Treasury, 1942-45. *Address:* 79 Bryanston Court, W.1. *Club:* Union. [*Died* 30 *March* 1955.

HOPKINS, Robert Thurston; author and journalist; *m.* 1912, Sybil, *d.* of Doctor Godfrey Bately; one *s.* *Educ.:* University College School and College, Gower Street. Founded Society of Sussex Downsmen. Group Officer (Sussex) Local Defence Volunteers, 1940. *Publications:* Rudyard Kipling, 1914; Kipling's Sussex, 1921; The Kipling Country, 1925; Old English Inns, 1927; Lure of Sussex, 1928; This London, 1929; English Watermills and Windmills, 1931; Small Sailing Craft, 1932; The Man Who Was Sussex, 1933; The Romance of the Bank of England (with Kate Rosenberg), 1933; Life and Death at the Old Bailey, 1934; English Moated Houses, 1935; The London-underneath-London, 1935; Famous Bank Robberies, 1936; Odd Corners in Sussex, 1937; The Scarlet Girdle, 1938; Sussex Rendezvous, 1938; Tales of the Grand Express (with Godfrey Thurston Hopkins), 1938; Weird and Uncanny Stories, 1944; Haunted Houses, 1944; The Adventures of Valentine Vaughan, 1945; Sussex; The Amber Girl; Adventures with Phantoms, 1946; The City of London and St. Paul's Cathedral, 1949; Bedside Book of Ghosts; The Heart of London; Ghosts over England, 1950; The Spirit of Cornwall, 1951; The Romance and Mystery of Dreams, 1954; World's Strangest Ghost Stories, 1955; The Banker Tells All, 1955; Cavalcade of Ghosts, 1956; The Mystery of the Wizard's Cap, 1956, and numerous topographical works; has written articles for all leading newspapers and special features for London Evening News, Press Association, Reuters, 1912-40, etc. *Recreation:* ghost hunting. *Adress:* 11 Richmond Street, Brighton, Sussex. *T.:* Brighton 23038. *Clubs:* Savage; Southwick and Shoreham Yacht; Cowdray Park Polo; Brighton Sailing. [*Died* 23 *May* 1958.

HOPKINSON, Rev. Arthur John, C.I.E. 1938; *b.* 28 Nov. 1894; *s.* of late Canon Charles Girdlestone Hopkinson, formerly Rector of Whitburn; *m.* 1928, Eleanor, *d.* of J. Alaric Richardson; two *s.* two *d.* *Educ.:* Temple Grove; Marlborough; Exeter Coll., Oxford. Served European War, 1914-18, Captain 4th D.L.I. (despatches); I.C.S. 1919; Indian Political Service, 1924; served U.P., Kathiawar, N.W.F.P. and Tibet; Political Officer in Sikkim under the Crown until Aug. 1947, and continued in service under Govt. of the Indian Dominion; retired 1950. Deacon, 1950; Priest 1951. *Address:* Aislaby Vicarage, Whitby, Yorks. [*Died* 30 *Aug.* 1953.

HOPKINSON, Emilius, C.M.G. 1922; D.S.O. 1900; M.A., M.B.(Oxon.); M.R.C.S., L.R.C.P., F.Z.S., M.B.O.U.; *b.* 1869; *e. s.* of Jonathan Hopkinson, of Frant, Sussex. *Educ.:* Haileybury; Trinity College, Oxford; St. Thomas's Hospital. Served South Africa as Medical Officer 15th Batt. Imperial Yeomanry, 1900-1, Captain I.Y. (despatches, Queen's medal 4

clasps, D.S.O.); Protectorate M.O. Gambia, W. Africa, 1901-11; Travelling Commissioner, Gambia, 1911-29; retired. *Publications:* A Vocabulary of the Mandingo Language, 1912; Notes on Protectorate Laws, Gambia, 1925; Records of Birds bred in Captivity, 1926. *Address:* Balcombe, Sussex.
[*Died* 11 *June* 1951.

HOPKINSON, Rev. John Henry; 2nd *s.* of late Sir Alfred Hopkinson, K.C.; *m.* 1902, Evelyn Mary, *d.* of late Rev. H. T. Fountaine, Vicar of Sutton Bridge, Lincolnshire; four *s.* one *d.* *Educ.:* Dulwich College; University Coll., Oxford. Craven Fellow of Oxford University, 1899-1900; Lecturer in Greek in Birmingham University, 1901-4; Warden of Hulme Hall and Lecturer in Classical Archæology in the Victoria University of Manchester, 1904-14; Ordained, 1914; served as private in the R.A.M.C., European War; Vicar of Holy Trinity Church, Colne, 1915-1920; Rector of Christ Church, Moss Side, Manchester, 1920-21; Vicar of Burneside, Westmorland, 1921-28; Residentiary Canon of Carlisle, 1928-31; Vicar of Christ Church, Cockermouth, 1931-36; Archdeacon of Westmorland, 1931-44; Diocesan Organiser of Religious Education and Examining Chaplain to the Bishop of Carlisle, 1928-44; Vicar of Winster, 1936-44; Assistant Curate of St. Mary's, Battersea, 1944-50. *Publications:* The Roman Fort at Ribchester; articles in the Journal of Hellenic Studies and in the Annual of the British School of Archæology at Athens. *Address:* 5 Dalton Road, Kendal, Westmorland.
[*Died* 22 *Oct.* 1957.

HOPWOOD, Brigadier Alfred Henry, C.B. 1938; D.S.O. 1917; 6th *s.* of Rev. Canon Hopwood, of Louth, Lincolnshire; *m.* 1911, Gladys Mary Neill Hopwood, *er. d.* of 1st Baron Southborough, P.C., G.C.B., G.C.M.G., G.C.V.O., K.C.S.I.; one *s.* *Educ.:* Glenalmond. 2nd Lieut. 5th Royal Irish Rifles, 1901; 2nd Lieut. Lincolnshire Regt., 1902; Lieut. 1904; Captain, 1912; Major, 1916; Lieut.-Col. 1930; Bt. Col. 1933; Col. 1934; served South African War, 1901-2 (medal with 5 clasps); Somaliland, 1909-1910 (medal with clasp); World War, 1914-19 (D.S.O. and bar, British War Medal, Victory Medal, despatches four times); p.s.c. 1919; attached R.N.S.C., 1921-22; Commanded Depôt Lincolnshire Regt., 1922-24; General Staff 53rd (Welsh) Division, 1924-28; commanded 2nd Lincolnshires, 1930-33; Instructor Senior Officers' School, Sheerness, 1933-35; Commander Tientsin Area, 1935-39; retired, 1939; re-employed, 1939-41 and 1942-49 (despatches, N.W.E.F.). *Address:* Common Lane House, Battlers' Green, Radlett, Herts. *T.:* Radlett 5961.
[*Died* 25 *Oct.* 1956.

HOPWOOD, Professor Frank Lloyd, Hon. M.A. Cantab.; D.Sc. (Lond.), A.R.C.Sc., F.Inst.P.; Professor Emeritus of Physics, Univ. of London, since 1949 and Consulting Physicist to St. Bartholomew's Hospital, London; Hon. Fellow of Queens' Coll., Cambridge; *b.* 1884; *er. surv. s.* of late William Hopwood, M.I.M.E., and Elizabeth Hopwood of Buckley, Chester; *m.* 1909, Helen, *d.* of late John and Susannah Sproxton, Wood Green; one *s.* *Educ.:* Hawarden Grammar School; University College of N. Wales, Bangor; Royal College of Science and University College, London. Formerly Vice Dean, Professor of Physics, St. Bartholomew's Hospital Medical College (University of London), and Physicist to St. Bartholomew's Hospital, London. Member of Grand Council, 1923-, and Hon. Secretary British Empire Cancer Campaign; Hon. Associate of L'Associazione Italiana di Radio-Biologia; Past President, Silvanus Thompson Medallist and Memorial Lecturer, and Hon. Member, British Institute of Radiology and Röntgen Society; Hon. Member Faculty of Radiologists; Vice-Pres. Emeritus of 7th Internat. Congress of Radiology; Hon. Sec. British Cttee. for Radiolgoical Units, 1925-1950. *Publications:* scientific papers in Proc. Royal Society, Philosophical Magazine, Proc. Physical Soc. Trans. of Optical Soc., Journal of Röntgen Soc., etc. *Address:* 68 Chandos Avenue, Whetstone, N.20. *T.:* Hillside 7067.
[*Died* 2 *May* 1954.

HORABIN, Thomas Lewis; Chairman of Lacrinoid; business consultant; *b.* 1896; *m.* 1920, *d.* of Dr. Cargil Martin. *Educ.:* Cardiff High School. M.P. North Cornwall Division (Ind. L.), 1939-47, (Lab.), 1947-50; Chief Party Whip, Aug. 1945. *Address:* 24 and 26 Kingsland Road, E.2.
[*Died* 26 *April* 1956.

HORDER, 1st Baron, *cr.* 1933, of Ashford in the County of Southampton; **Thomas Jeeves Horder,** Bt. of Shaston, *cr.* 1923; G.C.V.O., *cr.* 1938 (K.C.V.O., *cr.* 1925); Kt., *cr.* 1918; M.D.; B.Sc.; Hon. D.C.L. (Dunelm.); Hon. M.D. (Melbourne and Adelaide); F.R.C.P.; Deputy Lieut. Co. of Hampshire; Extra Physician to the Queen (formerly Extra Physician to King George VI); Consulting Physician to St. Bartholomew's Hospital; K.G.St.J.; Order of Star of Ethiopia; Freeman of Shaftesbury; *b.* 7 Jan. 1871; *s.* of Albert Horder, Shaftesbury; *m.* 1902, Geraldine Rose (*d.* 1954), *o. d.* of Arthur Doggett, Newnham Manor, Herts.; one *s.* two *d.* *Educ.:* privately: University of London; St. Bartholomew's Hospital. Capt. (temp. Major) R.A.M.C. (T.); Adviser to Minister of Food and President of Food Education Society; Chairman of Committee advising Ministry of Labour and National Service on medical questions connected with Recruiting; Chairman of Shelter Hygiene Committee of Ministry of Home Security and Ministry of Health; Hon. Consulting Physician to Ministry of Pensions; Consulting Physician Cancer Hospital, Fulham; Ex-President, Harveian Society of London; Chairman of British Empire Cancer Campaign and Chairman Advisory Scientific Committee; Ex-Chairman of Advisory Committee, Mount Vernon Hospital; Ex-President of Fellowship of Medicine; Consulting Physician to the Royal Orthopædic Hosp., to the Royal Northern Hospital and to the Hospitals of Bury St. Edmunds, Swindon, Bishop's Stortford, Leatherhead, Beckenham and Finchley; Member: Central Council of Recreative Physical Training; Boy Scouts Assoc.; National Parks; Ex-President: Medical Society of London; Eugenics Society; Pres. Brit. Assoc. and Internat. Fed. of Physical Med., Family Planning Assoc., Marriage Guidance Council, and of the N.W. London Child Guidance Society; Soc. Individual Freedom; Smoke Abatement Soc.; Chairman: Noise Abatement League; Mobile Physiotherapy; President: National Amenities Council; Cremation Society; Inst. of Management; Society for Study and Treatment of Delinquency; Chm. Empire Rheumatism Council, 1936-53; Chairman: Greater London Provident Scheme for District Nursing, Nursing Reconstruction Cttee.; Henry Wood Memorial Trust; Wireless for Bedridden; Fellowship for Freedom in Medicine; formerly Physician to King Edward VIII (and as Prince of Wales) and to King George VI. *Publications:* Clinical Pathology in Practice; Cerebro-spinal Fever; Medical Notes; Essentials of Medical Diagnosis; Health and a Day; Obscurantism; 50 years of medicine. *Heir:* *s.* Hon. Thomas Mervyn Horder [*b.* 8 Dec. 1911; *m.* 1946, Mary Ross, *yr. d.* of late Dr. W.S. McDougall, Benloyal, Wallington, Surrey]. *Recreation:* gardening. *Address:* 45 Nottingham Place, W.1. *T.:* Welbeck 2200; Ashford Chace, Petersfield. *T.:* Petersfield 18. *Club:* Athenæum.
[*Died* 13 *Aug.* 1955.

HORDERN, Sir Samuel, K.B.E., *cr.* 1938; Kt., *cr.* 1919; *b.* Sydney, N.S.W., 24 Sept. 1876; *s.* of Samuel Hordern of Retford Hall, Sydney; *m.* 1900, Charlotte, (*d.* 1952), *e. d.* of Sir John See, K.C.M.G., Randwick, N.S.W.; one *s.* two *d.* *Educ.:* Sydney Grammar School; Bath College,

Bath, England. Vice-Patron Royal Automobile Club of Australia; Pres. New South Wales Club. *Recreations:* golf, motoring, racing, yachting. Part owner of Artilleryman, winner of Melbourne Cup, 1919, and owner of Violoncello, winner of Caulfield Cup, 1921, and Pilliewinkie, winner of Australian Cup, 1926. *Address:* Babworth House, Darling Point, Sydney, N.S.W.; Retford Park, Bowral, N.S.W. *Clubs:* New South Wales, Royal Automobile of Australia, Royal Sydney Golf (Sydney); Athenæum (Melbourne). [*Died* 3 *June* 1956.

HORDERN, Samuel, C.M.G. 1958; O.B.E. 1945; M.A.; President of Royal Agricultural Society of New South Wales, Australia, since 1954; *b.* 16 May 1909; *s.* of late Sir Samuel Hordern, K.B.E., Sydney; *m.* 1934, June, *d.* of late Clive Baillieu, Melbourne; one *s.* one *d.* *Educ.:* Cranbrook School, Sydney; Cambridge University. Until 1949, was Member of Sydney Stock Exchange; until 1956 Director of: Perpetual Trustee Co. Ltd.; Tooth & Co. Ltd.; Courtauld's (Australia) Ltd. Served War of 1939-45, Roy. Aust. Armoured Corps, Major (O.B.E.). *Recreations:* golf, horse racing, riding. *Address:* 14 Ginahgulla Rd., Bellevue Hill, N.S.W., Australia. *T.:* FM 3009. *Clubs:* Hawks, Leander; Union, Australian (Sydney). [*Died* 25 *July* 1960.

HORE-BELISHA, 1st Baron *cr.* 1954, of Devonport; **Leslie Hore-Belisha,** P.C. 1935; Barrister-at-law; *s.* of late Capt. J. I. Belisha and Lady Hore; *m.* 1944, Cynthia (B.E.M. 1944), *d.* of late Gilbert Elliot, Hull Place, Sholden, Kent. *Educ.:* Clifton College; Paris; Heidelberg; St. John's College, Oxford (M.A.). President of Oxford Union Society, 1919; served in Army during European War, France and Flanders, 1914-16, Salonika, 1916-18, Roy. Fusiliers Public Sch. Bn. and R.A.S.C.; Major (despatches); called to Bar, Inner Temple, 1923; M.P. (L. Nat. 1923-42; Ind. 1942-45), Devonport; Parl. Sec. to Board of Trade, 1931-32; Financial Sec. to Treasury, 1932-34; Minister of Transport, 1934-37, with seat in Cabinet from Oct. 1936; Sec. of State for War and President of Army Council, 1937-40; Member War Cabinet, 1939-40; Minister of National Insurance, 1945; Mem. of Westminster City Council, 1947. *Address:* 16 Stafford Place, S.W.1; The Old Warren Farm, Wimbledon Common, S.W.19. *Clubs:* White's, Beefsteak, Buck's. [*Died* 16 *Feb.* 1957 (*ext.*).

HORLER, Sydney, *b.* Leytonstone, Essex, 18 July 1888; *o. s.* of G. H. and A. M. Horler; *m.* 1916, Rosie E. Piper; no *c.* *Educ.:* Redcliffe and Colston Schools, Bristol. Intended for scholastic profession, but by an accident, which must have been fortunate for his prospective pupils, became a journalist, entering the office of the Western Daily Press and allied newspapers, Bristol, 1905; served as a reporter on the Western Daily Press until 1911, when left to take up appointment as special writer on the staff of E. Hulton & Co., Ltd., Withy Grove, Manchester; subsequently had Fleet Street experience on the staffs of the Daily Mail and the Daily Citizen; during last year of European War, 1918, held an appt. in Propaganda Section of Air Intelligence; upon demobilisation, joined editorial staff of George Newnes, Ltd., and appointed a sub-editor on John O' London's Weekly; left July 1919, in order to write fiction; since then has published over 150 novels, chiefly stories of sensational interest, beginning with The Mystery of No. 1, 1925; in addition many other books of miscellaneous interest, including an autobiography, Excitement, and two Diaries, Strictly Personal and More Strictly Personal; many books have been widely translated. *Address:* c/o A. P. Watt & Son, Hastings House, 10 Norfolk Street, Strand, W.C.2. [*Died* 27 *Oct.* 1954.

HORLICK, Sir Peter James Cunliffe, 3rd Bt., *cr.* 1914; *b.* 4 March 1908; *o. s.* of Sir Ernest Burford Horlick, 2nd Bt., and Jane (who *m.* 2nd, 1931, Sir Francis Oppenheimer, K.C.M.G.), *d.* of late Col. Cunliffe Martin, C.B.; *S.* father 1934; *m.* 1st, 1931, Rosemary Margaret (who obtained a divorce 1934), *e. d.* of Charles Nicholl, Wargrave-on-Thames; 2nd, 1934, Beryta Stewart Murray, *d.* of Roland Allport, Sydney, N.S.W.; two *d.*; 3rd, 1948, Jacqueline Mary Lurie, *d.* of Clement Walter Mander; re-married his 2nd wife, 1957. *Educ.:* Eton. *Heir:* *u.* Lt.-Col. James Nockells, O.B.E. *Club:* Bath. [*Died* 29 *Jan.* 1958.

HORN, Brigadier Robert Victor Galbraith, D.S.O. 1918; O.B.E. 1919; M.C.; *b.* 1886; *s.* of late John Galbraith Horn; *m.* 1926, Michelle, *d.* of J. S. Newborg, New York; one *d.* *Educ.:* Cargilfield; Charterhouse; R.M.C., Sandhurst. Served European War, 1914-19 (despatches four times, M.C., D.S.O., O.B.E., Legion of Honour (Chevalier), Bt. Major); Malabar rebellion, 1921-22; p.s.c. Camberley, 1920; Major, 1925; Bt. Lt.-Col. 1928; Lt.-Col. 1931; Col. 1931; commanded 2nd Battalion Royal Scots Fusiliers, 1931-34; A.Q.M.G., Scottish Command, 1934-38, retired pay, 1938; employed War Office, 1939; A.A.G. War Office, 1939-40; Brig. i/c A. Anti-Aircraft Command, April-Nov. 1940; D.A. and Q.M.G. of an A.A. Corps till Sept. 1941; reverted to retired pay, 1941; with B.B.C. 1941-43. *Address:* Chesham House, Lyall Street, S.W.1. *T.:* Sloane 2331. *Clubs:* Army and Navy; New (Edinburgh). [*Died* 11 *July* 1959.

HORNBY, Maj.-Gen. Alan Hugh, C.B. 1945; C.B.E. 1943; M.C.; *b.* 22 June 1894; *o. s.* of Edgar Christian and Eva Gertrude Hornby; *m.* 1923, Margaret Vera, *o. d.* of Edward John and Ethel Maitland; one *s.* one *d.* *Educ.:* Winchester. Served European War, 1914-19, in France and Belgium (wounded, despatches, M.C.); Iraq, 1919-20; p.s.c. 1932; War of 1939-45 in Middle East, Italy and Sicily (despatches, C.B.E., C.B.); retired pay, 1948. Col. Commandant, R.A., 1953-. Hon. Col. Kent A.C.F. Regt. R.A. American Legion of Merit (degree of Commander). Commissioner of St. John's Ambulance Brigade, Kent; C.St.J. *Recreations:* golf and yachting. *Address:* 2 Lochmore House, Cundy Street, S.W.1. *Clubs:* Army and Navy, M.C.C.; Royal Yacht Squadron; Royal St. George's (Sandwich). [*Died* 28 *Oct.* 1958.

HORNBY, Admiral Robert Stewart Phipps, C.M.G. 1906; J.P.; R.N.; *b.* 9 July 1866; *y. s.* of late Admiral of the Fleet, Sir Geoffrey Phipps Hornby, G.C.B.; *m.* 1895, Rose, *d.* of the late Henry O'Malley; one *s.* one *d.* Entered Navy, 1879; served in Egyptian War, 1882; European War, 1914-18; Rear-Adm. 1913; Vice-Adm., 1918; Admiral, 1922; Sinai Boundary Dispute (C.M.G.); retired list, 1922. *Address:* Lordington House, Chichester, Sussex. *T.:* Emsworth 2171. *Club:* United Service. [*Died* 13 *Aug.* 1956.

HORNE, Alderson Burrell; (Anmer Hall); Actor-Manager, late owner of Westminster Theatre, S.W.1; *b.* 22 Nov. 1863; *yr. s.* of Edgar Horne; *m.* 1st, Maud (decd.), *y. d.* of late Frederick William Porter, J.P., Moyle Tower, Hythe, Kent; one *s.* one *d.*; 2nd, Gillian Gamble (*née* Scaife). *Educ.:* Westminster; Pembroke Coll., Oxford. Founded The Londoner, 1900; associated with Sir Johnston Forbes-Robertson in opening of Scala Theatre, 1905, and later with Vedrenne and Eadie at the Royalty, 1911; during European War organized theatrical parties with Miss Lena Ashwell and Y.M.C.A.; produced A Month in the Country (Turgenev) at the Royalty in July 1926, reviving it at the Fortune in autumn of that year, when he also produced The Cradle Song by Sierra; after various productions including A Doll's House for Ibsen Centenary, the Kingdom of God by Sierra, Fortunato and The Lady from Alfaqueque by the Quintero Bros. at the Court, he took over the Festival Theatre at Cambridge in October 1929 and remained there for four terms; in 1931 he opened Westminster Theatre with Bridie's Anatomist, following it with Six Characters In Search Of An Author, A Pair of Spectacles, The Unquiet Spirit, Tobias And The Angel, Dizzy, Jonah And The Whale, Love's Labour's Lost, and lately, Waste, Heartbreak House, Uncle Vanya, A Month In the Country, Hamlet, Mourning becomes Electra, Volpone, Land's End (F. L. Lucas), The Zeal of Thy House, You Never can Tell, and Marriage (Gogol); productions elsewhere: Storm In A Teacup, Winter Sunshine, Busman's Honeymoon, Women of Property, and Surprise Item, Third Party Risk, The Gentle People. He conducts his theatrical activities under name of Anmer Hall, and acts as Waldo Wright. Master of Clothworkers' Company, 1927-28, Chm. of Trust Committee for 15 years. Chm. of Governors of Mary Datchelor Girls School for many years; Governor of Clifton College; on Councils of R.A.D.A. and Royal Academy of Dancing; Chm. of Morib Plantations Ltd. since the company was formed. *Recreations:* book collecting, tennis, cricket. *Address:* K2 Albany, Piccadilly, W.1; Ditton Place, Balcombe, Sussex. *Clubs:* Garrick, Beefsteak, M.C.C. [*Died* 22 *Dec.* 1953.

HORNE, (Walter) Jobson, M.A., M.D., B.C. (Cantab.); M.R.C.P. (Lond.) (Weber-Parkes Medallist); F.R.Soc.Med. (Pres., 1920-21, late Vice-Pres. and Hon. Sec. of Laryngological Section, and of Otological Section, late Vice-Pres. History of Med. Section, of the Soc.); late Chm. of Marylebone Division and late Pres., Section of Laryngology and Otology, British Medical Association; Senior Hon. Consulting Surgeon and late Hon. Treasurer to the Metropolitan Ear, Nose, and Throat Hospital; subsection of Millbank (Queen Alexandra's) Hospital during 1914-18 War; late Aural specialist Ministry of Pensions; late Chief Assistant, the Throat Department, St. Bartholomew's Hospital; Semon Lecturer on Diseases of the Throat and Nose, the Univ. of London; *b.* 2 Aug. 1865; second *s.* of William Horne, Matfield, Kent, and Emily, *d.* of J. Jobson, Shrewsbury; unmarried. *Educ.:* Tonbridge School; Clare Coll., Cambridge; St. Bartholomew's Hosp.; Univ. of Berlin. B.A. Nat. Sci. Tripos, 1887. Formerly Science Research Scholar of the British Medical Association; Hon. Secretary and Editor of Catalogue of Museum of the British Congress on Tuberculosis for the Prevention of Consumption, 1901; Hon. Sec. to Committee for Organising visit of French Physicians and Surgeons to London, 1904. *Publications:* Editor of Transactions of the Otological Society of the United Kingdom, 1904-7; Editor of Catalogue of Museum of Sixth International Otological Congress, London, 1899; Gun Deafness and its Prevention, The Lancet, 15 Aug. 1914; various communications on Diseases of the Throat, Nose, and Ear. *Recreations:* country life, ancient silver, and mediæval antiquities. *Address:* Mereworth, near Maidstone, Kent. *T.:* Wateringbury 82104. [*Died* 7 *March* 1953.

HORNE, Sir William Kenneth, Kt., cr. 1954; b. 1883. In Private Practice as Barrister, 1913-15, and 1919-25. Served European War, 1915-18. Chief Justice, Tonga, 1925; acted as Chief Justice, Fiji, and Chief Judicial Commissioner, Western Pacific, February-September 1929; Judge of Supreme Court, Gambia, 1929-33; Supreme Court Judge, Kenya, 1933-37; Puisne Judge, Strait Settlements, 1937-42. War Service, East Africa, 1942-44. Seconded as Supreme Court Judge, Kenya, 1944-48, retired 1948. Speaker of Kenya Legislative Council, 1948-1955, retired. *Publication:* Revised edition of Laws of Tonga, 1905-28, 1928. *Address:* Epwell Mill, Nr. Banbury, Oxon. [*Died* 8 *Feb.* 1959.

HORNER, Rev. Bernard, M.A., L.Th.; M.A. (hon.) Leeds 1923; b. Nottingham, 18 April 1873; s. of late W. Frederick Horner, manufacturer, Nottingham. *Educ.:* The High School, Nottingham; Hatfield Coll., Durham. Deacon, 1896; Priest, 1897; served Asst. Curacy of Jarrow on Tyne, 1896-1900, and of St. Andrew, Plaistow, E., 1900-3; joined the Community of the Resurrection, Mirfield, 1903; Warden of the College of the Resurrection, Mirfield, 1908-22; Prior of the London Priory, 1925-37; Chaplain of S. Mary's College, Paddington, 1924-37; Chaplain of St. Andrew's Deaconess Community, 1930-37; Prior of the House of the Resurrection, 1937-1940; Superior of the Community of the Resurrection, 1940-43. Chaplain-General of the Order of the Holy Paraclete, 1940-50. *Address:* House of the Resurrection, Mirfield, Yorks. [*Died* 23 *Sept.* 1960.

HORNER, Norman Gerald, M.A., M.D., F.R.C.P., F.R.C.S.; late Editor of British Medical Journal; *b.* 1 Jan. 1882; *s.* of Arthur Claypon Horner and Frances, *d.* of Edward Yalden Cooper; *m.* Grace Malleson Fearon (*d.* 1950); one *s.* *Educ.:* Tonbridge School; Gonville and Caius Coll., Cambridge; St. Bartholomew's Hospital. Resident appointments, Westminster and St. Bartholomew's Hospitals, 1906-7; Assistant Editor, The Hospital, 1908-10; Assistant Editor, the Lancet, 1911-15; served European War in France, 1915-1917, Captain R.A.M.C.; Assistant Editor, British Medical Journal, 1917-28, Editor, 1928-1946; past Vice-President, Section of History of Medicine, Royal Society of Medicine. *Publications:* papers on medical history. *Address:* c/o British Medical Association, Tavistock Square, W.C.1. *Club:* Savile. [*Died* 7 *March* 1954.

HORNIMAN, Rear-Adm. Henry, C.B. 1923; *s.* of late Paymaster-in-Chief William Horniman, R.N.; *m.* 1st, Alice (*d.* 1947), *d.* of late Edward Croker Dartnell of Callao; one *s.*; 2nd, 1948, Mary Rachel Elisa Spencer-Smyth W. Norwood. *Educ.:* Christ's Hosp.; Portsmouth Grammar School. Entered Navy, 1887; served S. African War, H.M.S. Barracouta, 1901-2; European War, 1914-18, H.M.S. Inflexible, Falklands, Dardanelles, Jutland; Paymaster Admiralty Controllers' Department, 1917-19; Post Armistice Operations, Black Sea, etc., H.M.S. Iron Duke, 1919-22; Fleet Accountant Officer, Mediterranean, 1912-14, 1919-22; retired list, 1925; Keeper of Virginia Water, 1925-36. *Address:* 151 Brighton Road, Worthing, Sussex. *T.:* Worthing 3091. [*Died* 21 *May* 1956.

HORNING, Professor Eric Stephen Gurney, M.A. (Oxon), D.Sc. (Melb.); Professor of Experimental Pathology (Histopathology), University of London, at the Chester Beatty Research Institute, Royal Cancer Hospital, London, S.W.3, since 1956 (Reader, 1947-56); *b.* 25 April 1900; *s.* of Henry William and Florence Clifton Horning, Sydney, N.S.W. *Educ.:* Barker Coll., Hornsby, N.S.W.; Hertford Coll., Oxford. B.A. 1925, M.A. 1948, Univ. of Oxford; Victoria Govt. Research Scholar in Biology, 1926, D.Sc. 1928, Univ. of Melbourne. Rockefeller Foundation Fellow for Med. Research at Kaiser Wilhelm Inst., Berlin, 1931, and later at Washington Univ. (St. Louis, Mo.) Sch. of Med., 1932-34. Beit Fellow for Med. Research tenable at Imperial Cancer Research Fund, 1934-37. F.R.Soc.Med.; Mem. Pathological Soc. of Gt. Brit. and Ire.; Mem. Roy. Microscopical Soc. Served with A.I.F. overseas, 1917-19; Aux. Air Force, 1938-40; served with R.N.V.R., 1943-45; Lieut. (sp.) R.N.V.R. Naval Intelligence Div., 1943; Lt.-Comdr. R.I.N., 1944-45. *Publications:* (with H. Burrows) Oestrogens and Neoplasia, 1952. Papers in various scientific and med. jls. *Recreation:* motoring. *Address:* 12 Tufton Court, Tufton Street, Westminster, S.W.1. *T.:* Abbey 5510. *Clubs:* Royal Automobile, R.N.V.R. [*Died* 14 *Nov.* 1959.

HORRIDGE, John; Barrister-at-Law; Master of Supreme Court, King's Bench Division, since 1937; *b.* 25 June, 1893; *s.* of late Thomas Mowbray Horridge; *m.* 1934, Brita Charlotta, *d.* of Ing. E. S. Persson, Malung, Sweden; two *s.* Served European War 1915-16 France, 1917-18 Mesopotamia, Capt.; Political Service, Persia, Assistant Political Officer, Kermanshah, 1918; Assistant Political Officer and Acting Vice-Consul Hamadan, 1918-19; Civil Administration Mesopotamia, Assistant Political Officer, Khanaqin, 1919-20; Called to Bar Lincoln's Inn, 1922; contested (L.) Sevenoaks Division, 1935. *Recreation:* golf. *Address:* Red Lane, Argos Hill, Rotherfield. *T.:* Rotherfield 81. [*Died* 27 *Dec.* 1951.

HORSBURGH-PORTER, Sir John; *see* Porter.

HORSEY, Captain Frank Lankester, C.B. 1931; O.B.E., D.S.C.; R.N. retired; *b.* 22 Jan. 1884; *y. s.* of late F. J. Horsey, Inland Revenue Service; *m.* 1917, Ada N. R., M.B.E., *y. d.* of late E. H. Hearn, Indian Civil Service; one *s.* Joined Navy, 1901; Captain (S), 1933; served European War, Grand Fleet, and in 10th Cruiser Squadron as Secretary to Commodore R. E. R. Benson C.B., and Rear-Admiral J. S. Luard, C.B. (O.B.E., D.S.C.); Secretary to Admiral of the Fleet Sir Frederick L. Field, G.C.B., K.C.M.G., in all appointments 1920-33; retired list, 1939; re-employed war of 1939-45, Secretary to Vice-Controller, 1939-42; Additional Naval Assistant to First Sea Lord, 1942-45. *Recreations:* cricket, tennis, golf. *Address:* The Hazard, Liphook. *T.:* Liphook 3231. [*Died* 19 *Aug.* 1956.

HORSFIELD, George; *b.* 1882; *s.* of Richard Marshall Horsfield and Sarah Ellis Smart; *m.* 1932, Hon. Agnes Conway (*d.* 1950), *d.* of late Lord Conway of Allington; no *c.* *Educ.:* Leeds Grammar School. Architect, 1901-14; in New York with Cram, Goodhue and Ferguson, 1908-14, Head of Design Section; war service in Gallipoli in the Naval Brigade and on the Somme with the 7th West Yorkshire Regt.; Consulting Architect to Military Works at Army Headquarters, first at Rawal Pindi, then Simla, with rank of Major attached R.E., 1918-21; in Transjordan, repairing the monuments of Jerash, and responsible for all the Antiquities of Transjordan under the Mandate, 1924-36; Directed first excavations at Petra, 1929. *Publications:* The First Excavations at Petra, Journal of the Royal Geographical Society, Nov. 1930; The Stele of Balua, Revue Biblique, July 1931; Le Temple de Ramm. R.P. Savignac et G. Horsfield, Revue Biblique, April 1, 1935; Sela-Petra, The Rock of Edom and Nabatine, Chapters I and II in Quarterly of the Department of Antiquities in Palestine, Vol. VII, 1937 (with Agnes Horsfield); The Excavations, Vol. viii., No. 3, 1938; The Finds, Vol. ix., Nos. 2, 3, 4, 1941 (all with Agnes Horsfield). [*Died* 13 *Aug.* 1956.

HORSFORD, Cyril Arthur Bennett; Specialist Ear, Nose and Throat; *b.* 25 Jan. 1876; *s.* of late Hon. S. L. Horsford of St. Kitts, West Indies; *m.* Edith Louise Sayers, adopted *d.* and ward of late Miss Lascelles-Jones; one *s.* one *d.* *Educ.:* Bedford Modern School; Edinburgh University, M.B., Ch.B. Edin. 1898, M.D. (Honours) 1902, F.R.C.S. England, 1903, and Hon. R.C.M. Late Hon. Surgeon Throat and Ear Department, Princess Beatrice Hospital, Kensington; formerly Clinical Assistant Throat Hospital, Golden Square, and Central London Throat and Ear Hospital; Laryngologist to Royal Choral Society, Royal College of Music, Royal Society of Musicians, etc.; Liveryman, Worshipful Co. of Musicians and Freeman City of London. *Publications:* An original method of facilitating intralaryngial operations, 1908; The Epiglottic suture—its value in Laryngoscopy, 1911; Why Voices Fail, 1912; Cancer of the Larynx, 1935, etc. *Recreations:* music, motoring. *Address:* 24 Harley Street, W.1. *T.:* Langham 1384. [*Died* 16 *Dec.* 1953.

HORSLEY, Rt. Rev. Cecil Douglas, M.A.; *b.* Gillingham, Kent, 1903; 2nd *s.* of Admiral Arthur John Horsley and Mary Vyse, *d.* of Thomas Wilberforce Stoughton. *Educ.:* The Downs School, Colwall, Malvern; Brighton College; Queens' College, Cambridge. In business, Head Office of the Royal Mail Steam Packet Co., 1921-23; Queens', Cambridge, 1924-27; Ryle Reading Prize, 1927; Westcott House, Cambridge, 1927-29; B.A. 1927; M.A. 1931; Deacon, 1929; Priest, 1930; Asst. Curate, Romsey Abbey, 1929-32; St. Saviour's, Ealing, 1933-1934; Vicar of St. John Evangelist, Upper Norwood, 1934-38; Bishop of Colombo, 1938-1947; Bishop of Gibraltar, 1947-53; Hon. Senior Chaplain Ceylon Defence Force, 1939-47; O.C.F. (Imperial), 1942-47. Chaplain and Sub-Prelate, Order of St. John of Jerusalem, 1948. *Address:* c/o Gibraltar Diocesan Office, 35 Great Peter Street, Westminster, S.W.1. *Club:* United University. [*Died* 10 *March* 1953.

HORT, Sir Fenton George, 7th Bt., *cr.* 1767; *b.* 1 May 1896; *s.* of Sir Arthur Fenton Hort, 6th Bt., M.A., and Helen Frances (*d.* 1946), *d.* of late Canon G. C. Bell; *S.* father 1935; *m.* 1922, Gwendolene, *d.* of late Sir Walter Alcock, M.V.O.; three *s.* two *d.* *Educ.:* Harrow; Trinity College, Cambridge, B.A. Served European War, 1916-1919, with the R.E. (T.F.). *Recreations:* fishing and shooting. *Heir:* *s.* James Fenton, *b.* 6 Sept. 1926. *Address:* Old Mountjoy, Omagh, N. Ireland. *T.:* Omagh 433. *Club:* Royal Aero. [*Died* 5 *March* 1960.

HORTHY DE NAGYBANYA, Admiral Nicholas Vitéz, H.S.H. the Regent of the Kingdom of Hungary, 1920-44; was deported to Germany, Oct. 1944; captured by the Allies, 1945; released, 1946; *b.* Kenderes, Hungary, 1868; 4th *s.* of late Stephen de Horthy (late Member of House of Magnates) and late Paulette de Halassy; *m.* 1901, Magdalene, 3rd *d.* of John Purgly de Joszáshely; one *s.* (and one *s.* killed on active service; two *d.* decd.). *Educ.:* Reformist College, Debreczen; Sopron (Hungary); Imperial and Royal Naval Academy, Fiume. Entered the Austro-Hungarian Navy, 1886; Lieutenant de vaisseau, 1900; commanding the Taurus, stationed at Constantinople, 1908-09; 1909, Corvette Captain and Naval A.D.C. to H.M. the Emperor and King Francis Joseph I. until 1914; Fregate Captain, 1911; Imperial and Royal Chamberlain, 1913; Captain, 1913; at the beginning of the War Captain battleship Habsburg for ten months, afterwards of cruiser Novara until 1917; engaged in the attack of the Austro-Hungarian fleet on the Italian Adriatic Coast, 1915; sunk the whole transports bound for the relief of Montenegro in the port of San Giovanni di Medua, 1915; battle of the Otranto Roads, 1917; where, as leader of the cruiser squadron, was severely wounded; Captain of the dreadnought Prinz Eugen, 1917; Rear-Admiral, in command of the fleet, 1918; Vice-Admiral, 1918; 1919, War Minister in the Hungarian Szeged Government, later Commander-in-Chief of the Hungarian National Army. Knight of the Maria Theresia Military Order, Grand Cross of the Hungarian Cross for Merit. Second Class Military Cross for Merit with the Swords, Grand Cross of the Egyptian Mehmet-Ali Order with the Chain, Order of the Knights of the Holy Sepulchre. *Publication:* Ein Leben für Ungarn, 1952 (Germany) (trans. into English, French, Italian, Finnish), 1953; Memoirs, 1956. *Recreations:* riding, hunting, shooting, tennis, yachting. *Address:* Vila de S. José, Rua Melo e Sousa, Estoril, Portugal. [*Died* 9 *Feb.* 1957.

HORTON, Frank, F.R.S.; Sc.D. (Cantab.); D.Sc. (Lond.); M.Sc. (Birm.); Emeritus Prof. of Physics and formerly Vice-Chancellor of Univ. of London; Prof. of Physics, 1914-1946; a Representative of Faculty of Science on Senate, 1925-45, a co-opted member, 1945-1951; Member of University Court, 1932-51; *b.* 20 Aug. 1878; *e. s.* of late A. Horton of Olton, Warwickshire; *m.* 1st, 1911, J. M. Vèra, *o. c.* of J. E. Fulton, M.I.Mech.E., Wellington, N.Z.; one *d.*; 2nd, 1939, Ann Catherine Davies, Fellow of Newnham College Cambridge, *o. d.* of Robert Davies of Cricklewood, and Llangybi, Cardiganshire. *Educ.:* King Edward's School, Birmingham; Mason University College, Birmingham; St. John's College, Cambridge. Associate Mason University College, Heslop Gold Medallist for an English Essay, 1900; 1851 Exhibition Research Scholar, 1900-3; Granville Research Scholar, London University, 1903; Mackinnon Research Student of the Royal Society, 1903; Allen Scholar, Cambridge University, 1904; Clerk Maxwell Scholar, Cambridge University, 1906-9; Fellow of St. John's College, Cambridge, 1905-13; Lecturer at the Cavendish Laboratory, Cambridge, 1905-14; Dean of the Faculty of Science, University of London, 1930-34; Chairman of the Academic Council of the University, 1935-39; Vice-Chancellor, 1939-1945. Chm. Governing Body, Chelsea Polytechnic, 1936-47. *Publications:* Experimental Researches on Elasticity and Electricity in the Philosophical Transactions of the Royal Society and other scientific journals; Joint-Editor (with late Sir J. J. Thomson) of Monographs on Physics; Jt. Ed. (with late Dr. N. R. Campbell) of A History of the Cavendish Laboratory, 1871-1910. *Address:* 9 Clarkson Rd., Cambridge. *Club:* Athenæum. [*Died* 31 *Oct.* 1957.

HORTON, Admiral Sir Max Kennedy, G.C.B., *cr.* 1945 (K.C.B., *cr.* 1939; C.B. 1934); D.S.O. 1914; Bath King of Arms since 1946; *b.* 29 Nov. 1883; *s.* of R. J. Horton, Minster, Thanet. Britannia 1898; entered R.N. 1900; served European War, 1914-18 (D.S.O. and 2 bars, promoted Commander); when in command of Submarine E9 torpedoed light cruiser Hela at Heligoland, Sept. 1914, and German cruiser Prinz Adalbert in Baltic, July 1915; also sunk 3 German destroyers besides 2 transports and several merchant ships; Captain, 1920; Rear-Admiral, 1932; Vice-Admiral, 1936; Admiral, 1941; Assistant Director of Mobilisation, Admiralty, 1926-28; Rear-Admiral 2nd Battle Squadron, 1933-35; Vice-Admiral Commanding First Cruiser Squadron, 1935-36; Vice-Admiral Commanding Reserve Fleet, 1937-39; Vice-Admiral commanding Northern Patrol, Sept. 1939-Jan. 1940; Flag Officer Submarines, 1940-42; C.-in-C. Western Approaches, 1942-45; retired, 1945. Holds Russian Order of St. George, 4th Class; silver medal for saving life on occasion of loss of the Delhi off Cape Spartel, 1911; Grand Officer Legion of Honour and Croix de Guerre (with Palmes); 4th Class Order of St. Vladimir with swords; 2nd Class St. Anne with swords and diamonds; 2nd Class St. Stanislaus of Greece; Grand Cross of Orange Nassau; Chief Commander of Legion of Merit (U.S.A.); Grand Cross of the Order of St. Olaf (Norway); Hon. Freeman of City of Liverpool, 1946; Hon. LL.D. of Queen's Univ., Belfast, 1947. *Club:* Travellers'. [*Died* 30 *July* 1951.

HORTON-SMITH, Lionel Graham Horton, M.A.; F.S.A.Scot.; of Lincoln's Inn, Barrister-at-law; *b.* 12 July 1871; 2nd *s.* of late R. H. Horton-Smith, K.C., and Marilla, *e. d.* of late John Baily, Q.C.; *m.* 1909, Nora Blanche, 4th *d.* and *co-h.* of late W. E. Dorrington; two *s.* two *d.* *Educ.:* Marlborough (Head of School and Cotton Exhibitioner to the University, 1890); St. John's Coll., Cambridge: Foundation Scholar, 1889; McMahon Law Scholar, 1896; Fellow, 1900; Double First (Classics and Philology), 1893-94; Hon. Men. Porson (Greek Iambic) Prize, 1893; Members' Latin Essay Prize, 1894; 1st Winchester Prize, 1895. Hon. Member Internat. Mark Twain Assoc., 1950. Called to Bar, 1897; S.-E. Circuit, Sussex, Middlesex, and N. London Sessions; a Referee 1928-51, Landlord and Tenant Act, 1927, and from 1931, Hon. Sec. the Referees (L. and T. Act, 1927) Assoc.; Commissioner for Trial of Municipal Election Petition, Lancs, 1933; appointed, 1946, Chm. of the First Tribunal established under the Furnished Houses (Rent Control) Act, 1946; and formerly a Deputy-Chm. under the U.I. Acts, 1920-27. Water-colour painting, Preparations for the Building of the Royal Courts of Justice, 1870, presented to the Law Courts, 1942. Joint-Founder (Jan. 1908) and Joint Hon. Sec. (1908-13) Imperial Maritime League; and Initiator and Joint-Organiser the I.M.L. Recruiting Campaign, 1914-16. Territorial Medal, 1909, and served European War, in 1914, London Scottish. Chief of the Scottish Clans Assoc. of London, 1912-14; and Joint Organiser the Clans' Scottish Prisoners of War Relief, 1916-18. A Life Governor, University College Hospital, London, from 1900; a Life Trustee, Royal Southern Hospital, Liverpool, from 1933, and a Life Governor, Royal Liverpool United Hosp. *Publications:* Sophocles and Shakspere (a Work in Latin), 1896; Oscan Word "Anasaket," 1897; Origin of Gerund and Gerundive, 1894-98; Establishment and Extension of Law of Thurneysen and Havet, 1899. Galileo, 1899; Undina, 1900; Gilboa, 1901. The Passing of the Great Fleet, 1909; The True "Truth about the Navy," 1909; Keep the Flag Flying, 1910; The Declaration of London: National Starvation in War, and Paralysis of Britain's Power and Rights at Sea, 1910-11: Britain's Imminent Danger, 1912 (the last five jointly); Passing Thoughts, 1915; Victory or Annihilation, 1915; The Value of Sea-Power, 1916; The Freedom of the Seas, 1916; Perils of the Sea: How we Kept the Flag Flying, 1920; The Fiery Fray, 1920. First Report on Working of Landlord and Tenant Act (1927), 1931; Second, 1932; and over 300 articles, etc., explanatory of such Act, 1931 onwards, including Shopkeeper Tenants, 1949, and Scintillæ Lucis, 1949 and Supplement to latter, 1951; also, on the Rent Control Act 1946, A Six Months' Retrospect, 1947, and on that Act and the Act of 1949, over 100 articles, etc., and Scintillæ Lucis Alteræ, 1951. Earliest Hymn by Lord Macaulay, 1902; In Memoriam, Raymond J. Horton-Smith, 1903; Biography, R. H. Horton-Smith, K.C., down to 1907; over 350 articles, etc., genealogical and antiquarian, 1895-1950, mostly listed in For Them that are Yet for to Come, 1950; Rhyming Relics of the Legal Past, 1950, with Supplement, 1951; The Baily Family of Thatcham, etc., Co. Berks, 1951; Dr. Walter Baily (1529-92), Physician to Queen Elizabeth, 1952; and George Acworth's Life and his Letters (of 1558-73), 1952. Recorded at College of Arms: Pedigrees of Smith, 1902, Horton, 1938, 1940 and 1952, Baily, 1941 and 1951, Lumley, 1947 and 1950. Contributor to Principal Poets of the World, 1932 and 1938, The Poetry Quarterly, The Spring Anthology, etc. *Recreations:* formerly hockey, shinty, swimming, fives (Capt., Johnian Fives Club, 1893-95), and Highland step-dancing (14 times Amateur Medallist) and, throughout, Philology and Family Historiology. *Address:* 26 Rivercourt Road, Ravenscourt Park, W.6; 5 Paper Buildings, Temple, E.C. 4. *T.A.:* 54 Temple. *T.:* Riverside 2536, City 3724-6. *Club:* Athenæum. [*Died* 9 *March* 1953.

HORTON-SMITH-HARTLEY, Sir Percival; *see* Hartley, Sir P. H. S.

HORWILL, Herbert William, M.A.; *b.* Sandown, 1864; *s.* of late Rev. James Horwill; *m.* 1898, Kate (*d.* 1949), *d.* of late Rev. F. W. Bourne. *Educ.:* Victoria College, Jersey; Bible Christian College, Shebbear; Wadham College, Oxford (Scholar). Dyke Exhibitioner; First class Classical Mods. 1884; second class Lit. Hum. 1886; Chancellor's Prize English

Essay, 1887; at London, M.A., with gold medal in Classics, 1887; Member of Standing Committee of Convocation, London University, 1914-23; entered ministry of Bible Christian Methodist (now included in Methodist) Church, 1887; delegate to Methodist Œcumenical Conference, 1891; classical tutor, Way College, Adelaide, 1892-93; became a minister without pastoral charge for reasons of health, 1896, and has since been mainly engaged on the press; assistant-editor Forum, and on reviewing staff Nation (N.Y.), 1901-5; London Correspondent, New York Evening Post, 1911-20, New York Nation, 1918-20, New York Times Book Review, 1924-43. *Publications:* The Old Gospel in the New Era, 1894; The Usages of the American Constitution, 1925; A Dictionary of Modern American Usage, 1935; American Variations, 1936 (Soc. for Pure English); An Anglo-American Interpreter, 1939; articles in English and American Reviews. *Recreation:* music. *Address:* Castilla, 49 Plaistow Lane, Bromley, Kent. *T.:* Ravensbourne 0213. [*Died* 28 *Feb.* 1952.

HOSE, Sir (John) Walter, Kt., *cr.* 1926; C.S.I. 1911; *b.* Camberwell, 1865; *s.* of John W. Hose; *m.* 1891, Madeline Mary, *d.* of Rev. R. C. Caswall. *Educ.:* Dulwich College; Christ Church, Oxford (Scholar). Entered Indian Civil Service, 1886; Registrar, High Court of Judicature, N.W.P., 1894-98; Financial Secretary, United Provinces, 1905-8; and Chief Secretary to Government, 1908-12; Member of Provincial Legislative Council, 1905-12; Commissioner, Agra, 1912-15; retired, 1916; employed at the India Office, 1916-26. *Address:* Speldhurst, Kent. [*Died* 17 *Dec.* 1958.

HOSIE, Lady, (Dorothea), M.A.; writer; lecturer; *b.* Ningpo, China, 1885; *d.* of late Professor W. E. Soothill; *widow* of Sir Alexander Hosie, M.A., LL.D., F.R.G.S., Consul-General Commercial Attaché China Consular Service. *Educ.:* Newnham College, Cambridge (Associate); Bedford College, London. President of National Free Church Women's Council, 1932-33; served on County Educational and Girl Guide Committees, Isle of Wight; Member of various China Relief Committees; Vice-Principal Brampton Down Girls' School, Folkestone and Taunton, 1938-46. *Publications:* Two Gentlemen of China, 1924; Portrait of a Chinese Lady, 1929; Brave New China, 1938; The Pool of Ch'ien Lung, 1944; Jesus and Woman, 1946 (revised edn., 1956) (American edn., 1954, as The Master Calleth for Thee); numerous contribs., mainly travel, to magazines and newspapers; edited, Passport to China, by Lucy Soothill; assisted with Analects of Confucius (Soothill) and Dictionary of Chinese Buddhist Terms (Soothill and Hodous); Hall of Light (Soothill); also Philip's Commercial Map of China (Hosie); Article on Sir John Jordan in Dictionary of Nat. Biog. *Address:* Appletree Cottage, Redlynch, nr. Salisbury, Wilts. *T.:* Downton 2187. *Club:* Guide. [*Died* 15 *Feb.* 1959.

HOSKIN, Theo. Jenner Hooper, M.A., M.D. (Cambridge), F.R.C.P. (London); Physician and Cardiologist, Royal Free Hospital; Consulting Cardiologist, St. Paul's Hospital for Genito-Urinary Diseases; Consulting Physician to Royal National Throat, Nose, and Ear Hospital; Lecturer of Medicine, University of London; late Examiner in Medicine Conjoint Board; late President, Med. Soc. of London; Chief Med. Officer to Pearl Assurance Co., and to Friends' Provident and Century Life Office; Liveryman of Skinners' and Past Master Worshipful Co. of Makers of Playing Cards; *b.* 1888; *s.* of late Dr. Theophilus Hoskin, J.P.; *m.* Mary Jane Finlay, *d.* of late William Stewart, Skelmorlie, Ayrshire; one *s.* two *d.* *Educ.:* Charterhouse; Trinity College, Cambridge; Middlesex Hospital. Served European War, 1915-19 (despatches). *Publications:* Observations on Rheumatic Heart, Practitioner, 1928; The Portable Electrocardiograph (with Dr. J. S. Goodall), Brit. Med. Jour., 1930; Diagnosis, Prognosis and Treatment of Coronary Disease, address before Hunterian Society, 1934; Cardiac Problems in Recruits, Post-Graduate Med. Jour., April 1942; Analysis of Fifty Normal Electro-cardiograms, including Lead IV (with Dr. P. Jonescu), British Heart Journal, 1940; Silent Dissection of the Aorta (with Dr. F. Gardner), British Heart Journal, 1946; Tachycardia, British Encyclopaedia of Medical Practice, 1947; The Value of Drugs in the Treatment of Heart Disease, 1948; Arrhythmias, Brit. Encyclopaedia of Medical Practice, 1949. *Recreations:* golf, motoring. *Address:* 112 Harley Street, W.1. *T.:* Welbeck 7041. *Club:* Athenæum. [*Died* 27 *Feb.* 1954.

HOSKING, Ethelbert Bernard, C.M.G. 1944; O.B.E. 1932; *b.* 22 Feb. 1890; *s.* of Ethelbert Hosking, J.P., M.R.C.S.; *m.* 1919, Mary Isabella Grant; one *s.* one *d.* *Educ.:* Fonthill, East Grinstead; King's School, Canterbury; Wadham College, Oxford. Asst. District Commissioner, East Africa Protectorate, 1913; District Commissioner, Kenya Colony; Acting Commissioner, Local Government, Lands and Settlement; Commissioner of Mines; Chief Native Commissioner, 1937-44; retired, 1944. Acted Hon. Secretary-General Royal Empire Society, 1945; Chairman Uasin Gishu District Council, 1949-55. *Recreation:* forestry. *Address:* Kendurr, Eldoret, Kenya. *Club:* Nairobi. [*Died* 29 *Sept.* 1960.

HOSKYNS, Sir John Chevallier, 15th Bt., *cr.* 1676; Barrister, Inner Temple, 1951; now at Cuddesdon College, Oxford; *b.* 23 May 1926; *s.* of Rev. Canon Sir Edwyn Clement Hoskyns, 13th Bt., M.C., D.D., and Mary Trym, *d.* of Edwin Budden, Macclesfield; *S.* brother 1945. *Educ.:* Marlborough College; King's College, Cambridge. Served in War of 1939-45, K.R.R.C., 1944-48; Palestine, 1946-47; Kenya, 1947-48. *Recreations:* cricket, fishing, tennis. *Heir:* *b.* Benedict Leigh, *b.* 27 May 1928. *Address:* 11 Millington Road, Cambridge. *T.:* Cambridge 4822. [*Died* 12 *April* 1956.

HOSKYNS-ABRAHALL, Bennet, C.B.E. 1918; *b.* 26 Aug. 1858; *e. s.* of T. B. Hoskyns-Abrahall, Barrister-at-law, Last Commissioner of the Court of Bankruptcy for Northumberland District, of Goldspink Hall, Newcastle-on-Tyne, and Kernock, Torquay; *m.*; two *s.* *Educ.:* St. Peter's School, York; Keble College, Oxford. Entered Civil Service as Clerk, Grade 1, Secretary's Office, G.P.O., 1881; Principal Clerk, 1904; Director of Investigation Branch, 1909-21; retired, 1921. *Address:* Hatt Farm, near Newbury, Berks. *T.:* Highclere 408. [*Died* 1 *Oct.* 1951.

HOTBLACK, George Finch; a Director of the Peninsular and Oriental Steam Navigation Co. and British India Steam Navigation Co. Ltd.; The Atlas Assurance Co. Ltd. (Chm. 1939-49); National Provincial Bank Ltd.; Australasian United Steam Navigation Co. Ltd.; partner in Gray, Dawes & Co.; Commissioner for Land Tax, and Commissioner for Income Tax for City of London; *b.* 19 Jan. 1883; *o. s.* of late George Snelling Hotblack of Brundall, Norfolk; *m.* 1939, Ruth Honor Skrine. *Educ.:* Pembroke College, Cambridge (M.A., LL.B.). Served European War (despatches). *Recreations:* shooting and fishing. *Address:* 130 St. James' Court, Buckingham Gate, S.W.1; Point House, Narborough, Norfolk. *Clubs:* United University, City of London. [*Died* 20 *June* 1951.

HOTCHKIN, Stafford Vere, M.C., D.L.; J.P.; M.P. (Co. U.) Horncastle Division, 1920-22; *b.* 1876; *o. s.* of Thomas John Stafford Hotchkin, J.P., of South Luffenham Hall, Stamford and Woodhall Spa, Co. Lincoln, and Mary C. E. Lucas, *e. d.* of late G. V. Braithwaite, of Edith Weston Hall, Rutland: *m.* 1906, Dorothy, *yr d.* of F. A. Arnold,

18 Netherhall Gardens, N.W.; one *s.* one *d.* (decd.). *Educ.:* Shrewsbury. Served Leicestershire Yeomanry; 21st (E. of I.) Lancers; R.H.A. (T.F.); Sheriff of Rutland, 1912, and J.P. for parts of Lindsey; Chairman Lindsey Small Holdings Committee. *Recreations:* hunting, shooting, and golf. *Address:* The Manor House, Woodhall Spa, Lincs. *T.A.:* Hotchkin, Woodhall Spa. *T.:* Woodhall Spa 16. *Clubs:* Carlton, Cavalry, Naval and Military. [*Died* 8 *Aug.* 1953.

HOTHFIELD, 2nd Baron, *cr.* 1881, **John Sackville Richard Tufton,** D.S.O. 1916; 3rd Bt. *cr.* 1851; late Maj., 3rd Bn. Roy. Sussex Regt.; *b.* 8 Nov. 1873; *e. s.* of 1st Baron and Alice (*d.* 1914), 2nd *d.* of late Rev. William James Stracey-Clitherow; *S.* father, 1926; *m.* 1st, 1896, Lady Ierne Hastings (*d.* 1935), *d.* of 13th Earl of Huntingdon; two *s.* two *d.*; 2nd, Sybil Augusta (*d.* 1950), *d.* of late John Sant, S. Wales. Served South African War, 1901-2 (Queen's medal and five clasps); European War, 1914-19 (despatches, D.S.O., G.S. Medal, 1914-15 Star, Victory Medal, Mérite Agricole, Order of Leopold of Belgium, Croix de Guerre); Mayor of Appleby, 1937-38 and 1938-39. *Heir:* *s.* Hon. Henry Sackville Hastings Thanet Tufton [*b.* 16 March 1897; *m.* 1918, Dorothy, *d.* of late William George Raphael, 9 Connaught Place, W. *Address:* Castle Hill, Englefield Green, Surrey]. *Address:* Hothfield Place, Ashford, Kent; 74 Albion Gate, Hyde Park, W.2; Appleby Castle, Westmorland; Skipton Castle, Yorkshire. *Clubs:* Carlton, M.C.C. [*Died* 21 *Dec.* 1952.

HO TUNG, Sir Robert, K.B.E., *cr.* 1955; Kt., *cr.* 1915; J.P.; Hon. LL.D., University of Hong Kong, 1915; financier; real estate owner; *b.* 22 December 1862; *m.* 1880, Margaret Mak (*decd.*), O.B.E. 1942; three *s.* (one adopted) eight *d.* *Educ.:* Central School (now Queen's College), Hong Kong. Indoor Staff, Imperial Chinese Maritime Customs, Canton, 1879-80; Assistant Manager, Chinese Department, Jardine, Matheson & Co., 1880; Chief Manager of Chinese Dept. 1894; retd., 1900; Chm., Industrial and Commercial Newspaper Co. Ltd.; Director of Hong Kong & Shanghai Hotels, Ltd., and various Companies; member of Court, University of Hong Kong; High Class Hon. Adviser to National Chinese Government; Chairman of the Committee to investigate into the economic resources of Hong Kong and its dependencies, 1920; acted as Hon. Commissioner representing Hong Kong at the British Empire Exhibition, Wembley, 1924 and 1925; holds 3rd class Order of Excellent Crop, 1914; 2nd class, 1916; 2nd Class with Brilliancy, 1921; 1st class with Grand Sash, 1922 (National Chinese Government); Silver Donat of St. John of Jerusalem, 1924; Knight of Grace, 1925; Knight Commander of the Ancient Order of Christ, Portugal, 1925, and Knight Grand Officer, 1930; Grand Officer, Order of Public Education, Portugal, 1952; Commandeur de la Légion d'Honneur, 1932; First Class National Red Cross Order of Germany, 1932; Kt. Commander of Crown of Italy, 1933; Knight Commander of Crown of Leopold of Belgium, 1934; Knight Commander of the Imperial Dragon of Annam, 1935; Grand Cordon with Brilliant Jade Decoration, 2nd Class (National Chinese Government), 1939; Gold Meritorious Medal (National Chinese Government), 1938; Coat of Arms—Justice and Truth. *Address:* Des Voeux Road Central, Hong Kong; Idlewild, Seymour Road, Hong Kong. *T.A:* Longevity, Hong Kong. [*Died* 26 *April* 1956.

HOUDE, Camillien, C.B.E. 1935; past Mayor of Montreal; *b.* Montreal, 13 Aug. 1889; *s.* of Azade Houde and Joséphine Frenette; *m.* 1st, 1913, Mignonne Bourgie; two *d.*; 2nd, 1919, Georgianna Falardeau; one *d.* *Educ.:* Collège de Longueuil. Graduated, 1906; employed with Bank of Hochelaga (now Banque Canadienne Nationale), 1906-19; elected Mem. Quebec Legislature, 1923-31; elected Mayor of Montreal, 1928, and since re-elected, 1930, 1934, 1938, 1944, 1947, 1950; retired, 1954. Elected member of Parliament for Papineau, 1949. Legion of Honour (France), 1935. *Address:* Station "H", P.O. Box 340, Montreal, Quebec, Canada. [*Died Sept.* 1958.

HOUGH, James Fisher, O.B.E. 1958; M.A., F.R.A.S.; Chairman, Brentwood Group of Hospitals Management Committee, 1948-1958, resigned; *b.* 9 January 1878; *e. s.* of late Joseph Hough, Codsall Wood, Staffordshire; unmarried. *Educ.:* Wolverhampton School; St. John's College, Cambridge. Second master, Brentwood School, 1903-13; Headmaster of Brentwood School, 1913-45. *Recreation:* golf. *Address:* Springfield, Brentwood. *T.:* 625. [*Died* 16 *Jan.* 1960.

HOUGHTON, Rev. Edward John Walford, D.D.; *b.* 11 Aug. 1867; *e. s.* of Rev. Canon Houghton, M.A., Vicar of Blockley, Worcestershire; *m.* 1895, Ethelwynne Mary, *e. d.* of Rev. H. H. Chamberlain, M.A., Vicar of Godmanchester and Rural Dean; one *s.* (and three *s.* decd.). *Educ.:* Sherborne School (scholar); Christ Church, Oxford—prox. acc. Abbott University Scholarship. 2nd Class Honours Classical Mods. 1889; 2nd Class Lit. Hum. 1891; B.A. 1891; M.A. 1894; Member of M.C.C.; played cricket for Worcestershire; Deacon, 1892; Priest, 1893; appointed Assistant Master in Bromsgrove School, 1891; Housemaster and Senior Chaplain, 1893; Headmaster of King Edward's School, Stratford-on-Avon, Chaplain of Guild of Holy Cross, Trustee of Shakspere Buildings, etc., 1895-1902; Head Master of St. Edmund's School, Canterbury, and Licensed Preacher in the diocese of Canterbury, 1902-1908; Head Master of Rossall, 1908-32; Examining Chaplain to Bishop of Sodor and Man, 1925-29; Hon. Canon of Blackburn, 1927-1932. *Recreations:* cricket, tennis, and fives. *Address:* St. Michael's, Headington Hill, Oxford. [*Died* 2 *March* 1955.

HOULDSWORTH, Sir Hubert Stanley, 1st Bt. *cr.* 1956; Kt., *cr.* 1944; Q.C. 1937; D.Sc.; LL.D. (Hon.) Leeds and Nottingham; Chm., National Coal Bd. since 1951; *b.* 20 Apr. 1889; *s.* of Albert Edward Houldsworth and Susannah Buckley; *m.* 1919, Hilda Frances, *d.* of Joseph Clegg and Annie Gomersal, Cleckheaton, Yorks; one *s.* *Educ.:* University of Leeds (B.Sc. with First Class Honours in Physics, 1911; M.Sc. 1912; D.Sc. 1925). Assistant Lecturer in University of Leeds, 1919-26; called to Bar, Lincoln's Inn, 1926; Bencher, 1943; Independent Chairman of District Co-ordinating Committee of Midland (Amalgamated) District (Coal Mines) Scheme 1930, from Sept. 1936 to July 1942; Joint Coal Supplies Officer for Midland Area (Mines Dept.), Sept. 1939-July 1942; Fuel and Power Controller (North-Eastern Region), Board of Trade, Nov. 1941-July 1942; Regional Controller (S. and W. Yorkshire), Ministry of Fuel and Power, 1942-44, Controller-General, 1944-45; Chm. E. Midlands Division, N.C.B., 1946-51; Recorder of Doncaster, 1946-48; formerly Deputy Chairman of West Riding Quarter Sessions; Pro-Chancellor, Leeds University; contested (L.) Pudsey and Otley, 1929. *Publications:* papers in Transactions of Ceramic Society and Journal of Society of Glass Technology. *Heir:* *s.* (Harold) Basil [*b.* 21 July 1922; *m.* 1946, Norah Clifford Halmshaw; one *d.*]. *Address:* 6 Stone Buildings, Lincoln's Inn, W.C.2. *Club:* Athenæum. [*Died* 1 *Feb.* 1956.

HOULDSWORTH, Colonel Sir William Thomas Reginald, 3rd Bt., *cr.* 1887; C.B.E. 1946; T.D.; D.L.; J.P.; M.A.; *b.* 1874; 2nd *surv.* *s.* of Sir William Henry Houldsworth, 1st Bt.; *S.* brother 1947; *m.* 1899, Ethel Mary Alberta (*d.* 1937), *d.* of late Capt. T. C. D. Whitmore, D.L., Orsett Hall, Essex; two *s.* one *d.* *Educ.:* Eton; Christ Church, Oxford. Hon.

Col. Ayrshire (Earl of Carrick's Own) Yeo., 1926; served European War (Ayrshire Yeo.), 1916-19: Order of Nile, 3rd Class; Lt.-Col. comdg. Ayrshire Yeo., 1920-23. *Heir*: *s.* Reginald Douglas Henry [*b.* 9 July 1903; *m.* 1934, M.M. Laurie; one *s.* two *d.*]. *Address*: Kirkbride, Maybole, Ayrshire. *T.A.*: Crosshill. *T.*: Crosshill 202. *Clubs*: Cavalry, Caledonian; New (Edinburgh). [*Died* 31 *Dec.* 1960.

HOULTON, Charlotte Leighton, C.B.E. 1939; *b.* 23 Oct. 1882; *d.* of John Houlton and Charlotte Leighton; unmarried. *Educ.*: Royal Free Hospital School of Medicine for Women. M.B., B.S., London University, 1911; M.D. 1917; F.R.C.O.G. 1937; Women's Medical Service, India, 1913-39; Medical Superintendent, Lady Reading Hospital, Simla; Medical Supt., St. Stephen's Hospital, Delhi; Principal and Professor of Gynæcology, Lady Hardinge Medical College, New Delhi; Fellow Punjab University; Chief Medical Officer Women's Medical Service, India; Secretary Countess of Dufferin's Fund Council; Physician and Medical Missions Secretary, S.P.G., 1939 (retired); Founded Tertiary Order of the Order of the Holy Paraclete, 1948. Kaisar-i-Hind Medal, First Class, 1925; Silver Jubilee Medal, 1935; Coronation Medal, 1937. *Recreation*: reading. *Address*: St. Francis, Sneaton Castle, Whitby, Yorkshire. [*Died* 13 *Dec.* 1956.

HOUSE, (Arthur) Humphry; Senior University Lecturer in English Literature, Oxford; Fellow of Wadham College; *b.* 22 May 1908; *s.* of William Harold House and Eleanor Clara Neve; *m.* 1933, Madeline Edith Church; one *s.* two *d.* *Educ.*: Repton; Hertford College, Oxford, 1st Class Litt. Hum., 1929; 2nd Class Mod. Hist., 1930; Assistant Master, Repton School, 1930; Fellow and Lecturer in English Literature, Wadham College, Oxford, 1931; Special Assistant Lecturer in Classics, University College, Exeter, 1933; Professor of English, Presidency College, Calcutta, 1936; Lecturer in English, University of Calcutta, 1937; William Noble Fellow, University of Liverpool, 1940; Trooper, R.A.C., 1940; after various General Staff appointments (j.s.c. 1943) invalided from service with rank of Major, 1945; Director of Studies in English, Peterhouse, Cambridge, 1947. Clark Lecturer, Trinity College, Cambridge, 1951-52. Examiner Cambridge English Tripos Pt. II, 1953. Member Exec. Committee Radiowriters' Association, 1948; Committee of Management, Society of Authors, 1949. Deacon in C. of E., 1931; but in 1932 retired into lay life. *Publications*: (Ed.) Notebooks and Papers of Gerard Manley Hopkins, 1937; The Dickens World, 1941; Three essays in Ideas and Beliefs of the Victorians, 1948; Introduction to Oliver Twist, 1949; Coleridge (Clark Lectures), 1953; The Collected Essays and Broadcast Talks of Humphry House, 1956 (posthumous). Contributions to New Statesman and Nation, Spectator, etc. Numerous Broadcasts for B.B.C. and All India Radio. *Address*: 61 Bateman St., Cambridge; Wadham College, Oxford. [*Died* 14 *Feb.* 1955.

HOUSMAN, Laurence; author and artist; *b.* 18 July 1865. *Publications*: The Writings of William Blake, 1893; A Farm in Fairyland, 1894; The House of Joy, 1895; Arthur Boyd Houghton, 1896; Green Arras, 1896; All-Fellows, 1896; Gods and their Makers, 1897; Spikenard, 1898; The Field of Clover, 1898; The Little Land, 1899; Rue, 1899; The Seven Young Goslings, 1899; An Englishwoman's Love Letters, 1900; A Modern Antæus, 1901; Aucassin and Nicolette; Bethlehem: A Nativity Play, 1902; Sabrina Warham, 1904; The Blue Moon, 1904; The Cloak of Friendship, 1905; Mendicant Rhymes, 1906; Prunella, or Love in a Dutch Garden, 1906; The Chinese Lantern, 1908; Selected Poems, 1909; Articles of Faith, 1909; Lysistrata (A Modern Paraphrase), 1910; Pains and Penalties, 1911; The New Child's Guide to Knowledge, 1911; John of Jingalo, 1912; The Royal Runaway, 1914; Lord of the Harvest; As Good as Gold; Nazareth; The Return of Alcestis; Bird in Hand, 1916; The Sheepfold, 1918; St. Francis Poverello, 1918; The Heart of Peace, 1919; The Wheel; 1919; Ploughshare and Pruning-hook, 1919; The Death of Orpheus, 1921; Angels and Ministers, 1921; Possession: A Peep-show in Paradise, 1921; Little Plays of St. Francis, 1922; Second Series, 1931; Dethronements, 1922: Moonshine and Clover, 1922; A Doorway in Fairyland, 1922; False Premises, 1922; Echo de Paris, 1923; Trimblerigg, 1924; Odd Pairs, 1925; Ironical Tales, 1926; Followers of St. Francis, 1925; The Comments of Juniper, 1926; Uncle Tom Pudd, 1927; Ways and Means, 1927; H.R.H. The Duke of Flamborough, 1928; The Love Concealed, 1928; Cornered Poets, 1929; War Letters of Fallen Englishmen, 1930; Turn-Again-Tales, 1930; Palace Plays, 1931; Ye Fearful Saints! 1932; The Queen's Progress, 1932; What-o'clock Tales, 1932; Victoria and Albert, 1933; Nunc Dimittis, 1933; Four Plays of St. Clare; Victoria Regina, 1934; The Unexpected Years, 1936; Palace Scenes, 1937; The Golden Sovereign, 1937; A. E. H., 1937; What Next?, 1938; Collected Poems, 1938; What Can We Believe? Letters between Dick Sheppard and Laurence Housman, 1939; The Preparation of Peace, 1940; Gracious Majesty, 1941; Palestine Plays, 1942; Samuel, the Kingmaker, 1944; Back Words and Fore Words, 1945; The Family Honour, 1950; Old Testament Plays, 1951; Illustrated Goblin Market; Weird Tales from Northern Seas; The End of Elfintown; The Were-Wolf; Jump to Glory Jane; The Sensitive Plant; The New Child's Guide. *Address*: Longmeadow, Street, Somerset. [*Died* 20 *Feb.* 1959.

HOUSTON, Maj.-Gen. John B.; *see* Blakiston-Houston.

HOUSTON, Lt.-Col. W. B. D.; *see* Davidson-Houston.

HOUSTOUN-BOSWALL, Sir (Thomas) Randolph, 5th Bt., *cr.* 1836; late Capt. 14th Batt. Royal Scots; *b.* 5 Feb. 1882; 2nd *s.* of 3rd Bt. and Phoebe, *d.* of Sir Hugh Allan; *S.* brother, 1915; *m.* 1912, Edith Mary, *y. d.* of Jarvis Salter, Wribbenhall, Worcester; (*o. surv. son* killed in action in War of 1939-45) three *d.* Owns about 5400 acres. *Heir*: *cousin*, Gordon [*b.* 15 March 1887; *m.* 1916, Daisy, *d.* of Edwin Copeland Waller; two *s.*]. *Address*: 22 Eastern Lane, Berwick-on-Tweed. [*Died* 4 *Dec.* 1953.

HOUSTOUN-BOSWALL, Sir William Evelyn, K.C.M.G., *cr.* 1949 (C.M.G. 1942); M.C.; *b.* 5 June 1892; *e. s.* of late Alfred Houstoun-Boswall; *m.* 1921, Margaret Dorothy, O.B.E. 1919 (*d.* 1957), *d.* of late George Anson Byron; one *d.* *Educ.*: Wellington Coll.; New Coll., Oxford. Formerly Capt., the Black Watch. Served European War, 1914-18 (despatches, M.C., Croix de Guerre); Third Sec. in Diplomatic Service, 1921; (Madrid, Paris, Foreign Office); Second Sec. 1925 (The Hague, Lisbon); seconded to Dominions Office for service in Union of S. Africa, 1929-32; First Secretary, 1933 (Budapest, Oslo); Counsellor of Embassy, 1940 (Bagdad, Tokyo); seconded and served on staff of Resident Minister in W. Africa, Minister, 1944; British political representative in Bulgaria, 1944-46; Minister at Beirut, 1947-51; retired, 1951. *Address*: 34 Evelyn Mansions, Carlisle Place, S.W.1. *Club*: Boodle's. [*Died* 2 *Aug.* 1960.

HOWARD, Brig. Sir Charles Alfred, G.C.V.O. 1957 (K.C.V.O., 1944); D.S.O. 1917, Bar 1918; King's Royal Rifles, retired; Sergeant-at-Arms, House of Commons, 1935-56, retired; *b.* 1878; *s.* of Hon. Greville Theophilus Howard, *s.* of 17th Earl of Suffolk and Berkshire and Lady Audrey Townshend, *d.* of 4th Marquis Townshend (who *m.* 2nd, late Rt. Hon.

Sir Redvers Buller); *m.* 1908, Miriam Eleanore, *d.* of Lt.-Col. E. M. Dansey, 1st Life Guards; one *s.* (and one *d.* decd.). *Educ.:* Eton; Sandhurst. Entered army, 1898; India, 1898-99; served South African Campaign, 1900; Special Service Officer, A.D.C. to Sir Redvers Buller; and with S. African Light Horse; on Staff, 1912-1916; appointed to command 16th K.R.R. 1916 (wounded Aug. 1916, despatches, D.S.O.); Commander 162nd East Midland Infantry Brigade, 1929-32; Commander 12th Infantry Brigade and Dover Garrison, 1932-35; Légion d'Honneur. *Recreation:* hunting. *Address:* Castle Rising, King's Lynn, Norfolk. *Clubs:* Brooks's, Pratt's. [*Died* 5 *Jan.* 1958.

HOWARD, Major Edmund, F.R.I.C.S.; R.A.; retd.; Surveyor; *b.* London, 14 Nov. 1881; *s.* of late James Henry Howard, Wanstead, Essex; *m.* Florence Ada Strange, *d.* of late Sir Henry Foreman, M.P., J.P., O.B.E.; no *c.* *Educ.:* privately; abroad. Senior partner of Howard, Fairbairn and Partners, Architects and Surveyors, 81 Piccadilly, W.1; served European War, 1914-18 (1914 Star and Clasp, War Medal, Victory Medal); Controller of Building Construction, Ministry of Supply, 1941-43. President Associated Owners of City Properties; Chairman City of London Real Property Co. Ltd.; Director of London County Freehold and Leasehold Properties Ltd., etc. *Recreations:* hunting, farming; Master Mid-Surrey Drag Hounds, 1926-39. *Address:* Downside, Leatherhead, Surrey. *T.:* Leatherhead 2161; 41 Arlington House, Arlington Street, S.W.1. *T.:* Hyde Park 3930, Mayfair 7546-7-8. [*Died* 1 *March* 1960.

HOWARD, Francis; Chm. National Portrait Soc.; Director National Loan Exhibitions; Chevalier of the Crown of Belgium; *b.* 1 Jan. 1874; *o. s.* of Francis Gassaway Howard, *g.-g.s.* of Benjamin Franklin; *m.* 1903, L. Chess of Louisville, Ky.; one *s.* *Educ.:* St. Edmund's and St. Augustine's Roman Catholic Colleges; Germany, Geneva, and Paris. Studied art Paris, London; for many years art-critic Weekly Sun, and contributor of art, dramatic, and literary criticism and verse to many periodicals; founded the International Society of Sculptors, Painters, and Gravers, 1898; and National Portrait Society, 1910; organized Art section of Woman's Exhibition at Earl's Court, 1901; Chm. British Art and Antiquarian Committee, Jamestown Exposition, 1907, and Special Commissioner; organized the Exhibition of Chosen Pictures, Grafton Galleries, 1909; National Loan Exhibitions in aid of National Gallery Funds, and of other objects, 1909-10, 1913-14, and 1914-15; National Portrait Society's Exhibitions at Bradford and Oldham, 1910; and its Inaugural London Exhibition, 1911; Inaugural Exhibition, Grosvenor Gallery, 1912; Albert Besnard Exhibition, 1913; International Society 29th London Exhibition at the Royal Academy, 1925; Masterpieces of English Art Exhibition, Vienna, 1927; Exhibitor in principal European and American Galleries; formerly Honorary Managing Director of the Grafton and Grosvenor Galleries, and Director of The Sun and other newspapers; presented collection of modern pictures to the Tate Gallery, and examples of Modern British Painting to the Luxembourg Gallery; National Portrait Gallery; Ashmolean Museum, Oxford, Glasgow Art Gallery, etc.; represented in the Walker Art Gallery, Liverpool. *Publications:* Illus. Cat. Second National Loan Exhibition and numbers of biographical and other catalogues. *Recreations:* tennis, riding (formerly in flat and hurdle races in England, Germany, and America); collector of pictures. *Club:* Chelsea Arts. [*Died* 4 *Oct.* 1954.

HOWARD, Rev. Robert Wilmot, M.A. (Cantab. and Oxon.); Hon. C.F.; Rector of Westonbirt with Lasborough, Tetbury, Glos., and Chaplain to Westonbirt School since 1955; *b.* 16 Sept. 1887; *s.* of late Rev. Charles Howard, M.A., Vicar of St. Philip's, Cambridge, and Helen Gertrude, *d.* of Rev. R. G. Bryan, Principal of Monkton Combe Sch., nr. Bath; *m.* 1923, Nora Katharine, *yr. d.* of Dr. D. W. Carr, of C.M.S., Persia; one *s.* four *d.* *Educ.:* Weymouth Coll. (Scholar); Trinity Coll., Cambridge (Classical Scholar); First Class, Classical Tripos, Part I., 1909; First Class, Theological Tripos, Part I., 1911, University Bell Scholar, 1907; Stewart of Rannoch Scholar (Classics), 1908; Ridley Hall, Cambridge; ordained, 1912; Select Preacher before the University of Cambridge, May 1928 and April 1947 and University of Oxford, Nov. 1947, Oct. 1948, and Feb. 1949; Tutor at St. Aidan's Theological College, Birkenhead, 1912-15; Chaplain (1919) and Vice-Principal (1920) of St. Aidan's College; Home Education Secretary of the Church Missionary Society, 1920-1923; Assistant Master at Eton College, 1924-28; Headmaster Liverpool College, 1928-45; Canon Diocesan of Liverpool Cathedral, 1943-45. Canon Emeritus since 1945; Rector of St. Peter-le-Bailey, and Master of St. Peter's Hall, Oxford, 1945-55; Hon. Fell., St. Peter's Hall, 1955-; Chaplain to the Forces, B.E.F., 1916-19. *Publications:* A Merry Mountaineer, 1931; Talks in Preparation for Confirmation, 1941; Should Women be Priests?, 1949; Author-Editor of Workers Together (C.M.S. Handbook), 1924. *Recreations:* golf, gardening, walking, cycling. *Address:* Westonbirt Rectory, Tetbury, Glos. *T.:* Westonbirt 202. [*Died* 23 *Nov.* 1960.

HOWARD, Brig.-Gen. Thomas Nairne Scott Moncrieff, C.B. 1926; D.S.O. and bar, 1917; *s.* of late Colonel Thomas Howard, R.E.; *m.* 1926, Margarita Constance, *d.* of B. Y. Bevan, J.P., Weald Chase, Cuckfield, Sussex. *Educ.:* Edinburgh Acad.; Dulwich Coll.; Sandhurst. Joined the West Yorkshire Regiment, 1892; served Uganda, Nandi Expedition, 1900; Lango Expedition, 1901 (wounded); Somaliland, 1902-1904 (wounded); European War, 1914-18; Kurdistan, 1923 (despatches nine times, D.S.O. and bar); Bt. Lt.-Col. 1915; Bt. Col. 1919; Commanded 161st (Essex) Infantry Brigade, 1924-28; retired pay, 1928. Commanded 4th Bn. Alresford (Hampshire) Home Guard, 1940-43. *Address:* Weald Acre, Cuckfield, Sussex. *T:* Cuckfield 18. [*Died* 29 *Dec.* 1960.

HOWARD, Tom Forrest, D.C.M.; *b.* 1888; *m.* 1913, Haidie Alice, *d.* of Henry Battley, Ipswich; two *s.* one *d.* Member Finsbury Boro Council, 1922-25; Member L.C.C. 1925-28, and 1931-34; M.P. (U.) South Islington 1931-35. *Address:* 4 Vernon Rise, King's Cross Road, W.C.1. *T.:* Terminus 1051; 8 Quernmore Road, N.4. *Club:* 1912. [*Died* 12 *June* 1953.

HOWARD, Rev. Wilbert Francis, M.A. (Manch.), B.A., B.D. (1st Cl. Hons.), D.D. (Lond.), Hon. D.D. (St. Andrews and Manchester); F.B.A. 1949; Tutor in New Testament Language and Literature at Handsworth College, Birmingham, 1919-51 (Principal, 1943-51); formerly Lecturer in Hellenistic Greek and New Testament studies for the University of Birmingham; *b.* 1880; *e. s.* of Rev. Joseph Howard; *m.* Winifred Worsley, *o. d.* of T. A. Bedale, Worsley; two *s.* two *d.* *Educ.:* King Edward's School, Birmingham; Manchester University; Didsbury College. Minister of Wesleyan Methodist Church in Glasgow, Bowes Park, N., Manchester, Handsworth, and Wallasey; visiting Professor of Hellenistic Greek at Drew Theological Seminary, Madison, New Jersey (1919); Dale Lecturer at Mansfield Coll., Oxford, 1940; Fraternal Delegate of British Methodist Conference to General Conference of Methodist Episcopal Church, U.S.A., 1932; President Conference of the Methodist Church, 1944; Jt.-Chm. Methodist Ecumenical Conf.: Springfield, Mass., 1947, Oxford, 1951. Select Preacher Camb. Univ., 1946-47, 1952-53; Burkitt bronze medal, Br. Acad., 1947. *Publications:* editor and joint-author of the late Dr. J. H. Moulton's Grammar of New Testament Greek, Vol. II., 1 and 2 Corinthians in the Abingdon Commentary; critical essay on Acts in Study Bible; The Fourth Gospel in Recent Criticism and Interpretation; Christianity according to St. John; The Romance of New Testament Scholarship; Commentary on St. John's Gospel (Interpreter's Bible); numerous articles in theological journals. *Address:* 580 Newmarket Rd., Cambridge. [*Died* 10 *July* 1952.

HOWARD, Captain William Gilbert, C.B.E. 1919, R.N., retired; *b.* 12 March 1877; *s.* of late A. J. Howard; *m.* 1912, Hon. A. C. S. Parnell, *d.* of 4th Baron Congleton; three *s.* two *d.* *Educ.:* H.M.S. Britannia. Served at home and abroad; during the War served in the Dardanelles campaign, present at the landings on the Peninsula; commanded armed merchant cruisers in the 10th C.S. and on ocean escort duty; retired list 1923. *Recreation:* farming. *Address:* The Oast House, Stonegate, E. Sussex. [*Died* 18 *Jan.* 1960.

HOWARTH, Sir Edward, K.B.E., *cr.* 1939 (C.B.E. 1927); C.B. 1932; Managing Director National Camps Corporation since 1939; Director London Hostels Association; Member of Council Central After Care Association (under the provisions of the Criminal Justice Act, 1948); Chairman County Federation of Young Farmers' Clubs for West Sussex; *e. s.* of late J. E. Howarth, Prestwich; *m.* 1947, Ingrid Prytz, M.B.E., 7 Lampard House, Royal Hospital Road, Chelsea. *Educ.:* Shrewsbury School; Trinity College, Oxford, M.A.; Berlin University. Head of Trinity College, Oxford, Settlement, Stratford, E., 1904-7; entered Board of Education, 1908; Principal Private Secretary to successive Presidents of the Board (Lord Halifax, Sir Charles Trevelyan, and Lord Eustace Percy); Secretary to Lord Lytton's Committee on Indian Students, 1921; Secretary to Royal Commission on Cross-River Traffic in London, 1926; Director of Establishments, Board of Education, 1926-28; Accountant-General, 1928-37; Deputy Secretary, Board of Education, Whitehall, 1937-39; served European War, 1915-19; Lieutenant Oxfordshire Yeomanry (despatches). *Recreations:* hunting and gardening. *Address:* Crimbourne Farm, Kirdford, nr. Billingshurst, Sussex. *T.:* Wisborough Green 218. *Clubs;* Boodle's, United Hunts. [*Died* 26 *Aug.* 1953.

HOWARTH, Osbert John Radclyffe, O.B.E. 1920; *b.* London, 18 Nov. 1877; *o. s.* of late O. H. Howarth and Mary Macfarlane, Manchester; *m.* 1909, Eleanor Katherine, *e. d.* of late Stephen Paget, F.R.C.S.; two *s.* one *d.* *Educ.:* Westminster; Christ Church, Oxford (exhibitioner). Scholar in geography, University of Oxford, 1901, and diploma in the same; M.A. Oxon; Hon. Ph.D. Leeds; Geographical Assistant to Editor of the Encyclopædia Britannica, 1904-11; Asst. Sec. (later styled Secretary), British Assoc. for the Advancement of Science, 1909-46; Resident, Down House (Darwin Memorial) under the Association, 1929-53; Pres., Section E (Geography), British Assoc., 1951; President, Geographical Assoc., 1953; Intelligence Dept., Naval Staff, 1915-19. *Publications:* Geographical text books; editor of the Oxford Survey of the British Empire with the late Prof. A. J. Herbertson; The British Association: a Retrospect, 1831-1931; editor of London and the Advancement of Science (British Association Centenary Publication), 1931; The Scenic Heritage of England and Wales (for C.P.R.E.), 1937. *Recreations:* music, gardening, fishing. *Address:* West Hill House, Downe, Kent. *T.:* Farnborough (Kent) 6. *Club:* Athenæum. [*Died* 22 *June* 1954.

HOWAT, Very Rev. R. H.; *see* Henderson-Howat.

HOWE, Rt. Hon. Clarence Decatur, P.C. 1946; B.Sc.; *b.* Waltham, Mass., 15 January 1886; *s.* of William Clarence Howe and Mary Hastings; became Canadian citizen, 1913; *m.* 1916, Alice Martha Worcester; two *s.* three *d.* *Educ.:* Massachusetts Institute of Technology (B.Sc.). Draughtsman and Designer, J. R. Worcester & Co., Boston, Mass., 1905-8; Assistant Instructor, Massachusetts Institute of Technology, Boston, 1907-8; Professor of Civil Engineering, Dalhousie University, Halifax, N.S., 1908-13; Chief Engineer, Board of Grain Commissioners for Canada, Fort William, 1913-16; Consulting Engineer C. D. Howe & Co., Port Arthur, Ont.; Minister of Railways and Canals and Minister of Marine, Canada, 1935; Minister of Transport, 1936; Minister of Munitions and Supply, 1940; Minister of Reconstruction and Supply, 1946. Minister of Trade and Commerce and Minister of Defence Production, Canada, 1951-57 (Minister of Trade and Commerce, 1948-57). Member: Engineering Institute of Canada, American Society of Mechanical Engineers, American Society of Civil Engineers, Association of Professional Engineers of Province of Ontario. Hon. Member Instn. Civil Engineers, etc. Holds numerous Hon. degrees in Laws, Engineering and Sciences, in Canada and the U.S.A. Medal for Merit (U.S.A.), 1947. *Address:* 3468 Drummond Street, Montreal 25, Quebec, Canada. [*Died* 31 *Dec.* 1960.

HOWE, George William Osborn, D.Sc. (Durham); Hon. D.Sc. (Adelaide); Hon. LL.D. (Glasgow); Hon. F.I.R.E. (Amer.); Whitworth Scholar; *b.* Charlton, Kent, 4 Dec. 1875; *s.* of W. J. Osborn Howe of Charlton; *m.* 1901, Sarah Alice (*d.* 1930), *y. d.* of late James Kinnear Maunder of Newcastle upon Tyne. *Educ.:* Roan School, Greenwich; Armstrong College, Durham Univ. Apprentice with Siemens Bros., Woolwich; electrical engineer with Siemens-Schuckert, Berlin, 1900-2; lecturer at Hull Technical College, 1903-1905; lecturer 1905-9, and Assistant-Professor of Electrical Engineering at Imperial Coll., South Kensington, 1909-20; Head of Department of Electrical Standards and Measurements, National Physical Laboratory, 1920-21; James Watt Professor of Electrical Engineering, University of Glasgow, 1921-46. Faraday Medal, I.E.E., 1956. *Publications:* Text-Book of Electrical Engineering (transl.); Exercises in Electrical Engineering (with T. Mather); numerous papers before Royal Society, Institution of Electrical Engineers, Physical Society, British Association, etc.; editor of the Radio Review, 1920-22 and The Wireless Engineer since 1926. *Recreations:* music, foreign travel. *Address:* Lismore House, Kelvin Drive, Glasgow, N.W. *T.:* Maryhill 1128. *Club:* Savile. [*Died* 7 *Nov.* 1960.

HOWE, Sir Gerard Lewis, Kt., *cr.* 1949; Q.C. (Nigeria) 1947; Chief Justice of Hong Kong since 1950; *b.* 3 June 1899; *s.* of late Gerard A. Howe, Dublin, and Nina, *d.* of late Henry Beasley, Monkstown, Dublin; *m.* 1927, Margaret, *e. d.* of late Francis Maguire, J.P., Bullough Castle, Dalkey, Ireland; one *d.* *Educ.:* Armagh Royal School; Trinity College, Dublin. On military service, 1916-20 (despatches); Barrister-at-law, King's Inns, 1923; Resident Magistrate, Kenya, 1930; Crown Counsel, Gold Coast, 1934; Straits Settlements, 1937; Solicitor-General, Nigeria, 1941, Attorney-General, 1946-50. *Recreations:* sailing, golf, horses. *Address:* The Supreme Court, Hong Kong. *Club:* West Indian. [*Died* 25 *May* 1955.

HOWE, John Allen, O.B.E., B.Sc., F.G.S.; Past President Inst.M.M.; late Assistant Director Geological Survey; *b.* 1869; *s.* of William Elliot Howe, of Matlock Bath; *m.* Isabel Sarah (*d.* 1948), *d.* of Thomas Bickley of Barlaston, Staffs; one *s.* *Educ.:* privately; Royal College of Science, London. *Publications:* The Geology of Building Stones; Stones and Quarries; The Stones of London; Handbook to the Collection of Kaolin, China-Clay and China Stone in the

Museum of Practical Geology. *Address:* West Lodge, Box Hill Road, Tadworth, Surrey. *T.:* Betchworth 2161. [*Died* 11 *Dec.* 1952.

HOWELL, Conrad Meredyth Hinds, M.A., M.D. Oxon; F.R.C.P. London; Consulting Physician St. Bartholomew's Hospital; Consulting Physician, National Hospital for Paralysis and Epilepsy, Queen Square, W.C.; *b.* April 1877; *s.* of Conrad Goodriche Howell, Barrister-at-law; *m.* 1905, Mabel (*d.* 1958), 4th *d.* of Charles Gulland, J.P., Falkland, Fife; three *s.* *Educ.:* Marlborough; Trinity Coll., Oxford; St. Bartholomew's Hosp. Marlborough College Cricket XI., 1894-96; represented Oxford for Fencing, 1898-1900; 1st class Final Honour School Nat. Science, Oxford, 1900; M.B., B.S. Oxford, 1903; M.R.C.P. London, 1905; M.D. Oxon, 1908; F.R.C.P. London, 1910. *Publications:* various contributions to medical papers and societies. *Recreations:* golf, shooting, fishing. *Address:* 149 Harley Street, W.1. *T.:* Welbeck 4444. *Club:* M.C.C. [*Died* 9 *May* 1960.

HOWELL, David Arnold, C.I.E. 1944; O.B.E. 1939; M.Inst.C.E.; M.I.Mech.E.; Principal, Punjab College of Engineering and Technology, Lahore, Pakistan, since 1951; *b.* 28 June 1890; *s.* of late Capt. John Howell, Pantymeillion, nr. Llanelly, Carmarthenshire; *m.* 1915, Gwladys, *d.* of late John Howell Jones, Pontneathvaughan, Glam.; one *s.* one *d.* *Educ.:* County School, Llanelly. Civil and Mechanical Engineer; Engineer on construction City of Baku Water-supply Works, Caucasus, Russian Empire, 1912-14; Resident Engineer, Llanelly Rural Watersupply Van Lake Scheme, South Wales. 1914-18; Lieut. Royal Marines, 1918; Engineer, Llanelly Rural Water-supply and Drainage, South Wales, 1919-20; Specialist Cadre, P.W.D., India, since 1920; Superintending Engineer, Public Health Circle, Punjab, P.W.D., 1932-42; Chief Engineer, Civil Defence and Public Health Dept., Punjab, 1942-43; Chief Engineer, Public Health Branch, P.W.D., Punjab, 1944-46; Sec. to Govt. Punjab, P.W.D., B. & R. (Public Health) Branch, 1945-46; retired 1946. Employed in South Africa on construction of Waterworks schemes, 1947-51. *Publications:* various technical papers. *Address:* c/o Grindlay's Bank Ltd., Lahore, Pakistan. *Club:* Punjab (Lahore). [*Died* 11 *May* 1953.

HOWELL, William Gruffydd Rhys, C.M.G. 1952; O.B.E. 1947; H.M. Foreign Service; *b.* 16 Feb. 1904; *s.* of John Howell, C.B.E., M.D., F.R.C.S., and Margaret Ida Rees; *m.* 1931, Ruth Adelaide Brauer, Los Angeles, California. *Educ.:* Cheltenham College; Trinity College, Oxford; and self. Entered H.M. Consular Service, 1927; served at New York, Paris, Los Angeles, San Francisco, Lourenço Marques, Lisbon, Funchal and La Paz. Consul, New York, 1943-47; Counsellor (Commercial) Buenos Aires, 1947-1950; Counsellor (Commercial), Stockholm, 1950-53; Consul-General, Barcelona, 1953-1955. *Recreations:* travel, gastronomy. *Clubs:* St. James', Royal Automobile. [*Died* 3 *Sept.* 1956.

HOWELLS, George, B.A. (Lond.); M.A. (Camb.); B.Litt. (Oxon); Ph.D. (Tübingen); D.D. (St Andrews, Wales, and Serampore); Principal Emeritus of Serampore College, Bengal, also Master and President of College Council (retd.); *b.* Glandafal Farm, Cwm, Mon., 11 May 1871; *s.* of G. W. Howells; *m.* 1897, Beebee Mary Sophia, *d.* of J. L. Phillips, M.D.; one *s.* one *d.* *Educ.:* Pengam Grammar School; Regent's Park and University Colleges, London; Mansfield and Jesus Colleges, Oxford; Christ's College, Cambridge; University of Tübingen. Appointed by the Baptist Missionary Society for Educational work in India, 1895; located at Cuttack, Orissa, engaged in High School and theological teaching, and general literary and Biblical translation work, 1895-1906; Principal of Serampore College, Bengal, 1907-29; Angus Lecturer (Regent's Park College), 1909; Fellow of the University of Calcutta, 1913-29; Member Bengal Legislative Council, 1918; Dean of Faculty of Arts, 1926; Professor of Hebrew, Rawdon College, Leeds, 1932-35; Hon. Lecturer in Comparative Religion, University College, Cardiff (retd.). *Publications:* various articles and pamphlets on Theological Education in India, and on Hinduism in relation to Christianity; Translations into Oriya; The Soul of India, An Introduction to the Study of Hinduism; (Angus Lectures) The Story of Serampore and its College (with Prof. A. C. Underwood). *Recreation:* reading. *Address:* 93 Gloucester Place, W.1; Serampore, Castleton, near Cardiff. *T.:* Castleton, Mon., 405. [*Died* 7 *Nov.* 1955.

HOWITT, Sir Alfred Bakewell, Kt., *cr.* 1945; C.V.O. 1928; M.A., M.D. (Camb.); Physician; *b.* 11 Feb. 1879; *y. s.* of Francis Howitt, M.D., Nottingham and Heanor, Derbyshire; *m.* Hon. Dorothy (*d.* 1942), 2nd *d.* of first Baron Marchamley, P.C.; three *d.* *Educ.:* Epsom College; Clare College, Cambridge; St. Thomas's Hospital. Fellow of Royal Society of Medicine; served in France in European War, Capt. R.A.M.C.; late Senior Casualty Officer, St. Thomas's Hospital; Resident Medical Officer, St. Thomas's Home, and Resident Medical Officer, West London Hospital; M.P. (U.) Reading, 1931-1945. Contested (C.) Preston at General Election and By-Election, 1929; an Esquire of St. John of Jerusalem; President of Institution of Hospital Almoners. *Address:* 52 Warwick Square, S.W.1. *T.:* Victoria 3031. *Clubs:* Carlton, United University. [*Died* 8 *Dec.* 1954.

HOWITT, Frank Dutch, C.V.O. 1929; M.A., M.D., B.Ch. (Cantab.); F.R.C.P. (London); Physician with Charge of Physical Medicine, Middlesex Hospital; Senior Physician to Arthur Stanley Institute for Rheumatic Diseases; *b.* Nottingham, 24 Aug. 1894; *s.* of Arthur Gibson Howitt, Burland, Magdala Road, Nottingham; *m.* 1945, Violet Norris Leverton, Glapthorn, Peterborough. *Educ.:* Uppingham; Trinity College, Cambridge. Served European War in Gallipoli and France in R.A.S.C. and R.A.F.; War of 1939-45, Brig. R.A.M.C. and Adviser to Joint War Organisation (Red Cross and St. John); Hon. Consultant in Physical Medicine to the Army; Member of Army Health Advisory Cttee.; Hon. Adviser in Rehabilitation to Minister of Labour; Director Disabled Persons Employment Corp. (Remploy Ltd.); Member of Nuffield Foundation Cttees. on Industrial Medicine and Rheumatism; Exec. Cttee. Empire Rheumatism Council; Council Roy. Institute of Public Health; Chm. Research Board for Correlation of Med. Science and Physical Education. *Publications:* contributions to Medical societies and journals. *Recreations:* shooting and fishing. *Address:* 87 Harley Street, W.1. *T.:* Welbeck 9020; Valley Farm, Duntisbourne Hill, Cirencester, Gloucestershire. *Clubs:* Bath, Garrick. [*Died* 15 *May* 1954.

HOWLES, Leonard, C.B.E. 1951; M.I.E.E., M.I.Struct.E.; Chairman South Wales Electricity Board since 1948; Member of Central Electricity Authority; *b.* 22 April 1896; *m.* 1920, Catherine Margaret Helen Smith; one *s.* one *d.* *Educ.:* Smethwick Technical College. Shropshire, Worcestershire and Staffordshire Electric Power Co., 1919-35 (General Manager of same from 1933); South Wales Electric Power Co., General Manager, 1935-48. Member, British Electricity Authority, 1950-51, and 1955-. O.St.J. *Address:* Garryricken, Llandennis Avenue, Cyncoed, Cardiff, Glam. *T.:* Cardiff 52391. *Clubs:* Devonshire; Cardiff and County (Cardiff). [*Died* 13 *May* 1957.

HOWLEY, Richard Joseph, C.B.E. 1919; Member Inst.C.E., Member Inst.T.; Director Birmingham and District Investment Trust

Ltd.; The Electrical and Industrial Investment Co. Ltd.; *s.* of Lt.-Col. John Howley, D.L., of Rich Hill, Co. Limerick; unmarried. *Educ.:* Oscott Coll.; Royal University, Dublin; B.E. (*h.c.*) 1942. Educated as a Civil Engineer, and was engaged for some years on railway and dock construction; joined the British Electric Traction Company, 1899; Joint Manager. 1912-1919; Director, 1923; Chairman, 1942-46; specialises in the establishment and operation of passenger transport systems providing railway, tramway, and omnibus services; member of the Tramways (Board of Trade) Committee and the Railways Priority Committee, 1917-19. *Address:* 49 Hallam St., W.1; Stratton House, Piccadilly, W.1. *Club:* Union.
[*Died* 2 *April* 1955.

HOWSON, Capt. John Montagu, C.B.E. 1944; *b.* 1 June 1893; *s.* of Edmund Whytehead Howson and Agnes Isobel, *d.* of Dr. H. M. Butler; *m.* 1922, Betty Frances Clare Luard; one *s.* two *d.* *Educ.:* Stonehouse, Broadstairs; St. Aubyns, Rottingdean; Royal Naval Colleges, Osborne and Dartmouth. Grand Fleet, 1914; Harwich Striking Force, 1914-17; Flag Lieut. to Admiral Sir Doveton Sturdee, 1918-20; Commander, 1928; Captain, 1936; attended Imperial Defence College, 1938; commanded Effingham, 1939-40; Staff of C.-in-C. Western Approaches, 1940-42; served in Madagascar, N. Africa and Italian Campaigns, 1942-43, as Chief of Staff to Admiral Commanding Force "H" (despatches thrice, C.B.E.); S.N.O. Persian Gulf, 1944, and Senior Officer, East Indies Fleet at Delhi (Commodore 2nd Class), 1944-45; retired from Royal Navy, 1946. *Recreations:* fishing, shooting. *Address:* Haye, Lyme Regis, Dorset. *T.:* Lyme Regis 101. [*Died* 19 *March* 1959.

HOYLAND, Harold Allan Dilke, C.B.E. 1945 (M.B.E. 1919); British Consul, Rhodes (Dodecanese), 1947-52; *b.* 26 July 1885; *s.* of late C. W. Hoyland; *m.* 1918, Winifred Helen, *d.* of late F. B. Wood, O.B.E., I.S.O., H.M. Consul at Patras. *Educ.:* Charterhouse School. Clerk Brit. Consulate-General, Constantinople, 1902-14; Inns of Court O.T.C., 1914; 2nd Lt. General List, 1915; Lieut. 1917; Capt. 1918; Major, 1919 (despatches twice, Greek Order of the Redeemer, Serbian Order of the White Eagle); Vice-Consul Thasos, 1915, transferred to Drama, 1916; Vice-Consul at Patras, 1919; Consul Patras, 1926; Consul at Kermanshah, 1931, at Shiraz, 1934, at Tangier, 1936; Consul-General at Patras, 1940; at Ismailia, Egypt, 1942; at Athens, 1944. Retired on pension, 1946. *Recreations:* shooting, golf. *Address:* Old Forge Cottage, Bierton, nr. Aylesbury, Bucks.
[*Died* 12 *Dec.* 1959.

HOYLAND, John S., M.A.; F.R.Hist. Soc.; Lecturer Emeritus, Woodbrooke College, Birmingham; *b.* Birmingham, 1887; *s.* of John W. Hoyland and Rachel Somervell, Kendal; *m.*; two *s.* one *d.* *Educ.:* King Edward's School, Birmingham; Christ's College, Cambridge; Hartford Seminary School of Missions, U.S.A. Principal, Friends' Mission High School, Hoshangabad, C.P., 1912-19; Lecturer in History and English, Hislop College, Nagpur, C.P., 1919-28; Kaisar-i-Hind Gold Medal for public service in India. *Publications:* Faith and History; History of Modern Europe; A Brief History of Civilisation; Builders of Europe; The Race Problem and the Teaching of Christ; The Fourfold Sacrament; The Sacrament of Common Life; A Book of Prayers for an Indian College; The Light of Christ; The Warfare of Reconciliation; The Empire of the Great Mogol; The Great Forerunner; The Case for India; History as Direction; Simon the Zealot; The Cross Moves East; The Commentary of Monserrate; Prayers for a One-Year-Old; Prayers for a Two-Year-Old; God in the Commonplace; The Divine Companionship; An Indian Peasant Mystic; The New Russia; The Man of Fire and Steel (ed.); Christ and National Reconstruction; Indian Dawn; Digging with the Unemployed; Gopal Krishna Gokhale (biography); Village Songs of Western India; Songs from Prison (ed.); The Way of St. Francis; Christ and Human Progress; John Doncaster Hoyland (ed.); The Sacrament of Nature; Digging for a New England; Experiments in Social Reconstruction (ed.); That Inferiority Feeling: Prayer and the Social Revolution; How Christ met Aggression; Arnold's The Early Christians (trans); C. F. Andrews, Minister of Reconciliation; The World in Union; The Indian Crisis, the Background; The Christ of the Future; Gandhi, in Defence; Federate or Perish; We Who are India; These saw Jesus; The Man India Loved; Denys; The Clump of Bushes; Dead?; Once More, Federate or Perish; Christ and the Saving of Civilization; Gandhi and World Government; They saw Gandhi; (ed.) The Quiet Room; World Government and the Kingdom of God, They met by night, etc. *Address:* Kentmere, Rednal, Birmingham.
[*Died* 31 *Oct.* 1957.

HUBAN, Maj.-Gen. John Patrick, C.S.I. 1946; O.B.E. 1920; K.H.S. since 1944; Principal Medical Officer, Cable & Wireless, Ltd., Electra House, W.C.2; *b.* 13 Feb. 1891; *s.* of Malachy and Elizabeth Huban; *m.* 1916, Aimee, *d.* of Frank Willett; (one *s.* killed in action, 1943). *Educ.:* University College, Dublin and London. Joined R.A.M.C., 1914; I.M.S., 1919. Served European War, 1914-18, Afghanistan, Waziristan, 1919-21 (despatches thrice); Civil Surgeon, New Delhi, 1923-29, Peshawar, 1929-31; D.M.S., Jaipur State, 1931-38; Admin. Med. Officer, Rajputana, 1939-40; Additional Deputy Director-General, I.M.S., 1940-41; Inspector-General, Civil Hospitals, N.W.F.P., 1941-44; Surgeon-General with Government of Madras. Hon. Surgeon to Viceroy of India, 1944. O.St.J., 1944. *Recreations:* music and travel. *Address:* c/o Grindlay's Bank, Ltd., 54 Parliament St., S.W.1. *Clubs:* Naval and Military; Madras (Madras); Adyar. [*Died* 4 *Sept.* 1957.

HUBBACK, Most Rev. George Clay, B.Sc. D.D.; *b.* 7 April 1882; *s.* of Joseph Hubback, J.P., Liverpool; unmarried. *Educ.:* Rossall; Univ. College, Liverpool. Civil Engineer on the Admiralty Harbour, Dover, 1902-5; in Port Trust, Calcutta, 1906-8; Oxford Mission to Calcutta, 1908-24, with two years as Curate of St. Anne's, S. Lambeth, 1910-12, and War Hospital Chaplain, Bombay, 1916-17; Bishop of Assam, 1924-45; Metropolitan of India and Bishop of Calcutta, 1945-50; Deacon, 1910; Priest, 1911. *Address:* 77 Epsom Road, Guildford. [*Died* 2 *Nov.* 1955.

HUBBARD, (Eric) Hesketh, P.P.R.B.A., R.O.I., R.B.C.; F.S.A.; landscape and architectural painter and etcher, writer and lecturer on art; founder of the Print Society and New Group; Hon. Treasurer of the Artists' General Benevolent Institution; Trustee Imperial War Museum; Past Master of the Art Workers' Guild; with Frank Whittington, founded the Forest Press, 1922; Cantor Lecturer, 1933; Silver Medal of Royal Society of Arts for lecture on Hogarth, 1932; de Laszlo Silver Medal, 1939; University Extension Lecturer in Art, London, Cambridge and Oxford Universities; *b.* 16 Nov. 1892; *s.* of Henry Pratt Hubbard. Represented in British Museum; Victoria and Albert Museum; Fitzwilliam Museum, Cambridge; Nat. Museum of Wales, Cardiff; Ashmolean Museum, Oxford; City Art Galleries and many galleries at home and abroad. *Publications:* Book-plates of Frank Brangwyn; On Making and Collecting Etchings; 66 Etchings; How to Distinguish Prints The Gateways of Salisbury Cathedral Close; Colour Block Print Making; Simple Colour Block Print Making; Craft of Etching; An Outline History of the Royal Society of British Artists;

Architectural Painting in Oils; Materia Pictoria—Oil Painting; Forgotten Methods of Painting; Some Victorian Draughtsmen; Notes on Colour Mixing; 100 Years of British Painting, 1851-1951; First Principles of Oil Painting; many magazine articles on art subjects. *Recreation:* collecting drawings and books. *Address:* E.4 Albany, Piccadilly, W.1. *T.:* Regent 4939. *Clubs:* Athenæum, Art Workers' Guild. [*Died* 16 *April* 1957.

HUBBARD, Rt. Rev. Harold Evelyn, D.S.O. 1918; M.C.; Canon of York Minster since 1948; *b.* 12 Feb. 1883; *e. s.* of late Hon. Evelyn Hubbard; unmarried. *Educ.:* Eton; Christ Church, Oxford. Deacon, 1907; Priest, 1908; Curate of S. Hilda's, S. Shields, 1907-10; S. Mary of Eton, Hackney Wick, 1910-11; Skelton-in-Cleveland, Yorks, 1911-14; Chaplain to Forces, 1914-19; served in France, 1914-15; 1916-18 (with Guards Division) (D.S.O. and M.C.); Rector of Gisborough-in-Cleveland, Yorks, 1919-22; Chaplain of Cheltenham Coll., 1922-30; Vicar of St. John's, Middlesbrough, 1931-38; Rural Dean of Middlesbrough, 1936-38; Suffragan Bishop of Whitby, 1939-46; a Chaplain to the King, 1937-39. *Recreation:* fishing. *Address:* 2 Minster Court, York. *T.:* York 54485. [*Died* 23 *May* 1953.

HUBBARD, Hesketh; *see* Hubbard, E. H.

HUBBLE, Edwin (Powell), Ph.D. (Chicago); Hon. D.Sc. (Oxford, Princeton and Brussels); Hon. LL.D. (Occidental College and Univ. of California); Astronomer, Mount Wilson Observatory since 1919; Trustee, Huntington Library and Art Gallery; *b.* 20 Nov. 1889; *s.* of John Powell Hubble and Virginia Lee James; *m.* 1924, Grace Burke; no *c.* *Educ.:* University of Chicago (B.S., Ph.D.); Queen's College, Oxford (Rhodes Scholar, B.A.). Student Officer, U.S. Army, 1917; Capt. of Infantry, 1917; Major, C.O. 2nd Bn. 343rd Infantry, 1918, A.E.F.; Chief Ballistician, Ballistic Research Laboratory, Ord. Dept., U.S. Army, 1942-45; Researches in field of Nebulae; National Academy of Sciences, R.A.S.; A.A.A.; A.S.P. (President 1933), etc.; A.A.A.S. Prize 1925; Halley Lecturer, 1934; Silliman Lecturer, Yale, 1935; Rhodes Memorial Lecturer, Oxford, 1936; Hitchcock Lecturer, Univ. of California, 1947; Hon. LL.D.: Occidental Coll., 1936; California, 1949; Hon. D.Sc.: Oxford, 1934; Princeton, 1936; Brussels, 1937; Barnard Medal for meritorious service to science, 1935; Bruce Medal, 1938; Franklin Medal, 1939; Gold Medal of R. Astronomical Society, 1940; Medal for Merit, 1946. Honorary Fellow; Vienna Acad. of Science, 1947; Queen's Coll., Oxford, 1949; Corresp. Member, Paris Acad. of Science, 1949. *Publications:* The Realm of the Nebulae, 1936; Observational Approach to Cosmology, 1937; contributions to the Astronomical Journals of England and U.S.A. *Recreations:* fishing, camping, etc. *Address:* San Marino, California, U.S.A.; Mt. Wilson Observatory, Pasadena, California, U.S.A. *Clubs:* Athenæum; Sunset (California). [*Died* 28 *Sept.* 1953.

HUDDLESTON, Captain Sir Ernest Whiteside, Kt., *cr.* 1939; C.I.E. 1916; C.B.E. 1919; J.P.; Royal Indian Navy(retd.); *b.* Murree, 18 Aug. 1874; 6th *s.* of late Major Graham Egerton Huddleston, 70th East Surrey Regiment; *m.* 1st, 1904, Elsie (*d.* 1931), 4th *surv. d.* of late John Barlow-Smith, Buenos Aires; one *s.* one *d.*; 2nd, 1932, Lorna K., *yr. d.* of late W. W. Box, Hampstead. *Educ.:* Bedford School. Entered Royal Indian Marine, 1895; served Egyptian Campaign, 1895-96 (Queen's medal and Khedive's medal); wrecked in Warren Hastings' troopship off Reunion, 1897; received Royal Humane Society's silver medal and Lloyd's silver medal for saving life on this occasion; Lieut. 1900; served China Expedition (Boxer Rising), 1901-2, as Assist. Marine Transport Officer; Marine Transport Officer, Somaliland Expedition, and was in charge of landing operations in Obbiat, 1902-4 (despatches thrice, medal and clasp, thanks of the Government of India); Delhi Durbar medal, 1912; Staff Officer Bombay Dockyard, 1911; promoted Acting Commander, 1912; Commander, 1913; Senior Marine Transport Officer, Bombay, 1914-18 (promoted Captain, 1918; C.B.E.).; Principal Marine Transport Officer, Bombay and Karachi, 1918; Presidency Port Officer of Madras, 1920-1924; Deputy Director of Royal Indian Marine, 1924-25 and officiating Director, Royal Indian Marine; retired, 1925; transferred to retired list of the Royal Indian Navy, 1934; Shipping Surveyor and Adviser to the H.C. for India, 1925-38. *Recreation:* fishing. *Address:* Little Church Park, Whitchurch, Tavistock, Devon. [*Died* 10 *Oct.* 1959.

HUDDLESTON, Sisley; author, lecturer and journalist; some years Paris correspondent of The Times, later European Editorial Correspondent of Christian Science Monitor; now retired from newspaper activities; naturalized in France under Vichy government; *b.* Barrow-in-Furness, 28 May 1883; *m.* Jeanne Poirier. *Educ.:* Manchester; Paris. Writer in The Weekly Review; contributed extensively to Atlantic Monthly, New York Times, Fortnightly Review, Contemporary Review, New Statesman; Pres. de l'Association de la Presse Anglo-Americaine, 1923. *Publications:* Peace-making in Paris, 1919; Poincaré: A Biographical Portrait, 1924; Those Europeans: Studies of Foreign Faces, 1924; La Politique Anglaise et La France, 1925; France and the French, 1925; Mr. Paname: A Paris Fantasia, 1926; France, in the Modern World Series, A Survey of Historical Forces, 1926; In and About Paris, 1927; Little Guide to Paris, 1928; Normandy, in the Kit-bag Series, 1928; Articles de Paris: A Book of Essays, 1928; Bohemian Literary and Social Life in Paris (American Title: Paris Salons, Cafés, Studios), 1928; Louis XIV: in Love and in War, 1929; History of France, 1929; Europe in Zigzags, 1929; What's Right with America, 1930; Between the River and the Hills: A Normandy Pastoral, 1930; Back to Montparnasse, 1931; The Captain's Table: A Transatlantic Log, 1932; War Unless . . ., 1933; chapter on English in De Quoi se compose Paris; Section on Present-Day France, in France: A Companion to French Studies, 1937; In My Time: An Observer's Record of War and Peace, 1938; Cities and Men (biography of Inman Barnard), 1939; chapters on France in Annual Register; Chapter on Paris in Entente Cordiale, 1940; Peace through Federation; A Study in European Reconstruction, 1940; Le Livre de St. Pierre, 1941; Lettres à un Ami Français, 1943; Le Mythe de la Liberté, 1943; Terreur, 1944, 1947; Avec le Maréchal, 1948; Elizabeth d'Angleterre, 1948; Mediterranean Blue, 1948; Pétain: Patriot or Traitor?—The Truth about France, 1939 to 1951, 1951; posthumous: Popular Diplomacy and War; France, The Tragic Years 1939-47, 1955 (New York). *Recreations:* No recreations, finding sufficient amusement and occupation in work. *Address:* Villa Graziella, Troinex, Geneva, Switzerland; Mon Moulin, St. Pierre d'Autils, Eure, France. *T.:* 4 St. Pierre d'Autils. [*Died* 14 *July* 1952.

HUDDLESTON, Captain Willoughby Baynes, C.M.G. 1916; R.I.N. (retired); *b.* 1866; 3rd *s.* of late Major Graham Egerton Huddleston; *m.* Mary Lawrence, *d.* of late Sir John Strachey, G.C.S.I., C.I.E.; one *d.* *Educ.:* Bedford Modern School; H.M.S. Conway. Entered Royal Indian Marine, 1887; Commander, 1904; Marine Survey of India, 1888-1893; awarded Royal Humane Society's Silver Medal; Stanhope Gold Medal, 1891; was present at Rapsch River Mekran Expedition; served with Somaliland Expedition (medal); commanded R.I.M.S. Dufferin, on occasion of King George's Coronation (Coronation Medal);

Presidency Port Officer, Madras; Hon. A.D.C. to Lord Pentland, Governor of Madras; served as Principal Marine Transport Officer, Mesopotamia, Dec. 1915, to fall of Kut-al-amara (despatches thrice, C.M.G.); on Staff of Principal Naval Transport Officer, France (despatches); Commander R.N., Jan. 1917. *Recreation:* fishing. *Address:* River View, Headington Hill, Oxford. *T.:* Oxford 6797. *Club:* Flyfishers'.

[*Died* 1 *May* 1953.

HUDLESTON, Colonel Wilfrid Edward, C.M.G. 1918; C.B.E. 1919; D.S.O. 1917; late R.A.M.C.; M.R.C.S., L.R.C.P. Lond.; *b.* 22 Aug. 1872; *s.* of late Lt.-Col. Wilfred Hudleston, Madras Staff Corps; *m.* 1908, Alice Maud Mary, *d.* of late William Ferguson, W.S., Edinburgh; one *s.* two *d.* *Educ.:* Middlesex Hospital. Late House Surgeon, Middlesex Hospital, and House Surgeon, Royal Berkshire Hospital; served Nile, 1898 (two medals); European War, 1914-18 (despatches 6 times, C.M.G., C.B.E., D.S.O.); retired pay, 1921. *Address:* 57 Inverleith Row, Edinburgh. *T.:* 83823.

[*Died* 24 *Oct.* 1952.

HUDSON, 1st Viscount, *cr.* 1952, of Pewsey; **Robert Spear Hudson,** P.C. 1938; C.H. 1944; *b.* 1886; *e. s.* of late R. W. Hudson; *m.* 1918, Hannah, *d.* of P. S. P. Randolph, Philadelphia, U.S.A.; one *s.* *Educ.:* Eton; Magdalen College, Oxford. Attaché in Diplomatic Service, 1911; First Secretary, 1920-1923; M.P. (U.) Whitehaven Div. of Cumberland, 1924-29; M.P. (U.) Southport, 1931-52; Parliamentary Secretary, Ministry of Labour, 1931-35; Minister of Pensions, 1935-36; Parliamentary Secretary to Min. of Health and representative of H.M. Office of Works in House of Commons, 1936-37; Secretary Department of Overseas Trade, 1937-40; Minister of Shipping, Apr.-May, 1940; Minister of Agriculture and Fisheries, 1940-45. Farmer; a Vice-Pres., Royal Agricultural Society of England; Pres. British Percheron Society, 1946-47; Pres. Brit. Friesian Soc., 1954-55. Director, Willoughbys Consolidated Co. Ltd.; Chm. Board of Governors, Imperial Institute. *Recreation:* yachting. *Heir:* *s.* Hon. Robert William Hudson, *b.* 28 April 1924. *Address:* 26 St. Leonard's Terrace, S.W.3; Fyfield Manor, Pewsey, Wilts. *T.:* Pewsey 3138. *Clubs:* Athenæum, Carlton.

[*Died* 2 *Feb.* 1957.

HUDSON, Sir Austin Uvedale Morgan, 1st Bt., *cr.* 1942; M.P. (C.) North Lewisham since 1950; *b.* 6 Feb. 1897; *s.* of late Leopold Hudson, F.R.C.S., and late Ethel Vaughan (who *m.* 2nd, Brig.-Gen. Edward Hall Stevenson, C.M.G.), *d.* of late Septimus Vaughan Morgan; *m.* 1930, Peggy, *o. c.* of late Harold Broadbent and Hilda, Viscountess Dillon. *Educ.:* Eton; R.M.C., Sandhurst. Served in Army, first in Royal Berkshire Regiment, then in Guards Machine Gun Regt., 1915-20; M.P. (U.) E. Islington, 1922-23; Hackney, N., 1924-45; Chairman, Morgan Bros. (Publishers) Ltd. Commanded 1st London Bn. Home Guard, 1943-45; Asst. Conservative Whip, 1931; Lord Commissioner of the Treasury, 1931-35; Parliamentary Secretary, Ministry of Transport, 1935-39; Civil Lord of the Admiralty, 1939-42; Parliamentary Secretary to Ministry of Fuel and Power, 1945; Chairman Metropolitan Area, National Union of Conservative and Unionist Associations, 1932-34. *Recreations:* golf, shooting. *Address:* 141 Marsham Court, Marsham Street, S.W.1; 28 Essex St., Strand, W.C.2. *T.:* Victoria 8181, Central 6565. *Clubs:* United Service, Carlton, Buck's.

[*Died* 29 *Nov.* 1956 (*ext.*).

HUDSON, Bernard, M.A., M.D. Camb.; M.R.C.P. Lond.; Holder of the Swiss Federal Diploma in Medicine; late Dep. Medical Supt. National Sanatorium, Benenden, Kent; *s.* of late Henry Arthur Hudson of York, and Edith Hey; *b.* 1877; *m.* 1st, 1910, Enid, *y. d.* of Col. Maxwell; 2nd, 1936, Laura Almon, *yr. d.* of Mr. Adlington, Bath. *Educ.:* Clare College, Cambridge; St. Bartholomew's Hospital; late Casualty Physician, St. Bartholomew's Hospital; Pathologist and Registrar, East London Hospital for Sick Children, Shadwell; Assistant Physician, Hospital for Diseases of the Chest, City Road, London; Visiting Physician to Queen Alexandra Sanatorium, Davos-Platz; formerly H.B.M. Consul at Davos; reappointed British Vice-Consul at Davos, 1937; resigned 1939. *Publications:* Mountain Climates in Health and Disease; Alpine Climate, its Physiology and Therapeutics; Artificial Pneumothorax in Tuberculosis of Lungs; Vaccine Therapy for Secondary Infections in Tuberculosis of the Lungs; Aids to Medicine; The Modern Surgical Treatment of Pulmonary Tuberculosis; and other medical publications. *Recreations:* golf, skating, ski-ing, motoring. *Address:* c/o Midland Bank, 19 High Street, Marylebone, W.1.

[*Died* 21 *March* 1957.

HUDSON, Brig. Charles Edward, V.C. 1918; C.B. 1940; D.S.O. 1917 and Bar; M.C.; D.L.; J.P.; p.s.c.; King's Own Scottish Borderers; *b.* 29 May 1892; *s.* of late Lt.-Col. H. E. Hudson; *m.* 1920, Gladys Elizabeth, *d.* of late Matthew Lee and Mrs. Lee, Allendale, Northumberland; one *s.* *Educ.:* Sherborne School; R.M.C., Sandhurst. Commnd Sherwood Foresters; served European War, 1914-18, N. Russia, 1919 (despatches, V.C., D.S.O. and bar, M.C., Croix de Guerre, Italian silver medal for valour); transf. K.O.S.B. 1928; Chief Instructor Royal Military College, 1933-37; commanded 2nd Bn. K.O.S.B., 1938; Comdr., 2nd Infantry Brigade, 1938; a Comdr. until retirement, Feb. 1946; A.D.C. to the King, 1944-46; County Commissioner, St. John Ambulance Brigade, 1949-54. J.P. 1949; D.L. Devon, 1956. K.St.J. *Address:* Denbury Manor, Newton Abbot, Devon. *T.:* Ipplepen 269.

[*Died* 4 *April* 1959.

HUDSON, Major-Gen. Corrie, C.B. 1927; C.I.E. 1920; D.S.O. 1904; F.R.C.S. Ed.; M.R.C.S. Eng.; L.R.C.P. Lond.; I.M.S., retired; *b.* 5 April 1874; *s.* of late Charles Thomas Hudson, M.A., LL.D., F.R.S.; *m.* 1904, Frances Edith (*d.* 1945), *d.* of late Alfred Barratt, Senior Examiner Education Board, Whitehall; one *d.* House Surgeon and House Physician at Charing Cross Hospital, London, 1897-98; entered I.M.S. 1899; Medical Officer 2nd Queen's Own Rajput L.I. 1899-1907; Staff-Surgeon, Bangalore, 1908-12; Capt., 1902; Major, 1910; Lt.-Col., 1918; Brevet Colonel and Colonel, 1925; Major-Gen. 1928; served China, 1900 (medal); East Africa, 1903-4, present at action of Jidballi (despatches, D.S.O., medal and clasp); Balkan War, 1912-13: France Nov. 1914 to June 1916 as D.A.D.M.S. 1st Indian Cavalry Division (despatches); A.D.M.S. L. of C. Waziristan Field Force, 1919-20 (despatches, medal, clasp, C.I.E.); A.D.M.S. Wana Column, 1920-21 (depatches, clasp); A.D.M.S. Razmak Field Force, 1922-23 (despatches, clasp); Director of Medical Organisation for War, A.H.Q., 1924-25; D.D.M.S., Eastern Command, 1928-32; Hon. Surgeon to the King, 1928-32; retired 1932. *Address:* Garth, Knowle Drive, Sidmouth. *T.:* Sidmouth 1154.

[*Died* 11 *July* 1958.

HUDSON, Rev. Canon Cyril Edward; Canon of St. Albans; Examining Chaplain to the Bishop; Proctor in Convocation; *b.* 27 May 1888; *s.* of Richard Plantagenet Hudson and Violet Ellen Dawber; *m.* Mary Ernestine, *e. d.* of W. J. Yapp. *Educ.:* St. Bees; Queen's College, Oxford. Assistant Curate of Berkhamsted, 1911-14; East Ham, 1914-17; St. Mary Abbots, Kensington, 1917-23; Director of Religious Education in the Diocese of St. Albans, 1923-27; Hon. Chaplain to the Archbishop of Canterbury, 1943-44; Select Preacher, Oxford, 1944-45, 1957-1958. *Publications:* (with Canon Lindsay Dewar) Manual of Pastoral Psychology, 1932; Preface to a Christian Sociology, 1935; Nations as Neighbours, 1943; (with others) Introduction to Pastoral Theology, 1937; (with M. B. Reckitt) The Church and The World, Vol. I., 1938, Vols. II and III, 1940; (with Canon L. Dewar) Christian Morals, 1946; contributor to Prospect for Christendom (Ed. M. B. Reckitt), 1945; editor, Outlines of Teaching Sermons (3 vols.), 1931, 1932, 1934. *Address:* 33 Lemsford Road, St. Albans, Herts. *T.:* St. Albans 53707. *Club:* United University. [*Died* 27 *Jan.* 1960.

HUDSON, Sir Frank; *see* Hudson, Sir W. F.

HUDSON, Harry Kynoch, C.B.E. 1918; *b.* 14 May 1867; *s.* of late Robert Hudson, Lapworth, Warwickshire, and Jessie (*d.* 1921), *d.* of late John Kynoch, Peterhead; *m.* Emily (*d.* 1942), *d.* of late Henry Hammerton, Coventry. *Educ.:* Ludlow Grammar School. Private Secretary to late Rt. Hon. Sir Charles W. Dilke, 1887-1911; Commissioner of the British Red Cross in Salonika, Russia, and Rumania during European War. Serbian Order of St. Sava. *Recreation:* reading. *Address:* 19 Glenferness Avenue, Bournemouth. [*Died* 6 *May* 1958.

HUDSON, Manley Ottmer; Bemis Professor of International Law, Harvard Law School, Cambridge, Mass.; *b.* St. Peters, Mo., 19 May 1886; *s.* of David O. and Emma Bibb Hudson; *m.* 1930, Janet Norton Aldrich; two *s.* *Educ.:* William Jewell College, Liberty, Missouri; Harvard University, Cambridge, Mass. Commissioner on Uniform State Laws, 1916-19; Special Assistant, Dept. of State, 1918-19; attached to International Law Division, American Commission to negotiate peace, Paris, 1918-19; Member Legal Section of Secretariat of League of Nations, 1919-21, and during summers of 1922-32; Legal Adviser to International Labour Conference, Washington, 1919, Genoa, 1920, Geneva, 1924; to International Conference on Russian Refugees, Geneva, 1922; Lecturer in Academy of International Law, The Hague, 1925; Reader in University of Calcutta, 1927; U.S. Technical Adviser, Conf. on Codification of Internat. Law, The Hague, 1930; Judge Permanent Court of Internat. Justice at The Hague, 1936-46; Member Permanent Court of Arbitration, 1933-45; Rep. of Permanent Court at San Francisco Conf., 1945; Mem. Internat. Law Commn., U.N., 1948-53 (Chm. 1949); Consultant in Internat. Law, Naval War Coll., 1946-; Editor American Journal of International Law, 1924-; Mem. Amer. Bar Assoc., Amer. Foreign Law Assoc., Amer. Soc. of Internat. Law (Pres. 1949-52), Internat. Law Assoc., Amer. Acad. of Arts and Sciences, Institut de Droit International. *Publications:* Current International Cooperation, 1927; Progress in International Organization, 1932; International Legislation, 9 vols., 1931-50; Permanent Court of International Justice, 1934, 1943; World Court Reports, 4 vols., 1932-1942; By Pacific Means, 1935; Cases on International Law, 3rd ed., 1951; International Tribunals, 1944. *Address:* Harvard Law School, Cambridge, 38, Mass., U.S.A. *Clubs:* Faculty (Cambridge); Harvard (New York); Cosmos (Washington). [*Died* 13 *April* 1960.

HUDSON, Colonel Percy, C.M.G. 1919; D.S.O. 1916; late commanding 1st Bn. East Lancashire Regt., late The King's Regt., Liverpool; *b.* 10 June 1876; *m.* 1923, Dorothy Lilian (*d.* 1950), *e. d.* of Frederick Deighton, M.A., M.B.; one *s.* Served S. African War, 1900-2 (Queen's medal three clasps, King's medal two clasps); European War, 1914-18 (despatches six times, C.M.G., D.S.O., Bt. Maj., Bt. Lt.-Col., Croix de Guerre, Order of Leopold of Belgium); retired pay, 1927. *Address:* Greenhill, Brading, I. of Wight. [*Died* 28 *Feb.* 1955.

HUDSON, Brig. Stanley Grey, C.B.E. 1945; *b.* 21 March 1902; *s.* of Dr. Frank Horace Hudson and Constance Mary Bolton; *m.* 1939, Constance Mary Bouchier; one *s.* two *d.* *Educ.:* Epsom College, R.M.A. Woolwich. Commissioned R.E. 1921, served with R.E. in 1st and 8th Armies, 1939-45; retired 1954. *Address:* Edgehill, Kingsway, Gerrards Cross Bucks. *T.:* 3130. [*Died* 27 *May* 1960.

HUDSON, Sir (Walter) Frank, K.C.I.E. *cr.* 1933 (C.I.E. 1922), *b.* 22 Aug. 1875; *e. s.* of late W. J. Hudson of Dulwich and Paignton; *m.* 1901, Alice Violet, *d.* of late Rev. C. T. Ward, Vicar of Chudleigh; one *s.* *Educ.:* Dulwich College; Brasenose College, Oxford (Scholar); 1st Class Classical Mods., 1896; 2nd Class Lit. Hum., 1898. M.A. 1936. Entered I.C.S., 1899; Assistant-Commissioner in Sind, 1904; Manager, Sind Encumbered Estates, 1907; Dep. Commissioner U.S.F. and Thar Parker; Collector of Hyderabad, Karachi, Larkana, Surat and Poona, 1909-1922; Acting Commissioner, 1921; Member of Legislative Assembly (Government Whip), 1924-26; Commissioner in Sind, 1926-29; Member of Executive Council of Governor of Bombay, 1929-33. *Recreations:* lawn tennis (Oxford Univ. VI. 1896-98), walking. *Address:* Dunromin, 52 Carew Road, Eastbourne. *T.:* Eastbourne 2052. *Club:* East India and Sports. [*Died* 5 *Sept.* 1958.

HUGGARD, Sir Walter Clarence, Kt., *cr.* 1933; Q.C. 1921; *e. s.* of late John Turner Huggard, Milltown, Co. Kerry; *m.* 1915, Kathleen Norah, *d.* of Dr. W. M. A. Wright, Dalkey, Co. Dublin; no *c.* *Educ.:* Methodist College, Belfast; Dublin University. First Honourman and Senior Moderator in Legal and Political Science; LL.D. 1907; called to Bar, King's Inns, Dublin, 1907; Magistrate, Nigeria, 1914; Solicitor-General, Trinidad and Tobago, 1920; Attorney-General, Trinidad and Tobago, 1922-26; Kenya Colony, 1926-1929; Straits Settlements, 1929-33; Chief Justice of S.S., 1933-36; retired 1936. Apptd. Judge of the High Courts of Basutoland, the Bechuanaland Protectorate and Swaziland, and Legal Adviser to the High Commissioner for Basutoland, the Bechuanaland Protectorate and Swaziland, 1937; Actg. High Comr. 1938, 1940, 1942, 1945 and 1946; resigned 1948. *Recreations:* riding, shooting, golf, tennis. *Address:* c/o Barclays Bank, Cape Town, S. Africa. *Clubs:* Royal Automobile; University (Dublin). [*Died* 21 *June* 1957.

HUGGETT, Mrs.; *see* Killick, E. M.

HUGGILL, Henry Percy, A.R.E. 1917; R.C.A. 1941; President Royal Cambrian Academy of Arts, 1954; *b.* 23 July 1886; *e. s.* of Henry and Henrietta Huggill; *m.* 1915, Gladys Mary Wynne Day; two *s.* *Educ.:* Royal College of Art, London. Nat. Schol. in Design, 1908; Brit. Inst. Schol. in Engraving, 1909; Dip., Roy. Coll. of Art, 1912; served European War 1914-19, Army (France and Italy); Head of Dept. of Decorative Art and Crafts, Liverpool, 1913-1921; Prin., Southport Sch. of Art, 1921-30; Curator, Southport Art Gallery, 1921-30; Prin., Liverpool Coll. of Art, 1930-51; Pres. Nat. Soc. for Art Education, 1938-41; Pres., Liverpool Acad. of Art, 1942-47 and 1951-; Member of the Court of Governors, National Museum of Wales, 1953. Exhibitor of paintings and engravings in prin. galls. in Gt. Brit. and Colonies. Hon. M.A. Liverpool, 1936. *Address:* Greengates, Dyserth, Flintshire. *T.:* Dyserth 47. [*Died* 8 *May* 1957.

HUGGINS, Brig.-Gen. Alfred, C.M.G. 1918; D.S.O. 1917; *b.* 1884. Formerly Brig.-Gen. R.A.F., Deputy Controller-General of Equipment at Air Ministry, a Director of Sunbeam Motor Car Co. (Ltd.) and of W. & G. Du Cros, Ltd. Served European War, 1914-19 (despatches, D.S.O., Bt. Maj.). [*Died* 30 *July* 1959.

HUGHES, Rt. Rev. Albert Edward, D.D.; *b.* 13 Feb. 1878; *m.* 1911, Marguerite Hall, *e. d.* of John Baker, Myrtlefield, Croydon and Ceylon; two *s.* one *d.* *Educ.:* Dublin University. B.A., R.U.I., 1902;

B.A., T.C.D., 1908; Inspector of Education, Dublin Diocese, 1909-17; Rector of Rathfarnham, 1917-21; Rector of Mariners' Church, Kingstown, 1921-23; Rector of Christ Church, Leeson Park, Dublin, 1923-39; Canon of Christ Church Cathedral, 1929-33; Preb. of Dunlavin (Canon) of St. Patrick's Cathedral, 1933-39; Bishop of Kilmore, Elphin and Ardagh, 1939-50. Chaplain to the Lord Lieutenant, 1920-21; Select Preacher, University of Dublin, 1927, 1939. *Recreations:* golf and Rugby football. *Address:* Kilmore, 3 Orwell Park, Rathgar, Dublin, Eire. *T.:* Dublin 97267. *Clubs:* Royal Empire Society; University (Dublin). [*Died* 11 *May* 1954.

HUGHES, Major Basil, D.S.O. 1918; M.A., M.B.; B.Ch. (Cantab.); B.Sc. (Lond.); F.R.C.S. (Eng.); Order of St. Sava, Serbia; Senior Surgeon Bradford Municipal General Hospital; Hon. Surgeon Bradford Royal Infirmary; Honorary Consulting Surgeon, Children's Hospital, Bradford; *b.* 1878; *s.* of John Edward Hughes (late Captain, R.N., and later Mathematical Scholar of St. Catharine's College, Cambridge) and Mary Anne Hughes of Daresbury Hall, Cheshire; *m.* 1932, Norah Blaney, *d.* of W. H. Cordwell, London. *Educ.:* Eastman's R.N. Academy; Selwyn College, Cambridge. Sambroke Scholar; Senior Scholar, King's College Hospital; Founder Fellow of Assoc. of Surgeons of Great Britain and Ireland; and of Internat. Coll. of Surgeons (Geneva); served European War, 1914-18, R.A.M.C. (despatches), first as Regimental Officer, later as Surgical Specialist, finally as Officer in Charge of Surgical Division at General Hospitals in France and Salonica. *Publications:* (with Capt. H. Stanley Banks) War Surgery from Firing-Line to Base, 1918; collaborator in Surgery of Modern Warfare, 1940; several contributions to the current medical journals. *Recreations:* farming, shooting, fishing, golf, riding. *Address:* Vounder Farm, Par, Cornwall. [*Died* 21 *Nov.* 1953.

HUGHES, Cecil Hugh Myddleton, O.B.E., M.B., B.S. (Lond.), F.F.A.R.C.S.; Consulting Anæsthetist to King's College Hospital; *m.* Anne Athol (*d.* 1958), *d.* of James Horne Stewart of Bathurst, N.S.W., and *widow* of W. Rivers Pollock, M.D., F.R.C.P. *Educ.:* Westminster School; Westminster Hospital, where he held appointments of Assistant House Physician, House Physician, and Resident Obstetric Assistant. Was Senior Honorary Anæsthetist, lecturer and teacher in anæsthetics, King's College Hospital; Consulting Anæsthetist to the Bethlem Royal Hospital; and Honorary Administrator of Anæsthetics to the Westminster, Seamen's (Greenwich), National Dental, Paddington Green Children's and Samaritan Hospitals, and the Hostel of St. Luke; late Fell. Roy. Soc. of Med. and Past President of Anæsthetic Section; served S. African War, 1900, with the Imperial Yeomanry Field Hospital; in European War was Consultant Anæsthetist and Temporary Surgeon-Commander, R.N., 1914-19; in war of 1939-45 served as Specialist in the E.M.S and temp. Hon. Anæsthetist to the Royal Sussex County and other Hospitals, 1939-1945. *Address:* 23 Brunswick Square, Hove. *T.:* Hove 36611. *Club:* Brighton Union (Brighton). [*Died* 2 *May* 1960.

HUGHES, Col. Cyril E., C.B.E. 1924 (M.B.E. 1919); *b.* 6 Sep. 1890; *s.* of J. Emerson Hughes, Tasmania; *m.* Phyllis, *o. d.* of A. Watson Murdoch, Alexandria, Egypt; no *c. Educ.:* Hobart; Sydney. Civil Engineer; enlisted trooper, 1st Australian Light Horse Regt., Gallipoli; Royal Engineers, Egypt, Sudan; Australian Engineers, Palestine; Deputy Director of Work, Imperial War Graves Commission, Gallipoli; Senior British Representative, Anglo-Turkish War Graves Commission; late Chief Administrative Officer, Imperial War Graves Commission, Eastern District; Member, British Delegation, Montreux Conference on Militarisation of Dardanelles, 1936; Australian Govt. Commissioner, Middle East, 1937; resigned Dec. 1939. Commissioned R.E.; served Middle East (despatches twice). Director Claims and Hirings, Middle East, retd., 1946, and apptd. Sec. Jockey Club of Egypt. *Address:* 39 Egerton Gardens, S.W.3. [*Died* 2 *March* 1958.

HUGHES, Capt. Edward Llewellyn, C.B.E. 1919; R.N. retired; *b.* 3 June 1875; 3rd *s.* of late George Martin Hughes, Kings Wick, Sunninghill. Berks. Served China, 1900; European War, 1914-19 (despatches, C.B.E.); War of 1939-45, 1943-45. *Address:* Over-Seas House, St. James's, S.W.1. [*Died* 14 *June* 1955.

HUGHES, Col. Edward Talfourd, C.B. 1904; V.D.; *o. s.* of Col. Sir Edwin Hughes, late M.P. for Woolwich; *b.* Woolwich, 29 Dec. 1855; *m.* 1883, Annie Sarah Gooch (*d.* 1922), *d.* of late William Smith; two *d. Educ.:* Greenwich Proprietary School; King's College School. Articled to his father, 1872; admitted a Solicitor, 1878; retired from business, 1924; member of Woolwich Local Board, 1882; Plumstead Vestry and District Board of Works; Baths Commissioner for Plumstead; elected an Alderman of first Woolwich Borough Council; Commissioner for Oaths, and a Land Tax Commissioner; 2nd Lieutenant in the 2nd Kent Volunteer Artillery, 1873; Lieut.-Col. and Officer Commanding, 1888; holds V.D. and rank of Colonel, 1893; Coronation medal, 1902; S.A. medal (C.I.V.) and Order of League of Mercy; Freeman of the City of London, and on Court of the Worshipful Company of Bakers. *Address:* 58 Leysdown Road, Eltham, S.E.9. [*Died* 15 *Dec.* 1943.
[*But death not notified in time for inclusion in Who Was Who 1941–1950, first edn.*

HUGHES, Rev. Ernest Richard, M.A.; retired; *b.* 5 Jan. 1883; *s.* of Alexander and Lucy Hughes; *m.* 1910, Katharine Lloyd; two *s.* one *d. Educ.:* City of London School; Lincoln Coll., Oxford; Mansfield College, Oxford. Religious work in a London slum, 1909-11; went to China as Missionary under London Missionary Society, 1911; Tingchow, Fukien Province, 1911-29; Shanghai with Literary and Students Departments of National Y.M.C.A. 1929-32; trustee on Board for Administration of British Boxer Indemnity Refund, 1931-34 and 1943-44; between 1927 and 1934 had three periods of research in Peiping; Reader in Chinese Religion and Philosophy, Univ. of Oxford, 1934-47, retired; Visiting Professor in Graduate School, Claremont, California, 1949-1952. Leverhulme Travelling Fellowship, 1942-44; Lowell Lecturer, Boston, 1950. *Publications:* The Invasion of China by the Western World, 1937; The Individual in East and West (editor and contributor), 1937; China Body and Soul (editor and contributor), 1938; Chinese Philosophy in Classical Times (Everyman Library), 1942; The Great Learning and The Mean-in-Action, 1942; The Spirit of Chinese Philosophy (with Y. L. Fung); The Art of Letters (A Chinese View), 1951. *Address:* Dorn Cottage, Blockley, Glos. [*Died* 20 *Oct.* 1956.

HUGHES, Evan, C.B.E. 1918; Regional Information Officer for Wales, Ministry of Information; *b.* 18 Jan. 1882; *s.* of late Evan Hughes of Llwydiarth Hall, Montgomeryshire; *m.* 1st, 1913, Dora Mary (*d.* 1941), *d.* of Edward Brady Patching, Brighton; one *s.* two *d.*; 2nd, Dolan Evans, L.R.A.M., A.R.C.M., Cardiff; one *s. Educ.:* Univ. Coll. of Wales, Aberystwyth (M.A.); Gonville and Caius College, Cambridge (B.A.). Until 1914-18 War, University Lecturer in Economics; Director of Organisation, National Savings Committee, 1919-33; Secretary, 1933-37; Public Relations Officer, National Fitness Council for England and Wales, 1938-39. *Address:* 111 Cathedral Road, Cardiff. [*Died* 14 *Dec.* 1951.

HUGHES, Gerald Stephen, M.B. Lond. (Hons. in Med.), B.S. Lond., F.R.C.S. Eng.; J.P. City of York; Consulting Surgeon, York County Hospital; Consulting Surgeon, Ampleforth College; Consulting Medical Officer, Yorkshire Insurance Co.; Member Church Assembly; *b.* 23 Feb. 1878; *s.* of late Henry Hughes, J.P., The Bower, Maidstone. *Educ.:* Maidstone; Middlesex Hospital, London. Fellow of Woodard Corporation; Member Magistrates' Association; Member Council Queen Victoria Clergy Fund; Hon. Treasurer Friends of York Minster. Late Demonstrator of Anatomy Middlesex Hosp.; Prosector Royal Coll. of Surgeons; Surgical Registrar, Bolingbroke Hosp. S.W.; Surgical Specialist, B.E.F., 1915-19, and Northern Command, 1919-23; Past Pres. York Medical Soc. *Publications:* Abdominal Surgery at an Advanced Operating Centre, 1917; Wounds of the Chest as seen at an Advanced Operating Centre, 1918; contributions on medicine and surgery to medical journals. *Recreations:* golf and travelling abroad. *Address:* 4 Minster Yard, York. *T.:* 23155. *Clubs:* Athenæum, Royal Automobile; Yorkshire (York). [*Died* 24 *Nov.* 1959.

HUGHES, Maj.-Gen. Henry Bernard Wylde, C.B. 1941; D.S.O. 1917; O.B.E. 1920; late Engr. in Chief, War Office; *b.* 8 May 1887; *s.* of late C. W. Hughes, Headley, Hants; *m.* Nora Beatrice, *d.* of late H. W. E. Hickson; two *s.* *Educ.:* Cheltenham. Entered R.E. 1906; Captain, 1914; Bt. Major, 1919; Major, 1924; Lt.-Col., 1931; Col., 1935; Temp. Major-General, 1941; Maj.-Gen., 1942; served European War, India, N.W. Frontier, 1914-16; Mesopotamia, 1916-18 (despatches twice, Bt. Major, D.S.O.); Afghanistan, 1919 (despatches); Waziristan, 1919-20 (despatches, O.B.E.); Assistant Adjutant-General, War Office, 1936-39; Chief Engineer, Western Command, 1939-40; Engineer in Chief, Middle East, 1940-43; Chief Engineer, Supreme H.Q. Allied Expeditionary Force, 1943-44; served War of 1939-45 (C.B.); retired pay, 1946. U.S. Legion of Merit; French Légion d'Honneur and Croix de Guerre. *Address:* The Garden House, Aldeburgh, Suffolk. [*Died* 22 *Feb.* 1953.

HUGHES, James John; M.Inst. of Transport; Member of the Transport Advisory Council, Road and Rail Traffic Act, 1933; Chairman of the Traders' Co-ordinating Committee; Chairman of the Traders' Panel; Member of the Council of London Chamber of Commerce; *b.* 19 May 1874. *Recreation:* cricket. *Address:* 15 St. Mildred's Road, Lee, S.E.12. *Club:* Surrey County Cricket (Kennington Oval). [*Died* 12 *Oct.* 1952.

HUGHES, Colonel John Gethin, C.M.G. 1916; D.S.O. 1900; V.D.; Col., Retired List, 1917, N.Z. Forces; late N.Z. Staff Corps; late attached to General Staff, Headquarters; *b.* 12 Mar. 1866; *m.* 1909, Marion de Vere, *d.* of Robert de Vere O'Connor, Carrigfoyle, Kerry; two *s.* one *d.* Served South Africa, 1899-1902 (despatches, medal with five clasps, D.S.O.); European War, 1914-16 (C.M.G.). *Recreation:* golf. *Address:* Canterbury Ridge, Island Bay, Wellington, S.2, N.Z. *T.:* 14-279. [*Died* 23 *July* 1954.

HUGHES, Rev. Levi Gethin, C.B.E. 1945 (M.B.E. 1919); *b.* 25 Jan. 1885; *s.* of late Rev. Henry Hughes, Briton Ferry; *m.* 1912, Irene, *d.* of Thomas Powell, J.P., Porthcawl. *Educ.:* Taunton School; Bristol University; The Baptist College, Bristol. Ordained at Sheffield, 1911; Temporary C.F. 1915; served in France, 1915-18 (despatches). Staff Chaplain War Office, 1918: Assistant Chaplain-General, Western Command, 1940-1943; Deputy Chaplain-General War Office, 1943-45. K.H.C. 1943-45; retired, 1945. *Recreations:* tennis, golf, travel. *Address:* The Breakers, West Dr., Porthcawl, S. Wales. [*Died* 9 *June* 1953.

HUGHES, Dame Mary Ethel, G.B.E., *cr.* 1922; *d.* of Thomas Campbell, Burrandong, New South Wales; *m.* 1911, Rt. Hon. William Morris Hughes, P.C., C.H., Q.C. (*d.* 1952), Premier of Australia, 1915-23. Rendered services in Australia, European War, 1914-18. Coronation Medal, 1937. *Address:* Gladswood House, Gladswood Gardens, Double Bay, N.S.W., Australia. [*Died* 2 *April* 1958.

HUGHES, Sir Robert Heywood, 12th Bt., *cr.* 1773; Land Agent managing several large Estates in West of England; *b.* 2 Nov. 1865; *e. surv. s.* of Sir Alfred Hughes, 9th Bt., of East Bergholt Lodge, Suffolk; *S.* nephew 1945; *m.* 1894, Edith Agnes Skinner; four *d.* *Educ.:* St. Peters, York. *Recreation:* hunting. *Heir:* *nephew* Richard Edgar [*b.* 1897; *m.* 1927, Angela Lilian Adelaide, *e. d.* of late Major Albert Julian Pell, J.P., D.L.; one *s.* one *d.*]. *Address:* Sowdens, Shedfield, Hants. *Club:* Royal Western Yacht (Plymouth). [*Died* 3 *Jan.* 1951.

HUGHES, Ronw Moelwyn, Q.C. 1943; Barrister-at-law; a Master of the Bench of the Inner Temple, 1950; retired from practice, 1952; *b.* Cardigan, October 1897; *s.* of late Rev. Dr. Moelwyn Hughes, M.A., Ph.D., one time Moderator of Welsh Presbyterian Church; *m.* 1929, Louise Mary, *o. d.* of late Baron Fairfield, P.C., K.C.; two *s.* one *d.* *Educ.:* Cardigan Council and County Schools; University College of Wales, Aberystwyth; Downing College, Cambridge. B.A. (Wales); B.A., LL.B. (Cantab.), First Class Honours Law Tripos; Chancellor's Gold Medal in English Law; Yarborough Anderson Scholar of Inner Temple; Bar and Northern Circuit, 1922; one time Lecturer in International Law, London School of Economics, Lecturer in Commercial Law, Law Society, Examiner for Council of Legal Education and Univ. of London; ex-Councillor, Birkenhead, Ealing; M.P. (Lab.) Carmarthen, 1941-45; Islington N., 1950-51; contested (L.) Rhondda W. 1929, Southport 1931 and (Lab.) Cardigan 1935, Carmarthen 1945. Comr. for Inquiry into Bolton football disaster, 1946; Chairman Greater London Water Inquiry, 1947; Chairman Cotton Manufacturing Commission, 1946-49; Special Assistant Commissioner for Wales under Local Government Boundary Commission, 1946-49; Chairman Catering Wages Comm., 1946-50; Recorder of Bolton, 1946-53; member Society of Labour Lawyers, Fabian Society and Society of Public Teachers of Law; active service W. Yorks Regt., 1916; R.F.C. and R.A.F., 1917-19. *Publications:* 7th ed. Lord Birkenhead's International Law, 1928; Agency, Bills of Exchange, Money and Moneylending in Halsbury's Laws of England, 2nd ed. 1931-1935; Road and Rail Traffic Act, 1933 (with Dingle Foot). *Address:* 63 Marlborough Mansions, Hampstead, N.W.6. *T.:* Hampstead 7755. [*Died* 1 *Nov.* 1955.

HUGHES, Rev. Samuel William, D.D.; Baptist Minister; Vice-President of Baptist Union, Great Britain and Ireland, 1948-49; President, 1949-50; Secretary, The Free Church Federal Council, 1940-46 (Secretary-Emeritus from 1946); Pastor-Emeritus of Walgrave Baptist Church since 1948; *b.* 11 July 1874; *m.* 1st, 1903, Edith Annie Walker (*d.* 1940); two *s.* one *d.*; 2nd, 1942, Winifred Walker. Associate of Manchester Baptist Coll.; Pastor of Walgrave Baptist Church, 1898-1901; Market Harboro', 1901-4; Christ Church, Birmingham, 1904-15: Westbourne Park, Porchester Road, Paddington, London, 1915-32; Gen. Sec. National Council of the Evangelical Free Churches, 1932-40. *Recreations:* swimming, golf. *Address:* The Laurels, Walgrave, Northampton. *T.:* Walgrave 237. *Club:* National Liberal. [*Died* 16 *Sept.* 1954.

HUGHES, Sir Thomas Harrison, 1st Bart., *cr.* 1942, of Denford in the County of

Berks; LL.D. Liverpool University (Hon.); Steamship Owner; Senior Partner of Thos. and Jas. Harrison of Liverpool and London; Member of Suez Canal Board from 1920, Vice-President from 1932; *b.* 13 April 1881; *s.* of late John William Hughes, Allerton, Liverpool; *m.* 1920, Gertrude Mary (*d.* 1949), *d.* of Joseph Bradley, Aughton Park, Ormskirk, Lancs.; one *d.*; *m.* 1952, Mme. Anne Van Voorst Evekink, *d.* of late John R. Humphreys, Llwyn Hall, Carmarthenshire, and *widow* of General D. Van Voorst Evekink, Military Attaché, Netherlands Embassy. *Educ.:* Rugby. Director of Liner Div., Min. of War Transport, 1939-42. *Recreations:* farming, orchids, fishing, and shooting. *Address:* 12 Hyde Park Gardens, W.2; Eddington House, Hungerford, Berks. *T.:* Hungerford 14. *Clubs:* Brooks's, City of London. [*Died* 31 *Oct.* 1958 (*ext.*).

HUGHES, Rt. Hon. William Morris, P.C. 1916; C.H. 1941; Q.C. 1919; M.P. for Bradfield, in Federal Parliament of Australia; Member Australian Advisory War Council; late Leader of United Australia Party; *b.* London, 25 Sep. 1864; *m.* 1st, 1886; 2nd, 1911, Mary Ethel, G.B.E., *cr.* 1922, *d.* of Thomas Campbell, Burrandong, N.S.W.; two *s.* three *d.* *Educ.:* Llandudno Grammar School; St. Stephen's Church of England School, Westminster. Pupil teacher, St. Stephen's Church of England School; came to Australia 1884; engaged in various occupations; elected to State Parl. of N.S.W. for Lang Div. of Sydney, 1894, re-elected three successive Parliaments resigned upon election to 1st Federal Parliament for W. Sydney, on Labour Party's platform; Minister for External Affairs, 1904; Chairman Royal Commission on the Navigation Bill; Delegate to Imperial Navigation Conference, 1907; Member of Imperial Cabinet and Delegate to Paris Peace Conference; Australian representative, League of Nations Assembly, Geneva, 1932; Master of Gray's Inn; Grand Officier de la Légion d'Honneur; Order Grand Crown, Belgium; D.C.L., Oxford; LL.D. Cardiff, Birmingham, Edinburgh, Glasgow; F.Z.S.; admitted to N.S.W. Bar; admitted to English Bar, 1921; organized Maritime Unions; Gen. Secretary of Wharf Labourers; President Carters' Union, N.S.W.; President, Waterside Workers' Federation; President, Transport Workers Federation. Attorney-General, 1908-1909, 1910-13, and 1914-21; Prime Minister of Australia, 1915-23; Minister for External Affairs, 1921-23; Vice-President of Executive Council, 1934-35 and 1937-38; Minister for Health and Repatriation, 1934-35 and 1936-37; Minister in charge of Territories, 1937-38; Min. for External Affairs, 1937-39; Minister for Industry, 1939-40; Attorney-General, 1939-41; Minister for the Navy, 1940-41. *Publications:* The Splendid Adventure: a Review of Empire Relations, 1929; The Price of Peace, 1934; Australia and War To-day, 1935; brochure (with W. T. Dick) on Federation of Australian States; Case for Labour; Crusts and Crusades, 1946; Policies and Potentates, 1950. *Recreations:* golf, riding. *Address:* 43 Nelson Road, Lindfield, Sydney, N.S.W. [*Died* 28 *Oct.* 1952.

HUGHES D'AETH, Rear-Admiral Arthur Cloudesley Shovel, C.B. 1916; *y. s.* of late Narbrough Hughes D'Aeth of Knowlton Court, Kent; *b.* 5 June 1875; *m.* 1903, Violet Hessie Evelyn, *d.* of Col. W. Kelly. Served European War, 1914-18, including Jutland Battle (C.B., Legion of Honour, despatches); Captain-in-Charge, Portland, 1922-23; retired list, 1923. *Address:* Knowlton Cottage, Fleet, Hants. [*Died* 23 *Aug.* 1956.

HUGHES-HUNTER, Sir William Bulkeley Hughes, 2nd Bt., *cr.* 1906; *S.* father, 1907; *b.* 20 April 1880; *o. s.* of 1st Bt. and Sarah Elizabeth (*d.* 1933), *o. c.* and *heiress* of W. Bulkeley Hughes, M.P., of Plas Coch and Brynddu. *Educ.:* Radley; Trinity College, Dublin (M.A.). J.P. D.L. Anglesey; Alderman Anglesey; Barrister-at-law, Middle Temple; Commander of Order of St. John of Jerusalem in England; Lord of the Manor of Cemaes. *Heir:* none. *Address:* Brynddu, Llanfechell, Anglesey. [*Died* 17 *June* 1951 (*ext.*).

HUGHMAN, Sir (Ernest) Montague, Kt., *cr.* 1922; M.I.E.(Ind.); formerly Chairman of W. T. Henley's Telegraph Works Co., Ltd., and associated companies; *b.* Leeds, 22 Oct. 1876; *s.* of late Capt. Newman Reeve Hughman, Yoxford, Suffolk; *m.* 1900, Florence Adeline Maude Smith (*d.* 1952); two *s.* *Educ.:* St. Mark's College, Chelsea. Assistant to Robert Hammond, M.Inst.C.E., Consulting Engineer, 1895-1907; engaged for many years in engineering and shipbuilding in India; has travelled extensively in many parts of the world, studying British, Foreign, and Colonial Administration, and the Development of Empire Trade; Vice-Pres. British Electrical and Allied Manufacturers Assoc. (Inc.); Vice-Pres. of Royal Society of Arts and Member of Council, 1937-40; one of the Founders and Hon. Organising Sec. Institution of Engineers (India), 1918-19; Member of Council, 1920-22; Hon. Secretary Indian Section of English Institution of Electrical Engineers, 1912-21. *Recreations:* travelling, fishing. *Address:* Quarries Hotel, Coombe Road, Croydon, Surrey. *T.:* Croydon 3911. *Clubs:* National Liberal, City Livery; Bombay (Bombay); New (Calcutta). [*Died* 23 *March* 1956.

HUGO, Lt.-Col. Edward Victor, C.M.G. 1917; M.D., B.S. (Lond.), F.R.C.S. (Eng.); late I.M.S.; late Member, Medical Board, India Office; late Professor of Surgery, King Edward's Medical College, Lahore; *b.* 1865; *m.* 1909, Helen Frances, *d.* of E. Newton, Peterborough. *Educ.:* Foyle Coll., Londonderry; St. Bartholomew's Hospital; London University. Served Waziristan Expedition, 1894-95 (medal and clasp); Chitral Relief Force, 1895 (medal and clasp); N.W. Frontier of India, 1897-98 (despatches, two clasps); European War (Dardanelles, Mesopotamia), 1915-19 (despatches, C.M.G.); Afghanistan and N.W. Frontier, 1919; retired, 1922. *Address:* 75 Queen's Road, Richmond, Surrey; c/o Lloyds Bank (King's Branch), 6 Pall Mall, S.W.1. [*Died* 24 *Dec.* 1951.

HULL, Cordell; Secretary of State of the United States, 1933-44; *b.* Overton (now Pickett) County, Tennessee, 2 Oct. 1871; *s.* of William and Elizabeth Riley Hull; *m.* 1917, Rose Frances Whitney (*d.* 1954); no *c.* *Educ.:* National Normal Univ., Lebanon, Ohio, 1889-90; B.L., Cumberland University Law School, Lebanon, Tennessee, 1891. Admitted to the Bar of Tennessee, 1891; practised law; Member of Tennessee House of Representatives, 1893-97; Captain, 4th Regt., Tennessee Volunteer Infantry, during Spanish-American War (service in Cuba); Judge 5th Judicial Circuit, Tennessee, 1903-07; Member U.S. House of Representatives, 60th to 66th Congresses, 1907-21; and 68th to 71st Congresses, 1923-31; Chairman, Democratic National Committee, 1921-24; elected United States Senator from Tennessee for term, 1931-1937; resigned as Senator upon appointment as Secretary of State; author of Federal Income Tax Legislation of 1913, the revised act of 1916, and the Federal Inheritance Act of 1916; Chairman of U.S. Delegation to the Monetary and Economic Conference, London, 1933; Chairman U.S. Delegation to the Seventh International Conference of American States, Montevideo, 1933; Chairman of United States Delegation to Inter-American Conference for Maintenance of Peace, Buenos Aires, 1936; Member of Nat. Archives Council; Nobel Peace Prize, 1945; received hon. degree of Doctor of Laws from Cumberland University, Notre Dame, Columbia University, George Washington Univ., Coll. of William and Mary, Williams College, Pennsylvania Military College, University of Wisconsin, University of Michigan, Lafayette College, Brown University, University of Pennsylvania and Yale University, 1937, Dartmouth College and Princeton University, 1938; hon. degree of Doctor of Humanities from Rollins College. *Publication:* The Memoirs of Cordell Hull, 1948 (2 vols.). *Address:* Wardman Park Hotel, Washington, D.C., U.S.A. [*Died* 23 *July* 1955.

HULLAH, John, C.S.I. 1923; *b.* 1876; *s.* of Robert Hullah, M.R.C.S., Grahamstown, S.A.; *m.* 1st, 1920, Kate (*d.* 1935), *d.* of W. L. Mugliston, Duffield, Derby; 2nd, 1936, Dorothy Maude, *d.* of late L. J. Greensmith, Derby. *Educ.:* Oundle; Caius College, Cambridge. Entered Indian Civil Service, 1899; served in Central Provinces till 1918; Secretary to Govt. of India, Revenue and Agriculture Dept., 1920-1923; retired, 1925. *Address:* Lansdown Court West, Cheltenham. [*Died* 20 *Dec.* 1955.

HULME, Edward Maslin, A.M.; Professor of History, Stanford University, 1921-37, Professor Emeritus since 1937; *b.* London, 17 Sept. 1869; *s.* of Thomas Hulme and Annie Louise Farmer; *m.* 1906, Gertrude May Jenkins; one *s.* two *d.* *Educ.:* Stanford University; Harvard University; Cornell University. Teacher of Literature and History in the High School, Portland, Oregon, 1897-1900; Professor of History, 1902-21, and Dean of the College of Letters and Science, 1917-21, University of Idaho; teacher in the Summer Sessions of the Universities of California, Oregon, Utah, Chicago, S. California, Duke, Nevada, and New York. *Publications:* Renaissance and Reformation, 1914: A History of the British People, 1924; The Middle Ages, 1929, revised edition, 1938; Wandering in France, 1941; History and its Neighbours, 1942. *Recreations:* walking, swimming, singing. *Address:* 638 Channing Avenue, Palo Alto, California, U.S.A. [*Died* 10 *July* 1951.

HULTON, Sir Roger Braddyll, 3rd Bt., *cr.* 1905; Landowner; J.P. Lancs; *b.* 30 March 1891; *o. s.* of Sir William Rothwell Hulton, 2nd Bt.; *m.* 1918, Hon. Marjorie Evelyn Louise de Montmorency, *o. c.* of 6th Viscount Mountmorres; one *s.* one *d.* *Educ.:* privately. *Recreations:* gardening, fishing, chess. *Heir:* *s.* Geoffrey Alan Hulton, Captain Royal Marines [*b.* 21 Jan. 1920; *m.* 1945, Mary Patricia, *e. d.* of P. A. de V. Reynolds, Farnborough]. *Address:* Caynham, Lansdown Road, Cheltenham, Glos. [*Died* 23 *April* 1956.

HUME, James Gibson, A.M. (Harvard), Ph.D. (Germany); Professor Emeritus of History of Philosophy in the University of Toronto, Canada; *b.* near Toronto, 1860; *s.* of James Hume and Marion Brown; *m.* 1892, Margaret Alice, *y. d.* of Thomas Bunting and Sarah Ward, St. Catharines; four *s.* one *d.* *Educ.:* University of Toronto; Johns Hopkins; Harvard; Freiburg in Baden. B.A., University of Toronto, 1887 with double Honours in Classics and in Philosophy; Governor-General's Gold Medal; in Johns Hopkins, Fellow elect., 1888; at Harvard, Thayer's Fellow and A.M., 1889; Roger's Fellow, 1890; Prof. of History of Philosophy in Univ. of Toronto, 1889, and of Ethics in Univ. Coll., Ph.D. Summa cum laude, Germany, 1891; visited Oxford, and the Scottish Universities, 1891; returning to University of Toronto, 1891-92. *Publications:* chiefly Articles and Reviews in American and Canadian journals; Value of a Study of Ethics; Political Economy and Ethics; Introduction to Works of Schopenhauer; Introduction to Psychology for Teachers (International Series). Evolution and Personality in Memorial Volume to Professor John Watson, Queen's University, Kingston. *Address:* 58 Spadina Road, Toronto, Canada. *Clubs:* Toronto, Harvard. [*Died* 28 *Jan.* 1949.

HUME, Brigadier (retired) Reginald Vernon, C.M.G. 1956; C.B.E. 1951 (O.B.E. 1943); T.D. 1947; retired from temporary service with Foreign Office Dec. 1955; *b.* 7 Sept. 1898; *s.* of late Colonel Charles Vernon Hume, R.A., and of late Mrs. Ursula W. Hume; *m.* 1929, Mary Katharine Emma, *d.* of late Archdeacon T. R. Sale and of Mrs. K. S. Sale; one *s.* one *d.* *Educ.:* Wellington; R.M.A. Woolwich. 2nd Lt. R.F.A., 1918; served France, Flanders, B.A.O.R., Brit. Mil. Mission in Berlin, 1920-21; Actg. Mil. Attaché, British Embassy, Berlin, 1921-27, retired; Member London Stock Exchange, 1929-45; special mil. appt. in M.E., 1939; served in Intelligence, M.E., 1939-44; Dir. of Mil. Intelligence, M.E., 1943-44; joined Mil. Govt. in Germany, at own request, 1944; 1 Airborne Corps, 1945; Comdr., Hanover, 1945-47; Dir. Educ. Branch, C.C.G., 1948-49, and Dep. Educational Adviser; Dep. Land Comr., Schleswig-Holstein, 1949-52, Land Comr., 1952-55; H.M. Consul, Kiel, 1954-55. Officer, Order of Merit (U.S.A.), 1944. *Recreations:* fishing; study of foreign affairs. *Address:* Thurland, Hildenborough, Kent. *Club:* M.C.C. [*Died* 4 *Oct.* 1960.

HUME, Sir William Errington, Kt., *cr.* 1952; C.M.G. 1919; M.A., M.B., B.C. (Cantab.), M.D. (Cantab.); F.R.C.P. (London); retired; Emeritus Professor of Medicine, Durham University; lately Physician, Newcastle upon Tyne; Consulting Physician, Royal Victoria Infirmary, Newcastle on Tyne; Adviser in Medicine, Region No. 1 E.M.S.; medical adviser to Northumberland and Durham Coalowners Protection Association; *b.* Newcastle on Tyne, 14 July 1879; *e. s.* of late George H. Hume, M.D.; *m.* Marie Elisabeth, *e. d.* of Col. Tisseyre, late Military Attaché, Court of Madrid; two *s.* three *d.* *Educ.:* Repton School; Pembroke College, Cambridge; London Hospital; Berlin. House Surgeon, Senior House Physician, and Secretary to the Hon. Staff, Royal Victoria Infirmary, 1904-7; Hon. Assistant Physician, 1908; Demonstrator in Medical Pathology, Durham University College of Medicine, 1908-22; late Consulting Physician, British Armies in France (despatches twice, C.M.G.); late Senior Censor, Member of Council, Royal College of Physicians; Bradshaw Lecture, Harveian Orator, Royal College of Physicians; late Orator, Medical Society of London; late Examiner in Medicine, Universities of Cambridge, Edinburgh, London, Liverpool and Leeds; late Examiner in Pharmacology, Birmingham and Belfast Universities; late Hon. Col. R.A.M.C. Units 50th Division. *Publications:* contributor to Medical History of the War, 1914-18; British Encyclopædia of Medicine and medical journals. *Recreations:* fishing, golf. *Address:* 10 Windsor Crescent, Newcastle upon Tyne. *T.:* Newcastle 81-4187. [*Died* 1 *Jan.* 1960.

HUME, Lieut.-Colonel William James Parke, C.M.G. 1921; *b.* 25 Jan. 1866; *s.* of late W. W. Hume, Ceylon Civil Service; *m.* Alice (*d.* 1952), *e. d.* of George Stevenson, Oakleigh, Bromborough; three *d.* *Educ.:* Haileybury College; and on the Continent. Malayan Civil Service, 1888-1921; Auditor General, F.M.S., 1906; Commissioner Trade and Customs, 1911; Acting British Resident, Perak, 1912; British Resident, Perak, 1920-21; Malay States Volunteer Rifles, 1907; Lieut. 1911; Captain, 1912; Captain 5th Royal Sussex Regiment, 1914; Major, 1915; Lieut.-Colonel, and D.A.A.G. in India, 1918. Home Guard, 1940-45. *Address:* Brinksway, Lynchmere, Sussex. *T.:* Haslemere 293. *Clubs:* East India and Sports; 3 Counties (Haslemere). [*Died* 26 *Dec.* 1952.

HUME-CAMPBELL, Sir John H.-P.; *see* Campbell.

HUMPHREY, Herbert Alfred, M.Inst.C.E., M.I.Mech.E., M.I.E.E., F.C.G.I.; Fellow of the Imperial College of Science and Technology; Mem. Roy. Soc.; Chairman South Staffordshire Mond Gas Co.; *b.* London, 1868; *m.*; three *s.* two *d.* *Educ.:* Finsbury Technical

Coll.; The Central Institution of the City and Guilds of London. Manager to Heenan and Froude, Manchester and Birmingham; Departmental Manager and Engineer to Brunner Mond and Company, Limited, Northwich, Cheshire; Consulting Engineer at 38 Victoria Street, Westminster; Consulting Engineer to Imperial Chemical Industries, Ltd., for all their Works and Factories; Inventor of the Humphrey Pump; U.S.A. Patent rights for Humphrey Pump sold for £100,000. *War work:* Technical Adviser at Explosives Supply Department, and charge of manufacture of Ammonium Nitrate for high explosives; Technical Adviser and Chief Engineer to Munitions Inventions Department. *Publications:* Papers on Large Gas Engines and Gas Producers and similar subjects, which have gained for the author the Telford Gold Medal, the Willans Gold Medal, the Watt Gold Medal, the Constantine Gold Medal; Melchett Medallist, 1939. *Recreations:* motoring, golf, wood working. *Address:* Chenies, Westcliff Road, Hermanus, C.P., South Africa. [*Died* 9 *March* 1951.

HUMPHREY, John, C.B.E. 1942 (O.B.E. 1919); *b.* 2 Aug. 1879; *s.* of late John Humphrey; *m.* Agnes Florence, *d.* of late Col. J. Beatson Bell, C.B.E.; three *s.* *Educ.:* privately. European War, 1914-18 (O.B.E.). Member Bombay Legislative Council, 1932-1937; Chairman Chamber of Commerce, Karachi, 1940, 1941 and 1943; Vice-Pres. Associated Chambers of Commerce, India, 1940, 1944. *Address:* St. Leonard's Lane, Lincoln. *Clubs:* East India and Sports; Sind (Karachi). [*Died* 11 *July* 1956.

HUMPHREY-DAVY, Francis Herbert Mountjoy Nelson, O.B.E. 1919; *e.* and *o. surv. s.* of Alfred Humphrey-Davy, M.D., M.Ch. (*d.* 1941), Bournemouth, and Evangeline Nelson (*d.* 1929), *d.* of late Wm. Johnstoun Nelson Neale, Recorder of Walsall. Pioneer of the All-British Industrial Movement by founding the Union Jack Industries League, 1905, becoming Hon. Secretary, 1908, and Vice-Chairman, 1911; entered journalism, 1905; a Sub-Editor London News Agency, 1908-14; joined the staff of The Times, 1914; a Private Secretary to late Viscount Northcliffe, 1915-22; associated with the British War Mission to the U.S.A. 1917; Assistant Social Editor of The Times, 1923; on Daily Mail staff and a Secretary to 2nd Viscount Rothermere, 1924-39. *Address:* The Red House, Bournemouth. *T.:* Westbourne 61697. [*Died* 17 *Feb.* 1953.

HUMPHREYS, Lt.-Gen. Sir (Edward) Thomas, K.C.B., *cr.* 1936 (C.B. 1923); C.M.G. 1919; D.S.O. 1916; late Leinster Regt.; *b.* 5 Nov. 1878; *m.* 1919, Dorothy Grace, *y. d.* of Captain F. T. Penton, 43 Portland Place, W.; one *s.* two *d.* *Educ.:* Charterhouse; Sandhurst. Entered Army, 1898; served S. African War, 1899-1902 (despatches, Queen's medal 2 clasps, King's medal 2 clasps); European War, 1914-18 (despatches four times, C.M.G., D.S.O., Bt. Lt.-Col. and Col.); Malabar, 1921-22 (C.B.); Deputy Director of Military Operations and Intelligence, War Office, 1925-28; Maj.-Gen. 1927; Commandant of Staff College, Quetta, 1928-31; Commander of 5th Division, 1931-34; Lt.-Gen. 1933; retired pay, 1937. *Club:* Army and Navy. [*Died* 15 *Jan.* 1955.

HUMPHREYS, Captain Kenneth Noël, C.B. 1927; late Royal Navy; Younger Brother of Trinity House; *b.* 10 Oct. 1881; *e. s.* of late Noel A. Humphreys, I.S.O., F.S.S., Assistant Registrar-General of England and Wales; *m.* 1907, Marie, *d.* of late Hon. Mr. Justice Condé Williams of Mauritius, and *widow* of Lieut. W. E. Oliver, Royal Navy; two *s.* (and two *s.* killed in action). *Educ.:* Farnborough Park, Hants; H.M.S. Britannia. Entered R.N., 1896; Commander, 1915; served China, 1900 (China Medal); Navigating Officer, H.M.S. Conqueror, 1914-1919, Grand Fleet; Squadron Navigating Officer, H.M.S. King George V, 2nd Battle Squadron, 1919, and Master of the Fleet in H.M.S. King George V, under Adm. Sir Henry Oliver, C.-in-C., Home Fleet, Southend Review, 1920; commanded Boys' Training ships H.M.S. Collingwood and Colossus at Portland, 1921, 1922; Commander of Dockyard, Deputy Supt. and King's Harbour Master, Sheerness, 1922-25; commanded tow of ex-German Floating Dock, Medway to Malta, 1925; twice received thanks of Lords of Admiralty for command of Dock towage; King's Harbour Master, Plymouth, 1925-27; retired list, 1927; Naval Instructor Chinese Maritime Customs, 1929-32; Captain of the Port, Holyhead, 1934-39. Recalled to active service, 1939-46; Routeing Officer under C.-in-C. Rosyth, 1939-41; Comd. H.M.S. Arbella, Boston, Lincs., 1941-42, for training crews for Landing Craft; 1943-45, rewrote Admiralty Publication, Ports and Anchorages of the World. Employed by Festival of Britain, 1951, and in General Register Office on 1951 Census. *Address:* The Lodge, Park Crescent, Worthing, Sussex. [*Died* 30 *Oct.* 1955.

HUMPHREYS, Lt.-Gen. Sir Thomas; *see* Humphreys, Lt.-Gen. Sir E. T.

HUMPHREYS, Rt. Hon. Sir Travers, P.C. 1946; Kt., *cr.* 1925; *b.* 1867; 4th *s.* of Charles Octavius Humphreys, solicitor, London; *m.* 1896, Zoë Marguerite (*d.* 1953), *e. d.* of Henri Philippe Neumans, artist, Antwerp; one *s.* (and one *s.* decd.). *Educ.:* Shrewsbury School; Trinity Hall, Cambridge, B.A. Called to Bar, 1889; Junior Counsel to Crown at Central Criminal Court, 1908; Senior, 1916; Bencher Inner Temple, 1922; formerly Recorder of Chichester; Recorder of Cambridge, 1926-28; Judge of the King's Bench Div., 1928-51. Médaille du Roi Albert (Belgian). *Publications:* Criminal Days, 1946; A Book of Trials, 1953. *Address:* 1 Temple Gardens, Temple, E.C. *Club:* Garrick. [*Died* 20 *Feb.* 1956.

HUMPHRIES, Albert, C.B. 1936; C.B.E. 1932; M.I.M.E.; late Chief Mechanical Engineer and Superintendent Building Works Department, Royal Ordnance Factories, Woolwich, since 1926; *b.* 23 May 1872; *s.* of Edwin Humphries and Jane Coleman; *m.* 1899, Henrietta, *d.* of Joseph Britter, late Headmaster of the Warspite; one *s.* *Educ.:* Woolwich Polytechnic. Engineering apprentice, Royal Ordnance Factories, 1888; manager, Royal Laboratory, 1914; Associate Member Ordnance Committee, 1916; Superintendent Royal Ammunition Factories, 1922. *Recreation:* golf. *Address:* Parkside, Silverston Avenue, Bognor Regis. [*Died* 10 *Feb.* 1951.

HUNGERFORD, Samuel James, C.M.G. 1946; *b.* 16 July 1872; *s.* of S. J. Hungerford and Mary Wilson; *m.* 1893, Alberta, *d.* of Jesse Demorest. Vice-President and General Manager, Canadian National Railways, 1922-23; Vice-President, Operation and Construction Departments, 1923; acting President, 1932, President, 1934-41, Canadian National Railways; Chairman, Board of Directors, 1936-42. *Address:* Farnham, Quebec. [*Died* 7 *Oct.* 1955.

HUNT, Albert, C.B.E. 1918; *b.* 1863; *s.* of late George Hunt of Redland, Bristol; *m.* 1893, Sarah, *d.* of late John Bainbridge; one *d.* *Educ.:* Horfield. Joined Donald Currie and Co.'s Staff, 1889; local manager Union-Castle Line at Southampton, 1901-11; Freights Manager in London, 1911-12, and Joint Manager and Chairman of Managers of the Union-Castle Mail S.S. Co. Ltd., 1912-23; a member of Executive Councils of Chamber of Shipping and of Shipping Federation, 1913-23; a member of War Committee of the Chamber of Shipping (Submarine Menace) during European War, and inventor of numerous popular war-games; assisted to organise Naval and Military Transport during South African and

European Wars, especially despatch of original Expeditionary Force to France, 1914. *Recreations:* yachting, gardening. *Address:* 52 Bedford Gardens, Kensington, W.8. *T.:* Park 7795. *Club:* Constitutional.
[*Died* 25 *Dec.* 1957.

HUNT, Frank William, C.V.O. 1923; *b.* 1870; *s.* of late Felix Hunt; *m.* 1896, Annie Edith (*d.* 1951), *d.* of late Charles Nurse Coote. Valuer to the London C.C., 1915-1937; member of Panel of Official Arbitrators under the Acquisition of Land (Assessment of Compensation) Act 1919, 1937-40 and 1941-46. *Address:* Brookside, Norbury Avenue, S.W.16. *T.:* Pollards 1961.
[*Died* 16 *Aug.* 1955.

HUNT, Capt. Roland Cecil C.; *see* Carew Hunt.

HUNTER, Admiral Cuthbert; *b.* 1 March 1866; *y. s.* of late J. J. Hunter of The Grange, Whickham, Co. Durham; *m.* 1895, Maude Isobel Gore (*d.* 1934), *y. d.* of late Commander William Grant Douglas, R.N. *Educ.:* Eastman's; H.M.S. Britannia. Joined as Naval Cadet, 1879; passed out of H.M.S. Britannia as Midshipman, and 1st of the term; Lieutenant, 1887; served as Gunnery Lieutenant on staff of H.M.S. Excellent; Commander, 1900; Captain, 1905; last Command afloat H.M.S. Hampshire; Vice-President of the Ordnance Committee, which he relinquished on promotion to Rear-Admiral, 3 April 1917; retired, 17 April 1917; Adm. 1925; Member of L.C.C. for Greenwich, 1928-34. *Address:* 6 Vanbrugh Terrace, Blackheath, S.E.3. *T.:* Greenwich 1292.
[*Died* 30 *April* 1952.

HUNTER, Colonel Evan Austin, C.B.E. 1949 (O.B.E. 1917); T.D. 1950; Legion of Honour; Member Royal Commission on Betting, Lotteries and Gaming, 1949; Secretary, British Olympic Association, 1925-48; *b.* 28 Sept. 1887; *e. s.* of late Frank Hunter, W.S., Dixons, Lockerbie, and Elizabeth Agnes Mein-Austin; *m.* 1st, 1913, Jane Ritchie Kay, Hill of Ruthven, Perth; one *s.* one *d.*; 2nd, 1940, Joan Pierrepont Hunter, Redland House, Chester. *Educ.:* Edinburgh Academy; Fettes College; Christ Church, Oxford (B.A., 1909); Edinburgh University. Writer to His Majesty's Signet, 1912; Hon. Sec., Achilles Club, 1923-1948; Hon. Sec. British Empire Games Federation, 1930-48, and Organiser of the British Empire Games held in London in 1934; Hon. Sec. Universities Athletic Union and Dominion Students' Athletic Union, 1931-48; rep. Scotland against Ireland, Athletic International, 1911; has taken great interest in athletics and University sport generally, and has been Hon. Manager of teams to Australia, Canada, New Zealand, South Africa, America and many European countries; represented Oxford University on the A.A.A. Committee, 1927-48; the Scottish A.A.A. on the British Olympic Council, 1923-48, and the South African A.A.A. on the International Amateur Athletic Federation, 1926-48; Vice-President, London Athletic Club; Hon. Life Member, Stade Français; served European War, 1914-19, Scottish Horse Brigade R.A.S.C., Staff Captain, War Office, 1917 (O.B.E., despatches); Major R.A.S.C. 1940; Lt.-Col. A.D.S.T., War Office, 1941; Colonel D.D.S.T. British Army Staff, Washington, U.S.A., 1943-45. *Publications:* numerous articles in Sports Journals. *Recreations:* golf and farming. *Address:* Ty Draw Farm, Nerquis, nr. Mold, Flintshire. *T.:* Mold 244. *Clubs:* Caledonian; Prestwick Golf (Prestwick). [*Died* 31 *Jan.* 1954.

HUNTER, John B., C.B.E. 1946; M.C., M.Ch., F.R.C.S.; Surgeon; *b.* 16 July 1890; *s.* of James Hunter; *m.* 1923, Hilda, *d.* of Dr. A. Whitfield; one *s.* one *d.* *Educ.:* Bedford; St. John's College, Cambridge. Captain R.A.M.C. 1914-19, France, Russia (M.C., despatches); Surgeon Royal Chest Hospital; Surgeon King's Coll. Hosp. Emergency Medical Service, 1938-45. Member of Senate, University of London, Dep. Vice-Chancellor, 1950-51. *Publications:* Part Editor Rose and Carless Manual of Surgery; various medical. *Recreations:* golf, fishing. *Address:* 39 Devonshire Place, W.1. *T.:* Welbeck 6561. *Club:* Savile.
[*Died* 16 *Sept.* 1951.

HUNTER, Louis Lucien, C.M.G. 1949; Ceylon Civil Service, retired; M.P., M.H.R., Ceylon, 1952; *b.* 3 Dec. 1889; *s.* of Louis Andrew Norman Hunter and Antoinette Brohier; *m.* 1915, Edith Constance, *d.* of Dr. Arthur Fretz and Agnes Stork; two *d.* Senator and Parl. Sec. to Minister of Finance, 1950-52; Govt. Agent, Western Province, Ceylon, 1948-50. *Recreations:* gardening and travel. *Address:* 100 Rosmead Place, Colombo, 7, Ceylon. *T.:* 9542. *Club:* Dutch Burgher Union (Colombo).
[*Died* 25 *July* 1959.

HUNTER, Captain Michael John; *b.* 15 July 1891; *o. s.* of Michael Joseph Hunter, J.P., Stoke Hall, Derbyshire; *m.* 1919, Clare Margaret, *o. d.* of Henry Randolph Trafford, D.L., J.P., Michaelchurch Court, Herefordshire; one *s.* three *d.* *Educ:* Rugby; Clare College, Cambridge (B.A.). Served Royal Field Artillery, European War, 1914-18; M.P. (C.) Brigg Division, Lincolnshire, 1931-35; M.F.H. Monmouthshire Hounds, 1947-50. *Recreations:* hunting, shooting. *Address:* Gissing Hall, Diss, Norfolk. *T.:* Tivetshall 222; Michaelchurch Court, Abergavenny, Mon. *T.:* Peterchurch 256. *Clubs:* Carlton, 1900; Norfolk (Norwich). [*Died* 9 *March* 1951.

HUNTER, Peter Sinclair, C.B.E. 1937; M.A., M.B., Ch.B., D.P.H.; *b.* Newmill, Banffshire, 12 Dec. 1883; *m.* 1913, Anne E. M. Walker; one *s.* *Educ.:* Mackie Academy, Stonehaven; Aberdeen University. Bacteriologist, Singapore Municipality, 1913-23; Health Officer Singapore Municipality, 1923-39; retd. Capt. Singapore Field Ambulance, 1913-16; Temporary Captain R.A.M.C., France, 1917-18. *Publication:* Chapter on Anti-Malarial Work in Singapore in Watson's Prevention of Malaria. *Recreations:* golf, fishing. *Address:* Wing Loong Road, Singapore. *Clubs:* East India and Sports; Singapore.
[*Died* 27 *March* 1954.

HUNTER, Philip Vassar, C.B.E. 1920; Hon. M.I.E.E.; Chartered Electrical Engineer; Director British Insulated Callender's Cables Ltd. (late Dep. Chm.); *b.* 1883; *s.* of late J. Hunter, Norfolk; *m.* 1904, Helen Maud, *d.* of Charles Golder, Finchley; two *d.*; *m.* 1947, Ruby Phyllis Hudson, Herne Bay, Kent; one *d.* *Educ.:* Wisbech Grammar School; Faraday House. Asst. Engineer to late Robert Hammond, M.I.E.E., 1903-4; with Merz & McLellan, Consulting Engineers, 1904-19; with Callender's Cable and Construction Co. Ltd., 1919-45 (Director since 1937). Engineering Director to Experiments and Research Section of Anti-submarine Division of the Naval Staff dealing with new methods of submarine location and destruction, 1915-18; inventor of the Buoyant Cable for use against enemy magnetic mines, 1939. Past President, Institution of Electrical Engineers; Member, Royal Institution. Fellow of American Institute of Electrical Engineers; Chm., Nat. Inspection Council for Electrical Installation Contracting; Pres. Brit. Electrical Power Convention, 1952. Has devoted special attention to the development of electrical transmission; invented several systems of automatic discrimination for electric power transmission systems and improved forms of transmission cable. *Recreations:* golf, shooting; President of the British Ice Hockey Association. *Address:* Springhurst, Shirley Church Rd., Addington, Surrey. *T.:* Springpark 4384; Surrey House, Temple Place, W.C.2. *T.:* Temple Bar 7722. *Clubs:* Athenæum, Savage, St. Stephen's. [*Died* 22 *Oct.* 1956.

HUNTER, Sir Thomas, Kt., *cr.* 1944; *b.* 2 Oct. 1872; *s.* of Thomas Hunter and Annabella Struthers; *m.* 1897, Janet (*d.* 1938), 2nd *d.* of late William Harris, Perth; one *s.* *Educ.:* Perth Academy. Journalist, Editor, and Newspaper Proprietor; Fellow of Institute of Journalists; J.P. for County of Perth; Councillor, Senior Bailie; Lord Provost City and Royal Burgh of Perth, 1932-35; Member of Education Committee County Council of Perth and Kinross; Director of County and City of Perth Royal Infirmary; M.P. (C.) Perth and Kinross (Perth Division), 1935-45; Chairman Perth Division Conservative and Unionist Association; Board of Scottish Central Ice Rink Ltd., Perth; Munro Melville Trust, Perth; President, Perth Burns Club; Head of various Masonic Orders; Past Grand Superintendent, Provincial Grand Royal Arch Chapter of Perthshire; Tay Valley District Grand Prior of the Order of the Temple; Moderator, Perth Society of High Constables. *Publications:* History of St. John's Kirk, Perth; Guide to Perth City and its environments. *Recreations:* cricket, bowling, swimming. *Address:* Balcanquhal House, Gateside, By Fife. *T.A.:* Hunter, Balcanquhal House, Glenfarg. *T.:* Glenfarg 261. *Club:* Constitutional.
[*Died* 19 *March* 1953.

HUNTER, Sir Thomas (Alexander), K.B.E., *cr.* 1939; M.A.; M.Sc., Hon. Litt.D. (N.Z.); Hon. Fellow British Psychological Society; Principal Emeritus, Victoria University College (Principal, 1938-51), retired 1951; Chairman, New Zealand Council for Educational Research since 1934; member Academic Board, 1929-51, Chairman, 1948-1951; member Entrance Board, 1929-51, Chairman, 1948-50; *b.* Croydon, London, 1876; 3rd *s.* of William Hunter, banker; *m.* 1905, Zella Pope (*d.* 1950); one *s.* two *d.* *Educ.:* Otago Univ., Dunedin. Senr. Scholar N.Z. Univ., and M.A. with 1st Class Hons. in Mental and Moral Philosophy; Lecturer on Mental and Moral Philosophy and Economics, Victoria University College, 1904; Professor of Philosophy and Economics, 1907-1909; Professor of Philosophy and Psychology, 1909-48; Chm. of the Professional Board, 1911-12, 1920-21; Vice-Chancellor University of N.Z., 1929-47; Chairman of Massey Agricultural College, N.Z., 1936-38; Chairman Council of Adult Education, 1938-48. *Address:* 10 Clermont Terrace, Wellington, New Zealand. [*Died* 20 *April* 1953.

HUNTER, Sir Thomas Anderson, K.B.E., *cr.* 1947 (C.B.E. 1916). Served European War, 1914-18, with N.Z.E.F., 1918-20, as Director of Dental Services; retired, 1930. Hon. life member British Dental Association, 1930; Hon. Member Fédération Dentaire Internationale, 1950. *Address:* Heretaunga, New Zealand. [*Died Dec.* 1958.

HUNTER, Thomas Briggs, C.B. 1933; O.B.E.; M.I.C.E. Late Civil Engineer-in-Chief, Admiralty; retired 1934. *Address:* 10 Layer Gardens, Acton Hill, W.3. *T.:* Acorn 3964.
[*Died* 2 *Oct.* 1957.

HUNTER, His Honour Trevor Havard, Q.C. 1928; retired; County Court Judge, 1939-50; Chancellor of Diocese of Swansea and Brecon, 1929-53; Bencher of Middle Temple, 1936; *y. s.* of William Havard Hunter of Briton Ferry House, Briton Ferry, Glamorganshire; *m.* 1905, Ethel Ruth, *d.* of John Griffiths, Neath; two *s.* *Educ.:* Wilson's School. Admitted a Solicitor, 1899; called to Bar, Middle Temple, 1911 (certificate of Honour); served European War in Royal Welch Fusiliers, and subsequently as Courts-Martial Officer. *Address:* 11 York Mansions, S.W.11. *T.:* Macaulay 2619. *Club:* Carlton.
[*Died* 9 *May* 1960.

HUNTER, Hon. Lord, (William Hunter), M.A., LL.D. (Edin. and Glas.); *b.* 9 Oct. 1865; *s.* of late David Hunter of Ayr, Advocate, 1889; M.P. (L.) Govan Division of Lanarks., 1910-11; K.C. 1905; Solicitor-General for Scotland, 1910-11; Senator of the College of Justice in Scotland, 1911-36. *Address:* 3 Randolph Cres., Edinburgh. *Club:* New (Edinburgh).
[*Died* 10 *April* 1957.

HUNTER, Sir William B. H. H.; *see* Hughes-Hunter.

HUNTER-RODWELL, Sir Cecil; *see* Rodwell, Sir C. H.

HUNTINGTON, Archer Milton, M.A., Litt.D., LL.D.; Knight Commander of the Orders of Alfonso XII. and Carlos III.; Chevalier Legion of Honour, 1927; Order of Carlos Manuel de Céspedes (Cuba), 1937; former President and now Member Council American Geographical Society; Trustee of American Museum of Natural History, The N.Y. Historical Society, etc.; Corr. Member, Spanish Academy, etc.; Founder and President of The Hispanic Soc. of America: Hon. President American Numismatic Soc.; Member American Academy of Arts and Letters, etc.; presented in 1927 to Palace of the Legion of Honor, San Francisco, art collection in memory of Collis P. Huntington and to Yale Univ. Museum collection in memory of Arabella D. Huntington; in 1931-32, art collection to Charleston Museum; 1932, to Syracuse Univ., the Archer and Anna Huntington Wild Life Forest Station (13,000 acres); building for National Academy of Design, New York, 1940, and former residence and 500 acres to Palisades Interstate Park Commission, 1943; to N.Y. State for State Teachers Coll. at Cortland, N.Y., Camp Pine Knot, consisting of 198½ acres as a memorial to Collis P. Huntington, 1949; Founder of The Mariners' Museum, Virginia, and of Brookgreen Gardens (Museum), S.C.; *b.* New York, 10 March 1870; *s.* of Collis P. Huntington; *m.* 1st, 1895, Helen Manchester Gates; 2nd, 1923, Anna Vaughan Hyatt. *Educ.:* New York and Spain, Member: British Numismatic Society. Royal Numismatic Soc., Royal Institution of Gr. Brit., Br. Institute of Philosophical Studies, R.S.A., Bibliographical Soc., London Library. Elector Hall of Fame. G. Melchers Medal, 1950, Artists' Fellowship. *Publications:* A Note Book in Northern Spain, 1898; Lace Maker of Segovia, poems, 1928; The Ladies of Vallbona, poems, 1931; Youth; Torn Sails of Faith; Moraima's Tower; The Lady of Elche; America; Polvo; The Sea, poems, 1933; The Silver Gardens; Alfonso the Eighth Rides By, poems, 1934; Vela Venenosa, Rimas, poems, 1936; A Flight of Birds, poems, 1938; Spain and Africa, poems, 1943; Recuerdos, poems, 1949; Turning Pages, poems, 1950; Tapestry, poems, 1951; Tapestry II, poems, 1952; Collected Verse, poems, 1953; various magazine articles, poems, etc.; editor of a number of texts of rare and curious Spanish books; Lady ——'s Travels into Spain (with Introduction), 1899; The Poem of the Cid (3 vols.), Text, Translation, and Notes, 1897; Spanish Initials and Miniatures of the Ninth, Tenth, and Eleventh Centuries, 1904; Editor of the Publications of The Hispanic Society of America. *Address:* Box 245, Bethel, Conn., U.S.A. *Clubs:* Royal Societies', Authors'; Harvard, Yale, and Columbia Universities, New York Yacht, Authors', Century, Grolier (New York).
[*Died* 11 *Dec.* 1955.

HURD, Sir Archibald, Kt., *cr.* 1928; Chairman of the Shipping World, Ltd.; *s.* of Wm. Hurd, solicitor; *m.* Anne Perrott (*d.* 1946), *o. d.* of Albert Groser; *m.* 1947, Beatrice Maude, 3rd *d.* of late Alfred Stair, Accountant and Comptroller of the Inland Revenue. Contributor of naval and other articles to the Fortnightly Review, Nineteenth Century, and other English and American publications; on editorial staff of Daily Telegraph, 1899-1928; Joint Editor of Brassey's Naval and Shipping Annual, 1922-1928; author of the official History of the

Merchant Navy in the War of 1914-19 (under the auspices of the Historical Section of the Committee of Imperial Defence); Freeman of Worshipful Company of Shipwrights; Hon. Freeman of City of London; Assoc. Member of Council of Institution of Naval Architects, 1942-45; Hon. Member, Royal United Service Institution; a Vice-President British Sailors' Society; Executive Cttee., National Library for the Blind. *Publications:* Naval Efficiency, the War-Readiness of the Fleet; German Sea-Power, its Rise, Progress, and Economic Basis (joint); The Command of the Sea; The New Empire Partnership (with Sir Percy Hurd); The British Fleet in the Great War; Sons of Admiralty (with Sir Henry Bashford); The Merchant Navy, vol. i. 1921, vol. ii. 1924, vol. iii. (with an introduction by the Prince of Wales, Master of The Merchant Navy and Fishing Fleets), 1929; The Sea-Traders; The Triumph of the Tramp Ship, 1922; The Reign of the Pirates, 1925; State Socialism in Practice, 1925; The Islanders, 1926; The Eclipse of British Sea Power: An Increasing Peril, 1933; The Battle of the Seas, 1941; Who Goes There?, 1942; Britannia Has Wings!, 1942. *Address:* The Shaw, Brasted Chart, Kent. *T.:* Brasted 363. *Club:* Athenæum. [*Died* 20 *June* 1959.

HURLEY, Col. Lionel James, C.M.G. 1918; Member Commonwealth Film Censorship Board, 1928 - 49, retired; late Deputy-Director, Migration and Settlement, Commonwealth of Australia; late A.D.O.S., Australian Imperial Force, London; *s.* of late John Hurley, M.P., New South Wales Parliament; *b.* Sydney, N.S.W., 1879; *m.* 1904, H. M. Bate, N.S.W.; no *c.* *Educ.:* Katoomba College, N.S.W. Mining Engineer, Australia; Trade Commissioner, London, for N.S.W. Government, 1911 till outbreak of war in 1914; joined Imperial Forces, France; 1914-15; service in army in England, 1916-17; invalided on special leave to Australia, 1918. *Address:* Brompton, Cremorne Point, Sydney, N.S.W. [*Died* 15 *Sept.* 1955.

HURLEY, Sir (Thomas Ernest) Victor, K.B.E. *cr.* 1950; C.B. 1945; C.M.G. 1917; M.D., M.S., F.R.C.S., F.R.A.C.S.; *s.* of Thomas Hurley, Geelong, Victoria, Australia; *b.* 3 Jan. 1888; *m.* 1919, Elsie, *d.* of late Dr. G. H. Crowther, Brighton, Victoria, Australia; four *s.* two *d.* *Educ.:* Wesley College, Melbourne; Queen's College, Melbourne (M.B. and B.S. 1909, M.D. 1911, M.S. 1913). F.R.C.S. England, 1919; Assistant Director Medical Services, Australian Imperial Forces, 1915-17 (C.M.G.); Director-General of Medical Services, Royal Australian Air Force, 1940-45; Pres., Victorian Branch of British Medical Association, 1931; Chm. Australian Red Cross Society, 1940; Consulting Surgeon Royal Melbourne Hospital, Pres. 1947; President R.A.C.S., 1951; Pres. Medico Legal Society of Victoria, 1948; Pres. Federal Council of British Medical Assoc., 1949. *Address:* 14 Parliament Place, Melbourne, C.2, Australia. *Clubs:* Melbourne, Naval and Military (Melbourne). [*Died* 17 *July* 1958.

HURRELL, Ven. William Philip, M.A.; Archdeacon of Loughborough, 1923-1940, Archdeacon Emeritus, 1940; Hon. Canon of Peterborough, 1916; Canon Treasurer of St. Martin's Collegiate Church, Leicester, 1922; Canon of Leicester Cathedral, 1927; *b.* Newton, 27 Jan. 1860; *s.* of William Hurrell, J P., and Charlotte Jane, *d.* of Philip Dykes; *m.* 1893, Harriette Mary, *d.* of Rev. Haydn Aldersey and Mary Taylor; no *c.* *Educ.:* Charterhouse; Oriel College, Oxford; Ely Theological College. Curate of Fen Ditton, 1883-84; Elm, 1884-86; St. Mark, Peterborough, 1886-92; Vicar of St. James, Northampton, 1892-1905; Vicar of Hinckley, 1905-22; Rural Dean, 1909; Secretary of Church Congress, 1902. *Address:* St. Heliers, Knighton Rise, Leicester. *T.:* Leicester 77576. [*Died* 15 *July* 1952.

HURREN, Samuel; Commissioner of the Salvation Army, retired; *b.* London, 1875; *m.* 1898, Emily Priest, Salvation Army Officer; one *s.* one *d.* Entered the Salvation Army as an Officer, 1891; has held important administrative posts at the International Headquarters, London, including that of Chancellor of the Exchequer, 1919-25; Managing Director of the Salvation Army Fire Insurance Corporation, Ltd., Managing Director of the Reliance Bank; Director of the Salvation Army Trustee Co.; command of the British Territory, 1925-1931, and Principal Wm. Booth Memorial Training College, 1931-41. *Address:* Salvation Army, Denmark Hill, S.E.5; Broadstairs, Kent. [*Died* 3 *Dec.* 1953.

HURST, His Honour Sir Gerald Berkeley, Kt., *cr.* 1929; Q.C. 1920; M.A., B.C.L. (Oxon.); T.D.; J.P. Kent; *b.* Bradford, 4 Dec. 1877; *m.* 1905, Margaret Alice, *d.* of late Sir Alfred Hopkinson, K.C.; (one *s.* killed in action 7 April 1941) five *d.* *Educ.:* Bradford Grammar School; Lincoln College, Oxford (scholar). 1st class Modern History, 1898; Arnold Historical Essay Prize, 1900; Barrister, Lincoln's Inn, 1902; Bencher, 1924; Treasurer, 1944; practised at the Chancery Bar till 1937; M.P. (C.) Manchester (Moss Side), 1918-23, and 1924-1935; Judge of County Courts, Circuit 56 (Croydon and West Kent), 1938-52; late Lt.-Col. commanding 7th Bn. Manchester Regiment; served in Sudan, Gallipoli, Egypt, Sinai, Flanders, 1914-18; conducted Maidstone Aliens Tribunal, 1939; Chairman of Conscientious Objectors Tribunals, 1940 and 1955; Commissioner for divorce cases, 1947-55. Chairman Home Office Cttee. on Adoption, 1953. *Publications:* books and articles on history and politics; Closed Chapters, 1942; Short History of Lincoln's Inn, 1946; Lincoln's Inn Essays, 1949. *Address:* 1 Chestnuts Royal, Chislehurst, Kent. *T.:* Imperial 1769. *Club:* Athenæum. [*Died* 27 *Oct.* 1957.

HURST, Colonel Herbert Clarence, C.B.E. 1935; D.S.O. 1916; V.D.; *b.* Opawa, Christchurch, N.Z., 22 Nov. 1884; *m.* 1920, Veronica Mary, *d.* of late Hon. James Holmes, M.L.C., of Hokitika, N.Z. *Educ.:* Opawa School. Continuous Military Service since April 1903; Active Service, 5 Aug. 1914-1918 (wounded four times, despatches five times, D.S.O., Order of the Nile, 4th Class); Lt.-Col. Canterbury Yeo. Cavalry, 1925-29; Commanded 3rd New Zealand Mounted Rifles Brigade 1929-35; retired 1935; on Reserve of Officers; Col. N. Z. Mounted Rifles, Reserve of Officers, 1935; Colonial Officers' Auxiliary Decoration, 1924; A.D.C. to Governor-General, 1930-35; J.P., N.Z., 1928. *Recreations:* active interest in all kinds of sport. *Address:* Hurst & Drake, Ltd., Oil and Colourmen, 22 Ferry Road, Christchurch, C.1, New Zealand. [*Died* 20 *June* 1951.

HURST, James Edgar, C.B.E. 1953; J.P.; M.I.Mech.E.; Director, The Staveley Coal & Iron Co., Ltd.; *b.* 1 Dec. 1893; *e. s.* of John and Annie Hurst, Hadfield, Derbyshire; *m.* 1916, Margery, *d.* of Benjamin Whiteley, Leeds; one *s.* one *d.* *Educ.:* Glossop Grammar School; Manchester School of Technology. President: Inst. of British Foundrymen, 1935; Staffordshire Iron and Steel Inst., 1944-47; British Cast Iron Research Assoc., 1950-52; Inst. of Vitreous Enamellers, 1950-52; National Trades Technical Socs. Founder Fell., Inst. of Metallurgists; Liveryman Worshipful Company of Founders; Freeman of City of London. Sheriff of Co. of City of Lichfield, 1946; J.P. City of Lichfield; Chm. Lichfield Johnson Society. Oliver Stubbs and E. J. Fox Gold Medals, Inst. of British Foundrymen. Hon. Degrees: D.Met., Sheffield Univ., 1939; Dr.Ingénieur, Univ. of Karlsruhe, 1956. *Publications:* Metallurgy of Cast Iron, 1926; Melting Iron in the Cupola, 1928. Papers on Metallurgical subjects in journals of Metallurgical Societies. *Recreation:* fly fishing. *Address:*

Tregonatha, Gaia Lane, Lichfield, Staffs. *T.:* Lichfield 2339. *Club:* Constitutional. [*Died* 21 *June* 1959.

HUSSEY, Edward Windsor, M.A. (Oxon); D.L., J.P.; *b.* 1855; *s.* of Edward Hussey of Scotney and Henrietta Sarah, *d.* of Hon. Robert Clive and Baroness Windsor; *m.* 1900, Mary Rosamond, *d.* of Lt.-Col. P. R. Anstruther, 94th Regt.; no *c.* *Educ.:* Eton; Christ Church, Oxford. Barrister, Inner Temple. High Sheriff of Kent, 1907. Late Lt.-Col. and Hon. Col. 2 Vol. Bn. The Buffs (V.D.). *Address:* Scotney Castle, Lamberhurst, Kent. *T.:* 261. *Club:* Carlton. [*Died* 17 *Oct.* 1952.

HUSSEY, Eric Robert James, C.M.G. 1938; Order of the Nile, 4th class; *b.* Blandford, Dorset, 26 April 1885; *s.* of Rev. James Hussey and Martha Ellen Hewett; *m.* 1922, Christine Elizabeth Justice, *d.* of late A. Noel Morley; one *s.* one *d.* *Educ.:* Repton (Scholar); Hertford College, Oxford (open exhibitioner). B.A. 1908 (Lit. Hum.), M.A. 1923; Sudan Civil Service as tutor, Gordon College, Khartoum, 1908; District Commissioner, 1912; Chief Inspector, Education Department, Sudan, 1918; Educational Mission to Somaliland, 1920; Educational Mission to Uganda, 1924; Director of Education, Uganda, 1925; Educational Mission to Kenya, 1928; Director of Education, Nigeria, 1929-36; Secretary, National Society, 1936-42; Educational Adviser to Emperor of Ethiopia, 1942-1944; Member, Board of Inspectors, Achimota College, Gold Coast, 1932; Heath Clark Lecturer (joint), University of London, 1939; Member Governing Body of School of Oriental and African Studies, 1939; of Advisory Committee on Education in the Colonies, 1940; Educational Mission to Eritrea, 1952; Fellow of Woodard Corporation, 1948, Governing Body, Lancing, Hurstpierpoint (Chm.), and Ardingley. Represented Oxford v. Cambridge (hurdles), 1904-8; President, O.U.A.C., 1907 and 1908; represented Great Britain, Olympic Games (hurdles) in London, 1908. *Recreations:* tennis and golf. *Address:* Painswold, Cuckfield, Sussex. *T.:* 263. *Club:* Athenæum. [*Died* 19 *May* 1958.

HUSSEY, Capt. Thomas Edgar Cyril, D.L.; J.P.; *b.* 3 Apr. 1884; *s.* of late Thomas Arthur Hussey, Norton Court, Norton Fitzwarren, Som.; *m.* 1919, Alice Mary Taylor Pope (*d.* 1958), *widow* of Col. Philip Pope, D.L., 4th Dragoon Guards, *d.* of late Charles Taylor, J.P., Horton Manor, Bucks., and *g.d.* of Sir George Elliot, 1st Bt., M.P.; no *c.* *Educ.:* Leamington Coll. Commissioned R.A. 1909, seconded to Colonial Office for service in W. Africa, 1913. European War 1914-19, France, Capt. 1916; retired 1921. Rejoined Regt. July 1939, and subsequently employed by Ministries of Supply and Information until end of war. J.P. Hampshire, 1943; High Sheriff of Hampshire, 1948-49; D.L. Hampshire, 1953. Serving on Visiting Committee H.M. Prison, and Board of Visitors, Borstal Instns. Mem. Magistrates' Assoc. Gen. Council and Cttees. Chairman Droxford P.S.D. Bench. *Recreations:* travelling and gardening. *Address:* Lithend, Bishops Waltham, Hampshire. *T.:* Bishops Waltham 99. *Clubs:* Royal Automobile; Hampshire (Winchester). [*Died* 10 *June* 1958.

HUSTON, Major D. W. W. D. M.; *see* Chapman-Huston.

HUTCHEON, Sir Alexander Byres, K.B.E., *cr.* 1949 (M.B.E. 1920); C.M.G. 1942; Adviser on Establishments, Foreign Office, since 1950; *b.* 17 Feb. 1891; *m.* 1947, Aileen Constance Elles Petersen; one *s.* Entered General Post Office, 1909; Estate Duty Office, 1911; Vice-Consul in Consular Service, 1913; Senior Inspector of H.M. Foreign Service Establishments abroad, 1947-50. *Address:* Foreign Office, 8 Carlton House Terrace, S.W.1. [*Died* 19 *Jan.* 1956.

HUTCHESON, Capt. Bellenden Seymour, V.C. 1918; M.C.; M.D.; late Canadian Army Medical Corps; engaged in the practice of medicine in Cairo, Illinois, U.S.A.; Member of Staff of St. Mary's Hospital, Cairo; Acting Asst. Surgeon U.S. Public Health Service; Member American Medical Association and Illinois State Medical Society; *b.* Mt. Carmel, Illinois, U.S.A., 16 Dec. 1883; *s.* of Bellenden Hutcheson and Luella Wiley; *m.* 1919, Frances Rand, *e. d.* of William Young and Margaret Rand Young, of Kentville, Nova Scotia; one *s.* *Educ.:* North-western University, Chicago. Graduated at Mound City, Illinois High School, 1901; entered North-western University Medical School, Chicago, 1902; graduated from Medical School, 1906, and served as House Surgeon in Alexian Brothers Hospital, Chicago, for one year; practised medicine and surgery first in Iowa, then in Illinois, until entering Canadian Army Medical Corps, 1915. *Address:* 3011 Park Place west, Cairo, Illinois, U.S.A. [*Died* 9 *April* 1954.

HUTCHESON, John, C.B.E. 1937; Woollen Yarn Spinner; Chairman South of Scotland Woollen Manufacturers' Mutual Insurance Corporation, Ltd.; Chairman Scottish Wool Spinners Association; Vice-President Scottish Amicable Life Assurance Society; Chairman of Merchiston Castle School; Vice-President Association of British Chambers of Commerce; *b.* Greenock, 4 July 1870; *s.* of John Mitchell Hutcheson; *m.* 1899, Mabel Lizzie Teacher (*d.* 1947); two *s.* (and *y. s.* killed on active service) one *d.* *Educ.:* Merchiston Castle School. Late Chairman National Association of Scottish Woollen Manufacturers; late Chm. Roxburgh and Selkirk Unionist Association. *Recreations:* gardening, golf, fishing. *Address:* St. Aidans, Melrose. *T.:* Melrose 24. *Clubs:* Junior Constitutional; Scottish Conservative (Edinburgh); Royal Scottish Automobile (Glasgow). [*Died* 17 *May* 1959.

HUTCHINGS, Sir Alan, K.B.E., *cr.* 1920 (O.B.E. 1918); Lord of the Manor of Sutton-cum-Seaford; *b.* 9 May 1880; *o. s.* of Alfred Blandford Hutchings and Emma, *d.* of late Captain William Greet, R.N. *Educ.:* Tonbridge School; Royal Agricultural College, Cirencester (Honour Diploma and Ducie Gold Medal, 1900). Temporary Paymaster Army Pay Dept., 1914-15; member, Surveyors' Institution; late Secretary of Dept. of Director-General of Voluntary Organisations (War Office), 1915-19; member of several Government committees in connection with the War of 1914-18; Director-General of Voluntary Organisations, 1939-40; contested (C.) Louth Div. Lincolnshire By-Election, 1921; General Election, 1922. *Recreations:* golf and agriculture. *Clubs:* Carlton, Constitutional, Farmers', White's. [*Died* 26 *June* 1951.

HUTCHINGS, Norman Edwin, C.B.E. 1939; retired as Chief Admin. Officer, Ministry of Works, New Zealand (1952-58); *b.* 19 June 1899; *s.* of Edwin Alfred and Mary Hutchings; *m.* 1928, Olive Carson Warin. *Educ.:* Whangarei High School. Joined Public Works Dept. as cadet in 1916; Private Secretary to Public Works Ministers, 1926-1936; rejoined P.W.D. as Head Office Chief Clerk, 1936; Assistant Under-Secretary, 1938; Under Secretary, 1943. *Address:* 9 Penrose Street, Lower Hutt, Wellington, N.Z. [*Died* 11 *Jan.* 1960.

HUTCHINSON, Christopher D. H.; *see* Hely-Hutchinson.

HUTCHINSON, Colonel Thomas Massie, D.S.O. 1917; O.B.E. 1919; M.I.A.E., M.I.Mech.E.; Director Hammond Engineering Co. Ltd., Chase Side, Enfield; *b.* Harpurhey, Lancs, 14 Feb. 1877; *s.* of Rev. T. W. Hutchinson, M.A., Vicar, Stoke Row, Henley-on-Thames; *m.* 1933, Alice Gwendoline *o.d.* of

late Thomas Dent, Barnard Castle, Durham. *Educ.:* private tutors; Cambridge; Engineering and Technical Training, City and Guilds Institute, London; Bronze Medal and 1st Class Honours. First commissioned in 4th Suffolk (Cambs.) Militia, 2nd Lieut. 1898; gazetted 1st East Surrey Regiment, 2nd Lieut. 1899; Lieut. 1901; transferred to A.S.C. 1901; Capt. 1905; Major, 1914; acting Lt.-Col. 1917; Lt.-Col. 1922; Col. 1926; went South Africa, 1899, and served through Boer War in Natal, Zululand, Pongola Bush, Transvaal, Orange Free State, and Cape Colony (Queen's medal four clasps, King's medal two clasps); returned England, 1902, and was one of the pioneer members of the A.S.C. Mechanical Transport; in charge all A.S.C. M.T. vehicles, Irish command, 1904-7; M.T. Instructor at A.S.C. Training Establishment, Aldershot, 1907-14; member of War Office Mechanical Transport Committee, 1913; Secretary, 1914; Chief Inspector of Mechanical Transport to British Expeditionary Forces in France and Flanders on Staff of Transport Directorate, 1915-20 (D.S.O., O.B.E., despatches four times, 1915 Star, Allied and Victory medals), and War Office, 1920-24; Mechanical Transport Adviser, India Office, 1926-30; retired pay, 1933; lately member of War Office M.T. Advisory Board; of Tank Technical Sub-Committee; of British Engineering Standards Automobile Committees; and of Engineering Board, Scientific and Industrial Research Department; Chairman Technical Mechanical Transport Committee (India). *Address:* Thickthorns, Winnersh, Berks. *T.:* Wokingham 730.
[*Died* 16 *Aug.* 1952.

HUTCHISON, Sir Robert, 1st Bt., *cr.* 1939; M.D., F.R.C.P.; Consulting Physician to London Hospital and Children's Hospital, Great Ormond Street, W.C.; and to Royal Dental Hospital; Ex-President Royal College of Physicians; Ex-President Royal Society of Med.; *b.* Kirkliston, Midlothian, 1871; *m.* 1905, Laetitia Norah, *d.* of late Very Rev. Dr. Moore-Ede; two *s.* one *d.* *Educ.:* Universities of Edinburgh, Strasburg, and Paris. M.D. Edinburgh, 1896; F.R.C.P. London, 1903, Hon. F.R.C.P. Ed.; Hon. LL.D. (Ed. and Birmingham); Hon. D.Sc. Oxon.; Hon. M.D. Melbourne; Stark and Ettles Scholar and Leckie Macktier Fellow, University of Edinburgh; Goulstonian Lecturer, Royal College of Physicians, 1904; Harveian Orator, 1931; Member of Committee on Corporal Punishment, 1937. *Publications:* Food and the Principles of Dietetics; Clinical Methods; Lectures on Diseases of Children; Applied Physiology; Lectures on Dyspepsia; For and Against Doctors, an Anthology (with Dr. G. M. Wauchope); papers in medical and scientific journals. *Heir:* *s.* Peter [*b.* 27 Sept. 1907; *m.* 1949, Mary Grace, *d.* of late Very Rev. Algernon Giles Seymour; one *s.* two *d.* *Educ.:* Marlborough College; Lincoln College, Oxford, B.A. Solicitor, 1933]. *Address:* Thurle Grange, Streatley, Berks. *T.:* Goring-on-Thames 228.
[*Died* 12 *Feb.* 1960.

HUTSON, Thomas; Assistant Under Secretary of State, Home Office, since 1950; *b.* 16 May 1896; *yr. s.* of late Guybon Hutson and of Annie (*née* Taylor). *Educ.:* Glasgow Academy; Glasgow University. M.A. 1915. Served European War, 1914-18, K.O.S.B., 1915-19; Capt., 1917; staff, 1917-19. Home Office, 1920; acting Asst. Under Sec. of State, 1941; Assistant Secretary, Royal Commission on Licensing, 1929-31; Secretary, Hailey Conference on Deep Shelters, 1940; Director of Internal Affairs, Control Commission for Austria, 1946-47. *Recreations:* continental travel, mountaineering, motoring, bridge. *Address:* 26 Earls Court Square, S.W.5. *Clubs:* Reform; Walton Heath; Rye.
[*Died* 19 *July* 1952.

HUTTEN, Baroness von; *b.* Erie, Pa., U.S.A., 1874; *d.* of John Riddle; *m.* 1897, Freiherr von Hutten zum Stolzenberg (divorced by mutual consent, 1909); two *s.* two *d.* *Educ.:* New York. In 1938 regained her U.S. nationality; lived in California until 1948, now living in Europe. *Publications:* Pam; What Became of Pam; Kingsmead; Sharrow, 1912; Mothers-in-Law, 1922; Pam at Fifty, 1923; The Halo; Our Lady of the Beeches; Julia; Mrs. Drummond's Vocation; Yellowleaf; Happy House; Eddy and Edouard; Pam's Own Story; Monkey Puzzle; Cora Pearl; Die She Must; The Elgin Marble; Cowardy Custard (in New York Gentlemen's Agreement); The Mem; What Happened is This; Mice for Amusement. *Recreations:* travel, reading, music. *Address:* c/o Revd. Mother Superior, Convent of Bon Secours, 166 Westbourne Grove, W.11.
[*Died* 26 *Jan.* 1957.

HUTTON, Lady, (Isabel Emslie), C.B.E. 1948; M.D.; Emeritus Consultant Psychiatrist British Hospital for Mental and Nervous Disorders; *o. d.* of James Emslie, Edinburgh; *m.* 1921, Major Thomas Jacomb Hutton, M.C., R.A. (later Lt.-Gen. Sir Thomas Hutton). *Educ.:* Edinburgh Ladies' Coll.; Edinburgh Univ. Graduated in Medicine at Edinburgh Univ., 1910; M.D. (Hons.), 1912; studied in Munich, Vienna and other European medical centres. Late Resident Physician Royal Sick Children's Hosp., Edinburgh; pathologist Stirling Dist. Mental Hosp.; Physician Royal Mental Hosp., Edinburgh; thereafter specialised (except during two world wars) in the study and treatment of mental and nervous disorders and has held many appointments in London Hospitals. Fellow of R.S.M.; mem. of Royal Medico-Psychological Assocn., etc. Served European War, 1914-18, 1915-20 with Scottish Women's Hosps. in Macedonia and Serbia, latterly as C.M.O.; C.O. Lady Muriel Paget Hosp., in Sebastopol, Crimea (White Eagle of Serbia, St. Sava of Serbia, Royal Red Cross, Serbia, Croix de Guerre, France, St. Anne of Russia, C.St.J.); War of 1939-45, Director of Indian Red Cross Welfare Service. *Publications:* With a Woman's Unit in Salonika, Serbia and Sebastopol, 1928; Mental Disorders in Modern Life, 1940; The Hygiene of Marriage, 9th edn. 1953; Woman's Change of Life, 1958; and contributions to medical journals. *Recreations:* music, languages and the ballet. *Address:* 5 Spanish Place, W.1. *T.:* Welbeck 8831. *Club:* University Women's.
[*Died* 11 *Jan.* 1960.

HUTTON, James Arthur; Chevalier de l'Ordre de Léopold; Vice-President Empire Cotton Growing Corp., and British Cotton Growing Assoc.; Vice-Pres. National Assoc. of Fishery Boards; Member Wye Board of Conservators; Council Salmon and Trout Assoc.; Council Anglo-Norwegian Fishermen's Assoc.; Director Atlas Insurance Co. (Chairman Manchester Local Board); *b.* Bowdon, 1862; 4th *s.* of late James F. Hutton, formerly M.P. for North Manchester; *m.* Emily Fenton, *d.* of late J. J. Armitage; no *c.* *Educ.:* St. Paul's College, Stony Stratford; Heidelberg. Was one of the founders of the British Cotton Growing Association, and devoted many years to the development of cotton growing in the British Empire, and has written numerous pamphlets on cotton growing; takes a great interest in the economic development of the salmon fisheries of the country, and has carried out scientific investigations in connection with the life-history of salmon and other fish, and has published several reports on the subject. *Publications:* The Work of the British Cotton Growing Association; Cotton Growing in the British Empire; Scale Examination; The Life-history of the Salmon; Rod-fishing for Salmon on the Wye; The Reminiscences of Halsten Muri; Our Fishing Diary; Wye Salmon and Other Fish. *Recreations:* fishing, photography. *Address:* Woodlands, Alderley Edge. *T.A.:* Hutton, Woodlands, Alderley Edge. *T.:* Alderley 3111. *Clubs:* Flyfishers'; Union (Manchester).
[*Died* 28 *Feb.* 1955.

HUTTON-WILSON, Col. Arthur Harry, D.S.O. 1917; Director, Egglescliffe Chemical Co. Ltd. and Blue Pool (Camberley) Ltd.; *b.* 10 Sept. 1873; *e. s.* of late R. Hutton-Wilson and Emily Margaret, *d.* of T. W. Waldy, of Egglescliffe, Co. Durham; *m.* 1st, Edith Alice (*d.* 1937), *e. d.* of late Lieut.-Gen. Sir H. S. G. Miles, G.C.B., G.C.M.G.; one *s.* two *d.*; 2nd, 1938, Constance Mary, *widow* of James Buckley, Prestwich. *Educ.:* Charterhouse; Royal Military College. Joined Wiltshire Regiment, 1893; served S. African War (Queen's medal with 4 clasps, King's medal and 2 clasps); graduated Staff College, 1902-03; A.D.C. to G.O.C. Cape Colony, 1903; Staff Captain at War Office, 1904; D.A.A.G. at War Office, 1905-09; Brigade Major 10th Infantry Brigade, 1911-14; General Staff, War Office, 1914-15; served European War, 1915-18 (despatches thrice, Bt. Lieut.-Col., D.S.O., Légion d'Honneur, Ordre de la Couronne); General Staff, France, 1915-17; A.A. and Q.M.G., France, 1917-18; Brig.-Gen. Commanding British Troops, Paris, 1919; A.A.G. War Office, 1919-20; A.A.G. British Army of the Rhine, 1920-24; Col. i/c Records, York, 1925-28; retired pay, 1928; Home Guard 1st Surrey Bn., 1940-43. *Recreations:* shooting, fishing and golf. *Address:* Crawley Lodge, Crawley Ridge, Camberley, Surrey. *T.:* 229. *Club:* Army and Navy. [*Died* 23 *Jan.* 1955.

HYAMSON, Albert Montefiore, O.B.E. 1931; F.R.Hist.S.; late Director, Dept. of Immigration, Gov. of Palestine; ret. 1934; Council and Executive Committee, formerly Hon. Treas., Palestine Exploration Fund; Treasurer: British School of Archæology in Jerusalem; Hon. Member Jericho Excavation Fund and Vice-President and Hon. Editor of Publications (President 1945-47), Jewish Historical Society; Vice-President Jewish Book Council; Archives Cttee., Spanish and Portuguese Jewish Community; Exec. Cttee. Anglo-Jewish Tercentenary Council; Exec. Cttee. Jewish Soc. for Human Service; Editorial Bd., Jl. of Jewish Studies; *b.* London, 27 Aug. 1875; *m.* 1911, Marie Rose Lavey, two *d.* (and two *s.* killed in War of 1939-1945). *Educ.:* Swansea Grammar School; Beaufort College, St. Leonards. Entered British Civil Service (Post Office), 1895; transferred to Government of Palestine, 1921; First Hon. Secretary and subsequently Vice-President Union of Jewish Literary Societies; Joint Hon. Secretary Whitehall Conference Celebration, 1906; Editor of Jewish Literary Annual, 1903-1906; Joint Editor of Zionist Review, 1917-1919, and of Vallentine's Jewish Encyclopædia, 1938; Editor of Jewish Year Book 1940-50. *Publications:* A History of the Jews in England, 1908 (Second Edition, 1928); The Story of the Whitehall Conference and the Return of the Jews to England, 1905; The Jubilee of Jewish Emancipation in England, 1908; Humour of the Post Office, 1909; Elizabethan Adventurers on the Spanish Main, 1911; The Buccaneers of the Spanish Main, 1912; A Dictionary of Universal Biography, 1915 (2nd edn. 1951); Palestine: The Rebirth of an Ancient People, 1917; A Dictionary of English Phrases, 1922; Palestine, Old and New, 1928; Judas Maccabaeus, 1935; David Salomons, 1939; The British Consulate in Jerusalem, Pt. I, 1939, Pt. II, 1941; Palestine: a Policy, 1942; a Dictionary of International Affairs, 1946; Palestine under the Mandate, 1950; The Sephardim of England, 1951, etc.; contributor to the Dictionary of National Biography, Encyclopædia of Religion and Ethics, Quarterly Review, etc. *Address:* 12A Faraday Mansions, Queen's Club Gardens, W.14. [*Died* 5 *Oct.* 1954.

HYDE, Sir Harry, Kt., *cr.* 1953; J.P.; *m.* 1902; three *s.* one *d.* Chairman Co-ordination Cttee. and Manchester Assizes Cttee.; Commissioner of Taxes, Middleton, Rochdale and Oldham div. J.P. 1929, Councillor 1922, Ashton-under-Lyne. J.P. 1937, C.A. 1948, Lancs; Vice-Chm. C.C. 1946; Chm. 1948-49. Chm. Conservative Group, Lancashire C.C.; Pres. Ashton-under-Lyne Conservative Assoc. *Address:* Sylvester House, Ashton-under-Lyne, Lancs. *T.:* 2410. *Club:* Union. [*Died* 2 *Jan.* 1957.

HYDE, Walter, Hon. A.R.C.M., F.G.S.M.; Professor of Singing, Guildhall School of Music, E.C.4; *b.* Birmingham; *s.* of Henry M. Hyde; *m.* 1905, Esmé Atherden. *Educ.:* Birmingham; Royal College of Music, London (open Scholarship). Studied under Gustav Garcia, Sir Charles V. Stanford, Sir Walter Parratt, Cairns James; started career in light opera; graduated through concerts to Wagnerian Opera; has appeared at Metropolitan Opera, New York, Chicago, Boston, Buda-Pesth and Covent Garden; also all leading provincial concerts and festivals, including Handel Festival (3 festivals). *Recreations:* golf, reading, walking. *Address:* 23 King's Gardens, West End Lane, N.W.6. *T.:* Maida Vale 4385. [*Died* 11 *Nov.* 1951.

HYDE, Walter Henry; *b.* 1864; *s.* of William and Susannah Hyde; *m.* 1892, Helen, *d.* of Walter and Elizabeth Spare; one *s.* Commenced his business career in the secretary's office, Great Eastern Railway; Chief Accountant, 1897; General Manager, Great Eastern Railway, 1910-14; lectured on railway accounts at the School of Economics, 1904-05; a member of Sub-Committee A of Board of Trade Conference, 1908-09; Freeman of the City of London, 1911; Member of Needlemakers Company, 1918. [*Died* 10 *Dec.* 1953.

HYDE PARKER; *see* Parker.

HYNARD, Sir William (George), Kt., *cr.* 1946; C.B. 1939; C.B.E. 1920; *b.* 1881; *s.* of late W. Hynard, East Bergholt, Suffolk; *m.* Lysbeth, *d.* of F. Byard, artist, Queen's Avenue, Finchley; no *c. Educ.:* Bancroft's School, Essex. Joined Civil Service, Admiralty 1899, Ministry of Shipping, 1917; Assistant Director of Naval Sea Transport, 1918; Director of Naval Sea Transport, 1920-21; Director of Sea Transport, Mercantile Marine Dept., Board of Trade, 1929-39; Ministry of Transport, 1939-44; Representative of Minister of Transport, in Canada, 1944-46. Chevalier Legion of Honour, 1920; Officer of the Order of the Crown of Italy, 1921. *Address:* 30 Aylmer Road, N.2. [*Died* 22 *May* 1953.

HYNE, Engineer-Rear-Adm. Arthur Edward, C.M.G. 1919; retired, R.N.; *b.* 1874; Engineer Overseer for the Admiralty in Scottish District, 1925. *Address:* 98 Burbage Rd., Herne Hill, S.E.29. [*Died* 10 *June* 1956.

I

IBBOTSON, Sir William, Kt., *cr.* 1944; C.I.E. 1934; M.B.E. 1919; M.C.; retired; *b.* 25 Jan. 1886; *s.* of Robert Ibbotson, Knowle, Warwickshire; *m.* 1921, Dorothea Jean, *d.* of Rev. R. G. Yates, Sevenoaks; one *s.* (and one *s.* decd.). *Educ.:* King Edward's Sch., Birmingham; Pembroke Coll., Camb. B.A. 1908; Senior Wrangler; M.A. 1919; entered Indian Civil Service, 1909. Indian Army R. of O., attached 17th Cavalry and 18th Lancers, 1915-19. Revenue Minister and Special Comr., Alwar, 1933-34; Director-General Civil Defence and Secretary Government of India, 1941-43; Adviser to Governor of U.P., 1943-45; retd. from I.C.S., 1945. *Address:* Karen, P.O. Ngong, Kenya. *Club:* Karen Country (Ngong). [*Died* 2 *May* 1956.

IDELSON, Vladimir Robert, Q.C. 1943; *b.* at Rostov on Don; *e. s.* of Robert Idelson and Mary Gordon; *m.* 1918, Taissa Lipkine; two *s.* *Educ.:* Taganrog Classical Gymnasium; Univ. of Kharkov (First Class Law Degree); Univ. of Berlin (Dr. Phil., M.C.L.). Called to Russian Bar, 1906; practised in Russia, until 1918; Dozent, Imperial Polytechnic Institute until 1918; Member of Council of Russian and English Bank and of Committee of Union of Russian Banks, 1914-17; Russian Treasury, 1917; practised in London as expert on Russian and International Law, 1919-26; called to English Bar, Gray's Inn, 1926; naturalised British subject, 1930. Bencher Lincoln's Inn 1947; Mem. Exec. Councils of Grotius Soc. and Soc. of Comparative Legislation; Member Law Advisory Committee of British Council. *Publications:* Contract of Insurance in Russian Law, 1903 (in Russian); Taxation of Insurance, 1905 (in German); contributions to English and foreign legal magazines on Banking, Insurance, and International Law. *Recreations:* travel, study of languages. *Address:* 20 Sandy Lodge Road, Moor Park, Herts. *T.:* Rickmansworth 3556; 13 Old Square, Lincoln's Inn, W.C.2. *T.:* Holborn 5682. *Clubs:* Reform, Royal Thames Yacht. [*Died* 29 *Nov.* 1954.

ILCHESTER, 6th Earl of, *cr.* 1756; **Giles Stephen Holland Fox-Strangways,** Baron Ilchester and Strangways, 1741, Baron Ilchester and Stavordale, Baron Redlynch (G.B.) 1747; G.B.E., *cr.* 1950 (O.B.E.); late Captain, R. of O.; Hon.D.Litt.; F.S.A.; Trustee of National Portrait Gallery, (Chm. since 1941); Trustee of British Museum since 1931; Chm. Royal Commission on Historical Buildings, 1943-57; President of London Library, 1940-52; *b.* 31 May 1874; *e. s.* of 5th Earl of Ilchester and Mary (*d.* 1935), *o. d.* of 1st Earl of Dartrey, K.P.; *S.* father, 1905; *m.* 1902, Lady Helen Stewart (*d.* 1956), *o. d.* of 6th Marquess of Londonderry; two *s.* one *d.* Late 2nd Lieut. Coldstream Guards. Chevalier French Legion of Honour, 1918. *Publications:* edited Life and Letters of Lady Sarah Lennox (with the Countess of Ilchester), 1901; Further Memoirs of the Whig Party, 1807-21, by 3rd Lord Holland; edited The Journals of Elizabeth, Lady Holland, 1908; Henry Fox, First Lord Holland, 1920; The Journal of Hon. Henry Edward Fox, 1818-30, 1924; (with Mrs. Langford-Brooke) Catherine the Great, and The Life of Sir Charles Hanbury-Williams, 1929; The Home of the Hollands, 1605-1820, 1937; Chronicles of Holland House, 1820-1900, 1937; Letters of Lady Holland, to her Son, 1946; Lord Hervey and His Friends, 1726-38, 1950; (with late Sir Henry Hake) Vertue MSS. (for Walpole Soc.) 7 vols. (reproductions etc.), finished 1955. *Heir:* *s.* Lord Stavordale, D.L. *Address:* 14 Montagu Square, W.1. [*Died* 29 *Oct.* 1959.

ILES, John Henry, O.B.E. 1944; J.P. (retd.); Officier d'Académie Française; Founder and Director, National Band Festival, Crystal Palace; *b.* Bristol; 2nd *s.* of late J. T. Iles, Clifton; *m.* Marion, 3rd *d.* of late Fredk. Bird, J.P., C.C., of Norton House, Midsomer Norton; three *s.* one *d.* *Educ.:* Ashville Coll., Harrogate. Founded weekly newspaper, British Bandsman; conducted World's Tours of Besses o' the Barn and other bands; introduced the American Amusements Parks to Europe, including Scenic Railways; Hon. Entertainment Director of Lord Kitchener Memorial Fund; President for twenty-seven years of London and Home Counties Band Association; First President of National Band Club; Past Chairman, London Press Club; Past President, Margate Rotary Club; Master of the Court of the Worshipful Company of Musicians, 1933. *Publication:* Editor-in-Chief, British Bandsman. *Recreations:* golf, played for Gloucestershire C.C. 1890-91. *Address:* 210 Strand, W.C.2. *Club:* London Press (Life Member). [*Died* 29 *May* 1951.

ILIFFE, of Yattendon, 1st Baron, *cr.* 1933, **Edward Mauger Iliffe,** G.B.E., *cr.* 1946 (C.B.E. 1918); Kt., *cr.* 1922; Officer of the Legion of Honour; Knight of Order of St. John; J.P. Warwickshire; Chairman of Guildhall Insurance Co. Ltd., Director of the London Assurance; President (formerly Chairman), Birmingham Post and Mail Ltd.; Director and principal shareholder, Coventry Evening Telegraph and Cambridge Daily News; a Member of Lloyds; President, Trustees of the Shakespeare Memorial Theatre, Stratford-on-Avon, 1933-58; President, International Lawn Tennis Club of Great Britain, 1945-59; *b.* 17 May 1877; *s.* of late Wm. Iliffe, J.P., of Allesley, Warwickshire; *m.* 1902, Charlotte, *d.* of late Henry Gilding, J.P., of Gateacre, nr. Liverpool; one *s.* one *d.* (and one *s.* decd.). M.P. (U.) Tamworth Div. of Warwickshire, 1923-29; Chm. of the Duke of Gloucester's Fifty-seven million Red Cross and St. John Fund, 1939-45; President of Assoc. of British Chambers of Commerce, 1932; Controller Machine Tool Dept., Ministry of Munitions, 1917-18; Master of Coach Makers' & Coach Harness Makers' Company, 1936, of Company of Stationers and Newspaper Makers, 1937 and of Clockmakers' Company, 1946; President Periodical Proprietors' Association, 1935-38; Hon. Air Commodore No. 916/7 (Co. of Warwick) Balloon Squadron, R.A.F., 1939-44. *Heir:* *s.* Hon. E. Langton Iliffe. *Address:* Yattendon Court, near Newbury, Berks. *T.:* Yattendon 207; 23 Carlton House Terrace, S.W.1. *T.:* Whitehall 8264. *Clubs:* Brooks's, Carlton, All England Lawn Tennis; Royal Yacht Squadron (Cowes). [*Died* 25 *July* 1960.

ILKESTON, 2nd Baron, *cr.* 1910; **Balthazar Stephen Sargant Foster;** Stipendiary Magistrate, Birmingham, 1910-50, retd.; *b.* 31 Aug. 1867; *s.* of 1st Baron and Emily M. (*d.* 1920), *d.* of W. L. Sargant, Edgbaston; *S.* father, 1913; *m.* 1901, Mildred Charlotte, *d.* of late Henry P. Cobb, M.P. *Educ.:* Uppingham School; Magdalen College, Oxford; B.A. 1890. Called to Bar, Inner Temple, 1892; Midland Circuit, Revising Barrister, 1906-10; Chairman, Warwickshire Quarter Sessions, 1921-50. *Heir:* none. *Publication:* A Guide to the Law of Licensing, 1898. *Address:* 23 High Street, Warwick.
[*Died* 4 *Jan.* 1952 (*ext.*).

ILLINGWORTH, Captain Sir (Cyril) Gordon, Kt., *cr.* 1949; R.N.R. Ex-Commodore Cunard White Star Line; retd.; *m.* 1950, Mrs. Marie R. Caldwell. *Address:* c/o The Manager's Office, Cunard White Star Co. Ltd., Cunard Buildings, Pier Head, Liverpool, 3; c/o Cunard White Star Line, 88 Leadenhall Street, E.C.3.
[*Died* 7 *Aug.* 1959.

ILLINGWORTH, Dudley Holden, J.P.; Chairman: Hanlith Estate Ltd.; *b.* 3 Feb. 1876; *s.* of late Alfred Illingworth, Bradford; *m.* 1902, Florence (*d.* 1957), *d.* of J. E. Holden, Rheims; two *s.* one *d.* *Educ.:* Giggleswick School; Victoria Univ., Manchester (M.Sc.). Director-General British Committee, French Red Cross, 1914-19. Formerly Director National Provincial Bank Ltd. (and Chairman Bradford and District local board); Director: The London Assurance, 1928-56; Lister & Co. Ltd., 1932-56. J.P. West Riding of Yorks, 1923. K.St.J. 1919. Officier de la Légion d'Honneur (France), 1919. *Address:* Hanlith Hall, Kirkby Malham, Skipton, Yorks. [*Died* 2 *Oct.* 1958.

ILLINGWORTH, Capt. Sir Gordon; *see* Illingworth, Capt. Sir C. G.

IM THURN, Vice-Admiral John Knowles, C.B. 1931; C.M.G. 1924; C.B.E. 1919; *b.* 1881; *s.* of J. C. im Thurn; *m.* Margaret Elizabeth Fleming, *d.* of John Fleming, C.S.I. Served European War, 1914-19 (despatches, C.B.E.); Assistant Director of Electrical Torpedo and Mining Department Admiralty, 1918-1920; Director Signal Department Admiralty,

1920-21; Commanded H.M.S. Ceres, 1921-23; H.M.S. Hood, 1923-25; Commanded H.M. Signal School. Portsmouth, 1925-28; Chief of Staff, Mediterranean Fleet, Commodore 1st Class, 1928-30; Rear-Adm., 1929; Asst. Chief of Naval Staff, 1931-33; commanding First Cruiser Squadron, Mediterranean Fleet, 1933-35; Vice-Adm., 1935; retired list, 1935; Commodore R.N.R. Convoys, 1940; Admiralty, 1941-44. Knight of Malta, 1936, Bailiff Grand Cross, 1950. *Address:* Stainforth, near Settle, Yorks. *T.:* Settle 3179. *Club:* Army and Navy. [*Died* 5 *July* 1956.

INCE, Charles Percy, R.B.A., R.I., landscape painter; Director of C.F. Ince & Sons, Ltd., Printers; *b.* London, 10 June 1875; *e. s.* of Charles Frederick Ince; *m.* 1923, Norah, *d.* of Robert Gozney of Shireoaks, Notts; one *d.* *Educ.:* Cowper Street and King's College, London; pupil of the late Henry George Moon, landscape painter. *Recreation:* music. *Address:* Purbrook House, Purbrook, Hants. [*Died* 8 *July* 1952.

INCHES, Cyrus Fiske, D.S.O. 1919; M.C.; Q.C. (Can.) 1923; barrister, Inches and Hazen; *b.* 21 Jan. 1883; *s.* of P. Robertson Inches, M.D., and Mary Dorothea Isabel Fiske Inches; unmarried. *Educ.:* Saint John High School; King's College Law School; Harvard Law School. B.C.L., LL.B., LL.D. In France with first Canadian Heavy Battery as Lieutenant, Captain, Major and O.C., 1915-1919 (D.S.O., M.C., despatches twice); Member St. Andrews, N.B. Barristers' and Saint John Law Societies; Member Albion Lodge, A.F. and A.M.; Presbyterian. *Address:* Saint John, New Brunswick, Canada. *Clubs:* Sevogle Salmon, Cliff, Union (St. John). [*Died* 29 *Feb.* 1956.

ING, Colonel George Harold Absell, C.M.G. 1919; D.S.O. 1915; late 2nd Dragoon Guards (Queen's Bays); *b.* 24 Apr. 1880; *e. s.* of late George Ing; *m.* 1930, Eileen, widow of Lt.-Col. C. Harwood Manger, M.C., and *e. d.* of late Brig.-Gen. T. A. H. Bigge, C.B., C.M.G.; one *d.* Entered army, 1900; Capt. 1904; Major, 1911; served South Africa, 1901-2 (wounded, Queen's medal 5 clasps); European War, 1914-18 (wounded twice, despatches five times, D.S.O. and bar, C.M.G.); commanded North Somerset Yeomanry, 1917-18 and 1922-26; Lieut.-Col. Queen's Bays, 1918; retired pay, 1920; commanded 3rd Somerset Bn H.G., 1940-45. D.L. Somerset, 1944; High Sheriff of Dorset, 1948-1949. *Address:* Jerards, Sandford Orcas, Sherborne, Dorset. [*Died* 9 *Dec.* 1957.

INGE, Very Rev. William Ralph, K.C.V.O., *cr.* 1930 (C.V.O. 1918); F.B.A. 1921; D.D.; *b.* Crayke, Yorkshire, 6 June 1860; *e. s.* of late Rev. William Inge, D.D., Provost of Worcester College, Oxford, and Mary, *d.* of Ven. Edward Churton, Archdeacon of Cleveland; *m.* 1905, Mary Catharine (*d.* 1949), *d.* of late Ven. H. M. Spooner, Archdeacon of Maidstone, and *g.d.* of Bishop Harvey Goodwin; two *s.* one *d.* *Educ.:* Eton; King's College, Cambridge. Bell Scholar and Porson Prizeman, 1880; Porson Scholar, 1881; Craven Scholar and Browne Medallist, 1882; Senior Chancellor's Medallist, 1883; 1st class Classics, 1882 and 1883; Hare Prizeman, 1885; Assistant Master at Eton, 1884-88; Fellow of King's, 1886-88; Fellow and Tutor of Hertford College, Oxford, 1889-1904; Bampton Lecturer, 1899; Paddock Lecturer, New York, 1906; Lyman Beecher Lecturer, Yale, 1925; Vicar of All Saints', Ennismore Gardens, S.W., 1905-7; Lady Margaret Professor of Divinity and Fellow of Jesus College, Cambridge, 1907-11; Dean of St. Paul's 1911-1934; Hon. Fellow of Jesus College, Cambridge, of Hertford College, Oxford, and of King's College, Cambridge; Gifford Lecturer, St. Andrews, 1917-18; Romanes and Hibbert Lecturer, 1920; Rede Lecturer, 1922; Hulsean Lecturer, 1926; Warburton Lecturer, 1932; Hon. D.D. Aberdeen, 1905; Oxford, 1928; Hon. D.Litt. Durham, 1920; Sheffield, 1924; Hon. LL.D. Edinburgh, 1923; St. Andrews, 1930; formerly Trustee National Portrait Gallery; President of the Classical Association, 1933; Herbert Spencer Lecturer, Oxford, 1934. *Publications:* Society in Rome under the Cæsars, 1886; Eton Latin Grammar (with F. H. Rawlins), 1889, 3rd edition, 1900; Christian Mysticism, 1899; two essays in Contentio Veritatis, 1902; Faith and Knowledge, 1904; Selections from the German Mystics, 1904; Studies of English Mystics, 1906; Truth and Falsehood in Religion, 1906; Personal Idealism and Mysticism, 1907; Faith, 1909; Speculum Animæ, 1911; The Church and the Age, 1912; Types of Christian Saintliness, 1915; The Philosophy of Plotinus, 1918; Outspoken Essays, 1919; Second Series, 1922; The Idea of Progress (Romanes Lecture), 1920; The Victorian Age (Rede Lecture), 1922; Personal Religion and the Life of Devotion, 1924; The Platonic Tradition, 1926; England, in Modern World Series, 1926; Lay Thoughts of a Dean, 1926; The Church in the World, 1927; Assessments and Anticipations, 1929; Christian Ethics and Modern Problems, 1930; Every Man's Bible, 1931; More Lay Thoughts of a Dean, 1931; Things New and Old, 1933; God and the Astronomers, 1933; Vale, 1934; The Gate of Life, 1935; Freedom, Love and Truth, 1936; A Rustic Moralist, 1937; Our Present Discontents, 1938; A Pacifist in Trouble, 1939; The Fall of the Idols, 1940; Talks in a Free Country, 1943; Diary of a Dean, 1949; England, 1953. *Address:* Brightwell Manor, Wallingford. [*Died* 26 *Feb.* 1954.

INGLEFIELD, Brig. Lionel Dalton, D.S.O. 1915; late R.A.S.C.; *b.* 15 Sept. 1881; *m.*; one *s.* one *d.* Entered army, 1903; Captain, 1911; Major, 1914; Lt.-Col., 1929; Col. 1933; Brig. 1939; served S.Africa, 1899-1902 (Queen's medal 2 clasps, King's medal 2 clasps); European War, 1914-18 (despatches, D.S.O.); Assistant Director of Supplies and Transport, Northern Command, 1934-36; Assistant Director of Supplies and Transport, Southern Command, 1936-38; retired pay, 1938; D.D.S.T. Southern Command, Sept. 1939-Oct. 1941. *Address:* c/o Messrs. Glyn, Mills & Co., Holt's Branch, Kirkland House, Whitehall, S.W.1. [*Died* 31 *Jan.* 1953.

INGLES, Rev. Dr. Charles William Chamberlayne; *b.* 25 Jan. 1869; *e s.* of late John Chamberlayne Ingles, Deputy Inspector-General of H. & F. Royal Navy; *m.* 1900, Marianne Clare Bailey; no *c.* *Educ:* Newton College, Newton Abbot; Jesus College, Cambridge, M.A. D.D. from Archbishop of Canterbury, 1918; ordained 1892; Curate of St. Matthews, Exeter, 1892-96; Archdeacon for R.N., Chaplain of the Fleet and Chaplain of Greenwich Hospital, 1917-24; retired list, 1924. Served in Collingwood, 1896; Royal Oak, 1897-99; Juno, 1899; Galatea, 1899-1900; Minotaur, 1900-3: Hibernia and Egmont, 1903-6 (for R.N. Hospital, Malta); Indus, 1906; R.N. Barracks, Portsmouth, 1906-10; St. Vincent, 1910-12; Fisgard, 1912-1914; R.M. Depot, Deal, 1914-17; Archdeacon for Royal Navy, Chaplain of the Fleet, 1917-1924; Rector of Cheddon Fitzpaine, 1924-31; Hon. Chaplain to H.M., 1923-. *Recreations:* boating, Rugby football, tennis, golf. *Address:* Mountswood, Trull Rd., Taunton, Somerset. *T.:* Taunton 2010. [*Died* 18 *Dec.* 1954.

INGLES, Brig.-General John Darnley, C.M.G. 1918; D.S.O. 1917; D.L. Devonshire, 1936; *b.* Torcross, S. Devon, 18 Dec. 1872; 2nd *s.* of late John Chamberlayne Ingles, D.I.G., R.N. *Educ.:* Cheltenham College; United Services College, Westward Ho! Entered army, the Devonshire Regt., 1894; Captain 1900; Major, 1914; Lieut.-Colonel, 1922; served South Africa, 1899-1902 (despatches, Queen's medal 4 clasps, King's medal 2 clasps); European War, 1914-18 (despatches five times; Bt. Lt.-Col. June 1915, D.S.O., C.M.G.); temporary Brig.-Gen., 1916; retired, 1926; J.P. Co. Devon, 1934. *Address:* The

Hermitage, Ashprington, near Totnes, S. Devon. *T.:* Harbertonford 211. *Club:* Army and Navy. [*Died* 9 *March* 1957.

INGLIS, Prof. Sir Charles Edward, Kt., *cr.* 1945; O.B.E.; F.R.S. 1930; Hon. LL.D., Edinburgh University; M.Inst.C.E.; M.Inst. Structural Engineers; Hon. M.I.Mech.E.; Hon. Member Instn. of Municipal and County Engineers; Vice-Provost King's College, Cambridge, 1943-46: Prof. of Mechanical Sciences, Cambridge University, 1919-43; *b.* 31 July 1875; *s.* of late Dr. Inglis, M.D., of Redhall and Auchindinny, Midlothian; *m.* 1901, Eleanor Mary (*d.* 1952), *d.* of late Lt.-Col. Moffat, S. Wales Borderers; two *d.* *Educ.:* Cheltenham College; King's College, Cambridge (scholar), 22nd Wrangler, first class Mechanical Sciences Tripos. Pupil to Sir John Wolfe Barry; assisted in Engineering School, Cambridge, under Sir. J. A. Ewing, 1901: subsequently University Lecturer in Engineering; Fellow, King's College, Cambridge; Telford Medal, Institution of Civil Engineers, 1924; Member of Council of Institution of Civil Engineers, of Institution of Naval Architects and of Institution of Structural Engineers; President of British Waterworks Association, 1935-36; President of Institution of Civil Engineers, 1941-42; Thomas Hawksley Lecturer, 1943; James Forrest Lecturer, 1944; Sir Charles Parsons Medallist, 1944. *Publications:* various papers and treatises on engineering subjects. *Recreations:* walking, motoring and boat sailing. *Address:* King's College, Cambridge; 10 Latham Road, Cambridge. *T.:* Cambridge 4790. *Club:* Athenæum. [*Died* 19 *April* 1952.

INGRAM, Sir Herbert, 2nd Bt., *cr.* 1893; Chairman of Companies; *s.* of 1st Bt. and Mary, *d.* of Hon. Edward Stirling, Adelaide; *S.* father, 1924; *b.* 26 Sept. 1875; *m.* 1908, Hilda Vivian, *d.* of late Col. Carson Lake, New York; two *s.* *Educ.:* Winchester; Exeter College, Oxford, B.A. Capt. East Kent Yeomanry, 1902. Served European War, 1914-19; Lt.-Cdr. R.N.A.S., Major, R.A.F. Hon. D.Litt. Oxford, 1958. *Heir:* *s.* Herbert [*b.* 18 April 1912; *m.* 1935, Jane Lindsay, *d.* of James Palmer-Tomkinson; one *s.* three *d.*]. *Recreation:* fishing. *Address:* Driffield Manor, Cirencester. *Clubs:* Bath, Lansdowne. [*Died* 1 *June* 1958.

INGRAMS, Leonard St. Clair, O.B.E. 1946; Managing Director, Continental Assets Realisation Trust Ltd.; *b.* 23 Jan. 1900; *s.* of Rev. W. S. Ingrams; *m.* 1st, 1923, June (marriage dissolved, 1933), *d.* of L. L. Dunham, New York; one *s.*; 2nd, 1935, Victoria Susan Beatrice, *d.* of Sir James Reid, 1st Bt.; four *s.* *Educ.:* Shrewsbury School; Pembroke Coll., Oxford (Scholar and Exhibitioner). Coldstream Guards, 1918-19; Pembroke College, Oxford, 1919-22 (Inter-Varsity sports, 1920, 21, 22); Investment Banking, New York City, 1923-24; European Representative, Chemical Bank and Trust Co. 1924-39; Ministry of Economic Warfare, 1940-45. *Address:* 18 Cheyne Row, S.W.3. *T.:* Flaxman 8526. *Club:* Boodle's. [*Died* 30 *Aug.* 1953.

INMAN, Arnold, O.B.E.; K.C. 1931; *b.* 1867; *s.* of Thomas Frederic Inman, Bath; *m.* 1896, Margaret Amy Hope (*d.* 1942), *d.* of E. A. Le Mesurier, Genoa; one *s.* three *d.* *Educ:* Clifton; Magdalen College, Oxford (Demy); 2nd Class Science Finals (Chemistry). Called to Bar, 1892. *Address:* Thorndyke, Hatch End, Middlesex. [*Died* 26 *Feb.* 1951.

INNES, Sir Andrew (Lockhart), K.B.E., *cr.* 1954; C.B. 1951; Q.C. 1954; Legal Secretary and Parliamentary Draftsman; Lord Advocate's Department, since 1949; *b.* 10 June 1898; *e. s.* of late John Lockhart Innes, Solicitor, Kirkcaldy, Fife; *m.* 1926, Irene Campbell Ross; one *s.* two *d.* *Educ.:* Fettes College, Edinburgh; Oriel College, Oxford; Edinburgh University. B.A.(Oxon.), 1921; LL.B., 1923. Served European War, 1914-18, in R.F.A., 1917-18. Admitted to Faculty of Advocates, 1924; Asst. Legal Secretary and Parliamentary Draftsman, 1934-49. *Address:* Phœnix Cottage, Effingham Common Road, Effingham, Surrey. *T.:* Bookham 2539. [*Died* 8 *Dec.* 1960.

INNES, Sir Charles (Alexander), K.C.S.I., *cr.* 1924 (C.S.I. 1921); C.I.E. 1919; *b.* 27 Oct. 1874; *s.* of late Deputy Surg.-Gen. C. A. Innes and Jessie, *d.* of General Marshall, Madras Army; *m.* 1900, Agatha Rosalie (Kaisar-i-Hind medal, 1st Class, 1933) (*d.* 1956), *d.* of Col. Kenlis Stevenson, Indian Army; four *s.* one *d.* *Educ.:* Merchant Taylors' School; St. John's College, Oxford (Hon. Fellow). Joined I.C.S. 1898; served in Madras in various capacities; Under-Secretary to Government of India, 1907-10; Collector of Malabar, 1911-15; Director of Industries and Controller of Munitions, Madras, 1916-18; Indian Foodstuffs Commissioner, 1919; Secretary to Government of India Commerce Dept., 1920-21; Member Governor-General's Council, India, 1921-27; Governor of Burma, 1927-32. *Publication:* Malabar District Gazetteer. *Club:* Athenæum. [*Died* 28 *June* 1959.

INNES, Guy Edward Mitchell; *b.* Ballarat, Victoria, 1882; *s.* of William Innes; *m.* 1913, Frances Blanche, *e. d.* of Edwin Gray; one *s.* *Educ.:* State School; Ballarat College; East Melbourne Grammar School. After commercial experience joined Melbourne Argus, 1900; Chief Sub-Editor, 1910-11; News Editor Melbourne Herald, 1911-18; Editor-in-Chief, 1918-21: Secretary Press Congress of the World, Honolulu, 1921; Special Representative Melbourne Herald and Sydney Sun, Washington Disarmament Conference, 1921-22; London Manager Melbourne Herald Special Cable Service, 1923-26; Deputy Manager Australian Newspapers Cable Service, 1926-35; Australian Associated Press, 1935-1940; formerly Empire Affairs Department, Dominions Office; Foreign Office, 1949-50; formerly Ministry of Information; F.J.I.; Foundation Member Australian Journalists' Association; Member Stationers and Newspaper Makers' Co.; has written numerous verses; represented Australia at International Press Conferences in Paris and Oslo. *Recreations:* chess, reading. *Address:* Sloane Avenue Mansions, S.W.3. *T.:* Kensington 7020. *Club:* Authors'. [*Died* 13 *Feb.* 1953.

INNES-KER, Major Lord Robert (Edward); Flight Lieut. late R.A.F.V.R.; late Irish Guards, *y. s.* of 7th Duke of Roxburghe; *b.* 1885; *m.* 1st, 1920, Charlotte Josephine Cooney (José Collins, the actress) (who obt. a divorce, 1934); 2nd, 1939, Marie Hadley (*d.* 1958). *Educ.:* Eton. Served European War, 1914-17 (wounded); re-employed, 1940; Flight Lieut., 1942. Hon. Major, Irish Guards. [*Died* 19 *July* 1958.

INNIS, Harold Adams, M.A., Ph.D., F.R.S.C. 1934; Professor and head of the dept. of political economy, University of Toronto; Dean of the School of graduate studies, 1947; *b.* 5 Nov. 1894; *s.* of W. A. and Mary Innis; *m.* 1921, Mary E. Quayle; two *s.* two *d.* *Educ.:* McMaster University, Toronto. Served with 4th battery, C.F.A., C.E.F., 1916-17; Ph.D. Univ. of Chicago, 1920; LL.D. Univ. of New Brunswick, 1944, McMaster Univ., 1945, Univ. of Manitoba, 1946; Glasgow Univ., 1948; D.Ec.Sc. Laval Univ., Univ. of Toronto, Dept. of Economics, 1920; Pres. section two of Roy. Society of Canada, 1943; Member Royal Commission Provincial economic inquiry, Nova Scotia, 1934; Pres. Canadian Political Science Association, 1937; Pres. Economic History Assoc., 1942; Tyrrell Medal in Canadian history, 1944; Pres. Royal Society of Canada, 1946; Member of Royal Commission on Adult Education, Manitoba, 1946; Member Royal Commission on Transportation, 1949; Pres. American Economic Assoc., 1952. *Publications:* A History of the Canadian Pacific Railway, 1923; Fur Trade of Canada, 1926; Select Documents in Canadian Economic History, Vols. I., II., 1929, 1933; Fur Trade in Canada, 1930; Peter Pond, 1930; Problems of Staple Production in Canada, Toronto, 1933; edited with A. F. W. Plumptre, Canadian Economy and its Problems, 1934; Settlement on the Mining Frontier, 1936; (ed.) Dairy Industry in Canada, 1937; (ed.) Labour and Canadian American relations, 1937; (ed.) The Japanese Canadians, 1938; The Cod Fisheries, 1940; ed. The Diary of Alexander James McPhail, 1940; ed. American Influence on Canadian Mining, 1941; ed. The British Columbia Fisheries, 1941; Political Economy in the Modern State, 1946; (ed.) The Diary of Simeon Perkins, 1949; Empire and Communication, 1950; Bias in Communication, 1951; The Strategy of Culture, 1952. *Recreation:* travel. *Address:* University of Toronto, Toronto, Canada. *T.:* Hudson 7455. *Club:* Faculty Union (University of Toronto). [*Died* 8 *Nov.* 1952.

INSKIP, Sir Arthur (Cecil), Kt., *cr.* 1947; C.B.E. 1942 (O.B.E. 1918); T.D.; Vice-Chm. and Dep. Managing Dir., The British India Corp. Ltd., Cawnpore, India; *b.* London, 7 Dec. 1894; *yr. s.* of late John Inskip, Hove, Sussex; *m.* 1917, Edith Anne, *y. d.* of Edward Churchill Harper, Brighton, Sussex; two *d.* *Educ.:* Brighton and London. Served European War, 1914-18 (wounded, despatches twice, O.B.E.); Comdt. Cawnpore Contingent Auxiliary Force, India, 1933-36. Member, Central Legislative Assembly, New Delhi, 1943-47; Adviser to Govt. of India for Tanning and Leather Industries, 1939-47; Dep. Pres. Associated Chambers of Commerce of India, 1949; Pres., Upper India Chamber of Commerce, 1948-49; Chm. European Assoc., U.P. Branch, 1945-1948; Chm. Tanners Fed. of India, 1939-43; Gen. Man., Messrs. Cooper Allen and Co., 1939-48; Dir. of various Cos. in India. *Recreations:* golf, riding, tennis. *Address:* Grassmere, Cawnpore, U.P., India. *T.A.:* Inskip, Cawnpore. *T.:* Cawnpore 2296. *Clubs:* Royal Automobile; Bengal (Calcutta); Cawnpore (Cawnpore); Gulmarg (Kashmir). [*Died* 24 *Dec.* 1951.

INSKIP, Sir John Hampden, K.B.E., *cr.* 1937; Alderman of City of Bristol; Solicitor; *b.* Dec. 1879; *s.* of late James Inskip, Clifton Park House, Clifton; *m.* 1923, Hon. Janet Maclay, 2nd *d.* of 1st Baron Maclay, P.C.; two *s.* three *d.* *Educ.:* Clifton; King's College, Cambridge. Lord Mayor of Bristol, 1931; Freeman of City of Bristol, 1954. Secretary of United Kingdom Pilots' Association, 1913-1953. Served European War in France as Lieut., R.F.C. and R.A.F., 1915-17. *Address:* The Chantry, Abbot's Leigh, near Bristol. *T.:* Bristol 31128. [*Died* 8 *April* 1960.

INVERCHAPEL, 1st Baron, *cr.* 1946, of Loch Eck; **Archibald John Kerr Clark Kerr,** P.C. 1944; G.C.M.G., *cr.* 1942 (K.C.M.G., *cr.* 1935); Farmer; 5th *s.* of late John Kerr Clark of Crossbasket, Hamilton, Lanarkshire, and late Kate Louisa, *d.* of Sir John Struan Robertson, K.C.M.G.; *m.* 1929, Maria Teresa Diaz Salas, *d.* of Javier Diaz Lira, Santiago de Chile. *Educ.:* privately. Entered Diplomatic Service, 1906; served at Berlin, Buenos Aires, Washington, Rome, Teheran; enlisted in the Scots Guards, 1918; appointed to Tangier, 1919, and to Cairo, 1922, where he acted as Counsellor, 1923-25; Envoy Extraordinary and Minister Plenipotentiary to Central American Republics, 1925-1928; to Chile, 1928-30; to Sweden, 1931-1935; Ambassador in Iraq, 1935-38; in China, 1938-42; in the U.S.S.R., 1942-46; in the U.S.A., 1946-48. Special British Envoy to Java, 1946. Hon. LL.D. Glasgow and (in the U.S.A.) Johns Hopkins, Hamilton and Dickinson. *Address:* Inverchapel, Loch Eck, by Dunoon, Argyll. *T.:* Kilmun 321. *Clubs:* Turf, Buck's, Pratt's. [*Died* 5 *July* 1951 (*ext.*).

INVERCLYDE, 4th Baron, *cr.* 1897; **John Alan Burns,** Bt., *cr.* 1889; Scots Guards (Reserve of Officers); *b.* 12 Dec. 1897; *S.* father, 1919; *s.* of 3rd Baron and Charlotte Mary Emily (*d.* 1951), *y. d.* of late Robert Nugent-Dunbar of Machermore Castle, Co. Kirkcudbright. *Educ.:* Eton; Sandhurst. Served European War, 1916-18 (wounded); A.D.C. to Governor-General, Gibraltar, 1920-21; Assistant Secretary (unpaid) to Secretary for Scotland, 1922; Member of Royal Company of Archers (Queen's Bodyguard for Scotland); M.F.H. Eglinton Hunt, 1932-35; M.F.H. Lanarkshire and Renfrewshire Hunt, 1935-49; a D.L. for County of City of Glasgow; Hon. Col. 74th Anti-Aircraft Regt. R.A.(T.A.), 1939-44; A.D.C. to G.O.C. Lines of Communication B.E.F. 1940; Captain, Scots Guards, 1941 (1939-45 Star); Hon. Air Commodore No. 946 Squadron, A.A.F., 1940-45; Chairman Scottish Advisory Cttee., British Sailors' Soc. since 1924, and Dep. Chm. of Society since 1951; West of Scotland Dist. Comr.'s Special Representative, 1941-44; President, Glasgow Batt. Boys' Brigade, 1938-44, since when Hon. President; Lord Dean of Guild, Glasgow, 1948-50; Pres. Scottish Amicable Building Society, 1949-; Pres. United Commercial Travellers' Association of Great Britain and Ireland, 1951-52; President (Chairman, Council of Management, 1956-) British Hotels and Restaurants Assoc. 1957-; President Franco-Scottish Society, 1949-54; K.St.J.; Commander Legion of Honour (France), 1955; La Médaille de Reconnaissance Française; Freeman: City of Brest; Veulettes-sur-Mer; Docteur (h.c.) Univ. de Dijon; La Médaille d'Or de Nancy, 1949; Grand Cordon of Star of Ethiopia, 1952. *Publication:* Porpoises and People, 1930. *Recreations:* yachting, shooting, hunting. *Heir:* none. *Address:* Castle Wemyss, Wemyss Bay, Renfrewshire. *T.:* Wemyss Bay 3104. *Clubs:* Turf, Guards; Western (Glasgow); Royal Northern Yacht (Oban); Royal Yacht Squadron (Cowes). [*Died* 18 *June* 1957 (*ext.*).

INVERFORTH, 1st Baron, *cr.* 1919 of Southgate, **Andrew Weir,** P.C. 1919; President, Andrew Weir Shipping and Trading Co., Ltd.; Hon. Pres., Cable and Wireless (Holding), Ltd.; Chm. United Baltic Corporation Ltd., The Bank Line Ltd., etc.; *b.* 24 Apr. 1865; *m.* 1889, Anne (*d.* 1941), *y. d.* of Thomas Kay Dowie; one *s.* four *d.* Was senior partner of Andrew Weir & Co., Shipowners and Merchants of London, Glasgow, and elsewhere; Surveyor-General of Supply at War Office, and Member of the Army Council, 1917-19; Minister of Munitions, January 1919-March 1921; first Chairman of the Liquidation and Disposals Commission until May 1921; awarded American D.S.M. 1919; Knight Grand Cross Order of the Dannebrog, 1937; Diploma of Grand Croix of Grand Duke Gedinimas, 1938 (Lithuania). *Heir:* *o. s.* Hon. Andrew Morton Weir. *Address:* The Hill, Hampstead Heath, N.W.3. *T.:* Hampstead 1324. [*Died* 17 *Sept.* 1955.

IRELAND, (Walter) Alleyne; Author and Lecturer; a British subject, resident in the United States; *b.* Bowdon, Cheshire; *s.* of late Alex. Ireland, author of The Booklover's Enchiridion; unmarried. *Educ.:* Manchester Grammar School. Has devoted himself to study of comparative government, having visited during past forty years Australia, India, China, Japan, Korea, Manchuria, the Philippine Islands, Borneo, Java, the Malay Peninsula, Canada, the British, French, and Spanish West Indies, British Guiana, Indo-China, Hong Kong, and has lived, at intervals, for twenty-five years in the United States; has lectured at the Universities of Cornell, Chicago, Harvard, Pennsylvania, Peiping, etc., and has spoken before the British Association for the Advancement of Science, the Royal Colonial Institute, the American Academy of Political and Social Science, the Lowell Institute, etc. *Publica-*

tions: Tropical Colonization, 1889; The Anglo-Boer Conflict, 1900; China and the Powers, 1901; The Far Eastern Tropics, 1905; The Province of Burma, 1907; Democracy and the Human Equation, 1921; The New Korea, 1926; has contributed signed articles to The Times, The Spectator, The Atlantic Monthly, The North American Review, The Century, The Forum, McClure's, The Metropolitan, The Cosmopolitan, The Journal of Heredity, etc. *Recreations:* photography, demography. [*Died* 23 *Dec.* 1951.

IREMONGER, Colonel Edgar Assheton, C.B.E. 1919; *b.* 4 July 1862; *s.* of late Colonel H. E. Iremonger, Indian Army; *m.* 1902, Winifred Mary, *d.* of late G. W. Fowler, Mossel Bay, C.P., S. Africa; two *s.* one *d.* *Educ.:* Sherborne; Jesus College, Cambridge. Gazetted 2nd Lieut. Durham Lt. Infy. 1887; Captain 1896; Major (for service S. African War, 1902); during European War with 16th D.L.I. and 8th Suffolk Regt. (C.B.E.); Lieut.-Col. commanding 50th Regt. Dist.; Colonel commanding No. 6 Dist. *Address:* Villa Rosa Park, Tampa, Florida, U.S.A. [*Died* 2 *Feb.* 1953.

IREMONGER, Very Rev. Frederic Athelwold, M.A.; D.D. Glasgow, 1938; Dean of Lichfield since 1939; *b.* 1878; 3rd *s.* of late W. H. Iremonger, J.P., late 32nd Foot, of Wherwell Priory, Hants. *Educ.:* Clifton Coll.; Keble Coll., Oxford; Wells Theological College. Deacon, 1905; Priest, 1906; Curate of All Saints', Poplar, E., 1905-11; Priest-in-charge of S. Nicholas, Blackwall, 1908-11; Head of the Oxford House in Bethnal Green, 1911-16; Vicar of S. James the Great, Bethnal Green, 1912-16; Rector of Quarley, 1916-22; Editor of the Guardian, 1923-27; Vicar of Vernham Dean with Linkenholt, 1927-33; Director of Religion, B.B.C., 1933-39; Chairman of the Life and Liberty Movement, 1919-21; President, 1922; Proctor, Convocation, London, 1922, 1924, and 1925; Chaplain to the King, 1927-39; Hon. Chaplain to Archbishop (Temple) of York, 1928-1939; Select Preacher, Univ. of Cambridge, 1939, Univ. of Oxford, 1943-44. *Publications:* Before the Morning Watch, 1917; Men and Movements in the Church, 1928; Each Returning Day, 1940; William Temple, Archbishop of Canterbury: His Life and Letters, 1948. *Address:* 9 The Close, Lichfield, Staffs. *Clubs:* Boodle's, M.C.C. [*Died* 15 *Sept.* 1952.

IRONSIDE, 1st Baron, *cr.* 1941, of Archangel and of Ironside; **Field-Marshal William Edmund Ironside,** G.C.B., *cr.* 1938 (K.C.B., *cr.* 1919); C.M.G. 1918; D.S.O. 1915; *b.* 6 May 1880; *s.* of Surg.-Maj. William Ironside, R.H.A., of Ironside, Aberdeenshire; *m.* 1915, Mariot Ysobel, *d.* of Charles Cheyne; one *s.* one *d.* *Educ.:* Tonbridge School, R.M.A. Entered R.A., 1899; Capt. 1908; Maj. 1914; Staff Capt. South Africa, 1908-9; Brig. Maj., 1909-12; General Staff Officer 3rd Grade, 1914; 2nd Grade, 1915; 1st Grade, 1916; Brig.-Gen. commanding 99th Inf. Bde., 1918; Commander-in-Chief Allied troops, Archangel, Northern Russia, Oct. 1918-Oct. 1919; commanded Ismid Force, 1920; North Persian Force, 1921; served South Africa, 1899-1902 (despatches, Queen's medal 3 clasps, King's medal 2 clasps); European War, 1914-19 (despatches, D.S.O., C.M.G., K.C.B., Brevet Lieut.-Colonel, Brevet Colonel, Croix de Guerre avec Palme, 2nd Class Order St. Vladimir, Croix d'Officier de la Légion d'Honneur); C.-in-C. British Forces in Russia, 1918-19; North Persia, 1920-21 (medal, clasp); Commandant, Staff College, Camberley, 1922-26; Commanded 2nd Division, Aldershot, 1926-28; Commander Meerut District, India, 1928-31; Lieut. of H.M.'s Tower of London, 1931-33; Quartermaster-General in India, 1933-36; General, 1935; General Officer Commanding-in-Chief Eastern Command, 1936-1938; A.D.C. General to the King, 1937-40; Governor and Commander-in-Chief, Gibraltar 1938-39; Inspector-General of Overseas Forces, 1939; Chief of the Imperial General Staff, 1939-1940; Commander-in-Chief, Home Forces, 1940; Field-Marshal, 1940. Col. Commandant Royal Artillery, 1932-46. Grand Croix de la Légion d'Honneur. *Publication:* Tannenberg: The First Thirty Days in East Prussia, 1925; Archangel, 1918-19, 1953. *Heir:* *s.* Hon. Edmund Oslac Ironside, Lieut. R.N. [*b.* 21 Sept. 1924; *m.* 1950, Audrey Marigold, *y. d.* of Col. Hon. Thomas Morgan-Grenville, D.S.O.; one *s.* one *d.*]. *Address:* Hingham, Norfolk. *Club:* United Service. [*Died* 22 *Sept.* 1959.

IRVIN, Sir John Hannell, K.B.E., *cr.* 1917; J.P. Aberdeen; Governing Director since 1920 of Richard Irvin and Sons, Ltd. (Partner, 1896-1908; Joint Managing Director, 1908-20); Director, A. J. Wares Ltd.; Manager since 1910 of the Aberdeen Savings Bank and Trustee since 1922; a Commissioner of Aberdeen Harbour since 1902 and Chairman of the Finance Committee since 1911; President, Aberdeen Steam Fishers' Provident Society since 1901; *b.* 16 March 1874; *s.* of late Alderman Richard Irvin; *m.* 1st, 1896, Mary (*d.* 1923), *d.* of Henry Boak; 2nd, 1924, Agnes Margaret, *d.* of late Alexander Watt; one *s.* two *d.* Adviser to Board of Trade and Ministry of Blockade on purchases of Fish and Food Supplies in foreign countries, 1915-16; captured on High Seas while on Government business and interned in Germany, 1916-18; represented East Coast of Scotland Ports in the Dock and Harbour Authorities' Assoc., 1927-29, 1934, 1936-37, 1945-46, Pres. 1941 and 1942, Vice-Pres. 1947-50; Vice-Pres., Scottish Liberal Federation, 1921-30; Pres., Aberdeen Liberal Association, 1918-31. *Recreation:* golf. *Address:* Firhillock, Banchory, Kincardineshire. *T.A.:* Irvin, Aberdeen. *T.:* Banchory 168. *Club:* Royal Automobile. [*Died* 25 *March* 1952.

IRVIN, Captain William Dion, C.B.E. 1919; R.N., retired; *b.* 1870; *s.* of David S. Irvin, Bombay; *m.* 1908, Winifred May, *d.* of C. H. Maxsted, Oakland, Windermere. Served European War, 1914-19 (despatches, promoted Comdr., C.B.E.). Represented South African Motor Trade Association at Motor Congress, Savoy Hotel, London, 1927. Served in R.N. Ferry Service in Command, 1942-45 (despatches). *Address:* care Standard Bank of S. Africa, 10 Clements Lane, E.C.4. *Club:* Naval and Military. [*Died* 13 *Sept.* 1956.

IRVINE, Sir James Colquhoun, K.B.E., *cr.* 1948 (C.B.E. 1920); Kt., *cr.* 1925; F.R.S. 1918; J.P., D.L. County of Dundee; Principal and Vice-Chancellor University of St. Andrews since 1921, formerly Professor of Science in the Univ.; Trustee Pilgrim Trust; Chm. Scottish Universities Entrance Board, 1920-44; Commissioner for 1851 Exhibition; Pres. Section B, British Assoc., 1922; For. Lecturer, Inst. of Politics, Williamstown, Mass., 1926; Vanuxem Lecturer, Princeton, 1929; Woodward Lecturer, Yale, 1931; Chairman Adult Education Committee for Scotland, 1927-29; Chairman Forest-Products Research Board, 1927-39; Member Prime Minister's Committee on Training of Biologists, 1931; Chairman The Viceroy's Committee on the Indian Institute of Science, 1936; Member of Commission on Higher Education in the Colonies, 1943; Chairman Committee on Higher Education in the West Indies, 1944; Chairman Inter-University Council on Higher Education in the Colonies, 1946-51; Chm. Advisory Council Scottish Education Department, 1925-31; *b.* Glasgow, 9 May 1877; *m.* 1905, Mabel Violet, *y. d.* of John Williams, late of Dunmurry, Co. Antrim; (one *s.* died on active service, 1944) two *d.* *Educ.:* Allan Glen's School and Royal Technical College, Glasgow; Universities of St. Andrews and Leipzig; Ph.D. (Leipzig). D.Sc. (St. Andrews), LL.D. (Glasgow, Aberdeen, Edinburgh, Wales, Toronto, Columbia, and New York); Hon. D.Sc. (Liverpool, Princeton, and McGill); Hon. Sc.D. (Cambridge, Penn., and Yale); Hon. D.C.L. Oxford and Durham; F.R.S.E.;

Freeman of the City of St. Andrews; Hon. Member: Amer. Chem. Soc.; Amer. Philosophical Soc.; Franklin Inst.; Davy Medallist of the Royal Society; Willard Gibbs Medallist of American Chemical Soc.; Elliott Cresson Medallist of Franklin Institute; Longstaff Medallist, Chemical Society, London; Gunning Victoria Jubilee Prize, Royal Society of Edinburgh. Order of Polonia Restituta (Officer, Grand Cross), 1944; King Haakon VII Cross of Freedom (First Class), 1946. *Publications:* numerous papers, principally on the Chemistry of Sugars, in scientific journals. *Recreations:* formerly: tennis, golf, swimming; now: fishing and reading. *Address:* The University, St. Andrews, Fife. *Clubs:* Athenæum; Royal and Ancient (St. Andrews). [*Died* 12 *June* 1952.

IRVINE-FORTESCUE, Colonel Archer, D.S.O.; D.L., J.P. Kincardineshire; late Army Medical Service; *b.* 6 July 1880; *s.* of late William Irvine-Fortescue, M.B., C.M., J.P. of Kingcausie, Kincardineshire, and Swanbister, Orkney; *m.* 1916, Ruth Olive, *d.* of late Henry Boddington, J.P., of Pownall Hall, Cheshire; one *s.* one *d.* *Educ.:* Aberdeen Grammar School and Aberdeen University. Liddell Bursar and Duthie Scholar of Marischal College, Aberdeen; M.B., Ch.B. Honours, Aberdeen, 1904; B.Com. Edinburgh, 1932; Curator, Royal Herbarium, Calcutta, 1904-5; Lieut., R.A.M.C., 1907; Captain, 1910; Major, 1919; Lieut.-Col., 1931; Col. 1935; served European War, 1914-21 (despatches four times, D.S.O., Lion and Sun of Persia, 2nd Class, St. Stanislaus of Russia, 2nd Class with swords; 1914-15 star, General Service medal, Victory medal); acting Lieut.-Colonel commanding 141st Field Ambulance and 9th C.C.S.; member Anglo-Persian Military Commission, 1919-21; S.M.O. 7th Brigade Waziristan operations 1922-23 (despatches, medal and clasp); Inspector Medical Services, Iraq Army, 1926-29; served in Kurdistan, 1927 (Iraq active service medal); O.C. Military Hospital, Rawal Pindi, Punjab, 1934-37; Officiating Assistant Director of Medical Services, Rawalpindi District, 1937; retired, 1937; European War, 1939-45 (Gen. Service Medal, Victory Medal); recalled to service Aug. 1939 as D.D.M.S. Scottish Command; A.D.M.S. Polish Mission, 1940; A.D.M.S., H.Q. Advisory Staff Polish Resettlement Corps, 1946-48; retired, 1948. Jubilee Medal, 1935; Coronation Medal, 1937; awarded Polish Distinction Odznaka Sluzby Zdrowia, 1941; passed Higher Standard Examination in Urdu, Persian, and Pashtu languages; passed interpreter in German, Arabic, and Turkish; passed preliminary interpretership French, Russian, Italian. *Recreations:* the study of foreign languages, travel. *Address:* Kingcausie, Maryculter, Aberdeen, Scotland. *T.A.:* Peterculter. *T.:* Culter 3226. *Club:* English-Speaking Union. [*Died* 10 *March* 1959.

IRVING, Captain Charles Edward, C.B. 1922; R.D., R.N.R. (retired); Chairman, Thames Motor Boat Company (Westminster) Ltd.; President of Sunbury and Walton Sea Cadet Corps; *b.* 1871; *s.* of Major John Irving, Havering, and Caroline Oliphant Irving, *d.* of Hon. Jane Carter. Early sea training Clipper ship Cutty Sark. Entered P.&O. Service, 1889; Comdr. of many of the largest liners including Maloya sunk by enemy action, March 1916. Owing to large number lives saved under difficult conditions had audience with King George V to receive his thanks, also those of Queen Mary. Commission R.N.R. 1898; Commanded H.M. Trent 1918, sent in this ship to Bremen, Christmas 1918 to report on conditions regarding repatriation of British and French troops; H.M. Excellent as Administrative Commander-in-charge of Reserves, 1919; Led Reserves in Peace March, London, July 1919; R.N.R. Advisory Committee, Admiralty, 1921-22. Younger Brother of Trinity House. War Medals: S. Africa, European War, 1914-18. *Address:* 53A Eccleston Place, S.W.1. *T.:* Sloane 3008. *Club:* Royal Empire Society. [*Died* 18 *Nov.* 1955.

IRVING, Kelville Ernest, Hon. R.A.M.; Composer and Conductor; Musical Consultant of Ealing Film Studios; *b.* Godalming, Surrey, 6 Nov. 1877. Has been Musical Director of nearly all the West End theatres; has written the music for eighteen plays, including the modern Hamlet, Macbeth, Twelfth Night, Merry Wives of Windsor, The Taming of the Shrew, Yellow Sands, The Circle of Chalk, The Two Bouquets, and Elephant in Arcady; also seventy-one motion pictures; directed many operas and light operas in London, Paris and Madrid; for 30 years an officer of Roy. Philharmonic Soc., and now its only English Hon. Memb. *Recreations:* chess and music. *Address:* The Lawn, Ealing Green, W.5. *T.:* Ealing 2110. *Club:* Savage. [*Died* 24 *Oct.* 1953.

IRVING, Captain Sir Robert Beaufin, Kt., *cr.* 1943; O.B.E.; R.D.; D.L., County of Dumfries; R.N.R. (retired); late Commodore Captain of Cunard White Star Ltd.; *b.* 16 July 1877; *s.* of late Col. John Beaufin Irving, Bonshaw Tower, Kirtlebridge; *m.* 1902, Florence, *y. d.* of Joseph Brown, The Grove, Oxton, Cheshire. *Educ.:* Fullands College, Taunton; Ashbourne Grammar School; Training Ship Conway. *Address:* Bonshaw Tower, Kirtlebridge, by Lockerbie, Dumfriesshire. *T.:* Kirtlebridge 248. *Club:* Master Mariners. [*Died* 28 *Dec.* 1954.

IRWIN, Alfred, C.M.G. 1912; *b.* 20 Sept. 1865; *s.* of William Charles Irwin. *Educ.:* London and King's College. Coronation medal, 1902; official interpreter to Algeçiras Conference, 1906; granted rank of 3rd Secretary in Diplomatic Service, 1907; 2nd Secretary, 1921; Member of the Morocco Customs Commission, 1907-22; British Delegate on Commission for the examination and settlement of British claims, 1910; Diplomatic Delegate on Moorish Customs Committee, 1914-24; Interpreter and Dragoman to H.M. Legation, Tangier, 1895-1925; retired, 1925. *Address:* El Ksaibi, Tangier. [*Died* 5 *June* 1951.

IRWIN, Rt. Rev. Charles King, D.D.; *b.* 30 Mar. 1874; *s.* of late Charles King Irwin, D.D., Archdeacon of Armagh, and Mary Waller Crossle; *m.* 1901, Louisa Jane, *d.* of late Rev. T. H. Royse; two *s.* one *d.* *Educ.:* Royal School, Armagh; King's School, Warwick; Trinity College, Dublin. Curate of Armagh, 1897-1903; Incumbent of Brantry, 1903-16; Incumbent of Derrynoose (Middletown from 1922), 1916-34; Provincial Registrar of Armagh, 1898-1924: Archdeacon of Armagh, 1924-34; Hon. Secretary General Synod of Church of Ireland, 1922-34; Bishop of Limerick, Ardfert and Aghadoe, 1934-42; Bishop of Down and Connor and Dromore, 1942-44; Bishop of Connor, 1945-1956. *Address:* 1A Tullybrannigan Road, Newcastle, Co. Down. [*Died* 15 *Jan.* 1960.

ISAACS, Edward Maurice, O.B.E. 1953; Mus.B., Hon. M.A. University of Manchester, 1944; Hon. F.R.M.C.M., Pianist, Composer; Director of Manchester Tuesday Midday Concerts since 1923; *b.* 14 July 1881; *s.* of Isaac A. Isaacs and Annie Harris; *m.* 1907, Amy Florence Jordan; one *s.* one *d.* *Educ.:* Manchester Grammar School; Victoria Univ., Manchester. Mus.B. Manchester University 1901; Assoc. Royal Manchester College of Music, 1903, Hon. Fellow, 1910; Student at Royal Manchester College of Music 1894-1903 (Hallé Scholar, 1900); Further study Germany and Austria until 1905; settled in Manchester, 1907, since when many professional activities, touring, broadcasting, teaching, lecturing, etc.; Founded International Chamber Concerts in Manchester 1922; became totally blind through accident, 1924, but still carries on all former duties and professional activities. *Publications:* Various musical works; and

Monograph, The Blind Piano Teacher, 1948. *Recreations:* General interest in sport, but naturally greatly curtailed by loss of sight; much reading. *Address:* 19 Amherst Road, Fallowfield, Manchester, 14. *T.:* Rusholme 4429. [*Died* 31 *July* 1953.

ISEMONGER, Frederick Charles, C.I.E. 1931; C.B.E. 1921; *b.* 5 July 1876; *s.* of Edwin Empson Isemonger; *m.* 1909, Theodora (*d.* 1959), *d.* of James Myers Danson, D.D., Dean of Aberdeen and Orkney; two *d.* Entered Indian Police, 1898; District Superintendent of Police, Punjab, 1905; Principal, Police Training School, Phillour, 1916; Chief Civil Intelligence Officer, Punjab, 1919; Senior Superintendent of Police, 1920; Deputy Inspector-General of Police, Criminal Investigation Department, Punjab, 1921; acting Director of Intelligence Bureau, Home Department, Government of India, April-Nov., 1928; raised and commanded a Police Bn., 3/30th Punjabis, 1918; Inspector-General of Police, N.W. Frontier Province, 1925-30; retired from Indian Service, 1931; Chief of Police, British Municipal Council, Tientsin, 1931-35; Additional Inspector of Constabulary with Headquarters at Wales Civil Defence Region, 1940-44; Control Commission for Germany, Nov. 1944-Oct. 1946; retired, 1946. *Address:* Flat 3 Kingston House, Odiham, Basingstoke, Hants. [*Died* 11 *Dec.* 1960.

ISHAM, Lieut.-Colonel Ralph Heyward, C.B.E. 1919; F.R.G.S.; Financier; *b.* New York City, 2 July 1890; *o. s.* of Henry Heyward Isham and Juliet Calhoun Isham. *Educ.:* Cornell and Yale Universities. Big game shooting in Mexico, Malay Peninsula; entered British Army during European War; served three years; retained rank of Lieut.-Colonel upon discharge (C.B.E.); business interests and managing landed estates in America; secured James Boswell's private papers and MSS. from Lord Talbot de Malahide in 1927; Vice-President Johnson Society. *Publications:* Private Papers of James Boswell; Articles on Big Game Shooting in Malaya. *Recreations:* shooting, fishing, book collecting. *Address:* 342 Madison Avenue, N.Y.C., U.S.A. *Clubs:* Garrick, Royal Societies, Hurlingham; Union League, Grolier, Elizabethan, Nassau (New York). [*Died* 13 *June* 1955.

ISHERWOOD, Albert Arthur Mangnall, C.M.G. 1942; O.B.E. 1926; M.A.; *b.* 2 Nov. 1889: *er. s.* of late Rev. A. Isherwood, Staverton, Trowbridge; *m.* 1st, 1928, Agnes Theodosia (*d.* 1930), *yr. d.* of late Reginald Thompson, Loftus Hill, Knaresborough, Yorks; 2nd, 1932, Dorothy Helena, *y. d.* of late Rt. Rev. J. J. Pulleine, Bishop of Richmond. *Educ.:* St. John's, Leatherhead; University College, Oxford. Education and Administrative Service, N. Nigeria, 1913; served with Nigerian Land Contingent, 1914-17; Political Officer German East Africa, 1917; joined Civil Administration, 1919; Acting Senior Commissioner, Tanganyika Territory, 1923-24; Deputy Director of Education, 1924; Director of Education, 1931; Information Officer and Chief Censor, Tanganyika Territory; retired Sept. 1945; Member of Governing Board of School of Oriental and African Studies, 1945-. *Address:* P.O. Moshi, Tanganyika. *Club:* Constitutional. [*Died* 19 *Aug.* 1957.

ISMAIL, Sir Miras M., Amin-ul-Mulk, K.C.I.E., *cr.* 1936 (C.I.E. 1924); Kt., *cr.* 1930; O.B.E. 1923; *s.* of Aga Jan, Bangalore; *b.* 1883; *m.* 1906, Zeebeenda Begum, *d.* of Mahomed Mirza Shirazi, Bombay; one *s.* two *d.* *Educ.:* with the late Maharaja of Mysore, under Sir Stuart Fraser, K.C.S.I.; Central College, Bangalore; Madras University (B.A. 1905). Asst. Sec. to the Maharaja of Mysore, 1906; Huzur Sec., 1914; Private Sec., 1922; Dewan of Mysore, 1926-41; Prime Minister of Jaipur, 1942-46; Prime Minister of Hyderabad, 1946-47; Amin-ul-Mulk, 1920; Delegate to the Indian Round Table Conference held in London, Nov. 1930, representing the South Indian States of Mysore, Travancore, Cochin and Pudukotah; Delegate to the Second Indian Round Table Conference representing the States of Mysore and Jodhpur; Member of the Consultative Committee of the Indian Round Table Conference; Delegate to the Third Indian Round Table Conference and Delegate to the Joint Parliamentary Committee on Indian Reforms; Leader of Indian Delegation to Rural Hygiene Conference in Java, 1937; Associate C.St.J. 1937. Hon. LL.D.: Univs. of Mysore and Allahabad. *Publication:* My Public Life, 1954. *Recreation:* gardening. *Address:* Bangalore, India. [*Died* 5 *Jan.* 1959.

IZYCKI DE NOTTO, Sir Matthew, K.C.B., *cr.* 1949 (Hon. K.C.B. 1945); Air Vice-Marshal, retired; *b.* 22 Feb. 1899; *s.* of late Aleksander and late Sophie Izycki; *m.* 1927, Christine Mary Sophie Jackowski; one *d.*; became naturalised British subject, Feb. 1949. *Educ.:* University and Staff College, Warsaw, Poland. Regular soldier in Polish Army, 1925, transferred to the Air Force between European War, 1914-18, and War of 1939-45; Officer commanding various units, squadrons, and Wings; Military and Air Attaché with Polish Embassy, Ankara, Turkey, 1927-30; Professor of Tactics Air and War Staff Colleges, Warsaw, 1932-34; Air Officer commanding Air Force of 2nd Polish Army, 1939; after campaign, 1939-40 in France, spent 3 years with Western Desert Air Force, 1943-; Air Officer commanding-in-chief, Polish Air Force with R.A.F., 1943-47; Air Vice-Marshal, 1943. Inspector-General, Polish Resettlement Corps, R.A.F., 1947-48. Knight Commander of Sovereign Order of Malta; Grand Officer of Royal Dutch Order of Orange-Nassau, 1947; Commander of Legion of Merit, 1947; French Légion d'honneur, Croix de Guerre, Virtuti Militari, etc. *Recreations:* polo (played for his country in 1924-25); won several prizes in international air displays. *Address:* 46 Water Lane, Brixton Hill, S.W.2. *T.:* Brixton 5329. *Club:* St. James'. [*Died* 12 *Feb.* 1952.

J

JACK, Brigadier Evan Maclean, C.B. 1928; C.M.G. 1918; D.S.O. 1917; *b.* 31 July 1873; 2nd *s.* of late Evan A. Jack; unmarried. *Educ.:* Crediton and Hastings Grammar Schools; R.M.A., Woolwich. Commissioned in Royal Engineers, 1893; served in Gibraltar, St. Helena (during S.A. War), and on Ordnance Survey, York and Southampton; Assistant Commissioner on Anglo-Congolese Boundary Commission, 1907-9; Chief British Commissioner, Anglo-German-Belgian Boundary Commission, 1911-12; Geographical Section, War Office, 1912-14; to France on G.H.Q. Staff, Aug. 1914, as officer in charge Topographical Section, to 31 Dec. 1918 (Bt. Lieut.-Col., D.S.O., C.M.G.); Belgian Ordre de la Couronne, Belgian Croix de Guerre, French Legion of Honour, American Disting. Service Medal, Founder's Medal, R. Geographical Society, 1919; Chief of Geographical Section, General Staff, War Office, Sept. 1920; Director-General, Ordnance Survey, 1922-30; retired, 1930. *Publication:* On the Congo Frontier. *Recreations:* motoring, sketching. *Address:* 26 Winn Road, Southampton. *T.:* 55752. *Club:* United Service. [*Died* 10 *Aug.* 1951.

JACK, John Louttit, C.B.E. 1936; F.R.S.E.; *b.* 3 July 1878; *s.* of Donald Jack, Thurso, Caithness-shire, and Margaret Louttit; *m.* 1904, Flora Webster, *d.* of James Lind, Pernambuco; three *d.* *Educ.:* Miller Institution, Thurso; Edinburgh University. Solicitor and Town Clerk, Wishaw, 1906; Solicitor and Town Clerk, Dunfermline, 1910; Joint Clerk and Treasurer, Dunfermline District

Committee, 1918; Director of Housing, Local Government Board for Scotland and Scottish Board of Health, 1919; Deputy Secretary Department of Health for Scotland, 1929-41. *Publication:* Handbook of Town Planning as applicable to Scotland, 1910. *Recreations:* fishing, golf, and curling. *Address:* 18 Campbell Avenue, Edinburgh. *T.:* 61185.
[*Died* 5 *June* 1954.

JACK, Richard, R.A. 1920 (A.R.A. 1914); R.I.; A.R.C.A.; portrait and landscape painter; *b.* Sunderland, 15 Feb. 1866; *m.*; one *s.* one *d.* *Educ.:* York. Studied at York School of Art; won National Scholarship to South Kensington, 1886; there gained the gold medal travelling scholarship; afterwards studied in Paris at the Académie Julian; was hors concour 1890 and 1891, winning two medals in each year; also medallist at Academie Colorossi; regular exhibitor at Royal Academy, New Gallery, Liverpool, Pittsburg, and Rome, etc.; at the Paris International Exhibition of 1900 was awarded the silver medal for Portraiture; a member of Royal Society of Portrait Painters; picture, Rehearsal with Nikisch, purchased under the terms of the Chantrey Bequest for the nation, 1912; Silver Medal at Pittsburgh for String Quartette, 1914. *Recreations:* golf, singing, and all sports.
[*Died* 30 *June* 1952.

JACKMAN, Professor William T., M.A.; Prof. Emeritus of Transportation, Univ. of Toronto, since 1942; *b.* 8 Jan. 1871; *s.* of James and Beatrice Mitchell Jackman; *m.* 1915, Vera M. Tryon; no *c.* *Educ.:* University of Toronto; University of Pennsylvania; Harvard University; University of London. Assistant Professor of Commerce and Economics, University of Vermont, 1901-15; Lecturer in Political Economy, University of Toronto, 1915-1917; Assistant Professor, 1919-23; Professor of Transportation, 1923-41; Chairman of Ontario Commission on Rural Credit, 1920; Chairman of Manitoba Commission on Rural Credit, 1922-23; Member of Canadian Industrial Traffic League since 1918, and Chairman of its Committees on Education and Control of International Rates; Hon. Pres. Canadian Industrial Traffic League, 1946; Member Newcomen Soc. of Great Britain and U.S.; Hon. Member Institute of Traffic Administration (London, England). Founder Member of the American Society of Traffic and Transportation. *Publications:* Development of Transportation in Modern England, 2 Vols., 1916; Economics of Transportation, 1926; Economic Principles of Transportation, 1935; Report to Canadian Government on Organization of the Canning Industry, 1919; Reports to Ontario and Manitoba Governments on Rural Credit, 1920, 1923; Critical Analysis of The Canadian Railway Problem, 1939; The St. Lawrence Project, 1940; Development of the Great Lakes—St. Lawrence Route—Traffic, Service Finance Relations with Railways, 1941; frequent contributor to technical journals on transportation. *Recreations:* golf, walking, gardening. *Address:* 171 St. Leonards Avenue, Toronto, 12, Canada. *T.:* Mohawk 2156. *Clubs:* Transportation, Toronto Railway, Sigma Chi Fraternity (Toronto).
[*Died* 8 *Nov.* 1951.

JACKS, Lawrence Pearsall; Principal of Manchester Coll., Oxford, 1915-1931; Professor of Philosophy Manchester College, Oxford, 1903; retired 1931; Editor of the Hibbert Journal from its foundation, 1902, to his retirement, 1947; *b.* Nottingham, 1860; *m.* 1889, Olive Cecilia (*d.* 1945), *d.* of Rev. Stopford Brooke; five *s.* one *d.* *Educ.:* University School, Nottingham; Univ. of London (M.A. 1886); Manchester Coll.; Göttingen; Harvard, U.S.A.; Hon. M.A. Oxford; Hon. LL.D. Glasgow; Hon. D.Litt. Liverpool; Hon. D.D. Harvard; Hon. LL.D. McGill; Hon. LL.D. Rochester, U.S.A. Entered ministry as assistant to Rev. Stopford Brooke in Bedford Chapel, 1887; subsequently at Renshaw Street Chapel, Liverpool, and the Church of the Messiah, Birmingham. *Publications:* Life and Letters of Stopford Brooke; Mad Shepherds, and other Human Studies; The Alchemy of Thought; Among the Idolmakers; All Men are Ghosts; From the Human End; The Country Air; Religious Perplexities; Philosophers in Trouble; The Life of Charles Hargrove; The Legends of Smokeover; A Living Universe: The Challenge of Life; Realities and Shams; Responsibility and Culture; The Faith of a Worker; The Heroes of Smokeover, 1926; Constructive Citizenship, 1927; My Neighbour the Universe, 1928; The Inner Sentinel, 1930; The Education of the Whole Man, 1931; Education through Recreation, 1932; My American Friends, 1933; Elemental Religion, 1934; the Revolt against Mechanism, 1934; Co-operation or Coercion, 1938; The Stolen Sword, 1938; The Last Legend of Smokeover, 1939; Construction Now, 1940; The Confession of an Octogenarian, 1942; Near the Brink, 1952; many articles in British and American Reviews; trans. works by Alfred Loisy, 1948 and 1950. *Address:* Far Outlook, Headington, Oxford. *T.A.:* Headington. *T.:* Oxford 6983.
[*Died* 17 *Feb.* 1955.

JACKSON, 1st Baron, *cr.* 1945, of Glewstone; **William Frederick Jackson;** County Councillor Herefordshire since 1931; *b.* 1893; *s.* of late George Jackson, J.P., Birmingham, and Minnie Jackson; *m.* 1923, Hope H. F. Gilmour. *Educ.:* King Edward High School, Birmingham. Served European War in 14th Warwickshire Regt. until Battle of the Somme when invalided home with rank of Sergeant; at the end of the war took charge of his firm's properties, the Glewstone Farms and Fruit Plantations, near Ross-on-Wye, Herefordshire, which he has managed ever since; M.P. (Lab.) Brecon and Radnor, 1939-45. *Recreations:* cricket, golf, Rugby. *Heir:* none. *Address:* Glewstone, Hereford. *T.:* Peterstowe 14. *Club:* Farmers'. [*Died* 2 *May* 1954 (*ext.*).

JACKSON, Basil Rawdon; Chairman British Petroleum Co. Ltd. 1956-57; *b.* 1892; 3rd *s.* of Sir Henry Moore Jackson, G.C.M.G.; *m.* 1918, Marjorie Violet, 3rd *d.* of Auchie Warner, K.C.; no *c.* *Educ.:* Downside; London University. Law student, 1911-14. Served European War, 1914-18 (1914-18 medal). Joined British Petroleum Co. Ltd., 1921; Director, 1948; Deputy Chairman, 1950. *Recreations:* golf, motoring. *Address:* 20 Kingston House, Princes Gate, S.W.7. *T.:* Kensington 4322. *Clubs:* Bath; Links (New York).
[*Died* 29 *March* 1957.

JACKSON, Sir Edward Arthur Mather-, 4th Bt. *cr.* 1869; attached to Foreign Office since 1940; *b.* 8 Jan. 1899; 2nd *s.* of Sir Henry Mather Mather-Jackson, 3rd Bt., and Ada Frances (*d.* 1949), *d.* of late Gen. Edward Somerset, C.B.; *S.* father 1942; *m.* 1932, Cecilia (*d.* 1949), *d.* of late Capt. Christopher Balfour; no *c.* *Educ.:* Eton. Formerly Lieut. Scots Guards; served European War, 1917-18; is an Underwriting Member of Lloyds; Deputy Chairman of Resident Board of British Argentine Railways, 1945-48. *Publications:* in U.S.A. and U.K. *Heir: cousin,* George Christopher Mather-Jackson [*b.* 1896; *m.* 1941, Victoria Emily Ford]. *Clubs:* Pratt's, Brooks's.
[*Died* 8 *Nov.* 1956.

JACKSON, Rev. Canon Frank Hilton, M.A., D.Sc. (Cantab); J.P. Co. Durham; Canon Emeritus of Durham Cathedral, 1957; *b.* 16 Aug. 1870; *s.* of William and Alice Jackson, Hull; *m.* 1912, Elizabeth Lucy Bernarda, (*d.* 1954), *d.* of Edward Bernard Mulhern, Tunbridge Wells; no *c.* *Educ.:* Hull Grammar School; Peterhouse, Cambridge (Wrangler). Curate of Bemerton, Salisbury, 1896-98; Chaplain and Naval Instructor, Royal Navy, 1898-1907 (Medal, China, 1900 Boxer Rebellion); Curate, Christ Church, Isle of Dogs, 1908-9; Featherstone, Yorks, 1910-12; Vicar of Thornton-le-Street and North Otterington, Yorks, 1912-18; Instructor Commander Royal Navy attached to R.A.F., Calshot, 1918-19; Rector of Chester-le-Street, 1919-35; Rural Dean, 1925-35; Hon. Canon of Durham, 1930. *Publications:* Mathematical Memoirs, Proceedings of Royal Society, London Mathematical Society Quarterly Journal of Mathematics, etc. *Recreations:* walking, investigating local Roman British Archæology. *Address:* Hartbarrow, 4 Mavis Avenue, Cook-ridge, Leeds 6. [*Died* 27 *April* 1960.

JACKSON, Major Frank Whitford, C.B.E. 1941; D.S.O. 1918; *b.* 23 June 1886. Educational Department, L.C.C., 1905-14; European War, served overseas, 1914-19 (despatches thrice, D.S.O.); London Fire Brigade, 1920-39; Officer commanding the London Fire Service, 1939-41; Regional Fire Officer, later Chief Fire Commander of London Regional Fire Forces, 1940-48; Adviser on Fire Problems, Dept. of Scientific and Industrial Research, 1943-47; Technical Services Supervisor, Fire Offices' Committee Fire Protection Association, 1947-51. *Address:* 11 Tudor Close, Hook, Surbiton. *T.:* Elmbridge 9151. [*Died* 15 *June* 1955.

JACKSON, Major-General George Hanbury, C.B. 1926; C.M.G. 1917; D.S.O. 1900; late Border Regiment; *b.* 20 Dec. 1876; *s.* of Rev. R. N. Jackson, Rector of Manor of Sudeley in Glos.; *m.* 1917, Eileen (*d.* 1953), *y. d.* of late J. Hume Dudgeon, Merville, Booterstown, Co. Dublin; one *s. Educ.:* Neuenheim College, Heidelberg; R.M.C., Sandhurst. Entered Army, 1897; Captain, 1907; Major, 1915; Bt. Lt.-Col., 1915; Bt.-Col., 1919; Col., 1920; Maj.-Gen., 1931; served South Africa, 1899-1902 (despatches twice, Queen's medal 6 clasps, King's medal 2 clasps, D.S.O.), European War, including Dardanelles, 1914-18 (despatches eight times, Bt.-Col. and Col., C.M.G., bar to D.S.O., Legion of Honour); commanded 7th Infantry Brigade, Tidworth, 1923-27; A.D.C. to the King, 1930-31; Commander 49th (West Riding) Division T.A. 1931-35; retired pay, 1935; rejoined Army, 1941-44; on General list with rank of Lieut. *Address:* Kapkong, P.O. Turbo, Kenya Colony. [*Died* 4 *Sept.* 1958.

JACKSON, Major Sir George Julius, 3rd Bt., *cr.* 1902; *b.* 4 June 1883; *s.* of Sir Thomas Jackson, 1st Bt.; *S.* brother, 1954; *m.* 1909, Nesta Katherine, *d.* of Hedworth Barclay, Gaddesby Hall, Leicestershire; four *d.* (one *s.* killed on active service, 1944). *Educ.:* Rugby; R.M.C. Sandhurst. Major, late King's Royal Rifle Corps; invalided out, 1929. *Heir: b.* (Walter David) Russell [*b.* 8 Mar. 1890; *m.* 1915, Kathleen, *d.* of Summers Hunter, Tynemouth; one *s.*]. *Address:* Great Posbrooke, Titchfield, Fareham, Hants. *T.:* Titchfield 3335. [*Died* 21 *Feb.* 1956.

JACKSON, Sir Gilbert Hollinshead Blomfield, Kt., *cr.* 1934; late Chairman Conscientious Objector Appellate Tribunal; late Puisne Judge, High Court, Madras; *b.* 26 Jan. 1875; *s.* of Rev. Prebendary Blomfield Jackson; *m.* Dorothy S. Clough; two *s* one *d. Educ.:* Marlborough College; Merton College, Oxford. *Publication:* Maxwell on the Interpretation of Statutes, 8th Ed. 1937, 9th Ed. 1946. *Recreation:* chess. [*Died* 11 *March* 1956.

JACKSON, Lieut.-Col. Guy, D.S.O. 1943; T.D.; D.L. Warwickshire; late Warwickshire Yeomanry; *b.* 8 May 1903; 2nd *s.* of late G. F. Jackson; *m.* 1947, Audrey Elizabeth, *o. d.* of late Brig. C. F. K. Marshall, D.S.O.; one *d. Educ.:* Rugby; Trinity Coll., Cambridge. Served War of 1939-45, Middle East and Italy (D.S.O.). Joint Master North Warwickshire Foxhounds, 1929-40; Master Exmoor Foxhounds, 1946. *Address:* Exemead, Exford, Minehead, Som. *T.:* Exford 288. [*Died* 28 *April* 1960.

JACKSON, Captain Henry Leigh, C.B.E. 1919; R.N., retired; *b.* 1886; *m.* 1926, Mary Ursula, *y. d.* of late E. A. Smithers, Brighton, and Mrs. Talbot, Trehills, Hassocks, Sussex. *Address:* St. Donat's, 20 Albany Rd., Southsea, Hants. [*Died* 23 *May* 1956.

JACKSON, Major-General James, C.I.E. 1916; M.B., late I.M.S.; *b.* 1866; *s.* of late Very Rev. W. O. Jackson, Dean of Killala; *m.* 1904, Kathleen Edith Anderson, *d.* of Reginald Hooper, Southbrook, Starcross; one *s.* one *d. Educ.:* Queen's College, Cork (senior Scholar, Anatomy, etc.); M.B., B.Ch. (1st Hons.) R.U.I. Entered Indian Medical Service, 1890; Superintendent Central Prison, Hyderabad, 1894-8; Yeravda, 1898-1908; Inspector-General Prisons, Bombay, 1909; Additional Member Legislative Council, 1909-17; Col., 1918; A.D.M.S., 1919; Member India Jail Committee, 20 April 1919; D.D.M.S. in India, 1921; Maj.-Gen., 1923; D.D.M.S. Eastern Command; retired, 1924. *Address:* Little Orchard, Cofton Starcross, S. Devon. [*Died* 13 *Dec.* 1957.

JACKSON, John, C.B.E. 1950; F.R.S. 1938; F.R.S. (S. Africa) 1934; M.A., D.Sc.; F.R.A.S.; *b.* 11 Feb. 1887; *s.* of Matthew Jackson and Jeanie Millar; *m.* 1920, Mary Beatrice Marshall; no *c. Educ.:* Glasgow Univ.; Trinity College, Cambridge. Wrangler, 1912; First Smith's Prizeman, Mackinnon Research Student of the Royal Society, 1913; Chief Assistant, Royal Observatory, Greenwich, 1914-33; H.M. Astronomer, Cape of Good Hope, 1933-50; retired, 1950; during European War served as a Survey Officer, Royal Engineers; Pres. Royal Astronomical Soc., 1953-55 (Hon. Sec., 1923-1929); Editor of The Observatory, 1919-27; Pres. Roy. Soc. S. Af., 1949; Gold Medal of Roy. Astronomical Soc., 1952. *Publications:* papers on dynamical and fundamental astronomy in Monthly Notices of the Royal Astronomical Society; in conjunction with Dr. Knox-Shaw and W. H. Robinson, Reduction of Hornsby's Observations at Oxford, 1774-1798. *Address:* 30 Arundel Avenue, Ewell, Surrey. *T.:* Ewell 3303. [*Died* 9 *Dec.* 1958.

JACKSON, Col. Lambert Cameron, C.M.G. 1908; D.S.O. 1917; R.E., retired; *b.* 28 Sept. 1875; *s.* of late Henry Jackson of Shirley Hall, Southampton; *m.* 1910, Olive Margaret, 3rd *d.* of late Sir Howard Elphinstone, V.C., K.C.B., C.M.G.; two *s.* (and one *s.* decd.). *Educ.:* Clifton College; Woolwich. Entered Army, 1895; Capt., 1904; Major, 1914; Bt. Lt.-Col., 1916; Col. 1920; employed on Survey duty Sudan-Abyssinian Frontier, 1899-1900; served South Africa, 1900-2 (Queen's medal with 3 clasps, King's medal with 2 clasps); served on Anglo-German Yola-Chad Boundary Commission, 1903-4; in charge of Military Survey of the Orange River Colony, 1905-8 (C.M.G.); General Staff Officer at War Office, 1909-11; Staff College, Camberley 1911-1913; European War, as Regimental Officer and General Staff Officer (1st, 2nd, and 3rd Grades), on Western Front, 1914-19 (despatches six times, Bt. Lt.-Col., D.S.O., Order of the Crown of Roumania (Officier), 1914 Star with clasp and medals); General Staff Officer (1st Grade) G.H.Q. Army of the Rhine, 1919; General Staff Officer (1st Grade) Burma Div., 1920; Asst. Quartermaster-General, A.H.Q., India, 1920-1924; Deputy Chief Engineer Eastern Command, 1925-28; Chief Engineer, British Army of the Rhine, 1928-29; Chief Engineer, Western Command, 1930-32; A.D.C. to the King, 1930-32; retired pay, 1932. Served War of 1939-45 with Home Guard and Civil Defence (Defence Medal). *Address:* Parsonage Farm, Bentworth, near Alton, Hants. *Club:* Army and Navy. [*Died* 7 *Nov.* 1953.

JACKSON, Alderman Robert Frederick; Director Ipswich Town Football Club, Ltd.; *b.* Ipswich, 1880; *s.* of Henry and Emma Jackson; *m.* 1910, Rosa Emily, *d.* of Robert

Garrod, Ipswich; one *s.* two *d.* *Educ.:* District National School, Ipswich; Ipswich Technical Coll. Stone and Marble Mason; Mem. Ipswich Town Council since 1911; Mayor of Ipswich 1932-33 and 1940-42; studied social conditions in Germany and France; Director of Ipswich Town Football Club Ltd.; M.P. (Lab.) Ipswich, 1923-24; contested Ipswich, 1918, 1922. Hon. Freeman, Borough of Ipswich. *Recreations:* gardening, choral singing, cycling. *Address:* 79 Beechcroft Rd., Ipswich. *T.:* 3012. [*Died* 28 *Jan.* 1951.

JACKSON, Robert H.; Justice, United States Supreme Court, since 1941; Chief of Counsel for United States at Nürnberg trial Axis War Criminals; *b.* 13 Feb. 1892; *s.* of William Eldred Jackson and Angelina Houghwout; *m.* 1916, Irene Gerhardt; one *s.* one *d.* *Educ.:* Public Schools; Albany Law School; Union University. Private practice of Law, 1913-34; General Counsel U.S. Bureau Internal Revenue, 1934-36; Asst. Attorney-General of U.S., 1936-38; Solicitor-General, 1938-40; Attorney-General of U.S. Cabinet, 1940-41. Representative of U.S.A. to negotiate Agreement of London, signed 8 Aug. 1945, for trial of war criminals. Hon. Bencher Middle Temple, 1946. *Publications:* The Struggle for Judicial Supremacy, 1941; Full Faith and Credit—the Lawyer's Clause of the Constitution, 1945; The Case Against the Nazi War Criminals, 1946; The Nürnberg Case, 1947; many articles and addresses. *Recreations:* riding, gardening. *Address:* United States Supreme Court, Washington, D.C. [*Died* 9 *Oct.* 1954.

JACKSON, Sir Russell; *see* Jackson, Sir W. D. R.

JACKSON, Brig.-General Sir Thomas Dare, 2nd Bt., *cr.* 1902; D.S.O. 1902; M.V.O. 1912; late The King's Own Royal Regt.; *b.* 14 June 1876; *e. s.* of Sir Thos. Jackson, 1st Bt., and Amelia Lydia Dare; *S.* father, 1915; *m.* 1919, Mary Lilian Vera, *d.* of late Brig.-Gen. S. E. Massy Lloyd, C.B.E.; one *d.* (one *s.* killed in action, 1944, and one *s.* decd.). Entered Army, 1897; Captain, 1901; Major, 1914; Lt.-Col. 1919; retired with hon. rank of Brig.-Gen. 1919; served South Africa, 1901-2 (despatches, Queen's medal with 5 clasps, D.S.O.); European War, 1914-18 (despatches, Bt. Lt.-Col., bar to D.S.O.). *Heir:* *b.* Major George Julius Jackson [*b.* 1883; *m.* 1909, Nesta Katherine, *e. d.* of Hedworth Barclay; one *s.* four *d.*]. *Address:* Herringfleet Hall, Lowestoft. [*Died* 7 *Feb.* 1954.

JACKSON, Sir (Walter David) Russell, 4th Bt., *cr.* 1902; retired; *b.* 8 March 1890; 3rd *s.* of Sir Thomas Jackson, 1st Bt., and Amelia Lydia (*d.* 1944), *d.* of George Julius Dare; *S.* brother 1956; *m.* 1915, Kathleen, *d.* of Summers Hunter, C.B.E., Tynemouth; one *s.* *Educ.:* Rugby. Served apprenticeship as Mechanical Engineer, 1909-14; served in Royal Artillery, 1914-19; Group Warden and Instructor, A.R.P., 1938-45. Now interested in local government, Bullingdon R.D.C. *Heir:* *s.* Michael Roland Jackson, *b.* 20 April 1919. *Address:* Guy's, Drayton St. Leonard, Oxford. *T.:* Warborough 68. [*Died* 15 *Dec.* 1956.

JACOBSTHAL, Paul Ferdinand, M.A., Dr.phil. (Bonn); Corr. F.B.A.; Hon. F.S.A.; *b.* 23 Feb. 1880; *e. s.* of late Martin and late Ida Jacobsthal; *m.* 1915, Emma Auguste Dorothée, *d.* of late Theodor and late Elisabeth Braeunig. *Educ.:* Luisenstädtisches Gymnasium, Berlin; Universities of Berlin, Göttingen, Bonn. Lecturer in Göttingen Univ., 1908-12; Prof. of Classical Archæology in Marburg Univ., 1912-35; formerly Student of Christ Church and Reader in Celtic Archæology, Oxford University. *Publications:* Der Blitz in der orientalischen und griechischen Kunst, 1906; Göttinger Vasen, 1912; Ornamente griechischer Vasen, 1927; (with A. Langsdorff) Die Bronzeschnabelkannen, 1929; Die melischen Reliefs, 1931; Early Celtic Art, 1944; Greek Pins and their European and Asiatic Setting, 1956; and articles in various periodicals; with Prof. Sir John Beazley, Joint Editor of Oxford Monographs on Classical Archæology. *Address:* Christ Church, Oxford. [*Died* 27 *Oct.* 1957.

JACOBY, Felix, M.A. (Oxon.); Dr. phil. (Berlin); F.B.A.; Mem. Faculty of Literæ Humaniores, Univ. of Oxford (Christ Church), since 1939; *b.* 19 March 1876; *s.* of late Oscar Jacoby and late Gertrud (*née* Loewenthal); *m.* 1901, Margarethe Johanne, *d.* of late Prof. Dr. Alfred von der Leyen and late Louise (*née* Kapp); two *s.* (two *d.* decd.). *Educ.:* Paedagogium zum Kloster U.L. Frauen, Magdeburg; Universities of Freiburg im Breisgau, München and Berlin. Professor (emeritus) and Hon. Senator Univ. of Kiel; Deutsche Akademie d. Wissenschaften (Berlin); Akademie d. Wissenschaften, Göttingen, etc. Lecturer, Breslau, 1903-06; Prof. of Classics, Kiel, 1906-39. Ehrenkreuz für Frontkämpfer, 1914-18. D.Litt. *h.c.* (Oxon.). Member of Deutsch. Archæol. Inst., 1956. *Publications:* Apollodors Chronik, 1902; Das Marmor Parium, 1904; Die Fragmente der Griechischen Historiker, I-III, 1923-58; Hesiodi Carmina I, 1930; Atthis (The Local Chronicles of Ancient Athens), 1949; papers on various subjects, mostly in the Classical Quarterly, Journ. Hellenic Studies, Hermes, etc. *Recreation:* detective stories. *Address:* 3a Archivstr., Berlin-Dahlem. [*Died* 10 *Nov.* 1959.

JACQUES, Brigadier Leslie Innes, C.B. 1953; C.B.E. 1945; M.C. 1918; *b.* 11 Dec. 1897; *s.* of late H. I. Jacques, Clifton, Bristol; unmarried. *Educ.:* Clifton; R.M.A. Woolwich. Commissioned Royal Engineers, 1916; served European War: B.E.F. (France and Belgium), 1916-19; Egypt, 1919-21; Adjutant 50 Northumbrian Div. Engineers (T.A.), 1925-29; Q.V.O. (Madras) Sappers and Miners, India, 1930-40; C.R.E. 10 (Indian) Div., 1940-42 (India, Iraq, Syria, Persia, M.E.F.); C.E. 21 (Indian) Corps, 1942-43 (Persia and Iraq); C.E. 15 (Indian) Corps, 1943-45 (Arakan and Burma); C.E. Northumbrian Dist. (U.K.), 1946-48; C.E. West Africa Command, 1948-50; retired 1953. *Address:* North Way, Pinner, Middlesex. *T.:* Pinner 1036. *Club:* United Service. [*Died* 28 *Dec.* 1959.

JAFFRAY, Sir William Edmund, 4th Bt., *cr.* 1892; T.D.; *b.* 29 July 1895; 2nd *s.* of 2nd Bt. and Alice Mary, *d.* of Francis Galloway; *S.* brother 1916; *m.* 1950, Anne, *o. d.* of late Captain J. Otho Paget, M.C., and of Mrs. Paget; one *s.* *Educ.:* Eton; Royal Military College, Sandhurst; Lieut.-Colonel commanding Warwickshire Yeomanry, 1935-1939. J.P., D.L., Warwickshire. *Heir:* *s.* William Otho, *b.* 1 Nov. 1951. *Address:* Manor House, Priorsdean, Petersfield, Hants. *T.:* Hawkley 26. *Club:* Buck's. [*Died* 24 *Oct.* 1953.

JAFFREY, Sir Thomas, 1st Bt., *cr.* 1931; Kt., *cr.* 1920; Hon. LL.D. Aberdeen; *b.* 11 April 1861; *s.* of late Thomas Jaffrey, Great North of Scotland Railway Company, Aberdeen; *m.* 1st, 1887, Margaret (*d.* 1930), *d.* of late George Tough, Culsalmond, Aberdeenshire; 2nd, 1932, Agnes Helen, 2nd *d.* of late Alexander Reid Urquhart, M.D., F.R.C.P.E., LL.D., Perth. *Educ.:* Public Schools, Aberdeen. Entered North of Scotland Bank, Limited, 1877; Actuary Aberdeen Savings Bank, 1892-1929 (now Consulting Actuary of Bank); Lord Rector's Assessor, Aberdeen University Court, 1924-37; Chairman of Aberdeen Art Gallery Committee; (res. 1951); Chairman Royal Horticultural Society, Aberdeen (res. 1946); founded (1921) Jaffrey Chair of Political Economy in University of Aberdeen; established Fund for Annual Prizes to Trustee Savings Banks Officers for encouragement of educational pursuits; Freeman of the City of Aberdeen. *Address:*

Edgehill, Milltimber, Aberdeenshire. *T.:* Culter 2142. *Club:* Royal Northern (Aberdeen). [*Died* 23 *July* 1953 (*ext.*).

JAGGER, David, R.P., R.O.I.; Portrait Painter. Member of Council of Royal Institute of Oil Painters. Exhibits at the Royal Academy. *Address:* 9 Netherton Grove, Chelsea, S.W.10. [*Died* 26 *Jan.* 1958.

JAISALMER, Maharajahdhiraj of, H.H. Maharawal Sir Jawahir Singhji Bahadur, K.C.S.I., *cr.* 1918; *b.* 18 Nov. 1882; succeeded, 1914; *m.*; two *s.* *Educ.:* Mayo College, Ajmer. *Address:* Jaisalmer, Rajputana. [*Died Jan.* 1949. [*But death not notified in time for inclusion in Who Was Who 1941–1950, first edn.*

JALLAND, Arthur Edgar, Q.C. 1950; Chairman, Lancashire County Quarter Sessions, since 1950; Recorder of Preston and Judge of Preston Borough Court of Pleas since 1950; *b.* 1889; 4th *s.* of Wm. Hy. and Mary S. Jalland; *m.* 1914, Elizabeth Hewitt, *e. d.* of Alderman W. H. Wainwright, J.P.; one *s.* one *d.* *Educ.:* Manchester Grammar School; Manchester University; Gray's Inn. LL.B. 1910. Called to the Bar, 1911. J.P. Lancashire County, and Preston Borough, 1950. Served European War, with H.M. Forces, 1915-19; Lieut. R.G.A. (S.R.). Contested (L.) Knutsford Parl. Div., 1929. *Recreations:* chess, swimming. *Address:* Redcote, Heaton Mersey, near Stockport. *T.:* Heaton Moor 1543. *Club:* Reform (Manchester). [*Died* 21 *Jan.* 1958.

JAMES, Arthur, M.B.E. 1952; D.L., J.P. Co. of Monmouth; Retired Works Manager; *b.* Llanover, Mon., 1871; *s.* of late John James *m.* 1897, Sarah Louisa (*d.* 1953), *d.* of John Edmunds, Coed-y-paen, Mon.; no *c.* *Educ.:* Llanover; King Henry VIII Grammar School, Abergavenny. Member of Monmouthshire County Council, 1921-46; of Newport (Mon.) Harbour Commissioners since 1920 (Chairman, 1929); Chairman of Executive Committee of Monmouthshire Branch of National Playing Fields Assocn. since 1933; Monmouthshire Representative of King George's Jubilee Trust Fund; Member of Pontypool Urban District Council, 1935-46 (Chairman 1942-43); Governor of Jones' West Monmouthshire School, 1930-49, (Vice-Chairman, 1932-49); of Pontypool Girls County School since 1922 (Chairman, 1923); of Abergavenny Grammar School, 1931-46; Governor South Wales and Mon. University Coll., Cardiff; Senior Officer of Griffithstown Baptish Church for many years; for work done on behalf of Belgian Refugees during European war was awarded Medal (Palms in Silver) of the Order of the Crown of Belgium; Local Fuel Overseer (Unpaid) for Pontypool Urban District Council, 1939-53; Director of Wales and Monmouthshire Industrial Estates Ltd., 1939-1947; Chm., Monmouthshire Agricultural Wages Committee since 1941; High Sheriff of Monmouthshire, 1941-42; Chairman: Pontypool A.T.C. Committee; Monmouthshire County Committee; Member of Air Cadet Council, 1951; Member National Insurance Advisory Cttee. for Mon. and Brecon; Gen. Commissioner for Income Tax. A.T.C. *Recreations:* Rugby football, cricket and golf. *Club:* Monmouthshire County (Newport, Mon.). [*Died* 19 *Feb.* 1959.

JAMES, Arthur Godfrey, C.B.E. 1920; M.A.; *b.* 22 Oct. 1876; 5th *s.* of John Henry James, Kingswood, Watford, Herts; *m.* 1910, Helen (*d.* 1958), *yr. d.* of Thomas Maitland, Broughty Ferry, Forfarshire; two *s.* two *d.* *Educ.:* Eton; Trinity College, Oxford (Scholar). Admitted a Solicitor, 1903; Lieut. R.A.S.C., 1915; served in Egypt; Staff Captain and D.A.A.G., War Office, 1916; in Ministry of National Service, 1917-18. *Recreations:* bicycling—preferably in France—golf. *Address:* Upwood Park, Abingdon, Berks. *T.:* Frilford Heath 258. *Club:* Leander. [*Died* 3 *Feb.* 1959.

JAMES, Charles Holloway, R.A. 1946 (A.R.A. 1937); F.R.I.B.A., F.R.S.A.; Partner in firm of James & Bywaters; *b.* Gloucester, 1893; *s.* of Thomas James and Clara Holloway; *m.* Margaret Bernard, *d.* of Harry Bernard Calkin, Member of Lloyds; two *d.* *Educ.:* Sir Thomas Rich's School, Gloucester; Taunton School, Taunton. Articled in Gloucester; served in various offices, including those of Sir Edwin Lutyens, P.R.A., and Barry Parker and Raymond Unwin; served European War, 1914-17; Architect for much domestic work and, with partners, for City Hall at Norwich, Town Hall, Slough, and County Hall at Hertford, and other public buildings; Freeman of, and Architect to, the Company of Goldsmiths; twice Vice-Pres. Architectural Association; Silver Medallist Paris Exhibition, 1925; R.I.B.A. London Architecture Medal 1950, and Ministry of Housing and Local Government Medal, 1950 and 1952. *Publications:* (with F. R. Yerbury) The Modern English House, Small Houses for the Community; (with S. Rowland Pierce) A Plan for Norwich; Royal Leamington Spa: A Plan for Development; various papers and articles. *Recreations:* gardening and snooker. *Address:* 5 Bloomsbury Street, W.C.1. *T.:* Museum 9952. *Club:* Arts. [*Died* 8 *Feb.* 1953.

JAMES, Lieutenant-Colonel Edmund Henry Salt, C.I.E. 1921; C.B.E. 1926; *b.* 26 June 1874; *y. s.* of late Lt.-Col. L. H. S. James, Royal Artillery; *m.* 1908, Muriel Hume, *d.* of late Charles Fowler, architect; (one *s.* killed in action, 1944). *Educ.:* privately. Entered Army, 1894; joined the Somerset Light Infantry; exchanged to the Indian Cavalry, 1897; served with the 5th Punjab Cavalry Frontier Force and commanded Khyber Rifles; joined the Indian Political Department, 1901; raised the Tonk Border Police, N.W.F.P., 1902; served in various appointments on N.W. Frontier, Baluchistan, Kashmir, Gilgit and Mysore, including Revenue Comr., N.W.F. Province (1922); took part in operations against Mahsuds, 1901-2 (medal and clasp); European War (medal and despatches); Chief Political Officer in Black Mountain Expedition, 1920 (C.I.E.); Malakand, 1925 (C.B.E.); Chief Camp Officer, Baluchistan Camps, King's Delhi Durbar, 1911; Revenue and Judicial Commissioner in Baluchistan, 1926; Agent to the Governor-General and Chief Commissioner in Baluchistan, 1928 and 1929; retired, 1929; Liaison Officer, Home Guard, 1940; resigned Major's Commission in H.G. under age limit and joined Civil Defence Service, 1942 (Victory medal). *Recreations:* shooting, fishing, ski-ing, and golf. *Address:* c/o Grindlay's Bank Ltd., 54 Parliament Street, S.W.1. *Club:* Junior United Service. [*Died* 27 *Oct.* 1952.

JAMES, Captain Sir Fullarton, 6th Bt., *cr.* 1823; C.B.E. 1926 (O.B.E. 1918); *b.* 15 May 1864; 5th *s.* of late Francis Edward James of Kerelaw Ayrshire; *m.* Penel, M.B.E. (*d.* 1954), *d.* of late J. K. J. Hichens, Beechgrove, Sunninghill, Berks; one *d.* *Educ.:* Magdalene Coll., Cambridge, M.A. Captain 3rd Battn. Royal Scots Fusiliers; called to bar, 1891; Chief Constable of Radnorshire, 1897; Chief Constable of Northumberland, 1900-35; King's Police Medal, 1916. *Heir:* cousin, Gerard Bowes Kingston, *b.* 4 Feb. 1899. *Address:* Beech Grove, Sunninghill, Berks. *T.:* Ascot 371. *Club:* Oxford and Cambridge. [*Died* 19 *July* 1955. *Baronetcy dormant.*

JAMES, Col. Lionel, C.B.E. 1924; D.S.O. 1918; *b.* 1871; *s.* of late Lt.-Col. L. H. S. James, R.A.; *m.* *Educ.:* Cranleigh. Reuter's special correspondent in the Chitral campaign, 1894-95; Mohmund, Malakand, and Tirah campaigns, 1897-98; Soudan, 1898; on staff of Times, 1899; Times special correspondent in Egypt, 1899, and S. Africa; 1899-1901; America and Macedonia, 1903; Japan and Manchuria, 1904; frequent short foreign missions, 1904-13; retired from journalism and the staff of the Times, 1913;

commanded K.E.H. with B.E.F., France and Italy, 1915-18 (despatches twice, D.S.O., Crown of Italy); Manager Racing Stable and Stud Farm, 1929-31; a Governor of Imperial Service College, Windsor, 1930, of Haileybury and I.S.C., 1942; Berkshire C.C., 1940; retired from Public Services, 1946; occasional Broadcasts for B.B.C.; reviews serious and sporting books for several leading journals. *Publications:* four or five volumes of short stories; With the Chitral Relief Force, 1895; Indian Frontier War, 1897-98; On the Heels of de Wet, 1902; The Boy Galloper, 1903; The Yellow War, 1905; A Study of the Russo-Japanese War, 1906; A Subaltern of Horse, 1908; Side Tracks and Bridle Paths, 1909; With the Conquered Turk, 1913; The History of King Edward's Horse, 1921; High Pressure, 1929; Times of Stress, 1929; Green Envelopes, 1929; collaborated on the Times History of the War in S. Africa, vols. ii. and iii. *Address:* Fieldridge Wood, Shefford, Woodlands, Newbury, Berks. *T.:* Great Shefford 244. *Club:* Cavalry. [*Died* 30 *May* 1955.

JAMES, Rt. Rev. Melville Charles, D.D.; *b.* 13 May 1877; Deacon, 1901; Priest, 1902; Vicar of St. Peter, Ballarat, 1913-17; Archdeacon of Maryborough, 1917-21; Archdeacon and Canon of Ballarat, 1921-26; Bishop of St. Arnaud, 1926-50; retired, 1950. *Address:* 21 Rose Street, Box Hill, Victoria, Australia. [*Died* 4 *April* 1957.

JAMES, Hon. Robert, J.P.; Managing Director of the Barrow Hæmatite Steel Coy. Ltd. since 1933; *y. s.* of 2nd Lord Northbourne; *b.* 1873; *m.* 1st, 1900, Lady Evelyn Kathleen Wellesley (*d.* 1922), *d.* of 4th Duke of Wellington; one *s.*; 2nd, 1923, Lady Serena Mary Barbara Lumley, *d.* of 10th Earl of Scarbrough, K.G., G.B.E., K.C.B.; two *d.* *Educ.:* Harrow; Trinity College, Cambridge. *Address:* St. Nicholas, Richmond, Yorks. *Club:* Brooks's. [*Died* 13 *Dec.* 1960.

JAMES, Rolfe A. S.; *see* Scott-James.

JAMES, Thomas David, C.B.E. 1920; *b.* 1871; *m.* Pauline, *d.* of late Sir Francis Xavier Frederick MacCabe. *Educ.:* Christ College, Brecon; Christ's College, Cambridge; 1st Class Honours Classical Tripos, 1893; M.A., 1897. Entered Civil Service, 1894; Assistant Accountant-General, 1914; Deputy Accountant-General of the Navy, 1921-31. *Address:* 78 Waterloo Road, Dublin. [*Died* 23 *Feb.* 1955.

JAMESON, Alexander Hope, M.Sc., M.Inst.C.E., F.K.C.; Professor of Civil Engineering, University of London, King's College, 1912-1935, Emeritus Professor since 1935; *b.* Highbury N., 15 Oct. 1874; *s.* of John W. and Jessie M. Jameson; *m.* 1911, Mary A. Martindale, Kendal; no *c.* *Educ.:* Home at Accrington; Owens College, Manchester. Bishop Berkeley Fellow and Demonstrator in Whitworth Engineering Laboratory, 1894-97; Draughtsman Lancashire and Yorkshire Railway, Manchester, and Assistant to Resident Engineers, Halifax and Wakefield, 1897-1901; Engineering Assistant, Derwent Valley Water Board, and Resident Engineer on Derwent Aqueduct, 1901-9; Resident Engineer on Thirlmere Aqueduct (Third Pipe Line), 1909-1912; External Examiner Bristol Univ. 1920-1921, London University 1927 and 1930-33; Dean of Engineering Faculty, London University, 1932-1935. Hon. Sec, Worthing Branch, Over-Seas League, 1947-50, Hon. Treasurer, 1946-51. *Publications:* paper, Testing the Strength of Materials, in Proceedings Institute Civil Engineers (awarded Miller prize and James Forrest medal); paper on Theory and Practice in Air Lift Pumping, 1917, Non-Uniform Flow in Uniform Channels, 1919, The Venturi Flume 1925, Proceedings Institution of Water Engineers; Flow over Sharp-edged Weirs, Nov. 1948, Journal Inst. C.E.; Contour Geometry, 1931; Advanced Surveying, 2nd ed. 1948; Fluid Mechanics, 1937, 2nd ed. 1942; (Joint) Mathematical Geography, Vol. I., 1927; Vol. II., 1929. *Address:* 24 Cissbury Ave., Findon Valley, Worthing. [*Died* 23 *Dec.* 1952.

JAMESON, Lt.-Col. John Bland, C.I.E. 1919; M.B.; I.M.S., ret.; *s.* of J. Jameson, Heywood Hall, Lancs, and Armathwaite, Cumb.; *m.* 1900, Charlotte Ethel, *d.* of B. W. Jones of Brookhurst, Leamington. *Educ.:* Rossall; Edinburgh University, M.B., C.M. Served Miranzai Expedition, 1891 (medal and clasp); N.W. Frontier of India, 1897-98 (despatches, medal and clasp); Tirah Campaign, 1897-98 (clasp); European War, 1914-19 (despatches, C.I.E.). *Address:* c/o Lloyds Bank, Winchester. [*Died* 27 *Oct.* 1954.

JAMESON, John Gordon; Sheriff, Substitute of Lothians, 1923-46; Advocate-Scottish Bar; Barrister, English Bar; *b.* 13 Apr. 1878; *s.* of Andrew Jameson, Lord Ardwall, Scottish Judge; *m.* 1913, Margaret, 5th *d.* of A. L. Smith, Master of Balliol; two *d.* (and one *s.* decd.). *Educ.:* Edinburgh Acad.; St. Andrews Univ.; Balliol Coll., Oxford, B.A.; Intervarsity Boxing Champion (Middleweight), 1898; Edinburgh University, LL.B. Served S. African War, 1901; 19th Company Imperial Yeomanry (Queen's medal 2 clasps); Captain Scottish Horse, 1914; Major, 1916; Captain, 710th Labour Company, 1918; Unionist Candidate for Edinburgh, 1912; M.P. (Co. U.) Edinburgh (West), 1918-22. *Publications:* The Good News, 1921; The Way of Happiness (The Beatitudes), 1946; Why Jesus Died (The Trial of Jesus), 1948; The Kingdom of Heaven in the Parables, 1949. *Address:* 34 Great King Street, Edinburgh. *T.:* 28090. *Club:* New (Edinburgh). [*Died* 26 *Feb.* 1955.

JAMIESON, Rt. Hon. Lord; Douglas Jamieson, P.C. 1935; K.C. 1926; Senator of College of Justice in Scotland since 1935; *b.* 14 July 1880; *s.* of late William Jamieson, merchant, Glasgow; *m.* Violet, *d.* of late H. W. Rhodes, Stratheden House, Blackheath; one *s.* two *d.* *Educ.:* Cargilfield and Fettes College, Edinburgh; Glasgow and Edinburgh Universities. Admitted to Faculty of Advocates, 1911; M.P. (U.) Maryhill Division of Glasgow, 1931-1935; Solicitor General for Scotland, 1933-35; Lord Advocate for Scotland, 1935; contested (U.) Stirling and Falkirk Burghs, 1929. *Recreation:* fishing. *Address:* 34 Moray Place, Edinburgh. *Club:* University (Edinburgh). [*Died* 31 *May* 1952.

JAMIESON, Sir Archibald (Auldjo), K.B.E., *cr.* 1946; M.C.; *b.* 1884; *s.* of George Auldjo Jamieson and Susan Oliphant; *m.* 1917, Doris (*d.* 1947), *d.* of Capt. Henry Pearce, R.N.; two *s.* two *d.*; *m.* 1956, Margretta Stroup Austin. *Educ.:* Winchester; New College, Oxford. Chartered Accountant, Edinburgh, 1911; served European War, 1914-18 (despatches, M.C.); Director, Robert Fleming & Co., Ltd. *Recreation:* fishing. *Address:* 6 Smith Square, Westminster, S.W.1. *Club:* Broks's. [*Died* 23 *Oct.* 1959.

JAMIESON, Vice-Adm. Douglas Y.; *see* Young-Jamieson.

JAMIESON, Edgar George, C.B.E. 1926; *b.* 9 Oct. 1882; *s.* of late George Jamieson, C.M.G.; *m.* 1910, Mabel Armitage; two *d.* *Educ.:* Fettes College, Edinburgh. Student Interpreter in China, 1902; Consul-General, 1935; retired from Consular Service in China, 1940. *Address:* Rossway, Painswick, Glos. [*Died* 11 *June* 1958.

JANION, Edwin Manifold; Director English, Scottish, and Australian Bank, 1932-1945; *b.* 24 Jan. 1863; *s.* of Edwin Janion, Liverpool, and Elizabeth Bowers Robinson, Liverpool; *m.* 1905, Georgette Marie, *y. d.* of Mr. Justice Rossignon, Brussels; one *s.* one *d.* *Educ.:* Merchant Taylors', Crosby. Was 30 years with Chartered Bank of India, Australia, and China, and Manager of some of their important branches in the East; has been Chairman of Chamber of Commerce in Singapore and Penang, and a J.P. in those Settlements; Manager of the English, Scottish, and Australian Bank, London, 1913-32; served on Committees of British Bankers, British Overseas Banks, and Australian and New Zealand Banks' Association, and from 1923 to end of 1932 Chairman of the last-named. *Recreation:* fly-fishing. *Address:* Malaya, Sanderstead, Surrey. *T.:* Sanderstead 1348. [*Died* 12 *Jan.* 1952.

JANSEN, Hon. Ernest George, B.A., LL.B.; LL.D. (Hon.); Governor-General of the Union of South Africa since 1951; *b.* 7 Aug. 1881; *m.* M. M., *d.* of S. Pellissier and *g.d.* of Rev. J. P. Pellissier, a French Missionary; one *s.* *Educ.:* at home on farm near Dundee; Ladysmith; Durban. B.A., LL.B. (Cape) private study; Admitted as Attorney, 1906, and a few years later as Advocate in Pietermaritzburg, Natal, where he took active part in politics. In 1915 joined National Party, which was established that year, and contested Umvoti seat. Member of Independence Deputation to England, 1919; contested Vryheid seat, 1920; gained Vryheid seat from General Emmett, 1921, and for 22 years represented Vryheid in House of Assembly. On assumption of office by Hertzog Govt., 1924, became Speaker; Leader of S. African Parl. Party which toured Canada, 1928; Minister of Native Affairs, 1929; again took office as Speaker, 1933-43; was defeated in Vryheid and Zululand Constituencies, respectively, 1943 and 1947. After death of General Kemp, was elected National Party M.P. for Wolmaransstad, Transvaal, 1947; Minister of Native Affairs, 1948-50. Has always played leading rôle in cultural sphere; since 1906 has taken a prominent part in all movements in Natal for promoting the cause of Afrikaners; served for many years on Councils of Natal Univ. College and Univ. of S. Africa; until recently was a member of Council of Univ. of Pretoria; Chm. of Voortrekker Centenary Cttee., 1938; Chm. Voortrekker Monument Inauguration Cttee., 1949. One of original members of S. African Acad. for Science and Arts (Afrikaans), founded in 1909; recently apptd. hon. life mem.; Chairman of Central Nat. Monuments Commn., 1931-. Hon. Degrees: LL.D. Witwatersrand and Natal Universities. *Publications:* Die Natalse Boerekongres; Die Voortrekkers in Natal; Die Voortrekkertyd; many articles in Die Huisgenoot and other periodicals; editor of the National Party's English newspaper New Era (now defunct). *Recreations:* was a good athlete and cricketer. *Address:* Government House, Cape Town and Pretoria, S. Africa. [*Died* 25 *Nov.* 1959.

JARDINE, Brig. Christian W. B.; *see* Bayne-Jardine.

JARDINE, Maj.-General Sir Colin A., 3rd Bt., *cr.* 1916; C.B. 1940; D.S.O. 1914; M.C.; D.L.; *b.* 24 Sept. 1892; *s.* of 1st Bt., K.C.I.E., LL.D., and Minnie Dunbar (*d.* 1941), *d.* of Jabez Hogg, F.R.C.S.; *S.* brother, 1924; *m.* 1919, Jean Evelyn Livesey, *d.* of late Maj.-Gen. Sir W. A. Liddell, K.C.M.G., C.B.; one *s.* two *d.* *Educ.:* Charterhouse; R.M.A., Woolwich. R.A., 1912; Bt. Maj. 1929; Bt. Lieut.-Col. 1933; Lieut.-Col. 1939; Col. 1939; Major-Gen. 1942; served European War, 1914-18 (thrice wounded, despatches four times, D.S.O. and bar, M.C.); Brigade-Major, 7th Indian Infantry Brigade, Razmak, 1926-27; Military Sec. Dept., at the War Office, 1930-34; Military Secretary to C.-in-C., B.E.F., France, 1939-1940 (despatches twice); Deputy Fortress Commander, Gibraltar, 1942; Director of Army Welfare, War Office, 1943-44; retired pay, 1945; Member of Charterhouse School Governing Body; Chairman Friends of the Poor, Ebury Street, London; Chairman of Church Army Board; Chairman Family Welfare Association; Chairman Royal United Kingdom Beneficent Association; Member of Church Assembly. D.L. Hampshire, 1954. *Heir:* *s.* Ian Liddell, M.C., Major Coldstream Guards [*b.* 13 Oct. 1923; *m.* 1948, Priscilla Scott-Phillips, *y. d.* of D. M. P. Phillips, Halkshill, Largs, Ayrshire; two *d.*]. *Address:* Vallenders, Isington, Alton, Hants. *Club:* United Service. [*Died* 24 *Sept.* 1957.

JARDINE, Douglas Robert; *b.* 23 Oct. 1900; *s.* of Malcolm Robert Jardine and Alison Moir; *m.* 1934, Irene Margaret, *d.* of Sir Harry Peat, *q.v.*; one *s.* three *d.* *Educ.:* Winchester College; New College, Oxford. B.A. Oxon., 1923; qualified solicitor, 1926; Chairman N.S.W. Land Agency Co. Ltd.; Director The Scottish Australian Co. Ltd. Played cricket for England, captaining M.C.C. teams to Australia and New Zealand, 1932-33, and to India, 1933-34. Served War of 1939-45, Royal Berkshire Regt., France, Belgium, India. *Publications:* In Quest of the Ashes, 1933; Cricket, 1936. *Recreations:* cricket, fishing, shooting, stalking. *Address:* Holland Moor, Gills Hill, Radlett, Herts. *T.:* Radlett 5507. *Clubs:* United University, East India and Sports, M.C.C. [*Died* 18 *June* 1958.

JARDINE, Brigadier-General James Bruce, C.M.G. 1916; D.S.O. 1901; D.L. Roxburghshire; 5th Lancers; Officer Legion of Honour; *b.* Edinburgh, 6 Jan. 1870; *e. s.* of late M. L. P. Jardine, late 86th and 67th Regts.; *m.* 1908, Agnes, *e. d.* of late Sir A. Hargreaves-Brown, 1st Bt.: two *d.* *Educ.:* Charterhouse; Sandhurst. Joined 5th Lancers as 2nd Lieut. 1890; Lieut. 1892; Capt. 1901; Maj. 1907; Lt.-Col. 1917; served South African War, 1899-1902; was Staff Officer to Col. Callwell's Column for the latter part of the time; present at Elandslaagte, Reitfontein, Lombard's Kop, Defence of Ladysmith, Belfast, General French's operations in S.E. Transvaal and Cape Colony (despatches twice, D.S.O., medal with 5 clasps, King's medal 2 clasps); attached to Japanese Army, 1903; was with General Kuroki's army, as Military Attaché, during all the operations in Manchuria, 1904-5 (medal with clasp); European War, 1914-17 (despatches four times, Bt. Lt.-Col., C.M.G.); 4th Class Order of Sacred Treasure, Japan; Member, Royal Company of Archers, Queen's Bodyguard for Scotland. *Address:* Chesterknowes, by Selkirk. *Clubs:* Cavalry; New (Edinburgh). [*Died* 17 *March* 1955.

JARRATT, Sir Arthur (William), K.C.V.O. 1958; Kt. 1946; Capt. R.N.V.R.; Hon. Pres. Kinematograph Renters' Society since 1958; lately Deputy Chairman Royal Naval Film Corporation; Chairman and Managing Director George Humphries & Co. Ltd.; *b.* 22 Sept. 1894; *s.* of John Jarratt; *m.* 1920, Dorothy Veronica Cross; one *d.* *Educ.:* London. Master, Company of Gold and Silver Wyre Drawers, 1936; Warden Company of Drapers. Life Governor of St. Bartholomew's, St. Thomas's and Prince of Wales Hospitals and others. *Recreation:* music. *Address:* Royalty House, 72/3 Dean Street, W.1. *T.:* Gerrard 4383. *Clubs:* City Livery, Royal Automobile. [*Died* 14 *Dec.* 1958.

JARRETT, George William Symonds; *b.* 15 Dec. 1880; *m.* 1912, Janet Mary, *d.* of late Major R. H. Dunning, 17th Regt., of Putsborough, N. Devon. Assistant architect Devon Education Committee, 1905-1907; secretary and surveyor Lancing College, 1908-10; organiser, National Service League, 1913-15; Army, 1915-17; chief organiser, National Democratic Party, 1917-1920; Editor, British Citizen, 1918-20; Managing Director, The Dryden Press, 1924-1934; Director, Davy Gravure, Ltd., 1932-1937; Administrator, Embankment Fellowship Centre, 1935-46; Editor Fellowship, 1936-46. Contested Mansfield, 1918; Edmonton, 1924; East Ham North by-election, 1926; Edmonton, 1929; M.P. (C.), Dartford Division of Kent, 1922-23; Director, Combined Products, Limited, Continental Comestibles, Limited, 1942-53. Surrey County Council, 1949-52. Exec. Cttee. and Hon. Treas. National Society for Epileptics, 1954-1959. Médaille Reconnaissance Française,

1947. *Address:* 41 Riverview Gardens, S.W.13. *T.:* Riverside 5347.
[*Died* 6 *Dec.* 1960.

JARVIS, Very Rev. Alfred Charles Eustace, C.B. 1928; C.M.G. 1918; M.C.; D.D.; Provost Emeritus of Sheffield since 1948; Chaplain of the Order of St. John of Jerusalem, 1927; *b.* 14 Nov. 1876; *m.* Muriel (*d.* 1938), *y. d.* of Rev. Thomas Orton; three *s.* one *d.* *Educ.:* privately; Handsworth Theological College, Birmingham. Wesleyan Minister, 1901-8; served Birmingham Mission, Transvaal, and Guards' Depôt, Caterham; Deacon Church of England, 1908; Priest, 1909; Curate All Saints, South Lambeth, 1908-9; Chaplain to the Forces, 1909; served at Woolwich, 1909-11; Jamaica, 1911-13; Portsmouth, 1913-14; Lichfield, 1914-15; served European War, Assistant to Principal Chaplain Mediterranean Expeditionary Force (Gallipoli, Salonika, Egypt), 1915-1917; Principal Chaplain Mesopotamia, 1917-19 (despatches three times and specially promoted, M.C. C.M.G., Serbian Order of the White Eagle); Aldershot (St. George's), 1919-20; Assistant Chaplain-General, Northern Command, 1920-25; Chaplain-General to the Forces, 1925-31; Chaplain of the Tower of London, 1927-31; Provost of Sheffield, 1931-48; Vicar of Sheffield, 1931-48; Archdeacon of Sheffield, 1931-33 and 1934-38; Rural Dean of Sheffield, 1939-42; D.D. conferred by Archbishop of Canterbury, 1925; Select Preacher, Cambridge, 1928; Hon. Canon of Sheffield, 1931-36; Chaplain-in-Ordinary to King George V., 1925-31; Chaplain to King Edward VIII., 1936; to King George VI, 1937-52. *Address:* 22 Benslow Lane, Hitchin, Herts.
[*Died* 26 *March* 1957.

JARVIS, Lieut.-Colonel Charles Francis Cracroft, O.B.E.; Member of Lloyd's; D.L. Lincolnshire; J.P. Kesteven; formerly of the Yorkshire Regt.; late commander 12th Lindsey Home Guard Bn.; *s.* of late Rev. Canon F. A. Jarvis; *m.* 1st, Helen Constance (*d.* 1948), 3rd *d.* of Sir Edward Hunter-Blair, 4th Bart.; one *s.*; 2nd, 1949, Mme. T. Holtorp. Served S. African War (Queen's medal 7 clasps) European War, 1914-18 (despatches, Brevet Major); High Sheriff of Lincolnshire, 1930. *Address:* Doddington Hall, Lincoln. *T.:* Doddington 227. *Clubs:* Carlton City of London.
[*Died* 18 *Jan.* 1957.

JARVIS, Major Claude Scudamore, C.M.G. 1936; O.B.E.; *b.* 20 July 1879; *s.* of John Bradford Jarvis and Mary Harvey; *m.* 1903, Mabel Jane, *d.* of Charles Hodson of the American Embassy, London; one *d.* Served in South African War in Imperial Yeomanry, 2nd Lieutenant 3rd Dorset Regiment (Special Reserve) 1902; European War, France, Egypt and Palestine; Joined Egyptian Government in 1918; Governor, Sinai Peninsula, 1923-36; awarded Lawrence Memorial Medal by Royal Central Asian Society, 1938. Orders of Nile and Qaddara (Egypt), Phoenix (Greece), Istiklal (Trans-Jordan). *Publications:* Yesterday and To-Day in Sinai; Three Deserts; Desert and Delta; The Back Garden of Allah; Oriental Spotlight; Arab Command; Scattered Shots; Heresies and Humours; Happy Yesterdays; Gardner's Medley. *Recreations:* shooting and fishing. *Address:* Chele Orchard, Ringwood, Hants. *T.:* Ringwood 340.
[*Died* 8 *Dec.* 1953.

JAYAKAR, Rt. Hon. Mukund R., P.C. 1939. *Educ.:* Elphinstone High School and College, Bombay. Started a charitable public school called Aryan Education Society High School, in Bombay; worked there four years; practised as a Barrister in the Bombay High Court; took to public life in 1916; elected to Bombay Legislative Council, 1923; Leader of Council, Swaraj Party and Leader of Opposition until he resigned, 192; M.L.A. 1926; Deputy Leader of Assembly, Nationalist Party, 1927-30; Leader of Opposition in Simla Session, 1930; Judge, Federal Court, India, 1937-39; member of Judicial Committee of Privy Council, 1939-41; a Delegate to Round Table Conference, London, and Member of Federal Structure Sub-Committee; first hon. Vice-Chancellor of Poona Univ., 1948-6; Social-Reformer; President Social Reform Conference, Nasik, 1917. *Publication:* Aspects of Vedanta Philosophy. *Address:* Malabar Hill, Bombay 6, India. *Clubs:* Athenæum, National Liberal; Orient (Bombay).
[*Died* 10 *March* 1959.

JAYNE, Ronald Garland, C.B.E. 1938; formerly a Director of Garland Laidley & Co. Ltd., Oporto and Lisbon; Hon. Member of The British Chamber of Commerce in Portugal (Incorporated); *b.* Oxford, 1877; *s.* of late Rt. Rev. Francis John Jayne, late Bishop of Chester and Emily Sarah, *e. d.* of Watts John Garland, Lisbon; *m.* 1901, Mary Salkeld, *d.* of James Salkeld Robinson, Rochdale; one *s.* *Educ.:* Private. Was President for three years and Chairman for 25 years of The British Chamber of Commerce in Portugal; a Vice-President and Hon. Life Member of The Anglo-Portuguese Society; O.B.E. for services during European War. *Address:* Quinta das Pedras Altas, Canas de Senhorim, Beira Alta, Portugal.
[*Died* 6 *July* 1951.

JEBB, Geraldine Emma May, C.B.E. 1952; M.A. Cantab.; retired; 2nd *d.* of late Rev. H. H. Jebb and G. C. Jebb; unmarried. *Educ.:* Newnham College, Cambridge (Economics Tripos). Civil Service (Employment Department of the Ministry of Labour), 1913-17; Director of Studies and Lecturer on Economics at Newnham College, Cambridge, 1917-19; Lecturer on Economics at Armstrong College, Newcastle on Tyne, 1919-29; Principal of Bedford College, 1930-1951, retired, 1951. Fellow of Bedford College, Associate of Newnham College. *Address:* Stapleton's Chantry, N. Moreton, Didcot, Berks. *Club:* University Women's.
[*Died* 28 *Dec.* 1959.

JEBB, Richard, M.A., J.P.; *b.* 1874; *e. s.* of late Arthur Trevor Jebb of The Lyth, Ellesmere, Salop, and Eglantyne Louisa, *d.* of late Robert Jebb of Killiney, Ireland; *m.* 1900, Margaret Ethel (*d.* 1949), *d.* of George Lewthwaite of Littlebank, Settle; two *s.* one *d.* *Educ.:* Marlborough Coll.; New Coll., Oxford. Travelled in Egypt, North America, Australia, New Zealand, Japan, India, 1897-1901; Captain 2nd V.B. K.S.L.I., 1905-08; travelled in Canada, Australasia, South Africa (1906), West Indies (1909); contested East Marylebone as Independent Tariff Reformer, 1910; military service, 1914-19. *Publications:* Studies in Colonial Nationalism, 1905; The Imperial Conference, a History and Study, 2 vols., 1911; The Britannic Question, 1913; The Empire in Eclipse, 1926; various papers on Imperial Questions. *Recreations:* fishing, shooting, etc. *Address:* The Lyth, Ellesmere. *T.:* Ellesmere 39.
[*Died* 25 *June* 1953.

JECKELL, George Allen; Controller, Yukon Territory, from 1913; Agent, Department of Public Works; Inspector of Income Tax, Yukon Territory; *b.* 25 July 1880; *s.* of William Jeckell and Essy Case; *m.* 2nd, Anna Theresa Boyle: three *s.* *Educ.:* Public and High Schools, Province of Ontario. Teacher, Public and High Schools, Province of Ontario, North West Territories, and Yukon Territory; the position of Gold Commissioner of Yukon Territory was abolished, and the duties of Office merged with that of Controller, 1932. *Address:* Dawson, Yukon Territory, Canada.
[*Died* 30 *May* 1950.
[*But death not notified in time for inclusion in Who Was Who 1941–1950, first edn.*

JEFFERS, William Martin; Vice-Chairman, Board of Directors, since 1946- and Director, Union Pacific Railroad Company; *b.* North Platte, Nebraska, 2 Jan. 1876; *s.* of William Jeffers and Elizabeth Gannon; *m.* 1900, Lena A. Schatz (*d.* 1946);

one *d.* *Educ.:* Public schools, North Platte, Nebraska. Began career with Union Pacific Railroad in 1890, as call boy, telegrapher, clerk, maintenance of way dept. until 1894; clerk and telegrapher, 1894-95; train dispatcher, 1896-1900; chief dispatcher, 1900-1905; trainmaster, 1905-8; Asst. Supt. Utah Div. and Supt. Wyoming and Nebraska Divs., 1908-15; Gen. Supt., 1915-16; Gen. Man., 1916-17; Vice-Pres. and Gen. Man., 1917-28; Vice-Pres., 1928-32; Exec. Vice-Pres., 1932-37; Pres., 1937-46, upon his retirement elected Vice-Chm. Served as Nat. Rubber Director, Washington, D.C., 1942-43. *Recreations:* participates actively in civic and national affairs in interest of public welfare; Boy Scouts of America, etc. *Address:* (home) Huntington Hotel, Pasadena, Calif., U.S.A.; (office) Union Pacific Building, 422 West 6th St., Los Angeles, Calif., U.S.A. *T.:* Trinity 9211. *Club:* California (Los Angeles, Calif.).
[*Died* 6 *March* 1953.

JEFFERY, George Barker, M.A., D.Sc., F.Coll.H.; F.R.S. 1926; Director of Institute of Education, University of London, since 1945; Member of the Senate of the University of London since 1935; Member: Advisory Cttee. on Educ. in Colonies since 1945; Secondary Sch. Examinations Council since 1946; Chm. South West Middlesex Hosp. Management Cttee. since 1948; Member, Nat. Advisory Council on Training and Supply of Teachers since 1949; Chm. Exec. Cttee. Nat. Foundn. for Educ. Research in Eng. and Wales since 1949; Dean of the College of Handicraft since 1952; President: English New Education Fellowship since 1952; Association of Teachers in Colleges and Depts. of Education since 1954; *b.* 9 May 1891; *s.* of George and Elizabeth McDonald Jeffery; *m.* 1915, Elizabeth Schofield, Blackburn; one *s.* two *d.* *Educ.:* Strand Sch., King's Coll.; Wilson's Gram. Sch., Camberwell; Univ. Coll., London. B.Sc. (Lond.), 1911; M.A. (Lond), 1914; Fell. Univ. Coll., London, 1916; D.Sc. (Lond.), 1921; Hon. Fell. Coll. of Handicraft, 1952. Asst. in Applied Mathematics, 1912, University Reader in Mathematics, 1921, Univ. Coll., London. Professor of Mathematics at King's Coll., London, 1922-1924; Astor Prof. of Mathematics at Univ. Coll., 1924-45. Pro-Provost, Univ. Coll., London in Bangor, 1939-44. Swarthmore Lectr. to Society of Friends, 1934; Pres. Lond. Mathematical Soc., 1935-37; Pres. London Soc. for the Study of Religion, 1937-38; Vice-Pres. Royal Society, 1938-40; Pres. Mathematical Assoc., 1947; Chm. W. African Educ. Study Group, 1951. *Publications:* Papers on mathematics and mathematical physics published in Proc. Roy. Soc., London Mathematical Soc., Philosophical Magazine, etc. *Recreations:* cabinet making and silversmithing. *Address:* Institute of Education, Malet St., W.C.1; Balnagall, Potter St., Pinner, Middlesex. *T.:* Pinner 937. *Club:* Athenæum.
[*Died* 27 *April* 1957.

JEFFERY, Colonel Walter Hugh, C.S.I. 1924; C.M.G. 1949; C.I.E. 1914; *b.* 15 Dec. 1878; *m.* 1911, Cicely Charlotte Cowdell. *Educ.:* Blundell's School; Plymouth College; R.M.C., Sandhurst. Entered Army, 1898; Bt. Lt.-Col., Indian Army, 1919; Lt.-Col., 1921; Colonel, 1923; retired, 1935. *Address:* 29 Stafford Court, W.8. *T.:* Western 2823. [*Died* 27 *April* 1957.

JEFFERYS, Charles William, R.C.A.; LL.D. Queen's; O.S.A.; *b.* Rochester, Kent, 1869; *e. s.* of C. T. and Ellen Jefferys; *m.* 1st, 1894, Jane M. F. Adams; one *d.*; 2nd, 1907, Clara A. B. West; four *d.* *Educ.:* Public Schools, Hamilton and Toronto. Studied art under late C. M. Manly, A.R.C.A., and G. A. Reid, R.C.A.; engaged in illustration and commercial design; to New York, 1893; artist on New York Herald and American magazines; exhibited in numerous Canadian and American art exhibitions; returned to Canada, 1900; made many pictures illustrating American and Canadian history for the Makers of Canada, The Chronicles of Canada, The Pageant of America, The Chronicles of America (assistant editor), and School Histories of Canada; numerous illustrations in Canadian magazines and books, including 102 illustrations for works of T. C. Haliburton (Sam Slick); A.R.C.A., 1913; artist attached to the Canadian War Records, 1917; pictures in the National Gallery of Canada at Ottawa, the Art Gallery of Toronto, the Collegiate Institute, Saskatoon, Normal School, Ottawa, Public Library, Sarnia, Ont., and private collections; mural decorations in The Manoir Richelieu, Murray Bay, Quebec, in the Château Laurier, Ottawa, The Royal Ontario Museum, Toronto, and in private houses; historical consultant in reconstruction of Habitation of Port Royal, 1605-1613; author and illustrator of Dramatic Episodes in Canada's Story, Canada's Past in Pictures, The Picture Gallery of Canadian History, vols. I, II and III. *Address:* York Mills, Ontario, Canada. *T.:* Hudson 0895 W. Toronto. *Club:* Arts and Letters (Toronto).
[*Died* 8 *Oct.* 1951.

JEFFES, Maurice, C.M.G. 1939; *s.* of Thomas Edward Jeffes, late British Consul, Brussels; *m.* 1953, Susan Mildred, *d.* of late Captain T. H. Southam, Indian Army. *Educ.:* Brussels; Heidelberg. Served with the armies in France, 1916-19, Royal West Surrey Regiment and Intelligence Corps; Medal of King Albert of Belgium, 1919; entered Passport Control Service, F.O., 1919; formerly Director of Passport Control Dept. *Address:* The Grange, Thwaite, nr. Eye, Suffolk. *T.:* Mendlesham 314. *Clubs:* Savile, Royal Automobile.
[*Died* 8 *Nov.* 1954.

JEFFREY, Robert; Manager and Actuary, Scottish Amicable Life Assurance Society, retired 1948; *b.* 7 March 1884; *s.* of late Robert Jeffrey and Catherine Wishart; *m.* 1915, Mabel Inglis, *o. d.* of late Wm. Inglis Clark, D.Sc., Edinburgh; two *s.* *Educ.:* Edinburgh. Fellow of the Faculty of Actuaries in Scotland; Associate of the Institute of Actuaries. *Recreations:* mountaineering, ski-ing, golf. *Address:* The Lea, Bridge of Allan, Stirlingshire. *T.:* Bridge of Allan 2353. *Clubs:* Caledonian, Alpine; Western (Glasgow); New (Edinburgh); Prestwick Golf (Prestwick, Ayr).
[*Died* 19 *March* 1956.

JEFFREYS, 1st Baron, *cr.* 1952, of Burkham; **George Darell Jeffreys,** K.C.B., *cr.* 1932 (C.B. 1918); K.C.V.O., *cr.* 1924; C.M.G. 1916; J.P., D.L. and C.A., Hampshire; General, retired; Colonel of Grenadier Guards since 1952; *b.* 8 March 1878; *o. s.* of late Rt. Hon. A. F. Jeffreys, M.P., of Burkham, Hants; *m.* 1905, Dorothy (*d.* 1953), Viscountess Cantelupe, *widow* of Lionel, Viscount Cantelupe, and *d.* of J. P. Heseltine of Walhampton, Hants (one *s.* killed in action, 1940). *Educ.:* Eton; R.M.C., Sandhurst. Served with Grenadier Guards in Nile Expedition, 1898, including battle of Khartoum (Queen's medal and Khedive's medal with clasp); South African War, 1900-2 (Queen's and King's medals, 5 clasps); Commandant of the Guards' Depôt, 1911-14; served European War in France and Flanders, Aug. 1914 (at Mons) to Nov. 1918; Lt.-Col. commanding 2nd Batt. Grenadier Guards, 1915; commanded 58th, 57th, and 1st Guards Brigades, 1916-17; 19th Division, 1917-19 (severely wounded, despatches 9 times, Bt. Lieut.-Colonel 1915, Bt. Colonel 1917, C.M.G., C.B.; Major-General, June 1919); 2nd class Order of St. Stanislaus (Russia); Commander Ordre de la Couronne (Belgian); Croix de Guerre (Belgian); Commander Legion of Honour; Croix de Guerre (France); Knight of Norwegian Order of St. Olaf; Grand Officer Order of Leopold

(Belgium); 2nd class Order of the Rising Sun (Japan); Grand Cross Order of the Crown (Roumania); Commanded Light Division, Army of the Rhine, 1919; London District, 1920-24; Wessex Area and 43rd (Wessex) Division T.A., 1926-30; G.O.C.-in-C. Southern Command, India, 1932-36; A.D.C. General to the King, 1936-38; Hampshire C.C., 1926-32 and from 1937, Alderman, 1941; Chm. Hampshire and I.O.W. T.A. Assoc., 1938-48; Chm. Hampshire County Civil Defence Cttee. 1938-54; County Organiser Hampshire Home Guard, 1940; Chm. Basingstoke County Bench, 1925-1932 and 1936-52; Lieut.-Gen., 1930; General, 1935; retired pay, 1938. Colonel of Royal Hampshire Regt., 1945-48; Hon. Col. 583 (Hampshire) H.A.A. Regt. R.A. (late 48th S.L. Regt.), 1938-48; M.P. (C.) Petersfield Div. of Hants., 1941-51. *Recreations:* hunting, shooting. *Heir:* *g. s.* Mark George Christopher Jeffreys, Major Grenadier Guards, *b.* 2 Feb. 1932. *Address:* Burkham House, Alton, Hants. *T.:* Herriard 211. *Clubs:* Guards, Carlton. [*Died* 19 *Dec.* 1960.

JEFFREYS, W. Rees; Chairman, Roads Improvement Association, Inc.; Member Permanent International Commission, Assoc. of Road Congresses; Member, Statutory Panel of Experts, Ministry of Transport; Member, Council T.P.I.; Chairman, Roads and Public Works, Ltd., Surrey Motors, Ltd.; *b.* London 1871. *Educ.:* privately. Board of Trade, 1891-1903; organised the Motor Union of Great Britain and Ireland, 1903-10, the Commercial Motor Users Assoc., and the Institution of Automobile Engineers, 1906-10 (Hon. Treasurer, 1910-33); Secretary, Road Board, 1910-18; an authority on Highway Administration at Home and Abroad; secured appointment of a Departmental Committee in 1903 to inquire into Highway Administration in England and Wales; travelled extensively to examine transport conditions; a representative of Great Britain at the official Conference (Paris, 1909) on the international circulation of Motor Cars; associated with efforts to solve the dust problem; Chairman, British Committee Fourth Congress (Seville), 1923, Fifth Congress (Milan), 1926, Sixth Congress (Washington), 1930, Seventh Congress (Munich), 1934, and Eighth Congress (The Hague), 1938; Member of Treasury Committee on Motor Car Licence Duties, 1916; Member of the Departmental Committee on the Taxation and Regulation of Road Vehicles, 1920-22; Founder and Director (1906-28) of the Motor Union Insurance Co., Ltd. Has established a Studentship at London School of Economics, for Research into the Economics of Transport and a Triennial lecture under the auspices of the Town Planning Institute on Roads and Transport; has organised and endowed a Road Trust to promote the construction of new roads and bridges. *Publications:* The King's Highway, 1949, articles and pamphlets on Public Administration, Transport and Labour questions. *Recreation:* collecting modern pictures. *Address:* Wivelsfield Hall, near Haywards Heath, Sussex. *T.:* Wivelsfield Green 223. *Clubs:* Royal Automobile; Royal Scottish Automobile (Glasgow). [*Died* 18 *Aug.* 1954.

JEGER, Santo Wayburn, M.R.C.S., L.R.C.P.; M.P. (Lab.) S.E. St. Pancras, 1945-50, Holborn and St. Pancras South since 1950; *b.* 20 May 1898. *Educ.:* University College, Cardiff; London and St. Mary's Hospitals. Elected to Borough Council, 1925; Mayor of Shoreditch, 1930; Member of L.C.C., 1931-46. Visited Spain twice during Civil War 1937 on Medical Aid work for Republicans; during War was in charge of Mobile Ambulance Unit and First Aid Post as Medical Officer. Helped to found Socialist Medical Association. Contested S.E. St. Pancras 1935. Practised Medicine since 1923. *Publication:* London's Borough Councils, 1937; Austria, 1946. *Recreations:* Socialism and medicine, chess and the arts. *Address:* 31 Nottingham Place, W.1. *T.:* Welbeck 2602. [*Died* 24 *Sept.* 1953.

JEHU, Ivor Stewart, C.I.E. 1944; Chief Information Officer, Ministry of Aviation; *b.* 21 Oct. 1908; *s.* of late Professor Thomas John Jehu, Regius Professor of Geology, Edinburgh Univ., and Annie Meston, 2nd *d.* of late Very Rev. Principal Alexander Stewart, D.D.; *m.* 1944, Joan Mary Rose, *er. d.* of late Lt.-Col. J. L. R. Weir, C.I.E., and *widow* of Major G. B. Neale; one *s.* one *d.* *Educ.:* Edinburgh Academy; Edinburgh Univ.; St. John's College, Cambridge. Sub-Editor, Glasgow Herald, 1931-32; Junior Assistant Editor, Times of India, 1932; War Correspondent on North-West Frontier in Mohmand Operations 1935, and Waziristan Operations 1938; Special Representative of Times of India at Headquarters, Govt. of India, 1938; acted as correspondent for Times, Daily Mail, Daily Telegraph and Christian Science Monitor. Director of Public Relations, Defence Dept., Govt. of India, June 1940, with rank of Lt.-Col. (Indian Army); promoted Brigadier as head of Inter-Services Public Relations Directorate, India Command, 1942; released from military service July 1945 to resume duty as Editor, Times of India; Editor: The Sunday News of India, Evening News of India; Dir., Messrs. Bennett, Coleman & Co. (India), 1948-50; retired, 1950. Chief Information Officer, Ministry of Supply, 1952-59. *Recreations:* travel, golf, tennis. *Address:* 29 Bramham Gardens, S.W.5. *Clubs:* Oriental; Willingdon (Bombay). [*Died* 7 *Oct.* 1960.

JELF, Brig.-General Rudolf George, C.M.G. 1919; D.S.O. 1915; late the King's Royal Rifle Corps; *b.* 19 Aug. 1873; *m.* 1919, Kathleen, *y. d.* of W. Rowe Geen. Entered Army, 1893; Captain, 1901; Major, 1910; Col., 1920; A.D.C. to Viceroy of India, 1907-11; served Chitral, 1895 (medal with clasp); S. African War, 1899-1902 (Queen's medal 3 clasps, King's medal 2 clasps); European War, 1914-18 (despatches five times, C.M.G., D.S.O., Bt. Lt.-Col.); retired pay, 1926. *Recreations:* hunting, fishing, shooting, golf. *Address:* The Rough, Chobham Road, Camberley. *T.:* 738. [*Died* 22 *Oct.* 1958.

JENKIN, H(enry) A(rchibald) Tregarthen, O.B.E., 1919; *b.* 27 Feb. 1886; *s.* of John Jenkin and Ann Gamble Cooper; *m.* Dagmar, *d.* of William Leggott; one *s.* two *d.* *Educ.:* King's School, Canterbury; Jesus College, Cambridge. 1st class Classical Tripos, Historical Tripos. Board of Education, 1909; H.M. Inspector of Schools, 1914; Divisional Inspector, 1934; Prison Commission (Home Office), 1946; formerly Director of Education and Welfare, Prison Commission. *Recreations:* archæology, philately. *Address:* The Firs, Norton, nr. Worcester; 13 Old Court, Kensington, W.8. *Clubs:* Athenæum, Oxford and Cambridge, Authors'. [*Died* 1 *June* 1951.

JENKINS, Rev. Canon Alfred Thomas; Residentiary Canon and Custos of Lichfield Cathedral since 1955; *b.* 17 Feb. 1893; *s.* of David and Eveline Jenkins; *m.* 1922, Doris Cecelia Hutchings; one *s.* one *d.* *Educ.:* St. David's College School and St. David's College, Lampeter; University College, Oxford. B.A. 1923; M.A. 1928. Curate: Ystradyfodwg, 1917-19; St. Clement, Oxford, 1919-23; St. Martin, Birmingham, 1923-26. Vicar: Broxbourne, Herts, 1926-32; Sparkhill, Birmingham, 1932-44; Walsall, Staffs, 1944-55. Rural Dean: Ware, Herts, 1931-1932; Bordesley, Birmingham, 1932-43; Walsall, Staffs, 1943-55. Hon. Canon of Birmingham, 1941-43; Canon Emeritus of Birmingham, 1943-; Prebendary of Lichfield, 1952-55. Proctor in Convocation, for Diocese of Lichfield, 1950-. *Publications:* History of Birmingham Parish Church, 1925; S. Martinus Turonensis, 1925; History of Sparkhill Parish Church, 1936. *Recreations:*

ornithology, gardening, golf. *Address:* The Close, Lichfield. *T.:* Lichfield 2566. [*Died* 4 *June* 1960.

JENKINS, Rev. Canon Claude, D.D.; Canon of Christ Church and Regius Prof. of Ecclesiastical History, Oxford, 1934; Sub-dean Christ Church, 1943-57; Chaplain St. John of Jerusalem, 1933; Lambeth Librarian, 1910-29 (Hon. Librarian, 1929-); *b.* 26 May 1877; *e. s.* of late Oswald Jenkins, F.S.I., Little Aston, Staffs, and Sarah, *d.* of late William Palmer. *Educ.:* King Edward's School Birmingham; New College, Oxford. Open Classical Exhibitioner; 2nd Class Mods., 1898; B.A. (2nd Class Lit. Hum.), 1900; 2nd Class Theol., 1901; Denyer and Johnson University Scholar, 1902; Assistant Master Magdalen College School, Oxford, 1902-3; M.A. 1903; D.D. 1924; Deacon, 1903; Priest, 1904; Curate of St. Martin-in-the-Fields and Assistant Chaplain of Charing Cross Hospital, 1903-29; Lecturer in Ecclesiastical History, King's College for Women, 1905-11; Lecturer in Patristic Texts, King's College, London, 1911-34; Fellow, 1921; Prof. of Ecclesiastical History, King's College, London, 1918; and in Univ. of London 1931-1935; Reader in Greek and Latin Palæography, Univ. of London, 1925-35; Member of Senate, 1930-38; Dean of Faculty of Theology, 1933-34; Canon of Canterbury, 1929-34; Chaplain to the Archbishop of Canterbury, 1911-; Examining Chaplain to Bishop of Gloucester, 1923-45; Select Preacher, Cambridge, 1924-5, 1930-31; Sub-Editor, Church Quarterly Review, 1903-18, Joint Editor, 1921-7; F.S.A. 1917; Member of Council of Society of Antiquaries 1924-26, 1932-34, of King's College, London, 1944, of Canterbury and York Society, of Kent Record Society; Vice-President, Royal Historical Society, 1935; and S.P.C.K., 1937-; Hon. Librarian Church House, London; late Chairman of the Central London Federation of Working Men's Clubs; Curator of Bodleian Library, 1936-52; Senior Librarian Oxford Union Society, 1939-. *Publications:* Origen on 1 Corinthians, 1908-09; an unpublished Visitation of Archbishop Parker (1573), 1911; Cranmer's Collectiones de Divortio in Dibdin and Healey's English Church Law, 1912; editor, Index to Lambeth Act Books, 1916-1937; The Monastic Chronicler, 1922; an Unpublished Act Book of the Archdeaconry of Taunton, 1929; (with K. D. Mackenzie) Episcopacy, Ancient and Modern, 1930; Introduction to the Register of Simon Sudbury, Bishop of London, 1933; Sir Thomas More, 1935; English translation of Duchesne's History of the Christian Church, Vol. III., 1924; F. D. Maurice and the New Reformation, 1938; Supervisor, Wordsworth and White's edition of Vulgate, 1938-54. *Recreations:* walking, climbing, and collating MSS. *Address:* Christ Church, Oxford. *Club:* Athenæum. [*Died* 16 *June* 1959.

JENKINS, Ven. David, B.A.; Canon of Bangor, 1934; Archdeacon of Merioneth, 1940-52, now Emeritus; *b.* Llanfair Clydogau, Cards., 1876; *s.* of Daniel and Sarah Jenkins; *m.* 1st, 1911, Mary (*d.* 1946), *d.* of late Archdeacon Morgan, Bangor; one *s.* one *d.*; 2nd, 1949, Mildred Gertrude Bowyer, Criccieth. *Educ.:* St. David's College School; St. David's Coll., Lampeter; St. Michael's Coll., Aberdare. Vicar Choral of St. David's Cathedral, 1912-16; Surrogate, 1918; Member of the Governing Body and Representative Body, and the General Purposes Cttee. of the Church in Wales; Prebendary of Llanfair in Bangor Cathedral, 1934-40; O.C.F. 1941. High Sheriff's Chaplain, 1943. Vicar of Portmadoc with Tremadoc, 1916-47. Rural Dean of Eifionydd, 1929. *Address:* Min-y-Nant, Criccieth, N. Wales. *T.:* 2121. [*Died* 25 *May* 1960.

JENKINS, Sir (Edward) Enoch, Kt., *cr.* 1946; *b.* 8 February 1895; 2nd *s.* of late John William Jenkins, Rhiwbina, Cardiff; *m.* 1929, Muriel Alice, *d.* of late Audley Harold Ackermann, Que Que, S. Rhodesia; one *s.* one *d.* *Educ.:* Howard Gardens Grammar School, Cardiff; Cardiff Univ. Coll.; Peterhouse, Cambridge. B.A., LL.B.(Cantab.)1922; M.A. 1927; called to Bar, Gray's Inn, 1924; South Wales Circuit. Served European War, France, 1914-19; Lieut. R.F.A. Cadet, Nyasaland, 1925; Acting Attorney-Gen., Apr.-July 1927; Acting Asst. Attorney-Gen., July-Oct. 1927; Asst. Registrar, High Court, N. Rhodesia, Nov. 1927; Crown Counsel, Apr. 1930; Acting Attorney-Gen. various occasions, 1931-37; Acting Judge, High Court, 1934. Solicitor-Gen. 1936; Attorney-Gen. Fiji, 1938; Acting Chief Justice, 1939-40; Chief Justice, Nyasaland, 1945-53; Judge of Appeal, Rhodesia and Nyasaland Court of Appeal, 1948-53; Justice of Appeal, East African Court of Appeal, 1953-56. Chairman Fiji Hurricane Commn., 1941; Chm. Zomba Prison Riot Commn., 1948; Member Judicial Commn. on Central Africa Federation, 1952; Commissioner for the Revision of the Laws of the Leeward Islands, 1958. Gov. National Heart Hosp., London, 1958. *Recreations:* cricket, tennis. *Address:* c/o Secretariat, St. John's, Antigua, Leeward Is., W.I.; 84 Northway, N.W.11. *T.:* Speedwell 7883. [*Died* 25 *Feb.* 1960.

JENKINS, Evan David Thomas; Emeritus Prof. of Classics, University College of Wales, Aberystwyth, since 1947; *b.* 27 Feb. 1882; 2nd *s.* of late Rev. David Jenkins, Vicar of Llangwyryfon, Cardiganshire; *m.* 1921, Maggie, *e. d.* of late Hugh Dalrymple, Annan and Liverpool. *Educ.:* Christ College, Brecon; Keble College, Oxford (Scholar). 1st Class Classical Moderations, 1903; prox. acc. Gaisford Prize (Prose), 1904; 1st Class Lit. Hum. 1905; Assistant Lecturer in Classics, University College of Wales, 1906; Lecturer, 1918; Warden, Plynlymon Hall of Residence for Men Students, 1919-25. Head of the Department of Greek, 1923-38; Prof. of Classics, 1938-47. Temporary 2nd Lieutenant K.O. Yorkshire L.I. Dec. 1915; Lieut. June 1917; served with 9th (Service) Bn. in France, June-July 1916 (severely wounded 1 July); attached 25th Bn. Durham L.I. and in command of Works Detachments in Northern Command, 1917-19; Examiner Higher Certificate Central Welsh Board, 1927-35, and 1938, also Higher Certificate Oxford and Cambridge Joint Board; Member of Governing Body of Church in Wales, 1935; Member of Court, University of Wales, 1936-39; Member of Academic Board, 1942-45; Representative of Senate on Council of U.C.W., 1944-47; Life Governor of U.C.W.; Governor of Dr. Williams' School, Dolgelley, 1929-57; Member of Commission of Inquiry and Advice, St. David's College, Lampeter, 1939-40 and Examiner in Classics, 1942-48; Examiner for Univ. of London 1947-56; External Examiner in Latin, Sheffield Univ., 1949-52, Leeds Univ., 1953-55. Platoon-Comdr., 1940, Capt., 1st Cardiganshire Battn. Home Guard, 1941; Major, 1942. *Publications:* contribution to New Edition of Encyclopædia Britannica; reviews in Classical Review. *Address:* Deva, Marine Terrace, Aberystwyth, Cards. [*Died* 4 *May* 1960.

JENKINS, Hon. Sir George (Frederick), K.B.E., *cr.* 1946; Member, House of Assembly for Newcastle, S. Australia, 1938-55; *b.* Terowie, 24 June 1878; *m.* 1907, Ruby, *d.* of Hopkin Bowen; three *s.* two *d.* *Educ.:* Terowie Public School; Roseworthy Agricultural College. M.H.A. South Australia for Burra Burra, 1918-24, 1927-30 and 1933-38; Minister of Agriculture and Repatriation, 1922-23; Commissioner of Public Works and Minister of Local Government and Marine, 1923-24; Commissioner of Crown Lands and Minister of Local Government, 1927-30; Minister of Agriculture and Minister of Forests, South Australia, 1944-54. *Address:* 10 Godfrey Terrace, Leabrook, South Australia. [*Died July* 1957.

JENKINS, His Honour George Kirkhouse, Q.C. 1931; County Court Judge for Bath and Wiltshire, 1935-57, retired; Neutral Referee South Wales Coalfield; Divorce Commissioner; *yr. s.* of late Richard Jenkins, Mining Engineer, and late Margaret Jenkins, Llansamlet; *m.* 1924, Alice Dorothy (J.P. Somerset 1943), *y. d.* of late Cornelius Biddle, surgeon, and Mabel M. Biddle, Merthyr Tydfil; two *d. Educ.:* Swansea Grammar School. Admitted Solicitor, 1907; called to Bar, Middle Temple, 1914, and South Wales and Chester Circuit; enlisted Inns of Court O.T.C., 1915; Gazetted Welsh Regiment, 1915; served in Egypt and Palestine; Chairman: Somerset Quarter Sessions; Bath Licensing Planning Committee; Conscientious Objectors Tribunal, South Western Area. *Publications:* contrib. to Encyc. of Laws of England; Ed. 10th edn., Bullen and Leake's Precedents of Pleadings. *Address:* Glen Avon, Lansdown, Bath. *T.:* Bath 3749. [*Died* 10 *May* 1957.

JENKINS, Gilbert Henry, F.R.I.B.A.; Architect and Landscape Architect; *b.* Torquay, 22 July 1875; *s.* of Henry Tozer Jenkins and Elizabeth Lucy Pountain; *m.* 1902, Beatrice Estelle Langdon; three *s.* two *d. Educ.:* Queen's College, Taunton. Architect with late W. H. Romaine-Walker for Additions to Tate Gallery; Buckland, Berks; Derby House; Exbury, Hants; Great Fosters; Holme Lacy; Knowsley, and many town and country houses, gardens and estates; served (or serving) on Councils of Architectural Association, R.I.B.A., I.L.A., London Society, etc. for several years; Past Pres. Inst. of Landscape Architects; P.P. Architectural Assoc.; during European war, 1914-18, volunteered under Derby Scheme and was graded C.3 so joined Trench Warfare Dept. and served in it or Ministry of Munitions, first as Supply Officer, then Materials Allocation Officer and finally as Asst. on Production Programme until November 1918; Civil Defence Post Warden, 1940-45. Since 1945 engaged in restoring various Churches, including St. Paul's, Shadwell, St. Mary, Paddington and St. Stephen, Edinburgh. *Publications:* Many articles on Landscape Architecture and gardening in Technical Press. *Recreation:* golf. *Address:* 24 Daleham Gardens, Hampstead, N.W.3. *T.:* Hampstead 7769. *Club:* Chelsea Arts. [*Died* 24 *May* 1957.

JENKINS, Walter Allen, C.I.E. 1942; D.Sc.; LL.D.; Vice-Chancellor, Dacca University, since 1953; *b.* 1 April 1891; *e. s.* of William D. Jenkins, Rotherham; *m.* 1915, Kate Camburn Hobkinson, Rotherham; two *d. Educ.:* Rotherham Grammar School; Sheffield University; Emmanuel College, Cambridge. Senior Science Master, Mill Hill, 1915; joined I.E.S., 1916; Prof. of Physics, Dacca Univ., 1921-26, Vice-Chancellor, 1932. Divisional Inspector of Schools, 1926. Special Officer Government of Bengal, 1933; Director of Public Instruction, Bengal, 1943-45; Director Organisation and Method and Secretary to Govt. of Bengal, 1945-47; Administrative Adviser, Machinery of Government, The Treasury, 1948-49. Registrar, University College of North Staffordshire, 1949-53; Director of Studies, 1953. *Publications:* research papers and special reports upon University Finance, Primary and Adult Education. *Recreations:* cricket, football, golf. *Address:* The University, Dacca, East Pakistan. *Clubs:* Overseas; Bengal United Service (Calcutta). [*Died* 26 *Sept.* 1958.

JENKINS, Sir Walter (St. David), Kt. *cr.* 1936; C.B. 1921; C.B.E. 1918; *b.* 1 March 1874; *s.* of late Walter and Margaretta Jenkins; *m.* 1906, Dora, *d.* of G. N. Jacob, J.P., Dublin; one *s.* two *d. Educ.:* Carmarthen Grammar School; Oswestry School; Jesus College, Oxford (Meyricke Exhibitioner, 1893); B.A., 1897; 1st Class Clerk Admiralty, 1898; Assistant Director of Navy Contracts, 1912; Director of Navy Contracts, 1919-36; Sec. Oil Fuel Committee, 1902-6; Mission to India and Burma, 1905-6; Secretary to Admiralty Committee of the Royal Commission on Oil Fuel and Engines, 1913; Admiralty Secretary to the Railway Communications Board, 1912; superintended the supply of coal from South Wales to the British, French, and Russian Navies, 1914; member of Commission for State Control of the South Wales Collieries, Dec. 1916; Mission to Rome to confer with Italian Government on the supply of coal, 1917; chairman of the Shipping and Coal Co-ordinating Committee Ministry of Shipping, 1917; member of Admiralty Reconstruction Committee, 1918; Admiralty representative on the Surplus Government Property Advisory Council, 1918; Government Director of the Anglo-Persian Oil Co., Ltd., 1918-19; Chairman National Federation of Iron and Steel Merchants, 1938-44; Member Consultative Committee Iron and Steel Control, 1939; Officer of the French Legion of Honour, 1918; Officer of the Order of the Crown of Italy, 1918; Order of St. Anne of Russia; Silver Jubilee Medal, 1935. *Address:* 8 Rutland Court, Knightsbridge, S.W. *T.:* Kensington 9933. *Clubs:* United University, Royal Thames Yacht, Roehampton. [*Died* 7 *June* 1951.

JENKINS, Sir William John, Kt., *cr.* 1945; C.I.E. 1939; M.A., B.Sc.; *b.* Edinburgh, Scotland, 27 Oct. 1892; *s.* of late William Jenkins, M.A.; *m.* 1924, Kathleen Lilian Margaret, *d.* of late Richard Wilson. *Educ.:* George Watson's Boys' College, Edinburgh; Edinburgh Univ., M.A., B.Sc. (Agric.) 1919. Joined Indian Agricultural Service as Deputy Director of Agriculture in 1920, after serving from 1914-18 in Royal Field Artillery in France, Mesopotamia and Palestine; Deputy Secretary, Indian Central Cotton Committee, Bombay, 1925; Officiating Secretary, Central Cotton Committee, 1926 and 1928; Offg. Director, Institute of Plant Industry, Indore, 1927; Chief Agricultural Officer in Sind, 1930; Director of Agriculture, Bombay Province, 1936; Agricultural Commissioner, Bombay Province, 1946-47; retd. 1947. *Publications:* numerous departmental publications, etc., on agriculture and allied subjects. *Recreations:* golf and fishing. *Address:* Adamsrib, Netherstreet, Bromham, Wilts. *Club:* East India and Sports. [*Died* 16 *March* 1957.

JENNER, Lieut.-Colonel Sir Albert Victor, 3rd Bt., *cr.* 1868; C.M.G. 1918; D.S.O. 1888; J.P., Hants; Rifle Brigade, retired; *b.* 19 Dec. 1862; *s.* of Sir William Jenner, 1st Bt., G.C.B., F.R.S., M.D.; *S.* brother, 1948. *Educ.:* Winchester. Entered Rifle Brigade, 1882; Major, 1899; served Burmese Expedition, 1886-88 (despatches, D.S.O., medal with two clasps); South Africa, 1896 (despatches, brevet of Major, medal); South Africa, 1900-2 (brevet Lieut.-Colonel; Queen's medal 4 clasps, King's medal 2 clasps); General Staff Officer, War Office, 1915-19. *Heir:* none. *Address:* Greenwood, Durley, Hampshire. [*Died* 4 *Nov.* 1954 (*ext.*).

JENNER, Lieut.-Col. Leopold Christian Duncan, C.M.G. 1919; D.S.O. 1916; late K.R.R.C.; *b.* 24 Oct. 1869; 5th and *y. s.* of Sir William Jenner, 1st Bt.; *b.* and *heir-pres.* to Sir Albert Victor Jenner, 3rd Bt., *q.v.*; *m.* 1899, Nora Helen Gertrude (*d.* 1952), *y. d.* of Field-Marshal Sir Donald Stewart, 1st Bt.; no *c. Educ.:* Marlborough; Sandhurst. 2nd Lieut. King's Royal Rifles, 1888; Adjutant, 1891-95; won Army Fencing Championship, Royal Military Tournament, 1894-95; Captain, 1896; Adjutant 3rd London Rifles, 1899-1904; retired 1904; Joint Polo Manager, Ranelagh Club, 1904-1911, when resigned; won Roehampton Cup, 1905, 1907-10; Open Cup, Ranelagh, 1908; Champion Cup, 1907; Public Schools' Cup, 8 years; selected to play for England *v.* Ireland, 1907; rejoined Army on mobilisation in Aug. 1914; served Egypt, April-July 1915, Gallipoli, Aug.-

Dec. 1915 (despatches, D.S.O.), France, June 1916-April 1919 (despatches three times, C.M.G., Officer of the Order of the Crown of Roumania, promoted to Lt.-Col.). *Address:* 9 The Circus, Bath. *Club:* Royal Automobile. [*Died* 20 *Oct.* 1953.

JENNEY, Brigadier Reginald Charles Napier, C.B.E. 1960; Director, Field Survey, Ordnance Survey, since 1957; *b.* 24 Jan. 1906; *s.* of late Col. G. W. Jenney, I.M.S., and late Mrs. K. G. Jenney (*née* Bythell); *m.* 1932, Violet Rochfort, *e. d.* of late George Flowers, I.C.S.; four *s.* one *d.* *Educ.:* Dover College; R.M.A. Woolwich; Cambridge Univ. (B.A.). Commissioned as 2/Lt. Royal Engineers, 1926; India, 1929; seconded to Survey of India, 1930. War Service with survey units in India, Iraq and Persia (despatches, 1942). Director-General, Survey of Pakistan, 1947-50; Deputy Director of Military Survey, War Office, 1952; Ordnance Survey, 1955-. *Recreations:* cricket, hockey and tennis in the past; gardening now. *Address:* 68 Hillcrest Gardens, Hinchley Wood, Esher, Surrey. *T.:* Emberbrook 5948. [*Died* 1 *June* 1960.

JENNINGS, Edward Charles, C.B.E. 1919; D.L.; Lieut.-Colonel late commanding 6th Bn. (S.R.) Royal Fusiliers; *b.* 17 July 1877; *s.* of R. E. Jennings, M.A., J.P., of Gelli-deg, Carmarthenshire, and Margaret, *d.* and *co-heir* of R. Luther Watson of Calgarth Park, Westmorland; *m.* 1906, Ethel Anita Dawes (*d.* 1948), *d.* of late Thomas T. Whitehurst, The Mount, Shrewsbury; one *s.* one *d.* *Educ.:* Eton. 2nd Lieut. (Militia) Royal Lancaster Regt., 1895; transferred to Royal Fusiliers (regular army), 1898; served in Chinese Regt. and China Expeditionary Force, 1901; retired (on retired pay) with rank of Captain, Royal Fusiliers, 1906; transferred to Special Reserve, 1906; Major, 1914; Lieut.-Colonel, 1917; served European War, 1914-19 (C.B.E., despatches). J.P. 1911-50. *Recreations:* motoring, golf. *Club:* Devonshire (Eastbourne). [*Died* 13 *Jan.* 1955.

JENNINGS, Gertrude E.; Dramatic Author. *Publications:* one-act plays—Between the Soup and the Savoury, 1910; Our Nervous System, 1911; Acid Drops, 1914; The Rest Cure, 1914; Five Birds in a Cage, 1915; The Bathroom Door, 1916; Elegant Edward, 1916; Poached Eggs and Pearls, 1917; Waiting for the Bus, 1919; Me and My Diary, 1922; The Voice Outside, 1923; Richmond Park, 1927; The Bride, 1931; In the Black-Out 1942; Good Neighbours, 1942; Too much Bluebeard, 1944; Happy as a King; Puss in the Corner, 1946; I'll Pay Your Fare, 1951; three-act plays—The Young Person in Pink, 1920; Love Among the Paint Pots, 1921; Money Doesn't Matter, 1922; Isabel, Edward and Anne, 1923; These Pretty Things, 1928; Family Affairs, 1934; Our Own Lives, 1935; Pantomime Whiskers and Co., 1943; Pantomime: Sleeping Beauty, 1944; Aladdin, 1945; Bubble and Squeak, 1947; The Olympian, 1954; Happy Memories, 1955. *Address:* c/o Samuel French, Ltd., 26 Southampton Street, Strand, W.C.2. [*Died* 28 *Sept.* 1958.

JENNINGS, Lieut.-Col. James Willes, D.S.O. 1899; late R.A.M.C.; *b.* 25 Feb. 1866; *s.* of late Robert Jennings, Woodlawn, Cork. *Educ.:* Monmouth. L.R.C.S., L.M. Ireland; L.R.C.P. and L.M. Ireland; L.M. Rotunda; Senior Gold Medalist Operative Surgery, 1887-88, R.C.S.I. Entered Army Medical Dept., 1891; Egypt, 1892-95; served with Dongola expedition, 1896 (medal); seconded for service with Egyptian army, 1897; Nile expedition, 1897-99 (despatches, 2 clasps, 4th class Mejidieh); Gedaref Relief Force, 1898 (clasp); defeat of Ahmed Fedil's army, Rosaires, 26 Dec. 1898 (Gedaref clasp, despatches, D.S.O.); senior Medical Officer of Blue Nile District, Soudan, 1898-99; served South Africa, 1899-1902 with 2nd West Yorks Regt.; operations in Natal, Zululand and Swaziland (despatches, Queen's medal with 5 clasps, and King's medal with 2 clasps); with the Abyssinian Army against the Mullah, 1903-4 (despatches, medal and clasp); serving on Army H.Q. Staff, India, 1905-7; Burma, 1907-9; Lt.-Col. Comd. 56 Field Ambulance, B.E.F., France, 1915-16; Mediterranean, 1917-18; and No. 5 Native Stationary Hospital, B.E.F., France, 1919. *Publications:* Cordite Eating, 1903; With the Abyssinians in Somaliland, 1906. *Recreations:* shooting, fishing, phonography, photography, etc. *Club:* United Service. [*Died* 25 *Nov.* 1954.

JENNINGS, Leonard, O.B.E.; sculptor; studied at Lambeth School of Art, Glasgow School of Art, Royal Academy of Arts; employed in India by Government of India on Sculptures for Public Buildings, 1907-09; enlisted in Surrey Yeomanry, Sep. 1914; commissioned in Northumberland Hussars, 1915; served in France and Flanders, 1916-19 (despatches twice). Re-commissioned General List, 1940; served War of 1939-45, at Home, 1940-45. *Principal Works:* Statue of King Edward VII., Bangalore; Thackeray Memorial, Calcutta; Imperial Service Cavalry Brigade war memorial, Delhi; statue of Prince of Wales, Bombay; statue of King George V, Patna. *Club:* Chelsea Arts. [*Died* 5 *Oct.* 1956.

JEPSON, Captain Rowland Walter, M.A.; Officier d'Académie; *b.* 7 Nov. 1888; *s.* of J. W. Jepson, late Headmaster of Mr. Allatt's School, Shrewsbury; *m.* Margaret, *er. d.* of late G. R. Brace, Horam, Sussex; two *s.* two *d.* *Educ.:* Shrewsbury School; Magdalene College, Cambridge (Exhibitioner and Organist); 2nd Class Classical Tripos Pt. I, 1910; 2nd Class Historical Tripos Pt. II, 1911; B.A., 1910; M.A., 1926. Assistant Master, Liverpool College, 1911-1915; served 3rd Cheshire Regt. and R.A.F., 1915-19; President, Examinations Board R.A.F. Cadet Brigade; Chief English Master and School Librarian, Dulwich College, 1919-26; Headmaster, County School for Boys, Bromley, Kent, 1926-29; Headmaster, Mercers' School, Holborn, 1929-46; Gresham Lecturer in Rhetoric, 1946-47. *Publications:* Writer's Craft, 1927; First Steps in Writing English, 1933; Further Steps, 1934; English Exercises for School Certificate, 1935; Clear Thinking, 1936; English Grammar for To-day, 1936; A New Guide to Précis Writing, 1936; Exercises in Interpretation, 1937; Teach Yourself to Think, 1938; Teach Yourself to Express Yourself, 1944. *Recreations:* gardening, bridge. *Address:* The Elms, Iron Bridge, Shropshire. *T.:* 2152. [*Died* 29 *March* 1954.

JERROLD, Mary; Actress; *b.* 4 Dec. 1877; *m.* 1905, Hubert Harben; one *s.* (one *d.* *decd.*). *Educ.:* Gower St. School; Church of England High School, London. Two years and a season at St. James's Theatre with Mr. and Mrs. Kendal. Created character of Rose in Milestones, 1912; parts played include: Fraülein Schroeder in The Man Who Stayed at Home; Mrs. Morland in J. M. Barrie's Mary Rose; Susan Throssel in revival of Quality Street, Haymarket; played Martha Brewster in Arsenic and Old Lace, Strand, 1942-46; Miss Mabel in R. C. Sherriff's play of that name; Lucy in The Old Ladies, New Theatre, 1934, and in revival, Lyric, Hammersmith, 1950; Mrs. Simmons in And This Was Odd, Criterion, 1951; Miss Teresa Browne in The Living Room, Wyndhams, 1953; Laura Anson in A Day by the Sea, Theatre Royal Haymarket, 1954. First appeared in films, 1931. *Recreation:* the theatre. *Address:* 1 Beaumanor Mans., Queensway, W.2. *T.:* Bayswater 2091. [*Died* 3 *March* 1955.

JERVIS, Lt.-Col. Hon. St. Leger Henry, D.S.O. 1900; *b.* Godmersham Park, Canterbury, Kent, 7 Sept. 1863; 5th *s.* of 3rd Viscount St. Vincent; *m.* 1905, Hilda Maud (*d.* 1942), *d.* of Thomas Collier; two *d.* Entered army, K.R.R.C., 1885; Captain, 1893; served South Africa, 1899-1902, including Ladysmith (severely wounded, despatches twice, Queen's medal 4 clasps, King's medal 2 clasps, D.S.O.); Major, 1903; D.A.A.G.,

South Africa, 1901-4; retired, 1904; served T.R. Batt. Northern Command and Censor Newcastle (Cables). *Address:* Pittminster Lodge, Taunton. *Club:* Royal Automobile.
[*Died* 11 *April* 1952.

JERVOISE, Francis Henry Tristram, T.D., D.L., J.P., F.S.A., F.L.A.S. (an original member); landowner; *b.* 31 December 1872; *e. s.* of late F. M. E. Jervoise, M.A., J.P., D.L.; *m.* 1908, Beatrice A. L. (*d.* 1944), *d.* of late Capt. William Savile, 9th Lancers; *m.* 1946, Aileen Margaret, *er. d.* of G. W. Harrap, Marsh House, Bentley. *Educ.:* Winchester; Christ Church, Oxford. Succeeded to settled estates on death of father, 1903; owns between 7000 and 8000 acres in Hampshire and Wiltshire; High Sheriff of Hants, 1912; Major (retired) late Hampshire C. Yeomanry. *Recreations:* hunting, shooting, archæology. *Address:* Seymour House, 13 Hertford Street, W.1; Herriard Park, Basingstoke; The Fishing Lodge, Britford, Salisbury. *T.A.:* Jervoise Herriard. *T.:* Hyde Park 4749, Herriard 252. *Club:* Junior Carlton. [*Died* 27 *May* 1959.

JESSE, F. Tennyson; *d.* of late Rev. Eustace Tennyson d'Eyncourt Jesse, a nephew of Alfred, Lord Tennyson; *m.* 1918, H. M. Harwood, *q.v.* Started to train as a painter at the age of fifteen with Mr. Stanhope Forbes, R.A., and his wife, at Newlyn; exhibited two or three pictures at Liverpool and Leeds, and illustrated a book; came to London; worked for the Times and the Daily Mail as a reporter, and wrote book reviews for the Times Literary Supplement and the English Review; was at European War, 1914-18, as a newspaper correspondent also for the M.O.I., the National Relief Commission, and French Red Cross. F.R.S.L. *Publications:* The Milky Way; Secret Bread; Beggars on Horseback; The White Riband; The Happy Bride; Murder and its Motives; Tom Fool; Moonraker; Many Latitudes; The Lacquer Lady; Solange Stories; A Pin to See the Peep-show; Sabi Pas; Act of God; London Front, 1940 and While London Burns, 1942 (with H. M. Harwood); The Saga of San Demetrio; The Story of Burma; Comments on Cain, 1948; The Alabaster Cup; The Compass; The Dragon in the Heart. Plays produced: The Mask; Billeted; The Pelican; How to be Healthy though Married (with H. M. Harwood); sole author of Quarantine and Anyhouse; (with H. M. Harwood) A Pin to see the Peepshow (play from the novel). Editor (for Notable British Trials) of: Trial of Madeleine Smith, S. H. Dougal, Sidney Fox, Rattenbury and Stoner, Ley and Smith, Evans and Christie. *Recreations:* conversation and reading. *Address:* Pear Tree Cottage, 11 Melina Place, St. John's Wood, N.W.8.
[*Died* 6 *Aug.* 1958.

JESSON, Major Thomas Edward; *b.* 28 July 1883; *s.* of Thomas and Charlotte Jesson; *m.* 1921, Beatrice Holding (*d.* 1941); no *c.* *Educ.:* Charterhouse. Solicitor 1906, practising at Birmingham, later at Ashby de la Zouch, and after the war at Blackpool; joined up in Aug. 1914 and saw active service in France; retired from active legal practice, and entered into commercial life, 1929; M.P. (C.) Rochdale, 1931-35. J.P. *Recreations:* hunting and outdoor sports generally. *Address:* Rivoli, South Drive, St. Anne's-on-Sea, Lancs. *T.:* St. Anne's-on-Sea 108. [*Died* 23 *July* 1958.

JESSOP, Gilbert Laird; *b.* Cheltenham, 19 May 1874; *s.* of Dr. Henry Edward Jessop; *m.* Millicent Osborne (*d.* 1953), Moss Vale, N.S.W.; one *s.* *Educ.:* Beccles College, Suffolk; Christ's College, Cambridge University. Played cricket for Gloucestershire, 1894-1914; for Cambridge Univ., 1896-99, captain 1899; for England, 1899-1914. *Publications:* A Cricketer's Log, 1923; Cresley of Cressingham, 1923; Cricket and How to Play It, 1925. *Recreation:* golf. *Address:* St. George's Vicarage, Fordington, Dorchester, Dorset. [*Died* 11 *May* 1955.

JEVONS, Herbert Stanley, M.A., B.Sc. (Lond.), F.G.S., F.S.S.; Adviser to the Ethiopian Embassy since 1942; *b.* 8 Oct. 1875; *s.* of late William Stanley Jevons, author, and Harriet Ann (*d.* 1911), *d.* of J. E. Taylor, founder of Manchester Guardian; *m.* 1902, Alice (*d.* 1949), *e. d.* of Harry Beardsell, Huddersfield; one *d.* (one *s.* decd.). *Educ.:* Giggleswick Grammar School; Univ. Coll., London; Trinity Coll., Cambridge; Geological Institute, Heidelberg University. Demonstrator in Petrology, Cambridge, 1900-1901; Lecturer in Mineralogy and Geology University of Sydney, 1902-4; returned by China coast, Japan, U.S.A., and Canada, 1905; Lecturer, and later Fulton Professor of Economics and Political Science in the University College of South Wales and Monmouthshire, Cardiff, 1905-11; engaged in housing reform in South Wales Coalfield, 1911-14; Professor of Economics, University of Allahabad, 1914-23; editor Indian Journal of Economics, 1916-22; Professor of Economics, University of Rangoon, 1923-30; Member of Council of Royal Statistical Society, 1932-37; founder and first Hon. Secretary Abyssinia Association, Treasurer until 1951; Treasurer, Anglo-Ethiopian Society, 1952-54, now Editor of its Proceedings. Chairman of Bombing Restriction Committee, 1943-45. *Publications:* Essays on Economics, 1905; The British Coal Trade, 1915; Economics of Tenancy Law and Estate Management, 1921; Money, Banking, and Exchange in India, 1922; The Future of Exchange and the Indian Currency, 1922; The Students' Friend, 1923; Economic Equality in the Co-operative Commonwealth, 1933; and numerous papers and articles on Petrology, Mineralogy, Economics, Politics, Housing Reform, Co-operation, Peace and War, Utopia, Economic Development, etc.; also edited W. S. Jevons' Theory of Political Economy, Investigations in Currency and Finance. *Recreations:* country walks and listening to music. *Address:* 95 Raglan Court, Wembley, Middlesex. *T.:* Wembley 4527. [*Died* 27 *June* 1955.

JEX-BLAKE, Arthur John, M.A., M.D., F.R.C.P.; late Physician to St. George's Hospital, and Assistant Physician, Brompton Hospital for Consumption; 2nd *s.* of late Very Rev. T. W. Jex-Blake, D.D.; *m.* 1920, Lady Muriel Katherine Herbert (*d.* 1951), *sister* of 15th Earl of Pembroke, *q.v.*; one *d.* *Address:* P.O. Box 45, Nairobi, Kenya Colony.
[*Died* 16 *Aug.* 1957.

JEX-BLAKE, Henrietta; *d.* of late Very Rev. T. W. Jex-Blake, D.D., J.P., formerly Dean of Wells, and Headmaster of Rugby School. *Educ.:* at home; studied music at the Leipzig Conservatoire, Dresden, and Vienna; Second Mistress at St. Margaret's School, Polmont, N.B., 1898; Head Mistress, 1899-1909; Principal of Lady Margaret Hall, Oxford, 1909-21. *Address:* Nettlesworth, Hurstpierpoint, Sussex. *Club:* University Women's.
[*Died* 21 *May* 1953.

JEX-BLAKE, Katharine; *b.* 1860; *d.* of late Very Rev. T. W. Jex-Blake, D.D. *Educ.:* home; Girton College, Cambridge. Classical Tripos, Cambridge, 1882; Classical Mistress, Notting Hill High School, 1884; Resident Lecturer, Girton College, 1885-1916; Vice-Mistress, 1903-16; Mistress of Girton College, 1916-1922. *Publications:* Translation (with Mrs. S. A. Strong) of Latin text in The Elder Pliny's History of Art. *Address:* Nettlesworth, Hurstpierpoint, Sussex. *Club:* University Women's.
[*Died* 26 *March* 1951.

JHA, Sir Mahamahopadhyaya Ganganath, Kt. 1941; D.Litt.; LL.D.; Ph.D.; *b.* 1871; *s.* of Tirthanath Jha. Indian Educational Service, retired; late Vice-Chancellor, Allahabad University, India. Corresponding Fellow of British Academy; Hon. Fellow of Royal Asiatic Society. *Address:* George Town, Allahabad, India.
[*Deceased.*

JIBOWU, Hon. Sir Olumuyiwa, Kt. 1958; **Hon. Mr. Justice Jibowu;** Chief

Justice of High Court of Western Region of Nigeria, 1958; *b.* Lagos, Nigeria, August 1899. *Educ.:* Abeokuta Grammar School, Nigeria; Oxford University. Called to the Bar, Middle Temple, 1923. Practised in Nigeria, after which was appointed a Police Magistrate, Nigeria, 1931; Assistant Judge of the High Court, Nigeria, 1942; Judge, High Court, Nigeria, 1944; Puisne Judge, Supreme Court of Nigeria, 1945; Federal Justice, Federal Supreme Court, Nigeria, 1956; Chief Justice of High Court of Lagos and Southern Cameroons, 1957. *Address:* High Court, Ibadan, Western Region, Nigeria. [*Died* 1 *June* 1959.

JIMÉNEZ (MANTACON), Juan Ramón; Spanish poet and lecturer; *b.* Moguer, Andalusia, 24 Dec. 1881; *m.* 1916, Zenobia Camprubi (*d.* 1956), New York. *Educ.:* Jesuit School, Puerto de Santa Maria; University of Seville. First poems published in 1898; spent early years in Andalusia and Madrid; after Spanish Civil War went into voluntary exile in Cuba, 1936; visited many South American countries with his wife, 1940-47; Visiting Professor (with wife), University of Maryland, 1947; has made many recordings of his work for Library of Congress since 1949; Visiting Professor, College of Humanities, University of Puerto Rico, 1951-. Member: Hispanic Society of America; Sociedad Argentina de Escritores. Nobel Prize for Literature, 1956. *Publications:* Almas de Violeta (Violet Souls), Ninfas (Nymphs), 1898; Platero y Yo (Silver and I), 1914; Diariò de un poeta recién casada (Diary of a Newlywed Poet), 1917; Second Poetry Anthology, 1922; Que Cerca va del Alma (How Near My Soul), 1944; numerous articles and critical essays in Spanish journals. *Address:* 461 Padre Berrios Street, Floral Park, Hato Rey, Puerto Rico. [*Died* 29 *May* 1958.

JOAD, Cyril Edwin Mitchinson, M.A.; D.Lit.; author; University Reader in Philosophy; Head of Dept. of Philosophy, Birkbeck College, University of London, since 1930; Farmer since 1946; *b.* 12 August 1891; *s.* of late Edwin Joad and Mary Smith. *Educ.:* Blundell's, Tiverton; Balliol College, Oxford. John Locke Scholar in Moral Philosophy, University of Oxford, 1914; entered Civil Service, Board of Trade (later Ministry of Labour), 1914; retired, 1930; D.Lit. (Lond.) 1936. *Publications:* Matter Life and Value; Philosophical Aspects of Modern Science; Guide to Philosophy; Guide to the Philosophy of Morals and Politics; Philosophy for our Times; Philosophy; Journey through the War Mind; God and Evil; Essays in Common Sense Philosophy; Common Sense Ethics; Common Sense Theology; Guide to Modern Thought; Return to Philosophy; Mind and Matter; The Mind and its Workings; The Future of Life; The Meaning of Life; Great Philosophies; The Book of Joad; The Testament of Joad; Why War?; Guide to Modern Wickedness; Counter Attack from the East; Liberty To-day; The Present and Future of Religion; The Future of Morals; Diogenes; The Babbitt Warren; Samuel Butler; The Bookmark; After Dinner Philosophy; The Highbrows; Priscilla and Charybdis; A Charter for Ramblers; The Horrors of the Countryside; The Story of Civilization; The Dictator Resigns; The Story of Indian Civilization; (with A. Lunn) Is Christianity True?; The Adventures of the Young Soldier in search of the Better World; About Education; The Untutored Townsman's Invasion of the Country; Decadence, A Philosophical Enquiry; A Year More or Less; Shaw; A Critique of Logical Positivism; The Pleasure of Being Oneself; The Recovery of Belief; (posthumous) Folly Farm, 1954. *Recreations:* tennis, riding, walking, chess, bridge. *Address:* 4 East Heath Road, N.W.3. *T.:* Hampstead 6128; The Hills, Stedham, Midhurst. *T.:* Midhurst 174. [*Died* 9 *April* 1953.

JOCELYN, Captain Arthur Cecil, C.V.O. 1955; retired; *b.* 25 Dec. 1880; *o. s.* of Rev. Nathaniel Jocelyn and Edith Mary Elinor (*née* Straton); *m.* 1st, Elsie Olivia Bligh, *e. d.* of Arthur St. George; 2nd, Margaret, *widow* of Col. W. H. Lawes; no *c.* *Educ.:* Cheltenham College. Served in South African War 1899-1902, and in 1914-18 War; Political Parliamentary Secretary to several Members of Parliament. Captain R.F.A. Retired, 1929. Compiled historical record and detailed description of the Orders, Decorations and Medals of the world, comprising 75 countries together with specimens of their ribands. The descriptive text of the compilation together with the complete collection of ribands numbering 6000 were presented by the compiler to the Queen, which gift is now deposited in the Central Chancery of the Orders of Knighthood. *Publications:* Orders, Decorations and Medals of the British Empire, 1933; Awards of Honour, 1956. *Recreations:* miniature painting and gardening. *Address:* 4/13 Embankment Gardens, Chelsea, S.W.3. *Club:* Naval and Military. [*Died* 26 *March* 1959.

JODHPUR, Maharaja of; H.H. Raj Rajeshwar Saramad Raja-i-Hind Maharajadhiraj Shree Hanwant Singhji Sahib Bahadur; *b.* 16 June 1923; *s.* of H.H. the late Air Vice-Marshal Maharajadhiraj Shree Sir Umaid Singhji Bahadur, G.C.S.I., G.C.I.E., K.C.V.O., and H.H. Maharaniji Shree Badan Kunwarji Sahiba; *m.* 1943, Princess Shree Krishna Kunwar Ba Sahiba; one *s.* two *d.* *Educ.:* Mayo College and Government College, Ajmer. Trained in State Administration, worked as one of Council of Ministers and in charge of important portfolios, such as Education, Public Works, Customs, Electrical, Aerodrome and Development Depts. and the Ijlas-i-Khas (Highest Court of Appeal in State); Sovereign of the Marwar State; Head of the Rathor Rajput Clan and one of the leading ruling Princes in India; the younger offshoots of this family are the ruling Princes of Bikaner, Kishangarh, Idar, Rutlam, Sailana, Sitamau and Jhabua. Ascended the Gadi on 21 June 1947. *Recreations:* golf, tennis, shooting, fishing, flying, motoring, photography and mechanics; visited Europe on three occasions in 1925, 1928, 1932; Egypt in 1939 and Afghanistan in 1943. *Address:* Jodhpur, Rajputana, India. [*Died* 26 *Jan.* 1952.

JODRELL, Dorothy L. R.; *see* Ramsden-Jodrell.

JOHN, Sir Goscombe; *see* John, Sir W. G.

JOHN, William; *b.* Cockett, nr. Swansea, 6 Oct. 1878; *m.* 1908, Anna, *d.* of George and Catherine Brooks. Financial Secretary to Rhondda Miners, 1911-12; Miners' Agent for Rhondda since 1912. M.P. (Lab.) Rhondda West, 1920-50; Parliamentary Private Sec. to Parl. Sec. to Ministry of Labour, June 1929-Aug. 1931; Welsh Whip, Nov. 1935; Comptroller, H.M. Household, 1942-44; a Lord Commissioner of the Treasury, 1944-45; Deputy Chief Whip Parl. Labour Party, 1942-50. [*Died* 27 *Aug.* 1955.

JOHN, Sir (William) Goscombe, Kt., *cr.* 1911; R.A. 1909; Membre Correspondant de l'Institut de France; Commandeur de l'ordre de Léopold II of Belgium; Hon. LL.D. Univ. of Wales; Associate Royal Academy of Belgium; Hon. Associate of R.I.B.A.; Sculptor; *b.* Cardiff, 1860; *s.* of late Thomas John, Cardiff; *m.* 1890, Marthe (*d.* 1923), *d.* of late Paul Weiss, Neuchâtel, Switzerland; one *d.* Studied in Cardiff School of Art; City and Guilds of London School of Art, Kennington; Royal Academy Schools; Royal Academy Gold

Medal and Travelling Studentship, 1889; Paris, 1890-91; mention honorable, Paris Salon, 1892; Gold Medal, Paris Salon, 1901; Gold Medal of Royal Society of British Sculptors, 1942; Hon. freedom of Cardiff. 1936. *Principal works:* King Edward VII. at Cape Town; King George V. and Queen Mary at Liverpool; Queen Alexandra, in Sandringham Church; Prince Christian Victor, at Windsor; The Duke of Devonshire, at Eastbourne; Duke of Beaufort, at Badminton; Thomas Sutton, founder of Charterhouse, at Charterhouse, Godalming; The Rt. Hon. David Lloyd George, O.M., M.P., at Carnarvon, etc. *Equestrian Statues:* King Edward VII. at Liverpool; Viscount Wolseley, Horse Guards Parade, London; Earl Minto at Calcutta; Sir Stanley Maude at Bagdad; Viscount Tredegar at Cardiff. *Memorials:* The Marquess of Salisbury, in Westminster Abbey and also in Hatfield Church; Earl of Cromer, in Westminster Abbey and also in Cairo Cathedral; Memorial Altar in Crypt, Hereford Cathedral; Dean Vaughan, Llandaff Cathedral; Sir Arthur Sullivan, in St. Paul's Cathedral and also in the Embankment Gardens; The Coldstream Guards, in St. Paul's Cathedral; The King's Regiment, at Liverpool; Engine-room Heroes, at Liverpool; Port Sunlight War Memorial; Renwick War Monument, at Newcastle-on-Tyne; Royal Welch Fusiliers, Wrexham, etc. Works in the Tate Gallery, London; Glasgow Art Gallery; National Museum, Cardiff, and in other Art Galleries; designed the Regalia for the Investiture of the Prince of Wales at Carnarvon, 1911, and King George V Silver Jubilee Medal, 1935. *Address:* 24 Greville Road, N.W.6. *T.:* Maida Vale 1321. *Club:* Athenæum. [*Died* 15 *Dec.* 1952.

JOHNS, Richard Henry, C.B.E. 1956 (O.B.E. 1946); Consellier of the States of Guernsey; President of Board of Administration (States), 1946; Jurat Royal Court, Guernsey; *b.* 8 June 1878; *s.* of Samuel and Selina Johns; *m.* 1900, Helen Harriet Ozanne; one *s.* one *d.* (and one *d.* decd.). *Educ.:* Vale Wesleyan, Guernsey. Wholesale and retail meat trader 1899; retired 1940. *Recreation:* gardening. *Address:* Lowlands, Vale, Guernsey. *T.:* Guernsey, St. Sampsons 4523. [*Died* 20 *June* 1960.

JOHNSON, 1st Baron; *see* Webb-Johnson.

JOHNSON, Bernard Richard Millar; late Dean of Faculty of Anæsthetists, Royal College of Surgeons of England; Cons. Anæsthetist and Lecturer in Anæsth., Middlesex Hospital; Cons. Anæsthetist, War Office; *b.* 25 April 1905; *s.* of Henry Charles Johnson and Julia Anne Watts; *m.* 1933, Barbara Grace Scriven; one *d.* *Educ.:* Brighton College; Middlesex Hospital, W.1. M.R.C.S. Eng., L.R.C.P. Lond., 1927; D.A. Eng., 1938; F.F.A.R.C.S. Eng., 1948; F.R.C.S. 1956. Formerly: Senior Resident Anæsthetist and House Surgeon, Middlesex Hospital. Late Mem. Council of Roy. Coll. of Surgeons of England. Lieut. Col. R.A.M.C. (despatches 1944); Adviser Anæsthetist, C.M.F. Examiner and late Chairman, Board of Examiners, F.F.A.R.C.S.; Fell. Assoc. Anæsthetists of G. Brit., F.R.Soc.Med. (Pres. Anæsth. Sect.); Hon. F.F.A.R.A.C.S., 1953; Hon. Fell. Assoc. Greek Surgeons. *Publications:* contribs. to medical books and literature. *Address:* Middlesex Hospital, W.1. *T.:* Museum 8333. [*Died* 18 *May* 1959.

JOHNSON, Brig. Charles Reginald, C.M.G. 1919; D.S.O. 1902; late R.E.; *b.* 23 Dec. 1876; *s.* of late Lieut.-Colonel C. Hargitt Johnson, J.P., Thorngumbald, Yorks; *m.* 1904, Ida, *d.* of F. A. Hutchinson of Preston, Yorks; two *s.* Entered Army, 1896; served S. Africa, 1899-1902 (despatches, Queen's medal 5 clasps, King's medal 2 clasps, D.S.O.); European War, 1914-18 (despatches, Bt. Lt.-Col., C.M.G.); Chief Engineer, Eastern Command, 1928-32; retired pay, 1932; Order of St. Stanislas, 3rd Class; Chevalier of the Legion of Honour. *Address:* Thorn, Down Road, Tavistock. [*Died* 11 *March* 1953.

JOHNSON, Rear-Admiral (S) Cyril Sheldon, D.S.O. 1916; Royal Navy, retired; *b.* 23 Jan. 1882; *s.* of Rev. Arthur Johnson, M.A. and Bessie Barford. *Educ.:* Berkhamsted. Assistant Clerk, 1900; Paymaster, 1914; Paymaster-Commander, 1920; Paymaster-Captain, 1930; Secretary to Admiral Sir Doveton Sturdee, Bt., 1904-21; served China War, 1900; European War, 1914-18 Falkland Islands, Jutland (D.S.O., despatches); Fleet Accountant Officer, West Indies, 1922-23; Resident Naval Officer, Colombo, 1924-26; Fleet Accountant Officer, China, 1928-31; Mediterranean, 1932-34; Senior Accountant Officer, Devonport, 1935; Port Accountant Officer and Port Librarian, Plymouth, 1935-37; retired list, 1937. Mayor of Beccles, 1945. *Address:* Crochdantigh, Muckadilla, Queensland. *Club:* United Service. [*Died* 21 *Sept.* 1954.

JOHNSON, Sir (Edward) Gordon, 5th Bt., *cr.* 1755; *b.* 17 March 1867; *s.* of Archibald Kennedy Johnson, 3rd *b.* of 4th Bt.; *S. u.* 1908; *m.* 1902, Violet Eveline, *d.* of late Thomas Edward Hayes, M.D., of Dublin; no *c.* *Heir: cousin,* Major John Paley Johnson, M.B.E. [*Died* 15 *April* 1957.

JOHNSON, Sir Gordon; *see* Johnson, Sir J. N. G.

JOHNSON, Brig. Guy Allen Colpoys Ormsby, C.B.E. 1940 (O.B.E. 1919); M.C.; R.A.P.C.; *b.* 25 May 1886; *s.* of late Major Frederick Colpoys Ormsby Johnson, R.M.; heir-presumptive to Sir Edward Gordon Johnson, *q.v.*; *m.* 1911, Mary Isabella Humfrey, Cavanacor, Co. Donegal; three *d.* *Educ.:* Cheltenham College. Bedfordshire Regt. and Royal Army Pay Corps; served European War, 1914-19 (despatches twice, O.B.E., M.C.); Col. and Chief Paymaster, 1930. Served in War of 1939-45 (despatches-twice, C.B.E.): B.E.F. France, 1939-40; Malta, U.F.; retired pay, 1946. *Recreations:* golf, fishing. *Address:* Downings, Fleet, Hants. *T.:* Fleet 436. [*Died* 30 *Jan.* 1957.

JOHNSON, John, C.B.E. 1945; M.A., Hon. D.Litt.; Hon. Fellow of Exeter College; printer to the University of Oxford, 1925-46; *b.* 17 May 1882; *s.* of late Rev. J. H. and Mrs. A. B. Johnson; *m.* Margaret Dorothea, *d.* of Charles Cannan; one *s.* one *d.* *Educ.:* Magdalen College School and Exeter College, Oxford (Open Scholar). First Class Hon. Mods. and Second Class Lit. Hum.; Sub-Inspector of the Interior in Egyptian Civil Service, 1905-7; Senior Demy, Magdalen College, 1908-11; editing papyri and conducting expeditions to Egypt for excavation on the sites of the ancient Heracelopolis, Aphroditopolis, Antinoe and elsewhere, on behalf of the Greco-Roman Branch of the Egypt Exploration Fund, 1908-14; Acting Assistant or Assistant Secretary to the Delegates of the University Press, 1915-25. Hon. Fell. Imp. Coll. of Science and Technology. Trustee Oxford Preservation Trust; Governor Dorset House School of Occupational Therapy; Pres. Oxford Bibliographical Soc.; Governor Magdalen College School, Oxford. *Publications:* Catalogue of Greek and Roman Papyri in the Rylands Library of Manchester, Vol. II; Two Theocritus Papyri; The First Minute Book of the Delegates of the Oxford University Press, 1668-1756; Print and Privilege at Oxford to the Year 1700; The Printer, His Customers and his Men. *Address:* Bare Acres, Old Headington, Oxford. *T.:* 6959. [*Died* 15 *Sept.* 1956.

JOHNSON, Sir (John Nesbitt) Gordon, Kt., *cr.* 1937; C.S.I. 1936; C.I.E. 1928; late I.C.S.; *b.* 25 Feb. 1885; *s.* of late Rev. Canon Johnson, Carbury, Co. Kildare; unmarried. *Educ.:* Rossall; Queen's College, Oxford (Senior Scholar). Entered

Indian Civil Service, 1909; Under Secretary to Govt. United Provinces, 1915-16; Indian Army Reserve of Officers, attached 1/3 Gurkhas, 1918-1919; Registrar Allahabad High Court, 1919-1924; Officiating Deputy Secretary to the Govt. of India, Industries and Labour Dept., 1925; Deputy Commissioner, Delhi, 1924-32; on special duty Education, Health and Lands Dept., Govt. of India, 1928-29; officiated as Chief Commissioner Delhi, 1928 and 1930; Member Council of State, India, 1932-37; Chief Commissioner, Delhi Province, 1932-37; retired, 1939; Red Cross and St. John War Organisation, 1939; Ministry of Home Security, 1941-43; Administrative Director, Petroleum Warfare Dept., 1943-46; Control Office for Germany and Austria, 1946. *Club:* East India and Sports. [*Died* 9 *June* 1955.

JOHNSON, Sir Nelson King, K.C.B., *cr.* 1943; D.Sc., A.R.C.S.; *b.* 1892; 2nd *s.* of J. G. Johnson, Canterbury; *m.* 1927, Margaret, *d.* of J. Taylor, Blackburn; one *s.* one *d.* *Educ.:* Simon Langton School, Canterbury; Royal College of Science, London University. Assistant to Sir Norman Lockyer at Sidmouth Observatory, 1914-15; Royal Flying Corps, 1915-19; Meteorological Office, Air Ministry, 1919-28; Chemical Defence Research Dept., War Office, 1928-38; Director of the Meteorological Office, 1938-53. President International Meteorological Committee, 1946-51; Pres. World Meteorological Organisation, 1951. *Publications:* various Scientific Papers. *Address:* Air Ministry, Kingsway, W.C.2. [*Died* 23 *March* 1954.

JOHNSON, Owen; *b.* New York, 27 Aug. 1878; *s.* of late Robert Underwood Johnson; *m.* 1st, 1901, Mary Galt Stockly (*d.* 1910); one *s.* two *d.*; 2nd, 1912, Esther Cobb; 3rd, 1917, Cecile Denis de Lagarde (*d.* 1918); one *s.*; 4th, 1922, Catherine Sayre Burton (*d.* 1924); one *d.*; 5th, 1926, Gertrude Bovee, *widow* of John A. Le Boutillier. *Educ.:* Lawrenceville (N.J.) School; Yale, 1900. Founder and first editor Lawrenceville Literary Magazine; Chairman Yale Literary Magazine for class of 1900; Chevalier, Legion of Honour, 1919. *Publications:* Novels—Arrows of the Almighty, 1901; In the Name of Liberty, 1905; Max Fargus, 1906; The Eternal Boy, 1909; The Humming Bird, 1910; The Varmint, 1910; The Tennessee Shad, 1911; Stover at Yale, 1911; The Sixty-first Second, 1912; Murder in Any Degree, 1913; The Salamander, 1914; Sacrifice, 1929; Coming of the Amazons, 1931; Drama—The Comet, 1908; Comedy for Wives, 1912; Return from Jerusalem (adapted) 1912; The Salamander, 1914; The Spirit of France, 1915; The Woman Gives, 1916; Virtuous Wives, 1917; Children of Divorce, 1927; numerous magazine articles and stories. *Address:* Stockbridge, Mass., U.S.A. *Club:* Authors' (New York). [*Died* 27 *Jan.* 1952.

JOHNSON, Hon. Sir Reginald P. C.; *see* Croom-Johnson.

JOHNSON, Sir Robert Stewart, Kt., *cr.* 1942; O.B.E.; Chairman since 1940 and Managing Director, 1922-51, Cammell Laird and Co., Ltd., Shipbuilders and Engineers, Birkenhead; Member of Mersey Docks and Harbour Board; Director: La Mont Steam Generator Ltd., Metropolitan Cammell Carriage and Wagon Co. Ltd., Midland Railway Carriage and Wagon Co. Ltd.; *b.* 7 Aug. 1872; *s.* of Charles and Elizabeth Johnson; *m.* 1909, Lillian Edna White; one *s.* two *d.* *Educ.:* Foyle College, Londonderry. Served Apprenticeship with Harland and Wolff, Ltd., Belfast; later transferred to Workman, Clark and Co., Belfast, and eventually became Managing Director; entered service of Cammell Laird and Co., Ltd., Birkenhead, as Director, 1920. *Address:* The Garth, Waterford Road, Birkenhead. *T.A.:* c/o Camellaird Birkenhead. *T.:* Birkenhead 623. [*Died* 28 *Aug.* 1951.

JOHNSON, Sir Sidney Midlane, Kt., *cr.* 1937; *b.* 1885; *o. s.* of late John Johnson, Agden House, Agden, Cheshire; *m.* 1st, 1916, Vera Louise (*d.* 1950), *o. d.* of W. S. Pirie; no *c.*; 2nd, 1951, Margaret Kathleen Wallace, (*d.* 1957), *o. d.* of L. W. Saunders. *Educ.:* King's School, Chester. Solicitor: Asst. Solicitor, Chester, 1909-11; Asst. Secretary, County Councils Assoc., 1911-18; Secretary, 1918-50. *Publication:* British Bridges (jt.). *Address:* 100 Clarence Gate Gardens, Regent's Park, N.W.1. *T.:* Ambassador 1347. *Club:* Reform. [*Died* 11 *June* 1960.

JOHNSON, Thomas, D.Sc. (Lond.); F.L.S.; Ex-Vice-President, Royal Irish Academy; *b.* Barton-on-Humber, 1863; *m.* Bessie Stratton (*decd.*), *d.* of late Rev. W. Rowe, formerly of Toronto; one *s.* (elder son died on active service) one *d.* *Educ.:* Elmfield College, York; Royal College of Science, London. Demonstrator of Botany, 1885-90, Professor of Botany, 1890-1928, College of Science, Dublin, (1925-28 in University College, Dublin); Keeper and Founder of Botanical Division, National Museum Dublin, 1891-1928; First Director of Seed-testing and Plant Disease Stations (Department of Agriculture), 1900-10. Life-member British Association for the Adv. of Science, Royal Irish Academy and Royal Dublin Society. *Publications:* The Inometer: a new form of Food Chart; papers on seaweeds, parasitic plants, plant diseases, seed-testing, fossil plants of Ireland, and on the golfers' rush question. *Address:* 64 Terenure Road East, Rathgar, Dublin. *T.:* 905554. [*Died* 9 *Sept.* 1954.

JOHNSON, Rt. Rev. Thomas Sylvester Claudius, O.B.E. 1947; M.A., B.D. (Durham); *b.* 23 Sept. 1873; *s.* of Jas. B. and Nancy Johnson; *m.* 1903, Marian R. Johnson; four *s.* two *d.* *Educ.:* Fourah Bay College, Sierra Leone. Headmaster, C.M.S. School for Mohammedans, Freetown, 1896; Headmaster Fourah Bay College Practising School, Freetown, 1898; Headmaster Cathedral model School, Freetown, 1903; Deacon, 1909; Tutor Fourah Bay College, Freetown, 1911; Priest, 1911; Diocesan Inspector of Schools, 1914; Principal C.M.S. Grammar School, Freetown, 1933; Archdeacon of Sierra Leone, West Africa, 1934; Assistant Bishop of Sierra Leone and Sub-Dean St. George's Cathedral, Freetown, 1937-48; retired, 1948. *Publication:* The Fear-fetish: Its Cause and Cure, 1949; History of the Sierra Leone Church, 1952. *Recreation:* horticulture. *Address:* Benguema, Sierra Leone. [*Died* 22 *Oct.* 1955.

JOHNSON, Sir Walter Burford, Kt., *cr.* 1935; C.M.G. 1933; M.B., B.S., F.R.C.S.; Medical Adviser to the High Commissioner for Basutoland, Bechuanaland Protectorate and Swaziland; *b.* 20 Dec. 1885; *s.* of James Nowell Johnson and Elizabeth Burford. *Educ.:* City of London School; St. Thomas's Hospital (Surgical Registrar, 1911). West African Medical Staff, 1912; seconded for investigation under Yellow Fever Commission, 1913; served as Temporary Captain in Cameroons, 1914-15; seconded for service on Tsetse Fly Investigation in Nigeria, 1921; Director of Medical and Sanitary Services, Nigeria, 1929-36; retired, 1936. *Publications:* The Trypanasome Infection of Tsetse Flies in N. Nigeria (with Lloyd), Bull. Entom. Res. 1924; Experiments in Control of Tsetse Fly (with Lloyd and Ramson), Bull. Entom. Res. 1927; Recent Advances in the Knowledge of Yellow Fever, B.M.J. Aug. 1932. *Recreations:* travel and fishing. *Address:* The Thatch, Penhill Estate, Eerste River, C.P., South Africa. *Club:* Royal Empire Society. [*Died* 5 *July* 1951.

JOHNSON, Rt. Rev. William Herbert, B.A., Th.D.; Bishop of Ballarat since 1936; *b.* 12 May 1889; *e. s.* of Samuel Johnson, M.A., Brighton, South Australia; *m.* Dymphna, *d.* of late Lieut. Ernest de Chair, R.N., and *niece* of Admiral Sir Dudley de Chair, sometime Governor of New South Wales; three d. *Educ.:* St. Peter's College, Adelaide, Adelaide University; St. John's College, Melbourne. Graduated at Adelaide University in 1911 and at St. John's College, Melbourne, in 1913; Deacon, 1913; Priest, 1914; Curate of Holy Trinity, Kew, Melbourne, 1913-17; Chaplain with the A.I.F. in France, 1917-19; Rector of St. Cuthbert's Church, Prospect, Adelaide, 1919-28; Dean of Newcastle, New South Wales, 1928-36. Acting-Metropolitan, Province of Victoria, 1957. *Publication:* The Life of George Merrick Long. *Address:* Bishopscourt, Ballarat, Vic., Australia. [*Died* 15 *July* 1960.

JOHNSON-FERGUSON, Sir Edward Alexander James, 2nd Bart., *cr.* 1906; T.D., D.L., formerly Lt.-Colonel commanding Lanarkshire Yeomanry, Brev. Col.; *b.* 3 Mar. 1875; *o. s.* of Sir J. E. Johnson-Ferguson, 1st Bt., and Williamina, *d.* of W. A. Cunningham, Manchester; *S.* father, 1929; *m.* 1904, Hon. Elsie Dorothea McLaren, *d.* of 1st Lord Aberconway; three *s.* *Educ.:* Harrow; Trinity College, Cambridge. Served European War in Gallipoli, Palestine, France (despatches). *Heir: s.* Neil Edward [Lt.-Col. Royal Corps of Signals; *b.* 2 May 1905; *m.* 1931, Sheila Marion, *er. d.* of Col. H. S. Jervis, M.C.; four *s.*]. *Address:* Springkell, Eaglesfield, Dumfriesshire. [*Died* 27 *Dec.* 1953.

JOHNSON-WALSH, Sir H. H. A.; *see* Walsh, Sir H. H. A. J.-.

JOHNSTON, Alexander, C.M.G. 1934; LL.D.; Retired; *b.* 24 April 1867; *s.* of Donald Johnston and Mary Campbell; *m.* 1913; one *s.* one *d.* *Educ.:* Public School and St. Francis Xavier University, Antigonish. Elected to Nova Scotia Legislature 1897; Resigned in 1900 to contest Federal election and elected; re-elected in 1904, and sat until 1908; Deputy Minister of Marine and Fisheries 1910-32; Headed the Canadian delegation to the International Convention on Life Saving at Sea held in London, 1913-14; Headed the Canadian delegation to the International Conference on Radio Telegraphy, in Washington 1927; Again at the head of the Canadian delegation to the International Conference on Life Saving at Sea in London 1929, and to the International Conference on Load Line held in London, 1930. *Recreations:* Never had time for recreation, until it was too late. *Address:* 204 Clemow Avenue, Ottawa, Canada. *T.:* Carling 2670. *Clubs:* Rideau, Royal Golf, Country (Ottawa); Montreal (Montreal). [*Died* 30 *Nov.* 1951.

JOHNSTON, Colonel David Seton, C.I.E. 1933; *b.* 7 Aug. 1886; *s.* of John Leitch Johnston and Margaret Davidson. *Educ.:* Sherborne School; R.M.A., Woolwich. 2nd Lieutenant, R.E., 1906; Chatham, 1906-08; Military Works Services, India, 1908-09; Bombay Public Works Dept., 1909-42; Indian Expeditionary Force, France, 1914-18 (despatches, Bt. Major); Chairman, Aden Port Trust, 1924-34; Chairman, Karachi Port Trust, 1934-42; retired 1942. *Address:* Riverside, Aboyne, Aberdeenshire. *Club:* Junior Army and Navy. [*Died* 27 *Nov.* 1960.

JOHNSTON, Francis Alexander; Hon. Pres., Globe Telegraph & Trust Co.; *b.* Brighton, 18 Nov. 1864; 2nd *s.* of late Francis John Johnston of Dunsdale, Westerham, Kent; *m.* 1893, Audrey Beatrice (*d.* 1946); *y. d.* of Ernest Alers Hankey of Notton House, Chippenham, Wilts; no *c.* *Educ.:* Charterhouse; privately in France and Germany. *Address:* 11 Rutland Court, S.W.7. *Clubs:* Brooks's, City of London. [*Died* 12 *May* 1958.

JOHNSTON, Hon. Sir Harold Featherston, Kt., *cr.* 1947; Judge of the Supreme Court and Court of Appeal of New Zealand, 1934-47; *b.* 19 April 1875; *s.* of Hon. Sir Charles John Johnston, M.L.C., New Zealand, and Alice Margaret Featherston; *m.* 1900, Margaret Sara (*d.* 1946), *e. d.* of Rt. Hon. Sir Francis Bell, G.C.M.G.; two *s.* one *d.* *Educ.:* French Farm, Wanganui Collegiate School; Trinity College, Oxford, B.A. Called to Bar, Lincoln's Inn, 1897; Barrister and Solicitor N.Z. 1898; K.C., 1930; Judge of the Court of Review, 1935-39; served with London Scottish. European War (1st Battalion, France 1916 and 1917). *Address:* Mahia, Wairoa, New Zealand. *Clubs:* Oxford and Cambridge, Reform; Wellington, Christchurch (N.Z.). [*Died* 27 *July* 1959.

JOHNSTON, Rev. James B., M.A., B.D.; F.R.Hist.S.; Minister of the Church of Scotland; *b.* Edinburgh, 1862; *m.* 1888, Catherine E. Macmichael; one *s.* two *d.* *Educ.:* Royal High School, University and New College, Edinburgh. Cunningham Fellow, New College, 1886; Assistant in St. Matthew's Free Church, Glasgow, 1886-88; Minister of Falkirk Free Church, now St. Andrew's, Church of Scotland, 1888-1928; in charge of Scots Church, Biarritz, 1907-8; on the staff of New English Dictionary at Millhill, 1883; 1884-1915 and 1926-27, honorary member of the staff; on the staff of Scottish National Dictionary from 1931; has taken a prominent part in defence of the Lord's Day. *Publications:* Place-Names of Scotland, 1892, revised 1934; Place-Names of Stirlingshire, 1903; Place-Names of England and Wales, 1914; The Scottish Macs, 1922; Place-Names of Berwickshire, 1939; also revised the names in several Scottish topographical works; articles in Contemporary Review and Scotsman on the palæontological evidence unfavourable to Natural Selection; articles on Scottish Surnames in Chambers' Journal. *Address:* 63 Cluny Gardens, Edinburgh. *T.:* 53497. [*Died* 26 *Aug.* 1953.

JOHNSTON, James Wellwood, B.A.; Sheriff-Substitute of Lanarkshire, Lanark, since 1940; *b.* 5 April 1900; *er. s.* of late Sir Christopher Nicholson Johnston, Lord Sands, LL.D., D.D.; *m.* 1934, Kathleen Edith, 3rd *d.* of John Duncan, Edinburgh; one *s.* one *d.* *Educ.:* Edinburgh Academy; Cargilfield; Rugby; New College, Oxford. Called to Scottish Bar, 1924; Advocate Depute, 1935-39; M.P. (U.) East Stirlingshire and Clackmannan, 1931-35. *Recreations:* shooting, fishing, golf, tennis. *Address:* Old Parsonage, Lamington, Lanarkshire. *T.:* Lamington 206. *Club:* New (Edinburgh). [*Died* 18 *Sept.* 1958.

JOHNSTON, Sir John, Kt., *cr.* 1945; D.L.; *b.* 16 Sept. 1873. M.P. (U.) North Armagh, Parliament of Northern Ireland, 1929-45. *Address:* The Stone House, Portavoe, Donaghadee, Co. Down. *Clubs:* Constitutional; Ulster Reform (Belfast); Armagh County (Armagh). [*Died* 9 *March* 1952.

JOHNSTON, Major John Alexander Weir, Q.C. Northern Ireland, 1923; M.A., B.A.I., Barrister-at-Law (England); Member of the Panel of Referees for England and Wales under the Landlord and Tenant Act 1927, 1928-54; Director of Convoy Woollen Co. Ltd. since 1910, and of Sezincote Stud, Ltd. since 1932; Guardian Pari Mutuel, Ltd., since 1929; *b.* 17 Nov. 1879; *o. s.* of late Sir John Johnston, Boom Hall, Londonderry, Ireland; *m.* Enid Mary, *o. d.* of W. Simpson, Catteral Hall, Settle, Yorkshire; one *d.* *Educ.:* Foyle College, Londonderry; Shrewsbury School; Dublin University (Trinity College). B.A. 1902; called to Irish Bar (King's Inns), 1903; B.A.I. 1904; M.A. 1907; North-West Circuit, Ireland, 1903-20; Unionist Candidate South Down, 1910 and 1918; Director Londonderry Shipbuilding Co. Ltd. 1913-15, Standing Counsel, 1915-22. Served European War, Lieutenant R.A.O.C., 1914; Captain, 1915, Major, 1918 (twice mentioned for special services); in charge British Ordnance Mission, Canada, 1914-15-16, called to English Bar, Inner Temple, 1919; Northern Circuit of Ireland, 1920-24; Crown Prosecutor for County Tyrone, 1919-24; Hon. Consul to the Irish Free State for the Republics of Latvia and Bolivia; South-Eastern Circuit,

England. *Publication:* Londonderry as an Industrial Centre. *Recreations:* fishing, racing, hunting, travelling. *Address:* Flaunden House, Flaunden, Herts. *T.:* Bovingdon 3246. *Clubs:* Carlton, 1900, Royal Automobile, Leander (Henley-on-Thames); University (Dublin). [*Died* 3 *June* 1957.

JOHNSTON, Brig. Robert, C.B. 1935; D.S.O. 1916; O.B.E. 1922; Indian Army, retired; *b.* 9 April 1879; *s.* of late Maj. Robert Johnston, A.P.D., Drumahaire, Co. Leitrim; *m.* 1912, Maysie Fairbanks, *d.* of late Frank Egerton Gibbs, Port Arthur, Ont.; one *s.* one *d.* *Educ.:* privately; R.M.C. I.A. 1898. Served European War, 1914-18 (despatches, D.S.O.); A.A. and Q.M.G. Mhow District, 1928; A.A.G. India, 1919-22 and 1928-32; D.A. and Q.M.G., Eastern Command, India, 1932-36; retired, 1936. Col. 2 Royal Lancers (Gardners Horse), 1939-48. *Address:* Dower House, Elvaston Place, S.W.7. [*Died* 25 *Nov.* 1956.

JOHNSTON, Major Robert Douglas, C.B.E. 1923; late The Roy. Hampshire Regt.; *b.* 31 Dec. 1882; *m.* 1909, Cecil (*d.* 1918), *d.* of late Sir Alex. Shaw, Limerick; *m.* Grace, *d.* of late Capt. F. Papillon, R.N., and *widow* of Lt.-Col. C. E. A. Jourdain, D.S.O., The Loyal Regt. Served European War, 1914-18 (wounded, 1914 Star, British War Medal, Victory Medal); Malabar, 1921-1922 (C.B.E.); retired pay, 1931. *Address:* Moorlands, Boat of Garten, Inverness-shire. *Club:* United Service. [*Died* 28 *Sept.* 1959.

JOHNSTON, Sir Thomas Alexander, 12th Bt. of Caskieben. *cr.* 1626; Civil Engineer; Chief of Plant and Service Branches, Operations Division, Corps of Engineers, U.S. Army (Mobile, Ala., District), since 1951 (Chief of Service Branch, 1949-51); *b.* 3 May 1888; *e. s.* of Sir Thomas Alexander Johnston, 11th Bt. and Mary Ann (*d.* 1949), *d.* of William Thomas Norville, Mobile, Alabama; *S.* father, 1950; *m.* 1915, Pauline Burke, *d.* of Leslie Bragg Sheldon, Mobile; one *s.* two *d.* *Educ.:* Barton Academy (Public School); Mobile Military Institute, Ala.; Alabama Polytechnic Institute, Auburn, Ala. Member, American Society of Military Engineers. Recorder and surveyor, Corps of Engineers, 1909-18; Field Civil Engineer, Alabama Dry Dock and Shipbuilding Co., 1918-20; engineering and valuation of Railroads, 1920-32; Corps of Engineers, 1932-. *Recreations:* boating, fishing. *Heir:* *s.* Thomas Alexander Johnston, Attorney-at-Law [*b.* 7 Sept. 1916; *m.* 1941, Helen Torrey, *d.* of Benjamin Franklin DuBois; two *d.*]. *Address:* 53 South Carlen St., Mobile, Alabama, U.S.A. *T.:* 6-9663. *Club:* The Propeller Club of the United States (Port of Mobile). [*Died* 12 *April* 1959.

JOHNSTON, Prof. (Emeritus) Thomas Baillie, C.B.E. 1945; M.D.; Editor of Gray's Anatomy, 1928 - 58; *b.* July 1883; *s.* of late Major A. Johnston, Edinburgh; unmarried. *Educ.:* George Watson's College, Edinburgh; Edinburgh University, M.B., Ch.B. (1st class hons.), 1906, M.D. (Gold Medal), 1937. Demonstrator and Lecturer on Anatomy, Edinburgh University, 1907-14; Lecturer on Anatomy, University College, London, 1914-1919; temp. Capt. R.A.M.C., 1916-18; Professor of Anatomy, University of London, Guy's Hospital Medical School, 1919-48, and Superintendent of the Hospital, 1937-48; Group Officer, Sector X, E.M.S. 1939-46. *Publications:* Medical Applied Anatomy, 1915; Manual of Surgical Anatomy (with Lewis Beesly, F.R.C.S. Edin.); Synopsis of Regional Anatomy, 8th edn., 1957; Contributions to the Journal of Anatomy, etc. *Recreation:* golf. *Address:* Guy's Hospital, S.E.1; The Covert, Wood Drive, Elmstead Lane, Chislehurst. *T.:* Imperial 134. *Club:* Athenæum. [*Died* 8 *Oct.* 1960.

JOHNSTON, Thomas Harvey, M.A., D.Sc., C.M.Z.S.; Professor of Zoology, University of Adelaide, since 1922; *b.* 9 Dec. 1881; *s.* of Thomas Johnston, Belfast; *m.* Alice Pearce, Petersham, Sydney, N.S.W.; one *s.* one *d.* *Educ.:* University of Sydney. Lecturer in Zoology and Physiology, Sydney Technical College, 1907-8; Assistant Government Microbiologist, Sydney, 1909-11; Lecturer in charge, Biology Dept., University, Brisbane, 1911-19; W. and E. Hall Fellow in Economic Biology, University, Brisbane; Chairman of Queensland Government Scientific Travelling Commission to inquire into Prickly Pear Control in foreign lands, 1912-14; Scientific Controller, Commonwealth Government Prickly Pear Control Investigations (laboratories in Queensland, New South Wales, Argentine, Florida and Texas, U.S.A.), 1920-23; Prof. Biology, Univ., Brisbane, 1919-22; Hon. Prof. Botany, Univ., Adelaide, 1928-34; Hon. Director South Australian Museum, 1927-30; Chief Biologist, British, Australian and New Zealand Antarctic Research Expeditions, 1929-30, 1930-31; Syme Research Prize and Medal, University of Melbourne, 1913; President Royal Society of Queensland, 1915; President Royal Society of South Australia, 1931-32; Member of Australian National Research Council; Polar Medal, 1934; Verco Medal for Research, Royal Society of South Australia, 1935; Fellow since 1937, and Mueller Medal, 1939, of Australian and N.Z. Assoc. Adv. Science. *Publications:* about 280 papers dealing chiefly with Australian Parasitology; Control of Prickly Pear Pest; Economic Entomology. *Address:* Yeronga, Esplanade, Henley Beach, South Australia; University, Adelaide, South Australia. [*Died* 30 *Aug.* 1951.

JOHNSTON, Thomas Kenneth; *b.* Spalding, Lincolnshire, 20 July 1878; *s.* of David Johnston, formerly Manager, Capital and Counties Bank Ltd.; *m.* 1919, Margaret, *d.* of H. C. King, formerly H.M. Inland Revenue Dept.; two *s.* (eldest son killed in action). *Educ.:* Boston School; Trinity College, Cambridge. Entered Indian Civil Service, 1901; served in United Provinces and Eastern Bengal; retired, 1923; admitted as solicitor, 1924; Lecturer in Law, Armstrong College (afterwards King's College), Newcastle-upon-Tyne, 1927-44. *Publications:* articles in the Law Times. *Recreations:* golf, fishing. *Address:* The Corner House, Sheringham, Norfolk. [*Died* 21 *Feb.* 1953.

JOHNSTON, Sir William (Ernest George), Kt., *cr.* 1951; D.L. City of Belfast, 1951; Director James Johnston & Co. Ltd., 34 Donegall St., Belfast, Flax Merchants; *b.* 31 Oct. 1884; *s.* of Rt. Hon. Sir James Johnston, Belvoir Park, Belfast; *m.* 1912, Olive, *d.* of Rev. Dr. Wm. Patterson, Cooke Church, Toronto; one *s.* *Educ.:* Campbell College; Queen's University, Belfast (B.A.). High Sheriff, City of Belfast; Lord Mayor of City of Belfast, May 1949-May 1951. *Address:* 16 Wellington Park, Malone Road, Belfast. *Club:* Ulster Reform (Belfast) (Pres. 1946-47). [*Died* 26 *Oct.* 1951.

JOHNSTON, Lieut.-Col. William Hamilton Hall, D.S.O. 1918; M.C.; D.L.; late Middlesex Regt.; *e. s.* of late W. N. Johnston and Mrs. Johnston, of Plumbley, Cheshire; *m.* 1923, Hyllarie Mabel, *o. d.* of late Yates Williams, Manchester; two *d.* *Educ.:* Leys, Cambridge. Served European War, 1914-18 (despatches twice, M.C., D.S.O.); Pioneer Corps, 1940-41; Home Guard, 1941-45. High Sheriff of Merioneth, 1937-38; D.L. Merioneth, 1948. *Address:* Bryn-y-Groes, Bala, Merioneth. *T.:* Bala 35. *Club:* Junior United Service. [*Died* 11 *Aug.* 1952.

JOHNSTONE, Sir Alexander Howat, Kt., *cr.* 1950; O.B.E. 1946; Q.C. (New Zealand); barrister; *b.* Milton, Otago, 12 June 1876; *s.* of John Johnstone, contractor; unmarried. *Educ.:* Tokomairiro Dist. High Sch., Otago; Victoria Univ. Coll., Wellington, N.Z. B.A. 1903; LL.B. 1905; K.C. (N.Z.) 1934; Q.C. (N.Z.) 1952. Practised at New Plymouth until 1919, subsequently at Auckland. Member Council Taranaki Dist. Law Soc., 1907-19 (Pres. 1913); Council Auckland Dist. Law Soc. since 1920 (Pres. 1924-25); Vice-Pres. N.Z. Law Soc., 1933-50; Foundation Member: Committee of Management, Solicitors' Fidelity Guarantee Fund; Disciplinary Committee of N.Z. Law Society, and Council of Legal Education. Former Member: New Plymouth Borough Council; New Plymouth High School Board; Mem. Senate University of N.Z., 1938-48; Member Auckland University College Council, 1937-52; Council Auckland Inst. and Museum (Pres., 1942-43). Aliens Authority at Auckland and Special Tribunal relating to Conscientious Objectors during War. *Club:* Northern (Auckland). [*Died* 28 *May* 1956.

JOHNSTONE, Major David Patrick, C.I.E. 1923; O.B.E. 1919; late R.A.M.C.; *b.* 27 Feb. 1876. *Educ.:* Queen's College, Cork; Edinburgh University, L.R.C.S., L.R.C.P. Entered army, 1904; Major, 1915; served European War, 1914-19 (despatches, O.B.E.); retired pay, 1924; Surgeon to the Governors of Madras, 1929-39. [*Died* 11 *May* 1951.

JOHNSTONE, Sir George Frederic Thomas Tankerville, 9th Bt., of Westerhall, Dumfriesshire, *cr.* 1700; *s.* of late Col. G. C. K. Johnstone; *b.* 1 Aug. 1876; *S.* uncle, 1913; *m.* Ernestine, *d.* of Col. Porcelli-Cust; one *s.* three *d.* *Educ.:* Eton. Served R.N.V.R., 1914-18. *Heir: s.* Frederic Allan George, *b.* 23 Feb. 1906. *Address:* Claymore, The Parade, Cowes, I. of W.; South Kyme, Lincoln. *Clubs:* Royal Thames Yacht; Royal Southampton Yacht; Island Sailing (Cowes). [*Died* 9 *Jan.* 1952.

JOHNSTONE, Lewis Martin, Q.C. (Can.); Member of Johnstone, Ritchie & Huckvale, barristers and solicitors, Lethbridge, 1908; retired; *b.* Halifax, Nova Scotia, 29 August 1870; *s.* of Henry Wentworth and Teresa Frances Johnstone; *m.* 1902, Emily Mary, *d.* of Charles Rigby, M.D., Halifax; no *c.* *Educ.:* Stonyhurst College and Mount St. Mary's College, England; Dalhousie University, Halifax, Nova Scotia; Harvard University Law School. Practised Halifax, 1893; Alberta, 1901; served with Princess Patricia's Canadian Light Infantry in France, 1917-18 (despatches); member of Board of Governors, University of Alberta, resigned, 1936; Vice-President, Alberta Law Society; Director number of local companies; Roman Catholic. *Address:* Point Colville, Saanichton, Vancouver Island, B.C., Canada. *Clubs:* Bath; Union, Royal Victoria Yacht, Victoria Golf (all of B.C.). [*Died* 8 *May* 1960.

JOHNSTONE-WALLACE, Denis Bowes, M.Sc. (Dunelm), N.D.D.; Civil Servant, retired, 1957; lately, General Advisory Officer, National Agricultural Advisory Service, Ministry of Agriculture and Fisheries, attached to Royal Agricultural College, Cirencester, Gloucestershire; *b.* 25 March 1894; *e. s.* of late Colonel Sir Johnstone Wallace, K.B.E., D.L., J.P., Parkholme, Newcastle upon Tyne; *m.* 1918, Nancy, *e. d.* of late James Smith of Gainesville, Gowland Avenue, Newcastle upon Tyne; one *d.* *Educ.:* Royal Grammar School, Newcastle upon Tyne; Armstrong (now King's) College, Newcastle upon Tyne, in University of Durham; West of Scotland College of Agriculture and the Dairy School for Scotland, Kilmarnock; Univ. of Florida, U.S.A. Recorder of Experiments, Cockle Park Agricultural Experimental Station, Northumberland, 1914-15; Military Service, 1915-19, Capt. R.G.A.; Leeds University Lecturer in Agriculture for North Riding of Yorkshire, 1919-22; Organiser of Agricultural Education for Devonshire, 1922-24; Principal, East Anglian Institute of Agriculture, Chelmsford, 1924-29; Agrostologist in Experiment Station of New York State College of Agriculture, and Asst. Prof. of Agrostology, Cornell University, Ithaca, N.Y., U.S.A., 1931-47 (during War of 1939-45, on leave of absence for war service as Dep. Dir. National Institute of Agricultural Engineering, Ministry of Agriculture and Fisheries, 1943-44). *Publications:* include Cornell University Experiment Station Bulletins, 538, 567, 570, 600, 612, 630, 639, 755, and Extension Bulletin 393, on pasture improvement and management. *Recreations:* fishing, shooting, hunting, etchings. *Address:* Kemble Lodge, Kemble, Nr. Cirencester, Gloucestershire. *T.:* Kemble 288. *Club:* Farmers'. [*Died* 5 *Jan.* 1960.

JOHORE, Sultan of, Major-Gen. H.H. Sir Ibrahim, D.K.; S.P.M.J. (Darjah Karabat; 1st cl. Order of Crown of Johore); Hon. G.C.M.G., *cr.* 1916 (Hon. K.C.M.G., *cr.* 1897); Hon. G.B.E., *cr.* 1935 (Hon. K.B.E., *cr.* 1918); Major-General, Johore Military and Volunteer Forces; Hon. Major-General in the British Army, 1947; *b.* 17 Sept. 1873; *o. s.* of late Sultan Abu-Bakar; *m.* 1940, Marcella, *d.* of late Edgar Mendl. Visited Europe as Crown Prince, 1890, and as Sultan, 1904-5 and 1929; touring round the world, via China, Japan, and America in 1934; proclaimed Sultan in succession to his father, 7 Sept. 1895; crowned 2nd Nov. 1895. Celebrated Diamond Jubilee, 1955. Holds numerous foreign decorations. Hon. F.Z.S. (Scots.). *Heir: s.* Prince Ismail, Crown Prince of Johore. *Recreations:* big-game shooting, riding, driving, is a keen automobilist. *Address:* Istana Bukit Serene, Johore Bahru, via Singapore. [*Died* 8 *May* 1959.

JOLIOT-CURIE, Professor Jean Frédéric; Commandeur de la Légion d'Honneur; Croix de Guerre; Professor at the Collège de France since 1937, also Director of the Laboratory of Nuclear Physics and Chemistry; Professor, and Director of Curie Laboratory of Radium Inst., Faculty of Sciences, Univ. of Paris, since Oct. 1956; Membre du Conseil de l'Enseignement de l'Institut National des Sciences et Techniques Nucléaires, 1956; Member: Academy of Sciences; Nat. Acad. of Medicine; *b.* Paris, 19 Mar. 1900; *s.* of Henri Joliot; *m.* 1926, Irène (*d.* 1956), *d.* of late Pierre and Marie Curie; one *s.* one *d.* *Educ.:* Lycée Lakanal; École de Physique et de Chimie Industrielles; Univ. of Paris (L. ès S., D. ès S.). Asst. to Mme. Curie, 1925; Asst., Faculty of Sciences, 1932; Maître de Recherches, Caisse Nationale des Sciences, 1933; Lectr., Sorbonne, 1935; Dir.-Gen., Centre National de la Recherche Scientifique, 1944; High Comr. for Atomic Energy, 1946-50. Member Economic Council; member Consultative Assembly, 1944. Nobel Prize for Chemistry (jointly, with wife), 1935. Stalin Peace Prize, 1951. *Publications:* Le Noyau des Atomes, 1933; Le Neutron, Le Positron et la Radioactivité Artificielle; and other articles, some with wife, on artificial radioactivity, etc. *Address:* Collège de France, Place Marcellin Berthelot, Paris Ve.; 76 avenue Le Nôtre, Antony, Seine. [*Died* 14 *Aug.* 1958.

JOLLEY, Maj.-Gen. Norman Kempe, C.B.E. 1944; Royal Marines, retired; Secretary and Administrative Officer, Imperial Defence College, since 1945; *b.* 29 Nov. 1894; *s.* of Dr. C. E. Jolley; *m.* 1923, Jean M. Finlaison; one *s.* one *d.* *Educ.:* Richmond County School. Joined Royal Marines, 1912; R.M. Brigade, 1914; Grand Fleet, 1914-18; G.S.O. 3 Intelligence, 1918-1920; Adjutant, Plymouth Div., 1923-27; Passed Army Staff College, 1930; Military Instructor, 1931-33; Instructor Royal Naval Staff College, 1933-35; D.A.A.G. R.M., 1935-1939; A.A.G. R.M., 1940; Commander, 103 R.M. Brigade, 1940-42; Commandant,

Depot, R.M., Deal, 1943-44; retired Oct. 1943. *Address:* 32 Kensington Court, W.8. *Club:* Army and Navy. [*Died* 15 *Nov.* 1951.

JOLLIE, Mrs. Tawse; *see* Colquhoun, Ethel M.

JOLLY, William Alfred, C.M.G. 1927; *b.* Spring Hill, Brisbane; *s.* of late Alexander Jolly; *m.* Maude Moorehouse; seven *s.* First Mayor of Greater Brisbane, 1925-30; first Lord Mayor, 1930-31; M.H.R. for Lilley, 1937-43. *Address:* 351 Queen Street, Brisbane, Queensland, Australia. [*Died* 30 *May* 1955.

JOLOWICZ, Herbert Felix, LL.D., D.C.L.; Regius Professor of Civil Law in the University of Oxford since 1948; Editor, Journal of the Society of Public Teachers of Law; Major, late Intelligence Corps; *b.* London, 16 July 1890; 2nd *s.* of late Hermann Jolowicz; *m.* 1924, Ruby, *o. d.* of late Joseph Wagner; two *s.* one *d.* *Educ.:* St. Paul's School; Trinity College, Cambridge (Scholar); Leipzig and Freiburg Universities. 1st class, 1st division Classical Tripos Part 1, 1911; 1st class, Law Tripos Part 1, 1913; Inns of Court O.T.C., September 1914; Commissioned Bedfordshire Regt., 1915; served Gallipoli, Egypt, France; called to Bar, Inner Temple, 1919; All Souls Reader in Roman Law, University of Oxford, 1920-1931; Lecturer in Roman Law and Jurisprudence, University College, London, 1924; Professor of Roman Law in the University of London, 1931-48; Dean of the Faculty of Law, University of London, 1937-38; Intelligence Corps, War of 1939-45. Hon. D.C.L. Tulane University, Louisiana. *Publications:* Historical Introduction to the Study of Roman Law, 1932, reprinted with corrections, 1939, 2nd edn., 1952; Digest xlvii. 2 (De Furtis), Edited with Introduction, Notes and Translation, 1940; and articles in periodicals and collections. *Address:* Hurstcote, Cumnor, Oxford; All Souls College, Oxford. *Club:* Oxford and Cambridge. [*Died* 19 *Dec.* 1954.

JOLY DE LOTBINIÈRE, Brig.-Gen. Henri Gustave, D.S.O. 1902; late R.E.; *b.* 10 March 1868; *s.* of late Sir Henry J. de Lotbinière; *g.s.* of Gaspard Joly, Seignior of Lotbinière; *g.-g.s.* of last Marquis de Lotbinière; *m.* 1902, Mildred Louisa (*d.* 1953), *d.* of late C. S. Grenfell; two *s.* Entered Army, 1888; Captain, 1899; Major, 1900; Lt.-Colonel, 1915; Brevet Colonel, 1916; served N.W. Frontier, India, 1897-98 (medal with 3 clasps); S. Africa, 1899-1902 (despatches twice, brevet of Major, Queen's and King's medals 5 clasps, D.S.O.); Somaliland, 1903-1904 (medal); European War, 1915-18 (despatches five times, Belgian Croix de Guerre, Bt. Col.); retired pay, 1921; J.P. Suffolk. *Address:* Brandon Hall, Brandon, Suffolk. [*Died* 15 *Feb.* 1960.

JONES (Alfred) Ernest, M.D., B.S., F.R.C.P., (Lond.), Hon. D.Sc. (Univ. of Wales); D.P.H. (Cantab.); Hon. Consultant to Graylingwell Mental Hospital; Hon. President, International Psycho-Analytical Association, American Psychoanalytic Assoc., British Psycho-Analytical Society and of the Institute of Psycho-Analysis; Consulting Physician (late Director) to London Clinic for Psycho-Analysis; Founder and late Editor of the International Journal of Psycho-Analysis; Hon. Fellow Royal Medico-Psychological Assoc., American Psychiatric Assoc., American Psychopathological Assoc., British Psychological Society and of the American, French, German, Hungarian, and Italian Psycho-Analytical Societies; F.R.S.M., F.R.S.A., F.R.A.I.; *m.* 1919, Katherine Jokl; two *s.* one *d.* *Educ.:* University Colleges, Cardiff and London; Munich, Paris, and Vienna; double first-class honours, with two Gold Medals at M.B., London; Gold Medal at M.D., London. After filling several hospital posts in London, Professor of Psychiatry at the University of Toronto, and Director of the Ontario Clinic for Nervous Diseases; before and after this spent two years on Continent in research work; returned to England 1913, confining work to Medical Psychology; introduced study of Psycho-Analysis into England and America. *Publications:* 12 books and three hundred monographs on Neurology, Psychology, and Anthropology; edited Social Aspects of Psycho-Analysis, 1924; Sigmund Freud, Life and Work, 3 vols., 1953-57; Free Associations, 1960 (autobiography, posthumous). *Recreations:* chess, figure-skating. *Address:* The Plat, Elsted, Midhurst, Sussex. *T.:* Harting 261. *Club:* Athenæum. [*Died* 11 *Feb.* 1958.

JONES, Arthur G. M.; *see* Maitland-Jones.

JONES, Sir Arthur P. P.; *see* Probyn-Jones.

JONES, Very Rev. Arthur Stuart D.; *see* Duncan-Jones.

JONES, Rev. Canon Benjamin; retired; Vicar of Llanfairisgaer, Port Dinorwic, Caerns., resigned, 1948; Residentiary Canon of Bangor Cathedral, 1930-37, Chancellor, 1937-40, Chancellor Emeritus since 1940; *b.* 1865. Rural Dean of Arvon 1935; Editor of Church monthly organ, Haul, 1913-20; Editor of the Welsh Church organ, Y Llan, 1920-38. *Educ.:* Bangor School of Divinity; Marcon's Hall, Oxford. *Publication:* St. David's Day Sermon preached at St. Paul's Cathedral, 1932. *Recreation:* fishing. *Address:* Vron, Port Dinorwic, Carnarvonshire. *T.A.:* Port Dinorwic. *T.:* Dinorwic 266. [*Died* 16 *Dec.* 1955.

JONES, Bernard Mouat, D.S.O. 1917; Hon. D.C.L. (Durham), Hon. LL.D. (Wales and Leeds); Hon. Freeman of Company of Clothworkers; *b.* London, 1882; 4th *s.* of Alex. Mouat Jones. *Educ.:* Dulwich Coll.; Balliol Coll., Oxford. 1st Class Final Honour School of Natural Science (Chemistry), and 1st classes in Mineralogy and Crystallography, 1904; B.A. 1905; M.A. 1908. Research Assistant in Mineralogical Chemistry, Imperial Institute, 1905; Professor of Chemistry, Government College, Lahore, 1906; Assistant Professor Imperial College, 1913; Warden, University Hall of Residence, Chelsea, 1913; Private, London Scottish, 1914; Captain and Assistant Director Central Laboratory, G.H.Q. 1915; Major, 1918; Lieut.-Col. and Director, 1918 (D.S.O., despatches thrice); Professor of Chemistry and Director of the Edward Davies Laboratories, University College of Wales, Aberystwyth, 1919; Principal, Manchester College of Technology, 1921-38; Vice-Chancellor, Leeds University, 1938-48; Member of Advisory Committee on Education in the Colonies; President, Manchester Literary and Philosophical Society, 1930; Past Chairman, Association of Principals of Technical Institutions; Past Chairman, Association of Technical Institutions; Pres. Assoc. of Technical Institutions, 1943; Chairman, Northern Branch, National Library for the Blind, 1936-39; Member of Makerere-Khartoum Education Commission, 1937; of Commission on Higher Education in West Africa, 1944; Cttee. on Higher Technological Education; Cttee. on Higher Commercial Education. *Publications:* Papers in Journal of Chemical Society, Mineralogical Magazine, Proceedings of the Royal Society. *Recreation:* walking. *Address:* Waverley Abbey House, Farnham. *Club:* Athenæum, [*Died* 11 *Sept.* 1953.

JONES, Sir Cadwaladr Bryner, Kt., *cr.* 1947; C.B. 1936; C.B.E. 1920; LL.D., M.Sc., F.H.A.S.; *b.* 1872; *s.* of late E. Jones of Cefnmaelan, Dolgelley, and Jane, *d.* of Lewis Jones of Maesybryner; grandfather Congregationalist minister and first Editor of Dysgedydd; unmarried. *Educ.:* Dolgelly Grammar School; Agricultural Coll., Aspatria. Was County Lecturer at Univ. Coll., Bangor, and subsequently Lecturer in Agriculture, Armstrong (now King's) College, Newcastle upon Tyne; Prof. of Agriculture and

Director of College Farm, Univ. College of Wales, Aberystwyth, 1907-12; Chm. of Council of Royal Welsh Agricultural Society, 1944-53; Pres., 1954; Hon. Director of Show, 1908, 1909, 1910; Chm. of Governors of Dr. Williams' School, Dolgelley; Agricultural Comr. for Wales, and Chairman of Welsh Agricultural Council, 1912-19; Welsh Secretary, Ministry of Agriculture, 1919-44; President Welsh Mountain Sheep Flock Book Society, 1913-19; President of Welsh Black Cattle Society, 1944-45. *Publications:* Handbook on Manuring; numerous Reports on Experiments, and articles on agricultural topics; Editor of Live Stock of the Farm, 1915. *Address:* 12 Laura Place, Aberystwyth. *T.:* 7116. *Club:* Farmers'. [*Died* 10 *Dec.* 1954.

JONES, Charles Edward Irvine, C.B.E. 1950; Comptroller and Accountant General of the Post Office since 1950; *b.* 30 June 1899; *s.* of Charles Edward Jones; *m.* 1924, Daisie Foster; no *c.* *Educ.:* Owens. Served European War, 1914-18, in R.N.A.S. and R.G.A., 1917-19. Exchequer and Audit Department, 1919-39; Ministry of Supply, 1939-44; Treasury Officer of Accounts, H.M. Treasury, 1944-50. A.S.A.A. (Gold Medal, 1929). *Address:* Fenners, Esher, Surrey. [*Died* 8 *Nov.* 1951.

JONES, Sir Charles (Ernest), Kt., *cr.* 1950; C.M.G. 1947; Ceylon Civil Service, retired; *b.* 13 March 1892; *s.* of E. H. Jones, Southsea; *m.* 1923, Hilda Yorath, Ross-on-Wye, Herefordshire; one *s.* *Educ.:* Royal College of Science, London University. Royal Scholarship in Physics, B.A., B.Sc. (Lond.). Cadet, C.C.S., 1914; Asst. Censor, 1916-18; European War, 1914-18, served 1918-19; returned to C.C.S. and held various administrative and judicial posts, 1919-38; member of Retrenchment Commission, Ceylon, 1938-1939; Controller of Imports, Exports and Exchange, 1939-41; Dep. Financial Sec., Ceylon, 1941-45; Actg. Dep. Chief Sec., Actg. Financial Sec., Acting Chief Sec., 1946 and 1947; Permanent Sec. Ministry of Finance and Sec. to the Treasury Ceylon, 1947-50. Govt. Dir., Bank of Ceylon, 1947-50; Chm., Currency Bd., 1947-50; Nominated Member: Monetary Bd., Ceylon Central Bank, 1950; Chairman Housing Loans Bd., Ceylon, 1949-1950. *Recreations:* golf, billiards. *Address:* Murvagh, Sandford Road, Cheltenham. *T.:* Cheltenham 55405. *Clubs:* Royal Empire Society, East India and Sports; New (Cheltenham); Colombo (Ceylon). [*Died* 17 *Aug.* 1953.

JONES, Charles Evan William, C.I.E. 1924; *b.* 1879; *s.* of David Jones, Cardiff. *Educ.:* Llandovery; Brasenose College, Oxford (Scholar); Second Class Classical Moderations; First Class History Finals. Entered Indian Educational service, 1906; Principal, Morris College, Nagpur, Central Provinces, 1906-13; Director of Public Instruction, North West Frontier Province, 1913 and 1915 (officiating), 1917-1921; Director of Public Instruction, and Secretary for Education to the Government of the Central Provinces, India, 1922-34; retired from Indian Educational Service, 1934; Registrar, Indian Institute of Science, Bangalore, India, 1937-39. *Address:* c/o Lloyds Bank, 6 Pall Mall, S.W.1. [*Died* 13 *Oct.* 1951.

JONES, Lieut.-Col. Charles Herbert, C.M.G. 1916; T.D. B.A., Th. A. (Aus.); commanded 5th Battalion Leicestershire Regiment, 1913-17; 20 years House Master and 13 years Comdt. O.T.C. at Uppingham School; *b.* 1865; *m.* Kathleen, *o. d.* of Lt.-Col. J. Liddell, V.D., J.P., Huddersfield; one *s.* three *d.* Served S. African War, 1900-1 (Queen's medal 4 clasps, Hon. Lieut. in Army); European War, 1914-17 France (despatches twice, wounded twice, C.M.G., Officer Legion of Honour); Military Member Leicester and Rutland Territorial Association, 1908-25; Senior Range Officer N.R.A. Bisley, 1925; Australian Migration Scheme, 1926. *Address:* 64 Murdoch Street, Cremorne, N.S.W.; Barclays Bank, Highfields, 68 Evington Road, Leicester. [*Died* 9 *June* 1953.

JONES, Sir Charles Lloyd, Kt., *cr.* 1951; artist; Chairman David Jones Ltd., Sydney; *b.* Strathfield, N.S.W., 28 May 1878; *s.* of Edward L. and Helen A. Jones; *m.*; two *s.* one *d.* *Educ.:* Manor House School. One of the founders and Hon. Member Board of Control, Australian National Publicity Assoc.; Treasurer Chamber of Commerce, 1915-16, Cancer Research Fund for Univ. of Sydney; First Chm. Australian Broadcasting Commn.; Past Pres. Austr. branch, Chartered Inst. of Secretaries. One of Founders of Art in Australia, Ltd.; Trustee, National Art Gallery, New South Wales; paintings exhibited by Society of Artists, Sydney, N.S.W. Commodore (retd.) Roy. Sydney Yacht Squadron. Officer, Legion of Honour (France), 1953; Knight, Royal Order of Vasa (Sweden), 1955. *Address:* 86 Castlereagh St., Sydney, N.S.W., Australia; 95 Ocean Street, Woollahra, N.S.W., Australia. *Clubs:* Royal Automobile; Australian, Royal Sydney Golf, Royal Sydney Yacht (Sydney). [*Died* 30 *July* 1958.

JONES, Sir Crawford D. D.; *see* Douglas-Jones.

JONES, David Lewis; Local Director Barclays Bank Ltd.; *b.* 31 Jan. 1889; *s.* of late Lewis Morris Jones, Rhiwgoch Fawr, Anglesey, and Mrs. Owen, Glanafon, Pwllheli; *m.* 1919, Rachel Emily, *y. d.* of late Richard James Mathias, J.P., Public Works Contractor and Civil Engineer, and Mrs. Mathias, The Garth, Pontypridd, Glamorgan; one *d.* Sheriff of Caernarvonshire, 1941-42. *Recreation:* Captain, Pwllheli Golf Club. *Address:* Glenafon, Abererch. Pwllheli. *T.:* Pwllheli 100. [*Died* 26 *July* 1953.

JONES, Sir David T. R.; *see* Rocyn-Jones.

JONES, Dudley William Carmalt, M.A., D.M.Oxon; F.R.C.P.Lond.; F.R.A.C.P.; Emeritus Professor of Systematic Medicine, University of Otago, N.Z.; Consulting Physician, Westminster and Dunedin Hospitals; *b.* London, 30 Aug. 1874; *e. s.* of late T. W. Carmalt Jones, F.R.C.S. Ed., of the Middle Temple, Barrister-at-law, and Evelyn Danvers, *d.* of late W. T. Thornton, C.B.; *m.* 1907, Mabel Gertrude (*d.* 1955), 2nd *d.* of Captain F. L. Tottenham, one *s.* one *d.* *Educ.:* Uppingham; Corpus Christi College, Oxford; St. Mary's Hospital. Asst. Physician, Seamen's Hospital, Greenwich, 1908; Assistant Physician 1908, Physician 1913, Director, Department of Bacteriotherapeutics, Westminster Hospital, 1910-13; Dean, Westminster Hospital Medical School, 1912; Active Service, France, 1915-1918; Temp. Major, R.A.M.C.(T.); Egypt, 1918-19; Consulting Physician, E.E.F.; Temp. Colonel A.M.S. *Publications:* An Introduction to Therapeutic Inoculation, 1911; Organic Substances, Sera and Vaccines in Physiological Therapeutics, 1924; Elementary Medicine in Terms of Physiology, 1929; Annals of the University of Otago Medical School, 1945; Diversions of a Professor in New Zealand, 1945; papers on medical subjects. *Address:* 31 Ashcombe Gdns., Edgware, Mx. *Clubs:* Athenæum; Dunedin (Dunedin, N.Z.). [*Died* 5 *March* 1957.

JONES, Sir Edmund Britten, Kt., *cr.* 1953; F.R.C.P.; Hon. Cons. Physician, Adelaide Children's Hospital since 1947; Pres. Medical Board, S.A., since 1950; *b.* 8 Oct. 1888; *s.* of E. Britten Jones; *m.* 1915, Hilda Madeline, *d.* of Francis Joseph Fisher; one *s.* two *d.* *Educ.:* Christian Brothers Coll.; Adelaide Univ.; Magdalen Coll., Oxford (Rhodes Scholar). M.B., B.S. Adelaide 1910; M.A. Oxon, 1926; M.R.C.P. Lond. 1926; F.R.C.P. Lond. 1942; F.R.A.C.P. 1938. Served European War with R.A.M.C., 1914-1920; War of 1939-45, Middle East, 1940-41.

Lt.-Col., A.A.M.C. *Recreation:* golf. *Address:* 80 Molesworth St., N. Adelaide, S.A. *Club:* Adelaide (Adelaide). [*Died* 30 *Sept.* 1953.

JONES, Ernest; *see* Jones, A. E.

JONES, (Frederic) Wood, F.R.S., D.Sc., M.B., B.S., F.R.C.S., F.R.A.C.S., L.R.C.P., F.Z.S.; Hon. Curator of Hunterian Collection of Human and Comparative Anatomy, Royal College of Surgeons, since 1952; *b.* London, 23 Jan. 1879; *m.* Gertrude Clunies, 4th *d.* of late George Clunies-Ross, Governor of the Keeling-Cocos Islands. Demonstrator of Anatomy, London Hospital and at St. Thomas's; Lecturer on Anatomy, University of Manchester; wanderings as medical officer in the Far East; Anthropologist to Egyptian Government; Archæological Survey of Nubia; Arris and Gale Lecturer, Royal College of Surgeons 1914, 1915, 1916, and 1919; late Professor of Anatomy, the London School of Medicine for Women; Professor of Anatomy in the University of Adelaide, 1919-26; Rockefeller Professor of Physical Anthropology, the Univ. of Hawaii, Honolulu, 1927-30; Professor of Anatomy, University of Melbourne, 1930-37; Prof. of Anatomy, Manchester University, 1938-45; temp. Director Anatomy, Peiping Union Med. Coll., 1932-33; Sir William H. Collins Professor of Human and Comparative Anatomy in the Royal College of Surgeons in England, 1945-1952; late Examiner in Anatomy to London University, the Conjoint Board of the Royal Colleges of Physicians and Surgeons, and to the Society of Apothecaries; Captain R.A.M.C. during European War. *Publications:* Coral and Atolls: various articles on corals and coral islands; Arboreal Man; The Principles of Anatomy as seen in the Hand; Unscientific Essays; The Mammals of South Australia; The Matrix of the Mind; Man's Place among the Mammals, 1929; Sea Birds Simplified, 1934; Unscientific Excursions, 1934; Life and Living, 1939; Design and Purpose, 1942; Habit and Heritage, 1943; Structure and Function as seen in the Foot, 1944; Hallmarks of Mankind, 1948; Trends of Life, 1953; various articles on archaic anatomy and pathology, and articles of strictly anatomical interest in various scientific publications. *Address:* The Royal College of Surgeons, Lincoln's Inn Fields, W.C.2. [*Died* 29 *Sept.* 1954.

JONES, Sir George L.; *see* Legh-Jones.

JONES, Sir George William Henry, Kt., *cr.* 1928; Q.C. 1943; Recorder of Colchester, 1937-47; Barrister-at-law; *s.* of George Jones, Stamford Hill; unmarried. L.C.C. for North Hackney, 1910-18; LL.B. (Hon.) London; first in First Class Honours at Inter. LL.B. in Roman Law and Jurisprudence; first class in all Bar examinations; Senior Student at Bar Examination in Constitutional Law and Legal History; Certificate of Honour at Bar Final; M.P. (U.) Stoke Newington, Dec. 1918-23 and 1924-45; candidate for West Leeds, Dec. 1910; candidate for Haggerston, 1911-18, when the constituency was merged into Shoreditch; Candidate for Stoke Newington, 1945. *Address:* 47 St. Mary Abbott's Court, Kensington, W.14. *T.:* Western 9416; 2 Harcourt Buildings, Temple, E.C. *T.:* Central 7202. *Clubs:* Carlton, Constitutional. [*Died* 3 *Jan.* 1956.

JONES, Commodore Gerald N., C.B.E. 1941; D.S.O. 1917; Master Mariner, retired; R.N.R., retired; *b.* Llanarmon, near Ruthin, North Wales, 30 May 1885; *s.* of Humphrey Bradley Jones, schoolmaster, and Lucy George, Belper, Derbyshire; *m.* 1916, Flora, *d.* of James McGregor, Tain and North Wales; no *c.* *Educ.:* Home, under father. Apprenticed to the sea and sailed from Liverpool on first voyage in the clipper ship, Glenesslin, 1902; was second mate and first mate in sailing-ships and later joined White Star Line as an officer; late Master Cunard White Star Ltd., retired from sea employment, 1948; commissioned in the Royal Naval Reserve; served during European War on Belgian Coast, Gallipoli, North Sea, and other areas in command of destroyers (D.S.O.); awarded Liverpool Shipwreck and Humane Society's silver medal and illuminated address, 1919, for gallantry in saving life at sea. Commander R.N.R. 1929; Captain, 1935; studied at R.N. War College, Greenwich, 1930; lectured on naval history before the Royal United Service Institution, Whitehall; Nautical Assessor under the Central Court of Passage, Liverpool; Lecturer on Nautical Subjects and free-lance journalist. Served as Commodore R.N.R. (Second Class) in charge of convoys, Jan. 1940-June 1945 (despatches). *Address:* Westwinds, Deganwy, North Wales. *T.:* Deganwy 83558. [*Died* 29 *May* 1958.

JONES, Gwilym Arthur, C.M.G. 1938; J.P.; *b.* 1887; *m.* 1910, Ivy Estelle, *d.* of Hon. Christopher Musgrave, Dominica. *Educ.:* University College, Bangor (Diploma in Agriculture, William Griffith prize). Agricultural Dept., Dominica, 1909-19; Commissioner of Agriculture, Imperial College of Tropical Agriculture, Trinidad, 1933-38; Director of Agriculture, Jamaica, 1938-44; retired 1944. *Address:* 9 Lyttleton Road, Liverpool 17. [*Died* 13 *Nov.* 1957.

JONES, Sir Harold Spencer, K.B.E., *cr.* 1955; Kt., *cr.* 1943; F.R.S. 1930; M.A., Sc.D. (Cantab.); Hon. D.Sc. (Paris, Brussels, Delhi, Durham, Oxford, Calcutta); Hon. D.Phil. (Copenhagen); Hon. LL.D. Glasgow); F.R.A.S.; F.B.H.I.; F.I.N.; Hon. F.R.S.E.; Astronomer Royal, 1933-55; retired 31 Dec. 1955; *b.* Kensington, 29 Mar. 1890; *e. s.* of H. C. Jones, Harrow; *m.* 1918, Gladys Mary Owers; two *s.* *Educ.:* Latymer Upper School, Hammersmith; Jesus College, Cambridge. 1st Cl. Math. Tripos. Pt. i. 1909; 1st Cl. Math. Tripos, Pt. ii. 1911; 1st Cl. Nat. Sc. Tripos, Part ii. 1912; Isaac Newton Student and Smith's Prizeman; Fellow Jesus College, Cambridge, 1914; Hon. Fellow, 1933; Chief Asst. Royal Observatory, Greenwich, 1913-23; H.M. Astronomer at Cape of Good Hope, 1923-33; during war period, Assistant Director of Inspection of Optical Supplies for Ministry of Munitions; Secretary of Royal Astronomical Society, 1923; President, 1937-39, Treasurer, 1946, Foreign Secretary, 1955-. Secretary General, Internat. Council of Scientific Unions, 1956-58; President, British Astronomical Association, 1934-36; President, British Horological Institute, since 1939; President Internat. Astronomical Union, 1945-48; Pres. Institute of Navigation, 1947-49; Pres. Sec. A. British Assoc., 1949; Sec., Royal Instn. of Gt. Britain, 1958-; Master, Clockmakers' Company, 1949 and 1954; Editor of the Observatory, 1914-23; Gold Medal of Royal Astronomical Society, 1943; Royal Medal of Royal Society, 1943; Janssen Medal, Société Astronomique de France, 1945; Gold Medal of British Horological Institute, 1947; Bruce Gold Medal, Astronomical Society of the Pacific, 1948; Gold Medal, Stoke-on-Trent Assoc. of Engineers, 1950; Lorimer Medal of Ast. Soc. of Edinburgh, 1953; Rittenhouse Medal, Rittenhouse Astronomical Soc., Philadelphia, 1955; Joykissen Mookerjee Gold Medal, Indian Association for Cultivation of Science, 1957. Hon. Fellow Brit. Optical Assoc.; Hon. Mem. Roy. Ast. Soc. Can.; Roy. Ast. Soc. N.Z.; Ast. Soc. of S. Africa; Amer. Ast. Soc. Hon. Fell.; Roy. Soc. N.S. Wales. Foreign Assoc. or Mem. of U.S. Nat. Acad. of Sciences; Amer. Phil. Soc.; Amer. Acad. of Arts and Sciences; Acad. des Sciences, Institut de France; Acad. Royale des Sciences de Belgique; Soc. Royale des Sciences de Liège; Roy. Swedish Acad. of Sciences; Roy. Danish Acad. of Sciences; Austrian Acad. of Sciences; Accad. Nazionale dei Lincei, Rome; Instituto de Coimbra, Portugal. *Publications:* General Astronomy, 1922; Worlds Without End, 1935; Life on Other

Worlds, 1940; *translation:* Atlas of the Sky, by Vincent de Callatay, 1958; Astronomical papers and articles contributed to Monthly Notices R.A.S., Science Progress, etc. *Address:* Carlekemp, East Parade, Bexhill-on-Sea, Sussex. *T.:* Bexhill 4514; 40 Hesper Mews, S.W.5. *T.:* Fremantle 0676. *Club:* Athenæum. [*Died* 3 *Nov.* 1960.

JONES, Colonel Harry Balfour, C.B. 1915; late R.E.; *b.* 22 Sept. 1866; *m.* 1914, Edith (*d.* 1921), *widow* of H. F. Matthews, I.C.S. Entered Army, 1885; Captain, 1894; Major, 1902; Lt.-Col. 1910; Col. 1913; served South African War, 1899-1902 (despatches twice, Bt. Major, Queen's medal 3 clasps, King's medal 2 clasps); European War, 1914-18 (despatches thrice, C.B.); retired pay, 1922. *Club:* Junior United Service. [*Died* 28 *Dec.* 1952.

JONES, Brig.-Gen. Herbert Arthur, C.B.E. 1942; Chm. Campbell Praed & Co. Ltd., Wellingborough, and Eldred Everard-Wills, Kettering; Director, Smith & Co., Oundle; *s.* of Rev. G. H. D. Jones. *Educ.:* Jesus College, Cambridge. Entered Army, 1900; subsequently on the staff of Lord French, Sir William Robertson, and Lord Haig respectively (despatches twice, Bt. Lt.-Col. and Bt. Col., Legion of Honour, Croix de Guerre); retired, 1920; Food Commissioner for Eastern Counties; Food Commissioner, London and Home Counties; Chm. of Committees on R.A.F. Organisation and Administration. *Recreations:* shooting, fishing, cricket, lawn tennis. *Club:* United Service. [*Died* 20 *Oct.* 1955.

JONES, Rt. Rev. Herbert Gresford, D.D.; Canon Residentiary of Liverpool, 1935-1956; Hon. Asst. Bishop in Diocese of Liverpool since 1946; *b.* 7 April 1870; *s.* of Canon William Jones, Vicar of Burneside; *m.* 1900, Elisabeth, 2nd *d.* of late Dr. Thomas Hodgkin, D.C.L., of Barmoor Castle, Northumberland; one *s.* *Educ.:* Haileybury; Trinity College, Cambridge. Ordained to Curacy at St. Helen's Parish Church, 1894; Vicar of St. Michael's-in-the-Hamlet, Liverpool, 1896; Vicar of St. John's, Keswick, 1904; Vicar of Bradford and Rural Dean, 1906; Archdeacon of Sheffield and Vicar of Sheffield, 1912; Bishop of Kampala, 1920-23; Vicar of Pershore, 1924-27; Rector of Winwick, 1927-35; Bishop of Warrington, 1927-45; Hon. Canon, Sheffield, 1914. *Publications:* Friends in Pencil, 1893; Foreign Missions and the Modern Mind, 1905; Uganda in Transformation, 1926. *Address:* Sefton Court, Liverpool 17. [*Died* 22 *June* 1958.

JONES, Bt. Col. Henry M. P.; *see* Pryce-Jones.

JONES, Rev. Howard W.; *see* Watkin-Jones.

JONES, Ifano, M.A. (Hon.) University of Wales; *b.* Aberdare, Glam., 15 May 1865; *m.* 1913, Jessie Mary, 2nd *d.* of Thomas and Mary Charles, Havod House, Blaenavon, Mon.; no *c.* *Educ.:* Local elementary and private schools. Reader in a book and magazine publishing establishment, 1885-96; Cardiff's Welsh Librarian, 1896-1926; National Eisteddfod Literary adjudicator since 1901; National Eisteddfod prize-winner for dramas and poetry, 1902, 1904, and 1929; Editor of poetry and criticism column in The South Wales Weekly News, 1905-28; Lecturer on literary and historical subjects, etc. *Publications:* A Classified Catalogue of the Cardiff Welsh Library (jointly), 1898; Llenyddiaeth Hanner Ola'r Ddeunawfed Ganrif, 1902; Rhys ap Tewdwr Mawr (a tragedy in three acts), 1905; The Bible in Wales (jointly), 1906; Dan Isaac Davies and the Bilingual Movement, 1908; The Early Nonconformists of Cardiff and District, 1912, 2nd edition, 1924; Bibliography of Wales (periodically), 1899-1912; Sir Matthew Cradock and some of his Contemporaries, 1919; W. T. Samuel; ei fywyd a'i lafur (a biography), 1920; History of Printing and Printers in Wales and Monmouthshire, 1925; poems, tunes, articles, reviews, special bibliographies, etc., in Welsh and English periodicals and anthologies. *Recreations:* walking and light gardening. [*Died* 7 *March* 1955.

JONES, Group Captain James Ira Thomas, D.S.O. 1918; M.C., D.F.C., M.M.; R.A.F.; Commanding a Fighter O.T.U.; *b.* 1896; *m.* O. G. Edmund-Davies. Served European War, 1914-1918 (despatches, D.S.O., M.C., D.F.C. and bar, M.M., Medal of St. George); North Russian Campaign, 1919; Signal duties Iraq, 1923-25, and Egypt, 1925-27; O.C. Home Communication Flight, 1928-29; Experimental Section, S. Farnborough, 1930-31; Signal Staff duties No. 1 Air Defence Group H.Q., 1932-35; Air Ministry (D.S.D. Department), 1935-36; R.A.F. Depot, Uxbridge, 1936; retired list, 1936; officially credited with destroying 28 enemy aircraft, 3 balloons, and sending 10 enemy aircraft down out of control during war of 1914-18. *Publications:* King of Air Fighters: the biography of Maj. Mick Mannock, V.C., D.S.O., M.C.; An Air Fighter's Scrapbook: an autobiography. *Recreation:* Rugby football—R.A.F., London Welsh, Richmond, Bristol, Northampton. *Club:* Bath. [*Died* 29 *Aug.* 1960.

JONES, Rt. Rev. John Charles; Bishop of Bangor since 1949; *b.* 3 May 1904; *s.* of Benjamin Jones, Llansaint, Carmarthenshire; *m.* Mary, *d.* of William Lewis, Carmarthen; one *d.* *Educ.:* The Grammar School, Carmarthen; University of Wales, Cardiff; Wadham College, Oxford. University College of South Wales and Mon., Cardiff, B.A. (Hons. in Semitic Langs. Cl. I), 1926; Wadham Coll., Oxford, Hody Exhibitioner, 1926; Hall-Houghton Septuagint Prize, 1927, Pusey and Ellerton Scholar, 1927, B.A. (Hons. in Theology, Class I), 1928, Kennicott Scholar, 1928; Wycliffe Hall, Oxford, 1928; M.A. 1932; D.D. (Lambeth) 1950; Curate of Llanelly, 1929; of Aberystwyth, 1933; Missionary of Church Missionary Society in Uganda, 1934-1945; Warden of Bishop Tucker College, Mukono, Uganda, 1939; Vicar of Llanelly, 1945; Examining Chaplain to Archbishop of Wales, 1948. *Address:* Llys Esgob, Menai Bridge, Anglesey. *T.:* Menai Bridge 17. [*Died* 13 *Oct.* 1956.

JONES, John David Rheinallt, Hon. M.A. (Rand); Adviser on Native Affairs to Anglo-American Corporation since 1947; formerly Senator elected by African Electoral College, Transvaal and Orange Free State, 1937-42; a Founder, Life Member, and Director of S.A. Institute of Race Relations, 1930-47; formerly Lecturer in Native Law and Administration, now Hon. Lecturer on Race Relations, Univ. of Witwatersrand; Secretary Witwatersrand Council of Education, 1919-46; Editor, South African Quarterly, 1915-26; was associated in various capacities with establishment and development Univ. of the Witwatersrand, 1919-29; Founder and former Editor, Bantu (now African) Studies, 1921-44; Founder and former Editor, Race Relations (quarterly) and Race Relations News (monthly), publications of Institute of Race Relations; Chief Scout's Commissioner for Pathfinder Scouts (African); Member of: National Council for Adult Education; Consumers' Advisory Cttee. of Nat. Marketing Council; Nat. Liaison Cttee. of F.A.O.; Cttee. on Minimum Accommodation Standards; President Sections E (1926) and F (1947) and Member of Council S.A. Assoc. for Advancement of Science, and member several other public bodies; more especially engaged in inter-racial activities for uplift of Africans and other non-European sections of population; *b.* 1884; *y. s.* of late Rev. J. Eiddon Jones, Llanrug, N. Wales; *m.* late Edith Beatrice, *o. c.* of late Charles Barton, Keighley, Yorks; one *d.*; *m.* 1947, Helen Clare Norfolk Francis (*née* Verley). *Educ.:* Friars School, Bangor; Grammar

School, Beaumaris. *Publications:* has written much on economic, social, and educational aspects of racial problems. *Address:* 1 Lothbury Road, Auckland Park, Johannesburg. [*Died* 30 *Jan.* 1953.

JONES, John E. E.; *see* Emlyn-Jones.

JONES, Sir John E. L.; *see* Lennard-Jones.

JONES, John Richard; *b.* 1881; *s.* of John Jones, Mayfield, Wavertree, Liverpool; *m.* 1912, Mary, *d.* of John Hughes, Moneivion, Wavertree; one *d.* *Educ.:* Liverpool. Served European War, 1917-19 (Croix de Guerre); Member Liverpool City Council, 1936-37 and 1942-45; J.P. 1936, Liverpool; Member: Nat. Eisteddfod Gorsedd; Liverpool Public Entertainments and Theatres Cttee.; Vice-Chm. Temperance Council of Christian Churches of Wales; Vice-President: Lancs. Cheshire and North Western Liberal Federation; Wales League of Youth; Cambridge Archæol. Society; Anglesey Antiq. Soc.; Life member Cymmrodorion Soc.; Lanc. and Ches. Historic Soc.; President Wavertree Division Liberal Assoc.; formerly President New Wales Union; Joint Treas. Free Church Federal Council; formerly Treasurer North Wales Temperance Union. High Sheriff of Anglesey, 1940-41. *Publication:* The Welsh Builder on Merseyside. *Recreations:* travel and social work. *Address:* Cintra, 109 Menlove Av., Liverpool 18. *T.:* Childwall 1476. *Club:* Lyceum (Liverpool). [*Died* 28 *Jan.* 1955.

JONES, Sir Lawrence John, 4th Bt., *cr.* 1831; *b.* 16 Aug. 1857; *S.* father, 1884; *m.* 1st, 1882, Evelyn Mary (*d.* 1912), *d.* of J. J. Bevan, Bury St. Edmunds; two *s.* one *d.* (and two *s.* and one *d.* decd.); 2nd, Paula, *d.* of late Francis Joseph Schuster, London, S.W. *Educ.:* Eton; Trinity Coll. Cambridge (scholar, 1879, M.A.). President, Society for Psychical Research, 1928-29; Vice-Chairman of Council Charity Organisation Society, 1917-1934. *Heir:* *s.* Lawrence Evelyn, M.C. *Address:* 39 Harrington Gardens, S.W.7. *T.:* Fremantle 3958. *Club:* Athenæum. [*Died* 21 *Oct.* 1954.

JONES, Maj.-Gen. Leslie Cockburn, C.B. 1919; C.M.G. 1916; M.V.O. 1911; late 5th Cavalry and 7th Lancers, Indian Army; *b.* 14 Jan. 1870; *m.* Adelaide Girdwood Low (*d.* 1929); one *d.*; *m.* 1943, Edith Violet Eastwood. Entered Army, 1890; Capt., Indian Army, 1901; Maj.-Gen. 1922; retired, 1922; served Isazai Expedition, 1892, and in S. Africa, 1900-2 (despatches, Brevet Major, Queen's medal 3 clasps, King's medal 2 clasps); European War, including Mesopotamia, 1914-18 (C.M.G., C.B., Bt. Col.). *Address:* Cross Cottage, Dolton, Winkleigh, Devon. [*Died* 7 *May* 1960.

JONES, Rev. Maurice, D.D. (Oxon); Canon of St. David's, 1923; *b.* Trawsfynydd, Merioneth, 21 June 1863; *s.* of William and Catherine Jones; *m.* 1st, Emily, *d.* of Col. C. M. Longmore, J.P., Gosport; 2nd, Jennie Bell, *d.* of Sidney Smith, Gosport; three *s.* two *d.* *Educ.:* Christ College, Brecon; Jesus College, Oxford, B.A. (1st Class Honours, 1886); M.A., B.D. (1907), D.D. (1914). Ordained, 1886; Chaplain to the Forces, 1890-1915; Rector of Rotherfield Peppard, Oxon, 1915-23; Principal of St. David's College, Lampeter, 1923-38; Rural Dean of Lampeter, 1928-29; served S. African War as Chaplain on H.Q. Staff (Queen's medal with three clasps); Chaplain at Aldershot, Gosport, Chatham, Plymouth, Colchester, Curragh Camp, Malta, and Jamaica; Select Preacher at Oxford, 1920-21; Public Examiner at Oxford, 1921 and 1932; Examiner for B.D., University of Wales, 1922; member of Departmental Committee on Teaching of Welsh, 1925; Fellow of Jesus Coll., Oxford, 1923., Hon. Fellow 1953. *Publications:* St. Paul the Orator, 1910; The New Testament in the Twentieth Century, 1914; St. Paul's Epistle to the Philippians (Westminster Commentary), 1918; The Four Gospels, 1921; St. Paul's Epistle to Colossians, 1923; has written much for Welsh journals. *Recreation:* bowls. *Address:* 27 Gravel Hill, Addington, Surrey. *T.:* Addiscombe 9370. [*Died* 7 *Dec.* 1957.

JONES, Rt. Rev. Norman Sherwood; Assistant Bishop of Lagos since 1944; *b.* 23 April 1911; *yr. s.* of Rt. Rev. T. S. Jones, *q.v.*, and Muriel Edith Lockhart Jones; *m.* 1949, Doreen Mary Bottone, M.B., Ch.B., *o. c.* of R. A. R. Bottone, Sanderstead, Surrey; one *d.* *Educ.:* Trent Coll.; Christ's Coll., Camb.; Wycliffe Hall, Oxford. Tutor of Wycliffe Hall, Oxford, 1935-37; Curate-in-charge St. Peter's, Rugby, 1937-41; Vicar of Radford, Coventry, 1941-44; Examining Chaplain to Bishop of Coventry, 1943. *Recreations:* music, golf, tennis. *Address:* C.M.S., P.O. Box 26, Kano, Nigeria. *Club:* National. [*Died* 8 *March* 1951.

JONES, Owen Daniel, J.P., D.L., Merioneth; V.D.; Sheriff of Merioneth, 1930; Major retired, 1st Durham Royal Engineer Volunteers; late Edinburgh General Manager, North British and Mercantile Insurance Company; *b.* 1861; *e. s.* of J. D. Jones of Ruthin; *m.* Esther (*d.* 1945), 2nd *d.* of Edward Lawrence, of Sunnybank, Chorley; one *s.* one *d.* *Educ.:* City of London School. In insurance business fifty years; Fellow of the Chartered Insurance Institute. *Recreation:* gardening. *Address:* Talgarth, Pennal, Merionethshire. *T.:* Pennal 203. *Club:* Northern (Edinburgh). [*Died* 26 *Nov.* 1951.

JONES, Hon. Percy Sydney T.; *see* Twentyman-Jones.

JONES, Rt. Rev. Richard William; Assistant Bishop of the Province of Wales since 1946; Archdeacon of Llandaff since 1938; Rector of Peterston-super-Ely, Cardiff, since 1938. *Educ.:* University of Wales, B.A.; St. Michael's College, Aberdare. Deacon, 1903; Priest, 1904. *Address:* The Rectory, Peterston-super-Ely, Cardiff. [*Died* 2 *June* 1953.

JONES, Robert Edmond; stage designer and director; Member of National Institute of Arts and Letters; *b.* 12 Dec. 1887; *m.* *Educ.:* Harvard University. Designer of The Man who Married a Dumb Wife; The Jest, Hamlet, Richard III, with John Barrymore; The Birthday of the Infanta; The Green Pastures; Lute Song; Oedipus Rex; Director of Desire under the Elms, Fashion and Love for Love. *Publications:* Drawings for the Theatre; The Dramatic Imagination. *Clubs:* Players, Harvard, Century (New York). [*Died* 26 *Nov.* 1954.

JONES, Robert Walter; Fellow and Dep. Chairman of Council, Institute of Bankers; Manager, Trustee Dept., Westminster Bank, Ltd. since 1948; *b.* 1890; *o. s.* of Robert George Jones and P. J., *d.* of G. Corker; *m.* 1915, Muriel Joyce Gare; one *s.* two *d.* *Educ.:* Friern L.C.C. School; Haberdashers' School. Commenced Banking Career, 1907; joined 2/5th Buffs, 1916; Commissioned 9th London Regt. 1917; attached North Russia Expeditionary Force, 1918; retired with Hon. Rank of Captain, 1920. Rejoined Bank, 1920; Lecturer to Institute of Bankers, 1925-35; Gilbart Lecturer, Univ. of London, King's College, 1932-35, 1947-48-49; Joint editor of Chitty on Contracts; Editor Dictionary of Banking. *Publications:* Bankers and the Property Statutes; Studies in Practical Banking; Contributions to various Banking Periodicals. *Recreations:* golf, book collecting. *Address:* 53 Threadneedle Street, E.C.2; 99 Wood Vale, S.E.23. *T.:* Forest Hill 5035. *Club:* Savage. [*Died* 16 *Nov.* 1951.

JONES, Sir T. Barry, 2nd Bart., *cr.* 1917; M.A., M.I.C.E.; Director Topham, Jones & Railton, Ltd., Civil Engineering Contractors, since 1927; *b.* 1 Oct. 1888; *s.* of Sir Evan Davies Jones, 1st Bt., and Cecilia Ann (*d.* 1913), *d.* of Jacob Evans; *S.* father, 1949; *m.* 1922, Jean, *widow* of Lieut. Herbert Costain, R.A.F.; no *c.* *Educ.:* Haileybury

College; Trinity College, Cambridge, M.A. Served European War, 1914-18, Lt. Royal Fusiliers; Prisoner of War, 1917. *Heir:* none. *Address:* 74 Princes Court, Brompton Rd., S.W.3; Pentower, Fishguard, Pembrokeshire. *T.:* Kensington 3509. *Club:* United University. [*Died* 29 *May* 1952 (*ext.*).

JONES, Thomas, C.H. 1929; LL.D.; Secretary of the Pilgrim Trust, 1930-45, a Trustee, 1945-54 (elected Chairman for 2 years, Nov. 1952); member Unemployment Assistance Board, 1934-40; late Deputy Secretary, Cabinet, and Secretary, Economic Advisory Council; *b.* Rhymney, 1870; *m.* Eirene Theodora (*d.* 1935), *d.* of late R. J. Lloyd, D.Lit.; one *s.* one *d.* *Educ.:* Pengam County School; University College, Aberystwyth; Glasgow Univ. Clarke Scholar Glasgow University; Russell Student, London School of Economics; Barrington Lecturer in Ireland, 1904-5; Assistant to Professor of Political Economy and Lecturer in Economics, Glasgow University; Special Investigator, Poor Law Commission, 1906-9; Prof. in Economics, Queen's University, Belfast, 1909-10; Secretary Welsh National Campaign against Tuberculosis, 1910-11; Secretary National Health Insurance Commissioners (Wales), 1912-16; Governor of National Library and of the National Museum of Wales; a Commissioner of the Exhibition of 1851; President, Coleg Harlech; Chairman, Gregynog Press; Chairman, York Trust; Chairman, Royal Commission on Ancient Monuments in Wales and Mon., 1944-48; Hon. Trustee of the Observer; formerly Pres., Univ. Coll., Aberystwyth; late Deputy Chairman C.E.M.A.; Hon. LL.D. Glasgow, 1922; Wales, 1928; St. Andrews, 1947; Birmingham, 1955; awarded medal of Cymmrodorion Soc., 1944. *Publications:* Reports on Outdoor Relief; A Theme with Variations; Rhymney Memories, 1939; Leeks and Daffodils, 1942; Cerrig Milltir, 1942; The Native Never Returns, 1946; Lloyd George, 1951; Welsh Broth, 1951; A Diary with Letters, 1931-1950, 1954; The Gregynog Press, 1954; edited Mazzini's Essays; Smart's Second Thoughts of an Economist; Sir Henry Jones's Old Memories. *Address:* Manor End, St. Nicholas-at-Wade, Birchington, Kent. *Club:* Athenæum. [*Died* 15 *Oct.* 1955.

JONES, Sir Tracy French Gavin, Kt., *cr.* 1936; late Managing Director Cawnpore Chemical Works; late President Economic Reform Club, London; *b.* India, 1872; *s.* of Gavin S. Jones and Margaret French, Kent; *m.*; one *d.* *Educ.:* Clifton. Trained as Mechanical and Mining Engineer; served as Mining Engineer in Rhodesia, 1895-96; founded Empire Engineering Co., Cawnpore, 1898; British India Corporation, 1919-24; founded Cawnpore Chemical Works, 1928; served Matabele War, Rhodesia Horse, 1896; United Provinces Horse, Officer Commanding, 1912-18; President, Upper Indian Chamber of Commerce, 1921-23, 1934, and 1935; Member United Provinces Council, 1922-25; Member Legislative Assembly, 1926-29; M.L.C. Upper House United Provinces Legislatures, 1937-44; Round Table Conference London, 1930 and 1931; Deputy President Associated Chambers, 1929-30. *Publication:* Origin of World Crises and Britain's Task. *Address:* Pages Farm, Mayfield, Sussex; 10 Broadwater Down, Tunbridge Wells. *T.:* Tunbridge Wells 1754. *Clubs:* Constitutional; Cawnpore (Cawnpore). [*Died* 14 *May* 1953.

JONES, Vernon Stanley V.; *see* Vernon-Jones.

JONES, William Hugh, Q.C. 1924; *b.* 1866; *s.* of Hugh Jones, Cardiff; *m.* 1st, 1892, Jeannie (*d.* 1923), *o. d.* of David Lewis, Park View, Aberayron, and Barn Hall, Ombersley, Worcs.; one *s.*; 2nd, 1946, Eva, *e. d.* of David Morris, Elm Ho., Penally, Pembrokeshire. *Educ.:* University College of South Wales and Monmouthshire; London University. Called to the Bar, Gray's Inn, 1892; practised on the S. Wales Circuit; has acted as Deputy County Court Judge on Circuits 24, 28, and 31, as Deputy Recorder of Cardiff and Carmarthen, and as Commissioner of Assize on South Wales and Chester Circuit; Chm. of Court of Referees under the Unemployment Insurance Acts for the Rhymney Valley District, Glamorgan and Monmouth, 1928-31; Stipendiary Magistrate for the City of Cardiff, 1930-45; Hon. Legal Adviser to Regional Commissioners for Wales Civil Defence, 1941-45. *Publication:* Guide to the Liquor Licensing Acts; Prize Essay awarded by the Merthyr Incorporated Law Society at the Welsh National Eisteddfod at Merthyr, 1901, on the liability of employers for accidents to workmen. *Recreation:* walking. *Address:* 30 Park Road, Whitchurch, Glam. *Club:* Cardiff and County (Hon. Life Mem.). [*Died* 21 *Sept.* 1960.

JONES, Rt. Rev. William S.; *see* Stanton-Jones.

JONES, William Sydney, C.B.E. 1951; Chief Registrar, Chancery Division, Supreme Court of Judicature, since 1948; *b.* 8 March 1888; *s.* of William Darby Jones and Annie Jones, of Bromley, Kent, and Parkstone, Dorset; unmarried. *Educ.:* privately. 2nd Lieut. 2/10 London Regt., 1914; Machine Gun Officer, 1915; Bde. Machine Gun Officer, 175 Inf. Bde., 1916; Capt., 1916; France, 1916-17; Adjt. 2/10 London Regt., 1917; invalided home, 1917; Staff Capt. 207 Inf. Bde., 1918-19. Admitted a Solicitor, 1919; Chancery Registrars' Office, 1921; Registrar, 1931. Assistant Editor, Law Journal, 1925-31; Editor, 1941-45. *Publications:* Editor Lawyer's Remembrancer, 1923-28; Consulting Editor, Encyclopædia of Court Forms and Precedents. Contributions to Law Journal, 1924-48. *Recreation:* golf. *Address:* Royal Courts of Justice, W.C.2; 80 Redcliffe Square, S.W.10. *T.:* Fremantle 7456. *Club:* Royal Automobile. [*Died* 31 *March* 1959.

JONES, Sir William Y.; *see* Yarworth-Jones.

JONES, Wood; *see* Jones, F. W.

JONES-DAVIES, Henry, C.B.E. 1936; J.P.; Retired; *b.* Bremenda, Llanarthney, Carmarthen, 2 Jan. 1870; *s.* of Thomas and Elizabeth Davies; *m.* 1903, Winifred A. Ellis, *sister* of late T. E. Ellis, M.P., former Chief Liberal Whip; one *s.* *Educ.:* Carmarthen Grammar School. Farmer; County Councillor; Chairman of Carmarthen County Council, 1902; Chairman of County Education Committee, 1908; a pioneer of Agricultural Co-operation in Wales; a Member of the Development Commission, 1910-36; a life member of Welsh Agricultural Organisation Society (Pres., 1948-49), and Member of its Exec. Cttee.; Member of Irish Agricultural Organisation Society's Committee, 1914-21; President Carmarthen County Federation of Young Farmers Clubs, 1946-49. *Recreations:* shooting and gardening. *Address:* Glyneiddan, Nantgaredig, Carms. *T.:* Nantgaredig 217. [*Died* 16 *June* 1955.

JONSSON, Prof. Einar; sculptor; *b.* on the farm Galtafell, Iceland, 11 May 1874; father farmer there. *Educ.:* Royal Academy of Fine Art, Copenhagen. Travelled in Germany, Austria, Italy, Hungary, Holland, England, and America; made a statue in Philadelphia, U.S.A., in 1918, of the first white settler in America, Thorfinnur Karlsefni, an Icelander; presented all his works to his native State, Iceland, which has had a Museum built for them. *Publication:* an Essay on his Works in English, Danish, Icelandic, and German, with over 100 illustrations, 1925. *Address:* Reykjavik, Iceland. [*Died* 18 *Oct.* 1954.

JOPSON, Sir (Reginald) Keith, K.C.M.G., *cr.* 1955 (C.M.G. 1949); O.B.E. 1937 (M.B.E. 1929); H.M. Ambassador to Republic of Uruguay since 1955; *b.* 25 October 1898; *s.* of William Knowles Jopson and Ellen Butters; *m.* 1st, 1922, Frances Fifield, *d.* of Henry C. Barlow, Chicago, Ill., U.S.A.; one *s.* one *d.*; 2nd,

JONES, William Ernest, C.M.G., J.P. See page xxix.

1945, Barbara, *d.* of Ronald Ransom, Vice-Chairman, Board of Governors, Federal Reserve System, Washington, D.C. *Educ.:* privately and at University College, London; London School of Economics. Served European War, 1914-18, Lieut., London Rifle Brigade. Entered Foreign Service, 1920; H.M. Vice-Consul, Chicago, 1920-1923; Vice-Consul, Colon and Panama City, 1923-26; Vice-Consul, Cologne, 1926-1929; Actg. Consul-General, Cologne, in each year, 1926-29; Second Sec. of Legation and Vice-Consul, Montevideo, 1929-30; acted as Chargé d'Affaires, Montevideo, 1930; Commercial Sec., British Embassy, Buenos Aires, 1930-33; Commercial Sec., British Legation, Helsingfors, 1933-38; Dept. of Overseas Trade (Director Foreign Division), 1939-40; Counsellor (Commercial) British Embassy, Washington, D.C., 1941-1945; seconded from Foreign Service to serve as U.K. Trade Commissioner (Grade I) at Montreal, Canada; Economic Adviser to U.K. High Commissioner at Ottawa and Senior U.K. Trade Commissioner in Canada, 1948-53; Ambassador to Republic of Colombia, 1953-55. *Recreations:* sailing, ski-ing, swimming, golf, and gardening. *Address:* c/o British Embassy, Montevideo, Uruguay. *Clubs:* Jockey, Country (Bogotá). [*Died* 27 *May* 1957.

JORDAN, Alfred Charles, C.B.E. 1920; M.D., Camb.; M.R.C.P., London, etc.; Hon. Radiologist, Queen Alexandra's Hospital for Officers, Highgate, and Fishmongers' Hall Hospital for Officers, 1915-18; Medical Radiographer, Guy's Hospital, 1907-13, and Royal Hospital for Diseases of the Chest, 1907-20; F.R.S.M.; Ex-President Hunterian Society; 3rd *s.* of late Albert Jordan, merchant, of Manchester; *b.* Hale, Cheshire, 29 May 1872; *m.* 1911, Christina (*d.* 1941), *y. d.* of late Charles Brumleu; one *s.* (elder son killed in action, 1940), one *d.* *Educ.:* Manchester Grammar School (Langworthy Scholar); Sidney Sussex College, Cambridge (scholar); St. Bartholomew's Hospital; Berlin. 1st class Natural Sciences Tripos; R.M.O. and Pathologist, Sussex County Hospital, Brighton, 1900; House Physician (to Sir T. Lauder Brunton), St. Bartholomew's Hospital, 1901; in medical practice in the city of London, 1901-7; Medical Officer, Electrical Department, Metropolitan Hosp. and Queen's Hospital for Children, 1905-7; Diploma in Medical Radiology and Electrology, Cambridge; Founder, and Hon. Sec. 1929-39, Men's Dress Reform Party. *Publications:* Chronic Intestinal Stasis: a Radiological Study, 1923, 2nd edition, 1926; numerous papers. *Recreations:* music, lawn tennis, figure skating, cycling, swimming. *Address:* 38 Moss Hall Grove, N. Finchley, N.12. *T.:* Hillside 4501. *Clubs:* Royal Skating, Finchley Lawn Tennis. [*Died* 17 *March* 1956.

JORDAN, Mrs. Arthur; *see* Ashton, Helen.

JORDAN, H. E. Karl, F.R.S. 1932; Ph.D.; Director of the Zoological Museum, Tring, 1930-1939, Curator of Entomology, 1893-1939, retired; *b.* Almstedt, Province of Hanover, 7 Dec. 1861; *m.* 1891, Minna (*d.* 1925); two *d.* *Educ.:* Andreanum at Hildesheim; University of Göttingen, Ph.D. 188; Exam. pro facultate docendi, 1886; Master at the Progymnasium and Privatdocent at the Academy of Forestry at Münden, 1887-92; Master for Mathematics and Natural History at the Agricultural School at Hildesheim, 1892. *Publications:* essays on variation and entomological subjects (Morphology and Anatomy of Physopoda; Mechanical Selection; Contradistinction between geographical and non-geographical variation, etc.). *Address:* British Museum, Zoological Museum, Tring, Herts. *T.:* Tring 3346 [*Died* 12 *Jan.* 1959.

JORDAN, Canon James Henry; Prebendary and Canon Residentiary of Hereford Cathedral since 1940; Precentor since 1945; *b.* Worcestershire, 1882; *s.* of William Jordan; *m.* 1915, Alice Martin Unwin; two *d.* *Educ.:* King Edward's School, Birmingham; Hertford College, Oxford. Curate of St. John's, Waterloo; Vicar of St. Mark's, Haydock; Vicar of Fairfield, Liverpool; Vicar of Allerton, Liverpool; Diocesan Canon of Liverpool Cathedral; Rural Dean of Childwall. *Recreations:* golf, gardening. *Address:* The Canon's House, Hereford. *T.:* Hereford 3509. [*Died* 27 *Aug.* 1959.

JORDAN, Philip Furneaux, C.B.E. 1950; Public Relations Adviser to the Prime Minister since 1947; *b.* 10 Aug. 1902; *s.* of John Furneaux and Mildred Jordan; *m.* 1927, Ruth Castberg, Oslo. *Educ.:* Royal Naval Colleges, Osborne and Dartmouth. Joined staff of News Chronicle as columnist, 1936; later Features Editor and foreign corresp.; War of 1939-45, correspondent in Europe, Africa, U.S.S.R. and Asia. Foreign correspondent for Daily Mail, 1945; First Sec. at Embassy, Washington, 1946-47. *Publications:* various novels (under various names), 1921-36; There Is No Return, 1938; Say That She Were Gone, 1940; Russian Glory, 1942; Jordan's Tunis Diary, 1943. *Recreations:* watching other people garden; reading. *Address:* 8 Chester Place, Regents Park, N.W.1. *Clubs:* Travellers', Savile. [*Died* 6 *June* 1951.

JORDAN, Sara M., M.D.; **(Mrs. Penfield Mower);** Dir. (1922), Dir. Emerita (1958), Dept. of Gastroenterology, Lahey Clinic, Boston, Mass., U.S.A.; *b.* 20 Oct. 1884; *d.* of Patrick Andrew Murray and Maria Murray (*née* Stuart); *m.* 1st, 1914, Sebastian Jordan; one *d.*; 2nd, 1935, Penfield Mower. *Educ.:* Radcliffe Coll. (A.B.); Univ. of Munich (Ph.D.); Tufts Coll. Med. Sch. (M.D.). Pres. Amer. Gastro-enterological Assoc., 1942-44; Chairman: Women's Cttee. on Procurement and Assignment Service, War Manpower Commission, 1942-46; Trustee: New England Baptist Hospital; Tufts University; Museum of Science, Boston. Elizabeth Blackwell Citation for achievement in medicine, 1951; Julius Friedenwald Medal for outstanding achievement in gastroenterology, 1952; Jane Addams Medal for distinguished service, 1958. Hon. Degrees: Doctor of Science: Smith College, 1935; Tufts University, 1943; Wilson Coll., 1946; Doctor of Humanities, Suffolk Univ., 1954; Dr. of Medical Sciences, Women's Medical Coll. of Pennsylvania, 1956. *Publications:* (Co-author) Good Food for Bad Stomachs, 1952; author of numerous articles on medical subjects. *Recreation:* golf. *Address:* (Home) Foster Street, Marblehead Neck, Mass., U.S.A. *T.:* Neptune 2-2368. *Club:* Cosmopolitan (New York City). [*Died* 21 *Nov.* 1959.

JORDAN, Rt. Hon. Sir William Joseph, K.C.M.G., *cr.* 1952; P.C. 1946; Hon. LL.D.: St. Andrews, 1946, Cambridge, 1951; J.P. (N.Z.); retd.; *b.* Ramsgate, Kent; *s.* of Captain W. Jordan; *m.* 1st, Winifred Amy (*d.* 1950), *d.* of Louth Bycroft; one *s.* one *d.*; 2nd, Mrs. Elizabeth Ross Reid. *Educ.:* St. Luke's Parochial School, Old Street, London. Postal Service London; short term in Metropolitan Police; migrated to N.Z., 1904; engaged farming; First Secretary N.Z. Labour Party, Wellington, 1907, Pres. 1932; served in France with N.Z. Forces (wounded); M.P. Manukau, New Zealand, 1922-36; High Commissioner for New Zealand in London, 1936-51. Represented N.Z. at Coronation of King George VI. Chairman Imperial Economic Cttee., 1937-38; Pres. Council of League of Nations, 1938; N.Z. rep. at Nine Power Conf., Brussels, 1939; N.Z. rep. to Paris Peace Conf., 1946; signed peace treaty with Italy, Bulgaria, Hungary, Roumania, Finland, 1947. Member Worshipful Company of Girdlers, 1941; Member Worshipful Company of Butchers, 1947; Freeman City of London, 1941 (Master of Guild, 1947); Freeman of Ramsgate, 1937. *Address:* St. Helier's, Auckland,

N.Z.; N.Z. House, 415 Strand, W.C.2. *Clubs:* Devonshire, City Livery. [*Died* 8 *April* 1959.

JOSE, Very Rev. George Herbert, M.A.; Dean of Adelaide, 1933-53, Dean Emeritus since 1953; *b.* Clifton, Bristol, 15 Dec. 1868; *s.* of late W. W. Jose, J.P., merchant, Alderman; *m.* 1890, Clara Ellen (*d.* 1925), *d.* of late T. J. Sturt, M.D., F.R.C.S. (Lond.); one *s.* (one killed France, 1917, and one killed at Singapore, 1942). *Educ.:* Clifton College; Monkton Combe School; Worcester College, Oxon; B.A. Oxon (2nd Cl. Theol. Sch.), 1903; M.A. 1906; ad eund., Adel. 1906. To Australia, 1888, Surveyor; to China, 1891, Lay Missionary; Ordained, 1893; C.M.S. Missionary at Taichow, 1893-99; Curate of Coates, Glouc., 1899-1901; St. Giles', Oxon, 1901-2; Priest in Charge of St. Cyprian's, N. Adelaide, 1903-5; Rector of All Souls, St. Peters, 1905-6; Rector of Christ Church, N. Adelaide, 1907-33; Past Senior Grand Warden and Past Grand Chaplain of Grand Lodge F., S.A.; Chaplain, A.M.F., 1915-19; Deputy Senior Chaplain, 1916-18; General Secretary, Australian Church Congress, 1928; Examining Chaplain to Bishop of Adelaide, 1906-29; Canon of St. Peter's Cathedral, 1918-29; Archdeacon of Mt. Gambier 1927-29, of Adelaide 1929-33; Commissary during Bishop's absence, 1934, 1948, 1953; Dean Admin. Dioc. Adel., 1940-41. *Publications:* Annals of Christ Church, 1921; The Story of Jesus Christ, 1936; The Church of England in South Australia, 1836-56, 1937; The Church of England in South Australia, 1856-81, 1954; The Church of England in South Australia, 1882-1905, 1955. *Recreations:* reading, writing, gardening. *Address:* Kingsmead, Brougham Place, N. Adelaide, South Australia. [*Died* 26 *Nov.* 1956.

JOSEPH, Sir Francis (L'Estrange), 1st Bt., *cr.* 1942; K.B.E., *cr.* 1935 (C.B.E. 1918); Kt., *cr.* 1922; K. St. J., 1945; J.P.; D.L.; M.Inst.Min.E.; Hon. Colonel 71st A.A. Searchlight Regt. R.A. (T.A.), 1940-47; Chairman and Managing Director, Settle, Speakman & Co., Ltd., and its subsidiary cos.; Chm. Timber and Wood (Merseyside), Ltd.; ex-Chairman of U.K. Commercial Corp.; Director: Blaw-Knox Ltd.; and other public Cos.; *b.* Liverpool, 31 July 1870; *yr. s.* of late Thomas and Elizabeth Joseph, Liverpool; *m.* 1917, Violet, 2nd *d.* of Joel and Margaret Caroline Settle, Alsager, Cheshire; two *d.* *Educ.:* Caledonian Schools, Liverpool. Left school at twelve and commenced work as railway messenger; Member Liverpool City Council, 1903-13; J.P. Liverpool, 1910-24; J.P. County of Chester, 1920; County of Stafford, 1927; High Sheriff, Staffordshire, 1932-33; contested (L.) Walton Division, Liverpool, Jan. 1910; Fairfield Division, Liverpool (Coal. Lib.), Dec. 1918; Staff-Captain War Office, 1916-1917; Assistant Secretary Ministry National Service, 1917-18; Deputy Director-General National Labour Supply, 1918; President North Staffordshire Chamber of Commerce, 1922-32, Federation of British Industries, 1935; Society of British Gas Industries, 1939-46, and National Conference on Commercial Education, 1939; Government Director of Imperial Airways Ltd. from 1937 until purchased by Govt.; formerly director Midland Bank, Ltd.; Midland Bank Executor and Trustee Co. Ltd.; Pres. Institute of Industrial Administration, 1940-48; Founder (and Chm. 1928-33) of Central Pig Iron Producers Assoc. and Basic Iron Producers Assoc.; Member of Overseas Trade Development Council, 1930-44; British Govt. Economic Mission to S. Africa, 1930; Royal Commission on Location of Industry, 1937-1940; received Freedom of Stoke-on-Trent, 1936; Chairman Spitfire Mitchell Memorial Fund; Chairman Order of St. John for Staffs.; Pres. Coal Trade Benevolent Assoc. Member of Livery Goldsmiths Company. King's Jubilee Medal, 1935. *Address:* The Hall, Alsager, Cheshire. *T.A.:* Joseph Alsager *T.:* Alsager 24. *Clubs:* Carlton, City Livery, Royal Automobile. [*Died* 8 *Feb.* 1951 (*ext.*).

JOSEPH, Michael; Chairman and Managing Director of Michael Joseph, Ltd.; *b.* London, 26 Sept. 1897; *m.* 1st, 1918; two *s.*; 2nd, 1926, Edna Victoria Frost (*d.* 1949); one *s.* one *d.*; 3rd, 1950, Anthea, *d.* of Rt. Hon. Lord Justice Hodson, P.C., M.C.; one *s.* one *d.* *Educ.:* City of London School; Univ. of London. Served European War, 1914-1918; gazetted to Wiltshire Regiment, 1915; Lieut. and Captain, Machine Gun Corps, 1916-19; Lieut. and Captain, The Queen's Own Royal West Kent Regt., 1940-41; Director, Curtis Brown, Ltd., 1926-35; President of the Siamese Cat Society of the British Empire. *Publications:* Short Story Writing for Profit, 1923; Journalism for Profit, 1924; The Commercial Side of Literature, 1925; The Magazine Story, 1928; Cat's Company, 1930, new edns., 1946 and 1957; This Writing Business, 1931; Puss in Books (with Elizabeth Drew), 1932; Heads or Tails (with Selwyn Jepson), 1933; Discovery (play), 1934; The Sword in the Scabbard, 1942; Charles: The Story of a Friendship, 1943; The Adventure of Publishing, 1949; (ed.) Best Cat Stories, 1952. *Recreation:* cats. *Address:* Brown's Farm, Old Basing, Hants. *Club:* Savage. [*Died* 15 *March* 1958.

JOSHI, Narayan Malhar; Kaisar-i-Hind (Silver) Medal: (C.I.E. offered in 1921, but refused on the ground of his being very poor); *b.* Goregaon, Kolaba District, Bombay Presidency, 1879; Hindu (Brahmin); *m.* 1900; two *s.* one *d.* *Educ.:* Deccan College, Poona; Bombay University. Served in several high schools as an assistant teacher; joined Mr. Gokhale's Servants of India Society, 1909; for nearly two years was the Manager of a Marathi daily paper, Dnyan Prakash; Secretary of the Social Service League in Bombay since 1911; Secretary of the Bombay Presidency Social Reform Association, 1915-30; a Member of the Bombay Municipal Corporation, 1919-22; nominated by Government to represent labour interests in India at the International Labour Conference held at Washington, 1919, and nominated a Member of the Indian Legislative Assembly to represent labour interests, 1920, 1923, 1927, 1931, 1935 and 1946; attended Internat. Labour Conferences held at Geneva as rep. of Indian Labour, 1921, 1922, 1925, 1929, 1934, 1946 at Paris, and 1947 at Geneva; Member of Governing Body of the I.L.O., 1934-44 and again, 1945-48; General Secretary of the All-India Trade Union Congress, 1925-1929 and 1940-, now retd. President National Trades Union Federation, 1937; Member Royal Commission on Indian Labour; Delegate, Indian Round Table Conf. in London, 1930-32; Delegate, Joint Parliamentary Cttee. on Indian Constitutional Reform. Pres., Bombay Civil Liberties Union, 1937; Member of Pay Commission, 1946-47. *Address:* Model House, A/4, Proctor Rd., Girgaum, Bombay 4, India. [*Died* 30 *May* 1955.

JOUHAUX, Léon; French trade union leader; President: Economic Council of Republic of France since 1946; C.G.T. Force Ouvrière since 1947; Vice. Pres. Internat. Confederation of Free Trade Unions since 1949; Nobel Peace Prize for 1951; *b.* Paris, 1 July 1879. Sec.-gen. Confédération Générale du Travail, 1909-40 and 1945-47; Member: Gen. Council of Bank of France, 1936-; Workers Gp. of Governing Body of I.L.O.; Workers Vice-Chm., Governing Body, I.L.O., 1945-. French Deleg. to League of Nations for economic questions and disarmament, 1925-28. Former Vice-Pres. Internat. Fed. of Trades Unions; Pres. Internat. Council European Movement, 1949. Arrested and made prisoner in France, Dec. 1941; deported to Germany, 1943;

re-entered France, 1945. *Publications:* Organisation Internationale du Travail; Le Désarmament; La Fabrication Privée des Armes; Le Mouvement Syndical en France. *Address:* Confédération générale du Travail Force Ouvrière, 198 Avenue du Maine, Paris XIV, France. [*Died* 28 *April* 1954.

JOURDAN, Rev. George Viviliers; Professor of Ecclesiastical History, University of Dublin (T.C.D.), since 1933; *yr. s.* of John Jourdan, London and Dublin, and *g.s.* of Major John Jourdan, of the French Imperial Artillery. *Educ.:* privately; Trinity College, Dublin. Curate of Larah, Kilmore, 1896; Mullingar (Meath), 1896-1900; St. Paul's, Cork, 1900-2; Midleton, Cloyne, 1902-6; Rector of Rathbarry, Ross, 1906-1915; Rector of S. Mary Shandon, Cork, 1915-40; Rector of Dunboyne and Maynooth, 1942-44; Prebendary of Clonmethan in St. Patrick's Cathedral, Dublin, 1931-44; D.D. (T.C.D.), 1914; Litt.D. (T.C.D.), stip. cond., 1935; M.R.S.A.I.; M.R.I.A. *Publications:* The Movement Towards Catholic Reform in the Early Sixteenth Century, 1914; The Stress of Change, 1931; 7 Chapters in vols. ii. and iii. of The History of the Church of Ireland, 1933; articles and papers in Church Quarterly Review, History, Journal of Bibl. Lit. (U.S.A.), Irish Church Quarterly, Church of Ireland Gazette; Erasmus, and New Schaff-Herzog Encyclopedia. *Recreations:* golf, music, reading. *Address:* Castlewood Park, Rathmines, Dublin; 10 Trinity College, Dublin. *Club:* Dublin University (Dublin). [*Died* 9 *Dec.* 1955.

JOWETT, Percy Hague, C.B.E. 1948; R.W.S. 1936; F.R.C.A.; Hon. R.W.A.; Citizen and Liveryman of the Worshipful Company of Goldsmiths; *b.* 1 June 1882; *s.* of Smith Jowett, Halifax, Yorks; *m.* 1912, Enid Ledward; one *d.* *Educ.:* privately; Leeds School of Art; Royal College of Art; Italy. Travelling scholarship in painting, 1909; exhibits at New English Art Club, Royal Soc. of Painters in Water-Colours, Imperial Gallery, Chicago, and provincial galleries; Member of New English Art Club; Hon. Fellow Roy. Coll. of Art, 1952; held one-man shows at St. George's Gallery in 1923, 1925, 1927, 1929; pictures acquired for permanent collections at Oldham Art Gallery, Birmingham City Art Gallery, Leeds City Art Gallery, Brighton Art Gallery, Gloucester Guildhall, Bradford City Art Gallery, Manchester Whitworth Collection, Hanley Art Gallery, Aberdeen Art Gallery, Southport Art Gallery, Laing Art Gallery, Preston Art Gallery, Newcastle upon Tyne; National Gallery, New Zealand. War service as Lieutenant R.G.A. in France and Flanders, 1916-18; Principal of the L.C.C. Central School of Arts and Crafts, 1930-35; Principal of Royal College of Art, 1935-47. *Address:* 28 Drayton Gardens, S.W.10. *T.:* Fremantle 2736. *Club:* Athenæum. [*Died* 4 *March* 1955.

JOWITT, 1st Earl, *cr.* 1951; **William Allen Jowitt,** P.C. 1931; Kt., *cr.* 1929; Viscount Stevenage, *cr.* 1951, Viscount Jowitt, *cr.* 1947, Baron Jowitt, *cr.* 1945, of Stevenage; *b.* 1885; *o. s.* of late Rev. William Jowitt, Rector of Stevenage; *m.* 1913, Lesley, 2nd *d.* of J. P. M'Intyre, 45 Princes Gardens, S.W.; one *d.* *Educ.:* Marlborough College; New College, Oxford. Hon. D.C.L. (Oxf.); Hon. LL.D. (Columbia, Chicago, Toronto, New York, Sydney, and Univ. of São Paulo, Brazil). Called to Bar, Middle Temple, 1909, Treasurer, 1951; K.C. 1922; M.P. (L.) The Hartlepools, 1922-24; (Lab.) Preston, 1929-31; Attorney-General, 1929-32; member Royal Commission on Lunacy, 1924; M.P. (Lab.) Ashton-under-Lyne, 1939-45; Solicitor-General, 1940-42; Paymaster-General, 1942; Minister without Portfolio, 1942-44; First Minister of National Insurance, 1944-45; Lord Chancellor, 1945-51. Trustee of the National Gallery, 1946-53; Trustee of the Tate Gallery, 1947-53 (Chm. 1951-53). President of British Travel and Holidays Association; President of Queen Charlotte's Hospital; General Editor of Dictionary of English Law. *Address:* 121 Ashley Gardens, Westminster, S.W.1; West Lodge, Bradfield St. George, Bury St. Edmunds. *Clubs:* Athenæum, Beefsteak. [*Died* 16 *Aug.* 1957 (*ext.*).

JOYCE, Maj.-Gen. Hayman John H.; *see* Hayman-Joyce.

JUKES, John Edwin Clapham, C.S.I. 1930; C.I.E. 1921; I.C.S., retired; *b.* 12 Nov. 1878; *s.* of late Edward C. Jukes, of the London Stock Exchange; *m.* 1912, Marguerite Jessie, *d.* of late James Searle, Reigate, Surrey; one *s.* one *d.* *Educ.:* Aldenham School; Pembroke College, Cambridge. Porson University Prizeman, 1899; Second Chancellor's Classical Medallist, 1902; at different periods, Under, Deputy, Joint and Additional Secretary and four times officiating Secretary to the Govt. of India, Finance Dept.; officiated as Auditor-General in India in 1925 and 1926; temporary Finance Member of the Governor General's Executive Council in 1930; retired 1933. *Recreation:* gardening. *Address:* Lea Hurst, Wray Park Road, Reigate, Surrey. *T.:* Reigate 3818. [*Died* 4 *Jan.* 1955.

JULIUS, Very Rev. John Awdry, M.A.; *b.* Norwich, England, 1874; 2nd *s.* of late Most Rev. Churchill Julius; *m.* 1906, Alice, *d.* of Archdeacon Bowen. *Educ.:* Grammar School, Melbourne; Christ's College, Christchurch; Keble College, Oxford. Deacon, 1897; Priest, 1898; Curate of Kettering, 1897-1901; Vicar of Papanui, 1904-14; Waimate, 1914-20; Timaru, 1921-27; Dean of Christchurch, 1927-40; Archdeacon of Timaru and Westland, 1922-27; of Rangiora and Westland, 1928-34; of Christchurch, 1934-37. *Address:* St. Andrews Hill, Sumner, Christchurch, N.Z. [*Died* 18 *July* 1956.

JUNAGADH, Col. H.H. Sir Mahabatkhanji Rasulkhanji, Nawab Saheb of, G.C.I.E., *cr.* 1931; K.C.S.I., *cr.* 1926; *b.* 2 Aug. 1900; accession 1920; *m.* H.H. Senior Begum Sahiba Munavvarjehan of Bhopal. *Educ.:* Preparatory School in England; Mayo Coll., Ajmer. Visited England, 1913-14; celebrated Silver Jubilee, 1945. State legally and constitutionally acceded to Dominion of Pakistan, 1947; left State, 1947. [*Died* 7 *Nov.* 1959.

K

KALLAS, Madame Aino Julia Maria; *d.* of late Dr. Julius Krohn, Professor at the University in Helsinki, Finland, and Minna Lindroos; *m.* 1900, Dr. Oskar Kallas (*d.* 1946); two *s.* two *d.* Has lectured in different countries: Great Britain, Canada, United States, Netherlands, Hungary, Estonia, and Finland. *Publications:* novels, essays, plays and several volumes of short stories, which have been translated from the Finnish into Estonian, English, French, German, Italian, Swedish, Danish, Dutch, and Hungarian. English translations: The White Ship, 1924; Eros the Slayer, 1927; The Wolf's Bride, 1930. *Recreations:* change of work, travelling. *Address:* Parnu Maantee 28, Tallinn, Estonia. [*Died* 8 *Nov.* 1956.

KANDATHIL, Most Rev. Dr. Augustine; Archbishop-Metropolitan of Ernakulam since 1923; Assistant at the Pontifical Throne since 1936; *b.* Chemp, Vaikam, Travancore, 25 Aug. 1874. *Educ.:* Papal Seminary, Kandy, Ceylon. Priest, 1901; Parish Priest for some time; Rector of the Preparatory Seminary, Ernakulam, and Private Secretary to the first Vicar Apostolic of Ernakulam to end of 1911; Bishop of Arad and Coadjutor, 1911-19; Vicar Apostolic of Ernakulam, 1919-23. *Address:* Archbishop's House, Ernakulam, India. [*Died Jan.* 1956.

KANIA, Hon. Sir Harilal Jekisundas, Kt., *cr.* 1943; Chief Justice of India since 1947; *b.* 3 Nov. 1890; *s.* of Jekisundas; *m.* 1925, Kusum, *d.* of Sir Chunilal Mehta; one *d.* *Educ.:* B.A. Samaldas College, Bhavnagar; LL.B. Govt. Law College, Bombay; passed the High Court. Advocate (O.S.)'s Examination, 1915. Judge High Court, Bombay, 1933-46; Acting Chief Justice in 1944 and 1945; Judge, Federal Court, India, 1946-47. *Recreations:* golf, tennis, and cricket. *Address:* Supreme Court of India, New Delhi, India. *Clubs:* Willingdon (Bombay); Delhi Gymkhana (New Delhi). [*Died* 6 *Nov.* 1951.

KARANJIA, Sir Behram (Narosji), Kt., *cr.* 1946; J.P.; F.C.I.S.; Merchant; Director of many Companies; J.P. Bombay; Member Bombay Legislative Council; Trustee Bombay Port Trust; Chairman Chartered Institute of Secretaries India Association (Bombay Section); *b.* Sept. 1876; *m.* 1905, Piroja, *d.* of Pestonji Framji Talati; two *s.* one *d.* *Educ.:* Elphinstone High School; Sir J. J. P. B. Institution. Secretary War Loan and Food Control Committees, 1914-19; Governor's Sind Relief Fund, 1930-31; Quetta and Bihar Earthquake Relief Funds; Treasurer Hospital Maintenance Committee; Vice-Pres. St. John Ambulance Assoc.; Advisory Committee G.I.P. and B.B. & C.I. Railways; President Indian Merchants Chamber, 1932; Society of Hon. Pres. Magistrates, 1932, and Railway Passengers and Traffic Relief Assoc.; Silk Merchants' Assoc.; Chairman of Public Holiday Enquiry Committee, 1939; Kaisar-i-Hind Medal; Jubilee Medal, 1935; Coronation Medal, 1937. *Address:* Shengre-La, 4 Carmichael Road, Bombay 26. *T.A.:* Mazda. *T.:* 40792 and 20845. *Clubs:* Rotary (Pres. 1944-45). Willingdon Sports (Bombay), etc. [*Died* 13 *July* 1957.

KAUFFER, Edward McKnight; artist-designer; *b.* Great Falls, Montana, U.S.A. *Educ.:* American Public Schools. Began in America as a scene painter in the theatre; studied art in night classes; six months Art Institute of Chicago; six months in Munich; two years in Paris; settled in London early in 1914; began poster designing with Underground Railways; work represented in South Kensington Museum, Corcoran Art Gallery (Washington D.C.), and in Milan; made a fellow of the British Institute of Industrial Art; exhibition of work held in Ashmolean Museum, Oxford, 1926; Member of Council for Art and Industry, Board of Trade; retrospective exhibition of posters held in New York Museum of Modern Art, 1937; Hon. R.D.I. Royal Society of Arts, 1937. *Publications:* books illustrated: Burton, Anatomy of Melancholy; Herman Melville, Benito Cereno, Billy Budd; Cervantes, Don Quixote; Arnold Bennett, Elsie and the Child, Venus Rising from the Sea; Carl Van Vechten, Nigger Heaven; Lord Birkenhead, The Year 2030. *Address:* 40 Central Park South, New York, U.S.A. [*Died* 22 *Oct.* 1954.

KAVANAGH, Col. Sir Dermot; *see* McMorrough Kavanagh.

KAY, Sir Herbert, Kt., *cr.* 1946; C.B.E. 1936; F.C.I.S.; retired; *b.* 1 June 1879. *Address:* Kingsway Hotel, Worthing, Sussex. *Club:* Royal Automobile. [*Died* 11 *Jan.* 1957.

KAY, Sir Joseph Aspden, K.B.E., *cr.* 1947; Kt., *cr.* 1927; Managing Director W. H. Brady & Co., Ltd., Bombay and Manchester; *b.* Bolton, Lancs, 20 Jan. 1884; *m.* 1928, Mildred, 2nd *d.* of late J. G. and R. A. Burnett, Rowsley, Derbyshire; one *d.* *Educ.:* Bolton. Managing Director and Director of numerous joint-stock companies in Bombay and elsewhere; Chairman, Bombay Millowners Association, 1921, 1922 and 1935; Employees' representative International Labour Conference at Geneva, 1923; Hon. Presidency Magistrate and J.P.; Officer Bombay Light Horse; served on many public Boards in Bombay; Vice-President Bombay Chamber of Commerce, 1925, and President 1926; Member Legislative Council, 1925 and 1926; Vice-President Indian Central Cotton Committee, 1925, 1926, 1931, and 1932; Chairman Back Bay (Kay) Enquiry Committee, etc. *Recreations:* riding, tennis, golf. *Address:* Royal Insurance Buildings, Veer Nariman Road, Bombay. *T.A.:* Brad, Bombay; 16 John Dalton Street, Manchester. *T.A.:* Brads, Manchester. [*Died* 1 *Oct.* 1958.

KAY, Ven. Kenneth; Archdeacon of Bradford, 1953-57, resigned; Vicar of Heaton since 1945; Hon. Canon of St. Hilda in Bradford Cathedral since 1948; *b.* 1902; *m.* 1933, Blanche, *d.* of Frank Jones, Saltburn; two *d.* *Educ.:* Durham Cathedral Choristers' School; St. Chad's College, Durham. B.A. 1924; Dipl. in Th. 1925; M.A. 1927. Deacon 1925, Priest 1926, Durham; Curate of Herrington, 1925-27; Chaplain of St. Oswald, Lahore, 1927-30; R.N. Chaplain, H.M.S. Curaçoa, 1931-33; Vicar of Queensbury, 1933-44; Rural Dean of Bradford, 1953. Chaplain, R.N.V.R., 1940-. *Address:* Heaton Vicarage, Bradford, Yorks. *T.:* Bradford 43308. [*Died* 30 *Aug.* 1958.

KAY, Alderman Sir William, Kt., *cr.* 1922; *b.* 1868; *m.* 1892, Lila (*d.* 1951), *d.* of James Gresty, Manchester. Three times Lord Mayor of Manchester; Director Manchester Ship Canal Co. *Address:* Oakholme, Wilbraham Road, Manchester, 16. [*Died* 16 *Jan.* 1955.

KAY, Colonel William Martin, C.M.G. 1916; C.B.E. 1941; D.L.; *b.* 18 Aug. 1871; *s.* of James Cunninghame Kay, Solicitor, Hamilton, Co. Lanark, and Elizabeth Stevenson Crawford; *m.* 1903, Christina Russell (*d.* 1917), *d.* of James Smart, Coalmaster, Hamilton; one *s.* one *d.* *Educ.:* Glasgow Academy and University. Joined 2nd V.B. Scottish Rifles, 1889; T.D. 1910; commanded 6th Scottish Rifles, T.F., 1912-19; served European War, 1914-19 (despatches, C.M.G., wounded); Colonel, 1918; Hon. Sheriff Substitute of Lanarkshire. [*Died* 27 *Jan.* 1948.
[*But death not notified in time for inclusion in Who Was Who 1941–1950, first edn.*

KAY-MOUAT, Professor John Richard, M.A. (Oxon and Hon. M.A. Adelaide), M.Sc., M.B., B.Ch., D.P.H. (Bristol); L.M.S. Singapore; late R.A.A.M.C.; *b.* 2 May 1881; *s.* of late R. J. Kay and Margaret, *d.* of late John Fawcus; unmarried. *Educ.:* Bedford School; Hertford Coll. Oxford. Assistant Demonstrator in Physiology, Oxford University, 1905-8; Demonstrator of Pathology, Bristol University, 1912-21; Temporary Surgeon R.N.D., 1914-18; Acting Surgeon-Lieut.-Commander for anti-malarial duties at Sierra Leone; acting Professor of Pathology, Bristol University, 1918; Assistant Principal, then Professor of Physiology, College of Medicine, Singapore, 1921; Lecturer in Pharmacology, 1922. Captain, R.A.A.M.C., 1942-52. *Address:* The Grove, Gosford, N.S.W., Australia. *Clubs:* Royal Empire Society, Overseas League. [*Died* 11 *Dec.* 1952.

KAYE, Captain and Flight Commander Sir Henry Gordon, 2nd Bt., *cr.* 1923; late K.O.Y.L.I. and R.F.C.; *b.* 24 Feb. 1889; *s.* of 1st Bt. and Emily, *d.* of Alfred Crowther, J.P., of Greenroyd, Huddersfield; *S.* father, 1923; *m.* 1916, Winifred, *d.* of late W. H. Scales of Verwood, Bradford: three *s.* *Educ.:* Rugby: Oriel College, Oxford, M.A. Director, Huddersfield Building Society; Local Director Sun Insurance Office, Leeds; J.P. County Borough of Huddersfield. *Heir:* *e. s.* Stephen Henry Gordon Kaye, *b.* 24 March 1917. *Address:* Belwethers, Cranleigh, Surrey. *T.:* Cranleigh 457. *Club:* Junior Carlton. [*Died* 19 *Feb.* 1956.

KAYE, Sir Kenelm Arthur Lister; *see* Lister-Kaye.

KAYE, Robert Walter, J.P.; *b.* 23 Aug. 1871; 3rd *s.* of late Walter Kaye of Lofthouse, Yorks; *m.* 1897, Marion (*d.* 1946), *e. d.* of Charles S. Robinson, Eastfield, Leicester; four *s.* two *d.*; *m.* 1947, Vera Sybil Maudslay, Parsonage Green, Aldworth, Berks., *y. d.* of late Capt. E. R. Maudslay. *Educ.:* privately: Dr. Carter, LL.B. Leicester; High Sheriff of Leicestershire, 1928-29; M.F.H. South Notts Hounds, 1924-27; Joint M.F.H. Rufford Hounds, 1930-31; Joint M.F.H. Woodland Pytchley, 1933-35; Joint Master of Ross Harriers, 1955-56. *Recreations:* hunting, shooting. *Address:* How Caple Frith, Hereford. *T.:* How Caple 251. *Club:* Royal Automobile. [*Died* 27 *April* 1957.

KAYE-SMITH, Sheila; *d.* of late Edward Kaye-Smith, M.R.C.S., L.R.C.P., St. Leonards-on-Sea; *m.* 1924, Theodore Penrose Fry (later Sir Penrose Fry, 3rd Bt.; *S.* 1957). *Publications:* novels, including Sussex Gorse, 1916; Green Apple Harvest, 1920; Joanna Godden, 1921; The End of the House of Alard, 1923; Susan Spray, 1931; The Valiant Woman, 1938; Ember Lane, 1940; Tambourine, Trumpet and Drum, 1943; The Lardners and the Laurelwoods, 1948; The Treasures of the Snow, 1950; Mrs. Gailey, 1951; The View from the Parsonage, 1954. *Address:* Little Doucegrove, Northiam, Rye, Sussex. [*Died* 14 *Jan.* 1956.

KEALY, Sir (Edward) Herbert, Kt., *cr.* 1932; C.I.E. 1926; M.A. Oxon., Indian Civil Service, retired; *b.* 7 June 1873; 4th *s.* of J. R. Kealy, M.D., Alverstoke, Hants; *m.* 1905, Florence Tempe, *e. d.* of late Sir Charles Bayley, G.C.I.E.; three *s.* two *d.* *Educ.:* Felsted (Exhibitioner); University Coll., Oxford. 2nd class Classical Mods. and Lit. Hum.; B.A. 1896; M.A. 1900; entered Indian Civil Service (Bengal), 1897; officiating Collector Dinajpur, 1901; entered Government of India Foreign and Political Dept., 1902; Asst. Sec., 1905; Special Duty, 1905-07; Asst. Comr. Ajmer, 1907; Divisional and Sessions Judge, Derajat, 1909; Superintendent Census Operations, Rajputana and Ajmer-Merwara, 1910-13; Secretary N.W.F. Province, 1915-20; Divisional and Sessions Judge, Peshawar, 1920-21; Political Agent, Baghelkhand and Bundelkhand, 1922; British Resident, Gwalior, 1922, Baroda, 1923-27; Agent to the Governor-General, Central India, 1927; Agent to the Governor-General in Western India States, 1927-32; retired, 1932. *Publications:* Report (3 vols.) on Census Operations in Rajputana and Ajmer-Merwara, 1911; revised Aitchison's Treaties, India, 1909. *Address:* c/o Grindlay's Bank Ltd., 54 Parliament Street, S.W.1; 13 Lathbury Road, Oxford. *T.:* Oxford 58134. [*Died* 19 *Aug.* 1953.

KEANE, Lt.-Col. Sir John, 5th Bt., *cr.* 1801; D.S.O. 1916; late R.F.A.; D.L.; Barrister-at-law, Middle Temple, 1904; *b.* 3 June 1873; *e. s.* of 4th Bart. and Adelaide Sidney, *e. d.* of John Vance, M.P.; *S.* father, 1892; *m.* 1907, Lady Eleanor Hicks-Beach, *e. d.* of 1st Earl St. Aldwyn; one *s.* three *d.* *Educ.:* R.M.A., Woolwich. Entered army, 1893; Captain, 1900; Major, 1916; Temp. Lt.-Colonel, 1917; Private Secretary to Governor of Ceylon (Sir A.H. Blake), 1902-5; High Sheriff of Waterford, 1911; served South Africa, 1899-1902 (despatches, medal with 3 clasps); European War, 1914-18 (despatches, D.S.O., Legion of Honour); Councillor of State to Republic of Ireland; Director, Bank of Ireland. *Publications:* various articles and a pamphlet on national accounts. *Heir:* *s.* Richard Michael [*b.* 29 Jan. 1909; *m.* 1939, Olivia, *y. d.* of Oliver Hawkshaw, Chisenbury Priory, Wilts.]. *Address:* Cappoquin, Co. Waterford, Ireland; 47 Sandford Road, Dublin. *Clubs:* Army and Navy; Kildare Street (Dublin). [*Died* 30 *Jan.* 1956.

KEARSLEY, Brig.-Gen. Sir (Robert) Harvey, K.C.V.O., *cr.* 1952 (C.V.O. 1939); C.M.G. 1918; D.S.O. 1915; late 5th Dragoon Guards; *b.* 28 March 1880; *s.* of late Major Robert Wilson Kearsley; *m.* 1908, Evelyn Molly, *d.* of late Samuel Arthur Peto, Downs Court, Sandwich; one *d.* *Educ.:* Harrow; R.M.C., Sandhurst. Entered Army, 1899; Captain 1904; Major, 1912; Lt.-Col. 1919; Col. 1919; served South African War, 1899-1902 (Queen's medal 4 clasps, King's medal 2 clasps); European War, 1914-1918 (despatches, D.S.O., Bt. Lt.-Col., C.M.G., Bt. Col.); retired pay, 1922; one of H.M.'s Hon. Corps of Gentlemen at Arms, 1922-55, Clerk of the Cheque and Adjutant, 1935-45, Lieutenant, 1945-55; Extra Equerry to the Queen since 1955. *Publication:* His Majesty's Bodyguard of the Honourable Corps of Gentlemen-at-Arms, 1937. *Address:* 29 Kensington Square, W.8. *T.:* Western 1486. *Clubs:* Cavalry, Boodle's. [*Died* 9 *May* 1956.

KEAY, Herbert O.; Consultant Consolidated Paper Corporation, Limited, Three Rivers, P.Q.; *b.* Laconia, New Hampshire, U.S.A., 15 Aug. 1875. *Educ.:* Mass. Institute of Technology, Boston. Assistant to chie engineer, Pennsylvania Steel Co., 1901-2; mechanical engineer, Boston and Maine Railway, 1902-06, Assistant Professor mechanical engineering, McGill University, 1906-8; Head of Railway Dept., McGill University, 1908-17. *Publications:* various articles on railway subjects in engineering publications. *Address:* Consolidated Paper Corporation, Ltd., Three Rivers, P.Q., Canada. [*Died* 14 *May* 1958.

KEEBLE, Prof. Sir Frederick William, Kt., *cr.* 1922; C.B.E. 1917; F.R.S. 1913; Sc.D. Cantab.; *b.* 2 March 1870; *m.* 1st, 1898, Matilde Marie Cecile Maréchal (*d.* 1915); one *d.*; 2nd, 1920, Lillah McCarthy, *q.v.* *Educ.:* Alleyn's School, Dulwich; Caius College, Cambridge. Controller of Horticulture Food Production Department, Board of Agriculture, 1917-19. Assistant Secretary Board of Agriculture 1919; Director, Royal Horticultural Society's Garden, Wisley, 1914-19; Sherardian Professor of Botany and Fellow of Magdalen College, Oxford, 1920-27; Fullerian Professor Royal Institution, 1938; 1941; late Adviser in Agriculture, Imperial Chemical Industries. *Publications:* Scientific Memoirs in Proceedings of Royal Society, etc.; Plant Animals; Practical Plant Physiology; Life of Plants; Fertilizers and Food Production; Polly and Freddie; Science Lends a Hand in the Garden, 1939; (jointly) Hardy Fruit Production. *Address:* Cranley Mansion, Brechin Place, S.W.7. *Club:* Athenæum. [*Died* 19 *Oct.* 1952.

KEEBLE, Lady; *see* McCarthy, Lillah.

KEEL, James Frederick, F.R.A.M.; Baritone Vocalist, Teacher of Singing; Composer; late Professor and Lecturer on the Teaching of Singing at the Royal Academy of Music; *b.* London, 1871; *e. s.* of James Frederick and Mary Anne Keel; *m.* 1902, Dora, 2nd *d.* of late E. T. Compton, Alpine and Landscape Painter; one *s.* two *d.* *Educ.:* Wells Cathedral School and privately. Assistant Master in various private schools till 1895; entered R.A.M. 1895; studied singing with Frederick King and Frederick Walker; composition with Frederick Corder; went to Milan, 1896, and continued singing studies with Frederico Blasco; went to Munich, 1897, and studied German Lieder with Eugen Gura; Début in London at Queen's Hall, 1898; has sung in numerous concerts in London and the provinces, and given many recitals; has made a special study of old and traditional songs; formerly Editor of the Folk-song Society's Journal. *Publications:* Some pieces for Violin and Piano; vocal studies; many songs; edited two books of Elizabethan Songs, and one of 18th Century Songs. *Recreation:* gardening and the countryside. *Address:* Fridland, Bethersden, nr. Ashford, Kent. *T.:* 203. [*Died* 9 *Aug.* 1954.

KEELING, Sir Edward (Herbert), Kt., *cr.* 1952; M.C.; M.P. (C.) Twickenham since 1935; D.L.; Barrister-at-law; *y. s.* of late Rev. Wm. Hulton Keeling; *m.* 1929, Martha Ann Darling, 2nd *d.* of late Henry Dougherty, New York; one *s. Educ.:* Bradford; University College, Oxford, M.A. (2nd class honours, Jurisprudence). F.S.A. Served European War, 1914-19, in India, Mesopotamia (wounded twice, despatches, M.C.), Russia, Anatolia (MacGregor Medal for reconnaissance), Kurdistan; retired with rank of Lt.-Col.; formerly General Manager of Turkish Petroleum Co.; Conservative candidate, Central Southwark, 1929; Parliamentary Private Secretary to Parliamentary Secretary, Ministry of Labour, 1937; to Under Secretary of State for Air, 1937-38; to Under-Secretary of State for India and Burma, 1938-39; R.A.F., 1939-45; Hon. Secretary-General, International Exhibition of Persian Art, Royal Academy, 1931; Hon. Secretary, British School of Archæology in Iraq (Gertrude Bell Memorial); Mayor of City of Westminster, 1945-46; Chairman: London Advisory Council for Smoke Abatement; Income Tax Payers' Society; Deputy Chairman, Georgian Group, Executive Committee, National Trust, Statute Law Committee. Freeman of Twickenham. *Publications:* An Escape from Turkey-in-Asia, 1918; In Russia under the Bolsheviks, 1920; Adventures in Turkey and Russia, 1924. *Address:* 20 Wilton Street, Grosvenor Place, S.W.1. *T.:* Sloane 1937. *Clubs:* Brooks's, Beefsteak. [*Died* 23 *Nov.* 1954.

KEELING, Sir Hugh Trowbridge, Kt., *cr.* 1923; C.S.I. 1915; M.I.E. (India); F.Z.S.; *m.* Edith, *d.* of late Colonel T.O. Underwood, 4th Punjab Cavalry; one *s.* one *d. Educ.:* Marlborough; R.I.E. Coll. Assist. Engineer, Madras Public Works Dept., 1887; Prof. at Civil Engineering Coll., Madras, 1896-97; Executive Engineer, 1898; Principal, Civil Eng. Coll., Madras, 1904-5; Superintending Engineer, 1910; Chief Engineer and Sec. to the Chief Commissioner, Delhi, 1912; retired, 1920; re-employed for five years from 1920; member of Delhi Imperial Committee, 1913-25. *Address:* 17 Wetherby Gardens, S.W.5. *T.:* Fremantle 4192. *Club:* East India and Sports. [*Died* 3 *Feb.* 1955.

KEEN, Frank Noel; Barrister formerly practising at the Parliamentary Bar; *b.* London, 3 November 1869; *m.* 1903, Rosalie Muirhead (*d.* 1952); one *s.* one *d. Educ.:* City of London School. Trained as accountant; Final Examination Institute of Chartered Accountants in England and Wales (Certificate of Merit), 1892; LL.B. (Lond.) 1897; called to Bar, Middle Temple, 1897; retired from active practice, September 1954; one of the founders of the League of Nations Society, 1915; Member of Executive, 1915-18, and of League of Nations Union Executive, 1918-28. *Publications:* Tramway Companies and Local Authorities, 1902; Markets, Fairs, and Slaughterhouses, 1904; Urban Police and Sanitary Legislation, 1904; Local Legislation, 1909-1911, 1912, and 1913; The World in Alliance, 1915; Towards International Justice, 1923; The Law relating to Public Service Undertakings, 1925; Real Security against War, 1929; a Guide to Public Works Facilities Act, 1930 (with H. R. Askew), 1931; A Better League of Nations, 1934; Crossing the Rubicon, 1939; Guide to Liabilities (War-Time Adjustment) Act, 1941; The Abolition of War, 1955; numerous pamphlets and articles. *Recreation:* golf. *Address:* Nuffield Lodge, Shepherd's Hill, N.6. *T.:* Mountview 3580. [*Died* 30 *April* 1957.

KEEN, Brigadier Patrick Houston, C.B. 1929; *b.* 19 Sept. 1877; *s.* of late Col. Sir Frederick John Keen, K.C.B.; *m.* 1907, Ethel (*d.* 1953), *d.* of Bishop Whitley; one *s.* one *d. Educ.:* Haileybury; Sandhurst. 2nd Lieut., York Regt., 1898; Lieut., Indian Army, 1900; served European War, 1914-18 (despatches, Bt. Major, Bt. Lt.-Col.); Afghanistan, 1919; Waziristan, 1920-21 (despatches); North West Frontier, 1930-31; Commander Kohat Brigade, 1929-32; retired 1932. *Address:* Brampton Abbotts, Ross-on-Wye, Herefordshire. *T.:* Ross-on-Wye 136. [*Died* 10 *Feb.* 1954.

KEEN, Lt.-Col. William John, C.I.E. 1916; C.B.E. 1920; late Political Department Govt. of India; *s.* of late Colonel Sir Frederick John Keen, K.C.B., and Lady Keen of Talnotrie, Woking; *m.* 1899, Marion Beatrice (*d.* 1937), *d.* of Col. A. Mc.L. Mills, 37th Dogras; one *s.* one *d. Educ.:* Haileybury College; R.M.C., Sandhurst. Gazetted to R. Welch Fusiliers, 1892; transferred to Indian Army, 37th Dogras, 1894; served Chitral Relief Expedition, 1895; joined Punjab Commission, 1898; Political Dept., Govt. of India, 1901; served in N.W. Frontier Province; Kabul Khel Expedition, 1902; Mohmand Expedition, 1908; European War, 1914-18 (C.I.E.); Afghan war, 1919 (C.B.E.); Officiating Chief Commissioner N.W.F.P., 1925-1926; retired, 1928; J.P., Eastbourne, 1928; Reader, Diocese of Chichester. *Recreations:* usual. *Address:* Down Cottage, Magham Down, Hailsham, Sussex. [*Died* 26 *July* 1958.

KEENAN, Hon. Sir Norbert, Kt., *cr.* 1948; Q.C. (W.A.); M.L.A. for Nedlands, W.A., 1930-50; *b.* 1866; *e.* and *o. surv. s.* of Rt. Hon. Sir Patrick Keenan, K.C.B., K.C.M.G., P.C.; *m.* Rose, *d.* of Sir Henry Parker; one *s. Educ.:* Downside College, Somerset; Trinity College, Dublin; Middle Temple, Inns of Court. Called to Bar, King's Inn, Dublin, and Inns of Court. Arrived in W.A., 1895; admitted to W.A. Bar, 1895; Mayor of Kalgoorlie, 1901-5; M.L.A. for Kalgoorlie, 1905-11, when he retired from politics; Attorney-General, 1906-10, when he resigned office; Chief Secretary, 1930-32, when he resigned office; K.C., 1908, at W.A. Bar. *Recreations:* horse racing, yachting, bowls, football. *Address:* 71 Mount Street, Perth, Western Australia. *Clubs:* Junior Carlton, Leander; Weld (Perth, W.A.). [*Died* 24 *April* 1954.

KEENAN, William, O.B.E. 1946; J.P.; an official of Transport and General Workers' Union; *m.* 1937, Catherine Barker; one *s.* M.P. (Lab.) Kirkdale Division of Liverpool, 1945-55. *Address:* 7 Worcester Road, Liverpool 20. *T.:* Bootle 3326; Guilford Hotel, Guilford Street, Russell Square, W.C.1. *T.:* Terminus 7553. [*Died* 15 *Dec.* 1955.

KEENS, Sir Thomas, Kt., *cr.* 1934; D.L. Bedfordshire; Chairman Lee Catchment Board; *b.* Luton, Beds., 1870; *s.* of Thomas Keens and Emma Keens (*née* Hailstone); *m.* 1896, Ella, *d.* of Joseph and Elizabeth Batchelor, formerly of The Lee, Great Missenden; one *s.* one *d.* (and *er. s.* decd.). *Educ.:* private school. Councillor (for Luton North Ward 1) of Bedfordshire County Council, 1901-10; Alderman, 1919; re-elected, 1925, 1931, 1937, and 1949; Chairman, 1935-52; Chairman, Finance Committee; Member Standing Joint Committee; Senior Partner Keens, Shay Keens & Co., Incorporated Accountants, of Bilbao House, New Broad Street, E.C., and at Luton, Bedford, Aylesbury, Leighton Buzzard and Hitchin; Pres. of Society of Incorporated Accountants and Auditors, 1926-29; contested Aylesbury Div. 1922, 1924, and 1929; M.P. (L.) Aylesbury Div. of Bucks., 1923-24; contested Pontypool Div. (Nat. Lib.), 1931. *Recreation:* bowls. *Address:* Highfield, Luton. *T.:* Luton 372. *Clubs:* National Liberal, City Livery. [*Died* 24 *Nov.* 1953.

KEITH, Rev. Canon Archibald Leslie, M.A.; Canon Emeritus since 1953; Canon of Salisbury, 1929; retired, 1946; *b.* 20 Feb. 1871; *s.* of F. T. Keith, solicitor, Norwich, and Gertrude, *d.* of Minor Canon Butterfield, St. George, Windsor; *m.* Margaret Layard, *d.* of

Colonel Gordon Reeves, Ceylon; three *s.* (also three killed or died of wounds in 1943 and one in 1941) one *d.* *Educ.:* Haileybury College; Corpus Christi College, Cambridge; Ely Theological College. Served curacies at Winchester and Haslemere, 1896; Vicar of Fernhurst, 1901; Chaplain to Tea Planters in Ceylon, 1906; Vicar of St. Peter's, Colombo, 1910; Assistant Chaplain to Forces; returned to England 1915; served curacies in London; Vicar of Wimborne Minster, 1919; Prebendary of Salisbury Cathedral; Rural Dean of Wimborne, 1928. *Recreation:* golf. *Address:* Manormead Nursing Home, Hindhead, Surrey. [*Died* 9 *Aug.* 1956.

KEITH, Sir Arthur, Kt., *cr.* 1921; F.R.S. 1913; M.D., F.R.C.S., LL.D. (Aberdeen, Birmingham, Leeds), D.Sc. (Durham, Manchester, Oxford); Master, Buckston Browne Research Farm; *b.* Old Machar, Aberdeen, 5 Feb. 1866; *s.* of John Keith and Jessie Macpherson; *m.* 1899, Cecilia (*d.* 1 93), *d.* of Tom Gray, M.A., artist. *Educ.:* Aberdeen University; University College, London; Leipzig University. Secretary Anatomical Society of Great Britain, 1899-1902; President Royal Anthropological Institute, 1912-14; Rector, University of Aberdeen, 1930-33; Member Société d'Anthropologie de Paris, 1913; Fullerian Professor of Physiology, Royal Institution, 1917-23; Secretary of the Royal Institution, 1922-26; Treasurer of the Royal Institution; 1926-29; President of British Association, 1927. *Publications:* Introduction to Study of Anthropoid Apes, 1896; Human Embryology and Morphology, 1901; edited Hughes' Practical Anatomy, 1902; Asst. Editor of Treves' Surgical and Applied Anatomy; Ancient Types of Man, 1911; The Human Body, 1912; Antiquity of Man, 2nd ed. 1925; Menders of the Maimed, 1919; Engines of the Human Body, 2nd ed. 1925; Nationality and Race, 1920; Religion of a Darwinist, 1925; Concerning Man's Origin, 1927; New Discoveries relating to the Antiquity of Man, 1931; Darwinism and its Critics, 1935; Stone-age of Mt. Carmel Human Fossil Remains (with T. D. McCown), 1939; Essays on Human Evolution, 1946; A New Theory of Evolution, 1948; An Autobiography, 1950; Darwin Revalued, 1955 (posthumous). *Address:* Homefield, Downe, Kent. *Club:* Athenæum. [*Died* 7 *Jan.* 1955.

KEITH, James, C.B.E. 1945; *b.* 2 March 1879; *s.* of Alexander Keith and Margaret Milne; *m.* 1915, Mary Chalmers Hay. *Educ.:* Gordon's College, Aberdeen. Trained as Civil Engineer but took up farming at 24; farms extensively in Aberdeenshire and Norfolk; Governor North of Scotland College of Agriculture; has travelled extensively in Dominions, U.S.A., and on Continent studying agricultural affairs; served in 5th Gordon Highlanders T.F. and in European War with R.F.A., France. *Publications:* numerous contributions to agricultural journals. *Address:* Pitmedden, Udny, Aberdeenshire. *T.:* Udny Green 22. *Club:* Royal Northern (Aberdeen). [*Died* 21 *July* 1953.

KEITH-ROACH, Edward, C.B.E. 1935 (O.B.E. 1927); K.St.J.; late District Commissioner, Palestine Govt.; *b.* Clifton, 31 March 1885; 7th *s.* of late Rev. Thomas Roach, M.A., and Emily Maria, *d.* of Thomas Croome; assumed surname of Keith-Roach on coming of age; *m.* 1st, 1912, Violet Oliva (*d.* 1938), *y. d.* of late Edward Barnard; one *s.*; 2nd, 1939, Philippa Barnard, *d.* of L. F. Massey; one *s.* one *d.* *Educ.:* privately by father. Banking, 1902-08; Exchange Banking in India, 1908-14; 2nd Lieut. 7th Lancashire Fusiliers, Aug. 1914; Capt., Nov. 1914; Major, 1915; seconded, General Staff, G.H.Q., E.E.F., 1915; Bimbashi, Egyptian Army, 1916, and seconded Sudan Govt. as Intelligence Officer; Inspector, Port Sudan, 1916; appointed First Inspector, Umkedada; District Commissioner, Eastern Darfur, 1917; Public Custodian Enemy Property in Palestine, 1919; First Asst. Secretary, Palestine Govt., 1920; Acting Principal, Colonial Office, 1924; Asst. District Commissioner, Northern Palestine, 1925; Administered Jerusalem Division, 1926-31; Northern Dist., 1931-37; Jerusalem District, 1937-43; Chairman of the Palestine Central Censorship Board for Films and Plays; Member Advisory Council, 1931; Sultan of Egypt's Medal and bar; Order of the White Lion of Czechoslovakia, 1929; Commander of the Order of Al Rafidain (Iraq), 1934. *Publications:* Darfur, a Province of the Anglo-Egyptian Sudan; Adventures among the Lost Tribes of Islam; The Pageant of Jerusalem; Changing Palestine; Joint Editor, Handbook of Palestine and Trans-Jordan, 1922, third edit., 1934; Editor, first edit., General Regulations, Palestine Government. *Recreations:* acting, tennis, writing. *Address:* 13 Lypiatt Terrace, Cheltenham; Barnards, Burleigh, near Stroud, Glos. *Club:* New (Cheltenham). [*Died* 15 *Nov.* 1954.

KELLAND, Sir (Percy) John (Luxton), Kt., *cr.* 1937; M.R.C.V.S.; Chief Veterinary Officer, Ministry of Agriculture and Fisheries, 1932-38; retired, 1938. *Address:* Carita, Steyne Road, Seaview, I.o.W. [*Died* 24 *Sept.* 1958.

KELLAWAY, Charles Halliley, F.R.S. 1940; Director-in-Chief, Wellcome Research Institution, since 1944; *b.* 16 Jan. 1889; *s.* of Rev. Alfred Charles Kellaway; *m.* 1919, Eileen Ethel, *d.* of Dr. G. J. Scantlebury; three *s.* *Educ.:* Melbourne Church of England Grammar School; Melbourne University. M.B., B.S. 1911; M.D. 1913; M.S. 1914; M.R.C.P. 1922; F.R.C.P. 1929; F.R.A.C.P. 1939; Resident Medical Officer, Melbourne Hospital, 1912; Registrar, 1913; Resident Medical Tutor, Trinity College, Melbourne, 1914; Acting Professor Anatomy, Adelaide University, 1915; served in European War, 1915-18, Captain A.A.M.C. 1915; Major, 1918 (M.C.); acting Professor Physiology, Adelaide Univ., 1919; Foulerton Student Royal Society, 1920-23, at National Institute for Medical Research, Physiology School, Oxford, and at University College Hospital Medical School; Assistant Medical Unit University College Hospital, 1923; Director of the Walter and Eliza Hall Institute of Research in Pathology, Melbourne, 1923-1944; Specialist Physician Royal Melbourne Hospital, 1925-43; Director of Hygiene Australian Army H.Q. 1927-31 and 1939-40; Col. 1940; Director of Pathology, Australian Army H.Q., 1940-42; Brig. 1944. Chairman Royal Commission of Enquiry into fatalities at Bundaberg, 1928; Chairman State Cancer Advisory Committee, 1929; Walter Burfitt Prize Royal Society, N.S.W., 1932; Dohme Lectures, Johns Hopkins Medical School, 1936. *Publications:* Papers on the Adrenal Glands, 1919-24, on Anaphylaxis and Immunity, 1922-32, on ascending renal infection, 1926, on hydatid antigens, 1928, on the pharmacology of staphylococcal toxin, 1930, on Australian Snake venoms, 1929-36, and on the liberation of pharmacologically active substances in various forms of cell injury, 1937-1940. *Recreation:* fishing. *Address:* The Wellcome Research Institution, 183 Euston Road, N.W.1. *Club:* Athenæum. [*Died* 13 *Dec.* 1952.

KELLER, Hon. (Laurence) John Walter, C.B.E. 1945; M.P. (Lab.) Raylton, Bulawayo, 1928-58; *b.* 15 June 1885; *s.* of John B. Keller; *m.* 1946, Elizabeth Mollett, Edinburgh, Scotland. *Educ.:* County Council School, London, England. Started part-time work in London at age of 9. Left school at 13 years of age; worked on L. & N.W. Rlys. as Brakesman at Camden. Left England for Rhodesia, 1912, for employment on Rhodesia Railways. Created Rhodesia Railway Workers Union: built Unity Club. Headquarters of Union, in 1924. Founded Rhodesian Railways Review which he edited for nearly 20 years; General Secretary of Union, 1920-45. Represented workers of Rhodesia as Adviser on railway matters to Terms of Union Delegation in Capetown, 1922; Rhodesian and South African representative at first Empire Labour Conference, London, 1924. Served in France with Artists' Rifles during European War (wounded and prisoner); returned to Rhodesia 1919. In Cabinet of Sir Godfrey Huggins (now Lord Malvern) as Minister without Portfolio, 1940-43, with responsibility for Labour matters and rehabilitation of returned soldiers. Founded Rhodesia Labour Party, 1920, and became its first Chairman. *Publication:* Rhodesian Railway Review (speeches, articles and reminiscences). *Recreations:* keen supporter of all sport. *Address:* Oakdene, Greendale, Salisbury, S. Rhodesia. *T.:* 44374. *T.A.:* P.O. Greendale, Salisbury. *Clubs:* British Empire; Salisbury, City (Salisbury, Rhodesia). [*Died* 10 *Sept.* 1959.

KELLER, Maj.-Gen. Rodney Frederick Leopold, C.B.E. 1944; retired; *b.* Tetbury, Glos., 2 Oct. 1900; *o. s.* of Dr. H. L. A. and Ada Elizabeth Keller, Kelowna, B.C.; *m.* 1928, Barbara Beresford Sinclair (*née* Allan), Winnipeg, Man.; two *s.* *Educ.:* Chesterfield School, Kelowna, B.C.; Royal Military College, Kingston, Ont. (graduate 1920). Lieut. Cdn. M.G. Bde. 1920; transferred P.P.C.L.I. 1921; Bt. Capt. P.P.C.L.I. 1925; Temp. Capt. 1928; Staff College, Camberley, 1935-36, p.s.c.; G.S.O. 3 Cdn. Mil. District No. 2, 1937; G.S.O. 2 Cdn. Mil. District No. 12, 1938; Temp. Major, 1938; Major, 1939; Bde. Major 2 Cdn. Inf. Bde., Sept. 1939; Overseas to England, Dec. 1939; G.S.O.1 1 Cdn. Div. 1940, Lt.-Col.; O.C. P.P.C.L.I., Aug. 1941; Brig. commanding 1 Cdn. Inf. Bde., Sept. 1941; Maj.-Gen. commanding 3 Cdn. Inf. Div., Sept. 1942; comd. 3 Cdn. Div. N.W. Europe, 1944 (wounded, despatches); retired (ill-health). 1946. Hon. A.D.C. to Gov.-Gen. of Canada; Officer, Legion of Honour, Croix de Guerre avec Palme (France). *Recreations:* shooting, fishing, athletic sports. *Address:* Kelowna, British Columbia, Canada. [*Died* 21 *June* 1954.

KELLETT, Colonel John Philip, D.S.O. 1918; M.C.; *b.* 1890; *s.* of late John Kellett, Foxdale, I. of M.; *m.* 1st, 1921, Dorothy (*d.* 1936), *d.* of late Charles Bland, Cheshunt, Herts; one *s.* three *d.*; 2nd, 1941, Evelyn, *d.* of late Frank Tingle, Cheshunt, Herts. Served European War, 1914-19; in comd. 2nd Bn. London Regt., Royal Fusiliers, from April 1917 to Sept. 1919 (wounded twice, despatches five times, M.C., D.S.O. with bar); Staff College, Camberley, 1926-27; War Office, 1928-30; G.S.O. Eastern Command, Horse Guards, 1930-31; Brigade Major Razmak Brigade, India, 1933-36; G.S.O. Eastern Command, India, 1936-37; comd. 1st Bn. Wiltshire Regt., 1939-41; Air Ministry and S.A.S.O. (Col.) 72 Group, R.A.F., 1942-43; War Office, 1943-44; in comd. (Brig.) 1945, at Trincomalee, and, 1946, at Colombo, Ceylon; retd. 1947. O.St.J. *Address:* New Amberden Hall, Debden Green, Saffron Walden, Essex. *T.:* Henham 272. *Club:* Army and Navy. [*Died* 20 *Jan.* 1959.

KELLY, Sir Dalziel; *see* Kelly, Sir G. D.

KELLY, Sir David (Victor), G.C.M.G., *cr.* 1950 (K.C.M.G., *cr.* 1942; C.M.G. 1935); M.C. 1916; *b.* 14 Sept. 1891; *s.* of David Frederick Kelly, of Trinity College, Dublin, and Clare College, Cambridge, and Sophie Armstrong d'Arenberg; *m.* 1st, 1920, Isabel Adela (*d.* 1927), *d.* of Henry Maynard Mills; one *d.*; 2nd, 1929, Marie-Noële (author of Turkish Delights, 1951; Mirror to Russia, 1952; Picture Book of Russia, 1952; This Delicious Land Portugal, 1956). *d.* of late Comte de Jourda de Vaux, Brussels; two *s.* *Educ.:* St. Paul's School; Magdalen Coll., Oxford (Demy); B.A. 1st Cl. Hist. Nominated for Foreign Office, 1914; served in France, 1915-19; Brigade Intelligence Officer, 110th Infantry Brigade, from 1915; M.C. 1917; entered Diplomatic Service, 1919; served at Buenos Aires; Foreign Office; Lisbon; Mexico; Brussels; Stockholm; Foreign Office, 1931; Cairo, 1934; Minister in Egypt (local rank), 1937; Counsellor in Foreign Office, 1938-39; Minister in Berne, 1940-42; Ambassador in Buenos Aires, 1942; Ambassador to Turkey, 1946-49; Ambassador to the U.S.S.R., 1949-1951. Knight of Malta, 1954. Has made European lecture tours and spoken on B.B.C., TV, etc. President: British Atlantic Cttee., Anglo-Turkish Soc.; Chairman: British Council, 1955; Britain in Europe Cttee., 1958; Director, National Bank, 1955. *Publications:* Thirty-Nine Months, 1930; The Ruling Few, 1952; Beyond the Iron Curtain, 1954; The Hungry Sheep, 1955. *Clubs:* Athenæum, St. James', Beefsteak; Dublin Universities. [*Died* 27 *March* 1959.

KELLY, Sir (George) Dalziel, Kt., *cr.* 1938; *b.* Melbourne, 1891; *s.* of George Colman Kelly, Montalto, Toorak, Victoria, Australia; *m.* 1918, Beryl Gwendolene, *d.* of late Dr. R. L. McAdam, St. Kilda, Melbourne; no *c.* *Educ.:* Edinburgh Academy, Scotland; Melbourne Church of England Grammar School; Trinity College, Melbourne University. LL.B., 1914; rejected for active service in European War; articled to T. C. Alston, of Hedderwick, Fookes and Alston; managed Barwidgee, Caramut, Victoria, for family partnership, 1915-20; completed articles with Hedderwick, Fookes and Alston, 1920; Barrister and Solicitor of Supreme Court of Victoria; with partners bought and took over the management of Caramut North, Caramut, Victoria, 1924-1934; Vice-Chairman, Australian Woolgrowers' Council, 1930-35, Chairman, 1935-39; Chairman Australian Wool Board, 1936-43; Member of Graziers Federal Council of Australia, 1923-37, President, 1929 and 1933; Member of Council of Graziers Association of Victoria since 1922, President, 1925-37; Chairman, Australian Pastoral Research Trust since 1939; Member of Victorian State Committee, Council for Scientific and Industrial Research since 1930; Chairman Empire Wool Board Conference, 1937; Chairman, International Wool Publicity and Research Executive, 1937-43; Director of Colonial Mutual Life Assurance Society Ltd., Herald and Weekly Times Ltd., Perpetual Executors and Trustees Association of Australia Ltd. and Chevron Ltd.; Local Director Australia of Guardian Assurance Ltd.; Director Australian Foundation Investment Co., National Reliance Investment Co., Capel Court Investment Co., Jason Investment Co., Repco Ltd., H. C. Sleigh Ltd., Bradford Cotton Mills Ltd., etc. *Recreations:* golf and tennis. *Address:* 59 Marne Street, South Yarra, Melbourne, S.E.1, Victoria, Australia. *Clubs:* Australian, Melbourne, Royal Melbourne Golf (Melbourne). [*Died* 18 *Feb.* 1953.

KELLY, Maj. Henry, V.C. 1916; M.C.; Surveyor and Valuer; late Cheshire Regt. and Claims Commission, War Office; *s.* of late Charles Kelly, Sandyford, Co. Wicklow, Eire; *m.* 1926, Eileen, *d.* of Denis Guerin, Glenbeigh, Co. Kerry; one *s.* one *d.* *Educ.:* St. Patrick's Schools and Xaverian College, Manchester; National University, Dublin (B.A., B.Sc.). Chartered Surveyor (Eire). Served European War (V.C., M.C. and bar); late Maj.-Gen., Chief of Staff for Overseas Operations, Irish Free State Army, 1922; Commandanté Generalé, International Brigade, Spanish Civil War, 1936-38. Grand Laurelled Cross of San Ferdinando, Spain, 1937. [*Died* 18 *Jan.* 1960.

KELLY, Admiral Sir (William Archibald) Howard, G.B.E., *cr.* 1934; K.C.B., *cr.* 1931 (C.B. 1915); C.M.G. 1917; M.V.O. 1913; *b.* 6 Sept. 1873; 3rd *s.* of Lt.-Col. H. H. Kelly, R.M.A.; *m.* 1907, Nora (*d.* 1951), *d.*

of Adm. Sir Edmund Poë, G.C.V.O., K.C.B.; one *s.* one *d.* Entered Navy, 1886; Lt. 1894; Comdr., 1904; Captain, 1911; Rear-Admiral, 1922; Vice-Admiral, 1927; Admiral, 1931; served Somaliland, 1902-4 (medal and clasp); Naval Attaché, Paris, 1911-14; served European War, 1914-18; Comd. H.M.S. Gloucester, 1914-16; Commodore commanding 8th Light Cruiser Squadron, 1917; Commodore, 1st class, commanding British Adriatic Force, 1918-19; Head of British Naval Mission to Greece, with rank of Vice-Admiral in Greek Navy, 1919-21; Rear-Admiral First Battle Squadron, Atlantic Fleet, 1923-24; commanded 2nd Cruiser Squadron, 1925-27; Admiralty Representative on League of Nations, 1927-29; Vice-Admiral commanding the First Battle Squadron, and Second in Command of the Mediterranean Fleet, 1929-30; Commander-in-Chief China Station, 1931-33; retired list, 1936; recalled to active service 1940; British Naval Representative, Turkey, until July 1944 (1939-45 Star, Africa Star, 1940-43, Defence and War Medals); Retired List, Dec. 1944. Chm. Royal Central Asian Soc., 1950. Member of French Académie de Marine, 1937; Officer of Legion of Honour, 1911; Commander of Legion of Honour, 1917; French Croix de Guerre, 1917; Officer of the Italian Military Order of Savoy, 1918; American Distinguished Service Medal, 1919; Greek Order of Military Merit, 1st class, 1919; Jubilee Medal, 1935; Coronation Medals, 1911 and 1937. *Address:* 51 Ashley Gardens, S.W.1. *T.:* Victoria 4115. *Club:* United Service. [*Died* 14 *Sept.* 1952.

KELLY, Hon. Sir (William) Raymond, K.B.E., *cr.* 1952; Chief Justice of Commonwealth Court of Conciliation and Arbitration since 1949; *b.* Calcutta, 2 Dec. 1898; *s.* of late William A. St. L. Kelly, I.C.S., and Ethel Marion (*née* Johnston); *m.* 1928, Judith Ellen Fayres Nesbit; two *s.* *Educ.:* St. Xavier's College, Calcutta; Christian Brothers College, Adelaide, S.A.; University of Adelaide (LL.B.). Mayor, Yorkstown, S.A., 1924-26; President Industrial Court of S.A., and Chairman Board of Industry of S.A., 1930; Royal Commissioner on Waterfront, S.A., 1931; and on Agricultural College, S.A., 1932; Justice of Commonwealth Arbitration Court, 1941. *Address:* 468 Lonsdale St., Melbourne, Victoria, Australia. *T.:* MU 3245. *Clubs:* Melbourne, Melbourne Savage, West Brighton (Victoria); University (Sydney); Commonwealth (Adelaide). [*Died* 26 *July* 1956.

KELWAY, Albert Clifton, F.J.I.; F.R.H.S., F.R.G.S.; *b.* Hakin, Milford Haven, 20 Dec. 1865; 2nd *s.* of late Henry Kelway, Belgian Vice-Consul. *Educ.:* Flushing and Probus, Cornwall. Assistant-editor, Church in the West, 1889-90; sub-editor of the Western Daily Mercury (Plymouth), 1890-97; Managing Editor of the Sun, 1897-98; Editor of the Church Review, 1899-1908; Editor of Goodwill, 1908-10; Appeal Secretary, King's Coll. Hospital, and Secretary, King's Coll. Hosp. Med. School, 1910-15; Appeal Sec. C.E.M.S., 1915; General Secretary, Church Reform League, 1917; Secy. New Sees Committee of the National Assembly, 1921; Secy., Incorporated Church Building Society, 1922-46; Official Lecturer for the War Office, Victoria League, Y.M.C.A., etc.; Diocesan Lay Reader (London, Southwark, Truro, and Rochester); member of National Church Assembly, 1924-47; member of London, Swansea and St. Davids Diocesan Conferences; Chm., Additional Curates Soc., 1940-47. *Publications:* Life of George Rundle Prynne, M.A., 1905; A Franciscan Revival, 1908; Memorials of Old Essex, 1908; The Story of Christ Church, St. Leonards 1909; The Catholic Revival of the Nineteenth Century, 1914; The Story of Kikuyu, 1915; History of the Church of England Men's Society, 1949; pamphlets; numerous articles in English, Colonial, and American journals, etc. *Address:* St. Peter's Vicarage, Fulham, S.W.6. *T.:* Fulham 2045. [*Died* 28 *Nov.* 1952.

KEMP, Sir John, Kt., *cr.* 1951; M.E. Hon. Causa, Qld. Univ.; M.I.C.E.; M.I.E.Aust. (Pres. 1932); Co-ordinator-General Public Works, Queensland, 1939-54; Senator, Univ. of Queensland, since 1944; Dep.-Chm. Qld.-British Food Corporation; Director, Queensland Refineries Pty. Ltd. from 1954; *b.* 6 Oct. 1883; *s.* of John Winterburn and Elizabeth Kemp; *m.* 1913, Iva Lilley (*d.* 1952); *m.* 1954, Annie Janet, *d.* of late James Lawrance Tulloch. *Educ.:* Victorian State Schools and Technical College; Melbourne University. Shire and Cons. Civil Engineer, Vic., 1909-13; Engineer, Victorian County Roads Bd., 1913-20; Chm. Main Roads Bd., Qld., and subs. Comr. of Main Roads, 1920-49; Mem. Bureau of Industry, Qld., and Chm. of its Construction Bds. for Bridge, Reservoirs, and building of University; Chm. Roy. Commn. on Electricity, Qld., 1936-37; Mem. Roy. Commn. on Transport, including Harbours, 1936-37; Aust. Commonwealth deleg. to Internat. Road Cong., The Hague, 1938; Chm. Bureau of Investigation, Land and Water Resources, Qld.: Dep.-Dir.-Gen. Allied Works Council, 1939-45; Mem. Aust. National Security Resources Bd. since Dec. 1950. Kernot Memorial Medal of Melb. Univ., 1932; Peter Nicol Russell Medal for distinguished engineering service, 1942; Jubilee Medal, 1935 Coronation Medal, 1937. *Publications:* papers on road engineering; addresses, reports, etc. *Recreations:* reading and country life. *Address:* Marron, Elystan Rd., New Farm, Brisbane, Qld. *Clubs:* Queensland, Johnsonian (Brisbane); Rockhampton (Rockhampton). [*Died* 28 *Feb.* 1955.

KEMP-WELCH, Lucy Elizabeth, R.I. 1917; painter of animals, especially horses; *b.* Bournemouth; *e. d.* of Edwin Buckland-Kemp-Welch. *Educ.:* studied art at the Herkomer School, Bushey. Exhibited first at the Royal Academy, 1894, and each succeeding year; Colt Hunting in the New Forest, 1897 (bought by the trustees of the Chantrey Bequest); Harvesters; Summer Drought; Horses bathing in the Sea, 1900 (bought for National Gallery of Victoria); Lord Dundonald's dash on Ladysmith, 1901 (Exeter Permanent Gallery); Timber Hauling, 1904 (Bristol); The Riders, 1911; Forward, the Guns (bought by Trustees of Chantrey Bequest, 1917); R.B.A. 1902-10; President of Society of Animal Painters formed in 1914; Member of the Pastel Society, 1917; Royal British and Colonial, 1920; Royal Cambrian Academy, 1919; Paris Salon, 1921, awarded bronze medal, and, 1922, awarded the silver medal; presented to the Imperial War Museum a large picture of a remount camp entitled The Straw Ride, 1920; large Wall Panel for the Royal Exchange, entitled Women's Work during the War; one-man Exhibition, Bond Street, 1938. *Recreations:* riding, cycling. *Address:* Kingsley, Bushey, Herts. *T.A.:* Kemp-Welch, Bushey. *T.:* Bushey Heath 1845. *Club:* Empress. [*Died* 27 *Nov.* 1958.

KEMP-WELCH, Brig.-Gen. Martin D.S.O. 1916; M.C.; *b.* Sunningdale, Oct. 1885 4th *s.* of late C. D. Kemp-Welch, J.P., D.L *Educ.:* Charterhouse. Joined The Queen's Royal Regt. from Militia, 1907; Captain, 1915; temp. Lt.-Col. 1916; temp. Brigadier-General, 1918; Major and Bt. Lt. Col. York and Lancs Regt., 1921; Lt.-Col. Royal Tank Corps, 1929; Colonel, 1932; served European War (D.S.O. and bar, M.C., despatches); Commandant Senior Officers' School, Belgaum, India, 1932-1935; Commander 12th Infantry Brigade, 1935-1936; retired pay, 1937; Commandant, O.C.T.U. Sandhurst, 1939-41; County Commandant, Ulster Home Guard, Belfast, 1941-44. *Recreations:* fishing, shooting, golf. *Address:* 134 St. Cross Road, Winchester. *Club:* Army and Navy. [*Died* 16 *July* 1951.

KEMPE, Lieut.-Colonel Frederick Hawke, C.B.E. 1938; M.C.; Retired; *s.* of F. A. Kempe, Barnstaple, Devon; *m.* 1910,

Ada Mary Jones; two *s.* one *d.* *Educ.:* Privately; King's College, London. Postmaster Surveyor, Liverpool; Controller, London Postal Service; Regional Director, London Postal Region; Retired, 1938; Lieut.-Col. Supplementary Reserve (retired); War Service, 1915-19, Dardanelles, Egypt, Palestine, (M.C., despatches twice); Postmaster Surveyor, Liverpool, 1940; commanded 92nd County of Lancaster Bn. Home Guard; retired, 1943. *Recreations:* golf, shooting. *Address:* Sunny Bank, Rhiwderin, Newport, Mon. *T.:* Rhiwderin 282. [*Died* 11 *July* 1954.

KENDALL, Guy, M.A.; *b.* 1876; 4th *s.* of late H. J. B. Kendall, Hatfield, Herts; *m.* 1902, Ada (*d.* 1959), *d.* of J. Sampson, Withington, Lancashire; one *s.* one *d.* *Educ.:* Eton Coll. (King's Scholar; Newcastle Medallist, 1895); (Demy) Magdalen College, Oxford. 1st Class Mods. 1897, 1st Class Lit. Hum. 1899, 1st Class Theology, 1900; Warden, University Settlement, Ancoats, Manchester, 1901; Assistant Master, Charterhouse School, 1902-16; Borough Councillor of Godalming, 1908-12; Headmaster, University College School, Hampstead, 1916-36. *Publications:* The New Schoolmaster (published anonymously); The Call, and other books of verse; A Headmaster Remembers, 1933; A Headmaster Reflects, 1937; A Modern Introduction to the New Testament, 1938; Christianity and the Future Life, 1938; Robert Raikes, 1939; Charles Kingsley and His Ideas, 1947; Religion in War and Peace, 1947; The Social Application of Christianity, 1948. *Address:* Little Hanger, Wormley, Godalming. *Club:* Authors'. [*Died* 28 *Sept.* 1960.

KENDALL, Major John Kaye; *s.* of late Rev. Edward K. Kendall, M.A., D.C.L.; *g.s.* of E. N. Kendall, R.N., of Pelyn, Cornwall, and of Colonel Peard (Garibaldi's Englishman), Trenython, Cornwall; *m.* K. G. Sowerby; one *d.* *Educ.:* Portsmouth, for Army; Woolwich. Entered Royal Artillery, 1888; Captain, 1899; retired, 1904; Major, Reserve of Officers, 1917; as Dum-Dum his first appearance was in The Times of India, 1900; invited to contribute to Punch, 1902; began that year, and on being invalided home in 1903 became a frequent contributor; wrote Mrs. Bill, a comedy in 3 acts, 1908; Laughter in Court, a play in 1 act, 1909; Dad, 1911; Fond of Peter, 1913; Bingo, 1922. *Publications:* Dum-Dum: His Selected Verses, 1947; Dum-Dum: His Book of Beasts, 1943; Short Doses, 1932; Says He, 1932; Oh, Helicon, 1928; The Seventh Hole, etc., 1924; Odd Creatures, 1914; Odd Numbers, 1913; A Fool's Paradise, 1910; The Crackling of Thorns, 1906; Rhymes of the East, 1905; In the Hills, 1903; At Odd Moments. *Recreation:* amusement. *Address:* c/o Barclay's Bank, 108 Queen's Gate, S.W.7. *Club:* Garrick. [*Died* 11 *Jan.* 1952.

KENDALL, Lieut.-Colonel Sydney Robert Gordon, C.B.E. 1921 (O.B.E. 1919); Indian Army, retired; *b.* 18 Apr. 1879; *s.* of late Surg.-Gen. H. Kendall; *m.* 1907, Constance Alice, *e. d.* of Sir Joseph Leese, 1st Bt.; one *d.* (and one *d.* decd.). *Educ.:* Bedford; Sandhurst. Entered 1st Battalion Wilts Regiment 1899, Indian Army, 1903; served North-West Frontier of India, 1914-15; German East Africa, 1917-1918; Afghanistan, 1919 (O.B.E.); Waziristan, 1920-21 (C.B.E.); retired, 1929. *Address:* 4 Lowther Road, Bournemouth. *T.:* Boscombe 36067. [*Died* 19 *March* 1959.

KENDALL, William Henry, C.B.E. 1923 (O.B.E. 1918); *s.* of late John Kendall; *m.* Alice (*d.* 1940), *d.* of Nathaniel Roberts, of Southwater, Sussex; one *s.* two *d.* *Educ.:* private school; King's College, London. Entered Home Office (Second Division Clerk), 1877; transferred to Metropolitan Police Office, 1884; Secretary to Committees on Post Office Wages, 1902, and on Taxi Cab Fares, 1911; Chief Clerk, 1912; Secretary, Metropolitan Police Office, New Scotland Yard, 1918-25; Member of Church Assembly 1932-35, and 1939-45. *Recreations:* walking and reading. *Address:* Beacon Lodge, West Malvern, Worcestershire. *Club:* National Liberal. [*Died* 16 *Nov.* 1951.

KENDON, Frank; M.A.; Fellow of St. John's College, Cambridge; *b.* 1893; *s.* of Samuel Kendon and Ellen Susan Todman; *m.* 1930, Elizabeth Cecilia Phyllis Horne; three *s.* one *d.* *Educ.:* Goudhurst; St. John's Coll., Cambridge. *Publications:* Poems and Sonnets, 1924; Mural Paintings in English Churches, 1924; Arguments and Emblems, 1925; A Life and Death of Judas Iscariot, 1926; The Small Years, 1930; The Adventure of Poetry, 1932; Tristram, a poem, 1934; The Cherry Minder, 1935; The Interrupter, 1940; The Flawless Stone, 1942; The Time Piece, 1945; Each Silver Fly, 1946; Cage and Wing, 1947; Martin Makesure, 1950; Jacob and Thomas, 1952. *Address:* Beechcroft, Harston, Cambridge. [*Died* 28 *Dec.* 1959.

KENDRICK, Albert Frank; Keeper in the Victoria and Albert Museum, in charge of Textiles, 1897-1924; also Ceramics, 1899-1902, and Woodwork, 1904-8; *b.* 1872; *m.* 1900, Ada Layard (*d.* 1951), *d.* of late Rev. R. V. Dunlop. Fellow of Royal Society of Arts; Mem. of Anglo-Swedish Society. *Publications:* Lincoln Cathedral, 1897; English Embroidery, 1905; Burlington Fine Arts Club, catalogue of English Embroidery, 1905; A Book of Old Embroidery (Studio, 1921); Oriental Carpets, 1922; contributions to the Annual of the Walpole Society; Art History Society of Stockholm, 1920; Festschrift for Prof. Strzygowski, Vienna, 1922, and the Journal of the Art Congress, Paris, 1922; articles in the Encyclopædia Britannica, Times, Journal of Royal Society of Arts, Burlington Magazine, Art Workers' Quarterly, Architectural Review, Needlework, etc.; catalogues and guides of the Victoria and Albert Museum, including Tapestries, Carpets, Costumes, Embroideries, Coptic Textiles, etc. *Address:* Chilliswood, Newbury, Berks. *T.:* Newbury 355. [*Died* 17 *July* 1954.

KENDRICK, Sydney Percy; *b.* London, 17 Sept. 1874; *m.* Emily Annie Cowburn (*d.* 1949). *Educ.:* King's College, London. Was apprenticed to a well-known artist for 3 years and afterwards continued studies in Paris; has exhibited portraits and subject pictures in the Royal Academy, also in several municipal exhibitions; bronze portrait plaque for the Birchenough Bridge; bronze portrait plaque for the Sir Otto Beit Bridge over Zambesi River in Rhodesia, 1939. *Publications:* Her Choice; Twilight; The Mirror; Autumn Roses; etc. *Recreation:* billiards. *Address:* 12 Woodchurch Rd., West Hampstead, N.W.6. *T.:* Maida Vale 2622. [*Died* 27 *Aug.* 1955.

KENILWORTH, 1st Baron, *cr.* 1937, of Kenilworth; **John Davenport Siddeley,** Kt., *cr.* 1932; C.B.E. 1918; F.R.Ae.S.; Hon. M.I.M.E.; Past Pres., Society of British Aircraft Constructors, Engineering and Allied Employers Federation, Society of Motor Manufacturers and Traders; Master Coachmaker and Coach Harness Makers Company, 1933; *b.* 1866; *m.* 1893, Sara Mabel (*d.* 1953), *d.* of James Goodier, High Sheriff of Warwicks, 1932; J.P. for Coventry and Warwicks., 1933-38. *Heir:* *s.* Lt.-Col. Hon. Cyril Davenport Siddeley, C.B.E., T.D. *Address:* Rockmount, Gorey, Jersey, C.I. *T.:* Gorey 161. [*Died* 3 *Nov.* 1953.

KENMARE, 7th Earl of (*cr.* 1800), **Gerald Ralph Desmond Browne;** O.B.E. 1923; Bt. 1622; Viscount Kenmare, Baron Castlerosse, 1689; Viscount Castlerosse, 1800; Baron Kenmare of Killarney (United Kingdom), 1856; Major (retired), 1st Royal Dragoons; *b.* 20 Dec. 1896; *s.* of 5th Earl of Kenmare and Hon. Elizabeth Baring (*d.* 1944), *d.* of 1st Baron Revelstoke; *S.* brother, 1943. *Educ.:* Oratory School; R.M.C., Sandhurst. Served European War, 1916-18, France and Belgium; A.D.C. to

Lord Lt. of Ireland, 1921-22. *Heir:* none. *Address:* Kenmare House, Killarney, County Kerry, Ireland. *T.:* Killarney 41. *Clubs:* Cavalry, Buck's; Kildare Street (Dublin). [*Died* 14 *Feb.* 1952 (*ext.*).

KENNAN, John Melville; His Honour Judge Kennan; County Court Judge, Bradford, Circuit No. 12, since 1958; *b.* 9 August 1904; *s.* of William Kennan and Ellen Scott Robinson; *m.* 1939, Vera Duncan French; one *s.* *Educ.:* Liverpool Institute; Keble College, Oxford (B.A.). Open Classical Scholar, Keble Coll., 1923; 1st Cl. Hon. Mods., 1925; 1st Cl. Literæ Humaniores, 1927; Scholar of Inner Temple, 1928; called to Bar, 1930; Northern Circuit, 1930-40; Royal Corps of Signals, 1941; Captain, Military Dept., Judge Advocate-General's Office, 1942; Major, Dep. Judge Advocate, Palestine and Transjordan, 1945; Northern Circuit, 1946. *Recreation:* golf (Capt. Childwall Golf Club, 1949). *Address:* Ingleton, Aigburth Hall Road, Liverpool 19. *T.:* Garston 4777. *Club:* Union (Bradford). [*Died* 21 *April* 1960.

KENNARD, Sir Howard William, G.C.M.G., *cr.* 1938 (K.C.M.G., *cr.* 1929; C.M.G. 1923); C.V.O.1923; *b.* Brighton, 23 March 1878; *s.* of Arthur Challis Kennard, 17 Eaton Place, S.W., and Anne Homan Mulock; *m.* 1908, Harriet (*d.* 1950), *d.* of Jonathan Norris, New York; one *s.* *Educ.:* Wixenford; Eton. Entered Diplomatic Service, 1901; Rome, 1902; 3rd Secretary, 1903; transferred Tehran, 1904; 2nd Secretary, 1907; transferred Washington, 1907; Chargé d'Affaires, Havana, 1911; transferred Tangier, 1912; 1st Sec., 1914; transferred F.O., 1916; to Rome, 1919; Counsellor, 1919; British Minister in Yugoslavia, 1925-29; Sweden, 1929-31; Switzerland, 1931-35; Ambassador Extraordinary and Plenipotentiary to Poland, 1935-41. *Address:* 20 The Circus, Bath. [*Died* 12 *Nov.* 1955.

KENNAWAY, Sir Ernest Laurence, Kt., *cr.* 1947; F.R.S. 1934; F.R.C.P. 1937; M.A.; M.D. Oxon, D.Sc. London; Professor Emeritus of Experimental Pathology, University of London; *b.* 23 May 1881; *s.* of late Laurence James Kennaway, Exeter; *m.* 1920, Nina Marion, *d.* of late William Derry, Edgbaston. *Educ.:* Univ. Coll., London; New College, Oxford; Middlesex Hospital. Hulme Student, Brasenose College, Oxford; Radcliffe Travelling Fellow, University of Oxford; William Julius Mickle Fellow, University of London; Walker Prize, Royal College of Surgeons; Baly Medallist, 1937; Hon. Fellow, New York Academy of Medicine; Anna Fuller Memorial Prize (with others), 1939; Royal Medal, Royal Society, 1941; Hon. Fellow, New College, Oxford, 1942; Hon. Member, Amer. Assoc. for Cancer Research; Garton Medal and Prize, British Empire Cancer Campaign, 1946; formerly Director, Chester Beatty Research Institute of the Royal Cancer Hospital (Free), London; Osler Memorial Medal, 1950; Hon. Foreign Mem. Roy. Acad. of Medicine of Belgium, 1954; Hon. Associate, Rationalist Press Assoc.; Hon. F.Roy.Soc.Med. *Publications:* Some Religious Illusions in Art, Literature and Experience, 1953; Papers on Biological Chemistry and Cancer. *Address:* Department of Pathology, St. Bartholomew's Hospital, E.C.1. *Club:* Athenæum. [*Died* 1 *Jan.* 1958.

KENNAWAY, Sir John, 4th Bt., *cr.* 1791; M.A. (Oxon.); *b.* 7 Apr. 1879; *o. s.* of Rt. Hon. Sir John Henry Kennaway, 3rd Bt., P.C., C.B.; *S.* father, 1919; *m.* 1931, Mary Felicity, *yr. d.* of late Rev. Chancellor Ponsonby; two *s.* one *d.* *Educ.:* Harrow; Balliol College, Oxford. Called to Bar, Inner Temple, 1906; late Capt. 4 Bn. Devon Regt.; late Hon. Col. 8 Bn. Devon Regt. (1939); Member House of Laity, Church Assembly; J.P., D.L. Devon; Alderman, Devon C.C. *Heir:* *s.* John Lawrence, *b.* 7 Sept. 1933. *Address:* Escot, Ottery St. Mary, Devon. *T.:* Whimple 231. *Club:* Travellers'. [*Died* 3 *Aug.* 1956.

KENNEDY, Professor Alexander, M.D. (Lond.), M.B., B.S., F.R.C.P. (Lond.), F.R.C.P.E., F.B.Ps.S., D.P.M.; Professor of Psychological Medicine, University of Edinburgh, since 1955; Physician to Royal Infirmary, Edinburgh, and Clinical Director Royal Edinburgh Hospital for Mental and Nervous Diseases; Psychiatric Adviser and Clinical Director for Research to S.E. Scotland Regional Hosp. Bd.; Pres. Alfred Adler Medical Soc.; Pres., Scottish Assoc. of Psychiatric Social Workers; Vice-President: Eugenics Soc.; Roy. Medico-Psychological Assoc.; Lebanon Hospital, Beirut; Hon. Member Australasian Assoc. of Psychiatrists; Mem. Roy. Soc. of Health; Pres. International Medical Commission on Boxing; F.R.Soc.Med.; *b.* 16 Jan. 1909; *s.* of John Kennedy, Engineer, and Nora Sykes; *m.* 1st, 1934, Helen Emily Mary Walter; three *s.*; 2nd, 1944, Joanna Birkett; one *s.* *Educ.:* City of London School; St. Thomas's Hospital Medical School, Univ. of London; Johns Hopkins Univ. Medical School, U.S.A. Rockefeller Travelling Fellowship in Neuropsychiatry, 1936; Gold Medal Royal Medico-Psychological Assoc., 1938, Bronze Medal, 1936. During War of 1939-45, General Staff Officer, Intelligence, with rank of Lt.-Col. and Scientific Adviser, Intelligence Branch, C.G.C. Formerly Senior Physician, Maudsley Hosp. and Physician for Psychological Medicine, Maida Vale Hosp. for Nervous Diseases; Pres., British Medical Students' Assoc.; Professor of Psychological Medicine, Univ. of Durham, 1947-55, and Chm. No. 28 Hosp. Group. Pres. Electro-physiological Technologists' Assoc., 1959. *Publications:* The Organic Reaction Types, 1948; The Modern Approach to Juvenile Delinquency, 1948; Report on the Mental Hygiene Services of the State of Victoria, 1949; Hysteria and its Treatment, 1950; and numerous technical papers. Also (as Kenneth Alexander) radio plays: Dangerous Drugs; Life History of a Delusion; Area Nine, etc. *Address:* 2 Arboretum Road, Edinburgh 3. *T.:* Granton 83854; 2 George Square, Edinburgh 8. *T.:* Edinburgh 45411; Tosson Mill, Thropton, Northumberland. *Clubs:* Special Forces; Turf (Cairo). [*Died* 11 *June* 1960.

KENNEDY, Professor Alex. Mills, M.D., Ch.B.; F.R.C.P. (Lond.); Emeritus Professor of Medicine, University of Wales; Hon. Consulting Physician to the United Cardiff Hospitals; *s.* of late Alexander Kennedy, O.B.E., J.P., F.S.A. (Scot.), of Bothwell, Lanarkshire. *Educ.:* Allan Glen's School and the University of Glasgow, M.D., with highest honours. Has held at various periods the offices of Examiner in Medicine in the Univs. of Wales and Glasgow, Director of Medical Unit and Senior Hon. Physician, Cardiff Royal Infirmary, and Hon. Consulting Physician to other Hosps. in South Wales; Senior Assistant to the Professor of Medicine in the University of Glasgow, Senior Assistant to the Professor of Pathology in the University of Glasgow, Assistant Physician, Senior Assistant Pathologist, Assistant Medical Electrician, and Resident Physician to the Glasgow Royal Infirmary; formerly Dean of the Faculty of Medicine, Univ. of Wales; Director of the Research Department, Royal Maternity and Women's Hospital, Glasgow; served 1914, with the British Red Cross, and 1915 onwards in the R.A.M.C. (despatches). *Publications:* *books:* Cerebro-spinal Fever, The Etiology, Symptomatology, Diagnosis and Treatment of Epidemic Cerebro-spinal Meningitis; Parasitology for Medical Students; Medical Case-taking. Also numerous original papers in scientific and medical journals. *Address:* c/o Midland Bank Ltd., Queen Street, Cardiff. [*Died* 24 *Sept.* 1960.

KENNEDY, Brigadier-General Henry Brewster Percy Lion, C.M.G. 1918; D.S.O. 1916; late 60th Rifles; late commanding

2nd Rhine Brigade; *s.* of late Vice-Admiral J. J. Kennedy, C.B.; *m.* 1913, Ruby, *y. d.* of late Clarence Trelawny, and *cousin* of Sir W. Lewis Salusbury Trelawny, 10th Bart.; one *d.* *Educ.:* Eton College. Joined 60th Rifles, 1898; served S. African War, 1899-1902 with regiment, and on staff of Lt.-Gen. Sir W. Pitcairn Campbell, K.C.B., and late Major General F. V. Wing, C.B. (King's and Queen's medals 6 clasps); European War, in command of 21st London Regt., and commanding 140th Infantry Brigade, and 2nd Rhine Brigade (despatches seven times, D.S.O., C.M.G., Bt. Lt.-Col., Brevet Col., Grand Officer Military Order of Avis and Grand Officer Tower and Sword of Portugal, Croix de Guerre with palm); retired pay, 1927; re-employed 1939-42 as King's Messenger. *Recreations:* hunting, polo, racing. *Address:* 11 Pelham Court, S.W.3. *T.:* Kensington 6009. *Clubs:* White's, Bath, Queen's; Newmarket; Sandown.
[*Died* 8 *Dec.* 1953.

KENNEDY, Hon. Sir James Arthur, Kt., *cr.* 1950; M.L.C.; F.C.I.S.; F.I.C.A.; *b.* 5 Feb. 1882; *s.* of James Kennedy, Carlton, Victoria, Australia; *m.* 1913, Ann Taylor Higgins; two *d.* *Educ.:* Scotch College, Melbourne. Melbourne Electricity Supply Co. Ltd., 1903; Chief Accountant, 1920; Secretary, 1927-40; Secretary Melbourne Investment Trust Ltd., 1927-40. M.L.C. for Higinbotham, Victoria, 1937-; Minister for Transport and Works, and Vice-President Board of Lands and Works, Victoria, 1943-1945; Minister for Public Works, Victoria, 1947-50. *Address:* 28 Cosham Street, Brighton, Victoria, Australia.
[*Died* 19 *Nov.* 1954.

KENNEDY, Sir John Macfarlane, Kt., *cr.* 1943; O.B.E.; M.Inst.C.E., M.I.E.E.; *b.* 12 Oct. 1879; *s.* of late Sir Alexander B. W. Kennedy, LL.D., F.R.S., and late Elizabeth Veralls Smith; *m.* 1904, Dorothy Farrer; one *s.* one *d.* *Educ.:* Trinity College, Cambridge. Partner in Kennedy and Donkin, Consulting Engineers, 1908-34; Electricity Commissioner, 1934-48. *Address:* Woodstock, Shalford, Surrey. *T.:* Guildford 61486. *Club:* Athenæum.
[*Died* 31 *Aug.* 1954.

KENNEDY, John Robert, M.V.O. 1942; M.B., C.M.; J.P.; Medical Practitioner (retd.); *b.* 2 July 1871; *s.* of late Dr. William Kennedy, Tain, Ross-shire; *m.* 1895, Cecilia Ann Vicars Duff Walker, Elgin, Morayshire; three *s.* two *d.* (and two *s.* decd.). *Educ.:* Tain Royal Academy; Aberdeen University (M.B., C.M. 1893). Practised in Argyllshire, Shetland, and Caithness. Bronze Medal Royal Humane Society, 1927. *Recreations:* ornithology, yachting. *Address:* Dunbeath, 6 Couper Street, Thurso, Caithness.
[*Died* 8 *July* 1956.

KENNEDY, Bt.-Col. and Hon. Col. Norman, C.B.E. 1942; D.S.O. 1917; T.D., D.L., J.P.; Governing Director, James Kennedy & Company Ltd., Glasgow; *b.* 17 Mar. 1881; *e. surv. s.* of late James Kennedy, Doonholm, Ayr; *m.* 1915, Sylvia, O.B.E., *y. d.* of late Brig.-Gen. E. G. H. Bingham, R.A., and Mrs. H. P. Hickman; two *s.* two *d.* *Educ.:* Rugby School; University College, Oxford, B.A. Ayrshire Yeomanry, 1899-1928; commanded Regiment, 1924-28; served European War, Gallipoli, Egypt, Palestine (D.S.O., despatches twice); owns herd Pedigree Aberdeen Angus cattle; played Rugby football for Oxford, 1901-02, for Scotland, 1903; Past President Glasgow Chamber of Commerce; Director Glasgow Merchants' House; ex-Mem. Scottish Cttee., L.M.S. Ry. Co.; Bank of Scotland; Consul in Glasgow for the Republic of Honduras, etc. Hon. Col. Ayrshire (Earl of Carrick's Own) Yeomanry. *Recreations:* shooting, fishing, golf, etc. *Address:* Doonholm, Ayr. *T.:* Alloway 206. *Club:* Western (Glasgow). [*Died* 15 *Jan.* 1960.

KENNEDY, Rt. Hon. Thomas, P.C. 1931; General Secretary, Social Democratic Federation, and Editor of the Social Democrat; *b.* 1876; *m.* 1919, Annie, *d.* of G. S. Michie, Aberdeen; one *s.* M.P. (Lab.) Kirkcaldy, 1921-22, 1923-31 and 1935-44; Scottish Labour Whip, 1921-22 and 1923-25; a Lord Commissioner of the Treasury, 1924; Chief Whip of Labour Party, 1927-31; Deputy, 1925-27; Parliamentary Secretary to the Treasury, 1929-31; now retired. *Address:* Ivy Bank, Lumsden, By Huntly, Aberdeenshire.
[*Died* 3 *March* 1954.

KENNEDY, Sir Thomas Sinclair, Kt., *cr.* 1942; Director, Glenfield & Kennedy, Ltd., Kilmarnock, since 1944; *b.* Kilmarnock, 11 Feb. 1884; *s.* of late Thomas Kennedy, J.P., Managing Director of Glenfield & Kennedy, Ltd., and Jane McGregor; *m.* 1916, Jean Campbell Hunter, *er. d.* of William Middlemas, Solicitor and Town Clerk, Kilmarnock; no *c.* *Educ.:* Speirs School, Beith; Seafield House, Broughty Ferry; Fettes College, Edinburgh. Trained as Engineer with Glenfield & Kennedy, Ltd., 1901-7; Asst. Resident Engineer Robinson Deep Gold Mine, Johannesburg, 1907-8; returned to Glenfield, 1908. Travelling representative of Glenfield & Kennedy, Ltd., in India at Bombay, 1911. Toured India, Burma, Ceylon, Straits Settlements, Siam, Java, China, Formosa and Japan, 1911-14; European War, 1914-18. Lieut. and Capt. Royal Scots Fusiliers; transferred as Capt. to R.E., 1915; served in France, 1915-18, during which was two years on Staff of 2nd Army H.Q. as D.A.Q.M.G. J.P., Hon. Presidency Magistrate, Bombay City and Island; Member Bombay Legislative Council and Leader of European Group, 1933-35; Sheriff of Bombay, 1941. *Recreations:* golf, shooting, and philately. *Address:* Bendochie, Cove, Dunbartonshire. *Clubs:* Constitutional; Conservative (Glasgow); Royal Bombay Yacht, Willingdon Sports, Bombay Gymkhana (Bombay). [*Died* 20 *March* 1951.

KENNET, 1st Baron, *cr.* 1935, of the Dene; **Edward Hilton Young,** P.C. 1922; G.B.E., *cr.* 1927; D.S.O.; D.S.C.; Chairman: Treasury Capital Issues Cttee. 1939-1959 (Chairman Foreign Transactions Advisory Committee 1937-39); Companies (Restriction) Panel; *b.* 1879; 3rd *s.* of Sir George Young, 3rd Bt., of Formosa Pl., Cookham; *m.* 1922, Kathleen (*d.* 1947), *widow* of Captain Robert Falcon Scott, C.V.O., R.N.; one *s.* *Educ.:* Eton; Trinity Coll., Cambridge (M.A. 1907); Hon. D.C.L. Durham, 1934; Hon. Fellow University College. Called to Bar, Inner Temple, 1904; practised in the King's Bench Division and on the Oxford Circuit; contested East Worcester and Preston, 1910; M.P. (L.) Norwich, 1915-23 and 1924-29; and (C.) Sevenoaks, 1929-35; Lieutenant R.N.V.R. and appointed to H.M.S. Iron Duke, Aug. 1914; Naval Mission in Serbia, 1915; Obilich Medal (Semendria, Oct. 1915), and Karageorge Order, 4th class with swords; H.M. Centaur (Harwich), 1916; actions of 22 Jan., 11 May 1917, etc.; R.N. guns on Flemish Front, 1917 (D.S.C. and Croix de Guerre); served in Vindictive at Zeebrugge Mole, 1918 (wounded and special promotion to Lieut.-Commander); in command of armoured train in Archangel campaign, 1919 (D.S.O. for services in action); Financial Secretary to the Treasury, 1921-22; Secretary of the Overseas Trade Department, 1931; Minister of Health, 1931-35; British Representative at The Hague Conference on International Finance, 1922; Financial Missions for British Government to India, 1920, Poland (Grand Cordon of Order of Polonia) 1924, Iraq, 1925 and 1930 (Order of Rafidain, first class); Chairman of following Royal Commissions, Inquiries etc.; Custom's Law Codification (1951); C.S. Manpower (1940-46); Iron Ore Areas, 1939; East African Closer Union, 1928;

Indian Currency and Finance, 1926; Constitution of University of London, 1925; Organisation of Board of Trade, 1920; Free Places in Schools, etc.; British Delegate to the Assembly of the League of Nations, 1926, 1927, 1928, and 1932; has been President of Gas Federation of G.B., 1939-44; Crown Member of the General Medical Council; President, Royal Statistical Society, 1936-38, Association of Technical Institutes, 1937, and Poetry Society. *Publications:* Foreign Companies and other Corporations, 1911; The System of National Finance, 3rd ed., 1935; A Muse at Sea, 1919; Verses, 1935; By Sea and Land, 2nd ed., 1924; A Bird in the Bush, 1937. *Heir:* *s.* Hon. Wayland Hilton-Young [*b.* 2 Aug. 1923; *m.* 1948, Elizabeth, *d.* of Captain B. F. Adams, D.S.O.; one *s.* four *d.*]. *Address:* Leinster Corner, W.2. *T.:* Ambassador 4187.
[*Died* 11 *July* 1960.

KENNEY, J. C. F.; *see* Fitzgerald-Kenney.

KENNING, Sir George, Kt., *cr.* 1943; J.P.; Managing Director of Kennings Ltd., Midland Motor Finance Co., Kennings Estates, Pirelli Ltd., and other companies; Member of Lloyds; *b.* 1880; *m.* 1911, Catherine, *d.* of John Buchanan, Londonderry; three *s.* *Address:* Stumperlowe Hall, Fulwood, Sheffield 10. [*Died* 6 *Feb.* 1956.

KENNINGTON, Eric Henri, R.A. 1959 (A.R.A. 1951); F.A.M.S.; *m.* 1922, Edith Celandine, *d.* of Lord Francis Cecil; one *s.* one *d.* Pictures: Costardmongers, 1914; Kensingtons at Laventie, 1916; Official War Artist, 1916-19, 1940-43. Sculpture; Memorial to 24th Division, Battersea Park; British Memorial at Soissons, France; carving in the School of Tropical Medicine and Hygiene, Gower Street; Memorial to Thomas Hardy, Dorchester; Brick-carving, Shakespeare Memorial Theatre, Stratford-on-Avon; The earth child, Tate Gallery; panel on the Nag's Head, Bishop's Stortford; Bronze head of T. E. Lawrence, St. Paul's Cathedral; Art editor to the Seven Pillars of Wisdom, subscribers edition, 1926, and to Jonathan Cape's edition, 1935; Lawrence medal and Sykes medal Royal Central Asian Society; stone pillar for the Comet Inn, Hatfield; Colossal figure-sculpture outside Cohen Library, Liverpool, 1937; recumbent effigy of T. E. Lawrence, St. Martin's, Wareham, 1939; memorial to Geoffrey de Havilland, Hatfield Aerodrome, 1947, relief carving in Hammerwood Church, Sussex, 1949; baptismal font, Betchworth Church, Surrey, 1951; medal for Danish Bacon Co., 1952; Archangel Gabriel, Mid-South Primary School, Reading, 1953; Recumbent Effigy of T. E. Lawrence, Tate Gallery, 1954, and Art Gallery, Aberdeen, 1955; large mural painting, Technical College, Birkenhead, 1955; "1940" stone memorial to the R.A.F., purchased by Glasgow, 1955; Coker Memorial, Bicester Church, Oxon, 1956; Robson Tombstone, Hangleton Church, Hove, Sussex, 1956. *Publications:* Drawing the R.A.F., 1942; Tanks and Tank Folk, 1943; Britain's Home Guard, 1945. *Address:* Homer House, Ipsden, Oxon. *T.:* Checkendon 240. [*Died* 13 *April* 1960.

KENNY, Elizabeth; nursing sister; research worker on infantile paralysis since 1911; chief, teaching centre, Jersey City, U.S.A.; *b.* Australia, 20 Sept. 1886; *d.* of Michael Kenny and Mary (*née* Moore); unmarried. *Educ.:* privately; St. Ursula's College, Australia. Nursing in Australian Bush, 1911-14. European War, 1914-18, nurse in Australian Army. Went to U.S.A., 1940, to present to research institute a concept of symptoms of disease of infantile paralysis. Clinics in many countries have been established to treat polio on the lines advocated by Sister Kenny. *Publications:* Infantile Paralysis and Cerebral Diplegia, 1927; Treatment of Infantile Paralysis in Acute Stage, 1941; The Kenny Concept of Infantile Paralysis and its Treatment, 1942; (with Martha Ostenso) And They Shall Walk (autobiography), 1943. *Address:* Elizabeth Kenny Institute, 1800 Chicago Avenue, Minneapolis 4, Minnesota, U.S.A.
[*Died* 30 *Nov.* 1952.

KENRICK, Frank Boteler, M.A., Ph.D. (Leipzig); F.R.S. (Can.); Head of Dept. of Chemistry, 1937-44; Prof. of Chemistry, Univ. of Toronto, 1919-44, now Prof. Emeritus; *b.* Send, England, 4 Feb. 1874; *s.* of John Bridges Kenrick, M.A.; *m.* 1907, Hilda, *y. d.* of John Boulton Boulton of The Grange, Toronto. *Educ.:* Upper Canada College; University of Toronto; Leipzig; Berlin. Graduated University of Toronto, 1894; 1851 Exhibition Scholar, 1894-97; Assistant, University of Toronto, 1897-1900; Lecturer, 1900-7; Associate-Professor, 1907-19. *Publications:* with R. E. De Lury, An Elementary Laboratory Course in Chemistry, 1905; An Introduction to Chemistry, 1932; various articles in chemical journals (mainly Physico-Chemical). *Address:* 73 Oriole Road, Toronto 12, Ont., Canada.
[*Died* 19 *June* 1951.

KENRICK, George Harry Blair, Q.C. 1909; late Advocate-General, Bengal; Member of Legislative Council of Viceroy of India, 1910-1916; *s.* of late George Kenrick, Nant Clwyd Hall, Denbighshire. *Educ.:* Cheltenham; University of London (LL.B., First Class Honours); LL.D. 1899. First Class Scholarships of the Middle Temple, 1891, 1892; First Class Honoursman of Council of Legal Education, and Prizeman of Middle Temple, 1893; called to Bar, Middle Temple, 1893; member of South-Eastern Circuit; member of Board of Examiners for Final Bar Examination; Law Examiner of the University of London for four years; Assistant Legal Adviser to Secretary of State for Foreign affairs during Hague Conference, 1907; Advocate-General for the Presidencies of Bengal and Eastern Bengal and Assam, and Principal Law Officer of the Government of India, 1909; member of Senate and Syndicate, University of Calcutta, 1910. *Publications:* Strahan and Kenrick's Digest of Equity (joint author); assistant editor of the 18th edition of Rogers on Elections; a large number of articles in Encyclopædia of the Laws of England; and article Habeas Corpus in Lord Halsbury's Laws of England, etc. *Address:* Caer Rhun Hall, Conway, Caernarvonshire.
[*Died* 23 *Aug.* 1952.

KENT, Albert Frank Stanley, M.A., D.Sc. Oxon; late 2nd Lieut. in Territorial Army; Quartermaster and Musketry Instructor to local Home Guard; engaged in physiological research; lately conducting special Government inquiry into conditions of industrial occupations; Editor-in-Chief for Great Britain of the Journal of Industrial Hygiene; *b.* 26 Mar. 1863; *s.* of Rev. George Davies Kent, B.D., Fellow of C.C.C., Oxford, and Anne, *d.* of William Rudgard, Newland House, Lincoln; *m.* 1904, Theodora (*d.* 1957), *d.* of W. H. Hobson. *Educ.:* Magdalen Coll. School, Oxford; Magdalen College, Oxford. Final Honours School of Natural Science, 1886; Demonstr. of Physiology in Owens Coll., Manchester and the Victoria Univ., 1887-89; University of Oxford, 1889-91; St. Thomas' Hospital, London, 1891-95; Professor of Physiology in University College, Bristol, 1899-1909, and in the University of Bristol, 1909-18; an early worker on X-rays (1896); developed the X-ray Dept. at St. Thomas' Hospital; founded and for about eight years carried on the Clinical Research Laboratory (now the Public Health Laboratory) in University College; Lecturer in Bacteriology, and Bacteriologist to the Bristol Royal Infirmary; took active part in foundation of Bristol University; organised, and for some years directed, the Dept. of Industrial Administration, Manchester Municipal Technical Coll. *Publications:* numerous papers on scientific subjects, especially on the structure of the heart, 1890 onwards; White Paper (1915) and Blue Book (1916) on Industrial Fatigue;

Edited English Edition of Professor Amar's Physiology of Industrial Organisation, 1918. *Recreations:* foreign travel, golf, fishing, rowing, rifle shooting. *Address:* Cliffe Tyning, Murhill Lane, Limpley Stoke, Bath. *T.:* Limpley Stoke 2123.
[*Died* 30 *March* 1958.

KENT, Charles Weller, Q.C. 1922; *b.* 19 Sept. 1864; *o. s.* of late George Weller Kent; *m.* 1914, Winifred, (*d.* 1946), *widow* of Ernest Edwards; no *c. Educ.:* privately. Parliamentary journalist for many years on the Staff of The Times; called to Bar, Middle Temple, 1895. Joined the South-Eastern Circuit; Chairman, Assessment Committee, Eastbourne, 1932-40; Director of City Lands Investment Corp., E.C.2; Life Member, Soc. of Sussex Downsmen. *Publications:* Make Friends of the Wise, 1940; Happiness Haven, 1941; Pathway to Happiness, 1942; A Splendid Inheritance, 1946. *Address:* 34 Milnthorpe Road, Eastbourne, Sussex.
[*Died* 5 *June* 1952.

KENT, Chris Shotter, C.B.E. 1919 (O.B.E. 1918); *b.* 1887; *m.* Irene Muriel, *e. d.* of late Arthur David Rees; two *s.* one *d.* Member of British War Mission to U.S.A., 1917-18; Financial Controller of Department of Propaganda in Enemy Countries, 1918. Manager of The Times, 1937-49. *Address:* 13 Morpeth Mansions, S.W.1. *Club:* Devonshire.
[*Died* 30 *July* 1954.

KENT, Col. Sir John; *see* Kent, Col. Sir W. J.

KENT, Sir Stephenson Hamilton, K.C.B., *cr.* 1917; *b.* 22 Feb. 1873; 2nd *s.* of late Henry Kent of Bishopsbourne, Eastbourne; *m.* 1902, Beatrice Alexandra (*d.* 1939), *e. d.* of late Charles O'Flanagan, Co. Roscommon; *m.* 1940, Eileen Mary, *widow* of Kenneth Richards, Sydney, New South Wales. *Educ.:* Harrow. Director-General, Munitions Labour Supply; Member of Council of Ministry of Munitions; went on a Government Mission to America, 1917; Controller-General of Civil Demobilisation and Resettlement, Ministry of Labour, 1918-19; High Sheriff of Sussex, 1924. *Recreations:* shooting, fishing, golf. *Address:* Hills End, Sunningdale, Berks. *T.:* Ascot 462. *Clubs:* Buck's, St. James', Boodle's. [*Died* 28 *March* 1954.

KENT, Col. Sir (William) John, Kt., *cr.* 1952; C.B.E. 1943; T.D., D.L., J.P.; O.St.J. 1950; *b.* 20 Dec. 1877; *o. s.* of George Charles Kent, J.P., Stone, Staffs; *m.* 1902, Winifred Violet Ada (*d.* 1948), *er. d.* of I. Westley, Steephill, Isle of Wight; one *d.* (and one *s.* decd.). *Educ.:* Privately. Admitted a Solicitor 1899, and practised till 1913; joined 1st Shropshire and Staffordshire R.G.A., 1899; raised 2nd Staffs Battery R.F.A. (T.), 1908, and promoted Major; Member Staffs T.F. Assoc., mobilised Aug. 1914; served European War, 1914-18; Lt.-Col., 1916, to command 237th Brigade R.F.A. (T.); seconded to R.F.A., 1916, to command 87th Brigade, R.F.A.; Hon. Col. 61st Regt. R.A., 1945. Chairman Nat. Council Pottery Industry, 1926-28; J.P. Staffs, 1927; President British Pottery Manufacturers Federation, 1950 (Vice-Chm. 1931); Pres. N. Staffs Chamber of Commerce, 1932-46; apptd. Mem. Parl. Court of Inquiry into dispute in Hull Fishing Industry, 1935; Member Home Office Committee on Hours of Labour of Young Persons in Unregulated Occupations, 1936; Chairman N. Staffs Advisory Cttee. to Assistance Bd., 1934-49; Mem. Staffs Standing Joint Cttee., 1931-52; D.L. Staffs; County Controller Civil Defence for Staffs, 1940-45; High Sheriff of Staffs, 1942-43. *Address:* Hough Hall, Hough, nr. Crewe, Cheshire. *T.A.:* Hough, Crewe. *T.:* 349 Wybunbury. [*Died* 5 *March* 1960.

KENTISH, Brigadier-General Reginald John, C.M.G. 1919; D.S.O. 1914; late The Royal Irish Fusiliers; *b.* 29 Dec. 1876; *s.* of George Kentish; unmarried. *Educ.:* Malvern; Sandhurst. Entered Army, 1897; Captain, 1902; Adjutant, 1905-8; A.D.C. to G.O.C., 2nd Division, 1910; Brigade Major, 6th London Infantry Brigade, 1912-14; Bt. Lt.-Col., 1916; Brig.-Gen., 1916-19; Col., 1919; served South Africa, 1899-1902 (Queen's medal 4 clasps, King's medal 2 clasps); European War, 1914-18 (despatches five times, C.M.G., D.S.O., 1914 Star, Victory medal, Allied); Officer Legion of Honour; organised the Army School System in France and subsequently organised and became Commandant of the Senior Officers' School, Aldershot, 1916; V.P. Army Football Assoc., Army Fencing Union, Army Athletic Assoc., etc.; Member of the British Olympic Council and of Governing Body, Dockland Settlements; author of many papers on matters affecting the training and welfare of the soldier; a strong advocate of the policy of placing the private soldier on his honour, which led to the abolition of picquets in the Aldershot command, 1910, and subsequently in the whole army; originated at Aldershot in 1908 the scheme for providing adequate recreation grounds for the troops; in 1914 officially appointed by the Army Council to extend the scheme in Great Britain and Ireland; In 1919 he continued the scheme until he retired from the Army, 1922; and in 1925 he founded the National Playing Fields Association. *Address:* c/o Barclays Bank, 160 Piccadilly, W.1.
[*Died* 5 *July* 1956.

KENWARD, Rev. Herbert; *b.* Lewes, Sussex; *s.* of A. T. Kenward, Glengariff, Kingston Road, Lewes; *m.* Florence Mary Letheren, Grantham; two *s.* two *d. Educ.:* Castle Gate School, Lewes; Nottingham College. Minister Magdalen Road Congregational Church, Norwich, 1899-1905; Supt. Crossway Central Mission (of London Congregational Union), 1905-25; Minister Cricklewood Congregational Church, 1925-30; Commissioner for Church Extension (London Congregational Union), 1930-39; Sec. London Congregational Union, 1935-39; Norfolk Union, 1900-05; Chm. Surrey Union, 1919-20; Colonial Missionary Society, 1953-54. *Publications:* Articles, etc. *Recreations:* golf, fishing. *Address:* Hillside, Marine Drive, Bishopstone, Seaford, Sussex. *T.:* Seaford 3009. [*Died* 24 *May* 1954.

KENWORTHY, John Dalzell, A.R.C.A. 1914; J.P. 1919; President: West Cumberland Club; Whitehaven Art Club, 1948; *b.* 5 Nov. 1858; *m.* 1883, Dinah Towerson (*d.* 1950), *d.* of William Porter, Egremont; one *s.* one *d.* (and one *s.* killed 1916). *Publication:* A Fisherman's Philosophy. *Address:* Sea-croft, St. Bees, Cumberland. *T.A.:* St. Bees. *T.:* St. Bees 80.
[*Died* 4 *March* 1954.

KENYON, Sir Frederic George, G.B.E., *cr.* 1925; K.C.B., *cr.* 1912 (C.B. 1911); T.D. 1918; Director and Principal Librarian, British Museum, 1909-30; M.A., D.Litt. (Oxford, Durham, and Athens), Litt.D. (Cambridge and Dublin), LL.D. (St. Andrews, Wales and Princeton), L.H.D. (Kenyon Coll., Ohio), Ph.D. (Halle); Doctor hon. Univ. of Paris (1927) and Brussels (1930); Corr. Member of Roy. Irish Acad. and numerous foreign academies; Fellow of British Academy, 1903, Pres. 1917-21, Sec., 1930-50, Hon. Fellow, 1950; Prof. of Ancient History in the Royal Academy, 1918; Pres. of Society of Antiquaries, 1934-39 (F.S.A. 1926); President of the Society for Promotion of Hellenic Studies, 1919-24; Hon. A.R.I.B.A. 1923; Fellow of Winchester College, 1904, Warden, 1925-30; Fellow of Magdalen College, Oxford, 1888; Hon. Fellow, 1906; Hon. Fellow, New College, Oxford, 1913; President of British School of Archæology at Jerusalem since 1920; of the Bibliographical Society, 1924-26 (Gold Medal, 1935); of the Navy Records Society, 1924-48; Chairman of Soc. for Protection of Science and Learning, 1938-44; Pres. Surrey Record Soc.

1943-50, and of Surrey Archæological Society, 1944-50; Chairman of Friends of the National Libraries, 1931-50; of National Central Library; Trustee of War Museum, 1920-46; Gentleman Usher of the Purple Rod of the Order of the British Empire, 1918-52; *b.* London, 15 Jan. 1863; *s.* of John Robert Kenyon, Q.C., D.C.L., Vinerian Professor of Law in Oxford Univ.; *m.* 1891, Amy (*d.* 1938), *d.* of Rowland Hunt, J.P.; two *d.* *Educ.:* Winchester; New College, Oxford. Chancellor's English Essay, 1889; Conington Prize, 1897; Asst. in Brit. Museum, 1889; Asst. Keeper of MSS., Brit. Museum, 1898-1909; Rede Lecturer, Cambridge, 1915; Romanes Lecturer, Oxford, 1927; David Murray Lecturer, Glasgow, 1934; Lt.-Col. in Territorial Force (Inns of Court); served with Expeditionary Force in France, Aug.-Sept. 1914, and with his regiment till 1919; Adviser to Imperial War Graves Commission, 1917-48; University Grants Cttee., 1919-47; Chairman of Departmental Cttee. on Public Libraries, 1924-27; Home Guard, 1940-42. *Publications:* Aristotle's Constitution of Athens, 1891; revised edns., 1904, 1920; Classical Texts from Papyri in the British Museum (Herodas, Hyperides, etc.), 1891; Hyperides, Orations against Athenogenes and Philippides, 1892; Catalogue of Greek Papyri in the British Museum, vol. i. 1893, vol. ii. 1898, vol. iii. 1907; Our Bible and the Ancient Manuscripts, 1895, revised edition, 1939; The Brownings for the Young, 1896; joint-editor of R. Browning's Poems, 1896; Bacchylides, 1897; Letters of E. B. Browning, 1897; Poems of E. B. Browning, 1897; Palæography of Greek Papyri, 1899; Facsimiles of Biblical MSS. in the British Museum, 1900; Handbook to the Textual Criticism of the New Testament, 1901 (new edition, 1912); Robert Browning and Alfred Domett, 1906; Hyperides (text), 1907; editor of Centenary Edition of R. Browning, 1912; the Buildings of the British Museum, 1914; New Poems of R. and E. B. Browning, 1914; articles in Hastings' Dictionary of the Bible; Ancient Books and Modern Discoveries, 1928; Libraries and Museums, 1930; Books and Readers in Ancient Greece and Rome, 1932; Recent Developments in the Textual Criticism of the Greek Bible, 1933; The Chester Beatty Biblical Papyri, parts i.-ii., 1933; parts iii., iv., 1934; part v., 1935; part iii. (suppl.) 1936; parts vi., vii., 1937; part viii., 1941; Locke on Education (Roxburghe Club), 1934; The Story of the Bible, 1936; The Text of the Greek Bible, 1937; The Bible and Archæology, 1940; The Reading of the Bible, 1944; The Bible and Modern Scholarship, 1948. *Recreations:* walking, reading. *Address:* Kirkstead, Godstone, Surrey. *T.:* Godstone 335. *Club:* Athenæum. [*Died* 23 *Aug.* 1952.

KENYON, Sir Harold (Vaughan), Kt., *cr.* 1937; M.B.E. 1931; J.P.; F.T.C.L.; *b.* 7 Feb. 1875; *s.* of James Harold and Sarah Lea Kenyon; *m.* 1899, Minnie (*d.* 1943), *d.* of late Thomas Ridgway; two *s.* three *d.*; *m.* 1947, Millicent Charlotte May, *d.* of late Chas. Hamilton Jackson. *Educ.:* Philological School, St. Marylebone. Kensington Borough Council, 1908; Mayor, 1931-34; Alderman, 1933; Paddington Borough Council, 1910; Mayor, 1920-24 and 1935-37; Alderman, 1915; Pres. Metropolitan Mayors' Assoc., 1958; Chairman: Trinity College of Music, London; Paddington Bench of Magistrates, 1942-46; Metropolitan Boroughs Standing Joint Cttee. 1918-53; Leader of the Municipal Reform Party for several years, Chairman 1924-25: Member of Standing Joint Cttee. for County of London, 1937-46; Metropolitan Special Constabulary, 17 Aug. 1914; Commandant F Division), 1926-35 (M.B.E.); formerly Treas. of St. Mary's Hosp.; Chm. Central Council for District Nursing in London, 1945-54. Founder-Pres. of Paddington and St. Marylebone Rotary Club, 1924, also of Paddington Rotary Club, 1948; Master of the Cooks' Co., 1944-45 and 1949-50; Freeman of City of London, 1919; Freeman of Borough of Paddington; President of Paddington and Bayswater Chamber of Commerce, 1925-46, etc.; Chairman of Paddington Tuberculosis Dispensary; Chairman of the Assessment Committees of Paddington and Kensington for several years, and a number of other Municipal and Social Organisations; Representative for S. Paddington on L.C.C. 1931-1946; formerly Alderman of Kensington and Paddington. *Address:* Connaught Court, W.2. *T.:* Paddington 7518; Westmyllmead, Dogmersfield, Hants. *T.:* Fleet 807. *Clubs:* City Livery, County of London Magistrates. [*Died* 22 *Sept.* 1959.

KENYON, Major-Gen. Lionel Richard, C.B. 1917; late R.A.; *s.* of J. R. Kenyon, K.C., D.C.L., of Pradoe, Shropshire; *b.* 26 July 1867; *m.* 1896, Elizabeth Jane (*d.* 1946), *d.* of P.C. Sutherland, M.D., F.R.G.S., etc., Surveyor-General of Natal; one *s.* *Educ.:* Winchester; R.M. Academy, Woolwich. 2nd Lieut. R.A. 1887; Capt. 1897; Major, 1906; Bt. Lt.-Col. 1913; Lt.-Col. 1914; Bt. Col. 1915; Brig.-Gen. 1917; Col. 1919; Maj.-Gen. 1921; Staff Officer Artillery College, 1896-98; Staff Capt., Headquarters, 1899-1904; Military Assist. to Chief Supt. Ordnance Factories, 1905-7; Secretary, Ordnance Board, 1907-10; Deputy Director, Ordnance Factories, India, 1911-16; Director of Munitions Inspection in U.S.A., 1916-19; Director-General of Ordnance in India, 1919-24; Deputy Master-General of Supply, April-Oct. 1924; retired pay, 1925; Hon. LL.D. Kenyon College, Ohio, U.S.A. Church of England. *Address:* The Valley House, Stratford St. Mary, Colchester. *T.:* Dedham 2141. [*Died* 23 *Feb.* 1952.

KENYON, Myles Noel, C.B.E. 1953; President James Kenyon & Son Ltd.; retired 1960; *b.* 25 Dec. 1886; *s.* of James Kenyon, Walshaw Hall, Bury, Lancs.; *m.* 1909, Mary, *d.* of James Moon, Bidston, Birkenhead; one *s.* one *d.* (and one *d.* decd.). *Educ.:* Eton; Trinity College, Cambridge (M.A.). Served European War, 1914-18, with 2nd Duke of Lancaster's Own Yeomanry. High Sheriff, Lancashire, 1935; D.L. Lancs., 1935. Capt. Lancs. County Cricket Club, 1919-22, Pres., 1936-37. Honorary Freeman, Bury, 1936; Hon. M.A. Manchester University. *Recreations:* cricket and hunting when younger. *Address:* Kidside House, Milnthorpe, Westmorland. *T.:* Milnthorpe 23. [*Died* 21 *Nov.* 1960.

KENYON, Sir Norris (Vaughan), Kt., *cr.* 1955; J.P.; Director of J. H. Kenyon Ltd. since 1924; Chairman London Municipal Society since 1952; *b.* 5 June 1903; *s.* of Sir Harold Kenyon, *q.v.*; *m.* 1927, Marjorie Frances Henderson, *d.* of Thomas H. Beale, Holloway, N.7; two *s.* one *d.* *Educ.:* St. Marylebone Grammar School; London Univ. B.Sc. (Econ.) 1923. Member Paddington Borough Council, 1927. Alderman, 1938, Mayor 1950-52; J.P. County of London, 1940. Chairman Paddington Bench, 1945-1950. Chairman Metropolitan Juvenile Courts, 1946-. Member L.C.C. (S. Paddington), 1946-; Leader Conservative Party L.C.C., 1952-58. Chm. Paddingtom Chamber of Commerce, 1932; Chm. Paddington Boy Scouts Assoc., 1951-; Mem. Bracknell New Town Development Corporation (Dep. Chm. 1953-). Freeman of the City of London, 1924; Master of the Cooks' Company, 1952-53. F.R.S.A. 1952. *Recreations:* music and gardening. *Address:* 10 Connaught Court, W.2. *T.:* Ambassador 6513. *Clubs:* Constitutional, City Livery. [*Died* 28 *April* 1958.

KEOWN, Anna Gordon; Writer; *y. d.* of Robert Keown and Sarah White; *m.* 1st, 1921, W. H. Seymour (marriage dissolved); 2nd, Philip Gosse, *q.v.* *Educ.:* Cheltenham Ladies' College; Dresden. *Publications: Poetry:* The Bright of Eye; The Winds. *Novels:* The Cat who saw God; Mr Thompson in the Attic; Mr Theobald's Devil; Wickham's Fancy; Collected Poems (with foreword by Siegfried Sassoon), 1953; various short stories. *Recreation:* conversation. *Address:* 15 Grantchester Street, Cambridge. [*Died* 29 *Jan.* 1957.

KEOWN-BOYD, Sir Alexander William, K.B.E., *cr.* 1936 (C.B.E. 1920; O.B.E. 1918); C.M.G. 1928; *b.* 19 June 1884; *e.s.* of late William Keown-Boyd, late of Ballydugan, Co. Down, and Isabella Campbell; *m.* 1st, 1911; Joan Mary (*d.* 1913), *d.* of late M. D. D. Dalison, 2nd, 1921, Joan Mary, M.B.E. 1944, *d.* of late John Croker Partridge; three *s.* *Educ.:* Merchant Taylors' School; St John's Coll., Oxford. Sudan Civil Service, 1907-16; Private Secretary to the High Commissioner for Egypt, 1917-19; Oriental Secretary to the High Commissioner for Egypt, 1919-22; Director-General Foreign Affairs, Egyptian Government, 1922; Director General, European Department, Ministry of the Interior, Egyptian Government till 1937; Grand Cordon Order of the Nile; Grand Officer Belgian Order of the Crown; Grand Officer Italian Order of the Crown; Order of the Phoenix (Greece). *Recreations:* shooting and fishing. *Address:* Pontrilas Court, Hereford; 5 Sharia Ayoub, Zamalek, Cairo. *Clubs:* St. James', White's. [*Died* 26 *Dec.* 1954.

KER, Major Allan Ebenezer, V.C., late The Gordon Highlanders; *e. s.* of Robert Darling Ker, Writer to Her Majesty's Signet. *Educ.:* Edinburgh Academy and University. V.C., St. Quentin, 21 March 1918, while attached to 61 Bn. Machine Gun Corps. [*Died* 12 *Sept.* 1958.

KER, Major Lord Robert E. I.; *see* Innes-Ker.

KERMODE, Rev. Sir Derwent William, K.C.M.G. 1952 (C.M.G. 1948); Rector of Cocking with Bepton, since 1959; *b.* 19 June 1898; *s.* of late Frederick Bishop Kermode, Eastbourne, Sx., and Florence Amy Isabel (*née* Marshall); *m.* 1925, Barbara Nell Thorn, Norwich, Norfolk; two *s.* two *d.* Served European War, 1914-18. Entered Consular Service, 1921; served at various posts in Asia; Ambassador at Djakarta, Indonesia, 1950-53; Ambassador to Czechoslovakia, 1953-55; Ordained deacon, 1956; priest, 1957. *Address:* The Rectory, Cocking, Midhurst, Sussex. *T.:* Midhurst 281. [*Died* 12 *Jan.* 1960.

KERR, Prof. Douglas James Acworth; Regius Professor of Forensic Medicine, University of Edinburgh, since 1953; Medical Referee and Principal Police Surgeon, Edinburgh Corporation; Medical Referee Edinburgh Crematorium Co.; Fellow Royal College of Physicians, Edinburgh; Representative on General Medical Council; *b.* 21 Aug. 1894; *s.* of late James Kerr; *m.* 1935, Phyllis M. McGregor; two *s.* one *d.* *Educ.:* St. Paul's School, London; Edinburgh University. R.F.A. attached R.F.C. 1914-18; M.B., Ch.B., Edinburgh, 1920; D.P.H. 1922; M.D. Commended, 1927; F.R.C.P. Edin. 1927; Alison Prize, Edin., 1922; F.R.S.Ed. 1944. *Publications:* Forensic Medicine, a textbook, 1935, 6th Edition, 1957; Papers on Toxicology and Legal Medicine. *Address:* 14 Rothesay Terrace, Edinburgh. *T.:* Caledonian 6923. [*Died* 23 *March* 1960.

KERR, Sir John Graham, Kt., *cr.* 1939; F.R.S. 1909; Hon. Fellow, Christ's College Cambridge; Hon. LL.D (Edin. 1935, (St. Andrews) 1950; *b.* 18 Sept. 1869; *s.* of late James Kerr, M.A., Principal of Hoogly Coll., Calcutta; *m.* 1st, 1903, Elizabeth Mary (*d.* 1934), *d.* of T. Kerr, W.S.; two *s.* one *d.*; 2nd, 1936, Isobel, *d.* of A. Dunn Macindoe, and *widow* of Alan E. Clapperton, LL.D. *Educ.:* Universities of Edinburgh and Cambridge. Spent two years in zoological explorations in South America, especially on the Pilcomayo River, 1889-91; made special expedition to the Gran Chaco to investigate the habits and life-history of South American Lungfish (Lepidosiren), 1896-97; Demonstrator in Animal Morphology in the University of Cambridge, 1897-1902; Regius Professor of Zoology, University of Glasgow, 1902-35; Walsingham Medallist, 1898; Fellow of Christ's College, Cambridge, 1898-1904; Neill Prize, Royal Society of Edinburgh, 1904; Pres. Royal Physical Soc., Edinburgh, 1906-9; originated and communicated to Admiralty in Sept. 1914 protective coloration of ships by countershading and strongly contrasting patches ('dazzle'); Council of Royal Society, 1920-22 and 1937-1938; Vice-President, 1938; Pres. Royal Philosophical Society of Glasgow, 1925-28; Vice-Chairman, 1926-27, Chairman, 1928-30, Glasgow Unionist Association; Convener Western Divisional Council Scottish Unionist Association, 1933-34; President Scottish Unionist Association, 1934-35; M.P. (Scottish Universities), 1935-50; Vice-President Zoological Society of London, 1943-46; Associate Royal Belgian Academy, 1946; Chairman Advisory Committee on Fishery Research, 1941-49. Linnean Gold Medal, 1955. *Publications:* various papers on zoological subjects: Primer of Zoology; Textbook of Embryology; Zoology for Medical Students; Evolution: An Introduction to Zoology; A Naturalist in the Gran Chaco. *Address:* Dalny Veed, Barley, Herts. *T.:* Barkway 243 *Club:* Athenæum. [*Died* 21 *April* 1957.

KERR, (John Martin) Munro, Hon. Fellow Royal College of Obstetricians and Gynæcologists; Hon. Fellow of the Royal Academy of Medicine in Ireland; Hon. Fellow Edinburgh Obstetrical Society; Hon. Fellow American Gynæcological Society; *b.* Glasgow, 5 Dec. 1868; *s.* of George Munro Kerr, shipowner, Glasgow; *m.* 1899 (wife *d.* 1957), *d.* of August Johanson, Gothenburg, Sweden; one *s.* three *d.* *Educ.:* Glasgow Acad.; Univs. of Glasgow and Berlin. M.B., C.M. 1890; M.D. 1908; F.R.F.P.S. (Glasg.), 1895; F.R.C.O.G.; LL.D.; formerly President of the Royal Faculty of Physicians and Surgeons, Glasgow; President (Obstetrical and Gynæcological Section Royal Society of Medicine; Obstetric Surgeon Glasgow Maternity Hospital; Muirhead Professor of Midwifery and Gynæcology, Glasgow University, 1911-27; Regius Professor of Midwifery, Glasgow University, 1927-34; Examiner in Universities of London, Edinburgh, Manchester and Liverpool; first Blair Bell Medallist, Roy. Soc. Med. 1950. *Publications:* Operative Obstetrics, 5th edition, 1949; Clinical and Operative Gynæcology, 1922; Maternal Mortality and Morbidity: A Study of their Problems, 1933. *Address:* 5A Ethelbert Road, Canterbury, Kent, *T.:* Canterbury 2723. [*Died* 7 *Oct.* 1960.

KERR, Robert Bird, M.A., LL.B.; Editor, Malthusian, 1949; *b.* East Lothian, 21 May 1867; *s.* of Rev. Samuel Kerr and Margaret Bird; *m.* 1895, Dora (*d.* 1935), *d.* of Rev. H. B. Forster. *Educ.:* Craigmount, Edinburgh; Edinburgh, Bonn, and Berlin Universities. Advocate, Scottish Bar, 1891; practised in British Columbia as Barrister and Solicitor, 1893-1921. *Publications:* Is Britain Overpopulated?, 1927; Our Prophets, 1932. *Recreations:* chess, walking. *Address:* 335 Sydenham Road, Croydon. [*Died* 23 *April* 1951.

KERR, Sir Russell James, Kt., *cr.* 1934; D.L., J.P. Glos; *b.* 23 Jan. 1863; *e. s.* of Russell J. Kerr and R. M. A. Griffiths; *m.* 1888, Miriam M. (*d.* 1931), *e. d.* of J. R. Pine-Coffin of Portledge, Devon; two *d.* *Educ.:* Eton; Christ Church, Oxford. Barrister-at-law, Inner Temple, 1887; Hon. Major 3rd Bn. Glos. Regt.; Hon. Lt.-Col. in the Army since 1917. *Address:* Hill House, Newnham-on-Severn, Gloucestershire. [*Died* 13 *May* 1952.

KERR, Sir William, Kt., *cr.* 1954; C.B.E. 1944; D.L. 1949; J.P.; Town Clerk of Glasgow since 1939; Civil Defence Controller for Glasgow; Hon. Secretary, Glasgow Local

Savings Cttee.; *b.* 1895; *s.* of late James and late Margaret Loudon Kerr; *m.* 1922, Katherine Cameron, *d.* of late Matthew Marshall; one *s.* one *d.* *Educ.:* Queen's Park School; University of Glasgow. Solicitor, Certificated Practitioner in City of Glasgow; Mem. Roy. Faculty of Procurators in Glasgow; Served European War, 1914-18, Black Watch; served War of 1939-45, Civil Defence Controller, Glasgow; formerly Deacon, Incorporation of Bonnetmakers and Dyers; member of various government cttees. *Address:* City Chambers, Glasgow. *T.:* Central 9600; Broomwood, 17 Broompark Drive, Newton Mearns, Renfrewshire. *Club:* Royal Automobile. [*Died* 21 *Aug.* 1959.

KERR, Admiral Sir William Munro, K.B.E., *cr.* 1935 (C.B.E. 1920); C.B. 1929; *b.* 4 March 1876; 2nd *s.* of George Munro Kerr, Shipowner, Glasgow; *m.* 1907, Madeline Beatrice, *d.* of Albert Addison, Southsea; one *s.* Entered Britannia, 1890; served in Mediterranean, Australia, West Indies, Atlantic and Home Fleets; served European War, 1914-18, and post-war operations in Baltic and Black Sea, 1918-19 (C.B.E., Order of St. Vladimir 4th class); commanded H.M.S. Caradoc, 1917-19; Acting Consul-General, Odessa, 1919; Captain of Dockyard and King's Harbourmaster, Rosyth, 1921-23; Senior Officer Reserve Fleet, The Nore, 1924-25; commanded Aircraft Carrier Eagle, 1925-26; A.D.C. to the King, 1926; Rear-Admiral, 1927; Rear-Admiral 1st Battle Squadron Mediterranean, 1928-29; First Naval Member of Royal Australian Naval Board, 1929-31; Vice-Admiral, 1931; Vice-Admiral commanding Reserve Fleet, 1932-34; Admiral, 1936; retired list, 1936. *Address:* Afon Lodge, Lymington, Hants. [*Died* 26 *Oct.* 1959.

KERR, Rt. Rev. William Shaw, D.D.; Bishop of Down and Dromore, 1944-55, retd.; *b.* 1873; *s.* of James Heron Kerr, J.P., and Rose Shaw; *m.* Amy, *d.* of Thomas Smith, J.P., London; one *s.* three *d.* *Educ.:* privately; Dublin University. Archbishop King Prizeman, Bishop Forster Prizeman, Ecl. History Prizeman, Elrington Prizeman, 1st Theological Exhibitioner. Rector of Banbridge, 1916-32; Archdeacon of Dromore, 1929-32; Vicar of Belfast and Dean of St Anne's Cathedral, 1932-45. *Publications:* Memoir of Rev. Andrew Boyd, M.A.; The Independence of the Celtic Church in Ireland; History of Banbridge; Walker of Derry; Who Persecuted?; A Handbook on the Papacy. *Recreations:* fishing, controversy. *Address:* 76 Sandown Rd., Belfast. [*Died* 2 *Feb.* 1960.

KETCHEN, Major-General Huntly Douglas Brodie, C.B. 1918; C.M.G. 1917; late General Officer Commanding Military District No. 10 Canadian Local Forces; Member Legislative Assembly Province of Manitoba, as Conservative Member for City of Winnipeg since 1932; *b.* 1872; *s.* of Maj. James Ketchen, Indian Army; *m.* 1895, Margaret Elizabeth, *d.* of James Robinson, Listowel, Ontario; three *s.* Served South African War, 1901 (Queen's medal three clasps); European War, 1914-18 (despatches, C.M.G., C.B., 1914-15 Star, General Service and Victory medals, Legion of Honour, Belgian Croix de Guerre); Hon. Comdt. Corps of Imperial Frontiersmen, Canada, 1943; Member Grand Council Legion of Frontiersmen, London, Eng., 1943; Hon. President, Winnipeg Jockey Club, since 1925; Hon. President of Manitoba Command, Canadian Legion B.E.S.L. since 1920; President, Manitoba Provincial Rifle Association; Vice-President, Dominion of Canada Rifle Association (representing Manitoba); Hon. Pres. Manitoba Conservative Assoc.; Pres. Gold Shore Mines Ltd.; Coronation Medal, 1911; Jubilee Medal, 1935; Coronation Medal, 1937. *Address:* 1301 Wellington Crescent, Winnipeg, Canada. [*Died* 1959.

KETHLEY, Andrew H. V. P.; *see* Pitt-Kethley.

KETTERING, Charles Franklin; engineer and research consultant, U.S.; retired; Director, General Motors Corporation and of various other corporations and companies; Chairman Board of Trustees, Charles F. Kettering Foundation; Pres. Thomas A. Edison Foundation; Hon. Chm. The Winters National Bank and Trust Co.; Director National Geographic Society and Flexible Co.; *b.* 29 Aug. 1876; *s.* of Jacob Kettering and Martha Hunter; *m.* 1905, Olive Williams (*d.* 1946); one *s.* *Educ.:* Ohio State University, Columbus. Electrical designer, Nat. Cash Register Co.; designed first electric cash register, 1904; organised (with E. A. Deeds) the Dayton Engineering Laboratories Co. (Delco) and invented Delco battery ignition system for automobiles, 1907; invented electric self-starting lighting and ignition system for automobiles, 1911; organised Dayton Wright Airplane Co., 1917; Pres. Gen. Motors Research Corp., 1920; developed (with Thomas Midgley, jun.) tetraethyl lead anti-knock for gasoline, 1921; in charge of devel. of high-speed two-cycle engine with uni-flow scavenging and unit injector, 1932; in charge of devel. of first commercial process for producing triptane 2-2-3 trimethylbutane, 1941. Member several clubs and associations. Has very numerous hon. degrees from Colleges and Universities. *Publications:* author of numerous technical and semi-technical articles in various magazines. *Address:* Ridgeleigh Terrace, Dayton, Ohio, U.S.A. [*Died* 25 *Nov.* 1958.

KEYS, Rear-Adm. (S) John Anthony, C.B. 1917; *b.* 24 Dec. 1863; *s.* of Henry Gamble Keys; *m.* 1902, Agnes Aston (*d.* 1954), *d.* of late Thomas Brown of Ardmore, Campbeltown, Argyllshire; one *s.* one *d.* Joined R.N., 1880; Clerk of Thalia during Egyptian War, 1882 (medal, bronze star); Naval Sec. to Admiral Lord Charles Beresford, G.C.B., 1900-9, when in command of Mediterranean, Atlantic, and Channel Fleets respectively; Fleet Paymaster of H.M.S. Erin, Grand Fleet, 1914-17; present at Battle of Jutland (despatches); retired list, 1921; King Edward VII Coronation Medal; Russian Order of St. Stanislas, 2nd class with swords, 1917. *Address:* Ardmore, Shortheath, Farnham, Surrey. [*Died* 25 *Jan.* 1955.

KEYSER, Lionel Edward; *b.* 23 Oct. 1878. *Educ.:* Uppingham; Caius College, Cambridge (B.A.). Student Interpreter, China, 1902-4; Vice-Consul, Boston, 1906; Caracas, 1907; Beira, 1908; Consul, Bucarest, 1920; Consul-General, Zürich, 1924; Rotterdam, 1930; Quito, 1933-34; Marseilles, 1934-37. [*Died* 18 *Oct.* 1955.

KHALIL, Mohammed Bey, M.D. (Egypt), Ph.D. (London), M.D. (Brussels), M.R.C.P. (Lond.), D.P.H. (Oxon.), D.T.M. & H. (Eng.); Under-Secretary of State, Ministry of Health, Egypt, 1950; *b.* 23 May 1895; *s.* of Khalil Eff. Abdel Khalik; *m.* 1935, (Sit) Farida Hamdy; two *s.* one *d.* *Educ.:* Cairo; England; and Belgium. Cairo School of Medicine, 1913-1918 (Golden Sultan's Gift); Clinical Assistant at the Kasr-el-Aini Hospital, 1918; House Surgeon for one year; the Egyptian Government sent him to England to specialise in Tropical Medicine at the London School of Tropical Medicine, 1920; Sub-Director of the Parasitic Diseases Research Department of the Public Health Laboratories, 1922-25; lecturer for Parasitology at the Cairo School of Medicine, 1924-25; External Professor of Veterinary Parasitology at the School of Veterinary Medicine, Cairo, since 1924; Professor of Parasitology, Faculty of Medicine, Cairo, 1925, and Director, Research Institute and Endemic Diseases Hospital, P.H.D., Cairo, 1932; Controller-General of Endemic Diseases, Min. of Public Health, 1939; Member of the Medical Research Committee for the investigation of Ankylostomiasis in the Cornish Mine, 1920; Member of the

Filariasis Expedition of the Colonial Office for the West Indies, 1922. Recipient of several Egyptian and foreign Decorations. *Publications:* The Bibliography of Schistosomiasis (Bilharziosis), 1931; The Specific Treatment of Human Schistosomiasis (Bilharziosis), 1931; Dermal Leishmaniasis, a study of an endemic focus in Egypt, 1934. *Address:* Ministry of Public Health, Cairo, Egypt. *T.:* 190 Maadi. [*Died* 7 *Oct.* 1950.

[*But death not notified in time for inclusion in Who Was Who 1941–1950, first edn.*

KHAN, Ghaanfar Ali, C.I.E. 1932; O.B.E. 1918; B.A. (Cantab.); *b.* March 1875; unmarried. *Educ.:* Calcutta Madrasa; Presidency College, Calcutta; University College, London; Christ's College, Cambridge. Entered Indian Civil Service, 1899; Deputy-Commissioner, 1915; Commissioner, 1926; Member of Legislative Assembly, Sept. 1928-Sept. 1929; Commissioner, Nagpur Division, 1929-33; retd., 1934. *Address:* Birahimpore, Sylhet, East Pakistan. [*Died April* 1959.

KHAN, Liaquat Ali, (Hon.); Prime Minister, Pakistan, since 1947; *b.* 1 Oct. 1895; *s.* of late Ruknuddaullah, Shamsher Jang, Nawab Rustam Ali Khan; *m.* 1933, Raana Begum; two *s.* *Educ.:* M.A.O. College, Aligarh; Allahabad University; Exeter College, Oxford; Inner Temple, London. Joined Muslim League, 1923; Advocate of Punjab High Court, 1922- ; Member U.P. Legislative Council, 1926-40; Member Central Legislative Assembly, 1940-47; Dep. Pres. U.P. Legislative Council, 1931-36; Member Indo-British Trade Deleg., London, 1937; Hon. Gen. Sec. All-India Muslim League, 1936-47; Dep. Leader Muslim League Party in Central Legislature of United India, 1941-47; Member Court and Executive Council, Muslim Univ., Aligarh, 1941-46; Chairman of Central Parliamentary Board, All-India Muslim League; Rep. of Muslim League, Simla Conf., 1945, 1946 convened by Viceroy for settlement of Indian Question; Member Viceroy's Exec. Council, 1946; held portfolio of Finance, 1946-47; Member on behalf of Muslim League of London Conf., Dec. 1946, called by H.M. Govt. regarding grant of Independence to India; appointed member of Partition Council to represent future Government of Pakistan. *Recreation:* tennis. *Address:* 10 Victoria Road, Karachi, Pakistan. *T.:* (Office) 5420. [*Died* 16 *Oct.* 1951.

KHER, Shri Bal Gangadhar, B.A., LL.B.; High Commissioner for India in London, 1952-54; also Indian Ambassador to the Republic of Eire, 1952-54; *b.* 24 August 1888; *s.* of G. S. Kher and Yamuna Bai Kher. *Educ.:* Wilson College. Vurjeewandas Sanskrit Scholar, Bhawoo Daji Prizeman, Dakshina Fellow. Enrolled as Vakil, 1912; partner, Manilal, Kher Ambalal & Co., Solicitors. Formerly Director, Bombay Mutual Life Assurance Soc. Ltd.; Founder Bombay Legal Aid Society. Active in politics from 1922; Sec. Swaraj Party, etc.; Imprisoned for political reasons several times from 1930. Prime Minister, 1937-39; M.L.A. Bombay (Univ. constituency); Leader, Bombay Legislative Congress Party, 1946; Member, Constituent Assembly, 1946-50. Chief Minister, Bombay, 1946-52. Elected to the Council of States, 1952. Chairman, Official Language, Commission, 1955-56; Chairman Gandhi Memorial Trust, 1956. *Address:* Alaka, 14th Road, Khar, Bombay 21, India. [*Died* 8 *March* 1957.

KIDD, Beatrice Ethel; President of the British Union for Abolition of Vivisection; *b.* Bangor Isycoed, North Wales, 12 Oct. 1867; *d.* of John Howard Kidd. *Educ.:* Brighton; Germany. For 25 years engaged in Secretarial work for the Anti-Vivisection cause at the urgent request of Miss Frances Power Cobbe, foundress of the movement; has debated with leading physiologists and medical experts; previous years spent in tutorial work. *Publications:* Hadwen of Gloucester (with M. E. Richards); The Cassowary, a novel under the pseudonym Mark Winterton; articles in the Nineteenth Century and After and other Magazines, innumerable Anti-Vivisection pamphlets and contributions to The Abolitionist, the organ of the British Union. *Recreations:* country walks, reading. *Address:* Hoe Cottage, Peaslake, Surrey. *T.:* Abinger 187. [*Died* 26 *June* 1958.

KIDD, Rt. Rev. John Thomas, D.D., LL.D.; Bishop of London, Ont. (R.C.), since 1931; *b.* Athlone, Ont., 28 Aug. 1868. *Educ.:* Common School; De La Salle High School; St. Michael's College, Toronto; Propaganda and Gregorian Universities, Rome. Priest, 1902; returning to native diocese of Toronto, was appointed Assistant, Pastor, Episcopal Secretary and Chancellor, Administrator of Diocese during vacancy of the See, 1911-12; President of St. Augustine's Seminary, Toronto, 1913; Bishop of Calgary, 1925-31; LL.D. (Hon.) University of Ottawa, 1923; University of Western Ontario, 1934. *Address:* 90 Central Ave., London, Ontario, Canada. [*Died* 2 *June* 1950.

[*But death not notified in time for inclusion in Who Was Who 1941–1950, first edn.*

KIDSTON, George Jardine, C.M.G. 1918; *b.* 1873; *m.* 1911, Lilian Frances (*d.* 1953), *d.* of Sir G.F. Bonham, 2nd Bart.; one *s.* four *d.* Served Diplomatic Service, 1898-1921; Envoy Extraordinary and Minister Plenipotentiary to the Republic of Finland, 1920-21; retired, 1921; Sheriff of Wiltshire, 1936. *Publication:* A History of the Manor of Hazelbury, 1936. *Address:* Hazelbury Manor, Box, Wilts. [*Died* 26 *Dec.* 1954.

KIEK, Rev. Edward S., M.A., D.D.; Principal of Parkin Congregational College, Adelaide, 1920-57, now Emeritus; *b.* London, 1883; *s.* of late Sidney Kiek, Bookseller; *m.* 1911, Winifred Jackson (B.A. Manchester, M.A. Adelaide, B.D. Melbourne, now ordained Congregational Minister, author of Child Nature and Child Nurture); two *s.* one *d.* *Educ.:* Central Foundation School, London; Wadham and Mansfield Colleges, Oxford. B.A. First Class Honours Modern History, Second Class Honours Theology; B.D. (Lond.); M.A. (Oxon); B.D. Second Cl. Hons. in Biblical Theology; D.D. (Melb.); Minister of Newcastle-under-Lyme Congregational Church, 1909-13; Minister of Square Church, Halifax, 1913-20; served in France, European War, Y.M.C.A., and War Office Education Scheme (Lecturer in History); W.E.A. Lecturer in History and Political Science, 1921-39; temporary Lecturer in History and Political Science (Adelaide University), 1925-26; Examiner for B.D. (Melbourne) since 1924; Member of Public Libraries Board of South Australia, 1940-57; Pres. of S. Australia Council of Churches, 1927-28 and 1948-49; Pres. Sociological Society, 1920-57; Pres. of S. A. Congregational Union, 1929-30, 1950-51; Pres. of Congregational Union of Australia and N.Z., 1946-48; Vice-Pres. of Australian Institute of Sociology, 1942; President Federal Union Movement in S.A., 1943; Australian Army Education Service Lecturer; 1943-46; Livingstone Lecturer, Sydney, 1943; Bevan Memorial Lecturer, Adelaide, 1944. Chm. of U.N.R.R.A. Regional Cttee., S.A., 1946-48; Pres. of S.A. United Churches Social Reform Bd., 1946-57; Vice-Pres. World Council of Churches (Australia), 1947-49; Pres. S.A. Cttee. of the Council, 1954-56. Actg. Minister S. Brisbane Congregational Church, 1957-58. *Publications:* Sin and Forgiveness; Biblical Criticism; Modernism and Fundamentalism; The Modern Religious Situation; An Apostle in Australia; The Christian Ethic of Sex; The Battle of Faith; Group Psychology and the Contemporary Situation, 1943; The International Jungle and the Way Out, 1944; The New Psychology and the Old Faith, 1944; Congregationalism Then and Now, 1947; Lactantius, 1950; Centenary History of S. A. Congregational Union, 1950. *Recreations:* Freemasonry, journalism. *Address:* Box 1207 K., G.P.O., Adelaide, S. Australia. [*Died* 24 *April* 1959.

KIELBERG, Sir Michael; *see* Kroyer-Kielberg, Sir F. M.

KIERKELS, Most Rev. Archbishop Leo Peter; Consultor of the S. Congregation of Extraordinary Ecclesiastical Affairs, since 1953; *b.* Baexem, Holland, 12 Dec. 1882; *s.* of Lawrence Kierkels and Catherine Ronckers. *Educ.:* Tournai, Belgium; Rome, Italy. Entered in Passionist Order, 1898, ordained priest, 1906; Secretary General of Passionist Order, 1915-20; Procurator Gen., 1920-25; Superior General, 1925-31; Titular Archbishop of Salamis and Apostolic Delegate in India, 1931-48; Papal Internuncio in Delhi, 1948-52. Commander, Order of Orange-Nassau (Holland), 1947. *Address:* Piazza SS. Giovanni e Paolo, 13, Rome. [*Died* 7 *Nov.* 1957.

KIGGELL, Lieut.-Gen. Sir Launcelot Edward, K.C.B., *cr.* 1916 (C.B. 1908); K.C.M.G., *cr.* 1918; LL.D. (Hon.) St. Andrews; *b.* Wilton House, Ballingarry, Co. Limerick, 2 Oct. 1862; *s.* of Launcelot John Kiggell, J.P., and Meliora Emily, *d.* of Edward Brown; *m.* 1888, Eleanor Rose (*d.* 1948), *d.* of Colonel Spencer Field; three *s.* *Educ.:* Ireland; R.M.C., Sandhurst. Entered Royal Warwickshire Regt., 1882; Adjutant of 2nd Battalion, 1886-90; p.s.c., 1893-94; Instructor R.M.C., 1895-97; D.A.A.G. South Eastern District, 1897-99; served S.A. War, 1899, until peace declared; first on Sir R. Buller's Staff until he went home; then on H.Q. Staff, Pretoria, for 6 months; A.A.G. Harrismith District until end of War; A.A.G. Natal (despatches, brevet Lieut.-Col., Queen's medal 6 clasps, King's medal 2 clasps); D.A.A.G., Staff College, 1904-7; G.S.O., Army H.Q., 1907-9; Brig.-Gen. i/c Administration, Scottish Command, 1909; Director of Staff Duties, War Office, 1909-13; Commandant Staff College, Camberley, 1913-14; Director of Home Defence, War Office. 1914-1915; Chief of General Staff to British Armies in France, Dec. 1915-Jan. 1918 (prom. Lt.-Gen., 1917); G.O.C. and Lt.-Gov., Guernsey, 1918-20; retired 1920; Legion of Honour (Grand Officier); Belgian Order of the Crown (Grand Cordon); Italian Order of St. Michael and St. Lazarus (Grand Officier); Obilitch gold medal and Order of Danilo, 1st Class, Montenegro, 1917; Japanese Order of the Sacred Treasure (Grand Cordon). *Publication:* Revised Sir E. Hamley's Operations of War for 6th edition. *Address:* Camas, Croutel Road, Felixstowe. [*Died* 23 *Feb.* 1954.

KILEY, James Daniel; *b.* 1865. M.P. (L.), Tower Hamlets (Whitechapel), 1916-22; former Mayor of the Metropolitan Borough of Stepney. *Address:* 40 Broadwater Down, Tunbridge Wells, Kent. *Clubs:* National Liberal, Royal Automobile. [*Died* 12 *Sept.* 1953.

KILKELLY, Surg.-Lt.-Col. Charles Randolph, C.M.G. 1900; M.V.O.; J.P. (Hants and Co. Galway); late Grenadier Guards; late House Governor and Medical Superintendent Officers' Convalescent Home, Osborne; *b.* 7 Apr. 1861; *s.* of late Surgeon-General C. E. Kilkelly, F.R.C.S., of Drimcong, Co. Galway; *m.* 1893, Florence Petre, *d.* of late Hon. Henry William Petre; (two *s.*, both killed in action Germany) one *d.* *Educ.:* Downside College; Trinity College, Dublin; Vienna Allgemein Krankenhaus. M.B., B.Ch., University of Dublin, D.P.H. (Lond.); Surgical Travelling Prizeman; Gold Medallist Nat. Sci. Univ. Dub.; Personal Staff Field-Marshal H.R.H. the Duke of Connaught in India; Egyptian Campaign, 1898 (despatches, 2 medals and clasp); South African War (despatches, 2 medals 3 clasps, C.M.G.), 1899-1902; European War, 1914-18; Principal Med. Officer, Portland and Imperial Yeomanry Hospitals, Transvaal. *Publications:* Trans. Antiseptic System in Bilroth's Clinic; Report I.Y. Hospitals, S. Africa. *Address.* Menengai, Kenya. *Clubs:* Royal Automobile; University (Dublin). [*Died* 14 *July* 1953.

KILLICK, Esther Margaret; (Mrs. Huggett); Sophia Jex-Blake Professor of Physiology in the University of London, Royal Free Hospital School of Medicine since 1941; *b.* 3 May 1902; *d.* of Dr. Arthur Killick; *m.* 1938, A. St. G. Huggett, D.Sc., F.R.S.; two *d.* *Educ.:* Leeds Girls' High Sch.; Univ. of Leeds. Physiological Investigator to Safety in Mines Research Board (attached to Department of Physiology, Univ. of Leeds), 1929; Lecturer in Industrial Medicine and Hygiene, Univ. of Birmingham, 1935; Lecturer in Applied Physiology, London School of Hygiene and Tropical Medicine, 1939. *Publications:* Scientific papers in Journal of Physiology, Journal of Hygiene, etc. *Recreation:* gardening. *Address:* 31 Mapesbury Road, N.W.2. *T.:* Gladstone 5328. [*Died* 31 *May* 1960.

KILLICK, John Spencer, C.B.E. 1920; M.Inst.C.E.; *b.* 8 Sept. 1878; *m.* Lizzie Sheldon, *d.* of late Sir Henry Maybury, G.B.E., K.C.M.G., C.B.; one *s.* three *d.* *Educ.:* Cranleigh. *Address:* 34 Ennismore Gardens, S.W.7. *Clubs:* Arts, Constitutional. [*Died* 8 *Dec.* 1952.

KILNER, Major Sir Hew Ross, Kt. *cr.* 1947; M.C. 1918; *b.* 9 Sept. 1892; *s.* of Col. Charles Harold Kilner, D.S.O., R.A. and Helen MacGregor; *m.* 1919, Elizabeth, *d.* of John Harmstone Coulson; one *d.* *Educ.:* Cheltenham College; R.M.A., Woolwich. Commissioned R.A. 1911; served in France, European War, 1914-19 (M.C.). Instructor of Gunnery, 1919-23. Staff Captain, War Office, 1923-27; p.a.c. Military College of Science, 1929; retired, 1930; Director of Vickers-Armstrongs, 1936-53; Director of Vickers Ltd. 1945-53; Pres. of Soc. Brit. Aircraft Constructors, 1943-45. *Recreations:* fishing, golf. *Address:* Harwood, St. Georges Hill, Weybridge, Surrey. *T.:* Byfleet 3029. *Club:* Army and Navy. [*Died* 2 *Aug.* 1953.

KILPATRICK, Sir James (MacConnell), Air Marshal (Ret.), K.B.E. 1953 (O.B.E. 1946); C.B. 1952; Dean of London School of Hygiene and Tropical Medicine since 1957; *b.* 1 March 1902; *s.* of James Kilpatrick, Belfast; *m.* 1928, Marjorie, *d.* of Charles Drean, Belfast; two *s.* *Educ.:* Sullivan Upper School, Holywood; Royal Belfast Academical Institution; Queen's University, Belfast. Joined R.A.F. (medical Branch), 1925. Served War of 1939-45 in U.K. and West Africa. Director of Hygiene and Research, Air Ministry, 1947-49; Deputy Director-General, Medical Services, 1950; Principal Medical Officer, Middle East Air Forces, 1951; Director-General, Medical Services, R.A.F., 1951-57; Q.H.P. 1952-57. Hon. Physician to King George VI, 1951-52. Hon. LL.D. (Belfast), 1957. *Address:* Kynance, Upper Warlingham, Surrey. *T.:* Upper Warlingham 66. [*Died* 4 *April* 1960.

KIMBER, Lieut.-Col. Edmund Gibbs, C.B.E. 1919; D.S.O. 1915; T.D.; late 13th (County of London) Princess Louise's Kensington Battalion, The London Regt., Territorial Force; *b.* 6 Aug. 1870; *s.* of late Edmund Kimber, Shooter's Hill; *m.* 1913, Maud, *d.* of W. B. Wilson. *Educ.:* University College, London. Barrister, Lincoln's Inn and Middle Temple, South Eastern Circuit, Surrey, and South London Sessions; served European War, 1914-17 (despatches 4 times, D.S.O.); Prosecutor and Judge-Advocate Courts-Martial Irish Rebellion, 1916; Staff Captain, War Office, 1917; D.A.A.G. War Office, 1918; A.A.G. War Office, 1919. *Address:* 6 Yale Court, Honeybourne Road, W. Hampstead, N.W.6. [*Died* 23 *July* 1954.

KIMMINS, Dame Grace (Thyrza), D.B.E., *cr.* 1950 (C.B.E. 1927); D.St.J.; Founder and Hon. Secretary, Heritage Craft Schools and Hospitals for Cripples, Chailey, Sussex; The Guild of the Brave Poor Things; Guild of Play; *d.* of James and Thyrza Hannam; *m.* 1897, Dr. Charles William Kimmins (*d.* 1948); two *s.* *Educ.:* Wilton House School; abroad. Whole life since leaving school spent in work for cripples and poor children. *Publications:* Polly of Parker's Rents; Series of Guild of Play Books; pamphlets, etc. *Recreations:* reading, walking. *Address:* The Old Heritage, Chailey, Sussex. *T.:* Newick 111. *T.A.:* Kimmins, Chailey. *Clubs:* English-Speaking Union, Overseas.
[*Died* 3 *March* 1954.

KINANE, Most Rev. Jeremiah, D.D., D.C.L.; Archbishop of Cashel, (R.C.), since 1946; *b.* Upperchurch, Thurles, 1884. *Educ.:* St. Patrick's College, Thurles; Maynooth Coll.; Sant' Apollinare Univ., Rome. Priest, 1910; Professor of Canon Law at Maynooth, 1911-33; R.C. Bishop of Waterford, 1933-1942; Titular Archbishop of Dercos, and co-adjutor Archbishop of Cashel, 1942-46. *Address:* Archbishop's House, Thurles, Co. Tipperary, Ireland. [*Died* 21 *Feb.* 1959.

KINCAID, Charles Augustus, C.V.O. 1911; Officier d'Instruction Publique, 1923; Medallist Revue des deux Mondes, 1937; *b.* 8 Feb. 1870; *s.* of General Kincaid (*d.* 1909); *m.* 1904, Katherine Seddon; one *d.* (two *s.* decd.). *Educ.:* Sherborne School; Balliol College, Oxford. Passed I.C.S. examination, 1889; came out to India, 1891; served as Assistant-Collector in Sind, 1891-94; Assistant Judge, Satara, 1896-98; Judicial Assistant in Kathiawar, 1898-1905; agent for Sardars in the Deccan, 1905-9; political Secretary, 1910; agent for Sardars in the Deccan, 1914; Member of Viceroy's Council, 1917; Judicial Commissioner of Sind, 1920; Acting Judge of the Bombay High Court, 1921; Judicial Commissioner of Sind, 1925; retired, 1926; Vice-Consul at Cherbourg, 1927-31; Consul at Berne, 1931-33; Vice-Consul at St. Malo, 1934-35; *Publications:* Outlaws of Kathiawar, The Tale of a Tulsi Plant; Deccan Nursery Tales, 1914; The Indian Heroes, 1915; Ishtur Phakde, 1917; Tales from the Indian Epics, History of the Maratha People, 1918; Tales of the Saints of Pandharpur, 1919; Shri Krishna and Other Stories, 1920; Tales of King Vikrama, 1921; Tales of Old Sind; The Anchorite, 1922; Tales from the Indian Drama, 1923; Folk Tales of Sind and Gujarat, 1924; Teachers of India, 1927; Successors of Alexander, 1929; Cherbourg and the Colentin; Our Hindu Friends, 1930; The Land of Ranji and Duleep, 1931; Tales of a Throne, 1932; Indian Lions, 1933; Forty-Four Years a Public Servant, 1934; A verse translation of Ovid's Heroides, 1937; Indian Cavaliers, 1937; Indian Christmas Stories, 1939; Heroines of India, 1941; Hindu Gods; Our Parsi Friends, 1942; Shivaji, 1946; Laxmibai Rani of Jhansi, 1946. (Joint) A History of the Maratha People, 1925; a life of Shivaji. *Recreation:* watching cricket. *Address:* c/o Grindlay's Bank Ltd., Parliament Street, S.W.1. *Club:* East India and Sports.
[*Died* 15 *Aug.* 1954.

KINDERSLEY, 1st Baron, *cr.* 1941, of West Hoathly; **Robert Molesworth Kindersley,** G.B.E., *cr.* 1920 (K.B.E., *cr.* 1917); Officer of the Legion of Honour; Commander of the Order of Leopold; Grand Cross of the Order of Leopold II; Grand Cross of the Order of the Crown (Belgium); Grand Cross of the Crown of Italy; a Director of the Bank of England, 1914-46; Governor Hudson's Bay Company, 1916-25; Lieutenant City of London; Member of Court of Fishmongers Co.; Pres. National Savings Cttee., 1920-46; Chairman Trade Facilities Act Advisory Committee, 1921-25; Member of the Bankers' Committee on German Finance, 1922; Senior British representative on the Dawes Committee, 1924; High Sheriff, Sussex, 1928-29; *b.* 21 Nov. 1871; *s.* of Captain E. N. M. Kindersley and Ada Good; *m.* 1896, Gladys Margaret, *d.* of Maj.-Gen. J. P. Beadle, R.E., of 6 Queen's Gate Gardens, S.W.; two *s.* two *d.* *Educ.:* Repton. *Heir:* *s.* Brig. Hon. Hugh K. M. Kindersley, C.B.E., M.C. *Address:* Plaw Hatch Hall, Sharpthorne, Sussex. *Club:* Carlton.
[*Died* 20 *July* 1954.

KINDERSLEY, Lieut.-Col. Archibald Ogilvie Lyttelton, C.M.G. 1919; D.L.; late commanding 3rd Batt. The Highland Light Infantry; retired, 1924; Army Recruiting Officer for the Isle of Wight September 1939; *b.* 1869; *e. s.* of late Capt. H. W. S. Kindersley, late 29th and 99th Regts., of Tranmere, Lymington; *m.* 1st, 1908, Edith (*d.* 1936), *d.* of T. Craven, J.P., of Kirklington Hall, Notts; two *s.* one *d.*; 2nd, 1937, Hon. Emily Seely, *e. d.* of 1st Baron Mottistone, P.C., C.B. Served in W. Africa Brass River Expedition, 1895; S. African War, 1900-2; Hon. Attaché British Embassy, Tokio, Japan, 1911-13; served European War, 1914-19, Salonika, 1916-19; Commanded 1st Garr. Batt. Seaforth Highlanders and 11th (Service) Batt. Cameronians (despatches thrice, C.M.G., Ordre de l'Étoile Noire, France); County President of the Isle of Wight Boy Scouts Association. *Recreation:* yachting. *Address:* Hamstead Grange, nr. Yarmouth, Isle of Wight. *T.:* Yarmouth 230. *Clubs:* Royal Cruising; Royal Lymington Yacht (Lymington); Royal Solent Yacht (Yarmouth); Island Sailing (Cowes). [*Died* 19 *June* 1955.

KINDERSLEY, Major Guy (Molesworth), O.B.E. 1918; partner in Montagu, Loebl Stanley & Co., Stockbrokers; *s.* of late Captain E. N. M. Kindersley, Wanstead, Essex; *b.* 28 Feb. 1877; *m.* 1903, Kathleen (*d.* 1950), *e. d.* of late Sir Edmund Harry Elton, 8th Bt., Clevedon Court, Somerset; two *s.* two *d.* *Educ.:* Marlborough. Clerk in Lord Chancellor's office; afterwards Secretary to the Registrar H.M. Office of Land Registry; called to Bar at Lincoln's Inn; retired from Civil Service and became member of the London Stock Exchange; M.P. (C.) Hitchin Division of Herts, 1923-31; J.P. (Herts); Director of Clerical, Medical, and General Life Assurance Society; General Reversionary and Investment Co.; Trust Houses, Ltd.; Walker and Homfrays, Ltd. (Chairman); Manchester Brewery, Ltd. (Chairman); Eyre and Spottiswoode (Publishers) Ltd.; Wilson & Walker Breweries Ltd. (Dep. Chm.); served in European War as Inspector of Q.M.G.'s Services, France, 1917-18 (despatches twice, O.B.E.); retired with rank of Major. *Publication:* Work on Land Registration. *Recreations:* golf, fishing, lawn tennis. *Address:* Flat 4, 10 Berkeley Street, Piccadilly, W.1. *T.:* Mayfair 9849. *Clubs:* Athenæum, Carlton, City of London.
[*Died* 30 *Nov.* 1956.

KING, Alfred Hazell, C.B.E. 1952; Counsellor and Consul-General, Buenos Aires, since 1952; *b.* 21 Apr. 1896; *s.* of late F. H. King, Winchester; *m.* 1925, Mary Eileen, *d.* of late Dr. J. H. Lowry, Chinese Customs Service; two *s.* one *d.* *Educ.:* Peter Symonds' School, Winchester; Emmanuel College, Cambridge. Levant Consular Service, 1920; Probationer at Athens, Durazzo, and Corfu, 1921-24; Vice-Consul at Salonica, 1924; Acting Consul-General there July-Nov. 1925, and in 1927, 1928, and 1929; transferred to Casablanca, 1929; Fez, 1930; Consul at Cairo, 1934; Actg. Consul-Gen. in each year, 1934-38. Actg. Consul, Shiraz, 1938, Consul 1939, Ahwaz, 1940; Iskenderun (Alexandretta); 1942 (local rank Consul-Gen.); Paris, 1944; Salonica, 1945 (actg. Consul-Gen.); seconded to C.C.G. and appointed Consul-General for British Zone of Germany, 1945; Counsellor and Consul-General, Cairo, 1948. *Recreations:* walking, shooting, golf. *Address:*

British Embassy, Buenos Aires. *Club:* Royal Automobile. [*Died* 18 *June* 1956.

KING, Sir Carleton (Moss), Kt., *cr.* 1935; C.I.E. 1926; *b.* 17 July 1878; *s.* of late Robert Moss King, I.C.S., J.P., D.L., of Ashcott Hill, Somerset; *m.* 1909, Fanny Helen, *d.* of late A. W. Cruickshank, C.S.I., I.C.S., of Brooklands, Crowborough; three *d.* *Educ.:* Brighton College; Balliol College, Oxford. Joined Indian Civil Service, 1902; Legal Remembrancer and Judicial Secretary to United Provinces Government, 1921; Puisne Judge of the High Court, Allahabad, 1929-34; Chief Judge of the Oudh Chief Court, 1934-37. *Recreations:* gardening and bridge. *Address:* Wildacres, Fleet, Hants. *T.:* Fleet 590. [*Died* 26 *Nov.* 1954.

KING, Charles Montague, C.S.I. 1922; C.I.E. 1915; *b.* 1872; *m.* 1899, Agnes Bertha (*d.* 1933), *d.* of A. C. Clark, Haileybury. *Educ.:* St. Paul's School; Balliol College, Oxford. Entered I.C.S. 1890; Deputy Commissioner, 1901; Commissioner, Punjab, 1918; Financial Commissioner and Revenue Secretary to Government, Punjab, 1923; retired, 1928; member Alton Rural District Council, 1930-46; Hampshire County Council, 1930-46. *Address:* Walldown, Whitehill, Hants. [*Died* 23 *April* 1956.

KING, Colonel Sir Edwin (James), K.C.B., *cr.* 1944 (C.B. 1939); C.M.G. 1916; A.D.C. to the King, 1931-41; Bailiff Grand Cross of the Order of St. John of Jerusalem (Chancellor, 1945-51); F.S.A.; F.R.Hist.S.; F.R.N.S.; D.L., J.P., Middlesex; Liveryman of Pattenmakers Company and a Freeman of City of London; comd. 7th Middlesex Regt., 1907-19, and Hon. Col., 1925-49; *b.* 1877; *e. s.* of late Edwin King of The Elms, Highgate, and Susannah, *e. d.* of late James Johnston of Buckhurst Hill; *m.* 1st, 1905, Mildred (*d.* 1935), D.G.St.J., *y. d.* of late Richard Ashby of Scarborough; 2nd, 1937, Geneviève Ghislaine Marthe, D.St.J. (Jun. Comdr. A.T.S. (Army Welfare Officer), Pres. Women's Branch British Legion (Finchley) since 1941), *d.* of Alfred Henry, Tilques, France. *Educ.:* Cheltenham College; Christ Church, Oxford (M.A.). Member of Lincoln's Inn. Entered T.A., 1896; Lieut. 1897; Capt. 1901; Lieut.-Col. 1907; Col. 1918; retired, 1934; reappointed Col. 1940; retired, 1949. Served S. African War with Colonial Forces in 1900 (medal and three clasps); European War, 1914-18, at Gibraltar and in France and Flanders; (despatches thrice, C.M.G., promoted Colonel); Commander, Lille and Ypres Sub-Areas, March-Oct. 1919; Zone Commander Middlesex Home Guard, 1940-41; has been a Military Member of Middlesex Territorial Army Association, 1908-47; Vice-Chairman Middlesex Territorial Army Association, 1925-36, Chairman, 1936-45; Chairman Middlesex Cadet Committee, 1930-45; Pres. Hornsey Central Hospital, 1931-36; Chairman Middlesex Army Welfare Committee, 1939-45; Army Welfare Officer, 1940-48; Pres. British Legion (Finchley) since 1930; High Sheriff of Middlesex, 1935-36; King George V. Coronation Medal, 1910; Order of Mercy, 1912; Territorial Decoration, 1918; Conspicuous Service Medal of the Order of St. John, 1935; King George Jubilee Medal, 1935; King George VI. Coronation Medal, 1937. *Publications:* The Knights of St. John in England; The Pilgrimage of 1926; The History of the Seventh Middlesex; The Knights Hospitallers in the Holy Land, 1931; The Seals of the Order of St. John of Jerusalem, 1932; Records of the Family of King; The Rule Statutes and Customs of the Hospitallers, 1099-1310, 1934; Official History of the Order of St. John of Jerusalem, 1935; The History of the Middlesex Territorial Army and Air Force Association; various pamphlets and articles. *Address:* The Old House, East Finchley, N.2. *T.:* Tudor 1336. *Clubs:* Athenæum, Junior Army and Navy. [*Died* 11 *July* 1952.

KING, Ernest Gerald; Chairman and Director, Louis Cassier Co. Ltd., publishers of trade and technical works; *m.* Louise (*d.* 1952), *y. d.* of Andrew Dickson, Newry, Co. Down; (one *s.* killed in action) two *d.* *Educ.:* privately. Accompanied expedition to Northern Nigeria, 1898 on the staff of Rt. Hon. Lord Lugard, G.C.M.G. *Address:* Dorset House, S.E.1. *T.:* Waterloo 3333; Ashley, Park Drive, Middleton-on-Sea, Sussex. *Club:* Constitutional. [*Died* 23 *Oct.* 1955.

KING, Fleet Admiral Ernest Joseph, G.C.B. *cr.* 1946; U.S. Navy; *b.* 23 Nov. 1878; *s.* of James Clydesdale King and Elizabeth Keam; *m.* 1905, Martha Rankin Egerton; one *s.* six *d.* *Educ.:* Lorain (Ohio) High School; U.S. Naval Academy, Annapolis Maryland; Naval War College, Newport, Rhode Island. Midshipman, U.S. Navy, during Spanish-American War; Commissioned Ensign, U.S. Navy, 1903; Asst. Chief of Bureau of Aeronautics, 1928-29; advanced through grades to Rear-Adm. 1933; Chief of Bureau of Aeronautics, 1933-36; (Vice-Adm.) comdg. Aircraft, Battle Force, U.S. Fleet, 1938-39; Member, General Board, Navy Dept., 1939-40; Commander Patrol Force, U.S. Fleet, 1940; (Adm.) C.-in-C., U.S. Atlantic Fleet, 1941; C.-in-C. U.S. Fleet, and also Chief of Naval Operations, 1942-45. *Publication:* (with W. M. Whitehill) Fleet Admiral King, 1953. *Clubs:* Army and Navy, Army and Navy Country (Washington). [*Died* 25 *June* 1956.

KING, Dame Ethel Locke, D.B.E., *cr.* 1918; *b.* Govt. House, Tasmania; *d.* of Col. Sir Thomas Gore Browne, K.C.M.G.; *m.* Hugh Fortescue Locke King (*d.* 1926), *s.* of Hon. P. J. Locke King; no *c.* *Educ.:* home. Was Vice-President of the North Surrey Division and Assistant County Director, British Red Cross and Order of St. John. *Address:* Caenshill, Weybridge, Surrey. *T.:* 18. *Club:* Bath. [*Died* 5 *Aug.* 1956.

KING, Sir George Adolphus, 5th Bt., *cr.* 1815; *b.* 3 Sept. 1864; *s.* of late George King, 7th *s.* of 2nd Bt. and Frances Julia Andrews; *S. cousin*, 1920. *Heir:* *n.* Alexander William [*b.* 25 Nov. 1892; *m.* 1924, Dorothy Alice, *d.* of H. W. Champion; one *s.*]. *Address:* c/o Bank of London and South America, Tokenhouse Yard, E.C.2. [*Died* 15 *Aug.* 1954.

KING, Sir George H. J. D.; *see* Duckworth-King.

KING, Harold, C.B.E. 1950; F.R.S. 1933; *b.* 24 Feb. 1887; *s.* of late Herbert and Ellen Elizabeth King, Bangor, N. Wales; *m.* 1923, Elsie M. Croft; one *s.* *Educ.:* Friars Grammar School and University, Bangor. M.Sc. Wales, 1911; 1851 Industrial Bursary, 1911-12; Chemist with the Tar and Ammonia Products, Beckton, 1911-12, Burroughs Wellcome & Co., 1912-19; Head of Chemistry Division, National Institute for Medical Research, 1919-50. D.Sc. Wales, 1920; Hanbury medallist, 1941; Addingham Gold Medallist, 1952. *Publications:* Chemical papers, chiefly in Journal of Chemical Society and Biochemical Journal. *Recreations:* entomology, ornithology, music. *Address:* Birchwood, Brierley Avenue, West Parley, Dorset. [*Died* 20 *Feb.* 1956.

KING, Hon. James H., P.C. (Canada); M.D., C.M., LL.D.; F.A.C.S.; Member of Canadian Senate since 1930, Speaker 1946-1949; Leader of Govt. in Senate and Minister without Portfolio, 1942-46; President, King Lumber Mills Co. Ltd.; *b.* Chipman, N.B., 18 Jan. 1873; *s.* of late Hon. G. G. King and Esther Briggs; *m.* 1st, 1907, Nellie Sadler (*d.* 1949), Maple View, N.B.; 2nd, 1951, Flora Evans. *Educ.:* St. Martin's Academy; McGill University. Practised Medicine Andover and St. John, N.B., 1895-98; went to British Columbia, 1898, practised in Cranbrook; C.P.R. Chief Surgeon,

Crow's Nest Line; Vice-President, Graduates' Society, McGill University, 1908; attended Western Congress of Medicine and Surgery, Budapest, 1909; represented Cranbrook, British Columbia Legislature, 1903-9; candidate for Kootenay to House of Commons, 1911; elected to British Columbia Legislature, 1916; Minister of Public Works, 1916; re-elected for Cranbrook, 1920; Minister of Public Works for Canada, 1922-1926; Minister of Pensions and National Health for Canada, 1926-30; M.P. for Kootenay East, 1925; re-elected for Kootenay East, 1926; Delegate to World Security Conference, San Francisco, 1945. One of the original Founders and Governors of the American College of Surgeons at Chicago, 1913; Knight of Grace St. John Ambulance Association; Hon. LL.D., Acadia Univ., 1923; LL.D. Ottawa University, 1924. Liberal; Baptist. *Recreation:* golf. *Address:* Ottawa, Canada. *Clubs:* Country (Ottawa); Union of British Columbia (Victoria, B.C.); Vancouver (Vancouver). [*Died* 14 *July* 1955.

KING, Louis Vessot, F.R.S. 1924; M.A. (Cantab.); D.Sc. (McGill); Macdonald Professor of Physics, McGill University, Montreal, 1920, retd. *b.* Toronto, April 18, 1886; *s.* of Alonso King, M.A., Woodstock, Ontario, and Louisa Vessot, Joliette, Quebec; *m.* Lillian Dorothea R. N., *d.* of John Neville, Postwick, Norfolk; no *c.* *Educ.:* McGill University, Montreal; Cambridge. Assistant Professor of Physics, McGill University, 1912; Associate, 1915; investigated submarine acoustics for the Electrical and Submarine Committee of the British Inventions Board, 1915-20; Howard N. Potts Gold Medal of the Franklin Institute for the invention of the hot-wire anemometer, 1919; awarded the Flavelle Medal of the Royal Society of Canada for conspicuous scientific achievement, 1934; Sectional President of the Royal Society of Canada, 1919; Fellow of the American Physical Society; Member of the American Mathematical Society; American Astronomical Society, etc.; engaged at intervals since 1913 on researches on fog-alarms and the measurement of sound at sea; measurement of air velocities by hot-wire method; studies on the intensity and distribution of light from the sky; monograph on the numerical computation of elliptic integrals and functions; more recently engaged in researches in theoretical physics molecular structure, electron theory, distribution and penetration of radio waves into the earth, radiation field and electromagnetic properties of wireless antennae, etc. *Publications:* On the Numerical Calculations of Elliptic Functions and Integrals, 1924; Memoirs on various scientific topics communicated to Royal Society of London, Philosophical Magazine, and other scientific journals. *Recreations:* golf, tennis, riding, swimming, etc. *Address:* McGill University, Montreal, Quebec, Canada. *Clubs:* University (Montreal); Summerlea Golf. [*Died* 6 *June* 1956.

KING, Maurice John, Q.C. (Scot.) 1934; *b.* 1880. *Educ.:* Glasgow Academy; Trinity College, Glenalmond; Glasgow University (M.A., LL.B.). Sheriff of Roxburgh, Berwick, and Selkirk, 1944-51. *Address:* 8 Nelson Street, Edinburgh. [*Died* 11 *Jan.* 1952.

KING, Bt. Col. Norman Carew, T.D.; Registrar General Medical Council, 1911-33, and Registrar Dental Board of the United Kingdom, 1921-33; *b.* 19 Feb. 1871; *s.* of late George William King and Ellen Elizabeth, *d.* of late Wm. Tamplin, Brighton; *m.* 1914, Melita Lilian Marie, *d.* of late John Macintosh Macintosh, R.B.A.; no *c.* *Educ.:* Haileybury College. Joined London Rifle Brigade, 1892; served European War, 1914-1918; Lt.-Col. 1916 (Bt. Col., despatches, 1914 Star); commanded 3rd L.R.B. June 1915 to demobilisation, 1919; Director, Tamplins Licenced Properties; formerly Director Tamplins Brewery, Brighton. Member of Council of Haileybury College. *Publications:* (Ed.) History of L.R.B., 1921; (Ed.) Haileybury Register, 1946. *Recreations:* cricket, football, real tennis, etc. *Address:* 7L Hyde Park Mansions, N.W.1. *T.:* Paddington 4380. *Clubs:* Junior Carlton, M.C.C. [*Died* 21 *Aug.* 1953.

KING, Very Rev. Richard George Salmon, M.A.; Hon. D.Litt. (Q.U.B.); Hon. C.F. 3rd Class; Dean of Derry, 1921-46; and late Rector of Templemore (Derry City); *s.* of Rev. Robert King, Irish Scholar and Historian; *m.* Dorothea, *d.* of Very Rev. A. F. Smyly, M.A., Dean of Derry. Late Hon. Sec. General Synod of the Church of Ireland; served as S.C.F. 36th Div., B.E.F., 1914-16 (despatches). *Address:* Harberton, Swanage, Dorset. [*Died* 23 *Oct.* 1958.

KING-FARLOW, Sir Sydney Nettleton, Kt., *cr.* 1924; *b.* 13 Dec. 1864; *s.* of late John King-Farlow, D.L., of Wood Lee, Virginia Water, Surrey, and *g.s.* of late John King Farlow, solicitor, of Ely Place, E.C.; *m.* 1897, Alys (*d.* 1955), *d.* of G. H. Sprules, Manse Field, Reigate, Sy.; two *s.* one *d.* [Assumed under will, 1918, name of Nettleton. Resumed patronymic, 1936.] *Educ.:* Harrow; Trinity College, Oxford, M.A.; Public School Gold Medallist, Royal Geographical Society; F.R.G.S.; called to Bar, Middle Temple, 1889; went S.E. circuit; a Liberal Unionist; contested Attercliffe at by-election, 1909, and 1910, and South Hackney, 1910; Puisne Judge of High Court of Uganda, 1912; and Member of H.M.'s Court of Appeal for Eastern Africa, 1912; Acting Chief Justice of Uganda, 1913; of Sierra Leone, 1919; and of the Gold Coast, 1921; Senior Judge of Supreme Court of the Gold Coast, 1920; Puisne Judge, 1915; Chief Justice of the Bahamas, 1922-24, of Cyprus, 1924-27; Chief Justice of Gibraltar, 1927-31; retired, 1931. *Publications:* Gold Coast Judgments, 1915-17; The Masai Case, 1913; Ice Hockey (Isthmian series); Articles on the Empire; A Ballad of Downing Street, 1934-44, and War Verses. *Recreations:* travelling, all open-air sports, books. *Address:* c/o Midland Bank, Hill Str., Jersey, C.I. *Club:* Carlton. [*Died* 26 *Nov.* 1957.

KINGDOM, Thomas, M.A. Cantab.; Headmaster, Wyggeston Grammar School for Boys, Leicester, 1920-47; *b.* 13 Dec. 1881; *s.* of James Kingdom; *m.* Amy, *d.* of Joseph Doyle; two *s.* one *d.* *Educ.:* St. Olave's, Southwark, King's College, Cambridge, 1st Class Classical Tripos, Parts I. and II. Assistant Master at St. Olave's School, 1905-19; Member I.A.H.M., Simplified Spelling Soc. (Committee). *Recreations:* swimming (formerly Pres. of Cambridge Univ. Swimming Club) and golf. *Address:* 19 Stoneygate Court, Leicester. *T.:* Leicester 77850. [*Died* 3 *July* 1957.

KINGDON-WARD, F., O.B.E. 1952; M.A. (Cantab.); Hon. F.R.G.S.; F.L.S.; V.M.H.; plant explorer, botanist, and author; *b.* 6 Nov. 1885; *s.* of late Prof. Marshall Ward, F.R.S., Sc.D.; *m.*; two *d.*; *m.* 1947, Jean Macklin. *Educ.:* St. Paul's School; Christ's Coll., Camb. School teacher, Shanghai Public School, 1907-09; travelled in Western China and S.E. Tibet, 1909-13; on N.E. Frontier of Burma, 1914, 1919, 1926, 1930-31, 1937, 1938-39, 1942, 1953; Mount Victoria, W. Burma, 1956; W. China, 1921-23; interior Tibet, 1924, 1933, 1935; Assam Frontier, 1928, 1935, 1938, 1943, 1949; across French Indo-China, 1929; Thailand, 1941; East Manipur, 1948; Mishmi and Naga Hills, 1949; Assam-Tibet Frontier, 1950. Cuthbert Peek Grant, R.G.S., 1916 and 1924; Royal Medal, 1930; Victoria Medal of Honour in Horticulture, 1932; Veitch Memorial Medal, R.H.S., 1933; George Robert White Memorial Medal Massachusetts Hortl. Soc., 1934; Livingstone Gold Medal, Roy. Scottish Geog. Soc., 1936; Hon. Freeman, Worshipful Company of Gardeners of London, 1957. *Publications:*

On the Road to Tibet, 1910; The Land of the Blue Poppy, 1913 (Penguin edition, 1941); In Farthest Burma, 1921; The Mystery Rivers of Tibet, 1923; The Romance of Plant Hunting, 1924; From China to Hkamti Long, 1924; Rhododendrons for Everyone, 1925; The Riddle of the Tsangpo Gorges, 1926; Plant Hunting on the Edge of the World, 1930; Plant Hunting in the Wilds, 1931; The Loom of the East, 1932; A Plant Hunter in Tibet, 1934; The Romance of Gardening, 1935; Plant Hunter's Paradise, 1937; Assam Adventure, 1940; Modern Exploration, 1945; About this Earth, an Introduction to the Science of Geography, 1946; Commonsense Rock Gardening, 1947; Rhododendrons and Azaleas, 1948; Burma's Icy Mountains, 1949; Footsteps in Civilization, 1950; Plant Hunter in Manipur, 1952; Berried Treasure, 1954; Return to the Irrawaddy, 1956; articles in various journals. *Recreation:* walking. *Address:* c/o Natural History Museum (Botanical Dept.), S.W.7.
[*Died* 8 *April* 1958.

KINGSLEY, Hyman Herbert; Hon. Mr. Justice Kingsley; Puisne Judge, Sierra Leone, since 1947; *b.* Manchester, 28 Oct. 1897; unmarried. *Educ.:* Manchester Grammar School; Manchester University (Adams Scholar). Served European War, King's Own Regt. (Lieut., despatches, Afghan War, 1919); War of 1939-45 as Paymaster Lieut. in Tanganyika Naval Volunteer Force. Called to Bar, Gray's Inn, 1936. Practised Northern Circuit until Aug. 1940 when appointed Crown Counsel, Tanganyika. First Chairman Joint Cttee. on Teachers' Salaries, etc. in Sierra Leone (Kingsley Revision); Chairman Enquiry into Freetown Waterworks Dept., 1948. *Recreations:* walking, reading, theatre-going. *Address:* Law Courts, Freetown, Sierra Leone. *T.:* Freetown 2849. *Club:* Overseas.
[*Died* 29 *Nov.* 1956.

KINGSMILL, Lt.-Col. Andrew de Portal, D.S.O. 1917; O.B.E.; M.C.; Deputy Lieutenant for Hampshire; Alderman of Hampshire County Council; J.P. Hampshire; Deputy Chairman of Ind Coope & Allsopp Ltd. and director of other companies; partner in firm of Kingsmill & Hollingsworth, stockbrokers; *b.* 7 June 1881; *s.* of late W. H. Kingsmill of Sydmonton Court, Newbury, and Constance Mary, *e. d.* of late Sir Wyndham Portal, Bt., of Malshanger, Basingstoke; *m.* 1st, 1904, Gladys Frances Johnson (whom he divorced, 1920); one *s.* three *d.*; 2nd, 1930, Olga, *widow* of Capt. Herbert Flemming. *Educ.:* Eton; Christ Church, Oxford. Grenadier Guards, Feb. 1902-Dec. 1908; Reserve of Officers, Grenadier Guards, Aug. 1914-36. *Recreation:* shooting. *Address:* North Sydmonton House, Newbury. *T.A.* Kingsclere. *T.:* Headley 266. *Club:* Guards.
[*Died* 6 *May* 1956.

KINGSMILL, Lieut.-Colonel Walter B., D.S.O. 1918., V.D., Q.C. (Can.); Barrister; *b.* 6 May 1876; *s.* of Nicol Kingsmill, K.C. and Lavinia Thomson; *m.* 1906, Freda Puddicombe, London, Ont.; two *s.* one *d.* *Educ.:* Bishops College School, Lennoxville, P.Q.; Royal Military College, Kingston; Osgoode Hall, Toronto; Graduated from Royal Military College 1898; called to Bar, 1901; Gazetted to Royal Grenadiers, Toronto, as Junior Lieutenant 1898; served in all ranks eventually commanding Regt. in 1915; organized for services overseas 123 Battalion C.E.F.; served in France and Belgium 1917 and 1918 (despatches thrice, D.S.O.); Member of Law firm Kingsmill, Mills, Price and Fleming. K.C. (Can.) 1930. *Recreations:* golf, squash racquets. *Address:* 74 Castle Frank Road, Toronto, Canada. *T.A.:* Kingsmill, Toronto. *T.:* Midway 9214. *Clubs:* Toronto, Toronto Golf (Toronto).
[*Died* 10 *Jan.* 1957.

KINLEY, John; M.P. (Lab.) Bootle, 1929-1931 and 1945-55. Contested Bootle, 1924; served Bootle Town Council. *Address:* 32 Merton Rd., Bootle, Lancs.
[*Died* 13 *Jan.* 1957.

KINLOCH, James Laird, C.I.E. 1918; retired; *b.* 15 Jan. 1878; 4th *s.* of late Robert Kinloch, Kilmacolm, Renfrewshire, and Cardiff; *m.* 1920, Margaret Reid Houston, R.R.C., Blantyre, Lanarkshire. Late Engineer-in-Chief, Construction and Surveys, South India Railway. *Address:* Hillside, Raleigh, Bideford, N. Devon. *T.:* Bideford 279. *Club:* Royal North Devon Golf (Westward Ho!).
[*Died* 26 *June* 1952.

KINNEAR, Sir Norman (Boyd), Kt., *cr.* 1950; C.B. 1948; *b.* 11 Aug. 1882; 2nd *s.* of C. G. H. Kinnear, architect, Edinburgh, and Jessie Jane, *d.* of Wellwood Maxwell, Munches, Galloway; *m.* 1913, Gwendolen Beatrice, 2nd *d.* of Dr. William Millard, Edinburgh; two *d.* *Educ.:* Edinburgh Academy; Trinity College, Glenalmond. Volunteer Assistant Royal Scottish Museum, 1905-7; Curator Bombay Natural History Museum, 1907-19; Assistant Zool. Department British Museum Natural History, 1920; Assistant Keeper, 1928; Deputy Keeper, 1936; Keeper of Zoology, 1945; Director, 1947-50; Assistant Editor Bombay Natural History Society Journal, 1908-19; Editor Bulletin British Ornithological Club, 1925-30; President British Ornithological Union, 1943-48. *Publications:* various papers on Ornithology in Scot. Nat. Ibis., Bull. Brit. Orn. Club, Linnean Soc. and Jour. Bombay Nat. Hist. Soc. *Recreation:* gardening. *Address:* 2 Burghley Road, Wimbledon, S.W.19. *T.:* Wimbledon 5924. *Club:* Athenæum.
[*Died* 11 *Aug.* 1957.

KINNEAR, Sir Walter Samuel, K.B.E., *cr.* 1918; F.C.I.I.; *b.* 8 March 1872; *m.* 1913, Iris Mary (*d.* 1935), *d.* of Dr. W. Young Orr, Kenmore, Putney; one *d.* *Educ.:* Univ. Coll., Dublin; Graduate and First Class Honourman, Mental and Moral Science, Royal University of Ireland; Deputy-Chairman Irish Insurance Commission, 1911-19; Controller of Insurance Dept., Ministry of Health, 1919-36; Deputy-Chairman National Health Joint Committee, Ministry of Health, 1920-38; Chairman Navy and Army Fund, 1917-20. Chairman, Mission to Lepers; Vice-Chm. Empire Rheumatism Council, 1939-50. *Address:* 12 Parkside Gardens, Wimbledon Common, S.W.19. *T.:* Wimbledon 2434. *Club:* Reform.
[*Died* 4 *April* 1953.

KIPPENBERGER, Maj.-Gen. Sir Howard Karl, K.B.E., *cr.* 1948 (C.B.E. 1944); C.B. 1944; D.S.O. 1941 (Bar 1943); Solicitor; Editor-in-Chief, New Zealand War Histories; *b.* 1897; *m.* 1922, Ruth Isobel, *d.* of Joseph Flynn, Lyttelton, New Zealand. *Educ.:* Christchurch Boys' High School, New Zealand. Served European War, 1914-18, in France and Belgium (wounded); War of 1939-45 in Middle East (wounded twice, D.S.O. and Bar, C.B.E., C.B., American Legion of Merit). *Publication:* Infantry Brigadier, 1949. *Address:* Wellington, N.Z.
[*Died* 5 *May* 1957.

KIRBY, Bertie Victor, C.B.E. 1947; D.C.M. 1917; J.P.; Member, Liverpool City Council, since 1924 (when he won the Everton Ward from the Conservatives); Elective Auditor in 1924 for City of Liverpool; Alderman since 1939; J.P. (City of Liverpool), since 1929; *b.* Cheltenham, 2 May 1887; *m.* 1916, Alice Elizabeth Richmond, Ashchurch, Glos. *Educ.:* Abbey School, Tewkesbury (elementary education). Served European War, 1914-19 in R.H.A. in France and Belgium; served in R.A. Anti-Aircraft Defences, 1939-41, in all ranks to Captain. M.P. (Lab.) Everton Division of Liverpool from 1935 (when he won the seat from the Conservatives) until 1950 when constituency ceased to exist owing to a redistribution of seats; Member Select Cttee. on National Expenditure, 1941-45; Member

Public Accounts Cttee., 1946-50; Chairman Select Cttee. on Estimates, 1946-50; Deputy Chairman, Liverpool Educ. Cttee. *Address:* 710 Queens Drive, Stoneycroft, Liverpool 13. *T.:* Stoneycroft 3904. [*Died* 1 *Sept.* 1953.

KIRBY, Admiral Francis George; retired; late temp. Captain R.N.R.; *b.* 18 Aug. 1854; *s.* of late Rev. H. T. M. Kirby, vicar of Mayfield, Sussex; *m.* 1st, 1887, Mary Grey (*d.* 1915), *e. d.* of late John Burn Murdoch of Gartincaber, Perthshire; no *c.*; 2nd, 1916, Margaret, *o. d.* of late Thomas Henderson Hamilton, Lanarks. *Educ.:* Lancing College. Served constantly until promoted to Rear-Admiral, 1905; retired, 1908; Temp. Capt., R.N.R., of H.M. yacht Sapphire II., 1915-16; served Suakin, 1884; member Naval Intelligence Dept., 1888-90. *Address:* Enfield House, Ventnor, I. of W. [*Died* 13 *Jan.* 1951.

KIRBY, Group Capt. Frank Howard, V.C., C.B.E., D.C.M.; late Royal Air Force; *b.* 12 Nov. 1871; *s.* of William Henry and Ada Kirby; *m.* 1909, Kate Jolly; two *s.* three *d.* *Educ.:* Alleyn's School, Dulwich. Enlisted in Royal Engineers, 1892; proceeded to S. Africa with Field Troops, Royal Engineers, on mobilisation, 1899; gained medal for distinguished conduct in the field in action at Bloemfontein, March 1900; Victoria Cross for action East of Pretoria, June 1900; Troop Sergt.-Major from Corporal for services in the field, July 1901; Warrant Officer, Dec. 1906; commissioned from the ranks, April 1911; posted to Air Batt. Royal Engineers, South Farnborough; gazetted to Royal Flying Corps, 1912; served European War, France, 1916-18; Captaincy for services in the Field, 1917; Major for services connected with the War, 1918; retired with rank of Group Captain, R.A.F., 1926. *Address:* 3 Crescent Road, Sidcup, Kent. *T.:* Foots Cray 4671. [*Died* 8 *July* 1956.

KIRBY, Brig.-General Stuart Rodger, C.M.G. 1915; late 6th Dragoon Guards; *b.* 20 Oct. 1873; *m.* 1930, *widow* of Capt. T. Nelson Paisley. Entered Army, 1893; Captain, 1900; Major, 1905; Lt.-Col. 1914; served S. African War, 1899-1902 (despatches, Queen's medal 6 clasps, King's medal 2 clasps); European War, 1914-18 (despatches, Order of St. Anne C.M.G.); temp. Brig.-Gen. *Address:* Heath House, Milton-under-Wychwood, Oxon. *Club:* Cavalry. [*Died* 20 *Jan.* 1959.

KIRK, John, M.B., Ch.B., F.R.C.S.; Courtauld Professor of Anatomy, University of London, at Middlesex Hospital Medical School, 1937-49, Professor Emeritus of Anatomy since 1949; *b.* 27 Nov. 1881; *s.* of late Rev. John Kirk and late Eliza Walker Lewis, Edinburgh; *m.* 1908, Norah Elizabeth Hughes; two *s.* one *d.* *Educ.:* George Watson's College; University of Edinburgh. M.B., Ch.B. 1904; F.R.C.S. Edinburgh 1914; F.R.C.S. Eng., 1952. House Surgeon Mildmay Mission Hospital, London, 1904-1906; Resident Medical Officer, New Zealand Pres. Mission Hospital, Canton, China, 1907-28; late Senior Demonstrator of Anatomy and Senior Tutor University of London, University College; late Examiner in Anatomy for R.C.S. of England on the Conjoint Board, and Primary F.R.C.S., Eng. and Edin., and for Universities of London, Edinburgh, Cambridge, Aberdeen, and Birmingham, and Nat. Univ. of Ireland. Vice-President Anatomical Society of Great Britain and Ireland, 1947-49. Visitor of Examinations and of Medical Schools in subject of Anatomy, rep. Gen. Med. Council, 1953-57. F.R.S.M. 1944. *Publications:* Papers in Journal of Anatomy, and Annals of R.C.S. of England. *Recreations:* golf and fishing (Edinburgh Univ. Golf Blue, 1903; Scottish Universities Champion Foursome, 1904). *Address:* 12 Winscombe Way, Stanmore, Middlesex. *T.:* Grimsdyke 2180. [*Died* 26 *Sept.* 1959.

KIRK, Rt. Rev. Kenneth Escott, D.D.; Bishop of Oxford since 1937; Hon. C.F. (3rd Class); Hon. Fellow, S. John's Coll., Oxford, 1938, and Trinity Coll., 1943; *b.* Sheffield, 21 Feb. 1886; *e. o. surv. s.* of late F. H. Kirk, Director of Samuel Osborn & Company, Sheffield; *m.* 1921, Beatrice (*d.* 1934), 2nd *d.* of late His Honour Judge Radcliffe, K.C.; two *s.* three *d.* *Educ.:* Sheffield Royal Grammar School; St. John's College, Oxford (Casberd Scholar). First class Hon. (Class.) Mods., 1906; 1st class Lit. Hum., 1908; B.A., 1908; M.A., 1911; Senior Denyer and Johnson Scholar, 1913; B.D., 1922; D.D., 1926; Assistant to Professor of Philosophy, University College, London, 1909-12; Warden of University College Hall, Ealing, 1910-12; deacon, 1912; priest, 1913; Curate of Denaby Main, Yorks, 1912-14; Tutor, Keble College, Oxford, 1914-22; Chaplain of the Forces, 1914-19; Fellow of Magdalen College, Oxford, 1919-22; Fellow, Chaplain and Lecturer of Trinity College, Oxford, 1922-33; Six Preacher in Canterbury Cathedral, 1922-33; Controller of Lodgings, Univ. of Oxford, 1921-33; Select Preacher, 1925-27; Examiner in the Final Honour School, Theology, 1926-28; University Reader in Moral Theology, 1927-33; Regius Prof. of Moral and Pastoral Theology and Canon of Christ Church, Oxford, 1933-37. Examining Chaplain to the Bishop of Sheffield, 1914-37, and to the Bishop of St. Albans, 1924-37; Bampton Lecturer, 1928; Select Preacher, Cambridge, 1933, 1939, and 1950; White Lecturer, St. Paul's Cathedral, 1935; Maurice Lecturer, King's Coll., London, 1937; Forwood Lecturer, Univ. of Liverpool, 1938; Mond Lecturer, Univ. of Manchester, 1945; Provost of Lancing, 1937-1944; Fellow of Woodard Corporation, 1926-1945, President, 1946; Life Governor Marlborough College. *Publications:* A Study of Silent Minds, 1918; The Way of Understanding, 1919; Some Principles of Moral Theology, 1920; Ignorance, Faith and Conformity, 1925; Contributor to Essays Catholic and Critical, 1926; Conscience and its Problems, 1927; Contributor to Essays on the Trinity and Incarnation, 1928; The Vision of God: the Christian Doctrine of the Summum Bonum (Bampton Lectures), 1931; The Threshold of Ethics, 1933; Marriage and Divorce, 1933 (2nd ed., largely rewritten, 1948); The Vision of God (abridged ed.), 1934; editor of and contributor to Personal Ethics, 1934; The Fourth River, and other sermons, 1935; The Crisis of Christian Rationalism, 1936; The Epistle to the Romans (Clarendon Bible), 1937; The Story of the Woodard Schools, 1937 (2nd ed., revised, 1952); editor of and contributor to A Study of Theology, 1939; editor, A Directory of the Religious Life, 1943; editor of and contributor to The Apostolic Ministry, 1946; Church Dedications of the Oxford Diocese, 1946; The Ministry of Absolution, 1947; The Coherence of Christian Doctrine, 1950. *Address:* 88 St. Aldates, Oxford. *T.:* 47319. [*Died* 8 *June* 1954.

KIRKBY, Lieut.-Col. Henry McKenzie, M.I.E.E.; Senior Partner in Dolby and Williamson, Consulting Engineers; Hon. Treasurer R.A.O.C. Assoc.; *b.* 10 June 1877; *s.* of late Henry William Kirkby and Isabella Urquhart, 2nd *d.* of Colin Gordon McKenzie of Invergordon; unmarried. *Educ.:* Kensington Grammar School; Central Technical College, London; pupil of late Professors W. C. Unwin and W. E. Ayrton; with Dolby and Williamson since 1897; Consultant to Oxford Univ. Bodleian Library, Westminster Abbey, Canterbury Cathedral, Sheffield Cathedral, London School of Economics, Redhill Hospital, Hellesden Hospital, Air Ministry, War Office, etc.; joined London Scottish Regt., 1897; served European War, 1914-20; joined R.A.O.C., 1915; served as D.A.D.O.S. 4th Div., 1916-17; A.D.O.S. 4th and 6th Corps, 1917-20; retired, 1920 (M.C., D.C.M., despatches, Territorial Long Service Medal). *Publications:* Electric Thermal Storage, 1941; Post War Planning,

1942; and other engineering publications. *Recreations:* rifle shooting, cricket, motoring. *Address:* 64 Riggindale Road, Streatham, S.W.16. *T.:* Streatham 3967. [*Died* 4 *Dec.* 1952.

KIRKE, Claud Cecil Augustus, C.B.E. 1926; *b.* 13 June 1875, *o. s.* of late Augustus Kirke, Leicester; *m.* 1st, 1904, Mabel (*d.* 1927), *y. d.* of late F. R. Wilson, Alnwick, Northumberland; one *s.* two *d.* (and one *s.* killed on active service 1941); 2nd, 1929, Sybil Esmé, 2nd *d.* of late Rev. Edward Theodore Sandys, Canon of Calcutta Cathedral, Stapleford Rectory, Herts; two *s.* Appointed China Consular Service, 1898; China Medal and Clasp for the Defence of the Legations at Peking, 1900; Vice-Consul at Peking, 1905-10; Hankow, 1911-12; Acting Consul at Chefoo, 1912-14; Nanking, 1914; Acting Consul-General at Canton, 1915; Consul at Wuchow, 1916; Kiukiang, 1918-19; Acting Consul-General, Hankow, 1920-21; Consul at Chefoo, 1922-23; Swatow, 1924-1927; H.M. Consul-General in China (for provinces of Yünnan and Kweichow), 1927-32. *Address:* Bedlings, Milton Clevedon, Shepton Mallet, Somerset. *T.A.:* Milton Clevedon, Evercreech. *T.:* Evercreech 245. [*Died* 20 *Aug.* 1959.

KIRKPATRICK, Major-General Charles, C.B. 1924; C.B.E. 1922; Indian Army, retired; *b.* 1879; *s.* of late Dep. Surg.-Gen. James Kirkpatrick, H.E.I.C.S.; *m.* Elsie, *d.* of late H. J. H. Fasson, I.C.S.; one *s.* one *d.* *Educ.:* Edinburgh Academy; R.M.C., Sandhurst. Commissioned, 1898; attached 1st Bn. South Wales Borderers; Q.V.O. Corps of Guides, Frontier Force, 1900; Chitral Scouts, 1907-8; Comdt. 1st Bn. Khyber Rifles, 1908-9; D.A.A. and Q.M.G. Derajat Brigade, 1914-15; Commandant 3/12th F.F. Regiment, 1924-26; Commander Rawal Pindi Brigade, 1926; and Kohat Brigade, 1927-30; Major-General, 1929; Commander Sind (Ind.) Brigade Area, 1931-35. War 1914-18 (despatches four times); G.S.O.1 Waziristan Field Force, 1920-23 (despatches four times, C.B., C.B.E.); N.W. Frontier, 1930; A.D.C. to the King, 1927-29; retired, 1935. *Address:* Larchwood, Pitlochry, Perthshire. [*Died* 23 *Jan.* 1955.

KIRKPATRICK, Sir Cyril Reginald Sutton, Kt., *cr.* 1922; M.I.C.E.; Chartered Civil Engineer, retd., 1951; *b.* 17 Oct. 1872; *s.* of late Captain Thomas Sutton Kirkpatrick, 3rd Dragoon Guards, and Mary Ann Rosa, *d.* of Frederick Marriott; *m.* 1st, 1897, Pauline (*d.* 1946), *e. d.* of Rev. J. Last of Geneva; two *s.* two *d.*; 2nd, 1947, Leslie, *d.* of A. J. P. Thompson, Heswall, Cheshire. *Educ.:* Repton; Crystal Palace School of Engineering. Pupil on the L. and N.W.R. to Mr. E. B. Thornhill, M.I.C.E., Chief Engineer; an Assistant Engineer on the L.N.W.R.; Engineer in charge of various railway contracts; Engineer for Cleveland Bridge and Engineering Co., Ltd., upon King Edward VII. Bridge over the river Tyne; City Engineer, Newcastle on Tyne, 1906-10; Chief Assistant Engineer, 1910-13, and Chief Engineer, 1913-24, Port of London Authority; Past President of the Institution of Civil Engineers, 1931-32; Colonel, Engineer and Railway Staff Corps, R.E. (T.F.), retired; Member of the Central Rhine Commission, 1934; Member of the International Technical Consultative Commission of the Suez Canal Company, 1935-53. *Chief Works:* Bridge over the Severn at Shrewsbury, King Edward VII. Bridge over the Tyne; Quay Improvement Works, Newcastle on Tyne; King George V. Dock at North Woolwich, and many other large works at the London Docks and on the river Thames; also foundations and subaqueous tunnels for Tir John Power House at Swansea, and Ford Power House at Dagenham; Galway Harbour Development, Eire; Harbour works and seawall at Maryport, Water Supply and Sewerage for many villages in Norfolk; Power Station, Cyprus, etc.; responsible for construction of 33 concrete caissons for Mulberry Harbour, with K.C.D. group. *Publication:* King Edward VII. Bridge, Newcastle on Tyne, in Proceedings of Institution of Civil Engineers. *Address:* Westside, Burton's Lane, Chalfont St. Giles. *T.:* Little Chalfont 2157. [*Died* 25 *Aug.* 1957.

KIRKPATRICK, Frederick Alex., M.A., F.R.H.S.; *b.* 10 June 1861; 3rd *s.* of A. R. Kirkpatrick of Donacomper, Co. Kildare and Katherine Louisa, *d.* of Thomas Trench of Millicent, Co. Kildare; *m.* 1914, Violet, *d.* of H. Herbert, Cahirnane, Killarney; no *c.* *Educ.:* Wellington; Trinity College, Cambridge University Extension Lecturer, 1898-1919; Reader in Spanish in the University of Cambridge, 1919-33. *Publications:* Imperial Defence and Trade (Prize Essay of Royal Empire Society); A History of Argentina; The Spanish Conquistadores; Latin-America, a brief history; annotated editions of some Spanish classics. *Recreations:* walking, travel. *Club:* Royal Empire Society. [*Died* 14 *Jan.* 1953.

KIRKPATRICK, Lieut.-Colonel Henry; Ophthalmic Surgeon; *b.* 1871; *s.* of Rev. George Kirkpatrick; *m.* Edith Mary, *d.* of Henry Eames, M.D.; two *d.* *Educ.:* Marlborough College; Trinity College, Dublin, M.B. Indian Medical Service, 1898-1921; Honorary Fellow American Academy Ophthalmology and Oto-Laryngology; late Lecturer in Ophthalmology, London School of Hygiene and Tropical Medicine; Ophthalmic Surgeon to London Hospital for Tropical Diseases; Supt. Govt. Ophthalmic Hospital, Madras; Professor Ophthalmology, Medical College, Madras. *Publications:* Cataract and its Treatment; Diseases of the Eye; many papers relating to eye disease in scientific publications. *Recreation:* fishing. *Address:* Sandy Rise, Yateley, Hants. *Club:* East India and Sports. [*Died* 11 *May* 1958.

KIRKPATRICK, Sir James Alexander, 10th Bt., *cr.* 1685; Assistant Game Warden, Kenya Colony; Squadron Leader R.A.F.V.R.; *b.* 24 Oct. 1918; 2nd *s.* of late Lt.-Col. Harry F. Kirkpatrick, D.S.O., 2nd *s.* of 8th Bt.; *S.* uncle, 1937; *m.* 1941, Ellen Gertrude Elliott; two *s.* *Educ.:* Wellington College. Served War of 1939-45 (despatches). *Heir:* *s.* Ivone Elliott, *b.* 1 Oct. 1942. *Address:* Game Dept., Nairobi, Kenya Colony. [*Died* 4 *April* 1954.

KIRKPATRICK, T. Percy C., M.D., Litt.D. Dublin; D.Litt. (Hon.) N.U.I.; F.R.C.P. London; M.R.I.A.; Fellow and Registrar, Royal College of Physicians of Ireland; Physician to Steevens' Hospital, Dublin; *b.* Dublin, 1869; *s.* of John Rutherfoord Kirkpatrick, M.D. *Publications:* History of the Medical School, Trinity College-Dublin, 1912; The Book of the Rotunda Hospital; History of Dr. Steevens' Hospital, 1720, 1920, 1924, etc. *Address:* 11 Fitzwilliam Place, Dublin. *Club:* Royal Irish Yacht (Kingstown). [*Died* 9 *July* 1954.

KIRKPATRICK, William MacColin; Director Equity & Law Life Ass. Soc., Sons of Gwalia, Ltd., Central European Mines, Ltd. (Yugoslavia), Bank Insce. Trust Corp., etc.; *b.* 1878; *o. s.* of Colin Kirkpatrick; *m.* 1902, Marion, *o. d.* of late Conrad Cooke, and *g.d.* of E. W. Cooke, F.R.S., R.A.; two *s.* Merchant in Calcutta (partner Bird & Co.) and Director of Indian Railway, Telephone Co., Jute Mills, and Mining Co's till 1923; contested Preston (C.) 1923; M.P. (C.) Preston, 1931-37; Member of Councils of Asiatic Society of Bengal, European Association of India and Zoo. Soc.; Hon. Magistrate, Delhi, 1905-7; Co-operative Credit Societies movement in Bengal; Capt. Artillery India Defence Force; financial missions to Japan for Viscount Bearsted, 1924-26, for Oriental Telephone Co., to Hong Kong, 1927; to Chile on behalf of Bank of England and London Banks, relating to Nitrate industry, 1933; to Athens, 1935; Member of Committee Mexican Eagle Oil Co. 1935; Mission to

China for Board of Trade Export Credits, 1937-38; to Ankara, 1939; negotiated purchase and transfer of Turkish Public Utilities from Germans to Turkish Govt.; to Belgrade, 1939. Chilean Order of Merit; Kt. Comdr. *Publications:* several years, regular weekly finance articles in leading newspapers of India; Papers to Asiatic Society on Indian Gypsies; and to Hog Hunters Annual, English Review, Asiatic Quarterly, etc. *Recreation:* shooting. *Address:* 62 London Wall, E.C. *T.:* Monarch 3266; Barnston, Peaks Hill, Purley. *T.:* Uplands 3244. *Club:* Caledonian. [*Died* 3 *Dec.* 1953.

KIRKPATRICK-CALDECOT, Ivone; *b.* Jan. 1867; *s.* of late J. Kirkpatrick, J.P., Monks Horton Park, near Hythe, Kent; *m.* 1st, 1911, Margaret Elizabeth (*d.* 1913), *d.* of Rev. G. G. MacLean, late Vicar of Wadhurst, Sussex; 2nd, 1917, Je'nnet Elizabeth, *d.* of late W. H. J. Richards of Wollston, Worcs. *Educ.:* Haileybury College. Entered Sarawak Civil Service, 1892; First Divisional Resident, 1910; administered the Government during absence of the Rajah, 1910-11, 1912-13, 1913-14; retired, 1915. *Address:* Clare Grange, Ashburnham Road, Eastbourne. [*Died* 22 *April* 1951.

KIRKUP, Brig. Philip, D.S.O. 1918; O.B.E. 1938; M.C.; T.D.; mining engineer; *b.* 26 Sept. 1893; 2nd *s.* of late Philip Kirkup, J.P., of Low Fell, Co. Durham; *m.* 1925, Kathleen, *y. d.* of W. L. Scott, Corbridge, N'bland.; one *s.* one *d.* *Educ.:* Marlborough. Served European War, 1914-19 (M.C., D.S.O. with bar, despatches); Comdg. Inf. Bde., 1939-42 (despatches); hon. Brig. 1943. D.L. Co. Durham, 1942. *Address:* Healeyfield, North Lodge, Chester-le-Street, Co. Durham. [*Died* 9 *June* 1959.

KIRKUP, Thomas Henry; late Secretary London Football Association, and Football Combination; retired, 1947; *b.* Benfieldside, Co. Durham, 8 July 1864; *s.* of Michael and Margaret Kirkup; *m.* 1891, Mary (*d.* 1938), *d.* of David Lewis, Swansea; one *s.* *Educ.:* private school. *Recreations:* cricket, football, bowls. *Address:* 6 Woodhouse Grove, Manor Park, E.12. *T.:* Grangewood 0598. [*Died* 19 *Sept.* 1951.

KIRKWOOD, 1st Baron, *cr.* 1951, of Bearsden; **David Kirkwood,** P.C. 1948; J.P.; *b.* 1872; *m.* 1899, Elizabeth, *d.* of Robert Smith, Parkhead; three *s.* two *d.* Educated and trained as engineer on Clydeside. Early engineering career in managerial capacity; became very strong Trade Unionist and leader of the Engineers in Scotland; deported as leader of the Clyde workers for organising protest against increase in house rents, 1916; active member of the Glasgow Town Council, 1918-22. A typical Scottish engineer in his outlook. M.P. (Lab.) Clydebank Dumbarton Burghs, 1922-50, E. Dunbartonshire, 1950-51; formerly Chm., Engineering Group, House of Commons; represented most important shipbuilding centre in the world. Was responsible for the Government financial support of building of Queen Mary and Queen Elizabeth. *Heir:* *s.* Hon. David Kirkwood, *b.* 5 Oct. 1904. *Address:* Karleen, Roman Road, Bearsden, Dunbartonshire. *T.:* Bearsden 1358. [*Died* 16 *April* 1955.

KIRKWOOD, Lieut.-Col. James George, C.M.G. 1919; D.S.O. 1916; M.L.C., Kenya, since 1927; *b.* Greymouth, N.Z., 8 Aug. 1872; *m.* 1942, Gertrude, *widow* of late Sebastian Z. de Ferranti, D.S.O., F.R.S.; one *s.* Served European War, 1914-18 (despatches, D.S.O., C.M.G.). *Address:* P.O. Box 32, Naro Moru, Kenya. *Clubs:* Nairobi, Kitale (Kenya). [*Died* 20 *March* 1955.

KIRWAN, Lieut.-General Sir Bertram Richard, K.C.B., *cr.* 1934 (C.B. 1918); C.M.G. 1916; *b.* 17 May 1871; 4th *s.* of late Rev. R. Kirwan, Rector and Rural Dean, Gittisham, Devon; *m.* 1897, Helen, *d.* of Col. T. W. Hogg, late Indian Army; one *s.* one *d.* *Educ.:* Felsted; R.M.A., Woolwich. Entered army, 1890; Captain, 1900; Major, 1908; Lieut.-Colonel, 1915; Colonel, 1917; Major-Gen. 1925; Lieut.-General, 1932; Staff Captain at War Office, 1908-12; 1st Class Instructor in Gunnery, 1913-14; Staff Officer to Maj.-Gen. R.A. General Headquarters, France, 1914-16; Brig.-Gen. 1916; served European War, 1914-18 (despatches seven times, Chevalier of Legion of Honour, Croix de Guerre, C.B., C.M.G., Bt. Col.); Director of Artillery, War Office, 1920-1923; President of Ordnance Committee, 1923-1927; half pay, 1927-29; Inspector of Artillery in India, 1929-30; Master General of the Ordnance, India, 1930-34; retired pay, 1934; Colonel Commandant R.A., 1933-44. *Address:* c/o Lloyds Bank Ltd., 6 Pall Mall, S.W.1. [*Died* 5 *April* 1960.

KISCH, Harold, M.B., B.S. Lond.; F.R.C.S. Eng.; retired; *s.* of Dr. Albert Kisch; *m.* Sybil Hyman; no *c.* *Educ.:* St. Thomas's Hospital. Musgrave Scholar, Cheselden Medallist, Surgery Prizeman, late House-Surgeon and Casualty Officer, etc.; Consulting Surgeon to Univ. Coll. Hosp., Nose, Throat and Ear Dept.; Consulting Surgeon, Royal National Throat, Nose and Ear Hospital; Consulting Surgeon Nose, Throat and Ear Dept., London Jewish Hosp., etc.; Fellow Royal Society of Medicine, Medical Society; Past Pres., Otological Section, late Vice-President, Laryngological Section, Royal Society of Medicine. *Publications:* various contributions to the literature of Diseases of the Nose, Throat and Ear; Transactions of the Royal Society of Medicine, Journal of Laryngology, etc. *Address:* 15 Montagu Place, W.1. [*Died* 31 *July* 1959.

KITCHIN, Arthur James Warburton, C.I.E. 1917; *b.* 31 Jan. 1870; *s.* of Rev. J. L. Kitchin, Heavitree, Exeter; *m.* 1907, Mildred (*d.* 1957), *d.* of Rev. F. W. Murray, Stone, Kent; no *c.* *Educ.:* Clifton College; Pembroke College, Cambridge, B.A. Entered I.C.S. 1893; Commissioner, Punjab, 1918; retired, 1921. *Address:* 24 Coleherne Court, S.W.5. [*Died* 22 *April* 1957.

KITCHIN, John, J.P.; *b.* 16 Jan. 1869; *s.* of late Alexander Kitchin, farmer, The Clune, Cullen, Banffshire; *m.* E. A., *e. d.* of late John Garden, J.P., Greystone, Banff; two *s.* two *d.* *Educ.:* Cullen Public School. From the time he left school until 25 years assisted his father on his farm; gave up right to farm and struck out for himself; went to James Carters & Co., Royal Seedsmen, High Holborn, to gain experience in office work and agricultural seeds; went to C. W. Soper Whitburn, Addington Park, West Malling, Kent, to manage his estate and was there for 9 years; hired Boughton Place, bought it 1920, sold it, 1939. *Recreations:* hunting, shooting, cricket, and tennis. *Address:* Hunt Street Farm, Crundale, nr. Canterbury, Kent. *T.A.:* Kitchin, Crundale. *T.:* Chilham 329. [*Died* 31 *Dec.* 1951.

KITCHING, Rt. Rev. Arthur Leonard, M.A.; Assistant Bishop of Portsmouth, 1939-59; *b.* 18 Aug. 1875; *s.* of John Austen Kitching, merchant, London; *m.* 1st, M. B. Lloyd, Leicester (*d.* 1914); one *s.*; 2nd, E. E., *d.* of late Col. W. E. Dudley, R.A.M.C., Bath; one *d.* *Educ.:* Manor House, Hastings; Highgate School (Scholar); Emmanuel College, Cambridge (Exhibitioner); B.A., 1897; M.A., 1901; Ridley Hall, Cambridge, 1898-99. Ordained, 1899; Curate of St. Martin's, Birmingham, 1899-1901; To Uganda as C.M.S. missionary, 1901; Archdeacon of Bukedi, 1915-22; of Busoga, 1919-22; of Uganda, 1922, and Examining Chaplain and commissary to Bishop of Uganda; Bishop on the Upper Nile, 1926-36; Rector of All Saints', Dorchester, 1936-38; Vicar of Holy Trinity, Fareham, 1938-45; Asst. Bishop of Portsmouth, 1939-59. Archdeacon of Portsmouth, 1945-52; Hon. Canon of Portsmouth Cathedral, 1952-; Hon. Asst. Bishop of Portsmouth, 1959-. *Publications:* On the Backwaters of the Nile, 1912; Outline Grammar of the Gang Language.

1907; Handbook of the Ateso Language, 1915; Luganda Dictionary (in collaboration), 1925; From Darkness to Light, 1935; translations: 4 Gospels into Gang, 1906; New Testament into Ateso, 1930. *Address:* 9 Selsey Ave., Southsea. *T.:* Portsmouth 31412. [*Died* 24 *Oct.* 1960.

KITCHING, Elsie; *b.* 15 Aug. 1870; *d.* of John Austen Kitching, merchant, London; unmarried. *Educ.:* at home; at various schools. London Inter. Arts, 1893; Private Secretary to Miss Charlotte M. Mason, 1893-1923; Secretary to the House of Education and to the Parents' Union School, 1893-1923; Director of the Parents' Union School, 1923-1948; Editor of the Parents' Review, 1923-1949. *Publications:* various articles on the educational Philosophy of Charlotte M. Mason; articles on birdwatching. *Recreations:* reading, birdwatching, and the study of pictures. *Address:* Low Nook, Ambleside, Westmorland. [*Died* 29 *Dec.* 1955.

KITIYAKARA, Prince Nakkhatra Mangala, Kt. Comdr. of Chula Chom Klao, 1931; Comdr. of Crown of Siam, 1931; Officier de la Légion d'Honneur (France), 1928; Siamese Ambassador to the Court of St. James's since 1948; also Minister to Denmark since 1947; *b.* Bangkok, Siam, 4 Jan. 1898; 3rd *s.* of Prince Kitiyakara of Chandaburi and Princess Absara Smarn, *e. d.* of Prince Devawongse; *m.* 1928, Mom Luang Bua Snidvongse, *d.* of Gen. Chao Phya Wongsa; two *s.* two *d.* *Educ.:* England; France, Lycée de Caen (B. ès Sc.); Saint-Cyr; École Supérieure de Guerre à Paris. Officer in Siamese Army, attached to various regts. of different arms, in France, then Equerry to Prince Prajadhipok of Sukhodaya (the late King Prajadhipok), 1920-23; Lieut. 1923; Capt. 1925; Major, 1926; Officer comdg. 1st Bn. of 1st Guard Regt., 1927; attached to the Gen. Staff, 1927-31; Lt.-Col., 1929; Col., 1930; Dep. Chief of Gen. Staff, 1931; 1st Sec. of Siamese Legation, Washington, 1932-35; resigned from Service, 1935. Minister at the Court of St. James's, 1946; Minister to Denmark, 1947; Minister to France, 1947, while retaining the post in Denmark. *Recreation:* reading. *Address:* The Royal Siamese Embassy, 23 Ashburn Place, S.W.7. *T.:* Frobisher 2983. [*Died* 11 *Feb.* 1953.

KITSON, Vice-Admiral Sir Henry Karslake, K.B.E. *cr.* 1935; C.B. 1929; *s.* of late Major Edward Kitson, of Paynsford, Newton Abbot, Devon; *b.* 22 June 1877; *m.* 1926, Marjorie, *d.* of late Sir E. A. de Pass, K.B.E.; two *s.* H.M.S. Britannia, 1891; Comdr. 1912; Capt. 1917; Rear-Adm., 1928; Vice-Adm. 1932; served Persian Gulf, 1910; European War (despatches twice); Commanding 3rd Battle Squadron, 1929-30; Adm. Supt. H.M. Dockyard, Portsmouth, 1931-35; retired list, 1933; Flag Officer-in-Charge, Coast of Cornwall, 1940-42. *Address:* Monk's Hill, Farnham, Surrey. *T.:* Runfold 266. *Club:* United Service. [*Died* 19 *Feb.* 1952.

KITSON, Hon. William Henry; Agent-General for Western Australia since 1947; *b.* Leeds, England, 20 Nov. 1886; *s.* of late James and Ellen Kitson, Leeds; *m.* 1915, Mabel, *d.* of late A. B. Alport, York; three *s.* one *d.* *Educ.:* Higher Grade School, Leeds. M.L.C., W.A., 1924-47; Minister without portfolio, 1928-30; Hon. Minister, 1933-36; Chief Sec. W.A., 1936-47; Minister for Education 1939-43, for Police 1939-47; Member Rottnest Island Board of Control, 1925-47, Pres. 1933-47; Chairman of War Funds Council of W.A., 1939-46. *Recreations:* cricket, football, fishing, motoring. *Address:* West Australian Government Office, Savoy House, 115-116 Strand, W.C.2. *T.A.:* Karrakatta Rand, London. *T.:* Temple Bar 8601. [*Died* 13 *Dec.* 1952.

KITTO, John Vivian, C.B. 1946; C.B.E. 1942; *b.* 17 Nov. 1875; *s.* of late Prebendary J. F. Kitto, Vicar of St. Martin-in-the-Fields; *m.* 1908, Nettie Catherine, *d.* of Lt.-Col. H. Ryves; one *s.* one *d.* *Educ.:* Trinity Coll., Glenalmond; Balliol College, Oxford. History Hons., 1898; schoolmaster; History lecturer; Assistant Librarian, House of Commons, 1908-37; Librarian, 1937-46. Served European War, 1915-19, Capt. and Adjt. R.G.A. *Publications:* Churchwardens' Accounts of St. Martin-in-the-Fields (1525-1603), 1901; Registers of St. Martin-in-the-Fields (1619-1639), 1936. *Address:* 185 The Avenue, Sunbury-on-Thames, Middx. *T.:* Sunbury 3246. [*Died* 9 *Nov.* 1953.

KLEIBER, Erich; orchestral conductor, professor, general music director; *b.* 5 Aug. 1890; *s.* of Otto Kleiber and Veronica Schöppel; *m.* 1926, Ruth Goodrich; one *s.* one *d.* *Educ.:* Vienna and Prague (Universities). Court Theater, Darmstadt, 1912-18; Barmen-Elberfeld, 1918-21; Düsseldorf, 1921-22; Mannheim, 1923; Director of Berlin State Opera, 1923-35. Became an Argentine citizen, 1936. Conductor, State Opera, East Berlin, 1955, resigned, Guest appearances in Europe, North and South America, 1935-. Commandeur Ordre de Léopold, Belgium; Commendatore della Corona d' Italia; Commandeur Orden del Sol, Peru; Comendador del Merito, Chile, etc. *Address:* Poste Restante, Zürich, Switzerland. [*Died* 27 *Jan.* 1956.

KLEIN, Abbé Felix; writer and lecturer in French and English; *b.* Château Chinon, Nièvre, 1862. *Educ.:* Petit Séminaire of Meaux; St. Sulpice, Paris; courses at the Institut Catholique and Sorbonne. Priest, 1885; taught philosophy at Meaux Diocesan College; Prof. of French Literature at the Institut Catholique of Paris, 1893; was during the war chaplain of the American Ambulance at Neuilly, Paris, except during three months in 1918, when he was sent to U.S.A. by the French Government. *Publications:* Le Cardinal Lavigerie et ses œuvres, d'Afrique; Life of Mgr. Dupont des Loges, bishop of Metz; Autour du dilettantisme; Le Père Hecker, 1896, withdrawn from circulation, 1898; L'Église et le siècle; Quelques motifs d'éspérer; Le Fait religieux et la manière de l'observer, 1903; Au pays de la vie intense, 1905; L'Amérique de demain, 1910; Discours de mariage; Noces chrétiennes; Dieu nous aime; La Guerre vue d'une ambulance and Les Douleurs qui espérent; En Amérique à la fin de la guerre, 1919; Mon Filleul au jardin d'enfants: Une Expérience religieuse, Madeleine Sémer convertie et mystique, 1923; L'Amérique et le Cartel des Gauches, 1924; Les Paraboles évangéliques; Histoire de Joseph et de ses onze frères; Contes choisis de Perrault; S. François d'Assise et les Fioretti; Sept Comédies du moyen âge; La Sainte Vierge d'après l'Évangile; Histoires de jeunes martyrs; Jésus et ses Apôtres, 1931; L'Enfance du Christ et sa vie cachée; La Vie humaine et divine de Jésus-Christ Notre-Seigneur, 1933; Nouvelles Croisades de jeunes ouvriers, 1934; le Dieu des Chrétiens, notre foi en la Trinité, 1938; Notes d'un réfugié, l'exode, l'armistice, la politique de Vichy, 1945; La Route du Petit Morvandiau: Souvenirs, tome I, Enfance et jeunesse 1947; tome II, Dans le sillage de Lavigerie et de Léon XIII, 1948, tome III, A l'Institut Catholique et en Angleterre, tome IV, Une Hérésie-fantôme: l'Américanisme, tome V, Sans arrêt; tome VI, Au début du siècle, 1950. Many of the above awarded prizes by French Academy and translated into English; contributor to Vie Catholique, Revue des Deux Mondes, Atlantic Monthly, and other periodicals; Correspondent, Catholic World. *Address:* Meudon, Seine-et-Oise, France. [*Died June* 1954.

KLICKMANN, Flora, (Mrs. Henderson-Smith); *m.* 1913, E. Henderson-Smith (*d.* 1937). Started editorial work on the Windsor Magazine; edited Woman's Magazine and Girls'

Own Paper, 1908-30. *Publications:* The Ambitions of Jenny Ingram; The Flower-Patch among the Hills; Between the Larchwoods and the Weir; The Lure of the Pen; The Trail of the Ragged Robin; The Shining Way, Mending your Nerves; The Carillon of Scarpa; The Path to Fame; Flower-Patch Neighbours; Many Questions; Visitors at the Flower-Patch, The Lady with the Crumbs; Mystery in the Windflower Wood; Delicate Fuss; The Flower-Patch Garden Book; edited The Garden that we Made and In Our Flower-Garden, both by late Crown Princess of Sweden; Weeding The Flower-Patch. *Address:* The Flower-Patch, Brockweir, Chepstow. *T.:* Tintern 215. [*Died* 20 *Nov.* 1958.

KNAPP, Sir Arthur Rowland, K.C.I.E., *cr.* 1924; C.S.I. 1922; C.B.E. 1919; Indian Civil Service (retired); 2nd *s.* of late Lieut.-Colonel Charles Barrett Knapp; *m.* Florence Annie, *d.* of late Dr. E. Moore, Canon of Canterbury; one *s.* one *d.* *Educ.:* Westminster; Christ Church, Oxford. Entered Indian Civil Service, 1891; served in Madras, Under Secretary to Government, 1897-1903; Collector and District Magistrate, 1903-17; Revenue Secretary to Government, 1917; in charge of Special (War Activities) Department in Madras, 1917-19; Chief Secretary, 1919; Reforms Commissioner, 1920-21; Finance Member of Government (temp.), 1921; Special Comr. for Malabar Rebellion, 1921-22; Member and Vice-President, 1922, of Executive Council; resigned, 1925; a Governor of Westminster School. *Club:* Public Schools. [*Died* 22 *May* 1954.

KNIGHT, A. Charles, J.P. Co. London; F.S.A.; *s.* of late Athro Alfred Knight; *m.* Violet Evelyn (O.St.J.), *d.* of late John Bunce Turner; one *d.* Under-Sheriff of the City of London, 1919-21, 1924-25; Member of the City Corporation since 1916; one of H.M. Lieuts. of City of London; Deputy of the Ward of Cheap; Chm. of the Guildhall Library, 1923 and 1951; one of the founders and President, 1927-28, of the City Livery Club; on Council of London Topographical Society, and on Executive Committee of the London Society; a Director of the French Hospital; Deputy Governor of the Honourable The Irish Society, 1930; Chm. of City Police Cttee., 1941; formerly Senior Partner firm of Mackrell, Ward & Knight, Solicitors, 10 Ironmonger Lane, E.C.2; Commissioner in England for Australasia, India, Canada and Africa; Master of the Worshipful Company of Fletchers, 1933-34; of the Scriveners' Company, 1943-44; of the Tallow Chandlers' Company, 1947; of the Barber Surgeons Company, 1949-50; C.St.J. of Jerusalem. *Address:* Herne Place, Sunningdale, Ascot, Berks. *T.:* Ascot 439. *Clubs:* County of London Magistrates', Guildhall. [*Died* 10 *May* 1958.

KNIGHT, Captain Charles William Robert, M.C., F.R.P.S., F.Z.S.; Explorer, Author, Photographer, Lecturer; *b.* Sevenoaks, Kent, 25 Jan. 1884; 3rd *s.* of Charles John and Emily Knight; *m.* 1924, Eva Olive Margaret Bennett (*d.* 1926); one *d.* *Educ.:* Sevenoaks School. Devotee of Natural History generally; Pioneer of Photography of birds and animals inhabiting tall trees; later producer of films: Wild Life in the Tree-tops; The Filming of the Golden Eagle, Sea Hawks, etc.; many publications on Falconry; selected as Sniper for 1st Batt. H.A.C., 1914; Captain Queen's Own Royal West Kent Regt., 1915-19; proceeded U.S.A. with British Military Mission, 1917; now Lecturer Great Britain, Canada, United States; leader of National Geographic Society's Expedition to South Africa, 1937. *Publications:* Wild Life in the Tree-tops; The Filming of the Golden Eagle; Aristocrats of the Air; Mr. Ramshaw, My Eagle; The Adventures of Mr. Ramshaw; Knight in Africa; also articles in Field, Country Life, etc. *Recreation:* falconry. *Address:* Quebec Cottage, Montreal Park, Sevenoaks. *T.:* Sevenoaks 2960. [*Died* 19 *May* 1957.

KNIGHT, Clifford; Puisne Judge, Singapore, since 1951 (Tanganyika Terr., 1948-51); *b.* 1 Sept. 1909; *s.* of Clifford Hume Knight and Edith Frances Knight, both British; *m.* 1932, Pauline Bruce Steel; one *s.* one *d.* *Educ.:* Bishops, Capetown; Brasenose Coll., Oxford (B.A.). Called to the Bar (Inner Temple), 1932; Magistrate, Tanganyika, 1935-40. Served in Army, 1940-44. Assistant Judge, Nyasaland, 1947-48. *Address:* c/o Supreme Court, Singapore. [*Died* 23 *July* 1959.

KNIGHT, Sir George, Kt., *cr.* 1944; *b.* Delabole, 23 Sept. 1874; *s.* of William Knight, Delabole, Cornwall; *m.* Gertrude, 2nd *d.* of Ald. Bovey, Torquay; one *d.* *Educ.:* Camelford Grammar School. Began business career as a draper, purchased business of Williams & Hopkins in 1900 and retired in 1928. A Methodist lay preacher for over 50 years; Circuit Steward of Bournemouth Circuit for over 20 years; representative to conference 22 times; Treasurer Methodist Preacher's Connexional Committee for over 15 years. *Recreations:* bowls, golf, fishing. *Address:* Briarfield, Portarlington Road, Bournemouth. *T.:* Bournemouth 1020. *Clubs:* Royal Automobile, National Liberal. [*Died* 23 *Sept.* 1951.

KNIGHT, Sir Henry Foley, K.C.S.I., *cr.* 1944 (C.S.I. 1941); C.I.E. 1936; *b.* 19 Jan. 1886; *s.* of John Henry Knight, Weybourne House, Farnham; *m.* 1926, Jessie Spence, *d.* of Sir Robert Duncan Bell, K.C.S.I., C.I.E.; one *s.* one *d.* *Educ.:* Haileybury Coll.; Caius College, Cambridge. Indian Civil Service, 1910; Assistant Collector, Bombay Presidency; Indian Army Reserve of Officers, 1916-19; Royal Flying Corps, Royal Air Force; various appointments in Bombay Presidency including Deputy Secretary, Finance Dept.; Director of Commercial Intelligence; Director of Industries; Secretary to Govt. of Bombay, Home Dept.; Secretary to Govt. of Bombay, General Dept.; Commissioner of Excise, Bombay; acting Governor of Bombay March-May 1945; acting Governor of Madras, Feb.-May 1946; acting Governor of Burma, June-Aug. 1946; acting Governor of Assam, Sept.-Dec. 1946; Adviser to Secretary of State for India, Feb.-Aug. 1947; Assistant Secretary, Ministry of National Insurance, 1947-50; U.K. Representative on the Advisory Commission to the United Nations Relief and Works Agency for Palestine refugees in the Near East, 1950-53. *Publication:* Food Administration in India 1939-47, 1954. *Address:* Appletree Cottage, Staplecross, Robertsbridge, Sussex. *T.:* Staplecross 273. *Clubs:* Circle of 19th Century Motorists; Royal Bombay Yacht (Bombay). [*Died* 8 *July* 1960.

KNIGHT, Rt. Rev. Leslie Albert; *b.* York, West Australia, 4 Aug. 1890; *s.* of George Edward and Clara Knight, Wandering, W.A.; *m.* 1919, Mary Bertha Moore, Timaru, New Zealand; no *c.* *Educ.:* Boys' High School, Christchurch; University of New Zealand, B.A. 1913, M.A. 1914; Univ. of London (Inter. Divinity 1921). Deacon, 1914; priest, 1915; Curate of Fendalton, Christchurch, 1915-16; Vicar of Hororata, West Malvern, 1916-17; Chaplain to N.Z.E.F in France, 1917-19; Vicar of Leithfield, 1919-1921; Vicar of Kaiapoi, 1921-23; Rector and Chaplain of St. Saviour's Boys' Orphanage, Timaru, 1923-28 (all in N.Z.); Warden of St. Barnabas Theological College, and special preacher St. Peter's Cathedral, Adelaide, 1928-38; Bishop of Bunbury from 1938. *Recreations:* golf; painting in oils and water-colour, photography (pictorial). *Address:* Bishopscourt, Bunbury, Western Australia. *T.A.:* Bunbury, W.A. *T.:*

Bunbury 163. *Clubs:* South Western (Bunbury, W.A.); Weld (Perth, W.A.). [*Died* 31 *Dec.* 1950.

[*But death not notified in time for inclusion in Who Was Who 1941–1950, first edn.*

KNIGHT, William Lowry Craig, C.M.G. 1945; *b.* Cookstown, Co. Tyrone, 1 Oct. 1889; *er. s.* of late W. J. R. Knight, M.D., and Annie Berkeley Craig; *m.* 1916, May, *d.* of late Uvedale Barrington Tristram; two *s.* two *d.* *Educ.:* Royal School, Dungannon, Pembroke College, Cambridge. Student Interpreter in the Levant, 1909; Acting Vice-Consul, Salonica, 1913-19, and Acting Consul-General in 1919; Vice-Consul, Volo, 1920-24 and at Corfu in 1924; Consul at Trebizond, 1924-27; Second Secretary, H.M. Embassy in Turkey, in 1927 and 1928, and First Secretary, 1930-36; Acting Consul and Acting Consul-General, Alexandria, 1936-37; Acting Judge of H.M. Supreme Court in Egypt, in 1936; Consul - General, Tunis, 1937 - 40; Basra, 1942-1946; Athens, 1946; Salonica, 1946 - 49; retired from H.M. Foreign Service. Chief U.K. delegate to U.N. Special Cttee. on the Balkans, 1949-52 (when Cttee. was dissolved by Gen. Assembly). *Address:* 2 East Street, Rye, Sussex. [*Died* 31 *Dec.* 1955.

KNIGHT - ADKIN, Reverend Walter Kenrick, C.B. 1932; O.B.E. 1919; D.L.; Hon. Canon of Portsmouth, 1929; *b.* 17 Aug. 1880; *s.* of late Canon Harry Kendrick Knight-Adkin, B.A., and Georgina Elizabeth, *d.* of J. P. Knight, Cheltenham; *m.* Elsa Cuff, *d.* of Alexander Napier, M.D., Glasgow; no *c.* *Educ.:* Cheltenham College; St. Edmund Hall, Oxford; Wells Theological College. Curate of Kentish Town, 1908-10; served H.M.S. Lancaster, 1910-12; Victory, 1912-13; Conqueror, 1913-16; Victory, 1916-19; H.M.S. Revenge, 1919-20; R.N. Coll., Dartmouth, 1920-23; H.M.S. Queen Elizabeth, 1923-24; H.M.S. Victory, 1924-29; Archdeacon and Chaplain of the Fleet, 1929-33; K.H.C. 1929; retired list, 1933; Dean of Gibraltar, 1933-41; Vicar of Sparkwell, 1942-45; Chaplain to Lord Mayor of Bristol, Chapel of St. Mark, College Green, 1945-56. D.L. City and County of Gloucester and City and County of Bristol, 1950. *Recreation:* photography. *Address:* 17 Miles Road, Bristol 8. *T.:* 37783. [*Died* 24 *May* 1957.

KNIGHTS, Henry Newton, M.B.E.; J.P.; late Mayor of Camberwell; Engineer; *m.* Grace (*d.* 1946), *d.* of Joseph Mitchell. M.P. (Co-U.) North Camberwell, Dec. 1918 - 22; Sheriff, City of London, 1920-21. *Address:* Blake's Corner, 1 Bolters Lane, Banstead, Surrey. *T.:* Burgh Heath 2533. [*Died* 31 *Oct.* 1959.

KNOTT, Rev. Alfred Ernest, C.B.E. 1919; D.S.O. 1917; Methodist Minister; late Chaplain to the Forces, 1st Class; *b.* 1869; *s.* of Thomas Knott; *m.* 1897, Florence Mildred Constance, *d.* of T. G. Sweeney. Served Tirah Campaign, 1897-98; France, 1914-15; Mesopotamia, 1916-19 (despatches thrice, D.S.O., C.B.E.). *Address:* Homeleigh, Kiln Road, Fareham, Hants. *T.:* Fareham 3314. [*Died* 20 *Dec.* 1951.

KNOTT, John Espenett, C.M.G. 1918; D.S.O. 1916; late Royal Inniskilling Fusiliers; *s.* of Herbert Knott, J.P., of Wilmslow, Cheshire, and Ada, *d.* of late Thomas Birkbeck Wakefield of Hall, Moate, Co. Westmeath; *m.* 1915, Dorothy, *d.* of late Maurice Spring-Rice Bayly; one *s.* (and one killed in action, Libya, 1942). Temp. Lt.-Col. Aug. 1917; command of 2nd Batt. R. Inniskilling Fusiliers, Apr. 1918; served European War, Feb. 1916 to Sept. 1918 (C.M.G., D.S.O., despatches, wounded). Comd. 2 Herefordshire H.G., 1941-44. J.P. Herefordshire. *Address:* Birchyfields, Bromyard, Herefordshire. [*Died* 1 *Nov.* 1959.

KNOWLES, Arthur Richard, C.B.E. 1950 (O.B.E. 1942); Export Secretary, The British Electrical & Allied Manufacturers' Association, since 1958; *b.* Dursley, Glos., 18 April 1899; *s.* of Ezra Knowles, Manchester; *m.* 1922, Alice Leonora, *d.* of John Taylor, Manchester; one *d.* *Educ.:* Manchester Central High Sch. Commissioned in R.F.C. from Artists' Rifles, 1917. Employed in Chefoo, North China, 1919-25; Hon. Sec., Brit. Chamber of Commerce, Chefoo, 1922-25; Asst. Sec., Manchester Chamber of Commerce, 1927-34; Sec., Sheffield Chamber of Commerce, 1935-45; Founder Director of Joint Iron Council, 1945-46; Secretary-General, Association of British Chambers of Commerce, 1946-56. Hon. Secretary of Association of Secretaries of British Chambers of Commerce, 1946-56. Member: War Export Trade Investigation Cttee., 1940; Cttee. on the Practice and Procedure of the Department of Overseas Trade, 1944; Census of Production Advisory Committee, 1955-56. F.C.I.S.; F.B.I.M.; M.I.Ex. *Recreation:* gardening. *Address:* Meersbrook, Highfield Avenue, Pinner, Middlesex. *T.:* Pinner 6688. *Club:* Reform. [*Died* 28 *Feb.* 1960.

KNOWLES, Sir Francis Howe Seymour, 5th Bt., *cr.* 1765; *b.* 13 Jan. 1886; *s.* of 4th Bt. and Mary, *d.* of C. Thomson, Halifax, Nova Scotia; *S.* father, 1918; *m.* 1914, Kathleen, *d.* of late W. Lennon; one *s.* *Educ.:* Oriel College, Oxford. B.A., 1908; Diploma in Anthropology, 1909; B.Sc., 1911; M.A., 1911; sometime Physical Anthropologist to Geological Survey, Canada. *Publications:* The Physical Anthropology of the Roebuck Iroquois; The Manufacture of a Flint Arrow-head; other research papers on anthropology. *Recreations:* fishing and croquet. *Heir:* *s.* Francis Gerald William [*b.* 1915; *m.* 1948, Ruth (Hulse), *d.* of late Rev. Arthur Brooke-Smith; one *s.* two *d.*]. *Address:* 3 Bradmore Road, Oxford. [*Died* 4 *April* 1953.

KNOX, Sir Geoffrey George, K.C.M.G., *cr.* 1935 (C.M.G. 1929); *b.* 11 March 1884. Student Interpreter Levant, 1906; Second Secretary, 1920; First Secretary, 1923; Counsellor of Embassy, 1931; Chairman of the Saar Governing Commission, 1932-35; Envoy Extraordinary and Minister Plenipotentiary to Hungary, 1935-1939; British Ambassador to Brazil, 1939-41; served European War, 1917-19 (despatches, Chevalier of Order of Redeemer, Greece). *Club:* St. James'. [*Died* 6 *April* 1958.

KNOX, Brigadier Hon. Sir George Hodges, Kt., *cr.* 1945; C.M.G. 1918; V.D.; M.P., Parl. of Victoria, since 1927; *b.* 17 Dec. 1885; *e. s.* of late Hon. Wm. Knox, M.P., J.P., Melbourne, Australia; *m.* 1st, 1909, Kathleen, *o. d.* of late Robert MacPherson, Victoria; one *s.* one *d.*; 2nd, 1921, Ada Victoria, *o. d.* of late W. H. Harris, Halwill Manor, Beaworthy, N. Devon; one *s.* *Educ.:* Scotch College, Melbourne. Commission Commonwealth Military Forces, 1909, Victorian Scottish Regiment; World War, 1914-18: served with this regiment, left Australia as 2nd in command, 23rd Batt. A.I.F.; commanded 23rd Batt. A.I.F. during operations and evacuation of Gallipoli Peninsula; operations on Suez Canal, France, and Belgium (despatches twice, C.M.G.); A.D.C. to State Governor, 1918; Special Service Duty, 1919; commanded 52nd Bn. Australian Military Forces (Gippsland Regt.,) 1921-27; Unattached List, 1927-32; Reserve of Officers, 1932, World War, 1939-45: posted to command Victorian Scottish Regt.; Col. commanding an infantry brigade, 1940-41; commanded Brigade Group, 1941-42; Sec. to Cabinet, State of Victoria, 1929; Hon. Minister and Executive Councillor, 1929; and again in 1935; Speaker of Legislative Assembly, Victoria, 1942-47; is Life Mem. Polo Assoc. of Victoria; hon. inspector fisheries and native game, and hon. forest officer, in State of Victoria, etc. *Recreations:* farming and reading. *Address:* Greenlaw, Ferntree Gully, Victoria, Australia. *Clubs:* Australian, Naval and Military (Melbourne). [*Died* 11 *July* 1960.

KNOX, Brig.-General Henry Owen, C.M.G. 1915; C.I.E. 1917; C.B.E. 1919; *b.*

16 Jan. 1874; *s.* of late Rt. Hon. Sir Ralph Henry Knox, P.C., K.C.B., V.D.; *m.* 1st, 1899, Muriel Lucy (*d.* 1909), *d.* of late Sir Owen Roberts of Henley Park, Guildford, and Dinas, Carnarvon; two *s.*; 2nd, Elsie Caroline, *d.* of late Harry Harker of Hurlingham Lodge, Hurlingham; one *d.* *Educ.:* Dulwich College. Assistant in Court of Worshipful Company of Skinners; Master, 1923-24; joined A.S.C. from 4th Batt. South Stafford Regt. 1896; served S. Africa, 1899-1901 (Queen's medal with 4 clasps, despatches); appointed Quartermaster-General, New Zealand Forces, 1911-14; served European War, 8 Aug. 1914-Dec. 1914 (despatches); A.Q.M.G. to Australian and New Zealand Army Corps, Dec. 1914, was present at landing in Gallipoli, and remained until evacuation (wounded, despatches twice, C.M.G.); A.Q.M.G., G.H.Q., H.F., March-Aug. 1916; D.Q.M.G. Mesopotamia, Aug. 1916-Sep. 1917 (recapture of Kut and taking of Bagdad) (despatches twice, C.I.E., Order of St. Anne, 2nd class, with swords); granted hon. rank Brig.-Gen. 17 Nov. 1917; joined Civil Engineer-in-Chief's Dept. Admiralty, 1918; Chief of Staff thereof, 1919, and Representative of Civil Engineer-in-Chief on Naval Inter-Allied Commission, Heligoland, 1920; thanked by the Lords of the Admiralty; raised 22nd (Tunbridge Wells) Bn. Kent Home Guard. *Recreations:* cricket, tennis, golf. *Address:* High Trees, Forest Road, Tunbridge Wells. *T.:* Tunbridge Wells 1303. *Club:* United Service. [*Died* 5 *May* 1955.

KNOX, Rt. Reverend Monsignor Ronald Arbuthnott; a Protonotary Apostolic since 1951; a Member of the Pontifical Roman Academy of Theology, since 1957; *b.* 17 Feb. 1888; 4th *s.* of late Rt. Rev. E. A. Knox. *Educ.:* Eton (1st Scholarship); Balliol College, Oxford (1st Scholarship). Hertford Scholarship, 1907; 2nd in Honour Moderations, 1908; Ireland and Craven Scholarship, 1908; 1st in Litt. Hum., 1910; Fellow and Lecturer at Trinity College, Oxford, 1910; Chaplain, 1912; resigned, 1917; received into the Church of Rome, Sept. 1917; Catholic Chaplain at the University of Oxford, 1926-39; Domestic Prelate to His Holiness, 1936; Hon. Fellow of Trinity College, Oxford, 1941; Hon. Fellow of Balliol College, Oxford, 1953. F.R.S.L. 1950. Hon. D.Litt. Nat. Univ. of Ireland, 1954. *Publications:* Some Loose Stones, 1913; Reunion All Round, 1914; A Spiritual Aeneid, 1918; Memories of the Future, 1923; Sanctions, A Frivolity, 1924; The Viaduct Murder, 1925; Other Eyes than Ours, 1926; An Open Air Pulpit, 1926; The Three Taps, 1927; The Belief of Catholics, 1927; The Footsteps at the Lock, 1928; The Mystery of the Kingdom (sermons), 1928; Essays in Satire, 1928; On Getting There, 1929; Caliban in Grub Street, 1930; (with Arnold Lunn) Difficulties, 1932; Broadcast Minds, 1932; The Body in the Silo, 1933; Still Dead, 1934; Heaven and Charing Cross (sermons), 1935; Barchester Pilgrimage, 1935; The Holy Bible, an Abridgement and Rearrangement, 1936; Double Cross Purposes, 1937; Let Dons Delight, 1939; Captive Flames (sermons), 1940; In Soft Garments (sermons), 1942; God and the Atom, 1945; Translation of the New Testament, 1945; A Retreat for Priests, 1946; The Mass in Slow Motion, 1948; The Creed in Slow Motion, 1949; On Englishing the Bible, 1949; Translation of the Old Testament, 1949; Enthusiasm, a Chapter in the History of Religion, 1950; The Gospel in Slow Motion, 1950; Stimuli, 1951; The Hidden Stream (sermons), 1953; A Commentary on the Gospels, 1953; Off the Record, 1954; New Testament Commentary II, 1954; A Retreat for Lay People, 1955; The Window in the Wall (sermons), 1956; New Testament Commentary III, 1956; (posthumous) Literary Distractions, 1958; Ed. Philip Caraman: The Pastoral Sermons of Ronald A. Knox, 1960, Occasional Sermons of Ronald A. Knox, 1960; The Layman and his Conscience, 1962; several pamphlets, also Detective Stories. *Relevant publication:* The Life of Ronald Knox, by Evelyn Waugh, 1959. *Address:* The Manor House, Mells, Frome, Som. [*Died* 24 *Aug.* 1957.

KNOX, Lt.-Col. Stuart George, C.S.I. 1917; C.I.E. 1909; *b.* 7 Oct. 1869; *e. s.* of late Sir George Edward Knox; *m.* 1st, 1893, Ethel Laura, O.B.E. 1918 (*d.* 1934), *e. surv. d.* of Rt. Hon. Sir John Edge, P.C.; one *s.* (and one *s.* decd.); 2nd, 1934, Ethel Rose, O.B.E., R.R.C. and bar, *y. d.* of late James Collins. *Educ.:* Elizabeth Coll., Guernsey; Repton; R.M.C. Sandhurst. Entered Army, 1888; Indian Political Dept., 1894; Actg. Consul, Basra, 1894-95; Polit. Agent, Malwa, 1896; Asst. Agent to Gov.-Gen., Baluchistan, 1896-97; Polit. Agent, Kalat, 1897-1900; Capt. I.A. 1899; Attaché for Baluchistan to Delhi Coronation Durbar and Polit. Agent Thal Chotiali, 1903; 1st Asst. to Resident and Consul-Gen., Bushire, 1904; Polit. Agent, Koweit, 1904-09 and at Bahrein, 1910-11. Major I.A. 1906; Polit. Agent and Consul, Muscat, 1911-14; Lt.-Col. 1914. Polit. Resident and Actg. Consul-Gen., Bushire, 1914-15. Served European War, 1915-19: in Mesopotamia as Judicial Officer, 1915-17 (despatches, C.S.I.); Senior Judicial Officer, Basra, 1915-18; Pres. Court of Appeal, Mesopotamia, 1918-19; officiated as Resident, Mysore, 1921; Resident of Hyderabad, 1921-23, when apptd. Polit. Res. and Consul-Gen. at Bushire. Pres. Kuwait Conf., 1923-24; retired, 1924. *Address:* Mont-Fleuri Hotel, Parsonage Road, Bournemouth. *T.:* Bournemouth 190. [*Died* 11 *Dec.* 1956.

KNUTHSEN, Sir Louis (Francis Roebuck), K.C.V.O., *cr.* 1936 (C.V.O. 1934); O.B.E. 1919; M.D.; Physician in Ordinary to The Princess Royal, 1935, Extra Physician since 1951; *b.* Santa Cruz, West Indies; *s.* of Francis Knuthsen and Anne Roebuck; *m.* 1901, Mildred Helen Howell (*d.* 1946). *Educ.:* Edinburgh Academy; Edinburgh University M.D. (Honours); Paris, Berlin, and Vienna Universities; Fellow of Royal Society of Medicine; Member Section of Dermatology; late Consulting Physician, London Skin Hospital, Fitzroy Square; Warden, Queen's Chapel of the Savoy; Vice-Pres. British Hospitals Assoc.; served European War (Mons Star, 1914; British War medal, Victory medal, despatches twice, O.B.E.); Knight of Grace Order of St. John of Jerusalem; Médaille des Epidémies en Vermeil; Médaille de Reconnaissance avec Bouton. *Publications:* Treatment of Scabies in France, British Medical Journal, 1907; Notes on 150 cases treated by 606, Practitioner, 1911; Pruritus Ani, Lancet, 1930. *Recreation:* riding. *Address:* 33 Chesham St., Belgrave Sq., S.W.1. *T.:* Sloane 1470. *Club:* Travellers' (Paris). [*Died* 7 *July* 1957.

KOMISARJEVSKY, Theodore; theatrical producer, architect, artist, writer; *s.* of Professor Theodore Komisarjevsky, sen., and Princess Marie Kourzevich; *m.* Ernestine Stodelle; one *d.* *Educ.:* Petersburg Academy of Architecture and University, D.Ph. Since 1906 working in the theatre as designer and producing director: Theatre Vera Komisarjevsky in Petersburg, Nezlobin Theatre in Moscow, Moscow Private Opera, Russian Imperial Theatres, Russian Soviet State Theatres, own theatre and school of Dramatic Art in Moscow; productions in Italy, Paris, Vienna, New York, London, Glasgow, Edinburgh, etc.; since 1919 living permanently in London working as producer of plays, theatrical designer, as interior decorator, teacher of acting and writer; British subject since 1932; designed in England the interiors of Granada Cinemas at Woolwich, Clapham Junction, Harrow, Cheam, East Molesey, Greenford, and Greenwich. *Publications:* In English: Myself and the Theatre; The Costume of the Theatre; The Theatre and a changing Civilization, 1935; articles in the Encyclopædia Britannica and periodicals. In Russian: Theatrical Preludes; The Costume;

The Art of the Actor, etc. *Recreations:* tennis, music, travels. [*Died* 17 *April* 1954.

KON, George Armand Robert, F.R.S. 1943; M.A. Cantab.; D.Sc. Lond.; Professor of Chemistry, Chester Beatty Research Institute, Royal Cancer Hospital (Free) since 1942; *b.* 18 Feb. 1892; *s.* of Isidore Kon and Marie Antoinette Fleuret; *m.* 1st, 1926, Anne Hadfield Pollock (marriage dissolved 1937), *d.* of late James Watts, Abney Hall, Cheadle, Cheshire; 2nd, 1938, Mary Primrose, *d.* of late W. Maxwell Tress; no *c.* *Educ.:* privately; Gonville and Caius Coll., Cambridge (Nat. Sci. Tripos). Research in Organic Chemistry at Imperial College of Science and Technology, 1913; served in the Anti-gas Dept., 1916-19 (despatches); Capt. R.E., 1918; on British Gas Mission to U.S.A., 1918; returned Imperial College, 1919; joined staff as Lecturer in 1925, Assistant Professor in 1934. *Publications:* numerous scientific papers. *Recreations:* lawn tennis, golf. *Address:* 7 Astell Street, S.W.3. [*Died* 15 *March* 1951.

KONSTAM, His Honour Edwin Max., C.B.E. 1920 (O.B.E. 1918); Q.C. 1919; *b.* London, 1870; *m.* 1918, Mary Beatrix, *d.* of late Rev. Lewis Haig Loyd. *Educ.:* Marlborough; King's College, Cambridge. Indian Civil Service, 1890; retired, 1902; Barrister, Inner Temple, 1899; commenced to practise, 1902; Bencher, 1925; Treasurer, 1948; served in Food Production Department, Board of Agriculture, 1917-19; A Judge of County Courts, 1932-45; Member Treasury Committee on Codification of Income Tax Law, 1927-36; Chairman of Selection Committee, Charles II Exhibition, 1932, and Queen Elizabeth Exhibition, 1933; Chairman, Home Secretary's Advisory Committee for House to House Collections Act, 1939. *Publications:* The Law of Income Tax, and other works on similar subjects. *Address:* 19 Chapel Street, S.W.1. *T.:* Sloane 1143. *Club:* Athenæum. [*Died* 7 *April* 1956.

KORDA, Sir Alexander, Kt., *cr.* 1942; Chairman London Film Productions, Ltd.; Alexander Korda Film Productions Ltd.; *b.* Turkeve, Hungary, 16 Sept. 1893; *s.* of Henry and Ernestine Korda; became a British Subject, in 1936; *m.* 1st, 1919, Maria Farkas; one *s.*; 2nd, 1939, Estelle Merle O'Brien Thompson (who acted as Merle Oberon) (marriage dissolved); 3rd, 1953, Alexandra Irene Boycun. *Educ.:* Reformist College and Royal University, Budapest. Newspaper man in Budapest. Later film producer in Budapest, Vienna, Berlin, Hollywood and Paris. Founded London Film Productions, in London, 1932; Alexander Korda Film Productions, 1939. His 112 films include: The Private Life of Henry VIII, 1933; The Scarlet Pimpernel, 1935; The Third Man, 1950; Richard III, 1955. Former Director of United Artists' Corporations of America. Officier Légion d'Honneur (France), 1950. *Address:* 146 Piccadilly, W.1. *Club:* Royal Thames Yacht. [*Died* 23 *Jan.* 1956.

KORNGOLD, Erich Wolfgang; *b.* Brünn, Moravia, 29 May 1897; *s.* of Dr. Julius Korngold, Musical Critic of the Neue Freie Presse, Vienna; Professor Staatsakademie für Musik, Vienna. *Compositions:* Der Schneeman, 1908; Ring des Polycrates; Violanta, 1916; music to Shakespeare's Much Ado about Nothing, 1918; Tote Stadt, 1920; songs, chamber music, orchestral works; Das Wunder der Heliane, 1927; Operetten Bearbeitungen Strauss und Offenbach; Klaviersonate Op. 25; Baby-Serenade f. Orch. op. 24, 1931-32; Opera: Die Kathrin; Violin concert, op. 35; Cello Concerto, op. 37; Silent Serenade, music comedy, op. 36; Symphonic Serenade for strings, op. 39; Symphony in F Sharp, op. 40; 1937-46, picture-music in Hollywood: Antony Adverse, Prince and Pauper, Robin Hood, Juarez, Sea-hawk, Sea-wolf, King's-Row, The Constant Nymph, Devotion, Of Human Bondage, Deception, Escape me never, etc.; musical supervision of Magic Fire (Richard Wagner picture), 1954-55. *Address:* 9936 Tolucalake Av., N. Hollywood, Calif., U.S.A. [*Died* 29 *Nov.* 1957.

KOTZÉ, Sir Robert Nelson, Kt., *cr.* 1918; Honorary D.Sc. and D.C.L.; Honorary Member and Gold Medallist of the Institute of Mining and Metallurgy; *b.* 1870; 3rd *s.* of Rev. J. J. Kotzé, of Darling, Cape Province; *m.* 1898, Maria Beatrix (*d.* 1944), *e. d.* of Rev. D. P. Faure, of Cape Town; two *d.* *Educ.:* S.A. College, Cape Town (B.A. in Science, gold medallist); Royal School of Mines, Clausthal, Germany (diplomas in mining and metallurgy with distinction). Assistant engineer and consulting engineer to the Transvaal Goldfields, Ltd., and subsidiary companies, 1896-1907; Government Mining Engineer, Transvaal, 1908-10, Union of South Africa, 1910-26; Vice-Chancellor of the University of the Witwatersrand, 1922-25 and 1937-38; M.P. for Springs in Union Parliament, 1929-1939; Director, De Beers Consolidated Mines, Ltd., African Explosives and Industries, Ltd., Geduld Proprietary, East Geduld. *Publications:* (philosophical) The Scheme of Things; sundry papers read before technical Societies in Johannesburg; annual reports on mining industry. *Recreation:* chess. *Address:* Chartley, Park Road, Rondebosch, C.P., S. Africa. *Clubs:* Rand (Johannesburg); Civil Service (Cape Town); Kimberley (Kimberley). [*Died* 14 *March* 1953.

KOUSSEVITZKY, Serge; Conductor emeritus (of Boston Symphony Orchestra, U.S.A. 1924-49); *b.* Tver, Russia, 26 July 1874; *s.* of Alexander Koussevitzky and Anne Barabeitchik; *m.* 1905, Natalie Ouchkoff (*d.* 1942); *m.* 1947, Olga Naumoff. *Educ.:* Philharmonic Conservatory, Moscow. Master of Free Arts, Philharmonic Conservatory, Moscow, 1894; LL.D., Harvard, 1929; Mus. Dr. Brown Univ., 1926; Rutgers, 1927; Yale, 1928; Rochester, 1940; Williams College, 1943; Boston Univ., 1945; Princeton, 1947; double-bass virtuoso and soloist, Imperial Theatre Orchestra, Moscow, 1894-97; Professor in Moscow Conservatory, 1897; first European appearance as double-bass soloist, Berlin, 1898; début as Conductor with Berlin Philharmonic Orchestra, 1907; founded, with wife, publishing firm of Éditions Russes de Musique (entire profits of which went to Russian Composers), 1909; founded Koussevitzky Symphony Orchestra of 85 musicians, Moscow, 1910, Conductor until 1918; Director of State Symphony Orchestra, Russia, 1917; Director of Grand Opera, Moscow, 1918; founded Concerts Koussevitzky, Paris, 1921, Director and Conductor until 1928; directed Berkshire Symphonic Festival, 1936-41; initiated Berkshire Music Center, 1938, Director since 1940; in memory of wife, founded Koussevitzky Music Foundation to assist composers and for other cultural and educational needs, 1942; compositions: Concerto for double-bass and Orchestra; transcriptions from classical works; many pieces for double-bass and piano. Twice decorated by Czar of Russia, 1903; Knight of the Legion of Honor (France), 1924, Officer 1930, Commander 1936; Cross of Commander of Order of White Rose (Finland); Hon. Member of Am. Acad. of Arts and Sciences, 1934. *Publications:* Poetry and Music; Concerning Interpretation; Remarks About American Orchestras; Essays on Brahms and Debussy. *Recreations:* reading, drama and philosophy. *Address:* (home) 191 Buckminster Road, Brookline, Mass., U.S.A.; Lenox, Mass., U.S.A.; "Casa Serena," Scottsdale, Arizona, U.S.A. *Clubs:* Harvard, Tavern (Boston); Bohemians, Lotos (New York). [*Died* 4 *June* 1951.

KRAUSE, Hon. Frederick Edward Traugott, B.A., LL.D. (Cape Univ.), LL.D. (Univ. of Amsterdam), Barrister-at-law, Middle

Temple; Q.C., J.P.; b. District of Bloemfontein, Orange Free State, 29 April 1868; m. Annette Bowyer (d. 1957). *Educ.:* Grey College, Bloemfontein; Victoria College, Stellenbosch; University of Amsterdam; Inns of Court, London, Cambridge, etc. Called to Bar, 1893; started practice as Advocate in Pretoria; appointed, 1896, State Prosecutor and Acting Attorney-General for Witwatersrand under Republican Government, Transvaal; Special Commandant and Military Governor of Johannesburg during Boer war; surrendered Johannesburg to Lord Roberts, 31 May 1900; Member of Parliament for Vrededorp, 1907-10, under first Responsible Government; Judge of the Supreme Court of S. Africa, Transvaal Provincial Division, 1923-33; Judge President, Orange Free State Provincial Division of Supreme Court of S. Africa, 1933-38; Acting Judge of High Court, South-West Africa, Oct. 1944-Jan. 1945; Acting Judge of Supreme Court of S.A., Natal, Prov. Div., Feb.-May 1945; Acting Judge, O.F.S. Prov. Div. and Griqualand West local Div. of Supreme Court, 1946; President of S.A. Association for Advancement of Science, 1945-46; Chairman of various Commissions, e.g. Mining Regulations Commission, 1907; Johannesburg Hospital Inquiry Commission; Mem. of Witwatersrand School Bd., Public Library, etc.; Life and Hon. Member of S.A. Association for Advancement of Science; Hon. Member S.A. Akademie vir Wetenskap, Letteren en Kuns, and Life Vice-President of Witwatersrand Agricultural Society. *Address:* P.O. Box 1363, Pretoria; 359 Murray Street, Brooklyn, Pretoria. *Club:* Pretoria. [*Died* 23 *Aug.* 1959.

KRISHNA RAU, Sir Mysore Nanjundiah, Kt., cr. 1934; Diwan Bahadur 1925, Rajakaryaprasakta, 1922; retired member of council, Government of Mysore; b. 27 Jan. 1877; s. of Mysore Nanjundiah; m.; two s. two d. *Educ.:* Maharaja's College, Mysore. Held the following appointments under the Government of Mysore: Comptroller, Financial Secretary, President, Mysore State Life Insurance Committee, Member of Council, Chairman of the Board of Management of the Mysore Iron Works, and Dewan. *Address:* Basavangudi, Bangalore City, South India. [*Died* 2 *Feb.* 1958.

KRISHNASWAMI AYYAR, Diwan Bahadur Sir Alladi, Kt., cr. 1932; B.A., B.L.; Advocate-General for Presidency of Madras, 1929-44; b. 13 May 1883; m. 1906, Venkatalakshmamma; three s. four d. *Educ.:* Madras Christian College; Madras University. B.A. 1904; B.L. 1906; Enrolled as High Court Vakil, Madras, 1907; studied in the Chambers of late Justice P. R. Sundara Aiyer; Kaisar-i-Hind (silver medal) 1926 for philanthropic and public services; Title Diwan Bahadur, 1930; served on Expert Committee of the Govt. of India for drafting the Sale of Goods and Partnership Bills; served on the Syndicate of the Madras University for two terms; a member of the Committee of the Sanskrit College, Mylapore; Convocation Address, Andhra University, 1930. *Address:* Ekamra Nivas, Luz, Mylapore, Madras, India. *T.:* 3246. [*Died* 3 *Oct.* 1953.

KROYER-KIELBERG, Sir (F.) Michael, K.B.E., cr. 1947; Grand Cross of Dannebrog (Denmark); b. Skanderborg, Denmark, 2 Jan. 1882; s. of late Orlaf August Kielberg; m. 1910, Dora Margaret, d. of Thomas Corfe, Thornton Hough, Cheshire; two s. one d. *Educ.:* Skanderborg and Brockske, Copenhagen. Formerly Chm. United Molasses Co. Ltd., Athel Line Limited, and Tankers Ltd.; formerly Director, Anchor Line Ltd. *Address:* Flat 45, Orchard Court, W.1.; Sefton Lodge, Leighton Buzzard, Beds. *Club:* Danish. [*Died* 19 *May* 1958.

KYLE, Emily Escher, B.A. Hons. Lond.; Governor of Bedford College for Women; Hon. Sec. Church Teachers' Fellowship, 1939; Hon. Mem. of Staff, Inst. of Christian Education; d. of late J. W. Kyle, Coatham and Middlesboro'. *Educ.:* Middlesboro' High School, Girls; Bedford Coll., Women, London (entrance Scholar). Gilchrist Exhibition, London University, Pfeiffer Scholar, Bedford College. Assist.-Mistress, Princess Helena College, Ealing, 1896-98, Stroud Green and Hornsey High School, 1898-1901; Headmistress, Sunderland Girls' High School, 1901-05; Headmistress, Highbury Hill High School, N., 1905-38; Vice-Principal Home and Colonial Highbury Training College, 1905-12. *Publications:* various educ. papers. *Recreations:* study, philosophy. *Address:* 54 Princes Square, W.2. [*Died* 12 *Feb.* 1958.

KYLE, Henry Greville, M.A., M.D. (Oxford); consulting surgeon, Bristol General Hospital; late Surgeon, Southmead Hospital; Captain R.A.M.C. (T.). *Educ.:* Cheltenham; Oxford; Birmingham. *Address:* 31 Westbury Road, Bristol. *T.:* Bristol 62.6857. [*Died* 21 *March* 1956.

L

LACY, Francis Brandon; Fellow of the Institute of Bankers; Editor and Proprietor of The Tea and Rubber Mail; Chairman of Tidman and Son Ltd.; b. 25 Jan. 1872; s. of C. J. Lacy, private banker; m. 1896, L. Gertrude Jackson (d. 1951). *Educ.:* Haileybury College. *Recreations:* shooting, fishing. *Address:* 12 Portarlington Road, Bournemouth, Hants. *T.:* 63880 Westbourne. [*Died* 17 *Dec.* 1954.

LACY, Sir Pierce Thomas, 1st Bt., cr. 1921; b. 16 Feb. 1872; s. of late John Pierce Lacy of Oakmount, Edgbaston, Birmingham; m. 1898, Ethel Maud (d. 1955), d. of late James Finucane Draper, of St. Heliers, Jersey; one s. five d. *Educ.:* St. George's College, Weybridge. Chairman Birmingham Stock Exchange; has carried on the business of a stockbroker for many years in Birmingham, and has interested himself in British industrial undertakings; founded the British Shareholders Trust (B.S.T. Ltd.) and British Trusts Association, Ltd.; formerly a Dir. of several important financial and industrial companies. High Sheriff of Suffolk, 1927; J.P. Suffolk. K.C.S.G. (recd. from the Pope). *Recreations:* tennis, shooting, golf. *Heir:* s. Maurice John Pierce [late Lt., 2nd Life Guards, b. 2 April 1900; m. 1st, 1932, Primrose (who obtained a divorce, 1939), yr. d. of late F. E. V. Russell-Roberts; one d.; 2nd, 1940, Jean, d. of late Myrddin Evans, Bangor; two s. one d.]. *Address:* Ampton Hall, Bury St. Edmunds. *T.A.:* Ampton. *T.:* Culford 232. *Clubs:* Carlton, Boodle's; West Suffolk County; Country (Cannes). [*Died* 25 *Dec.* 1956.

LAFLECHE, Maj.-Gen. Hon. Léo-Richer, P.C. (Can.) 1942; D.S.O. 1917; Canadian Ambassador to Argentine, 1952-1955; Deputy Minister of National Defence, 1932; M.P. Outremont Division of Montreal, 1942; Minister of National War Services, Canada, 1942-45 (Deputy Minister, 1940-42); Canadian Ambassador to Greece, 1945-49; Canadian High Commissioner to Australia, 1949-50. Canadian Infantry Reserve of Officers; Hon. A.D.C. to Governor-General of Canada. Served European War, 1914-18 (despatches, D.S.O., Legion of Honour). *Address:* Department of External Affairs, Ottawa, Ontario, Canada. [*Died* 7 *March* 1956.

LA FOLLETTE, Robert M., jun.; Author; Economic Research Consultant; b. Madison, Wis., 6 Feb. 1895; s. of Robert Marion La Follette and Belle Case; m. 1930, Rachel Wilson Young; two s. *Educ.:* Public Schools of Madison, Wis.; Univ. of Wisconsin, Madison. Sec. to Senator Robert M. La Follette 6 years; elected to fill unexpired term of father in U.S. Senate, 1925; re-elected, 1928, 1934, 1940; term expired, 1947. *Address:* National Press Bldg., Washington, D.C., U.S.A.; Maple Bluff Farm, Madison, Wis. *Clubs:* Cosmos, Congressional Country, Metropolitan (Washington); Maple Bluff Country (Madison, Wis.). [*Died* 24 *Feb.* 1953.

LAFONE, Ven. Henry Pownall Malins; *b.* 1867; *e. s.* of late Hy Lafone, Knockholt, Kent; *m.* 1895, Gertrude (*d.* 1905), *d.* of late Sir William Henry Broadbent, Bt.; two *s.* one *d.* (and one *s.* one *d.* decd.); *m.* 1907, Marion Russell (*d.* 1955), *d.* of Dr. J. Watson, Dorman's Park, Surrey; one *s.* (and one *s.* decd.). *Educ.:* Trinity Coll., Cambridge (M.A.); Wells Coll. Curate of Portsea, 1890-96; Vicar of Ambleside, 1896-1902; Vicar and Lecturer, St. Cuthbert's, Carlisle, 1902-09; Chaplain H.M. Prisons, Carlisle, 1904-09; Vicar of Kendal, 1909-12 and 1923-1931; Hon. Canon of Carlisle, 1911-12; Vicar, St. George's, Barrow, 1912-19; Cartmel, 1919-23, Archdeacon of Furness, 1912-23; of Westmorland, 1923-31, retired, 1931. J.P., Kendal, 1934. *Address:* Hylands, Kendal. *T.:* Kendal 403. [*Died* 23 *March* 1955.

LAING, Bertram Mitchell, M.C.; Lecturer in Philosophy, Sheffield University, 1919-45; Professor of Philosophy, 1945-49, retired; Professor Emeritus, 1950; *m.* 1921, Jessie, *o. d.* of Edward Stanton, Smethwick, Staffs. *Educ.:* Aberdeen University, D.Litt. 1923; Berlin; Leipzig. *Publications:* A Study in Moral Problems, 1922; David Hume (Leaders of Philosophy Series), 1932; Articles in various philosophical magazines. *Address:* 88 Knowle Lane, Ecclesall, Sheffield 11. [*Died* 16 *May* 1960.

LAING, Air Vice-Marshal Sir George, K.C.B., *cr.* 1945 (C.B. 1941); C.B.E. 1928 (O.B.E. 1919); R.A.F., retired; *b.* 1884; *m.* 1908; two *s.* Served European War, 1914-19 (despatches, O.B.E.); Deputy Director of Equipment, Air Ministry, 1931-1938; Principal Deputy Director, 1938-39; Commanded No. 41 Group, 1939-44; retired 1945. *Address:* Mill House, Blackheath, S.E.3. [*Died* 1 *April* 1956.

LAIRD, Brigadier Kenneth Macgregor, D.S.O. 1917; *b.* 1880; *s.* of William Laird, Birkenhead; *m.* 1911, Ethel, *d.* of William M'Dowel Aikin Wright, M.D.; one *d.* *Educ.:* Charterhouse; R.M.C. Late Argyll & Sutherland Highlanders and Roy. Tanks Corps; p.s.c.; served S. African War, 1899-1902 (Queen's medal with three clasps, King's medal with two clasps); European War, 1914-18 (despatches, D.S.O, Bt. Lt.-Col.); retired pay, 1935. *Address:* c/o Standard Bank of S. Africa, Adderley Street, Cape Town, S. Africa. *T.:* 7-5813. *Club:* Civil Service (Cape Town). [*Died* 10 *Jan.* 1954.

LAISTNER, Max Ludwig Wolfram, Litt.D.; Hon. Fellow of Jesus College, Cambridge; Corresponding Fellow of the Mediæval Academy of America, 1935; John Stambaugh Prof. of History, Emeritus, Cornell University; *b.* London, 10 Oct. 1890; *s.* of late Max Laistner; unmarried. *Educ.:* Merchant Taylors' School; Jesus Coll., Cambridge Univ. (Senior Open Scholar); Craven Studentship, 1912 Studentship of the British School at Athens, 1913; Assistant Lecturer in Classics, Birmingham University, 1914; Lecturer in Archæology and Ancient History, Queen's University, Belfast, 1915; served in H.M. Forces, 1916-19; Lecturer in Classics, Manchester University, 1919; Reader in Ancient History, London University (King's College), 1921-25; Sather Professor of classical literature, Univ. of California, 1946; James W. Richard Lecturer in History, University of Virginia, 1950; *Publications:* Greek Economics, 1923; Philoxeni Glossarium, 1926; Glossarium Ansileubi (with W. M. Lindsay and others), 1926; Isocrates, De Pace and Philippus, 1927; A Survey of Ancient History, 1929; Thought and Letters in Western Europe, A.D. 500-900, 1931; (rev. edn. 1957); Greek History, 1932; A History of the Greek World 479-323 B.C., 1936; Bedae Venerabilis Expositio Actuum Apostolorum et Retractatio, 1939; A Hand-list of Bede MSS 1943; The Greater Roman Historians, 1947; Christianity and Pagan Culture in the Later Roman Empire, 1951; The Intellectual Heritage of the Early Middle Ages, 1957; numerous articles; Mem. bd. of editors, Amer. Hist. Rev., 1942-47. *Recreations:* walking, music. *Address:* 216 Wait Avenue, Ithaca, N.Y., U.S.A. *Club:* Authors'. [*Died* 10 *Dec.* 1959.

LAKIN, Sir Richard, 2nd Bt., *cr.* 1909; J.P. Warwickshire; *b.* 30 May 1873; *s.* of 1st Bt. and Alice Emma (*d.* 1927), *d.* of David Dewing of Norwich; *S.* father, 1931; *m.* 1903, Mildred Alice, *d.* of Geoffrey Joseph Shakerley; one *s.* one *d.* *Heir:* *s.* Henry [*b.* 8th Oct. 1904; *m.* 1927, Bessie, *d.* of J. Anderson; one *s.* one *d.*]. *Address:* Ready Token, Cirencester, Glos. [*Died* 14 *Feb.* 1955.

LALIQUE, René; artiste décorateur; maître de verrerier; Commandeur de la Légion d'Honneur; Membre du Conseil Supérieur des Beaux Arts; *b.* Ay, Marne, 6 avril 1860; *m.* Alice Lysiane Ledru. *Œuvres:* Objets d'art. *Recreation:* escrime. *Address:* 40 Cours Albert-Ier, Paris. *T.:* Elysées 77-51. [*Died* 5 *May* 1945. [*But death not notified in time for inclusion in Who Was Who 1941–1950, first edn.*

LALL, Sir Shankar, Kt., *cr.* 1946; Managing Director, Delhi Cloth and General Mills Co. Ltd., Delhi; *b.* 17 Feb. 1901; *s.* of Lala Madan Mohan Lall Kotwalwala, Banker, Landlord and Millowner; *m.* 1915, Sh. Birmo Devi; two *d.* *Educ.:* Government High School, Delhi; St. Stephen's College, Delhi. President Punjab Chamber of Commerce, 1943-45 and 1948-49; Senior Vice-Pres. Delhi Municipal Cttee., 1940; Member Exec. Council Delhi Univ.; Vice-Pres. All India Central Sugarcane Cttee., 1942-47; Member Central Cotton Cttee.; Pres. All India Sugar Mills Assoc.,1945-46; Pres. of the Delhi Pinjrapole; Pres. Delhi Olympic Assoc.; Vice-Pres. Assoc. Chambers of Commerce, 1945-46 and 1947-48; Member Advisory Board, B.B. and C.I. Rly. and E.P. Rly.; Chm. Ramakrishna Mission, Delhi; Pres. Boy Scouts Assoc.; Treasurer Gandhi Memorial Fund. *Address:* Shankar Niwas, 20 Curzon Road, New Delhi. *T.A.:* Care of Yarn, Delhi. *T.:* 7612. *Clubs:* Chelmsford, Imperial Delhi Gymkhana, Roshanara, Constitution (Delhi); Gulmarg (Gulmarg, Kashmir). [*Died* 14 *April* 1951.

LAMB, David C., C.M.G. 1934; Hon. LL.D. (Aberdeen); Commissioner of the Salvation Army (retd.); Director of the Salvation Army Assurance Soc., Ltd.; *b.* 26 Oct. 1866, Friockheim, Angus; *m.* M. Clinton, (*d.* 1939), Salvation Army Officer; one *s.* three *d.* Entered Salvation Army as an Officer, 1884; Chief Secretary in South Africa, 1891; Private Secretary to General Bramwell Booth, then Chief of Staff, 1895; Governor Hadleigh Farm Colony, 1898-1903; authority on Emigration Poor Law and Vagrancy; Member Rochford Board of Guardians, 1900-30; witness before Poor Law Royal Commission, 1906, Dominion Royal Commission, 1912; Royal Commissions on Licensing, England and Wales and Scotland, 1930; Member English-Speaking Union; Fellow Royal Empire Society; Member of the Government Empire Settlement Committee, 1917; has travelled widely on Salvation Army affairs (round the world 5 times); toured the British Overseas Dominions in the interests of Migration and Settlement, 1925-26; unofficial goodwill tours, U.S.A., Canada (eight times), Central and South Africa, Australia and N.Z., 1941-51. International Social Secretary, 1920-1932; Director of Salvation Army Emigration Dept., 1903-30; Intelligence Office, 1932-40. *Publications:* Social Maladies: Causes Conditions, Cures, 1938; several pamphlets on Social Problems. *Address:* 23 Canonbury Square, N.1. *T.:* Canonbury 3116 [*Died* 7 *July* 1951.

LAMB, Henry, M.C.; R.A. 1949 (A.R.A. 1940); L.M.S.S.A.; artist; a trustee of National Portrait Gallery since 1942 and of Tate Gallery, 1944-51; *b.* 1883; *s.* of late Sir Horace Lamb, F.R.S.; *m.* 1928, Lady Margaret Pansy Felicia Pakenham (author of August, 1931; Charles I., 1936), *sister* of 6th Earl of Longford, M.A.; one *s.* two *d.* *Educ.:* Manchester Grammar School; Manchester University Medical School; Guy's Hospital; (painting) La Palette, Paris. Served European War of 1914-18, R.A.M.C., France, Macedonia, Palestine, France (M.C.); official war artist for the Army, 1940-44; exhibitions, Alpine Gallery, 1922. Leicester Galleries, 1927, 1929, 1931, 1933, 1935, 1938, 1945, 1949, 1956; Pictures in Imperial War Museum, Tate Gallery, Public Galleries of Manchester, Cardiff, Southampton, Belfast, Aberdeen, Sheffield, Rochdale; at many Colleges at Oxford and Cambridge, and at Manchester and Leeds Univs. *Address:* Coombe Bissett, Salisbury, Wilts. *T.:* Coombe Bissett 220. [*Died* 8 *Oct.* 1960.

LAMB, Sir John, K.C.B., *cr.* 1926 (C.B. 1915); LL.D. (Aber.); *b.* 1871. Advocate, 1897; Legal Secretary to Lord Advocate, 1906-9; Assistant Under-Secretary, Scottish Office, 1909-21; Under-Secretary, 1921; Under-Secretary of State for Scotland, 1926-33. *Address:* Murlingden, Brechin, Angus. *T.:* Brechin 85. *Club:* New (Edinburgh). [*Died* 3 *July* 1952.

LAMB, Sir John Edward Stewart, Kt., *cr.* 1952; C.M.G. 1943; Political Liaison Officer, Tanganyika Territory, since 1947; *b.* 3 June 1892; *s.* of John Fuller Lamb and Lizzie Blee Stewart; *m.* 1921, Ada Emmeline Nuttall; one *s.* Served European War, 1915-19, 60th Rifles and King's African Rifles, France and East Africa; Colonial Administrative Service, Tanganyika, 1919; Provincial Commissioner, 1939; Administrative Secretary, 1942. *Address:* c/o The Secretariat, Dar-es-Salaam, Tanganyika. [*Died* 13 *April* 1954.

LAMBE, Admiral of the Fleet Sir Charles Edward, G.C.B. 1957 (K.C.B. 1953; C.B. 1944); C.V.O. 1938; Lord Commissioner of the Admiralty, First Sea Lord and Chief of Naval Staff, 1959-60; Extra Equerry to the Queen since 1952 (to King George VI, 1939-52); *b.* 20 Dec. 1900; *o. s.* of late Henry Edward Lambe and late Lady Lambe of Grove House, Semley, Shaftesbury, Dorset; *m.* 1940, Lesbia Rachel, *d.* of late Sir Walter Corbet, Bt., formerly wife of Victor I. H. Mylius, R.N.; one *s.* one *d.* *Educ.:* R.N. Colleges. Cadet, 1914; Midshipman H.M.S. Emperor of India, 1917-19; Specialised in Torpedoes, 1926; Staff College, 1930; Comdr., 1933; Equerry to King Edward VIII, 1936, to King George VI, 1936-1938; Actg. Rear-Adm., 1945; Rear-Adm., 1947; Vice-Admiral, 1950; Admiral 1954; Admiral of the Fleet, 1960; Assistant Chief of Naval Staff (Air), 1945-46; Flag Officer Flying Training, 1947-49; Flag Officer Commanding 3rd Aircraft Carrier Squadron, 1949-51; Flag Officer, Air (Home), 1951-53 (Flag Officer Royal Yacht for T.R.H. Visit to Australia and New Zealand, 1952); Commander-in-Chief, Far East Station, 1953-54; Second Sea Lord, 1955-57; Commander-in-Chief, Mediterranean, and N.A.T.O. Comdr.-in-Chief, Allied Forces, Mediterranean, 1957-1959. *Recreations:* painting and music. *Address:* Knockhill House, Newport, Fife; 21 Stafford Place, S.W.1. *Club:* Naval and Military. [*Died* 29 *Aug.* 1960.

LAMBE, Air Vice-Marshal Sir Charles Laverock, K.C.B. *cr.* 1931 (C.B. 1919); C.M.G. 1918; D.S.O. 1917; late R.A.F.; late Capt. R.N. Served Benin Expedition, 1897 (medal and clasp); European War, 1914-18 (despatches, D.S.O., C.M.G., Order of Leopold of Belgium, Belgian Croix de Guerre, Legion of Honour, Order of the Crown of Belgium, French Croix de Guerre, American Distinguished Service Medal); commanded R.N.A.S. units on the Belgian Coast; Director of Equipment, Royal Air Force, Air Ministry; commanded R.A.F. Halton, 1924-28; Air Officer commanding Coastal Area, 1928-31; retired list, 1931. *Address:* Hillcrest, Hindon, Salisbury, Wiltshire. [*Died* 25 *April* 1953.

LAMBERT, 1st Viscount, *cr.* 1945, of South Molton, **George Lambert,** P.C. 1912; *b.* Devon, 25 June 1866; *m.* 1904, Barbara, *d.* of late G. Stavers of Morpeth; two *s.* two *d.* *Educ.:* privately. J.P. Devon. Member Devon County Council for 62 years; member Royal Agricultural Commission, 1893; Royal Commission on Fuel and Engines for the Navy; Foundation Chairman Seale Hayne Agricultural College, Newton Abbot; M.P. (L.) S. Molton, 1891-1924, 1929-31, (L. Nat.) 1931-45; Civil Lord of the Admiralty, 1905-15; Chairman Liberal Parliamentary Party, 1919-21. *Recreation:* golf. *Heir:* *s.* Hon. George Lambert, T.D. *Address:* 35 Millbank, S.W.1. *T.:* Victoria 3636; Spreyton, Crediton, N. Devon. *Club:* Reform. [*Died* 17 *Feb.* 1958.

LAMBERT, Ven. Charles Edmund, M.A.; Rector of St. James's, Piccadilly, since 1922; Archdeacon Emeritus, since 1950; *b.* 4 April 1872; *s.* of late William Lambert of Banstead; *m.* 1927, Helena Mary, *er. d.* of late Preb. J. H. J. Ellison, C.V.O.; two *s.* one *d.* *Educ.:* High School, Newcastle-under-Lyme; Christ's College, Cambridge (Scholar); First Class, Classical Tripos; B.A. 1894, M.A. 1898; Theol. Coll. Sarum. Deacon, 1898; Priest, 1900; Curate of Leeds, 1898-1901; Domestic Chaplain to Archbishop of York (Maclagan), 1901-4; Sub-warden of Bishop's Hostel and Tutor of the Scholae Cancellarii. Lincoln, 1904-11; Select Preacher, Univ. of Cambridge, 1913, 1917, 1930, 1941; Examining Chaplain to Bishop of Rochester, 1914; also to Bishop of Salisbury, 1919; Principal of the Clergy Training School (Westcott House), Cambridge, 1911; Vicar of Allhallows Barking-by-the-Tower, E.C.3, and Warden of the Mission College of Allhallows, 1917-22; Archdeacon of Hampstead, 1920-50. Examining Chaplain to Bishop of London, 1920-50. *Publications:* Devotional Address at Pan-Anglican Congress, 1908; Editor of Letters of Rev. H. H. Jeaffreson, 1916; Life in the Spirit, 1951. *Recreations:* golf, gardening. *Address:* St. James's Church Room, Jermyn Street, S.W.1. *T.:* Regent 5244. *Club:* Athenæum. [*Died* 1 *April* 1954.

LAMBERT, Constant; composer, conductor, and critic; *b.* London, 23 Aug. 1905; *s.* of late G. W. Lambert, A.R.A., and *b.* of Maurice Lambert, R.A.; twice married; one *s.* *Educ.:* Christ's Hosp.; Roy. Coll. of Music. At the age of twenty was commissioned by Serge Diaghlieff to write a ballet for the Russian Ballet, first English composer to be so honoured; this ballet, Romeo and Juliet, was produced in Monte Carlo, 1926; a second ballet, Pomona, produced in Buenos Aires in 1927; most generally known work is the Rio Grande for chorus, pianoforte, and orchestra; late musical dir. Vic-Wells ballet; has been regular contributor to Figaro, New Statesman and Nation, Sunday Referee, Lilliput. *Publications:* in addition to above works publications include a piano sonata, a piano concerto, Eight Chinese Songs and Music for Orchestra; Music Ho! A Study of Music in Decline, 1934; Summer's Last Will and Testament: a masque for chorus and orchestra, 1936; Horoscope, a ballet, produced Sadlers Wells, 1938; Suite, Merchant Seamen, 1943, Tiresias, produced Covent Garden, 1951. *Recreation:* Russian billiards. *Address:* c/o Royal Opera House, Covent Garden, W.C.2. [*Died* 21 *Aug.* 1951.

LAMBERT, Ernest, C.B.E. 1937; Clerk to the Justices acting for the Division of Dickering. East Yorks etc.; *b.* 13 July 1874; *s.* of Robert

John and Sarah Lambert; *m.* 1st, 1895, Edith Annie Atkinson; one *s.* (and one killed in action) one *d.*; 2nd, 1936, Julia Letitia Conyers. *Educ.:* private. First Hon. Freeman of Borough of Bridlington; Bridlington Town Council since 1906, Alderman since 1922, three times Mayor of Bridlington; Member of East Riding of Yorks County Council since 1931; Governor Bridlington School; Governor Girls High School, Bridlington; Commissioner Bridlington Piers and Harbour; Chairman East Yorkshire United Friendly Society since 1911; Chairman East Yorks Association of Rural Friendly Societies; Vice-President National Association of Rural Friendly Societies; Hon. Secretary Buckrose Conservative and Unionist Association since 1906; Past Master Londesborough Lodge of Freemasons and other public offices; Clerk to the Lords Feoffees and Assistants of the Manor of Bridlington; Clerk to the Bridlington Charity Trustees; Chairman Bridlington Town Football Club; President Bridlington Town Cricket Club. *Address:* Broadgate, Bridlington. *T.A.:* Bridlington. *T.:* 3030. *Club:* County (Bridlington). [*Died* 6 *Feb.* 1951.

LAMBERT, Dame Florence Barrie, D.B.E., *cr.* 1938 (C.B.E. 1920); J.P.; M.B., B.S., D.P.H. Officer Sister of Order of St. John of Jerusalem; late Hon. Director Central Council for Infant and Child Welfare; late Hon. Sec. Central Committee for the Care of Cripples; Member Council Invalid Children's Aid Assoc.; Medical Women's Federation; formerly Member S.E. Regional Hospital Board; formerly Vice-President of Medical Defence Union; *d.* of late Henry Thomas Lambert, Solicitor. *Educ.:* France; London School of Medicine for Women; Univ. College; Stockholm. Served in S. Africa with the Imperial Yeomanry Hospital, 1899-1901; late physician in charge Mechano-Therapeutic Department, Charing Cross; Inspector Military Massage and Electrical Services, 1915-19; affiliated R.A.M.C. (Major); Member Electro-Medical Committee, War Office; Medical Officer, Ministry of Health, 1919-21. *Address:* 1 Langton Ridge, Tunbridge Wells. [*Died* 11 *Dec.* 1957.

LAMING, Richard Valentine, C.B.E. 1932 (O.B.E. 1920); Economic Consultant and Director of Anglo-Dutch companies; Chairman British Importers Association; *b.* Rotterdam, 30 Dec. 1887; *s.* of William Laming and Josephine Elizabeth Field; *m.* 1934, H. Lagewaard. *Educ.:* Gymnasium Erasmianum, Rotterdam; Univ., Amsterdam. Studied Medicine but took no degree; rowed for Univ. 1907-10; successful twice in Dutch Univ. boat race and many other events on the Continent; took up a business career and established a Rhine shipping service, which was forced to terminate at outbreak of the war; declared unfit to serve in H.M. forces on account of eyesight; appointed representative of Restrictions of Enemy Supplies Department under the Ministry of Blockade, 1916. Commercial Counsellor, H.B.M. Embassy, The Hague. Retired, 1948. *Publications:* the usual Annual Reports on Economic Conditions in the Netherlands. *Recreations:* rowing, sailing. *Address:* 1A Helmstraat, Scheveningen, The Hague, Holland. [*Died* 26 *Jan.* 1959.

LAMINGTON, 3rd Baron (*cr.* 1880); **Capt. Victor Alexander Brisbane William Cochrane Baillie,** late Scots Guards; *b.* 23 July 1896; *o. s.* of 2nd Baron and Hon. Mary Haughton Hozier (*d.* 1944), *y. d.* of 1st Baron Newlands; *S.* father, 1940; *m.* 1922, Riette, *d.* of late D. A. Neilson, Wentbridge House, Pontefract. *Educ.:* Eton. Retired pay, 1927. *Address:* Lamington, Lanarkshire. [*Died* 20 *Sept.* 1951 (*ext.*).

LAMONT, Brig.-Gen. John William Fraser, C.B. 1919; C.M.G. 1917; D.S.O. 1916; Officier de la Légion d'honneur, 1918; *b.* Kinross-shire, 11 Sept. 1872; *s.* of late Charles Lamont of Crambeth, Kinross-shire, and Agnes, *e. d.* of late William Fraser of Inverkeithing; *m.* Kathleen, *d.* of Charles Enderby, Burgh, Lincs.; one *s.* one *d.* *Educ.:* Merchiston Castle School, Edinburgh; R.M.A., Woolwich. Joined R.A., 1893; served with R.H.A., S. African War, 1899-1902 (despatches, Bt. Major, Queen's medal 5 clasps, King's medal 2 clasps); Natal Native Rebellion, 1906 (medal with clasp); European War, France and Belgium, 1914-18; Brig.-Gen., 1916-19 (despatches, Brevet-Colonel, C.B., C.M.G., D.S.O., Officier Légion d'Honneur, 1914 Star, British War Medal, Victory); Mesopotamia, 1920 (medal and clasp); Anglo-Persian Military Commission, 1920; C.R.A. 18th Division, Mesopotamia; C.R.A. 50th (Northumbrian) Division, 1921; retired, 1923, hon. rank Brig.-Gen. *Address:* South Terrace, Littlehampton, Sussex. [*Died* 26 *May* 1956.

LAMPEN, Graham Dudley, C.M.G. 1956; C.B.E. 1950; *b.* 7 April 1899; *e. s.* of late Canon H. D. Lampen, Rector of Toppesfield, Essex; *m.* 1937, Lola Joan, *d.* of late Col. D.M. Corbett, O.B.E.; one *s.* three *d.* *Educ.:* Merchant Taylors' School; The Queen's College, Oxford (Scholar; Hons. Lit. Hum.). Served European War, 1917-1919; R.F.A., Salonica and Caucasus. Sudan Political Service, 1922-49: Dist. Comr., Blue Nile, Darfur and Kordofan Provinces; Dep.-Governor, Kassala Province, 1939-44; Governor, Darfur Province, 1944-49; Sec., Jerusalem and the East Mission, 1949-50; Member, Sudan Terms of Service Commn., 1950-51; Deputy Sudan Agent in London, 1951-54; Adviser to Governor-General of the Sudan in London, 1954-55; Foreign Office, 1956-57; Order of the Nile (4th Class), 1934. *Publications:* articles in Sudan Notes and Records. *Recreations:* reading, travel. *Address:* South Cottage, The Warren, Ashtead, Surrey. *T.:* Ashtead 3862. *Club:* Travellers'. [*Died* 21 *May* 1960.

LAMPITT, Leslie Herbert, D.Sc., F.R.I.C., M.I.Chem.E.; Director and Chief Chemist, J. Lyons and Company Limited; *b.* 30 Sept. 1887; *s.* of Daniel Lampitt and Eliza Haywood; *m.* 1915, Edith Potter Potts, B.Sc.; one *s.* *Educ.:* University of Birmingham, 1906-11. Chief Chemist La Meunerie Bruxelloise, Bruxelles, 1911-14; Army Service, France, 1914-19; Hon. Sec. British National Committee for Chemistry; Past Pres. Society of Chemical Industry (Society Medallist, 1943, International Medallist, 1949); Hon. Treasurer International Union of Pure and Applied Chemistry; Vice-President Société de Chimie Industrielle (Lavoisier Medallist, 1950); Hon. Foreign Member, Chemists Club, New York, 1950. *Publications:* Scientific papers in Biochemical Journal, Journal of Society Chemical Industry, Jl. of Science of Food and Agriculture, Analyst, Chimie et Industrie, etc. *Recreation:* gardening. *Address:* Thornlea, Mount Park, Harrow-on-the-Hill, Middlesex. *T.:* Byron 2423. *Club:* Athenæum. [*Died* 3 *June* 1957.

LAMPSON, Curtis Walter, C.B.E. 1920; Commissioner of Taxes for City of London; late of C. M. Lampson & Co., 64 Queen Street, E.C.4; *b.* 18 Aug. 1875; *m.* 1908, Hilda (*d.* 1946), 2nd *d.* of Sir David Baird, 3rd Bt.; two *d.* *Educ.:* Eton; Magdalen College, Oxford, B.A. Director London Assurance, 1904-51. *Address:* Willinghurst, Shamley Green, Guildford. [*Died* 9 *Aug.* 1952.

LAMPSON, Commander Oliver S. L.; *see* Locker-Lampson.

LANCASTER, John Roy; *b.* 29 Nov. 1871; *s.* of late Sir William John Lancaster and Sarah Harriet Roy; *m.* 1896, Margaret Parkes; three *d.* *Educ.:* Charterhouse School. Partner in firm of Horne and Co., Auctioneers and Surveyors for over 25 years; Chartered Surveyor. Formerly Director: Prudential Assurance Co. (for 20 years); British Mutual Bank; retired. Past Master Carpenters Co.; J.P. Surrey. *Recreations:* coaching, riding. *Address:* Tapleys, Chiddingfold, Surrey. *T.:* Chiddingfold 153. *Club:* Royal Automobile. [*Died* 14 *Feb.* 1951.

LANCHESTER, Frank, C.I.Mech.E.; Joint Founder, with his brothers, in 1899, of The Lanchester Motor Company; *b.* 22 July 1870; 3rd *s.* of H. J. Lanchester, A.R.I.B.A., Architect, Hove, Brighton; *m.* 1903, Minnie, *d.* of William Thomas, Oakridge, Llandaff, Glam.; two *d.* *Educ.:* Brighton Preparatory School. Dr. Walker's College (coaching for the Services), Hove, Sussex. After an early business career, joined his two brothers in Gas Engine Industry, 1892-97; undertook secretarial and business work, later becoming London Sales Director and, in 1930, Managing Director of the Lanchester Motor Company, his brothers having been responsible for design and production, respectively. In 1931 the Lanchester Motor Co. was acquired by The Birmingham Small Arms Co. Ltd., Birmingham, as a Subsidiary Company; has remained an active Director up to the present time. Founder and first Hon. Sec., Midland Automobile Club, 1899; an original Mem. first Council and Cttee. of Soc. of Motor Manufacturers & Traders Ltd., 1903 (Vice-Pres., 1917-19, Pres., 1919-20, Chm. Brit. Car Manufacturers Section, 1923-27); Rep. and thrice Pres. (for Gt. Brit.) of Bureau d'Automobiles International, Paris, 1912-36; Chm. Bond Street (London) Traders Assoc., 1924-1928; Pres. Motor Trade Assoc., 1923-35 and 1940-45; a Vice-Chm. of Royal Automobile Club, 1938-41 (and on that Cttee. 1920-); Pres. Fellowship of the Motor Industry, 1939-1943; acting as Director and Sales Consultant to Lanchester Co. at Coventry, 1946-1958. *Recreations:* spare time given up to serving on trade committees and associations in honorary capacity for over 40 years. *Address:* The Porch, Wilmcote, Nr. Stratford-on-Avon, Warwicks. *Clubs:* Royal Automobile; (Founder) Midland Automobile (Birmingham); Royal Motor Yacht (Poole). [*Died* 28 *Aug.* 1960.

LANCHESTER, Henry Vaughan, Hon. Litt.D. (Leeds), 1936; architect, of Lanchester and Lodge, 10 Woburn Square, W.C.1; *b.* 9 Aug. 1863; *m.* 1909, Annie Gilchrist, *d.* of Robert Martin, of Holmhill, Lanark; one *s.* *Educ.:* privately. Commenced practice as architect, 1889; Royal Gold Medal for Architecture, 1934; principal works—Cardiff City Hall and Law Courts; Deptford Town Hall; The Wesleyan Central Hall, Westminster; Council Hall, Lucknow: Leeds Univ.; St. Bartholomew's Hospital; Birmingham Hospital Centre; H.H.'s Palace, Jodhpur; Town planning schemes for the North Tees Area, Derby Civic Centre, Delhi, Madras, Gwalior, Lucknow, Rangoon, and Zanzibar. A.R.I.B.A., 1889; Fellow, 1906; Vice-President, 1913 and 1927; Examiner, T.P. Joint Board, President 1922-23; President, Franco-British Union of Architects, 1936-37; formerly on National Housing and Town Planning Council; Editor of the Builder, 1910-12; Writer and Lecturer on Civic Design at University College and elsewhere; Examiner in Civic Design, Liverpool, 1910-12; Examiner for Diploma in Architecture, Scotland, 1913; appointed to advise Government of India as to site of Delhi, 1912; Hon. Director of the Civic Surveys, sanctioned by H.M. Government, 1915; Town Planning Adviser to the Government of Madras, 1915-16; the United Provinces, 1918; of Burma, 1921; Protectorate of Zanzibar, 1922; Consulting Architect to the University of London, 1929-31. *Publications:* Fischer Von Erlach; Talks on Town Planning; Town Planning in Madras; The Art of Town Planning, 1925. *Address:* 10 Woburn Square, W.C.1. *T.:* Museum 0846. [*Died* 16 *Jan.* 1953.

LANE, Charles Macdonald, C.S.I. 1935; Indian Service of Engineers (Retd.); late Chief Engineer and Secretary to Government, Public Works Dept., Bombay; *b.* 1882; *s.* of late James Horsburgh Lane; *heir-pres.* to 29th Earl of Mar; *m.* 1914, Jessie Helen Grant; one *s.* one *d.* (and one *s.* killed in action in Burma, 1944). *Educ.:* Marlborough; R.I.E. College, Coopers Hill. *Address:* Rafters, Waldron, Sussex. *T.:* Horeham Rd. 147. [*Died* 30 *April* 1956.

LANE, Ernest Frederick Cambridge, C.M.G. 1920; J.P.; *b.* 1882; *s.* of Frederick George Alexander Lane, Bloxworth House, Wareham, Dorset; *m.* 1911, Jessie Maud, *d.* of George Heys, Pretoria. Formerly in public service of Union of S. Africa. Sheriff of Dorsetshire, 1943. *Address:* Poxwell House, near Dorchester, Dorset. *T.:* Warmwell 254. *Clubs:* Junior Carlton; Civil Service (Cape Town); Bulawayo (Bulawayo). [*Died* 6 *Jan.* 1958.

LANE, Harry George; Newspaper editor, retired; editor Daily Sketch, 1919-1928; editor in chief, Northcliffe Newspapers, Ltd., 1928-32; editor Sunday Dispatch, 1932-33; Director Hull and Grimsby Newspapers Ltd., 1930-46; *b.* Swindon, 1881; *m.* 1906, Edith Webb (*d.* 1951), Birmingham; one *d.* *Educ.:* Worksop. *Address:* 41 Queen's Avenue, Dorchester, Dorset. [*Died* 22 *April* 1957.

LANE, Herbert Allardyce, C.I.E. 1927; *b.* 1883; *s.* of late Col. C. T. Lane, C.I.E.; *m.* 1909, Hilda Gladys Duckle Wraith; two *s.* one *d.* *Educ.:* Wellington Coll.; New College, Oxford. Appointed to Indian Civil Service, United Provinces, 1908; Assistant Settlement Officer, 1916; Deputy Commissioner and Settlement Officer, 1918; Magistrate and Collector, 1924; Secretary to Government, 1925; Settlement Commissioner, 1929; Secretary to Government, 1931; President, Court of Wards, United Provinces, 1934; retired from I.C.S., 1940. *Address:* Hillfield, Putley, Ledbury, Herefordshire. *T.:* Trumpet 238. [*Died* 11 *Sept.* 1959.

LANE, Brig. Hugh Robert Charles, C.B. 1940; D.S.O. 1925; O.B.E. 1921; *b.* Lucknow, 20 Dec. 1885; *e. s.* of late Colonel A. L. Lane, R.A.; *m.* Gwendolen Frances Badcock; one *s.* one *d.* *Educ.:* Wellington College; R.M.C., Sandhurst. Unattached List, I.A., 1905; served Zakka Khel Expedition, 1908; Special Service N.-E. Frontier, 1912; 3rd Afghan War, 1919; Iraq, 1920 (O.B.E. and despatches); Waziristan, 1922-23 (D.S.O., despatches); Commandant 1st Bn. 5th Royal Gurkhas, Frontier Force, 1931; Commander 6th (Lucknow) Infantry Brig., 1936; Commander 10th (Jubbulpore) Infantry Brig., 1937; retired, 1940; Col. 5th Royal Gurkha Rifles, 1945. *Recreations:* riding, usual games, shooting. *Address:* Doddington, Pondtail Road, Fleet, Hants. *Club:* United Service. [*Died* 2 *June* 1953.

LANE, Lupino; Actor-Manager; *b.* 16 June; *m.* Violet Blyth; one *s.* *Educ.:* Worthing. First stage appearance at 4 years of age, Prince of Wales' Theatre, Birmingham. First London appearance, London Pavilion, 1903; subsequently at Hippodrome, Palace, Empire, etc.; in Paris, principal cities of U.S. and Canada. London, 1915-19, in: Watch Your Step, Follow The Crowd, We're All In It, Extra Special, What a Catch, Afgar; Aladdin (Manchester). Went to U.S.A., 1920, and appeared at Century Theatre, N.Y., as Coucourli in Afgar; returned to London, 1920; played in: Aladdin, The League of Notions, Brighter London; Ziegfeld Follies, New Amsterdam Theatre, N.Y., 1924; Ko-ko in The Mikado, 44th St. Theatre, 1925; played, London, 1926-36, in: Turned Up, Hearts and Diamonds, Silver Wings, Aladdin, The One Girl, Please, The Golden Toy, Twenty To One (as Snibson), Cinderella; produced and presented Me and My Girl,

Victoria Palace, 1937 (appeared for 1550 consecutive performances and created celebrated dance, The Lambeth Walk), revived, Winter Garden, 1949; 1942-44: Babes in the Wood, La-di-da-di-da, Meet Me Victoria; Wishing Well, Comedy, 1952. Began film career, 1913; appeared in numerous silent and talking films, including: Lady of the Rose, The Love Parade, The Lambeth Walk. Has directed several films including: Love Lies, The Love Race, The Maid of the Mountains. A member of famous Lupino family of dancers and acrobats connected with the stage for nearly two centuries. *Publication:* How to Become a Comedian, 1945. *Relevant Publication:* Born to Star, by James Dillon White, 1957. *Address:* 11 Grosvenor Cottages, Eaton Terrace, S.W.1. *T.:* Sloane 5717. *Club:* Savage. [*Died* 10 *Nov.* 1959.

LANE, Rhona Arbuthnot; *d.* of Sir William Arbuthnot Lane, 1st Bart., C.B. *Educ.:* Francis Holland Church of England High School, Baker Street; St. Hugh's College, Oxford; St. Mary's College, Paddington. Sixteen years as English Specialist at Clifton High School for Girls, Clifton, Bristol; and head of the Senior Boarding House for Girls; six years Second Mistress; Head Mistress of Wycombe Abbey School, 1925-27. *Publications:* An Anthology of the Seasons; Poems of Praise (an anthology). *Address:* c/o Williams Deacon's Bank Ltd., 20 Birchin Lane, E.C.3. [*Died* 3 *Sept.* 1953.

LANE-ROBERTS, Cedric Sydney, C.V.O. 1942; M.B., M.S. (London); F.R.C.S. (Eng.); F.R.C.O.G.; Consulting Gynæcological Surgeon, Royal Northern Hosp.; Consulting Obstetric Surgeon to Queen Charlotte's Hospital; Consulting Obstetric Surgeon, Queen Mary's Maternity Home, Hampstead; Hon. Gynæcologist, Gerrard's Cross Cottage Hospital; 3rd. *s.* of late Lieut.-Col. A. S. Roberts, Gordon Highlanders and I.C.S., and Jane, *d.* of Brigade Surgeon B. Lane, A.M.S.; *m.* Nell Miles-Sharp, (*d.* 1954), *d.* of late D. W. Bain. *Educ.:* Cheltenham Coll.; Guy's Hosp. (Entrance Scholarship in Arts, Treasurers Gold Medal in Clinical Surgery). Late Senior Demonstrator of Anatomy Guy's Hospital; Qualified, 1913; M.S., F.R.C.S., 1920; Late Obstetric Tutor, Leeds Maternity Hospital, and St. Bartholomew's Hospital, Chief Assistant Maternity Department; Temporary Captain R.A.M.C., 1915-1919 (despatches); Examiner Central Midwives Board. *Publications:* Sterility and Impaired Fertility (jointly); Royal Northern Operative Surgery (jointly); The Queen Charlotte Practice of Obstetrics (jointly); various articles on Obstetric and Gynæcological subjects. *Recreations:* formerly Rugby Football, International Trials, Played for England 4 times 1909-13, played for Guy's Hospital (Captain 1913) six years. *Address:* Mill House, Tewin, Herts. [*Died* 25 *Dec.* 1959.

LANG, Archibald Orr; formerly Dep. Chairman and Man. Director Peninsular and Oriental S.N. Co., and the British India Steam Navigation Company; *b.* 22 March 1880; *s.* of late James Lang, Greenock; *m.* 1910, Elma, *d.* of late William McNaughton Love, 24 Palace Court, London, W., and Campbeltown, Argyllshire; one *s.* Prior to 1927 resided for a number of years in Far East and was a partner in China of Mackinnon, Mackenzie and Co., and Gibb, Livingston and Co.; and a member of the Executive and Legislative Councils of Hong Kong. *Address:* Southwood, Dittons Road, Eastbourne. *Club:* Oriental. [*Died* 10 *July* 1957.

LANG, Col. Elliott Brownlow, C.B.E. 1919; Indian Army, retired; *b.* 10 Aug. 1862; *s.* of Col. Arthur Moffatt Lang, C.B.; *m.* 1900, Jessie Thornhill. *Educ.:* Haileybury. Served Burma, 1885-86 (medal with clasp); European War, 1914-19 (despatches, C.B.E.); retired, 1919. *Address:* c/o Westminster Bank, Taunton, Somerset. [*Died* 21 *Nov.* 1955.

LANG, Lieut.-Col. Lionel Edward, C.I.E. 1921, M.C.; Indian Political Service, retired; *b.* Bombay, 1 Nov. 1885; *s.* of late Walter Lang, broker, Bombay; *m.* 1st, 1910, Constance de Chouilly, *d.* of late Colonel Burgess, Royal Artillery; one *d.*; 2nd, Constance Mayne, *yr. d.* of G. N. Mackay Cameron, Bexhill-on-Sea. *Educ.:* Berkhampsted School; Royal Military College, Sandhurst. Commissioned in Indian Army, 1905; attached 1st Bn. Manchester Regiment, India, 1905-6; appointed to the 106 Hazara Pioneers, 1906; Bombay Political Department, 1909; reverted temporarily to Military Employ, 1914; took part in operations in the Kalat State, 1915; served with General Dyer's Column in the Sarhad (Persia), 1916-17 (M.C.); served on Mohmand Blockade Line, 1917; commanded Seistan and Khorasan Levy Corps, 1917-19; took part in Afghan War of 1919 (C.I.E.). *Recreations:* won the Salmon Pony Pigsticking Cup in 1911; polo, pigsticking, shooting, fishing. *Address:* Turi, Kenya Colony, East Africa. [*Died* 29 *March* 1956.

LANG, Very Rev. Marshall B., M.A., B.D., D.D. (Glas.), 1930; T.D., F.S.A. (Scot.); Moderator of Church of Scotland General Assembly, 1935; *b.* 1868; 5th *s.* of Very Rev. John Marshall Lang, D.D., LL.D., C.V.O., Minister of Barony Parish, Glasgow, and Principal of Aberdeen University, and Hannah Agnes, *d.* of Rev. P. H. Keith, D.D., Hamilton; *m.* 1896, Mary Eleanor (*d.* 1954), *d.* of W. W. Farquharson, Edinburgh; one *s.* three *d.* *Educ.:* Albany Academy, Glasgow; Glasgow Academy and University; Göttingen and Leipsic Universities. Minister of Meldrum Parish, Aberdeenshire, 1895; translated to S. John's Cross Parish Church, Dundee, 1909; new church built, and opened 1914; retired as Senior Minister of Whittingehame, 1939; Chaplain to 3rd Highland Field Ambulance, R.A.M.C. (T.F.); served European War as Chaplain (First Class) in 2nd General Scottish Hospital, Forth Coast Defence, Aberdeen Coast Defence (T.D.); retains rank as Hon. Chaplain (First Class); Delegate to Pan-Presbyterian Council in Pittsburg, 1921, Cardiff, 1925, to General Assembly of Presbyterian Church of Wales, 1922; and to Reformed Church, U.S.A., 1928; Editorial Convener, Church Service Society, 1925, President 1942; President East Lothian Antiquarian Society, 1937; Member of East Lothian Education Committee, 1931; President Scottish Ecclesiological Society, 1936-37, and Sons of the Ministers Society, 1939; Sub-Chaplain of Order of St. John of Jerusalem, 1942. *Publications:* The Story of a Parish, 1897; Whittingehame, or the Seven Ages of a Parish, 1929; The Evolution of the Kirk, in Transactions of the Scottish Ecclesiological Society, 1932; St. Magnus Cathedral, Kirkwall, 1938. *Recreations:* gardening, angling, golf. *Address:* Gifford, Haddington, East Lothian. [*Died* 3 *Oct.* 1954.

LANG, Rt. Rev. Norman Macleod, D.D.; *b.* 1875; *m.* Monica (*d.* 1918), *d.* of Edward Crosfield, Liverpool. *Educ.:* Christ Church, Oxford (M.A.); Cuddesdon College. Curate of Portsea, 1900-03; Bloemfontein Cathedral, 1903-5; Vicar of Kroonstadt, 1905-06; Curate of Christ Church, Lancaster Gate, 1906-09; Vicar of St. Martin's, Leicester, 1909-13; Bishop Suffragan of Leicester, 1913-27; Archdeacon of Northampton and Canon of Peterborough, 1919-36; Assistant Bishop of Peterborough, 1926-45; Archdeacon of Oakham and Canon of Peterborough, 1936-45. *Address:* Rectory House, Wappenham, Towcester, Northants. [*Died* 5 *May* 1956.

LANG, William Henry, F.R.S. 1911; M.B., D.Sc.; LL.D.; late Barker Professor of Cryptogamic Botany, University of Manchester. *Publications:* papers (botanical) in scientific publications. *Address:* Westfield, Storth, Milnthorpe, Westmorland. [*Died* 29 *Aug.* 1960.

LANGDON, George; Commissioner of the Salvation Army (retd.); *b.* Watchet, Somerset, 1867; *m.* Clara Coles, Salvation Army Officer; four *s.* three *d.* Entered the Salvation Army as an Officer, 1888; appointed to command Scotland Sub-Territory, 1923; transferred to National Headquarters, London, as Chief Secretary, 1929. Formerly Governor of Men's Social Work, Great Britain and International Travelling Commissioner. *Address:* 4 Crossgate, Greenford, Middlesex. [*Died* 13 *Aug.* 1957.

LANGDON-DAVIES, Bernard Noël, M.A.; Literary Consultant, Bookselling Dept., Welwyn Stores; *b.* Anerley, Surrey, 7 Dec. 1876; 3rd *s.* of Charles Langdon-Davies, Electrical Engineer; *m.* Ethel May, *d.* of George Michael Silley, Architect; one *s.* one *d.* *Educ.:* St. Paul's School (Foundation Scholar); Pembroke Coll., Cambridge; Tancred Student, Lincoln's Inn; President Cambridge Union Society; First Class Classical Tripos; University Extension Lecturer, Cambridge and London; Examiner Cambridge Locals, Scottish Board of Education, etc.; private tutor chiefly for Oxford and Cambridge, 1902-12; joined Garton Foundation as lecturer on Internationalism, 1912; lectured in America, Germany, etc.; in 1914 joined the Independent Labour Party; in 1940 resigned from Labour Party; managed the Labour Publishing Co., the Theosophical Publishing House, Noel Douglas and Williams and Norgate, 1920-1932; managed a hotel in Corsica, 1934; Publicity Manager, Cresta Silks Ltd., 1936-39; Urban District Councillor, Welwyn Garden City, 1938; Executive Cttee. Nat. Book League and Booksellers' Assoc.; Chm., London Branch of Associated Booksellers, 1947-48. *Publications:* edited Young England, 4 novels by Disraeli; The Practice of Bookselling, etc. *Address:* 61 Valley Road, Welwyn Garden City, Herts. *T.:* Welwyn Garden 966.
[*Died* 28 *Dec.* 1952.

LANGFORD, 7th Baron, *cr.* 1800; **Clotworthy Wellington Thomas Edward Rowley;** *b.* New Zealand, 1 June 1885; *s.* of late Hon. Randolfe Thomas Rowley, 3rd *s.* of 3rd Baron; *S.* uncle, 1931; *m.* 1922. Served European War with New Zealand Expeditionary Force in Egypt and France. *Heir: kinsman* Sir Arthur (Langford Sholto) Rowley (later 8th Baron Langford, *q.v.*).
[*Died* 15 *July* 1952.

LANGFORD, 8th Baron, *cr.* 1800; **Arthur Langford Sholto Rowley,** Kt., *cr.* 1932; C.M.G. 1928; *b.* 10 Dec. 1870; 2nd *s.* of Col. Hon. H. L. B. Rowley, D.L., J.P., of Marley Grange, Rathfarnham, Co. Dublin, and Louisa Jane Campbell, *sister* of first Baron Blythswood; *S.* kinsman, 1952; *m.* 1st, 1908, Margarita Inez (*d.* 1928), *d.* of late Hugh Jameson, London; no *c.*; 2nd, 1929, Alice Maude, 2nd *d.* of Henri Lelacheur, formerly of Guernsey. *Educ.:* abroad. Vice-Consul at Valparaiso, 1899; acting Consul-General, 1903-06; Vice-Consul at Santo Domingo, 1906; Acting Consul-General at Port-au-Prince, 1907-08; Vice-Consul Toulon, 1907; Consul at Tahiti, 1908; Deputy Commissioner for the Western Pacific, 1909; Consul Bordeaux, 1912; Consul-General, Barcelona, 1919-23; Antwerp, 1923-30; H.M. Consul-General for Consular District of Paris, 1930-32; retired from H.M. Consular Service, 1932. *Recreations:* riding, boating, golf. *Heir: kinsman* Lt.-Col. Geoffrey Alexander Rowley-Conwy, O.B.E. 1943 [*b.* 8 March 1912; *m.* 1939, Ruth St. John, *d.* of Albert St. John Murphy, The Island House, Little Island, Co. Cork. *Educ.:* Marlborough. Served War of 1939-45, Singapore and Burma, 1942-45 (despatches, O.B.E.)]. *Address:* c/o Lloyds Bank, 222 Strand, W.C.2. *Club:* St. James'.
[*Died* 19 *Aug.* 1953.

LANGHAM, Sir (Herbert) Charles Arthur, 13th Bt., *cr.* 1660; *b.* 24 Mar. 1870; *s.* of 12th Bt. and Anna, 2nd *d.* of 3rd Lord Sandys; *S.* father, 1909; *m.* 1893, Ethel Sarah, *e. d.* of Sir W. Emerson-Tennent, 2nd Bt. (ext.); one *s.* *Educ.:* Eton. Was Lieut. 3rd Bn. Northants Regt. *Heir: s.* John Charles Patrick [*b.* 30 June 1894; *m.* 1930, Rosamond Christabel, *yr. d.* of Arthur Rashleigh, Holy Well House, Malvern Wells]. *Address:* Tempo Manor, Co. Fermanagh. [*Died* 3 *Oct.* 1951.

LANGLEY, Alexander, C.S.I. 1927; C.I.E. 1918; *b.* 22 May 1871; *m.* Gertrude Langrishe Mare, *o. d.* of Sir Edward Shea; one *d.* *Educ.:* Christ's Hospital; Pembroke College, Oxford. Entered I.C.S. 1894 Deputy Com., Punjab, 1909; Com., 1923; retd. 1930. *Address:* Savoy Hotel, Cheltenham.
[*Died* 4 *Jan.* 1952.

LANGLEY, Beatrice (Beatrice Cordelia Auchmuty Langley — Mrs. Basil Tozer); violinist; *b.* in Devonshire, 1872; *e. d.* of late Colonel W. S. Langley, R.A.; *m.* Basil Tozer, author and journalist (*d.* 1949); two *s.* *Educ.:* privately. Was pupil of Josef Ludwig and Wilhelmj. During her public career as a soloist appeared frequently at Queen's Hall Promenade and Sunday Concerts; also at the Crystal Palace Saturday Concerts where she made her debut under the conductorship of Sir August Manns, 1893. Made extensive concert tours in Canada, America and S. Africa and appeared with much success in Berlin and elsewhere on the Continent. Joint founder of series of mid-day London concerts known as "The Thursday Twelve o'clocks" and as leader of her string Quartet was recognized as a notable Chamber-music player. Since her early retirement from public playing owing to arthritis in her left hand, she has founded and conducted a String Orchestra and worked for increase in appreciation of music in Devon. Kreisler Award of Merit for distinguished service to Music, 1953. *Address:* Eastbrook House, Teignmouth, S. Devon. *T.:* Teignmouth 712. [*Died* 11 *May* 1958.

LANGLEY, George Harry, M.A.; late Indian Educational Service; *b.* 14 July 1881; *s.* of Leveson and Matilda Emma Langley; *m.* 1913, Eveline Mary Biggart, Armagh. *Educ.:* The University, Reading; Scholar in Logic and Psychology, London University, 1906; M.A. in Philosophy (London), 1909, with special mark of distinction. Indian Educational Service, 1913; Professor, Presidency College, Calcutta, 1913; Professor of Philosophy, Dacca College, 1913; Professor of Philosophy and Provost of Dacca Hall, University of Dacca, 1921-25; acting Vice-Chancellor, Dacca University, July to Sep. 1925; Vice-Chancellor of Dacca University, 1926-34; Pres., Seventh Indian Philosophical Congress, 1930; Chairman Inter-University Board, India, 1933-34; Pres., Third Conference of Indian Universities, Delhi, 1934; Member of Council of East India Association, 1949. *Publications:* articles in Mind, Proceedings of Aristotelian Society, Hibbert Journal, Monist, Philosophy, Dacca University Bulletin, Indian Philosophical Review, Indian Journal of Philosophy, Quest, Proceedings of Victoria Inst., etc. *Address:* 16 Ainsworth Avenue, Ovingdean, Sussex.
[*Died* 14 *Feb.* 1951.

LANGMAID, Lieut.-Comdr. Rowland, John Robb, R.N. (retd.); painting marine subjects in Mediterranean since demobilisation in 1946; *b.* 1 Dec. 1897; *e. s.* of Engineer Capt. J. Langmaid, R.N., and Louise Mary Robb; *m.* 1931, Cherry Ina, *o. d.* of Lieut.-Col. Herbert-Stepney, D.S.O., D.L., Derby. *Educ.:* Royal Naval Colleges, Osborne and Dartmouth; Trinity Hall, Cambridge. Went to sea at beginning of European War, 1914-18 (1914-15 Star, General Service and Victory Medal 1918); serving at Dardanelles in H.M.S. Agamemnon, made official sketches for landings; later served in first Commission H.M.S. Renown; retired, 1922. Studied at Royal Academy School and Royal College of Art; exhibited Royal Academy and at exhibitions in London, New York, and Paris. Collaborated with W. L. Wyllie, R.A., in Sea

Fights of the Great War, 1914-18. Has painted and engraved mostly marine subjects. Served in War of 1939-45, as official Admiralty Artist, Mediterranean Fleet, on the Staff of C.-in-C., Mediterranean (1939-45 Star, Africa and Italy Stars, General Service and Defence Medals). A number of his works are in Imperial War Museum. *Publications:* author and illustrator: The King's Ships through the Ages, 1937; The Med, 1948; illustrator: Bartimeus's East of Malta, West of Suez, 1943; The Mediterranean Fleet, Part II, 1944. *Recreations:* travel, nautical research. *Address:* Calle de la Bolsa 4, Malaga, Spain. *Club:* Goat.
[*Died* 11 *Feb.* 1956.

LANGMAN, His Honour Thomas Witheridge, O.B.E. 1919; Judge of County Courts Circuit No. 22 (Worcester, etc.), 1945-55; *b.* 1882; 2nd *s.* of Joseph Langman, Carmarthen; *m.* 1930, Mary Gwenda, *e. d.* of Henry G. Lewis, Porthkerry, Glamorgan. *Educ.:* Llandovery College; Jesus College, Oxford. Called to Bar, Gray's Inn, 1910; Judge of County Courts Circuit No. 17 (Lincolnshire), 1929-1945; Chairman of Kesteven (Lincs) Quarter Sessions, 1932-46; Chairman of the Lindsey (Lincs) Quarter Sessions, 1938-45; Chm. Herefordshire Qr. Sessions, 1951-57 (Dep. Chm., 1946). Served European War, 1914-1919 (despatches); Capt., 1915; Staff Capt., 1916. Hon. Freeman Carmarthen, 1926. *Address:* Parkfield, Hallow, nr. Worcester.
[*Died* 14 *Aug.* 1960.

LANGMUIR, Irving, Met.E., Ph.D., LL.D., D.Sc., D.Ing.; Consultant of the Research Laboratory of the General Electric Company, New York, 1950; *b.* 31 Jan. 1881; *s.* of Charles Langmuir and Sadie Lunt Comings; *m.* Marion Mersereau; one *s.* one *d.* *Educ.:* Columbia University; University of Göttingen. Instructor in chemistry at Stevens Institute of Technology, 1906-09; Research Laboratory of G.E.C. since 1909; retd. as Assoc. Director, 1950. Recipient of Nichols medal, 1915 and 1920, given by N.Y. Section of American Chemical Society; Hughes medal, awarded by Royal Society of London, 1918; Rumford medal by American Academy of Arts and Sciences, 1921; Cannizzaro Prize, awarded by Royal National Academy of the Lincei, Rome, 1925; The Perkin medal by the American Section of Society of Chemical Industry, 1928; School of Mines medal, Columbia University, 1929; Chandler medal, 1929; Willard Gibbs medal, 1930; Popular Science Monthly Award, 1932; Nobel Prize in Chemistry, 1932; Holley Medal Am. Soc. of Mechanical Engineers, 1934; Franklin Medal, 1934; Foreign Member of Royal Society, 1935; Award under Johns Scott Medal Fund, Philadelphia, 1937; Pilgrim Trust Lecturer, London, 1938; Eglestot Medal, Bd. of Managers of Columbia Eng. Schools Alumni Assoc., 1939; Nat. Modern Pioneer Award, Nat. Assoc. of Manufacturers, 1940 (for achievements in science and invention); Pres. Am. Assoc. for the Advancement of Science, 1941; Corr. Mem., Académie des Sciences, Paris, 1951. Faraday Medal Award, 1943; Hitchcock Foundation Lecturer, Univ. of California, 1946; Medal for Merit, presented by U.S. Army and U.S. Navy, 1948; John Carty Medal, Nat. Acad. of Sciences, 1950. *Publications:* extensive contributor to various scientific journals. *Recreations:* winter sports, mountain climbing, music, flying. *Address:* 1176 Stratford Road, Schenectady, N.Y., U.S.A. *T.:* Schenectady 4-7810. *Clubs:* Mohawk, Chemist (New York).
[*Died* 16 *Aug.* 1957.

LANGTON, Bennet, B.A.; *e. s.* of late Bennet Rothes Langton and Lucy Katharine, *d.* of Rev. Langhorne Burton Burton, Rector and Lord of the Manor of Somersby, Lincolnshire; *b.* 1870. *Educ.:* Repton; Clare College, Cambridge. Lord of the Manor of Langton; Patron of one living. *Address:* Langton Hall, Langton, nr. Spilsby, Lincolnshire.
[*Died* 20 *Sept.* 1955.

LANKTREE, Colonel Charles Joseph Dane, C.B.E. 1940; E.D.; Principal Collector of Customs, Government of Ceylon; *b.* 20 Nov. 1895; 4th *s.* of late Barnaby Dane Lanktree, Cork, Ireland; *m.* 1922, Margaret Lily (*d.* 1943), *o. d.* of late Frank Moncrieff Simpson; one *d.*; *m.* 1950, Elizabeth Catharine, *widow* of William Loring Kindersley, C.C.S. (retd.). *Educ.:* Univ. Coll., Cork; King's Inns, Dublin. Commissioned to Royal Munster Fusiliers, Sept. 1914; served with B.E.F., France and Belgium, 1915-19 (wounded); called to Irish Bar, 1920; appointed to Ceylon Civil Service, 1921; served in Ceylon Planters' Rifle Corps, Ceylon Light Infantry and Ceylon Army Service Corps. Is Colonel, Ceylon Defence Force (Gen. Reserve). *Address:* H.M. Customs, Colombo, Ceylon. *T.A.:* Customs, Colombo. *T.:* 4487. *Clubs:* Naval and Military, Royal Empire Society; Colombo, etc.
[*Died* 16 *Jan.* 1951.

LANSELL, Colonel Hon. Sir George (Victor), Kt., *cr.* 1951; C.M.G. 1937; V.D.; J.P.; Member Legislative Council of Victoria, 1928-52; proprietor of Bendigo Advertiser, and Stock and Station Journal; Managing Director Bendigo Mutual P. Land and B. Society; Chairman: S. and N.D. Trustee Co.; Australian Swiss Watch Co.; Riverina Herald, Echuca; Rochester Irrigator (Newspaper); Hanro Knitting Mill. Pres. since 1920 of Returned Soldiers' League of Bendigo, and Y.M.C.A. Bendigo; Mem. Australian Council Y.M.C.A.; State Counsellor Returned Soldiers League; Director, 3cv. Broadcasting Station, Bendigo; Member Bendigo Legacy Club; *b.* Bendigo, Victoria, 3 Oct. 1883; *s.* of George Lansell, Margate, Kent, England; *m.* Gwen Frew (*d.* 1952), Mount Gambier, South Australia; three *d.* *Educ.:* Church of England Grammar School, Melbourne. Served European War with 38th Bn. Australian Imperial Force in France and Belgium; served War of 1939-45 as Group Commander V.D.C. Past Pres.: Rotary Club, Bendigo; School of Mines and Industries, Bendigo. Attended Imperial Press Conferences in England, Canada and Australia. Past Commissioner Boy Scouts for Bendigo District. F.Inst.D. *Publication:* History of Bendigo. *Recreations:* golf, tennis. *Address:* Denderah, 268 View Street, Bendigo, Victoria, Australia. *T.:* Bendigo 1. *Clubs:* Overseas; Sandhurst, Soldiers (Bendigo); R.A.C. of Victoria (Melbourne).
[*Died* 9 *Jan.* 1959.

LARDNER-CLARKE, Colonel J. de W., C.B.E. 1919; retired pay; *b.* Royal Military Academy, Woolwich, 19 May 1858; *s.* of Maj. J. Lardner-Clarke, R.A.; *m.* 1903, Mary Elizabeth Augusta (*d.* 1950), *widow* of A. E. Chambré; two *s.* one *d.* *Educ.:* St. James's Collegiate School, Jersey; R.M. Academy, Woolwich. Lieut., R.A., 1877; served at home and abroad as regimental officer and sundry regimental and staff appointments; temporary A.D.C. to Governor-General of Canada; Adjutant of Artillery Volunteers; Instructor of Range-Finding, and, finally, O.C. Militia and Volunteer Artillery and C.R.A., North Western District; retired as Brevet-Colonel, 1908; served European War in Military Intelligence Dept., 2 Aug. 1914–10 Aug. 1919 (despatches, O.B.E., C.B.E.). *Recreations:* yachting, motoring, and fishing. *Address:* Parkholme, 97 Bainton Road, Oxford. *T.:* Oxford 58038. *Club:* Army and Navy.
[*Died* 27 *Sept.* 1951.

LARGE, Tennyson J. D., C.B.E. 1938 (O.B.E. 1928); *b.* Dublin, 25 Oct. 1879; *s.* of Thomas David Large; *m.* 1906, Margaret (*d.* 1945), *d.* of Joseph Fairbanks; no *c.* *Educ.:* High School, Dublin; London University (B.A. 1907). Entered Customs Service in 1899; Principal, Secretaries Office, Customs and Excise, 1920-25; Higher Collector, Belfast, 1925-28; Glasgow, 1928-29; Liverpool, 1929-42; Ministry of Food, 1942-

1945. *Address:* Eastville, Dowhills Road, Blundellsands, Liverpool. [*Died* 6 *June* 1959.

LARKE, Sir William James, K.B.E., *cr.* 1921 (C.B.E. 1920; O.B.E. 1917); D.Sc. (hon. Durham); M.I.E.E., F.Inst.F., M.I.Mech.E.; Vice-President, Iron and Steel Institute (Bessemer) Medal, 1947; The Director, British Iron and Steel Federation, 1922-46 (retd.); Pres. British Standards Institution, 1949, 1950; Chairman Advisory Committee Non-Ferrous Minerals, Ministry of Supply, 1940; Controller Non-Ferrous Mineral Development, 1942-45; Pres. Institute of Welding, 1938-42 (Hon. Mem. 1955); Pres. Junior Institution of Engineers (Incorporated), 1936-37; Pres. Institute of Fuel, 1933-34; a member of the Advisory Council to the Comm. of the Privy Council for Scientific and Industrial Research, 1927-31; *s.* of late William James Larke, London and Sidcup; *m.* 1900, Louisa Jane (*d.* 1959), *d.* of late James Taylor Milton, Blackheath, Kent; one *s.* one *d.* *Educ.:* privately; Colfe's School, Blackheath; Engineering School. Training H. F. Joel & Co., and Siemens Bros. & Co., Ltd., Woolwich; joined the British Thomson-Houston Company, 1898; Engineer and Manager of Power and Mining Dept., 1899-1912; Exec. Engineer, 1912-15; Min. of Munitions as Volunteer, July 1915, in charge of various depts.; Director General of Raw Materials, Member of Disposal Board, 1919-22; member of the Co-ordinating (Supply and Demobilisation) Committee, July 1919. *Recreation:* reading. *Address:* Steel House, Tothill Street, S.W.1. *T.A.:* Irostelfer, Parl, London. *T.:* Whitehall 1030; Cray Hill, Rectory Lane, Sidcup, Kent. *T.:* Footscray 2369. *Club:* Athenæum. [*Died* 29 *April* 1959.

LARKEN, Lieutenant-Colonel Edmund, C.B.E. 1919 (O.B.E. 1918); *b.* 1876; *s.* of late Francis Roper Larken, Lincoln; *m.* 1908, Leila Mary, *d.* of late Alfred Barrand Burton, Lincoln; one *s.* one *d.* *Educ.:* Winchester. Admitted a solicitor, 1900; Member of the legal firms of Toynbee, Larken, and Co., Lincoln, and Larken and Co., of Newark; served European War, 1914-19 (despatches, O.B.E., C.B.E.). *Address:* The Old Rectory, Lincoln. *T.:* Lincoln 156. [*Died* 28 *April* 1951.

LARKEN, Admiral Sir Frank, K.C.B., *cr.* 1932 (C.B. 1925); C.M.G. 1916; *b.* 15 Nov. 1875; 2nd *s.* of late Francis Roper Larken of Cantelupe Chantry, Lincoln; *m.* 1909, Victoria Alexandrina, *d.* of late Commander W. Rawson; one *s.* two *d.* Naval Intelligence Dept. 1910; War Staff Officer, 1921; Naval Secretary to First Lord of the Admiralty, 1925-27; commanded 2nd Cruiser Squadron Atlantic Fleet, 1927-29; commanded Reserve Fleet, 1930-32; retired list, 1933; served European War (Dardanelles), 1914-18 (despatches, C.M.G.); Rear-Admiral, 1924; Vice-Admiral, 1929; Adm., 1933; Commander Order of Crown of Belgium; Commander Order of Redeemer of Greece; Officer of Legion of Honour, France; Croix de Guerre with palm, France. *Address:* Annery, Roehampton, S.W.15. *Club:* United Service. [*Died* 21 *Jan.* 1953.

LARKINS, Laurence Brouncker Southey, C.M.G. 1950; O.B.E. 1942; *b.* 11 August 1891; *s.* of late Major William Robertson Larkins and of Edwina Fanny Larkins (*née* Thring); *m.* 1927, Margaret Cecilia (*née* Leak); one *s.* one *d.* *Educ.:* King's School, Grantham; St. Paul's School, London; privately abroad. Went to Canada, 1911; employed real estate business, in Vancouver; Canadian Militia, Vancouver Island, 1913; volunteered Aug. 1914; First Canadian Contingent, 7th Bn. Can. Inf., Flanders, 1915; Battle of Neuve Chapelle, 2nd Battle of Ypres (wounded, prisoner); exchanged to Switzerland, Dec. 1917; North Russian Relief Force, Archangel, 1919 (1914-15 Star, General Service and Victory Medals). Dept. of Overseas Trade, London, 1920; Asst. to Commercial Sec., Cairo, 1920; Commercial Sec. (Grade II), Cairo, 1930; Commercial Agent to Batavia, N.E.I. (with rank of Consul), 1934; re-appointed Commercial Sec. (Grade II), Cairo (local rank of C.S. Grade I), 1942; Dept. of Overseas Trade, London, 1944; Counsellor (Commercial), Santiago, Chile, 1945; Counsellor (Commercial) at H.M. Embassy, The Hague, 1948-1951; retired from For. Service, 1951. *Publications:* series of Economic Reports on Commercial Conditions in Netherlands East Indies (Indonesia), and in 1949 in Holland. *Recreations:* tennis, fishing. *Address:* The Chestnuts, Shere, Nr. Guildford, Surrey. *Club:* Royal Empire Society. [*Died* 23 *Nov.* 1953.

LASCELLES, Sir Alfred (George), Kt., *cr.* 1913; Q.C.; *b.* 12 Oct. 1857; 2nd *s.* of Hon. George Edwin (*d.* 1911) and Lady Louisa Lascelles; *m.* 1911, Isabel Carteret, *d.* of late Francis John Thynne of Haynes Park, Bedford; three *d.* *Educ.:* University College, Oxford (2nd class modern history). Called to Bar, 1885; served in Cyprus as District Judge at Papho, Larnaca, and Nicosia; Acting Puisne Judge, 1895; Queen's Advocate, 1898; Attorney-General, Ceylon, 1902; K.C. (Ceylon), 1906; Chief Justice, 1911-14. *Address:* The Cliff, Terrington, York. *Club:* Yorkshire (York). [*Died* 9 *Feb.* 1952.

LASCELLES, Edward Charles Ponsonby, O.B.E. 1920; *b.* 8 Oct. 1884; *s.* of late Lieut.-Col. H. A. Lascelles; *m.* 1911, Leila, *d.* of late Sir Vincent Kennett Barrington; one *s.* one *d.* *Educ.:* Winchester; abroad. 2nd Lieut., 3rd Batt. York and Lancaster Regt., 1901-02; served South African War; called to Bar, 1911; Chairman of Trade Boards, Courts of Referees and of other tribunals; Deputy Umpire under the Unemployment Insurance Acts; Member of the Royal Commission on Unemployment Insurance, 1930. *Publications:* Granville Sharp (biography), 1928; The Life of Charles James Fox, 1936; in collaboration with others—Unemployment in East London (edited for Toynbee Hall); Dock Labour and Decasualisation (with S. S. Bullock), 1924; A Guide to the Unemployment Insurance Acts (with H. C. Emmerson), 1927; Poverty, a Survey (with J. J. Mallon), 1930; contributions to New Survey of London Life and Labour; Early Victorian England, etc. *Address:* Woolbeding, Midhurst, Sussex. *T.:* Midhurst 70. [*Died* 3 *Feb.* 1956.

LASCELLES, Lieut.-Colonel Edward ffrancis Ward, C.B.E. 1920; *b.* Hawkes Bay, New Zealand, *e. s.* of late Henry Rohde Lascelles; *m.* Margaret Hawdon (*d.* 1956), *e. d.* of John Hawdon Davison, St. Leonards, Culverden, New Zealand; one *s.* Volunteered for service in South Africa, 1899; Sergeant, New Zealand Mounted Rifles, 1900; commissioned 3rd Dragoon Guards, 1900; A.D.C. to Lord Kitchener of Khartoum, commanding Coronation Troops, 1911; General Staff, New Zealand, Anzac, Cape Helles, War Office, India; Special employ Ministry of Food (Managing Director, National Meat Products Ltd.) 1917-18; Ministry of Labour (Deputy Controller, Appointments Dept.) 1918; initiated, organised, and administered Overseas Sailor and Soldier Scholarships, 1917-19; retired, 1930; contested Colne Valley (Unionist) 1931; Sales Organiser, L.M.S. Railway, 1933-41; Chairman, New Zealand War Services Assoc., London, 1939-45; British Information Services, U.S.A., 1943-44; Member of Council, League of Brit. Commonwealth and Empire. Chairman, Society of Yorkshiremen in London, 1948-49; a vice-President Over-Seas League. *Address:* P.O. Box 1479, Salisbury, S. Rhodesia. [*Died* 1 *Aug.* 1959.

LASKY, Jesse L.; Producer; *b.* San Francisco, Calif., 13 Sept. 1880. After starting as reporter, San Francisco, joined early gold rush to Alaska; became professional musician, San Francisco; later, soloist Royal Hawaiian Band, Honolulu; then three years in vaudeville with Lasky Military Musicians; (with B. A. Rolfe) producer vaudeville musical acts; (with late Henry B. Harris) built Folies Bergère (now Helen Hayes Theatre, New York), 1911; (with Samuel Goldwyn, Arthur S. Friend, and Cecil B. DeMille as dir.-gen.) organised Jesse L. Lasky Feature Play Co.; estab. jointly one of earliest studios in Hollywood and prod. The Squaw Man, etc.; organised Jesse L. Lasky Productions, 1932; formed, and named pres., Pickford-Lasky Corp., 1935; prod. radio programme, Gateway to Hollywood, 1938-40; joined Warner Bros. as prod., 1941; (with Walter MacEwen) formed Jesse L. Lasky Prods., Dec. 1944; to M.G.M. as prod., 1950. Member, M.P. Pioneers. Films (since sound) include: Zoo in Budapest, Berkeley Square, The Power and the Glory, Here's to Romance, One Rainy Afternoon, Gay Desperado, Sergeant York, The Adventures of Mark Twain, Rhapsody in Blue, Without Reservations, Miracle of the Bells, The Great Caruso. *Address:* Paramount Pictures Corp., Hollywood, California, U.S.A. [*Died* 13 *Jan.* 1958.

LAST, Hugh Macilwain, M.A.; Hon. LL.D. (Edin.); Hon. Litt.D. (Dublin); Principal of Brasenose College, Oxford, 1948-1956; an Emeritus Fellow of Brasenose College, since 1956; Hon. Fellow, Lincoln College; Corresp. Member, Istituto Lombardo di Scienze e Lettere, and Académie des Inscriptions et Belles Lettres; Fellow of St. John's College, 1919-36; Camden Professor of Ancient History and Fellow of Brasenose College, Oxford, 1936-49; Pres. of Soc. for the Promotion of Roman Studies, 1934-37; Pres. of Classical Assoc., 1949-50. *Address:* Strathmore, Mulberry Green, Harlow, Essex. [*Died* 25 *Oct.* 1957.

LATHAM, Brigadier Francis, D.S.O. 1916; *b.* Woolwich, 25 Aug. 1883; 4th *s.* of late Colonel Hugh Latham, R.A., and late Emily Dallas Baker; *m.* 1st, 1915, Muriel (*d.* 1946), *o. d.* of late John Henry Humphreys, M.D., London, and late Helen Jacquina Harratt; one *d.*; 2nd, 1948, Helena Beatrice Joan, *widow* of Brig. Bernard Howlett, D.S.O., and *o. d.* of late H. O. Whitby, Little Judde, Tonbridge. *Educ.:* Tonbridge School. Joined 4th Batt. Yorkshire Regt., 1901; served South Africa, 1902 (Queen's medal with 2 clasps); West India Regt., 1904; Lieut., 1906; transferred to Leicestershire Regt. 1907; Capt. 1913; Adjutant, 1914-15; Maj., 1921; Lieut.-Col. 1931; Colonel, 1935; Temp. Brigadier, 1937; Hon. Brig., 1939; served European War (twice severely wounded, Bt. Major, despatches six times, D.S.O. and Bar, Officier de l'Ordre de la Couronne, Belgian Croix de Guerre); commanded 1st Bn. Leicestershire Regiment, 1931-35; commanded 165th Infantry Brigade, T.A. 1935-40; retired, 1939; Comd. Sub-Area, 1940-43; Comd. Sub-District, 1943. *Address:* Tonlow, Tonbridge, Kent. *T.:* Tonbridge 2630. [*Died* 28 *June* 1958.

LATHAM, Sir (Herbert) Paul, 2nd Bt., *cr.* 1919, of Crow Clump; *b.* 22 Apr. 1905; *o. s.* of Sir Thomas Paul Latham, 1st Bt., and Florence Clara (*d.* 1950), *d.* of William Henry Walley, Manchester; *S.* father, 1931; *m.* 1933, Lady Patricia Doreen Moore (who obtained a divorce, 1943, she died 1947), *o. d.* of 10th Earl of Drogheda, *q.v.*; one *s.* *Educ.:* Eton; Magdalen Coll., Oxford. Contested (C.) Rotherham, 1929; M.P. (C.), Scarborough and Whitby Division of North Riding of Yorkshire, 1931-41; London County Councillor (M.R.) for East Lewisham, 1928-34. *Heir:* *s.* Richard Thomas Paul, *b.* 15 Apr. 1934. *Address:* Herstmonceux Place, Sussex. *T.:* 2156. [*Died* 24 *July* 1955.

LATIFI, Almá, C.I.E. 1932; O.B.E. 1919; M.A., LL.M. Cantab.; LL.D. Dublin; Barr.; I.C.S. (retired); *b.* 12 Nov. 1879; *e. s.* of late C. A. Latif, J.P., Bombay; *m.* 1908, Nasima (Kaisar-i-Hind Medal, 1937, etc.), *d.* of late Justice Badruddin Tyabji, Bombay; two *s.* two *d.* *Educ.:* Bombay; London; Paris; Heidelberg; Cairo; St. John's College, Cambridge (scholar and Macmahon Law Student). Cambridge: 1st class in 1st year exam. for Oriental Langs. Tripos; 1st class Honours in both parts of Law Tripos and 2nd class in Modern Langs. Tripos; Senior Whewell Scholar; Inns of Court: Barstow Scholar, 1902; 1st cl. Degree of Honour in Arabic (Govt. India), 1908; joined as Assistant Commissioner in Punjab, 1903; since held administrative, judicial, secretariat, and political offices; inquired Punjab industries, 1909-10; duty with Press Camp, Delhi Coronation Durbar, 1911 (*medal*); District Judge, Delhi, 1911-12; Director of Public Instruction, Hyderabad State, 1913-16; Deputy Commissioner, Hissar, 1918-21; secretary transfd. depts., also M.L.C., Punjab, 1921-24; Deputy Commissioner, Karnál, 1924-27; Commissioner, Ambálá, also member Council of State, 1927; Delegate, International Law Conference, The Hague, March 1930; substitute delegate and adviser, International Labour Conference, Geneva, June 1930; Delegate, Inter-Parliamentary Conference, London, July 1930; duty with 1st, 2nd, and 3rd Indian Round Table Conferences, London, 1930, 1931, 1932; Secretary Consultative Committee of Round Table Conference, Delhi, Jan. 1932; Commissioner Multan, March 1931, and Lahore, Jan. 1933; Financial Commissioner, Revenue, Punjab, 1934-37, retd. Mem. Defence Services Selection Committee, Bombay, 1942-45; Adjudicator in various Industrial Disputes, Bombay, 1942-44. *Publications:* Effects of War on Property: being studies in International Law and Policy, 1908; The Industrial Punjab, 1911; various addresses, articles, reports. *Address:* Latifia, Harkness Road, Malabar Hill, Bombay 6. *T.:* 42904. *Club:* Athenæum. [*Died* 16 *Aug.* 1959.

LATTA, Sir Andrew Gibson, K.B.E., *cr.* 1921; *s.* of late William Latta, Darmalloch, Old Cumnock; unmarried. *Educ.:* Hamilton Academy. Rendered voluntary service in the Ministry of Shipping and Assistant Director of the Ship Management Branch, 1918-21. *Address:* 71 Braid Avenue, Edinburgh. [*Died* 10 *Aug.* 1953.

LATTEY, Rev. Cuthbert Charles, S.J., M.A. (Oxon), Doctor of Philosophy and Theology (papal); Professor of Hebrew, etc., Heythrop College, since 1926; *b.* 12 May 1877; *s.* of late James Lattey, London doctor, and late Charlotte Cumming. *Educ.:* Beaumont College, Old Windsor; Campion Hall, Oxford (1st cl. classical Mods. and Greats). Professor Holy Scripture at St. Beuno's College, N. Wales, 1911-26; helped to found the Catholic Conference of Ecclesiastical Studies, 1920, the Catholic Biblical Association, 1940, and the Cambridge Summer School of Catholic Studies, 1921, to the lecture-books of which latter he has contributed many prefaces and papers; General Editor of the Westminster Version of the Sacred Scriptures, contributing 1-11 Thess., 1 Cor., Romans, Acts and other matter to the New Testament, and Ruth, Malachy, Psalms and Daniel, etc., to the Old; on Cttee. of Oxford Soc. of Historical Theology, 1934-49, and of Society for Old Testament Study, 1937-8 (Pres. 1947); Editorial Board of Catholic Biblical Assoc. of America for Revision of New Testament, 1939. *Publications:* Back to Christ, 1919; Thy Love and Thy Grace (retreat manual), 1923; First Notions of Holy Writ, 1923; Readings in First Corinthians, 1928; Paul, 1939; Back to the Bible, 1945; many pamphlets, articles, etc.; chiefly on biblical subjects. *Address:* Heythrop College, Chipping Norton, Oxon. *T.A.:* College, Enstone. *T.:* Enstone 38. [*Died* 3 *Sept.* 1954.

LAUDER, Lieut.-Col. Sir John North Dalrymple Dick-, 11th Bt., *cr.* 1688; late 6th D.C.O. Lancers, Indian Army; D.L. and Vice-Lieut., County of Ross and Cromarty, since 1945; *b.* 22 July 1883; *s.* of George Dick-Lauder, 10th Bt., and Jane Emily Clifford (*d.* 1921), *d.* of W. P. Woodward; *S.* father 1936; *m.* 1914, Phyllis Mary, *d.* of late Brig.-Gen. H. A. Iggulden, C.I.E.; one *s.* one *d.* Retired from Indian Army, 1934. *Heir:* *s.* George Andrew [*b.* 17 Nov. 1917; *m.* 1945, Hester Marguerite, *y. d.* of late Lt.-Col. G. C. M. Sorell-Cameron, C.B.E.; two *s.* two *d.*]. *Address:* Arabella House, Nigg, Ross-shire. *Clubs:* New (Edinburgh); Highland (Inverness). [*Died* 19 *Sept.* 1958.

LAUDERDALE, 15th Earl of, *cr.* 1624, **Ian Colin Maitland,** Baron Maitland, 1590; Viscount Lauderdale, 1616; Viscount Maitland, Baron Thirlestane and Boltoun, 1624; Baronet of Nova Scotia, 1672; *b.* 30 Jan. 1891; *e. s.* of 14th Earl and Gwendoline Lucy (*d.* 1929), *y. d.* of late Judge Vaughan-Williams of Bodlonfla, Flintshire; *S.* father, 1931; *m.* 1912, Ivy, *e. d.* of late J. J. Bell Irving; one *d.* *Educ.:* Eton. Served European War, 1914-1918; Major late 3rd Res. Bn. Q.O. Cameron Highlanders; A.D.C. to Lord-Lieutenant of Ireland, 1915-16 and 1918; Member of Royal Company of Archers, Queen's Bodyguard for Scotland; President Southampton Conservative Association, 1931-35; Hon. Pres. Assoc. of Certified and Corporate Accountants, 1939-45; D.L. Berwickshire; Representative Peer for Scotland, 1931-45. *Heir:* *cousin* Rev. Alfred Sydney Frederick Maitland [*b.*1904; *m.* 1st, 1938, Norah Mary (*d.* 1938), *d.* of late William Henry La Touche; 2nd, 1940, Irene Alice May, *d.* of late Rev. C. P. Shipton, Halsham, Yorkshire]. *Address:* Thirlestane Castle, Lauder, Scotland. *Club:* New (Edinburgh). [*Died* 17 *Feb.* 1953.

LAUGHTON, George Christian, C.I.E. 1942; M.Inst.T.; *b.* 26 Jan. 1887; *s.* of Lt.-Gen. G. A. Laughton, Indian Army, and Annie Barbara Beaumont; *m.* 1912, Anne Ruth Grundy; one *s.* one *d.* *Educ.:* Seafield Park College; City and Guilds Central Technical College, London University. Joined Indian State Railways, 1910; Assistant and Executive Engineer, Oudh & Rohilkhand Railway, 1910-21; Superintendent, Kalka-Simla Railway, 1921-25; Divisional Engineer and Divisional Superintendent, North-Western Railway, 1925-28; Deputy Director, and Director, Civil Engineering, Indian Railway Board, 1928-32; Secretary, Indian Railway Board, 1932; Senior Government Inspector of Railways, Bangalore, 1932-38; Agent and General Manager, B.B. & C.I. Railway Company, 1938-42; General Manager, Bombay, Baroda, and Central India Railway, Bombay, 1942; retired, 1944; Dep. Chief Controller, Railway Branch Transport Div., C.C.G., 1945-46. *Recreations:* golf and bridge. *Address:* Home Farm House, Elvetham, Basingstoke, Hants. *T.:* Hartley Wintney 222. [*Died* 13 *April* 1952.

LAURIE, Lieut.-Col. Sir John Dawson, 1st Bt., *cr.* 1942, of Sevenoaks; Kt., *cr.* 1936; T.D., J.P.; one of H.M. Lieutenants, City of London; Rep. London Court of Arbitration; Rep. London Museum; Treas. of the Lieutenancy; Partner in Laurie Milbank and Co.; Alderman, 1931; Sheriff, 1935-36, and Lord Mayor, City of London, 1941-42; *b.* 12 Sept. 1872; *s.* of Alfred St. George MacAdam Laurie, J.P., and Ellen Catherine Dawson; unmarried. *Educ.:* St. Leonards School, St. Leonards; Harrow. Entered Stock Exchange, 1896; Director of Public Companies; joined West Kent Volunteers, 1896; Commanded 2/4 Royal West Kent Regt. (despatches, 1916, Croix de Guerre, France); Master Woolmen Co. 1917 and 1943; Prime Warden Saddlers Co. 1931, Master 1941; J.P. Kent, 1922; Governor of Sevenoaks School, Christ's Hospital, St. Bartholomew's, St. Thomas's, Bridewell Hosps.; Trustee, Morden Coll., Blackheath; Member Court of Arbitration, London; Chm. Rowland Hill Benevolent Fund; Past Grand Warden Grand Lodge of England; Past Grand Warden Mark Masons; Vice-Pres. British Empire League; Representative of Ministry of Pensions on Bromley war pensions and civil pensions. Hon. Sec. Metropolitan Hospital-Sunday Fund. *Address:* Rockdale, Sevenoaks. *Clubs:* Constitutional, City Livery, Guildhall, City of London, Royal Automobile. [*Died* 20 *July* 1954 (*ext.*).

LAURIE, Emeritus Professor Robert Douglas, M.A.; Hon. General Secretary, Association of University Teachers, since 1920; *b.* Birkenhead, 27 Oct. 1874; *o. s.* of late Robert Laurie and Eleanor Ord; *m.* 1912, Elinor Beatrice, *d.* of late George Ord, Durham; one *d.* *Educ.:* Birkenhead School; University College, Liverpool, 1900; Merton College, Oxford (Exhibitioner), 1901-5; B.A. (Oxon.) 1905. On staff of Bank of Liverpool, 1891-99; Assistant Demonstrator in Department of Comparative Anatomy, Oxford, 1905-6; Demonstrator and Assistant Lecturer in Zoology in the University of Liverpool, 1906-1918; Lecturer in Embryology and Genetics in the University of Liverpool, 1911-18; Head of the Department of Zoology in the University Coll. of Wales, Aberystwyth, 1918; Prof. of Zoology, Univ. Coll. of Wales, Aberystwyth, 1922-40; Recorder of Zoology Section of British Association, 1921-23; Convener and Chm. of Conference of Univ. Lecturers, 1917-1919; First Pres. Assoc. of Univ. Teachers, 1919; Hon. Sec.-Gen. Internat. Assoc. of Univ. Professors and Lecturers since 1943; has travelled in Europe and Australia, partly for zoological purposes and partly for comparative study of University systems; 'Ami de Paris,' 1948. *Publications:* Papers on Crustacea, Genetics, and Ecology in scientific periodicals. *Recreation:* travelling. *Address:* Ty'n y Gongl, Caradoc Road, Aberystwyth, Cardiganshire. *T.:* Aberystwyth 225. *Club:* Authors'. [*Died* 7 *April* 1953.

LAUTERPACHT, Sir Hersch, Kt., *cr.* 1956; Q.C. 1949; M.A., LL.D., F.B.A.; LL.D. (Hon., Geneva); LL.D. (Hon., Aberdeen); Judge of the International Court of Justice, The Hague; Member, Permanent Court of Arbitration; Whewell Professor of International Law, Univ. of Cambridge, 1938-55; Mem. of the Institute of International Law; Hon. Fellow, London School of Economics, 1958; *b.* 16 Aug. 1897; 2nd *s.* of Aaron Lauterpacht; *m.* 1923, Rachel, 3rd *d.* of Michael Steinberg; one *s.* *Educ.:* Lwów; Vienna; University of London. Asst. Lecturer, London School of Economics, 1927; Reader in Public International Law, University of London, 1932; Gray's Inn: Barrister-at-Law; Master of the Bench, 1955; Professor at The Hague Academy of International Law, 1930, 1934, 1937 and 1947; Carnegie Endowment Visiting Professor in U.S., Oct.-Dec. 1940; Mary Whiton Calkins Visiting Prof., Wellesley Coll., Oct.-Dec. 1941; Charles Inglis Thompson Visiting Professor, University of Colorado, June-July 1948; Member: British War Crimes Executive, 1945-46; Inter-Departmental Cttee. on Immunities of Foreign Governments, 1950; United Nations International Law Commission, 1951-55; President Permanent French-Swedish Conciliation Commn., 1951-, and President Permanent Norwegian-Portuguese Conciliation Commn. *Publications:* Private Law Sources and Analogies of International Law, 1927; The Function of Law in the International Community, 1933; The Development of International Law by the Permanent Court of International Justice, 1934; Règles générales du droit de la paix (Lectures delivered at the Hague Academy of International Law, 1938); An International Bill of the Rights of Man, 1945; Recognition in International Law, 1947; International Law and Human Rights, 1950; Development of International Law of the International Court, 1958. Editor of Oppenheim's International Law, 1935-55; Editor of Annual Digest and Reports of Public International Law Cases, and International Law Reports; Editor of British Year Book of International Law 1944-1955; Joint Editor of Cambridge Series of International and Comparative Law; Contributor to Cambridge History of the British Empire; articles in various legal publications. *Recreations:* walking, gardening. *Address:* 6 Cranmer Rd., Cambridge. *T.:* 54622; Peace Palace, The Hague. *Club:* Athenæum. [*Died* 8 *May* 1960.

LAVARACK, Lieut.-General Sir John (Dudley), K.C.M.G., *cr.* 1955 (C.M.G. 1919); K.C.V.O., *cr.* 1954; K.B.E., *cr.* 1941; C.B. 1937; D.S.O. 1918; Governor of Queensland, 1946-57; late Royal Australian Artillery; *b.* 19 Dec. 1885; *s.* of late Cecil Wallace Lavarack, Consentes, N. Queensland; *m.* 1912, Sybil Nevett, 2nd *d.* of Dr. E. G. Ochiltree, Ballarat; three *s.* Joined Royal Australian Artillery, 1905; Capt. 1912; Major, 1919; Lt.-Col. 1926; Brevet Col. 1926; Maj.-Gen. 1935; Lt.-Gen. 1939. Served European War, 1914-18 (D.S.O., C.M.G., Bt. Maj. and Lieut.-Col.); Director of Military Training, Australia, 1925-27; Director of Military Operations and Intelligence (Australia), 1929-32; Comdt., Royal Military College of Australia, 1933-35; Chief of General Staff, 1935-39; commanded Southern Command Australian Military Forces, 1939-40; served Middle East, 1941 (K.B.E.); commanded 7th Aust. Div. 1940-41, Cyrenaica Command, April 1941, 1st Aust. Corps, A.I.F., 1941-42; 1st Aust. Army, 1942-44; Head of Australian Military Mission, Washington, 1944-46; Australian Rep. on Far Eastern Commission, Washington, during 1946. *Address:* Government House, Brisbane, Queensland. *Clubs:* Melbourne, Melbourne Savage, Naval and Military of Victoria, Royal Melbourne Golf (Melbourne). [*Died* 4 *Dec.* 1957.

LAW, Albert; *b.* 28 Dec. 1872; parents natives of Bolton, Lancs; father a brewer, mother a weaver; *m.* 1900, Mary Ann Jenkinson, *d.* of hand-loom weaver; four *d.* (one *s.* decd.) *Educ.:* Pikes Lane Elementary, Bolton. M.P. (Lab.) Bolton, 1923-24, and 1929-31; Member of E.C. of Amalgamated Operative Spinners, 1911-14; President of Bolton Operative Spinners Association, 1916-18, and 1920-22; Local Preacher 30 years; 15 years Bible Christian Methodist Church; 15 years Wesleyan Methodist Church; completed 60 years as local preacher, 1891-1951. *Address:* The Gables, Cox Green Road, Egerton, nr. Bolton, Lancs. [*Died* 22 *Oct.* 1956.

LAWFORD, Lieut.-General Sir Sydney Turing Barlow, K.C.B., *cr.* 1918 (C.B. 1915); Royal Fusiliers; *b.* 16 Nov. 1865; *m.* May Somerville, *d.* of Colonel F. W. Bunny, late Royal Berkshire Regt., and *g.d.* of late General Arthur Courtney Bunny, Royal Artillery. Entered Army, 1885; Captain, 1894; Major, 1900; Brevet Lieut.-Colonel 1902; Brevet Colonel, 1908; Colonel, 1912; Lieut-Gen., 1923; Commandant, School of Mounted Infantry, Longmore, 1912-13; Brigade Commander Essex Infantry Brigade, 1913; served South African War, 1901-2 (Queen's medal 3 clasps; Brevet Lieut.-Col.); European War, 1914-18 (despatches, C.B., promoted Maj.-Gen., K.C.B.; Commandeur of Legion of Honour, Commander of Order of Leopold I., French Croix de Guerre, Belgian Croix de Guerre, Russian Order of St. Vladimir); G.O.C. Lahore District, 1920-23; retired pay, 1926. *Club:* Army and Navy. [*Died* 15 *Feb.* 1953.

LAWFORD, Capt. (S) Vincent Adrian, C.M.G. 1919; D.S.O. 1916; Royal Navy, retired; *b.* 6 January 1871; 9th *s.* of late John Lawford, of Blackheath; *m.* 1904, Agnes Jane, 2nd *d.* of William Batty Mapplebeck, of Hampton-in-Arden, Warwickshire; four *s.* one *d.* *Educ.:* Tottenham; Blackheath. Entered Royal Navy as Assistant Clerk, 1887; Assistant Paymaster, 1892; Flete Paymaster, 1910; served as Secretary to Commodores, Hong-Kong and S.E. coast of America, to Rear-Admiral, 2nd in command, Mediterranean, to Rear-Admiral Commanding 4th Cruiser Squadron, to Admiral Commanding Coastguard and Reserves, to Rear-Admiral Commanding 10th Cruiser Squadron to Naval Adviser, Foreign Office; Naval Liaison Officer, Foreign Office; received Order of Crown of Italy and Messina Medal, 1908 (D.S.O. or services in patrol cruisers); Member of British War Mission to U.S.A., 1917; retired list, 1922; Civil Defence Controller, Chorley Wood, 1939-45. J.P. Herts. *Address:* Quickley, Chorley Wood, Herts. *T.:* Chorley Wood 35. [*Died* 11 *March* 1959.

LAWN, James Gunson, C.B.E. 1920; A.R.S.M.; Hon. D.Sc. (Eng.) Univ. of Witwatersrand, 1933; late Director of and Consulting Engineer in England to the Johannesburg Consolidated Investment Co., Ltd.; also late Director of a number of other companies in South Africa and in England since 1924; now retired from active work; Member of various technical institutions and societies; *b.* Dalton-in-Furness, North Lancashire, 4 Jan. 1868; *s.* of John Webster Lawn and Eleanor Gunson; *m.* 1st, Mary Searle; three *s.* one *d.*; 2nd, Mary Beatrice Good; one *d.*; 3rd, Grace, *d.* of late Joseph Thomas of St. Michael's Mount, Cornwall. *Educ.:* Private School; Royal School of Mines, London. Surveyor, Mines of Barrow Hematite Steel Co., 1891-92; Lecturer on Mining, Cumberland County Council, 1892-93; Lecturer, Royal School of Mines, 1893-96; Principal and Professor of Mining, So. African School of Mines, 1896-1902; Assistant Consulting Engineer, Johannesburg Consolidated Investment Co., 1903-6; Head of Mining Department, Camborne School of Mines, 1907-9; Principal and Professor of Mining, So. African School of Mines and Technology, now University of the Witwatersrand, 1909-10; Consulting Engineer, Johannesburg Consolidated Investment Co., 1910-15; Explosives Department of Ministry of Munitions, various positions, finally Controller, 1915-19; Joint Managing Director in Johannesburg of Johannesburg Consolidated Investment Co., 1919-24; has always been interested in Education, and has served on various bodies connected therewith. *Recreations:* walking and travelling. *Address:* Eshowe, Zululand, S. Africa. *Clubs:* Mining and Metallurgical; Rand (Johannesburg). [*Died* 21 *Oct.* 1952.

LAWRENCE, Professor Ernest O.; Professor of Physics since 1930 and Director of Radiation Laboratory since 1936, University of California, Berkeley, California, U.S.A.; *b.* 8 Aug. 1901; *s.* of Carl Gustavus Lawrence (President Emeritus Northern State Teacher's College, Aberdeen, South Dakota) and Gunda Jacobson Lawrence; Ancestry Norwegian; *m.* 1932, Mary Kimberly Blumer; two *s.* four *d.* *Educ.:* University of South Dakota; University of Minnesota; Yale University (Ph.D. 1925). National Research Fellow, Yale Univ., 1925-1927; Asst. Prof. of Physics, Yale, 1927-28; Assoc. Prof. of Physics, Univ. of Calif., 1928-1930. Member Solvay Conference, Brussels, 1933; Board of Trustees of Carnegie Institution of Washington, 1944-; Director: Yosemite Park & Curry Co.; Monsanto Chemical Co. *Medals and Prizes:* Elliott Cresson Medal of the Franklin Inst., Research Corp. Prize and Plaque, Comstock Prize of Nat. Acad. of Sciences, Hughes Medal of Royal Society, 1937; Nobel Prize for Physics, 1939; Duddell Medal, The

Physical Soc., 1940; William K. Dunn Award, Amer. Legion, 1940; Holley Medal, Amer. Soc. of Mechanical Engineers, 1942; Wheeler Award, 1945; Medal for Merit, 1946; Medal of Trasenster, Assoc. of Grad. Engineers of Univ. of Liége, Belgium, 1947; Faraday Medal, 1952; American Cancer Society Annual Award, 1954; Enrico Fermi Award, 1957; Sylvanus Thayer Award, 1958. Hon. Member: U.S.S.R. Acad. of Sciences, 1943; Royal Irish Acad. of Science, 1948; Hon. F.R.S.E., 1946; Hon. F.Phys.S., 1948; For. Mem. Roy. Swedish Acad. of Sciences, 1952; Hon. Fell. Indian Acad. of Sciences, 1953; Fell. Amer. Phys. Soc.; Fell. Amer. Acad. of Arts and Sciences; Fell. Amer. Soc. for Advancement of Science; Member: Nat. Acad. of Sciences; Amer. Phil. Soc.; Phi Beta Kappa; Sigma XI. Hon. Degrees: Sc.D. Univ. of South Dakota, 1936, Princeton Univ., Yale Univ. and Stevens Institute of Technology, 1937; Harvard, Chicago, and Rutgers, 1941; McGill, 1946; Br. Columbia, 1947; Southern Calif., and San Francisco, 1949; LL.D. Univ. of Michigan, 1938, of Pennsylvania, 1942, of Glasgow, 1951. Officier de la Légion d'Honneur, 1948. *Recreations:* tennis, music. *Address:* Radiation Laboratory, University of California, Berkeley, California, U.S.A. *T.:* Ashberry 3-6000, Local 476. *Clubs:* Faculty, (Hon.) Bohemian (Cal.). [*Died* 27 *Aug.* 1958.

LAWRENCE, Gertrude; Actress; *b.* 4 July 1898; *d.* of Arthur Lawrence Klasen and Alice Louise Banks; *m.* 1st, Francis Gordon-Howley (marriage dissolved); 2nd, 1940, Richard Stoddard Aldrich, Lieut.-Comdr. U.S.N.R. *Educ.:* Convent of the Sacré Coeur, Streatham. Studied dancing under Madame Espinosa and acting under Italia Conti; first appearance on stage, 1908, as a child dancer in pantomime, Dick Whittington; Repertory Theatre, Liverpool, 1912; played lead at most London Theatres and in New York since 1921; joint lead in Charlot's Revues, 1924 and 1925; parts include Kay in Oh, Kay, New York, 1926 and His Majesty's, 1927; Amanda Prynne in Private Lives, Phoenix, 1930 and New York, 1931; Evangeline in Nymph Errant, Adelphi, 1933; Josephine in Moonlight is Silver, Queen's, 1934; toured with Noel Coward in To-Night at 7.30, 1935; co-starred with Noel Coward in To-Night at 8.30, London and New York, 1936; starred in Susan and God, 1937-39; Skylark, 1939-40; Lady in the Dark, 1941-43; Blue Network radio star, 1943-44; entertained Armed Forces Europe for E.N.S.A. 1944; Pacific for U.S.O., 1945; starred in G. B. Shaw's Pygmalion, 1945-46-47; Stella in September Tide, Aldwych, 1948; Anna in the King and I, New York, 1951. Entered films, 1929; starred in film Glass Menagerie, 1950. Vice-Pres., American Theatre Wing; Pres. American Branch, E.N.S.A.; Director, British Actors' Orphanage. Hon. Member, Phi Beta Fraternity. Hon. Doctor of Fine Arts, Ithaca Coll., N.Y., 1948. *Publication:* A Star Danced, 1945. *Relevant publication:* Gertrude Lawrence as Mrs. Aldrich, by Richard Stoddard Aldrich, 1955. *Address:* 36 West 44th Street, New York City; 17 W. 54th Street, New York City, U.S.A. *Clubs:* Cosmopolitan (New York); Tavern (Chicago); Press (San Francisco). [*Died* 6 *Sept.* 1952.

LAWRENCE, Captain Henry Walter Neville; *b.* 26 Oct. 1891; *s.* of Sir Walter Lawrence, Bart., G.C.I.E., G.C.V.O., C.B.; *m.* 1933, Sarah, *o. c.* of late Nicholas Murray Butler, President Columbia University; one *s.* *Educ.:* Wellington College; Balliol College, Oxford. Joined Coldstream Guards, 1915, antedated 1914 (War Medals); Egyptian Army, 1922-26. Stockbroker, 1926-1949, retd., with an interval during War of 1939-45, when joined and started local Home Guard at Hook Heath, Woking; rejoined Coldstream Guards, 1941. High Sheriff of Surrey, 1949. *Recreations:* shooting, fishing, and golf. *Address:* Grey Walls, Hook Heath, Woking. *T.:* Woking 473. *Clubs:* Guards, Boodle's, Pratt's; Woking Golf. [*Died* 24 *May* 1959.

LAWRENCE, Rt. Hon. Sir Paul Ogden, P.C. 1926; Kt., *cr.* 1919; *b.* 8 Sept. 1861; 2nd *s.* of late Philip Henry Lawrence, of Lincoln's Inn, Barrister-at-law; *m.* 1887, Maude Mary (*d.* 1947), *d.* of late John Turner of Oaklands, Wimbledon Park. Called to Bar, Lincoln's Inn, 1882; Q.C. 1896; Bencher, 1900; Judge of the High Court of Justice, Chancery Division, 1918-26; a Lord Justice of Appeal, 1926-34; Chairman of the General Council of the Bar, 1913-18; Chairman of the Incorporated Council of Law Reporting for England and Wales, 1917-19; Member of the Rule Committee of the Supreme Court, 1910-27; Conservator of Wimbledon Common, 1901. *Address:* Dunarden, Wimbledon Park, S.W.19. *T.:* Putney 7607. [*Died* 26 *Dec.* 1952.

LAWRENCE, Sydney Boyle; author and journalist. Late special correspondent and leader writer, Standard, Evening Standard, Morning Post; late assistant editor and dramatic critic, Daily Express; late dramatic critic, Daily Mail, Evening News. Plays: Her Own Rival; A Promise; A Man of His Word; The First Kiss; The Heel of Achilles (with Louis N. Parker); The Popinjay (with Frederick Mouillot); Decameron Nights (with Robert McLaughlin); author and editor of Celebrities of the Stage; contributor of lyrics to the Beecham Opera Book. *Address:* Bowling Green Cottage, Plaistow Lane, Bromley, Kent. *T.:* Ravensbourne 3165. *Club:* Royal Automobile. [*Died* 30 *Dec.* 1951.

LAWRIE, Maj.-Gen. Charles Edward, C.B. 1915; D.S.O. 1898; J.P.; late R. A.; *b.* London, 7 Dec. 1864; *y. s.* of late Andrew Lawrie of Mount Mascal, Bexley, Kent, and 1 Chesham Place, London, and Eleanor, *d.* of late Rev. E. Johnson; *m.* Constance, *o. d.* of F. B. Salomons, 1898. *Educ.:* Cheam; Eton; Royal Military Academy, Woolwich. Joined Royal Artillery, 1884; promoted Captain, 1893; Major, 1900; employed with Bechuanaland Border Police Force, 1889-92; special service Lagos Jebu Expedition (medal and clasp, despatches), wounded slightly; Expedition to Dongola (despatches, Brev. of Major, Khedive's medal 2 clasps). 1896; operation Sudan (clasps), 1897; battle and cavalry reconnaissance of Atbara (clasp, 4th class Osmanieh); battle of Omdurman (despatches, D.S.O. clasp, Sudan medal); employed with Egyptian Army, 13 Oct. 1893 to 1899; served S. Africa, 1899-1900 (despatches, medal three clasps); European War, 1914-15 (despatches, C.B.); retired pay, 1920. *Address:* Copsefield, Ryde, I. of W. *Clubs:* Naval and Military; Royal Victoria Yacht, (Ryde). [*Died* 12 *April* 1953.

LAWS, Lieut.-Col. Henry William, C.M.G. 1919; D.S.O. 1915; *b.* 1876; *s.* of Richard William Laws; *m.* 1905, Grace Margaret, *d.* of Thomas Davidson of Tulloch. A member of Institute of Mining and Metallurgy; served Antwerp, 191; Gallipoli, 1915 (despatches, D.S.O.). *Address:* Queenswood, Victoria, B.C. [*Died* 19 *Dec.* 1954.

LAWSON, Sir Digby, 2nd Bt.; *cr.* 1900; J.P. Som.; T.D.; B.A. (Camb.); Major Yorkshire Hussars; Director, formerly Chairman, of Fairbairn, Lawson, Combe Barbour, Ltd., of Leeds and Belfast. Chairman of Urquhart Lindsay and Robertson Orchar, Ltd., Dundee; *b.* 3 Sept 1880; *s.* of 1st Bt. and Louise Frederica Edith Augusta (*d.* 1939), *d.* of John Stacpoole O'Brien, of Ennis, Co. Clare, and Tanderagee, Co. Armagh; *S.* father, 1915; *m.* 1st, 1909, Iris Mary (from whom he obtained a divorce, 1919; she *m.* 2nd, 1920, Major Eric Loder), *e. d.* of Hon. Eustace R. S. FitzGerald; two *s.* one *d.*; 2nd, 1922, Hon. Victoria Frances Maud (*d.* 1931), *o. d.* of late Col. J. E. B. Baillie, M.V.O.; one

s. (and one killed on active service, 1946); 3rd, 1933, Ruth Mary, 2nd *d.* of late T. W. Gimson of Fenton, Staffordshire; one *s.* *Educ.:* Winchester; Trinity Hall, Cambridge, B.A. Served European War, 1914-18 (despatches thrice); Captain and Adjutant, Yorkshire Hussars, 1916-17; 9th Bn. West Yorkshire Regt., 1917; 19th Royal Hussars, 1918; Pres. Summary Courts, Army of the Rhine, 1919-26. *Heir:* *s.* John Charles Arthur Digby, D.S.O. 1943, M.C., Lt.-Col. XI Hussars [*b.* 24 Oct. 1912; *m.* 1st, 1945, Rose (from whom he obtained a divorce, 1951), *widow* of Pilot Officer William Fiske, R.A.F., and *er. d.* of Lady Rosabelle Brand; 2nd, 1954, Tresilla Anne Eleanor, *e. d.* of Major E. B. L. Popham, Hunstrete House, Pensford, Bristol; she *m.* 1st, John Garland de Pret Roose (from whom she obtained a divorce, 1954)]. *Address:* North Cheriton Manor, Templecombe, Somerset. *T.:* Wincanton 3265. *Clubs:* Carlton, Cavalry, Royal Automobile. [*Died* 9 *Feb.* 1959.

LAWSON, Hon. Sir Harry Sutherland Wightman, K.C.M.G., *cr.* 1933; *b.* Dunolly, 1875; *s.* of Rev. J. W. Lawson; *m.* 1901; three *s.* four *d.* (and one *s.* killed, War of 1939-45). *Educ.:* State Schools; Grammar School, Castlemaine; Scotch College, Melbourne; University of Melbourne. Elected Member of Municipal Council of Castlemaine, 1899; Mayor, 1905-6; Member Legislative Assembly for Castlemaine, Victoria, 1899; for enlarged constituency of Castlemaine and Maldon, 1904; for again enlarged constituency of Castlemaine and Kyneton, 1927; sat continuously in State Parliament, 1899-1928; Minister of Lands, 1913-15; Attorney-General and Minister of Education, 1915-17; Premier, Attorney-General, Solicitor-General, and Minister of Labour, 1918-19; Premier, President of the Board of Land and Works and Commissioner of Crown Lands and Survey, 1919-20; Premier and Minister of Agriculture, 1920; Premier, Minister of Agriculture and Water Supply, 1921-23; Premier and Minister of Water Supply, 1923-24; Premier and Treasurer, 1924; resigned office, 1924; President National Federation, Victoria (5 years); resigned from Legislative Assembly, 1928; Senator for the State of Victoria, 1928-35; Assistant Minister (Treasury), Commonwealth Government, 1933; Acting Postmaster-General, 1934; Minister in charge of External Territories, 1934; resigned Oct. 1934; Chairman Colonial Mutual Life Assurance Soc.; Perpetual Trustees Co. (Melbourne); Robert Harper & Co., Ltd.; Hartleys, Ltd.; Permewan Wright, Ltd.; Dir., Bryant & May Pty., Ltd.; Mt. Lyell Mining and Railway Co., Ltd.; Federal Match Co., Sydney; Commonwealth Fertilizers and Chemicals, Ltd. Barrister and Solicitor. *Address:* 1088 Malvern Rd., Malvern, S.E.3, Victoria, Australia; 314 Collins St., Melbourne, Australia. *Club:* Australian (Melbourne). [*Died* 12 *June* 1952.

LAWSON, Major Sir Hilton, 4th Bt., *cr.* 1831; late Royal Fusiliers; *b.* 18 April 1895; *s.* of late Mordaunt Lawson (3rd *s.* of 2nd Bt.) and Adelaide Mary, *d.* of Col. Archibald Wybergh; *S.* uncle, 1937. *Educ.:* Repton; R.M.C., Sandhurst. Served European War, 1915-18; War of 1939-45 (prisoner). High Sheriff of Cumberland, 1952. *Address:* Isel Hall, Cockermouth, Cumberland. [*Died* 6 *Nov.* 1959 (*ext.*).

LAY, Brig. William Oswald, D.S.O. 1939; Bursar, Ardingly College, since 1948; *b.* 26 Nov. 1892; *e. s.* of late Amcy Lay, Imperial Chinese Customs; *m.* 1921, Margaret Davidson; one *s.* one *d.* *Educ.:* Lancing Coll.; R.M.C., Sandhurst; Graduate Staff College Camberley. 2nd Lieut. Border Regt., 1911; Brevet Major, 1919; Adjutant, 1919-22; General Staff Malaya, 1929-31; Staff Officer Local Forces, Malaya, 1931-34; Lieut. Colonel Comdg. 1st. Bn., 1936-39; Colonel, 1939; Temp. Brig. Comdg. 6th Lucknow Inf. Bde, 1939-42; P.O.W. Jap. 1942-45. Served European War, Gallipoli, 1915, France and Flanders, 1917-19 (despatches twice); Waziristan, 1920 and 1922; Palestine, 1937-39 (despatches twice, D.S.O.); awarded, 1919, French Silver Gilt Medal of Honour with swords; War of 1939-45: India, 1939-40; Malaya, 1940-42; P.O.W. Fall of Singapore, 15 Feb. 1942; A.D.A.W.S. Eastern Command, 1946-47; retd., 1948, with Hon. rank of Brigadier. *Address:* Little Saucelands, Ardingly, Sussex. *T.:* Ardingly 202. *Club:* United Service. [*Died* 31 *Dec.* 1952.

LAYARD, Austen Havelock, C.S.I. 1947; C.I.E. 1937; *b.* 20 Feb. 1895; *y. s.* of late Sir Charles P. Layard, Chief Justice of Ceylon; *m.* 1927, Irene, (*d.* 1943), *d.* of late F. H. King, Liss, Hants; two *d.*; *m.* 1948, Mrs. Elizabeth Sylvia Mary Byrne (*d.* 1953). *Educ.:* Rugby; King's Coll., Camb. (M.A.). Called to Bar, Gray's Inn, 1926; served European War, 1914-18; Royal Sussex Regt. and att. 2nd East Surrey Regt., Egypt and Salonica (Capt.); I.C.S. (Central Provinces), 1920; Deputy Comr., 1926; Deputy Commissioner, Delhi, 1932-38; Deputy Commissioner, Nagpur, 1942; Officiating Commissioner, 1943-45; Offg. Chief Secretary, 1946; Sec. to Governor of Central Provinces, 1946-1947; retired, I.C.S., 1948; held appointments in Office of High Commissioner for U.K. in India, at Delhi and Calcutta, 1948-49. *Address:* c/o Grindlay's Bank, 54 Parliament Street, S.W.1. *Clubs:* Athenaeum, Oriental. [*Died* 24 *March* 1956.

LAYCOCK, Brig.-General Sir Joseph (Frederick), K.C.M.G., *cr.* 1919 (C.M.G. 1917); D.S.O. 1900; Nottinghamshire Horse Artillery (Territorial Army); *b.* 12 June 1867; *o. s.* of late R. Laycock, M.P., and Annie, 2nd *d.* of Christian Allhusen, of Stoke Court, Bucks; *m.* 1902, Katherine M., 3rd *d.* of late Hon. Hugh Henry Hare; two *s.* two *d.* *Educ.:* Eton; Oxford. Served S. Africa, 1899-1900 (despatches twice, Queen's medal 6 clasps, D.S.O.); European War, 1914-18 (despatches, Bt. Lt.-Col., C.M.G.); Zone Commander, Home Guard, Notts.; D.L. Notts.; Lord High Steward of Retford. *Recreations:* fox-hunting and shooting. *Address:* Wiseton, Doncaster. *T.:* Wiseton 24. *Clubs:* Turf, White's, Royal Automobile; Royal Yacht Squadron (Cowes). [*Died* 10 *Jan.* 1952.

LAYNG, Rev. Thomas Malcolm, C.B.E. 1945 (M.B.E. 1924); M.C. 1916; Bar to M.C. 1940; Chaplain to the Queen since 1952 (to King George VI, 1940-52); Hon. C.F. (1st Class); *b.* 23 April 1892; *s.* of Henry Layng, M.R.C.S., L.R.C.P., Swatow, China; *m.* 1927, Mabel Kathleen, *d.* of John Hayward, Badley Hall, Essex; one *s.* one *d.* *Educ.:* Clifton College; Balliol College, Oxford. B.A. 1914, M.A. 1936. Commissioned in Indian Army (10th Jats), 1913; served European War, 1914-18 (despatches twice); Afghanistan, 1919, Iraq, 1920, Waziristan, 1923-24. Ordained, 1932; Rector of Duloe, Cornwall, 1934; Chaplain and Fellow of Balliol College, Oxford, 1938; War of 1939-45 (despatches four times) Royal Army Chaplains Dept.; Asst. Chaplain-Gen. 10th Army, 1942, 14th Army, 1943, Allied Armies in Italy, 1945; Dep. Chaplain-Gen., C.M.F., 1945. Archdeacon of York, 1946-47; Canon of York, 1946-48; Rector of Burnby and Nunburnholme, 1946-48; Vicar of St. James, Gloucester, 1948-50; Vicar of Kemble with Poole Keynes, 1950-55. D.L. East Riding, 1947-. *Address:* Deenhurst, Church Rd., St. Mark's, Cheltenham. *T.:* Cheltenham 52838. [*Died* 21 *April* 1958.

LAZAROVICH-HREBELIANOVICH, H.H. Princess, (Eleanor Calhoun); author; *g.g.-n.* of the statesman John C. Calhoun, *d.* of late Judge E. E. Calhoun and Laura Butler Davis Calhoun, biol. writer; *b.* Visalia, California; *m.* 1903, Prince Lazarovich-Hrebelianovich (*d.* 1941), descendant of Czar Lazar Hrebelianovich of

Serbia; one *d.* decd. (three step-*c.*). *Educ.:* San José, London, Paris. Originated the idea of giving pastoral plays in the open forest, as "Rosalind," Coombe Wood, Surrey, joint production with Lady A. Campbell ("Orlando"); acted in London, Haymarket Theatre (Theatre Royal); leading rôles, Shakespeare and modern; Lady Macbeth at Stratford-on-Avon Memorial; in French: Paris, at Odéon National Theatre, Comédie Parisienne, and Théatre d'Orléans, Racine, Shakespeare and modern; starred with Paul Mounet-Sully and Coquelin; shared her husband's work for Balkan freedom; promulgated for him and financed his Danube-Aegean Waterway Project; ex-President of the Woman's Chamber of Commerce of New York; Member Pi Gamma Mu; Hon. Officer of Old Guard of Georgia. *Publications:* The Serbian People, their Past Glory and their Destiny (with her husband), 1910; Pleasures and Palaces, European Memoirs, 1916; The Way: Christ and Evolution, a theory of human emergence on earth into a Higher Creative Order, 1927; The Way: The Creative Order, 1930; The Organic Character of Christ and of Democracy, 1931. *Recreations:* riding, driving, dancing, and travelling. *Address:* 3 East 84th Street, New York, U.S.A. [*Died* 9 *Jan.* 1957.

LEA, Right Rev. Arthur; Missionary, Japan, from 1897; *b.* Birmingham, 8 Dec. 1868; *s.* of Joseph and Eliza Lea; *m.* 1st, Miss M. L. Gregory; 2nd, Miss G. A. Reid; two *s.* five *d.* *Educ.:* University of Toronto (M.A., Hon. D.D.); Wycliffe College, Toronto. Ordained, 1894; Curate of Rothesay, New Brunswick, 1894-95; Rector of St. George's, New Glasgow, 1895-97; C.M.S. Missionary at Nagoya, Japan, 1897-1900; Gifu, 1900-05; Tokyo, 1905-09; Bishop of Kyushu, 1909-1935; *locum tenens*, St. Mark's, Palatka, Fla., 1939; St. Paul's, Quincy, Fla., 1940; Ch. of the Good Shepherd, Jacksonville, Fla., 1941-43; St. Paul's-by-the-Sea, Jacksonville Beach, Fla., 1944-45; Kobe, Japan, 1947-49; Principal Shŏ-in Junior Coll., Kobe, 1948-50; Melrose, Florida, 1950; Chaplain, Ruge Hall, Tallahassee, 1951; Mandarin, Florida, 1952-54; Momoyama, Gakuin, Osaka, Japan, 1954-55. *Address:* 1325 Ocean Front, Atlantic Beach, Florida, U.S.A. [*Died* 19 *Jan.* 1958.

LEA, Frederick Charles, O.B.E.; D.Sc. (London); M.Sc.; Hon. Fellow Imp. College; M.Inst.C.E.; Hon. M.I.Mech.E.; M.Inst.St.E.; Associate R.C.S.; Wh. Sc.; Consulting Engineer; Emeritus Professor, University of Sheffield; late Prof. of Civil Engineering, University of Birmingham; *s.* of Measham Lea and Sarah, *d.* of William Kiddy; *m.* 1st, 1899, Alice (*d.* 1942), *d.* of Rev. W. R. Sunman; two *d.* (one *s.* decd.); 2nd, 1944, Mrs. E. M. Taylor, St. Albans. *Educ.:* Owens Coll., Manchester; Royal Coll. of Science, London. Whitworth Scholar; Past President I.Mech.E.; Past President Birmingham and District Inst.C.E.; President Engineering Section British Association, 1929; Past Chairman Yorkshire Branch I.Mech.E., Yorkshire Branch Inst. C.E., and Pres. Whitworth Soc.; Vice-Chairman Yorkshire Council of Social Service Centres. Telford Prize and Crampton Prize, Inst.C.E.; medal Concrete Institute; T. Bernard Hall Prize, Institute Mechanical Engineers. Served apprenticeship in L. and N.W. Railway Works, Crewe; afterwards Assistant in Civil Engineering Department; Chief Assistant in Civil and Mechanical Engineering Dept., City and Guilds College, London; H.M.I. (Engineering); Officer in the Univ. of Birmingham O.T.C.; Lieut., R.N.V.R.; Captain, R.A.F. *Publications:* Hydraulics; Hardness of Metals; Cutting Tools for Metal Machining; The Machining of Steel: Civil Engineering Building Educator; Pioneer of Mechanical Engineering, Sir Joseph Whitworth; various papers in the Proceedings Royal Society and other journals. *Address:* Wayside, Dore, Sheffield. *T.:* 70383. [*Died* 30 *Sept.* 1952.

LEA, John, M.A.; *b.* 1871; *m.* 1914, Elsie Ida Gifford (*d.* 1956). *Educ.:* Gonville and Caius Coll., Cambridge; Heidelberg; London Hosp.; travel. First Cl. Nat. Sciences Tripos, 1892. Demonstrator in Biology, 1893; several years a Lecturer at University of London Holiday Courses for Foreign Students, School Inspector, Univ. of London, and representative of the University on the Secondary School Examinations Council (Board of Education); on Administrative Staff of Univ. of London from 1907; University Extension Registrar in the Univ. of London, 1912-36; Member of the Adult Education Committee, Board of Education, of various other Educational bodies, and of the Royal Institution; Hon. Member of the Art Teachers' Guild. *Publications:* The Romance of Bird Life; other books on natural history; articles on various subjects of art and science; short stories, etc. *Recreations:* field natural history, handicrafts; apragmosynism. *Address:* 3 Cadwallader, Park Crescent, Llandrindod Wells. *T.:* 2516. *Club:* Athenæum. [*Died* 14 *May* 1958.

LEACH, Rt. Hon. Sir (Alfred Henry) Lionel, P.C. 1949; Kt., *cr.* 1938; Q.C. 1949; Member of the Judicial Committee since 1949; *b.* 3 Feb. 1883; *e. s.* of late Robert Alfred Leach, Rochdale and Southport, Barrister-at-law; *m.* 1908, Sophia Hedwig (*d.* 1954), *d.* of Prof. Dr. Heinrich August Kiel, Bonn; one *s.* *Educ.:* privately. Called to Bar, Gray's Inn, 1907; Judge of High Court, Rangoon, 1933; Chief Justice, High Court, Madras, 1937-47; Official Referee, Supreme Court of Judicature, 1948-56; Chairman, Singapore Riots Inquiry Commission, 1951; served in Indian Defence Force; Indian Army Reserve of Officers. *Recreations:* fishing, shooting. *Address:* 3 Gray's Inn Square, W.C.1. *T.:* Chancery 4339. *Clubs:* Carlton, Flyfishers'; Madras (Madras). [*Died* 26 *Jan.* 1960.

LEACOCK, Sir Dudley Gordon, Kt., *cr.* 1951; Member of the Executive Council and late Pres. Legislative Council, Barbados; *b.* 1880; *s.* of John Henry Cutting Leacock, Bridgeton, Barbados; *m.* 1902, Edith Maud Hawkins, Barbados. *Address:* Harvale, Navy Gardens, Christ Church, Barbados. [*Died* 11 *Dec.* 1954.

LEAHY, Fleet Adm. William D., Hon. G.C.B., *cr.* 1945; N.C.; D.S.M.; on special duty under President; *b.* 6 May 1875; *s.* of M. A. Leahy and Rose Hamilton; *m.* 1904, Louise Tennent Harrington (*d.* 1942); one *s.* *Educ.:* Naval Academy, B.S., 1897. Commissioned in U.S. Navy, 1899; Rear-Admiral, 1930; Vice-Admiral, 1935; Admiral, 1936; Fleet Admiral, 1944; Chief of Naval Operations, 1937; Gov. of Puerto Rico, 1939; Ambassador to France, 1940; Chief of Staff to the President of the U.S. and member of Joint Chiefs of Staff, 1942-49; Hon. Diploma Naval War College; Hon. LL.D., University of Puerto Rico, Univ. of Wisconsin, Northland College, and Cornell College, Ia.; Hon. Sc.D.Mil., Georgetown Univ. *Publication:* I Was There, 1950. *Address:* Navy Department, Washington, D.C. *Club:* Army and Navy (Washington, D.C.). [*Died* 20 *July* 1959.

LEAKE, Lt.-Col. Arthur Martin-, V.C. 1902; F.R.C.S., L.R.C.P.; late R.A.M.C., Administrative Medical Officer of the Bengal-Nagpur Railway; *b.* 4 Apr. 1874; 5th *s.* of late Stephen Martin-Leake, Thorpe Hall, and late Isabel, *d.* of William Plunkett; *m.* 1930, Winifred Frances (*d.* 1932), *widow* of C. W. A. Carroll and 2nd *d.* of William Alfred Nedham. C.P. Commission, India. Served South Africa 1900-2 (despatches, severely wounded, V.C.); Balkan War, 1912-13; European War, 1914-18 (despatches, clasp to V.C.). *Address:* Marshalls, High Cross, near Ware, Herts. *Club:* Junior Carlton. [*Died* 22 *June* 1953.

LEATHAM, Admiral Sir Ralph, K.C.B., *cr.* 1942 (C.B. 1938); *b.* 1886; *y. s.* of S. Gurney Leatham; *m.* 1910, Enid May, *d.* of H. W. Birks; one *s.* one *d.* H.M.S. Britannia, 1900; Capt., 1924; Commands: H.M.S. Yarmouth, H.M.S. Durban, H.M.S. Ramillies and Valiant; Rear-Admiral First Battle Squadron, 1938-39; Vice-Admiral, 1939; Commander-in-Chief East Indies Station, 1939-41; Flag Officer in Charge, Malta, 1942-43; Deputy Governor, Malta, 1943; C.-in-C. Levant (temp.), 1943; Adm. 1943; C.-in-C. Plymouth, 1943-45; retired list, 1946; Governor and C.-in-C. Bermuda, 1946-49; Commander Legion of Merit (U.S.A.) and Legion of Honour (France); K.St.J. *Address:* Fairfield House, Lymington, Hampshire. *Club:* Army and Navy. [*Died* 10 *March* 1954.

LEATHES, John Beresford, F.R.S. 1911; M.A., M.B. Oxon; F.R.C.P., F.R.C.S., Hon. D.Sc. Sheffield; Hon. D.Sc. Manchester; Emeritus Professor of Physiology in the University of Sheffield since 1933; Hon. Fellow of New College, Oxford; *b.* London, 1864; *s.* of Rev. Stanley Leathes, D.D. *Educ.:* Winchester (Scholar); New College, Oxford; Guy's Hospital. Demonstrator in Physiology, 1894; worked at Berne under Drechsel, 1895-97; Strassburg under Schmiedeberg, 1897-99; Lecturer on Physiology, St. Thomas's Hospital, 1899-1909; Assistant at Lister Institute, 1901-9; Professor of Pathological Chemistry, Toronto, 1909-14; Professor of Physiology, Sheffield, 1915-33. *Publications:* Problems in Animal Metabolism; Biochemistry of Fats (with H. S. Raper); papers in Scientific and Medical Journals. *Address:* c/o National Provincial Bank, West Southbourne Branch, Bournemouth, Hants. [*Died* 14 *Sept.* 1956.

LEAVER, Noel Harry, A.R.C.A. (Lond.); A.R.C.A. Design (Lond.); Water-Colour Painter; Designer and Decorative Artist; *b.* Austwick, Yorks, 1889; *s.* of Peter Leaver, Schoolmaster; *m.* 1924, Jane Simpson, Burnley; no *c.* *Educ.:* St. James Day Schools, Burnley; Burnley School of Art (Burnley Art Exhibition to R.C.A.); Royal College of Art, South Kensington; awarded National Exhibition in Painting, 1906; Associateship in Design, Royal Coll. of Art, 1909; Roy. Coll. of Art Scholar, 1909-11; Full Associateship Roy. Coll. of Art, 1910; Travelling Studentship Roy. Coll. of Art, 1910; Travelling Studentship Royal Institute British Architects, 1911; Art Master Halifax Tech. Coll., 1912-15; engaged in water colour drawing since 1918; works exhibited in several public collections and galleries in England and America; drawing in Queen's Dolls House. *Publications:* works reproduced: Scenes in Algeria, Holland, Italy, Normandy, France; Cathedrals of England; Mediæval Cities and decorative landscapes. *Recreations:* wireless, gardening, golf. *Address:* Rowan Cottage, Burnley, Lancs. *T.:* Burnley 4379. *Club:* Burnley Golf (Lancs.). [*Died* 24 *July* 1951.

LEBUS, Sir Herman Andrew Harris, Kt., *cr.* 1946; C.B.E. 1920; J.P. County of London; Chairman and Managing Director of Harris Lebus Ltd.; *b.* 1884; *s.* of late Harris Lebus, London; *m.* 1912, Ethel, *d.* of late Charles Hart, Chicago, U.S.A.; two *s.* one *d.* *Address:* 18 Grosvenor Square, W.1. *T.:* Mayfair 1535. *Clubs:* St. James'. Royal Automobile. [*Died* 15 *Dec.* 1957.

LECHE, Sir John Hurleston, K.C.M.G., *cr.* 1949 (C.M.G. 1937); O.B.E.; *b.* 1889; *e. surv. s.* of late John Hurleston Leche, of Carden Park, Chester, and late Kathleen Marie, *d.* of Charles Donaldson Hudson, M.P., of Cheswardine, Market Drayton; *m.* 1st, 1916, Amy Violet (*d.* 1927), *y. d.* of Col. C. W. J. Unthank of Intwood Hall, Norwich; one *d.*; 2nd, 1928, Helen Morris (*d.* 1952), *y. d.* of late Francis Allison Janney, Philadelphia, U.S.A.; two *s.* two *d.*: 3rd, 1953, Mrs. Helen Margaret Kerrison (*d.* 1957), *y. d.* of late Lt.-Col. R. C. Donaldson-Hudson, D.S.O., Cheswardine. *Educ.:* Eton. R.M.C., Sandhurst. Entered 12th Lancers, 1910; retired and entered Special Reserve of same regiment, 1913; served European War, in France, August 1914-June 1919, G.S.O. 3 (Intelligence) (O.B.E., Crown of Belgium, 1914 Star, Victory and Allied Medals, despatches twice); entered Diplomatic Service, 1919, and has served at Paris, Rio de Janeiro, Buenos Aires, Foreign Office, Berne, Madrid, Guatemala; Chargé d'Affaires, as Minister Plenipotentiary, to Spanish Republican Govt., Valencia and Barcelona, 1937-1938; Minister and Consul-General to Central America, 1939-45; Ambassador to Chile, 1945-49; retired, 1950. Formerly Captain Regular Army Reserve of Officers. *Address:* Stretton Hall, Malpas, Cheshire. *T.:* Tilston 261. *Club:* White's. [*Died* 12 *May* 1960.

LECLÉZIO, Sir Jules, K.B.E., *cr.* 1942 (C.B.E. 1934); an elected Member of Council of Government and an Unofficial Member of Executive Council, Mauritius; *b.* 1877; *s.* of late Hon. Sir Henri Leclézio, K.C.M.G.; *m.* 1915, Inès, *d.* of Edgar Piat, Mauritius. *Address:* Curepipe, Mauritius. [*Died* 13 *Feb.* 1951.

LECOMTE, Georges; de l'Académie Française; Prés. d'honneur de la Soc. des Gens de Lettres de France; Grand Croix de la Légion d'Honneur, et de plusieurs ordres étrangers; *b.* Mâcon (Saône et Loire), 9 Juillet 1867; *m.*; deux enfants (un troisième fils mort pour la Patrie). *Educ.:* au Lycée Lamartine, à Mâcon; Études de droit à Dijon et à Paris. *Publications:* La Meule, comédie en 4 actes, 1891; Mirages, drame en 5 actes, 1893; L'Art impréssionniste, 1892; Espagne; Les Valets, roman; Suzeraine, roman; La Maison en Fleurs, roman; Les Cartons Verts, roman; Le Veau d'Or, roman; Les Hannetons de Paris, roman; L'Espoir, roman; Les Allemands chez eux; Pour ceux qui pleurent, pour celles qui souffrent; Les Lettres au Service de la Patrie; Jours de Bataille et de Victoire; Clemenceau; Bouffonneries dans la Tempête, roman; La Lumière retrouvée, roman; Le Mort saisit le Vif, roman; La Vie Amoureuse de Danton; Lamartine; Camille Pissarro; Albert Besnard; Auguste Delaherche; Guillaumin; Louis Charlot; J. F. Raffaëlli; La Vie héroique et glorieuse de Carpeaux; Les Prouesses du Bailli de Suffren; Au Chant de la Marseillaise; Les Forces d'amour, roman; Steinlen et son temps; Je n'ai menti qu'à moi-même, roman; Thiers; Gloire de l'Ile de France, etc.; La Rançon, roman; Servitude Amoureuse, roman; Ma Traversée, mémoires; Le Goinfre Vaniteux, roman. *Address:* 82 rue du Ranelagh, Paris, XVIe. *T.:* Auteuil 52-53. *Club:* Cercle de l'Union Interalliée (Paris). [*Died* 27 *Aug.* 1958.

LECONFIELD, 3rd Baron (*cr.* 1859), **Charles Henry Wyndham,** G.C.V.O., *cr.* 1935; Lord-Lieutenant of Sussex, 1917-1949; *b.* 17 Feb. 1872; *s.* of 2nd Baron and Lady Constance Evelyn Primrose (*d.* 1939), sister of 5th Earl of Rosebery; *m.* 1911, Beatrice Violet, *d.* of late Col. R. H. Rawson and Lady Beatrice *d.* of 2nd Earl of Lichfield; *S.* father, 1901. J.P. (1897) Sussex; J.P. (1905) Cumberland. Master of Lord Leconfield's foxhounds, 1901-42. Lt. 1st Life Guards, 1892-98; Lt.-Col. Comdt. (Hon. Col. 1906) Sussex Yeomanry, 1901-8 and Major and Hon.-Col. since 1914; Hon. Col. Home Countries Divl. T. and S. Col., A.S.C., 1910-25; Lt.-Col. and County Comdt. Sussex Volunteer Regt., 1917-20; Hon. Col. 5th batt. Border Regt. (T.F.), 1920; 98 (Surrey and Sussex Yeomantry) Bde. since 1922; C.A. West Sussex, formerly Chairman County Council. *Heir:* *b.* Hon. Hugh Archibald Wyndham. *Address:* Petworth House, Petworth, Sussex; Cockermouth Castle, Cumberland. [*Died* 16 *April* 1952.

LEDWARD, Gilbert, O.B.E. 1956; R.A. 1937; (A.R.A. 1932); President, Royal Society of British Sculptors, 1954-56; Trustee of the Royal Academy; *b.* 1888; 2nd *s.* of Richard Arthur Ledward, Sculptor; *m.* 1911, Margery Beatrix Cheesman; one *s.* one *d.* Studied Sculpture at Roy. Coll. of Art and Roy. Academy Schools and abroad; awarded the first British School of Rome Scholarship in Sculpture, 1913, and the Royal Academy Travelling Studentship and Gold Medal in the same year; Prof. of Sculpture, Royal College of Art, London, 1926-29; served as Lieut. R.G.A. during European War (despatches). *Chief works:* Guards' Division Memorial, Horse Guards Parade, designed in collaboration with H. Chalton Bradshaw, F.R.I.B.A.; War Memorials at Abergavenny, Blackpool, Harrogate, Stockport, Stonyhurst College, Grahamstown, S. Africa; marble panel for Reredos in Kilkenny Cathedral to the memory of the Marquis of Ormonde; Memorial to Dean Spence, Gloucester Cathedral; Memorial to Alfred Viscount Milner, Westminster Abbey; The Sunflower, group in Portland stone in the permanent collection Glasgow Institute of Fine Arts; Monolith, purchased by the Chantrey Bequest Fund for the Tate Gallery, 1936; Statue of Dr. A. C. Woolner, late Vice-Chancellor of the Panjab University, Lahore, 1937; Statues of the King and Queen in the restored Cloister of Norwich Cathedral, 1938; Bronze Statue of King George V at Kampala, Uganda, 1939, also at Nairobi, Kenya, 1940; Bronze statue King George VI, Hong Kong, 1947; Memorials in the cloister of Westminster Abbey to the Submarine Service, Commandos and Airborne Forces, 1948; Bronze figures of St. Nicholas (1952) and St. Christopher (1955), Hosp. for Sick Children, Gt. Ormond St.; Coronation Crown Piece and Great Seal of the Realm, 1953; Sloane Square Fountain, 1953; Memorial to 2nd Duke of Westminster in Eccleston Church, Cheshire, 1957; The Awakening of Africa (stone frieze on new building for Barclays Bank D.C.O., in Old Broad St., E.C.2). *Recreation:* sailing. *Address:* 6 Pembroke Walk, Kensington, W.8. *T.:* Western 6184. *Clubs:* Chelsea Arts; Tamesis (Teddington). [*Died* 21 *June* 1960.

LEE, Lieut.-Col. Arthur Neale, D.S.O. 1917; O.B.E. 1919; J.P.; T.D.; Director, Walker & Hall, Ltd., Sheffield, since 1920, and Seacroft Hotel Co. Ltd., Nottingham, since 1908; President, Sheffield Master Silversmiths Assoc. since 1934; *b.* Nottingham, 14 Aug. 1877; *y. s.* of William Henry Lee, Nottingham, and Jane Presbury Neale; *m.* Ethel Margaret Greer, 3rd *d.* of James Connell, London; one *s.* one *d.* *Educ.:* Uppingham School; Trinity College, Cambridge; B.A. 1899; M.A. 1931. 7th Bn. Notts and Derby Regt. (T.F.), 1899; solicitor, Nottingham, until 1914; Brigade Major 139 Infantry Brig. (Dublin Rebellion, 1916); III. Corps and G.S.O. 3, G.H.Q., France, 1916, G.S.O. 2, 1917; G.S.O. 1 "I" G.H.Q. 1918 (D.S.O., O.B.E., despatches three times; Sacred Treasure of Japan, Crown of Belgium, Croix de Guerre, Belgium, Commander of Crown of Siam, White Eagle of Serbia with swords); Wing-Comdr. Sheffield A.T.C., 1941-44; County Controller, V.A.D., Notts, 1924-34; Master of Cutlers Company, Sheffield, 1932-33; Member Board of Trade Commission on Trade Marks Act, 1933; Member of Championship Committee, R. and A. Golf Club, 1919-38; President: Sheffield Union of Golf Clubs and Notts Golfing Alliance, 1938-39; Yorkshire Union of Golf Clubs, 1947; Sheffield British Legion, 1935-1945. *Recreations:* shooting, golf. *Address:* Repton Lodge, Worksop, Notts. *T.:* Worksop 2679. *Clubs:* Royal and Ancient (St. Andrews); Borough (Nottingham). [*Died* 12 *Oct.* 1954.

LEE, Ernest Markham, M.A., Mus. Doc. Cantab.; F.R.C.O.; composer, author, lecturer, pianist; *b.* 8 June 1874; *m.* Eileen Marion, *o. c.* of G. Bishop Francis, Belgrave Road, S.W.; (son killed on Italian front) two *d.* *Educ.:* Perse School, Cambridge; Emmanuel College, Cambridge (Organ Scholar). Organist, All Saints, Woodford Green, 1896-1911; sometime Examiner in Music to University of London; Director Woodford Green Chamber Concerts; Examiner to Associated Board, Royal Schools of Music; University Extension Lecturer to Oxford, Cambridge, and London Universities; Adjudicator for various musical festivals; much engaged in musical-literary work and in various forms of composition; President Incorporated Society of Muscians, 1927-28; visited Canada as Examiner, 1929, New Zealand as Examiner and Lecturer, 1929-30, Jamaica and Canada, 1933; India, 1934; Canada and New Zealand, 1937-38; Ceylon, 1938; Malta and Gibraltar, 1939. *Publications:* The Story of Opera; The Story of Symphony; On Listening to Music; Tchaikovsky; Grieg; Brahms, the Man and his Music; Brahms's Orchestral Works; Musical Theory and Knowledge; A Course in Music; The Music-Lover's Ear-Tests, etc.—Compositions; numerous works, including church music, choral music, works for string orchestra, pianoforte pieces and albums, songs; Paris in Spring (Light Opera), 1939. *Address:* 61 Summerdown Road, Eastbourne. *T:* Eastbourne 2161. [*Died* 13 *Nov.* 1956.

LEE, Frank Herbert, B.A. Oxford; *b.* 1869; *s.* of Rev. Richard Lee, M.A., Rector of Stepney, and Maria Hayes; *m.* 1899, Ruth May Daisy Fox; one *s.* two *d.* *Educ.:* St. Edward's School, Oxford; Keble College, Oxford. Vth Batt. Royal Sussex Regt. (Territorials); H.M. Superintending Aliens Officer Liverpool, Tilbury, Gravesend, 1915-19; Instructor Imperial Naval College, Etajina, Japan, 1919; Retired, 1925; Interned in Tokyo, Dec. 1941-July 1942; evacuated on Exchange ship to India, July 1942; served in P.O.W. Censorship, 1942-3 in Bombay; Tutor to the Jam Sahib family, 1943-44; Monitoring section of the M.O.I. in New Delhi, 1944-45; returned to England, 1946. Order of Crown of Belgium; 5th Class Rising Sun; 4th Class Sacred Treasure. *Publications:* The English Country Calendar; A London Chronicle; The Tokyo Calendar; Days and Years in Japan. *Address:* Hermitage Pootings, Edenbridge, Kent. [*Deceased.*

LEE, Lt.-Col. H. R.; *see* Romer-Lee.

LEE, Maj.-Gen. Sir Richard Phillips, K.C.B., *cr.* 1919 (C.B. 1915); C.M.G. 1919; F.R.G.S.; D.L. Co. Southampton; late R.E.; Col. Comdt. R.E., 1931-35; *b.* 4 Sept. 1865; *s.* of Rev. T. J. Lee; *m.* 1898, Winifred (*d.* 1950), *o. d.* of T. M. Lord Claremont, Milbrook, Southampton; (*s.* killed on Service, 1941) one *d.* *Educ.:* Clifton; R.M.A., Woolwich. Entered Army, 1885; Capt., 1894; Major, 1902; Lt.-Col., 1910; Staff Capt. Headquarters, 1902-4; D.A.Q.M.G. 1904-6; served China, 1900 (despatches, Brevet Major; medal with clasp); European War, France and Flanders, 1914-18 (despatches six times, wounded, C.B., prom. Maj.-Gen.); retired pay, 1923. *Address:* Woodlands House, Woodlands, near Southampton. *T.:* Ashurst 12. [*Died* 24 *March* 1953.

LEE, Robert Warden, F.B.A.; Rhodes Prof. of Roman-Dutch Law, and Fellow All Souls College, Oxford, 1921-56; Reader to the Council of Legal Education; Président de l'Académie Internationale de Droit Comparé; docteur de l'Université de Lyon (honoris causa); Hon. LL.D., Witwatersrand and Ceylon; *b.* 14 Dec. 1868; 3rd *s.* of Rev. M. H. Lee, Canon of St. Asaph, and Louisa, *d.* of Robert Warden of Parkhill, Co. Stirling; *m.* 1914, Amice, *er. d.* of late Sir John Macdonell, K.C.B.; one *d.* *Educ.:* Rossall; Balliol Coll., Oxford; Scholar, 1st Class Classical Mods.; 1st Class Litt. Hum.; M.A. 1894; D.C.L. 1917. Ceylon Civil Service, 1891-1894; Barr. Gray's Inn, 1896, Bencher, 1934, Treasurer, 1945; Advocate, Transvaal, 1911; Quebec, 1917; K.C., Quebec, 1920; Professor of Roman-Dutch Law, University College, London, 1906-1915; Fellow Worcester Coll., Oxford, 1908-

LEE, Joseph Johnston. See page xxix.

1914; Dean, Faculty of Law, McGill University, Montreal, 1914-21. *Publications:* Law of Contract, 3rd ed. 1938 (in Dr. E. Jenks's Digest of English Civil Law); Introduction to Roman-Dutch Law (5th ed.), 1952; Grotius, Jurisprudence of Holland, translation and commentary, 1926, 1936; Elements of Roman Law with translation of Justinian's Institutes, 1944, 4th ed. 1956; (co-editor and part author) South African Law of Obligations, 1950; Law of Property, etc, 1953. *Address:* 11 Gray's Inn Square, W.C.1. *T.:* Holborn 1519; 2 Hare Court, Temple, E.C.4. [*Died* 6 *Jan.* 1958.

LEE, Brig. Stanlake Swinton, C.B.E. 1945; D.S.O. 1917; *b.* 18 June 1890; *s.* of Stanlake William Henry Lee and Emily Harriet Swinton; *m.* Kathleen McMaster; one *s.* one *d.* *Educ.:* Harrow; R.M.A., Woolwich. 2nd Lieut. R.F.A., 1910; operations N.W.F. India with M. Battery R.H.A., 1915; to Mesopotamia, June 1916; Captain and Acting-Major, 1916; (wounded 13 Mar. 1917, above Bagdad, D.S.O.); commanded M. Battery R.H.A. in operations, Afghanistan, 1919 (bar to D.S.O.); Deputy Assistant Director Territorial Army, 1927-30; Major, 1929; retired pay, 1931; recalled to the colours, 1939: France 1939-40 and 1944-45; Lt.-Col., 1941; Brig. 1942; demobilised, 1945. Legion of Honour, Croix de Guerre and Bronze Star. *Recreations:* polo, hunting, shooting. *Club:* Naval and Military. [*Died* 23 *Nov.* 1952.

LEE-ELLIOTT, David Lee, M.A.; *b.* 1869; *s.* of W. O. Elliott, J.P.; *m.* 1900, Winifred Theyre (*d.* 1939), *e. d.* of G. W. Willett, D.L., J.P., and *g.d.* of Canon Theyre Townsend Smith, M.A., Hulsean Lecturer, and Preacher at the Temple sixteen years; two *s.* one *d.* *Educ.:* privately; Cambridge University. Curate of Pembury, Kent, 1894-96; Stagsden, Beds., 1896-1898; St. George's, Brighton, 1898-1900; Rector of Southover, Lewes, 1900-6; Blakeney, Glandford, and Cockthorpe, Norfolk, 1906-15; Vicar of Maxstoke, 1918-20; Rector of Blakeney and Corkthorpe, 1923-24; relinquished Orders, 1943. *Address:* Blakeney, Norfolk. [*Died* 14 *March* 1956.

LEE-HANKEY, W., R.W.S. 1936 (A.R.W.S. 1925); *b.* Chester, 28 March 1869; *m.* 1917, Edith Mary Garner. *Educ.:* King Edward's School, Chester. On active service in Flanders with Artists' Rifles Feb.-June 1915, when gazetted 2nd Lieut.: Lieut. Nov. 1916; Capt., Nov. 1917. *Principal Works:* By the Sea; A Tangled Well; A Rustic Toilet, 1902 (purchased by French Govt.); In the Meadows; Young am I; Speak not of Poverty Here, 1906; The Kiss, 1907; The First Born; painting, Old Woman's Head, 1904; La Leçon de Tricot (purchased by French Govt.); Sur Le Digne; Boulogne Ville; First Steps; etching, Dawning Intelligence; The Houses of Parliament, painted for the King's Christmas Card, 1934; Portrait (Mrs. John de la Valette), exhibited R.A. 1934 (purchased for Nat. Gallery, Glasgow); Portrait of C. F. A. Voysey, 1935; Christ and the Twelve Apostles, painted for reredos at Wroughton Parish Church, 1935; portrait of Prince Arthur of Connaught, 1937; The performing Bear, and Poverty, 1938; The Wheelbarrow, 1939; The Butter Market Concarneau, 1939 (purchased by Newcastle Art Gallery); works purchased for numerous British and foreign galleries and museums, etc. *Publications:* An Old Garden; At the Well, Illustrations to Goldsmith's Deserted Village, and Isaak Walton's Complete Angler. *Address:* 9 Trafalgar Studios, Chelsea, S.W.3. *T.:* Flaxman 1860. *Clubs:* Arts, Savage, Chelsea Arts. [*Died* 10 *Feb.* 1952.

LEE-HOLLAND, Hetty, M.A.; *d.* of John T. Lee, F.R.I.B.A.; *m.* 1924, R. Holland, C.B.E. (*d.* 1942). *Educ.:* North London Collegiate School for Girls; Newnham College, Cambridge (Foundation Scholar). Mathematical Tripos, Class II.; Mistress at High School, Manchester; Lecturer at Manchester Kindergarten Training College; Lecturer at Avery Hill L.C.C. Training College; Examiner to National Froebel Union; Organiser in Religious Teaching to the National Society, 1909-36. *Publications:* New Methods in the Junior Sunday School; Talks to the Training Class; The Teacher's Craft (joint author); Lessons on the Life of our Lord; The Way of Worship; Characters and Scenes from Hebrew Story; More Characters and Scenes from Hebrew Story; The Sunday Kindergarten; More Stories for the Sunday Kindergarten; Children at Church, 1915; Present Day Problems in Religious Teaching, 1920; Self-Teaching in the Sunday School, 1926; I Say unto You, 1928; Songs of Life's Way, 1930. *Address:* Holmwood Cottage, Maynards Green, Horam, Sussex. [*Died* 2 *Nov.* 1954.

LEE STEERE, Sir Ernest (Augustus), Kt., *cr.* 1948; Pastoralist; *b.* 19 March 1866; *s.* of Augustus Frederick Lee Steere, Jayes Park, Surrey, Eng., and Ellen Elizabeth Roe; *m.* 1909, Bridget Yelverton, *d.* of C. Y. O'Connor, late Engineer-in-Chief, W. Aust.; one *s.* (and two *s.* missing on active service, 1940 and 1944) three *d.* *Educ.:* High School (now Hale School), Perth, W.A. From School to the land; leasehold land from the Govt. on the Murchison; purchased (with partner who later retired) Belele Station, 1890, with 3 flocks of shepherded sheep; today Belele has been built up to 990,000; Belele Pastoral Co. has developed; Chilimony is now a good Merino Stud; also Bowes property in Northampton District. Pres. Pastoralist Assoc. for 14 years; Chm. W.A. Turf Club for many years and owned several good race horses. Associated with several Directorates; Chairman Elder Smith & Co.; Instigator of underwriting to establish W.A. Meat Exports Co. (now Govt. owned); first Chm. W.A. Worsted and Woollen Mills (Albany). *Recreations:* fond of all sports, mainly racing; supporter of racing and polo. *Address:* (residence) 52 Mount St., Perth, W.A. *T.:* B 4548; (office) C. M. L. Bldgs., St. Georges Tce., Perth. W.A. *T.:* B7037. *Clubs:* Weld (Perth); Albany (Albany). [*Died* 22 *Dec.* 1957.

LEECH, William Thomas, C.B. 1928; *b.* 1869; *s.* of late Charles William Leech. Director of Telegraphs and Telephones, General Post Office, 1927-31. *Address:* Ridgecote, Sheiling Road, Crowborough, Sussex. *T.:* Crowborough 600. *Club:* Royal Automobile. [*Died* 13 *Jan.* 1953.

LEEDS, Katherine, Duchess of; *d.* of 2nd Earl of Durham; *m.* 1884, Marquis of Carmarthen (afterwards 10th Duke of Leeds); one *s.* (11th Duke of Leeds) one *d.* (and three *d.* decd.). *Address:* Selva Dolce, Bordighera, Italy. [*Died* 6 *Dec.* 1952.

LEEDS, Edward Thurlow, B.A. (Cantab.); M.A. (Oxon); F.S.A.; Hon. A.R.I.B.A.; *b.* 29 July 1877; 2nd *s.* of late Alfred N. Leeds, F.G.S., of Eyebury, Peterborough; *m.* 1925, Alice Marjory, *e. d.* of late James Blomfield Wright, Norwich. *Educ.:* Uppingham School; Magdalene College, Cambridge (Scholar). Cadet, Federated Malay States Civil Service, 1900; Assistant-Keeper, Department of Antiquities, Ashmolean Museum, 1908; Keeper of the Ashmolean Museum, 1928-45; Vice-President Society of Antiquaries, 1929-1932; Rhind Lectr., 1935; Fellow of Brasenose College, 1938-45; Hon. Fellow, 1946; Hon. Fellow, Magdalene College, Cambridge, 1955. Gold Medallist, Society of Antiquaries, 1946. *Publications:* The Archæology of the Anglo-Saxon Settlements; Celtic Ornament in the British Isles; Early Anglo-Saxon Art and Archæology (Rhind Lectures); Corpus of Anglo-Saxon Great Square-headed Brooches, and numerous archæological papers. *Address:* 88 Woodstock Road, Oxford. *T.:* Oxford 55602. [*Died* 17 *Aug.* 1955.

LEES, Arthur John, C.B.E. 1934; Solicitor and Parliamentary Agent, retired; former Senior partner in Lees and Co., Palace Chambers, Bridge Street, Westminster; *b.* 4 Oct. 1867; *e. s.* of John Lees, Slade Hill, Wolverhampton; *m.* 1st, 1896, Gertrude May (*d.* 1937), *e. d.* of Charles Horsley, R.B.A.; one *s.* three *d.*; 2nd, 1938, Ethel Marian (*d.* 1942), *widow* of Dr. F. H. Kyngdon and *er. d.* of late Dr. G. F. de la Cour; 3rd, 1943, Ragnhild, *widow* of Dr. Guy Hughes and *d.* of late Colonel Seeberg, Oslo. *Educ.:* Rugby. Secretary of the Urban District Councils Association, 1903-50; Joint Secretary, 1896-1904; Secretary of the Rural District Councils Association, 1901-23; Past Pres., Soc. of Parliamentary Agents. *Address:* Zinnia, Kettlewell Hill, Woking, Surrey. *Club:* St. Stephen's. [*Died* 17 *March* 1956.

LEES, Charles Herbert, D.Sc., F.R.S.; Emeritus Professor of Physics, University of London; Fellow and formerly Vice-Principal of Queen Mary College, London; *b.* Glodwick, Oldham, 28 July 1864; 2nd *s.* of John Lees of Glodwick, and of Jane, 3rd *d.* of David Ogden of Barrowshaw; *m.* 1902, Evelyn May, B.A., *e. d.* of Henry Savidge, Streatham Hill, S.W.; three *s.* two *d.* *Educ.:* private school; Owens College, Manchester (Berkeley Fellow, 1888); Univ. of Strassburg; City and Guilds College, London. Senior Assistant Lecturer and Demonstrator in Physics, Owens College, 1891; Lecturer in Physics and Assistant Director of the Physical Laboratories, University of Manchester, 1900; Hon. Sec. Literary and Philosophical Society of Manchester, 1901-6; President Physical Society of London, 1918-20; Vice-President Institute of Physics, 1921-23; lately Member of Kent Education Committee, Tunbridge Wells District Education Committee, of Delegacy for managing Goldsmiths' College, Univ. of London, of Food Investigation Board, of Road Research Board; Chairman of Tonbridge District Education Committee, and of Engineering Committee of Food Board; formerly Member of Safety in Mines Research Board, and of Air Inventions Committee. *Publications:* Text-Books on Practical Physics (joint); contributions to Dictionary of National Biography, etc. *Recreations:* gardening and handicrafts. *Address:* Greenacres, Dry Hill Road, Tonbridge, Kent. [*Died* 25 *Sept.* 1952.

LEES, Sir Clare; *see* Lees, Sir W. C.

LEES, Donald Hector, C.S.I. 1924; Indian Civil Service, retired. *Educ.:* St. John's College, Cambridge. Entered Indian Civil Service, 1890; retired 1925. *Address:* 53 Fairfield Road, Inverness. [*Died* 4 *March* 1953.

LEES, Edith Mabel Lucy, M.A.; *b.* 22 Oct. 1878; *d.* of late John Lees, Slade Hill, Wolverhampton, and Elizabeth M. Bate. *Educ.:* Beckenham Hall School; Somerville College, Oxford. Headmistress, Birkenhead High School (G.P.D.S.T.), 1917-23; Headmistress, Sutton High School (G.P.D.S.T.), Surrey, 1923-39. *Address:* 26 Cecil Road, Cheam, Surrey. [*Died* 16 *Nov.* 1956.

LEES, George Martin, M.C.; D.F.C.; F.R.S. 1948; Ph.D.; J.P.; F.R.G.S.; F.G.S. (President, 1951-53); F.Inst.Pet.; Consulting Geologist; *b.* 16 April 1898; *s.* of George Murray Lees; *m.* 1931, Hilda Frances (*née* Andrews); one *s.* *Educ.:* St. Andrew's College, Dublin; Royal Military Academy; Royal School of Mines; Vienna University. Commissioned R.A., 1915; served European War, 1914-18; in France, 1916-17; in Iraq, 1918. Joined Civil Administration, Iraq, and served in Kurdistan as political officer, 1919-20; joined Geological Staff, Anglo-Iranian Oil Co. Ltd., 1921, Chief Geologist, 1931-53; seconded to Petroleum Div., Min. of Fuel and Power, 1941-43. Member Geological Survey Board; Member Colonial Geological Survey Board; Geological Adviser to Anglo-Iranian Oil Co. Ltd., Burmah Oil Co. Ltd., and Iraq Petroleum Co. Ltd. Bigsby Medallist, Geological Soc., 1943; Sidney Powers Gold Medallist, American Assoc. Petroleum Geologists, 1954. *Publications:* numerous scientific articles in learned journals. *Recreation:* geology. *Address:* The White House, Ongar, Essex. *T.:* Ongar 22. *Club:* Athenæum. [*Died* 25 *Jan.* 1955.

LEES, Sir Jean (Marie Ivor), 6th Bt., *cr.* 1804; *b.* 30 March 1875; 7th *s.* of Sir Harcourt James Lees, 4th Bt., and Harriet Ellen Constance, 2nd *d.* of Henry Morgan Howard; *S. half-b.* (Sir Arthur Henry James Lees) 1949; *m.* 1st, 1898, Beatrice Nora Mary (*d.* 1927), *d.* of late E. E. Davis, Kingston-on-Thames, Surrey; one *s.* two *d.*; 2nd, 1927, Gladys Isobel, *d.* of F. W. Bull, Bassett, Southampton. *Heir:* *s.* Charles Archibald Edward Ivor [*b.* 6 March 1902; *m.* 1924, Lily, *d.* of A. Williams; one *s.* (one *d.* decd.)]. *Address:* 186 Gordon Road, Camberley, Surrey. [*Died* 2 *April* 1957.

LEES, Col. Sir John (Victor Elliott), 3rd Bt., *cr.* 1897; D.S.O. 1918; M.C.; late K.R.R.C.; *b.* 11 Dec. 1887; *s.* of 1st Bt. and Florence, *d.* of late Patrick Keith; *m.* 1915, Madeline, 2nd *d.* of Sir Harold Pelly, 4th Bt.; one *s.* (*er. s.* Capt. James Lees, K.R.R.C., killed in action, 1945) five *d.*; *S.* brother, 1915. *Educ.:* Eton; Sandhurst. Entered army, 1907; Capt. K.R.R.C., 1915; Bt.-Maj., 1919; temp. Lt.-Col., 1918-19; served European War (wounded twice, D.S.O., M.C., Croix de guerre); retired 1922. Comdg. 4th (T.) Bn. Dorset Regt., 1927-32; Comdg. 5th Bn. Dorset Regt. 1939-40; Col. T.A. 1932. One of H.M. Body Guard of Hon. Corps of Gentlemen-at-Arms, 1938-51. *Heir:* *s.* Thomas Edward, *b.* 31 Jan. 1925. *Address:* Post Green, Lytchett Minster, Poole. *T.A.:* Lytchett-Minster. *T.:* Lytchett Minster 219. *Club:* Army and Navy. [*Died* 16 *April* 1955.

LEES, Sir (William) Clare, 1st Bt., *cr.* 1937; Kt., *cr.* 1924; O.B.E.; LL.D.; J.P. Cheshire; Chairman Bleachers' Association, Limited; Director Manchester Ship Canal Company, Lloyd's Packing Warehouses, Limited; Deputy Chairman of Martin's Bank, Ltd.; Chairman Phœnix Assurance Company (Manchester Board); and Martin's Bank, Ltd. (Manchester District Board); Vice-President of Court of Arbitration, International Chamber of Commerce and of Federation of British Industries; President Manchester and District Bankers' Institute, 1939-43; Treasurer, Manchester University; *b.* 9 Dec. 1874; *s.* of William Lees, Birkdale, and Emma, *d.* of Dr. William Clare; *m.* 1901, Kathleen, *d.* of John Nickson, Liverpool; one *s.* one *d.* Deputy Chief Executive Officer, War Department (Cotton Textiles), 1917-19; Commercial Adviser to British Delegation, International Conference on Customs Formalities, League of Nations, 1923; President Manchester Chamber of Commerce, 1922-24; President Association of British Chambers of Commerce, 1931-32; President Manchester Statistical Society, 1925; President of the Textile Institute 1933 Member of President of the Board of Trade Advisory Council, 1924-27 and 1931-33, and of Balfour Committee, 1924-29; Member of British Economic Mission to South America, 1929; Chairman of Textile Mission to India, 1933; Chairman of Lancashire Committee on Indian Trade Relations; Member of Lord Weir's Conference on War Damage to Property, 1939. *Heir:* *s.* William Hereward Clare [*b.* 6 March 1904; *m.* 1930, Dorothy Gertrude, *d.* of Francis Alexander and Gertrude Florence Lauder; one *s.* one *d.*] *Address:* Etherow House, Hollingworth, Cheshire. *Clubs:* Conservative; Clarendon (Manchester). [*Died* 26 *May* 1951.

LEES READ, Bertie, O.B.E. 1950; Clerk to the Governors, Guy's Hospital, since 1937;

b. 9 April 1903; *m.* 1956, Mrs. Lydia Leonora Beecham; two step *d.* *Educ.:* Burnley Secondary School, Lancs. Articled, J. W. Kneeshaw and Co., Chartered Accts., Burnley, until 1932; United Birmingham Hospitals, 1932-37. Associate of Institute of Chartered Accountants, 1931; Fellow of Institute of Hospital Administrators. *Recreation:* gardening. *Address:* 104 Priory Lane, Roehampton, S.W.15. *T.:* Prospect 3558. [*Died* 19 *Nov.* 1960.

LEESON, Rt. Rev. Spencer; Bishop of Peterborough since 1949; *b.* 9 Oct. 1892; *s.* of Dr. J. R. Leeson, M.D., J.P., Charter Mayor of Twickenham, and Caroline, *d.* of F. Gwatkin of Lincoln's Inn; *m.* 1918, Mary Cecil, *d.* of Dr. Montagu Lomax; one *s.* three *d.* *Educ.:* Dragon School, Oxford; Winchester (scholar); New Coll., Oxford (scholar). 1st Classical Mods., 1913; B.A. (War Degree) 1916; M.A. 1918; D.D. (Oxon) 1950; St. John's College, Oxford, 1929; war service, 2nd Lieut. 1/8th Battalion Middlesex Regiment (Gibraltar and Flanders); and Intelligence Division, Naval Staff, Lieut. R.N.V.R.; Assistant Principal, Board of Education, 1919-24; Private Secretary to the Parliamentary Secretary and the Permanent Secretary of the Board; called to Bar, Inner Temple, 1922; Assistant Master, Winchester, 1924-26; Headmaster of Merchant Taylors' School, 1927-35; Headmaster of Winchester, 1935 - 46; ordained Deacon, 1939; Priest, 1940; Rector of St. Mary, Southampton, and Rural Dean of Southampton, 1946-49; Canon and Wiccamical Prebendary of Windham in Chichester Cathedral, 1940-49; Select Preacher, Oxford Univ., 1952, Cambridge Univ., 1941, 1951; Member of Council, Southampton Univ. College, 1935-49, Hon. Lecturer in philosophy of religion, 1943-49; University Examiner in Education, Oxford, 1928-1931; Chairman: Church of England Schools Council; Trustees, Oakham School; Headmasters' Conference, 1939-45; Council, S. Swithin's School, Winchester, 1941-49; Vice-Chm. of Council King Alfred's Training College, Winchester, 1937-49; Pres., Queen's Coll., Birmingham; Chairman of Governors, King Edward VI School, Southampton, 1946-49; Bampton Lecturer, Oxford Univ., 1944; Citizen, Salter (Court of Assistants, 1939), and Merchant Taylor of London. Proctor in Convocation, 1948-49. *Publications:* miscellaneous papers on religious education and education for citizenship; ed. R. L. Nettleship's Essay on Plato's educational theory; A Study of the Gospel of Christ, 1941; The Holy Communion, 1942; Christian Education (Bampton Lectures), 1946; Public Schools Question and other essays, 1947; The Parish Priest in Dockland, 1951; The Church and the Welfare State, 1953. *Address:* Bishop's House, Peterborough. *Club:* Athenæum. [*Died* 27 *Jan.* 1956.

LEFFINGWELL, Russell Cornell; retired banker, lawyer, Treasury official; *b.* New York City, 10 Sept. 1878; *s.* of Charles Russell Leffingwell and Mary Cornell Leffingwell; *m.* 1906, Lucy Hewitt (*d.* 1959); one *d.* *Educ.:* Yonkers Military Academy, Yonkers, N.Y.; Halsey School, N.Y. City; Yale University, New Haven, Conn. (A.B. 1899; Hon. M.A. 1919; LL.D. 1950); Columbia Law School, N.Y. City (LL.B. 1902). Law clerk with Guthrie Cravath & Henderson, 1902-07; Partner, Cravath Henderson & deGersdorff and Cravath & Henderson, 1907-17; Special Asst. to Sec. of Treasury in flotation of U.S. Treasury Liberty Loan, 1917; Asst. Sec. of Treasury, 1917-20; Partner, Cravath Henderson Leffingwell & deGersdorff, 1920-23; Partner J. P. Morgan & Co., 1923-40; Director, J. P. Morgan & Co. Incorporated, 1940-59 (one-time Chairman); Member, Directors' Advisory Council Morgan Guaranty Trust Company of New York, 1959-; Trustee, Carnegie Corporation of New York, 1923-59; Director, formerly Chm., Council on Foreign Relations. *Publications:* essays on fiscal, monetary and economic subjects in American learned and general publications. *Recreations:* country life and books. *Address:* 23 Wall Street, New York 8, N.Y. *T.:* Rector 2-6400; 38 East 69th St., New York 21, N.Y. *T.:* Rhinelander 4-7792; Yellowcote Road, Oyster Bay, Long Island. *T.:* Walnut 2-5464. *Clubs:* Knickerbocker, Century, University, Pilgrims, Yale, Down Town (New York); Piping Rock, Seawanhaka-Corinthian Yacht (Long Island); Metropolitan (Washington). [*Died* 2 *Oct.* 1960.

LEFROY, Sir Anthony Langlois Bruce, Kt. 1952; M.C.; J.P.; formerly President W.A. Pastoralists' Assoc.; Chairman: W.A. Turf Club Cttee.; W.A. Trustee Bd.; Bd. of Advice, Bank of N.S.W.; W.A. Div. of Red Cross Soc.; Dep. Chm. W.A. Newspapers Ltd.; *b.* Perth, W.A., 20 Apr. 1881; *s.* of late Sir Henry B. Lefroy, Walebing, W.A.; *m.* Callista, *d.* of Leon Couroublé, France. *Educ.:* High (now Hale) Sch., Perth, W.A.; Haileybury Coll., Hertford, Eng. Manager Jackeroo F. Wittenoom's Boolardy Station, W.A., 1903; owner Coodardy Station and Hill View Farm, Chittering, W.A. European War, 31 Div. Train. Eng., 1915, Adj., Capt. After War became Gen. Man. F. Wittenoom's Cos., Boolardy Pastoral Co. Ltd. Badja Ltd., later, Man. Dir. War of 1939-45; organised and comd. 19th Garrison Bn., Geraldton, W.A., retiring as Lt.-Col. Capt. and Pres. Perth Polo Club; Vice-Pres. W.A. Hunt Club. *Address:* 258 St. George's Tce., Perth, W.A. [*Died* 2 *Nov.* 1958.

LEFROY, Walter John Magrath; founder and Editor of the weekly journal Canada until its amalgamation, 1934; *b.* 6 April 1870; *e. s.* of late Capt. B. L. Lefroy, R.N., of Gratwicke House, Littlehampton, *g.s.* of Capt. B. L. Lefroy of Cardenton House, Athy, Co. Kildare; *m.* 1913, Ella Christina, *e. d.* of Col. J. W. A. Michell, Indian Army. *Educ.:* Royal Naval School; Giggleswick; Queen's College, Oxford. First visited Canada 1891, and after six years' residence returned to England and contributed articles to leading publications concerning the resources and development of Canada and its growing importance in the Empire. *Publications:* established the British Columbia Review, a weekly journal which he edited until he founded the larger weekly publication Canada in 1906; established Canada To-day, a popular illustrated Canadian annual, and The Canadian Export Pioneer. *Recreations:* fishing, shooting, fencing. *Address:* The Green Lodge, St. Mary Bourne, Andover, Hants. *T.:* 244. *Club:* Savage. [*Died* 29 *Jan.* 1955.

LEGARD, Brigadier-General D'Arcy, C.M.G. 1919; D.S.O. 1918; retired; *b.* 5 June 1873; *s.* of Rev. F. Digby Legard, Rector of Stokesley; *m.* 1908, Lady Edith Foljambe, *d.* of 4th Earl of Liverpool; three *s.* *Educ.:* Winchester; New College, Oxon. Joined 17th Lancers, 1896; served S. Africa, 1899-1902 (wounded, despatches, Queen's medal 4 clasps, King's medal 2 clasps); P.S.C.; G.S.O.3 War Office, 1907; Bde.-Major 2nd Cavalry Brigade; rejoined regiment in India, 1911; G.S.O. 1 Indian Cavalry Corps, 1914-15; commanded 17th Lancers European War, 1915-16; and commanded Hussar Brigade, 1916-19 (despatches, D.S.O., C.M.G., Chevalier Legion of Honour); Colonel, 1919; commanded 6th (Midland) Cavalry Brigade, 1920-24; retired pay, 1924. *Publication:* Translated from the German General von Pelet-Narbonne's book, Cavalry on Service. *Recreations:* fruit growing, gardening. *Address:* Maes Court, Tenbury, Worcs. *T.:* Newnham Bridge 203. *Club:* Army and Navy. [*Died* 9 *March* 1953.

LEGAT, Harold, C.M.G. 1948; Assistant Headquarters Commissioner for Oversea

Boy Scouts and Migration; m. Gertrude Eliza Johnson (d. 1950). *Address:* 37 Evelyn Mansions, Carlisle Place, S.W.1. *T.:* Victoria 5560. [*Died* 27 *Sept.* 1960.

LEGG, Ven. Richard Wickham; b. 23 July 1867; e. s. of late Rev. William Legg, Rector of Hawkinge, Kent; unmarried. *Educ.:* Harrow; New College, Oxford; Cuddesdon Theological College. Deacon, 1892; Priest, 1893; Assistant Curate of Aylesbury, 1892-95; Lecturer and Chaplain of Cuddesdon Theological College, 1895-1900; Vicar of St. John's, Newbury, Berks., 1900-12; Vicar of St. Mary's, Reading, 1912-26; Archdeacon of Berkshire, 1922-42; Proctor in Convocation, 1921-22; Vicar of Sonning, 1926-42; Hon. Canon of Christ Church, Oxford, 1929. *Address:* The Old Vicarage, Twyford, Berks. [*Died* 18 *Jan.* 1952.

LEGGATE, Hon. William Muter, C.M.G. 1924; M.A. (Hons.); b. 27 Oct. 1879; s. of James Leggate of Broadlees, Chapelton, Lanarkshire; m. 1947, Ellen B. Orr, M.B., F.R.F.P.S. (G.). *Educ.:* Edinburgh Univ. Served in S. African War, 1900-2; Clerk in Estate Duty Office, Inland Revenue, Edinburgh; resigned, 1904; came to S. Rhodesia in 1910; President Rhodesia Agricultural Union, 1919: represented Salisbury District, 1920-33; and Hartley District, 1940-46, in Legislative Council and Legislative Assembly; formed part of the delegation of elected members which proceeded to London to interview the Colonial Secretary on the Constitutional issue, 1921; Minister of Agriculture and Lands in the First Cabinet under Responsible Government, 1923-25; Colonial Secretary, or Minister of Internal Affairs, 1925-33; Chairman of Food Production Committee, 1942-46. *Address:* 64 Glencairn Drive, Glasgow, S.1. [*Died* 30 *Aug.* 1955.

LEGGATT, Captain Charles William Stares, C.B.E. 1919; Royal Navy, retired; b. 5 Aug. 1864; s. of S. Bethune Leggatt of Crofton Manor, Fareham, Hants; m. Gertrude Elizabeth (d. 1944), d. of late J. B. Walmsley, Liverpool; one s. *Educ.:* Mr. Foster's, Stubbington; H.M.S. Britannia. Joined H.M.S. Britannia at Dartmouth, 1877; Commander, 1899; retired with the rank of Captain, 1913; served with the Naval Transport Department at Liverpool and Plymouth for the duration of European War (C.B.E.). *Recreation:* gardening. *Address:* Wynscote, Crowborough, Sussex. *T.:* Crowborough 220. [*Died* 29 *April* 1954.

LEGGE, Rear-Admiral Montague George Bentinck, D.S.O. 1916; b. 16 Dec. 1883; 3rd s. of late Lieut.-Col. Hon. Edward Henry Legge and Cordelia Twysden, 3rd d. of Walter Hele Molesworth. Served European War, 1914-18; including Battle of Jutland (despatches, D.S.O.); Commander, 1917; Capt. 1925; Rear-Adm., 1936; comdg. Seventh Flotilla, 1926-27; Second Flotilla, 1927-28; Naval Attaché to H.M. Missions in China and Japan, 1930-33; commanded H.M.S. Centurion, 1933-34; Senior Officer, Reserve Fleet, and King's Harbour Master Rosyth, 1935-36; retired list, 1936. Served during War of 1939-45. *Address:* c/o National Provincial Bank, Portsea, Hants. [*Died* 11 *Feb.* 1951.

LEGGE, Brig.-General Reginald Francis, C.B.E. 1919; D.S.O. 1917; Companion I.E.E. 1932; Director: Radio and Television Trust Ltd., Airmec Ltd., A. & M.P. (Wimbledon) Ltd., Cable & Electric Industries Ltd.; 4th s. of Heneage S. Legge; m. Hélène, d. of Arthur Vrancken; two d. *Educ.:* St. Paul's School; R.M.C., Sandhurst. Joined Prince of Wales Leinster Regiment; served in Nigeria, West Africa, 1898-99 (medal and 2 clasps); South Africa, 1900-2 (Queen's medal 3 clasps, King's medal 2 clasps); European War in France, 1914-18 (despatches six times, C.B.E., D.S.O., Bt. Lt.-Col.); retd. pay, 1920; Pres. Office of Reparation Commn., Wiesbaden, 1920-22; Treasury Director North Wales Power Company Ltd., and Electricity Distribution Co. of N. Wales, 1925-48; Director and General Manager British Power and Light Corporation and its subsidiary Companies, 1929-48. Member Council Incorporated Association Elec. Power Companies, 1925-48 (Pres. 1943 and 1944); Member of N. Wales and S. Cheshire Joint Electricity Authority, 1926-48; Member of Council of Electrical Development Association, 1931-48; Member Council, Institute of Electrical Engineers, 1935-38. Croix de Chevalier Légion d'Honneur; Officier Ordre de Leopold (Belgium); Croix de Guerre (Belgium); Grand officier Order of Aviz (Portugal); Commander of Order of St. Maurice and Lazarus (Italy); Officier Ordre Instruction Publique (France). *Publications:* various guides to promotion and other military handbooks; Editor of the quarterly magazine Helios, 1929-39. *Club:* Army and Navy. [*Died* 24 *Aug.* 1955.

LEGH, Lieut.-Colonel Hon. Sir Piers (Walter), G.C.V.O., cr. 1948 (K.C.V.O., cr. 1942; C.V.O. 1937; M.V.O. 1919); K.C.B., cr. 1953; C.M.G. 1925; C.I.E. 1922; O.B.E. 1919; J.P.; Extra Equerry to the Queen since 1952 (Equerry to King George VI, 1936-46, Extra Equerry, 1946-52); b. 12 Dec, 1890; 2nd s. of 2nd Baron Newton, P.C.; m. 1920, Sarah Polk, d. of late Judge Bradford of Woodstock, Nashville, Tennessee, U.S.A., and *widow* of Captain Hon. Alfred Shaughnessy; one d. Entered Grenadier Guards, 1910; A.D.C. to Duke of Connaught, Governor-General of Canada, 1914-15; Equerry to Prince of Wales, 1919-1936; Master of Her Majesty's Household, 1952-Dec. 1953 (of the Household of King George VI, 1941-52). Served European War, 1915-18 (O.B.E., despatches twice). *Address:* St. James's Palace, S.W.1. *Club:* Turf. [*Died* 16 *Oct.* 1955.

LEGH-JONES, Sir George, Kt., cr. 1950; M.B.E.; Managing Director "Shell" Transport and Trading Co. Ltd.; Director: Shell Petroleum Co. Ltd.; Anglo-Saxon Petroleum Co. Ltd.; de Bataafsche Petroleum Mij.; Chairman: Canadian Eagle Oil Co. Ltd.; Eagle Oil & Shipping Co. Ltd.; Director Lloyds Bank Ltd.; b. 24 March 1890; e. s. of Edward and Emily Legh-Jones; m. 1915, Margaret Ethel, d. of late Samuel Boucher; one d. *Educ.:* Oswestry and Welshpool Schools. Served in Sea Transport Department, Admiralty, 1915-17; British Mission, Washington, 1918-19; with Royal Dutch/Shell Group, London and Hague, 1919-22; Director, Shell Union Oil Corporation, San Francisco and St. Louis, 1922-34; one of the Managing Directors, Royal Dutch/Shell Group, 1938, and served on a number of Government Committees since 1939. *Recreations:* shooting, fishing. *Address:* 33 Eaton Square, S.W.1. *T.A.:* Cleghjones, London. *T.:* Sloane 2700; The School Farm, Lockerley, nr. Romsey, Hants. *T.:* Lockerley 287. *Clubs:* White's; Pacific Union (San Francisco); Mid-Ocean (Bermuda). [*Died* 30 *April* 1960.

LEICESTER-WARREN, Cuthbert, J.P.; D.L. Cheshire; 2nd s. of Sir Baldwyn Leighton, 8th Bart., and Hon. Eleanor, d. of 2nd Baron de Tabley; b. 6 Nov. 1877; m. 1904, Hilda Marguerite, d. of Edmund Henry Davenport, of Davenport; one s. one d. (Changed name to Leicester-Warren by royal licence in 1898.) Late Captain and Adjutant 16th Batt. London Regt.; served World War; High Sheriff Co. Chester, 1921-22; Hon. Maj. R.A.S.C.(M.T.V.); War of 1939-45, Army Welfare Officer. *Address:* Davenport House, Bridgnorth, Shropshire. [*Died* 2 *Jan.* 1954.

LEIGH, Sir John, 1st Bt., cr. 1918; J.P. County Palatine of Lancaster; a Trustee of the Manchester Academy of Fine Arts, and Proprietor of the Pall Mall Gazette until its amalgamation with Evening Standard in

1923; *b.* 3 Aug. 1884; *s.* of John Leigh, J.P., of Brooklands, Cheshire; *m.* 1908, Norah Marjorie (*d.* 1954), C.B.E., *d.* of John Henry New, Melbourne; three *s.* one *d.* *Educ.:* Manchester Grammar School. M.P. (C.) Clapham Div. of Wandsworth, May 1922–July 1945. *Heir: e. s.* John Leigh, *b.* 23 March 1909. *Address:* Juniper Hill, Mickleham, Surrey. *Clubs:* Carlton, St. James'. [*Died* 28 *July* 1959.

LEIGHTON, Major Bertie Edward Parker, D.L., J.P.; *b.* 26 Nov. 1875; *s.* of Stanley Leighton of Sweeney Hall, Oswestry; 2nd *s.* of Sir Baldwyn Leighton, Bt., of Loton Park, M.P. for North Shropshire, and Jessie Marion, *d.* of H. B. Williams Wynn of Howbery Park, Wallingford; *m.* 1936, Margaret Evelyn, *er. d.* of Rev. Hugh Hanmer, The Mount, Oswestry. *Educ.:* Eton; Sandhurst. Served in 1st Royal Dragoons; South African War; European War (severely wounded); Adjutant, Shropshire Yeomanry, 1908-11. M.P. (C.) Oswestry Division, 1929-45. *Address:* Sweeney Hall, Oswestry, Shropshire. *T.:* Oswestry 498. *Club:* Cavalry. [*Died* 15 *Feb.* 1952.

LEIGHTON, Gerald, O.B.E., M.D., D.Sc., C.M., F.R.S.E., L.R.C.P. and S.E.; temp. hon. Lieut.-Col. Royal Army Service Corps (retired); Medical Officer (Foods) Department of Health for Scotland, retired; late Professor of Pathology and Bacteriology, Royal Veterinary Coll. Edinburgh; late Editor Field Naturalists Quarterly; *b.* Bispham, Lancs, 12 Dec. 1868; *o. surv. s.* of late Rev. J. Leighton, Kilpeck, Hereford; *m.* Clara, 2nd *d.* of late Bernard Gordon of Moston, Manchester; one *d.* *Educ.:* Nelson College, N.Z.; Manchester Grammar School; Edinburgh University. Spent early life in New Zealand; came to England, and from Manchester went to Edinburgh University; practised in Herefordshire until 1902, then went to Edinburgh to devote whole time to Zoology and Comparative Pathology; appointed interim Professor of Pathology at Royal Veterinary College, 1902; founded The Field Naturalists' Quarterly, 1902; Fellow of Royal Physical Society, Edinburgh, 1902; Hon. Member Woolhope Naturalists' Club, 1903. *Publications:* Botulism and Food Preservation, 1923; British Serpents; British Lizards; Reptile Studies; The Greatest Life; Scientific Christianity; The Modern Veterinary Adviser (Editor), 1909; Meat Inspection and the Meat Industry (Leighton and Douglas), 1910; Huxley, His Life and Work, 1912; Embryology, 1912; Snake-Bite in Great Britain (Encyclopædia Medica); Life of James Leighton; Handbook of Meat Inspection, 1924; The Principles and Practice of Meat Inspection, 1927; The Reptilia of the Monnow Valley (M.D. Thesis), and other papers. *Recreations:* cricket, sea-fishing, gardening. *Address:* Sharston, Port Lewaigue, Ramsey, Isle of Man. [*Died* 8 *Sept.* 1953.

LEIGHTON, Brevet Colonel Sir Richard Tihel, 10th Bt., *cr.* 1692; T.D., D.L., J.P. Salop; *b.* 13 Feb. 1893; *s.* of 9th Bt. and Margaret Frances (*d.* 1944), *d.* of late John Fletcher of Saltoun, Haddingtonshire; *S.* father, 1919; *m.* 1932, Kathleen Irene Linda, *o. d.* of Major A. E. Lees, Rowton Castle, Shrewsbury; one *s.* three *d.* *Educ.:* Eton; Royal School of Mines. Joined Westmorland and Cumberland Yeomanry, 1911; served European War, France, 1915-19; last three years with R.F.C. (wounded and prisoner); late commanding Shropshire Yeomanry; War of 1939-45, Squadron Leader R.A.F.V.R. High Sheriff of Shropshire, 1956. Owns about 4100 acres. *Heir: s.* Michael John Bryan, *b.* 8 March 1935. *Address:* Loton Park, Shrewsbury. *Clubs:* White's, Bath. [*Died* 26 *Sept.* 1957.

LEIGHTON, Sir Robert, Kt., *cr.* 1946; **Chairman and Managing Director of Leighton-Straker Bookbinding Co. Ltd., Director of The Nonesuch Library, Ltd., and Fletcher & Son, Ltd.; *b.* 15 June 1884; *e. s.* of Thomas and Edith Jane Leighton; *m.* 1918, Janet Welsh (*d.* 1951), *d.* of late J. M. Wotherspoon; two *s.* one *d.* *Educ.:*** Dulwich Coll. Managing Director of Leighton, Son & Hodge, 1908. (later Leighton-Straker Bookbinding Co. Ltd.). Served European War, 1914-18. Chm. Master Binders Assoc., 1921-24; Pres. British Federation of Master Printers, 1942-1945; Chm. Council of Printing and Allied Trades Research Assoc., 1945-47, Chairman of Joint Industrial Council, 1950-51. *Address:* Standard Road, N.W.10. *T.:* Elgar 7624. [*Died* 24 *July* 1959.

LEITH, Lieut.-Col. Sir Alexander, 1st Bt., *cr.* 1919; M.C., J.P., D.L.; *b.* 24 Sept. 1869; *e. s.* of late Walter Leith, J.P., of The Manor House, Ashby-de-la-Zouch, and Hints Hall, Tamworth, Staffs; *m.* 1st, Mary Caroline (*d.* 1934), 2nd *d.* of James F. Maguire, Boston, U.S.A., and Melbourne, Australia; 2nd, 1955, Mrs. Mary Holroyd, *d.* of late Leonard Asquith, Brook House, Cleckheaton, Yorks; no *c.* *Educ.:* Harrow; Brasenose College, Oxford. Merchant; Director of various Public Companies; Captain in Northumberland Hussars Yeomanry; Commandant 1st, 3rd, 4th, and 9th Bns. Durham County Volunteer Corps, 1917-20; European War, 1914-16, 7th Division, France; Gallipoli, 1915, D.A.Q.M.G. Suvla Bay (despatches, M.C.); Food Commissioner, Northumberland and Durham, 1917-19; High Sheriff of Northumberland, 1923-24; Chairman: Northern Counties Conservative Area, 1930-36; Nat. Unionist Assoc., 1922-23; Trustees of Hosp. of St. Mary the Virgin, Newcastle upon Tyne. *Address:* The Grey Cottage, Humshaugh, Hexham, Northumberland. *Clubs:* White's; Northern Counties (Newcastle upon Tyne). [*Died* 9 *Nov.* 1956 (*ext.*).

LEITRIM, 5th Earl of (*cr.* 1795), **Charles Clements;** late H.M. Lt. Co. of City, Londonderry; Baron Leitrim, 1783; Viscount Leitrim, 1793; Baron Clements (U.K.), 1831; *b.* 23 June 1879; *e. s.* of 4th Earl and Lady Winifred Coke, (*d.* 1940), 5th *d.* of 2nd Earl of Leicester; *S.* father, 1892; *m.* 1st, 1902, Violet Lina (who obtained a divorce, 1932; she died 1943), *d.* of late Robert Henderson of Sedgwick Park; 2nd, 1939, Hon. Anne Mary Chaloner (who *m.* 1st, 1915, Percy Rygate Borrett, from whom she obtained a divorce, 1939), *sister* of 5th Baron Huntingfield, K.C.M.G., and *y. d.* of late Hon. William Arcedeckne Vanneck. Lieut. 9th Lancers (resigned); served with Imperial Yeomanry in South Africa; Major in 11th Battalion Royal Inniskilling Fusiliers, 1914; Private Secretary to Secretary of State for the Colonies, 1917. *Heir:* none. *Address:* Mulroy, Co Donegal. [*Died* 9 *June* 1952 (*ext.*).

LELEAN, Percy Samuel, C.B. 1916; C.M.G. 1919; Order of the Nile, 1919; F.R.C.S., D.P.H.; Professor of Public Health, Edinburgh University, 1926-44; Bt. Colonel, late R.A.M.C.; Emeritus Prof. of Hygiene, Royal Army Medical College; *b.* Canada, 23 July 1871; *s.* of Wm. Cox Lelean, Canada; *m.* 1902, Mary Ellen (*d.*1956), *d.* of the late John Gillam of Penrhyn, Stourbridge; two *d.* *Educ.:* Hart House; St. Mary's Hospital (demonstrator in physiology). Civil surgeon in the S. African War, 1900 (commission R.A.M.C., and four clasps); served with the Anglo-French Boundary Commission—River Niger to Lake Tchad—1903; served in India, 1906-12; served European War, 1914-18 (despatches four times, C.B.); retired, 1922. *Publications:* Bilharzia hæmatobia, Trans. of Med. Society. London; Quinine as a Malarial Prophylactic, R.A.M.C. Journal; Sanitation in War; Anti-typhoid Inoculation, Trans. of Royal Institution; Myiasis, B.M. Journal. *Address:* 44 Edith Road, W.14. [*Died* 6 *Nov.* 1956.

LELONG, Lucien; Chevalier Légion d'Honneur, 1926; Honorary President of the Paris Couture since 1945; *b.* 11 Oct. 1889; *m.* 1954, Sanda Dancovici; one *d.* *Educ.:* Faculté de Médecine, Paris. Served European

War, 1914-18 (Croix de Guerre). Opened the Couture House, Lucien Lelong, 1918; started the Perfume Company, Lucien Lelong Parfums, 1920, of which he is Président du Conseil. Diplomé Hautes Études Commerciales Paris Promotion, 1908. *Address:* Domaine de Courbois, Anglet, Basses-Pyrenées, France. *T.:* Anglet 590-03. *Clubs:* Yacht Club de France; Saint-Cloud, Mortefontaine and Biarritz golf clubs. [*Died* 10 *May* 1958.

LE MAISTRE, Charles, C.B.E. 1920; F.C.G.I.; Kt. Commander of Order of the Vasa (Sweden), 2nd cl.; former Chairman of the Executive, British Standards Institution; General Secretary, Internat. Electrotechnical Commn.; *m.* 1926, Violet Katherine Maria, *d.* of late Major Henry Hobart Culme-Seymour. *Address:* Lea Gate House, Bramley, nr. Guildford. *Clubs:* Athenæum, Royal Automobile. [*Died* 5 *July* 1953.

LE MAITRE, Sir Alfred (Sutherland), K.B.E., *cr.* 1951; C.B. 1945; M.C. 1916; Civil Service, retired; *b.* 13 June 1896; *s.* of late Alfred George Le Maitre, St. Andrews; *m.* 1931, Evelyn Elsie, *d.* of late Ernest Martelli, K.C.; two *s.* *Educ.:* Fettes; St. John's Coll., Cambridge (scholar). Served in 7th Bn. Black Watch in France; 1st Class Classical Tripos, Cambridge, 1920; entered Admiralty, 1920; served as Under-Secretary Admiralty Delegation, Washington, 1944; Under-Secretary, Admiralty, 1946; Controller of Ground Services, Ministry of Transport and Civil Aviation, 1948-57; Member of Economic Planning Board, 1947. Retired, 1957. *Address:* Mill Cottage, Polstead, Suffolk. *T.:* Nayland 363. *Clubs:* United University; Royal and Ancient (St. Andrews). [*Died* 22 *March* 1959.

LE MAITRE, Ella Katharine Irving, M.A.; retired; *b.* 13 June 1896; *d.* of Alfred George Le Maitre and Katherine Cadell Bell. *Educ.:* St Leonard's School, St. Andrews (Scholar); Newnham College, Cambridge (Scholar). Assistant Classical Mistress, Roedean School, Brighton, 1918-20; Head of Classical Department 1920-33; Exchanged a year at The Baldwin School, Bryn Mawr, U.S.A. 1927-28. Headmistress, Roedean School, South Africa, 1933-Dec. 1958. *Address:* 52 1st Street, Marendellas, S. Rhodesia. *Clubs:* English-Speaking Union; Country (Johannesburg). [*Died* 30 *March* 1960.

LE MARCHANT, Brig.-General Sir Edward Thomas, 4th Bt., of Chobham Place, Surrey, *cr.* 1841; K.C.B., *cr.* 1943 (C.B. 1938); C.B.E. 1919; *b.* 23 Oct. 1871; 2nd *s.* of Sir Henry D. Le Marchant, 2nd Bart., of Chobham Place, Surrey, and Hon. Sophia Strutt, *e. d.* of 1st Lord Belper; *S.* brother, 1922; *m.* 1899, Evelyn Brooks, *er. d.* and *co-heiress* of late R. Millington Knowles of Colston Bassett Hall, Notts; two *s.* (twins) two *d.* *Educ.:* Eton. Formerly served in the Royal and Royal Welch Fusiliers and on the Staff; occupation of Crete; South African and European wars; Sheriff of Nottinghamshire, 1930-31; J.P. Notts, 1904; D.L., 1925; County Councillor, Notts, 1928-37; Chairman, Notts Territorial Army Association, 1931-46; County Army Welfare Officer, 1940-45; Deputy Chm. Nottingham Quarter Sessions, 1933-45. *Heir: e. s.* Denis Le Marchant [*b.* 28 Feb. 1906; *m.* 1933, Elizabeth Rowena, *y. d.* of Arthur H. Worth, Hovenden House, Fleet, Lincs; two *s.* one *d.*]. *Address:* Chobham Place, Surrey. *Clubs:* M.C.C., United Service. [*Died* 17 *Nov.* 1953.

LEMIEUX, Auguste, Q.C. for Ontario and Quebec; LL.B.; Barrister, Solicitor, Province Ontario and Quebec, Ottawa, Ont. Hon. Member Bar of Port-au-Prince. Haiti; *b.* Montreal, 20 Feb. 1874; *s.* of H. A. Lemieux and Marie Anne Philomène Bisaillon; *m.* 1899, Esther, *d.* of Henry Barbeau; two *d.* (one *s.* decd.). *Educ.:* L'Assomption Coll.; St. Mary's Jesuits Coll., Montreal; Laval Univ., Quebec (LL.B.). Called to Quebec Bar, 1898; K.C. Quebec, 1908; K.C. Ont., 1921. Formerly: Lecturer on Comparative Law, Ottawa Univ.; Bâtonnier (and presently Dean) of Hull Bar, and of French-speaking Bar of Ontario. F.R.E.S. Officier d'Académie (Academic Palms); Hon. mem. Bar of Port-au-Prince, Haiti; Mem. l'Association Internationale des Jurisconsultes de Paris. *Address:* Strathcona Apt., 404 Laurier Ave. East. Ottawa, Canada. [*Died* 9 *Feb.* 1956.

LEMON, Sir Ernest John Hutchings, Kt., *cr.* 1941; O.B.E. 1918; M.I.Mech.E.; *b.* 1884. *Educ.:* Heriot Watt College, Edinburgh. Works Manager, Carriage and Wagon Dept., Derby, 1917; Div. Carriage and Wagon Supt., 1923; Carriage and Wagon Supt. L.M.S.R., 1927; Chief Mechanical Engineer L.M.S.R., 1931; Vice-President (Operating and Commercial) L.M.S.R., 1932-1943; Director-General of Aircraft Production, Air Ministry, 1938-40; Special Adviser to Ministry of Production, 1942. *Club:* Athenæum. [*Died* 15 *Dec.* 1954.

LEMON, Lieutenant-Colonel Frederick Joseph, C.B.E. 1927; D.S.O. 1918; Chief Constable of Nott., retd. 1949; *b.* Aug. 1879; *y. s.* of Colonel R. S. Lemon, West Yorkshire Regiment; *m.* 1910, Laura, *y. d.* of John Miles Dawson of Brook Hall, Tadcaster, Yorks; one *s.* *Educ.:* Bedford School; Royal Military College, Sandhurst. Served in West Yorkshire Regt., 1899-1919; South African War, 1899-1902 (Queen's medal with 5 clasps, King's medal with two clasps); European War (severely wounded, despatches thrice, D.S.O., 1914 Star, British war medal, Victory medal); Chief Constable of City of Leeds, 1919-22. King's Police Medal, 1944. *Recreations:* shooting, tennis, and golf. *Address:* 23 Second Avenue, Hove, Sussex. *T.:* Hove 30553. *Club:* Naval and Military. [*Died* 17 *April* 1952.

LEMPFERT, Rudolph Gustave Karl, C.B.E. 1918; M.A. Cantab; *b.* Manchester, 1875; *m.* 1916, Marjorie Olive (Marjorie Hayward) (*d.* 1953), *d.* of late George Olive Hayward, Master Mariner; one *d.* *Educ.:* Manchester Grammar School; Emmanuel College, Cambridge. Assistant Master Rugby School, 1900-1902; joined staff of Meteorological Office, 1902; Assistant Director, Meteorological Office, 1919-38; Pres. Royal Meteorological Society, 1930. *Publications:* Life History of Surface Air Currents (joint author), 1906; Meteorology, 1920. *Recreation:* music. *Address:* 35 Fitz-James Avenue, W.14. *T.:* Fulham 6961. [*Died* 24 *June* 1957.

LEMPRIERE, Rev. Philip Charles; *b.* 12 April 1890; *s.* of late Rev. Philip Alfred Lempriere and of Janet Lempriere; *m.* 1915, Kate McKenzie (*decd.*); no *c.* *Educ.:* George Watson's College, Edinburgh; Edinburgh University; Edinburgh Theological College. Assistant-Curate St. Mary's, Hamilton, 1913-20; Rector, All Saints, Bearsden, 1920-23; St. James', Glasgow, 1923-27; St. Bride's, Glasgow, 1927-35; St. John's, Girvan, 1935-41; St. Mary's, Hamilton, 1941-46. In Diocese of Glasgow and Galloway; Examining Chaplain from 1921; Synod Clerk, 1938-43; Dean, 1943-46; Principal of Edinburgh Theological College, and Pantonian Professor of Theology, 1946-1948; Canon of St. Mary's Cathedral, Edinburgh, 1946-48; Examining Chaplain to the Bishop of Edinburgh, 1947-48; retired 1948. T.C.F. 1917-18. *Recreation:* chess. *Address:* 45 Falcon Gardens, Edinburgh 10. [*Died* 26 *Feb.* 1949.

[*But death not notified in time for inclusion in Who Was Who 1941–1950, first edn.*

LENANTON, Sir Gerald, Kt., *cr.* 1946; Chairman Foy Morgan & Co. Ltd. and subsidiaries; Director Yorkshire Insurance Co. Ltd.; Vice-President of the Timber Trade Federation; Governor Royal Hospital and Home for Incurables; *b.* 28 September

1896; *e. s.* of late W. R. Lenanton, J.P., Richmond, Surrey; *m.* 1922, Carola Oman, C.B.E. 1957; no *c. Educ.:* Winchester College; Royal Military Academy, Woolwich; Christ Church, Oxford. Served European War, 1914-18; Lieutenant, then Captain, R.H.A., 1915-18. Deputy Timber Controller, 1939; Director of Home Timber Production, 1941-46; Controller-General North German Timber Control, 1946-47. *Address:* Bride Hall, Welwyn, Herts. *Club:* Cavalry.
[*Died* 21 *Oct.* 1952.

LENMAN, Rt. Rev. Thomas; Rector of Hinxhill with Brook, 1954; An Assistant Bishop of Canterbury since 1955; *b.* 17 Feb. 1883; *s.* of Henry Lenman; *m.* 1913, Elsa Helen Louise Danielson; two *s.* one *d. Educ.:* Church Missionary College, Islington. Deacon, 1906; Priest, 1907; C.M.S. Missionary, India, 1907-43; to France with Indian Labour Corps, 1917-18; Member of Bihar Legislative Council, 1927-29; Hon. Canon of Calcutta, 1938-43; Archdeacon of Bhagalpur, 1939-43; Bishop of Bhagalpur, 1943-54. *Publications:* vernacular only. *Address:* Hinxhill Rectory, Ashford, Kent.
[*Died* 10 *Nov.* 1959.

LENNARD-JONES, Sir John (Edward), K.B.E., *cr.* 1946; F.R.S. 1933; Sc.D. (Cantab.); D.Sc. (Manchester); Principal of the University College of North Staffordshire since 1953; Life Fellow of Corpus Christi College, Cambridge; *b.* 27 Oct. 1894; *m.* 1925, Kathleen Mary, *d.* of late Alderman S. Lennard, Leicester; one *s.* one *d. Educ.:* Manchester University; Trinity College, Cambridge. Formerly Lecturer in Mathematics at Manchester University; Reader in Mathematical Physics at Bristol University; Professor of Theoretical Physics at Bristol University; Dean of Faculty of Science, Bristol University, 1930-1932; Plummer Professor of Theoretical Chemistry in the University of Cambridge, 1932-53. Served European War, 1914-18, Flying Officer (Pilot) in R.F.C. and later Experimental Officer at Armament Experimental Station, Orfordness; War of 1939-1945: successively Key Scientist, Chief Superintendent of Armament Research, Chief Scientific Officer and Director-General of Scientific Research (Defence) at Ministry of Supply; Advisory Council, Dept. of Sci. and Ind. Research, 1942-47; President, Faraday Society, 1948-50; Chairman Scientific Advisory Council, Ministry of Supply, 1947-53; Scientific Advisory Cttee., National Gallery. Hopkins Prize (Camb. Philosophical Soc.), 1953. Davy Medal of the Royal Society, 1953. Hon. D.Sc. Oxon, 1954. *Publications:* papers on Electronic Structure of Molecules, Theories of Chemical Interactions at Surfaces, Theories of Liquid Structure, Interatomic Forces. *Recreations:* golf, tennis, etc. *Address:* The Clock House, Keele, Staffordshire. *Club:* Athenæum.
[*Died* 1 *Nov.* 1954.

LENOX-CONYNGHAM, Colonel Sir Gerald Ponsonby, Kt., *cr.* 1919; F.R.S.; M.A.; Fellow of Trinity Coll. Camb.; *b.* 21 Aug. 1866; 5th *s.* of late Sir William Fitzwilliam Lenox-Conyngham, K.C.B., of Spring Hill, Co. Londonderry; *m.* 1890, Elsie Margaret, O.B.E., *e. d.* of late Surg.-Gen. Sir A. F. Bradshaw, K.C.B.; one *d. Educ.:* Edin. Academy. Commission, R.E. 1885; Col. 1914; Superintendent of the Trigonometrical Survey of India, 1912-21; Reader in Geodesy in the University of Cambridge, 1922-47. Represented H.M.'s Government at the 2nd Pan-Pacific Science Congress, held in Australia in 1923, and at the 3rd, held in Japan, in 1926. *Address:* Desertlyn, Grange Road, Cambridge. [*Died* 27 *Oct.* 1956.

LENTAIGNE, Major-General Walter David Alexander, C.B. 1947; C.B.E. 1945; D.S.O. 1942; i.d.c., p.s.c.; retired; *b.* 15 July 1899; *er. s.* of late Hon. Mr. Justice Lentaigne, Burma High Court and Stackallen, Navan, Eire; *m.* 1st, 1928, Suzanne Catherine Marsden; one *s.* two *d.*; 2nd. 1948, Hermione Constance, *y. d.* of late Sir Alfred Lascelles, Q.C.; one *s. Educ.:* Oratory Schl., Edgbaston. 2nd Lt. 4th Gurkha Rifles, 1918; Staff Coll., Camberley, 1935-36; D.A.Q.M.G., G.H.Q., India, 1938-41; Instructor Staff College, Quetta, 1941-42; comd. 1st Bn. 4th P.W.O. Gurkha Rifles, 1942; Brig. 1943; Maj.-Gen. 1944. Served Afghanistan, N.W.F. 1919; Waziristan, 1919-21 and 1921-24 (despatches); N.W. Frontier, 1930; Waziristan, 1936-37 (despatches) and 1938-39; Burma, 1942-45 (C.B.E., D.S.O. and despatches); i.d.c. 1946; G.H.Q. India, Dir. of Mil. Ops. & D.Q.M.G. 1947; Comdt. Indian Staff Coll., 1948-55, retired 1955. *Recreation:* shooting. *Address:* Lloyds Bank, Ltd., 6 Pall Mall, S.W.1. *Club:* United Service.
[*Died* 24 *June* 1955.

LENTON, Rev. Charles H., M.A.; Canon Emeritus of Lincoln; *b.* 1873; *s.* of late Edward C. Lenton; *m.* 1899, Eleanor, *d.* of late L. W. Stephenson; one *s.* three *d. Educ.:* Blairlodge School, Polmont; Pembroke College, Oxford. Master Grammar School, Dorchester, 1893-96; Theological College, Lincoln, 1896-98; Curate of Holy Trinity, Gainsborough, 1891-1901; of Marcham and Garford, Berks, 1902-4; Curate in Charge of Heapham, Upton and Kexby, 1904-5; Rector, 1905-7; Vicar of Nettleham, 1907-9; Vicar of S. Andrew's, Grimsby, 1909-16; Rector of Louth and Rural Dean of Louthesk W., 1916-1928; Vicar of Hessle, 1928-43; Prebendary of Lincoln, 1920-49. *Recreations:* tennis, golf, fishing, formerly Scotch International Trials Rugger, and Lincolnshire cricket. *Address:* Sutton Courtenay, Abingdon, Berks.
[*Died* 20 *Oct.* 1951.

LEONARD, Robert Galloway Louis, Q.C. 1918; *b.* 25 Oct. 1878; *m.* 1904, Mary Geraldine, *e. d.* of R. C. Millar, C.E. *Educ.:* High School, Dublin; Trinity College, Dublin (Classical Scholar, Reid Law Scholar, Senior Moderator). Called to Irish Bar, 1899; a Member of the Connaught Bar; Reid Professor of Law, University of Dublin, 1904-9; Junior Crown Prosecutor for Co. Sligo, 1908-18, and for King's Co., 1916-18; Senior Crown Prosecutor for Co. Sligo 1918-22; Bencher King's Inns, 1928, Treasurer 1949; Chairman Incorporated Council of Law Reporting. Chancellor of dioceses of Dublin, Glendalough and Kildare, Meath, Killaloe and Kilfenora, Clonfert and Kilmacduagh. *Address:* 27 Pembroke Park, Dublin. *Club:* St. Stephen's Green (Dublin). [*Died* 22 *June* 1957.

LEONARD, Colonel William Hugh, C.B. 1933; F.R.C.S.; Indian Medical Service, retired; *b.* 12 Feb. 1876; *s.* of Wm. Leonard, Paull, Hull. *Educ.:* Hull and East Riding College, Hull; St. Bartholomew's Hospital, London. M.R.C.S., L.R.C.P. (Lond.), 1899; House Surgeon Huntingdon County Hospital; entered I.M.S., 1901; retired, 1933; served Tibet Expedition, 1903-4 (medal and clasp); European War, 1914-18, in Mesopotamia (Brevet Lt.-Col., despatches twice). *Address:* Thorngumbald, Hull. *Club:* East India and Sports.
[*Died* 21 *Oct.* 1960.

LEPAILLEUR, Rt. Rev. Alfred, C.S.C.; First Bishop of Chittagong, (R.C.), since 1927; *b.* Lachine, Montreal, Canada. 1886. *Educ.:* St. Laurent College, Montreal; Gregorian University, Rome. Priest, Rome, 1911; went to India, 1914; mission work at Noakhali and Dacca, Bengal. *Publications:* Editor of the Bengali Monthly Dhorma Jyoti, 1918-26. *Address:* Bishop's House, Chittagong, Bengal, East Pakistan. [*Died* 12 *April* 1952.

LE QUESNE, Charles Thomas, Q.C. 1925; *b.* St. Heliers, Jersey, 3 Nov. 1885; *e. s.* of late Charles John Le Quesne; *m.* F. E. Eileen, 3rd *d.* of late Sir Alfred Pearce Gould, K.C.V.O., F.R.C.S.; four *s.* one *d. Educ.:* Victoria College, Jersey; Exeter College, Oxford (1st class Hon. Mods. 1906, 1st class

Lit. Hum. 1908, Senior Scholar, 1908). Called to Bar, Inner Temple, 1912; President of the Baptist Union of Great Britain and Ireland, 1946-47; Commander of Order of Orange Nassau. *Address:* Rickford Lodge, Admiral's Walk, Hampstead, N.W.3. *Club:* Reform. [*Died* 22 *Nov.* 1954.

LE ROSSIGNOL, Colonel Alfred Ernest, C.B. 1917; *b.* 1869; *s.* of Alfred Le Rossignol, 14 Vicarage Gate, Kensington; *m.* 1901, Mary Strathearne (*d.* 1946), *d.* of Robert Darling, Bonally, Helensburgh. *Educ.:* Marlborough; Hanover. Lt.-Col., London Divisional Electrical Engineers, R.E. (T.F.) 1914-18; Col. T.F. 1918; Superintendent Searchlight Experimental Establishment R.E. 1918-23; retd. 1926. Hon. Member Institution of Royal Engineers; M.Inst.C.E.; M.I.E.E. *Address:* Headon Cottage, Tilford Road, Farnham, Surrey. *T.:* Farnham 5957. *Clubs:* Argentine, Constitutional, Union. [*Died* 21 *March* 1951.

LE ROSSIGNOL, James Edward; Professor of Economics since 1911, and Director of the School of Commerce, 1913-19; Dean of the College of Business Administration, 1919-41; Dean Emeritus, 1941; University of Nebraska; *b.* Quebec, Canada, 24 Oct. 1866; *s.* of Peter Le Rossignol and Mary Gillespie; *m.* 1898, Jessie Katherine Ross, Montreal; one *s.* one *d.* *Educ.:* Montreal High School, McGill Univ. (B.A., LL.D. (hon.)); Univ. of Leipzig (Ph.D.); Clark Univ. (Fell. in Psychology); Prof. Psychology and Ethics, Ohio University, 1892-94; Prof. Economics, University Denver, 1894-1911; Special Lecturer in Economics, McGill University, 1900; Lecturer in Political Science, Univ. Wisconsin. summer session, 1903; Acting-Professor of Economics, Stanford Univ., summer term, 1923; Professor of Economics, Univ. of California, summer term, 1926; Chairman Lincoln Committee British War Relief Society, 1941-45; Pres. American Association of Collegiate Schools of Business, 1925-26; Member of American Economic Association; Member of Nebraska Writers Guild. *Publications:* The Ethical Philosophy of Samuel Clarke, 1892; Monopolies Past and Present, 1901; Taxation in Colorado, 1902; History of Higher Education in Colorado, 1903; Orthodox Socialism, 1907; Little Stories of Quebec, 1909; State Socialism in New Zealand, 1910; Jean Baptiste, 1915; What is Socialism?, 1921; Economics for Everyman, 1923; First Economics, 1926; The Beauport Road, 1928; The Flying Canoe, 1929; The Habitant-Merchant, 1939; From Marx to Stalin, 1940; Inflation and how to Scotch It, 1943; numerous articles on economic subjects; also short stories, chiefly of French Canada. *Recreations:* trout fishing, chess. *Address:* University of Nebraska, Lincoln, Nebraska. *Clubs:* The Club, Lincoln Rotary, Round Table (Lincoln, Neb.) [*Died* 2 *Dec.* 1959.

LE ROY, Édouard (Louis Emmanuel Julien); Officer of the Legion of Honour, 1939; Member of Académie française since 1945 and of Académie des Sciences morales et politiques since 1919; Hon. Professor, Collège de France; *b.* 18 June 1870; *e. s.* of Georges Le Roy and Eugénie Sauvage; *m.* 1902, M. T. Gernez; four *s.* one *d.* (and one *s.* decd.). *Educ.:* École Normale supérieure. Agrégé des Sciences mathématiques, 1895; docteur ès sciences, 1898. Deputy for M. Bergson at the Collège de France, 1914-20; Professor of Philosophy, Collège de France, 1921-41; Columbia Univ. (New York), 1923. *Publications:* Dogme et critique, 1907; Une Philosophie nouvelle: Henri Bergson, 1912; L'Exigence idéaliste et le fait de l'évolution, 1927; Les Origines humaines et l'évolution de l'intelligence, 1928; La Pensée intuitive, 1930; Le Problème de Dieu, 1929; Introduction à l'étude du problème religieux, 1944. *Address:* 27 rue Cassette, Paris 6e, France. *T.:* Littré 7556. [*Died* 10 *Nov.* 1954.

LESLIE, John Robert, J.P.; *b.* Lerwick, Shetland Isles, 1873; *m.* 1898; two *s.* two *d.* *Educ.:* Anderson's Institute, Lerwick. Grocery Manager; Organiser for Shop Assistants Union; Editor Shop Assistant; General Secretary; in public life was member of Finchley Urban District Council for twelve years; M.P. (Lab.) Sedgefield Division of Durham, 1935-50; retired, 1950; member of Labour Advisory Com., League of Nations Union. *Recreations:* in young days Rugby football player, rower and sprinter, now gardening as principal hobby. *Address:* 46 Grosvenor Road, Muswell Hill, N.10. *T.:* Tudor 5179. [*Died* 12 *Jan.* 1955.

LESLIE, Robert, M.A.; Professor of Political Economy, University of Cape Town, 1914-49, resigned, 1949; *b.* Buckie, Banff, 1885; *s.* of late Rev. J. R. Leslie, D.D.; *m.* 1912, Florence Ferriman, Lechlade; one *s.* *Educ.:* George Watson's College, Edinburgh; Edinburgh University. Assist. to Prof. Nicholson, Edinburgh University, 1909-13; Asst. Professor of Political Economy, Calcutta University, 1913. *Publications:* papers in Journal Economic Society of South Africa, and in South African Journal of Science. *Address:* Waldeck, Newlands Road, Claremont, Cape Town. [*Died* 5 *Feb.* 1951.

LESLIE, Major-General Robert Walter Dickson, C.B. 1941; C.B.E. 1946 (O.B.E. 1919); Hospital Officer, 1941, Medical Officer, Ministry of Health, 1948-54; *b.* 31 Jan. 1883; *s.* of late T. C. Leslie; *m.* 1911, Eleanor Violet, *d.* of late Roundell Palmer Jackson and Annie Norrington Field, widow of Admiral of the Fleet Sir Frederick L. Field, G.C.B., K.C.M.G. *Educ.:* Michaelhouse, Natal S.A.; Royal Coll. of Surgeons, Ireland. Entered R.A.M.C. 1906; Capt. 1910; Major (Brev.), 1917; Major (Subst.) 1918; Lieut.-Col. 1930; Col. (Brev.) Jan. 1934; Col. (Subst.) May 1934; Maj.-Gen. 1937; served European War, 1914-18 (despatches, Brev. of Major, O.B.E.); A.D.M.S. France, 1918-19; D.A.D.M.S. India, 1930-32; D.D.M.S. Palestine and Transjordania, 1936; Commanding The Queen Alexandra Military Hospital, Millbank, London, 1935-37; D.D.M.S. Northern Command, York, 1937-41; Hon. Physician to the King, 1939-41; Retired 1941. *Publications:* Improvements in Motor Ambulance Construction, Journal of the Royal Army Medical Corps, Nov. 1917 (with Capt. G. A. Child); Improvised Ambulance Trains, Journal of the Royal Army Medical Corps, May 1920; The Medical Services in Palestine, 1936. Journal of the Royal Army Medical Corps, Nov. 1937; R.A.M.C. Field Training—The casualty card Scheme, Journal of the Royal Army Medical Corps, March 1939. *Recreation:* golf. *Address:* Glenferrie, East Leake, nr. Loughborough. *T.:* East Leake 245. *Club:* Army and Navy. [*Died* 31 *Jan.* 1957.

LESLIE, Seymour Argent Sandford, C.M.G. 1949; D.L.; *b.* 9 June 1902; *s.* of Rt. Hon. James Graham Leslie, P.C., and Grace (*née* Brodie); *m.* 1930, Eleanor Mary, *d.* of James Stuart, Somerset, Coleraine; one *s.* one *d.* *Educ.:* Eton College; Trinity College, Cambridge. Nigeria: Asst. District Officer, 1925; District Officer, 1935; Acting Principal Asst. Secretary, 1941-44. Tanganyika: Dep. Financial Secretary, 1944; Actg. Chief-Sec. 1952-53; Financial Secretary, 1945-53. *Recreations:* shooting, racing, forestry. *Address:* Leslie Hill, Ballymoney, N. Ireland. [*Died* 18 *July* 1953.

LESLIE, of Warthill, William; *see* Arbuthnot-Leslie.

LE SOUEF, Albert Sherbourne, C.M.Z.S.; Retired Curator, Taronga Zoological Park, Sydney; *b.* 1877; *s.* of late Albert A. C. Le Souëf; *m.* 1908, Mary E. L. Greaves; no c. *Educ.:* Carlton College; Melbourne Veterinary Coll. Assistant Director Zoological Gardens, Melbourne, 1896-1903; Director Zoological Gardens, Sydney, 1903-39. Vice-Pres. Royal Zoological Society of N.S.W. *Publications:* Wild Animals of Australasia, 1926; A Modern View of Evolution, 1947; Silent Feet in the Forest, 1948; (with T. S. Gurr) Our Vanishing Wild Life, 1948; numerous scientific articles in Australian

Zoologist, The Emu, etc. *Recreations:* zoological field work, trout fishing. *Address:* Raraku, Mosman, Sydney, Australia. *T.A.:* Zoology, Sydney. *T.:* XM 1791. [*Died* 30 *March* 1951.

LESSORE, Frederick; Art expert; founder Beaux Arts Gallery; Sculptor; *b.* Brighton, 19 Feb. 1879; *o. s.* of late Jules Lessore, R.I., artist; *m.* 1934, Helen Brook; two *s.* Studied Paris and London; medallist, Royal Academy Schools, 1906; has modelled many statues and busts in Canada and England, including Duke of Connaught, Viscount Reading, Lord Mountstephen, Lord Strathcona, Sir Charles Tupper, Sir William Van Horne, Matthew Maris, etc.; *Address:* 7 Bruton Place, W.1. *T.:* Mayfair 2573. [*Died* 14 *Nov.* 1951.

LESTER, Eng.-Rear-Admiral Arthur Ellis, D.S.O. 1915; O.B.E. 1919; *b.* 1878. Served Falkland Islands and Dardanelles, 1914-18 (D.S.O. for services in engineroom when mined); Jutland, 1916 (commended, promoted Commander); Eng.-Rear-Adm. and retired list, 1930; recalled for service, 1939; reverted to retired list, 1947. *Address:* c/o Admiralty, Whitehall, S.W.1. [*Died* 5 *May* 1956.

LESTER, Sean, LL.D., University of Dublin, 1947; LL.D., National University of Ireland, 1948; *b.* 27 Sept. 1888; *s.* of Robert J. and Henrietta Mary Lester; *m.* 1920, Elizabeth Ruth Tyrrell; three *d.* Journalist until 1922; Dept. of External Affairs, Dublin, 1922-29; Irish Permanent Delegate accredited to League of Nations, 1929-34; represented Ireland at many League conferences, committees, and on Council of League; presided Council Committees on Peru-Colombia and Bolivia-Paraguay disputes. High Commissioner at Danzig, 1934-37; Deputy Secretary-General, League of Nations, 1937-40; Secretary-General, League of Nations, 1940-47; Woodrow Wilson Foundation Award, 1945; Pres. Permanent Norwegian-Swiss Conciliation Commission. *Recreations:* fishing, gardening. *Address:* Station House, Recess, Co. Galway. *T.:* Recess 7. *Club:* Stephen's Green (Dublin). [*Died* 13 *June* 1959.

L'ESTRANGE, Mrs. Julian; *see* Collier, Constance.

LETHBRIDGE, Marion Eva, C.B.E., 1918; *b.* 1879; *d.* of late Christopher Lethbridge; a Dame of Grace of Order of St. John of Jerusalem; was Commandant General Service V.A.D.'s, France, during European War. *Address:* Cruck Meole House, Hanwood, Shrewsbury, Shropshire. *Club:* V.A.D. Ladies. [*Died* 19 *March* 1959.

LETTS, Malcolm (Henry Ikin); solicitor (retired); *b.* 10 Jan. 1882; *y. s.* of John Letts, solicitor, London; *m.* 1913, Olive Mary, *d.* of Alfred Wilson of Sunderland. *Educ.:* Privately and abroad. Admitted solicitor, 1905; F.S.A.; President, Hakluyt Society, 1949-55. Officer, Order of Leopold II; corresponding member of the Royal Belgian Academy. *Publications:* Bruges and its Past, 1924; Francis Mortoft, his Book, 1926; Travels and Adventures of Pero Tafur, 1926; The True History of Hans Staden, 1928; The Diary of Jorg von Ehingen, 1929; A Wayfarer on the Rhine, 1930; A Wayfarer in Central Germany, 1931; As the Foreigner Saw Us, 1935; The Old House, 1942; The Travels of Arnold von Harff, 1946; Sir John Mandeville, 1949; Mandeville's Travels, Texts and Translations, 1953; Rozmital's Travels, 1956; Translation of Hampe's Nuremberg Malefactors' Books, and Cartellieri's Court of Burgundy; contributions on historical subjects to various periodicals. *Recreations:* books and motoring. *Address:* 27 West Heath Drive, N.W.11. *T.:* Speedwell 3921. *Club:* Athenæum. [*Died* 27 *June* 1957.

LETTS, Sir William Malesbury, K.B.E., *cr.* 1922 (C.B.E. 1918); High Sheriff of Caernarvonshire, 1922; a Director of several companies; *b.* 26 Feb. 1873; *s.* of William E. Letts; *m.* 1901, Edith Annie (*d.* 1943), *d.* of late William Pearson, Mexborough, Yorks. One of the pioneers of the British Motor industry and one of the founders of the Automobile Assoc.; supplied motor transport and aeroplanes to the Government during the war 1914-18, and built No. 3 National Aeroplane Factory at Heaton Chapel, near Stockport; President of Society of Motor Manufacturers and Traders, Ltd., 1925-26. Master of Coach Makers' and Coach Harness Makers' Company, 1944. *Recreations:* golf, shooting. *Address:* Eryl Fryn, Llandudno, North Wales. *T.A.:* Letts, Llandudno. *T.:* Penrhynside 39120. *Club:* Royal Automobile. [*Died* 25 *Feb.* 1957.

LEVAME, Mgr. Albert; Titular Archbishop of Chersonese; Apostolic Nuncio in Ireland since 1954; *b.* Monaco, 19 Jan. 1881. *Educ.:* Visitation's College, Monaco; Turin; Rome (Ph.D., D.C.L.). Ordained Priest, Monaco, 1905; Secretary of Nunciature, Bogotá, Colombia, 1916, Vienna, 1919; Auditeur of Nunciature, Caracas, Venezuela, 1924; Chargé d'Affaires, Buenos Ayres, 1925; Auditor and Chargé d'Affaires, Budapest, 1927; Counsellor and Chargé d'Affaires, Paris, 1928; consecrated Archbishop, Rome, 1934; Apostolic Nuncio: Salvador and Honduras, 1933; Guatemala, 1936; Montevideo, 1940; Cairo, 1949. Hon. D.Litt. Nat. Univ. of Ireland, 1958. Grand Officer Quetzal (Guatemala), Merito (Paraguay), Commandeur, Légion d'Honneur (France), Libertador (Venezuela); Grand Croix Mérite (Egypt). *Address:* Apostolic Nunciature, Phoenix Park, Dublin. [*Died* 5 *Dec.* 1958.

LEVERTOFF, Rev. Paul Philip, D.D., Director of Diocesan Council for Work among Jews (Bishop of Stepney's Fund), since 1922; *b.* 14 Oct. 1878; *s.* of Saul Levertoff and Judith Levertoff; *m.* 1911, Beatrice Adelaide, *d.* of late Dr. Spooner-Jones; two *d.* *Educ.:* Russian and German Schools and Universities. Professor of Old Testament and Rabbinics at the Delitzsch College, Leipzig, 1912-18; Librarian and Sub-Warden St. Deiniols Library, Hawarden, 1919-1922; Examiner in Hebrew for Leeds University, 1919-23; Charles Boys Lecturer, 1926-29; Hon. D.D. Lambeth, 1930; Boyle Lecturer, 1932-34, 1938-40; naturalised British subject. *Publications:* *In Hebrew:* Life of S. Paul, 1907; 4th ed., 1910; The Religion of Israel, 1908, 4th ed., 1909; The Son of Man, 1906, 4th ed., 1911; Thomas Carlyle, 1909; The Christian Doctrine of God, 1931; Trans. of the Confessions of St. Augustine, 1908, 2nd ed., 1928. *In German:* Die religioese Denkweise der Chasidim, 1918. *In English:* Love and the Messianic Age, 1924; Notes upon an important Collection of Hebraica, 1924; Sifre, 1925; Commentary on S. Matthew (with Canon Goudge), 1928; S. Paul in Jewish Thought; Hebrew Christian Liturgy in Hebrew and English, 1925, 2nd ed. 1929; Synagogue Worship in the time of Christ, 1931, etc.; contributed to New Standard Biblical Encyclopaedia, and to periodicals; Editor of The Hebrew Library of the Christian Faith, and of The Church and the Jews; contributor to Bishop Gore's Commentary on Holy Scripture, to the Teachers' Commentary, Liturgy and Worship, 1932; The Shekinah and the Christ, 1937; The Messianic Hope, 1938; The Infant Church, 1940; St. Matthew, Commentary for Schools, 1940; translator of Jesus—Jeshua, 1929; the Zohar, 1933; Orte und Wege Jesu, 1935; Pesikta Rabbati, 1953; Schlatter's Die erste Christenheit, 1953, etc. *Recreations:* translation of drama, etc., book collecting. *Address:* 5 Mansfield Road, Ilford, Essex. *T.:* Ilford 2366. [*Died* 30 *July* 1954.

LEVESON-GOWER, Colonel Charles Cameron, C.M.G. 1916; O.B.E. 1919; *b.* 30 June 1866; *e. s.* of Capt. H. B. B. Leveson-Gower; *m.* Beatrice, *d.* of late H. F. Makins; one *s.* one *d.* *Educ.:* Cheltenham College. Joined Berkshire Militia, 1884;

served in Punjab Frontier Cavalry and 31st D.C.O. Lancers, I.A.; Comdt. The Body Guard, Bombay; retired, 1906; Commanded 3rd N.M. Brigade Field Artillery T.F.; served in R.F.A. European War, 1914-18 (despatches, C.M.G.).; Insp. of Guns, Woolwich Arsenal, 1919; Home Guard Staff, 1940. *Address:* 13 Cottesmore Gardens, W.8. *T.:* Western 4936. [*Died* 26 *May* 1951.

LEVESON GOWER, Frederick Neville Sutherland; *b.* 31 May 1874; *o. s.* of late Lord Albert Leveson Gower, 3rd *s.* of 2nd Duke of Sutherland and Grace Emma Townshend, *d.* of Sir T. N. Abdy, 1st Bart.; *heir-pres.* to 5th Duke of Sutherland; *m.* 1916, Blanche Lucie Gillard. *Educ.:* Eton; Christ Church, Oxford. M.P. (L.U.) Sutherland, 1900-6. *Address:* Hinata, Avenue du Roi Albert, Cannes, A.M., France. *Club:* Travellers'. [*Died* 9 *April* 1959.

LEVESON GOWER, Sir George (Granville), K.B.E., *cr.* 1921; M.A. (Oxon); formerly Chairman, Lilleshall Co.; *b.* London, 19 May 1858; *o. s.* of late Hon. Frederick Leveson Gower and Margaret, 2nd *d.* of 2nd Marquess of Northampton; *m.* 1898, Hon. Cicely, *y. d.* of 8th Baron Monson; two *d.* (and one *d.* decd.). *Educ.:* Eton; Balliol Coll., Oxford 2nd cl. Moderations (Classics); 2nd class Final Classical Schools, M.A. Private Secretary to Mr. Gladstone when Prime Minister, 1880-85; Spanish Mission, 1881; M.P. (L.) North-West Staffordshire, 1885-1886; contested East Marylebone, 1889; M.P. Stoke-upon-Trent, 1890-95; Junior Lord of Treasury, 1885-86; Comptroller of H.M.'s Household, 1892-95; Second Church Estates Commissioner, 1892-95; Commissioner of Woods and Forests, 1908-24; Director Metropolitan District Railway, and of the Whitechapel and Bow Railway, 1925; Member of London School Board, 1897-99; European Editor of the North American Review in England, 1899-1908; Secretary to the American Delegation to the First International Conference on Radio-telegraphy at Berlin. 1906; Chairman, Home Counties Liberal Federation, 1905-8; first Hon. Secretary to the Keats-Shelley Memorial Association; Chairman of the Lilleshall Co. *Publications:* Poems, 1902; Haryo, Letters of Lady Harriet Cavendish, 1940; Years of Content (1858 to 1886), 1940; Years of Endeavour (1886-1908), 1942; Odds and Ends, 1947; co-editor (with Lord Monson) Memoirs of Captain George Elers, 1903. *Address:* 18 York House, Kensington Church Street, W.8. *Clubs:* M.C.C., Athenæum. [*Died* 18 *July* 1951.

LEVESON GOWER, Sir Henry Dudley Gresham, Kt., *cr.* 1953; Chairman Surrey County Cricket Club; *b.* 8 May 1873; *o. surv. s.* of late Granville Leveson Gower of Titsey Place, Surrey, and late Hon. Sophia Leveson Gower, *y. d.* of 1st Lord Leigh of Stoneleigh Abbey; *m.* 1908, Enid, *e. d.* of late R. S. B. Hammond-Chambers, K.C. *Educ.:* Winchester; Magdalen Coll. Oxford. Captain of Winchester Coll. Cricket XI. 1892; of Oxford Univ. Cricket XI. 1896; of Surrey XI. 1908; Member of Lord Hawke's Cricket Team to West Indies, Jan. 1897; Member of Cricket Team to America, Sept. 1897; Member of M.C.C. Team to South Africa, 1905-06; Capt. M.C.C. Team to South Africa, 1909-10; took Cricket Team to Malta, Gibraltar and Portugal between 1928 and 1934; served European War, 1914-18, Major in R.A.S.C. (despatches); Pres. of the Surrey County Cricket Club, 1929-40; Vice-President, 1940; Pres. of the Harlequins Cricket Club, 1946; presented with the Honorary Freedom of the Borough of Scarborough, 1930. *Publication:* Cricket Personalities. *Address:* 30 St. Mary Abbots Court, Kensington, W.14. *T.:* Western 1339. *Clubs:* East India and Sports, Albany, United Hunts. [*Died* 1 *Feb.* 1954.

LEVI, T. Arthur, M.A., B.C.L., LL.B., of the Inner Temple; Barrister-at-law; 1st Prof. of English Law in the University of Wales from 1901; *b.* Swansea, 13 Dec. 1874; *s.* of Rev. Thomas Levi, Minister of the Presbyterian Church of Wales. *Educ.:* Aberystwyth College; Lincoln College, Oxford; Inner Temple; graduated early in Arts and Law at London University; entered Lincoln College, Oxford, 1893; Carrington Law Prize, 1897; First Class Honours in Law, 1897; First Class Honours B.C.L. Examination, 1900; First Class and Certificate of Honour at the Bar Examination, 1900. Called to the Bar, 1900; delivers public lectures upon English Law; President Aberystwyth Liberal Club, 1910 and 1911; one of the promoters of the Board of Legal Education for Wales, 1911; Hon. Permanent Chairman of University College of Wales Liberal Society since 1922. *Publications:* An Edition of the Poems of Wales, 1896; The Opportunity of a Faculty of Law, 1901. *Address:* Arfron, St. David's Road, Aberystwyth. [*Died* 24 *Jan.* 1954.

LEVICK, Claude Blaxland, O.B.E. 1943, M.B., Ch.M., F.R.C.P.; Physician to In-Patients and Physician-in-Charge of Heart Dept. St. George's Hosp.; Senior Physician, Victoria Hospital for Children; Consulting Physician to County of Hertfordshire; Cardiologist, Ministry of Pensions; Lecturer in Clinical Medicine, University of London; Physician L.C.C. Cardiac Clinic; Visiting Physician, Shrodells Hospital, Watford, and Southall-Norwood Hospital; Examiner in Medicine, Univ. of London, M.R.C.P. and Conjoint Board Royal Colleges of Physicians and Surgeons; Medical Referee various insurance cos.; *b.* 17 Nov. 1896; *s.* of Sydney Levick and Lucy Blaxland; *m.* 1934, Stella Kent. *Educ.:* Sydney Grammar School; University of Sydney (Aitken Scholar, Cooper Scholar in Classics, John West Medallist, Grahame Medallist); post-graduate study; Sydney, Manchester, Vienna, London. War service, U.K. and M.E.F. 1939-45 (despatches twice). *Publications:* on medical and cardiological subjects. *Recreations:* lawn tennis, squash racquets, ice-skating. *Address:* 22 Harley Street, W.1. *T.:* Langham 3616; Hyde Heath, Bucks. *T.:* Chesham 318. *Clubs:* Athenæum, St. Stephen's. [*Died* 31 *May* 1953.

LEVICK, Surg.-Commander G. Murray, R.N.; F.R.G.S., F.Z.S.; *s.* of George Levick, Shinuton Hall, Monmouthshire; *m.* 1918, Audrey, 2nd *d.* of late Sir Mayson Beeton, K.B.E. one *s.* Accompanied Captain Scott's Antarctic Expedition as Medical Officer and Zoologist, 1910-13; served European War North Sea and Gallipoli and War of 1939-45, Naval Intelligence staff and Commando Training. Founded Royal Navy Rugby Union; Fellow, Royal Society of Medicine and Brit. Orthopædic Association; electrologist to St. Thomas's Hospital; Consultant Physio-Therapist, and Member, Committee of Management, Victoria Hospital for Children; Medical Director, Heritage Craft Schools for Crippled Children, Chailey; Consultant for physical treatment to East Sussex County Council; Member London University Advisory Committee on Physical Education; Founder and Leader Public Schools Exploring Society; Member of Council, Royal Empire Society; Executive Committee, Grenfell Assoc.; Council Lucas Tooth Boys Training Fund and Committee Nat. Cadet Training Assoc.; awarded, 1942, Beck Grant by Royal Geographical Society for services to Exploration. *Publications:* The Social Habits of Antarctic Penguins; A Monograph on Adelie Penguins; Young Explorers in Northern Finland; and various medical works. *Address:* Whitewater House, Budleigh Salterton, Devon. *T.:* Budleigh Salterton 5. *Club:* Army and Navy. [*Died* 30 *May* 1956.

LEVICK, Thomas Henry Carlton, C.B.E. 1921 (O.B.E. 1918); *b.* 1867; *s.* of late Frederick Levick, J.P., Pinner; *m.* 1895, Evelyn Constance, *d.* of George F. Quinton, J.P.; one *s.* one *d.* *Educ.:* University College School;

abroad. Retired, 1926, as Managing Director of Harris and Dixon, Shipowners of London. Attached to Staff of General Officer American Expeditionary Force in London during European War, 1914-18; sent on Special Mission abroad for Foreign Office and Ministry of Shipping; Army Welfare Officer, 1940-45. *Clubs:* M.C.C., Royal Societies; Royal Motor Yacht. [*Died* 19 *Oct.* 1957.

LEVIEN, John Mewburn; *b.* 3 May 1863; *s.* of late Edward Levien, M.A., F.S.A., of Balliol College, Oxford, and the British Museum; unmarried. *Educ.:* Birkenhead School; Chatham House, Ramsgate; St. John's College, Cambridge. On the advice of Sir Charles Santley, studied singing under late H. C. Deacon; subsequently studied under Manuel Garcia, Salzédo (Conservatoire de Paris), and Vannuccini (of Florence); Hon. R.A.M.; Liveryman Company of Musicians; a Vice-President, The London Society; successively Hon. Co.-Treasurer, Hon. Treasurer and Hon. Secretary, Royal Philharmonic Society, 1910-1929; late Professor of Singing, Guildhall School of Music and Trinity College of Music; Hon. Treasurer, Concerts at the Front, 1914-15. *Publications:* Beethoven and The Royal Philharmonic Society, 1927; Sir Charles Santley, 1930; The Garcia Family, 1932; Some notes for Singers, 1940; Impressions of W. T. Best, 1942; Santley and some famous singers of his time, 1943; The Singing of John Braham, 1944; Six Sovereigns of Song, 1947; and contributions to dictionaries and periodicals. *Address:* Chestnut Lodge, 57 Rosslyn Hill, N.W.3. *T.:* Hampstead 6800. *Clubs:* Athenæum, Savage. [*Died* 2 *July* 1953.

LEVINGE, Sir Edward Vere, K.C.I.E., *cr.* 1916; C.S.I. 1911; B.A., J.P.; *b.* 24 May 1867; *s.* of late H. C. Levinge, J.P., of Knockdrin Castle, Mullingar; *m.* 1900, Alys Adèle Thomas (*d.* 1952), *d.* of Maj.-Gen. Thomas; one *d.* *Educ.:* Cheltenham College; Balliol College, Oxford. Entered Indian Civil Service, 1887; Under-Secretary, Bengal; Under-Secretary to Government of India; Collector of Murshedabad; Secretary to the Board of Revenue, Bengal; Collector of Customs, Calcutta; Commissioner of Patna; Commissioner of Orissa; Member of the Board of Revenue, Bihar and Orissa; Member of the Executive Council and Officiating Lieutenant-Governor of Bihar and Orissa; retired from I.C.S. 1918. *Address:* Tara Farm, P.O. Wilton, Marandellas, Southern Rhodesia. [*Died* 24 *Jan.* 1954.

LEVINSTEIN, Dr. Herbert, M.Sc., Ph.D., F.R.I.C.; M.I.Chem.E.; *s.* of late Ivan Levinstein, M.Sc. Tech. (hon.) Manchester; *m.* 1914, Isabella Forrest Crawford, *d.* of late Prof. William Stirling, M.D., LL.D.; no *c.* *Educ.:* Rugby School; Manchester Univ.; Zürich. Formerly Man. Director of Levinstein Ltd., and the British Dyestuffs Corporation, Ltd.; President of the Institution of Chemical Engineers, 1935-36; President: Society of Chemical Industry, 1929-30, Society of Dyers and Colourists, 1928-29, British Assoc. of Chemists, 1923-24, 1949-50 (Hinchley Medallist, 1953); and Manchester Literary and Philosophical Society, 1925-26; gold medallist of the Society of Chemical Industry, 1931; served on Chemical Warfare, 1917-19, and other Government Committees; Peace Conference Delegation, 1919; Freeman of City of London, 1923; Prime Warden of Dyers Company, 1947. *Publications:* numerous patents and papers and addresses on technical subjects. *Recreations:* hunting and yachting. *Address:* Baddow, Pinkney's Green, near Maidenhead, Berks. *Clubs:* Royal Thames Yacht, Chemical, Royal Automobile. [*Died* 3 *Aug.* 1956.

LEVITA, Lieut.-Colonel Sir Cecil Bingham, K.C.V.O., *cr.* 1932 (M.V.O. 1901); Kt., *cr.* 1929; C.B.E. 1919; late Royal Horse Artillery; *b.* 18 Jan. 1867; *s.* of late E. Levita, 27 Ennismore Gardens, S.W.; *m.* 1917, Florence Woodruff, *o. c.* of late William Robb, Park Quadrant, Glasgow; one *s.* (one *d.* decd.). *Educ.:* R.M.A., Woolwich. Lieut., R.A. 1886; Captain, 1897; Major, 1902; served Matabele War (medal); South Africa; A.D.C. to Lieut.-Gen. Sir Baker Russell, G.C.B., 1899-1900; special service officer, South African War, and D.A.A.G., 5th Division, Natal Field Force (despatches, medal and 3 clasps); Reserve of Officers, 1909; recalled to service in Regular Forces, Aug. 1914; General Staff Officer, 1st Grade (despatches); contested (C.) St. Ives Division, Cornwall, 1910; Mem. L.C.C. (M.R.), North Kensington, 1911-37; Chairman L.C.C., 1928-29; D.L., County of London, J.P., 1920-50; Commander of the Legion of Honour, 1929; Commander Order of St. John of Jerusalem, 1930; originator of King George Hospital, Ilford. *Address:* 6 Brunswick Square, Hove. *Club:* Carlton. [*Died* 10 *Oct.* 1953.

LEVY, Thomas; *s.* of Lewis Levy, Oakleigh, Denmark Hill, S.E.; *m.* 1901, Maud Benjamin; two *d.* *Educ.:* City of London School. Assistant Executive Officer of Food Control, Bournemouth, European War of 1914-18; Officer commanding the transport during strike, 1919; M.P. Elland Division of Yorkshire, 1931-45; Chairman Parliamentary Textile Committee, 1919-33; Chm. Parliamentary Tariff Policy Committee, 1934-40; Chairman British Wool Central Advisory Committee, 1939-40. *Recreations:* golf, etc. *Address:* Flat 1, 28 Hyde Park Gardens, W.2. *T.:* Ambassador 2297. *Clubs:* Constitutional, Roehampton. [*Died* 14 *Feb.* 1953.

LEWIN, Brig.-General Arthur Corrie, C.B. 1916; C.M.G. 1916; D.S.O. 1902; late Colonel 3rd Batt. Connaught Rangers; late Captain the 19th Hussars; *b.* 26 July 1874; *s.* of Frederic T. Lewin, D.L., of Castlegrove, Co. Galway, and Cloghans, Co. Mayo, and Lucy, *d.* of William B. Corrie, Cheltenham; *m.* 1st, 1900, Norah Constance (*d.* 1931), *d.* of late William Higgin, of Rosganna, Carrickfergus; two *s.*; 2nd, 1933, Phyllis Mary Noel, *widow* of John Stanning and *d.* of late David Marriage. *Educ.:* Cheltenham College; Trinity Hall, Cambridge. Gazetted to King's Regiment, 1895; Capt. 1900; 19th Hussars, 1905; served with the Mounted Infantry in S. Africa, 1899-1902 (despatches twice, Queen's medal and five clasps, King's medal and two clasps, D.S.O.); European War, 1914-18 (despatches six times, C.M.G., C.B., Bt. Col., Russian Order St. Anne's). *Address:* Cloghans, Tuam, Co. Galway; Njoro, Kenya Colony. *Clubs:* Bath; Kildare Street (Dublin). [*Died* 16 *Sept.* 1952.

LEWIN, Octavia Margaret Sophia, M.B., B.S. Lond.; Consulting Rhinologist; Member of Convocation, London University; Member: Federation of Medical Women, British Homœpathic Society; International Federation of University Women; School Mnaager, L.C.C.; Member of the Royal Institution; Member and Lecturer for Women's Freedom League; Hon. Rhinologist to Soc. of Women Journalists; unmarried. *Educ.:* Queen's Coll., London (Arnott scholar); Girton Coll., Cambridge (Goldsmith scholar); London School of Medicine and Royal Free Hospital; Rotunda Hospital, Dublin. Late Rhinologist to the L.C.C. and to the Roll of Honour Hospital; Assistant Surgeon to English Military Hospital, Dieppe, 1914; Médecin Chef, French Military Hospital, Charenton, 1915-16; Aural Surgeon to the Women's Hospital Corps, Endell Street Military Hospital, 1917-18; Medical Adviser to the Westminster Health Centre. Governor of Bedford College, London Univ. *Publications:* Various articles on Personal Hygiene, on Nasal Hygiene, Education and Training of Children in Personal Hygiene, Breathing and Human Welfare, Sneezing, the Breathing Alphabet; various letters to medical periodicals. *Address:* 8 Manchester Square, W.1. *T.:* Welbeck 3430. [*Died* 27 *Dec.* 1955.

LEWIN, Percy Evans, M.B.E.; Librarian, Royal Empire Society, 1910-46; *b.* Boston, Lincs, 3 April 1876; *m.* 1st, 1906, Léontine Berthe (*d.* 1934), *d.* of J. Dorman, Cherbourg, France; three *d.*; 2nd, Winifred Caroline, *d.* of Herbert Charles Hill. *Educ.*: Boston Grammar School. Assistant-Librarian Woolwich Public Libraries, 1901-3; Port Elizabeth (Cape Colony), 1903-7; South Australian Public Library, 1908-9; was attached to the Admiralty Intelligence Division (Geographical Section), 1918-19; and prepared a Report for the Foreign Office on German administration in Africa, 1918. *Publications*: Catalogue of Port Elizabeth Library, 2 vols., 1906; History of the Prairie Provinces, 1913; History of Canada, 1914; The People of Australia (Oxford Survey), 1914; The Germans in Africa (Oxford Pamphlet), 1914; The Germans and Africa, 1915; The German Road to the East, 1916; Australia (International Information Series), 1917; German Rule in Africa, 1918; West Africa, a handbook (Editor), 1921; A Geography of Africa, 1923; The Resources of the Empire, 1924; Catalogue of the Royal Empire Society, 4 vols., 1930-37. *Address*: 4 Oxford Court, Queen's Drive, W.3. *T.*: Acorn 0489. [*Died* 24 *July* 1955.

LEWIS, Sir Andrew Jopp Williams, Kt., *cr.* 1929; D.L.; LL.D.; *b.* 18 Apr. 1875; *s.* of John Lewis and Elizabeth Williams; *m.* 1901, Anne Walker (*d.* 1940); two *s.* five *d.* *Educ.*: Grammar School, Old Aberdeen. Senior partner of firm of John Lewis & Sons, Ltd., shipbuilders and engineers, Aberdeen; large trawler owner; entered Board of Aberdeen Harbour Commissioners, 1910; Town Council, 1919; Baillie, 1920; Lord Provost of City and Royal Burgh of Aberdeen, 1925-29; LL.D. Aberdeen University, 1928; Director National Bank of Scotland Limited and Chairman Millom Askam, Hemitite Co.; Chairman Aberdeen, Edinburgh and London Trust; North Eastern Ice Co. Ltd. and John Lewis Ltd., Coal Factors; Vice-Chairman Aberdeen Mutual Insurance Co. *Recreation*: golf. *Address*: 11 Queen's Road, Aberdeen. *T.A.*: Boiler. *T.*: 7000. [*Died* 2 *Feb.* 1952.

LEWIS, Arthur King, C.M.G. 1914; *b.* on H.M.S. Ascension Island, 21 Jan. 1867; *s.* of late J. Lewis, R.N.; unmarried. *Educ.*: Royal Naval School, New Cross; Christ's Hospital; Trinity Coll., Oxford. Classical Master, St. Edward's School, Oxford, 1892-95; Egyptian Ministry of Public Instruction, 1895-97; Inspector of Finance, 1897-1900; Controller of Direct Taxes, Ministry of Finance, 1900-6; Director-General of Egyptian Customs, 1906-19. [*Died* 24 *Feb.* 1954.

LEWIS, Professor B. Roland, M.Sc.; M.A.; Litt.D.; D.Litt.; Professor of English, 1915-50, Emeritus since 1950, and Director of Shakespeare Laboratory, University of Utah, Salt Lake City, Utah; *b.* St. Mary's, Ohio, 3 Dec. 1884; *s.* of Samuel Lewis and Katherine Fox; *m.* 1906, Bessie Blanche Collins; one *d.* *Educ.*: Ohio Northern Univ.; Univ. of Chicago (Graduate Sch.); Harvard Univ. (Graduate Sch.). Prof. of English, Grand Island Coll., 1906-7; Professor of English, Ellsworth College, 1907-13. Research in Bodleian, Trinity Coll., British Museum, etc., 1913-. Shakespeare Research Scholar, Folger Shakespeare Library, Washington, D.C., 1933-1934, and Huntington Library, summers of 1927, 1929, 1930, 1931, 1937, 1939, 1942, 1947; Visiting Professor of English, Univ. of Arkansas, Fayetteville, 1926, Graduate School, Catholic Univ. of America, Washington, D.C., 1933-34. Vice-President of The Shakespeare Association of America; Hon. Mem., Institut de Littérature et Science de France, 1937. Is an international authority on Shakespeare Documents. *Publications*: The Life of William Shakespeare; The Technique of the One-Act Play, 1918; Contemporary One-Act Plays, 1922; Effective Writing, 1923; University of Utah Plays, 1928; Creative Poetry, 1931; The Shakespeare Documents, two vols. 1941. Critical reviews in New York Times, Times Literary Supplement. *Recreations*: motoring, fishing, ferreting out the backgrounds of the rare Shakespeare documents. *Address*: 1272 East Fifth South Street, Salt Lake City, Utah; The Shakespeare Laboratory, The University of Utah, Salt Lake City, Utah, U.S.A. *T.*: 4-0283. *Clubs*: Harvard (New York); Timpanogos (Salt Lake City). [*Died* 19 *July* 1959.

LEWIS, Ernest Harry, C.B.E. 1920 (M.B.E. 1918); Chartered Accountant (S.A.); F.R.E.S.; King's Jubilee Medal, 1935; Coronation Medal, 1937; *b.* 1877; *s.* of late Edwin Lewis; *m.* 1913, Mabel, *o. d.* of late John Jardine, Pietermaritzburg; one *s.* one *d.* Formerly Financial Adviser, Department of Defence, Union of South Africa; retired. *Address*: 587 Vermeulen Street E., Arcadia, Pretoria, Transvaal. *T.*: Pretoria 2.8913. *Club*: Pretoria. [*Died* 29 *Jan.* 1951.

LEWIS, Francis John, D.Sc., F.R.S.E., F.R.S.C., F.L.S.; Fellow Faraday Soc.; Prof. of Botany, Fouad I Univ., Cairo, 1935-1946; *b.* London, 1875; *m.* 1st, 1901, Gwendolen Elizabeth Meacock (*d.* 1927); no *c.*; 2nd, Mitta, *d.* of Gordon Dickson, Demonstrator in Botany, Univ. of Liverpool, 1900-5; Lecturer in Geographical Botany, 1905-12; Prof. of Botany Univ. of Alberta, Canada, 1912-35; Visiting Lecturer Plant Physiology, Royal Holloway Coll., London Univ., 1947-48; Advisory Ed. Chambers's Encyclopædia, 1947-48, and other scientific publications. Cuthbert Peek Fund, R.G.S., 1905; Neill Gold Medal, R.S.E., 1910. *Publications*: scientific papers in Transactions of Royal Society, Edinburgh, Geographical Journal, Annals of Botany, Science Progress, etc., chiefly on Physiology and Ecology. *Recreations*: camping, climbing. *Address*: c/o The Linnean Society, Burlington House, W.1. [*Died* 24 *May* 1955.

LEWIS, Howell Elvet, C.H. 1948; *b.* parish of Conwil Elvet, Carmarthenshire, 14 April 1860; *m.* 1st, 1887; two *s.* three *d.*; 2nd, 1923; 3rd, 1930. *Educ.*: Presbyterian Coll., Carmarthen. Held Congregational Pastorates at Buckley, Hull, Llanelly, Harecourt (Canonbury), and Welsh Tabernacle, King's Cross; at the National Eisteddfod of Wales received bardic crown, 1888, and chair, 1894; Hon. M.A., Univ. of Wales, 1906; Hon. D.D. (Univ. of Wales), 1933; LL.D. 1949. Chm. of the Union of Welsh Independents, 1925; Arch-druid of Wales, 1923-27; Pres. of National Free Church Council, 1926-27; President Welsh Union of League of Nations, 1927-28; Chairman Congregational Union of England and Wales, 1933-34: Worshipful Master Dewi Sant Lodge, 1934-35. *Publications*: Sweet Singers of Wales; My Christ, and other Poems; Dr. Herber Evans: Life and Letters; The Gates of Life; By the River Chebar; Jeremiah (Devotional Commentary); Encouragement (Devotional Addresses); Songs of Victory; With Christ among the Miners; Israel and Other Poems, Songs of Assisi; The Approach to Christ; The Book still speaks; The Book speaks again; besides several Welsh volumes in poetry and prose. *Address*: Erw'r Delyn, Penarth, Glam. [*Died* 10 *Dec.* 1953.

LEWIS, Mabel Terry; actress, miniaturist; *d.* of Arthur James Lewis and Kate Terry; *m.* 1904, Captain R. C. Batley of Crewkerne, Somerset. *Educ.*: home. First appearance on the stage as Lucy Lorimer in Mr. John Hare's revival of A Pair of Spectacles; since then with Mr. John Hare as Mary Faber in The Master, Blanche Haye in Ours, Bella in School, and Muriel Eden in The Gay Lord Quex; in The Mistress of Craignairn and Gudgeons; as Gloria Clandon in You never can Tell, and Barbara Quinton in English Nell; in A Woman in the Case and Women

are so Serious; in After All; as understudy to Miss Winifred Emery in Caste and There's many a Slip and The Unforeseen, playing all three parts; in Mrs. Gorringe's Necklace; and as the Lady of Rosedale, (with Sir Charles Wyndham); retired from stage on her marriage; returned to the stage after Major Batley's death, and has since played in The Grain of Mustard Seed, The Ninth Earl, with Norman McKinnel, Getting Married, at The Everyman, in Dear Brutus, with Gerald du Maurier; three seasons in New York in If Winter Comes, and Aren't We All, with Cyril Maude; Easy Virtue, with Jane Cowl, The Constant Wife, with Ethel Barrymore; also in London, The Pelican, Easy Virtue, The Golden Calf, Mud and Treacle, A Hundred Years Old, The Stag, and The Black Ace; The Skin Game (revival); The Importance of being Earnest (revival); The Mouthpiece and Charles the 3rd; Death Takes a Holiday; Windows; Faces; Cold Blood; Playground; Dinner at 8; Battle Royal; Frolic Wind; The Admirable Crichton; Distinguished Gathering; Bitter Harvest; Kind Lady; Victoria Regina; They came to a City; Lady Windermere's Fan (revival). *Films:* The Scarlet Pimpernel; Dishonour Bright; The Squeaker; Stolen Life; Jamaica Inn; The Adventures of Tartu; They came to a City. Has exhibited miniatures at Royal Academy, Grafton and New Galleries, and at Liverpool, Glasgow, and Manchester. *Address:* 7 The Parade, Epsom, Surrey.
[*Died* 28 *Nov.* 1957.

LEWIS, Malcolm Meredith, M.C., M.A., LL.B. (Camb.); Professor of Law and Pro-Vice-Chancellor, University of Bristol (Dean of Faculty of Law, 1932-54); *b.* 19 July 1891; *s.* of late Rev. H. Elvet Lewis, C.H., and Mary Taylor; *m.* 1917, Eileen Aitken; one *s.* *Educ.:* City of London School; Downing College, Cambridge (Foundation Scholar). Served European War, 1914-19, with 9th R.W.F. (M.C. and bar); Middle Temple, Barrister-at-law, 1921. *Publications:* various essays in British Year Book of International Law and in Law Quarterly Review. *Address:* Denehurst, Southfield Road, Westbury-on-Trym, Bristol. *T.:* Bristol 66942. [*Died* 23 *May* 1955.

LEWIS, Mary; *see* Milne, Mrs. Leslie.

LEWIS, Mary W.; *see* Wolseley-Lewis.

LEWIS, Sinclair; author; *s.* of late E. J. Lewis, M.D.; *b.* U.S.A., 7 Feb. 1885; *m.* 1st, 1914, Grace Livingstone Hegger; 2nd, 1928, Dorothy Thompson, (marriage dissolved, 1942); one *s.* *Educ.:* Yale University. Journalist, magazine sub-editor; literary adviser to the publishers Stokes & Doran, New York; has acted professionally, 1937-40; Nobel Prize for Literature, 1930; Litt. D. (hon. Yale), 1936; Member American Academy of Arts and Letters (U.S.). *Publications:* Our Mr. Wrenn, 1914; The Trail of the Hawk, 1915; The Job, 1917; Free Air, 1919; Main Street, 1920; Babbitt, 1922; Martin Arrowsmith, 1925; Mantrap, 1926; Elmer Gantry, 1927; The Man who Knew Coolidge, 1928; Dodsworth, 1929; Ann Vickers, 1933; Work of Art, 1934; It Can't Happen Here, 1935; The Prodigal Parents, 1938; Bethel Merriday, 1940; Gideon Planish, 1943; Cass Timberlane, 1945; Kingsblood Royal, 1947; The God-Seeker, 1949; World So Wide, 1951; *plays:* Hobohemia, 1919; (with Lloyd Lewis) Jayhawker, 1934; dramatic version of It Can't Happen Here, 1938; (with Fay Wray) Angela Is Twenty-Two, 1939; published plays: Dodsworth (dramatic version with Sidney Howard) and Jayhawker, both 1934; It Can't Happen Here, 1938; Selections from Short Stories, 1935. *Recreations:* motoring, walking, travel. *Address:* c/o Random House, 457 Madison Ave., New York 22. *Club:* Cosmos (Washington). [*Died* 10 *Jan.* 1951.

LEWIS, Thomas, M.A., B.D.; Principal, Memorial College, Brecon, 1908, now Emeritus; *b.* Con-wil-Elvet, Carms., 14 Dec. 1868; parents, farmers; *m.* *d.* of Jacob Williams, Whalley Range, Manchester; three *s.* three *d.* *Educ.:* Alun School, Mold; University College, Bangor; Owens College, Manchester; Marburg, Germany; Lancashire College, Manchester. Tutor, Lancashire College, 1894-98; Memorial College, Brecon, 1898; Director L.M.S. Society; Member of the Congregational Council; Member of the Breconshire Education Committee; Governor of the Intermediate School; Member of the Court of Governors, Cardiff; Member of the Welsh National Library Committee. *Publications:* Commentary on Amos; Prophecy and Judaism (Welsh); Literature and Theology of the Prophets; The Message of the Old Testament, 1931. *Recreations:* golf, music. *Address:* Memorial College, Brecon, South Wales. [*Died* 22 *May* 1953.

LEWIS, William Cudmore McCullagh, F.R.S. 1926; Brunner Professor of Physical Chemistry in the University of Liverpool 1913-47. *Educ.:* Queen's College (now the Queen's University) of Belfast. Graduated 1st Hons. B.A. (Royal University of Ireland), 1905; M.A. 1st Hons. and University Studentship in Experimental Science, 1906; Research in Chemistry at Liverpool University, Heidelberg, and Univ. College, London; Lecturer and Demonstrator in Chemistry, University College, London, 1910. *Publications:* System of Physical Chemistry, 3 vols.; papers on Physical Chemistry in various journals. *Address:* The University, Liverpool. *Club:* University (Liverpool). [*Died* 11 *Feb.* 1956.

LEWIS, Wyndham; author and artist; adviser to Library of Congress, U.S.A.; *b.* 1884 in America; *m.* 1929, Anne Hoskyns. *Educ.:* Rugby; Slade School. Hon. Lit.D. (Leeds), 1952. Work represented in Tate Gallery (5 works), Victoria and Albert Museum, also Durban, Ottawa, Toronto and Detroit City Art Museums and Museum of Modern Art, New York. *Publications:* Tarr, 1918; The Art of Being Ruled, 1926; The Lion and the Fox, 1927; Time and Western Man, 1928; Paleface, 1929; The Apes of God, 1930; The Wild Body, 1931; Hitler, 1931; The Diabolical Principle and the Dithyrambic Spectator, 1931; Filibusters in Barbary, 1932; Doom of Youth, 1932; Snooty Baronet, 1932; One Way Song, 1933; Men Without Art, 1934; Left Wings Over Europe, 1936; The Revenge for Love, 1937; Count your Dead: they are Alive, 1937; Blasting and Bombardiering, 1937; The Mysterious Mr. Bull, 1938; The Jews—Are they Human? 1939; The Hitler Cult, 1939; The Vulgar Streak, 1941; Anglo-saxony, 1942; America and Cosmic Man, 1948; Rude Assignment, 1950; Rotting Hill, 1951; The Writer and Absolute, 1952; Self Condemned, 1954; Trilogy, The Human Age: The Childermass, 1928; Monstre Gai, 1955; Malign Fiesta, 1955; The Red Priest, 1956. [*Died* 7 *March* 1957.

LEWISOHN, Frederick, C.S.I. 1925; C.B.E. 1922; *b.* 28 July 1878; *s.* of Leon Lewisohn; *m.* 1st, 1908, Edith Lilian Clementson (*d.* 1934); 2nd, 1935, Alice Theresa Burnett. *Educ.:* St. Paul's School; Trinity College, Oxford. Gaisford Prizeman and Craven Scholar, 1901; went to Burma in I.C.S., 1902; retired 1926; Gunner in Canadian Field Artillery, 1917; Lieut. attached 63rd Royal Naval Div., 1918; Assistant Master, Dulwich College, 1926; subsequently with Iraq Petroleum Co. *Club:* East India and Sports. [*Died* 13 *Feb.* 1951.

LEYEL, Mrs. C. F.; (Hilda Winifred); *d.* of late Edward Brenton Wauton of Uppingham School; *m.* 1900, Carl Fredrick Leyel (*decd.*); one *s.* *Educ.:* Halliwick Manor. Founder and Chairman of the Society of Herbalists and the Culpeper shops; initiated and organised The Golden Ballot, the total sum raised amounting to over £350,000, for the benefit of ex-service men and hospitals; was prosecuted under the Lottery and also the Betting Act in connection with these schemes and won both cases, thereby legalising ballots for charity; Life Governor of St. Mary's, the West London and the Royal National Orthopædic Hospitals; Given the Palme Academique by French Government, 1924. Fellow of Royal Institution. *Publications:* The Magic of Herbs; Herbal Delights; Compassionate Herbs; Elixirs of Life; The Truth about Herbs; Diet and Commonsense; The Lure of Cookery; with Olga Hartley) The Gentle Art of Cookery; Editor of Grieve's Modern Herbal; Heartsease; Green Medicine; Cinquefoil; Intoxicating Herbs. *Recreation:* travelling. *Address:* 21 Old Buildings, Lincoln's Inn, W.C.2; 17 Manchester Square, W.1; Shripney Manor, Shripney, Sussex. [*Died* 15 *April* 1957.

LEYLAND, Sir A. Edward H. N.; *see* Naylor-Leyland.

LIBERTY, Captain Ivor Stewart-, M.C., J.P., D.L.; Chairman of Liberty & Co. Ltd.; retired Captain in H.M. Army, 2nd Bucks Batt., Oxfordshire and Buckinghamshire Light Infantry; *b.* Nottingham, 16 March 1887; *e. s.* of late Dr. Donald Stewart of Nottingham and *nephew* of late Sir Arthur Lasenby Liberty; *m.* 1913, Evelyn Katharine, *e. d.* of late Rev. Canon C. O. Phipps; two *s.* three *d. Educ.:* Winchester; Christ Church, Oxford M.A. Barrister, Inner Temple; served European War, 1914-16 (M.C., wounded, lost a leg); Painter-Stainers Company; member of Council of the Bucks Architectural and Archæological Society; Lord of the Manor of The-Lee, Bucks; Chairman of The-Lee Parish Council; High Sheriff, 1922; owns about 3000 acres. *Publication:* A Record of the 2nd Bucks Battalion T.F., 1914-18. *Recreation:* shooting. *Address:* The-Lee Manor, Bucks. *T.A.:* The-Lee. *T.:* The-Lee 342; 25 Gt. Marlborough Street, W.1. *T.:* Regent 1234. *Club:* Ye Sette of Odd Volumes. [*Died* 13 *April* 1952.

LICHFIELD, 4th Earl of (*cr.* 1831), **Thomas Edward Anson;** Viscount Anson and Baron Soberton, 1806; late (Acting) Master of the Horse and A.D.C. to the Lord-Lieutenant of Ireland; *b.* 9 Dec. 1883; *e. s.* of 3rd Earl of Lichfield, and Lady Mildred Coke (*d.* 1941), *d.* of 2nd Earl of Leicester; *S.* father, 1918; *m.* 1st, 1911, Evelyn Maud (*d.* 1945), *e. d.* of late Colonel E. G. Keppel, M.V.O.; two *d.* (*yr. s.* killed on active service, 1943; *er. s.* died, 1958); 2nd, 1949, Mrs. Violet Margaret Phillips, *d.* of late Henry Dawson-Greene. *Educ.:* Harrow; Trinity College, Cambridge. Dep.-Lieutenant and J.P. Staffordshire; owns about 20,000 acres in Staffordshire. *Heir: g.s.* Viscount Anson. *Address:* Shugborough Hall, Stafford. *T.:* Milford (Staffs) 22. *Club:* Carlton. [*Died* 14 *Sept.* 1960.

LICHNOWSKY, Princess Mechtilde; writer; *b.* 1879; 3rd *d.* of Count Arco; *m.* 1st, 1904, Prince Lichnowsky, German Ambassador in London, 1912-14 (*d.* 1928); two *s.* one *d.*; 2nd, 1937, Major Ralph Harding Peto (*d.* 1945). *Publications:* Gods, Kings and Animals in Egypt, 1913; The Piano Tuner, 1915 (Der Stimmer), novel; Ein Spiel vom Tod (a play produced in Berlin Lessing Theatre, 1917); Geburt (a novel), 1918; Der Kinderfreund (a play produced Berlin Kammerspiele, 1919); Gott betet; Fighting the Expert (Der Kampf mit dem Fachmann), 1924; Half and Half (Halb und Halb) (a booklet of drawing and fine-lined funny verses about animals), 1926; The Rendez-vous at the Zoo, a novel, 1928 (Das Rendez-Vous im Zoo); On the Leash (An der Leine), 1930; Kindheit (childhood), 1934; Delaïde (a novel) 1935; Der Lauf der Asdur (a novel), 1936; Gespräche in Sybaris, 1947; Worte über Wörter, 1948; Zum Schauen bestellt (short stories and plays), 1953; Heute und Vorgestern (one year's diary), 1957. *Address:* Flat 2, 33 Ennismore Gardens, S.W.7 *T.:* Kensington 0148. *Club:* Stafford. [*Died* 4 *June* 1958.

LIDDELL, General Sir Clive Gerard, K.C.B., *cr.* 1939 (C.B. 1935); C.M.G. 1918; C.B.E. 1919; D.S.O. 1915; *b.* 1 May 1883; *s.* of late John Liddell, Huddersfield; *m.* 1st, 1914, Clare Lambert Roberts (*d.* 1917); 2nd, 1918, Hilda Jessie Bisset, *widow* of Lieut. Maurice Cane; one *s.* one *d. Educ.:* Uppingham; R.M.C., Sandhurst. Entered Army, 1902; Adjutant, 1908-11; Captain, 1908; Staff-Capt. 6 District, Northern Command, 1912-14; D.A.A. and Q.M.G., 1914; A.A. and Q.M.G., 1916; A.A.G., War Office, 1917-18; served European War, 1914-18 (despatches 6 times, D.S.O., C.M.G., C.B.E., Bt. Lieut.-Colonel); Instructor, Staff College, 1919-22; Deputy Administrator British Empire Exhibition, 1923-25; Imperial Defence College, 1927; General Staff Officer, 1st grade, War Office, 1928-31; Commander 8th Infantry Brigade, 1931-34; Maj.-Gen. 1933; Commander 47th (2nd London) Division T.A., 1935; Commander of 4th Division, 1935-37; Lt.-Gen., 1938; Adjut.-Gen. to the Forces, 1937-39; Governor and Commander-in Chief, Gibraltar, 1939-41; Gen., 1941; Inspector-General for Training, 1941-42; Col. Royal Leicestershire Regt., 1943-48; Director of Ambulance, Order of St. John, 1943-48; Acting Chief Commissioner, St. John Ambulance Bde., 1943-47; Governor, Royal Hospital, Chelsea, 1943-49. Chairman; 1st County Finance Co., 1948, A. H. Fuller Ltd., 1950, Wessex Central Concentrator Plant Ltd., 1952, Eureka Scientific Co. Ltd., 1954, Wilchester Permanent Building Society, 1955, Southall and Wembley Laundries, 1945. Bronze Medal, Royal Humane Soc., 1926. *Address:* 14 Sloane Court East, Chelsea, S.W.3. *Club:* United Service. [*Died* 9 *Sept.* 1956.

LIDDELL, Guy Maynard, C.B. 1953; C.B.E. 1944; M.C. 1918; Civil Assistant, War Office; *b.* 8 Nov. 1892; *s.* of late Captain Augustus Frederick Liddell, C.V.O., and late Emily (*née* Shinner); *m.* 1926, Hon. Calypso Baring (marriage dissolved, 1943), *d.* of 3rd Baron Revelstoke; one *s.* three *d.* Served European War, 1914-19, Royal Field Artillery (despatches, M.C.). *Address:* c/o War Office, S.W.1. [*Died* 2 *Dec.* 1958.

LIDDLE, Henry Weddell, M.A. (Cantab.); *s.* of John Liddle, North Shields; *b.* 6 Apr. 1885; *m.* Anna Cynthia, *d.* of N.D.F. Pearce, Grantchester, Cambridge; one *s.* two *d.* (and *yr. s.* decd.). *Educ.:* Royal Grammar School, Newcastle on Tyne; Downing College, Cambridge. Assistant Master King Edward VIth School, Aston, Birmingham, and King Edward VIIth School, Sheffield; House Master, St. Peter's School, York; Headmaster, Bedford Modern School, 1922-46; Tutor, Workers' Educational Association, Birmingham; 2nd Lt. K.R.R.C., 1917-18; Hon. Scout Commissioner; J.P. Bedford, 1942-46; Major, Home Guard. *Recreation:* music. *Address:* 36 Lensfield Road, Cambridge. *T.:* 54953. [*Died* 5 *Feb.* 1956.

LIDGETT, Rev. John Scott, C.H. 1933; M.A.; Hon. D.D. (Aberdeen, 1909; Oxford, 1932; Edinburgh, 1933); LL.D. (Lond., 1946); Member of the London School Board (Southwark Div.) since 1897; Alderman of the L.C.C., 1905-10; Member of the L.C.C. for Rotherhithe, 1910-1922; Alderman, 1922-28; Leader of the Progressive Party on the L.C.C., 1918-28; Warden of the Bermondsey Settlement, 1891-1949; Editor of the Methodist Times, 1907-18; Joint-Editor of the Contemporary Review since 1911; *b.* Lewisham, 1854; *s.* of late John Jacob Lidgett, Blackheath, and Maria Elizabeth, *d.* of Rev. John Scott; *m.* 1884, Emmeline Martha (*d.* 1934), 2nd *d.* of Andrew Davies, M.D., Newport, Mon.; one *s.* (killed in the War) one *d. Educ.:* Blackheath Proprietary School; University Coll., London. Entered Wesleyan ministry, 1876; stationed at Tunstall, Southport, Cardiff, Wolverhampton, and Cambridge; founded, in connection with late Dr. Moulton, the Bermondsey Settlement, 1891; President of the National Council of the Evangelical Free Churches of England and Wales, 1906-7; President Wesleyan Methodist Conference,

1908-9; President of the Free Church Commission, 1912-15; Hon. Secretary of the National Council of the Evangelical Free Churches of England and Wales since 1914; Moderator of the Federal Council of the Evangelical Free Churches, 1923-25; Joint President of the Temperance Council of the Christian Churches, 1924-28; Member of the Royal Commission on Venereal Diseases, 1913-15; Member of Senate of the Univ. of London, 1922-46; Dep. Vice-Chanc. of the Univ., 1929-30, Vice-Chancellor, 1930-31 and 1931-32; Member of the Court of the University, 1929-44; Chairman of the Executive Committee of the Central Council for Nursing, 1922-28; Governor of Royal Holloway College since 1931; Governor of Queen Mary College since 1934; Chairman, Universities China Committee, 1933-36; President of the Uniting Conference of the Methodist Churches, and first President of the United Church, 1932. *Publications:* The Spiritual Principle of the Atonement (Fernley Lecture), 1897; 7th ed. 1923; The Fatherhood of God in Christian Truth and Life, 1902; 2nd ed. 1913; The Christian Religion: Its Meaning and Proof, 1907; 2nd ed. 1908; Apostolic Ministry, 1909; God in Christ Jesus: A Study of St. Paul's Epistle to the Ephesians, 1915; Sonship and Salvation: A Study of the Epistle to the Hebrews, 1921; God, Christ, and the Church, 1927; (with Bryan H. Reed) Methodism in the Modern World, 1929; The Victorian Transformation of Theology, 1934; My Guided Life, 1936; The Idea of God and Social Ideals, 1938; The Cross seen from Five Standpoints, 1941; The Crowns of Jesus, 1941; God and the World, 1943; God and Man, 1944; Jesus Christ is Alive, 1946; Salvation, 1952. *Address:* Print Stile, Bidborough, Kent. [*Died* 16 *June* 1953.

LIDSTONE, George James, F.I.A., F.F.A., F.R.S.E., LL.D. (Edinburgh); Director (1930-46) and formerly Manager and Actuary (1913-29) of Scottish Widows' Fund and Life Assurance Society; Director (1919-46) of Royal Bank of Scotland and formerly (1927-42) of Scottish Consolidated Trust Ltd.; *b.* London, 11 Dec. 1870; *y. s.* of late William Thompson Lidstone; *m.* 1901, Florence Mary (*d.* 1942), *e. d.* of late Robert Gay; no *c.* *Educ.:* Kingsland Birkbeck School. Assistant Actuary (1893-1902), Joint Actuary (1902) and Actuary (1902-5) of the Alliance Assurance Co. Ltd.; Actuary and Secretary of the Equitable Life Assurance Society, 1905-13; Elected a Fellow of the Actuarial Society of America, 1910; was a member of the Actuarial Advisory Committee of the National Health Insurance Joint Committee, 1912-14; President of the Faculty of Actuaries in Scotland, 1924-26; Presented Oct. 1929, jointly by the Institute of Actuaries and the Faculty of Actuaries in Scotland, with a special Gold Medal (designed and executed by Gilbert Bayes, R.S.B.S., H.R.I., *q.v.*) in recognition of his services to actuarial science; member of the General Claims Tribunal, 1939-42. *Publications:* numerous papers in actuarial and mathematical journals. *Recreations:* lawn tennis, music, foreign travel. *Address:* 23 Wester Coates Avenue, Edinburgh 12. *T.:* Edinburgh 62322. [*Died* 12 *May* 1952.

LIFFORD, 7th Viscount (*cr.* 1781), **Evelyn James Hewitt,** D.S.O. 1916; Baron Lifford, 1768; late 1st Batt. Dorsets Regiment; *b.* 18 Dec. 1880; *e. s.* of 6th Viscount and Helen Blanche (*d.* 1942), *d.* of late C. S. Geach; *S.* father, 1925; *m.* 1919, Charlotte Rankine (*d.* 1954), *yr. d.* of late Sir Robert Maule, and *widow* of Capt. E. W. Walker, East Yorks Regt. *Educ.:* Haileybury; Dresden; Geneva. Studied with a view to the Diplomatic Service, but obtained commission in Worcestershire Militia, 1900; joined 1st Dorsets, 1902; transferred to 5th Dorsets, 1915; Capt., 1910; served S. Africa, 1902 (Queen's medal two clasps); European War, 1914-18, including Dardanelles (till evacuation), Egypt, and France (despatches, D.S.O. and bar); retired pay, 1923. *Recreations:* hunting, fishing, shooting. *Heir: kinsman,* Alan William Wingfield Hewitt [*b.* 11 Dec. 1900; *m.* 1935, Alison Mary Patricia, *d.* of T. W. Ashton; two *d.*]. [*Died* 5 *April* 1954.

LIGHTFOOT, Prof. Robert Henry, D.D.; Hon. D.D. (Aberdeen); F.B.A. 1953; **Ireland Professor of Exegesis of Holy Scripture, Oxford University, 1934-49, Professor Emeritus since 1949; Fellow, New Coll., Oxford, 1921-50; Fellow of Lincoln College, Oxford, 1950; *b.* Wellingborough, Northants, 30 Sept. 1883; *y. s.* of late Ven. R. P. Lightfoot, D.D., Archdeacon of Oakham, and Alice Gordon, *d.* of Rev. George Robbins, M.A., Vicar of Courteenhall, Northants. *Educ.:* Eton (Scholar); Worcester College, Oxford (Exhibitioner); Bishop's Hostel, Farnham. 1st Class Theological Honours, 1907; Liddon Student, 1907; Senior Greek Testament Prize, 1908; Senior LXX Prize, 1908; Curate of Haslemere, 1909-12; Bursar of Wells Theological College, 1912-13; Vice-Principal, 1913-16; Principal, 1916-19; Examining Chaplain to** the Archbishop of Canterbury, 1913-53; Fellow and Chaplain of Lincoln Coll., Oxford, 1919-21; Bampton Lecturer, 1934; Hon. Fellow of Worcester Coll., Oxford, 1938; **Six** Preacher at Canterbury Cathedral, 1948-53. ***Publications:* History and Interpretation in the Gospels, 1935; Locality and Doctrine in** the Gospels, 1938; The Gospel Message of St. Mark, 1950. *Address:* 3B Norham Gardens, Oxford. [*Died* 24 *Nov.* 1953.

LIGHTHALL, William Douw, Q.C. (Can.); LL.D., F.R.S.L., F.R.S.C.; Barrister, author, publicist; *b.* 27 Dec. 1857; *e. s.* of Wm. Francis (Schuyler-) Lighthall, Notaire, Montreal, and Margaret, *d.* of Captain Henry Wright of Chateauguay; *m.* 1890, Cybel, *d.* of John Wilkes and Alice Sabine, and *g.d.* of Rev. Henry Wilkes, D.D.; one *s.* two *d.* *Educ.:* High School of Montreal; McGill University. B.A., 1880; B.C.L. 1881; M.A. 1885; Representative Fellow, 1910; called to Bar, 1881; LL.D. (Hon.) 1921; Mayor of Westmount, Montreal, 1900-1-2; founded the Union of Canadian Municipalities, 1901; Honorary President; Metropolitan Parks Commissioner for Greater Montreal, 1910; Pres. Antiquarian Society of Montreal, 1912-28, Hon. President from 1928; President Royal Society of Canada, 1917; founded Chateau de Ramezay Museum, 1895; founded Great War Veterans' Association movement, 1915, now Canad. Legion B.E.S.L.; President Canadian Authors Association, 1930-1931; has introduced much municipal legislation into Parliament; received Civic Distinguished Service Award, 1939. *Publications:* numerous in verse and prose, 1887-1922; The Person of Evolution, 1930; Prehistoric Montreal; Resemblances between Chinese and Maya Civilization; The Diffusion Controversy: Astronomy Decides it? 1938; Origin of the Iroquoian Stock; General Statement of new Instinctivistic Philosophy (Evolutionary, Cosmic, Christian) in the Italian Symposium La Fase Attuale, 1936: The Law of Cosmic Evolutionary Adaptation, 1940; Yale University Philos. Symposium, 1944; and many ethical, historical, and literary pamphlets. *Recreation:* antiquarianism. *Address:* Westmount, Montreal, Canada. [*Died* 3 *Aug.* 1954.

LILLEY, His Hon. Cecil William; *b.* 23 March 1878; *s.* of Joseph Edward Lilley, J.P., barrister of the Middle Temple; *m.* 1936, Margaret Blanche, *y. d.* of late W. Herbert Williams. *Educ.:* Harrow. After travelling abroad, called to Bar 1900; Junior Counsel for Ministry of Labour, 1921; Bencher of the Middle Temple, 1932; Judge of County Courts, 1934-45. *Recreations:* fishing, golf. *Address:* Cleeve House, Goring-on-Thames. *Club:* Union. [*Died* 31 *March* 1953.

LILLEY, Thomas; Chairman Saxone, Lilley & Skinner (Holdings) Ltd., since 1957; Chm.

Lewis Berger & Sons Ltd. since 1948; *b.* 27 July 1902; *s.* of Thomas Lilley, late Chm. of Lilley & Skinner Ltd., and Florence Knight; *m.* 1940, Mrs. Vera Cottingham (*née* Sklarevskai). *Educ.:* University College School, Hampstead; Queens' College, Cambridge (M.A.). Joined Lilley & Skinner Ltd., 1925; Director Dec. 1927; Chm. Lilley & Skinner (Holdings) Ltd., 1951-57. Director of Lewis Berger & Sons Ltd., 1940; Vice-Chairman, 1942. *Recreations:* golf, tennis, shooting; interested in bloodstock breeding in connection with Irish Stud and Woolton House Stud, nr. Newbury, Berks. *Address:* Woolton House, nr. Newbury, Berks. *T.:* Highclere 328. *Club:* Bath. [*Died* 27 *Nov.* 1959.

LIMBERT, Roy; Theatre Director and Producer; *s.* of Charles Alberic William Limbert and Florence Isabel Strahan Campbell. *Educ.:* Blackheath; Bedford School. London Productions include: The School for Husbands, Royal Court Theatre, 1932; She Shall Have Music, Saville, 1934; Barnet's Folly, Haymarket, 1935; The Last Trump, Duke of York's, 1938; Geneva, Saville, 1938, and St. James's, 1939; Worth a Million, Saville, 1939; Music at Night, Westminster (with London Mask Theatre), 1939; In Good King Charles's Golden Days, New, 1940; Rookery Nook, St. Martin's, 1942; Mr. Bolfry, Westminster, 1943, and subsequently Playhouse; It Depends What You Mean, Westminster, 1944; The Forrigan Reel, Sadler's Wells, 1945. With Reandco the following: Dr. Angelus, Phœnix, and School for Spinsters, Criterion, 1947; The Anatomist, Westminster, 1948; Miss Mabel, Duchess, subs. Strand, 1948; Two Dozen Red Roses, Lyric, 1949; Black Chiffon, Westminster, 1949, 1950; Background, Westminster, 1950; Journey's End, Westminster, 1950; Lace On Her Petticoat, Ambassadors', 1950; Beauty And The Beast, Westminster, 1950 (Christmas); The Martins' Nest, Westminster, 1951; Taking Things Quietly, Ambassadors', 1951; Winter Sport, on tour, 1951; The Day's Mischief, Duke of York's, 1951-52; with Jack Hylton: Buoyant Billions, Lady Audley's Secret, Princes, 1949. With Sir Barry Jackson founded Malvern Festival in 1929, and was joint Director nine years until 1938 when he assumed sole control; at Malvern, 1938: Music at Night, Alexander, Coronation Time at Mrs. Beam's, St. Joan, Geneva, The Last Trump; and in 1939: In Good King Charles's Golden Days, What Say They, Professor from Peking, Dead Heat, Big Ben, Old Master. In 1932 formed Malvern Repertory Company which he still directs personally; presented ten special Malvern summer seasons at Arts Theatre, Cambridge, 1940-49. In 1944, 1945 and 1946, special Malvern seasons at Memorial Theatre, Stratford-upon-Avon. In 1948, first Harrogate High Season of Plays by Shaw. Responsible for many touring companies. In 1949, revived Malvern Festival with The Apple Cart, The Tressinghams, The Stars Bow Down, In Good King Charles's Golden Days, Max, and Buoyant Billions; Treasure on Pelican (J. B. Priestley), 1952; Not a Clue!, 1953; Not a Clue! (South Africa), 1954. Is a Director of Theatres, Cinemas and other undertakings; Pres., Malvern Canine Soc. *Address:* Wellington, Malvern, Worcs; 25 Haymarket, S.W.1. *T.:* Malvern 777, Whitehall 3332. *Clubs:* Savage, Royal Automobile, Green Room, Stage Golfing; Malvern (Malvern). [*Died* 29 *Nov.* 1954.

LIMPENNY, Eng.-Rear-Admiral Charles Joseph, C.M.G. 1946; D.S.O. 1918; R.N., retd.; *b.* 8 May 1881; *m.* Dorothy; two *d.* *Educ.:* Douai Abbey Coll., Midgham, nr. Reading. Served European War, 1914-18 (despatches, D.S.O.); A.D.C. to the King, 1933; Eng. Rear-Adm. and retired list, 1933. *Club:* Naval and Military. [*Died* 1 *March* 1952.

LINDLEY, Charles Gustaf; Retired Gen. Sec. Transport Workers Union, Sweden; retired Member of Parliament after 34 years; still Hon. Member of Transport Work Executive and retired Pres. International Transport Workers Federation; Editor of Swedish Transport Workers Trade Journal since 1897; *b.* Stockholm, 14 Oct. 1865; *m.* 1899; Elin Josefine Jonsson; no *c.* *Educ.:* Common school at Stockholm. Went to sea in 1881; sailed 13 years in British ships; joined the National Secular Society; took part in starting the Sailor and Firemen's Union in England; returned Sweden, 1894; started organising; Founder of Swedish Transport Workers Union, 1897; took part in starting the International Transport Workers Federation, 1896; Candidate for Swedish Parliament, 1895; elected, 1896; sat in the lower House until 1911 and was then placed in the Senate; now writing memorials and the 50 years' history of the transport workers' organisation. A Bust of Charles Lindley erected near Göteborg quay, 1952. *Recreations:* no time for recreations. *Address:* Önskeringsvagen 37, Smedslätten, Stockholm. *T.A.:* Transportarbete Stockholm. *T.:* 25 11 58. [*Died* 12 *Oct.* 1957.

LINDLEY, Sir (Mark) Frank, Kt., *cr.* 1944; C.B. 1937; LL.D., B.Sc.; *b.* Burgess Hill, Sussex, 20 Feb. 1881; *m.* 1913, Razel Elizabeth Hargreaves, B.A., L.R.A.M.; one *s.* one *d.* (and one *d.* decd.). *Educ.:* Brighton Science School; Univ. Coll., London; Hons. in Physics at B.Sc., Hons. and Univ. Scholarship at LL.B. (Lond.). Barrister-at-law, Barstow Law Scholar and King Edward VII Research Scholar (Middle Temple); joined the Examining Staff of the Patent Office, 1903; transferred to the Trade Marks Branch as Assistant Comptroller, 1926; Comptroller-General of Patents, Designs, and Trade Marks, and Comptroller of the Industrial Property Department of the Board of Trade, 1932-44; Member Enemy Debts Committee, Trade Marks Committee; Scientific Adviser to Appointments Dept. of Ministry of Labour and National Service, 1944-45. *Publication:* The Acquisition and Government of Backward Territory in International Law. *Recreation:* the countryside. *Address:* Holly Tree Cottage, East Gardens, Ditchling, Sussex. *T.:* Hassocks 669. [*Died* 15 *Aug.* 1951.

LINDNER, Ingram Joseph, Q.C. 1953. Called to the Bar, Middle Temple, 1935. *Address:* 1 New Square, Lincoln's Inn, W.C.2. *T.:* Holborn 5011; 26 Albert Court, Kensington, S.W.7. *T.:* Kensington 5980. [*Died* 26 *May* 1959.

LINDON, John Benjamin, O.B.E. 1919; Q.C. 1943; M.A., LL.M.; Bencher of Lincoln's Inn; *b.* 14 Sept. 1884; *m.* 1912, Myleta Fenton, *d.* of Sir William Corry, 2nd Bt.; one *s.* one *d.* *Educ.:* Harrow School; Gonville and Caius College, Cambridge (Mediæval and Modern Language Scholar and Law Scholar, 1st Class Law Tripos Parts I. and II.). War Trade Intelligence Dept. (Chief Intelligence Officer), 1915-1918; Ministry of Economic Warfare, 1939-1944. *Recreations:* sea-bathing, skating, walking, and Shakespearean research. *Address:* 12 New Square, and 19 Old Buildings, Lincoln's Inn, W.C.2. *T.:* Holborn 4596; St. Werstans, Malvern. *Clubs:* Oxford and Cambridge, Beefsteak. [*Died* 13 *July* 1960.

LINDRUM, Walter, O.B.E. 1958 (M.B.E. 1951); billiards champion; British Professional Champion, 1933; retired, 1950; *b.* 29 Aug. 1898; *m.* 1956, Beryl Russell. *Publication:* Billiards, 1930. *Address:* Walter Lindrum's Billiard Hall, 317 Flinders Lane, Melbourne, Australia. [*Died* 30 *July* 1960.

LINDSAY OF BIRKER, 1st Baron, *cr.* 1945, of Low Ground; **Alexander Dunlop Lindsay,** C.B.E. 1919; Hon. LL.D. Glasgow, Hon. LL.D. St. Andrews, Hon. LL.D. Princeton: Principal of University College of North Staffordshire since 1949; *b.* 1879;

m. 1907, Erica, *d.* of F. Storr; two *s.* one *d.* *Educ.:* Glasgow University; University College, Oxford. Shaw Fellow of the University of Edinburgh; Lecturer in Philosophy, Victoria University; Fellow of Balliol, Classical Tutor, 1906; Jowett Lecturer in Philosophy, 1911; Professor of Moral Philosophy, Glasgow University, 1922-1924; Master of Balliol College, Oxford, 1924-49, Hon. Fellow since 1949; Vice-Chancellor, Oxford University, 1935-38; served European War, 1914-19 (C.B.E., despatches). *Publications:* Translation of Republic of Plato; The Philosophy of Bergson; Karl Marx's Capital, 1925; The Nature of Religious Truth, 1927; The Essentials of Democracy, 1929; Christianity and Economics, 1933; Kant, 1934; The Churches and Democracy, 1934; The Moral Teaching of Jesus, 1937; The Two Moralities, 1940; The Modern Democratic State, 1943. *Recreation:* fishing. *Heir:* *s.* Hon. Michael Francis Morris Lindsay [*b.* 24 Feb. 1909; *m.* 1941, Hsiao Li, *d.* of Colonel Li Wen Che, Chinese Army, of Lishih, Shansi; one *s.* one *d.*]. *Address:* Keele Hall, Stoke-on-Trent, Staffs. [*Died* 18 *March* 1952.

LINDSAY, Major-Gen. George Mackintosh, C.B. 1936; C.M.G. 1919; C.B.E. 1946; D.S.O. 1917; p.s.c.; late Royal Tank Corps; *b.* 1880; *s.* of late Lieut.-Col. and Hon. Mrs. Lindsay, of Glasnevin House, Dublin; *m.* 1907, Constance, *d.* of George Stewart Hamilton; one *d.* *Educ.:* Sandroyd and Radley. Joined Royal Monmouthshire Royal Engineers (Militia), 1898; joined The Rifle Brigade, 1900; served S. African War, 1900-2 (despatches, Queen's medal and four clasps, King's medal and two clasps); European War, 1914-19 (despatches, Brevet Lt.-Col., C.M.G., D.S.O., Croix de Guerre, Order of Leopold of Belgium); Adjutant Customs and Docks Rifle Volunteers, 1907-08, and of 17th (County of London) Bn. The London Regt., 1908-11; Instructor School of Musketry, Hythe, 1913-15; Instructor, G.H.2 Machine Gun School, Wisque, 1915; G.S.O.2 Machine Gun Corps Training Centre, Grantham, 1915-16; Bde. Major, 99th Inf. Bde., 2nd Div., 1916-17; Chief Instructor G.H.2 Machine Gun School, 1917-18; Army Machine Gun Officer, 1st British Army in France, 1918; commanded 41st Bn., Machine Gun Corps, Germany, 1919; Staff College, 1920; commanded No. 1 Armoured Car Group, Irak, 1921-23; transferred from Rifle Bde. to Royal Tank Corps (now Royal Tank Regt.), 1923; Lt.-Col. in Tank Corps, June 1923, and Chief Instructor Royal Tank Corps Central Schools, Aug. 1923; Bt. Col., 1925; Subst. Col., 1925; Inspector Royal Tank Corps War Office, 1925-1929; Member Mechanical Warfare Board, 1926-29; B.G.S., Egypt Command, 1929-32; Comdr. 7th Inf. Bde., 1932-34; Comdr. Presidency and Assam Dist., India, 1935-39; retired pay, 1939; Director British Nat. Cadet Assoc., 1939; Commander 9th (Highland) Divn., 1939-40; A.D.C. to the King, 1928-34; Dep. Regional Commissioner for S.W. Civil Defence Region, 1940-44; Col. Comdt. Royal Tank Regt., 1938-47; Commissioner of British Red Cross and Order of St. John in N.W. Europe, 1944-46; K.J.St.J. 1947; Vice-Pres. Educational Interchange Council; President Machine Gun Corps Old Comrades Association and Chairman M.G.C. Officers' Club; Chm. Exec. Cttee. Army Boxing Assoc., 1928-29 (Navy and Army Middleweight Boxing Champion, 1909). Gold Kaisar-i-Hind Medal, 1939; Victory Medal, France-Germany Star and War Medal for British Liberation Army, 1944-45 Campaign in N.W. Europe; Cross of Merit, Netherlands Red Cross; Medals of: Belgian Red Cross, 1st Class; French Red Cross; Danish Red Cross; Swedish Red Cross; Silver Medal Am. Red Cross. Lees-Knowles Lecturer, Camb., 1942. Member of Council of Anglo-Danish Society and of Anglo-Netherlands Society. Vice-Pres. Army Boxing Assoc. *Publication:* The War on the Civil and Military Fronts, 1942; The Soviet-Communist Menace, 1952. *Recreations:* special interests: history and world affairs; sports: riding and shooting. *Address:* c/o Lloyds Bank, Cox & King's Branch, 6 Pall Mall, S.W.1. *Clubs:* Army and Navy, Royal Automobile; Kildare Street (Dublin). [*Died* 28 *Nov.* 1956.

LINDSAY, Philip, F.S.A. Scotland; Historical Novelist and film story writer; *b.* Sydney, N.S.W., 1 May 1906; *s.* of Norman Lindsay; *m.* Isobel Day; one *d.* *Educ.:* Church of England Grammar School, Queensland. Journalist in Sydney; Came to England to try to have his MSS. published 1929. *Publications:* *monographs:* Morgan in Jamaica, 1930; On Some Bones in Westminster Abbey, 1935; *novels:* Panama is Burning, 1932; One Dagger for Two, 1932; Here Comes The King, 1933; London Bridge is Falling, 1934; The Little Wench, 1935; The Duke is Served, 1936; Gentleman Harry Retires, 1937; The Bells of Rye, 1937; Bride for a Buccaneer, 1938; The Nutbrown Maid, 1939; Pudding Lane, 1940; The Fall of the Axe, 1940; The Gentle Knight, 1942; The Devil and King John, 1943; Jack Laughs at Locksmiths, 1943; He Rides in Triumph, 1945; Sir Rusty Sword, 1946; Whither Shall I Wander, 1947; The Queen's Confession, 1948; Heart of a King, 1948; The Loves of My Lord Admiral, 1949; There is no Escape, 1949; All that Glitters, 1949; Beauty or the Beast, 1950; Queen Honeypot, 1951; The Merry Mistress, 1952; The Shadow of the Red Barn, 1952; A Piece for Candlelight, 1953; An Artist in Love, 1954; The Counterfeit Lady, 1954; *history:* King Richard III, 1933; King Henry V, 1934; Kings of Merry England, 1936; Crowned King of England, 1937; Mirror for Ruffians, 1939; Hampton Court, 1948; For King or Parliament, 1949; The Great Buccaneer, 1950; The Loves of Florizel, 1951; The Queen Maker, 1951; The Secret of Henry the Eighth, 1953; The Haunted Man, 1953; *boy's book:* Knights at Bay, 1933; *autobiography:* I'd Live the Same Life Over, 1941; *biography:* Don Bradman, 1951. *Recreations:* studying English History and Criminal Records, watching cricket, reading almost anything. *Address:* c/o Curtis Brown, Ltd., 6 Henrietta Street, Covent Garden. W.C.2. [*Died* 4 *Jan.* 1958.

LINEHAM, Joseph, Ph.D., B.A.; Supernumerary 1943; Methodist Minister; *b.* 23 April 1869; *s.* of Joseph and Alice Lineham; *m.* 1st, 1896, Jane Brown, Sunderland (*d.* 1898); 2nd, 1901, Harriet Edith Brown (*d.* 1934); 3rd, 1940, Winifred Marie Jones, Antwerp. *Educ.:* Wesleyan Day School, Rochdale. Left school at 12 years; started work as errand boy; learned joinery in machine works; attended evening classes; became a Local Preacher; passed Entrance Examinations for Denominational College; after probationary period was received into Full Connexion. Circuits: Middlesbrough, Birmingham, London, North Shields, Heywood, Bristol, Newcastle-on-Tyne; Free Church Chaplain, Papworth Village Settlement; Home Mission Secretary, 1928 (ex-U.M. Section); studied Philosophy at Manchester and Birmingham; graduated by research, Bristol, 1920; admitted to degree of Ph.D. 1922; President of United Methodist Conference, 1924-25. *Address:* Tara, Nyetimber Lane, Bognor Regis. [*Died* 10 *Feb.* 1952.

LINEHAN, William, C.M.G. 1947; M.A., D.Litt.; Malayan Civil Service, retired; *b.* 6 August 1892; *s.* of late Senator Thomas Linehan, Whitechurch, Co. Cork; *m.* 1921, Mary, *d.* of D. O'Sullivan, Limerick; three *s.* one *d.* *Educ.:* Christian Brothers College and University College, Cork. Cadet, Malayan Civil Service, 1916; Asst. British Adviser,

Kelantan, 1931; Asst. Adviser, Johore, 1934; Sec. to British Resident, Perak, 1937; Director Education, Straits Settlements, and Adviser on Education, Malay States, 1938; Pres., Internat. Conf. of Pre-Historians of Far East, 1938. Interned in Changi Gaol and Sime Rd. Internment Camp, Singapore, 1942-45. Constitutional Adviser, Malayan Union, 1946; retd. from Malayan Civil Service, 1948; Director of Museums, Federation of Malaya, 1949-51. Asst. Director of Research in Oriental Languages, Univ. of Cambridge, 1955. *Publications:* History of Pahang, 1936; and various papers of **archæological interest published in Journal of Royal Asiatic Society, Malayan Branch.** *Address:* Fernlea, Barnhill Road, Dalkey, Co. Dublin. [*Died* 19 *Oct.* 1955.

LING, Brig. Christopher George, C.B., 1937; D.S.O. 1918; M.C.; p.s.c.; late Royal Engineers; *b.* 1880; 3rd *s.* of Christopher Ling, Wetheral, Cumberland; *m.* 1st, 1910, Frances Mary, *e. d.* of William Mitchell, Srinagar, Kashmir; one *s.* one *d.*; 2nd, 1928, Pamela Louise Archer, *widow* of Col. James Blair, C.M.G., C.B.E., D.S.O. *Educ.:* Bradfield College; R.I.E.C., Coopers Hill. Served European War, 1914-18 (despatches, M.C., D.S.O.); was Chief Instructor Royal Military Academy, Woolwich; a General Staff Officer in France and Germany; Director of Military Operations, A.H.Q. India, 1931-1933; Commander 10th (Jubbulpore) Infantry Brigade, India, 1933-37; retired, 1937; recalled Sept. 1939 and employed as General Staff Officer, War Office, until 1942, when again retired. *Address:* c/o Lloyds Bank, Ltd., 6 Pall Mall, S.W.1; Maybury House, Frimley, Surrey. *Club:* Naval and Military. [*Died* 21 *May* 1953.

LINLITHGOW, 2nd Marquess of (*cr.* 1902), **Victor Alexander John Hope,** K.G. 1943; K.T. 1928; P.C. 1935; G.C.S.I., *cr.* 1936; G.C.I.E., *cr.* 1929; O.B.E. 1919; D.L.; T.D.; Earl of Hopetoun, 1703; Viscount Aithrie, Baron Hope, 1703; Baron Hopetoun (U.K.) 1809; Baron Niddry (U.K.), 1814; Captain King's Body Guard for Scotland, Royal Company of Archers; Lord Lieutenant of West Lothian; Chancellor of Edinburgh University; Chairman, Midland Bank Ltd.; Chairman Board of Trustees, National Gallery of Scotland; *b.* 24 Sept. 1887; *e. s.* of 1st Marquess and Hon. Hersey de Moleyns (*d.* 1937), 3rd *d.* of 4th Lord Ventry; *S.* father, 1908; *m.* 1911, Doreen Maud, C.I. 1936, Kaiser-i-Hind Medal 1st Class, 2nd *d.* of Rt. Hon. Sir F. Milner, 7th Bt.; twin *s.* three *d.* *Educ.:* Eton. Served European War, 1914-18 (despatches); and commanded 1st Lothians and Border Armoured Car Company, 1920-26; Civil Lord of the Admiralty, 1922-24; Viceroy and Governor-General of India, 1936-43; Deputy Chairman of Unionist Party Organisation, 1924-26; President of Navy League, 1924-31; Chairman Departmental Committee on Distribution and Prices of Agricultural Produce, 1923; Chairman of Edinburgh and East of Scotland College of Agriculture, 1924-33; Chairman, Royal Commission on Indian Agriculture, 1926-28; Chairman Joint Select Committee on Indian Constitutional Reform, 1933; Chairman of Market Supply Committee, 1933-36; late Chm. Meat Advisory Committee, Board of Trade; Chm. of Medical Research Council, 1934-36; Chm. Governing Body, Imperial Coll. of Science and Technology, 1934-36; Lord High Commissioner to General Assembly of the Church of Scotland, 1944 and 1945. F.R.S.E. *Recreations:* golf, shooting. *Heir: s.* Earl of Hopetoun, M.C. *Address:* Grove House, Park Road, N.W.8. *T.:* Primrose 0970; Hopetoun House, South Queensferry, West Lothian. *T.:* South Queensferry 317. *Clubs:* Carlton; New (Edinburgh). [*Died* 5 *Jan.* 1952.

LINTON, Rt. Rev. James Henry, D.D. Lambeth, 1919; D.D. (Hon.) Durham; Asst. Bishop of Birmingham, 1937-Nov. 1954; Rector of Handsworth, 1935-Nov. 1954; Hon. Canon of Birmingham Cathedral since 1936; *s.* of Alexander Linton of Hawick, Scotland; *b.* Hawick, 9 Feb. 1879; *m.* Alicia Pears, *d.* of Rev. J. C. P. Aldous, late Chaplain and Chief Instructor H.M.S. Britannia; four *s.* one *d.* *Educ.:* St. John's College; Durham University, B.A.; C.M.S. College, Islington; 1st Class Prelim. T.E. 1904. Ordained, 1904; Vice-Principal C.M.S. Training College, Oyo, 1904-6; Home Organisation C.M.S., 1906-8; C.M.S. Missionary at Isfahan, Persia, 1908-19; Principal Stuart Memorial College, Isfahan, 1910-19; Bishop in Persia, 1919-35. *Publications:* Persian Sketches; Jesus Christus Heiland und Herr. *Address:* 109 Copse Hill, Wimbledon, S.W.20. *T.:* Wimbledon 3056. [*Died* 2 *June* 1958.

LINTON, Ralph, Ph.D.; **Sterling Professor of Anthropology, Yale University, since 1946; *b.* 27 Feb. 1893; *s.* of Isaiah W. Linton and Mary Gillingham; *m.* 1934, Adelin Briggs Hohlfeld; one *s.* *Educ.:* Swarthmore College (B.A. 1915); Univ. of Penn. (M.A. 1916); Columbia Univ., New York; Harvard (Ph.D. 1925). Anthropologist B.P. Bishop Museum, 1920-22; Assistant Curator of Ethnology, Field Museum, 1922-28; Professor Anthropology, Univ. of Wisconsin, 1928-37; Professor Anthropology Columbia University, 1937-46. Field work American Southwest, Guatemala, Polynesia, Madagascar, East and South Africa. Past member Social Science Research Council, National Research Council. Editor American Anthropologist, 1939-45. U.S. National Academy of Sciences, 1945; President American Anthropological Assoc., 1946.** *Publications:* **The Tanala, A Hill Tribe of Madagascar, 1932; The Study of Man, 1936; Acculturation in Seven American Indian Tribes, 1940; The Cultural Background of Personality, 1945; Arts of the South Seas, 1946; numerous articles.** *Recreations:* **reading and conversation.** *Address:* **346** Willow Street, New Haven. Conn., U.S.A. [*Died* 24 *Dec.* 1953.

LINTON, The Hon. Sir Richard, Kt., *cr.* 1936; *b.* 7 Feb. 1879; *s.* of James Linton; *m.* 1909, Ethel Bannister, Wellington, N.Z.; two *s.* *Educ.:* Terrace End School and Kenneth Wilson's High School, Palmerston, N. Retired paper, machinery, and general merchant; founder of Big Brother Movement in Australia, 1924, and was its Chairman; M.L.A. Victoria for Boroondara, 1927-33; Hon. Minister, 1929; Secretary to Argyle Cabinet, 1932-33; Agent-General for Victoria, 1933-36; Hon. Defence Liaison Officer, Voluntary Organisations, 1940; Hon. Defence Services Enquiry and Advice Officer until 1946. *Recreations:* tennis, golf; donor of the Linton Tennis Cup for Australian Juniors. *Address:* 233 Kooyong Road, Toorak, Melbourne, Victoria, Australia. [*Died* 21 *Sept.* 1959.

LINTON, Robert George, Ph.D., M.R.C.V.S.; *b.* 16 Feb. 1882; *s.* of late Rev. G. Linton, Corsham, Wilts; *m.* 1913, Gwendoline, *e. d.* of late A. Baird, Coveyheugh, Reston, Berwickshire; two *s.* *Educ.:* Royal (Dick) Veterinary College, Edinburgh. Vice-Principal and Professor of Hygiene, Royal (Dick) Veterinary College, Edinburgh; retired, 1944. *Publications:* Veterinary Hygiene, 2nd ed. 1934, 3rd ed. 1940, 4th edn., 1952; Animal Nutrition, 1927, 2nd edn., 1942, 3rd edn. 1950; various papers in scientific journals. *Recreations:* gardening, fishing. *Address:* Fairlaw Farmhouse, Reston, Berwickshire. *T.:* Reston 242. [*Died* 28 *Jan.* 1960.

LION, Flora, R.P.; *b.* London. *Educ.:* Royal Academy Schools and Paris under Jean Paul Laurens. Picture entitled My Mother, purchased for Tate Gallery, 1915; awarded Silver Medal Société des Artistes Français, Paris, 1921; twenty Lithographic Portraits acquired by the British Museum Print Room, 1923; has exhibited in R.A. Salon, Paris, Germany, Venice, etc.; Portrait of Madame Merry del Val, Royal Academy, 1920; portrait group of The Duchess of York, The Lady Elphinstone, The Lady Rose Leveson-Gower, Royal Academy, 1924; Portraits of Princess Alice, Countess of Athlone, Sir Henry Wood, and Mrs Duncan MacLeod of Skeabost, Isle of Skye, N.B., R.A., 1937; The Duchess of Kent, R.A., 1939; held own exhibition at Alpine Art Gallery of thirty-three portraits; also one-man exhibitions at Barbizon House of portraits and landscapes, 1929; Fine Arts Gallery, New Bond Street, 1937; Knoedler's Gallery, Old Bond Street, 1940, portrait of Her Majesty the Queen, Field Marshal The Earl Alexander of Tunis, The Countess Alexander, and other portraits; Two murals for Great Westminster House: Sir John Evelyn crossing the frozen Thames at Horse Ferry, 1683, The Fast Frost Fair, 1814. Gold Medal Société des Artistes Français, Paris, 1949. *Address:* 3 Avenue Studios, 76 Fulham Road, S.W.3. *T.:* Kensington 3719; 1A Sydney Close, S.W.3. *T.:* Kensington 6494. [*Died* 15 *May* 1958.

LIPSON, Ephraim, M.A.; Economic Historian; *b.* 1 Sept. 1888; *s.* of H. R. Lipson and Eva, *d.* of Michael Jacobs; unmarried. *Educ.:* The Royal Grammar School (now King Edward VII School), Sheffield; Trinity Coll., Cambridge. First Class Honours in both parts of the Historical Tripos (1909-10). Engaged in literary work and in historical teaching at Oxford, 1910-31; Reader in Economic History in the University of Oxford, 1921-31; has examined at Univs. of Oxford, Edinburgh, Aberdeen, Belfast, etc.; Lowell Lecturer at Boston (U.S.A.), 1932; Visiting Lecturer at University of California (summer sessions 1933). Went round the world, 1932-34. *Publications:* The Economic History of England: Vol. I. The Middle Ages, 1915 (12th ed. revised and enlarged, 1958); Vols. II. and III. The Age of Mercantilism, 1931 (6th ed. revised and enlarged, 1956); Europe in the Nineteenth Century, 1916 (10th ed. 1957); Europe, 1914-39, 1940 (7th ed. 1957); The History of the English Woollen and Worsted Industries, 1921; Increased Production, 1921; A Planned Economy or Free Enterprise—the Lessons of History, 1944 (2nd ed. 1946); The Growth of English Society—A Short Economic History, 1949 (4th ed. 1958) translated into Japanese; A Short History of Wool and its Manufacture, 1953; Reflections on Britain and the United States, 1959. Founded (and first editor of) The Economic History Review. Contributor to the Transactions of the Royal Historical Society, the English Historical Review, the Fortnightly Review, various encyclopædias, etc. *Recreation:* travel. *Address:* c/o New College, Oxford. [*Died* 22 *April* 1960.

LISTER-KAYE, Sir Kenelm Arthur, 5th Bt., *cr.* 1812; Sqdn. Ldr. (temp.) R.A.F.; Capt. late 3rd Bn. The West Yorkshire Regt.; *b.* 27 March 1892; *s.* of Sir Cecil Lister-Kaye, 4th Bt., and Lady Beatrice Adeline Pelham-Clinton, *d.* of 6th Duke of Newcastle; *S.* father, 1931; *m.* 1949, Jean, *widow* of Major R. E. Balders, M.C., Boulderwood, Halifax, N.S. *Educ.:* Eton; Trinity College, Oxford. *Heir: cousin,* Lister, *b.* 19 Dec. 1873. *Address:* Meares-Court, Mullingar, Eire. *Clubs:* R.A.F.; Kildare Street (Dublin). [*Died* 28 *Feb.* 1955.

LITAUER, Stefan; Doctor of Law; Professor at Warsaw Academy for Political Sciences and broadcaster on international affairs at Polish Radio in Warsaw; *b.* 31 May 1892. *Educ.:* Studied law and history at Univs. of Paris, Heidelberg, and Erlangen. In pre-war Polish Govt. and Diplomatic Service, 1918-1929; served as Secretary at Polish Diplomatic Mission in Charkov (Ukraine), 1922-23; Second Secretary at Polish Legation at Moscow, 1924; Counsellor at Russian section of Polish Ministry for Foreign Affairs in Warsaw, 1925-27; Assistant Chief of Press Department of Polish Ministry for Foreign Affairs, 1928-29; Chief London Corresp. of Polish Telegraph Agency, 1929-44; Pres. of Foreign Press Association in London, 1936-1941; in charge of Press Service of Polish Ministry of Information in London, 1941-44; Official Liaison Officer between British and Polish Ministries of Information; left Polish Emigré Government service, May 1944, and joined Editorial Staff of London News Chronicle as Special Correspondent for Eastern Europe; appointed by new Polish Govt. (Oct. 1945), Minister-Counsellor and Chargé d'Affaires at Polish Embassy, Washington, 1945-46; appointed Polish Minister in Canberra but appt. not taken up. Member Polish Deleg. to third session U.N. Gen. Assembly, Paris, 1948; now on leave from diplomatic service for scientific work and research. *Address:* Polna 3B, Warsaw, Poland. [*Died* 23 *April* 1959.

LITHGOW, Sir James, 1st Bt. of Ormsary, *cr.* 1925; G.B.E., *cr.* 1945; C.B. 1947; M.C., T.D., D.L., J.P.; Hon. LL.D. (Glasgow); Vice-Lieutenant of Renfrewshire since 1943; *b.* 1883; *e. s.* of late W. T. Lithgow of Drums, Renfrewshire; *m.* 1924, Gwendolyn Amy, *d.* of late John Robinson Harrison of Scalesceugh, Cumberland; one *s.* two *d.* *Educ.:* Glasgow Academy; Paris. Shipbuilder; Chm., Lithgows Ltd. and other Companies; commissioned Renfrew and Dumbarton R.G.A., 1902; served European War, 1914-19 (despatches, wounded), France; seconded to Admiralty as Dir. of Shipbuilding Production, 1917; Lt.-Col. 1917; Hon. Col. Clyde Heavy Batt. R.A. (T.A.), 1924; Member of Board of Admiralty, 1940-46, as Controller of Merchant Shipbuilding and Repairs; Member County of Renfrew T.A. & A.F.A. Pres., Clyde Shipbuilders' Assoc., 1908; Shipbuilding Employers' Fed., 1922; British Employers' Confed., 1924; British Employers' Deleg. at Internat. Labour Conf. (League of Nations) and Member of Governing Body, 1922-28 and 1933-35; Pres.: Fed. of British Industries, 1930-31-32; Institution of Engineers and Shipbuilders in Scotland, 1929-31; Member of Central Electricity Board, 1927-30; Pres.: British Iron & Steel Fed., 1943-44-45; The Iron & Steel Research Assoc.; Chm., Scottish Development Council, 1931-39. *Recreation:* shooting. *Heir: s.* William James, *b.* 10 May 1934. *Address:* Ormsary House, Ormsary, by Ardrishaig, Argyllshire; Gleddoch House, Langbank, by Port Glasgow, Renfrewshire. *Clubs:* New (Glasgow); Royal Scottish Automobile. [*Died* 23 *Feb.* 1952.

LITTLE, Eng. Rear-Adm. Henry Augustus, C.B. 1935; R.N., retired; *b.* Feb. 1883; *s.* of late Eng. Rear-Admiral Edwin Little and Bessie H. Little; *m.* 1932, Diana, *d.* of Dr. W. H. Cheetham, Guiseley, Yorks.; one *d.* *Educ.:* Porstmouth Grammar School; R.N.E.C., Devonport; R.N. College, Greenwich. Eng. Capt. 1928; A.D.C. to the King, 1934; Eng. Rear-Adm., 1934; served European War, 1914-19; retired list, 1937; served on retired list, 1937-41. *Address:* Downsclose, Ottery St. Mary, Devon. [*Died* 28 *July* 1954.

LITTLE, John Carruthers, C.B.E. 1941; *b.* 9 Sept. 1874; *s.* of William Little and Elizabeth Carruthers, Farmers, Penton, Cumberland; *m.* 1899; one *s.* one *d.* *Educ.:* Board School; Evening Classes. Engineer; became Trade Union Official in 1922 before which date was actively engaged in Heavy Production in Engineering; from 1897 until 1939 played an active part in Local, National and International Trade Union Affairs; National President Amalgamated Engineering Union, 1933-39; Member of Cttee. Investigating use of skilled men in the Services, 1941; Industrial Commissioner, Ministry of Labour and National Service, 1940-45; Member of Admiralty Manpower Economy Cttee., 1947; Member of Cttee. on Houses of Outstanding Historic and Architectural Interest. *Address:* 12 King George Road, Fawdon Park, Gosforth, Newcastle upon Tyne.

[*Died* 13 *Sept.* 1957.

LITVINOV, Maxim; (né **Meer Wallach**); Russian diplomat; *b.* Poland, 17 July 1876; *s.* of Maxim Litvinoff and Anne Perló; *m.* 1916, Ivy, *d.* of Walter Low; one *s.* one *d.* *Educ.:* Bialystok Real School. Member of Kiev Committee of Russian Social Democratic Labour Party; Delegate of same party to International Socialist Bureau; Editor of daily paper, New Life, in Leningrad. Lived 10 years in Britain, working as printer, clerk, commercial traveller and teacher of Russian. Appointed as the first diplomatic representative of Soviet Republic to Britain, 1917, for a short period; returned to Russia, 1918; employed there in Foreign Office; during 1920's headed Russian delegates to disarmament commns.; at Disarmament Conference, 1927; Foreign Minister, 1930-39; Ambassador to U.S.A., 1941-43; Deputy Minister of Foreign Affairs during 1946; retired, 1946. Deputy to the Supreme Soviets of the U.S.S.R. and of the R.S.F.S.R. *Publications:* The Bolshevik Revolution; Pamphlets; Tracts. *Recreations:* cycling, ski-ing, riding, walking.

[*Died* 31 *Dec.* 1951.

LIVINGSTON, Sir Noel (Brooks), Kt., *cr.* 1941; Custos Rotulorum for Parish of Kingston, Island of Jamaica, 1936-52; also Solicitor of Supreme Court of Judicature of Jamaica and first President of new Legislative Council, 1945; *b.* 9 Nov. 1882; 2nd *s.* of late Ross Jameson Livingston and Ellen Campbell Harris; *m.* 1924, Amy Blanche (*d.* 1945), *widow* of Surgeon-General Sir Charles McD. Cuffe, K.C.B.; no *c.*; *m.* 1948, Dr. Olga Josephine McDonagh, *d.* of late Alfred Ellen, Sticklepath, Devon, England. *Educ.:* Kingston Church of England Grammar School, Jamaica. Solicitor, 1906, and Notary Public, 1916; Ex-Officio Member of Kingston and St. Andrew Corporation, Kingston, Jamaica. *Publication:* Sketch Pedigrees of some of the Early Settlers in Jamaica, 1909. *Recreation:* West Indian Historical Research. *Address:* Callendar, 10 King's House Rd., Half Way Tree, Jamaica; Airy Castle, Stony Hill, Jamaica. *T.A.:* Lival.

[*Died* 17 *Jan.* 1954.

LIVINGSTONE, Sir Richard Winn, Kt., *cr.* 1931; M.A.; Hon. D.Litt. Cambridge, Belfast, Toronto, Durham, Manchester, London, Columbia and Yale; Hon. LL.D. St. Andrews, Dublin; Hon. Fellow Corpus Christi College, Oxford; President, 1933-50, late Fellow, Tutor, Librarian; Hon. Fellow, New College; *b.* 1880; *e. s.* of late Rev. Canon Livingstone of Liverpool and Hon. Mrs. Livingstone; *m.* 1913, Cécile, *e. d.* of late George Maryon-Wilson, J.P.; one *s.* two *d.* (and one *s.* killed, 1944). *Educ.:* Winchester; New College, Oxford. Hertford Scholarship, 1900; 1st Class Mods.; Latin Verse, 1901; 1st Lit. Hum. 1903; Arnold Essay Prize, 1905; temporary Assistant Master at Eton College, 1917-18; Vice-Chancellor of the Queen's Univ., Belfast, 1924-33. Chairman of the Council of St. Hugh's College, Oxford, 1935-37; Pres. Educational Section of British Association, 1936; President of the Hellenic Society, 1938; President of Classical Association, 1940-41; Member of the Appellate Tribunal for Conscientious Objectors, 1941; Vice-Chancellor, Oxford University, 1944-47. Member of the Prime Minister's Committee on Classics, 1920; Editor of Classical Review (with J. T. Sheppard), 1920-22; General Editor of, and originator of the method employed in, The Clarendon Series of Greek and Latin Authors. Member, American Philosophical Soc. Has given following lectures at Univs. in the U.S. and Canada: Martin (Oberlin Coll.), 1934; Burwash (Toronto), 1945; Pitcairn-Crabbe (Pittsburgh), 1946; Dunning (Queen's University, Kingston), 1952; Vanuxem (Princeton), 1952; Sarah Vanderbilt (Smith Coll.), 1956. Commandeur, Légion d'Honneur; King Haakon VII Liberty Cross (Norway). *Publications:* The Greek Genius and its Meaning to Us (2nd ed. 1915, translated into Greek, Japanese, Spanish); A Defence of Classical Education (2nd impression, 1917); (with C. E. Freeman, Caesar's Gallic War, Books IV. and V., 1920; Books VI. and VII., 1921; Editor and Contributor The Legacy of Greece, 1921 (trans. into Spanish, Italian, Arabic) The Pageant of Greece, 1923; The Mission of Greece, 1928; Greek Ideals and Modern Life, 1935 (trans. into German, Spanish and Greek); Portrait of Socrates, 1938; Selections from Plato (World's Classics), 1940; The Future in Education, 1941 (trans. into German, Polish, Greek, Italian, Danish and Arabic); Education for a World Adrift, 1943 (translated into German, Polish and Italian); On Education (American ed. of two volumes above), 1944; Thucydides (World's Classics), 1943; Plato and Modern Education (Rede Lecturer), 1944; Some Tasks for Education, 1947 (trans. into Greek and Italian): Education and the Spirit of the Age, 1952; The Rainbow Bridge, 1959. Essay in Warburg Vorträge, 1930-31; various articles. *Address:* 14 Rawlinson Road, Oxford. *Club:* Athenæum.

[*Died* 26 *Dec.* 1960.

LJUNGBERG, Göta; Opera Singer; *b.* Sundsvall, Sweden. *Educ.:* Royal College of Music, Sweden; Mme. Cahier and Professor Daniel in Berlin. Engaged at Royal Opera House, Stockholm, 1918-26; Staatsoper, Berlin, 1927; Covent Garden, 1924, 1926, 1927, 1928, 1929; New York Metropolitan Opera, 1931-35; singing the parts of: Elsa in Lohengrin; Kundry in Parsifal; Elisabeth in Tannhäuser; Sieglinde in Valkyrie; Eva in Meistersinger; Bryunhilden and Isolde; Senta in Holländer; Tosca; Santuzza in Cavalleria Rusticana; Leonore in La forza del destino; Salome; Crysothemis in Elektra; Anita in Jonny spielt auf; Asteria in Nero; created Judith in Goossens' first performance at Covent Garden, 1929. *Address:* 26 E. 93rd Street, New York City, N.Y.

[*Died* 28 *June* 1955.

LLEWELLIN, 1st Baron, *cr.* 1945, of Upton; **John Jestyn Llewellin**, P.C. 1941; G.B.E., *cr.* 1953 (C.B.E. 1939; O.B.E. 1926); M.C., T.D., M.A.; D.L. Dorset; Governor-General and C.-in-C. Federation of Rhodesia and Nyasaland, since 1953; Knight Commander of the Commandery in Central Africa of the Venerable Order of the Hospital of St. John of Jerusalem; *b.* Chevening, nr. Sevenoaks, 6 February 1893; *s.* of William Llewellin of Upton House, Poole, Dorset, and Frances Mary Wigan; unmarried. *Educ.:* Eton; Univ. Coll., Oxford. Commissioned in Dorset R.G.A., Sept. 1914; served in France, 1915-19; called to Bar, 1921; late Col. commanding Dorset Heavy Brigade; M.P. (U.) Uxbridge Division Middlesex, 1929-1945; Parliamentary Private Secretary to P.M.G., Sept.-Oct. 1931, and to First Commissioner of Works, 1931-35; Assistant Government Whip, 1935-37; Civil Lord of the Admiralty, 1937-39; Parliamentary Secretary, Ministry of Supply, 1939-40; Parliamentary Sec., Ministry of Aircraft Production, 1940-41; Parliamentary Secretary, Ministry of War Transport, 1941-42; President of the Board of Trade, 1942; Minister of Aircraft Production, Feb.-Nov. 1942; Minister Resident in Washington for Supply, 1942-43; Minister of Food, 1943-1945; Member B.B.C. Gen. Advisory Council, 1952. Chairman Dorset Quarter Sessions, 1950-53; President: Royal Society Prevention of Accidents, 1945-53; Fedn. of Chambers of Commerce of British Empire, 1948-51. *Address:* Upton House, Poole, Dorset. *Clubs:* Carlton, Leander.

[*Died* 24 *Jan.* 1957 (*ext.*).

LLEWELYN, Sir Charles L. D. V.; *see* Venables-Llewelyn.

LLOYD, Lieut.-Col. Charles Geoffrey, C.I.E. 1919; M.C.; J.P.; now employed by Board of Agriculture, Kenya Colony; *b.* 12 March 1884; *s.* of late Rt. Rev. John Lloyd, D.D., Bishop of Swansea, and Mrs. Lloyd, *née* Miss Bishop of Dolygarreg, Carmarthenshire; *m.* 1920, Nora Evelyn, *y. d.* of W. B. Jameson, of the Roundel, Wittersham, Rye; two *d.* *Educ.:* Repton; Cambridge. The Essex Regiment, 1904-12; subsequently Indian Army; war service, 1914-20, France, Dardanelles, Egypt, Mesopotamia, Kurdistan, and Northern Persia; retired 1935; re-employed, 1940, 1st E.A. Pioneers. J.P. Nairobi. *Publications:* Warlike Snips and Snaps; Matrimonial Weals and Woes; From an Indian State; Babu Piche Lal in Europe; Higgledey-Piggledey, etc. *Address:* Karen House, Ngong, Kenya. *Club:* Bath. [*Died* 12 *Dec.* 1953.

LLOYD, David John, M.A.; *b.* 6 March 1886; *s.* of Daniel Lloyd, J.P., and Jane Peregrine; *m.* 1914, Olwen, *d.* of Rev. D. J. Beynon, Southampton; three *s.* one *d.* (and one *s.* died on active service). *Educ.:* Swansea Grammar School; University College, Cardiff (Exhibitioner); Oriel College, Oxford (Exhibitioner). Assistant Classical Master, Liverpool Collegiate School, 1911-17; R.N.A.S. and R.A.F. 1917-19; Head Master, Port Talbot County School, 1919-20; Head Master, Newport (Mon.) High School, 1921-35; Head Master, Grove Park School, Wrexham, 1935-46; Ex-Member I.A.H.M. H.M.C., Welsh Secondary Schools Assoc. (Ex-Pres.); Classical Assoc. (Life); Oxford Union Society. Examiner: Oxf. Delegacy, Camb. Syndicate, Joint Matric. Board, and Central Welsh Board; Member: Menai Bridge U.D.C., 1947-51; Court of Governors and Council, University Coll., Bangor; Board of Managers, Menai Bridge Primary and Secondary Schools. *Recreation:* gardening. *Address:* Maes-yr-Awel, Menai Bridge, Anglesey. [*Died* 2 *Nov.* 1951.

LLOYD, Eric Ivan, M.A.; M.B.; B.Ch. (Cantab.); F.R.C.S. (Eng.); Orthopaedic Surgeon to Hospital for Sick Children, Great Ormond Street; and Consulting Orthopaedic Surgeon to Royal Northern Hospital; *b.* Birmingham, 1 July 1892; 3rd *s.* of John Henry and Gertrude E. Lloyd, Edgbaston Grove, Birmingham; *m.* 1926, Antoinette Marie, *o. d.* of A. S. Roux, Pretoria, S. Africa; one *s.* one *d.* *Educ.:* Leighton Park, Reading; Trinity Coll., Cambridge; St. Bartholomew's Hospital. During European War, 1914-18, after some service abroad with Friends Ambulance Unit, qualified and spent two and a half years as Surgeon.-Lt. R.N. (temp.); two years in H.M.S. Shannon; three years at St. Bartholomew's Hospital as House Physician, House Surgeon and Demonstrator of Anatomy; two and a half years a resident medical officer at the Hospital for Sick Children, Great Ormond Street, to the honorary staff of which he was appointed in 1926; visited many of the Surgical Clinics of Canada and U.S.A., 1923; F.R.S.M.; (late Pres. Orth. Section); Member Internat. Society of Orthopædic Surgeons; Fellow of British Orthopædic Association; Vice-Pres. Orthopædic Section, British Medical Association, 1934. *Publications:* many papers in medical periodicals. *Recreations:* Half blue for Athletics (½ mile), Cambridge, 1914. *Address:* Hammonds End House, Harpenden, Herts. *T.:* Harpenden 650. [*Died* 26 *Nov.* 1954.

LLOYD, Brig.-General Frederick Charles, C.B. 1918; *b.* 1860; *y. s.* of late Bartholomew Clifford Lloyd, Q.C.; *m.* Millicent (*d.* 1948), *d.* of Thomas Garnett; one *s.* one *d.* *Educ.:* Haileybury. Served South African War, commanding 7th Mounted Infantry, 1900-02 (despatches, Queen's medal 5 clasps, King's medal 2 clasps); European War, commanding N. Wales Infantry Brig., 1914-18 (C.B.); commanded 2nd Lincolnshire Regt., 1908-12. *Address:* 10 Cromwell Rd., Hove, Sx. [*Died* 3 *June* 1957.

LLOYD, Major-Gen. Herbert William, C.B. 1919; C.M.G. 1917; C.V.O. 1920; D.S.O. 1915; E.D. 1946; p.s.c.; *b.* 24 Nov. 1883; *s.* of William Lloyd, Victoria, Australia; *m.* 1914, Meredith, *d.* of Col. W. B. Pleasents, Victoria; two *s.* one *d.* *Educ.:* Wesley College, Melbourne. Captain and Adjutant Victorian Field Artillery, 1908-9; Administrative and Instructional Staff, 1910; Royal Australian Field Artillery to 1919; Director of Artillery, Australian Army H.Q., 1920; Staff College, Quetta, India, 1920-21; General Staff until 1925; G.O.C. 2nd Division, New South Wales, Australian Military Forces, 1940; Director-General A.I.F. Recruiting, 1940 and 1941; Adm. Comd. Second Aust. Army, 1943-46; served European War, 1915-18 Gallipoli, France, and Belgium (despatches, 4th Class Order of White Eagle of Serbia, Bt. Major and Bt. Lieut.-Col. D.S.O., C.M.G., C.B., C.V.O.); M.L.A., N.S. Wales, 1929-30 and 1932-41. *Address:* 32 Darling Point Road, Darling Point, Sydney, Australia. *Club:* Union (Sydney). [*Died* 10 *Aug.* 1957.

LLOYD, Sir Howard Watson, Kt., *cr.* 1937; formerly Chairman, Bank of Adelaide, and Chairman of many other companies; *b.* North Adelaide, 3 March 1868; *s.* of late John Sanderson Lloyd and Charlotte Emily, *d.* of Henry Watson; *m.* 1898, Mary, *d.* of late H. L. Ayers; two *s.* one *d.* *Educ.:* St. Peter's College, Adelaide, S.A. *Address:* 24 Trinity Street, College Town, South Australia; 22 King William Street, Adelaide. *T.A.:* Orpheus Adelaide. *T.:* F1548 and Cent. 994. *Club:* Adelaide (Adelaide). [*Died* 20 *May* 1955.

LLOYD, J. A. T., LL.B.; author and journalist; *s.* of Arthur Rickard Lloyd; *g.s.* of Thomas Lloyd of Beechmount, Co. Limerick, J.P., D.L.; *m.* 1st, 1904, Isabel Keith (*d.* 1913), *d.* of David Campbell, Glasgow; 2nd, 1917, Jeanne, *d.* of Antoine de Testenoire and Gabrielle, *d.* of Charles, Marquis de Peyronny. *Educ.:* Rugby; Trinity College, Dublin. Was for some time on the staff of the Toronto Week; Assistant Editor of T.P.'s Weekly, 1903-8. *Publications:* The Lady of Kensington Gardens, 1908; Sappho (anonymous), 1910; Two Russian Reformers, 1910; A Great Russian Realist, 1912; The Three Destinies, 1912; The Real Canadian, 1913; Quis? 1917; The Uprooters, 1918; Prestige, 1920; The Atheist, 1921; Leila Braddock, 1923; The Skein, 1925; Eros, 1926; Good-Better-Best, 1926; The Staircase, 1927 Proximity, 1928; The Murder of Edgar Allan Poe, 1931; Ivan Turgenev, 1943; Fyodor Dostoevsky, 1947; several translations from the French; several short stories. *Address:* 23 Gwydyr Mansions, Hove 2, Sussex. [*Died* 18 *Sept.* 1956.

LLOYD, Sir John Buck, Kt., *cr.* 1928; partner in the firms of Shaw Wallace & Co., India, Ceylon, and R. G. Shaw & Co., of London; *b.* 17 Nov. 1874; *s.* of late John Buck Lloyd, Tunbridge Wells; *m.* 1913, Flora Marguerite (*d.* 1942), *d.* of late Frederick Carlisle, Sunningdale; (one *s.* killed in action 5 Feb. 1943) three *d.* *Educ.:* Harrow. Went to India in 1897 to join the firm of Shaw Wallace & Co.; returned to England to become a Director of Anglo-Persian Oil Co. Ltd., 1919; retired, 1946; Member of Reorganisation Commission for Fat Stock Industry, 1932. *Address:* Waterton House, Cirencester, Glos. *Clubs:* Oriental, City of London. [*Died* 30 *Oct.* 1952.

LLOYD, Lt.-Col. Sir John Conway, Kt., *cr.* 1938; M.C.; *b.* 1878; *m.* 1903, Marion Clive, *yr. d.* of Maj.-Gen. William Clive Justice, C.M.G.; one *s.* one *d.* *Educ.:* Eton; Christ Church, Oxford. Sheriff of Brecknockshire, 1906; served European War, 1914-19. *Address:* Abercynrig, near Brecon. [*Died* 30 *May* 1954.

LLOYD, Brig.-Gen. John Hardress, D.S.O. 1917; Legion of Honour; D.L., J.P. King's Co.; Captain 21st Lancers, retired; *b.* 14 Aug. 1874; *s.* of John Lloyd, D.L., of Gloster, King's Co., and Susan, *d.* of Rossborough Colclough, D.L., of Tintern Abbey, Co. Wexford; *m.* 1903, Adeline (*d.* 1933), *d.* of late Sir Samuel Wilson, M.P.; no *c.* *Educ.:* Wellington; Sandhurst. Joined 4th Dragoon Guards; served Tirah, N.W. Frontier, 1897; S. Africa, 1901-2, as A.D.C. to Lt.-Gen. Sir E. L. Elliot; went out with 4th Dragoon Guards, Aug. 1914; Gallipoli, May 1915-Jan. 1916, with 29th Div.; commanded 1st Inniskilling Fusiliers, May 1916-Jan. 1917; joined Tank Corps, Jan. 1917; Brigade Commander, April 1917; 1st Tank Group Commander, Sept. 1918 (D.S.O. and bar, despatches six times). *Recreations:* polo, hunting, ski-ing; captained English Polo Team, America, 1911; Irish Team *v.* England on several occasions. *Address:* Glasderrymore, Roscrea, Ireland. *T.A.:* Shinrone. *Clubs:* Cavalry, Hurlingham, Roehampton; Kildare Street (Dublin). [*Died* 28 *Feb.* 1952.

LLOYD, Ven. John Walter, B.A.; Archdeacon of Montgomery and Vicar of Llansantffraid since 1944; *b.* 11 March 1879; *s.* of Rev. Canon Joseph Lloyd and Mary Lloyd; *m.* 1907, Elin Katherine Myvanwy, *d.* of Meilir Owen, J.P., Mysevin, Denbighshire; one *s.* one *d.* *Educ.:* Llandovery School; St David's College, Lampeter; St. Michael's, Aberdare. Curate of Denbigh, 1902-07; Rector of Pontfadog, 1907-1913; Vicar of Broughton, 1913-17; Vicar of Chirk, 1917-44; Rural Dean of Llangollen; Prebendary of Meifod (Sacrist) in St. Asaph Cathedral. *Address:* Llansantffraid Vicarage, Mont., N. Wales. *T.:* Llansantffraid 44. [*Died* 9 *July* 1951.

LLOYD, Col. Langford Newman, C.M.G. 1916; D.S.O. 1901; O.St.J. 1943; V.H.S. 1926; M.R.C.S., L.R.C.P.; late Dep. Dir. Medical Services Joint War Organisation British Red Cross Society and Order of St. John of Jerusalem; Member of Council and Vice-President National Rifle Association; Member of many International Rifle Teams; *b.* 28 Dec. 1873; *s.* of late Colonel E. G. K. P. Lloyd; *m.* Lilian May (*d.* 1946), *d.* of late Surgeon-General Sir W. R. Hooper, K.C.S.I., K.H.S.; *m.* 1949, Sylvia Margaret (*née* Hughes-D'Aeth), *widow* of Brig.-Gen. C. E. Macquoid, C.I.E., D.S.O., I.A. *Educ.:* St. Paul's School; Charing Cross Hosp.; London Univ. Entered Army, 1899; Lt.-Col. 1915; Col. 1919; Lt. and Captain London Irish Rifles Volunteers, 1891-1899; served South Africa, 1899-1901 (despatches twice, Queen's medal 7 clasps, D.S.O.); European War, 1914-18 (despatches five times, C.M.G., French Croix de Guerre avec Palme, Belgian Croix de Guerre); Asst. Director Medical Service, 41st Div. B.E.F., 1917-19, also of 3rd Div. and Salisbury Plain Area, 1927-30; retired pay, 1930. *Recreations:* cricket, shooting of all kinds, hunting. *Address:* The Well House, Firbank Lane, Woking, Sy. *T.:* Woking 229. *Club:* Army and Navy. [*Died* 20 *April* 1956.

LLOYD, Llewelyn Southworth, C.B. 1921; *b.* 1876; *e.s.* of late John Lloyd of Cheadle Hulme, Cheshire; *m.* 1902, Margaret Christine (*d.* 1951), *y. d.* of late William and Henrietta Parker; one *d.* *Educ.:* King William's Coll., I. of M.; Christ's Coll., Cambridge; 9th Wrangler, 1898, First Class Nat. Sci. Tripos, Part I. 1899. H.M. Inspector of Schools, Secondary Schools Branch of the Board of Education, 1905-16; Assistant Secretary, Department of Scientific and Industrial Research, 1917, Principal Assistant Secretary, 1935-43. *Publications:* Music and Sound (2nd. ed. 1951); The Musical Ear, 1940; various papers on musical acoustics, and (organ music) Four Hymn-Tune Preludes. *Address:* 11 St. James Road, Edgbaston, Birmingham 15. [*Died* 14 *Aug.* 1956.

LLOYD, Brig.-General Samuel Eyre Massy, C.B.E. 1919; retired; Sheriff, County of Suffolk, 1928; *e. s.* of Eyre Lloyd, Barrister-at-law, Middle Temple; *b.* 1867; *m.* 1890, Nancy (*d.* 1934), 4th *d.* of E. Madoc Jones, J.P., of Glentworth, Oswestry, Salop; two *d.* *Educ.:* Private School. Entered Militia, 3rd Suffolk Regt. 1885; Regulars Suffolk Regt. 1887; served South African War, 1899-1902 with Suffolk Regt. (despatches, Brevet Major); Major retired pay, 1910; Lt.-Col. commanding Reserve Batt. Suffolk Regt. 1910-17; Brigade Commander, 1917-19 (despatches, Brevet Colonel, 1917); D.L.; J.P. Suffolk; Hon. Colonel 3rd Suffolk Regt., 1920. *Address:* Westwood House, Ipswich. *T.:* 2725. *Club:* Army and Navy. [*Died* 1 *Aug.* 1952.

LLOYD, T. Alwyn, O.B.E. 1958; Hon. LL.D. (Wales); J.P.; P.P.T.P.I.; F.R.I.B.A. (distinction in T.P.); F.S.A. Architect and Town Planner; *b.* 11 Aug. 1881; *s.* of Thomas and Elizabeth Jones Lloyd; *m.* 1914, C. Ethel Robarts, M.A.; no *c.* *Educ.:* Liverpool College; University of Liverpool. Assistant to late Sir R. Unwin at Hampstead Garden Suburb, 1907-12; Consulting Architect to Welsh Town Planning and Housing Trust; designed many new villages in England and Wales; municipal housing at Fishguard, Sedgley, Dunstable, Llanidloes, Menai Bridge, Lampeter, Holyhead, and Llangefni. Educational buildings, halls, hospitals, Forestry Commission and Coal Board housing in Wales, and private houses; now in partnership with A. J. Gordon, A.R.I.B.A.; Joint Author South Wales Outline Plan for Minister of Town and Country Planning, 1947; Mem., S. Wales Regional Survey Departmental Cttee., 1920; Minister of Health's Advisory Committee on Town and Country Planning, 1933-40; Lord Reith's Consultative Panel on Reconstruction, 1941-42; Hon. Lecturer, Welsh School of Architecture; President, Town Planning Institute, 1933-34; Chairman National Housing and Town Planning Council, 1933-35; Fellow, Institute of Landscape Architects; Chairman, Council for Preservation of Rural Wales; Pres., S. Wales Institute of Architects, 1929-31; Central Advisory Council on Education (Wales), 1945-48; Pres. Cambrian Archæological Assoc., 1958-59; Chairman: P.M.G. Welsh Stamp Cttee., 1957-58; Royal Commn. on Ancient Monuments (Wales), 1949-. *Publications:* Planning in Town and Country, 1935; Brighter Welsh Villages and Towns (C.P.R.W.), 1932; S. Wales Outline Plan, 1949; Sundry Articles and Broadcasting. *Recreations:* pottering in the garden, studying buildings, and country travel. *Address:* 6 Cathedral Road, Cardiff. *T.:* Cardiff 30454; 11 Heol-wen, Rhiwbina, Glam. *T.:* Rhiwbina (Glam.) 157. [*Died* 19 *June* 1960.

LLOYD, Theodore Howard, J.P.; *b.* 2 Oct. 1872; *s.* of Alfred Howard Lloyd; *m.* 1906, Beatrice Mary, *d.* of Sir Henry Randall; no *c.* *Educ.:* Eton; Christ Church, Oxford. Formerly Director of Flower and Sons Ltd., Brewers, Stratford-on-Avon; High Sheriff of Surrey, 1939. Presented the 2000-acre Outwood estate, Surrey, to National Trust, 1955. *Recreations:* hunting, shooting, racing. *Address:* Harewoods, Outwood, Surrey. *T.A.:* Outwood, Surrey. *T.:* Smallfield 224. *Club:* Boodle's. [*Died* 23 *March* 1959.

LLOYD-ROBERTS, Sir Richard, Kt., *cr.* 1951; C.B.E. 1944; Chief Labour Officer, I.C.I. Ltd., 1927-48, retired; *b.* 22 June 1885; *m.* 1915, Sarah Lilian, *d.* of A. B. Davies, Swansea; one *d.* *Educ.:* Liverpool College. Civil Servant, Post Office and Labour Exchanges, 1903-16. Labour Officer, Brunner, Mond & Co. Ltd., 1916-27. Civil Servant, Ministry of Labour, 1948-51; Member, Industrial Disputes Tribunal, 1952-. *Recreation:* golf. *Address:* Morants Court, Sevenoaks, Kent. *T.:* Dunton Green 229. *Club:* Junior Carlton. [*Died* 29 *July* 1956.

LO, Hon. Sir Man-kam, Kt., *cr.* 1948; C.B.E. 1941; Member Executive Council of Hongkong; Senior Partner Lo and Lo, Solicitors and Notaries Public, Hongkong; *b.* 21 July 1893; *e. s.* of late Lo Cheung Shiu, J.P., and late Mrs. Lo (*née* Shi Sheung Hing); *m.* 1918, Victoria, *d.* of late Sir Robert Ho Tung, K.B.E.; one *s.* three *d.* *Educ.:* Private School in England. Passed Solicitors' Final, 1915 (1st in First Cl. Hons.); started legal firm of Lo and Lo with brother, Hon. M. W. Lo, C.B.E., J.P., as partner; Hon. Legal Adviser to numerous bodies; Director of various leading Companies in the Colony; held positions of Pres. and Chm. of various organisations and associations; ex-member Council and member Court of Univ. of Hongkong; member innumerable Cttees. appointed by Govt. to enquire into various matters; member Salaries Commission, 1947; Past Pres. and Cttee. member Law Society of Hongkong; J.P. 1921. Silver Jubilee Medal, 1935; Coronation Medal, 1937. *Recreations:* tennis and swimming. *Address:* 107 Robinson Road, and Jardine House (office), Hongkong. *T.A.:* Deodand Hongkong. *T.:* 24213. *Clubs:* Hongkong Jockey, Chinese, etc. (Hongkong). [*Died* 7 *March* 1959.

LOCH, Major-Gen. Stewart Gordon, C.B. 1920; C.S.I. 1919; D.S.O. 1901; A.D.C. 1925; late R.E.; *s.* of late Capt. Robert Gordon Loch, 20th Hussars and I.S.C.; *b.* 13 Apr. 1873; *m.* 1902, Kate Alice Muriel (J.P. Beds. 1936), *o. d.* of John Rathbone, Highcroft, Sevenoaks; two *s.* one *d.* *Educ.:* Westward Ho!; Merchant Taylors' School; R.M.A., Woolwich. Entered Army, Royal Engineers, 1893; served China, 1900-1 (despatches, medal with clasp, D.S.O.); European War (N.W.F.), 1914-18 (Bt. Lt.-Col. and Brevet-Col., C.S.I.); Afghan War, 1919 (C.B.); Major-General, 1925; retired, 1926; Colonel, Q.V.O. Madras Sappers and Miners, 1935-43; H.G., 1940-45; Chm., Bedfordshire British Legion, 1930-45; Hon. Pres. St. John's Ambulance Brigade for North Beds., 1937, 1951; O.St.J., 1948; D.L. County of Bedfordshire, 1938. *Address:* Pertenhall Manor, Bedford. *T.:* Kimbolton 223. *Club:* Army and Navy. [*Died* 27 *March* 1952.

LOCHORE, Sir James, Kt., *cr.* 1925; *b.* 1874; *m.* 1914, *d.* of Alex. Thomson of Burgie, Forres; (2nd *s.* killed by enemy action H.M.S. Barham 25 Nov. 1941; *er. s.* killed in action July 1944); one *d.* Member Executive Council of Ceylon, 1921-27; Chm. Ceylon Chamber of Commerce, 1918-21. *Address:* Burgie House, Forres, Morayshire. [*Died* 21 *Aug.* 1953.

LOCK, Major-General Sir Robert Ferguson, K.B.E., *cr.* 1944; C.B. 1937; *b.* 13 Dec. 1879; 4th *s.* of late Major F. E. Lock, 15th Regt.; *m.* 1910, Kathleen Beryl, *d.* of late Maj.-Gen. A. P. Penton, C.B., C.M.G., C.V.O.; (one *s.* killed in action, 1944) two *d.* *Educ.:* Cheltenham; Woolwich. Entered R.A. 1898; Capt., 1904; Major, 1914; Lt.-Col., 1923; Col., 1927; served European War, 1916, France and Belgium (wounded, despatches); President Ordnance Committee, 1936-37; Air Raids Precautions Officer, Isle of Wight C.C., 1939; British Supply Board, Canada, 1939-40; Chairman Joint Inspection Board U.K. and Canada, 1941-43; Ministry of Supply, London, 1944-45. *Address:* Valley Gate, Milford on Sea, Hants. *T.:* Milford on Sea 451. [*Died* 25 *July* 1957.

LOCKE KING, Dame Ethel; *see* King.

LOCKER-LAMPSON, Commander Oliver Stillingfleet, C.M.G. 1917; D.S.O. 1918; R.N.A.S.; *b.* 1880; *s.* of Frederick Locker, poet, and Jane Lampson, *d.* of Sir Curtis Lampson, 1st Bt.; *m.* 1st, 1923, Bianca Jacqueline Paget (*d.* 1929), of Pasadena, California; 2nd, 1935, Barbara Sophia, *d.* of late Reginald Goodall of Chobham; two *s.* *Educ.:* Cheam Private School; Eton; Trinity College, Cambridge. Winner of Prince Consort's Prize, German, 1898; Honours Tripos Degree in Modern Languages, 1902, and in History, 1903; B.A., 1903; edited Granta, 1900; President of Amateur Dramatic Company, 1903; called to the Bar, 1907; conducted Empire Review; wrote for leading magazines; commission as Lieut.-Commander in R.N.A.S., Dec. 1914; promoted Commander, July 1915; received Cross of Officer of the Order of Leopold, Dec. 1915; Order of St. Vladimir, 1916; St. Anne, 1917, and Roumanian orders; served with armoured cars in France, Belgium, Lapland, Russia, Turkey, Persia, Roumania, Caucasus, Austria, during the European War, 1914-18; appointed Russian representative of Ministry of Information, 1918; M.P. (C.) North Huntingdonshire, 1910; (C.U.), 1918-22; (C.) Handsworth Division of Birmingham, 1922-45; Parliamentary Private Secretary to Chancellor of Exchequer, March 1919; accompanied Austen Chamberlain to Peace Conference; conducted Victory Loan, 1919; Parliamentary Private Sec. to Leader of the House, and Lord Privy Seal, 1921. *Publication:* Preference Debate. *Recreations:* refusing honours; winner of weight-putting, Eton. *Clubs:* Royal Automobile, Carlton. [*Died* 8 *Oct.* 1954.

LOCKHART, Sir Charles Ramsdale, K.B.E., *cr.* 1948 (C.B.E. 1935); Kt., *cr.* 1944; Member of Overseas Food Corporation since 1948; *b.* 1892; *m.* 1923, Dorothy Clayton, Chesterfield. Served European War, 1914-19, Gallipoli, Egypt, and E. Africa (despatches twice); Asst. Treas., Tanganyika Territory, 1919; Dep. Treas., N. Rhodesia, 1931; Treasurer, 1933; Financial Sec., 1937; Fin. Sec., Kenya, 1938; Fin. Sec., Nigeria, 1942; Chairman, East African Production and Supply Council, 1943; Chief Sec. E. African Governors' Conf., 1944. *Address:* 61 Warwick Square, S.W.1. [*Died* 13 *July* 1954.

LOCKHART, Sir Graeme D. P. S.; *see* Sinclair-Lockhart.

LOCKHART, John Gilbert, C.B.E. 1952 (O.B.E. 1946); Secretary United Kingdom Branch of Commonwealth Parliamentary Association since 1949; *b.* 12 April 1891; *s.* of Alexander Francis Maxwell Lockhart and Ida Elizabeth Lockhart; *m.* 1937, Margaret Colette Mary Gordon; two *s.* *Educ.:* Marlborough and Trinity College, Oxford. Served European War, 1914-18, with 1/4th Wiltshire Regt. in India and Palestine. Publisher, 1922-39, with Philip Allan & Co. Ltd. and Geoffrey Bles Ltd.; served War of 1939-45, Camp Commandant, 43rd Division, 1939-40; Major, General Staff, War Office, 1940-42; Private Secretary to Earl of Halifax, British Ambassador at Washington, 1942-46; Asst. Sec., U.K. Branch of Commonwealth Parliamenttary Assoc., 1947-49. *Publications:* The Peacemakers, 1932; Cecil Rhodes, 1933; Viscount Halifax, 1935; Cosmo Gordon Lang, 1949; Winston Churchill, 1951; also several books about the sea, curiosities of history and contemporary personalities; two novels and two books for children. *Address:* 185 Ashley Gardens, S.W.1. *T.:* Victoria 5539. *Club:* Athenæum. [*Died* 7 *Jan.* 1960.

LOCKHART, John Harold Bruce, M.A.; Headmaster of Sedbergh School, 1937-1954; *b.* Beith, Ayrshire, 4 March 1889; *s.* of R. Bruce Lockhart, lately of Eagle House, Sandhurst and Florence Stuart Macgregor; *m.* 1913, Mona, *d.* of Henry Brougham, late of Wellington College; four *s.* *Educ.:* Sedbergh School (Head of Modern VIth, Head of Schoolhouse, Captain of Football, Captain of Cricket); Jesus College, Cambridge; Hons 2nd class Mod. Langs. Tripos (distinction in French Oral). Blue for Rugby Football, Blue for cricket; Rugby International for Scotland,

1913 and 1920. Played cricket for Scotland, 1909 and 1910; served in Intelligence Corps B.E.F. France (despatches); Assistant Master Rugby School, 1912; House Master Rugby School, 1923-30; Headmaster of Cargilfield School, 1930-36; Member of Lake Artists Society; has exhibited at the R.A., R.S.A., R.S.W., etc. Scottish Cttee. of Arts Council; Governor of Welbeck College; Council of National Youth Orchestra. Chevalier de la Légion d'Honneur. *Recreations:* sketching, fishing, music. *Address:* Drum Mhor, Bemersyde, Melrose, Roxburghshire. *Club:* Public Schools. [*Died* 4 *June* 1956.

LOCKHART-MUMMERY, John Percy, F.R.C.S. Eng.; F.A.C.S.; M.A., M.B., B.C. Cantab.; Consulting Surgeon St. Mark's Hospital for Cancer, Fistula, and other Diseases of the Rectum, Hon. Consulting Surgeon Queen's Hospital for Children; Hon. Surgeon King Edward VII. Hospital for Officers; Jacksonian Prizeman and late Hunterian Professor Royal College of Surgeons; Fellow and late President section of Proctology and Children's Diseases, Royal Society of Medicine; Chairman Executive Committee, British Empire Cancer Campaign; *b.* 1875; *e. s.* of J. Howard Mummery of Islips Manor, Northolt; *m.* 1st, 1915, Cynthia, *d.* of R. A. Gibbons; two *s.*; 2nd, 1932, Georgette, *d.* of H. Polak, Paris. *Educ.:* Caius College, Cambridge; St. George's Hospital. *Publications:* Diseases of the Colon; Diseases of the Rectum and Colon; The Origin of Cancer; numerous other writings upon surgical subjects; After Us; Nothing New Under the Sun. *Recreations:* golf and fishing. *Address:* 149 Harley Street, W.1. *T.:* Welbeck 4444. *Club:* Junior Carlton. [*Died* 24 *April* 1957.

LOCKWOOD, Francis William; Headmaster of Plymouth College since 1953; *b.* 31 Jan. 1908; *e. s.* of Ralph Edwin Lockwood, and Blanche (*née* Lovell), Bristol; *m.* 1941, Molly, *d.* of H. B. Secker, Golders Green, London; one *s.* two *d.* *Educ.:* Perse School, and St. Catharine's College, Cambridge. B.A. (both parts Classical Tripos), 1930; M.A. (Cantab.), 1934; M.A. (London), 1935; Assistant Master, Forest Hill School, London, 1931-32; Senior Classics Master, Wilson's Grammar School, London, 1932-40; Headmaster, Queen Elizabeth's Grammar School, Gainsborough, Lincs., 1940-44; Headmaster, William Ellis School, London, 1945-53. *Recreations:* chess and golf. *Address:* The Headmaster's House, Plymouth College, Devon. *T.:* Plymouth 3353. [*Died* 19 *Feb.* 1955.

LOCKYER, Cuthbert H. J., M.D., B.S., F.R.C.P., F.R.C.S.; F.R.C.O.G.; retired 1930; late Councillor Royal College of Physicians; late President of Obstetrical and Gynæcological Section, and Vice-President of the Royal Society of Medicine; Vice-President and Consulting Obstetric Physician, Charing Cross Hospital; Consulting Gynæcological Surgeon, Samaritan Hospital for Women; Consulting Obstetric Physician, Royal Northern Hospital; Consulting Gynæcologist, National Hospital, Queen's Square; Senior Consulting Gynæcologist, St. Mary's Hospital for Women and Children, Plaistow; late Examiner in Obstetrics and Gynæcology, University, Cambridge, and Conjoint Board; late Examiner in Universities of London, Leeds, Birmingham, and Sheffield; membre correspondant de la Société d'Obstet. et Gynécol. Belge; late Consulting Physician Royal Society of Musicians; *b.* 13 April 1867; *s.* of Cuthbert Lockyer, Evercreech, Somerset; *m.* 1st, Minnie Marie Coombs; two *s.* (one *d.* killed air raid St. Thomas' Hosp. S.E., 1940, whilst on duty as physiotherapist during Battle of Britain); 2nd, Violet Gwendoline Morton. *Educ.:* Charing Cross Hospital, Bonn and Vienna. *Publications:* Fibroids and Allied Tumours; (joint) Gynæcology, a Text-Book for Students and Practitioners; joint-editor of New System of Gynæcology; Chapters 17-19, Vol. XI, on Myoma, Adenomyoma and Sarcoma, Lewis' Practice of Surgery, 1929; author and editor of Catalogue of Lockyer Collection of Obstetric and Gynæcological Specimens in Charing Cross Hospital Museum, 1930. Foreword in Historical Review of British Obstetrics and Gynæcology, 1809-1950, 1954. *Recreations:* etching, gardening, and travel. *Address:* Alverton Cottage, Penzance. *T.:* Penzance 3266. [*Died* 28 *Aug.* 1957.

LOCOCK, Sir Guy Harold, Kt., *cr.* 1942; C.M.G. 1918; *b.* 10 July 1883; *o. s.* of late Col. Herbert Locock, C.B., R.E.; *m.* 1906, Esther Mary Eleanor (*d.* 1955), *o. c.* of W. J. Reade; (one *s.* died on active service) one *d.* *Educ.:* Wellington College. Foreign Office, 1906-18; Private Secretary to successive Under-Secretaries for Foreign Affairs, Nov. 1913-Jan. 1918; Acting Assistant Director in charge of the Foreign Section of the Department of Overseas Trade, 1918; Sec. Gen. of Internat. Conf. on safety of life at sea; Assistant Director Federation of British Industries; representative of the International Chamber of Commerce on the Statistical Conference of the League of Nations; member of the Government Committees under Lord Chelmsford and Sir Gilbert Garnsey on the British Industries Fair; member of the British Committee on Empire Trade; alternate Industrial Adviser in connection with the World Economic Conference, 1933; Member of the British Industrial Mission to Japan and Manchoukuo, 1934; Delegate at Joint Anglo-German Industrial Conference at Düsseldorf, March 1939; Member of Joint Anglo-French Industrial Council Feb. 1940; Board of Trade Representative on London and South Eastern Area Munitions Board; Member of Ministry of Supply Mission to India, 1940-41, and Delegate at Eastern Group Conference at New Delhi; F.B.I. representative on Central Joint Advisory Committee to the War Cabinet Production Executive, 1941; Member of Government Committee on Regional Boards; Member of National Production Advisory Council, 1942; Director of the Federation of British Industries, 1932-45, Vice-President, 1946; Member Reconstruction Joint Advisory Council; Member of Committee on admission of women to the Foreign Service; Chm.; of Advisory Cttee. to Bd. of Trade on Fairs and Exhibitions, 1946-56; of Statutory Cttee. under Merchandise Marks Act; a Director of the Trade Indemnity Co. Ltd. and Vice-Chm. of Doulton and Co.; is a Commander of the Greek Order of the Redeemer and of the Royal Danish Order of the Dannebrog. *Address:* 40 Alexandra Court, Queen's Gate, S.W.7. *T.:* Kensington 6856. *Clubs:* Boodle's, M.C.C. [*Died* 25 *Aug.* 1958.

LODER-SYMONDS, Vice-Adm. Frederick P. L.; *see* Symonds.

LODGE, Alfred, M.Sc. (Lond.); A.Inst.P.; Rector of Dumfries Academy since 1931; *b.* 2 April 1893; *y. s.* of John Lodge, Feltham, Middlesex; *m.* 1916, Gertrude Rose, *d.* of F. W. A. Robson, Clapham Common. *Educ.:* Henry Thornton School; King's College, London. B.Sc. Hons. Physics, 1913; M.Sc. Physics by Research, 1926. Assistant Master, Southend High School, 1914-21; Senior Physics Master Haberdashers' School, 1921-24; Chief Physics Master Oundle School, 1924-26; Headmaster Haslingden Grammar School, Lancs, 1926-31; served European War, 1914-19, Bedfordshire Regiment (O.C. A. Coy. 9th Bedf. R., 1916) and R.E. (Chief Wireless Officer XVIII. and VIII. Corps, B.E.F., 1917-18); Vice-President Dumfries Rotary Club, 1932. *Publications:* Theory of the Quadrant Electrometer; Thermionic Currents in Vacuo: various Physical Papers on Piezo-Electrification of Di-Electrics other than Crystals. *Recreations:* Amateur and Community Drama, hockey, lawn tennis, golf, and swimming. *Address:* 89 Castle Street, Dumfries. *T.:* Dumfries 512. [*Died* 24 *Jan.* 1957.

LODGE, Lieut.-Colonel Francis Cecil, C.M.G. 1918; D.S.O. 1917; late Royal Norfolk Regiment; *b.* 1868; *s.* of Colonel F. Lodge, late R.A.; *m.* Nora Margaret, *y. d.* of late A. Bryans, Holmwood Cottage, S. Holmwood, Dorking, Surrey; two *s.* one *d.* Served South African War, 1899-1902 (despatches, Queen's medal and 3 clasps, King's medal and 2 clasps); European War (Mesopotamia) 1915-18 (despatches, C.M.G., D.S.O.); retired pay, 1921. *Address:* Cull Lane Cottage, New Milton, Hants. *T.:* New Milton 1208. [*Died* 12 *Jan.* 1951.

LODGE, John; Headmaster, Nantwich and Acton Grammar School, 1932-50, retd.; *b.* Feltham, Mx., 29 Sept. 1890; *er. s.* of late John Lodge and Alice F. Lowman; *m.* 1917, Winifred A. Tier, Emsworth; one *s.* *Educ.:* Palmer's School, Grays; Christ's Hospital; King's College, London (Sambrooke Exhibitioner in Classics. Warre Memorial Prize); A.K.C. 1911; B.A.Hons. Classics, 2nd Class, 1910; B.A.Hons. English, 2nd Class, 1926; M.A. (with distinction) English Language and Literature, 1928; Assistant Master Hawarden County School, 1911-13, Kilburn Grammar School, 1913-25; Second Master, Chiswick County School, 1925-30; Headmaster Leominster Grammar School, 1930-32; served European War, Rifleman, Queen's Westminster Rifles, 1914-15; Lieutenant, 8th Bn. Bedfordshire Regt. 1915-19. *Publications:* (with Prof. A. A. Cock) Songs from Camp and College, 1915. *Recreations:* Amateur Acting and Play-Producing, ornithology. *Address:* 17 The Avenue, Summersdale, Chichester, Sussex. [*Died* 1 *April* 1954.

LODGE, Oliver William Foster; *b.* Brampton House, Newcastle under Lyme, Staffordshire, 11 Aug. 1878; *e. s.* of late Sir Oliver Lodge, F.R.S., LL.D.; *m.* 1st, 1914, Winifred (*d.* 1922), *o. d.* of late Sir William Atkinson, I.S.O., LL.D.; one *s.*; 2nd, 1932, Diana, *o. d.* of Thomas Uppington; two *s.* one *d.* *Educ.:* Eastbourne College; Liverpool University. *Publications:* The Labyrinth, a Tragedy in one act, 1911; Summer Stories, 1911; Spurgeon Arrives, a Comedy in one act, 1912; Six Englishmen, 1915; Poems, 1915; The Schooling of Trimalchio, a tragi-comedy in three acts, 1920; Love in the Mist (poems), 1921; The Pindar of Wakefield, one-act version, 1921; The Case is Altered, a Comedy in one act, 1921; What Art Is, 1927; The Candle, 1938; Love's Wine Corked, 1946; The Betrayer, 1950. *Address:* Cud Hill House, Upton St. Leonard's, Glos. *Club:* Chelsea Arts. [*Died* 17 *April* 1955.

LODGE, Sir Ronald Francis, Kt., *cr.* 1947; *b.* 8 April 1889; 4th *s.* of late George Oxland Lodge and Harriet Elizabeth Lodge, Liverpool, England; *m.* Elsie Helene, (*d.* 1958), *d.* of William Henry King, of S. Africa; one *s.* one *d.* *Educ.:* Liverpool Institute; King's Coll., Cambridge (Foundation Scholar). Passed examination for I.C.S. in 1912; arrived in India in 1913; officiated Judge, High Court, Calcutta, in 1935; Puisne Judge, High Ct., Calcutta, 1941-48; Chief Justice, High Court of Assam, 1948-49; Governor of Assam, 1949; retired Apr. 1949. *Recreation:* golf. *Address:* Brahmaputra, Crowborough Hill, Crowborough, Sussex. [*Died* 3 *March* 1960.

LODGE, Thomas, C.B. 1920; *b.* 23 May 1882; *s.* of late George and Harriet Lodge, Liverpool; *m.* Isobel, *d.* of late John and Margaret Scott, Liverpool; two *d.* (and one *d.* decd.). *Educ.:* Liverpool Institute; Trinity College, Cambridge (22nd Wrangler, 1903; 2nd Class Part II. Historical Tripos, 1904). Entered Home Civil Service as Upper Division Clerk Board of Trade, 1905; Principal Clerk Board of Trade, 1917; Assistant Secretary Ministry of Shipping. Feb. 1918; Secretary Ministry of Shipping, July 1919; represented Ministry of Shipping at Peace Conference, 1919; resigned, March 1920; Hon. financial adviser to Dr. Nansen, 1921-30 in connection with his philanthropic work for League of Nations and Russia; member of the Commission of Government of Newfoundland, 1934-37; Chevalier of the Order of the Crown, Belgium; Officier of the Légion d'Honneur, France; Officer of the Order of the Crown of Italy. *Publication:* Dictatorship in Newfoundland, 1939. *Address:* Blunham Grange, Blunham, Beds. *T.:* Blunham 220. *Club:* Reform. [*Died* 10 *Feb.* 1958.

LODWICK, John Alan Patrick; author; *b.* 2 March 1916; *s.* of late Capt. John Thornton Lodwick, D.S.O., Indian Army, and Kathleen, *d.* of Sir Henry Ashbrooke-Crump, K.C.S.I.; *m.*; two *s.* two *d.* *Educ.:* Cheltenham College; R.N.C., Dartmouth. Served War of 1939-45: Croix de Guerre (palmes), 1940; despatches, 1945. *Publications: novels:* Brother Death, 1948; The Cradle of Neptune, 1951; Somewhere A Voice Is Calling, 1953; The Butterfly Net, 1954; The Starless Night, 1956; Equator, 1957, etc.; *war:* The Filibusters, 1946; *travel:* The Forbidden Coast, 1956; *biography:* Gulbenkian, 1958; *autobiography:* Bid The Soldiers Shoot, 1958. *Recreations:* climbing, smuggling. *Address:* c/o William Heinemann Ltd., 99 Great Russell Street, W.C.1. [*Died* 18 *March* 1959.

LOFTUS, Pierse Creagh; late Capt. Suffolk Regt. T.F.; J.P. Suffolk; Alderman East Suffolk C.C.; Chairman Adnams & Co. Ltd., Southwold, Brewers and Hotel Proprietors; *b.* Mount Loftus, 29 Nov. 1877; *m.* 1910, Dorothy Reynolds (*d.* 1943); two *s.*; *m.* 1945, Eileen, *widow* of Brigadier-General Robert Elkington, C.B., C.M.G., D.S.O. *Educ.:* St. Augustine's School, Ramsgate; Oratory School, Birmingham. Worked in S. Africa, 1899-1902 (Maritzburg Defence Force, 1899); took interest in Adnams & Co., Ltd., Southwold, 1902; in 1914 joined 5th Suffolks T.F.; in France end 1916 to spring 1919 (despatches); member of East Suffolk County Council, 1922; M.P. (Nat. C.) Lowestoft Division, 1934-45; Vice-President Lowestoft Conservative Assoc., 1923; spoke for party at all elections in Lowestoft and neighbouring divisions; Alderman East Suffolk County Council 1930; High Steward of Borough of Southwold, 1945; Chm. Rural Reconstruction Assoc., 1948. *Publications:* The Conservative Party and the Future, 1912; The Creed of a Tory, 1923; The Main Cause of Unemployment, 1932. *Recreations:* walking, reading. *Address:* Reydon Covert, Southwold, Suffolk. *T.A.:* Loftus Southwold. *T.:* Southwold 3141; 12 Montpelier Square, S.W.7. *T.:* Kensington 3112. *Clubs:* Carlton; County (Ipswich). [*Died* 20 *Jan.* 1956.

LOGGIN, George Nicholas, C.M.G. 1932; M.Inst.C.E.; *b.* 1882; *s.* of Arthur Cole Loggin, Woolfardisworthy, N. Devon; *m.* 1st, 1915, Emily Adams (*d.* 1943), *d.* of Rev. J. Prankerd; one *s.* two *d.*; 2nd, 1946, Mary Katharine Helen, *widow* of Frederic Penny and *d.* of William Calthorpe Mallaby. *Educ.:* private schools; University College, London. Appointed to Public Works Department of Ceylon, 1908; Captain Local Defence Force, and Secretary, Ministry of Munitions Local Priority Authority, 1915-18; Director of Public Works, Uganda Protectorate, 1922-24; Chairman of Committee to report on proposed extension of Kenya-Uganda Railway; Deputy Director of Public Works, Nigeria, 1924-26; transferred from Colonial Service and appointed Director of Works, Sudan Government, 1926-36; a member of Governor-General's Council, 1932-36; President Sudan Board of Economics and Trade, 1935-36; Adviser to Ministry of Communications and Works, Iraq Govt., 1938-43; Director-General, Iraq State Railways, 1939-40; President Imports Committee and Member Iraq High Supply Council, 1941-43; Adviser on Engineering Appointments, Colonial Office, 1944-46. Second class Order of the Nile

(Egypt), 1936; 2nd class Order of the Rafidain (Iraq), 1945. *Address:* 23 Calverley Park, Tunbridge Wells. *T.:* Tunbridge Wells 2711. [*Died* 27 *Nov.* 1955.

LOGUE, Lionel, C.V.O. 1944 (M.V.O. 1937); Specialist in Speech Defects; *b.* Adelaide, South Australia, 1880; *s.* of George Edward Logue, Adelaide; *m.* 1907, Myrtle (*d.* 1945), *o. d.* of Francis Gruenert; three *s.* *Educ.:* Prince Alfred College, Adelaide. Specialist in Speech Defects and Speaking Voice; has had world experience in curative speech work; came to London permanently in 1924; one of original founders of British Society of Speech Therapists, 1935; Founder Fellow of College of Speech Therapists; Speech Therapist to Royal Masonic School, Bushey; attended King George VI (M.V.O.); Coronation Medal, 1937; Defence Medal. *Recreations:* gardening, walking. *Address:* 146 Harley Street, W.1; 68 Princes Court, Brompton Road, S.W.3. *T.:* Welbeck 2378; Kensington 2174. [*Died* 12 *April* 1953.

LOMAS-WALKER, Sir G. Bernard, K.B.E., *cr.* 1937; Solicitor since 1903; Director of Companies; Member, Harrogate Town Council; *b.* 31 Jan. 1881; *s.* of James Walker, Jr., Leeds; *m.* 1909, Phyllis Emelie, *d.* of late William Edward and Louisa Scharff, Bradford and Harrogate; one *s.* two *d.* *Educ.:* Harrogate College, Harrogate. Served European War, France, 1915-19; Major and Staff Paymaster; Registrar of Diocese of Ripon and Notary Public, 1931; retired, 1949; Member of West Riding County Council, 1913-39 and Chairman, 1933-39; J.P. Borough of Harrogate, 1922. Chevalier of the Order of Christ (Portugal). *Address:* St. Albans, 12 Granby Road, Harrogate. *T.:* Harrogate 2863. [*Died* 26 *Feb.* 1960.

LONDON, Sir George Ernest, Kt., *cr.* 1942; C.M.G. 1936; *b.* 6 April 1889; *s.* of Frederick Henry London and Sarah Goode; *m.* 1916, Helen Mary, *d.* of Lt.-Col. F. P. Reger; one *s.* one *d.* *Educ.:* Warwick; Downing Coll., Cambridge. Natural Science Tripos, 1910; History Tripos, 1911; B.A. 1911; Cadet, F.M.S. 1911; on military service, 1916-19; Under-Sec. to Government, F.M.S. 1934; Colonial Secretary, Gold Coast Colony, British West Africa, 1935-44; Member of Commission of Government of Newfoundland, 1944-45. *Address:* Wentworth, Milvil Road, Lee-on-Solent. *Club:* Royal Empire Society. [*Died* 20 *July* 1957.

LONDON, Hugh Stanford, F.S.A.; F.S.G.; F.H.S.; Norfolk Herald Extraordinary, 1953; Member of Royal Commission on Historical Monuments (England); Assistant Editor of New Dictionary of British Arms (Papworth); *b.* 3 April 1884; *er. s.* of late Sir Stanford London, C.B.E.; *m.* 1913, Edith Madeleine, F.R.H.S., *e. d.* of late Charles William Wilkins, Edgbaston. *Educ.:* Dulwich College; Clare Coll., Cambridge (M.A.). Vice-Consul at Zanzibar, 1908; at Algiers, 1912; Acting Consul-General at Paris, 1919-20; Consul at Geneva, 1920; Chargé d'Affaires at Managua, Nicaragua, 1928; Consul-General at Marseilles 1930-34; Chargé d'Affaires and Consul-General at Quito, 1934-35; Minister Resident, 1935-37; Consul-General at New Orleans, 1937-38; Consul-Gen. at Paris, 1938-1940. *Publications:* The Queen's Beasts, 1954; Royal Beasts, 1956; Papers on heralds and heraldry in Archaeologia, Complete Peerage, Antiquaries' Journal, Archives Héraldiques Suisses, Miscellanea Genealogica, etc. *Recreation:* Heraldic research. *Address:* Coldharbour, Buxted, Uckfield, Sussex. *T.:* Buxted 2271. *Club:* Athenæum. [*Died* 20 *Jan.* 1959.

LONDONDERRY, 8th Marquis of, *cr.* 1816; **Edward Charles Stewart Robert Vane-Tempest-Stewart,** Baron Londonderry, 1789; Viscount Castlereagh, 1795; Earl of Londonderry, 1796; Baron Stewart, 1814; Earl Vane, Viscount Seaham, 1823; sits as Earl Vane; b. 18 Nov. 1902; *o. s.* of 7th Marquess of Londonderry, K.G., P.C., M.V.O. and Hon. Dame Edith Chaplin (*see* Dowager Marchioness of Londonderry), *d.* of 1st Viscount Chaplin; *S.* father 1949; *m.* 1931, Romaine (*d.* 1951), *er. d.* of Major Boyce Combe, Great Holt, Dockenfield, Surrey; one *s.* two *d.* *Educ.:* Eton; Christ Church, Oxford, B.A. Was Hon. Attaché, British Embassy, Rome. M.P. (U.) County Down, 1931-45. Served War of 1939-45, R.A. (1941-42 in Middle East). J.P., D.L. Co. Down; J.P., D.L. Co. Durham; Hon. Col. 12th Bn. (Cadet) D.L.I. Member of Church Assembly, 1950-55. *Heir:* *s.* Viscount Castlereagh. *Address:* 101 Park Street, W.1. [*Died* 17 *Oct.* 1955.

LONDONDERRY, Marchioness Dowager of, (Edith Helen), D.B.E., *cr.* 1917; J.P.; LL.D.; *b.* 3 Dec. 1879; *e. d.* of 1st Viscount Chaplin and Lady Florence Sutherland Leveson Gower, *d.* of 3rd Duke of Sutherland, K.G., *m.* 1899, 7th Marquess of Londonderry, K.G., P.C., M.V.O. (*d.* 1949); three *d.* (one *s.* one *d.* decd.). Founder and Director-General Women's Legion, European War, 1915-19 (first woman given mil. D.B.E.); President Women's Legion, and served during War of 1939-1945. President Northern Ireland Council Branch B.R.C.S. J.P. Co. Durham, J.P. Co. Down, Northern Ireland (first woman), 1919. Member of Advisory Committee to advise the Lord Chancellor on appointment of women Justices of the Peace, 1918. Hon. LL.D. Queen's Univ., Belfast, 1949. *Publications:* Henry Chaplin: a Memoir prepared by his daughter, 1926; The Magic Inkpot, 1928; (Ed. with H. M. Hyde) The Russian Journals of Martha and Catherine Wilmot, 1803-1808; More Letters from Martha Wilmot, 1819-1829; Retrospect, 1938; Frances Anne, 1958. *Recreations:* writing, gardening. *Address:* Londonderry House, Park Lane, W.1. *T.:* Grosvenor 1617; Mount Stewart, Newtownards, Co. Down, N.I. *T.:* Newtownards 3270. [*Died* 23 *April* 1959.

LONG, Lt.-Col. Albert de Lande, D.S.O. 1918; D.L.; late Gordon Highlanders; *b.* 1880; *m.* Nan (*d.* 1946), *d.* of late Arthur Paterson; one *s.* one *d.* Served European War, 1914-18 (D.S.O., Bt. Maj., despatches thrice); retired, 1926. *Educ.:* Winchester; New Coll., Oxford. *Address:* Lisle Court, Wootton Bridge, Isle of Wight. *Clubs:* Bath, Leander; Royal Yacht Squadron (Cowes); Highland Brigade Yacht, Royal Victoria Yacht (Ryde); Bembridge Sailing (Bembridge). [*Died* 19 *April* 1956.

LONG, Alfred James, Q.C. 1938; Recorder of Wolverhampton since 1951; *b.* 1890; *s.* of late Alfred Long, West Bromwich. *Educ.:* King Edward's High School, Birmingham. LL.B. University of London; Called to Bar, Lincolns Inn, 1915 during absence on Army Service; Bencher, 1946; Practised at Bar since demobilisation in 1919; Member of Oxford Circuit; Recorder of Smethwick, 1937-39; West Bromwich, 1939-51. *Address:* 4 Brick Court, Temple, E.C.4. *T.:* Central 4870. [*Died* 7 *July* 1952.

LONG, Edward Ernest, C.B.E. 1921 (O.B.E. 1919); F.R.G.S.; F.J.I.; journalist and author; *b.* Sutton Valence, Kent; *o. s.* of Edward Long; *m.* Mabel Edith (*d.* 1941), 2nd *d.* of Andrew Benjamin Leicester, Straits Settlements Medical Service. *Educ.:* Sutton Valence School; abroad. Travelled in U.S.A. and Canada, and contributed articles London papers; joined staff of the Echo, London; went to Singapore, Straits Settlements, on Staff of Singapore Free Press; there acted as correspondent of the Daily Express, Assistant Editor Indian Daily Telegraph, Lucknow; Editor Rangoon Times, Burma,

1905; Correspondent of the London Standard; Editor Indian Daily Telegraph; The Times Correspondent in Northern India; represented Press of India at Conference of Overseas Journalists, 1910; resigned editorship Indian Daily Telegraph, 1915, to take Commission in Royal Field Artillery; later placed in charge of Eastern and Moslem Propaganda as Director, firstly under Foreign Office, then Ministry of Information; Foreign Office, as Officer-in-Charge Eastern Section, News Department, 1918-21; in charge of propaganda work for Government of India until Dec. 1923; Special Correspondent, touring British Malaya, Siam, Java, Celebes, Bali, the Moluccas, and Dutch New Guinea, 1924-25; contributor (1929) Articles, Dutch East Indies, to Encyclopædia Britannica (new edition); special correspondent touring Dutch and British Guiana, Colombia, Venezuela, Bermuda and West Indies, 1931-32; special correspondent touring the United States, Canada and Bermuda, 1938; formerly Travel Adviser to Illustrated London News, Tatler, Sketch, and Sporting and Dramatic News. *Publications:* Numerous articles in the London daily, weekly press, and in reviews, magazines, etc., dealing with Eastern and Far-Eastern problems; The King-Emperor's Activities in War-Time (published in seven Indian languages); The Anarchist, a one-act play; occasional verse. *Recreations:* travelling, exploring, walking, and stamp collecting. *Address:* 4 Ruskin Mansions, Queen's Club Gardens, W.14. *T.:* Fulham 0924. *T.A.:* Long, Savage Club, London. *Club:* Savage. [*Died* 3 *Nov.* 1956.

LONG, (Margaret) Gabrielle; writer of fiction, historical studies, plays and biographies. *Pseudonyms:* Marjorie Bowen, George R. Preedy, Joseph Shearing; *b.* Hayling, Hampshire, 1888; *d.* of Vere Campbell, 2nd *s.* of Hugh Campbell, M.D., and Josephine Elizabeth, *d.* of Rev. Charles Bowen Ellis; *m.* 1st, 1912, Zeffirino Emilio Costanzo (*d.* 1916); one *s.*; 2nd, 1917, Arthur L. Long; two *s.* *Educ.:* by self and others; Paris, Rome, and London. *Publications:* As Margaret Campbell: The Debate Continues (autobiography), 1939. As Marjorie Bowen: The Carnival of Florence, 1915; The Viper of Milan, 1917; The Netherlands Display'd, 1926; The Third Mary Stewart, 1929; Mary, Queen of Scots, 1934; Patriotic Lady (Lady Hamilton), 1936; The Cockney's Mirror (William Hogarth), 1936; Wrestling Jacob (John Wesley), 1937; trilogy of novels on the Renaissance, The Golden Roof, The Triumphant Beast, 1934, Trumpets at Rome, 1937; trilogy of novels on aspects of English spiritual life, God and the Wedding Dress, 1938, Mr. Tyler's Saints, 1939, The Circle in the Water, 1939; and some sixty other novels and historical studies. As George R. Preedy: *novels:* General Crack, 1928; The Rocklitz, 1930; Bagatelle, 1930; Tumult in the North, 1931; Violante, 1932; The Knot Garden, 1933; Dr. Chaos, 1933; The Devil Snar'd, 1933; Double Dallilay, 1934; Cornelius Blake, the Autobiography of a Banker, 1934; Laurell'd Captains, 1935; The Poisoners, 1936; My Tattered Loving, 1937; Painted Angel, 1938; Dove in the Mulberry Bush, 1939; Primula, 1940; Finderne's Flowers, 1941; Black Man—White Maiden, 1942; Lady in a Veil, 1942; The Fourth Chamber, 1943; Nightcap and Plume, 1945; The Sacked City, 1949; No Way Home, 1950; *plays:* General Crack; Captain Banner; The Rocklitz; *biographies:* This Shining Woman: a Life of Mary Wollstonecroft Godwin, 1937; Child of Chequer'd Fortune (Maurice de Saxe), 1938; Paul Jones, 1940; John Knox, 1941; The Courtly Charlatan (St. Germain), 1942. Contributed to Sketch, Pall Mall, Nash's, Illustrated London News; in U.S.A. to Collier's Weekly. As Joseph Shearing: Forget-me-not, 1932; Album Leaf, 1933; Moss Rose, 1934; Angel of Assassination (Charlotte Corday), 1935; Golden Violet, 1936; Lady and the Arsenic (Marie Capelle), 1937; Orange Blossoms, 1938; Blanche Fury, 1939; Laura Sarelle, 1940; The Fetch, 1942; Airing in a Closed Carriage, 1943; The Abode of Love, 1944; Mignonette, 1947; Within The Bubble, 1950; To Bed at Noon, 1951; other novels, prize winner, Contrib. to Ellery Queen, etc. *Recreations:* painting, needlework, and the theatre. *Address:* c/o Barclays Bank, Bloomsbury Branch, 10 Southampton Row, W.C.1. [*Died* 23 *Dec.* 1952.

LONG, Sydney (Sid Long), A.R.E., R.B.C.; artist; President of the Australian Painter Etchers; Member Royal Art Society, N.S.W.; Trustee National Art Gallery of N.S.W., 1933-49; *b.* Goulbourne, N.S.W. Australia, 1878; *s.* of Rev. John Long, Belfast. *Educ.:* Goulborne High School. Exhibited Royal Academy from 1913; studies under Julian Ashton, and A. J. Dalyn; Kennington Art Sch. and Central School of Arts; took up etching, 1919; Foundation Member of Society of Graphic Arts, of which he was the first Hon. Secretary; returned to Australia 1925; is represented in the Sydney, Melbourne and Adelaide Galleries, the British Museum, Victoria and Albert Museums, Montreal and Capetown Galleries. *Works:* Exhibited Scottish Academy, Edinburgh, Royal Glasgow Institute, by special invitation; his best known fantasies are: Fantasy, Spirit of the Australian Plains, Pan and Pastoral, Imaginative Creations. *Address:* National Art Gallery, Sydney, New South Wales. [*Died* Jan. 1955.

LONG, Col. Walter Edward Lionel, C.I.E. 1938; O.B.E. 1944; Indian Army, retired; *b.* Dublin, March 1884; *s.* of Walter E. Long, Barrister, and Jane, *d.* of Rev. T. MacNeece, D.D.; *m.* 1912, Mary Elizabeth Beresford Heelas (*d.* 1952); one *s.* *Educ.:* Marlborough; R.M.A., Woolwich. Commissioned in Garrison Artillery, 1903; seconded to Indian Army Ordnance Corps, 1911; served European War, Mesopotamia and Persia; became Inspector of Ordnance Services for India and promoted Colonel, 1934; Deputy and acting Director of the Corps, 1935; re-employed as A.D.O.S. Salisbury Plain District, 1940-45. *Address:* 28 The Crescent, Alverstoke, Hants. [*Died* 15 *April* 1960.

LONG, Lt.-Col. Wilfred James, C.M.G. 1918; late K.R.R.C.; *b.* 1871; *s.* of late Rear-Admiral S. Long and Mrs. Long of Blendworth Lodge, Horndean. Served Burma, 1891-92; S. African War, 1899-1902 (despatches twice, Queen's medal 6 clasps, King's medal 2 clasps); European War, 1914-1918 (despatches, twice, C.M.G., Bt. Lt.-Col.); retired pay, 1920. *Address:* Maytree, Josephine Avenue, Lower Kingswood, Surrey. [*Died* 24 *May* 1954.

LONG, Rev. William Joseph, Ph.D. (Heidelberg); *b.* North Attleboro, Mass., 3 April 1866; Irish parentage—on mother's side from Edmund Burke; *m.* Frances Marsh, *d.* of Professor Cecil F. P. Bancroft, LL.D., Andover, Mass. *Educ.:* Harvard; Andover Theological Seminary; Heidelberg; Paris Univ.; Rome. Became prominent as a preacher and liberal theologian, 1898; for many years a well-known naturalist and writer, which work is taken up as a recreation during vacations. *Publications:* Ways of Wood Folk, Wilderness Ways, Beasts of the Field, Fowls of the Air, Following the Deer, School of the Woods, A Little Brother to the Bear, Northern Trails; Whose Home is the Wilderness, 1907; A History of English Literature, 1908; American Literature, 1913; Brier-Patch Philosophy; How Animals Talk, 1919; Wood Folk Comedies; America, a History of Our Country; Mother Nature, a Study of Animal Life and Death, 1923; Fields of English Literature, 1947; Heart of the Woods, 1951; several magazine articles and books published under a pen-name. *Recreations:* camping, canoeing, exploring, salmon fishing. *Address:* Stamford, Conn., U.S.A. [*Died* 9 *Nov.* 1952.

LONGCROFT, Air Vice-Marshal Sir Charles Alexander Holcombe, K.C.B. *cr.* 1938 (C.B.1923); C.M.G. 1919; D.S.O. 1918; A.F.C.; late R.A.F.; a Gentleman Usher of the Scarlet Rod in the Order of the Bath, 1932-48; Registrar and Secretary of the Order, 1948-54; *b.* 13 May 1883; *e. s.* of late Charles Edward Longcroft of Llanina, Cards., J.P.; *m.* 1921, Marjory, *widow* of Capt. W. D. Hepburn, Seaforth Highlanders, and *d.* of late J. W. McKerrell - Brown, J.P.; one *s.* *Educ.:* Charterhouse; R.M.C. Served Welsh Regt. 1903-12; R.F.C. and R.A.F. 1912-30; European War, 1914-19 (Brevet Lt.-Col., Temp. Major-Gen., 5 despatches, C.M.G., D.S.O., A.F.C.); Legion of Honour (France); Order of St. Stanislas (Russia). 1st Commandant R.A.F. College, Cranwell, 1920-23; Director of Personal Services, Air Ministry, 1924-26; commanded Inland Area, 1926-29; retired list, 1930; President of the Aerodrome Board, 1934-45. *Address:* 6 Connaught Square, W.2. *T.:* Paddington 5850. *Club:* Army and Navy. [*Died* 20 *Feb.* 1958.

LONGDEN, Major Alfred Appleby, D.S.O. 1917; O.B.E. 1930; Director Wernher Collection, Luton Hoo; 4th *s.* of late James Appleby Longden, Sunderland, and Annie Walker Morley, York; *m.* 1917, Betty Marie Ahlberg (writer and journalist), *e. d.* of Peter Kronborg Sorensen, Elsinore; one *d.* *Educ.:* Durham School; Royal College of Art (medallist). Exhibited in Royal Academy and other exhibitions; British Government Representative for Fine and Applied Art, New Zealand International Exhibition, 1906-7; Director Aberdeen Corporation Art Gallery and Museum, 1909-1911; Exhibitions Branch, Board of Trade, 1912; Director, British Institute of Industrial Art, 1919-25; Assistant Director (Applied Art) British Empire Exhibition, 1924; Director of Art for Great Britain, Paris Exhibition, 1925; Secretary General of the winter exhibitions of Dutch, Italian, and Persian Art, at Burlington House, 1929-30-31; Representative for Fine Art, Empire Exhibition, South Africa, 1936; Director of Fine Art, Empire Exhibition, Scotland, 1938; Art Director for XIV Olympiad, 1948; served in the R.G.A. throughout European War (D.S.O., despatches twice); Director of Fine Art dept. of British Council, 1940-47; formerly Art Adviser to Dept. of Overseas Trade. Cavaliere of the Grand Cross of the Crown of Italy, 1938; Officer of the Legion of Honour, 1926; Commendatore of St. Maurice and St. Lazarus, 1930; Officer of the Order of Orange Nassau, 1929. *Publications:* British Cartoon and Caricature, 1944; Articles on Fine and Applied Art in magazines and papers. *Recreations:* fishing and sketching. *Address:* Luton Hoo Collection, Luton, Beds.; 7 Sion Hill Pl., Bath. *T.:* Luton 2955. *Club:* Arts. [*Died* 20 *Sept.* 1954.

LONGDEN, Clifford; *see* Longden, H. C.

LONGDEN, Fred; M.P. (Co-op. and Lab.) Deritend Div. of Birmingham, 1929-31 and 1945-1950, Small Heath Div. of Birmingham since 1950; Lecturer in the Co-operative, W.E.A., and Labour Movements; *b.* Ashton-under-Lyme, 1894; mother originally a silk weaver, father an iron-moulder; *m.* 1914, Alice Sherlock, Cadishead, now Alderman and J.P. of Birmingham; one *d.* *Educ.:* Elementary schools in many towns; under the W.E.A.; Ruskin Coll., Oxford. Left school at 13 and was a railway nipper till 13½, when he became a moulder-apprentice, remaining at this occupation till 1914; entered the Independent Labour Party in early teens, and has served the National Council of this body for three years; joined the Moulders' Union at 20, as well as the Co-operative Society at Irlam, and was prominent in debating, Trade Union, and Social Services; during the War was arrested for appealing (as a speaker and organiser for the Union of Democratic Control) for immediate Peace negotiations, and was imprisoned as a "C.O." for over two years, though offered exemption on trade and health grounds; since then has been a Clarion Vanner for five years; in 1912 the Manchester University and W.E.A. recommended him for Preparatory Tutorship; won the Hodgson Pratt Travelling Scholarship, 1913; won first place for residence at Ruskin College from the Club Union Examinations, 1914; whilst there he won first-class certificates in Citizenship, Economics, and Industrial History for the Co-operative Union, and gained the Diploma, with distinction, in Economics and Political Science. *Publications:* Co-operation and the New Orientation; Essentials of Public Speaking; Co-operative Politics Inside Capitalist Society; The Proletarian Heritage; Booklet on Apprenticeship in Iron-Foundry in England and Belgium; many articles on Social Science, and pamphlets including Remember, Unemployment, A Reply to Joseph Bibby, Why a Feud between Co-operation and Labour?, Peace at Once. *Recreations:* reading, writing, walking, gardening, swimming. *Address:* 58 Ansell Road, Erdington, Birmingham. *T.:* 0411. [*Died* 5 *Oct.* 1952.

LONGDEN, (Harry) Clifford, M.V.O. 1923; *b.* 18 June 1869; *s.* of late John Longden of H.M. Privy Purse Office. *Educ.:* Felsted. Clerk and Accountant to Duke of York, 1892; Chief Clerk to Prince of Wales (King George V), 1902; Assistant Secretary H.M. Privy Purse, 1910; Serjeant at Arms to H.M., 1926-35; retired, 1935. *Address:* c/o Coutts & Co., 440 Strand, W.C.2. [*Died* 18 *Nov.* 1953.

LONGDEN, Vice-Adm. Horace Walker, C.M.G. 1917; *s.* of late Sir James Longden, G.C.M.G.; *b.* 1877; *m.* 1902, Emily, *d.* of late Alfred Hewitt, J.P., of Lisle Court, Wootton, Isle of Wight; one *s.* *Educ.:* Cheltenham Coll. Entered Navy, 1890; Lt., 1898; Comdr., 1910; Capt., 1916; Naval A.D.C. to the King, 1926; Rear-Adm. and retired list, 1927; Vice-Adm., retired, 1932. *Address:* The Crossways, Wickham, Hants. *Club:* (Hon.) Royal Yacht Squadron (Cowes). [*Died* 4 *Jan.* 1953.

LONGHURST, Colonel Arthur Lyster, C.B.E. 1924; late Indian Army; J.P. County of Southampton; *s.* of late Dr. A. E. T. Longhurst, formerly Surgeon-Major, Crimea and Mutiny; *b.* 1872; *m.* 1900, Madeline, *d.* of W. H. Allen, LL.D., J.P., Bedford; one *d.* *Educ.:* Westminster; Trinity College, Cambridge. Gazetted in 1893 to Border Regt.; transferred to Indian Staff Corps, 1897; p.s.c., 1908; Staff Captain and G.S.O.3 and 2 Quetta Division and A.H.Q., India, 1908-12; War, 1914-18, Bde.-Major, 28th Indian Infantry Brigade, Egypt, Aden, Mesopotamia; G.S.O.1 A.H.Q., India; Commandant, 2/7th Gurkha Rifles, Palestine (twice wounded, despatches four times); Bt. Lt.-Col., 1916; G.S.O.1 Inter-allied Commission of Control, Berlin, 1919-22 and 1923-24; A.A. and Q.M.G., Waziristan Field Force, 1922-23 (despatches, C.B.E.); retired, 1924. *Address:* 6 Park Road, Winchester. *T.:* 3640. *Club:* Naval and Military. [*Died* 27 *Feb.* 1952.

LONGHURST, Margaret Helen; Civil Service, retd.; *b.* 5 Aug. 1882. *Educ.:* Privately. Asst. Victoria and Albert Museum, 1926; Keeper Department of Architecture and Sculpture, Victoria and Albert Museum, 1938-42. *Publications:* Catalogue of Carvings in Ivory, pt. 1 (1927), pt. 2 (1929), Victoria and Albert Museum publication; English Ivories, 1926; Part Author Catalogue of Italian Sculpture, 1932; V. and A. Museum publication; various articles for Burlington Magazine, etc. *Recreations:* travel and gardening. *Address:* Wayside, Aldbourne, Wilts. [*Died* 26 *Jan.* 1958.

LONGLAND, Rev. Sydney Ernest, M.A.; Canon Emeritus of Coventry; formerly Hon. Canon of Coventry Cathedral; *b.* 1873; *m.* 1908, Emily, *o. d.* of Frederick

Rigby of Frodsham, Cheshire; one *d.* *Educ.:* St. Albans School; Christ's College, Cambridge; Cuddesdon Theological College. Assistant Master, Felsted School, 1897-1900; Wellington College, 1901-1913; Warden, Trinity College, Glenalmond, 1913-23; Assistant Master, Rugby School, 1923-27; Vicar of Leek Wootton, 1927-43; Vicar of Beeley, Derbyshire, 1947-53; Editor of Coventry Diocesan Gazette and Chairman of Diocesan Council for Moral Welfare, 1927; Secretary of Coventry Ordination Candidates Fund, 1928; Examining Chaplain to Bishop of Coventry, 1929; Senior Examining Chaplain, 1936; Member of Council of Leamington Girls' High School, 1932; Lecturer under Central Advisory Council for Adult Education H.M. Forces, 1941. *Publications:* educational works. *Address:* Merryfield Cottage, Storrington, Sussex. [*Died* 17 *Dec.* 1957.

LONGLEY, Maj.-Gen. Sir John Raynsford, K.C.M.G., *cr.* 1919 (C.M.G. 1918); C.B. 1916; Col. The East Surrey Regiment, 1920-39; *b.* 7 March 1867; *s.* of late Charles Thomas Longley, Indian Civil Service; *m.* 1896, Iva Kathleen, *d.* of late Major Wm. Mills Molony, D.L., of Kiltanon, Co. Clare; one *s.* (and one *s.* killed in action at Jutland, 1916). Joined East Surrey Regiment 1887; Adjutant 1890; Capt. 1895; Major, 1903; Lt.-Col. 1911; Col. 1914; served S. Africa, 1902 (Queen's medal 4 clasps); European War, France, Macedonia, Egypt, Palestine, 1914-19 (despatches eleven times, Bt. Col., C.B., prom. Maj.-Gen., C.M.G., K.C.M.G.); retired pay, 1923. *Address:* West Knoyle, Warminster, Wilts. *Clubs:* Naval and Military, M.C.C. [*Died* 13 *Feb.* 1953.

LONGMORE, Brig.-Gen. John Constantine Gordon, C.B. 1921; C.M.G. 1917; C.B.E. 1919, D.S.O. 1915; late R.A.S.C.; *b.* 8 Aug. 1870; *m.* 1897, Nita, *d.* of late Thomas Davis. Entered army (East Lancs. Regt.), 1892; Captain A.S.C. 1898; Major, 1904; Lt.-Col., 1913; Deputy Assist. Director Supplies and Transport, Southern Command, 1910-13; served S. African War, 1899-1901 (Queen's medal 5 clasps); European War, 1914-19 (despatches, D.S.O., C.M.G., C.B.E.); Col. R.A.S.C. from 1913; A.Q.M.G. Aldershot Command, 1919-20; Brig.-Gen. in charge of Administration, Egypt, 1920-21; retired pay, 1921. *Address:* Mellands, Powderham, Exeter. [*Died* 21 *Feb.* 1958.

LONGMORE, Philip Elton, C.B.E. 1941; D.L. and J.P. (Herts); *b.* 13 Oct. 1884; *e. s.* of late Sir Charles Longmore, K.C.B., Hertford; *m.* 1916, Marjory Caldecott, West Chiltington, Sussex; three *d.* *Educ.:* Rugby; Exeter College, Oxford. Solicitor, 1910; Clerk of Peace and C.C. for Hertfordshire, 1930-48; Member of Welwyn Garden City and Hatfield Development Corporations, 1948-52; Late Major 1st Herts Regt. T.A.; D.A.A.G. Second Army B.E.F. and G.H.Q., Italy, 1916-18 (despatches twice); T.D. *Address:* Whyke Grange, Chichester, Sussex. *T.:* Chichester 3972. *Club:* United University. [*Died* 17 *March* 1954.

LONSDALE, 6th Earl of (U.K.), *cr.* 1807; **Captain Lancelot Edward Lowther,** O.B.E., J.P., D.L.; Bart. 1764; Viscount and Baron Lowther, 1797; Hereditary Admiral of Coasts of Cumberland and Westmorland; *b.* 25 June 1867; *s.* of 3rd Earl and Emily, *e. d.* of St. George Caulfeild, Donamon Castle, Co. Roscommon; *S.* brother, 1944; *m.* 1st, 1889, Gwendoline Sophia Alice (*d.* 1921), *d.* of Sir R. Sheffield, 5th Bt.; two *d.* (one *s.* decd.); 2nd, 1923, Sybil Beatrix, *d.* of Maj.-Gen. Edward Feetham, C.B., C.M.G.; one *s.* Formerly Capt. Border Regt.; served European War, 1914-19 (O.B.E., despatches twice, Mons 1914 Star, Order of the Nile, War medal, Military medal); was Field-Master of the Quorn and Cottesmore. *Heir:* *g.s.* Viscount Lowther. *Address:* Glebe House, Lowther, Penrith; Ashwell Hill, Oakham, Rutland. *Club:* Turf. [*Died* 11 *March* 1953.

LONSDALE, Frederick; Dramatic author; *b.* 5 Feb. 1881; *m.* Leslie Brooke Hoggan; three *d.* *Publications:* The King of Cadonia; The Balkan Princess; The Early Worm; The Best People; Betty; Maid of the Mountains; The Lady of the Rose; Aren't We All?; The Fake; The Street Singer; Spring Cleaning; The Last of Mrs. Cheyney; On Approval; The High Road; Canaries Sometimes Sing; Never Come Back; Once is Enough; Another Love Story; But for the Grace of God; The Way Things Go. Films, The Devil to Pay; Lovers Courageous. *Recreations:* golf, tennis, motoring. *Clubs:* Beefsteak, St. James'. [*Died* 4 *April* 1954.

LOOKER, Herbert William; *b.* St. Ives, Hunts., 2 Dec. 1871; *s.* of John Looker, Hunts.; *m.* 1st, Muriel Jessie Lloyd, *d.* of Tom Thomas, Yokohama; one *s.* one *d.*; 2nd, Stella May, *d.* of Basil Sharp, Brentwood, Essex; one *d.* *Educ.:* privately. Articled to a London firm of solicitors; managing clerk in London, 1894-95; proceeded to Hong-Kong and joined firm of solicitors there, 1895; admitted a partner, 1900; retired, 1919; firm Deacon, Looker & Deacon; contested Central Hull, 1922; M.P. (U.) S.E. Essex, 1924-29; East Sussex C.C., 1933, retd., 1950. *Recreations:* shooting, fishing, golf, tennis. *Address:* Chapel Meadow, Forest Row, Sussex. *T.:* 267. *Club:* Junior Carlton. [*Died* 13 *Dec.* 1951.

LORD, Captain S(ydney) Riley; President Sedgefield Conservative and Unionist Association since 1949; *b.* 14 June 1884; *s.* of late Albert Lord and *g.s.* of late Sir Riley Lord, Highfield Hall, Gosforth; *m.* 1914, Eva (*d.* 1956), *d.* of late William Jackson, Elmwood, Harrogate, Yorks; one *s.* three *d.* *Educ.:* Abbotsholme; Cologne University. Served European War, 1914-1919, with 3rd Bn. Duke of Wellington's Regiment, and 3rd Bn. Grenadier Guards, Captain, 1916. Commanded 20th Bn. (Durham) Home Guard, 1940-45. D.L. (Durham), 1947; High Sheriff of County Durham, 1949-50. *Recreations:* hunting, racing, shooting. *Address:* Newbus Grange, Neasham, nr. Darlington, Co. Durham. *Clubs:* Guards, Junior Carlton. [*Died* 5 *Nov.* 1959.

LORING, Frederick George, O.B.E.; Commander R.N.; retired, 1910; M.I.E.E.; Director International Marine Radio Company; Younger Brother of Trinity House; *b.* 11 March 1869; *e. s.* of late Admiral Sir William Loring, K.C.B., of Stonelands, Ryde, Isle of Wight; *m.* 1896, Charlotte (*d.* 1933), *d.* of late Hon. James Edward Arbuthnot of Mauritius; two *d.* *m.* 1949, Margaret Mackenzie, *d.* of late Montague S. Napier. Entered Navy, 1882; Sub-lieutenant, Royal Yacht, 1891; Lieutenant of H.M.S. Victoria when she was rammed by H.M.S. Camperdown and sunk off Tripoli, 22 June 1893 (bronze medal of R.H.S. for saving two lives); qualified in Torpedo, 1896; in charge of Admiralty shore Wireless Telegraph Stations, 1902-8 (letter of thanks from Admiralty on relinquishing appointment); Admiralty Delegate to the International Conference of Wireless Telegraphy at Berlin, 1906; Post Office Delegate to Conference, London, 1912, and Washington, 1927; represented International Marine Radio Company at International Radio Conferences, Copenhagen, 1931, Madrid, 1932, Lisbon, 1934, Bucharest, 1937, Cairo, 1938, Stockholm, 1948; Assessor Wireless Telegraphy, Board of Trade at Safety of Life at Sea Conferences, London, 1914 and 1929; Inspector of Wireless Telegraphy, Post Office, 1908-30. *Address:* The Old House, Foots Cray, Sidcup, Kent. *T.:* Foots Cray 2637. *Club:* United Service. [*Died* 7 *Sept.* 1951.

LORNIE, James, C.M.G. 1931; M.A., B.Sc.; Malayan Civil Service (retired); *b.* 10 May 1876; *m.* 1913; no *c.* *Educ.:* Perth Academy; Edinburgh University. Cadet S.S., 1899; Commissioner of Lands, Straits

Settlements, 1922-26; British Resident at Selangor, 1926-31; retired, 1931. *Address:* Lyndene, 1 Chiltern Hills Road, Beaconsfield, Bucks. [*Died* 30 *March* 1959.

LORY, Frederic Burton Pendarves, C.I.E. 1930; *er. s.* of late Rev. F. A. Pendarves Lory, vicar of Bagshot, Surrey; *b.* 23 March 1875; *m.* 1914, Mary Katharine, *er. d.* of Col. A. W. Alsager Pollock, late Somerset Light Infantry. *Educ.:* Marlborough; Exeter College, Oxford, M.A. Asst. Master, Temple Grove, East Sheen, 1901; joined Indian Educational Service, 1901; Director of Public Instruction, Bombay Presidency, 1921-30; retired 1930; served European War with Indian Army Reserve of Officers (Cavalry) 1916-19. *Recreations:* oriental art, especially Persian and Indian; formerly shooting and pig-sticking. *Address:* 51 Hurlingham Court, S.W.6. *Club:* East India and Sports. [*Died* 24 *Oct.* 1954.

LOUDOUN, Countess of, 12th in line (*cr.* 1633), **Edith Maud Abney-Hastings;** Baroness Botreaux, 1368; Baroness Hastings, 1461; Baroness Stanley, 1456 revived, 1921; Lady Mauchline, Campbell of Loudoun and Tarringean; *b.* 13 May 1883; *d.* of late Hon. Paulyn Rawdon-Hastings, *bro.* of 11th Earl and Lady Maud Grimston, *d.* of 2nd Earl of Verulam; *S.* uncle, 1920, in Earldom; and to Baronies of Botreaux, Stanley and Hastings (in her own right) on determination of abeyance, 1921; *m.* 1916, Major Reginald Mowbray Chichester Huddleston, Royal Scots (who together with his wife, assumed by Royal Licence, 1918, the surname of Abney-Hastings; she obtained a divorce 1947); five *d.* *Heir* (to Scottish Earldom and Scottish Baronies only) *d.* Lady Barbara Greenwood [*b.* 1919; *m.* 1st, 1939, Capt. W. S. Lord (marriage dissolved, 1945); one *s.*; 2nd, 1945, Capt. Gilbert Greenwood (*d.* 1951); one *s.* one *d.*; 3rd, 1954, Peter Griffiths (who assumed, with his wife, by deed poll, the surname of Abney-Hastings); one *d.*]. *Address:* Loudoun Castle, Galston, Ayrshire; The Manor House, Ashby-de-la-Zouch. [*Died* 24 *Feb.* 1960.

LOUGH, Lieut.-General Reginald Dawson Hopcraft, D.S.O. 1916; O.B.E. 1919; *b.* 1885. Served European War, 1914-19 (despatches five times, D.S.O., 1914 Star, Croix de Guerre with palm, O.B.E.); Bt. Lt.-Col., 1930; Lt.-Col. 1933; Col. 1936; Royal Marine A.D.C. to the King, 1938-39; Maj.-Gen., 1939; Lt.-Gen., 1940; retired list, 1941. *Address:* c/o Barclays Bank Ltd., Deal, Kent. [*Died* 22 *March* 1958.

LOUGHER, Sir Lewis, Kt., *cr.* 1929; *b.* 1 Oct. 1871; *s.* of Thomas Lougher, of Llandaff, Glamorgan, and Charlotte, *d.* of David Lewis, of Radyr, Glamorgan. *Educ.:* Cardiff Secondary School and Cardiff Technical College. Chairman, Lewis Lougher & Co., Ltd., Whitehouse Precast Concrete Ltd., and Danybryn Estates Ltd.; Director of Ben Evans & Co. Ltd., Swansea; a Member of Glamorganshire County Council, 1922-49; Member and Past Chm. Cardiff Rural District Council; was Chairman of Cardiff and Bristol Channel Shipowners Association, 1919, and of Shipping Federation (Cardiff District), 1918-19; of the National Trimming Board, of the Court of Inquiry *re* Hours of Labour of Coal Tippers and Trimmers under the Industrial Courts Act 1919; represented Cardiff Chamber of Commerce at the Conference of Chambers of Com. of the British Empire at Toronto, Canada, 1920, at Cape Town, South Africa, 1927 and Wellington, New Zealand, 1936; M.P. (C.) East Division of Cardiff, 1922-23; Central Cardiff, 1924-29; Member of Visiting Commission of M.P.'s to the Baltic States, 1923; Liveryman Worshipful Company of Wheelwrights; J.P., Glamorganshire, High-Sheriff, 1931. *Address:* Dany-Bryn Park, Radyr, Glamorgan. *Clubs:* Royal Automobile; Cardiff and County (Cardiff). [*Died* 28 *Aug.* 1955.

LOUGHNANE, Norman Gerald, C.B. 1924; LL.B. (Lond. Univ.); late Principal Asst. Secretary and Director of Milk, Ministry of Food; retd. 1946; *b.* 4 April 1883; *m.* 1913, Frances Mary, *y. d.* of late John Henry Smalpage, The Firs, East Sheen; one *d.* Barrister-at-law, Middle Temple; Colonial Office representative in Irish Free State, 1923-24; Member of Financial Commission of Enquiry, Mauritius, 1931; Member of British Food Mission in North America, 1943. *Address:* 11 Seymour Road, East Molesey, Surrey. *Club:* Reform. [*Died* 19 *March* 1955.

LOVE, Sir (Joseph) Clifton, Kt., *cr.* 1925; Chairman and General Manager, Clifford Love & Co., Ltd., manufacturers and merchants, Sydney, Melbourne, and Brisbane, Australia; *b.* Brisbane, 18 Jan. 1868; *s.* of late Harry Clifford Love of Gordon, Sydney, New South Wales; *m.* 1897, Maggie Drummond, 2nd *d.* of Captain James Matthew Banks of Sydney; one *s.* *Educ.:* Brisbane Grammar School; Sydney Grammar School. One of the founders of Chamber of Manufacturers of N.S. Wales, 1895; Vice-President Chamber of Manufacturers of N.S. Wales, 1915-20, President 1920, 1921, 1922; Vice-President Associated Chambers of Manufacturers of Commonwealth of Australia, 1921-22, President, 1922-23; President of the First Australian Exhibition in New South Wales, 1922; Commissioner, Government Savings Bank, New South Wales, 1931-33; Commissioner, Rural Bank of New South Wales, 1931-33; Chairman of Directors Manufacturers' Mutual Insurance Co.; Chairman Scottish Hospital; Chairman Carpet Manufacturers Ltd.; President Sydney City Mission. *Address:* Dunaird, Shirley Road, Wollstonecraft, Sydney, N.S. Wales. *Clubs:* Australian, Royal Automobile, Royal Sydney Yacht, Avondale Golf (Sydney). [*Died* 26 *Aug.* 1951.

LOVEGROVE, Edwin William, M.A. (Oxon), M.R.I.A.; F.S.A.; F.R.Hist.S.; *b.* 1868; *e. s.* of late Rev. E. Lovegrove, M.A., T.C.D., English Chaplain at Barcelona; *m.* 1st, 1899, Septima Jane (*d.* 1928), *d.* of late Rev. G. Roberts and sister of late Prof. W. Rhys Roberts, Litt.D., LL.D.; (one *s.* who fell at Dunkirk) two *d.*; 2nd, Kathleen Agnes, *d.* of late Brig.-Gen. G. A. F. Sanders. *Educ.:* Merchant Taylors' School, Crosby; New Coll., Oxford (Scholar), 1st Class Mathematics. Master at Giggleswick School; Friars' School, Bangor; Trent College. Headmaster of Humberstone Foundation School, Clee, Grimsby, Stamford School, and Ruthin School, 1913-30; Past President, Bristol and Gloucestershire Archæological Society; served on Council, Society of Antiquaries. *Publications:* St. Asaph Cathedral, St. David's Cathedral, Valle Crucis Abbey, Llanthony Priory, etc. (Arch. Camb.); St. David's Cathedral (Historical Monuments Commission); St. David's Cathedral (Archæological Journal); Llandaff Cathedral; Church Architecture of the Carolingian Age, etc. (Journal of British Archæological Association); Influence (Bristol and Gloucestershire Transactions). *Address:* Common Hill, Fownhope, Hereford. *T.:* Fownhope 57; Weobley, Hereford. *Club:* Royal Societies. [*Died* 11 *March* 1956.

LOVERIDGE, Charles William, C.B. 1929; retired assistant secretary, Admiralty; *b.* Portsmouth, 1 Oct. 1869; *s.* of John Loveridge; *m.* Alice Annie (*d.* 1952), *d.* of J. T. French, Sheerness; two *s.* *Address:* Maytree Cottage, Holtwood Road, Oxshott Surrey. [*Died* 14 *Sept.* 1957.

LOVETT, Rt. Rev. Ernest Neville, C.B.E. 1920; D.D.; late Chaplain to the King; Proctor in Convocation; *b.* 16 Feb. 1869; 3rd *surv. s.* of Rev. Robert Lovett and Elizabeth, *d.* of Hugh Lumsden of Pitcaple Castle, Aberdeen; *m.* Evelyn (*d.* 1937), *y. d.* of Commander Osmond Brock, R.N.; five *d.* *Educ.:* Sherborne School; Christ's College, Cambridge. Ordained 1892; Curate of Christ Church, Clifton, and of Wymynswold, Kent; Rector of Bishop's Caundle,

1895-98; St. Saviour's-on-the-Cliff, Shanklin, 1898-1908; Rural Dean of East Wight, 1905-1908; Rector of Farnham, 1908-12; Rector of St. Mary's Parish Church, Southampton, 1912-24, and Rural Dean; Hon. Canon of Winchester, 1916-27; Archdeacon of Portsmouth, 1924-27; Vicar of St. Thomas, Portsmouth, 1924-27; Bishop of Portsmouth, 1927-36; Bishop of Salisbury, 1936-1946. *Address:* Meon Lea, Droxford, Hants. *T.:* Droxford 19. *Club:* Athenæum. [*Died* 8 *Sept.* 1951.

LOW, A. M., A.C.G.I. (Lond.), E.I.M.M., F.C.S., F.R.G.S., F.G.S. (U.S.A.); F.I.Arb., F.F.Sc.; Pres. Brit. Institute of Engineering Technology; Pres. Inst. of Patentees; Consulting Engineer and Research Physicist; *b.* 1888; *s.* of John S. Low, Broughty Ferry, Dundee, and Gertrude Stewart, Trinidad; *m.* 1911, Amy (*d.* 1953), *d.* of Paymaster W. F. Woods, R.N.; two *s.* *Educ.:* St. Paul's School; Skerry's College, Glasgow; Central Technical College, South Kensington; Imperial College, London. Founded Low Accessories Co.; Major R.A.F. and Lt.-Comdr. R.N.V.R. (War of 1914-18); qualified as flying observer, R.A.F.; graded Experimental Officer, 1st Class; Major Pioneer Corps, attached H.Q. Southern Command, 1942-44. Hon. Asst. Prof. Physics, R.A. Coll., 1919-22; inventions include: system of radio signalling, a television system, 1914; Electrical Rocket Control, 1917; coal fuel engine, radio torpedo control gear, vibrometer and audiometer; formerly Vice-Pres. Radio Assoc. and Pres. British Instn. of Radio Engineers; Technical Adviser, Armchair Science; Chairman and Vice-Pres. Auto Cycle Union. *Publications:* Sparking Plug Design; Photography by Heat Rays; The Two-Stroke Engine; The Future; Wireless Possibilities; Cinematograph as an aid to the study of Engineering Design; Novel Methods of Chassis Testing; The Sound Proof House; Future of Motoring; Television; The Importance of Noise; Sound and Wireless; The Wonder Book of Invention; Scientific Tendencies; The Wonderful World of To-morrow; A Scientific Fantasy; Future of Motor-cycling; Experiments and Tricks; Recent Inventions; Science in Wonderland; Peter Down the Well; Modern Achievements; Modern Electric Invention; The Story of Life; Low's Book of Home Experiments; Science in the Home; Adrift in the Stratosphere; The Romance of Transport; What New Wonders; Mars Breaks Through; Science in Industry; Armaments; Science Looks Ahead; How Everything Works; How we find out; Mine and Counter Mine; Stand Easy; Submarines in War; Romance of Fire; Our Own Age; Tanks; Parachutes in Peace and War; Musket to Machine Gun; The Benefits of War; Tick-Tock; Six Scientific Years; Your World To-morrow; How Secrets Work; They made your World; Look, Listen, and Touch; It's Bound to Happen; Electronics Everywhere; The Past Presented; Wonderful Wembley; Thanks to Inventors; Modern Homes; Space Encounter. Contributor to daily and technical papers on subjects of original research. *Recreation:* the encouragement of original research. *Address:* The Yews, Woodstock Road, W.4. *T.:* Chiswick 2162. *Clubs:* Royal Automobile; British Automobile Racing (Vice-Pres. and Chm.). [*Died* 13 *Sept.* 1956.

LOW, Sir Austin, Kt., *cr.* 1928; C.I.E 1919; J.P. Co. of London; J.P. Co. of Bucks; *b.* 1862; 3rd *s.* of late S. P. Low, D.L., J.P., Kent; widower. *Educ.:* privately. Formerly Director London Assurance. *Address:* The Old House, Wexham, nr. Slough. *T.:* Slough 22867. [*Died* 12 *Jan.* 1956.

LOW, George Carmichael, M.A., M.D., C.M.; F.R.C.P.; retired; late Senior Physician, Hospital Tropical Diseases, Endsleigh Gardens, W.C.1, and Director, Div. of Clinical Tropcal Medicine, London School of Hygiene and Tropical Medicine; *b.* 14 Oct. 1872; 3rd *s.* of S. M. Low, Monifieth, Angus; *m.* 1906, Edith, *d.* of Joseph Nash. *Educ.:* Madras College, St. Andrews; St. Andrews University; Edinburgh University, 1st class honours in Medicine; Thesis gold medalist; Straits Settlements gold medalist in Tropical Medicine, 1912; Mary Kingsley Medallist, Liverpool School of Tropical Medicine, 1929; Vienna and London. Served on the Royal Society's Sleeping Sickness Commission in Uganda; Craggs Research Scholar for the Study of Filariasis, in the West Indies; Malaria-Mosquito Experiments in the Roman Campagna; late Superintendent of the London School of Tropical Medicine; (War Service, 1914-18 temp. Major I.M.S.); late President Royal Society of Tropical Medicine and Hygiene; late Member of Colonial Advisory Med. Committee; F.Z.S.; F.R.G.S.; M.B.O.U.; discovered the escape of Filaria bancrofti through the proboscis of the mosquito; B.M.A. Round the World Tour, 1935. *Publications:* Tropical Diseases (with Sir Neil Hamilton Fairley) in Price's Text Book of the Practice of Medicine, 1941; various papers on Filariasis and other Tropical Diseases; The Literature of the Charadriiformes, 2nd Edition, 1894-1928, 1931; Aves, in Centenary Volume, Zoological Society, 1929. *Recreations:* ornithology and walking. *Address:* 7 Kent House, Kensington Court, W.8. *T.:* Western 5060. [*Died* 31 *July* 1952.

LOW, Sir Stephen Philpot, Kt., *cr.*, 1938; *b.* 17 Sept. 1883; *o. s.* of late Hon. Mr. Justice Low; *m.* 1906, Bertie Faith, *d.* of R. Crosse; three *s.* *Educ.:* Dragon School, Oxford; Winchester Coll. (Exhibitioner); Magdalen Coll., Oxford (Demy, B.A. 1906). Called to Bar, Middle Temple, 1906; in practice, 1906-1914; served European War, Major (9th Hamps. Regt.), 1914-19; entered Solicitor's Dept., Ministry of Labour, 1920; Asst. Solicitor, Ministry of Labour, 1925-33; Solicitor to the Board of Trade, 1934-48; also Solicitor to the Ministry of Fuel and Power, 1942-48; Editor of Statutory Instruments, 1948-50; Director and Editor, Statutory Publications Office, 1950-54. *Address:* Little Company of Mary, Sudbury Hill, Harrow-on-the-Hill, Middlesex. *Club:* Oxford and Cambridge. [*Died* 25 *Oct.* 1955.

LOW, Sir Walter (John) Morrison-, 2nd Bt., *cr.* 1908; Director General Accident Fire and Life Assurance Corporation, Ltd., Tayside Floorcloth Company, Ltd., Newburgh; *b.* 27 May 1899; *s.* of 1st Bt. and Katherine, *d.* of Wm. Munro; *S.* father, 1923; *m.* 1924, Dorothy Ruth (*d.* 1946), *er. d.* of late Richard de Quincey Quincey, of Inglewood, Chislehurst, Kent; two *s.*; *m.* 1948, Henrietta Wilhelmina Mary, *o. d.* of Major R. W. Purvis, Gilmerton, Fife. *Educ.:* Harrow. Assumed by deed poll (enrolled at College of Arms), 1924, the additional surname of Morrison; Lieut. 1st Scots Guards during European War; Capt. Scots Guards, attached Provost Service as Major. J.P. Co. Fife. *Heir:* *s.* James Richard [*b.* 3 Aug. 1925; *m.* 1953, Anne Rawson, *d.* of Air-Cdre. R. Gordon; one *d.*]. *Address:* Kilmaron Castle, near Cupar, Fife. *T.:* Cupar 2248. *Clubs:* Guards; Royal and Ancient (St. Andrews). [*Died* 19 *July* 1955.

LOW, Ven. Walter Percival, O.B.E. 1942; M.A., Hon. C.F.; Archdeacon of Nairobi, 1921-25 and 1930-45; Archdeacon Emeritus and Hon. Canon, 1945; Examining Chaplain to Bishop of Mombasa, 1937-48; *b.* 29 Aug. 1876; *s.* of Francis Low, banker, College Green, Dublin, and Annie Elizabeth Curry; *m.* 1908, Ellen Mary, *d.* of John Cobham, Waterloo; two *s.* one *d.* (and two *s.* decd.). *Educ.:* Shrewsbury School; Christ's College and Ridley Hall, Cambridge. Deacon, 1901; Priest, 1902; Assistant Curate Walcot, 1901-03; C.M.S. Missionary Nigeria, 1903-09;

Assistant Curate Bitterne, 1909-11; Chaplain Kenya, 1911-25; Rector of Elmley Lovett, 1925; Rector of Bentham, 1926-30; Diocesan Inspector of Schools; Commissary to the Bishop of Mombasa, 1925-30; Member of Highland's Board, Kenya, 1939; Despatches Colonial Office, 1909; Temp. Chaplain Forces, 1914-15; Lance Corporal East African Medical Services, 1915-16; Temp. C.F. 1916-18 (despatches); Staff Chaplain H.Q. East Africa Command, 1939-45 (despatches, O.B.E.). *Address:* P.O. Naivasha, Kenya. *Clubs:* Nairobi (Nairobi); Nakuru, Rift Valley Sports (Nakuru). [*Died* 12 *July* 1960.

LOWE, Edward Cronin, M.B.E., M.B., B.S. (London); Pathologist and Bacteriologist; *b.* 1880; *s.* of John Henry Lowe and Charlotte Cronin; *m.* 1907; three *d.* *Educ.:* Wellington College, New Zealand; Guy's Hospital. General practice, Southport, 1907-15; Medical Officer in charge Southport Cottage Hosp., 1910-16; Pathologist to New Zealand Division, 1916-19; Capt. N.Z.M.C.; Consg. Clinical Pathologist, Liverpool and Southport, 1920-33; Consultant Bacteriologist and Pathologist, Southport Infirmary. *Publications:* Foci and Nature of Infection in Rheumatism, B.M.J., 1929; Study of Colitis, J. of State Med., 1932; Causes of Failure in Vaccine Therapy, B.M.J., 1932; Modified Bendien Reaction in Diagnosis of Cancer, B.M.J., 1933; Serodiagnosis in Cancer, British Journal Radiology, 1933; The Therapy of Cancer, Med. World 1944, 1946, 1950. *Address:* 31 Church St., Southport. *T.:* 5447; 41 Rodney St., Liverpool. *T.:* Royal 1220. [*Died* 12 *April* 1958.

LOWE, Dr. Edwin Ernest; *b.* Macclesfield, 1877; *s.* of Edwy W. R. Lowe and Mary Johnson Lowe; *m.* 1st, 1902, Maude (*d.* 1934), *d.* of John Roberts and Louisa Griffiths, Warrington; two *s.* one *d.*; 2nd, 1941, Millicent May Cross. *Educ.:* Warrington British School; Manchester Univ. Assistant in Warrington Museum, 1891-1901; Curator, Plymouth Museum and Art Gallery, 1901-7; Curator, Leicester Museum, 1907-1918; Director, City Museum, Art Gallery and Libraries, Leicester, 1918-40; Hon. Secretary of The Museums Association, 1908-1918; President of The Museums Association, 1922. *Publications:* The Igneous Rocks of Mountsorrel, 1926; Report on American Museum Work for Carnegie Trustees, 1928; Papers on Museum Administration in the Museums Journal. *Recreations:* gardening, entomology. *Address:* 17 Southfield Road, Westbury-on-Trym, Bristol. *T.:* 626349. [*Died* 7 *Dec.* 1958.

LOWE, Mrs. Eveline M., J.P.; LL.D.; *m.* Dr. George C. Lowe (*decd.*). Member L.C.C. for West Bermondsey, 1922-46; Dep.-Chm., L.C.C., 1929-30, Chm., 1939-40; Chm. Educ. Cttee., 1934-37, and Establishment Cttee., 1937-39. Hon. LL.D. London, 1950. *Address:* 30 Dulwich Common, S.E.21. [*Died* 30 *May* 1956.

LOWE, Herbert John, C.B.E. 1943; M.R.C.V.S.; Director of Veterinary Services, Tanganyika, 1938, retd., 1948; *b.* 8 Oct. 1892; *o. s.* of late John Lowe, Dublin and Ballynahinch, Co. Down; *m.* 1924, Rita, *o. d.* of Wilson Knipe, Armagh; one *s.* *Educ.:* St. Andrews College; Royal Veterinary College, Dublin. Lieut. R.A.V.C. 1914-15; Capt. R.A.V.C. 1915-18; Colonial Veterinary Service, Tanganyika Territory, 1918; Senior Veterinary Officer, 1923. *Publications:* Annual Reports of Dept. of Vet. Science and Animal Husbandry, Tanganyika Territory; articles in jls. *Recreations:* tennis and golf. *Address:* Old Dromore, Mallow, Co. Cork, Eire. [*Died* 4 *Aug.* 1960.

LOWE, Rev. John, D.D. (Tor.); Dean of Christ Church, Oxford, 1939-59; Vice-Chancellor, Oxford University, 1948-51; *b.* Calgary, Alberta, 9 Jan. 1899; *e. s.* of late Rev. H. P. Lowe, Rector of St. Luke's Pro-Cathedral, Calgary, and of Hilda, *d.* of late John Carter, Toronto; *m.* 1929, Ruth Maud, *d.* of late L. J. Burpee; two *s.* one *d.* *Educ.:* St. Catharine's Collegiate Inst.; Trinity College, Toronto; Christ Church, Oxford. Served European War, 1917-18; B.A. (Tor.) 1921; M.A. 1922; Rhodes Scholar for Ontario, 1922; 1st Class Lit. Hum. 1924; Liddon Student, 1924; 1st Class Theology, 1925; B.A. (Oxon) 1924; M.A. 1929; Grad. Student, General Theol. Sem. New York, 1925-26; Fellow and Tutor, 1926-27; Deacon 1926; Priest 1927; Asst. Curate, Grace Ch. Toronto, and Lecturer in N.T., Trinity Coll. 1927-29; Prof. of New Testament Language and Literature, Trinity Coll., 1929-39; Dean of the Faculty of Divinity, 1934-39; Rhodes Trustee, 1940; D.D. (hon. causa) of Trinity Coll., Toronto, 1939, General Theol. Seminary, New York, 1949 and Univ. of Durham, 1950; LL.D. Toronto, 1949. Commandeur de la Légion d'Honneur, 1951. *Publications:* St. Peter, 1956; Associate Editor Canadian Journal of Religious Thought, 1929-32; various articles and reviews in theological journals. *Recreations:* skating, bridge. *Address:* 14 Parks Road, Oxford. *T.:* Oxford 56231. *Club:* Athenæum. [*Died* 11 *Aug.* 1960.

LOWE, Sir Lionel (Harold Harvey), Kt., *cr.* 1951; Chairman H.M. Hudson & Co. Ltd., 1940; Director, Milford Docks Company, 1954; ex-Mem., Hops Marketing Board; *b.* 28 Dec. 1897; *s.* of late Lionel Harvey Lowe; *m.* 1925, Marjorie, *d.* of late Arthur Forward; one *s.* *Educ.:* Westminster; Trinity Coll., Camb. Articled to Thomson McLintock & Co., Chartered Accountants, 1921; A.C.A. 1925; Partner of Thomson McLintock & Co., 1935-46; F.C.A. 1940; Dir. of Finance, Cereals Division, Ministry of Food, 1939-42; Director of Finance, Ministry of Fuel and Power, 1942-45; Member of National Coal Board, 1946-51. *Address:* Newlands, St. George's Road West, Bickley, Kent. *Club:* Bath. [*Died* 30 *Aug.* 1960.

LOWE, Rouxville Mark, C.B. 1946; M.A.; *b.* 21 Oct. 1881; *yr. s.* of late David Lowe; *m.* 1944, Nancy Marian, *d.* of late Capt. W. E. Warde. *Educ.:* University College School, London; Brasenose College, Oxford (First Class Hons. in Law). Called to Bar, Lincoln's Inn, 1906; practised at Chancery Bar until 1915; served European War, 1915-18, R.G.A. two years in France; entered Land Registry, 1919; Chief Land Registrar, H.M. Land Registry, 1941-47. *Address:* 540 Holdenhurst Road, Bournemouth, Hants. *Club:* Oxford and Cambridge. [*Died* 27 *Jan.* 1957.

LOWE-BROWN, William Lowe, M.Sc., D.Eng., M.I.C.E., M.A.S.C.E., M.Cons.E.; Consulting Chartered Civil Engineer, retired 1953; *b.* 13 February 1876; *s.* of late W. D. and Martha Brown, Wigan; *m.* 1911, Mary, *d.* of late Rev. E. S. Carter, M.A. (double blue), Thwing Rectory, Yorkshire; no *c.* *Educ.:* University of Liverpool. Asst. Eng. to Sir Benjamin Baker, on construction of Central London Railway, 1897, and 1st Aswan Dam, 1899-1905; Res. Eng. Pennsylvania Rly. on construction tunnels under Hudson River, N.Y., 1905-10; Buenos Aires Western Rly., 1910-1924, successively Eng. Underground Lines, Chief Eng., Asst. Gen. Manager and Actg. Gen. Manager; served European War, 1914-1918, Lt.-Col. R.E. as O.C. Construction Richborough Train Ferry and Lt.-Col. R.M.E. as O.C. Construction Mystery Towers, Southwick, 1917-18; consulting C.E. in private practice, London, Technical Adviser, British North Borneo (Chartered) Co., Liverpool Corp. Water Supply (Vernwy Supply), tunnel under River Mersey, secret govt. schemes, 1924-43; partner in firm of Sir M. MacDonald & Partners, 1943-50, Consulting C.E. Engineers for Egyptian Govt. for Esna Barrage (Remodelling) and project, for Aswan Dam Third Heightening, River Great Ouse Catchment Board Flood Protection, North of Scotland Hydro-Electric Board, etc., 1943-; Investigation of possible Irrigation Projects for the Kingdom of Jordan, 1949; Consulting Civil Engineer. Member of Smeatonian Society; formerly M.Inst.W.E.; James Forrest Medal, Telford Premium, Miller Prize (all awarded by I.C.E.); Thomas Fritch Rowland Prize (awarded by A.S.C.E.); Order of Mejidiah (Egypt). *Publications:* An Introduction to Soil Mechanics; numerous articles and papers for professional societies and journals. *Recreations:* golf and engineering. *Address:* 81 Campden Hill Court, Kensington, W.8. *T.:* Western 6720. *Club:* Athenæum. [*Died* 20 *March* 1956.

LOWINGER, Victor Alexander, C.B.E. 1932; *b.* London, 26 Jan. 1879; *s.* of Charles Lowinger, Civil Engineer, and Mary Heath. *Educ.:* Pietermaritzburg, Natal; South African College, Cape Town. Royal Observatory, Cape Town, 1895-1904; Trigonometrical Survey, Transvaal and Orange River Colony, 1904-06; Survey Department, F.M.S., and S.S., 1906-32; Surveyor-General, Federated Malay States and Straits Settlements, 1922-1932; Agent for Malaya in United Kingdom, 1933-38; late Chairman International Tin Research Council. *Publications:* Primary Triangulation, Malaya, and various official technical reports and papers. *Address:* 19 Berkeley Square, Main Road, Rondebosch, Cape, S. Africa. *Clubs:* East India and Sports; Civil Service (Cape Town). [*Died* 9 *Aug.* 1957.

LOWNDES, Col. William Selby-, O.B.E., T.D., J.P., D.L.; *b.* 27 June 1871; *s.* of late William Selby-Lowndes and Jessie Mary, *d.* of Lieut.-General Lechmere Worral, and *widow* of Eyre Coote of West Park, Hants; *m.* 1st, 1894, Florence (*d.* 1923), *o. d.* of Frederick Norton of Auckland, New Zealand, and *widow* of Sir Edwin Abercromby Dashwood, 8th Bart.; 2nd, 1924, Maud, *e. d.* of Commander H. L. Wilson, R.N., *widow* of late T. Glen Wotherspoon, of Glenholm, Ayrshire. *Educ.:* Eton. Served South African War with Bucks Yeomanry Cavalry, European War with Beds. Yeomanry 1st Cavalry Div. (Legion of Honour, Croix de Guerre, despatches twice, O.B.E., T.D.); Director of West End Branch Royal Insurance Co.; Chairman of the County Gentlemen's Assoc.; patron of one living; Sheriff of Buckinghamshire, 1939. *Address:* Winslow, Bletchley, Bucks. *T.:* 147. *Clubs:* Carlton, Orleans, Royal Automobile, Hurlingham. [*Died* 24 *July* 1951.

LOWRIE, Rev. Walter, D.D.; retired priest of the Protestant Episcopal Church; *b.* Philadelphia, 26 April 1868; *s.* of Rev. Dr. Samuel T. Lowrie and Elizabeth (*née* Dickson); *m.* 1918, Barbara Armour; no *c.* *Educ.:* Lawrenceville School; Princeton University; Princeton Theological Seminary; Universities of Greifswald and Berlin, American Academy in Rome. Rector of Trinity, Newport, and of the American Church in Rome; Hon. Canon of Trinity Cathedral, Trenton, Diocese of New Jersey. Knight of the Order of Dannebrog (Denmark). *Publications:* Doctrine of St. John, 1899; Monuments of the Early Church, 1901; The Church and its Organization, 1904; Gaudium Crucis, 1905; Abba, Father, 1908; Problems of Church Unity, 1924; Birth of the Divine Child, 1926; Jesus According to St. Mark, 1929; Religion of Faith, 1930; Our Concern with the Theology of Crisis, 1932; Kierkegaard, 1938; Peter and Paul in Rome, 1940; Short Story of Kierkegaard, 1942; The Short Story of Jesus, 1943; Lord's Supper and the Eucharist, 1943; Ministers of Christ, 1945; Religion of a Scientist (Fechner), 1946; Art in the Early Church, 1947; Action in the Liturgy; Enchanted Island; What is Christianity?, 1953; Trans.: from Albert Schweitzer, The Mystery of the Kingdom of God, 1914; from Kierkegaard, 13 vols. (1939-44). *Address:* 83 Stockton St., Princeton, New Jersey, U.S.A. *T.:* Princeton 1866. [*Died* 12 *Aug.* 1959.

LOWRY, Charles Gibson, M.D., F.R.C.S.I.; F.R.C.S.I.; Hon.D.Sc. (Belfast); Pro-Chancellor and Emeritus Professor of Midwifery and Gynæcology, Q.U.B.; Cons. Surgeon, Ulster Hospital for Women, Royal Maternity Hospital, Belfast; Consulting Gynæcologist, Royal Victoria Hospital, Belfast; ex-Hon. Pres. Glasgow Obstetrical and Gynæcological Soc.; Hon. Fellow and ex-Pres., Ulster Medical Soc.; Hon. Fellow and ex-Vice-Pres., R.C. of Obstetricians and Gynæcologists; Hon. Fellow Obst. Soc. of Edin.; *b.* 1880; *e. s.* of Samuel Lowry, White Hill, Limavady, Co. Derry; *m.* Grace, *y. d.* of M. Crymble, Belfast; one *d.* *Educ.:* Foyle College, Londonderry; Queen's College, Belfast. Late Temporary Captain, R.A.M.C., General Medical Council, 1938-46 (Crown Nominee for N. Ireland). *Publications:* papers on various subjects connected with Obstetrics and Gynæcology. *Recreation:* gardening. *Address:* Greenlaw, Ballywilliam, Donaghadee, Co. Down. *T.:* Donaghadee 146. *Clubs:* Royal Societies; Union (Belfast). [*Died* 9 *Sept.* 1951.

LOYD, Rt. Rev. Philip Henry; *b.* 8 July 1884; *s.* of Rev. Lewis Haig and Emily Harriett Loyd. *Educ.:* Eton; King's College, Cambridge; Cuddesdon College, B.A., 1st Class Classical Tripos, 1906; M.A. 1911; Deacon, 1910; Priest, 1911; Curate, S. Mary of Eton, Hackney Wick, 1910-12; Vice-Principal, Cuddesdon College, 1912-15; Miri, India, 1915-17; Domestic Chaplain to Bishop of Bombay, 1917-19; Ahmadnagar, 1919-25; Asst. Bishop of Bombay, 1925-29; Bishop of Nasik, Deccan, 1929-44; Bishop of St. Albans, 1944-50. *Publications:* The Way according to S. Mark, 1935; By Faith with Thanksgiving, 1936; The Life according to S. John, 1936; The Treasures of the Heart of Jesus, 1938; Doers of the Word, 1939; Teach Me Thy Statutes, 1941. *Club:* Oxford and Cambridge. [*Died* 11 *Jan.* 1952.

LUBBOCK, Cecil; one of H.M.'s Lieutenants for the City of London; ex-Director of Bank of England and other Companies; ex-Chairman City of London Income Tax Commissioners; *b.* 15 Feb. 1872; 2nd *s.* of late Frederic Lubbock; *m.* 1898, Edith, *d.* of late Ven. Charles Wellington Furse, Archdeacon of Westminster; one *s.* four *d.* *Educ.:* Eton; Trinity College, Oxford. *Address:* 32 Malvern Court, S.W.7. [*Died* 18 *Jan.* 1956.

LUBBOCK, Brig.-Gen. Guy, C.M.G. 1917; D.S.O. 1916; late R.E.; *b.* 9 Oct. 1870; *s.* of late Frederic, 6th *s.* of Sir J. W. Lubbock, 3rd Bart. and *b.* of 1st Baron Avebury; *m.* 1912, Lettice Isabella, 3rd *d.* of R. H. Mason, J.P., Necton Hall, Norfolk; one *s.* *Educ.:* Eton; Woolwich. Served in Burma, Chitral, South Africa, German East Africa, France, Egypt, and Mesopotamia Campaigns (C.M.G.; Bt.-Col.); retired, 1921; Chev. Légion d'Honneur; Servian Order of the White Eagle with Swords; a Director of the Peruvian Corp., 1923-50. *Address:* The Glebe House, Westerham, Kent. [*Died* 3 *March* 1956.

LUBBOCK, Hon. Maurice Fox Pitt; Director of Lloyds Bank; *b.* 17 Oct. 1900; *s.* of 1st Baron Avebury; *heir pres.* to 3rd Baron; *m.* 1926, Hon. Adelaide Stanley, *sister* of 6th Baron Stanley of Alderley; one *s.* one *d.* *Educ.:* Eton; Balliol College, Oxford. *Address:* 75 Onslow Square, S.W.7. [*Died* 26 *April* 1957.

LUBBOCK, Samuel Gurney, M.A.; *s.* of late Frederic Lubbock of Ide Hill, Kent; *nephew* of first Lord Avebury; *m.* 1915, Irene Scharrer; one *s.* one *d.* *Educ.:* Eton (King's Scholar); King's College, Camb. (Scholar). 1st Class Classical Tripos, 1895; Hon. Sec. of the C.U.A.C., 1895-6; Assistant Master, Eton College, 1897-1934; Chevalier of the Order of Leopold. *Publication:* A Memoir of Montague Rhodes James, 1939. *Address:* 48 London

Road, Tunbridge Wells. *T.:* Tunbridge Wells 425. *Clubs:* M.C.C., Leander, Achilles, Oxford and Cambridge. [*Died* 29 *Jan.* 1958.

LUCAS (*cr.* 1663) **and DINGWALL** (*cr.* 1609), Baroness; **Nan Ino Herbert-Cooper**; *b.* 13 June 1880; *d.* of Hon. Auberon Herbert and Lady Florence Amabel, *d.* of 6th Earl Cowper; *S.* brother 1916; *m.* 1917, Lt.-Col. Howard Lister Cooper, A.F.C., R.F.C; two *d.* *Heir: d.* Hon. Anne Rosemary [*b.* 28 April 1919; *m.* 1950, Hon. Robert Palmer, *s.* of 3rd Earl of Selborne]. *Address:* Woodyates Manor, Salisbury, Wilts. *T.:* Handley 321. [*Died* 23 *Nov.* 1958.

LUCAS, Brig.-Gen. Cecil Courtenay, C.B.E. 1945; M.C. 1914; *b.* 17 Oct. 1883; *s.* of late Henry Frank Egbert Lucas, Lt.-Col. 3rd Dragoon Guards; *m.* Amelia Meliora, *y. d.* of John Adlercron, Moyglare, Co. Meath. *Educ.:* The Dragon School, Oxford; Blundells; R.M.A., Woolwich. R.F.A. 1902; R.H.A. 1910; Capt. 1914; Bt. Major, 1916; Bt. Lt.-Col. 1917; served European War, 1914-18 (M.C., despatches); retired 1926; Inspector of Remounts, 1926-37: entered Home Office, 1938; Asst. Sec., -1952. Legion of Honour, Crown of Italy, Anne of Russia. *Recreations:* hunting, shooting, cricket, football, etc. *Address:* Well House, nr. Eversley, Hants. *T.:* 2151. *Club:* Union. [*Died* 18 *Jan.* 1957.

LUCAS, Maj.-Gen. Cuthbert Henry Tindall, C.B. 1921; C.M.G. 1918; D.S.O. 1917; *b.* 1 March 1879; *s.* of late William Tindall Lucas of Foxholes, Hitchin; *m.* 1917, Joan, *d.* of late Arthur F. Holdsworth, Widdecombe, Kingsbridge; one *s.* one *d.* (and one *s.* decd.). *Educ.:* Marlborough; Sandhurst. Joined the 2nd Batt. Royal Berks Regt. 1898; served S. African War; served in the Egyptian Army and Sudan Civil Service, 1905-1909; entered the Staff College, 1913; served European War with the 1st Batt. R. Berkshire Regt. and on the Staff; 1914-18, Brevet Major and Brevet Lt.-Col. (D.S.O., C.M.G.); Bt. Col. 1 Jan. 1919; retired pay, 1932; D.L., J.P. Hertfordshire. *Address:* Northwood, Stevenage, Herts. *Club:* Army and Navy. [*Died* 7 *April* 1958.

LUCAS, Preb. Egbert de Grey; Archdeacon of Durham and Canon Residentiary of Durham Cathedral, 1939-53; Sub-Dean, 1943; Wiccamical Prebendary of Chichester Cathedral since 1953; *b.* 25 Sept. 1878; *s.* of late Henry Frank Egbert Lucas, Lt.-Col. 3rd Dragoon Guards; *m.* 1924, Joan Mary, *d.* of late Bishop Randolph, Dean of Salisbury; two *s.* two *d.* *Educ.:* Winchester; Christ Church, Oxford. Deacon 1903; Priest 1904; Curate St. Anne's, Wandsworth, 1903; Chaplain Hertford Coll., Oxford, 1906; Winchester College Mission, 1908; Vicar of Church of the Ascension, Lavender Hill, 1924; Rector of St. Nicolas, Guildford, 1930. *Address:* Randolph's, Steeple Aston, Oxfordshire. *T.:* Steeple Aston 216. [*Died* 25 *May* 1958.

LUCAS, Hon. Frank Archibald William; Judge of Appeal, High Commission Territories, South Africa, since 1955; *b.* Maritzburg, Natal, 8 Aug. 1881; *o. surv. s.* of Wm. Lucas and Fanny Agnes Greaves; *m.* Caroline Robertson, 3rd *d.* of Wm. Whittingham, London; one *d.* (two *s.* decd.). *Educ.:* Marist Brothers' School, Johannesburg; S.A. Coll., Capetown; Worcester Coll., Oxford. Gold Medallist in Arts, S.A. Coll. Studentship Inns of Court, London; Barrister-at-Law, Middle Temple, 1905; Advocate Supreme Court, S.A., 1906; K.C. 1924; Leader of Labour Party in Transvaal Provincial Council, 1914-17; Chm. of Wage Board of Union of S.A., 1926-35. Acting Judge, Transvaal Provincial Division, Supreme Court, 1946, 1947, 1948 and 1949; Judge, 1949-51. President, International Union for Land Value Taxation and Free Trade, 1955-. *Publications:* PEP Put an End to Poverty, 1935; South Africa as she might be, 1945. *Recreation:* golf. *Address:* The Sheiling, Campbell Road, Parktown West, Johannesburg. *T.:* 44-2318. *Club:* Pretoria (Pretoria). [*Died* 22 *April* 1959.

LUCAS, Brig. Reginald Hutchinson, C.B.E. 1944; M.C.; retd.; *b.* 18 Apr. 1888; *s.* of late Canon W. S. Lucas, Nelson, N.Z.; *m.* 1916, Kathleen Sibyl Reid, M.B.E. 1946; two *s.* *Educ.:* Nelson College, N.Z.; Guy's Hospital. Late Major R.A.M.C.; qualified Guy's Hospital, 1913; F.R.C.S.E. 1926; served war of 1914-18 (O.B.E., M.C., Cavaliera corona d'Italie, despatches twice); War of 1939-45, B.E.F., France, 9 months; M.E.F., 3½ years; B.L.A. 7 months (despatches); India, Malaya. Hon. Surgeon Kent and Canterbury Hospital, 1931-51; late M.O., King's School, Canterbury; Member, B.M.A. *Recreations:* tennis, golf, bridge. *Address:* 128 New Dover Road, Canterbury. *T.:* Canterbury 2020. [*Died* 5 *Feb.* 1956.

LUCE, Major-Gen. Sir Richard (Harman), K.C.M.G., *cr.* 1919 (C.M.G. 1918); C.B. 1916; M.B., F.R.C.S.; F.S.A.; Hon. Consulting Surgeon, Derby Royal Infirmary; *b.* 1867; *s.* of Col. C. R. Luce, D.L., of Halcombe, Malmesbury, Wilts; *m.* 1897, Mary Irene, *d.* of Dr. John Scott, Bournemouth; one *s.* three *d.* *Educ.:* Clifton College; Christ's College, Cambridge; Guy's Hospital. M.P. (C.) Derby, 1924-29; served European War, 1914-19 (K.C.M.G., C.B., C.M.G.); late Director, Medical Services, Egyptian Expeditionary Force; Mayor of Romsey, 1935-37; President Hants Field Club and Archaeological Society, 1939, 1943-45. *Recreations:* archæology and sketching. *Publication:* Pages from the history of Romsey and its Abbey, 1948. *Address:* Chirk Lodge, Romsey, Hants. *T.:* Romsey 2173. [*Died* 21 *Feb.* 1952.

LUCKHAM, Major Arthur Albert, C.B.E. 1930; Asst. Camp Adjutant, Mobilization Camp, Papakura, N.Z., 1940-41, Camp Adjutant since 1941; *b.* Bristol, 9 Jan. 1883; *s.* of Frederick James Luckham; *m.* 1937, Kittie Constance, *d.* of Edward George Boon, Auckland, N.Z.; no *c.* *Educ.:* Bishop's School, Glos. Twelve years 1st King's Dragoon Guards (South Africa and India); N.Z. Expeditionary Force, 1914-18, rank Capt.; Assistant Camp Adjutant, Trentham Camp, N.Z., 1915-17; Camp Adjutant, 1917-18; Camp Adjutant, Papakura Mobilisation Camp, New Zealand, 1940-44. Resident Commissioner, Niue Island, South Pacific, 1924-31; Resident Commissioner, Aitutaki, Cook Islands, 1920-24 and 1931-40. *Recreations:* tennis, badminton, cricket, football. *Address:* 27 Empire Road, Epsom, Auckland, N.Z. [*Died* 30 *May* 1957.

LUDLOW, Sir Richard (Robert), Kt., *cr.* 1950; Barrister-at-Law; *b.* 15 April 1882; *o. s.* of late James and Gertrude Howe Ludlow, Troy House, Ballycotton, Co. Cork; *m.* 1919, Katharine Guthrie, *o. c.* of James and Isabel Wood, Barclaven, Kilmacolm, Renfrewshire; one *s.* three *d.* *Educ.:* Cloyne College, Co. Cork; Marlborough College, Dublin; City of London College; Balliol College, Oxford. Inns of Court O.T.C. and 7th Duke of Cornwall's Light Infantry (7th), 1915-17, France (wounded). Balliol College, Oxford, 1917-19; B.A.Hons. (distinction) and Diploma in Economics and Political Science (distinction), 1918. Called to the Bar (Gray's Inn), and LL.B. (London) 1919; S.E. Circuit. Deputy Umpire (Unemployment Insurance Acts), 1928-47, and National Service and Reinstatement Acts, 1939-47; Umpire National Service and Reinstatement in Civil Employment Acts, 1947-55. *Publications:* Work and Labour in Halsbury's Laws of England (Hailsham edition), 1940; Random Notes (under name "Outlaw"), Law Journal, 1930, 1937; numerous articles (anonymous) on legal and general subjects in law and lay publications. *Recreations:* rowing, walking, golf, gardening. *Address:* Weston Green House, Thames Ditton, Surrey. *Club:* National Liberal. [*Died* 17 *Feb.* 1956.

LUGARD, Major Edward James, D.S.O. 1890; O.B.E. 1918; Indian Army; retired 1906; re-employed, 1915-19; *b.* Worcester, 23 March 1865; *y. s.* of Rev. F. G. Lugard, M.A., and Mary Jane, *d.* of Rev. Garton Howard; *m.* 1893, Charlotte Eleanor (*d.* 1939), *e. d.* of Rev. G. B. Howard, B.A.; one *s.* *Educ.:* Rossall. Passed first in competitive examination from Militia into Line. Farming in Canada, 1883-84; joined 3rd Worcestershire Regiment, 1885; joined Northumberland Fusiliers, 1886; transferred to Indian Army, 1888; Burmese Expedition, 1888-89 (medal with clasp); Chin-Lushai Expedition, 1889-90 (despatches, clasp, D.S.O.); Manipur Expedition, 1891 (slightly wounded, clasp); 2nd in command with British West Charterland Co.'s Expedition to Ngamiland, S. Central Africa, under Major F. D. Lugard (later Lord Lugard), 1896-97; in command of Expedition, 1897-99; S. African War, 1899-1900 (medal with 3 clasps); Political Assistant to the High Commissioner of Northern Nigeria, 1903-06; Secretary, Imperial Institute, 1908-12; Political Secretary to the Governor of Northern and Southern Nigeria, 1912-13, and to the Governor-General of Nigeria, 1914-15; served World War, 1915-19, in Naval Intelligence Division (O.B.E., War Medal). *Recreations:* gardening, shooting. *Address:* Furzen Wood, Abinger Common, Surrey. *T.A.:* Lugard, Abingercommon. *T.:* Abinger 124. [*Died* 3 *Jan.* 1957.

LUHRS, Lieut.-Colonel Henry Gordon-, C.M.G. 1917; T.D.; Managing Director, Carobronze, Ltd.; *b.* 1880; *s.* of late Hermann Luhrs, Dundee; *m.* 1918, Marion Gordon, *d.* of late Alexander Walker, Wallsend-on-Tyne; one *d.* Was Director in Gun Ammunition Filling Department, Ministry of Munitions; Regional Controller, Ministry of Supply, London and S.E. Served European War, 1915-16 (despatches, C.M.G.). *Address:* 5 Regina Court, 40 FitzJohn's Avenue, N.W.3. [*Died* 12 *Dec.* 1954.

LUKE, Brig.-Gen. Thomas Mawe, C.B.E. 1919 (O.B.E. 1918); D.S.O. 1905; *b.* 13 May 1872; *s.* of Colonel H. F. Luke, Kensington, W.; *m.* 1901, May Elizabeth, *d.* of J. Lamb, Penrith; one *s.* *Educ.:* private school. Entered Army, 1892; Captain, 1900; Major, 1913; Bt. Lt.-Col. 1915; Subst. Lieut.-Col. 1917; temp. Brig.-General, 1916; served N.W. Frontier, India, 1897-98 (medal with clasp); Thibet, 1903-4 (despatches, medal and clasp, D.S.O.); N.W. Frontier, India (Mohmund), 1908 (medal and clasp); European War, 1914-19 (despatches 4 times); Director of Administration Adjutant-General's Branch, Headquarters, India; retd. pay, 1920. *Address:* c/o Midland Bank, Ltd., 69 Pall Mall, S.W.1. [*Died* 29 *Sept.* 1952.

LUKIN, Brig.-Gen. Robert Clarence Wellesley, D.S.O. 1915; late 9th Hodson's Horse, Indian army; *b.* 22 Dec. 1870; *m.* 1909, Meriel, *d.* of Wellesley Taylor, Sherington Manor, Newport Pagnell. Entered Army, 1890, Captain Indian army, 1901; Major, 1908; Col. 1920; special service S. Africa, 1901-2; D.A.A.G. India, 1913; served Chitral, 1895 (medal with clasp); Tirah, 1897-98 (two clasps); South Africa, 1901-2 (Queen's medal 5 clasps); European War, 1914-16 (despatches, D.S.O.); Afghan War, 1919, and Arab Rebellion, 1919-20; retired, 1922. *Address:* Lockram House, nr. Mortimer, Berks. *T.:* Burghfield Common 18. *Club:* Lansdowne. [*Died* 23 *Oct.* 1955.

LUMB, Colonel Frederick George Edward, C.B. 1930; D.S.O. 1919; M.C.; late Royal Garhwal Rifles; *s.* of late Edward Henry Lumb and *g. s.* of late Edward Lumb, Wallington Lodge, Surrey; *b.* 1877; *m.* 1920, Eva Mary, *yr. d.* of late Robert Kennaway Leigh, Bardon, Washford. *Educ.:* Bedford School: R.M.C., Sandhurst. Served China, 1900-1901; European War (France, Egypt, Arabia, Mesopotamia, Kurdistan), 1914-1921 (despatches four times, D.S.O., M.C., Legion d'Honneur, Brevet Lieut.-Col.); Instructor Senior Officers' School, Belgaum, 1921-22; commanded Rangoon Brigade Area, 1925-26; A.A. and Q.M.G. Rawal Pindi District, 1927-29; retired, 1929. *Recreations:* cricket, polo, big game shooting. *Address:* Somerton Hill, Tangier, Morocco. *Club:* United Service. [*Died* 18 *March* 1958.

LUMSDEN, Thomas William; Director of Cancer Research, London Hospital, 1930-42; Pathologist in Emergency Medical Service, 1939-41; *b.* 20 Dec. 1874; *s.* of late Rev. Edward Lumsden, Midmar, Aberdeenshire, and Jessie, *d.* of Charles Downie, of Broomhill, Aberdeenshire. *Educ.:* Privately; Aberdeen Grammar School; Aberdeen University. M.B., Ch.B., Aberd. (honours) 1897; M.D. (Commendation) 1901, Fife Jamieson Gold Medallist in Anatomy 1895; Shepherd Gold Medal in Surgery 1897; Struthers Gold Medallist and Prizeman in Anatomy 1899; in private practice in Belgravia, 1900-25; Lieut. R.A.M.C.; Hon. Assistant Pathological Dept. Lister Institute, 1925-30; Cancer Researcher to British Empire Cancer Campaign, 1925-42; Director Cancer Research, London Hospital, 1930-42; Fellow Royal Society of Medicine; Fellow Physiological Society; Fellow Pathological Society; Discovered the four centres regulating Respiration, 1922-24; since then has been studying Anti-Cancer Sera and Immunity in relation to malignant tumours; has been Delegate to various scientific congresses at home and abroad. *Publications:* Physiology of the Respiratory Centres and the Regulation of Respiration, Journ. of Physiology, 1923-24; Various papers on Cancer Research in the Lancet, and Journal of Pathology, 1925-35; Monograph on Tumour Immunity in the American Journal of Cancer, 1931. *Recreations:* life drawing, violoncello, fishing, shooting, golf. *Address:* Stocking Pelham, Herts. *T.:* Brent Pelham 289. [*Died* 24 *Nov.* 1953.

LUND, Lieut.-General Sir Otto Marling, K.C.B., *cr.* 1948 (C.B. 1942); D.S.O. 1917; *b.* 28 Nov. 1891; *o. s.* of Albert Lund; *m.* 1922, Margaret Phyllis Frances Harrison; one *s.* one *d.* *Educ.:* Winchester Coll.; R.M.A., Woolwich. First Commission in Royal Artillery, 1911; served European War, 1914-18, in France in R.H.A. and R.F.A. (D.S.O., Brevet Major, despatches four times); A.D.C. to General Lord Rawlinson when C.-in-C. in North Russia, Aldershot Command, and India, 1919-22; Assistant Military Secretary Eastern Command, 1923-1924; Staff College, Camberley, 1924-25; General Staff Aldershot Command, 1926-27; Brig.-Maj. 2nd Infantry Brigade, 1928-30; G.S.O. 2, Staff College, Camberley, 1931-34; Military Asst. to Chief of Imperial General Staff, War Office, 1934-36; Imperial Defence Coll., 1936; G.S.O.1, War Office, 1937-39; mission in Turkey, 1939; Deputy Director of Operations, War Office, Sept. 1939; Major-General, Royal Artillery, Home Forces; and 21 Army Group till Feb. 1944; Director Royal Artillery, War Office, 1944-46; G.O.C.-in-C., Anti-Aircraft Command, 1946-48; retired. ex-Col. Comdt. R.A.; Col. Comdt. R.H.A.; Comr.-in-Chief, S.J.A.B.; K.St.J. *Address:* 33 Chesham Pl., S.W.1. *T.:* Sloane 1907. *Club:* United Service. [*Died* 15 *Aug.* 1956.

LUNDON, Thomas; *b.* 1883; *s.* of William Lundon, late M.P. for East Limerick. *Educ.:* Kilteely Classical Academy. M.P. (N.) Limerick County, East, 1909-18. *Address:* 17 Nassau Rd., S.W.13; Kilteely, Co. Limerick. [*Died* 28 *Oct.* 1951.

LUTOSŁAWSKI, Wincenty, M.A., Ph.D.; Professor Emeritus of Philosophy of the Stefan Batory University in Wilno, Poland, since 1929; *b.* Warsaw, 6 June 1863; *s.* of Franciszek Lutosławski and Maria Szczygielska; *m.* 1st, 1887, Sofia Casanova; four *d.*; 2nd, 1913, Wanda Peszyńska, *d.* of late Dr. med. Stanisław Peszyński; one *s.*

one *d.* *Educ.:* Mitau Gymnasium; Riga Polytechnicum; Dorpat University; Sorbonne, Paris. Privat docent of philosophy at Kazañ University, 1889; docent and State Examiner in the same University, 1891-93; research work in British Museum and Bibliothèque Nationale in Paris; teaching as privat docent at Cracow Univ. 1899-1900; privat docent in Geneva and Lausanne Universities, 1901-2; Lectures at University College in London, 1904-6; Lowell Lecturer in Boston, 1907; lectures at the Sorbonne, 1919; public lectures all over Poland, 1908-10; Ordinary Professor of Philosophy at the University of Wilno, 1919-29; settled since 1932 in Polish Silesia in order to create an institution called Forge (Kuźnica) for research; since Sept. 1934 moved to Cracow. Lectures at Cracow University, 1945-48 (these lectures stopped by the Govt. because of their anti-materialistic character, June 1948). *Publications:* Erhaltung und Untergang der Staatsverfassungen, 1888; The Origin and Growth of Plato's Logic 1897; The World of Souls, 1924; Pre-existence and Reincarnation, 1928, Italian edition Pre-esistenza e rincarnazione, 1931; The Knowledge of Reality, 1930; Seelenmacht, Abriss einer Zeitgemaessen Weltanschauung, 1899; Volonté et Liberté, 1913; Alternatives essentielles en Morale, 1939; Mlodzi Święci, 1948; many books in Polish; Polish Messianism in the East and West series, Karachi, India, 1939; Personality, 1946; articles in many English and Polish periodicals. *Recreations:* travel, friendship, extensive international correspondence, chiefly on postcards. *Address:* Szwedzka 10 m 2, Kraków XI, Poland. *T.A.:* Debniki, Kraków. [*Died Jan.* 1955.

LUXTON, Sir Harold, Kt., *cr.* 1932; *b.* 25 June 1888; *s.* of late Hon. Thomas Luxton, M.L.C., and Sarah Luxton; *m.* Doris Mary, *d.* of Walter Henry Lewis and Amy Francis Lewis; three *s.* one *d.* *Educ.:* Melbourne School. Chairman of Directors, McEwans Ltd. Served 1915-18, Austr. Field Artillery and Royal Air Force; Member for Caulfield of Legislative Assembly, Victoria, 1930-35, and Member of Melbourne City Council, 1919-43; Lord Mayor of Melbourne, 1928 - 29 - 30 - 31. *Recreations:* tennis, golf. *Address:* Elizabeth Street, Melbourne, C.1, Australia. *T.A.:* Sanmacew, Melbourne. *T.:* MU 8101. *Clubs:* Melbourne, Athenæum, Naval and Military (Melbourne). [*Died* 24 *Oct.* 1957.

LYALL, George, C.B.E. 1942; *b.* Macduff, Banffshire, 14 March 1883; *m.* 1913, Amy Beveridge, *e. d.* of late F. J. Jolly, J.P., Aberdeen; one *s.* Entered Consular Service in 1917; Vice-Consul at Riberalta, Bolivia; Para, Brazil, 1918-20; Consul at Tegucigalpa, Republic of Honduras, 1920, and held local rank of Consul-General and Chargé d'Affaires; Vigo, Spain, 1924; Berlin, 1926; Consul-General, Berlin, 1936-39; Consul-General and Chargé d'Affaires, Costa Rica, 1939; retired 1943. *Address:* 47 Hamilton Place, Aberdeen. *T.:* 27113. [*Died* 6 *Sept.* 1959.

LYALL GRANT, Sir Robert (William), Kt., *cr.* 1934; M.A.; LL.B.; T.D.; Norwich Diocesan Board of Finance, etc.; *b.* Aberdeen, 10 Sept. 1875; *s.* of John Lyall Grant, Richmondhill, Aberdeen; *m.* Annie Marie Tadman. *Educ.:* Aberdeen Grammar School; Aberdeen and Edinburgh Universities; Germany. Called to Scots Bar, 1903; Attorney-General, Nyasaland, 1909; M.E.C., M.L.C.; Judge of High Court, 1914; Attorney-General, Kenya, 1920; M.E.C., M.L.C.; Puisne Justice, Ceylon, 1926-32; Chief Justice of Jamaica, 1932-36; retired 1936; Capt. R.A. T.A.), retired. *Recreations:* reading, etc. *Address:* Elcot, Sheringham, Norfolk. *T.:* Sheringham 313. *Club:* Royal Cromer Golf. [*Died* 2 *Feb.* 1955.

LYGON, Lt.-Col. Hon. Robert, M.V.O. 1910, M.C.; formerly commanding 2/4th Batt. Loyal North Lancs Regt.; Lieut.-Col. Retired, late Grenadier Guards; *o. surv. s.* of 6th Earl Beauchamp; *b.* 9 Aug. 1879; *m.* 1903, Cecil Albinia, *o. d.* of late Sir G. Gough Arbuthnot; one *s.* *Educ.:* Eton; Sandhurst. Entered Grenadier Guards, 1898; Capt. 1905; Regimental Adjutant, 1909-11; retired 1914; A.D.C. to Governor of Madras, 1900-3; served South Africa, 1899-1900 (wounded, Queen's medal 5 clasps); European War, 1914-17 (despatches, Military Cross). *Recreations:* fishing, shooting. *Address:* c/o National Provincial Bank, 66 Trafalgar Square, W.C.2. *Club:* Guards. [*Died* 13 *Jan.* 1952.

LYLE OF WESTBOURNE, 1st Baron, *cr.* 1945, of Canford Cliffs; **Charles Ernest Leonard Lyle,** 1st Bt., *cr.* 1932; Kt., *cr.* 1923; J.P. Bournemouth; President Tate & Lyle, Ltd., sugar refiners; Chairman, West Indies Sugar Co.; Director, Lloyds Bank; Director, Canada & Dominion Sugar Refining Co.; Deputy President Queen Mary's Hospital for the East End; Treasurer, Royal Wanstead School; Vice-Pres. Lawn Tennis Association; *s.* of Charles Lyle and late Margaret Lyle; *b.* 22 July 1882; *m.* 1904, Edith L. (*d.* 1942), *d.* of John Levy, Rochester; one *s.* two *d.* *Educ.:* Harrow; Trinity Hall, Cambridge. M.P. (C.U.) Stratford Division of West Ham, Dec. 1918-22, (U.) Epping Division of Essex, 1923-1924; was Parliamentary Private Secretary to Right Hon. C. A. McCurdy, K.C., M.P., Food Controller; M.P. (C.) Bournemouth, 1940-45. *Recreations:* golf (Pres. Professional Golfers' Assoc.); an internat. lawn tennis player and has rep. England. *Heir:* *s.* Hon. Charles John Leonard Lyle [*b.* 8 March 1905; *m.* 1927, Joyce, *er. d.* of late Sir John Jarvis, 1st Bt.]. *Address:* Greystoke, Canford Cliffs, Bournemouth. *T.:* Canford Cliffs 77728. *Clubs:* Carlton; Royal Yacht Squadron; All England Lawn Tennis. [*Died* 6 *March* 1954.

LYLE, Herbert Willoughby, M.D., B.S. (Lond.); F.R.C.S. (Eng.), F.Z.S.; F.R.S.M.; Fellow, Associate and Member of the Corporation of King's College, London; Consulting Ophthalmic Surgeon to King's College Hospital and to Beckenham Hospital; Dean-Emeritus and Emeritus Lecturer on Ophthalmology in King's College Hospital Medical School; Consulting Surgeon, Royal Eye Hospital; Hon. Consulting Ophthalmic Surgeon to Royal School for Blind, and South London Institute for the Blind; *s.* of late Thomas Lyle, M.A.; *m.* 1924, Grace Kime, of Fulbeck, Lincoln; two *s.* three *d.* *Educ.:* King's College School and King's College (London University). Prizeman, Sambrooke Exhibitioner and Scholar in King's College, London; House Surgeon and Ophthalmic Assistant in King's College Hospital, and Resident Medical Officer at St. Peter's Hospital; Surgeon and Dean, Royal Eye Hospital; Ophthalmic Surgeon, Royal Ear Hospital; Senior Demonstrator of Anatomy and Tutor in the Sheffield Medical School; Assistant Demonstrator of Anatomy, and Senior Demonstrator of Physiology in King's College; became Lecturer on Physiology, Zoology, and Biology in King's College, London University; for 5 years was Examiner in Elementary Biology to the Conjoint Board in England, for ten years Examiner in Physiology for the Fellowship of the R.C.S. and for the Diploma in Ophthalmic Medicine and Surgery of the Conjoint Board; commenced the study of ophthalmology in 1893. Formerly J.P. in County of London. *Publications:* A Manual of Physiology (with Dr. David de Souza, 3rd Edition); Veratrine-like action of Glycerine on Muscle; Abnormal Circulation in the Frog; Eye-sight of Children attending Elementary Schools; Effect of Tobacco on the Eyes; Diseases of the Eye in Infants; Gumma of the Iris; Ocular Manifestations accompanying Influenza;

LUXTON, Brig. Daniel Aston, C.M.G., D.S.O.: See page xxix.

Glaucoma; King's and Some of King's Men, 1935, Addendum, 1950. Historical Articles in the Medical Press and Circular. *Recreation:* gardening. *Address:* Fircliff, Portishead, Somerset. *T.:* Portishead 3243. [*Died* 13 *March* 1956.

LYNAM, Alfred Edmund, M.A.; Master of the Dragon School, Oxford (with J. H. R. Lynam (son) as Headmaster); *b.* 29 Mar. 1873; *s.* of Charles Lynam, F.R.I.B.A., F.S.A., and *d.* of Robt. Garner, M.D., F.R.C.S., Stoke upon Trent; *m.* 1901; one *s.* one *d.* *Educ.:* Dragon School, Oxford; Rossall School (Scholar); Exeter Coll., Oxford (Scholar). Joined staff of Dragon School, 1895, as Classical Master for top form; became Bursar, and later, joint-Headmaster, with C. C. Lynam (eldest brother); sole Headmaster on latter's retirement, 1920; took G. C. Vassall and L. Wallace into partnership, later J. H. R. Lynam (son). *Publications:* Editor (with V. J. K. Brook, A. A. David, and W. H. Fyfe) of "A Short Bible", 1929; "Hymns and Prayers for Dragons", 1923 and 1950. *Recreation:* rowed in College VIII, 1894 and 1895, and won College sculls, 1895. *Address:* Dragon School, Oxford. *T.:* 55560 Oxford. [*Died* 14 *Oct.* 1956.

LYNCH, G(erald) Roche, O.B.E. 1919; M.B., B.S., London; L.M.S.S.A., D.P.H., F.R.I.C., F.C.G.I.; Senior Official Analyst to the Home Office, 1928-54; Director Department of Chemical Pathology, 1928-54, and Lecturer in Forensic Medicine, 1936-54, St. Mary's Hospital Medical School; *b.* 12 Jan. 1889; *s.* of late Jordan and late Marian Roche Lynch; *m.* 1917, late Sybil, *d.* of late George Pinnock; one *d.* *Educ.:* St. Paul's School; St. Mary's Hospital Medical School, Univ. of London; Central Technical College, South Kensington. Open natural science schol. St. Mary's, 1906; Demonstr. of Chemistry, St. Mary's, 1908. Surgeon, R.N., 1914-1918. Lecturer in Forensic Medicine and Toxicology, Westminster Hosp. Med. School, 1924-45. Junior Official Analyst to the Home Office, 1920-28. Member Poisons Board, 1933; Privy Council Visitor to Examinations of Pharmaceutical Soc., 1943; Examiner for D.P.H.: Roy. Coll. of Physicians, Roy. Inst. of Chemistry and Univ. of Lond. M.B. Past Pres.: Soc. of Public Analysts and Other Analytical Chemists, 1936-37; Medico-Legal Soc., 1939-41; Roy. Inst. of Chem., 1946-49. Past Master Soc. of Apothecaries of London. *Publications:* various, on Medicine, Toxicology and Chemistry. *Recreations:* horology, gardening and photography. *Address:* 81 Sussex Place, Slough, Bucks. *T.:* Slough 22232. *Club:* Savage. [*Died* 3 *July* 1957.

LYNCH, Sir Henry Joseph, Kt., *cr.* 1923; Senior partner, Davidson, Pullen & Co., Rio de Janeiro; *b.* 14 Apr. 1878; *s.* of Edward James Lynch, Rio de Janeiro. Ex-President, Chamber of Commerce, Brazil. F.R.G.S., F.Z.S., F.R.H.S. *Address:* 344 Praia do Flamengo, Rio de Janeiro, Brazil. [*Died* 16 *Jan.* 1958.

LYNCH-BLOSSE, Sir Robert C. L.; *see* Blosse.

LYNCH-ROBINSON, Sir Christopher Henry, 2nd Bt., *cr.* 1920; *b.* 18 Oct. 1884; *e. s.* of late Rt. Hon. Sir Henry Robinson, K.C.B., 1st Bt., and Harriet, *d.* of Sir R. Lynch-Blosse, 10th Bt., of Athavallie Balla, Co. Mayo; *S.* father, 1927; assumed by Deed Poll and Letters Patent the name of Lynch in addition to that of Robinson, 1947; *m.* 1st, 1912, Dorothy Warren (marriage dissolved, 1957), *d.* of Henry Warren, of Carrickmines, Co. Dublin; one *s.*; 2nd, 1957, Olive Louise, *d.* of George Bartholomew, Tonbridge. *Educ.:* Wellington College; R.M.C., Sandhurst. Entered Royal Fusiliers, 1904; Private Secretary to Lord Olivier, Governor of Jamaica, 1909-11; Member of Old Age Pensions Committee of Local Government Board for Ireland, 1911-12; Resident Magistrate for Counties Donegal, Louth, and Dublin, 1912-1922; Barrister-at-law, Irish Bar; Lieut. R.N.V.R., 1915-18. *Publications:* Intelligible Heraldry, 1949 (with brother); The Last of the Irish R.M.'s, 1950. *Heir:* *s.* Niall Bryan, D.S.C., Lieut. R.N.V.R. [*b.* 24 Feb. 1918; *m.* 1940, Rosemary Seaton, *e. d.* of Mrs. M. S. Eller; one *s.* one adopted *d.*]. *Address:* 20 Palmeira Court, Hove, Sussex. *Club:* United Service. [*Died* 22 *Nov.* 1958.

LYND, Sylvia; *b.* Hampstead, N.W.3, 1888; *d.* of late A. R. Dryhurst, I.S.O. and late N. F. Robinson of Dublin; *m.* 1909, Robert Lynd (*d.* 1949); two *d.* *Educ.:* King Alfred School; Slade School; Academy of Dramatic Art. Member Vie Heureuse Committee, 1923; Book Society Committee, 1929. *Publications:* The Chorus (novel), 1916; The Thrush and the Jay (miscellany); The Goldfinches (poems), 1920; The Swallow Dive (novel), 1921; The Mulberry Bush (stories), 1925; volume in Augustan Poets, 1928; The Yellow Placard (poems), 1931; edited The Children's Omnibus, 1932; The Enemies (poems), 1934; English Children, volume in Britain in Pictures, 1942; Collected Poems, 1944; Autobiography, 1952. *Address:* 5 Keats Grove, N.W.3. *T.:* Hampstead 0850. [*Died* 21 *Feb.* 1952.

LYNE, Robert Francis, O.B.E. 1950; Recorder of Hereford, 1935-55; *b.* 1885; *s.* of late Herbert Lyne; *m.* Veronica Cecil Earle (*d.* 1956), *d.* of C. W. Earle Marsh; one *s.* *Educ.:* Cranbrook School. Served with R.A. 1914-19, Gallipoli, Egypt, Palestine (despatches); called to bar, Inner Temple, 1922; joined Oxford Circuit; Lord Mayor of Bristol, 1951-52. *Address:* Woodlands, Wrington, Somerset. *T.:* Wrington 235. [*Died* 13 *April* 1957.

LYNE, Rear-Adm. Sir Thomas John Spence, K.C.V.O., *cr.* 1935; C.B. 1925; D.S.O. 1918; Royal Navy, retired; Director of Empire Service Club, Westminster; on Board of Governors, L.C.C. Nautical Schools; *b.* 1870; *s.* of late William John Lyne, R.N., and Janet, *d.* of late Colin Reid Cromarty; *m.* Ethel Louise (*d.* 1943), *d.* of late Ralph Stobbart, Newcastle and Rochester, Kent; one *d.* *Educ.:* Beers Private School, Stoke Damerel, Devon. Entered Navy as boy, 1885; promoted to Lieut. for services in South African War; passed through the various stages to rank of Captain in 1918, being the first ranker in modern times to have reached that rank; commanded many of H.M. ships at home and abroad; promoted to Commodore for Reserve Fleet Exercises, summer 1924; commanded the Central Reserves and Impregnable Boys' Training Establishment; retired list, 1925; despatches in S. African War and European War; Rear-Admiral, retired, 1931. *Publications:* Navigation of the Han Kiang, China; Something about a Sailor; From Sailor Boy to Rear-Admiral. *Recreation:* golf. *Address:* Hamilton House, Wolverstone, Ipswich. *Club:* Junior Army and Navy. [*Died* 25 *Dec.* 1955.

LYNN, Rev. Joseph, C.B.E. 1937; B.A., D.D.; Minister, West Church, Dollar; *b.* 30 Sept. 1887; *s.* of late Joseph Lynn, Londonderry; *m.* 1914, Alicia Martha, *d.* of late A. A. Clendinning, Belfast; one *s.* one *d.* *Educ.:* Foyle College, Londonderry; Queen's University, Belfast, B.A.; Magee College, Londonderry; New College, Edinburgh; Assembly's College, Belfast. B.D. (Lond.), 1911; Assistant, Malone Church, Belfast, 1911-12; Fortwilliam Church, Belfast, 1912-1913; Chaplain to the Forces, Aldershot, 1913-14, France, 1914-18 (despatches twice, 1914 Star, General Service and Victory medals); Senior Chaplain to the Forces, 1917-19; Assistant Chaplain-General, Scottish Command, 1933-34; Deputy Chaplain-General to the Forces, 1934-39; retired pay, 1940; D.D. (Hon.) Queen's University, Belfast, 1935; Jubilee medal, 1935; Coronation medal, 1937. *Recreations:* gardening, motoring, badminton. *Address:* West Manse, Dollar, Clackmannanshire. [*Died* 29 *Nov.* 1956.

LYNSKEY, Sir George Justin, Kt., *cr.* 1944; **Hon. Mr. Justice Lynskey;** Judge of High Court of Justice, King's Bench Division, since 1944; *b.* Knotty Ash, Liverpool, 5 Feb. 1888; *s.* of late George Jeremy Lynskey, Solicitor; *m.* 1913, Eileen, *y. d.* of John Edward Prendwille, Liverpool; two *d.* *Educ.:* St. Francis Xavier's College, Liverpool; Liverpool University, LL.B., 1907; LL.M., 1908; Hon. LL.D., 1951. Admitted a Solicitor, 1910; called to Bar, Inner Temple, 1920; K.C., 1930; Bencher, Inner Temple, 1938; Judge of Salford Hundred Court of Record, 1937-44. *Address:* Royal Courts of Justice, W.C.2; 6 Tower Grove, Oatlands Drive, Weybridge, Surrey. *T.:* Walton-on-Thames 2579. [*Died* 21 *Dec.* 1957.

LYON; *see* Bowes-Lyon.

LYON, Brig.-Gen. Charles Harry, C.B. 1919; C.M.G. 1918; D.S.O. 1916; late N. Stafford Regt.; *b.* 18 Mar. 1878; 2nd Lieut. N. Staffs. Regt. 1900; Capt. 1909; Major, 1915; Bt. Lt.-Col. 1917; Col. 1922. Served S. Africa, 1900-2 (despatches, Queen's medal 3 clasps, King's medal 2 clasps); European War, 1914-18 (despatches, C.B., C.M.G., D.S.O., Bt. Lt.-Col.); retired pay, 1927. *Address:* The Old Rectory, Ightfield, Whitchurch, Shropshire. [*Died* 3 *Dec.* 1959.

LYON, Brigadier Cyril Arthur, D.S.O. 1917; *b.* 11 Aug. 1880; 3rd *s.* of late C. W. Lyon, of Doveridge Manor, Derbyshire; *m.* 1909; one *d.* *Educ.:* Newton College. Served European War, 1914-19 (despatches thrice, Bt. Lt.-Col., D.S.O., Croix de Guerre); A.A.G. Artillery, War Office, 1930-34; Officer Commanding the Troops, Ceylon, 1934-37; retired pay, 1937; Private Secretary to Sir Winston Dugan, Governor of Victoria, Australia, June 1939; re-employed as Commander in an Eastern theatre of war, Nov. 1939-April 1942, when finally retired; employed in Ministry of Home Security, 1942-45. *Address:* Bullfield, Playden, Rye, Sussex. [*Died* 25 *Feb.* 1955.

LYON, David Murray, M.D., Ch.B., D.Sc., F.R.C.P. Ed., D.P.H., F.R.S. Ed.; Principal Medical Officer of Scottish Widows' Fund and Life Assurance Society, 1936-54; Editor Edinburgh Med. Jour.; *b.* 1888; *s.* of William Malcolm Lyon, M.R.C.V.S., Wooler, Northumberland, and E. Campbell; *m.* Edith Dona Lloyd; two *s.* one *d.* *Educ.:* George Watson's Coll., Edinburgh; Edinburgh University; Member Scientific Advisory Committee; President Royal Medical Society; Stark scholar in Clinical Medicine; Crichton scholar in Pathology; Lecturer in Pathology, Edinburgh University and School of Medicine of the Royal Colleges, Edinburgh; Christison Professor of Therapeutics, 1924-36; Prof. of Clinical Medicine University of Edinburgh, 1924-53; Resident Physician, Clinical Assistant, Assistant Pathologist, Assistant Physician, Physician Consultant, Royal Infirmary, Edinburgh; Pres. R.C.P., Edinburgh; Maj., Royal Army Medical Corps, Special Reserve (despatches). *Publications:* The Essentials of Medical Treatment, 1939; numerous papers in medicine, therapeutics and applied physiology. *Address:* 8 Hailes Gardens, Colinton, Edinburgh. *T.:* Colinton 87508. [*Died* 16 *Nov.* 1956.

LYON, Brig.-Gen. Francis, C.B. 1921; C.M.G. 1916; C.V.O. 1922; D.S.O. 1900; Commander of the Legion of Honour; late R.A.; *b.* 10 July 1867; *s.* of late Col. Francis Lyon, R.H.A., and Hon. Mrs. Lyon, *sister* of 11th Viscount Valentia; *m.* 1910, Jane, *e. d.* of Joseph C. Borwick; one *s.* two *d.* *Educ.:* Wellington College; R.M.A. Woolwich. Entered Army, 1887, Capt. 1898; Military Attaché, Sofia, Belgrade, Bucharest, and Athens, 1911-13; served N.W. Frontier, India, 1897-98 (medal with clasp); S. Africa, 1899-1900 (despatches, Queen's medal 3 clasps, D.S.O.); A.D.C. to Sir G. White, G.O.C. Ladysmith; Ashanti, 1900 (despatches, medal; p.s.c. 1902; N. Nigeria, 1903 (despatches, medal with clasp); Asst. Secretary to Committee of Imperial Defence, 1906-10; attached to Bulgarian Army in Balkan War, 1912, and to Rumanian Army in War against Bulgaria, 1913; European War, 1914-17 (despatches twice, C.M.G., Bt.-Col.); temp. Brig.-Gen. 1915; Military Attaché, Brussels, Copenhagen and Berne, 1918-22; retired from army, 1922. *Address:* Gorsehanger, Farnham, Surrey. *T.:* Farnham 5334. *Club:* United Service. [*Died* 21 *Feb.* 1953.

LYON, Kenneth, C.B. 1938; C.B.E. 1924; *b.* Rainhill, Lancashire, 7 Feb. 1886; *e. s.* of late William Lyon and Jessie Ellenor Lyon; *m.* 1st, 1913, Lucy (*d.* 1924), 2nd *d.* of late Rev. J. M. Geden, B.A., Rectory, Burrough; one *d.*; 2nd, 1929, Sybil Dorothy, *y. d.* of late Rev. W. Done Bushell, Harrow School. *Educ.:* Birkenhead School; Merton College, Oxford, Classical Postmaster, 1904-8, 1st class Lit. Hum. 1908. Entered Home Civil Service, 1909; Private Secretary to the Adj.-General to the Forces, 1912-16; served with H.M. Forces, 1916-19, Captain Royal Artillery (despatches twice); Private Secretary to successive Secretaries of State for War (The Right Hon. Sir L. Worthington-Evans; The Right Hon. the Earl of Derby, The Right Hon. Stephen Walsh), 1921-24; Assist. Sec., the War Office, Whitehall, S.W., 1924-36; Assistant Under-Secretary of State, 1936-46; Member of United Kingdom Delegation to the Disarmament Conference, Geneva, 1932. Is a Freeman of City of London; Master of Worshipful Company of Glass Sellers, 1951-52. Coronation medals 1911 and 1937, British War medal, Victory medal, Silver Jubilee medal, 1935; Defence Medal; Chevalier Legion of Honour. *Publications:* articles on literature and history, etc., in various journals. *Recreations:* wine, music. *Address:* The Old Barn, West Runton, Norfolk. *T.:* West Runton 101. *Club:* Authors'. [*Died* 3 *Aug.* 1956.

LYON, Percy Comyn, C.S.I. 1908; Emeritus Fellow of Oriel College, Oxford; M.A. Oxon (by decree of Convocation), 1918; I.C.S. (retired); J.P.; *b.* 9 Aug. 1862; *s.* of William Lyon, J.P.; *m.* 1890, Adeline (*d.* 1946), *d.* of late Henry Beverley, Judge of the High Court of Calcutta; one *s.* *Educ.:* King's School, Bruton, Somerset; Oriel College, Oxford. I.C.S. 1881; posted to Assam, 1883; to Bengal, 1888; held posts as District Officer, Private Secretary to Lieutenant-Governor, Settlement Officer, Director of Land Records, and Commissioner under the Government of Bengal, 1888-1905; Chief Secretary; Member of the Board of Revenue, Eastern Bengal and Assam, and Additional Member of the Legislative Council of the Governor-General, 1905-12; Member of the Executive Council of the Governor of Bengal, 1912; Vice-President of the Executive and Legislative Councils, Bengal, 1914-17; retired, 1917; Assistant Secretary in Scientific and Industrial Research Department, 1917-18; Fellow and Treasurer of Oriel College, Oxford, 1918-28; Treasurer (1926-32) and Chairman of the Council (1930-35) of St. Hugh's College, Oxford; Member, Oxford City Council, 1920-22 and 1927-29. *Address:* Wester Ogil, Headington Hill, Oxford. *T.:* Oxford 6910. *Club:* Reform. [*Died* 25 *Jan.* 1952.

LYONS, Most Rev. John, M.A., D.D.; *b.* 29 Nov. 1878; *s.* of Charles Lyons and Martha Croskery; *m.* 1st, 1908, Helena Barbara Bolton; two *d.*; 2nd, 1946, Margaret Isabel Tilley. *Educ.:* Toronto University; Trinity College, Toronto. Public School Teacher; Clerk, Canadian Pacific Railway, Montreal; Incumbent, Mission, Plevna, 1907; Rector, Parish Roslin, 1910; Burritt's Rapids, 1915; Elizabethtown,

1917; Picton, 1923; Vicar, St. Thomas' Church, Belleville, 1927; Rector, Prescott, 1931; Rural Dean of Leeds, 1922; Archdeacon of Frontenac, 1930; Bishop of Ontario, 1932-52; Metropolitan of Ontario, 1949-52; retired 1952. *Address:* St. George St., Deseronto, Ontario, Canada.
[*Died* 11 *June* 1958.

LYSAGHT, Gerald Stuart, J.P. Somerset; *b.* 1869; *y. s.* of late John Lysaght, of Hengrave Hall, Bury St. Edmunds; *m.* Nina Beatrice (*d.* 1947), *d.* of late J. L. Press, Clifton, Bristol; one *s.* *Educ.:* Cheltenham College. High Sheriff of Somerset, 1917. *Address:* Hunting Ball Lodge, Blue Anchor, Somerset. *Club:* Royal Automobile.
[*Died* 7 *Feb.* 1951.

LYSTER, Admiral Sir (Arthur) Lumley (St. George), K.C.B., *cr.* 1943 (C.B. 1941); C.V.O. 1936; C.B.E. 1942; D.S.O. 1919; *b.* 27 April 1888; *e. s.* of Arthur E. Lyster, M.D.; *m.* 1916, Daisy Agnes, 2nd *d.* of late Tankerville Chamberlayne of Cranbury Park, nr. Winchester; three *d.* *Educ.:* Berkhamsted; H.M.S. Britannia. European War, 1914-18, Gallipoli, Italy, Grand Fleet (D.S.O., Crown of Italy); H.M.S. Renown, 1919, during Prince of Wales' tour to Canada and Australasia; Captain, 1928; Naval Member of the Ordnance Committee, 1929-1930; H.M.S. Danae, 1932; Fifth Destroyer Flotilla, 1933-35; commanded R.N. Gunnery School, Chatham, 1935-36; commanded Gun Carriage, King George V.'s funeral, London, 1936 (C.V.O.); Director of Training and Staff Duties, Admiralty, 1936-1937; H.M.S. Glorious, 1938-39; A.D.C. to the King, 1939; Rear-Adm. 1939; Scapa Flow, 1939-40; Norway, 1940 (despatches); Aircraft Carriers, Mediterranean Fleet, 1940-1941; attack on Taranto, 11th Nov. 1940 (C.B.); Fifth Sea Lord and Chief of Naval Air Services, 1941-42; Aircraft Carriers, Home Fleet, 1942-43 (C.B.E.); Vice-Adm. 1942; Flag Officer Carrier Training, 1943-1945; retired, 1945. *Recreations:* gardening, shooting, fishing. *Address:* Hillside, Charminster, Dorset. *Club:* Royal Automobile.
[*Died* 4 *Aug.* 1957.

LYSTER, Robert Arthur, M.D., Ch.B., B.Sc. (Lond.), D.P.H.. B.Sc. (Pub. Health); M.S.A.; Lecturer in Public Health and in Forensic Medicine at St. Bartholomew's Hospital (London University), 1911-41; Member of Faculty of Medicine and Board of Studies in Hygiene in the University of London; V.P. Medical Defence Union, 1911-42; Member Medical Board, Lord Mayor Treloar's Hospital, Alton; Chairman Nat. Soc. for Prevention of Venereal Disease; Member Public Health Advisory Committee of Labour Party; contested (Lab.) Winchester, 1929 and 1931, Preston, 1935; Lab. Mem. Bournemouth Town Council, 1929-1946; Pres. Hants and Isle of Wight Federation Labour Parties, 1930-40; late County M.O., Hants; also Chief School M.O. and Chief Tuberculosis Officer, 1908-29; Editor of Public Health, 1918-25; Pres. Association of County Medical Officers of Health, 1926-27; Specialist Sanitary Officer for Barracks and Camps and Venereal Diseases Officer, in Winchester Area, S. Comd., 1914-18; Member Advisory Com. for the Welfare of Blind Persons (Ministry of Health); Member of Ministry of Health Com. on Sewage Disposal. *Educ.:* King Edward's School, Birmingham; Queen's College and Mason University College, Birmingham; Birmingham University and London University; Priestley Scholar in Chemistry, Exhibition in Hygiene; Associate of Mason University College; Fellow of various scientific societies; late Examiner in Public Health in University of Leeds, and in Forensic Medicine and for the Diploma in Public Health, University of Aberdeen, and Examiner in State Medicine in the University of London; late Examiner in Hygiene and Forensic Medicine, University of London and Glasgow; late Examiner in Public Health and Forensic Medicine, University of Birmingham; President Society of Medical Officers of Health, 1925-26; Bacteriologist to West Riding (Yorks) County Council, 1904-5; Medical Officer of Health, Urban District of Handsworth, Staffs., 1906-8; Lecturer in Public Health and Forensic Medicine, University of Birmingham, 1902-10. *Publications:* First Stage Hygiene; Second Stage Hygiene; School Hygiene; Prevention of Diphtheria; various articles and papers on scientific and other subjects in addition to official reports. *Address:* 33 Methuen Road, Bournemouth. *T.:* Boscombe 35064; St. Bartholomew's Hospital, E.C.
[*Died* 3 *June* 1955.

LYTTELTON, Commander Stephen Clive, O.B.E. 1919; D.S.C. 1916; R.N.; Chairman, Army and Navy Stores Ltd.; *b.* 17 June 1887; *yr. s.* of late Rt. Rev. Hon. Arthur Lyttelton, Bishop of Southampton; *m.* 1st, 1919, Maureen, *d.* of H. A. Smith; one *d.*; 2nd, 1938, Mary, *d.* of Sir Frederick Gascoigne; one *s.* one *d.*; 3rd, 1947, Hermione, *d.* of A. K. Graham; one *d.* *Educ.:* H.M.S. Britannia. Retired from H.M. Navy, 1912. Joined Gillanders Arbuthnot & Co., E. India Merchants, 1913; Member Calcutta Local Bd., Imp. Bank of India, 1937-39, Pres., 1938-39; Sheriff of Calcutta, 1938. Served European War, 1914-1919 (D.S.C., O.B.E., Croix de Guerre, France, promoted to Comdr.). Served Admiralty, Ops. Div. of Naval Staff, 1939-44. *Address:* The Oxdrove House, Burghclere, Nr. Newbury, Berks. *T.:* Newbury 785. *Clubs:* Oriental, Royal Automobile.
[*Died* 19 *Feb.* 1959.

LYTTON, 3rd Earl of, *cr.* 1880; **Neville Stephen Lytton;** O.B.E. 1918; Légion d'Honneur; artist-painter; *b.* 6 Feb. 1879; 4th *s.* of 1st Earl of Lytton; *S.* brother 1947; *m.* 1st, 1899, Judith Anne Dorothea, *o. c.* of late Wilfrid Scawen Blunt (who obtained a divorce, 1923; *see* Baroness Wentworth); one *s.* two *d.*; 2nd, 1924, Mlle. Sandra Fortel, St. Rambert-en-Bugey; one *d.* *Educ.:* Eton; graduate of University of Paris (école des Beaux Arts), 1899. Major Royal Sussex Regiment and General Staff; wounded in France, 1916 (despatches 4 times); contributor (by invitation) to International Exhibitions of Rome and Antwerp; regular contributor to all principal exhibitions in France and England; Balcombe Frescoes, 1923; Sociétaire of Société Nationale des Beaux Arts, Paris. Amateur Tennis Champion, 1911, 1913; International Amateur Tennis Champion and holder of the International Cup, Paris, 1911, 12, 13. *Publications:* Water Colour; The Press and the General Staff, 1921; The English Country Gentleman; Life in Unoccupied France, 1942. *Heir:* *s.* Viscount Knebworth. *Address:* 38 Oakley Street, S.W.3.
[*Died* 9 *Feb.* 1951.

LYWOOD, Air Vice-Marshal Oswyn George William Gifford, C.B. 1944; C.B.E. 1938 (O.B.E. 1918); F.R.S.A.; Chairman, Automatic Telephone & Electric Co. Ltd., Bridgnorth, Shropshire; Chairman and Joint Managing Director of O. G. Lywood Ltd.; *b.* 21 August 1895; *s.* of late Colonel E. G. Lywood, R.M., and late Ethel May Wells; *m.* 1915, Hilda Jessie Foster; two *s.* two *d.* *Educ.:* Stubbington House. 1st Batt. Norfolk Regiment (Suppl. Reserve of Officers), 1912; attached to R.F.C. 1914 (despatches); transferred to R.A.F. on formation, 1917; Squadron Leader, 1924; Wing Commander, 1930; Group Capt. 1938; Air Cdre. 1941; Acting Air Vice-Marshal, 1942; Temp. Air Vice-Marshal, 1943; C.S.O. H.Q. Inland Area, R.A.F. 1924; Air Ministry, Dept. of D.O.S.D. (Signals), 1930; H.Q. Coastal Area, 1934; Chairman Wireless Telegraphy Board, 1937; D.D. of S., Air Ministry, 1938; D. of S., Air Ministry, 1941; A.O.C. No. 26 Group 1942-46; retired, 1946. Comdr. Legion of Merit (U.S.A.), 1945. *Recreations:* yachting, shooting. *Address:* Woodlands Manor Farm,

Woodlands, nr. Sevenoaks, Kent. *T.:* Otford 386. *Club:* United Service. [*Died* 3 *Feb.* 1957.

M

McADAM, William; *b.* 7 Aug. 1886; *s.* of late Robert McAdam, ex-member of Hoddam Parish Council and School Board; *m.* 1913, Helen MacFarlane; one *d.* *Educ.:* Hoddam School, Ecclefechan. Clerk, soldier, railway porter, goods guard, yard foreman. National Executive Committee N.U.R. Scottish Executive Committee Labour Party. M.P. (Lab.) Salford North, 1945-50. *Publication:* Birth, Growth and Eclipse of Glasgow and South Western Railway Company, 1923. *Recreation:* golf. *Address:* 16 Overdale Gardens, Glasgow, S.2. [*Died April* 1952.

MacALISTER, Sir Ian, Kt., *cr.* 1934; M.A. Oxon; *b.* Liverpool, 1 April 1878; 2nd *s.* of late Sir John MacAlister and Elizabeth Batley; *m.* 1909, Frances Dorothy, *er. d* of late Robert Cooper Seaton, M.A.; one *s.* (and two killed on active service) four *d.* *Educ.:* St. Paul's School; Merton College, Oxford (Modern History Exhibition); Second Class Classical Moderations, 1899; Second Class Literæ Humaniores, 1901. Aide-de-Camp and Secretary to Major-General the Earl of Dundonald, General Officer commanding the Canadian Army, 1902-4; Secretary, R.I.B.A., 1908-43; Lt., Royal Defence Corps, 1916-19; Hon. A.R.I.B.A.; Honorary Member of American Institute of Architects, 1936. *Address:* Little Gables, Bourne Close, Tonbridge. *T.:* Tonbridge 3593. *Club:* Athenæum. [*Died* 10 *June* 1957.

McALLEN, Captain Thomas Wilfred, C.B.E. 1954; *b.* 24 Dec. 1888; *s.* of Daniel Courtis and Emily McAllen; *m.* 1913; one *d.* *Educ.:* Southampton. Joined U.C. Line, 1915, as Junior Officer; War Transport till end of European War, 1914-18; promoted through various grades to Chief Officer; subsequently Master: Durban Castle, Jan. 1940; Athlone Castle, May 1940; Llanstephan Castle, Aug. 1940 (S. and E. Africa; troops, evacuees, etc.); Dromore Castle Transport (lost by enemy action on voyage to Russia, Dec. 1941); Gloucester Castle, Jan. 1942; Roslin Castle Transport, June 1942; Llangibby Castle, 1944 ("D Day" landings and ferrying troops across Channel); Dunnottar Castle, 1945 (Channel trooping); again Llangibby Castle (trooping, Far East, etc.); Carnarvon Castle, 1947 (S. Africa, etc., with emigrants); Warwick Castle; Edinburgh Castle, 1948 (maiden voyage and subsequently); promoted to Commodore, 1950; Commodore Union Castle Mail S.S. Co. Ltd., 1950-53; retired Dec. 1953. *Recreation:* motoring. *Address:* St. Rumons, 86 West End Road, Southampton. *T.:* 89, 2525. *Club:* Master Mariners' (Southampton and Durban, S.A.). [*Died* 20 *Feb.* 1957.

MacALPINE, J(ohn) Warren, Ph.D. (Edin.); *s.* of Alexander and Frances MacAlpine (Scottish); *m.* Margaret MacMillan. *Educ.:* Universities of Toronto, Manitoba, Heidelberg and Edinburgh. Minister, Presbyterian Church in Canada, 1927. Postgraduate study, Edinburgh and Heidelberg, 1929-31 and 1933-34. Contested (Lab.) Maidstone, General Election, 1935; Research, Publicity and Marketing, 1935-41; British Broadcasting Corporation, 1941; Controller of Overseas Services, British Broadcasting Corporation, 1952-55, retired 1955. *Recreations:* horticulture, golf; (interests) French modern art, Georgian architecture. *Address:* 43 Kensington Square, W.8. *T.:* Western 6913. *Clubs:* Bath; University (Edinburgh); Burnham Beeches Golf. [*Died* 11 *June* 1956.

McANALLY, Sir Henry William Watson, Kt., *cr.* 1930; C.B. 1918; late Principal Assistant Secretary, Air Ministry; *b.* 1870; *s.* of late Arthur Acheson McAnally; *m.* 1906, Gertrude Hellen, *y. d.* of late Alfred Sandilands; one *s.* one *d.* *Educ.:* Dulwich College; Jesus College, Cambridge (Senior Classical Scholar). B.A. 1892; M.A. 1942; entered War Office, 1894; Private Secretary to Financial Secretary, 1896-99; Resident Clerk, 1899; Assistant Private Secretary to Secretary of State for War, 1899-1902; Secretary to Royal Commission on Militia and Volunteers, 1903; Principal Clerk, 1905; Assistant Secretary, Air Board, 1917; Asst. Secretary, Air Ministry, 1918; Chairman 1919-30, Air Ministry Industrial Whitley Council; retired, 1930; J.P. Co. of London, Kensington Division, 1931-39; Chairman Camberwell Local Employment Committee, 1933-40; Member London (No. 2) Conscientious Objectors Tribunal, 1940. *Publications:* The Irish Militia, 1793-1816; Alfieri's Vita, translated; articles in various journals. *Recreations:* Italian studies; Irish historical research. *Address:* 65 Barton Road, Cambridge. *Club:* Oxford and Cambridge. [*Died* 2 *April* 1952.

MACARTNEY, Sir Alexander Miller, 5th Bt., *cr.* 1799; *b.* 24 July 1869; *S.* brother, 1942; *s.* of 3rd Bt. and Catherine (*d.* 1904), *d.* of A. Miller, Merindindi, Victoria. *Heir:* *b.* John Barrington [*b.* 26 Oct. 1873; *m.* 1910 Selina, *d.* of W. Koch, Mackay, Queensland; one *s.* two *d.*]. *Address:* Kuttabul, Hampden, Mackay, Queensland, Australia. [*Died* 30 *Sept.* 1960.

MACARTNEY, Sir Edward Henry, Kt., *cr.* 1930; Solicitor; senior partner firm Thynne and Macartney; *b.* Holywood, Co. Down, Ireland, 24 Jan. 1863; *y. s.* of Wm. Isaac Macartney, Commissioner of Police, Ceylon; *m.* 1888, Caroline Tottenham Lucas, *d.* of Pollet Cardew, P.M.; one *s.* *Educ.:* Holywood, Enniskillen; Gracehill and Dublin. Four years business and legal training, Belfast; arrived Queensland, 1883; joined Queensland National Bank; admitted a Solicitor, 1891, and a Notary Public, 1894; national member for Toowong, 1900, 1902, 1904, 1907, 1911, 1912, 1915 and 1918; City of Brisbane, 1909-11; Minister for Lands, 1911; resigned portfolio, 1912; Leader of Opposition, 1915 and 1918; Agent-General for Queensland, 1929-31; Chairman Brisbane Board National Bank of Australasia, Ltd.; Chairman Directors Queensland Newspapers Proprietary Ltd.; Australian Chemical Co. Ltd., and Dry Ice Queensland Ltd.; Director British Traders Insurance Co. Ltd. *Address:* Lissanoure, Moray Street, New Farm, Brisbane. *T.A.:* Thymac. *T.:* B 2143. *Clubs:* Queensland, Brisbane (Brisbane). [*Died* 24 *Feb.* 1956.

MacARTHUR, Sir (William) Oliphant, Kt., *cr.* 1942; C.B.E. 1939; *b.* 24 Oct. 1871; *m.* 1929, Elisabeth Duff, *widow* of Edward Ellis Jackson. *Educ.:* City of London School; Queens' College, Cambridge; Divisional Food Commissioner, N. Midland Division, 1919-21; Divisional Food Officer, N. Midland Division, 1938-41; Chief Divisional Food Officer, North-East England, 1941-45. *Recreations:* cricket, bridge. *Club:* National Liberal. [*Died* 30 *April* 1953.

MACAULAY, Very Rev. James J., B.A., D.D., H.C.F., Senior Minister of Christ Church, Rathgar, Dublin; Ex-Moderator of the General Assembly of the Presbyterian Church in Ireland; *b.* 1870; *s.* of Rev. Matthew Macaulay; *m.* Margery, *d.* of H. W. Walker, Sugar Refiner, Greenock; one *s.* one *d.* *Educ.:* Queen's College, Belfast; Assembly's Theological College, Belfast; Edinburgh. Minister of Bangor, Co. Down; St. Mark's Church, Greenock. Served with forces in France as Chaplain during the War. *Address:* 11A Rothesay Place, Edinburgh, 3. *T.:* Edinburgh 31142. [*Died* 7 *Feb.* 1951.

MACAULAY, James Morison, B.Sc., Ph.D.; *b.* 26 Mar. 1889; *m.* 1947; no *c.* *Educ.:* Allan Glen's School; Royal Technical College, Glasgow; University of Glasgow. B.Sc. Eng. (Glasgow) 1911; Sapper R.E. and subsequently Captain (equipment) R.A.F., 1915-19; Professor of Physics, The Anderson College of Medicine, Glasgow, 1927-1943; Senior Lecturer in Natural Philosophy, Royal Technical College, Glasgow, 1943-53. Honorary Secretary, Royal Philosophical Society of Glasgow, 1953; Ph.D. University of Glasgow, 1927. *Address:* 5 Woodvale Avenue, Giffnock, Glasgow. *T.:* Giffnock 0135. [*Died* 16 *June* 1955.

MACAULAY, Dame Rose, D.B.E. 1958; Hon. Litt.D. (Camb.), 1951; author; writes Novels, Verse, Essays, etc. *Publications include:* What Not, 1919; Potterism, 1920; Dangerous Ages, 1921; Mystery of Geneva, 1922; Told by an Idiot, 1923; Orphan Island, 1924; Crewe Train, 1926; two Books of Verse, 1914, 1919; A Casual Commentary (essays), 1925; Keeping up Appearances, 1928; Staying with Relations, 1930; Some Religious Elements in English Literature, 1931; They Were Defeated, 1932; John Milton, 1933; Going Abroad, 1934; The Minor Pleasures of Life, 1934; Personal Pleasures, 1935; I Would be Private, 1937; The Writings of E. M. Forster, 1938; And No Man's Wit, 1940; Life among the English, 1942; They Went to Portugal, 1946; Fabled Shore, 1949; The World My Wilderness, 1950; Pleasure of Ruins, 1953; The Towers of Trebizond (James Tait Black Memorial Prize), 1956. *Rel. publ.:* Letters to a Friend, 1950-52, Ed. Constance Babington, 1961. *Address:* 20 Hinde House, Hinde Street, W.1. [*Died* 30 *Oct.* 1958.

McAULIFFE, Sir Henry T., Kt., *cr.* 1928; *b.* 1867; *yr. s.* of late Bartholomew McAuliffe; *m.* 1891, *y. d.* of late Henry Stevens, Greenwich; five *d.* *Educ.:* Greenwich. Formerly of McAuliffe, Davis & Hope, now amalgamated with Turquand Youngs, McAuliffe & Co. of London; formerly, Member of the Corporation of the City of London and of the L.C.C.; one of H.M. Lieutenants for the City of London; now retired. Officier de la Légion d'Honneur. *Address:* 2 King's Drive, Eastbourne. *T.A.:* McAuliffe, London. *T.:* Eastbourne 3335. *Clubs:* Athenæum, Guildhall, City Livery. [*Died* 22 *Nov.* 1951.

McBAIN, James William, F.R.S. 1923; Davy Medal of Royal Society, 1939; M.A. (Toronto); Ph.D. (Heidelberg); Hon. D.Sc. (Brown University, Bristol University); Capt. late T.F.; Professor Emeritus of Chemistry, Stanford University; Director, National Chemical Laboratory, Poona, 7, India. 1949-52; *b.* Chatham, New Brunswick, Canada, 22 Mar. 1882; *s.* of Rev. J. A. F. McBain, D.D.; *m.* Mary Evelyn, *d.* of David Laing; one *s.* one *d.* *Educ.:* Universities of Toronto, Leipzig, and Heidelberg. Lecturer, University College, Bristol, 1906; Leverhulme Professor of Physical Chemistry, University of Bristol; served Bristol University O.T.C., 3rd O.C. Bn. (mentioned, 1917); President of Association of Univ. Teachers, 1922-23; Member of Council of Editorial Boards of several scientific societies and journals; Fellow of Institute Physics and Institute Chemistry; Visiting Professor at the University of California, Berkeley, U.S.A., 1926; President of the Alumni Association of the University of Bristol, 1924-26; Member National Institute of Social Sciences, U.S.A.; Fellow of California Acad. of Sciences. *Publications:* The Sorption of Gases and Vapours by Solids, 1932; Colloid Science, 1950; over 400 original papers in scientific journals of England, Canada, United States, France, Russia, India, and Germany. *Recreations:* music, garden, swimming. *Address:* Box 1408, Stanford University, California, U.S.A. *Clubs:* Commonwealth, Rotary, Bohemian (San Francisco). [*Died* 12 *March* 1953.

MACBETH, Alexander Killen, C.M.G. 1946; M.A., D.Sc., F.R.I.C.; F.A.A.; F.C.S.; Emeritus Professor of Chemistry, University of Adelaide; 2nd *s.* of William Macbeth, Drumbuoy, Strabane, Co. Donegal; *b.* 11 Aug. 1889; *m.* Edythe Helena Patricia, *d.* of Rev. Andrew MacAfee, B.A., and Mrs. MacAfee, M.B.E., J.P., The Manse, Omagh, Co. Tyrone; one *s.* three *d.* *Educ.:* Queen's University Belfast (Junior and Senior Science Scholar, Andrews Student, and 1851 Exhibition Scholar). Sometime Senior Assistant in Chemistry, and Lecturer on Organic Chemistry, Queen's University, Belfast; Senior Lecturer on Chemistry, United College, Univ. of St. Andrews, 1919-24; Reader in Chemistry in the Durham Colleges, Univ. of Durham, 1924-28; Member of Australian Nat. Research Council; Member of Advisory Council on Food and Drugs, S. Australian Govt.; Dean of Faculty of Science, Member of Council of Univ. of Adelaide; Liversidge Research Lecturer, Univ. of Sydney, 1930; Chm. of the Board of Pharmaceutical Studies, Univ. of Adelaide; Hon. Commissioner S.A. Govt on Poisons Legislation, 1935; Pres., Sect. B. Australian and New Zealand Association for the Advancement of Science, Auckland Meeting, 1936; Sydney Meeting, 1952. *Publications:* upwards of one hundred papers in the scientific journals; Text-book of Organic Chemistry. *Address:* 12A Park Terrace, Eastwood, S. Australia. [*Died* 28 *May* 1957.

McBEY, James, Hon. LL.D. Aberdeen; Painter and etcher; *b.* Newburgh, Aberdeenshire, 23 Dec. 1883; *m.* 1931, Marguerite Huntsberry, *d.* of late Adolf Loeb, Philadelphia. *Educ.:* Village School. Entered North of Scotland Bank, Ltd., Aberdeen, 1899. Studied art privately, working in spare time; left Bank, 1910; first exhibition in London, 1911. Appointed Official Artist to the Egyptian Expeditionary Force, 1917, and accompanied it in advance through Palestine and Syria, making drawings and paintings of that campaign for the British Museum and the Imperial War Museum; citizen of U.S.A., 1942. *Publications:* etchings of Scotland, Holland, Spain, Morocco, France, Venice, Palestine and U.S.A. *Address:* El Foolk, The Mountain, Tangier, Morocco. *T.:* 15982. *Club:* Century Association (New York). [*Died* 1 *Dec.* 1959.

MACBRIDE, Alexander, R.I., R.S.W.; landscape painter; *b.* Cathcart, near Glasgow, 8 Mar. 1859; *o. s.* of James MacBride, writer, Glasgow; *m.* 1894, Jane Stewart, 2nd *d.* of Adam Houston, Helensburgh, Dunbartonshire. *Educ.:* Glasgow Academy; Craigmount House, Edinburgh; Glasgow University; Art in the Glasgow School of Art, and Atelier of M. Julian, Paris. *Address:* Sunnyside House, Cathcart, Glasgow. *T.:* Merrylee 1641. *Club:* Art (Glasgow). [*Died* 1 *Nov.* 1955.

McBRIDE, Vice-Admiral Sir William, K.C.B., *cr.* 1953 (C.B. 1951); C.B.E. 1947 (O.B.E. 1941); R.N. retired; *b.* 20 Feb. 1895; *s.* of John S. McBride; *m.* 1928, Juanita Marie Franco; one *s.* *Educ.:* Cork Grammar School. Joined Navy, 1912; H.M. Ships Weymouth, Monarch and Barham, European War, 1914-18; staff of: Flag Officer Cdg. 2nd Battle Sqdn., 1918-20; Flag Officer Cdg. Reserve Fleet, 1920-22; C.-in-C. China Station, 1922-24. H.M.S. Ganges and St. Vincent, 1925-28; China Station, 1928-30; Secretary to: Flag Officer Cdg. 2nd Cruiser Sqdn., 1931-33; Fourth Sea Lord, 1934-37; C.-in-C. China Station, 1938-40; C.-in-C. Western Approaches, 1940-1942; Head of Admiralty Deleg. U.S.A., 1942-44. Deputy Director-General, Supply and Secretariat Branch, 1944-46; Comd. Supply Officer (Air), 1946-49; Comd. Supply Officer (Nore), 1949-51; Director-General Supply and Secretariat Branch, Admiralty, 1951-54, retired 1954. *Recreations:* all outdoor recreations, gardening. *Address:* 166 Rivermead Court, Hurlingham, S.W.6. *Club:* Army and Navy. [*Died* 9 *Sept.* 1959.

McCABE, Joseph (formerly Very Rev. Father **Antony)**; author and lecturer; *b.* 11 Nov. 1867; *m.* 1899, Beatrice, *d.* of William Lee; two *s.* two *d.* *Educ.:* St. Francis's College, Manchester; St. Antony's, Forest Gate; Louvain University. Franciscan monk, 1883; Priest, 1890; Professor of Scholastic Philosophy, 1890-94; Rector of Buckingham College, 1895; left Church, 1896; afterwards private secretary, lecturer, journalist, and author. *Publications:* Twelve Years in a Monastery, 1897; Modern Rationalism, 1897; Can we Disarm? 1899; Peter Abélard, 1901; St. Augustine and his Age, 1902; Religion of Woman, 1904; Talleyrand, 1906; Life and Letters of George Jacob Holyoake, 1908; The Iron Cardinal, 1909; The Decay of the Church of Rome, 1909; The Evolution of Mind, 1910; The Empresses of Rome, 1911; The Story of Evolution, 1912; Goethe, 1912; A Candid History of the Jesuits, 1913; The Empresses of Constantinople, 1913; The Principles of Evolution, 1914; George Bernard Shaw, 1914; The Sources of the Morality of the Gospels, 1914; The Religion of Sir Oliver Lodge, 1914; Treitschke and the Great War, 1914; The Soul of Europe, 1915; The Kaiser, 1915; The Tyranny of Shams, 1916; The Influence of the Church on Marriage and Divorce, 1916; Crises in the History of the Papacy, 1916; The Pope's Favourite, 1917; The Bankruptcy of Religion, 1918; The Popes and their Church, 1918; The Growth of Religion, 1918; Georges Clemenceau, 1919; The End of the World, 1920; A.B.C. of Evolution, 1921; Evolution of Civilisation, 1921; Robert Owen, 1921; Ice Ages, 1922; G. J. Holyoake, 1922; The Twilight of the Gods, 1923; The Wonders of the Stars, 1923; Lourdes, 1925; The Marvels of Modern Physics, 1925; A Century of Stupendous Progress, 1925; 50 Little Blue Books, 1926; 40 Big Blue Books, 1927; Key to Love and Sex, 1929; The Story of the Catholic Church, 1929; The Rise and Fall of the Gods, 1930; The Hundred Men who moved the World, 1931; Spain in Revolt, 1931; The New Science, 1931; Edward Clodd, 1932; Can We Save Civilization? 1932; The Riddle of the Universe To-day, 1934; The Splendour of Moorish Spain, 1935; The Papacy in Politics To-day, 1937; A History of the Popes, 1939; A Rationalist Encyclopaedia, 1948; about 50 translations. *Recreations:* microscope, bridge, walking. *Address:* 22 St. George's Road, Golders Green, N.W. [*Died* 10 *Jan.* 1955.

McCALL, Charles William Home, C.B.E. 1919; *b.* 1877; *s.* of late Charles McCall and Jane, *d.* of late Robert Home; *m.* 1904, Dorothy Margaret, *d.* of late Dr. Joseph Kidd; five *s.* two *d.* Man. Dir. Ballantyne Press, London, 1908; Chm. 1913; Liverpool Scottish, 1915; Adjutant, Nov. 1915; Asst. Dir. Small Arms Ammunition, 1916; Dir. Non-Ferrous Rolled Metals, 1916; Dep. Cont. Non-Ferrous Metals, 1917; originated Officers Tech. Trng. Classes, 1917; Ministry of Labour, March 1918 as Controller Appointments Dept.; Member Officers Univ. and Technical Training Cttee.; the Officers Resettlement Cttee.; the Board of Agriculture Officers Resettlement Committee; Member of the East Suffolk C.C., 1922-25. *Address:* Sweetmeadows, Chislehurst, Kent. [*Died* 17 *Sept.* 1958.

McCALL, Lt.-Col. Hugh William, C.M.G. 1919, D.S.O. 1918; *b.* 28 Sept. 1878; *e. s.* of late Sir Robert McCall, K.C.V.O.; *m.* Elizabeth (*d.* 1944), *d.* of late Henry A. Lindgens, New York City. *Educ.:* Charterhouse; Trinity Coll., Cambridge, B.A. Joined Yorkshire Regt. 1900; Brevet of Lt.-Col., 1918; Lt.-Col. 1926 (D.S.O., C.M.G., Order of the Nile, 1918; Chevalier Légion d'Honneur, 1919); commanded 1st Batt. The Green Howards (Alexandra, Princess of Wales' Own) Yorkshire Regt. 1927-29; retd. pay, 1929. *Club:* United Service. [*Died* 15 *Dec.* 1957.

M'CALL, Brig.-Gen. J. B. P.; *see* Pollok-M'Call.

MACCALLAN, Arthur Ferguson, C.B.E. 1920 (O.B.E. 1918); M.D. (Camb.), F.R.C.S. (Eng.); Consulting Ophthalmic Surgeon, Westminster Hosp.; Consulting Surgeon, Royal Eye Hospital; *s.* of late Rev. J. Ferguson MacCallan, M.A., Vicar of New Basford, Notts; *m.* 1918, Hester McNeill Boyd, *d.* of late Rt. Rev. Bishop Boyd Carpenter, K.C.V.O.; two *s.* one *d.* *Educ.:* Charterhouse; Christ's College, Cambridge (Darwin Prize); St. Mary's Hospital (University Exhibitioner). Senior House Surg. and Chief Clinical Assistant, Royal London Ophthalmic Hospital; Civil Surgeon to War Hospitals in Egypt, 1914; Major, R.A.M.C. 1915-16 (despatches); Founder of Ophthalmic Hospitals of Egypt; Ophthalmic Surgeons of Egypt erected a bronze bust of him to commemorate his work, unveiled by British High Commissioner, 1931; President International Trachoma Organization; Member Société Française d'Ophtalmologie and Hon. Member Ophthalmological Society of Egypt. *Publications:* numerous contributions to ophthalmic literature. *Address:* The Downs, Hertford Heath, Hertford. *T.:* Ware 298. *Club:* United University. [*Died* 31 *March* 1955.

McCALLUM, Major Sir Duncan, Kt., *cr.* 1955; M.C.; D.L.; M.P. (C.) Argyllshire, since 1940; *b.* 24 Nov. 1888; 3rd *s.* of Colin Whitton McCallum and *g.s.* of Colin McCallum of Bunchrew, Inverness; *m.* 1925, Violet Mary, *d.* of James Louis Alexander Hope of Whitney Court, Hereford, and *widow* of Captain E. A. Hume, South Staffordshire Regt. and Barrister-at-Law. *Educ.:* Filey, East Yorks; Christ's Hospital, London and Horsham. Served European War, 1914-19 (despatches); Liaison Officer with French Army in Syria, 1920-24; Comdt. British Legation Guard, Peking, 1926-27; retired, 1928; R. of O. East Yorkshire Regt., 1928; Hon. Attaché British Legation, Bulgaria, 1932-34; Cairo, 1934-38; G.S.O.(1), G.H.Q., Middle East, Cairo, 1939-40. Mem. Highlands and Islands Advisory Panel, 1947-. Croix de Guerre with Palm (French); F.R.G.S., F.Z.S. *Publication:* China to Chelsea, 1930. *Address:* Ardanaiseig, Kilchrenan, Argyll. *T.:* Kilchrenan 212; 1 Cranmer Court, S.W.3. *T.:* Kensington 8094. *Clubs:* Carlton, International Sportsmen's; New (Edinburgh). [*Died* 10 *May* 1958.

McCALLUM, Sir William Alexander, K.B.E., *cr.* 1941 (C.B.E. 1938); M.I.Mech.E.; F.R.S.A.; Managing Director, The British Structural Steel Co. Ltd., 1923-49; Major, late Royal Engineers; *b.* Glasgow, 14 March 1883; *s.* of George McCallum and Helen Lyell Alexander; *m.* 1918, Gwendoline L'Estrange Wallace (*d.* 1957); five *s.* (and one killed in action, 1945) one *d.* *Educ.:* Woodside School and Royal Technical College, Glasgow; Institute of Technology, Manchester. Engineering apprenticeship with Clyde Structural Iron Co. Ltd., Glasgow; engineering experience with Edward Wood & Co. Ltd., Manchester, and with Frederick Braby & Co. Ltd., Glasgow; Chartered Engineer, M.I.Mech.E.; went to Buenos Aires, 1909; Resident Director of The British Structural Steel Co. Ltd. 1911-49; Chairman, British Chamber of Commerce in the Argentine Republic, 1927 and 1934-46; Chairman British Community Council in the Argentine Republic, 1939-44; President St. Andrew's Society of the River Plate, 1924 and 1945. Joined Royal Engineers, Chatham, 1915; served European War, Sinai and Palestine 1916-19 (despatches twice); R.A.R.O. 1920. *Recreations:* golf, rowing. *Address:* Calle Rawson 2682, Olivos, Argentine Republic. *T.A.:* McCallum, Britanica, Buenos Aires. *T.:* 791-2609. *Clubs:* Royal Commonwealth Society, Overseas; English, Strangers (Buenos Aires). [*Died* 22 *July* 1959.

MacCALMAN, Professor Douglas Robert, M.D.; Professor of Psychiatry, University of Leeds, since 1954; Hon. Physician, United Leeds Hosps., and Consultant Psychiatrist, St. James's Hospital, Leeds, since 1948; *b.* 4 Dec. 1903; *s.* of late Rev. D. M. MacCalman, Strachur, Argyll; *m.* 1935, Helen Grego, *o. d.* of J. M. Dawson, M.A., LL.D. late Dir. of Educn., Perth and Kinross; one *d.* *Educ.:* Glasgow Academy; Universities of Glasgow, Harvard and Johns Hopkins, Baltimore. M.D. (Glas.) 1933; M.R.C.P. (Edin.), 1948; F.R.C.P. (Ed.), 1952; F.B.Ps.S. Senior Resident Psychiatrist, Boston Psychopathic Hospital, 1930; Medical Director, Notre Dame Child Guidance Clinic, Glasgow, 1932; Asst. Physician, Victoria Infirmary, Glasgow, 1934; Gen. Sec., Child Guidance Council, London, 1935; Crombie-Ross Lecturer in Psychopathology, Univ. of Aberdeen, 1938; Physician Roy. Infirmary and Roy. Aberdeen Hosp. for Sick Children, 1938; Cons. Psychiatrist: E.M.S., 1939; Red. Cross Sanatoria of Scotland, 1946; Crombie-Ross Professor of Mental Health, 1946, Farquhar-Thompson Lecturer, 1947, Univ. of Aberdeen; Nuffield Prof. of Psychiatry, Univ. of Leeds, 1948. *Publications:* various sections of textbooks and articles on medical and psychological topics. *Recreations:* photography, gardening, ornithology. *Address:* Ridgefield, North Hill Road, Leeds 6, Yorkshire. *T.:* Leeds 55073. *Club:* Leeds (Leeds). [*Died* 31 *Jan.* 1957.

McCALMONT, Brig.-Gen. Sir Robert (Chaine Alexander), K.C.V.O. *cr.* 1952 (C.V.O. 1937); C.B.E. 1946; D.S.O. 1917; Col. ret., and Hon. Brig.-Gen.; *b.* 29 Aug. 1881; *o. s.* of late Col. James Martin McCalmont (M.P. Antrim E., 1885-1914); *m.* 1st, 1907, Mary Caroline (*d.* 1941), *o. c.* of late Andrew Skeen, Tarland, Aberdeenshire; three *d.*; 2nd, 1950, Iris Heather, *y. d.* of late J. J. Flinn, Belfast. *Educ.:* Eton. Served in South African War, 1900 (Queen's medal), as 2nd Lieut. 6th (M.) Batt. R. Warwickshire Regt.; 2nd Lieut. Irish Guards (on formation), 1900; Adjutant, Eton Coll. O.T.C., 1909-11; raised and commanded 12th (Central Antrim) S.B.R. Irish Rifles, 1914-15; commanded 1st Batt. Irish Guards, 1915-17 (D.S.O., despatches); 3rd Inf. Brigade, 1917 (despatches); Irish Guards Regt., 1919-24; 144th Inf., Brigade, 1924-25; an Exon of the King's Body Guard, 1925-37; Clerk of the Cheque and Adjt. 1937-45; Lieut., 1945-51; Comdr. No. 84 Group Nat. Defence Coys. 1939-40; 8th H.D. Battalion R. Berks Regiment, 1940-42; Comd. Welfare Officer, N. Ireland, 1943-46; M.P.(U.) Antrim E., 1913-1919; C.C. Glos. 1931-46; D.L., J.P., 1936-1946; Chairman Co. Antrim T.A. and A.F. Association, 1947-50; D.L. Co. Antrim, 1946-51. *Recreations:* yachting, shooting. *Address:* Glen Lodge, Strandhill, Sligo. *Clubs:* Guards; Kildare Street (Dublin); Ulster (Belfast); Royal Yacht Squadron (Cowes). [*Died* 4 *Nov.* 1953.

McCANDLISH, Emeritus Professor Douglas, M.Sc.; Hon. Director, Procter International Research Laboratory, since 1949; *b.* 1883; 2nd *s.* of David McCandlish, Straiton, Ayrshire and Leeds; *m.* 1910, Beatrice Alice Jackson; one *s.* *Educ.:* Leeds Modern School; University of Leeds. Leeds City Analyst's Laboratory, 1899-1902; Assistant to Prof. H. R. Procter, F.R.S., Leeds University, 1906-07; Chief Chemist Wm. Paul and Sons, Tanners, Leeds, 1908-1910; Chief Chemist A. F. Gallun and Sons, Milwaukee, U.S.A., 1907-08 and 1910-19; Professor of Leather Industries, University of Leeds, 1919-49, Dean of the Faculty of Technology, 1938-40; President International Society of Leather Trades' Chemists, 1926-27; President Leeds Caledonian Society 1930-38; President Sand Moor Golf Club, 1933-37; Chairman Appeal Tribunal, National Assistance Board (Leeds Area), since 1935; Chairman Advisory Committee on Leather Subjects City and Guilds of London Institute, 1920-49; Member, Conscientious Objections Tribunal (Military and National Service Acts), North Eastern Area, since 1939; Temp. Chairman Military Service (Hardship) Committee, 1943. *Publications:* various scientific and technical researches on leather subjects. *Recreations:* golf, motoring. *Address:* 152 Otley Road, Leeds 6. *T.:* 52400. [*Died* 18 *Dec.* 1954.

McCANN, Sir Charles Francis Gerald, Kt., *cr.* 1938; Agent General since 1934, and Trade Commissioner since 1931, for South Australia; *b.* 10 June 1880; *s.* of John Henry and Katherine McCann; *m.* 1909, Eileen Hammond; one *s.* one *d.* *Educ.:* Christian Brothers College and private tuition. Joined South Australian Civil Service, 1898; Trade Commissioner for South Australia in England, 1911; General Manager Smithfield and Argentine Meat Co. in South America, 1919; *Recreations:* shooting, fishing. *Address:* 13 Pembridge Villas, W.11. [*Died* 5 *June* 1951.

McCANN, Rt. Rev. Philip Justin, O.S.B., M.A.; Titular Abbot, 1949; Assistant Priest, St. Mary's, Warrington, since 1947; *b.* Manchester, 18 June 1882; *s.* of Philip McCann. *Educ.:* Ampleforth Coll., York; Oxford, First in Greats, B.A. 1907, M.A. 1911. Took the habit of St. Benedict, 1900, and final vows, 1904; Priest, 1909; Assistant Master at Ampleforth College, 1907-19; Claustral Prior, 1916-19; Master of St. Benet's Hall, Oxford, 1920-47. *Publications:* Commentary on the Rule of St. Benedict (Tr. from the French, 1921); Confessions of Father Augustine Baker, 1922; Cloud of Unknowing, 1924; Secret Paths of Divine Love, 1928; Resurrection of the Body, 1928; Spirit of Catholicism (tr. from the German, 1929); Vestments and Vesture (tr. from the French, 1930); Christ our Brother (tr. from the German, 1931); St. Augustine (tr. from the German, 1932); Life of Father Augustine Baker, 1933; Memorials of Father Augustine Baker (Catholic Record Society, vol. 33), 1933; St. Benedict, 1937; Rule of St. Benedict, tr. 1937; St. Benedict by St. Gregory the Great, tr. 1941; Rule of St. Benedict, Latin and English, 1952; Imitation of Christ (tr. 1952); various pamphlets. *Recreation:* walking. *Address:* St. Mary's Priory, Warrington. [*Died* 19 *Feb.* 1959.

McCARRISON, Maj.-Gen. Sir Robert, Kt., *cr.* 1933; C.I.E. 1923; M.D., B.Ch., B.A.O. (R.U.I.), D.Sc. (Q.U.B.), F.R.C.P., LL.D. (Belfast); M.A. (Oxon); Hon. Fellow College Physicians, Philadelphia; Indian Medical Service, retired, 1935; *b.* 15 March 1878; 2nd *s.* of late Robert McCarrison, Lisburn, County Antrim; *m.* 1906, Helen Stella, 3rd *d.* of late J. L. Johnston, I.C.S. *Educ.:* Queen's College, Belfast. Entered I.M.S., 1901; Foreign Department Government of India, 1904; Agency Surgeon, Gilgit, Kashmir, 1904-11; First Class Kaiser-i-Hind Gold Medal, 1911; Milroy Lecturer, R.C.P. of London, 1913; investigation of Goitre and Cretinism in India, 1913-14; and Deficiency Diseases, 1918-35, under Indian Research Fund Assoc.; Director, Nutrition Research I.R.F. Assoc., 1927-35; Prix Amussat, Academy of Medicine, Paris, 1914; on active service, 1914-17 (Bt. Lt.-Col.); Stewart Prize, B.M.A. 1918; Arnott Memorial Gold Medal, Irish Medical Schools and Graduates Association, 1922; Silver Medal, Royal Society of Arts, 1925; Bt. Col., 1928; K.H.P., 1928-35; Arnold Flinker and Julius Wagner-Jauregg Foundat. (Vienna) Prize, 1934; Mellon Lecturer, University of Pittsburgh, 1921; Mary Scott Newbold Lecturer, College of Physicians, Philadelphia, 1921; Hanna Lecturer, Cleveland, 1921; Mayo Foundation Lecturer, Rochester, Minn., 1921; De Lamar Lecturer, Johns Hopkins University, Baltimore, 1921; Cantor Lecturer, R.S.A., 1936; Lloyd Roberts Lectr., R.C.P. 1936;

Gabrielle Howard Lecturer, 1937; Sanderson-Wells Lecturer, 1939, Barclay Memorial Medal, R.A.S., Bengal, 1939. Group Officer, E.M.S., Oxford, 1939-45; Director, Post-Graduate Medical Education, Oxford Univ., 1945-55. *Publications:* various papers on experimental researches on Goitre and Deficiency Diseases; Etiology of Endemic Goitre, 1913; The Thyroid Gland, 1917; Studies in Deficiency Disease, 1921; The Simple Goitres, 1928; Food, 1928; Nutrition and National Health, 1946. *Recreation:* gardening. *Address:* 18 Linton Road, Oxford. *T.:* Oxford 58229.
[*Died* 18 *May* 1960.

McCARROLL, Col. James Neil, C.M.G. 1919; D.S.O. 1918; V.D.; *s.* of John McCarroll; *b.* Belfast, 1873; *m.* 1906, Janie, *d.* of John Hueston; two *d.* *Educ.:* Belfast Model School. Served European War, 1914-19 (despatches four times, C.M.G., D.S.O. and Bar, 1914-15 Star, two medals). *Address:* Whangarei, N. Auckland, N.Z.
[*Died* 26 *May* 1951.

MacCARTHY, Sir Desmond, Kt. *cr.* 1951; F.R.S.L., Hon. Litt D. Cambridge Univ., 1952; Hon. LL.D. Aberdeen Univ., 1932; author and literary critic; Pres. of English P.E.N. Club; late editor of Life and Letters, weekly contributor to Sunday Times; *s.* of Charles Desmond MacCarthy and Louise de la Chevallerie; *b.* 1877; *m.* 1906, Mary Warre-Cornish; two *s.* one *d.* *Educ.:* Eton: Trinity College, Cambridge. *Publications:* The Court Theatre; Remnants; Portraits; Criticism; Experience, 1935; Leslie Stephen, 1937; Drama, 1940; Shaw, 1950; (posthumous): *essays:* Humanities, 1953; Memories, 1953. Contributions to periodical literature and the Sunday Times. *Address:* Garrick's Villa, Hampton-on-Thames. *Clubs:* Athenæum, Beefsteak, Royal Automobile.
[*Died* 7 *June* 1952.

McCARTHY, Joseph R.; Senator, U.S.; Member firm of Eberlein & McCarthy, Shawano, Wis., since 1936; *b.* 14 Nov. 1909. *Educ.:* Marquette University. LL.B. Employed in chain grocery store, Manawa, Wis., 1929; practised law, Waupaca, 1935-36; Circuit Judge, 1939. Enlisted U.S. Marines, 1942; became Captain before discharge, 1945. Senator from Wisconsin, 1946-. Formerly: Vice-Chairman Joint Cttee. on Housing, Senate Banking and Currency, Senate Cttee. on Expenditures and Special Senate War Investigating Cttee., 1947-48, Chm. Senate Investigating Sub-Committee. Member of the Republican Party. *Address:* Senate, Washington, D.C., U.S.A.
[*Died* 2 *May* 1957.

McCARTHY, Hon. Leighton Goldie, Q.C. Canada, 1902; *b.* Walkerton, Ont., 15 Dec. 1869; *s.* of John Leigh Goldie McCarthy and Frances Olivia Irwin; *m.* 1900, Muriel Drummond (*d.* 1949), *d.* of Archibald H. Campbell, Toronto; one *s.* four *d.* Called to Bar, 1892; House of Commons, 1898; retired, 1908; Canadian Minister to the United States of America, Washington, D.C., 1941-1943, Ambassador, 1943-44; Director National Trust Company, Limited; Chairman of Board, Toronto Savings & Loan Co.; Vice-President and Director of Canadian National Carbon Company, Ltd.; Dominion Oxygen Co., Ltd.; Electro Metallurgical Co. of Canada, Ltd.; Union Carbide Company of Canada, Limited, and affiliated companies; Director, Central Canada Loan and Savings Company; Canada Life Assurance Co.; Aluminium Ltd.; Pres. Dominion Metallurgical Co. Ltd.; Trustee of Georgia Warm Springs Foundation; Hon. LL.D. Toronto University, University of Western Ontario, and Queen's Univ. *Recreations:* golf, fishing. *Address:* 45 Walmer Road, Toronto, Canada. *Clubs:* University, York, Toronto, Toronto Golf, Toronto Hunt, Ontario (Toronto); Rideau (Ottawa).
[*Died* 4 *Oct.* 1952.

McCARTHY, Lillah, O.B.E.; *b.* Cheltenham, 22 Sept. 1875; *d.* of J. McCarthy, F.R.A.S.; *m.* 1st, H. Granville Barker (whom she div. 1918); 2nd, 1920, Professor Sir Frederick Keeble, C.B.E., F.R.S. (*d.* 1952). *Educ.:* Cheltenham. Made her first stage appearance in A. E. Drinkwater's Company, 1895. Studied elocution with Hermann Vezin and voice production with Emil Behnke. Parts include: leading parts with Wilson Barrett in England, America, New Zealand, S. Africa and Australia. Returned to West End Theatre; at the Court: in 1905, Nora in John Bull's Other Island, Ann Whitefield in Man and Superman, in 1906, Gloria in You Never Can Tell, Jennifer in The Doctor's Dilemma; at the Royalty in 1908, Nan in Nan by John Masefield; at the Duke of York's, Madge Thomas in Strife; at the Court in 1911, Anne Pedersdotter in The Witch; Dionysus in The Bacchae (Euripides); assumed management of The Little Theatre in 1911, playing Margaret Knox in Fanny's First Play, Hilda Wangel in The Master Builder; appeared with Sir Herbert Tree as Lady Norma in The War God; at Covent Garden, 1912, appeared as Jocasta in Martin Harvey's production of Œdipus Rex; became manager of The Kingsway in 1912; played Iphigenia in Iphigenia in Tauris; Manager of the Savoy in 1912, appearing as Hermione in A Winter's Tale and Viola in Twelfth Night; played at the Haymarket theatre in Haddon Chambers' play, Tanta, The Impossible Woman; went to New York, December 1914 to June 1915, playing repertory under own management; became manager of Kingsway Theatre, 1919; produced there Judith, by Arnold Bennett; St. George and the Dragons, by Eden Phillpotts; played with Matheson Lang in The Wandering Jew and Blood and Sand; played Iphigenia, 1932; special tour to S. America to speak English Verse, visiting Buenos Aires, Rio de Janeiro, Uruguay, 1933. *Publication:* Myself and My Friends, 1933. *Recreations:* walking and outdoor sports. *Address:* Flat 6, Cranley Mansions, 160 Gloucester Road, S.W.7.
[*Died* 15 *April* 1960.

McCHEANE, Col. Montague William Hiley, C.M.G. 1916, C.B.E. 1919; late Royal Artillery and Royal Army Ordnance Corps; *b.* 27 Mar. 1872; *s.* of late Lt.-Col. W. H. McCheane, R.M.L.I.; *m.* 1922, Monica, *d.* of Dr. F. A. Mills; one *s.* two *d.* *Educ.:* Portsmouth; R.M.A., Woolwich. Entered R.A. 1892; Capt. 1900; Major, 1906, Lt.-Col. 1914; D.A.D. of Equipment and Ordnance Stores, War Office, 1913-15; retired pay, 1921; served South Africa, 1899-1902 (despatches, Queen's medal 2 clasps, King's medal 2 clasps); European War, 1914-17 (despatches four times, C.M.G., C.B.E.; Order of the White Eagle, Serbia; Order of the Nahda, Hedjaz). *Address:* 20 The Drive, Sevenoaks, Kent. *T.:* Sevenoaks 4532.
[*Died* 1 *July* 1955.

MacCHESNEY, Brig.-Gen. Nathan William; Lawyer, Author, Soldier, Diplomat, Judge U.S. Cts.; *b.* Chicago, Ill., 2 June 1878; *s.* of Alfred Brunson MacChesney, M.D., Lt.-Col. U.S.A., and Henrietta Milsom M.D., of Oxford and London; *m.* 1904, Lena Frost, Riverside, Ill., *d.* of William E. Frost; two *s.* *Educ.:* College of Pacific, A.B., 1898; University of Michigan, LL.B., 1902; Northwestern Univ., LL.M., 1922; Hon. LL.D. College of Pacific, 1926; Univ. of Michigan, 1934. Special Asst. Attorney-General of U.S., 1911-1912; Counsel for U.S. Senate in various investigations and War Dept. in U.S., Supreme Court; Judge Advocate-General, Illinois, 1911-17; Judge Advocate U.S. Army, G.H.Q., A.E.F. in France; Brig.-General; Citation by General Pershing; active duty U.S. Army, 1942-43, Yukon, Canada, Alaska, etc. U.S. Minister to Canada, 1932-33; High Commissioner for Canada, Century of Progress Exposition, Chicago, 1933-34; Consul-General for Thailand (Siam), 1924-. Cttee. Member, National Defense Advisory Commission; American Bar Assoc. (Vice-President 1925-26); Illinois State Bar Assoc. (Pres. 1915-16); American Institute Criminal Law and Criminology (Pres. 1910-11); Life Trustee, Northwestern Univ., Salvation Army; Presbyterian Church; Sons of American Revolution; Past Pres. of War of 1812; Mil. Order of World Wars. Past Comdr.; Order of the Coif; Mil. Order of Purple Heart, U.S.A.; Commendation Medal (2 stars), U.S. Army; Comdr. Order of White Elephant, Siam; Chevalier Order of Crown of Italy; Officer Legion of Honour, France. *Publications:* Abraham Lincoln, The Tribute of a Century, 1909; The Significance of the War of 1812; French Contribution to American Life, 1914; Military Policy and Laws of the U.S., 1914; Challenge to American Ideals, 1917; French Contribution to American Legal and Political Theory, 1920; Uniform State Laws, 1925; Principles of Real Estate Law; 1928; The Law of Real Estate Brokerage, 1938. *Recreations:* horseback riding, swimming. *Address:* 343 S. Dearborn St., Chicago 4, Ill.; Rockbridge Hall, Riverhill Farms, Belvidere Road, and Desplaines River, Libertyville, Ill.; 2350 Lincoln Park West, Chicago. *Clubs:* University, Union League, Chicago, Chicago Law, Chicago Literary, Knollwood (Chicago); Michigan Union, Lawyers, Ann Arbor (Mich.); Metropolitan (Washington). [*Died* 25 *Sept.* 1954.

McCLEAN, (Donald Francis) Stuart; Vice-Chairman, Daily Mail and Associated Newspapers; Chairman, Taylor Brothers Wharfage Co. Ltd.; Chm., Daily Sketch; Dep. Chm., Southern Television Ltd.; Director, Television Corporation Limited, Sydney, Australia, 1955; *b.* 21 Oct. 1909; *s.* of late Donald Stuart McClean and Mabel Clare McClean (*née* Burton), Kellyville, Athy, Co. Kildare; *m.* 1933, Marjorie Kathleen, *o. d.* of Arthur Franks; three *s.* two *d. Educ.:* The Abbey, Tipperary; Trinity College, Dublin. Joined Associated Newspapers, 1928. Major, Irish Guards, 1940-46. Dir., Associated Newspapers, 1948; Managing Director, Associated Newspapers, 1949; Chairman, Daily Sketch and Daily Graphic Ltd., 1957. Member of General Council of the Press, 1953. *Address:* The Doone, Silvermere, Cobham, Surrey. *Club:* Garrick. [*Died* 26 *June* 1960.

McCLEAN, Sir Francis Kennedy, Kt., *cr.* 1926; A.F.C.; F.R.Ae.S.; *b.* 1 Feb. 1876; *s.* of Frank McClean, F.R.S., LL.D.; *m.* 1918, Aileen, *d.* of W. H. Wale; two *d. Educ.:* Charterhouse; Clifton; R.I.E.C., Coopers Hill. Public Works Department, India; retired, 1902; Aviation, 1907-14; Astronomy; Royal Naval Air Service, 1914-18; Royal Air Force, 1918-19; Chairman (1923-24 and 1941-44) and Vice-Pres. 1945, Royal Aero Club; High Sheriff, Oxfordshire, 1932. *Address:* 64 Kingston House, Princes Gate, S.W.7. *Clubs:* Royal Aero, Garrick. [*Died* 11 *Aug.* 1955.

McCLEAN, Stuart; *see* McClean, D. F. S.

McCLEERY, Rt. Hon. Sir William Victor, P.C. (N. Ire.) 1949; Kt., *cr.* 1954; D.L.; J.P., M.P. (N. Ire.); *b.* 17 July 1887; *s.* of Rev. John Richard McCleery, M.A., and Henrietta McCleery (*née* Hodgins); *m.* 1913, Mary Williamson Alexander. *Educ.:* privately. Managing Director Hale, Martin & Co. Ltd., Flax Spinners, Ballymoney, 1920 (Chm. 1938). M.P. North Antrim, 1945-; Minister of Labour and National Insurance, 1949; Minister of Commerce, 1949-53, Northern Ireland. President Ballymoney Chamber of Commerce, 1921-46; Chairman N. Antrim Agricultural Association, 1922-45; President N. Antrim Unionist Assoc., 1931-46. Member of Grand Orange Lodge of Ireland; Grand Master of County Antrim, Imperial Grand Black Chapter of The British Commonwealth; Grand Master Grand Orange Lodge of N. Ireland, 1954; Grand Master of Imperial Grand Orange Council of the World, 1955. D.L. County of Antrim; J.P. Co. Antrim, 1921. *Recreation:* fishing. *Address:* Balnamore House, Ballymoney, Co. Antrim, N. Ireland. *T.:* Ballymoney 8. *T.:* Victoria 6949. *Club:* Ulster Reform (Belfast). [*Died* 30 *Oct.* 1957.

McCLELLAN, Frank Campbell, C.B.E. 1920; F.L.S.; Professor of Forestry and Estate-management, Royal Agricultural College, Cirencester; *b.* 1871. Director of Agriculture, Zanzibar, 1912-23. *Address:* 14 Warwick Square, S.W.1. *T.:* Victoria 6949. *Club:* St. James'. [*Died* 22 *March* 1957.

McCLENAGHAN, Herbert Eric St. George, C.I.E. 1944; M.A., LL.B.; I.C.S. (Retd); Partner, Cathcart and Hemphill, Solicitors, 11 Ely Place, Dublin, 1950; *b.* 5 Aug. 1896; *e. s.* of late Ven. Henry St. George McClenaghan; *m.* 1927, Charlotte Lane, 2nd *d.* of late Joseph Allison McGuinness, Lawrence Hill, Londonderry; one *s.* three *d. Educ.:* Royal School, Armagh; Trinity College, Dublin. 2nd Lt. 3rd Royal Irish Fusiliers, 1916; Lieut. 1917; Lieut. 2/129th D.C.O. Baluchis; Capt. 1920; retired from I.A. 1922, on appt. to I.C.S.; Capt. A.I.R.O., 1923; Asst. Commissioner, C.P. and Berar, 1923; Deputy Commissioner, 1926; Excise Commissioner, 1930; Major, A.I.R.O., 1931; retired from A.I.R.O., 1934; Collector of Salt Revenue, Bombay, 1939; Collector of Central Excise and Supt. of Lighthouses, Bombay, 1944; Chairman Persian Gulf Lighthouse Advisory Cttee., 1946; retired from I.C.S., 1949. Governor, Sir Patrick Dun's Hosp., 1947; Governor, Hosp. and Free School of King Charles II, Dublin, 1950; Adviser to Colonial Students in Ireland, 1950. *Recreations:* cricket, tennis, philately (F.R.P.S.L.). *Address:* Upton, Willow Bank, Dun Laoghaire, Co. Dublin. *T.A.* and *T.:* Dun Laoghaire 83526; c/o Lloyds Bank, 6 Pall Mall, S.W.1. *Clubs:* University, Royal Irish Automobile (Dublin). [*Died* 3 *May* 1955.

McCLURE, His Honour George Buchanan; retired; *b.* 21 April 1887; *s.* of James Howe McClure and Ellen Mary Collier; *m.* 1914, Doris Elizabeth, *d.* of George B. Tydd, Ascot; one *s.* one *d. Educ.:* Kelvinside Academy; Trinity College, Oxford. Called to Bar, Inner Temple, 1917; Bencher, 1938; served European War, 1914-19, France and Belgium; Captain, 1916, 9th London Regt. (despatches); Junior Counsel to the Treasury, Central Criminal Court, 1928-34; Third Senior Prosecuting Counsel, 1934-36; Second 1936-37; Senior, 1937-42; Recorder of Rochester, 1933-39, of Guildford, 1939-42; Chm. of Hertford Quarter Sessions, 1939-50; Judge of the Mayor's and City of London Court and Commissioner of the Central Criminal Court, 1942-53. *Publication:* joint editor of Russell on Crimes and Misdemeanours, 8th edn. *Address:* The Garth, West Clandon, Surrey. *T.:* Clandon 22. *Club:* United University. [*Died* 22 *Feb.* 1955.

McCLUSKEY, Alexander, Q.C. (Scot.) 1958; *b.* 25 October 1908; *s.* of Francis McCluskey, Glasgow; *m.* 1936, Mamie Mann; three *s.* two *d. Educ.:* St. Mungo's Academy, Glasgow; Glasgow University. Called to Scottish Bar, 1948; appointed standing junior counsel to Crown as *ultimus haeres*, 1949; Lecturer in Mercantile Law, Heriot-Watt College, Edinburgh, 1951-. *Address:* 32 Dundas Street, Edinburgh 3. *T.:* Edinburgh 30365. *Club:* Scottish Liberal (Edin.). [*Died* 14 *April* 1959.

MacCOLL, Sir Albert Edward, Kt., *cr.* 1949; Chief Executive Officer and Deputy Chairman North Scotland Hydro-Electric Board; *b.* 1882; *m.* 1916, Margaret, *d.* of Andrew Donald; one *s.* one *d. Educ.:* Dumbarton Academy; Royal Technical College, Glasgow, Glasgow University. Member of

Institution of Electrical Engineers. *Address:* 16 Rothesay Terrace, Edinburgh 3. [*Died* 14 *June* 1951.

McCOMBE, Brigadier John Smith, D.S.O. 1917; Retired; *b.* 9 April 1885; *s.* of Robert McCombe, Ealing, W.; *m.* 1919, Doris (*d.* 1946), *d.* of late George Maunsell-Smyth, and *widow* of Capt. Francis Leach, 2nd K.S.L.I.; *m.* 1951, Joyce, *widow* of 6th Baron Talbot de Malahide. *Educ.:* Queen's College, Belfast. M.B., B.Ch., B.A.O., R.U.I., 1907; Lieut. R.A.M.C. 1908; Lieut.-Colonel, 1933; Colonel, 1937; Royal Humane Society Certificate and Arnott Memorial Medal for life-saving, 1908; semi-final Army and Navy Boxing Championship, 1910; D.A.D.M.S. Mesopotamia, 1916-17; Army Headquarters, India, 1917-18; G.H.Q., Egypt, 1929-30; A.D.M.S. Southern Command, Salisbury, 1933-34; D.D.M.S. Malta Command, 1937-42; reverted to retired pay, 1944. Royal Humane Society Bronze Medal, 1916. *Address:* c/o Glyn, Mills & Co., Whitehall, S.W.1. *Clubs:* Army and Navy; Kildare Street (Dublin). [*Died* 19 *Oct.* 1959.

McCONNACH, James, C.B.E. 1954; Chief Constable of Aberdeen since 1933; *b.* 29 Jan. 1896; *s.* of late John McConnach and of Helen Cruickshank, *m.* 1920, Elsie Bruce; one *s.* two *d.* *Educ.:* Robert Gordon's College, Aberdeen. Grimsby Borough Police, 1913-15 and 1919-27. Scottish Horse and Imperial Camel Corps, 1915-19. Chief Constable of Newark-on-Trent, 1927-33. King's Police Medal 1944. *Publications:* Scottish Criminal Law, Police Duties and Procedure, 1950; Road Traffic Law, 1936, 1952. *Recreation:* golf. *Address:* 167 Great Western Road, Aberdeen. *T.:* Aberdeen 25580. *Clubs:* Royal Scottish Automobile (Glasgow); Sportsman's (Aberdeen). [*Died* 23 *Jan.* 1955.

McCONNAN, Sir Leslie James, Kt., *cr.* 1951; formerly Chief Manager, The National Bank of Australasia Ltd., 1935-52; *b.* 15 June 1887; *s.* of late Rev. A. C. McConnan, Benalla, Vic., Australia; *m.* 1921, Gladys A., *d.* of John B. Hay, Glasgow; one *d.* *Educ.:* North-eastern College, Benalla, Vic., Australia. Joined service of National Bank of Australasia Ltd., 1904; served continuously in various Australian States and London. Chairman of Associated Banks (Victoria) on various occasions over a period of 6 years. *Recreations:* reading and golf. *Address:* 189 Kooyong Road, Toorak, Melbourne, Victoria, Australia. *T.:* U. 2495. *Club:* Melbourne (Melbourne). [*Died* 22 *Dec.* 1954.

McCORKELL, Sir Dudley Evelyn Bruce, Kt. 1933; M.B.E.; J.P.; H.M. Lieutenant for County Londonderry, 1957; Chairman of Wm. McCorkell & Co. Ltd.; *b.* 1883; *e. s.* of late David Browne McCorkell, J.P., D.L., LL.B., Barrister-at-Law, of Ballyarnett, Londonderry; *m.* 1909, Helen Elizabeth, *d.* of Francis James Usher; three *d.* (one *s.* killed in action, 1944). *Educ.:* Shrewsbury; Pembroke College, Cambridge. An ex-officio Member of Senate of Northern Ireland whilst Mayor of Londonderry, 1929-1934; High Sheriff, Co. Londonderry, 1925; Director: Bank of Ireland; Industrial Finance Co. (N.I.) Ltd.; County Donegal Railways; Londonderry Gaslight Co.; Londonderry Port and Harbour (Commissioner); Member of Ulster Transport Authority; Chairman, Belfast Board of the London and Lancashire Insurance Co. Ltd. K.St.J. 1958. *Address:* Ballyarnett, Co. Londonderry. *T.:* Brookhall 239. *Club:* Kildare Street (Dublin). [*Died* 30 *May* 1960.

MacCORMACK, Charles Joseph, L.R.C.S. and P., and L.M. Ireland; late Medical Member, General Prisons Board, Ireland; late H.M. Inspector, Reformatory and Industrial Schools, Ireland; *b.* 9 Feb. 1861; 2nd *s.* of late Charles MacCormack, The Green, Castlebar, Co. Mayo; *m.* 1882, Mary, *d.* of John Duff, Ballaghaderin, Co. Mayo; four *s.* three *d.* *Educ.:* St. Mels College, Longford; Catholic University School of Medicine, Cecilia Street, Dublin. First Prizeman in Senior Anatomy and Physiology, and in Medicine, Midwifery, and Surgery; Exhibitioner in Medicine, Midwifery, and Surgery; Medical Inspector, Local Government Board Ireland, 1910-17; formerly Medical Officer of the Athlone No. 1 Dispensary District and Workhouse Infirmary. *Recreation:* cycling, shooting, and golf. *Address:* Suresnes, Bushy Park Road, Co. Dublin. [*Died* 15 *Dec.* 1952.

McCORMACK, Rt. Rev. Joseph; Bishop of Hexham and Newcastle, (R.C.), since 1937; *b.* Broadway, Worcestershire, 17 May 1887; *s.* of John McCormack and Hanora Graham. *Educ.:* St. Cuthbert's Grammar School, Newcastle upon Tyne; Ushaw Coll., Durham; Louvain Univ. Ordained, 1912; Curate St. Mary's Cathedral, 1914-17; Bishop's Secretary, 1914-27; Parish Priest at St. Teresa's, Newcastle, 1927-30; Administrator of St. Mary's Cathedral, Newcastle, 1930-36; Vicar General of Hexham and Newcastle, 1929-36; Canon Theologian, 1934; Vicar Capitular of Hexham and Newcastle, 1936. *Address:* Bishop's House, West Road, Newcastle upon Tyne 5. *T.:* Lemington 74556. [*Died* 2 *March* 1958.

McCORMICK, Anne O'Hare; Member of editorial board of The New York Times since 1936; *d.* of Thomas and Teresa Beatrice O'Hare; *m.* Francis J. McCormick. *Educ.:* St. Mary's College, Columbus, Ohio. Contributor to The New York Times since 1923; author of editorial column " Abroad " since 1937. Member of Advisory Cttee. on Post-War Foreign Policy of State Dept., 1942-43; U.S. Delegate to U.N.E.S.C.O. General Confs., 1946 and 1948. Pulitzer Prize for distinguished foreign correspondence, 1937; Laetare Medal, 1944. Member of National Institute of Arts and Letters. Chevalier of the Legion of Honour. *Publication:* The Hammer and the Scythe, 1928. *Address:* The New York Times, New York 36, N.Y., U.S.A. [*Died* 29 *May* 1954.

McCORMICK, Major James Hanna, D.S.O. 1917; Soldier, Pioneer, and Author; *b.* Belfast, 1875; *m.* Evelyne, *d.* of William Campbell, of Islandvale, Knock; two *s.* *Educ.:* Belfast Model School; Royal School of Instruction and Hythe School of Musketry. Commission in Canadian Militia Cavalry, 1907; served South African War, 1899-1902 (King's and Queen's medals with six clasps, wounded); with Barr Colonist Expedition to North-West Territories, 1903, 200 miles from railroad; Lloydminster Municipality founded; became its Deputy-Mayor, 1908; owner of 1200 acres of ranching and farm lands; was Deputy-Sheriff for the district surrounding; served with Canadian Expeditionary Force, European War (D.S.O., wounded five times, despatches twice); Administrative Comr. under Northern Govt. in Ireland, 1921-24; commanded a battalion of Ulster Police with rank of Lt.-Col. on the invasion of Ulster territory by Southern gunmen, 1922-26; M.P. (U.) St. Anne's Division of Belfast, Parliament of Northern Ireland, 1929-38; Chairman of Appeal Courts under Ministry of Labour, 1928-29; Official Lecturer, Canadian Pacific Railway Co. *Publications:* Lloydminster, or 5000 miles with the Barr Colonists; Annals of the Barrities; The Greater Saskatchewan; Fiscal Relations with our Colonies. *Recreations:* a past President, Irish Amateur Swimming Association; Vice-President Craigavad and Helens Bay Horse Association; hunting. *Address:* Vimy, Knock, Co. Down; Lloydminster, Sask., Canada. *Club:* Overseas. [*Died* 4 *May* 1955.

McCORMICK, Admiral Lynde Dupuy; Legion of Merit (two gold stars); U.S. Navy; President of the Naval War College, Newport, Rhode Island, since 1954; *b.* 12 Aug. 1895; *s.* of Rear-Adm. A. M. D. McCormick and Edith Lynde Abbot; *m.* 1920, Lillian

Addison Sprigg; two *s.* (and one *s.* decd.). *Educ.:* St. John's Prep. School and College, Annapolis; U.S. Naval Academy, B.S. 1915. Served European War, 1914-18 and War of 1941-45. Rear-Adm., 1942; Vice-Adm. 1947; Adm. 1950. Vice-Chief of Naval Ops., Navy Dept., 1950; C.-in-C. of the Atlantic Fleet, U.S.N., 1951-54; Supreme Allied Commander, Atlantic, N.A.T.O., 1952-1954. *Address:* Naval War College, Newport, Rhode Island, U.S.A.; (home) Clermont, Berryville, Va. [*Died* 16 *Aug.* 1956.

McCORMICK, Robert Rutherford; Editor and Publisher, Chicago Tribune; Chairman of Board, New York Daily News; *b.* Chicago, 30 July 1880; *s.* of Robert Sanderson McCormick and Katherine Van Etta Medill; *m.* 1st, 1915, Amie Irwin Adams (*d.* 1939); 2nd, 1944, Maryland Matheson Hooper; no *c.* *Educ.:* Ludgrove School, New Barnet; Groton School, Massachusetts; Yale College; Northwestern Law School. Alderman, Chicago, 1904, Member City Council, 1904-06; admitted to Ill. Bar, 1908; Member Chicago Bar Assoc.; Member Law firm, McCormick, Kirkland, Patterson and Fleming, 1908-20; President: Chicago Tribune, 1911; Washington Times-Herald, 1949-54; war correspondent with British, French and Russians, 1915; Major First Illinois Cavalry, Mexican Border, 1916; attached Gen. Pershing's staff, A.E.F. in France, Adj. 57th Artillery Bde.; Lt.-Col. 122nd Fd. Artillery, U.S. National Guard; Col. 61st Field Artillery, 1918; Col. Gen. Staff, 1919; Comdt. Fort Sheridan, Ill.; Distinguished Service Medal; recommended for rank of General Officer by General Pershing, 1919. LL.D. The Citadel of South Carolina, Colby College, Maine, and Northwestern Univ. Republican, Presbyterian. *Publications:* With the Russian Army, 1915; The Army of 1918, 1919; What is a Newspaper? 1924; Ulysses S. Grant, the Great Soldier of America, 1932; Freedom of the Press, 1936; How We Acquired Our National Territory, 1942; The American Revolution and Its Influence on World Civilization, 1945; The War Without Grant, 1949; The Founding Fathers, 1951; The American Empire, 1952. *Recreations:* deep-sea fishing; formerly polo, fox hunting, shooting. *Address:* 435 N. Michigan Avenue, Chicago; Wheaton, Illinois. *T.:* Superior 0100; Wheaton 8-0063. *Clubs:* Chicago, Chicago Golf, Chicago Racket (Chicago); Racket and Tennis (New York). [*Died* 1 *April* 1955.

McCOSH, Robert, O.B.E. 1919; M.C. 1918; J.P.; Member of the Queen's Body Guard for Scotland, The Royal Company of Archers; Deputy Governor, The Bank of Scotland; Director: Scottish Equitable Life Assurance Society, Scottish Insurance Corporation Ltd., Ailsa Investment Trust Ltd., Alva Investment Trust Ltd.; *b.* 14 April 1885; *s.* of late Andrew Kirkwood McCosh, D.L., Cairnhill, Airdrie, Lanarkshire; *m.* 1913, Agnes Dunlop, *yr. d.* of Bryce M. Knox, Redheugh, Kilbirnie, Ayrshire; two *s.* one *d.* (and one *s.* decd.). *Educ.:* Cargilfield, Fettes; Trinity Coll., Cambridge. B.A. 1907; played Rugby football for Camb., 1905-06-07. Writer to the Signet; partner in firm of Gillespie & Paterson, W.S., Edinburgh. Served European War in Lanarkshire Yeomanry, 1914-19; Gallipoli, Egypt and Palestine; Staff Captain, Desert Column and Eastern Force; D.A.Q.M.G. Palestine L. of C. (despatches twice, O.B.E., M.C., 1914-15 Star, Order of the Nile (4th Class)). *Recreations:* rural. *Address:* Hardington, Lamington, Lanarkshire. *T.:* Lamington 202; Southernwood House, Davidson's Mains, Edinburgh 4. *T.:* Davidson's Mains 77050. *Club:* New (Edinburgh). [*Died* 21 *Dec.* 1959.

McCOWAN, Lt.-Col. William Hew, C.B.E. 1925; D.S.O. 1917; D.L.; *b.* 1878; *s.* of late William McCowan of Roseneath, Whitehaven. *Educ.:* Rugby. Joined Cameron Highlanders, 1899; served European War, 1914-19 (despatches, D.S.O.); Commanding Khartoum District, 1920-25; Brevet Lt.-Col., 1919; retired list. *Address:* Kingston House, Whitehaven. *Club:* Naval and Military. [*Died* 20 *Dec.* 1958.

McCOY, Captain James Abernethy, D.S.O. 1940; Kommandör Royal Norwegian Order of St. Olav, 1947; Royal Navy, retired; British Vice-Consul, Kristiansand, South Norway, since 1951; *b.* 17 June 1900; *s.* of James Abernethy McCoy and Ethel Elizabeth Peet; *m.* 1936, Oretta, *er. d.* of Count Antonio Ghezzi-Morgalanti, Rome; three *s.* *Educ.:* Royal Naval Colleges, Osborne and Dartmouth; Christ's College, Cambridge. Entered Royal Navy; 1913; served in H.M.S. Lion, 1916-18; Commander, 1935; Capt. 1941; served war of 1939-45 (despatches four times); Senior Officer Destroyers, 2nd Battle of Narvik, 13 April 1940 (D.S.O.); retired, 1950. *Recreation:* hunting. *Address:* Roanmore, Co. Waterford, Eire. *T.:* Waterford 367. *Clubs:* Naval and Military; Royal Western Yacht Club of England (Plymouth). [*Died* 9 *March* 1955.

McCRAITH, Sir Douglas, Kt., *cr.* 1939; Solicitor and Notary; *b.* Nottingham, 1 Jan. 1878; *e. s.* of late Sir James William and Maria Elizabeth McCraith; *m.* 1915, Phyllis Marguerite, *d.* of late A. D'Ewes Lynam and Margaret C. F. H. Lynam; two *s.* *Educ.:* Harrow; Trinity College, Cambridge. B.A. 1899; Solicitor 1902 and became partner with father in firm Maples and McCraith; is Clerk to Commissioners of Taxes for Nottingham; Member Nottingham City Council 1904-30, Alderman 1920; was chairman Watch Committee and Estates Committee, Vice-Chairman Finance Committee; President East Nottingham Conservative Association for 30 years; President Nottingham and District Property Owners Assoc. since 1938; Chairman of Committee Notts County Cricket Club for over 30 years and was president 1937; President Nottingham Incorporated Law Society 1930, Chm. Nottingham Bench, 1951-52; J.P. 1928; Chairman of Lord Chancellor's Advisory Committee for Nottingham, 1936-51; Chm., Price Regulation Committee, North Midland Region, 1941-45, and Nottinghamshire P.O.W. Relatives Assoc.; Director Stoll Theatre Corporation, and other companies. *Publications:* By Dancing Streams, 1929; Dancing Streams in Many Lands, 1946. *Recreations:* golf, fly fishing; boxed heavyweight Cambs. *v.* Oxford, 1899. *Address:* Holme Lodge, Bingham, Notts. *Clubs:* Flyfishers'; Nottinghamshire (Nottingham). [*Died* 16 *Sept.* 1952.

McCREA, Charles, Q.C. 1921; Hon. LL.D. Univ. of Toronto, 1934; lawyer in practice at Toronto; Pres. Negus Mines, Ltd.; President of Toronto General Trusts Corporation; Chairman of Board of Mining Corporation of Canada, Ltd.; a Director of The Imperial Life Assurance Company of Canada; a Life Bencher of the Law Society of Upper Canada; *b.* Springtown, Renfrew County, Ontario, 27 Dec. 1877; of Irish-Scotch parentage; *s.* of James and Elizabeth Jervis McCrea; *m.* 1903, Edith Louise, *d.* of late M. H. Dent, Banker, Renfrew; three *d.* *Educ.:* Renfrew Separate School and High School; Osgoode Hall, Toronto. Called to Ontario Bar, 1901; practised at Sudbury, 1901-23; Member Ontario Legislature for Sudbury, 1911-34; Minister of Mines, Province of Ontario, 1923-34; Minister of Game and Fisheries, 1923-32; visited England in 1924 as Minister of Mines of Ontario Government; Progressive Conservative; Roman Catholic. *Recreation:* golf. *Address:* 410 Royal Bank Building, Toronto, Canada; 14 Edmund Avenue, Toronto. *Clubs:* Albany, Granite, Toronto Golf, Toronto Hunt, Royal Canadian Yacht, Rosedale Golf, York, Toronto (Toronto); Seigniory (Quebec). [*Died* 30 *Oct.* 1952.

McCUAIG, Maj.-Gen. George Eric, C.M.G. 1918; D.S.O. 1917; *b.* 2 Sept. 1885; 2nd *s.* of Clarence J. McCuaig, Montreal. *Educ.:* McGill University, Montreal. Served European War, 1915-18 (despatches five times, D.S.O. and bar, C.M.G.). Served War of 1939-45, 1940-45. Retired. *Address:* 276 St. James St. West, Montreal, Canada. [*Died* 21 *March* 1958.

M'CULLAGH, Francis; Knight Commander of the Royal Order of St. Sava; journalist, author; Captain, late of Royal Irish Fusiliers; *b.* Omagh, Tyrone, 1 May 1874; *s.* of James and Mary M'Cullagh; unmarried. *Educ.:* The Christian Brothers' Schools, Omagh; St. Columb's, Derry. Represented the New York Herald (Paris) in Bangkok and, afterwards, throughout the Russo-Japanese War; spent four years in Japan on a Japanese semi-official paper, then six months in Port Arthur on a Russian semi-official organ, the Novi Krai, having previously edited a French paper in Siam; prisoner of war in Japan; went to America when peace negotiations set afoot; expelled from Agadir by the Moors; taken prisoner by Bulgars outside Tchataldja Lines during Balkan War, being attached at that time to Turkish army; travelled in Servia; decorated by King Peter; in Russia on outbreak of European War, 1914; Lieut. in 12th Worcesters, Dec. 1914; transferred 8th Royal Irish Fusiliers, and sent to the Dardanelles, July 1915; acted as O.C. A Coy., 5th R.I.F. till 10th Div. sent to Serbia; acted in Serbia and Macedonia as a Divisional Intelligence Officer, being transferred to General List and Intelligence Corps; accompanied Gen. Knox's Military Mission to Siberia, July 1918, with rank of Captain; captured by Bolsheviks at Krasnoyarsk; brought to Moscow, where imprisoned by the Extraordinary Commission; released under the O'Grady-Litvinov Agreement and returned to England 22 May 1920; went again to Russia in 1922 for the New York Herald, but requested by the Soviet Government in April 1923 to leave; travelled extensively. *Publications:* With the Cossacks; The Fall of Abd-ul-Hamid; Italy's War for a Desert; Tales from Turkey (with Allan Ramsay); A Prisoner of the Reds, 1921; The Bolshevik Persecution of Christianity, 1924; Russia To-day, a pamphlet published by The Times and containing a series of articles which appeared in that paper, May-June 1923; The Bolsheviks and The Incas, a pamphlet published at Buenos Aires in 1926; Mexico under the Interdict, 1928; Red Mexico, 1928; In Franco's Spain (a description of his experiences as a war correspondent in Spain, 1936-1937), 1937. *Recreation:* travelling. *Address:* Butler Hall, 88 Morningside Drive, New York City, U.S.A. [*Died* 25 *Nov.* 1956.

McCULLOCH, Major-General Sir Andrew Jameson, (assumed surname of McCulloch, 1892), K.B.E., *cr.* 1937; C.B. 1934; D.S.O. 1918; D.C.M. 1901; D.L.; late H.L.I., 7th Dragoon Guards, and 14th Hussars; *b.* 14 July 1876; *e. s.* of late Andrew Jameson, Lord Ardwall, Scottish Judge, and Lady Ardwall of Ardwall, Gatehouse of Fleet; *m.* Esme Valentine, *d.* of late Colin Mackenzie, H.E.I.C.S., of Portmore, Peeblesshire; three *s.* (and one killed in action). *Educ.:* Edinburgh Academy, St. Andrews University; New College, Oxford (B.A.). Studied Law Inner Temple, 1898-99; Barrister-at-law, Inner Temple; served South Africa, 1900-2, including Paardeberg, Dreifontein, Johannesburg, Diamond Hill, Wittebergen (D.C.M., despatches); passed Staff College, Camberley, 1910; served European War, 1914-18 (D.S.O. with two bars, Legion of Honour, despatches thrice, wounded thrice; commanded 64th Infantry Brigade when it took Grandcourt, France, Aug. 1918; commanded 62nd Infantry Brigade, 1919; Chief Instructor, Staff College, Quetta, 1919-23; Brigadier 2nd Infantry Brigade, Aldershot, 1926-30; Comdt., Senior Officers' School, Sheerness, 1930-33; A.D.C. to the King, 1931-33; Temporary Command of Troops in Malta, 1935-36; Commander 52nd (Lowland) Division T.A., 1934-35 and 1936-38; Colonel of Highland Light Infantry, 1936-46; retired pay, 1938; Inspector of Oil Protection, 1941-44. *Address:* Ardwall, Gatehouse, Kirkcudbrightshire. *T.:* Gatehouse, 240. *Clubs:* Naval and Military; New (Edinburgh). [*Died* 19 *April* 1960.

MACCURDY, Edward Alexander Coles; *b.* 28 June 1871; *s.* of Rev. Alexander McCurdy; *m.* 1906, Sylvia Winifred Annette, *d.* of William Stebbing; two *s.* four *d.* *Educ.:* Loughborough; Balliol College, Oxford. 3rd Modern History, 1893; M.A. 1898; Barrister at Law Inner Temple, 1895; Resident at Toynbee Hall 1895 and 1896-98. *Publications:* Parva Seges (Poems) 1894; Roses of Paestum (Essays), 1900; Leonardo da Vinci (Great Masters Series), 1904; Leonardo da Vinci's Note Books, 1906; Thoughts of Leonardo, 1907; Essays in Fresco, 1912; Raphael Santi, 1917; Lays of a Limpet, 1920; Poems, 1925; The Mind of Leonardo da Vinci, 1928; Leonardo da Vinci The Artist, 1933; A Literary Enigma. The Canadian Boat Song: its authorship and associations, 1936; The Note Books of Leonardo da Vinci (in two volumes), 1938; Lyrics of Childhood, 1947. *Recreation:* the study of Gaelic. *Address:* Oakdene, Ashtead, Surrey. *T.:* Ashtead 484. [*Died* 15 *April* 1957.

McCURDY, Hon. Fleming Blanchard, P.C. (Can.); Publisher; *b.* Clifton, N.S., 17 Feb. 1875; *s.* of James McCurdy and Amelia J. Archibald; *m.* 1902, Florence Bridgeman, *d.* of late Hon. B. F. Pearson, M.P.P., Halifax; one *s.* *Educ.:* Public Schools, Nova Scotia. Governor and Hon. Treasurer, Dalnousie University, Halifax; Governor Ashbury College, Ottawa; Past Pres. Halifax Board of Trade; M.P. Shelburne-Queens, 1911-17; M.P. Colchester, 1917-21; Parliamentary Sec. of Department of Militia and Defence, 1916; Parliamentary Sec. of Department Soldiers' Civil Re-Establishment, Feb.-Nov. 1918; Minister of Public Works, Canada, 1920-21; President Eastern Trust Co. Eastern Utilities Ltd., Chronicle Company, and Halifax Insurance Co.; Vice-Pres. Bank of Nova Scotia; Director Canadian General Electric Co. Conservative; Presbyterian. *Recreations:* rod, gun, golf. *Address:* Fernwood, Francklyn Street, Halifax, Nova Scotia. *Clubs:* Royal Automobile; Halifax, Halifax Golf and Country (Halifax); St. James's, Mount Royal (Montreal); Rideau, Royal Ottawa Golf (Ottawa). [*Died* 29 *Aug.* 1952.

McCUTCHEON, Katharine Howard, M.A. (Camb.), Hon. LL.D. (St. Andrews); *b.* 7 Dec. 1875; *d.* of Rev. Oliver McCutcheon, D.D., LL.D. *Educ.:* Schools in Ireland; Girton Coll., Cambridge (Scholar). B.A. with Honours in Classics, Royal University of Ireland, Cambridge Classical Tripos, Part I Class 1, Cambridge Classical Tripos, Part II Class 1 (Ancient Philosophy); Classical Mistress, St. Leonards School, St. Andrews, 1900-10; Classical Tutor, Lady Margaret Hall, Oxford 1910-22; Headmistress, St. Leonards and St. Katharines Schools, St. Andrews, 1922-38; Member of Council Bedford College for Women, Univ. of London. *Publication:* (with G. Wynne Edwards) Notes on the Hebrew Prophets. *Address:* 12 Lancaster Close, St. Petersburgh Place, W.2. *T.:* Bayswater 5536. *Club:* University Women's. [*Died* 1 *March* 1956.

McDERMOTT, John Frederick; General Secretary, Amalgamated Society of Woodworkers, since 1949; *b.* 3 Sept. 1906; Irish; *m.* 1931, Mary Patricia Wallace, Dublin; one *s.* four *d.* *Educ.:* St. Stephen's, Dublin. Executive Council Member, Amalgamated Society of Woodworkers, 1947; Assistant General Secretary, 1948; Member of British Trade Union Congress, 1949-. *Recreations:*

yachting and tennis. *Address:* 9-11 Macaulay Road, S.W.4. [*Died* 14 *Aug.* 1958.

MACDIARMID, Duncan Stewart, B.A. (Cambridge); LL.B. (Glasgow); Advocate; Sheriff-Substitute of Lanarkshire at Glasgow (retired); *b.* 19 Nov. 1873; *m.* 1908, Robina Constance (*d.* 1939), *y. d.* of late George Moncrieff Grierson; two *d.*; *m.* 1946, Phillis Gray, *widow* of John Bartholomew, advocate, Glenorchard, Stirlingshire. Legal Secretary to the Lord Advocate for Scotland, 1910-12; Sheriff-Substitute of Stirling, Dumbarton and Clackmannan at Dumbarton, 1912-19; of Lanarkshire at Airdrie, 1919-24, at Glasgow, 1924-46. *Publication:* The Life of Lt.-Gen. Sir James Moncrieff Grierson. *Address:* Greenways, Crawley Drive, Camberley, Surrey. *T.:* Camberley 1766. [*Died* 1 *Aug.* 1954.

MACDONALD, Alexander, C.B.E. 1943; Managing Director of subsidiary of E.M.I. in Chile since 1948; *b.* Glasgow, 26 Sept. 1894; *s.* of Charles MacDonald and Elizabeth Shearer; *m.* 1922, Dorothy Lester Northcroft; (*o. s.* killed in War, 1945) one *d.* *Educ.:* Hutcheson's School, Glasgow. Served European War, 1914-18; commissioned to 6th Seaforth Highlanders; qualified as Chartered Accountant, Glasgow, 1919; Pres. British Legion, Santiago, 1934-1940; Chm. British Community War Effort, Santiago, Chile, 1939-42; Pres. Asociacion de Golf de Chile, 1947. *Recreations:* fishing, golf, and golf architecture; courses laid out: Pucon, Santo Domingo (Chile), Los Inkas Country Club (Peru). *Address:* Casilla 2651, Santiago de Chile. *Clubs:* Royal and Ancient (St. Andrews); Club de la Union, Golf, Country (Santiago). [*Died* 25 *July* 1954.

MACDONALD OF SLEAT, Sir (Alexander) Somerled (Angus Bosville), 16th Bt., *cr.* 1625; M.C. 1943; J.P., 1953; A.C.A. 1947; 23rd Chief of Sleat; Member of the Queen's Body Guard for Scotland, Royal Company of Archers; *b.* 6 Nov. 1917; *er. s.* of Sir Godfrey Macdonald of the Isles, 15th Bt., and Hon. Rachel Audrey Campbell, *yr. d.* of 1st Baron Colgrain; *S.* father 1951; *m.* 1946, Mary Elizabeth, *e. d.* of Lt.-Col. R. C. B. Gibbs; two *s.* two *d.* *Educ.:* Eton; Magdalen College, Oxford (B.A.). 2nd Lieut. Territorial Army, 1939; served War of 1939-45, B.E.F. France, 1940; M.E.F., 1941-43 (wounded, M.C.); Capt. 1942; retired through ill-health, 1943. *Recreations:* shooting, fishing. *Heir:* *s.* Ian Godfrey Bosville, *b.* 18 July 1947. *Address:* Thorpe Hall, Rudston, Driffield, Yorks. *T.:* Burton Agnes 39. *Club:* Flyfishers'. [*Died* 21 *Oct.* 1958.

MACDONALD, Rev. Allan John Macdonald, D.D.; Prebendary of St. Paul's, 1950; Rector of S. Dunstan-in-the-West since 1930; *b.* 1887; *e. s.* of late J. S. Macdonald, Bromley; *m.* 1915, Gertrude, *e. d.* of late Edward Lowe, Edgbaston; no *c.* *Educ.:* Private; Trinity College, Cambridge (Exhibitioner); Ridley Hall, 1st Class Historica' Tripos, 1908; B.A., 1909; M.A., 1913; Maitland Prize, 1915 and 1918; B.D., 1927; D.D., 1930. F.R.Hist.S. 1926; F.S.A. 1949. Hulsean Lecturer, 1931-32; ordained, 1910; Lecturer in Church History, C.M.S. College, Islington, 1910; Curate, Richard's Castle, Salop, 1911; Bury, Lancashire, 1914; Rector, Alyth-cum-Meigle, Perthshire, 1917; Chaplain, 15th (Scottish) Divisional Artillery, 1918; Hon. C. F., 1920; Vicar of S. Luke and Chaplain Royal Infirmary, Liverpool, 1920; Domestic Chaplain to Bishop of Madras and Joint-Chaplain Madras Cathedral, 1925; Boyle Lecturer, 1935-37; White Lecturer (S. Paul's), 1936; Golden Lecturer, 1941-42; Select Preacher at Oxford, 1944-45. Trinity College, Dublin, 1946; St. Andrew's, 1952; Rural Dean, City of London, 1943-57; Examining Chaplain to the Bishop of Southwark, 1937-51. *Publications:* Trade, Politics and Christianity in Africa and the East, 1916; The War and Missions in the East, 1919; Lanfranc, His Life, Work, and Writing, 1926; The Holy Spirit, 1927; Berengar and the Reform of Sacramental Doctrine, 1930; The Evangelical Doctrine of Holy Communion (Ed.), 1930; Hildebrand (Gregory VII), 1932; Authority and Reason in the Early Middle Ages, 1933; God, Creation and Revelation, 1938; With Jesus in Palestine, 1938; The Interpreter Spirit and Human Life, 1944. *Address:* S. Dunstan's Vestry, Fleet Street, E.C.4. *T.:* Chancery 6027. *Club:* Athenæum. [*Died* 21 *Feb.* 1959.

MACDONALD, Hon. Angus Lewis, P.C. (Can.); Q.C. (N.S.); B.A., LL.B., S.J.D., LL.D., D.C.L., M.L.A.; Premier of Nova Scotia; *b.* Dunvegan, Inverness County, N.S.; *s.* of Lewis Macdonald, Dunvegan, N.S., and Veronica (Perry) Macdonald, Tignish, P.E.I.; *m.* Agnes Mary Foley, Halifax, N.S.; one *s.* three *d.* *Educ.:* common schools of Nova Scotia; Port Hood Academy, N.S.; St. Francis Xavier Univ., N.S. (B.A., Gold Medallist); Dalhousie Univ., N.S. (LL.B.); Harvard Univ. (S.J.D.). Asst. Deputy Attorney-General, Halifax, 1921; Professor of Law, Dalhousie Univ., Halifax, 1924; Associate Editor, Dominion Law Reports, 1929. Contributor of various articles to Canadian Bar Review; unsuccessfully contested Inverness County in Federal election in Liberal interests, 1930; elected for Halifax South, Provincial election, 1933. Premier of Nova Scotia, 1933; re-elected for Halifax South, 1937; resigned as Premier of Nova Scotia, 1940, and appointed Minister of National Defence for Naval Services, Dominion of Canada; elected to House of Commons, 1940, by acclamation, as representative for Kingston; resigned portfolio Naval Services, 1945. Again leader Liberal Party, N.S., and again Premier, 1945. Re-elected for Halifax South, 1945, 1949 and 1953. Served with 25th Bn. as Lieut.; 185th Bn. Capt. *Address:* Winwick, Marlboro Woods, Halifax, N.S. *Clubs:* Halifax, Halifax Curling (Halifax); Ashburn Golf and Country. [*Died* 13 *April* 1954.

MACDONALD, Anne; late Principal St. Helen's School, Bridge of Allan; *e. d.* of Rev. George Macdonald, Aberdeen. *Educ.:* private schools; Aberdeen; Edinburgh; Germany. Founded St. Helen's School, Bridge of Allan, 1898. *Publications:* Lyrics: In Life's Garden, 1911; Echoes of Song, 1925; Spindrift, 1933; A Field of Wild Pansies, 1953; Chime of Flowers, 1954; (with Rev. H. Mayer) Lyric Psalms: Children's Verse: Dormer Windows, 1923; Through the Green Door, 1924; A Pocketful of Silver, 1927; Sung by the Sea, 1929; Girls' School Stories: Bud and Adventure, 1926; Dorty Speaking, 1927; Dimity Dand, 1928; Briony-Called Squibs, 1931; Jill's Curmudgeon, 1932; Lilt from the Laurels, 1934; The Deceiving Mirror, novel, 1935. *Recreations:* listening to music, reading, motoring. *Address:* Hamewith, 14 Marchhall Rd., Edinburgh. *T.:* 42754 Edinburgh. *Club:* P.E.N. [*Died* 9 *April* 1958.

MacDONALD, Anne Elizabeth Campbell Bard, (Betty MacDonald); Author; *b.* 26 March 1908; *d.* of late Darsie Campbell Bard, Mining Engineer, and of Elsie Thollimer Sanderson Bard, Artist; *m.* 1st, 1927, Robert Eugene Heskett (from whom she obtained a divorce, 1931); two *d.*; 2nd, 1942, Donald Chauncey MacDonald. *Educ.:* St. Nicholas School; Roosevelt High School; University of Washington. Private Secretary: American Smelting and Refining Co., 1931; Lumbe Research Inc., 1932; Labor Adjustor, National Recovery Administration, 1933-35; Chief Clerk, U.S. Treasury Dept., 1935-38; Publicity Director, National Youth Administration, 1939-41. *Publications:* The Egg and I, 1945; Mrs. Piggle Wiggle, 1947; The Plague and I, 1948; Mrs. Piggle Wiggle's Magic, 1949; Anybody Can Do Anything, 1950; Nancy and Plum, 1952; Mrs. Piggle-Wiggle's Farm, 1954; Onions in the Stew,

1955; contributions to magazines. *Recreations:* gardening, music and painting. *Address:* Carmel Valley, California, U.S.A. [*Died* 7 *Feb.* 1958.

MACDONALD, Sir Arthur, Kt., *cr.* 1946; J.P.; *b.* 12 October 1887; *s.* of Peter and Betsy Macdonald; *m.* 1920, Florence Annie Stephens; no *c.* *Educ.:* Rochdale Secondary School. Bank Manager C.W.S. Ltd., Newcastle, 1922; Administrative Officer-Bank Manager, Newcastle Branch C.W.S., 1930; Gen. Bank Manager C.W.S. Ltd., 1941; Asst. Sec.-Bank Manager of C.W.S. Ltd., 1944; Secretary and Executive Officer C.W.S. Ltd. Manchester, 1945 - 52. Commander of the Order of Dannebrog (Denmark), 1950. *Address:* Brentwood, Manchester Rd., Bury, Lancs. *T.:* Bury 703. [*Died* 24 *Sept.* 1953.

MACDONALD, Betty; *see* Macdonald, Anne E. C. B.

MACDONALD OF THE ISLES, Sir Godfrey (Middleton) Bosville, 15th Bt., *cr.* 1625; M.B.E. 1918; J.P.; 22nd Chief of Sleat; Clerk of the Peace and County Clerk of East Riding of Yorkshire, 1932-39; *b.* 25 Sept. 1887; *s.* of Sir Alexander Wentworth Macdonald Bosville, Macdonald of the Isles, 14th Bt., and Alice Edith (Author of The House of the Isles, All the Days of My Life, etc.; *d.* 1935), *d.* of John Middleton, Kinfauns Castle, Perthshire; *S.* father 1933; *m.* 1917, Rachel Audrey, *yr. d.* of Baron Colgrain; two *s.* two *d.* *Educ.:* Eton; Magdalen College, Oxford. Called to Bar, Inner Temple, 1912; served European War, 1914-18 (despatches, Mons Medal, M.B.E.), O.C. British Red Cross Stores Transport in France. *Recreations:* fishing, shooting, motoring. *Heir:* *s.* (Alexander) Somerled (Angus) Bosville, M.C. (who *S.* 1951, as Sir Somerled Macdonald of Sleat, 16th Bt., *q.v.*). *Address:* Thorpe Hall, Rudston, Yorks. *T.A.:* Rudston. *T.:* Burton Agnes, 39. *Clubs:* Flyfishers'; Yorkshire (York). [*Died* 3 *Aug.* 1951.

MACDONALD, Hugh, Hon. M.A. Oxon.; *b.* 15 Nov. 1885; *y. s.* of W. H. Macdonald, Marlborough; *m.* C. R. D. Young, sometime Fellow and Tutor of Somerville College, Oxford; one *d.* *Educ.:* Repton. Qualified as a Solicitor; served European War, 1914-18; Publisher (with Frederick Etchells) of The Haslewood Books, 1924-1931. *Publications:* England's Helicon, 1925 and 1949; The Phoenix Nest, 1926; A Journal from Parnassus, 1937; John Dryden, A Bibliography, 1939; Observations upon a late Libel (Halifax), 1940; On Foot, an anthology, 1942; Portraits in Prose, 1946; Arden of Feversham (Malone Society), 1947; Andrew Marvell's Poems, 1952 (2nd edn. corrected, 1956); Bibliography of Thomas Hobbes, 1952; and contributions to journals. *Recreation:* walking. *Address:* The Firs, Fyfield, nr. Abingdon, Berks. [*Died* 6 *Oct.* 1958.

MACDONALD, James, Q.C. (Scot.) 1924; Sheriff-Substitute of the Lothians and Peebles at Edinburgh, 1932-50; *b.* 10 March 1877; *s.* of James Macdonald, Blackmount, Argyllshire; *m.* 1909, Alice Elspeth (*d.* 1929), *d.* of late John Bell, Edinburgh; one *d.* *Educ.:* Edinburgh University, M.A., LL.B. Called to Bar, 1902; Chm. of Trade Boards; arbitrator in industrial disputes; Sheriff Substitute of Lanarkshire at Hamilton, 1928-32. *Address:* 19 Eglinton Crescent, Edinburgh. *T.:* 61497. *Club:* University (Edinburgh). [*Died* 9 *June* 1954.

MACDONALD, Major-General James Balfour, C.S.I. 1947; D.S.O. 1945; O.B.E. 1938; p.s.c.; I.A. retd.; *b.* 9 June 1898; *s.* of late Angus Graham Macdonald, O.B.E.; M.D.; *m.* 1923, Helen Marion Hyde Lay, one *s.* *Educ.:* privately. 2nd Lt., I.A., 1917; Capt. 1924; Maj. 1935; Lt.-Col. 1940; Brig. 1943; Maj.-Gen. 1947; retd. 1948. Afghanistan and N.W.F., India, 1919; Mahsud, 1919-20; Waziristan, 1919 (despatches), Iraq, 1920; N.W.F., India, 1935, 1936 and 1937 (despatches twice, O.B.E.); Italy, 1943-45 (D.S.O.). Dep. Adjutant-Gen., and Dir. of Organisation, G.H.Q., India, 1946-47. *Address:* Maxwell Place, Kelso, Roxburgh, Scotland. [*Died* 11 *Dec.* 1959.

MACDONALD, James Harold, C.V.O. 1953; T.D.; Writer to H.M.'s Signet since 1904; *b.* 1 March 1878; *s.* of late James Macdonald, President of S.S.C. Society, Edinburgh; *m.* 1907, Isa May (decd.), *d.* of Donald Kennedy, merchant, Edinburgh; one *d.* (two *s.*, in R.A.F., killed in Battle of Britain, Aug. and Sept. 1940). *Educ.:* George Watson's College; Edinburgh University (M.A., LL.B.). J.P. for County and City of Edinburgh. Served throughout European War, 1914-18 (wounded in France). *Recreations:* golf and literature. *Address:* Goodtrees, Murrayfield, Edinburgh. *T.:* 61902. *Clubs:* New, Royal Scots (Edinburgh); Hon. Company of Edinburgh Golfers, Muirfield, East Lothian. [*Died* 4 *Aug.* 1955.

MacDONALD, James Stuart; Chairman Commonwealth Art Advisory Board; *b.* Melbourne, 28 Mar. 1878; *s.* of late Hector MacDonald; *m.* 1904, Maud, *d.* of late H. P. Keller, New York City; one *s.* one *d.* *Educ.:* Kew High School and Hawthorn College, Victoria. Studied art at Melbourne National Gallery Art School, at Westminster, at Julians and Académie Carmen; for five years painted and taught, New York; served with Australian Imperial Force, European War; for six years art critic on Melbourne Herald, and contributor to many other papers; Director National Art Gallery of New South Wales, 1929-37; Director National Gallery of Victoria, 1937-41; Member, Victorian Artists Society and Yorick Club. *Publications:* Life of Frederick McCubbin; Art of G. W. Lambert; Art of David Davies; The Elliott Collection; Drawing for Watercolour; The Art of Charles Wheeler. *Recreations:* music, reading. *Address:* Yilleen, Montrose, Melbourne, Victoria, Australia. [*Died* 12 *Nov.* 1952.

MACDONALD, Rev. John Somerled, M.A., D.D.; *b.* 5 Sept. 1871; *s.* of late Rev. D. C. Macdonald, M.A., Kilmuir-Easter, Ross-shire. *Educ.:* Tain Academy; Aberdeen Grammar School; Aberdeen University. Graduated M.A., 1891, with First Cl. Hons. in Philosophy; D.D., Aberdeen, 1926. Taught mathematics 2 years Ayr Acad., Dingwall Academy, New College, Edinburgh, 1893-97; awarded First Cunningham Fellowship but obliged resign because ordained within year. Ordained, Stornoway, 1897; Nairn, 1901; Wemyss Bay and Skelmorlie, 1909; Dalkeith 1915; Sefton Park, Liverpool, 1921; First Presbyterian Church, Syracuse, N.Y., 1931; retired 1939. *Address:* 811 Ackerman Av., Syracuse, 10, N.Y., U.S.A. [*Died* 30 *May* 1956.

MacDONALD, Sir Kenneth Mackenzie, Kt., *cr.* 1933; M.C.; late Managing Governor, Imperial Bank of India; *b.* 19 Nov. 1879; *s.* of Duncan MacDonald and Margaret Elizabeth Cockburn; *m.* 1922, Enid Gladys, *d.* of late W. J. Stacey; one *s.* two *d.* *Educ.:* Allans School, Newcastle on Tyne. Hodgkin Barnett Pease Spence and Co.; Chartered Bank of India; Bank of Bengal; Imperial Bank of India; served in France with R.F.A., 1915-1918; demobilised as Major (M.C., despatches). *Address:* Viewfield, Aberlour, Banffshire. [*Died* 17 *Aug.* 1954.

MACDONALD, Sir Murdoch, K.C.M.G., *cr.* 1914 (C.M.G. 1910); C.B. 1917; M.Inst.C.E.; F.R.A.S.; Consulting Civil Engineer; *b.* 6 May 1866; *m.* 1899, Margaret (*d.* 1956), *d.* of Alexander Munro, Balmacarra; two *s.* Railway Construction in Scotland, 1888-96, on Aswan Dam, designed and carried out Protective Works, 1898-1905, and first heightening of Dam, 1907-12. Under-Secretary of State and Adviser Egyptian Public Works, 1911-21 (2nd Class Osmanieh; 2nd Class Mejidieh; Grand Officer, Order of the Nile, and Grand Officer, Cordon of the Nile, 1918). M.P. (L.-Nat.) Inverness, 1922-50. Twice Gold Medal for papers, Instn. Civil Engineers; President Inst. Civil Engineers, 1932-33; Freedom of Inverness, 1930. Formed firm of Sir Murdoch MacDonald & Partners, 1921: carried out re-modelling Esna Barrage; constructed 2nd Heightening Aswan Dam, 1929-33; designed and carried out Great Ouse Protection Works; two schemes North of Scotland Hydro Electric Works; Report on Irrigation Projects, Jordan; joint Consulting Engineer, Aswan Dam Power Scheme; designer four new Egyptian schemes, of which two include Barrages across the Nile, and two reservoir Dams across it, 1950-. *Publications:* Nile Control, 1921; article on Irrigation, Encyclopædia Britannica. *Address:* 72 Victoria Street, S.W.1. *T.A.:* Screetan, Sowest, London. *T.:* Victoria 7831. *Club:* St. James'. [*Died* 24 *April* 1957.

MACDONALD, Sir Percy, Kt., *cr.* 1941; J.P.; *s.* of late James Macdonald; *m.* 1st, Mabel Rushton (*d.* 1940); two *s.* one *d.*; 2nd, 1942, Jane Wilde, M.A., J.P., Chadderton. High Sheriff of Lancashire, 1946. Formerly Alderman, Lancashire County Council; Chairman, Standing Joint Committee. *Recreation:* yachting. *Address:* Garth-y-Don, Glyn Garth, Anglesey. *Club:* Royal Anglesey Yacht (Beaumaris). [*Died* 23 *July* 1957.

MACDONALD, Lt.-Col. Roderick William, C.I.E. 1927; D.S.O. 1916; Indian Army, retired; Apple Farmer; *b.* 22 April 1881; 3rd *s.* of late Malcolm Neil Macdonald of Tormore, Sleat, Isle of Skye; *m.* 1911, Hilda Gertrude Jones; one *d.* (adopted). *Educ.:* Inverness College; R.M.C., Sandhurst. 36th Sikhs, 1900-8, when seconded to Burma Police; reverted to military duty with 36th Sikhs, etc., 1914-19; (Mesopotamia, 1916-18 (despatches, D.S.O.); reverted to Burma Police, 1919; Commissioner of Police, Rangoon, 1921-1923; Inspector-Gen. of Police, Burma 1923-1932; retired 1932; re-employed in H.M. Army, August 1939; Group Commander, Pioneer Corps; returned to civil life, 1941; 7th Essex Bn. Home Guard. King's Police Medal, 1926; Indian General Service Medal, Burma 1930-1932 Clasp; Defence Medal and War Medal, 1939-45. *Address:* Lealane Wood, Great Braxted, Witham, Essex. *T.:* Wickham Bishops 279. [*Died* 7 *May* 1959.

McDONALD, Samuel, C.M.G. 1919; D.S.O. 1916; D.L.; LL.D.; Member, Faculty of Advocates, since 1920; Sheriff-Substitute of Aberdeen, Kincardine and Banff, at Aberdeen, since 1942; *b.* Macduff, Banffshire, 28 Nov. 1877; *s.* of James McDonald, house proprietor, and Margaret Reid; *m.* Jessie S., *o. d.* of late George Walker, J.P., shipowner, The Old Manse, Fraserburgh, Aberdeenshire; two *s.* *Educ.:* Gordon's College, Aberdeen; Aberdeen University; Edinburgh University. Interested in Territorial Forces; late Commanding 6th Seaforth Highlanders and 4th (Res.) Gordon Highlanders; served European War, 1914-18 (C.M.G., D.S.O. and two bars); Sheriff-Substitute of Angus at Forfar 1927-32, at Hamilton 1932-36; of Lanarkshire at Glasgow, 1936-42; Commander of the Order of D'Avis of Portugal. *Recreations:* golf and soldiering. *Address:* 42 Albyn Place, Aberdeen. *T.:* Aberdeen 27449. *Club:* University (Aberdeen). [*Died* 20 *Feb.* 1957.

MACDONALD OF SLEAT, Sir Somerled; *see* Macdonald of Sleat, Sir A. S. A. B.

MACDONALD, William Marshall, C.B.E. 1919; B.Sc. (N.Z.); M.D. (Edin.); M.R.C.P. (Lond.); Lt.-Col., N.Z. M.C. (R.); Member N.Z. Pensions Board since 1932; Consulting Physician, Dunedin Hospital; late Member, Otago University Council and High Schools Board; *b.* Edinburgh, 1872; *s.* of William Macdonald, LL.D.; *m.* 1912, Sadie, O.B.E. 1938, *d.* of John Murn, Gulgong, N.S.W.; two *s.* *Educ.:* Otago Boys' High School (dux 1889); Otago and Edinburgh Universities. Lecturer on Clinical Medicine, Otago Medical School; Pres. Otago Club; Life Mem. Wellington French Club; served with French Service de Santé, 1915-16; assistant neurologist IVth French Army District, N.Z.E.F., 1917-19; consulting neurologist and consulting physician, N.Z.E.F.; ex-member Otago Hospital Board; past-pres. Otago Div., B.M.A., N.Z. Trained Nurses' Assoc. Otago Univ. Court of Convocation, Otago Officers' Club, Dunedin Rotary Club, Medical Section Australasian Congress, Melbourne, 1923; past vice-pres. N.Z. Branch, B.M.A., Australasian Medical Congress; Cavaliere Ufficiale of Italian Order of Merit; Chevalier, Légion d'honneur, 1940; Officier de l'Instruction Publique, 1947. *Publications:* various articles in British Medical Journal and N.Z. Medical Journal. *Address:* 32 The Terrace, Wellington, N.Z. *Club:* Wellington (Wellington, N.Z.). [*Died* 26 *Aug.* 1956.

McDONNELL, Sir Michael (Francis Joseph), K.B.E., *cr.* 1949; Kt., *cr.* 1929; C.St.J. 1935; Chairman since Aug. 1940 of Appellate Tribunal for Southern England for Conscientious Objectors under National Service Acts, 1939-55, and, in addition, since Aug. 1947, Chairman of corresponding Appellate Tribunal for Northern England; *b.* 15 June 1882; *y. s.* of late Francis McDonnell; *m.* 1925, Muriel Coddington, *y. d.* of Robert F. Harvey, M.Inst.C.E. *Educ.:* St. Paul's School (Foundation Scholar); St. John's College, Cambridge (Scholar). B.A. 1904; M.A. 1920; Winchester Reading Prize, 1904; Pres. Cambridge Union, 1904; called to Bar, Inner Temple, 1908; Assistant District Comr., Gold Coast, 1911; Police Magistrate, Gambia, 1913; Legal Adviser, mem. Executive and Legislative Councils, Gambia, 1918; Solicitor-General, Sierra Leone, 1918; Attorney-General, and mem. Executive and Legislative Councils, Sierra Leone, 1920; Acting Chief Justice and Acting Judge of the Court of Appeal of Sierra Leone, on various occasions, 1920-26; Chief Justice of Supreme Court of Palestine, 1927-37; Ex-Officio Presiding Judge of H.B.M.'s Full Court of Appeal of Egypt, 1930-37; Member of Lord Chancellor's Committee, of the Palestine Conference, on the McMahon Correspondence, 1939; Ministry of Information, 1940. *Publications:* Ireland and the Home Rule Movement, 1908; A History of St. Paul's School, 1909; The Laws of Sierra Leone, 1925; The Law Reports of Sierra Leone, 1925; The Law Reports of Palestine, Vol. I. 1934, Vol. II. 1938. *Address:* 6 Mulberry Walk, Chelsea, S.W.3. *T.:* Flaxman 9551. *Club:* Athenæum. [*Died* 12 *April* 1956.

MACDOUGALL, Alexander James, of MacDougall and Dunollie; C.M.G. 1919; late Colonel of R.A.M.C.; 29th Hereditary Chief of the Clan MacDougall; *b.* 1872; *e. s.* of Surgeon General Henry R. L. MacDougall of MacDougall and Dunollie, 28th Hereditary Chief of the Clan MacDougall; *m.* 1901, Colina Edith, 3rd *d.* of Alex. W. MacDougall; three *d.* *Educ.:* Clifton College; Edinburgh University. Served in India, Ceylon, Ireland, England, and Scotland; European War, France, Egypt, Salonika, Palestine, Belgium, 1914-18 (C.M.G., despatches); Hon. Sheriff Substitute, D.L. and J.P. Argyll. *Address:* Dunollie Castle, Oban, Argyll. *T.:* Oban 12; Gylen Castle, Isle of Kerrera, by Oban. [*Died* 13 *March* 1953.

MACDOUGALL, Sir Alexander Maclean, Kt., *cr.* 1925; retired Chairman, Simpson & Co., Ltd.; *b.* 1878; *s.* of Alexander MacDougall, Glasgow; *m.* 1906, Marguerite, *d.* of Adrian de Jonge, Liverpool. Sheriff of Madras, 1923. Member Madras Legislative Council, 1920-23, 1925-27. *Ad-*

dress: 18 Bellevue Road, Prestwick, Ayrshire. *T.A.:* Almac, Prestwick. *T.:* 7424. [*Died* 24 *Jan.* 1953.

McDOUGALL, Alexander Patrick, C.B.E. 1919; Chairman of Directors and Managing Director, Midland Marts., Ltd., Banbury; *y. s.* of late Archibald McDougall, Milton, Ardtalnaig, Perthshire; *m.* 1920, Muriel (*d.* 1949), *e. d.* of late Rev. G. T. Cowper, M.A., Rathfriland, Co. Down; one *d.* *Educ.:* George Watson's School, Edinburgh. Vice-Chairman Scottish Farmers' Union, 1917; Live Stock Commissioner for Scotland under the Ministry of Food, 1917-20; bought the property of Prescote Manor near Banbury, 1920; was largely instrumental in founding the business of Midland Marts., Ltd., 1923; visited India as Expert Adviser to Indian Central Banking Enquiry Committee, 1930; J.P. for Oxfordshire, 1939. *Publications:* articles on agriculture in various newspapers and periodicals. *Address:* Prescote Manor, Banbury. *T.:* Cropredy 208. *Club:* Farmers'. [*Died* 6 *March* 1959.

McDOUGALL, Frank Lidgett, C.M.G. 1926; Economic Adviser to the Commonwealth Government in London; Australian Representative and Chairman, 1935-37, on the Imperial Economic Committee; *b.* 1884; 3rd *s.* of late Sir John McDougall; *m.* Madeline Joyce, 4th *d.* of F. W. Cutlack, Renmark, S. Australia; one *s.* one *d.* *Educ.:* Blackheath School; abroad. Lived in S. Africa, and fruit farming in Australia; one of the Economic advisers to Australian Prime Minister at Imperial Economic Conferences, 1923 and 1932, and Imperial Conferences, 1926, 1930 and 1937; Chairman, the London Agency of the Australian Dried Fruits Board; Member Economic Committee, League of Nations; Permanent Committee of International Institute of Agriculture, Rome. *Address:* Australia House, Strand, W.C.2. *T.:* Temple Bar 1567. *Club:* Reform. [*Died* 15 *Feb.* 1958.

McDOUGALL, James Currie, C.I.E. 1942; M.A.; B.Sc.; *b.* 5 Jan. 1890; *s.* of Archibald McDougall, Dunskeig Farm, Argyll; *m.* 1924, Eileen, *d.* of Lt.-Col. Biddulph; one *s.* two *d.* *Educ.:* George Watson's Coll.; Edinburgh Univ. Joined Indian Agricultural Service, 1920; Principal Agricultural College, Nagpur, 1928-35; Director of Agriculture, Central Provinces and Berar, 1935; retired, 1945. *Address:* Nant Bank, Taynuilt, Argyll. [*Died* 23 *Feb.* 1957.

MACDOWELL, Colonel Charles Carlyle, C.M.G. 1919; D.S.O. 1917; late Royal Artillery; *e. s.* of late C. W. MacDowell, M.D., F.R.C.S., M.A., of Otter Holt, Carlow, Ireland; *m.* Bertha Vere-Hopegood; one *s.* (and one *s.* killed in action, France 1917). *Educ.:* Cheltenham. Served South African War, 1900-02; Lieutenant R.A. and Captain and Adjutant, 18th Bn. (Sharpshooters) I.Y.; Brigade Major, Rhodesian Mounted Brigade (Queen's and King's medals, 5 clasps); raised 3rd London Yeomanry (Sharpshooters) as Adjutant, subsequently Major and Hon. Lt.-Col. in the regiment; served European War, 1914-18; joined on outbreak of war Aug. 1914, as Major second in command 6th Black Watch, 51st Highland Division; Lt.-Col. R.A., 12 Nov. 1915; commanded 281st Brigade, R.F.A., for three years on Western Front through all the principal engagements (despatches five times, C.M.G., D.S.O.); served in War of 1939-45, as Inspector of Armaments, Woolwich, and as Group Comdr. A.A.H.G. Defences, South London. *Address:* 18A Abercorn Place, N.W.8; Carlow, Ireland. [*Died* 16 *March* 1959.

MACDOWELL, Lieut.-Col. Thain Wendell, V.C. 1917; D.S.O. 1916; Canadian Local Forces; Mining Executive; *b.* La Chute, Quebec, 1890; *s.* of Rev. J. V. MacDowell; *m.* Norah Jean Hodgson, Montreal; two *s.* *Educ.:* University of Toronto; B.A. 1914, Hon. M.A. 1919. Served European War, 1915-18 (wounded twice, despatches, V.C., D.S.O.); he captured first three machine-guns and fifty prisoners, and later two machine-guns and seventy-five prisoners. *Address:* 354 Côte Saint Antoine Road, Westmount, P.Q. *Club:* University (Toronto). [*Died* 27 *March* 1960.

MACE, Commander (Acting Captain) Frederick William, C.B.E. 1937 (O.B.E. 1919); Royal Naval Reserve; Water Bailiff, 1902, Marine Surveyor, 1909, Mersey Docks and Harbour Board Liverpool, retired 1937; *b.* Weymouth, Dorset, 22 June 1872; *s.* of Capt. William Mace; *m.* 1902, Marguerite (*d.* 1950), *d.* of Edna Mary Ward; one *d.* *Educ.:* Salisbury Private School. Apprentice in Sailing Ships 1887; joined White Star Line as Junior Officer, 1897; trained in Royal Naval Reserve in H.M. Fleet, 1898; First Officer White Star Line, 1901; Younger Brother of Corporation of Trinity House, 1910; rank of Commander R.N.R. on the retired list, 1912; Acting Captain (Retired) R.N.R., 1918. *Recreations:* yachting and golf. *Address:* c/o Barclays Bank, Highgate High St., N.6. *Club:* Royal Lymington Yacht. [*Died* 21 *July* 1960.

McELROY, Robert, Ph.D.; LL.D.; F.R.Hist.S.; M.A., D.Litt. (Oxon); Harold Vyvyan Harmsworth Professor of American History at Oxford University, 1925-39, Emeritus since 1939; Civilian Mobilization Adviser and Historian to Federal Office of Civilian Defense, 1942-43; Editorial Consultant and Historian to War Department, Chemical Warfare Service, 1943- ; *b.* Kentucky, 1872. *Educ.:* Princeton; Oxford; Berlin. Instructor in history, Princeton, 1898; professor, 1909-25; head of Department of History and Politics, 1913-16; first American Exchange Professor to China, 1916-17; Member of Executive Committee of National Military Training Camps Association, 1915-1917; Educational Director, National Security League, 1917-18; associate editor, in charge of International Events, of New York Times Current History Magazine, 1924-25; Sir George Watson Lecturer, London, Cambridge, Manchester, Leeds, Edinburgh and Bristol, 1926; Fellow of Queen's College, Oxford, 1926-39; National Speaker for Republican Nat. Comm. in Presidential Campaigns, 1920, 1924, 1928; Lecturer for Hellenic Travellers' Club on the Cruise of 1930; Brooks-Bright Lecturer at Rugby, Charterhouse, Winchester, Stowe and other English Public Schools, 1926-30; Centennial Address, New York University, 1933. *Publications:* Kentucky in the Nation's History, 1909; Winning of the Far West, 1914; The Representative Idea in History: a sketch (Tsing Hua Lectures), 1917; Grover Cleveland, the Man and the Statesman, authorised biography, 2 vols., 1924; editor of the Addresses of Hon. William Bourke Cockran, under title, In the Name of Liberty, 1925; The Pathway of Peace (Watson Lectures), 1927; Associate Editor of new edition of Ramsay Muir's Historical Atlas, 1927 and 1938; The United States of America, in Benn's Sixpenny Series, 1928; Levi Parsons Morton, Banker, Diplomat and Statesman, 1930; Jefferson Davis, the unreal and the real, 1937; edited with Thomas Riggs, The Unfortified Boundary, a journal of the first survey of the American - Canadian boundary line, 1943; Contributor to Social and Political Ideas of the Revolutionary Era, 1931; and to the new edition of the Harmsworth Cyclopedia. *Address:* 2123 Grove Avenue, Richmond, Virginia, U.S.A. [*Died* 16 *Jan.* 1959.

McENTEE, 1st Baron, *cr.* 1951, of Walthamstow; **Valentine la Touche McEntee,** C.B.E. 1948; *b.* 16 Jan. 1871; *s.* of William Charles McEntee, Dublin, and Kate, *d* of Valentine Burchall; *m.* 1st, 1890, Elizabeth, *d.* of Edward Crawford; 2nd, 1920, Catherine, *d.* of Charles Windsor. *Educ.:* Elementary School; privately. Was on staff of London County Council; contested Walthamstow, West Division, 1918; M.P. (Lab.) Walthamstow, West Div., 1922-24 and 1929-50, retired; ex-Chm. of House of Commons Kitchen Cttee.; Alderman of Walthamstow Borough Council, Mayor, 1929-30 and 1951-52; Freedom of Borough of Walthamstow, 1948. *Heir:* none. *Address:* 57 Hillcrest Road, Walthamstow, E.17. *T.:* Larkswood 1313. [*Died* 11 *Feb.* 1953 (*ext.*).

McENTEGART, Air Vice-Marshal Bernard, C.B. 1944; C.B.E. 1942; R.A.F. retired; *b.* 1891; *s.* of William McEntegart, Liverpool: *m.* 1931, Anne Patmore; one *s.* Served European War, 1914-19; retired, 1945; despatches, 1945. *Address:* Lanehead, nr. Dunscore, Dumfriesshire. *T.:* Dunscore 270. [*Died* 25 *Sept.* 1954.

MACEWEN, Air Vice-Marshal Sir Norman Duckworth Kerr, Kt., *cr.* 1944; C.B. 1935; C.M.G. 1919; D.S.O. 1917; R.A.F. retd.; late Argyll and Sutherland Highlanders; *b.* 1881; *m.* 1907, Jean, *d.* of James Keswick, Dumfries; one *s.* (and one killed on active service 1941) two *d.* *Educ.:* Charterhouse; R.M.C., Sandhurst. Served S. African War, 1901-2 (Queen's medal and five clasps); European War, 1914-18 (despatches, D.S.O., C.M.G.); Afghan War, 1919 (despatches); Dep. Director of Training, Air Ministry, 1926-29, commanded No. 22 Group, Royal Air Force, 1929-31; Air Officer commanding Royal Air Force, Halton, 1931-34; Air Vice-Marshal, 1932; retd. list, 1935. Chairman Soldiers' Sailors' and Airmen's Families Assoc., 1936-49. *Club:* Army and Navy. [*Died* 29 *Jan.* 1953.

MACFARLAN, Brig.-Gen. Frederic Alexander, C.B. 1916; 2nd *s.* of late Lt.-Gen. D. Macfarlan, C.B.; *b.* July 1866; *m.* 1st, 1899, Nora Mary Woodhouse (*d.* 1938); one *d.*; 2nd, 1939, Fredericas Isabella de Lisle John, *widow* of Reginald John. *Educ.:* Loretto School, Edinburgh; Sandhurst. Lieut. Queen's Own Cameron Highlanders, 1885; served with the Regiment, commanded it 1909-13; served Egyptian campaigns, 1885 and 1898 (medal, bronze star, 4th class Mejidie); European War, in France, 1915 (despatches three times, C.B.); retired pay, 1920. *Recreations:* cricket and golf. *Address:* Glebe House, Chudleigh, Devon. [*Died* 7 *Oct.* 1954.

MACFARLAN, Hon. Sir James Ross, Kt., *cr.* 1938; *b.* 30 April 1872; *s.* of James Macfarlan, Glasgow and Melbourne, and Mary Nairn; *m.* 1903, Hilda Charlotte, *d.* of Hon. W. G. Gibson; four *s.* one *d.* *Educ.:* Wesley College; Queen's College, Melbourne University. Called to Bar, 1896; K.C. 1918; Professor of Law, University of Tasmania, 1898; Justice, Supreme Court of Victoria, 1922; Senior Puisne Judge, 1935-49. *Recreations:* shooting, golf. *Address:* 36 Collins Street, Melbourne, Victoria, Australia. *Clubs:* Melbourne, Royal Melbourne Golf; Barwon Heads Golf. [*Died* 12 *July* 1955.

McFARLANE, Sir Charles (Stuart), Kt., *cr.* 1955; O.B.E. 1936; *b.* 31 Oct. 1895; *s.* of Charles McFarlane, Glasgow; *m.* 1924, Jean Hart Kerr; one *s.* two *d.* *Educ.:* Glasgow. Served European War, 1914-19, with R.F.C. Director of J. & A. McFarlane, Ltd., Hardware Manufacturers, Glasgow. M.P. (C.) Camlachie Division of Glasgow, Jan. 1948-Feb. 1950. President, Scottish Unionist Assoc., 1954-55. *Address:* Cairnyard, Lochanhead, by Dumfries. *T.:* Lochfoot 218. *Club:* Conservative (Glasgow). [*Died* 4 *Feb.* 1958.

MACFARLANE, Very Rev. Dugald, D.D.; Parish Minister at Kingussie, Inverness-shire, since 1906; Moderator of General Assembly of Church of Scotland for 1937; *b.* Tobermory, Argyllshire, 10 July 1869; *s.* of Rev. Duncan Macfarlane, Baptist Minister, and Catherine MacLauchlan; *m.* 1902, Roma Constance (*d.* 1947), *e. d.* of Archibald James Campbell, Auchindarroch, Argyllshire; one *d.* *Educ.:* Royal High School, Edinburgh; Univ. of Edinburgh. Ordained to Parish of Glencoe, 1896; translated to Arrocher, 1901; formerly Convener of Royal Bounty Cttee. and of Highlands and Islands Committee of Church of Scotland; Convener of Bursary Committee of Inverness-shire; Chairman of Highlands and Islands Education Trust; Chaplain to Highland Division (51st) during European War, served in France, retired with rank of Major; Delegate from Church of Scotland to General Assemblies of Presbyterian Churches of Canada, Wales, and Ireland (Ulster), again in 1938 to General Council of the United Church of Canada, Toronto, and to General Assembly of the Presbyterian Church of New Zealand, Dunedin; Hon. D.D. St. Andrews, 1929, and Victoria University, Toronto, 1938; F.E.I.S., 1948; Hon. Secretary of Ladies Highland Bursary Association; Gaelic speaker; Judge at various Highland Mods. *Publications:* Annual Reports of Ladies' Highland Bursary Association 1910-43; Closing Address to General Assembly of 1938. *Recreations:* walking, sailing, and sea fishing. *Address:* Manse, Kingussie, Inverness-shire. *T.:* Kingussie 67. *Clubs:* Highland (Inverness); Scottish Conservative (Edinburgh). [*Died* 8 *Oct.* 1956.

MACFARLANE, Lieut.-Gen. Sir (Frank) Noel Mason-, K.C.B., *cr.* 1943 (C.B. 1939); D.S.O. 1940; M.C. and 2 bars; *b.* 23 Oct. 1889; *s.* of late Colonel David Mason-MacFarlane; *m.* 1918, Islay (*d.* 1947), *d.* of late F. I. Pitman; one *s.* one *d.* *Educ.:* Rugby; Woolwich. Served in South Africa and India; European War, 1914-18, France, Belgium, Mesopotamia; Afghan War, 1919; Staff College, Quetta, 1920; Imperial Defence College, 1935; Staff Appointments in France, India, and England; Military Attaché at Budapest, Vienna, and Berne, 1931-34, Berlin and Copenhagen, 1937-39; Brigadier Royal Artillery, Aldershot, 1939; D.M.I. with B.E.F. 1939-40; Gibraltar, 1940; Head of British Military Mission to Moscow, 1941-42; Governor and Commander-in-Chief, Gibraltar, 1942-44; Chief Commissioner Allied Control Commission for Italy, 1944; Col.-Comdt. R.A. 1944; retired pay, 1945 (disabled). M.P. (Lab.) North Paddington, 1945-46, Chiltern Hundreds, 1946. *Recreation:* writing. *Address:* Scarletts, Twyford, Berkshire. *T.:* Wargrave 108. *Club:* United Service. [*Died* 12 *Aug.* 1953.

MACFARLANE, James Waddell; Treasurer (General Manager) Bank of Scotland and Chairman, Committee of Scottish Bank General Managers, 1938-42; *b.* 19 Feb. 1877; *s.* of Rev. Robert Maxwell Macfarlane, Minister of Glenorchy and Inishail; *m.* 1917, Ada Cecilia (*d.* 1946), *d.* of Henry C. D. Rankin, Briarfield, Skelmorlie, Ayrshire; one *s.* one *d.* *Educ.:* Hutchesons' Grammar School, Glasgow; University of Glasgow. Called to Bar, Middle Temple, 1917. Served in Bank of Scotland, 1893-1942, Supt. of Branches, 1931, Manager at Glasgow, 1933, Secretary, 1937, Treasurer, 1938. Served European War, 1914-18, in Inns of Court O.T.C. and Argyll and Sutherland Highlanders, rank of Captain, 1914-19. Director Life Association of Scotland; Trustee and Member of Cttee. of Management, Edinburgh Savings Bank; Director National Bible Soc. of Scotland; Hon. Treasurer, Iona Community; President, for year 1941-42, of Glasgow Soc. of Sons of Ministers of the Church of Scotland (founded 1790). *Address:* 47 Dick Place, Edinburgh. *T.:* 41881. [*Died* 8 *Nov.* 1952.

MACFETRIDGE, William C.; Ophthalmic Surgeon; *b.* 16 June 1878; *s.* of late Archdeacon of Ross; *m.* 1912, Loui (*d.* 1951), *d.* of Major and Hon. Mrs. Carter; two *s.* three *d.* (and one *s.* killed in action). *Educ.:* Portora Royal School; Univ. of Dublin. Late Captain and Ophthalmic Specialist, R.A.M.C.; late University Examiner in Ophthalmic Surgery, University of Dublin and Ophthalmic Surgeon Sir Patrick Dun's Hospital, Royal Victoria Eye and Ear Hospital, etc.; Ophthalmic Surgeon to Ministry of

Pensions, Ireland. *Publications:* Conjunctivitis, ophthalmic papers, etc. *Address:* 4 Selborne Road, Hove. *Clubs:* University (Dublin); Union (Brighton).
[*Died* 23 *Feb.* 1957.

McGAVIN, Major-General Sir Donald Johnstone, Kt., *cr.* 1921; C.M.G. 1919; D.S.O. 1917; V.D.; M.D. (Lond.); F.R.C.S. (Eng.); Mem. of Prisons Board, 1924-57; F.R.A.C.S.; F.A.C.S.; *b.* 19 Aug. 1876; *s.* of John McGavin; *m.* 1903, Mary Allan (*d.* 1955), *d.* of John Cole Chapple; one *s.* *Educ.:* King Edward's High School, Birmingham; Univ. of Birmingham; London Univ. Scholar in Medicine (Gold Medal in Medicine and Obstetric Medicine). Served European War as A.D.M.S. to N.Z. Div. (despatches four times); Major-General, 1923; Director-General of Medical Services, N.Z., 1919-1924; Examiner in Surgery University of New Zealand; Consulting Surgeon Wellington Hospital; Hon. Surg. to Governor-General of New Zealand, 1920-24; Chairman Medical Council of N.Z., 1941. C.St.J. 1946. *Address:* 300 Oriental Parade, Wellington, E.1, N.Z. *Club:* Wellington (Wellington). [*Died* 8 *May* 1960.

McGAW, Andrew Kidd, C.M.G. 1937; Manager of Van Diemen's Land Co. at Burnie, 1903-46; retired 1946; *b.* 5 Oct. 1873; *s.* of late John McGaw, Aberdeen; *m.* Elsie Pringle, *d.* of late Dr. Henry Wotton, Ludlow; one *s.* two *d.* *Educ.:* Gordon's College, Aberdeen. *Address:* 19 Theodore Street, Mont Albert, E.10, Victoria, Australia. [*Died* 11 *Jan.* 1956.

McGHEE, Henry George; M.P. (Lab.) Penistone Division of Yorkshire since 1935; Dentist; *b.* 3 July 1898; *s.* of Richard McGhee and Mary Campbell; *m.* 1927, Edith Shelmerdine; two *s.* two *d.* *Educ.:* Lurgan; Glasgow. Parliamentary Private Secretary to Lord Privy Seal, 1951 (to Minister of Works, 1950-51). *Address:* 284 Millhouses Lane, Sheffield 11. *T.:* Sheffield 73203; 29 Burghley Avenue, New Malden, Surrey. *T.:* Malden 4088.
[*Died* 6 *Feb.* 1959.

McGIBBON, John E. G., O.B.E.; M.B., B.S. (Lond.), D.L.O.; Squadron-Leader R.Aux. A.F.; Aurist Laryngologist, Liverpool Ear, Nose and Throat Infirmary; Laryngologist, Royal Southern Hospital, Liverpool; Laryngologist Aintree Sanatorium and Alder Hey Children's Hospital; *s.* of John McGibbon, M.B., C.M., Edinburgh, and Lucy Shirtliff, Kingston-on-Thames; *m.* Elizabeth Pierce, Birkenhead; one *d.* *Educ.:* Liverpool College; University of Liverpool. Temp. Surgeon-Lieut. Royal Navy, demobilised 1919; Consulting and Hospital Practice since 1919; Member British Medical Association, Royal Society of Medicine. *Publications:* Articles on Medical Subjects, British Medical Journal, Journal of Laryngology, Lancet, etc. *Address:* 41 Rodney Street, Liverpool 1. *T.:* Royal 2712; Mere Brook House, Thornton Hough, Wirral. *T.:* Thornton Hough 276. [*Died* 25 *Oct.* 1959.

McGILLYCUDDY, John Patrick (The McGillycuddy of the Reeks); Director, Clayton Brothers, East Hill, Wandsworth, S.W.18; *b.* 20 Sept. 1909; *er. s.* of Lt.-Col. Ross Kinloch McGillycuddy, D.S.O. (The McGillycuddy of the Reeks); *m.* 1945, Elizabeth Margaret, *e. d.* of Major John E. Otto, Astrop Grange, King's Sutton, Banbury; one *s.* one *d.* *Educ.:* Eton. Commercial career, except for service in War of 1939-45, in 2nd Northamptonshire Yeomanry, Major (wounded twice, despatches). *Heir:* *s.* Richard Denis Wyer, *b.* 4 Oct. 1948. *Address:* The Reeks, Beaufort, Co. Kerry, Ireland. [*Died* 21 *Sept.* 1959.

MacGILLIVRAY OF MacGILLIVRAY, Angus Robertson, O.B.E. 1951; 29th Chief of the Clan MacGillivray; Managing Director Roberts, McLean & Co. Ltd.; Director Elliot Waud & Hill Ltd.; Chairman: Calcutta Import Trade Association; T. I. of India Ltd.; Member: Government of India Import Advisory Council; Calcutta Customs Advisory Committee; Jute Mill Stores Import Advisory Cttee.; *b.* 19 July 1892; *er. s.* of 28th Chief of the Clan MacGillivray; *m.* 1935, Ethel Georgina Southey; no *c.* *Educ.:* Dundee High School. Served European War, 1914-18; officer on special duty with 51st Highland Division. Came to India, 1919, and joined Messrs. Begg, Dunlop & Co. Ltd.; left in 1935 and joined Roberts McLean & Co. Ltd. During War of 1939-45 was Adjutant Calcutta Special Constabulary (Indian Police Medal). *Recreations:* golf, swimming, study of Celtic lore and Highland customs. *Heir:* *nephew*, John MacGillivray. *Clubs:* Bengal, Tollygunge, United Service, Saturday, Calcutta Swimming, Calcutta (Calcutta). [*Died* 22 *Sept.* 1955.

MACGILLIVRAY, Evan James, Q.C. 1939; *b.* 14 Sept. 1873; 2nd *s.* of William MacGillivray, W.S., Edinburgh; *m.* 1st, 1901, Maude (*d.* 1919), *e. d.* of Charles J. Turcan, merchant, Leith; 2nd, 1923, Margaret (*d.* 1940), 2nd *d.* of James Arthur Hilliard, solicitor, Cornhill; two *s.* *Educ.:* Edinburgh Academy; Trinity College, Cambridge, B.A., LL.B. Called, Inner Temple, 1896; Scottish Bar, 1897; Lieutenant R.N.V.R., Anti-Aircraft Corps, Dover Patrol and London Defences, 1914-18. *Publications:* Law of Copyright, 1902; Insurance Law, 1912, 1937, 1947, 1953; The Copyright Act 1911, 1912. *Address:* 1 Harcourt Buildings, The Temple, E.C.4. *T.:* Central 2214.
[*Died* 18 *Oct.* 1955.

McGILVRAY, Sir William, Kt., *cr.* 1950; C.B.E. 1941; *b.* 19 Jan. 1887; *s.* of Donald McGilvray and Jean Armour; *m.* 1927, Anne, *d.* of Robert Forster; one *s.* *Educ.:* Greenock Academy. Formerly Director Powell Duffryn Ltd., Stephenson Clarke Ltd., and associated companies. *Address:* 102 Albion Gate, W.2. *T.:* Paddington 2966. *Clubs:* Caledonian, East India and Sports. [*Died* 25 *Feb.* 1956.

McGRATH, Sir (Joseph) Charles, Kt., *cr.* 1933; Hon. LL.D. Leeds, 1939; Hon. Col. K.O.Y.L.I. Regt. 1944; Solicitor; late Clerk of the Peace of the West Riding of Yorkshire and Clerk to the County Council; County Solicitor; Solicitor to the West Riding of Yorkshire Asylums Board; Clerk to numerous County Committees; Clerk to the West Riding Licensing Compensation and Confirming Authorities; County Registration and Returning Officer; Clerk to the Lord Lieutenant's Advisory Committee; Deputy Regional Commissioner for Civil Defence, North Eastern Region, 1939-41; Clerk of War Zone Courts North East Region; President of Royal Artillery Association; Hon. Secretary of Officers' Association Branch of British Legion, West Riding District; Pres. of Institute of Public Administration, Central and North Yorkshire Regional Group, etc.; *b.* 1 Nov. 1875; *s.* of late Denis McGrath; *m.* 1907, Elsie, *d.* of Charles Arthur Beaumont; three *s.* Served European War, 1914-1919; Royal Artillery and General Staff. *Address:* Stanley Grange, nr. Wakefield, Yorks. *T.A.:* Magra, Wakefield. *T.:* Wakefield 2179. *Club:* Naval and Military. [*Died* 15 *Feb.* 1951.

McGRAW, Curtis Whittlesey; President and Chairman of the Board, McGraw-Hill Publishing Co., Inc., since 1950; *b.* 13 Oct. 1895; *s.* of James Herbert McGraw and Mildred Whittlesey; *m.* 1921, Elizabeth Woodwell; one *d.* *Educ.:* Lawrenceville School; Princeton University. Joined McGraw-Hill Book Company, 1920, asst. to Treas., 1922-25, Secretary and Asst. Treasurer, 1925, Vice-Pres., Treas. and Dir., 1927; Director of McGraw-Hill Publishing Co., 1930, Vice-Chm., 1948; Chm. McGraw-Hill Book Co., McGraw-Hill Internat. Corp., McGraw-Hill Co. of California; President and Director McGraw-Hill Building Corp.; Vice-Pres. and Dir. of Newton Falls Paper

Mill, 1948-. Dir. of Amer. Book Publishers Council, 1946-52, served as Pres. during 1948 and 1949; Treas. and Dir., Princeton Univ. Press; Pres. and Trustee Princeton Hosp.; Director: First National Bank of Princeton; Dragon Cement Co.; National Association of Magazine Publishers. Served European War, 1914-18, as Capt. and Major of Infantry, 320 Infantry, 80th Div., U.S. Army. *Recreation:* golf. *Address:* (office) 330 West 42nd Street, New York 36, U.S.A. *T.:* Longacre 4-3000; (home) 130 Hodge Road, Princeton, New Jersey, U.S.A. *T.:* Princeton 1036. *Clubs:* University, Union League, The Players (New York City); Springdale Golf (Princeton); Pine Valley Golf (Clementon, N.J.); Fishers Island (Fishers Is., N.Y.); Economic (New York); National Golf Links of America. [*Died* 10 *Sept.* 1953.

MACGREGOR, Sir Cyril Patrick M'Connell, 5th Bart., *cr.* 1828; *b.* 1887; *e. s.* of late Patrick Eugene Macgregor and Gertrude, *d.* of J. F. M'Connell; *S.* uncle, 1905. *Heir:* *b.* Robert James M'Connell [*b.* 1890; late Lt. R.A.F.; served European War, 1918]. *Address:* Box 1500, Val d'Or, Quebec. [*Died* 30 *Jan.* 1958.

MACGREGOR, David Hutchison, M.C.; Hon. LL.D. (Edin.); Emeritus Professor of Political Economy, University of Oxford; *b.* Monifieth, Angus, 1877; 2nd *s.* of Rev. Robert Macgregor, M.A., late Rector of Nithside Academy, Dumfries; *m.* 1914, Claire Nelson (*decd.*); one *d.* *Educ.:* George Watson's College, Edinburgh; Edinburgh University; Trinity College, Cambridge; President of the Union, 1902; Fellow of Trinity, 1904. Member of the Committee on Labour Exchanges, 1920, and of several Trade Boards; Member of the Agricultural Tribunal, 1923-24; Member of the Committee on Restraint of Trade, 1930, and of the Committee on Gift Trading, 1933; A.K. Travelling Fellow, 1911-12; Joint Editor of Economic Journal, 1925-37. Served with 49th Div. in France, and with General Staff in Italy (M.C., despatches). *Publications:* Lord Macaulay; Industrial Combination; Evolution of Industry; Enterprise, Purpose and Profit; Public Aspects of Finance; Economic Thought and Policy; The Thane of Cawdor (as David Baird); various contributions to economic and philosophical journals. *Address:* 3 Lucerne Road, Oxford. *T.:* Oxford 55590. *Club:* Authors'. [*Died* 8 *May* 1953.

MACGREGOR, David Sliman, C.B.E. 1925; F.S.A.A.; *b.* 19 Dec. 1864; *s.* of late Robert MacGregor, formerly of Dunkeld, Perthshire; *m.* 2nd, 1921; one *s.* *Educ.:* Glasgow. In business appointments Glasgow and West Indies; entered Colonial Government Service, 1895; served in Leeward Islands, Trinidad (on special mission to adjust accounts there), British Honduras, Mauritius, Ceylon and Nigeria; Treasurer of Nigeria; on temporary service in Baghdad, Dec. 1927-June 1928; retired, 1928; Member of Financial Commission to British Guiana, Feb.-May, 1931. *Recreations:* reading and motoring. *Address:* Auchingarroch, Bridge of Allan, Stirlingshire. *T.:* Bridge of Allan 3381. [*Died* 13 *Oct.* 1952.

MACGREGOR, James, M.A., F.R.I.B.A., F.S.A.; Director of School of Architecture, Cambridge University, since 1937; *b.* July 1889; *s.* of James and Janet Macgregor; *m.* 1930, Phyllis M. H. Bush (*d.* 1943); one *d.* *Educ.:* School of Architecture, Edinburgh College of Art; Heriot-Watt College, Edinburgh; in the offices of Williamson and Inglis Kirkcaldy, Mr. Hippolyte J. Blanc, A.R.S.A., Edinburgh, Sir Edwin Lutyens, R.A., London. In private practice London, 1919-33; Senior master in design and Lecturer in Mediæval Architecture, Manchester University School of Architecture, 1921-23; Studio Master, Architectural Association in London, 1926-33; Lecturer in Architectural History and Design, L.C.C. School of Building, Brixton, London, 1931-33; Head of School of Architecture, Edinburgh College of Art, 1933-1936; Member of Board of Architectural Education. *Address:* 1 and 2 Scroope Terrace, Cambridge. *T.:* Cambridge 54265. [*Died* 18 *March* 1953.

MACGREGOR of MacGregor, Sir Malcolm, 5th Bt., *cr.* 1795; C.B. 1919; C.M.G. 1917; *b.* Edinchip, Balquhidder, 3 Aug. 1873; *e. s.* of 4th Bt. and Lady Helen Laura M'Donnell (*d.* 1922), *o. c.* of 9th Earl of Antrim; *S.* father, 1879; *m.* 1925, Hon. Gylla Rollo, *yr. d.* of late Hon. Eric Rollo; one *s.* one *d.* Entered R.N. 1886; Midshipman, 1889; Sub-Lieut. 1893; Commander, 1904; Asst. to the Director of Naval Ordnance at Admiralty, 1907; retired Captain, 1911; served European War, 1914-18 as Commodore 1st Class and Principal Naval Transport Officer, France (despatches, C.B., C.M.G., Officer of the Légion d'Honneur, Croix de Guerre); Chm. Agric. Exec. Cttee., Perth W., 1939-47. *Heir:* *s.* Gregor MacGregor, Major Scots Guards [*b.* 22 Dec. 1925; *m.* 1958, Fanny, *o. d.* of C. H. A. Butler, Shortgrove, Newport, Essex]. *Address:* Edinchip, Lochearnhead, Perthshire. *T.:* Lochearnhead 204. [*Died* 5 *Dec.* 1958.

MacGREGOR, Robert Anderson, C.I.E. 1943; M.I.Mech.E.; late Chief Metallurgist to Govt. of India in Dept. of Supply; *b.* 9 Aug. 1888; *o. s.* of James MacGregor, M.I.Mech.E., Sheffield; *m.*, 1914, Gladys Neville Read (*d.* 1947), Sheffield; no *c.*; *m.* 1948, Helen Jones, Darlington. *Educ.:* Central High School and University, Sheffield. Twenty-five years Metallurgist with the Darlington Forge Ltd. and eight years with Govt. of India as Metallurgical Inspector, Director of Metals, and Deputy Director General (Chief Metallurgist), Dept. of Supply. Gold Medallist, N.E. Coast Inst. of Engrs. and Shipbuilders, 1930 and 1935, Member of Council, 1936; Bronze Medallist, 1937, of Mining, Geological and Metallurgical Inst. of India and President of same Inst. 1944; is Technical Director, Indian Special Steel Marketing Board, Calcutta. *Publications:* number of technical papers, mostly on effect of working stresses on steel parts. *Address:* 45A Gaulstaun Mansions, Calcutta 16, India. [*Died* *April* 1953.

MacGREGOR, Lieut.-Colonel Robert Forrester Douglas, C.I.E. 1939; M.C.; late I.M.S.; *b.* 5 Jan. 1885; *s.* of Robert Roy Macgregor, H.M.'s Exchequer, Edinburgh. *Educ.:* George Watson's College and Merchiston Castle School, Edinburgh; Edinburgh University, M.B., Ch.B., 1908. Joined Indian Medical Service, 1910; Captain, 1913; Bt. Major, 1919; Major, 1921; Lt.-Col., 1929; served European War, 1914-19 (M.C.), France, Iraq, Palestine and Syria; Chief Medical Officer, Baluchistan, 1929-31; Chief Medical Officer, Central India, 1931-33; Residency Surgeon Hyderabad, 1933-39; Deputy Director General, I.M.S., 1939-45. *Recreations:* golf, fishing. *Address:* c/o Lloyds Bank Ltd., 6 Pall Mall, S.W.1. [*Died* 22 *June* 1960.

MACGREGOR-MORRIS, John Turner, M.I.E.E., D.Sc. (Eng.) Lond.; Hon. Research Associate in Electrical Eng., University Coll. London since 1939; Professor Emeritus of Electrical Engineering, University of London, since 1938; Fellow of University Coll., and of Queen Mary Coll., London; *b.* London, 1872; *e. s.* of late Jas. Morris, M.D.; *m.* 1917, Annie Elizabeth Frances, B.A., B.D., (*d.* 1941), *e. d.* of late John MacGregor, M.A., Barrister-at-law, Author of The "Rob Roy" on the Jordan. *Educ.:* privately; at University College, London. Assistant to Professor Fleming at University College, 1894-98; has specialised in subjects connected with illumination and cathode ray oscillographs; June 1915, worked with A. F. Sykes at problem of submarine detection, and later with the co-operation of the

Admiralty produced a directional hydrophone, used in large numbers during the war; inventor of a Portable Direct Reading Anemometer; Director Electrical Engineering Section of Summer School for Engineering Teachers for the Board of Education, Oriel College, Oxford, July 1925, 1926, 1927, and 1928; I.E.E. Delegate at several International Commissions on Illumination; Faraday Centenary Celebration Lecturer at Loughborough, Sept. 1931; Faraday Lectures for I.E.E. local centres, 1932-33; Kerr Memorial Lecture, Television Society, 1937; Chairman, Meter and Instrument Section of I.E.E., 1934-35; Member of Academic Council London University, 1936 and 1937; University Professor of Electrical Engineering, Queen Mary College (formerly E. London College) up to 1938; Univ. of London delegate to High Tension Conference, Paris, 1939; Pres. Illuminating Engineering Soc., 1940-41; Inaugural Ambrose Fleming Lecture, Television Soc., 1946. *Publications:* Cathode Ray Oscillography with J. A. Henley, 1936; Sir Ambrose Fleming and the birth of the Valve, 1954; numerous papers to scientific journals and lectures to R.I. and Brit. Assoc. *Recreation:* music. *Address:* 3 Holly Mansions, Fortune Green Road, N.W.6. *T.:* Hampstead 4381. [*Died* 18 *March* 1959.

McGRIGOR, Admiral of the Fleet Sir Rhoderick Robert, G.C.B., *cr.* 1951 (K.C.B., *cr.* 1945; C.B. 1944); D.S.O. 1943; *b.* 12 April 1893; *s.* of late Major-General C. R. R. McGrigor, C.B., C.M.G., 60th Rifles; *m.* 1931, Gwendoline, *d.* of late Col. Geoffrey Glyn, C.M.G., D.S.O., and *widow* of Major Charles Greville, D.S.O., Grenadier Guards; twin *s.* (adopted). *Educ.:* R.N. Colls. Osborne and Dartmouth. Served European War, 1914-18, Mediterranean destroyers (Dardanelles campaign) and Grand Fleet (Jutland); Captain D, 4th Destroyer Flotilla, 1936-38; at outbreak of war of 1939-1945 was Chief of Staff to C.-in-C. China Station, and later commanded H.M.S. Renown (Malta convoys and operations in Mediterranean and Atlantic, 1941); a Lord Commissioner of the Admiralty and Assistant Chief of the Naval Staff, 1941-43; Naval Force Commander at capture of Pantellaria and Invasion of Sicily; Flag Officer Sicily during Sicilian and Calabrian Campaigns (wounded), and then Flag Officer Taranto and Adriatic; commanded 1st cruiser squadron, and Home Fleet aircraft carriers 1944-45 (operations off Norwegian coast and convoys to North Russia); a Lord Commissioner of the Admiralty and Vice-Chief of Naval Staff, 1945-47; C.-in-C., Home Fleet, 1948-50; Commander-in-Chief, Plymouth, 1950-51; First Sea Lord and Chief of Naval Staff, 1951-1955; First and Principal Naval A.D.C. to H.M. the Queen, 1952-53. Hon. LL.D. St. Andrews, 1953, Hon. LL.D. Aberdeen, 1955; Lord Rector of Aberdeen University, 1954-57. *Recreations:* shooting, fishing. *Address:* Hopewell Lodge, Tarland, Aberdeenshire. *T.:* Tarland 239. *Clubs:* United Service; Royal Northern (Aberdeen). [*Died* 3 *Dec.* 1959.

McGUFFIN, Samuel; *b.* Belfast, 18 Aug. 1863; *m.* 1894, Maggie, *d.* of William Haire, Derrykeevin, Portadown. *Educ.:* Belfast Model School. Pres. of Belfast No. 12 Branch Amalgamated Soc. of Engineers; Chairman of the Works Committee of the Belfast Water Commissioners; M.P. for North Belfast in the New Parliament for Northern Area, Ireland, 1921-25; M.P. (U.) Shankill Div. of Belfast, Dec. 1918-22. *Address:* Locksley, Martinez Avenue, Belfast. [*Died* 21 *Nov.* 1952.

McGUINNESS, Brigadier Edward, C.I.E. 1943; M.I.Mech.E.; late R.E.M.E.; *b.* 14 April 1883. Served European War, 1914-18. Director of Mechanisation, General Headquarters, India; retired pay, 1943, but re-employed until 1944. *Address:* Balmore, Gainsborough Rd., Bournemouth. [*Died* 23 *Jan.* 1958.

McGUIRE, Most Rev. Terence Bernard; *b.* Moree, N.S.W., 17 Sept. 1881. *Educ:* St. Patrick's Coll., Manly, N.S.W.; Propaganda Coll., Rome. Priest 1904; parish priest, Coraki, 1924-29; Grafton, N.S.W., 1929; R.C. Bishop of Townsville, 1930-38; Bishop of Goulburn, 1938-48; Archbishop of Canberra-Goulburn, 1948, retired. *Address:* c/o The Archbishop's House, Canberra, A.C.T. [*Died* 4 *July* 1957.

McHARDY, Major-General Alexander Anderson, C.B. 1918; C.M.G. 1916; D.S.O. 1900; M.B.E. 1946; *b.* 9 Nov. 1868; *s.* of late Lieutenant-Colonel Sir Alexander McHardy, K.C.B.; *m.* 1904, Lilian (*d.* 1936), *d.* of Coghlan McHardy, 1 Grenville Place, S.W. *Educ.:* Westminster School; R.M.A., Woolwich; Staff College. Joined R.A., 1888; Lt.-Col. 1915; Col. 1916; Maj.-Gen. 1924; served N.W. Frontier, India, 1897-98; S. African War, 1899-1902 (despatches, D.S.O.); Somaliland with Boer contingent, 1903 (despatches); European War, 1914-19 (despatches, Bt. Lieut.-Col. and Col., C.M.G., C.B.); Controller of surplus stores and salvage, W.O., 1919-22; Maj.-Gen. in charge of Administration, Constantinople, 1922; Director of Movements and Quarterings, War Office, 1923-27; Major-General in charge of Administration, Southern Command, 1927-1930; retired pay, 1930; Col. Commandant Royal Artillery, 1934-38. A.R.P. Sub-Controller, 1939-45; (Commandeur du Mérite Agricole, Officier de l'ordre de Leopold, Croix de Guerre avec Palme). *Recreations:* shooting, fishing. *Address:* The Thatched Cottage, Hickling, Norfolk. *Club:* United Service. [*Died* 11 *Nov.* 1958.

MACHARG, Sir Andrew Simpson, Kt., *cr.* 1947; *b.* 2 Nov. 1871; *s.* of late E. Simpson Macharg, Chartered Accountant, Glasgow; *m.* Isabel Miller, *d.* of late Sir Thomas Mason, D.L.; two *d.* Chartered Accountant; formerly Adviser to the Ministry of Supply on prices of Iron and Steel Products. *Address:* Bennochy, Helensburgh. *Club:* Western (Glasgow). [*Died* 7 *Aug.* 1959.

MACHELL, Lady Valda; *d.* of Admiral H.S.H. Prince Victor of Hohenlohe Langenburg, G.C.B., R.N., nephew of Queen Victoria, and Lady Laura Seymour, sister of 5th Marquis of Hertford; *m.* Lieut.-Col. Percy Wilfrid Machell, C.M.G., D.S.O. (adviser to Egyptian Ministry of Interior), of Crakenthorpe Hall, Appleby, killed in action, Battle of Somme, 1916; one *s.* *Publications:* various magazine articles on music, biographies, and travel. *Recreations:* music, travelling. *Address:* 18 Albert Court, S.W.7. *T.:* Kensington 6114. [*Died* 10 *Sept.* 1951.

McILQUHAM, Sir Gilbert, Kt., *cr.* 1937; Solicitor, McIlquham and Co., Cheltenham; Alderman of Gloucestershire County Council; *b.* 9 Sept. 1863; *e. s.* of James Henry McIlquham, Staverton House, Gloucestershire; *m.* 1st, Mabel Geraldine, *d.* of Thomas Gee, Hanley Castle, Worcestershire; 2nd, Maud Adeline (*d.* 1947), *d.* of James Lempriere Anley, Oakley, Cheltenham; one *s.* *Recreations:* shooting and hunting. *Address:* Staverton House, nr. Cheltenham. *T.A.:* Staverton Cheltenham. *T.:* Coombe Hill 229. *Clubs:* Gloucester County (Gloucester); New (Cheltenham. [*Died* 26 *Dec.* 1953.

McINDOE, Sir Archibald (Hector), Kt. 1947; C.B.E. 1944; M.B., Ch.B., M.S., M.Sc., F.R.C.S., F.A.C.S.; F.R.C.S.I. (Hon.), F.A.C.S. (Hon.), M.D. Uppsala (Hon.); Consultant in Plastic Surgery to R.A.F.; Surgeon-in-Charge Queen Victoria Plastic and Jaw Injury Centre, East Grinstead; Plastic Surgeon to St. Bartholomew's Hospital; Cons. Plastic Surgeon: Chelsea Hospital for Women; St. Andrew's Hospital, Dollis Hill; Royal North Staffs. Infirmary; Hospital for Tropical Diseases; *b.* Dunedin, N.Z., 4 May 1900; *s.* of John McIndoe and

Mabel Hill; *m.* 1st, 1924, Adonia Aitken; two *d.*; 2nd, 1954, Constance Belchem. *Educ.:* Otago Boys High School; Otago Medical School; Mayo Clinic; St. Bartholomew's Hospital. Medallist Clinical Medicine and Clinical Surgery, 1923; Mayo Foundation Fellow, 1924-28; William White Travelling Scholar, 1929; Assistant Surgeon, Mayo Clinic, 1929-30; Member Council of Royal College of Surgeons since 1948 (Vice-Pres. 1957-59); Bradshaw Lecturer, 1958; Hunterian Professor, 1939; Mem. Council, Brit. Assoc. of Plastic Surgeons, 1946-52 (Pres. 1951); Pres. Assoc. of Plastic Surgeons, 1946-52 (Pres. 1951); Pres., R.A.F. Reserves Club, 1956-; Life Pres., Guinea Pig Club. Freeman of City of London; Mem. Worshipful Co. of Pattenmakers. Comdr. Order of White Lion (Czecho Slovakia); Officer Order Polonia Restituta (Poland); Commander Order of Orange Nassau (Holland); Commander of the Legion of Honour (France). *Publications:* numerous on surgical and pathological subjects. *Recreations:* shooting, fishing, and sailing. *Address:* 149 Harley Street, W.1. *T.:* Welbeck 4444. [*Died* 12 *April* 1960.

MacINNES, Charles Stephen, C.M.G. 1917; K.C. 1908; Hon. LL.D. 1925; a Vice-Pres. Canadian Institute Internat. Affairs; Member Senate, Univ. of Toronto; Director Toronto General Trusts Corporation; *y. s.* of late Hon. Donald MacInnes and Mary A., *d.* of late Sir John Beverley Robinson, Bart., C.B., Chief Justice of Upper Canada; *b.* 5 May 1872; *m.* 1902, Rose Louise, *d.* of late T. C. Patteson. *Educ.:* Marlborough College (Leaf Exhibition); Trinity, Toronto (B.A., M.A., Fellow, 1893-94); Hon. LL.D., Toronto University, 1925. Called to Ontario Bar, 1897; Counsel for Canada before International Joint-Commission established under Treaty between Great Britain and U.S.A., 1913-15; European War: H.Q. Staff, Canadian Forces, Ottawa; A.A.G., 1915-17; Deputy Adjutant - General (Organization), 1917-19; Brevet Lieut.-Col. 1916; Colonel, 1917; mentioned for Services, and C.M.G. 1917. *Address:* 1 Admiral Road, Toronto, Canada. *Clubs:* Bath; Toronto, York (Toronto). [*Died* 20 *April* 1952.

MACINNES SHAW, Sir Douglas; *see* Shaw, Sir A. D. M.

McINTOSH, Annie, C.B.E. 1917; R.R.C.; *b.* 1871; *d.* of late Donald McIntosh, J.P. Seven years Matron's Senior Assistant at the London Hospital; Matron and Superintendent of Nursing at St. Bartholomew's Hospital, 1910-27 (R.R.C., 1st Class, 1917); a Member of Committee for Supply of Nurses by War Office, 1916; a Member of Royal College of Nursing (Limited); received médaille d'honneur (argent) l'assistance publique, Paris, 1924. *Address:* 5 Shellborne House, Marina, Bexhill-on-Sea. *T.:* Bexhill 1355. [*Died* 20 *Sept.* 1951.

McINTOSH, Arthur Johnston, C.B.E. 1955 (O.B.E. 1941); Chief Constable of Dunbartonshire since 1934; *b.* 17 April 1890; *s.* of James McIntosh and Mary Ann Muir Brown; *m.* 1918, Mary Hussey Tannahill; one *s.* *Educ.:* Brechin High School. Chief Constable, Paisley, 1931-34. King's Police Medal, 1937. *Publication:* Guide to Police Duties, 1936. *Recreations:* golf, fishing and shooting. *Address:* Netherby, Helensburgh, Dunbartonshire. *T.:* Helensburgh 349. *Club:* Royal Scottish Automobile (Glasgow). [*Died* 8 *March* 1956.

MACINTOSH, Douglas Clyde, M.A., Ph.D., D.D., LL.D.; *b.* 18 Feb. 1877; *s.* of Peter Macintosh and Elizabeth C. Everett; *m.* 1st, 1921, Emily Powell (*d.* 1922); 2nd, 1925, Hope G. Conklin; no *c.* *Educ.:* McMaster University, Toronto; University of Chicago. Instructor, Philosophy, McMaster University, 1903-4; Professor of Theology, Brandon College, Brandon, Manitoba, 1907-9; Assistant Professor of Theology, Yale Divinity School, 1909-16; Dwight Professor of Theology and the Philosophy of Religion, Yale University, 1916-33, Prof. of Theology and Philosophy of Religion, 1933; Chm. of the Department of Religion in the Graduate School, Yale University, 1920-38. Chaplain C.E.F., England and France, 1916; Y.M.C.A., Secretary A.E.F. France, 1918. *Publications:* God in a World at War, 1918; The Problem of Knowledge, 1915; Theology as an Empirical Science, 1919; The Reasonableness of Christianity, 1925; The Pilgrimage of Faith (Ghosh Lectures) 1931; Religious Realism, 1931; Is There a God?, 1932; Social Religion, 1939; The Problem of Religious Knowledge, 1940; Personal Religion, 1942; Thinking about God, 1942. *Recreation:* gardening. *Address:* 25 Woodlawn Street, Hamden, Conn., U.S.A.; c/o Yale Divinity School, 409 Prospect Street, New Haven, Conn., U.S.A. [*Died* 7 *July* 1948.
[*But death not notified in time for inclusion in Who Was Who* 1941–1950, *first edn.*

McINTOSH, Hon. Sir Malcolm, K.B.E. 1956; M.H.A. for Albert, S.A., since 1921; *b.* Branxholme, Vic., 3 March 1888; *s.* of late Malcolm and Catherine McIntosh; *m.* 1911, Bertha Chisholm, Geelong; one *s.* two *d.* *Educ.:* Flinders School, Geelong. Entered Law Office; accountancy practice, Adelaide, 1933-. Commissioner of Public Works and Minister for Education, S.A., 1927-30; Commissioner of Crown Lands and Minister of Repatriation, Irrigation and Afforestation, 1933-38; Commissioner of Public Works, Minister of Railways, Marine and Local Government, 1938-53; Minister of Works and Minister of Marine, State of South Australia, 1953-58. *Address:* 50 Hawker's Road, Medindie, South Australia. [*Died* 15 *Nov.* 1960.

MACINTYRE, Sir Alexander, Kt., *cr.* 1938; *b.* 20 Oct. 1879; *s.* of Donald MacIntyre, Laggan and Flowerburn, and Jessie Rhodes; *m.* 1910, Mary Louise Mackenzie; one *d.* (son in R.A.F. killed off Dunkirk, 1940). *Educ.:* Inverness Academy; Glasgow High School. Civil Engineering, 1898-1907; Manager Sudan Plantations Syndicate, 1907-19; ex-Director (Chm., 1923-49 and Managing Director, 1919-46), of Sudan Plantations Syndicate Ltd.; ex-Director (formerly Chm.), Kassala Cotton Co. *Recreation:* fishing. *Address:* Larkfield, Inverness. *T.:* Inverness 455. [*Died* 1 *April* 1952.

McINTYRE, Donald, M.B.E.; M.D. Glasg.; F.R.C.O.G., F.R.C.S.E., F.R.F.P.S.G., L.M., F.R.S.E.; Consulting Obstetrician and Gynæcologist, Royal Samaritan Hospital, Glasgow; Royal Samaritan Lecturer, University of Glasgow; Hon. Consulting Obstetrician and Gynæcologist, Paisley and District; Examiner, Roy. Coll. of Surgeons and University of Edinburgh; *b.* 29 July 1891; *s.* of Donald McIntyre, Greenock; *m.* 1922, Jean Gracie Menzies; one *s.* Hon. Major R.A.M.C.; served Dardanelles and East Africa (despatches). *Publications:* Part Author, Operative Obstetrics, 1937, and Combined Textbook of Obstetrics and Gynæcology, 1950; and many medical monographs. *Recreations:* golf, shooting, yachting. *Address:* 9 Park Circus, Glasgow, C.3. *T.:* Douglas 4741. *Clubs:* Royal Clyde Yacht, Royal Scottish Automobile (Glasgow); Greenock (Greenock). [*Died* 20 *Oct.* 1954.

MACINTYRE, Very Rev. Ronald George, C.M.G. 1926; O.B.E. 1918; M.A.; D.D. (Edin.); Hunter-Baillie Professor and Professor of Systematic Theology, St. Andrew's College, Sydney University, 1909-27; *b.* 30 Aug. 1863; *s.* of Angus Macintyre, Victoria, Australia; *m.* 1st, 1895, Christina Watson (*decd.*), *d.* of R. Cromb, Edinburgh; 2nd, 1935, Alice Mary, *d.* of Rev. Dr. J. N. Manning. *Educ.:* Fort William; University and New College, Edinburgh; received preliminary training in law, Minister St. Andrew's Church, Birkenhead,

1890-95; U.F. Church, Maxwelltown, Dumfries, 1895-1903; Woollahra Church, N.S.W., 1903-9; Moderator General of the Presbyterian Church of Australia, 1916-18; Director of Recruiting for New South Wales, 1916-18; Managing Director, Burnside Orphan Homes, Parramatta, 1926-34. *Publications:* Elijah and Elisha, 1901; The Other Side of Death, 1920; Christian Idea of Immortality, 1924; Courage and Comfort, 1927; The Substance of the Christian Faith, 1936; The Story of Burnside, 1947. *Address:* Invergarry, Springwood, N.S.W., Australia. [*Died* 22 *June* 1954.

MACK, Rear-Admiral Frederick Robert Joseph, C.B. 1954; C.B.E. 1945 (O.B.E. 1927); R.N. retired; a Gentleman Usher to the Queen, since 1954; *b.* 19 July 1897; *s.* of late R. F. Mack, Cork, Eire; *m.* 1933, Dorothie Mary, *d.* of late Rev. Dr. Thomas Young, Ellon, Aberdeenshire. Entered R.N. 1915; served on staff of Adm. of the Fleet Lord Beatty, 1915-22, and 1925-1927, in H.M. Ships: Lion, Iron Duke and Queen Elizabeth. During 1939-41 served in H.M. Ships Hood, Renown and Warspite (despatches); 1941-44, Sec. to 2nd Sea Lord, Admiralty (C.B.E.); Fleet Supply Officer, E. Indies Stn., 1947-48; Dep. Dir. Gen., Supply and Secretariat Branch, Admiralty, 1949-51; Command Supply Officer, The Nore, 1951-54; retired Aug. 1954. King Haakon VII Liberty Cross, 1946. *Recreations:* golf, Rugby football (from touch line!). *Address:* 58 Crompton Court, Brompton Road, S.W.3. *T.:* Kensington 3007. *Clubs:* Army and Navy; Royal Naval (Portsmouth). [*Died* 13 *May* 1959.

MACK, John David; *m.* 1943, Adèle Cywan. National Propagandist, Labour Party; formerly Life Assurance Agent and Representative of National Amalgamated Union of Life Assurance Workers; Contributor to Labour and Trade Unions journals; Liverpool City Councillor, 1928-1946; formerly Lecturer National Council of Labour Colleges; M.P. (Lab.), Newcastle-under-Lyme, 1942-51. *Address:* 26 Bryanston Square, W.1. *T.:* Ambassador 0898. [*Died* 9 *Feb.* 1957.

MACKAY, Hon. Lord; Alexander Morrice Mackay, M.A.; LL.D.; one of the Senators of the College of Justice in Scotland 1928-54; retd. from Bench; *b.* Aberdeen, 6 Sept. 1875; *s.* of Robert Whyte Mackay, wholesale warehouseman, and Isabella Christian, *d.* of Alexander Morrice, shipbuilder, Aberdeen; *m.* 1907, Alice Margaret (*d.* 1937), *d.* of Alexander Ledingham, Advocate, Aberdeen; two *s.* one *d.* *Educ.:* Aberdeen Grammar School; Aberdeen University (1st Class Honours Philosophy and Classics); Trinity College (Major Scholar), Cambridge (Moral Sciences Tripos, First Class and Star); Edinburgh University, Honours in Law. President Cambridge University Lawn Tennis, 1899; President Scottish Lawn Tennis Association, 1919-24; Scottish Lawn Tennis Champion, 1905-07; Hon. Pres. Scottish Lawn Tennis Assoc., 1947; called to Scottish Bar, 1902; K.C. 1920; Home Advocate Depute, 1927; Hon. LL.D. Aberdeen University, 1929; Chairman of Licensing (Scotland) Commission, 1930-31. *Recreations:* mountaineering, lawn tennis, golf, and curling; sketching in pastels; croquet. *Address:* 10 Coates Gardens, Edinburgh 12. *Club:* Northern (Edinburgh). [*Died* 2 *Nov.* 1955.

MACKAY, Donald G., C.B.E. 1937 (O.B.E. 1934); Grazier; *b.* Yass, N.S.W., 1870; *s.* of Alexander and Annie MacKay, both Scotch; *m.* 1902, Amy I. Little. *Educ.:* Oaklands, Mittagong, N.S.W. Prospector; Grazier; Explorer; Bicycle rider (rode bicycle round Australia, 1899); Traveller, visited America, Canada, China, Japan, England, Ireland, Scotland, Continent, New Zealand, Tasmania, New Guinea, Solomon Islands, New Hebrides, Java, New Caledonia; led and financed expeditions in Papua, 1908, by camel Central Australia, 1926, by Pack Horse Arnhem Land, 1928; also reconnaissance expeditions by Plane, 1930, 1933, 1935, 1937, presenting the Commonwealth Government with maps of 600,000 square miles of previously unmapped districts. *Recreations:* has been interested, and taken part, in nearly all forms of sport. *Address:* Tyreel Point, Port Hacking, N.S.W., Australia. *T.:* L.B. 7077. *Club:* Millions (Sydney). [*Died* 17 *Sept.* 1958.

MACKAY, Edward Fairbairn; Member of Lloyd's; *b.* 12 Feb. 1868; *s.* of late James Mackay and Mary Fairbairn; *m.* Lilian Maud, *d.* of late E. H. Lavers; three *s.* two *d.* *Educ.:* Edinburgh Merchant Company's Colleges, Edinburgh. North of Scotland Bank Ltd.; Broads Paterson and Co., C.A., London; Butterfield and Swire, China, 33 years (of which 15 years Chief Manager for China and Japan); Chairman Shanghai General Chamber of Commerce; Vice-Chairman Shanghai Municipal Council; retired 1925. Thereafter a Director of the Chartered Bank of India, Australia and China, 1925-43, and of P. & O. Banking Corporation. *Recreations:* golf, tennis, shooting. *Address:* Avalon, Tadworth, Surrey. *T.:* Mogador 2036. *Clubs:* Junior Carlton; Walton Heath Golf (Walton Heath); Kingswood Golf (Kingswood). [*Died* 30 *Aug.* 1953.

MACKAY, Rev. Canon Malcolm, M.A.; Canon of Zanzibar, 1913; *b.* 10 May 1873; 3rd *s.* of George M. Mackay, Solicitor, Shepton Mallet, Somerset; unmarried. *Educ.:* Lancing Coll.; Keble Coll., Oxford; Cuddesdon Theological Coll. Deacon, 1896; Priest, 1897; Asst. Curate of Henley-on-Thames, 1896-1900; joined the Universities Mission to Central Africa, 1900; worked in the islands of Zanzibar and Pemba, 1900-17; at Magila in the Tanganyika Territory, 1917-47; Domestic Chaplain to the Bishop of Zanzibar, 1908-24; Archdeacon of Zanzibar, 1913-17; Archdeacon of Magila, 1921-44; retired, 1947. *Address:* Homes of St. Barnabas, Dormans, Lingfield, Surrey. [*Died* 15 *Feb.* 1953.

MACKAY, Very Rev. Roderick John, M.A.; D.D. (Hon.) Edinburgh, 1944; Dean Emeritus of the Diocese of Edinburgh; Rector of St. Peter's Church, Edinburgh, 1921-54; Canon of St. Mary's Cathedral, 1928-54; *b.* Invergordon, 20 July 1874; *s.* of Roderick Innes and Margaret Mackay; *m.* 1905, Mary Louisa (*d.* 1951), *d.* of William Taylor; one *s.* two *d.* *Educ.:* Hatfield College, University of Durham. Theological Scholar, 1899; Barry Scholar, 1901; President of Union; Theological Prize and L. Th. (2nd Cl. Hons.) 1901; B.A. 1908, M.A. 1911. Univ. of Durham; Curate of St. Luke's, Sunderland, 1901-4; Priest in Charge, St. Matthew's, Edinburgh 1904-09; Rector of St. Martin's, Edinburgh, 1909-21; Synod Clerk, Diocese of Edinburgh, 1934-39; Dean of Edinburgh, 1939-54. Formerly: Member Edinburgh Education Committee; Convenor, Bursaries Committee; Gov. (Vice-Chairman) George Heriot's School; Member Council, Trinity College, Glenalmond; Mem. Edinburgh Educ. Authority, Edinburgh Merchant Co. Educ. Board, Convener Education Board of Episcopal Church and Bd. of Management Edinburgh College of Art; Prolocutor, Second Chamber, Provincial Synod, Episcopal Church, 1951. *Recreations:* motoring and gardening. *Address:* 20 Findhorn Place, Edinburgh 9. *T.A.* and *T.:* Edinburgh 43809. [*Died* 24 *Nov.* 1956.

MACKAY, Ronald William Gordon, M.A., LL.B.; *b.* 3 Sept. 1902; *s.* of Alexander William Mackay and Mary Knight Moulton; *m.* 1946, Doreen M. Armstrong, Linden Lodge, Frome; two *d.* *Educ.:* Sydney Grammar School; Sydney Univ. LL.B. 1926 and M.A. with Hons. in Education, 1927; Lecturer in Philosophy and History, St. Paul's College, Sydney University, and Lecturer in Economics, Tutorial Department,

MACKAWEE, Khan Bahadur Sir Mahomed Abdul Kader, K.B.E. See p. xxix.

Sydney University; admitted Solicitor in Sydney, 1926; came to England 1934, and admitted as Solicitor in England same year. Contested (Lab.) Frome (Somerset) 1935, (Independent Socialist) Llandaff and Barry 1942; M.P. (Lab.) Hull North-West, 1945-1950, North Division of Reading, 1950-1951. Has lectured and broadcast in this country, the U.S.A. and Australia before and during the War. Held war-time appointments with Ministry of Labour and Ministry of Aircraft Production. *Publications:* In Australia: Some Aspects of Education, 1929; The Industrial Arbitration Act of the Commonwealth of Australia, 1930. In England: Federal Europe, 1940; Peace Aims and the New Order, 1942; Coupon or Free ?, 1944; You Can't Turn the Clock Back, 1948; Britain in Wonderland, 1948; Western Union in Crisis, 1949; Heads in The Sand, 1950. *Recreations:* golf and walking. *Address:* 22 Elm Tree Road, St. John's Wood, N.W.8. *T.:* Cunningham 5494. *Club:* Reform. [*Died* 15 *Jan.* 1960.

MACKEAN, Rev. Canon William Herbert, D.D.: Canon Emeritus of Rochester since 1958; *b.* 20 January 1877; *s.* of Reverend W. S. Mackean; *m.* 1st, 1906, Beatrix Margaret Irene (*d.* 1921), *d.* of Sir Cyril Clerke Graham, 5th Bt. of Kirkstall; five *d.* (one *s.* decd.); 2nd, 1922, Hilda Gifford (*d.* 1960), *widow* of Harold de Carteret, and *d.* of Dr. Gifford Ransford. *Educ.:* Bristol Grammar School; Corpus Christi College, Oxford. 2nd class in Final Honours Schools of Theology and of Modern History; M.A., D.D.; B.D., University of Durham. Deacon, 1902; Priest, 1903; Curate of St. Peter's, Eaton Square, 1902-13; Vicar of Aldenham, Herts, 1913-14; Vicar of St. John's, Notting Hill, 1916-25; Rural Dean of Kensington, 1924-25; Proctor in Convocation, 1929-45; Select Preacher, Oxford, 1930-1932; Canon of Rochester, 1925-58; Treasurer of Rochester Cathedral, 1932-58; Librarian, 1925-54; Vice-Dean, 1943-58. *Publications:* Christian Monasticism in Egypt, 1920; Contributor to the Evangelical Doctrine of Holy Communion, 1930; The Eucharistic Doctrine of the Oxford Movement, 1933; Rochester Cathedral Library, 1953. *Address:* Princes Hotel, Folkestone, Kent. *Clubs:* Union, Athenæum. [*Died* 18 *Nov.* 1960.

McKEE, Major Hugh Kennedy, C.B.E. 1946; M.C. 1917 (Bar 1918); *b.* Sept. 1896; *s.* of late David and Mrs. H. McKee; *m.* 1922, Janet Wotherspoon Dick; one *s.* one *d.* *Educ.:* Airdrie High School. Served European War, 1914-19, 13th Royal Scots, 7/8th King's Own Scottish Borderers. Went to Northern Rhodesia, 1920; farming and commerce; owned Choma Trading Co., 1924-32, Kee's Ltd., Lusaka, 1934-46. Elected Member Legislative Council, 1940-47; Director Civil Supplies, 1942-47; Commissioner for Northern Rhodesia in the U.K., 1947-53. Member: Rhodesia Local Bd., Standard Bank of S.A. Ltd.; Federal Power Bd.; Central African Road Services Bd.; Ridgeway Hotel Bd.; Copperbelt Permanent Building Society Bd.; Roy. African Society. *Recreations:* golf, fishing. *Address:* Kabulonga House, Lusaka, Northern Rhodesia. *Clubs:* Royal Empire Society, Overseas League; Royal and Ancient (St. Andrews). [*Died* 14 *March* 1957.

McKEE, William Henry; Editor of the Belfast Newsletter, 1928-54; *b.* 5 Jan. 1881; *s.* of late James H. McKee, Belfast; *m.* 1913, Charlotte (decd.), *d.* of late Isaac Bradshaw, Belfast; one *s.* two *d.* *Educ.:* Methodist Coll.; Queen's College, Belfast. Sub-editor Belfast Newsletter, 1904-15; London Editor and Lobby Correspondent, 1916-28. *Address:* 9 North Parade, Belfast. *T.:* Belfast 42009. [*Died* 3 *July* 1956.

MACKELVIE, Colonel Thomas, C.M.G. 1915; Hon. Sheriff-Substitute for Argyll; *b.* 15 Feb. 1867; *m.* 1901, Agnes, *d.* of late Robert Greenlees; one *s.* *Educ.:* Campbeltown Grammar School; Royal High School, Edinburgh. Solicitor by profession; served European War (Dardanelles), 1914-15 (despatches, C.M.G.). *Address:* Jeaniefield, Campbeltown, Scotland. *T.:* Campbeltown 2368. [*Died* 3 *Jan.* 1952.

MACKENZIE, Agnes Mure, C.B.E. 1945; M.A., D.Litt. (Aber.); LL.D. (Aber.), 1951; *b.* Stornoway, Isle of Lewis, 1891; *e. d.* of Dr. Murdoch Mackenzie and Agnes Drake. *Educ.:* Home; Univ. of Aberdeen (1st cl. Hon. Eng. Language and Literature); Hon. President Saltire Soc. *Publications:* Without Conditions, 1923; The Women in Shakespeare's Plays, 1924; The Half Loaf, 1925; The Quiet Lady, 1926; The Playgoers' Handbook to the English Renaissance Drama; Lost Kinnellan, 1927; The Process of Literature, 1929; Keith of Kinnellan (*i.e.* Lost Kinnellan and The Falling Wind), 1930; Cypress in Moonlight, 1931; Between Sun and Moon, 1932; An Historical Survey of Scottish Literature to 1714, 1933; Single Combat, 1934; A History of Scotland to 1939 (The Foundations of Scotland: to 1286; Robert Bruce, King of Scots: 1286-1329; The Rise of the Stewarts: 1329-1513; The Scotland of Queen Mary and the Religious Wars: 1513-1638; The Passing of the Stewarts: 1638-1748; Scotland in Modern Times: 1720-1939), six volumes, 1934-41; I was at Bannockburn, 1939; The Kingdom of Scotland: A Short History, 1940; The Arts and the Future of Scotland, 1942; Scottish Principles of Statecraft and Government, 1942; Scottish Pageant, 80-1513, 1946; Scottish Pageant, 1513-1625, 1948; Scottish Pageant, 1625-1707; A History of Britain and Europe for Scottish Schools, 1949; Scottish Pageant, 1707-1802; Apprentice Majesty, 1950; articles, reviews, etc. *Recreation:* doing nothing. *Address:* 19 Lonsdale Terrace, Edinburgh 3. [*Died* 26 *Feb.* 1955.

McKENZIE, Alex., F.R.S. 1916; M.A., D.Sc., Ph.D., F.R.I.C., LL.D.; Prof. of Chemistry, University College, Dundee, University of St. Andrews, 1914-38, now Professor Emeritus; Member of the Deutsche Akademie der Naturforscher zu Halle; *b.* 6 Dec. 1869; *m.* 1906, Alice H. S. Sand; one *s.* *Educ.:* Dundee High School; Universities of St. Andrews and Berlin. Assistant, Chemistry Department, United College of St. Salvator and St. Leonard, 1893-98; Grocers' Company's Research Student, Jenner Institute, London, 1901-02; Lecturer in Chemistry, University of Birmingham, 1902-05; Head of the Chemistry Department, Birkbeck College, London, 1905-13. *Publications:* mainly on Stereochemistry. *Recreation:* golf. *Address:* 5 Invermark Terrace, Barnhill, Angus. [*Died* 11 *June* 1951.

MACKENZIE, Lt.-Col. Alexander D.; *see* Mackenzie, Lt.-Col. D. W. A. D.

MACKENZIE, Alexander Herbert, M.A.; Professor of Mathematics, University of Stellenbosch, formerly Victoria College, 1895-1940, retired; *b.* Helensburgh, Scotland, 1867; *m.* Mary Graham Russell; two *d.* (and two *s.* one *d.* decd.). *Educ.:* The Universities of Aberdeen and Cambridge. Taught in England and Scotland for five years; for fifteen years was a member of Council of the University of the Cape of Good Hope; represented that University at the Quatercentenary of the University of Aberdeen in 1906, and at the Universities' Congress and the celebration of the 250th anniversary of the Royal Society in London in 1912. *Address:* The University, Stellenbosch, South Africa. [*Died* 20 *Nov.* 1952.

MACKENZIE, Captain Cecil James Granville, C.V.O. 1938 (M.V.O. 1925); Royal Navy, retired; Secretary: Highlands and Islands and West of Scotland Areas, 1949-1957; King George's Fund for Sailors, Scotland; *b.* 26 February 1889; *e. surv. s.* of late Peter

Alexander Cameron Mackenzie, Count de Serra Largo of Tarlogie and Anita Do Amaral; *m.* 1945, Barbara, *o. d.* of late William Pontifex Allen, Calcutta, India; one *d.* *Educ.:* Inverness Coll.; Royal Acad., Tain; Lupton's Naval Prep. Sch., R.N.E. Coll., Devonport. Engineer Sub.-Lt., 1909; Engineer Lt., 1911; Engineer Lt.-Commander 1919; Engineer Commander, 1925; Engineer Captain, 1937; played for Navy at rugby, golf, hockey, and tennis; played for Scotland, rugby; Chief Cadet Captain R.N.E. College, Captain of Cricket XI, and honours cap for rugby; light and middle weights at boxing; Capt. R.N. and R.M. Golfing Soc., 1935-36; served in Donegal, Highflyer flagship E.I. Squadron, Victoria and Albert; Europa, Jupiter, Warspite, and Admiralty, 1914-18; Osborne College, 1918-19; Victoria and Albert, 1919-25; Durban, China Squadron, 1925-27; Dartmouth College, 1928-30; Fleet Engineer Officer A. and W.I. station in Despatch and Delhi, 1930-31; H.M. Yacht Victoria and Albert, 1932-38; Eng. Capt. i/c of R.N. Engineering College, Devonport, 1938-41; attached Staff C.-in-C. East Indies, C.-in-C. Eastern Fleet, Director-General Ship Repairs India, 1941-43; retired Nov. 1943; Staff F.O.I.C. Newcastle, June-Aug. 1944; Admiralty Engineer Overseer Wm. Denny Bros. Ltd., Dumbarton, 1944-47; finally retd., 1947. Hon. Secretary R.N. and R.M.R.U., 1920-25; arms traffic campaign, Persian Gulf, and three war medals 1914-18; Jubilee Medal, 1935; Coronation Medal, 1937; two war medals 1939-45. *Recreations:* all sports. *Address:* 77 Fullarton Drive, Troon, Ayrshire.
[*Died* 7 *Dec.* 1959.

MACKENZIE, Lieut.-Col. Charles, C.M.G. 1919; D.S.O. 1917; Indian Army, retired; *b.* 1869. Served N. W. Frontier of India, 1897-98; Mesopotamia, 1915-19 (despatches, D.S.O., C.M.G., French Croix de Guerre). *Address:* c/o Grindlay's Bank Ltd., 54 Parliament St., S.W.1. [*Died* 20 *March* 1953.

MACKENZIE, Major Charles Fraser, C.I.E. 1918; Indian Army, Political Dept., retired. Entered Army, 1899; Boundary Settlement Commission, Central India, 1905; Assist. to Political Resident, Persian Gulf, 1909; Political Agent, Bahrein, 1909; Assist. to Resident, Kashmir, 1912; special duty, Basrah, 1915 (C.I.E.); retired, 1921. *Publications:* Persian Wonder Tales, 1928; Drugs (Chemicals) Main Cause of Cancer; Citizens v. Doctors, 1944; A Citizens Chamber of Health, 1944; Common Sense about Cancer, 1945; Food for Health and Thought, 1946; Vitality from Within, 1946; Cancer is Curable, 1947; The Miracle of Homœopathy, 1948; How to avoid Cancer, 1952; Your Life is at Stake, 1955. *Club:* St. James'.
[*Died* 5 *Sept.* 1955.

MACKENZIE, Major-Gen. Sir Colin (John), K.C.B., *cr.* 1918 (C.B. 1900); late Seaforth Highlanders; *b.* 26 Nov. 1861; *e. s.* of late Maj.-Gen. Colin Mackenzie and Victoria, *e. d.* of Charles Mackinnon, Corry; *m.* 1898, Ethel (*d.* 1950), *d.* of Hercules Grey Ross, late I.C.S.; one *s.* *Educ.:* Edinburgh Academy; Sandhurst; passed Staff College. Entered Army, 1881; held appointments of regimental Adjutant; A.D.C. to Lord Roberts when Com.-in-Chief in India; D.A.A.-Gen., Quetta Dist., Baluchistan; D.A.A.-Gen., South Africa; Director of Military Intelligence, South Africa; Military Governor of Johannesburg; Command of Mobile Column, South Africa; C.S.O., S.E. District; Col., Gen. Staff, 5th Div.; A.A.G., Army Headquarters; commanded 6th Brigade, Aldershot; Chief of General Staff, Canada; commanded Highland Territorial Division; served Egypt, 1882 (medal, clasp, bronze star); Burma, 1886-1888 (medal 2 clasps); Hazara, 1888 (despatches, clasp); Hunza-Nagar, Gilgit, 1890-91 (despatches, brevet of Major, clasp); Waziristan, 1894-95 (despatches, clasp); Nile Expedition (including Khartoum), 1898 (two medals, clasp); South Africa, 1899-1902 (despatches thrice, brevet of Lieut.-Col., C.B., Queen's medal 4 clasps, King's medal 2 clasps); European War, 1914-18; commanded Highland Territorial Division, 9th (Scottish) Division, 3rd Division, 15th (Scottish Division), Director of Staff Duties, War Office, 1915, commanded 61st Division, 1916-18 (wounded, despatches five times, K.C.B.); retired, 1920; Col. of the Seaforth Highlanders, 1924-31. *Recreation:* golf; holds record for highest score for first wicket in India. *Address:* c/o Lloyds Bank, 6 Pall Mall, S.W.1. *Clubs:* M.C.C.; Nairn Golf (Nairn).
[*Died* 7 *July* 1956.

MACKENZIE, Lieut.-Colonel (Douglas William) Alexander Dalziel, C.V.O. 1937 (M.V.O. 1934); D.S.O. 1917; Extra Equerry to the Queen since 1952 (to King George VI, 1937-52); *b.* 20 Oct. 1889; *e. s.* of late W. R. D. Mackenzie, and *g.s.* of late W. Dalziel Mackenzie, of Farr; *m.* 1915, Patience Elizabeth, *e. d.* of late R. B. Hoare of 96 Eaton Place, S.W.; two *s.* one *d.* *Educ.:* Eton; Magdalen College, Oxford, B.A. Gazetted Seaforth Highlanders, 1911; Chevalier Order of Leopold, 1917; Croix de Guerre (Belgian), Jan. 1918; Brevet majority, Jan. 1919; retired pay, 1921; re-employed Cttee. of Imp. Defence with permanent rank of Lt.-Col., 1939-41, then released for work under Northern Counties Territorial Army Associations, 1941-43; H.M.'s Commissioner at Balmoral, 1926-37; D.L. and J.P. Inverness-shire; Chairman, Country Gentlemen's Assoc., 1952-55; Fellow of Land Agents Soc.; formerly Fellow Surveyor's Inst. *Recreations:* shooting, fishing. *Address:* Farr, Inverness-shire. *T.:* Farr 205. *Clubs:* Turf, Caledonian, M.C.C.; New (Edinburgh).
[*Died* 6 *Dec.* 1955.

MACKENZIE, Lady, (Faith Compton Mackenzie); *y. d.* of late Rev. E. D. Stone, sometime Master of Eton College; *m.* 1905, (Edward Montague) Compton Mackenzie, O.B.E., Hon. LL.D.; no *c.* *Educ.:* Francis Holland School for Girls, London. *Publications:* Mandolinata, 1931; The Sibyl of the North (Christina of Sweden), 1931; The Cardinal's Niece (Marie Mancini), 1935; (autobiographical) As Much as I Dare, 1938; More Than I Should, 1940; Always Afternoon, 1943; The Angle of Error (short stories), 1938; Napoleon at the Briars, 1943; William Cory, 1950; The Crooked Wall, 1953; Tatting, 1956; contributions to Time and Tide, New Statesman, Gramophone, etc. *Recreations:* Italy, music, birds. *Address:* 31 Drummond Place, Edinburgh 3.
[*Died* 9 *July* 1960.

MACKENZIE, Brig.-General George Birnie, C.B. 1919; C.M.G. 1918; D.S.O. 1916; *b.* 13 Jan. 1872; *s.* of late William Laurence Mackenzie of Inner Temple, Barrister; *m.* 1926, Eleanor Mabel, *e. d.* of late John Edward Dovey, C.A., Edinburgh. *Educ.:* Dulwich College; Royal Military Academy, Woolwich. 2nd Lieut. R.A. 1892; Col. 1921; was in New Zealand, Gibraltar, Hong Kong, and Peking; commanded the first British Siege Battery to fire in the European War; served 1914-18 (despatches six times, Bt. Lt.-Col., D.S.O., C.B., C.M.G., Officer of the Legion of Honour, Croix de Guerre); retired pay, 1925; employed under War Office, 1939, under Ministry of Information, 1940-42, under Director of Postal Censorship, 1943-45. *Address:* 62 Duke's Avenue, Muswell Hill, N.10. *T.:* Tudor 5338. *Club:* National. [*Died* 6 *Feb.* 1952.

MACKENZIE, Sir Hector David, 8th Bt. of Gairloch, *cr.* 1703; M.C.; J.P., D.L., Ross and Cromarty; Lord Lieutenant of Ross and Cromarty, 1936-55; Member of County Council of Ross and Cromarty; *b.* 6 June 1893; *o. s.* of Sir Kenneth Mackenzie, 7th Bt. and Lady Marjory Murray, C.B.E., *o. d.* of 10th Viscount Stormont, *sister* of 6th Earl of Mansfield and Mansfield; *S.* father, 1929. *Educ.:* Winchester. Served European War, 1914-18 (despatches, M.C.); British Liaison Officer, French Army of the Rhine, 1919-20. *Recreations:* shooting, hunting. *Address:* Conan House,

Cononbridge, Ross-shire. *Clubs:* Caledonian, Junior Carlton. [*Died* 10 *May* 1958.

MACKENZIE, Sir Hugh, Kt., *cr.* 1945; C.B.E. 1941; J.P.; Provost of Inverness, 1934-45; Director of Industrial and Commercial companies; Deputy Chairman of North of Scotland Hydro Electric Board; *b.* 11 January 1888; *s.* of Hugh Mackenzie, leather merchant, Inverness; *m.* 1911, Jane C. Clark; one *d. Educ.:* High and Central Schools. *Address:* Lethington, Inverness. *T.:* 1177. *Clubs:* Highland (Inverness); Conservative (Edinburgh). [*Died* 24 *Dec.* 1959.

McKENZIE, Very Rev. John, C.I.E. 1944; M.A., D.D. (Aberdeen.); Hon. F.E.I.S.; *b.* Turriff, Aberdeenshire, 13 June 1883; *s.* of Andrew McKenzie; *m.* 1912, Agnes Ferguson (Kaisar-i-Hind Medal, 1st Class, 1932), *d.* of Robert Dinnes, Mintlaw, Aberdeenshire. *Educ.:* Gordon's Coll., Aberdeen; Univ. of Aberdeen; New College, Edinburgh (Senior Cunningham Fellow); University of Tübingen. Ordained and appointed Professor of Philosophy, Wilson College, Bombay, 1908; Principal, 1921-44; President Bombay Anthropological Society, 1927-29; Vice-Chancellor of Bombay University, 1931-33; Vice-Chairman, National Christian Council of India, Burma, and Ceylon, 1937-1944; Moderator, United Church of Northern India, 1938-41; Moderator, General Assembly Church of Scotland, 1946-47. *Publications:* Hindu Ethics, 1923; edited Worship, Witness, and Work, by R. S. Simpson, D.D., 1928; edited The Christian Task in India, by various writers, 1929; Two Religions, 1950. *Address:* 21 Woodburn Terrace, Edinburgh. *T.:* 56234 *Club:* Overseas League. [*Died* 30 *Oct.* 1955.

MacKENZIE, Lt.-Col. John Alexander, C.M.G. 1918; retired; *b.* 1881; *s.* of John Campbell MacKenzie, Fort William, Inverness-shire; *m.* 1929, Laura, *d.* of Donald H. MacQueen, Leicester. *Educ.:* Lumsden School; Southland High School. Served European War, 1914-19 (despatches, C.M.G.). *Address:* Irwell-R.D., No. 3, Christchurch, N.Z. [*Died* 6 *Sept.* 1960.

McKENZIE, Sir John (Robert), K.B.E., *cr.* 1950; Managing Director McKenzie's Department Stores, Wellington, N.Z.; *b.* Yarrawalla, Vic., Australia, 5 Aug. 1876; *s.* of Hugh McKenzie; *m.* 1914, Annie May, *d.* of S. H. Wrigley; one *s.* (and one *s.* killed on active service, 1942). *Educ.:* Melbourne. Started business with Jacob Hart & Co., Melbourne and founded own business (now with many branches); Chairman: J. R. McKenzie, Ltd.; J. C. Williamson (Australia) Ltd.; founder of Rotary J. R. McKenzie Youth Educ. Fund of £10,000; Executive New Zealand Crippled Children Society; founder of J. R. McKenzie Charitable Trust of £100,000, now £1,000,000, for benefit of ailing children, N.Z. soldiers, sailors and airmen. Plunket Society. Served in South African War, 3rd Victorian Bushmen's Contingent. *Address:* (home) Roydon Lodge, 483 Yaldhurst Road, No. 1, Rural Delivery, Christchurch, New Zealand. *Club:* Canterbury (Christchurch). [*Died* 26 *Aug.* 1955.

McKENZIE, Thomas, C.B. 1945; C.B.E. 1941; Director Metal Industries Ltd., Hughes Bolckow Shipbreaking Co., Shipbreaking Industries Ltd.; *b.* 11 Dec. 1891; *s.* of late Daniel and Jessie Fenwick McKenzie; *m.* 1911, Isabelle McKenzie McMorland, Ayrshire; two *d. Educ.:* Glasgow. Commenced Salvage career, 1911, on completion of shipbuilding apprenticeship; work on own account, 1911-14; Clyde Navigation Trust, 1914-15; Admiralty Salvage Dept., 1915-19; Salvage and survey work abroad, 1920-23; Chief Salvage Officer on salvage of ex-German Fleet at Scapa, 1924-32; General Manager Metal Industries, Scapa, on ex-German Fleet Salvage, 1933-39; Admiralty Chief Salvage Officer, 1939; Managing Director Metal Industries Salvage Ltd., 1943; Director of Metal Industries Ltd., Shipbreaking Industries Ltd., Metal Industries (Metal Division); Commodore R.N.V.R. and Principal Salvage Officer to Allied Naval Commander Expeditionary Force (North Europe), 1945. *Recreations:* yachting, fishing. *Address:* Vista, Shandon, Dunbartonshire. *T.:* Gareloch-head 293. *Clubs:* Caledonian, Royal Automobile; Royal Clyde Yacht (Glasgow); Royal Northern Yacht (Rhu). [*Died* 25 *April* 1954.

MACKENZIE, William Cook, F.S.A. (Scot.); author; *b.* 1862; 3rd *s.* of late Colin Mackenzie of Stornoway, Island of Lewis; *m.* 1897, Gertrude Mary (*d.* 1941), *e. d.* of J. Parker Anderson, late of the British Museum. Was for a number of years the Managing Director in London of Carver Brothers, and Co., Ltd., Manchester, Liverpool, Alexandria, and London; retired from business, 1934; received freedom of the burgh of Stornoway, 1938. *Publications:* History of the Outer Hebrides, 1903; The Lady of Hirta, 1905; A Short History of the Scottish Highlands and Isles, 3rd ed. 1908; Life and Times of Simon Fraser, Lord Lovat, 1908; The Shirra: a Tale of the Isles, 1910; The Races of Ireland and Scotland, 1916; The War Diary of a London Scot, 1916; The Book of the Lews, 1919; The Life and Times of John Maitland, Duke of Lauderdale, 1616-1682, 1923; Scottish Place Names, 1931; The Western Isles: their history, traditions, and place-names, 1932; Lovat of the Forty-five, 1934; Andrew Fletcher of Saltoun: His Life and Times, 1935; The Highlands and Isles of Scotland: a historical survey, 1937 (re-printed, 1949). *Address:* Deargaill, St. George's Road, St. Margarets-on-Thames. [*Died* 1 *March* 1952.

MACKENZIE, William Mackay, M.A., D.Litt.; LL.D., Hon. R.S.A. 1942; *b.* Cromarty, 1871; *e. s.* of late A. H. Mackenzie, Sheriff-clerk, etc.; *m.* Ishbel Jane, *d.* of late C. E. Mackenzie, Charleston, S. Carolina, and Stornoway. *Educ.:* Cromarty Public School; Edinburgh University. Master, Glasgow Academy, Glasgow, 1896-1913; Editorial Staff War Trade Intelligence Dept., 1916-19; Rhind Lecturer in Archæology for 1925-26; Secretary to the Royal Commission on Ancient and Historical Monuments of Scotland, 1913-35; retired, 1935; Acting Head of Scottish History Department, Edinburgh University, 1940-44; Professor of Antiquities in Royal Scottish Academy, 1942; Rhind Lecturer in Archæology, 1945. Member of Royal Commission on Ancient and Historical Monuments of Scotland. *Publications:* Hugh Miller, a Critical Study, 1903; Outline of Scottish History, 1907; Pompeii, 1908; Edition of Barbour's Bruce, 1909; Bannockburn, a Study in Mediæval Warfare, 1913; Book of Arran, Vol. II. History and Folklore, 1914; The Mediæval Castle in Scotland, 1927; The Secret of Flodden, 1931; The Bannockburn Myth, 1932; Edition of the Poems of William Dunbar, 1933; William Dunbar, in Edinburgh Essays, 1934; Lothian, in Scottish Country, 1935; Castles and Towers, in The Stones of Scotland, 1938; Edition of The Kingis Quair, 1939; The Scottish Burghs, 1949; contributions to Proceedings of Society of Antiquaries of Scotland, Scottish Historical Review, etc. *Address:* 4 Barkly Street, Cromarty. *Club:* Scottish Arts (Edinburgh). [*Died* 4 *Aug.* 1952.

MACKENZIE, Major William Roderick Dalziel, D.L., F.S.A.; *b.* 2 Sept. 1864; *s.* of William Dalziel Mackenzie of Fawley Court, Henley-on-Thames and of Thetford Manor and Farr, Inverness-shire, and Mary Anna Baskerville; *m.* 1888; one *s.* one *d. Educ.:* Harrow; Christ Church, Oxford. Vice-Chairman 1904-09, Chairman 1909-13 Highways Committee; Vice-Chairman, Henley Rural District Council, 1904-13; Member Bucks County Council, 1907; Alderman since 1922; Vice-Chairman Education Committee; Chairman

Elementary Education Committee; Chairman Land Drainage Committee, all Bucks County Council; Represents Bucks C.C. on Thames Conservancy Board, since 1922 (Chairman River Purification Committee, 1936, Vice-Chairman, 1938); Vice-Chairman, Executive Committee, Chairman Home Committee, Gordon Boys Home; Vice-Chairman, 1906-10, Chairman, 1910-14, South Oxfordshire Conservative and Unionist Association; Chairman Marlow Water Co.; Chm. of Governors Henley Grammar School; served in 3rd Batt Q.O. Cameron Highlanders, 1887-1904, Captain 1896, Major 1900, Hon. Major in Army, 1900; Home Service in Great War with 6th and 8th Cameron Highlanders; J.P. Oxon, J.P. and D.L.Bucks, F.S.A. 1934. *Publications:* Fawley Court and Round About it; A Day in Kioto, etc., in English Illustrated and other magazines. Verses 1880-88. *Recreations:* voyaging, stamp collecting, browsing among books and in picture galleries. *Address:* Sunnyclose, Fawley, Henley-on-Thames. *T.:* Henley 735. *Club:* Junior Carlton. [*Died* 2 *Feb.* 1952.

MACKESY, Major-General Pierse Joseph, C.B. 1938; D.S.O. 1918; M.C.; *b.* 1883; *s.* of late Lt.-Gen. W. H. Mackesy; *m.* 1923, Dorothy, *o. d.* of James Cook, Enfield, Cults, Aberdeenshire; two *s.* Entered R.E. 1902; Major, 1917; Lt.-Col., 1928; Col., 1932 (1923); Maj.-Gen., 1937; employed on special Survey Duty in Ashanti and Northern Territories of the Gold Coast and as Deputy Director of Surveys, Gold Coast, 1911-14; served European War, Togoland, 1914-Cameroons, 1914, France, 1915-18, Murmansk, 1919; Military Mission in South Russia, 1919-20 (despatches twice, D.S.O., M.C., Brevet Lieut.-Col. 1919); Commander 3rd Infantry Brigade, Bordon and Palestine, 1935-38; Commander 49th (West Riding) Division and Area, T.A., 1938; commanded the Land Forces in the Narvik area, 1940; War Office, 1940; Offices of the War Cabinet, 1940-41; retd. pay, 1940. Councillor, Southwold Borough Council, 1946-53; Mayor of Southwold, 1949-1950-1951-1952; East Suffolk County Council, 1949-55. *Address:* Tudor Cottage, South Green, Southwold, Suffolk. *T.:* Southwold 2273. *Clubs:* Army and Navy, Royal Automobile.
[*Died* 8 *June* 1956.

McKIBBIN, Colonel Alan John, O.B.E. 1949; M.P. (U.U.) Belfast East (Imperial Parliament) since 1950; Managing Director John McKibbin & Son Ltd., Belfast; Chairman A.C.F. Association, N. Ireland; Hon. Col. A.C.F. Belfast, Antrim, and N. Down, 1956; Commandant A.C.F. (N.I.), 1957; J.P. (County Borough of Belfast); D.L. (Belfast); *b.* 2 February 1892; *m.* 1922, Kathleen Laura; one *s.* *Educ.:* Campbell College, Belfast. Served European War, 1914-18; Home Guard, 1939. *Recreations:* golf, sailing. *Address:* 22 Corporation Street, Belfast. *T.:* Belfast 20401; 28 Chiltern Court, Baker Street, N.W.1. *T.:* Welbeck 5544. *Clubs:* Ulster Reform (Belfast); Royal Ulster Yacht.
[*Died* 2 *Dec.* 1958.

MACKIE, Alexander; Principal of Teachers' College and Professor of Education, The University of Sydney, 1906, retd.; *b.* Edinburgh, 1876; *m.* 1914; one *s.* one *d.* *Educ.:* Daniel Stewart's College, Edinburgh; Edinburgh University. Lecturer, University College of North Wales, Bangor 1903-6; Lecturer, University of Edinburgh, 1906. *Publications:* Theory of Education; Groundwork of Teaching; Studies in Education, 1932. *Recreations:* walking, golf. *Address:* c/o The University, Sydney, N.S.W. *Club:* Australian (Sydney).
[*Died* 23 *Oct.* 1955.

MACKIE, Alfred William White, C.I.E. 1931; I.C.S. (retired); *b.* 20 Oct. 1877; *s.* of Alexander Mackie, of Arbroath, and Brucina Campbell, of Dundee; *m.* 1941, Cecilia Annie Staden. *Educ.:* Harris Academy, Dundee; High School, Dundee; St. Andrews University (M.A. 1898); Corpus Christi College, Cambridge (B.A. 1901). Settlement Commissioner and Director of Land Records and Inspector General of Registration, Bombay Presidency; Commissioner of Division, 1931; retired 1936. *Recreation:* golf. *Club:* East India and Sports. [*Died* 17 *Oct.* 1951.

McKIE, Helen Madeleine; Artist; *e. d.* of late Douglas Allan McKie and L. Anne McKie. *Educ.:* Studied Lambeth School of Art. On the permanent staff of The Bystander, 1915-29; contributor to The Graphic, The Queen, Autocar, etc.; Illustrated the de Luxe edition of Beau Geste and the translation of Pierre Mille's Barnavaux books; held exhibition at Brook Street Art Gallery, 1919, and also held exhibition at Walker's Galleries in June-July 1928, when H.M. Queen Mary purchased a picture; exhibited at the Paris Salon, 1934 and 1935; illustrated My Secret London and Romance of London River; exhibited in Paris Salon and Royal Hibernian Academy, 1936; decorated two new coaches for a Continental boat train for Southern Railway, 1939; Commissioned by late Lord Lloyd to visit naval bases to make sketches of the personnel and warships for publication in the "Navy"; painted a picture, 1943, of the Upper War Room, Admiralty, for a presentation to Mr. Churchill; series of paintings to decorate British Railways cross channel boat, S.S. Hotel, London and in Bahamas; series of paintings of Coronation personalities for Coronation Number of Country Life; series of six large panels of French Princesses, Queens of England, for French Govt. Tourist Office, 1953. *Publication:* wrote and illustrated, Travelling South under the Six King Georges, 1937. *Recreation:* travel. *Address:* 53 Glebe Place, Chelsea, S.W.3. *T.:* Flaxman 2473.
[*Died* 28 *Feb.* 1957.

MACKIE, John Hamilton; M.P. (C.) Galloway since 1931; *b.* 8 Jan. 1898; *o. s.* of William Murray Mackie (*d.* 1932) and Agnes Mary (*d.* 1927), *e. d.* of John Fildes of Barcaple, Kirkcudbrightshire. *Educ.:* Harrow; Christ Church, Oxford. Contested Central Edinburgh (C.), 1929. *Address:* Auchencairn House, Castle-Douglas, Kirkcudbrightshire. *Clubs:* Carlton; New (Edinburgh). [*Died* 29 *Dec.* 1958.

MACKIE, John Lindsay, C.B.E. 1926; Ph.D. (London), 1938; *s.* of John Mackie; *b.* 1864. Was Assist. Secretary Board of Customs and Excise. *Address:* 91 The Avenue, Muswell Hill, N.10. *T.:* Tudor 4135.
[*Died* 23 *Feb.* 1956.

MACKIE, Peter Robert McLeod, A.R.S.A. 1932; H.R.S.W.; 3rd *s.* of W. G. Mackie, and Anne, *d.* of Robert McLeod of Camoquhill, Stirlingshire. *Educ.:* Edinburgh; Paris. During European War gave service under the Earl of Lucan, Director of Wounded and Missing Department of the affiliated societies of the Red Cross, and the Order of St. John of Jerusalem. *Works:* pictures in the McKelvie Gallery, Auckland, New Zealand, Scottish Modern Arts Assoc., and in private collections; three-light stained glass windows in Temperley Church, Buenos Aires, S. America. *Recreation:* travel. *Club:* Scottish Arts (Edinburgh).
[*Died* 18 *Jan.* 1959.

MACKIE, Thomas Jones, C.B.E. 1942; Professor of Bacteriology, University of Edinburgh, since 1923; Dean of Faculty of Medicine since 1953; *b.* 5 June 1888; *s.* of late James Mackie, Hamilton; *m.* Edith, *d.* of late Joseph Warner, Birmingham; one *s.* one *d.* *Educ.:* Hamilton Academy; Glasgow Univ. (M.B., Ch.B. with Hons. and Brunton Memorial Prizeman 1910). House Surgeon and Physician, Western Infirmary, Glasgow, 1910-1911; Research Scholar and Fellow in Pathology, Glasgow Univ., 1911-14; D.P.H. Oxford, 1913; Asst. Bacteriologist, Middlesex Hosp. and Medical School, London, 1914; Lt. and Capt. R.A.M.C. (T.F.), 1914-18; O.C.

52nd Div. Sanitary Section; Officer in Charge Military Laboratory, Alexandria, E.E.F.; Wernher-Beit Prof. of Bacteriology, Univ. of Cape Town, 1918-23; F.R.S.S.Af.; M.D. (Hons. and Bellahouston and Straits Settlements Gold Medals for Thesis), 1921; Cons. Bacteriologist Royal Infirmary, Edinburgh; Consultant Bacteriologist to S.E. Regional Hospital Board, Scotland; lately Director of Bacteriological Services, City of Edinburgh and Regional Director (S.E. Scotland), Emergency Bacteriological Service; M.R.C.P.E., F.R.S.E.; Corr. Member Royal Acad. of Medicine, Rome; LL.D. Glasgow, 1947; Adviser in Bacteriology and Pathol., Dept. Health Scotland; Member, University Court and Curator of Patronage, Edinburgh University; a Director of Animal Diseases Research Assoc. (Scotland); Mem. Bd. of Management, Hill Farming Research Organization; formerly: Chm., Interdepartmental Committee on Furunculosis, Fishery Depts.; Mem.: Hill Sheep Farming Cttee. (Scotland); Agricultural Educ. Cttee. (Scotland); Scientific Advisory Cttee., Dept. of Health for Scotland; Chairman, Scottish Hill Farm Research Cttee. and Technical Cttee., Agricultural Advisory Council, Scotland; Member Agricultural Research Council; Mem. S.E. Regional Hosp. Bd., Scotland. formerly Examiner Universities of Aberdeen, St. Andrews, Glasgow, Durham and Sheffield. *Publications:* Textbook of Bacteriology (jointly), 1949; Handbook of Practical Bacteriology (jointly), 9th ed., 1953; Contributions to System of Bacteriology, M.R.C., 1929; and various scientific papers, articles, etc. *Address:* 22 Mortonhall Road, Edinburgh. *Club:* Caledonian United Services (Edinburgh). [*Died* 6 *Oct.* 1955.

MacKILLOP, Douglas, C.M.G. 1950; Consul-Gen.; employed in N.A.T.O. International Secretariat since 1952; *b.* 12 May 1891; *s.* of James MacKillop, Greenlaw, Berwickshire; *m.* 1st, 1919, Ethel Anne Baker (*d.* 1931); two *s.* one *d.* (and one *s.* died as prisoner of war, 1943, and one *s.* decd.); 2nd, 1935, Phyllis Selborne Jackson; two *s.* two *d.* *Educ.:* Manchester Grammar School, Manchester University, and in Lyons (France). Served in Army, 1914-19. Entered Diplomatic Service as 3rd Secretary, 1919, and served in various ranks in Sofia, Helsinki, Athens, Brussels, Moscow, Hankow, Riga, Berne, and in Foreign Office, 1919-49; British Consul-General, Munich, 1949-51, and British Land Observer, Bavaria, 1950-51. *Address:* Glenlea, Shillingstone, nr. Blandford, Dorset. *T.:* Childe Okeford 445. [*Died* 25 *Feb.* 1959.

MACKINLAY, Jean Sterling; Diseuse; *d.* of Antoinette Sterling and John Mackinlay; *m.* 1908, E. G. Harcourt Williams, *q.v.*; one *s.* (one *d.* decd.). *Educ.:* Roedean. Studied with Genevieve Ward; started on the stage with Sir Frank Benson; later joined Sir George Alexander; toured as "Sunday"; played with Sir John Hare in farewell London season; became a diseuse giving many recitals of folk songs and old ballads at the Little Theatre, at the Aeolian Hall, and all over the country; does much school and educational work; Originator of the Children's Theatre movement in this country; gave Children's Christmas Matinées for 27 seasons. *Recreations:* the theatre, reading, motoring. *Address:* 310 Clive Court, W.9. *T.:* Cunningham 0758; Ebony Cottage, near Tenterden. *T.:* Appledore 255. [*Died* 15 *Dec.* 1958.

MACKINLAY, Malcolm Sterling, M.A. Oxon; writer and vocal teacher; Lecturer to the Polytechnic (resigned); *b.* London, 7 Aug. 1876; *e. s.* of late Antoinette Sterling and John MacKinlay; *godson* of late Lord Mount Temple; *m.* 1908, Dagny (*d.* 1943), *y. d.* of Capt. Hansen, Oslo; one *d.* *Educ.:* Eton; Trinity Coll., Oxford. Learned singing under Manuel Garcia; *début*, Queen's Hall Ballad Concerts, Nov. 1900; gave over thirty London recitals; has appeared at Savoy Theatre, Lyric Theatre, Avenue Theatre, Duke of York's; founded the Sterling MacKinlay Players, 1912; 25th Light Opera revival, 1926. Produced Cabaresque with his Light Opera Singers at Easter, 1928; performed at concerts, cinemas, etc; Adjudicator for National Operatic Competition from the opening season, also for Musical Festivals; Adjudicator two years at Morecambe Drama Festival; critic for musical plays for the Play Pictorial, 1933. *Publications:* Antoinette Sterling and other Celebrities; Garcia the Centenarian and his Times; The Singing Voice and its Training; Light Opera (Technique); Origin and Development of Light Opera; English Diction for Foreign Students; Reparation (a novel); The Enemy Agent (a novel); Garden of Tradition (Jaunts in Great Britain); Supper for Three (a comedy); Paper on Expression of Emotion in Animals for the Zoological Society. *Songs:* Spring is the Time of Love, etc. *Recreations:* writing, reading, theatre-going. *Address:* 4L Portman Mansions, W.1. [*Died* 10 *Jan.* 1952.

MACKINNON, Doris Livingston, D.Sc., LL.D.; Professor Emeritus of Zoology, University of London; *b.* Aberdeen; *d.* of Lachlan Mackinnon, Advocate; unmarried. Graduated at the University of Aberdeen, 1906; Lecturer in Zoology at University College, Dundee, 1909-19, during which period served for two years as protozoologist to Military Hospitals in England; Lecturer and then Reader in Zoology at King's College, University of London, 1919-21; Professor, 1927-49. *Publications:* numerous papers on the Protozoa. *Address:* 44 St. Leonard's Terr., Chelsea, S.W.3. *T.:* Flaxman 8308. [*Died* 10 *Sept.* 1956.

MACKINNON, James Alexander Rudolf; Sheriff-Substitute of Perth and Angus at Dundee since 1946; of Forfarshire, 1932-46; *b.* Edinburgh, 1888; *o. c.* of late Prof. James MacKinnon and Pauline Klein; *m.* 1st, 1919, Patricia (*d.* 1938), *e. d.* of late J. Huntly MacDonald of Torbreck, Inverness-shire; (one *s.* killed in action, 1945) one *d.*; 2nd, 1942, Margaret Simpson Guild, *widow* of Andrew Lane, Glasgow. *Educ.:* Madras College, St. Andrews; George Watson's College, Edinburgh; St. Andrews and Edinburgh Universities; M.A., LL.B. (Edin.). Called to Scottish Bar, 1915; examiner in Edinburgh and Aberdeen Universities, and for the Police Examinations Board; Lecturer in Jurisprudence, Edinburgh University, 1927-1932; Advocate-Depute on the Glasgow Circuit, 1929-32. *Publication:* part author (with his father) The Constitutional History of Scotland, 1924. *Recreation:* golf. *Address:* Thornlea, Forfar. *T.:* Forfar 219. *Clubs:* New (Edinburgh); Eastern (Dundee); Forfar Golf (Forfar). [*Died* 21 *July* 1955.

MACKINNON, John, C.I.E. 1939; A.M.Inst.C.E.; Chief Engineer (retd.), Indian Rly. Service of Engineers; *b.* 30 Jan. 1886; *s.* of James L. Mackinnon and Anna M. Dow, Glasgow; *m.* 1914, May Dewar (*d.* 1957); three *s.* *Educ.:* Glasgow Academy; Fettes College, Edinburgh. Civil Engineer; A.M.Inst.C.E., 1912; Asst. Engineer, P.W.D. Indian State Railways, 1909, and served continuously in that Dept. till 1939 when Chief Engineer; also officiated as General Manager, and Director of Civil Engineering, Railway Board; European War, attached Railway Directorate, Mesopotamia, 1916-19, rank Captain. *Address:* 10 Queen's Gate, Glasgow, W.2. *T.:* Kelvin 1396. [*Died* 30 *Oct.* 1958.

MACKINNON, Sir Percy Graham, Kt., *cr.* 1928; Past-President of the Insurance Institute of London; an Hon. Member of the Honourable Company of Master Mariners; late Chairman of Lloyd's Patriotic Fund; a former Governor of Bryanston School; a Fellow of the Chartered Insurance Institute; late Chairman of

Edenbridge and District War Memorial Hospital; *b.* 6 Oct. 1872; 2nd *s.* of B. T. Mackinnon, Lloyd's, and East Park House, Lingfield, Surrey; *m.* Mabel (*d.* 1951), *d.* of George Locket; one *s.* three *d.* *Educ.:* Highgate School. Deputy Chairman of Lloyd's, 1924; Chairman of Lloyd's, 1925, 1927, 1928, 1932, and 1933; Underwriting Member of Lloyd's since 1894; Member of Committee of Lloyd's, 1918-45; awarded Lloyd's Gold Medal for services to Lloyd's, 1928; a trustee of National Maritime Museum, 1934-37; late Member Cttee. of Management of H.M.S. Worcester; late Chm. Salvage Assoc.; Member of Departmental Committee on Compulsory Insurance, 1936-37; a member of the West Indian Royal Commission, 1938-39. *Address:* High Quarry, Crockham Hill, Edenbridge, Kent. *T.:* Crockham Hill 313; Lloyd's, E.C.3. *Club:* City of London. [*Died* 21 *Nov.* 1956.

MACKINNON, Lieut.-Col. William Thomas Morris, C.M.G. 1919; B.L.; M.B.; M.D. (Toronto); Specialist in Eye, Ear, Nose and Throat; *s.* of Archibald Mackinnon, Amherst, N.S.; *m.* Elizabeth, *d.* of Charles McMillan, Pittston, Pa.; one *d.* *Educ.:* Dalhousie and Toronto Universities. Lt.-Col. re-employed Canadian Army Medical Corps, 1939-43; served European War, 1914-1919 (despatches, C.M.G.). Member of staff, Highland View Hosp., Amherst, N.S.; Member Amherst Board of Trade; Chairman Civil Defence Committee.; Member Amherst Town Council. *Address:* 112 Church St., Amherst, N.S., Canada. *Club:* Marshlands (Amherst, N.S.). [*Died* 30 *June* 1957.

McKINSTRY, Sir Archibald, Kt., *cr.* 1943; D.Sc., M.I.Mech.E., M.I.E.E.; Director Metal Box Co. Ltd. (ex-Vice-Chm.); *b.* 1877; *s.* of Robert McKinstry, Co. Antrim; *m.* 1914, Sarah Ogden Taylor Bark; one *s.* *Educ.:* Queen's College, Belfast; Royal University of Ireland. After graduating, joined British Westinghouse Company as junior engineer, 1902; connected with that company and the Metropolitan-Vickers Companies in various capacities (including that of Chairman, Metropolitan-Vickers Electrical Export Co. Ltd. and Director, Metropolitan-Vickers Electrical Co. Ltd.) till end of 1930 when resigned connection with these interests; went to Australia and New Zealand, 1911; Director of Munitions, Commonwealth Government of Australia, latter portion of European War; Electricity Commissioner, State of Victoria, Australia, 1918; visited U.S.A. and Canada on electrical matters, 1920 and 1921; Director of British Broadcasting Co., 1922-27; visited Spain as Member of F.B.I. Trade Mission, 1929; Member Industrial Panel of Ministry of Production, 1942; Representative of Ministry of Supply on Munitions Management and Labour Efficiency Committee of Ministry of Production, 1943; Member Appeal Tribunal (Road and Rail Traffic Act, 1933), 1947; Member Royal Commission on Awards to Inventors, 1947; Director, Managing Director, and Deputy Chairman, Babcock and Wilcox, Ltd., 1931-51. *Publication:* Notes on Electrical Calculations of High Voltage Transmission Lines, I.E.E. Journal, 1920. *Recreations:* golf, billiards. *Address:* Chesterfield House, 21 Ingram Avenue, N.W.11. *T.:* Speedwell 8960. *Clubs:* Union; Royal and Ancient (St. Andrews). [*Died* 6 *Oct.* 1952.

MACKINTOSH, Colonel Ernest Elliot Buckland, D.S.O. 1917; *b.* 3 Nov. 1880; *s.* of E. A. Mackintosh and Gina, *d.* of C. T. Buckland; *m.* 1923, Marion Constance, *o. d.* of late Maj. Edward F. Talbot-Ponsonby; (one *s.* killed in action 1944) one *d.* *Educ.:* Laleham; Temple Grove; Eton (King's Scholar); R.M.A., Woolwich. Commissioned Royal Engineers, 1899; Lt.-Col., 1925; Col., 1929; served with Egyptian Army, 1906-15 (4th Class Osmanieh); A.D.C. to Sirdar and Governor-General of Sudan, 1908-11; D.A.A.G. and A.A.G. 1911-15; European War, 1915-19 (despatches, D.S.O., Bt. Lt.-Col., Legion of Honour); Assistant Adjutant-General, War Office, 1930-32; Chief Engineer (Temp. Brig.), Eastern Command, 1932-33; retired pay, 1933; re-employed as Commandant S.M.E. Chatham, 1939-40; Director Science Museum, a Governor Imperial College of Science, a Trustee Imperial War Museum, 1933-45; Vice-President Royal Institution. *Address:* 24 Marlborough Place, N.W.8. *T.:* Maida Vale 1583. *Club:* Athenæum. [*Died* 25 *Nov.* 1957.

MACKINTOSH, Colonel George, C.B. 1911; C.B.E. 1919; Colonel, retired pay; 2nd *s.* of late Eneas Mackintosh, of Balnespick, Inverness-shire; *b.* Inverness, 28 Aug. 1860; *m.* 1912, Mary, *y. d.* of late G. B. Davy, Owthorpe, Notts, and Spean Bridge, Inverness; one *s.* (and one killed in action) three *d.* *Educ.:* Marlborough College, R.M.C., Sandhurst. Joined 78th Highlanders, 1878; Capt. Seaforth Highlanders, 1889; Major, 1897; Bt. Lt.-Col. 1900; Lt.-Col. 1905; Bt. Col. 1906; Col. half-pay, 1909; commanded 2nd Batt. Seaforth Highlanders, 1905-9; Commandant No. 1 District, Perth, 1912; served Afghan War, 1881 (medal); Hazara Expedition, 1888 (despatches, medal with clasp); occupation of Crete, 1897; South Africa, 1900-2 (despatches, Queen's medal with four clasps, King's medal with two clasps, Brevet Lt.-Col.); J.P., D.L., Inverness-shire. *Recreations:* shooting, fishing, sketching. *Address:* Balvraid, Tomatin, Inverness-shire; Bruach, Nairn. *T.:* Tomatin 204, Nairn 112. *Clubs:* Naval and Military; Highland (Inverness). [*Died* 10 *Feb.* 1954.

MACKINTOSH of Mackintosh (The Mackintosh), Vice-Admiral Lachlan Donald, C.B. 1945; D.S.O. 1943; D.S.C. 1918; D.L.; J.P.; 29th Chief of the Clan Mackintosh; *b.* 11 Nov. 1896; *s.* of D. H. Mackintosh; *m.* 1927, Margaret Elizabeth Darroch; one *s.* *Educ.:* Cheam School; Royal Naval Colleges, Osborne and Dartmouth. Midshipman 1914; served European War, 1914-18 (D.S.C.). Specialised as Naval Air Observer, 1922; learnt to fly, 1925; Captain 1938; war of 1939-45; commanded H.M.S. Charybdis, Eagle, Victorious and Implacable. Assistant Chief of Naval Staff (Air), 1944-45 (D.S.O., C.B., American Legion of Merit, Degree of Comdr.); Flag Officer Flying Training, 1945-1947; Rear-Adm. 1947. A.D.C. to the King, 1947; Vice-Controller (Air), Chief of Naval Air Equipment and Chief Naval Representative, at Min. of Supply, 1948-50; Flag Officer (Germany) and Chief British Naval Representative of the C.C.G., March-Nov. 1950; Vice-Adm. retd., 1950. D.L. Inverness-shire, 1952; County Councillor, Inverness-shire, 1952; J.P. Inverness-shire, 1954. Member of Queen's Body Guard for Scotland (Royal Company of Archers); Hon. Air Comdr., No. 3510 (County of Inverness) Fighter Control Unit, R.A.A.F., 1954. A.F.R.Ae.S. *Address:* Moy Hall, Moy, Inverness-shire. *T.:* Tomatin 211. *Club:* United Service. [*Died* 20 *March* 1957.

MACKWORTH, Vice-Adm. Geoffrey, C.M.G. 1920; D.S.O. 1918; R.N. retd.; *b.* 1879; 5th *s.* of Sir A. W. Mackworth, 6th Bt., and Alice, *d.* of Joseph Cubitt, C.E.; *m.* 1910, Noel Mabel, *d.* of William T. Langford, of Charford Manor, Avonwick, S. Devon; one *s.* two *d.* Served European War, 1914-18 (D.S.O., despatches, promoted); Baltic, 1918-20 (C.M.G.); Captain of the Dockyard, Devonport, 1924-26; Rear-Adm. and retired list, 1930; Vice-Adm., retired 1935. *Address:* Broomhill, Ivybridge, Devon. *Clubs:* Junior United Service; Royal Western Yacht (Plymouth). [*Died* 4 *March* 1952.

See also Colonel Sir Harry Mackworth, Bt.

MACKWORTH, Colonel Sir Harry Llewellyn, 8th Bt., *cr.* 1776; C.M.G. 1918; D.S.O. 1900; late R.E.; Royal Corps of Signals; *b.* 17 Mar. 1878; 4th *s.* of late Sir A. W. Mackworth, 6th Bt., and Alice, *d.* of Joseph Cubitt, C.E.; *S.* brother 1948; *m.*

1913, Leonie, *o. d.* of late Prof. Franklin Peterson. *Educ.:* Royal Military Academy, Woolwich. Entered Army, 1898; served South Africa, 1899-1902 (despatches twice. Queen's medal 6 clasps, King's medal 2 clasps, D.S.O.); European War, Dardanelles, 1914-15 (despatches); Egypt, 1916-18 (despatches, Bt. Lt.-Col. C.M.G.); retired pay, 1927. *Heir: nephew* David Arthur Geoffrey, Commander, R.N. [*b.* 13 July 1912; *m.* 1941, Mary Alice, *d.* of Thomas Henry Grylls, 36 Great Ormond Street, W.C.; one *s.*]. *Address:* Cliffend, Studland, Dorset. [*Died* 18 *Nov.* 1952.

See also Vice-Adm. G. Mackworth.

MACKWORTH, Air Vice-Marshal Philip Herbert, C.B. 1949; C.B.E. 1942; D.F.C.; R.A.F. retd.; *b.* 22 Oct. 1897; *m.* 1921, June, 3rd *d.* of William and Florence Moss; two *s.* one *d.* *Educ.:* Uppingham. Joined Royal Naval Air Service, 1916; transferred Royal Air Force, 1918; specialised Navigation, 1921; Cape to Cairo Flight, 1926; second attempt non-stop flight to India, 1927; Staff College, Andover, 1927-1928; commanded 216 Squadron, Egypt, 1935-36; Air Training Scheme, Canada, No. 1 Command, 1940-42; A.O.C. 225 Group, India, 1942-44; Comdt. Empire Central Navigation School, 1944-45; S.A.S.O., Coastal Command, 1945-47; A.O.A., H.Q., Transport Command, 1947-50; retired, 1950. *Recreations:* sailing, ski-ing, tennis, squash, skating, etc. *Address:* 83 Bridge Lane, Golders Green, N.W.11. *T.:* Speedwell 7969. *Club:* R.A.F. Yacht (Hamble). [*Died* 30 *Aug.* 1958.

MACLACHLAN, Alan Bruce, C.B. 1934; B.A.; *b.* 29 May 1874; *s.* of John Morton and Eleanor Charlotte Maclachlan; *m.* 1905, Cissie Alice Callieu. *Educ.:* Merchant Taylors' School; St. John's College, Cambridge. Entered Local Govt. Board as First Division Clerk 1897; Private Secretary to Parliamentary Secretary L.G. Bd., 1903-5; Assistant Secretary, Ministry of Health, 1919-28; Principal Asst. Secretary, Ministry of Health, 1928-37. *Recreation:* motoring. *Address:* St. John's, Hove Park Road, Hove, Sussex. *T.:* Brighton 53885. *Club:* Sussex County Cricket (Hove). [*Died* 27 *Dec.* 1955.

MACLACHLAN, Admiral Crawford, C.B. 1918; *b.* 11 July 1867; *s.* of late George Maclachlan of Maclachlan. Served Egypt, 1882 (medal, bronze star); China, 1900 (China medal); Member of Admiralty Committee on Berthing Accommodation of H.M. Ships at Home Ports, 1910; Commanded H.M.S. King Edward VII and H.M.S. Royal Oak, Grand Fleet, 1914-19; Rear-Admiral, Reserve Fleet, Rosyth, 1920-21; Senior Naval Officer, Yangtse, 1921-23; Vice-Adm., 1925; retired list, 1926; Adm. retired, 1930; Officer Legion of Honour; Order of the Rising Sun. *Address:* Ladymead, South Ascot. *Club:* Naval and Military. [*Died* 21 *April* 1952.

McLACHLAN, Herbert, M.A., B.D., D.D., Litt.D.; Fellow of Royal Historical Society; *b.* 22 Aug. 1876; *s.* of John McLachlan of Newchurch-in-Rossendale; *m.* 1st, 1906, Mary, *d.* of John Taylor of Longsight, Manchester; one *s.*; 2nd, 1942, Jane McWilliam. *Educ.:* Higher Grade School, Bacup; Manchester University; Unitarian College, Manchester; Durning-Smith Scholar, 1901-3; Hibbert Scholar, 1905-6; B.A. (1st Division), 1902; B.A. (1st Class Honours in History), 1903; M.A. 1905; B.D. (with distinction), 1906; D.D. 1920; F.R.Hist.S. 1932; Litt.D. 1944; Unitarian Minister, Leeds, 1906-9; Bradford, 1909-1911; Tutor and Warden, Unitarian College, Manchester, 1911-21, Lecturer in Hellenistic Greek, Victoria Univ. of Manchester, 1915-46; Dean of Theol. Faculty, 1925-27; Prin., Unitarian Coll., Manchester, 1921-44; Examiner in Hellenistic Greek, Manchester Univ., 1915-46; sometime Examiner in New Testament and Ecclesiastical History for Dr. Williams' Scholarship, also for Leeds and Birmingham Univs. *Publications:* St. Luke, Evangelist and Historian, 1912; The New Testament in the Light of Modern Knowledge, 1914; The Unitarian Home Missionary College, its Foundation and Development, 1915; The Methodist Unitarian Movement, 1919; St. Luke, the Man and his Work, 1920; The Letters of Theophilus Lindsey, 1920; The Story of a Nonconformist Library, 1923; Register of Students, Unitarian College, Manchester, 1854-1929; Education under the Test Acts (1662-1820), 1931; Alexander Gordon: A Biography, 1932; The Bible To-day, 1932; The Unitarian Movement in the Religious Life of England, 1934; Records of a Family, 1800-1933, 1935; Liberal Christianity and Modern Criticism, 1936; The Widows' Fund Association (est. 1764), 1937; The Unitarian College Library, 1939; Religious Opinions of Milton, Locke and Newton, 1941; Warrington Academy (Chetham Society), 1943; Sir I. Newton Theological Manuscripts (Selected and Edited, with an Introduction), 1949; Essays and Addresses, 1950; Sketch of Life and Work of R. Travers Herford (1860-1950), 1951; articles in Trans. Unitarian Hist. Soc. etc. *Address:* 11 Sydenham Avenue, Liverpool 17. *T.:* Sefton Park 3045. [*Died* 21 *Feb.* 1958.

MACLACHLAN, Thomas Banks. *Educ.:* George Watson's College; Prof. Masson's English Literature Class at Edinburgh University. Entered Press as Reporter; then Sub-Editor Evening Dispatch; Editor Edinburgh Evening Dispatch, 1909-43; Editor Weekly Scotsman. *Address:* Applegrove, Grantown-on-Spey, Moray. [*Died* 14 *April* 1952.

MACLAGAN, Sir Edward Douglas, K.C.S.I., *cr.* 1921 (C.S.I. 1909); K.C.I.E., *cr.* 1913; M.A.; *b.* 25 Aug. 1864; *s.* of late General Maclagan, R.E.; *m.* 1906, Edith Morony, Lady of Grace, St. John of Jerusalem; two *d.* *Educ.:* Winchester; New College, Oxford. Entered I.C.S., 1885; Under-Secretary, Government of India, Revenue and Agricultural Department, 1892; Chief Secretary to Government, Punjab, 1906; Secretary to the Government of India, Revenue and Agricultural Department, 1910-14; Secretary to the Government of India, Education Department, 1915-18; Lt.-Gov. of the Punjab, 1919-21; Governor, 1921-24; President of Royal Asiatic Society, 1925-28 and 1931-34. *Publication:* The Jesuits and the Great Mogul, 1932. *Address:* 39 Egerton Terrace, S.W.3. *T.:* Kensington 4075. [*Died* 22 *Oct.* 1952.

MACLAGAN, Sir Eric Robert Dalrymple, K.C.V.O., *cr.* 1945; Kt., *cr.* 1933; C.B.E., 1919; Hon. LL.D. (Birmingham); Hon. D.Litt. (Oxford); *b.* London, 1879; *s.* of late William Dalrymple Maclagan, Archbishop of York, and Augusta Anne, *d.* of 6th Viscount Barrington; *m.* 1913, Helen Elizabeth (*d.* 1942), *d.* of late Hon. Frederick Lascelles; one *s.* (and one *s.* killed in action 1942). *Educ.:* Winchester; Christ Church, Oxford. Entered Victoria and Albert Museum, 1905; lent to Foreign Office, 1916, and later to Ministry of Information: head of Bureau in Paris, 1917; Controller for France, 1918; attached to Press Section, British Peace Delegation in Paris, 1919; Deputy Keeper, Department of Architecture and Sculpture, Victoria and Albert Museum, 1921-24; Director and Secretary, Victoria and Albert Museum, 1924-45. Rhind Lecturer (Soc. of Antiquaries of Scotland) Edinburgh, 1926; Charles Eliot Norton Prof., Harvard Univ., 1927-28; Lecturer in Fine Arts (Sculpture), Belfast Univ., 1932-33; Hermione Lecturer, Alexandra College, Dublin, 1934 and 1935; Ferens Lecturer, University College, Hull, 1935; Vice-President of the Society of Antiquaries, 1932-36; President of the Museums Association, 1935-36; Chairman, Fine Arts Cttee., British Council; Chairman, National Buildings Record; Chairman, Listed Buildings Committee, Ministry of Town and Country Planning;

Honorary Secretary of Dilettanti Society; a Guardian of the Shrine of Our Lady of Walsingham; F.S.A.; Honorary A.R.I.B.A.; Officer de l'Instruction Publique; Order of St. Sava. *Publications:* Catalogue of Italian Sculpture (with Margaret Longhurst), 1924; Italian Sculpture of the Renaissance, 1935; various Museum catalogues, and articles in Burlington Magazine, the Antiquaries Journal, and elsewhere. *Address:* 5 Ashburn Gardens, S.W.7. *T.:* Frobisher 2050. *Clubs:* Athenæum, Beefsteak. [*Died* 14 *Sept.* 1951.

MACLAGAN-WEDDERBURN; *see* Wedderburn.

McLAGLEN, Victor; film actor; *b.* London; *s.* of Bishop McLaglen, Gunnersbury; *m.* 1919; one *s.* one *d.*; *m.* 1943, Suzanne Brueggemann. Enlisted in Life Guards at age of 14; rose to rank of captain; Assistant Provost Marshal Advanced Base, Baghdad. Academy award winner in 1935 (Informer). *Publication:* Express to Hollywood, 1934. *Address:* The McLaglen Ranch, Clovis, California. [*Died* 7 *Nov.* 1959.

McLAREN, Sir Charles Northrup, K.C.B., *cr.* 1941; M.I.Mech.E.; M.I.P.E.; Dir.-Gen. Ordnance Factories, Min. of Supply, 1940-51, retd. 1951; *b.* 14 Oct. 1898; *e. s.* of D. D. McLaren; *m.* 1949, Mrs. J. H. Jason-Smith, Brighton. *Recreations:* golf, yachting. *Address:* 31 Becmead Avenue, S.W.16. *T.:* Streatham 8865. *Clubs:* Carlton, Savage. [*Died* 8 *June* 1955.

M'LAREN, Rev. Douglas; Canon Residentiary of Exeter since 1913; Chancellor since 1938; *b.* 30 Jan. 1866; 4th *s.* of John Wingate M'Laren, 69 Addison Road, W., and 4 Fenchurch Street, E.C.; *m.* 1892, Elizabeth Maud (*d.* 1953), *d.* of W. H. Hinton, St. Briavels and Newnham-on-Severn, Glos. *Educ.:* abroad; King's College, London; Oriel College, Oxford, and Cuddesdon Theological College; B.A. 1889; M.A. 1892. Ordained, 1890; Curate of Newnham-on-Severn, 1890-91; Micheldean, 1891-92; Lower Guiting, 1893-94; St. Philip and St. James, Leckhampton, 1894-1900; Rector of Gidleigh, 1900-2; Vicar of Sourton, 1902-7; Vicar of Salcombe Regis, 1907-13; Sheriff of Exeter, 1923; Select Preacher Oxford University, 1925-26, 1926-27; Examining Chaplain to Bishop of Exeter, 1920-50. *Recreation:* fly-fishing. *Address:* The Close, Exeter. *T.:* Exeter 2498. [*Died* 22 *Feb.* 1956.

McLAREN, Jack; author and broadcaster; *b.* Melbourne, Australia, 13 Oct. 1887; *e. s.* of Rev. John McLaren, Presbyterian clergyman; *m.* 1st, 1924, Mrs. Ada Moore (author of Which Hath Been, etc.), widowed daughter-in-law of Notley Moore, Chief Police Magistrate of Melbourne; 2nd, 1951, Dorothy Norris, Chelsea. *Educ.:* Scotch Coll., Melbourne. Travelled extensively, and lived in the South Sea Islands; was Specialist in charge of Publicity About the Empire section, Min. of Information, London. *Publications:* My Civilised Adventure; New Love for Old; The Marriage of Sandra; Stories of the South Seas; Stories of Fear; My First Voyage; The Devil of the Depths; Blood on the Deck; My Odyssey; My Crowded Solitude; Isle of Escape; Songs of a Fuzzy-Top; The Skipper of the Roaring Meg; Red Mountain; The Savagery of Margaret Nestor; White Witch; On the Fringe of the Law; The Oil Seekers; Feathers of Heaven; Fagaloa's Daughter; Spear-Eye; Talifa; The Money Stones; The Hidden Lagoon; Sun Man; A Diver Went Down; The Crystal Skull; Their Isle of Desire; Gentlemen of the Empire. Many of his books appear in French, Spanish, Swedish, German and other languages; contributor of short stories and articles to many English and U.S.A. journals. *Address:* c/o John Farquharson, 8 Halsey House, Red Lion Square, W.C.1. [*Died* 16 *May* 1954.

McLAREN, Sir John (Gilbert), Kt., *cr.* 1935; C.M.G. 1925; B.A. (Sydney); J.P.; *b.* Parramatta, N.S.W., 15 Oct. 1871; *s.* of late William Burness McLaren, Summer Hill, N.S.W.; *m.* 1st, 1904, Emily F. S. (*d.* 1941), *d.* of late Capt. G. M. Wynn, Petersham, N.S.W.; three *d.*; 2nd, 1949, Lucie Adela Nash, Mosman, N.S.W. *Educ.:* Sydney High School; Sydney Univ. Entered N. S. W. Public Service as clerk, Money Order Office and Government Savings Bank, 1888; transferred Commonwealth Public Service, 1901; Commonwealth Electoral Officer for N S.W., 1904; Assistant Secretary, Prime Minister's Department, 1919; Secretary, Home and Territories Department, 1921-28; Secretary, Prime Minister's Department and Department of External Affairs, Commonwealth of Australia, 1929-33; Official Secretary in London to Commonwealth of Australia, 1933-36; Member Canberra University College Council, 1930-1933; Member Canberra University Association Council, 1928-33; Member, Commonwealth Public Service Board, 1928; Member of Commission which re-distributed the boundaries of the Commonwealth Electorates in New South Wales in 1911-12; Acting High Commissioner for Australia Feb.-June, 1934; represented Australia at International Labour Conferences, 1933 and 1934, and before Permanent Mandates Commission, Geneva, 1933, 1934, 1935 and 1936. *Recreations:* reading and walking. *Address:* 60A Raglan St., Mosman, N.S.W. *Clubs:* Millions, National (Sydney). [*Died* 27 *July* 1958.

MACLAUGHLIN, Colonel Arthur Maunsell, C.B.E. 1919; M.B., B.Ch. stip. cond., 1897; Director, Bamgaon, Derby, Isa Bheel, Noyapara and Longai Valley Tea Companies, Limited, Assam; 7th *s.* of Rev. Alexander MacLaughlin, Doone, County Limerick; *m.* 1923, Gertrude, *d.* of Richard Algernon Fry, London; two *d.* *Educ.:* Trinity College, Dublin. Resident Surgeon, Steeven's Hospital, 1898-99; entered R.A.M.C., 1899; served Boer War, 1900-2 Queen's medal (and three clasps, King's medal and two clasps); European War, 1914-18 (despatches, C.B.E.); retired pay, 1923. *Address:* 38 Gloucester Walk, W.8 [*Died* 10 *March* 1954.

McLAURIN, Eng.-Rear-Adm. John, C.B. 1919. Joined R.N. 1886; served European War, 1914-19; Engineer Rear-Adm., 1922; retired list, 1922. *Address:* Winhill, Reading Road, Fleet, Hants. [*Died* 13 *March* 1955.

MACLAY, 1st Baron *cr.* 1922, of Glasgow; **Joseph Paton Maclay,** P.C. 1916; Bt., *cr.* 1914; LL.D.; J.P. Glasgow; shipowner; *b.* 6 Sept. 1857; *m.* 1889, Martha (*d.* 1929), *d.* of William Strang, Glasgow; three *s.* two *d.* (and two *s.* decd.). *Educ.:* Glasgow. Minister of Shipping, 1916-21 and Member of War Cabinet; Mem. Cttee. on National Expenditure, 1921; D.L. of the City of Glasgow and of Renfrewshire; was given freedom of City of Glasgow, 1922; was Assessor in Glasgow University Court, Member of Glasgow Town Council, Magistrate of the City of Glasgow, and Member of Clyde Trust; was Commissioner of Taxes for City of Glasgow; was Member of Royal Commission on Coal Supplies, Member of Committee on Property and Endowments (Church of Scotland), 1922, and Member of Committee of Enquiry on Reformatory and Industrial Schools in Scotland. President of Orphan Homes of Scotland. *Heir:* *s.* Hon. Sir Joseph Paton Maclay, K.B.E. *Address:* Duchal, Kilmacolm. *T.:* 22. *Club:* New (Glasgow). [*Died* 24 *April* 1951.

McLEAN, Major Sir Alan, Kt., *cr.* 1933; *b.* 5 July 1875; *e. s.* of late David McLean, of Littlewood Park, Alford, Aberdeenshire; *m.* 1920, Elizabeth Blodwen, *d.* of late Rev. J. Jones. *Educ.:* Harrow; Trinity College, Cambridge. M.A., 1905. Barrister-at-law, Lincoln's Inn, 1902. Served European War, 1914-19; Major, Inns of Court O.T.C.; Chairman of Lamson Industries, Ltd., and other companies; Council, National Rifle Association, 1912-35; contested Caerphilly, 1922; M.P. (C.) S.W. Norfolk, 1923-29 and 1931-35; landowner. D.L. Aberdeenshire; Aberdeen C.C., 1938-56; Convener of Aberdeenshire, 1950-55; Chairman, Aberdeenshire National Service Committee, 1939. *Address:* Littlewood Park, Alford, Aberdeenshire. *T.:* Kildrummy 229. *Clubs:* Bath; Royal Northern (Aberdeen). [*Died* 9 *May* 1959.

MACLEAN, Dr. Catherine Macdonald, M.A., D.Litt., F.R.S.L.; *d.* of Kenneth Alexander Maclean, schoolmaster and Catherine Macdonald. *Educ.:* Muir-of-Ord and Dingwall Acad.; Edinburgh Univ.; Cherwell Hall, Oxford; Univ. Coll., London. Lecturer in English: Edinburgh University, 1917-19; Bristol University, 1919-21; The University of Wales, 1921-37. *Publications:* Dorothy and William Wordsworth, 1927; Dorothy Wordsworth, The Early Years, 1932; Born Under Saturn, 1943; Seven for Cordelia, 1941; Three for Cordelia, 1943; Farewell to Tharrus, 1944; Hazlitt Painted by Himself, 1948; Mark Rutherford, A Biography of William Hale White, 1955; introductions to The Round Table and Characters of Shakespeare's Plays (Everyman's Library), 1957. Contribs. to Mod. Lang. Review, The Observer, Review of English Studies, Times Literary Supplement, John O' London's Weekly, Essays and Studies by Members of the English Association, Essays by Divers Hands, etc. *Recreations:* walking and gardening, and the study of psychology, animal and human. *Address:* 10 Melbourne Mansions, Queen's Club Gardens, W.14. [*Died* 9 *Jan.* 1960.

MACLEAN, Sir Ewen (John), Kt., *cr.* 1923; T.D.; LL.D. (Edin.); D.Sc. (Hon.); M.D. (Hon.) Melbourne University; M.D., C.M., F.R.C.P. (Lond.); F.A.C.S. (Hon.); F.R.C.O.G. (Senior Past Pres.); Vice-Pres. British Medical Assoc. (Pres., 1928-29); Vice-Pres. Cardiff Royal Infirmary, 1946; LL.D. (Wales) 1947; F.R.S. (Edin.); D.L., J.P.; Pres. R. Coll. of Obstetricians and Gynæcologists, 1935-38, Hon. Fellow 1947; Hon. Member Cardiff Medical Society, 1948; Consulting Gynæcologist, Royal Infirmary, and Llandough Hosp., Cardiff; Member Board of Governors, Cardiff Teaching Hospitals; Emeritus Professor of Obstetrics and Gynæcology, Welsh National School of Medicine; a representative of Univ. of Wales on Board of Governors of United Cardiff Hospitals; Lt.-Col. late R.A.M.C. (T.); Officer Commanding 3rd Western General Hospital; President, Welsh Association of Insurance Committees; Chairman, Cardiff Insurance Committee since 1912; 2nd *s.* of late John Maclean, Kilmoluag, Tiree and Mounthill, Carmarthen. *Educ.:* Haverfordwest and Carmarthen Grammar Schools; University of Edinburgh. Registrar 3rd Western General Hospital, 1908-1918; Brevet Lieut.-Col., R.A.M.C. (T.), King's Birthday Honours, 1918; Commanding Officer Eaton Hall-Officers Military Hospital, 1917-19; Chairman, Welsh Consultative Council; Inspector of Hospitals for Wales B.R.C.S. and Order of St. John Joint War Organisation; Hon. Member Liverpool Medical Institution. *Publications:* various contributions British Medical Journal, British Journal of Obstetrics and Gynæcology, etc., Tuberculous Infection of Female Genitalia, Encyclopædia of Midwifery and Diseases of Women, Oxford Medical Publications. *Address:* 12 Park Place, Cardiff. *Clubs:* Brooks's, Bath; Cardiff and County (Cardiff). [*Died* 13 *Oct.* 1953.

MacLEAN, Hugh, M.D. (Aber.), M.Sc. (Liverpool), D.Sc. (Lond.); *b.* 1879; *s.* of Hector Maclean; *m.* 1913, Ida Smedley (*d.* 1944); one *s.* one *d.* *Educ.:* Aberdeen, Berlin, and London Universities. Formerly Lecturer on Physiological Chemistry, University of Aberdeen; Senior Assistant, Biochemical Department, Lister Institute of Preventive Medicine; Professor of Chemical Pathology, University of London, St. Thomas's Hospital; Professor of Medicine, Univ. of London, and Director of the Medical Clinic, St. Thomas's Hospital; Hon. Consulting Physician to the Ministry of Pensions and to St. Thomas's Hospital. *Publications:* Lecithin and Allied Substances; Albuminuria and War Nephritis in British Troops in France; Modern Methods in the Diagnosis and Treatment of Renal Disease, 1924; Modern Views on Gastric Disease, 1928; Lecithin and Allied Substances, 1926; many papers in scientific journals. *Recreations:* fishing, shooting, golf. *Address:* Heathdown, The Ridge, Woldingham, Surrey. [*Died* 18 *Sept.* 1957.

MACLEAN, Lachlan (Frederick Copeland), C.B. 1948; O.B.E. 1921; K.St.J., 1954; *b.* 14 Dec. 1885; *s.* of Lachlan W. B. Maclean, sometime Assistant Accountant General, G.P.O., and Agnes Lucy, *d.* of Lieut.-Col. W. C. R. Judd; *m.* 1st, 1907, Margaret, *o. c.* of Rev. W. Ireland Gordon; one *s.* one *d.*; 2nd, 1938, Isabel, *d.* of William Kelley, Deputy Accountant-General, India Office, and *widow* of Owen Monk of the Foreign Office. *Educ.:* Merchant Taylors School (Mod. Lang. Exhib.); King's College, London. Called to Bar, Inner Temple, 1919; Deputy Divisional Food Commissioner, S. Wales, 1920; Asst. Dir. of Emergency Services, Min. of Food, 1920; transferred to Bd. of Trade, 1921; Head of marketing branch, Empire Marketing Bd., 1926; Asst. Dir. Food (Defence Plans) Dept., 1937; Asst. Sec. Min. of Food, 1939; Principal Asst. Sec., 1940; Under-Sec. Jan. 1946, and Director of Establishments Nov. 1946; Regional Food Officer for London, 1948-51. Adviser to Cttee. appointed by High Commissioner of New Zealand on marketing of N.Z. dairy produce, 1934; Chairman: Cocoa & Coffee Cttee., and Dried Fruits Cttee., London Food Council, 1944-45; Cocoa & Spices Cttee. and Tea Cttee., Combined Food Board, 1945-46; Cocoa and Tea Cttees., Internat. Emergency Food Council, 1946-47; Cocoa Cttee., F.A.O., 1948-49; Member London and S.E. Regional Board for Industry, 1948-51. Served 4th (Militia and Special Reserve) Bn. Manchester Regt. 1905-35. European War, Aug. 1914-Nov. 1919, attd. 2nd Bn. Manchester Regt. B.E.F., 1916, served on Staff in France and North Russia (despatches, Chevalier du Mérite Agricole (Fr.), 3rd Cl. Order of St. Vladimir with Crossed Swords, and of St. Anne (Russia)); War of 1939-45, L.D.V. and Home Guard from May 1940, Lieut.-Col. Comdg. 11th Bn. Denbighshire Home Guard from formation to disbandment. Liveryman Merchant Taylors' Company; Hon. Treas. Highland Soc. of London; Hon. Fellow Institute of Certificated Grocers. *Publications:* book reviews, and articles in service and technical publications. *Address:* The Point, Church Island, Staines, Middlesex. *T.:* Staines 2161. [*Died* 13 *Sept.* 1957.

MACLEAN, Neil, C.B.E. 1946; Organiser of the Scottish Co-operative Wholesale Society; *s.* of Neil Maclean, Mull; *m.* Laura, *e. d.* of George Archibald, Glasgow. M.P. (Lab.) Govan, Division of Glasgow, Dec. 1918-Feb. 1950; a Labour Whip, 1919-21 and 1922-23; Chairman Parliamentary Labour Party, 1945-46. *Address:* 759 Mosspark Drive, Glasgow, S.W.2. [*Died* 12 *Sept.* 1953.

MACLEAN, Very Rev. Norman, D.D.; Chaplain-in-Ordinary to the King; *b.* The Braes, Portree, 3 May 1869; *s.* of Kenneth Maclean, Schoolmaster, and Alexandrina Macdonald; *m.* 1st, 1895, Shina (*d.* 1927), *d.* of Rev. Donald Macaulay, Minister of Reay; four *d.*; 2nd, 1929, Hon. Iona Macdonald, *o. d.* of 6th Baron Macdonald *Educ.:* his father's school, Inverness; Universities of St. Andrews and Edinburgh. Ordained Minister of Waternish, 1892; Minister of Glengarry, 1897; of Colinton, 1903; of the Park Church, Glasgow, 1910; of St. Cuthbert's Parish, Edinburgh, 1915-37;

retired 1937; travelled in Africa in 1913; served as Chaplain in the War; visited U.S.A. and Canada in 1921; the Near East in 1923, and appointed convener of Committee to erect Memorial Hospice and Chapel in Jerusalem; in 1926 officiated in Melbourne for four months; Moderator of the General Assembly of the Church of Scotland, 1927; contributed series of articles, In Our Parish, to The Scotsman; Convener of Life and Work Committee of Church of Scotland, 1928; preached the opening sermon in the Cathedral of Geneva of the 11th Assembly of the League of Nations, 1930; Hon. Sheriff-Substitute of Inverness-shire at Portree, 1938; Chaplain of St. Andrew's Church, Jerusalem, 1939-40. *Publications:* Fiction: Dwellers-in-the-Mist; Hills of Home; The Burnt Offering; Biography: Life of James Cameron Lees, K.C.V.O., D.D.; Social Questions: The Great Discovery; Stand up, ye Dead; Victory out of Ruin; Religious: God and the Soldier; The Message of Bethlehem; The Future Life; Death Cannot Sever; How Shall we Escape ?; His Terrible Swift Sword; The Former Days, Autobiography; Set Free. *Recreations:* golf, fishing. *Address:* Portree House, Isle of Skye. *T.:* Portree 63. *Club:* University (Edinburgh). [*Died* 15 *Jan.* 1952.

McLEAY, Hon. George; Minister of State for Shipping and Transport and Associate Minister for Commerce and Agriculture, Commonwealth of Australia; Dep. Leader of the Government in the Senate; *b.* 6 Aug. 1892; *s.* of late George McLeay, Port Clinton, Yorke Peninsula, S. Australia, and Margaretta Barton; *m.* 1924, Marcia Doreen, *d.* of Mark Weston, Crystal Brook; one *s.* one *d.* *Educ.:* Port Clinton Public School; Muirden College. Founded McLeay Bros., Wholesale and Retail Merchants, 1916. *Political:* Senator, 1934-47; Chairman of the Senate Regulations and Ordinances Committee, 1937; Government Whip, 1937; Vice-President Federal Executive Council, 1938-1939; Acting Minister for Trade and Customs, 1939; Minister for Trade and Customs, 1940; Minister for Commerce, 1939-40; Postmaster-General and Minister of Repatriation, 1940-41; Minister of Supply, 1941; Leader of Opposition in the Senate, Oct. 1941; Life Member, Liberal and Country League Executive, Vice-President, for 10 years. *Recreations:* golf, lacrosse, cricket, tennis. *Address:* 3 Broadway, Glenelg, S. Australia; 87 Grenfell Street, Adelaide, S. Australia. *T.:* X 4740, LA2637. [*Died* 13 *Sept.* 1955.

MACLEAY, John Thomson; Editor, Liverpool Daily Post, 1924-47; *b.* 28 July 1870; *s.* of W. A. Macleay, Inverness; *m.* Agnes Stein, *d.* of James Philip; one *s.* one *d.* *Educ.:* Inverness Academy; Edinburgh University. *Address:* 4A Ivanhoe Road, Liverpool 17. *T.:* Lark Lane 1180. *Club:* University (Liverpool). [*Died* 5 *May* 1955.

M'LELLAN, Alex. Matheson, R.B.A., 1909; R.S.W., 1911; *b.* Greenock, 23 Jan. 1872; *s.* of Thomas M'Lellan, engineer; *m.* 1905, Grace (*d.* 1947), *d.* of Captain Robert Hildreth. *Educ.:* Stirling and Greenock. Studied in the schools of the Royal Academy, London, and the Atelier of Gerôme; practised in Paris, London, Manchester, and New York, eventually settling in Glasgow. *Principal Works:* Burghers of Bruges (Salon); Heretics (Salon); The Ancient Mariner (Salon); Guests of the Borgias (R.S.A.); Lances for Ladies (R.S.A.); Launch of the Great Michael; Albigenses (R.A.); full length portraits of Provost of Greenock (portrait destroyed by enemy action) and Provost of Stirling for Municipal Galleries; Active Member of the Ecclesiological Society of Scotland; has painted frescoes and stained glass windows, and executed relievos for altars and reredoses in various churches; in the service of the Admiralty during the war as an inspector of shell. *Recreations:* archæology, botany, and music. *Address:* South Lodge, Larkfield Road, Gourock, Renfrewshire. [*Died* 12 *March* 1957.

MACLENNAN, Alexander, M.B., C.M. (Glas.), L.M. (Dublin); retired; *b.* Glasgow, 23 April 1872; *y. s.* of late Simon MacLennan, silk merchant; *m.* Helen Adamson, 2nd *d.* of late Rev. Thomas Adamson, D.D., of Duncrevie, Glenfarg, Perthshire, and Balmangan, Kirkcudbright. *Educ.:* Glasgow High School. Graduated M.B., C.M., Glasgow University in 1894, with first-class honours, and the Brunton Memorial Prize, awarded to the most distinguished graduate of the year. Formerly Consulting Surgeon, Dunoon and District Hospital; Hon. Consulting Surgeon, Royal Hospital for Sick Children, Glasgow, Royal Infirmary, Stirling and Falkirk and District Infirmary; Member of Consultative Council on Medical and Allied Services. *Publication:* Surgical Materials and their Uses, 1915. *Address:* Ardbeg, Kilmun, Argyllshire. *T.:* Kilmun 5. [*Died* 31 *May* 1953.

MACLENNAN, Kenneth; *b.* 24 April 1872; *s.* of Thomas and Dolina Maclennan, Maryburgh, Ross-shire; *m.* Mary (*d.* 1929), *d.* of Duncan Maclennan, Lybster; no *c.* *Educ.:* Maryburgh School, Ross-shire; Edinburgh University. Solicitor, 1894; Joint Secretary, World Missionary Conference, 1910; General Secretary and Editor, United Council for Missionary Education (Edinburgh House Press), 1908-31; Ministry of Munitions, Director of Gun Contracts and Assistant Liquidator, 1916-19; Secretary, Conference of Missionary Societies in Great Britain and Ireland, 1919-37; Director, Commonwealth Trust, Ltd., since 1919; Chairman, London Missionary Society, 1936; Director, Religions Division, Ministry of Information, 1939-40. *Publications:* Cost of a New World, 1926; Twenty Years Missionary Co-operation, 1927; (joint) East and West: Conflict or Co-operation, 1936. *Address:* 11 Pentland Terr., Edinburgh 10. *T.:* Edinburgh 54960. [*Died* 28 *March* 1952.

MACLEOD, Allan, C.I.E. 1933; Indian Civil Service, retired; *b.* 19 March 1887. *Educ.:* Edinburgh Academy; Merton College, Oxford. Entered I.C.S. 1910. *Address:* The Wick Cottage, Dover Road, Branksome Park, Bournemouth. [*Died* 20 *Oct.* 1955.

McLEOD, Lieutenant-General Sir (Donald) Kenneth, K.C.I.E., *cr.* 1942; C.B. 1937; D.S.O. 1917; D.L.; *b.* 1885; *s.* of late General Sir Donald J. S. McLeod, K.C.B., K.C.I.E., D.S.O.; *m.* 1923, Phœbe Scott-Elliot Macdonald of Redcliffe, Isle of Skye, *d.* of late John Macdonald; one *s.* one *d.* *Educ.:* Wellington Coll.; R.M.C. Sandhurst. Served N.W. Frontier of India, 1908 (medal with clasp); European War, 1914-18 (wounded, despatches thrice, D.S.O.); Kurdistan, 1919 (medal with clasp); p.s.c. Camberley 1920; General Staff, War Office, 1921-22; and Staff Coll. Camberley, 1923-26; commanded Guides Cavalry, 1928-32; graduated Imperial Defence College, 1932; commanded 4th and 1st Cavalry Brigades, India, 1933-36; D.A. and Q.M.G. Northern Command, India, 1937; General Officer Commanding Army in Burma, 1938-41; Col., 1933; Maj.-Gen., 1936; Lt.-Gen., 1941; retired 1942; Comr. British Red Cross in S. Europe, 1944-45; Hon. Sheriff Substitute, 1942; D.L. Inverness-shire, 1955; K.St.J. *Address:* Stratton Lodge, by Inverness. *Clubs:* United Service, M.C.C., Royal Automobile. [*Died* 25 *Oct.* 1958.

MACLEOD, John MacLeod Hendrie, M.A., M.D. Aberd., F.R.C.P. London; late President British Association of Dermatology, and Derm. Sect., Royal Society of Medicine; Consultant Physician St. John's Hospital; Consultant Physician for Diseases of the Skin, Charing Cross Hospital, Hospital for Tropical Diseases and Victoria Hospital for

McLEISH, Donald Alexander Stewart, O.B.E., LL.D. See page xxix.

Children; late Editor British Journal of Dermatology; President, Clan MacLeod Society (Lond. Br.); *b.* 1870; *e. s.* of late John Balmain MacLeod, M.D., Dundee, and Catherine, *d.* of John Hendrie, Galston, Ayrshire; *m.* Eva, *d.* of late Joseph Ruston, Monks Manor, Lincoln, and 5 St. George's Place, London; one *s.* one *d.* *Educ.:* St. Andrews and Aberdeen Universities; Paris, Hamburg, and University of Vienna. *Publications:* Textbook on the Diseases of the Skin, 1933; Handbook on the Pathology of the Skin; Burns and their Treatment; articles on the Anatomy and Bacteriology of the Skin in the Encyclopædia Medica; article on the Diseases of the Nail in Quain's Dictionary of Medicine; Article on Skin Diseases, Encyclopædia Britannica; and a number of contributions to the literature on Skin Diseases in various current journals. *Recreations:* shooting, fishing, sailing, etc. *Address:* Pannells, Lower Bourne, Farnham. *T.:* Frensham 479. *Club:* Athenæum. [*Died* 10 *Dec.* 1954.

McLEOD, Lt.-Gen. Sir Kenneth; *see* McLeod, Lt.-Gen. Sir Donald K.

MACLEOD, Lieut.-Col. Norman, C.M.G. 1919; C.B.E. 1953; D.S.O. 1917; Officer of the Legion of Honour; D.L., J.P.; chartered accountant; *b.* 14 June 1872; *s.* of Rev. Donald Macleod, D.D. *Educ.:* Fettes College, Edinburgh. Served Queen's Own Cameron Highlanders, 1914-19 (wounded, gassed, despatches thrice); Gentleman of Queen's Body Guard for Scotland, Royal Company of Archers; ex-Lord Dean of Guild, Glasgow; Joint Hon. Treasurer Officers Association and Earl Haig Fund, Glasgow and South West Area; Pres. Night Asylum; joint author of the History of the 7th Battalion of the Q.O. Cameron Highlanders. *Address:* Benview, Kippen, Stirlingshire. *Clubs:* Western, Mudhook Yacht (Glasgow); New (Edinburgh). [*Died* 27 *Feb.* 1960.

McLINTOCK, Sir Thomson, 2nd Bt. *cr.* 1934; Chartered Accountant; *b.* 30 April 1905; *s.* of Sir William McLintock, 1st Bt., G.B.E., C.V.O.; *S.* father 1947; *m.* 1929, Jean, *d.* of R. T. D. Aitken, New Brunswick; two *s.* *Educ.:* Loretto, Musselburgh; Pembroke College, Cambridge. Practising as a Chartered Accountant under the style of Thomson McLintock, Chartered Accountant, Kenwood House, Hardinge Street, Nairobi, Kenya, B.E.A. *Heir:* *s.* William Traven [*b.* 4 Jan. 1931; *m.* 1952, Andrée Lonsdale-Hands]. *Address:* Box 1112, Nairobi. [*Died* 28 *Dec.* 1953.

McLINTOCK, William Francis Porter, C.B. 1951; D.Sc., F.R.S.E., F.G.S.; *b.* Edinburgh, 2 February 1887; *e. s.* of Peter Buchanan McLintock; *m.* 1939, Maude Alice, *widow* of James McLean Marshall. *Educ.:* George Heriot's School and University, Edinburgh. Assistant Curator, Museum of Practical Geology, 1907-11; in charge of Geological Dept., Royal Scottish Museum, Edinburgh, 1911-21; Curator, Museum of Practical Geology 1921-45; Deputy Director, Geological Survey of Great Britain and Museum of Practical Geology, 1937-45; Director, 1945-50. *Publications:* Papers on mineralogical, petrographical and geophysical subjects. *Recreations:* shooting, golf. *Address:* Firgrove, Rosemount, Blairgowrie, Perthshire. *Club:* Caledonian. [*Died* 21 *Feb.* 1960.

McLOUGHLIN, Edward Patrick, B.A., Hon. M.D., LL.D., B.Ch., B.A.O.; Emeritus Prof. of Anatomy, University College, Dublin. *Educ.:* Rockwell College; University College, Blackrock; Catholic University School of Medicine, Dublin, and St. Thomas's Hospital, London. *Address:* 16 Villiers Road, Rathgar, Dublin, Eire. [*Died* 11 *March* 1956.

MACMAHON, Cortlandt, M.A. (Oxon), Instructor for Speech Defects and Breathing Exercises at St. Bartholomew's Hospital, 1911-39, Governor of the Hospital since 1940; *m.* 1912, Hilda Mary, *d.* of late Dudley D. Pontifex; no *c.* *Educ.:* Dulwich Coll.; Merton Coll., Oxford. Studied affections of the voice and speech, chest and abdomen; devised treatment of Empyema and Visceroptosis; treated many cases of gunshot wounds of the chest in the War and cases of speech affection due to the War for Ministry of Pensions, 1918-26; was Instructor for Speech Defects at the Queen's Hospital, Sidcup, and at Lord Knutsford's Special Hospital for Officers at Palace Green. *Publications:* Articles on:—Gunshot Wounds of the Chest in Lancet and Prophylactic Breathing exercises for pulmonary tuberculosis in N.A.P.T. Bulletin; papers to medical journals on Empyema, Visceroptosis and Stammering, etc. *Recreations:* fishing, golf, shooting. *Address:* The Croft, Trebor Avenue, Farnham, Surrey. *Club:* Vincent's (Oxford). [*Died* 30 *July* 1954.

MACMAHON, Ella; novelist; *b.* Dublin; *o. d.* of late Rev. J. H. MacMahon, M.A., Chaplain to Lord-Lieutenant of Ireland, and Frances (*d.* 1898), *e. d.* of T. S. Snagge; unmarried. *Educ.:* home. Served in Government Departments, including War Trade Intelligence Dept., 191-19; has written much for various magazines and periodicals, as well as in the daily press, and particularly on historical and archæological subjects; also written and broadcast talks and short stories for the B.B.C.; granted Civil List Pension for Literary services. *Publications:* A New Note, 1894; A Modern Man, 1895; A Pitiful Passion, 1896; The Touchstone of Life, 1897; An Honourable Estate, 1898; Fortune's Yellow, 1900; Such as have Erred, 1902; Jemima, 1903; The Other Son, 1904; Oxendale, 1905; An Elderly Person, 1906; The Heart's Banishment, 1907; The Court of Conscience, 1908; Fancy O'Brien, 1909; The Straits of Poverty, 1911; The Divine Folly, 1913; The Job, 1914; A Rich Man's Table, 1916; John Fitzhenry, 1920; Mercy and Truth, 1923; Wind of Dawn, 1927; Irish Vignettes, 1928. *Recreations:* travelling, art, the drama, and classical music. *Address:* The Watersplash Hotel, Brockenhurst, Hants. *T.:* Brockenhurst 2344. [*Died* 10 *April* 1956.

MACMAHON, Rt. Hon. James, P.C. Ireland, 1920; *b.* Belfast, 20 Apr. 1865; *m.* 1892, May, *e. d.* of John Rochford, C.E., Kingstown, Co. Dublin; one *s.* two *d.* *Educ.:* Christian Brothers' School, Armagh; St. Patrick's College, Armagh; Blackrock College, Co. Dublin. Assistant Secretary P.O. Ireland, 1913; Secretary to P.O. in Ireland, 1916; Under-Secretary to Lord-Lieutenant of Ireland, 1918-22; Captain, Portmarnock Golf Club, 1918. President, Royal Dublin Society, 1948. *Address:* St. John's, Island Bridge, Dublin. *T.:* Dublin 78439. *Clubs:* Stephen's Green, Royal Irish Automobile (Dublin); Royal Irish Yacht (Kingstown). [*Died* 1 *May* 1954.

MacMANAWAY, Rev. James Godfrey, M.B.E. 1945; *b.* 22 April 1898; *y. surv. s.* of late Rt. Rev. James MacManaway, D.D., Bishop of Clogher, and late Sarah Thompson MacManaway, 3rd *d.* of Thomas Ringwood, Castle Pierce, Co. Kilkenny; *m.* 1926, Catherine Anne Swetenham (*d.* 1951), *o. d.* of late Sir Thomas Lecky, Greystone Hall, Limavady, Co. Derry. *Educ.:* Campbell College; Trinity College, Dublin. Served European War, 1914-18, in Cavalry and in R.A.F. Ordained Curate-assistant of Drumachose (Derry), 1923; Incumbent Christ Church, Londonderry, 1930; resigned 1947; M.P. City of Derry, N.I. Parliament, 1947-1951. Elected to House of Commons as M.P. (U.U.) West Belfast, 1950, but disqualified. Served War of 1939-45 (despatches): Chaplain to 12th Royal Lancers, Senior Chaplain 1st Armoured Div., and finally as Chaplain 10 Corps. *Recreations:* travelling, riding, reading, and interested in most field sports. *Address:* Greystone Hall, Limavady, Co. Derry, N. Ireland; Red

Roof, Londonderry. *T.:* Londonderry 3083. *Clubs:* Cavalry; Ulster (Belfast); Royal Ulster Yacht (Co. Down); Northern Counties (Londonderry). [*Died* 3 *Nov.* 1951.

MacMANUS, Seumas; author; *b.* Donegal; *m.* 1st, 1901, Ethna Carbery, the poetess (*d.* 1902); 2nd, 1911, Catalina Violante Páez, Venezuela; two *d.* *Educ.:* at a mountain school of Donegal; Teachers' Trg. Sch., Enniskillen. Became a schoolmaster; contributed verse and prose to jls.; visited America, 1898; subseq. contributed to leading American magazines; now lives in (and publishes in) America; visiting lecturer to leading Universities and Colleges of U.S. (Hon.) LL.D. Notre Dame Univ., Ind., 1917. *Publications:* Shuilers (poems), 1893; The Leadin' Road to Donegal, 1895; 'Twas in Dhroll Donegal, 1897; Humours of Donegal, 1898; Bend of the Road, 1898; Through the Turf Smoke, 1899; In Chimney Corners, 1899; The Bewitched Fiddle, 1900; Donegal Fairy Stories, 1900; Lad of the O'Friels, 1903; The Red Poocher, 1903; Hard-Hearted Man, 1903; Irish Nights, 1905; Ballads of a Country Boy, 1905; The Irish Position (pamphlet), 1905; Yourself and the Neighbors, 1914; Ireland's Case, 1915; Lo, and Behold Ye, 1919; Top o' the Mornin', 1920; The Story of the Irish Race, 1921; The Donegal Wonder Book, 1926; O Do You Remember, 1926; Bold Blades of Donegal, 1935; The Rocky Road to Dublin, 1938; Well o' the World's End, 1939; Dark Patrick, 1941; Heavy Hangs the Golden Grain, 1950; (jointly) We Sang for Ireland, 1950; Bold Heroes of Hungry Hill, 1951. *Plays:* The Woman of Seven Sorrows; The Hard-Hearted Man; Orange and Green; The Lad from Largymore; Rory Wins; Bong Tong come to Balrithery; Mrs. Connolly's Cashmere; Nabby Harren's Matching; Dinny O'Dowd; Father Peter's Miracle; The Rale True Doctor; The Bachelors of Braggy; The Girl from Glen Easky; The Perverted Bachelor; The Last Will of Larry McGarry; The Little Mistress of the Eskar Mór. *Recreations:* walking and reading. *Address:* 1105 Park Avenue, New York City, U.S.A. [*Died* 23 *Oct.* 1960.

McMASTER, Sir Fergus, Kt., *cr.* 1941; Chairman of Directors of Qantas Empire Airways, Ltd. and of Queensland and Northern Territory Aerial Service, Ltd.; Managing Director McMaster Bros., graziers and woolscourers; *b.* 3 May 1879; *m.* 1st, 1911, Edith May (*d.* 1913), *d.* of W. E. R. Scougall; one *d.*; 2nd, 1922, Edna, *d.* of Alfred Faulkner; three *s.* *Address:* Tamilu, Rees Avenue, Clayfield, Brisbane, Queensland, Australia. [*Died* 8 *Aug.* 1950.
[*But death not notified in time for inclusion in Who Was Who* 1941–1950, *first edn.*

McMASTER, Sir Frederick Duncan, Kt., *cr.* 1934; J.P.; Governing Director, F. D. McMaster Ltd., Dalkeith, Cassilis, N.S.W.; *b.* 9 July 1873; *s.* of Duncan McMaster and Christina Cox; *m.* 1901, Muriel Evelyn Clara Sherlock; (*s.* died of wounds received in Battle of El Alamein, 1942) one *d.* *Educ.:* Sydney Grammar School. Commissioner for Affidavits N.S.W.; Director and Trustee N.S.W. Lawn Tennis Ground Coy.; Hon. Life Member English Speaking Union; Hon. Member Royal Agricultural Soc. of England, 1943; Vice-President Council of Royal Agricultural Soc. N.S.W.; Vice-Pres. Royal Empire Society, N.S.W.; Vice-Patron Royal Automobile Club of Australia; Member N.S.W. State Committee of the Council for Scientific and Industrial Research; gave £20,000 to found the F. D. McMaster Animal Health Laboratory, Sydney University 1929; gave N.S.W. Government 500 Merino Rams (value £4,000) for necessitous Graziers 1930; gave 400 Merino Rams (value 4000 gns.) to N.S.W. Govt. for distribution amongst returned A.I.F. settled on the land, 1947. Provided a Field Station at Hinchinbrook, 20 miles from Sydney, for Council of Scientific and Industrial Research in connection with the F. D. McMaster Animal Health Laboratory 1932. *Recreations:* engineering, polo, tennis. *Address:* Dalkeith, Cassilis, New South Wales, Australia. *T.:* Cassilis 1. *Clubs:* Australian, Australian Jockey, Royal Automobile of Australia (Sydney). [*Died* 28 *Nov.* 1954.

M'MEANS, Lt.-Col. Hon. Lendrum, Q.C. (Can.) 1909; *b.* Brantford, Ont., 30 July 1859; *m.* 1884; three *s.* one *d.* *Educ.:* Brantford; Toronto. Called to Bar of Ontario, 1881; Manitoba Bar, 1882; called to the Senate of Canada, 1917; President Autofinance, Limited; M.P.P. South Winnipeg, 1910-14; Lt.-Col. C.E.F., Feb. 23, 1916; recruited the 221st Batt. C.E.F. *Recreations:* golf, motoring, shooting, fishing. *Clubs:* Manitoba, St. Charles Country (Winnipeg). [*Died* 13 *Sept.* 1941.
[*But death not notified in time for inclusion in Who Was Who* 1941–1950, *first edn.*

McMICHAEL, Robert Clark, Q.C.; partner, McMichael, Common, Howard, Cate, Ogilvy, & Bishop; *b.* Windsor, Quebec, 5 June 1878; *s.* of Thomas McMichael and Margaret Clark; *m.*; one *s.* *Educ.:* St. Francis College, Richmond; McGill University (B.C.L.). Read Law with Hall, Cross, Brown and Sharp; called to Bar of Quebec, 1901; post-graduate course in France, 1901-1902; practising from 1902. *Recreation:* golf. *Address:* 1760 Cedar Avenue, Montreal, Canada. *Clubs:* Montreal, Forest and Stream, Mount Royal, Mount Bruno Country (Montreal). [*Died* 6 *Feb.* 1957.

MACMILLAN, Baron (Life Peer), of Aberfeldy, *cr.* 1930; **Hugh Pattison Macmillan,** P.C. 1924; G.C.V.O., *cr.* 1937; K.C. 1912; Hon. R.A.; Hon. F.R.I.B.A.; Liberty Cross of King Haakon VII (Norway); a Lord of Appeal in Ordinary, 1930-39 and 1941-47; a Lord of Appeal since 1947; *b.* 20 Feb. 1873; *o. s.* of late Rev. Hugh Macmillan, D.D., LL.D., Greenock; *m.* 1901, Elizabeth Katharine Grace, *d.* of late W. J. Marshall, M.D., Greenock. *Educ.:* Edinburgh Univ. (M.A., with First Class Honours in Philosophy, 1893) and Glasgow Univ. (LL.B. 1896, Cunninghame Scholar); F.R.S.E.; F.S.A. (Scot.); Hon. LL.D. Edin., 1924; Glasgow, 1930; Birmingham, 1930; McGill, Montreal, 1930; Columbia, 1930; London, 1931; St. Andrews, 1932; Queen's, Kingston, 1933; Manchester, 1934; Dalhousie, 1938; Nottingham, 1949; Hon. D.C.L., Western Reserve, 1938; Durham, 1950. Advocate, Scottish Bar, 1897; Examiner in Law, Glasgow Univ., 1899-1904; Editor Juridical Review, 1900-7; Asst. Director of Intelligence, Min. of Information, 1918; Senior Legal Assessor, City of Edinburgh, 1920-24; Lord Advocate of Scotland (non-political), 1924; Standing Counsel, Convention of Royal Burghs, Scotland, 1923-1930; Standing Counsel for Dominion of Canada, 1928, and for Commonwealth of Australia, 1929; Minister of Information, 1939-1940; Honorary Bencher, Inner Temple, 1924; Hon. Member of Bars of Brazil and Uruguay; Chairman: Royal Commission on Lunacy and Mental Disorder, 1924; Court of Inquiry, Coal-Mining Industry Dispute, 1925; Cttee. on British Pharmacopœia, 1926; Home Office Cttee. on Street Offences, 1927; Treasury Cttee. on Finance and Industry, 1929; Cttee. on Income Tax Law Codification: appointed as a Court of Inquiry, Wool Industry Wages Dispute, 1930; formerly Pres. of Ibero-American Inst. of Gt. Britain; Chm.: of Board of Management of Roy. Com. for Exhib. of 1851; of Pilgrim Trust, Mem. of Carnegie Trust for Universities of Scotland; Chm. Hospital for Sick Children, Great Ormond Street, 1928-34; Independent Chairman, Shipbuilding Industry Conferences, 1928-30; Chairman of Royal Commission on Canadian Banking, 1933; President of the British Gas Federation, 1934-35; President of Stair Society and formerly of Scottish Text Society; Chairman of the Court, Univ. of London, 1929-43; Pres. of Commission Permanente de Conciliation between the Netherlands and Norway; appointed by French Govt. a Corr. Mem. of Cttee. on For. Legislation and Internat. Law, 1936; Chm. Lord Chancellor's Cttee. on Advanced Legal Studies, 1938; Pres. Soc. of Comparative Legislation; Chm. Political Honours Scrutiny Comm.; Trustee: British Museum (1933-49), National Library of Scotland and Soane Museum; King George's Jubilee Trust; Dir., United Services Trustee, 1939-44; Hon. Prof. of Law, Royal Acad., 1941; Member of Council of National Trust for Places of Historic Interest, 1941; President, Society for Promotion of Nature Reserves: 1943-47; Chm., Cttee, on Post-War Restitution of Art Treasures; Chm. Scottish Land Registration Cttee., 1948; Hon. Corr. Member, American Academy of Arts and Letters; Hon. Member Inst. of C.E. and Inst. of Municipal and County Engineers; Rede Lecturer, Cambridge, 1934; Maudsley Lecturer, 1934; Sidgwick Memorial Lecturer, Cambridge, 1935; Andrew Lang Lecturer, St. Andrews, 1948; Hon. Burgess of the City of Edinburgh, 1938; a Freeman of the City of London. *Publications*: Law and Other Things; numerous articles in periodical press. *Address:* Moon Hall, Ewhurst, Surrey. *T.:* Ewhurst 39. *Clubs*: Athenæum; New (Edinburgh). [*Died* 5 *Sept.* 1952.

MACMILLAN, Archibald Morven, C.I.E. 1925; late I.C.S.; *b.* 25 April 1880; *s.* of Archibald M. Macmillan, J.P., Roseneath, Dumbartonshire. *Educ.:* Glasgow High School; Glasgow Univ.; Christ Church, Oxford. Entered Bombay Civil Service, 1903; served as Assistant Collector, various districts; as Manager, Encumbered Estates in Sind; as Collector and District Magistrate, Ratnagiri, West Khandish, Surat, Ahmednagar, Poona: Belgaum officiating Commissioner of Excise; retired, 1935. *Address:* 2 Merchiston Gardens, Edinburgh. *T.:* Edinburgh 63021. [*Died* 1 *April* 1954.

MACMILLAN, Rt. Rev. Mgr. John, D.D., Ph.D.; Rector of Ven. English College, Rome, 1939-51; *b.* Buenos Aires, 1899; *s.* of Hugh J. Macmillan, Glengarnock, Ayrshire. *Educ.:* in Rosario; Catholic Institute, Liverpool; St. Edward's, Liverpool; Gregorian University, Rome. Taught Philosophy at Upholland College, 1930-39; Domestic Prelate to the Pope, 1939; served in H.M.S. Royal Sovereign, 1917-18. *Address:* Upholland College, Nr. Wigan, Lancs. [*Died* 9 *July* 1957.

MACMILLAN, Rt. Rev. John Victor, O.B.E. 1919; D.D. (Lambeth); *b.* 2 May 1877; *s.* of late Alexander Macmillan, publisher; *m.* 1906, Anne (*d.* 1944), *d.* of late Major-General Sir Frederick Maurice, K.C.B.; one *s.* one *d.* *Educ.:* Eton College; Magdalen Coll., Oxford; 2nd class Classical Moderations; 1st class Modern History. Deacon, 1903; Priest, 1904; Curate of Farnham, Surrey, 1903-04; Resident Chaplain to Archbishop of Canterbury, 1904-15; Hon. Chaplain, 1915-21; temp. C.F., 1915-16 and 1917-19; Vicar of Kew, Surrey, 1916-21; Archdeacon of Maidstone and Canon of Canterbury, 1921-34; Suffragan Bishop of Dover, 1927-34; Bishop of Guildford, 1934-49; retired, 1949. *Address:* Corner House, Crouch House Road, Edenbridge, Kent. [*Died* 15 *Aug.* 1956.

MACMILLAN, W. J. P., O.B.E. 1943; F.A.C.S.; F.R.C.S.(Can.); M.D.; C.M.; M.L.A.; late Prime Minister of Prince Edward Island, Provincial Treasurer, and Minister of Education and Public Health; *b.* 24 March 1881; *s.* of Joseph MacMillan and Mary L. Hogan; *m.* 1st, 1909, Mary Bernadette Macdonald; 2nd, 1922, Mary Letitia Roberts; three *s.* three *d.* *Educ.:* Kensington High School; Prince of Wales College; Charlottetown; McGill University, Montreal. Chief of Staff Charlottetown Hosp. and Red Cross Soc. (40 yrs.); Pres. P.E.I. Div., Can. Red Cross (11 yrs.); Exec. Mem. Can. Medical Assoc. (19 yrs.); Fellow Internal Coll. of Surgeons, 1948; Mem. Legislature of P.E.I. (28 yrs.). K.C.S.G. 1947. *Recreation:* fishing. *Address:* 205 Kent Street, Charlottetown, P.E. Island, Canada. *T.:* 520. *Club:* Rotary (Charlottetown). [*Died* 7 *Dec.* 1957.

McMORROUGH KAVANAGH, Col. Sir Dermot, G.C.V.O., *cr.* 1953 (K.C.V.O. *cr.* 1946; C.V.O. 1943); *b.* 9 January 1890; 2nd *s.* of late Rt. Hon. Walter McMorrough Kavanagh, P.C., M.P., D.L., Borris, Co. Carlow; *m.* 1920, Gaynor Phoebe Claude, *d.* of late Claude Baggallay, K.C.; one *d.* *Educ.:* Eton. Joined 11th Hussars (P.A.O.), 1909; served European War, 1914-18, France and Palestine (despatches); Asst. Mil. Sec. Eastern Command, 1926-30; Lt.-Col. 1932; commanded 11th Hussars (P.A.O.), 1932-36; Col. 1939; served in France, 1940; Equerry to George VI., 1937-41; Crown Equerry, 1941-55; Extra-Equerry to the Queen, 1957. *Address:* c/o Barclays Bank Ltd., 1 Pall Mall East, S.W.1. *Clubs:* Cavalry, Buck's. [*Died* 27 *May* 1958.

M'MULLEN, William Halliburton, O.B.E. 1918; M.B., B.S. (Lond.); F.R.C.S. (England); Consulting Ophthalmic Surgeon to Charing Cross Hosp.; Consulting Surgeon to The Moorfields, Westminster and Central Eye Hosp.; Consulting Ophthalmic Surgeon to the Miller General Hospital for S. E. London; Fellow of the Royal Society of Medicine (Past President of Section of Ophthalmology); late Vice-President of the Ophthalmological Society of Great Britain; *b.* London, 19 June 1876; *s.* of late Wm. M'Mullen, medical practitioner; *m.* 1906, Kate Constance, *d.* of G. Randell Higgins, J.P., of The Croft, Burcote, Oxon; three *s.* *Educ.:* City of London School, Herne House, Margate; King's College, London, and King's College Hospital. Ophthalmic Specialist to Central London Recruiting Depot, 1916-18; Ophthalmic Surgeon to Hospital for Sick Children, Great Ormond Street, 1912-20; Ophthalmic Surgeon to the Royal Northern Hospital, 1919-23. *Publications:* Migraine from the Ophthalmic Standpoint, Brit. Med. Journ., 1926; Post-operative Distress in Cases of Senile Cataract, Brit. Journal of Ophthalmology, 1936; and contributions to The Lancet, Trans. Ophthal. Soc., etc. *Address:* 30A Wimpole St., W.1. *T.:* Welbeck 6731. [*Died* 15 *April* 1958.

MACMUNN, Lt.-Gen. Sir George Fletcher, K.C.B., *cr.* 1917 (C.B. 1916); K.C.S.I., *cr.* 1919 (C.S.I. 1918); D.S.O. 1893; Warden of Sackville Coll., East Grinstead; *b.* Chelsea, 14 Aug. 1869; *e. s.* of J. A. MacMunn, M.D., and Charlotte Edith, *d.* of Rev. George Mathias; *m.* 1st, 1893, Alice Emily (*d.* 1934), *e. d.* of Col. J. R. Watson, I.S.C.; one *s.* one *d.*; 2nd, 1937, Kathleen, *d.* of late F. C. Woods, Ceylon. *Educ.:* Kensington School. Gold and Silver Medallist R.A. Institution. Joined R.A. 1888; Gold Medallist United Service Institution, India, 1904; p.s.c., 1903; served in Upper Burma on Irrawaddy column, 1892 (wounded, despatches; D.S.O. medal and clasp); Sima column, 1893 (clasp); Kohat Field Force, 1897 (medal and clasp); Tirah Expedition, 1897-98; in command of Imperial Service mountain battery (2 clasps); served South Africa with Artillery and on Staff, 1899-1902 (slightly wounded, despatches twice, brevet majority, Queen's medal and three clasps, King's medal); European War, 1914-19, Dardanelles, Mesopotamia (Bt. Col., despatches twelve times, prom. Maj.-Gen., C.B., K.C.B., C.S.I., K.C.S.I., Officer of Legion of Honour); Commander-in-Chief, Mesopotamia, April 1919-Jan. 1920; Q.M.G. in India, 1920-24; retired pay, 1925; Col. Commandant, R.A., 1927-39; Comr. The Royal Hospital, Chelsea, 1932-38; Home Guard, 1940-42. *Publications:* The Armies of India, 1911; Pike and Carronade, 1912; A Free Lance in Kashmir, 1915; The Official History of the World War, Egypt, 1914-17, 1928; Afghanistan, from Darius to Amanullah, 1929; Behind the Scenes in Many Wars,

1930; The Army (Life and Work Series), 1929; Gustavus Adolphus, 1930; The King's Pawns (War Stories), 1930; The Indian Mutiny in Perspective, 1931; The Religions and Hidden Cults of India, 1931; The Romance of the Indian Frontiers, 1931; Vignettes from the Indian Wars, 1932; The Underworld of India, 1932; Kipling's Women, 1933; Martial Races of India, 1933; Black Velvet, 1934; Prince Eugene, 1934; The Living India, 1934; Azizun the Dancer, 1934; Turmoil and Tragedy in India, 1914 and after, 1935; The Crimea in Perspective, 1935; Indian State and Princes, 1936; Rudyard Kipling, Craftsman, 1937; Slavery thro' the Ages, 1938; American War of Independence in Perspective, 1939; Always into Battle, 1952. *Address:* c/o Lloyds Bank, 6 Pall Mall, S.W.1. [*Died* 23 *Aug.* 1952.

MACMURCHY, Helen, C.B.E. 1934; M.D.; *b.* Toronto, 7 Jan. 1862; *d.* of Archibald MacMurchy, Argyle, and Marjory Ramsay, Linlithgow. *Educ.:* Toronto. Chief of the Division of Child Welfare, Department of National Health, Ottawa, 1920-33. *Publications:* The Almosts, 1920; The Canadian Mother's Book, 1921; Sterilization? Birth Control? A book for Family Welfare and Safety, 1934; many reports and pamphlets. *Address:* 122 South Drive, Toronto, Canada. *T.:* Midway 6313 *Clubs:* Canadian, University Women's (Toronto) [*Died* 8 *Oct.* 1953.

MACNAGHTEN, Hon. Sir Francis Alexander, 8th Bt., *cr.* 1836; 2nd *s.* of Baron Macnaghten, P.C., G.C.B., G.C.M.G., 4th Bt. and Frances Arabella, *d.* of Rt. Hon. Sir Samuel Martin of Crindle, Co. Londonderry; *b.* 18 May 1863; *m.* 1905, Beatrice, *d.* of late Sir William Ritchie, Chief Justice of the Supreme Court of Canada; *S.* nephew, 1916. *Heir: b.* Hon. Frederic Fergus Macnaghten (*see* Hon. Sir Frederic Fergus Macnaghten). *Address:* Dundarave, Bushmills, Co. Antrim. [*Died* 1 *Nov.* 1951.

MACNAGHTEN, Hon. Sir Frederic Fergus, 9th Bt., *cr.* 1836; Chief of the Clan Macnaghten; *b.* 19 May 1867; 3rd *s.* of Baron Macnaghten, P.C., G.C.B., G.C.M.G., 4th Bt. and Frances Arabella, *d.* of Rt. Hon. Sir Samuel Martin, Crindle, Co. Londonderry; *S.* brother (Hon. Sir Francis Alexander Macnaghten, *q.v.*) 1951; *m.* 1914, Ada, *d.* of late John Webster. *Educ.:* Eton College; Trinity College, Cambridge. Admitted solicitor, 1891. *Recreation:* fishing. *Heir: n.* Antony [*b.* 15 Nov. 1899; *m.* 1926, Magdalene, *e. d.* of late Edmund Fisher; three *s.* one *d.* *Educ.:* Eton; Trinity College, Cambridge]. *Address:* Mortimer House, Egerton Gardens, S.W.3. *T.:* Knightsbridge 1060. *Clubs:* St. James', Beefsteak. [*Died* 18 *Nov.* 1955.

MACNAGHTEN, Rt. Hon. Sir Malcolm (Martin), P.C. 1948; K.B.E., *cr.* 1920; Commissary of the University of Cambridge since 1926; 4th *s.* of Baron Macnaghten, P.C., G.C.B., G.C.M.G., 4th Bt.; *b.* 1869; *m.* 1899, Antonia Mary (*d.* 1952), *d.* of late Rt. Hon. Charles Booth; one *s.* three *d.* *Educ.:* Eton; Trinity College, Cambridge, Major Scholarship, 1890; B.A. (1st class Historical Tripos), 1891; Pres. of the Cambridge Union, 1890. Barrister, Lincoln's Inn, 1894; Bencher, 1915; K.C. 1919; Recorder of Colchester, 1924-28; M.P. North Derry, June 1922, and Nov. 1922-28, for the City and County of Londonderry (Ulster Unionist); Judge of the High Court of Justice, King's Bench Division, 1928-47. *Address:* 69 Campden Hill Court, W.8. *T.:* Western 5200; The End House, Portballantrae, Co. Antrim, Ulster. *T.:* Bushmills 213. *Club:* United University. [*Died* 24 *Jan.* 1955.

See also Hon. Sir F. A. and Hon. Sir F. F. Macnaghten.

MACNAGHTEN, Steuart; Director, late Manager and Actuary, Standard Life Assurance Co.; *b.* 7 July 1873; *s.* of late Capt. Elliot Henry Macnaghten, late 20th Hussars; unmarried. *Educ.:* Privately; Royal Military Academy, Woolwich. President of The Faculty of Actuaries, 1930-32; Chairman of The Associated Scottish Life Offices, 1926-27; Chairman, Scottish Actuaries Club, 1933-34; Member of Government Committee of Enquiry to examine and report on the law and practice relating to Industrial Assurance. *Recreations:* golf and tennis. *Address:* 4 Henderland Road, Murrayfield, Edinburgh. *T.:* Edinburgh 61566. *Club:* University (Edinburgh). [*Died* 9 *Dec.* 1952.

MACNAIR, Sir Robert Hill, Kt., *cr.* 1932; *b.* 3 Dec. 1877; *er. s.* of Alexander Hill Macnair, M.I.C.E.; *m.* 1918 Marion Aitken, *d.* of James Wylie, M. D., Glasgow; no *c.* *Educ.:* George Watson's College, Edinburgh; Edinburgh University. Barrister Middle Temple, 1921. Indian Civil Service, 1899; Central Provinces Commission, 1900; Judicial Commissioner, 1932-35; retired, 1935. *Address:* Culgrianach, St. Andrews. *T.:* 644. *Club:* Royal and Ancient (St. Andrews). [*Died* 17 *Aug.* 1959.

McNALLY, Most Rev. John Thomas; Archbishop of Halifax (R.C.), since 1937; *b.* 1871. *Educ.:* Prince of Wales College, Charlottetown, P.E.I.; Ottawa University; Canadian College, Rome. Priest, 1896; Bishop of Calgary, 1913-24; Bishop of Hamilton, 1924-37. *Address:* Archbishop's House, Halifax, Nova Scotia. [*Died Nov.* 1952.

McNALTY, Brig.-Gen. Arthur George Preston, C.M.G. 1916; C.B.E. 1919; *b.* 6 June 1871; *s.* of late Lt.-Col. George William McNalty, C.B.; *m.* 1905, Margaret Maud (whom he divorced, 1921), *o. c.* of late Harry De Windt; (one *s.* killed in action, 1944) one *d.* Served S. African War, 1899-1902 (King's and Queen's medals 5 clasps, despatches); D.A.A. and Q.M.G. Army of Occupation in Egypt, 1911-14; European War (Egypt, Dardanelles and France), 1914-19 (wounded, despatches six times, Bt. Lt.-Col., C.M.G., C.B.E.); Director-General Graves Registration and Enquiries, France, 1919-20; retired pay, 1920. *Address:* Penruddock, Wood Lane, Iver Heath, Bucks. *T.:* Iver 195. *Club:* United Service. [*Died* 2 *Sept.* 1958.

McNAMARA, George, C.B.E. 1932; J.P.; *b.* Invercargill, 1881; *s.* of J. J. McNamara, farmer; *m.* 1908, Tess G., *d.* of late J. J. Connor, journalist; no *c.* *Educ.:* Park School, Invercargill; private tutor. Joined Post Office, 1896; Superintendent Staff, 1916; Assistant Secretary, 1920; Secretary and Director-General, Posts and Telegraphs, New Zealand, 1926-39; Controller of Censorship, N.Z., 1939-1945; Registrar Motor Vehicles, New Zealand; Director Signal Services, New Zealand Corps Signals, rank Colonel, 1927-39. N.Z. delegate International Postal Congress, London, 1929, Cairo, 1934, Imperial Congress, 1937. *Address:* Woburn, Lower Hutt, New Zealand. [*Died* 11 *Jan.* 1953.

MACNAMARA, Rear-Admiral Sir Patrick, K.B.E., *cr.* 1946 (C.B.E. 1938); C.B. 1940; retired; *b.* 11 Jan. 1886; *y. s.* of N. C. Macnamara, F.R.C.S.; *m.* 1921, Ellen Floyd Nickerson, Boston, Mass., U.S.A.; one *s.* two *d.* *Educ.:* H.M.S. Britannia; R.N. Staff College; Imperial Defence College. Served European War, H.M.S. King Edward VII, H.M.S. Tiger; Paris Peace Conference, 1919; Assistant Director of Plans, Admiralty, 1926; Captain and Chief of Staff H.M.S. Effingham, East Indies, 1928; Imperial Defence College, 1930; Naval Attaché to U.S.A., 1931; Flag Captain H.M.S. Nelson, 1933; Chief of Staff, Plymouth, 1934. "A" license Air Pilot. War of 1939-45, served Admiralty. Chief of Staff Nore, Rear-Admiral Scapa, Admiral Superintendent Orkney. Chevalier Légion d'Honneur, France, 1916; Order of Sacred Treasure, 2nd class, Japan, 1922. *Recreations:* fishing, shooting, golf, chess. *Address:* Invercharron House, Ardgay, Ross-shire, Scotland. *T.:* Ardgay 274. *Club:* United Service. [*Died* 4 *April* 1957.

McNAUGHT, William; Editor, Musical Times, since 1944; *b.* 1 Sept. 1883; *s.* of W. G. McNaught, D.Mus., and Clara Waller. *Educ.:* University College School, London; Worcester College, Oxford (B.A.). Music Critic: Morning Post, 1908-26; Evening News, 1933-40. *Publication:* Modern Music and Musicians, 1937. *Address:* 26 Cleveland Gardens, W.2. *T.:* Paddington 8926. *Club:* Alpine. [*Died* 9 *June* 1953.

McNAUGHTON, Brig. Forbes Lankester, C.B.E. 1945; D.S.O. 1918; R.A.; *y. s.* of late D. Norman McNaughton; *b.* 1891; *m.* 1st, 1919, Betty, *d.* of late Rev. Arnold Pinchard, M.B.E.; two *s.*; 2nd, 1938, Dorothy Violet, *d.* of late Frederick Stevenson. *Educ.:* Loretto; R.M.A., Woolwich. Served European War, 1914-18 (wounded, despatches, D.S.O.); Adjt. Honourable Artillery Company, 1920-1923; Assist. Proof and Experimental Officer, Research Department, Royal Arsenal, 1926-29; Assistant Superintendent, Research Dept., Woolwich, 1929-30; Assistant Superintendent, Design Department, 1931-35; Senior Instructor Military College of Science, 1936-38; Chief Instructor Military College of Science, 1938-41; Commandant Military College of Science, 1941; retired pay, 1945; p.a.c. *Address:* Weavers, Lodsworth, Sussex. *T.:* Lodsworth 265. *Club:* Army and Navy. [*Died* 21 *Aug.* 1959.

McNEIL, Rt. Hon. Hector, P.C. 1946; M.P. (Lab.) for Burgh of Greenock since 1941; Member B.B.C. Gen. Advisory Council, 1952; *b.* 1907; *m.* 1939, Sheila, *y. d.* of Dr. James Craig; one *s.* *Educ.:* Woodside School, Glasgow; Glasgow University. Journalist; magistrate of Glasgow and served on Corporation of Glasgow, 1932-1938; opposed Walter Elliot, Kelvingrove, 1935, and Malcolm MacDonald, Ross and Cromarty, 1936; Parliamentary Private Secretary to P. J. Noel Baker, Parliamentary Secretary to Ministry of War Transport, 1942-45; Parliamentary Under-Secretary of State, Foreign Office, 1945-46; Minister of State, 1946-50. Secretary of State for Scotland, 1950-51, and member of Cabinet. Vice-President, United Nations Assembly, 1947; Leader of Delegation to Economic Commission for Europe, 1948. *Address:* 64 St. John's Wood Court, N.W.8. *Club:* Savage. [*Died* 11 *Oct.* 1955.

McNEIL, Eng. Rear-Adm. Percival Edwin, C.B. 1936; R.A.N. (retd.); *b.* 25 Sept. 1883; *s.* of late John McNeil, Melbourne; *m.* 1912, Emily Jean, *d.* of Thomas Leslie; one *s.* two *d.* *Educ.:* privately. Entered R.A.N., 1911; Eng. Comdr. 1918; Eng. Capt. 1926; Eng. Rear-Adm. 1934; Director of Engineering, R.A.N., 1931-40; 3rd Naval Member and Chief of Naval Construction, Aust. Naval Board, 1940-43; retired, 1943, Director of Merchant Shipbuilding, Australia, 1943-48. *Address:* 169 Orrong Road, Toorak, Victoria, Australia. *Club:* United Service (Brisbane). [*Died* 17 *April* 1951.

McNEILL, Sir Hector, Kt., *cr.* 1946; LL.D. (Glasgow) 1948; Hon. F.E.I.S. 1947; *b.* 31 Jan. 1892; *m.* 1927, Grace Stephen Robertson; two *s.* *Educ.:* Glasgow. First elected to Corporation, 1924, served till 1930; re-elected 1932; Lord Provost of Glasgow, 1945-49. Deputy District Commissioner for Civil Defence for Glasgow and the West of Scotland, 1941-45; Regional Port Director for Scotland, 1945-46. Chm. Glenrothes Development Corp., 1948; Member: Scottish Council (Development and Industry); Scottish Tourist Board; Docks and Inland Waterways Executive; Government Director David MacBrayne Ltd. D.L. of County of City of Glasgow, 1949. *Address:* Sanda, Larchfield Avenue, Newton Mearns, Renfrewshire. *T.:* Newton Mearns 2743. [*Died* 28 *Sept.* 1952.

MACNEILL, Murray; Professor of Mathematics, Dalhousie University, Halifax, N.S., 1907-42; Civil Service Commissioner, Nova Scotia, 1935-44; *b.* Maitland, N.S., 9 Jan. 1877; *s.* of Rev. L. G. Macneill, D.D.; *m.* Kathleen, *d.* of Hon. S. H. Holmes, Halifax; three *d.* *Educ.:* Pictou Academy; Dalhousie and Cornell Universities; Harvard University; Sorbonne, Paris. Assistant Professor McGill University, Montreal, 1902-1907. LL.D. Dalhousie Univ. *Publications:* articles on mathematics. *Address:* 102 Young Avenue, Halifax, N.S. *Clubs:* (vice-pres.) Royal Caledonian Curling Club of Scotland; Studley Quoit Club. [*Died* 16 *Feb.* 1951.

McNEILL, Robert Norman; an Assistant-Chief Clerk in the Supreme Court of Justice, Northern Ireland, since 1935; *m.* 1920, Helen Marjorie Calwell, M.B.; one *s.* one *d.* *Educ.:* Royal Academical Institution, Belfast; Queen's University, Belfast. Called to Irish Bar, 1913; Member of the Circuit of Northern Ireland. Served K.O.S. Borderers, 2nd Batt., 1915-19; Law Lecturer in Queen's University of Belfast since 1926; Commissioner of County Fermanagh for Government of Northern Ireland, 1922-1924; Junior Crown Prosecutor for Derry City and County; M.P. (Ind. Unionist), Queen's University of Belfast, Northern Ireland, 1929-1935. *Recreation:* walking. *Address:* Kilninver, Glenkeen Avenue, Jordanstown, Co. Antrim, Northern Ireland. *T.:* Whiteabbey 3195. [*Died* 28 *May* 1956.

McNEILL-MOSS, Major Geoffrey, (Geoffrey Moss); *s.* of Capt. Gilbert Moss, 7th Fusiliers; *m.* Hon. Esther Rose McNeill, *e. d.* of Lord Cushendun. *Educ.:* Rugby; R.M.C. Sandhurst. Gazetted 2nd Lieut. in Brigade of Guards, and served, 1905-19; retired with rank of Major; commanded a Bn. of the Gordon Highlanders in France, 1915; expert on Central European Affairs, and writer, since 1923. *Publications:* short stories: Defeat; The Three Cousins; Wet Afternoon; Standing up to Hitler; novels: Sweet Pepper; I Face the Stars, 1933, etc; satyric novel: Little Green Apples; modern history: The Epic of the Alcazar, 1937. Plays: Sweet Pepper; The Siege. *Recreations:* yachting, continental travel, European history, canoeing, and before the war, motor racing. *Address:* Drominagh House, Borrisokane, Co. Tipperary; Le Brouix, Ramatuelle, Var, France. *Clubs:* Boodle's; Royal Albert Yacht (Southsea). [*Died* 13 *Aug.* 1954.

MACNICOL, Nicol, M.A., D.Litt., D.D.; retired Missionary of the Church of Scotland; Wilde Lecturer in Natural and Comparative Religion in the University of Oxford, 1932-35; *b.* 26 Feb. 1870; *s.* of Rev. Duncan Macnicol and Margaret Clark; *m.* Margaret G. C. Brodie, L.R.C.P.S.E.; two *d.* *Educ.:* High School of Glasgow; Glasgow University. Missionary of the Church of Scotland at Bombay, 1895-1901; Poona, 1901-31; Secretary of the National Christian Council of India, Burma, and Ceylon, 1926-29; travelled throughout India, 1930-31 as a member of the Commission on Christian Higher Education in India, appointed by the International Missionary Council to inquire into the place of the Christian College in Modern India. *Publications:* The Religion of Jesus; Indian Theism from the Vedic to the Muhammadan Period; Psalms of Maratha Saints; The Making of Modern India; Pandita Ramabai (Builders of Modern India); Tom Dobson: a Champion of the Outcastes; India in the Dark Wood; What Jesus means for Men; The Living Religions of the Indian People, 1934; Is Christianity Unique? A Comparative Study of the Religions, 1936; C. F. Andrews, Friend of India, (Modern Christian Revolutionaries), 1945; two chapters in The Christian Task in India; one chapter in The Times' special India Number (reprint); joint author of Report of Commission on Christian Higher Education in India; editor of Hindu Scriptures) Everyman's Library), 1938. *Address:* 28 Millar Cres., Edinburgh, 10. [*Died* 13 *Feb.* 1952.

MACNUTT, Ernest Augustus, C.B.E. 1943; LL.D.; Director: Sun Life Assurance Co. of Canada; Consolidated Paper Corporation; *b.* 1876; *s.* of George Augustus Macnutt, M.D., and Isabel Ridge; *m.* 1903, Sophia Ewing Easter (*decd.*); two *s.* one *d.* *Educ.:* St. Edmund's College, London, England; Caulfield Grammar School, Melbourne. For some years in business in London, Paris, and on the Continent; with Royal Bank of Canada, 1899-1904; Sun Life Assurance Co. of Canada since 1904. Asst. Director, Imperial Munitions Board (Canada), 1915-16; Joint Chairman Victory Loan Committee (Que.), 1917-18; Joint Chairman National War Finance Committee (Quebec Division), 1941-45; Member: Committee Canadian Save the Children Fund; Executive Cttee. Canadian Red Cross Soc., Quebec Div.; Cttee. Protestant Employment Bureau. *Recreation:* golf. *Address:* C33, 3940 Cote des Neiges Rd., Montreal; Sun Life Building, Montreal, Que. *T.:* Fitzroy 2976. *Clubs:* St. James's, Royal Montreal Golf (Montreal). [*Died* 10 *May* 1955.

McPHEE, Hon. Sir John Cameron, K.C.M.G., *cr.* 1934; *b.* Yan Yean, Victoria, 4 July 1878; *s.* of Donald McPhee, farmer, and Elizabeth McLaughlin; *m.* 1911, Alice B. Dean, two *s.* five *d.* *Educ.:* State and private Schools, Victoria. Started life as farmer; later printer and reporter; Principal, Remington Business College, Hobart, 12 years; member House of Assembly, Tasmania, 1919-34; Chief Secretary of Tasmania, 1922-23; Premier and Treasurer of Tasmania, 1928-34; at present Company Director. *Recreations:* tennis, golf. *Address:* Chigwell, Claremont, Tasmania. *Club:* Tasmanian (Hobart). [*Died* 14 *Sept.* 1952.

MACPHERSON, Arthur Holte, M.A., B.C.L., Oxon.; Retired Solicitor; *b.* 4 Jan. 1867; 2nd *s.* of late Sir Arthur G. Macpherson, K.C.I.E.; *m.* 1910 Alice (*d.* 1943), *d.* of Rev. J. W. Shepard. *Educ.:* Marlborough; Trinity College, Oxford. A Director of Watney Combe Reid and Company Ltd., 1918-31. *Publications:* Comparative Legislation for the Protection of Birds (Gold Medal Essay of Royal Society for Protection of Birds); various papers on ornithological subjects, particularly London birds. *Recreation:* bird-watching. *Address:* 12 The Beacon, Exmouth, Devon. *T.:* Exmouth 2988. *Club:* United University. [*Died* 7 *Jan.* 1953.

McPHERSON, Sir Clive, Kt., *cr.* 1941; C.B.E. 1925; Chairman of Younghusband Ltd., Melbourne, Wool-brokers, since 1953 (Managing Director, 1938); also a Director of Union Trustee Co. of Australia, Ltd.; Member Cttee. of Management of Royal Melbourne Hospital; Member of State Employment Council since 1932; Member, Board of Nat. Bank of Australasia Ltd.; *s.* of William George McPherson; *b.* 1884; *m.* 1915. Acted as Hon. Adviser to Government of Commonwealth of Australia in organisation of Primary Industries; Member of Board of Commonwealth Bank of Australia, 1940-44; Australian Commissioner of British Phosphate Commission, 1927-46; Member of Royal Commission appointed by Government of Victoria, 1930, to investigate complaints of British Migrant Settlers under Government Settlement Scheme; Chairman Closer Settlement Commission, Victoria, 1933-38; Chairman of Australian Wheat Board, 1939-46; Commonwealth Government Representative, Australian Dairy Export, 1925-46; late Managing Partner of McPherson, Thom and Co., stock, station, and financial agents, of Collins Street, Melbourne. *Address:* 216 Domain Road, South Yarra, Melbourne, S.E.1, Australia. *Clubs:* Melbourne, Australian (Melbourne). [*Died* 9 *Nov.* 1958.

McPHERSON, Ewen Alexander, Q.C.; Chief Justice Appeal Court, Manitoba, since 1944; *b.* 27 Jan. 1879; *s.* of Peter McPherson and Ellen Wallace; *m.* 1904, Winnifred M., *d.* of Rev. F. M. Finn; three *s.* one *d.* *Educ.:* Portage la Prairie. Practised law at Portage la Prairie from 1903 as barrister and solicitor in firms of: Meighen and McPherson, McPherson, Williams and Garland, and McPherson and Porter; contested Portage la Prairie, 1910; elected 1914 and 1915; elected Dominion constituency of Portage la Prairie, 1926; for Rupert's Land constituency, 1931; Provincial Treasurer of Manitoba, 1931-36; Chief Justice Court of King's Bench of Manitoba, 1937-44; a bencher of the Manitoba Bar Association since 1915; Chairman of Winnepeg Foundation (a charity Trust fund), 1937. Hon. LL.D. University of Manitoba, 1948. *Recreation:* shooting. *Address:* Law Courts, Winnipeg, Manitoba, Canada. *Club:* Manitoba (Winnipeg). [*Died* 18 *Nov.* 1954.

MACPHERSON, Rev. Hector, M.A., Ph.D. (Edin.), F.R.A.S., F.R.S.E.; Minister of Guthrie Memorial Church, Edinburgh (Church of Scotland); *b.* Edinburgh, 1 Apr. 1888; *s.* of late Hector Macpherson, formerly Editor Edinburgh Evening News, and late Mary Janet Copland; *m.* 1917, Catherine Anne Chisholm; two *s.* two *d.* *Educ.:* privately; University of Edinburgh; New College, Edinburgh (Waterbeck Prizeman and Cunningham Fellow). Minister of Loudoun East Church, Newmilns, Ayrshire, 1916-21; Thomson Lecturer in Natural Science, Church College, Aberdeen, 1925-26; Lecturer to the Protestant Institute of Scotland, 1929-30 and 1954-55; Elder Lecturer on Astronomy, Royal Technical College, Glasgow, 1929-32, 1934-38, 1946. *Publications:* Romance of Modern Astronomy, 1910 (2nd ed. 1922); Practical Astronomy, 1912 (2nd ed. 1919); Herschel, in Pioneers of Progress series, 1919; The Covenanters under Persecution, 1923; Hector Macpherson, the Man and his Work, a Memoir, 1925; Modern Astronomy: its Rise and Progress, 1926; The Church and Science, 1927; The Church, the Bible and War, 1928; Modern Cosmologies, 1929; The Religion of Common Sense, 1930; The Cameronian Philosopher, Alexander Shields, 1932; Makers of Astronomy, 1933; The Heavens Declare, 1937; Guide to the Stars, 1943 (revised edn., 1953); also various articles and papers in scientific journals. *Recreation:* golf. *Address:* 7 Wardie Crescent, Edinburgh. *T.:* Edinburgh 83770. *Club:* University Union (Edinburgh). [*Died* 19 *May* 1956.

M'PHERSON, Sir Hugh, K.C.I.E., *cr.* 1924; C.S.I. 1919; *b.* 3 May 1870; *s.* of late Duncan M'Pherson, Paisley; *m.* 1897, Gertrude, *d.* of Dr. James Kelly; one *s.* two *d.* *Educ.:* Paisley Grammar School; Glasgow University; Balliol College, Oxford (Snell Exhibitioner). Passed open competition I.C.S., 1889; Assistant Magistrate, Bengal, 1891; Settlement Officer, Santal Parganas, 1898-1905; Director Land Records, Bengal, 1907-12; Revenue Secretary, Bihar and Orissa, 1912-15; Chief Secretary, Bihar and Orissa, 1915-19; Member, Board of Revenue, Bihar and Orissa, 1919; Secretary to Government of India, Home Department, 1919-20; Member Executive Council, Bihar and Orissa, 1921-25; Acting Governor, Bihar and Orissa, 1925; retired, 1926. *Address:* 171 Mayfield Road, Edinburgh 9. *T.:* 42478. [*Died* 17 *Dec.* 1960.

MACPHERSON-GRANT, Sir George, 5th Bt., *cr.* 1838; J.P., landed proprietor; *b.* London, 15 May 1890; *o. s.* of 4th Bt. and Mary (*d.* 1914), *d.* of Alexander Dennistoun of Golfhill; *S.* father, 1914. *Educ.:* Eton. Owns about 150,000 acres. Member of Royal Company of Archers. *Heir:* cousin Ewan George, [*b.* 29 Sept. 1907; *m.* 1937, Evelyn Nancy Stopford, *yr. d.* of Major Edward Spencer Dickin, Wolverley House, Goring-on-Thames; one *d.*]. *Address:* Ballindalloch Castle, Ballindalloch, Banffshire. *T.:* Ballindalloch 206. *T.A.:* Sir George, Ballindalloch. *Clubs:* St. James'; New (Edinburgh). [*Died* 12 *Feb.* 1951.

MACQUEEN - POPE, Walter James; theatre historian since 1945; lecturer; *b.* 11 April 1888; *e. s.* of Walter George Pope and Frederica Macqueen; *m.* 1912, Stella Suzanne Schumann; one *d. Educ.:* privately; Tollington School. Has been connected with every West End Theatre; Manager, of Queen's, Globe, Shaftesbury, Duke of York's and Whitehall; specialized in theatrical publicity for many years; gave up managerial activities for publicity, 1931. Manager and Secretary, Alexandra Palace, 1922-25; publicity representative for Theatre Royal, Drury Lane, 1935-56 (now historian; connection from 1906); authority on pantomime. *Publications:* Theatre Royal, Drury Lane, 1946; Carriages at Eleven, 1947; Haymarket, Theatre of Perfection, 1948; Twenty Shillings in the Pound, 1948; Indiscreet Guide to Theatreland, 1947; Gaiety, Theatre of Enchantment, 1949; The Melodies Linger On, 1950; Ghosts and Greasepaint, 1951; Ivor, The Story of an Achievement, 1951; Ladies First, 1952; Shirt Fronts and Sables, 1953; (with D. L. Murray) Fortune's Favourite: The Life and Times of Franz Léhar, 1953; Back Numbers, 1954; Pillars of Drury Lane, 1955; Nights of Gladness, 1956; Give Me Yesterday, 1957; St. James's: Theatre of Distinction, 1958; The Footlights Flickered, 1959; Goodbye Piccadilly, 1960 (*autobiography*, posthumous); articles for newspapers and Television programmes. *Recreation:* ornithology. *Address:* 9 Oakdale, Southgate, N.14. *T.:* Enterprise 1939. [*Died* 27 *June* 1960.

MACRAE, Major - General Albert Edward, C.B. 1944; O.B.E. 1928; *b.* 3 Aug. 1886; *s.* of Farquhar Macrae, Strathcarron, Scotland; *m.* 1912, Grace Kaye Billman (*d.* 1953), Halifax, N.S.; one *s.* one *d. Educ.:* Dover College; R.M.C., Kingston, Canada. Joined R.A. 1906; p.a.c. 1914; M.I.Mech.E., A.I.C.E., 1926; L.G.M., 1930; M.E.I.C., 1944; Bt. Major 1917; Bt. Lt.-Col. 1931; Bt. Col. 1934; Col. 1935; Brig. 1937; Maj.-Gen. 1938. Asst. Supt., Royal Arsenal, 1914 - 21; Asst. Supt. Design, Woolwich, 1921-28 and 1929-34; Supt. of Experiments, Shoeburyness, 1934-37; Chief Supt. of Design, Woolwich, 1937-39; Ministry of Supply Rep., Canada, 1939-41; Military Technical Adviser to Dept. of Munitions and Supply, Ottawa, Canada, 1941-45; Chief Engineer Canadian Arsenals Ltd., 1945-46; ret. pay, 1946. Director, Gun Division, Canadian Dept. of Defence Production, 1951. *Publications:* Overstrain of Metals, 1930. *Recreations:* fishing, golf. *Address:* c/o Lloyds Bank Ltd., 6 Pall Mall, S.W.1. *Club:* Army and Navy. [*Died* 10 *Jan.* 1958.

MACRAE of Feoirlinn, Col. Sir Colin William, Kt., *cr.* 1935; C.V.O. 1933; C.B.E. 1922; Vice-Lieutenant of the County of Bute; J.P.; Lieutenant of Queen's Body Guard of the Yeomen of the Guard; K.J.St.J.; Order of Mercy; Chamberlain to the Pope; Order of the Holy Sepulchre; Hon. Colonel 51st A.-T.R.; Hon. Secretary for Scotland, Order of St. John of Jerusalem; *b.* 1869; 3rd *s.* of Duncan MacRae of Conchra, D.L., J.P., and Grace, *d.* of Donald Stewart; *m.* 1909, Lady Margaret Crichton-Stuart (O.B.E., J.P., County Controller, B.R.C.S., Bute; D.J.St.J.; Order of the Holy Sepulchre); *o. d.* of the 3rd Marquess of Bute, K.T.; two *d.* (one *s.* killed in action, 1942). Major R. of O.; Member C.C. for Bute and Argyll; Commr. of Income Tax, Co. of Bute; Hon. Sec. Red Cross Society for Bute; National Savings Committee for County of Bute; President of League of Mercy for Argyll and Glasgow, Clan MacRae Society, London, and Celtic Society of Glasgow; Warden for County of Bute for King George's Jubilee Trust; Member of the Royal Company of Archers (The Queen's Body Guard for Scotland); late Major the Black Watch (42nd Royal Highlanders); served South Africa, 1899-1902 (Queen's medal five clasps, King's medal two clasps); European War; retired, 1905; Coronation Medal of George V.; Silver Jubilee Medal; Coronation Medal George VI. *Address:* Friary Court, St. James's Palace, S.W.1; Feoirlinn, Colintraive, Argyll. *T.:* Colintraive 6. *T.A.:* Colintraive; Ascog, Isle of Bute. *T.A.:* Ascog. *Clubs:* Bath, M.C.C.; Royal Scottish Automobile (Glasgow); Royal Yacht Squadron (Cowes). [*Died* 10 *Oct.* 1952.

MACRAE, Donald Mackenzie, C.B.E., M.D., C.M., F.R.G.S.; retired; *b.* Gress, Stornoway, 1869; *s.* of late Alexander MacRae and Mary Mackenzie; *m.* 1915, Edith Muriel, *d.* of late Rev. Canon Frederick Phipps, Vicar of St. Peter's, Devizes, Wilts; one *d. Educ.:* Knock and Lurebost Schools, Stornoway; Glasgow University; University College, Bristol; St. Thomas's Hospital. Practised in the Highlands of Scotland, Glasgow, and London; Surgeon, Castle Mail Steamship Co., 1897-99; Resident Surgeon, Provincial Hospital, Port Elizabeth, South Africa; later Senior Assistant Medical Officer, Wilts County Asylum, England; Civil Surgeon, South African Field Force (Queen's medal and three clasps); Surgeon-Captain, Bechuanaland Protectorate Police, 1903; Surgeon-Major, 1915; Principal Medical Officer, Bechuanaland Protectorate, 1917; Medical Officer to the Protectorate Section, South African Railways; Member of Malaria Commission, South African Railways, Mafeking to Victoria Falls; retired, 1929. *Publications:* articles in South African Medical Record: Benign Tertian Malaria; Tropical Neurasthenia; Food in relation to Health and Disease in the Tropics. *Address:* Southbroom Cottage, Nursteed Road, Devizes, Wilts. *Club:* Royal Societies. [*Died* 4 *Feb.* 1955.

MACRAE, Maj.-Gen. Ian Macpherson, C.B. 1939; C.I.E. 1931; O.B.E. 1919; M.B.; I.M.S., retd.; *b.* 2 Oct. 1882. *Educ.:* Edinburgh University. Served European War, 1914-19 (despatches twice, O.B.E.); Inspector-General of Prisons, Bihar and Orissa, 1926; A.D.M.S. India, 1933-37; D.D.M.S. Eastern Command, India, 1937-41; K.H.P., 1936-41; retired, 1941. Served War of 1939-45 (prisoner). [*Died* 14 *May* 1956.

MACRAE, Russell Duncan; *b.* 6 Sept. 1888; *s.* of Rev. Duncan Macrae and Alice Hawkins; *m.* 1919, Dorothy Clara (*d.* 1954), *d.* of Walter Clayton; one *s.* one *d. Educ.:* City of London School; Sidney Sussex College, Cambridge; Heidelberg University. Ordained Presbyterian Church of England, 1913; joined Royal Naval Division, 1914; Commissioned West Yorkshire Regt., 1914; discharged with rank of Capt. 1919; appointed Consular service 1919; posts: New York, Stuttgart, Königsberg; Dunkirk, Porto Alegre, Zagreb, Moscow; Consul General, Galatz; Consul at Bahia, 1941-45; British Minister to the Dominican Republic, 1945-48; retired, 1948. *Recreations* tennis, fishing. *Address:* Struan, Lamlash, Isle of Arran. *T.:* 283. *Club:* Royal Automobile. [*Died* 24 *Dec.* 1956.

McRAE, William, C.I.E. 1934; M.A., D.Sc., F.R.S.E., Indian Agricultural Service, retired; late Director, Imperial Institute of Agricultural Research, Pusa, India; *b.* 26 May 1878; *s.* of William McRae and Margaret Younie; *m.* 1914; one *s.* one *d. Educ.:* James Gillespie's School and University, Edinburgh; Munich University. Demonstrator, Royal College of Science, South Kensington; Indian Agricultural Service, 1908; Government Mycologist, Madras; Imperial Mycologist, Pusa. *Publications:* mycological subjects in the Agricultural Journal of India and in the memoirs of the Imperial Department of Agriculture in India. *Recreation:* golf. *Address:* Daramona, Gamekeepers Road, Barnton, Midlothian. [*Died* 8 *July* 1952.

McREA, Sir Charles (James Hugh), Kt., *cr.* 1937; *b.* 1874; *s.* of Samuel Hugh McRea, Walthamstow; *m.* 1907, Edith, *d.* of James Farnie; (one *s.*, Commander R.N., killed in action 1940) one *d.* Head of firm of T. H. Beattie & Co.; formerly Chairman of London Soc. of Coal Merchants and of City of London Branch of Royal National Lifeboat Instn.; Past Master, Carmen's Company. Elected to Common Council, 1927; Sheriff of City of London, 1936-37; Alderman of Bridge Ward, 1939, resigned 1947; J.P. 1939. *Address:* Arrandene, Wise Lane, Mill Hill, N.W.7. *T.:* Mill Hill 1200. [*Died* 19 *June* 1951.

MACREADY, Lieut.-General Sir Gordon (Nevil), 2nd Bt., *cr.* 1923; K.B.E. *cr.* 1945 (O.B.E. 1919); C.B. 1942; C.M.G. 1932; D.S.O. 1918; M.C. 1916; late R.E.; Col. Comdt. R.E., 1946-56; *b.* 5 April 1891; *o. s.* of General Rt. Hon. Sir Nevil Macready, 1st Bt., P.C. (Ire.), G.C.M.G., K.C.B.; *S.* father 1946; *m.* 1920, Elisabeth de Noailles, 2nd *d.* of the Duc de Noailles; one *s.* *Educ.:* Cheltenham; R.M.A., Woolwich. Served European War, 1914-18; A.A. and Q.M.G. 66th Div. Nov. 1917-May 1918; A.A. and Q.M.G. Supreme War Council, Versailles, May 1918-April 1919; A.A.G. British Military Mission, Berlin, April-Sept. 1919; Special Mission (to organise Police Force) in Poland, Oct. 1919 (despatches six times, Brevet-Major); Assistant Secretary to Committee of Imperial Defence, 1926-32; Imperial Defence College, 1933; G.S.O. 1 War Office, 1934-36; Deputy Director of Staff Duties, War Office, 1936-38; Chief of British Military Mission to Egyptian Army, 1938; Asst. Chief of Imperial General Staff, 1940-1942; Chief of British Army Staff at Washington, 1942; retired pay, 1946; Regional Commissioner for Lower Saxony, Control Commission, Germany, 1946-47; British Chairman of Economic Control Office for British and American Zones of Germany, 1947-49; Economic Adviser to U.K. High Commissioner in Germany, 1949-51. Commander: Legion of Merit (American); Legion of Honour (French); Grand Cross of Order of Orange-Nassau. *Heir: s.* Nevil John Wilfrid [*b.* 7 Sept. 1921; *m.* 1949, Mary, *o. d.* of Sir Donald Fergusson, G.C.B.; one *s.* two *d.*]. *Address:* 51 Boulevard de Montmorency, Paris. *Clubs:* Junior Army and Navy; Jockey (Paris). [*Died* 17 *Oct.* 1956.

MACREADY, Brig. John, D.S.O. 1915; O.B.E. 1937; *b.* 10 April 1887; *o. surv. s.* of J. F. C. H. Macready, F.R.C.S.; *m.* 1918, Marguerite Mary, *d.* of late Rev. J. Milling, Ashton Keynes, Wilts; one *s.* one *d.* Entered Bedfordshire Regt. 1907; Captain, 1913; Major, 1925; Lieut.-Col. 1933; Col. 1937; served European War, 1914-18 (despatches four times, D.S.O., Order of Leopold, Belgian Croix de Guerre, French Croix de Guerre); command 2nd Bn. Bedfordshire and Herts Regiment, 1933-37; served throughout Arab Rebellion in Palestine, 1936 (O.B.E.); Commandant Hythe Wing, Small Arms School, 1937-39; commanded 162 Inf. Brigade; retired pay, 1945. *Address:* Ridgeway, Bartholomew Close, Hythe, Kent. *Club:* Public Schools. [*Died* 27 *Dec.* 1957.

MACROBERT (of Douneside and Cromar), Lady; Rachel W.; J.P.; B.Sc., F.G.S.; Director British India Corporation; Chairman MacRobert Farms (Douneside) Ltd.; Pres. Spitfire-Mitchell Memorial Fund; *d.* of Dr. William Hunter Workman and Fanny Bullock Workman, the Himalayan explorers; *m.* 1911, Sir Alexander MacRobert, 1st Bt., K.B.E., LL.D., V.D. (*d.* 1922); (one *s.* killed flying and two killed in action, 1941). *Educ.:* Cheltenham Ladies' Coll.; Royal Holloway Coll.; Royal Coll. of Science; Royal School of Mines; Edinburgh Univ. Geologist; Agriculturalist (Breeding of Pedigree British Friesian Cattle and Pedigree Aberdeen Angus and Highland Cattle, etc.). Founder of Alastrean House for R.A.F. flying personnel (Rest Centre). Awarded Gold Medal of Honor by National Society of New England Women, 1942. *Publications:* various geological. *Recreations:* skating, gardening. *Club:* University Women's. [*Died* 1 *Sept.* 1954.

MACROSSAN, Hon. Neal William; Chief Justice of Queensland since 1946; *b.* 27 April 1889; *s.* of Hon. John Murtagh Macrossan, M.L.A.Qld.; *m.* 1921, Eileen Elizabeth, *d.* of Hon. T. C. Beirne, Qld.; one *s.* four *d.* *Educ.:* St. Joseph's College, Nudgee, Qld.; Magdalen College, Oxford. Rhodes Scholar, Qld., 1907; M.A. Oxon, 1914. Barrister, 1912; Senior Puisne Judge, Supreme Court, Qld., 1940; Acting Chief Justice, 1944-45; Warden, University of Qld., 1940-. *Recreations:* motoring, riding, golf. *Address:* Chief Justice's Chambers, Supreme Court, Brisbane, Australia; 36 Kitchener Rd., Ascot, Brisbane. *T.:* Brisbane M3826. *Clubs:* Johnsonian, Brisbane (Brisbane). [*Died* 30 *Dec.* 1955.

MACTAGGART, Sir John Auld, 1st Bt., *cr.* 1938; J.P. Glasgow; Director of several Property Companies; *b.* 30 Sept. 1867; *s.* of Neil Mactaggart and Ann Auld, Glasgow; *m.* 1st, 1897, Margaret, *d.* of Robert Curtis, Ramelton, County Donegal; one *s.*; 2nd, Lena, *d.* of Rev. David Orr, Elderpark Church, Govan. *Educ.:* Glasgow. Was educated for the Civil Service but became accountant to large building syndicate in Glasgow; started in 1897 for himself in the building trade; rapidly became the most extensive builder of house property in the West of Scotland, and in conjunction with his son's firm has built over 40,000 flats and houses in Glasgow, Edinburgh and London; President of Economic Research Council; Founder and Treas. American and British Commonwealth Assoc.; Pres. National Federation of Property Owners. Has always been interested in politics and has been Chairman in 6 elections over 70 years; has been asked to stand for Parliament on 3 occasions. *Publications:* various Articles, Lectures and Reports on Housing and Economic and Political subjects. *Recreations:* reading, travel, and health research. *Heir: s.* John Auld Mactaggart (*see* Sir John Mactaggart, 2nd Bt.). *Address:* Kelmscott, Pollokshields, Glasgow; 55 Park Lane, W.1. *T.:* Ibrox (Glasgow) 0650, Mayfair 5180. *Clubs:* City Livery; English-Speaking Union; Locarno (Glasgow). [*Died* 24 *Nov.* 1956.

MACTAGGART, Sir John (Auld), 2nd Bt. *cr.* 1938; Director of several Land and Property Companies; Hon. French Consul for the Bahamas; *b.* 27 June 1898; *o. s.* of Sir John Auld Mactaggart, 1st Bt.; *S.* father 1956; *m.* 1922, Betty (*d.* 1951), *e. d.* of Robert Thomson, Kilmarnock; three *s.* Served European War, 1916-19, with R.G.A. (T.F.) (wounded). J.P. Glasgow, 1933. *Recreations:* shooting, yachting. *Heir: s.* Ian Auld [*b.* 19 April 1923; *m.* 1946, Rosemary, *d.* of Sir Herbert Geraint Williams, 1st Bt., M.P.; two *s.* two *d.*]. *Address:* Daiquiri, Nassau, Bahamas. *Clubs:* Carlton, Royal Automobile; Royal Thames Yacht; Royal Motor Yacht; Porcupine (Nassau). [*Died* 8 *April* 1960.

McWHIRTER, William Allan; formerly: Man. Dir., Associated Newspapers, Ltd. and Northcliffe Newspapers Group, Ltd.; Chm. Hull and Grimsby Newspapers, Ltd., Gloucestershire Newspapers Ltd., etc.; *y. s.* of late William McWhirter, M.I.E.E., Longhurst, Clarkston, Glasgow; *m.* 1922, Margaret, *d.* of Wm. Williamson, Eastbank, Giffnock; three *s.* *Educ.:* High School of Glasgow. Associated with the late Lord Rothermere from 1907; Director of Daily Record (Glasgow) group, 1919-25; served during War with Ross Mountain Battery, 4th (Highland) Mountain Brigade, in Egypt and the Balkans. *Publications:* numerous articles on industrial and political subjects. *Recreation:* lawn tennis.

Address: Aberfoyle, Winchmore Hill, N.21. *T.:* Palmers Green 0148. [*Died* 16 *May* 1955.

MacWHITE, Michael, LL.D.; Retired Ambassador; *b.* Glandore, Co. Cork, Ireland, 8 May 1883; *m.* 1921, Paula Asta Grüttner, Hilleröd, Denmark; one *s.* Served with French Army during European War (three citations, wounded); visited U.S. with French Military Mission, Aug. 1918; Secretary Irish Delegation at Paris, 1920-21; Permanent Delegate from Irish Free State to League of Nations, 1923-29; Envoy Extraordinary and Minister Plenipotentiary of Irish Free State to United States of America, 1929-38; to Italy, 1938-50, given personal rank of Ambassador, 1950. Vice-President International Labour Conf., Geneva, 1928; Fellow Royal Society of Antiquaries of Ireland. *Address:* The Spa Hotel, Lucan, Co. Dublin. [*Died* 13 *Nov.* 1958.

MACY, George; book publisher; Editor of The Columbia Jester and The 1920 Columbian; *b.* New York, N.Y., 12 May 1900; *m.* 1927, Helen Kaplan; one *s.* one *d.* *Educ.:* De Witt Clinton High Sch.; Columbia Univ. Gen. Sec. Zeta Beta Tau Fraternity, 1923-28; Ed., Zeta Beta Tau Quarterly, 1922-28. Organized (and Pres. of each since inception): Limited Editions Club, 1929; Heritage Press, 1935; Readers Club, 1940. Managing Director Nonesuch Press, London, Eng., 1936-52. Honoured by special exhibitions in Bibliothéque Nationale, Paris, 1948; British Museum, London, 1952. Gold Medal, Amer. Inst. of Graphic Arts, 1953; Legion of Honour, France, 1949. His firm has published many famous special editions. *Publications:* The Collected Verses of George Jester. Editor: A Soldier's Reader, 1943; A Sailor's Reader, 1943. *Address:* 1185 Park Avenue, New York 28; (Office) 595 Madison Avenue, New York 22. [*Died* 20 *May* 1956.

MADDOCK, Lt.-Col. Edward Cecil Gordon, C.I.E. 1925; I.M.S., retired; *b.* 29 June 1876; *s.* of late Rev. Canon H. E. Maddock, Rector of Patrington, Yorks; *m.* 1915, Cecilia Cockburn Hood. *Educ.:* Rossall; Caistor; Edinburgh University. M.B., Ch.B. Ed., 1898; M.D. Ed., 1911; F.R.C.S. Ed., 1911; D.T.M., Liver., 1906; D.P.H. Cantab., 1906. Entered I.M.S., 1899; retired, 1926. *Address:* Wardour Lodge, Sunningdale, Berks. [*Died* 6 *Jan.* 1952.

MADEN, Henry; *b.* 31 March 1892; *s.* of late Sir Henry Maden, Bacup; *m.* 1923, Alice, *d.* of James Herbert Fletcher, Holmfirth. *Educ.:* Privately; Exeter Coll., Oxford, B.A. Called to Bar, Middle Temple, 1916; contested Lonsdale, 1922; M.P. (L.) Lonsdale, 1923-24. *Address:* 8 Lowther Terrace, Lytham, Lancs. [*Died* 17 *Nov.* 1960.

MAENAN, 1st Baron, *cr.* 1948, of Ellesmere; **William Francis Kyffin Taylor,** G.B.E., *cr.* 1929 (K.B.E., *cr.* 1918); K.C.; D.L.; J.P. Shropshire; Presiding Judge Liverpool Court of Passage, 1903-48; a Railway and Canal Commissioner from 1930; *b.* Liverpool, 9 July 1854; *e. s.* of Ven. William Francis Taylor, D.D., Archdeacon of Liverpool, and Anne, *d.* of late Rev. Hugh Evans, Vicar of Plemonstall; *m.* 1883, Mary Fleming, *o. d.* of Robert Crooks, Rosemount, Liverpool; one *d.* *Educ.:* Liverpool Coll.; Exeter Coll., Oxford (B.A.). Practised as a barrister on Northern Circuit at Liverpool, 1879-94; Q.C. 1895; Recorder of Bolton, 1901-03; Bencher of the Inner Temple, 1905; Treasurer, 1926; Master of the Garden, 1927; Chairman Emergency Compensation Committee, 1927; Commissioner for Ministry of Transport, 1928; Member of the General Council of the Bar, 1900-11; the Judge of Appeal for the Isle of Man, June 1918-21; Vice-Chairman Shropshire Quarter Sessions, 1920; Chairman Shropshire Quarter Sessions, 1927-47; H.M. Commissioner of Assize, Midland Circuit, 1919; Chester and South Wales Circuit, 1920; Northern Circuit, 1920; Midland Circuit, 1925; Northern Circuit, 1929; V.P. War Compensation Court, 1920-1928; V.P. Liverpool College, 1927; Member of Commission, Irish Deportees, 1923; Independent Chairman of Monmouthshire and South Wales Coal Trade Conciliation Board, 1927; Chairman Committee on Summary Appeals, 1932. *Heir:* none. *Address:* 7 Mansfield Street, Portland Place, W.1; Gadlas Hall, Ellesmere, Shropshire. *Club:* Conservative. [*Died* 22 *Sept.* 1951 (*ext.*).

MAGER, Sydney, C.B.E. 1918; *s.* of late Edmund Mager; *b.* 1877; Director of Land Acquisition, Ministry of Agriculture and Fisheries; Chief Commissioner Food Production Department during European War. *Club:* National. [*Died* 17 *March* 1952.

MAGHERAMORNE, 4th Baron U.K. (*cr.* 1887); 5th Bt. U.K., *cr.* 1846; **Ronald Tracey McGarel-Hogg;** *b.* 28 July 1865; *s.* of 1st Baron and Caroline, *d.* of 1st Lord Penrhyn; *S.* brother, 1946. *Heir:* (*to Baronetcy only*) *kinsman,* Lt.-Col. Kenneth Weir Hogg [*b.* 1894; *m.* 1936, Hon. Aline Emily Partington, *d.* of 2nd Baron Doverdale]. *Address:* 37 Knyveton Road, Bournemouth. *Club:* Constitutional. [*Died* 21 *April* 1957 (*ext.*).

MAGIAN, Anthony John Capper, M.D., B.Ch., F.S.A. (Scot.), F.R.G.S., F.R.E.S., F.R.I.P.H., F.Z.S., F.L.H.S.; Count of Ararat; Director of St. Margaret's Cancer Clinic; late Gynæcological Surg. to the Battersea General Hospital, London; *b.* London, 1878; *s.* of John Anthony Capper Magian, cotton merchant; *m.* 1920, Margery, *d.* of late Rev. S. B. Ainley, Manchester; two *s.* one *d.* *Educ.:* London, Manchester, Dublin, and Paris Universities. Freeman of City of London; awarded Palmes d'officier de l'Instruction Publique, Médaille de la Reconnaissance Française and Médaille du Roi Albert for special services to France and Belgium; Chevalier Grand Cross Ordre Ste. Margaret; Officer of Order of St. John of Jerusalem; Past Pres. Manchester Medico-Chirurgical and Obstetric Soc.; Fellow R. Soc. Med. (Obst. and Gynæc. Section); Fellow Med. Socs. of London, Edinburgh and Paris; Past Pres. Euston Med. Soc.; Pres. Cancer Society; late Asst. Demonstrator of Anatomy, Victoria Univ.; Corps Surgeon Lecturer and Examiner to the St. John's Ambulance Assoc.; Lecturer post-graduate clinics; Medical Examiner for Le Phénix, Sun, Caledonian, and other life assurancé societies. Corr. Member Society of Obstetrics and Gynæcology of Paris. *Publications:* Manual of Diseases of Women; Practitioner's Manual of Venereal Diseases in Women; Manual of Sex Problems in Women; Manual of Midwifery for Practitioners and Students; Operative Technique in Gynæcology; After-Results of Abdominal Operations; A Contribution to the Study of Chlorosis; Twilight Sleep; Sterility in Women; The Treatment of Cancer of the Uterus; a Review of Modern Opinions; The Causation and Diagnosis of Uterine Cancer; The Modern Treatment of Cancer of the Breast; The Use of X-rays and Radium in the Treatment of Cancer; The Nursing of Gynæcological Cases; Glandular Treatment of Cancer of the Uterus; Ovarian Grafting and the Rejuvenation of Women. *Recreations:* motoring and the theatre. *Address:* 41 Churchgate, Southport. *T.:* Southport 86002. [*Died* 30 *July* 1956.

MAGNAY, Major Sir Christopher (Boyd William), 3rd Bt., *cr.* 1844; M.C.; D.L. Suffolk; J.P. West Suffolk; late 4th Hussars and Queen's Bays; *s.* of 2nd Bt. and Margaret (*d.* 1950), *d.* of Matthew Soulsby; *b.* 27 Mar. 1884; *S.* father, 1917; *m.* 1925, Winifred Madeline, *d.* of late Rt. Hon. Arthur Frederick Jeffreys of Burkham House, Hampshire, and *widow* of Major Chandos Leigh, D.S.O. *Educ.:* Harrow; Pembroke College,

Cambridge. Major, Norfolk Yeomanry, 1916; High Sheriff of Suffolk, 1935. *Recreations*: cricket, shooting, golf, etc. *Heir*: none. *Address*: Saxham Hall, Bury St. Edmunds, Suffolk. *T.*: Barrow (Suffolk) 259. *Club*: Cavalry. [*Died* 4 *Sept.* 1960 (*ext.*).

MAGNIAC, Brig.-Gen. Sir Charles Lane, Kt., *cr.* 1923; C.M.G. 1916; C.B.E. 1919; late R.E.; *b.* 14 Dec. 1873; *e. s.* of late Major-General Francis Lane Magniac, Madras Staff Corps; *m.* 1900, Letitia Anne, 3rd *d.* of late T. H. W. Knolles of Oatlands, Kinsale, Ireland; no *c.* *Educ.*: U.S. College, Westward Ho!. In India (Indian Railways), 1896-1914; thanks of Government of N.W. Provinces in 1897 for Famine work; also of Government of India in 1898 for work on N. W. Railway in connection with Tirah campaign; Delhi Durbar medal; Agent, Madras and South Mahratta Railway; served European War, 1914-19 (despatches, C.M.G., Bt. Lt.-Col., C.B.E., Légion d'Honneur, Croix d'Officier); Director of Movements, India, Afghan War, 1919 (despatches); retired, 1922; Hon. Brig.-Gen. *Address*: Garden House Hotel, Folkestone, Kent. [*Died* 4 *June* 1953.

MAGOWAN, Sir John Hall, K.B.E., *cr.* 1946 (O.B.E. 1929); C.M.G. 1941; appointed Ambassador to Siam, 1951; *b.* 5 Oct. 1893; *e. s.* of late William Hall Magowan and Sara Ann Irvine, Mountnorris, Co. Armagh; *m.* 1917, Winifred Isabel, *yr. d.* of late John Titterington Ray and Isabel Lowry, Dublin; two *s.* one *d.* *Educ.*: Armagh Royal School; Trinity College, Dublin. B.A. 1915; Hon. LL.D. 1949. Served in R.F.A. and Intelligence Corps, 1915-19 (wounded, despatches); appointed to Consular Service, 1919; Vice-Consul at Hamburg and Bremerhaven, 1920-24; Consul for Saar Territory and Bavarian Palatinate with residence at Mainz, 1924-29; Chargé d'Affaires *en titre* and consul to the Republic of Hayti at Port au Prince, 1929-31; Commercial Secretary to H.M. Embassy at Washington, 1931-34, and at Berlin, 1935-37; Commercial Counsellor at Berlin, 1937-39; Employed at Treasury, 1939-40; Deputy Comptroller General Export Credits Guarantee Department, 1940-42; Minister, Commercial Adviser to H.M. Ambassador in Washington, 1942-48; Ambassador to Venezuela, 1948-1951. *Address*: Mountmorris, Co. Armagh, N. Ireland. [*Died* 5 *April* 1951.

MAHALANOBIS, S. C., B.Sc., F.R.S.E., I.E.S.; Emeritus Prof. of Physiology, Univ. of Calcutta and Carmichael Medical College; *b.* Calcutta, 1867; *m.* 1902, Monica Sen, *sis.* of late Maharani Sunity Devi, C.I., of Cooch Behar, and 4th *d.* of Kesub Chandra Sen. *Educ.*: University of Edinburgh. Worked in Research Laboratory, Royal College of Physicians, Edinburgh, 1896-97; Interim-Professor of Physiology, University College, Cardiff, 1898-99; Professor, Presidency College, Calcutta, 1900-1927; Fellow of the University of Calcutta since 1904; President of Board of Higher Studies in Physiology and Head of Post-Graduate Department in Physiology, Calcutta Univ., 1916-42; Hon. Member Physiological Society of India; Member Governing Body Univ. College of Science, 1920-35; Member of the Syndicate of the Calcutta University, 1907-28; Dean, Presidency College, 1916-18. *Publications*: Investigations on the Life-History of the Salmon; Muscle-Fat in the Salmon; Teachers' Manual Science Section; Science Text-Books, etc. *Address*: 90 Park Street, Calcutta 17, India. *T.*: Park 3233. [*Died* 31 *July* 1953.

MAINPRISE, Maj.-Gen. Cecil Wilmot, D.S.O. 1917; M.R.C.S., L.R.C.P. Lond.; R.A.M.C.; *b.* 23 June 1873; *s.* of late W. B. Mainprise, Paymaster-in-Chief, Royal Navy, and *g.s.* of late Capt. Thomas Pullen, R.N., Plymouth; unmarried. *Educ.*: Royal Naval School, Newcross; St. Bartholomew's Hospital. Qualified 1897; received a Commission in the Royal Army Medical Corps, 1898; proceeded to India; served Tibet Expedition in charge of the only British Field Hospital, 1903-04 (Tibet medal and clasp); served at home, 1905-09; went again to India; present at Delhi Durbar, 1911 (Coronation medal); commanded an Indian Cavalry Field Ambulance proceeding to France for active service, Sept. 1914 (despatches); commanded a Casualty Clearing Station, 1915 (despatches, D.S.O.); left France, May 1917; charge Military Hospital, Curragh, Ireland, six months, and then proceeded to Salonika as O.C. 80 General Hospital, April 1918; present in offensive against Bulgaria as A.D.M.S. Advanced Base and after the Bulgar defeat, went through to Sofia (Acting Deputy Director Medical Services, 16th Corps); returned home in April 1919 and proceeded to India and took part in Afghan War, 1919 (A.D.M.S.), Peshawar); on termination of hostilities was given Command British Station Hospital, Bangalore, India; returned to England, 1922; A.D.M.S. Northern Ireland District; A.D.M.S. Southern Area, Portsmouth; Commdt. R.A.M. College, 1924-26; Maj.-Gen. 1926; retired at own request, 1926. *Address*: Landfall, Reading Rd., Fleet, Hants. *T.*: Fleet 144. *Club*: Junior United Service. [*Died* 16 *Feb.* 1951.

MAINWARING, Brig. Guy Rowland, D.S.O. 1920; late Indian Army; *b.* 5 Aug. 1885; 2nd *s.* of late Col. E. P. Mainwaring, Indian Army; *m.* Sybil Iris, *widow* of Randle Brereton, *d.* of Col. H. J. J. Middleton, late Skinner's Horse. *Educ.*: Cranleigh; R.M.C., Sandhurst. Attached 1st Bn. The Somerset Light Infantry, 1905-06; joined 39th Garhwal Rifles, 1906; served in France and Flanders, 1914-15; Egypt, 1915-16; Mesopotamia and Kurdistan, 1919-21 (D.S.O.); Malabar Rebellion, 1921, commanding 1st Battn. Royal Garhwal Rifles and troops in Rebel Area in Malabar, 1922; Waziristan, 1926-28; Mahsud operations, 1930 (despatches); Commandant 2nd Batt. Royal Garhwal Rifles, 1930-34; Comdt. Small Arms School, India, 1934-36; Commander Delhi (Independent) Brigade Area, India, 1936-38; retired 1938; re-employed under War Office (Movement Control, Troopships), 1940-46. *Recreations*: shooting and fishing. *Address*: 94 Overstrand Mansions, S.W.11. *T.*: Macauley 5803. *Club*: United Service. [*Died* 24 *Jan.* 1956.

MAIRET, Ethel, R.D.I. 1938; Handloom Weaver and Head of Ditchling Weaving School; *b.* Barnstaple, N. Devon, 17 Feb. 1872. Lived some years in India; travelled Europe in connection with weaving and education. *Publications*: Vegetable Dyes, 1939 (7th ed.); Handweaving To-day, 1939; Handweaving and Education, 1940; Handweaving Notes for Teachers, 1948. *Recreations*: work and travel for work, education. *Address*: Gospels, Ditchling, Sussex. *T.A.*: Ditchling, Hassocks. *T.*: Hassocks 174. [*Died* 18 *Nov.* 1952.

MAITLAND, Sir A. J. D. R. S.; *see* Steel-Maitland.

MAITLAND, Lieut.-Colonel Sir (George) Ramsay, 7th Bt., *cr.* 1818; D.S.O. 1918; late 14th Jat Lancers; *b.* 20 Dec. 1882; *yr. s.* of Sir John Maitland, 5th Bt.; *S.* brother 1949; *m.* 1919, Jean Hamilton, M.B.E., *d.* of R. Findlay of Easterhill, Lanarkshire; three *s.* one *d.* *Educ.*: Cheltenham College; R.M.A., Woolwich; 2nd Lieut. R.F.A. 1900; Lieut. 14th Jat Lancers, 1905; Capt. 1909; Major, 1915; Lt.-Col. (temp.), 1917; passed Staff College at Quetta, 1914; served South African War (Queen's medal 5 clasps); European War, 1914-18 (Croix de Guerre (Belgian), D.S.O. despatches thrice); retired, 1920; commanded 9th Argyll and Sutherland Highlanders T.F. 1922-23; Zone Commander Angus/Dundee Home Guard. D.L., J.P. Angus. *Recreations*: shooting, fishing. *Heir*: *s.* Alexander Keith, late Major Q. O. Cameron Highlanders [*b.* 19

MAGUIRE, Maj.-Gen. Frederick Arthur, C.M.G., D.S.O., F.R.C.S. See page xxix.

Oct. 1920; *m.* 1951, Lavender Mary Jex, *d.* of late F. W. J. Jackson, Kirkbuddo; two *s.*]. *Address:* Reswallie, Forfar; 2 Douglas Gardens, Edinburgh. *Club:* New (Edinburgh).
[*Died* 1 *Nov.* 1960.

MAITLAND, Brig.-Gen. James D. H.; *see* Heriot-Maitland.

MAITLAND, Lt.-Col. Sir Ramsay; *see* Maitland, Lt.-Col. Sir G. R.

MAITLAND-JONES, Arthur Griffith, O.B.E.; M.C.; M.D., F.R.C.P.; Consulting Physician, Children's Department, London Hospital; Physician, Infants Hospital, Westminster; *b.* 1890; *e. s.* of late Rev. Joseph Maitland-Jones, M.A. and Jeannie Maitland; *m.* 1926, Miriam, *o. c.* of late John Ritchey, M.D., Oil City, Pa., U.S.A.; one *s.* one *d.* *Educ.:* Taunton School; London Hospital; Johns Hopkins Hospital. Served in European War as temporary Captain R.A.M.C. (despatches twice, Croix de Guerre); Late Assistant and Assistant Director on the Medical Unit, London Hospital; late Fellow in Research and Assistant Physician to Johns Hopkins Hospital, Baltimore, U.S.A.; Member Assoc. of Physicians of Great Britain and late Pres. of British Pædiatric Assoc.; sometime member of expert committee of League of Nations on infant and child nutrition. Late Sector Hospital Officer (Sector II) E.M.S. and Senior Hospital Officer, Southern Command. Past President Section Diseases of Children, R.S.M.; Consulting Physician, Dr. Barnardo's Homes, Royal Merchant Navy School, National Adoption Society, etc. *Publications:* Articles on diseases of Children in various text books. *Recreations:* shooting and fishing. *Address:* Glangrwyney Court, Crickhowell, Breconshire. *T.:* Crickhowell 175. *Clubs:* Athenæum, Flyfishers'. [*Died* 17 *May* 1957.

MAITLAND-MAKGILL-CRICHTON, Brig. H. C.; *see* Crichton.

MAJENDIE, Brig.-Gen. Bernard J., C.M.G. 1918; D.S.O. 1916; late King's Royal Rifle Corps; *b.* 27 April 1875; *s.* of late Rev. Arthur Majendie of Woodstock; *m.* Dorothy, *y. d.* of late G. W. Davidson, Queen's Gate, London; no *c.* *Educ.:* Winchester; Sandhurst. Joined 60th Rifles, 1896; Captain, 1901; Major, 1912; temp. Lt.-Col. 1915; Col. 1924; served in India and Mauritius; S. African War, 1899-1902 (Queen's medal 4 clasps, King's medal 2 clasps); European War, 1914-19 (despatches four times, D.S.O., Bt. Lt.-Col., Officer Legion of Honour); retired pay, 1928. *Address:* 6 Bereweeke Close, Winchester. *Club:* Army and Navy.
[*Died* 4 *Sept.* 1959.

MAJENDIE, Major-General Vivian Henry Bruce, C.B. 1941; D.S.O. 1917; D.L.; *b.* 20 April 1886; *s.* of late Prebendary H. W. Majendie; *m.* 1916, Evelyn Margaret Dickson, *d.* of late Col. Charles Dickson King, C.B.E.; two *s.* *Educ.:* Winchester College; Sandhurst. Served West African Frontier Force in S. Nigeria, 1908-13; India, 1913-June 1915; European War with B.E.F. 1915-19 (D.S.O.); commanded 1st Batt. Somerset Light Infantry, 1916-19; Brevet Major, 1919; Major, 1925; Bt. Lt.-Col., 1927; Lt.-Col. 1929; Bt. Col. 1931; Col. 1933; Maj.-Gen. 1938; Staff College, 1921; Brig.-Maj. 14th Infantry Brigade, Curragh, 1922; General Staff Officer, Royal Military College, Camberley, 1922-24; Staff Officer to the Inspector-General, West African Frontier Force, 1924-28; commanded 2nd Battalion The Somerset Light Infantry 1929-33; Imperial Defence College, 1932; G.S.O.1. Staff College, Camberley, 1933-36; Director of Military Training, Army Headquarters, India, 1936-38; Commander 55th (West Lancashire) Division T.A. 1938-41; G.O.C. Northern Ireland District, 1941-43; President, War Office Regular Commissions Board, 1943-46; retired, July 1946; Colonel Somerset L.I., 1938-47. D.L. Hertfordshire, 1951. *Address:* Chevrons, Goodyers Avenue, Radlett, Herts. *T.:* 6736. *Club:* Army and Navy. [*Died* 13 *Jan.* 1960.

MAJOR, Edith Helen, C.B.E. 1931; M.A (Cantab.); *b.* Lisburn, Co. Antrim, 15 Feb 1867; *d.* of Henry Major. *Educ.:* Methodis College, Belfast; Girton; Hons. in Historica Tripos. Head Mistress, Putney High School 1900-10; King Edward's High School for Girls, Birmingham, 1910-25; Mistress of Girton, 1925-31; late President of Head Mistresses Association; Hon. LL.D., Queen's University, Belfast, 1932. *Address:* c/o Mrs. E. K. Mack, Parkmount, Lisburn, N. Ireland.
[*Died* 17 *March* 1951.

MAJOR, Hon. Gerald A. G. H.; *see* Henniker-Major.

MAKINS, Brigadier-General Sir Ernest, K.B.E., *cr.* 1938; C.B. 1917; D.S.O 1902; *b.* London, 14 Oct. 1869; *e. s.* of late H. F. Makins, 180 Queen's Gate, S.W.; *m.* 1903, Florence, *d.* of late Sir J. R. Mellor; one *s.* (and two *s.* decd.). *Educ.:* Winchester; Christ Church, Oxford Joined 4th Batt. Essex Regt., 1889; The Royal Dragoons, 1892; Captain, 1898; Major, 1902; Lt.-Col. 1910; Col., 1914; served S. African War, 1899-1902 (despatches twice; Queen's medal 6 clasps; King's medal 2 clasps, D.S.O.); European War, 1914-18 (despatches, C.B.); Col. of The Royal Dragoons, 1931-46; M.P. (U.) Knutsford Division of Cheshire, 1922-45. Officer of the Italian Order of St. Maurice and Lazarus; F.R.G.S., M.R.I. *Address:* 180 Queen's Gate, S.W.7. *Clubs:* Carlton, Cavalry, M.C.C.
[*Died* 18 *May* 1959.

MALAN, Hon. Dr. Daniel François, M.A., D.D.; Prime Minister of the Union of South Africa and Minister for External Affairs, 1948-54, and formerly M.P. for Piquetberg; Chancellor of University of Stellenbosch; *b.* Riebeek W., C.P., 22 May 1874; *s.* of Daniel François Malan and Anna Magdalena du Toit, Riebeek West, Cape Province; *m.* Maria Louw; two *s.* *Educ.:* Victoria College, Stellenbosch; University of Utrecht (Holland). Late Leader of the Nationalist Party, also when it was in Opposition, in the Union Parliament. *Address:* Morewag, Stellenbosch, South Africa. [*Died* 7 *Feb.* 1959.

MALCOLM, Sir Dougal Orme, K.C.M.G. *cr.* 1938; President of the British South Africa Co., 1937; Director of several other companies; *b.* 6 Aug. 1877; *s.* of late William Rolle Malcolm and Georgina, *d.* of late Lord Charles Wellesley; *m.* 1st, 1910, Dora Claire (*d.* 1920), *d.* of late Hon. John Stopford; 2nd, 1923, Lady Evelyn Farquhar, *widow* of late Col. Francis Farquhar. *Educ.:* Eton; New College, Oxford. First Class Honours Classical Moderations and Literae Humaniores; Fellow of All Souls College, 1899; entered Colonial Office 1900; Private Secretary to Lord Selborne in South Africa, 1905-10; Secretary to Lord Grey in Canada, 1910-11; joined the Treasury, 1912; became a Director of the British South Africa Company, 1913; Chairman of Committee on Education and Industry appointed by the President of the Board of Education and the Minister of Labour, 1926-28; Member of the British Economic Mission to Australia, 1928; late Vice-Chairman of Court of Governors of London School of Economics and Political Science. Grand Cross, Military Order of Christ (Portugal). Hon. LL.D. Witwatersrand University. *Publications:* Nuces Relictae; The British South Africa Company, 1889-1939; Magazine articles. *Address:* 53 Bedford Gardens, Kensington, W.8. *T.:* Park 8784; Woodside, Liphook, Hants. *T.:* Liphook 2268. *Clubs:* Brooks's, Beefsteak. [*Died* 30 *Aug.* 1955.

MALCOLM, John, C.M.G. 1947; M.D., F.R.S.E.; Prof. of Physiology, Otago Univ., Dunedin, N.Z., 1905-44, now Emeritus Prof.; *b.* Caithness, 1873; *s.* of John Malcolm; *m.* 1912, *d.* of W. L. Simpson; two *s.* one *d.* *Educ.:* Edinburgh University. *Address:* 7 Royal Terrace, Dunedin, New Zealand.
[*Died* 17 *June* 1954.

MALCOLM, Maj.-Gen. Sir Neill, K.C.B., *cr.* 1922 (C.B. 1919); D.S.O. 1899; retired; Director and Chairman B.K.L. Alloys Ltd. and Neill Malcolm and Company Limited; *b.* 8 Oct. 1869; 2nd *s.* of late Col. E. D. Malcolm, C.B.; *m.* 1907, Angela (*d.* 1930), *o. d.* of late William Rolle Malcolm; two *s.* *Educ.:* St. Peter's School, York; Eton; Sandhurst. Princess Louise's (Argyll and Sutherland) Highlanders, 1889; Capt. 1898; Major, 1910; Lieut.-Col. 1916; served N.W. Frontier, India, 1897-98 (medal with clasp); Uganda, 1897-99 (despatches, medal with 2 clasps, D.S.O.); S. Africa, 1899-1900 (severely wounded, Paardeberg); Somaliland, 1903-4; European War, 1914-18 (despatches, C.B., prom. Bt. Lt.-Col., Bt.-Col. and Maj.-Gen.; severely wounded, 29 March 1918); British Military Mission, Berlin, 1919-21; G.O.C. Malaya, 1921-24; retired pay, 1924; High Commissioner for German Refugees, 1936-38; Order of the Nile, 3rd Class, 1916; Comm., Legion of Honour; Order of the Crown of Italy; Order of the White Eagle, Serbia; Croix de Guerre; British Mission to Fez, 1905; Editor of The Science of War. *Address:* 8 Evelyn Mansions, Carlisle Place, S.W.1. *T.:* Victoria 9696; The Mill House, Swallowcliffe, Wiltshire. *T.:* Tisbury 282. *Club:* Travellers'. [*Died* 21 *Dec.* 1953.

MALDEN, Very Rev. Richard Henry, B.D.; F.R.Hist.Soc.; *b.* 19 Oct. 1879; *e. s.* of late Charles Edward Malden, Recorder of Thetford, and Sarah Fanny, *d.* of Sir Richard Mayne, K.C.B.; *m.* 1918, Etheldred Theodora, *o. d.* of Canon H. A. Macnaghten, Rector of Tankersley. *Educ.:* Eton; King's College, Cambridge. Assistant Curate at St. Peter's, Swinton, Manchester, 1904-07; Lecturer at Selwyn Coll., Cambridge, 1907-10; Principal of Leeds Clergy School and Lecturer of Leeds, 1910-19; Acting Chaplain H.M.S. Valiant, Jan. 1916-Dec. 1917; Acting Chaplain R.N. 1916-18; Vicar of St. Michael's, Headingley, Leeds, 1918-33; Hon. Canon of Ripon, 1926-33; Dean of Wells, 1933-50; Examining Chaplain to the Bishop of Norwich since 1910; Proctor in Convocation, 1924-1933; Chaplain to the King, 1926-33; Pres. Somerset Archæological Society, 1943-44. Select Preacher, Cambridge, 1908, 1914, 1919, 1935, and 1939; T.C.D. 1932; Oxford, 1948-49. *Publications:* Foreign Missions, 1910; The Temptation of the Son of Man, 1913; Watchman, What of the Night?, 1918; The Old Testament, 1919; Problems of the New Testament To-day, 1923; The Church of Headingley in Four Centuries, 1923; Religion and the New Testament, 1928; This Church and Realm, 1931; The Roman Catholic Church and the Church of England, 1933; The Story of Wells Cathedral, 1934; The Inspiration of the Bible, 1935; The Apocrypha, 1936; The Promise of the Father, 1937; The Authority of the New Testament, 1937; Christian Belief, 1942; Nine Ghosts, 1942; The Growth of a Cathedral Church, 1944; Abbeys, their Rise and Fall, 1944. *Recreation:* walking. *Address:* 1 The Glen, Sunninghill, Berks. *Club:* Athenæum. [*Died* 19 *Aug.* 1951.

MÂLE, Emile; Professeur honoraire à la Sorbonne; Directeur honoraire de l'École française de Rome; *b.* 1862; *m.* Mademoiselle Marguerite Granier; un fils et une fille. *Educ.:* École Normale Supérieure. Membre de l'Académie française et de l'Académie des inscriptions et belles lettres; membre de la Société des Antiquaires de Londres, de l'Académie de Belgique, de l'Académie de Pologne, de l'Académie pontificale d'archeologie, de l'Académie de Lincei, etc. *Publications:* L'Art religieux du XIIe siècle en France; L'Art religieux du XIIIe siècle en France; L'Art religieux de la fin du moyen âge en France; L'Art religieux après La Concile de Trente; L'Art français et l'art allemand; Art et artistes du moyen âge; Rome et ses vieilles églises; L'art religieux du XIIe au XVIIIe siècle (pages choisies des volumes précédents); la Cathédrale de Chartres; La Fin du paganisme en Gaule et les plus anciennes basiliques chrétiennes; La Cathédrale d'Albi. *Address:* 11 rue de Navarre, Paris Ve. [*Died* 6 *Oct.* 1954.

MALIK, Sardar Bahadur Sir Teja Singh, Kt., *cr.* 1942; C.I.E. 1930; B.Sc., A.M.I.C.E.; Chief Engineer Public Works Dept., Jaipur State, since 1942; *b.* Rawalpindi; *s.* of Sardar Bahadur Mohansingh Malik, premier Rais of Punjab; *m.* 1905, Bibi Kaval Raj; two *s.* one *d.* *Educ.:* Gordon Mission College, Rawalpindi; University Coll., London. Acted as Assistant Engineer in Shillong (Assam), and on the construction of new capital of East Bengal Ramna (Dacca) Bengal up to March 1912; since then employed on the construction of various buildings and roads in the new capital at Delhi (India); from Aug. 1921 employed solely on the construction of Viceroy's House, New Delhi, as Executive Engineer; Superintending Engineer in New Delhi until 1940; Chief Engineer, Central Public Works Dept., New Delhi, 1940-42. *Recreation:* tennis. *Address:* Public Works Dept., Jaipur State, Rajputana, India. *T.:* 3162. *Clubs:* Imperial Delhi Gymkhana, Chelmsford, Roshanara (Delhi). [*Died* 3 *Feb.* 1953.

MALLABAR, Herbert John, F.R.P.S.; *b.* 18 Aug. 1871; *s.* of John Osborne and Anne Mallabar; *m.* Gertrude (*d.* 1932), *d.* of Hugh Jones, Barrow, Cheshire; three *s.* *Educ.:* Liverpool College. Manufacturer of photographic materials; carried out research work on cellulose acetate non-inflammable films, and on silver phosphate and hydroxylamine chloride photographic emulsions; patented processes for the manufacture of cellulose acetate; introduced into this country industry of baryta coating photographic base papers. *Publications:* Author of articles in technical press relating to photographic emulsions, cellulose acetate, photographic films, etc. *Recreations:* salmon fishing and photography. *Address:* 105 Cassiobury Drive, Watford, Herts. *Club:* Royal Automobile. [*Died* 23 *May* 1956.

MALLOCH, George Reston; Author; *b.* Elderslie, Renfrewshire; *s.* of John Malloch, The Glen, Elderslie. *Educ.:* Paisley Grammar School; privately. Several volumes of poetry; plays produced by Scottish National Theatre: Thomas the Rhymer, 1924; The House of the Queen, 1926; Soutarness Water, 1926; The Coasts of India, 1928; The Grenadier, 1929; Harvest, 1934; Known also as a writer of short stories in British, Dominion, Continental and American periodicals. *Publications:* Arabella, A Comedy, 1912; Lyrics and other Poems, 1913; Poems and Lyrics, 1917; Poems, 1920; Soutarness Water, A Tragedy, 1927; Human Voices (Poems), 1930; The Moments' Monuments (sonnets) 1932; Down in the Forest (Play), 1935. *Address:* 2 Suffolk Road, S.W.13. *Club:* Authors'. [*Died* 11 *Dec.* 1953.

MALONE, Mrs. L'Estrange; (Leah), M.A., J.P., L.C.C.; Chairman of L.C.C. Welfare Committee since 1949; *yr. d.* of Arthur and Regina Kay; *m.* Lieutenant-Colonel Cecil L'Estrange Malone; one *d.* *Educ.:* Somerville Coll., Oxford. Hons. degree in modern history. Private Sec. to late Lord Henry Cavendish Bentinck, M.P.; Vice-chm. and Chm. L.C.C. Public Assistance Cttee., 1934-1944; London C. Alderman and J.P., 1937; Vice-chm. L.C.C. Educ. Cttee., 1944-46; Member: Home Office (Morris) Cttee. on War Damaged Licenced Houses, 1942-43; Board of Trade Cttee. on Re-sale Price Maintenance, 1947-49; Welwyn Garden City and Hatfield Development Corporations. Almoner of Christ's Hospital; Hon. Sec. Labour Parl. Assoc.; Vice-chm. of Old Vic, Governor of Sadler's Wells; member Jt. Council of National Theatre and Old Vic; Chm. Sadler's Wells Ballet School. *Publications:* The Great Infanta, an historical monograph. *Recreations:* theatre, ballet, opera, travel. *Address:* 36 Buckingham Gate, S.W.1. *Clubs:* University Women's, Forum, Service Women's. [*Died* 4 *Sept.* 1951.

MAN, Col. Hubert William, C.B.E. 1919; D.S.O. 1916; late R.A.O.C.; *s.* of E. Garnet Man, J.P., and Catherine Jane, *d.* of J. H. Matthews; *m.* Beryl, *d.* of Colonel T. N. Holberton; one *s.* two *d.* *Educ.:* Rugby; Sandhurst. Joined Hampshire Regt., 1896; transferred to R.A.O.C., 1913; served S. African War, 1899-1901; Aden Hinterland, 1903-04; European War, 1915-18 and War of 1939-45, 1940-41; retired pay, 1933. *Address:* c/o Bank of Bermuda, Hamilton, Bermuda. *Club:* United Service. [*Died* 20 *June* 1956.

MAN, Captain Joseph, C.M.G. 1919; O.B.E. 1918; R.N.; *b.* March 1867; *s.* of late William Man, The Priory, Bromley, Middlesex; *m.* 1941, Winifred Nora Stirling, Coombe Dingle, Bristol. *Educ.:* privately; H.M.S. Worcester. Lieutenant R.N., 1895; retired with rank of Commander, 1912; served in Naval Transport Service, France; D.N.T.O. Dieppe, Calais (S.N.O.), Havre (S.N.O.), P.N.T.O. Antwerp; after Armistice P.N.T.O. Liverpool; Officer Legion of Honour; Commander Order of Leopold. *Recreations:* shooting, golf. *Address:* 20 Hill Court, Hill Road, Wimbledon, S.W.19. [*Died* 28 *May* 1951.

MANCHESTER, Sir William Edwin, Kt., *cr.* 1936; J.P. County of London; Director, Express Dairy Co., Ltd.; *b.* 1869; *s.* of late James Manchester, Holloway, N.; *m.* 1897, Maud Annie (*d.* 1953), *d.* of late John Graham, Barnsbury, N.; two *s.* Alderman Borough of Islington, 1909-19 and 1922-34; Mayor, 1929-1930; Member Metropolitan Water Board, 1928-40; Hon. Freeman of Islington, 1932. *Address:* 9 Page's Hill, Muswell Hill, N.10. *T.:* Tudor 7433. [*Died* 5 *May* 1956.

MANDER, Sir Charles Arthur, 2nd Bt., *cr.* 1911, B.A., D.L., J.P., T.D.; Major, late Staffordshire Yeomanry; a Managing Director of Mander Bros., Ltd.; Director of Manders (Holdings) Ltd., Manders Printing Inks Ltd., John Kidd & Co. Ltd.; *b.* 25 June 1884; *s.* of 1st Bt. and Mary Le Mesurier, *d.* of Henry Nicholas Paint, Halifax, N.S.; *S.* father, 1929; *m.* 1913, Monica Claire Cotterill, *d.* of late G. H. Neame; one *s.* two *d.* *Educ.:* Eton; Trinity College, Cambridge (B.A.). High Sheriff Staffs, 1926; President Rotary International, G. B. and I., 1929-30; Mayor of Wolverhampton, 1932-33 and 1936-37; Hon. Freeman, 1945. *Recreations:* music, shooting, golf. *Heir:* *s.* Charles Marcus [*b.* 22 Sept. 1921; *m.* 1945, Maria Dolores Beatrice, *d.* of late Alfred Broderman; one *s.*]. *Address:* Kilsall Hall, Shifnal. *T.A.:* Tong. *T.:* Albrighton 3. *Club:* Cavalry. [*Died* 25 *Jan.* 1951.

MANIFOLD, Major-General Sir Courtenay Clarke, K.C.B., *cr.* 1922 (C.B. 1914); C.M.G. 1917; M.B.; *b.* 3 April 1864; *s.* of Surg.-Gen. M. F. Manifold; *m.* 1904, Josephine Beaumont Manifold (*d.* 1941), *d.* of Captain Charles Montagu, Royal Engineers, London and Wisconsin; *m.* 1944, Christine F., 4th *d.* of late Preb. Scott, Tiverton. *Educ.:* Clifton College; University of Edinburgh. Entered Indian Medical Service, 1887; served in Central India Horse till 1893, and till 1899 in charge of Rampur State, with an interval in 1897 of active service on Tirah campaign (despatches, medal and clasp); deputed on mission to Western China, 1899 (received thanks of H.E the Commander-in-Chief in India); on active service on headquarters staff at Relief of Peking, 1900 (despatches, medal and clasp, specially promoted to Lieut.-Col.); in command of mission to Central and Western China, 1900-1 (received Macgregor medal for exploration and thanks of Lord Kitchener); in command of special mission to Tsu-chuan, 1904-05 (received thanks of H.M.'s Secretary of State for Foreign Affairs for work accomplished by mission); Inspector-General Hospitals, United Provinces, India, 1910-15; Member of Legislative Council, United Provinces, India, 1910-15; Director Medical Services A. and N.Z.A. Corps, B.E.F., 1916-17; D.M.S. Australians, 1918 (C.M.G., despatches twice, Belgian Croix de Guerre); Major-General, 1917; retired 1923; Hon. Physician to the King, 1918; Deputy Commissioner for Cyprus for War Organisation British Red Cross and Order of St. John since 1940. *Publications:* papers published by Royal Geographical Society on Explorations in China. *Address:* Harbour Heights, Kyrenia, Cyprus. *Clubs:* United Service, East India and Sports. [*Died* 7 *June* 1957.

MANIFOLD, Major-General John Alexander, C.B. 1943; D.S.O. 1919; M.D.; D.P.H.; late R.A.M.C.; *b.* 12 Dec. 1884; *s.* of John Manifold and Edith Cameron; *m.* 1909, Ella Mackintosh; (two *s.* both decd.). *Educ.:* George Watson's College, Edinburgh; Edinburgh University (M.B., Ch.B. 1907, M.D. 1942). Lieut. R.A.M.C. 1909; Capt. 1912; Bt. Major 1919; Major, 1921; Lt.-Col. 1933; Bt. Col. 1936; Col. 1937; Brig. 1940; Maj.-Gen. 1941. D.P.H. London (Conjoint), 1923; Montefiore Prize and Medal R.A.M. College, 1909; Leishman memorial prize and Medal, 1928; Asst. Professor Pathology R.A.M. College, 1921-1924; Deputy Asst. Director of Pathology, Poona District, 1924-26; Asst. Director of Hygiene and Pathology, Western Command, India, 1926-27; Asst. Director of Pathology, A.H.Q., India, 1927-31; O.C. British Military Hospital, Calcutta, 1934; Asst. Director of Hygiene and Pathology, Eastern Command, India, 1935; Deputy Director of Hygiene and Pathology, A.H.Q., India, 1936-39; Director of Hygiene, War Office, 1939-41; D.D.M.S., Scottish Command, 1941; K.H.P., 1941-44; retired pay, 1944. Served European War, 1914-1918, Mediterranean, Egypt, German and Portuguese East Africa (despatches twice, D.S.O., Bt. Major). Hon. Surgeon to Viceroy in India, 1937. Liberty Cross of Norway. *Publications:* articles in medical journals; *inter alia:* important features in the correct diagnosis of Dysentery in India; study of certain features in connection with Enteric Group Infections in the Army in India. *Address:* c/o Glyn, Mills & Co., Whitehall, S.W.1. [*Died* 27 *Feb.* 1960.

MANISTY, Rear-Admiral Sir (Henry Wilfred) Eldon, K.C.B. *cr.* 1932 (C.B. 1919); C.M.G. 1916; *b.* 1876; *e. s.* of late Henry Clayton Manisty, Tynemouth; *m.* 1911, Florence Henderson (*d.* 1956), *y. d.* of late David Henderson McCathie, Sydney, N.S.W.; two *s.* *Educ.:* Barnard Castle School. Entered Royal Navy, 1894; as Assist.-Paymaster served in Peking Relief Expedition, 1900 (medal and clasp); specially promoted to rank of Paymaster, 1903, for services in China; Barrister-at-law (Gray's Inn), 1908; Finance Member and Naval Secretary of Australian Naval Board of Administration, 1911-14; served European War, 1914-19 (Organising Manager of Convoy, Admiralty Naval Staff, 1917-19) (C.M.G., C.B.); Deputy Judge-Advocate of the Fleet, 1925-27; Port Accountant Officer at Portsmouth, 1927-29; Paymaster Director-General at Admiralty, 1929-32; retired list, 1932; recalled, 1936-46; Head of Convoy Sect., Ministry of War Transport, 1939-42. [*Died* 26 *Aug.* 1960.

MANLEY, Professor Edgar Booth, M.Sc.; F.D.S.R.C.S.Eng.; Professor of Dental Pathology, University of Birmingham, since 1949; *b.* 18 July 1897; *s.* of Richard Manley and Mary Alice Booth; *m.* 1937, Eleanor Margherite Holden; one *s.* one *d.* *Educ.:* Epworth College; University of Manchester. L.D.S. 1920; B.D.S. 1942; M.Sc. 1944; F.D.S.R.C.S.Eng. 1948. Lecturer in Dental Histology, also in Dental Anatomy, Univ. of Manchester, 1930-37; Hon. Dental Surgeon to Cheshire County Mental Hosp., Lectr. in

Dental Prosthetics and Director of Mechanics Dept., Edinburgh Dental Hosp. and School, 1937-39; Surgical Registrar, Birmingham Dental Hosp., 1939-45; University of Birmingham: Hon. Asst. Lectr. in Special Anatomy of the Teeth, 1940-45; Lectr. in Dental Anatomy and Histology and Dental Pathology, 1946-48; Reader in Dental Pathology, 1948-49. Member Dental Cttee. of Medical Research Council; Vice-Pres. Odontological Section of Roy. Soc. of Med.; Examr. in Dental Subjects to Roy. Coll. of Surgeons of England, and to Univs. of London and Durham; late Examr. to Univs. of Glasgow and Manchester. F.Z.S. *Publications:* An Atlas of Dental Histology, 1947 (2nd edn. 1955); numerous publications in scientific journals. *Recreations:* golf, gardening. *Address:* 10 Woodrough Drive, Moseley, Birmingham 13. *T.:* South 2805.
[*Died* 4 *April* 1959.

MANN, Cathleen; (Mrs. J. R. Follett) R.P.; (professional name Cathleen Mann); *d.* of late Harrington Mann and Florence Sabine Mann; *m.* 1st, 1926, 11th Marquess of Queensberry (from whom she obtained a divorce, 1946); one *s.* (12th Marquess of Queensberry) one *d.*; 2nd, 1946, John Robert Follett (*d.* 1953), *s.* of late Brig. Follett and of Lady Mildred Fitzgerald. *Educ.:* privately. Artist, represented in the Victoria and Albert Museum, and the Luxembourg, Glasgow Institute and San Diego, U.S.A., permanent collections; Member Nat. Soc., Women's International Society, Royal Society of Arts, and Roy. Soc. of Portrait Painters. *Recreation (and work):* painting. *Address:* 41 Montpelier Walk, S.W.7.
[*Died* 9 *Sept.* 1959.

MANN, Hon. Sir Frederick Wollaston, K.C.M.G., *cr.* 1937; Kt., *cr.* 1933; *b.* Mt. Gambier, S.A., 1869; *s.* of late Gilbert Cheke Mann, Glenelg, S. Australia; *m.* 1911, Adeline, *d.* of late William Raleigh, Melbourne; one *s.* three *d.* (and one *s.* decd.). *Educ.:* Mt. Gambier Grammar School; Melbourne Univ. Called to Bar, 1896; Justice of the Supreme Court of Victoria, 1919-35; Acting Chief Justice, 1933-34; Chief Justice, 1935-44; resigned from Bench, 1944; Lieut.-Governor of Victoria, 1936-1945; Lieut., 4th Vic. M.R., South Africa, 1900-01. *Address:* 176 Walsh Street, South Yarra, Melbourne, S.E.1, Victoria, Australia. *Club:* Melbourne (Melbourne).
[*Died* 29 *May* 1958.

MANN, Sir John, K.B.E., *cr.* 1918; chartered accountant; *b.* Glasgow, 8 Apr. 1863; *s.* of John Mann, C.A., Glasgow; *m.* 1894, Margaret, *d.* of James Henderson, Glasgow; two *s.* three *d.* *Educ.:* Glasgow University, M.A. 1885. Professional affairs in Glasgow, London, and abroad; interested in Experiments in Workmen's Housing, Public Management of Liquor Traffic, Educational affairs, University, Training of Teachers, Commercial Education, Industrial Psychology; Financial Adviser in Ministry of Munitions of War, 1915; Assistant Financial Secretary in Ministry, 1917; Controller of Munitions Contracts, Ministry of Munitions, 1917-19. *Publications:* various articles on Housing, Liquor Control, Cost Accounting, etc. *Address:* 8 Frederick's Place, E.C.2. *Club:* Reform.
[*Died* 3 *March* 1955.

MANN, Sir John, Kt., *cr.* 1955; C.B.E. 1948; J.P.; D.L.; Convener of Lanarkshire County Council since 1945. D.L. Lanarkshire, 1951. *Address:* 2 Coldwell Terrace, Carnwath, Lanarkshire. [*Died* 24 *Dec.* 1957.

MANN, Ludovic MacLellan; President, Glasgow Archæological Society, 1931-33; President, Provand's Lordship Club, 1934-36; F.S.A. (Scot.); Member of Prehistoric Society and other scientific societies in Scotland and England, on the Councils of several of which he has served; trained in accountancy and insurance; became by examination an Associate of the Institute of Chartered Accountants and Actuaries, 1898; Councillor of the Corporation of Insurance Brokers, London; Chairman of Mann, Ballantyne & Co., Ltd. Insurance Administrators and Brokers, Glasgow and London; *y. s.* of John Mann, C.A., Glasgow, and Mary Newton Harrington; unmarried. *Educ.:* Scotland; Continent. Invented in 1899 the now universally adopted system of Consequential Loss Insurance; inaugurated other forms of insurance; discovered a hitherto unrecognised astronomical culture in prehistoric times; discovered the long-period nutation; organised Exhibition at Glasgow of Prehistoric Relics, 1911; and of Italian Old Stone Age Relics, London, 1934. *Publications:* special articles to periodicals, etc.; The Barochan Cross, 1919; Archaic Sculpturings, 1914; Queen Mary of Scots, 1918; A Lost Civilization, 1927; Craftsmen's Measures in Prehistoric Times, 1930; Earliest Glasgow, 1935; Ancient Measures: Their Origin and Meaning, 1938; Appeal: The Druid Temple, Glasgow, 1938; The Druid Temple Explained, 1939. *Recreations:* large collection of Prehistoric, Mediæval, and Neo-Archaic relics. *Address:* 56 Kingsway, W.C.2; 183 West George Street, Glasgow; 4 Lynedoch Crescent, Glasgow. *Clubs:* Conservative, Art (Glasgow).
[*Died* 30 *Sept.* 1955.

MANN, Thomas; *b.* Lübeck, 6 June 1875; *m.* 1905, Katja Pringsheim; three *s.* three *d.* Won Nobel Prize for Literature, 1929; left Germany, 1933; in Switzerland until 1938; lived in the U.S.A., 1938-. Hon. LL.D. Cambridge University, 1953; Hon. Freedom of the City of Lübeck, 1955; German Order Pour le Mérite, 1955. *Publications:* Buddenbrooks, German Edn., 1901 (Eng., 1924); Der Zauberberg, 1924 (Eng.: The Magic Mountain, 1928); Lotte in Weimar, 1939 (Eng., 1940); Unordnung und Frühes Leid, 1926; Mario und der Zauberer, 1930 (Eng.: Early Sorrow and Mario and the Magician, 1953); Joseph in Aegypten, 1936 (Eng.: Joseph in Egypt, 1938); Stories of Three Decades, 1936, containing: (Little Herr Friedemann, Disillusionment, The Dilettante, Tobias Mindernickel, Little Lizzy, The Wardrobe, The Way to the Churchyard, Tonio Kröger, Tristan, The Hungry, The Infant Prodigy, Gladius Dei, Fiorenza, A Gleam, At the Prophet's, A Weary Hour, The Blood of the Walsungs, Railway Accident, The Fight between Jappe and Do Escober, Felix Krull, Death in Venice, A Man and his Dog, Disorder and Early Sorrow, Mario and the Magician); The Coming Victory of Democracy, 1938; This War, 1940; Joseph der Ernährer, 1943 (Eng.: Joseph the Provider, 1944); Essays of Three Decades, 1947; Doktor Faustus, 1947 (Eng.: Doctor Faustus, 1949); Der Erwählte, 1951 (Eng.: The Holy Sinner, 1952); Die Betrogene, 1953 (Eng.: The Black Swan, 1954); Felix Krull, 1954 (Eng.: 1955); posthumous, in English: A Sketch of My Life (first publ., 1930), Letters to Paul Amann (1915-1952), 1961; The Genius of a Novel, 1961. *Address:* Erlenbach, nr. Zürich. [*Died* 12 *Aug.* 1955.

MANNERS, Brig. Charles Molyneux Sandys, D.S.O. 1916; M.C.; I.A. retired; *b.* 24 Jan. 1885; *s.* of late Col. R. A. Manners; *m.* 1919, Maisie, *e. d.* of John J. Calder, Ardargie, Forgandenny; one *s.* one *d.* *Educ.:* Stonyhurst. 2nd Lt. 1905; Lt. 1907; Capt. 1914; Maj. 1920; Lt.-Col. 1930; Col. 1934; Brig. 1937; served European War, Mesopotamia, 1914-1916; P.O.W. 1916-18 (D.S.O., M.C., despatches twice); commanded 4th Batt. 13th Frontier Force Rifles, 1930-33; A.A.G. India, 1933-37; Commander Ferozepore Brigade Area, India, 1937-40; A.D.C. to the King, 1939-40; retd., 1940. *Address:* c/o Grindlay's Bank, 54 Parliament St., S.W.1.
[*Died* 13 *Nov.* 1954.

MANNERS, Rear-Admiral Sir Errol, K.B.E., *cr.* 1943; R.N., retired; *b.* 1883; 2nd *s.* of Herbert and Emma Manners,

Ilmasnugger, Tirhoot, India; *m.* 1st, 1908, Maud, *d.* of J. S. Harrison, Sydney, Australia; three *s.* one *d.*; 2nd, 1927, Kathleen, *d.* of James Miller Johnson, Newcastle, New South Wales. Joined Royal Navy 1898; served European War, 1914-18 (despatches); Capt. 1923; Rear-Adm. 1935; retd. list, 1935, recalled and employed as commodore ocean convoys (despatches, K.B.E.). *Recreations:* played for Navy at Rugby, hockey and lawn tennis. *Address:* Haddon, The Avenue, Fareham, Hants. [*Died* 23 *Oct.* 1953.

MANNING, Air Commodore Edye Rolleston, C.B.E. 1943; D.S.O. 1924; M.C.; R.A.F. (ret.); member of Sydney Stock Exchange; *b.* Sydney, New South Wales, Australia, 14 Feb. 1889; *s.* of late William Alexander Manning, solicitor, and Marion Manning of Sydney, N.S.W.; *m.* 1930, Phyllis Mary Louise, *o. d.* of C. A. Degenhardt, Killara, Sydney, N.S.W.; one *s.* two *d.* *Educ.:* Sydney Church of England Grammar School. Cavalry Aug. 1914; served B.E.F., 2nd Lt. 15th Hussars, France and Belgium; transferred R.F.C., 1915 (M.C.); Iraq and Khurdistan, 1922-24 (D.S.O); retired list, 1935; recalled to Active List, Aug. 1939; Service Malaya, Burma, India, Great Britain, 1939-43; Acting Air Commodore, 1942; reverted to retired list, 1945, rank Air Cdre. *Clubs:* R.A.F.; Australian, New South Wales (Sydney). [*Died* 26 *April* 1957.

MANNING, John Westley, Q.C. 1920; *b.* 1866; *s.* of late Wm. Manning, London; *m.* Eliz. Ada (*d.* 1922), *d.* of late Robt. Chapman of Littlebury, Essex. *Educ.:* University College School and University College, London; M.A. (London University), 1887. Called to Bar, Lincoln's Inn, 1891; Bencher, 1923. *Address:* The Red House, Barton-on-Sea, Hants. [*Died* 19 *Dec.* 1954.

MANNING, W. Westley, R.B.A.; A.R.E.; *s.* of late William Manning; *m.* Lisa Madeline (*d.* 1950), *d.* of late Capt. A. H. H. Johnstone, R.N.; no *c.* *Educ:* University College School; matriculated at London University. Landscape painter, etcher and aquatinter; studied at Académie Julian, Paris; exhibitor at the R.A., Paris Salon, Rouen, International Society, New English Art Club, Glasgow and Edinburgh; and International Exhibitions at Brussels, Munich, Mannheim, Barcelona, Venice, Budapest, Oslo, Madrid, Argentina, St. Louis, Chicago, Tokio and Osaka, Japan; works are included in the British Museum, Victoria and Albert Museum, Stockholm Academy, Moscow, Johannesburg, Los Angeles, and Bucharest. *Publication:* Etchings and Aquatints. *Address:* 26 Gledhow Gardens, S.W.5. *Club:* Arts. [*Died* 15 *April* 1954.

MANNINGHAM-BULLER, Lt.-Col. Sir Mervyn Edward, 3rd Bt., *cr.* 1866; *b.* 16 Jan. 1876; *s.* of late Maj.-Gen. Edward Manningham Manningham-Buller and Lady Anne Coke, 2nd *d.* of 2nd Earl of Leicester; *S.* uncle, 1910; *m.* 1903, Hon. Lilah Constance Cavendish (*d.* 1944), *o. surv. d.* of 3rd Baron Chesham; one *s.* four *d.* Contested Heywood Div. Lancs, 1906 and 1910; M.P. (C.) Kettering Division of Northamptonshire, 1924-29; Northampton, 1931-40; commanded 12th (S.) Battalion Rifle Brigade, 1914-16. *Heir: s.* Major Rt. Hon. Sir Reginald Edward Manningham-Buller, M.P. *Address:* 47 Lowndes Square, S.W.1. *Club:* Carlton. [*Died* 22 *Aug.* 1956.

MANNOOCH, Geoffrey Herbert, C.I.E. 1943; J.P.; *b.* 23 Aug. 1890; *o. surv. s.* of late Charles and Florence Mannooch; *m.* Dorothy Beatrice, *o. d.* of John Francis Cousins, Hove, Sussex; two *d.* by former marriage. *Educ.:* Brighton College. Indian Police, 1910; Indian Army Reserve Officers, India and Salonika, Capt. 1917-19; Principal Police Training Coll., Bengal, 1925-28; D.I.G. Dacca Range, 1932, Bakarganj Range, 1935-40, Rajshahi Range, 1940-42; Inspector-General of Police, Bengal, 1942-46; retired, 1947. King's Police Medal. *Recreations:* bookcollecting and bookbinding. *Address:* 29 King's Mansions, Durban, Natal. *Clubs:* East India and Sports; United Service, Saturday (Calcutta). [*Died* 6 *Oct.* 1959.

MANSBRIDGE, Albert, C.H. 1931; Hon. M.A. (Oxon); Hon. LL.D. (Cambridge, Manchester, Pittsburgh, Mount Allison); Hon. F.L.A.; *b.* Gloucester, 10 Jan. 1876; *s.* of Thomas Mansbridge, mechanic, and Frances Thomas; *m.* 1900, Frances Jane, *d.* of John Pringle, Dublin; one *s.* *Educ.:* Elementary schools and Battersea Grammar School. Founded Workers' Educational Association in England, 1903; in Australia, 1913; First Secretary, 1903-15; Member of Government Committees on Education, including the Consultative Committee of the Board of Education, 1906-12, 1924-39, and the Prime Minister's Committee on the Teaching of Modern Languages, 1915-1918; Member of the Royal Commission on the Universities of Oxford and Cambridge, 1919-22; Member of the Statutory Commission on Oxford, 1923; Member of the Selborne Committee on Church and State, 1914-16, and numerous Church Committees; Lecturer on the Lowell Foundation, Boston, U.S.A., 1922 and 1934; on the Earle Foundation, California, 1926; Expert Adviser to British and Australian Army Education Services, 1918-19; Founder, National Central Library, Seafarers Education Service, etc. *Publications:* University Tutorial Classes, 1913; An Adventure in Working Class Education, 1920; The Older Universities of England, 1923. Margaret McMillan, Prophet and Pioneer, 1932; Brick Upon Brick: The Co-operative Permanent Building Society, 1934; Talbot and Gore, 1935; The Trodden Road, 1940; The Kingdom of the Mind, 1944; Fellow Men, 1948. *Recreation:* walking. *Address:* Windways, Dartmouth Rd., Paignton, Devon. *T.:* Churston 81265. *Club:* Athenæum. [*Died* 22 *Aug.* 1952.

MANSON, Henry James, C.M.G. 1928; *b.* 1869; *m.* 1899, Miss Paton; one *s.* one *d.* *Educ.:* Scotch College, Melbourne. New Zealand Trade Commissioner and Government Agent in Commonwealth of Australia, 1906-30; retired 1930. *Address:* Mangoane, Raetihi, New Zealand. [*Died* 30 *Jan.* 1952.

MANSON, Rev. Thomas Walter, D.D., D.Litt. (Glas.); M.A. (Oxon, Cantab., Manc.); Hon. D.D. (Cantab., Dublin, Dunelm. Pine Hill, Halifax, N.S.); Hon. Dr. (Strasbourg); F.B.A. (Burkitt Medal, 1950); Rylands Professor of Biblical Criticism and Exegesis in the University of Manchester since 1936; Dean of the Faculty of Theology, 1941-52; Pro-Vice-Chancellor, 1945-49; *b.* 22 July 1893; *s.* of Thomas F. Manson and Joan Johnson; *m.* 1926, Nora, J.P., *d.* of J. R. W. Wallace; no *c.* *Educ.:* Private School; Tynemouth High School; Glasgow University; Christ's College (scholar) and Westminster College Cambridge. B.E.F. France (Lieut. R.F.A.) 1916 (wounded) and 1918; M.A. (Glas.) Hons. in Mental and Moral Philosophy Class 1 1919; Clark and Ferguson Scholarships; Oriental Languages Tripos Pt. 2 Class 1 1923, Burney Prize 1923, Tyrwhitt Scholarship and Mason prize 1924; Tutor of Westminster College 1922-1925; Minister of the Presbyterian Church of England at Bethnal Green, 1925-26 and Falstone, Northumberland 1926-32; Yates Professor of New Testament Greek and Exegesis, Mansfield College, Oxford, 1932-36, and University Lecturer in New Testament Studies, 1935-36; Russell Lecturer, Auburn Theological Seminary and Shaffer Lect., Yale, 1939; Grinfield Lect., Oxf., 1943-45; Ayer Lect., Colgate-Rochester Theol. Sem., Zenos Lect., MacCormick Theol. Sem., Chicago, 1952; T. V. Moore Lecturer, San Francisco Theol. Sem. 1955; Corresp., Mem. Göttingen Acad.; Moderator of General Assembly of Presbyterian Church of England, 1953; Operations Officer N.W. Regional H.Q. 1939-41; Capt. 61st (Manch. Univ.) Bn. Lancs.

H.G. *Publications:* The Teaching of Jesus, 1931; The Mission and Message of Jesus (with H. D. A. Major and C. J. Wright), 1937; A Companion to the Bible (Editor), 1939; God and the Nations, 1940; The Church's Ministry, 1948; The Sayings of Jesus, 1949; The Beginning of the Gospel, 1950; The Servant-Messiah, 1953; (with G. Zuntz) Editor of Manchester University Loose-Leaf Texts; contributions to theological journals. *Recreations:* music, painting, fishing. *Address:* Croft House, Carr Bank, Milnthorpe, Westmorland. *T.:* Arnside 258.
[*Died* 1 *May* 1958.

MANSON, Rev. William, B.A. (Oxon.); D.D. (Glasgow); *b.* 14 April 1882; *e. s.* of Alexander Manson, Cambuslang, Lanarkshire; *m.* 1914, Mary D., *yr. d.* of Arch. Ferguson, Writer, Glasgow. *Educ.:* The High School and University of Glasgow; Oriel College, Oxford (Scholar). First Class in Hon. Mods. and in Lit. Hum. at Oxford (1908); George A. Clark Classical Scholar, University of Glasgow; studied Theology at the United Free Church College (now Trinity College), Glasgow; ordained, 1911; held charges at Oban, 1911-14, and at Pollokshields East, Glasgow, 1914-19; Bruce Lecturer, 1914; Professor of New Testament Language and Literature in Knox College, Toronto, 1919-25; Professor of New Testament, New College, Edinburgh, 1925; and in Edinburgh University, 1935; Professor of Biblical Criticism in the University of Edinburgh, 1946-52; Cunningham Lecturer, 1940; Baird Lecturer, 1950. Vice-Pres., British Council of Churches, 1950-52; Scottish Chairman of Anglo-Scottish Conference on Inter-Communion; Pres. *Studiorum Novi Testamenti Societas*, 1952-53. *Publications:* Christ's View of the Kingdom of God: Bruce Lectures, 1918; The Incarnate Glory: an Expository Study of St. John's Gospel, 1923; The Gospel of Luke, in the Moffatt Commentary series, 1930; Jesus the Messiah, 1943; The Epistle to the Hebrews, 1951; The Way of the Cross, 1958; reviews and articles. *Address:* 21 Grange Terrace, Edinburgh 9. *T.:* Edinburgh, 44107.
[*Died* 4 *April* 1958.

MANTOUX, Paul Joseph, C.B.; Emeritus Director of the Graduate Institute of International Studies, Geneva; *b.* Paris, 14 April 1877; *m.* 1911, Mathilde Dreyfus; three *s.* *Educ.:* Lycée Condorcet, Paris; École Normale Supérieure. Agrégé d'histoire et de géographie, 1897; Docteur ès lettres, 1906; Professor of Modern French History and Institutions in the University of London, 1913; served in French Army, August 1914; Officer Interpreter on a special mission in England, 1915; Interpreter of the Supreme War Council, and of the Peace Conference, 1919; Director of the Political Section, League of Nations Secretariat, 1920-27; Professor at the Conservatoire National des Arts et Métiers, Paris, 1934-44; Officier de la Légion d'Honneur. *Publications:* La Crise du Trade-Unionisme (with M. Alfassa), 1903; La Révolution industrielle au XVIIIe siècle, 1906; 2nd ed. 1928; Notes sur les comptes rendus des séances du Parlement anglais au XVIIIe siècle, conservés aux archives des Affaires Étrangères, 1906; A travers l'Angleterre contemporaine, 1909; Les Délibérations du Conseil des Quatre (28.III-28.VI, 1919), 1955; Contribution to the history of the lost opportunities of the League of Nations (in The World Crisis, Geneva, 1938); articles in the Revue de Paris, Revue Historique, Revue d'Histoire moderne et contemporaine, Revue de Synthèse historique, Bulletin of the Royal Institute of International Affairs, etc. *Address:* 45 Rue Scheffer, Paris xvi. *T.:* Passy 26, 06.
[*Died* 13 *Dec.* 1956.

MANUEL, Stephen, C.B.E. 1920; *b.* 1880. Chief of Section of Raw Materials Department and Adviser on East Indian Tanned Hides and Skins. *Educ.:* Tonbridge. *Address:* Martlesham House, Martlesham, nr. Woodbridge, Suffolk. *T.:* Kesgrave 12.
[*Died* 26 *July* 1954.

MANVERS, 6th Earl (*cr.* 1806), **Gervas Evelyn Pierrepont,** M.C.; Viscount Newark and Baron Pierrepont, 1796; *b.* 15 April 1881; *s.* of late Hon. Evelyn Henry Pierrepont; *S.* cousin 1940; *m.* 1918, Marie-Louise Roosevelt, *d.* of late Sir Frederick Butterfield; one *d.* (and one *s.* one *d.* decd.). *Educ.:* Winchester; R.I.E.C., Coopers' Hill. Engineering Department, Bengal and North-Western Railway, 1903-1911; Meerut Divisional Cavalry, 1914-15; Claims Commission B.E.F., 1915-19 (M.C., 1914 Star, Belgian Order of the Crown and Croix de Guerre); Member L.C.C. for Brixton, 1922-46; Notts County Council, 1940-46; D.L. Notts; J.P. London and Notts. *Address:* Thoresby Park, Ollerton, Notts. *T.:* Edwinstowe 315 or 376; 14 South Terrace, S.W.7. *T.:* Kensington 2080. *Clubs:* Carlton, Junior Carlton; Notts County (Nottingham).
[*Died* 13 *Feb.* 1955 (*ext.*).

MAPP, Henry William; retd.; *b.* 1871; *m.* 1st (wife *d.* 1950); two *s.* one *d.*; 2nd, 1951. Officer of Salvation Army, 49 years; held rank of Commissioner for 23 years and Chief of Staff and second in command of the International Salvation Army for 8 years; served for years as an officer in India and Ceylon; held administrative positions in Great Britain and Canada; was in command of the Army in South America and then in Japan; subsequently pioneered the Salvation Army's work in Russia, and later acted as International Secretary; has travelled in most parts where the Salvation Army is at work; was Vice-President Reliance Bank, Ltd., Salvation Army Fire Insurance Corporation, Ltd., Salvation Army Assurance Society, Ltd., and Vice-Chairman Salvation Army Trustee Co.; Fellow Royal Empire Society. *Address:* 52 Nightingale Lane, Bromley, Kent. *T.:* Ravensbourne 1323. *Club:* Veterans (Beckenham).
[*Died* 2 *April* 1955.

MAR, 12th Earl of, *cr.* 1565, **and KELLIE,** 14th Earl of, *cr.* 1619, **Walter John Francis Erskine,** K.T., 1911; J.P.; 17th Baron Erskine, 1429; Viscount Fentoun, 1606; Lord Dirleton, 1603; Premier Viscount; Hereditary Keeper of Stirling Castle; Lord-Lieut. County of Clackmannan since 1898; Chancellor of Order of the Thistle, 1932-49; late Honorary Colonel 7th Battalion Argyll and Sutherland Highlanders; President County Territorial Association; *b.* 1865; *e. s.* of 11th Earl and Mary Anne, *e. d.* of William Forbes; *S.* father, 1888; *m.* 1892, Lady Violet Ashley (*d.* 1938), *d.* of 8th Earl of Shaftesbury; one *s.* (and *er. s.* and one *d.* decd.). Lord Clerk Register and Keeper of the Signet, 1936-44; Conservative. Anglo-Catholic. Representative Peer for Scotland, 1892-1950. *Educ.:* Eton. Lieut. Scots Guards, 1887-92. *Heir: g.s.* Lord Erskine (later 13th Earl of Mar and 15th Earl of Kellie). *Address:* Alloa House, Alloa; Kellie Castle, Fife. *Club:* Carlton.
[*Died* 3 *June* 1955.

MARCH, General Payton C.; *b.* Easton, Pa., 27 Dec. 1864; *s.* of Francis Andrew March and Mildred Stone Conway; *m.* 1st, 1891, Mrs. Josephine (Smith) Cuningham (*d.* 1904); two *d.*; 2nd, 1923, Cora Virginia, *d.* of Arthur McEntee, Brooklyn, U.S.A. *Educ.:* Lafayette Coll., A.B., A.M., LL.D.; LL.D. Amherst Coll. and Union Coll.; Mil. Sc.D. Pennsylvania Mil. Coll., 1934; B.S., U.S. Mil. Acad., West Point. Served Spanish American War, 1898; Philippine War, 1899-1901; A.D.C. to Gen. Arthur MacArthur; Bt. Maj., Lieut.-Col., Col.; Capt. on first General Staff, U.S. Army, 1903-1907; Mil. Attaché with Japanese Army, Russo-Japanese War, 1904; Texas Border, 1917; served France, Maj.-Gen. commanding A.E.F. Artillery, 1917-18; General and Chief of Staff, U.S., 1918-21; retired 1921.

Thanks of Congress, 1953; Distinguished Service Cross, Distinguished Service Medal, Silver Star Medal (with 5 Oak Leaf clusters); G.C.M.G.; Grand Officer, Legion of Honour; Knight of Grand Cross of Order of St. Maurizio e Lazzaro; Grand Cordon, Order of Crown of Belgium; Grand Cross of Order of George I (Greece); Grand Cross, Order of Crown of Rumania; War Cross of Czecho-Slovakia; Grand Cordon, Order of Chiao-Ho (China); Grand Cordon, Order of Polonia Restituta; Grand Cordon, Rising Sun of Japan. *Publication:* The Nation at War, 1932. *Address:* 1870 Wyoming Ave., Washington, D.C. *Clubs:* Army and Navy (Washington); Union League (New York). [*Died* 13 *April* 1955.

MARCHANT, Edgar Cardew; Sub-Rector of Lincoln College, Oxford, 1907-37 and 1942-47; *b.* Hertford, 19 Oct. 1864; *s.* of John Marchant, Solicitor; *m.* 1914, Ethel Winifred Mallet; two *s.* *Educ.:* Christ's Hospital; Peterhouse, Cambridge. Assistant Master, St. Paul's School, 1887-91; Fellow and Assistant Tutor, Peterhouse, 1891-94; Assistant Master, St. Paul's School, 1894-99; incorporated M.A. Trinity College, Oxford, 1895; fellow, Lincoln College, 1901; Alto singer in many choirs, 1887-1914, including Wells Cathedral and New College, Oxford. *Publications:* Xenophontis opera omnia; Xenophon, 2 vols. (Loeb Classics); editions of Thucydides; many school books; articles in Dictionary of National Biography. *Address:* 68 Staunton Rd., Oxford. *T.:* Oxford 61315. [*Died* 19 *June* 1960.

MARCHANT, Sir James, K.B.E., *cr.* 1921 (C.B.E. 1920); Hon. LL.D., F.R.S.Ed.; Ministry of Works and Ministry of Supply; formerly Chairman, Visual Education, Ltd.; Director Stoll Picture Productions, Ltd.; Secretary Cinema Commission of Enquiry, Cinema Psychological Enquiry, International Morals Congress; *b.* 18 Dec. 1867; *y. s.* of late John Marchant, London; *m.* 1895, Eleanor Jane, *d.* of George Gordon of South Shields. Social writer and worker, in East London and provinces for some years; Lecturer on Christian Apologetics to Bishop St. Albans, 1889-1893; Minister, Exeter Street Independent Church; Minister-in-charge, Trinity Presbyterian Church, London, 1895-97; Assistant Minister for St. Andrew's Church, Chatham, 1900-1902; Clerical Secretary Dr. Barnardo's Homes and Memorial, 1903-6; travelled round Continent with Dr. Barnardo's successor investigating conditions of child-life and rescue work, 1905; Secretary National Birth-Rate Commission 1913-1934. *Publications:* Life of Dr. Paton, 1909; The Memoirs of Dr. Barnardo (joint), 1907; Letters and Reminiscences of Dr. A. Russel Wallace, 1916; edited Reminiscences of Prof. Meldola, 1917; Life and Letters of Dr. John Clifford, 1924; The Master Problem, 1917: Birth-Rate and Empire, 1918; The Future of the Church of England, 1926; Anthology of Jesus, 1926; The Future of Christianity, 1927; Anthology of the Madonna, with Sir Charles Holmes, 1928; Deeds done for Christ, 1928; British Preachers (annual publication), 1925 and onwards; The Whitehall Series, being the Story of the Great Departments of State, 1925 and onwards; selected and edited 3 vols. of The Times Saturday Religious Articles, 1923-26; Editor The Reunion of Christendom, 1929; Editor Reports of the National Birth-Rate Commission, 1916-20; Reports of Cinema Commission, 1917 and 1925; V.D. report, 1921; Birth Control Reports, 1925-27; Medical Aspects of Birth Control, 1927; Medical Birth Control Report, 1928; Editor, The Way to God, 1932; Toward Evening, 1936; edited History Through "The Times," being selection of "The Times" leaders, 1800-1937; Post War Britain, A Survey of possibilities, 1945; Anthology of God, 1945; Report on the Revival of Family Life, 1945; Has the Church Failed?, 1946; What has Life Taught Me?, 1947; What I believe, 1953; (Editor) Eyes in Industry, 1952; (Editor) Birthday Presentation Volume of Tributes to Sir Winston Churchill, 1954. *Recreation:* astronomy. *Address:* Lenthay Lodge, Sherborne, Dorset. *Clubs:* Authors'; The Club (Bournemouth). [*Died* 20 *May* 1956.

MARCHANT, Brig.-General Thomas Harry Saunders, D.S.O. 1918; *b.* 27 Oct. 1875; *s.* of Robert Marchant, Dartford Kent; *m.* 1925, Mrs. Evelyn A. H. Forwood. *Educ.:* privately; Cambridge University. Joined 13th Hussars, 1898; served S. African War, 1899-1902 (King's and Queen's medals with clasps); European War, 1914-18; Lt.-Col. 2/4 South Lancashire Regt., 1916-17; Brig.-Gen. commanding 126th Infantry Brigade, 1917-18 (despatches, D.S.O., Brevet Lt.-Col.); Lt.-Col. 5th Dragoon Guards, 1921; retired with rank of Brig.-General, 1925. O.C. 2nd County of London Bn., Home Guard, 1940-42. *Address:* Arlington Lodge, Bibury, Glos. *Club:* Cavalry. [*Died* 17 *Nov.* 1952.

MARCHANT, William Sydney, C.M.G. 1942; O.B.E. 1937; *b.* 10 Dec. 1894; *m.* 1922, Marjorie Daisy, *d.* of William Bean; one *s.* one *d.* Served European War, 1915-18, Royal Sussex Regt. Entered Colonial Administrative Service, Kenya, 1919; Deputy Provincial Commissioner, Zanzibar, 1935-37; Deputy Provincial Commissioner, Tanganyika Territory, 1937-39; Resident Commissioner British Solomon Islands Protectorate, 1939-43; Chief Native Commissioner, Kenya Colony, 1943-47; Labour Adviser to Overseas Food Corporation, 1947-50. *Address:* c/o The Nairobi Club, Nairobi, Kenya. *Club:* East India and Sports. [*Died* 1 *Feb.* 1953.

MARCHWOOD, 1st Viscount, *cr.* 1945, of Penang and of Marchwood, Southampton; 1st Baron, *cr.* 1937; **Frederick George Penny,** 1st Bt., *cr.* 1933; K.C.V.O., *cr.* 1937; Kt., *cr.* 1929; J.P.; *b.* 10 March 1876; 2nd *s.* of late Frederick James Penny, Bitterne, Hants; *m.* 1905, Anne Boyle, *e. d.* of late Sir John Gunn. J.P., St. Mellons, Cardiff; one *s.* *Educ.:* King Edward VI Grammar School, Southampton. Senior partner Fraser & Co., Government brokers, Singapore, and formerly Managing Dir. Eastern Smelting Co. Ltd., Penang; represented Federated Malay States Government in negotiations with Netherlands Indies Government at Bandoeng, Java, regarding liquidation of war (1914-18) tin stocks. Master Mariner; Master of Hon. Company of Master Mariners, 1941-45; M.P. (C.) Kingston-upon-Thames, 1922-37; Parliamentary private secretary to Financial Secretary to War Office, 1923; Conservative Whip, 1926-37; Lord Commissioner of the Treasury, 1928-29 and 1931; Vice-Chamberlain of H.M. Household, 1931-32; Comptroller, 1932-35; Treasurer, 1935-37; Hon. Treasurer of Conservative Party, 1938-46. Freeman, City of London. Officer 1st Class of the Most Honourable Order of the Crown of Johore. *Heir:* *s.* Hon. Peter George Penny, M.B.E., Major, R.A. [*b.* 7 Nov. 1912; *m.* 1935, Pamela, *o. c.* of J. Staveley Colton-Fox, J.P., Todwick Grange, Yorks; two *s.* one *d.* *Educ.:* Winchester]. *Address:* The Old Rectory, Felpham, Sussex. *T.:* Bognor Regis 28. *Clubs:* Carlton, White's. [*Died* 1 *Jan.* 1955.

MARDEN, Major-General Sir Thomas Owen, K.B.E., *cr.* 1924; C.B. 1918; C.M.G. 1915; *b.* 15 Sept. 1866; *s.* of T. Marden, Weston Priory, Bath; *m.* 1st, 1901, Mabel, *d.* of Col. Nesbitt, C.B., Grahamstown, South Africa; two *s.*; 2nd, 1920, Enid Millicent Louise, *o. d.* of late Captain J. R. Minshull-Ford, 8th (King's) Regt., and Mrs. Minshull-Ford, Abbeyfield, Slough, Bucks. *Educ.:* Berkhamsted School; R.M.C. Sandhurst. Joined Cheshire Regt., 1886; Staff, India, 1903-4; War Office, 1904-9; Staff, S. Africa, 1910-11; served Burma, 1887-89 (medal with clasp); South Africa, 1900 (King's medal, despatches); European War, 1914-18; commanded 1st Batt. Welch Regt., 1912-15; 114th Infantry Brigade, 1915-17; 6th Division, 1917-1919; British Troops, Constantinople, 1920-23; Welsh Division, 1923-27; retired pay, 1927; Colonel of the Welch Regiment, 1920-41; Légion d'Honneur, Officier, 1917; Order of St. Vladimir 4th Class with swords, 1915; Croix de Guerre with Palm, 1919. *Address:* 7 Metropole Court, Folkestone. *Club:* Army and Navy. [*Died* 11 *Sept.* 1951.

MARE, Captain Philip Armitage, C.I.E. 1945; R.I.N., retired; *b.* 28 March 1891; *s.* of Charles Dennis Mare, Worth Park, Crawley, Sussex; *m.* 1922, Patricia Dunton, *d.* of Charles Toosey, Oxton, Cheshire; two *s.* (one *d.* decd.). *Educ.:* Hurstleigh, Tunbridge Wells; H.M.S. Conway. Sub.-Lieut. Royal Indian Marine, 1912. Served European War, 1914-18, in Royal Navy. Held staff appointments and commanded ships of The Royal Indian Marine and Royal Indian Navy, 1928-1943. Royal Naval Staff College, 1930. Chief of Administration, 1943-45. *Recreations:* golf and yachting. *Address:* Tylehurst, Sion Hill, Bath, Somerset. *T.:* Bath 60114. *Clubs:* Royal Empire Society; Bath and County (Bath); Royal Falmouth Yacht; Royal Naval Sailing Association. [*Died* 18 *Feb.* 1951.

MARGERISON, Sir Lawrence, Kt., *cr.* 1926; C.B. 1933; C.B.E. 1918; *b.* 16 Feb. 1872; 3rd *s.* of Joseph Margerison, Chester; *m.* 1896, Caroline Elizabeth (*d.* 1958), *e. d.* of Richard Henry Aldis, Chester; one *d.* *Educ.:* Modern School, Chester; St. John's College, Battersea. Schoolmaster, 1893-1914; Assistant Inspector of Schools, Board of Education, 1914; Seconded to War Savings Committee, 1916; Secretary, National Savings Committee, 1919; retired 1933. *Address:* 45 Lord Avenue, Ilford, Essex. *T.:* Wanstead 1654. *Club:* Savage. [*Died* 22 *Feb.* 1958.

MARGOLIOUTH, Herschel Maurice, M.A.; D.Litt.; *b.* Greenwich, 22 February 1887; *e. s.* of Rev. George Margoliouth, of the British Museum; *m.* 1917, Maude Lilian (*d.* 1958), *y. d.* of John Ogden, Manchester. *Educ.:* Rugby; Oriel College, Oxford. 1st Cl. Classical Moderations; 1st Cl. Lit. Hum.; assistant master, Marlborough College, 1911-13; Senior Demy Magdalen College, Oxford, 1913-14; War Service, 1914-19 (Captain, Northamptonshire Regiment), Tutor in English Literature at University College and St. Edmund Hall, Oxford, 1919-20; Lecturer in English Literature at King's Coll., London, 1919-20; Professor of English, University College of Southampton, 1921-25; Secretary of Faculties, Oxford University, 1925-47; Fellow of Oriel 1935-; Editor, Oxford Magazine, 1947-51. *Publications:* Wells of English (English Literature for Schools), 1926-29; Marvell's Poems and Letters, 1927 and 1952; Intimation and Other Poems, 1948; William Blake, 1951; Wordsworth and Coleridge, 1953; William Blake's Vala, 1956; Traherne's Centuries, Poems and Thanksgivings, 1958; Wordsworth, 1959. *Address:* 14 Bradmore Road, Oxford. [*Died* 20 *March* 1959.

MARILLIER, Henry Currie; Technical Adviser to the Ministry of Works, 1947; Managing Director of Morris and Company, 1905-48; *b.* Grahamstown, South Africa, 1865; *s.* of Capt. Charles H. Marillier, C.M.R.; *m.* 1st, 1893, Katherine (*d.* 1901), *d.* of John Pattinson, J.P.; two *d.*; 2nd, 1906, Christabel (composer of musical fantasy, The Rose and the Ring, 1928), *d.* of late Arthur Hopkins, R.W.S.; one *s.* *Educ.:* Christ's Hospital; Cambridge. Served some years in engineering works, and then adopted journalism, chiefly in connection with Pall Mall Gazette, from 1893 onwards. Was a partner for some years in the late W. A. S. Benson's metal works. Literary work mostly on subjects connected with art. *Publications:* Men and Women of the Century, 1896; Dante Gabriel Rossetti, A Memorial of his Art and Life, 1899; The Early Work of Aubrey Beardsley, 1899; University Magazines and their Makers, privately printed, 1899; The Liverpool School of Painters, 1904; Christies', 1766 to 1925, 1926; History of the Merton Abbey Tapestry Works, 1927; English Tapestries of the 18th Century, 1930; Guide to the Tapestries at Hampton Court Palace, 1931; The Teniers Tapestries, 1932. *Recreation:* tapestry research. *Address:* Westbrook House, Upperton, near Petworth, Sussex. [*Died* 27 *July* 1951.

MARIN, John C.; Artist; *b.* 23 Dec. 1870; *m.* Marie Hughes; one *s.* *Educ.:* Stevens Institute of Technology, U.S.A. Member American Institute of Arts and Letters, New York City. Hon. Doctor of Fine Arts: Yale, 1950, Univ. of Maine, 1950. Relevant publications: John Marin, The Man and His Work, 1932; Letters of John Marin, Ed. by Herbert Seligmann, 1935; John Marin, by McKinley Helm, 1947; Letters of John Marin, Ed. by Dorothy Norman, 1948. *Recreation:* piano. *Address:* 243 Clark Terrace, Cliffside Park, N.J., U.S.A. [*Died* 1 *Oct.* 1953.

MARK-WARDLAW, Rear-Adm. William Penrose, D.S.O. 1919; Royal Navy, retired; Commandant, R.A.F.V.R., Blackpool, with rank of Hon. Wing Commander, 1939; Commission, R.A.F.V.R. 1940; Wing Commander, 1944 (resigned commission); re-employed Admiralty, Admiral Commanding Reserves, 1944-45; *b.* 11 May 1887; *s.* of late Colonel William Lambert P. Mark-Wardlaw, late 3rd Battalion North Staffordshire Regiment; *m.* 1938, Agnes Nancy, *o. c.* of late Dr. Hugh Riddell, Wyresdale Park, Scorton, near Preston, Lancs; three *d.* *Educ.:* Foster's, Stubbington. Entered H.M.S. Britannia, cadets training ship, 1902; Lieut. 1907; Commander, 1919; Captain, 1927; Rear-Adm., 1938; served European War (D.S.O. for service in Q ship); Commodore in charge Naval Base, Singapore, 1934-36; retired list, 1938. *Publication:* At Sea with Nelson, being the life of great-grandfather William Mark. *Recreations:* fishing, riding, sailing. Obtained "A" Flying licence. *Address:* Alyscroft, Crowthorne, Berkshire. *T.:* Crowthorne 430. *Clubs:* United Service; (Naval Hon. Member) Royal Yacht Squadron (Cowes); Royal Singapore Yacht (Singapore). [*Died* 10 *Aug.* 1952.

MARKHAM, Sir Charles, 2nd Bt., *cr.* 1911; *b.* 28 Aug. 1899; *s.* of 1st Bt. and Lucy, C.B.E., *d.* of Capt. A. B. Cunningham, late R.A. (she *m.* 2nd, 1922, Lt. Col. James O'Hea); *S.* father, 1916; *m.* 1st, 1920, Gwladys (who obtained a divorce, 1927), *e. d.* of Hon. Rupert Beckett, *q.v.*; one *s.* two *d.*; 2nd, 1932, Anne (from whom he obtained a divorce, 1938), *e. d.* of Arthur G. Vanscolina, Labuan, North Borneo; one *s.*; 3rd, 1942, Mrs. Crawford, *e. d.* of late Lt.-Col. Hon. Christian Eliot. 2nd Life Guards, 1918; entered Diplomatic Service, 1919; Hon. Attaché, Cairo; attached High Commission to S. Russia, 1919-20; War of 1939-45, Major, East African Rifles. Capt. Derbyshire Yeomanry; Esquire of Order of St. John of Jerusalem. *Heir:* *s.* Charles John [*b.* 2 July 1924; *m.* 1949, Valerie, *o. d.* of Lt.-Col. E. Barry-Johnston; one *s.*]. *Address:* P.O. Box 2263, Nairobi; Limuru, Kenya Colony. *Club:* St. James'. [*Died* 7 *Sept.* 1952.

MARKHAM, Violet Rosa (Mrs. Carruthers), C.H. 1917; J.P.; *y. d.* of late Charles Markham, Tapton House, Chesterfield, and Rosa, *d.* of Sir Joseph Paxton; *m.* 1915, Lieut-Colonel James Carruthers, D.S.O., M.V.O. (*d.* 1936). Member Executive Committee National Relief Fund; ex-Chairman Central Committee Women's Employment; Deputy Director Women's Section National Service Department, 1917; contested Mansfield division of Notts (Independent Liberal), General Election, 1918;

Member of Lord Chancellor's Advisory Committee for Women Justices, 1919-20; Member of Industrial Court, 1920-46; member and Deputy Chairman certain Trade Boards; member Assistance Board, 1934-1946, Deputy Chairman, 1937-46; Member Home Office Aliens Advisory Committee, 1939; Chairman Government Committee to report on Welfare and Amenities in Women's Services, 1942; Chairman Advisory Council National Institute of Houseworkers, 1946; represented Canadian Government on Governing Body International Labour Office, Geneva (League of Nations), 1923; Town Councillor, Chesterfield, 1924; Mayor, 1927; Freedom of Borough, 1952; Founder-President Chesterfield Settlement; D.Litt. Sheffield University, 1936; LL.D. Edinburgh, 1938; F.R.Hist.S., F.R.G.S. *Publications:* South Africa Past and Present; The New Era in South Africa; The South African Scene; A Woman's Watch on the Rhine, 1921; Romanesque France, 1929; Paxton and the Bachelor Duke, 1935; May Tennant, 1950; Return Passage, 1953; Friendship's Harvest, 1956. *Address:* 8 Gower Street, W.C.1. *T.:* Museum 0799. *Club:* Ladies' Empire. [*Died* 2 *Feb.* 1959.

MARKS, Alexander Hammett, C.B.E. 1919; D.S.O. 1917; V.D.; Medical Practitioner, Brisbane; Colonel A.A.M.C.; *b.* 6 Aug. 1880; *s.* of Hon. C. F. Marks, M.D., Brisbane; *m.* Annie G. Rhodes, Dublin; one *s.* two *d.* *Educ.:* Brisbane Grammar School: Trinity College, Dublin. B.A., M.D., Ch.B., D.P.H. Dublin; served Australian Imperial Forces, 1914-19 (despatches twice, D.S.O., C.B.E., Croix de Guerre); A.D.M.S. 1st Australian Division; Colonel Commonwealth Military Forces. *Address:* 109 Wickham Ter., Brisbane, Australia. [*Died* 18 *Jan.* 1954.

MARKS, Leslie; Metropolitan Magistrate since 1947; *b.* 20 Nov. 1889; *s.* of Albert Marks and Elizabeth Cohen; *m.* 1916, Leah Viva Benjamin. *Educ.:* St. Paul's School; Queen's College, Oxford. M.A. Called to Bar, Nov. 1912; practised at Common Law Bar until 1947; served European War, 1914-1918; Private, Artists' Rifles; commissioned Royal Sussex Regt.; served in France with 9th K.R.R.C. and 24th Fusiliers, and later on Staff; served War of 1939-45, in England; commissioned to R.A.S.C.; O. i/c Southern Command, Legal Aid Section, with rank of Major, 1942-45. *Address:* 4 Fursecroft, George St., St. Marylebone, W.1. *Club:* United University. [*Died* 22 *Oct.* 1956.

MARLEY, 1st Baron (*cr.* 1930) of Marley in the County of Sussex, **Dudley Leigh Aman,** D.S.C., J.P.; *s.* of late Edward Godfrey Aman; *b.* Helsby, Cheshire, 16 May 1884; *m.* 1910, Octable Turquet, *d.* of late Sir Hugh Gilzean-Reid, D.L., LL.D., formerly M.P. for Aston Manor; one *s.* *Educ.:* Marlborough; Roy. Naval Coll., Greenwich. Entered the Roy. Marine Artillery as 2nd Lieut. 1902; after service in the Home and Mediterranean Fleets, specialised in Wireless Telegraphy and served on the staff of the late Admiral Sir Henry Jackson, and in H.M.S. Vernon; in 1912 passed into the Army Staff College at Camberley for two years (p.s.c. certificate); at outbreak of war joined staff of Admiral Tottenham in Third Fleet, but shortly afterwards took an Artillery Command in France, where he served over two years with Trench Mortars and Anti-aircraft Artillery (despatches, D.S.C. wounded); joined H.M.S. Tiger in Battle Cruiser Force and then was appointed to H.M. Signal School Portsmouth for experimental and research work; retired from Service at his own request in 1920 to devote himself to service with the Labour Party; Labour Candidate for Petersfield Division from 1919; Fought elections of 1922 and 1923; contested Thanet in 1924 and Faversham in 1928 and 1929; Lord-in-Waiting to the King, 1930-31; Under Secretary of State for War, 1930-31; a Deputy Speaker House of Lords, 1930-41; Chief Government Whip, 1930-31; Chief Opposition Whip, 1931-37; Member of Fabian Society since 1917; Member Magistrates Association; Chairman Rent Restriction Acts Committee, 1931; Chairman Garden Cities Committee, 1932; attached to Ministry of Aircraft Production, 1943-45; J.P. Hampshire and Sussex; D.L. Hampshire, 1930-50. *Publications:* many articles on Russia, Siberia and Far East, Fascism and German Refugees. *Heir:* *s.* Major Hon. Godfrey Pelham Leigh Aman, R.M., *b.* 6 Sept. 1913. *Address:* 50 South Audley Street, Grosvenor Square, W.1. *T.:* Grosvenor 1073. [*Died* 29 *Feb.* 1952.

MARLEY, Brig. Cuthbert David, D.S.O. 1940; M.B.E.; T.D.; D.L., Durham County; Marketing Director, Durham Division, National Coal Board, since 1950 (Northern Div., 1947-50); *b.* 23 July 1897; *s.* of late T. W. Marley, J.P., Darlington. *Educ.:* Durham School. Served European War (wounded); Brevet Lt.-Col. 1936; served 5th D.L.I. (Territorial Army), 1920-39; Commanded 1/5 D.L.I., 1938; mobilised, 1939; Commanded 10th Bn. Durham Light Infantry, 1940-41; Commanded Infantry Brigade, 1942-44; Partner, Feetham & Grieveson, coal factors, Newcastle upon Tyne, 1924-36; Member Durham Sales Control Committee (Coal Mines Act, 1930), 1936; Controller-General North German Coal Control, Control Commission for Germany, 1945-46. *Recreations:* shooting, golf. *Address:* Castle Hill, Middleton St. George, nr. Darlington. [*Died* 24 *April* 1960.

MARLEY, James; schoolmaster; *b.* Shotts, Scotland, 1893; *m.* 1920, Alice Louise, *d.* of William Pilgrim. *Educ.:* St. Aloysius College, Glasgow; St. Mungo's Academy, Glasgow; St. Mary's College, Hammersmith; London School of Economics. M.P. (Lab.) N. St. Pancras, 1923-24, and 1929-31. [*Died* 11 *April* 1954.

MAROCHETTI, Baron; George Charles; Adviser to Chunilal & Co. Ltd. (Sir Chunilal B. Mehta), Cleveland Wine Co. Ltd., Prunier Wines Co. Ltd.; *b.* 22 July 1894; *s.* of Maurice, Baron Marochetti, Italian Ambassador to the Court of St. Petersburg, and of Mary Therese, Countess de Grandval; *g.s.* of Charles, 1st Baron Marochetti, R.A., the celebrated sculptor; *S.* father, 1916. *Educ.:* privately; Oxford. European War, 1914-18 (naturalised U.K. 1916); Intelligence Officer, 1914-15; Lieut. 11th P.A.O. Hussars, 1916; Captain General Staff and Assistant British Military Representative and then Asst. British Military Attaché, Vienna, 1919-1920; British Delegate to International Commission of Blockade (Hungary), 1921; Inspector of Shipping, Madagascar, 1925; Asst. Comdt. British Olympic Team at Amsterdam; entrusted with Mission to South America, 1929; New York Times, New York and London, 1930-32; Insurance Broker, 1932-39; Assistant Master for Modern History and Modern Languages, 1940-41, at Rugby and Eton; Interpreter and Liaison Officer for Ministry of Works in Northern Command, 1942-43; Commandant B.R.C. in Italy (Civilian Overseas Relief), 1943-45; Lt.-Col. 1945. Bronze Star U.S.A. 1945; Knight Grand Cross of Sovereign Military Order of Malta. *Publications:* Rich in Range, Autobiography, 1941; several articles to New York Times, 1930. *Recreations:* travel, golf, tennis, fishing, shooting, hunting. *Address:* Studio 5, The Village, 414 Fulham Road, S.W.6. *T.:* Fulham 4266. *Clubs:* Naval and Military, International Sportsmen's, Roehampton; Granton Golf (Scarborough). [*Died* 18 *Aug.* 1952.

MARQUAND, John Phillips, A.B., Litt.D.; Author; *b.* 10 November 1893; *s.* of Margaret Fuller and Phillip Marquand; *m.* 1st, 1922, Christina Sedgwick; one *s.* one *d.*; divorced, 1935; 2nd, 1937, Adelaide Hooker (marriage dissolved, 1958);

two *s.* one *d.* *Educ.:* Harvard University. *Publications:* Unspeakable Gentlemen, 1922; Four of a Kind, 1923; Black Cargo, 1925; Lord Timothy Dexter, 1925; Warning Hill, 1930; Haven's End, 1933; Ming Yellow, 1934; No Hero, 1935; The Late George Apley, 1937; Thank you, Mr. Moto, 1936; Think Fast, Mr. Moto, 1937; Wickford Point, 1939; H.M. Pulham, Esquire, 1941; Last Laugh, Mr. Moto, 1942; So Little Time, 1943; B.F.'s Daughter, 1946; It's Loaded, Mr. Bauer, 1949; Repent in Haste, 1949; Point of No Return, 1949; Melville Goodwin, U.S.A., 1951; Thirty Years, 1955; Sincerely, Willis Wayde, 1955; Stopover: Tokyo, 1957; Life at Happy Knoll, 1958; Women and Thomas Harrow, 1958. *Address:* Kent's Island, Newbury-port, Mass., U.S.A. *T.:* Newburyport 49. *Clubs:* Century (New York); Somerset (Boston). [*Died* 16 *July* 1960.

MARR, Sir Charles William Clanan, K.C.V.O., *cr.* 1934; D.S.O. 1918; M.C., V.D., J.P.; Chairman: Amalgamated Coffee Plantations Ltd., New Guinea; Vunalama Cocoa Plantations, New Guinea; Tavua Gold Developments Ltd., and Mineral Developments (Fiji); Forest Reefs Gold-mining, N.S.W.; Director: New Zealand Forest Products Ltd.; Hadfield's Steel Works; *b.* Petersham, N.S.W., 23 Mar. 1880; *s.* of James Clanan Marr, Hobart; *m.* Ethel May, *d.* of Samuel and Lydia Ritchie, Sydney, N.S.W.; two *s.* two *d.* *Educ.:* Petersham School; Newington Coll.; Engineering Course, Sydney Technical Coll. Joined Govt. Service as Asst. Engineer, Electrical Engineers Dept.; supervised the erection of first Wireless station in Australia for Commonwealth Govt. at Sydney, 1911; Officer, R.A.F., 1911; formed first Wireless Troops in Aust., 1912; served European War, 1914-18: comd. Australian and New Zealand Wireless Sqdn., Mesopotamia and Persia (D.S.O., M.C., despatches twice). Consulting Engineer, Sydney, after return from War. Member Commonwealth Parliament, 1919-29 and 1931-43; Whip to Hughes Govt., 1921; to Bruce Govt., 1923-1925; Minister and Acting Minister for Defence, 1926-27; Minister for Home and Territories, 1927-28; Leader of Australian Delegation, League of Nations Assembly, Geneva, 1929; Min. for Health, Min. for Repatriation, Min. for Works and Railways, and Min. for Territories, 1932-34; inaugurated Legislative Council for New Guinea, Rabaul, 1933; Director Royal Visit, 1934; Dep. Grand Master, United Grand Lodge of N.S.W. *Recreations:* bowls and golf. *Address:* Pymble, Sydney, N.S.W. *Clubs:* Masonic, Sydney (Sydney). [*Died* 20 *Oct.* 1960.

MARRIOTT, Charles, Hon. A.R.I.B.A.; art critic of The Times, 1924-40; *b.* Bristol, 1869; father a brewer; *m.* 1st. 1892, Dora M. I. M'Loughlin (*d.* 1917); one *s.* two *d.*; 2nd, 1919, Bessie (*d.* 1949), *y. d.* of late George Wigan, M.D., of Portishead. *Educ.:* by the Rev. Arthur Tooth, Woodside, Croydon, and N.A.T.S., South Kensington; worked at photography; qualified, at Apothecaries' Hall, as a dispenser in 1890; Dispenser and Photographer, County Asylum, Rainhill 1889-1901; Sydney Jones Lecturer in Art, Liverpool Univ., 1938-39. Occasional broadcaster. *Publications:* The Column, 1901; Love with Honour, 1902; The House on the Sands, 1903; Genevra, 1904; Mrs. Alemere's Elopement, 1905; The Lapse of Vivien Eady, 1906; Women and the West, 1906; The Remnant, 1907; The Wondrous Wife, 1907; The Kiss of Helen, 1908; A Spanish Holiday, 1908; The Happy Medium, 1908; When a Woman Woos, 1909; The Intruding Angel, 1909; Now, 1910; The Romance of the Rhine, 1911; The Dewpond, 1912; The Catfish, 1913; Subsoil, 1913; The Unpetitioned Heavens, 1914; Davenport, 1915; Modern Art, 1917; Augustus John, 1918; Modern Movements in Painting, 1920; The Grave Impertinence, 1921; An Order to View, 1922; Modern English Architecture, 1924; A Key to Modern Painting, 1938; British Handicrafts (for British Council), 1943. *Translations:* Perfection, from the Portuguese of Eça de Queiroz, 1923; Italian Paintings in America (with Comtesse Marie Vanden Heuvel), from the Italian of Lionello Venturi, 1933; History of Art Criticism from the Italian of Lionello Venturi, 1936. *Address:* 3 The Lindens, Woodhill Road, Portishead, Bristol. *T.:* Portishead 3067. [*Died* 13 *July* 1957.

MARRIOTT, Francis, C.M.G. 1934; retd.; *b.* 11 July 1876; *s.* of late William Kenaz Marriott and late Marie Maycock; *m.* 1907 Alice Maud, *d.* of late W. M. Harrison, M.A. Cantab.; four *s.* *Educ.:* Stamford Grammar School. Went to sea 1895; Superintendent street and street railroad U.S.A. and Scotland, 1897-1902; farming in Tasmania, 1903-36; served European War A.I.F. 1915-17; Lieut. 12th Bat. Egypt and France, totally blinded in action 26 Feb. 1917; M.H.A. Tasmania for Darwin 1922; re-elected 1925, 1928, 1931, 1934, 1937 and 1941; retired, 1946; Chief Commissioner Boy Scouts, 1928-32; Federal President Toc. H. Australia, 1931-34; Member Anglican Synod Tasmania and General Australia, 1922-49; Member Executive Councils R.S.S.I.L. Tasmania, 1917-1932; received in private audience by the King at Windsor Castle 1920 and at Buckingham Palace 1926; Jubilee Medal, 1935; Coronation Medals, 1937, 1953. *Address:* 5 Warneford Street, Hobart, Tasmania. *T.A.:* Hobart. *T.:* Hobart, Tas., B4219. [*Died* 10 *Feb.* 1957.

MARRIOTT, Ven. Henry; Archdeacon Emeritus, 1951; Hon. Canon, Bermuda Cathedral, since 1935; *b.* London, 17 July 1870; *y. s.* of Joseph William Marriott of St. John's, Newfoundland; *m.* 1909, Helen Mary, *d.* of Dr. J. H. Arton, Bermuda; one *s.* *Educ.:* Bishop Feild College, S. John's, N.F.; St. Augustine's College, Canterbury; Hatfield Hall, Durham (B.A.). Ordained 1893; Curate of Topsail and Foxtrap, Newfoundland, 1893-96; of Hamilton and Smiths, Bermuda, 1896-1902; Canon Res., Bermuda Cathedral, 1902-33; Archdeacan of Bermuda, 1925-51; Rector of Paget, Bermuda, 1933-51. *Address:* Dornoch, Hamilton, Bermuda. *Club:* Royal Bermuda Yacht. [*Died* 11 *April* 1952.

MARRIOTT, James William; Author, free-lance journalist, and lecturer on educational subjects; *b.* Codnor, Derbyshire, 1884; *e. s.* of late William Marriott; *m.* Margaret, *d.* of E. C. Waters, Chislehurst; two *d.* *Educ.:* Sevenoaks School. Under the pseudonym of Roger Wray, has published novels, short stories, essays, and articles. *Publications:* The Soul of a Teacher, 1915; Madcaps and Madmen, 1916; The Rayner Case, 1925; A Year's Work in English, 1921; Exercises in Thinking and Expressing, 1922; Matriculation English, 1928; also edited six volumes of One-Act Plays of To-day, and Great Modern British Plays, 1929; The Theatre, 1931; The Modern Drama, 1934; Modern Essays and Sketches, 1935; Arguments and Discussions, 1937; Q. E. D., 1944; Islands of Literature series, 1949. *Address:* 5 Montpelier Rise, N.W.11. *T.:* Speedwell 4081. *Club:* Savage. [*Died* 17 *March* 1953.

MARRIOTT, Brig.-Gen. John, C.B.E. 1919; D.S.O. 1900; M.V.O. 1909; late Norfolk Regiment; F.Z.S.; an authority on Big Game; *b.* 3 Nov. 1861; *s.* of late John Marriott of Stowmarket, Advocate-General, Bombay; *m.* 1902, Cordelia C. Nevers of St. Johnsbury, Vermont, U.S.A.; three *d.* Was captured by brigands in Asia Minor in Oct. 1896, who demanded a ransom of £16,000; was released by Turkish troops. Entered army, 1883; Capt. 1890; Major, 1904; Lieut.-Col. 1909; Col. 1912; served South Africa, 1900-2 (despatches twice, Queen's medal 3 clasps, King's medal 2 clasps, D.S.O.); specially employed on the Military Survey and Reconnaissance of Namaqualand and Bushmanland, South Africa, 1907; during European War Commanded the following

Infantry Brigades; The Surrey, 2/1 Surrey 112th in France, 200th and 221st Mixed Bde. specially mentioned for valuable services in connection with the War, 1918); retired Hon. Brigadier-General, 1919. *Address:* Clare Lodge, Ipswich. [*Died* 7 *May* 1953.

MARRIOTT, William Mason, C.B.E. 1943; Past Pres. Land Agents Society; *b.* 23 Feb. 1889; *s.* of W. H. Marriott, Sandal Grange, Wakefield, Yorks; *m.* 1916, Violet Helen Gordon; four *s.* *Educ.:* Rugby School; Leeds University. Agent to various owners except 1914-19 when in the Army; Chairman of Montgomeryshire War Agricultural Committee, 1939-44. High Sheriff of Montgomeryshire, 1955. *Address:* Park House, Welshpool. *T.:* Welshpool 2181. [*Died* 10 *Feb.* 1960.

MARRS, Robert, C.M.G. 1937; C.I.E. 1919; M.A. (Oxon.); Hon. LL.D. (Ceylon Univ.); Colonial Office (Directorate of Recruitment) since 1946; *b.* 21 Dec. 1884; *s.* of Rev. F. and Mrs. Marrs (*née* Mallinson); *m.* Nancy, *d.* of late A. H. A. Simcox, I.C.S.; (one *s.* killed on active service, 1941) one *d.* *Educ.:* Manchester Grammar School; Nottingham High School; Wadham College, Oxford. Formerly I.E.S.; Mesopotamian Expeditionary Force, 1915, in R.F.A.; Political Service, Mesopotamia, 1916-20 (rank Major); India Office, 1920-21; Ceylon from 1921; late Principal, Univ. Coll., Colombo; attached General Staff, War Office (civilian), Sept. 1939-40; Board of Trade, March 1940-Oct. 1945; to Malaya and Ceylon for Colonial Office. Nov. 1945 to end of Feb. 1946; Colonial Office, March 1946-. Member: Commission on Higher Education in the Colonies, 1943-45; Colonial University Grants Advisory Committee, 1950-. *Recreations:* gardening and books. *Address:* Heronden, Hawkhurst, Kent. *T.:* Hawkhurst, Kent 285. *Clubs:* Overseas League; Royal Bombay Yacht (Bombay). [*Died* 17 *Jan.* 1951.

MARRYSHOW, Hon. Theophilus Albert, C.B.E. 1943; Journalist; M.L.C. (Elected) for St. George's, Grenada (Dep. Pres., 1951-54); formerly M.E.C. Grenada; *b.* St. George's, November 1887. *Educ.:* St. George's Wesleyan School. Editor of St. George's Chronicle and Grenada Gazette, 1911; Founder and Editor of The West Indian, 1915-24. Formerly Member, St. George's District Board. President, Caribbean Labour Conference, 1946; Representative, West Indian Conference (Caribbean Commission), 1946; Adviser, Federation Conference, London, 1953. Advocate of closer unity of the West Indies. Jubilee Medal, 1935; Coronation Medal, 1937. *Publications:* articles in many journals. *Address:* St. George's, Grenada, T.W.I.; Commonwealth Parliamentary Association, Westminster Hall, S.W.1. [*Died* 20 *Oct.* 1958.

MARSDEN, Captain Arthur, C.B.E. 1960; R.N., retired; Chairman, Committee of Management, Shipwrecked Fishermen and Mariners' Royal Benevolent Society since 1952; *b.* 1883; *m.* 1921, Rachel Cecilia, *d.* of late Llewellyn and Lady Rachel Saunderson, and *widow* of late Brig.-General R. C. Gore. *Educ.:* Cheltenham; H.M.S. Britannia. Entered Royal Navy, 1898; Promoted Lieut. from H.M. Yacht Victoria and Albert, 1904; Commanded H.M.S. Ardent at Battle of Jutland, 1916; retired, 1920; Capt., 1939; Served in R.N. 1939-45. Contested N. Battersea (C.), 1929, and 1935; M.P. (C.) North Battersea, 1931-35, Chertsey Division of Surrey, 1937-50. Silver Medal of Royal Humane Society for saving life at sea, 1910. *Recreation:* living. *Address:* 7 Chelsea House, 24 Lowndes Street, S.W.1. *T.:* Belgravia 1737. *Clubs:* Carlton. United Service. [*Died* 26 *Nov.* 1960.

MARSDEN, Ven. E(dwyn) Lisle, M.A. (Lambeth) 1951; Archdeacon of Lindsey since 1948; 4th Canon Residentiary of Lincoln Cathedral since 1951; Canon and Prebendary of Centum Solidorum since 1938; *b.* 20 Sept. 1886; *s.* of late Edwin Bowen and Mary Eliza Marsden, Holywell, Flintshire, N. Wales; unmarried. *Educ.:* privately; The King's School, Chester. Clerk in Nat. Provincial Bank, 1903-12; 2nd Cl. Preliminary Theol. Exam., 1912. Deacon 1912, Priest 1913, Lincoln Diocese. Asst. Curate of Spalding, 1912-18; Temp. C.F., 1917-19 (despatches). Vicar of: Pinchbeck West, 1918-21; Haigh and Aspull, 1921-28; St. Michael and All Angels, Wigan, 1928-36; Vicar of Great Grimsby, 1936-51. Proctor in Convocation, 1942-48 and 1951-. *Address:* The Archdeaconry, Lincoln. *T.:* Lincoln 484. [*Died* 21 *June* 1960.

MARSDEN, Percy, C.I.E. 1942; I.C.S. retd.; Barrister-at-law; *b.* 26 Nov. 1888; *s.* of late Edmund Marsden; *m.* 1917, Helen Gladys, *d.* of Maj.-Gen. P. Carr-White, C.B.E., K.H.P.; one *s.* three *d.* *Educ.:* Cheltenham Coll.; St. John's Coll., Oxford. I.C.S., 1912; European War, 1918-19, attached Hodsons Horse and served with East Persian Cordon; Commissioner Ambala, 1935, Multan, 1937, Rawalpindi, 1938; Financial Commissioner, Punjab, 1945-47. *Recreations:* tennis, farming, riding. *Address:* Sutton Waldron House, near Blandford, Dorset. *Club:* Athenæum. [*Died* 16 *May* 1955.

MARSH, Sir Edward Howard, K.C.V.O. *cr.* 1937 (C.V.O. 1922); C.B. 1918; C.M.G. 1908; *b.* 18 Nov. 1872; *s.* of late Professor Howard Marsh, Master of Downing College, Cambridge, and Jane Perceval. *Educ.:* Westminster; Trinity College, Cambridge (Scholar). 1st class classical tripos, 1893; Senior Chancellor's medal for classics, 1895; 1st class with distinction classical tripos, Part II., and B.A., 1895; M.A., 1897; 2nd Class Clerk, Colonial Office, 1896; Assistant Private Secretary to Mr. Chamberlain, 1900; to Mr. Lyttelton, 1903; 1st Class Clerk, and Private Secretary to Mr. Churchill, 1905; accompanied Mr. Churchill on his visit to East Africa and Uganda, 1907-8; Assistant Private Secretary to Mr. Asquith, 1915-16, Private Secretary to Mr. Churchill, 1917-22, and 1924-29, to the Duke of Devonshire, 1922-1924, to Mr. J. H. Thomas, 1924 and 1929-1936, and to Mr. Malcolm MacDonald, 1936-37; Trustee of the Tate Gallery, 1937-44; Chairman of the Contemporary Art Society, 1937-52; Vice-Pres. R.S.L. 1943. *Publications:* Georgian Poetry, 1912-21; Memoir of Rupert Brooke, 1918; Fables of La Fontaine, 1931; A Number of People, 1939; Odes of Horace, 1941; Minima, 1947; Dominique (trans.), 1948; The Sphinx of Bagatelle (trans.), 1952; Oriane (trans.), 1952. *Relevant Publication:* Edward Marsh, by Christopher Hassall, 1959. *Address:* 86 Walton Street, S.W.3. *Club:* Brooks's. [*Died* 13 *Jan.* 1953.

MARSH, Brig.-Gen. Frank Graham, C.M.G. 1918; D.S.O. 1919; *b.* 1875; *m.* 1907, Ursula, *d.* of late J. P. Haslam, J.P. three *s.* two *d.* Passed Staff College, 1910; served N.W. Frontier of India, 1897-98; European War, 1914-19. *Publication:* The Godolphins, 1930. *Address:* Pinewood, Hordle, Hants. [*Died* 17 *Jan.* 1957.

MARSH, Rev. Fred Shipley, M.A., Hon. C.F.; F.K.C.; Lady Margaret's Professor of Divinity, Cambridge University, 1935-51, Emeritus since 1951; Fellow since 1920 and Tutor, 1922-35, Selwyn College, Cambridge; Canon of Lincoln since 1925; *b.* 4 June 1886; *s.* of James William Marsh and Elizabeth Shipley; unmarried. *Educ.:* Gainsborough Grammar School; Selwyn College, Cambridge (Scholar); Theological Tripos, part i. cl. 1, part ii. cl. 1; John Stewart of Rannoch (Hebrew), Tyrwhitt and Crosse Scholarships, Carus, Jeremie, Hebrew, and Mason Prizes. Tutor, House of the Sacred Mission, Kelham, 1909-11; Curate of Chiswick Parish Church, 1911-13; Tutor, St. Boniface College, Warminster, 1913-14; Lecturer in King's College, London, and Sub-Warden, King's College Theological Hostel,

1914-20; Examining Chaplain to the Bishop of Lincoln, 1921-46; Member of Council of King's College, London since 1937; Chaplain to the Forces (France), 1916-19; Lecturer of Selwyn College (1920 - 35), Dean (1920 - 24), Librarian (1920-29); Member of the Council, 1930 - 51. *Publications:* The Book of Holy Hierotheos (publications of the Text and Translation Society); articles in Hastings' Dictionary of the Apostolic Church and in the Encyclopædia Britannica. *Recreation:* fishing. *Address:* 31A Grange Road, Cambridge. [*Died* 26 *Oct.* 1953.

MARSH, William Waller, C.B.E. 1935; *b.* 29 March 1877; *s.* of Henry Marsh and Sophy Kiddell; *m.* 1915, Mary Hay Bogle; four *d.* Entered Civil Service, 1893; Ministry of Labour, Director of Establishment, 1926 1930; Trade Boards Division, 1931 - 37; Chairman of Court of Referees in London, 1937; Fuel and Power, Eastern Region, 1939-45 *Recreations:* fencing (amateur champion (sabre) 1908, 1909, Olympic Games 1908-12-20-24) and research. *Address:* Alladoon, Fairlight Cove, Nr. Hastings, Sussex. *T.:* Pett 3158. *Club:* East India and Sports. [*Died* 12 *Feb.* 1959.

MARSHALL, Archibald Cook, C.B.E. 1949; Director of Education of the County of Clackmannan and Clerk and Treasurer to the Governors of Dollar Academy Trust, 1925-1957; *b.* 27 April 1890; 3rd *s.* of Provost John Marshall, J.P., Cowdenbeath; *m.* 1918, Janet McKenzie, 2nd *d.* of Robert Grant, Polmont, Stirlingshire; one *d.* *Educ.:* Dunfermline High School; Edinburgh University. M.A., LL.B. (with Distinction, Edinburgh); LL.B. (Sheffield Univ.); F.R.S.E., F.E.I.S., J.P.; Barrister-at-law of Gray's Inn; school teacher in Beath Secondary School, Fifeshire, and Newbattle, Midlothian, 1911-18; Personnel Manager Messrs. Thomas Firth & Sons, Ltd., and Messrs. John Brown & Co., Ltd., 1918-25. Pres. of Inst. of Personnel Management, 1922-24; Pres. of Scottish Assoc. of Directors of Education, 1939-41. Member: Govt. Univ., and deptl. cttees. on training of Industrial Welfare Supervisors, 1922-24. Emergency Scheme for training Scottish Teachers, 1945-57; Cttee. for Education of Poles and their Families in Gt. Brit., 1946-54; Cttee. on Scottish Educl. Endowments, 1948-50; Chairman: Alloa Sea Cadets Cttee., 1952-57; Scottish Central Counties Musical Festival Assoc., 1935-57; Vice-Pres. Scottish Inst. of Adult Education, 1950-; Vice-Pres. Glasgow and West of Scotland Reg. Advisory Cttee. on Tech. Educ., 1951-57; Mem. Scottish Savings Cttee., 1957-; Mem. Scottish Advisory Cttee. on School Savings, 1928-(Chm. 1957-); Mem. Mining Qualifications Board, Divnl. Cttee. (Scot.), 1949-57; Hon. Trustee and Man. Falkirk and Counties Savings Bank, 1951-; Pres. Alloa Rotary Club, 1955-56; Chm. District 101 (Scottish Highlands) Rotary Internat. and Mem. R.I.B.I. Council, 1958-59. Actively engaged in youth and Community Service activities for many years. Served European War, Royal Scots and Army Cyclist Corps, 1914-17, in France and Salonika. *Publication:* (Jt.) The History of Firths, 1924. *Recreations:* golf, gardening, motoring. *Address:* Vernar, Alloa, Clackmannanshire. *T.:* Alloa 389. *Clubs:* Royal Scots (Edinburgh); Royal Scottish Automobile (Glasgow). [*Died* 12 *Dec.* 1959.

MARSHALL, Sir Arthur (Harold), K.B.E., *cr.* 1918; Barrister-at-law, Gray's Inn (North-Eastern Circuit); M.P. (L.) Wakefield, 1910-18, Huddersfield, 1922-23; was a Liberal Whip; *b.* Ashton-under-Lyne, 2 Aug. 1870; *s.* of Rev. H. T. Marshall, D.D.; *m.* 1896, Louie (*d.* 1948), 3rd *d.* of Joseph Hepworth, J.P., Leeds, and of Torquay and Harrogate. *Educ.:* privately at Leeds and Halifax; Yorkshire University. Called to Bar, 1904; has visited Canada, British Columbia, South and Central Africa, Egypt, etc. Formerly: a Vice-Pres. Yorkshire Liberal Federation; a member of the Harrogate Corporation for six years, and for two years was Chairman of the Wells and Baths Committee of that Corporation; a Vice-Chm. of the National Savings Committee. Chm. of Aston Construction Co. Ltd.; Pres., Sussex Brick Co. Ltd.; Chairman, Legal Insurance Co., the Charterhouse Finance Corp., Ltd., J. Hepworth & Son, Ltd., Bradford and District Newspaper Co. Ltd., G. Mallinson & Sons, Ltd., Beecham Group Ltd.; Trustee of the Wessex Trustee Savings Bank. *Recreations:* golf, travel, walking. *Address:* Redcourt, W. Overcliff Drive, Bournemouth. *T.:* Westbourne 61015. *Clubs:* Athenæum, Reform. [*Died* 18 *Jan.* 1956.

MARSHALL, Brig. Charles Frederick Keilk, D.S.O. 1918; M.C.; *b.* 13 Oct. 1888; *m.* 1st, 1919, Dorothy Margaret (*d.* 1936), *widow* of Alan S. Lloyd, M.C., R.F.A.; one *d.*; 2nd, 1944, Nora Elaine Macphail, *widow* of Douglas Ross Macphail, C.B.E. Served European War, 1914-1918 (wounded, despatches, D.S.O., M.C.); retired pay, 1944. [*Died* 17 *Oct.* 1953.

MARSHALL, Charles Jennings, M.L. M.D. (Lond.), F.R.C.S. (Eng.); Senior Surgeon, Charing Cross Hospital, Bromley Hospital, and Surgeon and Orthopædist, Victoria Hospital for Children; late Examiner in Surgery, London University and Society of Apothecaries; Surgical Consultant, London County Council; Director Surgical Section, Sutton Emergency Hosp.; *b.* 6 June 1890; *s.* of Charles William Marshall and Mary Jennings; *m.* Hope Embleton-Smith. *Educ.:* Charing Cross Medical School. Gold Medallist, London Univ., M.B., B.S., and M.S.; Murchison Scholar, Roy. Coll. of Physicians; formerly: Surgeon, Anglo-Russian Hosp., Petrograd, and Russian Front, 1915; Surgical Specialist, R.A.M.C.; Assistant Surgeon and Orthopædist, King's College Hospital, 1919; Surgeon, Manor House Hosp., 1919; Consultant, Ministry of Pensions, 1919-32; Consulting Surg., Surrey County Council, 1936-45. *Publications:* Text-book of Surgical Pathology (with A. Piney); The Surgeon; Text-book of Surgical Anatomy and Physiology; Text-book on Chronic Diseases of the Abdomen; Urological Section, in Text-book of Radiology; contrib. med. jls. etc. *Address:* 121 Harley Street, W.1. *T.:* Welbeck 6818. *Club:* Savage. [*Died* 29 *Dec.* 1954.

MARSHALL, Charles Robertshaw, M.D., M.A.; LL.D. (St. Andrews and Aberdeen); *b.* Bradford, 25 Dec. 1869; *e. s.* of late Henry Marshall; *m.* Mary Evelene (*decd.*), *e. d.* of Geo. B. Birdsall, J.P., Manchester; one *s.* two *d.* *Educ.:* The Owens College, Manchester. M.D. Vict. (gold medal) 1899; M.B. (honours) 1892; M.A. Cantab. (honoris causa) 1898. House Physician, Manchester Royal Infirmary; Hon. Research Fellow in Pharmacology, the Owens College, 1892-95; Assistant to the Downing Professor of Medicine, University of Cambridge, 1894 - 99; Professor of Materia Medica, University of St. Andrews, 1899-1919; Regius Professor of Materia Medica, University of Aberdeen, 1919-30. *Publications:* A Text-Book of Materia Medica; Manual of Prescribing; papers on Pharmacological subjects in various medical and scientific journals. *Address:* Annisholme, Manor Park, Burley-in-Wharfedale, Yorkshire. *T.:* 2186. [*Died* 2 *April* 1952.

MARSHALL, Frank, C.M.G. 1919; L.D.S., B.D.S., D.D.S.; *b.* 1886; *s.* of C. C. Marshall, J.P. Sydney, N.S.W.; *m.* 1918, Clarice J. Sandford; one *s.* one *d.* *Educ.:* Newington College; University of Sydney; University of Pennsylvania. Served European War with Australian A.M.C. 1915-19 (despatches); Staff Officer, Dental Services A.I.F. 1916-20; Lt.-Col. 1917; Member Faculty of Dentistry, University of Sydney. *Address:* Harley, 143 Macquarie Street, Sydney, N.S.W. *Club:* University (Sydney). [*Died* 16 *Jan.* 1952.

MARSHALL, Frederick Henry, M.A.; retd.; Koraes Prof. of Modern Greek and Byzantine History, Language and Literature, King's College, University of London, 1926-43; *b.* 1878; *s.* of late Henry Marshall, Underwriter at Lloyd's, and late Agnes Martha Westmorland; *m.* 1928, Priscilla Mary O'Meara (*d.* 1952). *Educ.:* Merchant Taylors' School, London. Fellow of Emmanuel Coll., Camb., 1901-07; Asst. in the Dept. of Greek and Roman Antiquities, British Museum, 1901-12; Fellow and Lecturer in Classics, Emmanuel College, Cambridge, 1912-1919; War Office, Postal Censorship, 1915-1919 (Assistant Censor in charge of Uncommon Languages Dept., 1918-19). *Publications:* Livy, Book vi., 1903; The Second Athenian Confederacy (Thirlwall Prize), 1905; Section Private Antiquities in Camb. Comp. to Latin Studies, 1910; Ancient Greek Inscriptions in the British Museum, Part iv. 2, 1916; Discovery in Greek Lands, 1920; Old Testament Legends, 1925; The Siege of Vienna in 1683, 1925; (with J. Mavrogordato) Three Cretan Plays, 1929; Articles in Encyclopædia Britannica, new edition, 1939; British Museum Catalogues, contributions to Journal of Hellenic Studies. etc. *Recreation:* horticulture. [*Died* 9 *Nov.* 1955.

MARSHALL, Engineer-Adm. Frederick William, C.B.E. 1924; R.N. retired; *b.* 24 July 1870; *s.* of late R. S. S. Marshall, Knaresborough, Yorkshire; *m.* Edith Ellis; one *d.* *Educ.:* Grammar School, Knaresboro; Westminster School; R.N.E. College. Assistant Engineer, 1890; Engineer Commander, 1907; Served in H.M.S. Monarch, European War, present at Jutland Battle; Engineer Admiral, 1923; retired, 1924. *Recreations:* golf, sailing, rowing, cycling, motoring. *Address:* 4 Wood's View Road, Winton, Bournemouth. [*Died* 21 *June* 1956.

MARSHALL, The Honourable George Catlett, G.C.B. (Hon.), 1945; D.S.M. and Oak Leaf Cluster, Silver Star (U.S.), Victory Medal, with 4 clasps (U.S.); a Consultant to President of the United States, Secretary of Defense, and United States Government officials; *b.* Uniontown, Pa., 31 December 1880; *s.* of late George Catlett Marshall and Laura Bradford; *m.* 1st, 1902, Elizabeth Carter Coles (*d.* 1927), Lexington, Va.; 2nd, 1930, Katherine Boyce Tupper Brown, Baltimore, Maryland. *Educ.:* Virginia Military Institute; U.S. Infantry-Cavalry School; Army Staff Coll. 2nd Lt. Infantry U.S.A., 1901; promoted through grades to Maj.-Gen., 1939; Gen., 1939; Gen. of the Army (permanent), 1946. Served in Philippines, 1902-03, 1913-16; Instructor Army Staff College, 1908-10; with A.E.F., 1917-19, General Staff 1st Division, Chief of Operations, 1st Army, Chief of Staff 8th Army Corps; participated in battle of Cantigny, Aisne-Marne, St. Mihiel and Meuse-Argonne operations; A.D.C. to Gen. Pershing, 1919-24; served in China, 1924-27; instructor Army War College, 1927; Asst. Comdt. Infantry School, 1927-32; Comdr. 8th Inf., 1933; Senior Instructor Illinois National Guard, 1933-36; Commanding General 5th Brig., U.S.A., 1936-38; Chief War Plans Division General Staff, July-Oct. 1938; Deputy Chief of Staff, U.S.A., 1938-1939; Acting Chief of Staff, July-Sept. 1939; General of the Army, 1944; Chief of Staff of United States Army, 1939-45; Special Representative of President to China, with personal rank of Ambassador, 1945-47; Secretary of State, United States, 1947-49. Chief Military Mission to Brazil, May-June 1939; Atlantic Charter Conf. at Sea, Aug. 1941; Casablanca Conf., Jan. 1943; Quebec Conf., Aug. 1943; Cairo and Tehran Confs., Nov. 1943; Quebec Conf., Sept. 1944; Yalta Conf., Feb. 1945; Potsdam Conf., July 1945; Council of Foreign Ministers, Moscow, Mar.-Apr. 1947; Inter-American Conf. for Maintenance of Continental Peace and Security, Brazil, Aug.-Sept. 1947; Gen. Assembly U.N., New York, Sept.-Nov. 1947; Council of Foreign Ministers, London, Nov.-Dec. 1947; Ninth Internat. Conf. of American States, Bogotá, Colombia, Mar.-Apr. 1948; Gen. Assembly U.N., Paris, Sept.-Nov. 1948; Secretary of Defense of the United States, 1950-51. Chm. Amer. Battle Monuments Commission, 1949-; Pres. American National Red Cross, 1949. Hon. degree at Oxford Univ. (Eng.) and at many other Univs.; numerous foreign decorations. Nobel Peace Prize, 1953. Episcopalian. *Recreations:* fishing, shooting, riding, gardening. *Address:* (office) The Pentagon, Washington, D.C., U.S.A.; (winter) Liscombe Lodge, Pinehurst, North Carolina; (summer) Dodona Manor, Leesburg, Va., U.S.A. *Clubs:* Army and Navy, University, Army and Navy Country, Alibi (Washington); Union League, University, Military-Naval, Metropolitan (New York). [*Died* 16 *Oct.* 1959.

MARSHALL, Sir Guy Anstruther Knox, K.C.M.G., *cr.* 1942 (C.M.G. 1920); Kt., *cr.* 1930; F.R.S. 1923; Hon. D.Sc. (Oxon); Director of the Imperial Institute of Entomology, 1913-42; *b.* Amritsar, Punjab, 20 Dec. 1871; *o. s.* of late Col. C. H. T. Marshall, Divisional Judge, Punjab, and *g.s.* of Rt. Hon. Sir Frederick Pollock, 1st Bart.; *m.* 1933, Hilda Margaret, *d.* of late David Alexander Maxwell and *widow* of James ffolliott Darling, Salisbury, Rhodesia. *Educ.:* Charterhouse. Scientific Secretary to the Entomological Research Committee (Colonial Office), 1909-12; Corr. Memb. American Acad. Sci. Philadelphia; Hon. Member of: Royal Soc. New Zealand, National Inst. Sci. India, Entomol. Soc. of Belgium, Russian Ent. Soc., etc. Officier de l'Ordre de la Couronne, Belgium. *Publications:* numerous papers on entomological subjects. *Address:* 31 Melton Court, S.W.7. *T.:* Kensington 7514. *Club:* Athenæum. [*Died* 8 *April* 1959.

MARSHALL, Rt. Rev. Henry Vincent, D.D.; Bishop of Salford (R.C.), since 1939; *b.* 19 July 1884; *s.* of Michael Marshall and Elizabeth Stack. *Educ.:* St. Michael's College, Listowel, Kerry; All Hallows, Dublin. Ordained 1908; Curate at St. Wilfrid's, Hulme, Manchester, 1908; Lent to the Old Newport Diocese, 1910; Curate St. Thomas of Canterbury, Hr. Broughton, Salford, 1911-1922; Parish Priest St. Malachy's, Manchester, 1928-34; St. Wilfrid's, Longridge, 1934-35; St. Anne's, Ancoats, 1935-39; Dean 1935; Vicar General of Salford, 1935; Vicar Capitular, 1938. *Address:* Wardley Hall, Worsley, Nr. Manchester. *T.:* Swinton 2188. [*Died* 14 *April* 1955.

MARSHALL, James Cole, M.D. Lond.; F.R.C.S. Eng.; L.R.C.P. Lond.; formerly Consulting Surgeon Western Ophthalmic Hospital; *b.* 3 Mar. 1876; *s.* of James Marshall, Blandford; *m.* 1905, Margaret, *d.* of E. T. Compton; three *d.* *Educ.:* Dean Close School, Cheltenham; St. Bartholomew's Hospital; Consulting Surgeon Western Ophthalmic Hospital; late Ophthalmic Surgeon to Lambeth Hospital; Honorary Ophthalmic Surgeon to the Royal Academy of Music; Hon. Consulting Ophthalmic Surgeon to Northwood and Pinner Cottage Hospital; Consulting Ophthalmic Surgeon, Royal Society for the Blind, Dorton, Bucks; Ophthalmic Surgeon, Sunshine Home, Nat. Inst. for Blind, Northwood; Hunterian Prof. Roy. Coll. of Surgeons, 1938; Middlemore Lecturer on Detachment of Retina, Birmingham Eye Hospital, 1935; late Capt. R.A.M.C.; Ophthalmic Specialist to Rhine Army and 2nd Army; late Ophthalmic Surgeon to Royal Waterloo Hospital; Chief Clinical Assistant and Assistant in L.C.C. Clinic Royal London Ophthalmic Hospital; Senior Clinical Assistant to Central London Ophthalmic Hospital; Fellow R.S.M. *Publications:* Detachment of the Retina, Technique in Treatment, 1936; contributions to R.S.M. and medical journals. *Recreation:* gardening. *Ad-*

dress: Compton Cottage, Sarratt Lane, Rickmansworth, Hertfordshire. *T.:* 2219. [*Died* 24 *Dec.* 1952.

MARSHALL, James Rissik, Q.C. (Scot.) 1937; T.D.; D.L.; *b.* 18 May 1886; *e. s.* of H. B. Marshall of Rachan; *m.* 1921, Eileen Margaret, *e. d.* of Patrick Chalmers Bruce of Baddinsgill, D.L.; two *s.* one *d.* *Educ.:* Marlborough; Trinity College, Oxford, B.A., 1909; Edinburgh University, LL.B., 1912. Called to Scotch Bar, 1912; served European War, France and Macedonia, with Lothians and Border Horse; Major Commdg. 19th (Lothians and Border Horse) Armoured Car Co., 1926-30; Lt. R.A. (A.A.L.O.), 1940-1942; Capt. 1943, Major, 1945, Gen. List (Legal Aid Section); Chairman, Edinburgh Territorial Army Assoc., 1945-47; Standing Junior Counsel in Scotland for Fishery Board and H.M. Customs and Excise, 1934-1935, and for Department of Agriculture for Scotland, 1935-37; Hon. Sheriff-Substitute of the Lothians and Peebles, 1937. *Publications:* War Record of the Lothians and Border Horse, 1920; Chapter on The County in the 19th Century, in History of Peeblesshire, 1925; Walter Scott, Quartermaster (Blackwood's Magazine, April, 1930). *Recreations:* Yeomanry history and bird-photography. *Address:* Baddinsgill, West Linton, Peeblesshire. *Clubs:* United University; New (Edinburgh). [*Died* 31 *Oct.* 1959.

MARSHALL, John; *s.* of George Marshall and Margaret Allen; *b.* 31 July 1860; *m.* 1888, Hannah (B.A. Queen's University), *d.* of Capt. William Givens, Kingston; one *s.* two *d.* *Educ.:* Queen's University, Kingston; Chicago University. B.A. 1886; M.A. 1889; Editor Kingston Daily News and Kingston correspondent of the Montreal Gazette, 1889-91; Lecturer Queen's University Extra Mural or University Extension Scheme, 1890-91; English Master, St. Thomas Collegiate Institute, Ont., 1892-97; Kingston Collegiate Institute, 1897-1901; Associate Professor of English Language and Literature, Queen's University, Kingston, 1901-10; one of the Editors of Queen's University Quarterly, 1905-1910; Principal of the Weyburn Collegiate Institute, 1910-15; Inspector of Schools, Province of Saskatchewan, Canada, 1915-27; superannuated, 1927. *Publications:* Editions of Poems for Schools, 1895, 1897, and 1901; articles in Queen's Quarterly and other Magazines; two series of newspaper articles on the Canadian West. *Recreations:* gardening, bee-keeping. *Address:* 612 Lansdowne Avenue, Saskatoon, Saskatchewan, Canada. [*Died* 19 *July* 1951.

MARSHALL, Sir John Hubert, Kt., *cr.* 1914; C.I.E. 1910; Commander of the Order of Leopold: M.A., Litt.D., Hon. D.Litt., Hon. Ph.D., Hon. A.R.I.B.A.; F.S.A.; Hon. Fellow of King's College, Cambridge; Fellow of the British Academy; Correspondent of the Institut de France; Hon. Member of the American and German Oriental Societies, La Société Asiatique, Royal Batavia Society, L'École Française d'Extrême Orient and Royal Asiatic Society of Bengal; Vice-Pres. of the Royal Asiatic and India Societies; Director-General of Archæology in India, 1902-1931; *b.* Chester, 19 Mar. 1876; *y. s.* of the late Frederic Marshall, K.C.; *m.* 1902, Florence, *y. d.* of late Sir Henry Longhurst, C.V.O.; one *s.* one *d.* *Educ.:* Dulwich; King's College, Cambridge (scholar). First-class Classical Tripos, parts i. and ii.; Porson prizeman, 1898; Prendergast Greek student, 1900; Craven travelling student; Birdwood Memorial Gold Medallist, Royal Society of Arts, 1922; Campbell Memorial Gold Medallist, Bombay Branch of Royal Asiatic Society, 1932; Triennial Gold Medallist, Royal Asiatic Society of Great Britain, 1944; Law Gold Medallist, Royal Asiatic Society of Bengal, 1947. *Publications:* A Guide to Sanchi; A Guide to Taxila; Mohenjo-Daro and the Indus Civilization; The Monuments of Sanchi; Taxila; The Buddhist Art of Gandhara; Editor and part author of Annual Reports of Archæological Survey of India, 1902-28. *Address:* Avondale, Sydney Road, Guildford. *T.:* Guildford 62511. [*Died* 17 *Aug.* 1958.

MARSHALL, Kenneth McLean, C.B.E. 1920; *b.* 16 May 1874; *s.* of late Francis Marshall; *m.* 1916, Gladys Kathleen, *d.* of late Charles Stonham, C.M.G., F.R.C.S. (England); two *s.* one *d.* *Educ.:* Rugby; Trinity College, Cambridge, B.A., LL.B.; Law Tripos, 1896. Called to Bar, Inner Temple, 1900; Metropolitan Police Magistrate, 1920-44. *Address:* 16 Abingdon Court, Kensington, W.8. *Club:* Union. [*Died* 21 *Nov.* 1954.

MARSHALL, Rev. Laurence Henry, B.A., B.D., Ph.D. Lond.; Principal of Rawdon College since 1948 (Tutor, 1936-48); *b.* Louth, Lincs, 8 Mar. 1882; *s.* of Henry Marshall; *m.*; one *d.* *Educ.:* Louth Grammar School; Rawdon College; Berlin and Marburg Universities. Minister of Prince's Gate Baptist Church, Liverpool, 1911-19; caught in Germany at outbreak of war in 1914, and detained 4 months; Minister of Queen's Rd. Baptist Church, Coventry, 1920-25; Professor of New Testament Interpretation, McMaster Univ., Toronto, 1925-30; Minister of Victoria Road Baptist Church, Leicester, 1930-36. *Publications:* Contributor to Studies in Religion and History, 1942; The Challenge of New Testament Ethics, 1946. *Recreation:* gardening. *Address:* The College, Rawdon, Leeds. [*Died* 22 *Jan.* 1953.

MARSHALL, Sir Robert C.; *see* Calder-Marshall.

MARSHALL, Rev. William, J.P., M.A. Camb.; Lord of the Manor and joint patron of Sarnesfield and Weobley Benefices; *b.* Hanley Court, Co. Worcs, Aug. 1875; 2nd *surv. s.* of George W. Marshall, LL.D., F.S.A., J.P., D.L., York Herald of Arms; *m.* 1912, Margaret Anne (*d.* 1955), *er. d.* of Thomas Davies Burlton, J.P., Eaton Hill and Luntley Court, Co. Hereford; one *s.* four *d.* *Educ.:* Uppingham; Peterhouse, Cambridge. Curate of High Ercall, Shropshire, 1901-3; Rector of Sarnesfield, Co. Hereford, 1905-19 and 1928-31; High Sheriff County of Hereford, 1937; C.C. for County of Hereford for 21 years and Hon. Sec. and Treas. of Radnor and West Hereford Hunt for 22 years. *Address:* Sarnesfield Grange, Weobley, Herefordshire. *T.A.* and *T.:* Weobley 204. *Clubs:* Oxford and Cambridge; County (Hereford). [*Died* 18 *June* 1955.

MARTEL, Lieut.-Gen. Sir Giffard Le Quesne, K.C.B., *cr.* 1944 (C.B. 1940); K.B.E., *cr.* 1943; D.S.O. 1916; M.C.; Col. Comdt. R.E. from 1944; i.d.c.; p.s.c.; M.I.Mech.E.; Director Greenwood and Batley Ltd., Leeds; *b.* 10 Oct. 1889; *s.* of late General Sir Charles Martel; *m.* 1922, Maud Mackenzie, *d.* of late D. F. Mackenzie, Collingwood Grange, Camberley; one *s.* (one *d.* decd.). *Educ.:* Wellington College. Served European War, France, 1914-18 (despatches five times, D.S.O., M.C., Brevet-Major); Brevet Lieutenant-Colonel, 1928; Lieut.-Col. 1933; Maj.-Gen. 1939; Lt.-Gen. 1942; Instructor at Staff College, Quetta, India, 1930-34; Imperial Defence College Course, 1935; Assistant Director of Mechanization, War Office, 1936-38; Deputy Director of Mechanization, War Office, 1938-39; Commander, 50th (Northumbrian) Division, T.A. 1939; Commander of the Royal Armoured Corps, 1940; Head of Military Mission at Moscow, 1943: retired pay, 1945. Chairman, Royal Cancer Hospital, 1945-50. *Publications:* In the Wake of the Tank; The Problem of Security; Our Armoured Forces; The Russian Outlook, 1947; An Outspoken Soldier, 1949; East Versus West, 1952. *Address:* Bulford Lodge, Heatherside, Camberley, Surrey. *T.:* Camberley 60. *Club:* Army and Navy. [*Died* 3 *Sept.* 1958.

MARTELLI, Major-General Sir Horace de Courcy, K.B.E., *cr.* 1937; C.B. 1928; D.S.O. 1917; *b.* 1877; *m.* 1904, Ethel Mary, *d.* of late Sir John Douglas,

K.C.M.G. Served European War, 1914-17 (despatches four times, D.S.O., 1914 Star, Order of St. Maurice and Lazarus, Italy, French Order du Mérite Agricole, Bt. of Lt.-Col. and Col.); Officer-Brother Order of St. John, 1947; Shanghai Defence Force, 1927; commanded R.A. 42nd (East Lancs) Division T.A. 1925-30; A.D.C. to the King, 1929-30; Major-Gen. in charge of Administration, Southern Command, Salisbury, 1930-34; Lieutenant Governor of Jersey, 1934-39; retired pay, 1939; commanded 8th Bn. Wilts Home Guard, 1941-42; Col. Comdt. R.A., 1940-47; County President St. John's Ambulance Brigade (Wilts.), 1943-51. *Address:* 32 Fowlers Road, Salisbury, Wilts. *Club:* United Service. [*Died* 11 *March* 1959.

MARTIN, Alfred James, C.B.E. 1936; *b.* 18 July 1875; *s.* of George Joseph Martin and Ann Alice Stalain; *m.* 1905, Isabella, *d.* of William Ferguson Hadden, Lurgacullion, Co. Tyrone; two *d.* Assistant Comptroller, The Patent Office, 1921-38; International Conference on Industrial Property, Washington, 1911; International Conference on Industrial Property and Copyright, Paris, 1916; Peace Conference Paris, 1919; International Conference on Industrial Property, League of Nations, 1924, and The Hague, 1925; International Conference on Copyright, Rome, 1928. *Address:* Holmwood, Sands, High Wycombe, Bucks. *T.:* High Wycombe 345. [*Died* 5 *Nov.* 1959.

MARTIN, Vice-Adm. Sir Benjamin Charles Stanley, K.B.E., *cr.* 1946 (C.B.E. 1944); D.S.O. 1941; *b.* 1891. *Educ.:* Royal Naval Hospital School, Greenwich. Served Somali Campaign, 1908; Persian Gulf, 1910; European War, 1914-18; War of 1939-45 (D.S.O., C.B.E., K.B.E.). Vice-Adm. on retired list, 1948. *Address:* Grantchester, P. Bag, Port Shepstone, Natal, S. Africa. *Club:* Durban (Natal). [*Died* 3 *June* 1957.

MARTIN, Dr. Charles F., B.A., M.D., C.M., McGill; LL.D. Queens, McGill and Harvard; D.C.L., Lennoxville; Starr Medallist, Can. Med. Assoc., 1953; Hon. Pres. Alexandra Hospital, Montreal; Hon. Vice-Pres., Royal Edward Laurentian Hospital. Trustee Children's Memorial Hospital; Emeritus Dean of the Medical Faculty, Emeritus Professor of Medicine, McGill University; Consulting Physician Royal Victoria Hospital; Hon. Pres. Montreal Museum of Fine Arts; *b.* Montreal, 1868; married; no *c.* *Educ.:* Montreal High School; McGill Univ., Montreal; Göttingen; Pasteur Institute, Paris. Member, and former President, Association of American Physicians; Master and former President American College of Physicians; former President: Association of American Medical Colleges; Canadian Medical Association. *Publications:* articles on Blood, Stomach, Heart, etc.; Metabolism; Medical Education. *Recreation:* travel. *Address:* 3504 Mountain Street, Montreal. *T.:* Plateau 2957. *Clubs:* Mount Royal, University, Forest and Stream (Montreal). [*Died* 28 *Oct.* 1953.

MARTIN, Sir Charles James, Kt., *cr.* 1927; C.M.G. 1919; M.B., D.Sc. Lond., D.Sc. Melb., D.Sc. *hon. causa* Sheffield and Dublin, LL.D. (hon.) Edin., D.C.L. (hon.) Durham; M.A. (hon.) Camb.; F.R.C.P., F.R.S. 1901; Fellow of King's College, London; *b.* London, 1866; *s.* of Josiah Martin; *m.* Edythe (*d.* 1954), *d.* of Alfred Cross of Hastings; one *d.* *Educ.:* private school; King's College, London; St. Thomas's Hospital; University of Leipzig. Exhibitioner, gold medal and Univ. Scholar in Physiology, London. Demonstrator Biology and Physiology, K.C.L. and evening lectr. in Comparative Anatomy, 1887; Demonstrator in Physiology, University of Sydney, 1891; Lecturer in Physiology, Univ. of Mel., 1897; Professor of Physiology, University of Melbourne, 1901; Director, Lister Institute of Preventive Medicine, 1903-30; Professor of Experimental Pathology, University of London, now Emeritus Professor; Chief of Division of Animal Nutrition of Australian Council for Scientific and Industrial Research, 1931-33; Professor of Bio-Chemistry and General Physiology, Adelaide University, 1931-33; late Lt.-Col. A.A.M.C. and Consulting Pathologist, A.I.F.; served Gallipoli, Egypt, Palestine Expeditionary Force, and France, 1915-19 (despatches twice, C.M.G.); Chairman War Office Committee on Anti-typhoid Inoculation, 1904-1907; Member Advisory Committee for investigation Plague in India, appointed jointly by India Office, Royal Society, and Lister Inst., 1905-13; went to India on behalf of Committee to organise investigation; Royal Medal of Royal Socy., 1923. *Publications:* numerous papers on biological, physiological, and pathological subjects in Proc. Royal Society, Journal of Physiology, Journal of Hygiene, Journal of Biochem., etc. *Recreations:* tinkering, boating. *Address:* Roebuck House, Old Chesterton, Cambridge. *Club:* Athenæum. [*Died* 15 *Feb.* 1955.

MARTIN, Chester, M.A. (Oxon.), Hon. LL.D., (Manitoba 1929; New Brunswick, 1930); Hon. D.Litt. (Toronto, 1952); F.R.Hist.S., F.R.S.C.; retired; Professor and Head of the Department of History, University of Toronto, 1929-52; *b.* Nova Scotia, Canada, 22 June 1882; *m.* 1912, Dorothy Payne-Evans, Brentwood, Essex; one *d.* *Educ.:* University of New Brunswick, Canada; Balliol College, Oxford (Rhodes Scholar), M.A. Modern History, Gladstone Prizeman, Brassey Student, Beit Prizeman. Staff of Public Archives of Canada, Ottawa, 1907; Chair of Modern History University of Manitoba, Canada, 1909; various government commissions; report on Natural Resources Claims, 1920; negotiations with Federal Government, 1920-28; provincial counsel before final Resources Commission, 1928-29; President Canadian Historical Association, 1928; President Section II, R.S.C., 1928. *Publications:* Canada and Its Provinces, Vol. XIX, 1914; Lord Selkirk's Work in Canada, 1916; The Natural Resources Questions, 1920; Empire and Commonwealth, 1929; The Kelsey Papers (with A. G. Doughty), 1929; The Story of Canada (with G. M. Wrong and W. N. Sage), 1929; sections in the Cambridge History of the British Empire, Vol. VI; The Book of Canada (ed. with W. S. Wallace), 1930; "Dominion Lands" Policy (Vol. II in Canadian Frontiers of Settlement Series), 1938; Simpson's Athabasca Journal, Introduction, 1938; Canada in Peace and War (ed.) 1941; Foundations of Canadian Nationhood, 1955; numerous articles, reviews, and papers, chiefly on Canadian history, for periodicals and learned societies. *Recreations:* walking, skating, fishing. *Address:* 24 Hawthorne Avenue, Toronto, Canada. *Clubs:* York, Faculty Union of University, Pen (Toronto). [*Died* 2 *April* 1958.

MARTIN, Christopher J. H.; *see* Holland-Martin.

MARTIN, Brig. Edwyn Sandys Dawes, D.S.O. 1918; O.B.E. 1940; M.C.; *b.* 1894; 2nd *s.* of late Edward Martin, Brackley Lodge, Brackley; *m.* 1923, Margaret (*d.* 1950), *d.* of late David Charles Guthrie of Craigie and East Haddon Hall; two *s.* one *d.* *Educ.:* Winchester. Served European War, 1914-18 (despatches, M.C., D.S.O.); D.A.Q.M.G., British Troops in Egypt, 1932-1936; commanded 5th Inniskilling Dragoon Guards, 1937; retired pay, 1946. *Address:* Sparkford Hall, Yeovil, Somerset. *Clubs:* Cavalry, Buck's. [*Died* 4 *Oct.* 1954.

MARTIN, Sir Ernest, Kt., *cr.* 1917; Chairman of Martin, Sons & Co., Fine Cloth Spinners, Huddersfield; *b.* 23 Dec. 1872; *s.* of late Henry A. Martin of Huddersfield; *m.* 1st, 1914, Ethel Tyrrell (*d.* 1936), *d.* of late A. Tyrrell Beck; one *s.* one *d.*; 2nd, 1938, Margharita Nina Amandini; one *s.* *Educ.:* Switzerland; Magdalen College, Cambridge, *Recreations:* motor-boat racing, fishing, golf.

etc. *Address:* Beechwood, near Huddersfield; Bureside, near Wroxham, Norfolk. [*Died* 1 *Oct.* 1957.

MARTIN, Col. Gerald Hamilton, C.M.G. 1918; D.S.O. 1916; O.B.E.; formerly K.R.R.C.; *b.* 1879; *m.* 1908, Mary Augusta, *d.* of late G. B. Rennie. *Educ.:* Harrow; R.M.C. Sandhurst. Served South African War, 1899-1902 (Queen's medal and four clasps; King's medal and two clasps); European War, 1914-18 (despatches, C.M.G., D.S.O., O.B.E., Bt. Lt.-Col.); Commanded 138th Lincolnshire and Leicestershire Infantry Brigade (T.A.), 1928-32; retired pay, 1932. *Address:* Oddington Top, Moreton-in-Marsh, Glos. *T.:* Stow-in-the-Wold 68. [*Died* 17 *Feb.* 1952.

MARTIN, Glenn L.; Airplane Manufacturer; President, 1909-49, Chairman Bd. of Directors since 1949, Glenn L. Martin Co.; *b.* Macksburg, Ia., 17 Jan. 1886; *s.* of Clarence Y. Martin and Minta DeLong; unmarried. *Educ.:* Kansas Wesleyan University. Began in 1907 to build gliders; designed and built pusher type airplane, 1908, and taught self to fly; established one of the first airplane factories in the U.S., 1909; constructed airplanes of various types, including monoplanes and water aircraft; one of world's outstanding pilots, held speed, altitude and endurance records, 1909-16; gave many exhibn. flights in U.S. and Can.; holds Aviation Certificate No. 56, and Expert Aviator's Certificate No. 2, Aero Club of Am.; incorporated Glenn L. Martin Co., Santa Ana, Calif., 1911; moved factory to Los Angeles, 1912; built airplanes for exhbn. flying and sport use until 1913, when first order was received from War Dept. for Model TT, which was later adopted by Army for training purposes; produced several new models for U.S. Army, and built for govts. of Holland and Netherlands East Indies, 24 airplanes; in 1917 merged interests with Wright Co., resulting in Wright-Martin Aircraft Corp., N.Y.; withdrew from Wright Martin Co., 1917, and organised Glen L. Martin Co. of Cleveland; designed first Am. designed airplane for Liberty engines and built Martin bombers; built China Clipper, Hawaian Clipper, Philippine Clipper, B-10, British Maryland, British Baltimore, B-26 Marauder, PBM and Mars airplanes, currently producing airplanes for Army and Navy and three types of commercial air transports, 1929-45; Two medals for over-ocean flight from Newport to Catalina (Calif.), 1912; Collier Trophy, 1932; Civic Award, Advertising Club of Baltimore, 1937; Daniel Guggenheim Medal, Inst. of Aeronautical Sciences, 1941; Lord and Taylor Annual Am. Design Award, 1942; Sports Afield Trophy, 1943. Wright Memorial Lecturer, R. Aeronautical Soc., London, 1931; Van Resselaer Lecturer, Drexel Inst., Philadelphia, 1938. Founded Glenn L. Martin College of Engineering and Aeronautical Sciences, Univ. of Maryland, 1945. Member: Izaak Walton League of Am., Ak-Sar-Ben Soc. (Nebraska), Maryland State Game and Fish Protective Assoc. *Address:* 3703 Greenway, Baltimore, Md., U.S.A. *Clubs:* Los Angeles Athletic (Vermejo, Los Angeles); Baltimore Country, (Hon. Commodore) Baltimore Yacht, Merchants, Early Birds, Maryland Flying, Maryland Sportsmen's Luncheon, Maryland Yacht (Baltimore); Annapolis Yacht (Annapolis); Touchdown (Washington). [*Died* 4 *Dec.* 1955.

MARTIN, Colonel Henry Graham, C.M.G. 1919; *b.* 5th May 1872; *s.* of late James Martin, land agent, Ballinasloe, Ireland, and Isabella Lawson, Stoney Groves, Forfar; *m.* 190, Beatrice Mabel Harris, *g.d.* of Samuel Harris, late High-Sheriff of Douglas, and Vicar-General, Isle of Man; no *c.* *Educ.:* private school; Royal College of Surgeons, Ireland; Dublin University. Qualified as a medical practitioner, 1895; general practice in Bristol for three years; commission in R.A.M.C. 1898; Captain, 1901; served throughout South African War, including defence of Ladysmith; served ten years in India; major, 1909; served European War in France and Belgium, 1914-18 (despatches three times, C.M.G.); held many appointments, including that of A.D.M.S. of the 55th (West Lancashire) Division, and the 3rd Cavalry Division; retired pay, 1926. *Address:* c/o Glyn, Mills & Co., Whitehall, S.W.1; Aranmore, Malone Park, Belfast. [*Died* 4 *Dec.* 1955.

MARTIN, Major-Gen. James Fitzgerald, C.B. 1935; C.M.G. 1915; C.B.E. 1919; M.B., late R.A.M.C.; Knight of Grace of the Order of St. John of Jerusalem, 1917; Chevalier de la Couronne of Belgium; late Hon. Surgeon to the King; late Hon. Surgeon to the Viceroy of India; *b.* 12 June 1876; *s.* of late Colonel W. T. Martin, A.M.S.; *m.* Mary Latimer, *e. d.* of late Colonel R. S. H. Moody, C.B., The Buffs and Royal Irish Fusiliers; one *d.* *Educ.:* Bath College; Edinburgh University; M.B., Ch.B., 1899; D.P.H., R.C.S. and P. London, 1911. Entered army, 1899; Captain, 1902; Major, 1911 Lieut.-Col. 1917; Col. 1927; Major-Gen., 1931; retired pay, 1935; served South Africa, 1900-2 (Queen's medal 4 clasps, King's medal 2 clasps); European War, 1914-18 (despatches 5 times, C.M.G., C.B.E., 1914 Star); employed, 1940-43, by Ministry of Health as Inspector of Hospitals and Assistant Hospital Officer No. 3 and No. 6 Regions; employed by Min. of Pensions, Southern Region, 1944-47. *Address:* Waverley Cottage, Waverley Avenue, Fleet, Hants. [*Died* 14 *Feb.* 1958.

MARTIN, James Rea, C.I.E. 1923; I.C.S. (retd.); B.A. (Royal University of Ireland); Barrister-at-Law (Middle Temple); *b.* 22 Aug. 1877; *m.* 1916, Francis Lily Elsie, *d.* of John Cother Webb; two *d.* *Educ.:* Queen's College, Belfast. Appointed I.C.S. 1901; Deputy Commissioner, Upper Sind Frontier, 1912; Collector of Karachi, 1918; of Surat, 1921; Secretary to Government of Bombay, Deputy Director of Development, and Commissioner Bombay Suburban Division, 1922-1925; Member Council of State, India, 1924; Chief Secretary, Government of Bombay, 1926-1930; Acting Home Member, Government of Bombay, July-Oct. 1928; Commissioner, 1931; Member Indian States Enquiry Committee (Financial). 1932; Chairman Wallingford Farm Training Colony Committee, 1936-38; General Secretary, British Empire Leprosy Relief Association, 1938-45. *Address:* 25 Kidderpore Avenue, Hampstead, N.W.3. *T.:* Hampstead 2041. *Club:* Athenæum. [*Died* 20 *June* 1951.

MARTIN, Maj.-Gen. Kevin John, D.S.O. 1914; *b.* Ootacamund, 3 July 1890; *s.* of late Lt.-Col. P. R. Martin, I.M.S.; *m.* 1915, Hilda, *y. d.* of C. W. Burkinshaw, Cotes Grange, Louth; (one *s.* killed in action, 1941) two *d.* *Educ.:* Beaumont Coll., Old Windsor, Berks. Entered R.E. 1910; served European War, 1914-15 (wounded, D.S.O., Officier de la Légion d'Honneur, Officier de l'Ordre de la Couronne, Croix de Guerre, despatches five times); General Staff C.-in-C. Allied Forces (Marshal Foch). 1918/19; Assistant Military Attaché, Paris, 1927-28; Military Attaché, Warsaw, 1928-31; C.R.E. Baluchistan District, 1934-36; General Staff, War Office, 1938-39; Acting Maj.-Gen., 1941; Temp. Maj.-Gen. 1942; A.D.C. to the King, 1942-45; retired, 1945. *Address:* Hillcote, Victoria Place, Budleigh Salterton, Devon. *Club:* Army and Navy. [*Died* 27 *Feb.* 1958.

MARTIN, Thomas Shannon; Director (Governor 1935-37) Bank of Ireland; Managing Director, T. and C. Martin, Ltd., Dublin; Director of National City Bank Ltd. and Chairman Dublin Artisans' Dwellings Co. Ltd.; on Local Board of Liverpool and London and Globe Insurance Co. Ltd.; *b.* 17 March 1891; *s.* of late Thomas P. Martin; *m.* 1924, Anne Mary Kenny; no *c.* *Educ.:* Downside School; Trinity College, Dublin. Served European War, 1914-

1918, and was Temp. Major in 5th Battalion The Connaught Rangers. *Recreations:* tennis and golf. *Address:* St. Brendan's, Ballsbridge, Dublin. *T.:* Dublin 63350. *Clubs:* Stephen's Green (Dublin); Royal Irish Yacht (Kingstown, Co. Dublin). [*Died* 29 *Jan.* 1954.

MARTIN, Prof. Dr. Willem; Director of the Mesdag Museum at The Hague; *b.* 20 June 1876; *s.* of late Prof. Dr. K. Martin, Prof. of Geology at Leyden Univ.; *m.* 1906, Maria Cornelia Visser, *d.* of late Prof. Visser van Yzendoorn, Member of the Dutch Parliament; one *s.* three *d.* *Educ.:* Gymnasium and University, Leyden. Doctor of Literature, Leyden, 1901; 2nd Director of the Royal Picture Gallery at The Hague, 1901; Privatdocent in Art History at Leyden University, 1904-7; lectured at London University College, 1906 and 1921, at the University of London (Courtauld Institute), 1935 and 1936, United States (Harvard, Princeton Universities, etc.), 1921 and 1938; late Director of the Royal Picture Gallery (Mauritshuis) and of the Printroom of Leyden University; Professor of Art History at the University of Leyden, Holland, 1907-45; Chevalier (Ridder) of the Order of the Dutch Lion and of the Order of Orange Nassau; Commander of the British Empire (C.B.E.); Commander of the Order of the Crown of Italy; Commander of the Order of the Crown of Belgium; Chevalier of the Dannebrog Order of Denmark; Chevalier of the St. Olaf Order of Norway; Chevalier 1st Class of the Pole Star Order of Sweden; member or trustee of scientific and artistic corporations, etc. *Publications:* G. Dou, 1901—also in French, Dutch, German; Oude Schilderkunst in Nederland; Altholländische Bilder; Catalogue of the Hoschek Collection, Prague, and of the Jansen Collection, Brussels—Joh. Bosboom (with G. H. Marius); Jan Steen, 1924, 1926 and 1953; Catalogue raisonné of the Royal Picture Gallery, 1914 and 1935; Holl. Schilderkunst, 2 vols., 1935 and 1936, third edition, 1944; articles in periodicals like the Burlington Magazine, Oud Holland, etc. *Address:* 11 Nassaulaan, The Hague, Holland. *T.:* 110169. *T.A.:* Prof. Martin, Hague, Holland. *Clubs:* Nieuwe of Literaire Societeit, Pulchri Studio (The Hague). [*Died* 10 *March* 1954.

MARTIN DU GARD, Roger; Homme de Lettres; Prix Nobel de Littérature, 1937; *b.* Paris, 23 March 1881; *m.* 1906, Hélène Foucault; one *d.* *Publications:* Novels: Devenir, 1908; Jean Barois, 1913; Les Thibault: (I, Le Cahier Gris, 1921; II, Le Pénitencier, 1922; III, La Belle Saison, 1923; IV, La Consultation, 1928; V, La Sorellina, 1928; VI, La mort du Père, 1930; VII, L'Été, 1914, 1936; VIII, Epilogue, 1940). Vieille France, 1933 (Eng. trans., The Postman, 1954); *essays:* L'Abbaye de Jumièges, 1909. 3 pièces de théâtre: Le Testament du Père Leleu, 1914; La Goufle, 1926; Un Taciturne, 1932. *Address:* à Bellême (Orne), France. [*Died* 23 *Aug.* 1958.

MARTIN-LEAKE, Lt.-Col. A.; *see* Leake.

MARTINDALE, Hilda, C.B.E. 1935; *b.* 1875; *d.* of late William Martindale and late Louisa Martindale, Horsted Keynes, Sussex. *Educ.:* Royal Holloway College, Englefield Green; Bedford College for Women, Regent's Park, N.W. Travelled extensively in Europe, India, Australia. New Zealand, and United States of America, enquiring into methods of dealing with State children; appointed one of H.M. Inspectors of Factories in 1901; Senior Lady Inspector, 1908, serving in Ireland, Midlands, and London; Superintending Inspector of Factories, 1921; Deputy Chief Inspector of Factories, 1925-33; Director of Women Establishments, H.M. Treasury 1933-37: retired 1937; Member of the Committee appointed by the Central Control Board (Liquor Traffic) in 1916 to enquire into excessive drinking among women in Birmingham; Member of the Departmental Committee on Factory Inspection, 1928; Member of th Committee appointed by the Secretary of State for Foreign Affairs in 1934 to review the question of the admission of women to the Diplomatic and Consular Services; Technical Adviser to the British Government Delegates to the Fifteenth, Sixteenth, Eighteenth and Twenty-third Sessions of the International Labour Conference, Geneva; Member of the Industrial Health Research Board, 1933-37, and appointed Member of two Trade Boards; Member of the Institute of International Affairs, and one of the Governors of Bedford College for Women; Dep. Chairman, Council of Dr. Barnado's Homes. *Publications:* Woman Servants of the State, 1870-1938; From One Generation to Another, 1839-1944; Some Victorian Portraits. *Recreations:* travelling, needlework. *Address:* 44 Coleherne Court, S.W.5. *T.:* Frobisher 6796. *Club:* University Women's. [*Died* 18 *April* 1952.

MARTINEAU, Lieut.-Col. and Hon. Col. Ernest, C.M.G. 1916; V.D., T.D., M.A.; Royal Warwickshire Regiment (T.F.); D.L. Warwickshire; late member of Ryland, Martineau & Co., Solicitors; *b.* 23 Feb. 1861; *s.* of late Sir Thomas Martineau, Kt., and Emily Kenrick; *m.* 1888, Margaret Lilla Kendrick (*d.* 1943); two *s.* one *d.* *Educ.:* Rugby; Trinity Hall, Cambridge. Served in Volunteers, 1878-1908; commanding 6th Batt. Royal Warwickshire Regt. (T.F.), 1908-15; Hon. Col. 1917-24; Birmingham City Councillor, 1900-45; Lord Mayor, 1912-14; Hon. Freeman, 1938. *Address:* Augustus Road, Birmingham. *Club:* Clef (Birmingham). [*Died* 25 *Nov.* 1951.

MARTYN, Colonel Anthony Wood, C.B. 1930; D.S.O.; O.B.E.; retired pay; *b.* 1864; *s.* of Lieut.-Colonel Anthony Martyn, Bradninch, Devon; *m.* 1887, Ethel Maud Grant (*d.* 1949), *d.* of William Grant of Alverstoke, Hants; one *d.* *Educ.:* Marlborough. 4th Devon Militia, 1881-84; 1st Batt. The Queen's Own Royal West Kent Regiment, 1885-1906; Volunteer Brigade Major and Secretary, Kent Territorial Army Association, 1906-30; served European War; raised and commanded 10th local battalion Royal West Kent Regt. (despatches five times, immediate award D.S.O., Order of Leopold of Belgium and Croix de Guerre). *Recreations:* all sports. *Address:* Lloyd's Bank Ltd. (Cox & King's Branch), S.W.1. [*Died* 20 *March* 1955.

MARTYN, Brigadier Athelstan Markham, C.M.G. 1918; D.S.O. 1916; *b.* 5 June 1881; *e. s.* of late J. G. Martyn, Armidale, New South Wales; *m.* 1916, Stella Godfrey, *o. d.* of late Frank Swift of Tasmania; two *d.* Served European War, 1914-18 (D.S.O., C.M.G.); Commander Field Troops and District Base Commandant, 5th Military District (Western Australia), 1932-35; Comdr. Field Troops, 4th Military District, S. Australia, 1936-39; Brigadier Administering Camps of Continuous Training, N.S.W., 1939-1940; retired, 1940. *Address:* 25 Highgate St. Rosefield, Adelaide, S.A. [*Died* 4 *Nov.* 1956.

MARTYN, Selwyn Rawlings; *b.* Bilbao, Spain. 23 Sept. 1892; *e. s.* of Samuel Thomas and Helena Martyn, Padstow, Cornwall; *m.* 1925, Nora, *y. d.* of Stephen O'Callaghan, Dros-y-Mor, Penarth, Glam; three *s.* *Educ.:* Forest School. Served European War, 1914-18, Capt. 1st Monmouthshire Regiment. High Sheriff of Glamorgan, 1944-45. *Recreation:* golf. *Address:* The Mount, Dynas Powis, Glamorgan. *T.:* Dynas Powis 3136; Trehuel, Constantine Bay, Padstow, Cornwall. *T.:* St. Merryn 326. *Clubs:* Bath, East India and Sports; Royal and Ancient (St. Andrews); Royal Porthcawl; Cardiff and County (Cardiff). [*Died* 8 *July* 1956.

MASCALL, Col. (Hon. Brigadier) Maurice Edward, D.S.O. 1917; O.B.E. 1919; R.A.; *b.* 1882; *s.* of Col. F. Mascall, R.E.; *m.* 1915, Esmée Maude, *d.* of late Col. Shafto

Longfield Cra'ster, C.B., C.I.E.; two *d.* *Educ.:* U.S. College, Westward Ho!; R.M.A. Served European War, 1914-19 (despatches four times, D.S.O., O.B.E.); N.W. Frontier (Afghan War), 1919-21 (despatches); Col. 1932; Chief Instructor (Commandant) Coast Artillery School, 1932-35; B.R.A. Western Command, 1935-39; retired pay, 1939, re-employed, Oct. 1939-Jan. 1942 as Commander S. Wales Area. *Address:* 19 The Avenue, Lewes, Sussex. *T.:* Lewes 1327. [*Died* 26 *April* 1958.

MASKELL, Ernest John, F.R.S. 1939; M.A., Ph.D. (Cantab.); Mason Professor of Botany, Birmingham Univ., since 1951; *b.* 1 February 1895; *s.* of J. Maskell, Camb.; *m.* 1922, Elisabeth Rose McCormick; one *s.* (decd.). *Educ.:* County High School, Cambridge; Emmanuel College, Cambridge. Frank Smart Student, Cambridge University, 1920-22; Physiologist, Horticulture Research Station, Cambridge, 1922-24; Rothamsted Experimental Station, 1924-26; Cotton Research Station, Trinidad, 1926-30; Lecturer and later Reader in Plant Physiology, Cambridge Univ., 1930-51; Fellow of Emmanuel College, 1945-51. Member Agricultural Research Council, 1952-57. *Publications:* papers on Plant Physiology. *Address:* 28 Wake Green Road, Birmingham 13. *T.:* South 2640. [*Died* 20 *Dec.* 1958.

MASON, John H., R.D.I. 1936; *b.* 13 June 1875; *s.* of Thomas James and Mary Dugan Mason; *m.* 1899, Edith Martha Rattee; two *s.* one *d.* *Educ.:* Elementary and then private tuition in the Greek and Latin classics. Diploma in the History of Art, London University; Apprenticed at the Ballantyne Press, London; the Doves Press, 1900-9; appointed by the London County Council to institute the printing classes at the L.C.C. Central School of Arts and Crafts, 1905 (part time), 1909 (full-time); retired Sept. 1940; assisted Count Harry Kessler to found the Cranach Press, Weimar, in 1913 and resumed in 1928 until 1929; co-founder of the Imprint and collaborated in designing that type, 1913; Diploma for services to the Empire Exhibition 1924 also 1925; Hon. Mem. Soc. of Scribes and Illuminators, 1922; Mem. Art Workers Guild, 1926, retired 1935; Vice-Pres. Arts and Crafts Exhibition Soc., 1941; Hon. Mem. Assoc. of Teachers of Printing and Allied Subjects, 1946. *Publications:* Notes on Printing considered as an Industrial Art; Articles and reviews in the Imprint, London Mercury, and Athenæum; Lucian's The Dream, and Lucian's Europa and the Bull, transl. from the Greek; Apuleius, Cupid and Psyche, transl. from the Latin; Virgil's Eclogues transl. from the Latin; Erasmus' Diversoria, transl. from the Latin; Maillol, by Count H. Kessler, transl. from the German; Typography, A Printer's Philosophy, in "Fifteen Craftsmen," 1945. *Recreations:* The study of art and linguistics, walking, sketching and nature study. *Address:* 12 Oxford Road, Putney, S.W.15. *Club:* Double Crown. [*Died* 15 *June* 1951.

MASON, Brig. Searle Dwyer, C.B.E. 1938; E.D.; J.P.; (Associated Registered Accountant, N.Z. Soc. of Accountants); N.Z. Military Forces, Retired List; *b.* 7 Sept. 1892; *s.* of John Joseph Mason; *m.* 1928, Lucy Margaret Hawkes; no *c.* *Educ.:* Timaru Boys' High School. Served European War 1914-18 with N.Z. Mounted Rifle Brigade, Royal Flying Corps and Somerset Light Infantry; Commanded 1st Canterbury Regiment, N.Z. Forces, 1930-36; Commanded 3rd Infantry Brigade, N.Z. Forces, 1936-37; Camp Commandant, Burnham Military Camp, N.Z., 1940-41; Commd. Brigade Group, 1941-43. *Recreations:* Rugby football (administrative side only, now), trout fishing, squash racquets. *Address:* 11 Montrose Terrace, Mairangi Bay, N.Z. *Club:* Midland (Christchurch, N.Z.). [*Died* 14 *Nov.* 1953.

MASON-MACFARLANE, Lt.-Gen. Sir Noel; *see* Macfarlane, Lt.-Gen. Sir F. N. M.-

MASSEREENE and FERRARD, 12th Viscount, *cr.* 1660; **Lieut.-Col. Algernon William John Clotworthy Skeffington,** D.S.O. 1900; late 17th Lancers; Baron of Loughneagh, 1660; Baron Oriel, 1790; Viscount Ferrard, 1797; Baron Oriel (U.K), 1821; H.M. Lieut. and Custos Rotulorum, Co. Antrim, 1916-38; *b.* 28 Nov. 1873; *s.* of 11th Viscount and Florence, *o. c.* of Maj. George John Whyte-Melville; *S.* father, 1905; *m.* 1st, 1905, Jean Barbara (*d.* 1937), *e. d.* of Sir John Ainsworth, 1st Bt.; one *s.*; 2nd, 1940, Mrs. Florence Clementina Vere Vere-Laurie, Carlton Hall, Newark, Notts. *Educ.:* Winchester; Sandhurst. Entered army, 1895; Captain, 1900; Adjutant, 1900; served South Africa, 1900-1902 (wounded, despatches twice, Brevet Major, Queen's medal 4 clasps, King's medal 2 clasps, D.S.O.); retired, 1907; Parliamentary Secretary of the Ministry of the Prime Minister, Northern Ireland, 1921-29; served European War, 1914-18 with North Irish Horse, and on the Staff in France, Egypt, Malta, and Mesopotamia (despatches twice). Owns several pictures by Lely, Godfrey, Kneller, Gainsborough, etc. *Heir:* *s.* Hon. John Clotworthy Talbot Foster Whyte-Melville-Skeffington [*b.* 22 Oct. 1914; *m.* 1939, Annabelle Kathleen, *er. d.* of late Henry D. Lewis, Combwell Priory, Hawkhurst, Kent; one *s.* one *d*]. *Address:* Clotworthy House, Antrim, Northern Ireland. *Clubs:* Carlton; Ulster (Belfast). [*Died* 20 *July* 1956.

MASSEY, Mrs. Gertrude; artist; *b.* 21 Feb. 1868; *m.* H. G. Massey, (*decd.*), Principal, The Heatherley Sch. of Fine Art; one *d.* *Educ.:* privately. Has painted miniatures of H.M. King George VI, T.R.H. the Duke of Windsor, the Princess Royal, and the Duke of Kent at the command of King Edward VII.; also painted miniatures of Queen Victoria, Queen Alexandra, King and Queen of Norway, and Prince Olaf, Princess Victoria, and for Dowager-Empress of Russia, etc.; has had many special exhibitions of portraits and landscapes. *Recreation:* bridge. *Publication:* Kings Commoners and Me, 1934. *Address:* Little Leas, Church Lane, Bognor Regis, Sussex. *T.:* Bognor 1724. [*Died* 7 *Dec.* 1957.

MASSINGHAM, Harold John; *b.* 25 Mar. 1888; *s.* of Henry William Massingham of Norwich and Emma, *d.* of John Snowdon, also of Norwich; *m.* 1933, Anne Penelope, *d.* of late A. J. Webbe. *Educ.:* Westminster School; Queen's College, Oxford (Exhibitioner). Journalist and Writer on Staff of Morning Leader, National Press Agency, and Athenæum, 1912-14; weekly contributor to Nation and Athenæum, 1916-1924, to Field, 1938-51 and to Spectator, 1951-. *Publications:* St. Francis of Assisi (paraphrase of French play), 1913; Letters to X, 1919; People and Things, 1919; A Treasury of Seventeenth-Century Verse, 1919; Dogs, Birds and Others; Natural History Letters from the Spectator, 1921; Some Birds of the Countryside, 1921; Poems About Birds (Anthology), 1922; Untrodden Ways, 1923; In Praise of England, 1924; Sanctuaries for Birds, 1924; H. W. M.: A Selection from the Writings of H. W. Massingham, 1925; Downland Man, 1926; Fee, Fi, Fo, Fum, 1926; Pre-Roman Britain, 1927; The Golden Age, the Story of Human Nature, 1927; The Heritage of Man, 1929; The Friend of Shelley, A Memoir of Edward John Trelawny, 1930; Birds of the Sea Shore, 1931; Wold Without End, 1932; London Scene, 1933; Country, 1934; Through the Wilderness, 1935; English Downland, 1936; Genius of England, 1937; Cotswold Country, 1937; Shepherd's Country, 1938; A Countryman's Journal, 1939; Country Relics, 1939; The Sweet of the Year, 1939; Chiltern Country, 1940; The Fall of the Year, 1941; Remembrance, An Autobiography, 1942; The English Countryman, 1942; The Tree of Life (an attempt at a synthesis between religion and nature), 1943; Men of Earth,

MASON, Thomas Godfrey, F.R.S. See page xxix

1943; Field Fellowship, 1943; This Plot of Earth, 1944; The Wisdom of the Fields, 1945; Where Man Belongs, 1946; The Cotswolds (Puffin Books); An Englishman's Year, 1948; The Curious Traveller, 1950; Faith of a Fieldsman, 1951; The Southern Marches, 1952; (with Edward Hyams), Prophecy of Famine, 1953; Chapter and introduction to the English Countryside, 1939; editor with Hugh Massingham of The Great Victorians, 1932; edited English Country, 1934, the Nonesuch Gilbert White, 1938, England and the Farmer, 1941, The Natural Order, 1945; The Small Farmer, 1947; Memoir on Thomas Hennell in his The Countryman at Work, 1947. *Recreations:* collecting rural antiquities and gardening. *Address:* Reddings, Long Crendon, Bucks. [*Died* 22 *Aug.* 1952.

MASSY, 8th Baron, *cr.* 1776; **Hugh Hamon Charles George Massy;** *b.* 13 July 1894; *s.* of 7th Baron and Ellen Ida Constance, *d.* of Charles W. Wise, Rochestown, Tipperary; *S.* father, 1926; *m.* 1919, Margaret, *d.* of late Richard Leonard of Meadsbrook, Ashbourne, Co. Limerick, and *widow* of Dr. Moran, Tara, Co. Meath; one *s.* *Heir: s.* Hon. Hugh Hamon John Somerset Massy, *b.* 11 June 1921. [*Died* 20 *March* 1958.

MASSY-GREENE, Hon. Sir Walter, K.C.M.G., *cr.* 1933; Chairman Associated Pulp and Paper Mills Ltd., Felt and Textiles of Aus., Bradford Cotton Mills Ltd., Electrolytic Zinc Co. of Australasia; Director Yarra Falls Ltd., Australian Knitting Mills Ltd., Dunlop Rubber Australia Ltd., and other companies; *b.* Wimbledon, 6 Nov. 1874; 2nd *s.* of John Greene and Julia Eamer, *d.* of Gen. Robert Sandeman; *m.* 1915, Lula May, *e. d.* of J. R. Lomax, Tenterfield Station, N.S.W., and Yandilla and Maxland, Queensland; two *s.* one *d.* *Educ.:* Lynton House Coll., Witney, Oxon. Emigrated to Australia, 1891; seven years in service of Bank of New South Wales, then engaged in farming and pastoral pursuits; nominated to Provisional Council, Terania Shire, N.S.W., 1906; represented A Riding, Terania Shire, 1907; President, 1907-9; represented Richmond, N.S.W., in Commonwealth Parliament, 1910; Whip Liberal Party in Cook Administration, 1913; Whip Coalition War Government, Hughes-Cook Administration, 1917; Member of the Board of Trade, 1918; Minister in charge of Prices Regulation and Food Control, 1918-1919; Minister of Trade and Customs, Commonwealth of Australia, 1919-21; Minister for Defence and Navy, 1921-23; Hon. Minister, Australia, 1932-33. Defeated, election 1922; Elected to the Senate, 1923, 1925 and 1931. *Address:* Collins House, Collins Street, Melbourne, C.1, Australia. *Clubs:* Athenæum, Melbourne (Melbourne). [*Died* 16 *Nov.* 1952.

MASSY-WESTROPP, Colonel John, C.M.G. 1902; late comdg. 5th R. Munster Fus. (Limerick County Regiment); *b.* 28 April 1860; *m.* 1st, 1890, Georgina (*d.* 1927), *d.* of Frederick William Kennedy, Limerick; two *s.*; 2nd, 1927, Mary, *d.* of M. O'D. Hogan, Limerick. *Educ.:* Windermere College; Portarlington. Entered the Clare Militia, 1880; served with the 12th Royal Lancers, 1882-88; Limerick City Artillery, 1888-90; Limerick County Regt., 1890-1906. *Address:* c/o Coutts & Co., 440 Strand, W.C.2. [*Died* 23 *July* 1951.

MASTER, Capt. Charles Edward Hoskins, J.P.; Chairman, Friary, Holroyd and Healy's Breweries Ltd., since 1928 (Director since 1902; Joint Managing Director, 1928-1959); *b.* 5 July 1878; *e. s.* of late Charles Hoskins Master, Sandgate, Kent; *m.* 1909, Beatrice Marie, *d.* of late Cyril Wilson; no *c.* *Educ.:* Eton; Oriel College, Oxford (M.A.). Captain Royal West Surrey Regt., 1906; retired, 1916. J.P. Surrey, 1936; High Sheriff, 1936. *Recreations:* caravanning, farming, yachting; generally gregarious. *Address:* Barrow Green Court, Oxted, Surrey. *T.:* Oxted 3300. *Clubs:* Carlton, Junior Carlton; Norfolk and Suffolk Yacht. [*Died* 3 *June* 1960.

MASTERMAN, Air Commodore Edward Alex. Dimsdale, C.B. 1923; C.M.G. 1919; C.B.E. 1918; A.F.C.; *b.* 15 April 1880; *s* of Edward Masterman, jun.; *m.* 1904, Heather Frances, *d.* of Rev. E. P. Gregg; one *s.* three *d.* *Educ.:* Evelyns, Uxbridge; H.M.S. Britannia. Entered Navy 1894; joined H M.S. Revenge as midshipman, 1896; Lieutenant R.N., 1900; specialised as Torpedo Lieut., 1904; qualified as Russian Interpreter, 1907; Staff Officer H.M.S. Vernon; Commander R.N., 1911; experiments with H.M. Rigid Airship No. 1 (Mayfly) at Barrow-in-Furness, March 1911; transferred to R.N.A.S. on formation; Command of Farnborough Airship Station, 1914; outbreak of war, serving in Director Air Department Admiralty; construction and trials of Rigid Airships, 1916; transferred to R.A.F., 1918; commanded No. 22 (operations) group; President of the Inter-Allied Aeronautical Commission of Control (Germany), 1919-22; Commanding No. 7 and No. 10 Group, R.A.F., 1922-1928; retired list, 1929; Commandant Observer Corps, 1929-36; Western Area Commandant, Royal Observer Corps, 1937-42. *Address:* Hook, nr. Basingstoke, Hants. *T.:* Hook 28. [*Died* 26 *Aug.* 1957.

MASTERSON, Most Rev. Mgr. Joseph, D.D., Ph.D., D.C.L.; Archbishop of Birmingham (R.C.), since 1947; *b.* 29 Jan. 1899; *s.* of William Masterson and Cecelia O'Toole. *Educ.:* Manchester; Douai School; Ushaw Coll.; Ven. English Coll., Rome. Late Vicar-General of Salford. *Address:* Archbishop's House, 6 Norfolk Road, Edgbaston, Birmingham 15. *T.:* Edgbaston 0564. [*Died* 30 *Nov.* 1953.

MATHER-JACKSON, Sir E. A.; *see* Jackson.

MATHEW, Lt.-Gen. George, C.B. 1930; *b.* Bombay, 11 Oct. 1879; *s.* of late Frank Mathew, C.E., B.B. and C.I.Rly.; *m.* Mary Johnston, M.B.E. 1945 (*d.* 1957) *d.* of R. W. Johnston, Wynberg, S.A.; (one *s.*, R.A.F., killed on active service 1943, and one, R.N. Fleet Air Arm, killed in action Aug. 1941) one *d* *Educ.:* Beaumont College; Eastman's R.N. Academy, Portsmouth. 2nd Lieut. Royal Marine Artillery, 1897; Lieut., 1898; Adjutant, Tipperary R.G.A. (M.), 1906-8; Captain, 1906; Officer Commanding Troops, St. Helena, 1911-1914; Major, 1916; R.M.A., Howitzer Brigade, France and Flanders, 1916-19; (despatches); Naval Staff, Admiralty, 1919-21; S.O.R.M. Staff of Naval C.-in-C., Portsmouth, 1921-23; Lieut.-Col., 1927; Colonel, 2nd Commandant, 1929 (C.B.); Colonel Commandant, 1931; Colonel Commandant (Temp. Brigadier) Depot, Royal Marines, Deal; A.D.C. to the King, 1933-34; Major-Gen. 1934; Lieut.-Gen. 1936; retired, 1937. *Publication:* part author, comedy, Divorce for Chrystabel. *Address:* c/o Standard Bank of South Africa, Adderley St., Cape Town. [*Died* 14 *Sept.* 1958.

MATHEWS, Basil Joseph, M.A. (Oxon); LL.D. (Univ. of B.C., Can.); *b.* Oxford, 28 Aug. 1879; *s.* of A. Mathews; *m.* 1st, H. Anne (*d.* 1939), *y. d.* of late W. H. Passmore; 2nd, Winifred Grace, *e. d.* of late John Wilson. *Educ.:* Oxford High School and Oxford University. Private Secretary to Principal Fairbairn, Mansfield College, Oxford, 1899-1904; Literary Staff of The Christian World, 1904-10; Editorial Secretary London Missionary Society, 1910-1919; Chairman and Secretary Literature Committee of Ministry of Information, 1917-1918; Editor of Outward Bound and Editor to the Far and Near Publications Company, Ltd.; Director of the Press Bureau of the Conference of Representatives of British Missionary Societies, 1920-24; International Literature Secretary, World's Committee of Young Men's Christian Associations (Boys'

Work), Geneva, 1924-29; Professor of Christian World-Relations in the University of Boston and Andover-Newton Theological Seminary, Mass., 1932-44; American Division, Ministry of Information, 1939-40; Prof. of World Relations, Union Coll., Univ. of British Columbia, Canada, 1944-49. *Publications:* The Splendid Quest, 1911; Livingstone the Pathfinder, 1913; John Williams the Shipbuilder, 1914; The Secret of the Raj, 1915; Paul the Dauntless, 1916; Three Years' War for Peace, 1917; Dr. Wardlaw Thompson, 1918; The Riddle of Nearer Asia, 1918; The Ships of Peace, 1919; Christian Fellowship in Thought and Prayer (with Rev. H. Bisseker), 1919; The Argonauts of Faith, 1920; The Clash of Colour: a Study in the Race Problem, 1924 (revised and largely rewritten, 1936); Wilfred Grenfell, the Master Mariner, 1924; Black Treasure, 1925; Young Islam on Trek, 1926; The Spirit of the Game, 1927; Jesus and Youth, 1929; A Life of Jesus, 1930; The Clash of World Forces: a Study in Nationalism, Bolshevism and Christianity, 1931; Yarns on Heroes of the Day's Work, 1932; A little Life of Jesus; World Tides in the Far East, 1933; John R. Mott, World Citizen, 1934; The Jew and the World Ferment (revised and partly rewritten, 1939); There go the Ships; Consider Africa, 1935; Shaping the Future, 1936; Ed. East and West: Conflict or Co-operation? 1936; Ed. Flaming Milestone: A Report of the World's Y.M.C.A. Conference, Mysore, 1937; India reveals Herself, 1937; The World in which Jesus Lived, 1937; The Church Takes Root in India, 1938; Yarns on Fighters of India's Foes, 1938; Through Tragedy to Triumph: the World Church in the World Crisis, 1939; Supreme Encounter, 1940; We Fight for the Future, 1940; Pattern for Living, 1942; United We Stand, 1943; Unfolding Drama in South-East Asia, 1944; The Adventures of Paul, 1945; Booker T. Washington: Educator and Inter-racial Interpreter, 1948, etc.; many of his books in foreign translations. *Recreation:* walking. *Address:* Triangle Cottage, Old Boar's Hill, Oxford. *T.:* Oxford 85587. *Club:* Athenæum. [*Died* 29 *March* 1951.

MATHEWS, Dame Vera Laughton, D.B.E., *cr.* 1945 (C.B.E. 1942; M.B.E. 1919); Adviser on Women's Affairs to the Gas Council; Life President Association of Wrens; *d.* of late Sir J. K. Laughton, R.N.; *m.* 1924, G. D. Mathews (*d.* 1943); two *s.* one *d.* *Educ.:* St. Andrew's Convent, England and Belgium; King's College, London. Director Women's Royal Naval Service, 1939-46; Chairman Domestic Coal Consumers' Council, 1947-50; President National Smoke Abatement Society, 1949-1951; Member of S.E. Gas Board, 1949-59; Pres. St. Joan's International Social and Political Alliance; Chm. Status of Women Cttee.; Pres. Mermaid Swimming Club; Mem. Council Girl Guides Association. Officer Cross of Orange Nassau, 1946. *Publication:* Blue Tapestry: The Story of the W.R.N.S., 1948. *Recreations:* music, bridge. *Address:* 14A Ashley Gardens, S.W.1. *T.:* Victoria 0970. *Clubs:* Forum, Service Women's, Royal Burnham Yacht. [*Died* 25 *Sept.* 1959.

MATISSE, Henri; French painter; *b.* Cateau, Nord, 31 Dec. 1869. *Educ.:* École des Beaux Arts; atelier de Gustave Moreau. Spent two years in Morocco; worked also in Southern France at Collioure and Nice; grand nombre d'œuvres à Moscou Musée d'État art occidental;—grand panneaux la Danse et la Musique,—aussi qu' à la Fondation Barnes à Merion (Pennsylvania), grande décoration murale—œuvres au Musée de Luxembourg et dans différents Musées d'Europe, d'Amérique, et du Japon; Illustrateur des œuvres de Stéphane Mallarmé, de l'Ulysse de James Joyce; Pasiphaë, de Henry de Montherlant. *Address:* 132 Bd. Montparnasse, Paris; Le Régina, Cimiez, Nice, A.M., France. [*Died* 3 *Nov.* 1954.

MATTERS, Leonard Warburton; London representative The Hindu Newspaper, Madras, 2-3 Salisbury Court, E.C.4; President (1943) Overseas Empire Correspondents' Assoc.; Chairman, Indian and Eastern Newspaper Society (London); *b.* Adelaide, S. Australia, 26 June 1881; *m.* 1910, Emilie M. Domela; one *d.*; 1939, Romana Kryszek. *Educ.:* South Australian State Schools. Journalist, Australian newspapers; for some years Managing Editor, Buenos Aires Herald, Argentina; trooper in S. African War; travelled and worked as journalist in United States, Canada, Japan, West Indies, and South America; M.P. (Lab.) Kennington Division of Lambeth, 1929-31; Member Overseas Trade Development Council, 1929; a delegate sent by the India League to investigate conditions in India, 1932; short story writer; translator of Argentine novels. J.P., 1934-50. *Publications:* The House of the Ravens (translation); The Mystery of Jack the Ripper; Through the Kara Sea, 1932; India, 1942. *Recreations:* gardening and golf. *Address:* Fiddler's Brook, Much Hadham, Herts. *T.:* Much Hadham 51. *Clubs:* Press, Publicity. [*Died* 31 *Oct.* 1951.

MATTHAI, John, C.I.E. 1934; D.Sc., B.Litt.; *b.* Calicut, S. India, 10 Jan. 1886; *s.* of Thomas and Anna Matthai; *m.* 1921, Achamma John; two *s.* *Educ.:* Madras Christian College; London School of Economics; Balliol College, Oxford. B.A. (Madras), 1906, B.L. 1910; D.Sc. (Lond.), 1916; B.Litt. (Oxon.), 1918. Officer on special duty, Co-operative Department, Madras, 1918-20; Prof. of Economics, Presidency Coll., Madras, 1920-25; Professor of Indian Economics, Madras University, 1922-1925; Member Madras Legislative Council, 1922-25; Member, Indian Tariff Board, 1925-31, President, 1931-34; Director-General of Commercial Intelligence and Statistics, 1935-40; retired from Govt. service and joined Tata Sons, Ltd., 1940, appointed Director, 1944; Member Governor-General's Exec. Council for Finance, 1946; for Industry and Supply, 1946-47; Minister, The Dominion Cabinet, for Transport and Railways, 1947-48; Minister for Finance in the Dominion Cabinet, 1948-50; resigned from Govt. 1950, and rejoined Tata Sons Ltd. as Director; resigned 1955; Chm. Indian Taxation Enquiry Commission, 1953; Vice-Chancellor, Bombay Univ., 1955-57; Vice-Chancellor, Kerala University, 1958. Chairman, State Bank of India, 1955-56; resigned 1956. *Publications:* Village Government in British India; Agricultural Co-operation in India; Excise and Liquor Control. *Address:* Aranatukara, Trichur, Kerala State. [*Died* 2 *Nov.* 1959.

MATTHEWS, A(lfred) E(dward), O.B.E. 1951; Actor; *b.* Bridlington, 22 Nov. 1869; *s.* of William Matthews; *m.* 1st, May Blayney; twin *s.* one *d.*; 2nd, Pat Desmond. Played various parts and was asst. manager at Princess's and Vaudeville Theatres, 1887-88; toured, and went to S. Africa with Lionel Brough, 1889; toured, 1891-93; Australia, 1893-96 (Jack Chesney in Charley's Aunt; Douglas Cattermole in The Private Secretary, etc.); many successful West End appearances, 1896-1909; went to America, 1910 (Algernon Moncrieffe in The Importance of Being Earnest, etc.); same part, St. James's, 1911; same part in Paris; continued West End appearances, 1911-20; went again to America, 1921; succeeded Gerald Du Maurier as Captain Hugh Drummond, in Bull-Dog Drummond, Comedy Theatre, 1922; continued in West End parts, with visits to New York in between (Ernest Steele, in Spring Cleaning; Charles, in The Last of Mrs. Cheyney; James Fraser in The First Mrs. Fraser), etc.; also toured 1942, 1945, 1946; Charles, in But for The Grace of God, St. James's, 1946; Lord Lister in The Chiltern Hundreds, 1948; The Gay Invalid,

Garrick, 1951; The Manor of Northstead, 1954; A Month of Sundays, 1957. Managing Director of the British Actors Film Co., 1916-18. Films include: The Chiltern Hundreds; Castles in the Air; Penny Princess; Something Money Can't Buy; Trial Marriage; The Iron Duke; Who Goes There; Galloping Major; Laughter in Paradise; Colonel Blimp; Man in Grey; Just William; Quiet Week-End; Mr. Drakes' Duck; Million Pound Note; The Weak and the Wicked; O'Leary Nights; Jumping for Joy. *Publication:* autobiography, 1952. *Address:* Prospect Cottage, Bushey Heath, Herts. *T.:* Bushey Heath 1265. *Clubs:* Garrick, Green Room. [*Died* 25 *July* 1960.

MATTHEWS, Sir (Alfred) Herbert (Henry), Kt., *cr.* 1916; *b.* 25 July 1870; *s.* of late Alfred Thomas Matthews; *m.* 1st, 1900, Ada Buckler (*d.* 1948), *d.* of Wm. Glover Mace of Tenterden, Kent; no *c.*; 2nd, Alma Gordon, *widow* of Major Clisdal, M.C. *Educ.:* Coll. House, Edmonton. Engaged in various positions in agriculture since 1890; Secretary, Central Chamber of Agriculture, 1901-27; Private Secretary to Parliamentary Secretary Ministry of Food, 1917-18; has travelled through all the Dominions studying Agriculture and Forestry; Pres. Inst. of Industrial Transport, 1925-53. *Publication:* Fifty Years of Agricultural Politics, 1915. *Address:* 12 Rochester Mansions, Leyds St., Johannesburg, S. Africa. *Club:* Farmers'. [*Died* 19 *July* 1958.

MATTHEWS, David, J.P.; *b.* Morriston, Swansea, 1868; *m.* 1892. Tinplate merchant, Swansea; elected Swansea Council, 1896; twice Mayor of Swansea; M.P. (Co.L.) East Swansea, 1919-22. *Address:* Windsor Lodge, Swansea. *T.:* 4220. [*Died* 26 *Feb.* 1960.

MATTHEWS, Sir Herbert; *see* Matthews, Sir A. H. H.

MATTHEWS, Hon. Robert Charles, P.C. Canada 1933; *b.* 14 June 1871; *s.* of George Matthews and Ann Smithson; *m.* 1895, Margaret Craig Spier. *Educ.:* McMaster University, Toronto; Harvard University. With A. E. Ames and Co. Brokers, Toronto; formed firm of R. C. Matthews and Company dealers in Government Bonds and Debentures, 1909; retired from business, 1923; elected House of Commons at General Election for Toronto East Centre, 1926; re-elected, 1930; Chairman Select Standing Committee on Banking and Commerce of House of Commons, 1931-33; Minister of National Revenue, Canada, 1933-35; sponsored and accompanied his Canadian cricket team to England, 1936; President, Canadian Chamber of Commerce, 1936-37; Pres., Federation for Community Service of Toronto, 1938-39; Pres. Toronto Humane Society, 1938-48; Member Governing Body Trinity College School. *Recreations:* cricket, golf, curling. *Address:* 134 Lyndhurst Avenue, Toronto, Canada. *Clubs:* Arts and Letters, Toronto, York, Albany, Toronto Cricket, Toronto Hunt, Toronto Golf (Toronto). [*Died* 20 *Sept.* 1952.

MATTHEWS, Sir Ronald (Wilfred), Kt., 1934; J.P., D.L.; M.Inst.T.; Knight, Order of St. John; Deputy Chairman, Independent Television Authority, since 1955; *b.* 25 June 1885; *s.* of Wilfred Arthur Matthews, 78 Eccleston Sq., S.W.1, and Julia Maud, *d.* of Henry Silvester, Beverley, Yorks; *m.* 1912, Vera, *d.* of W. B. E. Shufeldt, of Oconomowoc, Wisconsin, U.S.A.; (one *s.* killed in action 1942) three *d.* *Educ.:* Eton. Master Cutler, 1922-23: President, Sheffield Chamber of Commerce, 1929-31; President, Association of British Chambers of Commerce, 1940-42; Chairman: London and North Eastern Railway, 1938-48; General Refractories Ltd.; Phillips Furnishing Stores Ltd.; Deputy Chm. Legal & General Assurance Society Ltd.; Director: Thos. Cook & Son Ltd.; Gresham Life Assur. Soc. Ltd.; Gresham Fire & Accident Insur. Soc. Ltd.; Chm. and Managing Dir., Turton Bros. and Matthews Ltd.; served European War, King's Own Yorks Light Inf. (Capt.). D.L. West Riding of Yorks. *Recreation:* golf. *Address:* Albion Place, Doncaster. *T.:* Doncaster 61563; 146 Dorset House, N.W.1. *T.:* Welbeck 6844. *Clubs:* Junior Carlton, Transportation; Yorkshire (York). [*Died* 1 *July* 1959.

MATTHEWS, Sir Trevor Jocelyn, Kt., *cr.* 1947; Director of Grindlay's Bank Ltd.; *b.* 25 Nov. 1882; *s.* of James Henry Matthews; *m.* 1911, Christabel Stogdon; four *d.* *Educ.:* Harrow; Cambridge. Associated with Grindlay's Bank Ltd. since 1904. *Address:* 53 Albert Court, S.W.7. *Clubs:* Garrick, Oriental, M.C.C. [*Died* 6 *Nov.* 1954.

MATTHEWS, William Kleesmann, D.Lit., Ph.D., M.A., B.Com.; Professor of Russian Language and Literature in the University of London since 1948; Head of Department of Language and Literature at School of Slavonic and East European Studies and Editor of The Slavonic and East European Review since 1950; Corresponding Member of Finno-Ugrian Soc., Helsinki; Hon. Member of Slavistic Soc., Ljubljana; *b.* Narva, Viru, prov. of Estonia, Russia, 22 Feb. 1901; *e. s.* of Joseph Matthews, textile engineer, Hollinwood, Lancs. and Annie Marie Kleesmann, Nadalama, Viru; *m.* 1946, Naomi, *d.* of Ernest Charles, Kurku and Central Indian Hill Mission, Berar, India; no *c.* *Educ.:* Narva Gymnasium (Russian); Blackpool Grammar School; Univ. of Manchester; Univ. of London (King's Coll.); Univ. of Latvia. Lector in English Studies at State Institute of English, Riga, Latvia, 1926-32; Private Docent (Lecturer) in Eng. Lit., Univ. of Latvia, 1929-37; Lector in Eng. Lang., Univ. of Latvia and Kr. Barons People's College, 1934-37; Docent (Reader) in Eng. Philology, Univ. of Latvia, 1937-40, and Lector in Eng. Lit., People's Univ., Riga, 1939-40. Interpreter to Australian Mil. Forces censorship and U.S. Army censorship in Brisbane, Qld., 1940-45. Lecturer in German, Institute of Mod. Langs., University of Queensland, 1942-1944; Lecturer in Russian at School of Slavonic and East European Studies, Univ. of London, 1946-48. Order of the Three Stars (Latvia), 1939. *Publications:* (with K. Brants) A Latvian-English Dictionary, 1930; The Pronunciation of Literary English (in Latvian), 1936; Modern English Literature (in Latvian), 1936; The Tricolour Sun, 1936; The Influence of Byron on Russian Poetry, 1940; (with A. Eglitis), An Anthology of English Verse (in Latvian), 1940; Red Train (narrative poem trans. from Latvian), 1951; Earthbound (verse trans. from Estonian), 1951; Taras Shevchenko: the Man and the Symbol, 1951; Languages of the U.S.S.R., 1951; Pussy's Water Mill (story trans. from Latvian), 1952; Anthology of Modern Estonian Poetry, 1953; The Structure and Development of Russian, 1953; Flames on the Wind (verse trans. from Estonian), 1953; (with A. Slodnjak) Selection of Poems by France Prešeren (trans. from Slovene, 1954); Child of Man (verse trans. from Estonian), 1955; (with A. Slodnjak) The Parnassus of a Small Nation (versions of Slovene poetry); A Century of Latvian Poetry, 1957; Russian Historical Grammar, 1958; Studies in East European Linguistics, 1958. Articles and papers in several langs. on literary, linguistic and phonetic subjects, book reviews, poems (original and trans.) in European, British, Australian and American periodicals. Items in Latvian Encyclopædia (Riga); Cassell's Encyclopædia of Literature; Encyclopædia Britannica; Dictionary of Poetics and Poetry (New York). *Recreation:* travel. *Address:* School of Slavonic and East European Studies, University of London, Malet Street, W.C.1. *T.:* Museum 9782. [*Died* 3 *May* 1958.

MATTHIESSEN, Francis Otto; writer and teacher; Professor of History and Literature, Harvard University, since 1942; *b.* Pasadena, California, 19 Feb. 1902; *s.* of Frederic William Matthiessen and Lucy Orne Pratt; unmarried. *Educ.:* Hackley School, Tarrytown, New York; Yale University; New College, Oxford; Harvard University. B.A. (Yale), 1923; Rhodes Scholar, New Coll., Oxford, 1923-25 (B.Litt.); M.A. (Harvard), 1926, Ph.D. 1927; D.Litt. (Princeton), 1947; Cadet for Pilot, R.A.F., Toronto, Sept.-Dec. 1918; Instructor in English, Yale Univ., 1927-29; Instructor and Tutor in History and Literature, Harvard University, 1929-30, Asst. Prof. 1930-34, Associate Prof. 1934-42; Alexander Lecturer, Univ. of Toronto, fall 1944; Lecturer at Salzburg Seminär of American Studies, 1947; Visiting Lecturer, Charles Univ., Prague, fall 1947; Senior Fellow, Kenyon School of English, 1947-; member of Psi Upsilon, Skull and Bones, Phi Beta Kappa, Elizabethan Club, Yale, Signet Society, Teachers Union (A.F. of L.), Harvard, Massachusetts Civil Liberties Union; Vice-Chm. Progressive Party, Mass. *Publications:* Sarah Orne Jewett: A Critical Biography, 1929; Translation: An Elizabethan Art, 1931; The Achievement of T. S. Eliot, 1935 (enlarged ed. 1947); American Renaissance: Art and Expression in the Age of Emerson and Whitman, 1941; Henry James: The Major Phase, 1944; Russell Cheney: A Record of his Work, 1946; The James Family, 1947; From the Heart of Europe, 1948; editor, Selected Poems of Herman Melville, 1944; Stories of Writers and Artists by Henry James, 1944; The American Novels and Stories of Henry James, 1947; Editor (with Kenneth B. Murdock), The Notebooks of Henry James, 1947. *Address:* 87 Pinckney Street, Boston, Massachusetts, U.S.A.: Kittery, Maine, U.S.A. [*Died* 1 *April* 1950.

[*But death not notified in time for inclusion in Who Was Who* 1941–1950, *first edn.*

MAUDE, Cyril; Actor Manager; twice President R.A.D.A.; *b.* London, 24 April 1862; *e. s.* of Captain Charles Henry and the Hon. Mrs. Maude; *m.* 1st, 1888, Winifred Emery (*d.* 1924); one *s.* two *d.*; 2nd, 1927, Beatrice Mary, *d.* of late Rev. John Ellis, Hungorton Vicarage, Leicester, and *widow* of P. H. Trew. *Educ.:* Charterhouse. Began on stage in America, 1883; co-manager of Haymarket, 1896-1905; afterwards sole manager of The Playhouse (built by him), until Sept. 1915; played alternately in England and America, play Strange Cousins (with Peter Garland), produced 1934. Has appeared in films from 1913, notably: Peer Gynt, The Antique Dealer, Grumpy, These Charming People, Counsel's Opinion, Orders is Orders, Girls Will Be Boys, Heat Wave. *Publications:* The Haymarket Theatre, 1903; The Actor in Room 931; Behind the Scenes with Cyril Maude, 1927. *Recreations:* fishing, shooting, and riding. *Address:* Dundrum, Lower Woodfield Road, Torquay. *T.:* Torquay 3300. *Club:* Garrick. [*Died* 20 *Feb.* 1951.

MAUGHAM, 1st Viscount, *cr.* 1939, of Hartfield; Baron (Life Peer) *cr.* 1935; **Frederic Herbert Maugham,** P.C. 1934; Kt., *cr.* 1928; K.C. 1913; an Hon. Fellow of Trinity Hall; *b.* 1866; *s.* of Robert Ormond Maugham; *m.* 1896, Helen Mary (*d.* 1950), *d.* of Rt. Hon. Sir Robert Romer, G.C.B.; one *s.* three *d.* *Educ.:* Dover College; Trinity Hall, Cambridge (Scholar). Honours Math. Tripos, 1888; President Union Debating Society; rowed 7 in Cambridge University Eights, 1888, 1889; winner of various cups at Henley; Barr. Lincoln's Inn, 1890; Bencher, 1915; Judge of High Court of Justice, Chancery Division, 1928-34; a Lord Justice of Appeal, 1934-35; a Lord of Appeal in Ordinary 1935-38 and 1939-41; Lord Chancellor of Great Britain, 1938-39. *Publications:* The Case of Jean Calas; The Tichborne Case, 1936; At the End of the Day; Lies as Allies or Hitler at War (in a number of languages); The Truth about the Munich Crisis; U.N.O. and War Crimes. *Recreations:* pictures, golfing. *Heir:* *s.* Robin (Hon.), Robert Cecil Romer Maugham. *Address:* 73 Cadogan Square, S.W.1. *T.:* Sloane 1987. *Clubs:* Savile, Athenæum. [*Died* 23 *March* 1958.

MAUGHAM, Reginald Charles Fulke, C.B.E. 1927; F.R.G.S.; F.Z.S.; *b.* 19 Aug. 1866; *m.* 1st, 1894, Alice Anne Jane, *d.* of late Dr. T. Smith-Hewitt, Winkfield Lodge, Windsor (marriage dissolved 1906); 2nd, 1907, Hilda Wollaston, *y. d.* of late John Greene, of The Panels, Bury St. Edmunds, Suffolk. *Educ.:* privately. Served in Inniskilling Dragoons; Secretary to the Nyasaland Administration, 1894; British Vice-Consul at Blantyre, 1896; at Chinde, 1897; at Quilimane, 1898; Consul at Beira, 1902; at Lourenço Marques, 1908; and at Antofagasta (Chile), 1912; Consul-General, Liberia, 1913-20; Consul-General, Dakar, Sénégal, 1920-28; present at storming and capture of Chikala, 1894; took part in the Southern Angoni Expedition, 1896 (British Central African medal and clasp 1894-98, and Queen's South African war medal); Gold Medallist, Société d'Histoire Internationale, Paris. *Publications:* Portuguese East Africa, 1906; A Handbook of the Chi-Makua Language, 1909; Zambezia, 1910; Wild Game in Zambezia, 1913; The Republic of Liberia, 1920; Africa as I have Known It, 1929; Nyasaland in the Nineties, 1935; The Island of Jersey To-day, 1939; Les Bêtes Sauvages de la Zambézie, 1939; Jersey under the Jack Boot, 1946. *Recreations:* gardening, literature. *Address:* Spring Bank, Vallée des Vaux, Jersey, C.I. *T.:* Central 815. *Club:* St. James'. [*Died* 10 *Dec.* 1956.

MAUGHAN, Sir David, Kt., *cr.* 1951; Q.C. 1919; Barrister-at-law; *b.* Sydney, New South Wales, 5 Feb. 1873; *s.* of John Maughan, Chief Cashier of Bank of New South Wales; *m.* 1909, Jean Alice, *e. d.* of Rt. Hon. Sir Edmund Barton; one *s.* one *d.* (and one *d.* decd.). *Educ.:* The King's School, Parramatta (Broughton and Forrest Exhibition); Balliol College, Oxford. First Class Honours, School of Jurisprudence, 1895, and B.C.L. 1896; B.A. Oxford, 1895; M.A., B.C.L., 1909. Law Tutor, Balliol College, 1896; called to Bar, Lincoln's Inn, 1896; admitted to New South Wales Bar, 1896; Acting Justice of Supreme Court of New South Wales, 1924, 1936, and and 1937; Member of Queensland Bar; member and Q.C. Tasmanian Bar; *ad eundem* degrees at Sydney University B.A., M.A., LL.B.; sent to England twice to appear before the Judicial Committee of the Privy Council in cases relating to the abolition and reform of the Legislative Council of New South Wales; also appeared in many other cases before the Privy Council; Vice-President of the Oxford Society; Past-President Law Council of Australia; Vice-Chairman of Second Unofficial British Commonwealth Relations Conference, 1938; Director of the Royal Prince Alfred Hospital, Sydney; President of the Big Brother Movement; Pres. Athletic Assoc. of the Great Public Schools of New South Wales; Past President of The King's School Old Boys Union; Vice-President of N.S.W. Rugby Union; Vice-President N.S.W. Rowing Association; Hon. Counsel to the N.S.W. Cricket Association. *Publications:* The Statute of Westminster, 1938; Constitutional Revision in Australia, 1944. *Recreations:* mountaineering, walking. *Address:* 4 Fullerton Street, Woollahra, Sydney, N.S.W. *Clubs:* Australian, University, Royal Sydney Golf (Sydney). [*Died* 3 *Nov.* 1955.

MAULE, Col. Henry Noel St. John, C.M.G. 1918; late R.A.; *b.* 1873; *e. s.* of late Montagu St. John Maule; *m.* 1904,

Bessie Kate, *d.* of G. Martyn; one *d.* Served South African War, 1900-2 (Queen's medal four clasps, King's medal two clasps); European War (Mesopotamia), 1914-18 (C.M.G., despatches); retd. pay, 1921. *Address:* Rocklands, Weston Road, Bath. *T.:* Bath 7460. *Club:* Bath and County (Bath). [*Died* 3 *Sept.* 1953.

MAUND, Rear-Admiral Loben Edward Harold, C.B.E. 1941; retd.; Director of A. Kershaw & Sons, Ltd.; *b.* 26 Sept. 1892; *m.* 1932, Constance Alice Macartney Iredell. *Educ.:* R.N. Colleges, Osborne and Dartmouth; Gold Medal and Dirk. Served European War, 1914-18, Dover Patrol, Grand Fleet and Atlantic convoys. Commandant, Combined Operations Development Centre, 1938; Naval Chief of Staff, Narvik operations, 1940; in command H.M.S. Ark Royal, 1941, operation against Bismarck, and three convoys to Malta; Director of Combined Operations, Middle East and India, 1942-43; Rear-Admiral Landing Ships and Craft, 1944-45. *Publication:* Assault from the Sea, 1948. *Recreation:* farming. *Address:* Springs Farm, Fittleworth, Sussex. *T.:* Fittleworth 122; *Club:* United Service. [*Died* 18 *June* 1957.

MAUNG ME, C.I.E. 1925; I.S.O. 1918; received title of Kyet-Thaye-Zaung Shwe-Salwe-ya-Min, 1910; *b.* 2 May 1871; *s.* of U. Kaing; *m.* 1895, Daw Byaing, *d.* of U. Kin; three *s.* four *d.* *Educ.:* Govt. College, Rangoon. Subordinate Civil Service of Burma, 1894; Translation Depart., 1895-1900; Provincial Civ. Serv., 1908; Stamp Officer, Rangoon, 1919; Dep. Comr., Prome, 1922-27; special duty in Tharrawaddy District, Jan.-special duty in Tharrawaddy Dist., 1928; retd. as Dep. Comr.; life member Burma Research Soc. *Address:* Moulmein, Burma. [*Died* 6 *Feb.* 1952.

MAURICE, Maj.-Gen. Sir Frederick (Barton), K.C.M.G., *cr.* 1918; C.B. 1915; *b.* 19 Jan. 1871; *e. s.* of late General Sir F. Maurice, K.C.B.; *m.* 1899, Helen Margaret (*d.* 1942), *d.* of late Prof. Howard Marsh, Master of Downing College, Cambridge; one *s.* four *d.* Entered Army, 1892; Captain, 1899; Bt. Major, 1900; Major, 1911; Lt.-Col. 1913; Bt. Col. 1915; Maj.-Gen. 1916; General Staff Officer, 2nd grade, 1908; served Tirah, 1897-8 (medal, 2 clasps); S. African War, 1899-1900 (despatches, Bt. Major; Queen's medal 5 clasps); European War, 1914-18 (despatches 7 times, C.B., K.C.M.G.); Director of Military Operations, Imperial General Staff, 1915-18; Commander Legion of Honour; Croix de Guerre; Order of the Crown of Belgium, 2nd class; 1st Class Order of St. Stanislas of Russia; Principal, Working Men's College, St. Pancras, 1922-33; Principal of Queen Mary College (University of London), 1933-44; Hon. LL.D. Cambridge, 1926; Professor of Military Studies, London Univ., 1927; Chairman Adult Education Committee, Board of Education, 1928; D.Lit. London, 1930; Member of Senate, University of London, 1930; Hon. Treasurer British Legion, 1930; President, British Legion, 1932-47; Colonel, The Sherwood Foresters, 1935-1941; Hon. Fellow, King's Coll., Cambridge, 1944; Fellow Queen Mary College, 1946. *Publications:* Russo-Turkish War, 1877-78; Sir Frederick Maurice: a Record; Forty Days in 1914; The Last Four Months; Lord Wolseley (with Sir George Arthur), 1924; Robert E. Lee, the Soldier, 1925; Governments and War, 1926; An Aide-de-Camp of Lee, 1927; The Life of General Lord Rawlinson of Trent, 1928; British Strategy, 1929; The 16th Foot, 1931; History of the Scots Guards, 1934; Life of Lord Haldane, vol. I, 1937, vol. II, 1938; The Armistices of 1918-43; The Adventures of Edward Wogan, 1945; contributor to Cambridge Modern History. *Address:* 62 Grange Rd., Cambridge. *Club:* Athenæum. [*Died* 19 *May* 1951.

MAURRAS, Charles; *b.* Martigues (Bouches-du-Rhône), 20 avril 1868; homme nouveau d'une famille de petits fonctionnaires civils, et marins; célibataire. *Educ.:* Collège Catholique d'Aix en Provence. Écrivain et politique français; beaucoup de procés; de nombreux condamnations, dont il s'est moqué; 250 jours de prison qu'il a faits, en se moquant aussi; une couronne civique décernée par le Front national pour avoir empêché la guerre avec l'Italie en 1935; membre de l'Académie Française; co-directeur avec Léon Daudet du journal nationalist et royalist l'Action Française. Condamné à l'imprisonnement solitaire pour la vie, 1945; libéré à cause de mauvaise santé, 1952. *Publications:* Le Chemin de Paradis; Anthinéa; Les Amants de Venise; L'Avenir de l'intelligence; L'Enquête sur la monarchie; Kiel et Tanger; La Politique religieuse; L'Étang de Berre; Quand les Français ne s'aimaient pas; La Musique intérieure (poèms); Jeanne d'arc; Louis XIV; Napoléon; les Vergers sur la mer; la Balance intérieure (poèmes), etc. *Recreations:* séjours dans sa maison du Chemin de Paradis à Martigues pour la saison des Bains de mer. [*Died* 16 *Nov.* 1952.

MAVOR, O. H.; *see* Bridie, James.

MAWHINNY, Col. Robert John Watt, C.B. 1916; L.R.C.S.I. and R.C.P.I., L.M., D.P.H.; A.M.S.; *b.* Woodlawn House, Mount Nugent, Co. Cavan; *s.* of late Thomas Mawhinny, M.D., and Susan, *d.* of late Colonel Hugh McCalmont; *m.* Kathleen Sarah Rosa (*d.* 1950), *e. d.* of late Alexander Knox McEntire, B.L., Official Assignee, Ireland, Merrion Square, Dublin; one *d.* *Educ.:* Private School, Dublin; Carmichael School of Medicine, Dublin (Gold Medallist Operative Surgery). Joined R.A.M.C. 1890; served Isazai Expedition, 1892; Chitral Expedition, 1895; Punjab Frontier, 1897-98 (medal and clasp); South African War, 1899-1901 (despatches, Queen's medal 6 clasps); European War, 1914-1918; Punjab Frontier, 1915 (despatches, C.B.); A.D.M.S., L. of C. Indian Expeditionary Force "D," Mesopotamia, 1915-16; A.D.M.S., Mari Field Force B, 1918 (despatches) A.D.M.S., Abbottabad, Sialkot, and Kakul Brigades, 1918; A.D.M.S., 2nd (Rawal Pindi) Division, 1919 (1914-15 Allied and Victory medals); Colonel, 1921, antedated to 1918; AD.M.S., Bombay District, 1921; officiating D.D.M.S., Southern Command, India, 1922; A.D.M.S., Lahore District, 1922; retired pay, 1924; Retired Pay, Army Medical appointment, 1926-32; Civil Surgeon, Army Medical appointment, 1939-44. *Recreations:* hunting, shooting, dry-fly fishing, swimming, won Ormonde Cup for Ireland, 1888. *Address:* c/o Glyn, Mills & Co., Kirkland House, Whitehall, S.W.1. [*Died* 16 *July* 1953.

MAWSON, Sir Douglas, Kt., *cr.* 1914; O.B.E., F.R.S. 1923, D.Sc., B.E.; Emeritus Professor in Geology in the University, Adelaide; *b.* Bradford, Yorkshire, 5 May 1882; *s.* of R. E. Mawson, Otley, Yorkshire, and M. A., *d.* of T. Moore, Douglas, Isle of Man; *m.* 1914, Paquita, *d.* of late Guillaume D. Delprat, C.B.E., Melbourne, two *d.* *Educ.:* Sydney Univ. graduated Bachelor of Mining Engineering, 1901; Demonstrator Chemistry, Sydney University, 1902; Geological Exploration, New Hebrides Islands, 1903; Bachelor of Science, 1904; Lecturer Adelaide University, 1905; appointed to Scientific Staff, Sir Ernest Shackleton's Antarctic Expedition, 1907; ascent of Mt. Erebus and Magnetic Pole journey, 1908; graduated Doctor of Science for researches in Broken Hill mining area, 1909; leader of Australasian Antarctic Expedition, 1911-14; of British, Australian, and N.Z. Antarctic Expedition, 1929-1931; President of the Australian and New Zealand Association for the Advancement of Science 1932-37; Member Commonwealth Govt's. Antarctic Advisory Cttee., 1946-; Capt. E.S.O., 1916-17; temp. Hon. Major (Munitions), 1918-19. Member of many learned societies. Medals: R.G.S. Antarctic Medal, 1909; awarded Founder's

Medal R.G.S., 1915; King's Polar Medal (3 bars); Gold medals American, Chicago, and Paris Geog. Societies; Bigsby Medal, Geolog. Soc., London, 1919; Nachtigal Gold Medal of Gesellschaft für Erdkunde, Berlin, 1928; Von Mueller Memorial Medal, 1930; Sir Joseph Verco Medal, South Australian Royal Society, 1931; Founder's Medal, Royal Geographical Society, Australia (Queensland), 1931, etc.; O.B.E. and Order of SS. Maurice and Lazarus of Italy, 1920; Commander of Order of Crown of Italy, 1923. *Publications:* The Home of the Blizzard; Scientific Papers in Trans. of learned Societies; Ed. of and contrib. to, Scientific Reports of Australasian Antarctic Expedition (22 vols.) and Ed. of Reports of Banzar Expedition. *Address:* The University, Adelaide, Australia. *Clubs:* Adelaide (Adelaide); (hon. life member) Royal Thames Yacht; (hon. life member) Appalachian (Boston); (hon. life member) Explorers (New York). [*Died* 14 *Oct.* 1958.

MAXSE, General Sir Ivor, K.C.B., *cr.* 1917 (C.B. 1900); C.V.O. 1907; D.S.O. 1898; F.R.G.S. (elected for original exploration on the River Sobat, Upper Nile, Soudan), 1899; *b.* 22 Dec. 1862; *e. s.* of late Adm. Maxse; *m.* 1899, Hon. Mary Caroline Wyndham (*d.* 1944), *e. d.* of 2nd Baron Leconfield; two *s.* one *d.* *Educ.:* Rugby; Sandhurst. Joined 7th Fusiliers, 1882; Capt. Coldstream Guards, 1891; Major, 1897; Bt. Lt.-Col. 1900; Bt. Col. 1905; Brig.-Gen. 1910; Maj.-Gen. 1914; Lt.-Gen. 1919; Gen. 1923; served throughout Soudan campaigns, 1897-99, in Egyptian army (medal, six clasps, and D.S.O.); Boer War, 1899, as staff officer to mounted infantry and as Commander of Transvaal Constabulary after capture of Pretoria, 1900 (medal three clasps, C.B.); proceeded to France in command of 1st Guards Brigade, 12 Aug. 1914, and present at Retreat from Mons, and the Battles of the Marne and the Aisne; promoted Major-General to command 18th Division, Oct. 1914; on active service in France with this Division, 1915-17; Battles of the Somme and the Ancre; promoted to command 18th Army Corps, Jan. 1917, and engaged with it throughout the fighting in Flanders, July-Nov. 1917, and at St. Quentin, Jan. 1918-June 1918; Inspector-General of Training to the British Armies in France, June 1918-March 1919; employed on special duty at War Office, 1901; com. 2nd Batt. Coldstream Guards, 1903-7; Coldstream Regiment of Foot Guards, 1907-10; 1st Guards Brigade, 1910-14; 18th Division, 1914-17; 18th Army Corps, 1917-1918; 9th Army Corps on the Rhine (temporarily); G.O.C.-in-Chief, Northern Command, England, June 1919-23; fruit-grower, 1923-; Colonel of the Middlesex Regt., 1921-32; D.L. Sussex, 1932; Grand Cross of Crown of Belgium, Grand Cross of Crown of Rumania, Commandeur de la Légion d'Honneur, Military Medal with two bars (France), Military Medal (Belgium), despatches twelve times. *Publication:* Seymour Vandeleur, 1906. *Address:* Little Bognor, Fittleworth, Sussex. *T.:* Petworth 2120. *Club:* Guards. [*Died* 28 *Jan.* 1958.

MAXWELL, His Honour Alexander Hyslop; *b.* Liverpool, 1864; *s.* of late Maxwell Hyslop Maxwell of the Grove, Dumfries, and Liverpool; *m.* 1892, Elisa Amelia (*d.* 1955), *d.* of late Henry Holbrook Hammond, Liverpool; one *s.* one *d.* *Educ.:* Uppingham. Called to Bar, Middle Temple, 1889; joined Northern Circuit, and practised in Liverpool; Judge of County Courts Circuit No. 55 (Bournemouth), 1920-37. *Address:* 24 Oakwood Court, Kensington, W.14. *Club:* Union. [*Died* 7 *March* 1957.

MAXWELL, Col. Geoffrey Archibald Prentice, C.M.G. 1934; D.S.O. 1917; M.V.O. 1915; M.C.; late R.E.; late Chm. Railway Commission (Rhodesia) Bulawayo; *b.* 29 Oct. 1885; *y. s.* of late Capt. W. F. Maxwell, Royal Navy; *m.* 1918, Agnes Duncan, *o. d.* of late S. P. Ruthven, Parktown, Johannesburg. *Educ.:* St. Andrew's School, Tenby; Cheltenham College. Commission, 1904; Baro Kano Railway construction, Nigeria, 1908-11; East African Survey, 1912-14; European War, 1914-18 (Bt.-Major, Officer of the Order of Leopold with palm, Belgian Croix de Guerre, Officer of the Légion d'Honneur, Croix de Guerre with palm, despatches six times); Assistant Director-General of Transportation, Deputy Chairman, Communications Section, Supreme Economic Council, 1919-20; General Manager, Tanganyika Railways, East Africa, 1920-35; Chairman Rhodesian Railway Commission, 1939-40; War Service, 1940-42 (despatches twice). *Address:* Tinwald, Nanyuki, Kenya Colony. *Club:* Royal Empire Society. [*Died* 25 *April* 1953.

MAXWELL, Sir George; *see* Maxwell, Sir W. G.

MAXWELL, Wing-Comdr. Gerald Constable, M.C., D.F.C., A.F.C., A.E.M., Knight of Malta; D.L.; Member Royal Company of Archers (Queen's Body Guard for Scotland); Papal Chamberlain; *b.* 8 Sept. 1895; *s.* of late Hon. Bernard Constable Maxwell (*s.* of 15th Baron Herries) and late Hon. Alice Fraser, *d.* of 13th Baron Lovat; *m.* 1920, Carolyn, *d.* of George A. Carden, Dallas, Texas; one *s.* four *d.* (and one *s.* killed R.A.F. 1950). *Educ.:* Downside College. Joined Lovat Scouts Yeomanry, Aug. 1914; Royal Flying Corps, 1916; served in Gallipoli, Egypt, and France; brought down 30 German aeroplanes (M.C., D.F.C., A.F.C.); Major Royal Flying Corps; Permanent Commission as Sqdn. Ldr. R.A.F., Apr. 1918, resigned, 1922; rejoined R.A.F. at outbreak of War, 1939, as Wing Comdr. (despatches, A.E.M.); Wing Comdr. Tactics, Fighter Command, 1940; comd. Night Fighter Station, Ford, Sussex, 1941-45. Director several Public Companies. Prime Warden Fishmongers' Co., 1956-57; Third Warden, 1958. D.L. Southampton, 1957. *Address:* Old Alresford House, Alresford, Hants. *T.:* Alresford 86. *Clubs:* Turf, White's. [*Died* 18 *Dec.* 1959.

MAXWELL, James, C.B.E. 1954; M.Inst.T.; F.R.S.A.; General Manager, Thos. Cook & Son, Ltd., since 1947; Chairman: Association of British Travel Agents; England's & Perrott's Ltd.; Hernu, Peron & Stockwell Ltd.; Director: British Travel & Holidays Association; Dean & Dawson Ltd.; British Holiday Estates Ltd.; International Motorcoach Tours Ltd.; Thos. Cook & Son, A.B.; Thos. Cook & Son (Australasia) Pty. Ltd.; Thos. Cook & Son, Inc.; Thos, Cook & Son (South Africa) Ltd.; Thos. Cook & Son, S.A.; *b.* 1 Feb. 1905; *s.* of late James Black Maxwell; *m.* 1939, Cecilia Anne Wright: two *s.* *Educ.:* Shawlands Academy and Allan Glen's, Glasgow. Assistant to Managing Director, Prisoners of War Dept., British Red Cross, 1941-42. Chairman (1948-1953) and Founder Member, London Cttee., Scottish Council (Development and Industry). Chairman Association of British Travel Agents, from foundation, 1950-. Chevalier de la Légion d'Honneur (France), 1953; Officier de l'Ordre de Léopold (Belgium), 1956. *Recreation:* travel. *Address:* (business) 10 Mayfair Place, W.1. *T.:* Grosvenor 4000; 39 Fairacres, Roehampton Lane, S.W.15. *Clubs:* Caledonian, Royal Automobile, Roehampton. [*Died* 28 *Nov.* 1956.

MAXWELL, James Laidlaw, C.B.E. 1938; M.D., B.S. Lond. Univ.; Medical Supt., Kwang-Chi leper home and village, Hangchow; Prof. of Medicine, Chekiang Provincial Medical College, Hang-chow; Major late R.A.M.C.; late Director Institute of Hospital Technology, Union Hospital, Hankow, China; late General Secretary International Red Cross Committee for Central China; *b.* 9 June 1873; *s.* of James L. Maxwell, M.A., M.D., late of Formosa; *m.* 1901, Millicent Bertha Saunders; three *d.* *Educ.:* University College School, London; St. Bartholomew's

Hospital, London. Medical Superintendent, Tainan Mission Hospital, Tainan, Formosa, 1901-23; i/c King's Section, Graylingwell War Hospital, Chichester, Sussex, 1915-19; Secretary, China Medical Association, 1923-29; Editor, China Medical Journal, 1925-29; Head of Department of Field Research and Librarian, Henry Lester Institute of Medical Research, Shanghai, China, 1929-36; Associate Editor International Journal of Leprosy, 1932-48. *Publications:* The Diseases of China, including Formosa and Korea, 2nd Edition, 1929; Leprosy, A Practical Text Book for use in China, 1937. *Address:* The Barns, Clophill, Bedford. [*Died* 10 *Aug.* 1951.

MAXWELL, Sir John Maxwell Stirling-, 10th Bt., *cr.* 1682; K.T. 1929; LL.D. Glasgow, Aberdeen, and Edinburgh; Hon. R.S.A.; Hon. R.I.B.A.; Hon. R.W.S.; Hon. R.S.W.; D.L.; *b.* 6 June 1866; *e. s.* of 9th Bt. and Anna, 2nd *d.* of 10th Earl of Leven and Melville; *S.* father, 1878; *m.* 1901, Ann Christian (*d.* 1937), *d.* of Rt. Hon. Sir Herbert Maxwell, 7th Bt.; one *d.* *Educ.:* Eton; Trinity College, Cambridge (B.A.). M.P. (C.) College Division of Glasgow, 1895-1906; Chairman of Forestry Commission, 1929-32; late Chairman of Royal Fine Art Commission for Scotland; Trustee of Scots National Galleries; Chairman of Ancient Monuments Board (Scotland); lately Lieut. of King's Body Guard for Scotland. Owns about 10,800 acres. *Publication:* Shrines and Homes of Scotland, 1937. *Heir: g.s.*, John Ronald Maxwell Macdonald, *b.* 22 May 1936, eventual heir under terms of special remainder. *Address:* Pollok House, Glasgow, S.3, Scotland. *Clubs:* Carlton, Travellers'. [*Died* 30 *May* 1956 (*Btcy. Dormant*).

MAXWELL, Brig.-Gen. Laurence Lockhart, C.M.G. 1917; Indian Army, retired; *b.* 23 Oct. 1868; entered Lancs. Fus. 1889; Capt. Indian Army, 1900; Major, 1907; Lt.-Col., 1915; Col., 1920. Served Waziristan, 1894-5 (medal with clasp); Tirah, 1897-8 (medal, two clasps); S. Africa, 1900 (severely wounded, despatches, Bt. Major, Queen's medal three clasps); European War, 1914-18 (C.M.G., Bt.-Col.); retired, 1920. *Address:* Orchard Close, Theale, Reading. [*Died* 29 *April* 1954.

MAXWELL, William, J.P., F.R.S.E., LL.D.; Director, R. & R. Clark, Ltd., Printers, Edinburgh; *b.* 1873; *m.* 1898, Agnes Macniven (*d.* 1941); one *d.* (one *s.*, Fighter Pilot Royal Flying Corps, killed on active service, 1918). *Educ.:* Board School; Leith Science College; Heriot-Watt College, Edinburgh. Entered service of R. & R. Clark, 1892; Secretary, 1914; Director, 1920; Managing Director, 1926-49 (retired); President, Scottish Alliance of Master Printers, 1926-28; President, British Federation of Master Printers, 1929-1930; Chairman, International Typographic Congress, Cologne, Sept. 1928; Chairman, Scottish Joint Industrial Council for Printing and Kindred Trades, 1935-36; admitted Liveryman Worshipful Company of Stationers, 1929; Vice-Chairman of Board of Edinburgh College of Art (resigned 1952); on Board of Management Heriot-Watt College, 1926- (now Hon. Fellow of the College). Hon. LL.D. (Edin.), 1947. *Recreations:* book collecting, typography, fishing. *Address:* 14 South Inverleith Avenue, Edinburgh. *T.:* Edinburgh 84138. [*Died* 12 *Oct.* 1957.

MAXWELL, Lt.-Col. William Ernest, C.I.E. 1935; Indian Army, retired; *b.* 28 Nov. 1898; *m.* 1924, Mary, *d.* of Col. William Henry Savage, *q.v.*; one *s.* one *d.* Entered Indian Army, 1918; Capt. 1923; Major 1936; Lt.-Col. 1941; retired 1947. *Address:* Riverview, Bandon, Eire. *Club:* United Service. [*Died* 17 *Oct.* 1951.

MAXWELL, Sir (William) George, K.B.E., *cr.* 1924; C.M.G. 1915; *b.* 9 June 1871; *s.* of late Sir William Maxwell, K.C.M.G.; *m.* 1902, Evelyn (*d.* 1957), *e. d.* of late Walter F. Stevenson of Manila, and Westhorpe, Hendon; two *s.* *Educ.:* Clifton College. Colonial Civil Service, 1891; Barrister, Inner Temple; holds Royal Humane Society's Medal; has held various magisterial and judicial appointments in the F.M.S. and Straits Settlements Civil Services, including Sol.-Gen. S.S., and Acting Attor.-Gen. S.S.; British Adviser to the Kedah Govt. upon the transfer of the suzerainty of that State from Siam to Great Britain, 1909; Acting Colonial Sec., Straits Settlements, 1914-16; Acting British Resident, Perak, 1917; Acting Sec., High Commissioner, Malay States and Brunei, 1917; Vice-Chairman, Food Control, Straits Settlements and F.M.S.; General Adviser to Govt. of Johore, 1918; British Resident, Perak, F.M.S., 1919; Chief Secretary to the Government, Federated Malay States, 1920-26; retired, 1926; Vice-Chairman Slavery Committee, League of Nations. *Publications:* In Malay Forests; The Civil Defence of Malaya. *Address:* Chindles, High Salvington, Worthing, Sussex. *T.:* Swandean 571. [*Died* 22 *Aug.* 1959.

MAXWELL-ANDERSON, Capt. Sir M. H.; *see* Anderson.

MAXWELL-CARPENDALE, Major Frederic; *see* Carpendale.

MAXWELL-GUMBLETON, Rt. Rev. Maxwell Homfray; *b.* 17 June 1872; *s.* of Hon. Edward T. Smith, Barrister-at-law, Puisne Judge, Jamaica; assumed by Royal Licence surname of Maxwell-Gumbleton, 1916; *m.* 1897, Ella Maria, *d.* of Rev. S. G. Gillum, Vicar of Pucklechurch, Glos.; three *s.* one *d.* *Educ.:* Repton; Peterhouse, Cambridge, B.A. 1894; M.A. 1898; D.D. (hon.), 1916; Wells Theological Coll. Deacon, 1895; Priest, 1896; Curate of Pucklechurch with Abson, 1895-98; Vicar of Colerne, Wilts, 1898-1902; Rector of Colerne, 1902-4; Vicar of Chippenham and Rector of Tytherton Lucas, 1904-16; Rector of Hardenhuish, 1908-16; Hon. Canon of Bristol Cathedral, 1910-16; Rural Dean of Chippenham, and Surrogate, 1912-16; Chaplain to High Sheriff, Wilts, 1908 and 1910; Chaplain to Chippenham Workhouse, 1911-16; Bishop of Ballarat, 1917-27; Assistant Bishop in Diocese of St. Edmundsbury and Ipswich, 1931-34; Bishop Suffragan of Dunwich, 1934-45; Archdeacon of Sudbury, 1932-45; Rector of Hitcham, 1935-49. *Address:* 41 St. James's Square, Bath. *T.:* 3176. [*Died* 1 *Feb.* 1952.

MAXWELL-SCOTT, Major-General Sir Walter Joseph Constable, of Abbotsford, Melrose; 1st Bt., *cr.* 1932; C.B. 1923; D.S.O. 1915; *b.* 10 April 1875; *e. s.* of late Hon. Joseph and Mrs. Maxwell Scott, and *g.g.g.s.* of Sir Walter Scott, Bart.; *m.* 1st, 1918, Mairi Richmond (*d.* 1924), 3rd *d.* of late Lt.-Col. Steuart MacDougall of Lunga, Argyllshire; two *d.*; 2nd, 1928, Mme. de Sincay (*née* Marie Louise Logan of Youngstown, Ohio). *Educ.:* Stonyhurst. Entered Cameronians (Scottish Rifles), 1897; served Tirah, 1897-98 (medal with clasp); South African War, 1899-1902 (Queen's medal 2 clasps, King's medal 2 clasps); European War, 1914-18 (D.S.O., Bt. Lieut.-Colonel, Bt. Colonel, despatches 6 times); Kara Georg with swords (Serbian), 1916; Légion d'Honneur (Croix d'officier), 1917, Croix de Guerre, 1918; commander 52nd (Lowland) Division, and Area, 1930-34; retired pay, 1934; Zone Commander, Scottish Border Home Guard, 1940-42; Mem. Queen's Bodyguard for Scotland; D.L. Roxburghshire; Vice-President of the Royal Celtic Society; Hon. Life Member Scottish Branch, B.R.C.S., 1950; Hon. D.Sc. Fordham Univ.; New York, 1945; Hon. Member St. Andrew's Soc. of State of N.Y., 1945. *Address:* Abbotsford, Melrose, Roxburghshire. *Club:* New (Edinburgh). [*Died* 3 *April* 1954 (*ext.*).

MAY, John Cecil, C.M.G. 1955; O.B.E. 1918; Director, Empire Cotton Growing

Corporation, since 1949; *b.* 7 March 1890; *s.* of late Rev. J. C. May; *m.* 1921, Ellen Evelyn Collins; one *s.* one *d.* *Educ.:* Monmouth School; St. John's College, Oxford (B.A.). Asst. Resident, Nyasaland, 1914. Served European War, 1914-18: Nyasaland Volunteer Reserve, 1914; Lt. King's African Rifles, 1915-18. Asst. Political Officer, German East Africa and Tanganyika, 1916-20; Asst. Secretary, Empire Cotton Growing Corporation, 1921; Secretary, 1944. *Address:* The Cottage, 4 West Side, Wimbledon Common, S.W.19. *T.:* Wimbledon 5272. [*Died* 10 *Sept.* 1959.

MAY, General Sir Reginald Seaburne, K.C.B. 1935 (C.B. 1919); K.B.E. 1923; C.M.G. 1918; D.S.O. 1916; *b.* 10 August 1879; *e. s.* of late Admiral of the Fleet Sir William Henry May, G.C.B., G.C.V.O.; *m.* 1st, 1906, Marguerite Geraldine Ramsay (*d.* 1931), *o. d.* of John Ramsay Drake; three *s.*; 2nd, 1932, Jane, *er. d.* of late Sir John Wilson, Bt., Airdrie, and *widow* of Lieut.-Colonel J. C. Monteith. 2nd Lieut. Royal Fusiliers, 1898; Captain, 1903; Bt. Major, 1903; Major, 1915; Colonel, 1919; temp. Major-General, 1917-23; Major-Gen., 1929; Lieut.-Gen., 1934; General, 1938; served South Africa, 1899-1902 (despatches, Bt. Major, Queen's medal 5 clasps, King's medal 2 clasps); European War, 1914-18 (C.B., C.M.G., D.S.O., Officer of the Legion of Honour, French and Belgian Croix de Guerre with palm, Bt. Col., despatches, Commander of the Order of Leopold, American Order of Merit); Director of Movements, War Office, 1919-23; Director of Recruiting and Organisation, War Office, 1923-27; Brigadier i/c Administration, Northern Command, 1927-29; commanded 49th (West Riding) Division T.A. 1930-31; Commandant, Royal Military College, Sandhurst, 1931-34; Quarter-Master-General to the Forces, 1935-1939; retired pay 1939. Colonel The Royal Fusiliers, 1941-49. *Address:* 58 Kingston House, Princes Gate, S.W.7. [*Died* 26 *Oct.* 1958.

MAY, Major Thomas James, C.M.G. 1901; late Royal Field Artillery; *b.* 17 March 1864; *s.* of Chief Gunner James May, R.N. Served in 3rd Mounted Rifles, Bechuanaland Field Force, 1884-85; Victoria Rifles Kimberley, 1886; Diamond Fields Horse, 1889-1895; Matabeleland Relief Force, 1896; Mounted Infantry, D.E.O.V. Rifles, Bechuanaland Field Force, 1897 (despatches, medal, and clasp); South Africa, 1899-1902 (despatches twice, Queen's medal 2 clasps, King's medal 2 clasps, C.M.G.); was District Comdt. Barkly West District, 1900-1; Hay District, 1902; Reserve of Officers, Transvaal Horse Artillery, 1907-11; Major, Royal Field Artillery, 1914; served European War, 1914-18 (1914 Star, British war medal, Allied victory medal); Commissioner of the South African Section of the Imperial Exhibition and Festival of Empire, London, 1911; in charge of the educational, botanical, and chemical section, South African Pavilion, British Empire Exhibition, Wembley, 1924; Finance Officer Diamond Control, Ministry of Supply, 1942-43. 12th Batt. City of London Home Guard, 1940-44 (Defence Medal); Royal Navy Emergency Crew S.V.P., 1944-45 (1939-45 Star, France and Germany Star; B.W.M., 1939-45). *Address:* Swains Farm, Rochford, Essex. [*Died* 23 *Oct.* 1952.

MAYBURY, Bernard Constable, F.R.C.S. Eng., M.B., B.S. Lond., L.R.C.P. Lond.; Consulting Surgeon to St. Thomas's Hospital; Consulting Surgeon Queen Alexandra's Hospital, Worthing; Fellow of Assoc. of Surgeons of Gt. Britain and Ireland; F.R.S.M.; *b.* Feb. 1888; 3rd *s.* of late A. V. Maybury, M.D., Portsmouth; *m.* 1930, Isobel Wilson, *e. d.* of George Lyall, J.P.; one *s.* one *d.* *Educ.:* Epsom; St. Thomas's Hospital. Bracketed equal for Schol. in Anat. Intermed. M.B. Lond.; Musgrove Schol. and Cheselden and Treasurer's Gold Medals, St. Thomas's Hospital; Surg. Spec. British Red Cross Hospital, Netley, 1915; Surg. Spec. 9th Casualty Clearing Station, France and Italy, 1915-18. *Publications:* various contributions to medical literature. *Address:* 78 Wimpole Street, W.1; Weston Corbett House, Basingstoke. *T.:* Welbeck 3911, Upton Grey 38. [*Died* 15 *Nov.* 1953.

MAYERS, Very Rev. George Samuel. *Educ.:* Trinity College, Dublin. Ordained, 1885; Curate of Clonagam, 1885-86; Holy Trinity, Waterford, 1886-90; Vicar Tubrid, 1890-92; Incumbent of Killaloan, 1892-1900; Rector of Dungarvan, 1900-11; Rector of Lismore, 1911-13; Canon of Waterford, 1904-13; Dean of Lismore, 1913-1919; Dean of Waterford, 1919-37. *Address:* Upwey, Mount Hermon Road, Woking, Surrey. [*Died* 26 *Oct.* 1952.

MAYES, William, C.I.E. 1929; F.C.H.; *b.* 1 March 1874; *s.* of late George Mayes, Bedford; *m.* 1902, Florence, *d.* of late James Michael Calvert, Rochdale; one *s.* one *d.* *Educ.:* Bedford School; R.I.E. College, Coopers Hill, Entered Indian Forest Service, 1895; Conservator of Forests, 1918; Chief Conservator, 1924; retired from service, 1929. *Address:* Shalimar, 61 Pashley Road, Eastbourne. *T.:* Eastbourne 937. [*Died* 20 *Oct.* 1960.

MAYHEW, Lt.-Col. Sir John, Kt., *cr.* 1945; T.D., D.L., J.P.; Army Welfare Officer; *b.* 2 Oct. 1884; *e. surv. s.* of late Horace Mayhew, D.L., J.P., Broughton Hall, Flintshire; *m.* 1907, Guendolen (*d.* 1946), *d.* of late Capt. Francis Gurney, 91st Argyll and Sutherland Highlanders, Blaenau Hall, Merionethshire; two *s.* *Educ.:* King William's Coll., I.O.M. 2nd Lt. Denbighshire Hussars Yeomanry, 1902; Major, 1912; mobilised, 1914; served in France with Infantry, 1916-17 (wounded, mentioned by Secretary for War, 1917); Lt.-Col. 1918. Agriculturalist and Industrialist; M.P. (C.) East Ham (North Div.), 1931-45; contested (C.) Harwich Division of Essex, 1929, East Ham, North, 1945. Master of Company of Pattenmakers, 1944. *Recreations:* racing, shooting, swimming, and genealogy. *Address:* Newton Hall, Dunmow, Essex. *T.:* Dunmow 71; 2 North Court, Gt. Peter St., Westminster, S.W.1. *T.:* Abbey 3372. *Club:* Carlton. [*Died* 27 *Jan.* 1954.

MAYNARD, Harry Russell, C.V.O. 1932; Secretary of King Edward's Hospital Fund for London, 1906-38; Clerk to the General Council, 1938-41; Member of General Council since 1941; *b.* 1873; 3rd *s.* of late Robert Russell Maynard; *m.* 1907, Mabel, *e. d.* of late Thomas Carter, J.P., M.R.C.S., L.R.C.P., Richmond, Yorks. *Educ.:* Amersham Hall School; St. Catherine's Society, Oxford (1st Class Modern History, 1901); London School of Economics. Resident at Toynbee Hall, 1903-7; Hon. Secretary, Mansion House Unemployed Committee, 1903-4; Secretary, London Unemployed Fund, 1904-5; Clerk, Central (Unemployed) Body for London, 1905-1906; Ministry of Food (Rationing Dept.), 1918-19. *Address:* 24 Green Hill, Hampstead, N.W.3. [*Died* 8 *Feb.* 1954.

MAYNE, General Sir (Ashton Gerard Oswald) Mosley, G.C.B., *cr.* 1947 (K.C.B., *cr.* 1944; C.B. 1941); C.B.E. 1941; D.S.O. 1917; *b.* 24 April 1889; 2nd *s.* of late Major Mosley Mayne; *m.* 1916, Phyllis (*d.* 1949), *o. d.* of the late Lt.-Col. H. Tweddell (*o. s.* Capt. R.A., killed in action in Italy, 1943). *Educ.:* Wellington Coll.; R.M.C., Sandhurst. First Commission, 1908; joined 13th D.C.O. Lancers. 1910; Capt. 1915; Bt. Major 1919; 6th D.C.O. Lancers, 1921; Major, 1924; Bt. Lt.-Col. 1930; Lt.-Col. 1934; Brigadier 1936; Maj.-Gen. 1941; Lt.-Gen. 1942; General, 1944; served

European War, 1914-18 (despatches thrice, Bt. Maj., D.S.O.); G.S.O., 3rd and 2nd Grade, 1918 and 1919; D.A.Q.M.G. Army Headquarters (India), 1919 and 1920; Staff Coll. 1920-21; G.S.O., 2nd Grade, Army Headquarters (India), 1922-23; Chief Instructor, Equitation School (India), 1923-24; G.S.O.2 W.O., 1927-31; i.d.c. 1933; Comdt. Roy. Deccan Horse, 1934-36; Director of Military Operations, India, 1936-38; Comdr. of a Brigade in India, 1938-39; served in Middle East, 1940-43, as Comdr. 9 Indian Brigade, 5 Indian Division and 21 Corps (C.B., C.B.E.); G.O.C.-in-C., Eastern Command, India, 1943-44; Principal Staff Officer India Office, 1945-46; A.D.C. General to the King, 1944-1947. Colonel of Mahratta Light Infantry 1942-51, and of 6th D.C.O. Lancers, 1943; retired, 1947. F.R.S.A. 1948. Chairman S.S.A.F.A., 1950-53, Vice-Pres., 1953. *Club:* Army and Navy. [*Died* 17 *Dec.* 1955.

MAYNE, Horace Ardran, C.M.G. 1931; *b.* 10 Nov. 1876; *m.*; two *d.* Went to Egypt in 1892; joined department of Telegraphs and Telephones, Egyptian Ministry of Communications; retired, 1931, as Inspector General of Telegraphs and Telephones, Egyptian Ministry of Communications. Served European War, 1914-18 (despatches), Chief Censor on Suez Canal (Capt.), Grand Officer of the Order of the Nile; held Order of Ismail, also Order of Megidieh (Turkey). *Address:* Thornton House, Kenilworth, Cape Town, S. Africa. [*Died* 7 *Feb.* 1958.

MAYNE, Gen. Sir Mosley; *see* Mayne, Gen. Sir A. G. O. M.

MAYO, Robert Hobart, O.B.E.; M.A.; Assoc. M.Inst.C.E.; F.R.Ae.S.; M.Inst.T.; Major R.A.F. (Retd.), and Sqdn. Leader R.A.F.O. (Retd.); Consulting Engineer; Technical Adviser to various aircraft designing, manufacturing and operating companies; Director: Airtech, Ltd.; Superflexit, Ltd.; Past Chairman Air League of British Empire; Mem. Nat. Civil Aviation Consultative Council; Vice-Pres. Fédération Aeronautique Internationale and Hon. President of Commission Sportive; *b.* 25 Sept. 1890; *s.* of late Dr. James Mayo, LL.D.; *m.* 1924, Thorva Eyres Merrylees; one *d.* *Educ.:* Perse School; Magdalene College, Cambridge (Senior Scholar). 1st Class Mathematical Tripos, Pt. 1, 1910; 1st Class Mechanical Sciences Tripos, 1912; Head of Experimental Dept., Royal Aircraft Factory, 1914; served in France as Flying Officer, R.F.C., 1915-16; Senior Flight Commander, Testing Squadron, R.F.C., 1916-17; Head of Design (Aeroplane) Section, Air Ministry, 1917-19; Director of Ogilvie and Partners, Consulting Engineers, 1919-24, Consulting Engineer to Imperial Airways, 1925-36; European Representative of the Daniel Guggenheim Fund for the Promotion of Aeronautics, 1926-30; Consulting Engineer to the British Corporation Register and to the Joint Aviation Advisory Committee of Lloyds Register and the B.C. Register, 1926-35; Technical General Manager of Imperial Airways, 1936-39; and subsequently Technical Adviser to Imperial Airways and British Overseas Airways Corporation; Member of Cttee. and Chm. of Records, Racing and Competitions Cttee., Roy. Aero Club; former Member of Council, Inst. of Transport; Fellow Institute of the Aeronautical Sciences (U.S.A.); Inventor of the Short-Mayo Composite Aircraft, holder of the World's seaplane distance record; Silver Medal of Royal Aeronautical Society, 1939. *Publications:* Various papers on aeronautical and air transport engineering. *Recreation:* golf. *Address:* 806 Beatty House, Dolphin Square, S.W.1. *T.:* Victoria 8931. *Clubs:* Royal Aero; Walton Heath Golf. [*Died* 26 *Feb.* 1957.

MAZE, Sir Frederick (William), K.C.M.G., *cr.* 1944; K.B.E., *cr.* 1932; *b.* Belfast; *y. s.* of James Maze, Killultagh Cottage, Upper Ballinderry, and Mary, *d.* of Henry Hart, Ravarnette House, Lisburn, Ireland; *m.* Laura Gwendoline, *y. d.* of Edward Augustus Bullmore of Oakwood Station, Qld., and Rockton House, Ipswich, Australia. *Educ.:* Wesley Coll., Dublin, and privately. Entered Chinese Imperial Maritime Customs, closing period of Sir Robert Hart's régime; Acting Audit Secy., Inspectorate-General, Peking, 1899; Acting Commissioner, Ichang, 1900 (Boxer Year); Deputy Commissioner, Foochow, 1901; Deputy Commissioner, Canton, 1903-4; opened Custom House, Kongmoon, West River, 1904; subsequently Commissioner in Tengyueh (Burmah Frontier), Canton, Tientsin, Hankow and Shanghai consecutively; apptd., by Chinese Government, Deputy Inspector-General of Customs, 1928; Inspector-General of Chinese Maritime Customs, 1929-43; rank of Mandarin of 3rd Grade, conferred by Emperor of China, 1904; Order of Double Dragon, 3rd Division, 1st Class; Excellent Crop, 2nd Class; Excellent Crop in Gems; Conservancy Medal, 1st Class; Order of Wên Hu, 2nd Class; Imperial Order of the Sacred Treasure, 3rd Class, conferred by Emperor of Japan, 1920; appointed by Chinese Government, Adviser to National Board of Reconstruction, 1928; Member of the National Loans Sinking Fund Commission, 1932; Comdr. Order of Leopold, Belgium; Comdr. Order of Christ, Portugal; 1st Class, Order of Saint Olaf, Norway; Member of Chinese Government Monetary Advisory Committee, 1935; Knight Commander, First Class, Order of Dannebrog, Denmark; Order of the Brilliant Jade, with Sash, China; Commander Legion of Honour, France; Cross of the First Class of the Order of the Red Cross, Germany, 1937; Counsellor to accompany Dr. Kung, Envoy Extraordinary, at Coronation of King George VI., 1937; Membre d'Honneur l'Association des Amis du Musée de Marine, Paris; Knight Commander of the Order of Pius IX, Holy See. *Recreation:* yachting. *Address:* Ravarnette Lodge, Beach Drive, Victoria, B.C., Canada. *Clubs:* Athenæum, Junior Carlton, Royal Societies; Hong-kong; Shanghai, Shanghai Country (Shanghai); Union Club of British Columbia. [*Died* 25 *March* 1959.

MEACHEN, George Norman, M.D., B.S. London; Organist, 1941, and Lay Reader, 1951, Ringwood Parish Church; *b.* 17 April 1876; *o. s.* of George Buck Meachen, B.A., solicitor, of Beccles, Suffolk, and Isabella Mary, *d.* of William Leedes Fox, solicitor, of Harleston, Deputy Provincial Grand Master of Freemasons, Norfolk; *m.* 1913, Mabel Ethel, *e. d.* of Frederick Reis, Canonbury: one *d.* *Educ.:* private school; London University. Prizeman and Exhibitioner, Guy's Hospital; Member Royal College of Physicians, Edinburgh, 1901; Member of Royal College of Physicians of London, 1902; Chesterfield Silver Medallist in Dermatology 1901; Founder of Skin Department, Prince of Wales's General Hospital; formerly Tuberculosis Officer Essex and Durham County Councils and Southend Boro'; Physician, Blackfriars Skin Hospital; Dermatologist, Foundling Hospital; Physician, Eastern Dispensary; Joint Hon. Sec. Dermatological Society of Great Britain and Ireland, 1906-7; Fellow and late Member of Council of Dermatological Section Royal Society of Medicine; late Hon. Sec. New London Dermatological Society, 1911; Sub-Editor, Medical Press and Circular. *Publications:* Skin Diseases, their Nursing and General Management; A Short History of Tuberculosis, 1936; Human Physiology, 3rd ed. 1948; numerous papers, etc., in medical journals. *Recreations:* organ-playing (Assoc. Mus. Trinity College, London), literature, motoring. *Address:* Petherton Cottage, Ashley Heath, Ringwood, Hants. *T.:* Ringwood 450. [*Died* 12 *May* 1955.

MEAD, John Phillips, C.B.E. 1939; Lt.-Col. R.A.; *b.* 10 Aug. 1886; *s.* of late John Phillips Mead, 2 King's Bench Walk, Temple; *m.* 1917, Marjorie Lydia, *d.* of late G. E. T. Laurence; two *d.* *Educ.:* Charterhouse; R.I.E.C., Cooper's Hill;

Exeter College, Oxford (Diploma in Forestry). Entered Colonial Forest Service, 1907; served in Malaya, 1907-16; served with British Army (Lt. East Surrey Regt. in Gt. Britain, France, and Sudan), 1916-19; Conservator of Forests, Sarawak, 1919-28; reported on forests of Colony of Fiji, 1926-27; reappointed Malaya, 1928; Director of Forestry, Malaya, 1929-40; retired, 1940. Served with British Army in Royal Artillery (2nd Lt., Lt. 1940; Capt. 1942; Major, Lt.-Col. 1945) in Gt. Britain and S.E.A.C., 1940-46. Member, Governing Council, Empire Forestry Assocn. *Publications:* Mangrove Forests of the West Coast, F.M.S., 1911; Methods of Surveying in Flat Land, 1925; Report on the Forests of the Fiji Islands, 1927; various contributions to Empire Forestry Journal, Indian Forester and Malayan Forester. *Address:* The Elms, 22 Park Road, Teddington, Middx. *T.:* Molesey 1584. *Clubs:* East India and Sports, M.C.C. [*Died* 2 *Jan.* 1951.

MEADE, Major Harry Edward, O.B.E. 1919; *b.* 8 Oct. 1884; *s.* of Arthur William Meade and Grace Ellen, *d.* of George Maitland, Shotover Park, Oxford; *m.* 1909, Marion (who obtained a divorce, 1944), *d.* of Hon. Mr. Justice Chadwick, South Africa; one *s.* one *d.*; *m.* 1946, Elsie, *d.* of William Payne, London. *Educ.:* Eton Coll. 2nd Lt. Royal Fusilliers, 1904; retired, 1919; High Sheriff Berkshire, 1941; retired from directorships, 1947. *Recreations:* shooting, fishing. *Address:* St. George, Castel, Guernsey, C.I. *T.:* Guernsey 7500; Isoletta, Eze-sur-Mer, S. of France. *T.:* Eze-sur-Mer 24035. *Clubs:* Carlton, Army and Navy; Royal Yacht Squadron (Cowes). [*Died* 31 *Jan.* 1952.

MEADON, Sir Percival Edward, Kt., *cr.* 1937; C.B.E. 1930; M.A. (Oxon); Hon. LL.D. (Manchester); Hon. M.A. (Queensland); J.P. County of Lancaster; Director of Education for Lancashire (Lancashire County Council), 1924-45; *b.* Stoke-on-Trent, Staffs, 4 April 1878; *s.* of John Meadon; *m.* 1908, Alice Eliza (*d.* 1959), *er. d.* of Joshua Wilson Nelson, Liverpool; one *s.* one *d.* *Educ.:* St. Mark's College, Chelsea; St. John's College, Oxford. Assistant and Headmaster; Assistant Education Secretary, Oxfordshire County Council, 1908-15; Director of Education, Essex C.C., 1915-24. Pres. Assoc. of Directors and Secretaries of Education, 1932; co-opted Mem. Oxfordshire Educ. Cttee., 1953. *Address:* Southlea, Guildford Road, East Horsley, Surrey. *T.:* East Horsley 2591. [*Died* 17 *Nov.* 1959.

MEADOWCROFT, Lancelot Vernon, C.B. 1941; Director of Contracts, Air Ministry, 1937-44; *b.* 2 Jan. 1884; *s.* of Joseph Meadowcroft, Lancaster; *m.* 1911, Elizabeth Evelyne, *d.* of W. G. Wiltshire, Lancaster; two *d.* *Educ.:* Royal Grammar School, Lancaster; Manchester University (Dalton Scholar, 1903, 1st Class Honours School of Mathematics, 1904, Derby Scholar 1904, B.Sc. 1904, M.Sc. 1907); Trinity College, Cambridge (Major Scholar, 1906, 1st Class Natural Sciences Tripos, Part I, 1906, 1st Class Mathematical Tripos, Part I (10 Wrangler), 1907, Wrangham Gold Medal, 1907, Leigh Prize, 1907, Lees-Knowles Exhibition, 1907, B.A. 1907); M.A. 1944; entered Civil Service (Admiralty) as Clerk, Class I, 1908; Deputy Accounts Officer, 1911; Clerk to Commissioners of Income Tax, 1912; Superintending Clerk, 1914; transferred to Air Ministry, 1918; Principal (Old Style), 1918; Assistant Secretary, 1920; Principal Assistant Secretary (Director of Contracts), 1937. *Publications:* Papers in Mathematical Periodicals. *Recreations:* walking, reading. *Address:* 10 Hertford Avenue, East Sheen, S.W.14. [*Died* 3 *Aug.* 1952.

MEAKIN, Annette M. B.; *b.* Clifton, Bristol; *d.* of Edward E. Meakin. *Educ.:* in England and Germany. Studied music at Royal College of Music, Kensington Gore, and at Stern Conservatoire, Berlin; Classics at University College, London; first Englishwoman to cross Siberia by the Great Siberian Railway, 1900; qualified as chemist's assistant (Hall), Oct. 1916, to release a man for the Front. Lectured in Paris Sorbonne, and School of Medicine, and in Würzburg University, also often in England. *Publications:* A Ribbon of Iron (descriptive of above Journey), 1901; In Russian Turkestan, 1903; Russia: Travels and Studies, 1906; Woman in Transition, 1907; Galicia, the Switzerland of Spain, 1909; What America is Doing, 1911; Hannah More, 1911; Enlistment or Conscription, 1915; Nausikaa, Sixth Book of Odyssey in English Hexameters, 1926, 2nd Ed. 1938; Polyeuctes (from the French of Pierre Corneille), 1928; Inez de Castro (a tragedy in blank verse), 1930; Goethe and Schiller (3 vols.), 1931-32. *Recreations:* music and reading. *Address:* c/o National Provincial Bank, 69 Baker Street, W.1. [*Died* 26 *July* 1959.

MEAKINS, Brig. Jonathan Campbell, C.B.E. 1945; M.D., D.Sc., M.D. (Sydney), LL.D. (Ed.), F.A.C.P., F.R.C.P. (C.), F.R.C.P.E., Hon. F.R.C.S. (E.), F.R.C.P. (Lond.), F.R.S.E., F.R.S.C.; Hon. F.R.S.M., 1942; Deputy Director-General Medical Services (Professional) R.C.A.M.C.; *b.* Hamilton, Canada, 16 May 1882; *s.* of Charles William Meakins and Elizabeth Campbell; *m.* 1st, Dorothy (*d.* 1926), *d.* of late Fayette Brown, Montreal; one *s.* one *d.*; 2nd, 1928, Sara Caldwell Young. *Educ.:* Hamilton Collegiate; McGill University; M.D., C.M. Resident Physician, Royal Victoria Hospital, Montreal, 1904-6; Assistant in Medicine, Johns Hopkins Hospital, Baltimore, 1906-7; Resident Pathologist, Presbyterian Hospital, New York, 1907-10; Assistant Physician, Royal Victoria Hospital, Montreal; Lecturer in Medicine and Pathology, McGill University, Montreal; Director of Experimental Medicine, McGill University; Canadian Expeditionary Force, 1915-18; Medical Consultant, C.A.M.C., Montreal, 1918-19; Christison Prof. of Therapeutics, University of Edinburgh; Physician to the Royal Infirmary, Edinburgh, 1919-24; Editor, American Heart Journal, 1950-; formerly: Dean of the Faculty of Medicine; Emer. Professor of Medicine and Director of the Dept. McGill Univ.; Director of Univ. Clinic and Physician-in-Chief, Royal Victoria Hosp., Montreal; Pres. Roy. Coll. of Physicians and Surgeons of Canada, 1929-31; Pres., American College of Physicians, 1934-35; Pres. Canadian Medical Assoc., 1935-36. *Publications:* The Practice of Medicine, 1936, 6th ed., 1956; numerous scientific medical papers. *Recreations:* golf, travel. *Address:* 3640 University Street, Montreal 2. *T.A.:* McGill, Montreal. *Club:* University (Montreal). [*Died* 12 *Oct.* 1959.

MEARS, Sir Frank Charles, Kt., *cr.* 1946; R.S.A. 1943 (A.R.S.A. 1936; President, 1944-50); Hon. R.A.; Hon. LL.D.Edin.; F.R.S.E.; F.R.I.B.A.; M.T.P.I.; Architect and Planning Consultant; *b.* 11 July 1880; *s.* of William Pope Mears, M.A., M.D., and Isabella Bartholomew, L.R.C.P.I.; *m.* 1915, Norah, *d.* of Prof. Sir Patrick Geddes; one *s.* *Educ.:* George Watson's College; School of Applied Art; office of H. J. Blanc, R.S.A., Edinburgh. Pugin Student R.I.B.A. 1904. Designed Nat. Library Jerusalem and Scottish Zoological Park in association with Prof. Geddes. War service, 1916-1919, R.F.C. and R.A.F., Capt. Inv. parachute for aeroplanes, 1918. Architect for Highland Bridges; King George VI Bridge, Aberdeen; Sanderson Homes, Galashiels; Memorial to David Livingstone, Blantyre; Monument to the Royal Scots Regt., Edinburgh; restoration of Huntly House and Gladstone's Land, Edinburgh; Consultant, C. and S.E. Scotland Regional Planning Advisory Committee; Glasgow University; Greenock, Stirling and numerous Counties and Burghs. Mem. Scottish Coalfields, Housing, Hydro-

Electric Amenity and other committees. *Address:* Whitehouse, Inveresk, Musselburgh; 44 Queen Street, Edinburgh. *T.:* Musselburgh 2914, Caledonian (Edinburgh) 7441. *Clubs:* Scottish Arts (Edinburgh); Art (Glasgow). [*Died* 25 *Jan.* 1953.

MEASHAM, Paymaster Rear-Adm. Herbert Stanley, C.M.G. 1918; Royal Navy, retired; *b.* Croydon, 24 Jan. 1875; 2nd *s.* of late Rev. R. Measham, B.A., J.P.. R.N.; *m.* 1906, Muriel Mary, 2nd *d.* of late Colonel S. G. Huskisson, C.B.; one *s.* (and one *s.* decd.). *Educ.:* St. John's School, Leatherhead. Entered Royal Navy, 1892, as assistant clerk. Served in Benin expedition, 1897 (despatches, medal and clasp); served as Secretary to various Flag Officers, 1904-21; Secretary to Commander-in-Chief, Portsmouth, 1916-19; Paymaster Captain, 1923; Fleet Accountant Officer, Mediterranean Fleet, 1922-25; Superintendent Secretaries Course, 1925-27; Deputy Judge Advocate of the Fleet, 1927-30; retired list, 1930; J.P., Hampshire, 1934. *Address:* Woodcroft, Wallis Road, Waterlooville, Hants. [*Died* 23 *Aug.* 1954.

MEDD, Wilfrid, C.B. 1934; O.B.E. 1918; *b.* 12 Oct. 1877; *s.* of Charles Septimus Medd and Alice Maples; *m.* 1st, 1904, Elsie Mews; two *d.*; 2nd, 1922, Evelyn Natalie Powys Mathers; one *s.* one *d.* *Educ.:* Horris Hill; Winchester College (scholar); Queen's College, Oxford (Jodrell Scholar), M.A. Entered Department of the Accountant General of the Navy as Clerk Class 1 1901; Assistant Principal 1906; Assistant Accountant General (acting and confirmed), 1918-32; Principal Assistant Secretary, Admiralty, 1932-37; re-employed, 1939-45; District Air Raid Warden, Stanwell, 1938-42. Silver Jubilee Medal, 1935; Coronation Medal, 1937. *Recreation:* gardening. *Address:* Hillcrest, The Avenue, Farnham Common, Bucks. *Club:* Oxford Union. [*Died* 22 *Oct.* 1956.

MEDHURST, Air Chief Marshal Sir Charles Edward Hastings, K.C.B., *cr.* 1945 (C.B. 1942); O.B.E. 1919; Head of Air Force Staff, British Joint Services Mission at Washington, 1948-50; *b.* 12 Dec. 1896; 2nd *s.* of late Rev. C. E. Medhurst, Collingham; *m.* 1919, Christabel Elizabeth, *d.* of late Canon T. E. B. Guy, York; (one *s.* killed in action, 1944) two *d.* *Educ.:* Rossall; S. Peters, York; Sandhurst. 2nd Lt. R. Inniskilling Fusiliers, 1915; R.F.C., 1915-18 (Temp. Major, 1917); R.A.F., 1919; served France and Palestine, 1915-18 (M.C.); p.s.a., 1926; i.d.c., 1929; served Iraq, 1926-28; Instructor, R.A.F. Staff College, 1931-33; Deputy Director Intelligence, 1934-37; Air Attaché, Rome, Berne Athens, 1937-40; Asst. Chief of Air Staff (Intelligence), 1941; Asst. Chief of Air Staff (Policy), 1942; Commandant R.A.F. Staff College, 1943-44; Air Commander-in-Chief R.A.F., Mediterranean Middle East, 1945-48; retd., 1950. *Recreation:* squash. *Club:* Army and Navy. [*Died* 18 *Oct.* 1954.

MEDLEY, Dudley Julius; Professor of History, Glasgow University, 1899-1931, and now Emeritus Professor; Hon. LL.D., Glasgow, 1931; *b.* 31 Mar. 1861; *s.* of Major-Gen. J. G. Medley, R.E.; *m.* 1890, Isabel Alice (*d.* 1942), 2nd *d.* of Rev. J. L. Gibbs; three *s.* one *d.* *Educ.:* Wellington College; Keble College, Oxford. First Class, Honour School of Modern History, 1883; Lecturer at Keble College, 1884; Tutor, 1887. Sometime Examiner for Scottish Education Dept., Civil Service Commissioners and Oxford and Cambridge Univ. Examination Board, also for Universities of Oxford, Cambridge, Belfast, Birmingham, Durham, Glasgow and Sheffield; at Glasgow, for many years Chairman of Univ. Appointments Committee and of Military Education Committee (O.T.C.); Member of Glasgow City and County Territorial Army and Air Force Association; Chairman of Central Organization Military Education Committees (Senior Div. O.T.C.); during the last War, one of Y.M.C.A. lecturers and a sub-director under Army Scheme of Education in France. *Publications:* A Student's Manual of English Constitutional History (6th edition); Original Illustrations English Constitutional History (2nd edition); The Church and the Empire (in Church Universal Series); contributor to Constitutional Essays (2nd edition); and to Social England; co-editor of Bibliography of British History (18th Cent.). *Address:* 142 Newtown Road, Newbury, Berks. [*Died* 14 *Oct.* 1953.

MEDTNER, Nicholas; composer and pianist; *b.* Moscow, 24 Dec. 1879 (6 Jan. 1880); *m.* Anna Bratenski. *Educ.:* Moscow Conservatory (Gold medal). Professor at Moscow Conservatory, 1909-10 and 1918-21; lived in Berlin, 1922-24; United States, 1924-25; France, 1925-31; gave concerts in Canada, United States, Paris, Berlin, and England. *Publications:* 60 works. *Address:* 69 Wentworth Road, N.W.11. *T.:* Speedwell 2150. [*Died* 13 *Nov.* 1951.

MEEK, Lieut.-Colonel Arthur Stanley, C.M.G. 1919; formerly Foreign and Political Department, Government of India; *b.* Larne, Ireland, 7 Oct. 1883; *s.* of Rev. J. B. Meek of Larne, and later Rothesay Scotland; *m.* G. B. Leggatt, of Lee-on-the-Solent, *d.* of F. S. Leggatt; one *s.* *Educ.:* Bedford School; Sandhurst. First Commission, 1903; entered Bombay Political Department from Indian Army, 1907; Military Governor, Basrah, 1917-1919 (despatches); Special Mission in Tehama, Arabia (C.M.G.); Agent Governor-General Eastern States, 1934-37; retired, 1938. *Address:* c/o Lloyds Bank, 6 Pall Mall, S.W.1. [*Died* 14 *Aug.* 1955.

MEENAN, James Nahor, M.D., B.Ch.; B.A.O., R.U.I. 1903; D.P.H. 1905; L.M. Rotunda Hospital, Dublin, 1902; M.D., N.U.I., 1934; Physician St. Vincent's Hospital, Dublin; Consulting Physician St. Patrick's College, Maynooth; Professor of Systematic Medicine, University College, Dublin; Member of Governing Body, University College, Dublin; Member of the Medical Registration Council of Saorstat Eireann; *b.* Corhally House, Fintona, Co. Tyrone, 6 Sep. 1879; *m.* 1909, Mary E. Cleary, B.A.; three *s.* one *d.* *Educ.:* St. Macarten's Seminary. Monaghan; Clongowes Wood College; Catholic University Medical School, Cecilia Street. House Physician and Surgeon St. Vincent's Hospital; Assistant Medical Supt. Cork Street Fever Hospital, Dublin; Chancellor's gold medal Cecilia Street Medical School; gold medal Clinical Medicine St. Vincent's Hospital; medallist in Hygiene, Anatomy, Physiology, Materia Medica, and Chemistry Medical School, Cecilia Street. *Recreation:* golf. *Address:* 28 Fitzwilliam Square S., Dublin. *T.:* 62066. [*Died* 20 *Nov.* 1950.
[*But death not notified in time for inclusion in Who Was Who* 1941–1950, *first edn.*

MEES, C(harles) E(dward) Kenneth, F.R.S. 1939; D.Sc., F.C.S., F.R.A.S.; retired, in November 1955, from Eastman Kodak Company, Rochester, N.Y., U.S.A.; Director, Kodak Ltd., London, 1948-59; *b.* 26 May 1882; *s.* of Ellen Jordan and Charles Edward Mees; *m.* 1909, Alice Crisp (decd.); one *s.* one *d.* *Educ.:* Kingswood School, Bath; Harrogate Coll.; St. Dunstan's Coll., Catford; Univ. Coll. London. B.Sc. by research, 1903; D.Sc., 1906; Hon. D.Sc. Univ. Rochester, U.S.A., 1921, Alfred Univ., Alfred, N.Y., 1950; Managing Dir. Wratten and Wainwright, Ltd., Croydon, manufacturers of photographic plates, 1906-1912; made available commercial panchromatic and process panchromatic plates for photography, 1906-07; developed light filters for photography. Organized research lab. for Eastman Kodak Co., 1912; established dept. for manufacture and supply of synthetic organic chemicals for research, 1918; Silver medal Roy. Soc. Arts, 1908, 1934; Progress medal Roy. Phot. Soc. Gt. Brit., 1913 and

1953; John Scott medal, City Philadelphia, 1921; Janssen medal Soc. Franc. de Phot. 1923; Hurter and Driffield medal, Roy. Phot. Soc. 1924; Progress medal Society of Motion Picture Engineers, 1936; Henry Draper medal Nat. Acad. of Science, 1937; Rumford Medals, Am. Acad. Arts and Sciences, 1943; Adelsköld Gold medal, Swedish Phot. Soc., 1948; Progress medal, Phot. Soc. Amer., 1948; Hon. F.R.P.S.; Hon. Fellow, Photographic Society of America, 1940; Fellow, Amer. Acad. of Arts and Sciences, 1950; Patron, Amer. Astronomical Soc., 1950; Medal, Soc. Phot. Eng., 1954; Franklin Medal, 1954; Hon. mem. Soc. Franc. de Phot., Franklin Inst.; Fellow, Soc. Motion Picture and Television Engineers, A.A.A.S., Amer. Philosophical Soc.; Nat. Acad. Sciences, 1950; Fellow, Univ. Coll., London, 1950; Christmas lectr., Roy. Institution, London, 1935-36. *Publications:* Investigations on Theory of Photographic Process (with S. E. Sheppard), 1907; Organization Industrial Scientific Research, 1920, revised (with J. A. Leermakers), 1950; editor of six monographs on theory of photography; Photography, 1936; The Theory of the Photographic Process, 1942, revised, 1954; The Path of Science, 1946; From Dry Plates to Ektachrome Film (posthumous, U.S.A., 1961); over 100 scientific papers on photography and related subjects. *Address:* 4401 Kahala Avenue, Honolulu, Hawaii, U.S.A. *Clubs:* Athenæum; Chemists (New York City). [*Died* 15 *Aug.* 1960.

MEESON, Dora, R.O.I. 1919 **(Mrs. Geo. J. Coates);** Painter in oils, tempera and water colour; *d.* of John T. Meeson, M.A., Barrister-at-law, and Amelia Stuart-Kipling; *m.* 1903, George James Coates, Artist (*d.* 1930). *Educ.:* at home. Studied National Gallery, Melbourne; Slade School; Académie Julian, Paris. Exhibits R.A., London and provincial Exhibitions, Paris Salon (Hon. Mention); Member Women's International Art Club, 1929; has picture, Imperial War Museum; 5 in Port of London Authority Building; 1 in Greenwich Maritime Museum; 2 in Melbourne National Gallery, 3 in Sydney National Gallery, 2 in Adelaide Nat. Gallery, 1 Brisbane, 1 Perth, Australian War Museum, and other Australian Public Galleries; 2 Hobart Art Gallery; paints landscapes, flowers, children's portraits; Member of Tempera Society in 1912, 2 tempera panels at St. Anne's, Limehouse and at Danecourt, Sussex, and small tempera pictures. *Publications:* George Coates, his Art and his Life; Sunshine Farm, etc.; colour reproductions, Villefranche, Shipping in Pool of London, Hastings fishing fleet, Morning at La Rochelle, Sunset from Tower Bridge. *Recreations:* music, travelling. *Address:* 52 Glebe Place, Chelsea, S.W.3. *T.* Flaxman 2651. [*Died* 24 *March* 1955.

MEGAW, Major-General Sir John (Wallace Dick), K.C.I.E., *cr.* 1933 (C.I.E. 1926); *b.* 8 Feb. 1874; *s.* of late John Megaw, J.P., and Mrs. Megaw, Ballyboyland, Co. Antrim; *m.* 1912, Helen Esmée Ward. *Educ.:* Royal Academical Institution and Queen's College, Belfast. Hon. D.Sc., Belfast, 1934. M.B., B.Ch., R.U.I., 1899. Entered I.M.S. 1900; Principal and Professor of Pathology, King George's Medical College, Lucknow, 1917-21; Director and Professor of Tropical Medicine, Calcutta School of Tropical Medicine, 1921-28; Inspector-General of Civil Hospitals, Punjab, 1928-29; Surgeon-General with the Government of Madras, 1929-30; Director-General I.M.S. 1930-33; Hon. Physician to the King, 1930-34; retired 1933; President India Office Medical Board and Medical Adviser to Secretary of State for India, 1933-39; Editor of the Indian Medical Gazette, 1921-29; Comm. Ordre de Leopold II. *Publications:* Tropical Medicine (Rogers and Megaw); Chapters VI and VII Social Service in India, 1938; papers in the Indian Medical Gazette on the Short Fevers of India; Tick Typhus of India; Artificial Cooling of Rooms in India; The Population Problem of India, etc. *Address:* Tilden, Hawkhurst, Kent. *T.:* Hawkhurst 2231. [*Died* 24 *Oct.* 1958.

MEGHNAD SAHA, D.Sc. (Cal.); D.Sc. (Hon. Causa, Allahabad and Lucknow); F.R.S. 1927; F.R.A.S.B.; Hon. Fellow, American Academy of Sciences and Arts, Boston; Life Member of the Astronomical Society of France; Fellow and Founder President of the Academy of Sciences, United Provinces of Agra and Oudh, India; Organising Secretary and Foreign Secretary of the National Institute of Sciences, India, 1935; President, 1937; Pres. Indian Physical Society, 1937; General Pres., the 21st Indian Science Congress, 1934; Member of National Planning Committee of Indian National Congress; Member, Council of Scientific and Industrial Research, Government of India; Palit Professor of Physics, 1938-55; Dean of the Science Faculty, University of Calcutta, 1951-; Director: Institute of Nuclear Physics; Indian Assoc. for Cultivation of Science; Pres. Post-graduate Council in Science, Calcutta Univ., 1947-49; Member Univ. Commission of Govt. of India, 1948-49; M.P. Republic of India, 1952; *b.* 1893; *s.* of late Jagannath Saha; *m.* 1917; three *s.* four *d.* *Educ.:* Dacca College; Calcutta Presidency College. First or second in all University examinations; Premchand Raychand Studentship, 1920; Professor of Physics, Allahabad University, 1923-38; Carnegie Scholar of the British Empire, 1936. *Publications:* Theory of Thermal Ionisation of Gases, and Theory of Selective Radiation Pressure; many papers in Scientific Journals, the Philosophical Magazine of London, the Proceedings of the Royal Society, Zeitschrift fur Physik, Physikalische Zeitschrift, etc.; Six Lectures on Atomic Physics, a Treatise on Heat and Thermodynamics; Outlines of Modern Knowledge on Atoms, Molecules, and Nuclei; founder of the scientific journal, Science and Culture. *Address:* The University College of Science, 92 Upper Circular Road, Calcutta, India. [*Died* 16 *Feb.* 1956.

MEIER, Frederic Alfred, M.A., B.Sc., A.C.G.I., Senior Lecturer in the Physical Sciences at London University Institute of Education since 1946; Headmaster of Bedales School, 1935-46; *b.* 4 Feb. 1887; *m.* 1919, Sheena MacKinnon MacKenzie; two *d.* *Educ.:* Quernmore School; London University (B.Sc. Engineering with 1st Class Hons., John Samuel scholar); Bramwell Medal for Civil and Mechanical Engineering; Practical Engineering apprentice in Yarrow's shipbuilding works on Thames; Trinity College, Cambridge University (Exhibitioner); Maths. Tripos Part I. (1st Division), Natural Science Tripos Part II. (2nd Class); Science and Engineering Master at Trinity College, Glenalmond, 1910-13; Science and Maths. master at Marlborough College, 1913-14; Assistant Master, Rugby School, 1914-35; Head of Science department, 1928-35. *Address:* 28 East Street, Littlehampton, Sussex. *T.:* Littlehampton 73. [*Died* 13 *Feb.* 1954.

MEIGHEN, Rt. Hon. Arthur, P.C. 1920; Q.C.; B.A.; LL.D.; *b.* Anderson Post Office, Perth Co., Ontario, 16 June 1874; *m.* 1904, Isabel Cox of Birtle, Man.; two *s.* one *d.* *Educ.:* Toronto University (graduated with Honours in Mathematics, 1896). Raised on farm; taught Collegiate Institute, Caledonia, one year; then in manufacturing business and teaching in Winnipeg until 1900, when commenced study of law; called, 1903; practised in Portage la Prairie; elected to House of Commons, 1908; re-elected, 1911, 1913 and 1917; defeated, 1921; re-elected for Grenville, Ontario, 1922; re-elected for Portage la Prairie, Man., 1925; defeated, 1926; Solicitor-General of Canada, 1913; Secretary of State for Canada and Minister of Mines, 1917; Minister of

Interior and Superintendent General Indian Affairs, 1917; Prime Minister and Secretary for External Affairs, Canada, 1920-21; Prime Minister, July-Sep. 1926; Minister without Portfolio, Canada, 1932-35; Leader of the Government in the Senate, 1932-41; Leader of Conservative Party, Canada, 1941-42; Member of Imperial War Cabinet, 1918; attended Prime Ministers' Conference in London, 1921. *Address:* (office) 360 Bay Street, Toronto 1, Ontario, Canada. *Clubs:* Albany, National (Toronto). [*Died* 5 *Aug.* 1960.

MEIKLE, Capt. Archibald Robert, C.V.O. 1939; R.D.; R.N.R. (retd.); *b.* 27 April 1886; *s.* of Archibald Peter Meikle, Linlithgow, and Jessie Wallace, Langholm, Scotland; *m.* 1st, 1913, Elsie Gladys Griffiths (*d.* 1949); one *s.*; 2nd, 1950, Edna, *d.* of late J. M. Knight, Leigh-on-sea, Essex. *Educ.:* privately. Served apprenticeship in Barque, Falls of Halladale, 1902-6; joined Allan Line, 1908, and served in various vessels of that company till 1914; Commission as Sub-Lieut. R.N.R. 1914; called up on outbreak of war and appointed to H.M.S. Glory on mobilisation; served also in H.M.S. Swift and H.M.S. Repulse as Lieut. till end of war; rejoined Allan Line, then taken over by Canadian Pacific, and served in various ships of that company; Captain of Canadian Pacific Steamship Empress of Australia. Retired May 1946. Recalled R.N.R. and served 1940-46. *Recreations:* golf, railway signalling and general railway operations. *Address:* Silverhowe, Little Common, Bexhill, Sussex. [*Died* 22 *Sept.* 1958.

MEIKLE, Henry William, C.B.E. 1944; Hon. R.S.A. 1942; Hon. LL.D. (Edin.) 1946; Hon. Dr. de l'Université (Caen), 1957; Chevalier de la Légion d'Honneur, 1953; M.A., D.Litt.; H.M. Historiographer in Scotland since 1940; Librarian of the National Library of Scotland, 1931-46; Keeper of Manuscripts, 1927-31; a Crown Trustee since 1952; *b.* Edinburgh, 1880; *s.* of Thomas Meikle, Edinburgh; *m.* Jessie Mollison, *d.* of Thomas McLetchie, Edinburgh, formerly of Durban, Natal. *Educ.:* Daniel Stewart's Coll., and the University, Edinburgh, M.A.; 1st Class Hons. in English (1904); D.Litt. (1912); Lecteur d'Anglais, University of Lyons, 1904-1905; Master in George Watson's College, Edinburgh, 1905-8; Carnegie Scholar in History, 1908-9; Tutor in British History and Lecturer in Scottish History, University of Edinburgh, 1908-16; Administrative Officer in Ministry of Munitions and Ministry of Labour, 1917-22; Secretary and Librarian of the Institute of Historical Research and Adviser to External Research Students in History, University of London, 1923-27; David Murray Lecturer, Univ. of Glasgow, 1947; President Historical Assoc. of Scotland, 1947-50; Chairman Edinburgh University Library Cttee., 1946-55; Pres. Scottish History Soc.; Vice-President Franco-Scottish Society. Member of Scottish Records Advisory Council, Advisory Cttee. for National Portrait Gallery of Scotland, and Scottish Advisory Panel of British Council. *Publications:* Scotland and the French Revolution, 1912; The Works of William Fowler, vol. i. (Scottish Text Society), 1914, vol. ii. 1936, vol. iii. (joint), 1940; Correspondence of the Scots Commissioners in London, 1644-46 (Roxburghe Club), 1917; Calendar of State Papers relating to Scotland, vol. x. (joint), 1936; Catalogue of MSS. in the National Library of Scotland, vol. i. (joint), 1938; Diary of Sir William Drummond of Hawthornden (Scottish History Society), 1941; Scotland (ed.), 1947; Some Aspects of Later Seventeenth Century Scotland, 1947; Hume Brown's Short History of Scotland (rev. and ed.), 1951. Articles and reviews in periodicals. *Address:* 23 Riselaw Road, Edinburgh. *T.:* 52451. *Club:* New (Edinburgh). [*Died* 23 *May* 1958.

MELLANBY, Alexander Lawson, D.Sc., LL.D., Hon. M.I.Mech.E.; Emeritus Professor of Civil and Mechanical Engineering, The Royal Technical College, Glasgow; *b.* Hartlepool, 3 July 1871; *s.* of John Mellanby, shipyard manager, late of West Hartlepool; *m.* 1901, Annie W. Maunder of Newcastle-on-Tyne; two *s.* *Educ.:* Barnard Castle School; Armstrong College, Newcastle-on-Tyne; McGill University, Montreal. Apprenticeship at Central Marine Works, Hartlepool; after apprenticeship, entered Durham College of Science, obtained B.Sc. degree with honours, and was awarded 1851 Research Scholarship; entered McGill University for one year's research upon steam-engines, and passed another year in similar research at Newcastle; chief Technical Assistant at T. Richardson and Sons, engineers, Hartlepool, 1897; chief Lecturer in Engineering at Battersea Polytechnic, 1898; appointed to assist in designing the engineering equipment at Manchester School of Technology, and on completion of this work Lecturer in Engineering. *Publications:* The Relative Efficiencies of Multiple Expansion Engines (Royal Society of Canada); The Effects of Different Arrangements of Crank Angles upon the Efficiency of Quadruple Expansion Engines (North-East Coast Institute of Engineers); The Relative Efficiencies of Triple and Quadruple Expansion Engines (Manchester Association of Engineers); Steam Jackets (The Institution of Mechanical Engineers); Oil Fuel (Institution of Engineers in Scotland); Losses in Steam Nozzles (North-East Coast Inst. of Engineers). *Recreation:* golf. *Address:* Westwood, Bridge of Weir, Renfrewshire. [*Died* 26 *Nov.* 1951.

MELLANBY, Sir Edward, G.B.E., *cr.* 1948; K.C.B., *cr.* 1937; F.R.S. 1925; F.R.C.P.; Officier de la Légion d'Honneur (France) 1947; American Medal of Freedom with Silver Palm; Commander (1st Cl.) Swedish Royal Order of the North Star; Hon. F.R.C.S.E.; M.A., M.D. (Cantab.); Hon. Sc.D. (Cantab.); Hon. D.Sc. (Sheffield, Oxon, Belfast, Chicago, Oslo); Hon. LL.D. (Birmingham, Glasgow, St. Andrews, Melbourne); Hon. M.D. (Witwatersrand, Adelaide); Hon. Fellow, Danish Royal Academy of Science, 1947; Emeritus Prof. of Pharmacology, Univ. of Sheffield; Chm. Internat. Confs. for Standardization of Vitamins, 1931, 1934 and 1949; Chairman International Technical Commission on Nutrition; *b.* West Hartlepool, 1884; *s.* of late John Mellanby; *m.* 1914, May Tweedy, M.A., Sc.D., Hon.D.Sc. *Educ.:* Barnard Castle School; Emmanuel College, Cambridge (Scholar): St. Thomas's Hospital. Research Student of Emmanuel College, 1905-7; Walsingham Medal, 1907, Gedge Prize, 1908, Raymond Horton Smith Prize, 1915; Demonstrator of Physiology, St. Thomas's Hospital, 1909-11; Lecturer and later Professor of Physiology, London University (King's College for Women), 1913-20; Member of Medical Research Council, 1931-1933 (Secretary, 1933-49); late Fullerian Professor of Physiology Royal Institution; late Hon. Physician Sheffield Royal Infirmary; Oliver-Sharpey Lecturer, Royal College of Physicians, 1922; Stewart Prize for Medical Research, British Medical Association, 1924; Bissett-Hawkins Medal, Royal College of Physicians, 1929; Cameron Prize, Edinburgh University, 1932; Royal Medal, Royal Society, 1932; Croonian Lecturer, Royal College of Physicians, 1933; Linacre Lecturer, Cambridge, 1933; Charles Mickle Fellow, Toronto Univ., 1935; Moxon Medal, Royal Coll. of Physicians, 1936; Harveian Orator, Royal College of Physicians, 1938; Rede Lecturer, Cambridge Univ., 1939; Croonian Lecturer, Royal Society, 1943; Hon. Member Deutsche Akad. Naturf., Halle; Hon. Fellow: Emmanuel College, Camb., 1946; R. Soc. Med., 1947; Abraham Flexner Lecturer, Vanderbilt Univ., U.S.A. 1947; Buchanan Medal, Royal Society, 1947; Baly Medal, Royal College of Physicians, 1949; Withering Lecturer, Birmingham Univ., 1951. *Publications:* Nutrition and Disease, 1934; A Story of Nutritional

Research, 1950. Scientific publications of physiological, biochemical and medical nature. *Address:* 5 East Heath Road, Hampstead, N.W.3. *Club:* Athenæum. [*Died* 30 *Jan.* 1955.

MELLAND, Charles Herbert, M.D. (Lond.), F.R.C.P., B.Sc.; late Capt. R.A.M.C. (T.F.); Hon. Consulting Physician, Ancoats Hospital; Hon. Consulting Physician, The Royal Infirmary, Manchester; Hon. Physician National Association for the Feeble-minded; *b.* 20 Oct. 1872; *y. s.* of late Fredk. Melland, Surgeon, Manchester; *m.* 1906, Annie Dorothea (*d.* 1950), *o. d.* of L. C. E. Gee of Adelaide, S. Australia; one *s.* one *d.* *Educ.:* Manchester Grammar School and Owens College, Manchester; Universities of Vienna and Graz. 1st Class Honours, M.B. London University); Held Hospital Resident Posts, 1894-99; Consulting Physician since 1900; Director and Assistant Director of Clinical Laboratory, Manchester Royal Infirmary, 1901-1905; Medical Investigator for the Royal Commission on the Care and Control of the Feeble-minded 1906. *Publications:* Report on Feeble-mindedness and Epilepsy in Manchester, 1908; articles in medical journals. *Recreations:* walking, camping, cycling, botany, archæology. *Address:* 45 Parsonage Rd., Heaton Moor, Stockport. *T.:* Heaton 3445. [*Died* 8 *Jan.* 1953.

MELLERSH, Air Vice-Marshal Sir Francis John Williamson, K.B.E., *cr.* 1950 (C.B.E. 1945); A.F.C.; M.A.; retired; *b.* 22 September 1898; *s.* of late W. Francis Mellersh and Hilda E. Williamson; *m.* 1921, Mary Margaret Lee; one *s.* one *d.* *Educ.:* Cheltenham College. Royal Naval Air Service, 1916; Royal Air Force, 1918; Instructor to Oxford Univ. Air Squadron, 1929-33; Instructor R.A.F. Staff Coll., 1938-40; Air Commander, Strategic Air Force, Eastern Air Command (S.E.A.), 1944-1945; Commandant R.A.F. Staff College, Bulstrode, 1945-46; A.O.C. No. 91 Bomber Group, 1946-47; A.O.C. No. 21 Group, 1947-1948; A.O.A., H.Q. Air Force, Far East, 1948-49; A.O.C. Malaya, 1949-51; Air Officer in Charge of Administration, Bomber Command, 1951-52; Commandant-General of the Royal Air Force Regiment, and Inspector of Ground Combat Trg., 1952-54, retired. *Recreations:* golf, sailing. *Club:* R.A.F. [*Died* 25 *May* 1955.

MELLES, Major William Eugene, D.L. Staffs; *b.* 17 Jan. 1883; *e. s.* of late J. W. Melles of Gruline; *m.* 1932, Baroness Burton; no *c.* *Educ.:* Eton. High Sheriff of Staffordshire, 1943; J.P. Inverness-shire, 1944. *Address:* Dochfour, Inverness. *T.A.* and *T.:* Dochgarroch 2; Needwood House, Burton-on-Trent. *T.:* Hoar Cross 320. *Clubs:* Cavalry; New (Edinburgh). [*Died* 20 *Feb.* 1953.

MELLON, Rt. Rev. William H.; Bishop of Galloway, (R.C.), from 1943; *b.* Edinburgh, 6 Jan. 1877. *Educ.:* Blairs College; France; Rome. Ordained in Rome, 1902; nominated Coadjutor by Bulls of 21st August, 1935; consecrated in Edinburgh by Archbishop McDonald, O.S.B., 1935. *Address:* Candida Casa, Maxwelltown, Dumfries. *T.:* Dumfries 26. [*Died* 2 *Feb.* 1952.

MELLONE, Sydney Herbert; *s.* of late Rev. W. E. Mellone of Warrenpoint, Co. Down; *m.* Catherine Isabella, *d.* of late Rev. R. B. Drummond, Edinburgh; one *d.* *Educ.:* Univ. Coll., London; Univ. of Edinburgh; Manchester College, Oxford. Hibbert Scholar, 1894-97; graduated B.A. (London), 1890; D.Sc. (Edinburgh), 1895; M.A. (London), 1896; Minister, First Presbyterian Church, Holywood, County Down, 1898-1909; St. Mark's Chapel, Edinburgh, 1909-11; Lincoln Unitarian Church, 1930-39. Examiner in Philosophy, University of St. Andrews, 1899-1902; Univ. of London, 1902-6, 1930-33, 1940-53, 1955-56; Univ. of Edinburgh, 1907-10; in Psychology, Edinburgh, 1913-16; Principal, Unitarian Home Missionary College, Manchester, and Lecturer in the University of Manchester, 1911-21; Lecturer, Manchester College, Oxford, 1921-22, 1927-28; Editorial Adviser, Encyclopædia Britannica, 14th ed., 1928-29. *Publications:* Studies in Philosophical Criticism and Construction, 1897; Leaders of Religious Thought, 1902; Converging Lines of Religious Thought, 1903; Introductory Text-Book of Logic, 1903, 20th edit. 1945; Laws of Life, 1908; The Immortal Hope, 1911; Eternal Life Here and Hereafter, 1916; God and the World, 1919; Immortality and other articles in Hastings' Encyclopedia of Religion and Ethics; The New Testament and Modern Life, 1921; The Price of Progress, and other Essays, 1924; (with Miss M. Drummond) Elements of Psychology, 1907, 6th edition 1926; The Apocrypha: its Story and Message, 1927; Back to Realities, 1928; The Dawn of Modern Thought, 1930; Elements of Modern Logic, 1934; Western Christian Thought in the Middle Ages, 1935; Bearings of Psychology on Religion, 1939; Leaders of Early Christian Thought, 1954. *Address:* 50 Monkhams Drive, Woodford Green, Essex. [*Died* 16 *July* 1956.

MELLOR, Col. Robert Ramsden, C.B.E. 1919; T.D.; J.P.; *b.* 1870. Served European War, 1914-19, with 7th Bn. Duke of Wellington's Regt., T.A. (despatches); Col. 1922; J.P., W.R. Yorks, 1920; Divisional Commander, Huddersfield Division Special Constabulary, Yorkshire (West Riding); Chm., Mang. Dir. and Sec., B. Mellor & Son Ltd., Albert Mills, Holmfirth. *Address:* 103 Huddersfield Road, Holmfirth, Huddersfield, Yorks. *T.:* Holmfirth 97. *Club:* Huddersfield and County Conservative (Huddersfield). [*Died* 12 *Sept.* 1951.

MELVIN, Sir Martin John, 1st Bt., *cr.* 1933; Kt., *cr.* 1927; J.P.; LL.D.; Chairman of Ingall, Parsons, Clive & Co. Ltd.; of Charles Clifford & Sons, Ltd., and of Metallisation Ltd.; Chairman and Governing Director of Associated Catholic Newspapers (1912), Ltd.; Director, City Arcades, Ltd., Birmingham Rowton Houses Ltd.; *b.* 1879. *Educ.:* Mount St. Mary's College (Pres. of Coll. Assoc. 1917-18, Pres., 1941-42 Centenary year); Nantes. Raised large sums for War Charities, 1915-18; organised Finances and Supplies for Catholic Huts on the Western Front and at Home; as Chm., 1917-, of the Universe, founded the work of sending Catholic soldiers at the Front to Lourdes, 1918-19; a Governor of the Univ. of Birmingham, of St. Philip's Grammar School, and of St. Paul's High School; Chairman, 1930-32, Governor and Member of the Managing Board of the Birmingham General Hospital; Member of the Council of the Birmingham Chamber of Commerce; Chairman of Birmingham Catholic Reunions, 1916-19; Chairman of National Catholic Congress, 1923; President of the National Advertising Benevolent Society, 1933-34; *cr.* K.C.S.G. (Con Placca) by H.H. Benedict XV.; Knight Grand Cross of the Order of the Holy Sepulchre, 1917; G.C.S.G. 1921; Privy Chamberlain of Cape and Sword to H.H. since 1924. *Address:* Billesley Manor, Alcester, Warwickshire. *Club:* Carlton. [*Died* 11 *May* 1952 *(ext.)*.

MENCKEN, H. L.; *b.* Baltimore, 12 Sept. 1880; *s.* of August Mencken, cigar manufacturer; descendant of a line of professors of law and history at Leipzig, Halle, Helmstedt and Wittenberg; *m.* 1930, Sara Powell Haardt (*d.* 1935). *Educ.:* privately; Baltimore Polytechnic. Entered journalism at Baltimore, 1899; Chief Editor of Baltimore Herald at 25; on Staff of Baltimore Sun, 1906-41; War Correspondent for Sun, 1917; Political Correspondent; Literary Critic, The Smart Set, 1908-23; Editor, 1914-23; Contributing Editor, The Nation (New York), 1921-32; Editor, American Mercury, 1924-33; ex-Director, A. S. Abell Co., Publishers, and Baltimore Sun; ex-Director of Alfred A. Knopf, Inc., New York

Publications: Ventures into Verse, 1903; George Bernard Shaw: His Plays, 1905; The Philosophy of Friedrich Nietzsche, 1908; The Artist, 1912; A Book of Burlesques, 1916; A Little Book in C Major, 1916; A Book of Prefaces, 1917; In Defence of Women, 1917; Damn: a Book of Calumny, 1917; The American Language, 1918 (4th revised edition, 1936; Supplement I, 1945; Supplement II, 1948); Prejudices, six volumes, 1919, 1920, 1922, 1924, 1926, 1927; Notes on Democracy, 1926; Treatise on the Gods, 1930; revised ed., 1946; Making a President, 1932; Treatise on Right and Wrong, 1934; Happy Days, 1939; Newspaper Days, 1941; Heathen Days, 1943; Christmas Story, 1946; The Days of H. L. Mencken, 1947; (part author) Men v. the Man, 1910; Europe after 8.15, 1914; Heliogabalus, 1920; The American Credo, 1920; Civilization in the United States, 1922; Living Philosophies, 1931; The Sunpapers of Baltimore, 1937; I Believe, 1939; Editor: The Players' Ibsen, 1909; The Gist of Nietzsche, 1910; The Free Lance Books, 1919-22; Americana, 1925, 1926; The Charlatanry of the Learned, 1937; A New Dictionary of Quotations, 1942; A Mencken Chrestomathy, 1949; (translator) Nietzsche's The Antichrist. *Recreation:* music. *Address:* 1524 Hollins Street, Baltimore 23, U.S.A. *T.A.:* Baltimore; c/o Baltimore Sun, 40 Fleet Street, E.C. [*Died* 28 *Jan.* 1956.

MENDELSOHN, Eric, F.R.I.B.A.; A.I.A.; Architect; Lecturer, Graduate Class, University of California, Berkeley, 1947; *b.* 21 March 1887; *m.* 1915, Louisa Maas; one *d.* *Educ.:* Technical Universities, Berlin-Charlottenburg and Munich. Practice as Architect: Munich 1911, Berlin 1914-1933, London and Jerusalem 1933-41, New York 1941-45, San Francisco 1945; Main Buildings: Einstein Tower, Potsdam; Universum Cinema, Berlin; Schocken Department Store, Chemnitz; Columbus House, Berlin; De la Warr Pavilion, Bexhill; Hadassah University Medical Centre, Jerusalem; New Government Hosp., Haifa; Maimonides Hosp., San Francisco, 1948; Member Acad. of Arts, Berlin, 1930; Hon. member Internat. Arch. Soc., Japan, Mexican Inst. Arch. *Publications:* The International Conformity of the New Architecture—or Dynamics and Function, 1923; America—Architects Picture Book, 1925; Russia—Europe—America, An Architectural Section, 1928; The Creative Spirit of the World Crisis, 1932; Three Lectures on Architecture, 1942. *Address:* 627 Commercial Street, San Francisco 11, California. *T.:* Douglas 2-6346. [*Died* 15 *Sept.* 1953.

MENDL, Sir Charles, Kt., *cr.* 1924; *b.* 1871; *s.* of Jeanette Halford and Ferdinand Mendl; *m.* 1st, 1926, Elsie de Wolfe (*d.* 1950), of New York, U.S.A.; 2nd, 1951, Mme. Yvonne Reilly (*d.* 1956). *Educ.:* Harrow. Foreign Office, News Department since 1920; 25th Infantry Brigade, Sept. 1914; invalided out of Army, Feb. 1915 (1914 Star with bar); Work for Admiralty, 1918; Press Attaché British Embassy, Paris, 1926-40. *Address:* 1018 Benedict Canyon Drive, Beverly Hills, Cal., U.S.A. *Clubs:* St. James', Reform; Union (Paris). [*Died* 14 *Feb.* 1958.

MENENDEZ, Sir (Manuel) Raymond, Kt., *cr.* 1906; *b.* 4 July 1864; *m.* 1st, 1901, Hetty L. Tilyou (*d.* 1937), of Englewood, N.J.; 2nd, 1940, Mrs. Agnes Wilby, *widow* of Thomas W. Wilby. *Educ.:* privately; Emmanuel College, Cambridge (LL.B.); Barrister-at-law, Inner Temple. District Commissioner Lagos, 1894-7; Chief Judicial Officer Niger Coast Protectorate, 1897-1900, Puisne Judge, Southern Nigeria, 1900-5; Chief Justice of Northern Nigeria, 1905; retired, 1908; Chief Recruiting Officer, Wilts, 1915 to end of War; Hon. Major. *Recreations:* tennis, boating, golf. *Address:* Midford House, near Bath. [*Died* 1 *April* 1952.

MENGELBERG, Rudolf, Dr. Phil.; Composer, Musicologist; *b.* 1 Feb. 1892; *s.* of Heinrich Mengelberg, Krefeld, Germany. *m.* 1926, Eleonora Wubbe; one *s.* one *d.* *Educ.:* Krefeld; Geneva; Munich; Bonn; Leipzig. Artistic Adviser of the Concertgebouw, Amsterdam, 1917, Artistic Leader, 1925, Director, 1936-54. Chevalier Légion d'Honneur; Officier Oranje Nassau. *Publications:* Gustav Mahler (Biography), 1923; Holland as a Cultural Unity, 1928; Muziek, Spiegel des Tijds, 1948; numerous essays; Compositions for orchestra, choir, solo instruments, and many songs. *Address:* Schubertstr. 20, Amsterdam Z. *T.:* Amsterdam 26817. [*Died* 13 *Oct.* 1959.

MENNELL, George Gillies, C.B.E. 1937; late Staff Adviser to B.B.C.; *b.* 11 Feb. 1878; 2nd *s.* of late Zebulon Mennell, M.R.C.S., L.S.A., and late Jane Lilias Hudson, *yr. d.* of George Gillies; unmarried. *Educ.:* St. Paul's School; Worcester College, Oxford (Exhibitioner). Entered Civil Service by Open Competition (Class 1) and appointed to the Civil Service Commission, 1901; Assistant Secretary, 1915; Assistant Commissioner and Secretary, 1933-1941. Called to Bar, Lincoln's Inn, 1905. *Address:* 32 Hereford Square, S.W.7. *T.:* Fremantle 2848. *Club:* Oxford and Cambridge. [*Died* 11 *Feb.* 1959.

MENNELL, James Beaver; physician; *b.* 31 Jan. 1880; *y. s.* of late Zebulon Mennell, M.R.C.S.; *m.* 1912, Elisabeth Walton, *y. d.* of late George W. Allen of St. Louis, Missouri, U.S.A.; three *s.* *Educ.:* St. Paul's School; Pembroke College, Cambridge (Nat. Sci. Tripos, 1902); St. Thomas's Hospital. M.A. Cantab., 1907; M.R.C.S., L.R.C.P., 1908; M.B., B.C. Cantab., 1908; M.D., 1910; Consulting Physician in Physical Medicine, St. Thomas's Hospital; Consulting Physician B.R.C.S. Physical Treatment Centre, Kensington; past Member of Council of British Assn. of Physical Medicine; Life Governor St. Thomas's Hosp.; past Hon. Consultant Royal West Sussex Hospital, Chichester; Hon. Fellow Chartered Society of Physiotherapy; awarded Golden Key, American Congress of Physical Medicine, 1940; Hon. Member Netherlands Soc. of Physiotherapy, 1945; awarded Golden Key, American Physiotherapy Assoc., 1947; Past Pres. Section of Physical Medicine, R. Soc. Med., and Past Chairman Council of Chartered Soc. of Physiotherapy; Pres. Physio-Therapy Section Bi-lingual Congress of Radiology and Physiotherapy, 1922, and of the Section of Kinesitherapy of the International Congress of Physical Medicine, 1936; late Medical Officer in charge of the Physical-Therapy Dept. St. Thomas's Hospital and the Special Military Surgical Hospital, Shepherd's Bush. Late Casualty Assistant and Clinical Assistant, Physical Exercise Department; late Lecturer Physiotherapy Training School, St. Thomas's Hospital; Senior House Surgeon, St. Thomas's Hospital, and Resident Medical Officer, St. Thomas's Home, 1910-11. Visiting Associate Prof. of Physical Medicine Univ. of Southern California (Academic year 1947-1948). *Publications:* The Treatment of Fractures by Mobilisation and Massage; Physical Treatment by Movement, Manipulation and Massage (5th edition); Backache, 2nd edition; The Science and Art of Joint Manipulation (vol. I. The Extremities), 1939, (2nd Edn.), 1950; Vol. II. The Spinal Column, 1952. *Recreations:* golf, gardening. *Address:* Courts of the Morning, Rake, Liss, Hants. *T.:* Liss 2302; c/o Dr. Beauchamp, 119 Harley Street, W.1. *T.:* Welbeck 3088. *Club:* English-Speaking Union. [*Died* 2 *March* 1957.

MENNELL, Zebulon; Consulting Anaesthetist, St. Thomas's Hospital and National Hospital Paralysis and Epilepsy, Queen Square; *b.* London, 15 June 1876; *e. s.* of Z. Mennell, M.R.C.S., L.S.A., and Jane Lilias Hudson, *y. d.* of George Gillies; *m.* 1902,

Fanny Mabel (*d.* 1951), *o. d.* of William Arnold Lewis, Barrister, Inner Temple; three *d. Educ.:* St. Paul's School; St. Thomas's Hospital. M.B. Lond. 1901; F.F.A. R.C.S. Eng. 1948; M.R.C.S. Eng., L.R.C.P. Lond. 1900; D.A. Eng. 1935; (St. Thos.). Snow Medallist; Fell. Assoc. Anæsths. (Ex-Pres. and Treas. 12 years); Member B.M.A. (Ex-Pres. Sect. Anæsth. 1948, Vice-Pres. 1935); Fell. and Hon. Mem. Roy. Soc. Med. (Ex-Pres. Sect. Anæsth.; Life Fell. Med. Soc. Lond. (Councillor 6 years); Mem. Cent. Med. War Cttee.; Hon. Fell. Assoc. Anæsth. U.S. and Canada; Hon. Mem. Med. Soc. Anæsth. Australia; Embley Lect. Univ. Melb. 1935. Late Anæsth., Lect. Anæsth., Sen. Ho. Phys., Sen. Obst. Ho. Phys. and Clin. Asst. Ear and Throat Depts., St. Thos. Hosp.; Clin. Asst. W. London Hosp. and E. Lond. Hosp. for Childr. Shadwell; Mem. Standing and Case Cttee. Roy. Benev. Fund (12 years); Founding Mem. Harley Trust, London Clin. Capt. R.A.M.C., T., 1915-19. *Publications:* Chaps. Anæsthetics, Sargent & Russell's Emergencies of Gen. Pract.; Anæsthesia in Intra-Cranial Surgery, Proc. Roy. Soc. Med., 1922; Anæsthesia in Cerebral Surgery, Amer. Jl. Surg., 1924. Other communications to Medical Journals and Encyclopædias here and in U.S. and Australia. *Recreations:* fishing and golf. *Address:* Westways, Petworth, Sussex. *T.:* Petworth 3166. *Club:* Junior Carlton. [*Died* 20 *Jan.* 1959.

MENSFORTH, Sir Holberry, K.C.B., *cr.* 1923; C.B.E. 1918; M.Sc. (tech.); M.I.C.E., M.I.M.E.: Director of Tredegar Iron and Coal Co. Ltd., of Westland Aircraft Ltd., Yeovil, Somerset; A Vice-President of British Electrical and Allied Manufacturers Association; *b.* Bradford, Yorks, 1871; 2nd *s.* of Edward Mensforth, Bradford; *m.* Alice Maud (*d.* 1948), 3rd *d.* of William Jennings, Rossington, Yorks; two *s.* one *d. Educ.:* Bradford; privately. Pioneer installations in connection with Blast Furnace Gas; President Manchester Eng. Employees Association, 1919-20; Chairman Manchester District Armaments Output Committee; Director-General of Factories, War Office, 1920-26. *Address:* The Red House, Hazlemere, Bucks. *T.:* Penn 3133. [*Died* 5 *Sept.* 1951.

MENTETH, Sir William Frederick Stuart-, 5th Bart., *cr.* 1838; Member, Royal Company of Archers, the King's Bodyguard for Scotland; *b.* 18 June 1874; *s.* of 4th Bart. and Frances Octavia Moore (*d.* 1887), *d.* of Gen. Sir James Wallace Sleigh, K.C.B.; *S.* father, 1926; *m.* 1921, Winifred Melville, *d.* of Daniel Francis and *widow* of Capt. Rupert G. Raw, D.S.O.; two *s.* one *d. Heir: s.* James Wallace [*b.* 1922; *m.* 1949, Dorothy Patricia, *d.* of late Frank Grieves Warburton; one *s.*]. *Address:* Mansfield House, New Cumnock, Ayrshire. *T.:* New Cumnock 230. *Club:* New (Edinburgh). [*Died* 20 *Feb.* 1952.

MENZIES, George Kenneth, C.B.E. 1932; M.A.; *b.* 1869; *y. s.* of James Menzies; *m.* Mary Strathearn Gordon, *y. d.* of John Burnet, Advocate, Edinburgh. *Educ.:* St. Andrews University; Balliol College, Oxford. Assistant to Professor of Greek, St. Andrews University, 1893-96; Private Secretary to Sir William Dunn, Bt., M.P., 1896-1904; Secretary in Academic Department, University of London, 1904-8; Assistant Secretary Royal Society of Arts, 1908-17, Sec. 1917-35, a Vice-President, 1941-. *Publications:* Story of the Royal Society of Arts, 1935; for twenty years regular outside contributor to Punch, etc. *Address:* Upland Cottage, Marley Heights, Haslemere. *T.:* Haslemere 318. *Club:* Savage. [*Died* 12 *March* 1954.

MENZIES, Thomas Graham, C.B.E. 1919; M.I.C.E.; *b.* 1869; *s.* of Thomas Hunter Menzies, Edinburgh; *m.* 1909, Dorothy Frances, *d.* of Cornelius Horne, Kew Gardens. *Educ.:* Heriot-Watt College, Edinburgh. Director of Special Construction, Civil Engineer-in-Chief's Dept., Admiralty, 1917-19; a Chief Civil Engineer, Min. of Transport, 1919-21. *Address:* 26 Copse Hill, S.W.20. *T.:* Wimbledon 3570. [*Died* 5 *July* 1958.

MERCER, Maj. Cecil William; author, writes under name of Dornford Yates; *b.* 7 Aug. 1885; *o. s.* of late Cecil John Mercer, Solicitor King's Bench Walk, and Helen, *y. d.* of late W. H. Wall, Pembury, Kent; *m.* 1st, 1919, Bettine Stokes (whom he divorced, 1933), *e. d.* of late Robert Ewing Edwards, Philadelphia; one *s.*; 2nd, 1934, Elizabeth, *y. d.* of late D. M. Bowie, and late Mrs. Bowie, Virginia Water. *Educ.:* Harrow; University College, Oxford, M.A. President Oxford University Dramatic Society, 1906-7; Barrister Inner Temple, 1909; 2nd Lieutenant 3rd County of London Yeomanry, 1914; served Egypt, 1915-16; Salonica, 1916-17; O.C. Signals 8th Mounted Brigade, 1916-17; Captain, 1918; retired, 1925; recommissioned, 1942; served East Africa Command, 1942-43; S. Rhodesia Mil. Forces, 1944; Major, 1944. *Publications:* The Brother of Daphne; The Courts of Idleness; Berry and Co.; Jonah and Co.; Anthony Lyveden; Valerie French; And Five were Foolish; As Other Men Are; The Stolen March; Blind Corner; Perishable Goods; Maiden Stakes; Blood Royal; Fire Below; Adèle and Co.; Safe Custody; Storm Music; She Fell Among Thieves; And Berry Came Too; She Painted Her Face; This Publican; Gale Warning; Shoal Water; Period Stuff; An Eye for a Tooth; The House that Berry Built; Red in the Morning, 1946; The Berry Scene, 1947; Cost Price, 1949; Lower Than Vermin, 1950; As Berry and I Were Saying, 1952; Ne'er-do-well, 1954; Wife Apparent, 1956; B-Berry and I Look Back, 1958. *Recreations:* travelling, motoring. *Address:* Oak Avenue, Umtali, Southern Rhodesia. *Clubs:* Cavalry, Bath. [*Died* 5 *March* 1960.

MEREDITH, George Thomas; Recorder of West Bromwich since 1951; *b.* 11 September 1907; *s.* of George William and Edith Meredith; *m.* 1942, Ivy Lilian Hubbard; one *s.* one *d. Educ.:* King Edward's School, Birmingham; Trinity Hall, Cambridge. Called to Bar, Gray's Inn, 1932; Recorder of Ludlow, 1945-51. Member of Oxford Circuit. *Address:* 24 Temple Row, Birmingham. *T.:* Central 5771. *Club:* Union (Birmingham). [*Died* 3 *May* 1959.

MEREDITH, Sir Herbert Ribton, Kt., *cr.* 1947; Chairman, Central and Coast Rent Control Boards, Kenya, 1951; *b.* 8 April 1890; *s.* of F. W. Meredith, Dublin; *m.* 1929, Lorna, *d.* of R. D. Sandes; one *s.* two *d. Educ.:* Trinity Coll., Dublin (Wray prize for Mental and Moral Philosophy, B.A. with first place Senior Moderatorship, and large gold medal Mental and Moral Philosophy). Joined Indian Civil Service, 1914; District and Sessions Judge, 1931; Registrar Patna High Court, 1932; Legal Remembrancer and Judicial Secretary to Govt., 1934; Puisne Judge, Patna High Court, Bihar, 1940; Chief Justice Patna High Court, Jan. 1950; retired Apr. 1950. President Bihar Flying Club, 1941-42. *Recreations:* shooting, fishing, golf. *Address:* P.O. Box 3807, Nairobi, Kenya, East Africa. *Clubs:* Karen, Mombasa (Kenya). [*Died* 1 *May* 1959.

MEREDITH, Richard, C.S.I. 1919; C.I.E. 1914; *b.* 21 May 1867; *e. s.* of late Sir James Creed Meredith; *m.* 1st, 1892, Ada Louise (*d.* 1920), *y. d.* of Alfred Hancock Middleton, Athgoe Park, Shankill; 2nd, 1922, Eleanor Mary, *widow* of B. M. Samuelson, C.I.E. *Educ.:* Royal School, Armagh; Trinity College, Dublin; R.I.E. College. Assistant Superintendent, Indian Telegraph Dept., 1889; Superintendent, 1901; Director of Telegraphs, Eastern Bengal and Assam, 1910-11; of Construction, 1911-13; Dep. Director-General, Telegraph Traffic, 1914-1916; Chief Engineer, Telegraphs, 1916; retired

1922; served Burma, 1891 (medal and clasp); Chitral Relief Force, 1895 (medal and clasp). *Address:* 6 Clarence Crescent, Windsor. [*Died* 4 *Jan.* 1957.

MEREDYTH, Capt. Arthur Gwynn Moreton, C.B.E. 1919; R.N., retired as Capt., 1908; *s.* of late Rev. T. E. Meredyth; *b.* 1862; *m.* 1898, Daisy (*d.* 1952), *o. c.* of late Capt. W. R. Boulton, R.N. Served European War, 1914-15 as Captain, H.M.S. Imperieuse, Depot ship, and King's Harbour-Master of Scapa Flow, thereafter, 1915-19 was Senior Naval Officer, Thurso (despatches, C.B.E.). *Club:* Royal Naval (Portsmouth). [*Died* 13 *Dec.* 1955.

MEREZHKOVSKI, Dmitri Sergeievich; Russian novelist and critic; *b.* St. Petersburg, 14 Aug. 1865. The author died in Paris. *Publications:* The Death of the Gods, 1901; The Birth of the Gods, 1926; Akhnaton, King of Egypt; December the Fourteenth; The Life of Napoleon; The Secret of the West, 1928 (and later publications in different countries); Napoleon, a Study, 1929; Michael Angelo and other sketches, 1930; The Romance of Leonardo da Vinci, 1931; Jesus the Unknown, 1934; Jesus Manifest, 1935, etc. [*Died* 9 *Dec.* 1941.

[*But death not notified in time for inclusion in Who Was Who* 1941–1950, *first edn.*

MERRETT, Sir Herbert, Kt., *cr.* 1950; J.P.; *b.* 18 December 1886; *s.* of Lewis and Elizabeth Merrett; *m.* 1911, Marion Linda Higgins; two *d.* (and one *s.* decd.). *Educ.:* Cardiff. J.P. for County of Glamorgan; High Sheriff for Glamorgan, 1934-1935. President: British Coal Exporters' Federation, 1946-48; Cardiff Incorp. Chamber of Commerce, 1935-36; Glamorgan County Cricket Club; Cardiff City Assoc. Football Club; Chm. Post Office Advisory Committee for South Wales, 1936-; Member Court of Governors of University College of S. Wales and Monmouthshire. Chevalier de la Légion d'Honneur. *Publication:* I Fight for Coal, 1932. *Recreations:* farming, golf, fishing. *Address:* Cwrt-yr-Ala, nr. Cardiff. *T.:* Dinas Powis 3177. *Club:* Cardiff and County (Cardiff). [*Died* 3 *Oct.* 1959.

MERRINGTON, Rev. Ernest Northcroft, E.D. 1940; M.A. (Sydney); Ph.D. (Harvard); F.R.G.S.(A.); Pres., Dominion Council of the U.N.A. of New Zealand, 1945-49; Master of Knox College, Dunedin, 1929-41; formerly Minister of the First Church of Otago (Presbyterian), Dunedin; *b.* Newcastle, N.S.W., 27 Aug. 1876; *s.* of James Mayfield Merrington, merchant; *m.* Flora, *d.* of Neil Livingston, Sydney; one *s.* two *d.* *Educ.:* Universities of Sydney, Edinburgh and Harvard. Medallist at M.A. in Philosophy, Sydney University, and Woolley Travelling Scholar (Syd.); after completing Theological course in St. Andrew's College, Sydney, studied at Edinburgh University, Prizeman in Mental and Moral Philosophy Classes, 1904; also studied at New College, Edinburgh; studied at Harvard Graduate School (Ph.D. 1905); Pastorates at Kiama and Haberfield, N.S.W.; lectured in Philosophy at Sydney University, 1907-9; inducted St. Andrew's Church, Brisbane, Queensland, 1910; Convener of Committee that founded Emmanuel College, affiliated to University of Queensland; served on Theological Lecturing Staff, and also on Senate of the University of Queensland, 1916-23; Chaplain (1st Class) with Australian Imperial Force; served Egypt, Gallipoli, England and France; Moderator, General Assembly (Queensland), 1916-17; Examiner in Philosophy, University of New Zealand, 1924-25; N.Z. Delegate to Conference, Institute of Pacific Relations, Yosemite, U.S.A.; and Official Representative of University of Queensland at Harvard Tercentenary Celebration, 1936. *Publications:* The Possibility of a Science of Casuistry, 1902; The Problem of Personality, 1916; A Great Coloniser, Life of the Rev. Dr. T. Burns, 1930; Hymn for the Church Overseas. *Address:* 4 Papawai Terrace, Wellington, N.Z. [*Died* 26 *March* 1953.

MERRIVALE, 2nd Baron, *cr.* 1925, of Walkhampton, Co. Devon; **Edward Duke,** O.B.E. 1919; J.P., County of Devon, 1942; Deputy Chairman, Devon Quarter Sessions, 1947; *b.* 1883; *o. s.* of 1st Baron Merrivale, P.C., and Sarah (*d.* 1914), *d.* of late John Shorland, Shrewsbury; *S.* father, 1939; *m.* 1st, 1912, Odette (marriage dissolved, 1939), *d.* of Edmund Roger, Paris; one *s.* one *d.*; 2nd, 1939, Meta T., *d.* of Joseph H. Wolczon, Danzig. *Educ.:* Dulwich; Neuchatel. Served South African War, 1900-2; European War, 1914-19; A.P.M. to 24th Division, and Intelligence Dept. at War Office (O.B.E.); called to Bar, Gray's Inn, 1908; Secretary to President, P.D. and A. Division, Royal Courts of Justice, 1919-33. *Heir:* *s.* Hon. Jack Henry Edmond Duke [*b.* 27 Jan. 1917; *m.* 1939, Colette Wise; one *s.* [*b.* 16 March 1948) one *d.* Joined R.A.F. 1941]. *Address:* 9 Belle Vue Rd., Paignton, S. Devon. [*Died* 8 *June* 1951.

MERSEY, 2nd Viscount, *cr.* 1916, of Toxteth; **Charles Clive Bigham,** P.C. 1946; C.M.G. 1901; C.B.E. 1919; F.S.A.; Baron, *cr.* 1910; J.P., D.L. London; J.P. Sussex; a Deputy Speaker, House of Lords, since 1933, Deputy Chairman of Committees; formerly Director, National Provident Institution; *b.* 18 Aug. 1872; *e. s.* of 1st Viscount and Georgina (*d.* 1925), *d.* of late John Rogers, Liverpool; *S.* father, 1929; *m.* 1904, Mary, *d.* of late Horace Seymour, C.B. (nominated, but not invested, a K.C.B.); three *s.* one *d.* *Educ.:* Eton (King's Scholar); Sandhurst. Lieutenant Grenadier Guards, 1892; Captain Reserve of Officers, 1902; Brevet Major, 1918; Lt.-Col. 1919; Hon. Attaché, British Embassies, Petrograd, 1896; Constantinople, 1897; Peking, 1899; special correspondent for the Times with Ottoman army in Greco-Turkish War, 1897 (medal); British Delegate on the International Commission in Thessaly for Repatriation of Refugees, 1897-98; Intelligence Officer to Admiral of the Fleet Sir E. H. Seymour, G.C.B., in Peking Expedition, 1900 (despatches, medal and clasp); A.D.C. to Lord-Lieutenant of Ireland, 1901-2; attached Military Intelligence Div. General Staff, 1901-4; and to Commercial Dept., Board of Trade, 1905-9; Secretary to Royal Commissions, 1905-12; Brigade Major, Brigade of Guards, 1914; Provost Marshal Dardanelles Expedition and Military Attaché, Egypt, 1915 (2 medals, 1915 Star); General Staff Officer (1st grade) commanding Military Mission to French War Office, 1916-19 (despatches, Officer of Legion of Honour and Crown of Italy); specially attached to British Delegation, Paris Peace Conference, 1919; Member East Africa Joint Parliamentary Committee, 1930; a British Delegate, Burma Round Table Conference, 1931-32. Chairman: Royal Westminster Ophthalmic Hosp., 1935-46, and Westminster (St. George's) Bench, 1935-47; A Trustee of National Portrait Gallery, 1941-48. Pres. Sussex Archæological Society, 1947-50, and of Genealogists Soc., 1942-. Chief Liberal Whip, 1944-49. Chairman D.L. Territorials Committee for Westminster, 1951-. For many years a director of Gas, Light & Coke, Boots Pure Drug, Sea Insurance, & Mercantile Investment Cos.; K.St.J. *Publications:* A Ride through Western Asia, 1897; With the Turkish Army in Thessaly, 1897; A Year in China, 1901; The Prime Ministers of Britain, 1922; The Chief Ministers of England, 1923; The Kings of England, 1929; A Picture of Life, 1872-1940, 1941; Alexander of Macedon, 1946; Helen of Troy and Cleopatra, 1947; The Viceroys and Governors-General of India, 1747-1947, 1949; Journal and Memories, 1952. *Heir:* *s.* Hon. Edward Clive Bigham. *Address:* 22 Eaton Place, S.W.1; Bignor Park, Pulborough. *Clubs:* Brooks's, Beefsteak, Royal Automobile. [*Died* 20 *Nov.* 1956.

MESSER, Allan Ernest, C.B.E. 1937; M.A., late Senior Partner, Lawrance, Messer and Co., Solicitors, 16 Coleman Street; *b.* 4 Sept. 1865; *s.* of John Messer, J.P. Reading; *m.* 1893, Louise Ord (*d.* 1951), *d.* of Judge S. W. Holladay, San Francisco; one *d.* *Educ.:* Reading; St. John's College, Oxford (White Foundation Scholar), 1st Class Math. Mods. 2nd Class Law Finals, rowed in winning Trial Eight 1886. Articled as Solicitor to late W. J. Bruty 1887; admitted Solicitor 1891; practised at Georgetown, British Guiana 1892-1900 but had to leave the Colony owing to ill-health; took over the business of Lawrance and Webster 1901; during the war was Legal Adviser in the Ministry of Munitions; until 1941 was Secretary and Agent of the Administrative Trustees of the Chequers Trust under the Chequers Estate Act 1917; Director, Guildhall Insurance Co. Ltd. *Recreations:* yachting, fishing, golf. *Address:* Weald Edge, Seale Hill, Reigate. *T.:* Reigate 3755. *Clubs:* Royal Thames Yacht, Royal Corinthian Yacht (Vice-Commodore 1912-19), Royal Cruising, Leander, London Rowing, West Indian; Worplesdon Golf. [*Died* 4 *June* 1954.

METCALFE, Sir Aubrey; *see* Metcalfe, Sir H. A. F.

METCALFE, Major Edward Dudley, M.V.O. 1922; M.C. 1916; late D.Y.O. Skinner's Horse; *o. s.* of Edward Metcalfe, late I.C.S., Dublin Castle, Ireland; *m.* Lady Alexandra Curzon, *y. d.* of late Marquess Curzon of Kedleston; one *s.* twin *d.* *Educ.:* private; Trinity College, Dublin, B.A. 1907. Joined 3rd Bengal Cavalry, 1909; Adjutant to the Governor of Bombay's Bodyguard, 1914; served European War, France and Mesopotamia, 1914-18 (despatches, M.C.); Waziristan Campaign, 1919-21; A.D.C. to the Prince of Wales for Indian and Japanese Tours, 1921-1922; temp. Equerry to the Prince of Wales, 1923; A.D.C. to the Com.-in-Chief in India, 1925-26; retired, 1927; served France, 1939-40, as A.D.C. to the Duke of Windsor; joined R.A.F. 1940; *Recreations:* hunting, tennis, golf, etc. *Address:* St. James' Court, Buckingham Gate, S.W.1. *T.:* Victoria 2360. *Clubs:* White's, Buck's. [*Died* 18 *Nov.* 1957.

METCALFE, Sir (Herbert) Aubrey (Francis), K.C.I.E., *cr.* 1936 (C.I.E. 1928); C.S.I. 1933; M.V.O. 1922; I.C.S. (retired); *b.* 1883; *s.* of Captain G. J. Metcalfe; *m.* 1918, Joyce (*d.* 1956), *d.* of John Wilson Potter; two *s.* *Educ.:* Charterhouse; Christ Church, Oxford. Entered I.C.S., 1908; served in Punjab and Delhi Province till 1914; Assistant Private Secretary to Viceroy, 1914-17; served in Political Department in N.W.F. Province; Deputy Secretary, Foreign and Political Department, 1930-32; Foreign Secretary to Government of India, 1932-39; Resident and Chief Commissioner in Baluchistan, 1939-43. *Address:* Carrig, Caragh Lake, Co. Kerry, Eire. *Club:* Travellers'. [*Died* 27 *Sept.* 1957.

METHOLD, Sir Henry Tindal, Kt., *cr.* 1938; J.P.; The Master in Lunacy, 1928-44; *b.* 24 April 1869; *s.* of Thomas Tindal Methold, Barrister-at-law, Bencher of Lincoln's Inn, and Mary Ellen, *e. d.* of Rev. Edward James, Rector of Hindringham, Norfolk; *m.* 1st, 1904, Sybil Mary (*d.* 1932) *er.d.* of late Robert C. Antrobus; one *s.* two *d.*; 2nd, 1934, Daisy Emily, *o. d.* of A. R. Mackmin. *Educ.:* Eton College; Trinity College, Cambridge, LL.B. Called to Bar, Lincoln's Inn, 1894, Bencher, 1930, Treas., 1952. *Address:* 24 Old Buildings, Lincoln's Inn, W.C.2. *T.:* Holborn 0191; Bradfield House, Bradfield Combust, Bury St. Edmunds, Suffolk. *T.:* Sicklesmere 236. [*Died* 29 *Jan.* 1952.

MEWBURN, Maj.-Gen. Hon. Sydney Chilton, P.C.; C.M.G. 1917; Q.C. 1910; member of the firm, Mewburn & Marshall, Barristers and Solicitors, Pigott Building, Hamilton, Ontario; Vice-Pres.: Mutual Life Assurance Co. of Canada; Director: Steel Co. of Canada, Ltd., Roy. Trust Co., Bell Telephone Co. of Canada, Dominion Glass Co. Ltd.; formerly Director, Bank of Montreal; *b.* Hamilton, 4 Dec. 1863; *s.* of Thomas Chilton Mewburn, Inspector of Customs, Hamilton, and Rachel Amanda Cory; *m.* 1888, Mary Caroline (*d.* 1952), *d.* of John K. Labatt; one *s.* (*er. s.* killed in action, 1916) one *d.* *Educ.:* Public and High Schools, Hamilton; Osgoode Hall, Toronto. Called to Ontario Bar, 1885; represented East Hamilton, House of Commons, 1917-26; Minister of Militia and Defence for Canada, 1917-20; joined the 13th Royal Regiment as a private, 1881; Lieut.-Col. commanding the regiment, 1910; holds Long Service Decoration; Brigade-Major, 5th Infantry Brigade, for five years; Brigadier, 4th Infantry Brigade; Brigade-Major at Quebec Tercentenary Celebration; Assistant Adjutant-General, Military District No. 2, at Toronto, 1915; Director-General, Canadian Defence Force, at Ottawa, 1917; Acting Adjutant-General, Ottawa, 1917. *Address:* 65 Markland Street, Hamilton, Ont. *Clubs:* Canadian, Hamilton, Tamahaac (Hamilton); Mount Royal (Montreal). [*Died* 11 *Aug.* 1956.

MEYER, Eugene; Newspaper executive; *b.* Los Angeles, Calif., 31 Oct. 1875; *s.* of Eugene Meyer and Harriet Newmark; *m.* 1910, Agnes Elizabeth Ernst; one *s.* four *d.* *Educ.:* public schools of San Francisco; Univ. of California, 1892-93; Yale Univ. (A.B. 1895); nearly 2 yrs. in Europe studying languages and banking. LL.D. Yale 1932, Syracuse Univ. 1934, Univ. of California, 1942; Yale Medal, 1954. Head of firm of Eugene Meyer, Jr. & Co., New York, 1901-17 and dir. of many corporations until resigned in 1917 to enter Government service. Adviser on Non-Ferrous Metals to Advisory Commission of the Council of National Defense, 1917, and later had charge of the Division of Non-Ferrous Metals of the War Industries Board; also a Special Assistant to the Secretary of War in connection with aircraft production, 1918. Appointed Director of War Finance Corporation by President Wilson, 1918; re-appointed by President Harding, 1921, and by President Coolidge, 1925; Managing Director, 1919-20 and 1921-1929; Federal Farm Loan Commissioner, 1927-29. Governor of Federal Reserve Board, by appointment of Pres. Hoover, 1930-33; also first Chairman of Board of Directors of Reconstruction Finance Corporation, Feb.-July 1932; Member National Defense Mediation Board, by appointment of Pres. Roosevelt, 1941-42; Member, Newspaper Industry Advisory Comm. War Production Board, 1943-46; Vice-Chairman of President Truman's Famine Emergency Committee, March-June 1946. President, National Committee for Mental Hygiene, 1944-1946; First President, International Bank for Reconstruction and Development, June-Dec. 1946; Publisher, The Washington Post, 1933-40, and Editor and Publisher, 1940-46; Chairman of Board, The Washington Post Co., 1947-; Dir., Allied Chemical Corp.; Hon. Trustee, Cttee. for Economic Development; Councillor, Nat. Industrial Conf. Bd.; Mem. Amer. Soc. of Newspaper Editors, Council on Foreign Relations, Public Policy Cttee. of The Advertising Council, Inc. *Address:* The Washington Post and Times-Herald, 1515 L. St., N.W., Washington, 5, D.C. *T.:* Republic 7-1234; 20 Pine St., New York. *T.:* Whitehall 3-5145. *Clubs:* Players, Grolier, Recess, Yale (New York); Metropolitan, Cosmos, University, Burning Tree, National Press, Army and Navy Country (Washington). [*Died* 17 *July* 1959.

MEYERHOF, Professor Otto; Research Professor of Biochemistry, School of Medicine, Univ. of Pennsylvania, Philadelphia, since 1940; *b.* Hannover, 12 April 1884; *s.* of Felix Meyerhof, merchant, and Bettina May; *m.* 1914, Hedwig Schallenberg; three *c.* *Educ.:* Kgl. Wilhelmsgymnasium, Berlin. Dr. med. Heidelberg, 1909; Privatdocent, Universität

Kiel, 1913; Professor-Titel 1918 (Kiel); Assistent am physiolog. Institut, Kiel, 1915-24; Mitglied des Kaiser Wilhelm Instituts für Biologie Berlin, Dahlem, 1924-29; Director of the Kaiser Wilhelm Institute of Physiology, Heidelberg, 1929-38; Directeur de Recherche, Institut de Biologie, Paris, 1938-40; Nobel prize Laureate in Medicine, 1923; LL.D. (hon.) University, Edinburgh, 1927; Foreign Member of Royal Society (Lond.), 1937; corresponding member of the Royal Academy of Medicine, Rome, and Société de Biologie, Paris, biolog. Gesellschaft, Wien; foreign member, Max-Planckges. Göttingen, Akademie d. Wiss., Heidelberg, Germany; hon. member of the Societá biologia, Rome, Harvey Society New York and Virchow Society, New York; Member National Academy of Sciences, Washington, D.C.; Fraternity Sigma Xi. *Publications:* Respiration and Fermentation of Cells; Energy Transformation and Chemistry of Muscle; Enzyme Reactions, in Pflügers Arch. für Physiol. und Biochem. Z., 1909-37; Die chemischen Vorgänge im Muskel, 1930; English: Chemical Dynamics of Life Phenomena (Philadelphia, 1924); Chemical Studies on Muscle, Jour. of General Physiology, 1926 (Memorial Volume of Jacques Loeb); Nature, 1933 (p. 337 and 373); Jour. Biol. Chem. 1942-51; Archives of Biochemistry, 1945-51; Biolog. Symposia, Vols. 3 and 5, 1942, etc. *Address:* Hamilton Court Apts., C. 101 Chestnutstr/39th Street, Philadelphia 4, Pa., U.S.A. *T.:* Baring 2-0158. [*Died* 6 *Oct.* 1951.

MEYERSTEIN, Edward Harry William, M.A., F.R.S.L.; *b.* Hampstead, 11 Aug. 1889; *o. s.* of late Sir Edward William Meyerstein and late Jessy Louise Solomon. *Educ.:* Harrow School; Magdalen College, Oxford. Assistant, Dept. of MSS. British Museum, 1913-18; Pte. Royal Dublin Fusiliers, 1914. *Publications: poetry:* The Door, 1911; recent volumes: Selected Poems, 1935, New Odes, 1936, A Boy of Clare, 1937, Briancourt, 1937; The Elegies of Propertius done into English verse, 1935 Sonnets, 1939; Eclogues, 1940; The Visionary, 1941; In Time of War, 1942; Azure, 1944; Division, 1946; Three Sonatas, 1948; Quartets for four Voices, 1949; The Delphic Charioteer, 1951; *novels:* Terence Duke, 1935, Séraphine, 1936, Joshua Slade, 1938, Robin Wastraw, 1951, Tom Tallion, 1952; *Plays:* Heddon, 1921; The Monument, 1923; *short stories:* The Pageant and other stories, 1934; Four People, 1939; *biography:* A life of Thomas Chatterton, 1930. Ed. Coxere, Adventures by Sea, 1945. *Recreations:* walking, music, research. *Address:* 3 Gray's Inn Place, W.C.1. *Club:* Athenæum. [*Died* 12 *Sept.* 1952.

MEYNELL, Esther Hallam; (E. Hallam Moorhouse); *e. d.* of Samuel Moorhouse; *m.* Gerard Tuke Meynell; two *d. Educ.:* home. Received into Catholic Church, 1931. *Publications:* Nelson's Lady Hamilton, 1906; Samuel Pepys: Administrator, Observer, Gossip, 1909; Letters of the English Seamen, 1910; Wordsworth (Regent Library), 1911; Nelson in England: A Domestic Chronicle, 1913; Sea Magic, 1916; The Story of Hans Andersen, 1924; The Little Chronicle of Magdalena Bach, 1925; Grave Fairytale, 1931; Quintet, 1933; Bach (Great Lives), 1933; Time's Door, 1935; Sussex Cottage, 1936; Building a Cottage, 1937; Lucy and Amades, 1938; English Spinster: a Portrait, 1939; A Woman Talking, 1940; Country Ways, 1942; The Young Lincoln, 1944; Cottage Tale, 1945; Sussex (County Books), 1947; Portrait of William Morris, 1947; Tale Told to Terry, 1950; Small Talk in Sussex, 1954. *Address:* Conds Cottage, Ditchling, Sussex. [*Died* 4 *Feb.* 1955.

MEYNELL, Sir Everard Charles, Kt., *cr.* 1946; O.B.E. 1918; M.C.; *b.* 19 June 1885; *s.* of Hon. Frederick and Lady Mary Meynell; *m.* 1914, Rose Bulteel; one *s.* two *d. Educ.:* Christ Church, Oxford. Entered Baring Brothers & Co. Ltd. 1910, subsequently going out to Buenos Aires on their behalf. Joined North Midland Brigade R.F.A., T.F. Aug. 1914, subsequently served in France and in 1917 served as D.A.Q.M.G. 58th London Division, temp. Major (O.B.E., M.C.); demobilised in 1919; returned to Buenos Aires; partner in Leng, Roberts & Co. and later Roberts, Meynell & Co. Acted as representative of H.M. Treasury and Bank of England in Buenos Aires, Sept. 1939-April 1946. *Recreations:* golf, shooting. *Address:* Yewden Manor, Henley-on-Thames, Oxon. *T.:* Hambleden (Bucks) 222. *Clubs:* Brooks's, Bath. [*Died* 22 *May* 1956.

MEYNELL, Viola; novelist; 3rd *d.* of late Wilfrid Meynell, C.B.E., and late Alice Meynell; *m.* 1922, John Dallyn; one *s. Publications:* Alice Meynell, a Memoir, 1929; The Frozen Ocean and other Poems, 1931; editor of Friends of a Life-time, 1940, and The Best of Friends, 1955; author of many novels; First Love, short stories, 1947; Ophelia, 1951; Francis Thompson and Wilfred Meynell: a Memoir, 1952; Louise and other stories, 1954. Collected Short Stories, 1956. *Address:* Humphrey's, Greatham, Pulborough, Sussex. [*Died* 27 *Oct.* 1956.

MEYRICK, Major Sir George Llewelyn Tapps-Gervis-, 5th Bt., *cr.* 1791; D.L. Anglesey; J.P. Hants; late 7th Hussars; *b.* 23 September 1885; *e. s.* of Sir George Meyrick, 4th Bt., and Jacintha (*d.* 1938), *d.* of C. Phipps; *S.* father, 1928; *m.* 1914, Marjorie, *o. c.* of E. Hamlin, Ceylon; one *s.* one *d. Educ.:* Eton; R.M.C., Sandhurst. Served European War with Royal Horse Guards, 1914-19; Sheriff of Anglesey, 1939. *Heir: s.* George David Elliott, Lt.-Col. 9th Lancers [*b.* 15 Apr. 1915; *m.* 1940, Ann, *d.* of Clive Miller; one *s.* one *d.*]. *Address:* Hinton Admiral, Christchurch, Hants; Bodorgan, Isle of Anglesey. *Clubs:* Cavalry, Buck's. [*Died* 22 *April* 1960.

MEYSEY-THOMPSON, Hubert Charles, C.B.E. 1950; Lord Chancellor's Visitor, 1928-1955; *b.* 1883; *o. s.* of late Albert Childers Meysey-Thompson, Q.C.; *heir-pres.* to Capt. Sir Algar de Clifford Charles Meysey-Thompson, 3rd Bt.; *m.* 1936, Millicent Mary, *d.* of late Edmond Wallace Blake. *Educ.:* Marlborough; Trinity College, Cambridge. B.A. 1905. Called to the Bar, Inner Temple, Hilary Term, 1907, and practised on the North-Eastern Circuit. Joined Inns of Court O.T.C., 1914; served European War, 1914-18, commissioned in 2/4th Royal Berkshire Regt., 1914; transferred to 21st (S) Bn., K.R.R.C., 1916, and served in Flanders and France; Actg. Capt., 1917 (wounded). Pres. of Pensions Appeal Tribunal for England and Wales, 1924. *Recreations:* fishing, shooting, tennis, golf. *Address:* Chestnut House, Long Melford, Sudbury, Suffolk. *T.:* Long Melford 281. *Clubs:* Travellers', Leander, M.C.C.; Royal Tennis Court (Hampton Court). [*Died* 9 *Nov.* 1956.

MICHAEL, Rev. J. Hugh, M.A., D.D.; Prof. of New Testament Exegesis and Literature in Emmanuel College in Victoria Univ., Toronto (federated with the University of Toronto), 1913-43, Professor-Emeritus, 1943; *b.* 9 Aug. 1878; *s.* of late Thomas and Kate Michael, Port Dinorwic, N. Wales; *m.* 1913, Hilda, 2nd *d.* of late W. T. Clarke, of Eccles and Llandudno; one *s. Educ.:* National School, Port Dinorwic; the Friars School, Bangor; University College of North Wales, Bangor (Scholar) Didsbury College, Manchester; M.A. Wales, 1913; Hon. D.D., Queen's University, Canada, 1929. Entered Wesleyan Methodist Ministry, 1903; Assistant Tutor Headingley College, Leeds, 1903-7; Wakefield Circuit, 1907-10; Eccles Circuit, 1910-13; Associate Pastor of Timothy Eaton Memorial Church, Toronto, 1917-20; Member, Committee on Church Worship and Architecture of United Church of Canada. *Publications:* Philippians in the Moffatt New Testament Commentary, 1928; contributions to Journal of Theological Studies, Expositor, Expository Times, Harvard Theological Review, American Journal of Theology, Constructive Quarterly, American Journal of Semitic Languages and Literatures, Geiriadur Beiblaidd (Welsh Bible Dictionary), Faith for To-day (College Sermons), etc. *Address:* 127 Hilton Avenue, Toronto 10, Canada. *T.:* Lennox 2, 8076. [*Died* 4 *Jan.* 1959.

MICHELL, Anthony George Maldon, F.R.S. 1934; M.C.E. (Melb.); Engineer; *s.* of John Michell and Grace Rowse; unmarried. *Educ.:* State Sch., S. Yarra, Vic.; Perse Sch., Cambridge; Melbourne University Engineering School. Consulting Engineer, Melbourne, since 1903; James Watt International medallist, 1942; designer of numerous hydraulic and hydro-electric works; founded: Michell Bearings Limited, Newcastle upon Tyne, 1920; Michell Crankless Engineering Corporation, New York, 1928. Inventions: Water Turbine, 1903; Thrust bearing, 1905; Viscometer, 1917; Interconversion of rotary and harmonic motion, 1917; Opposed-piston crankless engine, 1924; Crankless diesel engines, 1933-39. *Publications:* The Limits of Economy in Frame Structures, Phil. Mag., 1904; The Lubrication of Plane Surfaces, 1905; Hydraulic Phenomena of Movable Weirs, Engineering, 1926; Lubrication, its Principles and Practice, 1951; Joint Author: The Mechanical Properties of Fluids, 1925. *Recreations:* various and variable. *Address:* 413 Collins St., Melbourne, C.1, Australia. *T.A.:* Miseg, Melbourne. [*Died* 17 *Feb.* 1959.

MICHELL, Rev. Gilbert Arthur, D.D.; Principal of St. Stephen's House, Oxford, 1919-1936; *b.* 1883; *s.* of late Rev. Arthur Tompson Michell, M.A., F.S.A., and Edith Margaret, *d.* of William Fox of Adbury Park, Newbury. *Educ.:* Rugby School; Lincoln College, Oxford (Scholar); Cuddesdon College. B.A. 1st Class Modern History, 1906; 2nd Class Honours School of Theology, 1907; M.A. 1909; B.D. and D.D. 1924; Deacon, 1909; Priest, 1910; Assistant Curate, St. Barnabas, Oxford, 1909-16 and 1918-19; St. Alban's, Holborn, 1917-18; Examining Chaplain to the Bishop of Zanzibar, 1914-43. *Address:* Champflower, Storrington, Pulborough, Sussex. [*Died* 24 *April* 1960.

MICHELL, Sir Robert Carminowe, K.C.M.G., *cr.* 1933; *b.* 2 Sept. 1876; *s.* of John Michell, I.S.O., many years H.B.M. Consul-General at Petrograd; *m.* 1st, 1903, Ethel (*d.* 1908), *d.* of Hon. Sir Lewis Michell, C.V.O.; (*s.* died on active service, 1942) one *d.*; 2nd, 1916, Margarita, *d.* of Don Domingo Gana, late Chilean Minister to the Court of St. James; one *s.* *Educ.:* Bath College. Served S. African War (medal and four clasps); Vice-Consul, Kertch, 1903; Rotterdam, 1908; H.B.M. Vice-Consul, Nyborg, 1912; Consul Nicaragua, 1913; Secretary of H.M. Legation, Santiago, Chile, 1915-21, rank of Second Secretary, Diplomatic Service; sent to Legation, Montevideo, as Chargé d'Affaires, 1921-22; rank of First Secretary, Diplomatic Service; H.B.M. Chargé d'Affaires and Consul-General in Ecuador, 1921-26; Minister in Bolivia, 1926-30; to Uruguay, 1930-33; Ambassador to Chile, 1933-37; retired, 1937. Served in Home Guard, 1940-44. *Recreations:* riding, shooting, fishing, tennis. *Clubs:* Travellers', Hurlingham; Club de la Union (Santiago de Chile). [*Died* 22 *Jan.* 1956.

MICKLEM, Major Charles, D.S.O. 1919; J.P., D.L. Surrey; Member of London Stock Exchange; *b.* 1882; *s.* of Leonard Micklem; *m.* 1920, Diana, *d.* of late W. Graham Loyd, J.P.; one *s.* four *d.* (and one *s.* decd.). *Educ.:* Wellington College; Hertford College, Oxford (M.A.). Served with Royal Marine Artillery, Howitzer Brigade, in Gallipoli and France, 1915-18 (despatches twice, D.S.O.); High Sheriff of Surrey, 1938. *Address:* Long Cross House, nr. Chertsey, Surrey. *Club:* Carlton. [*Died* 26 *Jan.* 1955.

MICKLEM, Comdr. Sir (Edward) Robert, Kt., *cr.* 1946; C.B.E. 1942; R.N. retd.; *b.* 5 June 1891; *y. s.* of late Leonard and Nannette Frances Micklem; *m.* 1922, Sibyl Ursula, *o. d.* of late J. R. Head; one *s.* one *d.* *Educ.:* R.N. Colleges, Osborne and Dartmouth. Royal Navy, 1903-19; served European War, Lieutenant, including two years in Submarine Service; retired, 1919; joined companies associated with Vickers Ltd.; Jt. Managing Dir. of Vickers Ltd.; Chm. and Managing Dir. of Engineering Works and Shipyards of Vickers-Armstrongs Ltd.; Chairman Regional Board Northern Area, Ministry of Production, 1942; services loaned by Vickers Ltd. to serve at Ministry of Supply, 1942; Chairman Tank Board and Chairman Armoured Fighting Vehicle Division, Ministry of Supply, 1942-44. *Address:* Landermere Hall, Thorpe-Le-Soken, Essex. *T.:* Thorpe-Le-Soken 297; 28 Kingston House, Prince's Gate, S.W.7. *T.:* Kensington 4284. *Clubs:* Boodle's, United Service; Northern Counties (Newcastle). [*Died* 13 *May* 1952.

MICKLEM, Brig.-Gen. John, D.S.O. 1916; M.C.; late Rifle Brigade; *b.* 13 Sep. 1889; *s.* of Leonard Micklem; *m.* 1917, Iris, *e. d.* of Comdr. Sir Trevor Dawson, 1st Bt.; three *s.* one *d.* *Educ.:* Winchester. 2nd Lt. Rifle Brigade, 1910; Lieut. 1911; Capt. 1914; temp. Lieut.-Col. attached Gloucester Regt., 1915; served European War, 1914-18 (wounded twice, M.C., D.S.O., despatches 5 times); Bt.-Major, June 1917; temp. Brig.-Gen., 1918; Commanding London Rifle Brigade, 1924-29. *Address:* Avenue Farm, Gosmore, Hitchin, Herts. *T.:* Hitchin 1693. *Club:* White's. [*Died* 26 *Feb.* 1952.

MICKLEM, Nathaniel, Q.C.; *b.* 1853; 2nd *s.* of T. Micklem; *m.* 1885, Ellen Ruth (*d.* 1952), *d.* of late Thomas T. Curwen; three *s.* M.A., B.C.L. (Oxford); B.A., LL.B. (Lond.); Fellow of University College, London. Called to Bar, Lincoln's Inn, 1881; Bencher, 1906; retired, 1923; a member of the Royal Commission on Lunacy and Mental Disorder, 1924; M.P. (L.) of Watford Division, Hertfordshire, 1906-10; Treasurer of Lincoln's Inn, 1930. *Address:* Northridge, Boxmoor, Herts. *T.:* Boxmoor 112. *Clubs:* National Liberal, Old Millhillians. [*Died* 19 *March* 1954.

MICKLEM, Comdr. Sir Robert; *see* Micklem, Comdr. Sir E. R.

MICKLETHWAIT, St. John Gore, K.C. 1927; M.A., B.C.L.; J.P. Monmouthshire and Middlesex; Deputy Chairman Middlesex Sessions, 1934, Chairman, 1936-45; *b.* 1870; *s.* of John Pollard Micklethwait, J.P.; *m.* 1898, Annie Elizabeth (*d.* 1948), *d.* of late Rev. F. Aldrich-Blake; four *s.* *Educ.:* Clifton College; Univ. College, Oxford. Barrister-at-law, Middle Temple, 1893; Bencher, 1921; Reader, 1930; Treasurer, 1933; Deputy Chm. Monmouthshire Quarter Sessions, 1935-50; at one time Chancellor of Diocese of Monmouth; Leader of the Oxford Circuit, 1940-46; Recorder of Reading, 1923-51; retired, 1951; Chairman of Merchandise Marks Act Cttee. of Ministry of Agriculture; war work: Aliens' Tribunal, Tunbridge Wells, 1939; Chm. of the Aliens Advisory Committee for the Southern Area, 1940. *Address:* 4 Temple Gardens, E.C.4. *T.:* Central 8549; Penhein, Chepstow, Mon. *T.:* Penhow 210. [*Died* 26 *April* 1951.

MIDDLETON, Alderman Sir Arthur Edward, Kt., *cr.* 1953; J.P.; a senior partner, Cole Dickin and Hills, Accountants, 18 Essex St., Strand, W.C.2., since 1928; Chairman of the London County Council since 1953; *b.* 2 Nov. 1891; 2nd *s.* of late Robert Jolly Middleton, Grovelands, Shinfield, Berks; *m.* 1918, Katie Louise Wilson;

no *c.* *Educ.:* Reading School. London County Council: co-opted Member of L.C.C. Cttees., 1937-42; Alderman, 1942-46; Councillor for Islington (North), 1946-52; Alderman, 1952-. Member Royal Commission on the Press, 1947-49; Minister of Agriculture's representative on Hops Marketing Board, 1950-; Member Council Society of Incorporated Accountants and Auditors, 1946-. F.S.A.A. 1922. J.P. 1950. *Recreation:* golf. *Address:* Beech Tree House, Laleham on Thames. *T.:* Staines 314; (office) Temple Bar 6791; (L.C.C.) Waterloo 5000. [*Died* 19 *Oct.* 1953.

MIDDLETON, Hubert Stanley, M.A., D.Mus.(Oxon.), Mus.D.(Cantab.), F.R.A.M. F.R.C.O.; Fellow, Trinity College, Cambridge, 1946: Organist of Trinity College, Cambridge, 1931-57; late University Lecturer in Music; late Fellow of Peterhouse, Cambridge; *b.* 11 May 1890; *m.* 1922, Dorothy May, *d.* of Dr. W. F. Miller; two *s.* *Educ.:* Imperial Services College, Windsor; Royal Academy of Music; Peterhouse, Cambridge. Organist and Master of the Choir, Truro Cathedral, 1920-26; Organist and Magister Choristarum, Ely Cathedral, 1926-1931. *Address:* 10 Trumpington Street, Cambridge. *T.:* 2778; Coxalls, Caxton Road, Bourn, Cambs. *T.:* Caxton 329. [*Died* 13 *Aug.* 1959.

MIDDLETON, Sir John, K.C.M.G., *cr.* 1931 (C.M.G. 1916); K.B.E., *cr.* 1924; *b.* 1870; *s.* of late James Middleton, M.D., Manorhead, Stow, Midlothian; *m.* 1920, Mabel (*d.* 1947), Commander of the Order of St. John of Jerusalem, *d.* of late Lieut.-Col. G. Wilbraham Northey, D.L., J.P., of Ashley Manor, Box, Wilts, and *widow* of R. K. Granville. *Educ.:* Sedbergh; Edinburgh University (M.A.). Assist. District Commissioner, Southern Nigeria, 1901; Acting District Commissioner, Warri, 1901; Assistant Sec., 1902; Senior Assistant Secretary, 1904; officiated as Secretary to Government and Divisional Commissioner, 1904-5; District Commissioner, 2nd Grade, 1906; Senior Assistant Colonial Secretary, 1907; Assist. Colonial Secretary, Mauritius, 1908; Acting Colonial Secretary, 1908-13; Colonial Sec., Mauritius, 1913; administered Government, 1914, 1916, and 1919; Governor and Commander-in-Chief, Falkland Islands, 1920-27; Gambia, 1927-28; Governor and Commander-in-Chief of Newfoundland, 1928-32. *Address:* The Red House, Lacock, Wiltshire. [*Died* 5 *Nov.* 1954.

MIDDLETON, Noel, Q.C. 1936; *b.* 1875; *e. surv. s.* of Clement Alexander Middleton. *Educ.:* Eton; New College, Oxford. Called to Bar, Gray's Inn, 1900; Bencher of Gray's Inn, 1930; Treasurer, 1942; Consulting Editor 4th Edn. Rayden on Divorce, 1942. *Address:* 7 King's Bench Walk, Temple, E.C.4. *T.:* Central 9789; 153 Sussex Gardens, W.2. *Club:* Athenæum. [*Died* 24 *June* 1955.

MIDGLEY, Rt. Hon. Harry, P.C. (N. Ire.), 1943; J.P., M.P. Northern Ireland, 1933-38 and since 1941; Minister of Education since 1950; enlisted Aug. 1914; served for four years on Western Front with Royal Engineers: Trade Union organiser, 1919-42; contested (Lab.) West Belfast, 1923 and 1924; Minister of Public Security, Northern Ireland, 1943-44; Minister of Labour, 1944-45. [*Died* 29 *April* 1957.

MIDGLEY, Lt.-Col. Stephen, C.M.G. 1916; D.S.O. 1902; *b.* M'Leay River, New South Wales, 29 May 1871; 4th *s.* of James Midgley, Queensland, Australia; *m.* 1916, Katharine Emily Mary, *widow* of Frank Evans, jun., of Bredwardine, Hereford; one *s.* one *d.* *Educ.:* privately. Served South Africa, 1900-1 and 1902; promoted from Lieutenant to Captain in the field when serving with the Pietersburg Light Horse (despatches, D.S.O., Queen's and King's medals); served as Lieutenant with Royston's Horse; Natal Rebellion, 1906 (medal); European War, 1914-17 (despatches twice, C.M.G., wounded). *Address:* Nambour, North Coast Line, Queensland, Australia. [*Died* 25 *Oct.* 1954.

MIDGLEY, Wilson; *b.* 1887; *s.* of John William Midgley and Jeannie Wilson; *m.* 1916, Helen Bamford. *Educ.:* Keighley Grammar School; Leeds University. On staff of Daily News, Manchester; American Correspondent Daily News, 1924-29; Deputy Editor, Star, London till 1941; Editor, John o' London's Weekly, 1943-53. *Publications:* Possible Presidents; From My Corner Bed; The Terrible Turk (for Children); Cookery for Men Only. *Address:* Crab Hill, Beckenham, Kent. *Club:* Authors'. [*Died* 23 *March* 1954.

MIGEOD, Frederick William Hugh; retired; *b.* Chislehurst, Kent, 9 Aug. 1872; *s.* of late Louis Frederic Migeod and late Rebecca Elizabeth Banks; *m.* 1925, Madeleine Marguerite Adrienne Charlotte Banks (*d.* 1933). *Educ.:* Folkestone. Royal Navy, Pay Dept., 1889-98; Colonial Civil Service (Gold Coast), 1900-19; undertook expeditions between 1919 and 1931,—across Africa twice, Lake Chad, Cameroons (two), Sierra Leone; Leader, British Museum East Africa Expedition, to excavate bones of dinosaurs, 1925-1927, 1929 and 1930; President, Worthing Archæological Soc., 1927 and 1938; F.R.G.S., F.R.A.I., etc.; Town Councillor, Worthing, 1932-35, and 1937-43; Alderman, 1943-49; Co. Councillor W. Sussex, 1934. Chm. of British Union for Abolition of Vivisection, 1950. *Publications:* Mende Language; Mende Natural History Vocabulary; The Languages of West Africa; Hausa Grammar; Earliest Man; Across Equatorial Africa; Through Nigeria to Lake Chad; Through British Cameroons; A View of Sierra Leone; Aspects of Evolution; Worthing, A Survey of Times Past and Present (Editor), 1938. *Address:* 46 Christchurch Road, Worthing, Sussex. *T.:* Worthing 4633. [*Died* 8 *July* 1952.

MIGHELL, Sir Norman (Rupert), Kt., *cr.* 1951; C.M.G. 1939; Chairman: Sulphide Corpn. (Pty.) Ltd.; Standard Telephones & Cables Pty. Ltd.; Consolidated Zinc Pty. Ltd.; Melbourne Board of Atlas Assurance Co. Ltd.; Director: Consolidated Zinc Corporation Ltd.; The Zinc Corporation Ltd.; New Broken Hill Consolidated Ltd.; Anglo-Australian Corp. (Pty.) Ltd.; *b.* 12 June 1894; *s.* of late A. W. Mighell; *m.* 1920, Marjorie, *d.* of late A. J. Draper; one *s.* *Educ.:* Nudgee College, Brisbane. Solicitor, Queensland, 1918; Barrister, 1929; served European War, 1914-18 with 15th Battalion Australian Imperial Force; Chairman Repatriation Commission, Australia, 1935-46, and Coal Commissioner for the Commonwealth, 1941-46. Deputy High Commissioner, for Australia in the U.K., 1946-49 (Actg. High Comr. 1949-50); retd., 1950. *Address:* 95 Collins St., Melbourne, Australia. *Clubs:* Melbourne, Athenæum, Victoria Racing, Victoria Amateur Turf (Melbourne). [*Died* 13 *April* 1955.

MILBORNE - SWINNERTON - PILKINGTON, Maj. Sir A. W.; *see* Pilkington.

MILBURN, Sir Leonard John, 3rd Bart., *cr.* 1905; late Lieut. Reserve Regt., Royal Horse Guards; J.P.; *b.* 14 Feb. 1884; *s.* of 1st Bt. and Clara Georgiana (*d.* 1936), *d.* of late Wm. C. Stamp; *S. b.* 1917; *m.* 1917, Joan, 2nd *d.* of Henry Anson-Horton of Catton Hall, Derbyshire; two *s.* two *d.* *Educ.:* Rugby School; Trinity College, Cambridge. High Sheriff of Northumberland, 1928-29. F.R.Z.S. *Heir:* *s.* John Nigel, Capt. Northumberland Hussars Yeo., M.F.H. [*b.* 22 Apr. 1918; *m.* 1940, Joan, *d.* of Leslie Butcher, Edlington Hall, Lincs; one *s.*]. *Address:* Guyzance Hall, Acklington, Northumberland. *T.:* Warkworth 247; Milburn House, Newcastle upon Tyne. [*Died* 17 *Sept.* 1957.

MILDMAY, Rev. Sir (Aubrey) Neville St. John-, 10th Bt., *cr.* 1772; Member Standing Council of the Baronetage, 1950; *b.*

14 Feb. 1865; 6th s. of late Rev. C. Arundell St. John-Mildmay, J.P., last resident lord of the manor of Queen Camel, and Harriet Louisa, d. of Very Rev. Hon. George and Lady Charlotte Neville-Grenville; S. g. nephew, 1949; m. 1902, Louisa Jane, d. of J. Barrett Maunder; one s. one d. (and twin sons decd.). *Educ.:* Winchester; New College, Oxford (scholar); Wells Theological College. B.A. (hons.) 1888; 1st class Theol. Gen., 1890; M.A. 1895. Deacon, 1890; priest, 1894; curate of St. Paul, Truro, 1890-91; of Witney, Oxon., 1893-95; of St. Andrews, Fife, 1895-96; of St. Peter, Vauxhall, 1897-98; Lecturer Father of Anglican Brotherhood, 1897-98; Head Master of Vernon C. of E. College, New Westminster, 1903-06; Vicar of Penticton, B.C., 1906-07; lecturer in classics, University of B.C., 1917-24. Hon. Treas. Vancouver Blind Institution, 1928-30. Hon. Sec. Vancouver Navy League, who then bought from Admiralty the Composite Sloop H.M.S. Egeria and started Training Ship for Boys, 1911. *Publications:* Laureates of the Cross, 1897; Horae Mediterraneæ, 1947; Poetical Works (under pseudonym Autremonde), 1894. *Heir:* (but not claiming Btcy.) s. Verus Arundell Maunder [b. 6 Jan. 1906; m. 1943, Marian, d. of Murdoch Ross]. *Address:* Little Manor, Ringmer, Lewes, Sussex. *T.:* Ringmer 56.

[*Died* 30 *March* 1955 (*abeyant*).

MILES, Alexander, M.D., F.R.C.S.; LL.D. Edin.; Consulting Surgeon, Royal Infirmary, Edinburgh, and Leith Hospital; Member Edinburgh Convalescent Hospitals Group, Board of Management; late Member University Court, and Curator of Patronage, University of Edinburgh; Member General Medical Council; b. Leith, Scotland, 1865; m. Helen Judith, e. d. of John Greig, Leith; one d. *Educ.:* Edinburgh University (Thesis Gold Medallist and Syme Surgical Fellow 1890). *Publications:* Surgical Ward Work and Nursing, 7th ed., 1943; (D. P. D. Wilkie) Manual of Surgery, 9th ed., 1939; (Sir James Learmonth) Operative Surgery, 3rd Ed. 1950; The Edinburgh School of Surgery before Lister, 1918; A Guide to the Study of Medicine, 1925. *Address:* 6 Blackford Road, Edinburgh; Cnoc-sualtach, Kirkmichael, Perthshire. *T.:* 52447.

[*Died* 9 *April* 1953.

MILES, Lieut.-Gen. Charles George Norman, C.M.G. 1918; D.S.O. 1917; b. 10 Nov. 1884; s. of Charles Stafford Miles, Brisbane; m. 1923, Marjorie, 2nd d. of M. Campbell Langtree, of Sydney, N.S.W.; one s. one d. *Educ.:* Toowoomba and Brisbane Grammar Schools. Served European War, 1914-18 (despatches, C.M.G., D.S.O). *Address:* 2 Forest Rd., Double Bay, Sydney, Australia.

[*Died* 18 *Feb.* 1958.

MILES, George Herbert, D.Sc.; Industrial Consultant; Experimental and Research work on Synthetic Training Devices since 1939; b. 12 Aug. 1880; s. of late G. R. Miles; m. Susanna, d. of late John Houlton; one s. *Educ.:* Westminster Coll.; London University. War Service: Chief Petty Officer, R.N., later 2nd Lieut., R.N.V.R., 1916-19; Sec., National Institute of Industrial Psychology, 1919; Assist. Director, 1921; Director, 1930-37. *Publications:* Two reports on American and German School and University Systems, 1907 and 1911; The Will to Work, 1927; Incentives in Industry, 1932; Industrial Psychology in Practice, 1932 (with H. J. Welch). *Recreations:* sailing, caravanning. *Address:* Orwell House, Hillside, New Barnet, Herts. *T.:* Barnet 2310. *Club:* Overseas. [*Died* 4 *April* 1955.

MILES, Gordon, C.B.E. 1954; Public Works Loan Commissioner, since 1959; b. 28 April 1891; 4th s. of late John Miles, Hove, Sussex; m. 1922, Nora Eunice, d. of late Horace Louth; two s. *Educ.:* Brighton Grammar School. Entered Finance Dept. of Metropolitan Asylums Board, 1911. Served European War, 1914-19, as private in Royal Fusiliers (M.M.). Associate Member of the Institute of Actuaries, 1919. Joined finance dept. of the London County Council, 1930, Deputy Comptroller, 1946; Comptroller of the London County Council, 1949-56; retired 1956. Fellow, Institute of Municipal Treasurers and Accountants, 1950. *Recreations:* tennis, badminton. *Address:* Keymer, Pembury, Kent. *Club:* Reform. [*Died* 3 *Nov.* 1959.

MILFORD, Sir Humphrey Sumner, Kt. cr. 1936; M. A., Hon. D.Litt. (Oxon); Publisher to the University of Oxford, 1913-45; b. 8 Feb. 1877; y. s. of late Canon R. N. Milford and Emily, d. of C. R. Sumner, Bishop of Winchester; m. 1st, 1902, Marion (d. 1940), y. d. of late Horace Smith; two s. one d.; 2nd, 1947, Rose Caroline, *widow* of Lt.-Col. Sir Arnold Wilson, K.C.I.E., D.S.O., M.P. *Educ.:* Winchester; New Coll., Oxford. 1st class Classical Moderations and Final School (Literæ Humaniores); Assistant to the Secretary to the Delegates of the Clarendon Press, Oxford, 1900-6; transferred to the London office of the Press, 1906; President of the Publishers' Association of Great Britain and Ireland, 1919-21. *Publications:* The Oxford Book of Regency Verse (joint-editor); editions of Cowper and Leigh Hunt in Oxford Poets; edition of Clough in Oxford Miscellany; etc. *Address:* The White House, Drayton St. Leonard, Oxford. *T.:* Stadhampton 68. *Club:* Athenæum.

[*Died* 6 *Sept.* 1952.

MILLAR, Henry James; Chairman A. Millar and Co. Ltd.; b. 30 Oct. 1878; s. of late Fitzadam Millar, Monkstown, Co. Dublin; m. Helen Christine, d. of late William Piper, Ackleton Hall, Shropshire; one s. *Educ.:* Corrig School, Kingstown; Dublin University. *Recreation:* golf. *Address:* Seacroft, Killiney, Co. Dublin. *Club:* Royal Irish Yacht (Kingstown).

[*Died* 17 *April* 1960.

MILLAR, Sir Jackson, Kt. 1957; C.B.E. 1943; D.L., J.P.; Director of Albion Motors Ltd., Leyland Motors Ltd., Royal Exchange Assurance, Ailsa Investment Trust Ltd., Edward McBean & Co. Ltd., Crittall Manufacturing Co. Ltd., South of Scotland Electricity Board, Scottish Aviation Ltd.; b. Singapore, 5 October 1888; s. of late Jackson Millar and late Elizabeth Goldie; m. 1920, Noreen Winifred Glynn; two d. *Educ.:* Ayr Academy. Past Chm. Conservative Club, Glasgow, and of Scottish Unionist Association; Partner Jackson Millar & Co., Engineers, Glasgow. Served European War, France, with R.A.S.C. (M.T.), 1914-18; G.H.Q. Staff (France), 1917-19. *Recreations:* fishing and shooting. *Address:* 78 St. Vincent Street, Glasgow. *T.A.:* Advantage. *T.:* Central 5938. *Club:* Conservative (Glasgow). [*Died* 15 *Dec.* 1958.

MILLARD, Charles Killick, M.D., D.Sc. (Pub. Health), Edin.; b. 14 Aug. 1870; s. of Rev. C. S. Millard, Rector of Costock, Notts.; m. Annie Susan, d. of Rev. John Longley, Vicar of Saltley, Birmingham; two s. two d. *Educ.:* Trent College; Edinburgh University. Medical Superintendent of City Hospital, Birmingham, 1897-99; M.O.H. for Burton on Trent, 1899-1901; M.O.H. for Leicester, 1901-1935; Past President Leicester Rotary Club, Society of Medical Officers of Health, Leicester Literary and Philosophical Society and Leicester Medical Society; for many years has held distinctive views on the question of vaccination in relation to the control of smallpox, but is not an anti-vaccinist; has frequently written and lectured on the subject; in 1931 brought forward the question of the legalisation of voluntary euthanasia (in Presidential Address to Society of Medical Officers of Health) and drafted a Bill with this object; a few years later founded the Voluntary Euthanasia Legalisation Society, of which he is the Hon. Secretary; is a life-long total abstainer and a Past-President of Leicester Temperance Society and Leicester Band of Hope Union; took up flying and obtained his Pilot's A Certificate at age of 63; took up motor cycling at age of 80. *Publications:* The Hospital Isolation of Scarlet Fever; An Appeal to Statistics, 1901; The Vaccination Question in the Light of Modern Experience, 1914; Population and Birth Control, 1917; Euthanasia, 1931; various articles on Vaccination and Smallpox, Cremation, Disposal of the Dead, Birthrate Control, and other subjects of Public Health interest; Annual Health Reports for Leicester, 1901-34. *Recreations:* gardening, bee-keeping, motoring. *Address:* The Gilroes, Leicester. *T.:* Anstey 83. [*Died* 7 *March* 1952.

MILLER, Arthur Hallowes, M.A., M.D. (Cambridge); M.R.C.P. (Lond.); late Senior Demonstrator of Pathology at University of Sheffield; Captain (temp.) R.A.M.C.; *b.* 21 April 1880; *e. s.* of late Ven. E. F. Miller, Parkstone, Dorset, Archdeacon of Ceylon and Warden of St. Thomas's College, Colombo; *g.s.* of W. H. Miller, F.R.S., formerly Professor of Mineralogy, Univ. of Cambridge. *Educ.:* Marlborough; Trinity College, Cambridge; Guy's Hosp.; Berlin. Late physician to out-patients, City of London Hospital for Diseases of the Chest, Victoria Park, E. *Publications:* The Biological Concept of Man, 3rd edition, 1933; papers in Pathology and on witch doctor's medicine as applied to the European. *Recreation:* golf. *Address:* c/o Lloyds Bank Ltd., Parkstone, Dorset. [*Died* 14 *Nov.* 1956.

MILLER, Lt.-Col. Charles Darley; Director, late Managing Director, of the Roehampton Club, S.W.; *b.* 1868; *s.* of late Edward Miller of Hoare, Miller & Co., merchants, Calcutta and London; *m.* 1904, Grace, *d.* of late F. H. Darley; one *s.* *Educ.:* Marlborough College; Trinity College, Cambridge, B.A. Went to Motihari, Behar, India, 1890; spent 12 years as Manager of Motihari Indigo Concern; came home, 1901; started Roehampton Club, 1902, and managed same from commencement until 1950; played for Eng. against Amer. at polo in 1904, and for Rugby team, 1902-14; joined army, Aug. 1914; France, 1915-19; Commanded Remount Depot, Rouen; later D.D.R. 5th Army, with rank of Colonel; demobilised 1919 with rank Lt.-Col. *Recreations:* hunting, shooting, polo, pig-sticking and big-game shooting in India. *Address:* Audley Lodge, Putney Park Avenue, S.W.15; *T.:* Prospect 1751. *Club:* Roehampton. [*Died* 22 *Dec.* 1951.

MILLER, Douglas Gordon; *b.* 5 Mar. 1881; *s.* of A. P. Schulze, yarn merchant, Glasgow, and Joanna Miller; *m.* Violet Edith, *d.* of J. W. Rose, solicitor, London; two *s.* two *d.* *Educ.:* Glasgow Academy; Fettes College, Edinburgh (Scholar); Merton College, Oxford (Classical Postmaster); 2nd Class Honours in Classical Moderations and Literæ Humaniores; Educational Diploma, Manchester University. Two years English Master R.N.C. Dartmouth; one year Christ College, Brecon; four years Uppingham School; eight years Rector, Kelvinside Academy, Glasgow; three years Rector, Aberdeen Grammar School; High Master, Manchester Grammar School, 1924-45; Oxford University Rugby Football XV., 1904; Scottish International XV., 1905-11. *Recreations:* Local Interests: Governor Fylde Farm Approved School, Past Chm. Dickens Fellowship. *Address:* 487 North Drive, St. Annes, Lancs. *T.:* St. Annes 1730. [*Died* 17 *May* 1956.

MILLER, Sir Eric; *see* Miller, Sir H. E.

MILLER, Sir Ernest Henry John, 10th Bt., *cr.* 1705, of Chichester, Sussex; *b.* 8 May 1897; *er. s.* of Sir Henry Holmes Miller, 9th Bt., sheep farmer, New Zealand, and of Caroline Matilda, *d.* of late Henry Joseph Greville, Pahiatua, New Zealand; *S.* father 1952; *m.* 1920, Mahalah Netta Bennett; two *s.* two *d.* *Heir:* *s.* John Holmes, *b.* 1925. *Address:* Ngaturi, Pahiatua, New Zealand. [*Died* 22 *April* 1960.

MILLER, Admiral Francis Spurstow, C.B. 1919; *b.* Litherland Park, Liverpool, 25 Nov. 1863; *e. s.* of late Francis B. Miller of Liverpool, and Charlotte, *d.* of Thomas Taylor; *m.* 1888, Amy Knowles (*d.* 1949), *e. d.* of William Stopford Ross of Port of Spain, Trinidad, W.I.; one *s.* (and two *s.* one *d.* decd.). *Educ.:* United Service Coll., Westward Ho! Entered R.N. 1877; Midshipman of Monarch at Bombardment of Alexandria, 1882 (Egyptian medal, Alexandria clasp, Khedive's bronze star); Sub-Lieut., 1883; Lieut., 1885; Comdr., 1897; Captain, 1903; Commanded Hawke, 1905-6; Sutlej, 1906-7; Goliath, 1907-9; Duncan, 1912-1913; Assistant Hydrographer Admiralty, 1909-1912; in administrative charge Scapa Naval Base, 1914-16 (1914-15 Star, British and Victory war medals); in charge of Northern Division Coast of Ireland, 1917-19; Rear-Admiral, 1913; Vice-Adm. 1918; retired, 1920; Admiral, 1922. *Address:* No. 1 Pine Mansions, Vale Road, Bournemouth. *T.:* Bournemouth 6593. [*Died* 6 *Feb.* 1954.

MILLER, George Waterston, D.S.O. 1917; T.D.; medical practitioner, retd.; late Hon. Col. R.A.M.C. 51st (Highland) Div. T.A.; *b.* Dundee, 1874; *s.* of Dr. J. W. Miller and Alice Waterston; *m.* 1901, Maria Louisa Gilbert; one *d.* (one *s.* decd.). *Educ.:* Dundee High School; Edinburgh Univ. B.Sc. 1895, M.B., Ch.B. 1898; Resident Physician, Edinburgh Royal Infirmary, 1898-99; Dundee Royal Infirmary, 1899-1900; Assistant Physician, 1908-19; Assistant Professor of Medicine, St. Andrews University, 1909-19; Officer of the Order of St. John of Jerusalem in England, 1927; 1st V.B.R.H. and Q.R.V.B.R.S., 1891-98; held Combatant Commission in 1st V.B.R.H., 1899-1904; Medical Commission 1st V.B.R.H., 1904-08; 3rd Highland Field Ambulance, R.A.M.C. (T.F.), 1908; Capt. 1908; Maj. 1914; Lt.-Col. 1920; commanded 152nd Highland Field Ambulance, 1920-24; Colonel and A.D.M.S. 51st (Highland) Division T.A., 1924-28; served in France with 51st Division, 1915-19; a./Lt.-Col. Comdg. 1/2nd H.F. Ambulance, 1918-19 (despatches twice, D.S.O., T.D., French Croix de Guerre with silver star); Col. late A.M.S., T.A.; Member of Council British Medical Association, 1922-29, 1930-35, and 1938-44; Chairman, Scottish Committee, B.M.A., 1927-29; President, Dundee Branch British Medical Association, 1922-23. *Address:* 6 Westfield Place, Dundee. *T.:* 2803. [*Died* 5 *Jan.* 1955.

MILLER, Capt. (S) Grenville Acton, C.B.E. 1919; M.V.O. 1925; R.N.; *s.* of late Commander W. E. Miller, R.N.; *m.* Clara Ainslie, *d.* of E. H. Mackay, Sydney, N.S.W.; one *s.* one *d.* Secretary to C.-in-C. Australian Station, 1905-8; Private Secretary successively to Admiral Sir Harry Rawson and Lord Chelmsford, Governors of N.S.W., 1908-10; Hon. Secretary Foreign Reception Committee at Coronations of King Edward VII. and King George V. 1902 and 1911 respectively; Secretary to C.-in-C. North America and West Indies Station, 1916-18; Secretary to V.A.C. 4th Battle Squadron, Grand Fleet, 1918; Secretary to Allied Naval Armistice Commission, 1918-19; retired list, 1926; Officer of Legion of Honour. *Address:* Uplands, Fareham, Hants. *T.:* 2153. [*Died* 31 *Oct.* 1951.

MILLER, Sir (Hans) Eric, Kt., *cr.* 1952; Chairman of Harrisons & Crosfield Ltd., East India Merchants, 1924-57, retired; a Director and a Life President since 1957; *b.* 12 June 1882. *Educ.:* Queen Elizabeth's, Darlington; Leipzig. Joined Harrisons & Crosfield in 1899. Chairman of numerous Rubber Plantation Companies and of International Rubber Research and Development

Boards. Member of Port of London Authority, 1936-. Commander Oranje-Nassau (Netherlands). *Recreations:* farming, book-collecting. *Address:* Oldhouse, Ewhurst Green, Cranleigh, Surrey. *T.:* Ewhurst 90. [*Died* 11 *July* 1958.

MILLER, Sir Henry Holmes, 9th Bt., *cr.* 1705; sheep farmer; *b.* 15 Dec. 1865; *s.* of Hon. Sir Henry John Miller (2nd *s.* of 6th Bt.), Fernbrook Oamaru, N.Z.; *S.* cousin, 1940; *m.* 1895, Caroline Matilda, Greville, Pahiatua; two *s.* three *d.* *Educ.:* Christ's College, Christchurch; Canterbury University. *Heir:* *s.* Ernest Henry John. *Address:* Tauroa, Pahiatua, New Zealand. *T.:* 88 R. *Club:* Gentlemen's (Pahiatua). [*Died* 13 *Nov.* 1952.

MILLER, Hugh; *see* Crichton-Miller.

MILLER, Brig. Hugh de Burgh, C.B.E. 1919; D.S.O. 1900; *b.* 4 June 1874; *s.* of Thomas de Burgh Miller; *m.* 1906, *d.* of Col. A. W. Baird, C.S.I., F.R.S.; one *s.* one *d.* Entered R.A. 1894; Captain, 1901; Major, 1911; Bt. Lt.-Col. 1915; served South Africa, 1899-1902 (despatches, Queen's medal 5 clasps, King's medal 2 clasps, D.S.O.). European War, 1914-17 (Bt. Col.); retired pay, 1922. [*Died* 2 *Feb.* 1951.

MILLER, Hugh Rodolph, C.E. Founder and editor Highways, Bridges and Aerodromes; Managing Director of Road Publications Ltd., originator and Editor Roads and Road Construction, 1923-34; Editor of Roads and Road Construction Year Book and Directory, 1931-34; Technical Editor, The World's Carriers and Carrying Trades' Review and The World's Carriers Year Book, 1919-34; *b.* 1875; 4th *s.* of late William Miller, Berkswell House, Berkswell, Warwickshire; *m.* 1900, Elizabeth Anne (Lily) (*d.* 1949), *d.* of late Thomas Heale, Cardigan; one *s.* three *d.* *Educ.:* Henry VIII School, Coventry; Mason's Engineering College, Birmingham. Cadet, Public Works Department, Jamaica; Assistant Engineer, Kingston and Liguanea Water and Gas Works, Jamaica; various engineering appointments at home; pioneer in mechanical road transport, 1903, organising services between industrial centres in the Midlands, also Liverpool and Manchester, and in 1910 demonstrated the advantage of transport by road of fruit and vegetables between Worthing and other market-gardening centres and Covent Garden. Originator of pedestrian barriers; instigator British Road Federation. Specialised in journalistic work mainly on subjects connected with road construction and road transport; has travelled extensively in Europe, Asia and Western Hemisphere. Served European War in France, Mesopotamia, India and Egypt, 1914-19. *Publications:* Running Costs of Motor Vehicles, 1911; How to make Motor Transport Pay, 1920; general contributor to the press on transport subjects. *Address:* Crescent House, Ashford, Middlesex. *T.:* Ashford Middlesex 2674. [*Died* 11 *Feb.* 1953.

MILLER, James, M.D., D.Sc., F.R.C.P.E., F.R.S.C.; late Prof. of Pathology, Queen's University, Kingston; late Consulting Pathologist, Ontario Dept. of Health; late Lecturer School of Medicine of Royal College, Edinburgh, and Edinburgh University; Pathologist, Royal Victoria and Royal Hospital for Incurables, Edinburgh; Captain R.A.M.C.(T.), Pathologist No. 2 Scottish General Hospital; Local Representative of India Office for Indian Students; *b.* 1875; *e. s.* of A. G. Miller, M.D., F.R.C.S.E.; *m.* 1907, Margaret Elizabeth, *d.* of T. H. Clare, Birmingham; one *s.* three *d.* *Educ.:* Edinburgh Academy; Universities of Edinburgh and Freiburg. B.Sc. 1896, M.B. (Honours) 1899, M.D. (Gold Medal) 1903, D.Sc. (Birm.) 1904; Fellow, Royal College Physicians, Edinburgh, 1910; Resident Physician, Royal Infirmary, Edinburgh, 1899-1900; served South Africa with Edinburgh and East of Scotland Hospital as Assistant Surgeon, 1900; Lecturer in Pathology and Bacteriology, Birmingham University, 1902-9; Visiting Pathologist, General Hospital, Birmingham, 1906-9; Examiner, University of Aberdeen, 1911-14. *Publications:* numerous articles in British and foreign medical publications, in Reports of Royal Commission on Tuberculosis, and in Report of Local Government Board; Manual of Post-mortem Technique and Practical Pathology. *Recreations:* walking, fishing. *Address:* Denmead, Painswick, Glos. [*Died* 21 *Sept.* 1958.

MILLER, Sir John Wilson Edington, K.B.E., *cr.* 1946; C.M.G. 1943; *b.* 20 June 1894; *s.* of late Rev. James Miller, Bridge-of-Allan, and Margaret, *d.* of John Wilson, Edington Mains, Berwickshire; *m.* 1927, Jessie Kathleen, *d.* of F. H. Reed, Wolverhampton; one *s.* one *d.* *Educ.:* Edinburgh Academy; Emmanuel College, Cambridge (B.A. 1920). European War, 1914-19, A. and S. Highlanders (Captain); Staff Capt.; France, Salonika, and Egypt (despatches, French War Cross with palms); Sudan Political Service, 1920; Assistant Financial Secretary, 1933; Deputy Financial Secretary, 1934; Financial Secretary and member of Governor-General's Council, 1944; Controller, Financial Division, the British Council, 1949; Secretary-General and Executive Member of the Iraq Government Development Board, 1950; retd. 1954. Order of the Nile (4th class 1930, 3rd class 1935). *Recreations:* golf and tennis. *Address:* Cairnbank, Duns, Berwickshire. [*Died* 6 *May* 1957.

MILLER, Brig. Laurence Walter, D.S.O. 1918; *b.* 3 June 1882; *s.* of late Dr. Henry Walter Miller, D.D., and late Sarah Nancy Miller; *m.* Olga Katrina Ronn; no *c.* *Educ.:* St. Paul's School. Served Boer war, 1901-02, South African Light Horse, rank corporal (Queen's medal and 5 bars); Civil Service, Pretoria, 1903-5; Zulu Rebellion 1906, Royston Horse, rank Lieut. (Medal); California and Mexico, ranching 1907-1910; enlisted Canadian Expeditionary Force Nov. 1914, 31st Infantry Battalion, Calgary, rank Lieut.; France June 1916, Nov. 1918, 2nd Canadian Rifles Battalion Adjutant 1916-17 and second-in-command 1917-18, 8th Brigade, 3rd Division (Captain and Major (2 medals) D.S.O., despatches thrice); in Canadian Permanent Force, 1920-42; District Officer commanding Military District No. 11, British Columbia (with rank of Brigadier), 1942; retired, Dec. 1942. *Recreations:* fishing, gardening. *Address:* 1970 Ernest Avenue, Victoria, B.C. *Club:* Union of B.C. (Victoria). [*Died* 24 *Aug.* 1958.

MILLER, Ralph William Richardson, C.M.G. 1944; Director of Agriculture, Tanganyika Territory, and Sisal Controller for East Africa, 1940-47; *b.* 25 Jan. 1892; *s.* of Wm. Miller; *m.* 1918, Jean, *d.* of D. Inglis, J.P., Musselburgh; three *d.* *Educ.:* Darlington; Trinity College, Cambridge. South Lancashire Regt. 1915-17; Special Brigade, R.E., 1917-19; Asst. Govt. Chemist, Kenya, 1919-25; Senior Agricultural Officer, Tanganyika, 1925-29; Director of Agriculture, Barbados, and Chairman, B.W.I. Sugar Cane Breeding Station, 1929-37; Director of Agriculture, Zanzibar, Member of Executive and Legislative Councils, 1937-40; Mem. for Agric. and Natural Resources, 1947-49; Unofficial M.L.C., 1951. *Address:* P.O. Lushoto, Tanganyika Territory. [*Died* 23 *April* 1958.

MILLES, Carl, Hon. R.A. 1940; Sculptor; *b.* 23 June 1875; *m.* Olga Granner, portrait painter, Graz, Austria. *Educ.:* Stockholm; Paris; Munich; Rome. Doctor of Honor of Bethany College; Rock Island University, Yale University, N.Y., North Western University, Chicago. Hon. Member of Archt. League New York (Gold Medal), Archt. League Vienna, Amer. Institute of Architects, Washington, D.C., Mark Twain Soc., etc. Has accepted invitation to live and

work at Cranbrook Acad. of Art, Michigan, U.S.A. Exhibitions: Paris, mention honorable, médaille d'argent, gold medal, Grand Prix, Légion d'Honneur; Munich Golden Médaille; Buenos Ayres Gold Medal; Archt. Assoc. Washington Gold Medal; Amer. Acad. of Arts Gold Medal; member: Amer. Acad. of Arts; Nat. Acad. of Arts and Letters; Nat. Acad. of Design, etc. *Works:* Upsala, Stockholm, Göteborg, Helsingborg, etc.; Chicago, St. Paul (Minn.), St. Louis (Mo.), Harrisburg (Penna.), Worcester (Mass.) Houston (Texas), Washington, D.C., etc. *In Museums:* Stockholm, Göteborg, Malmö, Berlin, Moskwa, Kopenhagen, London, Chicago, St. Louis, New York, Worcester, Lausanne, Zürich, Hamburg, etc. *Address:* Cranbrook, Bloomfield Hills, Mich., U.S.A. *Clubs:* Century, Architects League, (New York); Architect (Hon.) (Vienna); Member of honor of the American Institute of Architects (Washington, D.C.).
[*Died* 19 *Sept.* 1955.

MILLIGAN, Samuel, C.B.E. 1935; retired; *b.* 1874; *s.* of late James Milligan and Julia Agnes Farish; *m.* 1905, Elizabeth McLean; two *s.* *Educ.:* Wallace Hall School; Edinburgh University. M.A., B.Sc. Deputy Director of Agriculture, Punjab, 1905; Director of Agriculture, Bengal, 1916-20; Agricultural Adviser to Government of India, 1920-24; Representative in South Africa of Empire Cotton Growing Corporation, 1924-35. *Club:* Reform.
[*Died* 24 *July* 1954.

MILLIKAN, Robert Andrews; Director of the Norman Bridge Laboratory of Physics and Chairman of Executive Council, California Institute of Technology, 1921-45; Vice-Pres. Board of Trustees, 1945-; *b.* Morrison, Illinois, U.S.A., 22 Mar. 1868; *s.* of Rev. Silas Franklin Millikan and Mary Jane Andrews; *m.* 1902, Greta Ervin Blanchard; three *s.* *Educ.:* Maquoketa (Iowa) High School, 1885; A.B., Oberlin College, 1891; A.M., 1893; Ph.D., Columbia University, 1895; studied in Universities of Berlin and Göttingen, 1895-96. Assistant in Physics, University of Chicago, 1896-97; Associate, 1897-99; Instructor, 1899-1902; Assistant Professor, 1902-7; Associate Professor, 1907-10; Professor, 1910-21; recipient of honorary degrees from numerous American and European universities. M.N.A.S. and numerous foreign societies, Comstock Prize of National Academy of Sciences, Nobel Prize in Physics of Royal Swedish Academy, Hughes Medal of Royal Society of Great Britain, and many medals from American and foreign learned societies. Chevalier de l'Ordre National de la Légion d'Honneur (Commander, 1936), Chinese Order of Jade. *Publications:* Mechanics Molecular Physics and Heat, 1902; The Electron, 1917 (revised 1924); Science and Life, 1923; Evolution in Science and Religion, 1927; A First Course in Physics for Colleges, 1928 (with H. G. Gale and C. W. Edwards); Science and the New Civilization, 1930; Time, Matter and Values, 1932; Electrons (+ and −), Protons, Photons, Neutrons, Mesotrons, and Cosmic Rays, 1935, Revised 1947; New Elementary Physics (with H. G. Gale), 1936; Mechanics, Molecular Physics, Heat and Sound (with Duane Roller and Earnest C. Watson), 1937; Cosmic Rays, 1939; Autobiography, 1950; numerous papers in scientific periodicals. *Recreation:* golf. *Address:* California Institute of Technology, Pasadena, California. *T.:* Sycamore 3-2706. *Clubs:* Sunset, California (Los Angeles).
[*Died* 19 *Dec.* 1953.

MILLIKEN, Brigadier Robert Cecil, C.B.E. 1938; T.D., 1927; D.L. Middlesex; M.I.E.E.; *b.* 19 March 1883; *s.* of Robert Milliken; *m.* 1916, Florence, *d.* of Wm. Swannell; two *d.* *Educ.:* Aske's School; London University. Served European War, 1914-19 (despatches): Lt.-Col. Commanding Kent and Middlesex Group A.A. Searchlights and 29th (Kent) A.A. Bn. R.E. (T.A.), 1929-37; Col., 1933; Hon. Colonel 29th Kent A.A. Bn. and 564 S/L Regiment R.A. T.A., 1937-49; Brigade Commander 47th A.A. Brigade. T.A., 1938-40; Military Member Middlesex T.A. and Air Force Assoc., 1925-52. *Address:* 16 West End Avenue, Pinner, Middlesex. *T.:* Pinner 3005. *Club:* Royal Automobile.
[*Died* 30 *March* 1959.

MILLS, Arthur; *b.* 1887; *e. s.* of Rev. Barton Mills and Lady Catherine Mills; *m.* 1st, 1916, Lady Dorothy Walpole (Lady Dorothy Mills, *q.v.*, who obtained a divorce, 1933); 2nd, 1934, Monica Cecil Grant Wilson. *Educ.:* Wellington; Sandhurst. Gazetted Duke of Cornwall's Light Infantry, 1908; posted China station, 1912; served France, 1914; Palestine, 1917. *Publications: travel:* From Piccadilly to Devil's Island; *novels:* Ursula Vanet; Pillars of Salt; The Yellow Dragon; The Gold Cat; The Danger Game; Live Bait; White Snake; The Blue Spider; Pursued; The Apache Girl; Intrigue Island; Escapade; Stowaway; One Man's Secret; The Ant Heap; Paris Agent; Brighton Alibi; Café in Montparnasse; White Negro; Don't Touch the Body; Shroud of Snow; Last Seen Alive; Your Number is Up; The Jockey Died First; The Maliday Mystery; *short stories:* Modern Cameos; The Primrose Path. *Recreations:* golf, gardening. *Address:* Winds Cottage, Downton, nr. Lymington, Hants. *T.:* Milford on Sea 88. [*Died* 18 *Feb.* 1955.

MILLS, Arthur John, C.B.E. 1929; *b.* 1868; *m.* Margaret (*d.* 1946), *e. d.* of Geo. Hay, J.P.; four *s.* two *d.* *Educ.:* Bishopgate. Importer of Provisions, specialising in Dominion Dairy and Hog produce; Member of Ministry of Food during European War, 1914-18; sent to Canada and United States by Ministry of Food as buyer for Allies, 1917-1918. Formerly: Chairman A. J. Mills & Co. Ltd.; President of Provision Trade Benevolent Institution. Past President London Provision Exchange. *Recreations:* golf and other sports. *Club:* Constitutional.
[*Died* 7 *Sept.* 1956.

MILLS, Lady Dorothy R. M., F.R.G.S.; Hon. Member Portuguese Geographical Soc.; Author and traveller; *e. d.* of late 5th Earl of Orford; *m.* 1916, Arthur Mills, *q.v.* Has travelled extensively; in February 1923 was the first Englishwoman to visit Timbuctoo; made Expedition through Liberia, 1926; Expedition through Portuguese Guinea, 1929; several expeditions through the Sahara and the Middle East; Expedition up the Orinoco River, 1931. *Publications:* Card Houses, 1917; The Laughter of Fools, 1920; The Tent of Blue, 1922; The Road, 1923; The Road to Timbuktu, 1924; The Arms of the Sun, 1924; The Dark Gods, 1925; Beyond the Bosphorus, 1926; Phœnix, 1926; Through Liberia, 1926; Master! 1927; Jungle, 1928; The Golden Land, 1929; A Different Drummer, 1930; The Country of the Orinoco, 1932. *Recreation:* travelling. *Club:* Sesame Imperial and Pioneer.
[*Died* 4 *Dec.* 1959.

MILLS, Sir Frederick, 1st Bt., *cr.* 1921; J.P.; *b.* 1865; *m.* 1st, 1889, Edith Mary (*d.* 1916), *d.* of G. M. Topham, Tynemouth; one *s.* one *d.*; 2nd, 1918, Mary Kathleen, *o. d.* of E. Dawkins. M.P. (U.) Leyton, East, 1931-45. *Heir:* *s.* Major Frederick Leighton Victor Mills (*see* Sir Victor Mills, 2nd Bt.). *Address:* Hither Hyes, Rushlake Green, Heathfield, Sussex. *Clubs:* Royal Automobile, Constitutional. [*Died* 31 *Dec.* 1953.

MILLS, Major Sir (Frederick Leighton) Victor, 2nd Bt., *cr.* 1921; M.C.; Major R.A. retired; M.I.C.E.; *b.* 14 March 1893; *s.* of Sir Frederick Mills, 1st Bt., and Edith Mary (*d.* 1916), *d.* of George Marshall Topham, Tynemouth, Northumberland; *S.* father 1953; *m.* 1923, Doris Armitage,

Eastbourne; one *s.* *Educ.:* Cheltenham; R.M.A. Woolwich. Joined Royal Artillery, 1912; served European War, 1914-19 (despatches, M.C. and Bar, Belgian Croix de Guerre, three medals), Colonial Civil Service, 1922-47; appointed Director, Public Works Department, Sierra Leone, 1938, and Uganda, 1942; retired, 1947. *Heir:* *s.* Peter Frederick Leighton, *b.* 9 July 1924. *Address:* Long Acre, Botha's Hill, Natal, South Africa. [*Died* 21 *April* 1955.

MILLS, Geo. Percival, M.B., B.S.Lond.; F.R.C.S. Eng.; Consulting Surg. to the Gen. Hospital, Birmingham; Consulting Surg. to the Royal Cripples' Hosp., Birmingham; Consulting Surgeon to the Victoria Hospital, Lichfield; *b.* Walsall, 18 July 1883; *s.* of George Mills, Yew Tree House, Great Barr, Staffs., and M. E. Kettlewell, Howden, Yorkshire; *m.* 1913, T. M. Christabel, *d.* of Prof. J. Humphreys, F.S.A., Edgbaston; two *s.* two *d.* *Educ.:* Harrow School; Birmingham School of Medicine. Gold Medal of University of London in Anatomy, 1903; Qualified M.B., B.S., University of London, 1906 (Honours in Surgery); held resident surgical appointments in Manchester, London, and Birmingham; Temp. Major R.A.M.C. in charge of surgical division 36th Gen. Hosp., Salonika Army (despatches, Order of St. Sava, Fourth Class, Serbia. *Publications:* Surgery for Dental Students; Practical Hints on Minor Operations; articles in various surgical journals. *Recreations:* lawn tennis, rock climbing. *Address:* Glazenbridge, Shrawley, nr. Worcester. *T.:* Stourport 101. [*Died* 7 *March* 1952.

MILLS, James Philip, C.S.I. 1947; C.I.E. 1941; late I.C.S.; *b.* 1890; *s.* of James Edward Mills; *m.* 1930, Pamela, *d.* of J. F. Vesey-FitzGerald; two *d.* *Educ.:* Winchester; Corpus Christi College, Oxford. Entered I.C.S., 1913; posted to Assam; retd., 1947; Reader School of Oriental and African Studies, Univ. of London, 1948. Pres. Royal Anthropological Institute, 1951-1953. *Publications:* The Lhota Nagas; The Ao Nagas; The Rengma Nagas. *Recreations:* fishing and gardening. *Address:* East House, Sydling St. Nicholas, Dorchester. *T.:* Cerne Abbas 229. *Club:* Athenæum. [*Died* 12 *May* 1960.

MILLS, John Edmund; late Secretary Shop Stewards' Committee, Woolwich Arsenal; Joint Secretary, Woolwich Towns Committee for Alternative work; Alderman of Woolwich Borough Council; President National Housing Council. 1921; *b.* Fremantle, Western Australia; *s.* of Chief Inspector Charles Mills, W.A. Water Police. M.P. (Lab.) Dartford Division of Kent, 1920-22, 1923-24, and 1929-31; Parliamentary Secretary to Chancellor of Duchy of Lancaster, 1923-24. *Publications:* From the Back Benches; From Czardom to Genoa. *Recreations:* football, running, swimming. *Club:* Dartford Labour. [*Died* 11 *Nov.* 1951.

MILLS, Richard Charles, O.B.E. 1936; LL.M. (Melb.); D.Sc. (Econ.)(Lond.); Director, Commonwealth Office of Education from 1945; *b.* Ardmona, Victoria, 8 March 1886; *s.* of Samuel Mills; *m.* 1916, Helen Elizabeth, *d.* of Robert Crawford, Ballymena, Ireland; two *s.* two *d.* *Educ.:* Wesley College, Melbourne; Queen's College, Melbourne University (Wyselaskie Scholar in Constitutional History and Political Economy, Harbison-Higinbotham Scholar); London School of Economics, London University (Hutchinson Medallist). Acting Lecturer in Constitutional History and in Jurisprudence, Melbourne University; Tutor in History and Sociology; Lecturer in Economics, Sydney University; Professor of Economics and Dean of the Faculty of Economics, Univ. of Sydney, 1922-45; Member: of Victorian Royal Commission into High Cost of Living; of Economic Commission on Queensland Basic Wage; of Royal Commission on Monetary and Banking Systems; Chairman: Commonwealth Grants Commission; and Universities Commission. 61st Siege Battery, B.E.F., 1916-19 (wounded, despatches). *Publications:* The Colonization of Australia, 1829-1842, 1915; Money (part author), 1935. *Address:* 44 Raglan Street, Mosman, Sydney, N.S.W. *Clubs:* University (Sydney); Athenæum (Melbourne). [*Died* 6 *Aug.* 1952.

MILLS, Major Sir Victor; *see* Mills, Major Sir F. L. V.

MILLS, William Hobson, F.R.S., 1923; M.A. Cantab; Sc.D. Tübingen; Fellow and President, 1940-48, of Jesus College, Cambridge, Emeritus Reader in Stereochemistry in the University of Cambridge; *b.* 6 July 1873; *e. s.* of William Henry Mills, J.P.; *m.* 1903, Mildred, *d.* of George James Gostling, J.P.; one *s.* three *d.* *Educ.:* Uppingham School; Jesus College, Cambridge; University of Tübingen, 1899-1900. Head of the Chemical Department, Northern Polytechnic Institute, 1902-12; Longstaff Medallist of the Chemical Society, 1930; Davy Medallist of Royal Society, 1933; President of Section B of the British Association, York, 1932; Baker Lecturer, Cornell University, 1937; Member Advisory Council, Dept. of Scientific and Industrial Research, 1935-40; Pres. Chemical Society, 1941-44; Trustee of Uppingham School, 1933-48. *Publications:* papers in the Journal of the Chemical Soc. and elsewhere. *Recreations:* motoring, field-botany. *Address:* 23 Storey's Way, Cambridge, and Jesus College, Cambridge. *T.:* Cambridge 3915. [*Died* 22 *Feb.* 1959.

MILLSPAUGH, Arthur Chester, Ph.D., LL.D.; *b.* Augusta, Michigan, 1 Mar. 1883; *s.* of Hiram E. Millspaugh and Lydia H. Abbott; *m.* 1923, Mary Helen MacDonnell, Washington; one *s.* *Educ.:* Albion College; University of Illinois; Johns Hopkins University. Professor of Political Science, Whitman College, 1916-17; Instructor, Political Science, Johns Hopkins, 1917-18; in Drafting Office, State Department, 1918-21; Consul Class 4, and assigned to State Department, 1921; acting Foreign Trade Adviser, 1921-1922; Petroleum Specialist in State Department, 1920-22; Administrator General of the Finances of Persia, 1922-27; Financial Adviser General Receiver of Haiti, 1927-29; Participant and Director of Administrative Surveys, 1930-33; Administrator General of the Finances of Iran, 1943-45; Member, Sigma Nu, Phi Beta Kappa. *Publication:* Party Organisation and Machinery in Michigan since 1890 (thesis), 1917; The American Task in Persia, 1925; Haiti under American Control, 1930; Public Welfare Organization, 1935; Local Democracy and Crime Control, 1936; Crime Control by the National Government, 1937; Democracy, Efficiency, Stability, 1942; Peace Plans and American Choices, 1942; Americans in Persia, 1946. *Address:* Brookings Institution, Washington, D.C., U.S.A. [*Died* 24 *Sept.* 1955.

MILNE, Alan Alexander; Writer; assistant editor of Punch, 1906-14; Royal Warwickshire Regt., Feb. 1915-19; *b.* 18 Jan. 1882; *y. s.* of John Vine Milne; *m.* 1913, Dorothy (Daphne) de Sélincourt; one *s.* *Educ.:* Westminster; Trinity College, Cambridge. Edited The Granta, 1902; started journalism in London, 1903. *Publications:* The Day's Play, 1910; The Holiday Round, 1912; Once a Week, 1914; Once on a Time, 1917; Not that it Matters, 1919; If I May, 1920; The Red House Mystery, 1921; The Sunny Side, 1922; When We Were Very Young, 1924; Winnie-the-Pooh, 1926; Now we are Six, 1927; The House at Pooh Corner, 1928; By Way of Introduction, 1929; Two People, 1931; Four Days' Wonder, 1933; Peace with Honour, 1934; It's Too Late Now, 1939; Behind the Lines, 1940; Chloe Marr, 1946; The Norman Church, 1948; Birthday Party, 1949; A Table Near The Band, 1950; Year in, Year out, 1952; *plays:* Wurzel-Flummery, 1917; Belinda, Make-Believe, 1918; Mr. Pim Passes By;

1919; The Romantic Age, 1920; The Truth about Blayds, 1921; The Dover Road, 1922; The Great Broxopp, Success, 1923; To Have the Honour, 1924; Ariadne, 1925; The Ivory Door, 1927; The Fourth Wall, 1928; Michael and Mary; Toad of Toad Hall, 1930; Other People's Lives, 1932; Miss Elizabeth Bennet, 1936; Sarah Simple, 1937; Gentleman Unknown, 1938. *Address:* Cotchford Farm, Hartfield, Sussex. *T.:* Hartfield 17. *Club* Garrick. [*Died* 31 *Jan.* 1956.

MILNE, Charles, Q.C. (Scot.) 1932; Sheriff of Dumfries and Galloway since 1939; 2nd *s.* of late James Milne, M.D., L.R.C.S. (Edin.), bank agent, Huntly, Aberdeenshire; *m.* 1957, Hilda Christian Roberts, M.B., Ch.B. (Edin.); no *c.* *Educ.:* Edinburgh University, M.A., LL.B.; Advocate, 1904; Junior Counsel to the Secretary for Scotland under the Private Legislation Procedure (Scotland) Act, 1899, 1925-28; M.P. (U.) West Fife, 1931-35. *Address:* 9 Howe Street, Edinburgh. *Club:* Scottish Conservative (Edinburgh). [*Died* 17 *Feb.* 1960.

MILNE, David, C.I.E. 1927; B.Sc.(Agr.); Indian Agricultural Service, retired; *b.* 9 May 1876; *s.* of James Milne, Newmill, Drumlithie, Kincardineshire; *m.* 1912, Joan Annie (*d.* 1952), *d.* of Lieut.-Col. Spencer Cargill, Bengal Royal Artillery. *Educ.:* Aberdeen University. Agricultural Chemist to Corporation of Western Egypt, 1905-07; entered Indian Agricultural Service as Economic Botanist, 1907; Principal Agricultural College, Lyallpur, Punjab, 1921; member of Punjab Legislative Council, 1923-28; Director of Agriculture, Punjab, 1923-33; Dean of Faculty of Agriculture, Punjab University, Lahore, 1923-33; Member of Indian Central Cotton Committee, 1923-33; Member of Imperial Council of Agricultural Research, India, 1928-33; retired, 1933; as Economic Botanist gave the province many new and improved, types of cotton, wheats, and other crops, some of which are now grown on many millions of acres. *Publications:* Handbook of Field and Garden Crops of the Punjab; The Date Palm and its Cultivation in the Punjab; many Government reports, pamphlets, etc. *Address:* c/o National Bank of India, Ltd., 26 Bishopsgate, E.C.2. [*Died* 11 *Feb.* 1954.

MILNE, (J.) Maclauchlan, R.S.A. 1937 (A.R.S.A. 1933). Formerly resident in Nethergate, Dundee. Exhibited at Royal Scottish Academy, etc. *Address:* High Corrie, Isle of Arran, Scotland; c/o Aitken, Dott and Son, 26 Castle Street, Edinburgh. [*Died* 28 *Oct.* 1957.

MILNE, Sir James, K.C.V.O., *cr.* 1936; Kt., *cr.* 1932; C.S.I. 1923; formerly Director and General Manager Great Western Railway, 1929-47; Chairman: Ship Mortgage Finance Company; Director: Thos. Cook & Sons Ltd., Bentworth Trust, Bedford Insurance, Nyasaland Railway, Coast Lines Ltd., Belfast Steamship Co.; *b.* 1883; *s.* of late J. Milne, J.P., Dublin; *m.* 1912, Nora R., *d.* of late L. L. Morse, M.P.; two *s.* *Educ.:* Campbell College, Belfast; Victoria University, Manchester. Director of Statistics, Ministry of Transport, 1919-21; attached to (Geddes) Committee on National Expenditure, 1921-22, and India (Inchcape) Retrenchment Committee, 1922-23; Member of Committee of Inquiry into Coastguard Organisation, 1931; Chm. of Cttee. of Inquiry into Transport in Ireland, 1948; Deputy Chairman Railway Executive Committee, 1939-47. *Address:* Dildawn, Woldingham, Surrey. *T.:* Woldingham 3271. [*Died* 1 *April* 1958.

MILNE, James; *b.* Strathdon, 25 Sept. 1865. *Educ.:* Strathdon and Aboyne public schools, under old-time, scholarly Scots dominies; later, classes at Edinburgh Univ., including David Masson's English Literature Class. Grew up at Aboyne, in the Aberdeenshire Highlands; came to Fleet Street via Aberdeen Free Press and the Scottish Leader, Edinburgh; Literary Editor of the Daily Chronicle, 1904-18; editor and founder (1903) of the Book Monthly; contributor to the Daily Telegraph, the Scotsman, the Cornhill Magazine, the Strand Magazine, and other periodicals and papers, mostly on literary subjects, also under the pen names, Eliot Buckram and Elijah True. *Publications:* The Gordon Highlanders; The Romance of a Pro-Consul (Sir George Grey); The Epistles of Atkins; My Summer in London; John, Jonathan and Company; News from Somewhere; The Black Colonel, a novel; A New Tale of Two Cities, essays of the Great Wartime; A London Book Window; Pages in Waiting; The Love Letters of a Husband (anonymously); Travels in Hope, with colour drawings by Donald Maxwell; The Road to Kashmir; A Window in Fleet Street; The Memoirs of a Bookman; Over the Hills and Far Away; Printer's Devil: Or How Books Happen; Things People Do Not Tell. *Clubs:* Caledonian, Press. [*Died* 19 *March* 1951.

MILNE, James Mathewson, M.A., D.Litt.; *b.* Aberdeen, 1883; *m.* 1911, Jane Murray Crockart, M.A.; no *c.* *Educ.:* Aberdeen Grammar School; Aberdeen University; University of Rennes. Scholastic appointments in Campbeltown Grammar School, North Kelvinside H.G. School, Glasgow High School, Bell-Baxter School; Rector, Nairn Academy; retired, 1947; Military Service, 1915-19; Acting Captain, 5th Batt. Cameronians (Scottish Rifles). *Publications:* La Pomme d'Or, 1933; An Anthology of Classical Latin, 1952; numerous Latin and French text-books, e.g. Junior Latin Composition, Easy Latin Readings, etc. *Recreations:* golf, fishing, motoring. *Address:* c/o Mowat Nursing Home, Stonehaven, Kincardineshire; Salisbury, Torphins, Aberdeenshire. *T.:* Torphins 224. [*Died* 25 *Feb.* 1959.

MILNE, John Alexander, C.B.E. 1918; J.P. for Berks; Chairman and Managing Director, Henry Stone & Son, Ltd., London and Banbury; Chairman, Medici Society, Ltd.; Director Warner & Sons Ltd.; Vice-Pres. R. Soc. of Arts, Chairman of Council 1932-35; Vice-Chairman Royal Academy Exhibition of British Art in Industry, 1935; Pres. British Colour Council, 1934-44; Mather Lecturer Textile Inst., 1938; Member: of Council for the Preservation of Rural England; of Council, Royal India and Pakistan Society; Chairman, Golden Square Throat, Nose, and Ear Hospital, 1932-39; *b.* 1872; *s.* of late Rev. John Milne, Senior Chaplain to H.M. Forces; *m.* 1st, 1894, Isabel Mary (*d.* 1936), *d.* of late Theobald Theobald, M.F.H.; 2nd, 1936, Nellie Emma (*d.* 1952), *widow* of Kyrle Chatfield, H.M. Col. Service. *Educ.:* Rathmines School, Dublin; privately. Member Berks County Council, 1904-07; District Chairman North Berks Conservative Association, 1906-10; served R.N.V.R., 1914-15 (British War Medal); Member Admiralty Committee, War Trade Dept., 1915-16; Chairman Linen and Silk Committee, W.T.D., 1916-19; Special Foreign Office representative Allied Conferences on Blockade, Paris, 1916-17; Member Flax Control Board, 1917-20; Member Consultative Council Imports and Exports, 1919-20; King's Jubilee Medal; Albert Gold Medal, Royal Society of Arts, 1940. *Recreation:* golf (President of the Senior Golfers' Society). *Address:* 36 Bentinck Close, N.W.8. *T.:* Primrose 8522. *Clubs:* Carlton, Caledonian. [*Died* 5 *March* 1955.

MILNE, Joseph Grafton, M.A., D.Litt.; Deputy Keeper of Coins since 1931, Oxford University; *b.* Bowdon, Cheshire, 23 Dec. 1867; *y. s.* of William Milne and Ellen, *d.* of Joseph Smith Grafton; *m.* 1896, Kate, *y. d.* of James Edmondson Ackroyd, Bradford, Yorks. *Educ.:* Manchester Grammar School; Corpus Christ College, Oxford; British School at Athens. Sixth-form Master, Mill

Hill School, 1891-3; Junior and Senior Examiner and Assistant Secretary, Education Department and Board of Education, 1893-1926; retired 1926, and assisted in the organisation of the Coin Department at the Ashmolean Museum, Oxford; University Reader in Numismatics, 1930-38; Librarian of Corpus Christi College, 1933-46; received Annual Medal of Royal Numismatic Society, 1938, Archer M. Huntington Medal of American Numismatic Society, 1944. *Publications:* History of Egypt under Roman rule, 1898 (3rd edition, revised, 1924); Catalogue of Greek Inscriptions, Cairo Museum, 1905; Theban Ostraca, 1913; Greek Coinage, 1931; Catalogue of Alexandrian Coins, Ashmolean Museum, 1933; The First Stages in the development of Greek Coinage, 1934; Catalogue of Oxfordshire Tokens, Ashmolean Museum, 1936; The Development of Roman Coinage, 1937; Greek and Roman Coins and the Study of History, 1939; The Early History of Corpus Christi College, 1946; Finds of Greek coins in the British Isles, 1948; (with C. H. V. Sutherland and J. D. A. Thompson) Coin-Collecting, 1950; articles in various periodicals, mainly on the history of Græco-Roman Egypt and Greek coins. *Address:* 23 Belsyre Court, Oxford. *T.:* Oxford 4517.
[*Died* 7 *Aug.* 1951.

MILNE, Mrs. Leslie (Mary Lewis), Hon. M.A. Rangoon University, 1932; author; F.R.A.I.; M.R.A.S.; Hon. Member of The Burma Research Society; *b.* Kandy, Ceylon, 1 Aug. 1860; *e. d.* of late Alexander Harper, Torre al Prato, near Florence, and Ceylon, and Marion, *y. d.* of late Andrew Cross, Sheriff Substitute of Perthshire at Dunblane; *m.* Leslie Milne (*d.* 1897), M.A. Edin., M.D. Aber., *e. s.* of late Very Rev. A. J. Milne, LL.D., Minister of Fyvie. *Educ.:* privately at Naples, Edinburgh and Rome. Has travelled extensively in Europe and Asia; was five years in Cape Colony; spent some time in Kashmir and Burma; lived in Northern Shan States, 1906-8. *Publications:* Shans at Home, 1910; An Elementary Palaung Grammar, 1921; The Home of an Eastern Clan, 1924; A Dictionary of English-Palaung and Palaung-English, 1931. *Recreations:* painting, photography, reading, gardening, embroidery. *Address:* c/o Lloyds Bank Ltd., 39 Old Bond Street, W.1.
[*Died* 24 *Nov.* 1952.

MILNE, Colonel Thomas, C.B. 1936; D.S.O. 1919; *b.* 24 Feb. 1882; *s.* of Dr. Thomas Milne and Catherine Garland; *m.* 1st, 1913, Kathrine Elizabeth Garland (*d.* 1918); 2nd, 1923, Winifred Gertrude Hatton (*d.* 1955); two *d.* *Educ.:* Bedford Sch.; Sandhurst. 1st Commn. 1901; joined 62nd Punjabis 1903; 1/13th F.F. Rifles 1904; served N.W. Frontier of India, 1908; European War 1914-21 Egypt and Palestine 1918 (despatches twice, Order of Nile 4th Class, D.S.O.); Kurdistan, 1923; A.A. and Q.M.G. Western Command, 1932-34; commanded Wana Bde., 1934-36; retired, 1936. *Recreation:* fishing. *Address:* Greenhays, Barne's Lane, Milford-on-Sea, Hants. *Club:* Army and Navy. [*Died* 4 *Nov.* 1959.

MILNE, Sir William Robertson, Kt., *cr.* 1954; W.S.; N.P.; Member of the firm of Tait and Crichton, W.S., Edinburgh; Chairman of the General Trustees, Church of Scotland; Director of Gourock Ropework Co. Ltd. and other Cos.; Crown Agent for Scotland, 1941-45. *Address:* Birnam, Colinton, Edinburgh. [*Died* 31 *March* 1959.

MILNER, Viscountess; Violet Georgina; *d.* of late Adm. F. A. Maxse, Dunley Hill, Dorking, and Cecilia Steel; *m.* 1st, Lord Edward Cecil, K.C.M.G. (*d.* 1918); one *d.* (one *s.* killed in action); 2nd, 1921, 1st Viscount Milner, K.G. (*d.* 1925). Editor, National Review, 1932-48. D.G.St.J., 1901; Chevalier de la Légion d'Honneur, 1933. *Publications:* My Picture Gallery, 1951. *Address:* Great Wigsell, Hawkhurst, Kent.
[*Died* 10 *Oct.* 1958.

MILNER, Elizabeth Eleanor; Mezzotint Engraver; *d.* of Rector of Elton, Durham. *Educ.:* Silver Medallist South Kensington; Royal Academy School; Herkomer School. Plates engraved include Prince Octavius, and others in the Royal Collection at Windsor, Bonnie Prince Charlie at Holyrood, Pinkie by Lawrence, and Master Simpson by Devis, by permission of late Lord Duveen, and from pictures belonging to the Marquess of Londonderry, Lord Rothschild, Mr. James de Rothschild, Earl of Jersey, and The Duke of Buccleuch. Her latest engravings are The Duchess of Devonshire and Child (by permission of Duke of Devonshire), Prince Charles Edward and Cardinal York in Edinburgh, the Princesses Mary and Sophia, at Windsor, Prince James Francis Edward, Lord Burghersh and La Gamme d'Amour after Watteau. *Address:* Bourne Hall Cottage, Bushey, Herts. *T.:* Bushey Heath 1756. [*Died* 24 *Oct.* 1953.

MILNER, Frederic, C.M.G. 1955; H.M. Treasury Representative in the Middle East and Financial Counsellor, British Embassy, Beirut; *b.* 10 Jan. 1905; *s.* of David Milner, Bradford; *m.* 1931, Mina Wilkinson, Bradford; one *s.* one *d.* *Educ.:* Bradford Grammar School; St. John's College, Cambridge (Foundation Scholar). First Class Historical Tripos, Parts I and II. Asst. Dir. of Examinations, Civil Service Commission, 1930-39. Served in Min. of Information, Min. of Home Security, and Home Office, 1939-44. H.M. Civil Service Commissioner and Director of Examinations, Civil Service Commission, 1944-48. H.M. Treasury, 1948-. *Publication:* Economic Evolution in England, 1931. *Address:* Heatherview, Southside, Gerrards Cross, Bucks. *T.:* Gerrards Cross 3203; c/o British Embassy, Beirut. *Club:* St. George's (Beirut). [*Died* 4 *Sept.* 1957.

MILNER, Eng.-Rear-Admiral John William, C.B.E. 1943; M.V.O. 1920. Chief Engineer, Gibraltar Dockyard, 1923; Overseer for the North of England District, 1927; retired, 1928. *Clubs:* Junior United Service; Royal Naval (Portsmouth).
[*Died* 5 *May* 1953.

MILNER, Samuel Roslington, F.R.S., F.Inst.P., D.Sc. (Lond. and Bristol), Hon. D.Sc. (Sheffield); Emeritus Prof. of Physics, Univ. of Sheffield; *b.* 1875; *s.* of S. W. Milner, Retford; *m.* 1901, Winifred, *d.* of H. J. Walker, Bristol; one *s.* *Educ.:* King Edward VI. School, Retford; University Coll., Bristol; University of Göttingen. 1851 Exhib. Scholar, 1895-98; Demonstrator of Physics, University of Manchester, 1898; Lecturer in Physics, 1900, Acting Professor, 1917, Professor of Physics, 1921-40, University of Sheffield; Assistant Radiographer, 3rd Northern General Hospital, 1914-17. *Publications:* papers in scientific journals chiefly on Chemical Physics, Electricity, and Wave Theory. *Address:* 16 Keston Avenue, Mosman, N.S.W., Australia.
[*Died* 12 *Aug.* 1958.

MILNER, Sir William Frederick Victor Mordaunt, 8th Bt., *cr.* 1716; F.R.I.B.A.; F.S.A.; M.A. (Oxon); late member of Council of R.I.B.A.; Partner in Milner and Craze, architects, 120 Crawford St., W.1; a member of the College of Guardians of the National Shrine of Our Lady of Walsingham, Norfolk; *b.* 2 Oct. 1893; *o. s.* of Rt. Hon. Sir Frederick George Milner, G.C.V.O., 7th Bt., and Adeline Gertrude, *d.* of late William Beckett, M.P.; *S.* father, 1931. *Educ.:* Wellington; Christ Church, Oxford. Lieut. 2/1st Lothians and Border Horse (T.F.), 1915-19; Officer i/c Signals, Clyde Garrison, 1918-19; exhibited several times in Royal Academy. *Recreation:* gardening. *Heir:* cousin, George Edward Mordaunt Milner [*b.* 1911; *m.* 1935, Barbara (*d.* 1950), *d.* of H. Noel Belsham, Hunstanton, Norfolk; two *s.* one *d.*]. *Address:* Parcevall Hall, Appletrewick, Skipton, Yorks. *T.:*

Burnsall 213; 120 Crawford St., W.1. *T.:* Welbeck 0488. *Clubs:* Bath; Yorkshire (York); Leeds (Leeds). [*Died* 29 *March* 1960.

MILNES, W. H., R.B.A. 1905; A.R.E. 1899; A.R.C.A. 1898; late Headmaster, School of Art, Coventry; President National Society of Art, Coventry; President National Society of Art Masters, 1916 and 1923; *b.* 1865; *s.* of W. H. Milnes, J.P., Wakefield; *m. d.* of Colonel C. Jameson, late of Bombay Staff Corps; one *s.* two *d. Educ.:* Wakefield; Antwerp; London. Headmaster at Walthamstow School of Art, 1893-1906. *Club:* Chelsea Arts. [*Died* 6 *March* 1957.

MILWARD, Maj.-Gen. Sir Clement Arthur, K.C.I.E., *cr.* 1937 (C.I.E. 1920); C.B. 1931; C.B.E. 1925; D.S.O. 1917; *b.* The Holloway, Redditch, Warwickshire, 20 May 1877; *s.* of late Victor Milward, M.P., and Eliza Milward, Tamworth in Arden; *m.* 1907, Hestor Rose, *d.* of late William Lawson of Longhirst, Northumberland; one *d.* (one *s.* killed in action, Korea, 1951). *Educ.:* Rugby. p.s.c.; Comd. 9 K.O.Y.L.I. 1916-17, and 3rd Royal Battalion 12th F.F. Regiment (Sikhs), 1921-23; Brigade Commander Landi Kotal Brigade, Khyber Pass, 1927-30, Nowshera Brigade, 1930-31; A.D.C. to the King, 1926-31; Major-General, 1931; Commander Lucknow District, India, 1934-38; retired, 1938; Northumberland Home Guard, 1940-1942; Col. 3/17 Dogra Regt., 1933; Col. 3rd R. Bn. 12th F. F. Regt., 1938; on active service N.W.F. India, 1901-2 and 1908; European War, 1914—Mons to Ypres; 1915—Gallipoli, Helles and Suvla Bay landings, 1916, France, Somme; 1917, France; 1917-1918, Mesopotamia; 1920, Iraq Insurrection; N.W.F., 1922-24, Waziristan; 1930, operations v. Mohmands and Afridi Incursion: 1930-31, Khajuri Plain. *Address:* Lynn House, Wickham Market, Suffolk. [*Died* 31 *Dec.* 1951.

MINETT, Francis Colin, C.I.E. 1945; M.B.E. 1917; D.Sc. (Vet. Science), M.R.C.V.S.; Director Animal Health Trust's farm livestock research station, Houghton Grange, Huntingdonshire, since 1950; *b.* 16 Sept. 1890; *s.* of late Francis Minett, Corsham, Wilts; *m.* 1919, Iza, M.B.E., *d.* of late Robert Stitt, Belfast; one *s. Educ.:* King Edward's School, Bath; Royal Vet. College, London; Institut Pasteur, Paris. Captain Royal Army Veterinary Corps, 1914-1924; Director, Research Institute in Animal Pathology, Royal Veterinary College, London, 1927-39; Professor of Pathology, Royal Veterinary College, 1933-39; Director of Imperial Veterinary Research Institute, Mukteswar, India, 1939-47; Animal Husbandry Commissioner with Govt. of Pakistan, 1947-50. *Publications:* various papers concerning diseases of animals. *Address:* Animal Health Trust, Houghton, Huntingdon. [*Died* 26 *Dec.* 1953.

MINNS, Sir Ellis Hovell, Kt., *cr.* 1945; Litt.D., F.S.A., F.B.A., Hon. M.R.I.A.; Fellow of Pembroke Coll., Cambridge, since 1899, Pres. 1928-49; Disney Prof. of Archæology, 1927-39; Professor Emeritus since 1939; *b.* 16 July 1874; *s.* of George William Walter Minns, F.S.A., Vicar of Weston, Southampton; *m.* 1907 Violet (*d.* 1949), *d.* of F. Nalder, Falmouth; one *s.* one *d. Educ.:* Charterhouse; Pembroke College, Cambridge. Class I., Classical Tripos, Part I., 1896; Part II, 1897; Paris École des Chartes and École des Langues Orientales Vivantes, 1897-98; Russia, 1898-99; Craven Student in Russia, 1900-1; Librarian and Lecturer in Russian, Pembroke College, 1901-27; University Lecturer in Palæography, 1906-27; President Cambridge Antiquarian Society, 1912-14, and 1929-31; Postal Censorship, uncommon languages, 1915-18; Sandars Reader in Bibliography, 1925; Corr. Member of Russian Institute for History of Mat. Culture, 1925; of Bulgarian Archæological Institute, 1936; of Archæological Institute of America, 1950. *Publications:* Ed. Trans. Brückner's Literary History of Russia; art, Slavs, Scythians, etc., Encycl. Brit.; Scythians and Greeks, 1913; Parchments of the Parthian Period from Avroman, 1915; ed. with C. L. Feltoe, Vetus Liber Archidiaconi Eliensis, 1916; trans. and ed. N. P. Kondakov, The Russian Icon, 1927; The Art of the Northern Nomads, 1944. *Recreations:* study of languages, architecture and topography. *Address:* 2 Wordsworth Grove, Cambridge. *T.:* Cambridge 4731. [*Died* 13 *June* 1953.

MINOPRIO, Frank Charles; *b.* 1870; *s.* of late Francis Charles Anthony Minoprio, Liverpool, and *g. g. s.* of Aloysius Vincens Minoprio, Pavia, Italy; *m.* 1st, Leila (*d.* 1914), *d.* of James Mitchell Calder, Charleston, S.C. and Liverpool; three *s.* two *d.*; 2nd, 1920, Rachel, *d.* of Thomas Mann; two *s.* two *d. Educ.:* privately. High Sheriff of Caernarvonshire, 1934-5; President of the Hackney Horse Society, 1934; Past Member of National Coursing Club; Past Commodore of South Caernarvonshire Yacht Club. *Address:* Broadlands, Ascot, Berks. *T.:* Ascot 623; Haulfryn, Abersoch, Caernarvonshire. [*Died* 14 *Nov.* 1951.

MINTER, Percy, C.B.E. 1920; *b.* 1866; *s.* of John Minter, Norwood Green, Southall, Middlesex; *m.* 1889, Mary (*d.* 1933), *d.* of late Charles West, Pangbourne, Berks. *Educ.:* Philological School, Marylebone. Joined Contract Department of Admiralty, 1883; Assistant Director, 1912; Deputy Director of Navy Contracts, 1918; retired, 1926. *Address:* Staddleswood, St. Mary's Platt, Sevenoaks. [*Died* 7 *Sept.* 1955.

MINTON, (Francis) John; Artist and Illustrator; Tutor, Painting School, Royal College of Art, 1949-56; *b.* 25 December 1917; *s.* of Francis Minton, solicitor, and Kate Minton (*née* Key); unmarried. *Educ.:* Northcliffe House, Bognor Regis; Reading School, Berkshire. Studied painting at St. John's Wood Art Schools, 1935-38, and in Paris, 1938-39. Army service, 1941-43. (With Michael Ayrton) décor for Macbeth, Piccadilly Theatre, 1941. One-man shows: Leicester Galleries, 1942; Roland, Browse and Delbanco, 1945; Lefèvre, 1945, 1947, 1949, 1950, 1951, 1954, 1956. Teacher of Illustration, L.C.C. Camberwell School, 1943-1946; Teacher of Drawing and Illustration, L.C.C. Central School, 1946-48. *Publications:* Illustrations for: The Wanderer, 1946; Treasure Island, 1947; The Snail That Climbed The Eiffel Tower, 1947; Time Was Away, 1947; The Country Heart, 1949; Old Herbaceous, 1950; A Book of Mediterranean Food, 1950; French Country Cooking, 1951. *Address:* 9 Apollo Place, S.W.10. *T.:* Flaxman 0453. *Clubs:* Savile, Chelsea Arts. [*Died* 20 *Jan.* 1957.

MIRAJ (Junior), Chief of; Sir Shrimant Madhavrao Harihar, *alias* **Baba Saheb Patwardhan,** K.C.I.E., *cr.* 1936. *Address:* Miraj, Deccan States Agency, India. [*Died* 6 *May* 1950.

[*But death not notified in time for inclusion in Who Was Who* 1941–1950, *first edn.*

MISTINGUETT, (Jeanne Bourgeois); actress and dancer; *b.* Enghien-les-Bains (Seine-et-Oise), 1875. First stage appearance, Trianon Concert Hall, Paris; subsequently appeared in various revues, etc., including: Aux Bouffes on pouffe, L'Ane de Buridan, Tais-toi, mon cœur, Les Midinettes, Le Bonheur sous la main, La Vie parisienne, Madame Sans-Gêne, Bonjour Paris, Paris-Miss, Voilà Paris, etc.; appeared with Maurice Chevalier at the Folies-Bergère and Casino de Paris; first appearance on London stage, Casino, 1947. *Films include:* Fleur de Paris, Chignon d'or, La Double Blessure, La Glu, L'Ile d'amour, Rigolboche, etc. *Publications:* Mistinguett and her confessions, 1938; Mistinguett, 1954. *Address:* 24 Boulevard des Capucines, Paris 9e, France. [*Died* 5 *Jan.* 1956.

MITCHELL, Charles; late Chairman, Dorman, Long & Co. Ltd.; *s.* of William Mitchell and Margaret Greenwood; *m.* 1909, Catherine Mary Errington; two *s.* two *d.* *Educ.:* Glasgow Academy; Glasgow and West of Scotland Technical College. Chairman of the National Committee for the Iron and Steel Industry. *Recreations:* golf, tennis, fishing. *Address:* Atherstone, 21 Copthorne Road, Croxley Green, Rickmansworth.
[*Died* 8 *March* 1957.

MITCHELL, Edwin Laurence, C.B. 1942; C.B.E. 1933 (O.B.E. 1929); *b.* 1883; *y.s.* of late Henry Mitchell, Acton; *m.* 1915, Louise Alice, *widow* of Percy Barber, Knockdown, Tetbury; one *d.* *Educ.:* privately; King's College, London. Appointed to Board of Agriculture, 1903; Private Secretary to Lord Lucas, 1912, and Sir Harry Verney, Bt., M.P., 1914, as Parliamentary Secretaries to the Board of Agriculture; First Class Clerk, 1914; Principal, 1920; Assistant Secretary, 1929; Secretary, Royal Commission on Tithe Rent-charge, 1934-35; Prin. Assist. Secretary, Ministry of Agriculture and Fisheries, 1938-45; Government Director Agricultural Mortgage Corporation, 1944-59. *Address:* Ringers, Marsham, Norfolk. *T.:* Aylsham 3189. [*Died* 13 *July* 1960.

MITCHELL, Major-General Francis Neville, C.B. 1954; C.B.E. 1945; D.S.O. 1944; General Officer Commanding 6th Armoured Division since Oct. 1953; *b.* 11 Oct. 1904; *s.* of late Admiral F. H. Mitchell, C.B., D.S.O. and late Marion Mitchell; *m.* 1935, Ann Christian, *d.* of late Capt. N. J. Livingstone-Learmonth, 15th Hussars; three *d.* *Educ.:* Harrow; R.M.C. Sandhurst. 2nd Lieut. 15/19 Hussars, 1924; Lt.-Col. 1941; Col. 1946; Brig. 1954. Instructor Staff College, Camberley, 1940; G.S.O. 1, 9 Armoured Div., 1941; comd. 1 Roy. Gloucestershire Hussars, 1942; 2nd in comd. 23 Armoured Bde., 1943; comd. 26 Armoured Bde., 1944-45 (despatches). A.D.A.G. (o), A.F.H.Q., 1945-46; comd. 22 Armoured Bde. (T.A.), 1947-49; Brig. R.A.C., at H.Q., B.A.O.R., 1949-51; Chief of Staff, H.Q., 1st Corps, 1951-53. Officer Legion of Merit, U.S.A., 1944. *Address:* General Officer Commanding 6th Armoured Division, B.A.O.R.22. [*Died* 15 *Sept.* 1954.

MITCHELL, Sir Frank Herbert, K.C.V.O., *cr.* 1937 (C.V.O. 1934; M.V.O. 1928); C.B.E. 1918; Extra Groom-in-Waiting to the King since 1937; Secretary of Most Noble Order of the Garter since 1933; *b.* 13 June 1878; *s.* of late R. A. H. Mitchell, Eton; *m.* 1917, Grace Penelope, *d.* of late Thomas Maffey, Rugby; one *s.* one *d.* *Educ.:* Cheam; Eton (Captain of the Oppidans); Balliol College, Oxford. Served under Lord Milner in South Africa, 1901-4; Assistant Director of Official Press Bureau, 1915-1919; Press Secretary at Buckingham Palace, 1920; Assistant Private Secretary to the King, 1931-37; retired, 1937. *Recreations:* cricket (Eton XI, 1896 and 1897), golf (played for Oxford, 1898-1901, being Capt. in 1901; and three times for England *v.* Scotland). *Address:* Forest House, Crowborough. *Club:* M.C.C. [*Died* 27 *Nov.* 1951.

MITCHELL, Mrs. George J. (Maggie Richardson), A.R.C.A.; R.B.A. 1929; A.R.B.S., sculptor; *b.* London; *d.* of James Richardson and Lucy J. Hall, Campbeltown, Argyllshire; *m.* George J. Mitchell, A.R.C.A., London; one *d.* *Educ.:* Home; Goldsmiths' College and Royal College of Art, London (British Institute Sculpture Scholarship). Following works exhibited Royal Academy: Icarus, The Lizard, Love Bound; also exhibitor R.S.A. and Salon, Paris. *Portraits:* Dr. W. Gibson-Bott, William J. Locke, Thomas Hardy, O.M., Professor William Rothenstein, The Very Rev. Dean of Bath and Wells. Austin O. Spare; Mr. Justice Avory, 1930; Paul Harris, Rotary Founder (Salon 1930); portrait bust, bronze, Rt. Hon. Philip Snowden, 1931; portrait bust James G. Lawn, C.B.E., Mining Engineer, 1933; portrait bust Lord Snell, 1934; L. H. Pomeroy, Motor Engineer, portrait bust, 1936; Dr. Orr (Johannesburg, 1937); Paul Oppé, C.B. (R.A., 1938); Elizabeth Wallis bust (Women Artists), 1938); Africa, Bronze Bust, 1935; Charles E. Bedaux (R.A. 1940); James A. Richardson (R.A. 1941); "Liza" (R.A. 1947) (Honorable Mention, Paris Salon, 1949). *Recreations:* motoring, life drawing. *Address:* Norton-sub-Hamdon, Somerset. *T.:* Chiselborough 201. [*Died* 21 *Feb.* 1953.

MITCHELL, Hon. Sir James, G.C.M.G., *cr.* 1947 (K.C.M.G., *cr.* 1921; C.M.G. 1917); *b.* 27 April 1866; *s.* of William Bedford Mitchell, grazier, of Bunbury, W.A.; *m.* Clara (*d.* 1949), *d.* of Hon. W. Spencer, M.L.C., Bunbury; one *s.* *Educ.:* Bunbury, Western Australia. Entered Parliament, 1905; Minister, Agricultural Department, 1906-9. Minister for Lands, 1909-11; Minister for Railways, Water Supplies, etc., 1916-17; Premier, Western Australia, 1919-1924 and 1930-33; Lieutenant-Governor, 1933-48; Governor of Western Australia, 1948-51; retired 30 June 1951. *Clubs:* Weld (Perth); Northam (Northam).
[*Died* 25 *July* 1951.

MITCHELL, Lt.-Col. John Douglas, C.M.G. 1919; D.S.O. 1918; *b.* 1881; *s.* of late Thomas Mitchell, Chelsea; *m.* Lisa, 3rd *d.* of late James Murray Garden, Aberdeen; one *d.* *Educ.:* Eastbourne; Mill Hill. Served European War, 1914-19; commanded 1st Sherwood Foresters, 1918-19 (three times wounded, despatches twice, 1914 Star, D.S.O., Belgian Croix de Guerre, C.M.G.); President, The Old Millhillians Club, 1932-33; Vice-President The Northumberland and Newcastle Society; Freeman of the City of London; Liveryman of the Worshipful Company of Bakers; Gold Staff Officer at the Coronation of King George VI.; Coronation Medal, 1937. *Address:* The Mount, Park St. Village, St. Albans. *T.:* Park Street 2122. *Club:* Junior Army and Navy.
[*Died* 24 *Jan.* 1955.

MITCHELL, Sir Miles Ewart, K.B.E. *cr.* 1950; Kt., *cr.* 1934; J.P.; Alderman, City of Manchester, since 1927; M.A. Manchester Univ. (h.c.); *b.* 25 May 1875; *s.* of John Mitchell and Ann Bradbury Valentine; *m.* 1899, Annie Turner; one *s.* one *d.* *Educ.:* Roughton School, Mossley. Member of Manchester City Council, 1909; Lord Mayor of Manchester, 1925-26. Vice-Pres. Assoc. of Municipal Corporations. Hon. Freeman, City of Manchester, 1954. *Address:* 23 Yew Tree Lane, Northenden, Manchester 22. *T.:* Wythenshawe 4064. *Clubs:* National Liberal; Reform (Manchester).
[*Died* 15 *Dec.* 1955.

MITCHELL, Philip George Mylne; Captain, R.N.R. (Hon.); Director (formerly Man. Dir. and Dep. Chm.), Royal Mail Lines, retd. 1949; *b.* Southampton, 9 March 1875; *s.* of late Captain John Sumpter Mitchell (R.N. retired); *m.* 1894, Violet Lucy (*d.* 1952), *o. d.* of late Charles Patton Walker, I.C.S., Judge of Supreme Court of Ceylon; two *s.*; *m.* 1953, Mrs. Muriel Beatrice McLean Grant. *Educ.:* Bannisters, Southampton; Wood's, Southsea. Entered The Royal Mail Steam Packet Co., 1891; Head of Traffic Dept., 1912; Head of Freight Dept., 1916; Asst. Manager, 1918; Manager, 1923; General Manager, 1925-35; Director, 1929; Chairman, 1931-35; Managing Director, Royal Mail Lines, Ltd., 1932-49; Chairman of R.M.S.P. Transports, 1931-35, and of Marconi Steamship Co., 1941-43; late Director (formerly Dep. Chm.), Pacific Steam Navigation Co.; Chairman: Salter & Sons Ltd.; Andrew Low, Son and Co. Ltd.; Director of Marine and General Mutual Life Assurance Soc.; Director of Arthur Holland & Co., and other companies. *Recreations:* fishing, boating and swimming. *Address:*

The Lodge, Esher, Surrey; Lamorna, Southampton. *Clubs:* Argentine, Pilgrims. [*Died* 4 *Jan.* 1954.

MITCHELL, Stephen; *b.* 10 Mar. 1884; *o. s.* of Stephen Mitchell, Boquhan; *m.* 1910, Helen Beatrice Murdoch; one *s.* one *d.* *Educ.:* Loretto; Jesus College, Cambridge. Director of Imperial Tobacco Company, Limited; Major Fife and Forfar Yeomanry; served European War, 1914-18; M.P. (U.) Lanark Division of Lanarkshire, 1924-29; Member of Royal Company of Archers (King's bodyguard for Scotland). High Sheriff of Gloucestershire, 1945-1946. *Address:* 26 Wellington Court, Knightsbridge, S.W.1. *Club:* Carlton. [*Died* 7 *June* 1951.

MITCHELL, Sir Thomas, Kt., *cr.* 1943; D.L.; J.P.; LL.D. Aberdeen, 1947; Member of Town Council of Aberdeen since 1928, Lord Provost, 1938-47; *b.* 25 June 1869; *m.* 1st, 1894, Charlotte (*d.* 1925), *d.* of Robert Slessor, Builder, Aberdeen; three *d.*; 2nd, 1927, Elizabeth J. Mitchell, M.B., Ch.B., *d.* of Rev. William Innes, M.A., Skene, Aberdeenshire. Chm. of Aberdeen Parish Council, 1922-25; Deacon Convener of the Seven Incorporated Trades of Aberdeen, 1930-32; Pres. Scottish Assoc. of Master Bakers, 1933; Chairman Scottish Transport Assoc. 1935-36, Aberdeen Harbour Commissioners and Territorial Army and Air Force Assoc., Aberdeen; Member Aberdeen Univ. Court since 1938. Order of the White Lion, Czechoslovakia. *Recreations:* bowling, golf, billiards. *Address:* 6 Belvidere Street, Aberdeen. *Club:* University (Aberdeen). [*Died* 15 *Aug.* 1959.

MITCHELL, Col. Wilfrid James, C.M.G. 1918; D.S.O. 1917; Indian Army (retired); *b.* 5 March 1871; *s.* of Alexander Mitchell, Montreal, Canada; *m.* 1921, Louisa Monica, *d.* of N. Coulthurst, of Gargrave, Yorkshire. *Educ.:* R.M.C. Kingston, Canada. 47th L. North Lanc. Regiment, 1891; transferred Indian Staff Corps, 1893; 24th Baluchistan Infantry (Duchess of Connaught's Own); served Chitral Relief Expedition, 1895 (medal with clasp); British East Africa, 1896 (medal); Somaliland, 1903-4, with Mounted Infantry (despatches, medal with two clasps); European War, 1914-19, in France, German E. Africa, Waziristan, Mesopotamia and Palestine (despatches thrice, D.S.O., C.M.G.); Waziristan, 1921-1922; Col. Comdt. 21st Infantry Brigade (despatches, medal and clasp). *Recreations:* shooting, golf. *Address:* c/o Lloyds Bank, Guernsey, C.I. *Club:* United Service. [*Died* 30 *June* 1953.

MITCHELL-HEDGES, Frederick Albert; Explorer and Author; *b.* 22 Oct. 1882; *s.* of John Hedges, of Stewkley, Bucks; *m.* 1906, Lilian Agnes Clarke; one *s.* *Educ.:* Berkhampstead; University College School, London, F.R.G.S.; F.L.S.; F.E.S.; F.R.A.I.; F.R.S.G.S.; Mem. of Cttee. British Museum Maya Exploration; Life-Member Museum of American Indian, Heye Foundation, New York; Pres., the Shark Angling Club of Great Britain; holds numerous world's records for capture of giant fish, and has added largely to the knowledge of ichthyological science; penetrated unknown portion of hinterland of Panama, 1922-23, discovering new race of people; presented large collection of hitherto totally unrecorded specimens to British Museum, Museums of Oxford and Cambridge, etc.; penetrated interior of British Honduras with Dr. T. W. F Gann, discovering ruins of vast Maya city of Lubaantun, 1924; returned 1925 to clear and excavate the Maya city, which led to the discovery of an aboriginal stone building covering nearly 8 acres, also a stone-built amphitheatre, the first ever found on the American Continent, and returned with many specimens which are now at the British Museum; revisited British Honduras, 1926; transferred interests in exclusive concessions obtained from Government of British Honduras to the British Museum, 1927; Ichthyological specimens collected in the Caribbean, presented to the South Kensington Museum; in 1930 led an expedition from the United States to Central America, penetrated into the interior of the Mosquitia in the Republic of Honduras; discovered ruins of great antiquity; donated entire collection of fine pottery to the Museum of the American Indian (Heye Foundation); in 1932, under the joint auspices of the British Museum and the Museum of the American Indian, Heye Foundation, conducted an expedition to the Islas Bahia in the Caribbean off the coast of the Republic of Honduras and donated to the two museums the resulting specimens; returned on another expedition to the Bay Islands, 1934, resulting in the excavating of many more ethnological specimens which were donated to museums internationally. Expedition to the Seychelles, exploration of atolls south of Mahé, chiefly the Amirantes, 1950; expedition to Southern Province of Tanganyika for investigating and exploring Islamic ruins in Kilwa Masoko region, discovering new site at Songo Manara and a hitherto unknown ruined city at Sanji Ya Manjomo, 1951. *Publications:* Battles with Giant Fish; The White Tiger; Land of Wonder and Fear; Battling with Sea Monsters; Danger My Ally; journalistic work and scientific articles. *Recreations:* big-game fishing, exploring, yachting, entomology. *Address:* Shaldon House, Shaldon, Teignmouth, S. Devon. *T.:* Shaldon 3301. [*Died* 12 *June* 1959.

MITCHESON, Sir George Gibson, Kt., *cr.* 1936; J.P.; Solicitor (retired); *b.* 27 June 1883; *s.* of late Thomas and Mary H. Mitcheson; *m.* 1911, Eveline Anne, *d.* of Charles James Critchley, Colliery Proprietor, Batley. *Educ.:* Privately. M.P. (U.) South-west St. Pancras, 1931-45; Member of the Guild of Freemen of the City of London, and Member of the Court of Assistants of the Worshipful Company of Gardeners; Vice-Pres. of the National Assoc. of Building Societies; Vice-Pres. of the National Temperance Hosp.; Chairman, H.S.F. Research Trust; Chairman, Hosa Research Laboratories; Vice-President The National Chamber of Trade; a member of Metropolitan Board of Legal and General Insurance Co. Ltd.; Hon. Arbitrator, Hearts of Oak Benefit Society. *Recreation:* golf. *Address:* 2 Mansfield Street, W.1. *Club:* Constitutional. [*Died* 18 *June* 1955.

MITCHINER, Philip Henry, C.B. 1944; C.B.E. 1938; Q.H.S. since 1952; Consulting Surgeon, St. Thomas's Hospital; Maj.-Gen., A.M.S. (T.A.), late Consulting Surgeon M.E.F.; Member of Senate, Univ. of London (Deputy Vice-Chancellor, 1951-53); Member of Council (Vice-Pres., 1950-52), Royal Coll. of Surgeons; D.L. Co. London, 1939; *b.* 17 June 1888; *s.* of late Henry M. Mitchiner and Blanche Mitchiner; *m.* 1928, Margaret Philpott. *Educ.:* Reigate. Served with Serbian Army at Salonika (Knight of St. Sava, and gold medal for devoted service, Order of St. Stanislaus, Russia, despatches); Territorial Decoration, 1926; Surg., Serbian Relief Fund under Serbian Govt., 1920-21; Surgeon, Out-patients, Roy. Northern Hospital, 1921-26. K.St.J. 1952. *Publications:* Science and Practice of Surgery; Surgical Emergencies in Practice; Modern Treatment of Burns and Scalds; Surgery for Dental Students; Medical Organisation and Surgical Practice in Air Raids; A Pocket Surgery; articles to professional journals. *Recreation:* University Training Corps and T.A. *Address:* 6 Morpeth Mansions, S.W.1. *Club:* Athenæum. [*Died* 15 *Oct.* 1952.

MITROPOULOS, Dimitri; Greek-American conductor, composer, pianist; conductor, Metropolitan Opera, N.Y., since 1954; *b.* Athens, Greece, 18 Feb. 1896; American citizen, 1946. Studied at Athens Conservatory of Music, in Belgium, and in Germany. Formerly Asst. Conductor Staats-

oper, Berlin; Professor Odéon, Athens; Conductor Athens Symphony Orchestra. Musical Director and Conductor, Minneapolis Symphony Orchestra, Minneapolis, U.S.A., from 1937; Guest Conductor New York Philharmonic-Symphony Orchestra, beginning 1940; Appointed Conductor New York Philharmonic Symphony Orchestra, 1949; appointed Musical Director, 1951; took the orchestra to Edinburgh for 14 performances in the Festival of Britain, 1951 and on Tour in Europe, 1955. Has been guest conductor with many other orchestras. Holds various European decorations. Member Athens Academy. *Address:* c/o Philharmonic-Symphony Society of New York, 113 W. 57th St. New York 19. [*Died* 2 *Nov.* 1960.

MITTON, Geraldine Edith; author; 5th *c.* of Rev. H. A. Mitton (*d.* 1918) and Annie Eliza Dury (*d.* 1903); *m.* Sir J. George Scott, K.C.I.E. (*d.* 1935). *Educ.:* home; Durham High School. Came to London 1896 and worked under late Sir Walter Besant on The Survey of London, subseq. edited it, 1902-12; joined staff of A. and C. Black, 1899; visited Burma and Ceylon, 1906-7; Egypt, 1913; Ceylon and India, 1915-16; India, 1937-38; editor Englishwoman's Year-Book, 1907-16; Writers' and Artists' Year-Book, 1907-20; Editorial work, Who's Who, 1899-1920. *Publications: Guides:* Black's Guide to Scotland, 1903-, and many others; *miscellaneous:* The Book of London, 1903; The Dog, 1904; Jane Austen and Her Times, 1905; Normandy, The Scenery of London, The Thames and Berks and Bucks (Beautiful Books Series), The Fascination of London, 1905-6, and in the Peeps Series; A Bachelor Girl in Burma, 1907; Austria-Hungary, 1914; Cornwall, 1915; The Lost Cities of Ceylon, 1916; Durham, 1924; Scott of The Shan Hills, 1936; *boys' books:* The Book of Stars, 1907; The Book of the Railway, 1909; In the Grip of the Wild Wa, 1913, now Head Hunters; Round the Wonderful World, 1914; Whaup Castle, 1925; Danna: The Camel, 1933; The Book of Scotland, 1934; The Book of England, 1936; *novels:* A Bachelor Girl in London, 1898; Fire and Tow, 1899; The Gifts of Enemies, 1900; The Opportunist, 1902; Hawk of the Desert, 1917; The Two-Stringed Fiddle, 1919; (with Sir J. G. Scott), The Green Moth, 1921; A Frontier Man, 1923; Bitter Harvest, 1926; The Wife of the Pig Dealer, 1927; Hidden Corners, 1928; On Solway Bridge, 1929; The Judge's Daughters, 1931; Sisters (serial) 1932, short stories, articles, etc. *Recreations:* books and fruit gardening. *Address:* Thereaway, Graffham, nr. Petworth, Sussex. *Clubs:* Lyceum (life), London Library (life). [*Died* 25 *April* 1955.

MOBBS, Sir (Arthur) Noel, K.C.V.O. *cr.* **1948; O.B.E. 1918; Chairman: United Motor Finance Corporation Ltd., M.L. Holdings Ltd. and other Public Companies; *b.* 8 June 1880; *s.* of Oliver Linnell Mobbs and Elizabeth, *d.* of Colonel W. G. Hollis; *m.* 1st, 1903, Frances Mary Tanner (*d.* 1929); three *s.* one *d.*; 2nd, 1932, Helen Gertrude Cornish. *Educ.:* Bedford Modern School. Assistant Director (Hon.) Food Production Department, 1917-1918; Member of Advisory Committee of Ministry of Munitions, 1919; President Motor and Cycle Trades Benevolent Fund, 1933; High Sheriff of Buckinghamshire, 1945; Member of Stoke Poges Committee of National Trust; Chairman Nuffield Health and Social Services Fund; Member of National Council of Social Service; Founder of Slough Community Centre; Founder Slough Industrial Health Service; Hon. Pres. (formerly Chm.) Slough Estates Ltd.; Lord of the Manor, Stoke Poges. C.St.J. *Publication:* Curling in Switzerland, 1929. *Address:* Stanwix House, Westbourne, Bournemouth. *T.:* Westbourne 64985. *Club:* Portland. [*Died* 25 *Nov.* 1959.**

MOBERLY, Brigadier Archibald Henry, D.S.O. 1916; *b.* 3 Jan. 1879; *s.* of late Col. W. H. Moberly; *m.* 1908, Ethel Elizabeth (*d.* 1951), *d.* of late Col. A. Tracey, R.A.; one *d.* *Educ.:* Sherborne School; R.M. Academy, Woolwich. Commissioned in Royal Artillery, 1898; served European War (despatches five times, D.S.O., Brevet Lieut.-Col., Legion of Honour, Order of Savoia, Order of St. Maurice and Lazarus); Commandant School of Artillery, Kakul, N.W.F.P. India, 1923-27; Assistant Director of Artillery, War Office, 1927-30; Brigadier, R.A., Northern Command, India, 1930-34; retired pay, 1934. *Address:* Runnymede, Newland, Sherborne, Dorset. [*Died* 18 *Oct.* 1960

MOBERLY, Brig.-Gen. Frederick James, C.B. 1920; C.S.I. 1919; D.S.O. 1893 retired; employed Historical Section Committee of Imperial Defence, 1920-30; *b.* Madras 15 Sept. 1867; 2nd *s.* of late Col. C. M. Moberly, I.S.C.; *m.* 1901, May (*d.* 1950), *d.* of Rev. Thomas Johns, Manor Owen, Co. Pembroke; one *s.* one *d.* *Educ.:* Cheltenham; Edinburgh Academy; R.M.C., Sandhurst; Staff College, Camberley. 2nd Oxford L.I. 1888; 37th Dogras, 1891; 25th Punjabis, 1903; in India since 1888; on special duty under Foreign Dept. in Gilgit, 1892-96; on plague duty under Govt. of Bombay, 1899 (thanks of Govt. of Bombay); Assistant Secretary Government of India Military Department, 1902-6; D.A.A.G. Presidency Brigade, 1908-10; General Staff 9th Division, 1910-12; General Staff Officer, Hong Kong, 1914; General Staff, England, 1915-16; A.A. and Q.M.G. England, 1917; General Staff A.H.Q. India, 1917; Director of Military Operations, India, 1917-20; and Deputy Chief of General Staff, India, 1919-20; Member of Indo-Afghan Peace Delegation, July 1919. Served Burma 1891; Wuntho, served as Transport Officer (medal and clasp); N.E. Frontier of India, Manipur, served as Transport officer (clasp); N.W. Frontier of India Chilas (severely wounded, despatches, D.S.O.); Chitral, commanded at Mastuj during its investment and took part in Colonel Kelly's march (despatches, specially promoted to Capt., medal and clasp); N.W. Frontier, 1898 (clasp); South Africa, 1900 (despatches, medal with 6 clasps, Brevet of Major); N.W. Frontier, 1908, operations in Zakka Khel country (medal and clasp); British War medal, 1914-19; specially promoted to substantive Major or 13 Feb. 1905; retired, 1920. *Publications:* History of the Great War: The Campaign in Mesopotamia, 1914-18; Military Operations, Togoland and the Cameroons, 1914-16; Operations in Persia, 1914-19. *Recreations:* fishing, gardening. *Address:* Fairlea, Bideford, Devon. *T.:* Bideford 329. [*Died* 6 *April* 1952.

MOENS, Hon. Lt.-Col. Seaburne Godfrey Arthur May, C.I.E. 1917; C.B.E. 1918; Knight of Grace, Order of St. John of Jerusalem; F.R.G.S.; *b.* 25 Sept. 1876; *s.* of late Seaburne May Moens, Indian Civil Service, and late Emma Monteath, *d.* of General George Mytton Hill. *Educ.:* Charterhouse; Wren's. Travelling and private tutoring, 1898-1906; Headmaster, Down House, Rottingdean, Sussex, 1906-36. Served European War, 1915-19 (despatches). *Publication:* Rottingdean, the Story of a Village, 1952. *Recreations:* shooting, fishing. *Address:* Dene Cottage, Rottingdean, Sx. [*Died* 13 *Oct.* 1956.

MOFFAT, Graham; Scottish playwright, actor and producer; *b.* Glasgow, 21 Feb. 1866; *s.* of William Moffat and Helen Dobson; *m.* 1897, Maggie Liddel Linck; one *d.* *Educ.:* Rosemount Academy, Glasgow. Entered office of Buchanan, Wilson & Co.; took to elocution and photography as hobbies and made them professions, 1893; during winter months gave recitals with sister, Kate Moffat; during summer months employed by Valentine & Sons, Dundee, as landscape photographer; took to writing plays as a hobby, 1907, and made that a profession, 1910; Bunty Pulls the Strings, produced at the Playhouse, 4 July 1911, and afterwards ran at the Haymarket Theatre for over 600 performances; other plays, A Scrape o' the Pen, News from London, Granny, The Concealed Bed, Till the Bells Ring, etc. *Publications:* Towards Eternal Day (psychic experiences), 1948. Bunty Pulls the Strings; A Scrape o' the Pen; Susie Tangles the Strings; Granny. *Recreation:* psychical research. *Address:* Côte d'Azur, Camp Bay Drive, Cape Town, S. Africa. [*Died* 12 *Dec.* 1951.

MOFFAT, Hon. Howard Unwin, C.M.G. 1927; *b.* 13 Jan. 1869; *s.* of Rev. J. S. Moffat, C.M.G.; *m.* 1903, M. H. Meikle, Bulawayo; one *s* two *d.* *Educ.:* St. Andrew's College, Grahamstown. Joined Standard Bank, Grahamstown; joined the Bechuanaland Exploration Co., 1889; went up to Khama's Country, Bechuanaland; went into Matabeleland with Col. Gould Adam's column as interpreter for Khama's regt., 1893; General Supt. of B.E. Co., 1898; Lieutenant in Gifford's Horse, Matabele Rebellion, 1896; in Boer War was in Plumer's column, and in the relief of Mafeking; returned for Parliament for Victoria constituency, 1920; defeated for Gwelo, 1933; Minister of Mines and Public Works, 1923-27; Premier and Minister of Native Affairs, S. Rhodesia, 1927-33. *Address:* Ormiston, Shangani, S. Rhodesia. *Clubs:* Bulawayo (Bulawayo); Salisbury (Salisbury). [*Died* 19 *Jan.* 1951.

MOFFET, Stanley Ormerod, M.A.; Librarian, University College of South Wales and Monmouthshire, Cardiff, 1919-51; *b.* 19 May 1886; *s.* of late J. J. Moffet, Kendal; *m.* Barbara Mary, *d.* of C. R. O. Garrard, M.R.C.S.; two *s.* *Educ.:* Kendal Grammar School; Manchester University. Assistant Librarian, John Rylands Library, Manchester, 1909-19; On active service, 1915-19. *Address:* The Rossett, Rhiwbina, Cardiff. [*Died* 23 *Feb.* 1960.

MOGGRIDGE, Lieut.-Colonel Harry Weston, C.M.G. 1919; late Asst. Secretary, War Office; *b.* 1879; *m.* 1st, 1906, Isabel, *d.* of late Rev. William Cornish Hunt; 2nd, 1935, Helen, *d.* of late Allan Macnab Taylor; two *s.* *Educ.:* Radley; Corpus Christi College, Oxford. B.A. 1903; served South Africa, 1900-01 (Queen's medal with four clasps); European War 1916-18 (despatches, Bt. Major, C.M.G., Legion of Honour); retired, 1946. *Address:* 7 Park Crescent, Tonbridge. *T.:* Tonbridge 3899. [*Died* 23 *March* 1960.

MOHAMED AKBAR KHAN, Lt.-Col. Nawab Sir, K.B.E., *cr.* 1931; C.I.E. 1917; Landlord in N.W.F.P. (India); *b.* 27 Feb. 1885; *s.* of K. B. Khwaja Mohamed Khan. *Educ.:* Chief's College, Lahore; Imperial Cadet Corps, Dehra Dun. Joined the Indian Land Forces as 2nd Lieutenant, and accompanied Sir Louis Dane's Commission to Afghanistan, 1904-5; attended Prince of Wales, 1906; was on special duty with Amir of Afghanistan, 1907; Lieutenant, 1907; Orderly Officer to the Inspecting Officer, Frontier Corps, Peshawar, 1907-8; transferred to Malwa Bhil Corps, Indore, 1908-14; Captain, 1914; served with the Imperial Service Troops in Egypt, 1914; Suvla Bay (Gallipoli), 1915; A.D.C. to General Sir H. D. Watson at Elchatt, 1916; Somme Campaign with 3rd Ambala Cavalry Brigade, 1916; transferred to the Indian Army and posted with 1/1st Brahmins, 1917; Assist. Recruiting Officer, Rawalpindi, 1918; took part in Aden Field Force (1/1st Brahmins), 1918, and 3rd Afghan War in connection with the Relief of Thal (124 Baluchis), 1919 (despatches twice, Bronze Star, 1914-15; British War Medal, 1914-19; Victory Medal and Indian General Service Medal, 1908, with clasp inscribed Afghanistan, N.W.F., 1919); retired as Major, 1922; Additional District Magistrate, Mardan, 1921; President, Advisory Committee, Indian Territorial Forces, N.W.F.P.; Member of the Council of State, 1922; *cr.* Nawab, 1928. *Address:* Hoti, N.W.F. Province, India. [*Died* 6 *Oct.* 1952.

MOIR, Capt. Sir Arrol, 2nd Bt., *cr.* 1916; B.A., M.Inst.C.E., Hon. M.Brit.I.R.E. (Past Pres.); M.R.I.; late R.E.; Vice-Pres., Institute of Patentees; Vice-Pres. Isle of Thanet Conservative Association; *b.* 16 Sept. 1894; *o. s.* of Sir Ernest Moir, 1st Bt. (*d.* 1933), and Margaret Bruce (*d.* 1942), *d.* of late John Pennycook of Ravelstone, and Dalmeny, Midlothian; *S.* father, 1933; *m.* 1922, Dorothy Blanche, *d.* of late Adm. Sir Percy Royds, C.B., C.M.G.; one *s.* two *d.* *Educ.:* Repton; Caius College, Cambridge. Served European War, 1914-19. *Heir:* *s.* Ernest Ian Royds, *b.* 9 June 1925. *Address:* 9 Queens Elm Square, Church Street, Chelsea, S.W.3; Little Court, St. Peter's in Thanet. *Club:* Royal Automobile. [*Died* 8 *Aug.* 1957.

MOIRA, Gerald, R.W.S.; R.O.I.; R.W.A.; H.A.R.I.B.A.; President Royal Institute of Oil Painters; *b.* London; *s.* of Edward Moira and Eugina Moira, both Portuguese; *m.* Alice Mary, *d.* of late William Vicary, J.P., The Knoll, Newton Abbot; four *s.* *Educ.:* privately. Artist. Mural Decorations: Central Criminal Court, London; National Church House, Liverpool; United Kingdom Providence Institution, London; Lloyd's Register, London, and much other work as well as many pictures. *Recreations:* outdoor games. *Address:* The Chalfonts, 13 Dene Rd., Northwood, Middlesex. *Club:* Arts. [*Died* 2 *Aug.* 1959.

MOLAMURE, Sir (Alexander) Francis, K.B.E., *cr.* 1949; Speaker, House of Representatives, Ceylon, since 1947; *b.* 7 Feb. 1886; *s.* of A. F. Molamure, Ratemahatmaya and Molamure Kumarihamy; *m.* 1912, Adeline Meedeniya; two *d.* *Educ.:* St. Thomas College, Colombo. Called to Bar, 1910; went to England on deputation for Reforms, 1919; M.L.C., 1924; M.E.C., 1926; State Council, 1931; Speaker of State Council, 1931; M.H.R., 1947. Rep. Ceylon at Commonwealth Parliamentary Conf., 1948; rep. Ceylon as guest of House of Commons at ceremonial opening, 1950. *Recreations:* cricket, golf, tennis. *Address:* Mumtaz Mahal, Colombo. *T.:* 2262 (residence), 4656 (office). [*Died* 25 *Jan.* 1951.

MOLESWORTH, Hugh Wilson, C.B.E.; *b.* 9 Sept. 1870; *s.* of Lt.-Col. A. O. Molesworth, late R.A., and Annie Hope, *d.* of Major Hope Smith; *m.* 1903, Dora, *d.* of Sir R. Hanbury Brown; two *s.* one *d.* *Educ.:* Redland Hill House, Clifton; Bristol University; Royal Indian Engineering College, Coopers Hill. Joined the Egyptian Public Works Irrigation Service as Surveyor of Contracts, 1895; Inspector General of Irrigation, 1913; Assistant Under Secretary of State, 1917; served as temporary Lt.-Col. in Suez Canal Defence force (1915 Star, War and Victory medals, despatches); retired from the Egyptian Government Service, 1923; has the Defence Medal, 1939-45, Orders of the Nile, Osmanieh and Medjedieh. *Publication:* Irrigation Practice in Egypt. *Recreations:* fishing and shooting. *Address:* Broad Oak, Crawley Down, Sussex. *T.A.:* Copthorne. *T.:* Copthorne 82. [*Died* 5 *Jan.* 1959.

MOLESWORTH, Colonel William, C.I.E. 1914; C.B.E. 1918; V.H.S. 1916; I.M.S., retired; M.B., B.S. (Durham); M.R.C.S. (Lond.); L.R.C.P. (Eng.); *b.* Colombo, 30 Dec. 1865; *s.* of late Lt.-Colonel A. O. Molesworth, R.A., of Cruicksfield, Duns, Berwickshire; *m.* 1893, Winifred, *d.* of late T. Earle Weekes, J.P. of Hazledean, Co. Cork; one *s.* one *d.* *Educ.:* Redland Hill House, Clifton. Served Wuntho Field Force, 1890-91 (medal and clasp); Surgeon to the Governor of Madras, 1899-1905, and 1906-8; to the Viceroy, 1904; Presidency Surgeon, 1st District, Madras, 1912; late Senior Medical Officer, Govt. General Hospital, Madras; Acting Professor of Medicine, Medical College, Madras, and First Physician, General Hospital; D.D.M.S. in India, 1917-20; retired, 1921; late County Commissioner Boy Scouts, Berwickshire. *Publications:* Papers on Fishing in India. *Recreation:* fishing. *Address:*

Cruicksfield, Duns, Berwickshire. *T.:* Cumledge 29 (Borders). [*Died* 27 *Feb.* 1951.

MOLIN, C. Hjalmar V; Architect Etcher of architectonic subjects; *b.* 23 Feb. 1868; *s.* of J. P. Molin, Sculptor and Professor of the Royal Academy of Fine Arts in Stockholm, and Emma Broberg; *m.* 1904, Gerda Hahr. *Educ.:* The Polytechnical Institute and the High School of the Royal Academy of Fine Arts in Stockholm. After having practised as architect several years, began to etch, 1901; A.R.E., 1904-28; entered 1912 as member in the Swedish Artists' Association, 1913 in the Graphic Society in Stockholm (now retired), and 1914 as member of the Royal Academy of Fine Arts. *Recreations:* travels for studying art in England, France, Spain, Italy, Germany, Austria, Turkey, and Greece. *Address:* Gryt, Sweden. [*Died* 4 *March* 1954.

MOLLETT, Sir John, Kt., *cr.* 1946; Director of Potato and Carrot Supplies, Ministry of Food, 1939-50; Chairman of Potato Marketing Board, 1934-50; *b.* 7 June 1892; *s.* of Thomas and Mary Anna Mollett; *m.* 1918; two *s.* three *d.*; *m.* 1949, Nesta Kathleen, *er. d.* of Reginald W. Lone, Deep Dene, Buckhurst Hill, Essex. *Educ.:* privately. Royal Field Artillery, 1915-19; 49th (West Riding) and 17th Divisions; Captain and Adjutant 79th F.A. Brigade. Commander de l'Ordre de Mérite (agricole) (France), 1938. *Address:* Hay-a-Park, Knaresborough, Yorks. *T.A.* and *T.:* Knaresborough 3144. *Clubs:* Junior Carlton, Farmers'. [*Died* 12 *July* 1952.

MOLLISON, James Allan, M.B.E. 1946; F.R.G.S.; A.F.R.Ae.S.; Aviator; *b.* 19 April 1905; *s.* of Hector Alexander Mollison and Thomasina Macnee Addie; *m.* 1st, 1932, Amy Johnson (who obtained a divorce, 1938; she *d.* 1941); 2nd, 1938, Phyllis Louis Verley Hussey (from whom he obtained a divorce, 1948); 3rd, 1949, Maria Clasina Eva Kamphuis. *Educ.:* Glasgow and Edinburgh Academies. Commissioned Royal Air Force, 1923; transferred Reserve, 1928; subsequently air mail pilot in Australia; Australia-England record, 8 days 19 hrs. 28 mins., July/August, 1931; England-Cape record, first flight to Cape by West Coast route, March 1932, 4 days 17 hrs. 5 mins.; First solo Westward flight, North Atlantic, Aug. 1932; First solo Westward flight, South Atlantic, first flight England-South America, Feb. 1933; first flight United Kingdom to U.S.A. (together with wife), July 1933; England-India record 22 hours (together with wife) Oct. 1934; New York-Newfoundland-London (North Atlantic record crossing coast to coast, 9 hrs. 20 mins.) Oct. 1936; England-Cape by Eastern route, 3 days 6 hrs., Nov. 1936; Britannia Trophy and Johnston Memorial Air Navigation Trophy; Argentine Gold Medal for Aeronautics, twice awarded Gold Medal of City of New York; Freedom of Atlantic City; Lieut.-Col. Governor's Staff State of Texas, U.S.A. *Publication:* Death Cometh Soon or Late, Autobiography. *Recreation:* swimming. *Club:* Royal Aero. [*Died* 30 *Oct.* 1959.

MOLTENO, Vice-Admiral Vincent Barkly, C.B. 1918; *b.* 30 April 1872; 7th *s.* of late Sir John Molteno, K.C.M.G., first Premier of Cape Colony; *m.* Ethel Manwaring, *e. d.* of late Herbert Manwaring Robertson of Alice Holt, Farnham; one *d.* Lieut. with Naval Brigade, landed at Vitu, Zanzibar, 1893 (despatches, medal, clasp); in Controller's Depart., Admiralty, 1907-10; Flag Captain, 3rd Cruiser Squadron, 1913; served European War in Command of the following ships; H.M.S. Antrim, Flag Captain, 3rd Cruiser Squadron, H.M.S. Revenge (despatches), H.M.S. Warrior (despatches, Russian Order of St. Anne with Swords), H.M.S. King George V., Flag Captain, 2nd Battle Squadron, H.M.S. Minotaur, H.M.S. Shannon and H.M.S. Bellerophon; A.D.C. to the King, 1920; Rear-Adm. 1921; retired, 1921; Vice-Adm. retired, 1926. *Address:* Goldhill, Farnham, Surrey. *Club:* United Service. [*Died* 12 *Nov.* 1952.

MOLYNEUX, Major Hon. Sir Richard F., K.C.V.O., *cr.* 1935 (C.V.O. 1925); retd.; late Royal Horse Guards; late Extra Equerry to Queen Mary; *b.* 24 March 1873; 3rd *s.* of 4th Earl of Sefton. Entered Army, 1894; served North-West Frontier of India with Tirah Expeditionary Force, 1897-98 (medal with two clasps); Soudan, 1898, battle of Khartoum (severely wounded, despatches, British medal, and Khedive's medal with clasp); South African war, 1899-1901 (medal with three clasps); France and Belgium, 1914-1915, with Royal Horse Guards. *Address:* 25 Berkeley Square, W.1. *T.:* Grosvenor 1070. *Clubs:* Turf, Brooks's, Guards. [*Died* 20 *Jan.* 1954.

MONCK, (Walter) Nugent (Bligh), C.B.E. 1958 (O.B.E. 1946); F.R.A.M. 1935; Founder of the Maddermarket Theatre, Norwich; Director and producer of plays, 1911-1952, retired; *b.* Welshampton, Salop, 4 Feb. 1878; *s.* of Rev. George Gustavus Monck and Hester Isabella Nugent; unmarried. *Educ.:* Roy. Institution School, Liverpool; Roy. Acad. of Music. Educated in music from the age of 6; became a student of the R.A.M. in 1893; studied for the stage in 1895 under the late William Farren at the R.A.M.; toured the provinces, 1898-1900; started producing for amateurs, 1901; first mystery play revival, the Chester Plays, 1905; settled in Norwich, 1909; started the Norwich Players, 1911; was producer to the Abbey Theatre, Dublin, in 1912, and went to America with that company, 1913; returned to the Norwich Players, 1914; enlisted in the R.A.M.C., Sept. 1914; in Egypt, March 1915-18, where he produced five of Shakespeare's plays with the men; in Salonika, 1918-19; reconstructed the Norwich Players, Sept. 1919, at the old Music House, Norwich; in 1921 the Players opened their present Elizabethan playhouse; has produced 300 plays (including all of Shakespeare's) for the Norwich Players; also produced the following Pageants, Norwich, 1926; Northampton, 1930; Ipswich, 1930; Ramsgate, 1934; Nottingham, 1935; Chester, 1937; Manchester, 1938. *Publications:* The Masques of Anne Bolyn, 1909; Narcissus, 1910; The Mancroft Pageant, Norwich, 1912; The Masque of Revelry, 1921; The Norwich Pageant, 1926; King Robert of Sicily, Leeds, 1927; The Wolsey Commemoration Play, Ipswich, 1930. Produced Cymbeline, 1946, and Pericles, 1947, at Stratford-upon-Avon Shakespeare Festival; Merchant of Venice, Kingstown, Jamaica, 1950; The Masques of Cupid, Blickling Hall, Norfolk, 1957. *Recreations:* travelling, the stage. *Address:* Ninham's Court, Norwich. *T.:* Norwich 22573. [*Died* 21 *Oct.* 1958.

MONCREIFFE of that Ilk, Sir David Gerald, 10th Bt., *cr.* 1685; M.C. 1944; 23rd feudal Baron of Moncreiffe since 1247; Member Queen's Body Guard for Scotland (Royal Company of Archers); Captain Scots Guards, 1945; *b.* 29 July 1922; *s.* of Commander Sir Guy Moncreiffe of that Ilk, 9th Bt., and Mary, *o. d.* of late John Balli; *S.* father 1934. *Educ.:* Eton. Served war of 1939-45 (wounded twice). *Heir:* *cousin,* Rupert Iain Kay Moncreiffe. *Address:* Moncreiffe, Bridge of Earn, Perthshire. *T.:* Bridge of Earn 378; 12 Hyde Park Place, W.2. *T.:* Ambassador 4786. *Clubs:* Guards, Pratt's; Royal and Ancient Golf (St. Andrews). [*Died* 17 *Nov.* 1957.

MONEY, Maj.-Gen. Sir Arthur Wigram, K.C.B., *cr.* 1917 (C.B. 1908); K.B.E., *cr.* 1919; C.S.I. 1916; R.A.; retd. Mar. 1920; *b.* 23 Oct. 1866; *y. s.* of late Gilbert Pocklington Money, Bengal Civil Service; *m.* 1st, 1903, Cicely Frances Wedgwood (*d.* 1904); 2nd, 1911, Euphemia Mabel, *y. d.* of G. Drummond, Swaylands, Penshurst, and *widow* of Captain Alastair Brodie; three *s.* one *d.* *Educ.:* Charterhouse. Joined R.A., 1885; served Zhob Valley expedition, 1890; Isazai, 1892; N.-W. Frontier, 1897-98 (despatches, brevet Major, medal two clasps); South Africa, 1899-1902 (despatches, brevet Lt.-Col., Queen's medal three clasps, King's medal two clasps); Zakka Khel expedition, 1908 (despatches); Mohmand expedition, 1908 (despatches, C.B., medal and clasp); European War, Mesopotamia, Egyptian Expeditionary Force, 1915-19 (C.S.I., K.C.B., K.B.E., despatches). *Address:* Hungershall Park, Tunbridge Wells, Kent. *Club:* United Service. [*Died* 25 *Oct.* 1951.

MONEY, Brig.-Gen. Ernest Douglas, C.I.E. 1911; C.V.O. 1919; D.S.O. 1918; *b.* 11 Mar. 1866; *s.* of Major-General Robert Cotton Money and Selina Mary, *d.* of William Sholto Douglas, Lansdowne House, Bath; *m.* 1891, Winifred Mabel (*d.* 1937), 2nd *d.* of late Lt.-Col. H. Miles Burgess, R. A.; one *s.* one *d.* *Educ.:* Sherborne. Entered army, 1888; 2nd Lt. X. Lincolnshire Regt.; A.D.C. to Governor, United Provinces, 1889-90; Lieut. 1st P.W.O. Gurkha Rifles, 1891; Capt., 1899; Major, 1906; Lt.-Col., 1915; served Isazai, 1892; Waziristan, 1894-95 (medal with clasp); Tirah, 1895-98 (medal with clasp); Assist. Military Secretary to the King-Emperor, 1911-12; commanded 2/1st King George's Own Ghurka Rifles, 1915; operations against Swat and Boners, also Mohmand Expeditions, 1916-17 (despatches); Waziristan, Mahsud Operations, 1917; commanded unit and temporarily 45th Infantry Brigade; Brig.-Gen. Inspector Indian Depots, Quetta Division, 1918; selected Brig.-Gen., Indian Contingent, Peace Celebrations, 1919 (C.V.O.); Brig.-Gen. commanding 64th Infantry Brigade, 1919; 66th Infantry Brigade, Lahore Cant., 1919-20; retired, 1920. *Recreations:* racquets, lawn tennis, mountaineering, fishing, big-game shooting. *Address:* c/o Lloyds Bank, 6 Pall Mall, S.W.1. *Club:* Alpine. [*Died* 4 *Dec.* 1952.

MONEY, Col. Robert Cotton, C.M.G. 1917; C.B.E. 1919; retired pay; late K.O.Y.L.I.; *b.* 10 Jan. 1861; *s.* of late Maj.-Gen. R. C. Money, B.S.C., of Hopebourne, Canterbury, and Selina Mary, *d.* of William Douglas of Lansdown House, Bath; *m.* Geraldine Maria (*d.* 1947), *d.* of Frederick Wheeler, Worcester Park House, Surrey; one *s.* *Educ.:* Harrow. Entered Army, 1881; Lt. Col. 1904; Bt.-Col. 1907; retd., 1909; served European War, 1914-19 (despatches 5 times, C.M.G., C.B.E.). *Recreations:* shooting, fishing. *Address:* The Woodland, Glasbury-on-Wye, via Hereford. *T.:* Glasbury-on-Wye 2. *Club:* Flyfishers'. [*Died* 21 *Jan.* 1954.

MONIZ, Dr. Egas (Antonio Caetano de Abren Freire); Professor of Neurology, Faculty of Medicine, University of Lisbon, Portugal, since 1911; *b.* Avanca, Portugal, 29 Nov. 1874; *s.* of Fernando de Rezende and Maria de Rosario de Sousa; *m.* 1902, Elvira de Macedo Dias. *Educ.:* Universities of Coimbra, Bordeaux, Paris, Prof. Univ. of Coimbra until 1911. Dir. Institute of Neurology, for Scientific Investigations, Lisbon; Physician, Hosp. of Santa Marta, Lisbon. Served as Deputy, Portuguese Liberal Parl.; Minister of Portugal in Madrid, 1918; Pres. Portuguese Deleg. at Conf. in La Paz, 1918; Minister for Foreign Affairs, 1918-19. Member: Acad. des Ciencias, Lisbon (Pres. at various times); Acad. de Médecine, Paris; Acad. Brasileira de Letras; Acad. de Medicina, Madrid; Hon. Member, Roy. Soc. Med., etc. Grand Cross of: Isabel la Católica (Spain); Instrução Publica (Portugal); Santiago de Espada; Comdr. Legion of Honour. Nobel Prize (joint) for physiology, medicine, 1949 (discovered Cerebral Angiography and Pre-frontal Leucotomy). *Publications:* A Neurologia na Guerra, 1918; Tumeurs cérébrales, Encéphalógraphie artérielle, 1931; L'Angiographie cérébrale, (Paris) 1934; Tentatives opératoires dans le traitement de certaines psychoses, 1936; Die cerebrale Arteriographie und Phlebographie, 1940; Trombosas y otras obstrucciones de las Carotidas, (Barcelona) 1941, etc. *Address:* Avenida Cinco de Outubro 73, Lisbon, Portugal. [*Died* 13 *Dec.* 1955.

MONKHOUSE, Sir Edward (Bertram), Kt., *cr.* 1950; C.B.E. 1947; *b.* 28 Sept. 1890; *s.* of Joseph Monkhouse; *m.* 1917, Ethel Thompson; one *d.* *Educ.:* Liscard High School, Wallasey. Served European War, 1914-18, Liverpool Scottish T.F. President: Liverpool Timber Trade Association, 1930; Timber Trade Federation of the U.K., 1936-37; Timber Controller, Board of Trade, 1947-52. Joint Managing Director: Duncan Ewing Co. Ltd., Liverpool and London; Deodor-x Co. of England Ltd., Ellesmere Port. *Recreation:* walking. *Address:* 8 Huntingdon House, Cromwell Rd., S.W.5. *T.:* Fremantle 3365. *Clubs:* Constitutional, Royal Automobile. [*Died* 3 *Jan.* 1959.

MONRO, Alexander, C.I.E. 1931; *b.* 17 Feb. 1890; *s.* of Alexander Monro; *m.* 1929, Janet Elizabeth Carmichael, *d.* of David Monro; one *s.* *Educ.:* Charterhouse; Magdalen College, Oxford. Joined Indian Civil Service, 1912; arrived in India, 1913; served since then in various capacities in the executive branch of the service in the United Provinces; retired, 1939. Served Min. of Food during War of 1939-45, and until 1948. General Manager, Orient Airways, Pakistan, 1949-51. *Recreation:* shooting. *Address:* 49 Warwick Square, S.W.1. *Club:* Oxford and Cambridge. [*Died* 8 *May* 1953.

MONRO, Alexander William, C.B. 1919; late Ministry of Agriculture and Fisheries; *b.* 1875; *s.* of George Home, Binning Monro, New Zealand; *m.* 1910, Geraldine Marion, *d.* of M. Murray Johnson; one *s.* one *d.* *Educ.:* Radley. Private Secretary to successive Presidents of Ministry of Agriculture and Fisheries, 1915-19. *Address:* Walton House, Walton Street, S.W.3. *T.:* Sloane 1393. [*Died* 28 *April* 1960.

MONRO, Major-General David Carmichael, C.B. 1946; C.B.E. 1943; F.R.C.S. (Edinburgh); *b.* 19 May 1886; *s.* of late Charles John Monro, Craiglockhart, Palmerston North, N.Z.; *m.* 1942, Kathleen Noone; one adopted *d.* *Educ.:* Wellington College, N.Z.; Edinburgh Univ. (M.B., Ch.B. 1911, F.R.C.S.Ed. 1934). Temp. Commission R.A.M.C. 1914, Regular 1917; went to India 1918; Specialist in Surgery in India, U.K., and Malta; Personal Surgeon to C.-in-C. in India (F.M. Sir P. Chetwode), 1931; Asst. Professor Military Surgery, R.A.M. College, London, 1938; Consulting Surgeon to British Army and Prof. Mil. Surgery, R.A.M. College, 1940-45; Consultant Surgeon M.E.F., Cairo, 1941-42; Army Representative on Allied Surgical Mission to Moscow, June-July 1943; K.H.S.; retired pay, 1945, but re-employed as Consultant Surgeon M.E.L.F. until final retirement, Nov. 1948. External Examiner in Surgery, Fouad I Univ., Cairo, and Kitchener Medical School, Khartoum. Legion of Merit, degree of Commander (U.S.A.), 1947; King Haakon VII Liberty Cross (Norway), 1947. *Publications:* contributions to Medical Journals; The Medical Services in Burma (Surgery), Army Quarterly, 1946. *Recreations:* golf, swimming, yachting, fishing. *Address:* Fiftyone, Roehampton Lane, S.W.15. *T.:* Prospect 6087. *Club:* Roehampton. [*Died* 6 *Dec.* 1960.

MONRO, Edwin George, C.B.E. 1949 (O.B.E. 1930); Chairman and Managing Director Geo. Monro Ltd., Fruit Brokers, Covent Garden, since 1920; *b.* 1875; *e. s.* of late George Monro, Eagle's Nest, Hampstead, N.W.; *m.* 1897, Maude Mayfield, *d.* of late Alderman Thomas Gurney Randall; one *s.* two *d.* (and one *s.* decd.). *Educ.:* Private School; University College School, Hampstead. Joined London Scottish, 1898;

commnd., 1903; served European War: 1st Bn., France, Sept. 1914; Musketry Officer, Southern Command, 1916-17; gazetted out, rank Major, 1920. Member Coal Enquiry Board, 1939. Hon. Trade Adviser, Ministry of Food, and to War Office, during War of 1939-45; Member Empire Marketing Board; Managing Director, National Vegetable Marketing Board, 1941. *Recreations:* Rugby, hockey and rifle shooting (international shot, Capt. Scotland some years ago; Vice-Chm. Nat. Rifle Assoc., 1939-46, Chm., 1946-1952). *Address:* (business) 43 King St., Covent Garden. *T.:* Temple Bar 6761; (private) Woodview, Hempstead Rd., Watford. *T.:* Watford 3122. [*Died* 22 *May* 1954.

MONRO, George, C.B.E. 1927; Joint Managing Director, Geo. Monro, Ltd. (fruit broker); *b.* 24 March 1876; *s.* of George Monro, Hampstead; *m.* 1897, Helena, *d.* of Edward Oliver; one *s.* one *d.* *Educ.:* University Coll. School. Past Pres., Commercial Motor Users Association, British Chamber of Horticulture, British Florists Federation and International Horticultural Federation; Mem.of Council R.Hort.S.; Treasurer and Member of Executive Council, Automobile Association; Chevalier of Order of the Crown of Belgium; Chevalier of the Mérite Agricole of France; Victoria Medal of Honor, 1935. *Recreation:* shooting. *Address:* The Red House, Hendon Lane, N.3. *T.A.:* Monro, London. *Clubs:* St. Stephen's, Royal Automobile. [*Died* 14 *Nov.* 1951.

MONRO, Thomas Kirkpatrick, M.A. (Glasg.), M.D., Hon. LL.D.; Emeritus Regius Professor of Practice of Medicine, Glasgow University; Hon. Fellow (Ex-President) Royal Faculty of Physicians and Surgeons, Glasgow; Hon. Member (Ex-Pres.) Assoc. of Physicians of Great Britain and Ireland; Hon. Member (Ex-Pres.) Royal Medico-Chirurgical Soc. of Glasgow; Mem. B.M.A.; Mem. of Executive Cttee., Orphan Homes of Scotland and Colony for Epileptics; *b.* Arbroath, 6 Sept. 1865; *e. s.* of Wm. Monro, M.D., Arbroath, and Jane, *e. d.* of Thomas Kirkpatrick, Glasgow; *m.* 1905, Jane Christian (*d.* 1951), *e. d.* of Wm. Brand, Glasgow; two *s.* one *d.* *Educ.:* Arbroath High School; Glasgow Univ. After qualifying, studied in Vienna, Berlin, and Paris, and held office as Pathologist, Victoria Infirmary; Examiner in Pathology, Glasgow Univ.; Examiner in Medicine, Univs. of Dublin (T.C.D.), Durham, and St. Andrews; Physician and Clinical Lecturer, Glasgow Royal Infirmary; Manager of Glasgow Royal Infirmary; Director, Glasgow Royal Maternity and Women's Hospital; Professor of Medicine and Dean of the Medical Faculty, St. Mungo's College; Examiner for the Fellowship and for the License of the Royal Faculty of Physicians and Surgeons, Glasgow; Senior Editor, Glasgow Medical Journal: President Scottish Western Asylums Research Institute; Regius Professor of Practice of Medicine, Glasgow University, 1913-36; Senior Physician, Western Infirmary, Glasgow; Pres. Medical and Dental Defence Union of Scotland, Ltd.; Governor, Royal Technical College, Glasgow; Chairman Glasgow Workmen's Dwellings Co. Ltd.; Major Royal Army Medical Corps (T.F.). *Publications:* History of the Chronic Degenerative Diseases of the Central Nervous System, 1895; Raynaud's Disease, 1899; Manual of Medicine, 5th edition, 1925; The Physician as Man of Letters, Science and Action, 1933, revised and enlarged edn., 1951; An Unpublished Letter of Sir Thomas Browne, M.D. (Scottish Historical Review, Oct. 1921); The Early Editions of Sir Thomas Browne (Records of Glasgow Bibliographical Society, 1923); many contributions to periodical medical literature. *Recreation:* books. *Address:* 12 Somerset Place, Glasgow, C.3. *T.:* Douglas 2577. [*Died* 10 *Jan.* 1958.

MONROE, Hon. Walter S.; *b.* Dublin, 1871; *s.* of late Rt. Hon. Mr. Justice Monroe, P.C.; *m.* 1899, Helen Smith, St. John's, N.F.; one *s.* *Educ.:* Harrow. Came to Newfoundland, 1888; entered the mercantile business of his uncle, M. Monroe; formed the business known as the Monroe Export Co. Ltd., 1904; entered politics in 1923, being defeated for Bonavista Bay, and elected for that district in the General Election, 1924, as Leader of the Conservative Party; Prime Minister and Minister of Education, Newfoundland, 1924-28; Member of Newfoundland Legislative Council, 1929; attended Imperial Conference, London, 1926; D.C.L. Oxford and Edinburgh; LL.D. Trinity College, Dublin. *Recreations:* fishing and golf. *Address:* St. John's, Newfoundland. *Club:* City (St. John's). [*Died* 7 *Oct.* 1952.

MONSON, 10th Baron, *cr.* 1728; **John Rosebery Monson,** B.A.; Bt., *cr.* 1611; Barrister-at-Law; *b.* 11 Feb. 1907; *s.* of 9th Baron and Romaine, Lady of Grace Order of St. John of Jerusalem (*d.* 1943), *d.* of late Gen. Roy Stone and *widow* of late Lawrence Turnure of New York; *S.* father, 1940; *m.* 1931, Bettie Northrup, *d.* of E. Alexander Powell, *q.v.*; three *s.* one *d.* *Educ.:* Eton; Christ Church, Oxford. 2nd Lieutenant General List, 1940; Captain, 1942; Major, 1943. J.P. Lincs (parts of Lindsey) 1946-. C.St.J. *Heir:* *s.* Hon. John Monson [*b.* 1932; *m.* 1955, Emma Devas; one *s.*]. *Address:* The Manor House, South Carlton, Lincoln; 3 Capeners Close, Kinnerton Street, S.W.1. *Clubs:* Brooks's, Hurlingham. [*Died* 7 *April* 1958.

MONTAGU, Sir Ernest William Sanders, Kt., *cr.* 1923; *b.* 1862; *s.* of late John Edward Montagu. Late Secretary for Mines and Works, S. Rhodesia; retired on pension, 1924; M.L.A. Hartley Electoral District, Southern Rhodesia, 1924-28. *Address:* Salisbury, Rhodesia. [*Died* 20 *Nov.* 1952.

MONTAGU, Capt. Frederick James Osbaldeston, O.B.E.; M.C.; Coldstream Guards; *b.* 9 Feb. 1878; *e. s.* of James Montagu and Laura, *d.* of Ernest Thellusson; *m.* 1906, Louisa, *d.* of William Collier Angove; three *s.* one *d.* *Educ.:* Eton. Lieut. Coldstream Guards, 1899-1905; served South African War; European War, on Staff, in France. High Sheriff, Yorkshire, 1910. *Address:* The Manor, Upton, nr. Andover, Hampshire. *T.:* Hurstbourne Tarrant 250. *Clubs:* Guards, Carlton. [*Died* 12 *April* 1957.

MONTAGU, James Drogo, C.B.E. 1937; *y. s.* of late Capt. G. E. Montagu, J.P., late 84th Regt., Wilcot Manor and Stowell Lodge, Wiltshire. *Educ.:* Privately. Lieutenant 5th Royal Irish Rifles Boer War (Queen's Medal 2 clasps); served 1903-9 in Cape Mounted Police, Johannesburg Mounted Police and Rhodesian Police Commissioner of Police, Lagos, Nigeria, 1910-19; Local Commandant of Police, Cyprus, 1920-34; Commissioner of Nicosia and Kyrenia, Cyprus, 1934: Member Exec. Council; Member Legislative Council; Capt. 10th Bn. Wilts Home Guard, 1941; Major, 1944: Defence Medal; Jubilee Medal, 1935; Coronation Medal, 1937. *Recreation:* work. *Address:* 12 Elizabeth Place, St. Helier, Jersey, C.I. [*Died* 1 *Aug.* 1958.

MONTAGUE-BARLOW, Rt. Hon. Sir (Clement) Anderson, P.C. 1922; 1st Bt., *cr.* 1924; K.B.E., *cr.* 1918; LL.D., M.A.; F.S.A.; Barrister-at-law; *b.* 28 February 1868; *s.* of late Dean of Peterborough; *m.* 1934, Doris Louise Reed, late Dep. Administrator Women's R.A.F. *Educ.:* Repton (Head of the School); King's College, Cambridge. (Classical Exhibitioner; 2nd Class Classical Tripos, 1st Class Law, Senior Whewell Scholarship, Yorke University Prize Essay). Called to Bar, Lincoln's Inn, 1895; Scholarship, Middle Temple; Studentship, Inns of Court; practised mainly in educational and charity cases; sometime Lecturer, Law Society, Chancery Lane, also London School of Economics; also Examiner in Law, London University; L.C.C. (M.R.) East Islington, 1907-10, and Vice-Chairman Parliamentary Committee; for three years Secretary, Cambridge House Settlement, South London; Director or Chairman of Sotheby & Co., 1909-28. Raiser of the Salford Brigade of five Battalions (Lancs. Fuslrs.), clothing and equipping them on behalf of the War Office, and building a hut camp for them at Conway, 1914-16; M.P. (C.) S. Salford, Dec. 1910-Dec. 1923; Parliamentary Secretary to the Ministry of Labour, 1920-22; Minister of Labour, Oct. 1922-Jan. 1924, with seat in the Cabinet; Chairman of Select Committee on Soldiers' Pensions and of Int. Depart. Committee on Tuberculous Soldiers, 1919; Senior Govt. Representative at International Labour Conferences, Genoa, 1920, Geneva, 1921 and 1922; Chairman Royal Commission on Coal Industry in Alberta, 1935; Chm. Royal Commission on Location of Industry, 1938; Chm. Council Malvern Girls' College, 1932-45, Pres. since 1945; Chairman House of Laity, Church Assembly, 1945-46. *Publications:* Essays on Church Reform; Education Acts, 1902-3; Barlow Family Records, etc. *Recreations:* rowing, fishing, golf, shooting, etc. *Address:* 59 Kingston House, Princes Gate, S.W.7. *Clubs:* Athenæum, Leander.

[*Died* 31 *May* 1951 (*ext.*).

MONTAGUE - DOUGLAS - SCOTT; *see* Scott.

MONTEATH, John, C.I.E. 1937; *b.* 9 Oct. 1878; *s.* of late Sir James Monteath, K.C.S.I., I.C.S.; *m.* Bertha Geraldine, *d.* of late J. L. Johnston, I.C.S., Guildford; one *s.* *Educ.:* Clifton College; King's College, Cambridge (Scholar). Entered Indian Civil Service in 1902; Postmaster General Punjab and Madras; Home Secretary to Bombay Government; Commissioner Ahmedabad; Prime Minister Junagadh State, Kathiawar, India. *Recreation:* golf. *Address:* Three Corners, Honiton, Devon. *T.A.:* Honiton. *T.:* Broadhembury 207. *Clubs:* Royal Empire Society, East India and Sports.

[*Died* 11 *June* 1955.

MONTESSORI, Maria, M.D., D.Litt.; Educationalist; *b.* 30 August 1870; *o. d.* of Chevalier Alessandro Montessori. First woman to whom the degree of Doctor of Medicine was granted by the University of Rome; Assistant Doctor in Clinic of Psychiatry; took special interest in the mentally deficient; her lectures on this subject led to the foundation of the Scuola Ortofrenica for feeble-minded children; Directress, 1898-1900; studied philosophy at the University of Rome, and particularly the psychology of childhood; lectured on Pedagogical Anthropology at the University of Rome, 1900-7; controlled some tenement infant schools in Rome famous as the Casa dei Bambini; Government Inspector of Schools in Italy, 1922; Hon. degree of Doctor of Letters conferred at Durham University, 1923; held Training Courses in London every two years since 1919 and in alternate years in other parts of world, including Barcelona, Holland, Nice, India; F.E.I.S.; Hon. Member Academy of Science, Chicago; Hon. Member of Pedagogical Academy of Budapest. *Publications:* Pedagogical Anthropology; The Montessori Method; The Advanced Montessori Method; Montessori's Own Handbook, most of which have been published in Italian, French, German, Russian, Roumanian, Spanish, Catalan, Japanese, Dutch, Polish, Chinese, and Danish; The Mass Explained to Children; The Child in the Church; Psycho Geometry; Psycho Arithmetic; The Secret of Childhood, 1936. *Address:* The Montessori Centre, 33 Chepstow Villas, W.11. *T.:* Bayswater 2253.

[*Died* 6 *May* 1952.

MONTGOMERIE, Alexander, C.I.E. 1921; Member of Indian Civil Service (retired); Barrister-at-Law; *b.* 27 Feb. 1879; *s.* of John Montgomerie and Elizabeth Macnicol; *m.* 1908, Katherine MacDonald, *d.* of late William Rankin; one *s.* one *d.* *Educ.:* Glasgow High School; Glasgow Univ. Balliol College, Oxford. Joined Indian Civil Service in Bombay Presidency, 1903; officiated as Assistant Collector, Assistant Judge, and District Judge; Deputy Secretary to Government of Bombay Judicial and Political Departments, 1918; Political Secretary, 1919; Home Secretary, 1923-26; retired, 1929. *Recreation:* reading. *Address:* Gimmersmill House, Haddington, East Lothian.

[*Died* 5 *Dec.* 1958.

MONTGOMERY, George H. A., B.C.L., K.C., D.C.L., LL.D.; member of Montgomery McMichael, Common, Howard, Forsyth & Ker; *b.* Philipsburg, Quebec, 5 Feb. 1874; *s.* of Rev. Hugh Montgomery and Eliza M. Slack; *m.* 1909, Gwendoline M., *d.* of John Baptist, Three Rivers, Que.; one *s.* one *d.* *Educ.:* Bishop's College School, Lennoxville; University of Bishop's College, B.A., 1893; McGill University, B.C.L. 1897. Admitted to practice, 1898; member firm Smith, Markey & Montgomery, 1898-1905; Counsel for Montreal Light, Heat and Power Co., 1905-7; Batonnier Montreal Bar, 1927-28; President, Conference of Governing Bodies of Legal Profession in Canada, 1929-30; President for Canada of Canadian Bar Association, 1935-36; Hon. Member American Bar Association; Representative of Graduates' Society on Board of Governors of McGill Univ. 1928-31; Chancellor Univ. of Bishop's Coll., 1942-50; Dir. of many cos. F.R.S.A. *Recreations:* farming, pure bred live-stock; proprietor of Lakeside Farm, Philipsburg, Quebec. *Address:* The Royal Bank Building, Montreal. *T.A.:* Jonhall, Montreal. *Clubs:* Forest and Stream, Mount Royal, St. James's, University, Montreal, (Montreal); Garrison (Quebec); Rideau (Ottawa).

[*Died* 19 *June* 1951.

MONTGOMERY, Harold Robert, C.M.G. 1936; *b.* 8 May 1884; *s.* of Bishop Montgomery, K.C.M.G., and Maud, *d.* of Dean Farrar; *m.* 1st, 1926, Ursula (*d.* 1937), *d.* of G. Johnson, Vancouver; one *s.*; 2nd, 1941, Betty Galton Fenzi, *d.* of late J. M. Sandy, Sydney, Australia. *Educ.:* King's School, Canterbury. Imperial Yeomanry, S. Africa, 1902; S. African Constabulary, 1902-7; Assistant District Commissioner East Africa Protectorate, 1908; District Commissioner, 1914; Provincial Commissioner, Kenya, 1928; Chief Native Commissioner Kenya Colony, 1934-37. *Address:* Kigwa, Kiambu, Kenya Colony; Newpark, Moville, Co. Donegal. *Club:* East India and Sports.

[*Died* 17 *May* 1958.

MONTGOMERY, Henry Greville; *b.* London, 1864; *m.* 1st, Florence, *d.* of C. M. Shepherd; 2nd, Emily, *d.* of late David Lewis. Founded The British Clayworker, the organ of the Brick and Tile Trades, 1892; as an outcome the Institute of Clayworkers was inaugurated, 1895; revived Building Trades Exhibition at Royal Agricultural Hall, 1895, since held at Olympia; inaugurated the first Colliery Exhibition held in this country; M.P. (L.) Bridgwater Div., Somerset, 1906-10; is a Past Master of the Tylers and Bricklayers Co.; Member of Council of the Royal Drawing Society; Hon. A.R.I.B.A.; Patron of the living of Norton Malreward, Somerset; J.P. Norfolk. *Recreations:* golf, tennis. *Address:* Bacton Lodge, Nr. Norwich, Norfolk. *T.:* Walcott 275. *Clubs:* Reform, Savage.

[*Died* 2 *Dec.* 1951.

MONTGOMERY, Lt.-Col. Henry Keith Purvis-Russell-, O.B.E. 1944; Lord Lieutenant of Kinross-shire since 1944; *b.* 31 July 1896; *yr. s.* of Sir H. Purvis-Russell-Montgomery, 7th Bt., and *heir-pres.* to 8th Bt.; *m.* 1930, Cynthia Maconochie Welwood; one *s.* one *d.* *Educ.:* Rugby; Cambridge University; R.M.C.,

Sandhurst. Regular Army, Black Watch, 1915-36; Territorial Army, Black Watch, 1939-45. *Address:* Kinross House, Kinross, Scotland. *T.:* Kinross 3116. *Club:* New (Edinburgh). [*Died* 1 *Oct.* 1954.

MONTGOMERY, Major-Gen. Hugh Maude de Fellenberg, C.B. 1918; C.M.G. 1919; late Royal Artillery, *b.* 5 Dec. 1870; *e. s.* of late Rt. Hon. Hugh de F. Montgomery, P.C., of Blessingbourne, Fivemiletown, and Mary, *y. d.* of Rev. Hon. J. C. Maude; *m.* 1894, Mary Massingberd (*d.* 1950), *d.* of late Edmund Langton; three *s.* three *d.* *Educ.:* Eton; R.M.A. Served South African War, 1899-1900 (despatches); European War, 1914-18 (despatches); A.Q.M.G. of V Corps at end of War; served on staffs of Rhine Army and Southern Command after end of hostilities. Retired pay, 1925; J.P., D.L. County Tyrone. 3rd Class Russian Order of St. Anne; Legion of Honour; Croix de Guerre. *Address:* Blessingbourne, Fivemiletown, Northern Ireland. [*Died* 22 *Jan.* 1954.

MONTGOMERY, Kathleen; wrote (with her sister, Letitia who *d.* 1930), as K. L. Montgomery; they were daughters of late Robert Hobart Montgomery, of The Knocks, Co. Kildare; on maternal side connected with Oliver Goldsmith. *Publications:* The Cardinal's Pawn; Major Weir; Love in the Lists; The Ark of the Curse; Colonel Kate; The Gate-Openers; Maids of Salem; 'Ware Venice, 1927; translation of Histoire Littéraire du Sentiment Religieux en France, by Henri Bremond; and of Tirol Unterm Beil, by Dr. Reut Nicolussi, 1930; frequent contributor to Fortnightly, Cornhill, and various other magazines. *Address:* 81 Iffley Road, Oxford. [*Died* 22 *Dec.* 1960.

MONTGOMERY, Maj.-Gen. Sir Robert Arundel Kerr, K.C.M.G., *cr.* 1919; C.B. 1911; D.S.O. 1900; *b.* 21 Jan. 1862; *m.* 1887, Annie Rosalie, *e. d.* of John Lecky Phelps of Waterpark, Clare; one *s.* one *d.* Entered army, 1881; Captain, 1889; Major, 1899; Brig.-Gen. Southern Command, 1911; Professor Indian Staff College, 1906-9; passed Staff Coll.; served S. Africa, 1899-1902 (despatches twice; Bt. Lt.-Col.; Queen's medal 3 clasps, King's medal 2 clasps; D.S.O.); European War, 1914-1915 (despatches twice, promoted Maj.-Gen. and K.C.M.G.); retired 23 Feb. 1920; Col.-Commandant R.A. 1929-32. *Address:* Pinecroft, 2 Manor Way, Lee on Solent, Hants. *Club:* United Service. [*Died* 19 *Nov.* 1951.

MONTGOMERY, William Hugh, C.B.E. 1919; *b.* 14 Sep. 1866; *s.* of late Hon. William Montgomery and Jane Todhunter; *m.* 1902, Edina Mary, *d.* of late Hon. Sir James Allen, G.C.M.G., K.C.B.; one *d* (and one *d.* decd.). *Educ.:* Balliol College, Oxford. Barrister, Inner Temple, 1889; Member, N.Z. Parliament, 1893-1899; Assistant Director Base Records and Director of Vocational Training Defence Office, New Zealand, 1916-19. *Recreation:* art. *Address:* Little River, Canterbury, New Zealand. *Club:* Christchurch (Christchurch, N.Z.). [*Died* 26 *July* 1958.

MONTGOMERY-CUNINGHAME, Sir Andrew; *see* Cuninghame, Sir W. A. M. M. O. M.

MONTROSE, 6th Duke of (*cr.* 1707), **James Graham,** K.T. 1947; C.B. 1911; C.V.O. 1905; V.D. 1920; *cr.* Baron Graham before 1451; Earl of Montrose, 1505; Marquis of Montrose, 1645; Duke of Montrose, Marquis of Graham and Buchanan, Earl of Kincardine, Viscount Dundaff, Baron Aberuthven, Mugdock, and Fintrie, 1707; Earl and Baron Graham (Peerage of England), 1722; Hereditary Sheriff of Dunbartonshire; D.L. Stirling; Vice-Pres. Institution of Naval Architects; Younger Brother of Trinity House; Trustee for Royal Incorporation of Master Mariners; Member of H.M.'s Body Guard Royal Archers; Commodore of Sea Cadets in Scotland, 1942; *b.* 1878; *e. s.* of 5th Duke and Violet Hermione, G.B.E., LL.D. (*d.* 1940), 2nd *d.* of Sir Frederick Graham, 3rd Baronet of Netherby, Cumberland; *S.* father, 1925; *m.* 1906, Lady Mary Douglas-Hamilton, O.B.E., *o. c.* of 12th Duke of Hamilton and Lady Mary Louise Elizabeth Montagu, Duchess of Hamilton, *e. d.* of 7th Duke of Manchester; two *s.* two *d.* *Educ.:* Eton. Served in the Mercantile Marine (holds Master Mariner's Certificate), and A.S.C. in South Africa (medal and 3 clasps), 1900; served Aux. Naval Service, European War, 1914-19 (two medals); Comdr. of the Clyde Division R.N.V.R. and of East Coast of Scotland R.N.V.R.; Commodore R.N.V.R., 1921; retired list, 1927; was Assistant Private Secy. (unpaid) to Chancellor of Exchequer, 1905; Naval A.D.C. to H.M.; contested (C.) Stirlingshire, 1906; Eye Division, Suffolk, bye-election, 1906; same Division, 1910; joined Liberal Party, 1936; Lord-Lieutenant of Buteshire, 1920-53; President British Institution of Marine Engineers, 1911; President Junior Institution of Engineers, 1916 and 1917; Inventor and designer of first naval aircraft carrying ship; Designer and owner of first seagoing heavy oil motor ship. Obtained first film ever taken of Total Eclipse of Sun, R.A.S. Expedition, India, 1899; Mission for Lloyds to S. African Government to establish Wireless Telegraphic Stations on Coast, 1900; Commodore Royal Gourock Yacht Club, 1911; President Scottish Trade Mission to Canada, 1932; President Society of Scottish Artists; H.M.'s Lord High Commissioner to General Assembly of the Church of Scotland in Edinburgh, 1942 and 1943; Hon. LL.D. Glasgow, 1911. *Publication:* My Ditty Box (autobiography), 1952. *Heir:* *s.* Marquis of Graham. *Address:* Buchanan Castle, Glasgow. *T.A.:* Drymen 6; Brodick Castle, Isle of Arran, Scotland. [*Died* 20 *Jan.* 1954.

MOODIE, William, M.D., F.R.C.P., D.P.M. (Lond.); Consultant Physician, Department of Psychological Medicine, University College Hospital, London, since 1945; Honorary Consultant, London Child Guidance Training Centre, since 1928; *b.* 15 March 1886; *o. s.* of Robert Moodie, F.E.I.S., Arbroath, Angus, and Mary, *d.* of J. D. Mackintosh, Shotts, Lanark; *m.* 1922, Mary Enid, *d.* of William D. Hardy, R.M., Belfast; two *d.* (and one *d.* decd.). *Educ.:* Arbroath High School; St. Andrews University. Asst. Prof. of Physiology, 1909-10, of Pathology, 1911-12, Univ. Coll., Dundee; L.C.C. Mental Hospitals, 1913-28; Asst. Physician, University Coll. Hosp., Dept. of Psychological Medicine, 1935. Served European War, Capt. R.A.M.C., Pathological Specialist, 1914-20 (N. Russian Exped. with Regular Commission, 1919); War of 1939-1945, Lt.-Col. R.A.M.C. Specialist Physician, 1939-45. *Publications:* The Doctor and the Difficult Child, 1942; The Doctor and the Difficult Adult, 1946; Child Guidance, 1947; Hypnosis in Treatment, 1960. *Address:* 6 Abercorn Mansions, N.W.8. *T.:* Maida Vale 3337. [*Died* 24 *May* 1960.

MOODY, Admiral Sir Clement, K.C.B., *cr.* 1946 (C.B. 1944); *b.* 31 May 1891; *s.* of Rev. W. H. Moody, Vicar of Frensham; *m.* 1924, Rosalind, *d.* of R. E. Mitcheson; one *s.* one *d.* *Educ.:* R.N. Colls., Osborne and Dartmouth. Experimental Comdr., H.M.S. Excellent, 1926-27; Commanded H.M.S. Curacoa, 1935; Imperial Defence College, 1936; Commanded H.M.S. Eagle, 1937-39; Director of Naval Air Division, 1939-41; Rear-Adm. Naval Air Stations, 1941; Rear-Adm. Aircraft Carriers, Home 1943, Eastern Fleet, 1944; Vice-Adm. 1944; Flag Officer (Air) East Indies Station, 1944-46; C.-in-C. South Atlantic, 1946-48; retired, 1948. *Address:* Rushgrove, Fleet, Hants. [*Died* 6 *July* 1960.

MOON, Sir (Arthur) Wilfred Graham-, 4th Bt., *cr.* 1855; *b.* 24 June 1905; *o. s.* of late Major Wilfred Graham Moon, 4th *s.* of 2nd Bt., and Mary Frances (she *m.* 2nd late Lt.-Col. A. L. Crisp Clarke), *d.* of late Surg.-Maj.-Gen. Sir A. Frederick Bradshaw, K.C.B.; *S.* uncle, 1911; *m.* 1st, 1928, Constance (marriage dissolved 1934), *d.* of John William Abbott, Wellington, New Zealand; (one *d.* decd.); 2nd, 1934, Doris Patricia (marriage dissolved, 1947), *d.* of Thomas Baron Jobson, Dublin; one *s.*; 3rd, 1951, Mrs. Theodora Greaves (*widow*). *Educ.:* Eton; Magdalen College, Oxford. A.D.C. to Governor of Fiji, 1929-1931. *Heir: s.* Peter Wilfred Giles, *b.* 24 Oct. 1942. *Address:* Little Brook Farm, Newchapel, Lingfield, Surrey. *T.:* Lingfield 360. *Club:* Oxford and Cambridge. [*Died* 25 *Feb.* 1954.

MOON, Sir Cecil Ernest, 2nd Bt., *cr.* 1887; *b.* 2 Sept. 1867; *s.* of Edward Moon, *s.* of 1st Bt.; *S.* grandfather, 1899; *m.* 1912, Lilian Mary (*d.* 1950), *d.* of Rev. B. S. Darbyshire, M.A. Oxon, and *widow* of Dr. J. D. Preston. *Educ.:* Uppingham; Giessen. *Heir: cousin,* Richard Moon, *b.* 12 April 1901. *Address:* 11 Hartington Road, Buxton. [*Died* 22 *Feb.* 1951.

MOON, Robert Oswald, M.D., F.R.C.P.; J.P.; Consulting Physician to the National Hospital for Diseases of the Heart; Consulting Physician to the Royal Waterloo Hospital; *b.* 1865; *y. s.* of Robert Moon, Barrister-at-Law; *m.* Ethel (*d.* 1933), *d.* of General Waddington; one *s.* three *d.* *Educ.:* Winchester; New College, Oxford. Surgeon to the Phil-Hellenic Legion in Græco-Turkish War, 1897; Trooper in Hampshire Yeomanry in S. Africa, 1900; Civil Surgeon, Field Force, South Africa, 1901 (despatches); contested (L.) E. Marylebone, Jan. and Dec. 1910; Wimbledon, 1922; City of Oxford (L.), 1924, 1929; temp. Major, R.A.M.C., 1917-18; Chadwick Lecturer on Typhus in Serbia, 1915; Member of the Balkan Committee. *Publications:* The Relation of Medicine to Philosophy; Hippocrates in Relation to the Philosophy of his Time; Growth of our Knowledge of Heart Disease; Translation of Goethe's Autobiography; Translation of Jung Stilling's Autobiography; Medicine and Mysticism; Translation of Goethe's Wilhelm Meister; Translation of Eckermann's Conversations with Goethe. *Recreations:* riding, bicycling. *Address:* 21 Upper High Street, Winchester. *T.:* Winchester 2540. *Club:* Reform. [*Died* 28 *July* 1953.

MOON, Walter; Town Clerk, Liverpool, 1922-36; *b.* 16 Sep. 1871; *s.* of William Henry and Ellen Elizabeth Moon; *m.* 1903, Ada Caroline Florence Brooks Arnold; two *s.* two *d.* *Educ.:* Ilfracombe Collegiate School. Clerk and Solicitor, Metropolitan Water Board, London, 1904-22; Hon. Solicitor to the British Waterworks Association, 1908-35. *Recreation:* golf. *Address:* The Belmont Private Hotel, Ilfracombe, N. Devon. [*Died* 11 *Feb.* 1954.

MOONEY, His Eminence Cardinal Edward, D.D.; Archbishop of Detroit since 1937; *b.* Mt. Savage, Maryland, U.S.A., 9 May 1882; *s.* of Thomas Mooney and Sarah Heneghan. *Educ.:* St. Columba's School, Youngstown, O.; St. Charles College; St. Mary's Seminary, Baltimore, Md.; North American College, Rome. Priest, 1909; Professor, St. Mary's Seminary, Cleveland, Ohio, 1909-16; President, Cathedral Latin School, Cleveland, Ohio, 1916-22; Pastor, St. Patrick's Church, Youngstown, Ohio, 1922-23; Spiritual Director, North American College, Rome, 1923-26; Apostolic Delegate in India, 1926-31; Titular Archbishop of Irenopolis, 1926; Apostolic Delegate in Japan, 1931-33; Bishop of Rochester, N.Y., 1933-1937; Cardinal, 1946. *Address:* 1234 Washington Blvd., Detroit 26, Michigan, U.S.A. [*Died* 25 *Oct.* 1958.

MOOR, Rev. Edward, M.A.; Canon Residentiary, Winchester Cathedral, 1933-50; Canon Emeritus since 1950; *b.* 1880; *s.* of George Moor; *m.* Helen, *d.* of Lt.-Col. W. Drury Shaw; one *s.* Vicar of St. Michael's, Bournemouth, 1915-33; Rural Dean of Bournemouth, 1929-33; Hon. Canon of Winchester, 1930-33. *Educ.:* King Edward VI Grammar School, Morpeth; Hatfield College, Durham. *Address:* Chideock, Bridport, Dorset. [*Died* 11 *Feb.* 1953.

MOORE, Sir Alan (Hilary), 2nd Bt., *cr.* 1919; M.B., D.P.H.; *b.* 23 Jan. 1882; *s.* of Sir Norman Moore, 1st Bt., LL.D., M.D., F.R.C.P. (Pres. 1918-22), and 1st wife, Amy (*d.* 1901), *d.* of William Leigh Smith of Crowham, Sussex; *S.* father, 1922; *m.* 1922, Hilda Mary (*d.* 1950), *d.* of late Rt. Rev. Winfrid O. Burrows, Bishop of Chichester; two *s.* two *d.* *Educ.:* Eton; Trinity Coll., Cambridge; St. Bartholomew's Hosp. R.N.V.R. 1903-07, Sub-Lieut.; Temp. Surg. R.N., 1914-19. Formerly Medical Officer of Health of Battle Rural District and of Rye Borough; Assistant School Medical Officer, East Sussex Education Committee. One of the founders of the Society for Nautical Research; H.M.S. Victory, Technical and Advisory (1929) Committees, 1926-38; Vice-Pres. Soc. for Nautical Research, 1951; Battle Rural District Council, 1949-58, retd.; Vice-Chm. of Governors, Bexhill County Grammar School for Boys, 1953-58, retd. *Publications:* Last Days of Mast and Sail, 1925; Sailing Ships of War, 1800-60, 1926; several papers on nautical archæological subjects; many reviews of nautical books. *Recreations:* sailing, canoeing, and nautical research. *Heir: s.* Norman Winfrid [*b.* 24 Feb. 1923; *m.* 1950, Janet, *d.* of Mrs. Phyllis Singer]. *Address:* Hancox, Whatlington, Battle, Sussex. *T.:* Sedlescombe 209. *Clubs:* Oxford and Cambridge, Leander. [*Died* 13 *June* 1959.

MOORE, Arthur Collin; novelist and solicitor (retired); *e. s.* of John Collingham Moore, *nephew* of Henry Moore, R.A., and Albert Moore; *b.* Rome, 18 Mar. 1866. *Educ.:* Bradfield College; Queen's College, Oxford (B.A.). *Publications:* A Comedy of Masks (with late Ernest Dowson), 1893; Adrian Rome (do.), 1899; The Gay Deceivers, 1899; The Eyes of Light, 1901; The Knight Punctilious, 1903; Archers of the Long Bow, 1904. *Address:* 69 Springfield Road, N.W.8. *T.:* Maida Vale 1690. [*Died* 27 *Jan.* 1952.

MOORE, Ven. Arthur Crompton; Archdeacon of Norfolk and Canon of Norwich since 1934; Proctor in Convocation; Secretary, Standing Committee of the Church Congress; Examining Chaplain; *s.* of Henry Banks Moore, Liverpool; *m.* Annie Mildred, *d.* of Canon Symonds, Stockport. *Educ.:* Liverpool Coll.; Clare Coll., Cambridge; Wycliffe Hall, Oxford. Vicar of St. Peter, Hereford, 1917-34. *Address:* The Close, Norwich. [*Died* 5 *Oct.* 1954.

MOORE, Arthur Edward, M.D.(N.U.I.), B.Ch., R.U.I.; Emeritus Professor of Pathology, University College, Cork; *b.* 11 Jan. 1872; 3rd *s.* of Wm. Moore, merchant, Cork; *m.* Anna B., 3rd *d.* of late George Hollwey, Crumlin House, Dublin; one *d.* *Educ.:* Queen's College, Cork; University of Vienna; University of Prague. *Recreation:* golf. *Address:* Towerville, Blackrock, Co. Cork. [*Died* 24 *Jan.* 1951.

MOORE, Mrs. Beatrice Esther; Editor of Mothers in Council until 1950; *b.* London; *d.* of Rev. Michael Rosenthal, Vicar of St. Mark's, Aldgate, E., and Mary Margoliouth; *m.* Rev. Canon W. Moore (*d.* 1943); two *s.* one *d.* *Educ.:* St. John Baptist's School, Hamilton Terrace, N.W.; Member, House of Laity, Church Assembly, 1926-43. *Publications:* Verses and Carols; A Verse Kalendar, etc.; writes under name Beatrice Rosenthal; contributor to various magazines and journals. *Recreations:* gardening, motoring. *Address:* c/o Rev. R. G. C. Moore, Compton Abbas Rectory, Shaftesbury, Dorset. [*Died* 6 *Sept.* 1953.

MOORE, Charles Gordon, C.V.O. 1935; B.A., M.B., B.Ch. Camb., M.R.C.S., L.R.C.P. Lond.; *b.* 1884; *s.* of Wm. H. Moore, Malvern Wells, Worcs; *m.* 1911, Margaret, Dame of Order of St. John of Jerusalem, *widow* of W. B. Ogden; one *d.* *Educ.:* Sherborne; Caius College, Cambridge, B.A.; St. Bartholomew's Hospital. Served European War, Gallipoli, France, 1914-19; Officer Commanding Military Hospital, Gibraltar, 1917 (despatches); Deputy Commissioner of Medical Services, Ministry of Pensions, 1920-23; Physician-in-Ordinary to Princess Beatrice, 1928-44; Home Guard Med. Adviser, Bucks Sub-District, 1940-44; Chm. Bd. of Visitors, H.M. Prison, Reading. O.St.J. J.P. Bucks. *Address:* New Place, Sunningdale, Ascot, Berks. *T.:* Ascot 480. [*Died* 13 *Nov.* 1957.

MOORE, Clarence L., M.A.; *b.* Tatamagouche, N.S., 1869; *e. s.* of Edmund Moore, M.D., C.M.; *m.* 1906, Martha Jean Maxwell of Saltsprings, Pictou Co., N.S.; two *s.* two *d.* *Educ.:* Pictou Academy; Dalhousie University, Halifax; Johns Hopkins University, Baltimore, Md.; Harvard University, Cambridge, Mass. Science Master, King's Co. Academy, N.S., 1891; Science Master, Pictou Academy, 1892; Superintendent of City Schools, Sydney, N.S., 1907; Professor of Biology, Dalhousie University, Halifax, N.S., Canada, 1910. *Publications:* Rusts, with notes on Nova Scotian Species, Bull. Pictou Acad. Science Ass., Vol. 1, No. 2; Myxomycetes of Pictou Co., Trans. N.S. Institute of Sc., 1907; Nova Scotian Aquatic Fungi, Trans. N.S. Institute of Sc., 1908. *Recreations:* shooting, fishing. *Address:* Pictou, Nova Scotia, Canada. [*Died* 24 *Dec.* 1953.

MOORE, Eldon; *b.* 1901; *e. surv. s.* of late Judge Robert Ernest Moore. *Educ.:* Lancing; Trinity College, Cambridge. After some years in daily journalism, concentrated upon biology (genetics), and especially human biology, vital statistics, population, eugenics, sociology, etc.; Editor Eugenics Review, 1927-33; much lecturing for the Eugenics Society; Secretary of the British section of the International Union for the Scientific Investigation of Population Problems, and of Commission (on Differential Fertility, Fecundity, and Sterility) of that Union, 1928; Chief Officer of Imperial Bureau of Animal Genetics (attached Edinburgh Univ.), 1929-30; organised Second General Assembly (London, 1931) of Population Union; Member Public Assistance Sub-Committee (L.C.C.), 1931-33; Acting Editor, Everyman, 1933-34; Public Relations Department, London Press Exchange, 1937-40; Overseas Publicity, B.B.C., 1941-46. *Publications:* A Bibliography of Differential Fertility (Editor), 1933; Heredity — Mainly Human, 1934; The Magic Halibut, 1939; numerous and varied newspaper articles, but especially above subjects in Spectator, Nineteenth Century, Eugenics Review, Scientific Journals, etc. *Address:* c/o Lloyds Bank, Blackheath, S.E.3. [*Died* 16 *Nov.* 1954.

MOORE, Eva (Mrs. Henry V. Esmond); actress; *b.* Brighton; 8th child of Edward Henry Moore; *m.* 1891, Henry V. Esmond (*d.* 1922); one *s.* one *d.* *Educ.:* Brighton. Went on the stage, in Mr. Toole's company, 1888; afterward with Mr. Willard, Mrs. John Wood, Mr. Chudleigh, Mr. Ed. Terry, Mr. Sedger, Mr. Fred Kerr, Mr. Edwards, Messrs. A. and J. Gatti, Messrs. Maude and F. Harrison, Mr. Charles Hawtrey, Mr. Alexander in The Wilderness, Mr. Bourchier in My Lady Virtue, Mr. Alexander in Old Heidelberg, Mr. Charles Frohman in Billy's Little Love Affair, and Duke of Killiecrankie; John Glayd's Honor, 1907; Sweet Kitty Bellairs, 1907; The Explorer, 1908; Marriages of Mayfair; Little Lord Fauntleroy; Best People; House Opposite; Eliza Comes to Stay (joint management with H. V. Esmond); The Dangerous Age, 1914; When We were Twenty-one, 1915; The Title, 1918; Cæsar's Wife; Mummsie; The Bat; To-night or Never; The Holmeses of Baker Street; Without Motive; Hundreds and Thousands, 1939; A Star Comes Home, 1940; Wasn't it Odd, 1941; It happened in September, 1942. Films: Flames of Passion, Chu Chin Chow, I was a Spy, Never come Back, She Wanted her Man, The Old Dark House, The Flesh is Weak, Jew Süss, A Cup of Kindness, Vintage Wine, Annie Leave the Room, La Vie Parisienne, Old Iron, In Human Bondage; Hollywood, 1943, for various films; returned England, 1945. Produced St. John Ervine's play, Mary, Mary, Quite Contrary, on tour 1924, and later at the Savoy Theatre, 1925; Hay Fever; Cat's Cradle; Garden of Eden, 1927; Tin Gods, 1928; Getting Mother Married, 1929-30; The Swan; Grain of Mustard Seed; Cabbages and Kings; Pride and Prejudice, 1936-37. Retired from stage, 1945. *Publication:* Exits and Entrances: Eva Moore's Memories, 1924. *Address:* Apple Porch, Maidenhead, Berks. *T.:* Hurley 234. *Clubs:* Arts; Temple Golf (Maidenhead). [*Died* 27 *April* 1955.

MOORE, Lt.-Col. Francis Hamilton, C.B.E. 1919; D.S.O. 1916; *b.* 1876. Entered Royal Berkshire Regt., 1896; Major, 1915; Lieut.-Col., 1924; served S. African War, 1899-1902 (Queen's medal, 3 clasps, King's medal, 2 clasps); European War, 1914-19 (despatches, D.S.O., C.B.E.). [*Died* 6 *Oct.* 1952.

MOORE, Sir Fred Denby, Kt., *cr.* 1935; J.P. Ripon, W.R., 1922; *b.* 22 July 1863; *s.* of Richard Moore, Bradford; *m.* 1892, Edith May, *o. c.* of John Sugden, J.P., Oakworth, nr. Keighley; two *s.* *Educ.:* Bradford Grammar School; London International College; Abroad. *Address:* Mowbray House, Kirkby Malzeard, Ripon. *T.:* 3. *Club:* Bradford County Conservative (Bradford). [*Died* 5 *Oct.* 1951.

MOORE, Lt.-Col. Frederick Grattan, C.B.E. 1924; *b.* Burnham, Somerset, 26 April 1877; *m.* 1907, Marian (*d.* 1953), *d.* of Very Rev. W. Stone, M.A., Dean of Kilmore, Ireland; one *s.* one *d.* *Educ.:* King William's College, I.O.M.; R.M.C., Sandhurst. Joined Green Howards in India, 1897; transferred to Indian Army, 1898; served Tirah and N.W. Frontier, India, 1897-98; China, Boxer Rising, 1900-1; European War (severely wounded at Festubert, Nov. 1914); retired, 1928. *Address:* c/o Lloyds Bank, 6 Pall Mall, S.W.1. [*Died* 13 *June* 1955.

MOORE, Colonel George A., C.M.G. 1916; D.S.O. 1918; M.D.; A.M.S. (retired); Physician and Surgeon; *b.* 24 Mar. 1869; 4th *s.* of late Wm. Moore, J.P., M.D., F.R.C.P.I., Physician-in-Ordinary in Ireland to Queen Victoria and King Edward VII, of Moore Lodge, Co. Antrim and Fitzwilliam Square, Dublin; *m.* Helena Catherine Georgina (*d.* 1946), *d.* of Surg.-Gen. Whitla; three *s.* one *d.* *Educ.:* Charterhouse; Trinity College, Dublin. M.D., B.Ch., B.A.O., B.A. Univ. Dublin; entered R.A.M.C. 1892; specialist in diseases of throat, nose, and ear; served N.-W. Frontier India and Tirah Campaign, 1897-98 (medal and 2 clasps); South African War, 1899-1902 (Queen's medal 4 clasps, King's medal 2 clasps); European War (despatches thrice, C.M.G., D.S.O.); retired pay, 1921. *Publications:* contributions to medical journals. *Address:* 44 Harcourt Terrace, Redcliffe Square, S.W.10. *T.:* Fremantle 7945. [*Died* 29 *Jan.* 1955.

MOORE, George Edward, O.M. 1951; Litt.D. (Camb.), Hon. LL.D. (St. Andrews), Fellow of British Academy; Fellow of Trinity College, Cambridge; Emeritus Professor of Philosophy; *b.* 1873; 3rd *s.* of late D. Moore, M.D., and late Henrietta Sturge; *m.* 1916, Dorothy, *d.* of G. H. Ely; two *s.* *Educ.:* Dulwich College; Trinity College, Cambridge. First Class Classical Tripos, Part I., 1894; Craven University Scholar, 1895. First class Moral Sciences Tripos, Part II., 1896; Fellow of Trinity College, Cambridge,

1898-1904; University Lecturer in Moral Science at Cambridge, 1911-25; Editor of Mind, 1921-47; Professor of Philosophy at Cambridge, 1925-39; Visiting Professor at various Colleges and Universities in U.S.A., 1940-44. *Publications:* Principia Ethica, 1903; Ethics (Home University Library), 1912; Philosophical Studies, 1922; Some Main Problems of Philosophy, 1953. *Recreation:* reading. *Address:* 86 Chesterton Road, Cambridge. *T.:* Cambridge 56666.
[*Died* 24 *Oct.* 1958.

MOORE, Harry, A.R.C.S.; D.Sc. (Lond.); F.Inst.P.; F.S.G.T.; Professor of Glass Technology, University of Sheffield, 1946-1955; Professor Emeritus, 1955; *b.* 19 November 1887; *s.* of James Henry Moore and Sarah Ann (*née* Pollard); *m.* 1910, Beatrice Louisa Wright; two *s.* *Educ.:* Belle Vue School, Bradford; Royal College of Science, London. Lectr. in Physics, 1908-1915, Co-Manager, Munitions Trng. Dept., 1915-18, King's Coll., London; Tech. Supervisor W. of Eng. Area, Trng. Section, Min. of Munitions 1918-19; Chief Tech. Officer, S.W. Area, Trng. Dept., Min. of Labour, to Aug. 1919; Asst. Dir. of Research, 1919-33, Dir. of Research, 1933-37, Brit. Scientific Instrument Research Assoc.; Dir. of Research, Pilkington Bros. Ltd., 1937-45; Dean of Faculty of Engineering, Univ. of Sheffield (retd. Sept. 1951). Hon. Freeman, Worshipful Company of Glass Sellers, 1954. *Publications:* Textbook of Practical Physics (with H. S. Allen), 1915; Textbook of Intermediate Physics, 1923. Microscope and Microscopy (with Sir Herbert Jackson) Encyclopædia Britannica, 1933 Edition. Various papers, Phil. Mag., 1914, Proc. Roy. Soc., 1915, Proc. Phys. Soc., 1915, and many others in various Jls., particularly, J. Soc. of Glass Technology, 1939-55. *Recreations:* microscopy, cabinet-making, music. *Address:* 41 Torton Hill Road, Arundel, Sussex. *T.:* 2251. *Club:* Athenæum.
[*Died* 5 *Aug.* 1960.

MOORE, Captain Hartley Russell Gwennap, C.B.E. 1936 (O.B.E. 1918); Royal Navy (retired); *b.* 1881; *y. s.* of late John Gwennap Dennis Moore, Garlenick, Cornwall, and Mary (*née* Johnstone), of Alva; *m.* 1916, Lenore, *d.* of late Col. Euing Crawford, D.L., Auchentroig, Stirlingshire; two *d.* *Educ.:* Eastman's, Stubbington; H.M.S. Britannia. Entered Royal Navy, 1895; qualified in Torpedo, Wireless and Staff duties; Comdr., 1914; on Staffs of Admiral Commanding Channel Fleet, H.M.S. Lord Nelson, and of Admiral 2nd in Command Grand Fleet, Marlborough (Battle of Jutland) and Revenge, 1914-17; Admiralty, 1918, commanded H.M.S. Nairana, N. Russia, 1919; evacuated last British Troops from White Sea (despatches); Superintendent of Naval Mining and Anti-Mining Development, 1923-1935; Royal Humane Society's Bronze Medal; Vol. L.D.V. Coy. Comdr., Major, H.G., 1940-43; C.D. Service, 1943-45. *Address:* The Flint House, near Havant, Hants. *T.:* Havant 356. *Clubs:* United Service, Junior Army and Navy. [*Died* 26 *Dec.* 1953.

MOORE, Henry F., M.B., B.Ch., B.A.O. (1912, First Place, First Class Hons. and First Exhibition), M.D. (Published Research, 1917), D.Sc. (Published Research, 1920), F.R.C.P.I. (1930); M.R.C.P. (Lond.) by election 1937; F.R.C.P. (Lond.) 1939; Professor of Medicine, University College, Dublin (National Univ. of Ireland); Senior Physician, Mater Misericordia Hospital, Dublin; Consulting Physician, National Maternity Hospital, Dublin; *b.* Cappoquin, Co. Waterford, 1887; *m.* Frances L. Thomas (*d.* 1953), New York; one *s.* *Educ.:* Univ. College, Dublin; Post Graduate Scholar in Medicine, 1912, and Travelling Student in Medicine (Pathology and Bacteriology), N.U.I., 1913-15; Asst., Hosp. Rockefeller Inst. for Med. Research, New York, 1915-18; Extern Examiner in Medicine in Queen's Univ., Belfast, 1932-34; Member Medical Registration Council of Ireland; Member Medical Research Council of Ireland; F.R.S.M. and of the Royal Academy of Medicine in Ireland (Pres., Section Medicine, 1930-32); formerly Member of Editorial Bd., British Heart Journal; President, Section of Medicine, B.M.A., 1933; jt. Pres. Sect. Med. of B.M.A. and Irish Med. Assoc., 1952; Hon. Mem. Amer. Rheumatism, Assoc., 1953. M.R.I.A. Three Lectures on the results of Cortisone treatment: (Dublin; Mayo Clinic, Univ. of Minnesota; Univ. of Chicago), 1952 (request of Research Corporation of America). *Publications:* papers to Proc. Roy. Soc. Med., Practitioner, Brit. Encyclopædia of Med. Practice, Zeitschr. f. Immunitätsforschung, Brit. Med. Jn. Lancet, Quarterly Jn. of Med., Irish Jn. of Med. Sciences, Jn. of Med. Assn. of Ireland, Arch. of Internal Medicine and Jn. of Experimental Medicine; several papers on Cortisone, 1950-1951 (B.M.J. and Irish Jl. Med. Sc.). *Address:* 58 Fitzwilliam Square, Dublin, C.19. *T.:* Dublin 61834; Susquehanna, Killiney, Co. Dublin. *Club:* Royal Irish Yacht (Kingstown). [*Died* 25 *Jan.* 1954.

MOORE, Henry John, C.B.E. 1922; *s.* of late Henry John Moore, Longford; *b.* 1872; *m.* 1901, Ethel Clare, *y.d.* of late Rev. D. Moriarty, three *s.* one *d.* *Educ.:* Trinity College, Dublin (B.A., LL.B.). Royal Irish Constabulary, 1897-1920; seconded on appointment as Divisional Com., 1920-22. *Recreation:* golf. *Address:* Innisfree, Orwell Road, Rathgar, Dublin.
[*Died* 27 *Dec.* 1950.

MOORE, Colonel Herbert Tregosse Gwennap, C.M.G. 1919; D.S.O. 1915; R.E.; *b.* 12 March 1875; *e. s.* of late J. Gwennap D. Moore of Garlenick, Grampound, Cornwall; *m.* 1907, Ethel Freda, *d.* of late Griffiths Phillips, The Pines, Whitchurch; one *s.* two *d.* *Educ.:* Bradfield College; R.M.A., Woolwich. Entered army, 1894; Captain, 1904; Major, 1914; Asst. Commissioner, Yola-Cross River Boundary Commission, 1907-9; served South African War, 1899-1902 (Queen's medal 6 clasps, King's medal 2 clasps); South Nigeria, 1908 (despatches); European War, 1914-18 (despatches, D.S.O., Bt. Lt.-Col., C.M.G.); Col. 1922; Officer in charge of Records, Royal Corps of Signals, 1925-29; retired pay, 1929; Hon. Secretary S.S. and A.F.A., Bournemouth, 1939-45. *Address:* Harnham Croft Nursing Home, Salisbury, Wilts.
[*Died* 9 *Nov.* 1958.

MOORE, James Lennox Irwin, M.B., M.Ch. Edin.; Laryngologist and Aural Surgeon; Consulting Surgeon to Metropolitan Ear, Nose, and Throat Hospital; F.R. Soc. Med. (Vice-Pres. Laryngol. Sect. and Mem. Otol. Sect.); Hon. Fellow and Treas. Hunterian Soc.; Member: Med. Soc. Lond., Harveian Soc., W. Lond. Med.-Chir. Soc.; F.R.I.P.H.H.; late Aural Referee to Civil Service; Surgeon to Hospital for Diseases of Throat, Nose, and Ear, Golden Square; Surgeon to the London Throat Hospital for Diseases of the Throat, Nose, and Ear; Senior Assist. Surgeon to the Metropolitan Ear, Nose, and Throat Hospital, Fitzroy Square; Senior Assistant to the Professor of Laryngology, King's College Hospital; Laryngologist and Aural Surgeon to Princess Marie Louise's Military Hospital, Bermondsey; Consulting Throat Physician to the London Academy of Music; Honorary Throat Physician to the Actors' Association; *b.* London, April 1866; *s.* of late George Moore, M.D., Hertford Street, Mayfair; *m.* 1st, 1898, Georgina Roberta (*d.* 1919), 2nd *d.* of Maj.-Gen. R. H. Price-Dent, Bengal Staff Corps, J.P., The Manor House, Hallaton, Leic.; one *s.* (*d.* 1916); 2nd, 1938, Florence Rosina, 2nd *d.* of late T. H. Williams, Clifton, Bristol. *Educ.:* Westminster School; Edinburgh University; King's College Hospital. Spent five years in general practice at Market Harborough; settled in London in 1900; acted as Member of the Executive Committee of the British Congress on Tuberculosis, 1901; awarded the Royal Humane Society Diploma for life-saving. *Publications:* Intrinsic Cancer of the Larynx and the Operation of Laryngo fissure, 1921; The Tonsils and Adenoids and their Diseases, including the part they play in Systemic Diseases, 1928; Articles, The Neuroses and Neuronoses of the Larynx; Prolapse of the Laryngeal Ventricle, and Eversion of the Sacculus, Chevalier Jackson and G. M. Coates' American Text-book on The Nose, Throat, and Ear and their Diseases, 1929; also many contributions to medical journals on Ear, Nose, and Throat Diseases. *Recreations:* fishing, collecting antiques. *Address:* 30A Wimpole Street, W.1. *T.:* Welbeck 1950; Happy Creek, Painscastle, Radnorshire. *Clubs:* Knights of the Round Table, Savage; Edinburgh University. [*Died* 22 *March* 1953.

MOORE, Mary E. M.; *see* Rees, Mrs. Leonard.

MOORE, Ralph Westwood; Head Master of Harrow School, 1942–Jan. 1953. Member B.B.C. Gen. Advisory Council, 1952; *b.* 1906; *e. s.* of George Moore, Wolverhampton; *m.* 1931, Elsie Barbara, *d.* of W. H. Tonks, Wolverhampton; two *s.* *Educ.:* Wolverhampton Grammar School; Christ Church, Oxford (Scholar). First Class Honour Classical Moderations, 1926; First Class Literæ Humaniores, 1928; hon. ment. Hertford Scholarship, 1926; Assistant Master, Rossall School, 1928-31; Sixth Form Master, Shrewsbury School, 1931-38; Head Master, Bristol Grammar School, 1938-42; Member: Hispanic Council; Councils of St. Mary's and of Charing Cross Hospital Medical Schools. *Publications:* ed. Versus Wulfrunenses, 1929; Prose at Present, 1933; Greek and Latin Comparative Syntax, 1934; Idea and Expression, 1937; The Romans in Britain, 1938; editor of The Threshold, 1935-37, an annual anthology of prose and verse from the Schools of England; Where God Begins, 1941; The Roman Commonwealth, 1942; Christ the Beginning, 1944; ed. Education Today and Tomorrow, 1945; The Moving of the Spirit, 1947; The Furtherance of the Gospel, 1950; contributor to The Times, The Times Literary Supplement. *Address:* The Head Master's, Harrow-on-the-Hill. *Club:* Athenæum. [*Died* 10 *Jan.* 1953.

MOORE, Rev. and Rt. Hon. Robert, P.C. (N. Ire.) 1943; M.P. North Div. of Co. Londonderry (N.I. Parl.) since 1938; Minister of Agriculture, N.I., since 1943; Minister of Ringsend Presbyterian Church; *b.* 1886; *s.* of Kennedy Moore, farmer, Ballymacannon, Macosquin, Coleraine; *m.* 1933. *Educ.:* Queen's University, Belfast (B.A.). *Address:* Ringsend Manse, Macosquin, Coleraine, Co. Derry. [*Died* 1 *Sept.* 1960.

MOORE, Vice-Admiral Stephen St. Leger, C.B. 1938; C.V.O. 1937; *b.* 1884. Joined R.N., 1898; served War of 1914-18; Capt. 1924; Rear-Admiral, 1936; Chief of Staff and Maintenance Captain, Portsmouth, 1937-39; retired list, 1939. *Club:* Royal Yacht Squadron, Cowes (Naval hon. member). [*Died* 13 *Feb.* 1955.

MOORE-PARK, Carton; Painter—Portrait and Decoration and Animalier; *o. s.* of Robert Park, M.D.; *b.* 1877; *m.* Annette, *d.* of Samuel Hunter, of Dublin; one *s.* R.B.A., 1899; resigned 1905. Member: National Society of Portrait Painters, Zoological Society, England; Pastel Society, England; Society of Illustrators, America. *Publications:* A Book of Birds; An Alphabet of Animals; A Book of Dogs; The Child's Pictorial Natural History; A Child's London; La Fontaine's Fables for Children; The King of the Beasts; Series Mural Panels, Stencils—(I.) The Zoo; (II.) The Farmyard; Set Lithographs, Uncle Remus' Tales of the Old Plantation, second series; Brer Rabbit; The Anatomy of the Horse—a Series of Plates constituting a Basis for Students; Editor and Illustrator of the Lilliput series of books for a Child's Library (George Allen). Illus.: A Countryside Chronicle, S. L. Bensusan; The Love Family; The Bee; Biffel: The Story of a Trek-Ox. *Club:* Chelsea Arts. [*Died* 23 *Jan.* 1956.

MOORHEAD, Thomas Gillman, M.D., D.P.H., F.R.C.P.I., F.R.C.P.(Eng.); Hon. LL.D. National Univ. of Ireland and Queen's Univ., Belfast; Hon. F.T.C.D.; Consulting Physician to Mercer's Hosp., Dublin and Steevens Hospital, Dublin; Regius Professor of Physic, Univ. of Dublin, since 1926; Vice-Pres. of Council of Alexandra College; late President Royal College of Physicians of Ireland; President British Medical Association; President Irish Medical Schools and Graduates Association; Member General Medical Council; Member Irish Medical Council; Chairman Dublin Clinical Hospitals Joint Committee; Chairman Board of Governors Sir Patrick Dun's Hospital, Dublin; late Pres. Assocn. of Physicians of Great Britain and Ireland; Vice-Pres. Royal Irish Academy; late Director National Cancer Campaign (Ireland); late Visiting Physician, Sir Patrick Dun's Hospital, Dublin, and Royal City of Dublin Hospital; late Pres. Leinster Branch British Medical Association; Consulting Physician National Children's Hospital, Dublin, and Clonskeagh Hospital; late Hon. Consulting Physician to the Forces in Ireland; late temporary Lieutenant-Colonel R.A.M.C.; Professor of Medicine, Royal College of Surgeons; Censor in Medicine, Royal College of Physicians, etc.; King's Professor of Materia Medica and Member of Board, Trinity College, Dublin; *b.* County Tyrone, 1878; *s.* of Dr. W. R. Moorhead and Mrs. Moorhead, Bray, County Wicklow; *m.* 1st, 1907, Mai Beatrice, *d.* of Robert Erskine Quinn; 2nd, 1938, Sheila, *d.* of Stephen Gwynn. *Educ.:* Trinity College, Dublin; Vienna. *Publications:* Surface Anatomy; A Short History of Sir Patrick Dun's Hospital; numerous contributions to medical journals; late Joint-Editor Dublin Journal of Medical Science. *Recreations:* motoring, fishing. *Address:* 23 Upper Fitzwilliam Street, Dublin. *T.:* Dublin 61851. *Clubs:* Kildare Street (Dublin); Royal Irish Yacht (Kingstown). [*Died* 3 *Aug.* 1960.

MOORHOUSE, E. Hallam; *see* Meynell, E. H.

MOORSHEAD, Eng.-Rear-Adm. Herbert Brooks, C.B. 1925; C.B.E. 1919; *b.* 1870; *m.* 1905. Served European War, 1914-19 (despatches, C.B.E.). *Address:* 5 Penlee Gardens, Stoke, Devonport. [*Died* 28 *Feb.* 1955.

MORAN, Rev. Canon Walter Isidore, Hon. Canon of Newcastle since 1922; Examining Chaplain to the Bishop; H.C.F.; *b.* 9 June, 1865; *s.* of Patrick Thomas and Margaret Barton Moran; *m.* 1919, Alice Langdon Hoyle; no *c.* *Educ.:* Manchester Grammar School; Merton College, Oxford; Wycliffe Hall, Oxford. Postmaster of Merton College, Oxford, 1884-8; 1st Class Math. Mods., 1885; 2nd Class Final, 1888; B.A., 1889; M.A., 1892; Deacon, 1889; Priest, 1890; Asst. Curate of Totnes, 1889-91; Tutor Church Missionary College, Islington, 1891-96; Vice-Principal Elland Clergy Training School, 1896-97; Principal Bishop Wilson Theological School and Domestic Chaplain to Bishop of Sodor and Man, 1897-1907; Domestic Chaplain to Bishop of Newcastle, 1907-10; Vicar of Wooler, 1910-35; Examining Chaplain to the Bishop of Newcastle, 1907-15, 1916-27, 1927-41; T.C.F., 1917-19; H.C.F., 1921. *Recreation:* swimming. *Address:* Sunnybank, Felton, Northumberland. *T.:* Felton 235. [*Died* 5 *Feb.* 1958.

MORAUD, Hon. Lucien, K.C. 1922; *b.* Lotbiniere, Que.; *s.* of Camille and Marie (Paré) Moraud, Lotbiniere, Que. *Educ.:* Quebec Seminary; Laval University. B.A. 1905; L.LL. 1908; LL.D. 1932; called to Bar, 1909; barrister; firm, Moraud, Alleyn,

Grenier & Labrecque (Est. 1910) Quebec; Bâtonnier Gen. of Province of Quebec, 1936; Director and Member of Executive Canadian National Railways, 1930-33; Canadian Delegate to United Nations Conference, San Francisco, 1945; Canadian Delegate Commonwealth Parliamentary Conf., London, 1948; Lecturer, Law Faculty, and Member Bd. of Governors, Laval Univ.; President Les Prévoyants du Canada and various other corporations; Member of the Senate, Canada, 1933; Conservative; Catholic. Commander Order of St. Gregory, 1949. *Address:* Château St. Louis, Quebec. [*Died* 29 *May* 1951.

MORE, Lieut.-Col. James Carmichael, C.I.E. 1930; D.S.O. 1918; *b.* 1883; *m.* 1923, Helen Vera, *y. d.* of late H. S. Harington, Indian State Railways; one *s.* Served South Africa, 1902; European War, 1914-18 (despatches, D.S.O.); retired 1930. *Recreation:* travel. *Address:* BM/JCM, London, W.C.1. [*Died* 17 *Dec.* 1959.

MORE, John William; Retired as Sheriff-Substitute of Fife and Kinross, at Cupar, Fife (1939-59); *b.* 16 Oct. 1879; 2nd *s* of late Francis More, C.A., Edinburgh; *m.* 1910, Alice Muriel (*d.* 1947), *d.* of R. W. Hanson; one *s.* two *d.* *Educ.:* Edinburgh University, M.A. 1900; Trinity College, Oxford, B.A. 1903. Admitted Member of Faculty of Advocates, 1905; Lieut. Territorial Reserve, 1915-18; Sheriff-Substitute of Aberdeen, Kincardine, and Banff, at Banff, 1919-39. *Publication:* Trial of A. J. Monson (Notable Scottish Trials Series). *Recreation:* music. *Clubs:* New (Edinburgh); Royal and Ancient (St. Andrews). [*Died* 19 *Oct.* 1959.

MORE, Brig.-Gen. Robert Henry, C.M.G. 1918; C.B.E. 1919; 2nd *s.* of late R. Jasper More, M.P., Linley, Shropshire; *m.* 1919, Phyllis Blanche (*d.* 1943), 2nd *d.* of late Hon. Francis Parker. *Educ.:* Westminster. Served S. African War, 1900-1902; first in the Imperial Yeomanry and later attached to the Staff; joined the War Office, 1902; Assistant Military Secretary, 1917; Director of Air Personal Services, 1918; late Organising Secretary, United Services Fund; rejoined R.A.F. 1939, Wing Commander. *Address:* Chiltern House, Watlington, Oxon. *Club:* Royal Air Force. [*Died* 1 *Nov.* 1951.

MORESBY, Walter Halliday, C.B.E. 1920; M.A., LL.B.; Barrister, Inner Temple; Past Master, Makers of Playing Cards Company; Sometime Legal Adviser, Special Intelligence, War Office; *o. s.* of late Admiral John Moresby; *g.s.* of late Admiral of the Fleet Sir Fairfax Moresby, G.C.B.; *m.* 1897, Mary Graham, *d.* of Comdr. O. B. Niven, R.N. *Educ.:* Westminster School; St. John's College, Cambridge. *Address:* 61 Abingdon Villas, W.8. *T.:* Western 4628. [*Died* 24 *April* 1951.

MORETON, Hon. Algernon Howard; *b.* 2 May 1880; 2nd *s.* of 4th and *b.* and *heir-pres.* to 5th Earl of Ducie; *m.* 1913, Dorothy Edith, *d.* of Robert Bell, late of Rockhampton, Queensland; one *s.* three *d.* *Address:* Falfield, Nikenbah, Queensland. [*Died* 23 *June* 1951.

MORGAN, Angela; author and poet; *b.* Washington, D.C.; *d.* of Alwyn Morgan and Carol Baldwin. *Educ.:* public schools and under private tutors; Columbia; Chautauqua, N.Y. Began early as writer for Chicago American, later with Chicago Journal and New York and Boston papers; lived in England for three years and had some of her poetry published by the Spectator. Made several trips across the Continent of America, giving poetry readings at clubs and universities. Poet Laureate of General Federation of Women's Clubs, U.S.A., 1936. *Publications:* has published numerous volumes of poems, from 1914; The Imprisoned Splendour (fiction), 1915; Angela Morgan's Recitals (verse), 1930; Awful Rainbow (novel), 1932; Gold on Your Pillow (prose and poems), 1936-1941-1952; Behold the Angel (poems), 1945-1952); Rockets to the Sun (complete collection), 1956-1957. *Address:* 96 Washington Av., Saugerties, New York, U.S.A. *Clubs:* Hathaway Shakespeare (Hon.) (Philadelphia), MacDowell (hon.), Three Arts (New York). [*Died* 24 *Jan.* 1957.

MORGAN, Sir Arthur Croke, Kt., *cr.* 1945; Solicitor to Hon. Soc. of the Middle Temple, 1915-51; *e. s.* of late Joseph John Morgan, 134 Holland Road, Kensington; *m.* 1st, 1910, Dorothy Ethel (*d.* 1911), *d.* of Paul Forster, Malverleys, Newbury; one *s.*; 2nd, 1913, Gertrude Valentine (*d.* 1947), *y. d.* of Edwin Waterhouse, Feldemore, Holmbury St. Mary; three *d.* *Educ.:* Winchester; New College, Oxford. 2nd Class Honour School of Jurisprudence, 1900; partner in Park Nelson and Co. 1905; Member of Council of Law Society 1925-48, Pres., 1944-1945; Member of Disciplinary Cttee. under Solicitors Act, 1932-47; Lieut. (substantive) R.G.A. 1916-19; J.P. County of Hertford, 1930-36. *Address:* Kingsland House, Winchester; (Office) 11 Essex Street, Strand, W.C.2. [*Died* 18 *Aug.* 1955.

MORGAN, Sir Arthur E., Kt., *cr.* 1945; Commander Order of the Icelandic Falcon, 1947; *b.* 5 Jan. 1886; *e. s.* of David and Mary A. Morgan; *m.* 1912, Lilian, *d.* of William Francis; one *d.* Created Guildhall Insurance Co. Ltd., 1919; Pres. Insurance Institute of London, 1941-42; member mission to U.S.A. appointed by Treasury and Ministry of Economic Warfare, 1941; Chairman British Insurance Association, 1943-44; Pres. Chartered Insurance Inst., 1947-48; Pres. The Insurance Orphanage and Insurance Benevolent Fund, 1947-48. Late General Manager The London Assurance, 1933-49. *Address:* Lorne, Oxshott Way, Cobham, Surrey. *T.:* Cobham 545. *Clubs:* Pilgrims; New South Wales (Sydney). [*Died* 24 *Feb.* 1956.

MORGAN, Admiral Sir Charles Eric, K.C.B., *cr.* 1946 (C.B. 1945); D.S.O. 1919; Staff Captain, S.S. Clytoneus, 1948; *b.* 19 May 1889; *er. s.* of Conway John Morgan, Stafford; *m.* 1915, Winifred Eva James; one *s.* one *d.* *Educ.:* H.M.S. Conway. Midshipman, 1905, served European War as Navigating Officer of H.M.S. Pelorus, Bellona, Caledon, and Delhi (D.S.O., 1914-1915 Star, British War Medal with seven bars, Victory Medal, despatches). Navigating Officer of H.M.S. Repulse during World Cruise of Special Service Squadron; Fleet Navigating Officer, H.M.S. Nelson, Home Fleet, 1932; Capt. 1932; i.d.c. 1934; Capt. of H.M.S. Enterprise on E.I. Station, 1936-38; conveyed Emperor of Abyssinia after his abdication from Djbuti to Haifa; Jubilee Medal, 1935; Coronation Medal, 1937; Director of Navigation at Admiralty, 1938-40; Capt. of H.M.S. Valiant at bombardments of Valona, Bardia and Tripoli, and Battle of C. Matapan, 1940-42; Flag Officer Taranto and the Adriatic and Liaison with the Italians; Rear-Adm. 1942 (1939-45 Star, Africa Star, Italy Star, Defence Medal and British War Medal, despatches); Vice-Adm. 1945; Dep. Chief of Naval Personnel and Adm. Comdg. Reserves, 1945-47; Adm. on retired list, 1948; served in Merchant Navy, 1948. *Recreations:* represented Navy at golf, and Hampshire and Navy at hockey. *Address:* The White Cottage, Thakeham, Pulborough, Sussex. *T.:* Storrington 203. *Club:* United Service. [*Died* 1 *Aug.* 1951.

MORGAN, Charles Langbridge; Novelist; M.A. (Oxon); LL.D. (Hon., St. Andrews); F.R.S.L.; Docteur (Hon., Caen), (Hon., Toulouse); Membre de l'Institut de France; Officier de la Légion d'Honneur; President of the English Assoc., 1953-1954; International President, P.E.N., 1954-1956; *b.* 22 January 1894; *s.* of late Sir Charles Morgan, C.B.E.; *m.* 1923, Hilda Vaughan; one *s.* one *d.* *Educ.:* Royal Navy,

Brasenose College, Oxford. Entered Navy as Cadet, 1907; served in Atlantic and China, 1911-13, when he resigned; rejoined August 1914 and served throughout the War; Brasenose College, Oxford, 1919-1921; President O.U.D.S.; joined Editorial Staff of The Times, December 1921; Principal Dramatic Critic of The Times, 1926-1939. Sept. 1939-44 served at the Admiralty, with intervals in France (Nov. 1939) and U.S.A. W. P. Ker Lecturer (Glasgow), 1945; Zaharoff Lecturer (Oxford), 1948. *Publications:* The Gunroom, 1919; My Name is Legion, 1925; Portrait in a Mirror, 1929 (awarded the Femina-Vie Heureuse Prize, 1930); The Fountain, 1932 (awarded Hawthornden Prize for 1933); Epitaph on George Moore, 1935; Sparkenbroke, 1936; The Flashing Stream (play), 1938; The Voyage, 1940 (James Tait Black Memorial Book Prize, 1940); The Empty Room, 1941; Ode to France, 1942; The House of Macmillan, 1943; Reflections in a Mirror, 1944; Second Reflections in a Mirror, 1945; The Judge's Story, 1947; The River Line, 1949 (dramatised version produced Edinburgh Festival, 1952); Liberties of the Mind, 1951; A Breeze of Morning, 1951; The Burning Glass (play), 1953; Challenge to Venus, 1957; (posthumous) The Writer and His World, 1960. *Relevant publication:* The Novels and Plays of Charles Morgan, by H. C. Duffin, 1959. *Address:* 16 Campden Hill Square, W.8. *Club:* Garrick. [*Died* 6 *Feb.* 1958.

MORGAN, Clement Yorke; Rector of Michaelhouse, Natal, since 1952; *b.* 1 Jan. 1903; *s.* of late Rev. Samuel Morgan; *m.* 1939, Sheila Anne, *d.* of late C. J. Danby; two *s.* two *d.* *Educ.:* Christ's Hospital; Hertford College, Oxford. Open Classical Schol., Hertford Coll., Oxford, 1922; Hon. Classical Mods., 1924; Lit. Hum. 1926; B.A. 1926; M.A. 1928. Asst. Master, Liverpool College, 1926-28; Asst. Master, Radley College, 1928-52; Social Tutor, 1936; Sub-Warden, 1938. *Recreations:* Rugby football, travel. *Address:* Michaelhouse, Balgowan, Natal, Union of South Africa. *T.:* Balgowan 12. *Club:* Victoria (Pietermaritzburg, Natal). [*Died* 8 *April* 1960.

MORGAN, Capt. Frederick Thomas de Mallet, C.B.E. 1944; Royal Navy (retd.); *b.* 20 Aug. 1889; *m.* 1914, Joan Frances, *d.* of late W. H. Monckton, Southwell Manor, Nottinghamshire, and Mrs. Monckton, Rosemount, Jersey; one *s.* two *d.* *Educ.:* Cheltenham College. Entered Royal Navy 1904, H.M.S. Britannia; specialised in gunnery; entered Admiralty Dept. dealing with inspection, development, design, etc., 1919; Capt. Superintendent in Charge of R.N. Cordite Factory, Holton Heath, 1935-42; Superintendent, R.N. Torpedo Factory, Greenock, 1942-46, and Superintendent, Torpedo Experiment and Design, Torpedo Experimental Establishment, Greenock, 1945-1946. *Recreation:* fishing. *Address:* Bridge House, Britford, Nr. Salisbury, Wilts. *Club:* United Service. [*Died* 23 *Aug.* 1959.

MORGAN, Engineer Rear-Adm. (Ret.) Geoffrey, C.B.E. 1941; Consultant and Agent, Cairo; *b.* 4 Sept. 1889; *s.* of late John Richards Morgan and Elizabeth Mitchell; *m.* 1924, Shelagh de Courcy Hare; two *s.* *Educ.:* Dulwich College; Royal Naval Engineering College, Keyham. Engineer Sub-Lieut., 1909; Engineer Lieut., 1911; H.M.S. Warrior at Jutland Battle (despatches); specially promoted to Engineer Lieut.-Cdr., Italian Silver Medal for Military Valour; Engineer Cdr., 1921; lent Egyptian Govt. 1929-33; Order of the Nile 3rd Class; Engineer Capt., 1933; A.D.C. to King George VI, 1938-39; Eng. Rear-Adm., 1939; Engineer Manager, H.M. Dockyard, Malta, 1938-42; Staff of NCXF North Africa, 1942-1943 (despatches, Officer of Legion of Honour, Croix de Guerre); Staff of ANCXF, 1943-44 (despatches); Control Commission for Germany, 1944-45; retired Dec. 1945. Admiralty Regional Officer (London and S.E.), 1945-50. *Address:* 56 Abdel Khalek, Sarwat Pasha, Cairo, Egypt. *T.:* Cairo 78335; East Farleigh House, East Farleigh, nr. Maidstone, Kent. *T.:* Maidstone 86295. *Clubs:* Naval and Military; Turf (Cairo). [*Died* 21 *July* 1956.

MORGAN, George, C.I.E. 1928; F.R.H.S., F.Z.S.; K.I.H. gold medal, 1910; *b.* Kirkcaldy, Fifeshire, 1 Oct. 1867; *s.* of A. G. Morgan; *m.* 1901, Claire Loftus Weatherall; one *s.* one *d.* *Educ.:* Repton. Came to Calcutta to join the firm of George Henderson & Co., 1889; worked in Naraingunge, E. Bengal, till 1912; has been in Calcutta since 1912; a Director of Companies, Calcutta; Chairman of Naraingunge Municipality for eleven years; late Member: Legislative Council, E.B. and Assam; Legislative Assembly and Council, Bengal; Calcutta Corporation, Calcutta Improvement Trust; Member Central Legislative Assembly, 1930-37; President Royal Agri-Horticultural Society of India, 1924-35. *Recreation:* gardening. *Address:* Kalimpong, West Bengal, India. *Clubs:* Caledonian; Bengal, Tollygunge (Hon. Mem.) (Calcutta); Royal and Ancient (St. Andrews). [*Died* 26 *June* 1957.

MORGAN, Gladys Mary, M.A.; Warden of Manor Hall, and Special Lecturer to the Dept. of Education, University of Bristol, 1946-56, retd. *Educ.:* Blackheath High School; St. Hilda's College, Oxford. Headmistress of Colston's Girls' School, Bristol, 1927-45. *Address:* c/o Miss B. M. Dale, Allwood's Patch, Guiting Power, Nr. Cheltenham, Glos. *Club:* University Women's. [*Died* 22 *Nov.* 1957.

MORGAN, Sir Herbert (Edward), K.B.E., *cr.* 1917; F.R.S.L.; F.R.S.A.; Médaille du Roi Albert, 1920; Officer of St. John of Jerusalem; Chairman, Smith's Potato Crisps (1929), Ltd.; Smith's Potato Estates; Ebonestos Industries Ltd.; Crystalate Ltd., British Homophone Co., Ltd., Danubian Trading Co. Ltd.; The Economist's Bookshop Ltd.; Fillery's Toffees Ltd.; Dufay-Chromex Ltd.; Polyfoto (England) Ltd.; Coronet Ltd.; Old Jewry Trust Ltd.; Smith's Potato Crisps (Overseas) Ltd.; Spicer-Dufay (British) Ltd.; Standard Cameras Ltd.; Director Oddeninos Hotel and Restaurant Ltd.; President Licensed Victuallers' School, 1944; Chairman Animal Feeding Stuffs Advisory Com., London Division; Chairman Rationalisation of Wholesale Bread Deliveries, London and S.E. Division; Chm. Man Power Cttee. Wholesale Fish Distribution, London Div.; *b.* 1880; 2nd *s.* of Rev. A. R. Morgan. Attached to W. H. Smith & Son since 1906; Member Advisory Board to the War Office Employment Bureau; President: Printers' Pension Corporation, 1925; Czechoslovakia British Chamber of Commerce; lately Board of Governors and Chairman of Appeal Cttee., Middlesex Hospital; Member: Rebuilding Cttee., St. George's Hospital; Council of the Travel Association; Publicity Cttee., the National Trust Ltd.; Chm. Executive Committee King's College Hospital Centenary Fund; Vice-President Newspaper Press Fund; Member of Council, Malvern College; Member Governing Body, London School of Economics; Member Commerce Degree, University of London; one of the Founders and Chairman of the Governors of the Three Arts Club; Member of Council, Union Jack Club; President O.P. Club, 1923-25; Twice Master of the Masons Company, 1938 and 1939; Deputy Director National Labour Supply, Ministry of Munitions, 1915; attached Imperial Munitions Board in Canada, 1916, as Adviser on Labour Organisation; Deputy Director National Service for Wales, 1918; Adviser to Minister of Labour and Lord Privy Seal on National Service Propaganda, 1939; Chairman of Government

Committee National Service Review in Hyde Park, 1939. First President Society of Industrial Artists. *Publications:* The Dignity of Business, 1914; Munitions of Peace, 1916; Careers for Boys and Girls, 1926; Business and Organisation columns of the Daily Telegraph; articles in the Edinburgh Review, Fortnightly Review, etc.; lectures on Business subjects. *Recreations:* punting, golf. *Address:* 1 Carlton House Terrace, S.W.1. *T.:* Whitehall 6747. *Clubs:* American, Savage, Reform, Thames Punting (Pres.). [*Died* 4 *July* 1951.

MORGAN, Hyacinth Bernard Wenceslaus, M.D., Ch.B., D.P.H.; Medical Adviser and Consultant Specialist on Industrial Diseases, Trades Union Congress General Council; Physician, Manor House Hospital, N.W.; Advisory Medical Officer, Union of Post Office Workers, Federation of P.O. Supervisors, Assoc. of Cinematograph and Allied Technicians, etc.; Louis Sterling Lecturer on Industrial Diseases; Member Council of British Medical Assoc.; Fellow Royal Soc. of Medicine; Member, Exec. Committee Confederation of Health Service Employees; consulting physician; *b.* Grenada, B.W.I., 11 Sept. 1885; 2nd *s.* of L. F. Morgan, Accountant; *m.* 1930, M. L., *d.* of late David Powell of St. Harmon's, Radnorshire; two *d.* *Educ.:* Grenada Grammar Sch.; Glasgow Univ., M.B., Ch.B. (Glasgow Univ.), 1909; M.D. Thesis (Commendation), 1914; numerous medals and certificates in undergraduate course, winner, inter-University Scotch Competitive McCunn Research Scholarship, 1909; has held many hospital resident appointments; War service, 1914-19; finally Surgical Specialist Horton War Hospital; medical work, Ministry of Pensions, 1919-21; private practice, 1921-33; Labour candidate L.C.C. Election Greenwich, 1922 and 1925; Labour candidate (Parliamentary) North-West Camberwell, 1922, 1923, 1924; M.P. (Lab.) N.W. Camberwell, 1929-31, Rochdale, 1940-50, Warrington 1950-55. *Publications:* has written on medical, sociological, and political questions in various newspapers. *Recreations:* music, motoring, reading Tory newspapers. *Address:* 26 Hampstead Lane, N.6. *T.:* Mount View 6000. [*Died* 7 *May* 1956.

MORGAN, Most Rev. John, D.D.; Archbishop of Wales since 1949 and Bishop of Llandaff since 1939; *b.* Llandudno, 6 June 1886; *s.* of Ven. Archdeacon John Morgan, Archdeacon of Bangor and Anglesey, formerly Rector of Llandudno. *Educ.:* Hertford Coll., Oxford; Cuddesdon Coll. Hon. Fellow of Hertford College, Oxford, 1950. Curate of Llanaber, 1910-12; Resident Chaplain to Bishop of Truro and Hon. P.V. of Truro Cathedral, 1912-16; T.C.F., 1916-19; Vicar Choral of St. Asaph and Vicar of St. Asaph, 1917-19; Curate-in-Charge of Llanbeblig, 1919-20; Vicar of Llanbeblig with Carnarvon, 1920-33; Chaplain to H.M. Prison, Carnarvon, 1919-22; Rural Dean of Arfon, 1928-31; Rector of Llandudno, 1933-1934; Residentiary Canon of Bangor, 1931-1934; Bishop of Swansea and Brecon, 1934-1939; Sub-Prelate Order of St. John of Jerusalem, 1946. Select Preacher: Oxford, 1951 and 1952; Cambridge, 1953. D.D. Lambeth, 1934; D.D. Wales, Univ. of (*honoris causa*) 1952. *Address:* Bishop's House, The Green, Llandaff, Cardiff. [*Died* 26 *June* 1957.

MORGAN, Brig.-Gen. John Hartman, Q.C. 1926; M.A. (Lond.); M.A. (Oxon); Barrister-at-law; D.L., J.P. Wilts; British Member of the Académie Diplomatique Internationale; Legal Editor of the Encyclopaedia Britannica; Emeritus Professor of Constitutional Law in the University of London; Reader in Constitutional Law to the Inns of Court, 1926-36. Counsel: to the India Defence League, 1933-34, and Indian Chamber of Princes, 1934-37; for W. Australia at hearing before Parliament of Secession Petition, 1935; to State of Gwalior and Central India States, 1939-45; to Parliamentary Post-War Policy Group, 1942-45. Tagore Professor, Univ. of Calcutta, 1939; Member of Executive Council of International Law Association; Adviser to American War Crimes Commission at Nuremberg, 1947-49; *b.* 20 March 1876; *s.* of Rev. David Morgan, Congregational Minister, Ystrad Rhondda, and Julie, *d.* of Felix Wethli, Zürich, late Comdt. of No. 56 V.A.D. (Red Cross). *Educ.:* Caterham School; University College of South Wales (Scholar); Balliol College, Oxford (Scholar); University of Berlin. Graduated B.A. Lond., 1895; M.A. Lond. (Mental and Moral Science), 1896; B.A. Oxon 1900 in Honour School of Modern History; Research Scholar of University of London at Berlin, 1903-04; on literary staff of Daily Chronicle, 1901-03; leader-writer on Manchester Guardian, 1904-05; contested Birmingham (Edgbaston) as Liberal Candidate at General Election, Jan. 1910, and West Edinburgh, Dec. 1910; Rhodes Trust Lecturer to the University in the Constitutional Laws of the Empire, 1927-32; late A.A.G. Military Section of Paris Peace Conference; British Military Representative on Prisoners of War Commission, 1919; Deputy Adjutant-General and G.O.C. Effectives Sub-Commission on Inter-Allied Military Commission of Control in Germany, 1919-23; Vice-Chm. Govt. Committee of Enquiry into Breaches of the Laws of War; Home Office Commissioner with the British Expeditionary Force, 1914-15; Staff Captain on Adjutant-General's Staff (despatches, 1914-15 Star). *Publications:* The House of Lords and the Constitution, 1910; The New Irish Constitution, 1912; The German War Book, 1915; War, its Conduct and Legal Results, 1915; Leaves from a Field Note-Book, 1916; Gentlemen-at-Arms, 1918; The Present State of Germany, 1924; Viscount Morley: an Appreciation, 1924; Remedies against the Crown, 1925; What We Are Fighting For, 1941; Assize of Arms, 1945; The Great Assize, 1948; contributor to The Times, Quarterly Review, Revue des deux Mondes, The Dictionary of National Biography, etc. *Recreations:* walking, riding, tennis. *Address:* 2 Harcourt Buildings, Temple, E.C.4; Priory Cottage, Wootton Bassett, Wilts. *T.:* Central 8549. *Clubs:* Junior Army and Navy, Reform. [*Died* 8 *April* 1955.

MORGAN, Brig. Morgan Cyril, C.B.E. 1944; M.C.; p.s.c.; Chairman Council of Voluntary Welfare Work Committee, B.A.O.R., 1950-60; *b.* 1891; *s.* of late David Morgan, Henllys, Llandovery; *m.* 1917, Gertrude Mary, *d.* of late Comdr. R. Greey, R.N.R., Eastbourne; one *s.* one *d.* (and one *s.* killed flying accident, Cranwell, 1938). *Educ.:* Blundell's School. South Wales Borderers, 1913; served European War, 1914-18, Tsingtau (China), Gallipoli, France, Belgium (despatches four times); Staff College, 1921-22; Bt. Major 1918; Bt. Lt.-Col. 1936; retired, 1937 and appointed Secretary, City of London Territorial Army and Air Force Assoc.; recalled to Army, 1939, A.A. & Q.M.G. 2nd (Lond.) Div.; Dep. Dir. Army Welfare Services with rank of Brigadier, 1940; released from Army, 1945. French Croix de Guerre; Order of the Crown of Italy. *Publication:* Official History of Army Welfare, Second World War, 1939-1945 (by authority of the Army Council). *Address:* c/o Glyn Mills, Holts Branch, Kirkland House, Whitehall, S.W.1. *Clubs:* Army and Navy; Devonshire (Eastbourne). [*Died* 16 *Aug.* 1960.

MORGAN, Robert Harry; Parliamentary Secretary, National Union of Teachers; *b.* 25 Jan. 1880; 2nd *s.* of Robert Harry Morgan, Dudley; *m.* 1904, Mabel, *e. d.* of Alfred Henry Bailey, Dudley; one *s.* three *d.* *Educ.:* St. Thomas' Higher Grade School, Dudley; Saltley College, Birmingham. Headmaster of St. Thomas' Higher Grade School, Dudley; Headmaster of Dudley

Bluecoat Schools, 1907-31, resigned; M.P. (C). Stourbridge Division, Worcestershire, 1931-45; served European War in Royal Navy. *Address:* 371 Gillott Rd., Birmingham 16. *Clubs:* Midland Conservative, Engineers (Birmingham).
[*Died* 28 *Nov.* 1960.

MORGAN, R(obert) Orlando, F.G.S.M.; retired; Professor of Pianoforte and Composition, 1887-1951, at the Guildhall School of Music and Drama; *b.* Manchester, 1865; *s.* of Peter and Elizabeth Morgan; *m.* Annie Elizabeth Morley (*d.* 1952), singer; two *s.* *Educ.:* Privately; Guildhall School of Music (Merchant Taylors' Scholarship and Webster Prize); First Prize and Gold Medal Grand Concours International de Composition Musicale, Brussels, 1894; in 1910 his Comic Opera Two Merry Monarchs was produced at the Savoy Theatre, London; sometime Member of the Faculty and the Board of studies in Music in the University of London. *Publications:* Prize Cantata, The Crown of Thorns; two Cantatas for female voices;—Zitella, and The Legend of Eloisa; Song-Cycles for 4 voices: In Fairyland; Love Rhapsodies; Modern School of Pianoforte technique (6 vols.); Over 200 songs and pianoforte pieces; Edited Bach's 48 Preludes and Fugues from the original autographs; Bach's French Suites; Beethoven's Sonatas; Novelletten, Kinderscenen and Album für die Jugend, by Schumann, etc.; Rules of Harmony. *Address:* 9 Harvard Court, Honeybourne Road, N.W.6. *T.:* Hampstead 4829.
[*Died* 16 *May* 1956.

MORGAN, Walter, C.M.G. 1936; *b.* 14 Jan. 1886; *s.* of Henry and Ruth Morgan; *m.* 1st, 1920, Marjory Pearce (*d.* 1942); one *s.*; 2nd, 1943, Mavis Clara Griffiths (*d.* 1959), Woodside Cottage, Haslemere. *Educ.:* Merchant Taylors' School, London; Jesus Coll., Oxford. Assistant Resident Northern Nigeria, 1910; Station Magistrate, 1918; Resident, 1926; acted as Chief Commissioner Northern Provinces of Nigeria, Nov. 1934-May 1935 and again in 1936; Senior Resident, Administrative Service of Nigeria, 1932-37; retired, 1937; Divisional Petroleum Officer for Wales, Oct. 1939. *Address:* Woodside Cottage, Haslemere, Surrey. [*Died* 13 *April* 1960.

MORGAN-OWEN, Major-General Llewellyn Isaac Gethin, C.B. 1934; C.M.G. 1918; C.B.E. 1921; D.S.O. 1916; *b.* 31 March 1879; *s.* of T. Morgan-Owen, M.A., J.P., Bronwylfa, Montgom.; *m.* 1910, Ethel Berry (*d.* 1950), *d.* of J. B. Walford, The Chapel, Abergavenny; one *s.* *Educ.:* Arnold House, Llandulas; Shrewsbury School; Trinity College, Dublin. Joined Carnarvon Militia, 1899; passed into Army as University Candidate; 2nd Lieut. 24th South Wales Borderers, 1900; Captain, 1909; Major, 1915; Col. 1921; Maj.-Gen. 1933; served S. African War, 1900-02 (Queen's medal 3 clasps, King's medal 2 clasps); with N. Nigeria Mounted Infantry, 1905-09; Adjutant, 1908-09; p.s.c., 1915; Staff-Capt., Embarkation Staff, Southampton; Brigade-Major, 40th Infantry Brigade, 13th Division; General Staff Officer, 2nd Grade, 13th Division, 1916; General Staff Officer, 1st Grade, 13th Div., 1917-18; European War, 1915-18, France, Gallipoli (D.S.O.), Egypt, Mesopotamia (Bt. Lt.-Col., despatches 5 times, C.M.G.); operations in Waziristan, 1920-21 (Indian Gen. Service Medal with two clasps, despatches, C.B.E.); Director of Organisation, India, 1927-28, Col. on the Staff; commanded 160th (S. Wales) Infantry Brigade, T.A., 1929-31; Commanded 9th Infantry Brigade, 1931-33; (Temp.-Brig.); Colonel of the South Wales Borderers, 1931-44; Major-General in charge of Administration, Eastern Command, 1934-1938; retired pay, 1938; Maj.-Gen. i/c of Administration, 1939-40; Lieut.-Governor and Secretary, Royal Hospital, Chelsea, 1940-1944, Commissioner, 1945-58. *Club:* Army and Navy. [*Died* 14 *Nov.* 1960.

MORIARTY, Cecil Charles Hudson, C.B.E. 1938 (O.B.E. 1925); LL.D.; *b.* 28 Jan. 1877; 2nd *s.* of Rev. Thomas Alexander Moriarty, M.A., Rector of Millstreet, Co. Cork; *m.* 1906, Muriel Una, *o. d.* of George Tilson Shaen Carter, J.P., Belmullet, Co. Mayo; three *d.* *Educ.:* Trinity College, Dublin. B.A., Senior Moderator, Large Gold Medalist and Prizeman; LL.B. with honours, 1912; LL.D., 1932; District Inspector of Royal Irish Constabulary, 1902-18; Assistant Chief Constable of Birmingham, 1918-35; Chief Constable of Birmingham, 1935-41; Commander of Order of St. John of Jerusalem, 1936; King's Police Medal, 1929; King's Jubilee Medal, 1935; Coronation Medal, 1937. *Publications:* Police Law, 1929, now in 14th Edition; Police Procedure and Administration, 1930, now in 6th Edition; Questions and Answers on Police Duties, 1935; Further Questions and Answers on Police Duties, 1938; Emergency Police Law, 1940 (with J. Whiteside); Questions and Answers on Police Duties, Third Series, 1946 (Omnibus Edition, 1954). *Recreations:* formerly Rugby football and hockey; now fishing and gardening. *Address:* Tenbury Wells, Worcs.
[*Died* 7 *April* 1958.

MORIS, Rt. Rev. James, C.B.E. 1955; C.SS.R. (6th) Bishop of Roseau, Dominica, (R.C.), since 1922; *b.* Belgium, 10 March 1876; naturalized British in 1925. *Educ.:* St. Lambert's Coll. in his native town; St. Joseph's Coll., Hasselt. Entered Redemptorist Order, 1894; professed, 1895; ordained Priest, 1900; Professor of Classics at St. Trond, Belgium, 1902; attached to Roseau Cathedral, 1903; Secretary to late Bishop Schelfhaut, 1905; Vicar-General and Parish Priest of Cathedral, 1907; Parish Priest of St. Thomas, 1916; Parish Priest of Antigua, 1918; Vice-Provincial of Redemptorists in British West Indies, 1919. Assistant at the Pontifical Throne, 1950-. King's Jubilee Medal, 1935, Queen's Coronation Medal, 1953. *Publications:* Statuta Diœcesana, 1923; A Short History of the Catholic Church in the Island of Antigua, 1924; A Catechism of Christian Doctrine (I-II), 1938; The History of the Catholic Church in the Diocese of Roseau, in the Ecclesiastical Bulletin of Roseau, June 1923-Sept. 1932; also numerous articles for the same review. *Address:* Bishop's House, Roseau, Dominica, B.W.I. *T.A.:* Bishop, Dominica.
[*Died* 4 *June* 1957.

MORISON, Sir John, G.B.E. 1956; Kt. 1945; Chairman Iron and Steel Holding and Realization Agency since 1953; *b.* 25 Jan. 1893; *s.* of John Morison and Janet McKenzie; *m.* 1922, Rachel Wilson Campbell; three *s.* one *d.* *Educ.:* Greenock Academy. Chartered Accountant; partner in Thomson McLintock & Co., Chartered Accountants, London, etc.; Director-General (Finance and Contracts), Ministry of Supply, 1942-45. Member of McGowan Committee on Electricity, 1936; General Claims Tribunal, Compensation (Defence) Act, 1939-1942; War Damage Commission, 1941-48. *Address:* Highwood, Sundridge Avenue, Bromley, Kent. *T.:* Ravensbourne 0813; *Clubs:* Caledonian, Gresham, Union.
[*Died* 27 *March* 1958.

MORISON, John Lyle, M.A., D.Litt., LL.D.; Emeritus Professor of Modern History, in the University of Durham; *b.* Greenock, Scotland, 1 Oct. 1875; *s.* of George Morison and Jane Lyle; *m.* 1918, Maude Willes, R.R.C. (*d.* 1934). *Educ.:* Greenock Academy; Glasgow University; Post Graduate work at Oxford. Assistant Lecturer in the departments of History and Literature, Glasgow University and Queen Margaret Coll., Glasgow, 1901-7; Professor of History, Queen's University, Kingston, Canada, 1907-22; served in Canada and in the 52nd Lowland Division in Egypt,

Palestine and France, 1914-19; Professor of Modern History in King's College, formerly Armstrong College, Newcastle on Tyne, 1922-40; Fellow of the Royal Society of Canada. *Publications:* Reginald Pecock's Book of Faith, edited with introduction; Articles in Scottish and Canadian Historical Review, and in Cambridge Historical Journal; British Supremacy and Canadian Self-Government, 1839-54; The Eighth Lord Elgin, 1928; contributions to the Cambridge History of the British Empire, 1930 and 1940; Lawrence of Lucknow: a Life of Sir Henry Lawrence, 1934; Raleigh lecture to British Academy: From Alexander Burnes to Frederick Roberts, a survey of frontier policy, 1936. *Recreation:* walking. *Address:* The Park, Toward, Argyll. *T.:* Toward 205. [*Died* 26 *Nov.* 1952.

MORISON, John Miller Woodburn, M.D. Glas.; F.R.C.P. Edin. 1929; F.F.R.; D.M.R.E. Camb., 1924; late Prof. of Radiology and Examiner in Radiology, Univ. of London; late Director, Radiological Department Royal Cancer Hospital, London; *b.* Beith, Ayrshire, 13 Mar. 1875; *s.* of John M. Morison, M.D., and Elizabeth Woodburn; *m.* 1911, Elizabeth, *d.* of W. E. Radcliffe, Staley, Cheshire; two *s.* *Educ.:* Ayr Grammar School; Glasgow Univ. Hon. Member Deutsche Röntgen Gesellschaft, Wiener Gesellschaft f. Röntgenkunde, Societa Italiana di Radiologica Medica, Societas Radiologorum Terrarum Septentrionalium, Österreichische Gesellschaft f. Röntgenkunde, American Röntgen Ray Society; Past Pres. British Association of Radiologists; Past-Pres. Sect. Radiol. Roy. Soc. Med.; Past-Pres. Sect. Radiol. Brit. Med. Assoc.; Hon. Member, Société de Radiologie Medical de France. *Publications:* Elevation of the diaphragm, Archiv. Radiol. and Electrother., 1923; X-rays and Cancer diag., Brit. Jl. Radiol., 1927; Diaphragmatic Hernia, Proc. Roy. Soc. Med., 1930; Massive Collapse of the Lung, B.M.Jl., 1930; Recent Progress in Medicine and Surgery, 1919-33 (Section on Radiology) Edit. by Sir John Collie, 1933; Tumours of Bone, Brit. Jl. Radiol., 1934. *Address:* 9 Julian Road, Folkestone, Kent. [*Died* 3 *Sept.* 1951.

MORLAND, Dr. Andrew John, M.D., F.R.C.P.; Physician, University College Hospital and French Hospital, London; *b.* 6 May 1896; *s.* of John Coleby and Elizabeth Bracher Morland; *m.* 1928, Dorothy Saunders; one *s.* one *d.* *Educ.:* Sidcot School; University College and Hospital; Lausanne University. House Physician, Brompton Chest Hosp., 1924; Physician: Montana, 1924-28; Mundesley Sanatorium, 1928-35; French Hosp., 1935; University College Hosp., 1937. Chevalier Légion d'Honneur, 1950. *Publication:* Pulmonary Tuberculosis in General Practice, 1932. *Recreations:* ski-ing, fishing, farming. *Address:* 135 Harley Street, W.1. *T.:* Welbeck 1261. *Club:* Savile. [*Died* 13 *July* 1957.

MORLAND, Egbert Coleby, M.D., F.R.C.P., F.R.C.S., late Editor of the Lancet; *b.* 1874; 5th *s.* of Charles Coleby Morland, Croydon; *m.* 1903, Mary Windsor Latchmore (*d.* 1948), Leeds; two *s.* one *d.* (adopted). *Educ.:* Bootham School; Owens Coll.; St. Bartholomew's Hospital. Gilchrist Scholar at London Matriculation, 1st Class hons. in London B.Sc., Gold Medallist in physiology, M.B.; Swiss Federal Diploma, 1907; in practice at Arosa, Switzerland, and director of the Villa Gentiana, 1907-15; on staff of Lancet from 1915, Editor, 1937-44. *Publications:* Prize Essay for King Edward VII. Sanatorium; Alice and the Stork, 1950. Editor of Maternity and Child Welfare, 1917-1934. *Address:* Pell Croft, Wooldale, Holmfirth, Yorks. [*Died* 26 *April* 1955.

MORLE, Philip Bartlett, Q.C. 1948; *b.* 27 May 1876; *o. s.* of Samuel Morle; *m.* 1st, 1904, Mabel (*d.* 1945), *d.* of N. P. Marquetti, Teddington; one *d.*; 2nd, 1946, Annie Winifred, *d.* of William Boulton, Chichester. Student Middle Temple, 1896; called to Bar, 1899; joined South-Eastern Circuit. President of Hardwicke Society, 1903-04. *Address:* 1 Essex Court, Temple, E.C.4. *T.:* Central 6717. [*Died* 28 *Jan.* 1956.

MORLEY, 4th Earl of, *cr.* 1815; **Edmund Robert Parker,** J.P.; Viscount Boringdon, 1815; Baron Boringdon, 1784; late Capt. Royal 1st Devon (Yeo. Cav.); *b.* 19 April 1877; *e. s.* of 3rd Earl of Morley and Margaret, *d.* of late R. S. Holford, Weston Birt; *S.* father, 1905. A Liberal Unionist. *Educ.:* Eton; Trinity Hall, Cambridge. Owns about 8000 acres, and pictures by Sir Joshua Reynolds. *Heir:* *b.* Hon. Montagu Brownlow Parker. *Address:* Saltram, Plympton, Devon. *Club:* Travellers'. [*Died* 10 *Oct.* 1951.

MORLEY, Charles, M.A., F.R.C.M.; J.P.; *b.* 1885; 2nd *s.* of Charles Morley; *m.* 1st, 1912, Ruth Blackhall Eaton; two *s.*; 2nd, 1940, Martha, 4th *d.* of Doctor Anton Engel, Kitzbuhel and Elma Nobile de Ferrari. *Educ.:* Eton; Trinity College, Cambridge. A Vice-Pres. and Hon. Sec. R. C. M.; Sheriff of County of London, 1935-36; J.P. Wilts, 1942. *Address:* Shockerwick, Bath. *T.A.* and *T.:* Bath 88249. *Club:* Brooks's. [*Died* 19 *April* 1955.

MORLEY, Christopher; Author; *b.* Haverford, Penna., 5 May 1890; *e. s.* of Frank Morley, late of Woodbridge, Suffolk, and Lilian Janet Morley, late of Haywards Heath, Sussex; *m.* 1914, Helen Booth Fairchild, New York: one *s.* three *d.* *Educ.:* Haverford Coll., Penna.; New Coll., Oxford. Staff of Doubleday Page & Co., publishers, 1913-17; Evening Public Ledger (Philadelphia), 1918-20; New York Evening Post, 1920-24; Contributing Editor Saturday Review of Literature (New York), 1924-39; Theatrical Producer in Hoboken, New Jersey, 1928-30. Hon. D.Litt., Haverford College, 1933; Member National Institute of Arts and Letters. *Publications:* The Eighth Sin, 1912; Parnassus on Wheels, 1917; The Haunted Bookshop, 1919; Where the Blue Begins, 1922; Thunder on the Left, 1925; Poems, 1927; Essays, 1927; John Mistletoe, 1931; Human Being, 1932; The Trojan Horse, 1937; Kitty Foyle, 1939; Thorofare, 1942; The Middle Kingdom (poems), 1944; The Man Who Made Friends With Himself, 1949; and others. *Recreations:* second-hand book-stores, whisky and plain water, swimming and cooking. *Address:* Roslyn Heights, N.Y., U.S.A. [*Died* 28 *March* 1957.

MORLEY, Henry Seaward, M.D., F.R.C.P.; Senior Physician, The Royal West Sussex Hospital, Chichester, since 1932; Physician, St. Richard's Hospital, since 1954; Consulting Physician Graylingwell Hospital, Chichester, since 1945; Physician Haslemere Hospital since 1944; Crown Mem. of the Gen. Med. Council since 1952; *b.* 16 March 1897; *s.* of Dr. Henry Forster Morley, M.A., D.Sc., F.I.C., F.C.S., and Ida Rose Morley (*née* Tayler); *m.* 1934, Alison Kathleen, *d.* of late Major Rowland Hill, Cheshire Regt., and Mrs. Rowland Hill; two *s.* *Educ.:* Univ. Coll. School; Univ. Coll., London; Univ. Coll. Hospital. Active service in R.F.A., 1915-19 (Lieut.). Formerly: House Surgeon, House Physician, Obstetric Asst., Casualty M.O., Res. M.O. and Med. Registrar, Univ. Coll. Hosp., 1924-1932; Clin. Asst. Brompton and Gt. Ormond Street Hospitals. Master of Soc. of Apothecaries of London, 1953-54. F.R.C.P. 1948; F.R.Soc.Med. 1948. *Publications:* articles in Lancet, Brit. Med. Jl., etc. *Recreation:* sailing. *Address:* Church Hill House, Midhurst, Sussex. *T.:* Midhurst 232; Pwllcorn, Moylegrove, Pembrokeshire. *Clubs:* English-Speaking Union; Bosham Sailing. [*Died* 5 *July* 1960.

MORLEY, Lieut.-Colonel Lyddon Charteris, C.B.E. 1919 (O.B.E. 1918); *b.* 1877; *s.* of Lieut.-Colonel G. L. Morley, 79th Cameron Highlanders and R.A.S.C.; *m.* 1908, Gladys Vivienne, *d.* of late Sir Thomas de Multon Lee Braddell. Served Somaliland, 1902-04 (medal with clasp); European War, 1914-19 (despatches, O.B.E., C.B.E., Chevalier Legion of Honour). *Address:* Morwenstowe, Wellington Avenue, Fleet, Hants. [*Died* 15 *March* 1954.

MORLEY, Ralph, J.P.: M.A. (Reading); *b.* Chichester, 25 October 1882; *s.* of Thomas Walter, pharmacist, and Mary Morley; unmarried. *Educ.:* Southampton University Coll. Schoolmaster, Southampton, 1903-29 and 1931-45; Hon. General Secretary N.F.C.T., 1937-44; Chairman Itchen Urban District Council, 1920; President National Federation of Class-Teachers, 1928-29; Member of Court of Governors, Southampton University College; President N.U.T., 1946-1947. M.P. (Lab.) Southampton, 1929-31 and 1945-50, Itchen Division of Southampton, 1950-55. *Publications:* various articles in Socialist and Labour Press and Educ. Press *Recreations:* reading, walking, cycling. *Address:* 40 Athelstan Rd., Southampton. *T.:* Southampton 55710. [*Died* 14 *June* 1955.

MORNEMENT, Brevet Col. Edward, C.B.E. 1919; T.D.; *b.* 1867. Brevet Colonel, late R.E., 1918; Lt.-Col. late 4th Batt. Norfolk Regt. T.A., 1914; Royal Engineers,1916-1919. Member Norfolk County Council, 1904; County Alderman, 1924; J.P. Norfolk, 1914; served European War, Aug. 1914-May 1919. *Address:* East-Harling, Norfolk. *T.:* East-Harling 206. *T.A.:* East-Harling. [*Died* 6 *Feb.* 1956.

MORRICE, Humphrey Alan Walter, C.M.G. 1955; Adviser on Irrigation and Drainage to the Colonial Office since 1958; Irrigation Adviser to the Sudan Govt., 1953-58; *b.* 24 May 1906; *e. s.* of late Frederick Lancelot Hamilton Morrice, Brampton Hall, Suffolk; *m.* 1945, Margaret Alice, *er. d.* of late Rev. George Flint Seaton, Rector of Earsham, Norfolk; no *c.* *Educ.:* Wellington Coll., Berkshire; Corpus Christi Coll., Cambridge (M.A.). Worked on Argentine railways, 1927-33; joined Sudan Irrigation Dept., 1934, and worked there until 1958, except for service with Royal Engineers and Sudan Defence Force, 1940-44. Pres. Sudan Engineering Soc. 1953-55. M.I.C.E., M.A.S.C.E. *Publications:* various papers in Proceedings of Sudan Engineering Soc. and in Sudan Notes and Records; also various reports on irrigation in Africa published by Sudan Government. *Address:* Picknells, Stoke-by-Nayland, nr. Colchester. [*Died* 31 *Dec.* 1959.

MORRICE, Rev. Dr. James Cornelius, M.A.; B.Litt., D.Phil. (Oxon); Rector of Helmdon since 1949; *b.* 1874; *s.* of James and Margaret Morrice. *Educ.:* University College, Bangor; Corpus Christi Coll., Oxford. Lectr. on Celtic, Univ. Coll., Cardiff; Curacies at Mallwyd, Trefdraeth, and Amlwch; Minor Canonry, Bangor Cathedral; Rector of Festiniog and Maentwrog; Vicar of Bangor, 1913-20; St. Michael's, Oxford, 1920-25; Holyhead, 1925-27; Longbridge Deverill, Warminster, 1927-28; Rector of Stratton Audley, 1928-30; Vicar of Crowle, Lincolnshire, 1930-31; Rector of Letcombe Regis with Letcombe Bassett, 1936-38; Rector of Fairstead with Terling, 1931-33 and 1938-43; Vicar of Chrishall, 1943-46; Vicar of Ford End, Chelmsford, retired; Examiner to Oxford University, University of Wales, and St. David's College, Lampeter. *Publications:* The Poetical Works of Howel Swrdwal, Gruffydd ab Ieuan, William Llyn; A Manual of Welsh Literature; Wales in the Seventeenth Century; Social Conditions in Wales under the Tudors and Stuarts. *Recreation:* golf. *Address:* Helmdon Rectory, Brackley, Northants. [*Died* 22 *Jan.* 1953.

MORRIS OF KENWOOD, 1st Baron, *cr.* 1950, of Kenwood; **Harry Morris;** Solicitor; *b.* 7 Oct. 1893; *s.* of Jacob and Fanny Samuel; *m.* 1924, Florence Isaacs, Leeds; one *s.* one *d.* *Educ.:* Tivoli House School, Gravesend; privately. Solicitor, 1920-36; called to Bar, 1936. H.M. Forces, 1914-19 and 1940-45. Member Sheffield City Council, 1920-26, 1929-37; M.P. (Lab.) Sheffield Central, 1945-50, Neepsend Division of Sheffield, Feb.-March 1950. *Recreation:* golf. *Heir:* *s.* Hon. Philip Geoffrey Morris, *b.* 8 June 1928. *Address:* 4 Kenwood Avenue, Sheffield 7. *T.:* Sheffield 52315. [*Died* 1 *July* 1954.

MORRIS, Colonel Charles Temple, C.B.E. 1922; *b.* 9 Jan. 1876; 3rd *s.* of late Lieutenant-Colonel George Tomkins Morris, Bengal Staff Corps; *m.* 1901, Marie Willoughby Osborne (*d.* 1943); *m.* 1945, Dilys, *d.* of late Ven. D. G. Davis, Archdeacon, of Montgomery. *Educ.:* Bedford. Entered the 2nd Batt. Green Howards, 1897; transferred to Indian Army, 1901; served in N.W.F., 1897-98 (medal, 2 clasps), 1908 (medal, 1 clasp), 1915; European War, Mesopotamia, 1916 (despatches, 1915-16 Star, G.S. medal, Victory medal); N.W.F., 1919-21 (2 clasps to 1908 medal, C.B.E., despatches twice); commanded 5th Bn. 1st Punjab Regt., 1921-26; retired, 1931. *Address:* 83 Troy Court, Kensington, W.8. *T.:* Western 9991 *Club:* United Service. [*Died* 1 *June* 1956.

MORRIS, Colonel George Abbott, C.M.G. 1918; D.S.O. 1917; Director of Companies, 21 Stiemens St., Johannesburg; *b.* 1879; *s.* of J. W. Morris; *m.* 1908, Mabel Beatrice, *d.* of A. H. Stanford. Served Boer War; European War, 1914-18 (despatches, D.S.O., C.M.G.); War of 1939-45. *Clubs:* Union, Wanderers (Johannesburg). [*Died* 16 *July* 1957.

MORRIS, Brig.-Gen. George Mortimer, C.B. 1919; D.S.O. 1917; Indian Army, retired; *b.* 1868. Served European War, Mesopotamia, 1915-19 (despatches twice, D.S.O., Bt. Col., C.B.). [*Died* 24 *April* 1954.

MORRIS, Guy Wilfrid, M.A. Oxon; *b.* London, 21 Nov. 1884; *s.* of Rev. H. Morris, Assistant Master, Merchant Taylors' School, E.C. and Louisa Jane Britton; *m.* 1917, Hilda, *d.* of Capt. J. Brown, late Bombay Staff Corps; one *s.* one *d.* *Educ.:* Merchant Taylors' School; St. John's College, Oxford. Lecturer, St. John's College, Battersea, 1910-1914; Senior History and English Master, Bradford Grammar School, 1914-21; Headmaster, Penistone Grammar School, 1921-28; Headmaster, Colfe's Grammar School, Lewisham, S.E.13, 1928-47; Oxford University Extension Lecturer; served Artists' Rifles and War Office. *Publications:* The Golden Fleece; The English Speaking Nations (with L. S. Wood); Britain in the Nineteenth Century. *Recreations:* walking, gardening. *Address:* The Green, Northmoor, Oxford. *T.:* Standlake 267. *Club:* Royal Empire Society (Chairman Oxford Branch). [*Died* 27 *July* 1956.

MORRIS, Hon. Sir John Demetrius, K.C.M.G., *cr.* 1952; Kt., *cr.* 1943; Chief Justice of Tasmania since 1940; Chancellor of Univ. of Tasmania; *b.* 24 Dec. 1902; *s.* of James Demetrius and Margaret Jane Morris; *m.* 1930, Mary Louisa McDermott; one *s.* *Educ.:* St. Patrick's College, S.J., Melbourne; Melbourne Univ. B.A. 1924; LL.B. 1925; M.A. 1926; admitted to Victorian Bar, 1927; to Tasmanian Bar, 1930; acting Chief Justice of Tasmania, 1939-40. *Address:* Judges Chambers, Hobart, Tasmania. *Club:* Tasmanian (Hobart). [*Died* 3 *July* 1956.

MORRIS, Sir John N.; *see* Newman-Morris.

MORRIS, John T. M.; *see* Macgregor-Morris.

MORRIS, Ralph Clarence, C.M.G. 1941; *b.* 10 March 1889; *s.* of R. C. Morris and A. Dickins, Burdale, Tenbury Wells, Worcs; *m.* 1922, Sybil Hill; no *c.* *Educ.:* Ludlow Grammar School. Joined Indian Police (Burma), 1908; District Supt. 1914; Commandant Burma Military Police, 1917-19; Deputy Inspector-General, Administration, Apr.-Oct. 1928; Deputy Inspector-General, C.I.D. and Railways, 1931-37; Inspector-General of Police, Burma, 1937-42; King's Police Medal, 1935; India General Service Medal with clasp; Silver Jubilee and Coronation Medals. *Recreations:* riding and tennis. *Address:* 11 Queen's Gardens, Bournemouth, Hants. [*Died* 28 *May* 1959.

MORRIS, Sir Rhys Hopkin, Kt., *cr.* 1954; M.B.E. 1919; Q.C. 1946; M.P. (L.) Carmarthen since 1945; Dep. Chairman of Ways and Means since 1951; Barrister-at-law; *b.* 1888; *s.* of Rev. John Morris, Maesteg, Glam.; *m.* G. Perrie-Williams, O.B.E. 1942, M.A., Litt.D., Dinam, Llanrwst, N. Wales; one *d.* *Educ.:* Universities of Wales and London. Mem. of the Court of the Univ. of Wales; Gov. of the National Library and National Museum of Wales; served European War 1914-18 (despatches); M.P. (Ind. L.) Cardiganshire, 1923-32; Member of Parliamentary Delegation to East Africa, 1928; Member of Palestine Commission, 1929; Metropolitan Police Magistrate, 1932-36; Regional Dir. for Wales, B.B.C., 1936-45; formerly Member Central Advisory Cttee. to Minister of Pensions. Hon. LL.D. (Wales). *Address:* 1 Brick Court, Temple, E.C.4; 19 Hatherley Crescent, Sidcup, Kent. *T.:* Footscray 2609. [*Died* 22 *Nov.* 1956.

MORRIS, Thomas Joseph, C.M.G. 1931; *b.* 4 Feb. 1876; *s.* of Lieut. J. W. Morris, R.N.; *m.* Guendolen, *e. d.* of Commander C. B. Palmer, R.N. Served S. African War (medal and two clasps); entered Sudan Political Service, 1905; Deputy Assistant Financial Secretary, Sudan Government, 1917-19; Consul for Canary Islands, 1919; Chargé d'Affaires at Caracas, 1923-24; Chargé d'Affaires at Havana, 1924; Envoy Extraordinary and Minister Plenipotentiary (local rank) to Cuba, 1925-31; Special Ambassador in Cuba, 1929; Consul-General at Strasbourg, 1931-34; Envoy Extraordinary and Minister Plenipotentiary to Bolivia, 1934-37; British Delegate to International Conference on Emigration and Immigration at Havana, 1928; retired, 1937. Silver Jubilee Medal, 1935; Coronation Medal, 1937; Order of the Nile; Grand Cordon of Cuban Order of Merit. *Address:* Flemings Hall, Bedingfield, Suffolk. *Clubs:* Athenæum, Royal Automobile. [*Died* 4 *Sept.* 1953.

MORRISH, Rear-Admiral William Douglas Travers, C.B.E. 1936; R.N., retired; *b.* 19 April 1882; *s.* of late Captain William Douglas Morrish, R.N., and late Mariana Laura Travers; *m.* 1916, Dorothy Isabel, *d.* of A. G. Gordon, Hongkong; (one *s.* killed in action in M.T.B. 695, 1944). *Educ.:* Waltham College; Plymouth Grammar School. Entered Royal Navy, 1900; served Boxer Rebellion, China, 1900; Paymaster Commander of Cardiff, Rodney, Nelson; Assistant Paymaster Director General, Admiralty, 1930-33; Fleet Accountant Officer, Home Fleet, 1933-35; Paymaster Captain (S) R.N. Barracks, Chatham, 1935; Port Accountant Officer, Portsmouth (H.M.S. Victory) 1935-37; retired list, 1937; Served on Franco-Spanish Frontier with International Council for Non-Intervention in Spain, 1937-39; Ministry of Supply as Assistant Director of Storage, 1940-1942, Controller of Storage, 1942-46. *Recreations:* sailing, rowing (formerly football), hockey, tennis, motoring, etc. *Address:* The End House, Felpham Gardens, Bognor Regis, Sussex. *Clubs:* Royal Naval; Royal Naval Sailing Association. [*Died* 2 *Jan.* 1958.

MORRISON, 1st Baron, *cr.* 1945, of Tottenham; **Robert Craigmyle Morrison,** P.C. 1949; J.P.; D.L.; Parliamentary Secretary to the Ministry of Works, 1948-51; Alderman Tottenham Borough Council since 1934; *b.* 29 October 1881; *s.* of late James Morrison; *m.* 1910, Grace, *d.* of late Thomas Glossop; one *s.* M.P. (Co-op. and Lab.) North Tottenham, 1922-31 and 1935-45; Parliamentary Secretary to Prime Minister, 1929-31; Councillor for Wood Green, 1914-19; Middlesex County Councillor, 1919-25; joined army as a private in 1915, and served 3½ years in France; member Metropolitan Water Board, 1937-47; Chairman Waste Food Board, 1941-49; a Lord in Waiting to the King, 1947-48. D.L. (Middlesex), 1948. *Heir:* *s.* Hon. Dennis Morrison, *b.* 21 June 1914. *Address:* 41 Talbot Road, Tottenham, N.15. *T.:* Stamford Hill 1579. [*Died* 25 *Dec.* 1953.

MORRISON, Alexander Thomas, C.B.E. 1943; J.P.; Chairman Scottish Gas Consultative Council since 1949; Member Scottish Gas Board, 1949; *b.* 10 Sept. 1886; *er. s.* of Lewis Morrison, Aberdeen; *m.* 1921, Isobel, *e. d.* of Rev. John Livingstone; no *c.* *Educ.:* Robert Gordon's College, Aberdeen. Entered Aberdeen Town Council, 1931; Convener Housing Committee, 1932-35; District Commissioner for Civil Defence N.E. Scotland District, 1939-44; City Treasurer, Aberdeen, 1935-47; Trustee Aberdeen Endowments Trust, 1922-52; Governor Robert Gordon's College, 1931-53; Chairman National Joint Industrial Council for Local Authority Services (Scotland), 1944-51; Chairman Scottish Mental Hospitals Assoc. 1944-46. Member Whitley Council for Health Services, 1948-51; Member Board of Management, Aberdeen Gen. Hosps., 1948-1953. Deacon Convener Aberdeen Incorporated Trades, 1922-24. *Address:* 32 Craigie Park, Aberdeen. *T.:* 21125. *Clubs:* Scottish Conservative (Edinburgh); Royal Scottish Automobile (Glasgow). [*Died* 3 *March* 1954.

MORRISON, Arthur Cecil Lockwood, C.B.E. 1944; *b.* 27 Oct. 1881; *s.* of late Richard Morrison; *m.* 1927, Dorothy Gray; no *c.* *Educ.:* Strand School, London. Entered Civil Service, 1899, as 2nd Div. Clerk, W.O.; entered Metropolitan Police Courts Service, 1902; Chief Clerk, 1922; Chief Clerk of Juvenile Courts, 1929-37; Senior Chief Clerk, Bow St. Police Court, 1937-46. Member of Departmental Cttee. on Allowances to Witnesses in Indictable Cases, 1946; member of Departmental Cttee. on Depositions in Criminal Cases, 1948. Hon. member of Justices Clerks Soc. *Publications:* (with late Sir William Clarke Hall) Law relating to Children and Young Persons, 1934, 1942, 1947, 1951 and 1956; (with late Albert Lieck) Criminal Justice Acts, 1926 and 1927, also Matrimonial Jurisdiction of Justices, 1926 and 1932; (with E. L. Thackray) Outlines of Law for Social Workers, 1948; (with M. M. Wells and others) The Children Act 1948 and The Nurseries and Child-Minders Regulation Act, 1948; Domestic Proceedings, 1949; (with E. Hughes) The Criminal Justice Act 1948, 1949; Notes on Juvenile Court Law, 1952; joint editor of Paley on Summary Convictions (10th edn.), 1953; articles on legal and other subjects in various periodicals. *Recreations:* writing, reading and listening. *Address:* 40 Laburnham Road, Maidenhead, Berks. *T.:* Maidenhead 1016. *Club:* Authors'. [*Died* 26 *Nov.* 1960.

MORRISON, George Alexander, M.A., LL.D.; *b.* 30 Oct. 1869; *o. s.* of late Alexander Morrison, Dufftown, Banffshire; *m.* 1918, Rachel B., M.A., *e. d.* of late Malcolm Campbell, Grantown-on-Spey; two *s.* one *d.* *Educ.:* Mortlach Public School; Aberdeen University. Assistant Teacher, Robert Gordon's College, 1890-97; Principal Teacher of Classics, 1897-1910; Rector of Inverness Royal Academy, 1910-1920; Headmaster, Robert Gordon's College, Aberdeen, 1920-33; Convener of Secondary Education Committee, Educational Institute of Scotland, 1928-29; President E.I.S. 1930-31;

M.P. (L.N.) Scottish Universities, 1934-45; J.P. City of Aberdeen, 1929. *Publication:* Latin Course, Part I. 1930, Part II. 1931, Part III. 1932. *Recreation:* music. *Address:* 23 Albert Place, Dufftown, Banffshire.
[*Died* 8 *Sept.* 1956.

MORRISON, Sir William, Kt., *cr.* 1926; Member of the Privy Council of Jamaica, and Nominated Member of the Legislative Council since 1922; *b.* 14 Oct. 1877; *s.* of William Morrison, Banffshire, and Margaret Janet Duff; *m.* 1902, Amy D'Costa, Kingston, Jamaica; one *d.* *Educ.:* Kingston Collegiate School, Jamaica. Admitted to practise as a Solicitor of the Supreme Court of Judicature of Jamaica, 1899; Member of the Executive Committee of the Society for the Protection of Animals in Jamaica; Director of the Jamaica Mutual Life Assurance Society; President of the Jamaica Scottish Society; Member of the Managing Committee of the Jamaica Club; President of the Jamaica Cricket Council, and also of the Kingston C.C.; Member of the Law Council and of the Solicitors' Committee; senior partner of the legal firm of Morrison & Morrison. *Recreations:* cricket, bridge. *Address:* 85 Harbour Street, Kingston, Jamaica. *T.A.:* Lincora, Jamaica. *Clubs:* West Indian (Jamaica); Kingston Cricket (Kingston).
[*Died* 8 *Sept.* 1951.

MORRISON-BELL, Sir (Arthur) Clive, 1st Bt., *cr.* 1923; *b.* 19 April 1871; 2nd *s.* of late Sir Charles Morrison-Bell, 1st Bt., and *heir-pres.* to 3rd Bt; *m.* 1912, Hon. Lilah Wingfield, *y. d.* of 7th Viscount Powerscourt; two *d.* *Educ.:* Eton; Sandhurst. Joined Scots Guards, 1890; A.D.C. to Maj.-Gen. Hutton, commanding Militia in Canada, 1898-99; went to South Africa with Canadian Contingent, in charge of Maxim Gun Section (despatches); A.D.C. to Earl of Minto, Governor-General of Canada, 1900-4; Organising Secretary, under Earl Roberts, V.C., to Society of Miniature Rifle Clubs, 1906-8; rejoined Regiment, Aug. 1914; M.P. (C.) Honiton Division Devonshire, 1910-31. Home Guard, 1940-44. *Publication:* Tariff Walls, 1930. *Heir:* none. *Address:* 49 Montagu Square, W.1. *T.:* Paddington 6356. *Clubs:* Turf, Carlton, Alpine.
[*Died* 16 *April* 1956 (*ext.*).

MORRISON-BELL, Lieut.-Col. Ernest FitzRoy, O.B.E.; D.L.; J.P.; *b.* 19 April 1871; 3rd twin *s.* of Sir Charles Morrison-Bell, 1st Bt.; *m.* Maud Evelyn (*d.* 1960), 2nd *d.* of late Col. F. Henry, Elmestree, Tetbury; four *d.* *Educ.:* Eton. Joined Militia, 1889; 9th Lancers, 1891; served through war in S. Africa; Adjutant, 1899-1902 (despatches, Queen's medal 4 clasps, King's medal 2 clasps); Adjutant Yeomanry, 1903-6; contested Mid-Devon, 1906; M.P. (U.) Mid-Devon, 1908-10 and 1910-18; served European War, Aug. 1914-July 1919. *Address:* The Close, Tetbury, Glos. *T.:* Tetbury 26. *Club:* Cavalry.
[*Died* 20 *Oct.* 1960.

MORRISON-LOW, Sir Walter J. M.; *see* Low.

MORROGH, Brigadier Walter Francis, D.S.O. 1921; M.C.; M.I.Mech.E.; A.M.Inst.T.; *b.* 17 Sept. 1891; *s.* of Walter Morrogh, J.P., Rosetta, Blackrock; *m.* 1925, Violet Marjorie, *y. d.* of late J. Rushbrooke, J.P., Bulmershe Court, nr. Reading; one *s.* one *d.* *Educ.:* Beaumont. Joined Leinster Regt. 1912; served with them and M.G.C. in France during European war (badly wounded, M.C., despatches twice, 1914 star, G.S. and Victory medal); Waziristan, 1919-1922 (D.S.O., despatches twice, Indian G.S. medal and three clasps); transferred to Royal Tank Corps, 1923; Captain, 1916; Major, 1925; Bt. Lt.-Col., 1935; Lt.-Col., 1937; Col., 1939; Temp. Brig., 1939; retired pay, 1947. *Recreations:* hunting, tennis, golf. *Address:* Tangle Wood, Deepcut, Surrey.
[*Died* 19 *Aug.* 1954.

MORROW, George; book illustrator; *b.* Belfast, 1870. Contributor to Punch from 1906. Joined staff, 1924; Art Editor, 1932-1937. *Address:* Bardfield End Green, Thaxted, Essex.
[*Died* 18 *Jan.* 1955.

MORSE, Vice-Adm. Sir (John) Anthony (Vere), K.B.E., *cr.* 1945 (C.B.E. 1944); C.B. 1942; D.S.O. 1915; R.N. (retd.); *b.* 16 October 1892; *y. s.* of Sydney Morse; *m.* 1917, Mary Faith, *e. d.* of Rev. W. Howard Leeds, C.F.; one *d.* (*s.* killed in Battle of the River Plate, 1939). Joined Navy, 1905; Lieut. 1914; Comdr. 1927; Capt. 1934; Rear-Adm. 1943; Vice-Adm. 1947 (retd). Served European War, including Dardanelles, 1914-18 (despatches twice, D.S.O.); Head of British Naval Mission to China, 1934-37; War of 1939-45 (C.B., C.B.E., K.B.E.); Flag Officer, Malaya, 1945-46. *Club:* Union.
[*Died* 7 *May* 1960.

MORSE, William Ewart, J.P.; Director of Limited Company; *b.* 23 Nov. 1878; *s.* of late L. L. Morse, M.P. South Wilts; *m.* 1910, Alma, *o. d.* of Hawthorn Thornton, South Africa; one *s.* one *d.* *Educ.:* The High School, Swindon. Member of Swindon Town Council 20 years; Chairman of Finance Committee; Mayor of Borough of Swindon two years; Member of Wiltshire County Council 30 years; Ex-Pres. Swindon Chamber of Commerce; Mason for 40 years; P.M. Royal Sussex Lodge of Emulation 355; Provincial Grand Standard Bearer; lifelong member Primitive Methodist Church, now Methodist Church; elected Vice-Pres. for 1925-26; M.P. (L.) Bridgwater Div. Somerset, 1923-24. *Recreation:* golf. *Address:* The Croft, Swindon, Wilts. *T.:* Swindon 2701. *Clubs:* Reform, National Liberal.
[*Died* 18 *Dec.* 1952.

MORSE, Withrow, B.Sc., M.A., Ph.D.; Consulting Biochemist; *b.* Dayton, Ohio, 7 May 1880; *s.* of David Appleton Morse and Amanda Withrow; *m.* Winning Olga Allan, Island of Arran; one *s.* one *d.* *Educ.:* State University of Ohio; Columbia University. Formerly of the Faculties of the State Universities of Ohio, New York (Cornell, New York City), Wisconsin, Nebraska and West Virginia; Professor of Biology, Trinity College; Head of Department of Chemistry, Nelson Morris Memorial Institute for Medical Research, Chicago; Prof. of Biochem. and Toxicology, Jefferson Medical Coll., Philadelphia; Research, N.Y. State Psychiatric Inst.; Consultant: Röhm and Haas, Philadelphia; Lederle Laboratories, Inc., N.Y.; Kalak Co., Inc. N.Y.; Originator of Flugel, for War Wounds; Mem. Bioch. Soc. (Gt. Brit.); Amer. Soc. Biol. Chem. (life). *Publications:* Applied Biochemistry, 2nd ed., 1927; Treatise on Biochemistry (Anglo-Amer.), 1935; Media of the Body, 1950; Bibliographic Revs. over Mineral Metabolism, 1942; technical articles in Biochemical Jl. (Cambridge), and in American scientific periodicals. *Recreation:* Stereo-photography (Mem. Brit. Stereo. Assoc.). *Address:* Interlaken Gardens, Eastchester, via Tuckahoe, 7, N.Y., U.S.A.
[*Died* 10 *Feb.* 1951.

MORSHEAD, Lieut.-General Sir Leslie James, K.C.B., *cr.* 1942; K.B.E., *cr.* 1942 (C.B.E. 1941); C.M.G. 1918; D.S.O. 1917; E.D.; Légion d'Honneur; Virtuti Militari 5 (Poland); Medal of Freedom 2 (U.S.A.); President Bank of New South Wales; Chairman: Bank of N.S.W. Savings Bank; Bank of N.S.W. Unit Trust; David Jones Ltd.; Director: Mutual Life & Citizens' Assurance Co.; Amalgamated Wireless of Australasia; Trustees and Executors Agency Co.; Australian Consolidated Press; Pres. Boy Scouts Assoc., N.S.W.; Pres., Big Brother Movement; a trustee of Gowrie Scholarship Fund; *b.* 18 Sept. 1889; *s.* of late William Morshead, Ballarat, Vic.; *m.* 1921, *e. d.* of late William Woodside, Melbourne; one *d.* Served in European War with A.I.F. in Gallipoli and France 1914-19; comd. 33 Bn., 1916-19 (despatches 6 times). In Australia comd. 14 Inf. Bde., 1933, 15 Inf.

Bde., 1934-36, 5 Inf. Bde., 1937-39. Served War of 1939-45; comd. 18 Austr. Inf. Bde., 1939-41 (Austr., Eng. and Mid. East), 9 Austr. Div., 1941-42; Comdt. Tobruk Garrison, 1941; G.O.C., A.I.F., in Middle East, 1942-43; comd. 9 Austr. Div. at El Alamein, 1942; on return to Austr. comd. 2 Austr. Corps, 1943-44; G.O.C. New Guinea Force, 1944; Second Austr. Army, 1944; G.O.C. 1 Austr. Corps and was Task Force Comdr. for Borneo ops., 1945 (despatches thrice). Formerly General Manager in Australia of Orient Line. *Address:* 69 Wolseley Rd., Point Piper, Sydney, N.S.W. *Clubs:* Union (Sydney); Melbourne (Melbourne). [*Died* 26 *Sept.* 1959.

MORTEN, Frederick Joseph, C.M.G. 1938; B.A. (Oxon); *b.* 6 Oct. 1888; *s.* of Frederick Morten. *Educ.:* Lancing; Exeter College, Oxford. Eastern Cadetship, 1912 (Straits Settlements) now known as Colonial Administrative Service; held various posts finally being appointed Director of Education Straits Settlements and Adviser on Education F.M.S. 1932; acted as Colonial Secretary Straits Settlements, July 1937–Feb. 1938; retired 1938. *Address:* c/o Westminster Bank, Salisbury, Wilts. [*Died* 18 *May* 1960.

MORTENSEN, Theodor, Ph.D.; Director of the Department of Invertebrates of the Zoological Museum, Copenhagen, 1917-33; *b.* 1868; *s.* of late John G. Mortensen and Petra, *d.* of Jensen, Instructor; *m.* 1901, Valborg, *d.* of Blomberg, Copenhagen; one *s.* one *d.* *Educ.:* Frederiksborg; University, Copenhagen. Assistant at the Danish Biological Station, 1895-96; then at the Zoological Museum Copenhagen; Marine Zoological Expeditions to Siam in 1899-1900; to the West Indies in 1905-6; to the Pacific, 1914-16; to the Kei Islands, 1922; to Java, Mauritius, South Africa, and St. Helena, 1929-30; to the Red Sea, 1936 and 1937; member of numerous learned societies; awarded Prize Czar Nicolai II. at the International Zoological Congress Monaco, 1913; Linnean gold medal, Linnean Soc., Lond., 1951. *Publications:* Echinoidea of the Danish Ingolf Expedition, I.-II., 1903-7; Swedish South Polar, 1910; German, 1909; Echinodermenlarven of Plankton Expedition, 1898; Ctenophora of the Danish Ingolf Expedition, 1912; Studies of the development and larval forms of Echinoderms, 1921; Handbook of the Echinoderms of the British Isles, 1927; Discovery Reports, Echinoidea and Ophiuroidea, 1936; Monograph of the Echinoidea, I-V, 1928-52; numerous minor publications, mainly on Echinoderms, in Danish, English, French, American, Australian, German, Swiss, and Japanese periodicals. *Recreations:* music, literature, gardening, and sailing. *Address:* Zoological Museum, Copenhagen. [*Died* 3 *April* 1952.

MORTIMER, Sir Ralph George Elphinstone, Kt., *cr.* 1934; O.B.E. 1920; M.A. (Cantab), J.P.; owner of Milbourne and Holywell and Hartford Estates; *b.* 7 July 1869; *s.* of William Brook Mortimer and Caroline Jane Anne Bates Mortimer; *m.* 1907, Violet, *twin d.* of Major E. W. Stokes, King's Own Royal Lancaster Regiment; one *s.* (*yr. s.* killed in Burma, 1944) three *d.* *Educ.:* Elstree; Harrow; Trinity College, Cambridge. President and Chairman Northumberland County Cricket Club; played cricket for Lancashire and Northumberland; County Commissioner, Northumberland Boy Scouts; Holder of Silver Wolf; High Sheriff Northumberland, 1916-17; County Magistrate Lancashire and Northumberland. *Recreations:* cricket, football, shooting. *Address:* Milbourne Hall, Ponteland, Northumberland. *T.:* Ponteland 13. *Club:* Northern Counties (Newcastle upon Tyne). [*Died* 3 *May* 1955.

MORTISHED, Ronald James Patrick; Irish Correspondent, International Labour Office, 1953; *b.* London, 14 June 1891; *s.* of James Mortished, Limerick; *m.* Marie, *d.* of Adolphus Shields, Dublin; one *s.* two *d.* *Educ.:* London Council Schools; Strand School, King's College; Morley College; London School of Economics. Entered British Civil Service, 1909; Member Irish White Cross Reconstruction Commission, 1921; Secretary to Constitution Committee of Irish Free State, 1922; Assistant Secretary Irish Labour Party and Trade Union Congress, 1922-30; International Labour Office, 1930-46 and 1952-53; Chairman of Labour Court, Ireland, 1946-52. *Publication:* The World Parliament of Labour, 1946. *Club:* Stephen's Green (Dublin). [*Died* 16 *Aug.* 1957.

MORTON, Sir George, K.B.E., *cr.* 1952; Q.C. (Scot.) 1918; Sheriff of Aberdeen, Kincardine and Banff since 1932; *b.* 1870 *s.* of late George Morton, farmer, Auchengray, Lanarkshire; *m.* 1st, 1902, Isobel, *d.* of late William Martin, Montrose; 2nd, 1927, Hilda, *d.* of late R. J. Calver, Edinburgh. *Educ.:* Edinburgh University, M.A., LL.B. Admitted to Scottish Bar, 1895; Advocate-Depute, 1911-17; Sheriff of Dumfries and Galloway, 1917-24; of Forfar, 1924-32; Chairman General Board of Control for Scotland, 1936-39; contested South Lanarkshire, 1913. *Recreation:* walking. *Address:* 37 Moray Place, Edinburgh. *T.:* (Edinburgh) Caledonian 6452. *Clubs:* Scottish Liberal (Edinburgh); Royal Northern (Aberdeen). [*Died* 17 *July* 1953.

MORTON, Sir George Bond, Kt., *cr.* 1942; O.B.E. 1939; M.C.; Director, Bird & Co. (London), Ltd., National Bank of India, Ltd., Army & Navy Stores Ltd., Grindlays Bank Ltd.; *b.* 13 Feb. 1893; *s.* of late William and late Alice Maud Morton; *m.* 1929, Doreen Elizabeth O'Kinealy; one *s.* two *d.* *Educ.:* privately. Deloitte Plender Griffiths & Co., 1909-14; served European War, 1914-19; Temp. Commission Royal Fusiliers, 1914; Temp. Captain, 1915; active service, France, 1915-17 (wounded, M.C.). Ministry of Pensions, 1918-19; joined Bird & Co., Calcutta, 1919; Partner, Bird & Co., Calcutta, and F. W. Heilgers & Co., Calcutta, 1933-45; Senior Resident Partner, Bird & Co., Calcutta, and F. W. Heilgers & Co., Calcutta, 1938-45; Director Imperial Bank of India, 1936-45; Vice-Pres., 1939-41; Pres., 1942-1944; Hon. Sec. King George V. Memorial Fund, Bengal, 1936-39; Vice-Chairman, King-Emperor's Anti-Tuberculosis Fund for India, Bengal, 1938-39; Trustee Victoria Memorial, Calcutta, 1939-46; Adviser Eastern Group Conference, 1940; Munitions Production Advisory Committee, India, 1940-45; Vice-Chairman Provincial Advisory Committee for War Supplies, India, 1940-45; Chairman Bengal Telephone Corp. Ltd., 1940-1941; Pres. Bengal Chamber of Commerce, 1941-42; Vice-Pres., 1940-41; Pres. Associated Chambers of Commerce of India and Ceylon, 1941-42; Nat. Defence Council, India, 1941-45; Sheriff of Calcutta, 1941-42; Post-War Reconstruction Committees, India, 1942-46; British Economic Mission to Greece, 1946-47; Director of numerous Companies. *Recreations:* fishing, shooting, travel. *Address:* Rectory House, Ogbourne St. George, Marlborough, Wilts. *Clubs:* Oriental; Bengal (Calcutta). [*Died* 10 *April* 1954.

MORVI STATE, ex-Ruler of, H.H. Maharaja Shri Sir Lukhdirji Bahadur, G.B.E., *cr.* 1939; K.C.S.I., *cr.* 1930; LL.D. 1941; *b.* 26 Dec. 1876; *s.* of H.H. late Sir Waghji Rawaji, G.C.I.E. and Ba Shri Bajirajba, *d.* of the Thakore Saheb Shri Pratapsinhji of Palitana; two *s.* *Educ:* England; India under a special tutor Ascended the Gadi on the death of his father, 1922; the hereditary title of Maharaja was conferred on H.H. on His Majesty the King Emperor's birthday, 1926. Abdicated in

1948 in favour of his heir, Yuvraj Shri Mahendrasinhji, *b.* Jan. 1918. *Address:* Buckhurst Park, Ascot, Berkshire; Morvi, Kathiawar, India. [*Died* 4 *May* 1957.

MOSELEY, Geoffrey; Barrister-at-law; a Master of the Supreme Court of Judicature, King's Bench Division, 1926-51; *b.* 1882; *s.* of Charles Moseley. *Educ.:* Winchester; Christ Church, Oxford. Called to bar, Inner Temple, 1909. *Address:* Yeomans, Virginia Water, Surrey. *Club:* United University. [*Died* 23 *June* 1953.

MOSELEY, Herbert Harvey; *b.* 3 April 1873; *s.* of Rev. Herbert Henry Moseley and Mary Elizabeth, *d.* of John Harvey, Bristol; *m.* 1908, Marjorie Doris Furnivall; one *s.* *Educ.:* Marlborough College; Worcester College, Oxford. M.A., B.C.L. Oxford; Solicitor, 1897; Senior Solicitor to Prudential Assurance Co. Ltd. 1929-35; Director, 1935-1950, retd. 1950. *Recreations:* rowing, fishing, rifle shooting. *Address:* 10 Hillside, Wimbledon, S.W.19. *T.:* Wimbledon 4759. *Club:* Oxford and Cambridge. [*Died* 27 *May* 1959.

MOSELY, Sir Archie Gerard, Kt., *cr.* 1941; *b.* 6 March 1883; *s.* of Gerard Mosely, Solicitor, Clifton, Bristol, and Louisa Blankensee; *n.* of late Alfred Mosely, C.M.G., K.St.J., educationalist, philanthropist; *m.* 1908, Scylla Neame; one *d.* *Educ.:* Clifton College (Scholar); Wadham College, Oxford (Scholar). Honours Classical Moderations and Lit. Hum.; entered I.C.S., 1907; District and Sessions Judge, 1917; Puisne Judge, High Court of Judicature, Rangoon, Burma, 1932; retired, 1943. *Publication:* Crudities and Oddities, a book of Verses, 1930. *Recreations:* golf, fishing. *Address:* 6 Symonds Lane, George, Cape Province, S. Africa. [*Died* 21 *Jan.* 1951.

MOSER, Robert Oswald, R.I., R.O.I.; *m.* 1911; one *d.* *Educ.:* Margate; Highgate. Many things, then artist; Paris Salon, Mention Honorable, 1907, Silver Medal, 1922. The Girl in Red, purchased by Glasgow Corporation; Dixisti, The Last Supper, purchased by late Lord Winterstoke and now over the altar of the church at Blagdon, The Adoration of the Magi: now hanging in the parish church at Rye, Sussex, etc. *Publications:* Illustrated John Halifax, Gentleman, and other books. *Recreations:* anything and everything but golf, which he plays. *Address:* The Studio, c/o Wright & Pankhurst, Rye, Sussex. *Club:* St. John's Wood Arts. [*Died* 31 *March* 1953.

MOSS, Geoffrey; *see* McNeill-Moss, Major G.

MOSS, Sir George Sinclair, K.B.E. 1939 (C.B.E. 1929; M.B.E. 1918); *b.* Yokohama, Japan, 26 Apr. 1882; *s.* of Charles Davis Moss, Cirencester; *m.* 1916, Gladys Lucy Moore; two *s.* one *d.* *Educ.:* Germany; Switzerland; King's College, London. Entered Consular Service in China, 1902; District Officer and Magistrate at Weihaiwei, 1913-15; Secretary to the War Office Representative in charge of the Chinese Labour Corps in China, 1916-18; War Office representative in charge of Chinese Labour Corps Base at Tsingtao, 1918-21; Vice-Consul at Hankow, 1922-23; Acting Consul, Shanghai, 1923-24; served in the Foreign Office, 1925-26; H.B.M. Consul, 1926; Consul at Foochow, 1926-29; Acting Consul-General at Canton, 1929; Acting Consul-General at Nanking, 1931; Consul at Wei-hai-wei, 1932; Expert and Interpreter with the League of Nations Commission in Manchuria, 1932; Consul-General at Hankow, 1935-38; retired, from Consular Service, 1938; retired as farmer, 1956. *Recreation:* gardening. *Address:* The Old Glebe, Eggesford, Devon. *T.:* Chulmleigh 284. [*Died* 15 *Dec.* 1959.

MOSS, Sir Thomas E.; *see* Edwards-Moss.

MOSTYN, Sir Basil (Antony Trevor), 13th Bt., *cr.* 1670; *b.* 6 Feb. 1902; *s.* of George Trevor Basil Mostyn (*d.* 1913), 2nd *s.* of 8th Bt. and of Mary Hermione, *d.* of late Augustus Henry de Trafford; *S.* nephew 1955; *m.* 1931, Anita Mary, *d.* of late Lieutenant-Colonel Rowland Charles Feilding, D.S.O.; two *s.* two *d.* *Educ.:* Stonyhurst; Pembroke College, Cambridge. Formerly Lieutenant, Royal Army Service Corps. *Heir:* *s.* Jeremy John Antony Mostyn, *b.* 24 Nov. 1933. *Address:* Heart Say Garage, Biddenden, Kent. [*Died* 19 *March* 1956.

MOSTYN, Sir Pyers Edward, 12th Bt., *cr.* 1670; *b.* 12 July, 1928; *o. s.* of Captain Sir Pyers Mostyn, 11th Bt., and Margery, *o. d.* of late Alfred Stanley Marks, of Sydney, N.S.W.; *S.* father 1937. *Heir:* *u.* Basil Antony Trevor (*See* Mostyn, Sir Basil). [*Died* 11 *Feb.* 1955.

MOTEN, Brig. Murray John, C.B.E. 1944; D.S.O. 1941, and Bar, 1943; E.D.; General Manager The Savings Bank of S. Australia; *b.* Hawker, S. Australia, 3 July 1899; *s.* of John Moten, Flinders Park, Adelaide; *m.* 1926, Kathleen, *d.* of late P. Meegan, Dundalk House, Sandwell; two *s.* one *d.* *Educ.:* Mount Gambier High School; Adelaide University. Joined Staff, The Savings Bank of S.A., 1915; Associate Federal Institute of Accountants, 1924; Pres. S.A. Bank Officials Assoc., 1934-35; Cadet Lieut., 1916; 48 Bn. A.M.F., Lieut., 1923; Capt., 1926; Major, 1929; Lt.-Col. and Command 43/48 Bn., 1936; Comd. 48 Bn., 1938; Comd. 2/27 Bn., A.I.F., 1940; 17th Australian Inf. Bde., A.I.F., 1941; Temp. Comd. 11 Aust. Div., 1942; Comd. Kanga Force, N.W. New Guinea, 1943; Comd. 6 Aust. Div. 1945; Comd. Aust. Army, London Victory March Contingent, 1946; Comd. 9th Aust. Inf. Bde., C.M.F., 1948; Hon. Col. S. Aust. Scottish Regt., 1952. Served in Western Desert, Syria, Ceylon and New Guinea. Aust. Army representative on Imperial War Graves Commission, 1947. Hon. A.D.C. to H.E. the Governor General, 1953. *Recreations:* golf, tennis, gardening. *Address:* 17 Stanley St., Woodville, S. Australia. *T.:* M 7642. *Club:* Naval and Military (Adelaide). [*Died* 13 *Sept.* 1953.

MOTT, John R.; Hon. Chairman International Missionary Council, 1942 (Chairman, 1910-41); Hon. President of World Council of Churches; Hon. Canon, Washington Cathedral; *b.* Livingston Manor, N.Y., 25 May 1865; *s.* of John S. Mott and Elmira Dodge; *m.* 1st, 1891, Leila Ada White (*d.* 1952); two *s.* two *d.*; 2nd, 1953, Agnes Peter Mott. *Educ.:* Cornell University (Ph.B. 1888); hon. A.M. Yale, 1899; F.R.G.S.; Hon. LL.D. Edin., Princeton, Brown, Toronto; Hon. D.Litt. Upper Iowa University; Hon. D.D. Ecclesiastical Academy of Russian Orthodox Church, Paris; General Secretary of the World's Student Christian Federation, 1895-1920, Chairman, 1920-28; Chairman Executive Committee Student Volunteer Movement, 1888-1920; Chairman Continuation Committee of World Missionary Conference of Edinburgh, 1910-20; General Secretary of International Committee Y.M.C.A., 1915-1932; General Secretary of the National Council of the Young Men's Christian Association, 1924-28; Student Secretary, 1888-1915; Foreign Secretary, 1898-1915; made tour of world for Student Christian Movement, 1895-97; special tours to all parts of Europe, South Africa, South America, and Australia on similar missions, 1900-1; held Continuation Committee conferences and evangelistic meetings for students in Southern Asia and the Far East, 1912-13; member of Mexican Commission, 1916, and of the Special Diplomatic Mission to Russia in 1917; during European War was General Secretary of the National War Work Council, Y.M.C.A.; General Sec. United War Work Campaign, 1918; Pres. of the World Missionary Congresses in Edinburgh, 1910, Jerusalem, 1928, Madras,

1938; Pres. World's Alliance of Y.M.C.A., 1926-1947 (now Hon. Pres.); half share Nobel Peace Prize, 1946; The Star of the Hungarian Red Cross, 1923; The Order of the Estonian Red Cross; Order of Christ (Portugal), 1919; Order of the White Lion (Czechoslovakia); Order of the Crown (Siam), 1919; Officer of the Legion of Honour, France, 1949, holder, Distinguished Service Medal, America, the Imperial Order of the Sacred Treasure, Japan, Order of the Jade, China, Order of the Crown of Italy, Polonia Restituta, Poland, Prince Carl Medal of Sweden, 1946; Order of the White Rose of Finland, 1946. *Publications:* Strategic Points in the World's Conquest, 1897; Evangelisation of the World in this Generation, 1900; Christians of Reality, 1902; Pastor and Modern Missions, 1904; The Future Leadership of the Church, 1908; The Decisive Hour of Christian Missions, 1910; The Present World Situation, 1914; World's Student Christian Federation, 1920; Confronting Young Men with the Living Christ, 1923; Present-day Summons to the World Mission of Christianity, 1931; Liberating the Lay Forces of Christianity, 1932; Cooperation and the World Mission, 1935; Five Decades and a Forward View, 1939; Methodists United for Action, 1939; The Larger Evangelism, 1944; Six Volumes, Addresses and Papers of John R. Mott; many pamphlets and articles. *Address:* 528 East Washington Street, Orlando, Florida, U.S.A.; c/o Y.M.C.A., 291 Broadway, New York City, U.S.A. [*Died* 31 *Jan.* 1955.

MOTT, Hon. Major-Gen. (Bt. Lieut.-Col.) Stanley Fielder, C.B. 1918; late K.R.R.C.; *b.* 1873; *y. s.* of late Albert Mott, Scotswood, Sunningdale, and Emma, *d.* of late Henry Fielder; *m.* 1st, 1905, Ethel Harriet (*d.* 1906), *d.* of Oswald Robinson, Alderley Edge; one *s.* 2nd, 1909, Sophie Theresa (*d.* 1954), *d.* of Leopold Stern and *widow* of Captain H. F. Gaynor, R.E. *Educ.:* Eton; Sandhurst. Served throughout the Boer War in command of Mounted Infantry; granted brevet majority, 1902; retired, 1911; served throughout European War on staff of Yeomanry Mounted Division; in command of 158th Brigade in Gallipoli, and in command of 53rd Welsh Div. throughout the operations in Palestine; granted hon. rank of Major-General on retirement, 1919. *Address:* Spinney Close, Leamington-Hastings, nr. Rugby. *T.:* Marton (Warwickshire) 255. [*Died* 4 *Feb.* 1959.

MOUAT, Prof. J. R. K.; *see* Kay-Mouat.

MOULD, James, Q.C. 1948; *b.* 21 Sept. 1893; *s.* of John Thomas and Minnie Mould, Bury, Lancs; *m.* 1928, Alice May Hunt (decd.), Bedford; one *d.* *Educ.:* Bedford Modern School; Univ. Coll., London. B.Sc., Ph.D.; A.M.I.E.E. Called to the Bar, Gray's Inn, 1923, Bencher, 1950. Fellow, Univ. Coll., London. *Address:* New Court, Temple, E.C.4. *T.:* Central 4122; 4 Gray's Inn Square, W.C.1. *T.:* Chancery 3206. [*Died* 2 *April* 1958.

MOULE, Rev. Arthur Christopher; *b.* 18 May 1873; *s.* of George Evans Moule, D.D., Bishop in Mid-China, and Adelaide Sarah Griffiths; *m.* 1904, Mabel Benett Wollaston; no *c.* *Educ.:* King's School, Canterbury; Trinity College, Cambridge. After a short time as pupil of Mr. Walter Shirley (later Earl Ferrers) worked as an architect in China, 1898-1903; ordained, 1904, and worked with the S.P.G. in diocese of Shantung till 1908; various curacies in England, 1908-18; Vicar of Trumpington near Cambridge, 1918-33; Professor of Chinese Language and History in the University of Cambridge, 1933-38; Rector of Mundford, 1940-45; Fellow of Trinity College, 1937; Hon. Fellow School of Oriental and African Studies, London University, 1952. *Publications:* Christians in China before the Year 1550, 1930; Marco Polo (with late P. Pelliot), vols. I, II, 1938; Quinsai, 1956; The Rulers of China, 1957; many articles in the T'oung-pao, Journal of the Royal Asiatic Society, and other oriental periodicals. *Address:* 34 Chesterton Hall Crescent, Cambridge. *T.:* 56624. [*Died* 5 *June* 1957.

MOUNSEY, Rt. Rev. William Robert (Rupert), D.D. (Lambeth); C.R.; *b.* 20 September 1867; *s.* of W. Robinson Mounsey, of Lowther, Penrith, and Mary, *d.* of William Heskett, Plumpton Hall; unmarried. *Educ.:* Lichfield College. Ordained, 1890; Curate of St. Stephen's, Willenhall, 1890-94; St. James's, Wednesbury, 1894-96; St. James's, Sydney, N.S.W., 1896-1901; organising sec. New Guinea Mission, 1901-4; Curate of All Hallows Barking, 1904-9; Bishop of Labuan and Sarawak, 1909-16; in Charge Shiplake, Oxon, 1916-17; Alassio, Italy, 1917-19; Church of the Resurrection, Brussels, 1919; St. Dunstan's, Stepney, 1920; St. Paul's Vicarage-Gate, Kensington, 1920; Vicar St. Mark's, Regent's Park, 1921-24; Comm. Bishop, Wakefield, 1924, Truro, 1925-35; Assistant Bishop, Bradford, 1935-49; Canon of Bradford, 1937-49; Member Community of Resurrection, 1926; Licensed Preacher, Goulburn, N.S.W., 1928. *Address:* House of Resurrection, Mirfield, Yorks. *T.:* Mirfield 3318; 8 Holland Park, W.11. *T.:* Park 2300. [*Died* 18 *June* 1952.

MOUNT, Lieut.-Colonel Sir Alan Henry Lawrence, Kt., *cr.* 1941; C.B. 1931; C.B.E. 1919; Chief Inspecting Officer of Railways, Ministry of Transport, 1929-49, when appointed Consultant to Railway Executive on safety measures; *b.* 1881; *e. s.* of late R. C. Mount, Welwyn; *m.* Margaret Sybil, *y. d.* of late Colonel Edmond D'Arcy Hunt, 6th Inniskilling Dragoons; one *s.* one *d.* *Educ.:* Bradfield College; R.I.E.C., Coopers Hill. Commissioned R.E. 1902; S.M.E. Chatham, 1902-4; North-Western (State) Railway, India, 1905-14; served European War (France) as Deputy Chief Railway Construction Engineer, 1914-1919; retired 1923. Inspecting Officer of Rlys., Min. of Transport, 1919-29. *Address:* 6 Burghley Rd., Wimbledon. *T.:* 0608. *Club:* United Service. [*Died* 10 *Aug.* 1955.

MOUNTBATTEN OF BURMA, Countess, C.I. 1947; G.B.E. 1947 (C.B.E. 1943); D.C.V.O. 1946; *b.* 28 Nov. 1901; *m.* 1922 (as Hon. Edwina Cynthia Annette Ashley, *er. d.* of 1st Lord Mount Temple, P.C.) Lieut. the Lord Louis Mountbatten, R.N. (later Earl Mountbatten of Burma, K.G., P.C., G.C.B., G.C.S.I., G.C.I.E., G.C.V.O., D.S.O.); two *d.* *Educ.:* The Links, Eastbourne; Alde House, Aldeburgh, Suffolk. Supt.-in-Chief, St. John Ambulance Bde. Mem. Order of St. John and assoc. with its work, 1928-; joined St. John Amb. Bde., Dec. 1939; auxiliary nurse, Westminster Hosp.; i/c all St. John personnel working in C.D., London area, 1940-41; Dep. Supt.-in-Chief, Nursing Corps and Divisions, St. John Ambulance Bde., 1941; Supt.-in-Chief since 1942; Vicereine of India, 1947. Chairman St. John and Red Cross Service Hosps. Welfare Dept.; Governor Westminster Hosp. Council; Girl Guides Assn.; W.V.S. Advisory and Gen. Purposes Cttee., etc. Pres. Save the Children Fund, Dumb Friends League; Vice-Pres. Royal College of Nursing; Patron, Pres. and Chm. of many other organisations, cttees., etc. Hon. LL.D. Edinburgh University, 1954. G.C.St.J. 1945; American Red Cross Silver Medal, 1946; Belgian Red Cross 1st class, 1946, despatches, 1946; Brilliant Star of China, 1947; Netherlands Red Cross Medal, 1947; Freedom of City of Edinburgh, 1954. *Recreations:* swimming, riding, golf. *Address:* 2 Wilton Crescent, S.W.1. *T.:* Sloane 0081; Broadlands, Romsey, Hants. *T.:* Romsey 3333; Classiebawn Castle, Cliffoney, Co. Sligo. *T.:* Cliffoney 6. *Club:* International Sportsmen's. [*Died* 20 *Feb.* 1960.

MOUNTEVANS, 1st Baron, *cr.* 1945; of Chelsea; **Admiral Edward Ratcliffe Garth Russell Evans,** K.C.B., *cr.* 1935 (C.B. (Mil.), 1932; C.B. (Civil), 1913); D.S.O. 1917; LL.D. 1937; Freeman of Calgary, Canada, 1914; Freeman: of Dover, 1938; of Chatham, 1939; of Kingston-upon-Thames, 1945; of City of London, 1945; of Chelsea, 1945; Knight of Order of St. John of Jerusalem, 1937; *b.* 28 Oct. 1881; *s.* of Frank Evans, Barrister-at-law; *m.* 1st, Hilda Beatrice (*d.* 1913), *d.* of T. G. Russell, Barrister, Christchurch, N.Z.; no c.; 2nd, 1916, Elsa, *o. d.* of Richard Andvord, Christiania; two *s.* *Educ.:* Merchant Taylors' School; Training Ship Worcester. Entered Navy, 1897; Sub-Lieut., 1900; served in S.Y. Morning, relief ship to the Discovery Expedition, 1902-4; Lieut., 1902; awarded Shadwell Testimonial Prize by the Lords Commissioners of the Admiralty, 1907; joined British Antarctic Expedition as second in command, October 1909; specially promoted for Antarctic services to Commander, 1912; returned in command of expedition after death of Captain Scott, 1913; commanded Mohawk in bombardment of German Army right wing, Belgian Coast, 1914 (despatches); Commander H.M.S. Viking, 1915 (despatches); commanded H.M.S. Broke, 1917, when that ship with H.M.S. Swift engaged and defeated six German Destroyers; specially promoted Captain for services in action; commanded H.M.S. Carlisle, 1921-22; Patrol Minesweeping and Fishery Protection Flotilla, 1923-26; Battle Cruiser Repulse, 1926-27; Rear-Admiral commanding Royal Australian Navy, 1929-31; Commander-in-Chief Africa Station, 1933-35; Commander-in-Chief, The Nore, 1935-39; London Regional Commissioner for Civil Defence, 1939-45; Rector of Aberdeen University for 1937-39, re-elected 1939-42; Younger Brother of Trinity House; King Edward VII. and King George V. medals for Antarctic Exploration; Officer Legion of Honour; Commander of the Order of St. Olaf of Norway; Commander of Crown of Belgium, Croix de Guerre; United States Navy Cross; Médaille Civique of Belgium; 1st Class for saving life at sea, 1919; Board of Trade Silver Medal for saving life at sea, 1921; awarded special gold medal by Lloyd's for saving life at Hong Moh disaster in China seas, 1921; Officer of Order of Leopold, Belgium; Cavalier of the Military Order of Savoy, Italy; Croix de Guerre, France; Order of Tower and Sword, Portugal, 2nd Class; Norwegian War Medal for services during invasion of Norway; Gold Medallist of Royal Hungarian and Royal Belgian Geographical Societies; Livingstone Gold Medallist, Royal Scottish Geographical Society; awarded also gold medals from the city of Paris, city of Rouen, and from the Geographical Societies of Marseilles, Rouen, and Newcastle; Honorary Member of many Geographical Societies. *Publications:* Keeping the Seas, 1920; South with Scott, 1921; British Polar Explorers, 1944; Adventurous Life, 1946; The Desolate Antarctic, 1950; Arctic Solitudes, 1953; and numerous boys' books etc. *Heir: s.* Hon. Richard Andvord Evans [*b.* 28 Aug. 1918; *m.* 1941, Deirdré Grace, *d.* of Patrick O'Connell, Cork; two *s.* one *d.*]. *Address:* 30 Albert Court, Kensington Gore, S.W.7. *T.:* Kensington 2340. [*Died* 20 *Aug.* 1957.

MOUNTIFIELD, Engineer Rear-Admiral James, C.B.E. 1919; *b.* 28 May 1871; *s.* of Alfred Mountfield; *m.* 1908, Maud (*d.* 1947), *d.* of William Phillips, Tavistock; two *s.* *Educ.:* Royal Naval Colleges, Keyham and Greenwich. Passed special course of R.N. College, 1891-94; Engineer Lieut., 1894; Engineer-Comm. 1907; Engineer-Capt., 1917; Engineer Rear-Admiral, 1922; served in H.M.S. Blenheim, 1894-7; H.M.S. Melpomene, 1897-9; Assistant-Engineer Manager, Chatham, 1900-6; H.M.S. Diana, 1906-8; Assistant Manager, Hongkong 1908-9; Devonport, 1910-13; H.M.S. Indomitable, 1913-15 (Dogger Bank); Portsmouth Dockyard, 1915-17; Chief Engineer, Sheerness, 1917-19; Manager, Engineering Department H.M. Dockyard, Chatham, 1920-24; retired, 1925; Associate Member Institution of Civil Engineers. *Recreations:* motoring, golf. *Address:* The Myrtles, 9 Farncombe Road, Worthing, Sussex. [*Died* 14 *Aug.* 1957.

MOUNTMORRES, 7th Viscount, *cr.* 1763; **Rev. Arthur Hervé Alberic Bouchard de Montmorency,** M.A., T.C.D.; Bt. 1631; Baron Mountmorres, 1756; Hon. C.F. (for life); *b.* 6 Feb. 1879; *s.* of late Hon. Arthur Hill Trevor de Montmorency, M.D., 4th *s.* of 4th Viscount Mountmorres; *S.* cousin 1936; *m.* 1914, Katharine Sophia Clay, *d.* of late T. A. Warrand, Bridge of Allan; two *d.* *Educ.:* Trinity College, Dublin. Served as trooper in 29th Batt. I.Y. in Boer War (medal and 2 clasps); ordained, 1907; Curate of Armagh, 1907-10; Athlone, 1910-12; Curate of Tandragee, 1912-13; Curate-in-charge, Killeavy, 1913-14; Rector of Omeath, 1914-22; Rector of St. Modoc's, Doune, 1922-39; Rector of Lasham with Herriard, 1939-48, when he retired to private life. Bailie of Burgh of Doune, 1927; Parish Councillor, Kilmadock, 1928-30; Chaplain to the Forces, 1915-16 and Chaplain to R.A.F., 1942-47; Unionist. *Publication:* Some Observations on Filaroides Mustelarum, in the Scottish Naturalist, July-Aug. 1935. *Recreations:* shooting, zoology, handicrafts. *Address:* Windmill Cottage, Brill, Bucks. *T.:* Brill 57. [*Died* 15 *Oct.* 1951 (*ext. as to Viscountcy*).

MOWAT, Rev. Canon John Dickson, B.A. (Durh.) 1901; Hon. Canon St. Paul's Cathedral, Dundee, since 1953; Deacon, 1907; Priest, York, 1908; Lecturer in Div. Prov., Tr. College, Dundee, from 1912; Rector of St. Salvador, Dundee, 1918-29; Rector of St. Mary, Arbroath, 1929-53; retired. Canon of St. Paul's Cathedral, Dundee, 1935; Dean of Brechin, 1947-53. *Address:* Craigendarroch, Taylor Street, Forfar, Angus. [*Died* 13 *Aug.* 1955.

MOWAT, Brig.-Gen. Magnus, C.B.E. 1919; T.D.; F.R.S.E.; A.K.C., M.Inst.C.E., M.I.Mech.E., M.I.E.S.S., F.C.I.S.; Fellow of King's Coll., London; Emeritus Secretary, Institution of Mechanical Engineers; Fellow American Soc. of Mechanical Engineers; *b.* 10 Nov. 1875; *s.* of late Hon. M. Mowat; unmarried. *Educ.:* Aberdeen Grammar School, Blackheath School, and King's College, London (twice President of the Engineering Society, K.C.L.). Served an apprenticeship in the workshops of North British Railway at Cowlairs, Glasgow; Asst. Engr. on construction of the Great Central Rly. extension to London (Leicester Section); Asst. Engineer Indian Midland Railway, and Sub-Divisional Officer, Jhansi, N.W.P.; Resident Engineer on the G.I.P. Rlys. new works at Agra; contractor's engineer, Glasgow Main Drainage; Chief Engineer Millwall Dock Co., and later in charge of E. and W. India and Millwall Division under the Port of London Authority; Deputy Chairman and Administrative Member, Joint Roads Committee (War Office), 1919-20; Past President Old Students' Association of King's College, London; Member of Council of following; King's College, University of London, Roads Improvement Association, Battersea Polytechnic, Wandsworth Technical Institute, and Hon. Treasurer of the University of London Animal Welfare Society; served in the Infantry, R.G.A., and R.E.; during European War commanded R.E., of a Division for upwards of two years; Staff Officer to C.E.; Command Roads Officer and Director at the War Office. *Publications:* various papers read before scientific societies. *Address:* Ebor House, Sheen Gate Gardens, East Sheen, S.W.14 *Clubs:* National, Overseas, City Livery. [*Died* 19 *Jan.* 1953.

MOWER, Mrs. Penfield; *see* Jordan, Sara M.

MOWLL, Most Rev. Howard West Kilvinton, C.M.G. 1954; D.D.; Archbishop of Sydney since 1933, and Primate of Australia since 1948; Sub-Prelate of the Venerable Order of St. John of Jerusalem, 1934; *b.* Dover, Kent, 2 Feb. 1890; *e. s.* of late H. Martyn Mowll of Chaldercot; *m.* 1924, Dorothy A., O.B.E. 1956 (*d.* 1957), *d.* of late Rev. John Martin of C.M.S. in Fuhkien. *Educ.:* King's School, Canterbury; King's College and Ridley Hall, Cambridge. Tutor, Wycliffe Coll., Toronto, 1913-16; Pro., 1916-17; T.C.F. 1918-19; Dean, Wycliffe College, Toronto, 1919-22; Bishop in Western China, 1926-33; Assistant Bishop, 1922-26. Chm. Nat. Missionary Council of Austr. and Tasmania, 1946; Pres. World Council of Churches (Austr. Section) 1946. *Address:* Bishopscourt, Edgecliff, Sydney, Australia. [*Died* 24 *Oct.* 1958.

MOYER, L. Clare, D.S.O. 1918; Q.C.; Clerk of the Senate, Clerk of the Parliaments and Master in Chancery of Canada; *b.* 22 Oct. 1887; *s.* of Dr. Sylvester Moyer; *m.* 1934. *Educ.:* University of Toronto; Law Schools of Ontario and Saskatchewan. *Address:* The Senate, Ottawa, Canada. *Clubs:* Rideau, Royal Ottawa Golf (Ottawa); University (Montreal). [*Died* 4 *Oct.* 1958.

MUDALIAR, Dewan Bahadur V. Shanmuga, C.B.E. 1943; Director, Imperial Bank of India, Madras (Pres. of the Local Board); Director, United India Fire & General Insurance Co. Ltd., Consolidated Coffee Estates, Ltd., Pollibetta, Coorg; *b.* 31 Oct. 1874; *s.* of V. Thiagasubramania Mudaliar; *m.* 1897, V. Amirthammal; one *s.* two *d.* *Educ.:* Madras Christian College. Merchant, Dubash, South Indian Export Co. Ltd., Madras, for 42 years; Municipal Councillor, was connected with several public bodies; J.P.; Sheriff of Madras, 1927-28 and 1940-41. *Address:* Greenfield, Kilpauk, Madras. *T.:* 2518. *Clubs:* National Liberal; Cosmopolitan (Madras). [*Died* 12 *April* 1953.

MUDGE, Brig.-General Arthur, C.B. 1925; C.M.G. 1918; late of Queen's Royal Regt. and R. Berks Regt.; *b* 1871, *e. s.* of late Arthur Thomas Mudge, of Sydney, Plympton, S. Devon; *m.* 1st, 1898, Annie May (*d;* 1953), *e. d.* of late Surg.-Gen. D. R. McKinnon; 2nd, 1956, Charlotte Gordon Navelot, *e. d.* of late R. W. Urie, J.P., Largs, Ayrshire. *Educ.:* Marlborough College; Royal Military College, Sandhurst. Served N.W. Frontier of India, 1897-98 (medal and 2 clasps); European War, 1914-18 (despatches, Bt. Lieut.-Col., Bt. Col., C.M.G.): Inspector-General of West Indian Local Forces and Officer Commanding Troops in Jamaica, 1925-28; administered Govt. of Jamaica, Aug.-Oct. 1925; retired pay, 1928; Officer Legion of Honour, 1921; Order of White Eagle (Serbia) with swords, 1915; Order of the Nile, 1919; Patron Plympton Branch, British Legion; President, Plympton Conservative Club; Commissioner for Income Tax. *Address:* Villa Les Heures Claires, Route D'Almanarre, Hyères, Var, France. [*Died* 27 *Dec.* 1958.

MUIR, Sir (Alexander) Kay, 2nd Bt., *cr.* 1892; *b.* 20 April 1868; *s.* of 1st Bt. and Margaret, *d.* of Alexander Kay, Cornhill, Lanarkshire; *S.* father, 1903; *m.* 1st, 1910, Grace (*d.* 1920), *d.* of J. A. R. Newman of Newberry Manor, Co. Cork, and *widow* of Major H. Villiers-Stuart, of Dromana, H.M.L. for Co. Waterford; 2nd, 1924, Nadejda, *e. d.* of late Dimitri Stancioff, late Bulgarian Minister in London. *Heir: nephew* John Harling [*b.* 7 Nov. 1910; *m.* 1936, Elizabeth Mary, *e. d.* of Frederick James Dundas; four *s.* two *d.*]. *Address:* Blair Drummond, Perthshire. *T.A.:* Doune. *Clubs:* Carlton, St. James', Oriental. [*Died* 4 *June* 1951.

MUIR, Edwin, C.B.E. 1953; Litt.D., LL.D. and Ph.D. (*h.c.*); Author; *b.* Orkney, 1887; *s.* of James Muir and Elizabeth Cormack; *m.* 1919, Willa Anderson; one *s.* *Educ.:* Kirkwall Burgh School, Orkney. Clerk in various commercial and shipbuilding offices in Glasgow, later journalist, translator, author; Director of the British Institute of Rome, 1949; Warden of Newbattle Abbey College, Dalkeith, 1950-55; Charles Eliot Norton Professor of Poetry at Harvard University, 1955-56. Ph.D. h.c. (Charles Univ., Prague), 1947; LL.D. (Edin.), 1947; D. ès L. (Rennes), 1949; Litt.D.: (Leeds), 1955, Cambridge, 1958. F.R.S.L. 1953. Foyle Prize, 1949; Heinemann and Niven Prize, 1953; Russell Loines Prize and Saltire Society Prize, 1957. Visiting Winston Churchill Professor at Bristol University, 1958. *Publications: fiction:* The Marionette; The Three Brothers; Poor Tom; (transl. with Willa Muir) The Castle, The Trial, The Sleepwalkers; *poetry:* First Poems; Chorus of the Newly Dead; Six Poems; Variations on a Time Theme; Journeys and Places; The Narrow Place; The Voyage, 1946; The Labyrinth, 1949, Collected Poems, 1921-51, 1952; One Foot in Eden, 1956; (ed.) New Poets, 1959 (posthumous); *criticism:* Latitudes; Transition; Structure of the Novel; Scott and Scotland; Essays on Literature and Society, 1949; *biography:* John Knox; Scottish Journey, 1935; *autobiography:* The Story and the Fable, 1940 (rev. edn., An Autobiography, 1954). *Address:* Priory Cottage, Swaffham Prior, Cambridge. [*Died* 3 *Jan.* 1959.

MUIR, James; Chairman and President, The Royal Bank of Canada, since 1954; *m.* 1919, Phyllis Marguerite Brayley; one *d.* *Educ.:* Public and High Schools, Peebles, Scotland. Commercial Bank of Scotland, Ltd., Peebles, 1907; Chartered Bank of India, London, 1910; The Royal Bank of Canada: Moose Jaw, Sask., 1912; Supervisor's Department, Winnipeg, 1916; Accountant, Winnipeg, Grain Exch. Branch, 1916; Head Office, 1917; Inspector at Supervisor's Dept., Winnipeg, 1923; Asst. Superv., Supervisor's Dept., N.Y., 1925; Manager, Winnipeg, 1928; Gen. Inspector, Head Office, 1931; Asst. Gen. Man., 1935; Gen. Man. 1945; Director, 1947; Vice-Pres., 1948; Pres., 1949; Vice-Pres. and Mem. Exec. Cttee., Montreal Trust Co.; Director and Mem. Exec. Cttee., Algoma Steel Corp. Ltd.; Director: The Scotsman Publications Ltd., Edinburgh; Thomson Newspapers Ltd., London, Eng.; Standard Brands Inc. (also Member of Executive Committee); Canadian Pacific Railway Company; The Royal Bank of Canada Trust Co. (Vice-President); Sogemines Ltd.; Westcoast Transmission Co. Ltd.; Metropolitan Life Insurance Co.; Trust Corporation of Bahamas Ltd.; National Heart Foundation. Life Governor and Chairman Finance Committee, Verdun Protestant Hosp.; Governor: Montreal Gen. Hosp.; Roy. Edward Laurentian Hosp.; Roy. Victoria Hospital (also Member of Executive Committee); Lower Canada College; Dalhousie Univ.; McGill University. Hon. Chief Eagle Ribs of Blood Indian Tribe of Blackfoot Confederacy, Alberta, 1954; Life Member, National Trust for Scotland, 1954. Freeman of the Royal and Ancient Burgh of Peebles (Scotland), 1952; D.C.L. (Hon.) Bishop's University, 1953; LL.D. (Hon.): Dalhousie Univ., 1956, Univ. of Montreal, 1957. *Recreations:* golfing, fishing. *Address:* The Royal Bank of Canada, 360 St. James St., West, Montreal, Que., Canada; (Residence) 3495 Holton Ave., Montreal, Que. *Clubs:* St. James's, Montreal, Mount Royal, Mount Bruno Golf and Country (Montreal); The Brook (New York); Manitoba (Winnipeg); Toronto; York (Toronto); Royal and Ancient Golf (St. Andrews); Mattawin, Fishing; Seigniory; Royal St. Lawrence Yacht; Laval-sur-le-Lac Golf; Rideau (Ottawa); Lyford Cay (Nassau). [*Died* 10 *April* 1960.

MUIR, Lt.-Col. John Balderstone, C.B. 1938; D.S.O. 1917; D.L.; late Royal Highlanders. Served European War, 1914-18 (despatches, D.S.O., Croix de Guerre, Legion of Honour). *Address:* Holmstead, Craigie, Dundee. [*Died* 19 *Feb.* 1955.

MUIR, Sir Kay; *see* Muir, Sir A. K.

MUIR, Sir Robert, Kt., *cr.* 1934; F.R.S. 1911; Emeritus Professor of Pathology, University of Glasgow, since 1936; *s.* of late Rev. R. Muir, M.A., Allars Church, Hawick; *b.* 5 July 1864. *Educ.:* Edinburgh University. M.A. 1884; M.B., C.M. (1st Class Honours), 1888; M.D. (Gold medal Thesis), 1890; Sc.D. (Hon.); LL.D.; D.C.L.; F.R.C.P.E., 1896; F.F.P.S.G., 1901; F.R.C.P., 1935; senior assistant to the Professor of Pathology, Edinburgh University, and Pathologist to the Edinburgh Royal Infirmary, 1892; Lecturer on Pathological Bacteriology, Edinburgh University, 1894; Professor of Pathology, St. Andrews, 1898-1899; Professor of Pathology, University of Glasgow, 1899-1936; awarded Royal Medal of Royal Society, 1929; Lister medal for 1936. *Publications:* Manual of Bacteriology (10th edit.) (jointly with late Prof. J. Ritchie); Studies on Immunity; Text-book of Pathology (6th ed.); Scientific Papers, etc. *Recreations:* fishing, etc. *Address:* 163 Bruntsfield Place, Edinburgh 10. *T.:* Fountainbridge 3745. *Club:* New (Edinburgh). [*Died* 30 *March* 1959.

MUIR, Ronald James Samuel, C.M.G. 1956; General Secretary, Australian and Queensland Cane Growers' Councils, since 1938 (Assistant Secretary, 1930-38); *b.* Exeter, S. Australia, 12 Aug. 1899; *s.* of late James B. Muir, Paisley, Scotland; *m.* 1922, Margot (*d.* 1957), *d.* of late James B. Anderson; three *d.*; *m.* 1958, Gillian, *d.* of T. H. Clifton, Rustington, Sussex; one *d.* *Educ.:* Prince Alfred College, Adelaide, South Australia. Joined sugar-growing industry, 1918; Sec. Innisfail Dist. Cane Growers' Assoc. 1921, and has since taken a prominent part in organisations affiliated to and representing the industry; Member Commonwealth Power Alcohol Committee of Inquiry, 1940-41; Member Queensland Sugar Industry Roy. Commission, 1943 and 1950; Industry Adviser to Commonwealth Sugar Inquiry Cttee., 1952; Rep. Australian and Qld. Cane Growers' Councils on N.F.U. of Australia; an Australian rep. at Internat. Sugar Conf., London, 1953, New York and Geneva, 1956, Geneva, 1958; Mem. Australian Govt. Immigration Advisory Council; Rep., Aust., Brit. Commonwealth Sugar Agreement Talks, London, yearly 1949-. Contested: Innisfail Seat, State Elections, 1929; Federal Herbert Seat, 1934. Coronation Medal, 1953. *Publications:* articles on cane growing in The Producer's Review. *Recreation:* fishing. *Address:* Caradon, Stanley Terrace, East Brisbane, Queensland. *T.:* 4-1689. *Clubs:* Brisbane, Rotary (Brisbane). [*Died* 25 *April* 1960.

MUIRHEAD, Peter Haig, C.B.E. 1951; Director and General Manager of Vickers-Armstrongs Ltd., Newcastle upon Tyne; Director of British Clearing Machine Co. Ltd.; Director of George Mann and Co. Ltd.; Director of Martin's Bank Ltd. (North Eastern District Board); Director of Michell Bearings Ltd.; Director of Palmers Hebburn Company Ltd. *Address:* St. Leonards, Mitford, Northumberland; Messrs. Vickers-Armstrongs Ltd., Newcastle upon Tyne. [*Died* 27 *April* 1958.

MUKERJEE, Air Marshal Subroto; Chief of Air Staff, Indian Air Force, since 1954; *b.* 5 March 1911; *m.* 1941, Sharda Pandit; one *s.* *Educ.:* Presidency College, Calcutta; Royal Air Force College, Cranwell, England. Served with No. 16 Sqdn. R.A.F., 1932-33; No. 1 Sqdn. I.A.F., 1933-39; Staff Coll. Course at Quetta, 1941; comd. R.A.F. Station, Kohat, 1943-44; D.C.A.S. and Dep. Air Comdr., I.A.F., 1947; Imperial Defence College, London, 1953. *Recreations:* swimming, golf. *Address:* Air House, 23 Akbar Road, New Delhi, India. *T.:* Office 32517, Residence 47800. *Club:* Delhi Gymkhana (New Delhi). [*Died* 9 *Nov.* 1960.

MULFORD, Clarence Edward; *b.* Streator, Ill., 3 Feb. 1883; *s.* of Clarence C. Mulford and Minnie Grace Kline; married. *Educ.:* public and high schools, Streator; Utica Academy. *Publications:* Bar-20, 1907; The Orphan, 1908; Hopalong Cassidy, 1910; Bar-20 Days, 1911; Buck Peters, Ranchman, 1912; Coming of Cassidy, 1913; Man from Bar-20, 1918; Johnny Nelson, 1920; Bar-20 Three, 1921; Tex, 1922; Bring Me His Ears, 1922; Black Buttes, 1923; Rustler's Valley, 1924; Hopalong Cassidy Returns, 1924; Cottonwood Gulch, 1925; Hopalong Cassidy's Protégé, 1926; Bar-20 Rides Again, 1926; Corson of the JC, 1927; Mesquite Jenkins, 1928; Me an' Shorty, 1929; The Deputy Sheriff, 1930; Hopalong Cassidy and the Eagle's Brood, 1931; Mesquite Jenkins, Tumbleweed, 1932; The Roundup, 1932; Trail Dust, 1934; On the Trail of the Tumbling T, 1935; Hopalong Cassidy Takes Cards, 1937; Hopalong Cassidy Serves a Writ, 1941. *Address:* Fryeburg, Maine, U.S.A. [*Died* 10 *May* 1956.

MULLEN, Lt.-Col. J. L. W. F.; *see* Ffrench-Mullen.

MULLENEUX-GRAYSON, Lady L. M.; *see* Dale, Louise.

MULLENS, Major-General Richard Lucas, C.B. 1917; *b.* 25 Feb. 1871; 3rd *s.* of J. A. Mullens; *m.* Leonore, *e. d.* of A. de Wette, J.P., D.L., Middlesex; two *s.* one *d.* *Educ.:* Eton. Joined 16th Lancers, 1890; transferred to Queen's Bays, 1896; served in India, Egypt, and at home; was employed on special service in S. African War, and as Adjutant of Queen's Bays (severely wounded, 1902; despatches, brevet majority); Staff College, 1903-5; promoted to command 4th Dragoon Guards, 1911; brought this regiment out to France, Aug. 1914; selected to command 2nd Cavalry Brigade, Oct. 1914; Brevet. Col. Feb. 1915; commanded 1st Cavalry Division, B.E.F., Oct. 1915-April 1919 (Commander of the Crown, Belgium, Belgian and French Croix de Guerre, palmes); Major-General, 1918; retired, 1920. *Address:* The Beacon, Sidmouth, Devon. *T.:* 797. *Club:* Cavalry. [*Died* 26 *May* 1952.

MULLINGS, Frank Coningsby; Professor of Singing, Fellow of the Birmingham School of Music; *b.* Walsall, 1881; *s.* of Eugene Thomas Frank and Henrietta Mullings; *m.* Eleanora Vera Maud Ashbee; one *s.* Debut in Gounod's Faust, Coventry, 1907; has sung Canio in Pagliacci, Otello, Rhadames in Aida, Siegfried and Tristan. *Recreation:* philately. *Address:* (Home) 16 West Meade, Manchester, 21. *T.:* Chorlton 2490; (studio) 328 Oxford Road, Manchester. *T.:* Ardwick 5705. *Clubs:* Savage; Walsall, Walsall Unionist (Walsall). [*Died* 19 *May* 1953.

MULVEY, Anthony; *b.* 1882; *s.* of Gerald Mulvey, Ballinaglera, Co. Leitrim; *m.* 1921, Kathleen, *d.* of Thomas Tiernan, Ballinamore, Co. Leitrim; three *s.* one *d.* Former Editor, Ulster Herald. M.P. (Irish Nat.) Fermanagh and Tyrone, 1935-50, Mid-Ulster, 1950-51. *Address:* 2 Derry Road, Omagh, Co. Tyrone. *T.:* Omagh 143. [*Died* 11 *Jan.* 1957.

MUMMERY, J. P. L.; *see* Lockhart-Mummery.

MUNCEY, Rev. Edward Howard Parker, M.A.; Vicar of Haresfield and Rector of Harescombe since 1949; *b.* 12 Jan. 1886; *s.* of late F. W. Muncey and late Gertrude, *d.* of James Neal, Lathbury, Bucks; unmarried. *Educ.:* Highgate: St. John's College, Cambridge; Winchester Prize; Classical Tripos, 1908, M.A., 1912; Ely Theological College. Ordained, 1909; Curate of Chelsea, 1909; Minor Canon of

Windsor, 1910; Priest Vicar of Chichester, 1911; Chaplain of Magdalene College, Cambridge, 1913; Assistant Master at Wellington College, 1915; Headmaster of the King's School, Gloucester, and Precentor of Gloucester Cathedral, 1930-42; Licensed Preacher in the Diocese of Gloucester since 1942. *Address:* Haresfield Court, Gloucester. [*Died* 13 *Dec.* 1954.

MUNDAY, Major-General Richard Cleveland, C.B. 1919; M.R.C.S., L.R.C.P.; Surgeon-Captain R.N., retired; *b.* Valletta, Malta, 17 Dec. 1867; 2nd *s.* of Richard Munday, Paymaster-in-Chief, R.N., and Susan Elizabeth Munday; *m.* 1895, Olive Louise Burnard; one *s.* two *d.* *Educ.:* Plymouth College; St. Bartholomew's Hospital. House Physician, Royal Free Hospital; passed as Surgeon, R.N., 1890; China medal, 1900; Staff-Surgeon, 1902; Fleet Surgeon, 1906; Somali medal and clasp, 1908-10; Persian Gulf medal and clasp, 1910-14; P.M.O. E. Indies, 1909-11; served as Member of Admiralty Committee on Boys' Training Ships, 1912, and as Secretary and Member of Admiralty Committee on Ventilation of Warships, 1914; served during European War as Assistant Director-General Medical Department, Admiralty, and later as Medical Administrator, R.A.F.; Medical Member and subsequently Chairman, Pensions Appeal Tribunal, 1921-26; Chairman Recruiting Medical Board, Plymouth, 1939-46; Gilbert Blane Gold Medal, 1913; Chadwick Gold Medal and Prize, 1914; Order of the Liakat, 1908. *Publication:* A Report on Beri-Beri, 1912. *Recreation:* golf. *Address:* 17 Lockington Avenue, Hartley, Plymouth. *T.:* Crown Hill 71491. [*Died* 15 *July* 1952.

MUNDAY, Sir William Luscombe, Kt., *cr.* 1935; Solicitor practising in Plymouth; *b.* 1865; *s.* of Richard and Susan Elizabeth Munday; *m.* 1897, Mary Rosalind (*d.* 1946), *d.* of John Shelly. *Educ.:* Kelly College, Tavistock. Admitted Solicitor, 1887; Member of Plymouth Town Council, 1898-1930; Alderman, 1911-30; a Vice-President of University College of the South West, 1922-39; Deputy Pres., 1939-48; Chairman of Sutton Division (Plymouth) Conservative Association, 1922-44; President of Plymouth Institution, 1925-26; President of Plymouth Law Society, 1926-27 and 1936-37. *Recreations:* reading and foreign travel (when possible). *Address:* The Arches, Hartley, Plymouth. *T.:* Plymouth 71733. [*Died* 15 *April* 1952.

MUNDY, Sir Otto, K.B.E., *cr.* 1945; C.B. 1938; *b.* 9 Nov. 1887; *s.* of late William Lloyd Mundy, Malvern, Worcestershire. *Educ.:* Radley; Wadham College, Oxford. First Class Lit. Hum., 1909; entered Home Civil Service, 1910; Assistant Secretary Board of Customs and Excise, 1930; Commissioner and Secretary, 1936; Deputy Chairman, 1942; retired, 1949. *Address:* c/o Barclays Bank, Finsbury Pavement, E.C.2. [*Died* 29 *Aug.* 1958.

MUNIR BEY, Sir Mehmed, Kt., *cr.* 1947; C.B.E. 1939 (O.B.E. 1931); Barrister-at-law; Delegate and Director of Evcaf, Cyprus, 1925-48; Chairman of Governing Body of Moslem Secondary Schools, 1927-48; Chairman of Moslem Town School Committees, Cyprus, 1929-48; *b.* 27 Jan. 1890; *s.* of late Ahmed Djemal Effendi, Inspector of Moslem Schools; *m.* 1914, Vessime Hanim, *d.* of the Mufti of Cyprus; five *s.* *Educ.:* Turkish Schools and English School, Cyprus. Called to Bar, Gray's Inn, 1922; served in Cyprus Treasury, 1906-25; acted Judge, District Court, Kyrenia, 1923-25; acted additional Judge, District Court, Nicosia, July-Aug. 1925; Member Legislative Council, 1925-30; Member Executive Council, 1926-47; Member Advisory Council, 1932-47; served on several Commissions and Committees appointed to enquire into various questions in Cyprus; retired, 1948. Represented Colony of Cyprus at Coronation of King George VI, 1937. *Address:* P.O. Box 555, Nicosia, Cyprus. *Club:* Nicosia (Nicosia). [*Died* 20 *Sept.* 1957.

MUNNINGS, Sir Alfred J., K.C.V.O. *cr.* 1947; Kt., *cr.* 1944; P.P.R.A. 1949 (P.R.A. 1944; R.A. 1925; A.R.A. 1919); R.W.S. 1929 (A.R.W.S. 1921); Hon. LL.D. Sheffield University, 1946; *b.* 8 Oct. 1878; *s.* of John Munnings of Mendham, Suffolk; *m.* 1920, Violet, *d.* of Frank Golby Haines, Temple Fortune, Edgware, and *widow* of William McBride. *Educ.:* Framlingham College; Norwich School of Art; Paris. Exhibited Royal Academy 1898, and since then continually. President Royal Academy, 1944-49. *Works:* The Gravel Pit; Epsom Downs, City and Suburban Day, purchased by the Chantry Bequest; A Trooper in France; Arrival at Epsom Downs, Derby Week, purchased by City of Birmingham; Gipsy Life, purchased by City of Aberdeen; The Prince of Wales on Forest Witch, exhibited Royal Academy 1921; Changing Horses; The Fresian Bull; forty-five war pictures commissioned by Canadian Government exhibited Royal Academy, 1919, painted whilst attached to Canadian Cavalry Brigade and Canadian Forestry in France, 1917-18; won the Médaille D'or, Paris Salon, with his picture Changing Horses; judged at the International Art Exhibition, Pittsburgh, 1924; From My Bedroom Window, 1930, and Their Majesties return from Ascot, 1938, purchased by the Chantrey Bequest; equestrian statue of Edward Horner, Mells Church; "Brown Jack," Ascot Grand Stand. *Publications:* An Artist's Life, 1950; The Second Burst, vol. 2, 1951; The Finish, vol. 3, 1952; Ballads and Poems, 1957. *Recreations:* horses and riding, racing, reading. *Address:* Castle House, Dedham, Essex. *T.:* Dedham 2127; Beldon House, 96 Chelsea Park Gardens, S.W.3. *T.:* Flaxman 9236. *Clubs:* Athenæum, Arts, Garrick. [*Died* 17 *July* 1959.

MUNRO, Sir Arthur Talbot, 13th Bt., *cr.* 1634; *b.* 26 July 1866; *s.* of late Harry Munro, 2nd *s.* of 9th Bart.; *S.* brother, 1945; *m.* 1893, Frances Emily Emmeline, *d.* of William March; one *s.* *Heir:* *s.* Arthur Herman [*b.* 10 Sept. 1893; *m.* 1919, Violet Beatrice, *d.* of Henry Powles; one *s.*]. *Address:* Stanley Cottage, Mill Gardens, Wells Park, Sydenham, S.E.26. [*Died* 16 *Feb.* 1953.

MUNRO, Air Vice-Marshal Sir David, K.C.B., *cr.* 1930 (C.B. 1924); C.I.E. 1917; R.A.F., retired; M.A., LL.D. (St. Andrews); M.B., Ch.B., F.R.C.S. (Edin.); Chief Medical Officer of Ministry of Supply, 1940-43, Medical Adviser to the Ministry since 1943; Member of the Factory Welfare Board (1940) of the Ministry of Labour; Member of School Council of St. Thomas's Hospital; *b.* 23 June 1878; 12th *c.* of David Munro, schoolmaster, Elstree, Herts; *m.* 1905, Isabel, *d.* of Dr. J. Cunningham, Bellview, Campbeltown; one *s.* one *d.* *Educ.:* St. Andrews; Edinburgh University. Entered Indian Medical Service, 1901; Military Dept. and Bengal Civil Med. Department till 1914; served in France, Mesopotamia and Palestine, 1914-19; transferred to R.A.F., 1919; Director of Medical Services, Royal Air Force, 1921-30; Hon. Surgeon to the King, 1925-30; retired list, 1930; Chairman, No. 1365 A.T.C. Squadron, 1950-. Secretary, Industrial Health Research Board of Medical Research Council, 1930-42; Vice-Chairman of Board of Management, London School of Hugiene and Tropical Medicine, 1944-46; Rector of St. Andrews University, 1938-46; Master of Skinners' Company, 1942-43. *Publications:* It Passed too Quickly, autobiography, 1941; various in Medical Journals, and short stories in magazines, etc. *Recreations:* horses, golf. *Address:* Crosshill, Wendover, Bucks. *Club:* Athenæum. [*Died* 8 *Nov.* 1952.

MUNRO, Capt. Donald John, C.M.G. 1918; R.N. (retired) 1918; F.R.G.S.; *b.* 1865; *s.* of late Hector Munro, Home Civil Service; *m.* 1895, Isabel R., *d.* of late J. W. H. Sandell, I.C.S.;

two *d.* *Educ.:* Royal Academy, Inverness. Went to sea in the Merchant Service, 1880; joined the Royal Navy, 1895; served Burma War, 1885-87; on Geological Survey of Burma, 1890-91; Sierra Leone Rebellion; European War, 1914-18; author of various inventions for use in the Royal Navy, Inventor of anti-submarine defences for the protection of harbours, inventor of mine sweeping by trawlers, etc. *Publications:* The Roaring Forties and After; Scapa Flow, a naval retrospect, 1932; Convoys, Blockades, and Mystery Towers, 1932. *Recreations:* shooting and fishing. *Address:* Clearwell, New Galloway, Kircudbrightshire. *T.*: New Galloway 232. *Club:* Junior Army and Navy. [*Died* 11 *July* 1952.

MUNRO, Leo; *b.* 17 April 1878; *m.* Louise Douglas (*d.* 1950), *d.* of Wm. Cowderoy, Brighton. *Educ.:* privately; Royal Academy, Antwerp; Artist and journalist; studied art at Lambeth and Antwerp; has drawn for many illustrated papers, and written numerous articles and short stories, mostly sporting; editor of Golfing 1905-8; assistant editor of The Sportsman, 1911-24; Sunday Express sports cartoonist 1919-20; Daily Express sports writer: Rugby football, 1919-40; golf, 1925-40. *Recreation:* golf. *Club:* Press. [*Died* 28 *Feb.* 1957.

MUNRO, William Bennett, M.A.; LL.B.; Ph.D.; hon. LL.D.; hon. Litt.D.; Member of the board of trustees, California Institute of Technology; *b.* Almonte, Ontario, Canada, 5 January 1875; *s.* of John M'Nab Munro, J.P., and Sarah Bennett; *m.* 1918, Caroline Sanford, *o. d.* of Orren A. Gorton, M.D.; one *s.* *Educ.:* Queen's College, Canada; Univ. of Edinburgh; Harvard Univ.; Univ. of Berlin. A Member of Faculty of Harvard Univ., 1904-1930; President of the American Association of University Professors, 1929-31; Fellow of the American Academy of Arts and Sciences; Member Board of Overseers Harvard Univ., 1940-46; Trustee Henry E. Huntington Library and Art Gallery. Served in U.S. Army during European War, 1914-18, with rank of Major. *Publications:* Canada and British N. America, 1905; The Seigniorial System in Canada, 1907; Documents relating to the Seigniorial Tenure, 1908; The Government of European Cities, 1909; The Initiative, Referendum and Recall, 1912; The Government of American Cities, 1912; Bibliography of Municipal Government, 1914; Principles and Methods of Municipal Administration, 1916; The Government of the United States, 1919 (fifth edition, 1946); Social Civics, 1922; Municipal Government and Administration, two volumes, 1923; Current Problems in Citizenship, 1924; Personality in Politics, 1924; The Governments of Europe, 1925; The Invisible Government, 1928; American Influences on Canadian Government, 1929; Makers of the Unwritten Constitution, 1930; The Constitution of the United States, 1931; Municipal Administration, 1934; frequent contributor to historical and political reviews. *Address:* 268 Bellefontaine Street, Pasadena, Calif. *T.:* Sycamore 9-5382. *Clubs:* California (Los Angeles); Valley Hunt (Pasadena). [*Died* 4 *Sept.* 1957.

MUNROE, Sir Harry C.; *see* Courthope-Munroe.

MURCHISON, Sir (Charles) Kenneth, Kt. *cr.* 1927; Hon. Sec. since 1929 of the Farmer's Club 1795; Member of Committee appointed by Lord Chancellor, 1936, to report on jurisdiction of Quarter Sessions; formerly Chairman Committee of Management St. Andrews Hospital for Nervous and Mental Diseases, Northampton; *b.* 22 Sept. 1872; *y. s.* of late Charles Murchison, M.D., F.R.S., Physician to the Duke of Connaught, and Clara, *d.* of Robert Bickersteth of Liverpool and Casterton Hall, Westmorland; *m.* 1st, 1897, Evelyn (*d.* 1937), *d.* of Rev. George Rowe, M.A., Principal, Diocesan Coll., York; one *d.*; 2nd, 1938, Mary Lilian, *widow* of F. D. Crew, M.D., Higham Ferrers, and *d.* of late Rev. H. W. Richards, M.A., Rector of Stanwick, Northamptonshire. *Educ.:* Clifton; France and Germany. Partner in Basil Woodd & Sons, London, 1898-1915; Hertford Borough Council, 1900-5 (Mayor, 1902-3); Unionist Candidate Stirling Burghs, 1906; L.C.C. (M.R.) North Islington, 1907-10; with British Red Cross Society in France, 1915; Chairman Advisory Committee, Thrapston Division, Northamptonshire, 1916; attached to Military Intelligence Branch of the War Office, 1916-18; M.P. (Co. U.) East Hull, Dec. 1918-22 (C.) Huntingdonshire, Nov. 1922-Dec. 1923 and 1924-29; Member House of Commons Select Committee War-Wealth Increase, 1920; Parliamentary Private Secretary (unpaid) to Sir John Baird, Under-Secretary of State, Home Office, 1920 to 1922; Parliamentary Private Secretary (unpaid) to Major Rt. Hon. G. C. Tryon, Minister of Pensions, Nov. 1922, and 1924-29; Deputy Chairman Quarter Sessions, Northamptonshire, 1926-34; Chairman, 1934-47; Alderman, Northamptonshire County Council, 1927-46; Chairman Northamptonshire Standing Joint Committee, 1933-1948; High Sheriff Northamptonshire, 1942; Lord of the Manor and Patron of living of Hargrave, Northants. O.St.J. 1945. *Publications:* Account of Farmers' Club 1795, 1940; Family Notes and Reminiscences, 1940; Letters to my Grandsons, 1941; The Dawn of Motoring, 1942. *Address:* Sea View, Mudeford, Christchurch, Hants. *Club:* Travellers'. [*Died* 17 *Dec.* 1952.

MURDOCH, Hector B.; *see* Burn-Murdoch.

MURDOCH, Sir Keith Arthur, Kt., *cr.*, 1933; Chairman of Directors and late Managing Director of The Herald and Weekly Times, Ltd., Melbourne Herald, Sun News-Pictorial, Weekly Times, and associated publications; Director of Australian Newsprint Mills Pty. Ltd., The News, Adelaide and The Courier-Mail, Brisbane; former Chm., Australian section Empire Press Union; President of Trustees of National Gallery of Victoria (Trustee 1933); Past President of Australian-American Association, Victoria; Member of Reuters Trust; *b.* Melbourne, Australia, 12 August 1886; *s.* of late Rev. P. J. Murdoch, Camberwell, Australia, late of Aberdeenshire, and late Annie Brown Murdoch, Longhaven House, Aberdeenshire; *m.* 1928, Elisabeth, 3rd *d.* of Rupert Greene; one *s.* three *d.* *Educ.:* Camberwell Grammar School; London School of Economics. Journalist; began with Melbourne Age; in 1915 went to Gallipoli with mission from the Commonwealth Government and as war correspondent; proceeded to London, where reported to the British Government on the Gallipoli Campaign; was war correspondent with the Australian forces through the war; and Editor and Manager of the United Cable Service; represented Australian newspapers and the London Times on H.M.S. Renown on Prince of Wales's trip to New Zealand and Australia; Director-General of Information for the Commonwealth of Australia, 1939-40. Visited Great Britain, 1941-42, at invitation of British Govt. and again in 1944. Founded Australian Newsprint Mills in Derwent Valley, Tasmania. *Publication:* The Day—and After, a volume of Mr. Hughes's War speeches. *Recreations:* golf, riding. *Address:* The Herald and 39 Albany Rd., Toorak, Melbourne. *Clubs:* Athenæum; Melbourne (Melbourne); Adelaide (Adelaide); Queensland (Brisbane). [*Died* 5 *Oct.* 1952.

MURPHY, Emmett Patrick, C.M.G. 1946; LL.D.; D.Sc.; Consulting Engineer; Deputy Minister of Public Works, Canada, 1942; retired 1953; *b.* 1887; *s.* of Patrick Murphy, Ottawa, Canada. *Educ.:* Ottawa Collegiate; Queen's Univ., Kingston, Canada. Hon. LL.D. Ottawa, 1948; Hon. D.Sc. Laval, 1952. *Address:* 538-540 Chateau Laurier, Ottawa, Canada; 252 Metcalfe Street Ottawa, Canada. *Clubs:* Laurentian, Rideau, Royal Ottawa (Ottawa). [*Died* 17 *June* 1960.

MURPHY, Very Rev. Jeremiah Matthias, S.J.; C.M.G. 1954; Rector of Newman College, Carlton, University of Melbourne, Australia, since 1923. *Educ.:*

National University of Ireland (M.A.); University of Oxford; Milltown Park, Dublin. Entered Society of Jesus, 1901; ordained, 1916; went to Australia, 1920; attached to teaching staff of Xavier College, Kew, Victoria. Secretary to the Papal Legate, National Eucharistic Congress, Melbourne, 1934. *Address:* Newman College, Carlton, Victoria, Australia.
[*Died* 17 *May* 1955.

MURRAY, Alan James Ruthven-, C.M.G. 1954; Consultant Petroleum Technologist and Geologist in private practice since retiring as Managing Director, Trinidad Oil Co.; Company Director; *b.* 14 Mar. 1900; *s.* of late E. T. Ruthven Murray, M.I.M.E., M.I.E.E., and *g.s.* of Sir James Murray, Editor of the Oxford Dictionary; *m.* 1927, Marjorie, *d.* of late Dr. E. H. Cooper. *Educ.:* St. George's School, Harpenden; Hertford College, Oxford. R.N.A.S., 1917; R.A.F., Flying Officer, 1918; Oxford, 1919-21, also 1926-27 (M.A., B.Sc.). Geological work in S. America, 1921-28; Gen. Manager Kern Trinidad Oilfields, 1928-42; Trinidad Leaseholds Ltd.: General Manager, 1942-47, Asst. Managing Director, 1948-51, Managing Director, 1951-55. A Treasurer of the West India Cttee. F.Inst.Pet.; F.G.S. *Recreation:* golf. *Address:* Farm House, Tadworth, Surrey. *T.:* Tadworth 2328. *Clubs:* Royal Air Force, Royal Automobile.
[*Died* 14 *Sept.* 1959.

MURRAY, Alastair Campbell, M.C., F.F.A., F.R.S.E.; J.P.; Director: Scottish Equitable Life Assurance Society, Scottish Industrial Estates Ltd., Standard Property Investment Company, Ltd. and other Companies; *b.* 16 Oct. 1895; *s.* of late J. A. Murray, Edinburgh, and late Mary Campbell; *m.* 1923, Alexis Colburn Buchanan; four *s.* one *d.* *Educ.:* George Watson's College. Served European War, 1914-19, in Royal Scots and R.F.A., Western Front and Army of Occupation in Germany; Commanded 8th Bn. City of Edinburgh H.G., 1942-44; Manager and Actuary, Scottish Equitable Life Assurance Society, 1934-54; Chm. Associated Scottish Life Offices, 1942-44; Chm. Scottish Actuaries' Club, 1944-45. *Recreations:* fishing, golf. *Address:* 12 Glencairn Crescent, Edinburgh 12. *T.:* Edinburgh 61176. *Clubs:* New (Edinburgh); Western (Glasgow).
[*Died* 23 *May* 1957.

MURRAY, Sir Alexander Robertson, K.C.I.E., *cr.* 1936; Kt., *cr.* 1921; C.B.E. 1919; Knight of Grace of the Order of St. John of Jerusalem, 1924; *b.* 29 Nov. 1872; *s.* of Alexander Murray and Catherine Robertson; *m.* Margaret Allan Grant; (only son killed in action, 1944); two *d.* A Director of companies; Chairman Indian Jute Mills Association, 1913, 1917-19; Chairman Indian Mining Association, 1927; President, Bengal Chamber of Commerce, 1920; representative of that Chamber in Bengal Legislative Council 1919, Imperial Legislative Council 1920, and Council of State 1921-23; President Associated Chambers of Commerce of India and Ceylon, 1920, and their representative in Legislative Assembly, 1927; Delegate of Employers of Labour in India at International Labour Conferences, Washington 1919, Geneva 1924; Member Indian Retrenchment Committee, Delhi, 1922-23; a Governor of Imperial Bank of India, 1922-27; Member Royal Commission on Indian Currency and Finance, 1925-26; Member Royal Commission on Indian Labour, 1929-31; President Indian Special Tariff Board, 1935-36; Member Governing Body, School of Oriental and African Studies, 1935-. *Address:* Uplands, Hughenden, Bucks. *Club:* Oriental.
[*Died* 19 *March* 1956.

MURRAY, Admiral Arthur John Layard, C.B. 1940; D.S.O. 1919; O.B.E. 1919; *b.* 25 Nov. 1886; *e. s.* of late A. H Hallam Murray; *m.* 1912, Ellen Maxwell, *d.* of late Rev. W. A. Spooner; three *s.* three *d.* *Educ.:* Eton; H.M.S. Britannia; R.N. College. Greenwich. Midshipman, 1903; Lieut. 1908; served in H.M.S. Agamemnon (Channel Fleet and Dardanelles); Mining School, Portsmouth; and Dwina River Flotilla, N. Russian Campaign, 1919 (wounded, D.S.O., O.B.E., despatches twice); Commander, 1920; Captain, 1927; Commanding Anti-Submarine School, Portland, 1928-30; Commanding 6th Destroyer Flotilla, Atlantic Fleet, 1930-32; Director of Signal Dept., Admiralty, 1932-34 and 1941-42; commanded H.M.S. Dorsetshire, 1935-37; Captain of Signal School, Portsmouth, 1937-39; Rear-Admiral, 1939; Rear-Admiral Fifth and Fourth Cruiser Squadrons, 1939-40; Senior Naval Officer, Red Sea, 1940-41; Vice-Adm., 1942; F.O.I.C. Yarmouth, 1942; invalided, 1943. Petersfield R.D.C., 1946; Hon. Sec. Horndean Community Assoc. *Address:* Horndean, Hants.
[*Died* 26 *Dec.* 1959.

MURRAY, Colonel David Keith, C.B. 1947; D.L., V.D., B.L., J.P.; Solicitor and Factor, Thurso, since 1887; Bank Manager, 1893-1949; *b.* 8 Feb. 1865; *s.* of George Murray and Catherine Keith; *m.* 1891, Jessie, *d.* of James W. Galloway, J.P., Banker, Thurso; one *s.* three *d.* *Educ.:* George Watson's College and Edinburgh University. B.L. (with distinction), 1887; J.P. 1895; V.D. 1907; D.L., Caithness, 1926, Vice-Lieutenant, 1941; Hon. Sheriff-Substitute of Caithness, Orkney and Shetland, 1934; Convener of Caithness, 1919-30; Town Clerk, Thurso, 1905-35; Chm. Caithness Road Board, 1919-30; member Caithness C.C., 1896-1930; Chairman Trustees of Dunbar Hospital, Thurso, 1925-48; Chairman Agricultural Wages Committee for Caithness, Sutherland, Orkney and Shetland, 1940-47; Chm. Unemployment Assistance Board Advisory Cttee. for Caithness and Sutherland, 1935-47; Officer, 1887-1908, and Colonel Commanding 1st Caithness R.G.A. (Vols.), 1904-8; Lt.-Col. and Hon. Col. T.F., 1908; County Comdt. Caithness & Sutherland Volunteer Force, 1917-19; Military Member of Caithness Territorial Force Assoc., 1908-47, Chm. 1940-47. *Address:* Springbank, Thurso, Caithness. *T.A.:* Keith Murray, Thurso. *T.:* Thurso 137. *Club:* Scottish Conservative (Edinburgh).
[*Died* 29 *April* 1952.

MURRAY, Mrs. David L.; *see* Eyles, M. L.

MURRAY, Lieut.-Col. Sir Edward Robert, 13th Bt., *cr.* 1630; D.S.O. 1900; *b.* 22 June 1875; *e. s.* of Sir William Murray, 12th Bart., and Esther Elizabeth, *d.* of J. Body and *widow* of J. Rickard; *m.* 1st, 1904, Elsie Innes Macgeorge (*d.* 1935), *e. d.* of W. A. Brown; 2nd, 1938, Ruby, 2nd *d.* of Mr. Hearn, Helmdon, Northamptonshire; *S.* father, 1904. Served with 10th Batt. Imp. Yeo., S. Africa; Capt. and Adjt. 1st Regt. of 10th Yeo., and O.C. 2nd Regt. *Heir:* *n.* Rowland William Patrick, U.S. Army, *b.* 26 Oct. 1910.
[*Died* 14 *Jan.* 1958.

MURRAY, Brigadier Francis Mackenzie, C.B. 1934; *s.* of Francis Murray, late of Drummond Park, Inverness; *b.* 1880; *m.* 1916, Phoebe Millicent, *d.* of James Ross, Bath. *Educ.:* Inverness College; R.M.A. Woolwich. Joined R.A. 1899; employed with the West African Frontier Force, 1902-07; appointed to the Indian Ordnance Department 1908; served European War, Iraq 1918 (despatches), Iraq 1919-20 (despatches, Medal and clasp); transferred to I.A. for permanent employment with Indian Army Ordnance Corps, 1928; Director of Ordnance Services (India), 1931-35; Bt. Lt.-Col. 1919; Col. 1923; Brig. 1931; retired 1935. *Address:* Tynalt, Leebotwood, nr. Shrewsbury.
[*Died* 8 *April* 1958.

MURRAY, (George) Gilbert (Aimé), O.M. 1941; M.A., D.Litt., D.C.L., Oxford; LL.D. Glasgow; D.Litt. Birmingham; Litt.D. Camb.; D. ès Lettres, Lyons; F.B.A. and member of many other academies; F.R.S.L.; Regius Professor of Greek, Oxford University, 1908-36; Charles Eliot Norton

Professor of Poetry, Harvard University, 1926; Trustee of British Museum, 1914–1948; President: Society of Australian Writers, 1952; International Cttee. of Intellectual Co-operation, 1928–40; Chairman League of Nations Union, 1923–38, Co-President since 1938; *b.* Sydney, New South Wales, 2 January 1866; 3rd *s.* of late Sir Terence Aubrey Murray, President Legislative Council New South Wales; *m.* 1889, Lady Mary Henrietta Howard (*d.* 1956), *e. d.* of 9th Earl of Carlisle; one *s.* one *d.* (and two *s.* and one *d.* decd.). *Educ.:* Merchant Taylors' School, London; St. John's College, Oxford. Left Australia aged 11; Fellow of New College, Oxford, 1888; Professor of Greek, Glasgow University, 1889–99. Order Pour le Mérite, 1956. *Publications:* Carlyon Sahib, 1899, and Andromache, 1900, plays, both published and acted. *Verse translations:* Euripides: Hippolytus, Bacchae, Trojan Women, Electra, Medea, Iphigenia in Tauris, acted mainly at the Court Theatre, 1902–27; Rhesus, 1913; Alcestis, 1914; Ion, 1954; Sophocles: Oedipus Rex, 1910; Antigone, 1939; Oedipus Coloneus, 1948; Aeschylus: Agamemnon, 1920; Choephoroe, 1923; Suppliant Women, 1930; Prometheus Bound, 1931; Seven Against Thebes, 1935; Persians, 1939; Aristophanes: Frogs, 1902; Birds, 1949; Knights, 1955; Menander: Rape of the Locks, 1941; The Arbitration, 1945; History of Ancient Greek Literature, 1897; Euripidis Fabulae, adnotatione critica instructae, vol. i., 1901, vol. ii., 1904, vol., iii., 1910; Aeschyli Fabulae, adnotatione critica instructae, 1937; Rise of the Greek Epic, 1907, 1911, 1924; Hamlet and Orestes (Brit. Acad.) 1914; Stoic Philosophy, 1915; Five Stages of Greek Religion, 1913, 1925, 1951; Euripides and his Age, 1918; The Classical Tradition in Poetry, 1927; Aristophanes, a Study, 1933; Aeschylus, Creator of Tragedy, 1940; Stoic, Christian and Humanist, 1940, 1950; Greek Studies, 1946. Liberalism and the Empire (part author) 1900; The Foreign Policy of Sir Edward Grey, 1915; Faith, War, and Policy, 1918; The Problem of Foreign Policy, 1921; Collected Essays and Addresses, 1922; The Ordeal of This Generation, 1929; Liberality and Civilisation, 1938; From the League to U.N., 1947; Hellenism and the Modern World, 1953; An Unfinished Autobiography (posthumous), 1960 (with contributions from his friends). *Address:* Yatscombe, Boars Hill, Oxford. *T.:* Oxford 75261. *Clubs:* Athenæum, National Liberal. [*Died* 20 *May* 1957.

MURRAY, Most Rev. Gerald, C.SS.R., D.D. Consecrated, 1930. Coadjutor Archbishop of Winnipeg, (R.C.), from 1946. *Address:* 353 St. Mary's Avenue, Winnipeg, Canada. [*Died* 1951.

MURRAY, Gilbert; *see* Murray, G. G. A.

MURRAY, Lt.-Col. Herbert Edward, C.I.E. 1944; B.A., M.D., M.Ch., F.R.C.O.G.; L.M.S., retd.; Cons. Obstetrician and Gynæcologist, The Victoria Hospital, Cork, Eire; late Senior Obstetrician and Gynæcologist, the City General Hospital, Leicester; *b.* 19 May 1889; *s.* of late E. J. Murray, County Dublin, Ireland; *m.* 1933, Lylie Frances, *d.* of late C. H. Miller, Co. Dublin; no *c.* *Educ.:* private school; Dublin University. Entered Indian Medical Service, 1914; served in France, 1914–15. Held various posts in Military employ until 1925 in India and Hong-Kong; transferred, 1925, to Civil side of I.M.S., to Bengal, where several posts were held. Professor of Midwifery and Gynaecology, Medical College, and 1st Surgeon, Eden Hospital, Calcutta, 1940–46. Examiner to Central Midwives' Board. *Publications:* over one dozen short papers in various medical periodicals in the last fifteen years. *Recreations:* tennis, golf, billiards. *Address:* Shana Court, Castletownshend, Skibbereen, Co. Cork, Eire; Grindlay's Bank, Ltd., 54 Parliament St., S.W.1. *Clubs:* Oriental; Bengal (Calcutta). [*Died* 9 *Dec.* 1951.

MURRAY, Rear-Admiral Herbert Patrick William George, D.S.O. 1916; *b.* 8 Sept. 1880; *m.* 1914, Mabel (*d.* 1956), *d.* of Alderman W. Avens, Portsmouth; three *s.* Secretary to International Commission of Admirals administering Scutari, Albania, 1913; Secretary to Vice-Admiral and Senior Officer of International Squadron blockading coasts of Montenegro and Albania, 1913; War: Secretary to Vice-Admiral commanding Channel Fleet, 1914; Secretary to Vice-Admiral Second in Command Grand Fleet, 1914–16; present at Jutland action (despatches, D.S.O.); has been Secretary to Second Sea Lord, Admiralty, the Commander-in-Chief, Coast of Scotland, Commanders-in-Chief, Portsmouth, Africa Station, and The Nore, retired list, 1935; re-employed, 1939; Regional Petroleum Officer, South-Eastern Region, 1942–47. *Address:* Chilton, Uplands Road, Denmead, Hants. *T.:* Hambledon 9. [*Died* 29 *July* 1958.

MURRAY, John, O.B.E.; *b.* 12 May 1871; *s.* of Alexander and Barbara Murray, Gartymore, Sutherland; *m.* 1899, Annie Ball; one *s.* *Educ.:* Brecon. Entered service of Midland Railway Co., 1887; Superintendent of Freight Trains, 1911; Asst. General Supt. (Midland Div.) L.M. &. S. Railway Co., 1923; Outdoor Asst. to Chief General Supt., 1924; Asst. Chief General Supt., 1927; retired, 1932; High Sheriff of Breconshire, 1943–1944. *Recreations:* motoring, gardening, and photography. *Address:* Loan-Riavach, Llangorse, Brecon. *T.A.* and *T.:* Llangorse 39. *Club:* Brecon and County (Brecon). [*Died* 11 *Jan.* 1954.

MURRAY, John George, J.P. Co. Bedford; Sheriff of the County, 1923; D.L., 1926–43; *b.* 6 Aug. 1864; *e. s.* of Richard Murray, J.P. Benfieldside, Co. Durham; *m.* 1st, 1892, Isabella (*d.* 1946), *d.* of William Charleton, The Rigg, Northumberland; one *d.*; 2nd, 1947, Bridget, *d.* of late Col. John Blencowe Cookson, Meldon Park, Northumberland, and *widow* of Lt.-Col. H. B. des V. Wilkinson, The Durham Light Infantry. *Educ.:* privately. Solicitor (not in practice); Ex-Chairman, North-Eastern Breweries, Ltd.; Ex-Chairman, Kirkstall Brewery Co. Ltd.; Ex-Chairman, The Associated Breweries, Ltd.; Ex-Deputy Chairman, C. Vaux and Sons, Ltd.; Ex-Chairman, Seaton Burn Coal Co. Ltd.; Ex-Chairman, North Walbottle Coal Co. Ltd.; Ex-Chairman, Owners of Redheugh Colliery Ltd.; Chairman Gateshead Brick and Stone Co. Ltd.; Ex-Chairman Trustees and Governors of Richard Murray Hospital, County Durham; formerly Member Bedfordshire Standing Joint Committee; an Ex-President of Bedford Chamber of Agriculture; Ex-Master, Wrest Basset Hounds. *Recreations:* polo, shooting, hunting. *Address:* Coles Park, near Buntingford, Herts. *T.:* Buntingford 88. *T.A.:* Coles Park, Buntingford. *Club:* Carlton. [*Died* 11 *Aug.* 1953.

MURRAY, Lt.-Col. John Hanna, C.I.E. 1919; Indian Medical Service, retired; *s.* of Dr. John Murray of Wickham, Hants; *m. d.* (*decd.*) of Commander T. H. Hull, R.N.; one *d.* *Educ.:* Epsom College; University College, London. Formerly in the Fiji Medical Service; joined I.M.S., 1902; Inspector-General of Prisons, Bombay Presidency, 1924–29. *Address:* Mandeys, Brasted, Kent. *T.:* 408. *Club:* United Service. [*Died* 12 *March* 1959.

MURRAY, John Pears, C.B.E. 1925; *b.* 1866; *s.* of late Alfred Everitt Murray, Govt. Land Surveyor, East London, S.A.; *m.* 1900, Florence, *d.* of late D. R. Trollip, farmer, Aliwal North; three *s.* one *d.* *Educ.:* Muller's Private School, East London. Served in the Bechuanaland Border Police, 1885–87; Mercantile and Banking experience in Johannesburg, 1887–94;

Accounting clerk Basutoland Administration, 1894; Sub-Inspector Basutoland Mounted Police, 1895; Inspector, 1902; Financial Secretary, 1904; Assistant Commissioner, 1913; Govt. Secretary, 1918; Deputy Resident Commissioner, 1920; acted as Resident Commissioner, 1923, 1924, and 1926; retired, 1927. *Recreations:* fishing, shooting, ornithology. *Address:* 13 Nelson Avenue, Cambridge, East London, South Africa. *T.:* 3825. [*Died* 20 *April* 1947.

[*But death not notified in time for inclusion in Who Was Who* 1941–1950, *first edn.*

MURRAY, of Blackbarony, Sir Kenelm Bold, 13th Bt., *cr.* 1628; farming and mining in Chile since 1920; *b.* 26 May 1898; *s.* of Sir John Murray, 12th Bt., and Edith Mary (*d.* 1925), *d.* of George Raby of Valparaiso; *S.* father, 1938; unmarried. *Educ.:* St. Aubyn's prep. school, Rottingdean; Royal Naval College, Osborne. Served with 1st Cavalry Machine Gun Squadron (attached 1st Cavalry Brigade) as a Lieut., in France and on the Rhine, 1917-20; returned to Chile, 1920. *Recreations:* shooting, polo. *Heir:* *n.* Alan John Digby [*b.* 22 June 1909; *s.* of Alan Digby Murray (*s.* of 11th Bt.); *m.* 1943, M. E. Schiele, Argentina; four *s.*]. *Address:* Los Colorados, Vallenar, Chile. *T.A.:* Murray, Vallenar. [*Died* 16 *Aug.* 1959.

MURRAY, Philip, Medal of Merit (U.S.); President: Congress of Industrial Organizations since 1940; United Steelworkers of America since 1942; *b.* Lanarkshire, Scotland, 25 May 1886; *m.* 1910, Elizabeth Lavery; one *s.* *Educ.:* public schools in Pennsylvania. Arrived in U.S., 1902; worked in mines at early age; Vice-Pres. United Mine Workers, 1920-42; Congress of Industrial Organizations, 1936-: Chm. C.I.O. Political Action Cttee; Member: Advisory Cttee. to Nat. Security Resources Bd., 1950; President's Nat. Advisory Bd. on Mobilization Policy, 1951; Co-Chm. United Labor Policy Cttee. Positions with Public Service organizations in fields of charity, health, civil rights, etc.; American Red Cross, Nat. Assoc. for the Advancement of Colored People. Hon. degrees: Howard Univ.; Duquesne Univ.; Boston Coll.; Mem. Exec. Cttee. Internat. Confed. of Free Trade Unions. Member Ancient Order of Hibernians. *Publication:* (with Morris Llewellyn Cooke) Organized Labor and Production, 1942. *Recreations:* fishing, reading, athletics. *Address:* (office) 718 Jackson Place, N.W., Washington, D.C., U.S.A. *T.:* Executive 5581; 1500 Commonwealth Bldg., Pittsburgh, Pa. *T.:* Grant 1-5254; (home) 752 Berkshire Avenue, Pittsburgh, Pa. *Club:* Knights of Columbus (Washington, D.C.). [*Died* 9 *Nov.* 1952.

MURRAY, Robert Howson, C.M.G. 1934; *b.* 14 April 1882; *s.* of Robert Cuninghame Murray and Helen Annie Foulger; *m.* 1917, Elsie Rosamond Marsland (*d.* 1952); one *s.* (and one *s.* decd.). *Educ.:* Westminster School. Entered Colonial Civil Service, Nyasaland Protectorate, 1909; Administrative Officer (1st grade), 1923; Provincial Commissioner, 1928. *Recreations:* shooting, fishing, golf. *Address:* Garden Cottage, Horstead House, Norwich. *Club:* Flyfishers'. [*Died* 1 *Oct.* 1960.

MURRAY, T. C.; Headmaster, Inchicore Model Schools, retired; Director Authors Guild of Ireland; Member Irish Academy of Letters; *b.* County Cork, 1873. *Educ.:* St. Patrick's Training College. D.Litt. (Hon.), 1949. *Plays:* The Wheel of Fortune, 1909; Birthright, 1910; Maurice Harte, 1912; Sovereign Love; The Briery Gap, 1917; Spring, 1918; Aftermath, 1922; Autumn Fire, 1924; The Pipe in the Fields, 1927; The Blind Wolf, 1928; A Flutter of Wings, 1929; Michaelmas Eve, 1932; A Stag at Bay, 1934; A Spot in the Sun, 1938; Illumination, 1939. *Fiction:* Spring Horizon, 1937. *Address:* 11 Sandymount Avenue, Ballsbridge, Dublin. *T.:* Ballsbridge 680513. [*Died* 7 *March* 1959.

MURRAY, Lt.-Col. William Atholl, C.M.G. 1919; D.S.O., 1917; late R.A.; D.L. County of Southampton; *b.* 1879; *m.* 1905, Gladys Marion (*d.* 1948), *d.* of late William Herbert Peto. Served European War 1914-19 (wounded, despatches, D.S.O., Bt. Lt.-Col., C.M.G., Croix de Guerre). *Address:* Woodlands, Bembridge, Isle of Wight. [*Died* 13 *Nov.* 1953.

MURRAY, Sir William Keith, 9th Bt., *cr.* 1673; *e. s.* of 8th Bt. and 1st wife, Frances, *d.* of Anthony Murray, Dollerie, Perthshire; *b.* 8 April 1872; *S.* father, 1921; unmarried. *Educ.:* Harrow; Trin. Coll., Camb. (B.A. 1895). Entered Militia, 1894. Owns the estates of Ochtertyre and Fowlis Wester, about 11,000 acres. *Heir:* *n.* Patrick Ian [*b.* 28 Aug. 1904; *m.* 1929, Liska, *d.* of A. Creet, Ghusick, India]. *Address:* Aberturret, Crieff, Perthshire. *T.:* Crieff 16. *Club:* Royal Automobile. [*Died* 4 *Feb.* 1956.

MURRILL, Herbert Henry John, M.A., B.Mus., F.R.A.M.; Hon. Fellow of Trinity College of Music; Head of Music, B.B.C., since 1950; Professor of Composition, Royal Academy of Music, since 1933; *b.* 11 May 1909; *s.* of Herbert Walter Murrill and Kate Murrill (*née* Arnold); *m.* 1941, Veronica Catherine Canning; one *d.* *Educ.:* Haberdashers' Aske's School; Royal Academy of Music; Worcester College, Oxford. Organ Scholar of Worcester College, Oxford, 1928-1931. Held various London appointments as organist. Music master at London schools and Director of Music for the Group Theatre Season at Westminster Theatre, 1935-36. B.B.C. Music Department, 1936; Music Programme Organiser, 1942. Served War with Intelligence Corps, 1942-46. Acting Asst. Director of Music, B.B.C., 1947; Assistant Head of Music, 1948. *Publications:* Three Hornpipes (for Orchestra), 1932; Concerto for 'cello and orchestra, 1935; String Quartet, 1939; Concerto No. 2 for 'cello and orchestra, 1950; many smaller works for strings, pianoforte, etc.; incidental music for plays and films; contrib. to musical journals, Modern Home University and New Educational Library. *Address:* 16 Cavendish Avenue, St. John's Wood, N.W.8. *T.:* Cunningham 0368. [*Died* 25 *July* 1952.

MURRY, John Middleton, O.B.E. 1920; M.A.; author and farmer; *b.* Peckham, London, 6 Aug. 1889; *e. s.* of John Murry, Inland Revenue Dept.; *m.* 1st, 1913, Kathleen (Katherine Mansfield) (*d.* 1923), 3rd *d.* of late Sir Harold Beauchamp, Wellington, N.Z.; 2nd, 1924, Violet (*d.* 1931), *o. d.* of Charles le Maistre; one *s.* one *d.*; 3rd, Elizabeth, 2nd *d.* of Joseph Cockbayne; one *s.* one *d.*; 4th, 1954, Mary (*née* Gamble). *Educ.:* Christ's Hospital; B.N.C. Oxford. On staff of Westminster Gazette, 1912-13; Art Critic, 1913-14; Reviewer to Times Literary Supplement, 1914-1918; served in Political Intelligence Department of War Office, 1916-19; Chief Censor, 1919; Editor of the Athenæum, 1919-21; Editor of the Adelphi, 1923-48; Editor of Peace News, 1940-46; Clark Lecturer, Cambridge, 1924; William Noble Fellow, Liverpool, 1931. *Publications:* Still Life, 1917; Fyodor Dostoevsky, 1917; Poems, 1919; The Evolution of an Intellectual, 1920; Cinnamon and Angelica, 1920; Aspects of Literature, 1920; The Things We Are, 1922; The Problem of Style, 1922; Countries of the Mind, 1922; Pencillings, 1923; The Voyage, 1924; Discoveries, 1924; To the Unknown God, 1924; Keats and Shakespeare, 1925; Life of Jesus, 1926; Things to Come, 1928; God, 1929; Studies in Keats, 1930, 2nd edn. 1939; Son of Woman, 1931; Countries of the Mind (2nd series), 1931; The Necessity of Communism, 1932; William Blake, 1933; (with Ruth E. Mantz) The Life of Katherine Mansfield, 1933; Between Two Worlds, 1934; Shakespeare, 1936; The Necessity of Pacifism, 1937; Heaven and Earth, 1938; The Pledge of Peace, 1938; The

Price of Leadership, 1939; The Defence of Democracy, 1939; Europe in Travail, 1940; The Betrayal of Christ by the Churches, 1940; Christocracy, 1942; Adam and Eve, 1944; The Free Society, 1948; The Challenge of Schweitzer, 1948; Katherine Mansfield and Other Literary Portraits, 1949; The Mystery of Keats, 1949; The Conquest of Death, 1951; Community Farm, 1951; Jonathan Swift, 1954; ed. The Journal of Katherine Mansfield, 1904-22, 1954; Unprofessional Essays, 1955, Love, Freedom and Society, 1957; posthumous: Katherine Mansfield and other Literary Studies, 1959; Not as the Scribes (Ed. A. R. Vidler), 1960. *Relevant publications:* To Keep Faith, by Mary Middleton Murry, 1959; Selected Criticism, 1916-57 (chosen by Richard Rees), 1960. *Recreation:* gardening. *Address:* Lower Lodge, Thelnetham, nr. Diss, Norfolk. [*Died* 13 *March* 1957.

MUSGRAVE, Lt.-Col. Sir Christopher Norman, 6th Bt., *cr.* 1782; O.B.E. 1952; late R. Corps of Signals; Civil Engineer; *b.* 19 Oct. 1892; *e. s.* of late James Musgrave, M.I.C.E., *g. s.* of 3rd Bt., and Kathleen Const, *d.* of F. C. Barker of Blackrock, Dublin; *S.* cousin, 1930; *m.* 1918, Kathleen, 3rd *d.* of late Robert Chapman, Dartrey Lodge, Moy, Co. Tyrone; one *s.* one *d. Educ.:* Berkhamstead; Trinity College, Dublin. Served European War with Royal Engineers, 1914-18 (despatches twice). *Heir: s.* Richard James, *b.* 10 Feb. 1922. *Address:* Headfort Court, Kells, Co. Meath. *Clubs:* Kildare Street (Dublin); Ulster (Belfast). [*Died* 12 *May* 1956.

MUSGRAVE, Sir Courtenay; *see* Musgrave, Sir N. C.

MUSGRAVE, Ernest Illingworth, O.B.E. 1956; Director, Leeds City Art Gallery and Temple Newsam House, Leeds, since 1946; *b.* 16 Dec. 1901; *s.* of William Henry Musgrave; unmarried. *Educ.:* Leeds. Entered Art Gallery Service at Leeds, 1925; Director, City Art Gallery, Wakefield, 1934-. Served on Arts Panel of the Arts Council of Great Britain, 1946-52. F.M.A. *Publications:* Handbooks on Country Houses; articles and reviews in various art magazines. *Address:* 248 Shadwell Lane, Moortown, Leeds. *T.:* 662420. *Club:* Athenæum. [*Died* 18 *Nov.* 1957.

MUSGRAVE, Sir (Nigel) Courtenay, 13th Bt., *cr.* 1611; *b.* 11 Feb. 1896; *s.* of 12th Bt. and Hon. Eleanor Harbord (*d.* 1936), 7th *d.* of 5th Baron Suffield; *S.* father, 1926. Owns about 6900 acres. *Heir: cousin* Charles, *b.* 1913. [*Died* 19 *Feb.* 1957.

MUSKERRY, 5th Baron (*cr.* 1781), **Robert Matthew Fitzmaurice Deane-Morgan;** 10th Bt. *cr.* 1710; *b.* 14 Nov. 1874; *e. surv. s.* of 4th Baron and Flora (*d.* 1902), *d.* of Hon. Chichester Thomas Foster-Skeffington, 2nd *s.* of Viscount Ferrard and Harriet, Viscountess Massereene; *S.* father, 1929; *m.* 1906, Charlotte, *d.* of John Irvine, of Mervyne, Co. Wexford. *Heir: b.* Hon. Mathew Chichester Cecil Fitzmaurice Deane-Morgan (later 6th Baron Muskerry, *q.v.*). *Address:* Springfield Castle, Drumcollogher, Co. Limerick. *T.A.:* Muskerry, Drumcollogher. *T.:* Drumcollogher 5. *Clubs:* Kildare Street (Dublin); County (Limerick). [*Died* 12 *July* 1952.

MUSKERRY, 6th Baron, (*cr.* 1781), **Mathew Chichester Cecil Fitzmaurice Deane-Morgan;** 11th Bt. *cr.* 1710; *b.* 3 Nov. 1875; *s.* of 4th Baron and Flora (*d.* 1902), *d.* of Hon. Chichester Thomas Foster-Skeffington; *S.* brother 1952; *m.* 1915, Helen Henrietta Blennerhassett (*d.* 1952) *d.* of Brig.-Surgeon Lt.-Col. Rodolphe Harman, A.M.S. *Heir: kinsman* Matthew Fitzmaurice Tilson Deane [*b.* 30 July 1874; *m.* 1897, Mabel Kathleen Vivienne, *d.* of late C. H. Robinson, M.D.; two *s.* one *d.*]. *Address:* St. Ernan's, Co. Donegal. [*Died* 3 *May* 1954.

MUSSELWHITE, The Ven. William Ralph, C.V.O. 1952; Archdeacon of Lynn since 1953; *b.* 17 April 1887; *s.* of William and Fanny Keturah Musselwhite, Marlborough, Wilts.; *m.* 1911, Laura Mary, *d.* of Hugh John Veysey, Portsmouth; one *d.* (one *s.* decd.). *Educ.:* privately; Southsea; St. John's Hall, London. Deacon, 1910, priest, 1911, Southwell; Asst. Curate: St. Stephen, Nottingham, 1910; St. Jude, Southsea, 1914; Vicar: St. Paul, Upper Norwood, 1919; St. John, Bromley, 1931; St. Peter Wolferton and St. Felix Babingley, 1939; Rural Dean of Rising, 1942-53; Hon. Canon of Norwich, 1947-53. Hon. Sec. Rochester Dio. Conf., 1933-39. H.M. The Queen's Govr., King's Lynn High School, 1943; Govr. King Edward VII Grammar School, King's Lynn, 1948. *Address:* The Old Rectory, Anmer, Norfolk. *T.:* Hillington 278. [*Died* 28 *Sept.* 1956.

MUSSEN, Sir Gerald, Kt., *cr.* 1939; Director Associated Pulp and Paper Mills, Ltd., Melbourne; *b.* Dunedin, N.Z., 17 Oct. 1872; *s.* of Henry G. Mussen, Christchurch, N.Z.; *m.* 1900, Florence E. Gordon; two *s.* one *d. Educ.:* Southland High School, Invercargill, N.Z. Industrial Consultant Electrolytic Zinc Co. of Australasia, Ltd. and Broken Hill Associated Smelters, 1915-28; Chairman Federal Citrus Association, 1924-30; Victorian Central Citrus Association, 1924-30; Director various Proprietary Companies; one of two founders of The News, evening paper, Adelaide, 1922; ten years effort to establish successfully eucalyptus pulp and paper industry in Australia, 1926-36. *Publications:* The Humanizing of Commerce and Industry, 1919 (Fisher Lecture, Adelaide University); Australia's Tomorrow, 1944. *Recreation:* golf. *Address:* Associated Pulp and Paper Mills Ltd., Melbourne, Australia. *Club:* Metropolitan Golf (Melbourne). [*Died* 21 *March* 1960.

MUSSON, Dame Ellen Mary, D.B.E., *cr.* 1939 (C.B.E. 1928); R.R.C., LL.D., S.R.N.; Médaille en Argent de l'Assistance Publique de l'État Français, 1933; Florence Nightingale International Medal, 1939; Chairman General Nursing Council for England and Wales, 1926-43; *d.* of late W. E. Musson, Surgeon, Clitheroe, Lancs. *Educ.:* Home; Private School; France and Germany. Trained St. Bartholomew's Hosp., E.C.; certificate with Gold Medal; Night Superintendent, Ward Sister, Assist.-Matron in same Hospital; Matron Swansea General and Eye Hospital, 1906-9; Matron General Hospital, Birmingham, 1909-1923; Principal Matron Territorial Force Nursing Service, 1st Southern General Hospital, 1912-23; Royal Red Cross, 1st Class, 1916; Treasurer International Council of Nurses, 1925-47; Vice-Pres. Roy. Coll. of Nursing. *Address:* Badlesmere, Trinity Trees, Eastbourne. *Club:* Cowdray. [*Died* 7 *Nov.* 1960.

MYER, Lieut.-Colonel George Val., F.R.I.B.A.; portrait painter; *b.* 14 February 1883; *s.* of Grenville Myer and Ray Matilda Simmons; *m.* 1938, Betty Vera, *o. d.* of Lt.-Col. Cowell, Exmouth. *Educ.:* Univ. College School; Univ. College. Articled to John Belcher, R.A.; served in France in R.E. throughout European War, 1914-18; Assistant Architect to Government of Bengal, 1921; invalided home, 1922; resumed practice in London, 1924; took into partnership F. J. Watson-Hart, 1929; retired from practice of architecture, 1950. Served again in France in 1939-40 and later was camouflage officer for all London's "pill boxes," including the famous "Book Stall" and "Enquiry Bureau". *Principal Works:* Broadcasting House, Portland Place; Aldford House, Park Lane; Halifax House, Strand; Princes Court, Knightsbridge; Fountain House, Park Lane, W.; Russell Court, Woburn Place, W.C. *Address:* 3 Europa Rd., Gibraltar. [*Died* 25 *Feb.* 1959.

MURSHIDABAD, Nawab Bahadur of, K.C.S.I., K.C.V.O. See page xxix.

MYER, Sir Norman, Kt. 1956; Chairman and Managing Director, The Myer Emporium Ltd., Melbourne; Chairman Sidney Myer Charitable Trust; Chairman City Development Association; *b.* 1897; *m.* 1952, Pamela Margaret Sallmann. *Educ.:* Wesley College, Melbourne. Commissioned, Australian Imperial Forces, Western Front, European War, 1914-18. *Recreations:* tennis, golf, riding. *Address:* The Myer Emporium Ltd., Melbourne, Vic., Australia. *Club:* Naval and Military (Melbourne). [*Died* 17 *Dec.* 1956.

MYERS, Bernard, C.M.G. 1917; M.D., C.M.; F.R.C.P.; Lieut.-Colonel (Reserve) N.Z.M.C.; Consulting Physician to St. Thomas, Hospital; late-Consulting Physician to New Zealand Government, London, and to the Civil Service Sanitorium Soc.; formerly Commissioner in U.K. for New Zealand Red Cross; late Acting Director of Medical Services, 1st New Zealand E.F.; late Pres. Clinical Section Royal Society of Medicine, also of West London Medico-chirurgical Society; B.M.A. delegate to N.Z. Biennial Conference, 1935; Chadwick Lectr. Roy. Inst. of Public Health and Hygiene, 1937; *b.* 1872; *s.* of Louis and Catherine Myers; *m.* Violet Hayman (*d.* 1953); three *d.* *Educ.:* Wellington College, N.Z.; Edinburgh University; St. Bartholomew's Hospital. *Publications:* Practical Handbook on the Diseases of Children; Reminiscences of a Physician; Modern Infant Feeding; The Physician Investigates. *Address:* 4 Stockleigh Hall, N.W.8. *Clubs:* Savage; New (Edinburgh). [*Died* 9 *May* 1957.

MYERS, Most Rev. Edward, M.A. Camb.; Coadjutor Archbishop of Westminster and Titular Archbishop of Berea since 1951; Provost of Cathedral Chapter since 1938; Member of Education Advisory Cttee., Colonial Office; Apostolic Visitor to Roman Catholic Missions in West Indies, 1947; *b.* York, 8 Sept. 1875. *Educ.:* College St. Louis, Menin, Belgium; St. Edmund's College, Ware; Christ's College, Cambridge University; Oscott College, Birmingham. Priest, 1902; Professor of Ecclesiastical History and Patrology at St. Edmund's College, 1903; Dogmatic Theology, 1905-18; Vice-President of St. Edmund's College, 1916; Canon of Westminster Cathedral, 1919; Founder and Chairman of the Society of St. John Chrysostom, 1926; President of St. Edmund's College, Old Hall, Ware, 1918-32; Domestic Prelate to the Pope, 1929; Joint Editor of Clergy Review, 1931; Vicar Capitular of Westminster, 1943-44; Titular Bishop of Lamus and Bishop Auxiliary of Westminster, 1932-51. *Publications:* The Method of Theology (from the French of Archbishop Mignot), 1902; Historical Criticism and the Old Testament (from the French of Père Legrange) 1907; The New Psalter and its Use (1912) with Rev. E. Burton, D.D.; The Mystical Body of Christ, 1930; Lent and the Liturgy, 1948; Contributor to the Catholic Encyclopædia, the British Review, the Dublin Review, etc. *Address:* St. Mary's, Cadogan Gardens, S.W.3. *T.:* Kensington 5487. *Club:* Athenæum. [*Died* 13 *Sept.* 1956.

MYERS, Sir James Eckersley, Kt., 1950; O.B.E., D.Sc., A.R.I.C.; J.P. Cheshire; *b.* Bolton, 24 June 1890; *e. s.* of William and Sarah Myers; *m.* 1917, Elsie, *o. d.* of John Ingram, Colwyn Bay; (one *s.* decd.). *Educ.:* Manchester Grammar School; Manchester University. 1st Class Hons. in Chemistry; B.Sc. 1910; Beyer Research Fellow in Science, 1911; Senior Lecturer in Chemistry and Secretary and Tutor Faculty of Science, Univ. of Manchester, 1920-38; Asst. to Vice-Chancellor, 1930-38; Senior Tutor, 1933-38; Member of the Court of Governors and of the Council of the University of Manchester, 1923-27, 1929-32; Principal Manchester Municipal Coll. of Technology, Dean, Faculty of Technology, Manchester Univ., 1938-1951; Director, School of Education, Manchester University, 1951-55; Chairman, Joint Matriculation Board, 1938-41; Pres. Association of University Teachers, 1930; Governor, Macclesfield King's School; Member Norwood Committee on Secondary Education, 1941; Chm. Stockport Div., Juvenile Court, 1946-55; Mem. Council British Inst. of Management, 1947; Chm. N. W. Regional Academic Bd., 1949. *Publications:* various research publications in the Journal of the Chemical Society since 1910, including the Synthesis of Mustard Gas and Studies in Periodic Chemical Reactions; Monograph, The Problem of Physico-Chemical Periodicity (with Dr. E. S. Hedges). *Recreation:* cricket. *Address:* 28 Victoria Park, Colwyn Bay, N. Wales. *T.:* Colwyn Bay 2165. [*Died* 5 *Dec.* 1958.

MYLKS, Gordon Wright, M.D., C.M.; F.A.C.S.; F.R.C.S.(C.); *b.* Grenville County, Ontario, 14 Aug. 1874; *s.* of Manuel and Emily Helen Mylks; *m.* 1903, Lucy Hamilton Row, Louisville, Ky., U.S.A.; one *s.* *Educ.:* Collegiate Institute, Brockville, Ont.; Queen's University. Spent 14 months as House-Surgeon in Kingston General Hospital, after which spent some weeks at Johns Hopkins Hospital, Baltimore; and later, some months at London Hospital, Whitechapel Road, E.C., also at Vienna, in post-graduate work; located at Kingston, Ontario, 1899, and began practice of medicine; Demonstrator of Pathology, Queen's University, 1899; Demonstrator of Anatomy, 1902; Professor of Anatomy, 1904; Surgeon to Kingston General Hospital, 1905-12; practice limited to Surgery—Obstetrics and Gynaecology—since 1928; Emeritus Prof. Obstetrics and Gynaecology since 1939; Consultant Obs. and Gyn., Kingston Gen. Hospital, since 1939. *Address:* 122 Wellington Street, Kingston, Ontario. *T.:* 2-2801 Kingston. [*Died* 14 *Feb.* 1957.

MYRES, Sir John (Linton), Kt., *cr.* 1943; O.B.E. 1919; Hon. D.Litt.; Hon. D.Sc.; F.B.A.; F.S.A.; *b.* Preston, Lancs, 3 July 1869; *e. s.* of late Rev. W. M. Myres of Preston, and Jane, *d.* of late Rev. Henry Linton of Stirtloe, Hunts; *m.* Sophia Florence, *y. d.* of late Charles Ballance of Clapton, Middlesex; two *s.* one *d.* *Educ.:* Winchester (Scholar); New College, Oxford (Scholar); 1st Mods., 1890; 1st Lit. Hum., 1892. Fellow of Magdalen College, Oxford, 1892-95; Craven Travelling Fellow, 1892-94; Burdett-Coutts Geological Scholar, 1892; Student and Tutor of Christ Church, 1895-1907; Arnold Essay, 1899; Lecturer in Classical Archæology in University of Oxford, 1903-07; Junior Proctor, 1904-1905; Secretary to Committee for Anthropology, 1905-7; Examiner in Final Classical School, 1906-8, 1920-23, Modern Languages, 1920, 1940; Geography, 1933-34, 1941-44; Gladstone Prof. of Greek and Lecturer in Ancient Geography, University of Liverpool, 1907-10; Wykeham Prof. of Ancient History, 1910-39; Fellow and Librarian of New College, Oxford; Sather Prof. of Classical Literature in the University of California, 1914 and 1927; travelled in Greece and Asia Minor, 1893; Crete, 1893, 1895, 1898, 1903; conducted excavations in Cyprus, 1894 and 1913; and reorganised Government Museum, 1894; Hon. Sec. Royal Anthropological Institute of Great Britain and Ireland, 1900-3; President, 1928-31 (Huxley Memorial Medal 1933); Lt.-Commander (Acting Commander) R.N.V.R. 1916-19; General Secretary British Association for the Advancement of Science, 1919-32; President, Folklore Society, 1924-1926; Vice-Pres. Society of Antiquaries, 1924-1929 (Gold Medallist, 1942); Royal Geographical Soc., Victoria Medal, 1953. Pres. Hellenic Society, 1935-38; Chairman, British School at Athens, 1934-47; General Secretary, International Congress Anthropological and Ethnological Sciences, 1934-47; Frazer Lecturer, Cambridge, 1943; Hon. D.Sc. Wales, 1920; Manchester, 1933; Hon. D.Litt., Witwatersrand, 1929; Hon. Ph.D. Univ. of Athens, 1937; Hon. Fellow, Magdalen College, 1944, New College, 1946; Comm. R. Order of George I. of Greece, 1918; Officer, Order of St. Sava, 1930;

Commander, Order of the Dannebrog, 1939. *Publications:* A Catalogue of the Cyprus Museum, 1899; A History of Rome, 1902; The Dawn of History, 1911; Notes and Queries in Anthropology (edited), 1912: Handbook of the Cesnola Collection of Antiquities from Cyprus, 1914; The Political Ideas of the Greeks (Bennett Lectures), 1926; Who were the Greeks? (Sather Lectures), 1930; Mediterranean Culture (Frazer Lecture) 1943; Scripta Minoa II (edited), 1952; Geographical History, 1952; Herodotus, Father of History, 1953; (posthumous) Homer and his Critics, 1959; papers on Mediterranean geography, archæology, and anthropology. *Recreation:* study of antiquities. *Address:* 13 Canterbury Road, Oxford. *T.:* Oxford 3970. [*Died* 6 *March* 1954.

N

NABARRO, David Nunes, B.Sc., M.D. (Lond.), D.P.H., F.R.C.P.; Consulting Pathologist, formerly Director of the Pathological Department and Bacteriologist at Great Ormond Street (Children's) Hospital, 1912-39; Scientific Assistant in Pathology, University of London (1904-24); Jt. Sen. Fell. of Univ. College, London; Fellow of the Royal Society of Medicine; Hon. Mem. Brit. Paediatric Assoc., Osler Club; Member (Past President) of the Assoc. of Clinical Pathologists, London Jewish Hosp. Med. Soc., and of the Medical Society for the Study of Venereal Disease; Senior Member, Pathological Soc. of Great Brit. and Ireland; Corresponding Member of the Society of Tropical Pathology, Paris; Member of the Inner Temple; *b.* London, 27 Feb. 1874; *e. s.* of Jacob Nunes Nabarro, broker, London, and Hannah, *d.* of David Israel Ricardo, Amsterdam; *m.* 1914, Florence Nora, 2nd *d.* of Nathan Bell Webster, North Walsham; one *s.* one *d.* *Educ.:* Owen's School; University College and Hospital, London. Gold Medallist at M.D. Examination; Assistant Professor of Pathology and Bacteriology, Univ. Coll., London, 1899-1910; Pathologist to the Evelina Hospital for Children and to the West Riding Asylum, Wakefield; Member of the Royal Society's Sleeping Sickness Commission in Uganda, 1903, and discoverer (with Surg.-Gen. Sir David Bruce and Prof. A. Castellani) of the cause and mode of transmission of sleeping sickness. Pathologist in the E.M.S, 1940-1946. *Publications:* The Laws of Health, 1905; Translation and Amplification of Profs. Laveran and Mesnil's work, Trypanosomes et Trypanosomiases, 1907; Sleeping Sickness Commission Reports of the Royal Society, 1903-5; Congenital Syphilis, 1954; papers on medical and bacteriological subjects in various scientific journals. *Recreations:* gardening, philately. *Address:* 10 The Oaks, Woodside Avenue, Woodside Park, N.12. *T.:* Hillside 3121. *Club:* Maccabæans. [*Died* 30 *Sept.* 1958.

NAEF, Sir Conrad James, Kt., *cr.* 1931; C.B. 1923; C.B.E. 1918; J.P.; *b.* 28 July 1871; *o. s.* of Conrad Naef, Hausen am Albis, Switzerland. *Educ.:* City of London School; Merton College, Oxford. Entered the Department of the Accountant-General of the Navy, 1895; Superintending Clerk, 1898; Assistant Accountant-General, 1904; Deputy Accountant-General, 1906-21; Accountant-General of the Navy, 1921-32. *Address:* 7A Strawberry Hill Road, Twickenham, Middlesex. *T.:* Popesgrove 1849. *Club:* United University. [*Died* 11 *March* 1954.

NAHUM, Jack Messoud Eric di Victor, Q.C. 1953; *b.* 29 Nov. 1906; *s.* of Victor di Halfalla and Elise Nahum. *Educ.:* Clifton College; Merton College, Oxford. Called to Bar, Inner Temple, 1929. Served War of 1939-45, 7th Bn. The Cheshire Regt., 3rd Sept. 1939-Feb. 1943, India and M.E.F.; posted J.A.G. Branch, Iraq, 1943; D.J.A., M.E.F., as Major, Sept. 1944-Aug. 1948. *Recreations:* golf, tennis. *Address:* 4 Brick Court, Temple, E.C.4. *T.:* Central 4735; 59 Kensington Mansions, Trebovir Road, S.W.5. *T.:* Fremantle 5689. [*Died* 28 *March* 1959.

NAIRN, Rev. John Arbuthnot, Litt.D., B.D. Cantab.; D.Litt. Oxon (St. John's); Vicar of St. James's, Stubbings, Maidenhead, 1927-53; Chaplain of St. Mark's Hosp., Maidenhead, 1931-53; *b.* 1874; *s.* of J. Arbuthnot Nairn; *m.* Alison (*d.* 1942), *e. d.* of George Moxon; two *d.* *Educ.:* Trinity Coll., Cambridge (Pitt University Scholar, 1893; Members' Prizeman for Latin Essay, 1893; Classical Tripos, Part I., 1st Division, 1st Class, 1894; Part II., 1st Class with distinction, 1896; senior Chancellor's Classical Medallist, 1896); Fellow, 1896-1902; Headmaster of Merchant Taylors' School, 1901-26; Select Preacher, University of Cambridge, 1905, 1928; Officier d'Académie, 1926; Chevalier of the Legion of Honour, 1935. *Publications:* The Mimes of Herodas, with Introduction and Commentary, 1904; St. Chrysostom's treatise de Sacerdotio, 1906; Latin Prose Composition, 1925; Library Edition with Versions, 1926; Latin Translation of Buffon's Discours sur le Style, 1926; Greek Prose Composition, 1927, Library Edition with Versions, 1928; The Mimes of Herodas for the Budé Series of Classical Texts, 1928; Hand-List of books relating to the Classics and Classical Antiquity, 3rd edn., 1953; Record of Stubbings Parish, 1849-1950 (2nd edn.); Greek Through Reading, 1952; Threaded Beads of Memory, 1954. *Address:* Foxleigh Lodge, Holyport, Berks. *T.:* Maidenhead 4081. [*Died* 18 *Nov.* 1957.

NAIRN, Sir Michael, 2nd Bart., *cr.* 1904; *b.* 19 Feb. 1874; *s.* of 1st Bart. and Emily Frances, *d.* of Alfred Rimington Spencer, Weybridge, Surrey; *S.* father, 1915; *m.* 1901, Mildred Margaret, *e. d.* of G. W. Neish; one *s.* four *d.* *Educ.:* Edinburgh Academy; Sherborne; Marburg University; a director of the Bank of Scotland. *Heir:* *s.* Michael George [*b.* 30 Jan. 1911; *m.* 1936, Helen Louise, *yr. d.* of late Major E. J. W. Bruce, Melbourne, Australia, and of Mrs. L. Warre Graham-Clarke, 39 Hill Street, W.; two *s.*]. *Address:* Elie House, Elie, Fife. *Clubs:* Carlton; New (Edinburgh). [*Died* 24 *Sept.* 1952.

NAIRN, Major Sir Robert S.; *see* Spencer-Nairn.

NAIRN, Walter Maxwell; journalist and lawyer; *s.* of William Nairn, Elgin, and Forres, Scotland; one *s.* one *d.* Speaker, Commonwealth House of Representatives, 1940-43; Member for Perth, W. Australia, 1929-43. *Address:* 5 Regent Street, Mt. Lawley, W. Australia. [*Died* 12 *Dec.* 1958.

NAIRNE, Brig.-General Edward Spencer Hoare, C.B. 1918; C.M.G. 1916; J.P. (Bucks); D.L. (Oxfordshire); *b.* 1869; 2nd *s.* of late Rev. Spencer Nairne and Marion, *y. d.* of 1st Lord Curriehill; *m.* Lilias, *o. c.* of Stafford O'Brien Hoare, J.P., D.L. of Turville Park, Bucks; one *s.* two *d.* [Assumed prefix surname of Hoare by deed-poll, 1910.] *Educ.:* Haileybury; Royal Military Academy, Woolwich. Entered R.A., 1888; p.s.c., 1904; served N.W. Frontier, 1897-98; South Africa, 1900-1902 (despatches, Bt. of Major); European War, 1914-18 (despatches 6 times, C.M.G., Bt. of Colonel, C.B.); Military Attaché at Athens, 1919-23; retired, 1924, with hon. rank of Brig.-Gen. *Address:* Turville Lodge, Henley-on-Thames. *T.:* Turville Heath 234. *Clubs:* United Service, Cavalry. [*Died* 20 *Feb.* 1958.

NAISH, Rear-Adm. George Oswald, C.B. 1958; *b.* 4 August 1904; *e. s.* of Dr. A. E. Naish; *m.* 1926, Jean Mary Westropp, *d.* of late Capt. R. G. Westropp, of Cairo, Egypt; two *s.* one *d.* (and one *s.* decd.). *Educ.:* Dragon School, Oxford; R.N. Colleges, Osborne and Dartmouth; R.N. Engineering College, Keyham. Entered R.N. 1918; specialised in engineering, 1922; served as engineer-officer in various ships and in H.M. Dockyards, Portsmouth, 1932-1934, Alexandria, 1939, Malta, 1939-42 (despatches); Portsmouth, 1942-44; Admiralty, 1936-39, 1944-46, 1949-50; passed R.N. and Jt. Services Staff Colls., 1947-1948; Admlty. Ordnance Engineer Overseer, Northern Area, 1950-53; Fleet Engineer Officer, Mediterranean, 1953-55; Command Engineer Officer Portsmouth, 1955-58; retired 1959. M.I.Mech.E. 1951. *Recreations:* sailing, walking. *Address:* Moelfre, Garn Dolbenmaen, Caernarvonshire. *Club:* Royal Naval (Portsmouth). [*Died* 18 *May* 1960.

NALDER, Leonard Fielding, C.M.G. 1928; C.I.E. 1919; C.B.E. 1921; *b.* 1 Jan. 1888; *m.* 1936, Suzanne Elizabeth Gray, *d.* of Lt.-Col. A. P. Storm de Grave and of Jonkvrouwe S. E. Sandberg tot Essenberg of Bannink, Colmschate, Holland. *Educ.:* Rugby; Corpus Christi Coll., Oxford. Sudan Political Service, 1912; Red Sea Patrol, 1916-17; Political Service, Mesopotamia, 1917-22 (T/Lt.-Col. Special List); Anglo-Iraq Delegate, Turco-Iraq Frontier Commission, 1927; Governor, Mongalla Province, 1930; Equatorial Province, 1936; retired 1936. *Publication:* The Yacht Racing Rules, 1948. *Recreations:* fencing, sailing, motoring. *Address:* Donyland Lodge, Rowhedge, Colchester. *T.:* Wivenhoe 356. *Clubs:* Royal Automobile; West Mersea Yacht (Commodore, 1948-52). [*Died* 25 *March* 1958.

NALL, Colonel Sir Joseph, 1st Bt., *cr.* 1954; Kt., *cr.* 1924; D.S.O. 1918; D.L. (Lancs); D.L., J.P. (Notts); *b.* 24 Aug. 1887; *e. s.* of late Joseph Nall, Worsley, Lancs; *m.* 1916, Edith Elizabeth, *y. d.* of late J. L. Francklin and Hon. Mrs. Francklin, Gonalston, Notts; two *s.* three *d.* *Educ.:* privately. Director of several Transport undertakings; M.P. (U.) Hulme Division of Manchester, 1918-29 and 1931-45; President of the Institute of Transport, 1925-26; served European War (Egypt, Gallipoli, France), 1914-18 (wounded, despatches, D.S.O.). Retired from T.A. Reserve (Col.), 1948. High Sheriff of Nottinghamshire, 1952. *Heir:* *s.* Michael Joseph, Lt.-Comdr. R.N. [*b.* 6 Oct. 1921; *m.* 1951, Angela Loveday Hanbury, *e. d.* of Air Chief Marshal Sir (William) Alec Coryton, K.C.B., K.B.E., M.V.O.; two *s.* *Educ.:* Wellington. Served War of 1939-45]. *Address:* Hoveringham Hall, Notts. *T.:* Lowdham 3134. [*Died* 2 *May* 1958.

NAMIER, Sir Lewis Bernstein, Kt., *cr.* 1952; F.B.A. 1944; Hon. Fellow, Balliol College, Oxford, 1948; M.A.; Hon. D.Litt. Durham, 1952, Oxford, 1955, Rome, 1956; Hon. Litt.D. Cambridge, 1957; Hon. D.C.L. Oxford, 1960; Member, Editorial Board of History of Parliament; *b.* June 1888; *m.* 1947, Iulia de Beausobre. *Educ.:* Balliol College, Oxford. Private in the 20th Royal Fusiliers, 1914-15; worked in Propaganda Department, 1915-17; in Department of Information, 1917-18; in Political Intelligence Department of the Foreign Office, 1918-20; Lecturer in Modern History at Balliol College, Oxford, 1920-21; in business, 1921-23; 1923-29 engaged on historical research; Political Secretary of the Jewish Agency for Palestine, 1929-31; Prof. of Modern History, Manchester Univ., 1931-53. *Publications:* Germany and Eastern Europe, 1915; The Structure of Politics at the Accession of George III., 1929; England in the Age of the American Revolution, 1st vol., 1930; Skyscrapers, 1931; Additions and Corrections to Sir John Fortescue's Edition of The Correspondence of King George III. (Vol. I), 1937; In the Margin of History, 1939; Conflicts, 1942; 1848: The Revolution of the Intellectuals, 1946; Facing East, 1947; Diplomatic Prelude, 1938-39, 1948; Europe in Decay, 1936-40, 1950; Avenues of History, 1952; In the Nazi Era, 1952; Personalities and Powers, 1955; Vanished Supremacies, 1958. *Address:* 60 The Grampians, W.6. *T.:* Shepherds Bush 2445. *Club:* Athenæum. [*Died* 19 *Aug.* 1960.

NANSON, Group Capt. Eric Roper-Curzon, C.B.E. 1929; D.S.C., A.F.C.; *b.* 28 Feb. 1883; *y. s.* of late John Nanson and Lucy Roper-Curzon, Carlisle; *m.* 1929, Ida, *o. d.* of Mrs. Edward Foster. *Educ.:* Hawkshead Grammar School; H.M.S. Conway. Royal Naval Reserve, 1900-14; commenced flying, 1913; Lieut. R.N. 1914; Served European War, 1914-19; retired list, 1932; recalled to active list, Sept. 1939-March 1945; Inspector of Recruiting Royal Air Force, 1932-45. *Recreations:* fishing, motoring, shooting. *Address:* 222 Bickenhall Mansions, W.1. *T.:* Welbeck 8411. *Club:* Royal Aero. [*Died* 27 *Oct.* 1960.

NAPIER, 13th Lord, *cr.* 1627 (Scotland) **AND ETTRICK,** 4th Baron, *cr.* 1872, (U.K.); **Lieut.-Col. Sir William Francis Cyril James Hamilton Napier,** 10th Bt. of Thirlestane (*cr.* 1666); T.D.; *b.* 9 Sept. 1900; *e. s.* of 12th Baron Napier and 3rd Ettrick and Hon. Clarice Jessie E. (*d.* 1951), 3rd *d.* of 9th Baron Belhaven and Stenton; *S.* father, 1941; sits as Baron Ettrick; *m.* 1928, Muir, *d.* of Sir Percy Wilson Newson, 1st and last Bt.; four *s.* *Educ.:* Wellington Coll.; R.M.C. Sandhurst. Entered K.O.S.B. 1920; Lt.-Col. 1939; War of 1939-45, raised and commanded 6th Bn. of his Regt. 1939-41; A.A.G. War Office, 1943-44; retired, 1946. Member Royal Company of Archers (Queen's Body Guard for Scotland), 1930-. D.L. and J.P. Selkirkshire; County Councillor for Selkirkshire, 1946-48; Pres. Border Area Council, British Legion, Scotland; Joint Hon. Sec. Scottish Peers Association. *Recreations:* shooting and fishing. *Heir:* *s.* Master of Napier. *Address:* Thirlestane Castle, Ettrick, Selkirk. *T.:* Ettrick Valley 220. *Club:* New (Edinburgh). [*Died* 23 *Aug.* 1954.

NAPIER, Captain Sir Alexander Lennox Milliken, 11th Bt. of Napier, *cr.* 1627; late Grenadier Guards; *b.* 30 May 1882; *e. s.* of 10th Bt. and Mary, *d.* of Sir Thomas Fairbairn, 2nd Bt.; *S.* father, 1907; *m.* 1913, Joan, *o. c.* of late Edward Ashurst Morris; one *d.* Served S. African War, 1902; Lt. Grenadier Guards, 1904-8; Capt. Reserve of Officers, 1915-; A.D.C. to Governor-Gen. of Australia (Earl of Dudley), 1910-11; served European War, 1914-17 (twice wounded); A.D.C. Personal Staff since 1918. *Heir:* *b.* Robert Archibald [*b.* 19 July 1889; *m.* 1st, 1914, Violet (who obtained a divorce, 1929), *d.* of E. Payn; one *s.*; 2nd, 1929, Margaret Anne Searle Hinton, M.B.E., *o. surv. d.* of Thomas James Hinton, Horwell Lodge, Copplestone, Devon]. *Club:* Turf. [*Died* 15 *July* 1954.

NAPIER, Lionel Everard, C.I.E. 1942; F.R.C.P. (Lond.) 1940; Consultant on Tropical Diseases, Ministry of Pensions; Medical Editor, Caxton Publishing Co.; Cons. Editor Jl. Trop. Med. and Hyg.; *b.* 1888; *s.* of late Rev. J. R. Napier, Vicar of Old Windsor; *m.* Ella, *d.* of Arthur Ross. *Educ.:* St. John's School, Leatherhead; St. Bartholomew's Hospital. M.R.C.S. (Eng.), L.R.C.P. (Lond.) 1914. Served European War, 1915-18. Late Professor of Tropical Medicine and Director, School of Tropical Medicine, Calcutta. *Publications:* The Principles and Practice of Tropical Medicine, 1946; etc. *Address:* 25 St. George St., Hanover Sq., W.1.; Merchiston, Silchester, Hants. [*Died* 15 *Dec.* 1957.

NAPIER, Brigadier Vernon Monro Colquhoun, C.B. 1935; C.M.G. 1919; D.S.O.

1915; *b.* 9 Oct. 1881; *s.* of late Col. G.V.C. Napier, King's Dragoon Guards; *m.* 1919, Margaret, M.B.E., *widow* of Captain R. N. Phillips, Royal Welch Fusiliers, and *d.* of late H. R. Farmer, I.C.S., of Gatacre Park, Bridgnorth, Shropshire. *Educ.:* Wellington College, Woolwich. Entered Army, 1900; Captain, 1910; Adjutant, 1910-13; Major, 1914; Lieut.-Col., 1925; Col., 1928; D.A.A.G. 1914; served South Africa, 1902 (Queen's medal 4 clasps); European War, 1914-18 (despatches 5 times; Croix de Guerre, Belgium; Croix de Guerre, France; Order of the Rising Sun, Japan; C.M.G., D.S.O., Bt. Lt.-Col.); Commanded 1st Brigade, Royal Horse Artillery, 1925-28; A.A.G. War Office, 1928-30; Commander R.A. 3rd Division, Salisbury Plain, 1931-35; A.D.C. to the King, 1932-35; retired pay, 1935; recalled to the Army, Dec. 1939; A.A.G., War Office, 1939-42. *Address:* Horcott House, Fairford, Glos. *T.:* Fairford 253.
[*Died* 9 *May* 1957.

NAPIER, William Heathcote Unwin, C.B.E. 1931; *b.* Glasgow; *s.* of late William Heathcote Unwin Napier, Glasgow; *m.* 1903, Mary Teresa (*d.* 1953), *e. d.* of late Hugh McIntyre, Dublin; one *s.* one *d.* *Educ.:* Glasgow High Sch.; Glasgow Acad.; Greenock Acad. Held various positions with The National Telephone Co. Ltd. 1890-1912, when transferred to Civil Service; Senior Inspector of Telephone Traffic Secretary's Office, G.P.O., 1912; Deputy Controller, London Telephone Service, 1923; Controller London Telephone Service, General Post Office, 1929-36; Member of General Council, City of London Savings Association. *Publications:* various articles and correspondence class books on telephone traffic subjects. *Address:* Glannant, Wellington Road, Bush Hill Park, Middlesex. *T.:* Laburnum 1212.
[*Died* 3 *March* 1959.

NAPIER, Admiral William Rawdon, C.B. 1927; C.M.G. 1919; D.S.O. 1917; *b.* 13 June 1877; *o. surv. s.* of late Commander Lenox Napier and Ellin, 2nd *d.* of W. B. Buddicom of Penbeddw Hall, Flints; *m.* 1902, Florence Marie, *e. d.* of late James O'Reilly Nugent, Fareham; one *s.* one *d.* served European War; Superintendent of the Mining School, Portsmouth; decorated for mine-sweeping; awarded a good service pension, 1923; Rear-Adm., 1924; First Naval Member of Royal Australian Naval Board, 1926-29; Vice-Admiral and retired list, 1929; Adm., retired, 1933. *Address:* Catisfield Cottage, Fareham, Hants.
[*Died* 8 *April* 1951.

NARASIMHA GOPALASWAMI AYYANGAR (Sir), (Kt., *cr.* 1941; C.S.I. 1937; C.I.E. 1935); B.A., B.L.; Minister for Transport and Railways, Government of India, since 1948, and also for States since 1950; *b.* 31 March 1882; *m.* Shrimati Komalammal. Assistant Professor, Pachaiyappa's College, Madras, 1904; entered Madras Civil Service as Deputy Collector, 1905; Deputy Collector, 1905-19; Collector District Magistrate, 1920; Registrar-General of Panchayats and Inspector of Local Boards, 1921-28; Collector and District Magistrate, Anantapur, 1928-31; Inspector of Municipal Councils and Local Boards, 1931-32; Secretary to Government, P.W.D., 1932-34; Member, Board of Revenue, Madras, 1935-37; Prime Minister, Jammu and Kashmir State, 1937-43; Minister without Portfolio, Government of India, 1947-48; Leader of Indian Delegation to the U.N. Security Council on Kashmir Question, 1948; Member, Indian Legislative Assembly, 1927; Pres., Indian Officers' Assoc., Madras, 1935-37; elected Member, Council of State, 1943-47; Member, Sapru Cttee., 1944; Chm., Sub-Cttee. on Land Utilisation of Policy Cttee. No. 5 on Agriculture, Forestry and Fisheries, 1944-45; Chm., Armed Forces Nationalisation Cttee., 1947; Member: Constituent Assembly of India; Congress Assembly Party since 1947; Indian Constitution Drafting Cttee.; Member Council of States, 1952- (formerly Member of Parliament). *Address:* 5 Queen Victoria Road, New Delhi, India.
[*Died* 10 *Feb.* 1953.

NARES, Vice-Adm. John Dodd, D.S.O. 1919; R.N.; President of Directing Committee of the International Hydrographic Bureau at Monaco, 1932-1952, Director, 1952; *b.* 1877; *m.* 1904, Adeline Chaffey, *d.* of late Hon. Mr. Justice McIntyre, of the Supreme Court, Hobart, Tasmania; one *s.* (killed in action, 1942) one *d.* Served European War, 1914-19 (despatches, D.S.O.); Assistant Hydrographer of the Navy, 1924-1928, and 1930-31; Naval A.D.C. to the King, 1930-31; Rear-Adm. and retired list, 1931; Vice-Admiral, retired, 1936. Served as Naval Asst. to, and as Asst. Hydrographer of the Navy, 1940-45. *Address:* c/o International Hydrographic Bureau, Monte Carlo, Principality of Monaco. *Club:* United Service.
[*Died* 18 *Jan.* 1957.

NASH, Eveleigh; Lord of the Manor of Sutton Waldron in the county of Dorset; President of Our Society (The Crimes Club); *b.* 5 Nov. 1873; *s.* of Thomas Nash of Sutton Waldron and Susan, *e. d.* of James Robertson of Barbauchlaw, Midlothian; *m.* 1930, Lilian Gibson-Smith. *Educ.:* Edinburgh. Literary adviser to Constable & Company, publishers, 1900-2; founded the publishing house of Eveleigh Nash, 1902; founded and edited Nash's Magazine, in which second series of Kipling's Puck of Pook's Hill stories first appeared, 1909; has published stories and works by Thomas Hardy, Rudyard Kipling, Joseph Conrad, Hilaire Belloc, W. H. Hudson, George Gissing, Conan Doyle, O. Henry, Maurice Maeterlinck, Sir Sidney Lee, the Earl of Balfour, Visc. Haldane, Rider Haggard, A.E.W. Mason, Bishop Gore, Sir William Watson, George Saintsbury, and many other famous authors; retired from publishing world, 1929; during European War was Chief Civil Assistant to the Navy Controller for Armament Production. *Publications:* I Liked the Life I Lived, 1941; articles in the Fortnightly Review and other periodicals. *Recreations:* gardening and reading. *Address:* 12 Charles Street, W.1. *T.:* Grosvenor 1224. *Clubs:* Athenæum, Travellers'.
[*Died* 9 *July* 1956.

NASH-WILLIAMS, Victor Erle, M.A., D.Litt.; F.S.A.; Keeper of Archæology in the National Museum of Wales; Lecturer in Archæology in University College, Cardiff; Member, Royal Commission on Ancient Monuments in Wales and Monmouthshire, since 1955; *b.* 21 Aug. 1897; *m.* 1931, Margaret Elizabeth, *e. d.* of late William Luck, Liverpool; two *s.* *Educ.:* University College, Cardiff. Military service, 1915-19 (Infantry), and 1940-45 (R.A.S.C.). Seconded to the Historical Section (Military), War Cabinet offices, 1944-45. President Cambrian Archæological Assoc., 1953; Member Ancient Monuments Board for Wales, 1954-. *Publications:* The Roman Legionary Fortress at Caerleon, 1940; The Early Christian Monuments of Wales, 1950; The Roman Frontier in Wales, 1953; reports on excavations in Wales and Welsh antiquities in Archæologia Cambrensis, Antiquaries Journal, Archæologia, etc.; Ed. of Archæologia Cambrensis and of the Cambrian Archæological Association 1946 Centenary Volume: A Hundred Years of Welsh Archæology. *Address:* National Museum of Wales, Cardiff. [*Died* 15 *Dec.* 1955.

NASHIMOTO, Morimasa, Prince; The Grand Cordon of the Order of the Chrysanthemum; *b.* 9 March 1874; *m.* 1900, Princess Itsuko, 2nd *d.* of Marquess Nabeshima; two *d.* *Educ.:* Military Academy, France; attached to staff of General Oku during Russo-Japanese War. Arrested on suspicion of complicity in war crimes Nov. 1945 and released April 1946. *Address:* Mitakecho, Shibuya, Tokyo, Japan. [*Died* 1 *Jan.* 1951.

NASON, Col. Fortescue John, C.B. 1918; C.M.G. 1915; D.S.O. 1899; retired; *b.* 14 Sept. 1859; *s.* of late Major-Gen. John Nason. *Educ.:* Harrow. Entered Army 1880 (joined 26th Cameronians); Sudan, 1889, action of Arguin wounded (4th class Medjidie, medal, bronze star); Expedition to Dongola, 1896, as Brigade Major, 1st Brigade, operations of 7 June and 19 Sept. (despatches, Egyptian medal with 2 clasps); Nile Expedition, 1897 (clasp to Egyptian medal); Nile Expedition, 1898, battles of the Atbara and Khartoum, defeat of Ahmid Fedil's army (despatches three times, Brevet of Lieut.-Col., D.S.O., and 3 clasps to Egyptian medal); attached Egyptian Army, 1888-90 and 1896-1905 (3rd class Osmanieh, 2nd class Medjidie, and a Pacha in Egypt); retired from the army, 1905; served European War, 1914-18 (despatches thrice, C.B. and C.M.G., bronze star, 1914, Victory and War Medal). *Address:* The Red Cottage, Finchampstead, Berks. *T.:* Eversley 2239. *Club:* Army and Navy. [*Died* 16 *Jan.* 1952.

NATHAN, George Jean; Dramatic Critic Theatre Arts magazine and the King Features Syndicate; *b.* 14 Feb. 1882; *s.* of Charles Narét-Nathan and Ella Nirdlinger; *m.* 1955, Julie Haydon. *Educ.:* Cornell Univ. (B.A.); Univ. of Bologna, Italy, Indiana University (Lit.D.). Editor (with H. L. Mencken) Smart Set Magazine (also dramatic critic); founder and editor (with same) The American Mercury (also critic), and subsequently contributing editor and critic; founder (with Theodore Dreiser, Eugene O'Neill, James Branch Cabell, Sherwood Anderson and Ernest Boyd) and editor The American Spectator, also critic. Authority on American theatre since 1935 Encyclopædia Britannica and Britannica Book of the Year. Contributor to leading American periodicals. President N.Y. Drama Critics Circle, 1937-38-1939. Hon. member London Critics Circle. *Publications:* 40 books, including The Popular Theatre, 1918, The American Credo, 1920, The Critic and the Drama, 1922, Materia Critica, 1924, The House of Satan, 1926, Since Ibsen, 1933, The Theatre of the Moment, 1936, Encyclopædia of the Theatre, 1940, The Entertainment of a Nation, 1942, The Theatre Book of the Year, 1943-44, 45, 46, 47, 48, 49, etc. *Recreations:* wine, tobacco and work. *Address:* 44 West 44th St., New York City, 36, N.Y., U.S.A. *T.:* Murray Hill 2-8060. [*Died* 8 *April* 1958.

NAYLOR, Thomas Ellis, J.P.; retired; *b.* 5 Mar. 1868; *m.* 1899, Emily Fawcett; three *d.* *Educ.:* a London Board School; Working Men's College. From compositor to Corrector of the Press; afterwards journalist; M.P. (Lab.) S.E. Southwark, 1921-22, 1923-31 and, 1935-50. General Secretary London Society of Compositors, 7 and 9 St. Bride Street, E.C.4, 1906-38; Vice-Chairman Joint Industrial Council for Printing Industry, 1933-34; Chairman, 1934-35; Editor London Typographical Journal, 1906-38; Cobden Club Prizeman in Political Economy. Chairman London Labour Party, 1915-28. *Publications:* Rules and Conduct of Debate; A Compositor in Canada; Principles and Practice of Newspaper Make-up. *Address:* 10 Thornton Rd., Wimbledon, S.W.19. *T.:* Wimbledon 3552. [*Died* 24 *Dec.* 1958.

NAYLOR-LEYLAND, Sir (Albert) Edward (Herbert), 2nd Bt., *cr.* 1895; J.P.; late Hon. Attaché in H.M. Diplomatic Service; *b.* 6 Dec. 1890; *s.* of 1st Bart. and Jeanie (*d.* 1932), *d.* of William Selah Chamberlain, Cleveland, Ohio, U.S.A.; *S.* father, 1899; *m.* 1923, Marguerite Helene (*d.* 1945), 2nd *d.* of late Baron de Belabre; three *s.* one *d.* *Educ.:* Eton; Christ Church, Oxford. High Sheriff, Denbighshire. *Heir:* *s.* Vivyan Edward, *b.* 5 Mar. 1924. *Address:* 10 Dorset House, Gloucester Place, N.W.1; Nantclwyd Hall, Ruthin, North Wales. *Clubs:* Marlborough-Windham, Turf. [*Died* 23 *Sept.* 1952.

NEEDHAM, Colonel Alfred Owen, C.B.E. 1924 (O.B.E. 1919); M.C.; T.D.; *b.* 1883. Served European War, 1914-19 (despatches thrice, O.B.E., M.C.); commanded 8th Bn. The Worcestershire Regt.; J.P., Worcestershire. *Address:* Ankerdine View, Knightwick, Worcs.; 30 New Street, Worcester. *Club:* Union (Worcester). [*Died* 8 *Feb.* 1951.

NEEDHAM, Major Hon. Francis Edward, M.V.O. 1921; late Grenadier Guards; 2nd *s.* of 3rd Earl of Kilmorey, and *b.* and *heir-pres.* to 4th Earl; *b.* 6 Mar. 1886; *m.* 1911, Blanche Esther, *d.* of Richard Combe; two *s.* one *d.* *Educ.:* Eton. Served European War, 1914-19; retired pay, 1925; re-employed, 1941-1945. J.P. *Address:* Tocknells Court, Painswick, Stroud, Glos. *T.:* Painswick 2361. *Club:* Turf. [*Died* 24 *Oct.* 1955.

NEIL, James H.; *see* Hardie Neil.

NEILL, James Scott, C.M.G. 1941; *b.* 19 Nov. 1889; *s.* of late James Neill, Knock Belfast; *m.* 1920, Grace Constance (*d.* 1947), *e. d.* of Samuel Howard, Dungannon; one *s.* *Educ.:* Trinity College, Dublin; King's Inns, Dublin. Cadet, Fiji, 1914; District Comr., 1916; Registrar Supreme Court, 1922; Actg. Attorney-Gen., 1922-23; Actg. Prin. Asst. Colonial Secretary, 1924-26; Chairman Board of Examiners, Fijian language, 1926; British Agent and Consul, Tonga, 1927-37; special duty, Ocean Island, Gilbert and Ellice Island Colony, 1930; special duty, Pitcairn Island, 1937; Administrator, Dominica, 1938-45; Acting Administrator, St. Lucia, 1942; Acting Governor, Windward Islands, 1945; Commissioner of Public Utilities and Supply, Newfoundland, 1945-49; retired, 1949. *Publication:* Ten Years in Tonga, 1955. *Recreations:* tennis, walking. *Address:* 42 Warren Road, Reigate, Surrey. *T.:* Reigate 3924. [*Died* 3 *Oct.* 1958.

NEILL, Sir William (Frederick), Kt., *cr.* 1948; F.A.I.; F.R.I.C.S.; J.P.; *b.* 8 May 1889; 5th *s.* of John Neill, Belfast; *m.* 1912, Margaret Marshall (*d.* 1957); one *s.* (also one son missing, R.A.F.) two *d.*; *m.* 1957 Rhoda Eveline, *d.* of G. A. Kinning, 78 Somerton Road, Belfast. *Educ.:* Belfast Model School. Member of Belfast Water Commissioners, 1935-; Member of Belfast Corporation, 1938-; Lord Mayor, 1946, 1947 and 1948-49; Deputy Lord Mayor, 1955-56. M.P. (U.) Belfast North, 1945-50. D.L. for City of Belfast, 1949-; High Sheriff of Belfast, 1954. Freeman of the City of Belfast, 1949. Business—Estate Agent. Chairman, Bd. of Governors, British Water Research Association, 1946-58. *Recreation:* golf (Pres. Golfing Union of Ireland, 1953). *Address:* 35 Park Road, Belfast. *Club:* Reform (Belfast). [*Died* 3 *Jan.* 1960.

NEILSON, Lieut.-Col. John Beaumont, C.M.G. 1919; D.S.O. 1917; *b.* 1885; *s.* of John Neilson and Annie Blackie Steel; *m.* 1933, Myra Berry, *o. d.* of G. E. White, Kingsland, Herefordshire. *Educ.:* Harrow. Lieut.-Col. commanding 5th Battn. Highland Light Infantry, European War, 1914-18 (despatches twice, D.S.O., C.M.G.); Chairman: English and Scottish Investors Ltd. *Address:* The Middle Gate, Cross-in-Hand, Sussex. *Club:* Carlton. [*Died* 27 *July* 1957.

NEILSON, Julia (Mrs. Fred Terry), F.R.A.M.; Actress; *b.* London; *m.* Fred Terry (*d.* 1933); one *d.* *Educ.:* England; Wiesbaden; Royal Academy of Music, London (Llewellyn Thomas gold medal, Westmoreland Scholarship, and Sainton Dolby prize). First appeared on the stage as Cynisca in Pygmalion and Galatea at Lyceum Theatre, 1888; has since played in London at the Haymarket and St. James's; has toured the United States, Canada, and important towns of

Great Britain; her most noteworthy success is probably Rosalind in As You Like It, which she played during the longest run then on record in a London theatre; went into management with her husband, 30 Aug. 1900, and produced Sweet Nell of Old Drury, The Heel of Achilles, For Sword or Song, Sunday, The Scarlet Pimpernel. Dorothy o' the Hall, Matt of Merrymount, Henry of Navarre, The Popinjay, As You Like It, Much Ado about Nothing, Romeo and Juliet, The Duchess of Suds, The Marlboroughs, The Borderer, The Argyle Case, and The Wooing of Katherine Parr. *Publication:* This For Remembrance, 1940. *Recreation:* motoring. *Address:* 4 Primrose Hill Road, N.W.3. *T.:* Primrose 0850.
[*Died* 27 *May* 1957.

NEILSON, Richard Gillies, C.B.E. 1921; *b.* 1876; *yr. s.* of late Major Richard Neilson, V.D., Glasgow; *m.* Harriet Southwick. *Educ.:* Allan Glen's School, Technical College, Anderson's College, St. Mungo's College, Glasgow. Chemist, Burmah Oil Co. Ltd., Rangoon, 1901-10; Assistant Refinery Manager, 1910-13; Manager, Anglo-Iranian Oil. Co. Ltd., Abadan Refinery, Persian Gulf, 1913-21; Refineries Branch Manager, Anglo-Iranian Oil Co. Ltd., Britannic House, London, E.C.2, 1921-1927; F.C.S.; Member Society of Chemical Industry; Fellow, Institute of Petroleum. Member Central Asian Society. *Address:* Iona, 48 The Droveway, Hove, 4, Sussex. *T.:* Brighton 52351. [*Died* 28 *Feb.* 1956.

NELL, Sir Harry, Kt., *cr.* 1943; *b.* 27 May 1882; *s.* of William Nell, Brighton; *m.* 1914, Mary, *er. d.* of late Robert Lockhart. Qualified as solicitor, 1903; entered Estate Duty Office, 1904; seconded to Straits Settlements Govt. 1920-22; Controller of Death Duties, Board of Inland Revenue, 1938-44. *Address:* 12 Adelaide Mansions, Kingsway, Hove 3. *T.:* Hove 71866.
[*Died* 22 *May* 1958.

NELLES, Adm. Percy Walker, C.B. 1942; LL.D.; Royal Canadian Navy, retd.; *b.* Brantford, Ont., 7 Jan. 1892; *s.* of late Brig.-Gen. C. M. Nelles, C.M.G.; *m.* 1915, Helen Schuyler, *d.* of William Henry Allen of Bermuda; two *s. Educ.:* Lakefield Preparatory School; Trinity College, Port Hope. Formerly Senior Canadian Flag Officer (Overseas), London; Chief of Naval Staff and Chairman Chiefs of Staff Committee, Canada. Commander, Legion of Merit (U.S.); Commander, Legion of Honour (France); Cross of Liberation (Norway). *Address:* Wistowe, 620 St. Charles St., Victoria, B.C., Canada. *Clubs:* United Service (London, Eng.); Country, Rideau (Ottawa); Union Club of B.C. (Victoria, B.C.).
[*Died* 13 *June* 1951.

NELSON, 5th Earl (*cr.* 1805); **Edward Agar Horatio Nelson;** Baron Nelson of the Nile and Hilborough, 1798; Viscount Merton of Trafalgar and Merton, 1801; *b.* 10 Aug. 1860; 4th *s.* of 3rd Earl Nelson and Lady Mary Jane Diana Agar, *o. d.* of 2nd Earl of Normanton; *S.* brother, 1947; *m.* 1889, Geraldine (*d.* 1936), *d.* of late Henry H. Cave, Northampton; five *s.* three *d.* Lieut. 3rd Bn. Wilts Regiment, 1879-82; served in the Nile Expedition, 1884-85. Has always taken a great interest in agriculture and the management of landed estates. *Heir:* *s.* Viscount Trafalgar (*see* 6th Earl Nelson). *Address:* Richmond House, Rabling Road, Swanage, Dorset. *T.:* Swanage 2902.
[*Died* 30 *Jan.* 1951.

NELSON, 6th Earl (*cr.* 1805); **Albert Francis Joseph Horatio Nelson;** Baron Nelson of the Nile and Baron Hilborough of Hilborough, Norfolk, 1798; Viscount Merton of Trafalgar and Merton, 1801; F.R.G.S., F.R.A.S., F.R.S.A., F.R.Hort.S., F.Z.S.; *b.* 2 Sept. 1890; *e. s.* of 5th Earl Nelson and Geraldine (*d.* 1936), *d.* of late Henry H. Cave, Northampton; *S.* father 1951; *m.* 1st, 1924, Amelia, *widow* of John C. Scott (marriage dissolved 1925); 2nd, 1927 (in Scotland), 1942 (in England), Marguerite Helen, *d.* of late Capt. J. M. O'Sullivan, Tipperary, Eire. *Educ.:* Downside; abroad. Served with Australian Imperial Force, 1914-19, and with British Home Defence Forces, 1939-43. Has made a life study of Astronomy and Anthropology and lectures on these subjects. Carried out extensive mining prospecting in Queensland, N.S.W., and Western Australia, as well as in New Guinea, North Borneo, and Perak (Malay States). *Publications:* Life and the Universe. 1953; There is Life on Mars, 1955. *Recreations:* yachting, shooting, fishing. *Heir:* *b.* Hon. Henry Edward Joseph Horatio Nelson [*b.* 22 April 1894. *Educ.:* Maredsous, Belgium. Served European War, 1914-18, with A.I.F. in New Guinea and Europe; War of 1939-45, with Merchant Navy and I.A.]. *Address:* Merton Place, Dunsfold, Surrey. *T.:* Dunsfold 211.
[*Died* 23 *June* 1957.

NELSON, Donald Marr; Chairman, American Mollorizing Corp.; President, Pressure Dispensers, Inc.; *b.* 17 Nov. 1888; *s.* of Quincy Marr Nelson and Mary Ann MacDonald. *Educ.:* University of Missouri (B.S.); LL.D., Missouri, Harvard, North-western Univs., 1942; Dr. of Business Administration, Univ. of S. Calif., 1947. Chemical engineer, Sears, Roebuck & Co., 1912-21; Manager, Men's and Boys' Clothing Dept., 1921-26; Assistant in general merchandise office, 1926-27; general merchandise Manager, 1927-30; Vice-Pres. in charge of merchandising, 1930-39; Executive Vice-Pres. and Chairman Executive Committee, 1939; Co-ordinator of Purchases, National Defense Advisory Commission, 1940-41; Director of Purchases, Office of Production Management, 1941; Director of Priorities, Office of Production Management, and Executive Director of Supply, Priorities and Allocations Board, 1941-42; Chairman, War Production Board, 1942-44; Personal Representative of the President, 1944. *Publication:* Arsenal of Democracy, 1946. *Address:* (home) 9033 Briar Crest Lane, Beverly Hills, Calif., U.S.A.; (office) 9489 Dayton Way, Beverly Hills, California. *Clubs:* Commercial, Chicago, Metropolitan (Washington, D.C.). [*Died* 29 *Sept.* 1959.

NELSON, Sir James Hope, 2nd Bt., *cr.* 1912; *b.* 26 Feb. 1883; *e. s.* of 1st Bt. and late Margaret, *d.* of Michael Hope, of Gartlandstown, Co. Westmeath; *S.* father, 1922; *m.* 1st, 1913, Elizabeth, *d.* of Dr. Jules F. Vallee, St. Louis, U.S.A.; 2nd, 1923, Cathleen, *yr. d.* of ✠Lt.-Col. Loftus Bryan, Borrmount Manor, Co. Wexford. *Educ.:* Stonyhurst College. *Heir:* *n.* Major William Vernon Hope Nelson, O.B.E., 1952, 8th Hussars, [*b.* 28 May 1914; *m.* 1945, Elizabeth Ann Carey, *d.* of the Master of Falkland; two *s.* two *d.*]. *Address:* Knockbawn, Inch, Co. Wexford, Ireland.
[*Died* 5 *May* 1960.

NELSON, Rt. Rev. Robert, M.A.; Suffragan Bishop of Middleton since 1958; *b.* 26 June 1913; *s.* of John Nelson, Carlisle; *m.* 1942, Gabrielle Mary, *d.* of Frederick Hare, Scarborough; two *s.* one *d.* *Educ.:* The Grammar School, Carlisle; The University of Leeds. Curate, Grange-over-Sands, Lancs., 1936-38; Curate, Halton, Leeds, 1939-42; Vicar, St. Matthew's, Barrow-in-Furness, 1942-49; Rural Dean, Dalton-in-Furness, 1948-49; Rector of Liverpool, 1949-1958. Select Preacher, Univ. of Cambridge, 1953; Canon Diocesan of Liverpool, 1954-1956; Canon Residentiary of Liverpool, 1956-58; Chaplain to the Queen, 1956-58. *Publications:* contrib. to theological jls. *Address:* 8 Kersal Bank, Manchester 7. *T.:* Broughton 2390. *Clubs:* Royal Commonwealth Society; Old Rectory (Manchester).
[*Died* 3 *June* 1959.

NENK, David Moerel; Under Secretary for Finance and Accountant-General, Ministry of Education, since 1955; *b.* 6 Aug. 1916; *m.* 1941, Phyllis Winifred Yendoll; two *d.* *Educ.:* Haileybury; Gonville and Caius College, Cambridge. Entered Ministry (Board) of Education, 1938. War Service, Army, 1939-45. *Address:* Ministry of Education, Curzon St., W.1. [*Died* 24 *Jan.* 1960.

NEPAL, Ex-Maharaja of; H.H. Joodha Shamsher Jang Bahadur Rana; Ojaswi, Rajanya; Projjwala-Nepal-Tara; Atul-Jyotirmaya-Tri-Shakti-Patta; Ati-Pravala-Gorkha-Dakhshina-Bahu; Prithuladheesha Sri Sri Sri; G.C.B.(Hon.), *cr.* 1939; G.C.S.I.(Hon.) *cr.* 1935; G.C.I.E.(Hon.), *cr.* 1933 (K.C.I.E.(Hon.), *cr.* 1917); Hon. Gen. in British Army and Hon. Colonel of all Gurkha Rifle Regiments in Indian Army; Maharaja, Prime Minister and Supreme-Commander-in-Chief, Nepal, 1932-45; *b.* 24 April 1875; 10th *s.* of late Commander-in-Chief Dhir Shamsher Jang Bahadur Rana; *m.* 1888, H.H. Bada Maharani Padma Kumari Devi. Entered Army as a Colonel; Brigadier Patan, 1890; N. Command, March 1901; S. Command, June 1901; E. Command, 1907; W. Command and Acting Senior Commanding General, 1910; Senior Commanding General, 1914; Commander-in-Chief, 1929. Chief General of the Nepalese Staff during Maharaja Chandra Shamsher's state visit to Europe 1908 and visits to Nepal of King George V, 1911, and Prince of Wales, 1921; received First Class Star of Nepal, 1920; Grand Master, Most Glorious Order of Rajanya, Most Refulgent Order of the Star of Nepal, Most Illustrious Order of the Tri-Shakti-Patti, 1938, and Most Puissant Order of Gurkha Right Hand, 1932; Grand Cross Order of St. Maurice and St. Lazarus, 1933; Grand Cross Legion of Honour, 1934; First Class Order of Sacred Tripod (and highest rank in Chinese Army), 1934; Grand Cordon of Order of Leopold, 1935; Grand Cross of Order of German Red Cross, 1937; Grand Cross of Order of Netherlands Lion, 1939. *Address:* Nepal. [*Died* 23 *Nov.* 1952.

NEPEAN, Sir Charles Evan Molyneux Yorke, 5th Bt., *cr.* 1802; *b.* 24 Mar. 1867; *s.* of 4th Bt. and Maria, *d.* of Rev. Frederick T. Morgan-Payler, Rector of Willey, Warwickshire; *S.* father, 1903; *m.* 1896, Mary Winifred, *o. d.* of Rev. W. J. Swayne; one *s.* four *d.* Late Capt. and Hon. Major 3rd Batt. Princess Charlotte of Wales's (Royal Berks Regiment). *Heir:* *s.* Evan Yorke, Lt.-Col. Royal Signals [*b.* 23 Nov. 1909; *m.* 1940, Georgiana Cicely, *o. d.* of late Major N. E. G. Willoughby; three *d.*]. *Address:* The Warren, Uplyme, Lyme Regis, Dorset. [*Died* 1 *Jan.* 1953.

NEPEAN, Edith, author and journalist; *d.* of late John Bellis, C.C., Carnarvonshire; *m.* Molyneux E. Nepean (*d.* 1948), *s.* of late Sir Evan Nepean, C.B. *Educ.:* Home; Art under Robert Fowler, R.I. Exhibited at many exhibitions; since childhood has studied Welsh life, customs, and folklore and later Tzigan life in Transylvania; Commandant Kent 32 British Red Cross Society; Roumanian Order of Meritul Cultural for literature, 1935. *Publications:* Gwyneth of the Welsh Hills, 1917, filmed by Stoll; Welsh Love, 1919; Jewels in the Dust, 1920; Petals in the Wind, 1922; Cambria's Fair Daughter, 1923; The Valley of Desire, 1924; A Bundle of Myrrh, 1925; Moonlight Madness, 1926; Sweetheart of the Valley, 1928; Frail Lady, 1930; Fading Halos! 1931; Dangerous Diversion! 1932; Husbands and Lovers, 1933; Romance and Realism in the Near East, 1933; Waters of Separation, 1934; Gipsy Lover! 1935; Gay Penitents, 1936; Secret Lover 1937; Starlight Rapture, 1938; Another's Love Nest; Fires of Longing, 1940; Sinners with Wings, 1941; Perilous Waters, 1943 (Film rights acquired); Tinsel Paradise, 1944; Bryn came to the Valley, 1945; Forever in My Heart, 1947; Forbidden Rapture, 1948; Dreamer's Bliss, 1949; Return My Beloved, 1951; Come, Thou Stranger, 1952; Surrender Midnight, 1953; Telephone at Sunset, 1954; Starlit Folly, 1955; Gilt from the Charmer, 1957; Desires so Strong, 1958; contrib. largely to the Press. *Recreations:* music, painting. *Address:* Gunnersbury Manor, Ealing Common, W.5. *T.:* Ealing 1865. [*Died* 23 *March* 1960.

NEPEAN, Col. Herbert Dryden Home Yorke, C.I.E. 1945; D.S.O. 1917; formerly 5th Roy. Gurkha Rifles F.F. and 9th Gurkha Rifles; *o. s.* of late Brig.-Gen. H. E. C. B. Nepean, C.B., C.S.I, C.M.G.; *b.* 27 Nov. 1893; *kinsman* and *heir-pres.* of Lt.-Col. Sir Evan Nepean; *m.* Edith Florence, *d.* of late E. P. Woods. *Educ.:* Tonbridge School; Royal Military College, Sandhurst. Served European War, 1914-19 (wounded, D.S.O., despatches); 3rd Afghan War, 1919; N.W. Frontier, India, 1923; Bt. Lt.-Col. 1936; retd., 1940; employed with Gwalior State Forces; recalled, 1942 as Dep. Military Adviser-in-Chief, Indian State Forces; released, 1946; employed with the Hyderabad Army; Brig. Gen. Staff until 1948. Roy. Humane Soc. Bronze Medal, 1917. *Address:* c/o Lloyds Bank Ltd., (a/c 451246), 6 Pall Mall, S.W.1. *Club:* Naval and Military. [*Died* 25 *Jan.* 1956.

NEPEAN, Brig.-Gen. Herbert Evan Charles, C.B. 1921; C.S.I. 1919; C.M.G. 1917; Indian Army, retired; *o. s.* of Col. H. A. T. Nepean, Lansdowne Road, Worthing, and 1st wife, Alice, *d.* of Maj.-Gen. J. W. Bayley; *b.* 10 Oct. 1865; *m.* 1892, Alice Maude, (*d.* 1950), *d.* of late Surg.-Major Hamilton Ross; one *s.* one *d.* Served Soudan Field Force, 1885-86; Burmese War, 1887-89; operations in suppression of gun-running, Persian Gulf, 1910; European War, 1914-19; Mesopotamia Expeditionary Force (despatches five times, C.S.I., C.M.G.); retired, 1922. *Address:* c/o Grindlay's Bank, Ltd., 54 Parliament St., S.W.1. [*Died* 28 *March* 1951.

NESBITT, Major Randolph Cosby, V.C. 1896; *b.* 20 Sept. 1867; 4th *s.* of Major C. A. Nesbitt of Cape Colony; *m.* *y. d.* of T. J. Doherty, Newry, Co. Down, N. Ireland; no *c.* *Educ.:* St. Paul's School, London. Joined Cape Mounted Riflemen, 1885; expedition to Mashonaland, 1890; special service 1895, Gazaland 1896; J.P. 1895; Mashonaland medal, 1896; commanded a squadron of British South Africa Police serving with Generals Plumer and Baden-Powell in Transvaal (medal, and clasps for Rhodesia, Mafeking, and (Transvaal; Native Commissioner, 1909; retired. *Decorated* for rescuing party from Mazoe Valley beginning of Mashona rebellion. *Recreations:* shooting, fishing. *Address:* Waterways, Henley Road, Muizenberg, South Africa. *T.:* 8-1327. *Club:* Royal Automobile of South Africa (Capetown). [*Died* 23 *July* 1956.

NESS, Robert Barclay, M.A., M.B., C.M., F.R.F.P.S.G. (retd.); Hon. Fellow and Past Pres. Royal Faculty of Physicians and Surgeons, Glasgow; Hon. Consulting Physician to Western Infirmary, Glasgow, and Royal Hospital for Sick Children, Glasgow; Original Member of the Association of Physicians of Great Britain and Ireland; Hon. Member of the Royal Medico-Chirurgical Society of Glasgow; Captain R.A.M.C. (T.F.) retired; *s.* of Robert Ness, F.E.I.S., Glasgow; *m.* 1934, Elizabeth Birrell, *e. d.* of late William Brown, Rhuallan, Giffnock, Renfrewshire. *Educ.:* Glasgow Academy; Glasgow University. Has held following appointments: Professor of Materia Medica and Therapeutics in the Anderson College of Medicine, Glasgow; Professor of Practice of Medicine in the Anderson College of Medicine, Glasgow; Visiting Physician Western Infirmary, Glasgow, and Royal Hospital for Sick Children, Glasgow; Consulting Physician Bellefield Sanatorium, Lanark; Glasgow Ear, Throat and Nose Hospital and Ralston Red Cross Hospital for Paralysed Soldiers; Examiner in Materia

Medica and Therapeutics in University of Glasgow and University of St. Andrews, Examiner in Medicine, University of Glasgow; Examiner in medicine for the Fellowship of the Royal Faculty of Physicians and Surgeons, Glasgow. *Publications:* papers in medicine in various journals. *Address:* 19 Woodside Place, Glasgow, C.3. *T.:* Douglas 4304; Dunsunart, West Kilbride, Ayrshire. *T.:* West Kilbride 3159. [*Died 7 Sept.* 1954.

NETHERSOLE, Olga, C.B.E. 1936; R.R.C. 1920; Actress-manageress; Member of Consultative Council of Ministry of Food since 1940; *b.* London, 18 Jan. 1870; *y. d.* of late Henry Nethersole. *Educ.:* privately in London and Holland. Made her professional *début* at Theatre Royal, Brighton, in Harvest, March 1887; *début* in London at Royal Adelphi Theatre, June 1888; joined Garrick Theatre under Mr. John Hare's management, Apr. 1889; visited Australia on starring tour, Oct. 1890; was lessee and manager of the Court Theatre, London, in January 1894; several times visited U.S.A.; manager of Her Majesty's Theatre, 1898, when she produced The Termagant: Adelphi Theatre, 1902, where she produced Sapho; Shaftesbury Theatre, 1904; made her *début* in Paris, 1907, appearing in the leading rôles of the following plays—The Second Mrs. Tanqueray, La Dame aux Camelias, Adrienne Lecouvreur, Magda, Sapho, and Carmen. Created the part of Mary Magdalene in Maeterlinck's play in New York 1910, and also played Sister Beatrice, 1911. Joined British Red Cross 1916; on the Nursing Staff of the Hampstead Military Hospital as a V.A.D. 1916-19; founded The People's League of Health, 1917; a Trustee of the British Serbian Red Cross Fund; Life Governor of Denville Hall, Northwood; General Committee of Women's Section, British Empire Exhibition, 1924-25; Member of the Joint Parliamentary Advisory Council, 1924-25; V.P. of Medical Sociology Section of B.M.A.'s 97th Annual Conference, Manchester, July 1929; represents the People's League of Health upon the Council of the Central Chamber of Agriculture, 1931, and also upon the National Council of Women of Great Britain and Ireland—1930, 1931, 1932; V.P., Royal Institute of Public Health Congress, held at Eastbourne, June 1933 and June 1934; Member of International Association against Tuberculosis; represented People's League of Health at Conferences held in Brussels, 1920, Lausanne, 1924, Washington, U.S.A., 1926, Rome, 1928. Member of British Organizing Council, Ninth International Congress on Industrial Medicine, 1948. Member of National Farmers Union (Cornwall Branch). *Publications:* Inception of The People's League of Health, 1920; Milk Production and Distribution in Relation to Nutrition and Disease, 1933, the latter being a Paper delivered at the Meeting of The British Association (Agricultural Section) held at Leicester, Sept. 1933; also articles. *Recreations:* gardening, botany, dog fancier, motoring. *Address:* Heathland Lodge, Vale of Health, Hampstead, N.W.3. *T.:* Hampstead 2310; Trebarfoote Manor Farm, Poundstock, nr. Bude, N. Cornwall. *T.:* Widemouth Bay 2175; Headquarters of People's League of Health, 10 Stratford Place, W.1. *T.:* Mayfair 0386. [*Died 9 Jan.* 1951.

NETTLEFOLD, Sir Thomas Sydney, Kt., *cr.* 1945; O.B.E. 1935; *b.* 11 Nov. 1879; *s.* of Thomas and Susan Nettlefold, Oatlands, Tasmania; *m.* 1905, Gertrude Elizabeth, *d.* of Rev. Herbert Sargison; two *s.* one *d.* Lord Mayor of Melbourne, 1942-45. *Address:* Goliath House, 189 King Street, Melbourne, Victoria, Australia. *Clubs:* Athenæum, Royal Empire Society; Royal Automobile of Victoria, Victoria Amateur Turf, Victorian Racing (Melbourne). [*Died 20 July* 1956.

NEVE, Eric Read, Q.C. 1939; *b.* 11 March 1887; *s.* of David Edgar Neve, Blackheath, S.E.3; *m.* 1912, Nellie Victorine Uridge (*d.* 1943); one *s.* one *d.* *Educ.:* Brighton Grammar School. Private Sec., 1905-08; Newspaper Editor, 1908-14; served with Mech. Transport, Palestine and Egypt, 1915-1919; called to Bar, Middle Temple, 1921; Bencher, Middle Temple, 1948, South Eastern Circuit; Recorder of Canterbury, 1938-52. Chm. Middlesex Quarter Sessions, 1946-56, Chairman East Sussex Quarter Sessions, 1947-57. *Address:* 5 King's Bench Walk, Temple, E.C.4. *T.:* Central 4713-4. [*Died 12 Jan.* 1958.

NEVILL, Rev. Valentine Paul, C.B.E. 1953; O.S.B.; Headmaster of Ampleforth College since 1924; *b.* 17 Aug. 1882; 2nd *s.* of Henry William Nevill and Anne Mary Fenwick. *Educ.:* Ampleforth College; Hunter Blairs Hall, Oxford, now St. Benet's Hall. Entered the Benedictine Order, 1899, at Ampleforth Abbey; Priest, 1907; Sub-prior of Ampleforth, 1912-16; Chairman, Catholic Headmasters' Conference, since 1942. *Address:* Ampleforth College, York. [*Died 25 Jan.* 1954.

NEVILL, Commander Walter Howard, C.V.O. 1953; R.D. 1920; R.N.R. (Retd.); *b.* 5 Sept. 1887; *s.* of Thomas George Nevill, F.S.A., and Elizabeth Ann Nevill, Canonbury, London, N.; *m.* 1922, Violet Louie Luxton; one *s.* one *d.* *Educ.:* Merchant Taylors School. Bank of England, 1906-49; Secretary, Bank of England, 1944-1949. Mem. Transport Arbitration Tribunal, 1950-54; Vice-Chm. London Trustee Savings Bank, 1952-55; Hon. Treas. Star and Garter Home for Disabled Sailors, Soldiers and Airmen, 1950-; Royal Naval Reserve, Supply Branch, 1910-37; Sec. King George VI National Memorial Fund, 1952-53. *Recreation:* golf. *Address:* 2 Penlee, Cavendish Rd., Weybridge, Surrey. [*Died 11 Dec.* 1956.

NEVILLE, Brig. Alfred Geoffrey, C.B.E. 1944; M.C.; *b.* 27 Jan. 1891; 3rd *s.* of late Admiral Sir George Neville, K.C.B.; C.V.O.; *m.* 1923, Philippa, *d.* of Admiral Sir George Hope, *q.v.*; one *d.* *Educ.:* Eton; Magdalene College, Cambridge. 2nd Lt. R.A. 1911; R.H.A. 1915; European War, France; Adjt. R.H.A. Aldershot, 1923-25; Staff College; Asst. Military Attaché, Paris, 1928-1930; War Office, 1931-34; Military Asst. to C.I.G.S. 1935-37; i.d.c.; G.S.O.1 China, 1939-40; D.D.I.P. War Office, 1940-44; Brig. P. and P.W. 21 Army Group, 1944-45; retired pay, 1945. J.P., D.L., Somerset. *Recreations:* shooting, fishing, country life. *Address:* Parrisees Hayne, Howley, Chard, Somerset. *T.:* Chard 3196. *Club:* Cavalry. [*Died 3 March* 1955.

NEVILLE, Edith, O.B.E. 1937; Social worker; Hon. Secretary People's Theatre (London); Chairman St. Pancras Housing Society Ltd. for 14 years; Lecturer on the History of Painting, etc.; Hon. Director St. Pancras People's Theatre; *b.* 1874; *d.* of late Sir Ralph Neville, Judge of the High Court, Chancery Division. *Educ.:* Newnham College, Cambridge. *Recreations:* the theatre and picture galleries. *Address:* 17 Great Russell Mans., W.C.1. *Club:* Arts Theatre. [*Died 24 Feb.* 1951.

NEVILLE, Henry Allen Dugdale, C.B.E. 1948; M.A., B.Sc., F.I.C.; T.D.; Professor Emeritus, late Dean of Faculty of Agriculture, University of Reading; *b.* 13 Sept. 1880; *s.* of late Henry Neville and Emma, *d.* of late Thomas Holloway; *m.* 1908, Maud, *d.* of late William Grafton Curgenven, M.D.; one *d.* *Educ.:* Queen Elizabeth's Grammar School, Blackburn; University of Cambridge. On staff of Chemistry Departments of Technical College, Blackburn; School of Technology, University of Manchester; Institute of Agriculture, Chelmsford; School of Agriculture, University of Cambridge. *Publications:* many papers on organic chemistry and agricultural chemistry in journals of scientific societies. *Recreations:* travel and country life. *Address:* The University, Reading. *T.:* Reading 4422. [*Died* 17 *June* 1952.

NEVILLE, Kenneth Percival Rutherford, Ph.D., Litt.D., LL.D.; Dean of College of Arts, Univ. of Western Ontario, London, Can., 1927-47 (now emeritus); *b.* 26 Aug. 1876; *s.* of Chester Willison Neville and Mary Sharpe; *m.* 1912, Jean Thompson, M.A.; one *d.* *Educ.:* Queen's Univ., Kingston, Can. (M.A.); Harvard Univ. (M.A.); Cornell Univ. (Ph.D.). Queen's Univ. of Kingston, LL.D. (1947); Univ. of Western Ont., Litt.D. (1947); Assumption Univ. of Windsor, Ont., LL.D. (1957). Graduate Schol. in Classics, Cornell Univ., 1899-1900; Fell., 1900-1; Instr. in classics, Univ. of Illinois, Urbana, Ill., 1901-1908; former Registrar of Univ. of Western Ont. and Prof. of the Classics; United Church of Canada. *Publications:* Some Case Constructions after Comparatives in Latin; Letters of Robert Groseteste; a Latin Poetry Book; Selections from Latin Prose Authors. Editor, Yearbook of Canadian Universities, 1947-51. *Recreation:* golf. *Address:* R. R. 3, London, Ont., Canada. *T.:* 2-9776. [*Died* 1 *Oct.* 1957.

NEW, Charles George Morley, C.B.E. 1955; M.I.E.E.; *b.* July 1879; *m.* one *s.* one *d.* City Electrical Engineer, Cardiff, 1920-35; Electricity Commissioner, 1935-48; Member South-Eastern Electricity Board, 1948-55. Pres. Incorporated Municipal Electrical Association, 1931-32; Member H.M. Goodwill Trade Mission to Egypt, 1945. *Address:* Amberley, Llantrisant Road, Llandaff, Cardiff. *T.:* Cardiff 73850. [*Died* 10 *Dec.* 1957.

NEWALL, Norman Dakeyne, O.B.E. 1918; Landowner; Director of Companies; doing public work; *b.* 3 Nov. 1888; *y. s.* of late Frederick Stirling Newall, Wylam, Northumberland; *m.* 1913, Leslia, *y. d.* of late Charles Frank Forster, Southill, Co. Durham; one *s.* *Educ.:* Eton College. T.A. 1909-11; European War, 1914-18: attached French Army, Flanders, 1916; R.N.V.R. 1916-17; R.A.F. 1917-18; Major. Entered family business. High Sheriff of Northumberland, 1940; Vice-Chm. Royal Victoria Infirmary, Newcastle upon Tyne, 1941-48; Chm. United Newcastle upon Tyne Hosps., 1948-51; Chm. Newcastle Chamber Music Soc.; J.P. Northumberland, 1940. *Recreations:* shooting, fishing, motoring, travel. *Address:* Newbrough Lodge, Hexham, Northumberland. *T.:* Newbrough 21. *Clubs:* Carlton; Northern Counties, Union (Newcastle upon Tyne). [*Died* 12 *July* 1952.

NEWBOLT, Rev. Michael Robert; *b.* 1874; *o. s.* of late Canon W. C. E. Newbolt; *m.* 1917, Mary Caroline Butler; five *d.* *Educ.:* Radley; St. John's College, Oxford; Ely. Assistant Curate at Wantage, Berks; Vicar of Iffley, Oxford; Principal, Dorchester Missionary College; Vicar of St. Michael's, Brighton; Canon Residentiary of Chester Cathedral, 1927-46. *Publications:* The Manifold Wisdom of God; Healing; The Blessed Virgin; Edmund Rich; The Bible and the Ministry; The Book of Unveiling. *Address:* Cowley House, Bierton, Aylesbury, Bucks. [*Died* 7 *Feb.* 1956.

NEWBOROUGH, 5th Baron (*cr.* 1776), **Thomas John Wynn;** Bt. 1742; J.P.; *b.* 22 Nov. 1878; *g.s.* of 3rd Baron, *s.* of Hon. Thomas John Wynn and Anna, *d.* of Edwin Corbett, H.M. minister at Athens; *S.* brother, 1916; *m.* 1st, 1907, Vera Evelyn Mary (who obtained a divorce, 1938, *d.* 1940), *d.* of late Capt. P. Montagu, and *widow* of Henry Winch; one *d.*; 2nd, 1939, Deniza Braun (who obtained a divorce, 1947) one *d.*; 3rd, 1947, Katherine Rudkin, *d.* of Henry Stephen Murray, Victoria, Australia. *Heir:* *c.* R. V. Wynn, O.B.E. *Address:* 119A Mount Street, W.1. *Club:* Turf. *Died* 27 *April* 1957.

NEWBOULD, Alfred Ernest; *s.* of late J. J. Newbould, Tatenhill, Burton-on-Trent; *b.* Walsall, Oct. 1873; *m.*; one *s.* *Educ.:* Burton Grammar School. M.P. (L.), West Leyton, 1919-22. *Recreation:* fly-fishing. *Address:* Ocean Drive, Ferring-by-Sea, Sussex. [*Died* 25 *April* 1952.

NEWCASTLE, Kathleen, Duchess of, (Kathleen Florence May), O.B.E. 1920; *d.* of late Major Henry Augustus Candy, late 9th Lancers, and Hon. Mrs. Candy, *d.* of 3rd Baron Rossmore; *m.* 1889, 7th Duke of Newcastle (*d.* 1928). *Address:* Forest Farm, Windsor Forest. [*Died* 1 *June* 1955.

NEWCOMBE, Luxmoore, C.B.E. 1944; T.D., Hon. M.A. (Durham), Hon. Litt.D. (Manchester); *b.* 12 Jan. 1880; *s.* of Henry Newcombe, Crediton, Devon; *m.* Joan, *d.* of Sidney Stigings, Torquay; one *s.* one *d.* *Educ.:* Exeter School. Librarian (formerly Sub-Librarian) University College, London, 1922-26; Assistant Director of the University of London School of Librarianship, 1919-1926; Librarian and Secretary to the Trustees, National Central Library, 1926-44; formerly Vice-Pres. and Chairman of Council, Library Assoc.; Hon. Member Assoc. of Special Libraries and Information Bureaux; late Commanding the University of London Officers' Training Corps; Commandant of the School of Instruction for Officer Cadets, Perivale, Aug. 1914-March 1915; 4th Battalion (T.F.) The Green Howards, 1915-19; Brevet Colonel, 1931. *Publications:* The University and College Libraries of Great Britain and Ireland; Library Co-operation in the British Isles; contributed special chapters to books on librarianship, and articles to many professional and other journals. *Recreations:* architecture and walking. *Address:* 96 Avenue Road, Torquay. [*Died* 25 *May* 1952.

NEWCOMBE, Col. Stewart Francis, D.S.O. 1916; late Royal Engineers; interested in Arab affairs and in heating of buildings; *b.* 1878; *s.* of Edward Newcombe, M.I.C.E.; *m.* 1919, Elsie, 2nd *d.* of late M. and Mme. Chaki, of Nice; one *s.* one *d.* *Educ.:* Christ's Hospital; Felsted; Woolwich. Served South African War, 1899-1900 (Queen's medal and four clasps); Egyptian Army, 1901-11; European War, 1914-18, France, Gallipoli, Hejaz (despatches, D.S.O., Bt. Lt.-Col., foreign orders); escaped prisoner of war from Turkey; Chief Engineer, Malta, 1929-32; retired pay, 1932; late Hon. Sec. Royal Central Asian Society. *Publications:* Heat Insulation for Buildings (Journ. of R.I.B.A., Aug. 1944), etc. *Address:* 300 Woodstock Road, Oxford. *T.:* 58854. *Club:* United Service. [*Died* 18 *July* 1956.

NEWHAM, Lieut.-Col. Hugh Basil Greaves, C.M.G. 1919; M.D.; M.R.C.P., D.P.H.; (retired); late R.A.M.C.; late Curator of Museum and Warden of Studies, London School of Hygiene and Tropical Medicine; late Capt. in Home Guard (2nd Bn. Suffolk Regt.); *b.* 1874; *s.* of late Thomas Newham, M.D., Winslow, Bucks; *m.* 1st, 1900, Genevieve (*d.* 1932), *d.* of late James Byrne; 2nd, 1937, Nora Mary, *widow* of Douglas Mungo-Park. Served East Africa as Consultant in Tropical Diseases to the Forces, 1914-18 (C.M.G.). *Address:* Windrush, Market Weston, Diss, Norfolk. [*Died* 11 *Nov.* 1959.

NEWILL, Ven. Edward Joseph; Archdeacon of Dorking since 1936; *b.* Admaston, Shropshire, 26 Jan. 1877; 3rd *s.* of late R. D. Newill; *m.* 1907, Edith Sabine (*d.* 1945), *o. c.* of Richard Baring-Gould; no *c.* *Educ.:* King Edward's School, Birmingham; Hertford College, Oxford. Ordained, 1901; Curate successively of St. John-at-Hackney, Guildford and St. James, Norland; Vicar of Witley, Surrey, and Rural Dean of Godalming; Vicar and Rural Dean of Dorking, Hon. Canon of Guildford. *Address:* Trevelyan, Cranley Road, Guildford. *T.:* Guildford 62746. [*Died* 24 *July* 1954.

NEWLING, (Alfred) John, C.B. 1950; C.B.E. 1944; M.V.O. 1933; T.D. 1935; Under-Secretary, Ministry of Defence, since 1946; *b.* 11 Jan. 1896; 2nd *s.* of late J. A. Newling, Nottingham; *m.* 1955, Mrs. E. D. Watt, *d.* of late Rev. Sir Montague Fowler, 4th and last Bt., and of Lady Fowler, Inverbroom Lodge, Ross-shire. *Educ.:* Nottingham High School; Latymer Upper School; Jesus Coll., Cambridge. Commissioned 11th London Regiment, 1916-. Served European War (France), 1916-19. Asst. Principal, War Office, 1921; Private Sec. to Sir Herbert Creedy (Permanent Under-Sec. of State), 1923-34; Financial Adviser (Army) to Chatfield Commission on Indian Defence, 1938-39; Joint Secretary, Army Council Secretariat, 1941-46; Director of Finance, War Office, 1946. Served War of 1939-45, Sept. 1939-Apr. 1940; commanded 12th Light A.A. Regt. R.A. (T.A.), 1938-40 (Lieut.-Colonel). *Recreations:* tennis, swimming, classical music. *Address:* North Corner, Prince Edward's Road, Lewes, Sussex. *T.:* Lewes 1642. *Club:* Junior Army and Navy. [*Died* 18 *Aug.* 1957.

NEWMAN, Albert Gordon, C.B. 1956; C.B.E. 1948; a Principal Assistant Solicitor in Department of H.M. Procurator General and Treasury Solicitor since 1951; *b.* 18 Mar. 1894; 2nd *s.* of late Albert Augustus Newman, Town Clerk of Newport, Mon., and late Sarah Jane Gertrude Evans; *m.* 1921, Enid Maynard, *e. d.* of late Alfred M. James, J.P., Newport, Mon.; one *d.* *Educ.:* Blundell's School. Gazetted to 3rd Bn. Monmouthshire Regt., 1914. Served European War, 1914-1918 (despatches): Capt. 1916; demobilized, 1919. Admitted a Solicitor, 1920, and apptd. a Junior Legal Asst. in Dept. of H.M. Procurator General and Treasury Solicitor. Private Sec. to late Sir Maurice Gwyer, 1928. Served War of 1939-45, with 3rd Bn. Monmouthshire Regt., 1939-40. Governor of St. Helen's School for Girls, Northwood, 1952-. *Recreations:* golf, gardening. *Address:* Henllys, Maxwell Road, Northwood, Middx. *T.:* Northwood 646. *Clubs:* Union; Northwood Golf. [*Died* 29 *Oct.* 1956.

NEWMAN, Sir Cecil Gustavus Jacques, 2nd Bt., *cr.* 1912; Captain, 1st Norfolk Yeomanry; *b.* London, 9 June 1891; *s.* of Sir Sigmund Neumann, 1st Bt. and Anna Allegra (*d.* 1951), *d.* of late Jacques Hakim, Alexandria; *S.* father, 1916; *m.* 1922, Joan Florence Mary, *e. d.* of late Rev. Canon Hon. Robert Grimston; two *s.* three *d.* *Educ.:* Eton; Balliol College, Oxford. J.P. Herts; High Sheriff of Herts, 1939-40. *Heir:* *s.*, Gerard Robert Henry Sigismund, *b.* 19 July 1927. *Address:* Burloes, Royston, Herts. *T.:* 2150. *Club:* Boodle's. [*Died* 21 *May* 1955.

NEWMAN, Major-General Charles Richard, C.B. 1929; C.M.G. 1918; D.S.O. 1916; late R.A.; formerly D.L., Devonshire; *b.* 1875; *s.* of Major C. C. Newman, 14th Foot; *m.* 1922, Dorothy Sarah, 3rd *d.* of William Carr of Ditchingham Hall, Norfolk, J.P., D.L.; two *s.* one *d.* (and one *s.* decd.). Served N.-W. Frontier of India, 1897-98 (medal and clasp); European War, 1914-18 (despatches, C.M.G., D.S.O., Chevalier Legion of Honour, Croix de Guerre); Colonel on the Staff i/c Administration Scottish Command, 1924-28; Maj.-Gen. 1929; District Commander Madras, 1930-34; retired pay, 1934. *Address:* The Close, Barsham, Beccles, Suffolk. [*Died* 13 *Nov.* 1954.

NEWMAN, Brig.-Gen. Edward Harding-, C.B. 1929; C.M.G. 1918; D.S.O. 1915; R.A.; *b.* 30 July 1872; 2nd *s.* of B. Harding Newman of Nelmes, Essex; *m.* 1926, Violet Inez (*d.* 1948), *widow* of Col. Hubert Burton, R.A. *Educ.:* Cheltenham College. Entered army, 1893; Capt. 1900; Major, 1910; Lt.-Col. 1915; Brig. Gen. R.A., 1917-19; A.D.C. to Maj.-Gen., India; 1899-1902; Staff Capt. Irish Command, 1905-9; A.M.S. to G.O.C. Northern Command, 1911-14; served European War, 1914-18 (despatches five times, D.S.O., C.M.G., Bt. Col.); late commanding Royal Artillery, Southern Army, India; commanded R.A. Depôt and Garrison Commander, Woolwich, 1927-29; retired pay, 1929; J.P. Wilts, 1933; D.L. Wilts, 1942; High Sheriff of Wilts, 1934-35; holds Order of St. Stanislas. *Recreations:* shooting, golf. *Address:* Portway House, Warminster, Wiltshire. *T.:* Warminster 3070. *Club:* Army and Navy. [*Died* 21 *March* 1955.

NEWMAN, Ernest; Musical Critic, Sunday Times, etc., 1920-58; *b.* 30 Nov. 1868; *m.* 1st, Kate Eleanor (*d.* 1918), *d.* of H. C. Woollett; 2nd, Vera, *d.* of Arthur Hands; no *c.* *Educ.:* Liverpool Coll. and Liverpool Univ., Intended for Indian Civil Service, but health broke down; went into business in Liverpool, carrying on at same time musical and literary work; joined staff of Midland Institute, Birmingham, 1903; Musical Critic of Manchester Guardian, 1905; of Birmingham Post, 1906; resigned from latter, 1919, settling in London. Knight 1st Class, Order of White Rose of Finland, 1955; Knight Commander of the Order of Merit of the Federal Republic of Germany, 1958. *Publications:* Gluck and the Opera, 1895; A Study of Wagner, 1899; Wagner, 1904; Musical Studies, 1905; Elgar, 1906; Hugo Wolf, 1907; Richard Strauss, 1908; Wagner as Man and Artist, 1914 (revised and enlarged edition, 1924); A Musical Motley, 1919; The Piano-Player and its Music, 1920; A Musical Critic's Holiday, 1925; The Unconscious Beethoven, 1927; Fact and Fiction about Wagner, 1931; The Life of Richard Wagner, Vol. I., 1813-48, 1933; Vol. II., 1848-60, 1937; Vol. III., 1860-1866, 1945; Vol. IV, 1866-1883, 1946 (in America, 1947 in London); The Man Liszt, 1934; Opera Nights, 1943; Wagner Nights, 1949; More Opera Nights, 1954, etc.; translated: Über das Dirigieren, Weingartner; J. S. Bach, Schweitzer; Wagner's librettos for the Breitkopf and Härtel edition; Romain Rolland's Beethoven; edited The New Library of Music; From the World of Music, 1956; More Essays From the World of Music, 1958, etc. *Club:* National Liberal. [*Died* 7 *July* 1959.

NEWMAN, Colonel Richard Ernest Upton, C.B.E. 1938 (O.B.E. 1919), M.C.; retired; *b.* 18 Sept. 1883; *s.* of Richard Newman, Garryneel, Killaloe, Co. Clare, Ireland; *m.* 1922, Lucie M. Clément; two *d.* *Educ.:* Clifton College; Edinburgh Univ. M.B., Ch.B., Edin. 1905; Lt. R.A.M.C. 1906; European War, 1914-18 (O.B.E., M.C.); Bt. Lt.-Col. 1930; A.D.M.S. Waziristan, 1935-38; Ops. N.W. Frontier (Waziristan), 1936-37 (C.B.E.); A.D.M.S. West Lancs. Dist., etc., 1939-45; Mil. Govt. Det., Germany, 1945-46; retd. 1946. [*Died* 24 *Nov.* 1956.

NEWMAN, Trevor Clyde, LL.B. (Lond.); *b.* 19 Feb. 1882; *s.* of Edwin Bernard Newman and Elizabeth Ann Evans; *m.* 1910, Mary Phyllis, *d.* of Sidney W. Flamank, Richmond, Surrey; no *c.* *Educ.:* Newport (Mon.) High School; Warwick. Solicitor, 1905; Practised 1907-20; Treasury Solicitor's Department, 1920-36; Master of Supreme Court in Chancery, 1936-53; served European War, 1914-18, R.N.V.R. Anti-Aircraft Corps. *Recreations:* music, golf, gardening. *Address:* The Chantry, East Coker, Nr. Yeovil, Somerset. *T.:* West Coker 236. [*Died* 21 *April* 1955.

NEWMAN-MORRIS, Sir John, Kt., *cr.* 1948; C.M.G. 1938; M.B., B.S., F.R.A.C.S., F.A.C.S.; K.St.J.; Receiver-General, Priory of St. John in Australia; Cons. Surgeon, St. Vincent's Hospital, Melbourne; National Council Australian Red Cross Society; Pres. Medical Board of Victoria; Member of Council of Australian Flying Doctor Service (1st President, 1936-38); of Council of the University of Melbourne; of Executive of the Lord Mayor's Fund; President, Old People's Welfare Council; Vice-Pres. Victorian Soc. for Crippled Children; President Medical Defence Assoc.; Chm. Brit. Med. Ince. Co.; Chm. Automobile Fire & Gen. Insce. Co.; Trustee Med. Soc. of Victoria; Council of British Medical Association (Chairman for 17 years); Vice-Pres., Royal Empire Society (Pres. Victorian Branch); *b.* Melbourne, 2 March 1879; *s.* of W. A. Morris, Gloucs.; *m.* 1905, Eleanor (*d.* 1949), *e. d.* of William Jones, Melbourne; one *s.* one *d.* *Educ.:* Hawthorn College; Queen's College, University of Melbourne. Red Cross Mission to Britain, Canada, and U.S., 1942-43; Meeting of Board of Governors of League at Oxford and International Conference at Geneva, 1946. A Vice-Pres. of 17th Internat. Red Cross Conf. at Stockholm and Vice-Chm. of its General Commission in Aug. 1948; Pres. 8th Session Austr. Med. Congress, 1952; during War of 1939-45, Member Central Medical Co-ordination Cttee. and of Commonwealth Alien Doctors' Board (Nat. Security Regulations). Jubilee Medal, 1935; Coronation Medal, 1937 and 1953. *Publications:* Mackay Oration, Canberra, 1940; Stawell Oration, Melbourne, 1945; papers in Medical Journals. *Recreation:* gardening. *Address:* 46 Heyington Place, Toorak, S.E.2., Victoria, Australia. *Club:* Melbourne (Melbourne).

[*Died* 3 *Jan.* 1957.

NEWNES, Sir Frank Hillyard, 2nd Bt., *cr.* 1895; C.B.E. 1954; *b.* 28 Sep. 1876; *e. s.* of 1st Bt. and Priscilla, *d.* of Rev. J. Hillyard; *S.* father, 1910; *m.* 1st, 1913, Emmeline Augusta Louisa (Lena) (Lady of Grace of the Order of St. John of Jerusalem; *d.* 1939), *d.* of late Sir Albert de Rutzen; 2nd, 1946, Dorothy, *d.* of Everard Firebrace Darlot, Perth, W. Australia, and *widow* of Stephen Delmar-Morgan. *Educ.:* privately; Clare College, Cambridge; M.A., LL.B. On leaving university entered publishing business of George Newnes Ltd., of which he is President; also Chairman of Country Life, Ltd., Director C. A. Pearson, Ltd., Newnes and Pearson Printing Co. Ltd.; Director Westminster Gazette, Ltd., 1908-21; Director: Norwich Union Fire Insurance Society and Norwich Union Life Insurance Society (London Boards); 1st, 2nd, 3rd & 4th City & Commercial Investment Trusts Ltd. and Redeemable Securities Trust Ltd.; Chairman of Associated Weavers, Ltd. and Armoride Ltd.; Member of Committee of the Royal Free Hospital and Member of the Council of the Royal Free Hospital School of Medicine; Chairman of Committee of the Post-Graduate Institute of Dental Surgery; Eastman Dental Hosp.; Pres. Printers Pension Corp., 1948-1949; Vice-Pres. Periodical Proprietors Assoc., National Liberal Council. Called to Bar, 1899; M.P. (L.) Bassetlaw, Notts, 1906-10; Sub-Lt. R.N.V.R., April 1915; Capt. 12th Beds. Regt., Feb. 1917; C.St.J. *Heir:* none. *Recreation:* golf. *Address:* 66 Cadogan Square, S.W.1. *T.:* Kensington 1500. *Clubs:* Reform, Garrick; Walton Heath Golf (Hon. Mem.); Royal and Ancient Golf (St. Andrews).

[*Died* 10 *July* 1955 (*ext.*).

NEWTON, 3rd Baron, *cr.* 1892; **Richard William Davenport Legh,** T.D.; D.L., J.P.; *b.* 18 Nov. 1888; *e. s.* of 2nd Baron Newton and Evelyn (*d.* 1931), *d.* of late W. Bromley-Davenport; *S.* father, 1942; *m.* 1914, Hon. Helen Meysey-Thompson (*d.* 1958), 2nd *d.* of 1st Baron Knaresborough; two *s.* (and one *s.* decd.). *Educ.:* Eton; Oxford. Hon. Attaché, Embassy, Constantinople, 1911-13; Vienna, 1913-14; resigned, 1914; Lancashire Hussars (Yeomanry), 1910-1919 (despatches); Hon. Col. 7th Bn. The Cheshire Regt., 1939-50. *Heir:* *s.* Hon. Peter Richard Legh, M.P. *Address:* Timsbury Manor, Romsey, Hants. *T.:* Braishfield 314. *Clubs:* St. James', Turf.

[*Died* 11 *June* 1960.

NEWTON, George Percival, C.B.E. 1933; *b.* 23 June 1868; *s.* of Hibbert Newton, Barrister-at-law, and Catherine Elizabeth Liddiard; *m.* 1892, Marie Dupin; no *c.* *Educ.:* State School, and All Saints Grammar School. Had some experience in Banking in Victoria, and later went to New Zealand and entered the Public Service of that country becoming Under-Secretary of the Department of Internal Affairs, retiring from that position, 1931. *Recreations:* cricket football, some tennis, keen angler. *Address:* 24 Tollington Avenue, East Malvern, S.E.5, Victoria, Australia. *T.:* U 2505.

[*Died* 22 *July* 1951.

NEWTON, Sir Harry Kottingham, 2nd Bt., *cr.* 1900; O.B.E. 1919; Barrister-at-Law; M.A. (Oxon.); one of His Majesty's Lieutenants for the city of London; *s.* of Sir Alfred James Newton, 1st Bart., and E. Jane (Lily) (*d.* 1945), *e. d.* of Joseph Watson of Mill-house, Mitcham Common; *b.* 2 April 1875; *S.* father, 1921; *m.* 1920, Myrtle Irene, *e. d.* of Mr. and Mrs. Grantham, Balneath Manor, Lewes; two *s.* (*e. s.* killed in action 8 Feb. 1944). *Educ.:* Rugby; New College, Oxford. Captain School XV. at Rugby; Acting Hon. Secretary for the C.I.V. Regiment for service in South Africa; as Hon. Secretary Equipment Committee accompanied the Regiment to South Africa; contested Harwich Division of Essex, 1906; M.P. (C.) Harwich Division of Essex, Jan. 1910-Nov. 1922; has studied the principles and practice of small ownership and agricultural co-operation in Denmark, etc.; temp. Major A.S.C. 1914; Deputy Assistant Director Supply and Transport; Pl. Comdr. (Lieut.) Home Guard, 1941. *Publications:* descriptive articles and political essays. *Recreation:* yachting. *Heir:* *s.* Harry Michael Rex, *b.* 7 Feb. 1923. *Address:* Westfield Place, Sussex. *T.:* Seddlescombe 237. *Clubs:* Junior Carlton, Royal London Yacht.

[*Died* 22 *June* 1951.

NEWTON, Lieut.-Colonel Henry, C.B.E. 1920; D.S.O. 1916; T.D.; late 5th Sherwood Foresters (Notts and Derby Regiment) T.F.; *b.* 24 Feb. 1880; *s.* of Thomas Newton; *m.* 1917, Beryl Bertha, *d.* of Ernest Augustus Barford; one *s.* two *d.* *Educ.:* Derby School. Commission in the 5th Notts and Derbyshire Regiment T.F. 1902; served European War (France) 1914-17 (D.S.O.). Commanded an Infantry company 5th Notts. and Derby Regt. T.F. 1912-15; Officer Commanding II. Army R.E. workshops, 1915-17; Member of Trench Warfare Committee; Deputy Controller, Trench Warfare Department; chief of design Mechanical Traction Department, 1917-19; inventor of Nos. 107 and 110 Fuses (the first wire-cutting fuses ever used by British troops), Newton 6″ Trench Mortar, Newton Trench Mortar bomb, Newton Pippin rifle and hand grenades, ring charge (which employed with all British mortars reduced prematures and more than doubled their ranges), Newton Universal Military Tractor, among other devices, whilst serving with Infantry Royal Engineers and Artillery services. Placed at head of U.S.A. list of British war inventors with an award of 100,000 dollars. *Recreation:* horticulture. *Address:* Little Eaton, Derbyshire. *T.A.:* Little Eaton, Derbyshire. *T.:* Horsley 274.

[*Died* 20 *June* 1959.

NEWTON, Robert; actor; *b.* Shaftesbury, Dorset, 1 June 1905; *s.* of Algernon Newton, R.A. *Educ.:* Newbury Grammar School; Switzerland. Stage: Birmingham Repertory Theatre, 1920-23; toured S. Africa, 1923-24; London Life, Drury Lane, 1924; George Bristow in the Ring o' Bells, comedy, 1925; toured provinces for 3 years; Jacko Blaker in My Lady's Mill, Lyric, 1928; Paul Guisard in Her Cardboard Lover, 1928; John Murray and the Regent in Byron, 1929; Hugh Devon in Bitter Sweet, His Majesty's, 1929; succeeded Laurence Olivier as Victor Prynne in Private Lives, Times Square Theatre, N.Y., 1931; Mort in I Lived With You, Prince of Wales's, 1932; Jesse Redvers in the Secret Woman, Duchess, 1932; ran Grand Theatre as Shilling Theatre for 2 years; Patrick O'Leary in Once Upon a Time, Little Theatre, 1934; Boris in The Greeks Had a Word For It, Duke of York's, 1934; Jean in Miss Julie, Arts, 1935; Mark Gresham in Roulette, Duke of York's, 1935; Renny in

Whiteoaks, Little Theatre, 1936; toured in Saturday's Children; Horatio in Hamlet, Old Vic., 1937; Slim Grisson in No Orchids for Miss Blandish, Prince of Wales's, 1942; Randy Jollifer in So Brief the Spring, Wimbledon Theatre, 1946; in Gaslight, Vaudeville, 1950; Films: Major Barbara, 1940; Hatters Castle, 1941; They Flew Alone, 1941; This Happy Breed, Henry V, 1943; Night Boat to Dublin, 1945; Odd Man Out, 1946; Temptation Harbour, 1946; Snowbound, 1947; Oliver Twist, 1947; Obsession, 1949; Treasure Island, 1950; Waterfront, 1950; Tom Brown's Schooldays, 1951; Androcles and the Lion, 1951; Les Misérables, 1952; The Desert Rats, 1953; The Beachcomber, 1954; Long John Silver, 1954. *Recreations:* fishing and shooting. [*Died* 25 *March* 1956.

NEWTON, Sir Wilberforce (Stephen), Kt., *cr.* 1950; F.R.A.C.P. 1937; M.D. Melb. 1920; M.B., B.S., Melb. 1915; Physician to In-Patients, Alfred Hospital, Melbourne, Australia, 1933-48; Consultant Physician since 1948; *b.* 1890; *m.* 1926, Margaret W., *d.* of late Dr. W. Macansh; four *s.* Served European War, 1914-18, R.A.M.C. Med. Supt. Alfred Hosp., 1918-19; Med. Clin. Asst. to Out-Patients, 1920-21, Physician to Out-Patients, 1923-33; Stewart Lecturer in Med., Univ. of Melbourne, 1945-48; Member Board of Management Alfred Hosp., 1937-; Member Council Royal Australasian College of Physicians, 1944-54 (Vice-Pres., 1950-52); Member: British Medical Association; Consultant Physician to Royal Australian Navy; Special Tuberculosis Board, Repatriation Dept. *Publications:* contrib. on medical subjects to Austn. Med. Jl. and Austn. Jl. of Surgery. *Address:* 14 Parliament Place, Melbourne, C.2; 375 Glenferrie Road, Malvern, Vic., Australia. *Clubs:* Melbourne, Royal Melbourne Golf, Melbourne Cricket, Victorian Racing (Melbourne). [*Died* 4 *Oct.* 1956.

NEWTON, William James Oliver, C.B.E. 1941; formerly Chief Officer, Restaurants and Catering and Public Control Departments, L.C.C.; *b.* 24 Apr. 1884; *e. s.* of William Edward Newton; *m.* 1909, Charlotte, *d.* of Frank A. Davies, of Woolwich Arsenal. *Educ.:* Colfe's Grammar School, Lewisham. Formerly Assistant Education Officer, L.C.C.; served R.F.C. and R.A.F. (Captain) European War, 1914-18. *Address:* Bristol Court, Brighton. *Club:* Devonshire. [*Died* 14 *March* 1952.

NICHOLL, Air Vice-Marshal Sir Hazelton Robson, K.B.E., *cr.* 1942 (C.B.E. 1928); C.B. 1938; M.Inst.T.; *b.* Calcutta, 14 Jan. 1882; *s.* of William Nicholl, F.R.A.M.; *m.* 1st, Lulu Evans (*d.* 1925); 2nd, 1938, Lorna Margaret, *d.* of late Harry T. Henderson. *Educ.:* St. George's School, Ascot. Served in London Scottish Volunteers 1899-1902; S. Rhodesia Volunteers (Mounted), 1903-04; learned to fly at Brooklands, 1915; joined Royal Flying Corps, 1915; served in France, No. 8 Squadron, R.F.C., 1915; attached No. 6 Squadron, R.F.C., 1917; Commanding 110 Squadron, 1918 (Legion of Honour, despatches, O.B.E.); Permanent Commission, Royal Air Force, 1919; served in Iraq in Command of 70 Squadron, R.A.F., 1926-28 (C.B.E.); Deputy Director of Personal Services Air Ministry, 1929-30; Deputy Director of Manning, 1931-32; comdg. R.A.F. Base, Calshot, 1932-33, No. 23 Group, Grantham, 1933-34; Air Commodore, 1933; Commanded Central Area, R.A.F. 1934-1935; Member of Air Board of Royal Australian Air Force, 1935-37; Air Officer Commanding Royal Air Force, Middle East, 1938; Air Officer in Charge of Administration Fighter Command, 1939-42; retired, 1942; Controller of R.A.F. Benevolent Fund, 1944-47. *Address:* Minard Farm, Minard, Argyll. *Clubs:* R.A.F.; Roy. Northern Yacht. [*Died* 14 *Aug.* 1956.

NICHOLL, John Storer, C.B.E. 1939; Transport Consultant; *b.* 6 Sept. 1888; *s.* of late William Nicholl, F.R.A.M.; *m.* 1913, Constance Cornforth; one *d.* *Educ.:* Sutton Valence. Union Castle Line Head Office, 1904; subsequently served in Western Canada for a short time as office manager to Chief Engineer, Hudson Bay and Pacific Railway; qualified as Chartered Accountant and practised in Saskatchewan and Alberta; during 1914 war served with Imperial Munitions Board, Ottawa, eventually as Deputy Auditor and Controller; in 1920 joined McNamara & Co. as Chief Accountant; in 1921 joined the firm of Maxwell Hicks & Co., Chartered Accountants and Commercial Managers of McNamaras, of which firm he was a partner, being Vice-Chm. and Chief Executive Officer when McNamara was acquired by B.T.C. in 1948. Pres., Inst. of Transport, 1941-43; Member Canadian Institute of Chartered Accountants; Member Transport Advisory Council, 1934-43; National Joint Conciliation Board for Road Motor Transport Industry, 1934-1937; McLintock Committee of Enquiry into Public Transport System in Northern Ireland, 1938; Vice-President Commercial Motor Users Association; Member Road Transport Defence Advisory Committee, Road Haulage (Operations) Advisory Committee (Ministry of Transport); Committee on Emergency Conversion of Motor Vehicles to Producer Gas and Committee on Alternative Fuels for Internal Combustion Engines (Ministry of Mines); National Civil Aviation Consultative Council, 1947; formerly Chief Officer (Research and charges) Road Transport Executive; for a number of years Chairman Highways Transport Sub-Cttee. of British National Cttee. of International Chamber of Commerce; awarded Institute of Transport (Road Transport) Gold Medal, 1934. F.R.S.A. *Publications:* Papers on road transport matters. *Address:* 20 Park Avenue, Hove, Sussex. [*Died* 27 *Dec.* 1958.

NICHOLLS, Agnes; *see* Harty, Lady.

NICHOLLS, Frederick; *b.* Birmingham, 8 Jan. 1871; *m.* 1st, 1900, Catherine M. (*d.* 1924), *d.* of Thomas Cormack, Cellardyke, Fife; one *s.*; 2nd, 1929, Margaret A., *d.* of W. Johnston, Liverpool. Studied with Dr. R. W. Crowe of Liverpool; afterwards with Herr Krausse of Liverpool; subsequently alone; settled as a teacher of piano and composition in Liverpool, 1891; known as a composer chiefly of songs and piano music. *Publications:* Songs—Lyric Tone Poems, 1908; English Song-poems, 1910; Third Album, 1920; Five Songs from a Child's Garden of Verses, 1910; Songs in Sun and Shade; The Quest; Ariel's Songs; Love Songs of Tennyson; Eldorado, 1938; Piano—Fairy Gold; Carillon; Autumn Song; Whispering Leaves; Toccata; Water Colours; April Melody; Impressions and Arabesques; A Fairy Story; Whimsical Waltzes, 1927; Waltz Curios, 1928; Album of Miniatures, 1930; Homage to Brahms, Sonata for two pianos, 1934; Literature—The Language of Music, 1924; The Technique of the Piano Pedals; Adventures in Improvisation (with J. R. Tobin), 1938; miscellaneous articles on Harmony, Musical Form, etc. *Address:* 279 Brodie Avenue, Liverpool, 19. *T.:* Garston 4497. [*Died* 31 *Oct.* 1952.

NICHOLLS, Senator Rt. Hon. George Heaton, P.C. 1948; *b.* 1876; *m.* 1911, Ruby, *d.* of Capt. Hitchins, Durban; one *s.* two *d.* *Educ.:* Rotherham. Served in British Army in India; Burma and Tira Campaigns. Came to South Africa from Ceylon during South African War. District Commissioner, North-Western Rhodesia; Magistrate for Territory of Papua (New Guinea). Returned South Africa to engage sugar farming at Umfolozi. Elected to Union Parliament for the Zululand constituency in 1920. Leader of Natal Parliamentary Group during its existence. Senator 1939 and 1948-. Member: Indian Round Table

Conf., Cape Town; Indian Colonization Commission; permanent Native Affairs Commission; Administrator, Natal, 1942-1944; High Commissioner for Union of South Africa in London, 1944-47. Head S. African Deleg. to Prep. Conf. and Assembly U.N., London, 1946; Deleg. U.N. Assembly, New York; S. African Rep. at inaug. Dominion Parl., Ceylon, 1948 *Publications:* Bayete!; numerous pamphlets. *Address:* Mtubatuba, Zululand.
[*Died* 25 *Sept.* 1959.

NICHOLLS, Surgeon Vice-Admiral Sir Percival Thomas, K.C.B., *cr.* 1939 (C.B. 1934); F.R.C.S. Eng. 1940; *b.* 8 May 1877; *s.* of Harry and Ellen Nicholls; *m.* 1905, Hilda Boys Curry; two *d.* *Educ.:* Middlesex Hospital. House Physician Middlesex Hospital; entered Naval Medical Service, 1901; Order of Crown of Italy for services Messina earthquake, 1907; Staff Surgeon, 1909; served European War, 1914-18 (3 war medals); Fleet Surgeon, 1915; Surgeon Captain, 1926; P.M.O. R.N. Barracks, Portsmouth, 1927-29; Senior Medical Officer Medical Section R.N. Hospital, Haslar, 1929-32; Surgeon Rear-Admiral, 1932; Medical Officer in charge Royal Naval Hospital, Malta; Hon. Physician to King George VI, 1935-52; Surgeon Vice-Adm. 1937; Medical Director-General of the Navy, 1937-41; retired 1941; Medical Officer-in-Charge R.N. Auxiliary Hospital, Kilmacolm, 1942-46; retired, 1946; Commander (Brother) of Venerable Order of the Hospital of St. John of Jerusalem, 1937. *Recreations:* golf, tennis. *Address:* 10 King Street, Emsworth, Hants.
[*Died* 1 *March* 1959.

NICHOLLS, Colonel Stephen Charles Phillips, C.B.E. 1937; D.S.O. 1918; *b.* 17 July 1883; served European War, 1915-18 (despatches twice, D.S.O., two medals); O.C., Southern Command, New Zealand, 1931-37. *Address:* 49 Weston Road, Christchurch, New Zealand.
[*Died* 7 *July* 1959.

NICHOLS, Arthur Eastwood, C.B.E. 1948; M.C. 1918; Secretary, Headmasters' Conference and the Incorporated Association of Headmasters since 1955; *b.* 17 March 1891; *s.* of Rev. W. B. Nichols; *m.* 1918, Hilda Wyatt; one *s.* *Educ.:* Lady Hawkins School, Kington, Herefordshire; London University. B.A. 1913; M.A. 1923. Asst. Master, Harvey Grammar School, Folkestone, 1914-15; Asst. Master, Exeter School, Exeter, 1919-25; Headmaster, Kingston High School, Hull, 1925-28; Headmaster, Hele's School, Exeter, 1928-55. *Publications:* Report on Secondary Education in Mauritius, 1947; Report on Secondary Education in Sierra Leone, 1950; Editor of Review of the Incorporated Association of Headmasters; Assistant Editor of the Public Schools Year Book; editor of numerous memoranda on educational subjects. *Recreations:* local history, music, literature, travel, golf. *Address:* (Home) Adhurst St. Mary, Petersfield, Hants. *T.:* Petersfield 1053; (Business) 29 Gordon Square, W.C.1. *T.:* Euston 4995. *Club:* English-Speaking Union.
[*Died* 29 *June* 1959.

NICHOLS, Herbert John, C.I.E. 1947; D.Sc. (Lond.); M.Inst.C.E.; M.I.Mech.E., etc.; Member, Engineering Railway Board, Ministry of Railways, New Delhi, India, since 1945; *b.* 1 June 1895; 2nd *s.* of A. E. Nichols, M.Inst.C.E.; *m.* 1935, Helen Phyllis, *d.* of late Maj.-Gen. Sir Henry Freeland, K.C.I.E., C.B.; one *s.* *Educ.:* London University. Served European War, 1914-19, Mesopotamia and India, R.F.A. (T.), Indian Army. Joined Indian Rlys. as Asst. Engineer, 1920; B.B. & C.I. Rly.; Bridge Engineer, 1924-42; Dep. Gen. Manager, 1943; General Manager, 1944. *Publications:* numerous contributions on structural engineering to Technical Journals. *Recreations:* shooting, sailing, golf. *Address:* Railway Board, Secretariat of New Delhi, India. *T.:* New Delhi 2282. *Clubs:* Royal Bombay Yacht; New Delhi Gymkhana.
[*Died* 20 *Aug.* 1959.

NICHOLS, Joseph Cowie, C.B.E. 1918; sheep farmer; *b.* Launceston, Tasmania; *s.* of Charles Nichols, of Dalgety & Co.; *m.* Helen Hunter, *d.* of R. M. Ayre, Benduck Station, Hay, N.S.W.; one *s.* one *d.* *Educ.:* Otago Boys' High School; Christ's College, Christchurch; Jesus Coll., Cambridge. Sheep farming, N.S.W. and New Zealand; Volunteer Cadets and B. Battery; Lieut. North Otago Hussars, 1886; Capt. North Otago Mounted Rifles, 1900; Lt.-Col. Comd. 1st Regiment, Otago Mounted Rifles, 1903; V.D.: Col. Comd. Otago Mounted Rifles Brigade, 1911; A.D.C. to Governor-General; Senior Officer Territorial Force, 26 Jan. 1914; Commanding Otago Military District, Aug. 1914-Aug. 1919; Military Authority for Otago during the War (C.B.E.); Col., retired list, N.Z. Forces. *Address:* Kuriheka, Maheno, Otago, N.Z. *Club:* Otago.
[*Died* 27 *July* 1954.

NICHOLSON, Bt. Col. Arthur Falkner, C.B.E. 1936; T.D.; Chairman Brough, Nicholson and Hall, Ltd.; *b.* 9 June 1885; *er. s.* of late Sir Arthur Nicholson; *m.* 1918, Gwendolene Mary, (marriage dissolved, 1950), *e. d.* of A. E. Evans, Southport; *m.* 1950, Muriel Maxwell, *e. d.* of late Hugh Brown and of Mrs. Brown. *Educ.:* Oxford Preparatory School; Rugby. Served European War, 1914-18; served Territorial Army from 1908; commanded 61st (N.M.) Bde. R.A., T.A.; received T.D. for long service; High Sheriff of Staffordshire, 1924-25; Chairman Leek Urban District Council, 1926 and 1927; Brevet Colonel, 1928; transferred to Territorial Army Reserve, 1929; D.L. Staffordshire. *Recreations:* shooting, farming. *Address:* Bletchinglye Farm, Rotherfield, Sussex. *T.:* Rotherfield 459.
[*Died* 2 *Aug.* 1954.

NICHOLSON, Captain Bertram William Lothian, C.B.E. 1945; D.S.O. 1917; R.N. Retired; *b.* 3 June 1879; *s.* of Gen. Sir Lothian Nicholson and Hon. Lady Nicholson, *d.* of 1st Baron Romilly; *m.* 1915, Evelyn, 5th *d.* of Maj.-Gen. Montague Browne, Col. Royal Scots Greys. *Educ.:* H.M.S. Britannia, Dartmouth. Entered Britannia, 1893; served European War, 1914-18 (despatches, D.S.O.); Capt. 1919; retd. under reduction scheme, 1922. Joined Colonial Service, 1925; Kenya Education Dept.; Headmaster Nairobi School, 1925-31, Prince of Wales School, 1931-37. Recalled to R.N. Service at outbreak of War of 1939-45; comd. Armed Merchant Cruisers, 1939-41; Commodore, Ocean Convoys, 1941-45 (despatches). *Address:* Tiphams, Ockley, nr. Dorking, Surrey. *T.:* Capel 2219. *Club:* Lansdowne.
[*Died* 21 *Oct.* 1958.

NICHOLSON, Charles Ernest, O.B.E. 1949; M.I.N.A., 1901; R.D.I., 1944; First Hon. Freeman Borough of Gosport, 1934; Chairman, Camper & Nicholson's Ltd., Yacht Builders, Gosport and Southampton; *b.* 12 May 1868; 3rd *s.* of late Benjamin Nicholson, J.P.; *m.* 1895, Lucy Ella Edmonds; two *s.* two *d.* *Educ.:* Mill Hill; Brussels. Yacht design and building since 1885; designed 4 America's Cup Challengers: Shamrock IV, 1914; Shamrock V, 1930; Endeavour, 1934 and Endeavour II, 1937. Shamrock IV and Endeavour were the only challengers ever to win two races in series of five since 1851. Designed first two Diesel-engined yachts. 1914; both on war service, European War, 1914-18; designed Philante 1629 tons, 1937, largest motor yacht built in Great Britain, converted in 1948 to Norge, Norway's Royal Yacht; 12,000 tons of yachts of his design were on war service, War of 1939-45. Member (Hon. Mem. Council) Yacht Racing Assoc., 1945-; Liveryman Worshipful Co. of Shipwrights, 1936. *Recreations:* yachting and fishing. *Address:* Faringdon, Hill Head,

Hants. *T.:* Stubbingdon 2. *Clubs:* Royal Thames and nine other yacht clubs. [*Died* 27 *Feb.* 1954.

NICHOLSON, Lieut.-Colonel Edmund James Houghton, C.M.G. 1918; D.S.O. 1917; V.D., *b.* 1870; *s.* of Lt.-Colonel J. S. Nicholson; *m.* 1896, Anna Beatrice, *d.* of J. N. Taylor. Served European War, 1914-18 (wounded twice, despatches five times, D.S.O., C.M.G., 4th class Order of Karageorge of Serbia). *Address:* Glen Road, Darlington, West Australia. [*Died* 22 *June* 1955.

NICHOLSON, Commander Edward Hugh Meredith, D.S.O. 1898; R.N.; a Director of W. N. Nicholson & Sons, Ltd., Newark; *b.* 3 Sept. 1876; *e. s.* of Colonel E. H. Nicholson, Newark-on-Trent, Notts, and Sarah, *d.* of J. Prior, late of Shipton Manor, Shipton-on-Cherwell; *m.* 1904, Ethel, *o. d.* of R. L. Lambart; one *d.* *Educ.:* Eastmans, Stubbington, Fareham. Joined Britannia, 1890; served in Royal Sovereign, 1892-1893; Raleigh, 1893-94; St. George, 1894-96; R.N. College, 1896-97; Haughty, 1897; Hazard, 1897-99; Excellent, 1900-1, for gunnery course, Cambridge, 1902; Australia, 1902; Venus, 1903; Bulwark, 1904; midshipman Raleigh; served in Naval Brigade with Admiral Bedford at Bathurst, River Gambia, West Coast of Africa, February 1894; for the punishment of Fodi Silah, slave-raiding chief (African medal, Gambia, 1894, clasp); midshipman St. George, served with punitive expedition against King Koko of Nimbi, Brass River, West Coast of Africa, Feb. 1895 (Brass River, 1895, clasp); served with Naval Brigade under Admiral Rawson, C.B., at Mombasa, for the punishment of Mbaruk, an Arab chief; at the capture of Mwele, 17 Aug. 1895 (M'wele, 1895, engraved on General African medal); Sub-Lieut. Hazard, in command of company blue-jackets and marines, landed at Candia, 6 Sept. 1898, for the protection of the Dime Office and the quelling of disturbance (D.S.O.). *Address:* Green Lea, 73 Brook House Hill, Fulwood, Sheffield. *T.:* Sheffield 31535. *Club:* United Service. [*Died* 25 *Feb.* 1956.

NICHOLSON, Maj.-Gen. Francis Lothian, C.B. 1935; D.S.O. 1918; M.C.; Indian Army, retired; *b.* 1884; *s.* of late General Sir Lothian Nicholson, K.C.B; *m.* 1st, 1922, Dora Mary Loraine (*d.* 1923), *d.* of late Rear-Admiral the Hon. Walter Stopford; 2nd, 1927, Gwenllian, *d.* of late F. C. Faulkner, M.A.; two *d.* Served Mesopotamia, 1915-18 (despatches, D.S.O., M.C.); Afghanistan, 1919; Director of Personal Services, Army Headquarters, India, 1934-36; A.D.C. to the King, 1935-36; D.A. & Q.M.G. Eastern Command, India, 1937-38; Commander Lucknow District, 1938-41; retired, 1941. *Address:* c/o Lloyds Bank, 6 Pall Mall, S.W.1. [*Died* 18 *July* 1953.

NICHOLSON, Sir Frank, Kt., *cr.* 1943; C.B.E. 1937; D.L. Co. Durham, 1939; Chartered Accountant; Director of Brewery Companies; *b.* 1875; *s.* of Henry Nicholson, Sunderland, and The Butts, Stanhope; *m.* 1900, Amy (*d.* 1949), *d.* of John Storey Vaux, West Elms, Sunderland; one *s.* two *d.* *Educ.:* Privately. Chm. Durham County Agricultural Executive Cttee.; Chm. River Wear Commission; Chm. Agricultural Wages Board, Durham County; Vice-President, Brewers' Society; was for 24 years Chairman of Finance Committee, Sunderland County Borough; Chairman Sunderland Employment Committee of Ministry of Labour; Chairman Sunderland and District War Pensions' Committee; High Sheriff County of Durham, 1939-1940. *Address:* Southill Hall, Chester-le-Street, Durham. *T.:* Chester-le-Street 2286. *Clubs:* Constitutional, Royal Automobile. [*Died* 28 *Dec.* 1952.

NICHOLSON, Major Hugh Blomfield, D.S.O. 1918; J.P., C.A., Sheriff, Dorset, 1926; 5th *s.* of W. Nicholson, D.L., J.P., of Basing Park, Hants; *m.* 1st, Kathleen (*d.* 1936), *d.* of U. J. Burke, of Newton Valence Manor, Hants, Lady of Grace, St. John of Jerusalem; 2nd 1940, Eileen Dorothy, *o. d.* of late Captain Frank Northey. *Educ.:* Harrow; New College, Oxford. Joined K.R.R.C. 1888; retired 1902 (Captain) served with K.R.R.C., France and Salonika Force, 1914-19 (despatches, D.S.O.). *Address:* Clan House, Sydney Road, Bathwick, Bath. *Clubs:* Army and Navy; Dorset County. [*Died* 10 *Dec.* 1957.

NICHOLSON, Sir John (Gibb), Kt. 1944; *b.* 1 Nov. 1879; *s.* of James Nicholson, Glasgow; *m.* 1911, Jessie Ada, *d.* of T. H. Forgan, Northwich; two *s.* one *d.* Original Director of Imperial Chemical Industries Ltd. on its formation in 1926 and lately Deputy Chairman. Late Chairman British Nylon Spinners Ltd., Magadi Soda Co. Ltd., Plant Protection Ltd., and Director Scottish Agricultural Industries Ltd., Canadian Industries Ltd., Imperial Chemical Industries Australasia Ltd., etc. Late Member Board of Trade Export Advisory Council. *Address:* Medstead Grange, nr. Alton, Hampshire. *T.:* Medstead 2106. *Clubs:* Caledonian, Royal Automobile. [*Died* 13 *June* 1959.

NICHOLSON, Prof. John William, F.R.S. 1917; late Fellow and Tutor of Balliol College, Oxford, and Director of Studies in Mathematics and Physics; Professor of Mathematics in the University of London, 1912-21; *e. s.* of late John William Nicholson of Highcliffe, Redcar, Yorks, and late Alice Emily, *d.* of late John Kirton, of Darlington; *m.* 1922, Dorothy Wrinch (marriage dissolved, 1938); one *d.* *Educ.:* Univ. of Manchester; Trinity Coll., Camb. M.A. (Oxf. and Camb.); D.Sc. (Lond.); M.Sc. (Manchester); F.R.A.S.; Isaac Newton Student, 1906; Smith's Prizeman, 1907; Adams Prizeman, 1913 and 1919; Past President of the Röntgen Society; past Vice-President of the Physical Society of London; Past Member of Council of the Royal Society, the Royal Astronomical Society, the London Mathematical Society, and the Société Française de Physique; Member of other scientific societies; Chairman of British Association Committee on Mathematical Tables, and Member of Committee on Radio-telegraphic Investigations; Member of Council of British Scientific Instruments Research Association; Governor of Technical Optics Department, Imperial College of Science; formerly Lecturer at Cavendish Laboratory, Cambridge, and at Queen's University, Belfast. *Publications:* Scientific Papers of S. B. McLaren (with Sir Joseph Larmor and others), 1925; Problems of Modern Science (with Professor Dendy and others), 1921; The Theory of Optics (with Sir Arthur Schuster), 1924; papers in the Proceedings and Transactions of Scientific Societies, on various subjects of Mathematics, Physics, and Astronomy. *Recreations:* formerly mountaineering, golf, entomology, gardening. *Address:* c/o Balliol College, Oxford. [*Died* 10 *Oct.* 1955.

NICHOLSON, Lieut.-Colonel Mark Alleyne, C.I.E. 1941; Indian Medical Service (retired); *b.* 10 June 1885; *s.* of Brigade Surgeon Lt.-Col. F. C. Nicholson, I.M.S.; *m.* 1912, Anne, *d.* of Thomas Robinson, Danby, Yorks; one *s.* *Educ.:* Dulwich College; London Hospital. M.R.C.S., L.R.C.P., 1909; M.B., B.S. Lond., 1927; D.P.H. Lond., 1928; entered I.M.S., 1909; M.O., 6th Jats, 2/8 Ghurkas, and Laurence Military School, Sanawar; served European War, 1914-18; M.O., 22 Cav., Mesopotamia (wounded, despatches); Civil Surgeon, Mosul; entered Political Dept., 1922; M.O., Kurram and South Waziristan Militia; Residency Surgeon, Bushire; Civil Surgeon, Hazara and Ajmer; Chief Medical Officer, Central India, and Residency Surgeon, Indore. *Recreations:* fishing, shooting. *Address:* c/o Grindlay's Bank Ltd., 54 Parliament Street, S.W.1. *Club:* East India and Sports. [*Died* 4 *Jan.* 1952.

NICKERSON, Major-General William Henry Snyder, V.C.; C.B. 1919; C.M.G. 1916; late R.A.M.C.; *b.* 27 Mar. 1875; *s.* of Rev. D. Nickerson, Chaplain H.M. Forces (retired); *m.* 1919, Nan, *d.* of T. W. Waller, Baynard's Park, near Horsham; one *s.* one *d.* *Educ.:* Portsmouth Grammar School; graduated M.B., Ch.B. (Vict.), 1896, at Owens Coll., Manchester. Entered R.A.M.C. 1898; served S. Africa, 1899-1902 (despatches, promoted Captain, V.C.); European War, 1914-18 (despatches six times, C.M.G., Bt. Col., C.B.); Hon. Surgeon to the King, 1925-1933; Director of Medical Services in India, 1929-33; retired pay, 1933; Col. Comdt. R.A.M.C., 1933-45; served in an Atlantic Convoy, 1940; Port of London Authority River Emergency Service, 1941; Home Guard 1941 to end of war. *Address:* Cour, Kintyre, Argyllshire. *Club:* Naval and Military. [*Died* 10 *April* 1954.

NICOL, Jacob, Q.C. 1909; B.A., LL.M., D.C.L., LL.D.; M.L.C., 1929; late Minister without Portfolio and Leader of the Legislative Council; Treasurer, Province of Quebec, 1921-1929; President of the Legislative Council, 1930-35; Senator of Canada since 1944; Canadian birth and parentage; *s.* of Philippe Nicol and Sophie Cloutier; *m.* Emilie Couture; no *c.* *Educ.:* Feller Institute, Quebec; MacMaster University, Toronto; Laval University, Quebec. Practised law in Sherbrooke; head of Nicol, Lazure and Landry; founder and President of La Tribune; Pres. Stanstead and Sherbrooke Insurance Co., of Sterling Insurance Co. of Canada, and of the Missisquvi and Rouville Ins. Co.; Director, The Mutual of Commerce Fire Insurance Co., of the Wellington Fire Insurance Co., Toronto; The Mercantile Fire Insurance Co.; The General Trust of Canada; Sherbrooke Trust; Ex-Vice-Pres., La Banque Canadienne Nationale, Montreal; Pres. and Publisher: Le Soleil Ltée, Quebec, L'Evenement Ltée. Quebec; Le Nouvelliste Ltée, Three Rivers, etc.; Crown Prosecutor for fifteen years, etc. Knight of Legion of Honor, France, 1947. *Recreations:* motoring, fishing. *Address:* Sherbrooke, P.Q., Canada. *Clubs:* Reform (Montreal); Garrison (Quebec); St. George (Sherbrooke); The Hermitage (Magog). [*Died* 23 *Sept.* 1958.

NICOLAY, Colonel Bernard Underwood, C.B. 1924; *b.* 23 Dec. 1873; *s.* of late Lieut.-Col. F. W. Nicolay, 2nd P.W.O. Gurkha Rifles, of Rose Hill, Bideford, N. Devon; *m.* Alice Gertrude *d.* of late Rt. Hon. Sir E. N. C. Braddon, P.C., K.C.M.G.; (one *s.* lost on active service, H.M.S. Submarine Perseus, 1941) one *d.* *Educ.:* United Services College, Westward Ho!; R.M.C., Sandhurst. Gazetted 1st Batt. Hampshire Regt., 1894; transferred to Indian Army, 17th Bombay Infantry, 1898; to the 1/4 Gurkha Rifles, 1898; served N.-W. Frontier, India, 1897-98; China, 1900; European War, 1914-19, in Egypt and France (despatches, severely wounded); Afghanistan, 1919 (despatches); Waziristan, 1920-21 (despatches twice, Bt.-Col.); formed in 1916 the 4th Batt. 3rd Q.A.O. Gurkha Rifles, and disbanded the same, 1922; Deputy Military Secretary, A.H.Q., India, 1922-27; retired, 1928. *Address:* Birchcroft, Chobham Road, Camberley, Surrey. *Club:* United Service. [*Died* 8 *Dec.* 1960.

NICOLL, Gordon, R.I.; Free-lance artist; *y. s.* of William Ross Nicoll, Arbroath, Aberdeen; *m.* 1921, Lucy Olive Archer; one *s.* one *d.* *Educ.:* Taunton's, Southampton. Art training at Southampton Art School and Hornsey, N. London. Fellow of Royal Society of Arts, 1947. Served in London Scottish during European War, 1914-17, France, Egypt, Salonica. *Publications:* various articles of practice of water colour painting. *Recreations:* billiards, outdoor sketching, literature. *Address:* Studio Cottage, Hill Street, Totton, nr. Southampton. *T.:* Ower 298. *Club:* Savage. [*Died* 1 *Feb.* 1959.

NICOLL, Dr. Maurice; *b.* 1884; *s.* of late Sir William Robertson Nicoll; *m.* 1920, Catherine, 2nd *d.* of late Herbert Champion Jones, Mexico City, and Mrs. Champion Jones; one *d.* *Educ.:* Aldenham School; Caius College, Cambridge; St. Bartholomew's Hospital; Vienna, Berlin, Paris, Zürich. B.A., M.B., B.C., Camb., M.R.C.S. Lond.; formerly Medical Officer to Empire Hospital for Injuries to Nervous System; Lecturer in Medical Psychology to Birmingham University; Member British Psycho-Medical Society; and on editorial staff, Journal of Neurology and Psychopathology; served Gallipoli, 1915; Mesopotamia, 1916. *Publications:* Dream Psychology, 1917; The New Man, 1950; Commentaries on the Teaching of G. I. Gurdjieff and P. D. Ouspensky, 1952; Living Time, 1952. *Address:* 146 Harley Street, W.1. *T.:* Welbeck 2378. [*Died* 30 *Aug.* 1953.

NICOLSON, Sir Arthur John Frederick William, 11th Bart. of that Ilk and Lasswade, *cr.* 1629; O.B.E. 1944; Lord Lieutenant for the County of Zetland, 1948; *s.* of 10th Bt. and Annie (*d.* 1936), *d.* of late John Rutherford, Bruntsfield Place, Edinburgh; *b.* 8 June 1882; *S.* father, 1917. *Educ.:* Merchiston; Edinburgh University. Advocate, M.A., LL.B.; J.P., Zetland; Lt.-Col. i/c H.G. Bn. (O.B.E.); late Lieut. R.N.V.R. *Recreations:* shooting, fishing, golf. *Heir:* *b.* Harold Stanley, late Lieut. R.N.V.R., *b.* 22 Oct. 1883. *Address:* Brough Lodge, Fetlar, Shetland. *T.:* Fetlar 2. *Club:* Carlton. [*Died* 25 *April* 1952.

NIGHTINGALE, Sir Edward Manners, 14th Bt., *cr.* 1628; *b.* 30 Dec. 1888; *s.* of Edward Henry Nightingale, *s.* of 13th Bt. and Lily, *e. d.* of Captain Maitland Addison; *S.* grandfather, 1911; *m.* 1923, Alice Duncan, *e. d.* of late Robert Mackay Sutherland, of Solsgirth, Kinross-shire. Gazetted 1916; served in France, Germany, Egypt, and Palestine. *Heir:* *cousin* Geoffrey Slingsby, *b.* 24 Nov. 1904. *Address:* Selsfield Cottage, Turner's Hill, Sussex. *T.:* Turner's Hill 203. *Club:* Junior Carlton. [*Died* 26 *Aug.* 1953.

NIGHTINGALE, Maj.-Gen. Manners Ralph Willmot, C.B. 1923, C.M.G. 1918; C.I.E. 1920; D.S.O. 1915; Indian Army, retired; Col. of 5th Royal Gurkha Rifles, 1937-1945; *b.* Sidmouth, 15 April 1871; *s.* of Percy Nightingale, Inspecting Commissioner, Cape Civil Service; *g.-g.s.* of Sir Charles Nightingale, 11th Bt. of Kneesworth, Herts; *m.* 1st, 1907, Anna (*d.* 1924), *d.* of George Forestier Walker; one *s.* one *d.*; 2nd, 1930, Violet Marion, *d.* of late Lt. Col. H. M. E. Brunker, The Cameronians and *widow* of Capt. C. A. G. Cunningham. *Educ.:* Diocesan College, Rondebosch. 2nd Lt. Cheshire Regt., 1890; entered Indian Army, 1891; joined 5th Gurkha Rifles; Captain, 1901; Major, 1908; Lt.-Col. 1916; Col. 1920; Major-Gen. 1924; served Tirah, 1897-98 (medal and clasp); China, 1900 (medal); European War, 1914-18; Suez Canal, present at Turkish attack on Canal, 3-4 Feb. 1915, and minor operations; Dardanelles, battle at Krithia, 4 June 1915 (severely wounded. despatches, D.S.O.); N.W.F., 1916-17; Mesopotamia, 1917-18 (C.M.G., despatches six times); Kurdistan, 1919 (medal and clasp, C.I.E.); Iraq, 1920 (clasp); Waziristan, 1923-24 (medal and clasp); commanded 54th I. Infantry Brigade, 1917-22, and 5th Indian Infantry Brigade, 1923-24; G.O.C. Sind Independent Brigade Area, 1925-29; retired, 1929. Civil Defence, A.R.P., 1939-45. *Publications:* The Gates of Paradise, Pall Mall Magazine, 1910; various journalistic articles in press at odd times. *Recreations:* ordinary sports. *Address:* Trevince, Park Way, Camberley, Surrey. *T.:* 966. *Club:* United Service. [*Died* 8 *April* 1956.

NIMMO, Surgeon-Rear-Adm. Frank Hutton, M.V.O. 1922; R.N.; *b.* 18 June 1872; *s.* of late James Nimmo, Oakleigh Park, Whetstone, Herts; *m.* 1906, Anne J. R., *y. d.* of late Robert Mackirdy, Battery Place, Rothesay,

Bute; two *d.* *Educ.:* Mill Hill School; St. Bartholomew's Hospital (Jeaffreson exhibitioner). Entered Royal Navy as Surgeon, 1896; M.O. H.M. Yacht Osborne, 1908; M.O. of H.M. Yacht Alexandra on commissioning and recomm., 1908-14 and 1919-22; Surgeon-Capt., 1922; Surgeon-Rear-Adm. and retd. list, 1926. M.O. in charge of Casualty Service (Civil Defence) for Gosport (Hants) dist. in War of 1939-45. O.St.J. 1952. *Recreations:* outdoor sports. *Address:* Clifton Cottage, Alverstoke, Hants. [*Died* 15 *Nov.* 1954.

NIMMO, Henry, C.B.E. 1953; M.I.C.E., M.I.E.E., M.I.Mech.E.; Chairman of the Southern Electricity Board, since 1948; *b.* 28 July 1885; *e. s.* of late Gavin Nimmo; *m.* 1921, Una Kathleen, *er. d.* of late Richard Bankes Barron; two *d.* *Educ.:* Airdrie Academy; Coatbridge Technical College. Trained as Mechanical and Electrical Engr., 1900-06; Erection Engr., British Westinghouse Co., 1906-07; Chief Electr. Engr.: Oakbank Oil Co., 1907-09; Irrawaddy Flotilla Co., 1909-12; Asst. Engr., Rangoon Electric Supply & Tramway Co., 1912-14; Offg. Electr. Adviser to Govt. of Burma, 1914-15; Sapper to Capt. London Electr. Engrs., R.E. (T), 1916-19; Electr. Adviser to Govt. of Burma, 1920-29; Maj. O/C No. 2 Fld. Co., R.E. (A.F.I.), 1921-29; Chief Engrg. Inspector, Electricity Commn., 1929-45; Electricity Commr., 1945-47; Chm. Southern Electricity Bd. since 1948; Vice-Pres. and Mem. Council, Conf. Internationale des Grands Reseaux Electriques, since 1951; Mem. Council and Chm. Brit. Nat. Cttee. of Union Internationale des Producteurs et Distributeurs d'Energie Electrique since 1949. *Address:* Wingates, Matching Green, Harlow, Essex. *T.:* Matching 24. [*Died* 25 *Oct.* 1954.

NISBET, Brigadier-General Francis Courtenay, D.S.O. 1916; *b.* 18 Jan. 1869; *s.* of Harry Curtis Nisbet and Louisa Margaret Bruce; *m.* 1922, Helen Agnes, *y. d.* of late John MacFarlan, I.C.S. *Educ.:* Rugby; Sandhurst. Joined Gloucester Regt. 1890; served South African War (Queen's medal and three clasps); Major, 1913; Commanded 2nd Batt. Gloucesters in France, 1915; 8th Duke of Cornwall's Light Infantry, Macedonia, 1916-17; 84th Infantry Brigade in Macedonia, 1918, and Turkey, 1919 (despatches, D.S.O., Brevets Lt.-Col. and Col., Serbian Order of Karageorge); 1st Gloucester Regt., 1919-21; retired pay, 1921. *Recreations:* played Rugby football for the Harlequins and Surrey County, racquets, billiards, and chess. *Address:* 7 Bedford Gardens, Campden Hill, W.8. *T.:* Park 6816. [*Died* 8 *May* 1953.

NISBET, Noel L., R.I. 1925; *b.* Harrow, 30 Dec. 1887; *d.* of Hume Nisbet, author and artist, and Helen Currie; *m.* 1910, Harry Bush, *q.v.*; two *d.* *Educ.:* Convent of Notre Dame. Studied Art at Branch of South Kensington under L. C. Nightingale, winning three Gold Medals, Princess of Wales Scholarship, Bronze Medals, etc., 1912; illustrated following books, 1914: Russian Fairy Tales, Cossack Fairy Tales, Enchanted Logan, Legends of Saints and Sinners, World's Heritage, vols. I. and II.; Senior History, 1934; exhibitor at R.A. since 1914, at R.I. since 1921, also at R.O.I., Walker Art Gallery, Canada, Glasgow, Bristol, Bournemouth, Brighton, etc.; Evil Spirits, R.A., 1938, purchased for Newport (Mon.) Art Gallery. *Address:* 19 Queensland Avenue, Merton Park, Wimbledon, S.W. [*Died* 16 *May* 1956.

NISBET, Colonel Thomas, C.M.G. 1919; D.S.O. 1917; *b.* 1 Dec. 1882; *s.* of late T. M. Nisbet, Sunnybrae, Pitlochry; *m.* 1st, 1905, Barbara Frances, *d.* of Thomas Lawson; 2nd, 1920, Mary (*d.* 1931), *d.* of John Carter Clayden; 3rd, Jane Esther, *d.* of Patrick Moran. *Educ.:* Fettes College, Edinburgh; R.M.C., Camberley. Enlisted ranks Imperial Yeomanry and proceeded S. Africa, Jan. 1901; Lieut. 1 April 1901; 2nd Lieut. P.A. Somersetshire Light Infantry, 14 Sept. 1901 attached Mounted Infantry, 1902 (Queen's medal with 5 clasps); transferred 28th Lt. Cavalry, I.A., 1904; Adjutant Bihar Light Horse, 1911-14; Delhi Coronation Durbar Decoration; European War, served with Reserve Cavalry, Staff 13th Division, Gallipoli, 1915-16; Mesopotamia, 1916-18; General Maude's Staff and A.A. and Q.M.G., Cavalry Division; Palestine, 1918; A.A. and Q.M.G. 3rd Lahore Division; special duty Somaliland, 1919; operations round Urfa, 1919 (G.S. Medal, Kurdistan); Director-in-Chief Repatriation and Relief of Refugees, Syria and Palestine, 1919; A.Q.M.G., G.H.Q., E.E.F. 1920 (Brevet Lieut.-Colonel, C.M.G., D.S.O., Officier Légion d'Honneur, Croix de Guerre, despatches four times); Col. 1922; A.A.Q.M.G. Baluchistan District, 1924; retired, 1927; motored overland Europe-India 1925-27, and India-Europe (Calcutta-Beirut), 1927; F.R.G.S. 1925. *Address:* Brightwell, Wallingford, Berks. *T.A.:* Brightwell. [*Died* 24 *Feb.* 1956.

NIXON, Sir Edwin Vandervord, Kt., *cr.* 1951; C.M.G. 1935; F.C.A. (Australia); Senior Partner Edwin V. Nixon and Partners, Chartered Accountants (Australia), Melbourne; *b.* 31 March 1876; *s.* of Thomas and Jane Nixon; *m.* 1905, Amy Mabel Mackenzie; two *s.* one *d.* *Educ.:* Brisbane, Queensland. Senior Lecturer on Accounting, University of Melbourne, 1925-30; Member of Royal Commission on Taxation, 1932; and of Royal Commission on the Monetary and Banking Systems; Chairman of Advisory Accountancy Panel to advise Government on schemes of costing and profit control for production of munitions by private enterprise; Member of Board of Business Administration, Department of Co-Ordination; Director of Finance, Ministry of Munitions; Treasury Member, Dept. of Aircraft Production. *Publications:* contributor of numerous articles to Accountancy Journals. *Recreations:* motoring and golf. *Address:* 401 Collins Street, Melbourne, Australia. *T.A.:* Methodical, Melbourne. *T.:* MU 8895 and MU 8896. *Clubs:* Athenæum (Melbourne); New South Wales (Sydney). [*Died* 19 *Aug.* 1955.

NIXON, John Alexander, C.M.G. 1919; B.A., M.D. Cantab., F.R.C.P. Lond.; Emeritus Professor of Medicine, University of Bristol; Consulting Physician Bristol Royal Hospital; Southmead Hospital, Bristol; Bristol Mental Hospital, Hortham and Stoke Park Colonies, etc.; ex-Pres.: Assurance Medical Society; Assoc. of Physicians of Great Britain and Ireland; Bristol Medico-Chirurgical Society; Bath and Bristol branch of B.M.A., Bristol Division of B.M.A. Abernethian Society, London; Fellow Royal Society of Medicine; Temporary Colonel A.M.S.; Consulting Physician B.E.F. France; *b.* Edinburgh, 1874; *s.* of Robert Bell Nixon and Margaret Selina, *d.* of Surgeon-Major Alexander Hunter, Madras Army; *m.* 1924, Doreen Gennifer Constantia Walker, M.B., B.S., (Lond.), *o. d.* of W. A. Walker; one *s.* one *d.* *Educ.:* Hurstpierpoint; Gonville and Caius Coll., Cambridge; St. Bartholomew's Hospital, London. House Physician and Ophthalmic House Surgeon, St. Bartholomew's Hospital, 1900-1; House Surgeon, Metropolitan Hospital, 1901-2; House Physician and Senior Resident Officer, Bristol Royal Infirmary, 1902-6; formerly Editor Bristol Medico, Chirurgical Journal, and St. Bartholomew's Hospital Journal. *Publications:* The debt of Medicine to the Fine Arts, 1923; Text-book of Nutrition (with wife), 1938; various contributions to Journals on Medicine, Dermatology, and History of Medicine. *Address:* 7 Lansdown Place, Clifton, Bristol. *T.:* Bristol 34266. [*Died* 17 *March* 1951.

NIXON, Sir John Carson, K.C.I.E., *cr.* 1938 (C.I.E. 1932); C.S.I. 1936; B.Sc., A.R.C.S., L.C.P.; *b.* 21 Sept. 1887; *s.* of late John Albert Nixon; *m.* 1917, Madeleine Frances Graham; one *s.* *Educ.:* Royal College of Science and University College, London. Assistant Magistrate, 1912-14; Assistant and Director of Surveys, Bengal and Assam, 1914-16; Assistant and Controller of Munitions, Bengal, 1918; Under Secretary, Finance Dept., Govt. of Bengal, 1918-19; Commerce Dept., Govt. of India, 1919-20; Finance Dept., Govt. of India, 1920-21; Deputy Controller of the Currency, Bombay, 1923-25; Accountant General, Posts and Telegraphs, Madras and Bombay, 1925-30; Joint Secretary, Finance Dept., Govt. of India, 1932; Accountant General, Bengal, Government of India, 1934; Secretary Finance Department, Government of India, 1935-38; Acting Finance Member, Govt. of India, 1937; retired, I.C.S., 1941; Area Officer, Ministry of Aircraft Production, Birmingham, 1940-41; Assistant Secretary, Ministry of Supply, Adelphi, London, 1941-1942; Financial Adviser to British Economic Mission to Greece and Member of Greek Currency Committee, 1946. *Address:* Tideway, Wellington Parade, Walmer, Deal, Kent. *T.:* Kingsdown 135. *Club:* East India and Sports. [*Died* 15 *July* 1958.

NIZAMAT JUNG; *see* Ahmad, Maulvi Sir N.

NOBLE, Admiral Sir Percy Lockhart Harnam, G.B.E., *cr.* 1944; K.C.B., *cr.* 1936 (C.B. 1932); C.V.O. 1920 (M.V.O. 1901); LL.D. (Hon.) Liverpool and Belfast; Commander, Legion of Merit (U.S.A.); Grand Cross of Order of St. Olaf (Norway); Grand Officer, Legion of Honour (France); Grand Cross of the Dannebrog (Denmark); Rear-Admiral of the United Kingdom and of the Admiralty since 1945; *b.* 16 Jan. 1880; *s.* of Colonel Charles Noble; *m.* 1st, Diamantina (*d.* 1909), *o. d.* of Allan Campbell; 2nd, 1913, Celia Emily, *o. d.* of Robert Kirkman Hodgson and Lady Norah Hodgson. Entered Navy, 1894; Lieut. 1902; Commander, 1913. Served Grand Fleet, 1914-19 (promoted Capt. 1918); Commanded H.M. Ships Calliope, Calcutta and Barham, also Shotley and Forton Training Establishments; Director of Operations Division, Admiralty Naval Staff, 1928-30; Rear-Admiral, 1929; Director of Naval Equipment, 1931-32; Rear-Adm. Commanding 2nd Cruiser Squadron, 1932-34; Vice-Adm. 1935; Fourth Sea Lord, 1935-37; Commander-in-Chief, China Station, 1938-1940; Admiral 1939; Commander-in-Chief, Western Approaches, 1941-42; Head of British Naval Delegation in Washington, U.S.A., 1942-44; Naval A.D.C. to the King. 1929; First and Principal Naval A.D.C. to the King, 1943-45. *Address:* 66 Ashley Gardens, S.W.1. *T.:* Victoria 4553. *Clubs:* Boodle's, Royal Automobile. [*Died* 25 *July* 1955.

NOBLE, Thomas Paterson, M.D., F.R.C.S., F.R.S.E.; Emeritus Professor of Surgery, Chulalongchorn University, Bangkok, Siam; formerly Surgeon to the King of Siam; Surgical Specialist Ministry of Pensions; *b.* 12 March 1887; *s.* of Alexander Noble and Margaret Paterson; *m.* 1914, Cecilia Farmer; one *d.* *Educ.:* Edinburgh University; University College, London. Consulting Surgeon, specially orthopædic surgery. Order of Crown of Siam, 3rd class, 1935; Order of White Elephant, 4th class, 1934. *Publications:* Pseudocoxalgia; Myositis Ossificans; Klippel-Feils Syndrome; Coxa Vara; Acute Bone Atrophy. *Recreations:* fishing, photography. *Address:* c/o Glyn, Mills & Co. (Holt's Branch), 22 Whitehall, S.W.1. [*Died* 16 *Dec.* 1959.

NOBLE, T. Tertius, Mus. Doc. 1926; M.A., F.R.C.O., A.R.C.M.; organist emeritus, St. Thomas' Church, Fifth Avenue, New York; *b.* Bath, 5 May 1867; 5th *s.* of late Thomas Noble of Bath, and Sarah, *d.* of late William Jackson of Swaffham, Norfolk; *m.* Meriel Maude, *e. d.* of Rt. Rev. the Lord Bishop of Truro, 1897; one *s.* *Educ.:* private tutor; Colchester; Royal College of Music, London (Exhibitioner and scholar). Organist, All Saints', Colchester, 1881; St. John's, Wilton Road, S.W., 1889; assistant organist to Prof. Stanford at Trinity College, Cambridge, 1890; organist and master of the choristers, Ely Cathedral, 1892; organist, York Minster, 1907-13. *Publications:* Air and Variation for Organ; Solemn March, do.; Communion Service in A; The Music to The Wasps of Aristophanes performed at Cambridge, 1897; Service in B Minor; Songs and Violin Pieces; Service in A throughout; Services in A and G minor; Ten unaccompanied Anthems; Eight-part Motett and Anthem, The Soul Triumphant; Sacred Cantata, Gloria Domini; Introduction and Passacaglia for full orchestra, etc. *Address:* Old Garden Road, Rockport, Mass. [*Died* 4 *May* 1953.

NOEL, Andre Espitalier-, C.M.G. 1944; Controller of Supplies, Mauritius, since 1943; *b.* 20 June 1898; 4th *s.* of late Louis Espitalier-Noel, elected Member Mauritius Legislative Council; *m.* 1919, Laurence Leclezio, *g.d.* of late Sir Henry Leclezio, K.C.M.G.; one *s.* two *d.* *Educ.:* Paris; privately. Asst. Food Controller, 1939; Food Commodity Controller, 1942. *Address:* Clos Gentil, Curepipe, Mauritius. [*Died* 7 *Aug.* 1950.

[*But death not notified in time for inclusion in Who Was Who* 1941–1950, *first edn.*

NOEL-BUXTON, Lady, Lucy Edith; *d.* of late Major Henry Pelham Burn; *m.* 1914, 1st Baron Noel-Buxton (*d.* 1948); two *s* two *d.* (and one *s.*, one *d.* decd.). M.P. (Lab.) North Norfolk, 1930-31, Norwich, 1945-50. *Address:* Rayleigh Lodge, Frinton, Essex. [*Died* 9 *Dec.* 1960.

NOLAN, John J., M.A., D.Sc.; Professor of Experimental Physics, University College, Dublin, since 1920; Registrar, University College, Dublin, since 1940; *b.* Omagh, Co. Tyrone, 28 Dec. 1888; *s.* of Martin Nolan; *m.* 1914, Teresa, *d.* of J. Hurley, Coomhola, Bantry; three *s.* *Educ.:* Christian Schools, Omagh; St. Macarten's Seminary, Monaghan; U.C., lege, Dublin. Assistant in Physics, U.C., Dublin, 1909; Pres., R.I.A. since 1949; Member, Governing Body, U.C., Dublin; Mem., Senate, N.U.I.; Chm., Bd. of School of Cosmic Physics, Dublin Institute of Advanced Studies. *Publications:* Papers on ionization and atmospheric electricity. *Address:* 26 Cowper Rd., Rathmines, Dublin. *T.:* 92764. [*Died* 18 *April* 1952.

NONWEILER, Major-General Wilfrid Ivan, C.B.E. 1949; *b.* 27 August 1900; *s.* of late T. F. Nonweiler; *m.* 1926, Betty Evelyn, *d.* of late Brig.-Gen. F. V. Temple, C.M.G.; one *s.* one *d.* *Educ.:* Rossall School. 2nd Lt., R.M., 1918; Lt.-Col. 1941; Actg. Brig. 1943; Comd. 3 Commando Brigade, Burma, 1943; Comd. 117 Inf. Bde., Germany, 1945; Col. 1946; Maj.-Gen., 1950; Chief of Staff to Commandant General, Royal Marines, 1950-51; retired, 1951. *Recreations:* golf, gardening. *Address:* High Trees, Walmer, Kent. *T.:* Deal 470. *Clubs:* United Service, Royal Automobile. [*Died* 12 *Jan.* 1953.

NORBURY, 5th Earl of (*cr.* 1827); **Captain Ronald Ian Montague Graham-Toler**; Baron Norwood, 1797; Baron Norbury, 1800; Viscount Glandine, 1827; *b.* 11 Jan. 1893; *s.* of Lt.-Col. James Otway Graham-Toler, H.L.I., Beechwood Park, Nenagh, Co. Tipperary; *S.* cousin, 1943; *m.* 1932, Margaret Greenhalgh; two *s.* *Educ.:* H.M.S. Conway; Hannover; Dublin. Member of Management Committee H.M.S. Conway. Royal Enniskilling Fusiliers, 1912-1921; served European War, 1914-18 (3 medals, Mons Star); Chief Inter-allied Railway and Food Mission in Croatia, 1919-20; British Red Cross Mission to Greece, 1923; District Director Balkan Mission U.N.R.R.A., Cairo, 1944-45. Late Merseyside Manager International Paint Co., Ltd. *Recreations:* yachting and fishing. *Heir:* *s.* Viscount Glandine. *Address:* The Fishery, Maidenhead, Berks. *T.:* Maidenhead 2334; London Wall 4790. *Clubs:* Royal Automobile; Hibernian United Service (Dublin); Racquets (Liverpool). [*Died* 24 *May* 1955.

NORMAN, Brigadier Compton Cardew, C.M.G. 1919; C.B.E. 1937; D.S.O. 1917; late Roy. Welch Fusiliers; *b.* 1877; *m.* 1912, Grace Mary Comyns (*d.* 1953); one *s.* one *d.* Served S. Africa 1899-1902 (Queen's medal and five clasps, King's medal and two clasps, wounded); W. Africa, 1905 (medal and clasp, wounded); European War, 1914-1918 (twice wounded, despatches, C.M.G., D.S.O., Bt. Lt.-Col., Chevalier de la Légion d'Honneur); commanded 158th (Royal Welch) Infantry Brigade T.A., 1927-29; Inspector-General Royal West African Frontier Force, 1930-36, and King's African Rifles, 1931-36; retired pay, 1934. *Address:* c/o Lloyd's Bank, 6 Pall Mall, S.W.1. *Club:* Naval and Military. [*Died* 15 *Feb.* 1955.

NORMAN, Herman Cameron, C.B. 1920; C.S.I. 1919; C.B.E. 1917; *b.* 8 June 1872; *s.* of late Charles Loyd Norman of Bromley Common, Kent, and Julia, *d.* of Charles Hay Cameron. *Educ.:* Eton; Trinity College, Cambridge. Attaché in H.M. Diplomatic Service, 1894; 3rd Secretary, 1896; 2nd Secretary, 1900; 1st Secretary, 1907; Counsellor, 1914; Minister Plenipotentiary, 1919; British Minister, Tehran, 1920-21; Secretary of the International Conference in London on the Sleeping Sickness, 1907-8; Secretary-General of the International Naval Conference in London, 1908; Secretary of Turkey and Allied Balkan States Conference, 1912-13; Secretary of the British Delegation, Peace Conference, 1919; Coronation Medals, King Edward VII. and King George V.; attached to special mission to attend Coronation of the late Emperor of Japan, 1915, received the Order of the Sacred Treasure; Privy Chamberlain of Sword and Cape to Pope Pius XI., 1925-39 and since to Pope Pius XII.; has received the Silver Medal bene merenti and the Gold Cross bene merenti; Knight of Magistral Grace of the Order of Malta; Member of the Royal Commission on Local Government, 1926-29. *Clubs:* St. James', Beefsteak, Royal Automobile, M.C.C. [*Died* 8 *Sept.* 1955.

NORMAN BARNETT, Lt.-Col. Henry; *e. surv. s.* of late Charles William Barnett of Ballyagherty and Thornhill House, Knock, Co. Down, and Helen, *er. d.* of late Charles Mackenzie, of Fortree, Aberdeenshire; *m.* Jane Eleanor, *d.* of late Thomas Shaw, J.P., Colne Hall, Lancashire, and Hillside, Torquay; one *s.* two *d.* *Educ.:* privately; Queen's Univ., Belfast; Edinburgh; London. F.R.C.S. Edin. Served S. African War (transport) and European War, 1914-20 (B.E.F. France); raised, trained and commanded 3/2nd S.W. Mounted Bde. Field Amb.; O.C. 2/3 W. Riding Field Amb.; O.C. Chiseldon Military Hosp. (Special Div.); Assistant Commandant, Training Centre, Codford; Commanded Military Hospital and O.C. Troops, Warlingham; formerly Senior Surgeon, and largely responsible for the establishment of the modern hospital, Bath Ear, Nose and Throat Hospital; Resident Clinical Assistant, Registrar, Surg. Tutor and Anaesthetist, Royal Victoria Hospital, Belfast; Clinical Assistant and Anaesthetist Belfast Hospital for Sick Children and Ulster Ear, Nose and Throat Hospital; was a Member of the Ulster Legislative Assembly. Consulting Specialist to Ministries of Pensions and National Insurance; Consulting Ear, Nose and Throat Surgeon, Victoria Hospital, Frome and Shepton Mallet District Hospital; Fellow Royal Society of Medicine and Hunterian Society; Member of the National Assembly of the Church of England. *Publications:* Student's Textbook of Surgery; Accidental Injuries to Workmen; Legal Responsibility of the Drunkard; Sea Sickness, its true cause and cure in relation to the Inner Ear; Mastoiditis—its Diagnosis and Treatment; Modified Radical Operation for Chronic Mastoiditis; Deafness—its Cause and Treatment; Modern Trend of Treatment for Deafness, in Modern Treatment Year Book, 1950; The Approach of the General Practitioner to Diseases of the Ear, Nose and Throat. *Recreations:* riding, tennis, travel. *Address:* 27 The Circus, Bath; South Lynn, Weston, Bath. *T.:* 2462, 7461. *Clubs:* Junior Army and Navy, St. George's. [*Died* 24 *April* 1952.

NORMAN-WALKER, Colonel John Norman, C.I.E. 1933; M.R.C.P. (Lond.); D.T.M. and H. (Camb.); I.M.S., retd.; lately Director, Medical-Sanitary Dept., Hyderabad, Deccan, India; *b.* 30 March 1872; *s.* of Charles Walker; *m.* 1904; four *s.* one *d.* *Educ.:* Newcastle-under-Lyme; St. Thomas's Hospital. Entered I.M.S., 1899; Bt. Colonel, 1925; Colonel, 1927; Civil Surgeon, Delhi, 1921; Surgeon to the Viceroy, 1924; Inspector-General of Civil Hospitals, C.P., 1927; retired from Government service, 1929; served China, 1901; Waziristan, 1902; European War (despatches); C.C. Berks, Alderman, 1946. *Publications:* Indian Village Health; and articles on tropical diseases. *Address:* The Coombe, Streatley, Berks. *T.:* Goring 174. *Club:* East India and Sports. [*Died* 18 *June* 1951.

NORMAND, Alexander Robert, M.A., B.Sc., Ph.D., F.R.S.E.; Professor of Chemistry (retired), Wilson College, Bombay; *b.* Edinburgh, 4 March 1880; *s.* of J. H. Normand; *m.* 1909, Margaret Elizabeth, *d.* of Colin Murray; one *s.* *Educ.:* Royal High School and University, Edinburgh. *Address:* 33 Moray Place, Edinburgh 3. *T.:* Edinburgh Caledonian 6931. [*Died* 18 *July* 1958.

NORMANTON, Helena Florence, Q.C. 1949; *b.* Kensington; *d.* of William Alexander Normanton; *m.* 1921, Gavin Bowman Watson Clark (*d.* 1948); retains maiden surname as legal and only name. *Educ.:* B.A. 1st Class Hons. London, Modern History; Dijon Univ. Diploma in French language, literature, and history; Barrister-at-law; admitted as a Member of the Middle Temple, 24 Dec. 1919; called to Bar, 1922; first woman barrister briefed at High Court of Justice (1922) and at Central Criminal Court (1924), and at London Sessions (1926); Hon. Secretary of the Magna Carta Soc.,1921-53; Acting Jun. (=Secretary) and Hon. Treasurer, Bar Mess of the Central Criminal Court, 1942-49; formerly Senior Practising Woman Barrister of the English Bar; first woman barrister elected upon General Council of the Bar, 1945, re-elected 1947; Ex-Associate Grand Dean for Europe of the International Sorority of Women Lawyers (Kappa Beta Pi); formerly Lecturer to Post-Graduate Honours History Students of Glasgow University; Extension Lecturer London University; in 1925 elected member of New York Women's Bar Assoc.; a Founding Member of the Horatian Society; Former Chairman of the International Legislative Sub-Committee of International Federation of Business and Professional Women and ex-Vice-Pres. of same Federation for England; President of the Council of Married Women, 1952-53; retired from legal practice, Dec. 1950. Diploma, Ami de la Cité de Paris, 1951. *Publications:* Sex Differentiation in Salary; many articles; contributor to Ency. Brit. (13th and current edn.); Trial of Norman Thorne (Famous Trials Series); Trial of A. A. Rouse (Notable Trials Series); Everyday Law for Women. *Recreations:* gardening, Shakespeare. *Address:* 25 Aldersmead Road, Beckenham, Kent. *T.:* Sydenham 8768. [*Died* 14 *Oct.* 1957.

NORRIE, Colonel (temp. Brig.) Edward Creer, C.B. 1935; D.S.O. 1918; architect; *b.* 28 Sept. 1885; *s.* of late Frank Norrie; *m.* 1917, Jessie Frances Findlay White. *Educ.:* Scots College, Sydney. Served European War, 1915-19; Australian Imperial Force (D.S.O., despatches). Commanded 1st Div., N.S.W., 1934; retired, 1944. *Address:* c/o A.H.Q., Sydney, N.S.W., Australia. [*Died March* 1958.

NORRINGTON, Lieut.-Col. Reginald Lewis, C.M.G. 1916; *s.* of A. R. Norrington, Abbotsfield, Plymouth; *m.* Beryl, *e. d.* of Colonel George Hawkes, late commanding 5th Gurkha Rifles; two *d.* *Educ.:* Haileybury College; R.M.C., Sandhurst. Joined The Border Regt. 1907; with it in England, Gibraltar, India, and Burma; rejoined the Army at the outbreak of European War (despatches, C.M.G.); commanded 7th Batt. The Border Regiment, 1915-17. *Recreations:* shooting and fishing. *Address:* 1 Glenside, Manor Road, Sidmouth, Devon. [*Died* 14 *June* 1960.

NORRIS, Arthur Herbert, C.B.E. 1931; M.C.; M.R.C.S., L.R.C.P., D.P.H. (Vict.); Capt. R.A.M.C.(T.F.); (retired); formerly H.M. Chief Inspector Children's Branch, Home Office; *b.* 4 March 1875; *s.* of Rev. Chas. E. Norris, Vicar of Falinge, Rochdale; unmarried. *Educ.:* Ellesmere, Salop; Manchester Univ.; St. Thomas's Hospital, London. Resident Medical Officer, Manchester Chest Hospital, Bowdon; Crossley Sanatorium, Delamere; Senior Medical Officer, Children's Dispensary, Manchester; Assistant School Medical Officer, Tuberculosis Officer, Berkshire County Council; Capt. R.A.M.C. att. 1/6 Batt. Manchester Regt. 1909-17; served in Gallipoli, Egypt, and France (despatches, M.C.); Major Home Guard, 14th Bn. Devon Regt., 1940-42. Chairman Dawlish Urban District Council, 1946. *Address:* Speke, 5 Barton Terrace, Dawlish, Devon. [*Died* 20 *Feb.* 1953.

NORRIS, Henry, C.B.E. 1918; *b.* 1852; *s.* of Robert Norris; *m.* 1881; three *s.* Dock and Warehouse Manager, Port of London Authority; retired, 1919. *Address:* Homecroft, St. Michaels Road, Worthing, Sussex. [*Died* 23 *July* 1954.

NORRIS, Lieut.-Col. Henry (Everard DuCane), J.P.; late County Alderman; *b.* 27 April 1869; *e. s.* of late Col. Henry Crawley Norris, M.V.O., J.P., and Mary, *d.* of late Rt. Hon. Sir W. Bovill, P.C.; *m.* 1920, S. Eldrydd K., 2nd *d.* of Major Herbert Dugdale, 16 Lancers; no *c.* *Educ.:* Wellington College. Late Major 5th Bn. Royal Warwick Regt.; served South African War, 1899; European War, 1916, with Royal Naval Division; retired with rank of Lieut.-Colonel: High Sheriff Oxfordshire, 1939; J.P. 1896, D.L. 1935, V.L. 1948-54. Chm. Highways Committee County Council, 1937-46. K.St.J. *Address:* Cross Hill, Adderbury, Banbury, Oxon. *T.:* Adderbury 11. *Clubs:* Carlton, White's. [*Died* 14 *Jan.* 1960.

NORTH, Brigadier Harold Napier, D.S.O. 1917; late Royal Engineers; *b.* 11 June 1883; 5th *s.* of late Lt.-Col. Roger North, R.A.; *m.* 1921, Roberta Whitehead (*d.* 1940), *widow* of late Lt.-Col. F. O. Wyatt, M.V.O., R.G.A. *Educ.:* Harrow. 2nd Lieutenant R.E. 1900; served European War, 1914-18; operations Indian Frontier, 1915; Mesopotamia, 1916-21, including Arab Insurrection, 1920; Brigade Major, R.E., G.H.Q.; C.R.E. 14th Indian Division; 17th Indian Division (D.S.O. Brevet Lieut.-Colonel, despatches four times); Chief Engineer, Northern Command, 1931-33; Chief Engineer, Eastern Command, 1933-37; Technical member of Anglo-Egyptian Treaty Building Committee, 1937-39; Chief Engineer Southern Command, 1939-40; retired, 1940; A.D.C. to the King, 1935-40. Regional Director Ministry of Works (Midlands), 1945-48. *Recreations:* cricket, tennis, golf, polo, shooting. *Address:* c/o Lloyds Bank, Ltd., 6 Pall Mall, S.W.1. *Clubs:* Army and Navy, Queen's. [*Died* 13 *Feb.* 1957.

NORTHCROFT, Hon. Mr. Justice Sir Erima Harvey, Kt., *cr.* 1949; D.S.O. 1919; V.D.; Judge of Supreme Court, New Zealand, since 1935; Member representing New Zealand on International Military Tribunal for the Far East, Tokyo, for trial of major Japanese War Criminals; Member Council of Society of Comparative Legislation; *b.* 2 Dec. 1884; *s.* of Leonard Northcroft and Louisa Pellow James; *m.* 1908, Violet Constance, Mitchell; two *d.* *Educ.:* Hokitika High School; Wellington College; Auckland University College. Practised Law at Hamilton, N.Z., 1907-23; at Auckland, N.Z., 1923-35; Judge Advocate-General to New Zealand Military Forces, 1933-35; Director of Artillery, Southern Military District, 1940-42; Commander Christchurch Fortress Area, Jan.-Apr. 1942; formerly Mem. of Hamilton Borough Council and President Hamilton Law Society; Mem. Auckland University College Council until 1935; formerly Commodore Royal New Zealand Yacht Squadron; served European War with New Zealand Expeditionary Force (D.S.O., despatches); Long Service Medal. *Recreations:* yachting and golf. *Address:* Judge's Chambers, Christchurch, C.1, N.Z. *Clubs:* Northern (Auckland); Christchurch (Christchurch); Royal New Zealand Yacht Squadron. [*Died* 10 *Oct.* 1953.

NORTHEY, Major-Gen. Sir Edward, G.C.M.G., *cr.* 1922 (K.C.M.G., *cr.* 1918); C.B. 1917; *o. surv. s.* of late Rev. Edward William Northey, M.A., and Florence Elizabeth (*d.* 1928), *y. d.* of Sir John E. Honywood, 6th Bt.; *b.* 28 May 1868; *m.* 1897, Evangeline (*d.* 1941), 3rd *d.* of late Daniel Cloete, Wynberg, Cape Town; two *s.* two *d.* *Educ.:* Eton; Sandhurst. Served Hazara, 1891 (medal with clasp); Miranzai Expedition, 1891 (clasp); Isazai Expedition, 1892; S. Africa, 1899-1902 (despatches twice, Queen's medal 5 clasps, King's medal 2 clasps); European War, 1914-18 (despatches five times); battles of Mons, Marne, Aisne, and Ypres; at first in command of 1st King's Royal Rifles (Brevet Col. and A.D.C. to the King, Feb. 1915); later of 15th Infantry Brigade (twice wounded); Brigadier-General, March 1915; commanded Nyasa-Rhodesia Field Forces, 1916-18, in German East Africa (promoted Maj.-Gen. for distinguished service in the field 1 Jan. 1918, C.B., Commander Military Order of Avis (Portugal); 1st Class Brilliant Star of Zanzibar; Officer of French Legion of Honour); Governor and Commander-in-Chief of the Kenya Colony and H.M.'s High Commissioner for the Zanzibar Protectorate, 1918-22; Gen. Officer Commanding 43rd (The Wessex) Division T.A. and So.-Western Area, 1924-26; retired pay, 1926; F.R.G.S., F.Z.S. *Address:* Glebe Farm, Hinton Waldrist, Faringdon, Berkshire. [*Died* 25 *Dec.* 1953.

NORTHMORE, Hon. Sir John Alfred, K.C.M.G., *cr.* 1932; *b.* Adelaide, 14 Sept. 1865; *s.* of late John Alfred Northmore, Adelaide, S. Australia; *m.* Emily Agnes, *widow* of Arthur Ventris Murphy Ventris, I.S.O. *Educ.:* St. Peter's College, Adelaide; University of Adelaide, LL.B. Called to South Australian Bar, 1888; admitted to Western Australian Bar, 1896; K.C. 1911; Judge of the Supreme Court of Western Australia, 1914; Chief Justice, 1931-45; Lt.-Governor, 1932-33; Administrator of Government of Western Australia, 1931-33. *Address:* 25 Colin Street, West Perth, Western Australia. *Clubs:* Weld, Royal Perth Yacht (Perth). [*Died* 15 *May* 1958.

NORTON, Brig.-Gen. Cecil Burrington, C.M.G. 1919; D.S.O. 1916; 1st Batt. Duke of Cornwall's L.I.; Colonel retired pay; *b.* 1868; *s.* of Maj.-Gen. E. Nugent Norton; *m.* 1897, Charlotte Alexandra, *d.* of Col. F. R. Begbie, Bt. Lt.-Col.; two *d.* Served N.W. Frontier, India, 1897, with Tirah Expeditionary Force (medal, 2 clasps); European War, 1914-18 (despatches, D.S.O., C.M.G., Legion of Honour, 1917); Military Knight of Windsor, 1923. Retired, 1908. *Address:* c/o Secretary of Military Knights, Windsor. [*Died* 22 *Feb.* 1953.

NORTON, Brig.-General Charles Ernest Graham, C.B. 1922; C.S.I. 1919; *b.* 1869; *s.* of Joseph Norton, J.P., of Nortonthorpe Hall, near Huddersfield; *m.*

1906, Mary Darley (*d.* 1927), *y. d.* of late Arthur Leslie Boucicault, Queensland, Australia. *Educ.:* Harrow; Sandhurst. Joined 7th (Queen's Own) Hussars, 1889; Lt.-Col. 1915; served Matabeleland, 1896-97; S. African War, 1901-02 (despatches); European War, 1914-19; commanded 7th Cavalry Brig., Mesopotamia Exped. Force, 1917-19 (despatches); Assist. Director Remounts, War Office, 1920-21; Director of Remounts, War Office, 1921-25; retired pay, 1926; Aide-de-camp to the King, 1918-26. *Address:* 73 Park Street, W.1. *T.:* Mayfair 6310. *Clubs:* Army and Navy, Cavalry. [*Died* 13 *Jan.* 1953.

NORTON, Lieut.-General Edward Felix, C.B. 1939; D.S.O. 1918; M.C. 1914; Colonel Commandant R.A. since 1941; *b.* 1884; *s.* of late Edward Norton and Mrs. Norton, Belmore, Upham, Hants; *m.* 1925, Isabel Joyce, *yr. d.* of late Dr. William Pasteur, C.B., C.M.G.; three *s.* Awarded Founder's Medal of Royal Geographical Society, 1926. Served European War, 1914-1918 (despatches thrice, Brevet Major, M.C., D.S.O.); Instructor, Staff College, Quetta, 1929-32; Commander, Royal Artillery 1st Division Aldershot, 1932-34; Brigadier, General Staff, Aldershot Command, 1934-38; A.D.C. to the King, 1937-38; Commander, Madras District, 1938-40; Acting Governor of Hong Kong, 1940-41; Temp. Lt.-Gen., 1941; Commanded Western (Independent) District, India; retired pay, 1942. Colonel Comdt. R.H.A., 1947-51. Member Mount Everest Expeditions, 1922 and 1924. *Publication:* The Fight for Everest, 1924, 1925. *Address:* Morestead Grove, Morestead, nr. Winchester. [*Died* 3 *Nov.* 1954.

NORWAY, Nevil Shute, B.A. Oxon; F.R.Ae.S.; Author; *b.* 17 Jan. 1899; *s.* of Arthur Hamilton Norway, C.B., and Mary Louisa Gadsden; *m.* 1931, Frances Mary Heaton; two *d.* *Educ.:* Dragon School, Oxford; Shrewsbury School; R.M.A., Woolwich; Balliol College, Oxford. Served European War, 1918, Private, Suffolk Regt. Aeronautical career: Calculator, the de Havilland Aircraft Co. Ltd., 1922-24; Chief Calculator to Airship Guarantee Co. Ltd. on construction of Rigid Airship R. 100, 1925; Deputy Chief Engineer, 1928; flew the Atlantic twice in R. 100, representing the constructors, 1930; Managing Director, Yorkshire Aeroplane Club Ltd., 1927-30; founded Airspeed Ltd., aeroplane constructors, 1931; Joint Managing Director, 1931-38; commissioned R.N.V.R., 1940; Lieut.-Comdr., 1941; retired, 1945. *Publications:* Novels, under name Nevil Shute: Marazan, 1926; So Disdained, 1928; Lonely Road, 1932; Ruined City, 1938; What Happened to the Corbetts, 1939; An Old Captivity, 1940; Landfall, 1940; Pied Piper, 1942; Pastoral, 1944; Most Secret, 1945; Vinland the Good, 1946; The Chequer Board, 1947; No Highway, 1948; A Town Like Alice, 1949; Round The Bend, 1951; The Far Country, 1952; In the Wet, 1953; Slide Rule (autobiography), 1954; Requiem for a Wren, 1955; Beyond the Black Stump, 1956; On the Beach, 1957; The Rainbow and the Rose, 1958; Trustee from the Toolroom, 1960 (posthumous); Stephen Morris, 1961 (posthumous). *Recreations:* yachting, fishing. *Address:* Langwarrin, Victoria, Australia. *Clubs:* Oxford and Cambridge; Melbourne (Melbourne). [*Died* 12 *Jan.* 1960.

NORWICH, 1st Viscount, *cr.* 1952, of Aldwick; **Alfred Duff Cooper;** P.C. 1935; G.C.M.G., *cr.* 1948; D.S.O. 1919; late Grenadier Guards; *b.* 22 Feb. 1890; *o. s.* of late Sir Alfred Cooper, F.R.C.S., and late Lady Agnes Duff, *sister* of 1st Duke of Fife; *m.* 1919, Lady Diana Manners, *y. d.* of 8th Duke of Rutland; one *s.* *Educ.:* Eton; New College, Oxford (Honours Modern History). M.P. (U.) Oldham, 1924-29; M.P. (C.) St. George's Division of Westminster, 1931-45; Financial Secretary, War Office, 1928-29 and 1931-34; Financial Secretary to the Treasury, 1934-35; Secretary of State for War, 1935-37; First Lord of the Admiralty, 1937-38; Minister of Information, 1940-41; Chancellor of Duchy of Lancaster, 1941-43; Representative of H.M. Government with French Committee of National Liberation, 1943-44; Ambassador to France, 1944-47. Served European War, 1914-19 (D.S.O., despatches). *Publications:* Talleyrand, 1932; Haig, 1935, Vol. II, 1936; The Second World War, 1939; David, 1943; Sergeant Shakespeare, 1949; Operation Heartbreak, 1950; Old Men Forget, 1953. *Heir:* *s.* Hon. John Julius Cooper [*b.* 15 Sept. 1929; *m.* 1952, Anne, *d.* of Hon. Sir Bede Clifford, G.C.M.G., C.B., M.V.O.; one *d.*]. *Clubs:* White's, Buck's, Beefsteak, St. James'. [*Died* 1 *Jan.* 1954.

NORWOOD, Sir Cyril, Kt., *cr.* 1938; M.A. (Oxon); Hon. D.Lit. (Bristol); Hon. M.A. (Sydney); *b.* 15 Sept. 1875; *s.* of Rev. Samuel Norwood, Clerk in Holy Orders, Whalley, Lancashire; *m.* Catharine Margaret (*d.* 1951), *d.* of Dr. W. J. Kilner, Kensington; three *d.* *Educ.:* Merchant Taylors' School; St. John's College, Oxford; 1st class in Classical Moderations, 1896; 1st class in Literæ Humaniores, 1898; passed 1st into Home Civil Service, Class I, 1899. Clerk in Secretariat of Admiralty, 1899-1901; resigned, and accepted mastership of Classical VIth. Leeds Grammar School, 1901-06; Headmaster, Bristol Grammar School, 1906-16; Master of Marlborough College, 1916-25; Headmaster of Harrow School, 1926-34; President, St. John's College, Oxford, 1934-1946; Chairman of Secondary Schools Examination Council, 1921-46; Chairman, Allied Schools, 1934-54; Chairman of Committee on Curricula and Examinations after the war "Norwood Report"; President The Modern Churchmen's Union, 1937-47. *Publication:* (joint) Higher Education of Boys in England; English Educational System; The English Tradition in Education. *Address:* The Homestead, Iwerne Minster, Blandford, Dorset. *Club:* Athenæum. [*Died* 13 *March* 1956.

NORWOOD, Rev. Frederick William, D.D.; retired; devotes time to literature and special preaching and lecturing; *b.* Australia; *s.* of Edward and Mary Norwood, of Melbourne, Victoria, Australia; *m.* May Isabel Davis, Melbourne; two *s.* two *d.* *Educ.:* Ormond College, Melbourne; D.D. of Oberlin College, Ohio, and Ursinus College. Pennsylvania. Minister of churches at Canterbury (Victoria) Brunswick (Vic.), North Adelaide (South Australia); Minister The City Temple, London, England, 1919-36; Vancouver, B.C., 1939; Chairman, Congregational Union of England and Wales, 1930-31; Hon. Captain Australian Imperial Forces; Evangelist under auspices of National Free Church Council, 1936; Pastor of St. James' United Church, Montreal, 1943. *Publications:* The Cross and the Garden; Sunshine and Wattlegold; Moods of the Soul; The Gospel of the Larger World; The Gospel of Distrust; Indiscretions of a Preacher, 1932; Beaten by the Divine, 1933; Preaching in Our Generation; The Supreme Artist. *Address:* 3447 Walkley Avenue, Notre Dame de Grace, Montreal, Canada. [*Died* 14 *Feb.* 1958.

NORWOOD, Professor Gilbert, M.A. (Camb.); Hon. D.Litt. (Wales); F.R.S.C.; Professor Emeritus of Classics, Univ. Coll. Toronto; *b.* 23 Nov. 1880; *m.* 1st, Elizabeth, *d.* of Alexander Hepburn, Newcastle on Tyne; one *s.* five *d.*; 2nd, Frances, *d.* of Charles Hopkins Ould, London. *Educ.:* Duchess Road Board School and Royal Grammar School, Sheffield; St. John's Coll., Cambridge (Scholar and Fellow). Powis medal, 1900; Porson Prize, 1901, 1903; Members' Latin Essay Prize, 1901; Chancellor's medal, 1903; M.A., 1906; Assistant Lecturer in

Classics, University of Manchester, 1903-8; Professor of Greek, University College, Cardiff, 1908-26; Professor of Latin, 1926-28, Professor of Classics and Director of Classical Studies, 1928-51, Univ. Coll., Toronto; Sather Professor of Classical Literature, Univ. of California, 1943-44; Member of British Universities Delegation to Belgium, 1919. *Publications:* Edition of Euripides' Andromache, 1906; The Riddle of the Bacchae, 1908; Acting Edition of Aristophanes' Acharnians, 1911; Greek Tragedy, 1920 (4th ed., 1948); Euripides and Shaw, with other Essays, 1921; The Art of Terence, 1923; The Writers of Greece, 1925 (Spanish translation, 1928); The Wooden Man, 1926; Greek Comedy, 1931; Plautus and Terence, 1932; The Syntax of the Latin Gerund and Gerundive, 1932; Spoken in Jest, 1938; Pindar, 1945 (Italian translation, 1952); contributions to monthly reviews and classical journals. *Recreations:* novels, cross-words. *Clubs:* York, Faculty Union (Toronto).

[*Died* 16 *Oct.* 1954.

NOVELLO, Ivor; Actor-manager, Film Actor, and Composer; *b.* Cardiff, 15 Jan. 1893; *s.* of David Davies and Clara Novello Davies. *Educ.:* Magdalen College School, Oxford. Chorister of Magdalen College, Oxford, 1905-11. Served European War, 1914-18, in R.N.A.S. Studied composition under Dr. Brewer, of Gloucester; first song published when fifteen; Songs: Keep the Home Fires Burning, We'll gather Lilacs, and about 60 others; Musical Plays and Reviews: Theodore & Co.; Tabs; A to Z; Puppets; Golden Moth; The House that Jack Built; and part composer of Arlette, Who's Hooper, and Our Nell; Films: leading parts in The Call of the Blood, Miarka, Carnival, Bohemian Girl, The Man Without Desire, Bonnie Prince Charlie, White Rose, The Rat, The Lodger, the Triumph of the Rat, The Return of the Rat; and Downhill, The Vortex, The Constant Nymph, The South Sea Bubble, The Gallant Hussar, Symphony in Two Flats; made his debut as Armand Duval in Debureau, Ambassadors Theatre, 1921; Wu Hoo Git in The Yellow Jacket, Xavier in Spanish Lovers, Kingsway, 1922; Gaston in Enter Kiki, Playhouse, 1923; commenced actor manager 1924 with The Rat, written by himself in collaboration with Constance Collier; Prince Karl in Old Heidelberg; Lawrence Trenwyth in Iris, 1925; Benvenuto Cellini in the Firebrand, 1926; started management with Frank Curzon at Queen's Theatre in Down Hill; title-rôle in Liliom, 1926; Sirocco, 1927; resumed sole management with his own play, The Truth Game, Oct. 1928; continued management with his own play, Symphony in Two Flats, 1929, which after twelve months run was made into a talking film; appeared in The Truth Game, New York, 1930; 1931 went to Hollywood for writing and acting, 1931; returned to England and made his reappearance in his own play, I lived with You; author of Party, produced 1932; acted leading part of Bay in Party, toured I Lived With You; remade talking version of The Lodger, played Gaston in film Sleeping Car, filmed I Lived With You, 1933; played Seraphine in his own play Flies in the Sun; wrote Fresh Fields; resumed management as Gray Raynor in Proscenium; during run of Proscenium wrote and produced Sunshine Sisters; resumed actor-manager with Murder in Mayfair, Aug. 1934; Lord George Hell in the Happy Hypocrite, His Majesty's, 1936; title-role in King Henry the Fifth, Drury Lane, 1938; devised, wrote, composed and appeared in the leading part in Glamorous Night, 1935, Careless Rapture, 1936; Crest of the Wave, 1937; The Dancing Years, 1939 and Ladies into Action, 1939; wrote Full House, 1935; Comédienne, 1938; revived I Lived With You, 1940; toured entire Drury Lane production of The Dancing Years, 1940-41, resumed its London run, Adelphi Theatre, 1942; author of Breakaway, produced Theatre Royal, Windsor, 1941, and of We Proudly Present, produced Duke of York's Theatre, 1947; wrote and composed Arc de Triomphe, Phoenix Theatre, 1943; visited H.M. Forces in Normandy with Love from a Stranger, Aug. 1944; devised, wrote, composed and appeared in Perchance to Dream, London Hippodrome, 1945-47; paid first visit to S.A. with Perchance to Dream, His Majesty's Theatre, Johannesburg, 1947; wrote and composed: King's Rhapsody, Palace, 1949; Gay's the Word, Saville, 1951. *Recreations:* theatres, motoring, swimming. *Address:* 11 Aldwych, W.C.2.

[*Died* 6 *March* 1951.

NOVY, Frederick G., M.D., Sc.D., LL.D.; Dean Emeritus of the Medical School, Professor Emeritus of Bacteriology, University of Michigan; *b.* 9 Dec. 1864; Member of the National Academy of Sciences; American Philosophical Society; Hon. Member: Société de Pathologie Exotique of Paris, Soc. of Am. Bacteriologists, Am. Assoc. Immunologists, American Society of Tropical Medicine, Am. Trudeau Soc., Michigan Acad. of Science, Assoc. of Am. Physicians, and Philadelphia Pathological Soc.; Associate Member Société Royale des Sciences Médicales et Naturelles of Bruxelles; Corresp. Member Société de Biologie of Paris; Hon. Fellow New York Acad. of Medicine and of Internat. Coll. of Surgeons; Hon. Pres. 3rd Internat. Congress for Microbiology, New York City, 1939; Henry L. Russel Lecturer, 1927; George M. Kober Lecturer, 1931; Award of the 250,000th Bausch and Lomb microscope, Amer. Assoc. Adv. Sc., 1936; Chevalier of the Legion of Honour; Order of White Lion of Czechoslovakia. *Address:* 721 S. Forest Avenue, Ann Arbor, Michigan, U.S.A.

[*Died* 8 *Aug.* 1957.

NOWELL, Charles, Hon. M.A. (Manchester); F.L.A.; City Librarian, Manchester Public Libraries, since 1932; *b.* Kendal, 20 Nov. 1890; *s.* of Charles Nowell and Mary Craiston; *m.* 1922, Jessie, *d.* of Henry Dunt; one *s.* two *d.* *Educ.:* Kendal Grammar School. Deputy City Librarian, Norwich, 1913-22 (war service Artists' Rifles and Queen's Bn., London Regiment); City Librarian, Coventry, 1922-1932; examiner to and (since 1925) member Council of Library Assoc., Chairman, 1939-1945, Vice-Pres., 1946-47, Pres., 1948; Hon. Sec. North-Western Regional Library System; Pres. N.W. Branch of the Library Association, 1938-45; Pres. Soc. of Municipal and County Chief Librarians, 1948-53. *Publications:* Index Nominum: Norfolk Families, 1915; City of Coventry: Roll of the Fallen, 1927; Editor of Books for Club Libraries, 1926; Books to Read, 1930, and its Supplement, 1931; contributor to A Primer of Librarianship, 1931; Small Municipal Libraries: a manual of modern method, 1934; The Book World, 1935; and to various technical and professional books and journals on library practice. *Address:* Central Library, Manchester 2. *T.:* Manchester Central 1992, Chorlton-cum-Hardy 2332.

[*Died* 9 *Aug.* 1954.

NOYES, Alfred, C.B.E. 1918; LL.D.; Litt.D.; *b.* Staffs., 16 Sept. 1880; *s.* of late Alfred Noyes and late Amelia Adams Rowley; *m.* 1st, 1907, Garnett (*d.* 1926), *y. d.* of late Col. B. G. Daniels (U.S. army); 2nd, 1927, Mary, *widow* of Richard Weld-Blundell of Ince-Blundell Hall, Lancs, *d.* of late Captain J. G. Mayne, C.B.E., and *g.d.* of Sir Frederick Weld, G.C.M.G.; one *s.* two *d.* *Educ:* Exeter College, Oxford; Hon. LL.D., Glasgow University, 1927. Hon. Litt.D., Yale Univ., 1913; LL.D. Univ. of Calif. (Berkeley), 1944; Hon. L.H.D. Syracuse Univ. (N.Y.), 1942; gave the Lowell Lectures in America, on The Sea in English Poetry, 1913; elected to Professorship of Modern English Literature on the Murray Foundation, Princeton University, 1914; resigned, 1923; temporarily attached to Foreign Office, 1916; contributed to Blackwood's Magazine, Cornhill, Fortnightly Review,

Quarterly Review, etc. *Publications:* The Loom of Years (poems), 1902; The Flower of Old Japan (a tale in verse), 1903; Poems, 1904; The Forest of Wild Thyme, 1905; Drake (an English Epic), 1908; Forty Singing Seamen, 1907; Minstrelsy of the Scottish Border (editor), 1908; The Enchanted Island and other poems, 1909; Collected Poems, two volumes, 1910; third volume, 1920; William Morris (English Men of Letters), 1908; Tales of the Mermaid Tavern, 1912; The Winepress (a Tale of War, 1913); Rada (Play), 1915; A Salute from the Fleet, 1915; Walking Shadows (short stories), 1917; The Elfin Artist (new poems), 1920; Selected Verse, 1921; The Torchbearers, vol. i. 1922, vol. ii. 1925, vol. iii. 1930, in 1 vol. 1937; The Hidden Player (short stories), 1924; Aspects of Modern Poetry (essays), 1924; Songs of Shadow-of-a-Leaf (lyrics), 1924; Collected Poems, vol. iv., 1927; The Immortal Legions, and other poems; Robin Hood (a poetic drama), 1927; Ballads and Poems, 1928; The Return of the Scarecrow (novel), 1929; The Opalescent Parrot (essays), 1929; The Unknown God, 1934; Voltaire, 1936, 2nd Edition, 1938; Orchard's Bay, 1939; The Last Man, 1940; The Secret of Pooduck Island, 1943; The Edge of the Abyss, 1944; Shadows on the Down (verse), 1945; Portrait of Horace, 1947; Collected Poems in 1 vol., 1950; Two Worlds for Memory (autobiography), 1953; The Devil Takes a Holiday, 1955; A Letter to Lucian (new poems), 1956; The Accusing Ghost, or Justice for Casement, 1957. *Recreations:* chess, swimming. *Address:* Lisle Combe, St. Lawrence, Isle of Wight. *T.:* Ventnor 582. *Clubs:* Athenæum, Beefsteak. [*Died* 28 *June* 1958.

NUGENT, Vice-Admiral Raymond Andrew, C.M.G. 1918; R.N., retired; *b.* 1870; *s.* of Gen. Charles Lavallin William Nugent; *m.* 1st, 1906, Adelaide Georgina (*d.* 1920), *d.* of Maj. F. D. Forde; 2nd, 1922, Violet Graham (*d.* 1947), *d.* of T. F. Leadbitter and *widow* of A. J. Carew. Naval A.D.C. to H.M., 1919-20; Vice-Admiral, 1925. *Address:* The Field House, Lee-on-Solent, Hants. [*Died* 13 *Sept.* 1959.

NUGENT, Sir Walter (Richard), 4th Bart., *cr.* 1831; Senator, Irish Free State, 1928; M.P. (N.) S. Westmeath, 1907-1918; Director Midland Great Western Railway, Ireland; Deputy Chairman, 1913; Chairman Great Southern Railways Amalgamated Company, Ireland, 1925; Chairman Irish Railway Clearing House, 1926; Member of English Railways Clearing House and Railway Superannuation Committee, Euston; Deputy Chairman Fishguard and Rosslare Railways and Harbours Board, 1926; Pres., Dublin Chamber of Commerce, 1929; served on Royal Commission, 1916; Director Bank of Ireland, 1920, Deputy Governor, 1924; Director N. Assurance Co.; High Sheriff, Westmeath, 1922 and 1923; Peace Commissioner, I.F.S., 1924; J.P. and Deputy Lieut. Westmeath; on Agricultural Wages Board, Ireland; Steward Turf Club and National Hunt, 1923; *b.* 12 Dec. 1865; 3rd *s.* of 2nd Bt. and Maria More, *o. d.* of Rt. Hon. Richard More O'Ferrall; *m.* 1916, Aileen Gladys, *y. d.* of late Middleton Moore O'Malley, J.P., Ross, Westport, Co. Mayo; one *s.* two *d.* *Educ.:* Downside Coll.; Univ. Coll., Dublin. *Heir:* *s.* Peter Walter James [*b.* 26 Jan. 1920; *m.* 1947, Anne Judith, *o. d.* of Maj. R. Smyth; one *d.*]. *Address:* Donore, Multyfarnham, Co. Westmeath. *Clubs:* Reform, Turf; Irish Turf, Kildare Street (Dublin). [*Died* 12 *Nov.* 1955.

NUNAN, William, B.A., M.D., Psychotherapist; *b.* Limerick, 26 Jan. 1880; *m.* 1st; one *d.*; 2nd, 1949, Marjorie Reynolds, B.Sc., Psychologist. *Educ.:* Christian Brothers' Schools, and Crescent Coll., Limerick; Clongowes Wood Coll., Kildare; Royal Univ. of Ireland; Dublin University (T.C.D.); M.B., B.Ch., B.A.O., 1905; M.D. 1906. Acting Police Surgeon, Bombay, 1911; Acting Certifying Factory Surgeon, 1914; Kaisar-i-Hind medal, 1st class, 1932; Police Surgeon of Bombay and Professor of Medical Jurisprudence and Toxicology, Grant Medical College, Bombay, 1919-35; Examiner, University of Bombay; Administrative Medical Officer Bombay Port Trust; retired from India, 1935. Psychiatric Specialist Ministry of Pensions (Southampton and Portsmouth), 1946-48. Member, British Society of Medical Hypnotists, 1949; Fellow of Royal Academy of Medicine in Ireland, 1949. *Publications:* Lectures in Medical Jurisprudence; Suggestion as a Remedial Agent; The Mental Factor in Disease. *Recreations:* motoring, riding, travel. *Address:* 9 Fairholt Street, Knightsbridge, S.W.7. *T.:* Knightsbridge 1166; 83 Woodland Av., Hove 4, Sussex. *Clubs:* Authors'; University (Dublin). [*Died* 3 *May* 1955.

NUNN, Vice-Admiral Wilfrid, C.B. 1917; C.S.I. 1919; C.M.G. 1916; D.S.O., 1915. Served on staff R.N. War College, 1911-1912; War Staff Officer, 1912; European War, 1914-16 (D.S.O.); Amara (despatches); also present at capture of Nasiriyah (despatches), Baghdad (despatches); Naval General Service medal, Persian Gulf clasp, 1914; Mesopotamia (despatches several times, C.B., C.M.G., 1914-15 Star, British War Medal, 1914-18, Victory Medal); Commanded H.M. Ships Aurora and Curlew in Harwich Force, July 1917-April 1919; served in Training and Staff Duties Division at Admiralty, April to Nov. 1919; in Command of H.M.S. Ramillies, 1924-25; Rear-Adm. 1925; retired list, 1928; Vice-Adm., retired, 1930; a Naval A.D.C. to the King, 1924; a Nautical Assessor to the Court of Appeal, 1931-37. *Publication:* Tigris Gunboats, 1932. *Address:* Galphay Manor, Ripon, Yorks. *T.:* Kirkby-Malzeard 205. *Clubs:* Naval and Military; Royal Naval (Portsmouth). [*Died* 7 *April* 1956.

NUTT, Francis George, C.B.E. 1928; *b.* 1878; *s.* of late George Nutt, of Rugby, and late Diana Elizabeth, *d.* of Archdeacon Reynolds; *m.* 1940, Victoria Emily Symons, *d.* of late Arthur Weeks, Tenterden. *Educ.:* Winchester (Scholar); Hertford Coll., Oxford (Scholar). First Div. Clerk, Admiralty, 1901; Assist. Principal, 1906; O.B.E., 1918; Principal, Air Ministry, 1918; Assistant Secretary, Air Ministry, 1920-38. *Recreations:* book collecting and gardening. *Address:* Birchwood, Liphook, Hants. *T.:* Liphook 3109. [*Died* 11 *July* 1954.

NUTT, Major-Gen. Harold Rothery, M.D.(Lond.), F.R.C.S.; Indian Medical Service, retired; *b.* 28 Dec. 1876; *s.* of William Henry Rothery Nutt; *m.* 1909, Minnie McKerrow; one *d.* *Educ.:* Bedford Modern School. Entered Indian Medical Service, 1901; in Civil Medical employ as Civil Surgeon, United Provinces, India, 1908; Professor of Surgery, King George's Medical College, 1920-24; Inspector-General of Civil Hospitals, United Provinces, 1930-33; Surgeon-General with Govt. of Bombay, 1933-35; retired 1935; served European War in Egypt and Hospital ships. *Recreations:* gardening, motoring. *Address:* Warren Down, Upper Carlisle Road, Eastbourne, Sussex. *T.A.* and *T.:* Eastbourne 865. [*Died* 2 *Jan.* 1953.

NUTTALL, Ellis; *b.* 8 Dec. 1890; *e. and only surv. s.* of Alfred Nuttall, Blackburn; *m.* Muriel. *Educ.:* Rugby; Trinity Coll., Oxford; M.A. Called to Bar, Middle Temple, 1913; served R.F.A. (T.F.), 1914-19, Egypt, Gallipoli, and France; practised Northern Circuit; M.P. (C.) Birkenhead West, 1924-29; Joint Master Blackmore Vale Hounds, 1937-40; served War of 1939-45. *Address:* Camel Farm, Queen Camel, Yeovil, Somerset. *T.:* Marston Magna 221; Higher Thorne, Exford, Som. *T.:* Exford 226. [*Died* 1 *July* 1951.

NYGAARDSVOLD, John; *b.* Hommelvik, Trondelag, 6 Sept. 1879; *s.* of Anders Nygaardsvold and Andrea Ratvold; *m.* 1901, Albine Brandsleth; two *s.* two *d.* Sawmill, tile, and farm worker; railway construction worker in U.S.A., 1901-7; warehouseman; Member of Malvik Parish Council, later Chairman; Member of Norwegian Storting since 1916; later, President of Storting; President of Second Chamber of Storting; Minister of Agriculture, Jan.-Feb. 1928 in Hornsrud Govt. first Labour Govt. in Norway; Prime Minister of Norway, 1935-1945; Minister of Public Works, 1935-39; Member of a number of councils and committees; Member of National Executive Council of Norwegian Labour Party, since 1923; President Parl. Group of Norwegian Labour Party, 1932-35. *Recreations:* reading, including English and especially Swedish literature, both classical and modern. Outdoor life. *Address:* 35 St. Olav's Gate, Oslo; Hommelvik, Trondelag. [*Died* 13 *March* 1952.

O

OAKDEN, Sir Ralph, Kt., *cr.* 1931; C.S.I. 1925; O.B.E. 1919; B.A.; I.C.S., retired 1930; *b.* 1871; *s.* of late Rev. Roger Oakden, Rector of Bramshall, Staffordshire; *m.* 1899, Rosa Mary (*d.* 1948), *d.* of P. A. Eagles of Meophams Bank, St. Leonards-on-Sea; three *d.* *Educ.:* Cranbrook School; Hertford College, Oxford (Scholar). Entered I.C.S. 1894; went to India, 1895, and was posted to the United Provinces; from 1904 onwards held charge of various districts, Gorakhpur, Ballia (1904-08), Dehra Dun (1910-13), Shahjahanpur (1913-15), Aligarh (1915-20); Commissioner from 1920, successively at Lucknow, Jhansi, Fyzabad, and Meerut; Member, Board of Revenue and Legisl. Council, 1928; Financial Commissioner, Cyprus, 1934. *Publication:* Report on finances etc. of Cyprus, 1934. *Address:* Stowford House, Pit Farm Road, Guildford. *T.:* Guildford 2534. [*Died* 17 *Feb.* 1953.

OAKELEY, Sir Charles Richard Andrew, 6th Bt., *cr.* 1790; J.P.; head of firm of Oakeley, Vaughan & Co. Ltd., insurance brokers; *b.* 14 Aug. 1900; *s.* of Sir Charles Oakeley, 5th Bt., and 1st wife, Emily (*d.* 1932), *y. d.* of Col. Andrew Green, late Rifle Brigade; *S.* father 1938; *m.* 1st, 1924, Audrey Fairless Dampier (from whom he obtained a divorce, 1932), *er. d.* of Capt. Dampier Palmer, of Heronden Hall, Tenterden, Kent; 2nd, 1948, Marina (from whom he obtained a divorce, 1952; she *m.* 1952, Aubrey Baring), *er. d.* of Basil Bessel; 3rd 1957, Mrs. Anne Marie Rudd, London. *Heir: cousin* Edward Atholl [*b.* 31 May 1900; *m.* 1st, 1922, Ethyl Felice O'Coffey (marr. diss. 1929); 2nd, 1930, Patricia Mabel Mary (marr. diss.), *d.* of L. H. Birtchnell, Slough; one *s.*; 3rd, 1952, Doreen, *d.* of F. S. Wells, Southampton]. *Address:* Frittenden House, Cranbrook, Kent. [*Died* 22 *Nov.* 1959.

OAKES, Sir Cecil, Kt., *cr.* 1943; C.B.E. 1938; Deputy Chairman, East and West Suffolk Quarter Sessions since 1951; *b.* 9 February 1884. Formerly: Clerk of the Peace and of the County Council of East Suffolk; Chm. Agricultural Land Tribunal (Eastern Area); now an Alderman of that County Council; Member of Central Health Services Council since 1948; Vice-Chairman, 1957. D.L. Suffolk, 1952. *Publications:* Joint Editor (with W. I. Dacey) of Local Government and Local Finance (9th edition). *Address:* Burgh Cottage, nr. Woodbridge, Suffolk. *T.:* Grundisburgh 226. *Clubs:* Athenæum; County (Ipswich). [*Died* 14 *Jan.* 1959.

OAKESHOTT, Major-General John Field Fraser, C.B. 1954; C.B.E. 1940 (O.B.E. 1941); Director of Ordnance Services, Middle East Land Forces, since 1953; Col. Comdt., Royal Army Ordnance Corps, since 1957; *b.* 2 Sept. 1899; *s.* of late Dr. W. F. Oakeshott; *m.* 1922, Elaine, *d.* of late H. J. Criddle. Served European War, 1914-1918 in France and Belgium, 1914-19. Sometime A.D.C. to H.M. *Address:* Strangers Place, Brightwell, near Wallingford, Berks. [*Died* 4 *Oct.* 1957.

OAKLEY, Alfred James, F.R.B.S.; Practising Sculptor; *b.* 13 March 1880; *s.* of James and Emily Oakley; unmarried. *Educ.:* Wycombe School, Bucks. Exhibitor at leading galleries, International Exhibitions Paris, Brussels, Venice, Buenos-Aires, etc.; carved work in Tate Gallery purchased by the Chantrey Bequest, 1926; Decorative Panel and Group on Queen Mary, Cunard White Star S.S. and works on Public Buildings, etc., memorials. *Recreation:* walking. *Address:* Saint Michael's Abbey, Farnborough, Hants. *T.:* Farnborough 5. [*Died* 28 *April* 1959.

OAKLEY, Philip Douglas, C.B.E. 1936; M.R.C.S.; L.R.C.P.; D.T.M.; *b.* 25 March 1883; *s.* of John Oakley, Surgeon, Holly House, Halifax, Yorks; *m.* 1915, Beatrice Hilda Josephine Kirk; one *s.* *Educ.:* Shrewsbury School; Leeds University. Medical Officer, Gold Coast Colony, 1911; Director of Medical Services, Sierra Leone, West Africa, 1933-38. Medical Transport Officer and Medical Officer in Charge, Casualty Evacuation Trains, E.M.S., Ministry of Health, 1939-46. *Recreations:* shooting, fishing, golf. *Address:* Coasters Cottage, Roundabout, nr. Pulborough, Sussex. *T.:* West Chiltington 3200. *Club:* West Sussex Golf. [*Died* 16 *Aug.* 1958.

O'BRIEN, Hon. Donough; *b.* 29 Aug. 1879; 4th *s.* of 14th Baron Inchiquin, K.P., and 2nd wife, Hon. Ellen White, *d.* of 2nd Baron Annaly, K.P.; *m.* 1st, 1914, Patricia Fédora (*d.* 1926), *d.* of John Dowdeswell, Derby; no *c.*; 2nd, 1928, Mrs. Rose Ades, 66 Mount Street, W.1. *Educ.:* Winchester College; Christ Church, Oxford: M.A. 1905. Called to Bar, Inner Temple, 1905; Fellow: Society of Antiquaries; Irish Geological Research Society; Royal Society of Antiquaries, Ireland; Royal Society of Arts; Hon. member Roy. Soc. of Miniature Painters; Member of Executive Committee of Irish Trade Section of London Chamber of Commerce since 1927. Served European War, 1914-18, as 2nd Lt. in the Irish Guards. Diploma and Hon. Mem. Inst. Oriental Studies of Patriarchal Library, Alexandria, 1952. *Publications:* History of The O'Briens from Brian Boroimhe; Miniatures in the Eighteenth and Nineteenth Centuries. *Recreations:* cricket, golf, motoring. *Address:* Domaine Ades, Ras el Sodor, Alexandria, Egypt. *Clubs:* Bath, Royal Automobile, Curzon, Union, Royal Yacht Club of Egypt (Alexandria). [*Died* 23 *Sept.* 1953.

O'BRIEN, John, C.M.G. 1946; Retd.; *b.* 1895. *Educ.:* John Lyon's School, Harrow. Served European War, 1914-18; seconded 2nd Bn. King's African Rifles, 1918-20; Administrative Officer, Nyasaland, 1920; Deputy Provincial Commissioner, Zanzibar, 1937; Provincial Commissioner, 1939. [*Reported missing in South Africa, Dec.* 1947; *death legally presumed* 13 *Oct.* 1954.

O'BRIEN, Most Rev. Michael, D.D.; Bishop of Kerry, (R.C.), since 1927; *b.* 1877; *s.* of late Bryan O'Brien, Ardcanaught, Castlemaine, Co. Kerry. *Educ.:* Christian Brothers School, Tralee; Seminary, Killarney; Maynooth College; B.D., B.C.L. Ordained, 1901; returned to the Dunboyne Establishment, Maynooth, for two years, at the end of which received the S.T.L.; Professor of Sacred Scripture and Canon Law in All Hallows College, Dublin, 1903-10;

recalled to Kerry Diocese; served as Curate in Millstreet, Ballylongford, Dingle, and Killarney; Administrator, Killarney, 1926. *Address:* The Palace, Killarney, Co. Kerry, Ireland. [*Died* 4 *Oct.* 1952.

O'BRIEN, Michael, C.I.E. 1938; *b.* 1883; *s.* of Dr. M. O'Brien, Clare, Ireland; *m.* 1916, A. E. Hannigan (*d.* 1955), Donegal, Ireland; three *d.* *Educ.:* Queen's Colleges, Cork and Galway; National University of Ireland. Joined Public Works Department Madras, as Assistant Engineer, 1906; Executive Engineer, 1912; Superintending Engineer, 1930; Chief Engineer to Government of Madras, 1936-38; retired, 1938. *Address:* c/o Grindlay's Bank Ltd., 54 Parliament Street, S.W.1. [*Died* 10 *March* 1958.

O'BRIEN, Sir Robert Rollo Gillespie, 4th Bt., *cr.* 1849; *b.* 9 June 1901; *o. surv. s.* of Sir Timothy Carew O'Brien, 3rd Bt. and Gundrede, *d.* of Sir Humphrey De Trafford, 2nd Bt.; *S.* father 1948; *m.* 1925, Esther Ethel, *d.* of Norman Coghill, Almington Hall, Market Drayton; three *d.* *Educ.:* Oratory School. Formerly Flt.-Lieut. R.A.F.V.R. *Heir: cousin* John Edmond Noel O'Brien, M.C. [*b.* 23 Dec. 1899; *s.* of late Edmond Lyons O'Brien (*y. b.* of 3rd Bt.); *m.* 1st, 1928, Moira Violet (marriage dissolved, 1940), *d.* of Capt. R. B. Brassey; 2nd, 1940, Rosemary Brent Staniland, *d.* of Edgar Grotrian, Knapton Hall, Malton; one *d.*]. *Address:* Red House Farm, Monk Sherborne, Basingstoke, Hants. [*Died* 18 *April* 1952.

O'BRIEN-BUTLER, Pierce Essex; *b.* 15 Nov. 1858; *o. surv. s.* of late Pierce O'Brien-Butler, of Bansha, Co. Tipperary, and Inland Revenue, Somerset House; *m.* 1896, Mary Millicent, *e. d.* of T. J. O. Weatherston, Berwick-on-Tweed, and Chinkiang, China; two *d.* (and one *d.* decd.). *Educ.:* Germany. Student-Interpreter, China, 1880; Proconsul, Tainan, Formosa, 1888-93; called to Bar, Middle Temple, 1895; Consul Wenchow, 1899; Hangchow, 1902; Amoy, 1906; Consul-General, Chengtu, 1908; Yunnan-fu, 1909; Mukden, 1913; retired, Apr. 1919; Acting Consul, Vladivostok; Acting High Comr. for Siberia, then Acting Dep. High Comr. Vladivostok, Nov.-Dec. 1919. *Address:* Bansha, Plat Douet Road, Jersey, C.I. [*Died* 2 *Nov.* 1954.

O'BYRNE, Hon. Mr. Justice (John), Q.C. 1924; M.A.; Judge of Supreme Court of Justice of Eire since 1940; *b.* 24 Apr. 1884; 4th *s.* of Patrick and Mary O'Byrne of Seskin, Co. Wicklow; *m.* 1924, Marjorie, *er. d.* of John F. McGuire, Dublin; three *s.* two *d.* *Educ.:* Patrician Monastery, Tullow, Co. Carlow; University College, Dublin. Graduated Royal University of Ireland, 1907; First Place and First Class Honours, M.A. degree, 1908; Studentship in Mental and Moral Science, 1908; called to Irish Bar, 1911; Attorney-General Irish Free State, 1924-26; Judge of High Court of Justice of the Irish Free State, 1926-40; Member of Irish Free State Constitution Committee, 1922; Member of Judiciary Committee, 1923; Delegate to League of Nations, 1924. *Address:* St. Catherine's, Ballyboden, Co. Dublin. *T.:* 906036. [*Died* 14 *Jan.* 1954.

O'CONNOR, Arthur John; Chairman, Army Pensions Board, Ireland, since 1949; Circuit Court Judge for Cork City, 1947; *b.* 1888. Qualified, first as a Civil Engineer, then as a Barrister. M.P. (S.F.) South Kildare, Dec. 1918-22. *Address:* Elm Hall, Celbridge, Co. Kildare, Ireland. [*Died* 2 *May* 1950.
[*But death not notified in time for inclusion in Who Was Who* 1941–1950, *first edn.*

O'CONNOR, The Rev. Edward Dominic, S.J., M.A., F.R.A.S.; Professor at Manresa College since 1938; *b.* Trinidad, 1874; *s.* of late Leon Denis O'Connor, Crown Solicitor. *Educ.:* Beaumont; Campion Hall, Oxford. 1st Class Honours Maths., Mods. and Finals. Entered Society of Jesus, 1893; Professor, Mathematics and Physics at St. Mary's Hall Training College, 1902-7; theological studies, 1907-11; Priest, 1910; senior mathematical master at Stonyhurst College, 1912-16, and on the Observatory staff; Director of the Observatory, 1925-32; Rector of Stonyhurst, 1916-24, and again 1932-38. *Address:* Manresa College, Roehampton, S.W.15. *T.:* Putney 3285. [*Died* 23 *Feb.* 1954.

O'CONNOR, George Bligh; Judge of the Supreme Court of Alberta, 1941, Appellate Division, 1946, Chief Justice of Alberta since 1950; *b.* Walkerton, Ontario, 16 March 1883; *s.* of Frederick S. and Maria I. O'Connor; *m.* 1913, Hannah Margaret Fairlie; one *d.* *Educ.:* Walkerton Public and High Schools; Osgoode Hall, Toronto. Called to Ontario Bar, 1905; Alberta, 1905; K.C. 1913; LL.D. (Alberta), 1952; Member Griesbach, O'Connor and O'Connor, 1905-40; Bencher Law Society of Alberta, 1936-40; Chairman Western Labour Board, 1943-44; Chairman, Wartime Labour Relations Board (National), 1944-48; Chairman, Canada Labour Relations Board, 1948-53. *Address:* 36 St. George's Crescent, Edmonton, Alberta. *T.:* 82409. [*Died* 13 *Jan.* 1957.

O'CONNOR, Colonel Henry Willis-, C.V.O. 1946; C.B.E. 1935; D.S.O. 1916, *b.* 1886; *s.* of late Daniel O'Connor, K.C.; Barrister-at-Law, Ottawa; has assumed additional surname of Willis; *m.* 1921, Hyacinth, D.G.St.J., *d.* of late William Sismore Shaw, of Madras. Was Principal A.D.C. to Viscount Byng of Vimy, Marquis of Willingdon, Earl of Bessborough, Lord Tweedsmuir and Earl of Athlone; retired in 1945. European War, 1915-20; on Staff of 1st Canadian Div. as A.D.C. to Lt.-Gen. Sir Arthur Currie in France and Belgium (despatches twice, D.S.O., 1914-15 Star, two medals). K.St.J. 1954. *Address:* Byng House, Rockcliffe Pk., Ottawa, Canada. *Club:* Rideau (Ottawa). [*Died* 25 *April* 1957.

O'CONOR, Norreys Jephson, A.M.; author; *b.* New York, 31 Dec. 1885; *s.* of John Christopher O'Conor and Maria Jephson Post; *m.* 1st, 1917, Grace Edith Corson; one *d.*; 2nd, Evangelia Hawley Waller, M.A., M.S.S. *Educ.:* Cutler School, New York; Harvard University. With F. A. Stokes Company and John Lane Company, publishers, 1908-10; Assistant in English, Harvard, 1911-13; Instructor at Radcliffe College, 1918-19; Lectured at Harvard, Yale, Columbia and elsewhere in the U.S., 1917-1926; Assistant Professor English, Grinnell College, Iowa, 1922-23; Associate Professor English Literature, Mt. Holyoke College (Mass)., 1923-24; Associate Professor English, Bryn Mawr College (Pennsylvania), 1924-26; engaged in literary and research work in England, 1927-39; advisory editor Poetry Awards Foundation, 1948-50. Served A.R.P.; Chm. Language Corps, Pasadena O.C.D.; Arts and Skills Corps, Am. Red Cross. *Publications:* The Child's Hansel and Gretel, 1909; Celtic Memories and Other Poems, 1913; Beside the Blackwater, 1914; The Fairy Bride (play), 1916 and 1926; Songs of the Celtic Past, 1918; Battles and Enchantments, 1922; Changing Ireland, 1924; There was Magic in those Days, 1929; Memoir (with letters of Maarten Maartens), 1930; Godes Peace and the Queenes, 1934; A Servant of the Crown, 1938; weekly articles on United Nations to editorial page, Los Angeles Times, 1942-44; poems issued from the Handpress of Douglas Howell, 1947-; Late Offering, 1952. *Address:* 512 Plaza Rubio, Santa Barbara, California. *Club:* P.E.N. [*Died* 24 *Oct.* 1958.

O'DEA, William, M.B.E. 1933; Headmaster, St. Anne's, Ancoats, 1911-35; *b.* 1870. *Educ.:* St. Mary's, College, Hammersmith. Headmaster, SS. Peter and Paul's, Bolton, 1895-1911; Former President Catholic Teachers' Federation; Member of Catholic Education Council since 1908 and of the Executive; received Cross Pro Ecclesia et Pontifice for

Catholic educational services, 1932. *Address:* 19 Stretton Drive, Southport, Lancs. [*Died* 17 *Oct.* 1936.
[*But death not notified in time for inclusion in Who Was Who 1929–1940.*

O'DEIRG, Tomás, (Thomas Derrig); *b.* 26-adh Mí na Samhna 1897; *s.* of Pádraic Ó Deirg and Úna Ní Bhradáin; *m.* 1928, Sinéad Nic an tSaoir; two *d. Educ.:* Christian Brothers, Westport; University College, Galway (graduated 1919). Joined Irish Volunteers, 1914; deported, May 1916; imprisoned, 1918; interned, 1920-21; M.P. West Mayo, 1921; T.D., N. and W. Mayo, 1922; Carlow-Kilkenny, 1927-37, 1948; T.D. for Kilkenny since 1927; Minister for Education, 1932-39 and 1940-48; Minister for Lands, 1951-54 (also 1939-43). *Address:* 58 Cearnog Dartmouth, Baile Atha Cliath, Ireland. *T.:* 683021. [*Died* 19 *Nov.* 1956.

ODLE, Mrs. Alan; *see* Richardson, Dorothy M.

O'DOGHERTY, Engineer-Rear-Admiral Francis Blake, C.M.G. 1919. Served European War, 1914-19; with Caspian Flotilla (despatches, C.M.G.); Fleet Engineer Officer in China, 1923-25; Engineer Overseer for the Admiralty in the London district, 1925-29; a Naval A.D.C. to the King, 1928-29; retired list, 1929. *Address:* Old Fairfield, Chudleigh, Devon. [*Died* 4 *Sept.* 1952.

O'DONOGHUE, Thomas Henry, O.B.E. 1951; late Hansard Staff; *b.* 17 May 1886; *s.* of late Owen O'Donoghue, Belfast; *m.* 1918, Bridget Mary Ryan (*d.* 1935), Roscrea, Co. Tipperary; one *d.* Reporter on Irish News and Northern Whig, Belfast; joined Hansard Staff, 1921; Asst. Editor, 1944; Editor Official Report of Debates, House of Commons (Hansard) until 1951. *Recreations:* walking, golf. *Address:* 11 Farnham Road, Bangor, Co. Down. [*Died* 24 *May* 1957.

O'DONOVAN, William James, O.B.E.; M.D. Lond.; M.R.C.P.; Knight of St. Gregory the Great; Consulting Physician Skin Dept., London Hosp.; Consultant Whipp's Cross Hosp.; Dermatologist, St. Andrew's Hosp., Dollis Hill; Cons. Skin Physician, St. Paul's Hosp. and Queen Mary's Hosp., Stratford; late Pres. Dermatological Section and Chm. Marylebone Div., Brit. Med. Assoc.; Emeritus Dermatologist, St. James Hosp., Balham; ex-Pres. Dermat. Sec. Roy. Soc. Med.; late Col. R.A.M.C., Adviser in Dermatology, M.E.F.; Chairman Univ. of London Conservative Association, 1934-37, Pres. since 1937; Chm. London Conservative Union, 1947; Member Cttee. Convocation, Univ. of London; *b.* Tonbridge, Kent; *s.* of Patrick O'Donovan of Clonakilty and Beatrice Gibson of Eynsford; *m.* Ethel K. Smith; one *s.* two *d. Educ.:* Univ. of London; abroad. Formerly Medical Registrar, etc., London Hospital; Chief Medical Officer, Ministry of Munitions of War; Member T.N.T. Committee; Coroner's Pathologist for London; M.P. (U.) Mile End Division of Stepney, 1931-35. *Publications:* Dermatological Neuroses; Diseases of the Hair; Psycho-somatic Dermatoses; On T.N.T. Poisoning, Industrial Cancer, Industrial Dermatitis and Light Treatment, in Proceedings of Royal Society of Medicine, British Journal of Dermatology, British Medical Journal, and Lancet. *Address:* 130 Harley St., W.1. *T.:* Welbeck 3349. [*Died* 13 *Jan.* 1955.

O'DWYER, Lady; Una; D.B.E., *cr.* 1919; Lady of Grace St. John of Jerusalem; *b.* 27 April 1872; *d.* of late Monsieur Bord; *m.* 1896, Sir Michael O'Dwyer, G.C.I.E., K.C.S.I. (*d.* 1940); one *s.* one *d. Educ.:* Private. *Address:* 6 Empire House, Thurloe Place, S.W.7. *T.:* Kensington 3071. [*Died* 26 *Nov.* 1956.

OGDEN, C(harles) K(ay); Originator of Basic English; *b.* 1889; *s.* of late C. B. Ogden and late F. H. Ogden. *Educ.:* Rossall; Magdalene College, Cambridge (M.A., 1915). 1st Class Classical Tripos, 1910; represented Cambridge Univ. *v.* Oxford at Billiards, 1909; Founder and Editor, The Cambridge Magazine, 1912-22; visited schools and Univs. in France, Belgium, Germany, Italy, Switzerland, and India to study methods of language teaching, 1912-13; ditto in U.S.A. as Science Adviser, The Forum, New York, 1925-27; organized The Orthological Institute (1927) with Representatives in 30 countries (1939); Bentham Centenary Lecture, University College, London, 1932; gave evidence, October 1943, before Committee of Ministers established by Mr. Churchill on Basic English (Cmd. 6511, of 9 March 1944); bedevilled by officials, 1944-46; requested to assign General Basic Copyright to Crown (June 1946); Founder, The Basic English Foundation, with grant from Ministry of Education, April 1947; Editor, Psyche, Vol. XVIII, 1950. *Publications:* Various, on Debabelization, etc. *Recreation:* orthology. *Address:* Falcon Yard, Cambridge. *Clubs:* Athenæum, Reform, Oxford and Cambridge, Lansdowne, Royal Societies, Royal Automobile. [*Died* 20 *March* 1957.

OGG, Col. William Mortimer, C.M.G. 1919; D.S.O. 1916; late R.A.; *b.* 1873; *s.* of late Surgeon-General G. S. W. Ogg, I.M.S.; *m.* 1904, Evelyn, *d.* of E. E. Phillips. Entered R.A. 1893; retired, 1927; served European War, 1914-19 (despatches, D.S.O., C.M.G., Bt. Lt.-Col., Legion of Honour, Order of Aviz of Portugal). *Address:* Fernleigh, Larkfield, Maidstone, Kent. *T.:* West Malling 3439. [*Died* 3 *Feb.* 1958.

OGILVIE, Alan Grant, O.B.E. 1919; F.R.S.E.; Professor of Geography, University of Edinburgh, since 1931; *b.* Edinburgh, 1887; *s.* of late Sir Francis Ogilvie; *m.* 1919, Evelyn Decima (*d.* 1952), *d.* of Rev. G. E. Willes; one *d. Educ.:* George Watson's College; Westminster School; Magdalen College, Oxford, B.A. 1909, M.A., B.Sc.; Imperial College of Science, London; Universities of Berlin and Paris. Served in R.F.A., 1911-19 (despatches); and Peace Delegation, Paris, 1919; Captain, Home Guard, 1941-44; Demonstrator in Geography, University of Oxford, 1912-14; Reader in Geography, University of Manchester, 1919-20; Chief of Hispanic American Division of the American Geographical Society of New York, 1920-23; Lecturer, University of Edinburgh, 1923; Reader, 1924; Albert Kahn Travelling Fellow, 1914; awarded Cuthbert Peek Grant by Royal Geographical Society, 1915; Milne-Edwards Medal by the Paris Geographical Society, 1923; Royal Scottish Geographical Society; Hon. Sec. 1925-41, Research Medal and Hon. Fellow 1945, Livingston Medal 1951, and Pres. 1946-50; Pres. Inst. of British Geographers, 1951-52; Hon. Member Geographical Soc. of Belgrade, Frankfurt a/M., Leningrad, Stockholm, and Manchester; Assoc. of American Geographers; Contributing Editor, Geographical Review; Pres., Geographical Section of British Association, 1934, and of Physical Geography Section at International Geographical Congress, Lisbon, 1949. Serbian Order of St. Sava, 3rd Class and White Eagle, 5th Class. *Publications:* Some Aspects of Boundary Settlement at the Peace Conference, 1922; Geography of the Central Andes, 1922; editor and part author of Great Britain, 1928, 2nd Ed. 1930; various papers on geographical subjects. *Address:* 40 Fountainhall Road, Edinburgh 9. [*Died* 10 *Feb.* 1954.

OGILVIE, Lieutenant-Colonel Gordon, C.M.G. 1918; late R.G.A.; Consultant Canadian Arsenals Ltd. since 1948; *b.* 13 Mar. 1878; *s.* of late Rev. Alex. Ogilvie, LL.D., Aberdeen; *m.* 1905, Marion Mark, *d.* of late Arch. Cowan, Edinburgh; one *s. Educ.:* Gordon's College, Aberdeen; Royal Military Academy, Woolwich. 2nd Lieut. R.A., 1897; Capt. R.G.A., 1902; Major, 1914; Bt. Lt.-Col.,

1917; Lt.-Col., 1922; retired, 1923; Asst. Inspector, Woolwich, 1911-13; Inspector of Ammunition, Canadian Govt., 1913-15; Chief Inspector, Imperial Munitions Board, 1915-16; Chief Inspector and Deputy Director Inspection (Canada), Imperial Ministry of Munitions, 1916-19; Chief Inspector of Explosives, Dept. of Mines, Canada, 1919-37; Central Investigation Committee, Dept. of National Defence, 1937-39; Department of Munitions and Supply, Canada, 1940-46; on staff of War Assets Corporation, Canada, 1946-47. *Address:* P.O. Box 340, Valleyfield, P.Q., Canada. [*Died* 8 *Feb.* 1958.

OGILVIE-FORBES, Sir G. A. D.; *see* Forbes.

OGILVY, Gilbert Francis Molyneux; architect; *b.* 9 April 1868; 4th *s.* of Sir Reginald Ogilvy, 10th Bt., of Inverquharity, and Olivia, *d.* of 9th Baron Kinnaird; *m.* 1912, Marjory, *d.* of late M. B. Clive of Whitfield, Herefordshire; two *s.* three *d.* *Educ.:* Glenalmond; University College, Oxford. *Address:* Winton Castle, Pencaitland, East Lothian. *Club:* New (Edinburgh). [*Died* 17 *June* 1953.

OGILVY, Sir Herbert Kinnaird, 12th Bt., *cr.* 1626; Writer to the Signet; *b.* 29 June 1865; *s.* of 10th Bt. and Olivia Barbara, *d.* of 9th Baron Kinnaird; *S. nephew,* 1914; *m.* 1904, Lady Christian Bruce (*d.* 1940), 2nd *d.* of 9th Earl of Elgin. *Heir: n.* David John Wilfred Ogilvy, *b.* 3 Feb. 1914. *Address:* Baldovan House, Dundee; Pityoulish, Aviemore, Inverness-shire. *Clubs:* Brooks's, English-Speaking Union; New (Edinburgh); Highland (Inverness); Eastern (Dundee). [*Died* 1 *March* 1956.

OGILVY-WEDDERBURN, Sir John Andrew, 11th and 5th Bt., *cr.* 1704 and 1803; *b.* 16 Sept. 1866; *S.* cousin, 1918; *m.* 1909, Meta Aileen Odette (*d.* 1952), *e. d.* of Brig.-Gen. E. G. Grogan, C.B., C.B.E.; one *s.* three *d.* Formerly Major Scottish Horse Yeomanry; served European War, 1914-18. *Heir: s.* John Peter Ogilvy-Wedderburn, Comdr., R.N. [*b.* 29 Sept. 1917; *m.* 1946, Elizabeth Katharine, *d.* of late John A. Cox, Drumkilbo, Meigle; one *s.* (*b.* 4 Aug. 1952) three *d.*]. *Address:* Silvie, Alyth, Perthshire. [*Died* 10 *March* 1956.

OGLANDER, Brig.-Gen. C. F. A.; *see* Aspinall-Oglander.

O'GORMAN, Mervyn, C.B. 1913; D.Sc.; Lt.-Col. Royal Flying Corps, 1916; Chairman of Royal Aeronautical Society, 1921-22; Hon. F.R.Ae.S. 1950; M.I.C.E., M.I.Mech.E., M.Inst. Electrical Engineers: Vice-Chairman Royal Automobile Club, 1923-31; Vice-President Royal Automobile Club, 1952; Superintendent of H.M. Royal Aircraft Factory, 1909-16; on Government Mission with Admiral Sir M. Sueter to report on European Aeronautics, 1912; with Air Commodore Babington to report on Italian Front, 1917; C.E. to Director-General of Military Aeronautics, 1916-19; President Technical Commission of Federation Aeronautique Internationale; Chairman Accident Investigation and Civil Air Transport Committees of Air Ministry; Chairman of Adhesives Committee of the Dept. of Scientific and Industrial Research, 1919-29; Chairman League of Nations Sub-Committee on Rating Aeronautical Engines, 1931; Vice-President of the Association Internationale des Automobile Clubs Reconnus; Vice-President of the Fédération Internationale Aéronautique, Paris, 1910-37; Vice-Chairman, Royal Aero Club, 1928; Vice-President, 1934; *b.* Brighton, 1871; *m.* 1897, Florence Catharine (*d.* 1931), *y. d.* of late Arthur Rasch. *Educ.:* Downside; University Coll., Dublin. *Publications:* articles in Quarterly Review, Nineteenth Century, B.B.C., Fortnightly, Times, etc., on Aeronautics and Automobilism. *Recreations:* engraving, making lacquer. *Address:* 21 Embankment Gardens, Chelsea, S.W.3. *T.:* Flaxman 2726. *Club:* Athenæum. [*Died* 16 *May* 1958.

O'GRADY, Guillamore; Barrister-at-law, King's Inns, Dublin; Major, late South Irish Horse; Dublin Herald of Arms since 1908; *b.* 1879; 2nd *s.* of late Edward Stamer O'Grady, M.R.I.A., of Clenagh, Co. Clare. *Educ.:* Trinity College, Dublin, M.A. Called to Bar, Dublin, 1903; Auditor of College Historical Society, University of Dublin, 1901. *Recreations:* motoring and sailing. *Address:* 9 Marine Terrace, Kingstown, Ireland; Carnelly, Co. Clare. *Clubs:* Cavalry; Royal Yacht Squadron (Cowes); Royal Irish Automobile, Kildare Street (Dublin); Royal St. George Yacht (Kingstown). [*Died* 4 *Sept.* 1952.

O'HARA, Colonel Errill Robert, C.M.G. 1916; C.B.E. 1933; D.S.O. 1919; late R. Army Service Corps; 8th *s.* of Charles W. O'Hara, J.P. and D.L., of Annaghmore and Coopers Hill, Co. Sligo, and Annie Charlotte, *e. d.* of R. Shuttleworth Streatfeild; *m.* 1911, Moneen, *y. d.* of Capt. W. Bond, Newtown Bond, Co. Longford; (one *s.* decd.). Served S. African War, 1900-2 (despatches, Queen's medal 3 clasps, King's medal 2 clasps); East Africa, 1903-4 (medal with clasp); Somaliland, 1908-10 (clasp); European War, 1914-18 (despatches, C.M.G., Bt. Lt.-Col., D.S.O., Legion of Honour, Croix de Chevalier, 1917, 3rd Class Order of El Nahda, 1919); Assistant Director of Supplies and Transport, British Army on the Rhine, 1929; Malta, 1930-33; retired pay, 1933; re-employed with R.A.S.C., 1936-41. *Address:* Greatfield Lodge, Weyhill, Hampshire. *T.:* Weyhill 215. [*Died* 5 *June* 1956.

O'HARA, Francis Charles Trench; *b.* 7 Nov. 1870; 2nd *s.* of Robert O'Hara, Master in Chancery, Chatham, Ont., and Maria S. Dobbs; *m.* Helen R., *d.* of Senator H. Corby; one *d.* *Educ.:* Collegiate Institute, Chatham. Entered Canadian Bank of Commerce, 1888; entered journalism in Baltimore, Maryland, 1891; private Secretary to late Rt. Hon. Sir Richard Cartwright, Minister of Trade and Commerce, 1896-1908; Supt. of Trade Commissioner Service, 1904; Deputy Minister of Trade and Commerce for Canada, 1908-1931; Chief Controller Chinese Immigration Service, 1908-11; Local Officer for Canada for Dominions' Royal Commission, 1914-17; Priority Authority for Canada under H.M. Ministry of Munitions and U.S. War Trade Board, 1916-18; in charge Canadian purchase and shipment wheat, blankets and clothing for French and Italian Armies, 1914-1915; Wool Commission, 1917; officer in charge distribution of industrial diamonds for Canada under H.M. Diamond Committee, London, 1916-19; Member Ships' Licence Committee 1914-19; Member Editorial Committee on Government Publications, 1917-23; Deputy Commissioner of Patents, 1918-19; Chairman Canadian Trade Commission, 1920; Canadian Govt. delegate to first Pan Pacific Commercial Conference, Honolulu, 1922; made extensive tour of Latin America in interests of Canadian trade, 1927; retired, 1931. *Recreations:* golf, fishing. *Address:* 125 Wurtemburg Street, Ottawa 2, Canada. *T.:* 4-0056. *Clubs:* Country, Rideau, Royal Ottawa Golf, Denholm Angling (Ottawa). [*Died* 28 *July* 1954.

O'HEGARTY, Patrick Sarsfield; Secretary G.P.O., Dublin, 1922-45; *b.* Cork, 29 Dec. 1879; *m.* 1915, Wilhelmina Rebecca Smyth; one *s.* two *d.* *Educ.:* Christian Schools, Cork. Law clerk, 1895; P.O. clerk, 1897; resigned and took up business as bookseller, 1918. *Publications:* John Mitchel, an Appreciation, 1917; The Indestructible Nation, 1918; Sinn Fein, an Illumination, 1919; Ulster: a Brief Statement of Fact, 1919; A Short Memoir of Terence McSwiney, 1922; The Victory of Sinn Fein, 1924; A Bibliography of Standish O'Grady, 1930; a Bibliography of P. H. Pearse, 1931; Other Irish Bibliographies; A History of Ireland

Under the Union, 1801-1922, 1952; Editor An t- eireannach (London), 1913; Irish Freedom (Dublin), 1911-1914; The Irish World (Dublin), 1918-19; The Separatist (Dublin), 1922. *Recreations:* journalism, controversy, telling the truth. *Address:* Highfield House, Highfield Road, Dublin. *T.:* Dublin 905507. [*Died* 17 *Dec.* 1955.

O'KELLY, John Joseph; *b.* Valentia I., Co. Kerry; *m.* 1904, Nora, *y. d.* of Patrick O'Sullivan, Lisbawn, Kerry. M.P. (S.F.) Louth, Ireland, 1918-23; Member Dail for Cos. Louth and Meath, 1921-23; Chairman, Dail, 1919-21; Speaker, Dail, 1925-30; Chairman Executive Council Second Dail since 1930; Minister for Education, 1919-22; Editor Banba, Catholic Bulletin, An Camán; Hon. Secretary of Society for the Preservation of the Irish Language; President of Gaelic League, 1919-23; toured America and Australia, 1922-24; President Sinn Fein, 1926-30; Member of Council of Academy of Christian Art. *Publications:* over a score of books, in Irish and English, relating to history, folklore, drama, national biography, art, travel, economics; as well as a score of pamphlets on politics, polemics, architecture, education and art—the latest being O'Connell Calling, or the Liberator's Place in the World, and Ireland's Spiritual Empire: St. Patrick as a World Figure. *Address:* 173 Botanic Road, Glasnevin, Dublin. [*Died* 26 *March* 1957.

OLDFIELD, Major John William, C.M.G. 1932; O.B.E.; M.C.; E.D.; *b.* Georgetown, Demarara, 22 Oct. 1886; *s.* of late A. W. Oldfield, Birmingham and British Guiana Civil Service; *m.* 1st, 1910, J. G., *d.* of F. Vogan Harper, Edzell, Forfarshire, and Ceylon; one *s.* three *d.*; 2nd, 1954, Margaret Ella Dakeyne (*née* Bodington). *Educ.:* Royal St. Anne's Soc. School, Redhill. Planting in Ceylon, 1907-14; commissioned Cameronians, Aug. 1914; Brigade Machine Gun Officer, 1915; D.A.A.G., Divisional and Corps Staff, 1917-19 (despatches five times, O.B.E., M.C., Croix de Guerre, Chevalier of the Order of Leopold); Planting, Ceylon, 1919-26; Chairman, Planters' Association of Ceylon, 1924, 1925; European Member of Governor's Executive Council (Ceylon), 1926-31; Member of State Council, Ceylon, 1931-32, 1938-39, and 1943-46; M.P., Ceylon, 1947-52. Commanding (C.O.), Colombo Town Guard, 1939-45. *Address:* The Lido, Negombo, Ceylon. *Clubs:* Junior Carlton; Colombo (Colombo). [*Died* 1 *Dec.* 1955.

OLDFIELD, Dr. Josiah; physician; *b.* Shrewsbury; one *d.* *Educ.:* Newport Grammar School; Oxford Univ.; Lincoln's Inn. Took a second class in the Honour School of Theology at Oxford and then a second class in the School of Civil Law; entered at Lincoln's Inn, and was called to the Bar, and practised on the Oxford circuit; then joined St. Bartholomew's Hospital, and took his medical diploma, and later founded the Humanitarian Hospital of St. Francis, W.C.1, of which he was for some years chairman and senior physician; warden of and senior physician to the Lady Margaret Fruitarian Hospital, Sittingbourne, 1903; he was awarded the degree of Doctor in Civil Law (D.C.L.) at Oxford for his thesis on Capital Punishment; while at Oxford he adopted the Fruitarian diet, and has since then strenuously advocated its adoption by the higher classes for æsthetic and humane reasons; founded the Society for the Abolition of Capital Punishment, 1901; spent some time in India in the winter of 1901 studying the effect of the English Government on the people of India, and trying to discover the reality of their grievances, and at the same time to learn the cause of the modified success of Christian Missions in India; Chairman Romilly Society, 1910; admitted to Jamaican Bar, 1920; Fellow of the Royal Society of Medicine, 1920. *Publications:* Myrrh and Amaranth; Essays of the Golden Age; The Penalty of Death; Brother Pain and his Crown; Diet in Rheumatism; Diet in Indigestion; Diet and Appendicitis; Fasting for Health and Life; The Dry Diet Cure; Get Well and Keep Well; Eat and Get Well; Eat and Keep Well; Eat and Keep Young; Eat and Keep Happy; The Beauty Aspect of Life and Health; Eat and be Beautiful; Healing and the Conquest of Pain, 1944; The Mystery of Birth, 1948; The Mystery of Marriage, 1949; booklets and pamphlets. *Recreations:* raised and commanded a Casualty Clearing Station and a Field Ambulance European War (despatches, T.D.); invalided out with authority to retain his rank of Lt.-Col.; lecturing on Fruitarianism and humane reforms; tree-planting. *Address:* Harley Street, W.1; 5 Essex Court, Temple, E.C.4; Margaret Manor, Doddington, Kent. *T.:* Doddington 20311. *Clubs:* Overseas, English-Speaking Union. [*Died* 2 *Feb.* 1953.

OLDHAM, Henry Yule, M.A. *b.* Düsseldorf, 14 Dec. 1862; *y. s.* of late Thomas Oldham, LL.D., F.R.S., Director of the Geological Survey of India. *Educ.:* Rugby; Jesus Coll., Oxford. Tutor to Duc d'Orléans, 1886-87; studied in Paris, 1888; Assistant Master, Hulme Grammar School, Manchester, 1888-90; Harrow, 1890-91; Berlin University, 1891-92; Lecturer in Geography, Owens Coll. Manchester, 1892; Lecturer in Geography, Camb. Univ., 1893-98; Reader in Geography, Camb. Univ., 1898-1908. *Publications:* various papers in Journal of Royal Geographical Society, and other scientific publications. *Recreations:* golf, sailing, President Cambridge University Cruising Club. *Address:* King's College, Cambridge. *Club:* Athenæum. [*Died* 14 *March* 1951.

OLDROYD, Professor George, D.Mus. (Lond. and Lambeth), F.T.C.L.; King Edward VII Prof. of Music, Univ. of London since 1950; Prof. of Harmony and Composition, Lecturer and Examiner, Trinity College of Music, since 1921; *b.* 1 Dec. 1886; *s.* of Arthur Oldroyd; *m.* Olive, *d.* of A. D. Brown; one *s.* one *d.* *Educ.:* privately. Director of Music, St. George's Church, Paris, 1915; St. Alban's, Holborn, 1919; St. Michael's, Croydon, 1921. Member Corp. and Board Trinity Coll. of Music; Founder and Conductor Croydon Bach Soc., 1925; Dir. of Music, Whitgift Schools, 1933-48; Member Senate, Univ. of London, 1931; Dean of Faculty of Music, Univ. of London, 1944-48; Chm. Bd. of Studies in Music, Univ. of London, 1948; Examiner in Music, Univs. of London, Durham, Nat. Univ. of Ireland; Examiner Composition Prizes, R.A.M. *Publications:* The Accompanying of Plain-chant; The Technique and Spirit of Fugue, 1948; Polyphonic Writing for Voices, 1950; musical compositions published include: Stabat Mater Dolorosa, 1925; Paean of Remembrance for voices and orch.; Spiritual Rhapsody for voices and orch.; Mass of the Quiet Hour (incorp. in New American Episcopal Hymnary); Liturgical Preludes and Improvisations for Organ, etc.; anthems and services. *Recreations:* history, writing, wood-carving. *Address:* Haling Knoll, Nottingham Road, South Croydon, Surrey. *T.:* Croydon 5210. [*Died* 26 *Feb.* 1951.

O'LEARY, Daniel; Solicitor, retired; *b.* Glandart, Bantry 1878; *m.* , 1913, Sara, *d.* of late Patrick Laide, Tralee; one *d.* *Educ.:* Private schools in Cork; Queen's College, Cork; M.P. (N.) West Cork, 1916-18. *Address:* Glandart, Beaumont Drive, Ballintemple, Cork. [*Died* 23 *Dec.* 1954.

O'LEARY, Rev. De Lacy Evans; Lecturer in Bristol University; *b.* 1872; *s.* of H. E. O'Leary, formerly of Fort Shannon, Glin, Co. Limerick. *Educ.:* Trinity College, Dublin; Senior Moderator, History, Elrington Prize; Whately Prize, 1940; M.A., D.D. *Publications:* Apostolic Constitutions, 1906; Syriac Church, 1909; Coptic Theotokia, 1911; Life of St. Dominic, 1912; Studies in the Apoc. Gospels of Christ's Infancy, 1912; Characteristics of the Hamitic Languages, 1915; Arabic Thought and its place in

History, 1922; Short History of Fatimid Khalifate, 1923; Coptic Theotokia 1923 (text edited); Comparative Grammar of Semitic Languages, 1923; Islam at the Cross Roads, 1923; Fragmentary Coptic Hymns, 1924; Colloquial Arabic, 1926; Coptic Difnar, 1926: Arabia before Muhammad, 1927; Coptic Difnar II., 1928; Arabia (Antiquities), in Ency. Brit., 1929; Littérature Copte, in Cabrol-Leclercq Dict-d'arch. chrét., 1930; The Saints of Egypt, 1937; How Greek science passed to the Arabs, 1949. *Address:* 16 Nithsdale Rd., Weston-s.-Mare. [*Died* 22 *July* 1957.

O'LEARY, Rt. Hon. Sir Humphrey Francis, P.C. 1948; K.C.M.G., *cr.* 1947; Chief Justice of New Zealand since 1946; Hon. Master of Bench of Inner Temple, 1948; *b.* 12 Feb. 1886; *s.* of Humphrey John O'Leary and Mary Falvey; *m.* 1912, Lillian Patricia, *d.* of James and Honora Gallagher; one *s.* *Educ.:* Masterton Public School; Wellington Coll.; Victoria Univ. Coll. LL.B. 1908, and admitted as Barrister and Solicitor of Supreme Court. Practised for a time on own account and later until 1935 as member of firm of Bell Gully Myers & O'Leary. K.C. 1935; Past Pres. Wellington District Law Society and Pres. N.Z. Law Society, 1935-1946. Member since 1934 and Chairman, 1941-46, Victoria University College Council and Member Senate of University of New Zealand. *Address:* Chief Justice's Chambers, Supreme Court, Wellington, N.Z. *Club:* Wellington. [*Died* 16 *Oct.* 1953.

OLIPHANT, Capt. Henry Gerard Laurence, D.S.O. 1916; M.V.O. 1915; late R.N.; *b.* 22 Nov. 1879; *e. s.* of late Gen. Sir Laurence J. Oliphant of Condie and Newton, Perthshire, and Hon. Monica Mary Gerard, *e. d.* of 1st Baron Gerard; *m.* 1st, 1906, Ruth, *o. d.* of late Vice-Adm. Sir H. Deacon Barry, K.C.V.O.; one *s.* two *d.*; 2nd, 1934, Mrs. Jane Heywood Towse. *Educ.:* Fosters, Stubbington; Britannia. Served European War in command of Amazon during bombardment of German Army's right wing from coast, 1915 (despatches); patrol work, 1916 (D.S.O.); retired list, 1922; called up, Sept. 1939; commanded H.M.S. Circassia, Armed Merchant Cruiser, Northern Patrol, 1939-41; Coastal Force Base, Troon, 1941; Captain M.L., Portsmouth, 1941-45. *Address:* Little Havering, Milton, Lilbourne, Pewsey, Wilts. *T.:* Pewsey 3121. *Club:* Naval and Military. [*Died* 21 *March* 1955.

OLIPHANT, John Ninian, C.M.G. 1939; M.B.E. 1919; M.A. (Oxon); *b.* 7 May 1887; *s.* of T. T. Oliphant (of Rossie), St. Andrews, Fife; *m.* 1913, Amina, *d.* of H. Robert, Munich; one *d.* *Educ.:* Glenalmond; Christ Church, Oxford. Indian Forest Service, 1909-23; Conservator of Forests, British Honduras, 1924-29; Deputy Director of Forestry, Malaya, 1930-35; Director, Imperial Forestry Institute, Oxford, 1936-39; Chief Conservator of Forests, Nigeria, 1939-43; Adviser on Rural Development, Nigeria, 1944-46; retired. *Publications:* various writings on forestry and rural planning. *Address:* c/o National and Grindlay's Bank Ltd., 54 Parliament Street, S.W.1. [*Died* 23 *July* 1960.

OLIVER, Charles Pye, C.B. 1927; C.M.G. 1918; M.D. Lond. and M.D. State Medicine; Hon. Physician to the King; Consulting Physician West Kent General Hospital; and to Kent County Ophthalmic Hospital; Col. Army Medical Service, T.A. (retd.); ex-Hon. Col. R.A.M.C. 44th (Home Counties) Div. T.A.; Military Member of Kent T.A. and Air Force Association since formation; *b.* 18 March 1861; 4th *s.* of late Dr. Oliver, Maidstone, Kent; *m.* Agnes Charlotte (*d.* 1919), 4th *d.* of George Bensted of Ulcombe, Kent; four *s.* one *d.* *Educ.:* privately; Charing Cross Hospital; University College Hosp. Late Medical Officer of Health, Borough of Maidstone; commd. for sixteen years Maidstone Companies Medical Staff Corps; late A.D.M.S., Home Counties Division, and afterwards Southern Army (despatches 3 times, C.M.G.); late Pres. Kent Branch B.M.A.; C.St.J.; County Controller for Kent V.A.D.'s; J.P., D.L. Kent. *Publications:* Reports to Local Govt. Board on Health of Borough of Maidstone. *Address:* The Gables, Maidstone. *T.:* Maidstone 3032. *Club:* Junior United Service. [*Died* 28 *Jan.* 1951.

OLIVER, Francis Wall, F.R.S. 1905; D.Sc.; hon. LL.D. (Aberdeen); lately Professor of Botany, Egyptian University, Cairo; Quain Professor of Botany, University College, London, 1888-1929, now Emeritus Professor; *b.* Richmond, Surrey, 10 May 1864; *o. s.* of late Prof. D. Oliver, F.R.S.; *m.* 1896, Mildred Alice Thompson (*d.* 1932); two *s.* *Educ.:* Friends' Schools, Kendal and York; University College, London (Fellow); Trinity College, Cambridge (M.A.). Past President, Botanical Section, British Association, 1906; British Ecological Society, 1915-16; Egyptian Botanical Society, 1929-35; Linnean Medal, 1925. *Publications:* papers on morphological and fossil botany; on plant ecology, especially of deserts and the seashore; editor of Kerner's Natural History of Plants, Annals of Botany; Makers of British Botany; The Exploitation of Plants; Life and its Maintenance; co-author of Tidal Lands. *Recreations:* once mountaineering, now washing-up. *Address:* Ballard's Barn, Limpsfield Common, Surrey. [*Died* 14 *Sept.* 1951.

OLIVER, Sir John William Lambton, Kt., *cr.* 1944; C.B. 1924; C.B.E. 1920 (O.B.E. 1918); *b.* 1873; *s.* of J. P. T. Oliver; *m.* 1895, Nellie J., *d.* of Edward Bashford. Naval Store Officer, H.M. Dockyard, Devonport; Assistant Director of Stores and Senior Acting Deputy Director at Adm., 1918, Director of Stores, 1920-34; retired, 1934; Director of Supply, Air Raid Precautions Department, Home Office, 1936-38; Director of Stores, Ministry of Supply, 1939; Deputy Director-General of Equipment and Stores, 1939-46. *Address:* 59 Baronsmede, W.5. *T.:* Ealing 0222. [*Died* 21 *Dec.* 1952.

OLIVER, Philip Milner, C.B.E. 1920 (O.B.E. 1918); B.A.; Barrister-at-law; *b.* Manchester, 1884; *s.* of late J. R. Oliver. *Educ.:* Bowdon College; Manchester Grammar School; Corpus Christi College, Oxford. M.P. (L.) Blackley Division of Manchester, 1923-24, and 1929-31; Contested (L.) Blackley Division of Manchester, 1918, 1922, 1924, 1931, 1935, and 1945; Altrincham, 1933. *Publications:* Whatsoever Things; Genesis to Geneva. *Address:* Oakfield, Langham Road, Bowdon, Cheshire. *Club:* Reform (Manchester). [*Died* 12 *April* 1954.

OLIVER, Walter Reginald Brook, D.Sc., F.R.S.N.Z.; now retired; *b.* Launceston, Tasmania, 7 Sept. 1883; *s.* of Henry Oliver, Dorset, England; *m.* 1920, I. A. Cardno (*d.* 1954); one *s.* two *d.*; *m.* 1956, Helen C. Laing. *Educ.:* Tauranga High School, N.Z.; Victoria University College, Wellington, N.Z. Entered Customs Department, 1900; Assistant in Dominion Museum, 1920; Director 1928-47; Director Canterbury Museum, 1947-1948. Served European War, 1918, Canterbury Regt.; Sec. Wellington Meeting Australasian Association for Advancement of Science, 1923; Pres. Wellington Philosophical Soc., 1929-1930; Gov. rep. on Council of Roy. Soc. of N.Z., 1928-54; Pres., 1952-54; Hector Medallist, 1936 (Botany); Hutton Medallist, 1950 (Zool., Bot.); British Empire M.B.O.U.; Corresp. Fell. Amer. Ornithologists' Union; Hon. Mem. Swedish Phytogeographical Soc. and Fiji Soc.; President Wellington Botanical Soc., 1939, 1949; President N.Z. Association Scientific Workers, 1942. President Royal Australasian Ornithologists' Union, 1943. Travelled in U.S.A., Europe, Australia, Philippines, and Pacific Islands; Member of Scientific Expedition to Kermadec Islands, 1908; to

Southern Islands of N.Z., 1927; Fiordland, 1949. *Publications:* New Zealand Birds, 1930 (2nd edition, revised and enlarged, 1955); The Genus Coprosma, 1935; The Moas of New Zealand and Australia, 1949; also many papers on Zoology and Botany in scientific journals in N.Z., Australia and U.K. *Recreations:* botany, ornithology. *Address:* 26 Ventnor Street, Seatoun, Wellington, E.5, N.Z. *T.:* 17.568. [*Died* 16 *May* 1957.

OLIVIER, Herbert Arnould; Portrait painter; *b.* Battle, 9 Sept. 1861; 3rd *s.* of Rev. Henry A. Olivier, Potterne, Wilts, and Anne E. H. Arnould of Whitecross, Berks; *m.* 1903, Margaret, *o. d.* of Sir William Barclay Peat, of Wykeham Rise, Totteridge; one *s.* two *d. Educ.:* Sherborne. Creswick prize at Royal Academy, 1882, having exhibited at Burlington House for first time the previous year. *Principal Works:* Not Juno's Heartless Fowls; A Garden of Chances; Sumer is icumen in; Central Indian Chiefs, for the Daly College; Where Belgium greeted Britain; Merville, 1 Dec. 1914; The Supreme War Council, Versailles, July 1918, awarded Silver Medal in Salon, 1922; Premature Posthumous Exhibition of 300 collected works at Royal Institute Galleries, 1935 and in R.A. of 1944 two pictures of Bomber Command published for R.A.F. Benevolent Fund. All war work presented to the nation. *Recreation:* tidying. *Address:* 7 Airlie Gardens, W. *Clubs:* Athenæum, Arts. [*Died* 2 *March* 1952.

OLIVIER, Martin John, M.A.; T.D.; First Headmaster of Guthlaxton School, since 1955; *b.* 20 Feb. 1900; *s.* of late Canon Henry Olivier and Gertrude, *d.* of late Canon Capel Cure; *m.* 1949, Nancy Eden, *d.* of late Dr. J. E. Linnell, Sheringham; one *s.* one *d. Educ.:* Lancing; New Coll., Oxford. 2nd class Modern Languages (French and German); President Oxford University French Club, 1922; Assistant Master Rossall School, 1922-44, Head of Language Dept. Headmaster of Gresham's School, Holt, 1944-1955. Athletic Correspondent Yorkshire Post Berlin Olympic Games and till 1939; Eastern Daily Press, Wembley Olympic Games, 1948. Captain, Territorial General List, 1930-46. *Publications:* numerous articles on athletics and on education. *Recreations:* producing plays and coaching athletes. *Address:* Eden House, The Oval, Oadby, Leicestershire. *T.:* Oadby 2187. *Clubs:* London Athletic; Leicester County (Leicester). [*Died* 21 *Dec.* 1959.

OLNEY, Hon. Sir Herbert Horace, Kt., *cr.* 1942; Chairman Zoological Board of Victoria since 1927; Member Charities Board of Victoria; *b.* Ballarat, 26 Nov. 1875; *m.* 1898, Annie Lizzetta, *d.* of Richard Trudgeon; one *d. Educ.:* Ballarat College. M.L.C. Victoria, 1931-43. *Address:* Yantaringa, 47 Locksley Road, Ivanhoe, Melbourne, Australia. [*Died* 20 *July* 1957.

O'LOGHLEN, Sir Charles Hugh Ross, 5th Bt., *cr.* 1838; *b.* 6 July 1881; *s.* of Sir Bryan O'Loghlen, 3rd Bt. and Ella, *d.* of J. M. Seward, Melbourne; *S.* brother, 1934. *Educ.:* Xavier College, Melbourne, Australia. *Heir: b.* Henry Ross [*b.* 29 Nov. 1886; *m.* 1912, Dorris Irena, *d.* of late Major Percival Horne, R.A.; two *s.* two *d.*]. *Address:* Walsh Street, South Yarra, Melbourne, Australia. [*Died* 23 *July* 1951.

O'MALLEY, Major-General David Vincent, C.B. 1946; O.B.E.; *b.* 15 July 1891; *e. s.* of Henry Cusack O'Malley; *m.* 1927, Margaret Isabel, *d.* of George Toogood; no *c. Educ.:* Queen's College, Galway; University College, Dublin. M.B., B.Ch., B.A.O., 1916; Lieut. R.A.M.C. 1916; Capt. 1917; transferred I.M.S. 1922; Major 1927; Lt.-Col. 1935; Col. 1944; Maj.-Gen. 1945. War services: European War, 1914-18, Mesopotamia, 1916-1917; N.W. Frontier, India, June-Oct. 1917. Kuki Punitive Operations, 1918-19 (despatches, O.B.E.); N.W. Frontier, India, 1923-24 (despatches); N.W. Frontier, Mohmand Operations, 1933 (despatches); War of 1939-45, M.E.F., 1941-42. Appointments held: D.A.D.M.S. Shanghai Defence Force, Jan.-Oct. 1927; D.A.D.M.S. Western Command, India, 1929-32; A.D.M.S., G.H.Q., M.E.F., 1941-42; A.D.M.S. 5 Ind. Div. 1942-1943; Inspector Med. Services, India, 1943-1944; D.D.M.S., G.H.Q., India, 1944-45. D.D.M.S., Central Command, India, 1945-47; Southern Command, India, 1947; K.H.S. 1945-48; retired 1948. *Recreations:* golf, sailing. *Club:* United Service. [*Died* 8 *Dec.* 1955.

O'MALLEY, Hon. King; M.L.A., S. Australia, 1896-99; M.P. for Tasmania to 1st Federal House of Representatives, 1901-6; Darwin, 1906-17; Minister of Home Affairs, Federal Parliament, 1910-13 and 1915-1916; Member of Labour Party; Founder of Commonwealth Bank of Australia; Author of Australia House, London, 1906; moved, 19 July 1901, the Motion which secured 583,000 acres of inalienable land for Federal Capital Site, and was accepted by Rt. Hon. Sir Edmund Barton, 1st Prime Minister of Commonwealth; as Minister for Home Affairs was responsible for construction of Trans-Continental Railway commenced in 1910 and was in charge of the opening of the Commonwealth Capital at Canberra, March 1913. *Address:* 58 Bridport Street, South Melbourne, S.C.5, Australia. [*Died* 20 *Dec.* 1953.

OMMANNEY, Lt.-Col. Charles Vernon, C.B.E. 1920; Indian Army (retired); *b.* Peshawar, 29 Dec. 1872; 4th *s.* of late Col. Edward Lacon Ommanney, C.S.I.; *m.* 1904, Honoria Catherine, *o. d.* of late Dr. H. Cripps Lawrence; two *s.* two *d. Educ.:* Wellington College; Norwich Grammar School. Joined 4th Battalion Essex Regiment, 1893; Suffolk Regiment, 1895; transferred to 15th Madras Infantry, 1898, and to 109th Infantry, 1911; Aden operations, 1915-17 (despatches); Commandant 1/109th Infantry, 1918; raised 2/30th Punjabis at Lahore, 1918; Afghan War, 1919 (C.B.E., despatches); North-West Frontier with Waziristan Field Force, 1919-21 (*Medals:* 1914-15 Star, General Service Medal, Victory Medal, Indian General Service Medal, 1908, with clasps; Afghanistan, N.W. Frontier, 1919; Waziristan, 1919-21); retired 1922. *Recreations:* all usual games, etc. *Address:* Capel Cottage, Boundstone, Farnham, Surrey. *T.:* Frensham 206. *Club:* Junior United Service. [*Died* 11 *April* 1952.

O'NEIL, Bryan Hugh St. John, M.A., F.S.A. 1935; Chief Inspector of Ancient Monuments since 1945; Rhind Lecturer in Archæology, 1946; Member of Royal Commission on Historical Monuments (Eng.) since 1950; *b.* 7 Aug. 1905; *s.* of Charles Valentine O'Neil, F.L.A.A., and Mabel Meliora Rowe; *m.* 1939, Helen Evangeline Donovan. *Educ.:* Dulwich College Preparatory School; Merchant Taylors' School (Scholar); St. John's College, Oxford (Scholar). Hon. Secretary and President of the Oxford University Archæological Society, 1926; Excavations at Mancetter (Leicestershire), 1927; at the Roman *villa* near Camborne, Cornwall, 1931; at Titterstone Clee Hill Camp, Shropshire, 1932; at Breiddin Hill Camp, Montgomeryshire, 1933-35; at Caerau Ancient Village, Caernarvonshire, 1933-34; at Ffridd Faldwyn Camp, Montgomery, 1937-38-1939; at Porth Dafarch, Anglesey, 1939; and in the Isles of Scilly, 1947-54; Assistant Inspector of Ancient Monuments for Wales, 1930-35; Inspector of Ancient Monuments for Wales, 1935-45; Hon. Sec. of the Research Committee of the Congress of Archæological Societies, 1933-45; Vice-Pres. Soc. of Antiquaries of London, 1946-50. *Publications:* Reports on the above-mentioned excavations, other papers contributed to Archæologia, the Antiquaries Journal, Archæologia Cambrensis, Numismatic Chronicle, etc. *Recreations:* walking, various games. *Address:* 32 Blomfield Road, W.9. *Club:* Athenæum. [*Died* 24 *Oct.* 1954.

O'NEILL, Eugene (Gladstone); Dramatic Author; *b.* New York, 16 Oct. 1888; *s.* of James O'Neill, actor, and Ella Quinlan; *m.* 1929, Carlotta Monterey; one *s.* one *d.* (one *s.* decd.) by two previous marriages. *Educ.:* Princeton and Harvard Universities. Member American Academy of Arts and Letters, American Philosophical Society, Irish Academy of Letters; Litt.D. Yale University; Nobel Prize for Literature for 1936. *Plays:* The Moon of the Caribees, and other plays of the Sea, 1919; Beyond the Horizon, 1919; Diff'rent, 1921; The Emperor Jones, 1921; The Straw, 1921; Gold, 1921; Anna Christie, 1922; The First Man, 1922; The Hairy Ape, 1922; Welded, 1923; The Fountain, 1923; Desire Under the Elms, 1924; Marco Millions, 1924; The Great God Brown, 1925; Lazarus Laughed, 1926; Strange Interlude, 1927; Dynamo, 1928; Mourning Becomes Electra, 1931: Ah, Wilderness!, 1932; Days Without End, 1933; The Iceman Cometh, 1946; (posthumous): A Touch of the Poet, 1957; Long Day's Journey into Night, 1957; "Hughie" (one-act play), 1958. *Relevant publications:* Part of a Long Story, by Agnes Boulton, 1958; O'Neill, by Arthur and Barbara Gelb, 1962. *Address:* c/o Random House, Publishers, 20 East 57th Street, New York, U.S.A. [*Died* 27 *Nov.* 1953.

O'NEILL, Herbert Charles, O.B.E.; Strategicus of The Spectator. *Educ.:* The Victoria University of Manchester; Middlesex Hospital. Assistant at Shide Observatory, 1906-08; Daily Mail Editorial Staff, 1908-10; editor and literary adviser to Messrs. Jack; projected and edited The People's Books, The New Encyclopædia, The Nations' Histories, etc.; projected and wrote History of the War for the Foreign Office Dept. of Information, published month by month in French, German, Dutch, Danish, Norwegian, and Swedish, 1916-1918; Official in Charge of Scandinavian and Finnish Departments of the Ministry of Information; Clerk in Foreign Office, 1918-1920; Editor of the Financial News, 1920-21; Assist. Editor of the Westminster Gazette, 1922-28; Assistant Editor of the Observer, 1930-35. *Publications:* New Things and Old in St. Thomas Aquinas; Pure Gold, an Anthology; A History of the War; The Royal Fusiliers in the Great War. As Strategicus: The War for World Power; From Dunkirk to Benghazi; From Tobruk to Smolensk; The War moves East; To Stalingrad and Alamein; The Tide Turns; Foothold in Europe; The Victory Campaign (May 1944-Aug. 1945), A Short History of the Second World War, 1950; Men of Destiny, 1953, etc. *Recreations:* walking, desultory reading. *Club:* Reform. [*Died* 29 *Sept.* 1953.

O'NEILL, Most Rev. Hugh John, D.D.; D.C.L.; Titular Bishop of Bareta; Coadjutor Bishop of Dunedin, N.Z., (R.C.), 1943-49; *b.* Dunedin, N.Z., 29 June 1898; *s.* of Edward O'Neill and Elizabeth Alexander. *Educ.:* St. Mary's School (Sisters of Mercy), Mosgiel; Christian Brothers' High School, Dunedin; Holy Cross College, Mosgiel (Provincial Seminary). Priest, 1921; proceeded to Rome to study Canon Law at the Apollinare and was a student of the Irish College; D.C.L. 1923; Professor, Holy Cross College, N.Z., 1923-33; then became Parish Priest of Mosgiel; National Organiser of the Pontifical Mission Aid Works and Chaplain of St. Kevin's College, Oamaru, 1939. *Publications:* Editor of N.Z. edition of Catholic Missions, 1933-43. *Address:* 7 Paterson St., Wellington, C.4, N.Z. *T.A.:* Wellington, N.Z. *T.:* Wellington 54063. [*Died* 27 *Dec.* 1955.

O'NEILL, Most Rev. Patrick; Bishop of Limerick, (R.C.), since 1946; *b.* 8 Feb. 1891. *Educ.:* St. Munchin's, Limerick; Maynooth; Rome. Priest 1915; D.D. 1918; Doctorate of Canon Law, 1920; Professor of Theology and Canon Law, Maynooth, 1918-41, Vice-President, Maynooth, 1936-41; Parish Priest and Vicar General, diocese of Limerick, 1941-45. *Address:* Kilmoyle, N.C. Road, Limerick. *T.:* Limerick 294. [*Died* 26 *March* 1958.

O'NEILL, Joseph; *b.* December 1886; *s.* of Martin O'Neill and Mary Quigley; *m.* 1912, Mary Devonport O'Neill (Author of Prometheus and other Poems, etc.); no *c.* *Educ.:* Queens College, Galway; Victoria College, Manchester; University of Freiburg, Baden, Germany. M.A. (Hons.) Royal Univ. of Ireland; Post Graduate Research in Philology in Manchester University and University of Freiburg, 1906 and 1907; Govt. Inspector of Primary Schools for Ireland, 1907; of Secondary Schools for Ireland, 1909; Civil Service Commissioner for Irish Free State, 1923; Local Appointments Commissioner for Eire, 1926-46; Permanent Secretary to Department of Education, Irish Free State, 1923-44. Winner of Harmsworth Award of Irish Academy of Letters for best work of imaginative prose by an Irish Writer published 1934 (Wind from the North). Formerly Member of Irish Academy of Letters, 1936. *Publications:* Wind from the North (novel), 1934 (German translation, 1939); Land under England (novel), 1935 (French translation, Le Peuple des Tenèbres, 1938); Day of Wrath (novel), 1936; Philip (novel), 1940; Chosen by the Queen (novel), 1947. *Recreations:* winter sports, swimming, climbing. *Address:* 2 Kenilworth Sq., Rathgar, Dublin, Eire. [*Died* 2 *May* 1953.

ONKAR SINGH, Major-General Sir Apji, Kt., *cr.* 1939; C.I.E. 1918; of Palaitha, Kotah State; *b.* 1872. *Educ.:* Mayo College, Ajmer. Joined Kotah State Service in 1892, retired in 1942; held offices of General Supt. of Police, G.O.C. State Forces, Member Mahakma Khas and Prime Minister of the State. *Address:* Kotah State, Rajputana. [*Died* 27 *June* 1951.

ONRAET, Rene Henry de S., C.M.G. 1939; retired from army reserve of officers with rank of major; *b.* 6 April 1887; *s.* of Henry F. and Marie Onraet; *m.* 1914, Muriel Burghope; no *c.* *Educ.:* Stonyhurst. Cadet, Straits Settlements Police, 1907; studied Chinese and Malay, 1908-10; Superintendent of Police, Singapore, 1921; Inspector-General, Police, Straits Settlements, 1934; retired, 1939; Army, 1939-41; retired, 1941; Police Commission to British West Indies on behalf of Colonial Office, 1942; Police Adviser to the British Military Administration, Malaya, 1945-46; Police Mission to Cyprus, April-May 1946. *Publications:* Something about Horses in Malaya, 1938; Singapore Police background, 1946. *Recreations:* polo, golf. *Address:* Netherfield, Burley, Hants. *T.:* 2189. [*Died* 8 *March* 1952.

ONYON, Engineer-Captain William, M.V.O. 1912; R.N. (retired); *b.* Belvedere, Kent, 24 June 1862; *m.* 1891, Ada Annie (*d.* 1938), *d.* of late J. G. Barrow; one *s.* two *d.* *Educ.:* Christ's Hospital; H.M.S. Marlborough; R.N. College, Greenwich. Served in Alexandra, flag of H.R.H. the Duke of Edinburgh, in Mediterranean, and in Agamemnon in East Indies and Mediterranean, 1886-90; in charge of torpedo boats at Malta, 1891-94; in destroyers Dasher and Hasty, 1895-98; Chief Engineer of Jamaica Dockyard, 1898-1902; Engineer Overseer Clyde District, 1902-5; Engineer Commander H.M.S. Dreadnought, 1905-8; Engineer Inspector, Admiralty, 1908-11; Engineer Captain on staff of Sir Colin Keppel in Medina during Royal visit to India, 1911-12; was specially promoted to rank of Engineer-Captain for services in connection with management and construction of machinery of Dreadnought; retired, 1913: Past President Institute of Marine Engineers and Vice-President Institute of Engineers and Shipbuilders in Scotland; M.Inst.C.E.; Past

Member of Council, Inst. Naval Architects; member of Corrosion Cttee., Inst. of Metals, London representative of Vickers, Barrow, 1928-36. *Address:* Wrenholme, Pomphlett Road, Plymstock, Devon. [*Died* 19 *July* 1953.

OPPÉ, Adolph Paul, C.B. 1937; Hon. LL.D., Glas.: F.B.A.; *b.* London, 22 Sept. 1878; 3rd *s.* of late S. A. Oppé; *m.* 1909, Valentine (*d.* 1951), *d.* of late Rev. R. W. L. Tollemache; one *s.* one *d.* *Educ.:* Charterhouse; St. Andrews University; New College, Oxford (Exhibitioner), 1st Cl. Mods., 1st Cl. Lit. Hum. Lecturer in Greek, St. Andrews University, 1902; in Ancient History, Edinburgh University, 1904; entered Board of Education, 1905; Principal Assistant Secretary, 1930-38; Deputy Director, Victoria and Albert Museum, 1910-13. *Publications:* Raphael, 1909; Botticelli, 1911; Rowlandson, 1923; Cotman, 1923; Turner, Cox and de Wint, 1925; Art, in Early Victorian England, 1934; Sandby Drawings at Windsor Castle, 1947; Drawings of Hogarth, 1948; English Drawings at Windsor Castle, 1950; Alexander and John Robert Cozens, 1952; and various articles. *Address:* 17 Cheyne Walk, Chelsea, S.W.3. *T.:* Flaxman 0471. *Club:* Athenæum. [*Died* 29 *March* 1957.

OPPENHEIMER, Sir Ernest, Kt. 1921; *b.* Friedberg, Hesse, 22 May 1880; *s.* of Edward Oppenheimer and Nanette Hirschhorn; *m.* 1st, 1906, Mary Lina (*d.* 1934), *d.* of late Joseph Pollak; one *s.*; 2nd, 1935, Caroline Magdalen Harvey Oppenheimer, *widow* of Sir Michael Oppenheimer, 2nd Bt., and 2nd *d.* of Sir Robert Grenville Harvey, 2nd and last Bt. *Educ.:* private schools. Mayor of Kimberley, 1912-15; M.P. Kimberley in Parl. of Union of S. Africa, 1924-38; formed Anglo Amer. Corp. of S. Africa, Ltd., 1917, Chairman and Director since foundation. Chairman: African Explosives and Chemical Industries Ltd.; Anglo Amer. Investment Trust Ltd.; Bancroft Mines Ltd.; N'Changa Consol. Copper Mines Ltd.; Orange Free State Investment Trust Ltd.; The Rhodesia Broken Hill Devel. Co. Ltd.; Rhodesian Anglo Amer., Ltd.; Rhokana Corp. Ltd.; West Rand Investment Trust Ltd.; Consolidated Diamond Mines of South West Africa Ltd.; De Beers Consol. Mines Ltd.; De Beers Industrial Corp. Ltd.; The Diamond Corp. Ltd.; Premier (Tvl.) Diamond Mining Co. Ltd.; Rhodesia Copper Refineries Ltd.; Union Acceptances, Ltd.; Director: African & European Invest. Co. Ltd.; African Explosives and Chemical Industries (E. Africa) Ltd.; Central Reserves Ltd; Commonwealth Devel. Finance Co. Ltd.; Bultfontein Mines Ltd.; Gen. Mining and Finance Corp. Ltd.; Griqualand West Diamond Mining Co. (Dutoitspan Mine) Ltd.; Hambros Bank Ltd.; Tanganyika Concessions Ltd. Hon. D.C.L. Oxf. 1952; Hon. LL.D., Univ. of Witwatersrand and Rhodes Univ., 1953. K.St.J. *Address:* (home) Brenthurst, Federation Road, Parktown, Johannesburg, S. Africa; (office) 44 Main Street, P.O. Box 4902, Johannesburg, S. Africa. *Clubs:* Rand (Johannesburg); Kimberley (Kimberley); City (Cape Town); Salisbury (Salisbury); Bulawayo (Bulawayo). [*Died* 25 *Nov.* 1957.

ORANGE, Beatrice; M.A.; Warden, Women's Hall of Residence, Birmingham Univ., 1915-23; *d.* of late W. Orange, C.B., M.D. *Educ.:* Cheltenham Ladies' College; Brighton and Kensington High Schools; Girton College, Cambridge (Classical Scholar). Assistant Mistress, St. Margaret's, Polmont, 1899-1906; Sub-Warden, University House, Birmingham, 1908-13; Resident Tutor, Bedford College for Women, Regent's Park, London, 1913-15. *Publications:* article on Teaching as a Profession for Women; Four Little Latin Plays. *Address:* c/o Westminster Bank, Colmore Row, Birmingham. [*Died* 9 *Oct.* 1955.

ORANGE, Sir Hugh (William), K.B.E., *cr.* 1928; Kt., *cr.* 1919; C.B. 1914; C.I.E. 1906; *b.* 14 Apr. 1866; *s.* of late Dr. William Orange, C.B., M.D.; *m.* 1907, Mabel, *y. d.* of E. Ford of 69 Oxford Gardens, W.; one *s.* one *d.* *Educ.:* Winchester College; New College, Oxford. Visited Australia in service of Orient Line, 1891-93. Appointed Examiner in the English Education Dept., 1893; Director-General of Education in India, 1902-10; member Viceroy's Legislative Council, 1910; Chief Inspector, Elementary Schools, Board of Education, 1910; Accountant-General, Board of Education, 1912-1928. *Address:* Farrandene, Forest Row, Sussex. *T.:* Forest Row 127. [*Died* 24 *July* 1956.

ORCHARD, Rev. William Edwin; Catholic Priest; *b.* 20 Nov. 1877; *e. s.* of John Orchard, Rugby; *m.* 1904, Annie Maria (*d.* 1920), *widow* of Rev. Ellis Hewitt of Aldershot. *Educ.:* Board School; private tuition; Westminster College, Cambridge. Ordained, Enfield, 1904; B.D. London, 1905; D.D. London, 1909; Minister of the King's Weigh House Church, Duke Street, W., 1914-1932; received into Roman Catholic Church, 1932; ordained (sub conditione) Priest, 1935. *Publications:* Evolution of Old Testament Religion, 1908; Modern Theories of Sin, 1909; Problems and Perplexities, 1912; The Temple: A Book of Prayers, 1913; The Necessity of Christ, 1917; The Outlook for Religion, 1917; Divine Service: Order of Service for Public Worship, 1919; The Devotional Companion, 1921; Oracles of God, 1922; Various Volumes of Sermons, 1913-22; Foundations of Faith, 4 vols., 1924-27; Christianity and World Problems, 1925: The Present Crisis in Religion, 1929; Prayer, 1930; From Faith to Faith, 1933; The Inevitable Cross, 1933; The Way of Simplicity, 1934; The Cult of our Lady, 1937; The Necessity for the Church, 1940; Humanity: What? Whence? Whither?, 1944; Sancta Sanctorum: Prayers for the Holy of Holies, 1955. *Recreation:* painting. *Address:* St. Uriel's, Brownshill, nr. Stroud, Glos. *T.:* Brimscombe 2270. *Club:* Authors'. [*Died* 12 *June* 1955.

ORKNEY, 7th Earl of (*cr.* 1696), **Edmond Walter Fitz-Maurice,** D.L., J.P.; Viscount of Kirkwall and Baron of Dechmont, 1696; *b.* 24 May 1867; *s.* of late Captain Hon. Henry Warrender Fitz-Maurice (Seaforth Highlanders, 72nd) (2nd *s.* of 5th Earl) and Sarah, *d.* of George Bradley Roose, Bryntirion, N. Wales; *S. uncle,* 1889; *m.* 1892, Constance (*d.* 1946), *d.* of late David Gilchrist; (*o. d.* and *heiress* died 1950). *Educ.:* Cheltenham. Lt.-Col. comdg. 3rd Batt. Oxfordshire L. Infantry, 1898-1903; Provincial Grand Master, Bucks (Freemasons); M.F.H. Whaddon Chase, 1920-23. Owns about 11,000 acres. *Heir: Kinsman* Cecil O'Bryen Fitz-Maurice [*b.* 3 July 1919]. *Address:* The Tythe House, Stewkley, Bucks; Glanmore, Templemore, Tipperary. *Clubs:* Carlton, White's, Pratt's, Badminton; Kildare Street (Dublin). [*Died* 21 *Aug.* 1951.

ORME, Edith Temple, LL.D.; late Reader to Trussed Concrete Steel Co., Ltd., Reinforced Concrete Engineers; 2nd *d.* of late Temple Orme, of University College School. *Educ.:* privately; first woman to take LL.D. Degree, London University, and only woman awarded First-Class Honours in the LL.B. Examination. Has devoted herself to literary, educational, and philanthropical work; Secretary to the Froebel Society, 1907-14; Editor of Kahncrete Engineering (the official organ of the Trussed Concrete Steel Co.) from its commencement in 1914 until it was discontinued in 1936. *Publications:* a pamphlet upon Co-operation; article in The Child; several classified Educational Catalogues. *Recreations:* reading, music, and art. *Address:* c/o Truscon House, 35-41, Lower Marsh, S.E.1. [*Died* 16 *May* 1960.

ORME, Frederick George, O.B.E., F.C.I.S.; Secretary, James Powell & Sons

(Whitefriars) Ltd., 1919; Managing Director, 1921-48; Chairman, 1948; retired from the Board after 33 years, 1952. *s.* of late George Hill Orme, Hull; *m.* Wilhelmina, *er. d.* of John Rutgers, Amsterdam; one *s.* one *d.* *Educ.:* St. Paul's School. Joined the late National Explosives Co., Ltd.; spent eighteen years with the Coy. and for ten years was Secretary; Capt. 7th Middlesex Regt. (T.F.), 1915-16; Assistant-Inspector, 1916, and Inspector of High Explosives, Royal Arsenal, Woolwich, 1917-19. *Recreations:* golf, bridge, etc. *Address:* 76 Princes Park Avenue, Golders Green, N.W.11. *Club:* Royal Automobile. [*Died* 10 *Nov.* 1954.

ORMISTON, Lt.-Col. Thomas Lane; *b.* 30 May 1867; 2nd *s.* of late Thomas Ormiston, C.I.E.; *m.* 1904, Agnes Lucy Benniworth (*d.* 1942), *o. c.* of John Benniworth Parish, Toynton House, Lincs; no *c.* *Educ.:* Dulwich; Trinity College, Oxford, M.A.; Inner Temple, Barrister-at-law; R.M.C. 2nd Lt., K.O.S.B., 1890; entered I.A., 1893; Burma Commission, Asst. Commr., 1898, excise Commr., 1916, Commr. Arakan divn., 1919; retired, 1922; C.C. Devon, 1928-52; J.P., 1934; High Sheriff, 1940; a General Commissioner of Income Tax; Pres. W. of E. Institution for the Blind, 1931, 1932; F.R.Met.S. *Publications:* The Dulwich College Register, 1926; The Ormistons of Teviotdale, 1951. *Recreations:* genealogy and transcribing Church registers. *Address:* Trood House, Alphington, Exeter, Devon. *T.A.* and *T.:* Exeter 3411. *Clubs:* United Service; Devon and Exeter (Exeter). [*Died* 19 *June* 1954.

ORMSBY JOHNSON, Brig. Guy Allen Colpoys; *see* Johnson.

O'RORKE, Lt.-Col. George Mackenzie, C.I.E. 1919; M.B.E. 1918; R.E.; formerly Engineer, Bombay Development Dept.; *b.* 1883; *s.* of late Com. A. J. O'Rorke, R.N.; *m.* 1920, Belinda M.B., *d.* of John McRobert, J.P., Rademon, Crossgar, Co. Down; two *s.* Served European War, 1914-19. Last War, 1940-45. *Address:* Strathearn Hotel, Southsea. *T.:* Portsmouth 31223. *Clubs:* Royal Commonwealth Society; Royal Albert Yacht (Southsea). [*Died* 17 *Sept.* 1958.

O'RORKE, Rt. Rev. Mowbray Stephen, D.D.; *b.* Birmingham, 21 May 1869; *s.* of William Joseph and Annie Elizabeth O'Rorke; unmarried. *Educ.:* Wesley College, Sheffield; Univ. School, Nottingham. Engaged in commercial life in London, 1886-99; called to Bar, Middle Temple; graduated at Trinity College, Dublin, B.A. 1902, M.A. 1905, D.D. (hon.) 1912; Deacon in the English Church, 1902; Priest, 1903; served Assistant Curacies at St. Paul's, Jarrow, St. Margaret's, Durham, and St. Oswald's, Durham; in charge of St. Paul's Cathedral, Rockhampton, Central Queensland, 1910-11; Bishop of Accra, 1911-24; Rector of Blakeney with Langham Parva, 1924-34; Guardian of the Shrine of Our Lady of Walsingham, 1925; Chaplain of St. Audries School, West Quantoxhead, Somerset, 1934-35; Chaplain of King's College, Taunton, 1935-39. *Recreation:* chess. *Address:* Maristow, Roborough, S. Devon. *Club:* Church Imperial. [*Died* 15 *March* 1953.

ORR, John Wellesley, M.A., J.P.; *b.* Urmston, Lancs, 11 Sept. 1878; *o. s.* of Wm. Arthur Wellesley Orr and Annie Selina Mullady; *m.* 1905, Lilian Graham (*d.* 1954), ward of late C. H. Owles of Scarth House, Barnes, S.W.; two *s.* one *d.* *Educ.:* privately; Denstone; St. John's Coll., Camb. Called to Bar, Middle Temple, 1904; devilled for the late Sir Edward Marshall Hall, K.C., for many years; engaged in West Ham Guardians case, Seddon case, and many other important trials; Stipendiary Magistrate for the City of Manchester, 1927-51, retired, 1951; served as a Member of the H.O. Departmental Committee on Persistent Offenders, 1931. *Recreations:* golf, fishing, and motoring; founder and first hon. secretary of Middle Temple Golfing Society. *Address:* The Croft, Sutton, nr. Pulborough, Sussex. *Clubs:* Royal Empire Society; Union (Cambridge). [*Died* 12 *Feb.* 1956.

ORR EWING, Sir Ian Leslie, Kt., *cr.* 1953; M.P. (C. and Nat.), 1934-50, (C.) since 1950, for Weston-super-Mare Division of Somerset; *b.* 4 June 1893; *s.* of C. L. Orr Ewing, M.P., and Hon. Beatrice Ruthven; *m.* 1917, Helen Bridget Gibbs; one *d.* *Educ.:* Harrow; Oxford. Served European War, Royal Scots Fusiliers, A.D.C. to G.O.C. 20th Division, Scots Guards (wounded); Conservative candidate Gateshead, 1929; withdrew Conservative and National candidature St. Ives Division of Cornwall, 1931, in favour Rt. Hon. Walter Runciman; Parliamentary Private Secretary to Financial Secretary to the Treasury, 1935-36; to Minister of Agriculture, 1936-39; to Chancellor of Duchy of Lancaster, 1939; to Minister of Food, 1939-40, and to Postmaster-General, 1940. Member of the Rhodesia Nyasaland Royal Commission, 1938; Pres. Rural District Councils Assoc., 1957-. F.R.S.A. 1948. *Recreations:* sailing, fishing, golf, painting. *Address:* Christon, nr. Axbridge, Somerset. *Clubs:* Carlton, Caledonian, M.C.C.; Royal Highland Yacht (Oban). [*Died* 27 *April* 1958.

ORR EWING, Brig.-Gen. Sir Norman (Archibald), 4th Bt., *cr.* 1886; C.B. 1942; D.S.O. 1914; late Scots Guards; Hon. Colonel 7th Bn. Argyll and Sutherland Highlanders; Vice-Lieut. of Stirlingshire since 1931; Chm. of Stirlingshire Territorial Army Association since 1931; Army Welfare Officer for Stirlingshire since 1940; *b.* 23 Nov. 1880; *e. s.* of 3rd Bart. and Hon. Mabel Addington (*d.* 1942), *y. d.* of 3rd Viscount Sidmouth; *S.* father, 1919; *m.* 1911, Laura Louisa, 4th *d.* of Abraham John Robarts, D.L., Tile House, Lillingstone Dayrell, Bucks, and Hon. Edith, *d.* of 8th Viscount Barrington; two *s.* one *d.* *Educ.:* Eton. Entered army from Militia, 1900; Captain, 1907; Adjutant, 1910-12; employed with Egyptian army, 1907-10; served S. Africa, 1899-1901 (Queen's medal 2 clasps); European War, 1914-18 (twice wounded, despatches five times, D.S.O.); commanded 2nd Batt. Scots Guards, 1916-18; commanded a brigade May 1918 to Armistice; Bt. Lt.-Col., Légion d'Honneur, Croix de Guerre, Military Order of Savoy; retired, 1919; commanded the 154th Argyll Territorial Brigade, 1925-29; additional A.D.C. to the King, 1931-41; Home Guard Comdr. 1940, Adviser 1941; formerly Lieut. H.M. Royal Company of Archers; D.L. Co. Stirling; J.P. Perthshire; Grand Master Mason of Scotland, 1937-39. *Heir: s.* Ronald Archibald, Capt. The Scots Guards [*b.* 14 May 1912; *m.* 1938, Marion Hester, *yr. d.* of late Col. Sir Donald Cameron of Lochiel, K.T., C.M.G., and Lady Hermione Graham, *d.* of 5th Duke of Montrose; two *s.* two *d.*]. *Address:* Cardross, Port of Menteith, Stirling; Lennox Bank, Balloch, Dumbarton. *Clubs:* Carlton, Guards; New (Edinburgh); Western (Glasgow). [*Died* 26 *March* 1960.

ORTON, Major-General Sir Ernest Frederick, K.C.I.E., *cr.* 1935; C.B. 1926; p.s.c.; Col. 15th Lancers, Indian Army, 1928-45; *b.* Dinapore, India, 27 April 1874; 2nd *s.* of late Rev. F. Orton of Hope, Derbyshire; *m.* 1904, Alice Frances (*d.* 1948), 2nd *d.* of late F. H. Mickleburgh, late R. Indian Navy, and *g.d.* of Col. Edward Thomas Coke of Trusley, Derbyshire; (two *s.* decd.). *Educ.:* Derby; R.M.C., Sandhurst. 2nd Lieut. R. Dublin Fusiliers, 1894; transferred Indian Army (37th Lancers, Baluch Horse), 1897; served China Relief, Pekin, 1900-1 (despatches); Makran, capture of Fort Nodiz, 1901-2 (despatches); European War, 1914-19, Kalat and E. Persia, South Persia, Deputy Inspector-General and afterwards Inspector-General South Persia Rifles (despatches, Brevs. of Lieut.-Colonel and Colonel); Staff College, Camberley, 1906-7; 2nd I.

Brigade, Khyber, 1920-22; 22nd I. Infantry Brigade, Secunderabad, 1923-24; D.A. and Q.M.G., H.Q. Southern Command, India, 1926-1930; Major-General, 1926; Dy.Q.M.G., India, 1931-35; retired, 1935. *Publication:* Links with Past Ages, 1935. *Address:* Birtley House, Bramley, Surrey. [*Died* 25 *Oct.* 1960.

ORTON, James Herbert, F.R.S. 1948; D.Sc. (London); Emeritus Professor of Zoology, University of Liverpool (retired, 1949); Frank Buckland Professor, 1935; formerly Director, Marine Biological Station, Port Erin (retired, 1949); *b.* 11 March 1884; *s.* of late George Orton; *m.* Emma Teresa (*d.* 1941), *d.* of late Enoch Aykroyd, Bradford; one *s.*; *m.* 1942, Haidee Lodge. *Educ.:* Bradford; Royal College of Science, London (Associate, Marshall Scholar and Huxley Medallist); Naturalist at Marine Biological Laboratory, Plymouth, 1913; Biologist i/c Government Enquiry into Oyster Mortality Investigations, 1920-21; Chief Naturalist, Marine Biological Laboratory, Plymouth, 1922. *Publications:* Oyster Biology and Oyster Culture; publications in scientific journals on bionomics of marine animals. *Address:* c/o Dept. of Zoology, University, Liverpool. *T.:* Burton (Wirral) 266. [*Died* 2 *Feb.* 1953.

ORWIN, Charles Stewart, M.A., D.Litt. (Oxon); Hon. Fellow Balliol College; Hon. Fellow Wye College; *b.* 1876; *o. s.* of Frederick James Orwin, Warnham, Sussex, and Elizabeth, *d.* of Robert Campbell Stewart and *niece* of Col. George Gawler, Governor of South Australia, 1838-41; *m.* 1st, 1902, Elise Cécile (*d.* 1929), *y. d.* of late Edouard Renault, Cognac, France; three *s.* three *d.*; 2nd, 1931, Christabel Susan, *yr. d.* of late Charles Lowry, headmaster of Tonbridge. *Educ.* Dulwich College; South-Eastern Agricultural College, Wye (Scholar). Lecturer S.-E. Agricultural College, 1903-6; Agent for the Turnor Estates in Lincolnshire, 1906-13; Director, Agricultural Economics Research Institute, Oxford, 1913-45; Estates Bursar of Balliol College, 1926-47; Ed., Jl. Royal Agricultural Soc., 1912-27; Member Agric. Wages Board, 1917-21; President, Section M. (Agriculture) British Association, 1921; Agricultural Assessor on the Agricultural Tribunal of Investigation, 1922-24; Member of the Food Council 1925-33; Hon. Life Member of the Royal Agricultural Society, 1934; Citizen and Fruiterer of the City of London, 1915. *Publications:* A History of Wye Church and Wye College, 1913; Farm Accounts, 1914 (2nd ed. 1924); The Determination of Farming Costs, 1917 (2nd ed. 1920); The Tenure of Agricultural Land (with W. R. Peel), 1925 (2nd ed. 1926); Estate Accounts (with H. W. Kersey), 1926 (2nd. ed. 1936); The Reclamation of Exmoor Forest, 1929; The Future of Farming, 1930; Back to the Land (with W. F. Darke), 1935; The Open Fields (with Mrs. C. S. Orwin), 1938 (2nd ed. 1954); Speed the Plough (Penguin Special), 1942; Farms and Fields (with Mrs. C. S. Orwin), 1943, revised edn., 1951; Country Planning (ed.), 1944; Problems of the Countryside, 1945 (re-printed, 1946); A History of English Farming, 1949 (re-printed, 1952), etc. *Recreations:* seeing England and gardening. *Address:* The Red House, Blewbury, Didcot, Berks. *Club:* Farmers'. [*Died* 30 *June* 1955.

OSBORN, Sir (N.) Francis (B.), K.B.E., *cr.* 1928; C.B. 1921; *b.* 1872. *Educ.:* Merchant Taylors' School; St. John's College, Oxford (Scholar), First Class Honours Classical Moderations; First Class Honours Litt. Hum., Senior Scholar of St. John's College; M.A. 1898. Barrister-at-law, Inner Temple; Higher Division Clerk, War Office, 1895; Private Secretary to Sir R. H. Knox, Permanent Under-Secretary of State, 1898-1901; Assistant Principal, 1901-8; Principal, 1908-16; Deputy-Director of Army Contracts, 1916-21; Director of Finance, War Office, 1921-25; Director of Army Contracts, War Office, 1925-32; retired, 1932. *Address:* The Elms, Surbiton. *T.:* Elmbridge 6052. [*Died* 21 *June* 1954.

OSBORN, Sir Samuel, Kt., *cr.* 1941; J.P., LL.D.; Director Samuel Osborn and Co., Ltd., Sheffield; *b.* 11 July 1864; *s.* of Samuel Osborn and Eliza Fawcett; *m.* 1911; no *c.* *Educ.:* New College, Eastbourne. 2nd son of founder of Samuel Osborn and Co. Ltd. in which business his life has been spent; served in Sheffield City Council, 1903-35; Lord Mayor, 1912; Sheffield Education Committee, 1903-35; Liberal in politics; Member of Methodist Church; associated with many local philanthropic undertakings. *Recreations:* travel and walking. *Address:* 22 Hallamgate Road, Sheffield; Heatherleigh, Grindleford, nr. Sheffield. *T.:* Sheffield 62373, Grindleford 41. *Club:* Sheffield. [*Died* 10 *June* 1952.

OSBORN, Brig.-Gen. William Lushington, C.B. 1919; C.M.G. 1917; D.S.O. 1916; *o. s.* of late Lt.-Gen. W. Osborn, Indian Army; *b.* 30 July 1871; *m.* 1900, Ethel Marion, *d.* of late General Charles Elgee, 23rd Royal Welch Fusiliers; no *c.* *Educ.:* United Services Coll.; Westward Ho!; Sandhurst. Entered Royal Sussex Regt. in 1890; served Tirah Campaign, 1897-98 (medal and two clasps); Adj. 2nd Batt. 1899-1903; served in Thibet Mission Force, 1904 (medal); Brigade-Major, Sirhind Brigade, Punjab, India, 1905-9; 1st Batt. Royal Sussex Regt., India, till 1912; Commanding Depôt Chichester, 1912-14; served European War, 1915-18 (despatches six times, C.B., D.S.O., C.M.G., Bt. Lt.-Col., Order of Danilo 3rd Class); Commanded 7th Batt. Royal Sussex Regt., 1914-16; Temp. Brig.-General, 16th Infantry Brigade, 1916-17; 192nd Infantry Brigade, 1917-18; 5th Infantry Brigade, 1918-19; Lt.-Col. 2nd Batt. Royal Sussex Regt., 1919; Substantive Colonel, 1920: retired pay, 1921; Hon. Col. Royal Sussex Regt., 1926-41; Hon. Col. 4th Bn. Royal Sussex Regt., 1926-47. *Address:* Chichester, Sussex. [*Died* 10 *April* 1951.

OSBORNE, Vice-Adm. Edward Oliver Brudenell Seymour, C.B. 1935; D.S.O. 1918; Royal Navy, retired; *b.* 1883; 2nd *s.* of Capt. H. B. Osborne, 53rd Regt.; *m.* 1918, Joan Marion Herbert, *d.* of late Godfrey C. Chester Master, Rangeworthy Court, Yate; one *s.* (and one *s.* decd.). *Educ.:* The Grange, Folkestone. Entered Britannia, 1897; Lieut. 1904; Commander, 1915; Capt. 1920; Rear-Adm., 1933; Vice-Adm., 1937; Boxer Expedition, 1900 (despatches, early promotion, and 4th Order Crown Order of Prussia with Crossed Swords); Grand Fleet, 1914-18; Jutland, 1916; Dover Patrol Flag Comdr., 1918 (Zeebrugge, 1918, despatches, early promotion, D.S.O.); Captain of Gunnery School, Devonport, 1929-30; Commodore in command Destroyer Flotillas of Atlantic Fleet, 1930-32; commanded H.M.S. Excellent, 1932-33; Naval A.D.C. to the King, 1932; Vice-Pres. and Pres. Ordnance Board, 1936-40; retired list, 1937; President Air Gunnery Technical Board, Ministry of Aircraft Production, 1940-41; Home Guard, 1941-45. *Address:* Shadow Lawn, Stoke Poges, Bucks. *T.:* Farnham Common 412. *Club:* United Service. [*Died* 17 *Sept.* 1956.

OSBORNE, Sir George (Francis), 16th Bt., *cr.* 1629; M.C. 1918; retired Lt.-Col.; *b.* 27 July 1894; *s.* of Sir Francis Osborne, 15th Bt., and Kathleen, *d.* of George Whitfield, 3 Cornwall Gardens, S.W., and Modreeny, Co. Tipperary; *S.* father, 1948; *m.* 1938, Mary Grace, *d.* of C. Horn, Goring-by-Sea, Sussex; two *s.* two *d.* *Educ.:* Repton; R.M.C., Sandhurst. Commissioned Royal Sussex Regiment, 1913; served European War, 1914-18 (wounded twice, despatches twice, M.C.). Retired, 1938; re-employed, 1939. War of 1939-45; retired, 1945. *Heir:* *s.* Peter George, *b.* 29 June

1943. *Address:* Framfield Grange, Uckfield, Sussex. *T.:* Framfield 264. [*Died* 21 *July* 1960.

OSBORNE, Rev. (Henry James) Reginald, M.A.; Prebendary of St. Paul's Cathedral since 1920; Vicar of St. Saviours, Walton Street, S.W.3, since 1930; acting Rural Dean of Chelsea since 1951; Chairman of the Church Schools Company; *s.* of late J. H. S. Osborne, Exeter; *m.* Rose, niece of late J. F. Ellis, Pembroke House, Hampton, and the Rectory, Bow, N. Devon; two *d. Educ.:* Christ College, Cambridge; 3rd class Theological Tripos. Ordained, 1913; Curate of St. Mary, Twickenham, 1913-19; Assistant Diocesan Inspector of Schools, 1917-19; Chief Diocesan Inspector of Schools, 1919-30; Canon of Cantlers in St. Paul's Cathedral, 1920-30. *Address:* 7 Hans Place, S.W.1. *T.:* Kensington 2410. [*Died* 6 *April* 1952.

OSBORNE, Maj.-Gen. O. H. D.; *see* Delano-Osborne.

OSBORNE, Rev. Reginald; *see* Osborne, Rev. H. J. R.

OSBORNE, Rosabelle, C.B.E. 1918; R.R.C.; *y. d.* of late Dr. J. A. Osborne, J.P., Milford, Co. Donegal. *Educ.:* private schools. On completion of general training joined Queen Alexandra's Imperial Military Nursing Service as Sister, 1903; Matron, 1911; served European War in France, Egypt, Malta, Salonica and with the Army of the Black Sea, Aug. 1914–July 1920, as acting Principal Matron from March 1917 (despatches five times, R.R.C., C.B.E.); Principal Matron at War Office, 1924; Matron-in-Chief to 1930; Matron-in-Chief, Territorial Army Nursing Service, 1931-35; retired 1936; an honorary Serving Sister of St. John of Jerusalem; French decoration Médaille d'Honneur des Epidémies de la Marine (en vermeil); has travelled in Australia, South Africa and India. *Address:* 129 Queen's Gate, S.W.7. *Clubs:* United Nursing Services, Victory. [*Died* 8 *May* 1958.

OSBURN, Lieut.-Colonel Arthur, D.S.O. 1916; late R.A.M.C.; *y. s.* of Commander Francis Osburn, R.N.; *g.s.* of Captain Bushell, Royal Navy. *Educ.:* King's College; Guy's Hospital; B.Litt. Oxon. Served in Artists' Rifles; also in Dorsetshire Hussars (Dorsetshire Yeomanry); in the ranks, South Africa, 1900; Temp. Capt. 1900; M.R.C.S., L.R.C.P. Lond., 1902; Lieut. R.A.M.C. 1903; Capt. 1907; served with 4th Dragoon Guards, 2nd Cavalry Brigade, European War, Aug. 1914-Mar. 1915 and later (despatches five times, prom. Major and temp. Lt.-Col., D.S.O. and bar); retired pay, 1923; contested Walsall, General Election, 1923. *Publications:* Carrick-an-Arth; Must England lose India? 1930; Unwilling Passenger, 1932. *Recreations:* literature, travel. *Address:* c/o Holt & Co., Kirkland House, Whitehall, S.W.1. [*Died* 7 *March* 1952.

OSGOOD, Sir (Frederic) Stanley, Kt., *cr.* 1939; C.B.E. 1935 (O.B.E. 1918); M.V.O. 1911-late Secretary Lord Chamberlain's Office; a Serjeant-at-Arms to H.M., 1929-39; Officer, Order of St. John of Jerusalem; *b.* 1872; *m.* 1917, Doris Noel, *d.* of John Isaac Mullins; two *d. Address:* Child's House, Nutley, Sussex. *T.:* Nutley 152. [*Died* 4 *Nov.* 1952.

O'SHEA, Most Rev. Thomas, S.N., D.D.; Archbishop of Wellington (N.Z.), (R.C.) since 1935, and Metropolitan of New Zealand; *b.* San Francisco, California, 13 Mar. 1870; *s.* of Edmund O'Shea and Joan O'Sullivan. *Educ.:* St. Patrick's College, Wellington; St. Mary's Seminary, Napier. Priest, 1893; taught Philosophy and History at St. Mary's Seminary, 1894-96; Asst. Priest, St. Mary of the Angels Wellington, 1897-1901; Rector of St. Joseph's Parish, Wellington, 1903-13; Vicar General of Wellington, 1907; Consecrated Archbishop of Gortyna, and Coadjutor of Wellington with right of succession, 17 Aug. 1913; ex-officio Member the T. G. Macarty Education and Charitable Trust Board. *Recreation:* golf. *Address:* 7 Paterson Street, Wellington, E.1, N.Z. *T.:* 54,063 and 54,064 Central. [*Died* 9 *May* 1954.

OSMOND, Brigadier William Robert Fiddes, C.B.E. 1949 (O.B.E. 1941); *b.* 21 May 1890; *o. c.* of William Osmond and Margaret Laing; *m.* 1915, Cynthia Rosamond Emmeline, *o. c.* of late Col. Percy Hugh Hamon Massy, C.B.E., 6th Dragoon Guards, and *g.d.* of Sir Carey Knyvett, K.C.B.; one *s.* one *d. Educ.:* Marlborough College; University Coll. Oxford (M.A.); R.M.A. Woolwich. Called to the Bar, Inner Temple, 1915; served European War; joined (P Battery) R.H.A., 1915; Mesopotamia, 1916-17; Staff Capt. War Office, 1920; Mil. Asst. Judge Advocate General Office, 1923; D.J.A.G., Rhine Army, 1929; Brevet Major, 1932; D.A.A.G., 1934; D.J.A.G. International Force, Saar Territory, 1935; A.A.G., 1939; A.J.A.G., 1941; 2nd Military Deputy of J.A.G., 1944; Colonel, 1947; Military and Air Force Deputy of J.A.G. (Brig.), 1948; retired pay, 1950. *Publication:* a contributor to title Royal Forces in Halsbury's Laws of England (Hailsham Edn.). *Recreations:* shooting, fishing, golf. *Address:* Vine Cottage, Steyning, Sussex. *T.:* Steyning 2162. *Clubs;* Carlton, United Service. [*Died* 26 *Sept.* 1952.

O'SULLIVAN, Major-General Hugh Dermod Evan, C.B.E. 1919; The Royal Marines, retired; *b.* Gwalior, India, 11 Sept. 1874; 2nd *s.* of late Lt.-Col. Eugene O'Sullivan, R.A., and of Grace, *d.* of S. Patterson Evans, M.D., J.P., Co. Limerick; *m.* 1911, Flora, (*d.* 1946), *d.* of Hugh Campbell, of Eden Lodge, West Wickham; one *s.* one *d. Educ.:* The Inverness Coll.; Weymouth Coll.; Wimborne; Royal Naval Coll. Entered Royal Marines, 1892; Captain, 1899; served China War, 1900-1; Adjutant of Royal Marine Battalion of Naval Brigade (H.M.T.S. Jelunga) (medal); attached Egyptian Army, 1901-11; punitive measures Shad-Kadrug (Dar Nuba), and Jebel Daier (Kordofan), 1903; Sudan Government, 1903; Senior Inspector, Upper Nile Province, 1904, and Kordofan Province, 1906; Dar Messeria rising, 1906 (Order of Osmania); Governor and O.C. Troops, Upper Nile Province, 1909-11 (Order of the Mejidie); Major, Royal Marines, 1911; Senior Officer R.M., East Indies, 1912-1914; operations in Persian Gulf (Naval medal with clasp, Persian Gulf, 1912-14); European War, 1914-18; Senior Officer, R.M., East Indies and Egypt, 1914-15; Turkish attack on Suez Canal, 1915; Intelligence Officer to Naval C.-in-C. East Indies and Egypt, Flagship (H.M.S. Euryalus), operations at Smyrna, 1915; temp. Lieutenant-Colonel and General Staff Officer (1st Grade), Special Service in Egypt, Staff of Naval C.-in-C. East Indies and Egypt, 1916, and of Mediterranean, 1917; Hejaz operations, 1915-18 (General's despatches, Order of the Nile); Brevet Lt.-Colonel, 1918; Naval Political Officer (G.S.O.1), Egypt, 1918-19 (1914 Star, War and Victory medals, Naval clasps, Mediterranean, Dardanelles, Suez Canal, Red Sea, despatches emblem, C.B.E.); Lt.-Col. 1920; Col. 2nd Comdt., 1924; Retired List, 1926; (under Order in Council) Maj.-Gen. 1928. *Publication:* Dinka Laws and Customs (Royal Anthropological Institute). *Recreations:* travelling, study of general progress. *Address:* c/o Westminster Bank, St. James's Street, S.W.1. [*Died* 4 *Feb.* 1958.

O'SULLIVAN, Seumas; (James Sullivan Starkey, Litt.D., T.C.D.); Editor of The Dublin Magazine; *b.* 1879. Edited Tower Press, Booklets. Member of the Irish Academy of Letters; Gregory Medal, 1957. *Publications: poetry:* The Twilight People, 1905; Verses Sacred and Profane, 1908; The Earth Lover, 1909; Selected Lyrics, 1910; Collected Poems, 1912; An Epilogue, 1914; Requiem, 1917; The Rosses, 1918; The

Lamplighter and other poems, 1929. At Christmas (Poems), 1934; Personal Talk (Poems), 1936; Poems (1930-1938), 1938; Collected Poems, 1940; Dublin Poems (New York), 1946; *prose:* Mud and Purple, 1917; Common Adventures, 1926; Essays and Recollections, 1944; The Rose and Bottle (Essays), 1946. *Address:* 2 Morehampton Road, Dublin. [*Died* 24 *March* 1958.

O'SULLIVAN, Hon. Thomas; *b.* Ipswich, Queensland, 13 Dec. 1856; *m.* 1886, *d.* of L. T. Mellin of the firm of Cunninghame & Co., Pitt Street, Sydney, printers; three *s.* three *d.* *Educ.:* Ipswich State School; St. Mary's Boys' School, Ipswich. Admitted as solicitor at age of 21, 1878; practised at Ipswich till 1886; in 1886 entered into partnership with C. B. Lilley and carried on solicitors' firm of Lilley & O'Sullivan till about 1896, at Brisbane; carried on solicitors' business alone till 1900 at Brisbane; admitted to Bar, Queensland, 1900; M.L.C. and minister, without portfolio, 1903; Secretary for Public Works, 1906; Member for Warwick, 1906-8; Secretary for Agriculture, 1908; K.C. 1911; Member of Legislative Council of Queensland, Attorney-General of Queensland, 1908-15; Judge of District Courts, 1915-22; Judge of Supreme Court of Queensland, 1922-26; retired, 1926. *Publication:* The Insolvency Laws of Queensland (with F. G. Hamilton). *Recreations:* bowls, motoring. *Address:* Udale Toowong, Queensland, Australia. *T.:* Toowong 49. *Club:* Stock Exchange (Brisbane). [*Died* 22 *Feb.* 1953.

OSWALD, Felix, D.Sc. (London), B.A., F.S.A., F.G.S.; Hon. Reader in History of Roman Britain, the University, Nottingham; *b.* 3 Nov. 1866; *m.*; one *s.* In 1898 accompanied the late Mr. H. F. B. Lynch in an expedition to Turkish Armenia, made a survey and investigated the geology of the district between the Black Sea and Lake Van, published his results in a volume on the Geology of Armenia, 1906, printed by hand by himself in order to put on record the geological results of his journey; excavated the Roman camp of Margidunum near Nottingham, 1910-36, the collection of antiquities now exhibited in the University, Nottingham; investigated, on behalf of the British Museum, an important discovery of large Vertebrates of Mid-Tertiary age near the Victoria Nyanza, 1911; awarded Murchison Grant, Geol. Soc., 1905; Cuthbert Peek Grant, R.G.S., 1913; in 1915 travelled in the Caucasus, investigating the geology of oil-fields and locating oil-wells for The Anglo-Maikop Co.; reorganised and classified the Roman antiquities in the Leicester Museum; Probate Registrar for the districts of Nottingham, Leicester, Lincoln, and Derbyshire; retd., 1936; Home Guard, 1940. *Publications:* Geology of Armenia, 1906; Geological Map of Armenia, 1907; Geological Map of the Caucasus, 1914; Alone in the Sleeping Sickness Country, 1915; Terra Sigillata (Roman Provincial Red-glazed Ware), 1919; Margidunum, 1929; an Index of Potters Stamps on Terra Sigillata, hand-printed and published by the author, 1931; Index of Figure-types (over 3000 illustrations) on Terra Sigillata, 1936; Cursive Writing of Gaulish Potters, 1927; Origin of the Coritani, 1941; Margidunum Excavation Report, 1941; Mortaria of Margidunum, 1944; Borough-English in Notts, 1945; Decorated Ware of Lavoye Potters, 1945; Modiolo Aretino de Zaragoza, 1947; The Commandant's House at Margidunum, 1947; The Samian of Margidunum, 1947; St. Ann's Well Maze, Nottingham, 1947; Samian of the Trajanic potter Vibinus, 1948; Samian pottery of Leicester, 1948; Saxon Tympana of Notts churches, 1949; The Volute in Arretine and S. Gaulish Terra Sigillata, 1951; Ad Pontem, 1952; A Traverse of Margidunum, 1953; Week-day Gods at Margidunum, 1954; Last Days of Margidunum, 1956. Contrib. Jl. Roman Studies. *Address:* Highfields, Solva, Pembrokeshire. *T.:* Solva 283. [*Died* 3 *Nov.* 1958.

OTTLEY, Rev. Canon Feilding Hay, M.A.; Vicar of St. Luke's, Grayshott, since 1944; *b.* 1877; *s.* of Canon Bickersteth Ottley; *m.* 1901, Edith Matthey (*d.* 1954); one *s.* one *d.* *Educ.:* Christ Church, Oxford. Vicar of St. Matthias, Torquay, 1911; Diocesan Missioner for Exeter, 1921; Tait Missioner, Diocese of Canterbury, 1925; Preacher of Grays Inn, 1932; Hon. Canon of Canterbury, 1927-44, Canon emeritus since 1944; Member of the Ordination Commission, 1937. Six Preacher, Canterbury Cathedral, 1949; Chaplain to Drapers' Company, 1951-; Golden Lecturer, 1952-53. *Address:* Grayshott Vicarage, Hindhead, Surrey. [*Died* 30 *June* 1958.

OUDENDYK, William J., Hon. K.C.M.G., 1918; retired; *b.* 22 July 1874; *m.* 1911, Margaret Fuller (Dame Margaret Oudendyk, D.B.E.). *Educ.:* Leyden. Netherlands Minister in Teheran, 1910; Govt. Adviser in Batavia, 1913; Minister in Petrograd, 1917; in charge of British interests in Petrograd, 1918; Minister in Peking, 1919; retired, 1931. Grand Cross, or Commander, various orders (Netherlands, Belgian, French, Swedish, Russian, Austraian, Hungarian, Chinese and Persian). *Publications:* Ways and By-ways in Diplomacy (London), 1939. International Affairs (Journal of Royal Institute, Journal of Royal Central Asian Society, Fortnightly Review, etc.). *Club:* Sesame Imperial and Pioneer. [*Died* 22 *Nov.* 1953.

OULD, Hermon; Chevalier de la Légion d'Honneur, 1938; dramatist, poet, critic, etc.; General Secretary, International P.E.N. Club; General Ed. P.E.N. Books since 1941; *b.* London, 1885; *s.* of John and Alice Ould. Joint-Editor, Theatre-Craft, 1920-1923. *Publications:* Between Sunset and Dawn, a play, 1913; Domestic Interior, a play, 1913; Ada Wodderspoon, a play, 1914; What Fools these Mortals be! a play, 1915; Christmas Eve, a folk-music play, 1921; Candle-Ends: Verse, 1921; The Black Virgin, a play, 1922; The Dance of Life, a play, 1924; New Plays from Old Stories, 1924; Princess Mirabelle and the Swine-herd, 1924; Three Comedies, 1925; Plays of Pioneers, 1925; The Piper Laughs: a play, 1927; The Moon Rides High: a play, 1927; The Light Comedian: a play, 1928; Hoppla: an English version of Ernst Toller's play, 1928; Pierrot before the Seven Doors: an English version of Arthur Cantillon's play, 1928; Li Sui Yu, or Broken Jade: an English version of a play by C.K. Sie, 1928; Flames in Sunlight: a play, 1928; Ivan and the Firebird, and other tales, 1929; New Plays from Old Stories, 2nd series, 1930; The Shadow and the Substance, a play, 1930; The Miser of Rogafjord, a play, 1931; Shim Sham: a play for children, 1932; Which world, which way?, translation of Toller's Quer Durch, 1933; John Galsworthy: a study, 1934; New Plays from Old Stories, 3rd series, 1935; Tangled Skeins, an Early Victorian play, 1936; Ali Baba and his Son Hadji, a play with music by David Carver, 1936; The Meeting, a play, 1936; In the Country, a verse sequence, music by David Carver, 1937; Pathetic Symphony: English version of Klaus Mann's novel, 1938; The Art of the Play, 1938; Ed. Ten New One-Acters, 1936; Ed. Writers in Freedom: A Symposium based on the 17th International Congress of P.E.N. Club, 1942; My Spirit Walks Alone: a verse sequence, 1941; To One Who Sang: Verse, 1942; Time's Nemesis: Verse, 1943: The Way of Acceptance: Paraphrase of Lao Tse's Tao Tê Ching, 1943; Shuttle: An Autobiographical Sequence, 1945; Ed. Freedom of Expression: A Symposium based on the P.E.N. Areopagitica Conference, 1945; (Ed.) The Book of the P.E.N., 1950; many stories and verses for children. *Recreations:* music, travel. *Address:* 1 St. John's Gardens, W.11. *T.:* Park 5868; 62 Glebe Place,

S.W.3. *T.:* Flaxman 9549. *Clubs:* Savile, English-Speaking Union.
[*Died* 21 *Sept.* 1951.

OULD, Robert F.; *see* Fielding-Ould.

OULTON, Rev. John Ernest Leonard, D.D.; Regius Professor of Divinity in University of Dublin since 1935; Canon of St. Patrick's Cathedral, Dublin, since 1930; *b.* 22 March 1886; *s.* of Rev. Richard Charles Oulton, B.D., Incumbent of Glynn, Co. Antrim, and Katharine Jane Leonard, Listowel, C. Kerry; unmarried. *Educ.:* Campbell College, Belfast; Trinity College, Dublin. Junior Exhibitioner, 1904; Scholar in Classics, 1906; Vice-Chancellor's Latin Medal, 1907; Senior Moderator in Classics and Junior Moderator in Modern Literature, 1908; Berkeley Gold Medal in Greek, 1909; Divinity Testimonium (First Class), 1913; B.A., 1908; B.D., 1919; M.A., 1930; D.D., 1934; M.R.I.A., 1928; Member of General Synod of Church of Ireland, 1934; Curate-Assistant of Harold's Cross Parish, Dublin, 1913-16, of St. Stephen's, Dublin, 1916-27; Incumbent of Chapelizod, Dublin, 1927-29, of Monkstown, Co. Dublin, 1929-30; Assistant Lecturer in Divinity, T.C.D., 1924-30; Lecturer on the Bible, 1926-29; Archbishop King's Professor of Divinity, 1930-35; Deputy to the Regius Professor of Divinity, 1934-35; Select Preacher, Univ. of Cambridge, 1956. *Publications:* Contributor to The History of the Church of Ireland, 1935; Joint Editor of Eusebius, The Ecclesiastical History and the Martyrs of Palestine, 1927-1928, reprinted 1954; Editor of Eusebius, The Ecclesiastical History, Book vi-x, 1932, 2nd ed., 1938; The Cathedral Church of St. Patrick, Dublin, by the late J. H. Bernard, revised ed., 1940 and 1951; and of The Church Catechism Explained, by A. W. Robinson, revised ed., 1955; Author of Memoir of William Reeves, 1937, The Credal Statements of St. Patrick, 1940, The Study of Divinity in Trinity College, Dublin, 1941, Holy Communion and Holy Spirit, 1951 (2nd ed. 1954), Alexandrian Christianity (in part), 1954, The Mystery of the Cross, 1957, and of Articles in Journal of Theological Studies, Expository Times, Theology, Divinity, and Hermathena. *Recreation:* music. *Address:* Zion Lodge, Zion Road, Rathgar, Dublin; Trinity College, Dublin. *T.:* Dublin 909128.
[*Died* 2 *Feb.* 1957.

OUTEN, Roland Thomas; Senior Partner, Ashurst Morris Crisp & Co., Solicitors, 17 Throgmorton Avenue, E.C.2; *b.* 7 June 1900; *s.* of late Thomas Outen and of Frances Eleanor Outen (*née* Wingfield); *m.* 1927, Mary McLellan. *Educ.:* City of London School. Chairman: International Harvester Co. of Great Britain Ltd.; Quaker Oats Ltd.; The Fairey Aviation Co. Ltd.; Director: Smith & Nephew Associated Cos. Ltd. (Dep. Chm.); and other Cos. Mem. Council Institute of Directors and Chairman of its Legal Committee. *Recreations:* shooting (but little time for it); company law. *Address:* 17 Throgmorton Avenue, E.C.2. *T.:* London Wall 5581 (residence, Grosvenor 3581). *Clubs:* City of London, Devonshire.
[*Died* 9 *Feb.* 1957.

OUVRY, Ernest Carrington, M.B.E.; F.S.A.; Solicitor, lately Senior Partner, Ouvry and Co., 2 and 3 The Sanctuary, S.W.1; *b.* 2 July 1866; 3rd *s.* of Rev. Peter Thomas Ouvry, M.A., J.P., Vicar of Wing, Bucks, and Anne Louisa, *d.* of late John Grubbe, Horsenden, Bucks, J.P., D.L.; *m.* 1903, Elinor Southwood, *d.* of Charles Lee Lewes and Gertrude *sis.* of Octavia Hill; four *s.* one *d.* *Educ.:* Marlborough Coll.; Wadham Coll., Oxford. Vice-Pres. of Huguenot Soc. of London; Fellow of the Royal Society of Arts; a Director of the French Protestant Hosp., Victoria Park; Life Governor of the Marine Society; a Trustee of the French Protestant Church of London (Soho); Secretary to the Trustees of the French Protestant Episcopal Church of the Savoy; Hon. Treas. the Westminster French Protestant School Foundation; Hon. Solicitor to the British Trust for Ornithology and to the East London Nursing Society; retired, 1948 (after 50 years service), as Senior Member of the Council of the National Trust for Places of Historic Interest or Natural Beauty; Trustee and Council of The Universal Beneficent Society; Governor of Westminster Hospital; Commission 1st Volunteer Battalion Royal Fusiliers, 1886; served South African War 1900-1, 34th Co. Middlesex Imperial Yeomanry (medal and four clasps); late Cadet Lt.-Col. commanding 1st Cadet Bn., H.A.C. Secretary City of London Cadet Association. Member St. Stephens Club for 50 years; resigned Dec. 1948. *Address:* 2 and 3, The Sanctuary, Westminster, S.W.1; Crockham Hill, Kent. *T.A.:* Ouvry Parl. London. *T.:* Abbey 7206; Crockham Hill 218.
[*Died* 23 *Nov.* 1951.

OVERBURY, Sir Robert (Leslie), K.C.B., *cr.* 1950 (C.B. 1941); *b.* 26 July 1887; *m.* 1913, Ethel Stapleton; two *s.* Secretary of Commissions, Lord Chancellor's Office, 1923-30; Chief Clerk, Lord Chancellor's Office, 1930-34; Reading Clerk, Clerk of Outdoor Committees, House of Lords, 1934-1937; Clerk Assistant of the Parliaments, 1937-49; Clerk of the Parliaments, 1949-53. *Address:* Shovelstrode Manor Farm, East Grinstead, Sussex. *T.:* East Grinstead 965.
[*Died* 11 *Jan.* 1955.

OWEN, Sir Cecil; *see* Owen, Sir W. C.

OWEN, Colonel Charles Richard Blackstone, C.M.G. 1918; Order of St. Anne of Russia, 2nd Class, 1918; late R.A.; *b.* 17 Sept. 1870; *o. s.* of Charles Owen, Barrister-at-law, Field House, Marchington, Staffordshire; *m.* C. Gwendoline, 2nd *d.* of late Rev. Charles E. Hornby of Ashendene, Hertford; one *s.* three *d.* *Educ.:* Bedford; Royal Military Academy, Woolwich. Second Lieut. Royal Artillery, 1890; Col. 1921; retired pay, 1924. *Address:* Tre Evan, Llangarron, Ross-on-Wye. *T.:* Llangarron 225.
[*Died* 3 *Sept.* 1954.

OWEN, Brig.-Gen. Charles Samuel, C.M.G. 1918; D.S.O. 1915; late Royal Welch Fusiliers; *b.* 23 Jan. 1879; *s.* of late G. H. Owen, Ymwlch, Caernarvonshire; *m.* 1918, Violet Eva, *d.* of late Capt. George Fenwick, Royal Welch Fusiliers, Plas Fron, Wrexham; one *s.* one *d.* Entered army, 1899; Capt., 1906; Adjutant, 1913; Major, 1915; Lt.-Col. 1921; Col. 1925; served China, 1900 (medal with clasp), Relief of Pekin; European War, 1914-18 (despatches, D.S.O., C.M.G., Bt. Lt.-Col.); Waziristan, 1922-23; commanded 159th (Welsh Border) Infantry Brigade T.A., 1927-31; retired, 1931. *Address*; Plas Fron, Wrexham. *Club:* Naval and Military.
[*Died* 28 *Feb.* 1959.

OWEN, Collinson; author and journalist; *b.* 1882; *s.* of late William Owen, newspaper proprietor. Member of staffs of various London newspapers from 1901 onwards; resident correspondent in Paris, 1909-11; special correspondent in Europe and dramatic critic for Standard, 1911-15; Editor of Balkan News for British Salonica Forces and Official War Correspondent in Near East, 1916-19; special writer for Evening Standard under initials "C. O.", 1924-27; has contributed articles and stories to many leading newspapers and periodicals in England and America; special series include Monocle Monologues, The Letters of Lord Jesterfield and It Happened Last Week, a Sunday review of current events, 1932-38. *Publications:* The American Illusion; King Crime; C.O.'s Cameos: Salonica and After; and following novels; We Happy Few, Old Flames, Zero, The Adventures of Antoine, The Rockingham Diamond, The Battle of London (under pen name Hugh Addison), Hector Duval, The Perfect Friend, and The Riverton Wagers. *Clubs:* Savage, Athenæum.
[*Died* 15 *Sept.* 1956.

OWEN, Leonard Victor Davies; Professor of History, Nottingham University, 1920-51; *b.* 4 April 1888; *s.* of late John Owen of Cardigan; *m.* 1917, Gwen, *e. d.* of late E. O. Price, M.D., Bangor; one *s.* *Educ.:* Llandovery School; Keble Coll., Oxford (Scholar), Stanhope (Univ.) Prize, 1909, Class I., Mod. Hist.; B.A., 1911; M.A., 1914; Assistant Tutor, Keble College, Oxford, 1911-12; Assistant Lecturer in History, University College of North Wales, Bangor, 1912-14; Lecturer in Modern History, University of Sheffield, 1914-20; Captain, Oxford and Bucks Light Infantry; External Examiner at various times to Univ. of Sheffield, National University of Ireland, University of Wales, and Univ. of Reading; Member of Council, Pipe Roll Society; Lincoln Record Society. *Publications:* England and Burgundy, 1400-1450, 1909; England and the Low Countries, 1405-1413, in English Historical Review, 1913; Teaching of History in Elementary Schools, 1916; contributor to the Publications of the Pipe Roll Society, English Place-Name Society, History; Editor, Reports and Papers, Lincs. Archæological Society; Editor, British Section, International Bibliography of Historical Sciences, Vols. VI.-X., 1933-36; Joint Editor, Transactions of the Thoroton Society of Nottinghamshire; Articles on Robin Hood and Sir Roger Williams; The Gild Accounts of the Gilds of St. Peter's, Nottingham, 1939; Notts Manorial Records, 1946. *Address:* 12 Derby Road, Beeston, Notts. [*Died* 16 *Feb.* 1952.

OWEN, Maj.-Gen. Ll. I. G. M.; *see* Morgan-Owen.

OWEN, Sackville Herbert Edward Gregg, J.P. Pembs.; *b.* 1880; *o. s.* of late Sackville Herbert Owen, D.L., J.P., Pemb.; *m.* 1925, Dorothy Constance, O.B.E. 1951, *er. d.* of John St. Foyne Fair, Brendon, Winchester; one *d.* *Educ.:* Charterhouse; Pembroke College, Cambridge. Served in European War, 1914-19, in Egypt and Palestine, Lieut. Pembrokeshire Imperial Yeomanry, attached Camel Corps (wounded); J.P. Pembrokeshire, High Sheriff Pembrokeshire, 1941; Chairman Pembrokeshire County Council, 1946-47. *Recreations:* shooting, fishing. *Address:* Heywood, Tenby, Pembrokeshire. *T.:* Tenby 2053. [*Died* 7 *Jan.* 1960.

OWEN, Will; artist and lecturer; *b.* Malta, 1869; *s.* of Thomas Owen, R.N.; *m.* 1897, Margaret Florence (*d.* 1954), *d.* of Major Porteus; two *d.* *Educ.:* Rochester. Entered Civil Service, G.P.O. *Publications:* Old London Town; Potted London; Mr. Peppercorn; Illustrator W. W. Jacobs; humorous pages in illustrated papers and magazines, posters, etc. *Address:* Flat 90, Charterhouse Square, E.C.1. [*Died* 14 *April* 1957.

OWEN, Sir (William) Cecil, Kt., *cr.* 1930; *b.* 1872; *s.* of Lancaster Owen, M.Inst.C.E.; *m.* 1917, Ethel, *d.* of Charles Frederick Tanner, Exmouth, S. Devon, and *widow* of Charles Mackenzie Partington, Merklands, Perthshire; no *c.* *Educ.:* Marlborough; Trinity College, Cambridge, B.A. Called to Bar, Inner Temple, 1897; Personal Clerk in Treasury Solicitor's Department, 1903; an Assistant Solicitor to the Treasury, 1920; Chief Assistant Solicitor to the Treasury, 1926; retired, 1937. *Address:* Alltreoch, Blairgowrie, Perthshire. *Clubs:* Royal Cruising, Leander. [*Died* 25 *July* 1959.

OWEN, William Hugh, C.B.E. 1919; *b.* 16 Feb. 1886; *s.* of Thomas Owen, Holyhead, N. Wales; *m.* 1919, Enid Strathearn, *o. d.* of late Col. Sir John Strathearn Hendrie, K.C.M.G., C.V.O., former Lt.-Gov. Province of Ontario; three *d.* Lt.-Col., Royal Engineers, 1918. *Recreation:* hockey (Welsh International, 1910-11). *Address:* 3467 Ontario Avenue, Montreal, Canada. *Clubs:* White's; Mount Royal, Montreal Racket (Montreal). [*Died* 21 *Feb.* 1957.

OXENHAM, Elsie Jeanette; *e. d.* of late John Oxenham. *Publications:* some 84 books for girls, 1908-55. *Recreations:* tramps on the Downs, folk-dancing. *Address:* Inverkip, 45 The Glen, Worthing, Sussex. [*Died* 9 *Jan.* 1960.

OXLAND, Air Vice-Marshal Robert Dickinson, C.B. 1943; C.B.E. 1942 (O.B.E. 1929); *b.* 4 Apr. 1889; *s.* of late Charles Oxland; *m.* 1929, Ethel Barbara, *d.* of late Col. Henry David Williams, C.M.G.; two *d.* *Educ.:* Bedford Modern School. Joined R.F.C. 1915; R.A.F. 1918; retired, May 1946. Polonia Restituta 2nd Class, 1942. *Address:* Wingates, Boyn Hill, Maidenhead, Berks. *Club:* United Service. [*Died* 27 *Oct.* 1959.

OXLEY, Brig.-Gen. Reginald Stewart, C.B. 1916; C.M.G. 1919; *b.* 1863; *s.* of late John Stewart Oxley, Fen Place, Turner's Hill, Sussex; *m.* 1899, Margaret Grace Julia, *d.* of late George Banks Rennie; one *s.* three *d.* *Educ.:* Charterhouse; R.M.C., Sandhurst. Entered K.R.R.C. 1884; served Manipur, 1891 (medal); Brigade Major 12th Infantry Brigade, South African War, 1899-1900 (despatches, Bt. Major, Queen's medal 3 clasps); D.A.A.G., N.W. District; 1901-4; Lt.-Col. Comdg. Battn. K.R.R.C.; 1907-11; G.S.O.1, Staff College, 1912-14; G.S.O.1, B.E.F., France, 1914; Brig.-Gen. commanding an Infantry Brigade, B.E.F., France, 1915-16; D.A. and Q.M.G., 1916-19 (despatches twice, C.B., C.M.G.). *Address:* Queen Camel House, Queen Camel, nr. Yeovil, Somerset. *T.:* Marston Magna 331. *Club:* Army and Navy. [*Died* 4 *Oct.* 1951.

OYEBODE, Rt. Rev. David Richard; Bishop of Ibadan since 1956; *b.* 1 April 1898; *e. s.* of late Rev. R. S. and Mrs. Oyebode; *m.* 1926, Clara Adeline Sowunmi; one *s.* four *d.* *Educ.:* St. Andrew's College, Oyo, Nigeria; Fourah Bay College, Sierra Leone. B.A., L.Th. (Dunelm). School Teacher, 1918-27. Deacon, 1932, Priest, 1933; Army Chaplain, 1943-46; Archdeacon of Benin, 1946-54; Asst. Bishop, Ondo-Benin Diocese, 1954. Visited England, 1949-50, and spent a term at Wycliffe Hall, Oxford. *Recreations:* none specially. *Address:* Bishopscourt, Oke Are, P.O. Box 1075, Ibadan, Nigeria. [*Died* 13 *July* 1960.

P

PACE, Rev. Edward George; Reader in Divinity in the University of Durham, 1921-47; Proctor, 1927-31; Director of Extra-Mural Studies in the Durham Division of the University, 1925-47; Vice-Master and Chaplain of Hatfield College, Durham, 1917-47; and Vice-Master of University College, 1940-47; Hon. Canon of Durham, 1944; *b.* London, 15 Dec. 1881; *s.* of Edward Warren Pace; *m.* 1910, Blanche (*d.* 1948), *widow* of Rev. C. H. Venning and *d.* of Henry Newcombe; no *c.* *Educ.:* Central Foundation School, London; University College, London; University College, Durham. Scholar and Exhibitioner of Durham University; First Class Honours in Classics and in Theology; University Classical and Hebrew Scholar; L.Th. 1903; B.A. 1905; M.A. 1908; B.D. 1910; D.D. 1923; ordained, 1905; Assistant Curate of Christ Church, Albany Street, London, 1905-7; Fellow of University of Durham, 1906; Theological Lecturer, 1907; Hebrew Lecturer, 1917; J.P. Co. Durham, 1925. *Publication:* Ideas of God in Israel, 1924. *Address:* c/o Hatfield College, Durham. [*Died* 6 *Feb.* 1953.

PACELLI, Eugene; *see* Pius XII.

PACKE, Lieut.-Colonel Frederick Edward, C.V.O. 1945 (M.V.O. 1927); O.B.E. 1919; Equerry in Waiting to Princess Beatrice from 1921 to her death in 1944; an Extra Gentleman Usher in Ordinary to the

Queen since 1952 (Gentleman Usher in Ordinary, 1934 - 52, an Extra Gentleman Usher, Jan.-Feb. 1952, to King George VI); *b.* 1879; *s.* of late William Packe and Penelope, *d.* of Sir John Farnaby Lennard, Bart.; unmarried. *Educ.:* Marlborough. Joined Welch Regt., 1899; served S. African War, 1899-1902 (despatches, Queen's medal 5 clasps, King's medal 2 clasps); European War, France, 1914, with 2nd Bn. Welch Regt.; 1915, with 1st Bn. Welch Regt., 1916, commanded 13th Service Bn. Welch Regt. (twice very severely wounded); afterwards at War Office; retired, 1921. *Recreations:* shooting, fishing. *Address:* 13 Southwick Street, Hyde Park, W.2. *T.:* Paddington 6487. *Clubs:* Turf, Brooks's. [*Died* 2 *Nov.* 1953.

PADEL, Charles Frederick Christian, B.A.; *e. s.* of late Christian G. Padel, York; *b.* York, 20 July 1872; *m.* Mòrag, 3rd *d.* of late William Hunter, M.D., Rothesay; three *s.* one *d.* *Educ.:* St. Peter's School, York; Sidney Sussex College Cambridge (Scholar). 1st Class Classical Tripos, 1894; Assistant Master Merchiston Castle School, 1895; Rossall Preparatory, 1896; Leys School, 1899; Sherborne, 1950; Eastbourne College, 1901; Marlborough College, 1907; Headmaster, Ashby-de-la-Zouch, 1909; Headmaster Carlisle Grammar School, 1912-32. *Recreations:* instrumental music; literature, chess. *Address:* 34A Highfield Avenue, Headington, Oxford. [*Died* 11 *March* 1958.

PADWICK, Philip Hugh, R.B.A.; R.O.I.; *b.* 28 April 1876; *s.* of late Henry Padwick, M.A., J.P., of the Manor House, Horsham. *Educ.:* Repton; Slade School. *Address:* Redroof, Tripp Hill, Fittleworth, Sussex. [*Died* 16 *Oct.* 1958.

PAGE, Sir Arthur, Kt., *cr.* 1930; Q.C. 1922; *b.* 1876; *o. surv. s.* of late Nathaniel Page, J.P., Carshalton, Surrey; *m.* 1906, Margaret, Kaisar-i-Hind Gold Medal, 1935, *d.* of E. Symes Thompson, M.D., F.R.C.P.; one *s.* four *d.* *Educ.:* Harrow; Magdalen College, Oxford. Classical Honours Moderations, 1897; Literae Humaniores, 1899; B.A. 1899. Barrister-at-law, 1901; Judge of the High Court, Calcutta, 1923; Puisne Judge, 1924-30; Chief Justice of Burma, 1930-36; Conservative candidate, Derby Borough, Jan. 1910; served European War in France and Flanders, A.B., R.N.V.R. 1915; 2nd Lieut. Royal Marine Artillery; Captain, 1917; Arbitrator between Mysore and Madras concerning disputed water rights in River Cauvery, 1929; Chairman, Evidence Section, Blockade Intelligence, Ministry of Economic Warfare, 1939-40; Chairman, North Staffs Regional Coal Valuation Board, 1941; Vice-Chairman Special Cttee. Province of Canterbury Reorganisation Areas Measure, 1947. *Publications:* Licensing Bill, is it Just?, 1908: Shops Act (joint author), 1911; Legal Problems of the Empire in Oxford Survey of the British Empire, 1914; Imperialism and Democracy, 1913; War and Alien Enemies, 1914; Blood and Sweat: To What End?, 1944; The Citizen's Choice, 1947; Fifty Years of Sport at Eton and Harrow (jt.); various articles. *Recreations:* tennis, riding, shooting; Harrow School cricket and football elevens and fives player; Oxford University tennis player, 1897, 1899; British Team Olympic Games, 1908. *Address:* Crossways, Hildenborough, Kent. *Club:* Athenæum. [*Died* 1 *Sept.* 1958.

PAGE, Sir Leo Francis, Kt., *cr.* 1948; *b.* 2 April 1890; *y. s.* of late William Humphrey Page, Indian Civil Service, and Alice, *d.* of Richard Pope; *m.* 1916, Violet, *d.* of Captain F. C. Loder-Symonds, R.A., J.P.; two *s.* one *d.* *Educ.:* Beaumont; Royal Military Academy, Woolwich; University College, Oxford. Served in European War, Flight Commander Royal Flying Corps; invalided from Army, 1916; called to Bar, Inner Temple, 1918; Secretary of Commissions of the Peace, 1940-45; J.P. (Berks), 1925; High Sheriff of Berks, 1937; Member of Home Office Departmental Committee on Justices' Clerks; Member of Home Office Advisory Committee on Probation; Member of H.O. Council for Treatment of Offenders, 1944; Departmental Cttee. on Punishment in Prisons and Borstals, 1948. *Publications:* Justice of the Peace, 1936; Crime and the Community, 1938; For Magistrates and Others, 1939; First Steps in Advocacy, 1943; The Problem of Punishment, 1947; The Sentence of the Court, 1948; The Young Lag—A study in Crime, 1950. *Address:* Newton House, Faringdon, Berks. *T.:* Buckland 204. *Club:* Marlborough-Windham. [*Died* 31 *Aug.* 1951.

PAGE, Sir Thomas Spurgeon, Kt., *cr.* 1956; C.B.E. 1947; Speaker of the Legislative Council, Northern Rhodesia, 1948-56, retired; *b.* 19 Oct. 1879; *s.* of Thomas Collins Page and Caroline Louisa Spurgeon; *m.* 1st, 1910, Elsie Louisa, *d.* of late W. M. Harris, Long Sutton, Hants.; two *d.*; 2nd, 1943, Edith Ciceley, *d.* of late W. Ransom, Nailsworth, Glos.; *Educ.:* City of London School. Came to Northern Rhodesia, 1907; farming, cotton and tobacco growing, and transport. Member Legislative Council for N.E. Area, 1938-48, when elected Speaker; Price Controller for N. Rhodesia, 1942-48; Fuel Controller for N. Rhodesia, 1942-46. *Address:* P.O. Box 8022, Lusaka, Northern Rhodesia. [*Died* 10 *Feb.* 1958.

PAGE WOOD, Sir David (John Hatherley), 7th Bt., *cr.* 1837; Company Director since 1950; *b.* 6 Oct. 1921; *s.* of Sir John Stuart Page Wood, 6th Bt., and Barbara, *e. d.* of late Major E. J. Arundell Clarke. *S.* father 1955; *m.* 1947, Evelyn Hazel Rosemary, *d.* of Capt. George Ernest Bellville; one *s.* one *d.* *Educ.:* Westminster. Served War of 1939-45, Lieutenant R.N.V.R. (despatches). *Recreations:* golf, tennis, swimming, squash, etc. *Heir:* *s.* Anthony John Page Wood, *b.* 6 Feb. 1951. *Address:* 12 Astell Street, S.W.3. *T.:* Flaxman 9809. *Clubs:* Bath, M.C.C. [*Died* 28 *Nov.* 1955.

PAGET, Major Eden Wilberforce, C.B.E. 1918; *b.* 9 Sept. 1865; *s.* of late Rev. Edward Heneage Paget and Hon. Emma Mary Eden, *d.* of 3rd Baron Auckland; *m.* Gertrude, *d.* of late William Mawdsley Charnley; one *s.* *Educ.:* Rev. Stephen Hawtrey's, Windsor. Served European War, 1914-19 (despatches twice); Director of Transport for British Red Cross Society and the Order of St. John, during European War, 1914-18. *Address:* 183 Cromwell Road, S.W.5. [*Died* 20 *Nov.* 1955.

PAGET, Dame (Louise Margaret) Leila (Wemyss), G.B.E., *cr.* 1917; Grand Cordon of St. Sava, 1915; *d.* of late Gen. Rt. Hon. Sir Arthur Paget, G.C.B.; *m.* 1907, Rt. Hon. Sir Ralph Spencer Paget, K.C.M.G., C.V.O. (*d.* 1940), formerly Assist. Under-Sec. of State for Foreign Affairs and First Ambassador to Brazil. *Address:* Soames House, Coombe Hill Road, Kingston-on-Thames, Surrey. [*Died* 24 *Sept.* 1958.

PAGET, Sir Richard (Arthur Surtees), 2nd Bt., *cr.* 1886; F.Phys.S.; F.Inst.P.; F.R.A.I.; M.R.I.; Hon. A.R.I.B.A.; Hon. A.M.T.P.I.; barrister; *b.* 13 Jan. 1869; *s.* of 1st Bt. and Caroline (*d.* 1946), 2nd *d.* of H. E. Surtees, M.P., Redworth, Co. Durham, and Dane End, Herts; *S.* father, 1908; *m.* 1st, 1897, Lady Muriel Evelyn Vernon Finch-Hatton, C.B.E., 1938 (*d.* 1938), *o. d.* of 12th Earl of Winchilsea; one *s.* three *d.*; 2nd, 1939, Grace Hartley, *o. d.* of late Walter Herbert Glover of Birkdale and Grasmere. *Educ.:* Slough; Eton; Magdalen College, Oxford. Called to Bar, Inner Temple, 1895; Secretary Patent Law Committee, 1900; Secretary to Court of Arbitration, Grimsby Fishing Dispute, 1900; to Court of Arbitration under Metropolitan Water Act, 1902; to University College Transfer Commission, 1905; Assistant

Secretary Admiralty Board of Invention and Research, 1915-18. Pres. British Deaf and Dumb Assoc., 1953. Commander Icelandic Order of the Falcon. *Publications:* Papers in Proceedings of the Royal Society and Physical Society, Nature, proceedings of British Association and Encyclopædia Britannica on the Nature and Artificial Production of Speech; Partnership in Agriculture; Human Speech; Babel; This English. *Songs:* Farmer John, words and music; The House in the Woods, words and music; The Toy Band, words by Sir H. Newbolt. *Recreations:* music, acoustics, linguistics, Sign language for the education of the born deaf, arts and crafts. *Heir: s.* John Starr [*b.* 24 Nov. 1914; *m.* 1944, Nancy Mary, *d.* of late Lt.-Col. F. Woodbine Parish, D.S.O., M.C.; four *d.*]. *Address:* 9 Alexandra Court, Queen's Gate, S.W.7: *T.:* Knightsbridge 1849. *Clubs:* Athenæum, Royal Automobile, Royal Aero. [*Died* 23 *Oct.* 1955.

PAGET, Major Thomas Guy Frederick, D.L., C.A., J.P. Leicestershire and Northamptonshire; F.R.Hist.S.; *b.* 1886; *s.* of Thomas Guy Paget, J.P., of Ibstock, Leicestershire (*d.* 1894), and Frances Edith Nugent, *d.* of Thos. Nugent Vaughan and Viscountess Forbes; *m.* Bettine (a Lady of Grace of the Order of St. John of Jerusalem) 2nd *d.* of late Sir (Geo.) Wm. des Voeux, G.C.M.G., and Marion, *d.* of late Sir John Pender, G.C.M.G.; two *s.* *Educ.:* Eton. 2nd Lieut. Scots Guards, 1905; contested (U.) Mid-Northants, Jan. and Dec. 1910; rejoined S.R. Scots Guards in 1914; employed Captain and Adjutant, 7th Northants (which he helped to raise) (wounded), and as Major R.F.A., France and Palestine; retired as Major Scots Guards (S.R.), 1919; M.P. (Indpt. Tory) Bosworth Div. of Leicestershire, 1922-23; County Comr. Boy Scouts, Northants, 1930; Major L.D.V., 1940; Pilot Officer, R.A.F.V.R. (despatches); retired as Flt.-Lt. 1943; Master of the Company of Painter Stainers, 1945-46; High Sheriff of Leicestershire, 1947-48. *Publications:* The Raising of the 7th Northants Regt.; Chronicle of the Last Crusade; The Melton Mowbray of John Ferneley, 1931; Life of Edward IV (Rose of London, 1934, of Raby, 1937, of Rouen, 1940); Rum 'uns to Follow; The Flying Parson and Dick Christian; Wit and Wisdom of the Shires by Coronet; Bad Ones to Beat; The History of the Althorp and Pytchley Hunt, 1937; Mr. Mowbray returns to Melton; Britain in Pictures series, Sporting Pictures of England, 1945; Leicestershire (County Books); Life of Frank Freeman; articles on hunting and sporting pictures. *Recreations:* writing and hunting (Dep. Acting M.F.H. Fernie, 1939-45). *Address:* Wheler, Husbands Bosworth, Rugby, Northamptonshire. *T.:* Welford 227. *T.A.:* Welford. *Club:* Carlton. [*Died* 12 *March* 1952.

PAGET, Lord Victor (William); *b.* of 6th Marquess of Anglesey; *b.* 17 May 1889; *m.* 1st, 1913, Olive Mary Meatyard (stage name, Olive May, who *m.* 2nd, 1922, 10th Earl of Drogheda); one *s.* one *d.*; 2nd, 1922, Hon. Bridget Colebrooke (who obtained a divorce 1932), *yr. d.* of 1st Baron Colebrooke; one *s.* one *d.*; 3rd, 1935, Mavis, *d.* of William Crockford, and *widow* of Major Herbert Dawson, M.C. Capt. Royal Horse Guards; served European War, 1914-18. [*Died* 11 *Feb.* 1952.

PAGET-COOKE, Oliver Dayrell Paget, M.V.O. 1933; B.A.; Comptroller of the Household to late Princess Beatrice, 1934-1944; Senior Partner of Russell-Cooke and Co., Solicitors, 11 Old Square, Lincoln's Inn, W.C.2, since 1923; *b.* 26 Jan. 1891: *s.* of late Sir Henry Paget-Cooke and late Grace Bernard Paget-Cooke; *m.* 1917, Barbara Ponsonby Hughes Hutchinson; one *s.* *Educ.:* Cheltenham College; Christ Church, Oxford. Served in the Artists Rifles, Royal Army Service Corps and Grenadier Guards (Lieut.), 1914-18 (1914-15 Star, etc., wounded at Bienvillers, France, April 1918); Captain, Home Guard, 1941 (L.D.V. 1940); enrolled as a solicitor, 1920; Vice-Chairman and Hon. Treasurer of The Princess Beatrice Hospital, Kensington; Hon. Solicitor to Queen Mary's Maternity Home; travelled extensively since 1910; Jubilee Medal, 1935; Coronation Medal, 1937; Defence Medal. *Recreations:* tennis, shooting, golf, motoring, philately, travelling, fishing. *Address:* Flat 5, 76 Westbourne Terrace, W.2. *T.:* Paddington 8734. *Club:* M.C.C. [*Died* 15 *Aug.* 1954.

PAIGE, Lt.-Col. Cyril Penrose, C.I.E. 1917; D.S.O. 1921; *b.* 1882; *s.* of late Henry Paige, Broomborough, Totnes, Devon; unmarried. *Educ.:* Rugby; Oxford. First commission, D.C.L.I., 1902; transferred to Indian Army, 1905; served European War, 1914-19 (despatches, C.I.E.); Waziristan, 1920-21 (despatches, D.S.O.); commanded 2nd Bn. 4th Bombay Grenadiers, 1930-32; retired, 1932. *Address:* Cherfield, Minehead, Somerset. *Club:* United Service. [*Died* 18 *Aug.* 1958.

PAIGE, Col. (Hon. Maj.-Gen.) Douglas, C.B.E. 1943; M.C.; *b.* 18 April 1886; *s.* of R. E. Paige, J.P., and Emma Paige; *m.* 1st, Evelyn Ellen (*d.* 1919), *d.* of Col. P. S. Dyson; one *d.*; 2nd, Evelyn, *d.* of Thomas Wolferstan, Plymouth. *Educ.:* Plymouth College; R.M.A., Woolwich. 2nd Lieutenant R.A. 1907; Captain, 1914; Bt. Major, 1917; Major, 1917; Bt. Lieut.-Col. 1930; Lt.-Col. 1935; Col. 1938 (Seniority 1933); Brig., C.R.A. Malta, 1938-40; C.C.R.A. Corps Home Forces, June-Nov. 1940; Acting Maj.-Gen. 1940; Comd. A.A. Div.; Temp. Maj.-Gen. 1941; retired pay, 1942, with hon. rank Maj.-Gen.; Regional Petroleum Officer S. Wales Region, Cardiff, 1942-48. *Recreations:* normal. *Address:* Frogs Hall, New Romney, Kent. *T.:* New Romney 3271. [*Died* 17 *May* 1958.

PAINE, Hubert S.; *see* Scott-Paine.

PAINTER, Brig. Gordon Whistler Arnaud, D.S.O. 1917; Royal Artillery; *b.* 24 Feb. 1893; *s.* of late Brigadier-General Arnaud C. Painter, C.M.G.; *m.* Kathleen Hay Lannoy, *e. surv. d.* of Colonel J. L. Tweedie, D.S.O.; one *s.* two *d.* *Educ.:* Malvern College; R.M.A., Woolwich. Commission in R.G.A. 1913; Acting Major, 1916-19; Captain, 1917; Major, 1933; Bt. Lt.-Col., 1935; Col. 1939; Brig. 1940; G.S.O. 1st Grade, Rawalpindi District, India, 1939; served European War in France and Belgium, March 1915-July 1919 (despatches four times, D.S.O.); served War of 1939-45, Commanded Indian Infantry Brigade in India and Malaya, 1940-42 (despatches, prisoner); retired, 1948. *Address:* Cartref, Sycamore Rd., Farnborough, Hants. *T.:* Farnborough 363. [*Died* 28 *Sept.* 1960.

PAISH, Sir George, Kt., *cr.* 1912; *b.* 7 Nov. 1867; *m.* 1st, 1894, Emily Mary (*d.* 1933), *d.* of Thomas Whitehead, Liverpool; five *s.*; 2nd, 1936, Anita Carolyn Rouse-Rettig. Secretary to Editor of Statist, 1881-88; Sub-Editor, 1888-94; Assistant Editor, 1894-1900; Joint Editor, 1900-16; Member Departmental Committee of the Board of Trade on Railway Accounts and Statistics, 1906-8; Adviser to the Chancellor of the Exchequer and the British Treasury on Financial and Economic questions, 1914-16; Official Mission to American Government, Nov. 1914; Chairman Sound Currency Assoc.; Dep. Chm. Anglo-Austrian Economic Union; Fellow Royal Statistical Society; Royal Humane Society Bronze Medal, 1888. *Publications:* British Railway Position, 1902; Railways of Great Britain, 1904; Railroads of the United States, 1913; Capital Investments in other Lands, 1909 and 1910; Savings and the Social Welfare, 1911; A Permanent League of Nations, 1918; The Road to Prosperity, 1927; World Economic Suicide, 1929; The Way to Recovery, 1931; The Way Out, 1937; The World Danger, 1939; The

PAINE, Brig. Douglas Duke, C.B.E., D.S.O. See page xxx

Defeat of Chaos, 1941; World Restoration, 1944; Sound Currency, 1946; The Future of the £, 1948; The World of Danger, 1949. *Address:* 86 Kingsley Way, N.2. *Club:* Reform. [*Died* 1 *May* 1957.

PAKENHAM, Col. George de la Poer Beresford, C.M.G. 1918; C.B.E. 1922; D.S.O. 1915; *b.* 4 Dec. 1875; *s.* of Major Charles Pakenham and Blanche Harrison of Singapore; *m.* 1st, 1905, Elsie (*d.* 1921), 4th *d.* of late William Fowler, Broadlands, Liverpool; two *s.*; 2nd, 1923, Mimi, *widow* of Capt. Henri Joucla (French Army). *Educ.:* United Services College, Westward Ho! Entered army (I.S.C.), 1895; Captain, Indian army, 1904; Border Regt. 1904; Major, 1915; Lieutenant-Colonel, 1917; Colonel, 1921; Brigade-Major, 14th Brigade, Irish Command, 1909-13; served European War, 1914-18, as Brigade-Major and General Staff Officer (despatches six times, D.S.O., Bt. Lt.-Col. 1917, C.M.G.).; General Staff Officer, Southern District, Ireland, 1919; A.A.G., War Office, 1923-1927; Officer commanding the Preston Infantry Record and Pay Office, 1927-31; retired pay, 1931. *Address:* c/o Lloyds Bank Ltd., 6 Pall Mall, S.W.1. [*Died* 29 *Dec.* 1960.

PALAIRET, Sir Michael, K.C.M.G., *cr.* 1938 (C.M.G. 1923); *b.* 29 Sept. 1882; 2nd *s.* of late Capt. C. H. Palairet, Westhill, Ledbury, Herefordshire; *m.* 1915, Mary de Vere, *d.* of late Brig.-Gen. H. W. Studd, C.B., C.M.G., D.S.O.; one *s.* one *d.* *Educ.:* Eton. Attaché, 1905; appointed to Rome, 1906; 3rd Sec., 1907; transferred to Vienna, 1908; Paris, 1913; 2nd Sec., 1913; transferred to Athens, 1917; attached to Peace Delegation at Paris, 1918-19; First Secretary, 1919; transferred to Foreign Office, 1920; Paris, 1920; Counsellor of Embassy at Tokio, 1922; transferred to Peking, 1925; to Foreign Office, 1926; to Rome, 1928; Minister to Roumania, 1929-35; to Sweden, 1935-37; to Austria, 1937-38; to Greece, 1939-1942; Ambassador to Greece, 1942-43; Asst. Under-Secretary of State in Foreign Office, 1943-45. *Address:* Lynch Mead, Allerford, Minehead, Somerset. [*Died* 5 *Aug.* 1956.

PALANPUR, Nawab of, Lt.-Col. H.H. Zubd-tul-Mulk Dewan Mahakhan Taley Muhammed Khan Bahadur, G.C.I.E., *cr.* 1932 (K.C.I.E., *cr.* 1920); K.C.V.O., *cr.* 1922; Hon. A.D.C. to the King, 1936-47, Extra Hon. A.D.C. since 1946; *b.* 7 July 1883; succeeded, 1918; *m.*; one *s.* two *d.* *Recreations:* tennis, motoring, small and big game shooting. *Address:* The Palace, Palanpur, Rajputana, India. [*Died* 20 *May* 1957.

PALLIN, Colonel William Alfred, C.B.E. 1919; D.S.O. 1917; F.R.C.V.S.; F.R.S.E.; Army Veterinary Services (retired); *b.* Dublin, 6 June 1873; *e. s.* of late William Pallin, J.P., F.R.C.V.S., Athgarvan Lodge, Curragh Camp, Co. Kildare; *m.* Agnes Marthe Marie (*d.* 1954), *y. d.* of H. de Lenclos, Aubyn-Saint-Vaast, Pas de Calais, France; no *c.* *Educ.:* Cheltenham College; New Veterinary College, Edinburgh. Member Royal College of Veterinary Surgeons, 1894; Fellow, 1904; joined Army Veterinary Services, 1897; Captain, 1903; Major, 1912; transferred to Royal Horse Guards (The Blues), 1913; reverted to Army Veterinary Services, 1915; Lieut.-Colonel, 1921; Col., 1925; retired pay, 1929; Special Appointments, War Office staff, 1920-21; served China, 1900 (medal); World War, 1914-19 (C.B.E., D.S.O., despatches five times, Officier du Merit Agricole). *Address:* 5 Tower Gardens, Hythe, Kent. [*Died* 28 *Sept.* 1956.

PALLISER, Admiral Sir Arthur Francis Eric, K.C.B., *cr.* 1945 (C.B. 1943); D.S.C. 1917; *s.* of Arthur Palliser and Hester Brenda Boord; *m.* 1921, Margaret Eva, *d.* of J. J. King Salter; one *s.* one *d.* *Educ.:* Bradfield College; R.N. Colleges, Dartmouth and Greenwich. Midshipman, 1907; Admiral, 1947; Chief of Staff to Commander-in-Chief China, 1936-1938; H.M.S. Excellent, 1938-40; H.M.S. Malaya, 1940-41; A.D.C. to the King, 1940-1941; Chief of Staff to C.-in-C. Eastern Fleet, 1941-42; served at New Delhi, 1942-43; commanded 1st Cruiser Squadron, 1943-44; a Lord Commissioner of the Admiralty and Chief of Supplies and Transport, 1944-46; C.-in-C. East Indies Station, 1946-48; retired list, 1948. *Address:* 33 South Terrace, S.W.7. *Club:* Army and Navy. [*Died* 22 *Feb.* 1956.

PALLOT, Rev. Elias George, D.S.O., Croix de Guerre, 1918; Engineer Rear-Admiral, retired; *b.* 1876; *s.* of late E. N. Pallot; *m.* 1906, S. Winifred Kelly; one *s.* Eng.-Rear-Adm. 1928; Engineer Manager H.M. Dockyard, Chatham, 1927-32; retired list, 1932; ordained, 1933; Rector of Instow, 1935-38; Vicar of Nettlebed, Henley-on-Thames, 1938-47. Licensed to officiate, Dioceses of Oxford, St. Albans, Guildford. *Address:* 48 Okehampton Close, N. Finchley, N.12. *T.:* Hillside 1585. [*Died* 21 *March* 1954.

PALMER, Rt. Rev. Edwin James; Assistant to Bishop of Gloucester since 1929; *o. s.* of late Archdeacon Palmer, Oxford, and *nephew* of 1st Lord Selborne; *b.* 1869; *m.* 1912, Hazel (*d.* 1931), *y. d.* of Col. E. H. Hanning-Lee, Bighton Manor, Alresford. *Educ.:* Winchester (scholar); Balliol Coll., Oxford (scholar; Craven scholar; 1st Class Mods.; 1st Class Lit. Hum.). Ordained, 1896; Fellow Balliol College, 1891; Tutor, 1893; Chaplain, 1896; Examining Chaplain to Bishop of Southwell, 1899-1904; to Bishop of Rochester, 1904-5; to Bishop of Southwark, 1905-8; Bishop of Bombay, 1908-29. *Publications:* The Great Church Awakes, 1920; The Destiny of the Anglican Churches, 1931; The Challenge of an Indian Experience, 1933; Christ's Partners, 1947. *Recreations:* study of Architecture, travelling. *Address:* 37 Norham Road, Oxford. *T.:* Oxford 57800. *Clubs:* Church Imperial, Overseas. [*Died* 28 *March* 1954.

PALMER, Frederick; *b.* Pleasantville, Pa.; 29 Jan. 1873; *m.* 1st, 1896, Elsie Marie Wilbor; 2nd, 1924, Helen Talmadge Runkle. *Educ.:* Allegheny College, B.A., LL.D.; Litt.D. (Princeton University). London Correspondent, 1895-1897; Greek War, 1897; Klondike and Philippines, 1897-98; Relief of Pekin, 1900; Macedonian insurrection, 1903; First Japanese Army, 1904-1905; Turkish Revolution, 1909; Balkan War, 1912; European War; accredited correspondent for press of the United States B.E.F. 1914-16; Lt.-Colonel American Army in France, 1917-18 (Distinguished Service Medal); Correspondent B.E.F., France, April-May 1940; S.H.A.E.F., France; U.S. Army, and Fleet, Pacific, 1945. *Publications:* Going to War in Greece, 1897; In the Klondike, 1899; The Ways of the Service, 1901; The Vagabond, 1903; With Kuroki in Manchuria, 1904; Central America and its Problems, 1910; Over the Pass, 1912; The Last Shot, 1914; My Year of the War; The Old Blood, 1916; Battle of the Somme; America in France; Our Greatest Battle; Clark of the Ohio; Look to the East; Newton D. Baker: America at War; With My Own Eyes; Life of General John Pershing, 1948. *Clubs:* Century, Coffee House (New York); Cosmos (Washington, D.C.). [*Died* 2 *Sept.* 1958.

PALMER, Frederick William, V.C. 1917; M.M.; Wing Comdr., late R.A.F.V.R.; *b.* 11 Nov. 1891; *m.*; three *s.* one *d.* Enlisted as a private, 1914; given commission on active service, 22nd Royal Fusiliers; transferred to R.A.F., 1918; Director, Kyle, Palmer & Co., Ltd., Penang, Ipoh, Kuala Lumpur, Singapore; Director Kenneison Bros. Ltd., and other companies. *Address:* 2 Walton Road, Singapore. [*Died* 10 *Sept.* 1955.

PALMER, Lieut.-Col. Sir Geoffrey Frederick Neill, 11th Bt., *cr.* 1660; J.P., D.L.; late Coldstream Guards; *b.* 20 Sept. 1893; *er. s.* of 10th Bt. and Sibyll Caroline (*d.* 1933), *e. d.* of late Capt. W. J. Smith Neill; *S.* father, 1925; *m.* 1932, Cicely Kathleen, *o. d.* of late Arthur Radmall; two *s.* *Educ.:*

PAKENHAM-WALSH, Rt. Rev. Herbert Pakenham, D.D. See page xxx.

Repton; Trinity College, Cambridge. Entered Army, 1914; served European War, 1914-1917 (wounded); Capt. 1917; Major, 1928; retired, 1931; re-employed, 1939. *Heir:* s. Geoffrey Christopher John, b. 30 June 1936. *Address:* Carlton Curlieu Hall, Leicestershire. *Club:* Guards. [*Died* 22 *Nov.* 1951

PALMER, Maj.-Gen. (retd.) Geoffrey Woodroffe, C.B. 1948; C.B.E. 1944; R.A.O.C.; *b.* 1891; *s.* of late William Clayton Palmer, Greenhurst Park, Oxted, Surrey; *m.* 1919, Gretta, *d.* of late Col. F. W. McTier Burny, Royal Berks Regt.; one *s.* one *d.* *Educ.:* Uppingham. Served European War 1914-19, France and Belgium (1914 Star with clasp, 2 medals), 1st Bn. H.A.C., 1914-15, R.A.O.C., 1915-18; Lt.-Col. 1936; Palestine, 1936-39 (medal with clasp); War of 1939-45, France (despatches, C.B.E.); Brig. 1942; actg. Maj.-Gen. 1945; retd., 1948. *Address:* Durban, S. Africa. [*Died* 17 *Jan.* 1952.

PALMER, Sir (Herbert) Richmond, K.C.M.G., *cr.* 1933 (C.M.G. 1922); C.B.E. 1924; Barrister-at-law; Northern Circuit, Carlisle, Lancaster, Preston, Bolton, Blackburn, Wigan, Manchester, and Burnley Sessions; *b.* 20 April 1877; *m.* 1924, Margaret Abel, *d.* of late Reginald Abel Smith, Goldings, Herts; two *d.* *Educ.:* Oundle; Trinity Hall, Cambridge. Asst. Resident, Nigeria, 1904; Resident of Bornu Province, 1917; Lieut.-Governor, Northern Provinces, Nigeria, 1925-30; Governor and Commander-in-Chief, Gambia Colony, 1930-33; Governor and Commander-in-Chief, Cyprus, 1933-39. *Publications:* Monographs on the History of Northern Nigeria; The Bornu Sahara and Sudan. *Address:* 10A Winckley Street, Preston, Lancs.; 3 Cook Street, Liverpool. *Clubs:* Travellers'; Winckley (Preston). [*Died* 22 *May* 1958.

PALMER, Maj.-Gen. Robert John, C.V.O. 1947; D.S.O. 1944; S. African Police Officer; *b.* Grahamstown, S. Africa, 10 Feb. 1891; *s.* of Robert Palmer and Barbara Dyce; *m.* 1922, Henriette Muraour; two *d.* *Educ.:* Graeme College, Grahamstown, S.A. Matriculated, Graeme Coll., Grahamstown, S.A., 1907; Trooper, British S. Africa Police, S. Rhodesia, 1911; Constable, Orange Free State, 1913; with amalgamated S. African Police, 1913; Lt. S. African Police, 1924; Captain, 1931; Major, 1935; Lt.-Col. 1937; Commissioner (Brig.), 1945; Maj.-Gen. since 1946; retired from S. African Police, 1951; served European War, 1914-18; joined R.F.C.; Pilot Officer, R.A.F., 1918; returned to S. African Police as Corporal, 1919; served War of 1939-45, Bn. Comdr., 1/S.A.P., 6th Bde., 2nd Div., 1940; Brig., Bde. Comdr., 3rd Bde, 1st Div., 1942; Brig. Bde. Comdr., 12th Bde., 6th Div., S.A.A., 1943; Maj.-Gen. A/G.O.C., 6th S.A.A. Div., Feb.-March 1945; served with 8th Army in N. Africa and Italy, and with 5th American Army in Italy (D.S.O. and 2 bars, American Bronze Medal, 1944); amateur jockey, Rhodesia and Orange Free State, 1910-24; referee and judge, S. African Nat. Amateur Boxing Assoc.; judge, S. African Amateur Athletic Assoc.; successful competitor, Mounted Sports and Show Jumping, 1914-1937. *Address:* 34 Carbarra Court, 79 Quartz Street, Hillbrow, Johannesburg, S. Africa. [*Died* 25 *March* 1957.

PALMER, Sir Sydney Bacon, Kt., *cr.* 1949; C.B.E. 1941; Director of Rubber Companies; Chairman: Rubber Growers' Association, 1953; British Rubber Development Board, 1952; *b.* 4 May 1890; 3rd *s.* of late R. W. Palmer, Swafield House, nr. Norwich; *m.* 1915, Mary Maud, *e. d.* of late Dr. M. J. Wright, Malayan Medical Service. *Educ.:* Privately. Rubber Planting, 1909; Planting Mem., Perak State Council, 1932-42; Planting Member Federal Council of Federated Malay States, 1934-42; J.P. Perak. President, United Planting Association of Malaya, 1935, 1936, 1938, 1940-42, 1946, 1947, 1948; Chairman, Hon. Secretary and Treasurer, Far Eastern Relief Fund, South Africa and Southern Rhodesia, 1943-45; President, Malayan Association (Africa), 1943-45. Member Advisory Council Malayan Union, 1946, 1947. Member Legislative Council Federation of Malaya, 1948, 1949. *Recreation:* racing. *Address:* 35 Parkside, Knightsbridge, S.W.1; Asia House, Lime St., E.C.3. *Clubs:* East India and Sports; most Malayan. [*Died* 9 *March* 1954.

PALMER, Lt.-Col. William Legh, C.M.G. 1919; late R.E.; *b.* 1868; *m.* Ethel, *d.* of Major George Taylor; three *s.* Served European War, 1914-19 (despatches, C.M.G.). *Address:* Marston, 2 Westcote Road, Reading. [*Died* 29 *June* 1955.

PALMER, Colonel William Llewellen, M.C.; D.L.; 10th Royal Hussars (retired); commanded 4th Battalion Wilts Regiment, T.A., 1929-32; Hon. Colonel 5th Bn. Wilts Regt. T.A.; *b.* Sep. 1883; 2nd *s.* of Brigadier-General George Llewellen Palmer, C.B.; *m.* 1910, Lady Alexandra Carrington (for whom Queen Alexandra stood sponsor), 2nd *d.* of 1st Marquess of Lincolnshire, K.G.; two *s.* (and two *s.* killed in action, 1941 and 1942). *Educ.:* Harrow. Adjutant 10th Royal Hussars, 1908-11; served European War (despatches twice, M.C.); High Sheriff of Wilts, 1933 and 1944; D.L. Wilts, 1950. *Address:* Manor House, Great Somerford, Chippenham, Wilts. [*Died* 11 *Aug.* 1954.

PALMGREN, Selim; Composer, Pianist, Conductor; Professor of Honour, 1928; Doctor of Honour, 1950; Professor of Composition in Sibelius Academy, Helsingfors since 1939; *b.* Bjoerneborg, Finland, 16 Feb. 1878; *m.* 1st, 1910, Maikki Jaernefelt (*d.* 1929), Finnish singer; 2nd, 1930, Minna Talwik, Finnish singer. *Educ.:* National Conservatory, Helsingfors; Berlin; Weimar with Ferruccio Busoni; Professor of Composition in Eastman School of Music, Rochester, N.Y., 1921-26; music critic in Huvudstadsbladet, Helsingfors since 1930; Member of Honour of the following choral associations: Akademiska Sangforeningen Suomen laulu, M.M., Y.L. and several others; Member of Royal Academy of Music, Stockholm, since 1937; Member of Honour of Finnish Musicians Association, Finnish Composers Association, 1938; Chairman of the Sibelius Foundation, Member of Honour of the Sibelius Academy. *Works:* Opera, Daniel Hjort; 5 concertos for piano and orchestra: G-minor, The River, The Metamorphoses, April, A-major; about 200 compositions for piano solo; several compositions for violin and piano; 100 songs for voice and piano; 200 for chorus; several larger works for chorus and orchestra; several orchestral works, as The Seasons, Pastorale; Ballade; Ballet and Stage music; Concerto C-major for violin and orchestra. *Address:* Helsinki, Finland. [*Died* 13 *Dec.* 1951.

PALMSTIERNA, Baron Erik Kule, G.C.V.O.; *b.* 10 Nov. 1877; *s.* of late Baron C. F. H. Palmstierna and Hanna von Holst; *m.* 1899, Ebba, *d.* of Captain Alfred Carlheim-Gyllensköld; two *s.* *Educ.:* Stockholm. Passed through the Royal Naval Schools and was commissioned naval sub-lieutenant at the age of 19; early interested in public affairs, elected to the Karlskrona Council, in 1906 abandoned naval career, having received commission as Lieutenant Commander R.S.N. in order to take up a position as Secretary of the Central Association for Social Work; in the following year organised the Svenska Stadsforbundet, an association of Swedish townships constituted to promote common interests; retained this post until 1915, when member of the National Debt Board; soon after removal to capital, member of the City Council of Stockholm as well as of its Budget Committee and elected to the Riksdag by the Liberals and Social democrats; when a coalition government

was formed in 1917, entered it as Minister of Marine; in 1920 became Minister of Foreign Affairs in the Branting Government; Swedish Minister at the Court of St. James, 1920-37; Representative to the League of Nations on the Aaland Islands question in 1921. *Publications:* various publications on economic and political subjects and The World's Crisis and Faiths; God's Innocence; Rifts in the Veil; Horizons of Immortality. *Recreation:* gardening. *Address:* Via San Carlo 6, Bellosguardo, Firenze, Italy. *Club:* Athenæum.
[*Died* 22 *Nov.* 1959.

PAM, Major Albert, O.B.E., F.L.S.; Banker (J. Henry Schroder & Co.); *b.* London, 26 June 1875; *e. s.* of late Leopold Pam, Clapham Park, London; *m.* 1907, Maude Le Clerc, O.B.E., J.P., *e. d.* of late Lt.-General J. Faught, K.H.S.; one *d.* *Educ.:* City of London School; Frankfort and Lausanne. Travelled extensively in S. America; Mem. Council: 1907-32, Treas. 1932-1945, and Silver Medallist (1914) Zoological Soc. of London; Mem. Council: Roy. Horticultural Soc., 1946-; Medical Coll., St. Bartholomew's Hosp.; John Innes Horticultural Institution; High Sheriff of Hertfordshire, 1941-42. Served European War, 1915, under Admiralty; 1916-1918 France, D.A.D.G.T., H.Q. 3rd Army; member British Mission Permanent International Armistice Commission, Spa, 1918-19; (despatches three times, O.B.E. Chevalier Legion of Honour, Officer Crown of Belgium, Belgian Croix de Guerre). Victoria Medal of Honour from R. Hort. S. 1944; Hon. M.A. Oxford, 1944. *Recreations:* horticulture, aviculture. *Address:* Wormley Bury, Broxbourne, Herts. *T.:* Hoddesdon 2241. *Club:* Junior Carlton.
[*Died* 2 *Sept.* 1955.

PANET, Maj.-Gen. Henri Alexandre, C.B. 1919; C.M.G. 1916; D.S.O. 1900; *b.* Quebec, Canada, 24 July 1869; *s.* of late Col. Charles Eugene Panet; *m.* 1902, Mary A. (*d.* 1942), *y. d.* of late James Bermingham, Kingston, Ont., Canada. *Educ.:* graduated at Roy. Mil. Coll. of Canada. Served S. Africa, 1899-1900; Lieut. Royal Canadian Regiment; transferred as Captain to Royal Canadian Artillery at the relief of Mafeking (despatches, D.S.O., Brevet Major); Staff Adjutant, Royal Military Coll. of Canada, 1901-5; A.A.G. 1905-7; D.A.G. 1907-9; D.O.C. Military District No. 1, 1919-22; No. 2, 1922-23; Adjutant-General of the Dept. of National Defence, 1923-29; retired, 1930; European War, 1914-19 (wounded, despatches, C.M.G., C.B.); Hon. Colonel Commandant of the Royal Canadian Artillery, 1934-44. *Address:* 277 Stewart Street, Ottawa, Ont. *Clubs:* Rideau, Royal Ottawa Golf (Ottawa).
[*Died* 14 *Aug.* 1951.

PANETH, Friedrich Adolf, F.R.S. 1947; Director, Max-Planck-Institute for Chemistry, since 1953; *b.* Vienna, 31 Aug. 1887; 2nd *s.* of late Dr. Joseph Paneth, Lecturer in Physiology in Vienna Univ., discoverer of histological cells named after him; *m.* 1913, Else, *o. d.* of Dr. L. M. Hartmann, Prof. of History in Vienna University; one *s.* one *d.* *Educ.:* Universities of Vienna, Munich and Glasgow, in Laboratories of Z. Skraup, A. v. Baeyer and F. Soddy. Ph.D. Vienna, 1910; Asst., Institute for Radium Research, Vienna, 1912; Prof., Prague Institute of Technology, 1918; Prof., Hamburg Univ. 1919; Prof., Berlin Univ. 1922; Prof. and Director of Chemical Laboratories, Koenigsberg Univ. 1929; Guest, Imperial College of Science and Technology, London, 1933; Reader in Atomic Chemistry, London Univ., 1938; Prof. of Chemistry, Durham Univ., 1939; Head of Chemistry Division of Joint British-Canadian Atomic Energy Team in Montreal, 1943-45; Lieben prize, Vienna Acad. of Sciences, 1916; George Fisher Baker Lecturer, Cornell University, U.S.A., 1926-1927; Liversidge Lecturer, Chemical Society, 1936; Halley Lecturer, Oxford Univ., 1940; Schoenheimer Memorial Lecturer, New York, 1951; Hugo Müller Lecturer, Chemical Soc., 1952; Foreign Hon. Mem. Amer. Academy of Arts and Sciences, 1933; Hon. Member Soc. Austrian Chemists, 1950; Lavoisier Medal, Société Chimique de France, 1952; Corr. Mem. Austrian Acad. of Sciences, 1952; Stas Medal, Société Chimique de Belgique, 1953; Liebig Medal, Gesellschaft Deutscher Chemiker, 1957; Auer von Welsbach Medal, Verein Österreichischer Chemiker, 1957; President, Joint Commn. on Radioactivity, of Internat. Council of Scientific Unions, 1949-55. *Publications:* Radio-Elements as Indicators and Other Selected Topics in Inorganic Chemistry, New York, 1928; Manual of Radio-activity (with G. Hevesy), 2nd ed., 1938; The Origin of Meteorites, 1940; Papers on Radio-activity, Inorganic and Physical Chemistry. *Recreation:* photography. *Address:* Max-Planck-Institut für Chemie, Saarstrasse 23, Mainz, Germany. *Club:* Athenæum.
[*Died* 17 *Sept.* 1958.

PANK, Col. Cecil Henry, C.M.G. 1919; D.S.O. 1918; T.D.; *b.* 4 April 1876; 3rd *s.* of late Sir John Lovell Pank, D.L., J.P.; *m.* Dorothy Annie, *d.* of late W. Priestley, Offord D'Arcy, Hunts; one *s.* two *d.* *Educ.:* Haileybury College. Gazetted to 3rd Middlesex R.V. 1893; transferred to Territorial Force on its formation; retired, 1934; commanded 2/10th Middlesex Regiment, Gallipoli (Suvla Bay), Aug.-Dec. 1915; Egypt, Dec. 1915-July 1916; 8th Middlesex Regiment, France, Aug. 1917-Feb. 1919 (C.M.G., D.S.O., immediate award, despatches twice); Brevet Colonel, 1923; Col. 1924; commanded 141st (5th London) Infantry Brigade (T.A.), 1924-28; A.D.C. to the King, 1929-43; J.P., County of Hertford, 1923, and Middlesex, 1925; Sheriff of Middlesex, 1926; D.L., Middlesex 1932; Chm.: Barnet Petty Sessional Court, 1939-51; Herts. County Probation Cttee., 1940-51. *Address:* Eaton Socon, Huntingdon. *T.:* Eaton Socon 248. *Club:* United Service.
[*Died* 11 *Jan.* 1957.

PANKHURST, Dame Christabel, D.B.E., *cr.* 1936; LL.B.; *e. d.* of late Richard Marsden Pankhurst, LL.D., Barrister-at-law, and late Mrs. Emmeline Pankhurst. As one of founders and leaders of the Women's Social and Political Union worked for women's enfranchisement; declared suffrage truce upon outbreak of war in 1914 in order to co-operate in the national war effort. Religious propagandist. *Publications:* The Lord Cometh; Pressing Problems of the Closing Age; The World's Unrest; Seeing the Future. *Address:* c/o Westminster Bank, 63 Piccadilly, W.1.
[*Died* 13 *Feb.* 1958.

PANKHURST, (Estelle) Sylvia; author; editor of the Ethiopia Observer since 1956; Managing Director Lalibela House, Publishers since 1954; *b.* Manchester 1882; *d.* of Richard Marsden Pankhurst, LL.D. (*d.* 1898), and Emmeline Pankhurst (*d.* 1928); one *s.* *Educ.:* High School for Girls, Manchester; Municipal School of Art; Royal College of Art, S. Kensington. Father died when she was 16; obtained free studentship to Manchester School of Art, 1898, Lady Whitworth Scholarship, Proctor travelling Scholarship; went to Venice; took Diploma at Academia; won National Scholarship to R.C.A.; became Hon. Sec. of Women's Social and Political Union; was imprisoned on several occasions; formed East London Branches of W.S.P.U.; these developed a more democratic policy than parent body, became a separate organisation; founded Workers' Dreadnought (1914-24); was imprisoned several times, hunger struck thirteen times under forcible feeding and Cat and Mouse Act; Edited Workers' Dreadnought and Germinal; opposed the War; from 1914-19 opened and acted as Hon. Sec. for Mothers' Arms clinic, day nursery and Montessori School, and four other clinics, two cost-price restaurants, E. London Co-operative Toy Factory, founded League of Rights for Soldiers' and Sailors' Wives and Relatives and acted as Hon. Sec.; also National Labour Council for Adult Suffrage; fined for speeches against the War,

Derbyshire miners paid the fine; supported Russian Revolution; formed People's Russian Information Bureau; imprisoned in 1920 under D.O.R.A.; initiated Society of Friends of Italian Freedom to expose the atrocities of the Fascisti; Founder and Hon. Sec. Women's International Matteotti Cttee. to combat Fascism; Foundation Member Abyssinia Association; editor New Times and Ethiopia News, an organ of International Justice, 1936-56; supported War against Axis; founded Women's War Emergency Council to secure improved allowances for soldiers' wives and children and other measures; founder and Hon. Sec. 1942, of Princess Tsahai Memorial Hospital Council; Chairman of International Ethiopian Council for Study and Report, 1946. *Publications:* The Suffragette, 1912; Writ on Cold Slate, 1921; Soviet Russia as I Saw It, 1921; India and the Earthly Paradise, 1926; Delphos the future of International Language, 1927; The Suffragette Movement, 1931; Save the Mothers, 1932; The Home Front, 1933; translations from the Roumanian poet Eminescu, 1931; The Life of Emmeline Pankhurst, 1935; British Policy in Eritrea, 1945; British Policy in Eastern Ethiopia (Reserved Areas and Ogaden), 1945; Italy's War Crimes in Ethiopia; The Ethiopian People: Their Rights and Progress; The Ethiopian Cooperatives; Education in Ethiopia, 1946; Ex-Italian Somaliland, 1950; Eritrea and Ethiopia, 1950; Eritrea on the Eve; Why are we destroying the Ethiopian ports?; History of Ethiopia and Eritrea, 1953; Ethiopia, A Cultural History, 1955; Ethiopia Today, 1961. *Address:* P.O. Box 1896, Addis Ababa, Ethiopia. [*Died* 27 *Sept.* 1960.

PANNALL, Major J. Charles, D.S.O. 1919; O.B.E. 1941; M.C.; *b.* 1879. Served European War, 1914-19 (despatches, M.C., D.S.O.); Governor of Camp Hill Preventive Detention Prison, Isle of Wight, 1930-32; Governor of Dartmoor Prison, 1932-45. *Address:* 127 Old Christchurch Road, Bournemouth, Hants. [*Died* 28 *Jan.* 1960.

PANTON, Alexander Hugh, C.M.G. 1948; J.P.; M.L.A. (Lab.) for Leederville, Western Australia, since 1924; *b.* 20 March 1877; *s.* of Alexander Henry Panton and Jessie Miller; *m.* 1914, Ada Ethel Green; two *s.* one *d.* *Educ.:* Public School, Carisbrook, Victoria. Started as Gold Miner, later Sec. Shop Assistants Union. Entered Parl., 1919; still a Member. Went to S. African War, and European War, 1914-18. Speaker of Leg. Assembly 5 years; Minister for Mines and Health, 8 years; Minister of Lands and Labour, 1 year and 5 months; Minister for Civil Defence during war period, 1939-45. Member Royal Perth Hosp. Board, 19 years; also associated actively with R.S.S.L. Blind and Braille Societies and Industrial Unions for many years. *Recreations:* gardening and bowls. *Address:* 11 Morriston St. North, Perth, W.A. *T.:* B. 8843. *Clubs:* Anzac, Bowling (Perth, W.A.). [*Died* 25 *Dec.* 1951.

PAPALEXOPOULO, Rear-Admiral Dimitri, C.M.G.; Royal Hellenic Navy; Naval Attaché London and Paris, 1927 and 1928; *m.* 1921, Dorothy Elliadi; one *s.* two *d.* *Educ.:* Royal Hellenic Naval School, Piraeus. Officer, 1896; served in Greco-Turkish War of 1897 on battleships Hydra and Psara; Lieut. (Fleet Navigator) under Rear-Adm. Tufnell (organiser of Greek Fleet), 1911; Lieut.-Commdr. during Balkan Wars, 1912-13; took part in the two naval battles of Dec. 1912 and Jan. 1913 on board battle cruiser Averoff in capacity of First Lieutenant and Fleet Navigator; followed Veniselos in his Salonika expedition, 1916; Commander, 1917; C.O. of destroyer Ierax which acted as convoy, Oct. 1917–Feb. 1918 and formed part of the British Aegean Fleet under Rear-Admiral Lambert, Rear-Admiral Seymour and Admiral Calthorpe, Feb. 1918 to end of war (C.M.G.); Assistant Chief of Staff to Vice-Admiral Kelly (who was acting as organiser of the Greek Navy); Naval Attaché in Paris, 1924, resigned, 1930. *Address:* 22 Rue Beaujon, Paris. *T.:* Carnot 14.94. [*Died* 31 *Dec.* 1959.

PAPINI, Giovanni; Independent Writer; *b.* Florence, 9 Jan. 1881; *m.* 1907, Giacinta Giovagnoli; two *d.* *Educ.:* Florence. Editor of Review: Leonardo, 1903-7; La Voce, 1912; Lacerba, 1913-15; Vraie Italie, 1919; Conversion to Roman Church, 1920. *Publications:* Twilight of the Philosophers, 1906; The Tragic of Everyday, 1906; Twenty and Four Minds, 1912; A Finished Man, 1913; History of Christ, 1921; Bread and Wine, 1926; Saint Augustine, 1929; Gog, 1930; Dante Living, 1933; Storia della Letteratura Italiana, 1937; Cielo e Terra, 1943, etc.; Lettere agli Uomini di Papa Celestius VI, 1946; Santi e Poeti, 1947; Passato Remoto, 1948; Life of Michelangelo, 1949; The Black Book, 1951; The Devil, 1953; The World's Spy, 1955. *Address:* Via Guerrazzis 10 Florence (21). *T.:* 50.248. [*Died* 8 *July* 1956.

PARES, Richard, C.B.E. 1945; F.B.A. 1948; Fellow of All Souls College, Oxford, 1921-45, and since 1954; Hon. Fellow, Balliol College, Oxford; Joint Editor, English Historical Review; *b.* 25 Aug. 1902; *e. s.* of late Sir Bernard Pares, K.B.E., D.C.L.; *m.* 1937, Janet Lindsay, *yr. d.* of Sir Maurice Powicke, D.Litt.; four *d.* *Educ.:* Winchester (Scholar); Balliol College, Oxford (Scholar). B.A. 1924; M.A. 1928; Laura Spelman Rockefeller Memorial Student, 1928-1929; Lecturer, New College, Oxford, 1929-1940. Junior Proctor, 1938-39. Board of Trade, 1940-45; Professor of History, University of Edinburgh, 1945-54. Ford's Lecturer in English History, University of Oxford, 1951-52. Hon. LL.D. Edin. *Publications:* War and Trade in the West Indies, 1936; Colonial Blockade and Neutral Rights, 1938; A West-India Fortune, 1950; King George III and the Politicians, 1953; Yankees and Creoles, 1956; (posthumous) The Historian's Business and other Essays; articles and reviews in historical periodicals. *Address:* 97 Holywell, Oxford. [*Died* 3 *May* 1958.

PARFIT, Rev. Joseph Thomas, M.A.; *b.* Bethnal Green, 17 April 1870; *m.* 1st, 1897, Jessy S. King (*d.* 1898), Rushmere Hall, Ipswich; 2nd, 1902, Norah C. Stephens, Amberley, Glos.; four *s.* two *d.* *Educ.:* C.M. College, Islington; University College, Durham (Long Prize and Prox. Acces., Hebrew Scholarship). Ten years in Mesopotamia under C.M.S., where he opened the first British schools in Baghdad and Mosul; while Hon. Chaplain to German Consulate, and during frequent journeys in Turkey, obtained much valuable information, which he utilised as a writer and lecturer on the War Aims of the Central Powers; for 3 years was Vice Principal of the English College in Jerusalem, and became Chaplain to Bishop Blyth and Hon. Canon of St. George's Collegiate Church; for 7 years was Chaplain of Beyrout and Lebanon, with charge of work in Aintab and Marash; opened 23 schools for the Lebanon Druses and a Seamen's Institute at Beyrout; has lectured to British Troops in France, Germany, Italy, Egypt, Palestine, Syria, and Constantinople; has travelled much in Europe, Turkey, Persia, and India; is a lecturer in the British Isles on Near Eastern topics; in charge of the district church of Marlston, in the parish of Bucklebury, near Newbury, 1925-29; Rector of Frilsham, 1927-29; Vicar of Warfield, 1935-43. Founder of the Bible Lands Studio. *Publications:* Twenty Years in Baghdad and Syria; Among the Druses of Lebanon and Bashan; Marvellous Mesopotamia; Petra and Palmyra; Pamphlets on the War, St. George, The Bible Lands, etc. *Recreations:* football, tennis, and entomology. *Address:* Folly Close, Wantage, Berks. *T.:* Wantage 167. [*Died* 21 *July* 1953.

PARK, Sir Archibald (Richard), Kt. 1958; C.M.G. 1955; Metropolitan Transport Trust, Tasmania; Company Manager: A. R. Park and Son, Cartage Contractors; Hargrave Pty. Ltd., Shipping Agents; Mephalene (Tas.) Pty. Ltd.; *b.* 18 Sept. 1888; *s.* of Francis William D. Park; *m.* Vera Fanny, *d.* of Maurice Barnett; one *s.* Alderman, City of Hobart, 1934-, Deputy Lord Mayor, 1948-50, Lord Mayor, 1950-52, 1954-56, 1958-60. M.H.A., Franklin, 1949-55. Vice-President and State President, Royal Life Saving Society; State Pres., Tasmanian Road Transport Assoc., 1929; Warden Marine Board (past Master Warden); State Pres. and Life Mem. Ex-Navalman's Assoc.; State Pres., St. John Ambulance Assoc.; Rotarian (past Pres.). *Recreations:* bowls and farming; ex-Rugby player. *Address:* (home) 328 Macquarie Street, Hobart, Tasmania. *Clubs:* Athenæum, Masonic, Royal Automobile (Hobart). [*Died* 18 *Nov.* 1959.

PARK, Carton M.; *see* Moore-Park.

PARKER, Hon. Alexander Edward, O.B.E. 1949; late M.F.H. North Warwickshire; D.L., J.P., Warwickshire; 11th, but *o. surv. s.* of 6th Earl of Macclesfield; *b.* 1 July 1864; *m.* 1896, Winifred Florence, *d.* of late Albert O. Worthington, D.L., J.P., Maple Hayes, Staffs.; one *s.* *Educ.:* Eton. *Address:* Mill House, Warwick. *T.:* Warwick 163. [*Died* 2 *Sept.* 1958.

PARKER, Rear-Adm. (S) Alfred Ramsay, C.B. 1919; R.N. retired. Secretary to Admiral Sir Gerard Noel, 1898-1908; to Commander-in-Chief, Home Fleet, 1909-11; to Commander-in-Chief, Plymouth, 1911-16; War Staff, Admiralty, 1917; Admiralty Reconstruction Committee, 1918-19; retired list, 1923. *Address:* Oaklea, Bracknell, Berks. [*Died* 25 *Jan.* 1951.

PARKER, Alwyn, C.B. 1917; C.M.G. 1913; a Director of Lloyds Bank, Ltd., 1919-47; Editor of Lloyds Bank Review; *b.* 20 Apr. 1877; *s.* of late Alfred T. Parker of Fairlie, Ayrshire, and Aigburth, Liverpool; *m.* 1908, Sophia Dunbar (*d.* 1932), *d.* of late J. C. J. Brodie of Lethen, Nairnshire; one *s.* (and one son killed in action October 1944) one *d.* *Educ.:* Harrow. Studied in Germany. Attaché 1900; 3rd Secretary, 1902; Junior Clerk, 1906; Assistant Clerk, 1912; head of the Contraband Dept. Foreign Office, 1914-17; Librarian of the Foreign Office, 1918; has served in St. Petersburg; granted an allowance for knowledge of Russian and passed an examination in Public Law; commissioned as Counsellor of Embassy in H.M. Diplomatic Service while attending the Peace Conference at Paris in 1919; was Private Secretary to Lord Hardinge of Penshurst; resigned Foreign Office, 1919; Adviser on reorganisation of Communications Department, Foreign Office, Sept.-Dec., 1939. *Address:* Foldsdown, Thursley, Godalming. *T.:* Godalming 284. [*Died* 15 *Sept.* 1951.

PARKER, Admiral Edmond Hyde, C.B. 1917; *b.* 30 Jan. 1868; 3rd *s.* of late Sir William Parker, 9th Bart., of Melford Hall, Suffolk, and Sophia Mary, *d.* of late Nathaniel Barnardiston of The Ryes, Sudbury, Suffolk; *m.* 1908, Helen Margaret, *d.* of late Canon George Raymond Portal. *Educ.:* Stubbington House; Naval Colleges. Joined H.M. Navy, 1881; Commander, 1901; Captain, 1906; Rear-Adm., 1917; Vice-Adm., 1923; Adm., 1927; Senior Naval Officer, Crete (H.M.S. Minerva), Cretan Deputy disturbances, 1911-12; commanded Training Squadron, 1913-14; commanded H.M.S. Superb, Grand Fleet, 1915-18, Battle of Jutland (despatches); Director of Mobilisation Dept. Admiralty, 1918-20; commanded Portsmouth Division Reserve Fleet, 1921, and Reserve Fleet, 1922; retired, 1923; Order of St. Anne of Russia, 2nd class with swords, 1916. *Address:* Bodorgan House, Ramsbury, Marlborough, Wilts. *T.:* Ramsbury 204. *Club:* United Service. [*Died* 19 *Aug.* 1951.

PARKER, Eric; Author; Editor of the Lonsdale Library; *b.* The Grange, East Barnet, 1870; *e. s.* of Frederick Searle Parker and Elisabeth, *d.* of William Wilkieson of Woodbury Hall, Beds.; *m.* 1902, Ruth Margaret (*d.* 1933), 2nd *d.* of late L. Messel, Nymans, Crawley, Sussex; two *s.* two *d.* (and two *s.* killed in War of 1939-45). *Educ.:* Eton (King's Scholar); Merton College, Oxford (Postmaster). Assistant editor, St. James's Gazette, 1900-2; editor of the County Gentleman and Land and Water, 1902-7; Editor-in-Chief of the Field, 1930-37; shooting editor of the Field, 1911-37. *Publications:* The Sinner and the Problem, 1901; illustrations to A. K. Collett's British Inland Birds, 1906; Highways and Byways in Surrey, 1908; In Wind and Wild, 1909; A Book of the Zoo, 1909; Promise of Arden, 1912; A West Surrey Sketch-book (with William Hyde), 1913; Eton in the 'Eighties, 1914; Shooting Days, 1918; An Angler's Garland, 1920; Hawker on Shooting, 1921; Playing Fields, 1922; Floreat, An Eton Anthology, 1923; Elements of Shooting, 1924; Hesketh Prichard, A Memoir, 1924; Game Pie, 1925; Between the Wickets, 1926; edited Days on the Hill, 1926; Partridges Yesterday and To-day, 1927: Field, River, and Hill, 1927; edited Taverner's Certaine Experiments with Fish and Fruite, 1928; Shooting by Moor, Field and Shore, 1929; edited Rawstorne's Gamonia, 1929; English Wild Life, 1929; edited Fine Angling for Coarse Fish, and The Game of Cricket, 1930; edited Colonel Hawker's Shooting Diaries, 1931; The Lonsdale Anthology of Sporting Prose and Verse, 1932; An Alphabet of Shooting, 1932; edited the Book of the Golden Retriever, 1933; College at Eton, 1933; Ethics of Egg Collecting, 1935; Game Birds, Beasts and Fishes, 1935; new edition of Highways and Byways in Surrey, 1936; The Gardener's England, 1936; Sussex Woods, 1936; South West Surrey; East Surrey; North and Central Surrey (Highways and Byways); The Country Year; Memory Looks Forward, 1937; The Gardener's Week-end Book; Predatory Birds; An Anthology of the Bible, 1939; British Sport (Britain in Pictures); World of Birds, 1941; The Shooting Week-end Book, 1942; Oddities of Natural History; A Book of Comfort; Landmarks given to the People, 1943; The Countryman's Week-end Book; Surrey, 1947; Best of Dogs, 1948; The History of Cricket; The Dog-Lover's Week-End Book, 1950; Surrey Naturalist; The Cricketer's Week-End Book, 1952; Surrey Anthology, 1953; Surrey Gardens, 1954. *Recreation:* gardening. *Address:* Feathercombe, Hambledon, Godalming. *T.:* Hascombe 264. [*Died* 13 *Feb.* 1955.

PARKER, George Howard; Emeritus Professor of Zoology since 1935, Harvard University; *b.* Philadelphia, 23 Dec. 1864; *s.* of George Washington and Martha Taylor Parker; *m.* 1894, Louise Merritt Stabler; no *c.* *Educ.:* Harvard University. Assistant and instructor in Zoology, 1888-91; Parker Fellow in Europe, 1891-93; Instructor, 1893-99; Assistant Professor, 1899-1906; Professor, 1906-35; Fellow American Academy Arts and Sciences; Member American Philosophical Society; Member National Academy Sciences; William Brewster Clark, Lecturer, Amherst Coll., 1914 sent by U.S. Government to Pribilof Island to report on the fur-seal herd, 1914; Elliot Medal from Nat. Acad. Sciences for 1937; Lewis Prize from Amer. Philos. Society for 1941. *Publications:* Biology and Social Problems, 1914; The Elementary Nervous System, 1919; Smell, Taste, and Allied Senses, 1922; The Evolution of Man, 1922 (joint author); What Evolution Is, 1925; Creation by Evolution, 1928 (joint author); Human Biology and Racial Welfare (joint author), 1930; Humoral Agents in Nervous Activity, 1932; The Problem of Mental Disorder (joint); Color Changes in Animals in Relation to Nervous Activity, 1936; Chromatophores, 1946; The World Expands, 1946;

Animal Colour Changes and their Neurohumours, 1948; The Hormones (joint), 1951; numerous papers on the nervous system and the sense organs in various scientific journals. *Address:* 16 Berkeley St., Cambridge 38, Mass. *Clubs:* Faculty (Cambridge); Harvard (Boston). [*Died* 26 *March* 1955.

PARKER, John; Theatrical Historian and Journalist; Editor of Who's Who in the Theatre since 1912; *b.* 28 July 1875; *o. s.* of late David and Florence Parker; *m.* 1st, Edith Maud (*d.* 1942), *y. d.* of late Montague Belfield Pizey; one *s.* one *d.*; 2nd, 1944, Doris Mary, *y. d.* of George and Alice Margaret Sinclair. *Educ.:* London. Entered journalism, 1892, on Illustrated London News; subsequently on staff of Era, Free Lance, etc.; London Correspondent, New York Dramatic Mirror, 1903; London Correspondent, Critic and Manager, New York Dramatic News, 1903-20; Editor of Green Room Book, 1908-9; has contributed numerous biographies to each of supplemental issues of Dictionary of National Biography, since 1910; Hon. Editor of Critics' Circular since 1923; Hon. Secretary of Critics' Circle since 1924; President of Critics' Circle in its Silver Jubilee Year, 1937-38, and in that capacity, represented Great Britain at International Congress of Critics, Paris, 1937. *Publications:* The Green Room Book (Editor, 1908-9); Who's Who in the Theatre (Editor since 1912). *Recreations:* the theatre; collecting theatrical literature. *Address:* The Critics Circle, 2/4 Tudor Street, E.C.4. *Clubs:* Savage; Green Room; Surrey C. C. [*Died* 18 *Nov.* 1952.

PARKER, Hon. John (Holford); *b.* 22 June 1886; *y. s.* of 3rd and *heir-pres.* to 5th Earl of Morley; *m.* 1919, Hon. Marjory St. Aubuyn, *d.* of 2nd Lord St. Levan; three *s.* *Educ.:* Eton; Trinity College, Cambridge. *Address:* Pound House, Yelverton, South Devon. *T.:* Yelverton 162. [*Died* 27 *Feb.* 1955.

PARKER, Matthew Archibald, B.Sc.; LL.D., F.R.I.C., F.R.S.C.(R.); F.C.I.C.; Professor of Chemistry, University of Manitoba, 1904-37, Professor Emeritus since 1937; *b.* near Glasgow, 1871; *m.* 1904, Elizabeth Blackie; three *d.* *Educ.:* Glasgow; Heidelberg. Lecturer Glasgow and West of Scotland Technical College, 1894-1901; Lecturer Glasgow University, 1901-04. *Address:* 365 Waverley Street, Winnipeg, Canada. [*Died* 29 *Nov.* 1953.

PARKER, Col. Richard Cecil Oxley, O.B.E. 1944; T.D. 1935; Partner in Strutt & Parker, Lofts & Warner, Land Agents and Surveyors; *b.* 17 Sept. 1894; *o. s.* of late Charles Alfred Parker and Agnes, *d.* of Richard Durant, Sharpham, Devon, and High Canons, Herts.; *m.* 1918, Iris de Lautour, *o. d.* of late Capt. Sir Lionel de L. Wells, C.B., C.M.G., C.B.E., R.N., of Houghton, Hampshire. *Educ.:* Eton; Christ Church, Oxon. M.A. (Agric.) Oxon; 6th Dragoon Guards (Carabiniers) Spec. Res., 1914-20; 104th (Essex Yeomanry) Field Bde. R.A., 1920-38. Lt.-Col., 1934; Bt. Col., 1938; Colonel Essex Home Guard, 1940-45; Hon. Colonel Essex Yeomanry, 1950-55. J.P., Essex, 1929-39, Hants, 1940; D.L., Essex, 1934; High Sheriff of Essex, 1942; Chm. Hants branch C.P.R.E., 1958. Lay Reader, Dioceses of Chelmsford, Winchester and St. Andrews; F.R.I.C.S.; F.L.A.S. *Recreations:* shooting and deer stalking and photography. *Address:* Houghton Lodge, Stockbridge, Hampshire. *T.:* Stockbridge 2; Craiganour, Loch Rannoch, Perthshire. *T.:* Kinloch Rannoch 324. *Clubs:* United University, Farmers'. [*Died* 24 *March* 1959.

PARKER, Rev. Canon William; Hon. Canon of Rochester Cathedral, 1934-50, Canon Emeritus since 1950; *b.* 3 Feb. 1871; *e. s.* of Robert Parker, Fair View House, Lisnaskea, and Frances, *d.* of Robert Moore of Breagho, Enniskillen, Co. Fermanagh; *m.* 1st, Letitia (*d.* 1900), *d.* of Robert Masterson, Lisnaskea; 2nd, Laura Blanche (*d.* 1934), *d.* of Col. Henry Cowell, 27th Regt.; one *s.* one *d.* *Educ.:* Portora Royal School, Enniskillen; Trinity College, Dublin. Classical Scholar, Bedell Scholar in Irish, Vice-Chancellor's Medallist, B.A. (1st Sen. Mod. with Gold Med. in Classics), Tyrrell Memorial Medallist for Classical Compositions, M.A., B.D.; Deacon, 1901; Priest, 1902; Assistant Master at Highgate School, 1901-4; Warden of St. Columba's College, Rathfarnham, 1904-9; Assistant Master at Tonbridge School, 1910-12; Headmaster of King's School, Rochester, 1912-35; Rector of Longfield, 1935-45; T.C.F., 1914-19; Examining Chaplain to the Bishop of Rochester; Member of Headmaster's Conference and I.A.H.M., 1914-35; Freemason, Past Prov. Grand Chaplain of Kent. *Address:* 20 Hillside Avenue, Frindsbury, Rochester. [*Died* 23 *Feb.* 1952

PARKER, Sir William Stephen Hyde, 11th Bt., *cr.* 1681; *b.* 23 Jan. 1892; *er. s.* of Rev. Sir William Hyde Parker, 10th Bt., and Ethel (*d.* 1941), *o. d.* of John Leech, Gorse Hall, Dukinfield, Cheshire; *S.* father, 1931; *m.* 1931, Ulla Ditlef, *o. d.* of C. Ditlef Nielsen, Dr. of Philosophy, Copenhagen; one *s.* one *d.* *Educ.:* Malvern College; Magdalene College, Cambridge. France, India, Afghanistan, 1914-1921. *Heir:* *s.* Richard William Hyde, *b.* 5 April 1937. *Address:* Long Melford, Suffolk. *T.:* 384. *Clubs:* Cavalry, Farmers'. [*Died* 29 *July* 1951.

PARKES, Edward, C.M.G. 1941; M.V.O. 1934; I.S.O. 1932; Under-Secretary, Clerk of Executive Council and Chief Electoral Officer, Tasmania, since 1930; *b.* 8 June 1890; *s.* of late Edward Parkes; *m.* 1924, Gladys, *d.* of late A. T. Lipscombe; one *s.* one *d.* *Educ.:* By Rev. John Gray; Scotch College, Hobart. Entered Tasmanian Civil Service, 1906; Secretary to Premier's Office, 1925; State Secretary, Empire Parliamentary Association's Visit to Australia, 1926; Official Secretary, Tasmanian Agent General's Office, London, 1927-28; Returning Officer, Division of Franklin, 1921-1927; Deputy Chief Electoral Officer, 1922-30; State Director, Royal Visit, 1934; one of Commissioners of Salmon and Freshwater Fisheries, 1925-36; served European War, 2nd Australian Division, A.I.F. in Egypt, Gallipoli, and France, 1915-18; President, Hobart Branch, Returned Soldiers' League, 1942-43. *Recreation:* angling. *Address:* Lower Sandy Bay, Hobart, Tasmania. *Club:* Tasmanian (Hobart). [*Died* 24 *March* 1953.

PARKES, Major Harry Reeves, C.B. 1919; D.L.; late T.F. Res.; *b.* 4 Dec. 1873; *s.* of late F. W. Parkes, one of H.M. Inspectors of Schools; *m.* 1900, Lucy, *e. d.* of R. H. Parker, pottery manufacturer, Stoke-on-Trent; no *c.* *Educ.:* High School, Newcastle-under-Lyme; Univ. of Wales, Aberystwyth. Assistant Master at various Public Schools, 1898-1908; Volunteer Commission, 1900; Assistant Secretary, West Lancashire T.F. Association, 1909; Secretary, West Lancashire T.A. and A.F. Association, 1915-1938; various Hon. Secretaryships, including C.E.M.S. Federation, Liverpool. *Publication:* Essay on Recruiting for the Territorial Force. *Recreations:* outdoor sports. *Address:* Allandale, Aughton, Lancashire. *T.:* Aughton Green 2386. *Club:* Liverpool Press. [*Died* 1 *Jan.* 1949.

[***But death not notified in time for inclusion in Who Was Who 1941–1950, first edn.***

PARKES, Oscar, O.B.E., M.B., Ch.B.; Chevalier Ordre Mérite Maritime; *b.* 18 October 1885; *s.* of Dr. W. E. Parkes, J.P., Handsworth, Staffs; *m.* 1921, Natalie Randall; one *d.* *Educ.:* Berkhamstead; Birmingham Univ. M.B., Ch.B., 1914; Temp. Surg. Lt. R.N., 1914-18; Admiralty, 1918; Naval Intelligence Division; Naval Artist and Director Naval Photographic Section, Imperial

War Museum, 1919-20; Neurologist to Ministry of Pensions, 1920-24. *Publications:* Detection of Disease (jointly); Our Rheumatism; various contributions to Medical Press on Electro-Therapeutics and Ozone Therapy; editor of Fighting Ships, Naval Annual 1918-1935; British Navy, World's Warships, British Battleships, illustrated articles on Naval subjects to British and Foreign Press. *Recreations:* Collection of Naval photographs, photography, painting, gardening. *Address:* Craigavad, Co. Down, N. Ireland. [*Died* 24 *June* 1958.

PARKINSON, Brig. George Singleton, C.B.E. 1945; D.S.O. 1918; *b.* Oct. 1880; *s.* of late Henry Parkinson, M.A., B.L.; *m.* 1911, Hilda Lindsay Alexander, *d.* of late Thomas Chisholm Jack, Edinburgh. *Educ.:* Bath College. Served South African War, 1900-1 (Queen's medal 5 clasps); M.R.C.S., L.R.C.P., Lond. 1906; D.P.H. Lond. 1913; entered R.A.M.C. London, 1908; served European War, 1914-18, France and Belgium, Headquarters Staff First Army; Deputy Assistant Director of Hygiene, Assistant Director Medical Services, Acting Lt.-Colonel (D.S.O., despatches thrice, Chev. Order of St. Avis, French Croix de Guerre, Médaille de la Reconnaissance); served War of 1939-45: A.D.H.E. Comd., 1939-40; Dean and Dir. Public Health Dept., London, School of Hygiene and Tropical Medicine, 1940-43; Examiner D.T.M. & H. (Conjoint Bd.), 1936-39; Director Public Health Sub-Commission, A.M.G., A.C., North Africa, Sicily, Italy, 1943-45 (C.B.E., 1939-45, Italian Stars, and U.S.A. Typhus Commission Medal, 1944); Croce al merito, Italian Red Cross, 1947; Hon Brigadier; Technical Adviser to Greek Govenment, Athens, Feb.-Sept., 1951. Commander Order of St. John of Jerusalem; Hon. Life Mem. British Red Cross Society; Liveryman Painter Stainers Company. Medical Officer of Health, Gibraltar, 1919-23; Assistant Professor of Hygiene, and sometime Professor, Royal Army Medical College, Millbank, London; retired pay, 1928. *Publications:* Synopsis of Hygiene (9th edition), Jameson and Parkinson; British Red Cross Society Hygiene and Sanitation Manual No. 4 (5th edition). *Recreation:* gardening. *Address:* St. Kilda, Grove Avenue, Epsom. *Clubs:* Athenæum, Junior United Service, Savage. [*Died* 18 *Aug.* 1953.

PARKS, Mrs. G. R.; *see* Robins, Elizabeth.

PARMELEE, James Grannis, O.B.E.; *b.* 9 March 1875; 3rd *s.* of William Grannis Parmelee, I.S.O., and Marcella Whitney; *m.* Doris Olivia Stewart Hudson. *Educ.:* Provincial Model School, Ottawa; private tuition, Ottawa and Montreal. Inspection of Iron, Steel and other bounties for the Dominion Government, 1902; Administrative Branch, Dept. Trade and Commerce, Ottawa, 1911-21; Assistant Deputy Minister of Trade and Commerce for Canada, 1923-31; Deputy Minister of Trade and Commerce for Canada, 1931; visited Great Brit. and France, and investigated possibilities of increasing demand for Canadian products by means of publicity and exhibitions, 1928; Member National Film Bd. of Canada, 1939-41; Chm., Canadian Shipping Bd., 1939-41; served on number of War Committees, 1938-41, and missions for Government; retired 1941. Enlisted overseas European War, C.E.F., 27 Nov. 1914; Captain, promoted on the field as Major, 1916; demobilised, 4 Aug. 1919; served in France four and a half years, with Army of Occupation. Germany, 1918 (despatches twice, O.B.E., Croix de Guerre with bronze star): Fellow Canadian Geographical Soc.; Member: Brit. Columbia Historical Assoc.; United Services Institution of Vancouver Island; Hon. Citizen of City of New York, 1939; Jubilee Medal; Coronation Medal. *Recreation:* golf. *Address:* 963 Beach Drive, Victoria, B.C., Canada. *Club:* Victoria Golf (Victoria, B.C.). [*Died* 3 *April* 1953.

PARNALL, Eng. Rear-Admiral Walter Rudolph, C.B. 1927; C.B.E. 1945; *m.* 1930, Violet Lily Sands; no *c.* Served War of 1914-18 with Grand Fleet; joined staff of Engineer Inspectors, Admiralty, 1921; Asst. Engineer-in-Chief, 1923-27; Deputy Engineer-in-Chief, Admiralty. 1927-30; retired list, 1930; re-employed, 1939-44. *Address:* c/o Admiralty, S.W.1. *Club:* United Service. [*Died* 2 *March* 1954.

PARR, Olive Katharine, (Beatrice Chase); Foundress of the Crusade of White Knights and Ladies; *b.* Harrow on the Hill, 5 July 1874; *e. c.* of Charles Chase Parr. *Educ.:* Holy Child Convent, Cavendish Square, W. Organised the Catholic Children's Crusade for Cardinal Vaughan; is owner of a Catholic chapel on Dartmoor with full privileges, and is sole organiser of the Crusade for Chastity, which numbers among its members some of the most distinguished civilians, clergy, and officers in the Empire; Member of the Society of Authors, London. *Publications:* A Red-Handed Saint; A White-Handed Saint; My Heaven in Devon; Back Slum Idylls; The Little Cardinal; A Book of Answered Prayers; Daily Praise; Pearl, under real name; Through a Dartmoor Window; The Heart of the Moor; The Dartmoor Window Again; Gorseblossoms from Dartmoor; Pages of Peace from Dartmoor; Completed Tales of my Knights and Ladies; White Knights on Dartmoor; Lady Avis Trewithen; Lady Agatha; A Dartmoor Galahad; Patricia Lancaster's Revenge, 1928; The Twelfth an Amethyst, 1929; Dartmoor Snapshots, 1931; My Chief Knight, John Oxenham, 1943; The Corpse on the Moor, 1946; under pseudonym; (from author only) The Cry for a Heart; The Passing of the Rainbow Maker; The Dartmoor Window Forty Years After, 1948; The Voice of the River (Children's Book); Dartmoor the Beloved, 1951. *Recreation:* flower gardening. *Address:* Venton House, Widecombe-in-the-Moor, Newton Abbot, Devon. *T.:* Widecombe 217 [*Died* 3 *July* 1955.

PARR, Roger Charlton, J.P., D.L.; *o. s.* of late Joseph Charlton Parr; *b.* 3 Nov. 1874; *m.* 1906, Lady Julian Mary Jocelyn, *e. d.* of 7th Earl of Roden; one *s.* *Educ.:* Eton; Christ Church, Oxford, M.A. Late Lieut. Earl of Chester's Yeomanry Cavalry; High Sheriff of Herefordshire, 1905. *Heir:* *s.* Henry Charlton Parr [*m.* 1st, 1928, Elinor (divorced, 1934), *d.* of late Sir Archer Croft, 10th Bt.; 2nd, 1935, Margaret Cicely, *d.* of late Sir Alfred Fripp]. *Address:* The Weir, Hereford. *T.:* Bridge Sollars 229. *Clubs:* Junior Carlton, M.C.C., Royal Automobile. [*Died* 7 *Aug.* 1958.

PARRISH, Anne (Mrs. Josiah Titzell); Writer; *b.* Colorado Springs, Colorado, U.S.A.; *d.* of Thomas Clarkson Parrish and Anne Lodge; *m.* 1st, Charles Albert Corliss (*d.* 1936); 2nd, 1938, Josiah Titzell (*d.* 1943). *Educ.:* private schools. *Publications:* with Dillwyn Parrish (brother) wrote Knee High to a Grasshopper, 1923; Dream Coach, 1924, illustrated by ourselves; and Lustres, 1924; alone wrote A Pocketful of Poses, 1923; Semi-Attached, 1924; The Perennial Bachelor 1925 (winner of Harper Prize); Tomorrow Morning, 1927; All Kneeling, 1928; The Methodist Faun, 1929; Floating Island, 1930 (wrote and illustrated); Loads of Love, 1932; Sea Level, 1934; Golden Wedding, 1936; Mr. Despondency's Daughter, 1938; Pray for a Tomorrow, 1941; Poor Child, 1945; A Clouded Star, 1948; The Story of Appleby Capple (illustr. by the author), 1950; And Have Not Love, 1954. *Recreations:* travelling, gardening, and drawing. *Address:* Quantness, Peaceable Street, Georgetown, Conn., U.S.A. [*Died* 5 *Sept.* 1957.

PARRY, Hon. William Edward; Minister of Internal Affairs and Pensions, 1935-49; Minister of Social Security, 1938-1949; Minister in charge of Tourist and Health Resorts, 1941-49, New Zealand; M.P. for

Auckland Central, **1919-46**, for Arch Hill since 1946; *b.* at Orange, New South Wales, 1878; *m.* Georgina Fowke; two *d.* *Educ.:* Public Schools, New South Wales. Was a miner in early life; arrived in New Zealand about 1906 and was for three years in the Waihi Mines; President of the Waihi Miners' Union at the time of the strike, 1913; a Workers' Inspector and a member of the Royal Commission on Mines, in 1911; on executive of N.Z. Federation of Labour, and Vice-President until formation of the United Federation of Labour in 1913; on executive of the Social Democratic Party; an Organiser of the United Flax-workers' Union in Manawatu to 1914; Secretary of the Coal Miners' Federation in 1918; executive of the N.Z. Labour Party. *Recreations:* shooting, fishing, and physical culture; was a noted cyclist in early life. *Address:* Parliament House, Wellington, C.1, New Zealand. *T.:* 44-666, and 45-905.
[*Died* 27 *Nov.* 1952.

PARRY PRYCE, Ven. Thomas; Archdeacon of Newport, Mon., since 1948; Vicar of St. Mellons, Cardiff, since 1949; and Rural Dean. *Educ.:* St. David's College, Lampeter. B.A. 1906; deacon, 1906; priest, 1907. Curate of Blaenavon with Capel Newydd, 1906-12; Vicar of Dingestow, 1912-17; Rector of Aberystruth (or Blaina), 1917-21; Vicar of Pontypridd, 1921-23; Vicar of St. Paul, Newport, 1933. Hon. Canon of Monmouth, 1940-. *Address:* St. Mellons Vicarage, Cardiff.
[*Died* 15 *Jan.* 1953.

PARSONS, Lieut.-Colonel Alfred Woodis, C.M.G. 1919; D.S.O. 1915; late 19th Royal Hussars (Queen Alexandra's Own); *b.* 17 June 1878; *s.* of late John Parsons, Oxford; *m.* 1927, Margery, *d.* of late R. Hamilton-Stubber of Moyne, Queen's County. *Educ.:* Rugby; R.M.C., Sandhurst. Entered army, 1898; Captain, 1905; Major, 1912; served S. African War, 1899-1902 (despatches twice, Queen's medal 4 clasps, King's medal 2 clasps); European War, 1914-18 (despatches five times, D.S.O.); retired pay, 1923; Légion d'Honneur (Croix de Chevalier), 1917. *Address:* Kempsford House, Fairford, Glos. *T.:* Kempsford 209. *Club:* Cavalry.
[*Died* 26 *Aug.* 1954.

PARSONS, (Miss) Beatrice; Artist; Royal Academy Student; *d.* of Arthur W. Parsons. *Educ.:* King's College, London; Royal Academy Schools. Exhibited several times at the Royal Academy, and some other Galleries; has held 22 one-man shows of garden pictures, at Dowdeswell's in Bond Street, Greatorex in Grafton Street and since last War at the Bury Gallery, 30 Bury Street, St. James's; Queen Mary has bought a large number of her pictures. A large oil painting Hail Mary, exhibited at The New Gallery, has been engraved and sold in very large numbers. *Publications:* Illustrations to Gardens of England and other Garden Books; also large colour prints of garden subjects. *Address:* 63 Kingsfield Road, Watford, Herts. *T.:* Watford 4271.
[*Died* 17 *Feb.* 1955.

PARSONS, Hon. Geoffry Lawrence; *b.* 1874; *s.* of 4th Earl of Rosse; *m.* 1911, Margaret Betty (*d.* 1952), *e. d.* of Sir J. E. Gladstone, 4th Bt. *Educ.:* Winchester; Balliol College, Oxford, M.A. J.P. County of Southampton, 1919; A.M.Inst.C.E.; M.I.N.A.; Chairman The Parsons Marine Steam Turbine Co., Ltd., Wallsend-on-Tyne. Prime Warden, Worshipful Company of Shipwrights, 1951; Chm. Gardner's Trust for the Blind. *Publication:* (edited) Scientific Papers and Addresses of the Hon. Sir Charles A. Parsons, 1935. *Address:* Womersley Park, Doncaster, Yorks. *T.:* Wentbridge 282. *Clubs:* Athenæum; Northern Counties (Newcastle upon Tyne). [*Died* 13 *May* 1956.

PARSONS, Col. Sir John; *see* Parsons, Sir P. J.

PARSONS, Sir John Herbert, Kt., *cr.* 1922; C.B.E. 1919; F.R.S. 1921; M.B., B.S., D.Sc. (Lond.), Hon. D.Sc. (Bristol); F.R.C.S.; Hon. LL.D. Edin., 1927; Consulting Surgeon, Royal London Ophthalmic Hospital; Consulting Ophthalmic Surgeon, University College Hospital; Hon. Fellow and Past President, Royal Society of Medicine, 1936; Fellow of University College, London; temp. Col., A.M.S.; Member of Departmental Committee on Sight Tests, Board of Trade, 1910; on Factory Lighting, Home Office, 1913; on Causes and Prevention of Blindness, Ministry of Health, 1920; Glass-workers Cataract Committee, Royal Society, 1906; Advisory Medical Council, Air Ministry, 1919; Advisory Medical Council, Admiralty, 1922; Member of Medical Research Council, 1928-32; President, Illuminating Engineering Society, 1921; *b.* 1868. *Publications:* The Pathology of the Eye, 4 vols.; Diseases of the Eye, 10th edition, 1942; Elementary Ophthalmic Optics, 1901; Introduction to the Study of Colour Vision, 2nd edition, 1924; Mind and the Nation, 1918; Introduction to the Theory of Perception, 1927; etc. *Address:* 26 Bryanston Square, W.1. *T.:* Ambassador 0672. *Club:* Athenæum. [*Died* 7 *Oct.* 1957.

PARSONS, Col. Sir (Percy) John, Kt., *cr.* 1945; C.B.E. 1936; E.D.; J.P.; *b.* 26 Dec. 1881; 2nd *s.* of J. Salmon-Parsons, Weston-super-Mare, Somerset; *m.* 1st, 1930, Edith Mina Kemp (*d.* 1930); no *c.*; 2nd, 1947, Joyce Louise Donald. *Educ.:* privately. In firm of Shuttleworth & Co., Mincing Lane, 1898-1903; Bartleet & Co. Ltd., Colombo, tea and general brokers, 1903-51, retd., 1951. Colombo Town Guard, 1914; machine gun officer, 1915; Ceylon Garrison Artillery, 1917-36, in command from 1932; C.D.F. Reserve, 1936. *Recreations:* fishing, golf. *Address:* Millbrook House, Castle Cary, Somerset. *Clubs:* Colombo (Colombo), etc.
[*Died* 16 *Nov.* 1954.

PARSONS, Colonel William Forster, C.M.G. 1919; D.S.O. 1917; retired (late R.A.); *b.* 11 June 1879; *s.* of late Frederic James Parsons; *m.* Phyllis Blanche, *d.* of late General W. S. Pratt, C.B.; one *d.* *Educ.:* Harrow; R.M.A., Woolwich. 2nd Lieutenant R.A., 1898; served European War, 1914-18 (despatches three times, C.M.G., D.S.O., Officier Légion d'Honneur); Colonel, 1922; retired 1925. *Address:* 41 Prince's Court, Brompton Road, S.W.3. [*Died* 5 *Oct.* 1959.

PARSONS, Engineer Rear-Admiral William Roskilly, C.B.E. 1918; retired, 1920; *b.* 1865; *s.* of Rev. W. Parsons; *m.* Di Kedslie (*d.* 1947) *e. d.* of J. W. Watson, R.N.; no *c.* *Educ.:* private; R.N.E. College, Devonport; R.N. College, Greenwich. Served in H.M.S. Boomerang, Australian Fleet, 1891-94; specially promoted in 1904 to Engr.-Commander after serving with Admiralty Boiler Committee in H.M.S. Medea; specially promoted to Engr.-Captain for service on the Dover Patrol, 1917; promoted to Engr.-Rear-Admiral after duty as Head of Submarine Mining Inspection Dept., Admiralty, 1920. *Recreations:* sailing, tennis. *Address:* St. Margaret's, Emsworth, Hants. *T.A.:* St. Margaret's, Emsworth. *T.:* Emsworth 158. *Club:* Emsworth Sailing (Emsworth). [*Died* 16 *July* 1954.

PARSONS-SMITH, Basil Thomas, M.D., F.R.C.P.; Consulting Physician to the National Heart Hospital since 1948; *b.* 30 Aug. 1882; *s.* of Samuel Parsons-Smith, M.D., J.P.; *m.* 1910, Marguerite Ida, *d.* of Sir David Burnett, 1st Bt.; one *s.* one *d.* *Educ.:* Sir Roger Manwood's Gram. Sch., Sandwich; London Univ. M.D.Lond., 1909; F.R.C.P.Lond., 1929. Formerly House Phys. and Casualty Officer, St. Thomas's Hosp.; Anaesthetist London Throat Hosp.; Asst. Phys. Nat. Heart Hosp. and Dean of the Med. Sch. Med. Off. i/c Red Cross Convales. Home for Officers, 1915. Commnd. R.A.M.C., 1916; Med. Off. i/c Artillery Trg. Sch.,

PARSONS, Rt. Rev. Edward Lambe, D.D., LLD. See page xxx.

Aldershot, 1916; attached Field Amb. and Med. Off. Gloucester Regt. France, 1917; Heart Specialist: Convales. Depot, Cayeux, 1917-18; Mil. Hosp., Colchester, 1918-19; Min. of Pensions, 1919. Fell. Roy. Soc. Med. (Ex-Pres. Clin. Sect.); Fell. Med. Soc. Lond.; Fell. (Ex-Pres.) Hunterian Soc.; Mem. Cardiac Soc. of Gt. Brit. and Ire. St. Cyres Lectr., Nat. Heart Hosp., 1936; Lumleian Lectr., R.C.P., 1950. O.St.J. 1945. *Publications:* Intermittent Pulse, 1914 (Hunterian Medal); Cardiac Failure, 1934 (Hunterian Soc. Oration); Cardiology—Old and New, 1952 (Presidential Address Hunterian Soc.). Contrib. Jl. R.A.M.C. and other med. jls. *Address:* 23 Harley St., W.1. *T.:* Langham 2267; Tadworth Cottage, Tadworth, Surrey. *T.:* Tadworth 3264. *Clubs:* Athenæum; Walton Heath Golf. [*Died* 3 *Sept*. 1954.

PARTINGTON, Rev. Canon E. F. E.; *see* Edge-Partington.

PARTINGTON, Wilfred; Author and Journalist; *b.* 4 Nov. 1888; *m.* 1st, 1919; one *d.*; 2nd, 1947. *Educ.:* Ludlow Gram. Sch., etc. Sub-editorships, Birmingham, London, 1907-12; Assistant Editor, Bombay Gazette, 1912-14; Army service, 1914-15 and 1917-18; Editor, The Bookman's Journal, 1919-31; broadcast Talks, 1929-30; wrote the Rare Book Section of the American Bookman, 1931-33; ed. for Hazell's the Dickens and Famous Novels Series, research, and contributor to daily Press, 1933-39; secret War Service, 1939-42. *Publications:* Echoes of the Eighties, 1921; Smoke Rings and Roundelays, 1924; The Private Letter-Books of Sir Walter Scott, 1930; Sir Walter's Post-Bag, 1932; The Waverley Pageant, 1932, and Famous Stories of Five Centuries, 1934 (with Hugh Walpole); Forging Ahead, 1939 (U.S.A.); Thomas James Wise in the Original Cloth, 1947; several pamphlets, including The Identity of Mr. Slum, 1937 (identifying the Dickens character); and Charles Dibdin, 1944; much bibliographical work. *Recreations:* friendship, walking, talking, books, manuscripts, paintings, and objets d'art. *Address:* 12 Denmark Avenue, Wimbledon, S.W.19. *T.:* Wimbledon 2495. [*Died* 2 *April* 1955.

PARTON, Cyril John; Senior and Chief Registrar in Bankruptcy since 1949; *b.* 29 Nov. 1880; *s.* of G. A. and E. E. Parton; *m.* 1907, Katharine Ann Habberfield-Short; one *s.* three *d.* *Educ.:* Rugby School; University College, Oxford. Barrister-at-Law; called to the Bar, 1904; Registrar in Bankruptcy, 1936. *Recreations:* golf, and, until 1936, cricket. *Address:* Ebbsfleet, Ashley Road, Epsom. *T.:* Epsom 1207. [*Died* 22 *Nov.* 1953.

PARTRIDGE, Col. Sydney George, C.M.G. 1919; C.B.E. 1918; *b.* 1881; *e. s.* of Arthur Partridge, formerly of Painswick, Gloucester; *m.* 1912, Elsie, *d.* of Judson Mills; one *s.* three *d.* War Office, 1901-14 (Secretariat); served European War, France, Aug. 1914 to May 1919 (C.M.G., C.B.E., Chevalier of Legion of Honour, despatches 7 times); acting Deputy Controller of Information, Dept. of Controller-Gen. of Civil Aviation, 1919; Member of Standing Committee for Public Carriage Licences; Metropolitan Police Staff, New Scotland Yard, S.W., 1920-1928; appointed by Secretary of State Member of Committee to enquire into organisation of New Scotland Yard, 1927; retired on pension, 1928. *Publication:* Prisoners' Progress, 1935. *Address:* Meadfoot House, Torquay. *T.:* Torquay 3349. [*Died* 8 *Jan.* 1957.

PASCAL, Gabriel; Film Producer; *b.* Arad, Hungary, 4 June 1894. Boyhood years spent in Hungary and Italy. Sent to study agriculture, Nat. Economy Coll. Berlin; joined a theatrical stock company in Hamburg; two yrs. Mem. Imperial Hofburg Theatre, Vienna. Joined Hungarian Army, fighting against Russia, European War, 1914-18, ending as Capt. of a hussar cavalry regt. After the war, produced several silent films in Italy; then joined with Robert Reinert, dir. of UFA, to produce, co-direct and play lead in Popoli Morituri; made films in France and Germany, 1925-30; formed partnership with Prof. Max Reinhardt, 1930; but latter withdrew; continued venture alone, producing 12 films, last of which was Franz Lehar musical comedy, Frederica. Visited America, 1932, and subsequently Italy, Egypt, India; returned to England, 1935, making several quota films for British Paramount; produced: Pygmalion, 1938; Major Barbara, 1941; Cæsar and Cleopatra, 1944; returned to America, 1950; produced Androcles and the Lion for RKO Radio distribution, 1951. *Address:* RKO Studios, Los Angeles, Calif., U.S.A.; 1 Princes St., Cavendish Sq., W.1. *T.:* Mayfair 6832. [*Died* 6 *July* 1954.

PASCHALIS, Neoptolemus, O.B.E. 1937; Q.C. 1931; Solicitor-General, Cyprus, 1927-1940; Chairman of the Debt Settlement Board, Cyprus, 1940; *b.* 17 Feb. 1880; *s.* of Paschalis Constantinides, Advocate, and Helen Hava; *m.* Catherine Papadopoulos; one *s.* *Educ.:* Pancypriot Gymnasium, Nicosia; University of Athens; Middle Temple. Called English Bar, Middle Temple, 1902; journalist and Special Correspondent of the Athenian daily Hestia in London, 1899-1902; private practice as an advocate in Cyprus, 1903-27; Member of the Greek-Christian Board of Education, 1914-29; Member of the Legislative Council of Cyprus, 1916-21; Member of the Cyprus Deputations to England in 1918-19 and 1920; Acting Attorney-General on twelve occasions, 1927-38; Official Member of the Legislative Council on two occasions, 1928-29; Official Member of the Executive Council on eleven occasions, 1927-38. *Publication:* pamphlet entitled Facts and Figures about Cyprus. *Recreations:* golf, bridge. *Address:* P.O. Box 409, Nicosia, Cyprus. *T.A.:* Paschalis, Nicosia. *Club:* Nicosia (Nicosia). [*Died* 28 *Nov.* 1946.

PASSANT, Ernest James, C.M.G. 1953; M.A.; *b.* 12 March 1890; *s.* of late James Passant and late Elizabeth Ponting; *m.* 1925, Audrey Barrow; two *d.* *Educ.:* Dean Close School, Cheltenham; Downing Coll., Cambridge (Scholar). 1st in Hist. Tripos, Part I, 1910, and Part II, 1911; Members' Prize for English Essay, 1910; Lightfoot Scholar, 1914; Fellow and Lecturer in History, Sidney Sussex Coll., 1919-46; Univ. Lecturer in Fac. of Hist., 1926-46; Junior Proctor, 1925-26; Sec. of Fac. Bd. of Hist. and mem. of Gen. Bd. of Faculties; served in Dept. of Foreign Office, 1939-41; Naval Intelligence Div., Admiralty, 1941-45; Research Dept., Foreign Office (Head of German Section and Dep. Director), 1945-1946; Director of Research and Librarian and Keeper of the Papers, Foreign Office, 1946-55; Hon. Fellow of Sidney Sussex Coll., June 1946. *Publications:* Chapter in Cambridge Mediaeval History on Effects of Crusades on Western Europe, 1926; The Problem of Austria (Oxford pamphlets on world affairs), 1945; edited and wrote for official publications, 1942-46; (with others) A Short History of Germany, 1815-1945. *Address:* Crofter's Close, Little Milton, Oxford. *T.:* Great Milton 309. *Club:* Union Society (Cambridge). [*Died* 18 *Jan.* 1959.

PASSINGHAM, Col. Augustus M. O. A.; *see* Anwyl-Passingham.

PASTERNAK, Boris; poet and author; *b.* Moscow, 1890; *e. s.* of Leonid Pasternak, painter, and Rosa Kaufman-Pasternak, musician. *Educ.:* a Moscow high school; Moscow Univ. (law); Marburg Univ. (philosophy). During European War, 1914-18, worked in factory in Urals; after the Revolution worked in Library of the Commissariat for Education. Awarded but declined the Nobel Prize for Literature,

1958. *Publications: poetry:* Twin in the Clouds, 1912-14; Above the Barriers, 1916; My Sister, Life, 1917; Themes and Variations, 1923; The Year 1905, 1927; Lieutenant Schmidt, 1927; Spectorsky, 1932; Second Birth, 1932; collected verse (publ. Russia), 1933; In Early Trains, 1942; *prose works:* Five short stories, and Safe Conduct (an autobiographical sketch), 1931 (four of the short stories and Safe Conduct in English under title Collected Prose Works, 1945); Dr. Zhivago (Eng. trans., 1958); Essay in Autobiography (Eng. trans., 1959); (posthumous) Poems, 1955-59 (Eng. trans., 1960). *Relevant publication* (Ed. Cecil Hemley): Noonday I (Eng. trans., 1959) (includes short novel, The Last Summer). *Address:* Peredelkino, near Moscow, U.S.S.R.
[*Died* 30 *May* 1960.

PATERSON, Albert Rutherford, C.M.G. 1938; M.B., Ch.B. (Glasg.), D.P.H. (Camb.), D.T.M.&H. (Camb.); Colonial Medical Service; late Director of Medical Services, Kenya Colony; *b.* 1885; *s.* of late D. S. Paterson, Crieff, Scotland; *m.* 1931, Madeleine Ruth Alice, *y. d.* of late Paul von Bleichert of Leipzig; three *s.* one *d.* *Educ.:* High School, Glasgow; University of Glasgow. House Surgeon and House Physician, Glasgow Royal Infirmary; Resident Physician, Ruchill Fever Hospital, Glasgow; House Surgeon, Glasgow Maternity Hospital; joined West African Medical Staff, 1914; served with the Forces in West Africa (Cameroon Campaign), 1914-15, and in East Africa, 1916-18; transferred to East African Medical Service and appointed Chief Sanitation Officer, East African Protectorate, 1920. Served on Makerere College Council, 1938. *Publications:* various papers on Public Health subjects. *Address:* P.O. Box 24909, Karen, Nairobi, Kenya. *T.:* Karen 241. *Club:* Nairobi.
[*Died* 26 *Aug.* 1959.

PATERSON, George McLeod, C.B.E. 1939; B.A. (Cantab.); M.Inst.N.A.; Naval Architect, Cunard White Star Ltd., 1924-50; *b.* 1 April 1891; *s.* of Robert Ormiston Paterson; *m.* 1916, Grace Emily Muriel O'Callaghan; one *s.* *Educ.:* Cheltenham College; Pembroke College, Cambridge. Apprentice with John Brown and Co. Ltd., Clydebank, 1913-15; Temporary Asst. Constructor D.N.C. Dept. Admiralty, 1915-19; joined Naval Architects Dept., Cunard S.S.Co. Ltd., 1919; Asst. Naval Architect, 1924. *Recreation:* golf. *Address:* Westleigh, Montpelier, Weston-super-Mare. *Club:* Hawks (Cambridge).
[*Died* 29 *Nov.* 1953.

PATERSON, John Waugh, B.Sc., Ph.D.; *b.* 1869; *s.* of John Paterson, Skirling Mains, Peeblesshire; *m.* 1901, Agnes, *d.* of William Smith, Garrarie, Wigtownshire; six *s.* one *d.* *Educ.:* Edinburgh High School and Univ.; Göttingen; Leipsig, where he graduated with honours in Economics, Chemistry, and Agriculture. Free life member of the Highland and Agricultural Society and of the Royal Agricultural Society of England; for eight years Professor of Chemistry at the West of Scotland Agricultural College; Experimentalist to the Victorian Department of Agriculture, 1911; Professor of Agriculture in the University of Western Australia, 1913-34; Vice-Chancellor, 1918-21. *Publications:* Science in Agriculture (5th edn.), 1952 (trans. Serbo-Croat, 1954); Nature in Farming (6th edn.), 1951; Agriculture (Encyclopædia); numerous scientific papers on agricultural topics; translated Agricultural Botany (Frank). *Address:* Bilgoman Road, Glen Forrest, Western Australia.
[*Died* 5 *June* 1958.

PATERSON, Stronach, C.M.G. 1955; Company Director, New Zealand; *b.* Dunedin, N.Z., 24 Oct. 1886; *s.* of Alexander Stronach and Jean Paterson; *m.* 1913, Dorothy Lever; one *s.* two *d.* *Educ.:* Otago Boys' High School; Otago University. Joined A. S. Paterson & Co. Ltd., 1908; N.Z. Government Representative, Dairy Board, London, 1926-27; Director: Timaru Milling Co. Ltd., 1924, 1933-40 and 1954-; Distributors Ltd., 1933-37; Salmond & Spraggon Ltd., 1943-47; Bank of New Zealand, 1945-1951; South British Insurance Co. Ltd., 1938-; Golden Bay Cement Co. Ltd., 1941-, and other companies; Chairman of Directors: J. B. MacEwan & Co. Ltd.; MacEwans Machinery Ltd., 1941-47; Bond's Hosiery Mills (N.Z.) Ltd., 1935-; Gear Meat Co. Ltd., 1938-; Wholesale Trading Co. Ltd., 1946-; A. S. Paterson & Co. Ltd., 1948-. Consul for Denmark in New Zealand, 1932-. Vice-Pres. Fedn. of Chambers of Commerce of British Empire, 1947-53. Chancellor of the Priory in N.Z. of the Ven. Order of St. John of Jerusalem, 1955. Knight of Dannebrog, 1947; K.G.St.J. 1955. *Recreations:* tennis, golf, shooting, fishing. *Address:* G.P.O. Box 490, Wellington, New Zealand. *T.:* Wellington 70499. *Clubs:* Queen's (London); Dunedin (N.Z.); Canterbury (Christchurch); Wellesley (Wellington); Northern (Auckland).
[*Died* 11 *May* 1957.

PATERSON, Sir William, Kt., *cr.* 1944; Founder of The Paterson Engineering Company Limited; *b.* 5 Aug. 1874; *s.* of James Paterson, Rosslyn, Midlothian; *m.* Dorothy Isabel Steedman; one *d.* *Educ.:* Heriot-Watt College, Edinburgh. Founded the Paterson Engineering Co. Ltd. in 1902. *Address:* East Burnham Well, Farnham Royal, Bucks. *T.:* Farnham Common 189. *Club:* Junior Carlton. [*Died* 9 *Aug.* 1956.

PATERSON, William G. R., O.B.E. 1939; LL.D. Glasgow, 1944; B.Sc., N.D.A. (Hons.); F.R.S.E.; retd. 1944; Farmer; former Principal and Prof. of Agriculture, West of Scotland Agricultural College, Glasgow (1911-44); *b.* Buckrigg, Beattock, Dumfriesshire, 4 Dec. 1878; 7th *s.* of James Paterson, farmer, Buckrigg, and Mary Ann Rogerson; *m.* 1909; four *d.* *Educ.:* Kirkpatrick Juxta and Dumgree Public Schools; Moffat Academy; Edinburgh University; Glasgow University; West of Scotland Agricultural Coll. Asst. (Junior) to Principal in West of Scotland Agricultural Coll., 1905; Senior Asst. 1907; Extension Instructor and Organiser for the County of Dumfries, 1908; Hon. Member of Highland and Agricultural Society of Scotland in recognition of services to Agriculture and Allied interests, 1934. *Publications:* Farm Crops, 4 vols. (editor); author of numerous college bulletins and articles in the Highland and Agricultural Society Transactions, also in the Scottish Journal of Agriculture and the Agricultural Press, the Journal of the Ministry of Agriculture. *Address:* Buckrigg, Beattock, Dumfriesshire. *T.:* Beattock 28.
[*Died* 1 *Sept.* 1954.

PATON, Vice-Adm. William Douglas, C.B. 1927; D.S.O. 1917; M.V.O. 1908; 3rd *s.* of Major James Paton, Crailing, Jedburgh; *b.* 13 Aug. 1874; *m.* Gladys, *d.* of late H. W. Teschemaher, New Zealand; two *d.* Entered Navy, 1888; Commander, 1907; Capt. 1915; Rear-Adm. 1925; Vice-Adm., retired, 1930; served River Gambia, 1894 (medal, clasp); European War, 1914-17 (promoted Capt., D.S.O.); retired list, 1928. *Address:* Prickets Hatch, Nutley, Sussex. [*Died* 18 *Jan.* 1952.

PATRICK, Sir Neil J. K. C.; *see* Cochran-Patrick.

PATTEN, Rev. John Alexander, M.A. (Edin.); M.C.; Historian British and Foreign Bible Society since 1946; *b.* Rock, nr. Alnwick, 31 May 1883; *s.* of late Robert William Patten; *m.* Elsie Mary, *d.* of late Edward Lewis, J.P., Northampton; one *s.* one *d.* *Educ.:* Edinburgh University; Yorkshire Independent College, Bradford. Minister of Seacombe Congregational Church, Cheshire, 1910-14; served as chaplain in France, 1915-19 (despatches, M.C.); Minister of Tacket Street Congregational Church, Ipswich, 1919-29; Chairman of Suffolk Congregational Union, 1928; Minister of

Emmanuel Congregational Church, Dulwich, 1929-32; Editorial Sec., British and Foreign Bible Soc., 1932-48. *Publications:* Simon Peter's Ordination Day, 1915; The Decoration of the Cross, 1918; Faces through the Mist, 1924; Sir Walter Scott: A Character Study, 1931; The Martyr Church and its Book (part author), 1935; Salute to Tindale, 1936; The Unclouded Face, 1938; These Remarkable Men, 1945; John Smith's Book, 1948; and fifteen Popular Reports of Bible Society. *Recreations:* walking and reading. *Address:* Mill Burn, Bamburgh, Northumberland. *T.:* Bamburgh 15. [*Died* 9 *Feb.* 1952.

PATTENSON, Arthur Eric Tylden, C.S.I. 1939; *b.* 15 Nov. 1888; *m.* 1914, Dorothy Margaret, *e. d.* of John Alexander McIver, I.S.O. Joined Indian State Railways, 1908; Member (Traffic) Railway Board Government of India, 1935; Manager, London Railway Bureau, 1939-41. *Address:* Holme Cottage, West Horsley, Surrey. [*Died* 16 *Oct.* 1955.

PATTERSON, Robert Porter, D.S.M. (U.S.) 1945; D.S.C. (U.S.) 1918; *b.* Glen Falls, New York, 12 Feb. 1891: *s.* of Charles R. Patterson and Lodice E. Porter; *m.* 1920, Margaret T. Winchester; one *s.* three *d.* *Educ.:* Union College, Schenectady, N.Y. (A.B. 1912); Harvard Law School (LL.B. 1915). Admitted to New York Bar, 1915; served European War in France, 1918 (wounded, D.S.C.); Judge of United States District Court, Southern District of New York, 1930; Judge U.S. Circuit Court of Appeals for the Second Circuit, 1939; Assistant Secretary of War, July 1940; Under-Secretary of War, Dec. 1940; Secretary of War, United States, 1945 47. Pres. Bar Assoc. of City of New York, 1948-50; Chairman Exec. Cttee. of Cttee. for Marshall Plan, 1947-48. President: Freedom House; New York Soc. Military and Naval Officers World Wars; Practising Law Institute; Member: Century Assoc., Harvard Law School Assoc., Board of Trustees of Union College, Downtown Assoc. *Address:* Cold Spring, New York; 1 Wall Street, New York, U.S.A. *Clubs:* Harvard, Lawyers (New York). [*Died* 22 *Jan.* 1952.

PATTERSON, Admiral Sir Wilfrid Rupert, K.C.B., *cr.* 1947 (C.B. 1941); C.V.O. 1937; C.B.E. 1946; Director of Axia Fans, Ltd., 21 Pall Mall, since 1951 and Vent-Axia, since 1953; *b.* 20 Nov. 1893; *s.* of W. R. Patterson, Belfast; *m.* 1923, Maureen, *d.* of James Mahon, Belfast and New York; one *s.* one *d.* Joined Royal Navy, 1906; Admiral 1949; retd., 1950. *Address:* Northern Bank, Donegall Square, Belfast. *Clubs:* United Service; Royal North of Ireland Yacht (Cultra, Belfast). [*Died* 15 *Dec.* 1954.

PATTESON, John Coleridge, C.M.G. 1946; European General Manager, Canadian Pacific Railway since 1936; Director Canadian Pacific Steamships Ltd.; *b.* London, Ontario, 5 Dec. 1896; *s.* of Godfroy B. Patteson, Ottawa; *m.* 1921, Mary Nesbitt, *yr. d.* of late Herbert Ashley, Portsmouth, Hants; three *d.* *Educ.:* Ridley Coll.; Royal Military Coll. of Canada. Served European War, 1916-18. In Transportation, New York, 1920; Philadelphia, 1928, Chicago, 1934, Toronto, 1935, London, 1936. On loan to British Ministry of Supply, 1940-44. Member International Olympic Committee. *Address:* 62 Trafalgar Square, W.C.2. *Club:* Marlborough-Windham. [*Died* 10 *Jan.* 1954.

PATTINSON, Air Marshal Sir Lawrence Arthur, K.B.E., *cr.* 1945; C.B. 1938; D.S.O. 1919; M.C.; D.F.C., R.A.F. retd.; *b.* 8 Oct. 1890; *s.* of late H. L. Pattinson of Lowlynn, Beal, Northumberland, and late Mrs. H. P. R. Coode, Floriston Hall, Wixoe, nr. Halstead, Essex; *m.* 1923, Mabel Copeland, *e. d.* of late Col. William Capper, C.V.O.; one *s.* one *d.* *Educ.:* Rugby; Wesley College, Melbourne, Australia; Jesus College, Cambridge, M.A. 2nd Class Honours Historical Tripos, LL.B. 2nd Lieutenant 5th Durham Light Infantry T.F. 1914: seconded to R.F.C. 1915; proceeded to France with No. 11 Squadron as Pilot, 25 July 1915; Flight Commander and Temporary Captain, Oct. 1915; M.C. 1916; Squadron Commander and Temporary Major, 1916; proceeded to France in command of 57 Squadron, Dec. 1916; returned to Home Establishment, Nov. 1917; proceeded to France in command of 99 Squadron (Independent Force R.A.F.), May 1918 (D.F.C., despatches); assumed command of 41st Wing Independent Force, Oct. 1918, as temporary Lieut.-Col. (D.S.O.); Squadron Leader R.A.F., 1919; Wing Commander, 1922; Staff College, Camberley, 1922; Air Staff, H.Q. Royal Air Force, India, 1926-30; Group Captain, 1930; A.D.C. to the King, 1933-34; Deputy Director of Organisation, Air Ministry, 1930-34; Air Commodore, 1934; Air Officer Commanding Armament Group, Eastchurch, 1934-37; Air Vice-Marshal, 1937; Air Officer Commanding No. 23 (Training) Group, 1937-40; Air Officer Comdg.-in-Chief Flying Training Command, 1940-41; retired list, 1941; recalled to Active List, Oct. 1942, as Head of R.A.F. Training Mission to the Chinese Air Force. *Publication:* The History of 99 Squadron, R.A.F. *Recreations:* shooting, fishing. *Address:* Salkeld Hall, Little Salkeld, Penrith, Cumberland. *T.:* Langwathby 224. *Clubs:* United Service, Flyfishers'. [*Died* 28 *March* 1955.

PATTINSON, Sir Robert, Kt., *cr.* 1934; D.L., J.P.; Chairman Kesteven County Council since 1934; Chairman of the Witham Catchment Area Board; *b.* 1872; *s.* of William Pattinson, J.P., Ruskington; *m.* 1895, Catharine Lucy, *d.* of Henry Pratt, Lincoln; two *s.* one *d.* A Director of Pattinson & Co. Ltd.; M.P. (L.) Grantham Division of Kesteven and Rutlandshire, 1922-23; Sheriff of Lincolnshire, 1941. *Address:* The Fosse House, Lincoln. *Clubs:* National Liberal; City and County (Lincoln). [*Died* 2 *Dec.* 1954.

PATTON, Arnold Gordon, C.I.E. 1943; *b.* 2 Dec. 1892; *m.* 1st, 1916, Dorothy (marriage dissolved, 1934), *d.* of S. B. Bennett, Friern Barnet; 2nd, 1934, Coral Ogilvie (*d.* 1946), *d.* of late Dr. John Gordon, Aberdeen. *Educ.:* City of London School; St. John's College, Cambridge (B.A.). Entered Indian Civil Service, 1916; Secretary to Government of Assam, Finance and Revenue Departments, 1937-47. *Address:* 8 Elvaston Place, S.W.7. *Club:* East India and Sports. [*Died* 27 *April* 1960.

PATTON, Walter Scott, M.B., Ch.B. (Edin.): Major I.M.S. (retired); Dutton Memorial Professor of Entomology, Liverpool University and Liverpool School of Tropical Medicine, 1927-37; Professor Emeritus since 1938; *b.* 7 Oct. 1876; *s.* of late William Patton, J.P., Scott's Burn, Landour, N.W.P., India; *m.* 1906, Edith Mary, 2nd *d.* of late Rev. H. F. S. Gurney, Vicar Stoke St. Gregory, Somerset; five *s.* *Educ.:* Stoke's School, Mussoorie, India; Edinburgh and Marburg Universities. Resident Surgeon, Royal Maternity Hospital, Edinburgh, 1901; entered Indian Medical Service, 1902; Aden Boundary Commission operations, 1903-1904; special duty investigating etiology Kala-azar and Oriental Sore, 1905-7, 1912-14; Bacteriological Department, I.M.S., 1908-21; assistant director and director, King Institute Preventive Medicine. Madras, 1908-14: entomologist, Mesopotamian Expeditionary Force, 1917; director, Pasteur Institute, Southern India, 1919-21: lecturer, Medical Entomology, Edinburgh University, 1921-26; in charge Kala-azar Commission, Royal Society, North China, 1925-26; member, Psychological Association Great Britain and Ireland; Membre Correspondant Société Pathologie Exotique, 1908. *Publications:* Text-book of Medical Entomology.

1913 (jointly); Mycetoma, Parasites, Rabies, Undulant Fever, Encyclopædia Medica; The Blood-sucking Muscidæ in Practice of Medicine in the Tropics, Vol. I., Byam and Archibald (jointly); Insects, Ticks, Mites and Venomous Animals of Medical and Veterinary Importance, Part I., Medical (jointly); Part II., Public Health. *Address:* Wayside, 2 Mill Street, Torrington, N. Devon. [*Died* 23 *May* 1960.

PATTULLO, Hon. Thomas Dufferin, Q.C. (Can.); LL.D.; *b.* 19 Jan 1873; *s.* of George Robson Pattullo and Mary Rounds; *m.* 1899, Lillian, *d.* of O Reidemaster, Toledo, Ohio; one *d.* *Educ.:* High School, Woodstock, Ont. Secretary, Yukon Commission, 1897-98; Assistant Gold Commissioner, three years; Member, Dawson City Council; Past Alderman and Mayor of Prince Rupert; elected to British Columbia Legislature, 1916, 1920, 1924, 1928, 1933, and 1937; Minister of Lands, 1916-28; Leader of the Opposition, 1928-33; Prime Minister and President of the Council, Province of British Columbia, Parliament Buildings, Victoria, B.C., 1933-41; edited Galt Reformer, 1897; conducted general brokerage and financial business in Dawson and Rupert. *Address:* 951 Beach Drive, Victoria, B.C., Canada. [*Died* 29 *March* 1956.

PAUL, Sir (Charles) Norman, Kt., *cr.* 1938; M.B., Ch.M. (Syd.); F.R.A.C.P.; Dermatologist; *b.* 6 March 1883; *s.* of late John Paul, Wolseley Road, Point Piper, Sydney; *m.* 1914, Louie Millicent, *d.* of James Harris Morell, Sydney. *Educ.:* Sydney Grammar School; Univ. of Sydney. President Sydney Hospital; Hon. Consulting Dermatologist, Sydney Hospital and Royal Alexandra Hospital for Children (Sydney). Formerly Vice-Chairman of the Hospitals' Commission of New South Wales; formerly Hon. Major Military Forces of Commonwealth of Australia, A.A.M.C.; Vice-President St. John's Ambulance Association, New South Wales Centre. Hon. Member Brit. Assoc. of Dermatology. *Publications:* The Influence of Sunlight in the production of Cancer of the Skin, 1917; Cutaneous Neoplasms, 1933. *Address:* 143 Macquarie Street, Sydney, N.S.W., Australia. *Clubs:* Australian, Royal Sydney Golf (Sydney). [*Died* 25 *May* 1959.

PAUL, Elliot Harold; author; *b.* Malden, Mass., 13 Feb. 1891; *s.* of Howard Henry and Lucy Paul; *m.* five times. *Educ.:* High School, Malden; Maine University. Served European War, Sergeant, 317th Field Signal Battalion, A.E.F., 1914-18. Sec. Mass. Soldiers' and Sailors' Commission, 1919-21. Lit. editor, Chicago Tribune, Paris Edn., 1925, 1926; co-editor transition (international review), 1927, 1928; Lit. editor, New York Herald, Paris Edn., 1930. *Publications:* works include: Indelible (novel), 1922; Impromptu, 1923; Low Run Tide, 1928; Life and Death of a Spanish Town, 1937; Stars and Stripes Forever, 1939; (with Luis Quintanilla) All the Brave, 1939; Rhapsody in Blue (screen-play), 1946; Linden on the Saugus Branch, 1947; Ghost Town on the Yellowstone, 1948; My Old Kentucky Home, 1948; Springtime in Paris, 1950; Desperate Scenery, 1950. (Co-author) The Last Time I Saw Paris, 1942 (publ. in Gt. Brit. under title A Narrow Street). Films: Summer in December, 1945; Springtime in Paris, 1950; Desperate Scenery, 1955. *Address:* c/o Random House, Inc., 457 Madison Avenue, New York 22, U.S.A.; c/o Pearn Pollinger & Higham Ltd., 76 Dean St., Soho, W.1. [*Died* 7 *April* 1958.

PAUL, Sir (George) Graham, Kt., *cr.* 1943; Justice of Appeal, Appeal Court for Basutoland, the Bechuanaland Protectorate and Swaziland, 1955; *b.* 15 Nov. 1887; *e. s.* of late George Brodie Paul, of Friarton Grove, Dundee, and Pitpointie, Angus, and of Isabella Graham; *m.* 1916, Margaret Ann Alison (*d.* 1951), *e. d.* of Rev. Thomas Little, B.D., Lanark; no *c.*; 1952, Mary Featonby Branecka, *y. d.* of late Walter Saville, Entumein, Zululand, and of Mrs. Saville, Northridge House, Durban. *Educ.:* Clifton Bank School and the Univ., St. Andrews (M.A.); Edinburgh Univ. (LL.B.). Scots Bar, 1910; Nigerian Bar, 1914; Nigerian Land Contingent, 1914-17; Nominated Member Nigerian Council, 1920-23; Nominated Member Nigerian Legislative Council, 1923-33; Extraordinary Member Nigerian Legislative Council, 1933; Member ABA Commission of Enquiry, 1930; Puisne Judge, Nigeria, 1933; Chief Justice of Sierra Leone, 1939-45; Chief Justice, Tanganyika Territory, 1945-51; retd., 1951. *Publications:* Ed. Nigeria Law Reports, 1933-39. *Recreations:* golf, lawn tennis, played hockey for Scotland, 1910-12. *Address:* Flat No. 11, Northridge House, Northridge Rd., Durban, Natal, South Africa. *Clubs:* Constitutional; Royal Edinburgh Burgess Golfing Society. [*Died* 22 *Jan.* 1960.

PAUL, Sir Harisankar, Kt., *cr.* 1930; M.L.C.; Governing Director of firm of Butto Kristo Paul and Co., Druggists; *b.* Calcutta, 10 April 1888; *s.* of Butto Kristo Paul; *m.* 1st, 1906 (wife *d.* 1915), *d.* of Rai Bahadur Dr. Haridhan Dutt; one *s.*; 2nd, 1918; three *s.* one *d.* *Educ.:* University and Presidency College, Calcutta. Mem. Bengal Legislative Council, 1933-37, and again returned, to Bengal Legislative Assembly, 1937. Chairman or Director of numerous companies, etc. Mayor of Calcutta, 1936. *Address:* 1 & 3 Bonfield Lane, Calcutta, India. [*Died* 18 *June* 1951.

PAUL, Lieut.-Col. John William Balfour, D.S.O. 1919; Marchmont Herald since 1939; *b.* 1873; *s.* of late Sir J. Balfour Paul, K.C.V.O.; *m.* 1908, Muriel Cassells Monteith, M.B.E. 1939; three *s.* *Educ.:* Sedbergh. Was tea-planting in Ceylon; Lieut.-Colonel Ceylon Mounted Rifles (Res.); member of Queen's Bodyguard for Scotland (Royal Company of Archers); served in S. African War, lost arm (Queen's medal 6 clasps); European War (D.S.O.); Falkland Pursuivant, 1927-39; O. St. J.; Colonial Aux. Service Decoration; Jubilee and Coronation Medals, 1937, and; 1953 Defence Medal. V.L. Midlothian, 1951; County Commissioner, Boy Scouts, Midlothian, since 1930. Order of Polonia Restituta. *Address:* 14 Belgrave Crescent, Edinburgh, 4. *Club:* New (Edinburgh). [*Died* 3 *April* 1957.

PAUL, Sir Norman; *see* Paul, Sir C. N.

PAUL, Engineer-Rear-Admiral Oliver Richard, C.B.E. 1919; R.N. retd.; *b.* 1868. Was Engineer-Overseer for Scotland; served European War, 1914-19 (despatches, C.B.E.). *Address:* c/o Dr. J. E. Stevens, 127 Trinity Road, S.W.17. [*Died* 28 *Jan.* 1955.

PAUL, Capt. Sir Robert Joshua, 5th Bt. of Paulville, Carlow, *cr.* 1794; *b.* 6 June 1883; *s.* of 4th Bt. and Richenda Juliet (*d.* 1933), *d.* of H. E. Gurney, Nutwood, Surrey; *m.* 1919, Eveline Alice Wanda, O.B.E., *d.* of late Count Habdank Gorkiewicz, Warsaw, Poland; one *d.*; *S.* father, 1912. *Educ.:* Repton; Trinity College, Cambridge. Entered Egyptian Civil Service, 1906; served France, 1914, and with Egyptian Expeditionary Force, 1915 (despatches, croix de guerre); commanded Arab Gendarmerie, Aleppo province, Syria, 1919. *Heir:* *b.* Ven. William Edmund Jeffrey Paul, *b.* 23 Sept. 1885. *Address:* Ballyglan, Waterford, Ireland. [*Died* 9 *July* 1955.

PAUL, Maj.-Gen. Walter Reginald, C.B.E. 1919; *b.* 28 April 1882; *s.* of late Charles Paul, Clifton; *m.* 1911, Eileen, *d.* of late Colonel J. W. H. Potts, R.H.A. of New Court, Athlone, Ireland; three *d.* *Educ.:* Clifton; R.M.A., Woolwich. 2nd Lieut., R.F.A., 1900; Assistant Superintendent of Experiments, 1913; Assistant Director of Artillery, War Office, 1922; Member Ordnance

Committee, 1924; Director of Artillery, India, 1928-31; Deputy Master General of the Ordnance in India, 1931-35; retired pay, 1935; served European War, 1914-19 (despatches, C.B.E.). *Address:* Firhill, Totland Bay, I. of W. *T.:* Freshwater 355. [*Died* 8 *Jan.* 1953.

PAULET, Major Charles Standish, M.V.O. 1917; late Warwickshire Imperial Yeomanry; *b.* Oct. 1873; *e. s.* of late Col. Charles William Paulet, of Wellesborne, and Susan Amelia Georgina, 4th *d.* of William Standish Standish, of Duxbury; *heir-pres.* to 16th Marquess of Winchester; *m.* 1901, Lilian, *d.* of Major W. T. E. Fosbery; one *s.* two *d.* Served S.A., 1900-1 (medal 4 clasps); Order of the Rising Sun, Japan; Order of the Crown of Italy. *Address:* Brookhill, Ballyhogue, Co. Wexford, Ireland. [*Died* 18 *Sept.* 1953.

PAWAN, Joseph Lennox; Government Bacteriologist, Trinidad; served as a consultant, to W.H.O. of United Nations, on Rabies; *b.* Trinidad, B.W.I. 6 Sept. 1887. *Educ.:* St. Mary's Coll., Trinidad; Edinburgh University (M.B., Ch.B.); University College, London (D.P.H.); Germany. *Publications:* A new Medium for the differentiation of B. Coli in water analysis; The Type of Tubercle Bacillus in Human Sputa in cases of pulmonary tuberculosis in Trinidad; A comparative study of Sodium Citrate and Tartrate in the differentiation of B. Coli in water analysis; some aspects of the Colon Group of Organisms with special reference to the Water Supplies of Trinidad; An Outbreak of Rabies in Trinidad without history of bites and with symptoms of an Acute Ascending Myelitis; A Further Account of the Trinidad Outbreak of Acute Rabic-Myelitis—Histology of the Experimental Disease; The Serum Calcium of the Inhabitants of Trinidad; The transmission of paralytic rabies in Trinidad by the vampire bat (Desmodus rotundus murinus); Rabies in the vampire bat with special reference to the clinical course and the latency of infection. *Recreations:* tennis, swimming. *Address:* Government Bacteriological Laboratory, Port-of-Spain, Trinidad, B W.I. [*Died* 3 *Nov.* 1957.

PAWSON, Ven. Wilfrid Denys, M.A.; Archdeacon of Lindisfarne and Vicar of Eglingham since 1956; *b.* 26 Nov. 1905; s. of late Rev. Arnold Pawson, M.A., and late Susanna Felkin Pawson (*née* Chandler); *m.* 1932, Mary Elizabeth, *d.* of Dr. John Anderson, Pitlochry, Perthshire; one *s.* four *d.* *Educ.:* R.N. College, Osborne; R.N. College, Dartmouth; Jesus College, Cambridge. B.A. (Cantab.) 1928; M.A. 1932. Asst. Curate, St. Mary's, Barnsley, Yorks., 1929-34; Vicar of: Dodworth, Nr. Barnsley, 1934-38; Heckmondwike, 1938-1946; Brighouse, 1946-51; Rector of St. Mary's, Broughty Ferry, 1951-56; Canon of St. Paul's Cathedral, Dundee, and Synod Clerk of Diocese of Brechin, 1952-56. *Recreation:* golf. *Address:* Eglingham Vicarage, Nr. Alnwick, Northumberland. *T.:* Powburn 250. [*Died* 24 *Dec.* 1959.

PAXTON, Air Vice-Marshal Sir Anthony (Lauderdale), K.B.E., *cr.* 1950 (C.B.E. 1943); C.B. 1947; D.F.C. 1921; R.A.F.; *b.* 7 August 1896; *s.* of late James Thompson Tighe Paxton and late Beatrice Paxton; *m.* 1924, Phyllis Joan Bradford; two *s.* *Educ.:* Dulwich College. After leaving school lived in Mexico, cattle ranching. Joined R.F.C. in Vancouver, B.C., 1916; 2nd Lt. R.F.C. 1917; served in France, 1918, with R.F.C. and R.A.F. as pilot (despatches); permanent commission R.A.F. 1919; served in Egypt, Iraq, 1920-1924; U.K. 1925-34; Iraq, 1935; U.K., 1936-40; Director of Air Training, Canada, 1941-43; Senior Air Staff Officer, H.Q., Flying Training Command, 1943-45; A.O.C. No. 85 Group, 1945-46, A.O.C. No. 2 Group, 1946-47, Senior Air Staff Officer, Air H.Q., British Air Forces of Occupation (Germany), 1947; Director-General of Personnel, Air Ministry, 1947-49; retired from R.A.F., 1950. Commander Order of the Crown (Belgium). *Address:* No. 3 The Green, Barrowfield, Hove, 4, Sussex. *T.:* Brighton 57000. *Club:* R.A.F. [*Died* 25 *Sept.* 1957.

PAYNE, Vice-Adm. Christopher Russell, C.B.E 1919; *b.* 18 Sept. 1874; *s.* of Rev. S. W. Payne, LL.D., R.N.; *m.* 1921, Dorothy, *d.* of late Sir Arthur Whinney, K.B.E.; four *d.* *Educ.:* H.M.S. Britannia. Served European War, 1914-18; commanded H.M.S. Vindictive, 1914-15; Head of Signal Section Admiralty War Staff, 1916-17; commanded H.M.S. Suffolk, 1917-19, and acted as British S.N.O. Vladivostock with the rank of Commodore 2nd class (Commander Legion of Honour, 1918, Order of Rising Sun, Japan, 3rd class, 1919); commanded H.M.S. Vernon, 1920-22; H.M.S. Malaya, 1922-23; A.D.C. to the King, 1922-23; retired list, 1925. *Recreations:* usual. *Club:* Army and Navy. [*Died* 15 *Feb.* 1952.

PEACOCK, Colonel Pryce, C.M.G. 1919; R.M. Artillery (retired); *b.* 1868; *s.* of Rev. Ralph Peacock. *Educ.:* St. Columba's College, Rathfarnham. Served European War, 1914-19 (C.M.G., Officer of Order of Crown of Belgium, Croix de Guerre, Belgium). *Address:* 4 Tongdean Avenue, Hove. *Club:* United Service. [*Died* 24 *July* 1956.

PEACOCK, Sir Thomas, Kt. 1956; C.B.E. 1942; J.P.; *e. s.* of late Robert Peacock, Cotton Hall, nr. Chester. Mem. of Council Nat. Farmers' Union since 1934; Pres. 1939. 1940 and 1941; Member Milk Marketing Board for N.W. Region, 1944- (Vice-Chairman of Board, 1949; Chairman of Board, 1952-58); member of Cheshire County Council, 1931-45; member Cheshire County War Agricultural Committee; member Red Cross Agricultural Fund Committee, 1940; Chairman Chester Farmers Ltd. since 1924. Chairman XV International Dairy Congress, London, June 1959; Vice-Pres. Internat. Dairy Federation. Farmed all his life in Cheshire. *Address:* Dilwen, Whitchurch Road, Christleton, Chester. *T.:* Chester 35287. *Club:* Farmers'. [*Died* 19 *Aug.* 1959.

PEACOCK, Sir Walter, K.C.V.O., *cr.* 1924 (C.V.O. 1916; M.V.O. 1911); *b.* 24 May 1871; *s.* of late Right Hon. Sir Barnes Peacock; *m.* 1927, Irene Cynthia Humphreys (Author of Biographies of H.M. Queen Elizabeth II and Field Marshal the Viscount Montgomery of Alamein; T.R.H. Prince Charles and Princess Anne: An Authoritative Account; The Adventure of Cooking; Cooking is Exciting; Beating Austerity in the Kitchen); *d.* of late Lieut.-Colonel Thomas Augustus Le Mesurier. *Educ.:* Eton; Trinity College, Cambridge. Called to Bar, Inner Temple, 1894; Hon. A.R.I.B.A.; Resident Councillor and Keeper of the Records of the Duchy of Cornwall, 1908-30; Treasurer to Prince of Wales, 1910-15; Member of Prince of Wales' Council, 1910-1930; Member of Royal Fine Art Commission, 1930-34. *Address:* c/o Martin's Bank, Curzon Street, W.1. [*Died* 24 *Feb.* 1956.

PEAKE, Sir Charles (Brinsley Pemberton), G.C.M.G. 1956 (K.C.M.G., 1948; C.M.G. 1941); M.C.; *b.* 1897; *o. s.* of Col. W. P. Peake, Hildenborough, Kent; *m.* 1926, Catherine, *e. d.* of late W. G. Knight, C.I.E.; four *s.* *Educ.:* Wyggeston School, Leicester; Magdalen College, Oxford (B.A. 1921). Served in army, 1914-18, Capt. Leicestershire Regt. (M.C., despatches); Capt. P.A.O. Leicestershire Yeomanry, 1919-29; entered Diplomatic Service, 1922; 3rd Secretary, 1922; 2nd Secretary, 1925; 1st Secretary, 1934; Counsellor of Embassy, 1939; Head of News Department of Foreign Office, and Chief Press Adviser, Ministry of Information, 1939; temporarily attached to Viscount Halifax as Personal Assistant in Washington, 1941; British Representative to the French

National Committee, 1942-44; Political Adviser to the Supreme Commander, Allied Expeditionary Force, 1944-45; Consul-General at Tangier, 1945-46; British Ambassador at Belgrade, 1946-51; British Ambassador at Athens, 1951-57, retired. Has served in Sofia, Constantinople, Tokyo, Berne and Paris; British Plenipotentiary at Paris Conference on Tangier, 1945; Principal British Delegate to International Conference on the Danube, Belgrade, 1948. Assistant Missioner, Magdalen College Mission, 1921. Knight Grand Cross, Royal Order of King George I (Greece). *Recreations:* rowing and archæology. *Address:* 61 Eaton Terrace, S.W.1. *Clubs:* Brooks's, Pratt's, Travellers'. [*Died* 10 *April* 1958.

PEARCE, Right Hon. Sir George (Foster), K.C.V.O., *cr.* 1927; P.C. 1921; J.P.; Member Commonwealth Parliament of Australia, 1901-38; *b.* Mount Barker, S. Australia, 14 Jan. 1870; *s.* of James and Jane Pearce; *m.* 1897, Eliza Maude (*d.* 1947), *d.* of A. J. Barrett; two *s.* two *d.* *Educ.:* Public School, Redhill, South Australia. Began life as a carpenter and joiner; went to W. Australia, 1892; began public life by joining in organising trades unions and political associations; joined in the rush to newly discovered goldfields, Coolgardie, tramping from Perth, 400 miles, 1894; unsuccessful, returned to coast; head of various labour organisations; President, Trade Union Congress, 1899; elected Labour Councillor, Subiaco Municipality; a member of executive of Federal League, W.A., 1900; contested Legislative Council; Labour candidate, Federal Senate, first election; re-elected, 1906, 1913, 1914-1919, 1925 and 1931; a member of Executive, Parliamentary Labour Party; elected Chairman of Committees, Commonwealth Senate, 1907; Acting Prime Minister, 1916; Minister for Defence, 1908-9, 1910-13, 1914-21 and 1931-34; Minister for Home and Territories, 1921-26; Minister for External Affairs and Minister controlling Territories, 1934-37; Vice-President of the Federal Executive Council, 1926-29; Leader of Opposition in Federal Senate, 1929-31; Member of Commonwealth Grants Commission, 1939; Chairman Defence Business Board, 1940; Member Imperial Conference, 1911; became a member of National Party, 1916; re-elected to first Senate vacancy in West Australia, Dec. 1919, Dec. 1925, and Dec. 1931; visited Britain, 1919, to take control demobilisation Australian troops; signed Peace Treaty with Austria at St. Germains as representative of Australia; represented Australia at the Washington Conference for the Limitation of Armaments, 1921-22; Leader of Australian Delegation, League of Nations Assembly, Geneva, Sept. 1927; Commander Legion of Honour, 1924. *Publications:* From Carpenter to Cabinet, 1951; articles on The Trades Hall, Australian Review of Reviews, 1905; Free Trade from Labour Standpoint, in Free Trade Journal, 1904. *Recreations:* walking, bowls, golf. *Address:* Kingsley, 4 Drake Street, Elwood, Victoria, Australia. [*Died* 24 *June* 1952.

PEARCE, Seward, C.B. 1934; C.B.E. 1925; *b.* 1866; *s.* of James Pearce, Southampton; *m.* 1894, Winifred Williams; one *d.* *Educ.:* Southampton. Admitted a solicitor, 1889; joined Treasury Solicitor's Department, 1892; Assistant Director of Public Prosecutions, 1921-33; Instructor at law, Metropolitan Police College, 1934-35. *Address:* 6 Bedford Road, W.4. *T.:* Chiswick 1978. [*Died* 17 *Dec.* 1951.

PEARCE-SEROCOLD, Oswald, C.M.G. 1916; V.D.; D.L., J.P.; *b.* 24 July 1865; *e. s.* of Charles Pearce-Serocold, Taplow Hill, Bucks; *m.* 1901, Gwendolyn, *d.* of Charles Combe of Cobham Park, Surrey; two *s.* one *d.* *Educ.:* Eton; Trinity College, Cambridge; B.A. 1886. Lt.-Col. 1st V.B. Royal Berks Regt. 1902-6; Bt. Col. 4th Royal Berks Regt. 1910-16; served European War in Flanders and France, 1915-16 (despatches twice, C.M.G.). *Address:* 11 Boyn Hill Avenue, Maidenhead. [*Died* 7 *May* 1951.

PEARS, Charles, R.O.I.; President, Society of Marine Artists; *b.* 9 Sept. 1873; *m.* 1st, 1897, Miriam (*d.* 1931); three *s.*; 2nd, 1933, Mrs. D. H. Griffiths, *d.* of late Col. H. G. Kennard, C.B.E. *Educ.:* East Hardwick; Pomfret College. Official naval artist War of 1914-18; Painter of many pictures of the Navy in the War, for Imperial War Museum; several large pictures commissioned for records of Second World War; Illustrator of Two Years before the Mast; Masefield's Saltwater Ballads; The complete works of Dickens; writer of many sea articles illustrated by himself; painter of many posters for Empire Marketing Board, Underground Railway, etc. *Publications:* From the Thames to the Seine; From the Thames to the Netherlands; South Coast Cruising; Yachting on the Sunshine Coast; Going Foreign. *Recreation:* single-handed sailing. *Address:* Studio Polvarth, St. Mawes, Cornwall. *Club:* Royal Cruising. [*Died* 28 *Jan.* 1958.

PEARSE, Albert William, J.P.; F.R.G.S.; Managing Director of The Pastoral Review and Graziers' Record, Melbourne and Sydney; Liveryman of Hon. Company of Master Mariners and Freeman of the City of London; President and Founder and Vice-Pres., Ancient Mariners League, Sydney; Member Master Mariners Assoc. of Australia; Vice-Pres. Church of England Homes, Burwood; Vice-President Toc H (N.S.W.); Vice-President, Mission to Seamen, Sydney; Vice-President, N.S.W. Bush Brotherhood; Vice-President Dr. Barnardo's Homes; *b.* Hornsey, London, 6 April 1857; *s.* of L. B. Pearse, London; *m.* 1889, Emily Mary (*d.* 1949), *d.* of J. T. Mills, of Cookham, Bucks; two *s.* three *d.* (and *y. s.* killed 1918). *Educ.:* Islington Proprietary School; Deal College, Kent. Went to sea as a midshipman, 1875; passed for second and chief mate, and for master in mercantile marine in London; was for some years officer in Royal Mail Steam Packet Co., to West Indies and Brazil; then in Orient S.N. Co.; left sea in 1887; went to New Zealand and was gold mining there until 1891, when he left for Australia, and, with Mr. R. E. N. Twopeny, started The Pastoral Review in 1891; Fellow Royal Empire Society; Chief Commissioner in Egypt, Australian Comforts Fund, 1916-17; Rep. for Federal Gov. of Australia at Congress of Meat Refrigeration, Chicago, 1913, and also for all Meat Works of N.Z. and Austr., Paris, 1903, Chicago, 1913; Rep. Port of London Authority in Australia and N.Z., 1921-37. J.P., N.S.W. and Qld. King's Jubilee Medal, 1935. *Publications:* Our Great Rival (Argentina); Short Illustrated History of Australia's Wool Trade; Failure of State Owned Railways; Letting in Daylight in Frozen Meat Trade; The World's Meat Future, 1913; Recent Travel, 1914; Our Beef Rivals; A Windjammer Prentice, 1924; Windward Ho, 1932; Dawdling through Britain, 1937. *Recreation:* bridge. *Address:* 22 Loftus Street, Sydney, Australia; Empire House, St. Martin's le Grand, E.C. *T.A.:* Woolshed, London; Pastoral, Melbourne. *T.:* BU 1833 Sydney. *Club:* New South Wales (Sydney). [*Died* 12 *July* 1951.

PEARSE, Ronald Livian, A.I.N.A.; lately Editor and Managing Director, The Syren and Shipping; *b.* 1880; *s.* of Livian Francis Pearse; *m.* 1928, Edna Arnott; two *d.* *Educ.:* Thanet College, Margate; Whitgift Grammar School. *Publications:* The Last Survivors of a Glorious Era; A Chronicle of Deep Sea Sailing Ships; numerous articles and stories of the sea and ships. *Address:* 219 Upper Halliford Road, Shepperton, Middlesex. *T.:* Sunbury 3495. [*Died* 1 *May* 1960.

PEARSON, Rev. Andrew Forret Scott, D.Th., D.Litt., F.R.Hist.S.; Professor of Ecclesiastical History and Symbolics, Presbyterian College, Belfast, since

1942; Member Faculty of Theology, Queen's Univ., Belfast; *b.* Tayport, Fife, 25 Dec. 1886; *s.* of John Pearson and Agnes Forret; *m.* 1916, Jean Paxton, *d.* of James Kerr Love, M.D., Glasgow; two *s.* two *d.* *Educ.:* Ferry-Port-on-Craig H.G. School; Universities of St. Andrews, Marburg and Heidelberg. M.A., 1906; B.D., 1910; assisted in departments of Divinity and Church History, St. Mary's College, St. Andrews, 1910-12; studied under Herrmann in Marburg, 1908; under Weiss, Troeltsch and Von Schubert, in Heidelberg, 1910, 1911; awarded Doctorate of Theology, by thesis and examination, Heidelberg, 1911; Licensed by Dundee Presbytery, 1910; assisted ministers of First Charges, Cupar and Hamilton, 1912-14; served as Chaplain to Forces, 1918-20; D.Litt. (Glasgow), 1927; Parish Minister, West Kilbride, 1914-29, external examiner of theses for higher degrees; University of Manchester, 1929, 1951; Prof. of Ecclesiastical History Presbyterian Coll., affiliated to McGill Univ., Montreal, 1929-33; Minister of High Parish, Johnstone, Renfrewshire, 1934-42; Lectured History department, Oxford University, Trinity term, 1936; Special Preacher to Scots Church, Sydney, Australia, for six months from Dec. 1938; preached and lectured in Canada, 1939; Moderator, Presbytery of Paisley, Church of Scotland, 1940; Officiating Chaplain to Forces, 1941. External Examiner in Ecclesiastical History, St. Andrews University, 1946, Aberdeen University, 1948. Royal Historical Society's David Berry gold medal and prize for work on Anglo-Scottish Religious Relations, 1400-1600, 1943; Carey Lecturer, 1947; served in Germany for Christian Reconstruction of Europe Society, 1948 and 1949. *Publications:* Der Aelteste Englische Presbyterianismus, 1912; Thomas Cartwright and Elizabethan Puritanism, 1925; Church and State; Political Aspects of Sixteenth-Century Puritanism, 1928; Judgment, 1939; wrote introductory Chapter of Part 2 Vol. I. of Ekklesia, on the British Free Churches; Tercentenary of Westminster Assembly, 1943; Origins of Irish Presbyterianism, 1948; Alesius and the English Reformation, 1950; articles on Presbyterianism, etc., in Chambers's Encyc., 1950; contributions to Homiletic Review, etc.; conducted correspondence column in Scots Observer, 1928-29. *Recreations:* historical research and motoring. *Address:* 2 College Park, Belfast, N. Ireland. [*Died* 13 *Aug.* 1952.

PEARSON, Charles Child, C.B.E. 1920; was, prior to retirement from active business, sole partner Andrew Callender & Co., 15 Victoria Street, Liverpool, produce and provision importers, agents and brokers; *b.* Waterloo, near Liverpool, 1875; *o. surv. s.* of John Wyse and Caroline Child Pearson, of Waterloo, Liverpool; *m.* Mavis, 2nd *d.* of late William Powell, Allerton, Liverpool. *Educ.:* Cambridge House School, Seaforth; privately. During the European War appointed Official Brokers to Marshal of the Admiralty and other Government Departments; invited by Ministry of Food to join original Food Mission to U.S.A., 1917; Director of Allied Provisions Export Commission, New York; shortly after arrival in U.S.A. proceeded to Washington, D.C., to be in closer touch with Mr. Hoover, the American Food Controller; Director of Purchases of all American Packing House Products (other than fresh meat) for Great Britain and Allies; resident at Washington until end of 1919 as Official Representative of British Ministry of Food; returned Nov. 1919 and assisted Ministry of Food in London and on Continent in advisory capacity; retired to private business, March 1920. *Recreations:* all outdoor sports, music, literature. *Address:* Greenfields, Blundellsands, Liverpool. *T.:* Great Crosby 3283. [*Died* 22 *Nov.* 1955.

PEARSON, Ethel, Lady, D.B.E., *cr.* 1920; President of St. Dunstan's, 1921-47; Vice-Pres., National Institute for Blind; *d.* of William John Fraser, London; *m.* Sir Cyril Arthur Pearson, 1st Bt., G.B.E. (*d.* 1921); one *s.* *Address:* 17 Eresby House, Rutland Gate, S.W.7. *T.:* Kensington 4217. [*Died* 10 *April* 1959.

PEARSON, Sir Herbert Grayhurst, Kt., *cr.* 1931; *b.* 5 Aug. 1878; 2nd *s.* of late Lord Pearson, Edinburgh; *m.* 1905, Anne, 2nd *surv. d.* of late E. Erskine Scott; one *s.* one *d.* *Educ.:* Rugby. Barrister, Inner Temple, 1902, Advocate, High Court, Calcutta, 1902; Judge High Court, Calcutta, 1920-33; Legal Adviser to Secretary of State, India Office, 1933-38. *Address:* Levelis, Bulstrode Way, Gerrards Cross, Bucks. *Club:* Oriental. [*Died* 8 *Nov.* 1958.

PEARSON, James Rae, C.I.E. 1913; *b.* 2 Aug. 1871; *s.* of late David Ritchie Pearson, M.D., of Kensington and Beckley, Sussex, and of Jane, *d.* of late James Rae; *m.* Grace Carlton Crouchley, *y. d.* of Col. D. G. Pitcher, I.A.; two *d.* (one *s.* died on active service, 1944, and one *s.* decd.). *Educ.:* St. Paul's School; Clare College, Cambridge. Entered Indian Civil Service, 1892; Assistant Collector and Joint-Magistrate Muzaffarnagar, Agra, Bulandshahr, Meerut, 1892-1898; Deputy Commissioner, Naini Tal, 1899; Collector Azamgarh, 1902; Budaun, 1906; Meerut, 1910; Member Badshahi Mela Committee, Coronation Durbar, 1911; Officiating Opium Agent, 1917; Inspector-General, Police, and Member, Legislative Council, 1918; Commissioner, Agra, 1919, Meerut, 1922; Officiating Member Board of Revenue, 1922; Commissioner Kumaon, 1924; retired from I.C.S., 1925; Secretary to Government of Fiji for Indian Affairs, and Member of the Executive Council, 1927-32. *Recreation:* golf. *Address:* Auvesque, La Rocque, Jersey, C.I. [*Died* 28 *Aug.* 1951.

PEARSON, Lionel Godfrey, F.R.I.B.A., Partner in firm of Adams, Holden and Pearson, Architects, since 1911; *b.* Liverpool 29 Oct. 1879; *s.* of Rev. S. Pearson; *m.* 1932, Melinda Elizabeth Osborne; one *d.* *Educ.:* Manchester Grammar School. 2 years course at School of Architecture, Liverpool University; came to London in 1901 to office of Prof. E. S. Prior; Assistant to Adams and Holden, 1903-11; served with R.A.M.C. in France, 1914-18; resumed practice, 1919; carried out numerous hospitals including the new Westminster Hospital, Royal Westminster Ophthalmic Hospital, Southend Hospital, etc., and with A. Taylor, F.R.I.B.A. of Bath, the new Mineral Water Hospital, Bath; Member of Departmental Committee of Ministry of Health on Hospital Construction. *Publications:* Foreign Hospitals; Chadwick Lecture, Modern Hospital Planning; Numerous articles in periodicals on hospital details and planning. *Recreations:* sketching, gardening, push cycling. *Address:* University of London, W.C.1. *T.:* Museum 0383. *Club:* Athenæum. [*Died* 19 *March* 1953.

PEARSON, Rev. Marchant; *b.* 1 May 1871; *s.* of Daniel Pearson, Wesleyan Army Chaplain; *m.* Sybil Ruth Arnison (*d.* 1943), Penrith. *Educ.:* Kingswood School, Bath; Wren and Gurney's. B.A. London Univ.; formerly Assistant Science Master at Bradford Grammar School; Deacon, 1901; Priest, 1902; Headmaster of King Alfred's School, Wantage, 1903-11; Ardingly College, 1911-14; Worksop College, Notts, 1915-24; Vicar of Alfriston with Lullington, 1924-32; Rector of St. Paul's, St. Leonards-on-Sea, 1932-42. *Publications:* Notes on Volumetric Analysis; contrib. to the Press. *Recreation:* walking. *Address:* 22 Tennyson Rd., Bognor Regis, Sx. [*Died* 23 *Nov.* 1956.

PEARSON, Lt.-Col. Noel Gervis, D.S.O. 1918; M.C. 1916; late Sherwood Foresters South Wales Borderers and Queen's Westminsters; Engineer Iron Founder; *b.* 30 Sept. 1884; *y. s.* of late Henry John Pearson of Bramcote, Notts, and late Mrs. Pearson, The

Garden House, Ightham, Kent; *m.* 1914, Kathleen Mary (*d.* 1957), 3rd *d.* of late Rev. E. R. J. Nicolls, of Saxelbye Rectory, Leicestershire; two *s.* (and two killed in action, 1939-45 War) one *d.* *Educ.:* Aysgarth; Scarborough; and Charterhouse. Served European War, 1914-1918 (despatches twice, D.S.O., M.C.); High Sheriff, Notts, 1935; Chairman of the Nottingham No. 1 Hospital Management Cttee. *Address:* Bramcote, Notts; Gartland, Nordlands Banen, Norway. *T.:* Beeston 25-4052. *Clubs:* Junior Carlton, Royal Automobile.

[*Died* 26 *Nov.* 1958.

PEARSON, Sir Ralph Sneyd, Kt., *cr.* 1933; C.I.E. 1920; LL.D. (St. Andrews); F.L.S.; *b.* 8 Dec. 1874; *s.* of late Col. G. F. Pearson and Emma, *d.* of John Colvin, late Lieut.-Governor, N.W. Provinces; *m.* Constance H. G. Ommanney (*d.* 1938); two *s.* one *d.* *Educ.:* Royal Indian Engineering College, Coopers Hill, Joined Imperial Forest Service as Assistant Conservator of Forests, 1898; Deputy Conservator, 1906; Conservator, 1922; Forest Economist, Forest Research Institute, Dehra Dun, U.P., India, 1909-25; Director, Forest Product Research Laboratories, Dept. of Scientific and Industrial Research, 1925-33. *Publications:* Commercial Guide to the Forest Economic Products of India, 1912; A Further Note on the Antiseptic Treatment of Timber, 1922; Note on the Utilisation of Bamboo for Paper Pulp, 1916; Note on the Uses of Rosha Grass; Cymbopogon Martinii, 1916; Commercial Timbers of India, 2 vols. (Pearson and Brown) Government of India, 1932; etc. *Address:* Hazelton House, Thame, Oxon.

[*Died* 8 *Dec.* 1958.

PEARSON, Richard Francis Malachy, C.B.E. 1931; M.Inst.C.E.; *b.* 1872; *s.* of Richard Pearson; *m.* 1905, Kathleen Lucille (*d.* 1920), *e. d.* of Lionel Philip Payne-Gallwey; one *s.* one *d.* *Educ.:* Queen's College, Cork. Entered the Works Department of the Admiralty, 1899; served at Admiralty and Dockyards at home and abroad; Member of British Naval Mission to Greece, 1914-17 (4th class of the Order of Redeemer); attached to Air Ministry, 1918, as Assistant Director of Marine Works; Assistant Director of Works and Buildings, 1924; Deputy Director of Works and Buildings, 1928-33; retired. *Address:* c/o The Standard Bank of South Africa, Durban, Natal.

[*Died* 22 *Nov.* 1956.

PEARSON, Sir Robert Barclay, Kt., *cr.* 1944; M.A. Oxon; Hon. Fellow, Brasenose College, Oxford; *b.* 20 Nov. 1871; *y. s.* of David A. Pearson, Johnston, Laurencekirk, Kincardineshire; *m.* 1898, Margaret Ethel, *d.* of late James Stewart, Coatbridge, Lanarkshire; three *s.* two *d.* *Educ.:* Loretto; Brasenose College, Oxford. Advocate of Scottish Bar, 1898; Secretary of Royal Commission on Physical Training (Scotland), 1902-03; Legal Secretary to Lord Advocate, 1904-05; Conservative candidate for Kincardineshire, 1909-10; Member of London Stock Exchange, 1913; Member of Committee, 1929; Deputy Chairman, 1933; Chairman, 1936-47; retd. 1947. Member of Queen's Body Guard for Scotland (Royal Company of Archers). *Address:* 44 Bryanston Court, George Street, W.1. *Club:* Athenæum. [*Died* 12 *Feb.* 1954.

PEARSON, Thomas William, C.B. 1941; D.S.O. 1918; D.L.; *b.* 1872; *m.* 1897, Ada Isabel, *d.* of David Williams; two *d.* *Educ.:* Mill Hill School. Served European War, 1915-18 (despatches, D.S.O., Brevet Lieut.-Colonel). *Recreations:* Rugby football (thirteen times capped for Wales), cricket, golf, hockey. *Address:* Glenlyn, 7 Fields Road, Newport, Mon. *T.:* Newport 4513. *Club:* Monmouthshire County. [*Died* 12 *Sept.* 1957.

PEARSON, Colonel Walter Bagot, C.M.G. 1918; C.B.E. 1919; *b.* 19 Nov. 1872; 2nd *s.* of A. G. B. Pearson, Abbots Brow, Kirkby Lonsdale, Westmorland. *Educ.:* Dover Coll.; Liège University; King William's Coll., Isle of Man; R. Military Coll., Sandhurst. 2nd Lt. Lancashire Fusiliers, 1892; Lieut. 1893; Capt. 1899; Major, 1910; Lt.-Col., 1916; temp. Col. on the Staff, 1917; temp. Brig.-Gen., 1919; Col. 1920; served in India, 1892-98; in Egypt, 1898; took part in Soudan Campaign, 1898 (Queen's medal, Khedive's decoration and clasp); in Cretan Insurrection, 1898-99; South African Campaign, 1900-2, with Regt. and after on Staff as A.P.M. and as Staff Capt. Intelligence (Queen's S.A. medal and clasps, King's S.A. medal and clasps); served in Ireland, 1907-10; in India, 1910-14; on Staff as A.P.M. to 3rd Lahore Division at King George's Coronation Durbar, Delhi, 1911 (decoration); after outbreak of European War served at Aden and throughout Gallipoli Campaign, after in France with regt., 1914-17; on various Staff appointments as D.A.Q.M.G., A.A. and Q.M.G., and Base and District Commandant in France, 1917-20 (Chevalier of the Legion of Honour, C.M.G., C.B.E., 1914-15 Star, war medal and Allied decoration, despatches 5 times); on special duty at G.H.Q. Ireland, 1921-22; Officer-in-charge, Infantry Records, Warwick, 1922-26; retired pay, 1926. *Recreations:* gardening, fishing, shooting. *Address:* The Cottage, Kingsdown, Deal, Kent. *T.:* Kingsdown 94.

[*Died* 29 *March* 1954.

PEARSON, Major Wilfred John, D.S.O. 1918; M.C.; M.A., M.D. (Oxon.); F.R.C.P. (Lond.); retired; *b.* 23 June 1884; *m.* 1909, Charlotte Warrack; two *d.* *Educ.:* Rugby; University College, Oxford; University College Hospital, W.C. Served European War, 1914-18 (despatches, D.S.O.). Formerly Senior Physician, Hospital for Sick Children, Great Ormond St., W.C.; Physician in Charge, Children's Department, University College Hospital, W.C. *Publication:* (with Wyllie) Recent Advances in Diseases of Children (3rd edn.). *Address:* Kerry Cottage, Barton-on-Sea, Hants. [*Died* 27 *June* 1957.

PEART, Colonel Charles Lubé, C.I.E. 1919; Indian Army (retd.); late Adviser in Oriental Languages, Army Dept.; *b.* 2 April 1876; unmarried. *Educ.:* U.S.A.; Castleknock; Sandhurst. Entered Army, 1896; served in China, 1900-1. Relief of Pekin (despatches, medal and clasp); Waziristan, 1901 (medal with clasp); Staff Coll., Camberley, 1910-11; Great War, 1914-19, A.A. and Q.M.G. of a division (despatches twice, C.I.E.); retired 1930. Managing Director, Bengal Potteries, 1930-33. *Address:* Lou Mas de la Forêt, Mont Biron, Nice. *Club:* United Service. [*Died* 14 *Sept.* 1957.

PEASE, Edward R.; Secretary of the Fabian Society, 1890-1913, Hon. Secretary, 1914-38; *b.* 1857; *s.* of Thomas Pease of Westbury, Bristol; *m.* 1889, Marjory, (*d.* 1950), *d.* of Rev. G. Davidson of Perth; two *s.* *Educ.:* home. Entered merchant's office, 1874-78; member of London Stock Exchange, 1880-86; cabinet-maker and trade unionist in Newcastle, 1886-89; founded, with others, the Fabian Society, 1883; member of Executive of Labour Party from its start, 1900-13; a Governor from its foundation of London School of Economics. *Publications:* The Case for Municipal Drink Trade; Fifth Edition of Kirkup's History of Socialism; The History of the Fabian Society; Webb and The Fabian Society in The Webbs and their Work, 1949. *Recreation:* reading. *Address:* The Pendicle, Limpsfield, Surrey. *T.:* Limpsfield Chart 2217. [*Died* 5 *Jan.* 1955.

PEAT, Sir Harry (William Henry), G.B.E., *cr.* 1946 (K.B.E., *cr.* 1920); K.C.V.O. *cr.* 1952; M.A.; F.C.A.; chartered accountant; senior partner Peat, Marwick, Mitchell & Co., chartered accountants, London and other towns in Great Britain, Hong Kong, Japan, Malaya, S. Africa, Kenya and S. Rhodesia, and through associated firms in Canada, U.S.A., France and Belgium; Partner Price, Waterhouse, Peat

& Co., Egypt, India and South America; member of Needlemakers' Company (Master, 1920-21); member of Corporation of City of London, 1915-26; *b.* 4 May 1878; *e. s.* of late Sir William Barclay Peat; *m.* 1906, Alice Evelyn, 3rd *d.* of late Lieut.-Col. Eustace Jameson; two *s.* two *d.* *Educ.:* St. Paul's School; Trinity College, Oxford (played Rugby football for Oxford against Cambridge, 1898). Financial Secretary and Accounting Officer to Ministry of Food, 1917-20, and Financial Secretary (unpaid), 1939-46; Member of the Royal Commission on the Importation of Store Cattle, 1921; and Royal Commission on Food Prices, 1925; Member of Committee on Co-operative Selling in the Coal Industry, 1926; Member of National Mark Committee since 1928; Member of Standard Price Committee under the Wheat Act, 1935; Chairman, Board of Supervision, Pensioners' Savings Scheme, 1936; Chairman of Standard Price Committee under Wheat Act, 1939. *Recreations:* shooting, fishing and golf. *Address:* 11 Ironmonger Lane, E.C.2; Hillside, Bushey, Herts. *T.A.:* care Veritatem, Cent. London. *T.:* Monarch 8888, Bushey Heath 1266. *Clubs:* United University, Gresham, Athenæum. [*Died* 24 *June* 1959.

PECK, Col. Cyrus Wesley, V.C. 1918; D.S.O. 1917; *b.* 26 Apr. 1871; *m.* 1914, Kate E. Chapman, Kinora, Ont.; three *s.* Served European War, 1915-19 (despatches, D.S.O. with bar); member, House of Commons, Canada, 1917-21; member of Provincial Parliament, British Columbia, 1924. *Address:* Sidney, B.C., Canada. [*Died* 27 *Sept.* 1956.

PECK, Air-Marshal Sir Richard Hallam, K.C.B., *cr.* 1943 (C.B. 1941); O.B.E. 1919; *b.* 2 March 1893; *yr. s.* of Richard Edwards Peck; *m.* 1931, Lilian Fay Young; no *c.* *Educ.:* St. Paul's School; Brasenose College, Oxford (M.A.). Assistant Chief of the Air Staff (General), 1940-45; retired, 1946. A Governor of the B.B.C., 1946-49; a Vice-Chairman Nat. Savings Cttee., 1947; Pres. R.A.F. Assoc., 1949; F.R.S.A. *Club:* Army and Navy. [*Died* 12 *Sept.* 1952.

PEDDER, Sir John, K.B.E., *cr.* 1919; C.B. 1913; *b.* 27 Jan. 1869; 2nd *s.* of Rev. John and Harriet Pedder of Lancaster, Durham, and Bath; *m.* 1901, Frances Evelyn (*d.* 1952), *e. d.* of W. Arthur Sharpe, Highgate, N.; two *s.* *Educ.:* Somersetshire Coll., Bath; Bath Coll.; Oriel Coll., Oxford (Scholar). 1st Class Classical Moderations, 1889; 2nd Class Literæ Humaniores, 1891; B.A. 1891; entered Civil Service, 1892; first the Public Record Office, then Local Government Board and in 1895 the Home Office; Assistant Private Secretary to Home Secretaries Sir M. W. Ridley, 1898-1900, and C. T. Ritchie, 1900-2; Private Secretary to Home Secretary A. Akers-Douglas, 1902-4; Principal Assistant Secretary Home Office; retired 1932; Chairman of State Management Districts Council, 1921-32; Secretary and Member of various Departmental Committees; Delegate to International Congress on Alcoholism, The Hague, 1911; British Delegate to International Conference on Relief of Destitute Aliens, Paris, 1912; British Delegate to International Congress on White Slave Traffic, London, 1913; Member of Central Control Board (Liquor Traffic), 1915-21; Member of Royal Commission on Licensing, 1929-31; Officer of the Belgian Order of Leopold, 1919; Director of Watney, Combe, Reid & Co., 1932-49; an editor of Paterson's Licensing Acts, 1934-39. *Recreations:* rowing, lawn tennis, golf, etc. *Address:* Birtley House, Bramley, nr. Guildford, Surrey. *Club:* Athenæum. [*Died* 4 *Sept.* 1956.

PEEBLES, Major Herbert Walter, C.M.G. 1933; D.S.O. 1917; O.B.E. 1925; J.P. Barbados; *b.* 24 Dec. 1877; *s.* of Col. T. Peebles, Devonshire Regt., and Miss Chiappini, Cape Town, S. Africa; *m.* 1st, G. Davies (marriage dissolved 1934), Wrexham; 2nd, 1935, Marcella, *d.* of A. Cameron, Letterwalton, Barcaldine, Argyllshire. *Educ.:* Cheltenham College. Army and Colonial Civil Service; served South African War 2½ years (severely wounded, Queen's medal four clasps, King's medal two clasps); Somaliland Campaign 1903-1904 (medal, two clasps, despatches twice); European War, France, Oct. 1914-Oct. 1917 (despatches four times, Bt. Major, June 1919, D.S.O., O.B.E.); Commissioner and Treasurer of Montserrat, B.W.I., 1922-29; Administrator, St. Vincent, 1929-33; retired, 1933; acting Governor, Windward Islands, May-June 1930. *Address:* Bayleys, Barbados, B.W.I. [*Died* 24 *March* 1955.

PEEL, Hon. (Arthur) George (Villiers), M.A.; Major Bedfordshire Yeomanry; 2nd *s.* of 1st Viscount Peel; *b.* 27 Feb. 1868; *m.* 1906, Lady Agnes Lygon, *d.* of 6th Earl Beauchamp; one *s.* one *d.* *Educ.:* Harrow; New Coll., Oxford. D.L., Warwickshire; formerly Clerk in Treasury; Trustee of Gordon Coll., Khartoum. M.P. Spalding Division of Lincolnshire, 1917-18. Temp. Major Royal Marines, 1915; Head of War Trade Dept., Egypt, 1917; served European War (Gallipoli), 1918 (despatches thrice); Officer of Legion of Honour. *Publications:* The Enemies of England; The Friends of England; The Future of England, 1911; The Tariff Reformers, 1913; The Reign of Sir Edward Carson, 1914; The Private Letters of Sir Robert Peel, 1921; The Financial Crisis of France, 1925; The Economic Impact of America, 1928; The Economic War, 1930; The Economic Policy of France, 1937. *Address:* Blount's Court, Reading. *T.:* Kidmore End 3100. *Club:* Beefsteak. [*Died* 25 *April* 1956.

PEEL, Sir Arthur (Robert), K.C.M.G., *cr.* 1917; *b.* 15 Aug. 1861; *e. s.* of late Rev. Frederick Peel and Adelaide Frances Isabella, 3rd *d.* of 2nd Lord Sudeley; *m.* 1921, Grace, *e. d.* of Alberto Landsberg, Rio de Janeiro. *Educ.:* Eton. Attaché, 1886; appointed Petrograd, 1888; 3rd secy., 1889; Washington, 1891; 2nd secy., 1893; Buenos Ayres, 1894; The Hague, 1896; Lisbon 1900; 1st secretary, 1904; Monte Video, 1905; The Hague, 1906; Consul-General for Island of Crete, 1906; Envoy Extraordinary, and Minister Plenipotentiary at Bangkok, 1909-15; Brazil, 1915-20; Minister Plenipotentiary, Bulgaria, 1920-21. *Address:* Longwood, Torquay. *Club:* Carlton. [*Died* 7 *Oct.* 1952.

PEEL, Lt.-Col. Basil Gerard, C.B.E. 1923; D.S.O. 1916; *b.* 26 Dec. 1881; *s.* of Rev. Edmund Peel; *m.* 1907, Mildred Maud, *d.* of late Colonel W. J. Seaton, Conservator of Forests, Burma; two *s.* one *d.* (and one *s.* decd.). *Educ.:* Marlborough College. 3rd (Militia) Batt. Dorset Regt., 1899-1900; served South African War; 1st Batt. P.A. Somerset Light Infantry, 1900-8; 81st Pioneers, 1908-22; European War, 1914-18; G.S.O. 2, 6th (Poona) Division; captured at Kut-el-Amarah, and prisoner of war in Turkey (D.S.O.; despatches five times); D.A.A.G., Burma Division, 1919-20; D.A.A.G, Western Command, India, 1920-21; D.A.Q.M.G., Malabar Force, 1921-22 (C.B.E.); D.A.A.G., Southern Command, India, 1922-24; Commandant, 1st Bn. 1st Madras Pioneers (K.G.O.), Indian Army, 1924-28; retired 1930. *Address:* Tillington Cottage, Petworth, Sussex. [*Died* 18 *Jan.* 1954.

PEEL, Charles Lawrence Kinloch, C.B. 1944; *b.* 24 Jan. 1883; 2nd *s.* of E. L. Peel, of Liverpool and Bedford. *Educ.:* Bedford School; Balliol College, Oxford (Scholar). Craven Scholar, 1906; passed Higher Division Exam. for Civil Service, 1906, and entered Post Office; Asst. Secretary, 1929; Principal Asst. Secretary, 1939; retired, 1944. *Address:* 19 Park Hill, Ealing, W.5. *T.:* Perivale 3251. [*Died* 27 *April* 1954.

PEEL, Hon. George; *see* Peel, Hon. A. G. V.

PEEL, Colonel Herbert Haworth, C.B.E. 1919; *b.* 1866; *s.* of Frederick Peel of Highlands, East Bergholt; *m.* Monica (*d.* 1938), *d.* of Rev. J. E. Coulson of Long Preston, Yorkshire; two *d.* *Educ.:* Wellington College. Served European War, 1915-19. *Address:* Highlands, East Bergholt, Suffolk. [*Died* 22 *Oct.* 1956.

PEEL, William Croughton; *b.* 18 Oct. 1870; *s.* of Capt. William Henry Peel and Hester A. C. Croughton; *m.* 1894, Muriel Adeline Brudenell, 2nd *d.* of late Admiral Sir Algernon de Horsey, K.C.B.; one *s.* two *d.* *Educ.:* Winchester. 3rd Dragoon Guards, 1890-97; Remount Service, European War; in Home Guard, 1940-42. *Heir:* *s.* Gerard William Ernest Peel [*b.* 1895; *m.* 1921, Edith May, *d.* of F. Archer]. *Address:* Trenant Park, Duloe, Cornwall. *T.A.:* Peel, Sandplace. *T.:* 458 Looe. [*Died* 19 *May* 1957.

PEERS, Sir Charles Reed, Kt., *cr.* 1931; C.B.E. 1924; F.B.A., F.R.I.B.A., Litt.D., D.Litt., D.C.L., M.A.; Honorary Fellow, King's College, Cambridge; a Governor, the Charterhouse; Knight Commander, St. Olaf (Norway); Consulting Architect, York Minster, etc.; *b.* 22 Sept. 1868; *s.* of Rev. William Henry Peers; *m.* 1899, Gertrude Katherine Shepherd; three *s.* *Educ.:* Charterhouse; King's College, Cambridge. Pupil in office of Sir T. G. Jackson, architect, 1893-96; F.S.A., 1901; Architectural Editor, Victoria County Histories, 1903-10; Secretary, Society of Antiquaries, 1908-21; Director 1921-29; President, 1929-34; Inspector of Ancient Monuments, 1910-13, Chief Inspector, 1913-1933; Surveyor Westminster Abbey, 1935-51; Member of Advisory Boards on Ancient Monuments for England, Scotland, and Wales, 1914; Rhind Lecturer in Archæology, Edinburgh, 1922; Member of Royal Commission on Historic Monuments (England), 1921; Cantor Lecturer, Royal Society of Arts, 1926; Trustee British Museum, *ex-officio*, 1929, elected 1933; London Museum, *ex-officio* 1930, elected 1934; Member of Standing Commission on Museums and Galleries, 1931-51; President, International Congress of Prehistoric and Protohistoric Sciences, London, 1932; President Somerset Archæological Society, 1932; Antiquary to Royal Academy, 1933; Seneschal Canterbury Cathedral, 1933; Royal Gold Medallist, R.I.B.A., 1933; Member German Archæological Institute, 1933; Corr. Member Italian Institute of Human Palaeontology, 1933; Gold Medallist, Society of Antiquaries, 1938. *Publications:* Papers on Archæological Subjects in Archæologia, Proceedings of Society of Antiquaries, Antiquaries Journal, and publications of other learned societies. *Recreation:* archæology. *Address:* Woodcote Grove House, Woodcote Park, Coulsdon. *Club:* Athenæum. [*Died* 16 *Nov.* 1952.

PEERS, Edgar Allison, M.A. (Cambridge and London); Hon. LL.D. (Glasgow); Gilmour Professor of Spanish, University of Liverpool; Hon. Lecturer in Portuguese and Catalan; *b.* Leighton Buzzard; *o. s.* of John T. Peers and Jessie Dale, *d.* of late Charles Allison, Hampton Hill; *m.* 1924, Marion Young, Duryard Grange, Exeter. *Educ.:* Dartford Grammar School and abroad; Christ's College, Cambridge (Scholar and Prizeman); 1st Class Medieval and Modern Languages Tripos 1912 (distinction); Winchester Prize, 1912; Harness Prize, 1913; 1st Class Cambridge Teachers' Diploma, 1913 (double distinction) Members' Prize, 1914; Modern Language Master at Mill Hill and Felsted Schools and at Wellington College, 1913-19; Founder and (1918-29) Hon. Secretary Modern Humanities Research Association (President, 1931-32); Founder and Director, Bulletin of Hispanic Studies; University of Liverpool Summer School of Spanish; Institute of Hispanic Studies; Visiting Professor of English Literature, University of Madrid, 1928, 1929; of Modern Comparative Literature, Columbia University, 1929-30; of Spanish, Universities of New Mexico and California, 1930; Lecturer on Bernat Metge Foundation, Barcelona, 1928-1931; Rede Lecturer, Cambridge University 1932; Centennial Lecturer, New York University, 1932; Visiting Professor, Carnegie Endowment for International Peace, 1939; Taylorian Lecturer, Oxford Univ., 1940; Educational Director Hispanic Council, 1943-46; Member and Medallist Hispanic Society of America; Hon. Member Institut d'Estudis Catalans, American Academy of Arts and Sciences, Sigma Delta Pi and Amer. Assoc. of Teachers of Spanish; Corr. Member; Real Academia de Buenas Letras; Argentine Academy of History. *Publications:* Elizabethan Drama and its Mad Folk, 1914; Selected Poems of Alfred de Vigny, 1918; The Origins of French Romanticism (with M. B. Finch), 1920; The Poems of Manuel de Cabanyes, 1922; Book of the Lover and the Beloved, 1923; Rivas and Romanticism in Spain, 1923; Rivas, a Critical Study, 1924; Spanish Mysticism, 1924; El Romanticismo en España, 1924; Art of Contemplation, 1925; Studies in the Influence of Sir Walter Scott in Spain, 1926; Blanquerna, 1926; The Tree of Love, 1926; Studies of the Spanish Mystics, 2 vols. 1927-30; The Book of the Beasts, 1927; Ramon Lull: a Biography, 1929; Spain, a Companion to Spanish Studies (Editor and contributor), 1929; Spain, a Companion to Spanish Travel, 1930; A Book of Spiritual Exercises, 1930; Songs of the Lover and the Beloved, 1931; St. John of the Cross (Rede Lecture), 1932; The Pyrenees, 1932; The Romantics of Spain, 1934; Complete Works of St. John of the Cross (translation), 3 vols., 1934-1935; The Spanish Tragedy, 1936; Catalonia Infelix, 1937; Handbook to the Study and Teaching of Spanish (Editor and contributor), 1938; Our Debt to Spain, 1938; Spain, the Church and the Orders, 1939; History of the Romantic Movement in Spain, 2 vols., 1940 (abridged edition, 1949); Antonio Machado, 1940; Liverpool Studies in Spanish Literature (Editor), 4 vols., 1940-50; The Spanish Dilemma, 1940; Spirit of Flame, 1943; Spain in Eclipse, 1943; Spanish—now, 1944; Complete Works of St. Teresa (translation), 3 vols., 1945; "New" Tongues, 1945; Mother of Carmel, 1945; Fool of Love, 1946; St. John of the Cross and other lectures and addresses, 1946; Behind that Wall, 1947; Poems of St. John of the Cross, 1947; A Critical Anthology of Spanish Verse, 1948; Letters of St. Teresa (translation), 2 vols. 1950; The Mystics of Spain, 1951; Ascent of Mount Sion (translation), 1952; St. Teresa of Jesus and other essays and addresses, 1953; A Handbook to the Life and Times of St. Teresa and St. John of the Cross, 1953; A Skeleton Spanish Grammar, and other educational books. *Address:* The University, Liverpool; 12 Eddisbury Road, West Kirby, Cheshire. *T.:* Hoylake 1145. [*Died* 21 *Dec.* 1952.

PEET, Hubert William; editor, The Friend, the Quaker weekly, 1932-49; *b.* 18 March 1886; *s.* of William Henry and Margaret Peet; *m.* 1910, Edith Mary, *d.* of Rev. Harry Scott; two *s.* two *d.* *Educ.:* Dulwich College. Editorial staff, The Bystander, 1903, Daily Sketch, 1909, Daily News, 1909; editor, Sell's World's Press, 1913-15; during 1916-19, joint editor, The Ploughshare, and Secretary, Friends' Service Committee, and conscientious objector in prison; Secretary, Friends' Literature Committee, 1919-24; Editor, Far and Near Press Bureau, 1924-37. *Address:* 66 Gernon Rd., Letchworth, Herts. *T.:* Letchworth 1056. [*Died* 4 *Jan.* 1951.

PEIRSE; *see* Beresford-Peirse.

PELHAM, Major Hon. Dudley Roger Hugh, D.S.O. 1916; late 10th Hussars; *b.* 5 July 1872; 4th *s.* of 3rd Earl of Yarborough; *m.* 1907, Evelyn Elizabeth, *d.* of laté Montagu R. Waldo Sibthorp of Canwick Hall, Lincoln. *Educ.:* Eton; R.M.C., Sandhurst. Served S. Africa, 1899-1902 (despatches, Queen's medal 4 clasps, King's medal 2 clasps); European War, 1914-19 (D.S.O., despatches); Sheriff of Lincolnshire, 1938. *Address:* The Dower House,

Canwick, Lincoln. *T.:* Lincoln 467. *Clubs:* Cavalry, Naval and Military. [*Died* 13 *Sept.* 1953.

PELHAM-BURN, Brig.-Gen. Henry; *see* Burn.

PELHAM WELBY, Charles Cornwallis Anderson, C.V.O. 1945; *b.* 30 Sept. 1876; 2nd *s.* of late Hon. Evelyn Anderson Pelham; unmarried. *Educ.:* Uppingham. Secretary to Pytchley and Woodland Pytchley Hounds; Agent to The Cardigan, Biggin, Kedleston, Brocklesby and Sandringham Estates. Lt. in Leicestershire Yeomanry; Lt. Special Reserve XI Hussars; Temp. Capt. R.A.F.; A.D.C. in European War to Lord Trenchard and Sir John Salmond. *Address:* South Luffenham Hall, Oakham, Rutland. *T.A.* and *T.:* North Luffenham 234. *Club:* Cavalry. [*Died* 5 *Oct.* 1959.

PELLY, Brig.-Gen. Raymond Theodore, C.B. 1919; C.M.G. 1919; D.S.O. 1916; a Military Knight of Windsor, 1942; late The Loyal (North Lancashire) Regt.; *b.* 30 July 1881; *s.* of late Canon R. P. Pelly, M.A., Vicar of Great Malvern; *m.* 1910, Moriet Elsie Maxwell, *d.* of late Maj.-Gen. A. G. Creagh, C.B.; two *d.* *Educ.:* Ludgrove; Haileybury. Served S. African War (Queen's medal and 4 clasps) in Worcestershire I.Y.; granted commission in the Loyal North Lancashire Regt., and served in this regiment till Nov. 1912, transferring at that date to Special Reserve; emigrated to Canada, 1913, and came over as Major in Princess Patricia's Canadian Light Infantry; served European War, 1914-19; in command of P.P.C.L.I.; 8th Royal Irish Rifles; and 91st Brigade with temp. rank of Brig.-Gen.; Major, Loyal N. Lancs (Regulars), 1918 (despatches 7 times, Bt. Major and Lieut.-Col., D.S.O. and bar, C.M.G., C.B., Croce di Guerra); retired pay, 1921; Commander Order of St. Maurice and St. Lazarus, Italy, 1922. *Recreation:* music. *Address:* Henry VIII Gateway, Windsor Castle. *T.:* Windsor 1363. [*Died* 28 *June* 1952.

PEMBER, Francis William, M.A., D.C.L.; J.P.; *b.* 16 Aug. 1862; *o. surv. s.* of late Edward Henry Pember, M.A., K.C., J.P., of Vicar's Hill, Boldre, Hants; *m.* 1895, Hon. Margaret Bowen (*d.* 1942), *d.* of late Baron Davey of Fernhurst; one *d.* *Educ.:* Harrow; Balliol College, Oxford (Scholar). Fellow of All Souls College, 1884; called to Bar, Lincoln's Inn, 1889; practised as Equity and Parliamentary Draughtsman and Conveyancer; acted from time to time as temporary Assistant Legal Adviser to the Foreign Office; is an Honorary Bencher of Lincoln's Inn; Estates Bursar of All Souls College, 1910-14; Warden of All Souls College, Oxford, 1914-32; Hon. Fellow of All Souls and Balliol Colleges, 1932; a Governor of Harrow School, 1910-44; Vice-Chancellor of the University of Oxford, 1926-29; Officier Légion d'Honneur. *Recreations:* fishing, walking. *Address:* Broncroft Castle, Craven Arms, Shropshire. *T.:* Munslow 3. *Clubs:* Brooks's, United University. [*Died* 19 *Jan.* 1954.

PEMBROKE, 15th Earl of, *cr.* 1551, and 12th Earl of **MONTGOMERY,** *cr.* 1605; **Reginald Herbert,** M.V.O. 1918; Baron Herbert of Caerdiff, 1551; Baron Herbert of Shurland, 1604; Baron Herbert of Lea (U.K.), 1861; Hereditary Grand Visitor of Jesus College, Oxford; present Earl is a direct descendant of 1st Earl; *b.* 8 Sept. 1880; *e. s.* of 14th Earl and Lady Beatrix Louisa Lambton (*d.* 1944), *d.* of 2nd Earl of Durham; *S.* father, 1913; *m.* 1904, Lady Beatrice, C.B.E., *y. d.* of late Lord Alexander Paget; three *s.* one *d.* *Educ.:* Eton; R.M.C., Sandhurst. Major Royal Horse Guards; A.D.C. to General Sir Arthur Paget, Ireland, 1912; served European War, 1914-1917 (despatches); Mayor of Wilton, 1932-1933 and 1933-34. Owner of Wilton House, which contains pictures by Vandyke, Rubens, Sir Joshua Reynolds, etc., and much antique statuary; owns about 60,000 acres. *Recreations:* shooting, hunting, fishing. *Heir:* *s.* Lord Herbert, C.V.O. *Address:* Wilton House, Salisbury. *Clubs:* Turf, Carlton. [*Died* 13 *Jan.* 1960.

PENDLEBURY, Herbert Stringfellow, M.A., M.B., B.C. (Cantab.), F.R.C.S.; retired; Hon. Fellow, late Hon. Treasurer and Hon. Secretary, Royal Society of Medicine; first Hon. Secretary, Association of Surgeons; *b.* Wigan, 1870; *s.* of John Pendlebury, J.P.; *m.* 1st, Lilian Dorothea (*d.* 1921), *d.* of Sir Thomas Lane Devitt, 1st Bt.; 2nd, 1925, Mabel, *d.* of Richard Webb, Wanganui, N.Z. *Educ.:* Pembroke College, Cambridge (Prizeman, Exhibitioner, Scholar; Double First in the Natural Sciences Tripos); St. George's Hospital (University Scholar). Late Demonstrator of Anatomy, St. George's Hospital; Consulting Surgeon, Royal Waterloo Hospital for Children and Women; Consulting Surgeon to the Kensington Dispensary and Children's Hospital; Surgical Staff, St. George's Hospital, S.W.1; Lecturer on Surgery, St. George's Hospital Medical School; Member of Court of Examiners Conjoint Board for England; Examiner in Surgery, University of Cambridge and Society of Apothecaries. *Publications:* various papers to the medical and scientific journals. *Address:* c/o Westminster Bank, 249 Regent Street, W.1. [*Died* 21 *April* 1953.

PENDRED, Loughnan St. Lawrence, C.B.E. 1934; Editor of The Engineer, 1905-46; President Institution of Mechanical Engineers, 1930-31; President Newcomen Society, 1923 and 1930; Past-President Institution of Engineers-in-Charge; Hon. Mem. Inst. Mech.E.; M.I. and S.Inst.; Hon. Member Junior Institution of Engineers; *b.* 1870; 2nd *s.* of late Vaughan Pendred; *m.* 1900, Laura Mary Wildig; two *s.* *Educ.:* private school; Central Institution and Technical College, Finsbury. Served apprenticeship with Davey, Paxman & Co. Ltd., Colchester; improver at the works of Van den Kerchove, Ghent, and the Chemin de Fer de l'Ouest, Paris and Rouen; ordnance works of Sir W. G. Armstrong, Whitworth & Co., at Elswick, 1893-96; sub-editor of The Engineer, 1896. *Recreations:* reading and workshopping. *Address:* 28 Essex Street, Strand, W.C.2. [*Died* 20 *Nov.* 1953.

PENFOLD, Surg. Rear-Adm. Ernest Alfred, D.S.O. 1917; M.B.; R.N. (retd.); *b.* Portsmouth, 1866; *s.* of Alfred Penfold of H.M. Dockyard, Portsmouth; *m.* 1897, Ada, (*d.* 1947), *d.* of Richard Dixon, merchant, City of London, and of Grove Park, Kent; two *s.* two *d.* *Educ.:* Preparatory Schools at Portsmouth and Pembroke; The Grammar School, Portsmouth; Edinburgh University; M.B., C.M. 1889; St. Thomas's Hospital. Passed as Surgeon into the Royal Navy, 1891; Staff Surgeon, 1899; Fleet Surgeon, 1907; Surgeon Commander, 1918; Surgeon Captain, 1919; served in H.M.S. Goldfinch in Australia and New Zealand; with Royal Marines, Plymouth, 1897-99; in H.M.S. Crescent, North America and West Indies; in H.M.S. Aurora and Highflyer, training ships for Naval Cadets; in H.M.S. Terrible, when escort to Prince and Princess of Wales, in India, 1905-6; H.M.S. Hindustan, 1907-12; during the war served in Depot Ship for Destroyer Flotillas and in the Grand Fleet; present at the Battle of Jutland (despatches, recommended for early promotion, D.S.O.); retired list, 1922 (promoted Surg. Rear-Adm.); Order of St. Stanislaus, 2nd Class (with swords). *Publication:* A Battleship in Action, Journal of the Royal Naval Medical Service, Jan. 1917. *Recreations:* country walks, novel reading, gardening, etc. *Address:* Wolsdon House, Antony, Torpoint, Cornwall. *T.:* Torpoint 2148. [*Died* 6 *May* 1956.

PENIAKOFF, Lieut.-Col. Vladimir, D.S.O. 1945; M.C. 1942; Officier de l'ordre de la Couronne avec palme, Belgium, 1947; Croix de Guerre, 1940, avec palme, Belgium, 1947; F.R.G.S.; writer; *b.* 30 March

1897; *s.* of late Dmitri Peniakoff; *m.* 1st, Josette Ceysens (marriage dissolved); two *d.*; 2nd, 1948, Pamela Firth. *Educ.:* St. John's College, Cambridge. *Publication:* Private Army, 1950. *Address:* 31 Cliveden Place, S.W.1. *T.:* Sloane 5844.
[*Died* 15 *May* 1951.

PENLAKE, Richard; *see* Salmon, Percy R.

PENN, Sir Arthur (Horace), G.C.V.O., *cr.* 1953 (K.C.V.O., *cr.* 1949; C.V.O. 1946); M.C.; Groom in Waiting and Extra Equerry to the Queen; also Treasurer to Queen Elizabeth the Queen Mother; *b.* 20 April 1886; *s.* of late William and Constance Penn, Taverham Hall, Norwich; unmarried. *Educ.:* Eton College; Trinity College, Cambridge. Inner Temple, 1910. European War, 1914-18, Grenadier Guards, Adjutant 2nd Bn. (wounded, despatches, M.C., Croix de Guerre). Chairman, King & Shaxson Ltd., billbrokers; Steward of the Courts, Eton College; Groom in Waiting to King George VI, 1937; Extra Equerry, 1940; Acting Private Sec. to Queen Elizabeth the Queen Mother, 1940-1946. Rejoined Grenadier Guards, 1940; Regimental Adjutant, 1941-45. *Address:* Clarence House, S.W.1. *T.:* Whitehall 3141; Sternfield House, Saxmundham, Suffolk. *T.:* Saxmundham 2277. *Club:* Turf.
[*Died* 30 *Dec.* 1960.

PENNEFATHER-EVANS, Brig. Brian, C.I.E. 1946; O.B.E. 1941; M.C. 1918; Retired; *b.* 2 Jan. 1897; *yr. s.* of Lieutenant-Colonel Granville Pennefather-Evans, C.B.E.; *m.* 1st, 1918, Gracie Frances Elizabeth Gaussen; 2nd, 1949, Mary Agnes Kathleen Haynes. *Educ.:* Rossall School; Royal Military Academy, Woolwich. Commissioned R.F.A., 1914, and served European War, 1914-18, France, 1915-18. Transferred Indian Army Ordnance Corps, 1925; Brevet Lieut.-Col., 1935; War of 1939-45: D.O.S. Iraq, 1941-42; Dep. D.O.S. XIV Army, Burma, 1943-45. Brig. (temp.), 1941; Colonel (subst.), 1945; retired, 1947. *Recreations:* tennis, golf, squash. *Address:* Woodcrest, Greytown, Natal, South Africa.
[*Died* 13 *Aug.* 1954.

PENNY, Col. Frederick Septimus, C.M.G. 1916; D.S.O. 1918; M.B. Lond., D.P.H. Lond., M.R.C.S., L.R.C.P., F.R.G.S.; *b.* 4 Dec. 1869; *s.* of William Penny of Crewkerne, Somerset; unmarried. *Educ.:* Crewkerne Grammar School (scholar); King's College, London. Three scholarships, several prizes; Capt. Cricket Eleven; House Surgeon, King's College Hospital; House Surgeon, Sunderland Infirmary, 1896; joined Army Medical Service, 1897; proceeded Sierra Leone, where served in operations, 1898 (medal with clasp); South Africa, 1902; and served in Cape Colony (Queen's medal 2 clasps); India, 1902-1906; travelled and climbed in Kashmir and Baltistan, 1904-5; in England, 1907-10, travelling when on leave in France, Switzerland, Holland, Belgium, and Germany; Hong-Kong, 1910; travelled through Japan, Korea, Manchuria, and China, 1912; returned to England via Philippines, Australia, Tasmania, New Zealand, South Sea Isles, U.S.A. and Canada, 1913; was in Ireland till outbreak European War; served Flanders, Macedonia, and Bulgaria, 1914-19 (despatches four times, promoted Lieut.-Col., and temp. Col., C.M.G., D.S.O.); A.D.M.S., 26th Division, Macedonia, 1917; A.D.M.S. of S. Ireland Division, 1921; D.D.M.S., Gibraltar, 1922; retired pay, 1923; on scientific expedition to Pacific Islands, 1924-25. *Recreations:* travelling, cycling, sailing, skating, etc. *Address:* Anchorage, Netherton Road, Weymouth, Dorset. [*Died* 11 *May* 1955.

PENOYRE, John, C.B.E. 1918; M.A.; Hon. A.R.I.B.A.; Hon. Student of the British School at Athens; Life Member hon. causa Soc. for Promotion of Hellenic Studies; Corresponding Member of the German Archæological Institute; *b.* Clifton on Teme, 10 Feb. 1870; *s.* of Rev. Slade Baker; assumed patronym of Penoyre. *Educ.:* Cheltenham Coll.; Keble Coll., Oxford. Asst. Master Chigwell School, 1896-1900; Oxford University Extension Lecturer (classical art and archæology); Secretary and Librarian of the Society for the Promotion of Hellenic Studies, 1903-36; secretary of the British School of Athens, 1903-19; secretary of the British School at Rome, 1904-12; manager of Lord Roberts' Field Glass Fund, 1915-18; Keeper of the A.R.P. County Medical Stores, Witney, Oxon, 1939-42. *Publications:* Ante Oculos; Articles in Journal of Hellenic Studies, Annual of the British School at Athens, etc. *Address:* Greengates, 2 Hernes Rd., Oxford.
[*Died* 2 *Jan.* 1954.

PENSON, Sir (Thomas) Henry, K.B.E., *cr.* 1918; late Lecturer and Tutor in Modern History and Economics, Pembroke College, Oxford; Lecturer in Economics, Worcester Coll. (resigned 1922); *b.* 27 June 1864; *s.* of late John Whiteman Penson, Oxford (*d.* 1867); *m.* 1897, Sigrid (*d.* 1938), *d.* of late Dr. T. A. Säve, K.V.O., R.N.O., member of the First Chamber of the Swedish Riksdag. *Educ.:* City of London School; Worcester College, Oxford (M.A.). Chairman of the Trade Clearing House (War Trade Department), 1915; Chairman of the War Trade Intelligence Department, 1916-1919; Director of the Intelligence Branch of the British Delegation to the Paris Conference, 1919; a Knight Commander of the Swedish Order of the North Star, 1927. *Publications:* Economics of Everyday Life; Is Germany Prosperous?; Economics of Business Life; articles on various economic subjects contributed to papers and reviews. *Address:* c/o Barclay's Bank Ltd., Notting Hill Gate, W.11. [*Died* 14 *April* 1955.

PENTON, Cyril Frederick; T.D. 1955; *b.* 1886; 2nd *s.* of late Capt. Frederick Thomas Penton, D.L., J.P.; *m.* 1909, Gladys Lane, 4th *d.* of late Canon A. B. Thynne, formerly Vicar of Seend; one *s.* *Educ.:* Eton; Trinity College, Cambridge, M.A., 1908. Called to Bar, Inner Temple, 1912; served European War, 1914-18, with 8th Bn. Royal West Kent Regiment; Major, 1918; joined staff of Treasury Solicitors Department, 1920; transferred to Legal Branch of Board of Education, 1928; Commissioner, Board of Control, 1931; Legal Senior Commissioner until 1952; Hon. Col., 512th (Finsbury Rifles) Light A.A. Regt., R.A. (T.A.), retired 1955. *Recreations:* riding, golf. *Address:* 11 Albion Gate, W.2. *Club:* United Service.
[*Died* 13 *March* 1960.

PENZER, Norman Mosley, Litt.D., M.A., F.S.A., F.R.G.S., F.G.S.; author and Man of Letters; *b.* Mawdesley, Lancs, 30 Sept. 1892; *s.* of late Rev. Seymour Penzer, Vicar of Chapel Royal and Rural Dean of Brighton; *m.* 1950, Dorothy Cecilia, *e. d.* of John Croall Rcriston, Edinburgh. *Educ.:* Marlborough Coll.; Corpus Christi Coll., Cambridge. Commn. in 9th Royal Sussex, 1914; invalided out, 1917; Peace Conference work at War Trade Intelligence Dept.; Federation of British Industries (Intelligence Dept.); founded (with Dr. F. Grenfell Baker) the Richard Burton Memorial Lecture Fund at the Royal Asiatic Society; member of the Royal Asiatic, and the Hakluyt Societies; specialised in Comparative Anthropology, Mythology, Religion, and Folklore. *Publications:* Economic and geological works include—Cotton in British West Africa, 1920; The Tin Resources of the British Empire, 1922; The Mineral Resources of Burma, 1922; Non-Ferrous Metals and other Minerals, 1924, as well as numerous articles to the Encyclopædia Britannica and mining journals; works connected with the Burton Fund—An Annotated Bibliography of Sir Richard F. Burton, 1923; Selected Papers of Sir Richard F. Burton, 1924; The Ocean of Story, or Somadeva's Kathā Sarit Sāgara (Tawney's translation), ten vols., 1924, etc.; Nala and Damayanti, 1926; Travels of Marco

Polo, 1929 (Elizabethan version); Dialogues of Lucian (Tooke), 1930; The Pentamerone of Giambattista Basile (with Benedetto Croce) 2 Vols. 1932; The Harem, 1936; The Book of the Wine-Label, 1947; Poison, Damsels and other Essays, 1951; Paul Storr, the last of the Goldsmiths, 1954; contributor to the Connoisseur and Apollo, of articles on old silver; Editor of Argonaut Press (Sir Francis Drake, 1926, William Dampier, 2 vols., 1927, 1931, Chardin, 1927, Varthema, 1927, Ralegh, 1928; Cabot, 1929; Hamilton, two vols. 1930; Columbus, 1930; Spanish Voyage to Vancouver, 1930; Ralegh's Last Voyage, 1932, etc.); Editor of Library of Impostors (John Daniel, 1926; George Psalmanazar, 1926). *Recreations:* squash racquets, lawn tennis, music, collecting books, silver, furniture and Oriental works of art. *Address:* Oldlands Hall, Fairwarp, Uckfield, Sussex. *T.:* Nutley 12. [*Died* 27 *Nov.* 1960.

PEPLER, Sir George Lionel, Kt., *cr.* 1948; C.B. 1944; P.P.T.P.I.; F.R.I.C.S.; Hon. M.Inst.M.E.; Hon. A.R.I.B.A.; Planning Consultant; Vice-Pres. Instn. of Professional Civil Servants; Pres. Town and Country Planning Summer School; Hon. Pres. Internat. Federation for Housing and Town Planning; Chm. Town Planning Joint Examination Bd.; Member Royal Commission on Common Land; *b.* 24 Feb. 1882; *s.* of Harry Pepler, Somerleyton, Haling Park Road, Croydon; *m.* 1st, 1903, E. Amy (*d.* 1942), *d.* of A. E. Bobbett, solicitor, Bristol; one *s.* two *d.*; 2nd, 1947, Elizabeth E., L.C.C. (Dep.-Chm., 1956-57), *d.* of Eldred Halton, Kensington. *Educ.:* Bootham; Leys School, Cambridge. Articled to W. Hooker; laid out many large estates on Town Planning lines; two Gold Medals, Wolverhampton Model Housing Exhibition, 1908; one Gold Medal, S. Wales Model Housing Exhibition, 1910; Organiser Arterial Road Conferences, Greater London, 1914; Pres. Town Planning Inst., 1919-20 and 1949-50; member S. Wales Regional Survey Committee, 1920; Unhealthy Areas Committee, 1921; Vice-Chairman Aerodromes Advisory Board, 1934, President International Federation for Housing and Town Planning, 1935-38; and 1947-52; Chairman Institution Professional Civil Servants, 1937-1942; Chm. Inter-Allied Cttee. for Physical Planning and Reconstruction, 1942-45; Chief Town Planning Inspector, Ministry of Health, 1919-41; Chief Technical Adviser, Ministry of Town and Country Planning, 1943-46; Deputy Chairman Council for Architecture, Town Planning and Building Research, Festival of Britain, 1951; Planning Adviser to the Government of Singapore, 1950-54; Mem. of Royal Commission on Common Land. First Gold Medallist, Town Planning Inst., 1953. *Publications:* (Part) Town Theory and Practice; Paper on Greater London, R.I.B.A. Town Planning Conference, 1910; numerous papers on Town and Regional Planning at Conferences published in the Journals of Learned Societies. *Recreations:* golf, swimming, bonfires. *Address:* 49 Rivermead Court, Hurlingham, S.W.6; Little Bindon, West Lulworth, Dorset. *Clubs:* Athenæum, Hurlingham. [*Died* 13 *April* 1959.

PEPYS, George Digby, C.B.E. 1931; *b.* 7 June 1868; *e. s.* of late Hon. George Pepys; *m.* 1902, Margaret Mary Humphrey (*d.* 1954), *e. d.* of late G. W. Davidson; two *d.* *Educ.:* Winchester; Oriel College, Oxford. Formerly Chancery Bar; sometime Senior Official Receiver in Companies Liquidation. *Recreation:* fishing. *Address:* Taylors Mead, Sparsholt, Winchester. *T.:* Sparsholt 244. [*Died* 2 *May* 1957.

PERCEVAL, Major-General Sir Edward Maxwell, K.C.B., *cr.* 1922 (C.B. 1915); D.S.O. 1900; late R.F.A.; *b.* 18 Aug. 1861; *s.* of late General J. M. Perceval, C.B., J.P.; *m.* 1st, 1894, Marian, *d.* of R. L. Bowles, M.D., J.P.; one *s.*; 2nd, 1906, Norah (*d.* 1953), *y. d.* of late Rear-Admiral Richard Mayne, C.B., M.P.; one *s.* one *d.* *Educ.:* Royal Academy, Gosport; R.M.A., Woolwich. Passed Staff College; diploma, R. Geographical Society. Served in Royal Regt. of Artillery; first commissioned, 1880; Captain, 1888; Major, 1898; Lt.-Col. 1905; served in India and Burmah; South Africa, 1899-1902 (despatches, wounded, Queen's and King's medals 5 clasps, D.S.O.); European War, 1914-1917 (despatches five times, wounded, C.B., Maj.-Gen.); Professor at R.M.A. 1903-4; late Officer Commanding 1st Batt. Imperial Yeomanry; D.A.A.G. for Staff Duties at Headquarters, 1904-5; Officer Commanding 26th Brigade R.F.A., 1905-8; D.A.A.G. Staff College, 1908-9; General Staff Officer, 1st Grade, Staff College, 1909-12; Assistant Director of Movements at Headquarters, 1912-14; commanding R.A. 2nd Division, 1914-15; Sub-Chief of the Staff, G.H.Q., Jan. 1915; commanding a Division in France, 1915-17; commanding a Division at home, 1917-19; commanding Troops Folkestone and Shorncliffe, 1919; retired, 1920; commanded a Bn. of Home Guard, 1940-41. J.P. Surrey; Order of Vladimir 4th Class with swords; Commandeur de l'Ordre de Leopold; Military Order of Avis 1st Class; Belgian Croix de Guerre. *Recreations:* skating, golf, etc. *Address:* The Grange, Farnham, Surrey. *T.:* Farnham 5146. [*Died* 26 *Nov.* 1955.

PERCIVAL, Sir John Hope, K.B.E., *cr.* 1927; J.P.; *b.* 27 Dec. 1870; *e. s.* of late Edward Hope Percival, I.C.S., of Kimsbury House, Gloucester, and Louisa Jane, *d.* of Sir John Wedderburn, 2nd Bt.; *m.* 1901, Henrietta Lucilla, *d.* of late Maj.-Gen. Percival, Rifle Brigade; two *s.* one *d.* *Educ.:* Charterhouse; Trinity Hall, Cambridge (B.A. Senior Optime, 1893; LL.B. 1894). Barrister Inner Temple, 1894; went Oxford Circuit; Judge of Native Courts of First Instance, Egypt, 1903; Native Court of Appeal, 1909; Vice-President thereof, 1919; Legal Adviser to G.O.C. Egypt, 1919; Judicial Adviser to the Government of Egypt and Legal Adviser to the High Commissioner, 1925-28; Member of the Anglo-Mexican Special Claims Commission, 1929-30; Alderman, Gloucestershire County Council, 1937-49; holds Grand Cordon of the Order of the Nile and 3rd Class Osmanieh. *Recreations:* bowls, chess, bridge. *Address:* Kimsbury House, Gloucester. *T.:* Painswick 3219. [*Died* 7 *July* 1954.

PERCY OF NEWCASTLE, 1st Baron, *cr.* 1953, of Etchingham, Co. Sussex; **Eustace Percy,** P.C. 1924; Rector of Newcastle Division of the Univ. of Durham, 1937-Oct. 1952; *b.* 21 Mar. 1887; 7th *s.* of 7th Duke of Northumberland; *m.* 1918, Stella, *o. d.* of late Maj.-Gen. Laurence Drummond, C.B., C.B.E., M.V.O.; two *d.* *Educ.:* Oxford (M.A.). Was in Diplomatic Service; M.P. (U.) Hastings, 1921-37. Parliamentary Sec., Board of Education, March-May 1923; Ministry of Health, 1923-24; President of Board of Education, 1924-29; Minister without Portfolio, 1935-36. *Publications:* The Responsibilities of the League, 1920; Education at the Crossroads, 1930; Maritime Trade in War, 1930; Democracy on Trial, 1931; Government in Transition, 1934; John Knox, 1937; The Heresy of Democracy, 1954; Some Memories, 1958. (Editor), The Year Book of Education, 1932-1935. *Heir:* none. *Address:* The Old Rectory, Etchingham, E. Sussex. *Club:* Athenæum. [*Died* 3 *April* 1958 (*ext.*).

PERCY, Esmé; *see* Percy, S. E.

°PERCY, Maj.-Gen. Sir Jocelyn, K.B.E., *cr.* 1920; C.B. 1919; C.M.G., 1918; D.S.O. 1917; p.s.c.; East Lancs Regt.; *b.* 9 March 1871; *m.* 1902, Inez D'Aguilar (*d.* 1948), *d.* of late Col. A. W. Jamieson, I.A. (one *s.* killed with R.A.F., 1940) one *d.* *Educ.:* Queen Elizabeth's School, Sevenoaks; Royal Military College, Sandhurst. Served Waziristan Campaign, 1894, as Assist. Superintendent Army Signalling (medal with clasp); Chitral, 1895 (medal with clasp); S.

African War, 1899-1902 (despatches twice, Bt. Major, Queen's medal 4 clasps, King's medal 2 clasps); served in India as Brigade Major, Deputy Assistant Adjutant-General, and on the General Staff; served on the General Staff at the Royal Military College, Sandhurst; served European War, 1914-19; on General Staff of 27th, 48th and 31st Divs. B.G.G.S. IXth Corps, M.G.G.S. 5th and 2nd Armies (despatches six times, Bt. Lieut.-Col. and Col. C.B., C.M.G., D.S.O. 1914-15 Star, G.S. Medal, Allies' Medal); Comdr. Legion of Honour, Comdr. Order of Leopold of Belgium, Comdr. of the Star of Roumania, Order of the Sacred Treasure of Japan, 2nd class, Croix de Guerre, Belgium); served as M.G.G.S. Army of the Rhine, 1918-19; commanded 3rd London Brigade Army of the Rhine, 1919; served as B.G.G.S. British Military Mission with the Armed Forces of South Russia under General Denikine, 1919-1920; served as Comdr. of the British Military Mission with the Armed Forces of South Russia under General Wrangel (despatches twice, K.B.E., Order of St. Vladimir, 3rd class, Order of St. Stanislaus, 1st class); retired, 1920. Served as Inspector-General Albanian Gendarmerie, 1926-38. *Club:* Army and Navy. [*Died* 25 *Aug.* 1952.

PERCY, (Saville) Esmé; Actor; *b.* London, 8 Aug. 1887. *Educ.:* St. Mark's, Windsor; St. Louis, Brussels; Brussels and Paris Conservatoires. Studied under Sarah Bernhardt, Georges Berr, and Leloir. First London appearance, Royalty, 1905, as Romeo (William Poel's Production); played with F. R. Benson's Co., Beerbohm Tree, 1906; toured S. Africa, 1907; continued West End appearances; Manchester, 1910; formed touring repertory co. with Miss Kirsteen Graeme, 1913; played Hamlet, Little Theatre, 1914. Enlisted London Scottish, Dec. 1915; Commn. H.L.I., 1915; served in France and with Army of Occupation in Germany until 1923; Officer in charge Dramatic Co., British Army of the Rhine, producing over 140 plays. Asst. producer, Reandean, 1923; general producer Charles Macdona's Bernard Shaw Repertory Co., 1924; continued West End successes; intervals with Masque Theatre, Edinburgh, Glasgow, being producer and leading man, 1931; again produced and played lead in Shaw season, London, 1935; continuously in West End productions till Spring 1939, when toured with Bernard Shaw plays till outbreak of war; with Robert Atkins' Open-Air Theatre, Regent's Park, and Vaudeville Theatre, 1940. Of recent years played numerous leading parts in broadcast plays and television. Co-directed with John Gielgud, and played in, The Lady's Not for Burning, Globe Theatre, 1949. Produced Shaw's Buoyant Billions, Malvern Festival, 1949, and subs. Prince's, London. Produced James Joyce's Exiles, Q Theatre, 1950; The Praying Mantis, Q Theatre, 1954; played Gayeff in The Cherry Orchard, Lyric, 1954; Nicholas in The Burnt Flower Bed, Arts Theatre, 1955; 1st God in The Good Woman of Setzuan, Royal Court Theatre, 1956; Sir Jasper Fidget in The Country Wife, Royal Court Theatre, 1956; The Principal in the Apollo de Bellac, 1957. Played in many films, starting in Hitchcock's 2nd talking film, Murder. *Address:* 30 Warrington Crescent, W.9. *Clubs:* Savile, Savage, Arts Theatre. [*Died* 16 *June* 1957.

PEREIRA, Fredrick Linwood Clinton, C.V.O. 1946; O.B.E. 1935; *b.* 22 Dec. 1880; *s.* of late Godfrey Pereira Pereira; *m.* 1st, 1904, Louie A. B. Bowden; one *d.*; 2nd, 1931, Jessie May Cross. *Educ.:* Ottawa. Entered Civil Service of Canada as member of staff of office of Secretary to Governor-General, 1901; has served under ten Governors-General; Assistant Secretary to Governor-General of Canada, 1934; retired, 1948. *Recreations:* music, amateur acting, golf. *Address:* 128 Fourth Avenue, Ottawa, Canada. *Clubs:* Canadian, Ottawa Hunt and Golf (Ottawa). [*Died* 28 *Aug.* 1958.

PEREIRA, Richard Lionel, Q.C. (Ceylon), 1928; former Member of the Legislative Council, Ceylon; Member of the Municipal Council, Colombo since 1920; *b.* 19 Dec. 1880; *s.* of J. E. Richard Pereira, J.P. and Jeanie Wilson; *m.* 1908, Elsie Vivienne Koelman; one *d.* (one *s.* *decd.*). *Educ.:* Roy. Coll., Colombo. Joined the Bar, 1905; unofficial leader of the Bar on the Criminal Side. Steward of Ceylon Turf Club since 1936. *Recreations:* riding, motoring. *Address:* Anandagiri, Edinburgh Crescent, Colombo, Ceylon. *Club:* Orient (Colombo). [*Died* 8 *Aug.* 1960.

PERITZ, Rev. Ismar J., A.M., Ph.D.; Litt.D.; S.T.D.; Editor of Journal of Bible and Religion; Emeritus, since 1938; Professor of Semitic Languages and Biblical Literature, Syracuse University, 1896-1933; Prof. Emeritus since 1933; Willard Ives Professor of the English Bible since 1904; *b.* 8 Jan. 1863, Breslau, Germany; *s.* of Adolph Peritz and Sarah Wieluner; *m.* 1885, Caroline Louisa Irwin Cooper, of London. *Educ.:* Friederich's Gymnasium, Breslau; Drew Theological Seminary, Madison, N.J.; Harvard Univ. At the age of seventeen, while in Berlin, experienced a change in faith from Judaism to Christianity; moved to London; was called to New York City, 1883, to engage in mission work; studied theology in preparation for entering the ministry, 1884-87; ordained deacon, 1889; elder of the Methodist Episcopal Church, 1891; pastor of various churches of this denomination, 1887-1895; pursued advanced studies in Semitic Languages and Literature at Harvard University, 1892-95; A.M., 1893; Ph.D., 1898; resident lecturer at the Newman Biblical Institute, Jerusalem, 1913. *Publications:* Woman in the Ancient Hebrew Cult, in the Journal of Biblical Literature, 1898, pt. ii.; Critical and Exegetical Notes upon the International Sunday School Lessons in the Illustrative Lesson Notes for 1907 and 1908; contributor to the Encyclopædia Biblica and the Abingdon Bible Commentary; Old Testament History, 1915. *Address:* Lake Bluff, Wolcott, N.Y., U.S.A. (May-Sept.); 1121 Washington Avenue, Winter Park, Florida (Oct.-Apr.). [*Died* 16 *July* 1950.

[*But death not notified in time for inclusion in Who Was Who 1941–1950, first edn.*

PERKIN, Sir (Emil) Athol (Owen), Kt., *cr.* 1947; C.I.E. 1937; King's Police Medal, 1944; Indian Police (retired); *b.* Tiverton, Devon, 25 Sept. 1889; *s.* of E. S. Perkin, A.R.C.A. (Lond.); *m.* 1914, Marion Agnes Toogood; two *s.* two *d.* *Educ.:* Blundells. Entered Indian Police, 1909; various posts as Superintendent of Police, and Deputy Inspector-General, Bihar; Inspector General of Police, Orissa, 1936-44; Chairman of Joint Public Service Commission for Bihar, the Central Provinces and Berar, and Orissa, 1945-48. *Address:* 97 Lonsdale Road, Oxford. [*Died* 23 *Jan.* 1951.

PERKINS, Dr. Robert Cyril Layton, F.R.S. 1920; M.A., D.Sc. (Oxon), F.Z.S., F.R.E.S.; *b.* 1866; *s.* of Rev. C. M. Perkins, late Rector of Alderley, Glos.; *m.* 1901, Zoe L. S. A. (*d.* 1940), *d.* of A. T. Atkinson, Supt. of Public Instruction, Honolulu, Hawaiian Islands; three *s.*; *m.* 1942, Mrs. Clara M. J. Senior (*d.* 1949), Highweek, Newton Abbot. *Educ.:* Merchant Taylors' School; Jesus College, Oxford. Engaged in investigation of Land Fauna of Hawaiian Islands and in Economic Entomology of the same, 1892-1920. Gold Medal of Linnean Society, 1912. *Publications:* numerous works on the Hawaiian Fauna and on Economic Entomology. *Recreations:* fishing and entomology. *Address:* Wotton, Newton Rd., Bovey Tracy, Devon. [*Died* 29 *Sept.* 1955.

PEROWNE, Sir John Victor Thomas Woolrych Tait, K.C.M.G., *cr.* 1950

(C.M.G. 1944); K.St.J.; F.S.A.; British Minister to the Holy See since 1947; *b.* 30 July 1897; *e. s.* of Col. J. T. Woolrych Perowne, T.D., V.D.; *m.* 1933, Hon. Agatha Beaumont, *y. d.* of 1st Viscount Allendale; one *s.* *Educ.:* Eton; Corpus Christi Coll., Cambridge. Lt. Scots Guards, 1916-18; entered Diplomatic Service, 1920; Madrid, 1920-22; Lisbon, 1922-23; F.O. 1923-29; Copenhagen, 1929-31; F.O. 1931-36; Paris, 1936-38; F.O., 1938-47. *Recreations:* art, music, literature. *Address:* 1 Via del Parco Pepoli, Rome; Rivenhall Old Rectory, Witham, Essex. *T.:* Witham 2116. *Club:* St. James'. [*Died* 8 *Jan.* 1951.

PEROWNE, Ven. Archdeacon Thomas John; Archdeacon of Norwich, 1937-54; *b.* Aug. 1868; *s.* of Archdeacon T. T. Perowne; *m.* 1914, Joan Evelyn Patteson; two *d.* *Educ.:* Haileybury; Corpus Christi College, Cambridge, B.A., 1889; M.A. 1893; deacon 1892, priest 1893; Curate of Lowestoft 1892-1902; Brompton, 1902-4; Kelsale, 1904-5; St. Luke, Norwich, 1905-13; Vicar of Hindringham, 1913-22; Rector of Starston, Norfolk, 1922-45; Rural Dean of Redenhall, 1927-36; Hon. Canon of Norwich, 1929-37. *Address:* Old Hall, Framingham Earl, Norwich. *Club:* Norfolk County (Norwich). [*Died* 25 *Aug.* 1954.

PERREAU, Brigadier-General Arthur Montagu, C.B. 1919; C.M.G. 1916; R.A. retired; *b.* 4 Sept. 1870; *s.* of Col. M. C. Perreau; *m.* 1899, Nona Mabel (*d.* 1952), *d.* of late Col. H. R. B. Worsley, C.B.; one *d.* Served S. African War, 1899-1900 (wounded); European War, 1914-18 (despatches, C.M.G., C.B., Bt. Col.); retired, 1920. *Address:* West Flat, Hothfield Place, Nr. Ashford, Kent. [*Died* 28 *Feb.* 1953.

PERREAU, Colonel Charles Noel, C.M.G. 1918, retired; *b.* 19 Dec. 1874; *s.* of late Colonel M. C. Perreau, B.S.C., of Flexford House, Guildford; *m.* 1902, Emma Liddle, 3rd *d.* of J. Gordon, 46 Castle Hill Ave., Folkestone. *Educ.:* Harrow; Sandhurst. Joined Royal Dublin Fusiliers 1895; Lieut. 1897; Capt. 1900; Maj. 1914; Col. 1923; Temporary Colonel and G.S.O. I., 1916; temporary Brigadier-General Dec. 1918; Adjt. 10th Provisional Batt. 1901-2, 5th Royal Dublin Fusiliers 1902-7, 2nd Royal Dublin Fusiliers 1908-11; Staff-Adjt. R.M.C. of Canada, 1911-14; a/Cmdt. R.M.C. 1915-16; Comdt. 1916-19; Lt.-Col. I.R.D.F., 1919; commanded 166 Infantry Brigade (T.A.), 1923-27; retired pay, 1927; served S. African War (severely wounded at Talana, Queen's medal and 2 clasps); European War. *Address:* c/o Lloyds Bank, Ltd., 6 Pall Mall, S.W.1. [*Died* 10 *June* 1952.

PERRIN, Harry Crane, Mus.Doc. Trinity College, Dublin; F.R.C.O.; Dean Emeritus of Faculty of Music, McGill University, since 1930; *b.* Wellingborough, Northants, 19 Aug. 1865; *m.* 1896, Enid Hilda, *d.* of G. A. Pridmore, J.P., Brooklyn, Coventry; one *s.* one *d.* *Educ.:* Wellingborough School; Trinity College, Dublin. Studied music under Sir Robert Stewart and others; organist of St. Columba's College, Dublin, 1886-88; St. John's Church, Lowestoft, 1888-92; Coventry Cathedral, 1892-98; organist and master of choristers, Canterbury Cathedral, 1898-1908; Director McGill University Conservatorium of Music, and Professor of Music in Faculty of Arts, 1908-30; Dean of Faculty of Music, McGill University, Montreal, 1920-30. *Publications:* cantatas, anthems, church services, songs. *Address:* Hillstead, Streatham Drive, Exeter. [*Died* 6 *Nov.* 1953.

PERRING, William George Arthur, C.B. 1949; Director Royal Aircraft Establishment, Farnborough, Hants, since 1946; *b.* 16 Dec. 1898. *Educ.:* Royal Naval College, Greenwich. 1851 Research Scholar, 1923-25; joined Royal Aircraft Establishment, Dec. 1925; Superintendent, Scientific Research, 1940; Deputy Director Research and Experiment, 1941. Member Aeronautical Research Council; Member Council Royal Aeronautical Society. *Publications:* numerous contrib. various societies and international congresses. *Address:* Samarkand, Prior Road, Camberley, Surrey. [*Died* 8 *April* 1951.

PERRINS, Charles William Dyson, Hon. D.C.L.; D.L.; J.P.; F.S.A.; *b.* 25 May 1864; *o. s.* of late James Dyson Perrins; *m.* 1st, 1889, Catherine (*d.* 1922), *d.* of late A. A. Gregory, Inverness; two *s.* one *d.* (and one *d.* decd.); 2nd, 1923, Frieda, *y. d.* of late John Milne, Belmont, Cheadle. *Educ.:* Charterhouse; Queen's Coll., Oxford. Joined 4th Batt. Highland Light Infantry, 1888; retired (Capt.), 1892; Mayor of Worcester, 1897; High Sheriff of Worcestershire, 1899; Hon. Freeman of the City of Worcester, 1937; Life Governor of Birmingham University; a Member of the Council of Malvern College; collects illuminated manuscripts, early woodcut books, and Worcester china. Commander of Order of St. John of Jerusalem. *Address:* Davenham, Malvern. *T.:* 15 Malvern; Achandunie, Alness, Ross-shire. *Clubs:* Bath, Roxburghe, Royal Automobile. [*Died* 29 *Jan.* 1958.

PERRY, 1st Baron, *cr.* 1938, of Stock Harvard; **Percival Lea Dewhurst Perry,** K.B.E., *cr.* 1918 (C.B.E. 1917); LL.D.; F.R.G.S.; M.I.Mech.E.; Director: Ford Motor Co. Limited, Firestone Tyre & Rubber Co. Limited; President, Slough Estates Ltd.; *b.* Bristol, 18 March 1878; *m.* 1902, Catherine, *d.* of John Meals, Hull; no *c.* F.C.I.S. 1904; President Motor Trade Association, 1914; Director Food Production Dept., 1916; Director Agricultural Machinery Dept. Ministry of Munitions, 1917-1918; Deputy Controller Mechanical Warfare Department; Director of Traction, Ministry of Munitions, 1918-19; Business Adviser to Minister of Food, 1939-40. Officer of the Legion of Honour; Commander Order of Leopold II; Knight Commander of Royal Order of George I.; Commander of Order of Dannebrog; King Christian Xth Liberty Medal (Denmark); Commander of the North Star (Sweden); Grand Cross of the Finnish Lion Order. *Publications:* O.K. Verses, 1906; American Invasion, 1912; New Songs, 1925; Island of Enchantment, 1926; International Trade Balance, 1932; various pamphlets and papers. *Address:* 16 Berkeley Street, W.1; Nassau, Bahamas. *Clubs:* Brooks's, Reform, Royal Automobile, Portland. [*Died* 17 *June* 1956 (*ext.*).

PERRY, Major-General Aylesworth Bowen, C.M.G. 1909; Canadian Militia; late Commissioner, Royal Canadian Mounted Police; *b.* 21 Aug. 1860; *s.* of late W. H. Perry, J.P., and Eleanor Fraser; *m.* 1883, Emma Duranty Meikle (*decd.*); two *d.* (and one *s.* decd.). *Educ.:* Royal Military College, Canada. Lieutenant, Royal Engineers, 1880-1881; Librarian to Geological Survey, Canada, 1881-82; Inspector R.N.W.M. Police, 1882; Superintendent, 1885; served in N.W. Rebellion, rank of Major in Can. Militia (medal); commanded Diamond Jubilee Contingent (medal), and Coronation Contingent, 1911; Barrister in Provinces of Alberta and Saskatchewan. *Club:* Rideau (Ottawa). [*Died* 15 *Feb.* 1956.

PERRY, Bliss; Author; Francis Lee Higginson Professor of English Literature, Emeritus, Harvard University; *b.* Williamstown, Mass., 25 Nov. 1860; *s.* of Professor A. L. Perry, the political economist; *m.* Annie L. Bliss of New Haven, Conn. *Educ.:* Williams College; Berlin and Strassburg Universities. Professor of English, Williams College, 1886-93; Princeton University, 1893-1900; editor of the Atlantic Monthly, 1899-1909; Member of the National Academy of Arts and Letters; Fellow of the Royal Society of Literature of the United Kingdom; Chevalier of the Legion of Honour. *Publications:* The Broughton House; Salem Kittredge, and other stories; The Plated City; The Powers at Play; A Study of Prose

Fiction; The Amateur Spirit; Walt Whitman; Park-Street Papers; The American Mind; Carlyle; The American Spirit in Literature; A Study of Poetry; Life and Letters of Major H. L. Higginson; The Praise of Folly; The Heart of Emerson's Journals; Pools and Ripples; Emerson To-day; R. H. Dana (1851-1931); The Heart of Emerson's Essays; And Gladly Teach. *Recreations:* fishing, golf. *Address:* Exeter Inn, Exeter, N.H., U.S.A. *Club:* Tavern (Boston). [*Died* 13 *Feb.* 1954.

PERRY, Major-Gen. Henry Marrian, C.B. 1937; O.B.E. 1919; F.R.C.P. 1941; late R.A.M.C.; retd.; *b.* 11 March 1884; *s.* of late John Perry and late Katherine Hegarty; *m.* 1912, Mary Eleanor, 2nd *d.* of late Edward Griffith Brewer; no *c.* *Educ.:* Queen's Coll., Cork. Commissioned Royal Army Medical Corps, 1907; Captain, 1911; Major, 1919; Brevet Lieutenant-Colonel, 1921; Lieutenant-Colonel, 1931; Brevet Colonel, 1933; Colonel, 1934; Major-General, 1935; served Western Front 1914-18 as Regimental Medical Officer, Officer Commanding a Field Ambulance, and Assistant Adviser in Pathology; Professor, Royal Army Medical College, 1922-26; Director of Medical Scientific work under Egyptian Government, 1926-30; Hon. Surgeon to the King, 1933-40. *Publications:* Illustrations of Agglutination Method of Diagnosis, Lancet, April 1919; Medical Research Committee Report No. 24, 1919; Observations on Acute Infections in Egypt, Trans. Royal Society of Tropical Medicine and Hygiene, 1929; many articles on bacteriological and pathological subjects. *Recreations:* tennis, golf. *Address:* Burwood Park Cottage, Burwood Park, Walton-on-Thames, Surrey. *T.:* 1688. [*Died* 23 *March* 1955.

PERRY, Ralph Barton; Professor of Philosophy, emeritus, Harvard University, 1946; *b.* 3 July 1876; *s.* of George Adelbert Perry and Susannah Chase Barton; *m.* 1905, Rachel Berenson (*d.* 1933); two *s.* *Educ.:* Princeton University (A.B. 1896); Harvard University (A.M. 1897, Ph.D. 1899). Instructor in philosophy, Williams College, 1899-1900; Smith College, 1900-2; instructor in philosophy, Harvard University, 1902-5; assistant professor, 1905-13; professor 1913-1946; professor emeritus, 1946-. Major U.S. Army and secretary War Department Committee on Education and Special Training, 1918-19; Hyde lecturer in French universities, 1921-22; Gifford lecturer at Glasgow University, 1946-48. Chevalier Legion of Honor (France), 1936. Hon. degrees: Litt.D., Princeton University, 1936; D.H.L., Clark Univ. 1939; LL.D., Colby College, 1942, Univ. of Pennsylvania, 1944; Litt.D., Harvard Univ. 1944. *Publications:* The Approach to Philosophy, 1905; The Moral Economy, 1909; Present Philosophical Tendencies, 1912; The New Realism, 1912; The Present Conflict of Ideals, 1918; Annotated Bibliography of the Writings of William James, 1920; Ed. William James's Essays in Radical Empiricism, 1912; William James's Collected Essays and Reviews, 1920; Revision of Weber's History of Philosophy, 1925; Philosophy of the Recent Past, 1926; General Theory of Value, 1926; A Defense of Philosophy, 1931; The Thought and Character of William James (Pulitzer prize biography), 1935, briefer version, 1948; In The Spirit of William James, 1938; The Meaning of the Humanities (with others), 1938; Shall Not Perish From the Earth, 1940; On All Fronts, 1941; Our Side is Right, 1942; Puritanism and Democracy, 1944; One World in the Making, 1945; Characteristically American, 1949; The Citizen Decides, 1951; Realms of Value, 1954; The Humanity of Man, 1956. *Address:* 445 Widener Library, Harvard University, Cambridge 38, Mass. *Clubs:* Harvard (Boston, Mass.); Harvard (New York City). [*Died* 22 *Jan.* 1957.

PERRY, Samuel Frederick, J.P.; *b.* Stockport, 29 June 1877; *s.* of Samuel Perry; *m.* 1st (*d.* 1930); 2nd, 1931, Olive Elizabeth Gardner, Highgate. M.P. (Co-operative) Kettering, 1923-1924, and 1929-31; Parliamentary Private Secretary (unpaid) to the Minister of Health, 1924; Parliamentary Private Secretary (unpaid) to President Board of Trade, 1929; contested Stockport, 1920. *Address:* 223 Pitshanger Lane, W.5. [*Died* 19 *Oct.* 1954.

PERRY, Sir William, Kt., *cr.* 1933; sheep-farmer; *b.* 1863; *m.* 1891, Margaret (*d.* 1941), *d.* of William Bridson. Member of N.Z. Meat Control Board since 1923; President, Royal Agricultural Society, New Zealand, from 1924; Chairman Massey Agricultural College, 1934-36. *Publication:* Sheep-farming in New Zealand. *Address:* Penrose, nr. Masterton, N.Z. [*Died* 20 *May* 1956.

PERTH, 16th Earl of, *cr.* 1605; **(James) Eric Drummond,** P.C. 1933; G.C.M.G., *cr.* 1934 (K.C.M.G., *cr.* 1916); C.B. 1914; Baron Drummond of Cargill, 1488; Baron Maderty, 1609; Baron Drummond, 1686; Lord Drummond of Gilston, 1685; Lord Drummond of Rickertoun and Castlemaine, 1686; Viscount Strathallan, 1686; Hereditary Thane of Lennox, and Hereditary Steward of Menteith and Strathearn; Representative Peer of Scotland since 1941; Deputy Leader of Liberal Party in House of Lords, since 1946; *b.* 17 Aug. 1876; *S.* half-brother, 1937; *m.* 1904, Hon. Angela Constable-Maxwell, *y. d.* of 11th Baron Herries; one *s.* three *d.* *Educ.:* Eton. Entered Foreign Office, 1900; Private Secretary to Under-Secretary of State for Foreign Affairs, 1906-08 and 1908-10; Précis-Writer to Foreign Secretary, 1908 and 1910-11; one of the Private Secretaries to the Prime Minister, 1912-15; Private Secretary to Foreign Secretary, 1915-19; Secretary General to League of Nations, 1919-33; British Ambassador to Italy, 1933-39; Chief Adviser on Foreign Publicity, Ministry of Information, 1939-40. Hon. D.C.L. (Oxon); Hon. LL.D. (Liverpool). *Heir: s.* Viscount Strathallan. *Address:* Fyning House, Rogate, near Petersfield, Hampshire. *Club:* Travellers'. [*Died* 15 *Dec.* 1951.

PERY-KNOX-GORE, Colonel (Hon. Brig.) Arthur Francis Gore, C.B. 1937; D.S.O., 1917; R.A.S.C.; *b.* 1880; *m.* 1909, Evangeline, *d.* of Capt. John William St. John Hughes; (one *s.* Flying Officer R.A.F. killed 1943) two *d.* *Educ.:* Cheltenham. Served European War, 1914-18 (despatches, D.S.O., Order of Redeemer of Greece, Order of White Eagle of Serbia, Officer Legion of Honour, Military Medal of Greece); Lt.-Col. 1929; Col. 1930; A.A. and Q.M.G. 2nd Division, 1930-33; Brigadier in charge of Admin. Northern Command, 1934-37; A.Q.M.G. Aldershot, 1940. *Address:* Old Glass House, Countess Wear, nr. Exeter. *T.:* Topsham 3035. [*Died* 18 *Feb.* 1954.

PESHALL, Rev. Charles John Eyre, C.B.E. 1935; D.S.O. 1918; R.N. (retired); rejoined, 1940; re-retired 1943; *b.* Nov. 1881; *e. s.* of late Rev. Samuel Peshall, Oldberrow, Warwickshire; *m.* 1919, Beatrice (*d.* 1944), *e. d.* of late Ludford Docker, J.P., Alveston Leys, Stratford-on-Avon; one *d.* (one *s.* decd.) *Educ.:* Haileybury Coll.; Pembroke Coll. Cambridge. Ordained, 1904; Curate of Atherstone, 1904-7; Tormohun, 1907-8; Chaplain, R.N., 1908; Archdeacon Chaplain of the Fleet, 1933-35; Rector of Great Mongeham, Kent, 1936-40; Hon. Chap. to the King, 1934-35; Chap. to the Merchant Taylors' Company, 1951-52; has served in H.M.S. Black Prince, Encounter, St. George, Cornwallis, Repulse, Victory, and Royal Marine Barracks; present in Vindictive attack by night on Zeebrugge, April 1918 (D.S.O.). *Publication:* part-author The Immortal Gamble, 1917. *Address:* 52 Albert Hall Mansions, Kensington, S.W.7. *Club:* Army and Navy. [*Died* 18 *Oct.* 1957.

PÉTAIN, Philippe; Maréchal de France, 1918; Grand Cross of Legion of Honour; Médaille Militaire; membre de l'Académie des Sciences morales et politiques, 1919; member of the Académie Française, 1929-45; *b.* Cauchy le Tour, Pas-de-Calais, 24 April 1856; *m.* 1920, Madame Hardon. *Educ.:* École de St. Cyr, left in 1878 as a Lieutenant; passed through the École de Guerre. A Lieutenant and a Captain in the Chasseurs Alpins; was attached to the Staff of the 15th Corps, then to the Military Governor of Paris; as a Major, a teacher in the Firing School, Chalons, 1900; Teacher, Ecole de Guerre, 1901; Commandant le 33° régiment d'infanterie à Arras; at the head of the 4th Brigade at St. Omer, per interim, as a Colonel, 1914; Brigadier-General Aug. 1914 (Charleroi); commanded the 6th Division of Infantry (Marne), the 33rd Army Corps, 20 Oct. 1914; stormed Carency, May 1915; took command of the 2nd Army, June 1915; in charge of operations in front of Verdun, Feb.-May 1916; commanded a group of Armies, May 1916; General-in-Chief, May 1917; Inspector-General of the French Army, 1922-31; Secretary of War, France, 1934; French Ambassador to Spain, 1939-1940; Minister of State and Vice-Pres. of the Council, France, 1940; Chief of the French State, 1940-44; Prime Minister, France, 1940-42. In detention, after War of 1939-45, at the "Prison de Villedieu". *Publication:* Verdun, 1930.
[*Died* 23 *July* 1951.

PETERS, Arthur, C.B.E. 1918; J.P.; Alderman of Croydon County Borough Council; *s.* of James Peters, Brighton; *m.* 1894, Annie, *d.* of Alfred Lowe, Blakeney, Glos. Joint Hon. Secretary Parliamentary Recruiting Committee, 1914-17; Mayor of Croydon, 1935-37. *Address:* 1194 London Road, Norbury, S.W.16.
[*Died* 22 *March* 1956.

PETERSON, John Carlos Kennedy, C.I.E. 1919; B.A. (Oxon); *b.* Mahableshwar, India, 28 March 1876; *s.* of late Dr. Peter Peterson, LL.D., Bombay; *m.* Flora (*d.* 1953), *d.* of A. D. Campbell; four *s.* *Educ.:* Edinburgh Academy; Dulwich; Magdalen College, Oxford. Indian Civil Service, 1899-1919; Under-Secretary and officiating Secretary, Finance Department, Government of Bengal, 1906-8; special duty, Political Department, 1909; district judge, Purulia, 1910-12; first land acquisition collector, Calcutta, 1912-16; officiating Chairman, Calcutta Improvement Trust, 1917; Director of Industries and Controller of Munitions, Bengal, Government of India, 1917-19; Director, Tata Sons, Limited, Bombay, 1919-31. *Publications:* Burdwan District Gazetteer; Manual of Land Acquisition, Practice and Procedure; Her Daughter, a comedy in three acts; In the Clouds, a comedy in three acts; Mary of Scots, a tragedy. *Address:* Meadfoot, Carmen Sylva Rd., Llandudno, N. Wales.
[*Died* 9 *Feb.* 1955.

PETERSON, Sir Maurice Drummond, G.C.M.G., *cr.* 1947 (K.C.M.G., *cr.* 1938; C.M.G. 1933); Foreign Service, retired; Director, Midland Bank; *b.* 10 Mar. 1889; *yr. s.* of late Sir William Peterson, K.C.M.G., and late Lisa, *e. d.* of late Wm. Ross of Glencearn, Perthshire; *m.* 1927, Eleanor Angel, 2nd *d.* of late Rev. H. W. L. O'Rorke, The Manor, North Litchfield, Whitchurch, Hants; three *s.* *Educ.:* Rugby; Magdalen College, Oxford, B.A. (First Class Honours in Modern History, 1911; M.A. 1924). Entered Foreign Office, 1913; has served at Washington, Prague, Tokio, Cairo, and Madrid; Private Secretary to the Rt. Hon. A. J. Balfour at the Washington Conference on the Limitation of Armaments, 1921-22; acting High Commissioner for Egypt, 1934; H.M. Minister to Bulgaria, 1936-38; H.M. Ambassador to Iraq, 1938-39; H.M. Ambassador to Spain, 1939-40; Controller of Overseas Publicity, Ministry of Information, 1940-41; an Under-Secretary of State, Foreign Office, 1942; Ambassador in Ankara, 1944-46; in Moscow, 1946-49; retired, 1949. *Publications:* Both Sides of the Curtain, 1950; press articles. *Recreations:* fishing, golf. *Address:* Inglewood Lodge, Kintbury, Berks. *T.:* Kintbury 84. *Clubs:* St. James', Bath.
[*Died* 15 *March* 1952.

PETO, Major (Basil Arthur) John, King's Dragoon Guards; *b.* 13 Dec. 1900; 3rd *s.* of Sir Basil Peto, 1st Bt.; *m.* 1934, Patricia Geraldine, 3rd *d.* of late Gerald Macleay Browne, O.B.E.; one *s.* three *d.* *Educ.:* Harrow; Cambridge. B.A. Cantab. 1922, History and Political Economy; joined Royal Artillery, 2nd Lieut., 1924; transferred King's Dragoon Guards, Lieut., 1926; served British Army of the Rhine, 1926-1927; A.D.C. to Governor of Bombay, 1929-31; served with Regiment in Egypt 1932-35; Captain, 1932; Adjutant Scottish Horse, 1936-37; retired, 1939; rejoined outbreak of present war; M.P. (Nat. U.) King's Norton Division of Birmingham, 1941-45; Parliamentary Private Sec. to Chairman of Oil Board (Rt. Hon. Geoffrey Lloyd, M.P.), Dec. 1941-Feb. 1945. *Publication:* Escape from Now (Poetry). *Recreations:* fishing, shooting, and ski-ing. *Address:* Old Enton, Witley, Surrey. *T.:* Wormley 273. *Clubs:* Carlton, Cavalry, Queen's, M.C.C.
[*Died* 3 *Feb.* 1954.

PETO, Sir Geoffrey Kelsall, K.B.E., *cr.* 1939 (C.B.E. 1919); Chairman: Invalid Kitchens of London; Dorset House School of Occupational Therapy; Vice-Chairman Central Council for Care of Cripples; *b.* 1878; *s.* of W. H. Peto, Dunkinty, Elgin; *m.* 1903, Pauline (*d.* 1950), *d.* of William Quirin, Boston, U.S., and *widow* of Lt.-Col. R. Cokayne-Frith, 15th Hussars; one *s.* one *d.*; *m.* 1951, Edna (who *m.* 1st, 1922, Capt. Sir Denzil Cope, 14th Bt.; one *s.* (Sir Anthony Mohun Cope, 15th Bt.) one *d.* (wife of Sir Duncan Alexander Grant, 13th Bt.)), *d.* of late Edward B. Hilton, Paris and New York. *Educ.:* Eton (Scholar). Director Morgan Crucible Co., Ltd., 1903-47; late Captain, Royal Wilts Yeomanry; late Deputy-Controller of Contracts, Ministry of Munitions; M.P. (U.) Frome Division of Somerset, 1924-29, Bilston Div., Wolverhampton, 1931-35; Parliamentary Private Secretary to Colonel G. Lane-Fox, Secretary of Mines, 1926-27; to Earl Winterton, Under-Secretary of State for India, 1928-29; and to Rt. Hon. Walter Runciman, President of Board of Trade, 1931-35; Chairman of Gifts Coupons Committee, 1933; Chairman of International Copyright Committee, 1935; Chm. of Food Council and of Consumers' Committees and Mem. of Wheat Commission, 1936-39; Member of Committee on Pensions for Unmarried Women, 1938; Runciman Mission to Czecho-Slovakia, 1938; Regional Commissioner, S. W. England, 1940 (Deputy, 1939-40); Regional Controller, Ministry of Supply, Southern England, 1941-45. *Address:* 3 Wellesley House, Sloane Square, S.W.1. *T.:* Sloane 1580. *Clubs:* Carlton, Royal Automobile.
[*Died* 8 *Jan.* 1956.

PETO, Major John; *see* Peto, Major B. A. J.

PETO, Mrs. Ralph H.; *see* Lichnowsky, Princess Mechtilde.

PETRIDES, Sir Philip Bertie, Kt., *cr.* 1936; *b.* 1881; 3rd *s.* of late D. N. Petrides, Sydenham; *m.* Clare, *er. d.* of George Cosens, Sydenham; one *s.* one *d.* *Educ.:* Dulwich College, Brussels. Called to Bar, Middle Temple, 1906; practised at Common Law Bar, 1906-16; Legal Adviser and Crown Prosecutor, Seychelles, 1916; acting Chief Justice, Seychelles, July 1916-March 1917, May-Oct. 1918, and Dec. 1918-Nov. 1919; Chief Justice of Seychelles, 1920-24; administered the Government of Seychelles, March 1921-Sept. 1922; Attorney-

General of Nyasaland, 1924; Acting Judge of Nyasaland, June-Dec. 1925; Puisne Judge of Supreme Court of Nigeria, 1926-30; Chief Justice, Mauritius, 1930-36; Chief Justice, Gold Coast, 1936-44. *Publication:* Petrides' Students' Cases. *Recreations:* golf and bridge. *Address:* Grantchester, Tunbridge Wells. [*Died* 19 *April* 1956.

PETTER, Sir Ernest Willoughby, Kt., *cr.* 1925; President, British Engineers Association, 1923-24, 1924-25; Member of Executive, Federation of British Industries; Vice-President, Institution of Mechanical Engineers; *b.* 26 May 1873; *s.* of late James B. Petter, J.P., Yeovil. *Educ.:* Exeter and privately. In conjunction with brother, P. W. Petter, designed and built one of the first internal combustion engined motor cars made in this country; contested Bristol North (C.), 1918, 1923, St. George's, Westminster (Ind. C.) 1931. *Publications:* several pamphlets on Industrial Economics. *Address:* Bywell, Spencer Road, New Milton, Hants. [*Died* 18 *July* 1954.

PHEAR, Arthur George, C.B. 1919; M.D., F.R.C.P.; Consulting Physician to the Royal Free Hospital; late Consulting Physician to the Royal Chest Hospital, City Road, to the Royal National Hospital for Diseases of the Chest, Ventnor, to the Royal Hospital, Chelsea, and to the Queen Alexandra Military Hospital; late Examiner in Medicine, Cambridge University and Royal College of Physicians; late Lecturer in Medicine, London School of Medicine for Women; Member of Council Royal College of Physicians; temporary Colonel, A.M.S., and Consulting Physician, British Salonika Force, and Army of the Black Sea (C.B., despatches twice); *b.* 16 March 1867; *s.* of late Henry Carlyon Phear; *m.* 1897, Ellen Frances, *d.* of late Arthur Lister, F.R.S. *Educ.:* Charterhouse; Trinity College, Cambridge. *Publications:* on various medical subjects. *Address:* 16 Well Walk. Hampstead, N.W.3. *T.:* Hampstead 2902; Birch Copse, Brook, near Godalming, Surrey. [*Died* 26 *Feb.* 1959.

PHILBY, Harry St. John Bridger, C.I.E. 1917; F.R.G.S.; I.C.S. (retired); B.A.; *b.* St. John's, Badula, Ceylon, 3 April 1885; *s.* of late Henry Montague Philby, tea-planter in Ceylon, and May Beatrice, *d.* of late Lt.-Gen. John Duncan; *m.* 1910, Dora (*d.* 1957), *e. d.* of late A. H. Johnston, A.M.I.C.E., Public Works Department, India; one *s.* three *d.* *Educ.:* Westminster (Queen's Scholar and King's Scholar); Trinity College, Cambridge. Was Head Boy and Captain, Westminster School, 1903-4, obtaining Open Exhibition and Close Scholarship to Trinity College, Cambridge, in 1904, becoming Major Scholar (Classics) there in 1906; took Classical Tripos Part I. (Class II. Div. I.) in 1906, and First Class in Modern Languages Tripos and B.A. degree in 1907; in same year passed about 50th in Civil Service Examination; went to India to join I.C.S. (Punjab), 1908; served as Assistant Commissioner at Jhelum, Rawalpindi, Shahpur, Multan, Ambala, and Dera Ghazi Khan, becoming officiating Deputy Commissioner at Lyallpur, 1914; joined the Punjab Govt. Secretariat, 1914; Secretary to the Board of Examiners, Calcutta, 1915; in Nov. 1915 went to Mesopotamia as Political Officer, M.E.F., and served as Financial Assistant to Chief Political Officer, officiating Revenue Commissioner for Occupied Territories, Political Officer in charge of Amara district, and then on special duty at Baghdad; in charge of British Political Mission to Central Arabia, 1917-18; crossed the Arabian Peninsula from Uqair to Jidda, and carried out exploration in South Central Arabia, being first European to visit the Southern Provinces of Najd; Founder's Medal, R.G.S., 1920; Member of Royal Asiatic Society (Council, 1920); Royal Central Asian Society; was in political charge of Central Arabian Mission which visited England, 1919; Adviser to Ministry of Interior, Mesopotamia, 1920-21; Chief British Representative, Trans-Jordan, 1921-24; retired from I.C.S. 1925; elected to Council of R.G.S., 1925; awarded first Sir Richard Burton Memorial Medal by R.A.S., 1925; Resident Director in Arabia (Jidda) of Sharqieh, Ltd., 1926-46; then Director Mitchell Cotts (Sharqieh) Ltd., Jidda till 1955; from 1930 to 1940 carried out further extensive exploration of Arabian peninsula, including the crossing of the Rub' al Khali desert in 1932 and extensive travels in the Sheba country of S.W. Arabia in 1937; further explorations in Northern and Southern Arabia, 1946-55. *Publications:* The Heart of Arabia, 1922; Arabia of the Wahhabis, 1928; Arabia (Modern World Series), 1930; The Empty Quarter, 1933; Harun al Rashid, 1933; Sheba's Daughters, 1939; A Pilgrim in Arabia, 1943; The Background of Islam, 1947; Arabian Days, 1948. Arabian Highlands, 1952; Arabian Jubilee, 1952; Saudi Arabia (Nations of the Modern World Series), 1955; The Land of Midian, 1957; Forty Years in the Wilderness, 1957. *Address:* Riyadh, Saudi Arabia. *Club:* Athenæum. [*Died* 30 *Sept.* 1960.

PHILIP, Anne Glenday, C.B.E. 1930; Chief Woman Inspector of Schools, retired, 1938; *b.* 1878; *d.* of late William Philip, Dundee. *Educ.:* Dundee High School; Sorbonne; Glasgow University. Teaching, lecturing, and (during European war, 1914-18) administrative work in Ministry of Munitions. *Recreation:* conversation. *Address:* 3 North Charlotte Street, Edinburgh. [*Died* 19 *April* 1952.

PHILIP, Charles Lyall, C.I.E. 1933; I.C.S., retired; *b.* 10 Dec. 1881; *s.* of Pirie Philip and Mary Lyall; *m.* 1921, Ethel Leslie Carter; no *c.* *Educ.:* George Watson's College and University, Edinburgh. Political Agent and Commissioner, Orissa Feudatory States, 1921-27; Member, Board of Revenue, 1934-37. *Recreations:* fishing, shooting, golf. *Address:* Rosedene, 85 Hove Park Road, Hove, Sussex. *T.:* Brighton 54117. [*Died* 19 *April* 1951.

PHILIP, Sir (James) Randall, Kt., *cr.* 1953; O.B.E. 1946; Q.C. (Scot.) 1945; M.A., LL.B.; D.D.; Sheriff of Perth and Angus since 1955; Procurator of the Church of Scotland since 1949; *b.* 15 Feb. 1900; *s.* of late Very Rev. Adam Philip, D.D.; *m.* 1926, Ella Wallace, *e. d.* of late Robert Harbison Gray, Glasgow; two *d.* (one *s.* decd.). *Educ.:* Dundee High School; Edinburgh Univ.; Glasgow Univ.; Italy. Served R.A., 1918-19 (2nd Lt.); M.A. 1st class hons. Hist. (Edinburgh), 1921; LL.B. (Glasgow), 1923; called to Scots Bar, 1924; Junior Counsel in Scotland for Admiralty, 1938-39; for War Office and Air Ministry, 1939-45; Sheriff of Renfrew and Argyll, 1948-55; commissioner in Glenrothes and Cumbernauld New Towns enquiries and in Departmental enquiries; Chm. Scottish Milk Services Cttee.; member: War Damage Commission; Central Land Board; Slade Committee on Medical Partnerships; Standing Commission on Museums and Galleries; Chm. Cttee. on Scottish National Museum of Antiquities; Lord Advocate's Cttee. on Legal Reforms, 1938-54; Law Reform Cttee. (Scotland), 1955-; Trustee National Library of Scotland and Convener, Standing Cttee.; Scottish Regional Commissioner's Office, 1939-45; Trustee Scot. Nat. Museums of Antiquities; Commissioner, Northern Lighthouse Board, 1948-; Pres., Edinburgh University Graduates Assoc.; Member: British Council of Churches; Anglo-Scottish Church Conversations. Hon. D.D. (Aberdeen), 1955. *Publications:* Constitutional Law and History (Stair Society), 1936; Chapters on Constitutional Law (joint), 1930; Law Relating to Motor Cars, 1929; Gordon Philip, 1943; We Believe This (joint), 1953; various contributions and broadcasts. *Recreations:* travelling, photography, books, music. *Address:* 53 Great King Street,

Edinburgh 3. *T.:* Edinburgh Waverley 1759. *Clubs:* Athenæum, Caledonian; New (Edinburgh). [*Died* 2 *May* 1957.

PHILIPPS, Tracy, M.C., Hon. D.C.L. (Durham), M.A., B.Litt.; F.R.G.S., F.R.A.I.; late The Rifle Brigade; Secretary-General of International Union for Conservation of Nature and Natural Resources (World H.Q., Institut Royal des Sciences Naturelles, Brussels); Vice-President, the Hakluyt Soc., 1947-51, and 1952-58; Council, Church of England Council on For. Relations; (Brit. Mem.) Internat. Commission of Belgian Research Institute of African National Parks; *b.* Nov. 1890; *s.* of John Erasmus Philipps, M.A., and Margaret Viscountess Dillon. *Educ.:* Marlborough Coll.; Oxford; Durham Univ. (Pres. of Union, Pres. U.B.C.). Lt. R.O., 1913; Asst. Comr., B.E.A. (German frontier), 1913; Indian Expeditionary Force (B.), from 5 Aug. 1914, attached K.A.R. (wounded, despatches); Bukoba Expeditionary Force, 1915 (despatches); Capt., G.S.O. 3, 1916; Arab Bureau, Cairo, Jerusalem and Syria, 1918; Italian Front and Abyssinia, 1917-18; attached Embassy, Rome, 1918. Travelled on foot along Equator from E. to W. Africa, discovered the lutra paraonyx philippsi. British Relief Commissioner for South Russia (Red Cross and Nansen), 1921; Liaison Officer with French and Greeks in Turkey-in-Europe (Thrace), 1922; Administration, Khartoum and Cairo, 1923; Times War Correspondent Greco-Turkish War, 1922; Commissioner in Bahr el-Ghazal (French frontier), 1925; Dep. Provincial Comr., East Africa, in 1930; Foreign (Diplomatic) Corresp., on peoples of Moslem, Mediterranean and E. Europe, 1936-39; European Refugee Mission to Latin America, 1938; to Black Sea countries, to Canada and U.S.A., 1940. Chief of Planning Resettlement of Displaced Persons, U.N. Administration, Washington, D.C., and in Germany, 1944-45; Adviser to Cdn. Govt. (Dept. Nat. War Services) on immigrant European Communities in War Industry, 1941-43; Turkish Embassy Advisory Cttee. on Anglo-Turkish Cultural Relations, 1950. Chairman British Group of Union of Christian-Democrats of Europe (N.E.I.), 1947-56; Vice-President Internat. Inst. of Differing Civilisations (World-H.Q., Brussels), 1949-51; Mem. of Cttee., Internat. Centre for Regional Planning and Development (Brussels); Mem. of Council, Internat. Centre for Cultural and Art Exchanges (Rome), 1958-59. Fellow Académie des Sciences d'Outremer de France. Order of the Crown of Belgium; Medal of The Holy Redeemer of Greece. *Publications:* numerous Monographs and contribs. to Scientific Publications on Zoology, Linguistics, Islam, Social Reform, Ethnology, Refugee-and-Minority problems, and on international affairs. *Recreations:* ethnology, travel, natural history. *Address:* 46 Pall Mall, S.W.1. *Clubs:* Travellers'; Cercle d'Orient (Istanbul). [*Died* 21 *July* 1959.

PHILIPSON, Mrs. Hilton (Mabel Russell); *b.* 1 Jan. 1887; *m.* 1917, Hilton Philipson (*d.* 1941); two *s.* one *d.* M.P. (C.) Berwick-on-Tweed, 1923-29. *Address:* Limberlost, Ditchling, Sussex. [*Died* 8 *Jan.* 1951.

PHILIPSON-STOW, Sir E. P.; *see* Stow.

PHILLIMORE, Ven. Hon. Stephen Henry, M.C.; Archdeacon of Middlesex, 1933-53; Archdeacon Emeritus since Sept. 1953; Rector of St. George's, Hanover Square, 1940-55; Commander of Order of Orange Nassau; *b.* 14 Dec. 1881; *s.* of 1st Baron Phillimore; unmarried. *Educ.:* Winchester; Christ Church, Oxford. Curate of St. Michael and All Angels, Bromley-by-Bow; Vicar of Nakusp and Arrow Lakes, 1910-14; Vicar of Seaforth, Liverpool, 1915-26; Rector of Stepney and Rural Dean, 1926-33; Vicar of St. Thomas, Regent Street, 1934-40; Chaplain attached to the Brigade of Guards, 2nd Brigade, 1917-19; M.C. 1917, Houlthurst Forest; bar, Maubeuge, 1918. *Recreations:* lawn tennis, shooting, etc. *Address:* 110 Mount Street, W.1.; Shiplake House, Henley-on-Thames. *Club:* Oxford and Cambridge. [*Died* 16 *April* 1956.

PHILLIPPS, Henry Vivian; *s.* of Henry Mitchell and Louise Phillipps; *m.* Agnes Cassels, *d.* of James Ford, Edinburgh; one *s.* two *d.* *Educ.:* Charterhouse; Gonville and Caius College, Cambridge University. Called to Bar, 1907; Member of Northern Circuit; Private Secretary to Secretary for Scotland, 1912-16; Private Secretary to Rt. Hon. H. H. Asquith, 1917-22; contested Blackpool, 1906; Maidstone, 1910; Rochdale, 1918; M.P. (L.) West Edinburgh, Nov. 1922-Oct. 1924; Chief Whip of the Liberal Party, 1923-24; Chairman of the Liberal Party Organisation, 1925-27; J.P., Kent; Chm.: W. Kent Quarter Sessions, 1933-45; West Kent Unemployment Appeal Tribunal, 1934-40; Kent Agricultural Wages Committee, 1935-40; Board of Visitors Maidstone Convict Prison. *Address:* Upper Kennards, Leigh, Tonbridge. *Clubs:* Reform, Eighty. [*Died* 16 *Jan.* 1955.

PHILLIPS, Sir Beaumont; *see* Phillips, Sir F. B.

PHILLIPS, Eleanor Addison, M.A. Oxon; *b.* 2 Dec. 1874; *d.* of late Francis Phillips, C.B., Assistant Controller and Auditor, Exchequer and Audit Department, and Mary, *d.* of George Addison, of Temple Bar. *Educ.:* St. Mary's College, Paddington; St. Hugh's College, Oxford. Taught at St. Mary's Coll., Paddington; read for Honours School of Modern History at St. Hugh's College, Oxford, 1905-8; M.A. 1912; Headmistress of Clifton High School (Hon. M.A. Bristol University), 1908-33; President of Association of Headmistresses, 1929-31, now Vice-President; Hon. M.A. Bristol; founder, first Classification Club for Women (Venture Club now amalgamated with Soroptomists); served on Oxford and Cambridge Schools Examination Board, 1915-33, and on Panels of Investigation appointed by Secondary Schools Examination Council. Sometime Member Board of Management of Marie Curie Hospital; Member of Council of: Whiteland's Training College, Harrogate Ladies' College, Church Schools Co.; Hon. Officer of Institute of Christian Education. *Recreations:* reading, music, and drama, travel. *Address:* 17 Cleveland Sq., W.2. [*Died* 25 *June* 1952.

PHILLIPS, Colonel Eric Charles Malcolm, C.B. 1942; D.S.O. 1919; T.D.; D.L., J.P.; *b.* 7 Oct. 1883; *s.* of John Phillips; unmarried. *Educ.:* Eton; Brasenose College, Oxford. Served European War, 1914-19 (despatches, D.S.O.); A.D.C. to the King, 1931-41. *Address:* Earlshill House, Royston, Herts. [*Died* 7 *Jan.* 1957.

PHILLIPS, Ernest, M.B.E. 1939; *b.* 1870; Welsh parentage. Journalist, Sheffield, Lancaster, etc.; Conservative agent, Kent; Pres. Chamber of Trade; Chairman Conservative Assoc.; President Yorkshire Newspaper Society, etc.; Conservative candidate for Doncaster, 1929; Editor Doncaster Chronicle, 1908-46. *Publications:* How to become a Journalist; Trout in Lakes and Reservoirs; The Story of Doncaster; Float Fishing; The Golden Trout. *Address:* Edenholme, Thorne Road, Doncaster. *T.:* 2675. *Club:* Conservative (Doncaster). [*Died* 1 *Sept.* 1956.

PHILLIPS, Rear-Adm. Esmonde; *see* Phillips, Rear-Adm. P. E.

PHILLIPS, Sir (Frederick) Beaumont, K.B.E. 1956 (C.B.E. 1937); **His Honour Chief Justice Phillips;** LL.M. (Melb.); Chief Justice of the Supreme Court, Territory of Papua and New Guinea, since 1949 (Permanent Administration)

Judge of Central Court, Trust Territory of Nauru, since 1948; *b.* Ballarat, Victoria, 20 January 1890; *s.* of late J. B. Phillips, Camperdown, Victoria, and Mrs. C. A. Phillips, Camberwell, Vic.; *m.* 1943, Marie Jean Briton-Smith, Wellington, New Zealand. *Educ.:* Wesley College, Melbourne; Queen's College, Melbourne University. Admitted to Bar (High Court of Australia and Victorian), 1915; during European War, Asst. Censor 3rd M.D. and served overseas with A.I.F., first with A.A.M.C., later with Australian Flying Corps (Lieut. Observer); returned Australia, 1920; Special Commissioner of Inquiry to inquire into land disputes between non-natives and natives in the British Solomon Islands Protectorate, 1920-25; Stipendiary Magistrate, Rabaul, New Guinea, 1925; Judge of Supreme Court, Territory of New Guinea, 1928; Chief Judge, 1938; Senior Judge, Papua-New Guinea (Provl. Admin.), 1946; various occasions Acting or Deputy Administrator of the Territory of N.G. and P.-N.G. and P. and N.G.: *e.g.* during Native Strike at Rabaul in January 1929, and during volcanic eruptions at Rabaul, May 1937 (C.B.E.); granted leave of absence to serve with R.A.A.F., 1940-Feb. 1946; Group Captain, 1945; served overseas, U.K., 1941-44. *Recreations:* travel when possible; reading; interested in all arts. *Address:* Supreme Court, Port Moresby, Papua and New Guinea. *Clubs:* Savage, Royal Automobile Club of Victoria (Melbourne), Papua (Port Moresby). [*Died* 7 *June* 1957.

PHILLIPS, Frederick William, C.M.G. 1935; *b.* 11 Aug. 1879; *s.* of Hartley Phillips and Mary Grasby; *m.* 1906, Elizabeth Clara Chettle; two *s.* *Educ.:* Tottenham Grammar School. Entered Post Office, 1895; Assistant Secretary in charge of Overseas Telegraph Branch, 1925; Head of the British Delegation at the following International conferences:—Telegraph Conference at Brussels 1928, Broadcasting Conference at Prague 1929, Telegraph and Radio Conferences at Madrid 1932, and at Cairo, 1938; Broadcasting Conference at Lucerne, 1933; Director of Telecommunications, General Post Office, 1935-40; Deputy Chief Telegraph Censor, 1942-44. *Address:* 136 Purley Oaks Road, Sanderstead, Surrey. *T.:* Sanderstead 2629. [*Died* 5 *Dec.* 1956.

PHILLIPS, Gordon; Journalist; Lucio of the Manchester Guardian, 1910-50; *b.* Manchester, 13 July 1890; *s.* of Alfred Phillips and Mary Hague, *y. d.* of Robert Taylor, of Chadderton; *m.* 1922, Jess (*d.* 1945), *e. d.* of Thomas Hall; one *s.* *Educ.:* Manchester Grammar School. In business, Manchester; outside contributions to various magazines and journals; began to contribute verses over pen-name Lucio to Manchester Guardian, 1910; joined reporting staff, 1912; editorial staff, 1914; Inns of Court O.T.C. and Manchester Regt. (attached D.L.I.); miscellanist and leader writer Manchester Guardian since 1919; Assistant Editor, 1934-40; Hon. M.A. Manchester University, 1947. F.J.I. 1947. *Publications:* The Second Show, 1912; Brighter Intervals, 1923; High Explosive (novel), 1925; articles in prose and verse, Punch and elsewhere. *Recreations:* riding, golf. *Address:* Inglewood, Prestwich Park South, Prestwich, Manchester. *T.:* Prestwich 2587. *Clubs:* Savage; Manchester Press (Manchester). [*Died* 29 *Jan.* 1952.

PHILLIPS, Sir Herbert, K.C.M.G., *cr.* 1938 (C.M.G. 1928); O.B.E. 1918; *b.* 8 July 1878; *s.* of late Major Edward Phillips, 8th Hussars; *m.* 1913, Gertrude Georgina, *d.* of late Rodham Home Cook; one *s.* two *d.* Called to Bar, Middle Temple, 1914; Student Interpreter, China, 1898; China Medal, 1900; 1st class assistant, 1906; Acting Chinese Secretary, British Legation, Pekin, 1910; Vice-Consul, 1911; Consul at Shanghai, 1913-20; Foochow, 1921-22; Newchwang, 1922-23; Harbin, 1923-25; Inspector-General of Consulates in the Far East, 1926-1929; Consul-General, Canton, 1930-36; Consul-General, Shanghai, 1937-40; F.R.G.S. *Address:* Crockmore House, Fawley, Nr. Henley-on-Thames, Oxon. *T.:* Henley 367. *Club:* Phyllis Court (Henley). [*Died* 27 *March* 1957.

PHILLIPS, Colonel John Alfred Steele, C.I.E. 1934; M.B., Ch.B.; D.P.H.; Indian Medical Service retd.; late Director of Public Health, Bihar; *b.* 6 Oct. 1882; one *d.* Entered Indian Medical Service 1907; Director of Malariology, 1922-34; Inspector-General Civil Hospitals, United Provinces, India, 1936-1939; retired 1939; Officer of St. John's and Red Cross, 1939. *Address:* Dilkusha, Fowey, Cornwall. *Club:* Army and Navy. [*Died* 16 *Sept.* 1960.

PHILLIPS, Morgan Hector, M.A.Oxon; Director various private companies in London; Member London Labour Party since 1936; *b.* 14 March 1885; *y. s.* of late Rev. David Phillips, M.A., Rector of Radyr, nr. Cardiff; *m.* 1923, Jessie Whayman, *e. d.* of A. E. Percy Rae, Assistant Secretary to the Government of Burma (ret.); one *s.* *Educ.:* Christ's College, Brecon; Jesus College, Oxford (classical scholar). 21st Royal Fusiliers (Public School Batt.), 1914; Lieut. R.A.S.C. 1915-19; 1 year's Overseas Service, Italian Expeditionary Force; Assistant Master, University College School; Rector, Royal College, Mauritius and Head of Dept. of that Government, 1923-28; Headmaster, Ruthin School, North Wales, 1930-35; Delegate, Imperial Education Conference, 1927. *Recreations:* golf, fishing. *Address:* Rivelin, Berry Lane, Chorley Wood, Herts. *Clubs:* Royal Empire Society, National Trade Union. [*Died* 3 *March* 1953.

PHILLIPS, Rear-Admiral (Philip) Esmonde, C.B. 1945; D.S.O. 1917; D.L. Breconshire; *b.* 16 June 1888; *y. s.* of late P. S. Phillips, Crumlin Hall, Mon.; *m.* 1933, Mrs. Ellinor Curtis, *d.* of late Capt. Glen Kidston (marriage dissolved, 1950); one *s.* *Educ.:* H.M.S. Britannia. Served European War, 1914-18 (D.S.O. and bar); Chief Staff Officer to the Rear-Admiral of Submarines, 1927; Second Naval Member Commonwealth Naval Board, 1935-37; Chief of Staff and Maintenance Captain the Nore, 1937-38; A.D.C. to the King, 1938; retired list, 1938; served War of 1939-45, Flag Officer Milford Haven, and Senior British Naval Officer, Trinidad. *Address:* Woodberry Cottage, Itchenor, Sussex; c/o N.P. Bank, Builth Wells, Breconshire. *Clubs:* Naval and Military, Royal Yacht Squadron (Hon.). [*Died* 27 *Feb.* 1960.

PHILLIPS, Air Commodore Ronald Lancelot, C.B. 1955; C.B.E. 1946; Air Officer Commanding No. 27 Group since 1953; *b.* 19 Apr. 1909; *s.* of Philip Henry Phillips, F.L.A., and Francis Alice Phillips (*née* Wainwright); *m.* 1935, Ulla Eva, *d.* of Direktor Harry Wennerströn, Gothenburg; two *s.* *Educ.:* The College, Swindon; R.A.F. Electrical and Wireless School; R.A.F. College, Cranwell. Pilot Officer, 1929; India, 1930-32; Flying Officer, 1931; Afridi Campaign; specialised in signals, 1933; Flight Lieut., 1935; Aden, 1938-39; Mansuri Campaign; Sqdn. Ldr., 1938; Middle East, 1939-41; Wing Comdr., 1940; H.Q. Allied Expedn. Air Force, 1944; Group Capt. 1943; Western Europe, 1944; Air Cdre., 1945; Chief Signals Officer, Fighter Command, 1946-48; Air Ministry, 1949-53, Director of Radio, Director of Signals Policy. M.I.E.E. 1953. *Recreation:* horticulture. *Address:* Ebor House, Calne, Wilts. *T.:* Calne 3330. [*Died* 22 *Nov.* 1956.

PHILLIPS, Sidney, M.D. Lond., F.R.C.P.; Consulting Physician to St. Mary's Hospital, the Lock Hospital, the London Fever Hospital, and Paddington Green Children's Hospital; Treasurer, Royal College of Physicians, 1924-38;

late Examiner Royal College of Physicians and Surgeons, War Office, and University of London; late Brevet Col. R.A.M.C. *Educ.:* University College School and Hospital. *Publications:* article, Typhoid Fever, Cyclopædia of Medicine; numerous papers to medical journals and Transactions of Medical Societies. *Address:* 35-39 Queen's Gardens, W.2. [*Died* 19 *Jan.* 1951.

PHILLIPS, Wallace Banta, C.B.E. (Hon.) 1951; President Pyrene Manufacturing Co., New York, since 1950 (Director, 1915-); *b.* New York City, N.Y., 30 March 1886; *m.* 1915, Ann Lewis, New York. Chief of Circulation, G.2, American Exp. Force, France, 1917-19; Founder member, R. Soc. for Prevention of Accidents, 1923 (Vice-Pres., 1923, Hon. Treas., and Chm. Exec. Cttee., 1945-51); Chm. Monday Luncheon Club, 1937-51; Founder and first Dir.-Gen., Am. Ambulance, Great Britain, 1940; King's Medal; Special Asst. to Director of Naval Intelligence, U.S. Navy, Washington, D.C., 1940-41; Director Special Information Services, Office of Strategic Services, Washington and London, 1941-44. Chm. and Managing Dir., The Pyrene Co. Ltd., 1913-1951; Director, Avon India Rubber Co. Ltd., 1931-51; President American Chamber of Commerce in London, 1943-51; Treas. and Vice-Chm. Budget Commn. Internat. Chamber of Commerce, 1944-; Member Exec. Council Nat. Union of Manufacturers, 1936-51; Member Exec. Cttee., The Pilgrims of Great Britain, 1946-51; Member Council English-Speaking Union, 1941-51; Pres. American Soc. in London, 1950-51; Governor American Club, 1919-51. Trustee, Amer. Museum of Safety, 1950-; Director: Nat. Industrial Conf. Bd., 1951-; Nat. Safety Council, 1951-; Member Exec. Cttee. U.S. Council, Internat. Chamber of Commerce, 1951-. *Address:* 465 Park Avenue, New York 22, U.S.A. *T.A.:* Philrene, New York. *Clubs:* Bath, American, Royal Automobile; Links, Metropolitan, Recess, River (New York); Metropolitan, F. Street (Washington, D.C.); Travellers', St. Cloud Country (Paris). [*Died* 14 *April* 1952.

PHILLIPSON, Coleman, M.A., LL.D., Litt.D.; Professor of Law and Dean of Faculty of Law, University of Adelaide, 1920, 1925; of the Inner Temple, Barrister-at-law; *b.* Leeds, 1875; *e. s.* of Solomon Phillipson; Leeds; *m.* Eva Helen, *d.* of Mrs. Gottheil, London. *Educ.:* Central High School, Leeds, Yorkshire College (now University of Leeds); Victoria University of Manchester; Open Prizes for French, English Literature, Theory of Education, Debating; University College, London (Quain Prizeman in Comparative Law, 1906, 1907, and 1908). Was engaged for some years in educational work in Leeds, London, and Lincoln; called to Bar, 1907; spent much time in writing and research, chiefly on legal subjects; during European War did confidential work for various Government Depts., especially the Foreign Office, the Min. of Information, The Admiralty, and the War Cabinet; went with the British Delegation to the Paris Peace Conference, as Counsel and Legal Secretary to the Law Officers of the Crown; prepared the Handbook on War Indemnities for use of the British Plenipotentiaries. *Publications:* Studies in International Law, 1908; Effect of War on Contracts, etc., 1909; The International Law and Custom of Ancient Greece and Rome, 2 vols., 1911; co-author of Great Jurists of the World, 1913; Editor of 4th edition of Foote's Private International Jurisprudence, 1914; International Law and the Great War, 1915; Termination of War and Treaties of Peace, 1916; Editor of 5th English edition of Wheaton's International Law, 1916; The Question of the Bosphorus and Dardanelles, 1917; Alsace-Lorraine, 1918; Editor of 5th edition of Sir Frederick Smith's (afterwards Lord Chancellor) International Law, 1918; Editor of 8th edition of Taswell-Langmead's English Constitutional History, 1919; Editor of 9th edition of Mayne's Law of Damages, 1920; Three Criminal Law Reformers—a comparative study, 1923; Introductory Study on Albericus Gentilis (Classics of International Law, Washington); The Trial of Socrates, 1928. *Recreations:* reading, conversation, listening to music, walking. *Address:* 2 Kents Road, Torquay. [*Died* 11 *Dec.* 1958.

PHILLPOTTS, Eden; novelist; *b.* Mount Aboo, India, 4 Nov. 1862; *e. s.* of late Capt. Henry Phillpotts, 15th Native Infantry and Political Agent, States of Harowtee, Rajpootana; *m.* 1st, 1892 Emily (*d.* 1928), *y. d.* of late Robert Topham; one *s.* one *d.*; 2nd, 1929, Lucy Robina, *y. d.* of late Dr. Fortescue Webb. *Educ.:* Plymouth. Clerk in Sun Fire Insurance Office, 1880-90; on coming to London studied for the stage, but abandoned the art on finding his ability did not justify perseverance. *Publications:* Lying Prophets, 1896; Children of the Mist, 1898; The Human Boy, 1899; Sons of the Morning, 1900; The Striking Hours, 1901; The River, 1902; My Devon Year, 1903; The American Prisoner, 1904; The Secret Woman (dramatised, 1912); Knock at a Venture, 1905; The Portreeve, 1906; The Whirlwind; The Folk Afield, 1907; The Mother (dramatised, 1913); The Human Boy Again; The Virgin in Judgment, 1908; The Three Brothers; Fun of the Fair; The Haven, 1909; The Thief of Virtue; Tales of the Tenements; Wild Fruit, 1910; Demeter's Daughter; The Beacon; Dance of the Months, 1911; The Forest on the Hill, 1912; The Iscariot (poem), 1912; The Angle of Seventeen, 1912; Widecombe Fair; The Old Time before Them; The Joy of Youth, 1913; The Shadow (play), 1913; Curtain Raisers (short plays); The Judge's Chair, 1914; Brunel's Tower; Old Delabole, 1915; The Green Alleys; The Human Boy and the War; The Girl and the Faun, 1916; The Nursery; Plain Song (poems); The Farmer's Wife (play), 1917; Chronicles of St. Tid, 1917; The Spinners; A Shadow Passes, 1918; Storm in a Tea-Cup; Evander; St. George and the Dragons (play), 1919; Miser's Money; As the Wind Blows (poems); Orphan Dinah, 1920; Eudocia; The Bronze Venus, 1921; Pan and the Twins; Pixies' Plot (poems), 1922; Black, White, and Brindled; Children of Men; The Lavender Dragon, 1923; A Human Boy's Diary; A Comedy Royal; Cheat-the-Boys; The Treasures of Typhon; A Harvesting (poems); Redcliff, 1924; Up Hill, Down Dale; George Westover; Circé's Island, 1925; A Cornish Droll; Brother Man (poems); The Miniature; Yellow Sands (play) (with Adelaide Eden Phillpotts), 1926; The Blue Comet (play); The Jury, 1927; The Ring Fence; Arachne; Brother Beast (poems); Goodwill (poem); Three Short Plays, 1928; The Runaways (play); Tryphena; The Torch; One Hundred Sonnets; Buy a Broom (play), 1929; The Three Maidens; One Hundred Lyrics; Alcyone, 1930; Cherry Gambol (short stories), 1930; Stormbury; Jane's Legacy (play); Essays in Little, 1931; The Broom Squires, 1932; Bred in the Bone, 1932; Becoming (poems); They could do no other (short stories), 1932; Witch's Cauldron; A Shadow Passes, 1933; A Cup of Happiness (play); Song of a Sailor Man (narrative poem), 1933; The Oldest Inhabitant, 1934; Portrait of a Gentleman, 1934; Minions of the Moon, 1934; The Wife of Elias, 1935; Physician Heal Thyself, 1935; Ned of the Caribbees, 1935; Sonnets from Nature, 1935; The Owl of Athene, 1936; Woodnymph, 1936; Lycanthrope, 1937; A Dartmoor Village (Verse) 1937; Dark Horses, 1938; Portrait of a Scoundrel, 1938; Thorn in her Flesh; Golden Island, 1938; Saurus, 1938; Monkshood, 1939; Chorus of Clowns; A Mixed Grill; Goldcross, 1940; A Deed without a Name, 1941; Pilgrims of the Night, 1942; Flower of the Gods; A Museum Piece; The Changeling, 1943; The Drums of Dombali, 1945; Quartet, 1946; There was an Old Woman; Fall of the House of Heron; The Enchanted Wood (poem), 1948; Address Unknown; Dilemma, 1949; Waters of Walla, 1950; Through a Glass Darkly,

1951; From the Angle of 88; The Hidden Hand, 1952; His Brother's Keeper, 1953; One thing and another, 1954; The Widow Garland, 1955; Giglet Market, 1957; There Was an Old Man, 1958. *Address:* Kerswell, Broad Clyst, Exeter. [*Died* 29 *Dec.* 1960.

PHILLPOTTS, Admiral Edward Montgomery, C.B. 1916; *b.* 1871; *m.* 1911, Violet (*d.* 1949), *d.* of Col. G. W. Cockburn; one *s.* one *d.* Superintendent of Signal Schools, 1911; Naval Assistant to Second Sea Lord, 1912; to First Sea Lord, 1916; served Benin, 1897 (medal with clasp); European War, 1914-1917, including Jutland (despatches, C.B., Rear-Adm., 1918); President of Ordnance Committee, 1920-23; Retired List, 1923. *Address:* Beechwood, Speldhurst, nr. Tunbridge Wells. *T.:* Speldhurst 128. *Club:* United Service. [*Died* 9 *April* 1952.

PHILPS, (Alan) Seymour; Surgeon in Charge of Eye Department, St. Bartholomew's Hospital, since 1948; Surgeon to Moorfields, Westminster and Central Eye Hospital, since 1938; Lecturer in Ophthalmology to University of London; Examiner in Ophthalmology to the Royal Colleges; *b.* 28 Feb. 1906; *s.* of Francis John Philps, Editor of the Financial Times, and Matilda Ann Philps; *m.* 1st, 1934, Joan Wood Hill; three *d.*; 2nd, 1948, Dilys Bronwen Jones; two *s.* *Educ.:* Aldenham School; London University. Ho. Surg.: St. Bartholomew's, 1929, Moorfields, 1932; Chief Asst. to Eye dept. at St. Bartholomew's, 1934; Asst. Surg. to Moorfields, 1938; full Surg. to Moorfields, 1940; Ophthalmic Specialist R.A.M.C., 1942; Adviser in Ophthalmology to the War Office (Colonel), 1945; Adviser in Ophthalmology, Ministry of Transport, 1949. *Publications:* Ophthalmic Operations, 1950. Contributions to Brit. Jl. Ophthalmology, B.M.J., Lancet, etc. *Recreation:* fishing. *Address:* 104 Harley Street, W.1. *T.:* Welbeck 5900. [*Died* 26 *April* 1956.

PHIN, Sir John, Kt., *cr.* 1941; D.L., J.P.; LL.D. St. Andrews University, 1938; *b.* 24 Nov. 1881; *s.* of David N. Phin; *m.* 1909, Helena Halley Sharp. *Educ.:* Harris; High School, Dundee. Entered City Council, 1922; after having held various offices, *i.e.* Chairman of many Council Committees, Magistrate, Hon. City Treasurer, was elected Lord Provost, 1935-40; is also Chairman or Governor of many Philanthropic and Educational Institutions, and a Member of several Government Committees. District Commissioner for Civil Defence Eastern District, Scotland, 1939-44. *Address:* c/o Standard Bank of S. Africa, Commissioner St., Johannesburg, S. Africa. [*Died* 16 *Oct.* 1955.

PHIPPS, Brigadier Charles Constantine, C.B.E. 1940 (O.B.E. 1933); M.C.; Secretary, Institution of Royal Engineers; *b.* 17 Nov. 1889; *s.* of late Lt.-Col. E. V. A. Phipps, R.A.M.C., Richmond, Surrey; *m.* 1914, Alice Marjorie, *d.* of C. J. Copner, Laston, Ilfracombe; one *s.* *Educ.:* Cheltenham; Woolwich. Commissioned Royal Engineers, 1910; served European War, 1914-18, in France and Macedonia (M.C.); Dep. Chief Eng., N. Cmd., India, 1918; Afghan war, 1919; Technical Officer, Small Arms School, Hythe, 1920-24; Staff Capt. and D.A.D. Fortifications and Works, War Office, 1925-29; Chief Instructor, S.M.E., 1929-33; C.R.E. Canal Zone, Egypt, 1933-1936; C.R.E. Palestine, 1937; Dep. Chief Eng., Eastern Command, 1937-39; Chief Eng., Northern Command, 1939; Chief Eng. 2 Corps, B.E.F., France, 1939-40; Chief Eng. Scottish Command, 1940-44; retired pay, 1944. Commander Royal Order of St. Olav (Norway), 1947. *Address:* c/o Lloyds Bank, 6 Pall Mall, S.W.1. *Club:* Army and Navy. [*Died* 26 *July* 1958.

PHIPPS, Paul, F.R.I.B.A.; Architect; *b.* 3 March 1880; *s.* of William Wilton Phipps and Dame Jessie Phipps, D.B.E.; *m.* 1909; one *s.* one *d.* *Educ.:* Eton College; Balliol College, Oxford. *Address:* 315 Chelsea Cloisters, Sloane Avenue, S.W.3. *Club:* Brooks's. [*Died* 23 *Aug.* 1953.

PIBWORTH, Charles James, R.B.S.; R.W.A.; sculptor; *b.* Bristol, 1878; *m.* Geraldine MacMahon. *Educ.:* Royal Coll. of Art; The Royal Academy Schools. Awarded two Gold Medals for nude life studies in the National Competition of Schools of Art. *Principal Works:* the Turf Club War Memorial; four allegorical figures on the Law Society's building in Chancery Lane, London; three panels containing 21 life-size figures, representing the history of English Literature from the time of the Venerable Bede to that of Chaucer, on the Central Library, Bristol; four Abbots on the south side above Norman Arch, College Green, Bristol; ten silver figures and large silver knop ornament on Processional Cross, All Saints, Margaret Street, W.; the bronze decorations in the Entrance Hall of the Institute of Electrical Engineers; Euterpe, stone figure on the exterior of the Orchestral Musicians Association, Archer Street, Soho; statuettes of their Majesties King Edward VII., King George V., and Queen Mary; Prince of Wales and Princess Mary; also Beethoven and Calvin; portrait busts, King George V. and Queen Mary, Ex-President Hoover, The Prince of Wales, Viscount Runciman, Viscount Samuel, The Lord Stanmore, Sir Gilbert Parker, Bart., Sir J. Forbes-Robertson, Professor Lantéri, Professor Sir Patrick Geddes, Sir F. Handley Page, O.B.E., Sir Henry Gauvain, Professor Pomfret Kilner, Amelia Earheart; Medallion portrait of Sir Lindo Ferguson, M.D., in Dunedin Hospital, New Zealand; bas-relief portrait of Glyn Philpot, R.A.; exhibitor of many works at the Royal Academy, including life-size ideal statues of Andromeda and Diana; works in the permanent collections of the Royal West of England Academy, the Leicester Corporation Art Gallery, the Cheltenham Art Gallery, the Scottish National Portrait Gallery, Edinburgh, the Aberdeen Art Gallery. Mention Honorable for marble bas-relief, l'enfance Charmonte, Paris Salon, 1924; Bronze Medal for Gilt Terra-Cotta Statuette, Atalanta Tying Her Sandal, Paris Salon, 1937. *Address:* 295 King's Road, Chelsea, S.W.3. [*Died* 8 *Nov.* 1958.

PICCAVER, Alfred; Kammersinger; *b.* Long Sutton, Lincolnshire, 24 Feb. 1889; *m.*; one *s.* Went to America, 1890. *Educ.:* Troy, New York, under Allan Lindsay; School of the Metropolitan Opera, New York; Prague, under Proscie, Neuman Prohaska, also in Italy under Prof. Rosario. *Address:* 8 Putney Park Avenue, S.W.15. [*Died* 23 *Sept.* 1958.

PICK, Surgeon Rear-Admiral Bryan Pickering, C.B.E. 1938 (O.B.E. 1928); *b.* 13 Sept. 1879; *s.* of T. Pickering Pick, F.R.C.S., London; *m.* 1918, Annie Muriel, *d.* of George Frank, J.P., The Low Hall, Kirbymoorside, Yorks; one *s.* *Educ.:* Sherborne School; St. George's Hospital. Entered Royal Navy as Surgeon, 1904; Staff Surgeon, 1912; during European War served in Hospital Ships at Gallipoli and Eastern Mediterranean; Surgeon Commander, 1917, and later served as P.M.O. of R.N. College, Dartmouth, and as Surgical Specialist at R.N. Hospital, Chatham; Surgeon Captain, 1929; Professor of Surgery; Surgeon Rear-Admiral, 1934; Medical Officer-in-Charge, R.N. Hospital, Chatham, 1935-38; Honorary Surgeon to The King, 1936; retired list, 1938; House Governor and Medical Superintendent, King Edward VII's Convalescent Home for Officers, Osborne, Isle of Wight, 1939-46; Member of Council, B.M.A., President Kent Branch, 1936. *Publications:* Articles in Journal of Royal Naval Medical Service. *Recreation:* golf. *Address:* 1 Hyle House, Sherborne, Dorset. *T.:* Sherborne 328. [*Died* 3 *July* 1959.

PICKARD, Colonel Ransom, C.B. 1919; C.M.G. 1916; M.D., M.S., F.R.C.S.; A.M.S., T.A. (retired); *b.* 1867; *m.* 1912, Mabel Lucy Childe. Served European War, 1914-19 (C.M.G., C.B., despatches five times); Sheriff of Exeter, 1906-7; Mayor of Exeter, 1926-1927; Past President, Devonshire Association. *Address:* Rustholme, Streatham Drive, Exeter. [*Died* 9 *Feb.* 1953.

PICKARD-CAMBRIDGE, Sir Arthur (Wallace), Kt., *cr.* 1950; M.A., D.Litt. (Oxford and Sheffield); LL.D. (Edin.); F.B.A.; Hon. Fellow of Balliol College and of St. Hilda's College, Oxford; Member of the Governing Bodies of Rugby, Harrow, Stowe (formerly Chm.), Trent (Chm.), and Mill Hill (Chm.); Deputy Chairman Public Schools' Governing Bodies Association; Member of Executive Cttee., British Council; of Council of British Academy; and of London Tribunal for Conscientious Objectors; *b.* 20 Jan. 1873; *s.* of late Rev. O. Pickard-Cambridge, M.A., F.R.S.; *m.* 1901, Hilda Margaret, O.B.E. 1946, *d.* of late J. M. Hunt of Holmwood. *Educ.:* Weymouth College; Balliol College (Scholar and Jenkyns Exhibitioner); Craven Scholar, 1893. 1st Class. Mods. 1893; 1st Lit. Hum. 1895; Fellow of Oriel College, 1895-97; Fellow of Balliol College, 1897-1929; University Lecturer in Greek and Latin Literature, 1926-28; Member of the Hebdomadal Council, 1924-28; Joint-Secretary of the Oxford and Cambridge Schools Examination Board, 1915-19; Chairman of Council of St. Hilda's College, Oxford, 1920-28; Professor of Greek, Edinburgh University, 1928-30; Vice-Chancellor of Sheffield University, 1930-1938; Chairman of Northern Universities Joint Matriculation Board, 1936-38; Chairman of Government Commissions to inspect Achimota and Fourah Bay Colleges, etc., 1938; President Classical Association, 1938-1939; President Hellenic Society, 1941-44. Member of Church Assembly, 1935-45. *Publications:* Select Greek Comic Fragments, 1900; Translation of Demosthenes' Public Speeches, 1912; Demosthenes (in Heroes of Nations Series), 1914; Education, Science and the Humanities, 1916; Memoir of the Rev. O. Pickard-Cambridge, F.R.S., 1918; Dithyramb, Tragedy and Comedy, 1927; Chapters in Cambridge Ancient History, vol. vi., 1927; Chapter on Tragedy in New Chapters in Greek Literature III., 1932; Balliol and Edinburgh Compositions, 1936; The Theatre of Dionysus at Athens, 1946. *Recreations:* entomology and general natural history, gardening, travelling, motoring, music. *Address:* St. Catharine's, Marley, nr. Haslemere. *T.:* Haslemere 917. *Club:* Athenæum. [*Died* 7 *Feb.* 1952.

PICKARD-CAMBRIDGE, William Adair, M.A. (Oxford), Fellow Emeritus, Worcester College, Oxford; *b.* 14 Dec. 1879; *s.* of late Rev. O. Pickard-Cambridge, M.A., F.R.S.; *m.* 1917, Helen Ward, *d.* of late Daniel Richmond Henderson, Allahabad; one *d.* *Educ.:* Weymouth College (scholar); Balliol College, Oxford (scholar and Jenkyns Exhibitioner). 1st Class Mods. 1900; 1st Lit. Hum. 1902; hon. mention, Hertford Scholarship, 1900; Green Prize (Moral Philosophy), 1929; Assistant Master, Winchester College, 1902-5; Fellow of Magdalen College, 1904-12; Lecturer (Classics) Hertford College, 1906-12; Assistant Tutor (Classics and Philosophy), Jesus College, 1906-19; Lecturer in Philosophy, Bedford College for Women (London), 1915-20; Fellow and Tutor, Worcester College (Oxford), 1919-45. Organist of Manchester College (Oxford), 1917-19; of Balliol College, 1917-19; of Worcester College, 1919 and 1941-45; Conductor, Madrigal Group, Bournemouth Chamber Music Society, 1950-1954. *Publications:* Contributions to Mind, 1915-17-32, and to Aristotelian Society's Proceedings, 1917; Translation of Aristotle, Topica and Sophistici Elenchi (Oxford trans. of Aristotle Vol. I.), 1928; A Collection of Dorset Carols, 1926; Original Songs, Motets, Carols, and Carol-Arrangements. *Recreations:* music, motoring, cycling. *Address:* Brimlands, Water Tower Road, Broadstone, Dorset. *T.:* 348. *Club:* Oxford and Cambridge Musical. [*Died* 4 *March* 1957.

PICKEN, David Kennedy, M.A. (Camb., Glasg., Melb.); Master Emeritus of Ormond College; *b.* 27 July 1879; *m.* 1st, 1907; one *d.*; 2nd, 1911; five *d.* *Educ.:* Allan Glen's School, Glasgow; Glasgow University (1st class honours in Mathematics and Natural Philosophy, Metcalfe Fellowship); Jesus College, Cambridge (scholar); Ferguson Mathematical Scholarship of Scottish Universities, 1900; sixth wrangler, 1902. Lecturer on Mathematics, Glasgow Univ., 1903-7; Prof. of Mathematics, Victoria Coll., Wellington, Univ. of New Zealand, 1908-14; Master of Ormond Coll., Univ. of Melbourne, 1915-43; retd.; Member of London and Edinburgh Mathematical Societies and of the Mathematical Association, etc.; appointed by the Australian Federal Government to be Educational Director of the Commonwealth Educational Propaganda on War and Peace Issues, 1918; Chairman of the Australian Student Christian Movement, 1923-1932; Pres. of Mathematical Association of Victoria, 1937-44; Chm. Australian Editorial Cttee. of The Round Table, 1947-50. *Publications:* The Theory of Elementary Trigonometry; The Number-System of Arithmetic and Algebra; papers in L.M.S. and E.M.S. Proc. and Mathematical Gazette; Student Christian Movement publications; articles in the Australian Quarterly, etc. *Address:* c/o Ormond College, Melbourne, N.3., Victoria, Australia. [*Died* 17 *June* 1956.

PICKEN, Ralph Montgomery Fullarton, C.B.E. 1949; B.Sc. (Glasgow). M.B., Ch.B.Hons. (Glasgow), D.P.H. (Camb.), *b.* 25 July 1884; *s.* of David Picken, Glasgow; *m.* 1913, Jean Brand Watt; one *s.* two *d.* *Educ.:* Glasgow High School; Allan Glen's School, Glasgow; Glasgow University. Asst. and Divisional M.O., Public Health Dept., Glasgow, 1913-21; M.O.H. Cardiff, 1921-33; Mansel Talbot Professor of Preventive Medicine, Welsh National School of Medicine, 1933-49; Provost, Welsh National School of Medicine, 1945-55, retired. Member: Gen. Med. Council; Vice-Chm. Welsh Regional Hosp. Bd.; Mem. Bd. of Governors, Cardiff United Hospitals; Vice-President, B.M.A. Formerly: President Society of M.O.H.; Pres. Cardiff Medical Soc.; Chm. Public Health Cttee., B.M.A.; Vice-Chm. Medical Personnel Priority Cttee.; Member, Medical Advisory Council, Nuffield Provincial Hosps. Trust, General Nursing Council. *Publications:* contrib. to current medical literature on Public Health and Epidemiology. *Recreation:* golf. *Address:* 46 Palace Road, Llandaff, Cardiff. [*Died* 7 *Sept.* 1955.

PICKERILL, Henry Percy, C.B.E. 1923 (O.B.E. 1919); M.D., M.Ch. (Birm.), F.R.A.C.S.; Fellow Roy. Soc. Medicine; Membre d'honneur Société Belge de Stomatologie; Consulting Plastic Surgeon, Wellington Hospital, N.Z.; formerly Plastic Surgeon Royal North Shore Hosp., Sydney; foundation member, Brit. Assoc. Plastic Surgeons; Lieut.-Colonel N.Z.M.C. (retd.); *m.* 1st, Mable Louise Knott; 2nd, Cecily Mary Clarkson; three *s.* two *d.* Cartwright prizeman Royal Coll. of Surgeons, 1911. *Publications:* Stomatology, 1912; Facial Surgery, 1924; numerous papers on plastic surgery to Roy. Soc. Med., British and Aust. and N.Z. Journals of Surgery and Brit. Jl. Plastic Surgery. *Recreations:* fishing, gardening. *Address:* Beechdale, Silverstream, Wellington, N.Z. [*Died* 10 *Aug.* 1956.

PICKERING, Colonel Charles James, C.M.G., 1921; D.S.O. 1916; *b.* 1880; *m.* 1904, Eileen Rosetta, *y. d.* of Robert William

Cary Reeves, J.P., D.L., Besborough, Co. Clare; two *s.* *Educ.:* Mill Hill School; graduate of the Staff College and London School of Economics. 2nd Lieut. The Duke of Wellington's Regiment, 1900; A.D.C. to Lt.-Governor of Burma, 1901-3; Adjutant, 1908-11; Brigade Major, 1912-15; Commanding 4th Bn., temp. Lt.-Col., 1915; A.A. and Q.M.G., 1916-18; A.A.G. (Aldershot), 1918-19; (G.H.Q., Ireland), 1921-22; Commanding 2nd Bn., 1925-29; Colonel, 1929; A.A. and Q.M.G., 1st Division, 1929-1933; retired, 1933; employed Home Office from 1938; Colonel of The Duke of Wellington's Regt. 1938-47; Deputy Regional Commissioner for Civil Defence, 1941-45. Served European War, 1914-18 (severely wounded, despatches, C.M.G., D.S.O., Brevet Lt.-Col.). *Address:* 10 The Crescent, Alverstoke, Hants. *T.:* Gosport 89026. *Clubs:* United Service, Royal Automobile. [*Died* 15 *Feb.* 1951.

PICKUP, Sir Arthur, Kt. 1947; *b.* 14 December 1878; *s.* of John William and Margaret Pickup, Burnley, Lancashire; *m.* 1903, Florence, *d.* of John Knape, Burnley; three *s.* three *d.* *Educ.:* Church School, Burnley. Served European War, 1914-18, with Royal Artillery (T.A.). Became Public Accountant. Formerly: Director of the Manchester Ship Canal Company (1945-46); Director of the Co-operative Insurance Society, and President of the Co-operative Wholesale Society. *Address:* Burn Lea, 6 Dove Point Road, Meols, Wirral, Cheshire. *T.:* Meols 3430. [*Died* 9 *April* 1960.

PICKWORTH, Sir Frederick, Kt. 1957; Chairman: English Steel Corporation Limited and of its principal subsidiary Companies; Chairman: Security Rock Bits Limited; Director: British Acheson Electrodes Ltd.; High Speed Steel Alloys Ltd.; The Steetley Co. Ltd.; Vickers Ltd.; Master Cutler of Sheffield, 1957; *b.* 7 May 1890. *Address:* Southwood, Endcliffe Hall Avenue, Sheffield. [*Died* 14 *July* 1959.

PICTON-TURBERVILL, Edith, O.B.E.; *d.* of late Col. J. Picton-Turbervill of Ewenny Priory, Glamorgan, and Eleanor, *d.* of Sir Grenville Temple, Bart., of Stowe. *Educ.:* Royal School, Bath. Began her social work on the Vale of Glamorgan Railway to improve the conditions of the navvies; for ten years National Vice-President of the Y.W.C.A.; spent six years in India in social work, and secretary for the Student Movement in S. India; organised the war-time appeal for the Y.W.C.A., and raised £250,000 for its work; took part in the movement for admitting women into a wider ministry in the Church; Bishop of London's Certificate for Pastoral and Evangelistic Work; joined the Labour Party in 1918, and stood for Parliament in 1922 and 1924; M.P. (Lab.) Wrekin Division, 1929-1931; Member of Ecclesiastical Committee of the Lords and Commons, 1929-31; introduced successfully The Sentence of Death (Expectant Mothers) Bill, to prevent the passing of the sentence of death on expectant mothers, which was placed on the Statute Book; Leader of British Delegation to International Congress of Women Citizens at Istanbul, 1935 and at Copenhagen, 1939; Govt. Commissioner to inquire into the Mui Tsai Slavery in Malaya and Hong-Kong, 1936; Wrote and signed Minority report on Mui Tsai, published by Colonial Office, 1937, which has been accepted by the Governments concerned, 1939; attached to Ministry of Information, 1941-43. *Publications:* The Musings of a Laywoman; Christ and Woman's Power; Christ and International Life; (with Lady Oxford and others) Myself when Young, 1938; Life is good, an autobiography, 1939; In the Land of my Fathers, 1946; Should Women be Priests and Ministers?, 1953. *Recreations:* walking across country with a silent companion; swimming. *Address:* Woodend, Sandy Lane Road, Charlton Kings, Cheltenham. [*Died* 31 *Aug.* 1960.

PIDDUCK, Frederick Bernard; *b.* 17 July 1885. *Educ.:* Portland Street Elementary School, Southport; Bickerton House School, Southport; Manchester Grammar School; Exeter Coll., Oxford (Junior Mathematical Sch., 1905; Senior Mathematical Sch., 1907; 1st class Physics, 1907); Technical High School, Charlottenburg. Ballistic Research Officer, Woolwich Arsenal, 1918; D.Sc. 1923; Fellow Queen's Coll., Oxford, 1907; Tutor, Corpus Christi Coll., 1921-50; Univ. Lecturer, 1920. Univ. Reader in Applied Mathematics, 1927-34. *Publications:* A treatise on Electricity, 1916 (1921 Spanish translation), 1925; The Reform of Mathematics (Mathematical Gazette, 1937); Mathematical Theory of Electricity, 1937; Currents in Aerials and High-frequency Networks, 1946; The Semantic Discipline (New English Review, 1947); The Metre-Kilogram-Second System of Electrical Units (with Dr. R. K. Sas), 1947; mathematical and physical papers. *Recreations:* photography, swimming, travel. *Address:* c/o Barclay's Bank, Keswick. [*Died June* 1952.

PIERCY, Professor Norman Augustus Victor, D.Sc. Eng. (Lond.) 1920; M.I.C.E. 1936; M.I.Mech.E. 1934; F.R.Ae.S. 1928; University Professor of Aeronautical Engineering in the University of London, Queen Mary College, since 1949; Head of Aeronautical Department, Queen Mary College, since 1919; *b.* St. John's Wood, London, 10 Aug. 1891; *m.* Alma Piercy, M.A., LL.B. (Cantab.), M.Sc. (Lond.), of Lincoln's Inn, barrister-at-law, sister of 1st Baron Piercy, C.B.E. *Educ.:* Hampton Grammar School. Apprenticed to Yarrow and Co., Scotstoun, 1908-13; B.Sc. Hons. Eng. (Lond.), 1913; designed aircraft at Shoreham Aerodrome and experimented for Admiralty, Air Board and Min. of Munitions in University wind tunnel of own construction, 1914-18; chiefly responsible for introduction of aeronautics into B.Sc. (Lond.) 1922; mathematical and experimental research in aerodynamics and fluid mechanics since 1914; Keddy Fletcher-Warr Student, 1926; Univ. of London Reader in Aeronautics, 1934-49; member of Council R.Ae.S., 1935-39; T. Bernard Hall Prize, I.Mech.E., 1938; lecturer in Aeronautics and Fluid Mechanics, Univ. of Cambridge, 1939-44; Leverhulme Research Fellow, 1940; researches on laminar flow wings, 1936-44; service on many cttees. for aeronautical education. *Publications:* Aerodynamics, 1937; Elementary Aerodynamics, 1944; aeronautical articles in Encyc. Brit. and Chambers's Encyc.; papers in Proc. Roy. Soc., Phil. Mag., Advisory Cttee. for Aeronautics and Aeronautical Research Cttee. Reports and Memoranda, Aircraft Engineering, Proc. I.Mech.E., Jl. R. Ae. S. *Recreations:* golf, mountain walking. *Address:* 3 King's Bench Walk, Temple, E.C.4. *T.:* Central 8939; 14 St. Regis, Chesterton Road, Cambridge. *T.:* Cambridge 55536. *Club:* Gog Magog (Cambridge). [*Died* 1 *Feb.* 1953.

PIERIS, Sir Paulus Edward Deraniyagala, Kt., *cr.* 1952; C.M.G. 1933; Litt.D. (Cantab.); *b.* 16 Feb. 1874; *s.* of J. M. P. Pieris, Gate Mudaliyar and *d.* of Soloman Dias Bandaranaike, Gate Mudaliyar; *m.* Hilda, *d.* of Hon. J. P. Obeyesekere, M.L.C.; three *s.* one *d.* *Educ.:* St. Thomas' College, Colombo; Trinity College, Cambridge. 2nd Class Classical Tripos, 1895; M.A., LL.M.; called to Bar, Inner Temple, 1896; Cadet, Ceylon Civil Service, 1896; District Judge, Galle, 1914; Jaffna, 1915; Colombo, 1918; Kandy, 1921; Public Trustee, Ceylon, 1928-35; Trade Comr. for Ceylon in London, 1935-38; President R.A.S. (Ceylon), 1933-35. D. Litt. (*h.c.*), Ceylon. *Publications:* Ceylon, the Portuguese Era, 2 vols.; Ceylon and the Portuguese; Ceylon and Portugal; The Kingdom of Jafanapatam; Ribeiro's Ceilão (trans.); Ceylon and the Hollanders; The Growth of Dutch Influence in Ceylon; Notes on some

PICKERING, Loring, F.R.G.S. See page xxx.

Sinhalese Families (5 parts); Letters to Ceylon 1814-1824; Tri Sinhala, 1796-1815; Sinhale and the Patriots, 1815-1818; Law of Rei Vindicatio in Ceylon; numerous papers. *Address:* Nugedola, Pasyala, Ceylon. [*Died* 12 *April* 1959.

PIGGOTT, His Honour Judge Sir George Bettesworth, K.B.E., *cr.* 1919 (C.B.E. 1918); F.R.G.S.; J.P.; *b.* 30 April 1867; *o. surv. s.* of Fraser Piggott, J.P. (*d.* 1920), of Fitz-Hall, Sussex; *m.* 1st, 1904, Amy (*d.* 1909), *y. d.* of Major Harvey Spiller, and *g.d.* of late Robert Crawshay, J.P., of Cyfarthfa Castle, Glamorgan; 2nd, 1915, Nadine Sophie (whom he divorced, 1921), *d.* of late Sir Reginald Proctor-Beauchamp, 5th Bart., and Lady Violet, *o. c.* of 5th Earl of Roden; 3rd, 1927, Winifred (*d.* 1947), *d.* of Edward J. Dove, J.P., of Oaklands Park, Riding Mill, Northumberland; 4th, 1947, Constance Louise, *widow* of Enrique Juan Penard Fernandez and *d.* of Herbert E. Kennaird. *Educ.:* Westminster School. Called to Bar, Middle Temple, 1888; practised in London and on the South-Eastern Circuit, Sussex Sessions, North London, and Middlesex Sessions, and Central Criminal Court; appeared in several sensational cases, notably Regina *v.* Cater (threatening to shoot Her late Majesty), also in the Regent's Park Murder Case; Judicial Officer and Vice-Consul of the British Central Africa Protectorate, 1896; Chief Judicial Officer, 1898; Central African medal and clasp, 1894-98, as volunteer during the native wars; Senior Judge, Zanzibar, 1900-4; Assistant Judge H.M.'s Supreme Consular Court, Sublime Ottoman Porte, 1904-10, and Acting Judge; retired, 1911; sat in Appellate Jurisdiction as President of H.M. Appeal Court for Eastern Africa; also sat as Judge in Arab matters on the highest judicial tribunal of H.H. the Sultan of Zanzibar; was legal member of the East Africa Protectorate Council; contested Battersea Division for the London County Council as Municipal Reform Candidate, 1913; Member L.C.C. for Mile End, 1917-19; Clapham, 1919-22; a Member of the Appeal Tribunal for the County of London under the Military Service Act, and was Deputy Chairman and Secretary to that Tribunal, and served on a number of Government Committees. Has written on Central Africa. *Recreations:* shooting and travelling; has visited Baghdad, Lake Nyassa, and Lake Victoria Nyanza. *Clubs:* Carlton, St. James', M.C.C.; Travellers', Interalliée (Paris). [*Died* 14 *March* 1952.

PIGGOTT, Sir Henry Howard, Kt., *cr.* 1931; C.B. 1919; C.B.E. 1918; Deputy Metropolitan Traffic Comr. and Licensing Authority; *b.* 13 Sept. 1871; *s.* of late Rev. H. J. Piggott, Rome; *m.* 1916, Mary Tomlinson; one *d.* *Educ.:* Kingswood School, Bath; Corpus Christi College, Oxford. Assistant Master, Bradfield College, Berkshire, 1895-1902; H.M. Inspector of Schools, Board of Education, 1904-15; joined the Ministry of Munitions, 1915; Private Secretary to Minister of Munitions, 1916-17; Assistant Secretary, Ministry of Munitions, 1917-19; Assistant Secretary and Deputy Secretary, Ministry of Transport, 1920-34; Chairman of Traffic Commissioners and Licensing Authority for S.E. Traffic Area of Great Britain, 1934-39; War appointment: Regional Transport Commissioner for the Southern Region, with Headquarters at Reading, 1939-1946. *Address:* High Chimneys, Cholesbury, Tring, Herts. *T.:* Cholesbury 218. [*Died* 8 *April* 1951.

PIGOTT, Sir Stephen J., Kt., *cr.* 1939; D.Sc. (Columbia Univ. N.Y.); J. P. Glasgow; M.Inst.C.E., M.I.N.A.; *b.* Cornwall, New York, U.S.A., 30 Jan. 1880; *s.* of Patrick Pigott, Cornwall, New York, U.S.A.; *m.* 1907, Mary Thatcher Lewis (*d.* 1943), Chattanooga, Tennessee, U.S.A.; one *s.* four *d.*; *m.* 1951, Dorothy Quincy Wright, *widow* of Neil Matheson McWharrie. *Educ.:* Cornwall School; Columbia University, New York City (Degree in Mechanical and Marine Engineering, 1903). Became resident in Great Britain, 1908; Local Director of John Brown & Co. Ltd., Clydebank, 1920; Elected to Board, 1934; Director-in-Charge of John Brown & Co. Ltd., Shipyard and Engine Works, Clydebank, 1935; Managing Director, 1938-49; Member: Worshipful Company of Shipwrights, Institutes of Marine Engineers (Pres. 1937-38), Civil Engineers, Naval Architects, Mechanical Engineers; Institution of Engineers and Shipbuilders in Scotland; Medal for outstanding Leadership in Marine Propulsion and Construction, American Society of Mechanical Engineers, 1938. *Address:* Closeburn Castle, Closeburn, Thornhill, Dumfriesshire. [*Died* 27 *Feb.* 1955.

PIGOU, Arthur Cecil, M.A.; F.B.A. 1927-1945; Prof. of Political Economy, Cambridge, 1908-43; Member of Committee on Currency and Foreign Exchange, 1918; Royal Commission on Income Tax, 1919; Fellow King's College, Cambridge; *b.* 1877; *s.* of late C. Pigou, 15th Regiment. *Educ.:* Harrow; King's College, Cambridge. Ex-President Cambridge Union Society; Jevons Memorial Lecturer, University College, London, in 1903-4; Girdler's University Lecturer in Economics, Cambridge, 1904-7. *Publications:* Robert Browning as a Religious Teacher; The Riddle of the Tariff; The Principles and Methods of Industrial Peace; Protective and Preferential Import Duties; The Problem of Theism and other Essays; The Policy of Land Taxation; Wealth and Welfare; Unemployment; The Economy and Finance of the War; The Economics of Welfare, 1920; The Political Economy of War; Industrial Fluctuations, 1926; A Study in Public Finance, 1928; (with D. H. Robertson) Economic Essays and Addresses, 1931; The Theory of Unemployment, 1933; Economics in Practice, 1935; The Economics of Stationary States, 1935; Socialism versus Capitalism, 1937; Employment and Equilibrium, 1940; Lapses from Full Employment, 1945; Income, an Introduction to Economies, 1946; The Veil of Money, 1948; Essays in Economics, 1953; Alfred Marshall and Current Thought, 1953; various articles in the Journal of the Royal Economic Society and elsewhere. *Address:* King's College, Cambridge. *T.:* Cambridge 4305. *Club:* Alpine. [*Died* 7 *March* 1959.

PILCHER, Lieut.-Colonel (Hon. Col.) Alan Humphrey, C.I.E. 1944; M.C.; E.D.; Auxiliary Force (India); Managing Director J .Joule & Sons Ltd., Stone, Staffs.; *b.* 12 July 1898; *s.* of P. W. Pilcher, Shrewsbury; *m.* 1928, Dorothy Eileen, *d.* of R. S. Parrington, Liverpool; two *s.* one *d.* *Educ.:* Shrewsbury School. Served European War, 1914-18, with R.F.A., France, 1917-18 (M.C.); commanded Assam Valley Light Horse, 1935-1939; Hon. A.D.C. to Viceroy of India, 1937-1942; War of 1939-45; served Burma Campaign, 1942-43 (despatches, C.I.E.). Chm. Assam Branch Indian Tea Assoc., 1947. *Address:* Brookside, Blythe Bridge, Staffs. *T.:* Blythe Bridge 2149. *Club:* Bengal (Calcutta). [*Died* 15 *July* 1957.

PILCHER, Vice-Admiral Cecil Horace, D.S.O. 1920; *b.* 1877; *s.* of late H. C. Pilcher, Henley-on-Thames; *m.* Catherine Moraitinis, *g.d.* of Aristide Moraitinis, Regent and Prime Minister of Greece; one *s.* one *d.* Commanded H.M.S. Dauntless, 1919-21, employed in Baltic (despatches, D.S.O.); A.D.C. to H.M., 1928; Rear-Adm. and retired list, 1928; Vice-Adm., retd., 1933. *Address:* 5 Wilton Pl., Belgrave Sq., S.W.1. *T.:* Sloane 9719. [*Died* 4 *Feb.* 1953.

PILDITCH, Sir Philip John Frederick, 3rd Bt., *cr.* 1929; *b.* 10 Aug. 1919; *e. s.* of Sir Philip Harold Pilditch, 2nd Bt., and Frances Isabella, *d.* of J. G. Weeks, J.P., Bedlington, Northumberland; *m.* 1948, Phyllis Jean, *d.* of D. C. Stewart-Smith, M.B.E., The Pantiles, Weybridge, Surrey;

one *d.* *Educ.:* Winchester Coll.; Trinity Coll., Oxford. Served War of 1939-45, Lt. R.A. (invalided, 1942). *Recreations:* sailing and archæology. *Heir:* *b.* Richard Edward, *b.* 8 Sept. 1926. *Address:* Rowans Hill, Coulsdon Lane, Chipstead, Surrey. *T.:* Downland 4731. [*Died* 11 *May* 1954.

PILKINGTON, Major Sir Arthur William Milborne-Swinnerton-, 13th Bt., *cr.* 1635; M.C.; late 16th Lancers; *b.* 7 April 1898; *er. s.* of Sir Thomas Milborne-Swinnerton-Pilkington, 12th Bt., and Lady Kathleen Mary A. Cuffe (*d.* 1938), *o. c.* of 4th Earl of Desart; *S.* father, 1944; *m.* 1931, Elizabeth M., *d.* of Major J. F. Harrison, King's Walden Bury, Hitchin; one *s.* three *d.* *Educ.:* Eton; R.M.C. Sandhurst. *Heir:* *s.* Thomas Henry, *b.* 1934. *Address;* Little Belvoir, Melton Mowbray. *T.:* Nether Broughton 60; Chevet Park, Wakefield. *Club:* Buck's. [*Died* 24 *July* 1952.

PILKINGTON, Harry Seymour Hoyle, C.I.E. 1917; M.V.O. 1912; *b.* 1869; *s.* of late Henry Foster Pilkington, J.P., of Park Lane Hall, Doncaster; *m.* 1904, Constance Mary, *d.* of F. Nevill-May of Shanghai. Entered Indian P.O., 1890; Assistant Director-General, 1909-16; employed on famine duty, 1900; served with the Field Post Office in the China Expedition, 1900-2; took charge of postal arrangements during visits to India of Prince and Princess of Wales, 1905-6; the Ameer of Afghanistan, 1906-7; and King George and Queen Mary, 1911-12; Director Postal Services (Lt.-Col.) with the Indian Forces in France, 1914 (despatches, C.I.E.); Postmaster-General, 1916-24. *Address:* Wadenhoe, near Peterborough. [*Died* 11 *Jan.* 1954.

PILKINGTON, Colonel Herbert Edward, C.B.E. 1919; *b.* 1 Aug. 1877. Served S. Africa, 1900 (Queen's medal with four clasps); European War, 1915-19 (despatches, C.B.E., two medals); Director Ordnance Services, 1920-24; Q.M.G., N.Z. Military Forces, 1924-31; retired, 1931. *Address:* 46 McFarlane Street, Wellington, E.1, New Zealand. [*Died* 31 *May* 1956.

PILKINGTON, Colonel Lionel Edward, C.M.G. 1916; J.P.; Chairman of Richard Evans and Co. Ltd.; Hon. Col. 5th Bn. The Prince of Wales's Volunteers, 1934-45; *s.* of the late Colonel Richard Pilkington, C.B., M.P. Newton Div., Lancs, and Louisa Sinclair, Rainford Hall, St. Helens; *m.* 1902, Naomi Evelyn Beckett; two *d.* *Educ.:* Clifton Coll.; King's College, Cambridge. Joined 2nd V.B. now 5th South Lanc. Regt. 1896; commanded, 1912; served 71st I.Y. South Africa, 1900-1 (Queen's medal 5 clasps); European War (Flanders and France), 1914-16 (C.M.G.). *Recreations:* golf, shooting, fishing, etc. *Address:* 19 Greenbank Drive, Sefton Park, Liverpool. *T.:* Wavertree 2233. *Club:* Bath. [*Died* 9 *June* 1952.

PILKINGTON, M. Evelyn, C.B.E. 1925; J.P.; *b.* Oct. 1879; *yr. d.* of late Col. Richard Pilkington, C.B., M.P., and Louisa, *e. d.* of Arthur Sinclair, St. Helens. Contested (C.), St. Helens, 1923 and 1924; late Chm. Women's Unionist Association, St. Helens. *Recreation:* walking. *Address:* Crank House, St. Helens, Lancashire. *Club:* Forum. [*Died* 22 *Jan.* 1955.

PILLING, Sir (Henry) Guy, K.C.M.G., *cr.* 1941 (C.M.G. 1932); Brilliant Star of Zanzibar, First Class; Speaker of East Africa Central Legislative Assembly since 1949; *b.* East Dereham, 1886; *m.* 1912, Gladys Neville, *o. d.* of late J. H. Garrick, Suva, Fiji; (one *s.* killed in action 1942) one *d.* *Educ.:* King's School, Ely; Keble College, Oxford. Cadet, Fiji, 1907; Assistant Colonial Secretary, Fiji, 1921; Secretary, Western Pacific High Commission, 1926; Assistant to High Commissioner for Western Pacific, 1929; Colonial Secretary, British Honduras, 1929-34; Deputy Colonial Secretary, Kenya, 1934-37; Governor and Commander-in-Chief of St. Helena, 1938-41; British Resident Zanzibar, 1941-46; retired. *Address:* c/o Ngong Post Office, Nairobi, Kenya. [*Died* 13 *June* 1953.

PIM, Sir Alan William, K.C.I.E., *cr.* 1929 (C.I.E. 1918); K.B.E., *cr.* 1935; C.S.I. 1926; *s.* of late Jas. Pim, Monkstown, Co. Dublin; *m.* 1916, Nora Gordon, *d.* of late Sir John Scott, K.C.M.G., D.C.L. Entered I.C.S. 1894; retired, 1930; Financial and Economic Commissions Swaziland and Zanzibar, 1932; Bechuanaland, 1933; British Honduras, 1934; Basutoland, 1935; Kenya, 1936; Northern Rhodesia, 1937. *Address:* Ridgway, Harberton Mead, Headington, Oxford. [*Died* 28 *June* 1958.

PINK, Sir Harold (Rufus), Kt., *cr.* 1919; F.T.C.L.; F.I.D.; J.P.; Chairman W. Pink & Sons, Ltd., Portsmouth; Chairman Dear and Morgan Ltd., Cowes, I. of W.; Chairman, Portsmouth Water Company; Alderman of Portsmouth; Freeman of the City of Portsmouth, 1929; Vice-President of Royal National Life Boat Association; Lay Canon of Portsmouth Cathedral; *b.* 27 October 1858; *s.* of Sir William Pink, J.P., K.L.H.; *m.* 1st, 1879, Laura Kate Whitcher (*d.* 1929), Avon, Hants; 2nd, 1931, Blanche Marian Stares, Havant. *Educ.:* Warminster Grammar School, Wilts. Mayor of Portsmouth, 1899-1900, 1916-1917, 1917-18 and Lord Mayor, 1933-34. *Address:* Shrover, 1 Rothesay Road, Bournemouth, Hants. *T.:* Westbourne 61055. [*Died* 3 *Jan.* 1952.

PINSENT, Colonel John Ryland, C.B.E. 1949; D.S.O. 1918; *b.* 12 Aug. 1888; 3rd *s.* of Sir Richard Pinsent, 1st Bt.; *m.* 1915, Kathleen May Boyce; two *s.* *Educ.:* Winchester College; R.M.A., Woolwich. Royal Engineers, 1909-20. Served European War, Bt. Major, France, 1914-19. Royal Corps of Signals, 1920-24; Asst. Master, Winchester College, 1926-34; Councillor and Alderman Winchester City Council, 1931-45; Mayor of Winchester, 1937. Rejoined Army, comdg. 152 O.C.T.U. and Pres. No. 4 W.O.S.B., 1939-45; Chairman Civil Service Selection Board, 1945-50; Director, Birfield Ltd., 1954. Officier Légion d'Honneur, 1916. *Recreation:* gardening. *Address:* Priors Barton, Winchester. *T.:* Winchester 2615. *Club:* United Service. [*Died* 2 *Oct.* 1957.

PIPER, Mr. Justice Harold Bayard, LL.B.; O.St.J.; *b.* 26 April 1894; *s.* of late Mr. Justice Arthur William Piper and Edna Elizabeth Piper; *m.* 1922, Dorothy Edna Stow-Smith; one *s.* *Educ.:* Prince Alfred College, Adelaide; Adelaide University, LL.B., 1914. Admitted South Australian Bar, 1915; served with Australian Imperial Forces, Egypt, France, 1915-19; practised at South Australian Bar, 1919-38; Judge of Commonwealth Court of Conciliation and Arbitration, 1938; Chief Judge Commonwealth Court of Conciliation and Arbitration (Australia) since 1941-47; retired, 1947; Chairman Australian Red Cross Society, 1940-1942, Vice-Pres. 1942; Chm. Stevedoring Industry Commission, 1942-45. *Clubs:* Melbourne (Melbourne, Australia); Adelaide (Adelaide). [*Died* 10 *May* 1953.

PIPON, Philip James Griffiths, C.M.G. 1921; C.I.E. 1917; M.C.; Indian Civil Service, retired; *b.* 13 July 1874; *o. c.* of late Rev. J. C. C. Pipon, of Arnold House School, Llandulas and Toddington Rectory, Beds., and, till 1879, Seigneur de Noirmont, Jersey, and of Susan Augusta Griffiths; *m.* 1907, Harriet Nina. 2nd *d.* of G. L. Whately, of 17 Lincoln's Inn Fields and Ayres End, Harpenden, Herts; four *d.* *Educ.:* Arnold House and Cordwalles, Maidenhead; Charterhouse (scholar); Corpus Christi College, Oxford (open classical scholar). Entered I.C.S., 1897; employed N.-W. Frontier, Foreign and Political

Dept. Govt. of India. (Medal and Clasp, Mohmand Operations, 1908). Accompanied Sir Aurel Stein on Expedition to Mahaban, 1904; served European War, 1914-19, Interpreter with Indian Corps (M.C.), Military Intelligence (C.I.E.); 3rd Afghan War, 1919 (clasp); Sessions Judge, Peshawar Division, 1920; Additional Member Legislative Council; Member British Diplomatic Mission to Afghanistan, 1921; a signatory of Anglo-Afghan Treaty of 22 Nov. 1921; carried Treaty Kabul to Delhi (C.M.G.); Judicial Commissioner N.W. Frontier Province, 1922 and 1923. *Recreations:* lawn tennis (played Championship, Wimbledon, 1906 and 1907), and music. [*Died* 13 *July* 1960.

PIROW, Hon. Oswald; retired. Formerly M.P. for Gezina, Transvaal (S. African Nat. Party); Minister of Justice, 1929-1933, of Defence, Railways and Harbours, 1933-39, S. Africa. Q.C. (S.A.) ret. 1957. *Address:* Netherlands Bank Bldg., Pretoria, Transvaal, South Africa. [*Died* 11 *Oct.* 1959.

PITCHFORD, Lt.-Col. Herbert; *see* Watkins-Pitchford.

PITMAN, Alfred; *e. s.* of late Sir Isaac Pitman; *b.* 1862; *m.* 1909, Belinda Elizabeth (*d.* 1941), *o. d.* of late William Stuart Johnston, Dunboyne, Co. Meath; one *s.* one *d.* *Educ.:* Bath College. Until 1934 Governing Director, Sir Isaac Pitman & Sons, Ltd., Publishers, London, Bath, and Melbourne; Governor, Pitman's College, Southampton Row, London, W.C.1; President, Sir Isaac Pitman & Sons (Canada) Ltd., and Pitman Publishing Corporation, New York; Founder and first President of The Pitman Fellowship; Past President of The Soc. of Pitman's Certificated Teachers of Shorthand; Patron of the Incorporated Phonographic Society; Patron of The Incorporated Phonographic Society of Australia; also Patron of Shorthand and Educational Societies in India, America, and other parts of the world; Senior Member of The Publishers' Association; in 1932 he completed half a century's association with Commercial Education and Publishing; devoted his life's work to the advancement of Commercial Education and the publication of Commercial, Educational, Technical, Scientific, and other works; has addressed sundry organizations on aspects of business training, and been interviewed by important papers and periodicals for his views on modern business training; has travelled extensively in Europe and America. *Publication:* Half a Century of Commercial Education and Publishing. *Address:* Cranwells, Bath. *T.:* 4315. [*Died* 29 *Nov.* 1952.

PITT, Henry Arthur, C.M.G. 1934; O.B.E.; *b.* Colac, Victoria, 1872; *s.* of Mark A. Pitt, Wexford and County Clare; *m.* 1899, Gertrude Augusta, *d.* of J. R. Buxton; one *s.* two *d.* Manager Australian Wheat Board, 1916-22 (O.B.E.); Director of Finance, State of Victoria, 1923-37; Acting Agent-General for Victoria in London, 1927. *Address:* Bouleigh, 4 Bouleigh Avenue, Elwood, Melbourne, S.3, Victoria. [*Died* 3 *Aug.* 1955.

PITT-KETHLEY, Andrew Horace Victor; Editor of Wide World Magazine since 1901; founder of Wide World Brotherhood, 1949; *b.* 1879; *s.* of Andrew Pitt-Kethley, Barnard Castle, Durham; *m.* 1904, Nellie, *d.* of George Reed, Southend-on-Sea. *Educ.:* Dulwich College. During European War, 1914-18, Capt. and Assistant Adjutant, York and Lancaster Regiment. Joined staff of Strand Magazine, 1896; assisted to produce first number of Wide World Magazine, 1898, and has been connected with it ever since; served in H.A.C. and Essex Regt. *Publications:* several books; numerous stories and articles. *Recreation:* gardening. *Address:* Wayside, Amersham, Bucks. [*Died* 12 *May* 1955.

PITTMAN, Osmund, R.O.I.; Landscape Painter; *b.* London, 14 Dec. 1874; *s.* of Robert Pittman, A.C.A.; *m.* Caroline Mabel Waud Waud. *Educ.:* Palace School, Enfield; Royal Academy School. Exhibited Royal Academy, R.O.I., R.I. International Exhibition, Glasgow and Liverpool. *Address:* Twyford Abbey, Park Royal, N.W.10. [*Died* 25 *Oct.* 1958.

PIUS XII, His Holiness Pope, (Eugene Pacelli); *b.* Rome, 2 March 1876; *s.* of Philip Pacelli and Virginia Graziosi. *Educ.:* Gregorian Univ. and Roman Seminary; Capranica College. Ordained Priest, 1899; Attaché Secretariat of State; Prof. Academy of Noble Ecclesiastics; Sec. of Extraordinary Ecclesiastical Affairs; Nuncio in Bavaria and Germany; Archbishop of Sardes, 1917; Cardinal, 1929; Secretary of State to His Holiness, 1930-39; Archpriest of St. Peter's Basilica, 1930-39; Cardinal Camerlengo of the Holy Roman Church, 1935; Cardinal Legate to International Eucharistic Congress, Buenos Aires 1934, at Lourdes for *triduum* of intercession for world peace 1935, at Lisieux and Paris for the dedication of the Basilica of Sainte Thérèse de l'Enfant-Jésus, 1937, and to International Eucharistic Congress, Budapest, 1938; elected Pope, 1939. *Publications:* La personalità e la territorialità delle leggi specialmente nel diritto canonico, 1912; Gesammelte Reden, 1930; Triptyque, 1936; Discorsi e Panegirici, 2nd ed. (1931-1938), 1939; Discours et Panégyriques, 1939; Discorsi e Radiomessaggi, 17 vols., 1939-56 (selections translated into other languages). *Address:* The Vatican. [*Died* 9 *Oct.* 1958.

PLACE, Col. Charles Otley, C.M.G. 1917; D.S.O. 1902; late Royal Engineers; *b.* 3 Oct. 1875. Entered army, 1895; Capt. 1904; Major, 1914; Lt.-Col. 1921; Col. 1922; served South Africa, 1899-1902 (despatches, Queen's medal with five clasps, King's medal 2 clasps, D.S.O.); European War, 1914-17 (despatches, Bt. Lt.-Col., C.M.G.); Dep. Dir. Mil. Ops., 1921-22; retd. pay, 1923. *Club:* United Service. [*Died* 24 *Dec.* 1955.

PLACZEK, Mrs. A. K.; *see* Struther, Jan.

PLANT, George Frederick, C.B.E. 1927; *b.* 10 Nov. 1877; *s.* of late F. G. Plant, J.P., of Romiley, Cheshire; *m.* 1904, Frances Carrie Sophie Fisher; three *s.* two *d.* *Educ.:* Manchester Grammar School; Brasenose College, Oxford (Scholar). B.A. 1900; Ceylon Civil Service, 1901-18; Secretary, Oversea Settlement Committee, Dominions Office, 1918-36; Sec. Oversea Settlement Board, 1936-37; visited Canada on Government Oversea Settlement Missions, 1924 and 1928. *Publications:* Miscellaneous articles; Tales from Ceylon, 1948; Oversea Settlement, 1950; S.O.S. B.W.: A Survey of voluntary effort in Women's Empire Migration, 1951. *Address:* 73 Grove Park Road, S.E.9. *Club:* National. [*Died* 29 *March* 1954.

PLATT, Sir Frank, Kt., *cr.* 1943; Chairman (and formerly Man. Dir.), The Lancashire Cotton Corporation Ltd., 1932-41; Director, District Bank Limited; *b.* 9 June 1890; *s.* of Thomas and Rachel Platt; *m.* 1915, Mary, *d.* of Benjamin and Sarah A. Lord; one *d.* *Educ.:* Derby Street Board School, Rochdale; Central Higher Grade School, Rochdale. Cotton mill experience began at Clover Croft and State Mills, Rochdale, 1905-14; Higher Crompton Mills Ltd., Shaw, Manager and Director, 1914-21; various cotton spinning company directorates, 1914-32, in Oldham district; Deputy Cotton Controller, 1939-40; Cotton Controller, 1941-45; Executive Member Cotton Board, 1939-41; First Chairman British Overseas Cottons Ltd. (Export policy for Textiles), 1940. *Recreations:* Director Oldham Athletic Football Club, 1919-33; tennis. *Address:* Milverton, Bramhall, Cheshire. *T.:* Bramhall 435. [*Died* 8 *July* 1955.

PLATT, Rev. Frederic, M.A., D.D.; Methodist Minister, retired; formerly Principal of Handsworth Theological College, Birmingham; *b.* Bolton, Lancashire, 1 Jan. 1859; *e. s.* of James Bradshaw Platt; *m.* 1st, 1898, Lilian Rose, 4th *d.* of Robert Bell, Shieldfield, Newcastle on Tyne; 2nd, 1907, Marianne Bell, Newcastle on Tyne; one *s.* *Educ.:* Liverpool College; Durham University (M.A.); Didsbury Theological College; B.D. 1896; Hon. D.D. 1916, University of St. Andrews. Wesleyan Minister in Pastoral Work, 1882-1905; Tutor in Old Testament Languages and Literature, and in Philosophy, Didsbury College, Manchester, 1905-10; Tutor in Systematic and Pastoral Theology, Handsworth College, Birmingham, 1910-25; Fernley Lecturer, 1915; Member of Legal Conference, Wesleyan Methodist Church, 1916; Fraternal Delegate of British Conference to Conference of Methodist Episcopal Church, South, U.S.A., 1926, and to Council of United Church of Canada, 1926; Examiner in Theology, University of London. *Publications:* Miracles: An Outline of the Christian View, 1913; Immanence and Christian Thought, 1915; Certainty and Christian Faith, 1926. *Address:* The Bungalow, Walton Park, Clevedon, Somerset. [*Died* 24 *Jan.* 1955.

PLEDGE, Henry, C.B.E. 1918; late Assistant Director of Naval Construction, Admiralty. *Address:* 9 Prior Avenue, Sutton, Surrey. [*Died* 16 *Oct.* 1949.
[*But death not notified in time for inclusion in Who Was Who 1941–1950, first edn.*

PLEDGE, Humphrey Thomas, C.B.E. 1960; Keeper, Science Museum Library, South Kensington, since 1945; *b.* 6 Nov. 1903; *s.* of Thomas Pledge and of Isabella Allen; *m.* 1934, Ruth, *d.* of Rev. H. M. Brown; one *d.* *Educ.:* Tonbridge Sch.; Trinity Coll., Camb. (Exhibitioner, 1st Cl. Nat. Sciences Tripos). Asst. Master, Wrekin Coll., 1925-26; Asst. Keeper, Science Museum Library, 1927. *Publications:* Science since 1500, 1939; articles. *Address:* 30 Woodlands Road, Redhill, Surrey. [*Died* 28 *Dec.* 1960.

PLIMMER, Robert Henry Aders, D.Sc. Lond.; *b.* 25 April 1877; *e. s.* of Alfred Aders, Manchester; adopted name of stepfather, Henry George Plimmer, F.R.S.; *m.* Violet Geraldine Sheffield (*d.* 1949); one *s.* three *d.* *Educ.:* Dulwich College; University College, London; Universities of Geneva and Berlin. Grocers' Company Research Student, Lister Institute, 1902-4; Assistant at University College, London, 1904; Fellow of University College, London, 1906; Assistant Professor of Physiological Chemistry, University College, 1907; Reader in Physiological Chemistry, University of London, University College, 1912-19; Bio-chemist, Rowett Research Institute, Aberdeen, 1919-21; Professor of Chemistry in University of London at St. Thomas's Hospital Medical School, 1922-42; Professor Emeritus of Chemistry in University of London, 1944; lecturer Biochem. Dept. Postgraduate Medical School since 1943; co-editor of Monographs on Bio-chemistry, 1908; Hon. Secretary, 1911-19; Hon. Member, 1943, the Bio-chemical Soc. *Publications:* Chemical Constitution of the Proteins; Organic and Bio-chemistry; Vitamins and the Choice of Food; Food, Health, Vitamins (with Mrs. V. G. Plimmer), contributions to the Biochemical Journal, Journal of Physiology, Journal of the Chemical Society. *Address:* 18 Langside Avenue, S.W.15. *T.:* Prospect 1859. [*Died* 18 *June* 1955.

PLOWDEN, Lieut.-Colonel Charles Terence Chichele, C.I.E. 1933; *b.* 6 Feb. 1883; *s.* of late Lieut.-Col. Trevor John Chichele-Plowden, C.I.E., of Punjab Commission; *m.* 1914, Beatrice Stretton, *d.* of late Lieut. R. E. Liston, W. India Regt.; no c. *Educ.:* Cheltenham College; R.M.C., Sandhurst. First Commission, 1902; entered Indian Army, 1904; Indian, Political Department, 1908 (now Lieut-Col); Political Officer, N.W. Frontier Province, Central India, and Rajputana, 1908-14; Sec. to Resident in Mysore and Chief Commissioner Coorg, 1919-22; Vice-President Council of Regency, Cooch Behar State, 1923-26; Sec. to Agent to Governor-General in Baluchistan, 1928; Political Agent, Kalat, 1929-32; Resident in Mysore and Chief Commissioner, Coorg, 1933-37; retired, 1938; served European War, 1914-18. Press Reader, Russian Press Reading Dept., British Embassy, Moscow, 1944-45. *Address:* c/o Lloyds Bank, Ltd., Cox's & King's Branch, 6 Pall Mall, S.W.1. *Club:* Naval and Military. [*Died* 13 *July* 1956.

PLOWMAN, Sir Claude, Kt., *cr.* 1949; Chairman: Rajciph Ltd., Manufacturing Enterprises Ltd., Sealanes Pty. Ltd., Georgenia St. Pty. Ltd., etc.; Silverwater Rubber Co. Pty. Ltd., etc.; *b.* Hobart, 1895; British; *m.* 1925, Ruth, *d.* of Carl and Emma Hassel, Kil, Sweden; one *s.* one *d.* *Educ.:* Queen's Coll., Hobart, Tasmania. Trained as Engineer; served Merchant Marine, European War, 1914-18; Industrial Research Laboratory, California, U.S.A., 1919-24; organised and built firm of Airzone Ltd., in Sydney, which covered all States of the Commonwealth; sold his interests, 1946. Since 1946 has been adviser to a number of firms and sits on boards of many. *Recreations:* yachting, golf. *Address:* 8 Marathon Rd., Darling Pt., Sydney, Australia. *T.:* F.B. 2927. *Clubs:* Australian, Eleanora Country, Royal Sydney Golf, Royal Sydney Yacht Squadron (Sydney); Tasmanian (Hobart). [*Died* 5 *Sept.* 1954.

PLYMEN, Francis Joseph, C.I.E. 1929; late Indian Agricultural Service; *b.* 7 Feb. 1879; *m.* 1st, 1909, Muriel (*d.* 1931), *e. d.* of Cooper Wacher, Hoath, nr. Canterbury; one *s.*; 2nd, 1936, Joan Wacher (née Rigden), Ashford, Kent. *Educ.:* Royal Grammar School, Guildford; Central Technical College, London. Appointed to the Indian Agricultural Service in 1906 after some years on the staff of the South Eastern Agricultural College, Wye, Kent; held various scientific and administrative appointments, being subsequently promoted to be head of the Agricultural Department, Central Provinces; Director of Agriculture, of Central Provinces and Berar, Nagpur, India; retired 1934; formerly member of Central Provinces Legislative Council. *Publications:* various reports on agricultural subjects. *Recreations:* gardening and usual games. *Address:* Queens Lodge, Hurst Green, Etchingham, Sussex. *T.:* Hurst Green 328. [*Died* 10 *March* 1960.

POCKLINGTON, Geoffrey Richard, B.A.; *b.* 30 Oct. 1879; 4th *s.* of late Colonel Frederic Pocklington, 5th Fusiliers, and Alice Emmy, *d.* of Rev. R. W. Jelf, D.D., Principal of King's College, London, and Canon of Christ Church, Oxford; unmarried. *Educ.:* United Services College; Rossall School; Balliol College, Oxford. Educational work, 1902-5; joined literary staff of W. H. Smith & Son, 1906; in business as Publicity Writer, 1919-24; Editor Boy's Own Paper, 1924-33; Newsboy (afterwards Newsboy and Newsgirl), 1914-31; has been connected with a number of forms of work amongst boys, including Universities' Camps for Public Schools, Y.M.C.A. (Junior Section), Telegraph Messengers Christian Association, and (since 1909) Boy Scouts; County Alderman, West Suffolk; Chairman, West Suffolk Education Committee, 1942-57; Governor of King Edward VI Grammar School, Bury St. Edmunds, Framlingham College, Sudbury Grammar School and Sudbury High School. *Publications:* Chelsworth: the Story of a Little Suffolk Village; much publicity and propaganda matter; a good deal of rather light verse. *Address:* Red House, Chelsworth, Suffolk. *T.A.* and *T.:* Bildeston 241. [*Died* 22 *March* 1958.

POCKLINGTON, Henry Cabourn, F.R.S.; M.A., D.Sc.; *b.* Exeter, 28 Jan. 1870; *e. s.* of Henry Pocklington, Local Director of the Commercial Union Assurance Company, and Emma Janette Lilly; unmarried. *Educ.:* Yorkshire College, Leeds; St. John's College, Cambridge. Fourth Wrangler, 1892; Class

1 Div. 1 in Part II. of the Tripos; Smith's Prizeman; Fellow of St John's College. *Publications:* Various papers in the Philosophical Transactions, the Proceedings of the Cambridge Philosophical Society, the Philosophical Magazine, etc. *Recreations:* music, Chinese. *Address:* 6 Blenheim Crescent, Leeds, 2. [*Died* 15 *May* 1952.

POCOCK, Guy Noël, M.A.; author and editor; *b.* Hampstead, 1880; 2nd *s.* of late Noël Lewis Pocock; *m.* 1924, Dorothy Allcot Bowers, *d.* of late Bishop of Thetford; one *s.* *Educ.:* Highgate School; St. John's College, Cambridge. For ten years a master at Cheltenham College, and afterwards at the Royal Naval College, Dartmouth; made the teaching of English a special study; gave up teaching for writing, editing and lecturing, 1923; Cambridge University Extra-Mural lecturer, 1932; joined staff of B.B.C., 1934; retired 1940 and rejoined staff of Cheltenham College; Cambridge University, 1946. Visiting Committees of H.M. Borstal Institutions. *Publications: novels:* Knight's Gambit; Mrs. Clutterbuck Laughs; Somebody Must; Design for a Staircase; Period Programme, 1936; Stubbs at Fifty, 1937; Together We Go, 1938; Then They Pulled Down the Blinds, 1940; *essays:* The Little Room; Pen and Ink; also, The Essay Writer; *anthologies:* Modern Poetry, Modern Prose, and many others; editor with Sir Arthur Quiller-Couch of the King's Treasuries of Literature; author of many school-books for the teaching of English. *Recreations:* travel and music. *Address:* Frostlake Cottage, Malting Lane, Cambridge. *Club:* Authors'. [*Died* 19 *March* 1955.

POË, Col. William Skeffington, C.B. 1936; D.S.O. 1918; late R.M.A. and R.M.; *e. s.* of late Admiral Sir Edmund Poë, G.C.V.O.; *b.* 1878; *m.* 1909, Jean Rosina (*d.* 1947), *d.* of Col. C. P. Boyd of Crofton House, Titchfield, Hants. Served with Naval Brigade in S. Africa, 1899-1900 (medal and three clasps); European War, 1914-18, Royal Tank Corps, (severely wounded, despatches, D.S.O., brevet of Lt.-Colonel); Lt.-Col., 1927; Col. 1932; retired list, 1932; Chief Constable R. M. Police, 1932-36; employed on Administrative duties, 1940-45. *Club:* United Service. [*Died* 18 *March* 1958.

POË DOMVILE, Sir Hugo Compton Domvile, 2nd Bt., *cr.* 1912; *b.* 19 June 1889; *s.* of Sir Hutcheson Poë, 1st Bt., and Mary Adelaide (*d.* 1929), *d.* of late Sir Wm. Compton Domvile, Bt., of Santry Court, Co. Dublin; *S.* father 1934; assumed the additional surname of Domvile, 1939. *Heir:* none. *Address:* Blackhill, Abbeyleix, Leix, Eire. [*Died* 28 *July* 1959 (*ext.*).

POGANY, Willy, (William Andrew); painter, etcher, illustrator, sculptor; member Architectural League, Beaux Arts, Institute of Design Society of Mural Painters; *b.* Szeged, Hungary, 24 Aug. 1882; *s.* of Joseph S. F. Pogany and Helena Kolis; *m.* 1st, 1908, Lilian Rose Doris (decd.); two *s.*; 2nd, 1934, Elaine Cox. *Educ.:* Budapest Technical University; Art Schools, Budapest, Munich, Paris. Gold Medals, Budapest, Leipzig, Panama Pacific I. Exp.; Silver Medal, New York Soc. of Architects; illustrated over 100 books; magazine covers: Metropolitan Magazine, Town and Country, American Weekly, 1940-51; numerous stage designs including those for Metropolitan Opera House, Ziegfeld, Sigmond Romberg, James K. Hackett, John Golden, etc.; permanent stage setting, Convention Hall, Atlantic City, N.J.; Art Director, Motion Pictures: United Artists, Warner Bros., 20th Century - Fox, Universal, Charles Chaplin Studios, 1930-40; designed Ballets for Fokine and Adolph Bolm; notable mural works: William Randolph Hearst Estate at Wyntoon, Calif., John Ringling residence, Sarasota, Florida; Children's Theatre, N.Y., People's House, Niagara Falls Power Co.; architectural works, St. George Hotel Swimming Pool, St. George Hotel, N.Y.; stained glass windows, Forest Lawn Cemetery, Los Angeles, Calif. F.R.S.A. *Publications:* Willy Pogany's Drawing Lessons; Willy Pogany's Water-Colour Lessons; Willy Pogany's Oil Painting Lessons, etc. *Address:* 1 West 67th St., N.Y. City, U.S.A. [*Died* 30 *July* 1955.

POLE, Major David Graham; 3rd *s.* of Captain John Pole, Edinburgh; *m.* Jessie Hair, *e. d.* of late G. H. Pagan, Sheriff-Clerk of Fife. *Educ.:* Edinburgh School and University. Qualified and practised as a Solicitor in Edinburgh, 1900-14; admitted a member of the Society of Solicitors before the Supreme Courts of Scotland (S.S.C.), 1901; commissioned as Notary Public, 1903; practises as Solicitor in House of Lords and in the Privy Council; joined Edinburgh University Company of the Queen's Rifle Volunteer Brigade (The Royal Scots), 1899; 2nd Lieut., 1901; Lieut. and Capt. (T.A.); transferred to Reserve of Officers (T.A.) with rank of Captain, 1912; transferred to Northumberland Fusiliers (12th Service Bn.), Aug. 1914; served in France (wounded, battle of Loos); promoted Major Feb. 1915, and as Temp. Lt.-Col. commanded during War 12th (Service) Bn. Northumberland Fusiliers; permanently invalided; retired with rank of Major; M.P. (Lab.) South Derbyshire, 1929-1931; Parliamentary Private Secretary to Secretary of State for War, Jan.-Aug. 1931; Treasurer of the Commercial Cttee. of House of Commons, 1929-31; served as Member of the Burma Round Table Conf., 1931-32; Chairman: British Cttee. on Indian and Burman Affairs; Tribunal for Paddington and St. Marylebone under Furnished Houses (Rent Control) Act, 1946-49; South Paddington Rent Tribunal, 1949-52; Director: Ratsouris Ltd.; Max Arc Electrics Ltd.; M.M.M. Ltd. *Publications:* India in Transition, 1932; I Refer to India, 1929; (with B. Shiva Rao, M.A.), The Problem of India, 1926; Parliamentary Correspondent and Director of New India, Madras; London Correspondent of the Modern Review, Calcutta. *Recreations:* travelling, has toured India on seven different occasions studying political and industrial conditions; visited Palestine, Egypt, Turkey, France, Germany, Holland, Sweden, Russia, Finland, Belgium, Italy, Greece, Denmark, United States, Australia, New Zealand, St. Helena, etc. *Address:* 146 Palace Chambers, Westminster, S.W.1. *T.:* Whitehall 1811; Artillery Mansions, 75 Victoria Street, S.W.1. *T.:* Abbey 1966. *Club:* Junior Army and Navy. [*Died* 26 *Nov.* 1952.

POLE, Sir Felix John Clewett, Kt., *cr.* 1924; Chairman of Associated Electrical Industries Ltd., 1929-45, Director, 1945-55; *b.* 1 Feb. 1877; *s.* of late Edward Robert Pole, Great Bedwyn, Wilts; *m.* 1899, Ethel Maud Flack; one *s.* two *d.* *Educ.:* Ramsbury, Wilts. General Manager, Great Western Railway, Paddington, 1921-29; visited Sudan, 1923-24 and 1930-31, at invitation of Sudan Government to report upon the Sudan Government railways and steamers; Member of Committee to inquire into claims for pensions by Ex-ranker Officers, 1924; Committee on the Fishing Industry, 1932; 1933 Police Pay (New Entrants) Committee; Member of Industrial Court; Member: Colonial Development Advisory Committee; Coal Commission; Panel of persons representing Chancellor of Exchequer on Civil Service Arbitration Tribunal; reported to Northern Ireland Government on Transport Conditions in Northern Ireland, 1934; Chairman of Rural Housing Committee, 1936. *Recreation:* fishing. *Address:* Calcot Place, Reading. *T.:* Reading 67448. *Club:* Flyfishers'. [*Died* 15 *Jan.* 1956.

POLLARD, Claude, F.R.A.M.; Professor Royal Academy of Music. *Address:* Woodberry, Valley Road, Rickmansworth, Herts. [*Died* 10 *June* 1957.

POLLARD, Lt.-Col. George Chambers, C.M.G. 1918; D.S.O. 1915; late Royal Engineers (Territorial Force); served S. African War, 1900-1 (Queen's medal 5 clasps); European War, 1914-18 (D.S.O., despatches five times, wounded, C.M.G.). *Address:* Burnham Cottage, Sessay, Yorks. [*Died* 28 *April* 1954.

POLLEN, Sir John Launcelot Hungerford, 6th Bt. of Redenham, Hampshire, *cr.* 1795; *b.* 27 April 1884; 2nd *s.* of 4th Bt. and Frances Ann St. Aubyn Pollen; *S.* brother, 1930; *m.* 1928, Edith Muriel (*d.* 1949), 2nd *d.* of Rev. J. A. Lloyd; no *c.* *Educ.:* Eton; privately. Entered the publishing firm of Sands and Co., London and Edinburgh, and afterwards W. J. Ham Smith, London; Cadet Captain, London Diocesan Church Lads' Brigade, 1911-14; Lieut. R.F.A. (T.F.), 1915; demobilised, 1919; Active Service with 83rd Brigade R.F.A. 18th Division, 1916-18; Army of Occupation, 1919. *Recreation:* shooting. *Heir:* *kinsman*, John Michael Hungerford Pollen, Lieut. R.A. [*b.* 1919; *m.* 1st, 1941, Angela Mary Oriana, *d.* of Capt. F. J. Russi, M.C.; one *s.* one *d.*; 2nd, 1957, Diana Jubb (*née* Timbrell). *Educ.:* Downside; Merton Coll., Oxford]. *Address:* Rodbourne, Malmesbury, Wilts. [*Died* 14 *March* 1959.

POLLITT, Harry; Propagandist; Chairman Communist Party since 1956; *b.* 22 Nov. 1890. *Educ.:* Elementary School, Droylesden, Lancs. Boilermaker; Secretary Hands off Russia Movement, 1919; Secretary National Minority Movement, 1924-29; Secretary Communist Party, 1929-56. *Publications:* Serving My Time, 1940; How to Win the Peace, 1944; Answers to Questions, 1945; Looking Ahead, 1947; various pamphlets. *Address:* 31 Lodore Gdns., N.W.9. [*Died* 27 *June* 1960.

POLLOCK, Guy Cameron; *b.* 1878; *o. s.* of Walter Herries Pollock and Emma, *d.* of Col. Pipon, Seigneur de Noirmont, Jersey; *m.* 1901, Edith, *y. d.* of General Ingall, C.B.; no *c.* *Educ.:* Eton (K.S.). Took to journalism as a free lance, contributing verse to Punch and the Westminster Gazette, articles in various papers; joined the editorial staff of the St. James's Gazette under Lord Cushendun (Mr. Ronald McNeill), 1902; remained with the Evening Standard after the amalgamation of these two evening papers; became assistant editor; joined the Daily Express as leader-writer, 1911; served in anti-aircraft (Sub-Lt. R.N.V.R. and Captain R.G.A., 1914-19, in England and in Ireland (Sinn Fein Rebellion, 1916); rejoined Daily Express, 1919; Managing Editor, 1921; Managing Editor, Sunday Express, 1923; Managing Editor, The Morning Post, 1925-32; Editor, Navy League Publications, 1936-52. *Publications:* Hay Fever, novel (with W. H. Pollock); To See Ourselves, novel (with Anne Armstrong). *Recreations:* fishing, shooting, golf. *Address:* 36 Vallance Gardens, Hove, Sussex. *T.:* Hove 31509. *Club:* Garrick. [*Died* 1 *Feb.* 1957.

POLLOCK, Henry Brodhurst, D.S.O. 1918; ex-Commander, R.N.V.R.; Chairman Ferrier Pollock & Co. Ltd.; Director Bank of Ireland; Cairnes Ltd., Brewers Drogheda, Dublin South City Market Coy., Travel Goods Ltd., Ireland, and Local Director Liverpool and London and Globe Insurance Co. Ltd., etc.; *b.* 1883; *m.* 1916, Dorothy Margaret, *d.* of late Alexander Blood, K.C.; one *s.* one *d.* Served European War, 1914-19 (wounded, despatches, D.S.O. and bar). *Address:* Castleknock Lodge, Castleknock, Dublin. [*Died* 18 *Oct.* 1958.

POLLOCK, Hon. Sir Henry Edward, Kt., *cr.* 1924; Q.C.; *b.* 1864; *m.* 1906, Pauline Oakley, O.B.E. 1941. *Educ.:* Charterhouse. Called to Bar, Inner Temple, 1887; acted as Police Magistrate, Hong-Kong, 1888-89; acted as Puisne Judge, 1892; gold medal for plague services, 1894; acted as Attorney-General, Hong-Kong, for nearly three years, between 1896 and 1901; Q.C. 1900; Attorney-General, Fiji, 1902; Unofficial Member Legislative Council, Hong-Kong, for Chamber of Commerce, 1903-4; Unofficial Member for Justices of Peace since 1905; acted as Member of the Executive Council, 1911; acted as Attorney-General, Hong-Kong, 1919, 1925, and 1928; Senior Unofficial Member of both Councils from 1926; Life Member of the Court and Hon. LL.D. of the Hong-Kong University. *Publications:* Bill of Lading Exceptions; Regulations for Preventing Collisions at Sea. *Address:* Bank of Australasia, Sydney, N.S.W. [*Died* 2 *Feb.* 1953.

POLLOCK, Wm. Barr Inglis, M.D., F.R.F.P.S. Glasgow; Ophthalmic Surgeon; Hon. Consulting Surgeon, Glasgow Eye Infirmary; *b.* Glasgow, 1878; *e. s.* of late Dr. A. Barr Pollock; *m.* 1914, Elizabeth Campbell, *e. d.* of late J. M. Finlayson and *niece* of late James Finlayson, M.D. *Educ.:* Glasgow Academy; Hillhead High School; Universities of Glasgow, Berlin, and Vienna. (Glasgow Univ.) M.B. Ch.B. (Commend), 1900; M.D. Honours and Bellahouston Gold Medal (Eye Thesis), 1905; F.R.F.P.S. (Glasgow) 1910; Resident Physician, Resident Surgeon, Senior Resident, Western Infirmary, Glasgow, 1900-1901; House Surgeon, 1901-2; Clinical Assistant, 1903-6; Pathologist and Bacteriologist, 1906-9; Assist.-Surgeon, 1909-19; Extra-Surgeon, 1919-22; Surgeon, 1922-38; Glasgow Eye Infirmary; Ophthalmic Surgeon, Ayr County Hospital, 1907-38, Govan School Board, 1911-18, and Ayr School Board, 1915-19. *Publications:* numerous papers on Diseases of the Eye, and on research in connection with the same; Antiquity of Ophthalmology, Brit. Journ. Ophthm. 1945, Arabian Ophthalmology, *ibid.* 1946. *Recreations:* angling and golf. *Address:* 21 Woodside Place, Glasgow, C.3. *T.:* Douglas 0275. *Clubs:* Literary, Royal Scottish Automobile (Glasgow); Western Golf (Gailes). [*Died* 28 *March* 1953.

POLLOK-M'CALL, Brig.-Gen. John Buchanan, of Kindeace; C.M.G. 1916; D.S.O. 1918; 2nd *s.* of late R. M. Pollok-Morris of Craig, Kilmarnock; *b.* 1870; *m.* 1910, Frances, *d.* of Frederick M'Call of Lochbrae; one *s.* *Educ.:* Harrow; Oxford; Sandhurst. 2nd Lt. The Black Watch, 1891; Capt. 1900; Major, 1909; served as signalling officer Swat Movable Column, 1907, and as A.D.C. to Maj.-Gen. Sir Alexander Reid, K.C.B., in 1908; retired, 1910; commanded 5th Batt. Royal Scots Fusiliers, 1912-15; served S. African War with The Black Watch, and as Adjt. 6th (Scots) I.Y. (Queen's medal 3 clasps, King's medal 2 clasps); Tibet Expedition, 1904; action at Niani, operations at and around Gyantse, March to Lhassa (despatches, medal with clasp); European War, command of 1/5 R.S.F. Battalion (despatches four times, C.M.G., D.S.O. [Immediate Award]); Brigade Commander Gallipoli, Palestine and France, 1915-19; J.P., Ayrshire; D.L., Ross and Cromarty; contested (U.) Dumfries Burghs, 1910, also S. Ayrshire, 1918; Order of the Nile, 3rd Class. *Recreation:* sport. *Address:* Kindeace, Delny, Ross and Cromarty. *T.:* Kildary 233. [*Died* 30 *July* 1951.

POLSON, Hon. Sir William John, K.C.M.G., *cr.* 1951; M.L.C. 1950 (New Zealand); farmer; *b.* Wanganui, New Zealand, 6 June 1875; *s.* of Donald Gunn Polson, sheep farmer (arrived Otago, 1850, North Island, 1873); *m.* 1st, 1911, Florence Wilson (*d.* 1941), Melbourne; three *s.* one *d.*; 2nd, 1943, Mary Victoria Cracroft (*née* Wilson), M.B.E. 1946, M.P. (N.Z.), 1942-43, *widow* of A. N. Grigg, M.P. (N.Z.). *Educ.:* Wanganui Collegiate School, New Zealand. Farmed for some years and then became journalist; on staff of Evening Post, Wellington; Press, Christchurch (some years in charge of day work and also editing evening edition called Truth, and, later, Evening News); returned to farming, 1906, on father's property at Fordell, and took prominent part in public life; Member Wanganui County Council for many years (Chm. for some years); Wanganui Harbour Board; President of Farmers' Union (18 years) having resigned from local bodies; Director: Wanganui Woollen Co.; Feilding Freezing Co.; Fazackerley and Co. (sawmillers); Member Royal Commission on Rural Credits, 1926; Rural Credits Bd.; M.P. for Stratford (N.Z.), 1928-46, retired; Member of War Administration, 1942; Member Executive Council and Leader of Legislative Council, 1950. *Address:* Private Bag, Wanganui, New Zealand. [*Died* 8 *Oct.* 1960.

PONIATOWSKI, Prince Louis Leopold Charles Marie André; *b.* Paris, 2[?] Jan. 1864; *m.* 1894, Elizabeth Helen Sperry (*d.* 1942), Stockton, California; four *s.* *Address:* Paris, 15 rue Berton (XVI). *T.:* Aut. 32.50; Clos Baudoin à Vouvray (Indre et Loire); Speranza, Mougins (Alpes-Maritimes). *Clubs:* Nouveau-Cercle, Cercle Interallié, Automobile (Paris). [*Died* 16 *March* 1954.

PONSONBY, Brig. Henry Chambré, D.S.O. 1918, M.C.; late King's Royal Rifle Corps; *b.* 1883; *s.* of late C. B. Ponsonby and Hon. Mary Sophia Eliza Plunkett, *d.* of 16th Baron Dunsany; *m* 1923, Beatrice Maud Levinge; one *d.* *Educ.:* Eton; R.M.C., Sandhurst. Served European War, 1914-18 (despatches, D.S.O., M.C.); Deputy Assistant Adjutant General and Deputy Assistant Quartermaster-General at Peshawar, 1923-27; commanded 1st Batt. The Queen's Regt., 1928-32; Col. 1930; General Staff Officer 1st Grade 4th Division, 1932-35; Commander 6th Infantry Brigade, 1935-39; retired pay, 1939; Greek Military Cross. *Address:* Chicksgrove Mill, Tisbury, Wilts. *T.:* Tisbury 261. [*Died* 2 *Jan.* 1953.

PONSONBY, Maj.-Gen. Sir John, K.C.B., *cr.* 1927 (C.B 1918); C.M.G. 1915; D.S.O. 1900; late Coldstream Guards; *b.* 25 March 1866; *e. s.* of late Gen. Rt. Hon. Sir Henry Ponsonby; *m.* 1935, Mary, *d.* of late Thomas Robley, Ingleberg, Beckermet, Cumberland. Entered army, 1887; Capt., 1898; Maj., 1904; Lt.-Col. 1913; Bt. Col. 1916; served Matabeleland, 1893-94 (medal); Uganda, 1888-89 (medal); South Africa, 1899-1900 (despatches, two medals, D.S.O.); European War, 1914-18 (despatches 7 times, C.M.G., Bt. Col., C.B.); Brigadier-General commanding 2nd Guards Brigade, 1915-17; temp. Maj.-Gen. commanding 40th Division, 1917-18, and subsequently Major-Gen. commanding the 5th Div.; Major-Gen., 1919; G.O.C. Madras District, 1922-26; Colonel of the Suffolk Regiment, 1925-39; retired pay, 1927; commanded 7th Cumberland Bn. Home Guard, 1940-41. *Publication:* The Ponsonby Family, 1929. *Address:* Haile Hall, Beckermet, Cumberland. *Clubs:* Guards, Turf. [*Died* 26 *May* 1952.

POOL, Augustus Frank, C.B.E. 1935 (O.B.E. 1918); *b.* 14 Aug. 1872; *s.* of late William Pool, of Blackheath, S.E.; *m.* 1st, 1895, Harriette Maude Mary (*d.* 1940), *er. d.* of late Oliver Smith, Greenwich, S.E.: two *s.* one *d.*; 2nd, 1941, Olive, *widow* of George Blay, Surbiton, Surrey. *Educ.:* The Academy, Lowestoft; King's College, London. Entered Inland Revenue, Department, 1894; Deputy Chief Inspector of Taxes, 1926; President of Association of H.M. Inspectors of Taxes, 1917-18; retired from Civil Service, 1935. *Address:* Chart's Edge, Westerham, Kent. *Club:* Union. [*Died* 30 *Sept.* 1955.

POOLE, Brig.-Gen. Arthur James, C.B. 1923; C.M.G. 1917; R. Warwicks Regt., retired; *b.* 6 Nov. 1872; *m.* 1919, Margaret, *d.* of Percy C. Morris, 79 Elm Park Gardens, S.W., and *widow* of Major J. H. D. Costeker, D.S.O., Warwicks Regiment; one *s.* one *d.* 2nd Lieut. Royal Warwicks Regiment, 1892; Capt. 1900; Major, 1910; Lt.-Col. 1914; served N.W. Frontier, India, 1908 (medal with clasp); European War, 1914-18 (despatches six times, Bt. Col., C.B., C.M.G., Légion d'Honneur); Colonel Commandant, 16th Indian Infantry Brigade; retired pay, 1924. *Address:* St. Edmund's, Bury Road, Newmarket. [*Died* 8 *March* 1956.

POOLE, Major Cecil Charles; R.E.; *b.* Wellington, Salop, 1902; *s.* of Alexander and Mary Poole; *m.* 1926, Gertrude Carter; one *s.* three *d.* *Educ.:* Ludlow Grammar School. Member of Walsall Borough Council, 1931-38. M.P. (Lab.) Lichfield Div. of Staffordshire, 1938-50, Perry Barr Division of Birmingham, 1950-55. *Address:* Caverswall, Streetly Lane, Sutton Coldfield. [*Died* 2 *Feb.* 1956.

POOLE, Ernest; Writer; *b.* Chicago, 1880; American parents; *m.* 1907; two *s.* one *d.* *Educ.:* Princeton. Magazine writer of articles and short stories; often abroad as correspondent for magazines; twice in England, 1940, 1941; had three plays produced, two in New York. *Publications:* The Harbor; His Family (First Pulitzer Prize); His Second Wife; The Dark People; The Village; Blind, 1920; Beggar's Gold, 1921; Millions, 1922; Danger, 1923; The Avalanche, 1924; The Little Dark Man, 1925; The Hunters' Moon, 1925; With Eastern Eyes, 1926; Silent Storms, 1927; The Car of Crœsus, 1930; The Destroyer, 1931; Nurses on Horseback, 1932; Great Winds, 1933; One of Us, 1934; The Bridge (autobiography), 1940; Giants Gone, 1943; The Great White Hills, 1946; The Nancy Flyer, 1949. *Recreations:* horseback, tennis, mountain tramping. *Address:* Franconia, New Hampshire, U.S.A.; 139 E. 66th St., New York, N.Y., U.S.A. *Club:* Century (New York). [*Died* 10 *Jan.* 1950.

[*But death not notified in time for inclusion in Who Was Who 1941–1950, first edn.*

POPE, James Alister, C.I.E. 1931; Indian Civil Service, retired; *b.* 23 June 1883; *s.* of Rev. A. F. Pope, The Furlong, Tring, and C. I. E., *d.* of Major James Rose, Kilravock Castle, Nairnshire; *m.* 1921, Judith Chevallier, *d.* of Rowland Beevor, Framingham, Norwich; one *s.* one *d.* *Educ.*; Eton; Corpus Christi College, Oxford. I.C.S., Bombay Presidency, 1907; Under Secretary to Government of Bombay, 1915; Indian Army Reserve of Officers, 1916-18, in India; Excise and Opium Commissioner in Central India, 1923-31; President, Indian States Opium Committee, 1927-28; retired, 1934; Fellow and Bursar, Magdalene Coll., Cambridge, 1937-43. *Address:* Clephanton, Prestbury, Glos. [*Died* 27 *Oct.* 1954.

POPE, Mildred Katherine, M.A., Docteur de l'Université de Paris, Docteur de Bordeaux; Hon. D.Litt. Manchester; *b.* 28 Jan. 1872; *d.* of Edwin Pope, M.A., Clerk in Holy Orders, and Emily Frances Watson. *Educ.:* Edgbaston High School for Girls; Somerville College, Oxford. Modern Language Tutor at Somerville College, 1894; Reader in French Philology, Oxford University, 1928; Professor of Romance Philology, Manchester University, 1934-39, now Professor Emeritus. *Publications:* La Langue de Frère Angier (Thesis); edition of the Chandos Herald's Life of the Black Prince (with Miss E. C. Lodge, D.Litt.); From Latin to Modern French, with especial consideration of Anglo-Norman; edition with others of the A.N. text La Seinte Resurreccion, 1943; edition of The Romance of Horn by Thomas, vol. I, 1955; articles and Reviews. *Address:* Fant Cottage, Garford, Abingdon, Berks. [*Died* 16 *Sept.* 1956.

POPE, Maj.-Gen. Sydney Buxton, C.B. 1930; D.S.O. 1916; Indian Army, retired; p.s.c.; *b.* 9 Feb. 1879; *o. s.* of late John Pope, M.A.; *m.* 1925, Mrs. Dorothy Rolls. *Educ.:* St. Paul's School; Christ's College, Camb. Served N.W. Frontier, India, 1908; European War, 1914-18 (D.S.O.); commanded Bannu Brigade, India, 1926-29; Razmak Brigade, 1929-30; Maj.-Gen., 1930; Commander Waziristan District, India, 1931-1934. D.A. and Q.M.G., Southern Command,

India, 1934-38; retired, 1938. *Address:* Farthing Field, Wrotham, Kent. *T.:* Borough Green 470. *Club:* Naval and Military. [*Died* 24 *July* 1955.

POPE, Walter J. M.; *see* Macqueen-Pope.

POPE, Wilson; *b.* 1866. Editor of the Star, director Daily News, 1920-30; retired. *Address:* 11 Wool Road, Wimbledon, S.W.20. [*Died* 28 *Sept.* 1953.

POPHAM, Air Chief Marshal Sir (Henry) Robert (Moore) Brooke-, G.C.V.O., *cr.* 1935; K.C.B., *cr.* 1927 (C.B. 1919); C.M.G. 1918; D.S.O. 1915; A.F.C. 1918; K.St.J. 1937; F.R.Ae.S.; *b.* 18 Sept. 1878; *s.* of late Henry Brooke, Wetheringsett Manor, Suffolk, and Dulcibella, *d.* of late Rev. Robert Moore [asumed additional surname of Popham by Royal Licence, 1904]; *m.* 1926, Opal Mary, 2nd *d.* of Edgar Hugonin; one *s.* one *d.* *Educ.:* Haileybury; Sandhurst; Staff College. Entered army, 1898, Oxfordshire Light Infantry (now Oxford and Bucks L.I.); Captain, 1904; Air Bn. Royal Engineers, 1912; Royal Flying Corps, 1912; Bt. Major, 1913; Maj. 1915; Royal Air Force, 1919; D.A.Q.M.G. 1914; served European War, 1914-18 (Legion of Honour, Order of St. Stanislaus, D.S.O., C.B., C.M.G., Bt. Lt.-Col. and Col. A.F.C.); Director of Research, Air Ministry, 1919-21; Commandant of the Royal Air Force Staff College, 1921-26; Air Officer Commanding Fighting Area Air Defence of Great Britain, 1926-28; Air Officer commanding Iraq Command, 1928-30; Commandant. Imperial Defence College, 1931-33; Air Officer Commanding-in-Chief, Air Defence of Great Britain, 1933-35; Principal Air A.D.C. to the King, 1933-37; Inspector General of Royal Air Force, 1935; A.O.C.-in-C. Middle East, 1935-36; retired list, 1937; Governor and Comm.-in-Chief of Kenya, 1937-39; with R.A.F., 1939; C.-in-C. Far East, 1940-41; reverted to retired list, 1942; President N.A.A.F.I. Council, 1944-46. *Recreation:* hunting. *Address:* Cottisford House, Brackley, Northamptonshire. *T.:* Finmere 247. *Clubs:* Army and Navy, Royal Air Force. [*Died* 20 *Oct.* 1953.

PORRITT, Lieut.-Colonel Austin Townsend; T.F., retired; D.L., J.P.; T.D., 1935; Lancashire County Council, 1923; County Alderman, 1937; *b.* 3 Aug. 1875; *s.* of late Richard Millett Porritt of Green Mount, Stubbins, Lancashire; *m.* 1906, Annie Louise (*d.* 1943), *d.* of late George W. Law-Schofield of New-Hall, Hey, Rawtenstall, Lancs; (one *s.* killed in action, 1940). *Educ.:* Rossall; Germany. Commanded 2/5th Bn. East Lancashire Regt., 1914-17; T.F. Reserve, 1917-30; High Sheriff, Lancashire, 1932; Member of Council, Rossall School; Hon.-Colonel 4/5th Bn. The East Lancashire Regt.; Director, Porritts and Spencer, Ltd. *Recreations:* travel, shooting, motoring. *Address:* Yewbarrow Lodge, Grange-over-Sands; The Cliffe, Stubbins, Lancs. *Club:* Constitutional (Manchester). [*Died* 17 *Feb.* 1956.

PORTAL, Sir Spencer (John), 4th Bt., *cr.* 1901; Kt., *cr.* 1928; *b.* 14 May 1864; 2nd *s.* of Sir Wyndham Portal, 1st Bart.; *S.* to baronetcy of nephew, Viscount Portal, of Laverstoke, P.C., G.C.M.G., D.S.O., M.V.O., 1949; *m.* 1890, Mary Laura Florence (*d.* 1932), *d.* of late Colonel William Mure, M.P., of Caldwell; one *s.* one *d.* *Educ.:* Winchester; Christ Church, Oxford. Director of Royal Exchange Assurance and Portals Ltd. (till 1946); Vice-President of Trustee Savings Banks Association. *Recreations:* fishing, yachting. *Heir:* *s.* Francis Spencer Portal [*b.* 27 June 1903; *m.* 1st, 1930, Rowena (*d.* 1948), *o. d.* of Paul Selby, Johannesburg; two *d.*; 2nd, 1950, Jane Mary, *d.* of late A. H. Williams, and of Mrs. Selwyn, The Deanery, Winchester; one *s.*]. *Address:* Flat 19, 2 Mansfield St., W.1. *T.:* Langham 3469. *Clubs:* Travellers', Cavalry; Royal Yacht Squadron. [*Died* 25 *Nov.* 1955.

PORTARLINGTON, 6th Earl of (*cr.* 1785), **Lionel Arthur Henry Seymour Dawson-Damer;** Baron Dawson, 1770; Viscount Carlow, 1776; late Lt. Irish Guards; *b.* 26 Aug. 1883; *s.* of 5th Earl and Emma [who *m.* 2nd, 1901, Hon. Henry, afterwards Viscount, Portman], *d.* of late Lord Nigel Kennedy, *g.-g.d.* of 1st Marquess of Ailsa; *m.* 1907, Winnifreda, *o. c.* of G. S. Yuill, of Chesham Place; *S.* father, 1900. *Heir:* *g.s.* Viscount Carlow. *Address:* 34 Lyall Mews, S.W.1. *T.:* Sloane 7241. [*Died* 4 *July* 1959.

PORTER, Baron (Life Peer), *cr.* 1938, of Longfield; **Samuel Lowry Porter,** P.C. 1938; G.B.E., *cr.* 1951; Kt., *cr.* 1934; a Lord of Appeal in Ordinary, 1938-Oct. 1954; *b.* 1877; *s.* of Hugh Porter. *Educ.:* Emmanuel College, Cambridge. Called to Bar, Inner Temple, 1905; served European War, Captain General List (M.B.E.); K.C. 1925; Recorder of Newcastle-under-Lyme, 1928-32; of Walsall, 1932-1934; Judge of High Court of Justice, King's Bench Division, 1934-38; Hon. LL.D. Birmingham, 1940, Cambridge 1947, Queen's University, Belfast, 1949. *Address:* 46 Burton Court, S.W.3; Emmanuel College, Cambridge. *Clubs:* Athenæum, United University, Reform. [*Died* 13 *Feb.* 1956.

PORTER, Charles, M.D., B.Sc., M.R.C.P. Edin.; Barrister-at-law; retired; *b.* Edinburgh, 19 June 1873; 2nd *s.* of Alexander Porter; *m.* Jennie Leslie (*d.* 1937), *d.* of W. R. Chichester-McMillan, Belfast; one *s.* three *d.*; 2nd, Geraldine Maziere, *d.* of Dr. Edward Maziere Courtenay, Dublin. *Educ.:* Royal High School, Edinburgh; Universities of Edinburgh and Freiburg. Lecturer on Bacteriology, University of Sheffield, 1902-6; late Asst. Med. O.H., Leeds and Med. O.H., Finsbury, St. Marylebone, Greenwich, Paddington, Bethnal Green and Poplar; Lecturer on Public Health, Middlesex Hospital Medical School and London School of Hygiene and Tropical Medicine; Fellow (Pres., 1933-1934) Society of Medical Officers of Health; Vice-President (Chairman of Council, 1931-33) Royal Sanitary Institute; Hon. Fellow, American Public Health Association; Lecturer National Health Society; Member Board of Studies in Hygiene, London University; Examiner, B.A. (Architecture) University of London; Member of Council Queen's Institute of District Nursing; Member Royal Sanitary Institute and Sanitary Inspectors' Examination Joint Board. *Publications:* Sanitary Law and Practice (Robertson and Porter); Sanitary Law (Porter and Fenton); School Hygiene and the Laws of Health; Elements of Hygiene and Public Health; The Future Citizen and his Mother; Parkin Prize Essay on Cholera; contributions to various journals. *Recreations:* mainly literary. *Address:* 69 Clifton Hill, St. John's Wood, N.W.8. *T.:* Maida Vale 1326. *Clubs:* Devonshire, City Livery, English-Speaking Union. [*Died* 15 *Dec.* 1952.

PORTER, Brig.-Gen. Cyril Lachlan, C.B. 1925; C.M.G. 1918; D.S.O. 1918; late East Kent Regt.; *b.* 1872; *m.* 1905, Violet Ethel, *d.* of late E. T. Naylor, Dean House, Kilmeston, Hants. Served N.W. Frontier of India, 1897-98 (clasp); European War, 1914-18 (despatches, C.M.G., D.S.O., Bt. Lieut.-Col. and Col.); Area Commander Zhob Independent Brigade Area, 1925-29; retired pay, 1929. *Club:* Army and Navy. [*Died* 11 *Nov.* 1951.

PORTER, Alderman Edward, J.P. County of Lancaster and Borough of Blackburn; retired Trade Union Official; Alderman of Blackburn; *b.* Blackburn, 28 July 1880; *m.* (wife *d.* 1948); one *s.* *Educ.:* elementary. M.P. (Lab.) Warrington, 1945-1950. Chm. Blackburn Town Council Parliamentary Cttee.; member of Transport Users Consultative Cttee., North Western Area. Late Chairman Blackburn Corporation Electricity Department; Chairman Works Department. *Address:* 313 Preston Old

Road, Feniscliffe, Blackburn. *T.:* Blackburn 21239. [*Died* 31 *Aug.* 1960.

PORTER, Sir John (Scott) Horsbrugh-, 2nd Bt., *cr.* 1902; Senior Clerk in the House of Commons, retired 1934; *b.* 18 July 1871; *s.* of 1st Bart. and Agnes, *d.* of late Col. Horsbrugh, Peeblesshire [assumed additional name of Horsbrugh]; *m.* 1st, 1906, Elaine Maud (*d.* 1919), *y. d.* of Thomas Jefferies, J.P., of Newbay, Co. Wexford, and Los Ceibos, Buenos Ayres; one *s.*; 2nd, 1924, Edith Dorothy, *er. d.* of late Maj.-Gen. Richard Worsley, Indian Army; *S.* father, 1919. *Educ.:* Charterhouse; Brasenose College, Oxford. *Heir: s.* Lt.-Col. Andrew Marshall Horsburgh-Porter, D.S.O. *Address:* Keytes, Bourton-on-Hill, Glos. [*Died* 7 *March* 1953.

PORTER, Rt. Hon. Samuel Clarke, M.A., LL.B.; Lord Justice of Appeal, Supreme Court of Northern Ireland, since 1946; *b.* 14 June 1875; 3rd *s.* of W. J. Porter, Portrush, and Catherine Clarke; *m.* 1924, Laura Geraldine Holmes, 4th *d.* of late Rev. James Scott, Banbridge, Co. Down. *Educ.:* Coleraine Acad. Inst.; Methodist College, Belfast; Queen's College, Belfast (Exhibitioner and Senior Classical Scholar), B.A. (Hon.), M.A. (Hon.), LL.B. (Hon.). First Class Honours in Law, R.U.I.; called to Irish Bar, 1903; joined N.E. Circuit; K.C. 1933; Bencher of Inns of Court of Northern Ireland, 1939; Senior Crown Prosecutor for County Down, 1943; Senior Crown Prosecutor for City of Belfast, 1945; P.C. (N. Ire.), 1947; Lord Justice for Govt. of N. Ireland during absence of the Governor; Pres., N. Ireland Branch, Nat. Assoc. for Prevention of Tuberculosis. Vice-Pres. Irish Mountaineering Club. Sometimes lectr. in English Law and Constitutional History for the Workers Educational Association. Contested (Lab.) East Belfast, 1920. *Publication:* Workmen's Compensation, 1907. *Recreations:* mountaineering, yachting, golf. *Address:* 6 Castlehill Road, Belfast. *T.:* Belfast 53682. *Clubs:* Royal Portrush Golf; Portrush Yacht (Pres.). [*Died* 10 *July* 1956.

PORTSMOUTH, Percy, R.S.A. 1923 (A.R.S.A. 1906), F.R.B.S. 1927; Member of the Royal Glasgow Institute of the Fine Arts; *b.* Reading, 2nd Feb. 1874; *m.* Kate Emma Pope (*d.* 1941). After serving five years at engineering began to study Art at the University Extension College under Walter Crane and Morley Fletcher; following a short stay in Paris and Brussels, proceeded to London to pursue studies under Prof. Lanteri; exhibits at the Royal Academy, Paris Salon, Royal Scottish Academy, Glasgow Institute, Walker Art Gallery, etc.; amongst important works are The Captive, Vision, Labour, Il Penseroso, Calliope in marble, exhibited in the Royal Academy; Thurso Memorial, Memorial to late Rt. Hon. Lord Glentanar at Aboyne Church, Work on Scottish War Memorial, Madonna and Child in stone at St. Mary's Church, Rushden. *Address:* The Studio, Rushden, Buntingford, Herts. [*Died* 29 *Oct.* 1953.

POST, Emily, (Mrs. Price Post); American writer; President of Emily Post Institute (founded 1948); *m.* Edwin M. Post. *Publications:* The Flight of a Moth, 1904; Purple and Fine Linen, 1906; Woven in The Tapestry, 1908; The Title Market, 1909; The Eagle's Feather, 1910; By Motor to the Golden Gate, 1915; Etiquette, 1922; Parade, 1925; How to Behave Though a Debutante, 1928; The Personality of a House, 1930; Children are People, 1940. Began broadcasting, 1931. Has written columns in 152 daily papers since 1932; writes Sunday (long) column in same papers. Interested in good taste, manners, customs, also in architecture and interior decoration. *Address:* 39 East 79th Street, New York, N.Y., U.S.A. [*Died* 25 *Sept.* 1960.

POSTLETHWAITE, John Rutherfoord Parkin, C.B.E. 1933; *b.* 26 Nov. 1883; *s.* of John William Postlethwaite and Kate Desmond Foulger; *m.* Ellen Anna, *d.* of Lieut.-Col. H. Caddell; two *d.* *Educ.:* St. Clare, Upper Walmer; Haileybury College. Colonial Civil Service, 1909-32; Provincial Commissioner, Buganda Province, Uganda Protectorate; Member of Uganda Executive Council; served European War of 1914-18 (despatches twice); Deputy Divisional Food Officer, London Division, Ministry of Food; Divisional Food Officer, South-Eastern Division, 1940-42; Divisional Food Officer, London, 1942-44. U.N.R.R.A., 1944-45. Member of Council of Royal African Society, 1945. Trustee R. Hussey Slave Charity. Director of various companies. Lecturer and Author. *Publications:* African Roses, 1937; The Affairs of Men, 1938; A Broken Tooth, 1945; I Look Back, 1947; lecturer and contributor to various magazines. *Address:* Woodside, The Pilgrims Way, Guildford. *T.:* Guildford 3523. *Club:* Savage. [*Died* 12 *Jan.* 1956.

POTHECARY, Major Walter Frank, D.C.M. 1915; J.P.; LL.D.; *b.* 5 Sept. 1882; *s.* of Frank Pothecary, Fifehead Manor, Wallop, Hants; *m.* 1908, Amy, *o. d.* of Henry Nunn Aylward, Lockerley, Hants; one *s.* three *d.* (and one *s.* decd.). *Educ.:* Sherborne. Solicitor, 1905; enlisted London Rifle Brigade, 1911; King's Hundred (Bisley), 1913; active service France and Belgium, 1914-15, Sergt. (D.C.M.); commissioned to Hampshire Regt., 1915; Adjt. 3rd/5th Bn., 1915-16; Comdt. Southern Command Bombing Sch., Lyndhurst, 1917-1919; Bt. Major, 1919; transferred to London Rifle Bde., 1920; resigned 1924. Asst. Clerk to Clothworkers' Company, 1922; Clerk, 1933-50; retired, on promotion to Warden, 1950, Master, 1952, Assistant, 1953; J.P. (Surrey) 1937; organized Wallington Home Guard, 1940 and served continuously until disbanded. President Wallington Branch, British Legion, 24 years to 1948; Clerk to Mary Datchelor School, Camberwell, 1933-50; Joint Hon. Secretary City and Guilds of London Inst., 1935-52. Hon. LL.D. (Leeds), 1950; Officer Brother of Order of St. John of Jerusalem, 1950. *Recreations:* Layman's Church and Church Schools work; country pursuits. *Address:* 102 Manor Road, Wallington, Surrey. *T.:* Wallington 1251. [*Died* 28 *Jan.* 1958.

POTT, Sir (George) Stanley, Kt., *cr.* 1943; Solicitor; *b.* 13 Aug. 1870; *s.* of Ven. Alfred Pott, B.D., Archdeacon of Berks; *m.* 1920, Mildred Constance Bell Pitman; one *s.* (and one died in R.A.F. 1944). *Educ.:* Radley College; Magdalen College, Oxford. President of Law Society, 1942-43. Treasurer of Foundling Hospital. *Address:* Clifton Hampden, Abingdon. *Clubs:* United University, Leander. [*Died* 25 *Jan.* 1951.

POTTER, Frederick Felix, C.B.E. 1945; M.A., B.Sc.; Deal Town Council, 1948; Kent C.C., 1949; Coronation Baron of the Cinque Ports, 1953; *b.* Colchester, Essex, 11 Aug. 1882; 10th *c.* and 7th *s.* of Charles and Emily Potter; *m.* 1909, Emily Caroline, *e. d.* of G. E. Buckle, Isleworth, Middlesex; two *d.* *Educ.:* Colchester; London University. Lecturer, Borough Rd. Training College, 1904-7; Bolton Training College, 1907-9; Cheshire County Training College, 1909-19; Lt. R.N.V.R. in European War, 1918-19; H.M. Inspector of Schools, Technological Branch, 1919-22; Director of Education Cheshire County Council, 1922-1947; Mayor of Deal, 1950-54. *Publications:* numerous school books, *e.g.* Common Sense Arithmetic (Eight Books); Common Sense English (Eight Books); Anthology of Verse (Eight Books); New English Treasury (Eight Books); The Teaching of Arithmetic; Educational Journey (autobiographical), etc. *Address:* Holmwood, Marine Rd., Walmer, Kent. *T.:* Deal 932. [*Died* 11 *April* 1955.

POTTER, Harold, Ph.D., LL.D.; Barrister-at-Law; F.K.C., London; Prof. of English Law, University of London, since 1938; *b.* 12 Aug. 1896; *s.* of John James Potter and Maud Maria Howard; *m.* Beatrice Spencer, *y. d.* of C. Fairfax Crowder; two *s.* one *d.* *Educ.:* King's College, London. Admitted Solicitor, 1920; called to Bar, Gray's Inn, 1939. Member Editorial Board, Journal of Planning Law. *Publications:* Modern Law of Real Property (Goodeve and Potter); Historical Introduction to English Law; Principles of Registered Land Law; Principles of Liability in Tort; Key and Elphinstone's Precedents in Conveyancing, Vol. III: Registered Land, etc. General Editor, Chitty on Contracts (19th and 20th Eds.); General Editor, Clerk and Lindsell on Torts (9th and 10th Eds.), etc.; Jt. Ed., The Conveyancer (N.S.). *Address:* King's College, Strand, W.C.2; Barkway, Royston, Herts. *T.:* Temple Bar 5651, Barkway 212. [*Died* 3 *July* 1951.

POTTER, Colonel William Allen, D.S.O. 1917; R.A.S.C., T.F., 1910-22; T.A. (R), 1922-48; D.L. Notts, 1937; *y. s.* of late Tom Potter, J.P., Daybrook House; *m.* 1917, Margaret, *o. d.* of late James Forman; one *s.* two *d.* Served European War, 1914-18 (D.S.O.); J.P. Nottinghamshire, 1927; High Sheriff, 1944. Member Notts. T.A. and A.F.A., 1913-52, Vice-Chm., 1946-52. *Address:* Lambley House, Woodborough, Notts. [*Died* 11 *March* 1953.

POUISHNOFF, Leff; pianist; *b.* Russia, 1891; *m.* 1942, Dorothy Hildreth. *Educ.:* Petrograd Conservatoire (1st Class Diploma, Gold Medal and Rubinstein Prize). First appeared: Uman, 1896; Petrograd, 1910; London, 1921. Frequent subsequent appearances in London. *Recreations:* books, photography, motoring, snooker. *Club:* Royal Automobile. [*Died* 28 *May* 1959.

POUND, Sir Allen Leslie, 3rd Bart., *cr.* 1905; LL.B.; sole member of legal firm of Pound & Pound, of Egham; *b.* 31 Oct. 1888; *s.* of Sir Lulham Pound, 2nd Bart., and Julia Isabella (*d.* 1938), *d.* of Alfred Allen of Highbury New Park; *S.* father, 1937; *m.* 1st, 1916, Margery, 2nd *d.* of Stephen Hayworth of Clapton; one *s.* one *d.*; 2nd, 1925, Leonie May (*d.* 1950), *widow* of Stephen James Chapman. *Educ.:* Merchant Taylors' School; London University. *Heir: s.* Derek Allen, Lieut. Royal Artillery [*b.* 7 Apr. 1920; *m.* 1942, Joan Amy, *d.* of James Woodthorpe; one *s.* one *d.*] *Address:* 26 Whitehall Lane, Egham. [*Died* 15 *Nov.* 1952.

POWELL, E. Alexander; author and traveller; *b.* Syracuse, New York, 16 August 1879; *s.* of Edward A. Powell, L.H.D., and Lucy Caroline Smith Powell; *m.* 1st, Jessie, *d.* of late Hon. Milton H. Northrup; one *s.* one *d.*; 2nd, Florence Josephine, *d.* of Samuel Gale Taylor, Barrington, Ill. *Educ.:* Oberlin College; Syracuse Univ. American Foreign Service in Syria and Egypt, 1906-7; expedition to Russian Central Asia, 1908; to Equatorial Africa, 1909-10; Mexico, 1912; war correspondent of New York World, London Daily Mail and Scribner's Magazine with Allied armies, 1914-1917; Assistant to Chief of Staff, 91st Div., U.S. Army, 1917; served with American Expeditionary Forces in France, rank of Major, 1918; commissioned Lieut.-Col. Infantry (reserve), 1920; confidential mission for Italian Govt. in Balkans, 1919; expedition to Malaysia, 1920; to Arabia, Kurdistan, and Persia, 1922; to Abyssinia, Madagascar, and Congo, 1924; to the Sahara, 1925-26; to Nepal, 1927-28; to the Yukon, 1929; Political Analyst, Office of Naval Intelligence, 1941-42; Political Editor, Office of Censorship, Washington, 1942-43; Principal Administrative Officer, Foreign Economic Administration in Caribbean Area and the Guianas, 1943-44; Knight of Legion of Honour, France; Knight of Order of Leopold, Belgium; and other foreign orders. Awarded silver medal for literature by Commonwealth Club of California. *Publications:* The Last Frontier; Gentlemen Rovers; The End of the Trail; The Road to Glory; Fighting in Flanders; Vive la France; Italy at War; Brothers in Arms; The Army behind the Army; New Frontiers of Freedom; Where the Strange Trails go Down; Asia at the Cross-roads; Forgotten Heroes; By Camel and Car to the Peacock Throne; The Struggle for Power in Moslem Asia; Beyond the Utmost Purple Rim; The Map that is Half Unrolled; In Barbary; A Virginia Pilgrimage; Embattled Borders; The Last Home of Mystery, 1929; The Danger on the Danube, 1930; Thunder Over Europe; Marches of the North, 1931; Undiscovered Europe, 1932; Yonder Lies Adventure, 1932; Slanting Lines of Steel, 1933; The Long Roll on the Rhine, 1934; Red Drums, 1935; The Liberator (film), 1935; Aerial Odyssey, 1936; Free Lance, 1937; Gone are the Days, 1938; Adventure Road, 1954. *Recreations:* travel, history. *Address:* Riverain, Falls Village, Conn., U.S.A. [*Died* 12 *Nov.* 1957.
See also Baron Monson.

POWELL, Brig.-General Edward Weyland Martin, C.B. 1919; C.M.G. 1918; D.S.O. 1902; late R.F.A.; *b.* 3 Dec. 1869; *y. s.* of Lt.-Col. W. Martin Powell of Brooklands. Entered Royal Artillery, 1889; Captain, 1899; served South Africa, 1899-1901 (despatches, Queen's medal 4 clasps, D.S.O.); European War, 1914-18 (despatches, Bt. Lt.-Col., C.M.G., C.B., Legion of Honour). *Address:* Brooklands, Lyndhurst, Hants. [*Died* 25 *July* 1954.

POWELL, Vice-Admiral George Bingham, C.M.G. 1918; Royal Navy (retired); *s.* of late Captain G. C. B. Powell, Indian Army; *b.* 1871; *m.* 1911, Ada Patricia Fitzgerald, *d.* of late Major James Bower-Bower of Claremont, Teignmouth, Devon (one *s.*, Capt. Royal Marines, killed 1943, and second *s.*, Lieutenant R.N., killed 1942). As Lieutenant of H.M.S. Aurora landed with Sir Edward Seymour's Expedition for Relief of Pekin; severely wounded outside Tientsin June 1900 (despatches, China medal, Relief of Pekin clasp); appointed to command H.M.S. Kinsha for navigation of the Rapids of the river Yangtszi; specially promoted to Commander for services in North China, 1903; Captain, 1910; at commencement of European War was Chief of Staff to Vice-Admiral Sir A. Limpus, Senior Naval Officer at Malta; presented by the French Navy with a piece of Sèvres for services rendered to them; Officer of the Legion of Honour, 1916; Commander of the Order of the Crown of Italy, 1916; Liaison Officer on the Staff of the French Admiral of Patrols in the Mediterranean, 1917 (despatches of French Admiral, Croix de Guerre); appointed to command H.M.S. Devonshire employed in the North Atlantic Convoy Service, 1917; appointed to command H.M.S. Monarch, 1919; Rear-Admiral, 1921; retired, 1921; Vice-Admiral retired, 1926. *Address:* 5 Grand Parade, Portsmouth. *Club:* United Service. [*Died* 27 *May* 1952.

POWELL, Percival Herbert, M.Sc., M.Eng., M.I.E.E., M.A.I.E.E.; M.N.Z.Soc.C.E.; *s.* of James and E. M. Powell; *m.* Una K. Mayne; one *s.* *Educ.:* Liverpool College; University of Liverpool. Univ. course Honours Engineering; Scholar of Victoria University; David Rew Memorial Scholar; Fellow of Victoria Univ.; Siemens Bros. Works; Lecturer in Electrical Engineering, Canterbury Coll. Professor of Electrical Engineering, Canterbury College, Christchurch, N.Z., retired 1946. F.R.S.A. *Publications:* Hydrodynamical and Electromagnetic Investigation of Distribution of Magnetic Flux in Toothed Core Armature (part author); The Air-gap Correction Coefficient; Electric Power in New Zealand; Circuits of an Electrical Engineering Laboratory; Measurement of Power; Graphical Construction for Impedance of Parallel Circuits; Resistance of Induction Motor. *Recreations:* bowls, motoring, bridge. *Address:* 19 St. Albans Street, Christchurch, N.1., N.Z. *T.:* 56784. [*Died* 18 *Dec.* 1958.

POWELL, Lt.-Col. Philip Lionel William, C.B.E. 1918; D.S.O. 1916; late the Welch Regt.; Barrister-at-Law, Inner Temple, 1930; *b.* 21 April 1882; *s.* of late Col. L. L. Powell; *m.* 1904, Maud M. Wells-Dymoke (*d.* 1954); one *s.* *Educ.:* privately; Sandhurst. Served S. African War, 1901; European War, Aug. 1914-1918 (C.B.E., D.S.O., despatches, Bt. Lt.-Col.); Brigade-Major, 1915; D.A.A. and Q.M.G. 1916; A.A.G. 1918; G.S.O.1. Military Mission to Finland, 1924-25 (Order of the White Rose of Finland, Commander 2nd Class); retired pay, 1928. *Clubs:* Army and Navy, Travellers', United Service, Arthur's. [*Died* 31 *Dec.* 1959.

POWELL, Richard Albert Brakell, B.A. (Oxon.); Barrister-at-Law (retired); Governor of Queen Mary College, University of London and Hon. Treas. 1944-52; Governor of Liverpool College and other schools; *b.* 21 July 1892; *o. s.* of late Richard Ibbetson Powell and Sarah Brakell, of Liverpool; *m.* 1926, Stella Float, 2nd *d.* of late Percy Young; one *s.* one *d.* *Educ.:* Liverpool College; Hertford Coll., Oxford. Oxford Univ. O.T.C. 1913-14; Admiralty and Min. of Shipping, 1915-19; Member of British War Mission to U.S.A., 1917-19; called to Bar, Inner Temple, and practised King's Bench Division and Northern Circuit; sometime Deputy Judge of County Courts; H.M. Treasury, 1940-44. Freeman City of London; Drapers' Company: Liveryman, 1937; Clerk, 1944-52; Mem. Court of Assistants, 1952. *Publications:* edited (with Sir R. Burrows, K.C.) 3rd Ed. of Odgers on the Common Law; numerous contributions to the press. *Address:* Broad Eaves, Fetcham, Surrey. *Club:* Devonshire.
[*Died* 19 *April* 1957.

POWER, Admiral of the Fleet Sir Arthur (John), G.C.B., *cr.* 1950 (K.C.B., *cr.* 1944; C.B. 1941); G.B.E., *cr.* 1946; C.V.O. 1936; *b.* 1889; *s.* of E. J. Power; *m.* 1918, Amy (*d.* 1945), *e. d.* of Colonel D. A. Bingham; three *s.*; *m.* 1947, Margaret Joyce, Second Officer, W.R.N.S., *o. d.* of A. H. St. C. Watson, Penfold House, Hendon, N.W.4. Commanded Gunnery School, Portsmouth, 1935-37; commanded H.M.S. Ark Royal, 1938-40; a Lord Commissioner of the Admiralty and an Assistant Chief of Naval Staff, 1940-42; commanded 15th Cruiser Squadron, 1942; Vice-Adm., Malta, 1943; Second-in-Comd., Eastern Fleet, 1944; C.-in-C. East Indies Station, 1945; Admiral, 1946; Second Sea Lord and Chief of Naval Personnel, 1946-48; C.-in-C., Mediterranean Station, 1948-50; C.-in-C., Portsmouth, 1950-52, and Naval C.-in-C., Home (designate), 1951-52; Admiral of the Fleet, 1952; First and Principal Naval A.D.C. to King George VI, 1950-52, to the Queen, Feb.-Apr. 1952. Allied Commander-in-Chief Channel and Southern North Sea Command, 1952. *Address:* Lime Cottage, Brambridge, Hants. *Club:* United Service. [*Died* 28 *Jan.* 1960.

POWER, Air Vice-Marshal D'Arcy, C.B.E. 1945; M.C. 1916; M.R.C.S., L.R.C.P. 1914; retd.; *b.* 2 June 1889; *er. s.* of late Sir D'Arcy Power, K.B.E., F.R.C.S., F.S.A.; *m.* 1918, Cecilia Collins (*d.* 1958); one *s.* one *d.* *Educ.:* Merchant Taylors' School; St. Bartholomew's Hospital. Served with Montenegrin Contingent of B.R.C.S. during 2nd Balkan War, 1912-13; commissioned R.A.M.C. Special Reserve, 1911; served European War in France and Belgium, 1914-19; transferred to R.A.F. Medical Branch, 1918; Principal Medical Officer, Mediterranean, 1930-34; Principal Medical Officer India and South-East Asia Commands, 1942-45; Principal Medical Officer Transport Command, R.A.F., 1945; retired, 1946. House Governor Royal Masonic Hospital, 1945-49; ex-Member of Council, B.M.A.; ex-Chm. Board of Management, Metropolitan Convalescent Institution; Ex-Member of Borough Council, Kingston-upon-Thames; Ex-Member Executive Committee Samuel Pepys Club; M.R.I. 1935. Livery Merchant Taylors' Company, 1912. *Recreation:* motoring. *Address:* Bagdale, Gloucester Rd., Kingston-on-Thames, Surrey. *T.:* Kingston-on-Thames 1850. *Club:* Athenæum. [*Died* 26 *Dec.* 1958.

POWER, Ven. George Edmund; retired; late Archdeacon of Ardfert and Aghadoe; Prebendary of Effin in St. Mary's Cathedral, Limerick, 1924-41; Canon of St. Patrick's Cathedral, Dublin, 1929-41. *Address:* 97 Upper Leeson Street, Dublin.
[*Died* 6 *Jan.* 1950.
[*But death not notified in time for inclusion in Who Was Who 1941–1950, first edn.*

POWER, Harold Septimus; late official artist to Australian Imperial Forces (A.I.F.); Lieut.; *m.* 1st, 1904, Isabel Laura (*d.* 1935); one *s.*: 2nd, 1937, Margery Desmazurer; one *s.* *Educ.:* Melbourne; Julien's Academy, Paris. Exhibitor at Royal Academy; pictures in National Galleries of New South Wales, Victoria, South Australia; on Western front with Australian troops; Commissioned by the Federal Government to paint the Opening Ceremony of Parliament House, Canberra, by the Duke of York; Commissioned to paint mural decoration for the Public Library of Victoria in commemoration of the War. *Recreation:* music. *Address:* 11 Leadenhall Street, E.C.; 54 Crisp St., Hampton, S.7, Victoria, Australia. *Club:* Chelsea Arts. [*Died* 3 *Jan.* 1951.

POWER, Sir Ivan McLannahan Cecil, 2nd Bart., *cr.* 1924; Merchant Shipper and Company Director; *b.* London, 29 Nov. 1903; *e. s.* of Sir John Cecil Power, 1st Bart., and Mabel Katherine Louisa (*d.* 1945), *d.* of late J. Hartley Perks, J.P., Bramham Gardens, S.W.; *S.* father, 1950; *m.* 1st, 1927, Nancy Hilary (marriage dissolved, 1935), *d.* of late Rev. J. W. Griffiths, Wentworth, Virginia Water; one *s.* one *d.*; 2nd, 1935, Margret Mari (*d.* 1936), *d.* of William Henry Stevenson; 3rd, 1937, Kathleen Edyth, *d.* of late John Clarke Gloster. *Educ.:* Charterhouse; New College, Oxford (M.A.). Formerly: Diplomatic Service; Attaché at H.M. Embassy, Berlin, after European War, 1914-18; transferred to Prime Minister's Dept., Austr.; sometime Sec. to Speaker Austr. Fed. Parl. and on staff of Commonwealth Parl. Assoc.; widely travelled on Commonwealth Parl. liaison work, in the Commonwealth; held several correspondentships and editorships; several times Mem. Brit. Deleg. to League of Nations, Geneva; Priv. Sec. to Viscount Cecil of Chelwood, K.C.; Rep. Gt. Brit. on Af. Mandates Com.; Mem. L.C.C. for North Ken. Div. (Vice-Chm. Gen. Finance Cttee., etc.); Chm. Stepney Housing Trust; Dir. Brit. Housing Corp. and other finance and public Coys.; covered part of Spanish Civil War for London newspapers. Served War of 1939-45, R.A.F. at home and overseas. Chm. and Man. Dir. Power's Estates, Africa (Pty.) Ltd.; Director: Matabeleland Investment Co. (Pvt.) Ltd.; Selby Engineers (Pty.) Ltd.; Goodwood Investment Co. (Pty.) Ltd.; St. Clements Investment Trust Ltd.; Kuehne's Freight Services (Pty.) Ltd.; J. W. Kearsley (S.A.) (Pty.) Ltd. *Heir:* *s.* John Patrick McLannahan, *b.* 16 March 1928. *Address:* Kilfane House, 3 Cecil Avenue, Melrose, Johannesburg, S.A. *Clubs:* United University; Rand (Johannesburg).
[*Died* 13 *Feb.* 1954.

POWER, Rev. Patrick, D.Litt., M.R.I.A.; *b.* Callaghane, near Waterford, 8 March 1862. *Educ.:* Catholic University School and St. John's College, Waterford. Ordained 1885; attached for three years to St. Brigid's Church, Liverpool; for seven years Rector in succession of Cobar, Bourke and Wilcannia,

N.S.W.; on return to Ireland attached for three years to the Cathedral, Waterford; afterwards in succession — Diocesan Inspector of Schools (Waterford and Lismore), Chaplain to Training College and Curate of Portlaw; Lecturer in Archæology, Maynooth College, 1910-31. Professor of Archæology, University College, Cork, 1913-34. *Publications:* Manual of Religious Instruction (thirtieth edition); Place Names of Decies, 1907; Parochial History of Waterford and Lismore, 1912; Lives of SS. Declan and Mochuda, 1915 (Irish Texts Society); Place Names and Antiquities of S.E. Cork, 1917; Ardmore-Deaglain, 1919, 2nd ed. 1925, 3rd ed. 1929; Prehistoric Ireland, 1922, 2nd ed. 1925; Early Christian Ireland, 1925; The Ancient Topography of Fermoy, 1931; A Bishop of the Penal Times, 1932; Short History of Co. Waterford, 1933; Waterford and Lismore, 1937; Cathedral and Parish of Holy Trinity, Waterford, 1940; St. John's and Ballygunner, 1942; Lismore-Mochuda, 1946; author of a number of minor works (historical and archæological); Editor Journal of Waterford and South-East Ireland Archæological Society, 19 vols. *Address:* John's Hill, Waterford, Eire. [*Died* 16 *Oct.* 1951.

POWER, William; author and journalist; *b.* Glasgow, 30 Aug. 1873; *e. s.* of William Power, shipmaster. Bank clerk till 1907; on editorial staff of Glasgow Herald, mainly as literary editor and leader-writer, till 1926; Editor of The Scots Observer, 1926-29; President, Scottish P.E.N. Club, 1935-38; President, Scottish Convention; President, Scottish Ramblers' Federation. Contested Argyll in Scottish Nationalist interest, By-Election, 1940. *Publications:* Pavement and Highway; Prince Charlie; The World Unvisited, 1922; Robert Burns, and other Essays and Sketches, 1926; My Scotland; Scotland and the Scots, 1934; Literature and Oatmeal, 1935; Should Auld Acquaintance, 1937; The Face of Glasgow, 1938; The Face of Edinburgh, 1939; contributor to numerous journals in Scotland and England. *Address:* Corra Linn, Stirling. *Clubs:* Art, Press (Glasgow); Scottish Arts (Edinburgh) [*Died* 13 *June* 1951.

POWIS, 4th Earl of (*cr.* 1804), **George Charles Herbert,** D.L., J.P. Baron Clive of Plassey in Ireland, 1762; Baron Clive (U.K.), 1794; Viscount Clive, Baron Herbert, Baron Powis, 1804; *b.* 24 June 1862; *s.* of Lt.-Gen. Rt. Hon. Sir Percy Herbert, K.C.B., P.C., M.P. (*s.* of 2nd Earl), and Lady Mary Petty-Fitzmaurice, *o. c.* of Earl of Kerry, *g.d.* of 3rd Marquess of Lansdowne; *S. u.* 1891; *m.* 1890, Hon. Violet Ida Eveline Lane-Fox, 16th Baroness Darcy de Knayth (*d.* 1929), *d.* of 12th Baron Conyers and *de jure* 15th Baron Darcy de Knayth; (*er. s.* killed 1916, *yr. s.* killed in action 23 March 1943) one *d.* *Educ.:* Eton; St. John's College, Cambridge. Lord-Lieut. of Shropshire, 1896-1951. Owns upwards of 30,000 acres. Bailiff Grand Cross of the Order of St. John of Jerusalem. *Heir: cousin* Colonel Edward Robert Henry Herbert, C.B.E. [*b.* 19 May 1889; *m.* 1932, Ella Mary, *d.* of late Col. W. H. Rathborne]. *Address:* Powis Castle, Welshpool, Mont. *Club:* Carlton. [*Died* 9 *Nov.* 1952.

POWLES, Colonel (Charles) Guy, C.M.G. 1918; D.S.O. 1916; N.Z. Staff Corps; *s.* of late Charles Plummer Powles, Wellington, N.Z.; *b.* 15 Dec. 1872; *m.* 1903, Jessie Mary, *d.* of C. T. Richardson, Wellington, N.Z.; two *s.* one *d.* *Educ.:* Wellington College, N.Z. Served South African War, 1900-1 (Queen's medal four clasps); European War, 1914-18 (despatches, C.M.G., D.S.O., Order of the Nile); Colonel Commandant, Central Command, N.Z. Military Forces, 1924-27; A.D.C. to the King, 1921-28; retired list, 1934; Principal of Flock House Station, 1930-36; posted to Active List, N.Z.S.C., 1940; reposted retired list, Oct. 1944. *Publications:* History of the New Zealanders in Sinai and Palestine; The History of the Canterbury Mounted Rifles, 1914-19. *Address:* Te Horo, New Zealand. *Club:* Wellington (Wellington, New Zealand). [*Died* 17 *June* 1951.

POWNALL, Lieut.-Colonel Sir Assheton, Kt., *cr* 1926; O.B.E.; T.D.; D.L.; *b.* 3 Oct. 1877; *s.* of C. A. W. Pownall; *g.s.* of Ven. Assheton Pownall, Archdeacon of Leicester; *m.* Florence Helen (*d.* 1952), *d.* of Lt.-Col. Clayton-Cowell; one *d.* *Educ.:* Rugby. Underwriter on Lloyd's; M.P. (U.) E. Lewisham, 1918-45; on L.C.C. for Lewisham, 1907-10, Vice-Chairman Highways Committee; Unionist candidate Bermondsey, 1908-9; contested Rotherhithe, Jan. and Dec. 1910; Unionist candidate Tottenham, 1911-18; Lieut.-Col. 20th Batt. London Regiment, 1915. London District Welfare Officer, 1939; Chairman Public Accounts Committee, House of Commons, 1943-45. Master Vintners' Company, 1942 and 1947; member County of London Territorial Assoc., 1908-47. *Recreations:* shooting, ski-ing, golf, tennis. *Address:* 29 Palace Gate, W.8. *T.:* Western 3633. *Clubs:* Athenæum, Carlton. [*Died* 29 *Oct.* 1953.

POWYS, Theodore Francis; author; *b.* Shirley, in Derbyshire; *s.* of Rev. Charles Francis Powys; *m.* 1905, Violet Rosalie Dodds; one *s.* (and one *s.* decd.). *Educ.:* private schools. *Publications:* Fables; The House with the Echo, 1929; The Dew-pond; Mr. Weston's Good Wine, 1928; Soliloquies of a Hermit, 1926; Innocent Birds, 1926; Mr. Tasker's Gods; Mockery Gap, 1925; Mark Only, 1924; Black Bryony; The Left Leg; Hester Dominy; and Abraham Men, 1923; Kindness in a corner, 1930; The White Paternoster, 1930; The Only Penitent, 1931; When Thou Wast Naked, 1931; Unclay, 1931; The Two Thieves, 1932; Captain Patch, 1935; Make Thyself Many, 1935; Goat Green, 1937. *Recreations:* none. *Address:* The Lodge, Mappowder, Sturminster Newton, Dorset. [*Died* 27 *Nov.* 1953.

POYSER, Sir (Arthur Hampden) Ronald (Wastell), Kt., *cr.* 1952; C.B.E. 1941; The Master in Lunacy, 1944-56; *b.* 30 September 1884; *s.* of Arthur H. Poyser, K.C., of Sydenham; *m.* 1912, Dorothy, *o. d.* of Rev. Walter J. Latham, Holy Trinity, Beckenham, Kent; (one *s.* killed in action 1943) two *d.* *Educ.:* Eton; St. John's College, Oxford. Barrister, Middle Temple, 1908; Midland Circuit; served European War, 1914-19, Mesopotamia and Persia (despatches), Inns of Court and Machine Gun Corps; Maj. 1917. *Address:* Court of Protection, Staffordshire House, Store Street, Bedford Square, W.C.1; The Old Cottage, Arnull's Road, Streatham, S.W. 16. [*Died* 30 *June* 1957.

PRAEGER, Robert Lloyd, D.Sc. Belfast (Hon.); Sc.D. Dublin (Hon.); D.Sc. Nat. University Ireland (Hon.); B.E. Royal Univ. of Ireland; A.L.S.; Librarian, National Library of Ireland 1920-1924; *b.* Holywood, Co. Down, 25 Aug 1865; *s.* of Willem Emil Praeger of the Hague, linen merchant, and Maria Patterson, *d.* of late Robert Patterson, F.R.S., of Belfast; *m.* 1902, Hedwig Elena Ingeborg Meta, *d.* of Christian Carl Magnussen, artist, of Schleswig. *Educ.:* Royal Academical Institution, Belfast; Queen's College, Belfast. Graduated 1886; engaged in harbour and water engineering works and harbour defence works, 1886-92; appointed to National Library, 1893; President of Royal Irish Academy, 1931-34; President National Trust for Ireland, 1928-; much interested in Naturalists' Field Club Work. *Publications:* Open-Air Studies in Botany, 1897; Irish Topographical Botany, 1901; Tourist's Flora of the West of Ireland 1909; Weeds (Cambridge Nature Study Series), 1913; Aspects of Plant Life, 1920; Beyond Soundings, 1930; An Account of the Sempervivum Group, 1932; The Botanist in Ireland, 1934; The Way that I went, 1937; A Populous

Solitude, 1941; Natural History of Ireland, 1950; Some Irish Naturalists, 1950; numerous papers on Irish Botany and Geology, chiefly in Irish Naturalist, Journal of Botany, Proceedings Royal Irish Academy, Journal of Royal Horticultural Society, and Proceedings Belfast Naturalists' Field Club. *Recreation:* gardening (especially alpine and rock plants). *Address:* Rock Cottages, Craigavad, Co. Down. [*Died* 5 *May* 1953.

PRAEGER, S. Rosamond, M.B.E. 1939; Hon. M.A., Queen's University, Belfast; Hon. R.H.A.; *b.* Holywood, Co. Down; *d.* of William E. Praeger, of the Hague, Holland, and Belfast, and Maria, *d.* of Robt. Patterson, F.R.S., Belfast. *Educ.:* Holywood, Co. Down; London. Art Student at Slade School, London, 4 years, last year free scholarship; Silver Medal for drawing, Prize for modelling in clay; returned to Holywood, Co. Down, and practised as professional artist, illustrator, and sculptor; exhibited in Royal Academy, The Philosopher, The Waif, These Little Ones, etc. *Publications:* 15 children's picture books, such as The Three Bold Babes series, How They Went to School series, Wee Tony, etc. *Address:* Craigavad, Co. Down; (Studio) Holywood, Co. Down. *T.:* Craigavad 2394. [*Died* 16 *April* 1954.

PRAGNELL, Colonel Thomas Wykeham, C.B.E. 1945; D.S.O. 1917; (p.s.c.) late 4th Hussars; *b.* 12 Jan. 1883; *y. s.* of late George William Pragnell; *m.* 1st, 1915, Ida (*d.* 1932), *y. d.* of late Rt. Hon. Sir W. J. Goulding, 1st Bt.; one *s.* one *d*; 2nd, 1937, Elfrida, *d.* of G. Hume, Dunelm, Salford; one *s.* one *d.* 2nd Lt. 3rd Border Regt. 1900; 4th Hussars, 1902; Capt. 1912; Major, 1918; Bt. Lt.-Col. 1919; Lt.-Col. 1922; Col. 1923; served operations Northern Nigeria, 1911; European War, 1914-18 (despatches, D.S.O., Bt. Lieut.-Col.); (p.s.c.); retired, 1929. A.Q.M.G. Northern Command, 1926-29; A.Q.M.G. Southern Command, 1939-40; A.M.S. Western Command, 1941-45; a Director of Sphere Investment Trust, Trust Union Ltd., East Anglian Engineering Coy. and The Assam Coy. Ltd., Charles Kendall & Partner. *Address:* Red House, Shiplake, Oxon. *Clubs:* Cavalry, Royal Automobile. [*Died* 25 *Jan.* 1957.

PRASAD, Jagat, C.I.E. 1934; *b.* 16 May, 1879; *s.* of Ajudhya Prasad and Bhagirti bai; *m.* Rajkali Bai; four *s.* four *d.* *Educ.:* Muir Central College, Allahabad. Joined Indian Audit and Accounts Service, 1900; Comptroller, Assam, 1925; Accountant General, Bengal, 1926-27; Accountant General Posts and Telegraphs, 1928-34; retired, 1934. *Recreations:* tennis and bridge. *Address:* 19 Daryaganj, Delhi, India. [*Died* 29 *Jan.* 1957.

PRATER, Stanley Henry, O.B.E. 1943; British Museum (Natural Hist.), 1948-53, retd. 1953; *b.* Wynaad, Nilgris, South India, 12 March 1890; *s.* of Edward Prater, Planter; *m.* 1921, Emma Elizabeth Sharman; one *s.* two *d*; *Educ.:* St. Mary's High School, Bombay; St. Xavier's Coll., Bombay. Joined Bombay Nat. History Society as an assistant in 1907; Corresponding Member of Zoological Society of London, 1920; Joint Editor of Journal of Bombay Natural History Society, 1921; Curator, Prince of Wales Museum (Natural History), and of Bombay Natural History Society, 1923-47; sent to Great Britain, 1922; to United States, England, and Germany, 1926, to study principles of Museum technique and methods of popular education; Trustee of Prince of Wales Museum, Bombay, 1931; served on Committee of Anglo-Indian and Domiciled European Association, 1919-21; President Bombay Provincial Branch, 1932; Edited Anglo-Indian Review, 1920; served on Bombay Provincial Franchise Committee, 1932; Honorary Presidency Magistrate, 1934; Provincial Board of Education, 1934; Managing Committee, St. George's Hospital, 1935; Inter-Provincial Board for European and Anglo-Indian Education, 1937; Member of Senate of University of Bombay, 1937; Member Bombay Legislative Assembly, 1946; elected member Constituent Assembly, 1946. *Publications:* Various papers on Indian Natural History, published in Journal, Bombay Natural History Society, Wild Animals of the Indian Empire *Recreations:* painting, swimming. *Address:* 49 Drewstead Road, Streatham, S.W.16. *T.:* Streatham 6365. [*Died* 12 *Oct.* 1960.

PRATT, Maj.-Gen. Douglas Henry, C.B. 1944; D.S.O. 1918; M.C.; *b.* 7 Oct. 1892; *s.* of Charles Henry and Elizabeth Pratt; *m.* 1915, Agnes F. Docksey; one *s.* *Educ.:* Dover College; Sandhurst. Joined 1st R. Irish Regt., 1911; India, 1911-14; European War, France, 1914-18, transferred to Tank Corps, 1916 (D.S.O., M.C., despatches thrice); Ireland, 1919-22; Staff College, Camberley, 1923-24; G.S.O.2 42nd Div. (E. Lancs), 1926-28; Exchange Officer Australia at R.M.C. Duntroon, 1930, 1931, 1932; 6th Bn. R.T.C. Cairo, 1933; G.S.O.2, War Office, 1934-1935; commanded 2nd Bn. Royal Tank Corps, 1936-37; Asst. Director of Mechanization, War Office, 1938; Comdr. Army Tank Bde., 1939-40; France and Belgium, 1940, Dunkirk, May 1940; M.G. A.F.V. Washington, D.C., 1940-43; Dep. Dir.-Gen. B.S.M., Washington, D.C., 1943; A.D.C. to the King, 1944-46; retired 1946 as Maj.-Gen. Commander Legion of Merit (U.S.A.), 1946. *Recreations:* shooting, golf. *Address:* c/o Lloyds Bank Ltd., 6 Pall Mall, S.W.1. [*Died* 14 *May* 1958.

PRATT, Col. (Hon. Maj.-Gen.) Fendall William Harvey, C.B. 1948; C.B.E. 1943; D.S.O. 1940; M.C.; D.L.; late R.A.; *b.* 4 Nov. 1892; *s.* of late Col. James John Pratt, F.R.C.S., I.M.S.; *m.* 1938, Margaret Alice, *yr. d.* of late Brig.-Gen. W. St. C. Bland, C.B., C.M.G.; one *s.* one *d.* *Educ.:* Cheltenham College; R.M.A., Woolwich. R.A., 1912; served France and Flanders, 1916-18 (M.C., despatches); Army of the Black Sea, 1920-21; Instructor at Royal Military Academy, 1922-25, Artillery Schools Larkhill and India, 1926-33; served with Union Defence Force of South Africa, 1935-36; Brevet Lieut.-Colonel, 1936; Commander Corps Medium Artillery, 1st Corps B.E.F., 1939-40; Commander Corps R.A. 10th Corps, 1940-41; Brigadier, R.A., South Eastern Command, Home Forces, 1941-1942; Colonel, 1941; Commander Corps R.A. 5th Corps, Tunisia, 1942-43; Brig. R.A. 15 Army Group, Sicily and Italy, 1943-44; Maj.-Gen. R.A. Training, 1944-45; Pres., R.M.A. Sandhurst Selection Bd., 1946-1948; A.D.C. to the King, 1946-48; retd. pay, 1948; Rep. Col. Comdt. R.A., 1950; Colonel Commandant R.A., 1949-57. President Cheltonian Society, 1953-54. Pres. R.A. Cricket Club, 1945-55. D.L. County of Southampton, 1955. Mayor of Winchester, 1958-59. *Recreations:* cricket, Rugby football, refereeing, 1912-53. *Address:* c/o National and Grindlay's Bank Ltd., 54 Parliament Street, S.W.1; Warden Hill, Weeke, Winchester. *Clubs:* Army and Navy, I Zingari, M.C.C. [*Died* 26 *April* 1960.

PRATT, Sir Henry Sheldon, Kt., *cr.* 1928; *b.* 26 Jan. 1873; *s.* of Henry Pratt of Warwick; *m.* 1st 1902, Ma Win (*d.* 1935) of Bassein, Burma; two *s.* three *d.*; 2nd 1938, Mary, *d.* of Mrs. Willshaw, Winterbourne, Bristol. *Educ.:* Warwick School; Lincoln College, Oxford; M.A. Joined I.C.S. 1896; District Judge, 1905; Divisional Judge, 1914; Additional Judge, Chief Court, Lower Burma, 1917; Officiating Judicial Commissioner, Upper Burma, 1919-20; Judge, Chief Court, L.B., 1920; Judge, High Court, Rangoon, Dec. 1922; officiated as Chief Justice, Nov.-Dec. 1926, and April to Nov. 1928; retired, 1930. *Address:* 55 Bromley Heath Road, Downend, Bristol. [*Died* 8 *May* 1954.

PRATT, John Lhind; Metropolitan Magistrate, 1944-55, for West London since

1946; Barrister; a Bencher of Middle Temple, 1939; *b.* 7 Oct. 1885; *s.* of John Marchant Pratt, Pratshayes, Exmouth, and Ellen Abercromby; *m.* 1917, Anne Mary Mills, *d.* of Major A. J. Coghill; one *s.* one *d.* Called Middle Temple, 1909; Western Circuit; Recorder of Bournemouth, 1932-44. Judge Advocate of the Fleet, 1943-45. Served European War, 1914-19 (Capt. R.G.A., despatches). *Address:* 4 Branstone Road, Kew Gardens. *T.:* Richmond 0928. [*Died* 23 *Sept.* 1960.

PRATT, Sir John William, Kt., *cr.* 1922; *b.* South Shields, 9 Sept. 1873; *m.* 1895, Elizabeth (*d.* 1945), *d.* of Hugh Niven, Gosforth; one *s.* *Educ.:* South Shields Public School; Glasgow Univ. Warden of Glasgow Univ. Settlement, 1902-12; Member of Glasgow Town Council, 1906; a Lord Commissioner of the Treasury, 1916-19; Parliamentary Under-Secretary for Health, Scotland, 1919-22; M.P. (Co.L.) Linlithgow, 1913-18; Cathcart Division, Glasgow, 1918-22. *Address:* North Dene, Beckenham Place Park, Beckenham, Kent. [*Died* 27 *Oct.* 1952.

PREECE, Sir Arthur Henry, Kt. *cr.* 1932; LL.D.(Hon.) Hong Kong, 1924; M.Inst.C.E., M.Inst.E.E., M.Cons.E., Partner, Preece, Cardew & Rider, Consulting Engineers, Westminster; *b.* 16 Aug. 1867; 2nd *s.* of late Sir William Preece, K.C.B., F.R.S.; *m.* 1896, Annie Fairclough, *yr. d.* of late W. H. Butterworth Warrington; three *d.* *Educ.:* King's College School; Germany; King's College, London. Trained as engineer at Elwell Parker Ltd., Wolverhampton, and late Dr. Gisbert Kapp, M.Inst.C.E.; has been responsible for construction and advice upon numerous electrical undertakings including telegraph, telephone and electricity supply, also many hydro-electric works, in Great Britain, Ireland, India, Australia, New Zealand, South Africa, China and South America, also in all the Crown Colonies; various works carried out for Colonial Office, Crown Agents, India Office and Dominion Governments; Member Government Rating Committee, 1927-1928, under section 24 1925 Rating Act. *Publications:* Sundry papers, including 1898 Telford premium and medal Inst.C.E. for paper on Electricity Supply. *Address:* Quains, Virginia Water, Surrey. [*Died* 31 *Jan.* 1951.

PREEDY, George R.; *see* Long, Margaret Gabrielle.

PREMCHAND, Sir Kikabhai, Kt., *cr.* 1931; Senior Partner of the firm of Premchand Roychand and Sons, Financiers, Bombay; *b.* 1 April 1883; *s.* of Premchand Roychand; *m.* 1903, Lady Lily K. Premchand, J.P. *Educ.:* Bombay. Member of the Indian Legislative Assembly, 1927-30; Member of the Select Committee for the establishment of Reserve Bank; Member of the Indian Central Committee which co-operated with the Indian Statutory Commission appointed to enquire into and report on the Indian constitutional problem; Sheriff of Bombay, 1931-32. *Address:* Premodyn, Love Lane, Byculla, Bombay, India; The Lily, Juhu, Bombay. *T.A.:* Pronown Bombay. *T.:* 40802 and 30821. *Clubs:* Willingdon Sports, Cricket Club of India Ltd., Orient (Bombay); Royal Western India Turf (Poona); Calcutta, Royal Calcutta Turf (Calcutta); Roshanara (Delhi); Imperial Delhi Gymkhana (New Delhi); Chelmsford (Simla and New Delhi). [*Died* 5 *Dec.* 1953.

PRENTICE, Brig.-Gen. Robert Emile Shepherd, C.B. 1919; C.M.G. 1918; D.S.O. 1916; late The Highland Light Infantry; *b.* 17 Feb. 1872; *s.* of Robert Russell Prentice (*decd.*); *g.s.* of late George Prentice of Strathore, Fife; *m.* 1900, Violet Rosabelle, *e. d.* of Brig.-Gen. J. H. S. Craigie; one *s.* two *d.* *Educ.:* Loretto School, Musselburgh. 2nd Lieut. Highland Light Infantry, 1892; served in Indian Frontier Campaign, 1897-98 (medal with clasp); European War, 1914-18 (wounded, despatches five times, D.S.O., Brevet Lt.-Col., C.M.G., C.B.); has held following staff appointments: Staff Captain of a District, D.A.A. and Q.M.G. Div. (T.F.), Brig. Major and Brig. Commander in the field; Brigade Comm., E. Lancashire and Border Brigade, T.F., 1924-28; retired pay, 1928. *Recreations:* fishing, shooting. *Address:* c/o Glyn, Mills, Holts Branch, Kirkland House, Whitehall, S.W.1. [*Died* 22 *Feb.* 1953.

PRESCOTT, Sir Charles William Beeston, 6th Bt., *cr.* 1794; O.B.E. 1918; *b.* 1877; 2nd *s.* of Sir George Prescott, 4th Bt.; *S.* brother, 1942. *Educ.:* Wellington; Magdalen College, Oxford. Late Chairman National League of Young Liberals; contested (L.) St. Augustine's Div. of Kent, 1906; Private Secretary to President of Board of Agriculture, 1907-14, and subsequently served in same capacity two successive First Commissioners of Works; appointed interpreter and attached to 2nd Life Guards, 1914; present at 1st Battle of Ypres (wounded and invalided home). Attached as Personal Asst. to Director-General of War Trade Dept. and represented that Dept. in early stages of Peace Conference in Paris, 1919. Under editorship of late Filson Young was critic and leader writer in the Saturday Review. *Heir: cousin,* Lt.-Col. William Villiers Leonard Prescott-Westcar, D.S.O. 1916; J.P. [*b.* 18 Sept. 1882; *m.* 1925, Thora, *e. d.* of Henry Fielding, O.B.E.; one *d.* (one *s.* killed in action, Korea, 1951)]. *Address:* 52 Pont Street, S.W.1. *Clubs:* Brooks's, St. James', Travellers'. [*Died* 27 *Sept.* 1955.

PRESCOTT, Lieut.-Col. Henry Cecil, C.M.G. 1926; C.I.E. 1919; Chief of Police, retired, Southern Railway; Indian Army, retired, 1928; *b.* 1882; *s.* of A. E. Prescott; *m.* Mary Augusta, *d.* of Edward Chisholm, Nairn; one *s.* (and one *s.* killed on active service; 1939). *Educ.:* Bedford Modern School. Served Indian Army with rank Lieut.-Col.; S. Africa, 1901-2 (Queen's medal with five clasps); European War, 1914-1919, in Mesopotamia (despatches, C.I.E.); Iraq, 1920 (medal with one clasp); Inspector-General of Police, Iraq; retired, 1935; Defence Medal, 1939-45; 2nd Class Order Rafidain. *Address:* Les Augerez Farm, S. Peter, Jersey, C.I. *T.:* 400 Western. *Club:* East India and Sports. [*Died* 3 *Aug.* 1960.

PRESCOTT-DECIE, Brig.-Gen. C.; *see* Decie.

PRESCOTT-WESTCAR, Lieut.-Colonel Sir William (Villiers Leonard), 7th Bt. (Prescott of Theobald's Park), *cr.* 1794; D.S.O. 1916; J.P.; late Rifle Brigade (Prince Consort's Own); *b.* 18 Sept. 1882; 2nd *s.* of Charles William Prescott-Westcar (*d.* 1910), 2nd *s.* of 3rd Bt., of Strode Park, Kent, and Constance, *e. d.* of late John Carbery Evans, Hatley Park, Sandy, Cambs.; *S.* cousin, Sir Charles William Beeston Prescott, 6th Bt., 1955; *m.* 1925, Thora, *e. d.* of late Henry Fielding, M.B.E.; one *d.* (one *s.* killed in action, Korea, 1951). *Educ.:* Wellington; Sandhurst. Served in South African War, 1901-02; European War, 1914-1918 (despatches, D.S.O.); Indian Frontier, 1919; War of 1939-45 as Sub-Controller, Civil Defence, Borough of Sandwich. Mayor of Sandwich, 1935-45, Hon. Freeman, 1945; Senior Alderman Borough Council (Member, 1929-); Baron of the Cinque Ports, 1937-. *Publications:* Dhank and the Dholes, 1932; Big Game Boers and Bosches, 1934. *Recreations:* shooting, golf. *Heir:* none. *Address:* Incledon's Hay, Winsford, Somerset. *Club:* Calcutta Turf. [*Died* 3 *Feb.* 1959 (*ext.*).

PRESTAGE, Edgar, M.A., D.Litt. Oxon; F.B.A. 1940; F.R.G.S.; Grand Officer Portuguese Order of S. Thiago; Corr. Member Lisbon Academy of Sciences, Portuguese Academy of History, Lisbon Geographical Soc.; Emeritus Prof. of Portuguese language, literature, and history University of London; Norman Maccoll Lecturer, Cambridge, 1933; *b.* 1869; *o. s.* of John E. Prestage and Elisabeth Rose,

High Wycombe; *m.* 1st, 1907, M. Christina (*d.* 1918), *o. d.* of poet Gonçalves Crespo and of writer D. Maria Amalia Vaz de Carvalho; 2nd, 1924, Victoria, *d.* of Charles Davison Cobb. *Educ.:* Radley; Balliol Coll., Oxford. Press Officer attached British Legation, Lisbon, 1917-18. *Publications:* D. Francisco Manuel de Mello, esboço biographico; Registo de Sta. Cruz do Castello; Relação da embaixada a França em 1641; Frei Domingos do Rosario; O Dr. Antonio de Sousa de Macedo, Residente de Portugal em Inglaterra; (joint) Corresp. de Francisco de Sousa Coutinho durante a sua embaixada em Hollanda (vol. 3, 1950); A embaixada de T. de Mendonça Furtado a Hollanda em 1641; Registo da Sé de Lisboa; Correspondencia do Conde de Castelmelhor; Critica contemporanea á Cronica de D. Manoel de Goes; O Conselho de Estado; The Royal power and the Cortes; Portugal a pioneer of Christianity; Diplomatic Relations of Portugal with France, England and Holland; The Chronicles of F. Lopes and G. E. de Zurara; Albuquerque; Diplomatic Relations of Sweden and Portugal (with colleague); The Anglo-Portuguese Alliance; The Portuguese Pioneers; Portugal and the war of the Spanish Succession, a Bibliography; translator of various Portuguese works, including Zurara's Chronicle of Guinea (with colleague), and Brother Luiz de Sousa of Garrett; editor of and contributor to book on Chivalry; editor of Epanaphoras and Carta de Guia de Casados of D. Francisco Manuel de Mello and Ultimas acções del Rei D. João IV; editor of and contributor to Chapters in Anglo-Portuguese Relations. *Address:* 16 Holland Street, W.8. *T.:* Western 0348. *Club:* Athenæum. [*Died* 10 *March* 1951.

PRESTIGE, Rev. Canon George Leonard, D.D.; Canon of St. Paul's since 1950; *b.* 29 Nov. 1889; *er. s.* of G. E. and J. Prestige; *m.* 1915, Wilhelmina, *d.* of Wm. Atkinson, M.D.; one *s.* two *d.* *Educ.:* Merchant Taylors' School; Christ Church, Oxford (scholar, 1st class hons. in Classical Mods., Lit. Hum., and Theology; 1st eight and coxless four, and Rugby football XV); Cuddesdon Theological College. Took holy orders, 1913; Fellow of New College, Oxford, 1913-20; Rector of Upper Heyford, Oxon, 1920-44; did much research work for the Lexicon of Patristic Greek; regular contributor to The Church Times from 1925, assistant editor, 1931, editor 1941-47; Acting General Secretary, Church of England Council on Foreign Relations, 1949-50; Bampton Lectr., 1940; Select Preacher, Cambridge, 1941, 1953. *Publications:* Christian Verity, 1924; Pusey, 1933; The Life of Charles Gore, 1935; God in Patristic Thought, 1936; Fathers and Heretics, 1940; St. Paul's in its Glory: 1831-1911, 1955 (posthumous); and various articles and pamphlets. *Recreations:* reading, fiction. *Address:* 3 Amen Court, St. Paul's, E.C.4. *Club:* Athenæum. [*Died* 19 *Jan.* 1955.

PRESTON, Francis Noel Dykes; *b.* 17 Dec. 1888; *s.* of Charles Francis Preston, late Solicitor, and Town Clerk of Barrow-in-Furness, and Caroline Sybil, *d.* of late Dr. J. B. Dykes, Mus. Doc., composer of Church Music; *m.* 1950, Alice Marion Agnes Gee. *Educ.:* Bromsgrove School; Trinity Coll., Oxford; London Univ. (External Student). Admitted Solicitor of Supreme Court, 1912; LL.B. Lond., 1912; Assistant Solicitor to Doncaster Corporation, 1913; Dep. Town Clerk of Doncaster, 1916; served European War, 1914-18, 19th W. Riding Vol. Regt., 1915; 2nd Batt. H.A.C., 1917. Solicitor's Office, Inland Rev.: Asst. Chief Clerk, 1920; Chief Clerk, 1921; Asst. Solicitor of Inland Revenue, 1934. Member, Southwark Diocesan Conf., 1944-53; Vice-Chm. Wimbledon Ruri-Deaconal Conf., 1950-1953; Member Wimbledon Parochial Church Council, 1938-53. Special Commissioner of Income Tax, 1943-53; retired, 1953. Member Automobile Assoc., 1927. Member Law Society, 1930. *Recreations:* golf, etc. *Address:* 25 Dunmore Road, Wimbledon, S.W.20. *T.:* Wimbledon 6026. *Club:* English-Speaking Union. [*Died* 12 *Nov.* 1957.

PRICE, Sir Charles Frederick Rugge-, 7th Bt., *cr.* 1804; late Lt.-Col. Royal Field Artillery; *b.* 5 Feb. 1868; *s.* of 6th Bt. and Antonia (*d.* 1918), *d.* of William James Harvey, of Carnousie, Co. Banff; *S.* father, 1927; *m.* 1901, Isabella Napier Keith (*d.* 1947), *e. d.* of late Maj.-Gen. Sir J. Keith Trotter, K.C.B., C.M.G.; two *s.* two *d.* *Educ.:* Cheltenham; R.M.A., Woolwich. *Heir:* *s.* Charles James Napier, Major, R.A. [*b.* 1902; *m.* 1935, Maeve Marguerite, *y. d.* of E. S. de la Peña, Hythe, Kent; one *s.* (*b.* 7 Aug. 1936) two *d.*]. [*Died* 13 *Feb.* 1953.

PRICE, Maj. Sir Charles William Mackay, Kt., *cr.* 1932; *b.* 1872; *s.* of late James Price; *m.* 1897, Gwyndolin Louise Wolmer (*d.* 1951), *d.* of Major James Figuls; three *s.* one *d.* *Educ.:* privately. Admitted solicitor, 1893. Served European War, 1915-1919, Queen's Royal Regt.; M.P. (C.) Pembrokeshire, 1924-29; a Forestry Commissioner, 1929. D.L. Pembrokeshire. *Address:* Hermon's Hill House, Haverfordwest, Pembrokeshire. [*Died* 6 *July* 1954.

PRICE, Col. Cyril Uvedale, C.M.G. 1916; Indian Army, retired; *b.* 13 May 1868; 4th *s.* of late Gen. G. U. Price and Harriette Anne Wilhelmina, *d.* of Rev. C. R. Gayer; *m.* 1919, May Edith, *d.* of late Robert Lewis of Damaraland; one *s.* *Educ.:* U.S. Coll., Westward Ho!; R.M.C., Sandhurst. Served Zhob Field Force, 1890; Uganda, 1897-99 (despatches, medal with clasp); China, 1900 (medal); European War, 1914-17 (C.M.G., Bt. Col.); retired, 1920; Order of St. Anne (3rd class). *Address:* c/o Barclays Bank (D. C. and O.), Main Street, Paarl, C.P., S. Africa. [*Died* 3 *May* 1956.

PRICE, Dorothy Stopford, M.D., B.Ch., B.A.O., B.A. Dublin, L.M.; retired; *b.* Dublin, 1890; *d.* of Jemmett J. Stopford, Dublin; *m.* 1925, W. G. Price, Barrister-at-law, Justice of the District Court, Eire. *Educ.:* St. Paul's Girls' School, London; Trinity College, Dublin. M.O. Kilbrittain Dispensary, Co. Cork, 1921-23; Physician to St. Ultans Infant Hospital, Dublin, 1924; Consultant Physician to Royal National Hospital for Consumption for Ireland and to Children's Sunshine Home for Rickets. *Publications:* Tuberculosis in Childhood, 1942; articles on Tuberculosis in Children, in Med. Journals. *Address:* 8 Herbert Park, Dublin. [*Died* 30 *Jan.* 1954.

PRICE, Rev. Ernest Jones, M.A., B.D.; Minister of Broadway Congregational Church (Worcs), since 1947; *b.* Manchester, 21 Jan. 1882; *s.* of Philip Price, postal inspector, Manchester; *m.* Elsie, *d.* of George Brocklehurst, Manchester; one *s.* two *d.* *Educ.:* Ducie Avenue Higher Grade School, Manchester; Victoria Univ., Manchester; Lancashire Independent Coll. Six years in a Manchester business house: entered Lancashire Independent Coll. as Woodward Scholar, 1903; First Hope Chapel Scholar, 1905; Lewis Scholar, 1907; B.A., 1906; M.A. 1907; B.D., 1910; Bles Hebrew Prize (Manchester Univ.), 1906; First Graduate Scholar in Theology (Manchester University), 1910; Minister of Francis St. Congregational Church, Farnworth (near Bolton), 1910; Professor in Ecclesiastical History, Comparative Religion, and Historical Theology in the Yorkshire United Independent Coll., Bradford, 1914-32, Bursar, 1926-32; Principal, 1932-47, Emeritus, 1947-; in conjunction with Professorship, carried on temporary pastorates in Congregational Churches as follows: Horton Lane, Bradford, 1915-17 and 1944-46; Duckworth St., Darwen, 1917-19; Salem, Bradford, 1923-25; Founder and President of the Congregational Ministerial Fellowship Friendly Society; member of the Council of the Congregational Union of England and Wales and of Board of Directors of London Missionary Society; Chairman of the Board, 1934-35; Chairman Consultative and Finance Committee, 1942-1946. Member of the Editorial Board of the Congregational Quarterly; Chairman Congregational Union of England and Wales, 1937; Examiner in Ecclesiastical History (History of Doctrine) and Philosophy of Theism, Univ. of Bristol, 1945-47; Examiner in History of Doctrine and Christian Ethics, University of Wales, 1946-49. *Publications:* Handbook of Congregationalism, 1924; Baptists, Congregationalists, and Presbyterians, 1934; Can a man save himself?, 1935; (joint) John Milton, 1922; Articles in Congregational Historical Society Transactions, Hibbert Journal, Holborn Review, Congregational Quarterly; Editor and part author of the late Prof. E. Armitage's Riddle of Life, 1930; contributor to Essays Congregational and Catholic, 1931. *Recreations:* walking, gardening. *Address:* The Manse, Broadway, Worcs. *T.:* Broadway 3273. [*Died* 24 *July* 1952.

PRICE, Frederick William, M.D., C.M. (Ed.), F.R.S. (Ed.), F.R.C.P., (Lond.), Hon. M.D. (Belf.); F.R.S.M.; retired; formerly Consulting Physician to Royal Northern Hospital and to National Hospital for Diseases of the Heart; *m.* 1943, Hilda G. Price. *Educ.:* Univ. of Edinburgh. Formerly: Resident Physician to Edinburgh Royal Infirmary; Asst. Resident Med. Officer to Brompton Hosp.; Pathologist to City of London Hosp. for Diseases of the Chest; Medical Registrar to Westminster Hosp.; Physician and Hon. Pathologist to Mount Vernon Hosp. for Consumption and Diseases of the Chest (10 years); Examiner in Medicine to the Univ. of St. Andrews; Lecturer on Diseases of the Heart to the Medical Graduates' Coll. and Polyclinic. *Publications:* Diseases of the Heart: their Diagnosis, Prognosis, and Treatment by Modern Methods (two editions); Recent Advances in the Diagnosis, Prognosis, and Treatment of Heart Disease, Toronto Acad. of Medicine; Diseases of the Myocardium and Endocardium in The Practitioner's Encyclopædia of Med. Treatment; Bronchiectasis, Chronic Interstitial Pneumonia, Pneumokoniosis, and Pulmonary Aspergillosis, in A System of Treatment by Latham and English; Diseases of the Bronchi and Uræmia, in The Practitioner's Encyclopædia of Medicine and Surgery; The Pathology of Heart Failure, a contribution to the Discussion at International Congress of Medicine; papers in Proc. R.S.M., etc.; Ex-Editor of A Text-book of the Practice of Medicine, by various authors, 8 edns. (re-named Price's Text-Book of Medicine). *Address:* 32 Carlisle Mans., Carlisle Pl., S.W.1. [*Died* 19 *March* 1957.

PRICE, Major Hubert Davenport, M.C. 1917; J.P.; solicitor; *b.* 1890; *s.* of late Charles Frederick Price, Field View, Stoke Prior, Worcs; *m.* 1918, Valentine Mary, *d.* of late Theodore Pritchett, King's Norton; one *s.* two *d.* *Educ.:* Bromsgrove. Qualified as solicitor, 1911. Served European War, 1914-19, Staffs. Yeo. and Machine Gun Corps (M.C.). Chairman or Director of numerous publishing, investment and other companies. J.P. Worcs. 1944. *Address:* 105 Hallam St., W.1. *T.:* Langham 6102; Abbots Morton Manor, Nr. Worcester. *T.:* Inkberrow 253. [*Died* 8 *Nov.* 1958.

PRICE, Sir James (Frederick George), K.B.E., *cr.* 1938; C.B. 1927; *b.* London, March 1873; *o. surv. s.* of James Samuel Price; *m.* 1897, Elizabeth Ada (*d.* 1940), *d.* of Thomas Catterall, Preston, Lancs; one *d.* *Educ.:* Westminster City School. Entered Civil Service, 1888; served in various Public Departments; Deputy Secretary Ministry of Labour, 1935-38; retired, 1938. *Address:* 22 Cromwell Avenue, Bromley, Kent. *T.:* Ravensbourne 1503. [*Died* 1 *June* 1957.

PRICE, Sir Keith, Kt., *cr.* 1917; *b.* 16 Apr. 1879; *s.* of E. G. Price of Broadwater, Godalming; *m.* 1904, Gertrude, *d.* of Baldwyn Fleming, Godalming; two *s.* one *d.* *Educ.:* Charterhouse. Chairman Price & Pierce, Ltd.; joined Explosives Dept. 1914; Director Raw Material Section, 1915; Deputy Director-Gen. 1916-17; Member of Council Ministry of Munitions, 1917-19; Deputy Director-General, Ministry of Supply, 1939-45. Officer Legion of Honour, 1918; Officer Order of Leopold, 1917; Order of St. Anne (2nd class), 1916; Commander Order of White Rose, 1924. *Recreations:* hunting, yachting. *Address:* Wintershall, Bramley, Surrey. *T.:* Bramley 2167. *Clubs:* Royal Thames Yacht, City of London. [*Died* 18 *May* 1956.

PRICE, Seymour James; retired as Insurance Co. General Manager, 1957; *b.* Cirencester, Glos. 31 Aug. 1886; *s.* of William James Price; *m.* 1st, 1913, Nellie Hutchins; one *s.*; 2nd, 1944, Agnes Stevenson McGibbon; one *s.* *Educ.:* Acton. Fellow of Corp. of Insurance Brokers, 1914; Secretary, London Baptist Property Board Ltd., 1922; Vice-President, Baptist Historical Society, 1929, Sec., 1935, Pres., 1948; Acton Chamber of Commerce, 1930; Joint Editor Baptist Quarterly, 1931; Pres. London Baptist Assoc., 1933; Treasurer Dr. John Ward's Trust, 1934; Director of Baptist Insurance Co. Ltd., 1936, Dep. Chm. and General Manager, 1941; Deputation to Jamaica for Baptist Missionary Society, 1937; President London Baptist Missionary Union, 1939; Chairman Baptist Missionary Society, 1941, and Treasurer, 1942; Director Temperance Permanent Building Society, 1942. President Baptist Union of Great Britain and Ireland, 1944-45. Member of Councils of Baptist Union, London Baptist Assoc., Regent's Park and Rawdon Colleges. *Publications:* Popular History of Baptist Building Fund, 1927; Coming of Age of London Baptist Property Board Ltd., 1928; Laymen and Reunion, 1931; Upton, 1935; Bloomsbury, 1948; From Queen to Queen (Centenary of Temperance Permanent Building Society), 1954; Building Societies: Their origin and history, 1958. *Recreations:* mountaineering, golf, history. *Address:* Winbury, 39 Arlington Road, Eastbourne. *T.:* Eastbourne 1546. *Clubs:* Alpine; Royal Eastbourne (Eastbourne). [*Died* 28 *May* 1959.

PRICE, Hon. Brig.-Gen. William, C.B. 1915; C.M.G. 1902; C.B.E. 1918; late Royal Engineers Special Reserve, and 8th City of London (Post Office) Rifles; *b.* 1864; *m.* 1891, Mary, *d.* of late George Middleton of Cullisse House, Ross-shire; one *d.* Late Private Secretary to the Postmaster-Gen. Served with Army Post Office Corps in S. Africa, 1899-1902 (despatches, Queen's medal 3 clasps, King's medal 2 clasps, C.M.G.); European War, as Director Army Postal Services, 1914-19 (despatches five times, C.B., C.B.E., Officier Légion d'Honneur, Commander Military Order of Avis (Portuguese)); Secretary to the Post Office for Scotland, 1920-24. *Address:* c/o Barclays Bank (City Office), 170 Fenchurch St., E.C.3. [*Died* 9 *Dec.* 1952.

PRICE-DAVIES, Brigadier Charles Stafford, C.V.O. 1942; M.C.; T.D. 1949; *b.* 17 Aug. 1892; *o. s.* of late Lt.-Col. Stafford Davies Price-Davies, D.L., J.P. *Educ.:* Eton; Royal Military College, Sandhurst. Joined K.R.R.C., 1912; served European War, 1914-19; Captain K.R.R.C., 1916; G.S.O. 3, 1918; A.D.C. to Gov.-Gen. and C.-in-C., Canada, 1924-27; Lt.-Col. 7th Royal Welch Fusiliers (T.A.), 1929; Bt. Col., 1933; Col., 1937; Brig. (temp.), 1939-40; retd. from T.A. with hon. rank of Brig., 1949. Extra-Equerry, 1935-42, and Comptroller, 1940-42, to Field-Marshal The Duke of Connaught; J.P. Salop, 1931-55; High Sheriff, Montgomeryshire, 1944; D.L., Salop, 1952-55. *Address:* Oakhurst, Dixwell Road, Folkestone. *T.:* 4072. *Club:* Army and Navy. [*Died* 19 *Feb.* 1959.

PRICHARD, Herbert William; *b.* 1873; *s.* of late William Joseph Prichard; *m.* Louise Cécile, *d.* of Dr. E. F. Bour, Paris. *Educ.:* privately; Keble College, Oxford (scholar); B.A. Called to Bar, Gray's Inn, 1902; practised in London till 1910; Stipendiary Magistrate, Trinidad, 1910; Puisne Judge, Mauritius, 1915; Procureur-General, 1922; acting Colonial Secretary on several occasions; K.C., 1923; Judge of Supreme Court of Straits Settlements, 1927-35; retired, 1935. *Recreations:* mountaineering, golf. *Address:* Sound View Cottage, Tucker's Town, Bermuda. [*Died* 5 *July* 1951.

PRICKETT, Brig. Charles Henry, D.S.O. 1915; late Royal Corps of Signals; *b.* 23 July 1881; *s.* of M. Prickett, M.D., Bridlington, Yorks; *m.* 1914, Margaret (*d.* 1954), *d.* of James Kemp, Oakhurst, Woodhay. Entered army, 1900; Captain, 1910; Major, 1920; served S. African War, 1901-2 (Queen's medal 4 clasps); European War, 1914-18 (despatches five times, D.S.O., Bt. Lt.-Col., Serbian White Eagle); Chief Signal Officer, Aldershot Command, 1926-30; Commandant Signal Training Centre, Catterick Camp, 1930-1934; retired pay, 1934; Chief Signal Officer Southern Command, 1939-40. *Address:* Newlands, Montrose, Pietermaritzburg, Natal, S. Africa. [*Died* 24 *Sept.* 1958.

PRIDEAUX, Sir (Joseph) Francis (Engledue), Kt., *cr.* 1949; C.B.E. 1946 (O.B.E. 1941); *b.* 13 March 1884; *s.* of Dr. T. Engledue Prideaux, Wellington, Somerset; *m.* 1910, Lucy Roylance Clive; two *d.* *Educ.:* Epsom College; University Coll., London. Qualified M.R.C.S., L.R.C.P., 1907; Colonial Medical Service (Fiji), 1909-1916, and R.A.M.C. to 1919. Ministry of Pensions Medical Service, 1921-49, Director-General, 1947-49; retired, 1949. *Publications:* articles in medical journals and in Brain, Brit. Jl. of Psychology, etc. *Address:* Chell, Four Marks, Alton, Hants. [*Died* 15 *Nov.* 1959.

PRIDHAM, Colonel Geoffrey Robert, C.B.E. 1929 (O.B.E. 1919); D.S.O. 1917; R.E., retired; *b.* 1872; *e. s.* of late Col. F. Pridham; *m.* 1917, Mignonne Muriel Maude, *d.* of late C. L. B. Cumming, I.C.S., and *widow* of Major John Chrystie, R.G.A.; one *s.* Served Tirah Expedition, 1897-98 (medal and clasp); China, 1900; European War (despatches, D.S.O.); Chief Engineer in Egypt; President, Royal Engineer Board, 1927-29; retired, 1929. *Address:* Bonhurst, Fleet, Hants. [*Died* 22 *March* 1951.

PRIDHAM-WIPPELL, Admiral Sir Henry Daniel, K.C.B., *cr.* 1941 (C.B. 1939) C.V.O. 1929; Royal Navy; *b.* 12 Aug. 1885; *s.* of P. H. Pridham Wippell, Barrister-at-Law, Thorverton, Devon, and Clara, *d.* of Wm. Ascroft, Oldham; *m.* 1918, Elsie, *d.* of late J. H. Crouch, Hove, and *widow* of Lt.-Com. A. G. Onslow, D.S.C., R.N.; one *s.* one *d.* *Educ.:* The Limes, Greenwich; H.M.S. Britannia. Midshipman, 1901; Lieut. 1907; Comm. 1919; Capt., 1926; Rear-Adm. 1938; Vice-Adm., 1941; Adm. 1944; served European War in H.M.S. Audacious and Warspite, Grand Fleet, and in command of Destroyers at Gallipoli, Adriatic and Palestine coast (despatches, Order of Nile IV cl.); commanded H.M.S. Enterprise in East Indies, 1928-30; Sixth Destroyer Flotilla, Home Fleet, 1932-33; Director of Operations Division Admiralty, 1933-35; Commodore (D) commanding Home Fleet Destroyer Flotillas, 1936-38; A.D.C. to the King, 1937-38; Director of Personal Services, Admiralty, 1938; Second in Command Mediterranean Fleet, 1940; Flag Officer Commanding, Dover, 1942-45; Commander-in-Chief, Plymouth, 1945-47; retired list, 1948. *Recreations:* golf, shooting, fishing. *Address:* 1 Coastguards, Kingsdown, Deal. *Club:* United Service. [*Died* 2 *April* 1952.

PRIESTMAN, Bertram, R.A. 1923; A.R.A. 1916; *b.* Bradford, Yorks, 1868; *s.* of Edward Priestman, Bradford; *m.* 1896; one *s.* four *d.* *Educ.:* Friends' School, Bootham, York. Came to London, 1888; first exhibited at Royal Academy and Grosvenor Gallery, 1889; later at all principal London and provincial galleries; made Member of the New English Club, 1897; Associate of the International Society of Sculptors, Painters, and Gravers, 1900; and member of the Council, 1902; Hon. Mention, Paris, 1900; Gold Medal Munich International, 1901; Bronze Medal, Barcelona, 1911; Hon. Mention, Pittsburg, U.S.A., 1912; represented in the National collections of Canada (at Ottawa), New South Wales, Hungary, Bavaria, and Ireland, and in the municipal galleries of Magdeburg, Barcelona, Wellington, N.Z., Wanganui, N.Z., Liverpool, Bristol, Bury, Birmingham, Sunderland, Leeds, Bradford, Halifax, Cardiff, Belfast, Manchester, Hull, Blackburn, Rochdale, Doncaster, Ipswich, Southampton, Salisbury (Rhodesia), Newport (Mon.), Worthing, Whitworth Museum, Folkestone, the Society des Beaux-Arts, Ghent, the Canterbury Society of Fine Arts, New Zealand, Auckland, New Zealand, and the York Club, Toronto, exhibitor in America and most of the principal exhibitions in Europe. *Address:* St. Giles, The Green, Crowborough, Sussex. *T.:* Crowborough 502. [*Died* 19 *March* 1951.

PRIESTMAN, Harold Eddey, C.M.G. 1937; *b.* 1888; *s.* of late Henry Priestman, Hesket, Newmarket. *Educ.:* Trinity College, Dublin. Served European War, 1914-18; Capt. The King's (Liverpool) Regiment (wounded Mesopotamia); Deputy Asst. Military Secretary to Commander-in-Chief in India, 1918-19; Administrative Officer Ministry of Labour, 1919-1920; Administrative Officer, Nigeria, 1921; Clerk of Executive and Legislative Councils, 1927-30; Private Secretary to Officer Administering Govt. 1927 and 1929; Seconded Colonial Office, 1930-31, 1932-33; Acting Colonial Secretary, Gambia, 1931; Administrative Secretary to the High Commissioner for Basutoland, the Bechuanaland Protectorate and Swaziland, 1935-49; retd., 1949. *Club:* Naval and Military. [*Died* 14 *Oct.* 1956.

PRIMROSE, Sir William Louis, 2nd Bart., *cr.* 1903; *b.* 1 June 1880; *s.* of 1st Bt. and Margaret Jane (*d.* 1896), *d.* of James Adam, merchant, Glasgow; *S.* father, 1924; *m.* 1907, Elizabeth Caroline (against whom he was granted decree of divorce, 1943; she *d.* 1951), *d.* of Hugh Dunsmuir, Glasgow; two *s.* *Heir:* *s.* John Ure, *b.* 15 April 1908. *Clubs:* Arts, Royal Scottish Automobile (Glasgow). [*Died* 23 *Dec.* 1953.

PRINGLE, George Taylor, C.B.E. 1955; H.M. Senior Chief Inspector of Schools (Scottish Education Department) since 1948; *b.* 28 Aug. 1890; *s.* of George Cossar and Annie Hay Pringle; *m.* 1921, Madeline Charlotte Pringle (*née* Gibson); (one *d.* decd.). *Educ.:* Peebles High School; Edinburgh and Oxford Universities. Graduate (Hons. Classics) Edin. Univ., M.A. 1912; Sen. Schol. Lincoln Coll., Oxf., 1914; Pitt Club Schol. Edin. Univ., 1914; M.A. (Oxford) 1918; 2nd Cl. in Hon. Mods., 1st Cl. in Lit. Hum. Served European War with Siege Artillery in France, 1916-17. Principal Teacher of Classics in Hutchesons' Grammar School, Glasgow, 1920-23. Secretary Classical Association of Scotland, 1920-27. H.M. Inspector of Schools (Scottish Education Dept.), 1923-45; H.M. Chief Inspector of Schools (Northern Div.), 1945-48. *Address:* 26 Cluny Drive, Edinburgh, 10. *T.:* Edinburgh 57009. *Club:* New (Edinburgh). [*Died* 16 *July* 1955.

PRINGLE, Sir James (Scott), K.C.B., *cr.* 1943 (C.B. 1941); O.B.E., F.C.G.I.; Hon. Fellow, Imperial College of Science and Technology, M.I.E.E.; *b.* 21 July 1876; *e. s.* of James Pringle, Oxford; *m.* 1906, Laura Anne, 2nd *d.* of James Hull Hall, Bedford; two *s.* *Educ.:* Watford Grammar School; Central Technical College of City and Guilds

Institute, South Kensington. Held positions as Electrical Engineer with Evershed and Vignoles, Ltd., R. W. Blackwell & Co. Ltd., and Crompton & Co., Ltd., 1896-1903; appointed Deputy Borough Electrical Engineer, Salford, 1903; appointed to Admiralty Service, 1903. Served as Electrical Engineer in charge of Electrical Department at H.M. Dockyards at Malta, Gibraltar, and Rosyth, 1903-19; Assistant Director of Dockyards, Admiralty, 1919-37; Director of Electrical Engineering, Admiralty, 1937-45; Principal Electrical Adviser to Board of Admiralty, responsible for design and equipment of electrical installations in all H.M. ships. Designed and installed electrical equipment of H.M. Dockyard, Singapore. Member of Council of Institution of Electrical Engineers, 1940. Retired from Admiralty Service, 1945; Consulting Engineer to Metropolitan-Vickers Electrical Co. Ltd. 1945. *Recreations:* travelling, motoring, photography, swimming. *Address:* 88 York Mansions, S.W.11. *T.:* Macaulay 5174. *Club:* Athenæum. [*Died* 27 *Feb.* 1951.

PRINGLE, John Mackay, Q.C. 1945; I.C.S. retd.; Member of the Bar; *b.* 27 April 1888; *s.* of David and Agnes Pringle; *m.* 1st, 1916, May Downing; 2nd, 1936, Julia Beardsworth; one *s.* *Educ.:* Fettes College, Edinburgh; Merton College, Oxford (Senior Classical Postmaster). 1st Class Hons. Classical Mods. 1909; 1st Class Hons. Lit. Hum. 1911. Joined Indian Civil Service, 1911; Barrister, 1923; District Judge, Bengal, 1923-30; Practice before Judicial Committee of Privy Council, 1930-50. *Recreations:* reading, gardening. *Address:* 5 Roedean Crescent, Roehampton, S.W.15. *T.:* Prospect 1669. *Clubs:* Athenæum, Roehampton; Gridiron (Oxon.). [*Died* 22 *April* 1955.

PRINGLE, Seton Sidney, O.B.E.; M.D., B.A.O., B.A.; M.Ch.; retired; Consulting Surgeon, Rotunda Hospital, Dublin, 1932, Mercer's Hospital, 1935; Royal Victoria Eye and Ear Hospital, 1935; *b.* 6 July 1879; *m.* Ethel (*d.* 1938), *d.* of late Andrew M'Munn, M.D., of Ballymote; three *s.* two *d.* *Educ.:* Campbell College, Belfast. Trinity Coll., Dublin. Late Surgeon to Dublin Castle Red Cross Hospital, 1915; Lecturer in Special Pathology, T.C.D.; late Lt.-Col. R.A.M.C., O.C. Irish Counties War Hospital (1917-19); late Surgeon to Mercer's Hospital, Dublin, 1904-18; Surgeon to Cork Street Hospital, 1913-29; Surgeon to Royal City of Dublin Hospital, 1918; Surgeon to Drumcondra Hospital, 1915; Surgeon to Royal Hospital for Incurables, 1931; late Surgeon to Urgency Cases Hospital for France; late Examiner in Surgery, Royal College of Surgeons, Ireland; late Examiner in Surgery T.C.D.; ex-President Dublin University Biological Association, 1913; President Royal College of Surgeons in Ireland, 1934-36; President Royal Academy of Medicine in Ireland, 1940-42; Pres. St. John Ambulance Bde. of Ireland, 1946-55; Commander (Officer) of Order of St. John of Jerusalem. *Publications:* contributions to medical journals. *Address:* Ringlestown House, Kilmessan, Co. Meath. [*Died* 10 *Nov.* 1955.

PRIOLEAU, John Randolph Hamilton; Journalist and Author; *y. s.* of late Charles Prioleau, Charleston, South Carolina, and Mary, *d.* of Richard Wright, Liverpool; *b.* April 1882; *m.* 1947, Dorothy, *e. d.* of late Herbert Crawshay, Oaklands Park, Newnham. *Educ.:* Harrow; Christ Church, Oxford. Served European War, Lieut. R.N.V.R., 1915, R.N. Armoured Cars, 1915-1919, Naval Intelligence, Greece, Egypt and Red Sea; served, Major, Intelligence Corps, 1939-45; Chevalier, Royal Order of Cambodia, 1921. *Publications:* The Adventures of Imshi; Imshi in New Europe; Car and Country; The Open Road Abroad; Enchanted Ways; The Motorist's Companion. *Recreations:* fishing, motor-touring abroad. [*Died* 13 *April* 1954.

PRIOR, A. C. Vincent, M.A., LL.B.; *b.* 1881; *e. s.* of late Asher and Marian Prior, Colchester; *m.* 1925, Gwladys Haidée, *d.* of late Evan Powell, Mapperley, Nottingham; one *s.* one *d.* *Educ.:* Bishop's Stortford College; King's College, Cambridge. Called to Bar, Inner Temple, 1905; Attorney-General, St. Vincent, 1915; Attorney-General, Leeward Islands, 1918; Solicitor-General, Sierra Leone, 1920; Solicitor-General, Gold Coast, 1925; Attorney-General, Sierra Leone, 1927; Attorney-General of Nigeria, 1929-35. *Recreations:* walking, tennis and golf. *Address:* Moray Lodge, Saltwood, Hythe, Kent. [*Died* 27 *Feb.* 1954.

PRISTON, Rev. Stewart Browne; *b.* Gillingham, Kent, 1880; *s.* of Engineer-Rear-Admiral Priston; *m.* 1937, Hilda Beryl Hall; one *s.* *Educ.:* Christ's Hospital; Royal Naval Engineering College, Devonport; St. John's College, Cambridge; Ely Theological College; M.A. (2nd Class Nat. Sci. Tripos) Cantab. Asst. Curate, S. John's, Walham Green, 1903-9; Chaplain, Diocesan College, Rondebosch, South Africa, 1909-17; S. John's College, Johannesburg, 1918-20; Archdeacon of Stanley and British Chaplain, Valparaiso, 1922-25. Rector of Bacton, Suffolk, 1926-42, of Worsboro' Dale, Yorks, 1942-55, of Marwood, Devon, 1955-1957. Permission to Officiate London Diocese, 1957-59, Peterborough Diocese, 1959-. *Publications:* Prayers and Hymns for School Use, Capetown, 1916; The Holy Communion, 1924. *Address:* Oak Farm, Eydon, Nr. Rugby. [*Died* 26 *April* 1960.

PRITCHARD, Major-General Gordon Arthur Thomas, C.B.E. 1947; Director of Fortifications and Works, War Office, since 1955; *b.* 1902; *s.* of Thomas Pritchard, St. Margarets, Middx.; *m.* 1933, Lucie, *d.* of Major W. W. Whitburn, Sargodha, India; one *d.* *Educ.:* King's School, Chester; R.M.A. Woolwich. Commissioned into Corps of Royal Engineers, 1922; served in India, 1924-34 and 1936-41; Dep. Chief Engineer, Airfields, 14th Army and later H.Q. ALFSEA, 1944-45; Chief Engineer: Allied Land Forces, Netherlands East Indies, 1946; Burma Command, 1947-48; Cyprus, 1950-1951; Southern Command, 1953-54. *Address:* c/o Lloyds Bank Ltd., 6 Pall Mall, S.W.1. *Club:* Army and Navy. [*Died* 17 *Dec.* 1957.

PRITCHARD, Major-General Harry Lionel, C.B. 1923; C.M.G. 1917; D.S.O. 1898; *b.* 16 Nov. 1871; *s.* of late Colonel Hurlock Pritchard; *m.* 1902, Elizabeth Gilbert, *e. d.* of E. Furse of Alphington, Frimley; two *d.* *Educ.:* Charterhouse. 2nd Lieut. R.E., 1891; Captain, 1902; Major, 1911; Major-General, 1928; served Ashanti Expedition, 1895-96 (despatches, star); Dongola Expeditionary Force, 1896 (despatches, medal with clasp, 4th class Medjidie); Nile Operations, 1897 (clasp), and 1898 (despatches, D.S.O., British medal, and clasp to Khedive's medal); South African War, 1899-1902 (despatches, two medals, six clasps); European War, 1914-18 (despatches four times, very severely wounded, Brevet Lieutenant-Colonel and Colonel, C.M.G., Order of Redeemer, 1914 Star and clasp, Greek medal of Military merit, G.S. medal, Victory medal); Chief Engineer Northern Command, 1921-23; Assistant-Director Fortifications and Works, War Office, 1923-25; Chief Engineer Eastern Command, 1925-29; G.O.C. Malaya, 1929-31; A.D.C. 1926-29; Commandant School of Military Engineering, and Inspector of Royal Engineers and Commander Chatham Area, 1931-33; retired pay, 1933; Col. Comdt. R.E., 1932-41. *Publications:* The Sudan Campaign; Army Organisation and Administration; A.R.P. and High Explosive; A.R.P. organisation and its relation to Imperial Defence. *Address:* c/o Lloyds Bank, Ltd., 6 Pall Mall, S.W.1. [*Died* 14 *May* 1953.

PRITCHARD, Ivor Mervyn, R.C.A.; lately a Civil Servant; sometime Inspecting Officer Royal Commission on Welsh Historic Constructions; *b.* Beaumaris, Isle of Anglesey; *m.* 1922, Olwen, *d.* of W. Stanley-Jones, Stow Park, Newport. *Educ.:* Beaumaris Grammar School; University College of North Wales; London Architectural Association; Royal Academy School; Central School of Arts and Crafts, London. Served European War, with Royal Artillery (Territorial Force) Egyptian Expeditionary Force; Member of Council for the Preservation of Rural Wales; also the Society of Graphic Arts; Works and Engravings exhibited at: Kunsterhaus, Vienna International Exhibition, Los Angeles, Czechoslovakia, Royal Academy, London, Salon, Paris, etc. The Pritchard Collection of Antique Atlases in 80 Folio volumes has been acquired by National Library of Wales. A.R.I.B.A. until 1941. *Recreations:* art, travel, bibliopolism. *Address:* 12 Calais Gate, Myatts Park, S.E.5. [*Died* 10 *Feb.* 1948.
[*But death not notified in time for inclusion in Who Was Who 1941–1950, first edn.*

PROBYN-JONES, Sir Arthur Probyn, 2nd Bt., *cr.* 1926; *b.* 28 July 1892; *o. s.* of Sir Robert Jones, 1st Bt., and Susie, *d.* of William Evans, Liverpool; *S.* father, 1933; *m.* 1919, Eileen, *d.* of late James Evans of Birkdale, and Mrs. James Evans of The Old Hall. Helsby, Cheshire; one *d.* *Educ.:* Clifton (Exhibitioner); King's College, Cambridge. B.A., LL.B. (Honours) 1913, M.A. 1918; Bar, Inner Temple, 1919; served European War, 1914-19, Captain, King's (Liverpool) Regiment; with Ministry of Food, Tunbridge Wells, until May 1945; Chm. Medical Appeals Tribunal North Midland Region; Dep. Chm. Nat. Health Service Tribunal; J.P. Sussex. Contested (L.) West Derby Division, Liverpool, 1929. *Address:* High Seas, South Cliff, Bexhill-on-Sea. *T.:* Bexhill 1784; 199 Cromwell Road, S.W.5. *T.:* Frobisher 5235; 1 Plowden Buildings Temple E.C.4. *Club:* Royal Automobile. [*Died* 17 *Oct.* 1951 (*ext.*).

PROBYN-WILLIAMS, Robert James, M.D.; F.F.A., R.C.S.; Consulting Anæsthetist to the London Hospital; Hon. Fellow Assoc. of Anæsthetists; lately Instructor in Anæsthetics, and Lecturer on Anæsthetics in the London Hospital Medical College, Anæsthetist at Royal Dental Hospital of London and Lecturer on Anæsthetics at the London School of Clinical Medicine; late President of the Society of Anæsthetists; late Captain R.A.M.C. (T.) 2nd London General Hospital; *b.* London, 19 May 1866; *m.* Emily, *d.* of Rev. W. Anden, M.A., Church Broughton, Derby; one *s.* *Educ.:* Durham University; London Hospital. *Publications:* A Practical Guide to the Administration of Anæsthetics; Medical Papers. *Recreations:* golf, music, photography. *Address:* Chipping Manor, Wotton-under-Edge, Glos. *Club:* Royal Societies. [*Died* 14 *Dec.* 1952.

PROCTER, Henry Adam, M.A., LL.D.; *b.* 1883; *m.* Amy Bedford, 2nd *d.* of Richard Killey, Liverpool; three *d.* *Educ.:* Bethany Coll. W.Va., U.S.A.; Melbourne and Edinburgh Universities. Served European War, 1916-19; retired from Regular Army with rank of Major, 1922; M.P. (U.) Accrington, 1931-45; has patented numerous inventions in connection with pulverised fuel; called to Bar, Middle Temple, 1931. *Address:* Potterford Cottage, Billington, near Whalley, Lancs. [*Died* 26 *March* 1955.

PROCTER, Lt.-Col. James, C.B.E. 1923; *b.* 1884; *s.* of James Procter; *m.* 1911, Pauline Eugenie Emeric. Rendered services in connection with relief of refugees from Russia and Anatolia. *Club:* St. James'. [*Died* 30 *Jan.* 1955.

PROCTER, His Honour Sir William, Kt., *cr.* 1941; Chairman of Medical Appeal Tribunal for North-west Region under National Insurance (Industrial Injuries) Act; J.P. for Counties of Derby and Lancaster; *b.* 17 Nov. 1871; *m.* 1897; two *d.* Called to Bar, Gray's Inn, 1905; practised Northern Circuit; Judge of County Courts on Circuit No. 19, 1928-31; Circuit No. 6 (Liverpool, etc.), 1931-46; Commissioner of Assize, Northern Circuit, 1931, 1936, and 1941; Member of Standing Committee for framing Rules for County Courts, 1933-46; Hon. Independent Chairman of Sandstone Industry (Silicosis) Scheme for Derby, Notts., Staffs., Leics., Northants and Rutland, 1929-31. *Address:* 2 Beach Cliff, Promenade, Hoylake, Cheshire. [*Died* 26 *June* 1951.

PROCTOR, Alexander Phimister; Sculptor; *b.* Canada, 27 Sept. 1862; *m.* 1893, Margaret Gerow; four *s.* four *d.* *Educ.:* New York; London; Paris under Puech and Ingalbert. *Principal Works:* Heroic figure, Pioneer, University of Oregon, Eugene, Ore.; Equestrian, The Circuit Rider, Salem, Ore.; Indian Fountain Figure, Fort George, N.Y.; The Princeton Tigers, Princeton University; Equestrian, On the War Trail and Bronco Buster, Denver Colo. Civic Center, Theodore Roosevelt, Portland, Ore.; Colossal 4 Buffaloes on Bridge and 4 Tigers, Washington, D.C.; Pioneer Mother—Kansas City; Buffalo Reliefs; Artington Bridge, Washington; many portraits in bas relief and many smaller groups of figures and animals. *Address:* 39 West 67th Street, New York. *Club:* Century (New York). [*Died* 4 *Sept.* 1950.
[*But death not notified in time for inclusion in Who Was Who 1941–1950, first edn.*

PROCTOR, Mary, F.R.A.S.; Lecturer and Writer on Astronomical Subjects, Mythology and Folk Lore; *b.* Dublin; *d.* of late Richard A. Proctor, Astronomer, and Mary Mills, Ireland. *Educ.:* special course in astronomy at Columbia University, New York, 1897; Tutor for Mathematics. First literary contributions, Knowledge, 1886-88, under nom-de-plume Stella Occidens; first lecture contract signed with J. B. Pond Lecture Agency, N.Y., 1893; went to Bodo, Norway, to observe total eclipse of the sun, 1896; observed total eclipse of sun at Norfolk, Virginia, U.S.A., 1900; and in Burgos, Spain, in 1905, fine view of corona on each occasion; observed eclipse from aeroplane, Yorkshire, 29 June 1927; observed total eclipse of Sun at Magog, Canada, Aug. 31, 1932; observed total eclipse of sun at Greece, 19 June 1936; visited Yerkes Observatory in 1910; Mt. Wilson Observatory in 1911, 1926, and 1928; Lick Observatory in 1911; Sydney Observatory, 1912; Melbourne, 1912; Kodaikanal, S. India Observatory, 1913; has lectured in leading cities in U.S.A., Montreal, Canada; in Australia in 1912; New Zealand, 1912-13; and in Great Britain, 1919-38; Government work, 1915-19; lectured in France, 1919-20, and in Cologne, 1922, for Army of Occupation under auspices of Y.M.C.A.; has lectured in England, in North and South Wales and Scotland, 1920-37; Hon. Member Montreal Women's Club and New York Woman's Press Club. *Publications:* Stories of Starland, 1895; Giant Sun and his Family, 1896; Half Hours with the Summer Stars, 1911; Legends of the Stars, 1922; Children's Book of the Heavens, 1924; Legends of the Sun and Moon; Evenings with the Stars, 1924; Romance of Comets, 1926; The Romance of the Sun, 1927; The Romance of the Moon, 1928; Romance of the Planets, 1929; Wonders of the Sky, 1931; Our Stars from Month to Month, 1937, specially prepared for U.S.A., 1938; Comets, their Nature and Origin, 1937; Everyman's Astronomy, 1939; Comets, Meteors and Shooting Stars, 1940. *Recreations:* music, painting, travelling. *Address:* c/o Royal Astronomical Society, Burlington House, W.1. [*Died* 11 *Sept.* 1957.

PROKOFIEFF, Serge Sergeyevich; Soviet musician; *b.* S. Russia, 23 Apr. 1891. Toured world as pianist, presenting own works, 1918-38. Lived in U.S., 1918-22, in Paris until 1935. Works include: 5 symphonies, 3 cantatas, 8 concertos, songs, piano pieces, ballet music, film music; operas: The Love of Three Oranges, The Bethrothal in a Nunnery (based on Sheridan's The Duenna), War and Peace (based on Tolstoy's). *Address:* Moscow. [*Died* 4 *March* 1953.

PROSSER, Rt. Rev. Charles Keith Kipling; Bishop Suffragan of Burnley since 1950; *b.* 27 March 1897; *s.* of Charles Richard Prosser, Coleshill, Warwickshire; *m.* 1924, Mary Janet Ofield; three *s.* (one *d.* decd.). *Educ.:* King Edward's, Birmingham; Queens' College, Cambridge; Westcott House, Cambridge. Served European War, 1914-18, R.G.A., 1916-19 (despatches). Rector of Alert Bay, B.C., 1929-34; Vicar of Howe Bridge, 1934-50; Hon. Canon of Manchester, Rural Dean of Leigh, 1948-50. *Address:* Palace House, Burnley, Lancs. *T.:* Burnley 3564. [*Died* 27 *June* 1954.

PROTHEROE-BEYNON, Major Godfrey Evan Schaw, J.P., D.L., Carmarthenshire; *b.* Woolwich, 1872; *y. s.* of late Surgeon-General E. S. Protheroe, J.P., D.L., Dôl Wilym, Carmarthenshire; assumed additional surname of Beynon by Royal Licence, 1899; *m.* 1902, Emily Williama, M.B.E., *e. d.* of late Col. W. Lewes, J.P., D.L., Llysnewydd, Carmarthenshire; two *s.* *Educ.:* Bath. Tea Planter Ceylon, 1890-1900; served in Ceylon Mounted Infantry; joined Pembroke Yeomanry, 1901, retired 1913; rejoined 1914 and served on staff of 41st Recruiting Depot and with Pembroke Yeomanry until end of War; Hon. Sec. United Counties Hunters Society, 1910-22; Joint Hon. Sec. Carmarthen Hunt Club; High Sheriff, Carmarthenshire, 1907. *Recreations:* hunting, shooting, fishing. *Address:* Trewern, Whitland, South Wales. *T.A.:* Whitland. *T.:* Whitland 313. *Club:* Carmarthen and County. [*Died* 10 *Nov.* 1958.

PROUDFOOT, Alexander, R.S.A. 1932 (A.R.S.A. 1920); F.R.B.S. 1938; J.P.; sculptor; *b.* Liverpool, 1878, of Scottish parents *m.* 1955, Ivy H. Gardner. Head of the Sculpture Department, Glasgow School of Art, 1912-28; served European War, Artists Rifles, 1915-18, France, attached Machine Gun Corps; invented Protractor for Vickers Machine Gun, 1917. War Memorials: Greenock, Bearsden, Cambuslang, and Glasgow Cathedral. Marble Group: Thais and Paphnutius; Bronze Portraits: Roger Quin and Neil Munro in Kelvingrove Art Gallery, Frederic Lamond for Scottish National Academy of Music, James Bridie (Dr. O. H. Mavor) for Caird Art Bequest Trust, Greenock, etc. *Address:* 15 Woodside Terrace, Glasgow, C.3. *T.:* Douglas 2183. *Club:* Glasgow Art. [*Died* 10 *July* 1957.

PRYCE, Frederick Norman, M.A., F.S.A.; *b.* 19 Aug. 1888; *s.* of T. W. Pryce, Welshpool; *m.* Ruby, 2nd *d.* of late A. L. Sewell, Harrow. *Educ.:* Welshpool Grammar and County Schools; Univ. Coll., Aberystwyth. Entered British Museum, 1911; Dep. Keeper, 1934; Keeper of Greek and Roman Antiquities, 1936-39; served War 1914-18, Egypt, Palestine, Army of Black Sea (despatches twice), and 1940-44 (Intelligence); Editor, The Journal of Hellenic Studies, 1924-38; served War of 1939-1945, Intelligence Staff, War Office; Member of the German Archæological Institute. *Publications:* British Museum Catalogue of Sculpture, vol. 1 pt. 1 (Early Greek), 1928; pt. 2 (Cypriote and Etruscan), 1931; Corpus Vasorum, fascicules 2 (1926) and 7 (1932); various archæological and historical papers. *Address:* c/o 31 Erw Wen, Welshpool. [*Died* 14 *Oct.* 1953.

PRYCE, Ven. Thomas P.; *see* Parry Pryce.

PRYCE-JONES, Bt. Col. Henry Morris, C.B. 1943; C.V.O. 1952 (M.V.O. 1918); D.S.O. 1917; M.C. 1915; D.L. (County of London); late Coldstream Guards; *b.* 1878; *s.* of late Sir P. Pryce-Jones; *m.* 1905, Marion Vere, *d.* of late Lt.-Col. Hon. L. Payn Dawnay; two *s.* *Educ.:* Eton; Trinity College, Cambridge. Served South Africa, 1899-1902 (despatches twice); European War, 1914-19 (D.S.O., M.V.O., M.C., despatches six times); Commander Legion of Honour; commanded 2nd City of London Regt., 1922-26. Standard Bearer, H.M. Body Guard, Hon. Corps of Gentlemen-at-Arms, 1949-52 (Harbinger, 1938-49). *Address:* Henry VIII Gateway, Windsor Castle. *T.:* Windsor 1619. *Clubs:* Guards, Travellers'. [*Died* 5 *Nov.* 1952.

PRYDE, David Johnstone; M.P. (Lab.) Midlothian since 1955 (Peebles and Southern Midlothian, 1945-50, Midlothian and Peebles, 1950-55); J.P. Midlothian; Senior Bailie, of Bonnyrigg and Lasswade; *b.* 3 March 1890; *y. s.* of Matthew James John Maitland Pryde, Gorebridge, Midlothian; *m.* 1916, Marion, 3rd *d.* of Henry Rue Grandison, Edinburgh; one *s.* one *d.* *Educ.:* Lasswade Secondary School; Scot. Labour College. Colliery clerk (2 years); entered mines; studied under Jonn McLean, M.A., Private Tutor, Rev. Wm. Nicholson, M.A.; meteoric career as miners' T.U. Official, 1921-33, Mid and East Lothian Miners and Nat. Union of Scot. Miners; filled every position in both industrial and political organisation; victimised for T.U. activities, 1926. Entered Bonnyrigg and Lasswade Town Council, 1938. Twice election agent to J. Westwood; contested (Lab.) South Midlothian, 1935. *Recreation:* angler. *Address:* 66 Dobbie's Road, Bonnyrigg, Midlothian. *T.:* Lasswade 3386. [*Died* 2 *Aug.* 1959.

PRYKE, Sir (William Robert) Dudley, 2nd Bt., *cr.* 1926; *b.* 5 March 1882; *s.* of Sir William Pryke, 1st Bt., and Marguerite Harriott (*d.* 1925), *d.* of Robert Stiles, St. John's Wood, N.W.; *S.* father 1932; *m.* 1911, Marjorie (*d.* 1936), *d.* of late H. Greenwood Brown, Leytonstone; two *s.* one *d.* (and one *s.* died on active service in Burma, 1945). *Educ.:* City of London School. Chairman Pryke and Palmer Ltd. *Heir:* *s.* David Dudley Pryke [*b.* 16 July 1912; *m.* 1945, Doreen W., *er. d.* of R. B. Wilkins, Winchmore Hill; two *d.*]. *Address:* 93 Chandos Avenue, Whetstone, N. 20. *T.:* Hillside 2148. *Club:* Constitutional. [*Died* 23 *March* 1959.

PRYNNE, Colonel Harold Vernon, C.B.E. 1919; D.S.O. 1917; F.R.C.S. (Eng.), A.M.S.; late Chief Medical Officer, General Post Office, London; *s.* of late Lieut.-Col. John Basset Prynne, Royal Marines. Served China, 1900 (despatches, medal and clasp); European War, 1914-18 (despatches four times, C.B.E., D.S.O., Croix de Guerre with Gold Star); Officer of the Order of St. John of Jerusalem. *Address:* c/o Glyn, Mills & Co., Kirkland House, Whitehall, S.W.1. [*Died* 19 *Jan.* 1954.

PRYOR, Major-Gen. Sir Pomeroy Holland-, K.C.B., *cr.* 1926 (C.B. 1919); C.M.G. 1918; D.S.O. 1916; M.V.O. 1909; Col., 1st Duke of York's Own Skinner's Horse, 1923-1945; *b.* 7 July 1866. Entered army, 3rd Dragoon Guards, 1887; served Waziristan, 1894-1895 (medal); Mohmand, 1897-98 (medal); Tirah, 1898 (despatches, clasp); South African War, 1899-1902, A.A.G. and Assistant Military Governor, Orange River Colony (despatches twice, Queen's medal 3 clasps, King's medal 2 clasps, Brev. of Maj.); North-West Frontier, India, 1915-16 (despatches, D.S.O., Bt. Col.); European War, 1914-18 (despatches five times, C.B., C.M.G.); Afghan War, 1919; retired, 1928; in charge H.M.'s Indian Orderly Officers, 1910. *Recreations:* polo, shooting. *Club:* United Service. [*Died* 15 *March* 1955.

PRYSE, Gerald Spencer; Queen Victoria's Rifles, R. of O., K.R.R. (despatches, M.C., 1914 Star, Order of the Crown of Belgium, Croix de Guerre, twice wounded); R. of O., 1919; served with 1st Division, Defence Force, 1921; attached M. I. 1939; *b.* 1882; *m.* 1932, Muriel Anstace Theodora, 2nd *d.* of late Rev. Laurence Farrall, Rector of Holy Trinity, Chester, and *g. d.* of late Charles Millar, Melbourne; three *d. Educ.:* privately; studied Art, London and Paris. First exhibited Venice International Exhibition, 1907; examples of his work were purchased by the Italian Government and by the Comité des achats pour la Maison Royale d'Italie, 1910; since that time specimens have been acquired by the King for the Royal Collection at Windsor Castle, and by the Trustees of the British Museum, The Contemporary Art Society, the Victoria and Albert Museum, the Louvre Exhibition in 1914, the Public Authorities of Rome, Vienna, Zurich, Sydney, Ottawa, Venice, Brussels, Leipzig, Stuttgart, the Uffizi Gallery in Florence, and by the National Gallery of Australia in Canberra; illustrated the Book of the Pageant of Empire, the official souvenir of the British Empire Exhibition, 1924; visited the colonies of Nigeria and the Gold Coast on behalf of the Empire Marketing Board, 1928; a collection of paintings made in the Gold Coast purchased by the Colonial Government, 1930; collection of paintings made in the course of a tour in the colony of Nigeria purchased by the Imperial Institute, 1932. *Publications:* Through the Lines to Abd el Karim's Stronghold in the Riffs; Four Days. *Recreations:* field sports, farming. *Address:* Domaine de Trè'at, Souk'el'arba Durharb, Morocco. *Club:* Savile. [*Died* 28 *Nov.* 1956.

PUCKLE, Lt.-Col. Frederick Kaye, C.M.G. 1918; late R.A.S.C.; *b.* Worthing, 6 July 1880; *last surv. s.* of late Colonel H. G. Puckle, Madras Staff Corps; *m.* 1st, 1916, Lisa Geraldine (who obtained a divorce), *e. d.* of General Rt. Hon. Sir Nevil Macready, 1st Bt., G.C.M.G., K.C.B.; one *d.*; 2nd, 1925, Mary Helen, 3rd *d.* of late Gilbert Gostwyck Cory, Toowoomba, Queensland. *Educ.:* Eastman's Royal Naval Academy; Tonbridge School. Joined 3rd Batt. Border Regt. 1901; joined A.S.C. 1904; Capt. 1913; Major, 1917; served European War, France and Belgium, 1914-17; on British Mission to U.S.A., 1917-1918; at G.H.Q., American Expeditionary Force, 1918-19 (despatches thrice, American D.S.M.); operations in North Persia and Mesopotamia, 1919-21; Waziristan Operations, 1922-24 (despatches); retired pay, 1930. *Address:* Turramurra, Sydney, Australia. *Club:* United Service. [*Died* 23 *June* 1959.

PUGH, Sir Arthur, Kt., *cr.* 1935; C.B.E. 1930; J.P.; General Secretary of the Iron and Steel Trades Confederation and the British Iron Steel and Kindred Trades Association, 1917-36; Member Economic Consultative Committee League of Nations; Chairman, General Council of Trade Union Congress, 1925; Member Appellate Tribunal Military Service Act, 1939; *b.* 1870; *s.* of W. Valentine Pugh, Civil Engineer, and Amelia Rose Adlington, Malvern Link, Worcs; *m.* 1901, Elizabeth Morris (*d.* 1939), Port Talbot, Glam.; one *s.* two *d. Educ.:* Elementary School, Ross, Herefordshire. Lost parents in infancy; apprenticed to farmer and butcher at age 13; migrated to Wales, 1894, and took up trade of steel smelter; Assistant Secretary of British Steel Smelters' Association, 1906. *Address:* Grange Corner, Bromham, Beds. *T.:* Oakley 297. [*Died* 2 *Aug.* 1955.

PULBROOK, Sir Eustace Ralph, Kt., *cr.* 1943; Chairman of Lloyd's (1926, 1940-46 and 1948); *b.* 20 Sept. 1881; *s.* of Henry Pulbrook; *m.* 1907, Dorothy Fry (*d.* 1942); one *s.* one *d.*; *m.* 1947, Mrs. Susan L. O. Crowle, 14 Carlos Place, W. *Educ.:* Dulwich College. Entered Lloyd's, 1899; Chairman of Salvage Association, 1930 and 1931; Gold Medal for services to the Corporation, 1932; Grand Officer Order of Orange Nassau; Knight Commander of Royal Order of George I, Greece. *Recreations:* golf and billiards. *Address:* Datchet House, Datchet, Bucks. *T.:* 33. *Clubs:* City of London, Buck's. [*Died* 20 *Jan.* 1953.

PULLIBLANK, Engineer - Rear - Admiral John Blackler, D.S.O. 1917; O.B.E. 1919; *b.* 1879; *s.* of late Reverend Canon Joseph Pulliblank, Rector of Rampisham, Dorset; *m.* Ethel, *e. d.* of late Dr. C. C. Skardon of Evershot, Dorset; one *d.* Served European War, 1914-19, with Dover Patrol, and at Vladivostock (despatches twice, D.S.O., O.B.E.); Chief Engineer at the Dockyard and Naval Base at Simonstown, 1926; A.D.C. to H.M., 1931-32; Eng. Rear-Adm. and retired list, 1932; Admiralty Regional Officer, North Midlands, 1940-46. *Address:* c/o National Provincial Bank, Devonport. [*Died* 18 *Jan.* 1951.

PULLICINO, Sir Philip, Kt., *cr.* 1934; LL.D., B.Lit.; *b.* 21 Nov. 1885; *s.* of Judge Giovanni Pullicino and Giorgina, *d.* of Judge Pasquale Mifsud; *m.* Maude, *d.* of Col. Achilles Samut, C.B., C.M.G.; six *s.* five *d. Educ.:* St. Ignatius Coll. and Univ., Malta. Matriculated, 1900; one of His Majesty's Judges in the Superior Courts of Malta, 1928; Treasury Counsel and Public Prosecutor, Malta 1929; Legal Adviser to H.M's. Forces in Malta and Treasury Solicitor's Agent, 1934; Attorney General, Malta, 1937; retired, 1941. *Address:* The Bastions, Notabile, Malta. *T.:* Rabat 11. [*Died* 16 *July* 1960.

PULLIN, Victor Edward, C.B.E. 1933; Consulting Engineering Radiologist; Consultant on non-destructive testing to Ministry of Supply; late Director Radiological Research, Research Department, Woolwich. *Address:* 1 Paper Buildings, Temple, E.C. *Club:* Garrick. [*Died* 4 *Aug.* 1956.

PULSFORD, Rev. Edward John; Editor, New Church Magazine; Correspondence Tutor, New Church College; *b.* Jersey, C.I., 8 Jan. 1878; *er. s.* of Rev. E. M. Pulsford; *m.* 1906, Mabel M. Hardy; one *s.* two *d. Educ.:* Alloa Academy; New Church College, London. Ordained into the Ministry of the New Church, 1906; Pastorate at Whitefield, Manchester, 1905-12; Bath, 1912-20; Moseley, Birmingham, 1920-24; Salford, 1928-38; Woodlands Road, Glasgow, 1938-1951; retired from pastoral work, 1951; President General Conference of the New Church, 1920-21 and 1941-42; Chief Superintendent New Church Native Mission in South Africa, 1924-29. *Publications:* Rationalists should be Christians!, 1938; Can I help you, Dr. Joad?, 1945. *Address:* 113 Woodmancote, Dursley, Glos. [*Died* 20 *Aug.* 1952.

PUNCHARD, Mrs.; *see* Holme, Constance.

PURDON, Lt.-Col. David William, C.M.G. 1917; late I.A.; *b.* 17 July 1853. Entered army, 1878; U.S. List, 1908; served Burma, 1887-88 (medal with clasp); European War, 1914-17 (C.M.G.); J.P. Co. Meath. *Address:* Ardrums, Agher, Enfield, Co. Meath, Eire. *Club:* United Service (Dublin). [*Died* 3 *Jan.* 1948.
[*But death not notified in time for inclusion in Who Was Who 1941–1950, first edn.*

PUREY-CUST, Brig. Richard Brownlow, C.B.E. 1942; D.S.O. 1918; M.C.; late R.A.; *b.* 1888; *o. s.* of late Rev. Canon W. A. Purey-Cust; *m.* 1928, Gertrude Patricia Zoe, *o. d.* of late F. J. L. Birch; one *s.* one *d. Educ.:* Eton; R.M.A., Woolwich. Served European War, 1914-18 (wounded, despatches, M.C., D.S.O.); retired pay, 1942. Lt.-Comdr. R.N.V.R. 1944-45. *Address:* Martlets, Sedgehill, Shaftesbury, Dorset. [*Died* 6 *Feb.* 1958.

PURNELL, Christopher James, C.B.E. 1950; M.A. Oxford, F.R.S.L.; *b.* 7 Aug. 1878; *s.* of William Purnell, Oxford; *m.* 1912, Letitia Lucy Glanvill; one *s.* one *d. Educ.:* City of Oxford High School; Saint Catherine's Society, Oxford. Assistant, Bodleian Library, 1896; special assistant, London Library, 1905; assistant secretary and sub-librarian, 1909-40; Secretary and Librarian, 1940-50; retired, 1950. *Publications:* The log-book of William Adams (Japan Society), 1916; collaborated with late Sir C. Hagberg Wright in London Library's Catalogue and Subject Index, 1909-53. *Address:* c/o London Library, 14 St. James's Square, S.W. 1. [*Died* 31 *May* 1959.

PURSER, Maj.-Gen. Arthur William, O.B.E. 1918; M.C.; *b.* 21 Sept. 1884; *o. s.* of Edward Purser, Jr., Smyrna; *m.* 1913, Beatrice Mary Lynch; three *d.* *Educ.:* Marlborough; R.M.A., Woolwich. Commissioned R.F.A., 1903; Maj.-Gen., 1938; retired, 1940; served European War, France. *Address:* The Red House, Wilsford, Salisbury, Wilts. *Club:* United Service. [*Died* 21 *Dec.* 1953.

PURSSELL, Richard Stanley, C.I.E. 1933; O.B.E. 1918; Director, Calcutta Tramways Co. since 1944; *b.* 5 July 1882; *s.* of Richard and Susannah Purssell; *m.* 1925, Ruth Mary Scutt; two *s.* *Educ.:* Oundle School; Royal Indian Engineering College, Coopers Hill. Assistant Superintendent Indian Telegraph Dept., 1904; Chief Engineer, Indian Posts and Telegraphs, 1934; Officiating Director General Posts and Telegraphs, India, April-Oct. 1937; Member Indian Legislative Assembly, 1937-38; retired, 1938; Agent, Calcutta Tramways Co., 1939-45; Member Bengal Legislative Council, 1943-45. *Address:* Closeways, Snowdenham Links Road, Bramley, Surrey. *T.:* Bramley 3203. *Club:* Oriental. [*Died* 21 *May* 1954.

PURVIS, Tom, R.D.I.; Freelance Commercial Artist. Has designed posters and advertising material for leading commercial firms in England, on the Continent, and in America for exhibition all over the world. *Club:* English-Speaking Union. [*Died* 27 *Aug.* 1959.

PURVIS-RUSSELL-MONTGOMERY, Lt.-Col. H. K.; *see* Montgomery.

PUTNAM, Herbert; Librarian of Congress, Washington, 1899-1939, Librarian of Congress Emeritus since 1939; *b.* New York City, 20 Sept. 1861; *s.* of George Palmer Putnam and Victorine Haven; *m.* 1886, Charlotte Elizabeth Munroe (*d.* 1928), Cambridge. *Educ.:* public and private Schools, New York; Harvard (A.B.), 1883; Columbia Law School, New York. Librarian, Minneapolis (Minn.) Athenæum, 1884-87; Librarian, Minneapolis (Minn.) Public Library 1887-91; admitted to Minnesota Bar, 1885; Bar of Suffolk County, Massachusetts, 1892; practised law, Boston, 1892-95; Librarian, Boston (Mass.) Public Library, 1895-99; President, Massachusetts Library Club,1896-1897; President, Amer. Library Assoc., 1898, 1903-4; Member Board of Overseers, Harvard Univ., 1902-6; represented U.S. at United States Library Conferences, London, 1897, Paris, 1900, Rome, 1929, and at the celebration of the 500th anniversary of birth of Johann Gutenberg, Mainz, 1900; member Administrative Board on Congress of Arts and Sciences, Louisiana Purchase Exposition, 1904; General Director, American Library Association, Library War Service, 1917-19; Hon. Litt.D. Bowdoin, 1898; Brown, 1914; Princeton, 1933; Catholic University of America, 1939; Hon. LL.D. University of Illinois, 1903; Columbian (now George Washington) University, 1903; University of Wisconsin, 1904; Yale University, 1907; Williams College, 1911; Harvard, 1928; New York University, 1930; Knight, Royal Order of the Pole Star, Sweden, 1928; awarded Roosevelt distinguished service medal, 1929; received Joseph W. Lippincott award of American Library Association, 1939; author of various articles in magazines and periodicals, and in professional journals. *Address:* Library of Congress, Washington, D.C. *Clubs:* Century (New York); Tavern (Boston); Cosmos (Washington). [*Died* 14 *Aug.* 1955.

PYE, Sir David (Randall), Kt., *cr.* 1952; C.B. 1937; F.R.S. 1937; M.A., Sc.D., M.I.Mech.E., F.R.Ae.S.; *b.* 29 April 1886; 3rd *s.* of late William A. Pye, J.P.; *m.* 1926, Virginia Frances, *y. d.* of late C. Moore Kennedy; two *s.* one *d.* *Educ.:* Tonbridge School; Trinity College, Cambridge (Mechanical Science Tripos). Engineering experience with Mather and Platt; Lecturer in Engineering Science, Oxford University, 1909-14, and Fellow of New College; served European War as Experimental Officer with R.F.C. and R.A.F.; Fellow of Trinity College, Cambridge, and Lecturer in Engineering, 1919-25; Deputy Director of Scientific Research, Air Ministry, 1925-37; Director, 1937-43; Member of Aeronautical Research Council, 1943-46; Wilbur Wright lecturer, 1936; President Institution of Mechanical Engineers, 1952-53; Provost of Univ. Coll., London, 1943-51; Hon. Fellow, University College, London; Hon. Fellow, Inst. Aero. Sciences, U.S.A.; Trustee of National Central Library. *Publications:* The Internal Combustion Engine, 2 vols.; Heat and Energy; George Leigh Mallory, a memoir; The Mummers Play, edited, with a memoir of R. J. E. Tiddy; articles in Scientific and Technical Press. *Recreations:* music and mountaineering. *Address:* Cuttmill Cottage, Shackleford, Godalming. *T.:* Elstead 3229. *Clubs:* Athenæum, Alpine. [*Died* 20 *Feb.* 1960.

PYKE, Joseph, C.B.E. 1942; *b.* 20 April 1884; *e. s.* of late T. J. Pyke, of London, and H. Lewis; *m.* 1907, Phyllis, *y. d.* of late J. R. James, M.D., of Cardiff, and Ellen Phillips; one *s.* two *d.* *Educ.:* University College School, London. Vice-Consul, Baltimore, 1907; Galatz, 1909; Chargé d'Affaires, Port-au-Prince, 1911, with local rank of 1st Secretary in the Diplomatic Service; acting Consul-General, Paris, 1914; Tangier, 1917; Foreign Office, 1917; served in Welsh Guards, 1918; Vice-Consul, Liége, 1918; Consul, 1919; Consul-General, Lourenço Marques, 1926; Hamburg, 1931; Mexico, 1934; Strasbourg, 1938; Basle, 1940-45; retired, 1945. *Recreations:* gardening, motoring. *Address:* The Cottage, Rushlake Green, Heathfield, Sussex. *T.:* Rushlake Green 348. *Club:* Royal Automobile. [*Died* 15 *June* 1955.

Q

QADIR, Khan Bahadur Sheikh Sir Abdul, Kt., *cr.* 1927; Barr.-at-law; a Fellow Punjab Univ. Lahore; *b.* 1874; *s.* of late Sheikh Fatchaddin of Kasur, Punjab, India; *m.* Mohammad Umar, *d.* of late Sheikh Mohammad Umar, Barr.-at-law, Lahore; seven *s.* one *d.* *Educ.:* Forman Christian College, Lahore; Lincoln's Inn. Journalist, as editor The Observer and the Makhzan, Lahore, 1895-1904; study for the Bar in England, 1904-7; practice as advocate, 1907-20, during which period he worked as Public Prosecutor at Lyallpur for eight years; Additional Judge, High Court of Judicature, Lahore; member Punjab Legislative Council, Lahore, 1923 (Deputy President, 1924); the first elected President of the Punjab Legislative Council, Jan.-Sept. 1925, when he resigned the Chair on his appointment as Acting Minister for Education, Punjab; on termination of that duty sat on the Committee of Inquiry appointed to examine the Jails Administration in the Punjab; deputed as a full delegate to represent India at the 7th Assembly of the League of Nations at Geneva, 1926; acted as Revenue Member of the Executive Council, Punjab Government, 1927; as Member Public Service Commission, 1929; Member Council of the Secretary of State for India, 1934-37, Adviser, 1937-39; returned to India, 1939; Khan Bahadur, 1919. *Publications:* The New School of Urdu Literature (in English); Maqam i Khilafat (in Urdu). *Address:* 4 Temple Road, Lahore, Pakistan. [*Died* 9 *Feb.* 1951.

QUALTROUGH, Sir Joseph Davidson, Kt., *cr.* 1954; C.B.E. 1949; Speaker, House of Keys, Isle of Man, since 1937; Timber Merchant; *b.* 11 June 1885; *m.* 1923, Ethel Mary (*née* Qualtrough); one *s.* two *d.* (and one *d.* decd.). *Educ.:* King William's College, I.O.M. Served European War, 1915-19, R.A.O.C.; Lieut. 1916. Member, House of Keys, 1919-. *Recreations:* golf, yachting. *Address:* How Yngren, Castletown, Isle of Man. *T.:* Castletown 2200. [*Died* 14 *Jan.* 1960.

QUARLES, Donald Aubrey; Deputy Secretary of Defense, U.S.A., since 1957; *b.* Van Buren, Ark., 30 July 1894; *s.* of Robert Warren Quarles and Minnie Hynes Quarles; *m.* 2nd, 1939, Rosina Cotton; one *s.* two *d.* (by a former marriage), and one step *d.* *Educ.:* Yale University (B.A.). Enlisted in the Army, 1917, served two years in France and Germany (rank of Capt., Fd. Art.). Engineer, Engineering Dept. of Western Electric, 1920-25 (which became Bell Telephone Laboratories, 1925); subseq. in charge Outside Plant Devel. Dept.; Dir. Transmission Devel. Dept. (radar, etc.), 1940-44; Dir. Apparatus Devel., 1946; Mem. Cttee. on Electronics of Jt. Research and Development Bd., Dept. of Defense (apptd. Chm. cttee., 1949); Vice-Pres. Bell Telephone Laboratories, 1948; Vice-Pres. Western Electric, 1952: Pres. Sandia Corp. (a Western Electric subsid. which op. Sandia Lab. in Albuquerque, New Mexico, for Atomic Energy Commn.), 1952; Asst. Sec. of Defense (Research and Development), 1953; first Chairman, reorganized Air Navigation Devel. Bd., 1954; subseq. Mem. Nat. Advisory Cttee. for Aeronautics, 1954; Secretary of the Air Force, 1955-57. Mem. and Pres. Common Council Englewood, 1940-46; Mayor, 1946-48. Member: Phi Beta Kappa, Sigma Xi, Amer. Assoc. for the Advancement of Science, Yale Engineering Assoc., Telephone Pioneers of America, etc.; Fellow: Amer. Phys. Soc.; Inst. of Radio Engineers; Amer. Inst. of Electrical Engineers (Pres. 1952-53). Holds several hon. degrees in engineering, science and law. *Publications:* papers in technical journals (including Bell System Tech. Jl., and Electrical Engineering), 1930-. *Address:* (home) 3041 Porter Street, N.W. Washington 8, D.C., U.S.A.; (office) Department of Defense, Washington 25, D.C. *T.:* Liberty 5-6700, 56352. [*Died* 8 *May* 1959.

QUEENSBERRY, 11th Marquess of, *cr.* 1682; **Francis Archibald Kelhead Douglas;** Viscount Drumlanrig and Baron Douglas, 1628; Earl of Queensberry, 1633; Bt. (Nova Scotia), 1668; Capt. The Black Watch (Reserve of Officers); *b.* 17 Jan. 1896; *s.* of 10th Marquess and Anna Maria (*d.* 1917), *d.* of Rev. Thomas Walters; *S.* father, 1920; *m.* 1st, 1917, Irene (whom he divorced, 1925; she *m.* 2nd, 1926, Sir James Dunn, *q.v.*), *d.* of H. W. Richards, 16 Albert Road, N.W.1; one *d.*; 2nd, 1926, Cathleen (who obtained a divorce, 1946; she *m.* 2nd, 1947, J. R. Follett), *d.* of late Harrington Mann (*see* Cathleen Mann); one *s.* one *d.*; 3rd, 1947, Muriel Rowe Thornett, *d.* of late Arthur John Rowe Thornett, Monte Carlo; one *s.* *Educ.:* Harrow; Sandhurst. Served European War, 1915-17 (wounded). *Publication:* The Sporting Queensberrys, 1942; Oscar Wilde and the Black Douglas, 1949. *Heir:* *s.* Viscount Drumlanrig. *Clubs:* St. James', Carlton, Buck's, Portland, Turf; Northern Counties (Newcastle); Conservative (Birmingham); Union (Brighton); Travellers', Jockey (Paris). [*Died* 27 *April* 1954.

QUICKSWOOD, 1st Baron, *cr.* 1941, of Clothall; **Hugh Richard Heathcote Gascoyne-Cecil;** P.C. 1918; Hon. D.C.L. Oxon and Durham; LL.D. Edinburgh and Cambridge; Provost of Eton, 1936-44; *b.* 14 Oct. 1869; 5th *s.* of 3rd Marquess of Salisbury and Georgiana Caroline, *d.* of late Sir E. H. Alderson. *Educ.:* Eton; University College, Oxford; Fellow of Hertford. Was private sec. to his father; Lieut., Royal Flying Corps, 1915; M.P. (C.) Greenwich, 1895-1906, Oxford University, 1910-37. *Address:* 16 Beechwood Avenue, Bournemouth, Hants. *Clubs:* Carlton, Junior Carlton. [*Died* 10 *Dec.* 1956 (*ext.*)

QUILTER, Sir Cuthbert; *see* Quilter, Sir W. E. C.

QUILTER, Sir (John) Raymond (Cuthbert), 3rd Bt., *cr.* 1897; Chairman and Managing Director of G.Q. Parachute Co. Ltd., Stadium Works, Woking, Surrey, since 1934; *b.* 25 Feb. 1902; *o. s.* of Sir Cuthbert Quilter, 2nd Bt., and Hon. Gwynedd Douglas Pennant, 7th *d.* of 2nd Baron Penrhyn; *S.* father 1952; *m.* 1935, Margery Marianne, *d.* of late Sir J. Douglas Cooke, F.R.C.S.; one *s.* *Educ.:* Eton. Lieutenant, Grenadier Guards, 1922-27. *Recreations:* golf, flying. *Heir:* *o. s.* Anthony Raymond Leopold Cuthbert, *b.* 25 March 1937. *Address:* 6 Ringrone Court, Heathside Road, Woking, Surrey; Methersgate Hall, Woodbridge, Suffolk. *T.:* Woodbridge 16. *Clubs:* Boodle's, Guards, Royal Aero. [*Died* 7 *Feb.* 1959.

QUILTER, Roger; Composer; *b.* Brighton, 1 Nov. 1877; *s.* of Sir Cuthbert Quilter, 1st Bart. *Educ.:* Eton College; Frankfort-on-the-Main, under Professor Ivan Knorr. Compositions: Song cycle to Julia, 1905; Serenade (for small orchestra), 1907; Seven Elizabethan Lyrics, 1908; Three English Dances (for orchestra), 1910; Music to Children's Fairy Play, Where the Rainbow Ends, 1911; Suite for orchestra, Where the Rainbow Ends, 1912; A Children's Overture; Suite from As You Like It; Light Opera, Love at the Inn. *Address:* 23 Acacia Road, N.W.8. [*Died* 21 *Sept.* 1953.

QUILTER, Sir (William Eley) Cuthbert, 2nd Bt., *cr.* 1897; J.P.; M.P. (C.) South Suffolk, 1910-18; late Captain Suffolk Yeomanry; President Suffolk Horse Society; *b.* 17 July 1873; *e. s.* of Sir Cuthbert Quilter, 1st Bart., and Mary Anne, *d.* of late John Wheeley Bevington, of Brighton; *S.* father, 1911; *m.* 1899, Hon. Gwynedd Douglas Pennant, 7th *d.* of 2nd Baron Penrhyn; one *s.* three *d.* *Educ.:* Harrow; Trinity College, Cambridge: B.A. 1895. *Recreations:* shooting, fishing. *Heir:* *s.* John Raymond Cuthbert [*b.* 25 Feb. 1902; *m.* 1935, Margery Marianne, *d.* of late Sir J. Douglas Cooke, F.R.C.S.]. *Address:* 28 South Street, W.1. *T.:* Grosvenor 3228; Methersgate Hall, Woodbridge, Suffolk. *Clubs:* Carlton, Boodle's. [*Died* 18 *Sept.* 1952.

QUINAN, General Sir Edward Pellew, K.C.B., *cr.* 1946 (C.B. 1936); K.C.I.E., *cr.* 1942; D.S.O. 1938; O.B.E. 1920; p.s.c.; i.d.c.; *b.* 9 Jan. 1885; *m.* 1922, Moira, *widow* of E. Law, J.P., Great Freffans, Co. Meath; one *s.* Entered Indian Army, 1905; Captain, 1913; Major, 1919; Lt.-Col. 1929; Col. 1930; Commander 9th (Jhansi) Infantry Brigade, India, 1934-38; A.D.C. to the King, 1936; Major-General, 1937; a District Commander, Waziristan, 1938; Lt.-Gen. 1941; G.O.C. Iran and Iraq, 1941; General, 1942; G.O.C., Tenth Army, 1942-43; Cdr. North-Western Army in India, 1943; retired, 1943. Colonel 8th Punjab Regt., 1945. *Address:* Barrington, near Ilminster, Somerset. [*Died* 13 *Nov.* 1960.

QUINN, James, R.O.I., R.P.S.; artist; *b.* Melbourne, 4 Dec. 1870; *s.* of John Quinn; *m.* 1898, Blanche, *d.* of Louis Guernier of Paris; two *s.* *Educ.:* St. Peter's College, Melbourne. Gained Victorian Government gold medal and travelling scholarship, 1895; studied in Paris eight years under Jean Paul Laurens; Member of Royal Society of Portrait Painters and Royal Institute of Oil Painters; came to London; Exhibitor Royal Academy, Paris Salon, etc.; gained honourable mention Paris Salon, 1912; pictures bought for National Galleries—

Melbourne, Geelong, Switzerland, Sydney (Australia), Tokio; Liverpool Corporation Gallery (Walker Art Gallery); Lieutenant and official artist to the Australian Military Forces at the Front in France, 1917-18; painted General Birdwood and General Monash for the Australian Commonwealth; appointed official artist for the Canadian War Records, and painted four of their V.C.'s for them; painted official portrait of the Duchess of York, exhibited Royal Academy, 1931 (for Australia); second portrait of the Duchess of York exhibited Royal Academy 1933 (for England). *Recreation:* landscape sketching. *Club:* Chelsea Arts. [*Died* 19 *Feb.* 1951.

QUINTON, Hon. Herman William, C.M.G. 1949; Minister of Finance, Province of Newfoundland, Canada, since 1949; *b.* 26 Oct. 1896; *s.* of J. B. Quinton and S. J. Benger; *m.* 1921, Ella, *d.* of late Capt. George Blackmore and Elinor Blackmore, Port Blandford, Bonavista Bay; one *s.* (one *d.* decd.). *Educ.:* Anglican School; Open Hall Academy; private studies. *Address:* The Bank of Montreal, St. John's, Newfoundland, Canada; 62 Circular Rd., St. John's. [*Died* 2 *April* 1952.

QUIST, Sir Emmanuel Charles, Kt., *cr.* 1952; O.B.E. 1942; *b.* Christiansborg, Ghana; *s.* of a pastor of Basel Mission; *m.*; three *c.* *Educ.:* Basel Mission; Theological Seminar and Training College, Akropong, Ghana; Middle Temple. Called to Bar, 1913; Formerly: Member Accra Town Council (10 yrs.); Legal Adviser to Eastern Provinces Council of Chiefs. Actg. Puisne Judge, Cape Coast, 1948; Speaker of the Legislative Assembly, Ghana, West Africa, 1949-57. Judge at Accra Turf Club; Chm. Ghana Scouts Exec. Council; Achimota College Council; Ghana Br. B.R.C.S. *Address:* Accra, Ghana. [*Died* 28 *Feb.* 1959.

R

RABINO, H. Louis, C.M.G. 1937; O.B.E. *b.* 27 July 1877; *s.* of Joseph Rabino di Borgomale; *m.* M. Paule (*d.* 1947), *d.* of Col. R. J. Pagès des Huttes; one *s.* *Educ.:* privately. Acting Consul, Kermanshah, 1904 and 1905; Vice-Consul at Resht, 1906-1912; Mogador, 1912-16; Acting Consul and then Consul at Casablanca, 1915-22; Consul at Cairo, 1922-24; negotiated with the French Protectorate authorities in Morocco the settlement of the question of Crown and mosque property in British hands, 1917-19; H.B.M. Consul-General, Smyrna, 1924-28; Salonika, 1928-29; Cairo, 1929-37; Consul-General in North Africa and President of Naval Courts, 1943-45; and in France, 1945. Counsellor at the Embassy, Paris, in charge of War Claims Department, 1945-47. *Publications:* Le Guilan; Mazandaran and Astarabad; Le Monastère de Sainte-Catherine (Mont-Sinai); Coins, Medals and Seals of the Shahs of Iram, 1501-1943; Essai d'un Armorial de l'ancien Comté de Nice et de la Principauté de Monaco; numerous papers on Persia and Morocco, and genealogical studies. *Address:* c/o Westminster Foreign Bank Ltd., 18 Place Vendôme, Paris 1. [*Died* 26 *Sept.* 1950.

RADCLIFFE, Sir Frederick Morton, K.C.V.O., *cr.* 1925; Kt., *cr.* 1922; Hon. LL.D. (Liverpool), 1937; *b.* 16 Feb. 1861; *e. s.* of late Sir David Radcliffe, Liverpool; *m.* 1885, Margaret, *d.* of Alfred Horsfall of Hollenden, Exmouth; four *d.* (*s.* killed in war). *Educ.:* Liverpool Institute; Trent College, Nottingham; and privately. Hon. Secretary, Liverpool Constitutional Association, 1884-1901, and subsequently Vice-President; Hon. Sec. of the Liverpool International Exhibition, 1886; is one of the original members of the Committee for building the new Liverpool Cathedral, which has been in course of erection since 1903, and was first Treasurer (1901-13), Chm. (1913-34), and now President; Chm. of Committees of Queen Anne's Bounty, 1927-32; formerly Chairman Legal Board of Church of England. Officier d'Académie. *Address:* Tuesley Court, Godalming, Surrey. *T.:* Godalming 806. *Club:* Athenæum. [*Died* 23 *Sept.* 1953.

RADCLIFFE, Geoffrey Reynolds Yonge, D.C.L., F.S.A.; Emeritus Fellow of New College, Oxford; *b.* 3 April 1886; *s.* of Judge F. R. Y. Radcliffe, K.C., and Helen Lushington; *m.* Sylvia, *d.* of Ernest Capel Cure; one *s.* *Educ.:* Westminster; Christ Church, Oxford, 1st Class Lit. Hum., 1909; Eldon Scholar. 1911; called to Bar, Lincoln's Inn, 1913, served European War, 1914-18, with 23rd Bn; London Regt. and Staff, Bt. Maj., 1918. Fellow, Tutor and Law Lectr., New Coll., Oxf., 1920-24, Bursar 1924-56. Examiner in Honours, School of Jurisprudence, 1926-28 and 1950; Examiner in B.C.L., 1922-23 and 1932-33; Member Hebdomadal Council, 1926-28; Principal Law Society's School of Law, and Director of Legal Studies, 1928-40; Member of Lord Chancellor's Committee on Advanced Legal Studies, 1938; Pres. Soc. of Public Teachers of Law, 1938-39; Mem. Court of Weavers Co. (Upper Bailiff, 1929, 1941, 1952); a Governor of Westminster School and of Harpur Trust, Bedford; and a Trustee of the Whiteley Homes Trust; J.P. Herts. *Publications:* Students' Property Statutes, 1927; Real Property Law, 1933; (with Geoffrey Cross) The English Legal System, 1937. *Recreation:* shooting. *Address:* Glebe House, Knebworth, Herts. *T.:* Knebworth 2109. *Club:* Oxford and Cambridge. [*Died* 18 *July* 1959.

RADCLIFFE-BROWN, Alfred Reginald, M.A., F.B.A., F.R.A.I.; Emeritus Professor, Oxford University; *b.* 17 Jan. 1881; *m.* Winifred (marriage dissolved 1938), *d.* of Algernon Lyon, Cambridge; one *d.* *Educ.:* King Edward's High School, Birmingham; Trinity College, Cambridge. Fellow of Trinity College, Cambridge, 1908-14; Lecturer in Ethnology, University of London, 1909-10; Professor of Social Anthropology, University of Cape Town, 1921-25; Professor of Anthropology, University of Sydney, 1925-31; Professor of Anthropology, University of Chicago, 1931-37; Fellow of All Souls College and Professor of Social Anthropology, Oxford University, 1937-46; Professor of Social Science in the Farouk I University, Alexandria, 1947-49; President of Royal Anthropological Institute, 1939-40; Member Royal Acad. of Sciences, Amsterdam; Hon. Mem., New York Academy of Science. [*Died* 24 *Oct.* 1955.

RADCLYFFE, Major (Charles Robert) Eustace; late 1st Life Guards; High Sheriff, Dorset, 1925; J.P. Dorset; *b.* 1873; *e. s.* of late Charles James Radclyffe, of Foxdenton Hall, Lancs, and Hyde, Dorset; *m.* 1st, 1897, *o. d.* of S. J. Howard, Richmond, Surrey; four *d.*; 2nd, 1927, Kathleen, *o. d.* of J. B. Docherty, Thurso; one *d.* *Educ.:* private schools and army tutors. 2nd Lt. 1st Life Guards, 1893; A.D.C. to late Gen. Sir Redvers Buller, 1898; served South African War, 1900-1, on the Staff, and attached to 1st Royal Dragoons; European War, 1914-15; Egypt, 1915-16; temp. A.A.G. to the I.G.C. Egypt; a member of the British Military Mission in Roumania, 1918-19 (Star of Roumania); has travelled widely as an explorer and sportsman, chiefly in Arctic regions; Founder of the Shikar Club (or the Society of Big Game Hunters of England); for many years maintained the largest establishment of trained hawks and falconers in England, and a great votary of this ancient sport. *Publications:* Big Game Shooting in Alaska; Modern Falconry; Small Game Shooting in Hungary; Norwegian Angling; Round the Smoking Room Fire, 1933, etc. *Recreations:* falconry, shooting, fishing, formerly boxing and lawn-tennis. *Address:* Hyde, Wareham; Forss House, Thurso. [*Died* 1 *July* 1953.

RADFORD, Basil; Actor; *b.* Chester, 25 June 1897; *s.* of Arthur Radford and Florence Isobel Radford (*née* Cadell); *m.* 1926, Shirley Deuchars; one *s.* *Educ.:* St. Peter's, York. Served European War, 1915-1918. First London appearance, Ambassadors, 1924; toured in Australia and New Zealand, 1927-28; San Francisco and Los Angeles, 1929; played in Vancouver with British Guild Players, 1929-31; returned to London stage, 1932; toured 1933, 1946. Recent stage: The Astonished Ostrich, Clutterbuck, Blind Goddess, The White Falcon, Taking Things Quietly, Affairs of State. Recent films: Captive Heart, Dead of Night, Passport to Pimlico, Whisky Galore, Quartet, Chance of a Lifetime, The Galloping Major. *Recreations:* golf, cricket, shooting. *Address:* 4 Old Burlington Street, W.1; Old Mill Dene, Blockley, Glos. *Clubs:* Green Room, Savage, Garrick. [*Died* 20 *Oct.* 1952.

RADICE, Mrs. A. H., (Sheila Radice); *d.* of Colonel Alister Jamieson; *m.* 1913, Lt.-Col. A. H. Radice, D.S.O., Gloucestershire Regt., *s.* of Albert Hampden Radice, Thistleborough, Co. Antrim; one *s.* one *d.* Acting Editor The Times Educational Supplement, 1919-38; joint founder St. George's Home for Officers' Children and the Public Schools Careers Association. Entered University of Fribourg as a student, 1949. *Publications:* Not all Sleep (life of James Hammond the poet); and other works. *Address:* c/o Lloyds Bank (Foreign) Ltd., Boulevard des Capucines, Paris. [*Died* 20 *Nov.* 1960.

RADIN, Max, LL.B., Ph.D., LL.D.; Professor of Law, 1919-40; John H. Boalt Professor of Law, University of California, 1940-48; emeritus since 1948; *b.* Kempen, Poland, 29 March 1880; *s.* of Adolph M. Radin and Johanna Theodor; brought to United States, 1884; *m.* 1st, Rose Jaffe (*d.* 1919); one *d.*; 2nd, 1922, Dorothea Prall (*d.* 1948). *Educ.:* College of the City of New York; New York University; Columbia University. Instructor in Classics, High Schools, New York City, 1901; Lecturer in Roman and Civil Law, College of the City of New York, 1919; Instructor in History, Columbia University, 1918-19; Professor of Law, Stanford University Summer Session, 1931; Northwestern University Summer Session, 1936; Storrs Lecturer in Jurisprudence, Yale University, 1940; Hillman Lecturer, Pacific University, 1946; Visiting Prof. of Law, Columbia Univ., 1947; Member Institute for Advanced Study, Princeton, N.J., 1949, 1950; Visiting Prof. of Law, Duke Univ., Durham, N. Carolina, 1949. Member of New York and California Bars; Bar of U.S. Supreme Court; Member of American National Committee of International Congress of Comparative Law, 1932-37; American Council Institute of Pacific Relations, 1933; Vice-Pres. Social Science Research Conference of the Pacific Coast, 1932-33; President's Commission for Inter-American University, 1939; Chairman, American Bar Association Committee on Comparative Legal Philosophy; Chairman California Commission on Uniform State Laws; Draftsman Code of Administrative Ethics, State Bar of California, 1946; Member Societé d'Histoire du Droit, Paris; Stair Society, Edinburgh. *Publications:* The Legislation of the Greeks and Romans on Corporations, 1909; The Jews Among the Greeks and Romans, 1916; The Life of the People in Biblical Times, 1929; Handbook of Roman Law, 1927; The Lawful Pursuit of Gain, 1931; The Trial of Jesus of Nazareth, 1931; Handbook of Anglo-American Legal History, 1935; The Law and Mr. Smith, 1938; Marcus Brutus, 1939; Manners and Morals of Business, 1939; Law as Logic and Experience, 1940; The Day of Reckoning, 1943; The Law and You, 1948; Epicurus, My Master, 1949; various legal and classical articles. *Address:* 2683 Buena Vista Way, Berkeley, California, U.S.A. *T.:* Ashbery 3-2614. *Clubs:* Faculty (Berkeley); Commonwealth, Press (San Francisco). [*Died* 22 *June* 1950.

[*But death not notified in time for inclusion in Who Was Who 1941–1950, first edn.*

RADSTOCK, 5th Baron (*cr.* 1800), **Montagu Waldegrave;** *b.* 15 July 1867; *s.* of 3rd Baron and Susan (*d.* 1892), *d.* of John Hales Calcraft, M.P., Rempstone, and of Caroline, *d.* of 5th Duke of Manchester; *S.* brother, 1937; *m.* 1898, Constance Marian (*d.* 1936), *e. d.* of late J. C. J. Brodie of Lethen, Nairn; (one son killed on active service, 1944) two *d.* *Educ.:* Cambridge University, B.A. Chairman of the Executive of the Native Races and Liquor Traffic Committee, 1925-31. *Address:* 51 Princes Court, S.W.3. *T.:* Kensington 4016. *Club:* Travellers'. [*Died* 17 *Sept.* 1953 (*ext.*).

RAE, George Bentham Leathart, D.S.O. 1919; T.D. 1926; Bt.-Col. (T.A.); *b.* 19 October 1884; 2nd *s.* of Edward and Margaret Rae, Courthill, Birkenhead; *m.* 1914, Helen Margaret, *d.* of Edwin A. Beazley, J.P., Willaston, Wirral, Cheshire; one *s.* four *d.* *Educ.:* Mostyn House School, Parkgate, Cheshire; Winchester College. Served European War, 1914-18 (despatches, D.S.O.). War of 1939-45; O.C. 5th Bn. Cheshire Home Guard. High Sheriff of Cheshire, 1949. *Address:* The Lodge, Kirriemuir, Angus. [*Died* 15 *Aug.* 1958.

RAE, Sir James, K.C.B., *cr.* 1937; K.B.E. *cr.* 1933; J.P. Counties of Middlesex and Hertford, 1940; *b.* 6 March 1879; *s.* of James Rae and Christina Hyslop; *m.* 1916, Edith (*d.* 1957), *e. d.* of Joseph Lines and Jane Fitzhenry. *Educ.:* Owen's School, Islington. Entered Civil Service, 1895; Second Division Clerk, Board of Education, 1897; Staff Clerk, 1911; Insurance Commission, 1912; First Class Clerk, 1912; Acting Senior Clerk, 1914; H.M. Treasury, Principal, 1919; Asst.-Secretary, 1920; Principal Asst.-Sec. 1931; Under-Secretary (Third Sec.), H.M. Treasury, 1932; Secretary Royal Commission on Honours, 1922; Secretary to Political Honours Scrutiny Committee, 1923-1939; Visited India as Member of Committee appointed to examine procedure of Government of India's Secretariat under the new Constitution, 1935-36; Member Coronation Executive Committee, 1936-37; British Purchasing Commission in Canada, 1939; British Supply Board in United States and Canada, 1939-40; Member of Royal Commission on Awards to Inventors, 1946-56. *Recreations:* gardening, golf, and fishing. *Address:* Stocks, Hadley Green, Barnet, Herts. *T.:* Barnet 2121. *Club:* Union. [*Died* 1 *Nov.* 1957.

RAE, Sir James Stanley, Kt., *cr.* 1933; *b.* 1881. Called to Bar, Bahamas, 1904; Middle Temple, 1919; Attorney-General, St. Vincent, 1919; St. Lucia, 1920; Chief Justice, St. Vincent, 1923; Grenada, 1927; Leeward Islands, 1931-37; retired, 1937. *Publication:* Revised and consolidated Laws of St. Vincent, 1926 Edition. *Club:* Royal Empire Society. [*Died* 28 *Sept.* 1956.

RAEBURN, Agnes M., R.S.W.; Member of the Royal Scottish Water-Colour Society and Society of Scottish Women Artists; *y. d.* of late James Raeburn, Glasgow. Studied Glasgow School of Art. Subjects, landscapes and flowers; favourite sketching grounds, Scotland and England. *Address:* 11 Cranworth Street, Glasgow. *T.:* Kelvin 1015. *Club:* Lady Artists (Glasgow). [*Died* 3 *Aug.* 1955.

RAEMAEKERS, Louis, LL.D. (Hon.) Glasgow, 1922; cartoonist; formerly member of staff of De Telegraaf, Amsterdam; *b.* Roermond, Holland, 6 April 1869; *m.* 1902, Johanna P. van Mansvelt; one *s.* two *d.* *Educ.:* Roermond;

Amsterdam; Brussels. Honorary Member of the Royal Society of Miniature Painters, 1915, and of the Three Arts Club, 1916; Chevalier of the Légion d'Honneur, 1916; Officier, 1925; Honorary Fellow of the Royal Society of Literature, 1916; Hon. Member of the Saintsbury Club (First Edition Club); Chevalier de l'ordre de Leopold, 1920; Honorary Member of the Ligue des Poilus de France, 1922; Diplome d'honneur de la Ligue des Pays Neutres; Officer of the Order of Orange-Nassau; Commander of the Order of the Crown of Italy; Commander of the Order of Polonia Restituta; Commander of the Order of the Crown of Belgium; Commander of the Order of the Three Stars of Letland; Commander of the Order of St. Sava of Yougoslavia; Commander in the Order of Grand Duke Gediminas of Lithuania; painted portraits and landscape, and sometimes genre; about 1907 started making political cartoons; Member of the Arts Clubs at Amsterdam and The Hague; had several successful special exhibitions of his works in Holland, England, France, Italy, Spain, Switzerland, Belgium, U.S.A., etc.; made a great number of posters, etc. *Publications:* The Great War in 1916; The Great War in 1917; Devant l'Histoire, 1918; Cartoon History of the War, 1919; cartoons in the Amsterdam Telegraaf. *Address:* Klatteweg 1, The Hague (Scheveningen), Holland. [*Died* 26 *July* 1956.

RAFFERTY, His Honour Judge Michael Harvey, C.B.E. 1951; British Judge International Court, Tangier, Morocco, since 1932; *b.* 18 Jan. 1877; *o.s.* of Michael Rafferty of Colgath House, Kilcock, Co. Kildare, and Wilhelmina, *d.* of John Quinlan, formerly proprietor and editor of Dublin Evening Post; *m.* 1910, Yolande, *d.* of P. Ch. van Lennep, Dutch Diplomatic Agent in Cairo, and Maud Ogilvy. *Educ.:* privately. Licencié en droit de l'Université de Paris; Barrister-at-Law, Lincoln's Inn; British Judge in Native Courts of First Instance, 1912; Judge in Court of Appeal, Cairo, 1921-27; retired from Egyptian Government Service, 1927; Delegate to International Institute of Agriculture in Rome, 1929-32; Member of Jury, Milan Exhibition, 1906, section prévoyance sociale. *Publication:* author of monograph on Vico in Great Jurists of the World series. *Address:* International Court, Tangier, Morocco. [*Died* 3 *Oct.* 1953.

RAHIM, Sir Abdur; (Mr. Justice Rahim), K.C.S.I., *cr.* 1925; Kt., *cr.* 1919; D.C.L. (Oxford); D.L. (Dacca); *b.* Midnapore, Bengal, 1867; *m.* 1905, *d.* of late Moulvi Mohammad Yahia; three *s.* one *d.* *Educ.:* Midnapore Government High School; Presidency College, Calcutta. Called to Bar, Middle Temple, 1890; practised in the Calcutta High Court until 1908; Puisne Judge of the Madras High Court, 1908; a member of the Royal Commission on Public Services in India, 1913-15; a Member of the Bengal Executive Council and was in charge of the Portfolio of Administration of Justice and Jail and allied subjects, 1921-25, Member Bengal Legislative Council, 1926-30; Indian Legislative Assembly, 1930; Leader of the Independent Party; Leader of the Opposition, 1933-34; Member of the Indian Delegation to the Joint Parliamentary Committee on Indian Reforms, 1933; President of the Assembly, 1935; Leader and Member, Indian Delegations to the Empire Parliamentary Conferences in London, 1935 and 1937. *Publication:* Principles of Mohammedan Jurisprudence according to the Sunni School of Law. *Address:* 217 Lower Circular Road, Calcutta, India. [*Died* 15 *Aug.* 1952.

RAHMAN, Sir Ahmed Fazlur, Kt., *cr.* 1942; LL.D. Professor of History, M.A.O. College, Aligarh, and later Muslim University, Aligarh, 1914-21; Provost, Muslim Hall, University of Dacca, 1921-27; Vice-Chancellor, University of Dacca, 1934-36; Member, Federal Public Service Commission, India, 1937. [*Died* 25 *March* 1945.

[*But death not notified in time for inclusion in Who Was Who 1941–1950, first edn.*

RAIKES, Humphrey Rivaz; Principal, 1928, and Vice-Chancellor, 1948, University of the Witwatersrand, Johannesburg; retired, 1954; 3rd *s.* of late Canon W. A. Raikes; *m.* 1936, Joan, 2nd *d.* of W. A. Hardy, Norwich. *Educ.:* Tonbridge School; Dulwich College, Balliol College, Oxford (Williams Exhibitioner). Abbott Scholar, 1911; B.A., 1914; M.A., 1919; Hon. LL.D. (Bristol), 1948, (Toronto), 1949, (Cape Town), 1951 (Cantab.), 1953. Served European War, 1st Batt. The Buffs, R.F.C. and R.A.F., 1914-19 (A.F.C.); Fell. Exeter Coll. Oxf., 1919-27; Hon. Fellow, 1946; Demonstrator and Treasurer, Balliol and Trinity College Laboratory, 1920-27; Chief Instructor Oxford University Air Squadron, 1925-1927. O.St.J. *Publications:* Papers in the Journals of the Chemical Society and Faraday Society. *Recreations:* motoring, gardening. *Clubs:* Royal Air Force; Rand (Johannesburg); Pretoria (Pretoria). [*Died* 13 *April* 1955.

RAIKES, Admiral Sir Robert Henry Taunton, K.C.B., *cr.* 1941 (C.B. 1937); C.V.O. 1935; D.S.O. 1916; *b.* 23 Aug. 1885; 5th *s.* of late Robert Taunton Raikes, of Treberfydd, Brecons; *m.* 1917, Ida Guinevere, 4th *d.* of late David Evans, Ffrwdgrech, Brecons, and Mrs. Evans, Stoke Court, Shropshire; three *s.* *Educ.:* Radley. Entered R.N., 1900; Submarine service, 1908; Commander, 1917; Captain, 1923; Rear-Adm. 1935; Vice-Adm., 1939; served European War, 1914-17 (despatches, D.S.O. and Bar, Chevalier of the Legion of Honour); Director of R.N. Staff College, Greenwich, 1932-34; Commodore and Chief of Staff, Mediterranean, 1934-35; A.D.C. to the King, 1935; Adm.-in-Charge Alexandria (temp.), 1936; Rear-Admiral Submarines, 1936-1938; War of 1939-45 (King Haakon VII Liberty Cross); Vice-Admiral Commanding Northern Patrol, 1940; Commander-in-Chief, South Atlantic Station, 1940-41; Admiral, 1942; Flag Officer, Aberdeen, 1942-44; Retired List, 1942. *Address:* Mantley, Newent, Glos. *T.:* Newent 285. [*Died* 24 *May* 1953.

RAINES, Lieut.-Colonel Ralph Gore Devereux Groves-, D.S.O. 1915; Hon. M.A., Belfast; late The Buffs, East Kent Regiment; late Commanding Queen's University, Belfast, O.T.C.; *b.* 14 Aug. 1877; 3rd *s.* of late Lieutenant-Colonel John Percy Groves, 67th and 27th Regiments of Foot; *m.* Ellen, *d.* of late Thomas Workman, J.P., of Craigdarragh, Co. Down; two *s.* High Sheriff for the County of Down, 1932; Rear-Commodore Royal Ulster Yacht Club, 1927 and 1932; Royal Guernsey Artillery, 1894; Regular Army, The Buffs, 1898; Captain, 1903; Major, 1914; Adjutant, T.F., 1911-13; commanded Coy. Gentlemen Cadets, R.M.C., 1916-17; served European War, 1914-17 (despatches, D.S.O.); retired pay, 1921. Vice-Commodore, Roy. Ulster Yacht Club, 1951. *Address:* Ardview House, Killinchy, Co. Down. *Clubs:* Army and Navy; Union (Belfast); Royal Ulster Yacht; Royal North of Ireland Yacht; Royal Clyde Yacht. [*Died* 7 *Sept.* 1953.

RAINSFORD-HANNAY, Col. Frederick, C.M.G. 1919; D.S.O. 1917; J.P.; D.L.; *b.* St. Thomas Mount, Madras, 28 April 1878; *s.* of late Col. R. W. Rainsford-Hannay, Kirkdale, and Helen Jane, *d.* of John Brancker, Liverpool; *m.* 1910, Dorothea Letitia May, *y. d.* of late Sir William F. Maxwell, 4th Bt., of Cardoness; one *s.* (and one *s.* decd.). *Educ.:* Wellington College; Royal Military Academy, Woolwich. Wellington and R.M.A., Woolwich, Football Fifteens, 1894-1896; served South African War, 1899-1902 (despatches, slightly wounded, Queen's medal 6 clasps, King's with 2 clasps); in India and South Africa, 1906-15; Passed Staff College,

Quetta; served European War, 1915-18; Brigade-Major R.A., May 1915-Feb. 1916; Lt.-Col. (temp.), Feb. 1916 (wounded, D.S.O., C.M.G.); C.R.A. 52nd (Lowland) Division, 1924-28; retired pay, 1930. *Publication:* Dry Stone Walling. *Recreations:* usual field sports, cricket. *Address:* Cardoness, Gatehouse of Fleet, Kirkcudbrightshire. *Clubs:* Army and Navy, M.C.C.; New (Edinburgh). [*Died* 11 *Sept.* 1959.

RAISON, Rev. Herbert Chaplin, M.A.; Rector of St. Peter's, Doncaster, since 1936; *b.* Portland House, Wyke Regis, 13 Nov. 1889; *s.* of Frank Herbert Raison; *m.* 1929, Josephine Mary, *e. d.* of Percy Stops, Towcester, Northamptonshire; two *s.* *Educ.:* St. John's College, Oxford (Scholar); Ely Theological College. Ordained to Rugby Parish Church, 1913; Priested, 1914; Assistant Priest, St. George's, Leicester, 1915-17; Assistant Master and Chaplain, Malvern College, 1917-19; Vice-Principal and Bursar Warminster Theological College, 1919-22; Organising Secretary National Society, 1922; Principal, Queen's College, Birmingham, 1923-34; Warden, 1924-1934; Vicar of St. Luke's, Paddington, 1934-36; Hon. Chaplain to Bishop of Birmingham, 1924. *Recreations:* motoring, gardening. *Address:* Saint Peter's Rectory, Doncaster. *T.:* 53324. [*Died* 29 *Sept.* 1952.

RAIT, Miss Helen Anna Macdonald, C.B.E. 1919; R.R.C. Chief Superintendent Queen Alexandra's Military Nursing Service, India; retired, 1921; served European War, 1914-19 (R.R.C., C.B.E.); Kaisar-i-Hind medal, 1911. *Address:* Berryburn, Dunoon, Argyll. [*Died* 18 *July* 1955.

RAJADHYAKSHA, Hon. Mr. Justice Ganpat Sakharam, M.A. (Cantab.); Barrister-at-Law; I.C.S.; Judge High Court, Bombay, since 1943; *b.* 9 Sept. 1896; *s.* of Rao Bahadur S. V. Rajadhyaksha, formerly Executive Eng., P.W.D., Bombay Presidency; *m.* 1922, Champu Nabar; one *s.* one *d.* *Educ.:* Elphinstone High School and College, Bombay; St. Catharine's College, Cambridge (1st Cl. Hons. Nat. Sci. Tripos, 1918); School of Oriental Studies, London University. Called to Bar, Gray's Inn, 1920; second in Exam. for I.C.S. 1919; entered I.C.S. 1920; transferred to Judicial Dept., 1924; Deputy Secretary to Govt. of Bombay Legal Dept. and Secretary to Bombay Legislative Council, 1928; studied Parliamentary Procedure in England, 1930; one of Secretaries to Indian Round Table Conference, London, 1930-31; Deputy Secretary, Political Dept. of Govt. of Bombay, and Deputy Reforms Officer, 1931; Member Franchise Committee, 1932; Secretary to Govt. of Bombay, Legal Dept. and Remembrancer of Legal Affairs, 1934-37; District and Sessions Judge, Dharwar, 1935-37, Ahmedabad, 1938-42, Poona, 1942-43; Judge High Court of Judicature, Bombay, 1943; Member of Court of Industrial Arbitration, 1940-47; Adjudicator, Post and Telegraph dispute, 1946, Railway dispute, 1946-47; Member of Income Tax Investigation Commission appointed by Govt. of India, 1947-48; Chairman Air Transport Inquiry Cttee. appointed by Govt. of India, 1950; Sole Member, Fertiliser Inquiry Cttee. appointed by Govt. of India, 1951; Chm. Indian Press Commission, 1952-54. *Recreations:* tennis, golf, photography. *Address:* High Court, Bombay. *Clubs:* National Liberal; Willingdon, Orient, Cricket Club of India (Bombay). [*Died* 9 *Feb.* 1955.

RAJPIPLA, Maharaja of; Lieut.-Col. H.H. Maharana Shri Sir Vijayasinhji Chhatrasinhji, G.B.E., *cr.* 1945; K.C.S.I., *cr.* 1925; Ruler of first class State in Bombay Presidency, India; enjoys a permanent salute of 13 guns; area of the State 1600 square miles; population of the State about 249,032; *m.* 1940, Ella Devi (*née* Atherton); one *s.* one *d.* *Educ.:* Rajkumar College, Rajkot; Imperial Cadet Corps, Dehra Dun. *Recreations:* polo, racing (won the Derby with Windsor Lad, 1934). *Address:* The Manor, Old Windsor, Berks; Rajpipla, India. [*Died* 29 *April* 1951.

RALLI, Augustus John; Author; *b.* 6 Jan. 1875; *s.* of John Antony Ralli and Virginia Agelasto; *m.* 1927, Isabel Murray, *d.* of William Mackay. *Educ.:* Eton; Christ Church, Oxford, M.A. F.R.S.L. *Publications:* The Morning of Life, 1908; Christians at Mecca, 1909; Guide to Carlyle, 1920; Critiques, 1927; A History of Shakespearian Criticism, 1932; Later Critiques, 1933; Poetry and Faith, 1951. *Recreation:* walking. *Address:* 4 Royal Crescent, Bath. *T.:* 3875. *Club:* Athenæum. [*Died* 19 *March* 1954.

RALPH, Herbert Walter, M.A.; *b.* London, 24 May 1885; *s.* of George and Eleanor Anne Ralph; *m.* 1910, Augusta Louisa Sellwood; no *c.* *Educ.:* St. Olave's Gram. School; King's Coll., Cambridge (Classical Scholar), 1st Class Classical Tripos, Part I, 1907, 1st Class Part II, 1908, Cambridge Univ. Teaching Diploma, 1908, Powis Medal Proxime Accessit, 1907. Senior Classical Master, Llandovery College, 1908-13; Stonyhurst College, 1914-19; King Edward VI. School, Birmingham, 1920-24; Headmaster King's School, Chester, 1924-27; Headmaster Plymouth College, 1929-45; Lieut., R.G.A. 17th Siege Battery, 1916-18. *Address:* 3 South Drive, Cattistock, Dorset. [*Died* 17 *April* 1955.

RAM, Sir (Lucius Abel John) Granville, K.C.B., *cr.* 1938 (C.B. 1931); Q.C. 1943; M.A. (Oxon); J.P. (Herts. since 1923 and Cornwall since 1946); Chairman Statute Law Committee since 1947; Chairman Herts Quarter Sessions since 1946 (Deputy 1932-46) and of Appeal Cttee. and Licensing Cttee.; Church Commissioner since 1948; *b.* 24 June 1885; *s.* of late A. J. Ram, K.C., of Ballytegan, Co. Wexford, and Berkhamsted Place, Herts, and Hon. Mary Grace (*d.* 1912), *d.* of 13th Baron Inchiquin; *m.* 1924, Elizabeth, *y. d.* of late E. A. Mitchell-Innes, C.B.E., K.C.; three *s.* two *d.* *Educ.:* Eton; Exeter College, Oxford. Barrister, Inner Temple, 1910; Herts Yeomanry, 1910; served European War, 1914-19 (Egypt, Gallipoli, France), Captain Herts Yeomanry and Adj. S. Irish Horse; 3rd Parliamentary Counsel to Treasury, 1925-29; 2nd Parliamentary Counsel, 1929-37; First Parliamentary Counsel, 1937-47. *Recreations:* shooting, sailing. *Address:* Furze Park, Polruan by Fowey, Cornwall. *T.:* Polruan 72. *Clubs:* Travellers'; Royal Fowey Yacht (Fowey). [*Died* 23 *Dec.* 1952.

RAMSAY, Allen Beville, M.A.; Hon. Fellow of Magdalene Coll., 1948; Master of Magdalene College, Cambridge, 1925-Sept. 1947; Vice-Chancellor of Cambridge University, 1929-1931; *b.* 3 Aug. 1872; *s.* of Beville Ramsay, Croughton House, Brackley, Northants; unmarried. *Educ.:* Eton; King's College, Cambridge. Assistant Master at Eton College, 1895-1925; Lower Master of Eton College, 1916-25. *Publications:* Inter Lilia, 1919; Ros Rosarum, 1925; Frondes Salicis, 1935; Flos Malvae, 1946; Ros Maris, 1955. *Address:* Allan Bank, Graham Road, Great Malvern. *Club:* Union. [*Died* 20 *Sept.* 1955.

RAMSAY, Captain Archibald Henry Maule; *o. s.* of late Lt.-Colonel Henry L. Ramsay, *er. s.* of General the Hon. Sir Henry Ramsay, K.C.S.I., C.B.; *m.* Ismay Lucretia Mary, *o. d.* of 14th Viscount Gormanston, and *widow* of late Lord Ninian Crichton-Stuart, M.P.; three *s.* (and *e. s.* died on active service, 1943). *Educ.:* Eton; R.M.C. Sandhurst. Joined 2nd Bn. Coldstream Guards, 1913; to France 12 Aug. 1914; Captain, 1915; severely wounded, 1916; S.D.3 War Office, 1917; British War Mission in Paris, 1918; invalided, 1919; Member of H.M. Body Guard for Scot-

land, since 1920; M.P. (U.) Peebles, S. Midlothian, 1931-45; Parliamentary Member of Potato Marketing Board since 1936 (Mem. Nat. Exec. Council of Board, 1954); 23 May 1940, detained at Brixton Prison under Reg. 18b until 26 Sept. 1944. *Publications:* The Nameless War, 1953; A Short Life of Sir Alexander Ramsay of Dalwolsy. *Recreations:* shooting, cricket. *Address:* Kellie Castle, Arbroath, Angus. *Clubs:* Carlton, British Sportsmen's; New (Edinburgh).
[*Died* 11 *March* 1955.

RAMSAY, Major-Gen. Frank William, C.B. 1919; C.M.G. 1917; D.S.O. 1916; late Middlesex Regiment; *b.* Dec. 1875; *s.* of Brig.-Gen. W. A. Ramsay (late 4th Q.O. Hussars); *m.* 1929, Amy Frances, widow of Lieut.-Colonel A. St. Leger Glyn, Grenadier Guards, of Holbrook Hall, Sudbury, Suffolk. A.D.C. to the Governor of Madras, 1898-1900: 2nd in Command 2nd Mounted Infantry, 1907-1911; served S. Africa as Special Service Officer with Mounted Infantry, 1901-2 (Queen's medal 5 clasps); European War, France and Flanders, 1914-18, commanded 9th Kings, 1915-16, 48th (Irish) Bde., 1916-18 (Bt. Lt.-Col., Bt. Col., despatches seven times, C.B., C.M.G., D.S.O.); commanded 58th (London) Division, 1918-19; commanded 30th Division, 1919; commanded 6th Infantry Brigade, 1919-23; Quetta Infantry Brigade, 1925-29; retired pay, 1929; J.P. (1932), Suffolk. *Publication:* Polo Pony Training, with Hints on the Game, 1928. *Address:* Drinkstone Lodge, Bury St. Edmunds, Suffolk; Cattistock Cottage, Maiden Newton, Dorset. *Club:* United Service.
[*Died* 1 *Oct.* 1954.

RAMSAY, Graham Colville, C.I.E. 1937; O.B.E.; M.D.; D.T.M. and H.; *b.* 1889; *s.* of late A. W. Ramsay, Sleaford, Ayr; *m.* 1919, Muriel, *d.* of George Fulham; two *d.* *Educ.:* George Heriots School; Edinburgh University. M.B. Ch.B. 1912 (Medalist); M.D. 1924 (with Commendation); D.T.M. and H. (Eng.) with distinction, 1924; House Surgeon Edinburgh, Hartlepool and Birkenhead, 1912-14; served 1914-19 as Capt. R.A.M.C. in France, Mesopotamia, Hedjaz and Syria (despatches, O.B.E., Order of El Nahda); K.I.H. Gold Medal, 1931; carried out research on malaria in India. Was Principal India Br., Ross Inst., and Dep. Dir., Ross Inst. of Trop. Hygiene, London; retd., 1946; now settled in S.A. *Publications:* in medical journals, on malaria, yaws, hookworm disease and tropical hygene. *Recreations:* Natural history, fishing. *Address:* c/o Barclays Bank, D.C.O. P.O. Box 6, Sea Point, Cape Town, S.A. *Clubs:* Oriental; Bengal (Calcutta).
[*Died* 15 *May* 1959.

RAMSAY, Rev. Ivor Erskine St. Clair, M.A.; Dean of King's College, Cambridge, since Jan. 1949; Fellow since Nov. 1948; *b.* 1 Nov. 1902; *s.* of Alfred Alexander and Isabel Florence Ramsay, 10 Park Quadrant, Glasgow, W.; unmarried. *Educ.:* Ardvreck, Crieff; Uppingham, Rutland; Glasgow University; King's College, Cambridge; Cuddesdon College, Oxford. Asst. Curate, St. Paul's Cathedral, Dundee, 1925-31; Novice of the Community of the Resurrection, Mirfield, 1931-32; Chaplain of the Home of St. Francis, Dunfermline, Fife, 1932-33; Rector of St. John's Church, Jedburgh, Roxburghshire, 1933-36; Rector of Christ Church, Falkirk, with St. Mary's, Grangemouth, and St. Andrew's, Dunmore, Stirlingshire, 1936-44. Provost of St. Mary's Cathedral, Palmerston Place, Edinburgh, 1944-49. *Recreations:* travel, walking, art, and archæology. *Address:* King's College, Cambridge. *T.:* 4411. *Club:* Overseas League. [*Died* 22 *Jan.* 1956.

RAMSAY, James, C.M.G. 1951; O.B.E, 1946; *b.* 1905; *s.* of late William and Helen Margaret Ramsay; *m.* 1932, Edith Parmenter Tilly; one *s.* (and one *s.* decd.). *Educ.:* Whitehill School, Glasgow. Mem. Inst. of Accountants and Actuaries, Glasgow, 1928. Appointed General Manager of United Kingdom Commercial Corporation Ltd. (Portugal), 1941, and Chief Representative in Portugal, 1943. Admitted to Continental Partnership of Messrs. Barton, Mayhew & Co., Chartered Accountants, 1931, retired 1947. Director Cía Carris de Ferro de Lisboa, 1946; Chm. and General Manager of Cía de Ferro de Lisboa, 1949; resigned, 1950. Chm. Companhia Portuguesa de Radium Lda. Officer of the Ordem Militar de Cristo (Portugal), 1957. *Recreation:* golf. *Address:* Vivenda Fernando, Rua Algarve, 10, Estoril, Portugal. *T.:* Estoril 287. *Club:* Royal British (Lisbon).
[*Died* 11 *May* 1959.

RAMSAY, Sir J. Douglas, 11th Bt. of Bamff, *cr.* 1666; M.V.O. 1925; T.D., D.L., J.P., Co. of Perth; F.R.I.C.S., Chartered Surveyor; Hon. Col., late R.A., T.A.; raised 31st (Perth) Regt. Light A.A.R.A. Sept. 1939, with Batteries in Perth, Dundee, Aberdeen and Fife; late Scottish Horse; H.M. the King's Commissioner on the Balmoral Estates, 1919-1926; *b.* 19 Apr. 1878; *s.* of Sir J. H. Ramsay, 10th Bart., and Charlotte (*d.* 1904), *d.* of William Stewart of Ardvorlieh; *S.* father, 1925; *m.* 1908, Hope Anita Jane, *d.* of Lt.-Col. A. D. MacGregor of Verbeer House, Cullompton; one *s.* *Educ.:* Harrow; Trinity College, Cambridge. Served European War, 1914-1919; War of 1939-45 in A.A.R.A. Staff and Home Guard. *Recreations:* all out-of-door sports. *Heir:* *s.* Neis Alexander, *b.* 4 Oct. 1909. *Address:* Bamff, Alyth, Perthshire. *T.:* Alyth 82. *Clubs:* Caledonian, New (Edinburgh).
[*Died* 14 *March* 1959.

RAMSAY, Lieut.-Col. James Gordon, D.S.O. 1918; O.B.E.; late Queen's Own Cameron Highlanders; *b.* 1880; *y. s.* of late William Ramsay, of Bowland, Midlothian; *m.* 1924, Marian, *d.* of C. J. G. Nash-Leibrandt, of The Kloof, Langland Bay, Glamorganshire; one *s.* one *d.* Served S. Africa, 1901-2 (Queen's medal with five clasps); European War, 1914-18 (despatches, D.S.O., Croix de Guerre); War of 1939-45, re-employed as Lieut.-Col. Member of Royal Company of Archers (Queen's Body Guard for Scotland). *Address:* Farleyer, Aberfeldy, Perthshire. *Clubs:* United Service; New (Edinburgh). [*Died* 20 *Aug.* 1952.

RAMSAY, Mabel Lieda, M.D., F.R.C.S. (Edin.), D.P.H. (Cantab.), M.O.G.C., late Cons. Surgeon Gynæcologist City Hospital, Plymouth; late Consulting Surgeon, Public Dispensary; Consulting Obstetrician, the Three Town Maternity Home; late Cons. Obstetrician to Counties of Devon and Cornwall; Consulting Surgeon Gynæcologist, the Salvation Army Home; Past President Plymouth Medical Society; Past President Medical Women's Federation, Ex-Hon. Secretary; lecturer to Midwives for Plymouth Centre for Central Midwives Board; *b.* London; *d.* of Paymaster-in-Chief Andrew J. Ramsay, Royal Navy. *Educ.:* Edinburgh University; Leeds University; Manchester University; London Royal Free Hospital (School) of Medicine. Served Surgeon Women's Imperial Hospital Units at Antwerp and Cherbourg; Surgeon Salisbury Road Hospital, Plymouth; President, the Plymouth Medical Society, 1930-31; Hon. Treasurer, the Plymouth Panel Committee; late Hon. Secretary, Plymouth Local Medical Cttee.; Past President Plymouth Soroptimist Club. *Publications:* The Women's Imperial Service Unit, 1914-18; Sub-Arachnoid Hæmorrhage in a Child (B.M.J.); Hydatid Cysts of Liver-Empyema of Gall Bladder and Lung-Recovery (B.M.J.); Puerperal Sepsis, Sloughing Fibroid and subsequent Pregnancy, British Journal of Obstetrics and Gynæcology. *Recreations:* walking, swimming, motoring. *Address:* 4 Wentworth Villas, North Hill, Plymouth. *T.:* Plymouth 5572. *Club:* University Women's.
[*Died* 9 *May* 1954.

RAMSAY, Rt. Rev. Ronald Erskine, LL.D. (Bristol), M.A.; Chairman, Church of

England Pensions Board, 1936-49; *b.* 4 Nov. 1882; *s.* of Rev. Alexander Ramsay; *m.* Winifred Constance, *d.* of H. Partridge; two *s.* one *d.* *Educ.:* St. Edmund Hall, Oxford, second class theological honours; Wells Theological College. Curate of St. Paul's, Lozells, Birmingham, 1908-9; Warden of the Clifton College Mission, St. Agnes, Bristol, 1910-18; Chaplain to the Forces, 1916-17; Clerical Secretary, Bristol Board of Finance, 1918-27; Suffragan Bishop of Malmesbury, 1927-46; Vicar of All Saints, Bristol, 1927-35; Rector of Brinkworth, 1936-49; Archdeacon of Swindon, 1928-1947; Hon. Canon Bristol Cathedral, 1926; Hon. Chaplain to Bishop of Bristol, 1924-27; Examining Chaplain to Bishop of Llandaff, 1924-27. *Publication:* Editor Bristol Diocesan Review, 1922-27. *Recreations:* golf and tennis. *Address:* The Mansells, Minety, Wilts. *T.:* Minety 244. *Club:* National. [*Died* 26 *March* 1954.

RAMSAY, Thomas Bridgehill Wilson; *b.* 2 July 1887; *s.* of late A. W. Ramsay, Sleaford, Ayr. *Educ.:* Edinburgh University (M.A., LL.B.). Barrister-at-Law, Gray's Inn, 1910; Specialist in Privy Council Appeals; has been Secretary, Treasurer and Chairman of Indian Gymkhana Club; Past President and Past Chief of Scottish Clans Association of London; Past President of Gray's Inn Debating Society; Trustee, Elder and Session Clerk of St. Columba's Church, Pont Street, S.W.1; Treasurer and Convener Maintenance of the Ministry Fund of the Church of Scotland in England; life member of many Scottish Societies; M.P. (L.) Western Isles, 1929-31, (L. Nat.), 1931-35; contested Shettleston Division of Glasgow, 1922 and Western Isles, 1935. *Address:* 88 Ebury Street, S.W.1. *T.:* Sloane 7303; 10 King's Bench Walk, E.C.4. *T.:* Central 2775. [*Died* 20 *Oct.* 1956.

RAMSBOTTOM, Edmund Cecil, C.B.E. 1942 (O.B.E. 1929); *b.* 30 Sept. 1881; *s.* of Edmund and Jane Ramsbottom, Manchester; *m.* 1st, 1911, Annie Florence Sandon (*d.* 1956); two *d.*; 2nd, 1957, Dorothy Chipperfield. *Educ.:* Manchester Gram. School; London School of Economics. Entered Civil Service, 1899; Director of Statistics, Min. of Labour, 1929-45; Member of I.L.O. Committee of Statistical Experts, 1931-46; Member of Council, Royal Statistical Society, 1935-1940; British Government Delegate to various I.L.O. Conferences on Labour Statistics, and to Conf. of Brit. Commonwealth Statisticians, Ottawa, 1935; Member Advisory Cttee. on Nutrition, 1935-39; Member Economics Cttee. of Roy. Commn. on Population, 1944-49; Statistical Adviser, British Employers' Confederation, 1946-58, retd. *Publications:* statistical papers in Jls. of Royal Statistical Soc., and Manchester Statistical Soc. *Recreations:* golf and bridge. *Address:* 21 Sea Lane, Goring-by-Sea, Worthing, Sussex. *Club:* National Liberal. [*Died* 5 *Dec.* 1959.

RAMSDEN, 1st Baron, *cr.* 1945, of Birkenshaw; **Eugene Joseph Squire Hargreaves Ramsden,** 1st Bt., *cr.* 1938; Kt., *cr.* 1933; O.B.E.; J.P.; *b.* 2 Feb. 1883; *s.* of James Ramsden; *m.* 1919, Margaret, *d.* of F. E. Withey, *widow* of late Major George W. Farwell, U.S.A. *Educ.:* England, France, and Germany. Travelled extensively U.S.A., Europe, S. America, West Indies, China, Japan, etc.; contested Spen Valley, 1923; served European War, 1915-19 (despatches); M.P. (U.) Bradford North, 1924-29 and 1931-45; contested Bradford North, 1929; Chairman National Union of Conservative and Unionist Associations, 1938-39; Chairman National Executive Committee, 1938-1943; Chairman of Yorkshire Provincial Area, 1933-46; Pres. Nat. Union of Conservative and Unionist Assoc., 1951-52. Chairman U.K. Trade Mission to Poland, 1934; Chairman Departmental Committee on Education and Training of Overseas Students, 1933-34; Director, Lloyds Bank Ltd.; Chm., Crosthwaite Furnaces and Scriven Machine Tools, Ltd.; Underwriter at Lloyds. *Recreations:* sea-fishing, travel. *Address:* The Wheatleys, Gomersal, nr. Leeds. *T.A.:* Ramsden, Gomersal. *T.:* Cleckheaton 350. *Club:* Carlton. [*Died* 9 *Aug.* 1955 (*ext.*).

RAMSDEN, Brig. Sir Arthur Maxwell, Kt., *cr.* 1954; C.B. 1945; O.B.E. 1938; T.D.; D.L.; Royal Artillery, T.A.; *b.* 2 December 1894. Contested (C.) S. Leeds, 1945, Batley, 1949. D.L. for W. Riding of County of York, 1949. A.D.C. (Additional) to the King, 1940-51. *Address:* 4 Headingley Terrace, Leeds. *T.:* Leeds 52166. [*Died* 7 *Nov.* 1957.

RAMSDEN, Charles Frederick Ingram; retired; *b.* 4 May 1888; *o. s.* of Capt. F. W. Ramsden and Lady Maud (*née* Conyngham); *m.* 1922, Nathalia (*d.* 1945), *d.* of John Pykhatcheff. *Educ.:* Eton; New College, Oxford. Joined Diplomatic Service, 1910; retired as 3rd Secretary, 1919, after service in Spain, Persia, Roumania and Russia. Federation of British Industries, 1919-52, Overseas Director, 1929-52; retired 1952. *Publication:* French Bookbinders, 1789-1848, 1950; U.K. Bookbinders, 1953; London Bookbinders, 1956. *Address:* 11 Alexandra Court, 171 Queen's Gate, S.W.7. *T.:* Kensington 4332. *Club:* Pratt's. [*Died* 2 *April* 1958.

RAMSDEN, Sir John Frecheville, 6th Bt., *cr.* 1689; late Capt. Norfolk Yeomanry; *b.* 7 Jan. 1877; *s.* of 5th Bt. and Lady Helen Guendolen Ramsden (*d.* 1910), 3rd *d.* and *co-heiress* of 12th Duke of Somerset; *S.* father, 1914; *m.* 1901, Joan, *d.* of late G. F. Buxton, C.B.; one *s.* one *d.* *Educ.:* Eton; Trinity College, Cambridge. Owns about 620 acres. *Heir:* *s.* Geoffrey William Pennington, Major, Life Guards, (retired) [*b.* 28 Aug. 1904; assumed name and arms of Pennington by Deed Poll, 1925; *m.* 1927, Veronica Prudence Betty, *d.* of F. W. Morley, formerly of Biddestone Manor, Chippenham, Wilts; three *d.*]. *Address:* Forest Ridge, Sunninghill, Berks.; Ardverikie, Kingussie, Inverness-shire; Muncaster Castle, Ravenglass, Cumberland. *Club:* Royal Automobile. [*Died* 6 *Oct.* 1958.

RAMSDEN, Lieut.-Col. Josslyn Vere, C.M.G. 1919, D.S.O. 1915; M.A.; late Royal Artillery; *b.* 1 Dec. 1876; *s.* of John C. F. Ramsden, *g.-s.* of Sir J. Ramsden, 4th Bt., and Emma Susan, *d.* of Rev. Edward Duncombe; *m.* 1909, Olive Clotilde Bouhier, *o. d.* of F. W. Imbert Terry, late of Aston, Herts; one *s.* *Educ.:* Eton; New College, Oxford. Entered army, 1900; Captain, 1910; Adjutant, 1911-14; Major 1914; A.D.C. to Divisional Commander, India, 1908-9; served European War, 1914-18 (despatches twice, D.S.O., Bt. Lt.-Col., C.M.G.). *Address:* Offwell House, Honiton, Devon. *T.:* Wilmington 205. *Club:* Army and Navy. [*Died* 20 *July* 1952.

RAMSDEN-JODRELL, Dorothy Lynch, C.B.E. 1920; J.P. Derbyshire, 1937; *d.* of late Col. Sir E. T. D. Cotton-Jodrell, K.C.B., D.L., J.P.; *m.* 1902, Capt. H. Ramsden, R.A. (*d.* 1950), *s.* of late Capt. J. C. Ramsden, R.A.; assumed by Royal Licence additional name of Jodrell, 1920; three *d.* *Address:* Donhead Lodge, Shaftesbury, Dorset. *T.:* Donhead 264. [*Died* 24 *April* 1958.

RAMSEY, Arthur Stanley; President, 1915-37, Lecturer, 1897-1934, Tutor, 1912-27, Bursar 1904-13, Fellow since 1897 of Magdalene College, Cambridge; Member of the Financial Board of the University, 1912-34; University Lecturer in Mathematics, 1926-32; Examiner of the University of London, 1915-18, 1932-1934; Examiner of Queen's University, Belfast, 1942-44; *b.* Hackney, 1867; *e. s.* of Rev. A. Averell Ramsey, Congregational minister; *m.* 1902, Mary Agnes (*d.* 1927), *y. d.* of Rev. P. S. Wilson, Vicar of Horbling, Lincs; one *s.* two *d.*

(and one *s.* decd.). *Educ.:* Batley Grammar School; Magdalene Coll., Camb. Mathematical Master at Fettes College, Edinburgh, 1890-97. *Publications:* Modern Plane Geometry (Richardson and Ramsey); Hydromechanics (Besant and Ramsey); Hydrodynamics; Elementary Geometrical Optics; Dynamics; Statics; Hydrostatics; Electricity and Magnetism; Introduction to Newtonian Attraction. *Recreation:* gardening. *Address:* Howfield, Buckingham Road, Cambridge. *T.:* Cambridge 4729. [*Died* 31 *Dec.* 1954.

RANALOW, Frederick Baring, F.R.A.M.; professional singer, actor and teacher; Professor Royal Academy of Dramatic Art and Guildhall School of Music; *b.* Dublin, 7 Nov. 1873; *o. s.* of late J. G. Ranalow, Dublin; *m.* Lilian Mary, *d.* of late William E. Oates, of Gestingthorpe Hall, Essex; one *d.* *Educ.:* Westminster. Studied at the Royal Academy of Music; has sung at most of the principal Musical Festivals, including the Handel Festival, Norwich and Sheffield Festivals, and for several seasons for the Royal Choral Society Concerts at the Albert Hall; toured Australia and New Zealand with Melba; for many years a leading baritone in Sir Thomas Beecham's Opera Company, singing such rôles as Hans Sachs, Figaro, Falstaff, Papageno, King Mark, Capulet, Colline, etc., and creating such rôles as Ned Travers in Dr. Ethel Smyth's Bo'sun's Mate, Sir Walter Raleigh in Stanford's Critic, Mr. Pepys (Clifford Bax and Martin Shaw), Paragot in the Beloved Vagabond (Adrian Ross and Dudley Glass), and re-creating the part of Captain Macheath in the Beggar's Opera, a rôle he has played over 1600 times; also played Herr Feldmann in Autumn Crocus and Sir Lucius O'Trigger in a musical version of The Rivals; created the part of W. Gill, the Victorian father in The Two Bouquets; Father Christmas in The Land of the Christmas Stocking, 1945-46 (Duke of York's); appeared in several films, including Drake, Autumn Crocus, Who's Your Lady Friend, Uncle Silas. *Recreation:* golf. *Address:* 215 Cromwell Rd., S.W.5. *T.:* Frobisher 2774. *Club:* Garrick. [*Died* 8 *Dec.* 1953.

RANDALL, Group Captain Charles Russell Jekyl, C.B.E. 1919; R.A.F. (retd.); *b.* 12 Sept. 1879; *s.* of late Lieut.-Colonel R. H. Randall, Vauxlaurens, Guernsey; unmarried. *Educ.:* Elizabeth College, Guernsey; Lancing College. Entered R.N.E. College, 1896; Royal Naval College, Greenwich, 1901-4; appointed to No. 1 Naval Airship, 1911; appointed R.N. Aeroplane School, Eastchurch; Pilot's Certificate, Feb. 1912 (No. 182); Instructor Central Flying School, Upavon, 1912-13 (thanks of Army Council twice); Member of Airship Subcommittee of Committee of Imperial Defence, 1914; Admiralty Overseer in Charge of No. 9 Rigid Airship Building; special Service in France at outbreak of War (thanks of Army Council and appreciation of Lords Commissioners of Admiralty); Admiralty Deputy Superintending Captain Aircraft building, 1915-16; Air Board, 1917; O.C. Malta Group R.A.F., 1918; Lent to Greek Govt. for reorganisation of R.H.N.A.S., 1919; retired, 1923; Chevalier Legion of Honour, Chevalier of Order of Redeemer, Greek Order of Military Merit 2nd Class with Silver Palms; entered Cambridge University, Michaelmas Term, 1931; elected fellow Commoner, Downing College, Oct. 1931. During War of 1939-45 deported from Guernsey to Germany, returned March 1945. *Recreations:* polo, fencing, skating, golf. *Address:* Grange Cottage, Guernsey. *T.:* Guernsey 577. *Club:* Royal Air Force. [*Died* 5 *June* 1956.

RANDALL, J(ames) G(arfield); Professor of History (Emeritus), University of Illinois, since 1949; *b.* Indianapolis, Indiana, 24 June 1881; *s.* of Horace Randall and Ellen Kregelo; *m.* 1st, 1911, Edith Laura Abbott (*d.* 1913), Chicago; 2nd, 1917, Ruth Elaine Painter, Salem, Va.; no *c.* *Educ.:* Indianapolis Public Schools; Butler College; University of Chicago. Ph.D. in History, Chicago, 1911. Litt.D. Washington and Lee University, 1948; LL.D. Butler Univ., 1948. College teaching positions in history at Illinois Coll. (Jacksonville, Ill.), 1907-8; Univ. of Michigan, 1908-9; Syracuse Univ., 1910-11; Butler Coll., 1911-12; Roanok, Coll. (Salem, Va.), 1912-18; Richmond Coll. (Richmond, Va.), 1919-20; Univ. of Illinois since 1920. Special Expert, U.S. Shipping Board, 1918-19. Pres., Miss. Vall. Hist. Assoc., 1939-40. Pres., Illinois State Historical Soc., 1945-46. Pres. Amer. Historical Assoc., 1951-52. *Publications:* Constitutional Problems under Lincoln, 1926; co-editor of Diary of Orville H. Browning, 1927-33; The Civil War and Reconstruction, 1937; co-editor, Democracy in the Middle West, 1941; Lincoln the President, 2 vols., 1945; Lincoln and the South, 1946; Lincoln the Liberal Statesman, 1947; Lincoln the President: Midstream, 1952; Lincoln the President: Last Full Measure (completed by Prof. Richard N. Current), 1956; Abraham Lincoln in Dictionary of American Biography. Contributor to learned journals. *Address:* 1101 West Oregon St., Urbana, Ill., U.S.A. *T.:* Urbana Ill., 7-2123. *Club:* University (Urbana). [*Died* 20 *Feb.* 1953.

RANDELL, Wilfrid L.; Consulting Editor; *b.* 1874; *m.* (wife *d.* 1949); one *d.* Actg. Ed. of Academy and Literature, 1910-1915; Asst. Ed., Review of Reviews, 1922-23; Ed.-in-Chief, Electrical Press, 1925-35. *Publications:* a book of railway stories and one novel; handbooks on Clocks and Watches; Michael Faraday, Dr. Ferranti, Col. Crompton (biographies); Conveying the World's Messages; The Romance of Electricity; Messengers for Mankind; contributor to Ency. Brit., D.N.B., Times, Fortnightly, North American Review, Spectator, Punch, Chambers' Journal and many other papers. *Address:* 12 Trewsbury Road, Sydenham, S.E. *T.:* Sydenham 7542. *Club:* Press. [*Died* 5 *May* 1952.

RANDOLPH, Lieut.-Col. Algernon Forbes, C.M.G. 1919; D.S.O. 1917; D.L. Sussex; retired pay; *b.* 1865; *s.* of late Rev. Canon E. J. Randolph; *m.* 1912, Constance Mary (*d.* 1930), *sister* of Sir G. A. A. L. St. J. Mildmay, 7th Bart., and *widow* of J. A. B. Wallington. *Educ.:* Charterhouse; R.M.C., Sandhurst. Served European War, 1914-17 (despatches, C.M.G., D.S.O.). *Address:* Heathcote, Worthing, Sussex. *T.:* Worthing 687. *Club:* Army and Navy. [*Died* 7 *Feb.* 1953.

RANDOLPH, George Boscawen, O.B.E.; J.P. Oxfordshire; High Sheriff, 1924-25; C.C. Chairman of Oxfordshire Education Committee; *b.* 28 Oct. 1864; *s.* of late Rev. Leveson Cyril Randolph and Hon. Mrs. Randolph, *sister* of Viscount Falmouth; unmarried. *Educ.:* Marlborough. *Address:* Steeple Aston, Oxfordshire. *T.A.:* Steeple Aston. [*Died* 20 *Feb.* 1951.

RANK, James Voase; Chairman Ranks Ltd. and Joseph Rank Ltd. since 1943; Director, Imported Cereals Div. of Ministry of Food; *b.* 10 May 1881; *e. s.* of late Joseph and Emily Rank; *m.;* one *d.* *Educ.:* Hymers College, Hull. *Recreations:* racing, coursing, golfing. *Address:* Ouborough, Godstone, Surrey. *T.A.:* Ouborough, Godstone. *T.:* Godstone 358. *Club:* Bath. [*Died* 3 *Jan.* 1952.

RANKEILLOUR, 2nd Baron, *cr.* 1932, of Buxted; **Arthur Oswald James Hope;** G.C.I.E., *cr.* 1939; M.C.; *b.* 7 May 1897; *e. s.* of 1st Baron Rankeillour, P.C., and Mabel Ellen, O.B.E. (*d.* 1938), *d.* of late Francis Riddell of Cheeseburn Grange, Northumberland; *S.* father, 1949; *m.* 1919, Grizel (Kaiser-i-Hind Gold Medal, C.St.J.), *y. d.* of late Brig.-Gen. Sir R. Gordon Gilmour, 1st Bt., C.B., C.V.O., D.S.O.; four *d.* *Educ.:* Oratory School; Sandhurst. Joined Coldstream Guards, 1914; served in France, 1915-19 (M.C., Croix de Guerre, despatches, severely wounded); served in Turkey, 1922-1923; M.P. (C.) Nuneaton Division of Warwickshire, 1924-29; M.P. (U.) Aston Division, Birmingham, 1931-39; Parliamentary Private Secretary to Col. G. R. Lane Fox, Secretary of Mines, 1924-26; Assistant Whip (unpaid), 1935; a Lord of the Treasury (unpaid), 1935-37; Vice-Chamberlain of H.M. Household, May-October 1937; Treasurer of H.M. Household, 1937-39; Governor of Madras, 1940-46. *Recreations:* hunting, shooting, cricket. *Heir: b.* Lt.-Col. Hon. Henry John Hope [*b.* 20 Jan. 1899; *m.* 1933, Mary Sibyl, *yr. d.* of late Lt.-Col. Wilfrid Ricardo, D.S.O.; one *s.* one *d.* Scots Guards, retd.]. *Address:* Meriden Court, Chelsea Manor St., S.W.3. [*Died* 26 *May* 1958.

RANKIN, Lieut.-Colonel Allan Coats, C.M.G. 1919; M.D., C.M., D.P.H., LL.D. (Alta.); F.R.C.P. (Can.); R.C.A.M.C.; Professor Emeritus of Bacteriology, University of Alberta; *b.* Montreal, Canada, 1877; *s.* of late John and Louise Sophia Rankin of Montreal; *m.* 1926, Florence Caroline West; no *c.* *Educ.:* Private Schools; Montreal High School; McGill University, M.D., C.M., 1904; D.P.H. (McGill) 1909; Assistant Bacteriologist, Royal Victoria Hospital, Montreal, 1907-9; Assistant Medical Officer of Health (Bacteriologist) Ministry of Local Government, Bangkok, Siam, 1909-14; Prof. of Bacteriology and Hygiene, Univ. of Alberta, 1914-45; Dean of the Faculty of Medicine, 1921-45; Provincial Bacteriologist, Province of Alta., 1914-45; served with C.A.M.C. European War, 1914-19 (despatches twice, C.M.G.) and as A.D.M.S., A.M.D.5, Hygiene, Ottawa, R.C.A.M.C. 1939-43 in War of 1939-45. *Publications:* various professional articles. *Address:* 9005 112th Street, Edmonton, Alberta, Canada. *Clubs:* Royal Societies; University (Montreal). [*Died* 27 *May* 1959.

RANKIN, Archibald Aloysius, C.B.E. 1938; Pres. Royal Newcastle Hosp. from 1914; Pres. Newcastle Aero Club; *b.* 24 Nov. 1871; 2nd *s.* of Angus Rankin and Catherine Jane MacDonald, Bombowlee, Tumut, N.S.W.: *m.* 1910, Vera de Lauret, *d.* of Edward Percy Simpson, Solicitor, Sydney; two *s.* two *d.* *Educ.:* St. Ignatius College, Riverview, Sydney. Solicitor practising in Newcastle from 1899. *Clubs:* Newcastle (Newcastle, N.S.W.); Union (Sydney). [*Died* 9 *Oct.* 1951.

RANKIN, Ethel Mary, J.P.; Member of London County Council since 1949 (Vice-Chm. 1955); *b.* 28 Aug. 1893; *m.* 1917; one *s.* *Educ.:* Braintree, Essex. Member Fulham Borough Council, 1934-49; Member Central Health Services Council. J.P. Co. London, 1945-; Freeman Borough of Fulham, 1955. *Recreations:* camping, foreign travel. *Address:* 19 Burnfoot Avenue, Fulham, S.W.6. *T.:* Renown 3775. [*Died* 5 *Dec.* 1956.

RANKIN, James Stuart; 2nd *s.* of late John Rankin, St. Michael's Hamlet, Liverpool. *Educ.:* Sedbergh; University College, Oxford. Captain, R.F.A., B.E.F. and Mesopotamia Expeditionary Force. M.P. (U.) East Toxteth Division of Liverpool, 1916-24. *Address:* 10 Lord North Street, Westminster, S.W.1. [*Died* 20 *Oct.* 1960.

RANKIN, John Elliott; Ex-Member Congress, House of Representatives; *b.* Itawamba County, Miss., 29 March 1882; *s.* of Thomas Braxton Rankin and Venola Modest (*née* Rutledge); *m.* 1919, Annie Laurie Burrous; one *d.* *Educ.:* Common Schools and High School and Univ. of Mississippi. LL.B. Univ. of Miss., 1910; started Practice of Law at West Point, Miss., 1910; moved to Tupelo, Miss., 1910 (served 4 years as Prosecuting Attorney): served European War, 1914-18; Member of Methodist Episcopal Church South, Masonic Fraternity, and several other orders; nominated in Democratic primaries, 1920, and elected to 67th Congress as representative from First District of Mississippi, renominated and re-elected to 68th, 69th, 70th, 71st. 72nd, 73rd, 74th, 75th, 76th, 77th 78th, 80th, 81st, and 82nd Congresses; delegate to Democratic National Conventions, 1932, 1936 and 1940; one of leaders of the House for Administration Power Policies, and was Co-author with Senator George W. Norris, Nebraska, of bill to create Tennessee Valley Authority; succeeded in getting every county in his district connected up with T.V.A. and supplied electric energy from T.V.A. at "yardstick" rates, serving tens of thousands of farm homes with cheap electricity; Chm. of Public Power Bloc in House and has led fight for rural electrification (known as Father of rural electrification); Chairman House Cttee. on World War Veterans' Legislation (20 years); author of amendment to raise base pay of men in armed forces to $50 a month, author of amendment to Rules of the House creating permanent Cttee. on Un-American Activities. *Address:* Tupelo, Mississippi, U.S.A. [*Died* 26 *Nov.* 1960.

RANKIN, Rev. Professor Oliver Shaw, M.A., B.D., D.Litt. (Edin.), D.D. (Glasg.); Professor of Old Testament Language, Literature and Theology in Edinburgh University since 1937; *b.* 28 Jan. 1885; *s.* of late Rev. Robert Rankin, B.D., Lamington, Lanarkshire; *m.* 1912, Olivia Teresa, *d.* of late Charles Martin Shaw; two *s.* one *d.* *Educ.:* John Watson's Institution, Edinburgh; George Watson's College, Edinburgh; The Universities of Edinburgh and Berlin. Vans Dunlop Schol. in Hebrew, Arabic and Syriac, 1908. Parish Minister of Sorbie, 1912-37. Visiting Lecturer in Hebrew and Old Testament Studies in United Theological College, Montreal, 1931; Kerr Lecturer, Trinity College, Glasgow, 1933-36. C.F., 1918-20. *Publications:* The Origins of the Festival of Hanukkah, 1930; Israel's Wisdom Literature: its bearing on Theology and the History of Religion, 1936. Articles in A Theological Word Book of the Bible, 1950; also in Jl. of Jewish Studies, Hibbert Jl., Zeitschrift für Alttestamentliche Wissenschaft, Transactions of Glasgow Oriental Soc. *Address:* 7 Mayfield Terrace, Edinburgh. *T.:* 41325. [*Died* 7 *Feb.* 1954.

RANKIN, Sir Robert, 1st Bt., *cr.* 1937; *b.* 18 Oct. 1877; *er. s.* of late John Rankin, St. Michael's Hamlet, Liverpool; *m.* 1st, 1907, Renee Helen Mary (*d.* 1932), *o. d.* of late James Edmund Baker, Teheran, Persia; two *d.*; 2nd, 1940, Rachel Dupin, *d.* of Charles Dupin Drayson, Melton Court, S.W. *Educ.:* Sedbergh; Clare College, Cambridge. M.P. (U.) Kirkdale Div. of Liverpool, 1931-45; Pres., Lonsdale Unionist Division, 1937-47. Enlisted 1914 in 18th Royal Fusiliers (Public School Brigade); later Capt. R.A.S.C., H.T.; Vice-Pres.: Royal Commonwealth Society; Air League of the British Empire; Liverpool School of Tropical Medicine. J.P. Lancs., 1923-47; High Sheriff of Lancashire, 1948-49. *Address:* 82 North Gate, Regent's Park, N.W.8. *T.:* Primrose 5938. *Clubs:* Athenæum, Oxford and Cambridge, Carlton, Lansdowne. [*Died* 11 *Oct.* 1960 (*ext.*).

RANKIN, Thomas, O.B.E. 1919; Hon. Surgeon Dentist to the Queen in Scotland since 1953; *b.* 1884; *s.* of James Deans Rankin, cork merchant; *m.* 1913, Grace Barr Cooper; two *s.* one *d.* *Educ.:* St. John's, Hamilton; Anderson's Medical College; St. Mungo's Medical College, Glasgow. L.D.S., R.F.P.S. Glasgow. Served European War, 1914-18, as Dental Surgeon; Inspector of Dental Services, Aldershot Command, 1917; retired with rank of Major. Dep. Dir. of Medical Services (Dental), Ministry of Pensions, 1921-26; Pres. West of Scotland Branch, British Dental Assoc., 1929; Chm.

Public Dental Service Assoc. of Gt. Britain, 1939-42; Consultant Dental Surgeon, Plastic and Maxillo-Facial Injuries unit, Ballochmyle and Bangour E.M.S. Hosps., 1939-53. Town Councillor, 1937; Hon. Treas. 1941; F.D.S., R.C.S. Edin. 1951. *Address:* Auchingramont, Hamilton, Lanarkshire. *T.:* Hamilton 115. *Club:* Scottish Conservative (Edinburgh). [*Died* 2 *April* 1959.

RANKINE, Alexander Oliver, O.B.E. 1919; F.R.S. 1934; D.Sc. (Lond.); *b.* 1881; *s.* of late Rev. John Rankine, Guildford; *m.* 1907, Ruby Irene, *d.* of Samuel Short, Reading; two *s.* two *d.* *Educ.:* Royal Grammar School, Guildford; University College, London. B.Sc. (Lond.) 1904; D.Sc. 1910; Fellow of University College, London, 1912; Assistant in Department of Physics, University College, London, 1904-19; Chief Research Assistant, Admiralty Experimental Station, Harwich, 1917-18; Professor of Physics, Imperial College of Science and Technology, South Kensington, 1919-37, now Emeritus Prof.; Chief Physicist to the Anglo-Iranian Oil Co., Ltd., 1937-47; Recorder of Section A of British Assoc., 1921-24; Hon. Sec. of Physical Soc., 1923-29; Dir. of Dept. of Technical Optics, Imperial College, 1925-31; Hon. Secretary of Institute of Physics, 1926-31; President of the Optical Society, 1931-32; President, Section A, British Association, 1932; Pres. of the Physical Society, 1932-34; seconded for special work with Petroleum Warfare Department, 1942-45; Secretary of the Royal Institution of Great Britain, 1945-52. *Publications:* about sixty papers in various scientific journals, principally on the dimensions of gaseous molecules, the transmission of speech by light, and applied geophysics. *Address:* 14 Oak Avenue, Hampton, Middlesex. *T.:* Molesey 2494. [*Died* 20 *Jan.* 1956.

RANSOM, Rear-Admiral (S) Alfred Charles, C.B.E. 1925; *b.* 22 Aug. 1871; *y. s.* of C. Bayly Ransom. *Educ.:* Bedford. Entered R.N., assistant clerk, 1888; Paymaster Captain, 1923; retired Paymaster Rear-Admiral, 1926; served Gambia Expedition, 1894 (W. African medal); China, Boxer Rising, 1900 (China medal); European War, H.M.S. Dreadnought, Grand Fleet, Aug. 1914-16; Admiralty Cttee. on Accountant Branch, 1919-20. *Recreation:* golf. *Address:* Lincot, 82 Ilsham Road, Torquay. [*Died* 28 *June* 1953.

RANSOM, Herbert Charles, C.B.E. 1938 (O.B.E. 1923); late Head of Stores Dept., Crown Agents for the Colonies; *b.* 6 Aug. 1881; *s.* of George Ransom: *m.* 1909, Mabel Gertrude, *d.* of Andrew Crosby; two *d.* Entered Crown Agent's Office, 1901; retired 1945; Secretary Palestine Currency Board, 1926-30. *Recreations:* golf and literature. *Address:* Rydens, Mount Hermon Road, Woking. *T.:* Woking 1245. *Club:* Worplesdon Golf (Woking). [*Died* 9 *March* 1960.

RAPER, Professor Henry Stanley, C.B.E. 1919; F.R.S. 1929; F.R.C.P. 1938; Hon. LL.D. (Leeds) 1943; D.Sc., M.B., Ch.B.; Dean of the Medical School and Professor of Chemical Physiology, University of Manchester since 1946; 5th *s.* of James R. Raper, Bradford, Yorkshire, and Sarah Ann, *d.* of James Tankard; *m.* 1911, Edith, *d.* of Wright Rhodes, Allerton, Bradford; two *s.* *Educ.:* Technical College, Bradford; University of Leeds; Akroyd Scholar in 1902 and University Scholar in 1903; awarded an 1851 Exhibition Scholarship in 1904, and spent the ensuing three years in research work at the Lister Institute, London, and the University of Strassburg; medical education completed at the School of Medicine, Leeds, in 1910; Lecturer in Pathological Chemistry at the University of Toronto, 1910-13; Lecturer in Physiological Chemistry, and later Professor of Physiology and Biochemistry, at the Univ. of Leeds, 1913-23; Professor of Physiology, Univ. of Manchester, 1923-46. Member of Medical Research Council, 1933-39; War service, 1916-19; Lieut. R.A.M.C., 1916; Major R.A.M.C., 1917; Lt.-Col. R.E., 1918; O.C. R.E. Anti-Gas Establishment, 1918. *Publications:* (with J. B. Leathes, *q.v.*) The Fats; numerous papers in scientific journals on physiological and biochemical subjects. *Address:* The University, Manchester. [*Died* 12 *Dec.* 1951.

RAPER, Sir John Hugh Francis, Kt., *cr.* 1942; late Member, Transportation, Railway Dept. (Railway Board), Govt. of India; *b.* 23 Sept. 1889. Joined Indian State Railways, 1912. [*Died* 23 *Jan.* 1955.

RASCH, Brig. Guy Elland Carne, C.V.O. 1936; D.S.O. 1915; Gentleman Usher to the Queen since 1952 (to King George VI, 1938-52); *s.* of Sir Frederic Carne Rasch, 1st Bt., of Woodhill, Danbury, Essex; *b.* and *heir-pres.* to 2nd Bt.; *m.* 1916, Phyllis Dorothy Lindsay, *d.* of late Hon. Alwyn Greville, C.V.O.; two *s.* Entered army, 1905; Adjutant, 1912; Captain, 1914; Bt.-Major, 1919; Major, 1920; Lt.-Col., 1928; Col., 1932; served European War, 1914-18 (despatches, D.S.O., Croix de Guerre); Officer Commanding Grenadier Guards Regt. and Regimental District, 1932-37; retired pay, 1938; served War of 1939-45, 1939-44 (despatches). Extra Equerry to Duke of Connaught, 1938-1942. High Sheriff and D.L., Wilts., 1952. *Address:* 27 Swan Court, S.W.3. *T.:* Flaxman 1668; Avon Cottage, Lower Woodford, Salisbury, Wilts. *T.:* Middle Woodford 238. *Clubs:* Guards, Turf. [*Died* 3 *Sept.* 1955.

RASHLEIGH, Sir Colman Battie Walpole, 4th Bt., *cr.* 1831; *b.* 17 Nov. 1873; *e. s.* of 3rd Bt., and 1st wife, Geraldine, *d.* of Lieut.-Gen. Sir Robert Walpole; *S.* father, 1907. *Heir: kinsman* Harry Evelyn Battie, *b.* 17 May 1923. *Address:* Polmear, Tywardreath, Cornwall. [*Died* 22 *Feb.* 1951.

RATCLIFFE, Samuel Kerkham; Journalist and Lecturer, England and U.S.A.; *b.* 1868; *m.* K. M. Jeeves; one *s.* two *d.* Editor of The Echo, 1900; Acting Editor of The Statesman, Calcutta, 1903-6; of the Sociological Review, 1910-17; Lecturer, Bromley Foundation, Yale, 1926; Peterson Lecturer, New York City, 1939; Conway memorial lecturer, 1946. *Publications:* Sir William Wedderburn and the Indian Reform Movement, 1923; The Story of South Place, 1955; frequent articles in monthly reviews. *Address:* 1A Oakwood Road, N.W.11. *T.:* Meadway 2640. *Club:* National Liberal. [*Died* 1 *Sept.* 1958.

RATHDONNELL, 4th Baron (*cr.* 1868), **William Robert McClintock-Bunbury,** M.C. 1945; Major, 15th/19th Hussars; *b.* 23 Nov. 1914; *o. s.* of 3rd Baron and Ethel Synge (*d.* 1922), 2nd *d.* of late Robert Wilson Ievers, C.M.G.; *S.* father, 1937; *m.* 1937, Pamela (3rd Officer W.R.N.S.), *e. d.* of late John M. Drew and Mrs. Drew, Eversley, Milnthorpe, Westmorland; one *s.* three *d.* (and one *d.* decd.). *Educ.:* Charterhouse; Trinity College, Cambridge (B.A.). Served War of 1939-45 (M.C.). *Recreations:* hunting, shooting, racing. *Heir: s.* Hon. Thomas Benjamin McClintock Bunbury, *b.* 17 Sept. 1938. *Address:* Lisnavagh, Rathvilly, Co. Carlow. *T.:* Rathvilly 4. *Clubs:* Cavalry; Kildare Street (Dublin). [*Died* 13 *Oct.* 1959.

RATSEY, Col. Harold Edward, C.B.E. 1919; D.S.O. 1918; Naval Architect and Engineer, retired; *b.* 1861; *s.* of Michael Edward Ratsey, Cowes, Isle of Wight; *m.* 1922, Iris Warde Cox; two *s.* Served European War, 1914-19; Mesopotamia, 1916-19 (despatches five times, D.S.O., C.B.E.). *Address:* Knellstone House, Udimore, nr. Rye, Sussex. [*Died* 4 *Feb.* 1953.

RATTIGAN, (William) Frank (Arthur), C.M.G. 1920; *b.* 11 April 1879; *s.* of Sir William Rattigan, K.C., M.P.; *m.*; two *s.* *Educ.:* Harrow; Magdalen College, Oxford.

Passed into Diplomatic Service, March 1903; Attaché to Vienna, 1904; 3rd Secretary, 1905; 2nd Sec., 1909; served European War, 1914 (Mons Star, Allied and Roumanian War Medals); 1st Sec., 1916; Councillor of Embassy, 1920; Chargé d'Affaires in Roumania, 1919-20; Assistant High Commissioner, Constantinople; Acting High Comr. at Constantinople, May 1921; resigned from Diplomatic Service, 1922; a Gold Staff Officer at the Coronation of King George V (Coronation medal), and at the Coronation of King George VI (Coronation medal). *Publication:* Diversions of a Diplomat, 1924. *Recreations:* shooting, cricket, rackets, tennis, fishing. *Address:* 19 Stanhope Gardens, S.W.7. *Clubs:* Bath, M.C.C. [*Died* 9 *March* 1952.

RATWATTE, Sir Jayatilaka Cudah, Kt., *cr.* 1939; Member State Council, Ceylon. *Address:* Colombo, Ceylon. [*Died* 15 *March* 1940.

[*But death not notified in time for inclusion in Who Was Who 1929–1940.*

RAU, Sir Narsing, Kt., *cr.* 1938; C.I.E. 1934; Constitutional Adviser to the Constituent Assembly of India, 1946; *b.* 26 Feb. 1887; *s.* of Benegal Raghavendra Rau. *Educ.:* Presidency College, Madras; Trinity College, Cambridge. Indian Civil Service, 1910; Officiating Judge, Calcutta High Court, 1935; Puisine Judge, High Court of Judicature, Bengal, 1938-44; on special duty with Government of India for the revision of the Indian Statute Book, 1935; Chairman, Hindu Law Cttee., 1941; Indus Waters Commn., 1941-42; Member Indian Deleg. to U.N., 1948; Permanent Rep. of India to the United Nations, 1949; Leader, India Deleg. to 5th Session of Gen. Assembly of U.N., 1950-51; India's Rep. on Security Council, 1950-. *Recreations:* tennis, golf. *Address:* 3 East 64th Street, New York 21, N.Y., U.S.A. *Clubs:* National Liberal; Calcutta (Calcutta). [*Died* 29 *Nov.* 1953.

RAVEN, Edward, C.B. 1919; *b.* Greenwich, 10 Mar. 1874; *s.* of Frederick Edward Raven, Secretary Royal Naval College, Greenwich; *m.* 1st, 1903, Mary Elizabeth (*d.* 1932), *d.* of late Dr. E. R. B. Reynolds; three *d.*; 2nd, 1939, Mary Geraldine, *widow* of late Leonard Pailthorpe. *Educ.:* University College, London. Passed Open Competition for Upper Division Civil Service, 1896; entered Secretary's Office G.P.O., 1896; Second Secretary General Post Office, 1919-34. *Address:* The Spinney, Horsham Road, Cranleigh, Surrey. *T.:* Cranleigh 151. [*Died* 25 *May* 1952.

RAVEN, Rev. Edward Earle, M.A.; Dean of St. John's College, Cambridge, since 1927; *b.* 27 Dec. 1889; *s.* of John E. Raven, barrister-at-law; *m.* 1930, Esther Margaret, *o. d.* of William C. Brooks, Blackheath; one *s.* three *d.* *Educ.:* Uppingham; St. John's College, Cambridge (Scholar). Ordained, 1914; Army Chaplain, 1917-1918; Head of Maurice Hostel, Hoxton (St. John's College, Cambridge, Mission), 1918-1925; Chaplain St. John's College, Cambridge, 1921-1926; Fellow, 1923; Examining Chaplain to Bishop of Wakefield, 1924-28; Canon Theologian of Liverpool, 1930-35. *Publication:* The Heart of Christ's Religion, 1933. *Recreation:* cricket. *Address:* St. John's College, Cambridge; 255 Hills Rd., Cambridge. *T.:* Cambridge 5052 and 87485. [*Died* 2 *Dec.* 1951.

RAVENSHEAR, Ewart Watson, C.B. 1951; O.B.E. 1933; M.A. (Cantab.), B.Sc. (Lond.); *b.* 23 April 1893; *o. s.* of Albert Francis and Mary Watson Ravenshear, Dulwich, S.E.21; *m.* 1924, Mary Elizabeth, *yr. d.* of Alfred Herbert and Annie Louise Dykes, Shortlands, Kent; three *s.* *Educ.:* Dulwich Coll.; Clare Coll., Cambridge (1912-14 and 1919-20). Open Scholarship, Clare Coll, 1912; 1st class Pt. I Nat. Sci. Tripos, 1914. Served European War, 1914-19, Major, Royal Berkshire Regt. (despatches twice). 1st class Hons. B.Sc. London, 1919, 1st class Pt. II Nat. Sci. Tripos, 1920, Geology; Harkness Scholarship, Cambridge, 1920. Entered First Division Civil Service, 1920; H.M. Treasury, 1920-23; Mines Department, 1923-42. Ministry of Fuel and Power, 1942-54, and part-time, after retirement, 1954-58. Secretary Miners' Welfare Cttee., 1923-32; Secretary, Royal Commission on Safety in Coal Mines, 1935-38. *Recreation:* philately. *Address:* The Old School House, Poundgate, Crowborough, Sussex. *T.:* Crowborough 3304. [*Died* 26 *Oct.* 1959.

RAVERAT, Gwendolen Mary, (Mrs. G. Raverat), R.E. 1934; Member Society of Wood Engravers; *b.* 1885; *d.* of late Sir George Darwin, K.C.B., Plumian Professor at Cambridge; *m.* 1911, late Jacques Raverat; two *d.* *Educ.:* Slade School. *Publication:* Period Piece, 1952. *Address:* The Old Granary, Silver Street, Cambridge. *T.:* Cambridge 56178. [*Died* 11 *Feb.* 1957.

RAWDON SMITH, Edward Rawdon, O.B.E. 1919; M.A.; Public Relations Counsel, English Electric Group of Companies, since 1949; Director, Editorial Services Ltd., and New Scientist; *b.* 2 July 1890; *y. s.* of late F. Rawdon Smith, J.P., Ironbridge, Shropshire, and late Beatrice, *y. d.* of late George Melly, M.P., Liverpool; *m.* 1915, Agnes (*d.* 1957), *y. d.* of late Dr. John Grindal Brayton, Hindley, Lancs. *Educ.:* St. Edward's School, Oxford; The Sorbonne, Paris; Queen's College, Oxford. Called to Bar, Inner Temple, 1912; served with Rifle Brigade at home and abroad, 1914-16; Court Martial Officer, 1916; War Office, 1917; Asst. Secretary, Min. of National Service, 1917-18; Secretary to Labour Supply Sub-Cttee. of War Cabinet, 1918; Company Secretary, 1919-26; held various positions in Underground Group of Companies, 1926-33; London Passenger Transport Board: Asst. Secy., 1933; Public Relations Officer, 1934-39; Public Relations Director, British Overseas Airways Corp., 1939-43; Director of Public Relations, Dominions Office, 1940-42; Director, Empire Division, Ministry of Information, 1942-43; Public Relations Counsel to Edmundson's Electricity Corporation, 1944-1948; to Electricity Supply Cos. 1946-47. Médaille d'Or d'Education Physique, 1930; Fellow of Chartered Institute of Secretaries, 1931; Fellow of Inst. of Public Relations, 1949; served on several Government Departments' Publicity Advisory Committees; Vice-Chairman, London Hostels Association; Chairman of S.O.S. Society since inauguration in 1929; St. Marylebone Conservative Assoc., Vice-Chm., 1946-48; Chm., 1949; Member St. Marylebone Borough Council, 1949-53. *Recreations:* gardening, travelling. *Address:* John o' Gaddesden's House, Little Gaddesden, Herts. *T.:* Little Gaddesden 2144. *Clubs:* Athenæum, Pratt's. [*Died* 7 *Dec.* 1957.

RAWLING, Ven. John, B.A.; Archdeacon Emeritus; *b.* 20 Mar. 1869; *m.* 1902, Adrienne Loudon Wood; one *s.* one *d.* (and one *s.* killed, War of 1939-45). *Educ.:* S. Bees School; Queen's College, Oxford. Curate of S. Mary, Huntingdon; Rector of Wilcannia, N.S.W.; Urana, N.S.W.; Narrandera, N.S.W. *Address:* Narrandera, N.S.W., Australia. [*Died* 8 *Oct.* 1955.

RAWLINGS, Marjorie Kinnan; Writer and Citrus Grower; *b.* Washington, D.C., 8 Aug. 1896; *d.* of Arthur F. Kinnan and Ida M. Traphagen; *m.* 1919, Charles A. Rawlings (divorced, 1933); *m.* 1941, Norton Sanford Baskin; no *c.* *Educ.:* University of Wisconsin. *Publications:* South Moon Under, 1933; Golden Apples, 1935; The Yearling, 1938; When the Whippoorwill, 1940; Cross Creek, 1942; Cross Creek Cookery, 1942; The Sojourner, 1953; short stories and verses in magazines and anthologies. *Recreations:* fishing, hunting, cooking. *Address:* Cross

Creek, Hawthorn, Florida, U.S.A.; St. Augustine, Crescent Beach, Florida, U.S.A. [*Died* 14 *Dec.* 1953.

RAWLINS, Major-Gen. Stuart Blundell, C.B. 1945; C.B.E. 1944; D.S.O. 1945; M.C. 1917; *b.* 18 Aug. 1897; *s.* of James Ernest Rawlins, Syston Court, Gloucestershire; *m.* 1925, Millicent Olivia, *d.* of Lieut.-Colonel W. E. Burges, The Ridge, Chipping Sodbury; one *s.* *Educ.:* Clifton College; R.M.A. Woolwich. 2nd Lt. R.A. 1916; served in France and Belgium, 1916-1918 (wounded, M.C. and bar). Appointed R.H.A., 1917; A.D.C. to F.M. Lord Plumer, Gov. of Malta, 1920-21; King's African Rifles, 1922-24; G.S.O.3, War Office, 1927-1930; Staff College, Camberley, 1931-32; Regimental duty in India, 1933-35; G.S.O.3, War Office, 1935-37; S.O.R.A., Aldershot Command, 1938-39; G.2. R.A. 1st Corps in France, Belgium and England, 1939-40; G.S.O.1 R.A., West Africa, 1940-42 (April); Command 33 Fd. Regt., May 1942; C.R.A. 3rd Division, Sept. 1942, Brig.; C.C.R.A. 12th Corps, 1943; C.C.R.A. 30th Corps, 1944-45, France, Belgium, Holland and Germany; Maj.-Gen. 1945; Commander 49th (West Riding) Infantry Division, Holland and Germany, 1945; Commander British Military Mission to Greece, 1945 to April 1948; Director Royal Artillery, 1948-1950; Comdr. British Training Team, Iraq, 1951; retired pay, 1951. *Address:* St. George's Island, Looe, Cornwall. *Club:* Army and Navy. [*Died* 2 *April* 1955.

RAWLINSON, Rt. Rev. Alfred Edward John, D.D.; Bishop of Derby, 1936-59, retired; *b.* Newton-le-Willows, Lancashire, 17 July 1884; *e. s.* of late Alfred John and Anna Margaret Rawlinson; *m.* 1919, Mildred, *o. d.* of late Rev. P. A. Ellis, sometime Vicar of S. Mary's, Westminster, S.W.; one *s.* *Educ.:* Dulwich College; Corpus Christi College, Oxford (Scholar); Cuddesdon. 1st Class in Classical Mods., 1905; 1st Class Lit. Hum., 1907; Liddon Theological Student, 1907; 1st Class Honour School of Theology, 1908; Denyer and Johnson Scholar, 1909; B.A., 1907; M.A., 1910; B.D., 1921; D.D., 1925; Hon. D.D. Durham, 1931; Deacon, 1909; Priest, 1910; Tutor of Keble College, Oxford, 1909-13; Lecturer at Christ Church, Oxford, 1913; Student and Tutor of Christ Church, Oxford, 1914-29; Assistant Chaplain and Divinity Lecturer at Corpus Christi College, Oxford, 1920-29; University Lecturer in Biblical Studies, Oxford, 1927-29; Canon Residentiary of Durham and Archdeacon of Auckland, 1929-36; a Chaplain to the King, 1930-36; Examining Chaplain to the Bishop of Lichfield, 1913-1929; to Bishop of Durham, 1929-36; temporary Chaplain to the Forces, 1915-17; Priest-in-Charge, S. John the Evangelist, Wilton Road, London, 1917-1918; Bishop Paddock Lecturer in the General Theological Seminary, New York, 1923; Select Preacher, Oxford, 1923-25 and 1941-42; Select Preacher, Cambridge, 1924, 1928, and 1937; Bampton Lecturer, Oxford, for 1926; Hon. Fellow of C.C.C., Oxford, 1948. *Publications:* Dogma, Fact, and Experience, 1915; Religious Reality, 1918; Studies in Historical Christianity, 1922; Authority and Freedom (Paddock Lectures), 1924; The Gospel according to S. Mark (Westminster Commentaries), 1925; The New Testament Doctrine of the Christ (Bampton Lectures), 1926; The Church of England and the Church of Christ, 1930; The Church and the Challenge of To-day, 1937; Christ in the Gospels, 1944; The World's Question and the Christian Answer, 1944; Problems of Reunion, 1950; The Church of South India, 1951; Current Problems of the Church, 1956; contributor to Foundations, 1912; The Meaning of the Creed, 1917; Peake's Commentary on the Bible, 1919; Psychology and the Sciences, 1924; an Outline of Christianity, 1925; Essays Catholic and Critical, 1926; Mysterium Christi, 1931, etc. Editor of, and Contributor to, Essays on the Trinity and the Incarnation, 1928. *Recreation:* foreign travel. *Address:* 111 Corringham Road, N.W.11. *Club:* Athenæum. [*Died* 17 *July* 1960.

RAWLINSON, Rev. Bernard Stephen, C.M.G. 1916; O.B.E. 1918; O.S.B.; *b.* 27 June 1865; *s.* of late Thos. Rawlinson. *Educ.:* Downside School, nr. Bath; Rome. Priest, 1892; served as Acting Chaplain to the Forces during S. A. War, 1900-2 (despatches twice); European War, 1914 (despatches five times, C.M.G., O.B.E.); 2nd Class, 1915; 1st Class, 1916; Asst. to Principal Chaplain British Expeditionary Force, France, 1915-19; Senior R.C. Chaplain to the British armies in France, 1916-20; French Legion of Honour, 1918; Commander Portuguese Order of Christ, 1919; in charge of Settlement at Bermondsey, 1910-14, and 1920-1935; Private Chaplain to Lord Mayor of London (Sir Stephen Killik), 1934-35; Acting R.C. Chaplain to H.M.S. Impregnable, St. Budeaux, Plymouth, 1940-45. *Address:* Downside Abbey, near Bath. [*Died* 7 *Sept.* 1953.

RAWLINSON, Hugh George, C.I.E. 1933; M.A.,; F.R.A.S.; Indian Educational Service, retd.; late Principal, Deccan College, Poona; *b.* 12 May 1880; *s.* of late Rev. G. Rawlinson; *m.* 1910, Rose, *d.* of Lt.-Col. J. F. Fitzpatrick, I.M.S.; one *s.* *Educ.:* Emmanuel College, Cambridge (Exhibitioner and Scholar). 1st Class Classical Tripos, Hare University Prize; Ceylon Educational Service, 1903-8; Indian Educational Service, 1908-33; Principal and Professor of English and History, Karnatak College, Dharwar, 1917-1923; Member of Indian Historical Records Commission; Ministry of Information, 1939-40; Lecturer in Classics, Birkbeck College, 1944. *Publications:* Intercourse between India and the Western World; British Beginnings in Western India; Ovington's Voyage to Surat; Captain Basil Hall's Travels in India, Ceylon and Borneo; History of Napier's Rifles; History of Outram's Rifles; History of the Seventh (D.C.O.) Rajput Regiment; India, a Short Cultural History; The British Achievement in India; contributor to the Cambridge History of India, Chamber's Encyc., Encyc. Britannica, and Cassell's Encyc. of World Literature. *Address:* 32 Queen's Gate Terrace, S.W.7. *T.:* Western 2380. [*Died* 8 *June* 1957.

RAWS, Lieut.-Colonel Sir (William) Lennon, Kt., *cr.* 1926; C.B.E. 1918; Chm. I.C.I. of Australia and New Zealand, Ltd., 1934-47; Pres. Assoc. Chambers of Commerce of Australia, 1925-26; President Melbourne Chamber of Commerce, 1924-25; Chairman Australian Metal Exchange, 1915-23; Chairman Australian National Committee, International Chamber of Commerce, 1940-43; Australian Military Forces, Reserve; Deputy Chancellor Melbourne Univ., 1939-41; *b.* Kimbolton, Huntingdonshire, 7 Aug. 1878; *e. s.* of late Rev. John G. Raws; *m.* 1905, Elsie (*d.* 1946), *y. d.* of Mrs. William Rogers, Adelaide, South Australia; one *s.* three *d.* *Educ.:* Ellesmere, Harrogate. *Clubs:* Melbourne (Melbourne); Australian (Melbourne and Sydney); Adelaide (Adelaide). [*Died* 19 *April* 1958.

RAY, Major-General Kenneth, C.B. 1944; C.B.E. 1944; D.S.O. 1942; South African Forces; Director of Companies; *b.* 19 May 1894; *s.* of Spencer Ray, Cape Town; *m.* 1924, Grace Johnstone-Brown. *Educ.:* in England. Served European War, 1914-18; War of 1939-45 (D.S.O. and Bar, C.B.E., C.B.). *Address:* P.O. Box 5662, Johannesburg, South Africa. [*Died* 22 *Dec.* 1956.

RAYMENT, Instructor Captain Guy Varley, C.B.E. 1919; B.A.; R.N., retired; *b.* 27 Jan. 1878; *s.* of Henry Rayment; *m.* 1911, Laura Frances Ingram; one *s.* *Educ.:* Royal Naval School; Trinity

College, Cambridge. Gazetted Naval Instructor, 1901; has served on the staffs of the R.N. College at Greenwich and Dartmouth; Fleet Education Officer on the staff of Commander-in-Chief in the Mediterranean, 1927-31; Dean and Professor of Navigation, R.N. College, Greenwich, 1931-33; retired list, 1933. *Address:* Daisy Lodge, North Holmwood, Surrey. [*Died* 10 *Aug.* 1951.

RAYMOND, Lt.-Col. Maurice Claud, C.I.E. 1919; M.C.; Indian Army, retired; on active service in Burma; *b.* 2 Dec. 1884; *y. s.* of late Lt.-Col. E. A. Raymond, 44th Foot; *m.* 1912, Margaret Lilias Nancy, *d.* of A. F. G. Brown of Mazonet, South Devon; one *s.* two *d.* *Educ.:* Privately; R.M.C., Sandhurst. Joined Army, 1904; served in France and Belgium, 13 Oct. 1914-11 Nov. 1918 (despatches twice, M.C., C.I.E.); retired, 1934; King's Police Medal, 1934. *Recreations:* riding, golf. *Address:* Panthill, Barcombe, Sussex. *T.:* Barcombe 105. *Club:* Naval and Military. [*Died* 2 *April* 1959.

RAYMONT, Thomas, M.A. (Univ. of London); *b.* Tavistock, 27 Sept. 1864; *s.* of S., and E. Raymont; *m.* 1st, 1893, Constance Annette (*d.* 1899), *d.* of I. Backett, Brixton; 2nd, 1902, Christine Marion Morton, *d.* of W. E. Nance, Penarth, Glamorgan; four *d.* (and one *s.* killed in action). *Educ.:* Plymouth Road School, Tavistock; Borough Road College, London, S.E.; privately. Tutor at Borough Road College, 1886-89; Assistant Master at Central Foundation School, E.C., 1890; Lecturer in, afterwards Professor of Education, University College, Cardiff, 1890-1905; Vice Principal, and afterwards Warden, of Goldsmiths' College (University of London), 1905-27; Educational Adviser to National Froebel Union, 1927-35; Chairman of National Froebel Union, 1922-37; Member of Teachers' Registration Council, 1927; President of Training College Association, and of Froebel Society, 1928. *Publications:* Principles of Education, 1904; Use of the Bible in Education, 1911; Modern Education, 1931; History of Education of Young Children, 1937; Seven to Eleven: Problems of the Junior School, 1946; also articles in various journals including The Journal of Education, and Nature. *Address:* Carbis Bay, Cornwall. *T.:* St. Ives 197. *Club:* St. Ives (St. Ives). [*Died* 13 *Aug.* 1953.

RAYNES, Rev. Raymond Richard Elliott, M.A., C.R.; Father Superior of the Community of the Resurrection, 1943-1958; *b.* 6 Feb. 1903; *s.* of Herbert Alfred Raynes and Sarah Alice Raynes (*née* Sargent); unmarried. *Educ.:* Colet Court Preparatory School; S. Paul's School; Pembroke College, Oxford; Westcott House, Cambridge. Graduated at Oxford, 1925; ordained (Diocese of Manchester), 1926; Asst. Priest at Holy Trinity, Bury, Lancs, 1926-29; Novice, Community of the Resurrection, Mirfield, 1930-32; professed in the Community, 1932; Asst. Master and Chaplain, S. John's College, Johannesburg, S. Africa, 1932-34; Priest-in-Charge of Sophiatown with Orlando and Pimville Mission Districts. Diocese of Johannesburg (Mission House of C.R.), 1934-43; Provincial Superior of C.R. in South Africa, 1940-43; returned to Mother House at Mirfield, 1943. Proctor in Convocation of York for diocese of Wakefield, and Member of Church of Assembly, 1945-; Commissary to Bishop of Johannesburg, 1943-; Warden of Community of S. Mary the Virgin, Wantage, 1945-; Commissary to Bishop of Zululand, 1947-. Select Preacher Univ. of Cambridge, 1952. *Publications:* Conversations with Jesus, 1937; Concerning the Priestly Life, 1944; Called by God, 1946; The Apostolic Ministry and Reunion, 1955; theological and ecclesiastical articles for various journals and newspapers at home and abroad. *Recreations:* reading political philosophy and detective stories in the country; particular interests: Church Reform and South African Racial Problems. *Address:* House of the Resurrection, Mirfield, Yorkshire. *T.:* Mirfield 3318; Priory of S. Paul, 8 Holland Park, W.11. *T.:* Park 4300. [*Died* 12 *June* 1958.

REA, Alec Lionel, C.B.E. 1945; Chevalier de la Légion d'Honneur; High Sheriff of Westmorland, 1917; *b.* Liverpool, 30 Jan. 1878; *y. s.* of late Rt. Hon. Russell Rea, M.P., and Jane Philip, *d.* of late P. L. Mactaggart; *m.* 1st, 1900, Marguerite (*d.* 1946), *o. c.* of Charles H. Requa of New York; no *c*; 2nd, 1947, Elizabeth Collins, Barton, Cambs. *Educ.:* Univ. College School, London, and abroad. Contested (L.) W. Nottingham, 1922; Master of the Worshipful Co. of Pattenmakers, 1929 and 1939; Director of Rea Brothers, Ltd., merchant bankers; Director of State Assurance Co., Ltd. (London Board); Chairman of Reandco (formerly Reandean); Chairman of Council, Royal Academy of Dramatic Art, 938-39; Chairman Over-seas League, 1930-33. *Recreations:* travel and the theatre. *Address:* Hill House, Long Melford, Suffolk. *Clubs:* Garrick, Royal Automobile. [*Died* 11 *Feb.* 1953.

REA, Major John George Grey, C.B.E. 1953; D.S.O. 1918; Hon. D.Sc. Durham, 1943; Chairman Northumberland County Agricultural Executive Committee since 1939; *b.* 31 May 1886; *s.* of late George G. Rea, C.B.E., of Doddington, Wooler; *m.* 1919, Lavinia, *d.* of late Major-General Lambert and Mrs. Lambert, Bolton Hall, Alnwick. *Educ.:* Rugby; Jesus College, Cambridge. Farmer; served in France with the Northumberland Hussars Yeomanry, Oct. 1914, until wounded Aug. 1918 (despatches twice, D.S.O.). High Sheriff of Northumberland, 1947-48. *Recreations:* hunting, shooting, fishing. *Address:* Berrington House, Ancroft, Berwick-on-Tweed. *T.:* Ancroft 26. *Club:* Cavalry. [*Died* 25 *Aug.* 1955.

READ, Sir Alfred (Henry), Kt., *cr.* 1919; *b.* 1871; *e. s.* of late Col. Alfred Read, Chester. Member Port of London Authority, 1934-41; Member of the Mersey Docks and Harbour Board, 1904-20; Chairman of Liverpool Steamship Owners' Association, 1912; Director of Home Trade Services, Ministry of Shipping, 1916-20. *Address:* c/o Coast Lines Ltd., 35 Crutched Friars, E.C.3. [*Died* 8 *March* 1955.

READ, Bertie L.; *see* Lees Read.

READ, Sir Charles (David), Kt. 1957; M.B., Ch.B.; F.R.C.S., F.R.A.C.S., F.R.C.O.G.; Director Institute of Obstetrics and Gynæcology, British Post-Graduate Medical Federation, University of London; Pres. Roy. Coll. of Obstetricians and Gynæcologists; Hon. Fellow, American Association of Obstetricians, Gynæcologists and Abdominal Surgeons; Hon. Fellow, American Gynæcological Society; Hon. Fellow Athens Obstetrical and Gynæcological Society; Hon. Member S. African Assoc. of Obstetricians and Gynæcologists; Surgeon: Queen Charlotte's Maternity Hosp.; Chelsea Hospital for Women; Hammersmith Post Graduate Hospital; Consulting Gynæcological Surgeon to the Northwood and Pinner Memorial Hospital, the Passmore Edwards Hospital, Wood Green, and St. Luke's Hostel for the Clergy; Surgeon to Out-Patients, and Director of Post Graduate Studies, Chelsea Hospital for Women; Gynæcologist, Bolingbroke Hospital; Gynæcological Surgeon Victoria Memorial Hospital, Barnet, Beckenham Hospital, and Bromley and District Hospital; *b.* N.Z. 22 Dec. 1902; *o. s.* of J. J. Read, J.P., Dunedin, N.Z.; *m.* 1st; two *s.*; 2nd, 1939, Dr. F. Edna Wilson, of Dublin and London; two *s.* *Educ.:* Southland and Otago Boys' Schools; University of Otago, Dunedin (Medallist in Clinical Medicine). Entered Otago Medical School, 1920; qualified 1924; Medallist in Clinical Medicine; held posts of House Physician and House Surgeon, Dunedin Hospital; House Surgeon and Resident Surgical Officer to the Chelsea Hospital for Women, 1926; for three years was Gynæcological and Obstetric Registrar and Tutor, Charing Cross Hospital and Medical School, for four years was Obstetrical and Gynæcological Tutor at Westminster Hospital and Medical School, and for five years was Pathologist to the Chelsea Hospital for Women; Fellow of Royal Society of Medicine (Vice-President, late Secretary, of Obstetric Section); Fellow of Hunterian Society and Harveian Society; Examiner R.C.O.G. and for Central Midwives Board, Universities of Birmingham and Glasgow. *Publications:* various, in American and British literature on Obstetrics and Gynæcology. *Address:* Queens Gate Private Clinic, 31 Queens Gate, S.W.7. *T.:* Western 1597. *Clubs:* Union; Royal Thames Yacht. [*Died* 21 *Aug.* 1957.

READ, Professor Conyers Read; Professor Emeritus, University of Pennsylvania, U.S.A., since 1951 (Professor in English History, 1934-51); *b.* 25 April 1881; *s.* of William F. Read and Victoria Conyers Read; *m.* 1st, 1910, Edith C. Kirk; two *s.* one *d.*; 2nd, 1939, Evelyn P. Braun; one *d.* *Educ.:* Harvard University; Balliol College, Oxford. A.B., A.M., Ph.D., Harvard; B.Litt., Oxford. Instructor, Princeton Univ., 1909-10; Instructor to Professor, Univ. of Chicago, 1911-1920; Treas., Vice-Pres., then Pres., Wm. F. Read & Sons Co., Philadelphia, 1920-33. Served with American Red Cross overseas, 1914; Office of Strategic Services, Washington, D.C., 1941-45. Hon. degrees: Litt.D. (Ursinus) 1938; (Temple) 1954; (Dickinson) 1958; D.C.L. (Penn.) 1951. *Publications:* Mr. Secretary Walsingham and the Policy of Queen Elizabeth (3 vols.), 1925; The Tudors, 1936; Bibliography of British History (1485-1603), 1933; Mr. Secretary Cecil and Queen Elizabeth, 1955; Lord Burghley and Queen Elizabeth, 1960 (posthumous). *Recreations:* golf, bridge, gardening, motoring. *Address:* Wistar Road, Villa Nova, Pennsylvania, U.S.A. *T.:* La. 5-2724. *Clubs:* Royal Historical Soc., American Philosophical Soc. (Philadelphia); American Academy of Arts and Sciences (Boston); Merion Golf (Ardmore, Pa.). [*Died* 23 *Dec.* 1959.

READ, Francis Charles Jennings; City Surveyor, Corporation of London, 1931-1944; *b.* 16 Feb. 1875; *s.* of William Charles Read and Margaret Hogarth Moison; *m.* 1898, Clara, *d.* of late James Jiggens; one *s.* two *d.* Service with Corporation of London; Fellow of the Royal Institution of Chartered Surveyors; served with 4th City of London Regt. Egypt, Gallipoli and France. *Address:* Hilltops, Wood Ride, Petts Wood, Kent. *T.:* Orpington 22737. [*Died* 5 *Feb.* 1958.

READ, Dr. Grantly Dick-, M.A., M.D. Cantab.; retired from active practice, now lecturing (internationally), writing, etc.; *b.* 26 Jan. 1890; 6th *c.* of Robert John Read and Fanny Maria (*née* Sayer); *m.* 1st, 1921, Dorothea Cannon; two *s.* two *d.*; 2nd, 1952, Jessica Bennett (*née* Winters); two step *s.* (adopting name of Dick-Read). *Educ.:* Bishop's Stortford Coll., Hertfordshire; St. John's Coll., Camb.; London Hospital. R.A.M.C., 1914; D.A.D.M.S., Indian Cavalry Corps, 1917. Resident Staff, London Hosp., 1919. Private Practice, Harley Street and Woking, 1923-48. Private Practice, Johannesburg, S. Africa, 1949-53. Evolved theory of Natural Childbirth now accepted and universally taught. A film is shown throughout the World. *Publications:* Natural Childbirth, 1933; Revelation of Childbirth, 1942 (2nd edn. 1943, 3rd edn. 1954); Motherhood in the Post-war World, 1943; Childbirth Without Fear, 1944 (Amer. edn. of Revelation of Childbirth, by which title the book was universally published from 1950); Birth of a Child, 1947 (U.S. 1950); Introduction to Motherhood, 1950 (also in U.S.); Childbirth without Fear, 1953 (U.S., 3rd edn.); Antenatal Illustrated, 1955; No Time for Fear, 1955; No Time for Fear, 1956 (U.S.); Natural Childbirth Primer, 1956 (Amer. title for Antenatal Illustrated). Many books published in foreign languages. Contributions to: B.M.Jl., Lancet, Western Jl. of Surgery, Ob. and Gyn. (U.S.A.), Jl. of Ob. and Gyn. Brit. Emp., etc. Also to certain compiled vols. *Relevant Publication:* Doctor Courageous, by A. Noyes Thomas, 1957 (London and New York). *Recreations:* entomology, gardening, and travel. *Address:* c/o Barclay's Bank Ltd., 74 East Street, Chichester, Sussex. *Clubs:* Hawks (Cambridge); Incogniti and Cryptics Cricket. [*Died* 11 *June* 1959.

READ, John Gordon, C.M.G. 1944; *b.* 28 Apr. 1886; *s.* of John Read, Aylestone Park, Leicester; *m.* 1942, Esme Una, *d.* of William James Smith, Northampton; no *c.* *Educ.:* Wyggeston School Leicester; King's College, London. British South Africa Police (Southern Rhodesia), 1909-13; Colonial Service, Northern Rhodesia, 1913; Provincial Commissioner, Barotse Province, 1937-44; Chief Supervisor of Census, 1946-47; Building Authority, 1947; Chief Rationing Officer, N. Rhodesia, 1948; Assistant to Commissioner for Native Development, N. Rhodesia, 1949-51; Chief Supervisor of Census, N. Rhodesia, 1951; retd. March 1952; Regional Director of Census, N. Rhodesia, 1956. *Recreation:* chess. *Address:* Gorduna, Helderberg Street, Somerset West, Cape Province, Union of South Africa. *T.:* 1033. [*Died* 2 *May* 1958.

READE, Aleyn Lyell, Hon. M.A. Oxon., 1935, and Liverpool, 1939; *b.* Blundellsands, Lancs, 23 April 1876; *y. s.* of T. Mellard Reade, F.R.I.B.A., F.G.S. (Murchison Medallist, 1896), and Emma Eliza, *d.* of William Treleaven Fox; unmarried. *Educ.:* Merchant Taylors' School, Great Crosby. Has in his leisure time made a special study of Dr. Johnson's origins and early life; served as rifleman and afterwards post-corporal on Western Front, with 2/6 King's Liverpool Rifles, 1916-19; Hon. Member of Johnson Club, and of Johnson Society of Lichfield. *Publications:* The Reades of Blackwood Hill and Dr. Johnson's Ancestry, 1906; Johnsonian Gleanings, Part I. (1909), to XI. (1952); The Mellards and their Descendants, with Memoirs of Dinah Maria Mulock and Thomas Mellard Reade, 1915; Audley Pedigrees, Part I. (1929), to III. (1936); A Family News Letter, 1930 (all privately printed); contributions to Notes and Queries, etc. *Recreation:* foot-slogging. *Address:* Treleaven House, Blundellsands, nr. Liverpool. *T.:* Great Crosby 4239. [*Died* 28 *March* 1953.

READE, Sir John (Stanhope), 11th Bt., *cr.* 1661; *b.* 12 Sept. 1896; *s.* of 10th Bt. and Carrie Nixon; *m.* 1924, Alice Elizabeth, *d.* of L. Luke Llewellyn Dubber, Michigan and Berks; *S.* father, 1923. Served European War. *Heir: b.* Clyde Nixon, *b.* 1906. *Address:* Dexter, Michigan, U.S.A. [*Died* 18 *Jan.* 1958.

READING, 2nd Marquess of, *cr.* 1926; **Gerald Rufus Isaacs;** P.C. 1953; G.C.M.G. 1958 (K.C.M.G. 1957); C.B.E. 1945; T.D. 1945; Q.C. 1929; Earl, *cr.* 1917; Visc. Erleigh, *cr.* 1917; Visc. Reading, *cr.* 1916; Baron, *cr.* 1914; Bencher, Middle Temple, 1936; (Treas., 1958); Chairman, Council on Tribunals, since 1958; *b.* 10 Jan. 1889; *o. s.* of 1st Marquess of Reading, P.C., G.C.B., G.C.S.I., G.C.I.E., G.C.V.O., and Alice Edith, G.B.E., C.I. (*d.* 1930), 3rd *d.* of late Albert Cohen; *S.* father 1935; *m.* 1914, Eva Violet, C.B.E., J.P., *d.* of 1st Baron Melchett; one *s.* two *d.* *Educ.:* Rugby; Balliol College, Oxford. Served European War; Inns of Court O.T.C., Royal Fusiliers, Staff (M.C., Croix de Guerre); Lieutenant-Colonel commanding Inns of Court O.T.C. (T.A.), 1923-1925; Lieut.-Col. Commanding Pioneer

Corps Training Centre, 1939-41; Col. on Staff, 1941-43; Brigadier, Director of Labour H.Q. 21st Army Group, 1943-44; retired with hon. rank of Brig., Nov. 1944; Hon. Col. Inns of Court Regt., 1947-59. Barrister: contested (L.) Blackburn, 1929; Member of House of Lords Select Committee on the Prevention of Road Accidents, 1938-39; Chairman, Central Valuation Board, under Coal Act, 1938; Chairman, Departmental Committee on London Government, 1945-46. Chairman: Appeal Tribunal under Further Education and Training Scheme, 1945-51; Central Valuation Board and Panel of Arbitrators and Panel of Referees under Coal Industry Nationalization Act, 1946-51; Joint Select Cttee. on Consolidation Bills, 1947-51; Deptl. Cttee. on Copyright Law, 1951. Parl. Under-Sec. of State for Foreign Affairs, 1951-1953; Minister of State for Foreign Affairs, 1953-57. Assoc. K.St.J. 1948. D.L. County of London, 1950. Grand Cross of Merit of the Order of Duarte, Sanchez y Mella, Dominican Republic, 1957. *Publications:* The South Sea Bubble, 1933; Rufus Isaacs, 1st Marquess of Reading (vol. 1), 1943, (vol. ii), 1945. *Heir: s.* Viscount Erleigh. *Address:* Flat No. 8, 30 Cadogan Place, S.W.1. *T.:* Sloane 7755; Cumberland House, Thakeham, Sussex. *T.:* West Chiltington 2103. *Clubs:* Carlton, Beefsteak.
[*Died* 19 *Sept.* 1960.

REAY, Margaret Edith, C.B.E. 1929; J.P.; 2nd *d.* of late Rev. Canon Thomas Osmotherley Reay and Alice Julia Harriott Reay; *b.* 16 Oct. 1876. *Educ.:* Francis Holland School, Clarence Gate; Ladies' College, Cheltenham. Hon. Freeman, Borough of Southend. *Address:* 134 Alexandra Road, Westcliff-on-Sea, Essex. *T.:* Southend-on-Sea 43721.
[*Died* 25 *April* 1959.

REDDIE, Brig.-General Anthony Julian, C.M.G. 1919; D.S.O. 1915; late South Wales Borderers, retired; D.L. Perthshire; *b.* 27 Aug. 1873; *y. s.* of late Captain J. G. Reddie of Redhouse, Fife; *m.* 1906, Rose Robertson, *e. d.* of late Colonel R. D. Murray, retired I.M.S. *Educ.:* Cargilfield and Fettes College, Edinburgh; R.M.C., Sandhurst. Entered army, 1892; Adjutant, 1901-04; Captain, 1901; Major, 1913; Lt.-Col. 1919; Col. 1920; Adj. T.F., 1909-13; served European War, 1914-19 (despatches seven times, Bt. Lt.-Col., C.M.G., D.S.O.); Order of St. Stanislas, 3rd class; Legion of Honour pour Officier; temp. Brig.-Gen.; Com. 1st Inf. Brigade, Aug. 1915-Oct. 1917; Welsh Reserve Brigade, Nov. 1917-March 1918; 187th Infantry Brigade, April 1918-March 1919; commanded Black Watch and Gordon Territorial Infantry Brigade, 1924-1928: retired pay, 1928; Area Organiser Home Guard, Highland Area, later South Highland Area, 1940-41. *Address:* Ruthvenfield House, Perth. *T.:* Perth 932.
[*Died* 26 *Jan.* 1960.

REDDIE, Lt.-Col. Sir John Murray, Kt., *cr.* 1943; C.B. 1917; K.St.J. 1918; D.L., J.P. Worcs.; *b.* 27 June 1872; *e. s.* of late Captain J. G. Reddie, R.N., of Redhouse; *m.* 1897, Katharine, D.St.J. 1919, O.B.E. 1920 (*d.* 1954), *o. d.* of late Col. J. C. Carter, late 43rd L.I., of Ardington, Wantage, Berks. *Educ.:* Fettes College, Edinburgh; R.M.C., Sandhurst. Joined Worcestershire Regt. 1892; commanded N. Borneo Constabulary, 1897-99; served expeditions against Mat Salleh, 1897-98 (medal and clasp); Adjutant Worcestershire Regt. 1900; Adjutant 1st V.B. A. & S. Highlanders, 1904; Bde.-Major, A. & S. Highlanders, Vol. Bde., 1906; Major, 1907; retired, 1912; Secretary Territorial Army Association, County of Worcester, 1912-37; Secretary, Council of County Territorial Associations, 1936-47; Vice-Chairman, Council of Voluntary Welfare Work, 1939-1952; President Worcestershire Regiments' Assoc. since 1949. *Address:* The Lawns Hotel, Kempsey, Worcester.
[*Died* 7 *Sept.* 1954.

REDDY, Sir C. Ramalinga, Kt., *cr.* 1942; Pro-Chancellor, Mysore University, since 1949; Member, Legislative Council of Madras since 1935; nominated to Upper Chamber of New Provincial Legislature, 1937; *s.* of C. Ramaswami Reddy of Kattamuchi in Chittoor District; *b.* 1880; unmarried. *Educ.:* St. John's College, Cambridge, 1902-6; Government of India Scholarship to England; 1st Class in History Tripos. Vice-President of Cambridge Union Society, 1906, being the only Indian to be elected to that office; Secretary of Cambridge University Liberal Club; toured in America, 1906; second tour to England and America, and tour in Europe, Canada, Japan, Philippines, and Hong-Kong, 1913-14; Principal, Maharajahs College, Mysore, 1916-18; Inspector-General of Education in Mysore, 1918-21; resigned office, 1921; Vice-Chancellor, Andhra Univ., 1926-30 and 1936-49, having been elected five times in succession; member of the All India Advisory Board of Education, 1921 and 1940; All India Board of Scientific and Industrial Research, 1941; Deputy Leader and Organiser of the United Nationalist Party, 1924; Hon. D.Litt., 1936. *Publications:* Speeches on University Reform; Political Economy in Telugu, for which the Madras University Prize for a work of modern interest in Telugu was awarded; Enquiry into the Principles of Poetry; Collected Poems and Collected Essays (Telegu); Congress in Office, 1940; Democracy in Contemporary India (Madras Univ. Endowment Lectures). *Recreation:* tennis. *Address:* West Lake, Mysore, S. India; Padma Prabhasa Chittoor, N.A., South India. *Club:* Cosmopolitan (Madras).
[*Died* 25 *Feb.* 1951.

REDESDALE, 2nd Baron (*cr.* 1902), of Redesdale; **David Bertram Ogilvy Freeman-Mitford,** late Capt. Northumberland Fusiliers; *b.* 13 Mar. 1878; *s.* of 1st Lord Redesdale and Lady Clementine Gertrude Helen Ogilvy (*d.* 1932), *d.* of 9th Earl of Airlie; *S.* father, 1916; *m.* 1904, Sydney, *e. d.* of late T. G. Bowles, M.P.; (only son Maj. Hon. T. D. F.-Mitford killed in Burma, 1945) five *d.* Served South Africa, 1900-02 (dangerously wounded); European War (despatches). *Heir: b.* Capt. Hon. Bertram Freeman-Mitford, D.S.O. *Address:* Redesdale Cottage, Otterburn, Northumberland. *T.:* Otterburn 88; 4 Rutland Gate Mews, S.W.7. *T.:* Kensington 6476. *Clubs:* Carlton, Pratt's.
[*Died* 17 *March* 1958.

REDL, Lieut.-Colonel Ernest Arthur Frederick, C.M.G. 1919; C.I.E. 1917; late 113th Infantry; late Senior General Staff Officer with British Military Mission to Turkestan; *b.* 1 Aug. 1869; *m.* 1909, Mary Beatrice, *d.* of late Thomas Jones; one *s.* *Educ.:* Haileybury; R.M.C., Sandhurst. 2nd Lieut. The King's Own Royal Regt. (R. Lancs.), 1890; Capt. Indian Army, 1901; Major, 1908; with Egyptian Army, 1898-1903; Aden Hinterland Boundary Commission, 1903-4; served Nile Expedition, 1899 (medal with clasp); Aden, 1903-4 (despatches); Military Attaché, Meshed, 1909-13; European War, 1914-18, in France, Mesopotamia, and Persia (C.M.G., C.I.E., 1915 Star, General Service, Victory and 3rd Afghan War medals, despatches); retired, 1921. *Address:* The Sycamores, Newick, Sussex
[*Died* 23 *Feb.* 1954.

REDLICH, Rev. Canon Edwin Basil, M.A., B.D. (Cantab.), F.R.Hist.S.; Rector of Little Bowden, 1924-55; Canon Theologian Emeritus of Leicester Cathedral; Padre Market Harborough Old Contemptibles; Chm. Market Harborough Archæological Soc.; *b.* 2 Feb. 1878; *s.* of late Frederick James Redlich, Colombo; *m.* 1st, 1903, Maud (*d.* 1927), *d.* of J. Le B. Le Maistre, Jersey; one *s.* one *d.*; 2nd, 1931, Violet Katherine Louise, J.P., *d.* of William Hawkins and Mary Simms-Reeve, Sheringham; one *s.* *Educ.:* Wesley College,

Colombo; Christ's College, Cambridge. Mathematical Master, Pietermaritzburg College, Natal; Curate of Boston, 1908-10; St. John, Hampstead, 1910-17; Diocesan Inspector of Schools, London, 1910-18; Director of Religious Education, Diocese of Wakefield, 1918-20 and Diocese of Peterborough, 1920-27; Rector of Teigh, Oakham, 1920-24; Editor of Leicester Diocesan Calendar, 1932-46; Hon. Chaplain to Home Guard (7th Bn. Leicesters), 1940-1944; Rural Dean of Gartree, I., 1929-49. *Publications:* St. Paul and his Companions, 1913; Introduction to Old Testament Study, 1920; Old Testament Stories and how to teach them, 1922; The Church Catechism, its History and Meaning, 1924; History of Teigh, 1926; the Student's Introduction to the Synoptic Gospels, 1936; The Forgiveness of Sins, 1937; Let's Look at the Bible, 1938; Form Criticism, 1939; An Introduction to the Fourth Gospel, 1939; The Christian Heritage, 1940; St. Mark's Gospel, 1947; The Early Traditions of Genesis, 1951. *Recreation:* bowls. *Address:* Bowden Lodge, 72 Coventry Road, Market Harborough, Leics. *T.:* Market Harborough 2076. [*Died* 6 *Feb.* 1960.

REDMAN, George Herbert, C.B.E. 1941 (O.B.E. 1920); Managing Director J. E. Baxter and Co. Ltd., Rubber and Respirator Manufacturers, Leyland, Lancs.; *b.* 21 Sept. 1882; *e. s.* of late Rev. George Ormerod Redman, Vicar of Withnell, Lancs.; *m.* 1911, Fanny Ethel, *d.* of Eli Crook, Hoghton. *Educ.:* Rivington Grammar School; Owen's College, Manchester. J.P. retd., County of Lancaster. *Address:* Levens Lodge, Leyland, Lancs. *T.:* Leyland 81555. *Club:* Royal Automobile. [*Died* 7 *Sept.* 1959.

REDMAYNE, Sir Richard Augustine Studdert, K.C.B., *cr.* 1914 (C.B. 1912); Chevalier Legion of Honour, 1918; M.Sc., M.Inst.C.E. (Pres., 1934-35), M.Inst.M.E.; M.Inst.M.M. (past Pres.); F.G.S.; Consulting Mining and Civil Engineer; H.M. Chief Inspector of Mines, 1908-20; Assistant to Controller of Coal Mines, 1916-20; Chairman Governor Imperial Mineral Resources Bureau, 1918-25; *b.* South Dene, Low Fell, Co. Durham, 22 July 1865; 4th *s.* of late John Marriner Redmayne, J.P., and J. A. Fitzgerald Studdert Redmayne; *m.* 1898, Edith Rose (*d.* 1942), *e. d.* of Thomas Picton Richards, Swansea; one *s.* two *d.* *Educ.:* private tuition; the Durham College of Science, Newcastle on Tyne. Mining apprentice and an under-manager at the Hetton Collieries, Co. Durham, 1883-91; engaged in mining in South Africa, 1891-93; resident manager of the Seaton Delaval Collieries, Northumberland, 1893-1902; Prof. of Mining in the Birmingham Univ., 1902-8; formerly member of three Royal commissions and many departmental committees, and committees of experts, in connection with mining; Chm. of Bd. for Mining Examinations, 1912-50; acted as External Examiner in Mining for Universities of New Zealand, Wales, Birmingham, Royal School of Mines and Camborne School of Mines, and in Principles of Mining for Board of Education, and Mining and Ore Dressing for the City and Guilds, London; Member (Vice-Chm.) Coal Distribution Cttee. under Board of Trade, 1916-17; Mining Assessor to Council of Scientific and Industrial Research, 1915-20; Member of Fuel Research Board, 1916-20; Assessor to Chairman of Coal Industry Commission, 1919; Pres. Inst. of Professional Civil Servants, since 1922; Chairman Sectional Committee, Mining and Metallurgy, British Empire Exhibition, 1924; Chairman Advisory Council on Minerals to Imperial Institute, 1925-35, Acting Director (for six months, 1925) of the Institute; Member Mining Committee Industrial Health Research Board, 1928; Independent Chairman National Conciliation Board on Road Motor Haulage, 1934-38; Chairman Road Haulage Wages Board, 1938-41; Member Southern Regional Valuation Board under the Coal Commission, 1939-43; Chm. Agricultural Wages Cttee. for Essex, 1943-53; Member of Council Cornish School of Mines since 1946. C.St.J. 1917. *Publications:* works on mining and allied subjects; reports; contrib. to scientific and technical jls., etc. *Recreations:* fishing, walking, and natural history pursuits. *Address:* Lodge Farm, Little Hadham, Near Bishop's Stortford, Herts. *T.:* Aldbury 252. *Club:* Athenæum. [*Died* 27 *Dec.* 1955.

REDPATH, Robert, C.B.E. 1920; *b.* 1871; *s.* of late Robert Redpath, Newcastle on Tyne; *m.* 1st, Millie (*d.* 1936), *d.* of late A. J. Porter; 2nd, 1937, Hilda Marion, *d.* of late Harry Saxty Garland. *Educ.:* Royal Grammar School, Newcastle on Tyne. Was a member of Board of Inventions and Research, Admiralty, and Panels of Munitions Inventions Dept.; late Chief Designer, Coventry Ordnance Works, Ltd.; retired. *Address:* Twyford House, Leamington Spa. [*Died* 3 *Feb.* 1960.

REED, Sir (Albert) Ralph, Kt., *cr.* 1945; F.C.G.I. 1954; Paper Manufacturer (retired); Chairman, Albert E. Reed & Co. Ltd., 1920-1954; *b.* 1884; *s.* of Albert Edwin Reed; *m.* 1933, Constance Marjorie, *d.* of John Percy Smith, Nottingham. *Educ.:* Leys School, Cambridge; City and Guilds Technical College. Served European War, 1914-18, as Lieutenant R.E., in Anti-Gas Service. Member Board of Trade Advisory Council (for Industry), 1933-36; Paper Controller, Ministry of Supply (later Board of Trade), Sept. 1939-March 1951; Pres. Paper Makers Assoc., 1926-29. *Address:* Medway Farm, Rotherfield, Sx. *Club:* Athenæum. [*Died* 29 *May* 1958.

REED, Arthur William, M.A., D.Lit.; Professor-Emeritus of English Language and Literature, Univ. of London, King's College; *b.* 1873; *s.* of Lancelot George Reed, Durham; *m.* 1904, Esther, *d.* of Thomas Casson, Denbigh; two *s.* two *d.* *Educ.:* Cathedral School, Durham; St. Mark's College, Chelsea; King's College, London. Assistant Master St. Saviour's School, Everton, 1895; Tutor and afterwards Dean of St. Mark's College, Chelsea, and Lecturer at the Working Men's College, 1896-1917; Reader and afterwards Professor of English of the University of London, King's College, 1919-39; Member of the Senate of the University of London, 1925-46; Gresham Lecturer in Rhetoric, 1934-39; Fellow of King's College, 1934. *Publications:* Early Tudor Drama; Sir Thomas More's English Works (with W. E Campbell); contributions to the Transactions of the Bibliographical Society, The Library, The Year's Work in English Studies, etc. *Recreations:* motoring, golf, fishing. *Address:* Rosemary Cottage, 16 Church St., Hampton-on-Thames. [*Died* 5 *Oct.* 1957.

REED, Austin Leonard; Founder (ex-Dir.), Austin Reed Ltd.; *b.* 6 Sept. 1873; *s.* of William Bilkey Reed and Emily Florence Bowler; *m.* 1902, Emily Wilson (*d.* 1953); one *s.* four *d.* (and one *s.* killed on active service). *Educ.:* Reading School. Entered father's business (Retail Hosiers and Hatters) 1888; business experience in London and United States of America; founded business of Austin Reed in small shop in Fenchurch Street, 1900; business formed into private Ltd. Co. 1910, and public Co. 1920. *Address:* Garden Reach, Camp Road, Gerrards Cross, Bucks. *T.:* Gerrards Cross 3311. [*Died* 5 *May* 1954.

REED, Col. Charles, C.B. 1933; D.S.O. 1916; Indian Army, retired; *b.* 10 Aug. 1879; *s.* of late Talbot Baines Reed; *m.* 1909, Marion Ethel, 2nd *d.* of late Lt.-Col. S. E. Pemberton, R.A.; three *d.* *Educ.:* Haileybury College. Joined Royal Garrison Artillery from Militia, 1899; seconded for service with Indian Mountain Artillery, 1900; served with 26th (Jacob's) Mountain Battery till promoted Captain, 1906; joined Indian Ordnance Department, 1908; Major, 1914; proceeded to France as Deputy

Assistant-Director of Ordnance Services, Meerut Division, Sept. 1914; Mesopotamia, Dec. 1915-Jan. 1917; Assistant-Director of Ordnance Services (Provision), Mesopotamia Expeditionary Force, with acting rank of Lieut.-Col., 1917 (D.S.O., Bt. Lt-Col., Order of the White Eagle, 4th Class, Serbia); Brevet Lt.-Col. 1918; Iraq, 1920 (despatches, medal and clasp); Lieut.-Col. 1925; Col. 1928; transferred to Indian Army, 1928; Assistant Director of Ordnance Services, Northern Command, India, 1933-34; retired, 1934; Sub Controller (Civil Defence) Uckfield Rural District, 1939-45. *Recreation:* walking. *Address:* Loxley, Lordswell Lane, Crowborough, Sussex. [*Died* 30 *Jan.* 1958.

REED, Clinton Austin, C.B.E. 1943 (O.B.E. 1930); retd. civil servant; *b.* 12 Sept. 1876; *s.* of Clinton and Henrietta Reed; *m.* 1904, Ethel Mabel Edwards; one *d.* *Educ.:* Harrison College, Barbados. Water Works Dept. 1898-1910; Customs Dept. 1910-19; on active service with Egyptian Exped. Force, 1916-19; Inspector of Police, Barbados, 1919-23; Governor of the Prison, Barbados, 1923-32; Comptroller of Customs, Barbados, 1932-42. *Address:* One Acre, Rockley New Road, Christchurch, Barbados. *T.:* 8369. *Club:* Savannah (Barbados). [*Died* 14 *July* 1954.

REED, Edward, M.A.; Managing Director The Newcastle Breweries Ltd. and Subsidiary Companies; Director, the Northern Corporation Ltd., Northern and London Investment Trust Ltd., Greville Place Property Co. Ltd., Beech Hill Estate Ltd., Rock Building Society, Wilson & Walker Breweries Ltd., The Review Press Ltd.; *b.* 16 June 1902; *s.* of late Barras Ramsay Reed and Hilda Bramwell; *m.* 1928, Greta Milburn Pybus; one *s.* two *d.* *Educ.:* Rugby; Trinity College, Cambridge. Represented Univ. in Athletics and at Lawn Tennis; Rural District Councillor (Morpeth); Hon. Lieut.-Colonel The Black Watch (The Royal Highland Regiment). *Publications:* Sundry articles (technical and sporting). *Recreations:* shooting, fishing. *Address:* Ghyllheugh, Longhorsley, Northumberland. *T.:* Longhorsley 43. *Club:* Northern Counties. [*Died* 9 *Jan.* 1953.

REED, Herbert Langford (Langford Reed); Author and Journalist; *b.* Clapham, 1889; *m.* Hetty Elizabeth, *d.* of late K. Spiers; one *d.* *Educ.:* Clapham Collegiate School; Hove College. On London editorial staff of Daily Mail, 1910; on active service in France throughout 1917; R.A.F. Officer, 1940-41. *Publications:* The Chronicles of Charlie, 1916; The Picture Play and How to Write It, 1919; The Complete Limerick Book 1924 (U.S.A. 1925); The Anthology of Nonsense Verse, 1925 (U.S.A. 1926); Sausages and Sundials, 1927; Nonsense Tales for the Young, 1927; The Indiscreet Limerick Book, 1928; Further Nonsense Verse and Prose by Lewis Carroll (edited), 1927 (U.S.A. 1928); The Life of Lewis Carroll, 1932; The Child's Own Limerick Book, 1932; Limericks for the Beach, Bathroom and Boudoir, 1933; Mr. Punch's Limerick Book, 1934; The Complete Rhyming Dictionary, 1936; The New Limerick Book, 1937; The Nondamsense Ballads, 1937; My Limerick Book for Boys and Girls (also in U.S.A.), 1937; (with Countess of Warwick) The Prime Minister's Pyjamas, 1933; jointly, with wife, Potter's Clay, 1923, Daphne Grows Down, 1925, and The Mantle of Methuselah, 1939; American edn. of The Complete Rhyming Dictionary, 1950; King of the Jesters, 1952; My Lady's Treasure Book; The Complete Limerick Book (5th edn.); has contributed special articles, short stories and humorous poems, to The Times, Daily Mail, Evening Standard, News Chronicle, Star, Manchester Guardian, Radio Times, etc., and to monthly magazines; editor and originator of the Year Book, Who's Who in Filmland; author of many original plays for the screen; official editor of the Government propaganda films sent abroad during 1918; Lecturer for the L.C.C. and Middlesex C.C. on literary subjects. *Address:* 59 Carlton Hill, St. John's Wood, N.W.8. *T.:* Maida Vale 7506. [*Died* 11 *March* 1954.

REED, Hon. Sir John Ranken, Kt., *cr.* 1936; Q.C. 1913; C.B.E. 1919; V.D.; *b.* Ipswich, Queensland, 26 Dec. 1864; *e. s.* of late Rev. G. M. Reed, B.A.; *m.* 1889, Eliza de Villiers, *d.* of late Alfred Carew; one *s.* two *d.* *Educ.:* Grammar School, Auckland, N.Z.; Victoria College, Jersey; Clare College, Cambridge. Admitted to New Zealand Bar, 1887; under the New Zealand Territorial System of Defence was Lt.-Col. in command of the 3rd (Auckland) Infantry Regiment; retired with rank of Col., 1911; Judge Advocate-General for N.Z., 1911-1933; one of the Judges of the Supreme Court of New Zealand and of the Court of Appeal of New Zealand, 1921-36; retired when Acting Chief Justice in 1936; reappointed temporarily, 1937, 1938 and 1939; Pres. N.Z. Prisons Board, 1928-37; has held the positions of President of the Auckland Law Society, President of the Auckland Club, and President of the Auckland Garrison Officers' Club; has taken a prominent part in Freemasonry, having held for seven years the position of District Grand Master for Auckland under the English Constitution. *Address:* Chatswood, 437 Remuera Road, Remuera, S.E.2, Auckland, N.Z. *Clubs:* Northern, Auckland (Auckland). [*Died* 22 *April* 1955.

REED, Langford; *see* Reed, Herbert L.

REED, Sir Ralph; *see* Reed, Sir A. R.

REES, Lt.-Col. Evan Thomas, D.S.O. 1918; O.B.E. 1939; M.C.; *b.* 6 May 1883; *s.* of Thomas Rees, Barry, Glam.; *m.* 1916, Mary (*d.* 1950), *y. d.* of John Humphreys, Dafen, Carmarthen. Joined 4th Bn. Universities and Public Schools Brigade as private, Aug. 1914; obtained commission in 10th Battalion, South Wales Borderers, March 1915; Captain, 1915; Major, 1916; Lt.-Colonel, 1917, when given command of 7th Battalion The Norfolk Regiment; severely wounded and taken prisoner, 27 March 1918 (M.C., D.S.O., despatches 4 times); in Air Ministry, 1923-39; War Cabinet Offices, 1939-45. J.P. for Surrey. *Recreations:* golf and walking. *Address:* Sagamore, Weston Green, Thames Ditton, Surrey. *T.:* Emberbrook 1840. [*Died* 22 *Oct.* 1955.

REES, Eng.-Capt. John David, C.B.E. 1919; R.N., retired; *b.* 1861; *s.* of Griffith Rees; *m.* 1897, Florence Caroline (*d.* 1930), *o. d.* of late W. T. Sanders, Plymouth; two *s.* Served China, Boxer Rebellion (medal); European War, 1914-19 (despatches, C.B.E.). *Address:* 7 Normanton Avenue, Bognor Regis, Sussex. [*Died* 23 *Jan.* 1951.

REES, His Honour (John) Tudor, D.L., J.P.; Chairman Epsom County Bench; Lay Assessor, Dioceses of Canterbury and Southwark; *s.* of late I. J. Rees, of Maesteg; *m.* 1918, Dorothy, 2nd *d.* of late E. J. Sidebotham, M.A., of Bowdon; one *s.* two *d.* *Educ.:* University of Wales. Freeman, City of London, 1921, Epsom and Ewell, 1954; M.P. (L.) Barnstaple Division, Devon, 1918-1922, and 1923-24; formerly Judge of Uxbridge and Brentford County Courts; Chairman, Surrey Quarter Sessions; retired, 1955. Served in the Welch Regt. (Capt.) and Machine-Gun Corps, 1914-18. D.L. Surrey. *Publications:* Our Jury System; Disestablishment. *Address:* Katmos, Tadworth, Surrey. *T.:* Tadworth 3289. [*Died* 27 *Feb.* 1956.

REES, Mrs. Leonard (Mary Emily MacLeod Moore); regular contributor for many years Sunday Times (Pandora column), etc.; occasional contributor to numerous publications in Canada, New York, and London; *d.* of late Lt.-Col. W. J. B.

MacLeod Moore; b. near Montreal; m. Leonard Rees (*d.* 1932), sometime Editor of the Sunday Times. *Club:* Sesame.
[*Died* 26 *Feb.* 1960.

REES, Group Captain Lionel Wilmot Brabazon, V.C. 1916; O.B.E.; M.C.; A.F.C.; late Royal Air Force; *b.* 31 July 1884; *s.* of Col. Charles H. Rees, V.D., and Leonora Maria, *d.* of Smith William Davids of Carnarvon. *Educ.:* Eastbourne College; Royal Military Academy, Woolwich. Entered R.A. 1903; Lieut. R.F.C. 1914; Capt. 1914; R.A.F. 1918; served European War, 1914-18 (V.C., despatches, O.B.E., M.C., A.F.C., wounded, Bt. Lt.-Col.); A.D.C. to the King, 1925-31; retired list, 1931; re-employed during War of 1939-45, in Africa, 1941-42. Received the Freedom of Carnarvon Borough, 1919. *Address:* c/o Lloyds Bank (Cox's Branch), 6 Pall Mall, S.W.1. [*Died* 28 *Sept.* 1955.

REES, Sir Milsom, G.C.V.O., *cr.* 1934 (K.C.V.O., *cr.* 1923; C.V.O. 1911); Kt., *cr.* 1916; D.Sc. (hon.); F.R.C.S. Edinburgh; M.R.C.S., L.R.C.P. London; retired; *b.* Apr. 1866; *s.* of late John Rees, Neath, Glamorgans.; *m.* 1894, Eleanor Jessie, *d.* of late William P. Jones, Manor House, Finchley. Laryngologist to the King and Queen and Household, 1910-36; to the late Queen Alexandra and late Queen of Norway; to Royal Opera House, Covent Garden; to the Guildhall School of Music; and to the Woollen Drapers' Institution; Hon. Freeman of the Company of Musicians; Hon. Consulting Laryngologist and Audist, Musicians' Benevolent Fund; Consulting Surgeon, Throat and Ear Department, Prince of Wales General Hospital, Tottenham; Senior Honorary Surgeon, Sussex Throat and Ear Hospital, Brighton; Vice-Pres.: Charing Cross Hospital; King George V Hospital; West End Hospital for Nervous Diseases; Governor: St. Mary's Hospital; Royal Free Hospital; Royal Hospital Bridewell and Bethlehem; Medical College, St. Bartholomew's Hospital; University of Wales and Monmouthshire; Epsom College; Hon. Life Governor Middlesex Hospital; Life Governor: London Hospital; London Jewish Hospital; National Hospital Diseases of the Heart; Royal Surgical Aid Society; late Resident Medical Officer, Hospital for Diseases of Throat, Golden Square; Trustee of the Alfred de Rothschild Residuary Estate; The Milsom Rees Operating Theatre, St. Bartholomew's Hospital and Margate and Broadstairs Hospital; Vice-Pres. of London Welsh Rugby Football Club. Chairman of the Nyanza Salt Mines, East Africa; Chm. of the Tchenzema Mines, East Africa; late Chairman of Jones Bros., Holloway Road, N., and John Barnes, Ltd., Finchley Road, N.W. *Publications:* Care of the Vocal Chords in Singers and Speakers, 1937; Practical Hints on Singing in Preparatory Schools, 1938; The Role of the Labyrinth in Man and Animals, 1941. *Recreations;* big game investigations in Central Africa; Rugby football, cricket, boxing, golf, etc. *Address:* Arusha, Kingsgate, Broadstairs, Kent. *T.A.:* Milsomrees Broadstairs 909. *T.:* Broadstairs 909; 18 Upper Wimpole Street, W.1. *Clubs:* Royal Empire Society; North Foreland Golf (Broadstairs); Royal St. George's Golf. [*Died* 23 *April* 1952.

REES, Thomas James, C.B.E. 1943; J.P.; B.A.; Director of Education in Swansea, 1908-43; late Hon. Secretary of Federation of Education Committees in Wales and Mon.; *b.* 19 March 1875; *s.* of James and Mary Rees, Waun Wen, Swansea; *m.* 1902, Katie Davies, Gowerton; two *d.* *Educ.:* Universities of Wales and London. Member of: Board of Education Departmental Committee on Scholarships and Free Places, 1910; Consultative Committee of Board of Education; Advisory Committee of Board of Education; Advisory Committee of Ministry of Labour on Juvenile Employment; Ministry of Health Committee on Evacuation of Schoolchildren, 1938; Central Council for School Broadcasting; British Council; Executive Committee of Central Welsh Board; Council of University of Wales; Welsh National Council of Music; Treasurer of Univ. Coll., Swansea; Formerly member Welsh National School of Medicine; Welsh National Youth Cttee.; President of Rotary in Great Britain and Ireland, 1942-44. *Address:* Brynfield, Reynoldston, Swansea. *T.:* Reynoldston 9. [*Died* 24 *Dec.* 1957.

REES, Major-General Thomas Wynford, C.B. 1945; C.I.E. 1931; D.S.O. 1919; M.C.; D.L.; late I.A.; Chief Executive Officer and General Manager, Cwmbran New Town, South Wales; *s.* of late Rev. T. M. Rees; *m.* 1926, Rosalie, *o. d.* of Sir Charles Innes, *q.v.*; one *s.* one *d.* Served European War, 1914-19 (despatches, M.C., D.S.O., wounded); Waziristan, 1920, 1922-1924 (despatches), 1936-37 (Bt. Lt.-Col., despatches twice); Instructor at R.M.C. Sandhurst, 1926-27; Private Sec. to Gov. of Burma, 1928-30; D.A.Q.M.G., 1935-37, G.S.O. 2nd grade, Waziristan Dist., 1937-38; Comdt. 3rd Bn. 6th Rajputana Rifles, 1939; Lt.-Col. 1939; Col. 1940; Maj.-Gen. 1947; served war of 1939-45 (wounded twice, despatches, Bar to D.S.O., C.B.); Commander: 10th Indian Div., Iraq and N. Africa, 1942; 19th Indian Division (The Dagger Division), Burma, 1944-45; 4th Indian Div., 1945-47; Punjab Boundary Force, Aug.-Sept. 1947. Head of Military Emergency Staff to Emergency Committee of Cabinet, Delhi, Sept.-Dec. 1947; retired 1948. Colonel, The Rajputana Rifles, 1946; Hon. Col. 5th Bn. The Welch Regt., T.A. Hon. Pres. The Boys' Brigade (Wales). D.L. Monmouthshire, 1955; Vice-Pres. and Hon. Co. Comr., Boy Scouts, Monmouthshire; Civil Defence Controller, Cardiff Sub-Region of Wales. Hon. LL.D. Univ. of Wales. *Address:* Goytre Hall, nr. Abergavenny. *T.:* Nantyderry 223. *Clubs:* United Service; Royal Bombay Yacht (Bombay).
[*Died* 15 *Oct.* 1959.

REES, His Honour Tudor; *see* Rees, His Honour J. T.

REEVE, His Honour Judge Raymond Roope; *b.* 1875; *s.* of J. W. Reeve and Laura Lydia, *d.* of Lavington Roope, Hobart, Tasmania; *m.* 1897, Leonora, *d.* of Samuel Smith Travers of Hobart, Tasmania; one *s.* one *d.* *Educ.:* Christ's College, Hobart. Called to Bar, Lincoln's Inn, 1900; Transvaal Bar, 1906; K.C. 1922; Bencher Lincoln's Inn, 1926; Additional Judge at Westminster, Marylebone, and Clerkenwell County Courts, and Judge of Uxbridge County Court, 1926-27; Judge of County Courts Circuit No. 22 (Worcester, Hereford, etc.), 1927-45; retired 1945; formerly on General Council of the Bar; Committee Barristers Benevolent Association; sent to South Africa, 1905-6, as Special Commissioner under Royal Commission on War Stores in South Africa; served as Lieut. in Royal Field Artillery, France, Palestine, 1916-18 (once wounded). *Publication:* Gale on Easements, 8th edition. *Recreations:* hunting, fishing, (holder of what is believed to be world's record for trout killed on dry-fly—sea-trout 20½ lbs.), shooting. *Address:* Brynffynnon, Machynlleth, Mont. *T.A.* and *T.:* Machynlleth 148. *Club:* Flyfishers'. [*Died* 16 *Feb.* 1952.

REEVES, Vice-Adm. Edward, C.B. 1918; *b.* 1869; *s.* of late Herbert W. Reeves; *m.* Eleanor, *d.* of late James Hall, D.L., J.P., Tynemouth, Northumberland. Commanded H.M.S. Liverpool, 1913-15; H.M.S. Birkenhead, 1915-17; H.M.S. St. Vincent, 1917-19; present in the actions of the Heligoland Bight and Jutland; Commodore, Royal Naval Barracks, Devonport, 1919-21; retired list, 1921; Vice-Admiral retired, 1926. *Address:* Southleigh, Shawford, Winchester, Hants. [*Died* 4 *March* 1954.

REFORD, John Hope, C.M.G. 1928; M.D.; *b.* 1873; *s.* of Anthony B. Reford; *m.* Grace M. (*d.*

1942), *d.* of S.E. Parker. *Educ.:* Royal University of Ireland. Was Director of Medical and Sanitary Services, Uganda; served S. Africa 1900-2; European War 1915-17 in East Africa. *Publications:* The Play of the Cards (with Frank England), 1930; Contract Up-to-Date, 1931. *Address:* c/o Lt.-Col. Lewis Reford, M.C., Savalmore House, Ardaragh, Newry, Co. Down, Northern Ireland. [*Died* 13 *Nov.* 1957.

REGENER, Prof. Dr. Erich; Direktor des Max Planck Institutes für Physik der Stratosphäre in Weissenau, Kr. Ravensburg and Ord. Prof. Emeritus der Physik an der Technischen Hochschule, Stuttgart; *b.* 12 Nov. 1881; *s.* of Amandus Regener and Anna Urban; *m.* 1906; one *s.* one *d.*; *m.* 1949, Gertrud Heiter. *Educ.:* Gymnasium Bromberg; University of Berlin. Assistant to Professor P. Drude and H. Rubens at Berlin; Privatdozent University of Berlin; Ord. Prof. a. d. Landwirtschaftlichen Hochschule, Berlin; Ord. Prof. der Physik an der Technischen Hochschule, Stuttgart; Member of the Kaiser Wilhelm Gesellschaft zur Förderung der Wissenschaften; Vice-Pres. Max Planck Gesellschaft, Göttingen. *Publications:* Determination of Elementary charge of electricity by counting the *a*-Particles; Investigations of cosmic rays in deep water and in the stratosphere; Ozone in the stratosphere; Oxygen content of the air in the stratosphere; Condensation and sublimation of water vapour at low temperatures, etc. *Recreations:* sailing and archery. *Address:* Stuttgart, N. Wiederholdstr. 13. *T.:* Stuttgart 91114; Weissenau, Kreis Ravensburg, Württ. *T.:* Ravensburg 3621. *Club:* Yachtclub Friedrichshafen (Bodensee). [*Died* 27 *Feb.* 1955.

REID, Rachel Robertson, D.Lit.; F.R.Hist.S.; Fellow of University College, London; *b.* Jan. 1876; *d.* of James Monro Reid and Anné Bleloch; unmarried. *Educ.:* North Hackney High School; Bedford College for Women. History Mistress at private schools, 1899-1901; Exeter High School, 1903-1904; Geography and Mathematics Lecturer at the London Day Training College, 1905-6; History and Geography Lecturer at Avery Hill Training College, 1906-8; Director of Studies in History at Girton College, Cambridge, 1908-9; Senior Assistant to the Professor of Constitutional History at University College, London, 1909-19; Inspector of Schools under the L.C.C., 1919-40. Hon. Vice-Pres. and Member of Council, Historical Assoc. (Vice-Pres., 1924-47). *Publications:* Eng. Historical Review—Note on Redman's Life of Henry V., Articles on Barony and Thanage and The Office of Warden of the Marches; The King's Council in the North; The Italian Plebiscites in Peace Handbook No. 16; The Franco-Italian War, Syria and Poland, in The Cambridge History of British Foreign Policy; The Influence of the "North Parts" under the Later Tudors in Tudor Studies; General Editor of Philip's Junior (now Intermediate) Historical Atlas; (jointly) Planning of a History Syllabus for Schools, 1944; England 1413-1489, 1920, in Cassell's History of the British People, re-published 1947. *Recreations:* reading, playing patience. *Address:* 40 Cholmley Gardens, Hillfield Road, Hampstead, N.W.6. [*Died* 10 *May* 1952.

REID, Col. (Hon. Brig.) Walter Richard, D.S.O. 1915; D.L. Devon; late R.A.; *b.* 11 April 1880; *s.* of late Insp.-Gen. Walter Reid, R.N.; *m.* 1st, 1913, Theresa Mabel Johnson (*d.* 1930); 2nd, 1937, Ella Lucy (*d.* 1945), *widow* of G. W. F. Brown. *Educ.:* Malvern, Edinburgh University. Entered army, 1900; Capt. 1911; Maj. 1914; Lt.-Col. 1927; Col. 1931; served European War, 1914-18 (despatches five times, D.S.O., Bt. Lt.-Col.); Brigadier R.A. Western Command, India, 1932-36; retired pay, 1936. *Address:* Phayre House, Bideford, Devon. [*Died* 30 *Oct.* 1959.

REID, William Allan; *b.* 1865; *m.* 1917, Ethel Walker (*d.* 1943), *d.* of W. Walker Smith and *widow* of Dr. H. Boam. Admitted a solicitor, 1895; M.P. (U.) Derby, 1931-45; Chairman Derbyshire Children's Hospital, 1920-31. *Recreations:* shooting and golf. *Clubs:* Carlton, Constitutional. [*Died* 17 *March* 1952.

REID, William Clarke, T.D.; B.A.(Oxon); LL.B.; Sheriff Substitute of Ayrshire and Bute at Ayr, Dec. 1947; *b.* 3 June 1909; *s.* of William Clarke Reid, Flour Importer, Glasgow, and Margaret Gow, *d.* of Robert Nish, Dunclutha, Kirn, Argyll; *m.* 1941, Josephine, *widow* of Flying Officer C. Chope, R.A.F., and *d.* of late W. J. Leeman, Stock Exchange, London. *Educ.:* Warriston School; Rugby School; Oxford University; Glasgow University. Admitted to Faculty of Advocates, 1935. Practised at Scottish Bar, 1935-39, when mobilised with 51st Heavy Regt. R.A. (T.A.) as Lieut. Served with B.E.F. in France and Belgium, 1939-40; Capt. 1940; joined Military Dept., Judge-Advocate-General's Office, 1941; Major, 1944; released from Army, Nov. 1944; Sheriff Substitute of Roxburgh, Berwick and Selkirk at Jedburgh, 1944-47. *Recreation:* shooting. *Address:* Oakendean Cottage, Alloway, by Ayr. *Clubs:* New (Edinburgh); Royal Scottish Automobile (Glasgow); County (Ayr). [*Died* 23 *July* 1956.

REID, William Sydney; Chairman Commercial Bank of Australia since 1951 (Director, 1941); Director New Zealand Loan and Mercantile Agency Co. Ltd.; etc.; *b.* Geelong, Australia, 18 Feb. 1880; *s.* of William R. Reid, Geelong; *m.* 1909, Lilian E. (decd.), *d.* of G. S. Parsons; two *d.* *Educ.:* Geelong College, Australia. Joined Gollin and Co. Pty. Ltd., 1897; subsequently became Chairman and Managing Director; retired, 1948. *Address:* (business) La Mode Industries Ltd., 31 Victoria Street, Fitzroy, Vic., Australia; (home) 60 Broadway, East Camberwell, Vic. *Clubs:* Savage; Melbourne, Australian, Royal Melbourne Golf (Melbourne). [*Died* 12 *April* 1960.

REISS, Richard Leopold; Director Hampstead Garden Suburb Trust Ltd.; Kt. (1st cl.) Order of St. Olav of Norway; *b.* 20 May 1883; *s.* of late Charles A. Reiss and Florence, *d.* of late Lord Justice Baggallay; *m.* 1910, Celia, *d.* of late H. H. Butts, J.P.; three *s.* two *d.* *Educ.:* Marlborough; Balliol College, Oxford (Scholar). Lecturer, Magdalen College, Oxford, 1907-8; Barrister, Lincoln's Inn; contested Colchester (Lab.), 1922-29; Preston, 1935; Head Organiser of Rural Inquiry for Mr. Lloyd George's Land Inquiry, 1912-14; Capt. L. N. Lancs.; served Gallipoli and Mesopotamia (wounded); served on Ministry of Health Committee on Unhealthy Areas, 1919-20, and other Departmental Committees; member Housing Committee, L.C.C., 1930-38; Howard Medal for distinguished Services to Town Planning, 1948. Director, Welwyn Garden City Ltd., 1919-48; Vice-Chm. Welwyn Garden City and Hatfield Development Corps., 1948-52. *Publications:* The Home I Want; The New Housing Handbook; The Town Planning Handbook; Town Theory and Practice (Joint); British and American Housing; Municipal and Private Enterprise Housing, 1945. *Address:* 51 Brockswood Lane, Welwyn Garden City. *T.:* Welwyn Garden 231. [*Died* 30 *Sept.* 1959.

RELPH, George, C.B.E. 1959; Actor; *b.* 27 January 1888; *s.* of George and Elizabeth Relph; *m.* 1st, 1911, Deborah Nanson (marriage dissolved); one *s.*; 2nd, 1925, Mercia Swinburne. *Educ.:* High School, Whitley Bay, Northumberland. First appearance on stage, Grimsby, 1906; first London appearance, Hamlet, Lyceum, 1909. Toured Australia, 1910; in Kismet, Garrick, 1911 First appearance in New

York, Romeo in Romeo and Juliet, 1912; played in New York: The Yellow Jacket; The Garden of Paradise. Played in Joseph and His Brethren, and The Darling of the Gods, 1914. Served European War; 3rd Yorkshire Regt., 1917 (wounded). Toured S. Africa, 1924. Has appeared in The Man Who Came Back, Caesar's Wife, The Bat, The Green Goddess, Hamlet, The Squeaker. In recent years has played Blenkinsop in Doctor's Dilemma, and, joining new Old Vic Co., New Theatre, 1944, played wide range of parts including Clarence, Telyegan, Pistol, Worcester, Gloucester, Subtle, Dangle, Grumio, Sir Oliver Surface, Creon. Played in continental, Australian and New York seasons with Old Vic Co., and at the Comédie Française in Peer Gynt and Richard III; in Fading Mansion, 1949; Reedbeck in Venus Observed, St. James's, 1950; Giaconda Smile, New York, 1950; The General, in Ardele, Vaudeville, 1951; Duke of Applecross in The Mortimer Touch, 1952; The Dean in The Bad Samaritan, 1953; Mortmain in I Capture the Castle, 1954; Abbé Martignon in The Little Glass Clock, 1955. Old Ekdal in The Wild Duck, 1955; Peter Sorin in The Seagull, 1956; Billie Rice in The Entertainer, 1957; The Entertainer, New York, 1958. *Films include:* I Believe in you, 1952; The Titfield Thunderbolt, 1952; Davy, 1957. Has also appeared several times on Television in classic and other plays. *Recreations:* reading, gardening. *Address:* 18 Argyll Mansions, Kings Road, Chelsea, S.W.3. *T.:* Flaxman 9789. *Clubs:* Garrick, Green Room. [*Died* 24 *April* 1960.

REMIZOV, Alexei; Russian novelist; *b.* Moscow, 1877. *Educ.:* University of Moscow (Faculty of Science). Banished from Moscow, on ground of some connexion with revolutionary organisations; spent some time with fellow-exiles, in Vologda, North Russia; subsequently lived in St. Petersburg; emigrated to Berlin, 1921; settled in Paris, 1923. Had begun writing in 1896; first story in print, 1901; first book, 1907. *Publications: novels* (trans. Eng.); The Clock, The Pond, The Fifth Pestilence; other novels trans. into French and German; The Story of Ivan Semenovich Stratilatov, 1909 (was a basis for a great deal of modern Russian fiction); other works included: Round with the Sun; Sisters of the Cross; Tales of the Russian People; Mara; The Noises of the Town; The Chronicle of 1917; La Russie en tourmente, 1921; In a Field Azure; Russia in Writ (commentary on ancient MSS.), etc. [*Died* 26 *Nov.* 1957.

RENDALL, Richard Antony, C.B.E. 1951; *b.* 15 July 1907; *s.* of late Bernard and Lilian Rendall; *m.* 1932, Anne, *d.* of Cyril and Mary Moinet; two *s.* one *d. Educ.:* Copthorne; Winchester; Trinity Coll., Cambridge. Joined B.B.C. as announcer, 1928; Talks Dept., 1929; West Regional Programme Director, 1934; seconded to Palestine Government as Adviser on Broadcasting, 1935; Assistant Director, Television, 1937; Director of Empire Services, 1940; Acting Controller, Overseas Services, 1944; Controller, Talks Division, 1945-50. *Address:* 20 Park Square East, N.W.1. *T.:* Welbeck 2050. [*Died* 20 *March* 1957.

RENDALL, Vernon Horace; *b.* Great Rollright, Oxon, 1869; 7th *s.* of late Rev. H. Rendall; *m.* 1901, Jane (*d.* 1936), *d.* of Thomas Hey, Leeds. *Educ.:* Elstree School; Rugby School (Science Scholar, Classical Scholar, Tait Scholar in Divinity, Exhibitioner, Cricket XI.); Trinity College, Camb. (Major Scholar, 1889); 1st class Classical Tripos; Tripos verses; B.A. 1891. Cambridge Journalism since 1889; Assistant Editor, Athenæum, 1896-1900; Editor of the Athenæum, 1901-16; Notes and Queries, 1899-1907; Editor of Notes and Queries, 1907-12; Staff of Saturday Review, 1916-21; Literary Ed. English Review, 1926-31; Pension on Civil List, 1937, increased, 1942, and later; has been a publisher's "reader" and L.C.C. lecturer. *Publications:* The Profitable Imbroglio, 1910; The London Nights of Belsize, 1917; Hallowmead, Limited, 1927; Wild Flowers in Literature, 1934; Baker Street Studies (essay in), 1934; Anthology of Courtship and Wooing, 1936; articles in various magazines and papers. *Recreations:* chess, Greek, botany, etc. *Address:* Oxenwood, California Lane, Bushey Heath. Herts. [*Died* 13 *May* 1960.

RENDEL, H. S. G.; *see* Goodhart-Rendel.

RENDELL, Col. Walter Frederic, C.B.E. 1919; Newfoundland Representative, Canadian Dept. of Trade and Commerce, 1949; *b.* 1888; *s.* of late Frederick John Wood Rendell; *m.* 1920, Dorothy Evelyn, *d.* of Daniel Webster, Crosby, Liverpool; two *s. Educ.:* Bishop Feild College, St. John's. Served European War, 1914-19, C.B.E.). Organised and commanded Newfoundland Regt., 1939-41; Director of Recruiting, 1940-41; Secretary for Defence-Newfoundland, 1941-42; Trade Commissioner for Newfoundland in London, 1946-1949. *Address:* Dept. of Trade and Commerce, St. John's, Newfoundland. [*Died* 14 *Dec.* 1951.

RENISON, Most Rev. Robert John, M.A., D.D.; (Anglican) Archbishop; *b.* Cashel, Ireland, 8 Sept. 1875; *s.* of Rev. Canon Robert Renison, M.A., and Mary Elizabeth Kennedy; *m.* 1914, Elizabeth Maud, *d.* of George Everett Bristol, Hamilton, Ont.; two *s. Educ.:* Trinity Coll. Sch., Port Hope, Ont.; Univ. of Toronto. B.A. 1896, M.A. 1897. Ordained, 1896; Curate Ch. of the Messiah, Toronto, Ont. 1897; Missionary, Moose Fort and Albany, 1898; Archdeacon of Moosonee, Ont. 1907; Rector, Ch. of the Ascension, Hamilton, Ont., 1912; Archdeacon of Hamilton, 1924; Rector, Christ Ch., Vancouver, B.C., 1927; Dean, New Westminster, B.C., 1929; elected Bishop of Athabasca, 1931; Rector, St. Paul's, Toronto, Ont., 1932-43; Bishop of Moosonee, 1943; Archbishop of Moosonee and Metropolitan of Ont.. 1952-54. Hon. D.D.: Univ. of Manitoba, 1910; Wycliffe Coll., Tor., 1932; Univ. of Sask., 1932; Trinity Coll., Tor., 1952; Univ. of Ont., 1953. Served European War as Chaplain and Hon. Capt. 4th Inf. Bde., C.E.F., France and Belgium, 1917-19; Chaplain, 13th Roy. Regt., Hamilton, Ont., 1923-27; Hon. Wing Comdr., R.C.A.F.; first Air Force Chaplain in Canada. 1914-18 Overseas Medals: Jubilee Medal of King George V, 1935; 1939-45 Service Medal; Coronation Medal, 1933. Editorial Writer for Globe and Mail, Toronto. An authority on the lang. and hist. of Canadian Indians. Freemason. *Publications:* Indian Cree Hymn Book; Canada at War, 1919; Life of Bishop Sullivan, 1916; Wednesday Morning (sermonettes), 1943; For Such a Time as This (sermonettes), 1947; has also written numerous essays and articles. *Recreations:* fishing, shooting, golf. *Address:* 106 St. Leonards Ave., Toronto, Ontario, Canada. *Club:* York (Toronto). [*Died* 6 *Oct.* 1957.

RENNIE, Colonel (Brig.-Gen.) George Arthur Paget, C.M.G. 1918; D.S.O. 1900; retired; *b.* 6 Sep. 1872; *s.* of late G. B. Rennie of Denford, Hungerford; *m.* 1904, Florence Mary, *d.* of late Philip Wroughton; three *d. Educ.:* Marlborough. Entered army, 1893; Captain, 1902; Major, 1911; served South Africa, 1899-1902 (despatches twice, Queen's medal 6 clasps, King's medal 2 clasps, D.S.O.); European War, 1914-18 (despatches six times, Bt. Lt.-Col., C.M.G.); Commander of the Order of the Crown of Rumania. *Address:* Osmington House, Kintbury, Berks. *Club:* Army and Navy. [*Died* 22 *June* 1951.

RENNIE, William, C.B.E. 1941; M.A. (Edin. and Camb.); Hon. Litt.D. Liverp.

RENNIE, John, M.D. See page xxx.

1930; LL.D. (Edin.) 1933; LL.D. (Glasg.) 1947; sometime Fell. Trin. Coll., Camb.; Prof. of Humanity, 1927-34, of Greek, 1934-1946, Glasgow Univ. *Address:* 16 Glencairn Cr., Edinburgh 12. [*Died* 8 *Dec.* 1957.

RENNY, Colonel Lewis Frederick, C.M.G. 1918; D.S.O. 1915; late Royal Dublin Fusiliers; *b.* 4 July 1877; *y. s.* of William Renny, Southsea, Hants; *m.* 1908, Maud, 2nd *d.* of Rev. Canon Nicholson, M.A., Floraville, Cork. Entered army, 1897; Captain, 1904; Major, 1915; Col. 1920; A.D.C. to Major-General, S. Africa, 1900; employed with West African Frontier Force, 1904; Brigade-Major, Infantry Brigade, Malta, 1912-14; Expeditionary Force, 1914-18; served S. Africa, 1899-1902 (despatches; Queen's medal 4 clasps, King's medal 2 clasps); European War, 1914-18 (despatches seven times, D.S.O., Bt. Lt.-Col., C.M.G., Bt. Col.); Commandant, Machine Gun School, 1919-24; commanded 148th Infantry Brigade, 1924-25; Col. on Staff and Brigadier General Staff, India, 1925-29; retired pay, 1930. *Address:* 5 Armstrong House, Manor Fields, Putney, S.W.15. *T.:* Putney 0940. *Club:* Army and Navy. [*Died* 8 *June* 1955.

RENOUF, Winter Charles, C.I.E. 1920; *b.* 1868. *Educ.:* Victoria College, Jersey; Christ Church, Oxford. Entered I.C.S., 1887; Director of Land Records and Agriculture, Punjab, 1903; Director of Agriculture, 1906; Political Agent, Bahawalpur, 1916; retired, 1922. *Address:* Peverell, Greve d'Azette, Jersey, C.I. [*Died* 28 *June* 1954.

RENSHAW, John W., B.A., LL.D.; Principal, Shaftesbury House Tutorial College, Belfast, since 1911; *b.* 28 Dec. 1877; *e. s.* of John Renshaw, Newry; *m.* 1st, 1911, Esther (*d.* 1942), *d.* of Wm. Morton, Sec., Flax Spinners' Assoc., Belfast; 2nd, 1944, Evelyn M., *d.* of late Rev. E. B. Cullen, Belfast, ex-Pres. of Methodist Church in Ireland; no *c. Educ.:* Newry Intermediate School; Queen's College, Galway (Science and Literary Scholar); Queen's College, Belfast (Law Scholar and Prizeman), Senior Resident Master, High School for Boys, Croydon. M.P., Northern Ireland Parliament for Queen's Univ., 1943-45. Member Standing Committee of Convocation, Queen's Univ., Belfast, from 1930, and Member of Senate, Queen's Univ., since 1938. Member Overseas League. *Recreations:* golf and masonic activities. Past Captain Balmoral Golf Club and Belvoir Park Golf Club, Belfast. *Address:* 28 College Gardens, Belfast. *T.:* 23015 (Home), 23617 (Business) Belfast. *Clubs:* Balmoral Golf, Belvoir Park Golf, Belfast Rotary (Belfast). [*Died* 12 *Oct.* 1955.

RENWICK, Major Gustav Adolph; Ship Repairer and Transport Director; also farms extensively; *b.* 1883; 4th *s.* of Sir George Renwick, 1st Bt.; *m.* 1907, Mabel, *d.* of James Deuchar, Stichill House, Kelso; one *s. Educ.:* Giggleswick. Chairman: The Manchester Dry Docks Co. Ltd.; Fisher Renwick Investments Ltd.; Fisher Renwick Services Ltd.; Fisher Renwick Services (Manchester) Ltd.; Fisher Renwick Services (Wimbledon) Ltd.; Fisher Renwick Contracts Ltd.; French Renwick Ltd.; Beresford Atkinson Ltd.; "K" Garage Ltd.; Kingsway Garage (Manchester) Ltd.; Simpsons Motors (Manchester) Ltd.; Holystone Estates Ltd.; Shap Wells Hotel Ltd.; Director, Scammell Lorries Ltd.; former Member Executive Council: Shipping Federation; Chamber of Shipping of U.K.; former Dir. of Manchester Chamber of Commerce; Chm. Road Haulage (Operations) Advisory Cttee., Ministry of War Transport, 1941-. Served European War, 1914-18, with Northumberland Fusiliers (severely wounded, despatches). M.P. (Nat. Con.) Stretford Division of Lancashire, 1931-1935. *Recreations:* farming, shooting, racing, coursing, fishing. *Address:* Holystone Grange, Sharperton, Morpeth, Northumberland. *T.:* Hepple 223; Burnstones, Slaggyford, Carlisle. *T.:* Haltwhistle 235; Dilston House, Talbot Road, Old Trafford, Manchester, 16. *T.:* Trafford Park 3095. [*Died* 10 *Sept.* 1956.

REVELL, Daniel Graisberry, B.A., M.B.; Professor Emeritus of Anatomy, University of Alberta, Edmonton, Alta.; Member of American Association of Anatomists; Fellow, American Association for Advancement of Science; *b.* Ingersoll, Ont., Canada, 15 Aug. 1869; *s.* of James Charles Revell and Alice Dickson; *m.* 1896, Helen Rose, *d.* of Andrew Murray and Hannah Wright, Aylmer, Ont.; three *s.* one *d. Educ.:* Public Schools; Woodstock High School and Model; Guelph Collegiate Institute; Toronto University (B.A. 1894; M.B. 1900); Chicago University. Science Master, High School, Tillsonburg, Ont., 1889-91; Science Master, High School, Paris, Ont., 1894-97; Fellow in Anatomy, University of Chicago, 1900-2; Instructor in Anatomy, University of Chicago, and Rush Medical College, Chicago, Ill., 1902-1907; Provincial Pathologist and Bacteriologist, Government of Alberta, Edmonton, Alta., 1907-13; Professor and Head of Anatomy, University of Alberta, 1913-38. Has devoted much attention to criminology, examination of questioned documents, identification of handwriting (frequently called as handwriting expert in Supreme Court of Alberta and Court of King's Bench of Saskatchewan and for Royal Canadian Mounted Police) and to general principles of identification. Served with C.A.M.C., with rank of Captain, 1917-19, as pathologist to Edmonton Area of Mil. Dist. No. 13; Member of Strathcona Hospital Board, 1910-12, and of Edmonton Hospital Board, 1912-13; Director, Provincial Laboratory, 1907-14; Pres. Edmonton Med. Soc., 1910-11; Pres. Alberta Med. Association, 1917-18; Member of Canadian National Committee for Mental Hygiene, 1918-36; Member of Alberta Medical Council, 1919-22; Member Medical Council of Canada, 1920-28. Protestant. *Publications:* The Pancreatic Ducts in the Dog, in Amer. Jour. Anat.; Laboratory Manual of Anatomy (with Lewellys F. Barker and Dean D. Lewis), 1904; anatomical research; articles on public health and medicine. *Recreations:* nature study, books and art. *Address:* 9105 112th Street, Edmonton, Alberta, Canada. [*Died* 25 *Aug.* 1954.

REVELL-SMITH, Maj.-Gen. William Revell, C.B. 1946; C.B.E. 1944; D.S.O. 1940; M.C. and bar 1917; A.M.; *b.* Melbourne, Aust., 1894; *o. s.* of late Herbert Smith, 1 Pont St., S.W.1; *m.* 1920, Norma, F.A.N.Y. 1914-18 and 1939-45 (Order of Elizabeth (Belgium), Croix de Guerre with bronze star (France), despatches), *o. d.* of late J. G. Flowerdew Lowson, Quarwood House, Stow on the Wold; one *s.* one *d. Educ.:* Charterhouse. Served European War, 1914-1918, R.A., 1914-19 (despatches, M.C. and bar, A.M., Croix de Guerre avec Palme, France). Retired pay, 1949. Commander Legion of Merit (U.S.A.), 1946; Commander, Order of Crown with Palm, Croix de Guerre avec Palme (Belgium). *Address:* Devon Estates, Marandellas, S. Rhodesia. *Club:* Army and Navy. [*Died* 4 *June* 1956.

REYNE, Rear-Admiral Sir Cecil Nugent, K.B.E., *cr.* 1944; Rear-Admiral retired; *b.* 23 Dec. 1881; 2nd *s.* of late Major J. F. Reyne, Hampshire Regt.; *m.* 1917, Gladys Mary, *d.* of Capt. H. C. Savory, Seaforth Highlanders; one *s.* three *d. Educ.:* H.M.S. Britannia. Gunnery specialist; Gunnery and Executive Officer, H.M.S. Dreadnought, 1914-18; Commander H.M.S. Royal Oak, 1918-20; S.G.O. to late Admiral Sir R. Phillimore; Flag Captain and Chief Staff Officer 2nd Cruiser Squadron, 1923-25; Commanded H.M.S. Effingham, 1925; Senior Officer, Reserve Fleet, Devonport; 2nd Naval Member, New Zealand Naval Board, 1927-30; Commanded H.M.S. Berwick,

1933; A.D.C. to the King, 1934; retired with rank of Rear-Admiral, 1934; recalled 1939, served as Commodore Convoys (despatches). *Address:* Brookfield, Alverstoke, S. Hants. *T.:* Gosport 8437. [*Died* 19 *Feb.* 1958.

REYNOLDS, Cedric Lawton, M.A.; Headmaster of Nottingham High School, 1925-53; retd. Dec. 1953; *b.* 1888; *s.* of R. Reynolds, J.P., Wakefield; *m.* 1921, Margaret Aimée, *d.* of G. Muskett, Kemerton, Tewkesbury; two *d.* *Educ.:* Queen Elizabeth's Grammar School, Wakefield; Clare College, Cambridge. First class honours in mathematics (11th Wrangler) and natural science; late Head of Science Dept., Rugby School; previously for ten years Master at the R.N. College, Dartmouth. Member, Departmental Committee on Public Schools, 1942 - 44. *Address:* Overbrook, Godshill, Fordingbridge, Hants. *T.:* Fordingbridge 3176. [*Died* 23 *May* 1958.

REYNOLDS, Frank, R.I. 1903; *b.* London, 13 Feb. 1876; *s.* of late W. G. Reynolds; *m.* 1905, Winifred, *d.* of David Braick Milne, Liverpool; one *s.* two *d.* Joined Punch staff 25 June 1919; Art Editor of Punch, 1920-30; contributor to Illustrated London News and Sketch, etc.; illustrator of Dickens. *Publications:* Pictures of Paris, and other books. *Address:* Nyren, Giggs Hill Green, Thames Ditton, Surrey. [*Died* 18 *April* 1953.

REYNOLDS, Frank Neon, F.R.C.S.Ed., F.R.C.O.G., M.R.C.S.(Eng.), L.R.C.P.(Lond.); Hon. Surgeon Hosp. for Women, Soho Square; Hon. Obstetric Consultant to County of Herts, Hon. Obstetric Surgeon, Hospital for Women and Children, Harrow Road; Consulting Gynaecologist to Hackney Borough Council; Examiner to Central Midwives Board; *b.* 1895; *yr. s.* of late Robert Reynolds, R.D., R.N.R.; *m.* 1926, Freda, *yr. d.* of A. R. Wilson, Ingatestone, Essex; one *s.* two *d.* *Educ.:* Epsom College; St. Thomas's Hospital. Served with H.M. Forces, 1914-18; first with Mediterannean Forces (Dardanelles) and later as Surgeon-Lieutenant R.N.; with the Grand Fleet present at Battle of Jutland in H.M.S. Oak; transferred to Dover Patrol and present, in H.M.S. Broke at Blocking of Ostend; After the war held resident appointments at St. Thomas' s Hospital where he was Senior Obstetric House Physician; later Medical Superintendent, Hospital for Sick Children, Great Ormond Street; Registrar and Pathologist Hospital for Women, Soho Square; Chief Assistant to Gynæcological and Obstetrical Departments, St. Thomas's Hospital; Gynaecologist Southend General Hospital; Surgeon Emergency Medical Service, 1939-45. *Publications:* The Relief of Pain in Child-birth, 1934; contributions in Medical Journals on Pædiatrics and Obstetrics. *Recreations:* tennis, golf, fishing, shooting. *Address:* 147 Harley Street, W.1. *T.:* Welbeck 1598; 71 Harley House, N.W.1. *Clubs:* Bath, Hurlingham; Sunningdale Golf (Sunningdale). [*Died* 22 *Dec.* 1952.

REYNOLDS, Lieut.-Col. Sir John Francis Roskell, 2nd Bt., *cr.* 1923; M.B.E. 1945; J.P.; Irish Guards; partner Reynolds and Gibson, Liverpool, London and Manchester; Chairman Combined English Mills (Spinners) Ltd., Atherton; Dir.: Martin's Bank, Sea Insurance Co. Ltd., Harrods (Buenos Aires); *b.* 23 June 1899; *e. s.* of Sir James Philip Reynolds, 1st Bt., and Leila, 2nd *d.* of Nicholas R. Roskell, Kensington; *S.* father, 1932; *m.* 1st, 1921, Milicent (*d.* 1931), *d.* of late Major J. Orr-Ewing and late Lady Margaret Orr-Ewing; one *s.* one *d.*; 2nd, 1933, Constance, 2nd *d.* of late Col. J. H. E. Holford, C.M.G., D.S.O.; one *s.* one *d.* *Educ.:* Downside; Christ Church, Oxford. Served European War, Irish Guards: also War of 1939-45 (M.B.E.). High Sheriff, Lancashire, 1952. *Recreation:* sport. *Heir:* *s.* David James, *b.* 26 Jan. 1924. *Address:* 30 Exchange Street East, Liverpool; 67 Chelsea Square, S.W.3. *T.:* Flaxman 9574. *Clubs:* Guards, White's. [*Died* 20 *Aug.* 1956.

RHOADS, Cornelius Packard, M.D.; Director, Sloan-Kettering Institute for Cancer Research, since 1945; Scientific Director, Memorial Center for Cancer and Allied Diseases, since 1953; Professor of Pathology, Department of Biology and Growth, Sloan-Kettering Division of Cornell University Medical College, since 1952; *b.* Springfield, Mass., 20 June 1898; *s.* of George Holmes Rhoads and Harriet E. Barney; *m.* 1936, Katherine Southwick Bolman; no *c.* *Educ.:* Bowdoin Coll., graduated 1920 (A.B.); Harvard Medical Sch., graduated 1924 (M.D. *cum laude*). Various appts., 1924-28; Rockefeller Inst. for Med. Research: Associate, 1928-33; Pathologist (Hosp. of Inst.), 1931-1939. Dir., Memorial Hosp. for the Treatment of Cancer and Allied Diseases, N.Y. City, 1940-50; Dir., Memorial Center for Cancer and Allied Diseases, N.Y. City, 1950-1955. Professor of Pathology, Cornell Univ. Med. Coll., 1940-52. Colonel, Medical Corps, Army of the U.S.; Chief, Med. Division, Chemical Warfare Service, 1943 - 45. Member, Cancer Chemotherapy Commission, U.S.P.H.S., 1953-; also Consultant to other organisations and member of many committees and associations. Clement Cleveland Award, 1948; American Cancer Soc. Award, 1955; Walker Prize, 1951-56, Royal College of Surgeons; Fellow American Association for the Advancement of Science (Chairman, Section on Medical Sciences, 1953, Vice-Pres., 1953). Legion of Merit (U.S.), 1945. Holds honorary degrees. *Publications:* numerous contributions to American medical and scientific journals. *Recreations:* sailing and gardening. *Address:* Sloan-Kettering Institute for Cancer Research, 410 East 68th St., New York 21, N.Y., U.S.A. *T.:* Trafalgar 9-3000, ext. 251-2-3, and 544. *Clubs:* Army and Navy, University, Century Association (New York); Harvard (Boston), etc. [*Died* 13 *Aug.* 1959.

RHODES, Sir Edward, Kt., *cr.* 1921; J.P.; *b.* 10 Apr. 1870: *e. s.* of John William and Charlotte Rhodes, Manchester; *m.* 2nd, 1940, Marguerite, *d.* of William Dodd, Keldwith, Windermere. A deputy Chairman of the City of Manchester Advisory Committee National Service, 1915-1918; Chairman to the Board of Trade and Ministry of Shipping, Textile Exports Shipping Committee, 1917-18; Member of Board of Trade Advisory Council, 1934-37; Emeritus Director Manchester Chamber of Commerce; President, 1937; Vice-President of Associated British Chambers of Commerce, London, 1938-46. *Address:* Cairncroft, Didsbury, Manchester 20. *Club:* Reform (Manchester). [*Died* 18 *Dec.* 1959.

RHODES, Harold William, Mus.D. (Lond.); F.R.C.O., A.R.C.M.; *b.* Hanley, Staffs., 15 Sept. 1889; *m.* 1914; two *s.* *Educ.:* Royal College of Music. Acting-Assistant to Sir Walter Parratt at St. George's Chapel, Windsor, 1908-10; Music Master, Lancing College, 1910-12; Organist, St. John's, Torquay, 1912-28; Organist Coventry Cathdedral, 1928-33; Organist Winchester Cathedral, 1933-49; late Professor, Royal Academy of Music. *Publications:* Church Music, Songs and Part Songs. *Address:* 31 Church Way, Sanderstead, Surrey. *T.:* 3875. [*Died* 27 *Feb.* 1956.

RHODES, Col. Hon. Sir Heaton; *see* Rhodes Col. Hon. Sir R. H.

RHODES, Rev. Herbert A., M.A.; *b.* Uttoxeter, 8 June 1869; *s.* of T. E. Rhodes, M.A., head-master of Uttoxeter Grammar School and of Brewood Grammar School; unmarried. *Educ.:* Shrewsbury School, 1883-88; Christ Church, Oxford, 1888-92 (Exhibitioner). Assistant Master at Yarlet Preparatory School, N. Stafford; Felsted School, Essex, 1894-96; Giggleswick School, Yorks, 1896-99; Curate of Brewood (Staffs.), 1899-1900; Chaplain and Assistant

Master at Bilton Grange, Rugby, 1900-2; Senior Master of Christ's Hospital Preparatory School, 1902-4; Headmaster of Ardingly Coll., 1904-11; Headmaster of Cranleigh School, Surrey, 1911-1931; Vicar of Iford with Kingston-near-Lewes, 1932-45. *Address:* Downside, Kingston, Lewes, Sussex. *T.:* Lewes 197. [*Died* 23 *Jan.* 1956.

RHODES, Lt.-Col. Sir John (Phillips), 2nd Bt., *cr.* 1919; D.S.O. 1918; *b.* 19 July 1884; *er. s.* of Sir George Rhodes, 1st Bt., and Margaret Catherine, *o. d.* of John Phillips, Liverpool; *S.* father, 1924; *m.* 1st, 1913, Elsie Constance (who obtained a divorce, 1925), *d.* of late Lt.-Col. G. A. Maclean Buckley, C.B.E., D.S.O.; one *s.*; 2nd, 1926, Doris Mary, *o. d.* of William H. Adams. *Educ.:* Harrow; R.M.A., Woolwich. Entered Royal Engineers, 1904; served European War, 1914-18 (D.S.O., Croix de Guerre, Bt. Major); retired with rank of Lieut.-Col., 1919; M.P. (C.) Stalybridge and Hyde Division of Cheshire, 1922-1923; F.R.G.S. *Heir: s.* Christopher George [*b.* 30 April 1914; *m.* 1st, 1936, Mary, *o. c.* of Horace Kesteven; 2nd, 1943, Mary Florence (Maonie), *er. d.* of late Dr. Douglas Wardleworth; one *s.* (*b.* 24 May 1946).] *Address:* 26 Westminster Gardens, S.W.1. *T.:* Victoria 7005. *Clubs:* Boodle's, United Service. [*Died* 14 *Nov.* 1955.

RHODES, Colonel Hon. Sir (Robert) Heaton, K.C.V.O., *cr.* 1927; K.B.E., *cr.* 1920; V.D.; Hon. Colonel 1st N.Z. Mounted Rifles; *b.* Purau, Lyttelton, 27 Feb. 1861; *s.* of late Robert Heaton Rhodes, Christchurch, at one time M.P. for Akaroa; *m.* Jessie Cooper (*d.* 1929), *y. d.* of late Walter Clark, of Glenara, Victoria. *Educ.:* New Zealand, Brasenose College, Oxford. M.A. 1887; Barrister-at-law, Inner Temple, 1887; Member House of Representatives for Ellesmere 1899-1925; M.L.C. 1925-32 and 1934-41; served South African War with the 8th N.Z. Contingent; commanded the Canterbury Mounted Rifles Brigade of New Zealand Territorial Force; Postmaster-General and Minister for Public Health, Hospitals, and Tourist Resorts, 1912-15; N.Z. Red Cross Commissioner, in Great Britain and France, 1917-19; Special Commissioner to Egypt and Gallipoli to report on conditions *re* New Zealand Troops, 1915-16; Minister of Defence, 1920-26; Commissioner of State Forests, 1922-26; Member of Executive Council, without Portfolio, 1926-28, and Deputy Leader of Legislative Council of New Zealand, 1926-28; Bailiff Grand Cross, Order of St. John of Jerusalem, 1931. *Address:* Otahuna, Tai Tapu, Canterbury, N.Z. [*Died* 30 *July* 1956.

RHONDDA, 2nd Viscountess, *cr.* 1918, of Llanwern; **Margaret Haig Thomas;** Editor Time and Tide; Chairman Time and Tide Publishing Co., Ltd.; *d.* of 1st Viscount Rhondda and Sybil Margaret (*d.* 1941), *d.* of G. A. Haig, Penithon, Radnorshire; *S.* father, 1918; *m.* 1908, Sir Humphrey Mackworth, 7th Bt. (from whom she obt. a div., 1923, and who *d.* 1948). *Educ.:* St. Leonards Sch., St. Andrews; Somerville Coll., Oxford. Pres. University Coll. of S. Wales and Monmouthshire, 1950-55. Hon. LL.D., Wales, 1955. *Publications:* D. A. Thomas, Viscount Rhondda, 1921; Leisured Women, 1928; This was My World, 1933; Notes on the Way, 1937. *Address:* 70 Arlington House, St. James's, S.W.1; Churt Halewell, Shere, Surrey. *T.:* Shere 248. [*Died* 20 *July* 1958.

RHYS-WILLIAMS, Lt.-Col. Sir R.; *see* Williams.

RICE, Alexander Hamilton, M.A., M.D., D.Sc. (hon.); Founder, Organizer and former Director of Institute of Geographical Exploration, Harvard University; Prof. Emeritus of Geographical Exploration, Harvard University; Ex-Chm., Bd. of Trustees, Spanish Nationalist Relief Cttee.; Mem.: Bd. of Trustees, American Museum Natural History; many European and American learned socs.; *b.* Boston, Massachusetts, 29 Aug. 1875; *e. s.* of late John Hamilton Rice and Cora Lee Clark; *m.* 1st, 1915, Eleanor (*d.* 1937), *d.* of late William L. Elkins, and *widow* of George D. Widener, Philadelphia; 2nd, 1949, Mrs. Dorothy Farrington Upham, *d.* of late Robert I. Farrington, and *widow* of John P. Upham. *Educ.:* Noble and Greenough School; Harvard University, 1894-1903; Surgical interne Massachusetts General Hospital, 1903-05; Royal Geographical Society's School of Geog. Surveying and Field Astronomy, 1909-10; Member Surgical Staff of the Ambulance Americaine, Paris, 1914-15; Surgeon and Director of Hôpital 72, Paris, Aug. 1914-Jan. 1915. Commissioned Lieut. U.S.N.R.F., 8 Oct. 1917; Instructor of Navigation and Nautical Astronomy, 2nd Naval District Training School; appointed Director of same, Dec. 1917; Lecturer, Lowell Institute, Dec. 1922; Explored Napo River, Ecuador, 1901; crossed Venezuela and Colombia from Caracas to Bogota, 1906-07; explored, surveyed and mapped Caiari-Uaupés River of Colombia, Brazil, 1907-08; further explorations in the N.W. Amazons Basin of important tributary rivers of the Caqueta, Negro, and Orinoco Systems, 1911-13; ascended Amazons—Solimoēs River to Iquitos, Peru, in s. y. Alberta, Dec. 1916-May 1917; carried out survey of rio Negro; Medical Survey carried out in addition to geographical work, July 1919-May 1920; Exploration and mapping of rio Branco-Uraricuera-Parima to its source in Serra Parima, 1924-25; Patron's Gold Medal of Royal Geographical Society and Gold Medal of Harvard Travellers' Club, 1914; Hon. M.A., Harvard, 1915; Elisha Kent Kane Medal, Geog. Soc. Philadelphia, 1920; David Livingstone Centenary Medal, American Geog. Soc., 1920; Gold Medal, Mercator-Ortelius, Société Royale de Géographie d'Anvers, 1931; Gold Medal of the Society of Mayflower Descendants in the State of New York, 1934; Comdr. de la Légion d'Honneur, 1938; Grande Médaille de la Soc. de Geog., Paris, 1939; Gran Cruz Orden de Isabel la Catolica, 1940. *Publications:* Quito to Iquitos by the River Napo, 1903; The River Uaupés, with Map, 1910; Further Explorations in the N.W. Amazons Basin, with Map, 1914; Notes on the Rio Negro (Amazonas); The Rio Negro, the Casiquiare Canal, and the Upper Orinoco, with Map, 1921; Exploration at the Head Waters of the Branco and Orinoco; through Amazon Jungles with Radio and Hydroplane, 1925; The rio Branco-Uraricuera-Parima, with Map, 1928; El rio Negro (Amazonas) y sus grandes affluentes de la Guayana Brasileña; Exploration en Guyane Brésilienne; Air Photography in Geog. Exploration and in Topographical and Geological Surveying. *Address:* Miramar, Bellevue Avenue, Newport, Rhode Island, U.S.A.; 901 Fifth Avenue, New York; 22 rue Barbet de Jouy, Paris. *Clubs:* Boodle's, Hurlingham, International Sportsmen's; Geographical; Travellers'; Union Interalliée (Paris); Harvard, New York Yacht, Explorers', Ends of the Earth, Racquet, Knickerbocker Union, Brook, River, Turf and Field, Automobile (New York); Somerset, Tavern, Tennis and Racquet (Boston); Philadelphia (Phila.). [*Died* 23 *July* 1956.

RICE, Cale Young; poet, dramatist, novelist; *b.* Dixon, Kentucky, U.S.A., 7 Dec. 1872; *s.* of Laban M. and Martha Rice, *m.* Alice Caldwell Hegan (*d.* 1942). *Educ.:* A.B. Cumberland University, 1893; A.B. Harvard; 1895; A.M. 1896; LL.D. University of Kentucky, 1927; Litt.D., Rollins College, 1928; Litt.D. University of Louisville, 1937; Professor of English Literature, Cumberland University, 1896-97; has since devoted himself to writing, extensive travels, occasional lectures and readings; a founder and first President of the Arts Club of Louisville; Member of Board of Governors of J. B. Speed Memorial Art Museum; Member Advisory Council, Univ. of Louisville. *Publications:* (*Poems*) From Dusk to Dusk, 1898; With

Omar, 1900; Song-Surf, 1900; Nirvana Days, 1908; Many Gods, 1910; Far Quests, 1912; At the World's Heart, 1914; Collected Plays and Poems, 1915; Earth and New Earth (including Gerhard of Ryle, a drama), 1916; Trails Sunward, 1917; Wraiths and Realities, 1918; Songs to A.H.R., 1918; Shadowy Thresholds, 1919; Sea Poems, 1921; Mihrima (a drama) and other Poems, 1922; A Pilgrim's Scrip, 1924; A Sea Lover's Scrip, 1925; Bitter Brew, 1925; Selected Plays and Poems, definitive edition, 1926; Stygian Freight, 1927; Seed of The Moon, 1929; High Perils, 1933. *Poetic dramas*: Charles di Tocca, 1903; David. 1904; Yolanda of Cyprus, included in Plays and Lyrics, 1906, and produced as grand opera, music by Clarence Loomis, 1929; A Night in Avignon, 1907; The Immortal Lure (four one-act dramas), 1911; Porzia, 1913; (*short stories*) Turn About Tales (with Alice Hegan Rice), 1920; Winners and Losers (with Alice Hegan Rice) 1925; Passionate Follies (with Alice Hegan Rice), 1936; Youth's Way (novel), 1923; Early Reaping (novel), 1929; The Swamp-Bird (prose play), 1931; Love and Lord Byron (prose play), 1936; Bridging the Years, autobiography, including Poetry's Genii (criticism), 1939; Quadric Realism, a New Approach to Philosophy. *Recreations*: travel and golf. *Clubs*: Authors'; Arts (Louisville). [*Died* 23 *Jan.* 1943.

[*But death not notified in time for inclusion in Who Was Who 1941–1950, first edn.*

RICE, Lt.-Col. Sidney Mervyn, C.I.E. 1917; C.B.E. 1919; late 64th Pioneers, I.A.; *b.* 4 Mar. 1873; *s.* of late Lewis Rice, C.I.E., of Greenhalgh, Harrow; *m.* 1923, Dorothy Anna, *d.* of Lt.-Col. C. T. Sennett, Hove. Entered Army, 1893; Capt. Indian Army, 1902; Major, 1911; Lt.-Col. 1918; served Afghan War, 1919 (C.B.E.); retd., 1922. *Address*: Tudor Cottage, Hound St., Sherborne, Dorset. [*Died* 5 *Feb.* 1959.

RICE, Rev. William Ignatius, O.S.B., M.A.; Headmaster of Douai School, 1915-1952; retired July 1952; Titular Prior of Gloucester, 1954; *b.* 1883. *Educ.*: Douai; Oxford; St. Anselmo, Rome. *Address*: Douai School, Woolhampton, nr. Reading. *T.*: Woolhampton 414. [*Died* 22 *April* 1955.

RICH, Edmund Milton, C.B.E. 1941; F.C.G.I., B.Sc.; *b.* 12 July 1875; *s.* of Thomas Rich, Tetbury, Glos. and Elizabeth Cuddeford, Plymouth; *m.* Louisa Anne Grone; two *s.* *Educ.*: Aske's Hatcham School; Central Technical College, S. Kensington. Demonstrator, Central Technical College, 1895-96; Science Master, Owen's School, Islington and Colfe's Grammar School, Lewisham, 1896-99; organiser of science classes, Staffs C.C., 1899-1901; Inspector, Dept. of Agriculture and Technical Instruction (Ireland), 1901-05; Principal Assistant, Education Officer's Dept., L.C.C., 1905-07; Head of Technology Branch, 1907-10; Elementary Branch, 1910-28; Technology Branch, 1928-33; Assistant Education Officer, 1912; Senior Assistant Education Officer, 1928; Education Officer, 1933-1940; Vice-President Royal Soc. of Arts, 1948; Governor, The Covenantors Educational Trust, 1945; Educational Adviser, National Police Fund, 1946; Chm. Chadwick Trustees, 1950; Hon. Treas. Commonwealth Youth Sunday Cttee., 1948; Freeman and Liveryman Worshipful Company of Haberdashers, 1947; Pres. Old Centralians Assoc. (City & Guilds College), 1951-52; Pres. London Schools Swimming Assoc., 1953. *Publications*: various scientific and educational reports. *Recreations*: gardening, walking, cycling. *Address*: 69 Copers Cope Road, Beckenham, Kent. *T.*: Beckenham 1263. [*Died* 14 *April* 1954.

RICH, Edward Charles, M.A. (Oxon.); *b.* London, 15 July 1895; *m.* 1927, Alison Mary, *d.* of late Major R. M. Richardson, 14th King's Hussars, Amwellbury, Ware, Hertfordshire; one *s.* three *d.* *Educ.*: City of London School; Christ Church, Oxford (B.A. 1920, 2nd Class Hons. Theology, Liddon Student, M.A. 1923); Cuddesdon College. Deacon, 1921; Priest, 1922; Curate of St. Mary Redcliffe, Bristol, 1921-1923; Domestic Chaplain to Bishop (Burge) of Oxford, 1923-24; Priest-in-Charge of St. Mary's, Bourdon Street, W.1, 1924-28; Vicar of Batheaston with St. Catherine, 1928-31; Chief Diocesan Inspector of Schools, London, 1931-34; Prebendary of St. Paul's, 1931-35; Vicar of Chiswick, 1934-44; Rural Dean of Hammersmith, 1943-44; Professor of Theology, Queen's College, Harley Street, 1935-44. Director of Religious Education, Peterborough, 1944-50; Canon Residentiary of Peterborough Cathedral, 1944-51; Canon Emeritus of Peterborough, 1951-56; Chancellor and Chapter Librarian, 1946-51, resigned. Vicar of Padbury and Rector of Adstock, 1954-56, resigned. Received into the Catholic Church, 1956. *Publications*: Discipleship and Christian Worship, 1932; The Gift of the Spirit, 1934; Some Principles of Evangelism, 1948; The Church of England (in From Bible to Creed), 1949; Spiritual Authority in the Church of England, 1953. Editor, Church Teaching Quarterly, 1951-52. *Recreations*: walking, conversation. *Address*: 31 Yeomans Row, S.W.3. *T.*: Kensington 8401. *Club*: Reform. [*Died* 26 *May* 1959.

RICH, Rt. Hon. Sir George (Edward), P.C. 1936; K.C.M.G., *cr.* 1932; a Justice of Supreme Court of N.S.W., 1911-13, and of the High Court of Australia, 1913-50; (acting Chief Justice, 1940-41); Member of Judicial Cttee. of the Privy Council, 1936; *b.* Braidwood, N.S. Wales, 3 May 1863; *s.* of late Rev. C. H. Rich; *m.* 1st, (wife *d.* 1945), *d.* of late Hon. R. R. S. Bowker, M.D., F.R.C.S., M.L.C.; one *s.* one *d.* (one *s.* killed in European war, 1915); 2nd, 1950, Letitia Fetherstonhaugh Strong, *d.* of late Rowland Woodward, Melbourne. *Educ.*: Grammar School and University, Sydney; M.A. Called to the Bar (N.S.W.), 1887; sometime Challis Lecturer in Law within the University of Sydney; K.C. 1911; one of the Australian delegates at the League of Nations, Geneva, 1922. LL.D. (h.c.) Sydney, 1952. *Address*: 104 Elizabeth Bay Road, Sydney, New South Wales. *Clubs*: Athenæum (London); Australian (Sydney). [*Died* 14 *May* 1956.

RICHARDS, Sir Edmund Charles, K.C.M.G., *cr.* 1944 (C.M.G. 1937); Kt., *cr.* 1941; *b.* 6 Oct. 1889; *s.* of late Edmund Richards, Civil Servant, and Amelia Symes; *m.* 1926, Jean Margaret Joanna, *d.* of late George Barron Beattie, Bieldside, Aberdeenshire; one *d.* East African Protectorate, 1909-12; Nyasaland, 1912-14; King's African Rifles, 1914-17 (German East Africa, Croix de Guerre with palms, despatches); Assistant Political Officer, 1917; Tanganyika Territory Administrative Officer (1st Grade), 1922; District Commissioner, 1923; Assistant Secretary for Native Affairs, 1927; Deputy Provincial Commissioner, 1928; Provincial Commissioner, 1931; Deputy Chief Secretary, 1934; Acting Chief Secretary, 1934; Resident Commissioner, Basutoland, 1935-42; Governor and C.-in-C. of Nyasaland, 1942-48. *Recreations*: golf, shooting, fishing. *Address*: Kokstad, E. Griqualand, S. Africa. *Clubs*: Athenæum, East India and Sports. [*Died* 28 *June* 1955.

RICHARDS, Hon. Sir Frederick William, Kt., *cr.* 1946; LL.D. (Lond.); late Senior Puisne Judge of Supreme Court of South Australia; *b.* Gawler, South Australia, 3 Oct. 1869; *s.* of late William Richards; *m.* Ida Jane, *d.* of John Drayton, Exeter; one *d.* *Educ.*: Shebbear College, North Devon. Doctor of Laws, London University, 1896; admitted Solicitor (England), 1896; South Australia, 1897; Associate to C.J. (S.A.), 1901-8; Parliamentary Draftsman (S.A.), 1908-16; Crown Solicitor (S.A.), 1916-25; Acting Judge Supreme Court, 1925-27; Puisne

Judge, 1927-45. *Address:* Unley Park, South Australia. [*Died* 31 *March* 1957.

RICHARDS, Rev. George Chatterton, D.D.; *b.* Churchover, Warwickshire, 24 Aug. 1867; *s.* of John Richards, of St. Keverne Cornwall, and Mary Elizabeth, *d.* of George Chatterton of Brumby, Lincs; *m.* Annie Elizabeth, *d.* of W. D. Hughes, of St. Leonards; two *s.* five *d.* *Educ.:* Rugby (scholar); Balliol College, Oxford (scholar); 1st Mods. and Ireland and Craven Scholar, 1887; 1st Lit. Hum., 1889; Craven Fellow and Derby Scholar, 1890; Fellow of Hertford College, 1889-91; Prof. of Greek, University College, Cardiff, 1891-98; deacon, 1895; priest, 1897; curate of St. John the Baptist, Cardiff, 1895-98; assistant director British School at Athens, 1899; Fellow, Tutor and Chaplain, Oriel College, Oxford, 1899-1924; Senior Proctor, 1907; Class. Hon. Moderator, 1902-3, 1909-10; hon. secretary of the English Classical Association, 1920-26; Vicar of St. Mary-the-Virgin, Oxford, 1923-27; Canon of Durham and Professor of Greek and Classical Literature in Univ. of Durham, 1927-34; D.D. Oxon, 1924; Senior Fellow of Oriel College, 1926-32; Examining Chaplain to the Bishop of Durham, 1927-34; D.D. Durham, 1929. *Publications:* The Provosts and Fellows of Oriel College (with Dr. C. L. Shadwell), 1922; The Dean's Register of Oriel (with Rev. H. E. Salter), 1926; A Concise Dictionary to the Vulgate New Testament, 1934; More's Utopia translated into Modern English, 1923; Cicero, a study, 1935; Baptism and Confirmation, 1942; Translator of (from German) an Old Catholic view of Confession, 1905; Buschor's Greek Vase Painting, 1920; Wilamowitz, Erinnerungen, 1929; Wilcken's Alexander der Grosse, 1932; (from Danish) Poulsen's Delphi, 1919; Travels and Sketches, 1923; Sculpture in English Country Seats, 1922; (from Swedish) Brilioth's The Anglican Revival, 1924; Nilsson's Imperial Rome, 1926; Nygren's Der tyska Kyrkostriden, 1934; articles in Classical Review, Classical Quarterly, Journal of Theological Studies, Church Quarterly Review. *Address:* 2 Winchester Road, Oxford. [*Died* 27 *Jan.* 1951.

RICHARDS, Sir Henry Maunsell, Kt., *cr.* 1930; C.B. 1920; Chairman Council Grenfell Association; Member: Herts County Council Education Cttee.; Governor Stowe School, Haileybury College, and Hertford Grammar School; *b.* 17 Nov. 1869; *s.* of late Rev. J. Richards, M.A., Senior Chaplain, Bengal Establishment; *m.* Helen Margaretta, *d.* of late Col. D. O'Brien, R.E. *Educ.:* Merchant Taylors' School; St. John's College, Oxford. H.M. Inspector of Schools, 1902; Divisional Inspector, 1911; Chief Inspector for the Training of Teachers, 1917; Chief Inspector Elementary Schools, 1918; Senior Chief Inspector, 1926; retired, 1933; LL.D. University of St. Andrews, 1929. *Address:* The Dell, Hertingfordbury, Hertford. *T.:* Hertford 3625. [*Died* 9 *Dec.* 1957.

RICHARDS, Henry William, Mus. Doc.; F.R.C.O.; Hon. R.A.M.; Hon. R.C.M.; *b.* Notting Hill, 1865; *s.* of William and Helen Richards; *m.* 1894, Theodora C. (*d.* 1953), *d.* of Theodore Walrond, C.B.; one *d.* (and one *s.* decd.). *Educ.:* All Saints, Notting Hill Choir School. Organist, St. John's, Kilburn, 1880; Organist, Queen's Hall Choral Society, 1897; late organist and choirmaster Christ Church, Lancaster Gate; Examiner University of Durham, 1919-21; Warden of the Royal Academy of Music, 1924-34; late Member of the Committee of Management of the R.A.M.; Council of the R.C.O.; President of R.C.O., 1925-27; Representative of Music on the Teachers Registration Council, 1912-27; Chairman Board of Studies in Music, London University 1925, and External Examiner, 1940; late Director of the Royal Philharmonic Society; Examiner, R.C.O.; late Member of the Associated Board R.A.M. and R.C.M. *Publications:* Anthems; Lectures R.C.O.; Organ accompaniment of the Church Services; Church Choir Training. *Address:* The Slade, Mortimer West End, Berks. *T.:* Silchester 215. [*Died* 4 *Jan.* 1956.

RICHARDS, Herbert Arthur, C.B.E. 1929; Retired Consular Officer; *b.* Southsea, Hants, 30 Jan. 1866; *s.* of Lt.-Col. W. M. Richards; *m.* Elsie Stainton; one *s.* *Educ.:* Framlingham. An Assistant in the British Central Africa Protectorate, 1900-1; Oriental Secretary to the Legation at Tehran; H.M. Vice-Consul, Tehran, 1903; transferred to Bushire, 1904; to Zanzibar, 1906; to Abidjean, West Africa, 1907; Acting Consul at Loanda, 1908; Acting Consul-General at Dakar, 1908, 1909 and 1910; Acting Consul at Lorenzo Marques, 1910; Vice-Consul at Beira, 1910; Consul for the Society Islands, 1912; also a Deputy Commissioner for the Western Pacific, 1912; Acting Consul at Calais, 1916-19; in charge at Callao, 1919; Consul there, 1919; in charge of the Legation at Lima, 1922 and 1923; Consul-General, Chicago, 1923; retired, 1928. *Address:* c/o Midland Bank Ltd., 36 Old Bond Street, W.1. [*Died* 6 *March* 1957.

RICHARDS, John Eugene; Town Clerk and Clerk of the Peace for the City of Nottingham since 1936; *b.* 18 Nov. 1885; 2nd *s.* of William Lewis Richards, Holyhead, Anglesey, and Margaret, *d.* of William McCulloch, Pinwherry, Ayrshire; *m.* 1915, Sarah Annie, *d.* of H. Tomlinson, Gnosall, Staffs. *Educ.:* Alford Grammar School (Queen Elizabeths); Pocklington School, East Yorks. Articled to S. B. Carnley, Alford, Lincs; private practice, 1908-14. Served European War with Sherwood Foresters and Loyal North Lancs, 1914-19; Adjutant, Sherwood Foresters 3rd Bn., 1917-19; retired with rank of Captain. Assistant Solicitor, Nottingham Corporation, 1919-23; Deputy Town Clerk, 1923-36. *Address:* The Guildhall, Nottingham. *T.:* 43051; 13 Carisbrooke Drive, Mapperley Park, Nottingham. *T.:* 66135. *Club:* Borough (Nottingham). [*Died* 13 *Jan.* 1951.

RICHARDS, Very Rev. John Harold, M.A.; *b.* 1869; *s.* of William Richards, Llanafan, Cards.; *m.* 1st, 1902, Amy (*d.* 1912), *d.* of late Rev. T. H. Evans, Vicar of Llanrhaiadr, Mont.; four *s.* one *d*; 2nd, 1939, Gladys Marian, also *d.* of late Rev. T. H. Evans. *Educ.:* Wrexham Grammar School; Fitzwilliam Hall, Cambridge. Deacon, 1895; Priest, 1896; Curate, St. Matthew's, Cambridge, 1895-98, and Secretary Ely Diocesan C.E.T.S.; Secretary Worcester Diocesan C.E.T.S., 1898-1900; Vicar of St. Andrew's, Bordesley, 1900-1915; Maney, 1915-20; Coleshill, 1920-29; Rural Dean of Bordesley, 1913-15; Vicar of St. Augustine's, Edgbaston, Birmingham, 1929-37; Provost of Birmingham, 1937-48; resigned 1948; Archdeacon of Aston and Hon. Canon of Birmingham, 1920-38; Chairman, Anglican Evangelical Group Movement, 1926; Cromer Convention, 1928-33. *Recreations:* tennis, photography. *Address:* 54 Lichfield Road, Sutton Coldfield. *T.:* Sutton Coldfield 3492. [*Died* 23 *Aug.* 1952.

RICHARDS, Robert; M.P. (Lab.) Wrexham Division of Denbigh, 1922-24 and 1929-31, and since 1935; late regional comr. for the Welsh region under the civil defence scheme; Tutor in Economic and Political Science at Coleg Harlech since 1932; *b.* 1884; *m.* Mary Myfanwy Owen. *Educ.:* Elementary School; Cambridge University Lecturer in Political Economy, Glasgow University, 1909-11; Lecturer in Economics, University College, Bangor, 1911-22; Under-Secretary for India, 1924. *Address:* Brynglas, Llangynog, Oswestry, Salop. [*Died* 22 *Dec.* 1954.

RICHARDS, His Honour Whitmore Lionel; *b.* 1869; *y. s.* of late John Henry Richards (County Court Judge and Chairman of Quarter Sessions for County Mayo, Ireland) and *g.s.* of Rt. Hon. Baron Richards of the Irish Court of Exchequer; *m.* 1st, 1900, Ethel (*d.* 1905), *y. d.* of late Rt. Hon. Joseph Chamberlain, M.P.; one *d.*; 2nd, 1908, Emelyn Mary, *d.* of late Wm. B. Eastwood of Kingswood, Englefield Green, Surrey; two *s. Educ.:* Rugby School; Trinity College, Dublin, B.A. Called to Lincoln's Inn Bar, 1895; joined Midland Circuit and Birmingham Sessions; County Court Judge, Circuit No. 7 (Cheshire), 1922–42; Mid-Cheshire, 1925. *Publication:* joint Editor of Godefroi's Law of Trusts (3rd edition). *Recreations:* hunting, fishing, shooting, rowing. *Address:* Woodfield, Chester. *T.:* Chester 816. *Club:* Grosvenor (Chester).
[*Died* 21 *Nov.* 1954.

RICHARDSON, Air Marshal Sir (Albert) Victor (John), K.B.E., *cr.* 1939 (O.B.E. 1919); C.B. 1937; B.A., M.B., B.Ch., D.P.H.; *b.* 4 Sep. 1884; 2nd *s.* of late Thomas Ferdinand Richardson (Lieutenant-Colonel 5th Royal Irish Fusiliers) of Poplar Vale, Monaghan, Ireland, and late Margaret Mary Victoria Coote; *m.* 1st, Dulcie (*d.* 1929), 4th *d.* of Francis Fredk. Eld of Seighford Hall, Staffordshire; two *d.*; 2nd, Eileen Mary, *d.* of William H. Hornibrook, F.R.C.S. (I.), Gerrards Cross; one *d. Educ.:* Trinity College, Dublin. M.B., B.Ch., B.A.O., B.A., D.P.H.; Hudson Silver Medallist, Adelaide Hospital, Dublin, 1908; Entered Royal Navy, 1908; Served European War, Royal Navy, Royal Naval Air Service and Royal Air Force, 1914-18; Wing Commander R.A.F. 1919; Group Captain, 1927; Air Commodore, 1934; Air Vice-Marshal, 1938; Air Marshal, 1939; Director-General of Medical Services, Air Ministry, 1938-41; Hon. Surgeon to the King, 1935-41; retired list, 1941; Chief Casualty Services Officer, H.Q. London Civil Defence Region, 1942-45. *Recreations:* golf, fishing. *Address:* The Holt, Gerrard's Cross, Bucks. *T.:* Gerrard's Cross 3268. *Club:* Athenæum.
[*Died* 16 *Sept.* 1960.

RICHARDSON, Maj.-Gen. David Turnbull, C.B. 1945; M.C.; M.B.; late R.A.M.C.; *b.* 21 Dec. 1886. Lt. R.A.M.C. 1912; Capt. 1915; Major, 1924; Lt.-Col. 1934; Col. 1938; Maj.-Gen. 1941. Asst. Professor Royal Army Medical College, 1928-32; Asst. Director of Hygiene, War Office, 1935-38; Professor of Hygiene, 1938-39; Deputy Director of Hygiene, 1939-40; A.D.M.S. B.E.F. 22-29 June 1940; Director of Hygiene War Office, 1941; K.H.S. 1941; retired pay, 1946. *Address:* Aird House, Badachro, Ross-shire.
[*Died* 14 *Sept.* 1957.

RICHARDSON, Dorothy M. (Mrs. Alan Odle). *Publications:* The Quakers—Past and Present, 1914; Pointed Roofs, 1915; Backwater, 1916; Honeycomb, 1917; The Tunnel, Interim, 1919; Deadlock, 1921; Revolving Lights, 1923; The Trap, 1925; Oberland, 1927; Dawn's Left Hand, 1931; Clear Horizon, 1935; Pilgrimage (Omnibus Edition), including Dimple Hill, 1938; Poems, Essays, Short Stories. *Address:* c/o J. M. Dent & Sons, 10 Bedford Street, W.C.2.
[*Died* 17 *June* 1957.

RICHARDSON, Edward Gick, B.A. Ph.D., D.Sc.; Professor of Acoustics and Reader in Physics in Univ. of Durham; *b.* Watford, 1896; *s.* of Edward Gick and Ada Elizabeth Richardson. *Educ.:* Cooper's Company's School and University College, London. Royal Air Force, 1918-19; Assistant Master Kilburn Grammar School, 1919-22; Lecturer at University College, London, 1923-31; at King's College, Newcastle, 1931-40; Scientific Adviser at Admiralty, Mine Design Dept., 1940-42; at Royal and Marine Aircraft Establishments, 1942-45; Leverhulme Research Fellow, 1956. Member of the Physical and Acoustical Societies; Editor of Acustica. *Publications:* Sound, a Physical Text-book, 1927; Acoustics of Orchestral Instruments and of the Organ, 1929; Introduction to Acoustics of Buildings, 1933; Physical Science in Modern Life, 1938; Physical Science in Art and Industry, 1940; Dynamics of Real Fluids, 1949; Ultrasonic Physics, 1951; (editor) Technical Aspects of Sound, 1953, 1956; Relaxation Spectrometry, 1957; a number of original papers and essays on sound and fluid dynamics in the Proceedings of the Royal and the Physical Societies and in the Philosophical Magazine. *Recreations:* cycling, music. *Address:* King's College, Newcastle upon Tyne.
[*Died* 31 *March* 1960.

RICHARDSON, Lt.-Col. Henry Sacheverell Carleton, O.B.E. 1943; D.L.; Member of Senate, N. Ireland Parliament, 1949; *b.* 18 Jan. 1883; *s.* of Lt.-Col. J. M. A. C. Richardson, D.L., and Mildred, *d.* of G. Gartside-Tipping; *m.* 1918, Phyllis (*d.* 1955), *d.* of Lt. Comdr. H. Gartside-Tipping, R.N.; one *s.* one *d. Educ.:* Eton. Rifle Brigade 1905-20, Captain, retired with rank of Lt.-Col. *Recreations:* yachting and shooting. *Address:* Rossfad, Ballinamallard, N. Ireland. *T.:* Killadeas 205. *Club:* Army and Navy.
[*Died* 2 *Jan.* 1958.

RICHARDSON, Maj.-Gen. John Dalyell, D.S.O. 1918; V.D.; grazier; *b.* 23 April 1880; *s.* of John Richardson and Helen Melville Dalyell; *m.* 1905, Isabel Mary McKillop; two *s. Educ.:* Sydney Grammar School. Joined Australian Military Forces (Militia) as 2nd Lieutenant, 1911; embarked in 1914, Captain 7th Light Horse Regt.; Major, 1916; Brigade Major 2nd L.H. Brigade, 1917-18; Lt.-Col. commanding 7th L.H. Regt., 1918-19 when returned to Australia (despatches twice, wounded thrice, D.S.O., Commander of Order of the Nile of Egypt, 1914-15 Star, two medals); commanded: 16th Light Horse Regt. Australian Military Forces, 1920-23; 2nd Cavalry Brigade, 1923-28; 1st Cavalry Division, 1936-42; Commanded Volunteer Defence Corps of N.S.W. (Home Guard), 1942; retired, 1942; Member of N.S.W. Milk Board, 1937; Chairman of Directors Hunter Valley Co-op. Dairy Co., 1945; Director Dairy Farmers' Co-operative Milk Co.; Member Hunter Valley Conservation Trust, 1950. Coronation Medal, 1937. *Publication:* History 7th Light Horse Regiment, A.I.F. *Recreation:* tennis. *Address:* Roslyn, Raymond Terrace, N.S.W., Australia. *T.:* Raymond Terrace 105. *Clubs:* Old Sydneians, Imperial Service, Royal Sydney Yacht Squadron (Sydney).
[*Died* 30 *July* 1954.

RICHARDSON, Lewis Fry, F.R.S. 1926; D.Sc. Physics, 1926; Fellow Brit. Psychological Soc.; *b.* 1881; *s.* of David and Catherine Richardson of Newcastle on Tyne; *m.* 1909, Dorothy, *d.* of late Dr. William Garnett; two *s.* one *d. Educ.:* Bootham School, York; Durham Coll. of Science, Newcastle; King's Coll., Cambridge, Nat. Sci. Tripos, 1st Cl. Pt. 1, 1903. Three years at National Physical Laboratory; 3 years in charge of chemical and physical laboratory in a tungsten lamp factory; 4½ years at geophysical observatories (Superintendent, Eskdalemuir); 2½ years with Friends' Ambulance Unit attached to French Army formerly Hon. Secretary of Royal Meteorological Society; B.Sc. 1929 (Psychology); in charge of Physics Department, Westminster Training College, London, S.W.1, 1920-29; Principal of Paisley Technical College, 1929-40. *Publications:* original investigations on physics, mathematics, meteorology, and latterly psychology (including Weather Prediction by Numerical Process, 1922, Generalized Foreign Politics, 1939, Arms and Insecurity, 1949, a microfilm, Statistics of Deadly Quarrels, 1950, in microfilm). *Address:* Hillside House, Kilmun, Argyll. *T.:* Kilmun 8. [*Died* 30 *Sept.* 1953.

RICHARDSON, Maggie; *see* Mitchell, Mrs. George J.

RICHARDSON, Sir Owen (Willans), Kt., *cr.* 1939; M.A. (Cantab.), D.Sc. (London, Leeds (hon.)), Hon. LL.D. (London and St. Andrews); F.R.S.; Yarrow Research Professor of the Royal Society and Director of Research in Physics at King's College, London, 1924-44; Emeritus Professor of Physics, University of London, since 1944; *b.* Dewsbury, Yorks, 26 April 1879; *s.* of Joshua H. and Charlotte M. Richardson; *m.* 1st, Lilian Maud (*d.* 1945), *sister* of Harold Albert Wilson, F.R.S.; two *s.* one *d.*; 2nd, 1948, Henrietta Maria Rupp. *Educ.:* Batley Grammar School; Trinity College, Cambridge (ex-Fellow).; Hon. Fellow of Trinity College, Cambridge, since 1941, Institute of Physics since 1942; Fellow of King's College, London; Hon. F.Inst.P., 1925; Hon. Mem. American Phil. Soc.; Hon. Fellow Indian Academy of Sciences; Foreign Mem. Norwegian Academy of Arts and Sciences, Oslo, and Royal Swedish Academy of Sciences, Stockholm; Corresponding Member Prussian Academy of Sciences, Berlin; Wheatstone Professor of Physics, University of London, King's College, 1914-24; Prof. of Physics, Princeton Univ., U.S.A., 1906-14; awarded Hughes Medal, 1920, and Royal Medal 1930, of Royal Soc.; President of Section A of British Association, 1921; President of the Physical Society 1926-28, Hon. Foreign Secretary since 1928; Nobel Prize for Physics, 1928; Silliman Memorial Lecturer, Yale Univ., 1932; Pres. N. E. Hampshire Agricultural Assoc., 1948-49. *Publications:* Electron Theory of Matter, 1914; 2nd edition, 1916; The Emission of Electricity from Hot Bodies, 1916; 2nd edition, 1921; Molecular Hydrogen and its Spectrum, 1933; numerous articles theoretical and experimental physics, especially connected with Theory of Electrons. *Address:* Chandos Lodge, Alton, Hants. *T.:* Alton 2322. *Club:* Athenæum. [*Died* 15 *Feb.* 1959.

RICHARDSON, Lieut.-Col. Sir Philip Wigham, 1st Bt., *cr.* 1929; Kt., *cr.* 1921; O.B.E. 1919; V.D.; J.P. Surrey; *b.* Newcastle on Tyne, 26 Jan. 1865; *e. s.* of late John Wigham Richardson, Newcastle on Tyne; *m.* 1st. 1891, Rosa America, *d.* of late General C. Colorado of Spain; two *s.*; 2nd, 1909, Bertha Anne, 2nd *d.* of late J. E. Greenley, Dulwich; one *d.* *Educ.:* Rugby School, King's College, Cambridge. Served in Volunteers and Territorials, 1880-1919; Member of National Rifle Association Council, 1901; Vice-President, 1918, Vice-Chairman, 1920-28, 1931-39; Chairman, 1939-46; Comdt. N.R.A. School of Musketry; served European War, 1914-18; France, 1916-17; M.P. (Cons.) Chertsey Div. Surrey (By-election), March 1922-31; shipbuilder and shipowner; Director, Swan Hunter & Wigham Richardson, Ltd., Wallsend, President, P. Wigham Richardson & Co., Ltd., London. *Publications:* Exterior Ballistics; Systems and Chances; It Happened To Me (autobiography), 1952. *Recreations:* rifle shooting; Captain, British Teams to Canada and Australia, 1907, and S. Africa and Australia, 1920; British Olympic Team, Stockholm, 1912; English Eight, English Twenty, etc. *Heir:* *s.* William Wigham Richardson [*b.* 12 June 1893; *m.* 1921, Katharine Elizabeth (*d.* 1945), *d.* of late H. J. Elphinstone; no *c.*]. *Address:* Aldenholme, Ellesmere Road, Weybridge. *Clubs:* Carlton, Savage, Royal Automobile. [*Died* 23 *Nov.* 1953.

RICHARDSON, His Honour Thomas, O.B.E.; on Standing Joint Committee for Northumberland and Durham; *e. s.* of late Sir Thomas Richardson, M.P. for the Hartlepools, D.L. and Anna Constance Richardson, *d.* of late Rev. J. C. Faber, Rector of Chicklade, Wilts; *m.* 1913, Winifred Ernestine (*d.* 1954), *y. d.* of His Hon. Judge F. G. Templer, The Hall, Egglescliffe, Co. Durham; two *s.* two *d.* (and one *s.* decd.). *Educ.:* Rossall School; Clare Coll., Cambridge (Exhibitioner); B.A., LL.B.; History and Law Tripos (2nd Class Honours); Middle Temple Powell Prizeman. Called to Bar, 1905; contested (U.) Houghton-le-Spring, 1913; Member of North-Eastern Circuit and Northumberland, Durham, and North Riding Sessions; Judge of County Courts Circuit No. 2, 1927-37; No. 1, 1937-53; retired July 1953; formerly Chairman: Durham Quarter Sessions, Northumberland Quarter Sessions; Capt., Gen. List, European War; J.P. Northumberland and Durham. *Recreations:* shooting, golf, gardening, music, sketching, and fishing. *Address:* Cliffe, Corbridge, Northumberland. *T.:* 94. *Clubs:* 1900; County (Durham). [*Died* 22 *April* 1956.

RICHARDSON, Air Marshal Sir Victor; *see* Richardson, Air Marshal Sir A. V. J.

RICHARDSON-BUNBURY, Sir Mervyn William; *see* Bunbury.

RICHMOND, Sir Frederick Henry, 1st Bt., *cr.* 1929; formerly Chairman Debenhams, Ltd., and Harvey Nichols, Ltd.; *b.* 30 Nov. 1873; *s.* of Henry Richmond, Marnham; *m.* 1921, Dorothy Agnes, *d.* of Francis Joseph Sheppard; one *s.* one *d.* *Heir:* *s.* John Frederick, *b.* 12 Aug. 1924. *Address:* Westoning Manor, Bedfordshire. *Clubs:* Carlton, Canada. [*Died* 11 *Nov.* 1953.

RICHTER, Herbert Davis, R.O.I. 1917; R.B.A. 1910; artist, designer, and L.C.C. Lecturer; President The Pastel Society; President Bath Society of Artists; *b.* Brighton, 10 May 1874; 4th *s.* of Frederick W. Richter; *m.* Gertrude, 5th *d.* of Alderman W. L. Barber, J.P., Birmingham. *Educ.:* Bath. In practice at Bath as architect and designer, 1895-1906; in association with brother established the business of the Bath Cabinetmakers Co., Ltd., 1895; gold and silver medals Paris International Exhibition, 1900, for British-made cabinet work; Society of Arts medal, 1897; studied painting with late J. M. Swan, R.A., and Frank Brangwyn, A.R.A.; first exhibited Royal Academy, 1906, since when exhibits regularly at principal London and provincial galleries; Lectr. on interior decoration, Camberwell School of Arts and Crafts, 1909-21; elected The Pastel Society, 1916; The Royal Institute Water Colours, 1920; The Arts and Crafts Society, 1922; Royal British Colonial Society, 1927; Royal Scottish Society of Painters in Water Colours, 1937; one-man exhibition at the Leicester Galleries, 1925; works acquired for the permanent collections of the Victoria and Albert Museum, Southport, Doncaster, Leicester, Manchester, Harrogate, Cork, Bristol, Brighton, Oldham, Hull, Rochdale, Hanley, Glasgow, Bath, Bradford, Sunderland, Buxton, Ipswich and Dundee Art Galleries; National Gallery, Wellington, Auckland, and Nelson Galleries, N.Z.; silver medal, Paris Salon, 1930; Director of Bath Artcraft Ltd., and Bath Cabinetmakers Co. Ltd., 1902-42. *Publications:* Flower Painting in Oil and Water Colour: Floral Art-Decoration and Design; Paintings and Poems (with Lady Margaret Sackville). *Recreations:* music, reading. *Address:* 5 Redcliffe Square, S.W.10. *T.:* Fremantle 9575. *Club:* Arts. [*Died* 21 *Aug.* 1955.

RICKARD, Thomas Arthur, A.R.S.M., D.Sc., retired; *b.* Pertusola, Italy, 29 Aug.

1864; *s.* of Thomas Rickard and Octavia Rachel Forbes; *m.* 1898, Marguerite Lydia Rickard (cousin); one *s.* *Educ.:* Queen's College, Taunton; University of London; Royal School of Mines, London. Assayer and surveyor in Colorado, 1885; Manager of mines in Colorado and California, 1886-89; Travels in Australia and New Zealand, 1891; Consulting Engineer, Denver, Colorado, 1892; State Geologist of Colorado, three terms, 1895-1901; Editor, Engineering and Mining Journal, New York, 1903-05; Editor, Mining and Scientific Press, San Francisco, 1905-09; Editor, The Mining Magazine, London, 1909-15; Editor, Mining and Scientific Press, 1915-22; Travels through Central Africa and in the eastern Mediterranean, 1925-29. Awarded Gold Medal of Institution of Mining and Metallurgy, 1932. *Publications:* Journeys of Observation; Technical Writing; Through the Yukon and Alaska; The Copper Mines of Lake Superior; Stamp-milling of Gold Ores; The Sampling and Estimation of Ore in a Mine; Pyrite Smelting; A History of American Mining; Man and Metals; Retrospect; The Romance of Mining; Historic Backgrounds of British Columbia. *Clubs:* Union, Victoria Golf (Victoria, B.C.). [*Died* 15 *Aug.* 1953.

RIDDELL, Brig.-Gen. Sir Edward Pius Arthur, Kt., *cr.* 1945; C.M.G. 1919; D.S.O. 1916; late Rifle Brigade; *b.* 23 May 1875; 3rd *s.* of late John Giffard Riddell of Felton Park and Swinburne Castle, Northumberland, and 2nd wife, Victoria Henrietta, 5th *d.* of Peter Purcell of Halverstown, Co. Kildare; *m.* 1903, Frances Hygnia, *d.* of late Francis John Sumner of Park Hall, Derbyshire. Served S. Africa, 1901-2 (Queen's medal 3 clasps); European War, 1914-18 (D.S.O. and two bars, C.M.G., Bt. Lt.-Col.); retired pay, 1925. *Address:* Anick House, Hexham, Northumberland. *T.:* Hexham 2. [*Died* 3 *Aug.* 1957.

RIDDELL, Florence; Author; *b.* London; *d.* of Charles Napier and Ann McDonald; *m.* 1915, George Riddell (*d.* 1924); one *s.* Has lived in India and Kenya and travelled extensively elsewhere; wrote first book in Kenya, and used same setting for numerous following novels, serials and short stories; studied at school for deaf-born children while writing Silent World. *Publications:* Kenya Mist, 1924; Out of the Mist, 1925; Dream Island, 1926; Kismet in Kenya, 1927; What Women Fear, 1927; The Misty Pathway, 1928; Castles in Kenya, 1928; Can Women Forget, 1929; House of the Dey, 1929; Valley of Suspicion, 1930; Wives Win, 1931; Perilous Love, 1932; Floating Palace, 1933; Silent World, 1934; I Go Wandering, 1935; Royal Wedding, 1936. *Recreations:* travel, sketching. *Address:* c/o Barclay's Bank, 53 Maida Vale, W.9. [*Died* 14 *April* 1960.

RIDDELL, Rev. Professor John Gervase, M.A., D.D.; Professor of Divinity, University of Glasgow, since 1947; *b.* 22 Sept. 1896; *s.* of George Riddell, Edinburgh; *m.* 1924, Margaret Rolland Guthrie; one *s.* two *d.* *Educ.:* Edinburgh Academy; University of Edinburgh; New College, Edinburgh. Commission in Gordon Highlanders and R.E. Signal Service, 1915-19; Minister of High Church, Forres, 1924-29; Netherlee Church, Glasgow, 1929-34; Professor of Systematic Theology, University of Glasgow, 1934-47. *Publications:* What we Believe, 1936; Why did Jesus Die ?, 1938. *Address:* 12, The University, Glasgow, W.2. *T.:* Western 6435. [*Died* 7 *Sept.* 1955.

RIDDET, Professor William, C.B.E. 1954; B.Sc., N.D.A., N.D.D., C.D.A.D.; Logan-Campbell Professor of Agriculture, Massey Agricultural College, Palmerston North, New Zealand, since 1927, Vice-Principal since 1946; Director, Dairy Research Institute, New Zealand, since 1927; *b.* 16 March 1896; *s.* of Robert Lang Riddet and Lillias Tweed Millar Riddet, Dalry, Ayrshire; *m.* 1st, 1928, Mary Stuart McLean (*d.* 1945); one *s.* one *d.*; 2nd, 1948, Dorothy May Richards. *Educ.:* Dalry (Ayrs.) H.G. School, Irvine Royal Academy; Glasgow Univ. (B.Sc.); West of Scotland Agricultural College. N.D.A. (Hons.), N.D.D. (Hons.), C.D.A.D. (Hons.); Fream Memorial Prizewinner; Stevens Memorial Prizewinner; R.A.S.E.; H.A.S. Served European War, 1915-17: R.A.V.C., Lieut. (Actg. Capt.) 4th Bn. R.S.F. in Palestine, France, Belgium, Germany. Asst. County Agric. Organiser, 1921-22; Ayr County Agric. Organiser, 1923-24; Lectr. in Dairying, West Scotland Agricultural Coll., 1924-25; Pres. N.Z. Dairy Science Assoc., 1929-46; N.Z. Soc. of Animal Production, 1944; Palmerston North Rotary Club, 1943-1944; Member, N.Z. Research Council, 1934-53; U.K. Soc. Dairy Technology Gold Medallist, 1953; Coronation Medals, 1937 and 1953. *Publications:* author and joint author, technical papers on dairying. *Address:* Massey Agricultural College, Palmerston North, New Zealand. *T.:* P.N. 7269. *Clubs:* Manawatu (Palmerston North, N.Z.); Wellesley (Wellington, N.Z.). [*Died* 30 *Dec.* 1958.

RIDEOUT, Percy Rodney; Composer and Organist; retired, 1956 after 52 years as organist at West London Synagogue; *b.* London, 1868; *m.* Violet (*d.* 1926); two *s.* *Educ.:* Royal College of Music. Open Scholarship for Composition, and studied for three years under Sir Hubert Parry, afterwards receiving a special grant for travel in Germany; Doctor of Music, London University, 1896. Compositions include: Opera, Vita Nuova; Operetta, Cinderella. *Address:* Shandon, Dalewood Road, Orpington, Kent. [*Died* 18 *Dec.* 1956.

RIDGEWAY, Rev. Charles Spencer-Churchill FitzGerald, (F. Gerald Ridgeway); Headmaster St. Peter's Court School, Broadstairs, Kent, since 1898; *b.* 4 July 1872; *s.* of Charles John Ridgeway, late Bishop of Chichester, and Susan Jane FitzGerald; *m.* 1900, Jean Bland Campbell, *d.* of James Duncan Campbell, C.M.G.; one *s.* *Educ.:* Harrow; New College, Oxford (M.A.). Ordained by the Archbishop of Canterbury, 1898; Chaplain to Bishop of Chichester. *Recreations:* all games and fishing; amateur Doubles Racquets Championship, 1894. *Address:* St. Peter's Court, Broadstairs, Kent. *T.:* Thanet 62705. *Club:* Royal St. George's Golf. [*Died* 2 *Nov.* 1958.

RIDGEWAY, Ven. S., M.A.; Rector of Carlow since 1912; Prebendary of Stagonil in St. Patrick's Cathedral, Dublin; Archdeacon of Ossory and Leighlin since 1940; *b.* 1872; 2nd *s.* of late J. Ridgeway, J.P., Ballydermot, King's County, and Rosser, Manitoba; *g.s.* of late Rev. J. H. Ridgeway, M.A.; *m.* 1903, Flora Isabella, 3rd *d.* of J. J. McEacharn, Kelvinside, Glasgow; one *s.* one *d.* *Educ.:* Trinity Coll., Dublin; Theological College, Lichfield, Staffs. Curate of St. Margaret's, Leicester, 1900; New Ross, Co. Wexford, 1902; Rector of Gorey, Co. Wexford, 1905. *Address:* The Rectory, Carlow, Ireland. *T.A.:* Carlow. *T.:* Carlow 124. [*Died* 24 *Jan.* 1951.

RIDLEY, Henry Nicholas, C.M.G. 1911; F.R.S., M.A., F.L.S., F.R.H.S.; Corresponding Member Pharmaceutical Society and Zoological Society; Correspondent Moscow Anthropological and Ethnological Society; Corresponding Member Massachusetts Horticultural Society; *b.* 10 Dec. 1855; *s.* of Rev. Oliver Matthew Ridley and Louisa Pole, *y. d.* of Wm. Stuart of Aldenham Abbey, Herts; *m.* Lily Eliza Doran. *Educ.:* Haileybury School; Exeter College, Oxford. Second Class Honours in Science, 1877; Burdett-Coutts Geological Scholarship; Gold Medal Rubber Planters' Assoc., 1914; Frank Meyer Medal Foreign Plant Introduction, 1928; Linnean Medal, 1950; Hon. F.I.R.I., 1955; Colwyn Medal, 1955; Botanic Dept., British Museum, 1880; explored Island of Fernando de Noronha, Brazil, 1887; Director of Gardens, Straits

Settlements, 1888 - 1911; commenced research on cultivation of Para rubber, 1889; founded the industry, 1895: made numerous scientific expeditions to all parts of the Malay Peninsula, Sumatra, Java, Borneo, Cocos, and Christmas Island; Editor of the Agricultural Bulletin of the Straits Settlements and Federated Malay States, and Secretary and Editor, Journal of the Royal Asiatic Society, Straits branch, 1889-1911. *Publications:* over 400 papers and articles on zoology, botany, geology, etc., chiefly relating to Malay Peninsula, including Botany and Geology of Fernando de Noronha, Botany of Christmas Island, Flora of East Coast of Malay Peninsula, Materials for a Flora of the Malay Peninsula, Monocotyledons (3 vols.), Spices; Flora of the Malay Peninsula, 5 vols.; Dispersal of Plants; papers on tropical agriculture. *Recreations:* natural history, reading, motor trips. *Address:* 7 Cumberland Road, Kew. [*Died* 24 *Oct.* 1956.

RIDLEY, Hon. Sir Jasper (Nicholas), K.C.V.O., *cr.* 1946; O.B.E. 1919; Chairman Coutts & Co., and National Provincial Bank; a Director Standard Bank of South Africa and Bank of British West Africa; President London Life Assoc.; J.P. Suffolk; Fellow of Eton Coll.; a Trustee of Tate Gallery (Chm.); a Trustee of British Museum since 1947; *b.* 6 Jan. 1887; 2nd *s.* of 1st Viscount Ridley and Hon. Mary Georgiana Marjoribanks, *d.* of 1st Lord Tweedmouth; *m.* 1911, Countess Nathalie Benckendorff, *d.* of Russian Ambassador in London; three *s.* one *d.* (and one *s.* decd.). *Educ.:* Eton; Balliol College, Oxford (M.A. Honours, 1908). Called to Bar, 1912; contested Morpeth (U.), Jan. 1910; Newcastle, Dec. 1910; served European War, 1914-18, Northumberland Hussars Yeomanry (D.A.A.G., O.B.E., despatches, Chevalier Légion d'honneur); Secretary Ministry of Labour, Training Grants Committee, 1919-20; member of Reorganisation Commissions, Pigs and Pig Products, 1932 and for Fat Stock Industry, 1933-34; Member Livestock Commission, 1936, and Royal Commission on Equal Pay for Equal Work; late Trustee of National Gallery. *Address:* 4 Gloucester Place, Portman Square, W.1. *T.:* Welbeck 5769; Mockbeggars, Claydon, Suffolk. *Clubs:* Travellers', Beefsteak, Turf. [*Died* 1 *Oct.* 1951.

RIDSDALE, Rt. Rev. Charles Henry; *b.* 2 March 1873; *s.* of late Francis J. Ridsdale of Thornton Lodge, Clapham Park, S.W., and 5 Gray's Inn Square; *m.* 1915, Bertha Jessie, *e. d.* of late Alfred Field, of Hove; two *d.* *Educ.:* Malvern; Trinity College, Oxford. Formerly curate of Tideswell, S. Werburgh's, Derby, and Parish Church, Brighton; Head of Trinity College Oxford Mission, Stratford, E.; Vicar of St. Margaret's, Leytonstone, E.; Canon Missioner of Gloucester, 1909-17; Vicar of High Wycombe, 1917-20; Vicar of St. Mark's, Gloucester, 1920-21; Archdeacon of Gloucester, 1919-33; Canon Residentiary and Treasurer of Gloucester, 1921-33; Suffragan Bishop of Colchester, 1933-46; Archdeacon of Colchester, 1933-46. Chaplain to the Bishop of Gloucester, 1911-22; Proprolocutor, Lower House, Canterbury Convocation, 1943-46. *Address:* Crowborough, Sussex. *Club:* National. [*Died* 27 *Aug.* 1952.

RIDSDALE, Sir William, K.C.M.G., *cr.* 1954; (C.M.G. 1939); Head of Foreign Office News Department, 1941-1953, with rank of Counsellor in H.M. Foreign Service; *b.* 14 April 1890; *s.* of late Arthur S. Ridsdale, Gloucester; *m.* Margaret, *d.* of late Edmund J. Cullis, Gloucester; one *d.* War Correspondent for Daily News, 1914; Officer in Infantry, 1915-1918; joined Foreign Office, 1919; retired Dec. 1953. *Address:* 1 Kelsey Way, Beckenham, Kent. *T.:* 2368. *Club:* Reform. [*Died* 24 *Nov.* 1957.

RIND, Lt.-Col. George Burnet Abercrombie, D.L.; High Sheriff of Pembrokeshire, 1935; *b.* 30 Aug. 1880; *s.* of Burnet George and Elinor Amy Rind; *m.* 1909, Gladys May Cairns; one *s.* two *d.* *Educ.:* King's School, Bruton; Sandhurst. Indian Army. *Recreations:* tennis, cricket, horticulture. *Address:* Allenbrook, Dale, Pembrokeshire. *T.A.:* Dale. *T:* Dale 7. [*Died* 14 *Nov.* 1958.

RINEHART, Mary Roberts; *b.* Pittsburgh; *d.* of Thomas Beveridge Roberts; *m.* 1896, Stanley Marshall Rinehart, M.D. (*d.* 1932); three *s.* *Publications:* The Circular Staircase, 1908; The Man in Lower Ten, 1909; When a Man Marries, 1909; Adventures of Letitia Carberry, 1911; Case of Jennie Brice; Where There's a Will; The After House; The Street of Seven Stars, 1914; "K," 1915; Kings, Queens and Pawns, 1915; Tish, 1916; Bab—A Sub-Deb, 1917; Long Live the King, 1917; Tenting To-night, 1917; The Amazing Interlude, 1917; The Altar of Freedom, 1917; Dangerous Days, 1919; Love Stories, 1920; Affinities, 1920; A Poor Wise Man, 1920; Sight Unseen, and The Confession, 1921; The Breaking Point, 1922; The Out Trail, 1923; Temperamental People, 1924; The Red Lamp, 1925; Nomad's Land, 1926; Tish Plays the Game, 1926; Lost Ecstasy, 1927; Two Flights Up, 1928; This Strange Adventure, 1929; The Romantics, 1929; The Door, 1930; Mary Roberts Rinehart's Mystery Book, 1930; My Story, 1931; The Book of Tish, 1931; Mary Roberts Rinehart's Romance Book, 1931; Miss Pinkerton, 1932 (British Title, The Double Alibi, 1932); The Album, 1933; The State Vs. Elinor Norton, 1934; Mr. Cohen Takes a Walk, 1934; The Doctor, 1936; The Wall, 1938; The Great Mistake, 1940; Familiar Faces, 1941; Haunted Lady, 1942; Alibi for Isabel, 1944; The Yellow Room, 1945; A Light in the Window, 1948; Episode of the Wandering Knife, 1950; The Swimming Pool, 1952; The Frightened Wife, 1953; The Best of Tish, 1955; The Mary Roberts Rinehart Crime Book, 1957. *Plays:* Double Life, 1907; The Avenger (one-act play, with husband), 1908; Seven Days (farce, with Avery Hopwood), 1911; Cheer Up (farce), 1913; The Bat (with Avery Hopwood) 1920; Spanish Love, 1920; The Breaking Point, 1922. *Address:* 635 Park Av., New York 21. [*Died* 22 *Sept.* 1958.

RIORDAN, Very Rev. Father James John, C.M.G. 1949; League of St. Teresa; Director Marist Fathers' Maori Mission, New Zealand, from 1943, retired; *b.* 6 August 1896; *s.* of James Riordan and Mary (*née* Reail). *Educ.:* St. Patrick's College, Wellington; Mt. St. Mary's, Greenmeadows, Hawkes Bay. Priest (R.C.), 1922; Assistant, Jerusalem, Wanganui Maori Mission, 1923; in charge Maori Mission Otaki District, 1929; Parish Priest, Otaki, and Superior, Maori Mission, 1934; Parish Priest, Meeanee, and Superior, Maori Mission, Hawkes Bay, 1936. Professed Member of Society of Mary, 1919. Estab. Hato Paoro Maori Boys' Coll., Parorangi. 1947. *Recreation:* golf. *Address:* 62 Friend St., Karori, Wellington, N.Z. [*Died* 30 *Aug.* 1959.

RIPLEY, Lt.-Col. B., C.B.E. 1919; D.S.O. 1918; M.Am.Soc.C.E., M.E.I.C., Member Am. Rly. Eng. Assn.; Special Eng. Rep., Toronto Terminals Rly. Co., from 1944; in Consulting Practice, from 1945; *b.* Oxford, Nova Scotia, 29 Aug. 1880; *s.* of Robert Ripley and Nancy Angus; *m.* 1904, Edith Muriel Henson. Railway Service, 1897, with Great Falls and Canada Railway and Canadian North-West Irrigation Co.—serving in the following capacities consecutively to 1901—rodman, draftsman, instrumentman, etc.; Asst. Engineer, G.F and C. Rly. and Can. North-West Irrigation Co. in Alberta, Can. 1902-4; Engineer of Construction, St. Mary's River Rly. (now Can. Pacific) 1904-5; Resident Engineer of Construction, Grand Trunk Pacific

Rly. (now Canadian National) 1905-7; Resident Engineer, C.P.R. Lethbridge (Alberta) Viaduct, 1907-8; Assistant Engineer in charge, Old Man River Viaduct at Macleod, Alberta and Viaduct at Outlook Sask., 1908-9; Assistant Engineer, Dominion Atlantic Railway in Nova Scotia, 1910-12; Engineer of Grade Separation C.P.R. at Toronto, 1912-15; recruited and took First Canadian Railway Constr. Battalion overseas as Commanding Officer, 1916-19 (C.B.E., D.S.O., despatches 3 times); District Engineer, Ontario Dist., C.P. Rly., Toronto, 1919-38; Engineer Maintenance of Way, Eastern Lines, C.P. Railway, Toronto, 1938-43. Retired to Victoria, B.C., 1948. *Recreations:* golf, fishing, shooting. [*Died* 5 *July* 1958.

RIPLEY, Sir Geoffrey Arnold, 3rd Bt., *cr.* 1897; *b.* 4 Aug. 1883; *s.* of Sir Frederick Ripley, 1st Bt., and Kate, 2nd *d.* of David Little, Bradford; *S.* brother, 1945; *m.* 1908, Sybil (*d.* 1954), *d.* of late T. N. F. Bardwell, J.P., D.L., Bolton Hall, Yorks. *Educ.:* Eton; Oxford. Barrister Inner Temple, 1912; late Lieut. 1st (Royal) Dragoons; served European War, 1914-19; France and Belgium (1914-15 Star and 2 medals). *Heir:* none. *Address:* 50 Eresby House, Rutland Gate, S.W. [*Died* 16 *Nov.* 1954 (*ext.*).

RIPLEY, Gladys, (Mrs. E. A. Dick); contralto vocalist; *b.* 9 July 1908; *d.* of late Alfred Ripley and of Amy Ripley; *m.* 1st, 1928; one *d.*; 2nd, 1945, Sqdn. Ldr. F. Price (*d.* 1952), R.A.F.; 3rd, Flight-Lieut. E. A. Dick, R.A.F. *Educ.:* St. Edwards, East Ham, Essex. First important concert, 1925, at Royal Albert Hall in Elijah, conducted by Albert Coates; then successive years for Royal Choral Society, Principal Provincial Socs. and all important festivals, including Leeds, Norwich, Three Choirs, Three Valleys, etc. Toured France, Belgium, W. Africa, Holland, with troops, 1940-45; guest artist for New Zealand Centennial celebrations, 1940; N.Z. and Australia, 1949; Holland, 1950. First broadcast, 1926; since then all types broadcasts, operas, etc. Appeared 6 internat. seasons, Covent Garden, prior to war. Has appeared with many famous conductors. *Recreations:* swimming, gardening, knitting, ballroom dancing. *Address:* Oak Apple Lodge, Pagham Road, Bognor Regis, Sussex. *T.:* Pagham 2587. [*Died* 21 *Dec.* 1955.

RIPLEY, Sir Henry (William Alfred), 3rd Bt., *cr.* 1880; J.P.; Captain, late the Royal Dragoons; District Councillor; *b.* Sleningford Grange, near Ripon, 3 Jan. 1879; *e. s.* of 2nd Bt. and Eugenie Frederica, *d.* of Maj.-Gen. E. A. G. Emmott-Rawdon; *S.* father, 1903; *m.* 1911, Dorothy, *e. d.* of Hon. Mrs. Harley of Brampton Bryan, Herefords; two *s.* (and two killed on active service) one *d.* (and one *d.* decd.). *Educ.:* Eton. Received a commission in 1st Royal Dragoons, 1899; served 2½ years in South Africa and resigned as a Lieutenant, 1903; came into Bedstone and Hopton Castle estates, 1903; served as Captain 5th Reserve Cav. Reg., 1914-17; D.A.Q.M.G., XV. Corps, B.E.F., 1917-18; Major 7th Bn. Shropshire Home Guard, 1940-42. *Recreations:* hunting, shooting, fishing, golf, late Joint Master Teme Valley Hounds. *Address:* Bedstone Court, Bucknell, R.S.O., Shropshire. *T.:* Bedstone 204. *T.A.:* Bedstone. *Clubs:* Carlton, Overseas. [*Died* 14 *Dec.* 1956.

RISHWORTH, Frank Sharman; Professor of Civil Engineering, University College, Galway, 1910-47 (retired); *b.* 1876; *e. s.* of John Rishworth, Tuam, Ireland; *m.* Mary A., *d.* of late William Beecroft, Eastgrove, Keighley; no c. *Educ.:* Queen's Coll., Galway (Science Scholar). Exhibitioner Royal University of Ireland, B.E., 1898; M.A.I., Univ. of Dublin; LL.D.; M.Inst. C.E.; Asst. Engineer on Great Northern Railway in Derbyshire and at King's Cross, 1898-1902; Lecturer in Civil Engineering at School of Engineering, Giza, under Egyptian Ministry of Education, 1902-10; 3rd Class (Commander) Order of Medjidieh; Chief Engineer, Shannon Power Development; Member of the Senate, National University of Ireland, 1939-49; Member of Governing Body, University College, Galway, 1912-37; Past President Inst.C.E. Ireland. *Address:* 29 Leeson Park, Dublin. [*Died* 31 *March* 1960.

RISLEY, Sir John Shuckburgh, K.C.M.G., *cr.* 1922; C.B. 1912; Q.C. 1921; *b.* 22 Dec. 1867; 2nd *s.* of late Shuckburgh Norris Risley, barrister-at-law, of Elmore, Newbury, Berks; *m.* 1900, Elizabeth Cruger (*d.* 1950), *o. c.* of Henry Gordon, D.L., J.P., of Manar, Aberdeenshire; one *d.* *Educ.:* Marlborough (Scholar); Magdalen College, Oxford (classical exhibitioner). 2nd class classical mods., 1888; 2nd class jurisprudence, 1890; B.A. 1890; open studentship Inns of Court, 1892; called to Bar, Lincoln's Inn, 1893; M.A. and B.C.L. 1894; Colonial Office Legal Assistant, 1901-11, and Principal Legal Adviser, 1911-31; also Principal Legal Adviser to Dominions Office from its establishment, 1925-31. *Publications:* The Founding of St. Stephen's Golf Club, 1893; The Law of War, 1897; Notes and Echoes, 1902; regular contributor of light verse, etc., to Punch, 1894 - 1901; edited Dale's Clergyman's Legal Handbook, 7th ed., 1898; and Waterlow's Companies Acts Manual, 11th and 12th eds., 1899 and 1901. *Recreations:* interested in most games, especially rugby football [School XV., 1885], hockey [School XI, 1885 and 1886, Capt.] and cricket [Cock House XI., 1884 and 1885]; 1900-30 formed representative collection of old English Table Glass in use 1690-1820, (in old age) reading and writing (but not arithmetic!) Times crossword, a little classics, Homer, Virgil, Greek Anthology, etc. *Address:* c/o Coutts & Co., 440 Strand, W.C.2. [*Died* 22 *Feb.* 1957.

RITCHIE, Sir Adam (Beattie), Kt., *cr.* 1923; retired; *b.* 23 April 1881; 2nd *s.* of late George Ritchie of Nenthorn, Berwickshire; *m.* 1917, Vivienne, *o. d.* of late Hon. Mr. Justice Lentaigne, High Court, Burma; one *s.* two *d.* *Educ.:* Merchiston Castle School; Clare College, Cantab. Member of Society of Scottish Chartered Accountants, 1905. High Sheriff of Essex, 1945-46. *Address:* Boreham Manor, Chelmsford. *Club:* Oriental. [*Died* 24 *Dec.* 1957.

RITCHIE, Ven. Andrew Binny; *b.* 1880; *s.* of Alexander Ritchie, Solicitor, Edinburgh, and Charlotte Ritchie; *m.* 1918, Vera Crosbie Siordet; two *s.* one *d.* *Educ.:* Edinburgh Academy; Durham University (M.A.); Wells Theological College. Ordained 1904; Vicar of S. Frideswide, Poplar, 1914-18; Rector and Rural Dean of Poplar, 1918-20; Rector: Sudborough, 1920-22; S. Mary's Chester, 1922-25; Vicar: S. John's Margate, 1925-31; Kennington, 1931-34; Cranbrook, 1934-39; S. Mary, Dover, 1939-41; Rector of Haslemere, 1941-49; Archdeacon of Surrey, 1949-55. Hon. Canon of Canterbury, 1940 - 41. *Address:* Parkside, Wonersh, Surrey. *T.:* Bramley 3178. [*Died* 20 *Jan.* 1956.

RITCHIE, Major-Gen. Sir Archibald Buchanan, K.B.E., *cr.* 1927; C.B. 1919; C.M.G. 1915; *b.* 14 May 1869; *s.* of late Maj.-Gen. J. Ritchie, R.A.; *m.* Anna Orr (*d.* 1925), *d.* of late Andrew Stewart, LL.D., D.L., 17 Park Terrace, Glasgow; one *s.* one *d.* *Educ.:* Westward Ho!; R.M.C., Sandhurst. Entered Seaforth Highlanders, 1889; Captain, 1898; Major, 1905; Lt.-Col. 1913; Brevet Col. 1915 served Nile Expedition, 1898; S. African War, 1899-1902 (despatches twice, Queen's medal with clasp, King's medal 2 clasps); European War, 1914-19; Comdr. 26th Brigade 9th Division, 1915-16; Comdr. 11th Division, 1917, and 16th Division, 1918 (despatches six times, dangerously wounded C.M.G., C.B., Brevet Col.); Maj.-Gen. 1919; was A.D.C. to Maj.-Gen. Commanding Troops, Belfast District, 1895-98; G.O.C. 51st Highland Division (T.A.), 1923-27; retired, 1928;

Colonel The Seaforth Highlanders, 1931-39; Croix de guerre avec palme; St. Anne (Russia). *Address:* Donnington Hayes, Newbury, Berks. *Clubs:* Army and Navy, M.C.C. [*Died* 9 *July* 1955.

RITCHIE, Rev. Canon Charles Henry; Canon of St. George's Chapel, Windsor, since 1954; Chaplain to The Queen since 1953 (to King George VI, 1946-53); Chaplain, Heathfield School, Ascot, since 1954; *b.* 28 May 1887; *y. s.* of late John Macfarlane and Ella Ritchie, Dunedin, New Zealand; *m.* 1915, Marjorie Alice, *y. d.* of late Sir Charles and Lady Mary Stewart; two *s.* (one *d.* decd.). *Educ.:* Collegiate School, Wanganui, N.Z.; St. John's College, Cambridge; Leeds Clergy School. B.A. 1910; M.A. 1914; deacon 1911; priest 1912; Curate, St. Michael's, Chester Square, S.W.1., 1911-1914, 1919-20; acting Chaplain for temporary service R.N., 1914-19; All Saints, Dunedin, N.Z., 1920-22; St. Martin-in-the-Fields, 1922-1927; Rector of St. John the Evangelist, Edinburgh, 1927-39; Sandford Canon in Edinburgh Cathedral, 1937-39; Archdeacon of Northumberland and Canon of Newcastle Cathedral, 1939-54. *Address:* 6 The Cloisters, Windsor Castle. *Clubs:* Athenæum; Hawks (Cambridge). [*Died* 8 *Sept.* 1958.

RITCHIE, Rev. David Lakie, D.D.; Dean Emeritus, United Theological College, Montreal; *b.* Kingsmuir, Forfarshire, 15 Sep. 1864; *s.* of John Ritchie, builder, and Bella Lakie; *m.* 1890, Jane A., Inverarity, Forfar. *Educ.:* North Public School, Forfar; Forfar Academy; Edinburgh University; University Theological Hall. Ordained to Congregational Church, Dunfermline, Scotland, 1890; called to succeed Rev. J. H. Jowett at St. James's Congregational Church, Newcastle, 1896; Principal Congregational Theological Institute, Nottingham, 1904-19; deeply interested in education; member of Dunfermline and Newcastle on Tyne School Boards, and of Education Committee, Nottingham; lecturer Liverpool University, 1911-13, and Sheffield University, 1912, on Religious Pedagogy; Chairman of Notts Congregational Union; lecturer United Theological Colleges, Montreal, 1918; President National Sunday School Union, 1915; France, Y.M.C.A. Director of Education, 1916, and 1918-19; Principal of Congregational Theological College of Canada, Montreal, 1919-26; President Montreal and Ottawa Conference U.C.C., 1927; Life Governor British and Foreign Bible Society, and an Hon. Life Governor British and Foreign Bible Society in Canada. *Publications:* a volume of Sermons; Peace the Umpire; Why Grade?; Concerning Religious Education; Adolescence; The Teen Age and its Training; The Genius of Congregationalism; contributions to religious magazines. *Recreation:* golf. *Address:* Apt. 87, 1509 Sherbrooke Street West, Montreal, Canada. [*Died* 14 *Dec.* 1951.

RITCHIE, Captain Henry Peel, V.C. 1915; R.N.; *b.* Jan. 1876; *s.* of R. Peel Ritchie, M.D. Ed., and Mary, *d.* of James Anderson, of Bleaton Hallet, Perthshire; *m.* Christiana Lillias Jardine (*d.* 1951), *o. d.* of Jas. A. Aikman, Edinburgh; two *d.* Entered Navy; Commander, 1911; served East Africa, European War, 1914-15 (severely wounded, V.C. for operations at Dar-es-Salaam); retired, 1917; Captain 1921. [*Died* 9 *Dec.* 1958.

RITCHIE, James, C.B.E. 1948; Hon. LL.D. (Aberd.); P.R.S.E.; M.A., D.Sc.; Prof. (Emeritus, 1952-) of Natural History, Univ. of Edinburgh, 1936-52, and Dean of Faculty of Science, 1940-48; *b.* Port Elphinstone, Aberdeenshire, 27 May 1882; *s.* of late James Ritchie, schoolmaster; *m.* Jessie J. (*d.* 1933), *y. d.* of late Walter Elliot, Hollybush; one *s.* two *d.* *Educ.:* Robert Gordon's Coll. and Univ. of Aberdeen. M.A. 1904; B.Sc., with Special Distinction in Zoology, Botany, and Geology, 1906; Fullerton Research Scholar in Science, 1906; D.Sc. 1912; entered Civil Service by competitive examination as Asst., Natural Hist. Depart., Royal Scottish Museum, 1907; Assistant Keeper, 1919; Keeper, 1921-30; Regius Professor of Natural History, Aberdeen University, 1930-1936; Secretary and Editor of Proceedings, Royal Physical Society, 1911-16; Pres., 1924-1927, 1950-53; Vice-Pres. Roy. Zoological Soc. of Scotland; Sec. of meetings, Roy. Soc. of Edinburgh, 1928-31; Vice-Pres., 1931-34, 1940-43, 1951-54, Pres. 1954-; Pres. Conf. of Delegates of Corresponding Societies, British Association, 1937; Pres., Zoology Section, British Assoc., 1939; Pres. Assoc. of British Zoologists, 1939; Thomson Lecturer on Natural Science, U.F. Church College, Aberdeen, 1917-18; Silver Medal, Société Nationale d'acclimatation de France, 1920; Keith Medal, Royal Society Edinburgh, 1944; Governor Edinburgh and East of Scotland College of Agriculture; Member Scottish Office Advisory Cttee. on Wild Birds Protection, 1921-54, Chm. 1949-54; Member: Sanctuaries Cttee. for Royal Parks in Scotland since 1925, Chm. 1955-; Scottish National Parks Cttee., Chairman Scottish Wild Life Conservation Cttee., 1946-49; Scottish Cttee. of Nature Conservancy, and Scottish Office Deer (Close Seasons) Cttee., 1952-54; Hon. President Scottish Field Studies Assoc.; Vice-President Scottish Marine Biological Association; Chairman of Council Royal Scottish Geographical Soc. 1937-41; F.R.S.G.S.; F.S.A. Scot. *Publications:* Influence of Man on Animal Life in Scotland, 1920; Beasts and Birds as Farm Pests, 1931; Fossil Men—Elements of Human Palæontology, 1923, a translation (with his wife) of M. Boule's Hommes Fossiles; Design in Nature, 1937; revised edition Thomson's Outlines of Zoology, 1944; many papers on Hydrozoa and Scottish fauna in scientific journals; Editor of the Scottish Naturalist, 1921-35. *Recreations:* sketching, golf, archæology. *Address:* 31 Mortonhall Road, Edinburgh. [*Died* 19 *Oct.* 1958.

RITCHIE, Sir James Martin, Kt., *cr.* 1939; C.B.E. 1926; J.P.; Chairman and Managing Director, Andrew Ritchie & Son, Ltd., Bridgeton, Glasgow; Director The Eburite Corrugated Containers Co. Ltd., Park Royal, N.W.; Chairman of the Executive Committee of the Glasgow King's Roll Committee since 1932; General Commissioner of Income Tax for the Lower Ward of Lanarkshire since 1941; *b.* Mount Vernon, Lanarkshire, 7 May 1874; *s.* of late Andrew Ritchie, J.P., of Mount Vernon and Millport; *m.* 1912, Mary Dunbar, *e. d.* of late Wm. Gemmell, Glasgow; one *s.* *Educ.:* Hutcheson's Grammar School, Glasgow. Member of Paper Box Trade Board, representing Scotland, 1910-19; re-appointed, 1925; Chairman of Scottish Paper Box Manufacturers Association, 1910-19; re-elected, 1924; Chairman of British Paper Box Manufacturers Federation, London, 1916-18; Chairman of Local Employment Committee (Bridgeton Labour Exchange) since 1917; member of the King's Roll National Council; Collector of the Incorporation of Bonnet-makers and Dyers of Glasgow, 1927, 1928; Town Council of Glasgow Representative of the 22nd (Kelvinside) Ward, 1927-32; Governor of Hutcheson's Educational Trust, representing the Glasgow Town Council, 1929-38; Chairman of the Glasgow Municipal Society, 1932-35; Governor of Hutcheson's Hospital Trust since 1929; Deacon of Incorporation of Bonnetmakers and Dyers, 1929; Representative of the Glasgow Town Council on the Clyde Navigation Trust, 1930; Member of Executive Committee of the Scottish National Development Council; Chairman Executive Committee (Bridgeton Area) Community Service in Unemployment; Chairman Northern division (of Glasgow) Advisory Committee to the Assistance Board since 1936; Member Glasgow Ministry of War Pensions Committee; Member of Appeals Tribunal; Director, Glasgow Chamber of Commerce, since 1939; a Director of the Merchants'

House of Glasgow; Bailie of the River and Firth of Clyde Corporation of Glasgow, 1931-32. *Recreation:* golf, Captain Glasgow Golf Club, 1938-40. *Address:* Holmcroft, Craigmillar Avenue, Milngavie, Dunbartonshire. *T.A.:* Mabox, Glasgow. *T.:* 1502 Milngavie. *Clubs:* Conservative, Royal Scottish Automobile (Glasgow). [*Died* 16 *Aug.* 1951.

RITCHIE, Rear-Admiral James Stuart McLaren, C.B. 1945; *b.* 12 Mar. 1884; *s.* of late J. M. Ritchie, Dunedin, New Zealand; *m.* 1929, Joan, *d.* of late John Preston Karslake; one *s.* two *d.* *Educ.:* Wanganui Collegiate School, Wanganui, New Zealand. H.M.S. Britannia, 1899; joined Royal Navy, 1899; served European War, 1914-18; Captain, 1923; Commanded H.M.S. Diomede, N.Z. Division of Royal Navy, 1925-1927; Naval Attaché, Washington, U.S.A., 1928-31; Director of Training, Admiralty, 1931-33; Commanded H.M.S. Furious, 1933-1935; A.D.C. to the King, 1935; Rear-Admiral, 1935; retired, 1935; Commodore R.N.R. from outbreak of war, 1939; Rear-Admiral Flag Officer in Charge, Liverpool, 1941-44; Rear-Admiral Flag Officer, Norway, 1945. Commander of St. Olav, 1945. *Recreations:* golf, tennis, fishing. *Address:* Catts Place, Headley, Newbury. *T.:* Headley (Newbury) 233. *Club:* United Service. [*Died* 17 *May* 1955.

RITCHIE, John, M.B., Ch.B., F.R.C.P.E., D.P.H.; former Member National Insurance Advisory Cttee.; Medical Officer of Health, Dumfriesshire, 1925-47; retd.; *b.* 16 Feb. 1882; *s.* of Rev. T. L. Ritchie, Brechin, Angus, Scotland; *m.* 1912, Dorothy Ann Johnston; two *s.* one *d.* *Educ.:* Brechin High School; University of Edinburgh. City Hospital, Edinburgh, 1907-11; Deputy M.O.H. Dumfriesshire, 1911-25; Capt., R.A.M.C.; served in Macedonia, 1917-18; former Member of General Medical Council; former Pres. Scott. Branch Soc. Medical Officers of Health. *Publications:* History of the Laboratory of the Royal College of Physicians of Edinburgh, 1953; contributions to journals. *Recreations:* medical history and folklore. *Address:* 6 Blantyre Terrace, Edinburgh. *T.:* Edinburgh 53571. [*Died* 24 *Dec.* 1959.

RITCHIE, R. L. Græme, D.Litt., LL.D. (Aber.); Docteur de l'Université de Paris; Officier de la Légion d'Honneur; Lauréat de l'Académie Française; Doctor (Hon.) Univ. of Caen; D.Litt (Hon.) Univ. of Birmingham; *b.* Glasgow, 16 Nov. 1880; 2nd *s.* of late Rev. Robert Ritchie, Rector of St. Mary's, Inverurie; *m.* 1912, Marthe Yvonne, 2nd *d.* of Maître Armand Pillot, Censeau, Jura; one *s.* one *d.* *Educ.:* Grammar School and University of Aberdeen, 1st Class Classics, 1st Class Modern Languages, Liddel Prize for Latin Verse; Universities of Strasbourg, 1903, and Paris, École des Hautes Études, 1904-08. Carnegie Research Scholar, 1904-06, and Fellow, 1908-09; Lecturer in French in the University of Edinburgh, 1909-19; Prof. of French Language and Literature in the Univ. of Birmingham, 1919-46; Emeritus Professor, 1953-; Professor of French, University College, Exeter, 1946-52; Zaharoff Lecturer, Oxford, 1952; President Modern Language Association, 1954. *Publications:* Recherches sur la Syntaxe de la Conjonction "Que," 1907, awarded Prix Saintour by the French Academy; Les Vœux du Paon and The Buik of Alexander the Great, critical editions, Vols. I.-IV. 1921-29; papers in linguistic and literary journals; General Editor Modern Studies Series; Manual of French Composition, 1914 (Annotated Renderings, 1921; Supplement, 1922); Translation from French, French Prose from Calvin to Anatole France, 1918; French Verse from Villon to Verlaine, 1922; New Manual of French Composition, Essays in translation from French, 1941; The Normans in England before Edward the Confessor, 1948; The Normans in Scotland, 1953, etc. *Address:* Treoke, Radden Stile Lane, Exmouth. *T.:* Exmouth 3727. [*Died* 10 *April* 1954.

RITSON, Lieut.-Col. John Anthony Sydney, D.S.O. 1917; O.B.E. 1935; M.C.; T.D.; B.Sc. (Durh.); Consulting Mining Engineer; Emeritus Professor, University of London; *b.* Pelton House, Pelton, Co. Durham, 18 Aug. 1887; *s.* of late W. M. P. Ritson, Scottcrest, Gullane, East Lothian; *m.* 1920, Winifred Amy, *d.* of late Thomas Dickson, Bellfield, Banbridge, Co. Down; two *s.* *Educ.:* Uppingham School; Durham Univ. H.M. Inspector of Mines, Scotland, Yorkshire, South Wales; Professor of Mining, Univ. of Leeds, 1923-35; Professor of Mining, Royal School of Mines, 1936-52; Member of Board of Mining Examinations, 1935-50; Crown Mineral Agent, 1942; President of Institution of Mining Engineers, 1948-49; President, Institution of Mining & Metallurgy, 1952-53; Hon. A.R.S.M.; Hon. Fell. Imp. Coll. Durham L.I., T.F., 1906; served 8th Durham Light Infantry, 1914-16; 12th Royal Scots, 1916-19, as Lieut.-Colonel (D.S.O. and bar, M.C., T.D., despatches four times). *Publications:* Papers in Proc. of Institution of Mining Engineers and Institutions of Mining and Metallurgy and other technical journals. *Recreation:* English Rugby International, 1910-13. *Address:* Wykeham Park House, Frimley Green, nr. Aldershot, Hants. *T.:* Deepcut 102. *Club:* Athenæum. [*Died* 16 *Oct.* 1957.

RITSON, Rev. John Holland, M.A., D.D.; *b.* 21 Feb. 1868; *s.* of Caleb Ritson, of Bolton, Lancashire; *m.* Jane S. Lamplough (*d.* 1936); three *s.* one *d.* *Educ.:* Manchester Grammar School; Balliol College, Oxford; Headingley College, Leeds. Entered Wesleyan Methodist ministry, 1891; Assistant Tutor, Didsbury College, Manchester, 1891-94; Minister in Eccles and Blackheath Circuits, 1894-99; Secretary of the British and Foreign Bible Society, 1899-1931; has visited Agencies of Bible Society over the world; a Secretary of Edinburgh World Missionary Conference, 1910; for several years Chairman of Standing Committee of British Missionary Societies Conference, and Member of International Missionary Committees; elected Member of Legal Hundred of Wesleyan Methodist Church, 1910, and President of its Conference, 1925; Honorary D.D. of the McGill University, Montreal, and of Oxford University (1926); Treasurer of Methodist Ministerial Training Committee since 1926, and Secretary, 1931-34. *Publications:* Abroad for the Bible Society; Christian Literature on the Mission Field; The Bible among Men; The World is our Parish; Magazine Articles. *Address:* Arundel House, Chyngton Road, Seaford, Sussex. *T.:* Seaford 2452. [*Died* 28 *Aug.* 1953.

RITSON, Alderman Joshua, C.B.E. 1949; J.P. Sunderland; Member Sunderland Town Council; *s.* of Joshua Ritson, Brampton, Cumberland; *b.* 1874; *m.* 1900, Elizabeth, *d.* of Irvin Dinning, Cambois, Northumberland. M.P. (Lab.) Durham, 1922-31 and 1935-1945; ex-Mayor of Sunderland. *Address:* 21 Dale Terrace, Fulwell, Sunderland. [*Died* 5 *Feb.* 1955.

RIVERDALE, 1st Baron, *cr.* 1935, of Sheffield, **Arthur Balfour,** 1st Bt., *cr.* 1929; G.B.E., *cr.* 1942 (K.B.E., *cr.* 1923); LL.D.; J.P.; *b.* London, 1873; *m.* 1899, Frances Josephine Keighley, Officer Sister of the Order of St. John of Jerusalem, 1941, *d.* of Charles Henry Bingham; two *s.* three *d.* *Educ.:* Ashville Coll., Harrogate. Master Cutler of Sheffield, 1911-12; Mem. of the Royal Commission on Railways, 1913; Member of Industrial Advisory Committee to the Treasury during the War; Member of Advisory Council for Scientific and Industrial Research, 1916, 1929, 1933, 1935 and Chairman 1937-46;

Member of the Board of Trade Engineering Industries Committee, 1916; Member of Lord Balfour's Committee on Commercial and Industrial Policy after the War, 1916; Member of Man-power Committee, 1916; Member of Advisory Committee on War Munitions; President Sheffield Chamber of Commerce, 1919; Member of Coal Industry Commission, 1919; Member of Imperial Mineral Resources Bureau, 1920; Member of the Post Office Advisory Council, 1921; Member of Permanent Panel in connection with Safeguarding of Industries, 1922; Chairman Toy Industries Commission, 1922; Member of Therm Enquiry Commission, 1922; President of Association of British Chambers of Commerce, 1923; Board of Trade Advisory Council, 1923; Department of Oversea Trade Advisory Council, 1923; National Debt Commission, 1923; Delegate to International Conference on Customs on behalf of Brit. Govt., 1923; Member of Committee appointed by Brit. Govt. to draw up Agenda for Imperial Economic Conference, 1923; Member of Committee appointed to enquire into Census of Production for 1925, 1924; Member of Committee appointed to enquire into Imperial Wireless Telegraphy, 1924; Member of National Debt and Taxation Committee, 1924; Chairman Government Committee on Industry and Trade, 1924; Chairman of British National Committee, International Chamber of Commerce, 1926; Member of Com. on Standardisation and Simplification; Vice-President, International Chamber of Commerce; British Delegate to Economic Conference, 1927; Member of Economic Advisory Council, 1930; Imperial Economic Committee, 1930; Dept. of Overseas Trade Advisory Council, 1930; Chairman of Economic Mission to Egypt, 1931; Member of Chinese Govt. Purchasing Commission, 1931; Chairman of the London Council of the Australian Association of British Manufacturers, 1932; Vice-Chm. of the British Council for Relations with other Countries, 1935 (Pres. 1947-50); Mem. Grand Council of Federation of British Industries; Member of Anglo-Japanese Trade Relations Committee; Chairman of London Advisory Committee to Empire Exhibition, S. Africa; Member of Council Machine Tool Trades Assoc.; F.A.G.S.; Chairman Fire Brigades Committee, 1936; Chairman, Advisory Council to Committee of Privy Council for Scientific and Industrial Research, 1937; Member of Advisory Committee of Department of Overseas Trade for New York World's Fair, 1939, 1938; Chairman, United Kingdom Air Mission to Ottawa, Canada; ex-Chairman of R.A.F. Benevolent Fund and Chairman of the Appeals Committee; Local Director: Nat. Provincial Bank, Ltd.; Alliance Assurance Co. Ltd.; Chairman: Arthur Balfour & Co. Ltd.; High Speed Steel Alloys, Ltd., Widnes; C. Meadows & Co. Ltd., Sheffield; ex-Director: Halifax Building Soc.; Pres. Production Engineering Research Assoc. since 1948. Chevalier de l'ordre de Leopold Ier; Grand Officier de l'Ordre de la Couronne; Médaille civique de Iere Classe de Belgique; Commander (Grade II) of the Order of the Dannebrog; Officier de la Légion d'Honneur; Order of the Brilliant Jade of China; Is a Freemason, a Churchman, and a Conservative. *Publication:* Hints to Practical Users of Tool-Steel. *Recreations:* shooting, tennis. *Heir:* s. Hon. Robert Arthur Balfour, J.P. *Address:* Riverdale Grange, Sheffield. *T.:* Sheffield 31247. *Clubs:* Bath; Sheffield (Sheffield). [*Died* 7 *July* 1957.

RIVET, Raoul, C.M.G. 1946; M.B.E. 1941; Chief Editor Le Mauricien since 1922; *b.* 8 May 1896; *m.* 1931, Lydie Feillafé; one *s.* six *d.* (and one *d.* decd.). *Educ.:* private secondary school. Member of Municipal Council of Port Louis, 1924-46; Mayor of Port Louis, 1934, 1935 and 1944; member of Legislative Council, 1931-53; sat five years on Exec. Council. Member of Town Council of Curepipe under the new Mauritius Town Councils Constitution, Chairman, 1952. Mem. Société des Écrivains Mauriciens; member of Delegations to Réunion Islands, 1938, to Madagascar, 1947. Delegate for Mauritius to Empire Parliamentary Conf., 1948. Chevalier de la Légion d'Honneur; Commandeur de l'Ordre de l'Étoile d'Anjouan; Officier d'Académie. *Address:* Port Louis, Mauritius. [*Died* 29 *Nov.* 1957.

RIVIERE, Hugh Goldwin, R.P.; M.A.; portrait-painter; *b.* Bromley, Kent, 1869; *e. s.* of late Briton Riviere, R.A.; *m.* Winifred Elaine, *d.* of Charles Langdon-Davies; one *s.* one *d.* *Educ.:* St. Andrews Univ.; Royal Academy Schools. Has exhibited in the R.A. since 1892, and at Salon; bronze and gold medallist, Salon; Hon. Secretary of the Royal Society of Portrait Painters; has painted among others, Canon Ainger, Bishops of Ripon, Durham, Ely, Gloucester, Hereford, late Archbishop of Canterbury, Headmasters of Clifton, Shrewsbury, Winchester, Holt, Westminster, Dr. Spooner, Sir Adolphus Ward, Col. Sir Russell Kerr, Sir Hugh Fraser, Sir Squire Bancroft, Mr. Owen Nares, Lords Winterstoke, Ullswater, Blanesburgh, Sir Alfred Yarrow, Lord Justice Lawrence, Earl Beatty, Lady Betty Trafford, Miss Dorothy Lawrence, Countess of Leitrim, Lady Evelyn Guinness, Dame Mary Scharlieb. *Address:* 18 Mortlake Road, Richmond. *Club:* Arts (Life Member). [*Died* 14 *Jan.* 1956.

RIVINGTON, Madame Hill, (Lady Holmes); Composer and violinist; F.L.C.M.; *d.* of late Charles Robert Rivington; *m.* 1903, Sir Charles Holmes, K.C.V.O. (*d.* 1936); two *s.* *Educ.:* privately; Darmstadt, Hampstead Conservatoire, and the Royal Academy of Music. Sub-professor at Hampstead Conservatoire, 1902-03; Violin Recitals at Bechstein Hall, Steinway Hall, Salle Erard, etc.; Composer of the operas Nur Jahan, Pausanias, Ironhand, Aladdin, Mr. Bellamy Comes Home, and King Hildebrand. *Publications:* Violin pieces and songs. *Address:* 9 Hornton Court, Hornton Street, W.8. *T.:* Western 7574; Castle Bank, Appleby, Westmorland. [*Died* 30 *Aug.* 1957.

ROACH, Edward K.; *see* Keith-Roach.

ROAF, Herbert Eldon; Professor Emeritus, University of Liverpool; *b.* Toronto, Canada, 1881; *s.* of late James R. Roaf, K.C., Barrister-at-law; *m.* Beatrice Sophie, *d.* of late Sir W. A. Herdman, C.B.E., F.R.S.; two *s.* two *d.* *Educ.:* Upper Canada Coll., Toronto; Univ. of Toronto. Johnston Colonial Fellow Univ. of Liverpool, 1902-5; British Medical Association Research Scholar, 1905-6; Assistant Lecturer on Physiology, University Liverpool, 1906-11; Lecturer on Chemical Physiology, University Liverpool, 1909-11; Lecturer on Physiology, St. Mary's Hospital Medical School, W., 1911-20; Professor of Physiology, London Hospital Medical College, University of London, 1920-32; George Holt Professor of Physiology, University of Liverpool, 1932-44. M.D. Toronto; D.Sc. Liverpool; M.R.C.S. Eng.; L.R.C.P. Lond. *Publications:* Biological Chemistry, 1921; Text Book of Physiology, 2nd ed., 1936; Colour Vision, Physiological Review, July 1932; and numerous papers in Biochemical Journal, Journal of Physiology, Proceedings Royal Society, and Quarterly Journal of Experimental Physiology. *Address:* Woodend Corner, Woodend Lane, off Grassendale Road, Liverpool, 19. *T.:* Garston 1146. [*Died* 21 *Sept.* 1952.

ROBARTS, John, J.P.; Director National Provincial Bank, Ltd., 1920-50; *b.* 10 June 1872; *s.* of A. J. Robarts and of sister of 9th Viscount Barrington; *m.* 1898, Margaret Georgina Louisa, *e. d.* of Sir Hugh Cholmeley, 3rd Bt.; no *c.* *Educ.:* Eton; Christ Church, Oxford. *Address:* Tilehouse, Buckingham;

Manor House, Thornham. *Clubs:* Brooks's, Travellers'. [*Died* 22 *Jan.* 1954.

ROBB, Rt. Hon. John Hanna, P.C. 1937; Q.C. 1921; retired; *b.* Clogher, Co. Tyrone, 4 Nov. 1873; 2nd *s.* of Rev. J. Gardner Robb, D.D., LL.D.; *m.* Emily, *y. d.* of John Ritchie of Ulsterville, Belfast; one *d.* *Educ.:* Royal Belfast Academical Institution; Queen's College, Belfast (Scholar), Gray's Inn; King's Inns. Called to Irish Bar, 1898; some time Chairman of Trade Boards, Ireland; M.P. (U.) Queen's University in the Parliament of Northern Ireland, 1921-37; Parliamentary Secretary to the Ministry of Education, Northern Ireland, 1925-37; Minister of Education and Leader of the Senate, Northern Ireland, 1937-43; Chairman Departmental Committee on the Cost of Living, Ministry of Labour, Northern Ireland, 1922; Chairman Departmental Committee on Bankruptcy Law Reform, 1927. Father of the Bar of Northern Ireland, 1939-43; County Court Judge of Armagh and Fermanagh, 1943-Dec. 1954; retired 1954. *Publications:* The Law and Practice of Bankruptcy and Arrangements in Ireland, 1907; The History of the School, in the Centenary Volume of the Royal Belfast Academical Institution, 1912. *Recreations:* reading, bridge. *Address:* 6 Deramore Park, Belfast. *T.:* 65640. [*Died* 21 *June* 1956.

ROBBINS, Rowland Richard, C.B.E. 1920; J.P.; retired farmer; 4th *s.* of Rowland Robbins of Willersey, Hounslow, Mx.; *m.* 1st, 1896, Rosa Marion (*d.* 1910), *d.* of C. C. Harris, St. John's Wood, N.W.; 2nd, 1911, Estelle May (*d.* 1951), *d.* of C. C. Harris; two *s.* two *d.* *Educ.:* Taunton School. Member Middlesex County Council, 1913-28; Member Agricultural Wages Board, 1917-21, and 1924-31; Member Royal Commission on Agriculture, 1919; Member Linlithgow Commission on Prices of Agricultural Produce, 1923; Member Agricultural Advisory Committee, England and Wales, 1920-24; President National Farmers' Union, 1921 and 1925; Member Council and Executive Committee, 1918-31; National Institute Agricultural Botany, 1921-28; Member Royal Commission on Land Drainage, 1927; Chairman of Legal and Parliamentary Press and Publicity Committees National Farmers' Union, 1926-31; Member Transport Advisory Council, 1934-44 (Road and Rail Traffic Act, 1933); Member of Thames Conservancy, 1943-46; High Sheriff of Middlesex, 1945-46. *Club:* Farmers'. [*Died* 18 *Aug.* 1960.

ROBERTON, Sir Hugh S., Kt., *cr.* 1931; LL.D. (Aberdeen); Founder of The Glasgow Orpheus Choir, 1906, Conductor, 1906-51, retired, 1951; *b.* Glasgow, 1874; *s.* of James Roberton and Mary Sim; *m.* 1st, 1895; 2nd, 1909; seven *s.* two *d.* *Educ.:* Glasgow. Known as an adjudicator in Britain and in Canada, also as a lecturer and journalist; composer of many part songs, and arranger of many Scottish songs. *Publications:* Choir Training; Kirsteen (two plays); Curdies (humorous sketches). *Address:* 24 Briar Road, Glasgow, S.3. [*Died* 7 *Oct.* 1952.

ROBERTON, Bailie Violet Mary Craig, C.B.E. 1928; LL.D. (Glasgow 1943); J.P.; Town Councillor of City of Glasgow; Member, Roy. Comm. on Marriage and Divorce, 1951; first woman Preceptor of Hutchesons' Hospital, Glasgow, 1947; *b.* 5 March 1888; *d.* of William Craig Roberton, LL.B., Solicitor and Notary Public, and Jane Leney Reid, both of Glasgow; *g.d.* of Sir James Roberton, LL.D., Professor of Conveyancing, University of Glasgow. *Educ.:* private schools, and Queen Margaret College, Glasgow; Dresden. Member of Glasgow Parish Council and District Board of Control, 1912; J.P. of the County of the City of Glasgow, 1921; elected a Member of Glasgow Town Council, 1921; Commandant Women's Auxiliary Police Corps, 1939-44; Fellow Royal Sanitary Institute; Member of Scot. Central Probation Council; Chairman: H.M. Prison, Duke Street, Glasgow; Pres., Scot. Assoc. for Mental Health. *Address:* 22 Woodlands Terrace, Glasgow, C.3. *T.:* Douglas 4519. *Clubs:* Forum, W.V.S.; Kelvin (Glasgow). [*Died* 3 *Oct.* 1954.

ROBERTS, Countess (3rd in line, *cr.* 1901); of Kandahar, Pretoria and Waterford; **Ada Edwina Stewart Lewin;** O.B.E. 1918; Viscountess St. Pierre, 1901; *b.* 28 March 1875; 4th *d.* of F.M. Earl Roberts, V.C., and Nora Henrietta (*d.* 1920), *d.* of Capt. Bews, 73rd Regt.; *S.* sister, 1944; *m.* 1913, Brig.-Gen. Henry Frederick Elliott Lewin (*d.* 1946) (one *s.* Frederick Roberts Alexander, Lt. Irish Guards, *b.* 18 Jan. 1915, killed in action, May 1940). *Heir:* none. *Address:* The Camp, Ascot, Berkshire. *T.A.* and *T.:* Ascot 89. *Club:* W.V.S. [*Died* 21 *Feb.* 1955 (*ext.*).

ROBERTS, Rt. Rev. Basil Coleby, M.A.; D.D. 1951; Secretary of Soc. for the Propagation of the Gospel since 1944; *b.* Cheltenham, 23 Sept. 1887; *s.* of Rev. Henry Eugene and Beatrice Louisa Roberts; *m.* 1922, Dorothy Mary, O.B.E., M.B., Ch.B., *d.* of Alexander Somerville, Edinburgh; one *s.* three *d.* *Educ.:* Allhallows School, Honiton; Marlborough College; Pembroke College, Cambridge (Foundation scholar); Wells Theological College; a Stewart of Rannoch scholar; first class in both Classical and Theological Triposes. Deacon, 1911; Priest, 1912; Curate of St. Jude's, Salterhebble, 1911-13; Lecturer at St. Augustine's College, Canterbury, 1913-22; Fellow, 1914; Sub-Warden, 1920-22; temporary Chaplain to the Forces, 1915-19; served in Singapore and Siberia; Chaplain of Selangor, F.M.S., 1922-27; Bishop of Singapore, 1927-40; Hon. Canon of Canterbury Cathedral, 1941; Warden of St. Augustine's College, Canterbury, 1941-45; Asst. Bishop of Canterbury, 1942-55. *Recreations:* golf, tennis, billiards, music. *Address:* 15 Lower Camden, Chislehurst, Kent. *T.:* Imperial 3646. *Club:* Overseas. [*Died* 3 *Feb.* 1957.

ROBERTS, Cedric Sydney; *see* Lane-Roberts.

ROBERTS, Charles Henry; *b.* 22 Aug. 1865; *s.* of Rev. A. J. Roberts, late Vicar of Tidebrook, Sussex, and Ellen, *d.* of Rev. R. H. Wace, Wadhurst, Sussex; *m.* Lady Cecilia Maude Howard (*d.* 1947), *d.* of 9th Earl of Carlisle; one *s.* two *d.* *Educ.:* Marlborough College; Balliol College, Oxford (Scholar). Fellow and Tutor of Exeter College, Oxford; contested Wednesbury, 1895; Lincoln City, 1900; M.P. (L.) City of Lincoln, 1906-18; Borough of Derby, 1922-1923; Under-Secretary of State for India, 1914-15; Chairman National Health Insurance Joint Committee, 1915-16; Comptroller of H.M.'s Household, 1915-16; Chairman of Cumberland War Agricultural Committee, 1939-47; Chm. of Cumberland County Council, 1938-58; J.P. (Cumberland), 1900-1950; Deputy Chairman of Cumberland Quarter Sessions until 1950. *Address:* Boothby, Brampton, Cumberland. *Clubs:* Farmers', National Liberal. [*Died June* 1959.

ROBERTS, Rev. E. Berwyn; Ex-Chairman of the Second North Wales Methodist Synod, Ex-Pres. of the Welsh Methodist Assembly; *b.* 31 July 1869; *s.* of Morris and Jemima Roberts; Rhewl, Llangollen; *m.* Annie Roberts, Waterloo House, Caernarvon; two *s.* two *d.* *Educ.:* Wesleyan College, Richmond. *Publications:* Commentaries on Ephesians, I. and II. Peter, St. John's Gospel (2 vols); Handbook on the Life of Jesus. *Recreation:* golf. *Address:* Moelwyn, Llannerch Road, Colwyn Bay, North Wales. *T.:* 4717. [*Died* 26 *Jan.* 1951.

ROBERTS, Col. Sir George Fossett, Kt., *cr.* 1935; C.B. 1942; O.B.E. 1919; T.D. J.P., D.L.; Hon. LL.D. (Wales); Vice-President University College of Wales,

Aberystwyth; Chairman Mid-Wales Hosp. Management Cttee., 1948-51; *b.* 1 Nov. 1870; *s.* of David and Maria Roberts; *m.* 1896, Mary (*d.* 1947), *e. d.* of John Parry, Glanpaith, Cardiganshire; two *d.* *Educ.:* Private School, Cheltenham. Contested (C.) County of Cardigan, 1910; High Sheriff of Cardiganshire, 1910-11; Staff Officer, Embarkation Staff, 1914-19; Commanded 102nd Field Brigade R.A. (T.A.), 1921-25; Hon. Colonel 146th Medium Regt. R.A. (T.), 1933; Mayor of Aberystwyth on two occasions and a member of the Aberystwyth Town Council for 30 years; President National Library of Wales, 1944-50. *Address:* Glanpaith, Aberystwyth, Cardiganshire. *T.A.:* Glanpaith, nr. Aberystwyth. *T.:* Aberystwyth 249. *Club:* East India and Sports.
[*Died* 8 *April* 1954.

ROBERTS, Harold, C.V.O. 1951; J.P.; retired; *b.* 3 Mar. 1879; 3rd *s.* of late James Haworth Roberts, Bury, Lancs., Cotton Merchant; *m.* 1914, Nona Ruth, *d.* of late James Howard Walker, Wigan, Lancs., Mining Engineer; one *s.* one *d.* *Educ.:* Rossall; Exeter College, Oxford. B.A. 1901, Hons. in Jurisprudence; M.A. 1908. Called to Bar, Inner Temple, 1902; joined Northern Circuit; practised at Chancery Bar in Lancashire Palatine Chancery Court and High Court. Served European War, 1914-18, Lieut., R.A.S.C. Registrar of Lancashire Palatine Chancery Court, 1925-51; Deputy of Chancellor of Duchy of Lancaster during Vacations, 1947-52. J.P. Lancs. 1933-. *Recreations:* golf, fishing and gardening. *Address:* 18 Park Avenue, Southport, Lancs. *T.:* Southport 2660. *Clubs:* Union (Manchester); Union (Southport).
[*Died* 29 *June* 1959.

ROBERTS, Henry David, M.B.E. 1918; Hon. Curator, Thomas-Stanford Museum, Brighton, since 1935; *b.* Worcester, 6 Feb. 1870; *e. s.* of late Henry Wm. Roberts; *m.* 1895, Margaret Cuthbertson (*d.* 1948), *o. c.* of late Jas. Mackintosh, of Glasgow and Buenos Aires; one *d.* *Educ.:* Worcester Cathedral King's School (King's Scholar); Old Elvet School, Durham. Officier de l'Instruction Publique (France), 1910; Knight (1st Class) of the Royal Swedish Order of Vasa, 1911; Chevalier of the Order of the Crown of Italy, 1919; Chevalier of the Order of the Crown of Belgium, 1920; Officer of the Order of Orange-Nassau (Holland), 1920; Officer of the Order of Leopold II. (Belgium), 1930; Medal of the Serbian Red Cross Society, 1924; Dieppe Medal, 1922; Liege Medal, 1926; Medal of the City of Paris, 1932; Assistant in Public Library, Newcastle-on-Tyne, 1885-93; Librarian and Clerk, St. Saviour's Public Library, Southwark, 1893-1905; Consulting Librarian to Corporation of Hackney, 1905 - 1906; Director, Public Libraries, Museums, and Fine Art Galleries, Brighton, 1906-35; Director of the Brighton Publicity Department, 1912-1929; Director of the Royal Pavilion Estate, 1920-1935; Hon. Fellow, a Vice-Pres. (1929), and formerly one of the Examiners Library Assoc.; Member of Council and Vice-Pres. Museums Association, 1912-13; formerly Lecturer in Library Management and Bibliography, London School of Economics (University of London); Local Representative, and Member of Council, National Art Collections Fund; Life Governor, Royal Sussex County Hosp. and of the Royal Alexandra Hospital, Brighton; Member of Council of Management of New Sussex Hospital Brighton, 1936-44, later Vice-Pres.; President (and now hon. member), Brighton Rotary Club, 1920; Pres. Brighton and Hove Natural History Soc., 1942-43 and 1943-44, now a Vice-Pres.; organised at Brighton 19 special exhibitions of the work of modern foreign artists; Hon. Sec. Inter-Allied Exhibition on the Treatment and Training of Disabled Men (Ministry of Pensions), 1918. *Publications:* The Book of Brighton, 19th ed. 1929; Story of the Royal Pavilion, Brighton, 1915; compiler and editor of a Short History in English, Gurmukhi, and Urdu of the Royal Pavilion, Brighton, and a description of it as a Hospital for Indian soldiers, 1915; Souvenir of the reconstructed Dome and Corn Exchange, Brighton, 1937; History of the Royal Pavilion, Brighton, 1939; editor and annotator of Chatterton's works, Thomson's Seasons, and Castle of Indolence, 1906; editor Brighton Parish Register, 1558-1701, 1932, etc. *Address:* Preston Manor, Brighton, 6. *T.:* Brighton 52101. *Clubs:* Brighton Arts (Hon. Member), Brighton Municipal Officers' (Hon. Life Vice-Pres.), Sussex County Arts (Hon. Member)(Brighton).
[*Died* 6 *Jan.* 1951.

ROBERTS, Kenneth, Author; *b.* 8 Dec. 1885; *s.* of Frank Lewis Roberts and Grace Mary Tibbets; *m.* 1911, Anna S. Mosser, Boston, Mass. *Educ.:* Cornell University. Editorial staffs, Boston Post, Life (New York); Captain, M.I.D., Siberian Expeditionary Force; Staff correspondent, Saturday Evening Post, 1918-28, covering assignments in America, Europe and Asia; abandoned journalism in 1928 to write novels; given honorary D.Litts. by Dartmouth, Colby, Middlebury, Bowdoin and Northeastern; Member American Inst. of Arts and Letters; Hon. Mem.: Phi Beta Kappa (Dartmouth); Soc. of Cincinnati, N.J.; In partnership with Sir Stanley Spurling and Sir Howard Trott, in 1950, opened three fresh water springs in Bermuda, where fresh water wells had been unknown for 341 years. *Publications:* Europe's Morning After, 1921; Why Europe Leaves Home, 1922; Sun Hunting, 1923; The Collector's Whatnot (with Booth Tarkington and Hugh MacNair Kahler), 1923; Black Magic, 1924; A Study of Calvin Coolidge, 1924; Florida, 1926; Antiquamania, 1928; March to Quebec (the journals and records of Arnold's Expedition in 1775), 1938; the Kenneth Roberts Reader, 1945; translation, with Anna M. Roberts, of Moreau de St. Méry's Journey to the United States of America (1793-1798), 1947; I Wanted to Write, 1949; Henry Gross and His Dowsing Rod, 1951; The Seventh Sense, 1953 (all non-fiction); *novels:* Arundel, 1930; The Lively Lady, 1931; Rabble in Arms, 1933; Captain Caution, 1935; North-west Passage, 1937; Oliver Wiswell, 1940; Lydia Bailey, 1947; Boon Island, 1956. *Address:* Kennebunkport, Maine, U.S.A. *Club:* Royal Bermuda Yacht.
[*Died* 21 *July* 1957.

ROBERTS, Lancelot, R.C.A. (the lettering later became R.Cam.A.); Member of the Pastel Society, London. *Address:* Little Meadows, Eglwys Bach, Tal y Cafn, N. Wales; c/o The Royal Cambrian Academy of Art, Plas Mawr, High Street, Conway, North Wales.
[*Died* 4 *April* 1950.
[*But death not notified in time for inclusion in Who Was Who 1941–1950, first edn.*

ROBERTS, Owen Josephus; Assoc. Justice, Supreme Court of U.S., 1930-45; *b.* Philadelphia, Pennsylvania, 2 May 1875; *s.* of Josephus Roberts and Emma Lafferty; *m.* 1904, Elizabeth Caldwell Rogers; one *d.* *Educ.:* Germantown Acad.; Univ. of Pennsylvania; Law School of University of Pennsylvania. A.B., Univ. of Pennsylvania, 1895, LL.B. 1898; LL.D., Beaver Coll. 1925, Ursinus Coll. 1926, Univ. of Pennsylvania 1929, Lafayette Coll. 1930, Pennsylvania Military Coll. 1931, Dickinson Coll. 1931, Trinity Coll. 1931, Williams Coll. 1933, Princeton Univ., 1934, Temple Univ., 1946; Duke Univ., 1948; John B. Stetson Univ., 1949; D.C.L., Oxford Univ., 1951; began practice at Philadelphia, 1898; 1st Asst. District Attorney, Philadelphia County, 1901-4; Instructor, Asst. Prof., Prof. of Law, Univ. of Pennsylvania, 1898-1918; Director: City Trusts of Philadelphia, 1920-29; Bell Telephone Co. of Pennsylvania, 1920-29; Am. Telephone & Telegraph Co. 1927-29, Real Estate Title & Trust Co. 1920-27, Franklin Fire Insurance Co. 1923-29; appointed by Pres. Coolidge one of two attorneys to prosecute "Oil Cases," 1924; Trustee: Jefferson Medical Coll., 1921-24; Univ. of Pennsylvania (life) since 1943; Pres.: Pennsylvania Bar Assoc. 1947, House of Deputies, Gen. Convention (1946) of Protestant Episcopal Church; Member, Nat. Exec. Board, Boy Scouts of America; Chairman: War Dept. Advisory Board on Clemency 1945-47, Board for Award of Medals for Merit, 1945-48, Am. Commission for Protection and Salvage of Artistic and Historic Monuments in War Areas, 1943-46, Laws and Ordinances Cttee., President's Highway Safety Conference 1946-47, President's Amnesty Board, 1946-47, Personnel Security Review Board of U.S. Atomic Energy Commission, Jan.-Sept. 1948; Dean, The Law School, Univ. of Pennsylvania, 1948-51; President, American Philosophical Society, 1952-; Trustee, Lincoln University; Chairman: Fund for Advancement of Education; Ford Foundation. Member of Psi Upsilon, Phi Beta Kappa. *Publications:* various magazine articles. *Address:* Chester Springs, R.D., Chester County, Pennsylvania. *T.:* Phoenixville (Pa.) 3123. *Clubs:* Union League, (Hon.) University, Midday (Phila.). [*Died* 17 *May* 1955.

ROBERTS, Peter Burman Moir; London Correspondent of The Scotsman, 1906-41, now retired; *b.* Newtyle, Angus, 15 Aug. 1874; *m.* 1903, Elisabeth J. T. Storm, West Hartlepool; two *s.* two *d.* *Educ.:* Morgan Hospital, Dundee. Reporter, Dundee Advertiser, 1890-1893; Aberdeen Journal, 1894; joined Glasgow staff of The Scotsman, 1895; transferred to Edinburgh, 1901; Chairman of Parliamentary Press Gallery Committee, 1920; Member of Newspaper Press Fund Council (two years Chairman), 1918-40; Chairman of Newspaper Conference, 1929-38. *Recreation:* chess. *Address:* Yagden, Tilford, Surrey. *T.:* Frensham 184. *Club:* Hankley Common Golf (Farnham). [*Died* 13 *Dec.* 1956.

ROBERTS, Reginald Hugh; Director of Industrial and Commercial Finance Corporation Ltd.; Chairman: The Birmingham Guild Ltd., Super Oil Seals, Ltd., Bay Tree Hotels, Ltd.; *b.* 26 January 1883; *s.* of late Hugh Stewart Roberts; *m.* 1910, *d.* of late Arnold Duckworth, Oakhurst, King's Norton; two *s.* three *d.* *Educ.:* King Edward's School, Birmingham; Birmingham University. Member Board of Trade Advisory Committee, 1933-36; Member of Council of Art and Industry, 1935-37; Industrial Adviser to H.M. Comr. for Special Areas, 1937-39; Member of sub-committee, Production Executive Industrial Capacity Committee, 1939; Deputy Director-General of Equipment and Stores, Ministry of Supply, 1939; Director of Machinery Licensing, Board of Trade, 1940; Regional Port Director (South Western Area), Ministry of War Transport, 1941-45; Member of Lord Justice Scott Committee (Ministry of Works and Planning) on utilisation of land and dispersal of industry, 1942. Awarded medal of Freedom by President of U.S.A. *Recreation:* l'art d'être grand-père. *Address:* Dorsington Manor, nr. Stratford-on-Avon. *T.:* Bidford-on-Avon 13. *Clubs:* Union, Farmers'; Union (Birmingham). [*Died* 13 *Feb.* 1955.

ROBERTS, Richard Ellis; *b.* 26 Feb. 1879; *s.* of late Richard Roberts, J.P., Islington and Aberystwyth, and Anne Catherine Corbett; *m.* 1920, Harriet Ide, *o. c.* of late Herbert Ide Keen and Elizabeth Doebler, Philadelphia, U.S.A., and Paris. *Educ.:* Merchant Taylors' School; St. John's College, Oxford, B.A. 1901. On the Editorial Staff, Pall Mall Gazette, 1903-5; contributor to News-Chronicle, Observer, New Statesman, Guardian, Church Times, London Mercury, XIX. Century, etc.; 1st Div. Clerk in Admty., 1916-18. Literary Editor The New Statesman, 1930-32; Time and Tide, 1933-34; Editor Life and Letters, 1934-1935; F.R.S.L., 1931; F.R.S.A., 1937; Vice-Pres. P.E.N., 1934. *Publications:* Poems; Samuel Rogers and his Circle; A Roman Pilgrimage; Henrik Ibsen; Peer Gynt, trs.; The Other End; Life as Material; Reading for Pleasure; Prayer; Portrait of Stella Benson; Toller's Letters from Prison and Poems (translation); Life of Dr. H. R. L. Sheppard; Religion and Literature. *Recreations:* five-ten, walking. *Address:* The Edge, Stroud, Glos. *T.:* Painswick 3239; 11 New Square, Lincoln's Inn, W.C.2. *T.:* Holborn 2993; Carmel, Monterey County, Calif. *T.:* 2235 J. *Club:* Reform. [*Died* 5 *Oct.* 1953.

ROBERTS, Sir Richard L.; *see* Lloyd-Roberts.

ROBERTS, Robert Lewis, C.B.E. 1939; M.A. (Oxon.); Chairman of Governors Northern Polytechnic; Chairman of Governors Highbury School; *b.* 3 Nov. 1875; 2nd *s.* of late Richard Roberts, J.P., and late Anne C. Corbett; *m.* 1905, Muriel Grace (*d.* 1945), 2nd *d.* of late J. T. Henderson, Highbury; four *s.* one *d.* *Educ.:* Merchant Taylors' School; The Queen's College, Oxford. President, London Master Builders' Association, 1928; President, Institute of Builders, 1931-32, 1947-48; Past Chairman of Council of Assoc. of Technical Institutions. *Recreations:* lawn tennis, walking. *Address:* 29 Kingsley Way, N.2. *T.:* Speedwell 1742. *Club:* United University. [*Died* 12 *Jan.* 1956.

ROBERTS, Rev. Canon Roland Harry William; Canon Residentiary and Chancellor of Truro Cathedral since 1944; Director of Religious Education, Diocese of Truro, since 1944; Examining Chaplain to Bishop of Truro since 1944; Proctor in Convocation since 1945; Member of Cornwall County Education Committee since 1944; Chairman of Further Education Committee since 1949; *b.* 18 Sept. 1894; *s.* of Henry Arthur and Agnes Roberts; *m.* 1924, Christiana Hilda Swainson Dickson; one *s.* *Educ.:* Roan School, Greenwich; Durham University. Lieut. R. W. Kent Regt. attd. M.G.C., 1915-18; President of Durham Union, 1919; University Declamation Prize, B.A. and Diploma in Theology, 1920; M.A. 1923; Deacon, 1920; Priest, 1921; Curate of St. Andrews, Stockwell, 1920-23; Curate of St. Annes-on-Sea, 1923-24; Midland Director I.C.F., 1924; Vicar of St. Paul's, Peel, 1924-28; Member of Little Hulton U.D.C., 1925-28; Rector of Victoria Park, Manchester, 1928-32; Chaplain of Manchester Royal Infirmary, St. Mary's and Christie Cancer Hospitals, 1928-32; Chaplain of Langdale Hall (Univ. of Manchester) and Diocesan Rescue Shelter, 1928-32; Vicar of Burton, Hants, 1932-36; Warden of Lay-Readers, Diocese of Winchester, 1932-36; Diocesan Missioner, Diocese of Guildford and Chaplain to Bp. of Guildford, 1936-44; Residentiary Canon, Guildford Cathedral, 1937-44; C.F. 1939; Senior C.F. 1940-44. *Publication:* The Hungry Sheep, 1945. *Recreations:* billiards, bowls and motoring. *Address:* Benson House, Truro. *T.:* Truro 2697. *Clubs:* Overseas; Cornwall County. [*Died* 13 *March* 1951.

ROBERTS, Sir Samuel, 2nd Bt., *cr.* 1919; M.A., LL.B.; *b.* 1882; *e. s.* of Right Hon. Sir Samuel Roberts, 1st Bart., and Martha Susan (*d.* 1941), *o. d.* of late Archdeacon Blakeney; *S.* father, 1926; *m.* 1906, Gladys Mary, *d.* of W. E. Dring, M.D., Tenterden, Kent; one *s.* *Educ.:* Harrow; Trinity College, Camb. Solicitor, 1906; retired from practice, 1921; M.P. (Con.) Hereford, 1921-29; Ecclesall Division of Sheffield, 1929-35; elected to Sheffield City Council, 1910; Chairman of Health Committee, 1913-19; Lord Mayor, 1919-1920; Master Cutler, 1935. *Recreation:* shooting. *Heir:* *s.* Major Peter Geoffrey Roberts, M.P. *Address:* Cockley Cley, Swaffham, Norfolk; 6 Thorney Court, W.8. *Club:* Carlton. [*Died* 13 *Dec.* 1955.

ROBERTS, Rev. William Corbett; *b.* 7 Nov. 1873; *e. s.* of Richard Roberts, J.P., of Islington, N., and Anne Catherine, *d.* of William and Anne Corbett; *m.* 1909, Ursula, *y. d.* of Lt.-Col. R. J. H. Wyllie. *Educ.:* Merchant Taylors' School; St. John's College, Oxford. Scholar, 1st class in Classical Moderations; 2nd class in Literæ Humaniores; 1st class in Theology; obtained the Liddon Studentship at Oxford, 1897, and the Denyer and Johnson University Scholarship, 1898; Senior Scholar of St. John's College, 1897-1901; B.A. 1896; M.A. 1899; Deacon, 1899; Priest, 1900; Curate of Bow, London, E., 1899-1903; Principal of Dorchester Missionary College, 1904-9; Rector of Crick, Northants, 1909-17; Rector of S. George, Bloomsbury, 1917-38; Rector of Sutton, Bedfordshire, 1938-1946; Rural Dean of Holborn, 1932-34; Rural Dean of Finsbury and Holborn, 1934-38; Rural Dean of Biggleswade, 1940-45; Examining Chaplain to the Bishop of St. Albans, 1939-51; Staff of St. Saviours, Hitchin, 1946-51. Staff of St. Stephen's College, Delhi, 1915-16; Chairman of Association for Moral and Social Hygiene, 1923-31. *Address:* 21 Benslow Lane, Hitchin, Herts. *T.:* Hitchin 1036.
[*Died* 24 *Jan.* 1953.

ROBERTS, Brig. William Henry, C.I.E. 1939; D.S.O. 1918; O.B.E. 1921; M.C., R.E.; *b.* 1882. Served Mesopotamia, 1914-18 (D.S.O., despatches); Waziristan, 1920-1921 (O.B.E.); Chief Engineer, Northern Comd. India, 1935-39; retd. pay, 1939. *Address:* c/o Lloyds Bank, 6 Pall Mall, S.W.1.
[*Died* 17 *Jan.* 1954.

ROBERTSHAW, Sir Charles, Kt., *cr.* 1938; *b.* 13 March 1874; 2nd *s.* of late John Robertshaw, J.P., West Riding of Yorkshire, of Stansfeld Hall, Luddenden Foot, Yorkshire; *m.* 1901, Alice, *o. c.* of Abraham Hoyle, Summerfield, Hebden Bridge; no *c. Educ.:* University School, Southport. Formerly J.P. West Riding, 1919; Chairman W. R. Bench at Todmorden; late Chairman of Juvenile Court and Probation Court; retired, 1950; late Chm. of West Riding Standing Joint Committee, 1942-43; Chairman, Income Tax Commissioners for West Morley (Halifax) Division; late Pres. of Royal Halifax Infirmary, 3 years; late Pres. of Sowerby Division Conservative Association; Chairman of West Riding Licensing Compensation and Confirming Authority; late Commander of Todmorden Division of Special Constabulary (two medals); President Hebden Bridge and Calder Valley Agricultural Society. *Recreation:* shooting grouse. *Address:* Falling Royd, Hebden Bridge, Yorkshire. *T.:* Hebden Bridge 32. *Club:* Halifax (Halifax).
[*Died* 14 *March* 1960.

ROBERTSON, Rear-Admiral Albert John, M.V.O. 1925; R.N., retired; *b.* Wynnstay, Clonskeagh, Co. Dublin, 6 Jan. 1884; *s.* of late Maj. J. A. Robertson, Royal Artillery; *m.* 1909, Lorna, *y. d.* of late Lt.-Col. G. M. Cardew, Hampshire, Regt.; three *s.* two *d. Educ.:* Hill House, St. Leonard's-on-Sea; H.M.S. Britannia. Midshipman, 1900; Sub-Lieut., 1903; served in European War in 2nd Cruiser Squadron of the Grand Fleet (H.M.S. Achilles and H.M.S. Minotaur); Commander, 1917; served as Navigating Officer in H.M. Yacht Victoria and Albert, 1922-25; Captain, 1924; Captain of Dockyard, and King's Harbour Master, Portsmouth, 1931-1933; Rear-Adm. and retired list, 1936. *Address:* Abingdon House, Filsham Road, St. Leonards-on-Sea. *T.:* Hastings 2057. *Club:* United Service. [*Died* 8 *Jan.* 1954.

ROBERTSON, Brig.-Gen. Alexander Brown, C.B. 1934; C.M.G. 1918; D.S.O. 1916; late Cameron Highlanders; *b.* 1878; *s.* of late William Brown Robertson, J.P., of Coleburn, Morayshire; *m.* 1st, 1911, Anne Clare Carmichael (*d.* 1947), *d.* of late Major G. R. Cruden of Wellhouse, Shettleston; one *s.* one *d.* (and one *s.* died of wounds, 1940); 2nd, 1949, Gladys Mary Francis, *widow* of H. S. Manisty, M.C. Served South African War, 1900-2 (Queen's medal and four clasps, King's medal and two clasps, despatches); European War, including Egypt, 1914-18 (despatches, C.M.G., D.S.O., Bt. Lieut.-Col., 4th class White Eagle, and Chevalier Legion of Honour); A.Q.M.G. War Office, 1925-29; commander 10th (Jubbulpore) Infantry Brigade, 1929-33; retired pay, 1933. Member of League of Nations Chaco Commission, 1933-34. *Address:* Dunboylan, Kings Ride, Camberley, Surrey. *T.:* 46. *Club:* Naval and Military.
[*Died* 7 *Dec.* 1951.

ROBERTSON, Sir Benjamin, K.C.S.I., *cr.* 1911 (C.S.I. 1910); K.C.M.G., *cr.* 1914; C.I.E. 1898; Hon. LL.D. (Aberdeen), 1914; late Indian Civil Service; *b.* Dunphail, Morayshire, 16 Oct. 1864; *e. s.* of late B. Robertson of Dunphail, Morayshire; *m.* 1st, 1893, Charlotte, C.B.E. (*d.* 1931), *d.* of late W. Young of Londonderry; 2nd, 1938, Helen Leslie Poole (*d.* 1952), *er. d.* of late Capt. Michael Ramsay Spence, B.S.C. *Educ.:* Private school; Aberdeen University; Balliol College, Oxford. Passed into Indian Civil Service, 1883; landed in India, 1885; served as assistant magistrate and collector Bombay Presidency until 1890; superintendent of census in Central Provinces, 1890-92; deputy Commissioner and magistrate, Central Provinces, 1892-1902; Chief Sec. to Chief Commissioner, C.P., 1902-06; President Assam Labour Commission, 1906; Secretary, Government of India, Commerce Department, 1907; Temporary Member of Governor-General's Council, 1910; Chief Commissioner of the Central Provinces, 1912-20; was on special duty in South Africa, 1914, with Commission of Inquiry into grievances of Indians within the Union; on a similar mission in 1920, and also visited Tanganyika, Kenya and Uganda in connection with status of Indians in these countries; retired, 1921; deputed to Russia to report on Volga Famine, 1922; Member Council of India, 1922-27. *Address:* Relugas, Edgeborough Rd., Guildford. *T.:* 5571. [*Died* 14 *April* 1953.

ROBERTSON, Col. Colin MacLeod, C.B. 1929; D.S.O. 1918; T.D.; D.L., J.P., C.C. Buteshire; Member Buteshire Territorial Army Assoc. since 1908, Chairman, 1920-44; Vice-Chm. and Governor, Glasgow Veterinary College; Director Scottish Board, Phœnix Assurance Co. Ltd.; Member of the Royal Archers (King's Body Guard for Scotland); *b.* 1870; *s.* of late John Hepburn Robertson, Calvine, near Struan, Perthshire; *m.* 1931, Ann Marsali (*d.* 1951), *d.* of late Francis C. Buchanan, D.L., J.P., Clarinish, Rhu. Served European War, 1914-19 (despatches thrice, D.S.O., Croix de Guerre); Hon. Col. 26th (High) Pack Brigade R.F.A., 1923-29; County Welfare Officer (Buteshire), 1941-46; *Address:* Ardmoy, Rhu, Dumbartonshire; *T.:* Rhu 230. *Clubs:* Caledonian; Conservative (Glasgow); Royal Clyde Yacht (Hunter's Quay); Royal Northern Yacht (Rhu).
[*Died* 2 *July* 1951.

ROBERTSON, David, M.A., LL.B., S.S.C.; *b.* Stranraer, Wigtownshire; *m.* 1909, Margaret L. M. Low (*deed.*); one *s.* one *d. Educ.:* Stranraer Academy; Edinburgh University. Town Clerk, Leith; Town Clerk, Edinburgh, 1934-41. *Publications:* South Leith Records; Bailies of Leith; Castle and Town; Princes Street Proprietors; Edinburgh, 1329-1929. *Recreation:* golf. *Address:* Strathearn Place, Edinburgh 7. *T.:* 53888.
[*Died* 28 *Nov.* 1952.

ROBERTSON, Major-General Donald (Elphinston), C.B. 1932; D.S.O. 1920; late 11th King Edward's Own Lancers (5th Probyn's Horse); *b.* 1879; *o. s.* of late Lieutenant-Colonel Sir Donald Robertson, K.C.S.I.; *m.* 1st, 1909, Evalina Catharine (*d.* 1942), *e. d.* of late Sir J. O. Miller, K.C.S.I.; three *s.* two *d.*; 2nd, 1943, Mary Reed. Served European War, 1914-20 (despatches, D.S.O., Legion of Honour);

Chief Instructor Cavalry School, Saugor, 1921-23; A.A.G. Northern Command, India, 1924-28; Commanded 9th (Jhansi) Infantry Brigade, 1928; Bareilly Brigade, 1931-32; A.D.C. to the King, 1932-34; Officiating Officer Commanding, Presidency and Assam District, April-Nov. 1932; Director of Personal Services, Army Headquarters, India, 1933-34; Maj.-Gen. 1933; Commander Waziristan District, India, 1934-37; retired, 1937; Wing Commander R.A.F.V.R. 1939; resigned Commission, 1943. *Recreations:* consults undertakers and attends funerals. *Club:* United Service. [*Died* 23 *May* 1953.

ROBERTSON, Air Commodore Edmund Digby Maxwell, C.B. 1935; D.F.C. 1918; R.A.F. retired; *b.* 1887; *s.* of late Col. H. Maxwell Robertson, R.A., and Mary E. L. Campbell; *m.* 1912, Evelyn J. Simpson; one *s.* one *d.* (and one *s.* killed on active service, 1940). *Educ.:* H.M.S. Britannia. Entered Royal Navy, 1903; Lieut., 1907; Commanded H.M.S. Riviera, 1914-15 (despatches) and R.A.F. Station, Felixstowe, 1918; Lt.-Col. R.A.F. 1918; Group Captain, 1926; Air Commodore, 1931; A.D.C. to the King, 1931; Director of Personal Services, Air Ministry, 1930-35; Airport Superintendent, Croydon Airport, 1935-39; retired list, 1935; re-employed R.A.F., 1939-1945. Fellow Royal Empire Society. *Address:* 206 Nelson House, Dolphin Square, S.W.1. *T.:* Victoria 3800. *Club:* Royal Air Force. [*Died* 24 *July* 1956.

ROBERTSON, George; *b.* 4 Jan. 1883; *m.* 1909, Lilian S. Ross; one *s.* three *d.* (and one *s.* decd.). *Educ.:* George Watson's College, Edinburgh; Edinburgh University (M.A. 1903; LL.D. 1952). Balliol College, Oxford (Exhibitioner and Honorary Scholar); Ireland and Craven Scholar, 1906; Professor of Classics, Grey University College, Bloemfontein, 1907-13; Headmaster of Eltham College, 1914-26; Headmaster, George Watson's College, Edinburgh, 1926-43. *Address:* 31 Hatton Place, Edinburgh. [*Died* 3 *May* 1956.

ROBERTSON, Lt.-Col. Graham; *see* Robertson, Lt.-Col. J. H. G.

ROBERTSON, Granville Douglas, F.R.C.S., M.R.C.S., L.R.C.P.; Consulting Ear, Nose and Throat Surgeon to St. Mary's Hospital, W.2, and to London County Council; *b.* 21 May 1891; *s.* of late Col. Robert Robertson, I.M.S.; *m.* 1930, Louise, *o. d.* of late Alfred Kingsley Johnson; no *c.* *Educ.:* Charterhouse; St. Mary's Hospital, London. F.R.C.S. (Eng.), 1923; M.R.C.S., L.R.C.P. (London), 1914; late Surgical Registrar, St. Mary's Hosp.; Ear, Nose and Throat Surgeon Princess Louise Children's Hosp., London, Wembley Memorial Hosp., Maida Vale Hosp. for Nervous Diseases, Hanwell Cottage Hosp., Sevenoaks Fever Hosp.; served European War, 1914-18, Major R.A.R.O., R.A.M.C.; B.E.F. 1914-19 (despatches, 1916); War of 1939-45, Ear, Nose and Throat Surgeon, Base Hospitals, B.E.F. and U.K. *Recreations:* fishing, golf. *Address:* Robin Hill, Itchen Abbas, Winchester, Hants. *T.:* Itchen Abbas 316. [*Died* 7 *Aug.* 1951.

ROBERTSON, Lieut.-Gen. Sir Horace Clement Hugh, K.B.E., *cr.* 1950 (C.B.E. 1941); D.S.O. 1917; Commander-in-Chief, Australian Southern Comd., 1953-54, retd.; *b.* 29 Oct. 1894; *s.* of John Robertson and Annie Gray; *m.* 1917, Jessie Bonnar (*d.* 1956); no *c.* *Educ.:* Geelong Coll., Victoria; Royal Military College, Duntroon. Commissioned Australian Staff Corps, 1914; served European War, 1914-18, 10th Light Horse Regt.; Gallipoli, Egypt, Palestine, Syria, and Staff of Yeomanry Mounted Div. and Force in Egypt (D.S.O., Order of Nile 4th Class, despatches twice); Staff College, Camberley, 1923-24; Courses in England, 1925; Brigade Major; Chief Instructor, Small Arms School, 1926-29; General Staff Officer, 1933; Instructor in Tactics, R.M.C., 1934; Director of Military Art, R.M.C. Duntroon, 1935-38; Commandant 7th Military District, Northern Territory of Australia, 1939-40; commanded 19th Infantry Brigade of 6th Division, 2nd A.I.F., 1940-41; 1st Aust. Armoured Div., 1942-43; 5th Aust. Div., 1945; 6th Aust. Div., 1945; 1st Aust. Army, 1945; Commander-in-Chief British Commonwealth Occupation Forces, Japan, 1946-51, and Administrative C.-in-C. British Commonwealth Forces, Korea, 1950-51; Director-General of Recruiting, Australia, Dec. 1951-Jan. 1953; p.s.c. Pres. Victorian Br., Roy. Commonwealth Soc.; Chm. Exhibition Trustees, Melbourne; Comr., State Savings Bank of Victoria. Chief Commander Legion of Merit, U.S.A., 1951; Order of Military Merit (Taiguk), Republic of Korea, 1951. *Recreations:* riding, golf, rifle shooting, game fishing. *Address:* 226 Dandenong Road, East St. Kilda, Victoria. *Clubs:* Naval and Military, Athenæum, Melbourne, Savage (Melbourne). [*Died* 28 *April* 1960.

ROBERTSON, Rev. Professor James Alex., M.A., D.D., LL.D.; *b.* 26 November 1880; *s.* of late Rev. A. A. Robertson, Burnbank, Newburgh, Aberdeenshire; *m.* Edith Anne Stewart (E. A. S. Robertson); three *d.* *Educ.:* Inverness Royal Academy (Gold Medallist); Aberdeen University (First Class Honours, Mental Philosophy, Bain Gold Medallist, Hutton Prizeman, Fullarton Scholar); Glasgow United Free Church College (Freeland Scholar, Thompson Scholar, Clark Fellow); St. Andrews University; Marburg University; Ferguson Scholar in Philosophy (Scottish Universities); Minister of Glenlyon United Free Church, 1908; Forfar West, 1911; Edinburgh, Palmerston Place U.F. Church, 1914; Ballater United Free Church, 1918; Bruce Lecturer, Glasgow College, 1917; Professor of Divinity and Biblical Criticism, Aberdeen University, 1938; retired, 1945; Professor of New Testament Language and Literature in Christ's College, Aberdeen, 1920. *Publications:* The Spiritual Pilgrimage of Jesus (4 edits.); The Gospel and Epistles of St. John (Primer); The Hidden Romance of the New Testament (2nd ed.); Concerning the Soul, 1921; Divine Vocation in Human Life, 1925; Jesus the Citizen, 1927; Who was Jesus of Nazareth, 1929; Studies for a Portrait of Jesus, 1936; Joint Compiler of The Sayings of Jesus of Nazareth. *Recreations:* outdoor exercises, walking, etc. *Address:* Blythehill, Forfar, Angus. [*Died* 17 *Nov.* 1955.

ROBERTSON, Brig.-Gen. James Campbell, C.B. 1919; C.M.G. 1915; D.S.O. 1917; V.D. 1925; *b.* 24 Oct. 1878; *m.* Ada, *e. d.* of late Richard Godsall; one *s.* *Educ.:* Toowoomba Grammar School, Queensland. Commanded 11th Infantry Battalion, C.M.F., prior to War; joined A.I.F. 20 Aug. 1914; served European War, 1915-16, landing at Gallipoli with covering brigade, 25 April 1915 (wounded, despatches seven times, C.M.G.); served in France, 1916-18 (C.B., D.S.O.). *Address:* Struan, Toowoomba, Queensland, Australia. *Clubs:* Downs (Toowoomba); United Service (Brisbane). [*Died* 26 *Jan.* 1951.

ROBERTSON, Col. James F.; *see* Forbes-Robertson.

ROBERTSON, Lieut.-Colonel (James Herbert) Graham, C.B.E. 1919; V.D.; M.B., Ch.B., N.Z.; F.R.C.S.E.; F.R.S.M.; retired; Dermatologist, Actino-therapist; *b.* Dunedin, New Zealand; *m.* 1910, Gladys, *d.* of James Gear; one *d.* *Educ.:* Otago High School, Dunedin; Otago Univ.; Edinburgh. Practised medicine since 1904, several times visiting the Old Country and the Continent in pursuit of post graduate work; over three years service European War (C.B.E., despatches twice, Lieut.-Colonel); now on retired list; specialising in dermatology and physio-therapy; Hon. Dermatologist to Wellington Public Hospital; Hon.

Actino-therapist, Wellington Public Hospital; Hon. Consulting Dermatologist, Public Health Dept. Wellington. K.St.J. *Publications:* Sundry and various medical papers. *Recreations:* golf, tennis, etc. *Address:* c/o Department of Dermatology, Wellington Public Hospital, Wellington, N.Z. *Clubs:* Wellington; Hawkes Bay. [*Died* 3 *July* 1956.

ROBERTSON, Colonel John, C.B.E. 1919; V.D.; *b.* 1878; *s.* of R. J. Robertson, Q.C., Dublin; *m.* 1907. *Educ.:* Clifton College; Dublin University. Formerly Lieutenant-Colonel East Indian Railway Regiment. Served European War, 1914-19, as Colonel, R.E. (despatches, C.B.E.). *Address:* Stepaside, Wormley, Godalming, Surrey. [*Died* 15 *March* 1951.

ROBERTSON, John Charles, M.A.; Hon. LL.D., Toronto; Professor Emeritus of Greek since 1932, Victoria College, University of Toronto; *b.* Brampton, Ontario, 1864; *m.* 1889, Eleanor A., *d.* of B. B. Toye, Toronto; one *s.* *Educ.:* Goderich High School; University College, Toronto; Fellow in Classics, 1883-1886; Johns Hopkins, Baltimore (scholar 1888). Gold Medallist in Classics of University of Toronto at graduation, 1883; for some years engaged in secondary school teaching in Brampton, Owen Sound, and West Toronto; Lecturer in Greek in Victoria College, Toronto, 1894; Associate-Professor, 1899; Professor, 1902; Dean of the Faculty of Arts, 1910-22; a member of the Senate of the University of Toronto, 1906-22; delegate to Congress of Universities of Empire in London, 1912; a member of Massey Foundation Commission on Methodist Colleges, 1920-21. *Publications:* various school editions of Cæsar and Virgil; Primary Latin Book, 1892 and 1900; Latin Lessons for Beginners, 1906, High School Latin Book, 1917 and 1926; The Story of Greece and Rome, 1928; Latin Songs, New and Old, 1934 and 1937; Mixed Company (Classical Essays), 1939; Latin Songs and Carols, 1945. *Address:* 409 Brunswick Avenue, Toronto, Canada. *Club:* Madawaska (Toronto). [*Died* 24 *Feb.* 1956.

ROBERTSON, John James, J.P.; Sales Representative, Scottish Housing Group; *b.* Shetland Is., 23 May 1898; *m.* 1924, Agnes Leslie; one *d.* *Educ.:* elementary, Shetland Islands. First went to sea in sail at age of 14; joined Royal Navy at 16; served throughout European War, 1914-18, at sea, present at Jutland Battle; served in Red Sea, India and China; demobilised, 1919; Merchant Navy, 1920-35; Retail Fruit Merchant, Edinburgh, 1935-45. Ministry of Information Lecturer, 1940-45; Chief Labour Officer (Scotland) Ministry of Supply, 1941-1944. Member of Edinburgh Town Council, 1938-45; Commissioner of Leith Harbour and Docks, 1938-45; Governor of Leith Nautical College, 1938-45; Member Board of Management, Scottish Special Housing Assoc., 1944-46; M.P. (Lab.) Berwick and Haddington, 1945-50, Berwick and East Lothian, 1950-51; Jt. Parliamentary Under-Secretary of State, Scottish Office, 1947-50. Member British Medical Council, 1946-. J.P. Edinburgh. *Recreations:* won Naval Boxing Championship, 1918 (Middle-weight), yacht sailing and other sports. *Address:* Dunalastair, Eastfield Gardens, Joppa, Midlothian. *T.:* Portobello 5309. *Clubs:* Overseas League; Royal Forth Yacht; East Lothian Yacht. [*Died* 6 *Oct.* 1955.

ROBERTSON, Rt. Hon. Sir Malcolm Arnold, P.C. 1927; G.C.M.G., *cr.* 1930 (K.C.M.G., *cr.* 1929; C.M.G. 1915); K.B.E., *cr.* 1924; Chairman of Spillers, Ltd., 1930-47; Fellow of St. Catharine's College, Cambridge, 1940; *b.* 2 Sep. 1877; *s.* of late Charles Boyd Robertson of the Foreign Office; *m.* 1917, Gladys, *d.* of late Melville E. Ingalls of Hot Springs, Va., U.S.A.; one *s.* *Educ.:* Marlborough. Clerk Foreign Office, 1898; Coronation medal; 3rd Secretary Diplomatic Service, Berlin, 1903-4; 2nd Secretary Pekin, 1905; Madrid, 1907; Chargé d'Affaires, Bucharest, 1910-11; 1st Secretary, 1912; Chargé d'Affaires, Monte Video, 1912-13; Rio de Janeiro, 1913-15; 1st Secretary, Washington, 1915-18; Hague, 1918-19; Counsellor of Embassy and Deputy British High Commissioner on Inter-Allied Rhineland High Commission, 1919; British High Commissioner on same High Commission, 1920-21, with personal and local rank of Minister Plenipotentiary in the Diplomatic Service; Minister Plenipotentiary, 1921; H.M. Agent and Consul-General at Tangier, 1921-25; Envoy Extraordinary and Minister Plenipotentiary, Buenos Aires, 1925-27; Ambassador, 1927-29; retired, 1930; M.P. (C.) Mitcham Division of Surrey, 1940-45; Chairman of the British Council, 1941-45; Jubilee Medal, 1935; Coronation Medal, 1937. *Address:* 22 Rutland Court, Rutland Gardens, S.W.7. *T.:* Kensington 7356. *Clubs:* St. James', Beefsteak. [*Died* 23 *April* 1951.

ROBERTSON, Norman Charles, C.M.G. 1954; M.B.E. 1944; Deputy Managing Director, E. K. Cole Ltd., since 1945; *b.* 28 April 1908; *s.* of Charles Walter and Jessie Robertson; *m.* 1935, Joan Elizabeth Carr; two *s.* one *d.* *Educ.:* Southend High School; Regent Street Polytechnic. Apprentice, Sterling Telephone & Electric Co. Ltd. 1924-26; Marconi's Wireless Telegraph Co., 1926-28; Kolster-Brandes Ltd., 1928-30; E. K. Cole Ltd.: Executive, 1930-43; Director and General Works Manager, 1943-1945; loaned to Min. of Supply in capacity of Dir.-Gen. of Electronics Production, 1951-53. M.Brit.I.R.E.; A.I.E.E.; Sen. Mem. Inst. of Radio Engineers, U.S.A. *Recreations:* yachting and golf. *Address:* The Old Vicarage, Burnham-on-Crouch, Essex. *T.:* Burnham-on-Crouch 2151. *Clubs:* Royal Automobile; Royal Burnham Yacht (Cdre.); Royal Corinthian Yacht. [*Died* 1 *April* 1956.

ROBERTSON, Rae, M.A., F.R.A.M., concert pianist; *b.* Ardersier, Inverness-shire, 29 Nov. 1893; *s.* of Rev. Alexander and Mary Taylor Robertson; *m.* 1921, Ethel Bartlett; no *c.* *Educ.:* Inverness Academy; Edinburgh University (Bucher Scholarship); studied piano with Florence Hendery and Philip Halstead; at Royal Academy of Music under Tobias Matthay and Frederick Corder; Chappell Gold Medal for piano; served 3½ years with London Regiment during European War (twice wounded), after some years career as solo pianist, specialised in two-piano duet playing with wife, Ethel Bartlett, with whom has made tours in North and South America, Germany, Holland, Belgium, Sweden, Poland, Spain, and South Africa, as well as British Isles. *Recreations:* swimming and reading. *Address:* Essex House, 160 Central Park South, New York, N.Y., U.S.A. [*Died* 4 *Nov.* 1956.

ROBERTSON, Robert Spelman; Chief Justice of Ontario, 1938-52; *b.* 11 Dec. 1870; *s.* of William R. Robertson and F. A. Smith; *m.* 1900, Laura G. Segsworth; four *s.* one *d.* *Educ.:* usual schools; Osgoode Hall. Barrister at Stratford, Ont., until 1917; then at Toronto until 1938. LL.D. (Hon.) University of Toronto. *Address:* 53 Castle Frank Road, Toronto. *Clubs:* York, Royal Canadian Yacht (Toronto). [*Died* 28 *May* 1955.

ROBERTSON, Robin Haskew, C.M.G. 1949; *b.* 19 October 1898; *e. s.* of Rev. J. T. Robertson, Prince Edward Island, Canada; *m.* 1925, Dorothy May (*d.* 1947), *e. d.* of Thomas Edward Pickford, Exeter; one *s.* *Educ.:* abroad and London University. B.Sc. (Engineering). Assistant Engineer, Sudan Railways, 1924; Harbour Engineer, 1927; Maintenance Engineer, 1934; Asst. Chief Engineer, 1938; Chief Engineer, 1941; Dep. Gen. Manager, 1941; General Manager, 1946-50, retired. Order of the Nile (4th Class), 1940. *Address:* 36 Greenlands Rd., Staines. [*Died* 2 *Nov.* 1952.

ROBERTSON, Stuart; Film Executive; Singer and Actor; Lt.-Comdr. R.C.N.V.R.; 2nd *s.* of late Capt. H. W. Robertson; *m.* 1927, Alice Moxon; one *s.* one *d.* *Educ.:* Chigwell School, Essex. Studied singing at Royal College of Music, London; solo bass St. Paul's Cathedral at age of 19; resigned to accompany Dame Nellie Melba on farewell tour of Australia; first broadcast, 1924; first gramophone record made, 1926; first film (Bitter-Sweet), 1933. *Recreations:* golf, motoring, walking. *Address:* 59 Deacons Hill, Elstree, Herts. [*Died* 26 *Dec.* 1958.

ROBERTSON, Thomas Atholl, F.S.A. (Scot.); *e. s.* of late John Robertson, Snaigow, Dunkeld; *m.* 1st, Flora Campbell (*d.* 1943), *o. d.* of late James Cumming, L.D.S.; two *s.* four *d.*; 2nd, 1948, Agnes Christie, *d.* of late James Paterson, Redgorton, Perthshire. *Educ.:* Clunie Public School, Dunkeld, Perthshire. Began business career in Glasgow; completed training in Germany; travelled extensively in Europe and Near East, Canada, U.S.A., etc.; Ex-Chief Scottish Clans Association of London; Governor Royal Caledonian Schools, Bushey, Herts; President English League for Taxation of Land Values; Past Pres., London Perthshire Association; ten years 9th H.L.I. (The Glasgow Highlanders) Territorials; contested (L.) South Hammersmith, 1918; Finchley Div. of Middlesex, 1922, 1929 and 1935; M.P. (L.) Finchley Div. of Middlesex, 1923-24; contested Kinross and West Perthshire, 1931; Aylesbury Bucks By-Election, 1938. *Publications:* Articles on Scottish and Highland Customs; Folk Lore and Legends of Perthshire; Editor, The Scots Year Book. *Recreations:* fishing, bowls. *Address:* Dunvorlich, Ewanfield, Crieff, Perthshire. *Clubs:* National Liberal; Scottish Liberal (Edinburgh). [*Died* 14 *Dec.* 1955.

ROBERTSON-EUSTACE, Mrs. Marjory Edith, C.B.E. 1919; *d.* of late Major Thomas Leith, of Petmathen, Oyne, Aberdeenshire, and Lady Mary Isabella Leith; *m.* 1906, Major Charles Legge Eustace Robertson-Eustace, D.S.O. (*d.* 1908). Organiser and Administrator, First Rest Club for Q.A.I.M.N.S. in France during European War, 1914-19. *Address:* Merethold, Wrecclesham, Farnham, Surrey. [*Died* 12 *Oct.* 1957.

ROBEY, Sir George, Kt. 1954; C.B.E. 1919; *b.* 20 Sept. 1869; *m.* 1st, Ethel Haydon (marriage dissolved); one *s.*; 2nd, Blanche Littler, Theatrical Proprietor and Producer. Made first appearance on music hall stage Oxford, 1891, and in revue at Alhambra, 1916; recently appeared as Sir John Falstaff in Henry IV (Part I); films include Don Quixote, Chu Chin Chow, Southern Roses, A Girl Must Live, Salute John Citizen, Variety Jubilee, Falstaff in Henry V., Technicolour, Innkeeper in Waltz Time, The Trojan Brothers, etc.; served with Motor Transport Service during War, 1914-1918, and organised many entertainments for war charities when he raised £500,000 (C.B.E.); 1939-45, appeared in concerts and camps all over England for troops, etc., and was instrumental in inaugurating meetings on behalf of War Savings and thereby contributing over 2 million pounds towards same; celebrated his eightieth birthday, 1949; continued his professional activities in the Theatre, Music Hall, Concerts, and on behalf of charities, etc., broadcasting and televising in all principal programmes. Appearances as "Top of the bill" at Glasgow, Liverpool, Nottingham, Birmingham, etc.; Toby Weller in Dickens' Pickwick Papers (film). Has exhibited at Royal Academy, Institute of Painters in Water Colours (from which he holds a diploma). *Publications:* My Life up to Now, 1908; Pause, 1910; Mental Fireworks, 1925; Don't, 1926; Looking Back on Life, 1933. *Recreations:* cricket, football, cooking. *Club:* M.C.C. [*Died* 29 *Nov.* 1954.

ROBINS, Rt. Rev. Edwin Frederick, D.D., St. John's Coll., Winnipeg, Trinity Univ., Toronto, and Emmanuel Univ., Saskatoon; Asst. to Bishop of Norwich since 1931; Hon. Canon of Norwich, 1931; Commissary to Bishop of Athabasca and to Bishop of Ottawa; *b.* London, 11 Feb. 1870; *s.* of John Crawley and Elizabeth Robins; *m.* 1897, Florence Durnford (*d.* 1940), *d.* of late Rev. G. Iliff. *Educ.:* C.M. College, Islington. Deacon, 1894, Priest, 1897, St. Paul's Cathedral; C.M.S. Missionary at Dera Ghazi Khan, Punjab, 1894-1897; Curate of St. James, Paddington, 1897-98; Widcombe, 1898-1901; Organising Sec. C.M.S., 1901-2; Vicar of Thorpe-Le-Soken, 1902-10; Archdeacon of Athabasca, 1909-12; Bishop of Athabasca, 1912-30; Vicar of Wicklewood, 1931-47. *Address:* Gimingham, Norwich. *T.:* Mundesley 137. *Club:* Church Imperial. [*Died* 22 *March* 1951.

ROBINS, Elizabeth; Mrs. George Richmond Parks (C. E. Raimond); actress and author; principally known as an interpreter of Ibsen's characters; *b.* Louisville, Kentucky. *Educ.:* Zanesville, Ohio. *Publications:* George Mandeville's Husband, 1894; The New Moon, 1895; Below the Salt, 1896; The Open Question, 1898; The Magnetic North, 1904; A Dark Lantern, 1905; Votes for Women (Play); The Convert, 1907; Come and Find Me, 1908; The Florentine Frame, 1909; Where are You Going to? 1912; Way Stations, 1913; Camilla, 1918; The Messenger, 1920; Time is Whispering, 1923; Ancilla's Share, 1924; The Secret that was Kept, 1926; Theatre and Friendship, 1932; Both Sides of the Curtain, 1940; Raymond and I, 1956 (posthumous). *Address:* Backset Town, Henfield, Sussex; 6 Palace Gate, W.8. *Clubs:* American Women's, Writers'. [*Died* 8 *May* 1952.

ROBINS, Very Rev. Henry Charles; Dean Emeritus of Salisbury, since 1952; *b.* Beccles, Suffolk, 2 Feb. 1882; *s.* of Henry Lambley and Mary Ann Robins; *m.* 1915, Dorothy, *d.* of Sampson Zachary Lloyd, Areley Hall, Worcestershire; (son died P.O.W. Java, Sept. 1945) two *d.* *Educ.:* Fauconberge School, Beccles; Winchester College (Foundation Scholar) New College, Oxford (Scholar); Bishop's Hostel, Farnham. 1st Class Classical Mods., 1903; B.A., 2nd Class Lit. Hum., 1905; M.A. 1909; Master at Harrow School, 1905, and Winchester College, 1906; Deacon, 1907; Priest, 1908; Curate of S. John, Forton, Gosport, 1907-11; Assistant Chaplain, Khartoum, 1911-16; Vicar of Fleet, Hants, 1916-22; T.C.F., 1918; Vicar of Romford, Essex, 1922-30; Rural Dean of Chafford, 1925-30; Vicar of Barking, Essex, 1930-35; Hon. Canon of Chelmsford, 1931-35; Vicar of St. Mary's, Portsea, Hants, 1935-43; Rural Dean of Portsmouth, 1936-43; Hon. Canon of Portsmouth, 1935-43; Chaplain to the King, 1939-43; Dean of Salisbury, 1943-52; retired, 1952. Proctor in Convocation, 1932; Vice-President of Guild of Health. *Publications:* Fear, its cause and cure; Christian Joy; Leisure, Curse or Blessing; A Guide to Spiritual Healing, 1953; A Three Hours' Meditation, 1956; The Conquest of Fear, 1958. *Address:* 1 De Vaux Place, Salisbury, Wilts. *T.:* 2184. [*Died* 31 *July* 1960.

ROBINS, William Palmer, R.E. 1917; R.W.S. 1948; Member of: Print Makers Society, California; Chicago Society of Etchers; Honorary Member Australian Society of Etchers; Hon. Member Sheffield Society of Artists; *b.* 21 July 1882; *s.* of William Benjamin Robins; *married.* *Educ.:* Roans School, Greenwich; studied architecture under Prof. Banister Fletcher at King's College, London; Silver Medallist, History of Architecture, King's College; studied St. Martin's School of Art, London;

awarded Logan Medal for Etching by the Chicago Arts Institute, 1925; medal for Lithography, 1931, International Print Makers' Exhibition, Los Angeles; Exhibitor Royal Academy since 1912, New English Art Club, International Exhibitions, Venice, Florence, Leipzig, Stockholm, Zürich, Dunedin, Adelaide, Brooklyn. Work in permanent national collections, U.S.A.; Congress Gallery, Washington; Uffizi Gallery, Florence; British Museum, Victoria and Albert Museum, South Kensington. *Publications:* Etching Craft, a Guide for Collectors and Students, 1923. *Recreation:* gardening. *Address:* 3 St. Oswald's Studios, Sedlescombe Road, S.W.6. *T.:* Fulham 3734. [*Died* 14 *July* 1959.

ROBINSON, 1st Baron, *cr.* 1947, of Kielder Forest and of Adelaide; **Roy Lister Robinson;** Kt., *cr.* 1931; O.B.E., B.A. (Oxon.); B.Sc.; F.S.A.S.M. (Adelaide); Hon. LL.D. Aberdeen; Chm. of Forestry Commission, 1932-52 (Dir.-Gen., 1945-47); *b.* 8 March 1883; *e. s.* of late William Robinson, Perth, W.A.; *m.* 1910, Charlotte Marion, *y. d.* of late Harry Cust Bradshaw, formerly of Fair Oak Park, Hampshire; two *d.* (one *s.* killed in action, 1942). *Educ.:* St. Peter's College, Adelaide (State Exhibitioner and Scholar); School of Mines and University, Adelaide; Magdalen College, Oxford; Rhodes Scholar, South Australia, 1905; First class Honours School Nat. Science, Oxford, 1908; Burdett Coutts Scholar, 1908; Assistant Inspector Board of Agriculture and Fisheries, 1909; Inspector, 1910; Superintending Inspector, 1912; Ministries of Munitions and Agriculture, 1914-18; Technical Commissioner 1919-32, and Vice-Chairman Forestry Commission, 1929-32; Chairman British Empire Forestry Conference, South Africa, 1935 and Great Britain, 1947. Hon. Member Society of American Foresters; Hon. Member Institute of Foresters of Australia. *Publications:* Papers, etc. (Forestry) to Technical Journals. *Recreations:* golf, cricket, Oxford XI, 1908 and 1909, Athletic Teams, 1907-09, Lacrosse Team, 1906-09. *Heir:* none. *Address:* Forestry Commission, 25 Savile Row, W.1. *T.:* Regent 0221. *Club:* Brooks's. [*Died* 5 *Sept.* 1952 (*ext.*).

ROBINSON, Sir Arnold Percy, Kt., *cr.* 1934; *b.* 7 March 1879; *s.* of late Arnold Robinson, Berkhamsted, Herts; *m.* 1st, 1910, Eversley (*d.* 1949), *d.* of Dr. Chaning-Pearce, Ramsgate; one *d.*; 2nd, 1949, Violet Eileen, *widow* of George Kay and *d.* of late Wm. C. Ward, Victoria, B.C., and Harbourne House, High Halden, Kent. *Educ.:* Berkhamsted School. Admitted solicitor, 1905; went to Singapore, 1907; admitted Straits Settlements Bar and Federated Malay States Bar, 1908; senior partner Drew & Napier, Advocates and Solicitors, Singapore; retired, 1935; senior Unofficial Member of Executive Council and Unofficial Member Legislative Council, Straits Settlements, 1927-35; Member of Exec. Cttee. Raffles College, Singapore; 4 years Pres. of Straits Settlements Assoc.; 4 years Pres. of Royal Singapore Golf Club; many years member of Straits Settlements Bar Cttee.; represented Straits Settlements at Coronation of King George VI; Pres. of Assoc. of British Malaya (London), 1937; Jubilee and Coronation Medals. *Address:* Dene House, Milepath, Hook Heath, Woking, Surrey. *T.:* Woking 845. *Clubs:* East India and Sports; Royal Singapore Golf; Woking Golf. [*Died* 29 *Feb.* 1960.

ROBINSON, Arthur Leyland, M.D.; B.S. (Lond.), F.R.C.S. (Eng.), F.R.C.O.G.; Emeritus Professor of Midwifery and Gynæcology, University of Liverpool; *b.* 27 July 1887; *s.* of Joseph Henry Robinson and Caroline Sandford; *m.* 1914; one *d.*; *m.* 1959, Margaret Joan Worthy, Broadstairs, Kent. *Educ.:* privately; University of Liverpool; Univ. Coll. Hosp., London. Served European War with B.S.F., R.A.M.C.; late Hon. Surgeon, Women's Hosp., Liverpool, and Maternity Hosp., Liverpool; Fellow (Pres. 1933-34); North of England Gynæcological Society; Member (Pres. 1940-41); Liverpool Medical Institution; late Examiner Obst. and Gynæcol. Univs. of London, Manchester, Sheffield and Wales, and Conjoint Board of England. *Publications:* papers in the medical journals. *Recreations:* fishing, numismatics. *Address:* Longmeadow, Warsash, Hants. [*Died* 28 *May* 1959.

ROBINSON, Sir Christopher H. L.; *see* Lynch-Robinson.

ROBINSON, Rear-Adm. Sir Cloudesley Varyl, K.C.B., *cr.* 1945 (C.B. 1942); *b.* 10 June 1883; *s.* of late Commander C. N. Robinson, R.N.; *m.* 1921, Helen Marguerite, *y. d.* of late Roland Latreille, Kingston, Jamaica. *Educ.:* privately. Joined H.M.S. Britannia, 1897; Midshipman of Orlando during Boxer rising, 1900; landed for Admiral Seymour's expedition to Peking (despatches, China medal); Sub-Lieut. Royal Yacht, 1903; Coronation Medal; Lieutenant, 1903; specialised in gunnery; served H.M.S. Achilles, Grand Fleet, 1914 (promoted Commander, 1914); H.M.S. Edgar, Dardanelles and Eastern Mediterranean, 1915-17; Experimental Dept., Whale Island, and Western Front, 1917; Coastal Motor-Boat Base, Osea Island, 1918; commanded H.M.S. Empress, Eastern Mediterranean and Black Sea, 1919 (despatches thrice), (promoted Captain, 1921); Captain-in-Charge at Singapore, 1921-23; commanded H.M.S. Constance, America and West Indies, 1924-26; Naval Attaché to H.M. Embassy at Tokyo and to H.M. Legation at Peking, 1926-29; commanded H.M.S. Courageous, 1931-1932; Rear-Adm. 1933; retired list, 1934; Re-employed Sept. 1939 to Aug. 1945. *Club:* Royal Navy. [*Died* 24 *Dec.* 1959.

ROBINSON, Courtenay Denis Carew, C.B. 1944; *b.* Calcutta, 23 Nov. 1887; *s.* of late Courtenay Carew Robinson, formerly barrister-at-law Inner Temple, and of Gertrude Eliza Laurie; *m.* 1915, Phyllis Emily Hardy; one *s.* one *d.* *Educ.:* Winchester; Balliol College, Oxford. House of Commons, Clerk, 1911; Home Office, Clerk, 1912; Assistant Under-Secretary of State, 1938; Acting Chairman of Prison Commission, 1939-42; Assistant Under-Sec. of State, Home Office, 1942-47; retired 1947. *Recreations:* fishing, golf. *Address:* 9 Marlborough Court, Pembroke Road, W.8. *T.:* Western 8372. *Club:* Flyfishers'. [*Died* 6 *Nov.* 1958.

ROBINSON, David Moore, Ph.D., LL.D., Litt.D., L.H.D.; Hon. D.Phil. Univ. of Thessalonica, 1951; Professor of Archæology, Epigraphy and Greek, Johns Hopkins University, Baltimore, Md., 1905-48; Professor of Classics and Archæology, University of Mississippi, Oxford, Miss., since 1948; *b.* 21 Sept. 1880; *s.* of Willard H. Robinson; *m.* 1910, Helen Haskell; (one *d.* decd.). *Educ.:* Chicago, 1894-1901; American School, Athens, 1901-3; Halle, 1902; Berlin, 1903-1904; Bonn, 1909. Acting Director and Professor Greek Language and Literature, American School, Athens, 1909-10; Professor at Bryn Mawr, 1911-12; Prof. Classical Philology, Univ. of Columbia, summer 1919, Univ. of Calif., 1927; Professor Latin, Syracuse, summers 1929-33, Chicago, 1930; Prof. Greek, Notre Dame, Md., 1921-35; Lecturer Fine Arts, N.Y. Univ., 1926-31; on leave as annual Prof. of Greek and Archæology and Librarian, Am. School, Athens, Greece, 1946-47; Vice-Pres. Archæological Inst. of Am.; Fellow of Am. Acad. of Arts and Sciences; Member Am. Philos. Soc., Archæological Soc. of Athens and some 40 other socs.; Hon. Editor of Am. Journal of Philology; Hon. Director of Coll. Art Assoc.; Assoc. Editor of Am. Journal of Archæology, and Art Bulletin; former Pres. of Coll. Art Assoc., Classical

Assoc. of Atlantic States, Baltimore Archæological Soc.; Actg. Capt. Military Intelligence, 1916, etc.; Director Excavations at Pisidian Antioch, 1924, at Olynthus, 1928-1938; President Society for Promotion of Byzantine and Modern Greek. Director Odyssey Cruise, 1954. *Publications:* some thirty four books: Sinope, 1906; Sappho and her **Influence, 1924; Songs of Sappho (Greek text and trans.), 1925; Theocritus, 1926;** Deeds of Augustus, 1926; Greek and Latin **Inscriptions of** Sardis, 1932; Greek Vases at **Toronto (2 vols.), 1930;** Robinson Collection **of Vases (3 vols.), 1933-40; Olynthus (vols. i-xiv), 1930-52; History of Greece, 1936; Pindar, 1938;** The Dodecanese, 1940; **Baalbek and Palmyra, 1946; America in Greece,** 1948; Coins of Carystus, 1953; The Greek Way of Life, 1953; New Ancient Sculpture and Vases in Robinson Collection, 1955, etc., also about 400 articles on philological and archæological subjects. *Recreations:* tennis, swimming, bridge, collecting vases, coins, etc. *Address:* The University, Mississippi. *Clubs:* (Pres.) University, Bachelors', Cotillon, Country, Coin (Baltimore). [*Died* 2 *Jan.* 1958.

ROBINSON, Reverend Edward Colles, M.A.; *b.* 4 April 1877; *s.* of Maj.-Gen. C. G. Robinson, R.H.A., Lydd, Kent, and Mina Elizabeth Purefoy Colles; unmarried. *Educ.:* St. Paul's School, London; Queens' College, Cambridge (Mathematical Exhibitioner, Math. Tripos); Ridley Hall, Cambridge. Ordained, 1900; Curate of St. Paul's, Bournemouth, 1900-3; Rector of Corozal, British Honduras, 1903-5; Rector and Senior Canon of St. John's, Belize, 1906-10; Dean of the Cathedral, 1907; administered the Diocese in absence of the Bishop, 1907-8; late Rector of St. Mark's, Limon, and of the Railway Missions of Costa Rica; Archdeacon of Limon, 1910-13; Vicar of St. Martin's, Dover, 1913-26; St. Andrew's, Sheperdswell, 1926-31; Vicar of St. Nicholas-at-Wade with Saare, 1931-46. *Address:* 16 Hillcrest Road, Hythe, Kent. [*Died* 20 *Jan.* 1956.

ROBINSON, (Esmé Stuart) Lennox, Hon. D.Litt. (T.C.D.), 1948; Director, Abbey Theatre, Dublin, 1923; (Manager, Abbey Theatre, 1910-14 and 1919-23); *b.* Douglas, Cork, 4 Oct. 1886; *y. s.* of late Rev. A. C. Robinson; *m.* 1931, Dorothy Travers Smith. *Educ.:* Bandon Grammar School. Organising Librarian, Carnegie Trust, 1915-25; first play, The Clancy Name, produced Abbey Theatre, 1908. *Publications:* The Cross Roads, 1909; Two Plays, 1910; Patriots, 1912; The Dreamers, 1915; The Lost Leader, 1918; The Whiteheaded Boy, 1920; The Round Table, 1924; Crabbed Youth and Age, 1924; The White Blackbird and Portrait, 1926; Six Plays, 1928; Ever the Twain, 1930; The Far-off Hills, 1931; Is Life Worth Living ?, 1933; More Plays, 1935; Killycreggs in Twilight, 1937; Birds' Nest, 1938; Towards an Appreciation of the Theatre, 1945; Pictures in a Theatre, 1947; The Lucky Finger, 1949; Ireland's Abbey Theatre, 1951; Speed the Plough, 1954; Drama at Inish, 1953; I sometimes Think, 1957; *novel:* A Young Man from the South, 1917; *stories:* Dark Days, 1918; Eight Short Stories, 1919; *autobiography:* Three Homes, 1938; Curtain Up, 1941; *biography:* Bryan Cooper, 1931; Palette and Plough, 1948. Edited: Further Letters of J. B. Yeats, 1920; Golden Treasury of Irish Verse, 1925; Poems of Thomas Parnell, 1927; A Little Anthology of Modern Irish Verse, 1929; Irish Theatre, 1939; Lady Gregory's Journals, 1946; (with D. MacDonagh) The Oxford Book of Irish Verse, 1958. *Address:* 20 Longford Terrace, Monkston, Co. Dublin. *T.:* 83125. [*Died* 14 *Oct.* 1958.

ROBINSON, Sir Harold F.; *see* Cartmel-Robinson.

ROBINSON, Harold Roper, Ph.D. **Cambridge; D.Sc. Manchester;** F.R.S. 1929; Hon. Fellow of Indian Assoc. for the Cultivation of Sciences, 1943; Professor Emeritus of Physics, University of London; Deputy Vice-Chancellor, Univ. of London, March-June 1954; Vice-Chancellor, June 1954-Oct. 1955; Fellow, Queen Mary Coll., 1955; Mem. of Governing Body, Old Vic; Vice-President and Hon. Life Member, Vic-Wells Assoc.; *b.* 26 Nov. 1889; *e. s.* of late James Robinson, Ulverston; *m.* 1st, 1920, Marjorie Eve (*d.* 1939), *o. d.* of late T. E. Powell, Marchamley; one *s.* one *d.*; 2nd, 1940, Madeleine Jane Symons, J.P., *o. d.* of late G. T. Symons, Barnet. Formerly Lectr. and Asst. Director of Physical Laboratories, University of Manchester; Moseley Research Student of the Royal Society; Reader and Carnegie Teaching Fellow, University of Edinburgh; Professor of Physics, University College, Cardiff; Professor of Physics, 1930-53, and Vice-Principal, 1946-53, Queen Mary College, University of London; served France, 1915-19; Temp. 2nd Lt.—Captain R.A. (attached R.E.). *Publications:* original papers in Proc. Roy. Soc., Proc. Phys. Soc., Phil. Mag., etc., mainly on Radioactivity, Röntgen Rays and Atomic Structure. *Address:* 18 Pelham Crescent, S.W.7. *T.:* Kensington 5273. [*Died* 28 *Nov.* 1955.

ROBINSON, Henry Goland, C.B.E. 1955; Professor of Agriculture, Nottingham Univ. (late U.C. Nottingham), 1943-54; Emeritus Professor, 1954; *b.* 2 June 1896; *er. s.* of late George Goland Robinson and Edith Alice, *e. d.* of Daniel Pearson; *m.* 1st, 1922, Ruth Maude (*d.* 1943), *y. d.* of late Thomas May, Reading; one *s.* one *d.*; 2nd, 1944, Margaret Gemmell Dickie, *d.* of late John Taylor, Humberston, Grimsby. *Educ.:* Queen Elizabeth's School, Kirkby Lonsdale, Westmorland; Armstrong College, Newcastle upon Tyne (Westmorland Scholar). B.Sc. with distinction in Agriculture, 1917; Armstrong College Research Student and Record Keeper at Northumberland Agricultural Experimental Station, Cockle Park, Morpeth, 1917-1918; Lecturer in Agriculture, University College, Reading, 1919-25; M.Sc. Durham, 1919; Senior Lecturer in Agriculture, Midland Agricultural College, Sutton Bonington, 1925-35, and Director of the College Farm, 1929-35; Principal of Midland Agricultural College, Sutton Bonington, Loughborough, 1935-47; Member: Notts. War Agricultural Exec. Cttee. 1939-45, A.E.C. 1945-50; Dir. of the Nottingham Univ. School of Agriculture, Sutton Bonington, Loughborough, 1947-1954. Retired, 1954. *Publications:* Good Milk Farming, 1945; papers in agricultural and technical journals. *Recreations:* collecting old books of agricultural interest and antiques. *Address:* Green Bank, 347 Holyhead Road, Wellington, Shropshire. *T.:* Wellington 2742. [*Died* 20 *Feb.* 1960.

ROBINSON, James, M.B.E.; D.Sc., Ph.D., M.I.E.E., F.Inst.P., Technical Adviser to British Radiostat Corporation; *b.* Seghill Northumberland, 9 Sept. 1884; *s.* of Robert Robinson; *m.* 1914, Beatrice M., *d.* of W. Buckley, North Shields; two *d.* *Educ.:* Armstrong College, Newcastle on Tyne; University of Göttingen; Pemberton Fellow of the University of Durham, 1906. Lecturer in Physics at various Universities (Armstrong College, Sheffield University, London University), 1909-14; Commission in University of London O.T.C., 1914-15; Lieut. R.N.V.R., 1915-18; served in Mediterranean; transferred to R.N.A.S. for Wireless Duties, 1917; in charge of Research and Development Work in Wireless and Photography for the Royal Air Force, 1918-25, the laboratories being at Biggin Hill, 1918-22, and at Royal Aircraft Establishment, Farnborough, 1922-25. Pioneer of the Wireless Compass on Aeroplanes. Introduced the stenode system and the quartz crystal gate into radio. Ex-Vice-Pres. British Institute of Radio Engineers, Member of the Parliamentary and Scientific Committee. *Pub-*

lications: scientific papers in Physics, esp. in Photo Electricity, Acoustics, and the applications to Radio. *Recreation:* golf. *Address:* 12 Dainton Close, Upper Park Road, Bromley, Kent. *Club:* R.A.F. [*Died* 21 *Oct.* 1956.

ROBINSON, Sir John Beverley, 6th Bt., *cr.* 1854; *b.* 13 Jan. 1885; *s.* of late Christopher Conway Robinson, K.C. (*g.s.* of 1st Bt.), and late Jane, *d.* of Norman Torquil M'Leod, Toronto; *S.* kinsman, 1948; *m.*; one *s.* one *d.* *Heir:* *s.* John Beverley, *b.* 3 Oct. 1913. *Address:* 26 Park Road, Grimsby Beach, Ontario, Canada. [*Died* 8 *June* 1954.

ROBINSON, **Sir Joseph Benjamin,** 2nd Bt., *cr.* 1908; *b.* 11 March 1887; *s.* of 1st Bt. and Elizabeth Rebecca, *d.* of James Ferguson, Kimberley; *S.* father, 1929; *m.* 1935, Alice J. Cullen. *Educ.:* Eton; Cambridge. Member of S.A. Parliament, 1915-20; M.P. Wynberg, 1933-38. *Recreation:* golf. *Heir:* nephew Wilfred Henry Frederick, *b.* 24 Dec. 1917. *Address:* Hawthornden, Wynberg, Cape Colony. [*Died* 16 *Nov.* 1954.

ROBINSON, Laurence Milner, C.M.G. 1944; *b.* 6 Aug. 1885; *s.* of Rev. E. C. Robinson, Chadsmore, Malvern; *m.* 1933, Lesley; *d.* of G. A. Tomkinson. *Educ.:* Marlborough; Peterhouse, Cambridge. British Vice-Consul, New York, 1913; Santos, 1914; Calais, 1920; Consul, Budapest, 1921; Munich, 1922; British Assistant Delegate on International Commission of the Danube in 1921; British Deputy Commissioner on European Commission of the Danube, 1924-30; Consul-General, Galatz, Roumania, 1924-30; Amsterdam, 1930-34; Danzig, 1934-37; Hamburg, 1937-39; Basle, 1939-40; Philadelphia, 1940-45; retired, 1945. *Recreation:* golf. *Address:* The White House, 27 Deepdene Avenue, Dorking, Surrey. *T.:* Dorking 3683. [*Died* 15 *Sept.* 1957.

ROBINSON, Lennox; *see* Robinson, E. S. L.

ROBINSON, Leonard Nicholas, C.B.E. 1920; late Senior Physician, Hertford British Hospital; retired from practice; *b.* 24 Nov. 1869; *s.* of Samuel Henry Robinson of Howrah, Bengal; *m.* 1903, Victoria, *d.* of D. Hoef; one *d.* *Educ.:* Malvern College; Universities of Edinburgh (M.B., C.M. 1893, M.D. 1898) and Paris (M.D. 1899). Physician, Hertford British Hospital, Paris, 1900; Senior Member Egyptian Civil Service, Medical Board for France, 1908; President Paris Branch British Red Cross Society, 1914; President Paris Branch Overseas League, 1922; temporary Hon. Lieut.-Colonel R.A.M.C. (despatches); Knight of Grace of the Order of St. John of Jerusalem in England; Officier de la Légion d'Honneur; Third Class Order of the Nile. *Publications:* Étude sûr le Syndrome de Graves-Basedow consideré comme manifestation de l'Hysterie, 1899; Therapeutic Value of Extracts of certain Organs, Practitioner, 1901, etc. *Address:* Le Jardin des Roses, Biot, A.M., France. *T.:* Biot 490.62. *Club:* Travellers' (Paris). [*Died* 15 *March* 1955.

ROBINSON, Samuel, C.B.E. 1923; R.D.; Capt. (ret.), R.N.R.; superannuated and retired from active sea service in 1932, after 37 years in the Canadian Pacific Railways Pacific steamships, 29 years of which was in command; *b.* Hull, Yorkshire, 8 May 1870; *s.* of Captain Henry Robinson, Master Mariner of Hull, and Susan Pearson, Sykehouse, Yorkshire; *m.* 1901, Jessie Benten Nichols, of Searsport, Maine, U.S.A.; no *c.* *Educ.:* Hull Grammar School. Went to sea in 1884, and served as apprentice and officer in various lines of sail and steam until 1895, when joined the Pacific Service of the C.P.R. as junior officer, and was promoted to command, 1903; joined Royal Naval Reserve in 1896; Commander, 1916; in European War served in Empress of Asia as navigator and second in command, and in command s.s. Empress of Russia, transport work, North Atlantic; afterwards in command of s.s. Empress of Australia, Empress of France, and Empress of Canada, on the Pacific; took out new s.s. Empress of Japan, 1930; from which vessel retired; received the Siamese Order of the White Elephant, April 1931, when making the record crossing of the Pacific carrying the King of Siam and suite; C.B.E. for services during the great earthquake at Yokohama, 1 Sept. 1923; has Lloyd's Silver Medal for Meritorious Service, Life Saving Medal of the Order of St. John of Jerusalem (Silver) and Second class of the Order of Naval Merit from King Alfonso of Spain; Imperial Japanese Medal of Merit 1932. *Address:* 1154 Matthews Avenue, Shaughnessy Heights, Vancouver 9, B.C. [*Died Sept.* 1958.

ROBINSON, Sidney; *b.* 1863; *s.* of late John Robinson, Backwell House, Somerset; *m.* 1887, Catherine F. Grant (*d.* 1935). *Educ.:* Mill Hill. M.P. (L.) Brecknockshire, 1906-10; (Co. L.) Brecon and Radnor, 1918-22. J.P. Glam. 1907, Wilts. and Som., 1911. *Recreation:* gardening. *Address:* Cran Hill, Bath. [*Died* 6 *Dec.* 1956.

ROBINSON, Sir Thomas, K.B.E., *cr.* 1934 (O.B.E. 1919); Kt., *cr.* 1920; J.P. Lancs; *s.* of late Peter Robinson, Stretford; *m.* 1936, Emmeline Mary Standring. Chairman Salford Hundred Licensing Committee, 1916-41, Chairman, Manchester Port Health Committee, since 1927, Member since 1897; Pres. Allied Trades of Bleachers, Dyers and Printers; M.P. (Ind.) Stretford Division of Lancs, 1918-31; Member of the Stretford Urban District Council since 1894; Charter Mayor of the Stretford Borough, 1933; Chairman: Local Legislation Cttee. House of Commons, 1922-31; Dye Stuff Licensing Cttee. under the Act of 1921, 1923-34; Law and Parliamentary Cttee. of Stretford Corporation; Member: Council of the Manchester Victoria University; Lancashire Rivers Board; Mersey and Irwell Catchment Board (first Chairman). *Address:* Hawthorns, Edge Lane, Stretford, Lancs; Rockside, Trearddur Bay, Holyhead. [*Died* 30 *Dec.* 1953.

ROBJOHNS, Sydney, F.R.A.M.; Violinist; Professor, lecturer and examiner at Royal Academy of Music; Examiner for Associated Board of Royal Schools of Music, London; *b.* London, 25 March 1878; *s.* of late Sydney Robjohns and Ellen Crews; *m.* 1914, Janet, 2nd *d.* of R. Bruce Anderson, A.M.I.C.E. *Educ.:* Privately; Royal Academy of Music under Emile Sauret and Ebenezer Prout. Spent some years in solo playing and chamber-music, after wards specialising in teaching; in 1928, undertook a tour through Australia as Examiner for Associated Board of Royal Schools of Music, London; Adjudicator at principal musical Festivals. *Publications:* Violin Technique, 1930, reprinted 1946; Graded Studies for the Violin, 1941; The Forty-two Studies of Kreutzer: their technical instruction and musical interpretation, 1954. Many articles in Musical Press on the art of violin teaching and kindred subjects. *Recreations:* water-colour sketching. *Address:* 18 The Little Boltons, S.W.10. [*Died* 24 *Sept.* 1954.

ROBSON, Philip Appleby, F.R.I.B.A.; Consulting Architect, Surveyor, and Valuer, late of Westminster; *b.* Liverpool, 1871; *s.* of E. R. Robson, F.S.A., F.S.I., F.R.I.B.A., of Durham and Westminster, late Consulting Architect to the Board of Education, etc.; *m.* 1901, Gladys Dorothy (*d.* 1927), 2nd *d.* of late H. J. Hanson; one *s.* one *d.* *Educ.:* Blackheath School; St. Christopher's, Eastbourne; Lancing College; pupil of J. L. Pearson, R.A. Started in practice, 1893; succeeded to the practice of his father in 1917, and is consulting architect to many churches and schools; elected to Church Assembly (House of Laity), 1935; a few of his buildings are: St. George's Schools, Hanover Square; St. Gabriel's College, Camberwell; Cowper St. Council Schools Leeds; St. Andrew's Church, Catford; Grove

Church, Wantage; Honduras Cathedral, Belize; St. Clement's, Hull, and many other churches, schools and much domestic work including re-building Union Street, S.E.1 (Flats); Vice-President Kent County Hockey Association and Blackheath Hockey Club; Life Member: Surrey Archæological Soc.; Bibliographical Soc., London; Lancing Club. *Publications:* St. David's (Bell's Cathedral Series); School; Planning; Votarial Verse and Arabesques-Hockey (Isthmian Library, with J. N. Smith); S. David's Cathedral and See; and several others; Bows for Stringed Instruments; Architecture as a Career, 1929; A Manual of Hockey, 1934; House-Planning and Church-Planning (in preparation). *Recreations:* billiards, violin, philately, bibliography, etc. *Address:* Perceval House, S.E.10. *T.:* Tideway 4967. [*Died* 14 *Nov.* 1951.

ROCH, Colonel Horace Sampson, C.M.G. 1919; C.B.E. 1920; D.S.O. 1917; late R.A.M.C.; *b.* 13 Aug. 1876; *y. s.* of late Deputy Surgeon-General Sampson Roch of Woodbine Hill, near Youghal, Ireland; *m.* 1st, 1919, Marjorie (*d.* 1919), *e. d.* of late Robert Henry Power, Lismore, Co. Waterford; 2nd, 1931, Emily Helena, *y. d.* of Rev. Alexander Crone, Ryans Newry, Co. Down; one *d.* *Educ.:* King's College Hospital, London. M.R.C.S. Eng.; L.R.C.P. Lond. 1899; joined R.A.M.C. 1899; served S. African War, 1899-1902 (Queen's Medal 6 clasps, King's Medal 2 clasps); in India 1902-1905, while on leave walked and climbed in Kashmir; Adjutant R.A.M.C. School of Instruction, West Riding Division Territorial Force, 1908-11; Major, 1911; in S. Africa, 1911-1914; European War in France and Belgium, 1915-19, as D.A.D.M.S. 28th and 7th Divisions and A.D.M.S. 2nd Cavalry and 36th (Ulster) Divisions (C.M.G., D.S.O., Croix de Guerre, despatches three times); Lieutenant-Colonel 1915; D.D.M.S. Military Mission S. Russia, 1919-20 (C.B.E.; 2nd Class St. Anne, Russia with swords; Hon. Colonel in late Russian Imperial Army; despatches); Mesopotamia, 1921-23 including operations in Khurdistan 1923 (despatches); India, 1924-25, travelled home by China, Japan and United States; Colonel A.D.M.S. East Anglian Area, 1926; A.D.M.S. Lahore District, India, 1927-30; Hon. Surgeon Viceroy of India, 1928-30; walked and climbed in Kashmir, Ladak, Chilas and Hanza on leave in 1928 and 1930; retired, 1930; re-employed as Pres. Medical Boards, Northern Ireland, 1940-45. *Recreations:* travel, walking, mild mountaineering (Himalaya Club, 1929), and gardening. *Address:* c/o Glyn, Mills & Co. (Holt's Branch), Kirkland House, Whitehall, S.W.1; Woodbine Hill, near Youghal, Co. Cork, Ireland. [*Died* 23 *May* 1960.

ROCHE, Baron (Life-Peer), *cr.* 1935 of Chadlington; **Alexander Adair Roche,** P.C. 1934; Kt., *cr.* 1917; *b.* 24 July 1871; *m.* 1902, Elfreda Gabriel (*d.* 1955), *d.* of John Fenwick; two *s.* one *d.* *Educ.:* Wadham College, Oxford; Barrister, Inner Temple; K.C. 1912; Judge of King's Bench Division, High Court, 1917-34; a Lord Justice of Appeal, 1934-35; a Lord of Appeal in Ordinary, 1935-38; Chairman Oxon Quarter Sessions, 1932-47; Chairman Central Agric. Wages Board, 1940-43. *Recreations:* fishing, hunting, shooting. *Address:* Chadlington, Oxford. *Club:* Athenæum. [*Died* 22 *Dec.* 1956.

ROCHE, Most Rev. James J.; Bishop of Cloyne, (R.C.), since 1935; *b.* 1870; *s.* of late William Roche, Clerk to the Midleton Poor Law Union. Formerly Professor in St. Patrick's College, Carlow, and in St. Colman's College, Fermoy; served in Charleville, Whitechurch, and Mallow; R.C. Bishop of Ross, 1926-31; Apostolic Administrator of Ross since 1931; Coadjutor Bishop of Cloyne, 1931-35. *Address:* Bishop's House, Cobh, Co. Cork. [*Died* 31 *Aug.* 1956.

ROCHESTER, 1st Baron, of the 4th creation, *cr.* 1931, of Rochester in the County of Kent; **Ernest Henry Lamb,** Kt., *cr.* 1914; C.M.G. 1907; one of H.M. Lieutenants for the City of London; Member of the Port of London Authority and of the Central Advisory Water Committee of the Ministry of Housing and Local Government; *b.* Hornsea, E. Yorks, 4 Sept. 1876; *e. s.* of Benjamin Lamb (*d.* 1921), Windlesham, Surrey, and Shorne, Rochester, and Eliza Lowry (*d.* 1942); *m.* 1913, Rosa Dorothea, *y. d.* of late W. J. Hurst, J.P., Drumaness, Co. Down; three *s.* two *d.* (and one *d.* decd.). *Educ.:* Dulwich; Wycliffe College, Stonehouse, Glos. M.P. (L.) Rochester, 1906-10, and 1910-18; Paymaster-General, 1931-35; represented Ministry of Labour in House of Lords, 1931-35; Retired Transport Contractor; on Ministry of Transport Panel of Experts since 1920; J.P. Surrey since 1907; member of the City of London Corporation, 1903-31; a Vice-Pres. of the British and Foreign Bible Soc.; and of the National Children's Home and Orphanage; a Lay Representative to Methodist Conf., 1906-, and for 22 years Treasurer of Wesleyan Temperance and Social Welfare Department; Vice-Pres. of Methodist Conference, 1941-42 and of British Council of Churches, 1942-44; Chm. of the Distress Cttee. of the Central (Unemployed) Body for London, 1920-30; sometime Chairman of the City of London Schools Committee and of the City of London Police Committee. *Heir:* *s.* Capt. Hon. Foster Charles Lowry Lamb, M.A. (Cantab.), 23rd Hussars [*b.* 7 June 1916; *m.* 1942, Mary Carlisle, *yr. d.* of T. B. Wheeler, Sanderstead, Surrey; two *s.* one *d.*]. *Address:* Upfield Chase, Shirley, Croydon, Surrey. *Club:* National Liberal. [*Died* 13 *Jan.* 1955.

ROCKEFELLER, John Davison, Jr., F.R.S. 1939; A.B., M.A., LL.D., Brown University; *b.* Cleveland, Ohio, 29 Jan. 1874; *s.* of John Davison Rockefeller and Laura C. Spelman; *m.* 1st, 1901, Abby Greene (*d.* 1948), *d.* of Nelson W. Aldrich; five *s.* one *d.*; 2nd, 1951, Mrs. Martha Baird Allen. Associated with his father in business and philanthropic enterprises; former member (ex-Pres.) of the Board, Rockefeller Inst. for Medical Research; former Chm. of Board, Rockefeller Foundation. *Publication:* Personal Relation in Industry. *Address:* 30 Rockefeller Plaza, Rockefeller Center, New York 20. *Clubs:* University, Alpha Delta Phi, Brown University, Sleepy Hollow Country, Broad Street, Century, Rockefeller Center Luncheon, Union (New York). [*Died* 11 *May* 1960.

ROCKLIFF, Percy, O.B.E. 1954, F.F.I.; F.C.I.I.; Vice-Pres., Insurance Institute for London; Member Central Council for District Nursing, 1930-48; Joint Secretary, National Insurance Beneficent Society, Limited; Hon. Secretary, National Incorporated Beneficent Soc. and Counties Benevolent Association; *b.* Boston Spa, Yorks, 8 Dec. 1869; *s.* of Charles and Elizabeth Rockliff; *m.* 1938, Hilda Edith Mary Hayward. *Educ.:* Buxton College. Secretary New Tabernacle Provident Soc., 1896-1932; Sec. (now Trustee) of London and County Permanent Benefit Society since 1905; Secretary of New Tabernacle and London and County Approved Societies, 1912-48; Hon. Sec. Joint Committee of Approved Societies; Member of Dental Benefit Council and Ophthalmic Benefit Approved Committee, 1920-48; Secretary of the National Union of Holloway Friendly Societies Pooling Association and of the London and Counties Association of Approved Societies, 1912-48; Director of Supplies Ltd.; Parliamentary Agent, National Union of Holloway Friendly Societies, 1920-56; Fell. Roy. Statistical Soc.; Past Chm. Insurance Cttee. for County of London; Past Pres. Faculty of Insurance. *Publication:* Editor of Thrift. *Address:* 57 Silverdale Rd., Eastbourne; *T.:* Eastbourne 2751. *Club:* Royal Automobile. [*Died* 4 *Nov.* 1958.

ROCYN-JONES, Sir David (Thomas), Kt., *cr.* 1948; C.B.E. 1920; M.B.; Master of Surg. (Edin.); D.P.H. (Oxon.); J.P., D.L. County of Monmouth; K.G.St.J.; County Medical Officer for Monmouthshire since 1908; Director of Ambulance for Wales, St. John Amb. Bde.; Member: Court of Governors Univ. of Wales; Council of Welsh National School of Medicine; Vice-Pres. and Member of Court of Governors and of Council of Univ. Coll. of S. Wales and Monmouthshire; Member Chapter, Priory for Wales Ven. Order of St. John of Jerusalem; Chm. North Monmouthshire Hosp. Management Cttee.; *b.* 16 Nov. 1872; *s.* of David Rocyn-Jones, Rhymney, Mon.; *m.* 1901, Alla (*d.* 1950), *e. d.* of late Alderman S. N. Jones, O.B.E., J.P., Abertillery, Mon.; three *s.* *Educ.:* Lewis' School, Pengam; University Colleges, Cardiff and London; University of Edinburgh. Chief Surgeon, Powell's Tillery Collieries, Abertillery, 1899-1908; Member Territorial Force Association and County Controller, V.A.D. (T.F.A.) for Monmouthshire; late County Commissioner, Order of St. John Priory for Wales; Ex-Chairman South Wales and Monmouthshire Branch of the British Medical Association; Ex-Chairman, Monmouthshire Division, British Medical Association; Ex-Chairman Monmouthshire Congregational Union; Chairman of the Bedwellty Division of Monmouthshire Magistrates; Life Member and President of Welsh Rugby Football Union; Member, Consultative Council of the Ministry of Health for Wales; Fellow of the Society of Medical Officers of Health, of the Royal Sanitary Institute and of the Royal Institute of Public Health. Chairman Joint War Committee for Monmouthshire of British Red Cross and the Order of St. John. *Publications:* Outbreak of Glanders at Collieries of Ebbw Vale Iron and Steel Coal Co.; Special Reports dealing with Health matters in Monmouthshire. *Address:* Brynawelon, Llantarnam, Mon. *T.A.:* Comitatus, Newport, Mon. *T.:* Cwmbran 7674. *Clubs:* National Liberal; Monmouthshire (Newport). [*Died* 30 *April* 1953.

RODEN, 8th Earl of (*cr.* 1771), **Robert Soame Jocelyn;** Baron Newport, 1743; Viscount Jocelyn, 1755; a baronet of England, 1665; retired Captain North Irish Horse; An Irish representative Peer since 1919; *b.* 8 Sept. 1883; *e. s.* of the 7th Earl and Ada Maria (*d.* 1931), *e. d.* of late Col. Soame Gambier Jenyns, C.B., of Bottisham Hall, Cambridge; *S.* father, 1915; *m.* 1905, Elinor Jessie, 2nd *d.* of late Joseph Charlton Parr; one *s.* (*y. s.* killed in action, Nov. 1941) two *d.* *Heir:* *s.* Viscount Jocelyn, R.N. *Address:* White Lodge, Fareham, Hants. [*Died* 30 *Oct.* 1956.

RODWELL, Sir Cecil Hunter-, G.C.M.G., *cr.* 1934 (K.C.M.G., *cr.* 1919; C.M.G. 1909); J.P., Suffolk; Director of Companies; *b.* 29 Dec. 1874; *e. s.* of late William Hunter-Rodwell, Woodlands, Holbrook, and Constance, *d.* of late Sir S. Ruggles-Brise, K.C.B., of Spains Hall, Essex; *m.* 1908, Ethel Clarissa, *d.* of Herbert Ralland; three *s.* two *d.* *Educ.:* Eton (Scholar); King's College, Cambridge (Scholar, Class II, Div. I Classical Tripos, 1896; Editor of The Granta). Served with Suffolk Yeomanry in South Africa (Queen's medal 2 clasps); and on Lord Milner's Staff, 1901-03; Imperial Secretary South Africa, 1903-18; Governor of Fiji and High Commissioner for the Western Pacific, 1918-24; Governor of British Guiana, 1925-28; Governor of Southern Rhodesia, 1928-34; Controller of Diamonds (Ministry of Supply), 1942-45. *Recreations:* shooting, fishing, golf, lawn-tennis, chess. *Address:* Broom Hill, Holbrook, Ipswich. *T.:* Holbrook 245. *Clubs:* Marlborough-Windham, M.C.C. [*Died* 23 *Feb.* 1953.

RODZINSKI, Artur; Guest Conductor in Europe, S. America and U.S.A., with leading orchestras; records, E.M.I., etc.; *b.* 2 January 1894; *s.* of Polish parents, Josef Rodzinski and Jadwiga Wiszniewska; *m.* 1st; one *s.*; *m.* 2nd, 1934, Halina Lilpop Wieniawska; one *s.* *Educ.:* Vienna Univ. (LL.D.); Vienna Acad. of Music. Mus.D. (Oberlin), 1938. Came to U.S. 1925; naturalized, 1933. Began as conductor of chorus; in Lwow; conductor of Opera and Philharmonic Orchestra concerts in Warsaw, 4 years; Philadelphia Orchestra, 1926-29; at same time Director Orchestra and operatic dept. at Curtis Inst. of Music, Philadelphia; Musical Director of Los Angeles Philharmonic Orchestra, 1929-33; Cleveland Orchestra, 1933-43; on leave for 8 weeks, 1937; Conductor and Musical Director of N.Y. Philharmonic Symphony Orchestra, 1943-47 (resigned, 1947); Musical Director of Chicago Symphony Orchestra, 1947-48. Conductor Salzburg Musical Festival, 1936-37; same year conducted in Buda Pesth, Vienna and Paris. Diplôme d'Honneur, France, 1937; Medal Polonia Restituta, Poland, 1938. *Recreations:* photography, carpentering, stamp collecting. *Address:* Lake Placid, N.Y. [*Died* 27 *Nov.* 1958.

ROE, Sir Alliott Verdon-, Kt., *cr.* 1929; O.B.E. 1918; Hon. F.R.Ae.S., F.I.Ae.S. (U.S.A.); President, Saunders-Roe Ltd., Cowes; Chairman Aviation Developments Ltd.; Chairman Vero Precision Engineering Ltd.; *b.* 26 April 1877; 4th *c.* of Edwin Hodgson Roe, V.D., M.R.C.S., L.R.C.P., and Annie Sophia Verdon; *m.* Mildred E. Kirk; two *s.* (and *e. s.* and 3rd *s.* killed on air operations 1941 and 1943) five *d.* *Educ.:* St. Paul's School, King's College, Strand. Went to a civil engineer in British Columbia at the age of 14½ to learn surveying; returned to England at 15½; served apprenticeship at the L. and Y. Railway Locomotive Works; two years at sea as a marine engineer; entered the motor industry as a draughtsman and designer; won highest awarded prize in Daily Mail Model Aeroplane Competition, April 1907; built a full-size aeroplane on the lines of winning model driven by a 24-h.p. Antoinette engine, on which he left the ground for distances of 75 to 150 feet, on 8 June 1908, nearly a year before the first official flight; pioneered the tractor type of aeroplane; founded A. V. Roe & Co. Ltd., with his brother, H. V. Roe, 1910, and built Avro planes also; produced the first enclosed aeroplane in the world to fly early in 1912; Avros were used to bomb the Zeppelins at Friedrichshafen in that famous raid soon after the outbreak of war; Commander Bigsworth was flying an Avro when he brought down the first Zeppelin; bought an interest in S. E. Saunders, Ltd., one of the few firms building flying boats for the Air Ministry; the firm is now known as Saunders-Roe, Ltd., builders of Saro Flying Boats, helicopters, marine craft, etc. *Recreations:* bowls, motor-cycling, articles on monetary questions relating to the State regaining its prerogative over currency creation; a Vice-President of the Economic Reform Institute. *Address:* Long Meadow, Rowlands Castle, Hants. *T.:* 232. *Club:* Royal Aero. [*Died* 4 *Jan.* 1958.

ROE, Frederick Charles, M.A., LL.D., L. ès L.; Chevalier de la Légion d'Honneur; Officier de l'Instruction Publique; Doctor (Hon.) Universities of Rennes and Clermont Ferrand; Emeritus Professor in the University of Aberdeen, 1957; *b.* Hockley Heath, Warwickshire, 22 February, 1894; *s.* of Robert Roe; *m.* 1926, Claire Andrée, 2nd *d.* of André Frebault, Pougues-les-Eaux, Nièvre; three *s.* one *d.* *Educ.:* Solihull School, Warwickshire; Universities of Birmingham, Lyons, and Paris. 2nd Lieut., Royal Warwickshire Regiment, 1915-16; Lieutenant Machine Gun Corps, 1916-19. Served in France, 1916; Lecteur in English, University of Lyons, 1919-20, 1921-22; Licencié-ès-Lettres, 1920; Docteur de

l'Université de Paris, 1923; Lauréat de l'Académie Française, 1924; Lecturer in French at the University of Birmingham, 1920-21, 1923-25; Lecturer and Joint-Head of French Department University of St. Andrews, 1925-28; Professor of French, University College, Hull, 1928-32; Carnegie Prof. of French, Univ. of Aberdeen, 1932-57; Dean of the Faculty of Arts, Univ. Coll., Hull, 1931-32 and University of Aberdeen, 1945-1948; Director of French Summer School, McGill University, Montreal, 1937. Vice-President Fédération Internationale des Langues et Littératures Modernes, Paris, 1948-. Vice-Pres. Internat. Assoc. of Comparative Literature, 1955. Major, Home Guard, and Captain, Aberdeen University Contingent, University Training Corps (T.A.), 1940-50. *Publications:* Taine et l'Angleterre, 1923, awarded Prix Bordin by the French Academy; Modern France: An Introduction to French Civilization, 1955; edited La France Laborieuse, 1927; French Travellers in Britain, 1800-1926, 1928, and other works; articles on literary subjects, particularly comparative literature, in British, American and French reviews. *Address:* King's College, Aberdeen; The Dower House, Don Street, Old Aberdeen. *T.:* Aberdeen 43463. [*Died* 6 *Dec.* 1958.

ROFFEY, Edgar Stuart, C.I.E. 1933; solicitor; *b.* 23 Dec. 1875; *s.* of Thomas William and Maria Roffey, late of Blackheath and Broadstairs; *m.* 1904, Sibyl Mary, *d.* of Rev. Richard Ibbetson Porter; one *s.* one *d.* *Educ.:* Private. Solicitor, 1898; Attorney Calcutta High Court, 1903; practised with and subsequently Proprietor of Firm of Steel & Hadow, Solicitors, Assam, 1903-30; Member Assam Council, 1925-35; Member Indian Legislative Assembly, 1926; Secretary Assam Branch, Indian Tea Association, 1915-1935. Vice-Chairman Indian Tea Assoc. (London), 1935-47. *Address:* Manora, Swanage, Dorset. *T.:* Swanage 2556. [*Died* 7 *Feb.* 1957.

ROGERS, Sir Arthur Stanley, Kt., *cr.* 1947; F.C.I.I.; Chairman of London and Lancashire Insurance Co. Ltd. since 1947, and a Director since 1945; Chairman: Gracechurch Insurance Co. Ltd.; Standard Marine Insurance Co. Ltd.; British Fire Insurance Co., Law Accident Insurance Soc.; Dep. Chm. Law Union and Rock Insurance Co. Ltd.; Director of The Marine Insurance Co. Ltd., and several Overseas Insurance companies; *b.* Liverpool, 11 Jan. 1883; *s.* of Rev. Stanley Rogers; *m.* Christina Margaret, *d.* of Captain A. Moar, Liverpool; one *s.* one *d.* *Educ.:* Liverpool Coll. Joined London and Lancashire, Liverpool, 1899; Foreign Superintendent, 1919-21; Secretary, 1921-27; Assistant Manager, 1927-29; Dep. General Manager, 1929-36; General Manager, 1936-1947; Pres. Insurance Institute of London, 1938-39; Pres. Insurance Orphanage and Insurance Benevolent Fund, 1940; Member Mission to U.S.A. appointed by Treasury and Ministry of Economic Warfare, 1941; President Chartered Insurance Institute, 1943-44; Chairman British Insurance Assoc., 1945-46 and 1946-47. *Address:* Camden Place, Chislehurst, Kent. *Clubs:* Reform, Pilgrims; Chislehurst Golf. [*Died* 15 *Nov.* 1953.

ROGERS, Bertram Mitford Heron, B.A., M.D., B.Ch. (Oxon), M.R.C.S., L.R.C.P.; Consulting Physician to the Royal Hospital for Sick Children, Bristol; Lt.-Col. R.A.M.C. (T.A.); late Medical Referee under Workmen's Compensation Act; *b.* 25 Aug. 1860; *s.* of James E. Thorold Rogers, M.P., Professor of Political Economy Oxford Univ. and King's Coll., London, and Ann S. C. Rogers, *d.* of H. R. Reynolds, Solicitor to the Treasury; *m.* 1891, Agnes C. Fletcher (*d.* 1939); two *d.* *Educ.:* Westminster School; Exeter Coll., Oxford; University Coll., London. Blue for Association football, Oxford; 2nd class in Nat. Sc. School, Oxford; studied medicine in University College, London; practice as physician in Clifton; a past President of the Bristol Medico-Chirurgical Society; late Regional Medical Officer, Ministry of Health. *Publications:* numerous in medical papers. *Address:* 14 Northmoor Road, Oxford. *T.:* Oxford 58469. [*Died* 10 *Feb.* 1953.

ROGERS, Bruce, B.S. (Purdue), Hon. M.A. (Yale), 1928; Hon. L.H.D. (Purdue), 1932; Hon. M.A. (Harvard), 1939; designer of books; *b.* Lafayette, Indiana, U.S.A., 14 May 1870; *s.* of George and Ann Gish Rogers; *m.* 1900, Anne E., *d.* of Dr. M. H. Baker of Stockwell, Ind. *Educ.:* Purdue University, Lafayette, Ind. Designer, Indianapolis, 1891-94; Riverside Press, Cambridge (Mass.), 1895-1912; New York City, 1913-16; with Emery Walker, 1917; Printing Adviser to University Press, Cambridge (Eng.), 1918-19; Printing Adviser to Harvard University Press and Associate of Printing House of W. E. Rudge, Mt. Vernon, N.Y., 1920-28; independent designer of books since 1928; designed The Oxford Lectern Bible, 1935. *Publications:* The Odyssey, translated by T. E. Shaw, 1931; Letters of T. E. Shaw to Bruce Rogers, 1933; More Letters of T. E. Shaw, 1936; Paragraphs on Printing, 1943; Centaur Types, 1949; Pi: Miscellaneous papers, 1953; occasional introductions to printing pamphlets. *Recreation:* contemplation of nature. *Address:* October House, New Fairfield, Conn., U.S.A. [*Died* 18 *May* 1957.

ROGERS, Edwin John, C.M.G. 1927; J.P.; retired from business; *b.* 1858; 2nd *s.* of late Richard John Rogers and Anna Colbeck; *m.* 1884, Ada Alice, *y. d.* of late William Belbin, M.H.A.; one *s.* *Educ.:* Somerset House Academy, Hobart. Chairman of Hobart Public Cemetery Trust; a Member Executive of Hobart Benevolent Society and a Trustee; Mayor of Hobart, 1926-27, when the King and Queen, as Duke and Duchess of York, visited Tasmania. *Recreations:* music, and walking. *Address:* Albuera Street, Hobart, Tasmania. *T.:* 2289. [*Died* 23 *Feb.* 1951.

ROGERS, Lieut.-Col. Henry Schofield, C.M.G. 1919; D.S.O. 1916; R.E., retd.; Surveyor of Prisons, Prison Commission, Home Office, 1907-35; *b.* Peterborough, Canada, 1869; *s.* of late Col. H. C. Rogers, Canadian Militia; *m.* 1st, 1898, Aileen Mary (*d.* 1946), *d.* of late J. E. O'Conor, C.I.E., D.G. Statistics, India; one *s.* decd., one *d.* decd.; 2nd, 1947, Margaret Maclean, *y. d.* of late George Turnbull. *Educ.:* R.M.C. Kingston, Canada (Gold Medal Gen. Proficiency; Sword of Honour Military Subjects). Commissioned R.E. 1889; served in India in Military Works and Punjab Public Works, 1891-1904; Tirah Expedition, 1897-98 (medal, three clasps); Mahsud-Waziri blockade, 1899-1901 (clasp and thanks of Punjab Govt.); Staff-Capt. R.E. War Office, 1904-7; transferred for employment as Surveyor of Prisons, 1907, and retired from Army as Major, R. of O. 1909; recalled to colours and served in France as Staff Officer, R.E., L. of C., and VIIth Corps (1915); special duties Advance Water Supplies H.Qrs. 3rd and 4th Armies, 1916-17; C.R.E. XVIIth Corps Troops, 1917-19 (C.M.G., D.S.O., Chevalier Legion of Honour, despatches four times, three war medals, promoted Lt.-Col. R. of O. on retirement); President of Institution of Structural Engineers, 1938-39. *Publications:* articles to technical journals. *Address:* Hales, 78 Park Road, Woking. *T.:* Woking 1762. *Club:* Army and Navy. [*Died* 3 *Aug.* 1955.

ROGERS, Rear-Adm. Hugh Hext, M.V.O. 1920; O.B.E. 1919; R.N. retd.; *b.* 27 Oct. 1883; 2nd and *o. surv. s.* of late Reginald N. Rogers, of Carwinion, Falmouth; *m.* 1912, Agnes Helena Trevelyan (*d.* 1953), *d.* of late Rt. Hon. Sir Arthur Channell; one *s.* *Educ.:* The Old Ride, Bournemouth; H.M.S. Britannia. Lieutenant, 1904; served Persian Gulf operations in Philomel, 1910-12 (medal); Vanguard at commencement of European

War; Commander, 1916; Birmingham, 1917-19 (O.B.E.); Renown, 1919-21, including tours of Prince of Wales to Canada and Australasia (M.V.O.); Humane Society bronze medal, 1913; Commander, Royal Naval College, Dartmouth, 1921-23; Captain, 1924; Rear-Adm., 1935; has commanded Weymouth, Sandhurst, London, Frobisher, 4th Destroyer Flotilla, Ganges; retired list, 1935; J.P. (Cornwall), 1938; served as Commodore R.N.R. for convoy duty, 1939-42; Flag Officer in Charge, Harwich, 1942-44; Order of the White Lion of Czechoslovakia, 4th class, 1947. *Recreations:* golf, sailing, etc. *Address:* Carwinion, Mawnan Smith, Falmouth. *T.:* Mawnansmith 258. *Club:* Army and Navy.
[*Died* 16 *May* 1955.

ROGERS, Brig.-General Hugh Stuart, C.M.G. 1919; D.S.O. 1916; *b.* 1878; *s.* of late Rev. R. B. Rogers, Vicar of Sancreed, Cornwall; *m.* 1st, 1904, Katharine Mary (*d.* 1923), *e. d.* of Musgrave Ridley, Wylam-on-Tyne, Northumberland; one *s.* three *d.*; 2nd, 1925, Norah, *d.* of W. E. Robson, Penzance. *Educ.:* Wellington College; Queen's College, Oxford. Served European War, 1914-19 (despatches seven times, C.M.G., D.S.O., Bt. Major, Officer Legion of Honour, Chevalier Order of Agricultural Merit, France); Bt. Lt.-Col. 1918; Col. 1922. *Recreations:* at present shooting and fishing, formerly cricket, football, hockey. *Address:* The Coombe, Chyandour, Penzance, Cornwall. *T.A.:* Gen. Rogers-Penzance. *T.:* Penzance 566. *Club:* Army and Navy.
[*Died* 2 *Sept.* 1952.

ROGERS, Muriel A. G. C.; *see* Coltman-Rogers.

ROGERS, Philip Graham, C.I.E. 1924; B.A.; *s.* of John Charles Rogers, London; *m.* 1st, Eirene Scott O'Connor (*d.* 1930); one *d.*; 2nd, Janet Wales Smellie. *Educ.:* Christ's Hospital, London; Keble Coll., Oxford. Joined Indian Civil Service, 1901; served as Assistant Magistrate and Collector in Bengal; Personal Assistant and Under-Secretary to Chief Commissioner of Assam; Private Secretary to Lieut.-Governor Eastern Bengal and Assam; Under-Secretary to Government, Eastern Bengal and Assam; Postmaster-General successively of Central, Bengal and Assam and Punjab Circles; Deputy Director-General, Posts and Telegraphs, and Deputy Director, Postal Services, Field Army, India; Postmaster-General, Bombay; acting Director-General, 1928 and 1929; Dep. Director-Gen., Post Office, 1927; retd. 1931. *Address:* 5 Elizabeth Avenue, Route Orange, St. Brelade, Jersey, C.I. *Club:* Royal Channel Islands Yacht.
[*Died* 8 *Aug.* 1958.

ROHMER, Sax; Author. *Publications:* Dr. Fu Manchu, 1913; The Romance of Sorcery, 1914; The Sins of Séverac Bablon, 1914; The Yellow Claw, 1915; The Exploits of Captain O'Hagan, 1916; The Devil Doctor, 1916; Brood of the Witch Queen, 1917; The Si Fan Mysteries, 1917; The Orchard of Tears, 1918; Tales of Secret Egypt, 1918; Quest of the Sacred Slipper, 1919; Dope, 1919; The Golden Scorpion, 1920; The Green Eyes of Bâst, 1920; The Dream Detective, 1920; Batwing, 1921; Fire-Tongue, 1921; Tales of Chinatown, 1922; Round in 50 (play), 1922; The Eye of Siva (play), 1923; Grey Face, 1924; Yellow Shadows, 1925; Moon of Madness, 1927; She Who Sleeps, 1928; The Emperor of America, 1929; The Day the World Ended, 1930; Daughter of Fu Manchu, 1931; Yu'an Hee See Laughs, Tales of East and West, 1932; Fu Manchu's Bride, 1933; Trail of Fu Manchu, 1934; The Bat Flies Low, 1935; President Fu Manchu, 1936; White Velvet, 1937; Salute to Bazarada, 1938; The Drums of Fu Manchu, 1939; The Island of Fu Manchu, 1941; Egyptian Nights; Seven Sins, 1944; Shadow of Fu Manchu, 1948; Hangover House, 1950; Sins of Sūmurū, 1951; Slaves of Sūmurū, 1952; Virgin in Flames, 1953; The Moon is Red, 1954; Sand and Satin, 1955; Sinister Madonna, 1956; Re-enter Fu Manchu, 1957. *Address:* c/o A. P. Watt and Son, Hastings House, Norfolk Street, W.C.2.
[*Died* 1 *June* 1959.

ROLLS, Capt. Sir John C. E. S.; *see* Shelley-Rolls.

ROLPH, Sir Gordon Burns, Kt., *cr.* 1948; C.M.G. 1946; O.B.E. 1942; Governing Director W. R. Rolph & Sons Pty. Ltd., proprietors The Examiner (founded 1842), Saturday Evening Express, Radio 7EX; Chairman Australian Provincial Daily Press Ltd., 1948-56; Chairman of: Cleanquick Pty. Ltd.; The Walpamur (Aust.) Ltd.; Tasmanian Permanent Executors and Trustees Assoc. Pty. Ltd.; and of the Equitable Building Society; *b.* 28 January 1893; *s.* of late W. R. Rolph, Strathairlie, Elphin Road, Launceston; *m.* 1918, Dorothy Hope, *d.* of late A. W. Hardman, Waterhouse, Tasmania; three *d.* *Educ.:* Scotch College, Launceston; Leslie House School, Hobart. Delegate to Imperial Press Conference, London, 1930 and 1946, Canada, 1950, Australia, 1955, and to Federated Chambers of Commerce of British Empire, 1930; Mem. Commonwealth Newsprint Pool Cttee., 1939-1949; President Australian Provincial Press Association, 1942-51. Life Member 1951; Member Commonwealth Press Union Cttee., Aust. Sect., and Overseas Mem. London Council; State Pres. Australian Federation of Commercial Broadcasting Stations, 1940; Pres.: Launceston Chamber of Commerce, 1933-37 and 1944-50; Launceston Rotary Club, 1932-33, foundation Hon. Secretary; Mem. Launceston Hospital Board, 1933-50; Extra Territorial J.P.; Foundation Pres., now Patron, Roy. Soc. of St. George and R. Autocar Club of Tasmania (N. Section) (Life Mem.); President: Royal Empire Society (Tasmania), 1937; Hon. Justices' Assoc. of Tasmania, 1944-50 and Patron, 1950-; Nat. Agricultural and Pastoral Soc., 1952-54; Vice-Pres.: Soc. for Care of Crippled Children; Junior Farmers' Clubs of Tasmania; Patron: Scotch College Old Boys' Assoc.; Youth Drama Festival; Vice-Patron Launceston War Memorial Community Centre Assoc.; Trustee: N. Tasmanian Home for Boys; Tamar Yacht Club. Jubilee Medal, 1935; Coronation Medal, 1937, 1953. *Recreations:* fishing and golf. *Address:* The Examiner Office, Launceston, Tasmania; (private) Beringa, 142 Elphin Rd., Launceston; Como, Richmond Hill. *Clubs:* Launceston, Northern, Masonic (Launceston); Tasmanian (Hobart); Australian, Athenæum (Melbourne).
[*Died* 23 *March* 1959.

ROME, Brig.-Gen. Claude Stuart, C.M.G. 1919; D.S.O. 1918; late Queen's Bays; *b.* Queensland, 1875; *e. s.* of late Thos. Rome, J.P., Charlton House, Charlton Kings, Glos.; *m.* 1905, Hon. Grace Loudenne Blyth (*d.* 1952), 2nd *d.* of 1st Lord Blyth; two *s.* *Educ.:* Harrow; Sandhurst. Joined 11th Hussars, 1895; transferred to command Queen's Bays, 1920; served Tirah Campaign, 1897 (medal and clasp); South African War, 1900-2 (Queen's medal and four clasps, King's medal and two clasps); European War, 1914-18 (despatches, C.M.G., D.S.O.); retired pay, 1925. *Address:* c/o Barclays Bank, Bagshot, Surrey.
[*Died* 17 *May* 1956.

ROMER, Carrol, M.A., M.C.; *b.* 1883; *s.* of late Edgar Romer; *m.* 1910, Violet Louis Jacquier of Lyons; two *s.* two *d.* *Educ.:* Eastbourne College; Gonville and Caius College Cambridge (Scholar); Mechanical Sciences Tripos. Egyptian Civil Service, Survey Department, 1905-8; called to the Bar, Inner Temple, 1911; served in Royal Engineers, 1914-19. Editor of the Nineteenth Century and After, 1925-30; Assist. Registrar, 1931-33; King's Coroner and Attorney, Master of the Crown Office and Registrar of the Court of Criminal Appeal, 1933-46. *Address:* Glenelg, 269 Victoria Drive, Eastbourne. *T.:* 4330.
[*Died* 22 *March* 1951.

ROMER-LEE, Lieut.-Colonel H., C.M.G. 1919; D.S.O. 1918; late 20th Hussars; *b.* 21 July 1874; *m.* Clara Douglas Hilger, New York; two *s.* *Educ.:* Eton; Sandhurst. Served Army, 1895 to end of European War. *Recreations:* fishing, polo, shooting. *Address:* 9 Sloane Gate Mansions, S.W.1. *Clubs:* Cavalry, Hurlingham. [*Died* 8 *Oct.* 1955.

ROMILLY, Eric (formerly **Frederic) Carnegie,** J.P.; *b.* 10 Sept. 1886; 2nd *s.* of late Samuel Henry Romilly and late Lady Arabella Romilly; *m.* 1914, Constance Isabella, *d.* of late Duncan Macneill; two *s.* three *d.* *Educ.:* Eton; Balliol College, Oxford Barrister, Inner Temple, 1911; served European War, 1914-18, Lt. R.G.A., in England and France; contested (C.) Hereford Division, 1929; High Sheriff Herefordshire, 1941. *Publication:* Bleeding from the Roman, 1949. *Recreations:* shooting, golf. *Address:* Broadfield Court, Bodenham, Herefordshire. *T.:* 75. *Club:* Brooks's. [*Died* 30 *April* 1953.

RONALDSON, James Bruce, O.B.E. 1937; V.R.D., M.A., M.D., B.Ch. Cantab.; Cons. Physician, King Edward VII Hospital, Windsor; *b.* 15 Jan. 1886; *s.* of James Bruce Ronaldson, V.D., M.D., F.R.C.S.E., and Anne Macdonald; *m.* 1915, Irene Constance, *d.* of G. R. Bird, A.M.I.C.E., P.W.D. *Educ.:* Merchiston Castle School, Edinburgh; St. John's College, Cambridge; B.A. (Nat. Sci. Tripos); Charing Cross Hospital. Commissioned in R.N.V.R. as Surgeon, 26 Jan. 1912; Surgeon-Capt., London Division, 31 Dec. 1930; Hon. Physician to the King, 1933-36; mobilised for war, 3 Sept. 1939; retired list, 1944. *Address:* Innisfree, Little Chalfont, Amersham, Bucks. *T.:* Little Chalfont 2083. [*Died* 5 *April* 1952.

RONEY, Sir Ernest, Kt., *cr.* 1920; Solicitor; *b.* 7 Sept. 1871; 2nd *s.* of late John Roney and Helena Lucy; *m.* 1898, Emily Jane (Mayor of Wimbledon, 1933-34-35; J.P.), *e. d.* of late Richard Henry and Margaret Jones; two *s.* two *d.* *Educ.:* privately. Chevalier of the Order of the Crown, Belgium, 1920. *Recreations:* yachting, golf, tennis. *Address:* 42-45 New Broad Street, E.C.2. *T.:* London Wall 5445; 26 The Grange, Wimbledon Common, S.W.19. *T.:* Wimbledon 0580; Crespigny House, Aldeburgh, Suffolk. *T.:* Aldeburgh 234. *Clubs:* Reform, Pilgrims, Royal Wimbledon Golf, Royal Thames Yacht; Royal Harwich Yacht (Harwich); Aldeburgh Yacht, Aldeburgh Golf (Aldeburgh). [*Died* 22 *March* 1952.

ROOK, Air Vice-Marshal Sir Alan Filmer, K.B.E., *cr.* 1948 (O.B.E. 1937); C.B. 1946; F.R.C.P. Lond. 1939; M.R.C.S. Eng. 1915; D.P.H. Camb. 1919; retired as Senior Health Officer, Cambridge Univ. (1948-59); *m.* 1st, 1917, Dorothy Pearse (*d.* 1944); *m.* 2nd, 1946, Elizabeth Wilson. *Educ.:* Guy's Hospital. Late Royal Air Force Medical Branch; Consultant in Medicine, R.A.F.; K.H.P. 1944-48. *Address:* Crosby, Little Abington, Cambridge. [*Died* 26 *Aug.* 1960.

ROOK, Sir William (James), Kt., *cr.* 1942; *b.* Exeter, Devon, 20 May 1885; *s.* of Wm. Rook, Exeter; *m.* 1912, Millicent, *d.* of H. W. Baker, Exeter; one *s.* one *d.*; *m.* 1947, Beryl Mary Rosalie, *o. d.* of Frank Stalt-Gardner, Cromwell Road, Kensington. *Educ.:* University College, Exeter, and Continent. Chairman of City Company; Member of British Empire Producers' Organisation; prior to War, Member of Advisory Committee on Sugar, Colonial Office; Deputy Director of Sugar Supplies and Director of Purchases, 1939-40; Director of Sugar, 1941-50; Life Governor, Exeter University. Member of Pilgrims. Commander of Order of Orange Nassau, 1948; Officer Ordre de la Couronne (Belgium), 1948; Grand Officer Order of Duarte Sanchez y Mella (Dominican Republic), 1958. *Recreations:* tennis, golf. *Address:* Northfield, Chartwell, Kent; Princes Gate, S.W.7. *Clubs:* Travellers', Royal Automobile. [*Died* 29 *Nov.* 1958.

ROOKER, John Kingsley, C.B.E. 1945; M.C.; B.A., D.Lit. (Paris); Hon. Attaché British Embassy, Paris, since 1947; *b.* 10 Feb. 1887; *s.* of John Rooker and Adele Frances Thompson; *m.* 1922, Helen Frances Jaffray; no *c.* *Educ.:* Trent College; Balliol College, Oxford; Sorbonne, Paris. Honours, Modern History, Oxford, 1909. Served in France, 1914-18 (Mons Star, despatches, M.C., immediate award); Foreign Office, 1919; First Sec. Diplomatic Mission to Tiflis, Trans-Caucasia, 1920-21; International Chamber of Commerce, 1922-25; British Delegation Inter-Allied Claims Commission, Paris, 1925-27; joined firm of A. Johnson & Co., Stockholm, 1931; Chairman A. Johnson & Co., Paris. Director A. Johnson & Co., London, 1932; Director European Gas & Electric Co. 1933; Director British & Dominion Ferralloys, 1935; Foreign Office, First Secretary, Liaison Mission to General de Gaulle, 1941; Counsellor to His Majesty's Representative with the French Provisional Government, Algiers, 1944; Asst. Political Adviser to the Supreme Allied Commander, Nov. 1944; Counsellor British Embassy, Paris, 1945-47. *Publications:* Critical Study of Francis Thompson, 1913; articles in various periodicals. *Recreation:* fishing. *Clubs:* Travellers'; Travellers' (Paris). [*Died* 28 *Feb.* 1951.

ROPER, Edgar Stanley, C.V.O. 1943 (M.V.O. 1930); D.Mus. 1950; M.A., Mus.B. (Cantab.), F.R.C.O.; *b.* 23 Dec. 1878; *s.* of James Roper, Croydon; *m.* Mary Monica Margaret Western-Edwards; one *d.* *Educ.:* Westminster Abbey; Corpus Christi College, Cambridge (Organist Scholar). Hon. Assistant Organist, Westminster Abbey. *Address:* 41 Thornton Avenue, Streatham Hill, S.W.2. *T.:* Tulse Hill 6148. *Club:* Athenæum. [*Died* 19 *Nov.* 1953.

ROPER, Philip Hampden, C.V.O. 1954; Under-Secretary and Permanent Head, Premier's Department, New South Wales, since 1948; *b.* 24 April 1906; *s.* of late W. J. Roper; *m.* 1937, May Bullows, *d.* of G. B. Smith, Chatswood, N.S.W.; one *s.* two *d.* *Educ.:* University of Sydney, N.S.W. (LL.B.). Entered Public Service of N.S.W., 1924. *Recreations:* golf and bowls. *Address:* 13 Melbourne Rd., East Lindfield, N.S.W. *T.:* J.M. 4850 (Home), BO56 (office). *Clubs:* Tattersall's; Lindfield Bowling. [*Died* 6 *Oct.* 1956.

ROSE, Vice-Admiral Sir Frank Forrester, K.C.B., *cr.* 1936 (C.B. 1931); D.S.O. 1914; *b.* 1878; *y. s.* of late William Rose; *m.* 1st, 1911, Freda Edith, *o. d.* of late Walter Alwynne Gordon; (one *s.* killed in action, R.N., War of 1939-45); 2nd, 1923, Dorothy, *widow* of Lieutenant-Commander Barttelot, R.N., Stopham House, Sussex. *Educ.:* Stubbington House, Fareham. Entered Navy, 1892; Lieut. 1901; Commander, 1913; served European War, 1914-18; commanded H.M.S. Laurel in the action off Heligoland, 28 Aug. 1914 (wounded, despatches, D.S.O., prom. Captain, 1918); commanded Third Destroyer Flotilla of the Atlantic Fleet, 1921; Director of Operations Division, Naval Staff, 1925-27; Commanded Royal Naval Barracks, Portsmouth, 1928-29; Naval A.D.C. to the King, 1929; Rear-Admiral, 1929; Rear-Admiral commanding Destroyer Flotillas, Mediterranean Fleet, 1931-33; Vice-Adm. 1934; Commander-in-Chief, East Indies, 1934-36; invalided, 1937. *Address:* 117 Cranmer Court, S.W.3. *Club:* United Service. [*Died* 3 *March* 1955.

ROSE, Geoffrey Keith, M.C., M.A., LL.B.; Metropolitan Magistrate since 1934; *b.* 27 Oct. 1889; *y. s.* of T. H. Rose, J.P., Oxford; *m.* 1919, Gertrude Nesbyth, *d.* of Rev. N. B. Lodge, R.N., Paignton, Devon. *Educ.:* Dragon School, Oxford; Harrow (Scholar); King's College, Cambridge (Scholar). 1st Class Hist. Tripos, Pt. I., 1910, 2nd Class

RONAN, Very Rev. Myles V., D.Litt. See page xxx.

Law Tripos, Pt. II., 1911; 1st Class and certificate of honour, Bar Final Examination, 1912; Called to Bar, Inner Temple, 1913; Lincoln's Inn, 1940; joined Oxford Circuit, 1914; Recorder of Ludlow, 1932-34; J.P. Essex, 1934; Chairman: Studies Committee Working Men's College, Crowndale Road, N.W.1, 1927-32; Deptford and Woolwich Juvenile Courts, 1934; served European War with Oxford and Bucks Lt. Infy. (T.F.), 1914-1919 (M.C. and bar, despatches twice); Major, 1918-19, and in Home Guard, 1941. G.O.C.'s certificate of merit, 1945. *Publications:* History of 2/4th Oxford and Bucks Lt. Infy., 1920; Genealogical History Rose Family, 1945; war drawings in Imperial War Museum. *Recreations:* water-colour painting, figure skating, music. *Address:* 11 Marsham Court, S.W.1; Stone Farm, Ipsden, Oxon. *Clubs:* Athenæum, Arts. [*Died* 1 *June* 1959.

ROSE, Percy Jesse, C.B. 1925; *b.* 1878; *y. s.* of George Rose; *m.* 1926, Phyllis Helen, *y. d.* of late William Whitelaw, M.D., J.P., Kirkintilloch; two *d. Educ.:* Liverpool Institute; St. John's College, Cambridge. Private Secretary to Secretary for Scotland, 1909-12; Member of Departmental Committees on Reformatory and Industrial Schools, 1914, Scottish Fishing Industry, 1917, Lights on Vehicles, 1920; Scottish Local Government Legislation Consolidation, 1937; Assistant Under-Secretary for Scotland, 1921-42; King's and Lord Treasurer's Remembrancer in Scotland, 1942-48; Secretary, of Commissions for Scotland, 1949-52; retired, 1952. *Recreations:* gardening, golf. *Address:* 5 Murrayfield Gardens, Edinburgh 12. *T.:* 63508. [*Died* 27 *June* 1959.

ROSE, Sir Thomas Kirke, Kt., *cr.* 1914; D.Sc.; A.R.S.M.; Chemist and Assayer of the Mint, 1902-26; *b.* 14 Aug. 1865; *y. s.* of late Thomas Rose; *m.* 1890, Jenny (*d.*1938), *d.* of late J. B. Rundell; one *d. Educ.:* Dulwich College, Royal School of Mines and Univ.of London. Engaged in the treatment of gold ores in Colorado and elsewhere, 1887-90; in the Royal Mint, London, 1890-1926; President Institution of Mining and Metallurgy, 1915-16; Vice-President, Institute of Metals, 1916; Gold Medal of Institute of Mining and Metallurgy, 1921. *Publications:* The Metallurgy of Gold, 7th ed. 1937; The Precious Metals, 1909; and a number of communications to learned societies on gold and other metals. *Address:* Four Winds, Hindhead, Surrey. *T.:* Hindhead 23. [*Died* 10 *May* 1953.

ROSENBACH, Abraham S. Wolf; Secretary, The Rosenbach Company, dealers in rare books and manuscripts; *b.* Philadelphia, 22 July 1876; *s.* of Morris and Isabella Rosenbach; unmarried. *Educ.:* University of Pennsylvania, B.S. 1898, Ph.D. 1901, D.F.A. (hon.) 1927, Hon. D.H.L., Hon. LL.D., Hon. Fellow in English, 1900-03. Hon. Member Phi Beta Kappa; Pres. Pennsylvania Library Club; Hon. Pres.: American Jewish Historical Soc.; Shakespeare Assoc. of America; American Friends of the Hebrew Univ.; Hon. Vice-Pres. Jewish Publication Society of America; Trustee Free Library of Philadelphia; Corresponding Secretary of Historical Society of Pennsylvania; Trustee Gratz College; Trustee Philadelphia Museum of Art; Associate Trustee and Member Board of Graduate Education and Research, University of Pennsylvania; Member of American Antiquarian Society, Worcester, Mass.; American Philosophical Society, Philadelphia, etc.; Director American Shore and Beach Preservation Assoc.; Founder Fellowship in Bibliography Univ. of Pennsylvania, 1930. *Publications:* Catalogue of the Books and Manuscripts of Harry Elkins Widener in the library of Harvard College, five vols., 1913; The Unpublishable Memoirs, 1917; An American Jewish Bibliography, 1926; Books and Bidders, 1928; The All-Embracing Dr. Franklin, 1932; Early American Children's Books, 1933; The Libraries of the Presidents of the United States, 1934; A Book Hunter's Holiday, 1936; The First Theatrical Coy. in America, 1939, etc.; Editor, with Austin Dobson, of Dr. Johnson's Prologue, 1898; various articles on literary topics, bibliography, etc. *Recreation:* fishing. *Address:* 2010 De Lancey Street, Philadelphia, U.S.A.; Strathmere, Corson's Inlet, New Jersey; Office address, 1618 Locust Street, Philadelphia. *T.A.:* Rosebrook, Philadelphia; 322 East 57th Street, New York. *Clubs:* Grolier (New York); (President), Philobiblon (Philadelphia). [*Died* 1 *July* 1952.

ROSENHEIM, Otto, F.R.S., Ph.D., F.L.S.; *b.* 1871; *m.* Mary Christine (*d.* 1953), *d.* of William Tebb, Rede Hall, Burstow. *Educ.:* Univs. of Würzburg, Bonn, Geneva, Manchester. Research Student of Pharmacol. Chemistry, King's College, London, 1901; Lecturer, 1904; later, Assistant Professor of Physiology; Reader in Biochemistry, University of London, until 1920. *Publication:* Researches on Bio-Chemical subjects in various scientific journals. *Address:* 75 Hampstead Way, N.W.11. [*Died* 7 *May* 1955.

ROSENTHAL, Major-Gen. Sir Charles, K.C.B., *cr.* 1919 (C.B. 1915); C.M.G. 1917; D.S.O. 1918; V.D. 1922; *b.* N.S.W., 12 Feb. 1875; *m.* 1897, Harriet Ellen Burston of Melbourne, Victoria; three *s.* Architect by profession; F.R.I.B.A. London; Life Fellow R. Aust. Inst. of Architects; Past President Federal Council of Australian Institute of Architects, and of Institute of Architects, N.S.W. Joined Militia forces in Australia, 1903, and served continuously thereafter; left Australia with Australian Imperial Expeditionary Force, Sept. 1914; served through Gallipoli Campaign as Commanding Officer of 3rd Field Artillery Brigade, 1st Australian Division (twice wounded, despatches, C.B.); served in France and Belgium, at Armentieres, Ypres, Somme, Bullecourt, Messines as C.R.A. 4th Australian Division (wounded at Somme, despatches twice, C.M.G.); as G.O.C. 9th Australian Infantry Brigade served at Passchendaele, Hangard, Villers-Bretoneux and Morlancourt (gassed at Passchendaele, despatches twice, D.S.O., Belgian Croix de Guerre); as G.O.C. 2nd Australian Division served at Villers-Bretoneux and in final allied advance, including capture of Mt. St. Quentin (wounded at Villers-Bretoneux, despatches twice, K.C.B., French Croix de Guerre with palms, and French Légion d'Honneur (Officier)); Commanded A.I.F. Depots in U.K., Feb.-Sept. 1919; G.O.C. 2nd Division Australian Military Forces, N.S.W., 1921-26 and 1932-37; Administrator of Norfolk Island, Nov. 1937-Dec. 1945. M.L.A. Bathurst, N.S.W., 1922-25; Alderman Sydney City Council, 1923-26; M.L.C. (N.S.W.), 1936-37. *Address:* Norfolk Island. *Club:* Imperial Service (Sydney). [*Died* 11 *May* 1954.

ROSS, Brig.-General Arthur Edward, C.B. 1918; C.M.G. 1916; B.A., M.D., LL.D. (Queen's University, Canada, and Edinburgh University); *b.* June 1870; *s.* of late John and Leah Ross; *m.* 1st, 1902, Mabel Parker (*d.* 1916), Stirling, Ont.; one *s.*; 2nd, 1923, Anne Ethel Stinson, Ottawa. *Educ.:* Queen's University, Kingston, Canada. Mayor City of Kingston, 1908; Member of Ontario Legislature, 1911-21; Member House of Commons since 1921. Served South African War, 1900-2 (despatches, medal and 5 bars); European War; O.C. 1st Canadian Field Ambulance, 1914-15; A.D.M.S. 1st Canadian Division, 1915-17; D.D.M.S. Canadian Corps, 1917-18; D.M.S. Canadian Section, General Headquarters France (C.M.G., C.B., despatches seven times). *Address:* Kingston, Ontario, Canada. [*Died* 15 *Nov.* 1952.

ROSS, Edward Alsworth; sociologist; *b.* Virden, Ill., U.S.A., 12 Dec. 1866; *s.* of William Carpenter Ross and Rachel Alsworth; *m.* 1st, 1892, Rosamond C. Simons (*d.* 1932).

Washington; three *s.*; 2nd, 1940, Helen Forbes, New York City. *Educ.:* Coe College, A.B., LL.D.; University of Berlin, 1888-89; Johns Hopkins, Ph.D. Professor of Economics, Ind. U., 1891-92; Associate Prof. Political Economy and Finance, Cornell, 1892-93; Prof. of Sociology, Leland Stanford Jr. University, 1893-1900; Univ. of Nebraska, 1901-6; University of Wisconsin, 1906-37, Emeritus, 1937; Lecturer on Sociology, Harvard, 1902; University of Chicago, 1896, 1905, National Univ. of Mexico, 1928; Sec. American Economic Association, 1892-93; advisory editor of American Journal of Sociology since 1895; member Institut International de Sociologie; President American Sociolgoical Society, 1913-15; Chairman of American Civil Liberties Union, 1940-; Director of Education of the Floating University, 1928-29; has travelled in the Far East, South America, Russia, Mexico, Portuguese Africa, India, Tahiti, Australia, studying sociological problems. *Publications:* Honest Dollars, 1896; Social Control, 1901; The Foundations of Sociology, 1905; Sin and Society, 1907; Social Psychology, 1908; Latter Day Sinners and Saints, 1910; The Changing Chinese, 1911; Changing America, 1912; The Old World in the New, 1914; South of Panama, 1915; Russia in Upheaval, 1918; What is America?, 1919; Principles of Sociology, 1920, revised, 1930, 1938; The Russian Bolshevik Revolution, 1921; The Social Trend, 1922; The Social Revolution in Mexico, 1923; Outlines of Sociology, 1923, revised, 1933; The Russian Soviet Republic, 1923; Roads to Social Peace, 1924; Civic Sociology, 1925, revised, 1932; Report on Compulsory Labour in Portuguese Africa, 1925; Changes in Size of American Families (with Baber), 1925; Standing Room Only?, 1927; World Drift, 1928; Seventy Years of It (autobiography), 1936; New-Age Sociology, 1940; two hundred articles in economic and sociological journals and literary periodicals. *Recreations:* golf, canoeing, and fishing. *Address:* Shorewood, Madison, Wisconsin, U.S.A. [*Died* 22 *July* 1951.

ROSS, George Mabyn, C.I.E. 1937; retired; *b.* 30 Apr. 1883; *s.* of George Murray and Alice Jane Ross; *m.* 1912, Georgina Evelyn Stewart, *d.* of Canon Trotter; three *s.* *Educ.:* St. Andrews, Dublin; Rossall School; Trinity College, Dublin. B.A., B.A.I., 1904; joined Punjab Irrigation Branch of P.W.D., 1905; Under Secretary Punjab Govt., 1922-26; State Engineer, Bahawalpur, 1926-30; President, Central Board of Irrigation, India, 1936-37; Chief Eng. and Sec. P.W.D., N.W.F.P., 1934-1938; retd., 1938; Senior Regional Technical Adviser, Home Office, Civil Defence, Regional Office, Cardiff, 1939. *Recreations:* tennis, golf, fishing, shooting. *Address:* Sunnyside Lodge, Rosbeg, Westport, Co. Mayo. *Club:* Overseas. [*Died* 28 *Jan.* 1954.

ROSS, George Robert Thomson, M.A., D.Phil. (Edin.); Indian Educational Service (retired); *b.* 1 April 1874; *s.* of John Ross and Janet MacPherson MacDonald; *m.* 1911, Amy Sarah Fage (*d.* 1953); one *s.* one *d.* *Educ.:* Arbroath High School; Dundee University Coll.; Edinburgh University; Sorbonne. Tutor in Philosophy, University of Edinburgh; Classical Master, Hamilton Academy; Assistant to Professor of Logic and Metaphysics, University of St. Andrews 1900-5; Lecturer in Philosophy and Education, Hartley University College, Southampton, 1905-9; Professor of Philosophy, Govt. College Rangoon, 1909-21; Professor of Philosophy, Rangoon University, 1921-28. *Publications:* In the Highlands and other poems, 1901; Aristotle, De Sensu and De Memoria, edited with translation and commentary, 1904; The Philosophical Works of Descartes trans. 2 vols (with Miss E. S. Haldane), 1908; reprinted with corrections, 1931-34; Part of the Parva Naturalia, in Oxford translation of Works of Aristotle. *Recreations:* gardening, trout fishing. *Address:* 1 Townsend Drive, St. Albans, Herts. *T.:* St. Albans 2074. *Club:* Overseas League. [*Died* 2 *Aug.* 1959.

ROSS, Colonel George Whitehill, C.I.E. 1930; D.S.O. 1916; Indian Army, retired; *b.* 6 June 1878; 3rd *s.* of Colonel Sir Edward Ross, C.S.I.; *m.* 1903, Clare Josephine, *d.* of Lieutenant-Colonel Welman, Indian Army; one *s.* *Educ.:* Clifton College. Commissioned, 1898; served in India with 2nd Queen Victoria's Own Rajput Light Infantry; China Campaign, 1900-2; entered Military Finance Dept. 1903; Assistant Secretary to Govt. of India Finance Dept. Military Finance, 1911-13; European War, Field Disbursing Officer, Mesopotamian Expeditionary Force in Mesopotamia, Nov. 1914-March 1916 (D.S.O.); Deputy Financial Adviser Army Headquarters, India, 1920-23; Military Accountant General, Military Finance Branch, India, 1926-29; retired, 1929. *Address:* c/o Lloyds Bank, Ltd., 6 Pall Mall, S.W.1. [*Died* 15 *Dec.* 1952.

ROSS, Hon. Dame (Grace) Hilda, D.B.E. 1956; M.P. (N.) Hamilton, New Zealand, since 1945; Minister of Social Security and Welfare of Women and Children, 1949-59); Mem. Executive Council since 1949; *b.* Auckland, 1884; *d.* of Adam Nixon; *m.* 1904, Harry Campbell Ross, *s.* of Henry Ross; two *s.* *Educ.:* Sydney; Auckland. Promoter of children's health camp, Pt. Waikato, 1927, and associated with it since; President St. John Ambulance Nursing div. and Lady Galway Guild; Hon. Child Welfare Officer and mem. board of Waikato Hospital, 1941-; Mem. Hamilton Borough Council, 1944, resigned 1945; Deputy Mayor, 1945; received freedom of City of Hamilton, 1948. J.P. 1937. *Address:* 301 River Road, Hamilton, New Zealand. [*Died* 6 *March* 1959.

ROSS, Lieut.-Colonel Henry, C.I.E. 1921; O.B.E. 1917; Indian Medical Service, retired; *b.* 1877; *s.* of late William Ross, Cork; *m.* Betty, *d.* of late Christopher Mitchell; (son killed flying on active service, 1939), one *d.* *Educ.:* Queen's Coll., Cork. Joined Indian Medical Service, 1902; Major, 1914; Lt.-Colonel, 1922; served European War, 1914-19; M.B.; B.Ch., B.A.O., R.U.I., 1901; F.R.C.S.I., 1914; Assistant Director-General, Indian Medical Service, 1916-20; retired 1932; Commander of the Order of St. John of Jerusalem. Czechoslovak Military Medal of Merit, 1st cl., 1946. *Address:* c/o Lloyds Bank, Cox's Branch, 6 Pall Mall, S.W.1. [*Died* 24 *Aug.* 1958.

ROSS, Hon. Dame Hilda; *see* Ross, Hon. Dame G. H.

ROSS, Howard Salter, B.A., LL.B.; Q.C. (Can).; D.C.L.; Barrister and Solicitor; *b.* 10 July 1872; *s.* of Alexander Charles Ross, ex-M.P., Canada, and Marianne Peters; *m.* Susie Burton Murray; one *s.* three *d.* *Educ.:* Acadia College, Wolfville, Nova Scotia, B.A.; Cornell Law School. LL.B. Dalhousie University, 1900; D.C.L. Acadia University, 1922; in active practice of Law at Sydney, Nova Scotia, 1901-9; in active practice at Montreal Bar since that time; for some years was member of the Senate of Acadia University; one of the founders of People's Forum of Montreal and President for two years; Past President of Montreal Brotherhood Federation, and Chairman of Education Committee; toured Western Canada summer 1929 on circuit of Chautauqua, lecturing on World Unrest—A Suggested Cure, at 72 towns. Edited for 17 years a Forum in 4 weekly papers in Montreal; still contributes book reviews to those newspapers; advocates what is known as the Equitist Plan, the basis of which is a unit of exchange having as its basis one hour of adult human work; frequent speaker in Canada and U.S.A. at Church groups, Rotary, Kiwanis and other service clubs, women's clubs, forums, labor groups, Universities and High Schools; arbitrator of labor disputes. *Recreations:* until a few years

ago tennis, swimming; now walking, fishing. *Address:* (office) Apt. 609, Ten Rosemount Avenue., Montreal 6. *T.:* PL 4451; (home) Westmount, Que., Canada. *T.:* GL 2177.
[*Died* 9 *Feb.* 1955.

ROSS, Captain Hugo Donald, C.V.O. 1948 (M.V.O. 1937); M.C. 1918; Land Agent (late Resident Factor, Balmoral); *b.* 1880; *s.* of Hugh Ross, Dibidale, Ross-shire; *m.* 1920, Dorothy (*d.* 1960), *d.* of Ernest Latimer, Kirtle House, Knutsford, Cheshire; one *s.* one *d. Educ.:* George Watson's College, Edinburgh; Inverness Royal Academy. Inland Revenue, 1900-9; in Siam, 1910-14; served in European War, 1915-19, with Cameron Highrs., Adjutant 4th Bn., 1920-23; Resident Factor, Balmoral, 1930-48. J.P. Aberdeenshire, 1939. *Recreations:* golf and shooting. *Address:* c/o British Linen Bank, 41 High St., Inverness. [*Died* 2 *Oct.* 1960.

ROSS, Sir Ian; *see* Clunies-Ross.

ROSS, James, M.A. (Hon.) Bristol; F.R.S.L.; F.L.A.; City Librarian, Bristol, 1931-51; *b.* Newcastle on Tyne; *s.* of William Grey Ross and Elizabeth Sanderson; *m.* 1913, Kate Oxberry, York; one *s.* one *d.* Deputy City Librarian, Bristol, 1919-31; Vice-Pres. Library Association, 1947-52 (Pres. S.W. Branch, 1950-51); Chairman, S.W. Regional Library System, 1937-51; Pres. Assoc. of Assistant Librarians, 1916; Fellow, Tutor and Examiner, Library Association; Member of Cttee. and Examiner, School of Librarianship, Univ. of London; Member of Bristol Univ. Court and Art Lectures Cttee.; visited principal libraries of Canada and U.S.A., on invitation of Carnegie Corporation of New York; Member of Council of Friends of Bristol Cathedral. *Publications:* Bristol Cathedral: historical and descriptive handbook, 14th edn. 1951; An Eighteenth Century Playhouse (in Essays by Divers Hands, R.S.L.), 1945; and various select bibliographies and guides to reading. *Address:* 15 Oakfield Road, Clifton, Bristol. *T.:* Bristol 34186. *Clubs:* Royal Automobile, Royal Empire Society.
[*Died* 1 *June* 1953.

ROSS, Major-Gen. James George, C.M.G. 1917; V.D.; Chartered Accountant; *b.* Montreal, 18 Oct. 1861; *m.* 1891, Margaret Alice, *d.* of John Monk; two *d.* Served European War, 1915-17, as Chief Paymaster, Canadian Expeditionary Forces, and Paymaster-General, Overseas Military Forces of Canada (despatches, C.M.G.). *Address:* Woodlands, Province of Quebec, Canada.
[*Died* 11 *Sept.* 1956.

ROSS, Major-General John Munro, C.M.G. 1919; D.S.O. 1917; V.D.; Canadian Infantry; *b.* 1877; *m.* 1st, 1903, Anne, *d.* of John Duncan; one *s.* one *d.*; 2nd, 1938, Mary Gertrude, *d.* of Edmond Meredith, K.C. Served South African War, 1899-1900 (Queen's medal and two clasps); European War, 1914-18 (despatches, C.M.G., D.S.O. and bar). *Address:* St. Mary's Hospital, 35 Grosvenor Street, London, Ont., Canada. *Clubs:* Union (Victoria, B.C.); London (London, Ont.).
[*Died* 28 *Jan.* 1959.

ROSS, Sir John Sutherland, Kt., *cr.* 1954; C.M.G. 1926; Chairman of Ross and Glendining (Limited); Director National Insurance Co. of New Zealand; *b.* 1877; *e. s.* of late Sir John Ross, Morven, 3 Newington Avenue, Maori Hill, Dunedin; *m.* 1908, Muriel Amy Campbell (*d.* 1956), *d.* of late Samuel Macaulay Inkster, M.D. Sheffield; two *s.* two *d. Educ.:* Highgate School; Leipzig University. Chairman of Directors of New Zealand and South Seas Exhibition, 1925-26; Vice-Consul for Sweden at Dunedin, 1923-51; Chevalier Order of Vasa (Sweden), 1944. Fell. Roy. Commonwealth Society. Jubilee Medal, 1935; King of Saxony's Medal for Life-Saving, 1898. *Address:* 70 Belgrave Crescent, Roslyn, Dunedin, New Zealand. *Club:* Fernhill (Dunedin).
[*Died* 1 *Feb.* 1959.

ROSS, Major-General Robert Knox, C.B. 1945; D.S.O. 1918; M.C.; *b.* 23 Aug. 1893; *s.* of late Brig.-Gen. R. J. Ross, C.B., C.M.G.; *m.* 1933, Kathleen Ogden, *y. d.* of late Col. F. W. Fleming, Kansas City; two *s. Educ.:* Cheltenham Coll.; R.M.C., Sandhurst. Entered Army, 1913; Lt., 1914; Capt., 1915; Maj., 1931; Lt.-Col., 1937; Col., 1940; Acting Maj.-Gen., 1942; Maj.-Gen., 1944; G.S.O. 3rd Grade, 30th Div., B.E.F., 1916; Brig.-Major (22nd Infantry Brig., B.E.F.), 1916-18; Brigade Major, 233rd Brigade, E.E.F., 1918; G.S.O.2, 60th Div., Egyptian Expeditionary Force, 1918-19; Adjutant, 2nd Bn. The Queen's Royal Regt., 1919-22; served European War, 1914-18 (despatches thrice, D.S.O., M.C.); Waziristan, 1920-21 (medal and two bars); attached Egyptian Army and Sudan Defence Force, 1923-32; commanded 2nd Bn. The Queen's Royal Regiment (West Surrey), 1937-39; served War of 1939-45; Palestine 1939-40 (despatches, medal); Commander 160 (S.W.) Inf. Bde., 1940-42; Commander 53 (Welsh) Div., 1942-45; B.L.A. 1944-45 (despatches thrice, C.B., Legion of Honour, Croix de Guerre); Commander Aldershot and Hants District, 1945-46; retired pay, 1946. *Club:* Army and Navy. [*Died* 3 *Nov.* 1951.

ROSS, Lieut.-Colonel Sir Ronald Deane, 2nd Bt., *cr.* 1919; M.C.; D.L. Co. Tyrone. 1947; *b.* 13 July 1888; *o. s.* of Rt. Hon. Sir John Ross, 1st Bt., and Katharine Mary Jeffcock (*d.* 1932), *d.* of Colonel Deane Mann, D.L., Dunmoyle, Co. Tyrone; *S.* father 1935; *m.* 1921, Dorothy Evelyn Frances, *y. d.* of Rev. A. Dudley Ryder, Maresfield Rectory, Sussex. *Educ.:* Eton; Trinity College, Cambridge. B.A., 1910; Bar, Inner Temple, 1913; N.E. Circuit; Recorder of Sunderland, 1936-51. Served European War in France, Aug. 1914 to Armistice; Major late North Irish Horse; Brigade-Major 109th Infantry Brigade, 36th (Ulster) Division (M.C., Croix de guerre); contested (U.) Seaham Division, Durham, December 1923 and October 1924; M.P. (U.) Londonderry, 1929-51; Parliamentary Private Secretary (unpaid) to First Lord of the Admiralty, 1931-35; returned to North Irish Horse, war emergency commission, Sept. 1939; first C.O. of North Irish Horse when regiment was re-raised; Chm. Ulster Unionist members at Westminster, Oct. 1939-June 1941; resigned owing to military service. A.A.G. (Welfare), London District, 1943-45. British Deleg. to Assembly of First Council of Europe, Strasbourg, Aug. 1949 and to Second Council of Europe, 1950. Agent in Great Britain for the Government of Northern Ireland, 1951-57. *Recreations:* shooting, lawn tennis. *Heir:* none. *Address:* Dunmoyle, Six Mile Cross, Co. Tyrone; 49 Morpeth Mansions, S.W.1. *Clubs:* Carlton, Leander; Northern Counties (Londonderry); Ulster (Belfast).
[*Died* 31 *Jan.* 1958 (*ext.*).

ROSS-TAYLOR, Sir Joshua, Kt., *cr.* 1938; J.P.; *b.* Oct. 1878; 2nd *s.* of Very Rev. Walter Ross-Taylor, D.D., Glasgow, and Margaret Innes, *d.* of Dr. Joshua Paterson, Glasgow; *m.* 1908, Griselda Helen, *d.* of Robert Cochran, Verreville, Glasgow; one *s. Educ.:* Glasgow Academy; Leys, Cambridge. Farmer, H.M.'s Treasury Representative and a Director of Scottish Agricultural Securities Corporation. *Club:* Scottish Conservative (Edinburgh).
[*Died* 10 *Nov.* 1959.

ROSS TAYLOR, Walter, C.B.E. 1919; *b.* 1877; *e. s.* of late Rev. Walter Ross Taylor, D.D., of Glasgow, and *g.s.* of Rev. Walter Ross Taylor, D.D., of Thurso; *m.* 1910, Frances (*d.* 1957), *d.* of Robert Orr, of Kinnaird, Stirlingshire; two *s. Educ.:* The Leys, Cambridge; Glasgow and Edinburgh Universities, M.A., LL.B. Called to Scottish Bar, 1902; entered Egyptian Government Service, 1905; held judicial and administrative posts, finally appointed Counsel to the Sultan, and Legal

Adviser to the Ministries of Public Works, War, and Agriculture; during latter part of War was Chairman of Supplies Control Board, Egypt (despatches, 1919, Order of the Nile); retired, 1923; M.P. (U.) Woodbridge Division of Suffolk, 1931-45; J.P., Suffolk. *Recreations:* yachting, etc. *Clubs:* Royal Harwich Yacht (Harwich); Aldeburgh Yacht (Aldeburgh). [*Died* 12 *July* 1958.

ROSSMORE, 6th Baron, *cr.* 1796; **William Westenra;** *b.* 12 July 1892; *s.* of 5th Baron and Mittie, *d.* of Richard Christopher Naylor, Hooton, Chester; *S.* father, 1921; *m.* 1927, Dolores Cecil (served war of 1939-45, W.A.A.F.), *d.* of late Lt.-Col. J. A. Wilson, D.S.O., West Burton, Yorks; one *s.* one *d.* Lieut. R.N.V.R., Royal Naval Division, personal Staff; served war of 1939-45, Lieut. R.N.V.R. *Heir: s.* Hon. William Warner Westenra, *b.* 14 Feb. 1931. *Address:* Rossmore Castle, Monaghan, N. Ireland. [*Died* 17 *Oct.* 1958.

ROSTOVTZEFF, Michael I.; Sterling Prof. Ancient History and Archæology, Emeritus 1944, in Yale Univ., U.S.A.; *b.* Kiev, Russia, 10 Nov. 1870; *s.* of Ivan Y. Rostovtzeff, educator, and Marie I. Monakhoff; *m.* 1901, Sophie M. Kulczycki; no *c.* *Educ.:* Kiev; S. Petersburg, Russia. On scholarship in the classical lands, 1895-98; Doctor of Latin Literature, University of St. Petersburg, Russia; Doctor honoris causa, Leipzig, Oxford, Wisconsin, Cambridge, Harvard, Athens, Chicago; Professor of Latin, Univ. of St. Petersburg, 1898-1918; Ordinary member of the Russian Academy of Science, 1916; Vice-Pres. Imperial Archæological Soc. in S. Petersburg; left Russia in 1918; resided at Oxford, England, 1918-20; Prof. Ancient History in University of Wis., 1920-25; Yale University, 1925-44; Member of many American and foreign academies and learned societies. *Publications:* A Large Estate in Egypt in the III-d cent., B.C., 1922; The Iranians and the Greeks in South Russia 1922; Social and Economic History of the Roman Empire, 1926; A History of the Ancient World, Vols. I. and II., 1926-27; Inlaid Bronzes of the Han Dynasty in the Collection of C. T. Loo, 1927; Mystic Italy, 1928; The Animal Style in South Russia and China, Paris, 1929; Seleucid Babylonia, Yale Classical Studies III., 1932; The Caravan Cities, 1932; Out of the Past of Greece and Rome, 1932; Many Chapters in Cambridge Ancient History, Vols. VII., VIII., IX., XI., and in Excavations at Dura-Europos, I.-IX., 1928-43; Dura and the problem of Parthian Art, Yale Classical Studies V., 1935; Proletarian Culture, London, 1919; Dura-Europos and its Art, 1938; Social and Economic History of the Hellenistic World, Vols. I.-III., 1941; and several other books in German, French, Italian, Russian and Latin; more than 500 articles in various reviews, periodicals and encyclopædias. *Address:* 470 Whitney Avenue, New Haven, Conn., U.S.A. *Club:* Graduate (New Haven, Conn). [*Died* 20 *Oct.* 1952.

ROTH, George Kingsley, C.M.G. 1957; O.B.E. 1954; Hon. Keeper of Fijian collections, Cambridge University Museum of Archæology and Ethnology, since 1958; *b.* 30 March 1903; *yr. s.* of H. Ling Roth, Hon. Curator, Bankfield Museum, Halifax, Yorks; *m.* 1937, Jane Frances Violet, *er. d.* of Dr. G. W. Coats, Paisley. *Educ.:* Liverpool University (B.A. Hons.); Christ's College, Cambridge (M.Sc.). Administrative service in Fiji, 1928; Zanzibar, 1937; Fiji, 1939; Secretary for Fijian Affairs, 1954-57, retd. *Publications:* Fijian Way of Life, 1953. Contributions to scientific journals on Fijian ethnology. *Address:* 61 Maids' Causeway, Cambridge. *Clubs:* Royal Commonwealth Society, Junior Carlton. [*Died* 29 *June* 1960.

ROTHERWICK, 1st Baron, *cr.* 1939, of Tylney; **Col. Herbert Robin Cayzer,** 1st Bt., *cr.* 1924; Chairman: Union-Castle Mail Steamship Co. Ltd., Clan Line Steamers, Ltd., Cayzer, Irvine & Co. Ltd., Scottish Shire Line Ltd., Turnbull, Martin & Co. Ltd., B. and S.A. Steam Navigation Co. Ltd., Houstons (London) Ltd., Greenock Dockyard Co. Ltd., British Ship Adoption Society, Caledonia Investments Ltd., Clanair Ltd., Clan Engineering Patents Ltd., Sea Lion Investments Ltd., Scottish Lion Ship Repairing and Engineering Co. Ltd., Scottish Tanker Co. Ltd.; Scottish Lion Insurance Co. Ltd.; Cayzer Trust Co.; Huntley & Cook Ltd.; London American Maritime Trading Co. Ltd.; Thompson Steam Shipping Co. (1954) Ltd.; Hunting-Clan Air Holdings Ltd.; Director: Suez Canal Co., London General Shipowners' Association, English Coaling Co. Ltd., Steamship Owners' Coal Assoc. Ltd., Ceylon Wharfage Co. Ltd., Thames Nautical Training Coll.; Governor, Commercial Bank of Scotland; *b.* 1881; 5th *s.* of Sir Charles William Cayzer, 1st Bart. of Gartmore; *m.* 1911, Freda Penelope, *d.* of late Colonel William Hans Rathborne, formerly of Scripplestown, Co. Dublin, and of Kilcogy, Co. Cavan; two *s.* two *d.* *Educ.:* Rugby. At outbreak of European War was 2nd i/c. Q.O.R. Glasgow Yeomanry (1903-21); served European War, 1914-18; commanded 24th Div. Mounted Troops in France, 1915-17 (despatches); Hon. Col. R. Corps of Signals, 1939; raised and commanded 25th (Rotherwick) Bn. Hampshire Home Guard, 1940-43. M.P. (C.) Portsmouth (S. Div.), 1918-22 and 1923-39; Chm. H. of Commons Shipping Cttee., 1932-39 and of H. of Commons Naval Cttee., 1936-39; Member H. of Commons Select Cttee. on Estimates, 1934-36; Pres. Chamber of Shipping of the U.K. 1941-42; Pres. Institute of Marine Engineers, 1949-50; First Pres. Gen. Council of British Shipping, 1941; Alternate Chm. Shipping Advisory and Allocation Cttee. 1947. J.P. City of Glasgow, 1905; for Hampshire, 1944; D.L. for Hampshire, 1936-50; D.L. for Sussex, 1948. Pres. British Legion, Portsmouth Branch, 1918-39; Hook Branch, 1940-47; Master Garth Hunt, 1922-26; Joint Master 1931-39. Warden, Worshipful Co. of Shipwrights, 1957. *Recreations:* shooting and gardening. *Heir: er. s.* Hon. Herbert Robin Cayzer [*b.* 5 December 1912, late Royal Scots Greys; *m.* 1952, Sarah Jane, *o. d.* of Michael Slade, Castle Hill House, Nether Stowey, Somerset; two *s.* one *d.*]. *Address:* Sedgwick Park, Horsham, Sussex. *T.:* Lower Beeding 204; Lanfine, Newmilns, Ayrshire. *T.:* Darvel 207; 2 St. Mary Axe, E.C.3. *T.:* Avenue 2010. *Clubs:* Cavalry, Carlton, Bath, City of London. [*Died* 16 *March* 1958.

ROTHSCHILD, James A. de, D.C.M., D.L., J.P.; Trustee of the Wallace Collection, 1941-1955; *e. s.* of late Baron Edmond de Rothschild, Paris; *m.* 1913, Dorothy, M.B.E. 1949, *o. d.* of late Eugene Pinto. *Educ.:* Lycée Louis le Grand; Trinity College, Cambridge (M.A.); Harness Prize, 1900; served European War, 1914-18, France and Palestine; Major, Royal Fusiliers, 1918. M.P. (L.), Isle of Ely, 1929-45; Joint Parliamentary Secretary, Ministry of Supply, 1945. *Address:* 23 St. James's Place, S.W.1. *T.:* Hyde Park 2176; Waddesdon, Aylesbury, Bucks. *Clubs:* Reform, Turf; Jockey (Newmarket). [*Died* 7 *May* 1957.

ROUAULT, Georges; painter; Hon. Keeper of Musée Gustave Moreau, Paris; *b.* Paris, 27 May 1871; *m.* Marthe Le Sidaner; one *s.* three *d.* *Educ.:* École des Beaux-Arts, Paris (pupil of Gustave Moreau). *Works:* (Musée Colmar) L'Enfant Jésus parmi les docteurs; (Petit Palais) Tête de Vieille Femme; Paysages; Head of Christ, etc. *Address:* 14 rue de la Rochefoucauld, Paris, IXe. [*Died* 13 *Feb.* 1958.

ROUGHEAD, William; Writer to the Signet; author; *b.* 13 Feb. 1870; *o. s.* of late John Carfrae Roughead, Edinburgh, and late Amelia Shaw Nicol; *m.* 1900, Janey (*d.* 1940), *d.* of late Francis More, C.A., Edinburgh; two *s.* *Educ.:* Craigmount; Edinburgh University.

Admitted member of the Society of Writers to Her Majesty's Signet, 1893. *Publications:* Rhyme without Reason, 1901; Notable British Trials—Dr. Pritchard, 1906; Deacon Brodie, 1906; Captain Porteous, 1909; Oscar Slater, 1910; Mrs. McLachlan, 1911; Mary Blandy, 1914; Burke and Hare, 1921; Katharine Nairn, 1926; J. D. Merrett, 1928; J. W. Laurie, 1932; Twelve Scots Trials, 1913; The Riddle of the Ruthvens, 1919; Glengarry's Way, 1922; The Howdie (ed.), 1923; The Fatal Countess, 1924; A Rich Man (ed.), 1925; The Rebel Earl, 1926; Malice Domestic, 1928; The Evil that Men Do, 1929; Bad Companions, 1930; What is Your Verdict? 1931; In Queer Street, 1932; Rogues Walk Here, 1934; Knaves' Looking-Glass, 1935; Galt's Works (ed.), 1936; Mainly Murder, 1937; The Seamy Side, 1938; Neck or Nothing, 1939; Rascals Revived, 1940; Reprobates Reviewed, 1941. *Address:* 12 Belgrave Crescent, Edinburgh. *Club:* Caledonian United Service (Edinburgh).
[*Died* 11 *May* 1952.

ROUGHTON, Noel James, C.S.I. 1938; C.I.E. 1933; I.C.S. Ret.; *b.* 25 Dec. 1885; one *s.* *Educ.:* Winchester; New College, Oxford. Entered I.C.S., 1908; Deputy Sec. to Government of India, Commerce Dept., 1925; Finance Secretary to Central Provinces Govt., 1928-33; Chief Sec. to Government, 1933-36; officiated Revenue and Finance Member to C.P. Government, Nov. 1934-March 1935; officiated Home Member to C.P. Govt. May-Sept. 1936; Member Indian Tariff Board, May 1938; Commissioner Central Provinces, India; Chairman, Motor Vehicles Insurance Committee, 1937; Establishment Officer, Govt. of India, 1939; Chm. Jt. Public Service Commn., Bihar, C. P., and Orissa, 1941-45; retd. Apr. 1945.
[*Died* 14 *July* 1953.

ROUND-TURNER, Vice-Admiral Charles Wolfran, C.B. 1935; C.M.G. 1925; Royal Navy, retd.; *s.* of late Capt. H. L. Round-Turner, Grundisburgh, Suffolk; *m.* 1915, Janet Mary, *d.* of late Sir Jenner Verrall; two *s.* two *d.* *Educ.:* H.M.S. Britannia. Experimental Commander H.M.S. Excellent, 1914-16; Comdr. H.M.S. Ramillies, 1916-18; Director of Operations and Plans in Australian Navy, 1920-22; Captain H.M.S. Dauntless, 1922-24; World Cruise of Special Service Squadron, 1923-24 (C.M.G.).; Commodore Royal Naval Barracks, Devonport, 1926-28; Flag-Captain and Chief Staff Officer, H.M.S. Revenge, 1928-30; Admiral Superintendent, Chatham Dockyard, 1931-35; retired list, 1935; resumed service in Royal Navy, 1940-45; H.M.S. Lynx (for Folkestone), 1940; and H.M.S. Allenby in Command, 1944-1945. *Address:* 10 Cherry Garden Lane, Folkestone. *T.:* Folkestone 75280.
[*Died* 30 *Jan.* 1953.

ROUNDELL, Christopher Foulis, C.B.E. 1920; D.L., J.P.; *b.* 11 July 1876; *o. s.* of late Charles Savile Roundell: *m.* 1910, Lady Maude Vivian (*d.* 1932), *widow* of H. W. Vivian and *d.* of 4th Earl of Leitrim; two *s.* two *d.* *Educ.:* Harrow; Balliol College, Oxford; B.A. (Honour School of Natural Science). Coldstream Guards; served S. Africa (Queen's medal and clasp); Reserve of Officers; Barrister-at-law, Inner Temple; Assistant Private Secretary to Lord President of the Council, 1906; Inspector, Board of Agriculture and Fisheries, 1907; Chief General Inspector Ministry of Health, 1935-41; Chief of Staff, Civil Commissioners' Department; Senior Regional Officer, xii Region, 1939-40; London Hostels Board, 1940; Officer, St. John of Jerusalem; Commander Order of the Crown, Belgium; Officer Order of the Crown, Italy; Officer Order of the White Eagle of Serbia; Médaille (Argent) de la Reconnaissance Française. *Recreations:* shooting, fishing. *Address:* 53 Ashley Gardens, S.W.1. *T.:* Tate Gallery 8304. *Clubs:* Garrick, Beefsteak.
[*Died* 29 *Dec.* 1958.

ROUSE, Harold Lindsay; Director: Midland Bank Ltd. Midland Bank Executor and Trustee Co. Ltd., since 1951; Belfast Bank Ltd. since 1952; Director of London and Manchester Assurance Co. Ltd. since 1953; *b.* 26 March 1887; *s.* of Joseph and Margaret Rouse (*née* Corin); *m.* 1914, Gladys Mary (*née* Parker); one *d.* *Educ.:* Alleyn's School, Dulwich. Entered Midland Bank, 1903; Chief Accountant, 1930; Controller, 1932; Jt. Gen. Manager, 1936; Chief General Manager, 1946. *Recreation:* golf. *Address:* Howlettes Meade, College Road, Dulwich, S.E. 21. *T.:* Gipsy Hill 2886. *Club:* Constitutional.
[*Died* 2 *Nov.* 1959.

ROUTH, Harold Victor, M.A., D.Litt., F.R.S.L.; retired; *b.* 18 Oct. 1878; 4th *s.* of Dr. E. J. Routh, Peterhouse, Cambridge; *m.* 1922, Eleanor Constance Travell; no *c.* *Educ.:* Bath College; Cambridge University Classical Tripos, 1900; Sorbonne, Marburg and Munich. Lecturer in Modern Languages, University of Bishop's College, Province of Quebec, 1903-4; Professor of Latin, Trinity College, University of Toronto, 1906-12; Lecturer in English Goldsmiths' College and East London College, 1912-14; during European War Captain in R.F.A. and M.I.D.; University Reader in English at London University, 1919-37; First Incumbent of Byron Chair of English Literature and Institutions at University of Athens, 1937; founder and Director of first Institute of English Studies in Greece, 1938-39; Educational Adviser to The British Council, 1939 and 1940. Member of Council Royal Society of Literature 1943 and English Ass. 1944. *Publications:* Five Chapters in Cambridge History of English Literature, 1906-1912; God, Man, and Epic Poetry, 1927; England under Victoria, 1929; Money, Morals and Manners, 1935; Towards the Twentieth Century, 1937; Diffusion of English Culture outside England, 1941; English Literature and Ideas in XX. Century, 1946. *Recreations:* riding and mountain climbing. *Address:* Cheesecombe, Hawkley, Liss, Hants. *T.:* Hawkley 49. *Clubs:* Savage, Royal Automobile.
[*Died* 13 *May* 1951.

ROUTLEY, Frederick William, M.D.; Exec. Secretary-Treasurer, Ontario Hospital Assoc.; Hon. Consultant, Canadian Red Cross Soc.; Member of Board of Governors and of Exec. Cttee. of League of Red Cross Societies; *b.* 28 Dec. 1879; *s.* of Obadiah Routley and Eliza Silverwood; *m.* 1908, Gertrude, *d.* of James and Anne Fry. *Educ.:* Public and High School, Lindsay, Ont.; University of Toronto, graduated in Medicine, 1907; post-graduate studies, London, England. Practised Medicine in Toronto, Ontario, 1909-22; Nat. Commissioner of Canadian Red Cross Soc., 1937-48; Past Pres., Canadian Hosp. Council; spent four months as temporary Medical Director of League of Red Cross Societies, Paris, France, in 1926; Past President, York County Medical Soc.; Fellow of Academy of Medicine, Toronto, Ont.; Member of Canadian Medical Association; Sec., Ontario Hospital Assoc. since 1924; Pastmaster in Freemasonry; Member United Church of Canada. *Publications:* numerous articles on hospital and Red Cross activities in Canada. *Recreations:* riding, golf and music. *Address:* 135 St. Clair Ave. West, Toronto, Ont.; (home) Maple, Ontario. *Clubs:* York, Empire, Ontario, Rotary, Canadian, Granite (Toronto); Rosedale Golf, Beaumaris Golf.
[*Died* 13 *Feb.* 1951.

ROWE, Charles (William Dell), C.B. 1948; M.B.E. 1919; T.D., D.L., J.P.; Managing Dir. and Dep. Chm., London Brick Co., Ltd.; *b.* 2 Aug. 1893; *s.* of John William and Anne Georgina Rowe; *m.* Alison Barford (marriage dissolved, 1947); one *s.* one *d.* *Educ.:* Uppingham. Commissioned T.A., 5th Beds. Regiment, 1911; Hunts Cyclist Battalion, 1914; seconded R.F.C. 1915 (despatches twice); 5th

ROW, Brigadier Robert Amos, D.S.O. See page xxxi.

Norths. Regiment, 1919; commanded, 1924-1926. Commander Hunts and Soke of Peterborough Sector, Home Guard, 1941-45; County Comdt., Hunts Army Cadet Force, 1943-46; Vice-Chm. Hunts and Northants T. and A.F.A.; D.L. Hunts.; High Sheriff Cambs. and Hunts., 1947-48. *Recreations:* shooting, golf, flying, books, listening to music. *Address:* Orton Longueville, near Peterborough. *T.:* Peterborough 2370. *Club:* Royal Aero. [*Died* 1 *July* 1954.

ROWLAND, Francis George; I.C.S. (retired); *b.* 14 Aug. 1883; *s.* of William Rickford Rowland, Creslow, Aylesbury, Bucks; *m.* 1912, Frances Elizabeth, *d.* of Thomas Horwood, The Warren, Aylesbury, Bucks; two *s.* one *d.* *Educ.:* Harrow (scholar); Balliol College, Oxford (scholar). 1st cl. Class. Mods., 1903; 2nd cl. Lit. Hum., 1905; Indian Civil Service, Bengal, 1906; Magistrate, Bihar, 1912; appointed to act as District Judge, 1913; Deputy Secretary to Government of India, Legislative Department, 1917; Additional Legal Remembrancer to Government of Bihar, 1918; confirmed as a District Judge, 1919; appointed to act as a Puisne Judge of the High Court, Patna, 1929; Puisne Judge, High Court, Patna, India, 1936-44; appointed to act as a Judge of the Federal Court, India, 1943; retd. 1944. *Address:* Coombewood, Rignall Road, Great Missenden. *T.:* Great Missenden 2936. *Club:* Athenæum. [*Died* 30 *Dec.* 1957.

ROWLAND, Sir Frederick, 1st Bt., *cr.* 1950; Kt., *cr.* 1939; F.C.A.; Grand Officier Légion d'Honneur; Grand Officer of the Crown of Roumania; *b.* 25 December 1874; *s.* of late J. E. Rowland, Taunton, Somerset; *m.* 1903, Alice Blanche Reynolds; one *s.* two *d.* *Educ.:* The Temple, Taunton; Bristol. Articled to Wentworth H. Price, F.C.A., of Cardiff; qualified as a Chartered Accountant, 1901; Elected for Ward of Cordwainer as Common Councilman, 1922; Alderman, Coleman St., 1942; now serving on several Committees of Corporation, having served as Chairman of some in the past; now Trustee of Morden College; Commissioner of Taxes, City of London; Member London Airports Advisory Committee; Past Pres. City Livery Club; Master of Worshipful Company of Horners, 1935-36 and 1936-37; Sheriff of the City of London, 1938-39; Lord Mayor of London, 1949-50. *Publication:* Dairy Accounts, 1903, 2nd ed. 1928. *Recreation:* golf. *Heir:* *s.* Wentworth Lowe [*b.* 7 Nov. 1909; *m.* 1947, Violet Mary Elizabeth Macbeth Robertson; one *d.*]. *Address:* 56 Moorgate, E.C.2; The Hydro Hotel, Eastbourne, Sussex. *T.A.:* Unknot Stock, London. *T.:* Monarch 3788/9/3780. *Clubs:* Athenæum, City Livery. [*Died* 13 *Nov.* 1959.

ROWLANDS, Sir Archibald, G.C.B., *cr.* 1947 (K.C.B., *cr.* 1941); M.B.E.; Member of Economic Planning Board since 1947; *b.* 26 Dec. 1892; *m.* 1920, Constance May, *d.* of P. W. and M. Phillips; no *c.* *Educ.:* Penarth; Univ. Coll. of Wales; Jesus Coll., Oxford. Served European War, Mesopotamia (despatches); Asst. Principal, War Office, 1920; Private Sec. to Sec. of War Office (Sir Herbert Creedy), 1920-22; Principal, War Office, 1923; Principal Private Sec. to successive Secretaries of State for War (Viscount Hailsham, Viscount Halifax and Mr Duff Cooper); *i.d.c.* 1936; Financial Adviser, Military Finance, Govt. of India, 1937-39; Deputy Under Secretary of State, Air Ministry, 1939-40; Permanent Secretary, Ministry of Aircraft Production, May 1940-Nov. 1943; Member of Beaverbrook-Harriman Mission to Moscow, Sept. 1941; Adviser to the Viceroy on War Administration (India), Nov. 1943; Chairman of Enquiry into Bengal Administration, Oct. 1945; Finance Member of Governor-General's Executive Council, India, 1945-46; Permanent Secretary of Ministry of Supply, 1946-53; Financial and Economic Adviser to Quaid-i-Azam M. A. Jinnah (1st Governor General of Pakistan), Aug.-Dec. 1947. *Club:* Oriental. [*Died* 18 *Aug.* 1953.

ROWLANDS, Ernest B.; *see* Bowen-Rowlands.

ROWLANDS, His Honour Horace, M.A.; *b.* 3 June 1869; 2nd *s.* of late Joseph Rowlands of Evesbatch Court, Herefordshire and Birmingham, Solicitor; *m.* 1899, Edith Geraldine, *e. d.* of late C. H. Feiling, Southgate House, Middlesex and London Stock Exchange; no *c.* *Educ.:* Malvern College; Exeter College, Oxford; Honours in Law. Called to Bar, 1895, Inner Temple; Practised in London and on the Midland Circuit; Judge of the County Court, Clerkenwell, Middlesex, 1928-34, of Circuit 32 (Norwich), 1934-44. Chairman of: Norfolk Quarter Sessions, Rent Tribunal for Norwich and Area. *Recreations:* shooting, fishing, golf. *Address:* Fritton Old Rectory, Nr. Long Stratton, Norfolk. *Club:* Norfolk County. [*Died* 6 *Feb.* 1954.

ROWLATT, Charles James, M.B.E. 1920; Vice-Provost of Eton, 1952-59; *b.* 24 Aug. 1894; 2nd *s.* of late Rt. Hon. Sir Sidney Rowlatt, K.C.S.I.; unmarried. *Educ.:* Eton; University College, Oxford. Served European War, 1914-18, in 13th Bn. The Rifle Bde. and on General Staff. Assistant Master at Eton, 1920-52. *Address:* Eton College, Windsor. *T.:* Windsor 971. *Clubs:* Oxford and Cambridge, Leander. [*Died* 24 *May* 1959.

ROWLATT, Sir John, K.C.B., *cr.* 1954 (C.B. 1945); K.C.I.E., *cr.* 1947; M.C. 1918; Q.C. 1954; First Parliamentary Counsel to Treasury since 1953; *b.* 19 Nov. 1898; 3rd *s.* of late Rt. Hon. Sir Sidney Arthur Taylor Rowlatt, K.C.S.I.; *m.* 1928, Janet Peace Thompson; two *s.* three *d.* *Educ.:* Eton College; Christ Church, Oxford. 2nd Lt. Coldstream Guards, 1917-1918; Barrister-at-law, 1922; one of the Parliamentary Counsel to the Treasury, 1937; Second Parliamentary Counsel, 1947-1953. *Address:* 5 Bigwood Road, N.W.11. *Club:* Oxford and Cambridge. [*Died* 4 *July* 1956.

ROWLEDGE, A. J., M.B.E. 1920; F.R.S. 1941; Engineer, retired. Formerly Consultant Engineer to the Rolls Royce Company. *Address:* 21 Trowels Lane, Derby. [*Died* 13 *Dec.* 1957.

ROWLEY, Alec, F.R.A.M., F.R.C.O., F.T.C.L.; Composer, Organist, Pianist, Lecturer and Writer; Professor and Lecturer, Trinity College of Music, since 1920; *b.* London, 13 March 1892. *Educ.:* Royal Academy of Music. Studied composition there under F. Corder; Organist, St. John's, Richmond, 1912-21, St. Alban's, Teddington, 1921-34, St. Margaret's, Westminster (during War of 1939-45). Vice-Chm. Trinity Coll. of Music; member cttee. of management of Royal Philharmonic Soc., 1939-47. Three works produced at Promenade Concerts during war of 1939-45, and also at Cheltenham Festival after the war. Has broadcast since 1930 and has had many works performed by the B.B.C. *Publications:* has written a number of books on Music, including a Pronouncing Dictionary, Do's and Dont's for Musicians, etc. Mime Ballet (Carnegie Award), 1927; String Quartet, Piano Quartet, Five Trios, Sonatas and Suites, Miniature Concerto for Piano, 1947. Many works in all forms, including plays for children and a sacred cantata, The Garden and the Cross, 1948. *Recreations:* tennis (eight cups in various tournaments prior to War of 1939-45). *Address:* Anne House, 33 Broadlands Avenue, Shepperton, Middx. *T.:* Walton-on-Thames 2394. *Clubs:* Queen's, Savile, International Music Association. [*Died* 11 *Jan.* 1958.

ROWLEY, Capt. and Bt. Maj Sir George William, 5th Bt., *cr.* 1836; Essex

Regt. retd.; b. 10 May 1896; s. of 4th Bt. and Caroline, o. d. of Rev. John Cuming, M.A.; S. father, 1924; m. 1939, Mrs. Marjorie Alice Parker, d. of late John William Borchards Blagrave. *Educ.:* Repton; R.M.C., Sandhurst. Instructor, Small Arms School, India, 1930-32; Adjutant and Quartermaster, 1932-34; retired pay, 1934. *Heir:* u. William Joshua, Major Lancashire Fusiliers, b. 15 Apr. 1891. *Recreations:* cricket, tennis, golf. *Address:* Myrtle Cottage, Newlyn, Penzance, Cornwall. *T.:* Penzance 3104. [*Died* 8 *Aug.* 1953.

ROWLEY-CONWY, Rear-Adm. Rafe G.; *see* Conwy.

ROWNTREE, Arnold (Stephenson); Director, Westminster Press and Associated Papers; b. 1872; s. of John Stephenson Rowntree; m. Mary Katharine, d. of late William Harvey, Leeds; three s. three d. *Educ.:* Bootham School, York. M.P. (L.) York, 1910-18; Past President of the York Liberal Association; President Educational Centres Association; member of a well-known family of the Society of Friends. *Recreations:* travel, tennis. *Address:* Brook House, Thornton-Le-Dale, Pickering, Yorks. *T.:* Thornton-Le-Dale 221. *Club:* National Liberal. [*Died* 21 *May* 1951.

ROWNTREE, B. Seebohm, C.H. 1931; Hon. LL.D. (Manchester); Chairman of Rowntree & Co. Ltd., 1925-41; b. 1871; s. of late Joseph Rowntree; m. 1897, Lydia Potter (d. 1944); four s. one d. *Educ.:* Friends' School, York; studied Chemistry, Owen's College. Chairman Governors of York Citizens' Theatre Trust; Chairman of Floris Bakeries Ltd. Trustee of Nuffield Trust for Special Areas; Pres.: The Outward Bound Trust; The War on Want Cttee. *Publications:* Poverty, a Study of Town Life; Betting and Gambling, a National Evil; Land and Labour: lessons from Belgium, 1910; (with B. Lasker) Unemployment: A Social Study, 1911; (with May Kendall) How the Labourer Lives, 1913; The Way to Industrial Peace, 1914; The Human Needs of Labour, 1918, new and revised edition, 1936; The Human Factor in Business, 1921, new and revised edition, 1937; Poverty and Progress, 1941; (with G. R. Lavers) English Life and Leisure, A Social Study, 1951; (with G. R. Lavers) Poverty and the Welfare State, 1951. *Address:* Hughenden Manor, High Wycombe, Bucks. *T.:* High Wycombe 2326. *Club:* Reform. [*Died* 7 *Oct.* 1954.

ROWSON, Edmund, K.C. 1947; Recorder of Blackpool since 1948. Called to the Bar, Gray's Inn, 1913; Northern Circuit. *Address:* 1 Brick Court, Temple, E.C.4. *T.:* Central 1857; Lynwood, Gosforth Rd., North Shore, Blackpool. *T.:* North Shore 51543. [*Died* 18 *Dec.* 1951.

ROXBURGH, Alexander Bruce, M.A., M.B., F.R.C.S.; Fellow of the Royal Society of Medicine; Member of the Ophthalmological Society; Consulting Ophthalmic Surgeon (late Lecturer on Ophthalmic Surgery), London Hospital; s. of late William Roxburgh, M.D.; m. 1916, Edith Annie, d. of George Fletcher, M.D., J.P. *Educ.:* Exeter College, Oxford; London Hospital. *Recreation:* gardening. *Address:* Oaksleigh, Locks Heath, Hants. *T.:* Locks Heath 3148. [*Died* 17 *March* 1953.

ROXBURGH, Archibald Cathcart, M.A., M.D., B.Ch. Camb.; F.R.C.P. Lond.; M.R.C.S., Eng.; Emeritus Physician for Diseases of the Skin, St. Bartholomew's Hospital, London; Consulting Physician St. John's Hospital for Diseases of the Skin; Dermatologist to the Assoc. of Retired Naval Officers; late Dean and Joint Chesterfield Lecturer London School of Dermatology; late Dermatologist to Royal Masonic Hospital; Past Pres. British Assoc. of Dermatology, Section of Dermatology R. Soc. of Med. and St. John's Hospital Dermatological Soc.; Mem. Roy. Instn.; Assoc. Roy. Phot. Soc. Corresp. Mem. Belgian, Danish, French and Hungarian Dermatological Societies; late Consultant in Dermatology Sector III Emergency Medical Service; late Editor British Journal of Dermatology; late Vice-Pres. Dermatological Section British Medical Association; late Member of Council Royal Soc. of Med.; late Temporary Surgeon Royal Navy, 1914-19; b. Valparaiso, Chile, 17 Aug. 1886; er. s. of late Archibald Roxburgh, Valparaiso and Liverpool, and of late Janet Briggs, d. of John F. Cathcart, Edinburgh; m. 1916, Mary, d. of Lt.-Col. J. A. Lambert, Queen's Bays; three s. one d. *Educ.:* Charterhouse; Trinity College, Cambridge (Exhibitioner, 1st Class Nat. Science Tripos); St. Bartholomew's Hospital (Senior Entrance Scholar); Vienna. *Publications:* Common Skin Diseases, 10th edition, 1955; numerous articles on Diseases of the Skin. *Recreations:* photography, travel. *Address:* 121 Harley Street, W.1. *T.:* Welbeck 6818, 6819; 5 Redington Road, Hampstead, N.W.3. *Club:* Oxford and Cambridge. [*Died* 3 *Dec.* 1954.

ROXBURGH, John Fergusson, M.A., L. ès L.; Headmaster of Stowe from its foundation in 1923, retired 1949; b. Edinburgh, 5 May 1888; 2nd s. of Archibald Roxburgh, Glasgow and Liverpool, and Janet, d. of John Cathcart, Edinburgh; unmarried. *Educ.:* Charterhouse; Trinity College, Cambridge; University of Paris. Sixth Form Master at Lancing College, 1911-23; served with Corps of Signals (France) in War of 1914-18 (despatches). *Clubs:* Athenæum, Reform. [*Died* 6 *May* 1954.

ROY, Donald Whatley, M.A., M.B., B.Ch., Cantab.; F.R.C.S.Eng.; F.R.C.O.G., retd.; Consulting Obstetric Surgeon, St. George's Hosp.; Consulting Physician to General Lying-in Hosp.; Consulting Surgeon to Samaritan Hosp. for Women; late Senior Examiner in Obstetrics and Gynæcology, London Univ. and Society of Apothecaries; late Examiner in Obstetrics and Gynæcology Camb. Univ. R.C.S. and Coll. of Physicians, London; late Member Board of Advanced Studies, University of London, Mem. London Hosps. Representative Cttee., and Cons. Obstetrician L.C.C. Hosps.; late Hon. Sec. and Vice-Pres. Obstetric and Gynæcological Section, R.S.M.; Vice-Pres. Obstetrical Section B.M.A. Meeting, 1931; b. Appleton Roebuck, York, 1881; 4th s. of Rev. James Roy, Rector of Stockton-on-Forest, York, and Mary, d. of Thomas Denman Whatley, Barrister-at-Law; m. Beatrice Anne, d. of Henry Barstow, late Bengal Civil Service, Hazelbush, York; two s. one d. *Educ.:* St. Peter's School, York; Sidney Sussex College, Cambridge (Exhibitioner and Scholar); 1st Class Honours Natural Science Tripos Part 1, 1902, 1st Class Honours Part 2 Natural Science Tripos, 1903; University Scholarship and Brodie Prize for Clinical Surgery, St. George's Hospital. Asst. Surgeon Samaritan Hosp. for Women, 1913; Asst. Obstetric Surgeon, St. George's Hospital, 1919; Surgeon, R.N.V.R., Grand Fleet, 1914-16 (1914-1915 Star); Temp. Major, R.A.M.C., i/c Surgical Div. Northamptonshire War Hosp., 1917-18. *Publications:* articles, and other publications on Obstetrics, Gynæcology, Medicine, Surgery, and on Organisation of teaching of Midwives and Medical Students. *Recreation:* fly-fishing. *Address:* c/o Barclays Bank Ltd., Cavendish Square Branch, Vere St., Oxford Street, W.1. [*Died* 9 *Dec.* 1960.

ROY, Sir Satyendra Nath, K.C.I.E., cr. 1945 (C.I.E. 1932); Kt., cr. 1942; C.S.I. 1938; Partner, Bird & Co., Calcutta; b. 23 Sept. 1888; 3rd s. of late Kedarnath Roy; m. *Educ.:* Presidency College, Calcutta; Christ's College, Cambridge. Appointed I.C.S., 1913, and posted to Bengal; Under-Sec. Govt. of Bengal, Finance Dept.; Under-Secretary, General Department, Govt. of Bengal, 1918-19; Magistrate and Collector, Deputy Secretary, Political Dept.

Govt. of Bengal, 1925-27; Deputy Secretary, Home Department, Government of India, 1929-32; Joint Secretary, Home Department, 1931; Additional Secretary, Political Department, Govt. of Bengal, 1933-36; Joint Secretary, Department of Industries and Labour, 1936; Secretary, Dept. of Communications, Govt. of India, 1937-42; Acting Member Governor General's Exec. Council, 1942; Secretary, Dept. of War Transport, Govt. of India, 1942-45. Member Central Legislative Assembly, 1928-32, and of Council of State at Delhi, 1937-45; retired from I.C.S., Dec. 1946. *Clubs:* National Liberal, Overseas; Calcutta (Calcutta). [*Died* 26 *April* 1955.

ROYDEN, (Agnes) Maude; (Mrs. G. W. H. Shaw), C.H. 1930; D.D. (Glasgow University); *b.* 1876; *y. d.* of late Sir Thomas Royden, 1st Bart., of Frankby Hall, Birkenhead; *m.* 1944, Rev. George William Hudson Shaw (*d.* 1944). *Educ.:* Cheltenham Ladies' College; Lady Margaret Hall, Oxford. Worked at the Victoria Women's Settlement, Liverpool, for three years, and then in the country parish of Luffenham; Lecturer in English Literature to the Oxford University Extension Delegacy; joined the National Union of Women's Suffrage Societies, 1908; on Executive Committee, 1908; edited The Common Cause, 1912-14; wrote and spoke chiefly on the economic, ethical, and religious aspects of the Women's Movement; resigned Executive, 1914: Assistant Preacher at the City Temple, 1917-20; Founder with Dr. Percy Dearmer of the Fellowship Services at Kensington, 1920, and of the Guildhouse, 1921. *Publications: books*—Blessed Joan of Arc; The Hour and the Church; Sex and Commonsense; Prayer as a Force; Political Christianity; The Friendship of God; Christ Triumphant; The Church and Woman; Life's Little Pitfalls; I Believe in God; Here and Hereafter, 1933; The Problem of Palestine; A Threefold Cord, etc. *Recreations:* bathing and motoring. *Address:* 110 Hampstead Way, N.W.11. *T.:* Speedwell 1022. [*Died* 30 *July* 1956.

ROYDEN, Sir Ernest Bland, 3rd Bt., *cr.* 1905; J.P. Cheshire; *b.* 30 Jan. 1873; *s.* of Sir Thomas Bland Royden, 1st Bt., and Alice Elizabeth, *d.* of late Thomas Dowdall; *S.* to brother's baronetcy, 1950; *m.* 1901, Rachel Mary, *d.* of Jerome Smith, of Frankby; two *s.* four *d.* *Educ.:* Winchester. High Sheriff of Anglesey, 1920. *Heir: s.* John Ledward [*b.* 31 Dec. 1907; *m.* 1936, Dolores Catherine, *e. d.* of late Cecil J. G. Coward; two *s.* two *d.*]. *Address:* Hill Bark, Frankby, West Kirby, Cheshire. [*Died* 13 *Oct.* 1960.

ROYDS, Admiral Sir Percy (Molyneux Rawson), Kt., *cr.* 1938; C.B. 1924; C.M.G. 1917; *b.* 1874; *m.* 1898, Florence (*d.* 1948), *d.* of Sir A. F. Yarrow, 1st Bt.; one *s.* three *d.* *Educ.:* Eastman's, Southsea. Served China, 1900 (medal); European War, 1914-18 (despatches, C.M.G., Legion of Honour, Russian Order of St. Anne); Admiral Superintendent of Chatham Dockyard, 1923-1925; Vice-Admiral, 1927; Retired List, 1927; Admiral, retired, 1932; M.P. (U.) Kingston-on-Thames, 1937-45. Danish Order of Dannebrog, 1913. *Address:* 27 Westminster Gdns., Marsham St., S.W.1. *Club:* United Service. [*Died* 25 *March* 1955.

ROYDS, William Massy, M.A.; *b.* Reading, 22 June 1879; *e. s.* of Dr. W. A. S. Royds; *m.* 1914, Doris Mary Bromley; two *s.* one *d.* *Educ.:* St. John's College, Cambridge. Student Interpreter in Japan, 1902; Vice-Consul, 1912; on special service at Norfolk, Virginia, U.S.A., 1915-17; Consul, 1918; Consul-General at Kobe, 1926-31; Consul-General, Seoul, Korea, 1931-34; retired, 1934; Captain Home Guard. *Recreations:* rowing, tennis, shooting. *Address:* Dene End, East Dean, Eastbourne. *Clubs:* Overseas; Seoul (Seoul); Kobe (Kobe); Manila (Manila). [*Died* 16 *June* 1951.

ROYLE, Admiral Sir Guy Charles Cecil, K.C.B., *cr.* 1941 (C.B. 1936); C.M.G. 1919; R.N., retired; Yeoman Usher of the Black Rod since 1946; Secretary to the Lord Great Chamberlain since 1948; *b.* 1885; 2nd *s.* of Arnold Royle, C.B., Esher; *m.* 1915, Ellis (O.B.E. 1953), *d.* of Charles Gilmer. Naval Attaché, Brit. Embassy, Tokio, 1924-27; in command of H.M.S. Canterbury, 1927-29; H.M.S. Excellent, 1930-1932; H.M.S. Glorious, 1933-34; Naval Sec. to First Lord of the Admiralty, 1934-37; Vice-Admiral, Aircraft Carriers, 1937-39; Naval Secretary to First Lord, Lord Commissioner of the Admiralty and Chief of Naval Air Services, 1939-41; First Naval Member, Commonwealth Naval Board, 1941-45; retired list, 1946. Served European War, 1914-19 (despatches, C.M.G.). *Address:* Tricketts House, Ferndown, Dorset. *Club:* United Service. [*Died* 4 *Jan.* 1954.

RUDKIN, Brig.-General Charles Mark Clement, D.S.O. 1918; late R.A.; *b.* Collon House, Co. Louth, 12 Nov. 1872; *s.* of late Major H. W. Rudkin, 85th Regt.; *m.* 1939, Marie, *d.* of late Thomas Russell of Ascog, D.L. of Bute. Served South African War; A.D.C. to Lord Methuen, and finally commanded a composite Brigade of Artillery, 1899-1902 (Queen's medal 4 clasps, King's medal 2 clasps); commanded the Royal Artillery Reserve at the Coronation, 1911; Coronation Medals, 1902 and 1911; served European War, 1914-18, in France, Belgium, and Italy; commanded an Artillery Division at Ypres, the Somme, and on Asiago Plateau, Italy (wounded twice, despatches twice, D.S.O., 1914 Star, Medaglia al Valore and Croce di Guerra); Barrister-at-law, Lincoln's Inn, 1912; M.P. (L.) Chichester Division of West Sussex, 1923-24; contested S. Portsmouth, 1929; has travelled and shot in Africa, Australia, India, and Canada, and travelled in America, New Zealand, Tasmania, China, Burma, Fiji, Samoa, Japan, Hawaii, and Ceylon, and extensively in Europe, including Russia. Has travelled twice round the world since Nov. 1926; is a Freeman of the City of London; has instructed himself in the progress of agriculture in Holland, Sweden, Norway, Belgium, France, Canada, America, Australia, and New Zealand by travel and inspection. *Recreations:* motoring, mountaineering, ski-ing, skating, travelling. *Address:* c/o Lloyds Bank, 16 St. James' Street, S.W.1; Kincraig, Darlington, Umtali, S. Rhodesia. *Club:* Yacht Club de France. [*Died* 30 *Dec.* 1957.

RUDLER, Dr. Gustave; Agr. des Let., Doct. ès Let.; M.A.; Marshal Foch Professor of French Literature, University of Oxford, 1920-49, Professor Emeritus since 1949; Fellow of All Souls College, 1926-49; Officier de l'Instruction publique; Commandeur de la légion d'honneur; *b.* 1872; *m.* Madeleine (*d.* 1946). *Educ.:* École Normale Supérieure, Paris; University, Paris. Professor Lycées Caen, Charlemagne and Louis le Grand, Paris, successively, deputy lecturer at the Sorbonne; Prof. of French Literature, London University, 1913-20. *Publications:* L'Explication française; La Jeunesse de Benjamin Constant (ouvrage couronné par l'Académie française); Bibliographie des œuvres de B. Constant; B. Constant, Adolphe, Edition historique et critique; Les techniques en histoire et critique littéraire; Michelet, Jeanne d'Arc (édition critique, 2 vols.); Michelet, historien de Jeanne d'Arc, 2 vols.; B. Constant, Adolphe (exégèse); Le Français par l'observation et la raison, 3 vols.; Critique littéraire à la Revue Universitaire, 1907-13; joint-editor of the Revue Critique des Livres Nouveaux and of the French Quarterly. *Address:* 7 Rue Florence Blumenthal, Paris 16e. [*Died* 17 *Oct.* 1957.

RUDMOSE-BROWN, Robert Neal; Emeritus Professor of Geography, University of Sheffield; Professor, 1931-45; Lecturer, 1908-31; *b.* 13 Sept. 1879; *y. s.*

of Robert Brown of Campster and Friherreinde Kristiane Augusta Marie Eleonora Rudmose; *m.* Edith (*d.* 1950), *e. d.* of G. W. Johnstone, R.S.A.; one *d.* *Educ.:* Dulwich Coll.; Univ. of Aberdeen (D.Sc.); Université de Montpellier. Assistant Professor of Botany, University College, Dundee (University of St. Andrews), 1900-1902; Reader in Geography, University of Manchester, 1920-22; Naturalist, Scottish National Antarctic Expedition, Scotia, 1902-04; Assistant, Scottish Oceanographical Laboratory, 1904-05; Commissioner under Indian Government to Report on Pearl Oyster Fisheries of Lower Burma, 1907; Surveyor and Naturalist, Scottish Arctic Expeditions to Spitsbergen, 1909, 1914, 1919, and visited Spitsbergen on several other occasions; Intelligence Division, Naval Staff, 1915-19; medallist, Royal Scottish Geographical Society, 1904; Cuthbert Peek Grant, Royal Geographical Society, 1919; Vice-President, International Polar Congress, 1906; Pres., Sect. E, British Assoc., 1927; Recorder, 1920-25; Council Royal Geographical Society, 1925-28, 1945-46 and British Assoc., 1933-38; President Inst. British Geographers, 1937-38. Pres. Antarctic Club, 1932, Arctic Club, 1949. Commander, Norwegian Order of St. Olav. *Publications:* The Voyage of the Scotia, 1906; Report on the Pearl Oyster Fisheries of Mergui (with J. J. Simpson), 1907; Zoological Log of the Scotia (Editor), 1908; Scientific Results of the Scottish Antarctic Expedition, Botany, 1912; Spitsbergen, 1920; Principles of Economic Geography, 1920 (new ed. 1926, 1931, 1939, 1946); The Scope of School Geography (jointly), 1922; A Naturalist at the Poles, 1923; The Polar Regions, 1927; and many articles in scientific journals, reviews, Encyclopædia Britannica; Dictionary of National Biography, etc.; Editor, Harrap's Geographical Series. *Recreations:* walking, gardening. *Address:* 108 Westbourne Road, Sheffield. *T.:* Sheffield 62028.
[*Died* 27 *Jan.* 1957.

RUFFSIDE, 1st Viscount, *cr.* 1951, of Hexham; **Douglas Clifton Brown,** P.C. 1941; D.L., J.P.; High Steward of Cambridge University since 1951; Major, late 1st Dragoon Guards and Colonel late Northumberland Hussar Yeomanry; *b.* 16 Aug. 1879; *s.* of late Col. J. C. Brown; *m.* 1907, Violet Cicely Kathleen, *d.* of late F. E. A. Wollaston, of Shenton Hall, Nuneaton; one *d.* *Educ.:* Cheam; Eton; Trinity College, Cambridge (M.A.). M.P. (U.) Hexham Division of Northumberland, Dec. 1918-Nov. 1923, and 1924-51; Deputy Chairman of Ways and Means, and Deputy Speaker, House of Commons, 1938-43; Chairman of Ways and Means, Jan. 1943; Speaker, March 1943-Oct. 1951. Hon. D.Litt. Durham University, 1945; Hon. Litt.D. Cambridge University, 1946; Dr. Honoris Causa, Université de Caën, 1948. Hon. Col. Northd. Hussars (Yeomanry), 1949-55. Grande Croix Légion d'Honneur, 1947. *Heir:* none. *Address:* Ruffside Hall, Shotley Bridge, Consett, Co. Durham. *T.:* Edmondbyres 238. *Clubs:* Carlton, Travellers'. [*Died* 5 *May* 1958 (*ext.*).

RUGGE-PRICE, Sir Charles F.; *see* Price, Sir C. F. R.

RUMFORD, R. Kennerley; *b.* London, 2 Sept. 1870; *m.* 1st, 1900, Clara Butt (*d.* 1936); one *d.* (two *s.* decd.); 2nd, 1941, Dorothy Jane Elwin. *Educ.:* King's School, Canterbury. In 1896 entered the musical profession; served European War in France, 1914-17 (despatches twice); from 1917 to end of war on Special Intelligence Dept. at W.O. *Address:* North Stoke, Oxford. *Clubs:* Arts, Garrick. [*Died* 9 *March* 1957.

RUML, Beardsley; *b.* Cedar Rapids, Iowa, U.S.A., 5 Nov. 1894; *s.* of Wentzle Ruml and Salome Beardsley; *m.* 1917, Lois Treadwell; two *s.* one *d.* *Educ.:* Dartmouth (B.S.); University of Chicago (Ph.D.). Sec., The Scott Co., Philadelphia, 1919-21; Asst. to President, Carnegie Corp. of N.Y., 1921-22; Director Laura Spelman Rockefeller Memorial, 1922-29; Member Board of Trustees Spelman Fund of N.Y., 1929-49; Dean, Social Science Div. and Professor of Education, Univ. of Chicago, 1931-33; Treasurer, R. H. Macy & Co. Inc., 1934-45; Chm., 1945-49; Director, Federal Reserve Bank of N.Y. City, 1937-46; Chm. 1941-46. Director: Encyclopædia Britannica, Inc.; General American Investors Co. Inc.; Nat. Securities & Research Corp.; Peerless Insurance Co.; Govt. Development Bank for Puerto Rico; Enterprise Paint Mfg. Co. Economic Adviser to Govt. of Puerto Rico. Trustee: Committee for Economic Dev.; National Planning Association; Museum of Modern Art; National Bureau of Economic Research; Dartmouth Coll. (N.H.); Fisk Univ. *Publications:* Government, Business and Values, 1943; To-morrow's Business, 1945; Memo to a College Trustee, 1959. *Address:* 342 Madison Ave., New York 17, U.S.A. *T.:* Oxford 7-1750. *Clubs:* Links, Century, Dartmouth (N.Y.).
[*Died* 18 *April* 1960.

RUNCIMAN OF DOXFORD, Dowager Viscountess; Hilda; J.P.; 5th *d.* of late James C. Stevenson, M.P.; *m.* 1898, 1st Visc. Runciman of Doxford, P.C. (*d.* 1949); two *s.* two *d.* *Educ.:* Notting Hill High Sch.; Girton Coll., Camb. (schol., 1st cl., Hist. Tripos); first woman elected Newcastle on Tyne School Board, 1897; one of the original co-opted members of Northumberland County Education Committee, 1903; M.P. (L.) St. Ives, 1928-29; contested Tavistock, 1929. *Address:* 73 Portland Place, W.1. *T.:* Langham 2269. *Club:* Ladies' Empire.
[*Died* 28 *Oct.* 1956.

RUNCIMAN, Philip; Chairman Anchor Line Ltd.; Director Barberrys Steamship Co. Ltd.; Director Moor Line Ltd.; Director Runciman (London) Ltd.; Director United Mutual Steamship Assurance Association Ltd.; Director Walter Runciman & Co. Ltd.; Director West of England Steamship Owners Protection & Indemnity Association Ltd. *Address:* 52 Leadenhall Street, E.C.3; 12-16 St. Vincent Place, Glasgow, C.1.
[*Died* 5 *June* 1953.

RUNDALL, Lieut.-Col. Charles Frank, C.M.G. 1919; D.S.O. 1917; member Institution of Mechanical Engineers; retired; late Royal Engineers; *b.* 25th June 1871; *s.* of J. W. Rundall, Indian Public Works Department; *m.* 1901, Helen Agnes Townsend (*d.* 1937); one *s.* two *d.* *Educ.:* Oundle School; R.M.A., Woolwich, Thirty-two years' Regimental Service; served European War (despatches five times). *Recreation:* gardening. *Address:* Trezion, Fore Street, St. Ives, Cornwall. *T.:* St. Ives 437.
[*Died* 15 *Sept.* 1951.

RUNDLE, Rear-Admiral Mark, D.S.O. 1918; M.I.Mech.E.; retired from Navy, 1925; *b.* 1871; *m.* 1st, 1901, Elsie Cameron (*d.* 1935), *d.* of late Eng.-Rear-Adm. J. M. C. Bennett, M.V.O.; one *d.* (and one *d.* decd.); 2nd, 1938, Margaret (*d.* 1942), *d.* of late Mrs. Wilson, Braidwood, Ifield, Sussex, and late John Wilson; 3rd, 1944, Mildred Ellen (*d.* 1957), *widow* of R. B. Robinson. Entered Royal Naval Engineering College, Devonport, 1887; joined H.M. Navy as Asst. Eng., R.N., 1892; served European War as Engineer Officer of H.M.S. Lion, 1915-17; present at Battle of Jutland, May 1916 (despatches, D.S.O., Chevalier Legion of Honour); on the Staff of Vice-Admiral commanding Special Service Squadron, 1923-24. *Address:* Berigem, Maresfield Park, Sussex. *T.:* Uckfield 306. [*Died* 8 *Oct.* 1958.

RUSSELL, Hon. Sir (Alexander) Fraser, K.B.E., *cr.* 1943; Kt., *cr.* 1933; M.A., LL.B. Cantab.; *b.* 21 Oct. 1876; *e. s.* of late Rev. J. M. Russell, B.D., LL.D., V.D., Cape Town; *m.* 1904, Winifred, C.B.E. 1938, *e. d.* of late A. F. Robertson, Civil Service, Cape Colony; one *s.* (and one killed in action, 1941) two *d.* *Educ.:* Merchiston Castle School, Edinburgh; South African College, Cape Town (B.A. and Ebden Scholar,

1897); St. John's College, Cambridge (Law Tripos, 1900). Of the Middle Temple, Barrister-at-law, 1901; admitted to Cape Bar, 1901; member of the first Provincial Council of the Cape Province, 1910-13; Puisne Judge, S. Rhodesia, 1915; Chief Justice of S. Rhodesia, 1931-42; President of Rhodesian Court of Appeal, 1939-42; acting Governor of S. Rhodesia, Oct.-Dec. 1931, July 1934-Jan. 1935, Oct. 1936-Feb. 1937, and Jan.-Dec. 1942. *Publications:* joint editor, Supreme Court Reports (Cape Colony and Union of South Africa), 1902-15; The School Board Act (Cape Colony), 1906. *Address:* Woodville, Newlands Road, Claremont, Capetown. *Clubs:* Royal Empire Society, Overseas; Bulawayo (Bulawayo); Salisbury (Salisbury, S. Rhodesia); Royal Automobile of South Africa, Civil Service (Cape Town). [*Died* 28 *March* 1952.

RUSSELL, Colonel Sir Alexander James Hutchison, Kt., *cr.* 1939; C.B.E. 1925; Hon. LL.D. (St. Andrews), 1939; I.M.S. retd.; *b.* 30 Aug. 1882; *s.* of Walter Nicoll Russell, Dunfermline; *m.* 1910, Jessie Waddell, *d.* of W. Muir. *Educ.:* Dollar Academy; St. Andrews University (M.A., M.B. and Ch.B., M.D.); Cambridge University (D.P.H.). D.T.M. Liverpool, 1912; Medical Officer of Health, Madras City, 1913-1914, Professor of Hygiene and Bacteriology, Madras Medical College, 1912-17; Professor of Pathology, 1919-21; Director of Public Health, Madras, 1922; Medical Assessor with the Royal Commission on Labour in India, 1930-31; Officiating Deputy Director-General Indian Medical Service, 1933; Public Health Commissioner with the Government of India, 1933-39; K.H.S., 1936-39; retired, 1939; Additional Deputy Chief Medical Officer, Dept. of Health for Scotland, 1940-45. *Address:* Hazelwood, Chalton Road, Bridge-of-Allan, Stirlingshire. *T.:* 2176. *Club:* Royal and Ancient Golf (St. Andrews). [*Died* 22 *March* 1958.

RUSSELL, Major-General Sir Andrew Hamilton, K.C.B., *cr.* 1918 (C.B. 1917); K.C.M.G., *cr.* 1915; Hon. Col. Wellington East Coast Mounted Rifles and of Wellington Infantry Regiment; *e. s.* of Captain Andrew Hamilton Russell and Katharine Sarah, *d.* of late Thomas Tinsley; *b.* 23 Feb. 1868; *m.* 1896, Gertrude Mary, *d.* of late J. N. Williams, N.Z.; one *s.* three *d.* (and one *s.* killed at El Alamein). *Educ.:* Harrow; Sandhurst. Served European War (Dardanelles), 1914-18 (wounded, despatches, K.C.M.G., K.C.B.); President of New Zealand Returned Soldiers' Association, 1921-24 and 1926-35; Order of Danilo (Montenegro), 2nd Class, 1917; Legion of Honour, French Croix de Guerre; Commander, Order of Leopold, Belgian Croix de Guerre; Commander, Order of White Eagle, Serbia; retired list, N.Z. Military Forces, 1932; Inspector-General, N.Z. Forces, 1940-41; member of N.Z. War Council. *Address:* Tunanui, Hawkes Bay, New Zealand. *Club:* Naval and Military. [*Died* 28 *Nov.* 1960.

RUSSELL, Archibald George Blomefield, C.V.O. 1945 (M.V.O. 1929); B.A. Oxon; F.S.A.; F.R.Ent.S.; J.P. (Dorset); Clarenceux King of Arms, 1954; Lancaster Herald, 1922; Earl Marshal's Secretary; *b.* 20 June 1879; 4th *s.* of late Captain T. Stuart Russell, D.L., Chief Constable, W.R. Yorks; *m.* 1915, Janet Frances, *e. d.* of late Colonel John M. Kerr; (two *s.* killed, War of 1939-45). *Educ.:* Eton (King's Scholar); Christ Church, Oxford (Classical Scholar). Temporarily employed at the Colonial Office, 1917-18; temporary Secretary, His Majesty's Embassy, Madrid, 1918; acting Third Secretary, H.M. Embassy, Madrid, 1919; Rouge Croix Pursuivant of Arms. *Publications:* The Letters of William Blake, 1906; The Engravings of William Blake, 1912; Catalogue of an Exhibition of Blake's Works at the National Gallery, British Art, 1913; Drawings by Guercino, 1923; Hellas and a Renaissance, 1943. *Address:* College of Arms, Queen Victoria Street, E.C.4. *T.:* City 1991; Scar Bank House, Swanage, Dorset. *T.:* Swanage 2793. [*Died* 30 *Nov.* 1955.

RUSSELL, Rev. Charles Frank, M.A., B.D., F.S.A.; *b.* 8 May 1882; *o. s.* of late Rev. C. D. Russell, Vicar of Burscough, Lancs; *m.* 1908, Irene Kathleen, *d.* of late Rev. S. L. Dixon; three *d.* *Educ.:* Liverpool Coll.; Pembroke College, Cambridge (Scholar). Bell University Scholar, 1902; Double First in Mathematical Tripos, Parts I. and II., 1904 and 1905; Smith's Prizeman, 1906; Fellow of Pembroke College, 1906-12; Lecturer at King's College, London, 1905-6; Lecturer and Chaplain of Pembroke College, Cambridge, 1907-11; Assistant Master at Harrow, 1911-18; Headmaster of King Edward VI School, Southampton, 1918-29; Headmaster, Merchant Taylors' School, Great Crosby, 1929-42; ordained, 1907 and 1908; Select Preacher at Cambridge, 1909, 1912, 1921, 1934; Hulsean Lecturer in Cambridge University, 1922-23; Commissary in England to Bishop in Chekiang, 1908-28; Member of Archbishop of Canterbury's Commission on Christian Doctrine, 1923-38. *Publications:* Religion and Natural Law, 1923; translation of Moreux's Où en est l'Astronomie (title, Astronomy To-day), 1926; Crosby Songs, 1934; A History of King Edward VI School, Southampton, 1940; The Parish Registers of Sefton (Lancs. Par. Reg. Soc.), 1947; a number of papers on theological, mathematical, and antiquarian subjects; Hon. Editor, Lancs. and Cheshire Historic Society, 1945-48. *Recreations:* lawn tennis, fives, chess. *Address:* 18 Alexandra Road, Clifton, Bristol. [*Died* 17 *Feb.* 1951.

RUSSELL, Sir (Charles) Lennox (Somerville), Kt., *cr.* 1924; *b.* 10 July 1872; 2nd *s.* of late Capt. Stuart Russell, D.L., W.R. Yorks, and Louisa, *d.* of late Rev. Sir Thomas Blomefield, 3rd Baronet; *m.* 1907, Nina, *d.* of late Hon. Hugh Elliot; (two *s.* died on active service, 1941 and 1943). *Educ.:* Rugby; St. John's College, Cambridge (scholar). Entered Indian Civil Service, 1893; served in Behar, 1893-98; Under-Secretary to the Bengal Government, Political Department, 1898-1901; First Assistant to the Resident in Mysore and Secretary to the Chief Commissioner of Coorg, 1901-2; Under-Secretary to the Government of India, Foreign Department, 1903-04; Deputy Secretary to the Government of India, Foreign Department, 1904-6; Political Agent and Deputy Commissioner, Quetta and Pishin, 1906; Divisional Judge, Dera Ismail Khan, Bannu, and Kohat, 1907-1908; Resident at Indore, 1909-12, and again 1913-15; Resident at Udaipur, 1916; Secretary to Surrey War Agricultural Cttee., 1917; Resident at Baroda, 1918-19; Resident at Hyderabad, 1919-25. *Address:* Crooksbury Hurst, near Farnham, Surrey; *T.:* Runfold 2444. *Club:* Travellers'. [*Died* 31 *Jan.* 1960.

RUSSELL, Sir Claud Frederick William, K.C.M.G., *cr.* 1930; F.R.G.S.; F.Z.S.; 2nd *s.* of late Lord Arthur Russell and Laura, *d.* of Vicomte de Peyronnet; *b.* 9 Dec. 1871; *m.* 1920, Athenais Iphigenia, *d.* of late Shirley C. Atchley, C.M.G., O.B.E. *Educ.:* Balliol College, Oxford; M.A. Entered Diplomatic Service, 1897; has served in H.M. Embassies or Legations in Turkey, Egypt, China, France, Russia, Morocco, Argentine Republic, Paraguay, Spain, Greece, and in the Foreign Office; British Delegate and President International Financial Commission in Athens, and Treasury Representative Inter-Allied Financial Commission, 1919-1920; late Major Bedfordshire Yeomanry; served European War, 1914-18 (1914 Star); Minister to Abyssinia, 1920-25; to Switzerland, 1928-31; British Ambassador to Portugal, 1931-35; Coronation Medal, 1910; Jubilee Medal, 1935; in ranks Home Guard,

1940-44, Defence Medal. Grand Cross Portuguese Order of Christ. *Address:* Trematon Castle, Saltash, Cornwall. *Clubs:* Brooks's, White's, Beefsteak; Royal Yacht Squadron (Cowes). [*Died* 9 *Dec.* 1959.

RUSSELL, Sir David, Kt., *cr.* 1946; LL.D. (St. Andrews); F.R.S.E., F.S.A., F.L.S.; F.S.A. (Scot.); J.P.; Managing Director of Tullis, Russell & Co. Ltd., Paper Makers; *b.* 1872; *s.* of late David Russell of Silverburn, Leven; *m.* 1912, Alison, *d.* of Francis C. Blyth, Belvedere, Kent; one *s.* (and one died of wounds, 1944) two *d.* *Educ.:* Clifton Bank, St. Andrews; Univ. of Edinburgh. Chancellor's Assessor on Court of St. Andrews University, 1938-55; Trustee, The Walker Trust; Vice-Pres., the National Trust for Scotland. *Publications:* The Power of Prayer (edited jointly with the Very Rev. Professor W. P. Paterson, D.D.), 1920; The Great Palace of the Byzantine Emperors (editor), 1947. *Recreations:* archæology and photography. *Address:* Silverburn, Leven, Fife; Rothes, Markinch, Fife. *Clubs:* Athenæum; Royal and Ancient (St. Andrews); New (Edinburgh). [*Died* 12 *May* 1956.

RUSSELL, Edward Stuart, O.B.E.; M.A., D.Sc., F.L.S.; Director of Fishery Investigations, Ministry of Agriculture and Fisheries, 1921-45; Fisheries Scientific Adviser, 1945-47; Hon. Lecturer in Animal Behaviour, University Coll., London, 1932-47; *b.* 25 March 1887; *s.* of Rev. John Naismith Russell and Helen Cockburn Young; *m.* 1911, Jehanne Aurélie Minchin. *Educ.:* Greenock Academy; Glasgow University. Inspector of Fisheries and Naturalist-Inspector in the Ministry of Agriculture and Fisheries, 1909-21; Fisheries Adviser to Sec. of State for Colonies, 1943-44; Editor of Journal du Conseil international pour l'Exploration de la Mer (Copenhagen), 1926-40; President Section D (Zoology) British Association, 1934; President of Linnean Society, 1940-42; Hon. Member, Dutch Zoological Society. *Publications:* Form and Function, 1916; The Study of Living Things, 1924; The Interpretation of Development and Heredity, 1930; The Behaviour of Animals, 1934, 2nd edition, 1938; The Overfishing Problem, 1942; The Directiveness of Organic Activities, 1945. *Recreations:* walking, rowing. *Address:* The Orchard, Beauharrow Rd., St. Leonards-on-Sea, Sussex. [*Died* 24 *Aug.* 1954

RUSSELL, Hon. Sir Fraser; *see* Russell, Hon. Sir A. F.

RUSSELL, Rev. George Stanley, M.A. (Aberdeen), D.D. (Victoria University, Toronto) 1934, (Aberdeen) 1937; Minister, Deer Park United Church, Toronto, since 1929; *b.* Gt. Grimsby, Lincs, *s.* of Joseph and Isabella Wells Russell; *m.* Ethel Margaret Tait (B.A. Toronto), *o. d.* of D. M. Tait; no *c.* *Educ.:* Aberdeen Grammar School and University. Editor Alma Mater (Aberdeen University Magazine); Minister at Mirfield, 1907-11; St. Annes-on-the-Sea, 1911-15; Grafton Square Congregational Church, London, S.W.4., 1915-29; Chairman, London Congregational Union, 1928; President Congregational Ministers' Crusade Against War, 1927-29; Hon. Chaplain Tower of London and King George's Hospital, 1915-19; and Queen Alexandra Hospital Home for Paralysed Soldiers, Roehampton, 1919-29; Hon. Chaplain, Imp. Veterans Assn. of Toronto, 1938-50; studied Theology at United Coll., Bradford. F.R.S.A. 1950. *Publications:* The Faith of a Man today; The Monastery by the River; The Church in the Modern World; The Face of God, and other Sermons, 1935; The Road Behind Me (Autobiography), 1936; A Book of Worship, 1955; many articles and sermons. *Recreations:* walking, Boys' Organisations. *Address:* 150 St. Clair Av. W., Toronto, Ont., Canada. *Club:* English-Speaking Union. [*Died* 21 *June* 1957.

RUSSELL, Colonel Guy Hamilton, C.I.E. 1924; D.S.O. 1920; Indian Army, retired; *b.* 22 Oct. 1882; *s.* of late Lieut.-Col. Charles Russell, retired, R.A., Rosslyn, Sidcup; *m.* 1925, Jane, *d.* of late F. W. Portal, The Lodge, Forest Hill; one *s.* one *d.* *Educ.:* Westward Ho!; R.M.C., Sandhurst. 2nd Lieut. Indian Army, 1902; Captain, 1911 Major, 1917; Bt. Lt.-Col., 1925; Lt.-Col., 1926; Col. 1929; served World War, 1914-18 (Croix de Guerre); 3rd Afghan War, 1919 (severely wounded, D.S.O.); Waziristan, 1921-24 (Bt. Lt.-Col.); retired 1934. *Address:* Thorne's Cottage, Wareham, Dorset. *Club:* United Service. [*Died* 21 *Oct.* 1958.

RUSSELL, Harold G. Bedford, M.A. (Cantab.); F.R.C.S. (Eng.); Consulting Surgeon Throat Department, St. Bartholomew's Hospital; *b.* Horsham, Australia, 10 Oct. 1886; 2nd *s.* of late Francis Richard Russell; *m.* 1928, Lilian, *o. d.* of late Harold Longmore-Mavius; two *s.* *Educ.:* Geelong, Australia; Sidney Sussex College, Cambridge. Served France, 1914-18 (despatches, French Croix de Guerre); Major D.A.D.M.S. IX. Corps. *Publications:* The Nasal Aspect of Asthma, St. Bartholomew's Hospital Reports, 1939; The Nasal Aspect of Migraine, Proc. Roy. Soc., 1955. *Address:* 86 Harley Street, W.1. *T.:* Langham 3622. *Club:* Bath. [*Died* 30 *Dec.* 1957.

RUSSELL, Henry Norris, Ph.D., D.Sc.; Research Professor of Astronomy, 1927-47; Director of the Observatory, 1912-47, Princeton University; *b.* Oyster Bay, New York, 25 Oct. 1877; *s.* of Rev. Alexander G. Russell and Eliza Norris; *m.* 1908, Lucy May, *d.* of John H. Cole, New York; one *s.* three *d.* *Educ.:* Princeton University (A.B. 1897; Ph.D. 1900); King's College, Cambridge. Research Assistant, Carnegie Institution, stationed at the Cambridge Observatory, 1903-5; Instructor in Astronomy, Princeton University, 1905; Assistant Professor, 1908; Professor, 1911; Civilian Engineer, U.S. Air Service, 1918-19; Foreign member of Royal Society, 1937; Fellow of Royal Astronomical Society; Correspondant, Académie des Sciences, Paris; Associé, Académie Royale des Sciences, Bruxelles; Socio Straniero Accad. Nazionale dei Lincei, Roma; Member Nat. Acad. of Sciences, U.S.A.; Amer. Acad. of Arts and Sciences; Amer. Philosophical Soc.; Amer. Astronomical Soc.; Amer. Physical Soc.; Foreign Associate Royal Astronomical Soc., 1916; Gold Medal Royal Astronomical Society, 1921; Research Associate Mount Wilson Observatory, 1921; Henry Draper Medal, 1922; Lalande Medal, 1922; Bruce Medal, 1925; Rumford Medal, 1925; Franklin Medal, 1934; Janssen Medal, 1936; Pres. A.A.A.S., 1933; Research Associate, Lick Observatory, 1947; Harvard Observatory, 1947-52. *Publications:* Determination of Stellar Parallax, 1911; Astronomy, 1926; Fate and Freedom, 1927; The Solar System and its Origin, 1935; The Masses of the Stars, 1940; many papers on astronomical topics. *Recreations:* travel, climbing, boating. *Address:* 79 Alexander Street, Princeton, New Jersey, U.S.A. *T.:* 404. [*Died* 18 *Feb.* 1957.

RUSSELL, Rear-Admiral Sir (Henshaw) Robert, K.B.E., *cr.* 1935; C.B. 1925; C.M.G. 1918; R.N.; *s.* of late Lieut.-Colonel Hickman Rose Russell, 57th Regiment; *b.* 19 Jan. 1875. *Educ.:* Ipswich School. Joined Royal Navy, 1892; Assistant Paymaster, 1896; Paymaster Commander, 1910; Paymaster Captain, 1923; retired list as Paymaster Rear-Adm., 1929; served South African War, 1900-2; European War, 1914-18. *Address:* Scole Lodge Nursing Home, Scole, Nr. Diss, Norfolk. *Club:* Army and Navy. [*Died* 2 *Oct.* 1957.

RUSSELL, Air Commodore John Cannan, D.S.O. 1919; R.A.F., retired; *b.* 6 March 1896; *s.* of Wm. Russell, J.P., Ardluss, Helensburgh. *Educ.:* Fettes College, Edinburgh. Major, Royal Flying Corps, 1917; Squadron Leader Royal Air Force, 1918; served European War (despatches twice, Chevalier de Léopold, Croix de Guerre, D.S.O.); North-West Frontier, India, 1919 (despatches); Wing-Comdr., Royal Air Force, 1930; Commanded R.A.F., Amman, Transjordania; Senior Air Staff Officer, Air H.Q. Palestine and Transjordan; commanded 502 (Ulster) (B) Squadron, 1934-36; Group Capt. 1936; commanded R.A.F. Station, Scampton, near Lincoln, 1936-38; commanded R.A.F. Station, Thorney Island, Hants, 1938; Air A.D.C. to the King, 1938-1939; Air Commodore, 1939; Air Headquarters, Australia, 1939; India N.W.F., 1940; despatches; retired list, 1945. Representative, Herts County Territorial Assoc. Cttee., 1946-49. [*Died* 15 *Aug.* 1956.

RUSSELL, John F. R. V.; *see* Vaughan-Russell.

RUSSELL, Sir Lennox; *see* Russell, Sir C. L. S.

RUSSELL, Mabel; *see* Philipson, Mrs. Hilton.

RUSSELL, Hon. Sir Odo (William Theophilus Villiers), K.C.M.G., *cr.* 1926, K.C.V.O., *cr.* 1923 (C.V.O. 1909); C.B. 1916; 2nd *s.* of 1st Lord Ampthill; *b.* 3 May 1870; *m.* 1910, Countess Marie Louise Rex, *d.* of Count Rex, Saxon Minister at the Austro-Hungarian Court; three *s.* Nominated Attaché, 1892; 3rd Secretary, 1894; 2nd Secretary, 1898; 1st Secretary, 1905; has served in Rome, Athens, St. Petersburg, Berlin, Buenos Ayres, Vienna; in Foreign Office, 1905-8; Private Secretary to Sir E. Grey; Counsellor of Embassy at Vienna, 1909-15; Diplomatic Secretary to the Secretary of State for Foreign Affairs, 1915-19; British Minister at Berne, 1919-22; Minister Plenipotentiary to the Holy See, 1922-28; British Minister at The Hague, 1928-33; retired 1933. *Address:* 14 Culford Mansions, Culford Gardens, S.W.3. *T.:* Knightsbridge 2088. *Club:* Brooks's. [*Died* 23 *Dec.* 1951.

RUSSELL, Rear-Adm. Sir Robert; *see* Russell, Rear-Adm. Sir H. R.

RUSSELL, Sir Thomas Wentworth, K.B.E., *cr.* 1938 (O.B.E. 1920); C.M.G. 1926; Commandant Cairo City Police, Ministry of the Interior, Cairo, 1917-46, with rank of Lewa (Major-General) and civil rank of Pasha; Director, Egyptian Central Narcotics Intelligence Bureau, 1939-46; retired from Egyptian Civil Service, 1946; *b.* 22 Nov. 1879; *s.* of late Rev. Henry Charles Russell, *s.* of Lord Charles James Fox Russell, 6th *s.* of 6th Duke of Bedford and late Hon. Leila Louisa Millicent Willoughby, *d.* of 8th Baron Middleton; *m.* 1911, Evelyn Dorothea Temple, M.B.E. 1943, *d.* of Francis Moore; one *s.* one *d.* *Educ.:* Cheam School; Haileybury College; Trinity College, Cambridge. Entered Egyptian Civil Service as Inspector, Ministry Interior, 1902; Assistant Commandant Police, Alexandria, 1911; has 3rd Medjidie, 2nd Order of Nile, Commander Star of Roumania, 1st Class Order of Astaur (Afghanistan); Grand Officer, Crown of Italy, etc. *Publication:* Egyptian Service, 1949. *Recreations:* fishing and shooting. *Address:* 33 Chelsea Square, S.W.3. *Club:* Traveller '. [*Died* 10 *April* 1954.

RUSSELL, Rev. Vernon William, B.A.; *b.* 1861; 3rd *s.* of late Vernon Wm. Russell, J.P., of Rock Abbey, Cashel, Co. Tipperary. *Educ.:* Trinity College, Dublin; Trinity College of Music, London; Master of the Music, Westminster Cathedral, 1924-39. Chaplain of the Order of Knights of Malta, 1921; retired 1936. *Address:* Rock Abbey, Cashel, Co. Tipperary. [*Died* 24 *Jan.* 1953.

RUTH, Rev. Thomas E.; *b.* 17 Dec. 1875; *s.* of G. W. S. Ruth, Aveton Gifford, South Devon; *m.* Mabel, *er. d.* of W. M. Law, Bournemouth. *Educ.:* Bristol University. Pastorates at Portland Chapel, Southampton, and Princes Gate, Liverpool; Minister at Collins Street, Melbourne, Australia, 1914-23; Minister of the Pitt Street Congregational Church, Sydney, 1925-39; known for comprehensive churchmanship and progressive theology; weekly writings a feature of Australian newspapers. *Publications:* The Progress of Personality after Death; Playing the Game; Over the Garden Wall; Australia at the Cross-Roads; A Rendezvous with Life, etc. *Recreation:* golf. *Address:* 32 Karranga Avenue, Killara, N.S.W., Australia. [*Died* 29 *March* 1956.

RUTHERFORD, Very Rev. Claude Anselm, M.A.; Claustral Prior of Downside Abbey since 1946; *b.* 8 March 1886; *s.* of George Rutherford, late of Home Civil Service. *Educ.:* Dulwich College; King's College, Cambridge (Exhibitioner); Collegio Sant' Anselmo, Rome. Received into the Catholic Church by the late Monsignor R. H. Benson, 1906; joined the Benedictine Community at Downside, 1909; Priest, 1916; while Prior of S. John's Priory, Bath, 1923-32, built the Church of S. Alphege, Bath; First Prior of Worth Priory, Sussex, 1933-34; Headmaster of Downside School, 1934-39; Subprior of Downside Abbey, nr. Bath, 1939-40; Prior of Fort Augustus Abbey, Inverness, 1940-1944; Fourth Prior of Worth Priory, 1945-1946. *Publication:* Acts for Mental Prayer. *Address:* Downside Abbey, Bath. *T.:* Stratton-on-the-Fosse 295. [*Died* 25 *June* 1952.

RUTHERFORD, John Rutherford; Barrister-at-Law; Staff Capt. R.A.; farming Rutherford Burnside since 1946; *b.* 27 Aug. 1904; *s.* of John Rutherford Chalmers and late Almeria Edith Foster; changed name by Royal Licence to Rutherford, 1933; *m.* 1937, Doreen (marriage dissolved, 1947), *y. d.* of late C. F. Hilton and of Mrs. Hilton, Ashcombe, Devon; one *s.* one *d.* *Educ.:* Repton; Worcester College, Oxford. M.A. Hons., Law. Called to Bar, 1928; Municipal Reform candidate for Deptford, L.C.C. election, 1931; M.P. (U.) Edmonton, 1931-35. *Recreations:* boating, motoring. *Address:* Rutherford Lodge, Rutherford, Nr. Kelso, Roxburgh. *T.:* Maxton 7. *Clubs:* Carlton, Junior Carlton; New (Edinburgh). [*Died* 5 *July* 1957.

RUTHERFORD, Sir Thomas George, K.C.S.I., *cr.* 1943 (C.S.I. 1939); C.I.E. 1925; *b.* 25 Sept. 1886; *s.* of J. Rutherford, late H.M. Office of Works; *m.* 1926, Audrey Dickenson (*d.* 1955); one *d.* *Educ.:* George Watson's Coll., Edinburgh Univ.; Univ. College, London. Entered I.C.S. 1910 and served in Army, 1917-19 (East Persia); Collector and District Magistrate, Madras, 1921-38; Special Commissioner Agency operations, 1925; held various administrative posts, and acted as Secretary to Government, 1928-38; Governor's Secretary, Madras, 1938-39; Adviser to Governor, Madras, 1939-1943; Governor of Bihar, 1943-46; acted as Governor, Bengal, Sept. 1943-Jan. 1944. *Address:* Barwon Heads, Victoria, Australia. *Clubs:* East India and Sports; Melbourne. [*Died* 5 *Aug.* 1957.

RUTHERSTON, Albert Daniel, Hon. M.A., Oxford; R.W.S. 1942 (A.R.W.S. 1934); Artist and Designer; Ruskin Master of Drawing, Oxford University, 1929-49; *b.* Bradford, Yorkshire, 5 Dec. 1881; *s.* of Moritz Rothenstein and Bertha Dux; *m.* 1919, Marjory Holman; one *s.* (and one *s.* decd.). *Educ.:* Bradford Grammar School. Came to London in 1898 to study at Slade School, Univ. College, under Prof. Frederick Brown; worked there for four years. Served in Palestine, 1916-19, Lt. Northants. Regt. and Camp Commandant to H.Q. P.L. of C. Former member of N.E.A.C., where has exhibited pictures regularly since 1901; illustrated The Children's Blue Bird, by Mme. Maeterlinck; Cymbeline, for the Players' Shakespeare, the Cresset Herrick, the Soncino Haggadah, and other Fine Letter Press books; designer of decorations for The

Winter's Tale, Androcles and the Lion, Le Mariage Forcé, etc. Drawings and Paintings in public collections, Tate Gallery, National Portrait Gallery, British Museum, Victoria and Albert Museum Imperial War Museum, Ashmolean Museum, Bradford, Manchester, Newcastle, Gloucester, Sheffield, Brighton, Carlisle, Chicago, Melbourne, Leipzig, Dresden, etc. *Publications:* Decoration in the Art of the Theatre; Editor of Contemporary British Artists series; with John Drinkwater, a Memoir of Claud Lovat Fraser; Sixteen designs for the Theatre. *Recreation:* the Country. *Address:* 29 Burton Court, Lower Sloane Street, S.W.3. *T.:* Sloane 1922. *Club:* Athenæum. [*Died* 14 *July* 1953.

RUTHVEN, 9th Baron, Scotland, *cr.* 1651 (1st creation 1487); 2nd Baron, U.K., *cr.* 1919, **Walter Patrick Hore-Ruthven,** C.B. 1919; C.M.G. 1915; D.S.O. 1900; D.L., J.P.; Maj.-Gen.; *b.* London, 6 June 1870; *e. s.* of 8th Baron Ruthven and Lady Caroline Gore, *d.* of 4th Earl of Arran; *S.* father, 1921; *m.* 1st, 1895, Jean Leslie (*d.* 1952), *o. d.* of Norman Lampson, Pont St., S.W.; four *d.*; 2nd, 1953, Judith Gordon, *yr. d.* of late Bertie E. Bell. *Educ.:* Eton. Served South Africa, 1899-1901 (despatches thrice, Queen's medal with 9 clasps); European War, 1914-18 (despatches seven times, C.B., C.M.G., prom. Colonel); Commander Bangalore Brigade Area, 1920-24; G.O.C. London District, 1924-28; Lt.-Gov. of Guernsey, and commanding troops in Guernsey District 1929-1934; retired pay 1935. *Heir:* (to Scottish Barony only) *d.* Hon. Bridget Helen, C.B.E. 1947 [*m.* 1918, 11th Earl of Carlisle, J.P.; *m.* 1947, Sir Walter Monckton (later 1st Viscount Monckton of Brenchley, P.C., K.C.M.G., K.C.V.O., M.C., Q.C.)]; (to U.K. title), *g.n.* 2nd Earl of Gowrie. *Address:* Concora, Bembridge, Isle of Wight. *Club:* Royal Yacht Squadron (Cowes). [*Died* 16 *April* 1956.

RUTHVEN-MURRAY, Alan J.; *see* Murray, A. J. R.

RUTTLEDGE, Lieut.-Colonel Thomas Geoffrey, C.B.E. 1923; M.C.; *b.* 22 October 1882; *s.* of late T. F. Ruttledge, D.L., Westport Lodge, County Mayo; *m.* 1931, Phyllis Lilian, *d.* of W. Hopwood, of Great Barton, Suffolk; one *s.* one *d.* *Educ.:* Marlborough. Entered the Connaught Rangers, 1901; Major, 1916; transferred to the Green Howards, 1922; retired with rank of Lt.-Col. 1923; re-employed on staff, 1939-47; served South African war, 1902 (Queen's medal and 3 clasps); European War, 1914-18 (wounded, despatches four times, 1914 Star, War and Victory Medals, O.B.E., M.C., Chevalier Legion of Honour, Chevalier Belgian Order of Leopold, Belgian Croix de Guerre); War of 1939-45 (Defence and War Medals). *Address:* 3 Uplands Way, Highfield, Southampton. [*Died* 26 *June* 1958.

RUXTON, Major U. FitzHerbert, C.M.G. 1925; *b.* 8th Nov. 1873; *s.* of late Admiral W. F. Ruxton; *m.* 1906, Genevieve (*d.* 1942), *d.* of late Henri Rappin, Paris. *Educ.:* Wellington College. First Commission, Worcestershire Regiment, 1895; Captain, 1900; Major (Reserve of Officers), 1915; retired from the Army, 1911; seconded for service under the Royal Niger Company, 1898-1899; served South Africa, 1900 (severely wounded); entered Colonial Civil Service, 1901; served in Intelligence Division, Admiralty, 1915-18; Assistant Military Attaché, Berne, 1918; British High Commission, Constantinople, 1919-21; Lieutenant-Governor, Southern Provinces of Nigeria, 1925-29. *Publication:* Maliki Law, published by Government. *Club:* Royal Societies. [*Died* 2 *Sept.* 1954.

RYAN, Colonel Eugene, C.M.G. 1918; D.S.O. 1916; *b.* 1873. Entered R.A.M.C. 1901; Capt. 1904; Major, 1913; Brevet Lt.-Col. 1917; Brevet Colonel, 1926; served South African War, 1901-2; European War, 1914-18 (despatches 8 times, D.S.O., Legion of Honour, Brevet Lt.-Col., C.M.G.); Hon. Physician to the King, 1926-30; retired pay, 1930. *Address:* c/o Glyn, Mills & Co., Whitehall, S.W.1. [*Died* 11 *April* 1951.

RYAN, Mervyn Frederick, C.B.E. 1918; M.I.C.E.; M.I.E.E.; F.R.G.S.; late General Manager, Buenos Ayres and Pacific Railway; retired; *s.* of late Maj. C. A. Ryan, R.A.; *m.* 1st, Elizabeth (*d.* 1924), *d.* of late Francis Lochrane, Glasgow; two *s.*; 2nd, 1925, Muriel (*d.* 1938), *d.* of late H. N. Larden; 3rd, Mildred, *d.* of late John Cowes, Buenos Aires. *Educ.:* Stonyhurst; Univ. College, Nottingham. Engineering training M.R., General Electric Co., Schenectady & Pennsylvania R.R. Co.; Assistant Locomotive Works Manager, Midland Railway; Resident Locomotive Superintendent, Somerset and Dorset Railway; Assistant Chief Locomotive Engineer, London and South-Western Railway; Chief Mechanical Engineer, Central Argentine Railway; during European War Director of Munitions Gauges, Ministry of Munitions; Past Pres. of Inst. of Locomotive Engineers; ascended Mt. Aconcagua (23,080 ft.), Andes, 1925. *Recreations:* shooting, golf, fishing. *Address:* Quinta La Modesta, Bellavista, Buenos Aires. *Club:* Alpine. [*Died* 28 *April* 1952

RYAN, Most Rev. Richard, C.M.; Bishop of Sale, (R.C.), since 1926; *b.* Ireland, 1881. *Educ.:* St. Patrick's College, Armagh; St. Vincent's College, Castleknock; St. Joseph's College, Blackrock. Priest, 1907; Superior, House of Missions, Melbourne, 1919; Rector, St. Joseph's, Malvern, 1919; Bishop of Geraldton, 1923-26; Assistant at Pontifical Throne, 1948-. *Publication:* Eucharistic Hours. *Address:* St. Mary's Cathedral, Sale, Victoria, Australia. [*Died* 15 *June* 1957.

RYAN, Lieut.-Colonel Rupert Sumner, C.M.G. 1928; D.S.O. 1918; late R.A.; Member, Commonwealth House of Representatives for Flinders since 1940; *b.* 1884; *o. s.* of late Major-General Sir Charles Ryan, K.B.E.; *m.* 1924, Lady Rosemary Ferelith Hay (who obtained a divorce, 1935), *o. d.* of 21st Earl of Erroll; one *s.* *Educ.:* Harrow; R.M. Academy, Woolwich. Served European War (despatches five times, Brevet Lt.-Col., D.S.O.); British Deputy High Commissioner, Rhineland High Commission, Coblenz, 1920-29; retired pay, 1928. *Address:* Parliament House, Canberra, A.C.T. *Clubs:* Travellers', Flyfishers'. [*Died* 25 *Aug.* 1952.

RYAN, Wing-Comdr. William John, C.B.E. 1919 (O.B.E. 1919); late Royal Air Force; *s.* of William Ryan, Sligo; *b.* 1883; *m.* 1906, Gwendoline, *d.* of William Wood, A.S.C. Served South African War, 1901-02; European War, 1914-19 (despatches, M.B.E., O.B.E., C.B.E.); A.S.C., 1900-14; R.F.C. and R.A.F. 1914-31; retired list, 1931; War of 1939-45; Deputy Secretary R.A.F. Benevolent Fund, 1945-57. *Address:* Northendene, Court Dr., Hillingdon, Middlesex. *T.:* Uxbridge 3787. *Club:* R.A.F. [*Died* 1 *Feb.* 1959.

RYCROFT, Sir Nelson Edward Oliver, 6th Bt., *cr.* 1784; *b.* 19 Dec. 1886; *e. s.* of 5th Bt. and Lady Dorothea Hester Bluett-Wallop (*d.* 1906), *d.* of 5th Earl of Portsmouth; *S.* father, 1925; *m.* 1912, Ethel Sylvia (*d.* 1952), *d.* of Robert Nurton, Odcombe, Yeovil; one *s.* *Educ.:* Christ Church, Oxford; B.A.; Sheriff of County of Southampton, 1938. *Heir:* *s.* Richard Newton [*b.* 23 Jan. 1918; *m.* 1947, Ann, *d.* of late Hugh Bellingham-Smith and Mrs. Harvey Robarts; two *d.* *Educ.:* Winchester; Christ Church, Oxford. War of 1939-45 (despatches); Knights Cross of Royal Order of Phœnix with Swords]. *Address:* Clarks Hill Farm, Little Rissington, nr. Cheltenham, Glos. *T.:* Bourton on the Water 426. [*Died* 30 *Aug.* 1958.

S

SABATIER, Professor Paul; Professor of Chemistry, Toulouse University; Nobel Prize, 1912; Royal Society's Davy Medal, 1915; Membre Institut de France (Acad. Sc.), 1913; Foreign Member Royal Society, 1918. *Address:* Allée des Zéphyrs, 11, Toulouse. [*Died* 14 *Aug.* 1941.
[*But death not notified in time for inclusion in Who Was Who 1941–1950, first edn.*

SABIN, Arthur Knowles; writer, poet and printer; Officer-in-Charge of the Bethnal Green Museum, 1922-40; *b.* Rotherham, Yorks, 3 April 1879; 2nd *s.* of Thomas Sabin; *m.* 1st, 1903, Elizabeth Thompson; one *s.*; 2nd, 1919, Alma Otilie Kuher, Walmer (*d.* 1954); one *d.*; 3rd, 1959, Rose Wallace. Printed books by hand for the Samurai Press, of which he was one of the founders, 1907-09; several books for the Pear Tree Press, 1908-16; and for the Temple Sheen Press, which he owned from 1911; Technical Asst. in the Victoria and Albert Museum, 1909; Asst., 1917; Asst. Keeper, 1928; Keeper, 1935. Formerly: Trustee, Whitechapel Art Gallery; Hon. Consultant Geffrye Museum; Governor Parmiters Sch. and Charity. *Publications:* Typhon, and other Poems, 1902; The Death of Icarus, 1906; The Wayfarers, 1907; Dante and Beatrice, 1908; Medea and Circe, 1911; Five Poems, 1913; War Harvest, 1914; Christmas, 1914; a Poem; New Poems, 1915; War Posters (with Martin Hardie), 1920; East London Poems, 1931; several official publications of the Victoria and Albert and Bethnal Green Museums. *Address:* 26 Mountney Drive, Beachlands, Pevensey Bay, Sussex. [*Died* 19 *Oct.* 1959.

SACHSE, Sir Frederic Alexander, Kt., *cr.* 1938; C.S.I. 1935; C.I.E. 1930; I.C.S., retired; *b.* Liverpool, 27 Feb. 1878; *s.* of A. E Sachse; *m.* Hilda Margaret (*d.*1942), *d.* of Joseph Gatey, K.C.; one *s.* two *d.* *Educ.:* Liverpool College; Caius College, Cambridge. Entered I.C.S., 1902; was Settlement Officer, Mymensingh; Director of Land Records, Collector of Chittagong and Commissioner of Presidency Division; Member Board of Revenue, Bengal. *Publications:* Mymensingh Gazetteer and Mymensingh Settlement Report. *Address:* Annstead, Fleet, N. Hants. [*Died* 10 *Dec.* 1957.

SADLEIR, Michael; Author and Publisher; *b.* 25 Dec. 1888; *s.* of late Sir Michael Sadler, K.C.S.I., C.B.; *m.* 1914, Edith, 2nd *d.* of late Canon A. D. Tupper-Carey; one *s.* one *d.* (and one *s.* killed in action, 1940). *Educ.:* Rugby; Balliol College, Oxford, M.A. F.R.S.L. Director of Constable & Co. Ltd., 1920; Sandars Reader in Bibliography, Cambridge University, for 1937. President, Bibliographical Society, 1944 - 45. *Publications:* Political Career of Richard Brinsley Sheridan (Stanhope Essay), 1912; Privilege, 1921; Excursions in Victorian Bibliography, 1922; Desolate Splendour, 1923 (new ed. 1948); Daumier, 1924; The Noblest Frailty, 1925; Trollope: A Commentary, 1927 (new ed. 1945); Trollope: A Bibliography, 1928; Evolution of Publishers' Binding Styles, 1770-1900, 1930; Bulwer and his Wife, 1803-1836, 1931; Blessington-D'Orsay: a Masquerade, 1933 (new ed., 1947); These Foolish Things, 1927 (new ed., 1944); Fanny by Gaslight, 1940; Things Past, 1944; Forlorn Sunset, 1947; Michael Ernest Sadler; a Memoir by his Son, 1949; Nineteenth Century Fiction: a Bibliographical Record, 2 vols. 1951. *Clubs:* Garrick; Roxburghe, Grolier (N.Y.). [*Died* 15 *Dec.* 1957.

SADLER, Admiral Arthur Hayes, C.S.I. 1916; Commander Legion of Honour, 1916; *b.* 9 Oct. 1863; 3rd son of late Sir James Hayes Sadler, K.C.M.G. Entered Navy, 1877; Captain 1904; Rear-Admiral, 1915; Vice-Adm., 1919; Admiral, 1924; served Egyptian War, 1882 (medal with clasp, bronze star); European War, 1914-18 (C.S.I.); retired list, 1924. *Club:* Naval and Military. [*Died* 9 *Feb.* 1952.

SAINT AULAIRE, Comte de; *b.* 13 Aug. 1866; *m.* *d.* of Comte Balny d'Avricourt; one *s.* two *d.* *Educ.:* The Paris Law University; is a licencié en droit and diplomé de l'Ecole des Sciences politiques. Attaché to the Foreign Office in Paris, 1892; Secretary of Embassy at the French Legations in Chili, Peru, Cairo, Tangiers; First Secretary at Vienna, 1909-12; French Minister in Morocco, 1912-16; in Rumania, 1916-19; French Ambassador in Madrid, 1920; French Ambassador in London, 1920-24; Grand Officer of the Legion of Honour, 1924. *Address:* Avenue Rapp 19, Paris (viie). *Club:* Union (Paris). [*Died* 27 *Sept.* 1954.

ST. CLAIR, Major-Gen. George James Paul, C.B. 1945; C.B.E. 1944; D.S.O. 1917; R.A.; *b.* 1885; *e. s.* of late Hon. L. M. St. Clair; *m.* 1911, Charlotte Theresa Orme, *d.* of Major Archibald Cosmo Little; one *s.* three *d.* *Educ.:* Royal Military Academy, Woolwich. Served European War, 1914-17 (wounded, despatches, D.S.O.); Lt.-Col., 1933; Col., 1937; A.A.G. War Office, 1937-40; Temp. Maj.-Gen., 1941; retired pay, 1945. D.L. Glos. 1953; High Sheriff of Gloucestershire, 1954. *Address:* Upton House, Tetbury, Glos. *Clubs:* Cavalry, Naval and Military. [*Died* 13 *Nov.* 1955.

ST. GERMANS, 8th Earl of, *cr.* 1815; **Montague Charles Eliot;** K.C.V.O., *cr.* 1934 (C.V.O. 1928; M.V.O. 1923); O.B.E. 1919; Baron Eliot, 1784; *b.* 13 May 1870; 2nd *s.* of late Col. Hon. C. G. C. Eliot, C.V.O.; (6th *s.* of 3rd Earl); *S.* brother, 1942; *m.* 1910, Helen Agnes Post, *d.* of Lady Barrymore and late Arthur Post, U.S.A.; two *s.* one *d.* *Educ.:* Charterhouse; Exeter College, Oxford, B.A., Honours in Classics and Jurisprudence, called to the Bar, 1895 (Inner Temple); Director (St. James's Street Branch) of the Alliance Assurance Company; Senior Scholar and Exhibitioner, Charterhouse School; Classical Scholar, Exeter College, Oxford; Groom-in-Waiting to King Edward VII., 1908-10; Gentleman Usher, 1901-08; Gentleman Usher to King George V., 1911-36; Groom of the Robes, 1920-36; Extra Groom-in-Waiting to the Queen since 1952 (to King George V, 1924-36, to King George VI, 1937-52); Lt.-Commander, R.N.V.R., 1914. *Heir:* *s.* Lord Eliot. *Address:* 88 St. James's Street, S.W.1. *T.:* Whitehall 5886; Port Eliot, St. Germans, Cornwall. *T.:* St. Germans 221. *Club:* Turf. [*Died* 19 *Sept.* 1960.

ST. JOHN, Lieut.-Colonel Sir (Henry) Beauchamp, K.C.I.E., *cr.* 1930 (C.I.E. 1913); C.B.E. 1920; Indian Political Service (retired); *b.* 26 August, 1874; *s.* of Colonel Sir Oliver B. C. St. John, K.C.S.I., R.E.; *m.* Olive, *d.* of late Col. C. Herbert, C.S.I.; one *s.* *Educ.:* R.M. Coll. Sandhurst. Entered Army, 1893; attached 32nd Duke of Cornwall's Light Infantry; transferred to Indian Staff Corps, 1894, and served with 45th Rattray's Sikhs; entered Political Department, 1898; served on N.-W. Frontier of India, 1897-98 — Defence of Malakand, Relief of Chakdara, Malakand, action of Landakai, operations in Bajaur and in the Mamund country; Tirah, 1897-98; operations with the Bara Valley, 7 to 14 Dec. 1897 (medal with 3 clasps); Afghan War, 1919 (C.B.E., despatches); amongst many political appointments has held that of Agent to the Governor-General, Punjab States, 1925-27; Agent to the Governor-General and Chief Commissioner in Baluchistan, 1927-30; after retirement returned to India in 1933; Prime Minister Jaipur State, Rajputana, 1933-39. *Address:* Curtle Cottage, Beaulieu, Hants. *Club:* United Service. [*Died* 5 *Oct.* 1954.

ST. JOHN, Major-General Richard Stukeley, C.B. 1927; C.I.E. 1919; D.S.O.

1917; Indian Army, retired; *b.* 15 Jan. 1876; 2nd *s.* of R.F. St. A. St. John and Julia Louisa, *e.d.* of Rev. William Churchill; *m.* 1905, Edwardine Annie Georgina, *d.* of late Capt. L. A. Jourdier, 20th French Dragoons. Served European War, 1914-18 (despatches, D.S.O.); Japanese Order of the Sacred Treasure; India and China medals; Serbian Order of Karageorge (with crossed swords); commanded Lahore Brigade Area, 1922-26; Maj.-Gen., 1926; D.A. and Q.M.G., N. Command, India, 1926-29; retired, 1929. [*Died* 6 *June* 1959.

ST. JOHN-MILDMAY, Rev. Sir Neville; *see* Mildmay, Rev. Sir A. N. St. J.

ST. OSWALD, 3rd Baron (*cr.* 1885), **Rowland George Winn,** late Captain Coldstream Guards and R.A.F.; *e. s.* of 2nd Baron and Mabel, *d.* of Sir Charles Forbes, 4th Bt.; *b.* 29 July 1893; *m.* 1915, Eva Greene, *d.* of Charles Greene; two *s.*; *S.* father, 1919. *Educ.:* Eton. Served European War, 1914 (wounded). *Heir: s.* Hon. Rowland Denys Guy Winn, M.C., Major 8th King's Royal Irish Hussars [*b.* 19 Sept. 1916; *m.* 1st, 1952, Laurian (marriage dissolved, 1955), *o. d.* of Sir Roderick Jones, K.B.E.; 2nd, 1955, Marie Wanda, *y. d.* of Sigismund Jaxa-Chamiec]. *Address:* Hillhampton, Sunningdale, Berkshire. *T.:* Ascot 991. *Clubs:* White's; Royal Yacht Squadron. [*Died* 25 *Feb.* 1957.

SAIYID, FAZL ALI, Sir, Kt., *cr.* 1941; Chairman, States Reorganisation Commission; Governor of Orissa, 1952-54; *b.* 19 Sept. 1886; *s.* of Saiyid Nazir Ali; *m.* 1908; two *s.* three *d.* *Educ.:* London Mission High School, Benares; Queen's College, Benares; Muir Central College, Allahabad. B.A. Allahabad Univ. (stood first in the whole University); called to Bar, Middle Temple, 1912 (First Class in Bar Final); commenced practice in Behar in 1912; officiated as Chief Justice of High Court, Patna, for about two months in 1938; was sole member of Conciliation Bd., appointed to settle certain industrial disputes in Jamshedpur (Bihar), 1938; Puisne Judge, 1928-43; Chief Justice, High Court, Patna, 1943-47; Chm., R.I.N. Mutiny Commn., 1946; Member, Calcutta Disturbances Commn. of Enquiry, 1946-47; Judge, Federal Court, India, 1947; Member, Ind. Deleg. to U.N.O. Gen. Assembly, 1947, Chm. of Fifth Cttee. of U.N. Judge of the Supreme Court of India, 1950-52. Fellow of Patna Univ.; Member of Managing Committee of Patna Museum. *Recreations:* formerly cricket and tennis, now golf. *Address:* 32 Aurangzeb Road, New Delhi, India. [*Died* 22 *Aug.* 1959.

SAKLATVALA, Sir Sorabji Dorabji, Kt., *cr.* 1941; Member Bombay Legislative Assembly; Director Tata Sons, Ltd., Bombay. *Address:* Tata Sons, Ltd., Bombay. [*Died* 18 *Oct.* 1948.
[*But death not notified in time for inclusion in Who Was Who 1941–1950, first edn.*

SALAMAN, Redcliffe Nathan, F.R.S. 1935; F.L.S.; M.D., M.A. Cantab.; J.P., Herts; late Director of Potato Virus Research Station, University of Cambridge; Vice-President and Hon. Fellow, National Institute of Agricultural Botany; Trustee of Jews' College; Governor Hebrew University, Jerusalem; late Chairman of Justices, Odsey division of Herts; Commissioner of Taxes; Trustee Barley Parish Charities; *b.* 12 Sept. 1874; *s.* of late Myer Salaman, Mill Hill; *m.* 1st, Nina (*d.* 1925), *d.* of Arthur Davis; three *s.* two *d.*; 2nd, Gertrude, *d.* of Ernest D. Lowy. *Educ.:* St. Paul's School (exhibitioner); Trinity Hall, Cambridge (scholar; Hon. Fellow, 1955); London Hospital; House Physician, Clinical Assistant, Sutton Scholar. Director of Pathological Institute, London Hospital, 1901-04; temporary Captain R.A.M.C., 1914-19 (despatches); conducted research on the genetics of the potato and other subjects at Barley, 1906-26. *Publications:* Palestine Reclaimed, 1920; Potato Varieties, 1926; contributions relating to Pathology to Trans. Path. Soc., Proc. of Zoological Society and Lancet, etc.; Heredity in Journal of Genetics and Journal of Agricultural Science; the Anthropology of the Jews to Trans. Jewish Historical Society, Palestine Quarterly Statement, etc.; Virus Disease of Potato, Trans. and Proc. Royal Soc. B.; History of the Potato, Journal R.H.S., 1937; The Influence of the Potato on the Course of Irish History, Finlay Lecture, Dublin, 1943; The History and Social Influence of the Potato, 1949; Lucien Wolf Lecture, 1953. *Recreations:* walking, travelling. *Address:* Homestall, Barley, Royston, Herts. *T.A.:* Barley, Herts. *T.:* Barkway 252. *Club:* Athenæum. [*Died* 12 *June* 1955.

SALE, Hon. Mr. Justice Stephen Leonard, J.P.; *b.* 30 Sept. 1889; *s.* of late Sir S. G. Sale, K.C.I.E., and Lady Sale, Midhurst, Sussex; *m.* 1915, Edith Touche; two *d.* *Educ.:* Marlborough College; New College, Oxford. Entered Indian Civil Service, 1914. Barrister-at-Law. Judge, High Court, Lahore, 1939-48; retired, 1948. J.P. Oxon., 1949; Deputy Chairman, Quarter Sessions, Oxon., 1952; Chairman, Oxford and Area Rent Tribunal. *Address:* Rose Mount, 50 Rose Hill, Oxford. *T.:* Oxford 77224. [*Died* 11 *March* 1958.

SALMON, Balliol, artist; *b.* 1 June 1868; *s.* of Henry Curwen Salmon, F.C.S., F.G.S., Barrister, and Ellen Fennell; *m.* 1909, Dorothy Rodham; three *s.* one *d.* *Educ.:* privately; studied art under Prof. Brown, afterwards in Paris at Julian's. The pursuit of art has been his whole career; first as a pupil, for a short time as a teacher, and now for many years as a black-and-white artist on the Graphic and other papers. *Recreations:* golf and music. *Address:* 9 South Parade, Bedford Park, W.4. *T.:* Chiswick 0897; Sidegate, Sparke, Northiam, Sussex. [*Died* 3 *Jan.* 1953.

SALMON, Edward, O.B.E. 1928; *b.* 1865; *m.* Maud Mary Jeacock (*d.* 1942); two *s.* two *d.* *Educ.:* St. Mark's, Chelsea; privately. Editor Home News for India and Australia, 1889-99; Assistant Editor and Managing Director Saturday Review, 1899-1913; Edited the British Dominions Year-Book, 1916-24; Editor United Empire, 1920-37, hon. Editor, 1941-46; toured Canada as representative of the Royal Empire Society, 1928 and the Rhodesias, 1939; contributor Nineteenth Century, National, Fortnightly, Strand, Outlook, and other periodicals. *Publications:* Juvenile Literature as it Is, 1888; The Story of the Empire, 1900, 2nd edition, 1910; Lord Salisbury; Life of General Wolfe, 1909; Life of Admiral Sir Charles Saunders, 1914; Shakespeare and Democracy, 1917; The Literature of the Empire, 1924. *Address:* High House, Sewardstonebury, E.4. *Clubs:* Royal Empire Society, Savage. [*Died* 15 *Sept.* 1955.

SALMON, Col. Geoffrey Nowell, C.M.G. 1918; D.S.O. 1915; late the Rifle Brigade; *b.* 26 Nov. 1871; *s.* of late Admiral of the Fleet Sir Nowell Salmon, V.C., G.C.B., and Emily, *d.* of late Eramus Saunders of Westbrook Priory, Dorset; *m.* 1917, Gwladys, *e. d.* of Mrs. Francis Lawson, Pieta, Malta; one *s.* Entered army, 1894; Capt. 1900; Maj. 1912; Lt.-Col. 1915; Adjutant and Commandant Mounted Infantry, Malta, 1904-06; S. Africa, 1906-10; served S. African War, 1899-1902 (despatches, Queen's medal 3 clasps, King's medal 2 clasps); European War, 1914-18 (D.S.O., C.M.G., American Distinguished Service Medal, 1918); retired pay, 1926. *Address:* 24 St. Thomas Street, Winchester. *Club:* United Service. [*Died* 7 *Dec.* 1954.

SALMON, Percy R. (Richard Penlake), F.R.P.S.; Journalist and Photographic Expert; *b.* Waterbeach, 12 March 1872. *Educ.:* Cambridge. Sub-editor Practical Photographer, and Junior Photographer,

1895-98; Editor of the Photographic News, 1901-06; Editor of Year Book of Photography, 1901-05; Acting Editor, Photographic Dealer, 1907-09; Sub-editor Building World, 1917-18. *Publications:* Trick Photography, 1906; Photographic Formulæ and Recipes, 1907; A Photographic Expedition to Egypt, Palestine, Turkey, and Greece, 1903; Home Portraiture for Amateur Photographers, 1889; Developers, their Use and Abuse, 1895; The Artful Amateur, 1894; Colouring Photographs, etc., 1911; Book of Palestine for Boys and Girls, 1913; The Wonderland of Egypt, 1915; The Story of Our Empire, 1920; All about Photography, 1925; travelled extensively in France, Belgium, Italy, Asia Minor, Palestine, Lebanon, Turkey, Greece, and Egypt; now on the staffs of several journals (English, Australian, and American), contributing articles dealing with photography, travel, foreign and general matters. *Recreations:* countryside antiquities, folklore. *Address:* Fordham, Nr. Ely, Cambs. *Club:* Royal Photographic. [*Died* 23 *Aug.* 1959.

SALMOND, Robert Williamson Asher, O.B.E., M.D., Ch.M., D.P.H., D.M.R.E.; retired; Consulting Radiologist, University College Hospital, London; *b.* 1883; *s.* of late Robert Salmond, Aberdeen; *m.* Amelia Maude, *e. d.* of J. Thomlinson, late of Tonford Manor, Canterbury; one *d.* *Educ.:* Grammar School and Marischal College, Aberdeen; Cambridge University; St. Bartholomew's Hospital. Late Assistant to the Professor of Anatomy, Aberdeen University; Deputy Consulting Radiologist, British Armies in France (despatches); Director Radiological Dept., Univ. Coll. Hosp., London; Gen. Hosp. Barbados. *Publications:* numerous contrib. on medical X-ray subjects. *Address:* Landfall, Sandy Lane, St. James, Barbados, B.W.I. [*Died* 2 *Sept.* 1953.

SALOWAY, Sir Reginald (Harry), K.B.E., *cr.* 1954 (O.B.E. 1942); C.M.G. 1951; C.I.E. 1947; Controller of Operations, Colonial Development Corporation, 1955; *b.* 26 October 1905; *s.* of late Henry Saloway, Bridport, Dorset; *m.* 1930, Betty Louisa Jenkins, Kaisar-i-Hind Bronze Medal, *d.* of late Mrs. W. J. Cavill, Torquay, Devon; no *c.* *Educ.:* Exeter School; St. John's College, Cambridge. Entered I.C.S., 1928; Secretary Board of Revenue, U.P., 1936; Revenue and Finance Minister, Rampur State, 1937-44; Director General Resettlement and Employment, Govt. of India, 1946. Gold Coast: Sec. Rural Development, 1947-1950; Colonial Sec., 1950; Chief Secretary and Minister of Defence and External Affairs, and periodically acted as Governor, 1951-54. *Recreations:* shooting, fishing and tennis. *Address:* 18 Prince of Wales Terrace, W.8. *Clubs:* East India and Sports, Royal Commonwealth Society. [*Died* 1 *Oct.* 1959.

SALT, Sir John William Titus, 4th Bt., *cr.* 1869; Commander, R.N., retd.; *o. s.* of 3rd Bt. and Charlotte, *d.* of Very Rev. John Cotter MacDonnell, D.D., Canon of Peterborough, Rector of Misterton; *b.* 30 Nov. 1884; *S.* father, 1920; *m.* 1st, 1913, Dorothy (who divorced him, 1925), *e. d.* of Col. W. Baker Brown, late R.E.; 2nd, 1926, Stella Houlton, 2nd *d.* of Richard Houlton Jackson, M.R.C.S., L.R.C.P., Bakewell, Derbyshire; three *s.* *Heir:* *s.* David Shirley, *b.* 14th June 1930. *Address:* Park House, Cookham, Berks. *T.:* Bourne End 92. [*Died* 22 *Jan.* 1953.

SALTER, Rev. Herbert Edward, Hon. D.Litt.Oxon, 1933; M.A.; F.B.A.; *b.* London, 6 Feb. 1863; *s.* of Dr. Hyde Salter, F.R.S.; *m.* 1st, 1893, Beatrice Eva (*d.* 1932), *d.* of Rev. J. Ruddach; two *d.*; 2nd, 1933, Gladys Nina, *er. d.* of late Douglas Dewar. *Educ.:* Winchester College; New College, Oxford; 2nd class Classical Moderations, 1st class Lit. Hum., 1st class Theology, Cuddesdon College. Deacon, 1888; Priest, 1889; Curate of Sandhurst, Berks, 1888-91; Vice-Principal of Leeds Clergy School, 1891-93; Vicar of Mattingley, Hants, 1893-99; Vicar of Shirburn, Oxon. 1899-1909; Ford's Lecturer in English History, Oxford, 1934-1935; Research Fellow of Magdalen College, Oxford, 1918 - 39. Hon. Freeman City of Oxford, 1930. *Publications:* The Cartulary of Eynsham Abbey, 2 vols.; The Cartulary of the Hospital of St. John the Baptist, 3 vols.; A Subsidy in the Diocese of Lincoln, 1526; Hearne's Collections, vols. ix., x. and xi.; Balliol Oxford Deeds; A Survey of Oxford in 1772; Coroners' Rolls of Oxford; Munimenta Civitatis Oxon; The University Archives, 2 vols.; Snappe's Formulary; Registrum Collegii Mertonensis; Oxford City Properties; Oriel Records; Oxford Town Council Acts, 1583-1626; The Borstall Cartulary; The Cartulary of Oseney Abbey (6 vols.); Newington Longeville Charters; Oxfordshire Feet of Fines; Registrum Cancellarii Oxon (2 vols.); Churchwardens' Accounts of St. Michael's, Oxford; Lectures on the History of Oxford; A Map of Mediaeval Oxford; The Early History of St. John's College; Oxford Surveys and Tokens; Facsimiles of Oxford Charters; The Cartulary of Thame Abbey. *Address:* Broad Oak, Sturminster Newton, Dorset. [*Died* 23 *April* 1951.

SALTER DAVIES, Ernest, C.B.E. 1932; M.A. (Oxon); Hon. M.A. Adelaide, 1937; Chm., Carnegie United Kingdom Trust, 1946-1951, Life Trustee since 1924; Trustee and Member Exec. Cttee., and Chm. of Trustees, National Central Library; member Teachers Registration Council, 1946; *b.* 25 October 1872; *s.* of Rev. Thomas Davies, Haverfordwest; *m.* 1900, Evelyn May (*d.* 1951), *d.* of Captain William Lile, J.P., Tenby; two *s.* *Educ.:* Haverfordwest Grammar School; University College, Aberystwyth; Jesus College, Oxford (Classical Scholar). Master at Glasgow Academy, 1895-96; Cheltenham Grammar School, 1897-1904; Inspector for Higher Education, Kent Education Committee, 1904-18; Director of Education for Kent, 1918-38; President, Association of Directors and Secretaries for Education, 1924; President, New Education Fellowship (English Section), 1932-33; President Library Association, 1935; Expert Adviser (English), Army Education, 1918; Educational Adviser H.M. Prison, Maidstone, 1923-38; Chairman National Committee for Regional Library Co-operation until 1949; Member Ministry of Agriculture Committee on Higher Agricultural Education, 1940; Central Council for School Broadcasting (Chm. Rural Schools Committee) until 1948. *Publications:* The Aim of Education (National Adult School Union); The Reorganisation of Education in England (New Education Fellowship); Education for Industry and for Life; Technical Education (The Schools of England); etc. Editor, school editions of Kenilworth, The Fortunes of Nigel. Editor of the Journal of Education, 1939-. *Address:* Amen House, Warwick Square, E.C.4; 13 Chichester Road, East Croydon, Surrey. *Club:* English-Speaking Union. [*Died* 10 *June* 1955.

SALUSBURY, Frederic George Hamilton Piozzi; Editor, Greek Review, Athens; *b.* 17 Nov. 1895; *s.* of late F. H. Salusbury, Barrister-at-law, and Isabel, *d.* of Hon. W. H. Suttor, M.L.C., N.S.W.; *m.* 1922, Joan, *d.* of late Major H. A. Cummins, C.M.G.; one *d.* *Educ.:* Grammar Sch. and Univ., Sydney. Served with King's Shropshire Light Inf., 1915-19 (wounded); Judge's Associate, High Court of Australia, 1920-21; Free-lance journalist and film actor, 1922-23; joined Daily Express, 1924; Daily Herald, 1936, "The Showman"; War Corresp., France and Middle East, 1939-45; formerly Daily Herald Correspondent in Greece and Middle East; Editor Egyptian Gazette, 1952-54. *Publications:* King Emperor's Jubilee, 1935;

George V and Edward VIII, 1936. *Club:* Union. [*Died* 17 *April* 1957.

SALUSBURY-TRELAWNY, Sir J. W. R. M.; *see* Trelawny.

SALVEMINI, Gaetano; Lauro de Bosis lecturer in History of Italian Civilisation, Harvard, 1934; Emeritus, 1948; *b.* Molfetta, Italy, 8 Sept. 1873. *Educ.:* University of Florence. Secondary School teacher, 1895-1901; Professor of Modern History at the University of Messina, 1901-08; at the University of Pisa, 1910-16; at the University of Florence, 1916-25; at the University of Florence since 1950; Member of the Italian Chamber, 1919-21; arrested June 1925, as an opponent of the Fascist Dictatorship; left Italy, Aug. 1925; resigned his Chair, 5 Nov. 1925: dismissed as an absentee, Dec. 1925; deprived of Italian citizenship with confiscation of property, 30 Sept. 1926; visiting Professor, Harvard, 1930, Yale, 1932. *Publications:* La Dignità Cavalleresca nel Comune di Firenze, 1896; Magnati e Popolani nel Comune di Firenze, 1900; Mazzini, 1905 (Eng. trans. 1956); La Rivoluzione Francese, 1906 (Eng. trans. 1954); La riforma delle Scuola Media, 1908; Come siamo andati in Libia, 1913; La Questione dell' Adriatico, 1918; Il Partito Popolare e la Questione Romana, 1922; Dal Patto di Londra alla Pace di Roma, 1925; The Fascist Dictatorship in Italy, 1927; Mussolini Diplomate, 1931; Under the Axe of Fascism, 1936; Italian Fascism, 1938; Historian and Scientist, 1939; (with George La Piana) How to Deal with Italy, 1943; La Politica Estera dell' Italia dal 1871 al 1915, 1946; I Clericali e la Scuola, 1951; Prelude to World War Two, 1952; Scritti sulla Questione Meridionale, 1955. *Club:* Harvard Faculty (Cambridge, Mass.). [*Died* 6 *Sept.* 1957.

SAMMAN, Sir Henry, 2nd Bt., *cr.* 1921, of Routh; M.C.; *b.* 18 Feb. 1881; *s.* of 1st Bt. and Elizabeth, *d.* of John Sanders of Kiddington, Oxfordshire; *S.* father, 1928; *m.* 1914, Ellis Watson, *d.* of B. Boyes of King's Mill, Driffield. *Educ.:* Rugby. Lieut. R.F.A. (T.A.); served S. Africa, 1901-2 (Queen's medal five clasps); European War, 1914-19 (despatches, M.C.); patron of one living. *Heir:* none. *Address:* Browsholm, Cottingham, E. Yorks. [*Died* 1 *Dec.* 1960 (*ext.*).

SAMMONS, Albert E., C.B.E. 1944; F.R.C.M.; Hon. R.A.M.; Prof. of Violin, Roy. Coll. of Music, London; Solo Violinist, at the Sir Thomas Beecham, B.B.C., London Symphony Philharmonic, Hallé, and Scottish orchestras and leading festivals; late leader of the London String Quartette Chamber Music Players, Russian Ballet (Berlin and Covent Garden) and late leader and soloist of Monteux's orchestra, Dieppe; sometime member of H.M.'s private band; *b.* London, 23 Feb. 1886; *s.* of Thomas Sammons and Anne Jackson; *m.* Olive, *e. d.* of late Alfred and of Ethel Hobday; three *d.* *Educ.:* privately. *Works:* Secret of Technique and many violin solos. *Address:* Pembridge, North Avenue, Southdean, nr. Bognor Regis, Sussex. [*Died* 24 *Aug.* 1957.

SAMMUT, Oscar, C.B.E. 1943; *b.* 9 May 1879; *s.* of Enrico Sammut and Virginia Laferla; *m.* 1910, Emily, *d.* of Antoine Briffa, LL.D., and Louise Rutter; three *s.* *Educ.:* Lyceum, Valletta, Malta. Entered Malta Civil Service, 1899; Collector of Imposts and Lotto, Malta, 1937-45; Acting Director of Agriculture, Malta, 1940-1941; Land Valuation Officer, Malta, 1941-1945; Member of Council of Govt., Malta, 1945-47; a Director of Malta Hotels Co. Ltd., 1948-52. *Recreation:* gardening. *Address:* 38 Cathedral Street, Sliema, Malta, G.C. *T.:* 1250. *Club:* Casino Maltese (Valletta). [*Died* 24 *July* 1959.

SAMS, Sir Hubert Arthur, Kt., *cr.* 1931; C.I.E. 1919; *b.* 3 May 1875; *s.* of J. H. Sams; *m.* 1902, Millicent Helen Langford; two *s.* *Educ.:* St. Paul's School, London; Peterhouse, Cambridge. Entered I.C.S., 1899; Punjab Commission, 1899; Assistant Commissioner, 1899-1907; officiating Deputy Commissioner, 1903-7; Postmaster-General Bengal and Assam, 1907-8; Bengal, 1908-11; Burma, 1911-13; Bombay, 1913-14; Central Circle, 1914-17; Director of Postal Services M.E.F. Mesopotamia, 1917-19, Lt.-Col. R.E. (C.I.E., despatches thrice); Postmaster-General, Bombay, 1920-22; Deputy Director-General Posts and Telegraphs, 1922-27; Officiating D.-G., 1922-23, 1924, 1926; Director-General, 1927-31; Member, Indian Legislative Assembly, 1923-31; Bursar and Fellow of Peterhouse, Cambridge, 1932-40, Emeritus Fellow, 1940; Bursar, Steward and Fellow of Selwyn Coll., Cambridge, 1941-44; Cambridge Borough Council, 1932-40, 1942-1944; President, Cambridge Y.M.C.A., 1932-1940; A Governor of St. Paul's School and St. Paul's Girls' School, 1938-54. *Publications:* The Post Office of India in the Great War, 1922; Pauline and Old Pauline. *Address:* c/o Lloyds Bank Ltd., 6 Pall Mall, S.W.1. *Club:* Over-Seas. [*Died* 9 *June* 1957.

SAMSON, Colonel Arthur Oliver, C.B.E. 1943; T.D.; M.I.Mech.E.; Director of Companies; late Chief Electrical and Mechanical Engineer, No. 7 Base Workshops, M.E.F.; *b.* 21 Jan. 1888; *s.* of Arthur Alfred Samson, late of C.T.O., London; *m.* 1910, May Tyson Woodman; no *c.* *Educ.:* Friern Barnet Grammar School; London Univ. Wilson & Pilcher Ltd., Westminster; Sir W. G. Armstrong Whitworth & Co. Ltd. Raised and commanded M.T. Section 2nd London Div. T.F. in 1909 to outbreak of war 1914. Commanded M.T. Units throughout war, including Base Heavy Repair Workshops. Inspector of M.T., Egypt, 2½ years last war. 1939, created largest Tank Repair Workshop, under one roof, in the world and in command until disbanded in 1946. Past Asst. Grand Dir. of Ceremonies, United Grand Lodge of Eng. *Recreation:* yacht racing (2 yachts). *Address:* 57 Rue Lavison, Bulkeley, Ramleh, Egypt. *T.A.:* Arthur Samson, Alexandria, Egypt. *T.:* Ramleh 63612. *Clubs:* Royal Corinthian Yacht (Burnham-on-Crouch); Royal Yacht Club of Egypt, British Boat, Union, Sporting (Alexandria), etc. [*Died* 4 *Nov.* 1955.

SAMUEL, Colonel Frederick Dudley, C.B.E. 1938; D.S.O. 1917; T.D.; a Director of M. Samuel & Co. Ltd.; *s.* of late Joseph Samuel; *b.* 1877; *m.* 1909, Dorothy, *d.* of late Meyer Salaman. *Educ.:* City of London School. Served South African War, 1901-2 (medal with three clasps); European War, 1914-18 (wounded, despatches four times, D.S.O. with bar). *Address:* 15 Orchard Court, W.1. *T.:* Welbeck 6380; Loxboro House, Bledlow Ridge, High Wycombe. *T.:* Radnage 286. *Clubs:* Flyfishers', Savile. [*Died* 1 *Jan.* 1951.

SAMUEL, His Honour Judge Howel Walter, Q.C. 1931; Barrister-at-law; Judge of County Courts on Circuit No. 28 (Mid-Wales) since 1933; Chairman, Radnorshire Quarter Sessions; *b.* Swansea, 1881; *m.* 1911, Harriott Sawyer Polkinghorne (*d.* 1939); *m.* 1941, Lady Gregg, *widow* of Sir Henry Gregg. M.P. (Lab.) Swansea West, 1923-24 and 1929-31; Recorder of Merthyr Tydfil, 1930-33. *Address:* Llandrindod Wells; 24 Corrymore Mansions, Swansea. [*Died* 5 *April* 1953.

SAMUELS, Moss T.; *see* Turner-Samuels.

SAMUELSON, Sir Herbert, K.B.E., *cr.* 1922; a Knight of Grace of the Order of St. John of Jerusalem; *b.* 23 Jan. 1865; *s.* of late Rt. Hon. Sir Bernhard Samuelson, Bt., P.C., F.R.S.; *m.* 1896, Sybil Charlotte Eleanor, *d.* of Hon. Walter and Lady Eleanor Harbord; one *s.* (and one *s.* killed in action, 1917). *Educ.:* Rugby. Chairman and Treasurer University College Hosp., 1927-37. *Address:* 2 Greenaway Gardens, Hampstead, N.W.3. *T.:* Hampstead 5852. *Club:* White's. [*Died* 5 *Sept.* 1952.

SANDBACH, John Brown, K.C. 1925; Metropolitan Police Magistrate, 1926-47; 2nd *s.* of late Rev. Francis B. Sandbach; *m.* Helen Vawdrey Sandbach (*d.* 1951); two *s.* two *d.* *Educ.:* The Leys School and King's College, Cambridge. Called to Bar, Inner Temple, 1902; Northern Circuit. Retired, 1947. *Publications:* The Law of Motor Cars; This Old Wig. *Recreations:* golf, travel. *Address:* St. Yves, Northwood, Middlesex. *T.:* Northwood 580. [*Died* 27 *Aug.* 1951.

SANDEMAN, Christopher, F.L.S., F.R.G.S.; author, playwright, lecturer, traveller, plant-collector; *b.* 25 Nov. 1882; *s.* of late Walter A. Sandeman, Morden House, Royston, Cambs., and Constance Fenwick; unmarried. *Educ.:* Eton; Christ Church, Oxford. Resided many years in Germany, France and Spain (and speaks the languages of these three countries fluently). Has travelled widely. In Peru descended Huallaga River by raft, and in remote districts collected botanical specimens for Herbaria of Kew Gardens and Univ. of Oxford, each of which has received from him some 6000 specimens, many being unknown to science. Made journey of exploration from Rio de Janeiro to Lima, 1942. Served European War, 1914-18: Intelligence Corps, B.E.F., France, Aug. 1914; War of 1939-45: a regular during 1940 in War Dept. Constabulary, London. *Publications:* Hohenzollerndämmerung (illustr. Glyn Philpot), 1917; Private and Confidential, 1935; A Forgotten River, 1939; Thyme and Bergamot, 1947; A Wanderer in Inca Land (photographs by author), 1948. Plays include: The Widow's Might (with L. Huskinson), Haymarket, 1916; The Temptation of Eve (with Désirée Welby), Q Theatre and tour. Broadcasts, articles, lectures, etc. *Recreations:* gardening, photography, reading, play-going, visiting picture galleries, travelling any way except by aeroplane. *Address:* 51 Redcliffe Gardens, S.W.10. *T.:* Fremantle 8306. *Clubs:* St. James', Beefsteak. [*Died* 20 *April* 1951.

SANDEMAN, Edward, M.Sc., M.Inst. C.E., M.I.W.E.; F.R.M.S. consulting civil engineer; *b.* 8 Dec. 1862; 5th *s.* of late Wm. Sandeman of Hollin Bank, Church, Lancashire; *m.* Edith Mary, *d.* of William P. Vosper, Merafield, Plympton St. Mary, Devon; two *s.* Constructed works for supplying Plymouth with water from Dartmoor, whilst acting as Water Engineer to that town, 1891-1900; Chief Engineer to Derwent Valley Water Board, 1900; and during succeeding 12 years constructed works of water supply costing three millions sterling for supply of Leicester, Derby, Nottingham, Sheffield, and the county of Derby; subsequently responsible for design and construction of waterworks for numerous authorities in British Isles; Past President of Institution of Water Engineers, and for many years Assoc. Prof. at Victoria University, Manchester; Member of several technical committees. *Address:* Bay Cottage, Shaldon, Teignmouth, Devon. [*Died* 8 *Feb.* 1959.

SANDERS, Brigadier Geoffrey Percival, C.S.I. 1935; D.S.O. 1924; O.B.E. 1930; I.A., retired; *b.* 1880. Served Tibet, 1903-4 (Medal); N.W. Frontier of India, 1908 (Medal with clasp); European War, 1914-19; Waziristan, 1920-23 (D.S.O., despatches); retired, 1934. *Address:* c/o Lloyds Bank, 6 Pall Mall, S.W.1. [*Died* 3 *April* 1952.

SANDERS, Colonel Gilbert Edward, C.M.G. 1917; D.S.O. 1900; retired except for membership in various committees in connection with the war; late Police Magistrate at Calgary; late Superintendent Royal North-West Mounted Police; *b.* Fort Yale, British Columbia, 25 Dec. 1863; *e. s.* of E. H. Sanders, Judge of County Courts, British Columbia; *m.* Caroline, *d.* of Dr. Jukes, M.D.; two *d.* *Educ.:* King Alfred's School, Wantage; Royal Military College, Kingston. Entered Royal North-West Mounted Police as Inspector, 1884; served throughout Riel Rebellion, 1885 (medal); H.M.'s Representative to negotiate a Treaty between Indians, 1887; served: S. Africa in command of squadron of Canadian Mounted Rifles, 1900 (twice wounded); European War, France, 1915-17 (despatches, C.M.G.). *Recreation:* golf. *Address:* Calgary, Alberta, Canada. [*Died* 19 *April* 1955.

SANDERS, Sir John Owen, Kt. 1954; C.M.G. 1948; Member for Railways and Ports, 1951, and Gen. Man. Malayan Rly. since 1946; *b.* 30 Sept. 1892; *m.* 1933, Margaret M. Flachner, Ph.D. *Educ.:* Elstow School, Bedford; Owen's Coll., Manchester Univ. Training L. & N.W. Railway Company Loco. Works, Crewe. Army Service, 1915-20; Works Manager, F.M.S. Railways, 1924; Transportation Manager, F.M.S. Railways, 1930; Army Service, 1942-46, Royal Engineers; Director of Transport, Eritrea, 1942; War Office, Malayan Planning Unit, 1943; Technical Adviser to Chief Civil Affairs Officer, Malaya, 1944-45; Senior Civil Affairs Officer, Railway (Actg. Brig.), 1946; Hon. Col. M.Inst.T.; A.M.Inst.C.E. *Address:* c/o Malayan Railway, Kuala Lumpur, Malaya. *T.A.:* Railway, Kuala Lumpur. *Club:* Royal Automobile. [*Died* 21 *March* 1954.

SANDERSON - WELLS, John Sanderson, R.I.; artist; *b.* Aug. 1872. *Educ.:* Slade School; Juliens. Hon. Treasurer Royal Institute of Painters in Water-Colours. *Address:* 8 Bedford Park Mansions, W.4. *T.:* Chiswick 1285. *Club:* Arts. [*Died* 16 *March* 1955.

SANDERSON-WELLS, Thomas Henry, M.B.E. 1920; M.D., B.S.Lond., F.R.C.S.Ed.; M.R.C.S.Eng., L.R.C.P.Lond.; Vice-Pres. and Consulting Surgeon Weymouth and District Hosp.; Vice-Pres., late Chairman, Food Education Soc.; *b.* 12 March 1871; *s.* of J. S. Wells, Banbury, Oxon, and Ellen, *d.* of T. H. Saunderson, Abergavenny and Oxford; *m.* 1906, Agnes (Nan) (*d.* 1950), *d.* of James Macpherson Laurie, J.P., D.L., Dorset; no *c.* *Educ.:* Bloxham School; Middlesex Hosp., Univ. of London. Junior Demonstrator of Anatomy; House Physician and Casualty Medical Officer Middlesex Hospital; Senior R.M.O. Queen Charlotte's Lying-in-Hospital; Civil Surgeon South African Field Force; Surgeon British Red Cross Hospital, Giza, Egypt, 1915-16; Captain Dorset R.A.M.C. (vol.), 1917-18; late M.O. (Capt.) 13th Company XXth Middlesex H.G.; Medical Officer Westminster and St. James's Palace Red Cross Vol. Aid Detachment, 1942-48; 25 years J.P. Dorset; late Ruling Councillor Primrose League; President Conservative Association and President of Boy Scouts, etc.; Founder of Sanderson-Wells Lecture on Food and Health at Middlesex Hospital and of an occasional lecture and prizes for intermediate and senior students at University of London on soil fertility, nutrition and health. Founder Member The Soil Association. *Publications:* Substitute Feeding of Infants, 1905; Random Rhymes, 1910; Food and National Health, 1937; Sun Diet, 1939; (Poems) Grist, 1939; Articles in medical and contemporary journals in England and New Zealand. *Recreations:* politics, writing, travel. *Address:* Mellifont Abbey, Wookey, Wells, Somerset. *Club:* Junior Carlton. [*Died* 1 *Oct.* 1958.

SANDFORD, 1st Baron, *cr.* 1945, of Banbury in the County of Oxford; **Major Albert James Edmondson,** Kt., *cr.* 1934; D.L. Oxfordshire; *b.* 1887; *e.* and *o. surv. s.* of James and Isabelle Edmondson; *m.* 1911, Edith Elizabeth (*d.* 1946), *d.* of George James Freeman; two *s.* *Educ.:* University Coll. School. H.A.C., R.H.A., 1910; Staff Capt. R.A. Army H.Q., 1916; Staff appointment Headquarters Eastern Command, 1918; M.P. (U.) Banbury Division of Oxfordshire, 1922-45; Parliamentary Private Secretary Ministry of Pensions, 1925-35; Member, Oxfordshire County Council, 1922-37; Private Secretary to Chief Civil Commissioner, 1926; a Lord Commissioner of the Treasury, 1939; Government Whip, 1937-45; Deputy Chief Whip, 1942-45; Vice-Chamberlain of H.M.'s Household, 1939-42; Treasurer, H.M. Household, 1942-45. Chm. Carlton Club, 1946-56. Deputy Lieutenant Oxfordshire, 1945; High Steward of Banbury, 1947. C.St.J., 1949. *Heir:* *s.* Comdr. Hon. John Edmondson, D.S.C., R.N. [*b.* 22 Dec. 1920; *m.* 1947, Catherine, *d.* of Rev. Oswald Hunt; two *s.* two *d.*]. *Address:* 20 Eresby House, Rutland Gate, S.W.7. *Club:* Carlton. [*Died* 16 *May* 1959.

SANDFORD, Hon. Sir (James) Wallace, Kt., *cr.* 1937; Member Legislative Council, S. Australia, 1938-56; Chairman of Directors, A. W. Sandford and Co., Limited; *b.* 20 March 1879; *e. s.* of late Hon. A. W. Sandford, sometime Member Legislative Council; *m.* 1907, Kate Irene, *d.* of late John MacLeod, Raasay, Ballarat, Australia; one *s.* one *d.* *Educ.:* St. Peter's College, Adelaide; Science in London. President Royal Agricultural Society of S. Australia, 1920-24; President Taxpayers Assoc. of S. Australia, 1927-29; Representative of Employers of Australia at International Labour Conference, Geneva, 1928; Chairman Wine Overseas Marketing Board, 1929-33; Chairman S. Australian Committee of Enquiry into Education, 1930-31; Member of Commonwealth Grants Commission, 1933-36; President Adelaide Chamber of Commerce, 1938; Senior Vice-President Associated Chambers of Commerce, Australia, 1938; Director of several public companies. Knight Commander Royal Vasa Order, Sweden, 1939. *Recreation:* golf. *Address:* East Terrace, Adelaide, S. Australia. *Club:* Adelaide (Adelaide). [*Died* 9 *July* 1958.

SANDILANDS, Maj.-Gen. James Walter, C.B. 1919; C.M.G. 1916; D.S.O. 1902; late Cameron Highlanders; *b.* 6 Sept. 1874. *Educ.:* Harrow. 2nd Lieutenant, 1897; served Soudan Campaign, 1898 (Khedive's medal, two clasps); Atbara; Khartoum (Queen's medal, despatches); served South African campaign (despatches, Queen's medal 5 clasps, D.S.O.); European War, 1914-18 (despatches, C.B., C.M.G., Bt. Col.); General Staff, Western Command, 1905-9; Staff College, 1909-10; Commanded an Infantry Brigade, 1916-24; Military Attaché at The Hague, 1924-28; also Berlin, 1927-28; Maj.-Gen. 1928; General Officer Commanding British Troops in China, 1929-33; retired pay, 1933. Chairman, Naval and Military Club, 1940-46. *Address:* Drumalbin House, Camberley. *T.:* 559. *Clubs:* Naval and Military, M.C.C., Royal Automobile. [*Died* 23 *Sept.* 1959.

SANDYS, Lt.-Col. Edward Seton, D.S.O. 1915; late R.E.; *b.* 17 Sep. 1872; 3rd *s.* of Major E. W. Sandys, late R.A., of Fulford House, York. Entered army, 1892; Captain, 1903; Major, 1912; served European War, 1914-1918 (despatches four times, D.S.O., Bt. Lt.-Col., 1914 Star, British War medal, Victory medal, Greek Medal for Military Merit); wounded, Feb. 1915; Officer of Order of St. John, 1940. *Address:* 11 Onslow Av. Mansions, Richmond, Sy. [*Died* 3 *March* 1953.

SANER, Col. John Arthur, C.B. 1939; V.D.; M.I.C.E.; D.L., J.P. Cheshire; *b.* 1864; *m.* 1892, Ethel Maude (*d.* 1930), *d.* of late Robert Jameson; one *s.* two *d.* *Address:* Sandiway Heyes, nr. Northwich, Cheshire. *T.:* Sandiway 31. [*Died* 20 *Feb.* 1952.

SANGSTER, Maj.-Gen. Patrick Barclay, C.B. 1928; C.M.G. 1919; D.S.O. 1916; Officer of the Order of St. John of Jerusalem, 1933; *b.* Rogart, 28 Aug. 1872; *s.* of Patrick Williamson Sangster, J.P., of Rovie, Rogart, Sutherland; *m.* 1904, Jeanie Murphy (*d.* 1943), 2nd *d.* of Major Francis Eastwood of Castletown, Dundalk, Co. Louth; one *s.* one *d.* *Educ.:* Aberdeen Grammar School. Commissioned Indian unattached List, Indian Army, 1894; joined Hampshire Regt. in India, 1895; 2nd Lancers, 1896; served Tirah Campaign, 1897-98 (medal and two clasps); Adjutant 2nd Lancers, 1902-6; served as Brigade Major of Ferozepore Infantry Brigade in France, 1914-15, and later as D.A.A. and Q.M.G. Indian Cavalry Corps; commanded 29th Lancers in France and Palestine, 1916-20; latterly Brig.-Gen. commanding 11th Cavalry Brigade (C.M.G., D.S.O., despatches four times); Colonel Commandant, Equitation School, Saugor, C.P. India, 1921-24; Commanded Rangoon Brigade Area, 1924-26, and officiating Command Burma District, Mar. to Oct. 1925; Commanded 9th Jhansi Infantry Brigade, 1926-28 (overseas Shanghai Defence Force, Feb.-Sept. 1927); retired, 1928. *Address:* c/o Lloyds Bank Ltd., Cox and King's Branch, 6 Pall Mall, S.W.1. [*Died* 19 *June* 1951.

SANGSTER, Rev. William Edwin Robert, M.A.; Ph.D. (Lond.); Hon. LL.D. (Southern Methodist Univ.); Secretary Emeritus Home Mission Department of the Methodist Church; President of the Methodist Conference, 1950; *b.* London, 5 June 1900; 3rd *s.* of Henry George and Martha Elizabeth Sangster; *m.* Margaret, *d.* of John Conway; one *s.* one *d.* *Educ.:* Shoreditch Secondary School; Richmond College, Surrey; University of London. Served in Queens (Royal West Surreys), 1918-1919; ordained into Methodist Ministry, 1926; ministered at Bognor Regis, Colwyn Bay, Liverpool, Scarborough, Leeds, and at the Westminster Central Hall for 16 years. President of London Free Church Federation, 1944-46; Pres. of London Regional Council of U.N.A., 1947-48; Cato Lecturer, 1954; Mem. of Senate of Univ. of London, 1944-1956. *Publications:* Why Jesus never wrote a book, 1932; God does Guide us, 1934; He is Able, 1936; Methodism can be born again, 1938; These Things Abide, 1939; Ten Statesmen and Jesus Christ, 1941; The Path to Perfection, 1943; The Craft of Sermon Illustration, 1946; Methodism: Her Unfinished Task, 1947; Let Me Commend, 1949; The Craft of Sermon Construction, 1949; The Approach to Preaching, 1951; Teach Us to Pray, 1951; Doctrinal Preaching: Its Neglect and Recovery, 1953; The Craft of the Sermon, 1954; The Pure in Heart, 1954; They met at Calvary, 1956; The Secret of Radiant Life. 1957; Power in Preaching, 1958; Give God a Chance, 1959. *Address:* 52 Lyford Road, S.W.18; 1 Central Buildings, S.W.1. *T.:* Whitehall 5911. [*Died* 24 *May* 1960.

SANJIVA ROW, Kodikal, C.I.E. 1935; Kaisar-i-Hind Gold Medal 1947; *b.* 18 March 1890; *s.* of Kodikal Laxman Row; *m.* 1907, Uma Bai; three *s.* three *d.* *Educ.:* Government College, Mangalore; St. Aloysius College, Mangalore; Presidency College, Madras. Joined Accountant General's Office, Madras, 1914; Personal Assistant to Controller of Currency, 1925; Assistant Secretary to Government of India, Foreign and Political Department, 1927; Finance Department, 1928; Secretary to Federal Finance Committee, 1932; Budget Officer to Government of India, 1933; Deputy Secretary to Government of India, Finance Department, 1936; Representative of the Govt. of India on the Indo-Burma Financial (Application) Committee, 1936; Joint Secretary to Government of India, Finance Department, 1937-40; Member, Federal Public Service Commission, 1940-47 (Chairman, 1945); Financial Adviser to the Govt. of East Punjab, 1948-49; Nominated Official Mem. of Indian Legislative Assembly, 1927-1940; Govt. Dir. on the Central Bd. of the Reserve Bank of India, 1938; Hon. Treas., British Empire Leprosy Relief Assoc. since

1939, Indian Red Cross Society, St. John Ambulance Association, Lady Chelmsford Maternity and Child Welfare Bureau, Lady Reading Health School, Victoria Memorial Scholarship Fund, and Indian Soldiers' Medical Aftercare Fund since 1940; Hon. Treasurer, Univ. of Delhi, 1942-44; Member of Central Joint War Committee, 1944-46; Associate Knight of the Order of St. John, 1946. Silver Jubilee and Coronation Medals. *Recreation:* tennis. *Address:* Ishodyan, Dabadhai Road, Juhu, Bombay, 23, India. [*Died* 8 *Aug.* 1951.

SANKEY, Colonel Harold Bantock, C.B.E. 1944; M.C.; T.D.; D.L.; J.P.; *b.* 18 Feb. 1895; *s.* of late G. H. Sankey, Astley Abbotts, Bridgnorth; *m.* 1921, Doris Mary Higgs-Walker; three *s.* *Educ.:* Wolverhampton Grammar School; Trinity College, Cambridge, M.A. (Mech. Science Tripos). Served in France, Flanders, Italy, R.F.A., 1914-18; Cambridge, 1919-1921; joined firm Joseph Sankey & Sons Ltd., 1921, Managing Director since 1935. Chairman, 1951. Served in 67th Regt. R.A. (T.A.), 1919-34; retired, 1934, Bt. Col.; Regional Controller Ministry of Production (Midland Region), 1942-44; High Sheriff of Staffordshire for 1946-47. *Recreations:* farming, gardening. *Address:* Whiston Hall, Albrighton, nr. Wolverhampton. *T.:* Albrighton 229. *Club:* Union (Birmingham). [*Died* 27 *Aug.* 1954.

SANSOM, Charles Lane, C.M.G. 1917; F.R.C.S. (Edin.); M.R.C.S. (Eng.); D.P.H., L.S.A., A.K.C.; J.P.; Cross of Isabella of Spain; late Principal Medical Officer, Federated Malay States; *b.* 10 June 1862; *s.* of James Sansom, Civil Service, retired; *m.* Edith Elizabeth (*d.* 1948), 2nd *d.* of Henry Waring, Beenham House, Berks; two *s.* one *d.* *Educ.:* King's College, London. Resident Medical Officer, Royal Free Hospital, London; Member of several Royal Commissions; late Lt.-Col. commanding Transvaal Medical Corps (Queen's medal); Medical Officer of Health, Transvaal. *Publications:* contributions to medical journals. *Recreation:* tennis. *Address:* c/o Midland Bank, 25 Wigmore St., W.1. [*Died* 6 *Jan.* 1951.

SANTAYANA, George, M.A., Ph.D., Litt.D.; formerly Professor of Philosophy at Harvard College; *b.* Madrid, 16 Dec. 1863, of Spanish parents (Augustin Ruiz de Santayana and Josefina Borrás). *Educ.:* Harvard College. After graduating at Harvard in 1886, studied for two years at Berlin; taught at Harvard, mainly the history of philosophy, 1889-1911; an "advanced student" at King's College, Cambridge, 1896-97; Hyde Lecturer at the Sorbonne, Paris, 1905-6; Spencer Lecturer at Oxford, 1923. Nicholas Murray Butler Gold Medal of Columbia Univ., 1945, for The Realm of Being. *Publications:* The Sense of Beauty, being the outlines of æsthetic theory, 1896; Interpretations of Poetry and Religion, 1900; The Life of Reason, or the Phases of Human Progress, in five volumes; Reason in Common Sense, 1905; Reason in Society, 1905; Reason in Religion, 1905; Reason in Art, 1905; Reason in Science, 1906; Three Philosophical Poets—Lucretius, Dante, and Goethe, 1910; Winds of Doctrine, 1913; Egotism in German Philosophy, 1916; Little Essays, 1920; Character and Opinion in the United States, 1920; Soliloquies in England and later Soliloquies, 1922; Scepticism and Animal Faith, Introduction to a System of Philosophy, 1923; Dialogues in Limbo, 1925; Platonism and the Spiritual Life, 1927; The Realm of Essence, 1928; The Realm of Matter, 1930; The Genteel Tradition at Bay, 1931; Some Turns of Thought in Modern Philosophy, Five Essays, published under the auspices of the Royal Society of Literature, 1933; The Last Puritan, a Memoir in the Form of a Novel, 1935; Obiter Scripta, 1935; The Realm of Truth, 1937; The Realm of Spirit, 1940; The Realm of Being; Persons and Places: The Background of My Life, 1945. Verse: Sonnets and other verses, 1894; Lucifer, a theological tragedy, 1898; The Hermit of Carmel, and other poems, 1901; Poems, selected by the author and revised, 1923. *Address:* c/o Brown, Shipley & Co., 123 Pall Mall, S.W.1. [*Died* 26 *Sept.* 1952.

SAPELLNIKOFF, Wassily; concert pianist; has been a regular visitor to England for thirty years; *b.* at Odessa, 2 Nov. 1868; *e. s.* of Leon Sapellnikoff, violinist and conductor at Odessa and other parts of Russia. *Educ.:* Odessa; St. Petersburg. Conservatoire de Musique de la Société Imperiale at St. Petersburg; studied the violin, and subsequently the piano, with Louis Brassin and Sophie Menter, and theory and composition with various teachers; a great friend of Tschaikovsky, who brought him to England, where he played in London the Concerto for pianoforte and orchestra No. 1 in B flat minor in 1889; is an honorary member of the Royal Philharmonic Society, for whom he has played on fifteen occasions. *Publications:* over thirty works for piano. *Recreations:* chess, reading, and visiting beautiful places. [*Died* 17 *March* 1941.

[*But death not notified in time for inclusion in Who Was Who* 1941–1950, *first edn.*

SAPSWORTH, Capt. Charles Howard, C.V.O. 1939; lately in service of Canadian Pacific Steamship Co., now retd.; *b.* 1 Sept. 1883; *m.* 1936, Lillie Muriel, *d.* of late Henry Brown, J.P., Edinburgh; one *s.* Commanded R.M.S. Empress of Britain during return voyage of the King and Queen from Canada, 1939 (C.V.O.). *Address:* 24 Belgrave Crescent, Edinburgh 4. [*Died* 7 *April* 1958.

SAREL, Rear-Adm. Colin Alfred Molyneux, O.B.E.; Royal Navy, retired; *b.* Rollesby Hall, Great Yarmouth, 10 Aug. 1880; *s.* of late Lieut.-General Henry Andrew Sarel and Phyllis, *d.* of late Rev. More Molyneux of Compton, Guildford; *m.* 1907, Mabel, *d.* of late Howard Rumney, solicitor, London; one *d.* (and one *d.* decd.). *Educ.:* Stubbington, Fareham; H.M.S. Britannia, Dartmouth, 1904-06. Midshipman in Magnificent, Renown (Flag of Sir John Fisher), Pelican, and Cruiser; Sub-Lieut., 1900, Greenwich and Portsmouth Colleges, Fairy, Decoy; Lieut., 1902, Retribution, Gibraltar, Vernon, Ramillies, Africa; Lieut.-Commander, 1910, Actaeon, Berwick, Queen; Commander, 1914, Cornwallis in Dardanelles (wounded and invalided); Naval Mission in Greece, 1916; minelaying at Scapa Flow, Dover, and coasts of England and Scotland, 1917-18; in command of Espiegle in Persian Gulf, 1919-20; Capt. 1920, Assistance, 1922-24; Calypso, 1925-26; Captain-in-Charge, Bermuda Dockyard, 1926-28; Argus, Aircraft Carrier, 1929-30; Flag-Captain and Chief of Staff to Vice-Admiral Commanding Reserve Fleet, Constance and Frobisher, 1930-32; Rear-Admiral and retired list, 1932; Second Naval Member of Australian Naval Board and Captain Supt. of Training and in command of Flinders Naval Depot, 1932-34; stations served on Channel, Mediterranean, North America and West Indies, East Indies, Australia; served at sea as Commodore of Convoys, 1939-40; Naval Officer in charge at Leith, 1942-45; reverted to retired list, invalided, 1945. *Recreation:* golf. *Address:* Flinders, Cooden Beach, Bexhill. *T.:* Cooden 419. [*Died* 7 *June* 1954.

SAREL, Colonel George Benedict Molyneux, C.S.I. 1922 (retired); *s.* of late Lt.-Gen. H. A. Sarel, C.B.; *m.* Nan I. Ross; three *s.* one *d.* *Educ.:* Wellington College. Gazetted to Royal Scots Fusiliers, 1890; to 11th Bengal Lancers, 1894; commanded 11th K.E.O. Lancers, 1916-21; served Chitral Expedition, 1895; China Expeditionary Force, 1900-1; European War, 1914-18; N. Iraq 1919-21. *Re-*

creations: hunting, shooting, yachting, fishing. *Address:* Drynoch, Dorchester Rd., Hook, Basingstoke. *Club:* Royal Cruising. [*Died* 29 *July* 1953.

SARGANT, Walter Lee, M.A.; J.P. Rutland; *s.* of Henry Sargant, Barrister-at-law. *Educ.:* Rugby School; Trinity College Cambridge. Assistant Master at Fettes College, 1892-1901: Head Master of Oakham School, 1902-29. *Publications:* The Book of Oakham School; Oakham through the Centuries, 1950. *Address:* Torbay Hotel, Sidmouth. [*Died* 17 *July* 1956.

SARGANT-FLORENCE, Mary; *b.* 21 July 1857; *d.* of Henry Sargant, Barrister, and Catherine Emma Beale; *m.* 1888, Harry Smyth Florence, musician; one *s.* one *d.* *Educ.:* at home; Brighton; Paris; Slade School, London. Lived and worked in Paris, New York, and London; Member of the Mural Decorators and Painters in Tempera Society, The New English Art Club, and Hon. Member of the Women's International Art Club. Decorations in Fresco of the Old School at Oakham, Rutland; Decorations in Fresco of the Bournville Schools near Birmingham; Decorations in Fresco and in Tempera at Lords Wood, Marlow; Decorative Panel in Tempera in Chelsea Town Hall; Invention of the Harmonic Compass. Chantrey bequest, 1950. *Publication:* Colour Co-ordination, 1940. *Recreations:* gardening, walking. *Address:* Lords Wood, Marlow, Bucks. *T.:* Marlow 169. [*Died* 14 *Dec.* 1954.

SARKAR, Sir Jadunath, Kt., cr. 1929; C.I.E. 1926; M.A.; Hon. D.Litt.; I.E.S. (ret.); Hon. F.R.A.S.; Corresponding Member Royal Hist. Soc.; Hon. Fellow, R.A.S. Bengal and Bombay; Hon. life mem. Amer. Hist. Assoc.; Member, Legislative Council of Bengal, 1929-32; Member, Indian Historical Record Commission, 1919-41; Vice-Chancellor, Calcutta Univ., 1926-1928; *b.* Rajshahi District of Bengal, 10 Dec. 1870; *s.* of Raj-kumar Sarkar and Hari-sundari; *m.* 1893, Kadambini Chaudhuri; four *s.* six *d.* *Educ.:* Rajshahi College and Presidency Coll., Calcutta. Prof. of History at Presidency Coll., 1898-99, Patna, 1899-1917 and 1923-26, and Cuttack, 1919-23; Univ. Prof. of Indian History at Univ. of Benares, 1917-19; Reader in Indian History, Patna University, 1920-22 and 1931; Sir W. Meyer Lecturer (Madras University, 1928); winner of the Premchand Roychand Studentship and the Griffith Prize, Calcutta University, and of the Sir James Campbell Gold Medal (Royal As. Soc. of Bombay). *Publications:* History of Aurangzib, 5 vols.; Shivaji and his Times; Studies in Mughal India; Anecdotes of Aurangzib; Mughal Administration; India of Aurangzib (Statistics, Topography and Roads); Chaitanya; Economics of British India; India Through the Ages; Fall of the Mughal Empire, 4 vols.; Studies in Aur. Reign; House of Shivaji; Military History of India; ed. W. Irvine's Later Mughals, 2 vols.; Editor, Poona Residency Correspondence, Persian Records of Maratha History, 2 vols., Nawabs of Bengal, and Dacca University History of Bengal. *Address:* 10 Lake Terrace, Calcutta 29, India. [*Died* 15 *May* 1958.

SARMA, Sir (Ramaswami) Srinivasa, Kt., *cr.* 1936; C.I.E. 1926; Managing Editor The Whip, and Eastern Rly. Magazine; *b.* 1890. *Educ.:* Madras. Started life as Sub-editor of the Bengalee, Calcutta, 1913; left it to join as Calcutta Correspondent of Associated Press of India, 1916; visited Europe 1919, 1926, 1929, 1934, 1936, 1943, and 1951; went back to India as Associated Press and Reuter's Correspondent in Calcutta, 1920; Editor-in-Chief of Bengalee and New Empire, and Managing Director of Liberal Newspapers, Ltd.; started the Whip, Calcutta weekly political newspaper, 1934. Leader of India Government Delegation to U.K. and U.S.A. to publicize India's war effort, 1943. *Recreation:* tennis. *Address:* 20 British Indian Street, Calcutta; Kali Koti, Mavur, P.O. S. Rly., Madras Presidency. *T.A.:* Whip, Calcutta. *T.:* 22-6811, Ext. 48; 23-3300. *Clubs:* National Liberal, Overseas; Calcutta, Bengal Flying, Lake, Kalighat, 300 (Calcutta). [*Died* 26 *Sept.* 1957.

SAROLEA, Charles, D.Ph. and Litt. (Liège University), Hon. D.Ph. (Brussels), LL.D. Montreal, D. Juris (Cleveland), F.R.Hist.S. Lond. (Hon. Causa); Kt. Comdr., Royal Belgian Order of Leopold; Officer of the Order of the Crown; Royal Belgian Life Saving Medal; Belgian Civic Medal, First Class; Knight Commander of Saint Sava; Knight Commander of Polish National Order, Polonia Restituta; Officier de la Légion d'Honneur; First Consul Free Congo State; Foreign Member of Royal Acad. of Belgium; Member of Brazilian Acad. of Rio de Janeyro; late Professor of French Literature in the University of Edinburgh; First Belgian Consul-General, Edinburgh, and Doyen d'Age of Consular Corps of Edinburgh-Leith; *b.* Tongres, Belgium, 25 Oct. 1870; *s.* of late Jean Sarolea, M.D., and late Felicité Vrindts; *m.* 1st, 1895, Martha (*d.* 1901), *d.* of Prof. Van Cauwenberghe, Rector of Ghent Univ.; one *s.*; 2nd, 1905, Julia Frances (*d.* 1941), *d.* of late Charles Dorman. *Educ.:* Royal Athénée, Hasselt; Liège University, First Class Honours in Classics and Philosophy. Was awarded the Belgian Government travelling scholarship for memoir on Metaphysique de la Sensation, 1892; studied Paris, Palermo, Naples, 1892-93; First Lecturer and Head of French and Romance Department, Edinburgh University, 1894-1931; Founder of Revue Française d'Edimbourg, 1896; Founder, Editor and proprietor of Everyman, 1912-17; Belgian Consul for Edinburgh, 1901. Founder and first Chm. of Directors of French publishing firm, Georges Crès and Co.; War Correspondent of the Daily Chronicle, 1914; visiting Professor of Political History, Egyptian Univ., Cairo, 1926-1927; addressed many mass meetings in America, Great Britain and on Continent during two world wars; raised over £100,000 for Belgian relief; invited by King Albert of Belgium to accompany him as political adviser on his journey to Brazil and West Africa, 1920. *Publications:* H. Ibsen, 1891; La Liberté et le Déterminisme, 1893; Essais de Philosophie et de Littérature, 1898; The Russian Revolution, 1905; The Balkan Question, 1906; Essais de Littérature et de Politique, 2nd vol. 1906; Cardinal Newman and his Influence on Religious Thought, 1908; Victor Hugo, 1911; Life of Tolstoy, 1912; The Anglo-German Problem, 1912; How Belgium saved Europe; Europe's Debt to Russia, 1916; The Curse of the Hohenzollern; Nurse Cavell; The French Renascence, 1916; German Problems and Personalities, 1917; Le Reveil de la France; The Russian Revolution, 1917; Joan of Arc, 1918; Europe and the League of Nations, 1919; President Masaryk and Abraham Lincoln, 1920; Modern Brazil, 1921; Letters on Polish Affairs, L'occupation allemande de la Pologne, 1922; R. L. Stevenson and France; Impressions of Soviet Russia (translations in nine languages), 1924; five Chinese and Japanese translations for Anti-Bolshevist Propaganda, 1926; Daylight on Spain, 1938; General Editor of the Collection Nelson; General Editor of the Collection Gallia; has collected foreign library of 200,000 volumes. *Recreations:* travelling and learning languages. *Address:* 21 and 22 Royal Terrace, Edinburgh. *T.:* Edinburgh 25837. [*Died* 11 *March* 1953.

SATTERTHWAITE, Lt.-Col. Clement Richard, O.B.E. 1919; R.E. (retired); *b.* 21 Feb. 1884; *e. s.* of late Col. Edward Satterthwaite, C.B. *Educ.:* Rugby; Royal Military Academy, Woolwich. Royal Engineers, 1902-22; Adviser on Works Services to Director-General, Territorial Army, 1922-24; Deputy Secretary, Royal National Life-boat Institution, 1925-31; Secretary, 1931-46. *Address:* Lansdowne House, Alton, Hants. [*Died* 5 *May* 1953.

SAUNDERS, Sir Alan Arthur, Kt., *cr.* 1949; O.B.E. 1918; Chairman British Sugar Corporation Limited since 1949; Chairman National Research Development Corporation, since 1955 (Director 1954-55); Lately Co-ordinator of Building Supplies, Ministry of Health. *Address:* c/o British Sugar Corporation Ltd., 134 Piccadilly, W.1; Whiteleaf, Dyke Road, Hove 3, Sussex. [*Died* 26 *Feb.* 1957.

SAUNDERS, Lt.-Col. Cecil Howie, C.M.G. 1915; late Royal Army Ordnance Corps; *b.* 15 June 1881; *s.* of late Col. W. E. Saunders, C.B., R.A.M.C.; *m.* 1913, Muriel Vivian Stevens; one *s.* *Educ.:* Clifton College; R.M.A., Woolwich. Entered R.A. 1900; Captain, 1908; Major, 1914; Lt.-Col. 1929; Ordnance Officer, 4th class, 1910; 2nd class, 1928; p.a.c.; served European War, 1914-18 (despatches, C.M.G.); retired pay, 1936. [*Died* 3 *Nov.* 1954.

SAUNDERS, Hilary Aidan St. George, C.B.E. 1951; *b.* 14 Jan. 1898; *er. s.* of late Rev. G. W. St. George Saunders and late Sybil K. Somers Clarke; *m.* 1st, Helen Foley (*d.* 1937); 2nd, Joan, *d.* of J. P. Bedford; one *s.* one *d.* *Educ.:* Balliol College, Oxford. Welsh Guards, 1916-18; M.C., 1918; Secretariat League of Nations, 1920-37; Private Sec. to Doctor Fridtjof Nansen, 1921-23. Librarian House of Commons, 1946-50. *Publications:* The Battle of Britain, 1941, and other official publications of War of 1939-1945; Pioneers! O Pioneers!, 1943; Per Ardua, 1944; The Green Beret, 1949; The Red Beret, 1950; The Sleeping Bacchus, 1951. Numerous novels with the late John Palmer under the pen-name of Francis Beeding since 1924; The Seven Sleepers, The Six Proud Walkers, Death Walks in Eastrepps, Eleven were Brave, etc.; also with late John Palmer under pen-name of David Pilgrim; So Great a Man, 1938, No Common Glory, 1941, The Grand Design, 1944; The Emperor's Servant, 1946; Westminster Hall, 1951. *Recreations:* golf, conversation accompanied by the wines of France. *Address:* Old Holbans, Broad Oak, Heathfield, Sussex. *Clubs:* Athenæum, Garrick. [*Died* 16 *Dec.* 1951.

SAUNDERS, Major-General Macan, C.B. 1935; D.S.O. 1918; I. A., retired; p.s.c. Camberley; *b.* 9 Nov. 1884; *o. s.* of late Col. M. W. Saunders; *m.* 1914, Marjory, *d.* of Francis Bacon. *Educ.:* Malvern College; R.M.A., Woolwich. Lieut. Royal Field Artillery, 1903; Lieut. Indian Army, 1907; Captain, 1912; Major, 1918; Bt. Lieut.-Col. 1919; Colonel, 1923; Maj.-Gen. 1935; in India till 1914, except for a year in Russia; Staff Captain 2nd Royal Naval Brigade, 1914, operations in Belgium and siege of Antwerp; operations in Gallipoli, 1915, from first landing to evacuation; G.S.O.3 in Egypt to March 1916; Brigade-Major Eastern Persian Field Force to April 1917; G.S.O.2 and Intelligence Officer with Major-Gen. Dunsterville's Mission through N.W. Persia to the Caucasus, 1918; G.S.O.1, Caucasus Section, G.H.Q. British Salonika Force, 1919 (wounded, despatches five times, D.S.O., Bt. Lt.-Col.); Military Attaché, Tehran, Persia, 1921-24; Deputy Director, Military Intelligence, A.H.Q., India, 1924-29; Director, Military Operations, A.H.Q., India, 1929-30; Commander, Wana Brigade, Waziristan, 1930-34; A.D.C. to the King, 1932-35; Commander Delhi Independent Brigade Area, 1934-36; Deputy Adjutant-General A.H.Q., India, 1936-1938; Commander Lahore District, 1938; retired, 1940; Chairman, Central Interview Board for Commissions, 1941-43; President Services Selection Board, 1943-47. *Address:* Seagulls, Fauvic, Jersey, C.I. *Club:* Victoria (Jersey). [*Died* 2 *April* 1956.

SAURAT, Denis; Agrégé de l'Université, Docteur ès lettres (Paris); Officier de la Légion d'Honneur; Directeur, Centre international d'études françaises, Nice; Professor Emeritus in the University of London; Member of Vetenskaps-Societeten i Lund; Fellow of King's College, London; *b.* Toulouse, 1890; *m.* Ella, *d.* of William Bocquet-Smith, freeman of the City of London; one *s.* three *d.* *Educ.:* Universities of Lille, London, Paris. Lecteur, French Department, Univ. of Glasgow, 1918-19; Professeur au Lycée de Bordeaux, 1919-20, Lecturer, English Language and Literature, Bordeaux University, 1920-22; Professor, University of Bordeaux, 1922-24; Professor of French Language and Literature, University of London (King's College), 1926-50; Directeur de l'Institut français du Royaume Uni, London, 1924-45. *Publications:* La pensée de Milton, 1920; Blake and Milton, 1920; L'Actuel, 1922; Milton, Man and Thinker, 1925, New Edition, 1944; The Three Conventions, 1926; Milton et le Matérialisme chrétien; Tendances (Essais de critique), 1928; La Littérature et l'occultisme; La Religion de Victor Hugo, 1929; Blake and Modern Thought, 1929; Literature and Occult Tradition, 1930; Histoire des Religions, 1934; Modernes, 1935; La Fin de la Peur, 1937; Perspectives, The End of Fear, 1938; The Spirit of France, French War Aims, The Christ at Chartres, Regeneration, 1940; Watch over Africa, 1941; Le soldat romain, poème épique en vers blancs, 1944; Death and the Dreamer, 1946; Modern French Literature, 1946; Gods of the People, 1947; L'expérience de l'Audelà, 1951; Blake et le Catharisme anglais, 1954; L'Atlantide et le règne des géants, 1954; La religion des géants et la civilisation des insectes, 1955; Encaminament catar (poème épique en langue d'oc), 1955. *Address:* 504 Regina, Cimiez, Nice, France. *T.:* Nice 811.31. *Club:* Athenæum. [*Died* 7 *June* 1958.

SAVAGE, Sir Geoffrey Herbert, Kt., *cr.* 1952; *b.* May 1893; *s.* of late Frederic W. Savage, Port Elizabeth, S. Africa; *m.* 1923, B. Marjorie, *d.* of late Major H. N. Webb; three *s.* one *d.* *Educ.:* Bradfield College, Berkshire; Elizabeth College, Guernsey. Director of Rover Company, Meteor Works, Solihull, Birmingham. Interested in Engineering and Allied Employers Federation, London; works on various cttees. as appointed. Governor of Cranborne Chase School, Crichel, Nr. Wimborne. *Recreations:* real tennis and fishing. *Address:* Upper Fulbrook Farm, Nr. Stratford-on-Avon, Warwicks. *Club:* Junior Carlton. [*Died* 11 *Feb.* 1953.

SAVAGE, Lt.-Col. Morris Boscawen, C.B.E. 1919; D.S.O. 1915; late 2nd Batt. the South Staffs. Regiment; *b.* 14 Mar. 1879; *o. s.* of Lt.-Col. Harry B. Savage, R.M.A.; *m.* 1915, Helen Elise (*d.* 1951), 2nd *d.* of Rev. T. W. Tovil; one *s.* Entered army, 1899; Captain, 1908; Major, 1915; Bt. Lt.-Col. 1918; Lt.-Col. 1921; with Egyptian army, 1912-14; served European War, 1914-18, with 2nd S. Staffs. Regt. (severely wounded); Staff Captain 110th Infantry Brigade. D.A.A. & Q.M.G. 9th Scottish Div.; D.A.A.G. 19th Corps; A.A. & Q.M.G. 6th Div.; A.A.G. Scottish Command (despatches five times, D.S.O., C.B.E., Bt. Lt.-Col.); retd. pay, 1925; Member for North Battersea, L.C.C., 1928. *Publications:* A History of the Naval and Military Monuments, Memorials, and Colours in Lichfield Cathedral; contributor to various periodicals on Military History. *Address:* Langton House, Lichfield, Staffs. *Club:* Army and Navy. [*Died* 11 *June* 1958.

SAVAGE, Col. William Henry, C.M.G. 1917; Indian Army, retired; *b.* 18 Apr. 1863; *s.* of late Major G. W. Savage, 37th North Hants Regt.; *m.* Rosa Edith, *e. d.* of late Brig.-Surg. C. F. Oldham, I.M.S.; three *d.* *Educ.:* Wellington College. Joined 2nd Batt. Loyal N. Lancs. Regt. 1882; transferred to Indian Army, 1883; served with 3rd Q.A.O. Gurkha Rifles, and lately with 13th Batt. Royal Irish Rifles; Capt. 1893; Major, 1901; Lt.-Col. 1908; Col. 1912; served

Zhob Valley, 1884; European War, 1914-18 (C.M.G.); retired, 1919; J.P. Co. Antrim. *Address:* Rarkmoyle, Cushendall, Co. Antrim.

See also Lt.-Col. W. E. Maxwell.

[*Died* 21 *Feb.* 1951.

SAVI (née Bryning), Ethel Winifred; novelist; *b.* India, of English and American parents; *m.* 1884, late John Angelo Savi (British), of Italian and French ancestry; two *s.* two *d.* *Educ.:* privately at home. Married at eighteen; spent the first twelve years of her married life in rural Bengal (Udhua Nullah, on the Ganges); while in India she wrote short stories for English and Indian journals, and began the writing of long novels only after retiring to England in 1909. *Publications:* The Reproof of Chance, 1910; A Blind Alley, 1911; The Daughter-in-Law, 1912; Baba and the Black Sheep, 1913; Sinners All, 1914; Mistress of Herself, 1915; Banked Fires, 1919; When the Blood Burns; The Devil Drives; Rulers of Men; Mock Majesty; The Marquise Ring; A Fateful Escapade; Our Trespassers; Fruits of Desire; Neither Fish nor Flesh; Sackcloth and Ashes; Satan's Finds; The Acid Test; Vagrant Love; A Fool's Game; Making Amends: The Inconstancy of Kitty; Taken by Storm; Breakers Ahead; Daggers Drawn; The Other Man; Tree of Knowledge; A Prince of Lovers; White Lies; The Unattainable; The Beauty Market; On the Rack; Dog in the Manger; The Back o' Beyond; The Saving of a Scandal; A Man's a Man, 1927; The Great Gamble; A Forlorn Hope; The Maker of Dreams, 1928; On Trust, 1928; The Fatalist, 1929; Crashed; God-forsaken; The Law Divine; The Power of Love, 1929; The Door Between, 1930; The Everlasting Fraud, 1930; By Torchlight, 1931; Idol Worship, 1931; In Desperation, 1931; The Pendulum Swings, 1931; The Blunder, 1932; In Confidence, 1932; On the Knees of the Gods, 1932; Mixed Cargo (with Charles Barry), 1932; Glad Rags, 1932; At Close Quarters, 1933; A Flat in Town, 1933; Prisoners of Necessity, 1933; Sins of Commission, 1934; The Passionate Problem, 1934; The King's Proctor, 1935; The Tyranny of Freedom, 1935; The Insolence of Youth, 1935; The Glamorous East, 1936; A Fresh Deal, 1936; The Riddle of the Hill, 1936; Licensed to Kill, 1937; The Soothsayer, 1937; A Question of Honour, 1937; Ill-Gotten Gains, 1938; A Mad World, 1938; The Beloved Autocrat, 1938; The Human Element, 1939; Birds of Passage, 1939; The Way Thereof, 1939; Money and Power, 1940; The Laughter of Courage, 1940; The Devil's Playground, 1941; A Comedy of Endeavour, 1942; Clay and the Mould, 1943; No Other Choice, 1944; Lords of Creation, 1945; The Fragrance Lingers; My Own Story, 1947; Vanity of Vanities, 1948; The Human Heart, 1948; Pawns and Puppets, 1949; Labelled Dangerous, 1949; The Quality of Mercy, 1950; The Unvarnished Truth, 1950; Fame and Folly, 1951; The House Party, 1952; The Trouble Maker, 1953; The Price of Loyalty, 1953; No Greater Love, 1954; The Devil's Carpet, 1954; The Ewe Lamb, 1955, etc. *Recreations:* reading, gardening, and travel. *Address:* 16 Thanet Court, Queen's Drive, W.3. *T.:* Acorn 2705. [*Died* 6 *Oct.* 1954.

SAVIGE, Lt.-Gen. Sir Stanley George, K.B.E., *cr.* 1950 (C.B.E. 1941); C.B. 1943; D.S.O. 1919; M.C. 1917; E.D.; Retired List, A.M.F.; Managing Dir. S. G. Savige, Pty. Ltd., Melbourne; Commissioner State Savings Bank, Vic.; *b.* Morwell, Vic., 26 June 1890; *m.* 1919, Lilian, *d.* of Samuel Stockton. Served European War, 1915-19, in Gallipoli, Sinai, France, and Persia (despatches thrice, M.C., D.S.O.); War of 1939-45 in Middle East, New Guinea and Solomons (despatches, C.B.E., C.B.). *Publication:* Stalky's Forlorn Hope, 1920. *Address:* 9 Goldthorns Ave., Kew, Vic., Australia. *Clubs:* Melbourne, Navy, Army and Air Force, Savage, Legacy, V.R.C. (Melbourne). [*Died* 15 *May* 1954.

SAVILE, Sir Leopold Halliday, K.C.B., *cr.* 1929 (C.B. 1925); M.Inst.C.E.; M.I.E.Aust.; *b.* 31 Aug. 1870; *s.* of late Lieutenant-Colonel John Walter Savile, of Ballendrick, Scotland; *m.* 1st, 1904, Frances Evelyn (*d.* 1920), *d.* of late Frank Stileman, M.I.C.E.; one *d.*; 2nd, 1929, Lilith E. M., *o. d.* of late Brig.-Gen. Walter Clare Savile, C.B., D.S.O. *Educ.:* Marlborough; King's College, London. Pupil of Sir John Wolfe Barry and H. M. Brunel; Harbour, Dock, and Railway Engineer; late Partner of, now Consultant to, the Firm of Sir Alexander Gibb & Partners, Consulting Engineers; Past President of Institution of Civil Engineers; Member of Internat. Consultative Cttee. on Suez Canal; Hon. Member of Permanent International Commission of Navigation Congresses; Fellow of King's College, London; Dep. Chief Engineer, Bombay Port Trust, 1904-19; Civil Engineer-in-Chief, Admiralty, 1919-32. *Publications:* various papers on technical subjects. *Address:* 23 Pelham Crescent, S.W.7; Tawcroft, Belstone, Devon. *Club:* Junior Carlton. [*Died* 28 *Jan.* 1953.

SAVILL, Ven. Leonard, M.A.; *b.* 1869; *s.* of E. Savill, Eastern Terrace, Brighton. *Educ.:* Charterhouse; Cambridge; Cuddesdon. Deacon, 1892; Priest, 1894; Curate of St. Bartholomew's, Great Smithfield, 1892-1902; Vicar of Swanley, 1902-16; of Dartford, 1916-25; Rural Dean of Dartford, 1919-25; Archdeacon of Tonbridge, 1925-40; Archdeacon Emeritus, 1940; Hon. Canon of Rochester, 1919-25. *Address:* Fair View, West Lane, East Grinstead, Sussex. [*Died* 21 *Oct.* 1959.

SAWBRIDGE, Rear-Admiral Henry Richard, O.B.E. 1924; *b.* 11 March 1885; *s.* of late Canon J. S. Sawbridge, Coney Weston Hall, Suffolk. *Educ.:* Stubbington; H.M.S. Britannia. Served in European War as Lieut-Commdr. and Commander in H.M.S. Emperor of India, Grand Fleet, 1914-18; Anti-Submarine Division of Admiralty, 1918; First Lord's Mission to United States, 1918; on Staff of Admiral-of-Fleet Lord Jellicoe for Naval Mission to H.M. Dominions, 1919; Naval Inter-Allied Commission in Germany, 1920; in command H.M. Anti-Submarine School, 1921; Captain, 1924; Commanded H.M.S. Osprey, 1924; H.M.S. Champion, 1926; H.M.S. Comus, 1928; H.M.S. Sussex, 1930; Director of Torpedoes and Mining, 1931-34; Commanded H.M.S. Renown, 1934-36; A.D.C. to King George V. 1935; Rear-Admiral, 1936; awarded American Navy Cross, 1919. *Address:* Thrigby Hall, nr. Gt. Yarmouth. *T.:* Fleggburgh 62. *Club:* Naval and Military. [*Died* 15 *Jan.* 1956.

SAWKINS, Harold; Late Proprietor and Editor of The Artist; Art Review; The Artist's Year Book; retd.; *b.* 29 Jan. 1888; *s.* of George and Anne Elizabeth Sawkins; *m.* 1920; one *s.* *Educ.:* Barnard Castle. First twenty years of business career spent in building up an Advertising Agency; went into publishing business, 1931. *Publications:* The Artist; Art Review; The Artist's Year Book. *Recreation:* painting. *Address:* Brown Gates, Durrant Road, Bournemouth. [*Died* 22 *March* 1957.

SAWYER, Maj.-Gen. Henry Thomas, C.B. 1924; D.S.O. 1915; late R.A.V.C.; *b.* 12 Aug. 1871; *m.* 1913, Helen Constance (*d.* 1953), *d.* of late Edward Webb. Capt. 1900; Maj. 1906; Lt.-Col. 1914; Col. 1921; Maj.-Gen. 1925; Assistant Director-General, Army Veterinary Service, 1910-14; served Chitral, 1895 (medal with clasp); S. African War, 1899-1902 (despatches, Queen's medal 4 clasps, King's medal 2 clasps; promoted Vet. Captain); European War, 1914-17 (despatches, D.S.O.); Director of Veterinary Services, India; Director-General Army Veterinary Services, War Office, 1925-29; retired pay, 1929. *Address:* Laurel Lodge, Liss, Hants. [*Died* 15 *March* 1955.

SAWYER, James Edward Hill, M.A., D.M., B.Ch. Oxon; M.R.C.P. Lond.; F.R.G.S.; Lt.-Col. R.A.M.C.; retired; Administrator 1st Southern General Hospital, 1917-20; Registrar, 1st Southern General Hospital, 1908-1917; Brevet Lt.-Col. 1917; served European War, 1914-19; Capt. 19th Batt. E. Sussex Regt., 1941-43; *b.* Birmingham, 8 Sept. 1874; *s.* of late Sir James Sawyer; *m.* 1906, Margaret, *d.* of Lt.-Col. Ll. W. Longstaff, Ridgelands, Wimbledon; three *s.* one *d.* *Educ.:* Shrewsbury; Christ Church, Oxford (Hons. in Physiology, Natural Science Schools, 1897; qualified with the M.B., B.Ch. degrees, 1900); St. Thomas's Hospital, London (Solly Medallist, 1899; Bristowe Medallist, 1900; Hadden Prizeman, 1900). Has held the posts of Assistant Physician, Pathologist, General Hospital, Birmingham; Assistant to the Chair of Medicine, University of Birmingham; Assistant House Physician, House Physician, at St. Thomas's Hospital; House Physician, Bethlem Royal Hospital; and Physician to Out-patients, the Children's Hospital, Birmingham; formerly Editor, The Birmingham Medical Review, Sub-Editor, The British Journal of Children's Diseases. *Publications:* Chronic Interstitial Nephritis in Children (Thesis, 1904); Physical Signs of Diseases of the Thorax and Abdomen, 1908; numerous contributions to medical and other scientific journals. *Recreations:* scouting, gardening. *Address:* Little Holton, Burwash, Sussex. [*Died* 22 *Feb.* 1953.

SAYCE, George Ethelbert; Newspaper Proprietor, Companies' Director, etc.; *b.* 25 Dec. 1875. Read literary and commercial subjects, and trained for journalistic career; actively engaged in journalistic positions, gaining experience, 1898-1914; purchased Brecon and Radnor Express and Radnor Express (1914) and incorporated Brecon County Times (1933); Director, Principal and Partner of other commercial undertakings; F.J.I. 1917; Member Newspaper Society; J.P. County of Brecon; High Sheriff of Breconshire, 1940-41 and 1947-48. *Recreations:* golf, motoring, angling and horticulture. *Address:* Dineterwood, Pontrilas, Herefordshire. *T.:* Pontrilas 278; London House, Builth Wells, Breconshire. *T.:* Builth Wells 3288; Express Buildings, Brecon. *T.A.:* Sayce, Dineterwood, Pontrilas. *T.:* Brecon 32, Llandrindod Wells 2428. *Club:* Royal Automobile. [*Died* 7 *Oct.* 1953.

SAYE, Air Vice-Marshal Geoffrey Ivon Laurence, C.B. 1948; O.B.E. 1940; A.F.C. 1933; Air Officer Commanding No. 19 (Reconnaissance) Group, Royal Air Force, Mount Batten, since 1956; *b.* 1 March 1907; British; *m.* 1934, Pamela Ross-Hime; four *s.* *Educ.:* Repton; Royal Air Force College, Cranwell. Flying Boat Squadrons at Calshot and Mount Batten, 1926-34. First R.A.F. crew to fly to Iceland, 1930; Adjutant R.A.F. Heliopolis, Egypt, 1934-36; Specialist Navigation Course, 1936; Navigation Staff Officer No. 1 Bomber Group, 1937-39, H.Q. Advanced Air Striking Force, Rheims, France, 1939-40, H.Q. Bomber Command, 1940-42; Comdg. R.A.F. Waterbeach (Bombers), 1942-44; Comdg. Central Navigation School, Shawbury, 1944; Director of Navigation, Air Ministry, 1944-48; Officer i/c Organisation, H.Q. M.E.A.F., 1948-50; Director of Manning, Air Ministry, 1950-52; Imperial Defence College, 1953; Air Officer in charge of Administration, H.Q., M.E.A.F., 1954-56. Fellow Institute of Navigation, 1949. *Recreations:* motoring, sailing, swimming. *Address:* Monckswood, Wembury, Plymouth, Devon. *T.:* Wembury 234. *Club:* Seaview Yacht. [*Died* 6 *March* 1959.

SAYERS, Dorothy Leigh (Mrs. Fleming), M.A.; Hon. D.Litt. Durham; *b.* 1893; *d.* of Rev. Henry Sayers and Helen Mary Leigh; *m.* 1926, Capt. Atherton Fleming (*d.* 1950). *Educ.:* Somerville College, Oxford. *Publications:* *Verse:* Op. 1, 1916; Catholic Tales, 1919; (trans.) Tristan in Brittany, 1930; (trans.) Dante's Inferno, 1949, Purgatorio, 1955. *Fiction:* Whose Body? 1923; Clouds of Witness, 1926; Unnatural Death (U.S.A. The Dawson Pedigree), 1927; The Unpleasantness at the Bellona Club, 1928; Lord Peter views the Body, 1928; (with Robert Eustace), The Documents in the Case, 1930; Strong Poison, 1930; The Five Red Herrings (U.S.A. Suspicious Characters), 1931; Have His Carcase, 1932; Hangman's Holiday, 1933; Murder Must Advertise, 1933; The Nine Tailors, 1934; Gaudy Night, 1935; Busman's Honeymoon, 1937; In the Teeth of the Evidence, 1939. (With other members of the Detection Club): The Floating Admiral, 1931; Ask a Policeman, 1933. *Plays:* Busman's Honeymoon (with M. St. Clare Byrne), 1936; The Zeal of Thy House, 1937; The Devil to Pay, 1939; Love All, 1940; The Man Born to be King (Radio Drama), 1942; The Just Vengeance, 1946; Where Do We Go from Here? (Radio Drama), 1948; The Emperor Constantine, 1951. *Essays:* Begin Here, 1940; The Mind of the Maker, 1941; Even the Parrot, 1944; Unpopular Opinions, 1946; Creed or Chaos?, 1947; The Lost Tools of Learning, 1948; Introductory Papers on Dante, 1954; Further Papers on Dante, 1957. Edited Great Short Stories of Detection, Mystery and Horror (3 series), 1928, 1929, 1934. *Address:* 24 Newland Street, Witham, Essex; 24 Great James Street, W.C.1. *T.:* Witham 3157, Holborn 9156. [*Died* 18 *Dec.* 1957.

SAYERS, Dame Lucile Newell, D.B.E., *cr.* 1956 (C.B.E. 1952); *d.* of Charles Schiff, Lowndes Square, S.W.1, and Mary Ballard Burch, Nashville, Tennessee, U.S.A.; *m* 1910, Lorne Sayers (*d.* 1940), Major, R.A.S.C.; three *s.* two *d.* *Educ.:* Roedean. President Plymouth Br., Red Cross; Mem. Nat. Assistance Advisory Cttee., Western Region; Governor of Plympton Grammar School and of Plympton Modern School. Lecture tour in Germany at request of Foreign Office, 1950. Chairman Cons. Women's Advisory Committee, 1946-49; Chm. Nat. Union Cons. and Unionist Assocs., 1951-52. U.K. Delegate to Status of Women Commission of United Nations, 1955, 1956 and 1957. U.K. Delegate to General Assembly of United Nations, 1955. President National Union of Conservative and Unionist Associations, 1955-56. J.P. for Devon, 1935. *Recreations:* reading, gardening, travel. *Address:* Alston Hall, Holbeton, nr. Plymouth. *T.:* Holbeton 59. [*Died* 4 *Nov.* 1959.

SAYERS, William Charles Berwick; Chief Librarian of Croydon Public Libraries, 1915-47; President of the Library Association, 1938; Trustee of National Central Library; *b.* Mitcham, 23 Dec. 1881; *s.* of late Thomas Hind Sayers; *m.* 1915, Olive Emily, *d.* of R. Edwyn Clarke, F.G.S., Muswell Hill; three *s.* *Educ.:* St. Clement's, Bournemouth; pupil of late George C. Barter, M.A., 1896-1900; London School of Economics for Librarianship Courses, 1905-8. Sub-librarian, Bournemouth, 1900-4; Deputy Librarian, Croydon, 1904-15; Chief Librarian, Wallasey, 1915; won Greenwood prizes in librarianship, 1898 Hon. Secretary, Library Assistants' Association, 1905-9, and 1912-15; President, 1909-12; Hon. Editor, The Library Assistant, 1909; Fellow by hons. diploma of the Library Association, 1908; Councillor and Examiner since 1912; Hon. Fellow, 1947; Chairman of the Executive Cttee. 1937-45; Lecturer, University of London School of Librarianship, 1919-51; member of the B.B.C. Central Council on Broadcast Adult Education, 1928-34. *Publications:* The Children's Library, 1913; Over Some Alpine Passes, 1913; Canons of Classification, 1915; Samuel Coleridge-Taylor, Musician: his Life and Letters, 1915; new ed. 1927; An Introduction to Library Classification, 1918; 9th edition, 1958; The Story of

Croydon, 1925; A Manual of Classification, 1927, 3rd ed. 1959; The Revision of a Public Library Stock, 1929; Children's Libraries, 1932; Library Local Collections, 1939; Croydon and the Second World War (illustr.), 1949; Guide to Croydon, 1959; Editor of Brown's Manual of Library Economy, editions 3-6; Books for Youth, 1936, etc.; has written many songs for music, and other poems. *Address:* 52 Blenheim Crescent, South Croydon. [*Died* 7 *Oct.* 1960.

SAYWELL, Rev. Preb. George Frederick, M.A. Cambridge; Rector of St. Michael's, Cornhill, E.C.3, since 1944; Prebendary of St. Paul's Cathedral since 1942; Chaplain to the Queen since 1952 (to King George VI, 1948-52); *b.* 2 Aug. 1882; *s.* of Horace Hunt Saywell and Sarah Ann Burgess; *m.* 1914, Evelyn Neville Lea-Wilson; no *c.* *Educ.:* Toronto University (1st Class Oriental Languages); Christ's College, Cambridge (Exhibitioner and Scholar, 1st Class Oriental Languages, Tyrwhitt Hebrew Scholar). Deacon, 1912; Priest, 1913; Curate of St. Anne's, Toronto, 1912-14; Church of the Redeemer, Toronto, 1914-16; St. Paul's, Cambridge, 1916-18; in France with the Y.M.C.A., 1918; Chaplain, Christ's College, Cambridge, 1919-20; Foreign Secretary, Church Missionary Society, 1920, 1923; Editorial Secretary, 1923-25; Examining Chaplain to Bishop of Peterborough, 1924-26; Rector of Holy Trinity St. Marylebone, 1925-44; Rural Dean of St. Marylebone, 1926-31; Examining Chaplain to Bishop of Leicester, 1927-35, to Bishop of London, 1933-48; Chairman, Anglican Evangelical Group Movement, 1932; Chairman, Cromer Convention Council, 1934-36; Chairman, Executive Committee of Bible Reading Fellowship, since 1939, and Chairman of the Council since 1951. Select Preacher, Cambridge, 1945. *Publications:* contributor to The Call for Christian Unity, 1930; various religious articles and papers. *Recreations:* walking, riding, photography. *Address:* 84 Hallam Street, W.1. *T.:* Langham 6518. *Club:* Oxford and Cambridge. [*Died* 17 *July* 1956.

SCAFE, Lt.-Col. William Ernest, C.M.G. 1919; D.S.O. 1916; late Devonshire Regt.; *b.* 1878; *e. s.* of late Gen. C. H. Scafe, Royal Marines; *m.* 1914, Elizabeth Mary, *d.* of late James R. Shirreff of Joradah, Bengal; (one *s.* killed in action 1942). *Educ.:* St. Paul's School, London; Royal Naval School, Eltham. 2nd Lieut. 3rd Batt. Devon Regt. (Militia), 1897; Devonshire Regt. 1899; Captain, 1907; Major, 1915; Bt. Lt.-Col. 1917; Lt.-Col. 1927; graduated Staff College, 1914; served South African War, 1899-1902; European War (C.M.G., D.S.O.); retired pay, 1931. [*Died* 23 *Dec.* 1951.

SCARISBRICK, Sir Everard Talbot, 2nd Bt., *cr.* 1909; J.P. Lancashire; *b.* 10 Dec. 1896; *o. surv. s.* of Sir Tom Talbot Leyland Scarisbrick, 1st Bt., and Josephine Ethel (*d.* 1950), *d.* of W. S. Chamberlain, Cleveland, Ohio; *S.* father, 1933; *m.* 1919, Nadine, *d.* of Charles Brumm, Manchester, and Mrs. H. B. G. Warren; no *c.* *Heir:* none. *Address:* Wiveton Barn, Holt, Norfolk. *T.:* Cley 311. *Club:* White's. [*Died* 29 *Aug.* 1955 (*ext.*).

SCARLETT, Maj.-Gen. Hon. Gerald, C.B. 1941; M.C.; D.L.; *b.* 10 April 1885; *m.* 1928, Margaret Macdonald, *widow* of Col. William Alleyne Macbean, late R.A. *Educ.:* Wellington College, p.s.c. 1921. 3rd Bedfordshire Regt., 1904; Buffs, 1907; served in Command and on Staff, France and Belgium, 1914-19; Temp. Lt.-Col., 1918-19; War Office, G.S.O., 1922-23; Brig.-Major, Aldershot, 1923-26; G.S.O., Shanghai Defence Force, 1927-28; Brevet Lt.-Col., 1928; G.S.O., War Office, 1928-31; Lt.-Col., 1932; commanded 2nd Batt. The Buffs, 1932-34; Col., 1932; G.S.O.1 Western Command, 1934-36; Commander 12th Infantry Brigade and Deputy Constable Dover Castle, 1936-38; Maj.-Gen., 1938; Commander Deccan District, 1938; Commander 4th Indian Div., Egypt, 1939-40; Director of Mobilisation, 1940; Deputy Adjutant General (A), 1940; retired pay, 1942; Col. The Buffs (Roy. E. Kent Regt.), 1943-53. D.L. Kent 1949. Knight Grand Cross of the Dannebrog. *Address:* Stonegreen Hall, Mersham, Kent. *Clubs:* United Service, Carlton, Royal Automobile. [*Died* 5 *Oct.* 1957.

SCEALES, Colonel George Adinston M'Laren, D.S.O. 1917; late Argyll and Sutherland Highlanders, and Tank Corps; Member of Royal Company of Archers, Queen's Bodyguard for Scotland; *b.* 5 July 1878; *o. s.* of late James Sceales, Thornhill House, Stirlingshire, Brig.-General of the R.C.A., Q.B.G.S.; *m.* 1919, Evelyn Lily May, *d.* of A. P. Macewen, and *widow* of Brig.-Gen. H. B. Kirk, A. & S.H.; (one *s.* killed, Italy, 1944). *Educ.:* Charterhouse; Sandhurst. Joined Princess Louise's 91st Argyll and Sutherland Highlanders, 1898; and served with this battalion in South African War, 1899-1902 (Queen's medal 4 clasps, King's medal 2 clasps); Adjutant, 1908-11; and in European War, 1914-15; commanded 4th and 4/5th Black Watch, 1916-December 1917 (despatches thrice, D.S.O., Bt. Lieut.-Colonel); commanded 14th Battn. Tank Corps, 1917-18, and Brig.-Gen. Commanding 1st Tank Brigade, 1918-19; raised and commanded 5th Bn. Tank Corps, 1919-21; retired pay, 1921; re-employed as Assistant Records Officer, 1940-45. Gold-Staff Officer, King George V Coronation, 1911; Jubilee Medal, 1935; Gold-Staff Officer, King George VI Coronation, 1937; Coronation Medals, 1911, 1937, 1953; Home Defence Medal. Capt. Roy. St. George's Golf Club, 1938-39. President, Army Golfing Soc., 1947-50; Capt., Senior Golfers' Soc., 1950. *Address:* Cliffs End Hall, Isle of Thanet. *T.:* Thanet 51683. *Clubs:* Army and Navy, Royal Automobile, M.C.C.; Royal Highland Yacht (Oban); Royal St. George's Golf (Sandwich). [*Died* 2 *Aug.* 1956.

SCHIERWATER, Harry Turner; Member of Council: Chamber of Shipping of the United Kingdom (President, 1945-46); International Tanker Owners Assoc. (Chm. 1934-49); *b.* Grassendale, nr. Liverpool, 1 Sept. 1876; *s.* of A Schierwater; *m.* 1905, Ethel May Hughes; one *d.* (one *s.* decd.). *Educ.:* Liverpool College, Sefton Park. Past Pres. Seed, Oil & Cake Trade Assoc.; ex-Member, Shipping Defence Advisory Sub-Committee to Admiralty; ex-Mem. Shipping Cttees. London and Liverpool. *Recreations:* golf, gardening. *Address:* Longwood, Fairfield Rd., Eastbourne. *Clubs:* Royal Automobile; Royal Eastbourne Golf. [*Died* 7 *Aug.* 1952.

SCHMITT, Marchese A. F.; *see* Della Torre Alta.

SCHNABEL, Professor Artur; *b.* Lipnik, Austria, 17 April 1882; *m.* 1905, Therese Behr, Liedersinger and teacher; two *s.* *Educ.:* Vienna. Studied with Leschetizky and Mandyszewski in Vienna; began with concerts, 1896; played since then everywhere in Europe, America, and Australia; wrote songs, smaller pieces for piano, one concerto for piano and orchestra, five string quartettes, one quintette for piano and string quartette, one Sonata for violin solo, one Sonata for violoncello solo and one string trio, two Sonatas for piano, one Sonata for piano and violin, three symphonies, one Rhapsody for Orchestra, one Duodecimet, two pieces for Chorus and Orchestra, etc.; edited Sonatas by Mozart and Brahms for piano and violin together with Carl Flesch and almost all piano works by Beethoven. Leader of a class for piano-teaching at the State Academy of Music in Berlin, 1926-31; lectured at Universities of Michigan, Chicago,

Harvard. Hon. Doctor of Music, Manchester University, 1933; has recorded for H.M.V. all piano works by Beethoven and many works of other composers. *Publications:* Reflections on Music, 1935; Music and the Line of Most Resistance, 1942; Ed. E. Crankshaw: My Life and Music, 1961. *Address:* 2 West 86, New York City.

[*Died* 15 *Aug.* 1951.

SCHOENBERG; *see* Schönberg, Professor A.

SCHOFIELD, Wentworth, T.D.; Lt.-Col.; M.P. (C.) Rochdale since 1951; *b.* 17 Apr. 1891; *s.* of Edwin James and Mary Hannah Schofield, Failsworth, Lancs.; *m.* 1915, Sarah, *d.* of Joseph Twyerould, Oldham; one *d.* Cotton industry: Company Director; Member Management Committees. Oldham Master Cotton Spinners Assoc.; also of Federation Master Cotton Spinners Assocs. Hon. Vice-Pres. Oldham Chamber of Commerce; Mem. Brit. Nat. Cttee., Internat. Chamber of Commerce; Mem. Exec. Cttee., Brit. Empire Chambers of Commerce; Hon. Vice-Pres. Rochdale Chamber of Commerce. Served European War, 1914-18, Manchester Regiment; War of 1939-1945, Comd. 47 Roy. Tank Regt. *Recreation:* golf. *Address:* 6 Park Avenue, Southport, Lancs. *T.:* Southport 4554. *Clubs:* St. Stephen's; Royal Tank Regiment.

[*Died* 16 *Dec.* 1957.

SCHOLES, Frank Victor Gordon, C.M.G. 1939; M.D., B.S. (Melb.); D.P.H. (Camb.); F.R.A.C.P.; Medical Superintendent Infectious Diseases Hospital, Melbourne, 1910-48; retired, 1948; Member Commission of Public Health, State of Victoria; *b.* Victoria, 24 May 1885; *s.* of Albert and Sarah Scholes (British); *m.* 1918, Nancie Noble Millar; two *s.* *Educ.:* Grenville College, Ballarat; Queen's College, University of Melbourne. M.B.B.S. Melb. 1908; M.D., Melb. 1912; D.P.H. Cambridge 1913; F.R.A.C.P. 1938 (Foundation Fellow); Major A.A.M.C. Retired; Member Army Medical Directorate Consultative Committee, 1940-45; Member of several Consultative Councils and Committees. President, Section of Medical Science, Adelaide Meeting of Australian and New Zealand Association for the Advancement of Science, 1946. *Publications:* Prognosis in Diphtheria, 1912; Diphtheria, Measles, Scarlatina, 1920, 2nd Ed. 1927; Nursing in Infectious Diseases, 1940; numerous reports and papers. *Recreations:* music, reading, fishing, motoring. *Address:* 48 Lansell Road, Toorak, S.E.2, Melbourne, Austr. [*Died* 11 *Sept.* 1954.

SCHOLES, Percy Alfred, O.B.E. 1957; M.A.; D.Litt.; Hon. D.Mus. (Oxon.); Hon. Litt.D. (Leeds), Dr. ès Lettres (Lausanne); F.S.A.; F.R.Hist.S.; A.R.C.M.; Hon. R.A.M.; F.T.S.C.; Officer of the Star of Rumania, 1930; Author; *b.* Leeds, 1877; *s.* of Thomas Scholes; *m.* Dora Wingate, *d.* of Richard Lean, Gloucester. Hon. Fellow and Trustee, St. Edmund Hall, Oxford. Formerly Music Critic of Observer, Music Critic to B.B.C., and Musical Editor of the Radio Times; Extension Lecturer of Universities of Oxford, Cambridge, London and Manchester; lectured in many American universities, etc.; Inspector of Music in Schools to London University, and also inspected for Board of Education; Founder and General Secretary of Anglo-American Conference on Musical Education, Lausanne, 1929 and 1931; Corr. Member of American Musicological Soc.; Pres. Soc. of Recorder Players; Vice-Pres. Welsh Folk Song Soc. Vice-Pres. Vegetarian Soc., London Vegetarian Soc. and Patron of League for Prohibition of Cruel Sports. *Publications:* Oxford Companion to Music; Oxford Junior Companion to Music; Oxford Concise Dictionary of Music; The Great Doctor Burney (James Tait Black Memorial Prize, Edinburgh Univ., 1948); The Life and Activities of Sir John Hawkins, musician, magistrate, and friend of Johnson; The Mirror of Music, 1844-1944; The Puritans and Music in England and New England; God Save the Queen: the History and Romance of the World's First National Anthem; Listener's Guide to Music; Listener's History of Music (also in Dutch translation); Columbia History of Music by Eye and Ear (also in Japanese and Braille), and many other works. *Recreations:* music, reading and travel. *Address:* Hauterive, Ave. de Sully, La Tour de Peilz, Vaud, Switzerland. *T.:* 5.65.64. *Club:* Athenæum. [*Died* 31 *July* 1958.

SCHOLFIELD, Brig.-Gen. George Peabody, C.B. 1924; C.M.G. 1916; C.B.E. 1919; *b.* 1868; *m.* 1908, Helen Mary Goodall of Pine Ridge, Farnham; one *s.* one *d.* Entered R.E. 1887; Brevet Major, 1902; Lieut.-Colonel, 1914; Brevet Colonel, 1918; Colonel, 1919; served South African War, 1899-1902 (Queen's medal with five clasps, King's medal with two clasps, Brevet Major); European War, 1914-19 (despatches, C.M.G., Brevet-Colonel, Croix de Guerre, C.B.E.); retired, 1924. *Address:* c/o Lloyds Bank, Cox's and King's Branch, 6 Pall Mall, S.W.1. [*Died* 27 *Feb.* 1952.

SCHOMBERG, Rev. Edward St. George, M.A.; D.L. County of London; Master of the Charterhouse since 1935; Member of Central Housing Advisory Committee, 1936-1944; also Secretary of Bishop of London's Commission on the City Churches, 1943; *b.* 1882; *s.* of late Lieut.-Gen. Herbert St. George Schomberg, C.B.; *m.* 1919, Mary Alice, *d.* of Rev. Edward Samson; two *s.* *Educ.:* Haileybury; Hertford College, Oxford; Wells Theological College. B.A. 1906; M.A. 1908; Deacon, 1907; Priest, 1908; C.F. 1916-17 (despatches); Vicar of St. Andrew's, Westminster, 1917-35; Mayor of Westminster, 1931-33; Select Preacher, Cambridge University 1936; Member of Governing Body of Charterhouse School, 1935-; Member of Council of Haileybury College, 1936-49; Member of Council of Whitelands College, 1924-49. 3rd Class Order of the Rafidain (Iraq), 5th Class Order of St. Sava (Jugoslavia). *Address:* Glycine House, Hampton Court, Middlesex. *Club:* Athenæum. [*Died* 31 *July* 1952.

SCHOMBERG, Brig. Harold St. George, C.B.E. 1944; D.S.O. 1918; *b.* 24 Aug. 1886; *s.* of late Lieut.-General Herbert St. George Schomberg, C.B., R.M., and Sophia Elizabeth Hoare; *m.* 1917, Madeline Grace Stancomb; no *c.* *Educ.:* Kelly College, Tavistock. Joined East Surrey Regt., 1908; served, France, Aug. 1914-Oct. 1914 (twice wounded); France and Belgium, July 1916-Nov. 1917; Italy, Nov. 1917 to Armistice; Acting Major, 1/4th Oxford and Bucks L.I., 1916-17; Acting Lt.-Col. commanding 1/6th Gloucestershire Regt., 1917-19 (D.S.O., Brevet Majority, Italian Silver Medal for Military Valour, despatches four times); Commander 149th (Northumberland) Infantry Brigade, T.A. 1935-39; retired pay, 1939; recalled Sept. 1939; Commanding Shorncliffe Garrison to Nov. 1940; Comdr. of a Brigade, 1941; Sector Commander Home Guard, 1943-44. *Recreations:* shooting and fishing. *Address:* Seend Lodge, Seend, Wilts. *Club:* Army and Navy.

[*Died* 11 *July* 1954.

SCHOMBERG, Colonel Reginald Charles Francis, C.I.E. 1937; D.S.O. 1916 and Bar, 1917; late Seaforths; *o. s.* of late Reginald B. Schomberg; unmarried. *Educ.:* Oratory School; New College, Oxford (B.A.). Joined 1st Seaforth Highlanders, 1901; served in Egypt and India; Indian Frontier Expedition, 1908; European War (severely wounded twice, despatches, D.S.O. and Bar, Bt. Lt.-Col.); Commanding 1st Seaforth Highlanders, 1917-19; Commandant Singapore Vol. Corps, 1919-21; Inspector of Prisons, S.S., 1919-21; 2nd Batt. Seaforth Highlanders, India, 1922; retired pay, 1928; H.B.M. Consul-General in the French Establishments in India, 1936-37 and 1938-41; from Nov. 1939 in addition Consul-General for Portuguese Possessions in India; Consular Liaison Officer, Persia, 1942-43; Customs, Perso-Indian Frontier, 1943-44; Colonel, Force 136, China, 1944-45. *Publications:* Peaks and Plains of Central Asia, 1933; Between the Oxus and the Indus, 1935; Unknown Karakoram, 1936; Kafirs and Glaciers, 1938. *Address:* Chasewood Lodge, Ross, Herefordshire. [*Died* 2 *March* 1958.

SCHÖNBERG, Professor Arnold; Professor of Music Univ. of California at Los Angeles, 1936-44; retired; *b.* 13 Sept. 1874; *m.* 1st, 1901, Mathilde Zemlinsky (*d.* 1923); one *s.* one *d.*; 2nd, Gertrud Kolisch; two *s.* one *d.* *Educ.:* erst Autodidakt; Vienna, under von Zemlinszky. Leiter einer Meisterklasse für musikalische Komposition an der Akademie der Künste zu Berlin. *Works:* Klaviermusik: Op. 11, 19, 23, 25, 33; Kammermusik: 4 Streich-quartette, Op. 7, 10, 30, 36; Streichsextett Verklärte Nacht, Op. 4; Serenade Op. 24, Kammer-Suite Op. 29; Bläserquintett, Op. 26; String Trio, Op. 45; Fantasy for Violin (with piano accompaniment), Op. 47; Kammersymph. Op. 9; Arrangement for full orchestra, Op. 9B, 1936; 2nd Chamber Symphony, Op. 38 (version for two pianos, Op. 38B); Pierrot lunaire Melodramen, Op. 21; Lieder u. Gesänge, Op. 1, 2, 3, 6, 12, 14, 15, 20, 48; mit Orchester: Op. 8 u. 22; Chormusik: Op. 13, 27, 28, 35; 3 Folksongs 1 chorus, Op. 49; Dreimal tausend Jahre, Op. 50A; Psalm 130, Op. 50B; Der 151. Psalm, Op. 50C. Mit Orchester und Solis; Gurrelieder (1900) und Jakobsleiter (1917; noch unvollendet); Kol Nidre for Solo, Chorus and Orchestra Op. 39, 1938; A Survivor from Warsaw, Op. 46; Orchester, Pelleas u. Melisande, symph. Dicht., Op. 5; Fünf Orchesterstücke (new version, 1951), Op. 16; Variationen, Op. 31; Begleitungsmusik zu einer Lichtspielscene, Op. 34; Variations for Wind Band, Op. 43 and Op. 43B, Version for Full Orchestra; Prelude to the Genesis (for orchestra), Op. 44; Suite for String Orchestra, 1935; Concerto for Violin and Orchestra, Op. 37, 1937; Concerto for Piano and Orchestra, Op. 42; Variations on a Recitative, for Organ, Op. 40; Ode to Napoleon Buonaparte (by Lord Byron) for Recitation and Piano Quintet, Op. 41; Bearbeitungen Bachscher Orgelwerke: Concerto for Violoncello and Orchestra (after Monn), 1935; Concerto for String Quartet and Orchestra (after Handel), 1935; Orchestration of Brahms' Piano Quartet in G. Minor, 1938; Bühnenwerke; Monodram Erwartung, Op. 17; Die Glückliche Hand, Op. 18; Von heute auf morgen, Op. 32; Moses und Aron; Dichtungen: Der biblische Weg; Ein Band Texte; Moses und Aron, Oper; Schriften: Harmonielehre, 1911, trans. Theory of Harmony, 1949; two vols. of essays, Style and Idea, 1950, and Program Notes; Models for Beginners in Composition, 1942; Structural Functions of Harmony; Counterpoint in 3 vols.: Preliminary Exercises; Contrapuntal Composition; Counterpoint in homophonic music since 1750; one vol. in German containing: Dichtungen, Texte, Aphorismen, etc., also Der biblische Weg and Moses und Aron; Research Lecture: Composition with twelve tones. *Recreations:* tennis, ping-pong, bookbinding. *Address:* 116 N. Rockingham Avenue, Brentwood Park, Los Angeles 49, California. *T.:* Arizona 35077. [*Died* 13 *July* 1951.

SCHORR, Friedrich; Opera Singer; *b.* Hungary, 2 Sept. 1888; *m.* *Educ.:* Grammar School and University. Engagements at Berlin and Vienna State Opera; Metropolitan Opera House, New York; Covent Garden; Prague, Buenos Aires, Bayreuth, etc.; retired from operatic stage, March 1943. Head of Vocal and Opera Department at Manhattan School of Music, New York City. *Address:* Friedrich Schorr, 329 Forest Avenue, Rye, N.Y., U.S.A. [*Died* 14 *Aug.* 1953.

SCHREIBER, Colonel (Hon. Brig.-Gen.) Acton Lemuel, C.B. 1916; C.M.G. 1918; D.S.O. 1900; *b.* 30 March 1865; *s.* of Rev. John Edward Lemuel Schreiber; *m.* 1889, Evelyn Amy (*d.* 1947), *d.* of Lt.-Col. Edmond Darcy Hunt; one *s.* (and one *s.* decd.). Entered army, R.E., 1884; served North-West Frontier, India, 1897-98 (medal with clasp); South Africa, 1899-1902 (Queen's medal with 5 clasps, King's medal with 2 clasps); European War, 1914-18 (wounded twice, despatches six times, C.B., C.M.G.); A.D.C. to the King, 1915; retired, 1920; late J.P., D.L. *Address:* The Manor House, Sidmouth, Devon. [*Died* 11 *Jan.* 1951.

SCHUMANN, Elisabeth; leading soprano of the Vienna Staatsoper, Austrian and Bavarian Kammersängerin, hon. member of the Vienna Staatsoper and the Vienna Philharmoniker, and possessor of the ring of the Philharmoniker, also decorations from Austria, the King of Denmark, Bulgaria, Rumania, Greece, and the Légion d'honneur; *b.* Merseburg, Germany, 13 June 1885; *d.* of Alfred Schumann (Organist of the Merseburger Dom) and Emma Sonntag; one *s.* Studied firstly in Dresden with Natalie Haenisch, then in Berlin with Marie Dietrich from the Staatsoper, and later with Alma Schadow in Hamburg, where she made her début; visited America (Metropolitan Opera House), had many concert tours, a notable one in 1921 with Richard Strauss, who engaged her in 1919 for the Vienna Opera. London début, Covent Garden, Ariadne of Naxos by Richard Strauss and secondly as Sophie (Rosenkavalier), 1924; sang also Blonda (Entführung aus dem Serail), Zerlina (Don Giovanni), Susanna (Figaro), Eva (Meistersinger), Adèle (Fledermaus); has sung in concerts and operas in nearly all countries of the world; teaches voice at the Curtis Institute of Music, Philadelphia. *Recreations:* collecting antiques and driving. *Address:* c/o Annie Friedberg, Concert Management, 251 West 57th Street, New York City. [*Died* 23 *April* 1952.

SCHUSTER, 1st Baron, *cr.* 1944, of Cerne; **Claud Schuster,** G.C.B., *cr.* 1927 (K.C.B., *cr.* 1920); Kt., *cr.* 1913; C.V.O. 1918; Q.C. 1919; *b.* 22 Aug. 1869; *o. s.* of late Frederick Leo Schuster; *m.* 1896, Mabel Elizabeth (*d.* 1936), *d.* of late Rev. Dr. W. W. Merry; one *d.* *Educ.:* Winchester College; New College, Oxford. Called to Bar, Inner Temple, 1895; Bencher, 1925; Treasurer, 1947; Secretary to London Government Act Commission, 1899-1902; Legal Assistant, Board of Education, 1903-7, and Assistant Secretary, 1907-11; Principal Assistant Secretary (Legal Branch), Board of Education, 1911; Chief Registrar of Friendly Societies, 1911-12; Secretary and Legal Adviser, National Health Insurance Commission (England), 1912-13; Legal Member National Health Insurance Joint Committee and National Health Insurance Commission (England), 1913-1915; Clerk of the Crown in Chancery, and Permanent Secretary to Lord Chancellor, 1915-1944; Director Legal Division, Allied Commission for Austria (British Element), 1944-1946; J.P. County of London; Honorary Fellow of St. Catharine's College, Cambridge; Officier de l'Ordre de la Couronne, Belgium; Hon. Member Canadian Bar Association; Vice-Pres. Ski Club of Great Britain, 1931-32, Pres., 1932-34; Vice-Pres. Alpine Club, 1937, Pres., 1938-40; Sheriff of Dorset, 1941. *Publications:* Peaks and Pleasant Pastures, 1911; Men, Women, and Mountains: Days in the Alps and Pyrenees, 1931; Sweet Enemy 1934; Postscript to Adventure. *Recreations:* mountaineering, hunting. *Address:* 7 Campden Hill Court, Kensington, W.8. *T.:* Western 5603. *Clubs:* Alpine, Oxford and Cambridge, Travellers'. [*Died* 28 *June* 1956 (*ext.*).

SCLATER-BOOTH, Col. (Hon. Brig.-Gen.) Hon. Walter Dashwood, C.B.

1917; C.M.G. 1919; D.S.O. 1915; late R.A.; *b.* 15 Feb. 1869; 4th *s.* of 1st Baron Basing; *m.* 1918, Frances Mary (*d.* 1949), *d.* of late Rowland Burdon; one *s.* two *d.* *Educ.:* Wellington; Royal Military Academy, Woolwich. Commissioned Royal Artillery, 1887; retired, 1919; served European War, 1914-17 (wounded, despatches, D.S.O., C.B., C.M.G.). *Address:* Upton Grey Lodge, Basingstoke. *Club:* Army and Navy. [*Died* 10 *Jan.* 1953.

SCOBELL, Major-Gen. Sir (Sanford) John (Palairet), K.B.E., *cr.* 1942; C.B. 1935; C.M.G. 1919; D.S.O. 1916; *b.* 26 Sept. 1879; *o. surv. s.* of late Sanford George Treweeke Scobell and Edith Palairet of Walton House, Ashchurch, near Tewkesbury; *m.* 1910, Cecily Maude, *d.* of late C. C. Hopkinson; two *d.* (and two *s.* decd.). *Educ.:* Winchester; Sandhurst. Joined 1st Batt. Norfolk Regt. in India, 1899; went to Somaliland with a British M.I. Co., 1903-4; at the outbreak of European War was employed on embarkation duties at Southampton, subsequently becoming Brigade Major 35th Infantry Brigade on the formation of the New Armies; G.S.O.2 at Corps H.Q. and G.S.O.1 49th Div.; G.S.O.1 Mission to Baltic States, 1919; G.S.O.1 28th Div. in Turkey, 1920-23 (C.M.G., D.S.O.); Commanded 2nd Batt. The Norfolk Regiment, 1926-28; A.A.G. War Office 1928-30; Commandant, Senior Officers' School, Belgaum, India, 1930-32; Brigade Commander, India, 1932-34; District Comdr., India, 1935-39; retired pay, 1939; recalled, Oct. 1939; commanding Troops, Malta, 1939-42; retired pay, 1942; Lieutenant of the Tower of London, 1942-45. *Address:* Applethorpe, Blewbury, Berks. [*Died* 2 *March* 1955.

SCORGIE, Sir Norman Gibb, Kt., *cr.* 1945; C.V.O. 1935 (M.V.O. 1931); C.B.E. 1927 (O.B.E. 1919); M.A., LL.B. (Trinity, Cambridge), Barrister (Inner Temple); *b.* 6 Oct. 1884; *e. s.* of late Norman Scorgie, J.P., M.Inst.C.E.; *m.* 1912, Iza (*d.* 1945), *d.* of Henry Donnan, J.P. *Educ.:* St. Olaves; Cambridge. First in first class of Law Tripos, Part II, 1907; Whewell Scholar in International Law, 1908; served European War, France and Italy, 1915-19 (despatches three times, O.B.E.); Deputy Controller of H.M. Stationery Office, 1919-40; Deputy Director-General, Ministry of Information, 1940-41; Principal Assistant Secretary, Mines Department, 1941-42; Controller of H.M. Stationery Office and King's Printer, 1942-49; Chm. of B. Winstone & Sons Ltd., 1949-55. *Address:* Erindale, Knebworth, Herts. *T.:* Knebworth 3129. *Clubs:* Athenæum, Oxford and Cambridge; New (Edinburgh). [*Died* 26 *March* 1956.

SCORGIE, Professor Norman James; Professor of Veterinary Hygiene, Royal Veterinary College, University of London, since 1946; *b.* 7 June 1908; *s.* of Alexander Scorgie and Catherine Barnett; *m.* 1939, Beryl Alice Sack; two *d.* *Educ.:* Inverurie Academy; University of Aberdeen. M.A. 1929; B.Sc. 1931; M.R.C.V.S. 1934; Demonstrator in Dept. of Natural History, Univ. of Aberdeen, 1928-30; Royal Veterinary College; Research Asst. in Res. Instit. in Animal Pathology, 1934-35; Research Asst. in Preventive Medicine, 1935-36; Lecturer, 1937, and College Reader, 1937-46, in Animal Husbandry Dept. For. Mem., Sociedad Veterinaria De Zootecnia, Spain, 1951. *Publications:* Linton's Veterinary Hygiene, 1952. Contributions to Brit. Veterinary Jl., Veterinary Record Jl. Comp. Path., Veterinary Medicine (U.S.A.), etc. *Recreations:* tennis, fishing, racing. *Address:* Royal Veterinary College (University of London), Animal Husbandry Department, Royal College Street, N.W.1. *T.:* Euston 5321. [*Died* 10 *Feb.* 1958.

SCOTSON, Frederick Hector; Major R.A.M.C., T.A.R.O.; Consultant Surgeon Manchester Northern Hospital; Consultant Surgeon Crumpsall Hospital; lecturer and examiner in surgery, Manchester University; *b.* 28 Jan. 1900; *s.* of Frederick Charles Scotson and Winifred Connor; *m.* 1928, Annie Mollie Bradbury (*d.* 1940); two *s.* one *d.*; *m.* 1942, Leila M. B. O'Connell; one *s.* *Educ.:* Manchester Grammar School; Victoria University of Manchester. M.B. Ch.B. (Honours), M.B. B.S. London Univ., L.R.C.P. (Lond), M.R.C.S. (Eng.), F.R.C.S. (Eng.); Bradley Surgical Scholarship, Distinction in Anatomy and Medicine for the M.B. Ch.B. Examinations, Graduate Prize in Medicine; House Surgeon, Surgical Registrar, Assistant Resident Surgical Officer and Resident Surgical Officer at the Manchester Royal Infirmary; Pres. Middleton and N. Manchester Medical Soc.; former Vice-Pres. Manchester Pathological Soc.; Member: of Assoc. of Surgeons of Great Britain and Ireland; Medical Appeal Tribunal; Manchester Medical Society; Manchester Surgical Society. *Publications:* Traumatic Rupture of the Stomach, Brit. Medical Journal, 1929; Investigation of a Renal Case, Brit. Med. Journal, 1932; Progressive Post-operative Gangrenous Ulceration of the Skin, Lancet 1933; Calcified Cyst of the Spleen, Brit. Med. Journal, 1933; Treatment and Post-operative results of Perforated Peptic Ulcers, British Med. Journal, 1933; A Case of Myeloma, Lancet, 1934; Tumours of the kidney and testes, Brit. Med. Journal. *Recreations:* tennis, golf, swimming (Ex-President Manchester University Swimming Club), climbing, ski-ing. *Address:* Davenham, Wythenshawe Road, Northenden, Manchester; 2 St. John Street, Manchester. *T.:* Wythenshawe 2521; Blackfriars 9757 and 9758. *Clubs:* Reform, University Union (Manchester); Mere Golf and Country (Bucklow Hill); Didsbury Golf; Northern Lawn Tennis. [*Died* 23 *March* 1955.

SCOTT, Agnes Catharine, C.B.E. 1930; *b.* 26 Oct. 1875; 2nd *d.* of late Canon John Scott of Hull, Leeds and Wanstead. *Educ.:* Leeds Girls' High School; Yorkshire College, Leeds; London Royal Free Hosp. School of Medicine for Women. Qualified M.B. London, 1901; arrived in India, 1903; Cambridge Mission to Delhi, 1903-17; admitted to Women's Medical Service, 1917; Asst. to Inspector General, Civil Hospitals, Punjab, 1917-23; Chief Medical Officer, Women's Medical Service, India, and Secretary, Countess of Dufferin's Fund, 1924-32; Kaisar-i-Hind Medal 1st Class, 1925. *Address:* France Lynch, Stroud, Glos. *Club:* Overseas. [*Died* 22 *March* 1955.

SCOTT, Sir Angus Newton, Kt., *cr.* 1933; F.C.A.; D.L. County of London; J.P. County of Argyllshire; Chairman, Moran Tea Co. Ltd.; *b.* 1876; *yr. s.* of late Newton Scott, of Lloyd's; *m.* 1st, 1904, Frances Mary (*d.* 1934), *d.* of late C. A. Granlund; two *d.*; 2nd, 1936, Joyce Alexina, *d.* of C. J. March, Parkside Gardens, Wimbledon; one *d.* *Educ.:* City of London School. Served articles to Chartered Accountant; admitted to Institute of Chartered Accountants in England and Wales, 1899; Fellow, 1920; Freeman of City of London; Liveryman of Glaziers Company; Past Grand Deacon of the United Grand Lodge of Freemasons; Chairman of the Royal Commission on Local Government on Tyneside, 1935-37; a member of the Departmental Committee appointed by the Minister of Health on Thames flood prevention; a member of the London County Council for the Putney electoral division, 1922-34, for City of London division, 1934-41; Chairman of the London County Council, 1932-33; a representative of the Council on the Standing Joint Committee on Salaries of Teachers in Elementary Schools, 1923-31; on the London and Home Counties Traffic Advisory Committee, 1925-34; on the Greater London Regional Planning Committee, 1929-37; and on the Committee set up by the Minister of Health for the establishment of a post-graduate hospital and medical school; Chairman

Finance Committee of L.C.C. 1927-32. *Recreations:* fishing, yachting, and golf. *Address:* Anscombe Close, Worthing, Sussex. [*Died* 21 *Dec.* 1958.

SCOTT, Arthur, R.B.A., 1929; A.R.C.A. (Lond.); Painter Etcher; retired; *b.* Stoke-on-Trent, 1881; *s.* of George T. Scott, Potter; *m.* Eleanor Figgins; one *s.* *Educ.:* Wedgwood Institute; Burslem School of Art; Royal College of Art, South Kensington. Formerly Ceramic Artist at Doulton's Pottery; Premier National Scholar in Painting; 2 National Silver Medals for design for pottery; obtained 4 King's prizes for drawing from the life and drawing the antique; Master of Painting at Cambridge, 1913-16; Headmaster School of Arts and Crafts, Barnstaple, 1916-19; late Principal Watford School of Art and Crafts and Watford School of Printing; assisted on the decorations of the Peace Palace at the Hague; travelled in Holland, Belgium, and France; exhibited Royal Academy, The Salon, Paris, Liverpool, Manchester and other Provincial Galleries; Examiner to the Union of Educational Institutions. *Address:* 45 King's Way, Harrow. *Club:* Chelsea Arts. [*Died* 15 *Aug.* 1953.

SCOTT, Charles Thomas; Master of the North Cotswold Hounds, 1908-21; late Capt. Royal Gloucestershire Hussars; *b.* 4 Mar. 1868; 5th *s.* of Sir Walter Scott, Bart., and Ann, *d.* of John Brough, of Bromfield, Cumberland; *m.* Jane Davidson, *d.* of late James Milvain, Newcastle on Tyne; one *s.* *Educ.:* privately; Jesus College, Cambridge. *Address:* Buckland Manor, Broadway, Worcestershire. *Club:* Boodle's. [*Died* 14 *Jan.* 1953.

SCOTT, Christopher Fairfax, M.A.; retd.; *b.* 28 July 1894; *s.* of Reginald Fairfax Scott and Frances Louisa Lewis; *m.* 1932, Muriel Gladys Rowe. *Educ.:* Lancing College; Oriel College, Oxford. 2nd Lt. 8th Bn. The Rifle Brigade, 1914; invalided, 1915; English Instructor, Imperial Naval College, Etajima, Japan, 1917; Assistant Master, Radley College, 1920; Cheltenham College, 1920; Kelvinside Academy, Glasgow, 1920-21; Cheltenham College, 1921-27; Headmaster, Monmouth School, 1928-36; Headmaster, Brighton College, 1937-38; Headmaster, Cathedral School, Hereford, 1940-45. *Address:* Point House, Devoran, Truro, Cornwall. [*Died* 22 *Jan.* 1958.

SCOTT, David Russell, M.A. (Edin.); B.A. (Oxon); Ph.D. and Hon. D.D. (St. Andrews); Professor of Biblical Languages, Criticism and Exegesis, Congregational College, Edinburgh, since 1920, Principal, 1941-44; Examiner in Biblical Criticism, Univ. of St. Andrews; Pres. of the Congregational Union of Scotland, 1928-29; *b.* Airdrie, Lanarkshire; *s.* of late Rev. Adam Scott, Congregational Minister, Southport; *m.* Gertrude Mary, 3rd *d.* of late Edward Wellbank Robinson Mitchell, Manchester; one *s.* one *d.* *Educ.:* Manchester Grammar School; Edinburgh University; Mansfield College, Oxford; Germany. Pusey and Ellerton Scholar, Oxford; Dr. Williams Divinity Scholar; Assistant Lecturer, Mansfield College; Minister of the Congregational Church, Wick, 1897-1904; Montrose, 1904-18; of Castle Street Chapel, Dundee, 1918-20. *Publications:* Pessimism and Love, a Study in Ecclesiastes and Song of Songs; Christ, Sin and Redemption; articles in The Story of the Bible, 1938; joint author of Ecclesiastes and Song of Songs in the Study Bible; and of an Introduction to the Literature of the Old Testament; joint-editor of the Humanism of the Bible Series; articles in Encyclopædia of Religion and Ethics, Abingdon Commentary, Expository Times, etc. *Address:* 31 Dick Place, Edinburgh. [*Died* 10 *March* 1954.

SCOTT, Denis Herbert, C.B.E. 1956; D.Phil.; Chairman Revertex Ltd. since 1938; Deputy-Chairman Public Works Loan Board since 1948; and Director of other Public Companies; *b.* 17 Oct. 1899; *o. s.* of Cecil Scott, solicitor, St. Albans, and Lizzie Gertrude Reynolds; *m.* 1932, Laura Innes Foster; three *d.* *Educ.:* St. Lawrence College, Ramsgate; Balliol College, Oxford. Open Mathematical Schol., Balliol, 1917; 1st Cl. Maths. Mods., 1919; 1st Cl. Natural Science, 1921; D.Phil. 1923. Served European War, 1914-1918, 2nd Lieut. R.E., 1918; War of 1939-45, Flight Lt., R.A.F.V.R., 1939; Group Capt., 1945. Member Governing Body, and Hon. Treasurer, St. Lawrence Coll.; Chm. Governing Body, West Heath School, Sevenoaks. *Recreations:* lawn tennis, sailing; formerly hockey (O.U. Hockey Club, Capt. 1923; played for Hockey Assoc. XI *v.* Holland and Belgium, 1926). *Address:* Farley Grange, Westerham, Kent. *T.:* Westerham 3218. *Clubs:* Brooks's, City of London, United University; Vincent's (Oxford). [*Died* 10 *Feb.* 1958.

SCOTT, Sir Douglas Edward, 7th Bt., *cr.* 1806; *b.* 2 Feb. 1863; *g.-g. s.* of 1st Bt.; *S. cousin,* 1905; *m.* 1899, Florence Ada, *d.* of W. Wilderman; three *s.* two *d.* Ordained 1905; Curate of Birchington, 1905-6; Longbridge, Deverill, with Crockerton, 1906-8; Bere Regis with Winterbourne, 1908-13; Rector of Teffont-Ewyas, 1913-14. *Heir: s.* Edward Arthur Dolman, *b.* 14 Dec. 1905. [*Died* 22 *Aug.* 1951.

SCOTT, Ernest Findlay, D.D.; Union Theological Seminary, New York, since 1919; *b.* 1868; *s.* of Rev. E. F. Scott, Glasgow; *m.* Annie Roxburgh, *d.* of George Dunlop, Kilmarnock; one *d.* *Educ.:* Glasgow University; Balliol College, Oxford. Minister of South U.F. Church, Prestwick, Ayrshire, 1895-1908; Professor N.T. Literature, Queen's University, Kingston, Ontario, 1908-19. *Publications:* The Fourth Gospel: its Purpose and Theology, 1906; The Apologetic of the New Testament, 1907; The Kingdom and the Messiah, 1911; The Beginnings of the Church, 1914; The New Testament To-Day, 1921; The Epistle to the Hebrews, 1922; The Spirit in the New Testament, 1923; The Ethical Teaching of Jesus, 1924; The First Age of Christianity, 1926; The Gospel and its Tributaries, 1929; Commentary on Colossians and Ephesians, 1930; The Kingdom of God, 1931; The Literature of the New Testament, 1933; The New Testament Idea of Revelation, 1935; The Validity of the Gospel Record, 1937; The Nature of the Early Church, 1941; The Purpose of the Gospels, 1949; The Crisis in the Life of Jesus. *Address:* Union Theological Seminary, New York City, U.S.A. [*Died* 21 *July* 1954.

SCOTT, Ernest Newey; J.P. Stoke-on-Trent; F.R.S.A.; Editor Staffordshire Evening and Weekly Sentinel, Hanley, Stoke-on-Trent, 1927-48; Director, Staffordshire Sentinel Newspaper Ltd.; 2nd *s.* of late Samuel Scott, Walsall, and Paulina Newey, Birmingham; *m.* Fanny Bennett, Burslem. *Educ.:* Queen Mary's School, Walsall (school medallist, 1896). Journalistic appointments in the Midlands; Chief Sub-Editor and Art Critic Staffordshire Sentinel, 1911-27; correspondent of The Times, 1912-1927; Mayor, Ancient Corporation of Hanley, 1934-35. *Publications:* special articles in daily journals and magazines on industry (chiefly pottery and mining) and art (principally painting and ceramics). *Address:* Newstead, Harrowby Drive, Newcastle, Staffs. [*Died* 26 *Feb.* 1952.

SCOTT, Hon. Sir Ernest Stowell, K.C.M.G., *cr.* 1931 (C.M.G. 1912); M.V.O. 1905; *b.* 1 Nov. 1872; 2nd *s.* of 3rd Earl of Eldon; *m.* 1941, Winifred Brodrick; one *d.* (and one adopted *d.*). *Educ.:* Winchester College. Attaché, 1896; 3rd Secretary, 1898; British Agent on Newfoundland Claims Arbitration Tribunal, Paris, 1905; Acting Agent and Consul-General, Sofia, 1906; Chargé d'Affaires, Monte Video, 1909; Counsellor to the Legation, Tehran, 1916-19;

acted as Counsellor to the Residency, Cairo, 1920-23; Envoy Extraordinary and Minister Plenipotentiary at Monte Video, 1925-30. *Address:* Encombe, Wareham, Dorset. *T.A.:* Encombe Kingston-Dorset. *T.:* Corfe Castle 216. [*Died* 6 *Nov.* 1953.

SCOTT, Eustace Lindsay, C.M.G. 1933; O.B.E.; M.C.; *b.* 22 Oct. 1885; *s.* of late B. C. G. Scott, H.B.M.'s Consular Service, China, and Ada Elizabeth Tickell: *m.* 1926, Edith Gertrude, *er. d.* of late C. H. V. Hathorn; one *s.* one *d.* *Educ.:* Bradfield College; University College, Oxford, B.A. Assistant District Commissioner, Uganda, 1908; District Commissioner, 1918; seconded for Military service, 1914-19; Lieut., E.A. Carrier Corps, 1914; Deputy Assistant Director of Transport, E.A.E.F., 1916; Deputy Director of Military Labour, E.A.E.F., 1917; Labour Commissioner, Uganda Protectorate, 1921; Assistant Secretary for Native Affairs, 1922; Assistant Chief Secretary, 1924; Deputy Chie. Secretary, 1930; Chief Secretary, 1932-35; Acting Governor and C. in C., in 1932 and 1934; retired, 1935. *Address:* Little Stover, Camp Road, Gerrards Cross, Bucks. *T.:* Gerrards Cross 3177. [*Died* 15 *May* 1956.

SCOTT, Lt.-Col. Lord Francis (George Montagu-Douglas-), K.C.M.G., *cr.* 1937; D.S.O. 1915; late Grenadier Guards; *b.* 1 Nov. 1879; 6th *s.* of 6th Duke of Buccleuch; *m.* 1915, Lady Eileen Elliot (*d.* 1938), *e. d.* of 4th Earl of Minto; two *d.* *Educ.:* Eton; Christ Church, Oxford. Entered Army, 1899; Captain, 1908; A.D.C. to Viceroy of India, 1905-1910; served S. Africa, 1900-2 (Queen's medal 3 clasps, King's medal 2 clasps); European War, 1914-18 (despatches, D.S.O., Bt. Lt.-Col.); retired pay, 1920; rejoined Army, 1941, as A.M.S. to G.O.C. E.A. Forces; served in Ethiopian campaign (despatches). Late Member of Executive Council and of Legislative Council, Kenya Colony. *Recreations:* shooting, golf. *Address:* Deloraine, Rongai, Kenya Colony. *Clubs:* Guards, White's, Turf, M.C.C. [*Died* 26 *July* 1952.

SCOTT, Lieut.-Col. George, C.M.G. 1917; M.B.; C.M.; D.P.H.; R.A.M.C., retired; *b.* 1859; *m.* 1st, 1890; 2nd, 1920. Served in Jamaica, Burma, India, and Egypt. *Address:* 132 Hamilton Place, Aberdeen. *T.:* Aberdeen 23030. [*Died* 10 *Sept.* 1955.

SCOTT, Lady (George); *see* Mitton, G. E.

SCOTT, Sir Giles Gilbert, O.M. 1944; Kt., *cr.* 1924; R.A. 1922 (A.R.A. 1918); Hon. D.C.L. Oxford, 1933; Hon. LL.D. Liverpool Univ., 1955; Cambridge, 1955; Hon. Fellow, Trinity College, Toronto, 1958; *b.* 1880; *s.* of George Gilbert Scott; *g.s.* of Sir G. Gilbert Scott; *g.g.g.s.* of Rev. Thomas Scott, Commentator; *m.* 1914, Louise Wallbank Hughes (*d.* 1949); two *s.* *Educ.:* Beaumont Coll., Old Windsor. *Principal Works:* Liverpool Cathedral; new Chapel, Charterhouse School; new Nave, Downside Abbey; new Church, Ampleforth Abbey; St. Maughold's Church and Presbytery, Ramsey, Isle of Man; Restoration Works, Chester Cathedral; St. Paul's Church, Derby Lane, Liverpool; Church of Our Lady, Northfleet; New Buildings, Clare College, Cambridge; Wm. Booth Memorial Buildings, Denmark Hill; The New Whitelands Training College, Putney; additions to Magdalen College, Oxford; St. Mary's Church, Terriers, High Wycombe; New Buildings and Chapel, Lady Margaret Hall, Oxford; St. Andrew's Church, Luton; St. Alban's Church, Golders Green; New Library, Cambridge University; Extensions to Bodleian Library, Oxford; Waterloo Bridge; Rebuilding of the House of Commons; Reconstruction of London Guildhall and Precincts; Chapel of Trinity College, Toronto. P.R.I.B.A., 1933-1935. *Address:* 9 Gray's Inn Square, Gray's Inn, W.C.1. *T.:* Chancery 8388; Chester House, Clarendon Place, W.2. *Club:* Athenæum. [*Died* 8 *Feb.* 1960.

SCOTT, Guy Harden Guillum; Assistant Secretary, Church Assembly, 1920-1939, Joint Secretary, 1939-46; *b.* 1874; *e. s.* of late Sir Arthur Guillum Scott, Accountant-Gen. India Office; *m.* 1910, Anne Dorothea, (*d.* 1956), *e. d.* of late Rev. T. L. Tudor Fitzjohn, J.P., Salop; two *s.* one *d.* *Educ.:* Westminster; Christ Church, Oxon. Barrister-at-law, Inner Temple; Private Secretary successively to late Sir F. Seager Hunt, M.P., Lord Cochrane of Cults, and Viscount Chaplin; served in South African War with the C.I.V.M.I., and 1914-17 with the A.A.C. and Inns of Court Regt. Chancellor of Diocese: Peterborough, 1930-55; Winchester, 1930-58; Oxford, 1937-1958. *Publications:* The Law relating to the Prevention of Cruelty to Animals; The Diary of the C.I.V.M.I. *Address:* Drayton Beauchamp, Aylesbury. [*Died* 24 *Nov.* 1960.

SCOTT, Sir (Henry) Harold, K.C.M.G., *cr.* 1941 (C.M.G. 1936); M.D., F.R.C.P. Lond., D.P.H., D.T.M.H. Camb. F.R.S.E., F.Z.S.; late Member of Board of Directors of Chest Hospitals of London; Consultant Physician William Julien Courtauld Hospital; late Pres. Roy. Soc. of Tropical Medicine and Hygiene; *b.* 3 Aug. 1874; *s.* of Rev. Dr. Douglas Lee Scott, M.A., LL.D. Cantab.; *m.* 1st, Harriette (*d.* 1933), *d.* of Rev. d'Arcy Harrington Preston, Attleborough, Norfolk; (one *s.* decd.); 2nd, 1934, Eileen Anne, *d.* of Rev. R. P. Prichard, M.A. (Oxon.), Vicar of Wilburton, Cambs. *Educ.:* Mercers; City of London; Univ. Coll.; St. Bartholomew's and St. Thomas's Hosps.; Copenhagen. Resident M.O. Teignmouth, Dawlish and Newton Abbot Infirmary; House Physician St. Thomas's Hospital; R.A.M.C. Capt., South African War; M.O. i/c Hosp. for Women and Children, Fort Napier, Maritzburg; European War; Pathologist, Cambridge Hospital, Aldershot, in charge Mobile Laboratory No. 13; Milner Research Fellow in Comparative Pathology, London School of Hygiene and Tropical Medicine; Pathologist, Zoological Society of London; Govt. Bacteriologist, Jamaica, B.W.I.; Hong Kong; Lecturer on Bacteriology, Medical Jurisprudence, and Public Health, Victoria Univ.; Lecturer on Tropical Disease, Westminster Hospital Medical School; Director, Bureau of Hygiene and Tropical Diseases, 1935-42; late Mem. Tropical sub-committee, Royal Society; Chm. Anglo-Soviet Med. Cttee.; Examiner in Tropical Medicine and Surgery, Conjoin, Board of Royal Coll. Physicians and Surgeons. Medical Secretary, Colonial Medical Research Committee; Examiner for Diplomas in Tropical Medicine and Tropical Hygiene, and in Parasitology for the Diploma in Public Health, and the B.Vet.Sc. Liverpool University; FitzPatrick Lecturer, Royal Coll. of Physicians, London. *Publications:* British Red Cross Manual of Tropical Hygiene (with Maj.-Gen. D. T. Richardson), 1946; A History of Tropical Medicine, 2 vols., 1939; Some Notable Epidemics, 1934; Postgraduate Clinical Studies; Health Problems of the Empire (with Sir Andrew Balfour); Tuberculosis in Man and Lower Animals, Medical Research Council, Special Report Series; Ed. of Proc. of Ninth Internat. Congress on Industrial Medicine, 1948; papers on scientific subjects. *Recreation:* books. *Address:* Fox Meadow, Braintree, Essex. *T.:* Braintree 694. [*Died* 6 *Aug.* 1956.

SCOTT, Sir Henry Milne, Kt., *cr.* 1928; Q.C.; *b.* Levuka, Fiji, 1876; *s.* of late William Scott, Barrister; *m.* 1900, Nellie Weir Lindsay, *d.* of Chairman Methodist Mission; one *s.* one *d.* *Educ.:* Sydney Grammar School, Australia. Called to Bar of Fiji, 1899; President of Suva Chamber of Commerce, 1908-1922; took silk, 1912; Mayor of Suva, 1914-22; was Member of Executive and Legislative Council for many years; acting Attorney-General, Fiji, for several periods since 1913;

represented Fiji as its official representative at coronation of King George VI and Queen Elizabeth, 1937; Life Member Royal Empire Soc. *Recreations:* riding, fishing, lawn tennis, etc. *Address:* Eldon Chambers, Suva, Fiji. *Clubs:* Australian (Sydney); Fiji, Defence (Fiji). [*Died* 20 *May* 1956.

SCOTT, Sir Herbert Septimus, Kt., *cr.* 1948; C.M.G. 1935; *b.* 6 Sept. 1873; *m.* Ada Gertrude, *d.* of E. Latchford; one *s.* two *d.* *Educ.:* Eton; Hertford College, Oxford. Inspector of Schools, Transvaal, 1902; Secretary Transvaal Education Dept. 1911; Director of Education, Transvaal, 1924; Director of Education, Kenya, 1928-35; retired 1935; Member of Committee of Economic Advisory Council on Nutrition in the Colonial Empire; Member of Colonial Office Advisory Committee on Education in the Colonies. *Address:* 21 Boundary Road, Woking, Surrey. [*Died* 16 *Feb.* 1952.

SCOTT, Hugh, F.R.S. 1941; F.L.S.; F.R. Entomological S.; Sc.D.; *b.* 16 Sept. 1885; *er. s.* of late William Edward Scott (descendant of the family of Scot's Hall, Kent), and of late Edith Truscott, *er. d.* of late James Chapman Amos, M.Inst.C.E.; *m.* 1913, Beatrice Emily (*d.* 1947), *e. d.* of late Arthur Ogle Streatfeild; one *s.* one *d.* (and one *d.* decd.). *Educ.:* privately; Trinity College, Cambridge (Exhibitioner). Nat. Sciences Tripos, Part I, Class I; Curator in Entomology in University of Cambridge, 1909-28; Entomologist in Hygiene Dept., Royal Army Medical College, 1917-18; Entomologist in Dept. of Agriculture, Baghdad, Iraq, 1928; Assistant Keeper of Entomology in British Museum (Natural History), 1930-1948, retired; principal writer of official Handbook of Western Arabia and the Red Sea, for Naval Intelligence Division, Admiralty, 1942-46; Leverhulme Research Fellow, 1937; Member, 1911-28, of (Colonial Office) Entomological Research Committee (Tropical Africa), from 1913 called Hon. Committee of Management, Imperial Bureau (later Institute) of Entomology; Councils of Linnean Soc., 1933-36, and Roy. Entomological Soc., 1925-27 (Vice-Pres., 1926; elected Hon. Fell., 1954); editorial staff, Entomologists Monthly Magazine, 1923-; natural-history exploratory expeditions to Seychelles (mem. of the Percy Sladen Trust Expedition), 1908-9; central Abyssinia, 1926-27 (with J. Omer-Cooper, F.L.S.); S.W. Arabia, 1937-38; Southern Ethiopia (Gughé Highlands), 1948-49; Northern Ethiopia (high Simien), 1952-53; shorter journeys to West Indies, Basutoland, Kurdistan, and several European countries. *Publications:* In the High Yemen, 1942, 2nd edn. 1947; many entomological works in scientific journals from 1907 onwards: illustrated general articles on high Ethiopia (Proc. Linn. Soc., Vols. 163, 1952 and 170, 1958, and Webbia (Florence), vol. 11, 1955) and on the Yemen (Geographical Journal, Feb. 1939, and Journal of Royal Central Asian Society, Jan. 1940); also A Naturalist in Basutoland (Discovery, vol. 11, 1930); article on Early Clay Tobacco Pipes (Cambridge Antiquarian Soc., 1917). *Recreation:* gardening. *Address:* Ancastle Cottage, Gravel Hill, Henley-on-Thames. *T.:* Henley-on-Thames 593. [*Died* 1 *Nov.* 1960.

SCOTT, Maj.-Gen. John Walter Lennox, C.B. 1941; D.S.O. 1918; late R.A.M.C.; *b.* 30 Jan. 1883; *m.*; two *s.* Served European War, 1914-18 (despatches, D.S.O.); Deputy Assistant Director-General, War Office, 1926-30; Bt. Colonel, 1932; Col. 1934; Major-Gen., 1937; Assistant Director-General Army Medical Services, 1933-35; Deputy Director-General, Army Medical Services, 1935-37; K.H.P., 1934-41; Deputy Director of Medical Services Eastern Command, 1937-39; Director, 1939; retired pay, 1941. *Address:* c/o Glyn, Mills (Holt's Branch), Kirkland House, Whitehall, S.W.1. [*Died* 6 *Nov.* 1960.

SCOTT, Sir Lindsay; *see* Scott, Sir Warwick L.

SCOTT, Noel; dramatist and physician; *b.* 25 Dec. 1890; *e. s.* of Rev. John Hugh Scott, Hampstead; *m.* 1927, Elizabeth Colls (marriage dissolved, 1941). *Educ.:* Manchester Grammar School; Reading School; Trinity Hall, Cambridge; St. Bartholomew's Hospital. M.R.C.S., L.R.C.P. 1915; served in the Fourth Destroyer Flotilla, 1914-15; subsequently as a Captain in the R.A.M.C. in France, 1915-17 (wounded and invalided, 1917); after serving as surgeon in the Royal Mail and Cunard S.S. Cos. was appointed Medical Assessor, Ministry of Pensions; started private practice, 1920; specialised in physio-therapy, 1932; first began writing after the 1914-18 War, revue sketches at first, and subsequently plays. Served War of 1939-45, as Squadron Leader R.A.F. in Malta, West Africa, and N. W. Europe. *Publications: Revues* (part author), The Rainbow (with Edgar Wallace), 1923; The Odd Spot (with Dion Titheradge), 1924; Shake Your Feet, 1927; De La Folie Pure, 1930. *Plays* (author): The Broken Thread, 1925; Half-a-Loaf, 1926; The Joker, 1927; Dawn, 1927; Traffic, 1930; The Millionaire Kid, 1931; Playground, 1932; Ourselves Alone, 1932 (with Dudley Sturrock); And the Music Stopped, 1937; Life Goes On, 1940; Man from Heaven, 1943; Not Quite Herself, 1953; A Leap in the Dark, 1954. *Recreations:* reading, golf, motoring. *Address:* 4 Home Farm Close, Thames Ditton, Surrey. *T.:* Emberbrook 3942. [*Died* 20 *Nov.* 1956.

SCOTT, Lieut.-Col. Norman (Emile Henry), C.I.E. 1918; I.M.S., retired; *b.* Greenock, Dec. 1875; *y. s.* of John Scott, jr., of Finnart House, Greenock, Renfrew; *m.* 1902, Laura Elizabeth (*d.* 1943), 2nd *d.* of Hugh Roberts, Old Bank House, Llanrwst, North Wales; one *s.* *Educ.:* Sedbergh School; Glasgow and Paris Universities; M.B. Glasgow University, 1897. Entered Indian Medical Service, 1901; joined Political Dept. Govt. of India, 1906; served as Agency and Residency Surgeon at Muscat (Arabia) and Baghdad, Iraq, 1906-14; Vice-Consul, Baghdad, 1911; Acting Consul-General and Political Resident, Baghdad, June to Nov. 1914; served M.E.F. 1914-19, attached to Executive of Central Administration of Civil Commissioner at Baghdad (despatches, C.I.E). *Recreations:* golf and tennis. *Address:* c/o National Overseas and Grindlays Bank, Ltd., 54 Parliament Street, S.W.1. [*Died* 10 *Oct.* 1958.

SCOTT, Sir Oswald (Arthur), K.C.M.G., *cr.* 1951 (C.M.G. 1946); D.S.O. 1918; *b.* 1893; 2nd *s.* of Archibald Scott, Rotherfield Park, Alton, Hants.; *m.* 1st, 1917, Hermione Monica, *y. d.* of William Ferrand, St. Ives, Bingley, Yorkshire; one *s.* (and two killed in action 1940 and 1942), one *d.*; divorced 1933; *m.* 2nd, 1934, Ursula Margaret, *y. d.* of Rev. H. B. Wolryche Whitmore, Royal Hill, Tewkesbury. Served with Hampshire Regiment, European War, 1914-18 (despatches, D.S.O.); British Minister to Finland, 1947-51; Ambassador to Peru, 1951-53; retired 1954. *Address:* 47 Lowndes Square, S.W.1. *T.:* Belgravia 3561. [*Died* 19 *May* 1960.

SCOTT, Sir (Robert) Russell, K.C.B. 1922 (C.B. 1919); C.S.I. 1916; I.S.O. 1932; *b.* 30 Dec. 1877; *s.* of Rev. Adam Scott of Sale and Southport; *m.* 1904, Helen, *y. d.* of Principal Fairbairn of Mansfield College, Oxford. *Educ.:* Manchester Grammar School; Wadham College, Oxford (Scholar). First Class, Honour Moderations, 1897; First Class, Lit.Hum., 1900; Clerk, Class I. Admiralty, 1901; Private Secretary to Civil Lord of the Admiralty, 1904-7; Joint Secretary to Royal Commission on Indian Public Services, 1912-15; Member of Central Control Board (Liquor Traffic), 1915; Acting Assistant Secretary Admiralty, 1917; Deputy Controller of Establishments, H.M. Treasury, 1920; Controller, 1921-32; Permanent Under-

Secretary of State, Home Office, 1932 - 38. *Address:* Invererne, Forres, Morayshire.
[*Died* 16 *March* 1960.

SCOTT, Sir Samuel Haslam, 2nd Bt., of Yews, Westmorland, *cr.* 1909; *b.* 7 Aug. 1875; *s.* of 1st Bt. and Anne Jane, 2nd *d.* of late John Haslam, J.P., of Gilnow Hall, Bolton-le-Moors, and *nephew* of late Lt.-Col. G. F. Scott, D.L., of Penmaenucha and Arthog Hall, Merioneth; *S.* father, 1913; *m.* 1st, 1905, Carmen Estelle (*d.* 1919), *d.* of late Edmund Heuer, of Dunham Knoll, Dunham Massey, Cheshire; (one *s.*, died of wounds in Libya) one *d.* (and one *d.* decd.); 2nd, 1920, Nancy Lilian (*d.* 1935), *d.* of late William Charles Anderson, Hill House, Keston, Kent; one *s.*; 3rd, 1937, Marion Dorothy, *d.* of Charles Garnett, Hall Garth, near Carnforth. *Educ.:* at home on account of health; Oriel College, Oxford, M.A.; Heatherley's School of Art, 1899-1901. Chairman of Provincial Fire and Accident Insurance Office, 1913-46; J.P. Westmorland; High Sheriff, 1926; Chairman Westmorland Agricultural Soc., 1931-50 and Pres. of Fell Sheep Breeders Association; Chairman of Westmorland Cancer Commission which promulgated Sambon's theory of Virus Causation, 1929; a Vice-Pres. of Cumberland and Westmorland Antiquarian Soc. Formerly member of Exec. Committee of National Trust; gave Tarns near Coniston to National Trust and placed Glencoyne Park estate on Ullswater (2,000 acres) under restrictive covenant. Hon. Member of Johnson Club. *Publications:* A Westmorland Village, 1904; Supplément au Répertoire Bibliographique Strasbourgeois vers 1530, 1910; Memoir of Sir James William Scott, 1914; The Silver Ship, 1926; Vignettes of Childhood, 1927; Robino (translated from the Italian), 1932 and in U.S.A. 1933; The Exemplary Mr. Day, 1935; contributions to the Transactions of the Bibliographical Soc., Spectator, Nineteenth Century, and various journals. *Heir: s.* Oliver Christopher Anderson [*b.* 6 Nov. 1922; *m.* 1951, Phoebe-Ann, *d.* of Desmond O'N. Tolhurst. *Educ.:* Charterhouse; King's Coll., Cambridge (B.A., M.B., Ch.B.). *Club:* Brooks's]. *Address:* Yews, Undermilbeck, Windermere; Sand Aire House, Kendal, Westmorland. *Club:* Brooks's.
[*Died* 23 *June* 1960.

SCOTT, Rt. Rev. Thomas Arnold; *b.* 9 June 1879. *Educ.:* Christ's College, Cambridge (Scholar); Leeds Clergy School. Deacon, 1902; Priest, 1903; S.P.G. Missionary in North China, 1908; Principal of the Church of England School, Peking, 1913; Bishop of Shantung, 1921-40; Bishop of North China, 1940-50. *Address:* Cleeves, France Lynch, Stroud, Glos.
[*Died* 29 *March* 1956.

SCOTT, Colonel Wallace Arthur, C.M.G. 1918; B.A.; M.D. (Tor.); F.R.C.S.; C.A.M.C.; *s.* of Wm. Scott, B.A., Principal, Toronto Normal School; *m.* Evelyn (*d.* 1940), *d.* of late Hugh Byron Ronan, Ottawa; no *c.* *Educ.:* Ottawa Collegiate Institute; Toronto University; King's College, London. Served European War (C.M.G.). *Address:* 627 Sherbourne Street, Toronto, Canada.
[*Died* 4 *Jan.* 1949.

[*But death not notified in time for inclusion in Who Was Who* 1941–1950, *first edn.*

SCOTT, Major-Gen. Sir Walter J. C. M.; *see* Maxwell-Scott.

SCOTT, Sir Walter Lawrence, Kt., *cr.* 1939; C.I.E. 1929; I.C.S. (retired); *b.* Rangiora, New Zealand, 1880; *m.* 1910, Beatrix Mary, *d.* of J. H. Nicholson, Nelson, New Zealand; two *d.* *Educ.:* Christ's College Grammar School, Christchurch, N.Z.; Canterbury College, Christchurch, N.Z. Indian Civil Service, 1904; Assistant Magistrate and Collector, East Bengal and Assam, 1905; Assistant Commissioner, Assam, 1912; Settlement Officer, Cachar, Assam, 1913; Director of Department of Land Records, Assam, 1923; Commissioner, 1934; Member of Governor's Executive Council, 1935. *Address:* c/o Grindlay & Co. Ltd., 54 Parliament Street, S.W.1; 24A Bronte St., Nelson, New Zealand.
[*Died* 20 *Jan.* 1951.

SCOTT, Walter Samuel, K.C., J.P., LL.D.; *b.* 28 Feb. 1870; 5th *s.* of William Scott, M.D., J.P., F.R.C.S., The Bawn, Aughnacloy, Co. Tyrone, and Anne Atkinson Crossle; *m.* 1899, Annie Sidney, *d.* of William Smith, C.E., Dublin; one *s.* *Educ.:* The High School, Dublin; Trinity College, Dublin (a first Honoursman in Classics and English Literature, Classical Sizar and a Senior and Junior Exhibitioner); King's Inns, Dublin; Lincoln's Inn, London. Assistant Master, Royal School, Dungannon; Barrister-at-law, Lincoln's Inn; devilled for Sir P. S. Gregory, Conveyancing Counsel to the Court; on Editorial Staff of Halsbury's Laws of England; Editor in Chief of Western Weekly Reports Canada; Adviser on Legal Studies to University of Alberta; Legislative Counsel to Legislative Assembly of Alberta; one of the Commissioners for Uniformity of Legislation in Canada; Vice-President of Canadian Bar Association; Bencher of Law Society of Alberta. *Publications:* Keats' Poems, 1903; La Rochefoucauld's Maxims, 1904; Fitzgerald's Omar Khayyam and Salaman and Absal, 1902; London Pride (with Joan Stevenson and W. Sidney Scott), 1947; The Bluestockings, 1947; White of Selborne, His Life and Times, 1945; Torrens System Mortgages, 1917; Canadian Constitution, 1918; Homestead Exemptions, 1919; Chattel Exemptions, 1919; Contract, in Canadian Encyclopaedic Digest, 1918; By-Laws, in Encyclopaedia of English Law, 1935; Craies' Statute Law, 1936; and many contributions to Canadian Law Times, Canadian Bar Review, and Quarterly Review. *Recreations:* reading, gardening and golf. *Address:* The Limes, Selborne, Hampshire. *T.:* Selborne 203. *Clubs:* British Empire; University (Dublin). [*Died* 6 *March* 1951.

SCOTT, Sir (Warwick) Lindsay, K.B.E., *cr.* 1942; D.S.C. 1918; F.S.A.; Archæologist; a Director of Marine and General Life Assurance Society, of Power Jets (Research and Development) Ltd. and of Times Veneer Co.; *b.* 1892; *o. s.* of late Robert Lindsay Scott, Hampstead, and Isabella Helen, *y. d.* of William Reid, Aberdeen; *m.* 1920, Winifred, *y. d.* of late J. G. Turner; one *s.* two *d.* *Educ.:* St. Paul's School; Clare College, Cambridge. Enployed on mine-sweeping duties, 1914-19, Lt., R.N.V.R. Appointed to Colonial Office, 1919; transferred to Air Ministry, 1919; acting Deputy Under-Sec. of State, 1940; Second Secretary, Ministry of Aircraft Production, 1940-46, and of Ministry of Supply, 1945-46; President Prehistoric Society, 1946-50. *Publications:* papers in archæological journals. *Address:* Parslows Hillock, Princes Risborough, Bucks. *T.:* Hampden Row 371. *Club:* Oxford and Cambridge. [*Died* 17 *June* 1952.

SCOTT, Col. Sir William Dishington, Kt., *cr.* 1947; C.B.E. 1942; D.S.O. 1917; M.C.; T.D.; Chief Divisional Food Officer, Scotland; *b.* 1878; *m.* Served European War, 1914-19; Maj. 16 (S) Bn. H.L.I. 1916; Col. 1929; Hon. Col. 6 Bn. H.L.I.; Chm. H.L.I. (City of Glasgow Regt.) Regtl. Assoc.; mil. member Glasgow T.A. and A.F. Assoc.; Hon. Col. 15th Parachute Bn. (Scottish); J.P. 1928, D.L. 1932, Glasgow. *Address:* 40 High Craighall Rd., Glasgow. *T.:* Douglas 3261; 3 Whittingehame Drive, Glasgow. *T.:* Western 1940. *Clubs:* Conservative, Royal Scottish Automobile, New (Glasgow).
[*Died* 22 *Feb.* 1952.

SCOTT, Rev. William Morris Fitz-Gerald, M.A.; Principal St. Aidan's College, Birkenhead, 1950-58; Hon. Canon, Chester Cathedral, since 1956; *b.* 10 July 1912; *s.* of late Col. M. F. Scott; *m.* 1943, Nora

Compigné, *d.* of Canon C. L. Shaw; two *s.* one *d.* *Educ.:* King's School, Canterbury; Trinity College, Oxford; Wycliffe Hall, Oxford. Curate of Christ Church, Folkestone, 1937-40; Tutor and Chaplain, Wycliffe Hall, Oxford, 1940-44; Chaplain, Hertford College, Oxford, 1942-44; Vicar of Christ Church, Toxteth Park, Liverpool, 1945-50. *Publications:* The Hidden Mystery, 1942; The Creed of a Christian, 1947; I believe in God, 1951. *Address:* St. Aidan's College, Birkenhead, Cheshire. *T.:* Birkenhead 1247. [*Died* 11 *Jan.* 1959.

SCOTT, Lt.-Col. Lord William Walter Montagu-Douglas-, M.C.; *b.* 1896; 2nd *s.* of 7th Duke of Buccleuch, K.T., G.C.V.O.; *m.* 1937, Lady Rachel Douglas Home, *yr. d.* of 13th Earl of Home; one *s.* four *d.* *Educ.:* Eton; Royal Military College, Sandhurst. M.P. (U.) Roxburgh and Selkirk, 1935-50. *Address:* Eildon Hall, St. Boswells, Roxburghshire. *T.:* St. Boswells 2105. *Clubs:* Carlton, Cavalry, Buck's. [*Died* 30 *Jan.* 1958.

SCOTT, Winifred Mary; novelist (pen-name Pamela Wynne); *d.* of Samuel and Lily Watson; *m.* 1905, Herbert, *o. s.* of late Archdeacon Scott of Bombay; three *s.* *Educ.:* privately; Lausanne. Wrote a few short stories for the Bystander and Hutchinsons, 1920 and 1923; published her first novel, 1923. *Publications:* Ann's an Idiot, 1923; Warning, 1923; The Dream Man, 1924; Ashes of Desire, 1925; Penelope Finds Out, 1926; Concealed Turnings, 1927; A Passionate Rebel, 1927; Mademoiselle Dahlia, 1928; Under the Mosquito Curtain, 1928; Rainbow in the Spray, 1929; At the End of the Avenue, 1929; A Little Flat in the Temple, 1930; East is Always East, 1930; The Last Days of September, 1931; Love in a Mist, 1932; The Sealed Door of Love, 1933; Delight, 1933; All About Jane, 1934; Bracken Turning Brown, 1934; A Dream Come True, 1935; Priscilla Falls in Love, 1935; Love Begins at Forty, 1936; Leave it to Love, 1936; Valerie, 1937; Sunshine After Rain, 1938; Choose from the Stars, 1938; Love's Lotus Flower; Honey-Coloured Moon; Splendour of Love, 1939; Happiness Round the Corner, 1940; Life will be Different, 1942; Merry Widows, 1943; Diana's Last Day, 1945; Pine-apple Place, 1946; Do You See the Sun ?, 1946; Gift of a Daughter, 1947; A Knight in Mufti, 1948; Come with Me to the Stars, 1949; Forsaking All Others, 1949; Safe at Last, 1949; Long Corridors, 1950; A Sunday in June, 1953; Dandelions for Henry, 1954; The Tide Has Turned, 1954; Daughter of Daybreak, 1955; Search for Love, 1955; The Doctor Decided, 1956; Moonlight Behind Me, 1956; Secluded Situation, 1956; The Doctor and Mrs. Marlowe, 1956; Oh! What a Lovely Day; Climbing to Happiness, 1957; Carols by Candlelight, 1958; Throw Wide the Windows, 1959. *Recreations:* writing, befriending cats; indoor plants. *Address:* The Old Rectory, Crowhurst, Battle, Sussex. [*Died* 29 *Jan.* 1959.

SCOTT-BARRETT, Rev. Hugh, C.B. 1946; C.B.E. 1937; T.D.; *b.* 3 March 1887; *y.s.* of late Sir William Scott Barrett and Julia Louisa Colvile; *m.* 1916, Dorothy, *d.* of late Rev. A. E. Farrar; three *s.* one *d.* *Educ.:* Aldenham School; St. John's College, Cambridge. Called to Bar, Inner Temple, 1911; Northern Circuit; served European War, France, 1915-18 (O.B.E., despatches twice); D.A.A.G. 1919; Deputy Judge Advocate-General, Army of the Rhine 1920-23, China 1927-28, Egypt 1935, Palestine 1936, B.E.F. (France) 1939-40, M.E.F. 1941-43, 21 Army Group, 1944-46 (despatches 5 times); retired pay, as Brigadier, 1949. Chm. Pensions Appeal Tribunal (Special Review), 1949-50. Ordained Priest, 1952. *Address:* St. Nicholas, Kingswood, Surrey. *T.:* Mogador 2451. [*Died* 30 *July* 1958.

SCOTT-DUFF, Bt. Lieut.-Col. Arthur Abercromby, C.I.E. 1912; M.V.O. 1917; late 3rd Gordon Highlanders; *b.* 11 Apr. 1874; 2nd *s.* of late Rt. Hon. Sir Robert Duff, G.C.M.G., of Fetteresso Castle and Louisa, 3rd *d.* of Sir William Scott, 6th Bart. of Ancrum; *m.* 1928, Stella, *er. d.* of late Lieut.-Gen. Sir Stanley Maude; two *d.* *Educ.:* Harrow. Private Secretary to the Governor of the Bahamas, 1897; A.D.C. to Governor of Singapore, 1898-99; Assistant and Vice-Consul at the Legation in Abyssinia, 1901-3; served with the Abyssinian Expeditionary Field Force in Somaliland, 1903-4 (despatches, medal); A.D.C. Lt.-Governor of Transvaal, 1905; A.D.C. Governor of Madras, 1906-9; Military Secretary Governor of Madras, 1909-12; served with 1st Batt. and 6th Batt. Gordon Highlanders, Aug. 1914; served with British Expeditionary Field Force in France; A.D.C. to Duke of Connaught, Governor-General of Canada, Dec. 1914. *Recreations:* hunting, shooting, etc. *Address:* Woodhay Lodge, Newbury, Berks. *Clubs:* Turf, Buck's. [*Died* 3 *Dec.* 1951.

SCOTT-JAMES, Rolfe Arnold, Captain, O.B.E. 1955; M.C. 1918; Journalist and Author; *b.* Stratford-on-Avon, 21 Dec. 1878; *s.* of Rev. John Scott-James; *m.* 1905, Violet Eleanor (*d.* 1942), *d.* of Captain Arthur Brooks; one *d.* (and one *s.* one *d.* decd.); *m.* 1947, Paule Honorine Jeanne, *d.* of late P. E. Lagarde. *Educ.:* Mill Hill School; Brasenose Coll., Oxford (Scholar). Lived for some time at Canning Town and Toynbee Hall; joined staff of Daily News, Dec. 1902; Literary Editor of Daily News, 1906-12; Editor of the New Weekly, 1914; Leader-writer, Daily Chronicle, 1919-30; Leader-writer and Assistant Editor of The Spectator, 1933-35; Editor of London Mercury, 1934-39; returned to the Spectator, 1939-45; Editor of Britain To-day, 1940-Dec. 1954. Member Executive of Balkan Committee, 1903-14; 2nd Lt. R.G.A. 1916; Captain, 1918; served Siege Artillery, B.E.F., France (M.C.). *Publications:* Modernism and Romance, 1908; An Englishman in Ireland, 1910; Personality in Literature, 1913; The Influence of the Press, 1913; Housing Conditions in Mining Areas, in Coal and Power, 1924; The Making of Literature, 1928; Personality in Literature (1913-31), 1931; edited Education in Britain, 1944; The Day before Yesterday, 1947; Fifty Years of English Literature, 1900 to 1950, 1951; Thomas Hardy, 1951; Lytton Strachey, 1955; contributions to Reviews, etc. *Address:* The Forge, Upper Basildon, Berkshire. *T.:* Upper Basildon 209; 2 Linton House, 11 Holland Park Avenue, W.11. *T.:* Park 6596. *Club:* Reform. [*Died* 3 *Nov.* 1959.

SCOTT-PAINE, Hubert; Chairman, British Power Boat Co., Ltd., Canadian Power Boat Co., Ltd., Marine Design and Engineering Development Corp., U.S.A.; *b.* 11 March, 1891. First flew, 1910; designed and built land aircraft, 1910-14; from then developed marine aircraft; constructed first circular flying boat hull, 1913; patented many original developments for flying boats; built first quadruplane and one of first twin-engined land machines in England and first all-cabin flying machine, 1915; opened first Internat. flying boat route Havre - Southampton, 1920, subsequently Southampton-Channel Islands; financed, built and organised British Challenger which won Schneider Trophy, 1922; Managing Owner of Supermarine Aviation Works, Ltd., 1920-23; organised and financed British Marine Air Navigation Co., 1923; incorporated with Imperial Airways, 1924; founder Director of Imperial Airways, 1924-40; founded British Power Boat Co., 1927; designed, built and raced Panther I, II and Miss Britain I, II and III, to win many international races; designed and built original Motor Torpedo Boat and Motor Gun Boats for Admiralty and High-speed Air/Sea Rescue Craft for R.A.F., 1934-46; designed and built P.T. Boats in U.S. and

Canada, 1939-46. *Address:* Hythe, Hants.; Smythe House, Shore Road, Greenwich, Connecticut, U.S.A. *Clubs:* Royal Aero, Royal Motor Yacht; Royal Southampton Yacht (Southampton); Wings, Indian Harbor Yacht (U.S.A.). [*Died* 14 *April* 1954.

SCRIBNER, Charles; President: Charles Scribner's Sons New York, N.Y., since 1932; Charles Scribner's Sons, Ltd., London, England; Director, Grosset & Dunlap, Inc., Bantam Books, Inc.; *b.* 26 Jan. 1890; *s.* of Charles Scribner & Louise Flagg; *m.* 1915, Vera Gordon Bloodgood; one *s.* one *d.* *Educ.:* St. Paul's School, Concord, N.H.; Princeton University. With Charles Scribner's Sons since 1913; Secretary, 1918-26; Vice-President, 1926-32. Trustee Blair Academy; Director of American Kennel Club. Served overseas as a 1st Lieut. European War, 1917-18, in United States Remount Service. *Recreations:* tennis, hunting. *Address:* Far Hills, New Jersey, U.S.A. *T.:* Peapack 8-0023. *Clubs:* Century Assoc., Racquet and Tennis (N.Y.). [*Died* 11 *Feb.* 1952.

SCRIMGEOUR, H(ugh) Carron; (formerly) partner in J. and A. Scrimgeour; *b.* 26 Jan. 1883; *s.* of Walter Scrimgeour of Wisset Hall, Halesworth; *m.* Oonah, *d.* of Robert O'Callaghan, F.R.C.S.; one *d.* *Educ.:* Eton; New College, Oxford. Served European War, North Somerset Yeomanry and Coldstream Guards. *Recreations:* yachting, shooting, golf. *Address:* 9 Chelsea Park Gardens, S.W.3. *Clubs:* Boodle's, Royal Automobile; Royal Yacht Squadron (Cowes); Aldeburgh Yacht. [*Died* 27 *May* 1958.

SCROGGIE, Rev. William Graham, D.D. (Edin.); retired; *b.* 3 March 1877; Scotch; *m.* 1900, Florence Harriet Hudson; one *s.*; *m.* 1941, Joan Mary Hooker. *Educ.:* Exeter; Malvern; Bath; Spurgeon's College. Pastorates: Leytonstone, London, 1899-1902; Trinity Road, Halifax, 1902-5; Bethesda Free Chapel, Sunderland, 1907-16; Charlotte Chapel, Edinburgh, 1916-33; travelling ministry: South Africa, Australia, New Zealand, United States, Canada, British Isles, 1933-37; Minister of Spurgeon's Tabernacle, London, 1938-44; Hon. D.D. Edinburgh, 1927. *Publications:* The Fascination of Old Testament Story; Visions of Christ; The Great Unveiling (Book of the Revelation); Ruling Lines of Progressive Revelation; Is the Bible the Word of God?; Prophecy and History; Know Your Bible, 2 vols.; What About Heaven?; The Lord's Return; A Life in the Love of God; The Study of the Bible, A Lecture on Method; Method in Prayer, or How to Use the Devotional Hour; The Baptism of the Spirit, What Is It? And Speaking with Tongues; Paul's Prison Prayers; Tested by Temptation; Christ the Key to Scripture; A Simple Guide to Biblical Study; The Problem of Unanswered Prayer; A Note to A Friend; Lectures on the New Testament; Christ in the Creed; St. Mark's Gospel; St. John's Gospel; The Book of the Acts; The Psalms, 4 vols.; Facets of the Faith; The Love Life; Eight Things that Matter; Salvation and Behaviour; A Guide to the Gospels; The World Outlook of the Bible; The Land and Life of Rest; The Unfolding Drama of Redemption, 3 vols.; The New Testament Unfolded; A Bible Correspondence Course (closed), etc. *Address:* 15 Belvedere Drive, Wimbledon, S.W.19. *T.:* Wimbledon 1835. [*Died* 28 *Dec.* 1958.

SCROGGIE, Colonel William Reith John, C.I.E. 1918; M.R.C.S., L.R.C.P.; I.M.S. (retired); *b.* 1876; *s.* of late Dr. W. R. Scroggie; *m.* 1909, Florence Marjorie, *d.* of late William Ure; two *s.* one *d.* Served Somaliland, 1902-4 (medal); Mesopotamia 1914-18 (despatches, C.I.E.); A.D.M.S. Delhi Independent Brigade, 1931; A.D.M.S. 4th (Secunderabad) Division, 1932; retired, 1933; War of 1939-45, served in Civil Defence and Royal Observer Corps. *Recreations:* wood and metal turning, water-colour painting. *Address:* Abbotsford Lodge, Callander, Perthshire. *T.:* Callander 66. [*Died* 20 *Sept.* 1953.

SCROOPE, Arthur Edgar; *s.* of late Henry Scroope; *m.* Judith Agatha, *d.* of late T. H. Horwood, The Warren, Aylesbury. *Educ.:* Clongowes Wood College. District and Sessions Judge, Bihar and Orissa; Registrar of the High Court at Patna, 1923; Legal Remembrancer and Judicial Secretary to the Government of Bihar and Orissa, 1923-28; Judge of the High Court of Patna; retired, 1933. *Address:* c/o Grindlay's Bank, Ltd., 54 Parliament Street, S.W.1. [*Died* 17 *Oct.* 1954.

SCRYMGEOUR, Norval, J.P.; F.S.A. (Scot.); on reviewing staff of Dundee Courier and Advertiser, and Editor of Leng's novels series; *b.* 22 Oct. 1870; *yr. s.* of late James Scrymgeour; *m.* 1901, Helen Moncur Prain; one *s.* *Educ.:* West End Academy, Dundee. Started writing when sixteen; came through the "hards"; contributed to British Weekly, Great Thoughts, etc. *Publications:* City Songs; The New Theology and the Old Facts; numerous brochures on historical subjects; many serials; edited Bonnie Scotland Portfolio. *Recreation:* collecting gems and precious stones. *Address:* The Barn, Longforgan, Perthshire. [*Died* 26 *July* 1952.

SCULLIN, Right Hon. James Henry, P.C. 1930; *b.* 18 Sept. 1876; *s.* of late John Scullin, Ballarat, Victoria; *m.* 1907, Marie McNamara, Ballarat. *Educ.:* Mount Rowan School, near Ballarat; Night School, Ballarat. Joined Labour Party, 1903; won Corangamite (Victoria) seat in House of Representatives, 1910; defeated, 1913; became editor of evening newspaper published at Ballarat; re-entered House of Representatives, 1922, as member for Yarra Division, Melbourne; Leader of Federal Parliamentary Labour Party, 1928-35; Prime Minister of Australia and Minister of Industry, 1929-31. *Publications:* numerous Labour pamphlets. *Recreations:* walking, bowls, and reading. *Address:* 2 Urquhart Street, Hawthorn, Victoria, Australia. [*Died* 28 *Jan.* 1953.

SCUPHAM, Brigadier Sir William Eric Halstead, Kt. 1957; C.M.G. 1941; M.C. 1917; M.L.C., 1947-53; M.E.C. 1951-53; *b.* 1893; *s.* of late Herbert Scupham, Maidenhead, Berks. *Educ.:* St. Paul's School. Diploma in Anthropology, Cambridge. Served in European War, France and Belgium, 1914-19, in York and Lancaster Regt. and Tank Corps; Major, 1918 (despatches). Colonial Administrative Service, 1920-43; Provincial Commissioner, Tanganyika, 1936; Senior Provincial Commissioner, 1937; Administrative Secretary to Government, 1939. Served War of 1939-45, Middle East; Military Administrator, Italian Somaliland, 1941-43 (despatches twice). Member East African Central Legislative Assembly, 1947-53; Speaker of the Legislative Council, Tanganyika, 1953-58, resigned. *Address:* c/o Glyn, Mills & Co., Kirkland House, Whitehall, S.W.1. *Clubs:* East India and Sports, Royal Automobile. [*Died* 24 *Nov.* 1958.

SEABY, Allen W.; late Prof. of Fine Art, University of Reading; *b.* 1867; *m.*; three *s.* one *d.* *Publications:* Drawing for Art Students, 1921; Skewbald, The New Forest Pony, 1923; Lettering—The Roman Alphabet, 1924; Art in Ancient Times, 1928; Exmoor Lass and other Pony Stories, 1928; Birds of the Air, 1931; Dinah, the Dartmoor Pony, 1935; British Ponies, 1936; Sons of Skewbald, 1937; Sheltie, 1939; The White Buck, 1939; The Ninth Legion, 1943; Purkess the Charcoal Burner, 1945; Alfred's Jewel, 1948; Mona, the Welsh Pony, 1949; Pattern without Pain, 1949. *Address:* Culverwood, Shinfield, Reading. [*Died* 28 *July* 1953.

SEAGER, Captain John Elliot, M.C.; D.L.; J.P.; *b.* 30 July 1891; *e. s.* of late Sir William Seager; *m.* 1922, Dorothy Irene Jones; one *s.* three *d.* *Educ.:* Cardiff High School; Queen's College, Taunton. Shipowner; a past chairman of Cardiff and Bristol Channel Shipowners' Association, and a past President of Cardiff Institute for the Blind; a Fellow of Inst. of Chartered Shipbrokers; Vice-Chm. Cardiff Local Marine Board, and Chairman, Cardiff Pilotage Authority; on board of management of Cardiff Royal Infirmary, and a director of numerous business undertakings, including many shipping companies; Chairman of South Wales and Monmouthshire Discharged Prisoners' Aid Society; ex-Pres. Publicity Club of Cardiff; Vice-Pres. Cardiff Business Club; Vice-Chm. Ministry of Labour and Nat. Service, Cardiff and Dist. Employment Cttee.; Chairman, Government Business Training Scheme Panel for Wales; Member of Cardiff Appeals Tribunal, Ministry of National Insurance; formerly Hon. Adviser on Ships' Stores to Ministry of Food; Past President Cardiff Inc. Chamber of Commerce; Trustee, South Wales Federation of Boys' Clubs and Treasurer of the Charity of Sir David R. Llewellyn for Clergymen and Ministers; on Welsh National Council of Young Men's Christian Associations; a Governor of Queen's College, Taunton; Pres.: Cardiff Central Boys' Club and Hostel; Cardiff S.E. Div. Conservative and Unionist Assoc.; served European War (M.C.); High Sheriff of Glamorgan, 1937-38; takes an active interest in all youth movements. Member of Priory for Wales Headquarters Committee of the Order of St. John of Jerusalem. K.St.J. *Recreations:* motoring and billiards. *Address:* Ty Gwyn Court, Cardiff. *T.A.:* Seager Cardiff. *T.:* Cardiff 45340. *Clubs:* Royal Automobile, Junior Army and Navy; Cardiff Exchange, Cardiff Rotary, Cardiff and County. [*Died* 8 *Jan.* 1955.

SEAGRAM, Brig.-Gen. Tom Ogle, C.M.G. 1919; D.S.O. 1917; *b.* Aug. 1872; *o. s.* of late Lt.-Col. J. H. Seagram, Bathampton House, Wylye, Wilts; *m.* 1931, Sheila Stephanie Congreve, *er. d.* of late F. Bluett Duff. *Educ.:* Bath College; R.M.A., Woolwich. Entered Army, 1893; Captain, 1900; Major, 1910; Lt.-Col., 1915; served European War France, 1914-18 (D.S.O., C.M.G.; and promoted temporary Brigadier-General, 1918); late commanding 10th Brigade R.F.A., Colchester; retired pay, 1920. *Recreation:* shooting. *Club:* Naval and Military. [*Died* 17 *April* 1958.

SEALE, A. Barney, F.R.B.S.; G.M.C.; R.B.A. 1938; F.R.S.A.; Sculptor Modeller of conversation pieces for porcelain and Painter in Oil; *m.* Berenice (*d.* 1957), *d.* of Capt. F. W. Wood, M.V.O., Scots Guards; one *d.* Exhibitor Roy. Acad., Roy. Scottish Academy, Royal Cambrian Academy, Paris Salon and all principal galleries; One Man Shows, London and New York; Selected to represent Great Britain in International Competition for Equestrian Statue of His late Majesty King Fouad I of Egypt, placed among the finalists. Best known works: heroic size Portrait Head (Bronze) of Augustus John, exhibited Royal Academy, 1937 and purchased by National Museum of Wales; smaller bronze version of this portrait is in private collection of the Queen; 28 ft. high group of Perfect Man, Woman and Child for British Pavilion, British Empire Exhibition, Glasgow, 1938; 16 ft. Royal Lion for British Pavilion, World Fair, New York, 1939; bronze figure, Blue Riband of the North Atlantic, for the new Mauretania, 1939; bronze groups, for Cunard White Star liner Caronia, 1948; principal sculpture for International Gardens Exhibition, Olympia, 1949, including figure of goddess Ceres 38 ft. high with base; 22 ft. high carved and coloured totem pole for a decoration at Building Exhibition, Olympia, 1953. Best known porcelain conversation group, 'Boswell's first meeting with Dr. Johnson', first exhibited at Royal Society of Arts, and now in private collection of the Queen. Served European War, Artists' Rifles, Aug. 1914; Commissioned, 1915; later Pilot Royal Flying Corps. *Address:* 147 Old Church St., Chelsea, S.W.3. *T.:* Flaxman 6050. *Clubs:* Arts, Chelsea Arts, Savage. [*Died* 22 *July* 1957.

SEARLE, George Frederick Charles, F.R.S. 1905; Sc.D.; *b.* Oakington, Cambs, 3 Dec. 1864; *s.* of late Rev. W. G. Searle, M.A., formerly Vicar of Oakington, and Fellow of Queens' College, Cambridge; *m.* 1904, Alice Mary, *d.* of Thomas Edwards of Highbury, and *widow* of Thomas Parsons, of Wimbledon. *Educ.:* home; Peterhouse, Cambridge (Scholar). 28th Wrangler, Mathematical Tripos, 1887; Second Class in Part II. of the Natural Sciences Tripos, 1888; Assistant Demonstrator, 1888-90, and 1890-35 University Demonstrator of Experimental Physics at the Cavendish Laboratory; War-time Demonstrator, 1940-45; Fellow of Peterhouse, Cambridge, 1911-17; Technical Assistant Royal Aircraft Establishment, 1917-19; University Lecturer in Experimental Physics in the University of Cambridge, 1900-35. *Publications:* Experimental Elasticity, 1908; Experimental Harmonic Motion, 1915; Experimental Optics, 1925, Experimental Physics, 1934; Problems in Electric Convection, Philosophical Transactions of Royal Society, 1896; On the Steady Motion of an Electrified Ellipsoid, Philosophical Magazine, 1897; Studies in Magnetic Testing, Journal of the Proceedings of the Institution of Electrical Engineers, 1904; with J. J. Thomson, A Determination of "v," the Ratio of the Electro-magnetic Unit of Electricity to the Electrostatic Unit, Phil. Trans. Royal Society, 1890; with T. G. Bedford, The Measurement of Magnetic Hysteresis, Phil. Trans. Royal Soc., 1902; The Modern Conception of the Universe (Pan-Anglican Congress, 1908), etc. *Address:* Wyncote, 170 Hills Road, Cambridge. *T.:* Cambridge 87417. [*Died* 16 *Dec.* 1954.

SEARS, Rear-Admiral Harold Baker, D.S.O. 1918; *b.* 1880; 2nd *s.* of late R. H. Sears, Manea, Cambs.; *m.* May (*d.* 1958), *yr. d.* of late Dr. C. Skardon, Evershot, Dorset. *Educ.:* Oundle; Royal Naval Engineering Coll. Devonport. H.M.S. Royal Sovereign, 1902-4; H.M. Destroyers, Defender, and Raider. European War (despatches, D.S.O.); Engineer Commander (D), 3rd and Atlantic Flotillas Chanak operations, 1922-23; Principal Assistant to Chief Engineer, H.M. Dockyard, Hong Kong, 1924-26; Engineer Commander H.M.S. Hood, 1926-28; Engineer Captain, 1928; Chief Engineer, H.M. Dockyard, Hong Kong, 1929-1932; H.M.S. Effingham, 1933-34; Eng. Rear-Admiral and retired, 1934; returned to Active Service, 1939-45. *Address:* Downside, Ashford Rd., Tenterden, Kent. *T.:* 168. [*Died* 9 *May* 1959.

SEARS, John Edward, C.B.E. 1920; M.A.; late Superintendent Metrology Division, The National Physical Laboratory, Teddington; retired 1946; *b.* 1883; *s.* of late John Edward Sears, F.R.I.B.A., and late Selina Marianne Sears; *m.* 1919, Kathleen Lucy, *d.* of late Edward Wadsworth; one *s.* two *d.* *Educ.:* Mill Hill School; St. John's College, Cambridge (Scholar). University (John Winbolt) Prizeman. Deputy Warden of Standards, 1921-1931; President of International Committee of Weights and Measures, and member of British Standards Institution. *Publications:* various scientific papers. *Address:* Woodscme, Pelham's Walk, Esher, Surrey. *T.:* Esher 227. [*Died* 21 *Dec.* 1954.

SEATH, Major-Gen. Gordon Hamilton, D.S.O. 1916; R.M., retired; *s.* of late Captain Seath, Westmount, Jersey; *m.* 1910, Eleanor (*d.* 1940), *d.* of late Captain E. M.

Dayrell, R.N., J.P., Lillingstone Dayrell, Bucks; no *c.*; *m.* 1945, Beatrice Selina, *widow* of Frederick Charles Guy, Liverpool House, Walmer. *Educ.:* Victoria Coll., Jersey; R.N. Coll., Greenwich. Entered R.M.L.I. as 2nd Lieut., 1905; Lieut., 1906; Capt., 1915; Major, 1928; Lt.-Col., 1934; Maj.-Gen., 1941; posted to Chatham Div., 1907; served on H.M.S. Africa, 1908-11; H.M.S. St. George, 1911; H.M.S. Implacable, 1912-14 (despatches, D.S.O.); served Salonika Army, March 1916-Oct. 1918 (Bt. Major, despatches); appointed R.N. College, Greenwich, 1919; A.D.C. to the King, 1940-41; retd. list, 1942. *Recreation:* golf. *Address:* Liverpool Hse., Walmer, Kent. *T.:* Deal 340. [*Died* 30 *Aug.* 1952.

SEATON, 4th Baron, *cr.* 1839; **James Ulysses Graham Raymond Colborne-Vivian;** *b.* 20 Apr. 1863; *s.* of 2nd Baron; *S.* brother 1933; *m.* 1904, Caroline Mabel (*d.* 1948), *d.* of late Sir Arthur Pendarves Vivian, K.C.B.; took additional name of Vivian, 1927. *Educ.:* Royal Military College, Sandhurst. Formerly Capt. S. Staffordshire Regiment; served Soudan Expedition, 1884-85 (severely wounded); Soudan Field Force, 1885-86; S. Africa, 1899-1902; A.D.C. to Gen. Comdg. S.E. Dist. 1888-91, and to Lieut.-Gen. Comdg. troops in Canada, 1893-98; Major, 1915; Royal Humane Society's medal, 1896. *Heir:* none. *Address:* Beechwood, Plympton, Plymouth, S. Devon. *T.:* Cornwood 224. *Club:* Army and Navy. [*Died* 12 *March* 1955 (*ext.*).

SEBRIGHT, Lieut.-Col. Sir Giles Edward, 13th Bt., *cr.* 1626; C.B.E. 1954; late 4th Dragoon Guards; late O.C. 2nd Hertfordshire Regiment; on County Council, Hertford; J.P.; Steward of the British Boxing Board of Control; *b.* 12 Nov. 1896; *s.* of late Arthur E. S. Sebright, 5th *s.* of 8th Bt. and Emily Eva (*d.* 1921), *d.* of John Bowen and *widow* of W. Ingram; *S.* uncle, 1933; *m.* 1929, Margery Hilda, *d.* of Adm. Sir Sydney Robert Freemantle, *q.v.*; one *s.* Served European War, 1914-19; Equerry to the Duke of York, 1922-23. *Heir: s.* Hugo Giles Edmund, *b.* 2 March 1931. *Club:* St. James'. [*Died* 9 *Dec.* 1954.

SEDDON, Sir Harold, Kt., *cr.* 1951; M.L.C. of West Australia, 1922, President 1946, retired 1954; *b.* 6 March 1881; *s.* of William Seddon and Elizabeth Ann Seddon (*née* Davy), Openshaw, Manchester, England; *m.* 1932, Winifred Jean, *d.* of William Perry Dunstan, Southern Cross, W.A.; *twin s.* two *d.* *Educ.:* Primary School, Varna St., Manchester; Central Higher Grade School, Deansgate, Manchester; Manchester Institute of Technology. Apprentice Electrical Engineering, Great Central Railway, England, 1896; Electrical Supervisor W.A. Govt. Rlys., 1901; Councillor, Municipality of Kalgoorlie, 1920-22. Jubilee Medal, 1935; Coronation Medal, 1937 and 1953. *Recreations:* reading, walking. *Address:* 97 Circe Circle, Nedlands, West Australia. *Club:* Kalgoorlie (Kalgoorlie, W.A.). [*Died* 25 *Feb.* 1958.

SEDGWICK, Ellery; *b.* 1872; *s.* of Henry Dwight and Henrietta Ellery Sedgwick of Stockbridge, Massachusetts, U.S.A.; *m.* 1st, Mabel Cabot; two *s.* two *d.*; 2nd, Marjorie Russell, Stubbers, Essex, England. *Educ.:* Groton School; Harvard University. Teacher Groton School, 1894-96; Assistant Editor Youth's Companion, 1896-99; Editor American Magazine, 1899-1907; Literary Adviser D. Appleton & Company, 1907-08; Editor The Atlantic Monthly and President of the Atlantic Monthly Company, 1908-38; Member American Academy of Arts and Sciences; Member American Institute of Arts and Letters; Member Massachusetts Historical Society; Overseer Harvard University; President Boston Public Library; Litt. D. Tufts College, Dartmouth College; L.H.D. Syracuse Univ. *Publications:* The Happy Profession, 1946; Atlantic Harvest, 1947. *Address:* Long Hill, Beverly, Massachusetts. *Clubs:* Athenæum; Century (New York); Somerset, Tavern (Boston). [*Died* 22 *April* 1960.

SEDGWICK, Lieut.-Col. Francis Roger, C.M.G. 1919; D.S.O. 1916; late R.A.; *b.* Bombay, 5 July 1876; *s.* of late Roger Buttery Sedgwick, Froyle, Hants; *m.* 1st, Madeline Louisa (*d.* 1930), *d.* of late W. L. Jennings, M.P., Stockport; one *s.* one *d.*; 2nd, 1934, Marjorie Helen, *d.* of late Henry W. Fell, Knells, Cumberland. *Educ.:* Uppingham School; R.M. Acad., Woolwich. Entered Army, 1896; Lt.-Col. 1918; served S. African War (medal and 4 clasps); W. African Frontier Force, 1901-5; Royal Military College, Canada, 1910-13; retired 1913; served European War (wounded, despatches, D.S.O., Bt. Lt.-Col., C.M.G.); retired pay, 1922; J.P. Bucks. *Address:* The Little House, Stewkley, Bucks. [*Died* 3 *May* 1955.

SEDGWICK, Henry Dwight; Essayist and Historian; Fellow of the American Academy of Arts and Sciences; Member of the American Academy of Arts and Letters; Member of Massachusetts Historical Society; *b.* 24 Sept. 1861; *s.* of Henry Dwight Sedgwick; *m.* 1ts, 1895, Sarah Minturn; two *s.*; 2nd, 1953, Gabriella M. Ladd. *Publications:* Life of Francis Parkman; Essays on Great Writers; A Short History of Italy; The New American Type, and other essays; Italy in the Thirteenth Century; Apology for Old Maids, and other Essays; Dante; Marcus Aurelius; Pro Vita Monastica; Ignatius Loyola; Spain, 1926; Cortez; La Fayette; Henry of Navarre; Alfred de Musset, The Black Prince; The Art of Happiness; Dan Chaucer; In Praise of Gentlemen; Short History of France; House of Guise; Vienna, the biography of a bygone City; Madame Récamier, 1940; Memoirs of an Epicurean, 1942; Horace, 1947. *Address:* Dedham, Mass., U.S.A. [*Died Jan.* 1957.

SEGAR, Hugh William, M.A., F.R.S.N.Z., *b.* 1868; *s.* of Robert Segar, Liverpool; *m.* 1895, Elise Frederica, *d.* of Franz Otho Scherff, Auckland, N.Z.; one *s.* two *d.* (and one *s.* decd.). *Educ.:* Liverpool College; Trinity College, Cambridge; 2nd Wrangler and Yeats prizeman, 1890; Smith's prizeman, 1892; lecturer on Mathematics, University of Wales, Aberystwyth, 1893-4; Professor of Mathematics, University College, Auckland, N.Z., 1894-1934; Pres. of Auckland Institute, 1900, 1912, and 1932-1933; Member of Council, 1900-52; Governor of St. John's College, Tamaki, 1908-10; Original Fellow of N.Z. Institute, now Royal Society of N.Z.; Member of Council, 1914-46; President, 1933-35; Member of Auckland Univ. Coll. Council, 1913-29; of Senate, N.Z. Univ., 1913-27; of Council N.Z. University, 1927-29; of Senate N.Z. University, 1929-34; Chairman Board of Studies, 1915-27; Chairman of Academic Board 1927-34; Member of Auckland Grammar Schools Board, 1914-46; of City Council Library Committee 1915-35; Vice-President of Economic Society, 1930-31; Member of Council of W.E.A., 1915-37, and of Tutorial Class Committee, 1915-39; President, 1918 and 1924, Vice-Pres., 1934-37; Member of Dilworth Trust Board, 1930-52; Vice-President of Rotary Club, 1922-23, and President, 1923-24; President Remuera Bowling Club, 1938-39. *Publications:* various papers on subjects in Mathematics, Economics, and Statistics. *Recreations:* bowls, and music. *Address:* 4 St. Vincent Avenue, Auckland, S.E.2, N.Z. *T.:* 22514. [*Died* 18 *Sept.* 1954.

SÉGUEL, Dr. George Gregory M.; Ex-Medical Superintendent English Nursing and Convalescent Home, Château Mer et Mont, Mentone; *s.* of late Dr. M. Séguel, Councillor of State (Russia), Chief Medical Officer at Kertch (Crimea), Knight of St. Wladimir, and Anne Trojanowsky. *Educ.:* Kertch College, B.Sc.; German University of Dorpat, M.B.; Russian University of Kiev, M.D.; Paris University, M.D. (with honours). Attached to the Government's Medical Mission, fighting the great cholera epidemic of 1892-93; in the provinces of Orel and Kiev, 1892; in Borjom in Caucasus, 1893; practised in Paris as a specialist for obstetrics and gynæcology, 1895-1914; Deputy High-Commissioner for Russia and V.-President of the Intern. Jury for Spas, Climatic Stations, Sanatoria at Universal Exhibitions of Paris, 1900, 1904, Liège, 1905, Milan, 1906, Bordeaux, 1907; Hon. Secretary of the Internat. Congress of Thalassotherapy, 1903, at Biarritz; President of Congresses in Paris, Liège, Milan, Petrograd; Delegated by the French Prime Minister on special Mission to Russia, 1903-04; in 1915, delegated by the French Red Cross (U.F.F.) to the Russian Army, later joined the Army with the rank of a Colonel; C.O. of the Unit No. 1 at the Russian Front near Minsk, afterwards (1916) of the military hospitals of Teheran and Ispahan (Persia); Attaché to the Director General of the R.A.M.C. in Petrograd; in April 1917 sent by the War Minister as Medical Liaison Officer to the Allied Armies at the French Front; Official representative for Russia at the Interallied Conference for Asphyxiating Gases, Sep. 1917; President of the Trav. Med. Board for the Russian Troops in France, transferred to the Russian Military Mission in London, Oct. 1917; Col. Attached to H.M. Imperial Forces as Medical Officer i/c of Troops of Sevenoaks District, 1918; appointed on the Staff of Queen Alexandra Military Hospital, 1918-19; Knight of the Legion of Honour, 1905; Officer of the Legion of Honour, 1927; Knight of Leopold of Belgium; K.C. of St. Anne and St. Stanislas of Russia; K.C. of Black Star (French Colonial); Decorated with the Insignia of Red Cross of Spain, Russia, Medal of Honour for Epidemics (France); Officier d'Académie. *Publications:* On Obstetrical and Gynæcological Complications of Influenza, 1895; various papers on Obstetrics and Gynæcology in French, German, and Russian medical journals, and reports on medical work in Russia. [*Died* 8 *July* 1954.

SEILLIÈRE, Baron Ernest, Ph.D.; Commandeur de la Légion d'honneur, 1952; Member Institut de France since 1914; Permanent Secretary of Académie des Sciences Morales et Politiques of Institut de France since 1934; Member Académie française since 1946; Man of Letters and Philosopher; *b.* 1 Jan. 1866; *m.* 1895, Germaine Demachy; one *s.* one *d.* (and one *s.* killed on active service, 1918). *Educ.:* École St. Ignace; Collège Stanislas (Paris); École Polytechnique (Paris); Heidelberg University. Awarded grand prix for literary work, by Institut de France, 1951. Officer of Order of Leopold (Belgian), 1937. *Publications:* Ferdinand Lassalle, 1897; Le Parti socialiste allemand, 1898; La Philosophie de l'impérialisme, Le Comte de Gobineau, 1903; Nietzsche, 1905; Le Mal romantique, 1907; Schopenhauer, 1909; Barbey d'Aurevilly, 1910; Flaubert, 1914; Les Origines romanesques, 1918; George Sand, 1919; Jean-Jacques Rousseau, 1921; Balzac, 1922; Le Romantisme, 1925; Auguste Comte, Marcel Proust, 1931; Baudelaire, 1932; Anatole France, 1934; Jules Lemaitre, 1935; D. H. Lawrence, 1936; Paul Bourget, 1937; Henri Bataille, 1937; Carlyle, 1938. *Address:* 16 rue Hamelin, Paris 16e. *T.:* Passy 36.64. [*Died* 15 *March* 1955.

SELBY, 3rd Viscount, *cr.* 1905; **Thomas Sutton Evelyn Gully;** Ret. Paym. Lieut.-Comdr. R.N.R.; *b.* 16 Feb. 1911; *s.* of 2nd Viscount and Dorothy Evelyn (*d.* 1951), *y. d.* of late Sir William Grey, K.C.S.I.; *S.* father, 1923; *m.* 1933, Veronica, *er. d.* of Mrs. Briscoe-George, 46 Lowndes Square, S.W.1, and Starbotton, Yorks; two *s.* two *d.* *Educ.:* Bradfield; Chillon, Switzerland. *Heir:* *s.* Hon. Michael Guy John Gully, *b.* 15 Aug. 1942. [*Died* 18 *Sept.* 1959.

SELBY, Percival Marchant, O.B.E. 1953; President Theatrical Managers' Association; Proprietor of The Frederick Mouillot Offices; Deputy-Chairman Theatres Mutual Insurance Co. Ltd. and associated with various theatrical concerns; *b.* 1886; *s.* of Wilton J. Selby, a character actor of the 'nineties and early twentieth century; *m.* 1st, Marion Ada Rogers (*decd.*), of the Deal family; two *s.* one *d.*; 2nd, Minnie Rosina Sherlock. *Educ.:* privately. Achieved some fame as a boy actor, making first appearance at the age of five in a play entitled, A Yorkshire Lass; played a long round of boy's parts; reversed the usual theatrical procedure by playing girl's parts, and created a record by being assistant stage manager at the age of ten; joined the London offices of the theatrical firm of Morell and Mouillot and on the dissolution of that partnership became secretary to the late Frederick Mouillot, on whose death he became general manager and eventually proprietor; President of the Theatrical Managers' Association since 1929. *Publication:* (with James M. Glover) Theatre Manager's Handbook. *Address:* 22 Greville Park Road, Ashtead, Surrey. *T.A.:* Lutanist Epsom, Surrey. *T.:* Ashtead 2425. [*Died* 25 *Nov.* 1955.

SELBY-BIGGE, Sir (Lewis) Amherst, 1st Bt., *cr.* 1919; K.C.B., *cr.* 1913 (C.B. 1905); J.P. Principal Assistant Secretary Board of Education, 1908-11; Permanent Secretary, 1911-25; Member of Education Committee of East Sussex County Council; Member of Departmental Committee and Statutory Commission for London University, 1927-28; Chairman of Departmental Committee on Superannuation of Local Government Officers, 1925-27; Member of Committee on Growth of Education in India, auxiliary to the Statutory Commission, 1928; *b.* 3 April 1860; 2nd *s.* of Charles Selby-Bigge of Linden, Northumberland, and Ightham Mote, Kent; *m.* 1885, Edith Lindsay (*d.* 1939), *d.* of late Rt. Hon. J. R. Davison, M.P.; one *s.* two *d.* *Educ.:* Winchester; Christ Church, Oxford. Fellow and Lecturer in Philosophy, University College, Oxford, 1883; Hon. Fellow, 1930; Barrister, Inner Temple, 1891; Assistant Charity Commissioner, 1894; J.P. Sussex. *Publications:* The Board of Education, 1927; Hume's Treatise, Hume's Inquiries, British Moralists, etc. *Heir:* *s.* John Amherst, O.B.E., 1946 [*b.* 20 June 1892; *m.*; three *d.*]. *Address:* Kingston Manor, Lewes, Sussex. *T.:* Lewes 133. *Club:* Athenæum. [*Died* 24 *May* 1951.

SELBY-LOWNDES, Col. William; *see* Lowndes.

SELIGMAN, Sir Charles David, Kt., *cr.* 1933; late Senior Partner of Seligman Bros., Bankers, 18 Austin Friars, E.C.2; *b.* London, 31 Oct. 1869; *e. s.* of late Isaac and Lina Seligman; *m.* 1899, Eva Henriette, *e. d.* of late Henry B. and Alice G. Merton; three *s.* one *d.* *Educ.:* Harrow; Trinity Hall, Cambridge; M.A. Late Dir. Commercial Union Assurance Co. Ltd.; late Chm., National Discount Co. Ltd.; Vice-President, Royal Empire Society; Member of the Advisory Committee of the Export Credits Dept. of the Board of Trade, 1921-40; Member of Overseas Development Council of Board of Trade, 1933-39; Member of Federation of British Industries Mission to Japan and Manchoukuo, 1934; Hon. Consul-General for Austria in London, 1931-38. *Address:* 5 Acacia Place, N.W.8. *T.:* Primrose 9332. *Clubs:* Devonshire, Leander, Pilgrims', Royal Automobile. [*Died* 11 *Dec.* 1954.

SELIGMAN, Brig.-General Herbert Spencer, C.M.G. 1919; D.S.O. 1917; Hon. Col. 129th Field Regt. R.A. since 1939; *b.* 1872; *s.* of late Leopold Seligman, 179 Queen's Gate, S.W. *Educ.:* St. Paul's School; R.M.A., Woolwich. Served in the Royal Artillery, 1892-1919; formerly Lieut.-

Col. and Brevet Col. Royal Artillery; retired as Hon. Brig.-General, Sept. 1919; served S. African War, 1900 (Queen's medal with 3 clasps); European War, 1914-19 (despatches six times, D.S.O., French Legion of Honour, Brevet Lieut.-Col. and Brevet Col., C.M.G.); Hon. Col. 78th (Lowland) Field Brig. R.A. (T.A.) until 1935. *Recreations:* shooting, golf. *Club:* Army and Navy.
[*Died* 19 *March* 1951.

SELINCOURT, Hugh de; author; *b.* 15 June 1878; *s.* of C. A. de Selincourt and T. B. Bendall; *m.* Janet Wheeler, pianist; one *d.* *Educ.:* Dulwich College; University College, Oxford. Dramatic critic of the Star, 1910-12; literary critic of the Observer, 1911-14; contributed chapter to Cambridge History of English Literature, 1909. *Publications: Novels:* A Boy's Marriage, 1907; The Strongest Plume, 1907; The High Adventure, 1908; The Way Things Happen, 1909; A Fair House, 1911; A Daughter of the Morning, 1912; Realms of Day, 1915; A Soldier of Life, 1916; Nine Tales, 1917; Women and Children, 1921; One Little Boy, 1923; The Cricket Match, 1924; Young Mischief, 1925; Young 'Un, 1927; Never in Vain, 1929; Mr. Buffum, 1930; Game of the Season; Evening Light, 1931; Studies from Life, 1934. *Plays:* Loyalty, 1909; The Beetle, 1909; The Dream of Death, 1912; Getting What You Want, 1913; St. John and the Orphan, 1910; Beastie, 1911; Belles Lettres, Great Ralegh, 1908; Oxford from Within, 1910; Pride of Body, 1913; Over! 1932; More Over, 1934; The Saturday Match, 1937; Gauvinier Takes to Bowls, 1948. *Recreation:* bowls. *Address:* Sand Pit, Thakeham, near Pulborough, Sussex. *T.:* Storrington 3.
[*Died* 20 *Jan.* 1951.

SELLEY, Sir Harry Ralph, Kt., *cr.* 1944; J.P.; Governor of Battersea Grammar and Sir Walter Saint John's Schools, and Battersea Polytechnic; *b.* Topsham, Devonshire, 1871; *m.* 1st, 1896, Eleanor Kate (*d.* 1935), *d.* of Thomas Westcott, Newton St. Cyres; one *s.* one *d.*; 2nd, 1939, Margaret Avelyn (Sheila), *widow* of Joseph Hendrick. M.P. (U.) South Battersea, 1931-45; Member L.C.C., 1925-37; late Chairman of the Housing Committee and the Hospitals Planning and Development Sub-Committee. Pres. Fed. of Master Builders. *Address:* 60 Elmbourne Road, Tooting Bec, S.W.17. *T.:* Balham 3596. *Club:* Constitutional.
[*Died* 24 *Feb.* 1960.

SELTMAN, Charles Theodore, Litt.D.; formerly Fellow of Queens' College, Cambridge, and University Lecturer in Classics; *b.* 4 Aug. 1886; *e. s.* of late Ernest John Seltman and Barbara, *d.* of James Watson, Procurator-Fiscal of Linlithgowshire; *m.* 1917, Isabel (*d.* 1935), *d.* of late Col. Arthur Morris Dane, P.M.O. Central Provinces, India; one *s.* *Educ.:* Berkhamsted School; Queens' College, Cambridge. Lieut. Suffolk Regt. in France, 1917, and General List. Classical Tripos, Part II, Class I, 1921; Winter Warr Scholar, 1921; Diploma in Classical Archæology with distinction, 1922; Prendergast Student, 1922; Student of British School at Athens, 1922-23; Member Johns Hopkins Expedition at Olynthus, 1928; Norton Professor, American Archæological Institute, 1929; Martin Lecturer, Oberlin Univ., 1931; Librarian, Queens' College, 1936; Lecturer at Collège de France and acting Professor, Univ. of Paris, 1940; Senior Proctor, Cambridge University, 1940-1941; Director, Exhibitions of Greek Art, Royal Academy, London, 1942 and 1946; Medallist of Royal Numismatic Society, 1945; of Royal Society of Arts, 1946; Hellenic Red Cross Medal with gold laurels, 1951; Medallist of American Numismatic Society, 1954. *Publications:* The Temple Coins of Olympia, 1921; Athens, its History and Coinage, 1924; Greek Coins, 1933 (new ed., 1955); Attic Vase Painting, 1933; Cambridge Ancient History, Five Volumes of Plates, 1927-39; Greek Art (with Jacqueline Chittenden), 1947; Approach to Greek Art, 1948; Masterpieces of Greek Coinage, 1949; A Book of Greek Coins (King Penguins), 1952; The Twelve Olympians, 1952; Women in Antiquity, 1956; Twelve Olympians and their Guests, 1956; numerous articles in classical and other periodicals. *Recreations:* travel; cooking. *Address:* 11 Little St. Mary's Lane, Cambridge. *T.:* 59387.
[*Died* 28 *June* 1957.

SELWYN, Very Rev. Edward Gordon, M.A.; D.D.; Dean of Winchester, 1931-58, resigned; *b.* Liverpool, 6 July 1885; *e. s.* of late Rev. E. C. Selwyn, D.D.; *m.* 1st, 1910, Phyllis Eleanor (*d.* 1941), *d.* of late Sir Edwyn Hoskyns, Bishop of Southwell; two *s.* one *d.*; 2nd, 1942, Barbara, *widow* of Albert Henry Williams. *Educ.:* Eton College; King's College, Cambridge (Scholar). Newcastle Scholar; Bell Scholar; Porson Scholar and Prizeman; Waddington Scholar; Browne's Medallist; 2nd Chancellor's Medallist; Fellow and Lecturer of Corpus Christi College, Cambridge, 1909-13; Hon. Fellow, 1943; Exam. Chaplain to Bishop of London, 1911-13; Select Preacher at Cambridge, 1912, 1923, 1950, and at Oxford, 1924-26, 1951-53; Warburton Lecturer, 1954-55. Warden of Radley College, 1913-18; C.F. 1918-19 (despatches); Rector of Redhill, Havant, 1919-30; Proctor in Convocation, 1921-31; Hon. D.D. Aberdeen, 1927; Examining Chaplain to the Bishop of Portsmouth, 1927; Hon. Canon of Portsmouth, 1928-30. *Publications:* The Teaching of Christ; Forbes Irenicum, Book I.; The Approach to Christianity; The Story of Winchester Cathedral; Thoughts on Worship and Prayer; The White Horseman and other Sermons; The Epistle of Christian Courage; The First Epistle of St. Peter; Editor of Essays Catholic and Critical, and of History of Christian Thought; Editor of Theology, 1920-33. *Address:* The Quinton, Shawford, Hants. *Club:* Athenæum.
[*Died* 11 *June* 1959.

SELWYN, Rt. Rev. George Theodore; Lecturer, Meston College, Madras, since 1953; *b.* 30 July 1887; *s.* of Rev. W. M. Selwyn; unmarried. *Educ.:* S. Lawrence College, Ramsgate; Corpus Christi College, Cambridge (Theo. Tripos Cl. iii); Ridley Hall, Cambridge. Curate, S. Matthew's Church, Bayswater, 1910-12. Sent out to Tinnevelly by C.M.S. in 1912 and has worked there ever since; Principal of S. John's College, Palamcottah, 1936-45; Bishop in Tinnevelly, 1945-1953 (Church of S. India, 1947-). *Recreation:* tennis. *Address:* Meston College, Madras.
[*Died* 30 *May* 1957.

SELWYN, Rt. Rev. William Marshall, M.A.; Hon. C.F.; *b.* 1880; *s.* of Rev. Sydney A. Selwyn and Ellen M. Blake; *m.* 1916, Dorothy Mary Ross; no *c.* *Educ.:* Haileybury; Emmanuel College, Cambridge. Curate of All Saints, S. Lambeth, 1903-8; Vicar of S. Simon Zelotes, Upper Chelsea, 1908-21; Chaplain of the London Irish Rifles, 1912-17; Chaplain of the 2nd Cavalry Division, 1917-19; Chaplain of the British Embassy Church, Paris, 1921-29; Vicar of Holy Trinity Church, Bournemouth, 1929-31; Vicar of Brompton, 1932-38; Archdeacon of Bath, 1938-47; Rector of Bath, 1938-47; Prebendary of White Lakington in Wells Cathedral, 1938-47; Proctor for the Diocese of Bath and Wells, 1938-47; Rector of St. Anne and St. Agnes, Gresham St., E.C., 1947-49; Bishop Suffragan of Fulham, 1947-1949. *Address:* Alveston, Kettlewell Hill, Woking. [*Died* 29 *Sept.* 1951.

SEMPLE, Patrick, M.A., Hon. D.Litt. (N.U.I.), 1943; Professor of Latin, University College, Dublin, 1909-48; *b.* Derry, 1875; *s.* of late Robert Semple; *m.* 1913, Frances, 2nd *d.* of Surgeon Kennedy, Dublin; one *s.* four *d.* *Educ.:* St. Columb's College, Derry; University College, Dublin. B.A. (Royal University of Ireland), 1896; M.A. (with gold medal), 1897; Fellowship, R.U.I., 1901; Member: Royal Irish Academy;

Senate of National University of Ireland, and of Governing Body of University College, Dublin, 1908-48, retired. *Address:* Ballsbridge, Dublin. [*Died* 6 *July* 1954.

SEMPLE, Hon. Robert; Minister of Railways, N.Z., 1941-49; Minister of Works, 1942-1949; M.P. Wellington East, 1928-54; *b.* Sofala, New South Wales, 1873; *s.* of John Semple; *m.* Margaret, *d.* of Thomas M'Nair, of Victoria (formerly of New Zealand); three *s.* two *d.* *Educ.:* Sofala School. Worked for 26 years on coal and goldfields of Australia (first as trucker, then as miner); was in Coolgardie in the rough days of mining; at about 23 years of age became trades union official; associated with Unions in various States, chiefly Victoria and W.A.; arrived N.Z., 1903; engaged in State mines on W. Coast and formed first Miners' Union at Runanga (Pres. for some years); assisted to form first Miners' Federation of N.Z. about 1908 (Pres.); when this merged into Federation of Labour (better known as Red Federation) about 1910, became organiser; helped to organise, 1913, and took leading part in Unity Conference, out of which grew Social Democratic Party and United Federation of Labour; involved in waterside workers' strike, 1913; imprisoned and bound over to keep the peace for 12 months in bond of £2,000. remained in organisation until bond expired, and then engaged in co-operative tunnelling contracts at Otira tunnel (8 months); miners' agent and inspector for 5 years; lived at Wellington during war; sentenced to 3 years' imprisonment for resisting conscription of man-power, without conscription of wealth (served 12 months); M.P. Wellington South, 1918-19; Manager for Orongorongo co-operative tunnelling party, 1921-24; organiser for Freezing Workers and Related Trades, 1924; Minister of Public Works, 1935-41; Minister of Transport, 1935-42; Minister of Marine, 1935-40 and 1940, 1942; Minister of National Service, 1940-42; Minister for Rehabilitation, 1942-43; Wellington City Council and Harbour Board some years. Retired 1954. *Address:* Mill Road, Otaki, N.Z. [*Died* 31 *Jan.* 1955.

SEN, Sir Usha Nath, Kt., 1944; C.B.E. 1930; formerly Adviser, Press Trust of India, New Delhi and Managing Editor, Reuter's and Associated Press of India, Simla and Delhi, and Director Associated Press of India, from 1937; *b.* 6 Oct. 1880; *y. s.* of late Nobin Krishna Sen, Garifa, Bengal, India; unmarried. *Educ.:* Ripon College; Bangabasi College, Calcutta. Joint founder of Associated Press of India; Staff Correspondent with Prince of Wales in India, 1905-06 and 1921 and 1922; Member Indian Legislative Assembly, 1929; Special Correspondent at the Indian Round Table Conference in London, 1930 and 1931; Member Institute of Journalists, Great Britain; Hon. Secretary and Treasurer Central Committee, Indian League of Nations Union. Chief Press Adviser to Govt. of India for the duration of the War; Chairman Indian Red Cross Society. *Clubs:* Overseas; (first Indian Pres.) Delhi Gymnkhana (New Delhi). [*Died* 20 *April* 1959.

SENANAYAKE, Rt. Hon. Don Stephen, P.C. 1950; Prime Minister and Minister of Defence and External Affairs, Dominion of Ceylon, since 1947; *b.* 20 October 1884; *s.* of Mudaliyar Don Spater and Elizabeth Catherine Senanayake; *m.* 1909, Emily Maud Dunuwille; two *s.* *Educ.:* St. Thomas College, Mount Lavinia, Ceylon. An agriculturist by training and choice; has spent several years as a planter of coconuts and rubber and has owned and managed plumbago mines; a keen paddy cultivator and can take a hand behind a plough even to-day. Entered political field in 1924, when returned unopposed to Legislative Council of Ceylon as one of 3 territorial reps. for Western Prov.; in council 7 years; again returned unopposed, 1931 and 1936, and each time unanimously elected Minister of Agric. and Lands by Exec. Cttee. Leader of State Council and Vice-Chm. Bd. of Ministers, 1942, until became first Prime Minister of Ceylon, Sept. 1947, when Ceylon took her place as a member of the Commonwealth. *Publication:* Agriculture and Patriotism, 1935. *Recreation:* riding. *Address:* The Temple Trees, Colombo 3; Prime Minister's Office, Colombo. *T.:* 3492. [*Died* 22 *March* 1952.

SENIER, Sir Frederic William, Kt., *cr.* 1924; J.P. Essex and Southend-on-Sea; *b.* 1869; *s.* of Frederic Senier, Dalston; *m.* 1892, Tilley (*d.* 1935), *d.* of Edward Pilbrow, Dalston; one *s.* one *d.* *Address:* Terra Nova, Salisbury Road, Leigh-on-Sea. [*Died* 3 *Aug.* 1951.

SEROCOLD, Oswald P.; *see* Pearce-Serocold.

SERVICE, Robert William; author; *b.* Preston, England, 16 Jan. 1874; *s.* of Robert Service, manager, Preston Bank, and Emily Parker, of Preston; married. *Educ.:* Hillhead High School, Glasgow. Served apprenticeship with Commercial Bank of Scotland, Glasgow; emigrated to Canada and settled on Vancouver Island; engaged in farming; travelled up and down Pacific coast, following many occupations; finally joined the staff of the Canadian Bank of Commerce in Victoria, B.C., 1905; transferred to White Horse, Yukon Territory, and then to Dawson; spent eight years in Yukon and travelled extensively in the sub-arctic. *Publications:* Songs of a Sourdough; Ballads of a Cheechako; Trail of '98; Rhymes of a Rolling Stone; The Pretender; Rhymes of a Red Cross Man; Ballads of a Bohemian; The Poisoned Paradise; The Rough-neck; The Master of the Microbe; The House of Fear; Why not Grow Young?; Bar-Room Ballads; Bath Tub Ballads; Ploughman of the Moon; Harper of Heaven; Songs of a Sun-Lover; Rhymes of a Rough Neck; Lyrics of a Low Brow; Rhymes of a Rebel; Songs for my Supper; Carols of an Old Codger; More Collected Verse; Rhymes for my Rags. *Recreation:* motoring. *Address:* c/o Ernest Benn Ltd., Bouverie House, E.C.4. [*Died* 11 *Sept.* 1958.

SETH-SMITH, Brigadier Hugh Garden, D.S.O. 1918; late R.A.S.C.; *b.* 1885; *s.* of Frederick Seth Smith, Upton Grey Lodge, Basingstoke, Hants; *m.* 1912, Cicely, *d.* of Thomas Parnell Parnell; one *s.* Served European War, 1914-1918 (despatches, D.S.O.); D.A.Q.M.G. British Troops in Egypt, 1924-27; D.A.A. and Q.M.G. Home Counties Area T.A., 1928-31; Lt.-Col. 1932; Col. 1934; A.A. and Q.M.G. i/c of Administration, British Troops China, 1934-37; retired pay, 1937. *Address:* Little Chaffey, Bourton, Dorset. [*Died* 12 *April* 1958.

SETON, Mrs. Grace Gallatin Thompson; writer, explorer, lecturer, book designer, poet; Editor, Poetry Booklet, since 1950; *b.* Sacramento, Cal.; *d.* of Albert Gallatin and Nemie Rhodes; *m.* Ernest Thompson Seton (marriage dissolved, 1935; he *d.* 1946); one *d.* (Anya Seton). *Educ.:* Packer Collegiate Institute, Brooklyn; privately. President of the National League of American Pen Women, 1926-28 and 1930-1932; President, Pen and Brush, 1898-1913; Delegate to Women's Conference, Pan Pacific Union, 1928-38; Delegate from U.S. Council to International Council of Women, Triennial, Paris, France, 1934; Delegate and Chairman United States Exhibit at Dubrovnik, Jugo Slavia, 1936; Head of U.S. delegation, International Council of Women's Jubilee, Edinburgh, 1938: Vice-Convener of Letters International Council of Women, 1934-38; As Chairman of Letters to the United States Council of Women, she organized the International Women Writers Conclave and the First International Book Exhibit for the International Congress of Women, Chicago, 1933, in connection with the Century of Progress Exposition; Assembled Biblioteca

Femina (World Woman's Library) of over 3000 volumes of women's work from 41 countries, housed in Deering Library, North Western University, Evanston, Ill., 1933; has travelled in out-of-the-way places in Africa, South America and Asia studying the wild life and the manners and customs of native peoples; headed expeditions into the interior of Paraguay, into Assam and into interior of Indo-China; Delegate to Women's Centennial Congress, 1940; Director of Literary Activities, Pan American League, 1940-45; Chairman of Letters and of Women's Archives Committees of U.S. Council of Women, 1940-52; Contributor, Writer's War Board O.W.I., 1944; organised The Quills, Palm Beach, Fla., 1947; Connecticut Chairman National Poetry Day, 1950-1959; Hon. member: Theta Sigma Phi Women Journalists; Instituto de Cultura Americana, Argentine, 1948; Assosicao Intercambio Cultural, Brazil, 1949, New York Soroptimists, 1951; Nat. Inst. of Social Sciences, 1954; Fellow Am. Geog. Soc.; Mem. Internat. Soc. Woman Geographers; Poetry Award, Brooklyn Poetry Soc., 1950; 1st Poetry Award, New England Regional Conference, 1953. *Publications:* A Woman Tenderfoot in the Rockies; Nimrod's Wife; A Woman Tenderfoot in Egypt; Chinese Lanterns; Yes, Lady Saheb; Magic Waters; Log of the Look-See; Poison Arrows, 1939; Partial Survey of Women Writers of Seventeen Countries, 1940; Singing Traveller, 1946; The Singing Heart, 1958. Writer of over fifty lyrics and song suites, set to music by nine composers; Contributor to New York Times Magazine, Liberty, Poetry Digest, etc. *Address:* 61 Binney Lane, Old Greenwich, Connecticut, U.S.A. *Clubs:* Colony (New York City); Everglades (Palm Beach, Fla.).

[*Died* 19 *March* 1959.

SETON, Capt. Sir John Hastings, 10th Bt., *cr.* 1683; late Gordon Highlanders; serving as Temp. Capt. Gordon Hdrs., since 1940; *b.* 20 Sept. 1888; *s.* of 9th Bt. and Eva, *o. d.* of Gen. Sir Henry Hastings Affleck Wood, K.C.B.; *S.* father, 1914; *m.* 1923, Alice Ida (Lady Seton), *d.* of Percy Hodge, Cape Civil Service; one *s.* one *d.* Late Lieut. Royal Field Reserve Artillery; served European War, 1914-18. *Heir:* *s.* Robert James, *b.* 20 Apr. 1926. *Address:* 31 Millway, Mill Hill, N.W.7.

[*Died* 21 *June* 1956.

SETON-WATSON, Robert William; *b.* 20 Aug. 1879; *o. c.* of late William L. Watson, of Ayton, and Elizabeth Lindsay, *d.* of George Seton (author of Scottish Heraldry, and other works); *m.* 1911, Marion Esther, *d.* of late Edward Stack, Bengal C.S.; two *s.* one *d.* *Educ.:* Winchester; New College, Oxford (B.A. 1902, D.Litt. 1910). Stanhope Historical Essay, 1901; afterwards matriculated at Berlin, Paris, and Vienna Universities (1903-6). Has devoted the last 40 years to a study of Central European and Balkan history and politics, at first writing under the pseudonym of Scotus Viator; founder and joint-editor of the New Europe, 1916-20; joint-editor of the Slavonic Review (with Sir Bernard Pares), 1922-49; Hon. Secretary of the Serbian Relief Fund, 1914-21; Hon. Lecturer in East European History at King's College, London, 1915-22; Masaryk Professor of Central European History in the University of London, 1922-45; Creighton Lecturer in the University of London, 1928; Raleigh Lecturer, British Academy, 1932; Professor of Czechoslovak Studies in University of Oxford, 1945-1949; President Royal Historical Society, 1945-49; Hon. D.Phil. of Prague (1919), Zagreb (1920), Bratislava (1928), Belgrade (1928, not yet promoted), and Cluj (1930) Universities; Hon. Citizen of Cluj (Transylvania) and of Turčiansky Sv. Martin (Slovakia); Hon. Ph.D., Birmingham, 1946; Hon. Fellow, New College and Brasenose Coll., Oxford, 1949; F.B.A.; F.R.Hist.S. In European War was Mem. of Intelligence Bureau of War Cabinet, 1917, and of Enemy Propaganda Dept. at Crewe House, 1918; in War of 1939-45 of Foreign Research and Press Service, 1939-40, and of Political Intelligence Bureau of Foreign Office, 1940-42 *Publications:* Maximilian I., 1902; The Tombs of the Popes (trans. from Gregorovius), 1903; The Future of Austria-Hungary, 1907; Racial Problems in Hungary, 1908 (Bohemian translation, 1910); The Southern Slav Question, 1911 (greatly enlarged German edition, 1913); Corruption and Reform in Hungary, 1911 Absolutism in Croatia, 1912; The War and Democracy (jointly with A. E. Zimmern and others), 1914; Roumania and the Great War, 1915; The Balkans, Italy, and the Adriatic, 1915; German, Slav and Magyar, 1916 The Rise of Nationality in the Balkans, 1917; Europe in the Melting Pot, 1919; Serbia and Yugoslavia, in new volumes of Encyclopædia Britannica; edited Tudor Studies (in honour of A. F. Pollard), 1923; The New Slovakia, 1924; Sarajevo (a study in the Origins of the Great War), 1926; A Plea for the Study of Contemporary History, 1929; Slovakia Then and Now, 1931; Treaty Revision, 1934; History of the Roumanians, 1934; Disraeli, Gladstone, and the Eastern Question, 1935; Britain in Europe (1789-1914), 1937; Britain and the Dictators, 1938; Munich and the Dictators, 1939; From Munich to Danzig, 1939; Masaryk in England, 1943; History of the Czechs and Slovaks, 1943; Transylvania; A Key Problem, 1943; edited Prague Essays, 1949. *Address:* Kyle House, Kyleakin, Isle of Skye. *T.:* Kyleakin 17. *Club:* Athenæum.

[*Died* 25 *July* 1951.

SEWELL, Brigadier Edgar Patrick, C.B.E. 1943; *b.* 22 March 1905; *s.* of F. W. Sewell, Dartford, Kent; *m.* 1934, Elizabeth Cecily Mease, *e. d.* of S. M. Toyne, M.A.; two *s.* one *d.* *Educ.:* St. Peters School, York; R.M.C., Sandhurst. Joined Northampton Regt. 1925; Capt. in S.W. Borderers, 1935; Palestine, 1929 and 1936 (despatches); served War of 1939-45 (C.B.E., despatches 5 times). *Recreation:* gardening. *Address:* River Cottage, Amwell, Nr. Ware. *T.:* Stanstead Abbotts 47. *Club:* Army and Navy. [*Died* 8 *Jan.* 1957.

SEWELL, Col. Evelyn Pierce, C.M.G. 1919; D.S.O. 1916; late R.A.M.C.; M.B., B.Chir. Cantab., M.R.C.S., L.R.C.P. (Lond.), D.P.H.; *s.* of Rev. H. D. Sewell of Headcorn, Kent; *m.* (wife *d.* 1960), *d.* of late Lieut.-Colonel A. Crombie, C.B., I.M.S.; one *s.* two *d.* *Educ.:* Monkton Combe School; Pembroke College, Cambridge; St. Bartholomew's Hospital. Commission in R.A.M.C. 1900; served European War, 1914-18 (D.S.O., C.M.G.); retired pay, 1930. *Address:* Carbery, Hartley Wintney, Hants.

[*Died* 31 *Aug.* 1960.

SEWELL, Brig.-Gen. Horace Somerville, C.M.G. 1919; D.S.O. 1915 (bar, 1918); *b.* 10 Feb. 1881; 3rd *s.* of late Henry Sewell, Steephill Castle, Isle of Wight; *m.* 1916, Emma, 2nd *d.* of late J. Berre King, New York; one *s.* (one killed in action, 1940), one *d.* *Educ.:* Harrow, Trinity College, Cambridge. Entered army, 4th Dragoon Guards, 1900; Capt. 1907; Major, 1914; Lt.-Col. Commanding 7th Queen's Own Hussars, 1919-23; Colonel, 1924; Commanding 6th Cavalry Brigade, T.A., 1924-1928; retired pay, 1928; commanded 1st Cavalry Brigade as temporary Brig.-Gen., 1918-19; served European War, 1914-18 (despatches five times, D.S.O. and bar, Bt. Lt.-Col., C.M.G.); War of 1939-45, attached to British Information Services, New York. Chevalier of the Legion of Honour, 1915. *Address:* Arcadia, Duncan's P. O., Jamaica, B.W.I.; 23 East 74th St., N.Y. City, N.Y. *Clubs:* Cavalry; Century (N.Y.).

[*Died* 25 *Dec.* 1953.

SEXTON, Frederic Henry, C.B.E. 1943; LL.D.; D.C.L.; D.Eng.; D.Sc.; President

Emeritus, Nova Scotia Technical College, 1907-47; retired, 1947; *b.* New Boston, N.H., 9 June 1879; American parentage; *m.* 1st, 1904, E. May Best; one *s.* one *d.*; 2nd, 1931, Anne B. Grant. *Educ.:* Howe High School, Billerica, Massachusetts; Cambridge English High School, Cambridge, Mass.; Massachusetts Institute of Technology, Boston, Mass. Assistant to Prof. H. O. Hofman, Prof. Metallurgy, Mass. Inst. Tech., 1901-2; Research Metallurgist in Research Laboratory, General Electric Co., Schenectady, N.Y., 1902-4; Asst. Prof. Mining and Metallurgy, Dalhousie University, Halifax, N.S., 1904-07; President, Nova Scotia Technical College and Director of Technical Education for Nova Scotia, 1907-47; President Canadian Education Association, 1928-1930; Board of Governors, Nova Scotia Research Foundation, 1947-50; Regional Director for Nova Scotia Canadian Vocational Training, 1940-47. *Recreations:* angling, gardening, photography. *Address:* Westwood Ave., Wolfville, Nova Scotia. *T.:* 576. *Club:* Rotary (Halifax). [*Died* 12 *Jan.* 1955.

SEXTON, T. M., J.P. Co. Durham; *m.* 1902, Edith Longstaff; one *s.* *Educ.:* Bede College, Durham. Headmaster of Stanhope Council School, Co. Durham, 1909-35; M.P. (Lab.) Barnard Castle Division of Durham, 1935-45. *Address:* Dales Terrace, Stanhope, Co. Durham. *T. A.:* Sexton, Stanhope. *T.:* Stanhope 294; Waverley Hotel, Southampton Row, W.C.1. *T.:* Terminus 6292. [*Died July* 1946.
[*But death not notified in time for inclusion in Who Was Who* 1941–1950, *first edn.*

SEYLER, Clarence Arthur, D.Sc. (Wales), B.Sc. (Lond.), F.R.I.C.; General Consultant to the British Coal Utilisation Research Association and Head of Dept. of Coal Systematics and Petrology, 1943-57; now Hon. Consultant on retirement; former British representative on International Committee for Coal Petrology and 1st Hon. Pres., 1955; late Public Analyst and Official Agricultural Analyst for Counties of Glamorgan, Carmarthen and Pembroke and County Borough of Swansea; formerly Consulting and Analytical Chemist; later concentrating upon Coal Research, particularly Coal Petrography; *b.* London, 5 Dec. 1866; *e. s.* of Clarence H. Seyler and Clara Thies, both of London; *m.* 1895, Ellen Andrews; two *d.* *Educ.:* Priory House School, Clapton; Univ. Coll., London; City and Guilds Tech. Coll., Finsbury. Asst. to Dr. W. M. Tidy, water analyst at London Hosp., and later to Sir Wm. Crookes. Asst. to Dr. Wm. Morgan, Public Analyst, 1892, and on his death in 1895 succeeded to his practice and many of his public appointments. Became interested in Coal and read his first paper on chemical classification of Coal in 1900 before S. Wales Institute of Engineers. Since 1923 has developed methods of Study of Coal by means of microscope with aid of grant from Dept. of Scientific and Industrial Research; Gold Medal, 1931, and bar to gold medal, 1937, of S. Wales Institute of Engineers. Melchett Medal of Institute of Fuel, 1941. *Publications:* papers to Phil. Trans. Roy. Soc., etc. *Recreations:* historical and place-name investigation in study and field. Late member of Council of National Museum of Wales. Mem. Surrey Archæological Soc., 1948. *Address:* Gaywood, Chine Walk, Parley Cross, Ferndown, Dorset. [*Died* 24 *July* 1959.

SEYMOUR, Alfred Wallace, C.M.G. 1934; V.D. 1921; *b.* 14 Sep. 1881; *s.* of late William Wallace and Elizabeth Ann Seymour; *m.* 1923, Ruby, *d.* of R. Hayward; two *s.* one *d.* *Educ.:* Warwick School; St. Andrews University. Cadet Ceylon Civil Service, 1905; Asst. Government Agent of Mullaitivu, Trincomalie, Nuwara Eliya and Matale Districts, 1910-16; Commission in Ceylon Planters Rifle Corps, 1909; in Royal East Kent Yeo. 1916; served in Egypt, Palestine, France and Belgium, 1916-19; demobilised, 1919; returned to Ceylon and appointed District Judge Chilaw and Puttalam, 1919; Asst. Govt. Agent, Kegalle District, 1920; Govt. Agent North Central Province, 1921; Registrar General Ceylon, 1924; Colonial Secretary Colony of Fiji; various periods in 1927, 1928, 1929, 1932, 1933 and 1934 acted as Officer Administering the Govt. Fiji and High Commissioner Western Pacific Territories; Represented Fiji and W.P.H.C. at Colonial Office Conference, London, 1930; Colonial Secretary, Trinidad and Tobago, 1935-38; Acting Governor Trinidad and Tobago 31 March to mid-Sept. 1936 and mid-Feb. to mid-June 1938. F.R.S.A. 1950. *Recreations:* study of local history and archæology, fishing, music. *Address:* Underbank, Torquay. *Club:* Royal Torbay Yacht. [*Died* 2 *Oct.* 1960.

SEYMOUR, Mrs. Beatrice Kean; *m.* William Kean Seymour, F.R.S.L. *Publications:* Invisible Tides, 1919; Intrusion, 1921; Hopeful Journey, 1923; Romantic Tradition, 1925; The Last Day, 1926; Three Wives, 1927; Youth Rides Out, 1928; False Spring, 1929; But Not for Love, 1930; Maids and Mistresses, 1932; Daughter to Philip, 1933; Interlude for Sally, 1934; Frost at Morning, 1935; Summer of Life, 1936; The Happier Eden, 1937; Jane Austen, 1937; The Unquiet Field, 1940; Fool of Time, 1940; Happy Ever After, 1941; Return Journey, 1942; Buds of May, 1943; Joy as it Flies, 1944; Tumbled House, 1946; Family Group, 1947; The Children Grow Up, 1949; The Second Mrs. Conford, 1951; The Wine is Poured, 1953; The Painted Lath, 1955. *Address:* c/o Heinemann, Gt. Russell Street, W.C.1. [*Died* 31 *Oct.* 1955.

SEYMOUR, Prof. Henry J., B.A., B.Sc.; M.R.I.A.; Vice-President Royal Dublin Society; *b.* Co. Cork, 1876; *e. s.* of late M. S. Seymour, M.A., Senior Secretary Board of National Education of Ireland; *m.* 1910, Mabel, 2nd *d.* of late Daniel Murphy, Kanturk, Co. Cork; two *s.* two *d.* *Educ.:* Queen's College, Belfast; University College, Dublin; Prof. of Geology and Mineralogy, University College, Dublin (N.U.I.), 1909-47. *Recreations:* fishing and golf. *Address:* Hazelhurst, 166 Stillorgan Road, Dublin. *T.:* Dublin 69337. [*Died* 28 *Jan.* 1954.

SEYMOUR, Richard Sturgis, M.V.O. 1909; *b.* 21 Sept. 1875; *s.* of late Col. Leopold Seymour; *m.* 1911, Lady Victoria Alexandrina Mabel FitzRoy, *d.* of late Lord Charles Edward FitzRoy; two *s.* one *d.* *Educ.:* Eton; Magdalen College, Oxford. Entered Diplomatic Service, 1898; has served at Berlin, Paris, Teheran, Vienna, St. Petersburg, Copenhagen; Secretary in H.M. Legation, The Hague, 1915-18; British Minister to King of Siam, 1919-24; Minister Plenipotentiary and Envoy Extraordinary to Bolivia, 1924-26. *Publications:* Rhyme Unreasoned, 1938; Shaded Candles, 1939; The Marionettes; Selected Poems: Afterthoughts. *Address:* 108 Swan Court, Chelsea, S.W.3. *T.:* Flaxman 1792. *Club:* Turf. [*Died* 21 *April* 1959.

SFORZA, Count Carlo; Minister Secretary of State, Italy, since 1951; *b.* 25 Sept. 1873; *s.* of Count Giovanni Sforza; *m.* 1911, Countess Valentine de Dudzeele; one *s.* one *d.* *Educ.:* Pisa University. Minister of Foreign Affairs, 1920-21; Ambassador to France, 1922; Leader of Free Italians, 1942; Minister Secretary of State, 1944-46; Minister of Foreign Affairs, 1947-51. *Publications:* Diplomatic Europe after the Treaty of Versailles, 1929; Makers of Modern Europe, 1932; European Dictatorships, 1934; Europe and Europeans, 1934; Fifty Years of Wars in the Balkans, 1941; The Totalitarian War, and after, 1942; Machiavelli, 1942; The Real Italians, 1943; Contemporary Italy and its Intellectual and Moral Origins, 1943. *Heir:* *s.* Sforzino, *b.* 6 Sept. 1916. *Address:* 12 Via Linneo, Rome, Italy. [*Died* 4 *Sept.* 1952.

SHACKLETON, Sir Harry Bertram, Kt., *cr.* 1937; *b.* 1878; *s.* of late Tetley Shackleton; *m.* 1902, Eleanor Maude, *d.* of William Martello Gray; one *s.* Wool Controller, 1939-49; Chairman U.K.-Dominions Wool Disposals Ltd., 1946-51; Chairman, Wool Textile Delegation, 1931-46; President, Woollen and Worsted Trades Federation, 1916-46; hon. permanent President, 1946; President, Bradford Manufacturers' Federation, 1915-38; Hon. President, 1938-; President National Confederation of Employers' Organisations, 1933-34. LL.D. (Hon.) Leeds. *Address:* Greystones, Heaton, Bradford. [*Died* 15 *Jan.* 1958.

SHAHUB-UD-DIN, Khan Bahadur Sir Chaudhri, Kt. *cr.* 1930; formerly: Advocate, High Court; President, Legislative Council, Punjab; Speaker, Punjab Legislative Assembly. *Educ.:* Government College; Law College, Lahore (B.A., LL.B.). Member, Lahore Municipal Cttee., 1913; Pres., 1922-24; Minister of Education, Punjab Govt., 1936-37. *Publications:* The Criminal Law Journal of India: Indian Case and two Punjabi poems; founder and proprietor, Indian Cases, and Criminal Law Journal. [*Died Aug.* 1949.
[*But death not notified in time for inclusion in Who Was Who* 1941–1950, *first edn.*

SHANAHAN, Colonel Daniel Davis, C.M.G. 1918; D.S.O. 1917; late R.A.M.C.; *b.* 11 April 1863; *e. s.* of Jeremiah Shanahan of Cluen, Tralee, and Joan Davis; *m.* Henrietta (*d.* 1919), *d.* of late James Young and Mrs. Young, 2 Knapton Terrace, Kingstown, County Dublin. *Educ.:* Blackrock College, Dublin; Royal College of Surgeons, Ireland, and Trinity College, Dublin. Entered the Royal Army Medical Corps, 1891; served N.-W. Frontier, India, 1897; South African War, 1899-1902 (severely wounded, despatches, Bt. Major); went with the Expeditionary Force to France, Aug. 1914 (despatches); proceeded to Gallipoli; in July 1915 took part in landing at Suvla (despatches); after the evacuation of Gallipoli returned to France, took part in the battle of the Somme (despatches, D.S.O.); in the taking of Messines Ridge, the operations in Belgium ending with the taking of Paschendale (despatches, C.M.G.). *Recreations:* hunting, golf. *Address:* The Acacias, Oatlands Drive, Weybridge, Surrey. [*Died* 20 *Aug.* 1954.

SHAND, Philip Morton, M.A.; *b.* 21 Jan. 1888; *s.* of late Alexander F. Shand, 1 Edwardes Place, Kensington, W., and Augusta Mary Coates, Bath; *m.* 1931, Sybil Mary, *er. d.* of late R. J. Sissons, Weybridge; two *d.* *Educ.:* Eton; King's College, Cambridge; abroad. *Publications:* A Book of Wine, 1926; A Book of Food, 1927; Bacchus, 1927; A Book of French Wines, 1928; A Book of other Wines (than French), 1929; The Architecture of Pleasure: Modern Theatres and Cinemas, 1930; translation of Professor Walter Gropius's The New Architecture and the Bauhaus, 1935; Essays of Adolf Loos, 1936; various articles published in the architectural and technical press. *Address:* 9 Norland Square, W.11. [*Died* 30 *April* 1960.

SHAND, Samuel James, D.Sc. (St. Andrews); Ph.D. (Münster); F.G.S., F.R.S.E.; Emeritus Professor of Geology in Columbia University, New York (Prof., 1937-1950); *b.* 29 Oct. 1882; *s.* of late James Shand, Sandsting, Shetland; *m.* Anna (*d.* 1947), *d.* of Rev. George Davidson, B.Sc., Edinburgh. *Educ.:* St. Andrews Univ.; Univ. of Münster. Assistant in Geology in St. Andrews University, 1906-7; Officer-in-Charge Geological Department the Royal Scottish Museum, Edinburgh, 1907-11; Professor of Geology and Mineralogy in the Univ. of Stellenbosch, South Africa, 1911-1937. Draper Medallist, Geol. Soc. S. Africa, 1937; Lyell Medallist, Geological Soc. of London, 1950. *Publications:* Useful Aspects of Geology, 1925, 3rd ed. 1949; Eruptive Rocks, 1927, 5th ed. 1952; The Study of Rocks, 1931, 3rd ed. 1951; Earth-Lore, 1933 2nd ed. 1937; Rocks for Chemists, 1952; various papers on geological and related subjects. *Club:* New (Edinburgh). [*Died* 19 *April* 1957.

SHANKS, Edward (Richard Buxton); author; *b.* London, 11 June 1892; *o. s.* of E. L. Shanks; *m.* 1926, Dorothea Maryon, *e. d.* of R. H. Burbrook. *Educ.:* Merchant Taylors'; Trinity College. Cambridge (Senior Scholar in History; B.A. 1913). Editor of The Granta, 1912-13; 2nd Lieut. 8th South Lancs, 1914; invalided out of the Army, 1915; War Office, 1915-18; first winner of the Hawthornden Prize for Imaginative Literature, 1919; Assistant Editor London Mercury, 1919-22; Lecturer in Poetry in the University of Liverpool, 1926; chief leader-writer, Evening Standard, 1928-35. *Publications:* Songs, 1915; Poems, 1916; Queen of China and other Poems, 1919; The Old Indispensables, 1919; The People of the Ruins, 1920; The Island of Youth and other Poems, 1921; First Essays on Literature, 1923; The Richest Man, 1923; Bernard Shaw, 1924; The Shadowgraph, 1925; Collected Poems, 1926; The Beggar's Ride, 1926; Second Essays on Literature, 1927; Bo and His Circle, 1931; Queer Street, 1932; The Enchanted Village, 1933; Poems, 1912-32, 1933; Tom Tiddler's Ground, 1934; Old King Cole, 1936; Edgar Allan Poe, 1937; My England, 1938; Rudyard Kipling, 1939; Do You Know?, 1939; Elizabeth Goes Home, 1942; The Night Watch for England, 1943; The Universal War and the Universal State, 1946; Images from the Progress of the Seasons, 1947; The Dogs of War, 1948; Selections from Swinburne (ed.), 1950; Selections from Browning (ed.), 1952; Poems, 1939-1952, 1953. *Recreations:* conversation, golf, and playing with dachshunds. *Address:* Kilve, Park Copse, Dorking. *Clubs:* Beefsteak, International Sportsmen's. [*Died* 4 *May* 1953.

SHANKS, W(illiam) Somerville, R.S.A. 1933 (A.R.S.A. 1923); R.S.W. 1925; teacher of drawing and painting, Glasgow School of Art, 1910-39; *b.* Gourock, Renfrewshire, 28 September 1864; *s.* of John Shanks, portioner; *m.* 1909, Jessie (decd.), *d.* of John Anderson. Trained originally in design department of a chenile and tapestry curtain manufacturer; studied drawing in the evenings under F. H. Newbery, Glasgow School of Art; later in Paris under J. P. Laurens and Benjamin Constant; Hon. Secy. R.G.I., 1937-1941; Pictures in several public Galleries: Pipes of Pan, Portrait of John Q. Pringle, and the Chancel, St. Andrew's Parish Church, Glasgow, Kelvingrove Gallery, Glasgow; Pantry Shelf, Scottish Modern Arts Ass., Edinburgh; His Heritage, Portrait of Archibald Kay, R.S.A., also bronze bust of Ex-Provost Robert Cochran, Paisley Permanent Collection; Interior, Walker Art Gallery, Liverpool; Still Life, Bradford Art Gallery; awarded Médaille d'Argent, Société des Artistes Français, 1922. Exhibited in Prague and Munich with the Glasgow Group. *Address:* Glenacre, 18 Victoria Rd., Gourock, Renfrewshire. *Club:* Art (Glasgow). [*Died* 28 *July* 1951.

SHARP, Colonel Alexander Dunstan, C.B. 1918; C.M.G. 1916; T.D.; F.R.C.S.; Army Medical Service; late Hon. Surgeon to the King; Hon. Colonel 49th W. Riding Div. R.A.M.C.(T.); *b.* Keith, N.B., 6 Nov. 1870; *m.* 1909, Amelia, *d.* of late Henry Sutcliffe, J.P., Eastmoor, Ilkley; two *s.* one *d.* *Educ.:* Edinburgh (at Medical School won 4 medals (first) and 3 prizes (second)); London; Berlin; Vienna; Paris; Buda Pesth. Consulting Surgeon Ear, Nose, and Throat Dept., Dewsbury Infirmary; Leeds Education Committee; Hon. Surgeon Ear, Nose, and Throat Department, Leeds Public Dispensary and Hospital; Ear, Nose, and Throat Specialist, Seacroft Military Hospital; Membre Correspond. Soc. Laryngol., Paris; late H. Surgeon Ear and Throat Dept., Edinburgh Royal Infirmary; Surgeon S. African War,

1901-02 (medal and 4 clasps); at outbreak of European War was Major R.A.M.C. (T.F.), commanding 1st W.R. Field Ambulance; Lt.-Col. 1914; Col. A.M.S. 1915 - 18 (despatches, C.M.G., C.B.); Commander of the Military Order of Aviz, Portugal, 1919; Médaille de la Reconnaissance Française, 1926. *Publications:* various medical journals, Lancet, R.A.M.C. Journal, etc. *Recreation:* golf. *Address:* Hilly Ridge House, Grosvenor Road, Leeds. *T.A.:* Sharp, Park Square, Leeds. *T.:* Leeds 51523 (Hilly Ridge House). *Club:* Leeds.
[*Died* 18 *March* 1955.

SHARP, Air Vice-Marshal Alfred Charles Henry, C.B.E. 1953; D.S.O. 1944; A.F.C. 1947; R.A.F. (Retd.); Director, Foreign Sales, Martin Aircraft Company, Baltimore, Maryland; *b.* 13 Nov. 1904; *s.* of Charles F. and late Florence D. Sharp; *m.* 1st, 1929, Alison Scott Wollen (marr. diss. 1955); two *d.*; 2nd, 1955, Lynn Macready Fallon. *Educ.:* King's College School, Wimbledon; Selwyn College, Cambridge. Joined R.A.F., 1924; graduate R.A.F. Staff Coll., 1937; Dep. Dir. Organisation, Air Ministry, 1941; Dep. Chief of Staff, 8th U.S. Air Force, 1943; Base Comdr., R.A.F. Bomber Comd., 1944; A.O.A., India, 1944; Dir. of Accidents Air Ministry, 1945; grad. Imperial Defence Coll., 1948; A.O.C. No. 38 Group, 1949; Dir.-Gen. of Organisation, Air Ministry, 1950; Wing Comdr., 1940; Group Capt., 1941; Air Commodore, 1943; Air Vice-Marshal, 1944, Substantive 1951, and retired from R.A.F. at own request, in same rank, Feb. 1953. U.S. Legion of Merit (Comdr.), 1946; U.S. Silver Star, 1943. *Recreations:* cricket, golf, tennis, squash. *Address:* c/o Glyn, Mills & Co., Whitehall, S.W.1. *Clubs:* Royal Air Force; Army and Navy (Washington, D.C.).
[*Died* 7 *Feb.* 1956.

SHARP, Ven. Arthur Frederick, M.A.; retired; *b.* Holloway, 30 October 1866; 4th *s.* of William Sharp and Maria Louisa Perkins Chamney; *m.* 1893, Viva Bertha (*d.* 1928), *e. d.* of Captain Augustus Tabuteau, Royal Navy; two *s.* four *d.* (and one *d.* decd.). *Educ.:* Queen Elizabeth Grammar School; St. Mary Magdalene (Paddington) Choir College; Queen's College, Oxon. Matriculated Queen's College, Oxon, 1888; B.A. 1891; M.A. 1896; Deacon, 1891; Priest, 1892; Assistant Curate Chard, Som., Madeira, Teneriffe, 1891 - 92; Singapore, 1892-97; Hong-Kong, Japan, 1897; Archdeacon of Sarawak, 1900-10; Vicar and Missionary in charge of Kuching; Surrogate; Diocesan Registrar, 1897-1910; Vicar-Gen., 1909; Priest in charge, Finchampstead, 1911-12; Rector of Adisham, Canterbury, 1912-13; Vicar of St. Stephen's, Hampstead, 1913-48; retired, 1948; Rural Dean of Hampstead, 1921-35. *Publications:* The Wings of the Morning, Vol. I, 1954, Vol. II, 1957; The Spirit Saith, Vol. I, 1954, Vol. II, 1955; Where Thine Honour Dwelleth, 1955. *Recreation:* writing. *Address:* 16 Redington Road, Hampstead, N.W.3.
[*Died* 24 *Jan.* 1960.

SHARP, Dorothea, R.B.A. 1907; R.O.I. 1922; Past Pres. of Forum Club Art Section; *e. d.* of James Sharp of Dartford, Kent; unmarried. *Educ.:* (Art) Polytechnic, Regent Street; and at Paris. Exhibitor at R.A. and all provincial exhibitions, also abroad. *Chief Pictures:* The Cliff Top in Russell-Cotes Art Gallery, Bournemouth; The Primrose Way in Laing Art Gallery, Newcastle; Over the Hills and Far Away, in the National Museum and Art Gallery, Wales; The Sands, in Northampton Art Gallery; White Ducks, Doncaster Art Gallery; Where Children play and Sea Birds fly, Leamington Public Art Gallery; Lambs, Auckland Art Gallery, N.Z.; White Rocks-Cassis, Art Gallery, Rhodesia, S. Africa; Sea Bathers, Newport, Mon.; Low-Tide, Rochdale; Spring on the Sussex Downs, Worthing Art Gallery; The Yellow Balloon, Manchester Corporation Art Gallery; Summer Morning, Maidstone Art Gallery; Summer, Belfast. *Recreation:* reading. *Address:* 22 Blomfield Road, W.9. *T.:* Cunningham 0802; Balcony Studio, St. Ives, Cornwall. *Club:* Forum.
[*Died* 17 *Dec.* 1955.

SHARP, Evelyn, F.R.S.L.; author, journalist, and lecturer; contributor to Manchester Guardian, Christian Science Monitor, Observer, Home and Country, News-Chronicle, Contemporary Review, New Statesman, and others; *b.* London, 4 Aug. 1869; 9th *c.* of James and Jane Sharp; *m.* 1933, Henry W. Nevinson (*d.* 1941). *Educ.:* privately. Active part as speaker and demonstrator in militant suffrage movement, 1905-18, twice imprisoned; Lecturer and teacher in schools and privately 1893 onwards; on staff of Daily Herald and Herald, 1915-23; Speaker in humanitarian and international causes 1918 onwards; relief work under Quakers in Germany, 1920, and Russian famine, 1923. *Publications:* Unfinished Adventure; Selected Reminiscences, 1933; Hertha Ayrton: A Memoir; The London Child; The Child Grows Up; Here We Go Round, Story of the Dance; Daily Bread; The African Child. Novels—Somewhere in Christendom, 1919; At the Relton Arms, 1894; The Making of a Prig; Nicolete; Fairy Tales—Wymps; All the Way to Fairyland; The Other Side of the Sun; Round the World to Wympland; Children's Books—Young James; Who was Jane?; The Youngest Girl in the School; The Other Boy; The Making of a Schoolgirl; The Children who Ran Away; Lessons; Micky; The Child's Christmas; The Story of the Weathercock; The Hill that Fell Down; John's Visit to the Farm. Short Stories—Rebel Women. The Victories of Olivia, The War of all the Ages, A Communion of Sinners. Plays—The Loafer and the Loaf; The Poisoned Kiss (libretto of R. Vaughan Williams' Opera, produced 1936). Also edited H. W. Nevinson's Visions and Memories (essays and poems), 1944. *Recreations:* concerts, friendships, reading, walking. *Address:* 13 Russell Road, Kensington, W.14. *T.:* Western 0600. *Clubs:* M.M., P.E.N., University Women's.
[*Died* 17 *June* 1955.

SHARP, Sir Henry, Kt., *cr.* 1922; C.S.I. 1916; C.I.E. 1911; M.A.; F.R.S.L.; *b.* 1 June 1869; *s.* of Henry and Margaret Sharp. *Educ.:* Rugby; New College, Oxford, 1st Class Lit. Hum. Indian Educational Service, 1894, in the Central Provinces; employed as Relief Officer during famines of 1897 and 1899-1900 (Kaisar-i-Hind Medal, 1st class); Director of Public Instruction, Eastern Bengal and Assam, 1906-10; Joint Secretary to the Government of India in the Education Department, 1910-15; Member of Governor-General's Legislative Council, 1911-20; Knight of Grace, St. John of Jerusalem, 1913; Educational Commissioner with the Government of India, 1915; Secretary to the Government of India in Dept. of Education and Public Health, 1918; retired from service, 1922; Secretary to the Statutory Commission on Oxford, 1923-26; Secretary to the Statutory Commission on London University, 1927-28; Secretary to the Cathedral Commissioners for England, 1931-42; member of the Royal Commission on the Civil Service. *Publications:* Rural Schools in the Central Provinces; Indian Education, Quinquennial Reviews, 1907-12, 1912-17; Delhi, its Story and Buildings, 1921; Translation of the Agamemnon; Good-bye, India; *fiction:* The Devil's Tower; The Assassins, 1928; The Dancing God, 1928. *Address:* 16-17 Pall Mall, S.W.1. *T.:* Abbey 6394. *Club:* Athenæum.
[*Died* 24 *Jan.* 1954.

SHARP, Lauriston William, M.A., Ph.D., Librarian to the University of Edinburgh since 1939; *b.* 1 Jan. 1897; *s.* of W. L. Sharp and Lilias J. Stewart; *m.* 1928, Edith M. Hill, B.A.; two *s.* *Educ.:* Leith Academy; Edinburgh University; Cambridge University. M.A.

First Class Honours, Edinburgh University, 1920; Gray Scholar, 1920; Edmondstoune Aytoun Fellow, 1921; Ph.D. Cambridge University, 1927; Assistant in Manuscripts Edinburgh University Library, 1925; President of Scottish Library Assoc., 1949-50. *Publication:* Edited Early letters of Robert Wodrow, 1698-1709 (Scottish History Society), 1937. *Address:* Greenloaning, West Carnethy Avenue, Colinton, Edinburgh 13. *T.:* Edinburgh 87364. [*Died* 29 *June* 1959.

SHARP, Sir Percival, Kt., *cr.* 1938; LL.D. (Hon.) Sheffield University, B.Sc.; *b.* 12 Sept. 1867; *s.* of Henry and Catherine Sharp; *m.* 1891, Jessie, *d.* of Thomas Henderson Maclaren; three *s.* *Educ.:* Edward Walton's Endowed (Public Elementary) School, Bishop Auckland; Homerton Training College for elementary teachers. Assistant and Head Master in public elementary schools; Mathematical Master in School of Science, Hull; afterwards Director of Education in St. Helens (Lancs.), Newcastle upon Tyne and Sheffield; retired from local administration, 1932; Secretary Association of Education Committees (England, Wales and Northern Ireland), 1925-44; formerly Member of Governing Body of Armstrong University College, Newcastle upon Tyne; also Member of the Council and Finance Committee of Sheffield University; took prominent part in the inception of the Burnham Committee on Teachers' Salaries; Member from its establishment, 1919 until 1949; Hon. Sec. Authorities panel, 1925-45; Member of Departmental Committee on Teachers' Salaries, 1917; and of the Norwood Committee; formerly President of the Association of Directors and Secretaries for Education. *Address:* Kinbrae, Gyllyngvase Road, Falmouth. *Club:* National Liberal. [*Died* 8 *Feb.* 1953.

SHARPE, Charles W., R.C.A.; M.A.; Painter of landscape and genre subjects; Hon. Sec. Royal Cambrian Academy since 1946; exhibitor at Royal Academy, on the Continent, America, Canada, and in chief provincial galleries in England; represented in permanent collections of Liverpool, Southport and Birkenhead. Sometime Principal of Laird School of Art, Birkenhead. *Address:* Plas-y-Don, Deganwy, N. Wales; Glandon, Beddgelert, Caerns. [*Died* 27 *July* 1955.

SHARPE, Rev. Harold Stephen; Diocese of Exeter from 1956; *b.* Beddington, Surrey, 1886; *s.* of Rev. Clement Rene and Catharine Sharpe, Rectory, Beddington; *m.* 1912, Alma, *d.* of Rev. William and Julia Arbuthnot, Lea Marston Vicarage, Birmingham; two *s.* one *d.* *Educ.:* St. Edward's School, Oxford; Keble College, Oxford; Kelham. Ordained, 1910; Deacon, 1911; Assistant Priest, Aston Brook, Birmingham, 1910-12; S. Michael's Handsworth, 1912-15; Priest, Bloemfontein Cathedral, 1915; Director of Mafeteng Mission, 1916-23; Archdeacon of Basutoland, 1922-24; Director of Native Training School, Masite, 1923; Archdeacon of Pretoria and Director of Native Missions, 1924-31; Missioner for S.P.G., 1935; Archdeacon of Damaraland, 1932-36; Rector of Marsham, Norwich, 1936-39; of Ditchingham, 1939-43; of Blairgowrie, 1943-46; Rector of St Perrott with Mosterton and Chedington, 1946-51; Curate of Pinner, 1954-56. *Publication:* The Fascination of South African Missions. *Address:* Corner Cottage, Newton Ferrers, Plympton, Devon. [*Died* 18 *Oct.* 1960.

SHARPLES, Charles Norman, C.I.E. 1947; I.C.S. retired; farming in Cornwall; *b.* 29 Aug. 1906; *s.* of C. Sharples; *m.* 1937, Joan, *d.* of C. E. L. Gilbert, C.I.E., I.F.S., Chief Conservator of Forests, Poona; one *s.* one *d.* *Educ.:* Blackpool School; Selwyn College, Cambridge. B.A. 1927. Entered I.C.S., 1929; temporary Under Sec., Commerce Dept., Govt. of India, 1938-39 and Dep. Sec., 1939-42; Eastern Group Supply Council, 1944; late India Supply Comr., London. *Recreations:* fencing, riding, shooting. *Address:* Great Beer, Marhamchurch, nr. Bude, Cornwall. *T.:* Bridgerule 205. *Club:* East India and Sports. [*Died* 25 *Feb.* 1954.

SHARWOOD-SMITH, Edward; *b.* 1865; *s.* of Rev. Frederick Smith, Vicar of St. Mary's, Aston Brook, and Rector of Church Lench, near Evesham, and Sarah Annie Williams, Admaston, Shropshire; *m.* 1898, Lucy, *d.* of Rev. E. Evers, Rector of Preston and Vicar of Aldborough, Yorks; two *s.* three *d.* *Educ.:* King Edward's School, Birmingham; Jesus College, Cambridge. Assistant-masterships at Shrewsbury School, Cheam School, Hymers Coll., Hull; Head Master Whitchurch Grammar School, Shropshire, 1899-1902; Newbury Grammar School, 1903-24. *Publications:* In Black and Red (Cambridge and School verses), 1898; The beginnings of Western Philosophy, 1918; The Faith of a Schoolmaster, 1935; Storm in a Village and other verses, 1953. *Recreations:* walking, reading. *Address:* Glyne Hall, Bexhill-on-Sea. [*Died* 2 *May* 1954.

SHAW, Ven. Archibald, M.A.; Archdeacon Emeritus since 1940; *b.* 1879; 2nd *s.* of late Walter Shaw. *Educ.:* Bromsgrove; Emmanuel College, Cambridge; Ridley Hall, Cambridge. Curate, Walcot, Bath, 1903-05; went out under C.M.S. to Southern Sudan, 1905; Secretary of Gordon Memorial Sudan Mission, C.M.S., 1907-36; Archdeacon of Southern Sudan, 1922-40; Temporary Chaplain to the Forces, 1941-42. *Address:* P.O. Karen, Nairobi, Kenya. *Clubs:* National, Royal Empire Society; Rift Valley Sports, United Kenya (Kenya). [*Died* 26 *Aug.* 1956.

SHAW, Sir (Archibald) Douglas MacInnes, Kt., *cr.* 1953; D.S.O. 1918; D.L., J.P.; *b.* 15 March 1895; *s.* of late Sir A. MacInnes Shaw, C.B.; *m.* 1920, Dorothy Ada (J.P. Ayrshire, 1944), *d.* of P. MacLellan, Esq., Cormiston Towers, Biggar, Lanarks.; no *c.* *Educ.:* St. Ninian's, Moffat; Charterhouse; abroad. Joined army, Royal Scots Fusiliers, Sept. 1914 (despatches twice, D.S.O.); commanded Bn., 1918; entered Glasgow Town Council, 1921; contested Paisley, 1923; M.P. (U.) West Renfrewshire, 1924-29; assumed command 5/8 Cameronians, 1924; Bt.-Col. 1928; Commanding 64th Anti-Tank Regt. of Artillery, 1940; Commanding 7th A.A. 3 Regt. R.A. 1940-41; took over command of 19th Light A.A. Regt. R.A., 1941; served overseas (India) with 122 L.A.A. Regt., 1943-45. Convenor, County of Ayr, 1955. *Recreations:* fishing, shooting. *Address:* Symington House, By Kilmarnock, Ayrshire. *Clubs:* Carlton; Conservative (Glasgow). [*Died* 10 *June* 1957.

SHAW, Geoffrey Reginald Devereux; Barrister-at-law; *b.* 29 May 1896; 2nd *s.* of late James Edward Shaw and Adela Constance Alexandrina Durrant; *m.* 1924, Elizabeth Mary Margaret, *e. d.* of Adm. Sir Cyril Thomas Moulden Fuller, K.C.B., C.M.G., D.S.O.; two *s.* three *d.* *Educ.:* Cheltenham College; King's College, Cambridge. 5th K.O.Y.L.I. 23 Sept. 1914-2 Feb. 1916; East Riding Yeomanry, 2 Feb. 1916-27 May 1919; 5 K.O.Y.L.I., 1929-39; 57th L.A.A. RA., 1939-40 (Lt.-Col.) Cambridge B.A., LL.B., 1921; M.A., 1925; called to Bar, Inner Temple, 1923; joined N.-Eastern Circuit; M.P. (U.) Sowerby Division (W. Yorks), 1924-29; Sheriff of Northamptonshire, 1938. *Recreations:* golf, hunting, polo, tennis. *Address:* Scottow Hall, Norwich. *Clubs:* Carlton, St. Stephen's, Hurlingham; Northampton County; Norfolk County. [*Died* 8 *Sept.* 1960.

SHAW, George Ernest, C.M.G. 1931; O.B.E. 1919; *b.* 5 Jan. 1877; *s.* of A. G. Shaw, Shanagarry, Co. Cork; *m.* 1904, Dorothy, *d.* of R. G. Palmer; three *s.* Entered Malayan Civil Service, 1900; served in various posts; Federated and Unfederated Malay States; Adviser Lands, Kedah, 1911; Commissioner, Lands and Mines, Johore, 1922; Secretary for Agriculture, Straits Settlements and Federated

Malay States, 1924; British Adviser, Kelantan, 1926; General Adviser, Johore, 1927. *Address:* Dene House, Regent Road, Jersey. [*Died* 25 *Feb.* 1958.

SHAW, Mrs. G. W. H.; *see* Royden, A. Maude.

SHAW, Kathleen Trousdell, R.H.A.; sculptor; *b.* Middlesex, 1870; *d.* of late Dr. Alfred Shaw. *Educ.:* Dublin; Paris; Rome; Athens. *Works:* portraits of the late Earl Egerton of Tatton, the Duchess of Buckingham and Chandos, Lord Avebury, Cardinal Logue, Archbishop of Armagh, Primate of Ireland, Countess Annesley, and many others (all exhibited in R.A. and Salon); Archbishop Alexander, half figure in marble (in Armagh Cathedral); also ideal figures of Mowgli, A Nymph (exhibited R.A.), Myron (exhibited Salon), and a public memorial to the officers and men of the Royal Irish Fusiliers who fell in the South African War, at Armagh, Ireland; also Count Athos Romanos, and Countess Bokmet; has exhibited 18 works in the Royal Academy and 25 in Paris Salon; Hon. Royal Hibernian Academician; the first woman sculptor who is a member of an Academy in Great Britain. *Address:* Pitt Cottage, Cadmore, High Wycombe, Bucks. *Club:* Albemarle. [*Died* 13 *June* 1958.

SHAW, Martin Fallas, O.B.E. 1955; F.R.C.M., 1958; Mus. Doc.; composer, ed., and dir. of music; Director of Church Music for Dioc. of Chelmsford, 1935-45; *b.* London, 1875; *s.* of James Shaw, composer and organist; *m.* 1916, Joan, *d.* of A. Townshend Cobbold of Bramford House, nr. Ipswich; two *s.* one *d.* *Educ.:* R.C.M. under Sir Charles Stanford. Founded with Gordon Craig and conducted Purcell Operatic Society, 1899; toured as musical director for Isadora Duncan in Germany, Holland, Denmark, and Sweden, 1906-08; organist and choirmaster, St. Mary-the-Virgin, Primrose Hill, N.W., 1908; Co-founder League of Arts, 1918; Master of the Music St. Martin-in-the-Fields, W.C., 1920-24, and Guildhouse, S.W. 1920; wrote music to Ibsen's Vikings; Trio for pianoforte, violin, and 'cello; Ballad-operas with Clifford Bax, Mr. Pepys; Waterloo Leave; External Examiner in Music for University of Wales, 1934, and for Froebel Education Union, 1938. *Publications:* Songs of Britain, English Carol Book; Songtime, with Percy Dearmer; Brer Rabbit; Midsummer's Night's Dream; settings for soli, chorus, and orchestra of John Masefield's Easter and The Seaport and her Sailors; Mime at the Sign of the Star (Barclay Baron); music-editor with R. Vaughan Williams of hymn-book Songs of Praise and Oxford Carol Book; Up to Now (autobiography); suite for string quartet; Sonata for Flute (or Recorder) and pianoforte (or harpsichord); The Ungentle Guest (song sequence for voice, harp, and string quartet); Water-Folk (from Heine) for voice, pianoforte, and string quartet (Three Choirs Festival, 1932); cantatas for soli, chorus and orchestra, Sursum Corda (Laurence Binyon), Three Choirs, 1933, The Ithacans (Eleanor Farjeon), 1933, The Changing Year (Colchester Festival of Britain), 1951; Oratorio, The Redeemer, 1944; Opera, The Thorn of Avalon (Barclay Baron); Music to T. S. Eliot's The Rock, 1934; Royal Jubilee This England (Liverpool Cathedral, 1935); Master Valiant (Toc H Coming of Age, 1936); Six Men of Dorset, 1937; Judgment at Chelmsford, 1939; Thursday's Child (G.F.S. Pageant), 1939; O Light Invisible (T. S. Eliot), 1940; God's Grandeur (Aldeburgh Festival), 1948; (with R. Vaughan Williams) 20 Traditional English Carols arranged for Soprano and Alto, 1954-58; Church Music; Songs; etc. *Recreations:* sawing, and reading detective stories. *Address:* Long Island House, Southwold, Suffolk. [*Died* 24 *Oct.* 1958.

SHAW, Major Peter Stapleton-, O.B.E. 1918; Director of Walker Cain Ltd. and associated companies; *b.* 6 July 1888; *s.* of Henry Shaw, J.P., Ashton-under-Lyne, and Lena Alexandra, *d.* of late Robert Cain, Liverpool. *Educ.:* Loretto; R.M.C. Queen's Bays, Lancashire Hussars and Tank Corps; Chief Gunnery Instructor Royal Tank Corps; Commanded 5th County of London Yeomanry (Sharp-shooters), European War, 1914-19 (despatches, O.B.E.). M.P. (U.) Wavertree Division of Liverpool, 1935-45. *Address:* Nodes, Hailsham, Sussex. *Club:* Carlton. [*Died* 3 *Aug.* 1953.

SHAW, Reeves; Editor, Strand Magazine, 1931-41, and other publications; *b.* 7 March 1886; *y. s.* of William Bury Shaw, Dublin; *m.* Gladys, *o. d.* of F. H. Wales, Hove; two *d.* *Educ.:* Brighton Grammar School. Joined Editorial Staff of C. Arthur Pearson, Ltd., 1903; of George Newnes, Ltd., 1910; Editor of The Captain and other publications, 1910-22; Editor of The Humorist from foundation, 1922, to 1940; contributor of short stories to most of the principal magazines. *Recreation:* golf. *Address:* Woodways, Thames Ditton. *T.:* Emberbrook 1060. *Club:* Savage. [*Died* 16 *March* 1952.

SHAW, Wilfred, M.A., M.D. (Cantab.), F.R.C.S. (Eng.), F.R.C.O.G.; Surgeon in charge of Gynæcological and Obstetrical Dept., St. Bartholomew's Hospital; Gynæcologist, St. Andrew's Hospital, Dollis Hill; *b.* 12 Dec. 1897; *s.* of late Isaac Shaw, J.P., Birmingham; *m.*; three *s.* one *d.* *Educ.:* King Edward's School, Birmingham; St. John's College, Cambridge (Raymond Horton Smith Prize, Open Scholarship, Foundation Scholarship and Exhibition, Wrights Prize); St. Bartholomew's Hospital (Matthews Duncan Gold Medal, Lawrence Research Scholarship and Gold Medal, Cattlin Research Scholarship); Vienna; Dublin; Royal College Surgeons' Jacksonian Prize Certificate, 1931; Arnott Demonstrator, 1933; Late Examiner in Midwifery at Oxford and Cambridge; Examiner to Univ. of London; late Examiner to Conjoint Board; Fellow and Member of Council Obstetrics Section, Royal Society of Medicine. *Publications:* Text-book of Gynæcology, 5th Edition; Text-book of Midwifery, 3rd Ed.; Midwifery for Nurses; Articles on Ovarian Physiology and Pathology, and on Uterine Hæmorrhage in Journ. of Obst. and Gynæcology. *Recreation:* gardening. *Address:* Little Parndon House, Burnt Mill, Nr. Harlow, Essex. *T.:* Harlow 2152. [*Died* 9 *Dec.* 1953.

SHAWE, Lt.-Col. Charles, C.B.E. 1919; late Rifle Brigade; *b.* 1878; *y. s.* of late Henry Cunliffe Shawe of Weddington Hall, Nuneaton; *m.* 1916, Christabel, *y. d.* of J. C. N. Grigg, of Longbeach, New Zealand; one *s.* one *d.* (and one *s.* killed in action, 1940). *Educ.:* Eton; Sandhurst. Joined 3rd Battalion Rifle Brigade, 1898; A.D.C. to Commander of the Forces in Ireland, 1908-12; Military Secretary to Governor-General of New Zealand, 1912-14; retired pay, 1913; joined N.Z. Expeditionary Force, Aug. 1914; served in Egypt and Gallipoli; present at landing at Anzac Cove; in War Office latter part of War (two Brevets, C.B.E.). *Recreation:* cricket. *Address:* The Hermitage, Witham Friary, Frome, Somerset. *T.:* Upton Noble 22. *Clubs:* Army and Navy, M.C.C. [*Died* 9 *Feb.* 1951.

SHAWYER, Arthur Frederic; General Manager of Martins Bank, Ltd., and Director (London Board), 1926 until retirement 1933; Director of General Life Assurance Company; Chairman of Teasdale & Co. Ltd., Carlisle; *b.* Cockermouth, 16 Jan. 1876; *s.* of late Robt. Cort Shawyer, J.P.; *m.* Elizabeth Mary, *d.* of late R. J. Park, Hove; three *s.* *Educ.:* Giggleswick School. With Cumberland Union Bank, 1892-97; entered Bank of England, 1897; Second Auditor, Bank of England, 1907; General Manager: Lincoln and Lindsey Bank,

1908; Assistant General Manager, Midland Bank, 1918; Martins Bank, 1924. *Address:* The Manor, Upwey, S. Dorset. *T.:* Upwey 311. *Clubs:* Reform; Royal Dorset Yacht (Weymouth). [*Died* 12 *April* 1954.

SHEARING, Joseph; *see* Long, Margaret Gabrielle.

SHEDDEN, Rt. Rev. Roscow George, D.D.; Hon. Asst. Bishop of Oxford since 1947; *b.* 13 May 1882; *s.* of late Sir George Shedden of Spring Hill, East Cowes and Hardmead, Bucks. *Educ.:* Winchester; New College, Oxford, 2nd Class Mod. Hist.; Cuddesdon College. Ordained, 1907; Curate of St. Peter's, Leicester, 1907-09; All Saints', Margaret Street, 1909-19; Chaplain (1st City of London), Royal Fusiliers, 1909-19; Bishop of Nassau, 1919-31; Vicar of Wantage, Berks, 1931-52; Rural Dean of Wantage, 1944-51. *Publication:* Ups and Downs in a West Indian Diocese, 1927. *Address:* Woodstock House, Woodstock, Oxon. *Club:* Leander. [*Died* 11 *Dec.* 1956.

SHEEHY, Sir Christopher, Kt. 1959; O.B.E. 1951; Chairman, Australian Dairy Produce Board, since 1952; *b.* 25 December 1894; *s.* of late J. Sheehy, Gympie, Queensland; *m.* 1919, Ruby, *d.* of M. Barlow, Sydney; one *s.* two *d.* *Educ.:* Christian Brothers College, Gympie. Secretary, Queensland Wheat Board, 1920-21; Secretary and General Manager, Queensland Butter Marketing Board, 1928-; General Manager, Commonwealth Dairy Produce Equalisation Committee, 1938-; Commonwealth Controller of Dairy Products, 1942-47. *Recreations:* walking, swimming, reading. *Address:* 100 Hamilton Road, Wavell Heights, Queensland, Australia. [*Died* 31 *Aug.* 1960.

SHEEN, Eng.-Rear-Adm. Charles C., C.B. 1917; R.N. (retired); *b.* 1871; 2nd *s.* of late Alfred Sheen, M.D., of Cardiff; *m.* Alice (*d.* 1940), *d.* of late T. M. Richards, H.M. Civil Service; one *s.* one *d.* Landed with Naval Brigade for defence of Ladysmith (despatches twice, prom. Chief Engineer, medal and clasp); Engineer Commander of Neptune, 1914-15; Engineer Capt. Light Cruiser Squadrons, 1915-16, and Battle Cruiser Force, 1916-18 (C.B., Order of the Rising Sun of Japan, 3rd class); J.P. Surrey, 1930; retired list, 1923. *Address:* Nuneham, Pyrford, Surrey. [*Died* 23 *Dec.* 1952.

SHEILDS, Francis E. W.; *see* Wentworth-Sheilds.

SHEILS, George Kingsley, C.M.G. 1944; lately Gen. Man., Canadian Manufacturers' Association, Inc., Toronto; *b.* Gagetown, N.B., 22 April 1894; *s.* of John and Alice Sheils; *m.* 1919, Hazel Jean, *y. d.* of Geo. Teed, St. John, N.B.; two *s.* *Educ.:* Gagetown Primary and Grammar Schools; Saint John Business College; La Salle and Alexander Hamilton Institutes Extension Courses. Commenced work at age of 14 in St. John, as book-keeper. Then cashier in King Cole Tea Co. and their purchasers George E. Barbour Co. Ltd. Served European War: enlisted 6 Aug. 1914 as Private; proceeded to England Sept. 1914 and to France Feb. 1915, Royal Montreal Regiment, 3rd Canadian Infantry Bde., 1st Canadian Division (wounded); returned to duty, 1917; discharged 1919 with rank of Capt. Has subsequently held following positions: Assistant General Manager, Maritime Division, then Ontario Division, Ames, Holden, McCready Ltd.; Secretary and, later, Comptroller, Ames, Holden Tire & Rubber Co. Ltd., and their successors, Canadian Goodrich Co. Ltd.; Asst. to General Manager, Robt. Simpson Eastern Ltd., Toronto; Assistant General Manager, Robt. Simpson Western Ltd., Regina, Sask.; Asst. to Vice-Pres., Robt. Simpson Co., Ltd., Toronto; Merchandise Man., Robt. Simpson Mail Order Houses, Toronto; one year on independent Industrial Research and Business Reorganisation work; Vice-Pres. and Asst. Gen. Man., General Steel Wares Ltd., Toronto, until 1940; Dir. of Admin., War Supply Bd., Ottawa, Jan.-Apr. 1940; Dep. Minister of Munitions and Supply, Ottawa, Apr. 1940-Dec. 1945 (dept. closed). Chm. (first) Can. Section, Jt. War Production Cttee. of Canada and U.S., 1941-42; Executive Vice-President and Director, N.M. Davis Corporation Ltd., Toronto, Ont., 1946-53. Past Pres. Can. Manufacturers' Assoc. Inc.; Member The Canadian General Council and the Ontario Provincial Council; Hon. Metropolitan Commissioner, The Toronto Metropolitan Area, The Boy Scouts Assoc.; Mem. Exec. Cttee., Toronto Br., Can. Red Cross Soc.; Mem. Fort York Br., Can. Legion of Brit. Empire Service League; Dir. Toronto Veterans' Farms, Inc.; First Vice-Pres. St. Patrick's Protestant Benevolent Soc. *Clubs:* Royal Canadian Military Institute, Granite (Toronto); Canadian. [*Died* 22 *Nov.* 1953.

SHELDON, Sir Mark, K.B.E., *cr.* 1924; Kt., *cr.* 1922; *b.* Armidale, N.S.W., 13 Nov. 1871; *s.* of William Sheldon, M.D., Stratford-on-Avon, Warwickshire; *m.* 1897, Blanche Mary (decd.), *d.* of Hon. Thomas Dalton; two *s.* one *d.* (and two *d.* decd.). *Educ.:* Ushaw Coll., Durham. Entered Dalton Bros., merchants and shipping agents, Sydney, 1890; Manager, 1896; Managing Director Dalton Bros. of Sydney, Ltd., 1902; Chairman Carmichael & Co. Ltd.; Director of various public companies throughout Australia; Commissioner for the Commonwealth of Australia in the United States, 1919-22; Chairman of the Repatriation Board, 1917-19; Member of the Council of the Commonwealth Bureau of Commerce and Industry; Australian Commonwealth representative at the League of Nations, Geneva, 1922; President of Associated Chambers of Commerce of Australia, 1922-23; President of the Sydney Chamber of Commerce, 1923-4-5; Australian Representative on British Empire Economic Committee, 1925. *Address:* c/o Dalton Bros. of Sydney Pty. Ltd., Box 109, G.P.O., Sydney, N.S.W. *Clubs:* St. James'; Union, Royal Sydney (Sydney). [*Died* 13 *Oct.* 1956.

SHELLEY, Sir Percy Bysshe, 7th Bt., *cr.* 1806; *b.* 24 June 1872; *s.* of 5th Bt. and Lady Mary Jane Jemima Stopford; 3rd *d.* of 5th Earl of Courtown; *S.* brother 1951. *Educ.:* Wellington College. *Heir:* *b.* Sidney Patrick, *b.* 18 Jan. 1880. *Address:* Lovington, Alresford, Hants.; Parkside, Avington, Winchester, Hants. [*Died* 24 *Sept.* 1953.

SHELLEY-ROLLS, Capt. Sir John Courtown Edward, 6th Bt., *cr.* 1806; J.P., D.L.; late Scots Guards; High Sheriff for County of Southampton, 1928; A.D.C. to G.O.C. London District, 1914-18; *b.* 5 Aug. 1871; *s.* of 5th Bt. and Lady Mary Jane Jemima Stopford, 3rd *d.* of 5th Earl of Courtown; *S.* father 1902; *m.* 1898, Hon. Eleanor Georgiana Rolls, *o. surv. c.* of 1st Baron Llangattock. Served S. African War (medal 3 clasps); rejoined Scots Guards, Aug. 1914. Owns about 3000 acres. [In compliance with the will of John, 1st Baron Llangattock, assumed by Royal Licence the additional surname of Rolls, 1917.] *Heir:* *b.* Percy Bysshe, *b.* 24 June 1872. *Address:* Avington Park, Winchester, Hants; The Hendre, Monmouth; South Lodge, Knightsbridge, S.W.7. *T.:* Kensington 1896. *Clubs:* Guards, Army and Navy; Royal Yacht Squadron (Cowes). [*Died* 18 *Feb.* 1951.

SHELLSHEAR, Joseph Lexden, D.S.O. 1918; M.D., M.S.; *b.* Sydney, N.S.W., 31 July 1885; *s.* of Walter Shellshear, M.I.C.E., and Clara Mabel Eddis; *m.* Hildred Robertson, Melbourne; no *c.* *Educ.:* Sydney University (Renwick Scholar); Second Class Honours at graduation, 1906-7. Lt.-Col. Commanding 4th Australian Field Artillery Brigade, France (D.S.O., despatches twice); Rockefeller

Fellow, 1920-21; Senior Demonstrator, Department of Anatomy, University College, London; Prof. of Anatomy, Hong Kong Univ., 1923-36; Research Prof. of Anatomy, Univ. of Sydney, 1937-48. Radiologist. *Publications:* The Anatomy of the Brain of the Chinese, Australian, Bushman and Prehistoric Man; Memoirs on Anatomical Subjects dealing with development of the Peripheral Nervous System; contributions to study of blood supply of the brain, and to prehistory of Hong Kong; Surveys of Anatomical Fields. *Recreation:* golf. *Address:* 141 Macquarie Street, Sydney, N.S.W. [*Died* 22 *March* 1958.

SHENNAN, Sir Alfred (Ernest), Kt., *cr.* 1952; F.R.I.B.A.; J.P.; Chartered Architect; *b.* 26 Nov. 1887; 5th *s.* of late William and Sarah Shennan; *m.* 1916, Dorothy (*d.* 1955), *y. d.* of W. T. McCabe, Liverpool; two *d.* *Educ.:* Birkenhead. Hon. M.A. Liverpool Univ., 1940; Hon. Freedom of City of Liverpool, 1946; J.P. Liverpool, 1933-; Alderman, 1934-; Leader Conservative Party in City Council; Chairman: Mersey Tunnel Jt. Cttee., Finance, and Merseyside Co-ordination Cttees.; Civil Defence, Emergency, Parliamentary and Special Salaries Cttees.; Lancashire Industrial Development Assoc.; Commission to examine working of the Ecclesiastical Dilapidations Measures, 1923-1929, 1958-59. *Address:* Greystoke, West Derby, Liverpool, 12. *T.:* Stoneycroft 3729. *Clubs:* Athenæum, Constitutional (Liverpool). [*Died* 6 *May* 1959.

SHENTON, Edward Warren Hine, M.R.C.S. Eng.; L.R.C.P. Lond.; retired; Hon. Radiologist, St. Bartholomew's Hospital, Rochester, 1934; late Senior Surgical Radiographer, Guy's Hospital; Radiologist, Royal Air Force Central Hospital; *b.* 1872; *m.* 1900, Phœbe Hollis. *Educ.:* private school. Entered Guy's, 1893; some years Hon. Radiographer to St. Peter's Hospital; for one year Medical Officer in charge of Electrical Department of the Royal London Ophthalmic Hospital; mentioned for distinguished services and Gold Medal Red Cross for war services. *Publications:* Disease in Bones, its Detection by the X-rays; X-rays in Obstetric Practice; Co-editor of Atlas of Visceral Radiograms, 1926. *Recreation:* music (Hon. Member, Trinity Coll. of Music, London, 1944). *Address:* 2 Willifield Way, N.W.11; 126 Harley Street, W.1. *T.:* Speedwell 1888. [*Died* 12 *Oct.* 1955.

SHEPHARD, Cecil Yaxley, C.B.E. 1948; J.P., Ph.D., B.Sc.(Econ.); Executive Secretary (Agricultural Economics). Caribbean Commission, since 1953; Vice-Principal, 1947-53, and Carnegie Professor of Economics, 1925-53, Imperial College of Tropical Agriculture; Managing Director, Salvador (1951) Ltd., since 1951; Pres., 1957-58, Dir., 1955-58, The Cocoa Planters' Assoc. of Trinidad, Ltd.; *b.* 14 Mar. 1900; 3rd *s.* of late John James Shephard, Bridport, Dorset; *m.* 1st, 1924, Phoebe Florence Bark (*d.* 1926) no *c.*; 2nd, 1930, Phyllis Mae Pashley, Trinidad, B.W.I.; one *s.* one *d.* *Educ.:* Bridport Grammar School; Borough Road College; London School of Economics. B.Sc.(Econ.) 1st Cl. Hons. and Mitchell Student, 1923; Ph.D. 1937. Reader in Economics, 1924, Imperial Coll. of Tropical Agriculture. Editor of Tropical Agriculture, 1924-28; Founder, 1932, Sec.-Treas., 1932-1936, and Pres., 1936-49, Historical Soc. of Trinidad and Tobago; Pres. Trinidad Science Club, 1935-36; Member: Board of Education, 1935-43; Joint Sugar Bd., 1939-43; Cocoa Board, 1946-; Copra Cttee. 1946-49, Trinidad and Tobago; Pres., West Indian Limes Assoc., 1944-45. Lieut. 1937, Capt. 1938-40, 3rd Bn. Trinidad Vol. Director of Ground Training, 1940, The Director, 1941, Trinidad Air Training Scheme; Dist. Warden A.R.P., 1942-45. *Publications:* The Cacao Industry of Trinidad, 1932; The St. Kitts-Nevis Sugar Industry, 1935; Peasant Agriculture in the Gold Coast, 1936; British West Indian Economic History, 1939; Agricultural Policy for Fiji and the Western Pacific High Commission Territories, 1944; Peasant Agriculture in the Leeward and Windward Islands, 1945; The Sugar Industry of Fiji, 1945; The Sugar Industry of Barbados, 1946. *Recreation:* golf. *Address:* Caribbean Commission, Kent House, Port of Spain, Trinidad, T.W.I. *T.A.:* Censec, Port of Spain, Trinidad, T.W.I. [*Died* 16 *June* 1959.

SHEPHARD, Sidney, M.C.; Chairman and Managing Director of Bairns-Wear Ltd.; *b.* 29 March 1894; *s.* of late C. H. Shephard, Lenton, Notts; *m.* 1923, Lilly Jane Alexander, *d.* of late J. A. T. Shannon, Darjeeling, India; two *s.* one *d.* Served Sherwood Foresters, 1914-19; Master of South Notts Hounds, 1932-39; High Sheriff of Nottinghamshire, 1941; Army Welfare Officer, 1939-47; commanded Newark Home Guard Bn., 1940-43. M.P. (C.) Newark Division of Notts, 1943-50. *Recreations:* shooting, fishing. *Address:* Elston Hall, nr. Newark, Notts; Inchnadamph Lodge, Sutherland. *Clubs:* Bath; Nottinghamshire (Nottingham). [*Died* 25 *Nov.* 1953.

SHEPHERD, 1st Baron, *cr.* 1946, of Spalding; **George Robert Shepherd,** P.C. 1951; Chief Opposition Whip, House of Lords, since 1951 (Chief Government Whip, Oct. 1949-Oct. 1951); *b.* 19 Aug. 1881; *s.* of George Robert and Eleanor Sophia Shepherd; *m.* 1915, Ada Newton; one *s.* one *d.* *Educ.:* The Board School, Spalding, Lincs. Shop assistant, 1895; Labour Party Agent, Dundee, 1909-13; Labour Party Agent, Blackburn, 1913-19; Assistant National Agent, Labour Party, 1919-29; National Agent, Labour Party, 1929-46; in charge, as National Agent, of the General Elections 1929, 1931, 1935 and 1945; representative of Labour Peers on Parliamentary Cttee. of Labour Party, 1951; led delegation from British Parliament to Swedish Parliament, 1950; a Lord-in-Waiting to the King, Oct. 1948; Captain of the Yeoman of the Guard, 1949; Captain of Honourable Corps of the Gentlemen-at-Arms, Oct. 1949-Oct. 1951; a Deputy Speaker of the House of Lords. *Recreations:* gardening, motoring. *Heir:* *s.* Hon. Malcolm Newton Shepherd, *b.* 27 September 1918. *Address.* Elm Trees, Parkfield Gardens, Harrow, Middx. *T.:* Pinner 4242. [*Died* 4 *Dec.* 1954.

SHEPHERD, Arthur; School teacher East Ham since 1932; *b.* 7 Feb. 1884. *Educ.:* Birmingham Univ. Teacher; M.P. (Lab.) Darlington, 1926-31. *Address:* Theydon Bois, Essex. [*Died* 14 *April* 1951.

SHEPHERD, Lt.-Col. Claude Innes, D.S.O. 1917; O.B.E. 1944; *b.* 14 Jan. 1884; *s.* of late Major A. I. Shepherd, Kirkville, Aberdeenshire; *m.* 1st, 1911, Edith Ivy (*d.* 1911), *d.* of H. G. Reid, Punjab Police; 2nd, 1914, Evelyn Flora, *d.* of late H. Villars Margary, Ceylon. *Educ.:* Bedford School; R.M.C. Sandhurst. Joined Indian Army, 1902; served European War, 1914-18, Egypt and Mesopotamia; Lt.-Col. 1924; retired, 1931. Gold Staff Officer, Coronation, 1937. Served as Major, Home Guard, 1940-1942. County Director, Middlesex Red Cross, 1938-40; Hon. Secretary, Indian Comforts Fund, 1941-45; Deputy Commissioner, Indian Red Cross and St. John, 1942-45; Chairman, Punjab Frontier Force Assoc., 1954-57 (Vice-Pres. 1957-); Life Governor King Edward VII's Hospital for Officers. Order of the Nile, 3rd class, 1920. C.St.J. 1955. *Address:* 52 Barkston Gardens, S.W.5. *T.:* Frobisher 1514. [*Died* 15 *Feb.* 1960.

SHEPHERD, Gilbert David, M.B.E. 1941; J.P. 1932; F.C.A.; Chartered Accountant; Senior Partner in Gilbert Shepherd, Owen & Co., 22 St. Andrew's Crescent, Cardiff; *b.* 15 April 1880; *e. s.* of

David Shepherd, Cardiff; *m.* 1907, Florence Jessie, *e. d.* of W. R. Foster, Ilfracombe; two *s.* one *d.* *Educ.:* St. Mary's Hall School, Cardiff. Member Council Inst. Chartered Accountants, 1929-57 (Pres. Jan. 1947-June 1948; rep. Inst. in America, 1948, and at Australian Congress on Acctg., 1949); Member Panel of 3, 1947, to apportion £150,000,000 re British-Argentine Rlys.; also on Panel of 2, 1948, to apportion £7,150,000 re British-Uruguay Railways; Chairman Principality Building Society; Chm. South Wales Bd., Legal and General Assurance Soc.; Director Cardiff Pure Ice & Cold Storage Co. Ltd., Thos. Stevens, Confectioner, Ltd., etc. An Officer Cardiff Naturalists' Soc. 1901-51 (Pres. 1921-22); Founder Cardiff Chamber of Trade, 1910 (Pres. 1924-25); Member Bd. of Management of National Chamber of Trade, 1914- (Pres. 1934-36); a Founder, Rotary Club of Cardiff, 1917 (Sen. Mem.; Pres., 1921-22); a Founder, Prince of Wales' Orthopædic Hosp., Cardiff, 1917 (Hon. Sec. 25 years to 1942); Chairman Board of Governors United Cardiff Hospitals (the Teaching Hospitals attached to Welsh National School of Medicine), 1948-54. Chief Inspector Cardiff Special Constabulary, 1914-19; Chief Air Raid Warden, City of Cardiff, 1938-46. Member Post Office Advisory Council, 1934-; Member Cardiff Dist. Advisory Cttee. of the Assistance Bd., 1936-47; Member S. Wales Price Regulation Cttee., 1940-53; Commr. of Taxes for Cardiff Div., 1941-; Member Council Decimal Assoc. 1921-; Treasury Dir. on Bd. of Wales and Mon. Industrial Estates Ltd., 1941-47; Chairman of Nuffield Trust for Special Areas; Mem. Court and Council, Nat. Museum of Wales. Freemason, 1919-; Past Grand Deacon, Grand Lodge of England. *Recreations:* foreign travel, motoring, photography. *Address:* Oakhurst, Ty-Gwyn Road, Cardiff. *T.:* Cardiff 45343. *Clubs:* National Liberal; Cardiff and County (Cardiff). [*Died* 6 *June* 1958.

SHEPHERD, Sir (William) Walker (Frederick), Kt., *cr.* 1956; Chairman Turner and Newall Ltd. since 1944; *b.* 13 Oct. 1895; *e. s.* of late Walker Shepherd and Jane (*née* Cramp), Penrhyn Bay, N. Wales; *m.* 1930, Isabel Cromwell Ingham, *e. d.* of Frederick W. and Anne Ingham, Heatley Heath, Cheshire; no *c.* *Educ.:* privately. Served European War, 1914-18, Palestine and France, as officer of Cheshire Regt.; subs. held several minor commercial appointments; joined Turner and Newall Ltd.: Sec., 1927; Director, 1931; Jt. Man. Dir., 1938; Dep. Chm., 1942. *Recreation:* travel. *Address:* 4 Wilton Crescent, S.W.1. *T.:* Belgravia 3157. *Clubs:* Devonshire, Junior Carlton, Oriental; Clarendon (Manchester); Mount Royal (Montreal). [*Died* 28 *Feb.* 1959.

SHEPPARD, Admiral Sir Dawson L.; *see* Sheppard, Admiral Sir T. D. L.

SHEPPARD, Brig.-General Herbert Cecil, C.B. 1919; C.M.G. 1917; D.S.O. 1916; late R.A.; *s.* of late Col. T. D. Sheppard, and *brother* of late Col. G. S. Sheppard, and Adm. Sir T. D. L. Sheppard, *q.v.* Served W. Africa, 1899 (Benin Territories), and also 1900 (Ashanti) (despatches); S. Africa, 1900 (Queen's medal 3 clasps); European War, 1914-18 (C.B., C.M.G., D.S.O., Bt. Col.). *Address:* St. Nicholas House, Thetford, Norfolk. [*Died* 1 *Feb.* 1953.

SHEPPARD, Samuel Townsend; *b.* 9 Jan. 1880; *y. s.* of late Philip Sheppard, Bath; *m.* Lilian Agnes (Anne) Howard (*d.* 1934), *d.* of late John Howard Carpenter; one *d.* *Educ.:* Bradfield; Trinity College, Oxford. Secretary to the Editor of The Times, 1902; Assistant Editor of the Times of India, 1907-23; Editor, 1923-32; temporary Capt. in the army, and Staff-Capt. Bombay Brigade, 1917-18; Officer of the (Hellenic) Order of the Phœnix, 1933. Civil Assistant, War Office, 1939-45. *Publications:* Bombay Place-names and Street-names; A History of the Byculla Club; History of the Bombay Volunteer Rifles; edited Bombay in the Days of Queen Anne, for the Hakluyt Society; Bombay (a short history), 1932; Joint-Editor of the Indian Year-Book from the first issue until 1932; contributed to The Times History of the War in S. Africa. *Club:* Oriental. [*Died* 20 *April* 1951.

SHEPPARD, Maj.-Gen. Seymour Hulbert, C.B. 1918; C.M.G. 1917; D.S.O. 1902; *b.* 24 Dec. 1869; *e. surv. s.* of G. F. Sheppard, J.P. *Educ.:* Haileybury. Entered Army, 1890; Captain, 1901; Bt. Major, 1904; Bt. Lieut.-Colonel, 1913; Bt. Colonel, 1915; Brig.-General, 1916; Major-General, 1919; served Waziristan Expedition, 1894-95 (medal with clasp); North-West Frontier, India, 1897 (despatches); Tirah Expeditionary Force, 1897-98 (despatches, medal with two clasps); Mahsud Waziri operations, 1902 (despatches, D.S.O., clasp); operations against Cabul Khels, 1902; Tibet, 1903-4 (despatches, Brevet-Major, medal and clasp); European War, 1914-18 (East African Expeditionary Force, despatches 6 times, C.B., C.M.G.); 3rd Afghan War, 1919; Maj.-Gen R.E., India, 1921-22; retired, 1922; Col. Comdt. R.E., 1933-40. *Recreations:* Army Champion Rackets, Singles, 1903, 1906, and 1921; Amateur Champion Rackets, 1906. *Address:* 73 Wick Hall, Hove, Sussex. *T.:* Hove 2309. *Club:* Army and Navy. [*Died* 7 *Feb.* 1957.

SHEPPARD, Admiral Sir (Thomas) Dawson Lees, K.B.E., *cr.* 1922; C.B. 1918; M.V.O. 1906; *b.* 7 April 1866; *s.* of late Col. T. D. Sheppard, J.P., The Grange, Shanklin; *m.* 1904, Mona (*d.* 1945), *widow* of Major Holden, Berkshire Regiment. Entered R.N., 1879; Captain, 1904; Rear-Admiral, 1916; served in H.M.S. Renown during tour of the Prince and Princess of Wales in India, 1905-6; commanded 9th Cruiser Squadron, Dec. 1916-Jan. 1919; served European War, 1914-18 (C.B.); Commander of the Sword of Sweden, Spanish Naval Order of Merit, 2nd class; Vice-Adm. 1920; retired list, 1922; Adm. retired list, 1925; commanded Allied Naval and Military Forces in Slesvig during the taking of the Plebiscite, 1920. *Address:* Hayes Barton, Shanklin, Isle of Wight. *Club:* Naval and Military. [*Died* 24 *Feb.* 1953.

SHERA, Frank Henry, M.A., Mus.M. Cantab., F.R.C.O., Hon. A.R.C.M.; Emeritus Professor of Music, University of Sheffield; *b.* 1882; *er. s.* of late H. A. Shera, M.R.C.S., L.R.C.P. *Educ.:* Oakham; Jesus College, Cambridge (Scholar). 1st Class Classical Tripos Part I., 1904; Mus.B. Cantab., 1906; F.R.C.O. 1908; M.A. and Mus.M. Cantab., 1910; Assistant Master in Preparatory Schools, 1904-9; Highgate School, 1909-10; Bradfield College, 1911-13 and 1914-16; Director of Music, Malvern College, 1916-28; Rossiter Hoyle Professor of Music in the Univ. of Sheffield, 1928-48; Public Orator of the Univ., 1934-45; Pres. Sheffield Univ. Assoc., 1939-46; Chairman, Sheffield Philharmonic Society, 1935-47; Pres. Union of Graduates in Music, 1937-39; Vice-President Royal College of Organists since 1937; Member B.B.C. North Regional Advisory Committee on Music, 1936-39; North Regional Advisory Council, 1947-; Central Music Advisory Committee, 1947-50; Music Advisory Committee, British Council, 1946-; Lecturer, Royal Institution, 1936 and 1937; Univ. of London, 1938. *Publications:* Musical Groundwork; Debussy and Ravel; Elgar; The Amateur in Music; regular contributions to the Sheffield Telegraph, 1913-1914 and 1923-39; articles in the Journal of Education, The Listener, etc.; contributor to D.N.B. and to Grove's Dict. of Music and Musicians (5th edn.). *Address:* 21 Beech Hill Road, Sheffield. *T.:* 60730. *Club:* Public Schools. [*Died* 21 *Feb.* 1956.

SHERER, Brig.-Gen. James Donnelly, C.M.G. 1919; D.S.O. 1917; retired R.A.;

b. 1870. Served European War, 1914-19 (wounded, despatches, D.S.O., C.M.G.). *Club:* Army and Navy. [*Died* 27 *July* 1959.

SHERIDAN, Rear-Admiral (Retd.) Henry A., C.B. 1941; *b.* 15 April 1884; *s.* of James Sheridan, Superintending Engineer Post Office Telegraphs in Ireland; *m.* 1917, Marjorie, *o. d.* of W. Neilson Megaw; one *d.* *Educ.:* Dixon's Academy, Cork; R.N. Engineering College, Keyham. Entered R.N. 1900; served throughout European War, 1914-18, in H.M. Ships King Edward VII, Nicator and Tryphon, and after the war in H.M.S. Orion, Saumarez, Campbell, Cumberland and Valiant; Engineer Captain, 1932; served as Squadron Engineer Officer on staff of Commodore Commanding the Home Fleet Destroyer Flotillas and as Fleet Engineer Officer on staff of Commander-in-Chief Mediterranean; Engineer Rear-Admiral, 1939; served as Naval Member of British Supply Board in North America and later appointed Deputy Head of the British Admiralty Technical Mission with headquarters in Ottawa. *Recreation:* golf. *Address:* Somerset, Anglesea Road, Dublin. *T.:* Dublin 683074. *Club:* Royal Irish Automobile (Dublin). [*Died* 16 *Sept.* 1959.

SHERMAN, Most Rev. Louis Ralph, M.A., B.Litt., D.D.; LL.D.; Archbishop of Rupert'sland since 1943; *s.* of Louis Walsh Sherman and Alice Maxwell Myshrall; *b.* Fredericton, New Brunswick, 26 August 1886; *m.* 1919, Carolyn Gillmor; one *s.* two *d.* (and one *s.* killed in action). *Educ.:* Universities of New Brunswick and Lennoxville; Christ Church, Oxford; Cuddesdon. Deacon, 1912; Priest, 1913; Curate at Christ Church Mission, Poplar E., Notting Hill W., and Trinity Church, St. John, N.B., 1914-16, Priest-in-charge, 1916-17; Rector, Church of the Holy Trinity, Toronto, 1917-25; Canon of St. Alban's Cathedral, 1922; Dean of the Cathedral, Quebec, 1925; Bishop of Calgary, 1927-43. *Address:* Trinity Hall, Winnipeg, Canada. [*Died* 31 *July* 1953.

SHERRINGTON, Sir Charles Scott, O.M. 1924; G.B.E., *cr.* 1922; F.R.S.; M.A., M.D., D.Sc. Cantab., F.R.C.P., F.R.C.S.; Hon. D.Sc. Oxford, Paris, Manchester, Strasbourg, Louvain, Upsala, Lyon, Buda Pesth, Athens; LL.D. London, Toronto, Harvard, Dublin, Edinburgh, Montreal, Liverpool, Brussels, Sheffield, Berne, Birmingham, Wales and Glasgow; late Waynflete Professor of Physiology, Oxford; late Member of Medical Research Council of Privy Council; *b.* 27 Nov. 1857; *m.* 1892, Ethel Mary (*d.* 1933), *y. d.* of John Ely Wright, Preston Manor, Suffolk; one *s.* *Educ.:* Caius College, Cambridge. Late Brown Prof. of Pathology, Univ. of London; Lecturer on Physiology, St. Thomas's Hosp., London; Royal and Copley Medallist and Past-Pres. of the Royal Society; Baly Gold Medallist, Royal Coll. of Physicians; Retzius Gold Medal, Royal Swedish Academy; Hon. Member Royal Irish Academy; Soc. de Neurologie, Paris; associate member of the Institut de France; member Imperial Academy of Medicine, Vienna; Foreign Member of National Academy of Sciences, Washington, French Acad. of Sciences, Real. Accadem. d. Scienze, Rome, and of Imperial Academy of Sciences, Petrograd; Royal Acad. of Medicine of Belgium and of Madrid; Member of Royal Acad. of Holland, Amsterdam; Royal Acad. of Sweden; Hon. Mem. Royal Danish Academy of Science, Copenhagen; Société de Biologie, Belge; Foreign Mem. Real. Accad. d. Scienze, Bologna; Hon. Fellow of Magdalen Coll., Oxford; Hon. Fellow Caius Coll. Cambridge; Hon. Fellow Roy. Soc. of Edinburgh; Hon. Member Physiol. Soc. of America; Soc. Medica di Roma; R. Accadem. di Scienze, Turin; Papal Academy Rome; Anglo-American Secretary, International Congresses of Physiology, Liège, Berne, Cambridge, Turin, Brussels, Heidelberg; Vice-Pres. Brit. Child Study Assoc.; Pres. Physiol. Sect. Brit. Assoc. Cam. 1904; Dunham Lecturer, Harvard, 1927; Lister Oration, Canadian Medical Association, Toronto, 1927; Silliman Memorial Lecturer, Yale University, 1904; Page May Memorial Lecturer, University of London, 1910; Croonian Lecturer, Royal College of Physicians, 1913; Member of Board of Trade Committee on Sight Tests, 1910-12; Home Office Committee on Lighting of Factories and Workshops, 1913; War Office Committee on Tetanus, 1916-17; Scientific Com. of the Central Board of Control, Alcohol, 1916-17; Professor of Physiology, Univ. of Liverpool, 1895-1913; Fullerian Professor of Physiology, Royal Institution of Great Britain, 1914-17; late Chairman, Industrial Fatigue Research Board, 1918; Nobel Laureate for Medicine, 1932; Gifford Lecturer, University of Edinburgh, 1936-38; a Trustee, British Museum. *Publications:* The Integrative Action of the Nervous System; Mammalian Physiology, 1916; School Hygiene (part author), 1913; papers to the Royal and other scientific societies, especially on the brain and nervous system; Selected Writings, 1939; Assaying of Brabantius, and other Verse, 2nd ed. 1940; Man on his Nature: the Gifford Lectures, Edinburgh, 1940, 4th ed. 1946; The Endeavour of Jean Fernel, 1946. *Address:* Gonville and Caius College, Cambridge. *Club:* Athenæum. [*Died* 4 *March* 1952.

SHERWOOD, Robert Emmet; Author; Member Amer. Acad. of Arts and Letters; Hon. Litt.D. Harvard, Yale, Dartmouth; Hon. D.C.L., Bishop's University, Canada; *b.* 4 April 1896; *s.* of Arthur Murray and Rosina Emmet Sherwood; *m.* 1st, 1922, Mary Brandon; one *d.*; 2nd, 1935, Madeline Hurlock Connelly. *Educ.:* Harvard University. Joined 42nd Bn. Royal Highlanders of Canada (Black Watch) 1917; served at front in France; after discharge, 1919, entered upon editorial career in New York; Editor of Life, 1924-28; wrote criticism, essays, verse, plays, novels. Late Dir. Overseas Operations, Office of War Information, U.S. Govt., resigned 1944. *Publications:* The Road to Rome; Unending Crusade; Waterloo Bridge; This is New York; The Queen's Husband; Reunion in Vienna; The Petrified Forest; Idiot's Delight; Acropolis; Abe Lincoln in Illinois; There Shall Be No Night; The White House Papers of Harry Hopkins (2 vols.). Adaptation: Tovarich. Awarded Pulitzer Prize: Idiot's Delight (1936), Abe Lincoln in Illinois (1939), There Shall Be No Night (1941), Roosevelt and Hopkins (1949); awarded Gold Medal for Drama, American Academy of Arts and Letters (1940); awards for Best Screenplay of 1947, The Best Years of Our Lives, by Motion Picture Acad. and Internat. Film Festival, Brussels. *Address:* 25 Sutton Place, New York City 22. *Clubs:* Garrick, Buck's; Harvard (New York). [*Died* 14 *Nov.* 1955.

SHERWOOD, Will, C.B.E. 1938; late National Industrial Officer, National Union of General and Municipal Workers; Member of the General Council, Trades Union Congress; *b.* 1871; *s.* of John Sherwood and Amy Caister; *m.* 1895; four *s.* two *d.* *Educ.:* Board School, Hartlepool. Trade Union Official since 1900; President of the Federation of Engineering and Shipbuilding Trades, 1923-34; contested (Lab.), Hartlepools, 1918; Darlington, three times, 1922-23; Joint Chairman Committee of Inquiry Shipbuilding Industry, 1924; member of Government Departmental Committee Inquiry Shipbuilding Industry, 1923; Member Court of Inquiry into Mining Industry, 1925; Trade Union Congress Delegate to American Federation of Labour 1927; Trades Union Congress Delegate to Mexican Labour Movement, 1927; Member of the Metalliferous Mines Advisory Committee of Mines Department, and Member of the Committee of Engineering Industry Board of Education; National Trustee to Medical Expenses Fund—Workmen's Compensation (Silicosis Scheme) Act; an accepted authority on Engineering and Shipbuilding practice, wages and conditions; visited France, Belgium, Holland, Germany, America, Canada on research work. *Publications:* Report on Shipbuilding Engineering Industries on the Continent, 1926-27; Wages and machine operations, 1930; Contributor to Man and The Machine, 1935; articles, magazines and newspapers. *Recreations:* mineralogy, collecting minerals, spars, chrystals, literature. *Address:* 10 Monica Road, Narboro Road, Leicester. [*Died* 13 *March* 1955.

SHIELDS, Sir Douglas (Andrew), Kt., *cr.* 1919; LL.D. (Hon.) St. Andrews, 1922; M.D., M.B., Ch.B.; F.R.C.S.A. (Hon.) Administrator and Surgeon-in-Chief at Hospital, 17 Park Lane; *b.* Melbourne, 21 July 1878; *m.* 1900, Mary Ellen Shirrefs (*d.* 1939); one *s.* *Educ.:* Melbourne University. Consulting Surgeon, R.N.; Lecturer Clinical Surgery, Melbourne University. *Address:* 8 Upper Wimpole Street, W.1; Oakley, Merstham, near Redhill, Surrey. [*Died* 22 *Feb.* 1952.

SHIELS, Sir (T.) Drummond, Kt., *cr.* 1939; M.C.; M.B., Ch.B.; *s.* of James Drummond Shiels and Agnes Campbell, Edinburgh; *m.* 1st, 1904, Christian Blair Young (*d.* 1948), Gilmerton, Edinburgh; one *d.*; 2nd, 1950, Gladys L. Buhler, M.B.E. *Educ.:* Board School; Edinburgh Univ. (M.B., Ch.B.). Fellow and ex-Senior Pres. Roy. Med. Soc.; service in 1914-18 War, with 9th (Scottish) Division (despatches, M.C., Belgian Croix de Guerre); was a member of Edinburgh Town Council; M.P. (Lab.) East Edinburgh, 1924-31; Member of Special Commission on Ceylon Constitution, 1927; Parliamentary Under-Secretary of State, India Office, 1929; Parliamentary Under-Secretary of State, Colonial Office, 1929-31; Vice-President, Royal Empire Society; Former Member Governing Body of British Post-Graduate Medical Federation and of Secretary of State's Colonial Economic and Development Council. Sometime Deputy-Secretary Commonwealth Parliamentary Association; Public Relations Officer, General Post Office, London, 1946-49. British Group, Inter-Parliamentary Union, Houses of Parliament, Westminster. *Address:* 35 Coram St., W.C.1. [*Died* 1 *Jan.* 1953.

SHIGEMITSU, Mamoru; Vice-President of Japan Democratic Party since 1954; Deputy Prime Minister and Minister for Foreign Affairs, 1955-56; *b.* 29 July 1887; 2nd *s.* of Naomasa Shigemitsu; *m.* 1923, Kie Hayashi; one *s.* one *d.* *Educ.:* Faculty of Law of Tokyo Imperial University. Passed examinations for both Diplomatic and Civil Services; Attaché at Berlin, 1911; transferred to London as 3rd Secretary and later to Portland, U.S.A., as Consul; Member of Japanese Delegation to Paris Peace Conference, 1919; Counsellor and later Secretary of the Foreign Office; 1st Secretary of the Legation in China; Member of delegation to Special Conference on Chinese Customs and Member of Commission of Extra-territoriality in China, 1925; Counsellor of Embassy in Berlin, 1927; Consul-General, Shanghai, holding additional post of Counsellor to Embassy in China, 1929; Chargé d'Affaires in China, 1930; Envoy Extraordinary and Minister Plenipotentiary in China, 1931; Vice-Minister for Foreign Affairs, 1933; Ambassador Extraordinary and Plenipotentiary at Moscow, 1936; Japanese Ambassador to Court of St. James, 1938-41; to Nanking Government, 1942-43; Foreign Minister, Japan, 1943. Detained in Sugamo Prison, Tokyo, as one of the major war crime suspects, Jan. 1946; sentenced to 7 years' imprisonment by International War Crimes Tribunal, Nov. 1948, released on parole, 1950; Sentence expired, Nov. 1951. Pres. Progressive Party and M.P. (Japan), 1952. *Recreation:* swimming. *Address:* No. 345, 3 Chome, Harajuku, Shibuya-ku, Tokyo, Japan. [*Died* 25 *Jan.* 1957.

SHILLIDY, John Armstrong, C.S.I. 1932; I.C.S. (retired); *b.* 6 June 1882; *s.* of Rev. J. Shillidy, D.D.; *m.* 1917, Ethel Vera Halliday (*d.* 1919), *d.* of W. C. Hickie; one *s.* *Educ.:* School for Sons of Missionaries, Blackheath; Campbell College, Belfast; Trinity College, Dublin. Assistant Collector and Magistrate, Bombay, 1906; Municipal Commissioner, Ahmedabad, 1915-17; Assistant Commissioner in Sind, 1917-20; Deputy Secretary to Govt. of Bombay, Home Dept., 1922; Collector and Political Agent; officiating Joint Secretary to the Govt. of India, Home Dept., 1927-29; Secretary to the Government of India in the Dept. of Industries and Labour, 1929-33. *Club:* East India and Sports. [*Died* 16 *Nov.* 1952.

SHINE, Eustace Beverley, C.B. 1927; *b.* 9 July 1873; *s.* of George Shine, Trinidad; *m.* 1st, 1900, Mary Venables; one *s.*; 2nd, 1912, Ida J. Cornwell; three *d.* *Educ.:* King Edward VI. School, Saffron Walden; Selwyn College, Cambridge. Cambridge and Kent Cricket XI., 1896-97; Inspector Board of Agriculture, 1900; Private Secretary to late Sir Thomas Elliott, 1905-7; Private Secretary to late Marquess of Lincolnshire, 1907-11; Head of Live Stock Branch, 1911-20; Assistant Secretary, 1920-33, and Establishment Officer, 1921-33, Ministry of Agriculture and Fisheries; retd. *Address:* Belhurst, Ashley Rd., New Milton, Hants. [*Died* 11 *Nov.* 1952.

SHINE, Most Rev. Thomas; Archbishop-Bishop of Middlesborough, (R.C.), since 1955; Bishop of Middlesbrough, 1929; *b.* Tipperary, 1872. *Educ.:* Rockwell College; Thurles College; St. Joseph's Seminary, Leeds. Priest, 1894; curate at Leeds Cathedral, 1894-1904; pastor, Horsforth, 1904-8; Administrator of Leeds Cathedral, 1908-21; Canon of Leeds, 1914; Coadjutor to Bishop of Middlesbrough and titular Bishop of Lamus, 1921. Knight Commander of the Holy Sepulchre, 1924; Count of the Holy Roman Empire and Assistant at the Pontifical Throne, 1946. *Address:* Bishop's House, Middlesbrough. [*Died* 22 *Nov.* 1955.

SHIRCORE, John Owen, C.M.G. 1926; M.B., M.R.C.P.E.; M.O., Fort Johnston, 1946, Nyasaland Medical Service; retd. 1948; *b.* 1882; *s.* of late Capt. J. C. Shircore, I.M.S. *Educ.:* Edinburgh, London, and Camb. Appointed to the Colonial Service as Medical Officer, 1908; served in Nyasaland, Uganda, Kenya, and Tanganyika, since 1908; Capt. East African Medical Service, 1914-18 (despatches); Director of Medical and Sanitary Services, Tanganyika Territory; retired, 1932; Lt.-Col., East Africa Army Medical Corps; A.D.M.S. (M. Branch) E. A. Force Headquarters, Nairobi, 1941; unofficial M.L.C.; Tanganyika Territory, 1934-35; Medical Investigator, British North Borneo, 1936; M.O. Karonga, 1942. *Publications:* Epidem. Cerebro-Spinal Meningitis in Nairobi, Trans. Soc. Trop. Med. and Hy., 1914; Suggestions for the Limitation and Destruction of Glossina Morsitans, Bull. Entomol. Research, 1914; Report on Native Health with Special Reference to the Sociological and Economic Factors bearing on the Depopulation Problem of the Interior and West Coast, North Borneo, 1936. *Address:* c/o The Standard Bank of S. Africa Ltd., Zomba, Nyasaland. *Club:* East India and Sports. [*Died* 23 *June* 1953.

SHIRRAS, George Findlay, M.A.; Hon. F.S.S. 1920; *b.* Aberdeen, 16 July 1885; *e. s.* of late George Findlay Shirras, merchant, Aberdeen, and Anne Fiddes, *d.* of late John Cantlay, Aquaharney, Aberdeenshire; *m.* 1911, Amy Zara, *o. d.* of late George McWatters, Madras Civil Service; one *s.* *Educ.:* Robert Gordon's College, Aberdeen; Univ. of Aberdeen; Univ. Prizeman in Economics. Indian Educational Service as Prof. of Economics, Dacca Coll., 1909; Fellow of the Univ. of Calcutta since 1909, and Syndic. Univ. of Calcutta; on special duty under

Government of India, Finance Dept., 1910-1913; Reader in Currency and Finance in the University of Calcutta, 1914; Director of Statistics with the Government of India, 1914-21; Director, Labour Office, Government of Bombay, 1921-26; Principal and Professor of Economics, Gujarat College, Univ. of Bombay, 1926-39, Fellow, University of Bombay, 1927-39; Member Govt. of India Prices Enquiry Cttee.; on deputation Imperial Statistical Conference, London, on behalf of Govt. of India, Dec. 1919-Feb. 1920; on special duty India Office in connection with League of Nations work, March 1920; deputed to British Ministry of Labour and Board of Trade and International Labour Office, Geneva, 1924, by Govt. of Bombay; Major 4th Gordon Highlanders, 1920 (despatches); T.A. Reserve Regimental List, 1921; External Examiner in Political Economy, Glasgow Univ., 1940-45; formerly Member, Bombay Legislative Council; formerly Controller-Gen. of Public Revenue and General Finance, Finance Div., Control Commission for Germany (British Element), 1946; Formerly Deputy Chm., Wages Councils, Ministry of Labour and National Service, and Arbitrator under the Industrial Courts Act, 1919; Professor of Economics and Dean of Faculty of Economics and Commerce, Univ. College, Exeter, 1940-45; Professor of Political Economy in the University of Dublin, Trinity College, Dublin, 1950-51. Goldwin Smith Lecturer, Cornell Univ., Ithaca, N.Y., 1953; Visiting Professor of Economics, University of Illinois, Urbana, 1952-53 and 1953-54 (Graduate School of Commerce and Business Organization); Visiting Prof. of Economics, Univ. of Florida, Gainesville, Fla., 1953-54; Visiting Lecturer on Political Economy at Harvard Univ., 1954. Hon. Fellow, Royal Statistical Society, International Inst. of Statistics (membre titulaire); original member of Internat. Assoc. for Research in Income and Wealth: Mem. Internat. Inst. of Public Finance (Mem. Cttee. of Direction); Foreign member, Società Italiana di Economia, Demografia e Statistica, etc. *Publications:* Indian Finance and Currency, 3rd impression, 1920; The Science of Public Finance, 1924, 3rd ed., in 2 vols., 1936; Some Aspects of Indian Commerce and Industry, Annual Reviews of the Trade of India, 1913-14 to 1918-19; An Enquiry into the Wages and Hours of Labour in the Cotton Mill Industry, Bombay, 1923; An Enquiry into Working-Class Budgets in Bombay, 1923; An Enquiry into Agricultural Wages in the Bombay Presidency (1900-22), 1924; Some Effects of the War on Gold and Silver, 1920; Die Volkswirtschaftliche Theorie (Univ. of Vienna, 1927), The readjustment of Central and Provincial Finance (Publicationi della R. Universita di Pavia), 1930; Poverty and Kindred Economic Problems in India, 1932; 4th ed. 1936; Indian Finance and the Financial Relations of Provinces in the Dominion of S. Africa [Handbuch der Finanzwissenshaft]; The Burden of British Taxation (with Dr. L. Rostas), 1942, Amer. ed. 1943; Federal Finance in Peace and War, 1944; Sir Isaac Newton and the Currency, 1945; Planning towards Recovery (Univ. of Vienna), 1949; Newton, a study of a Master Mind (Archives Internat. d'Histoire des Sciences), 1951; The Economic Development in South and South East Asia and its Financial Requirements (International Inst. of Public Finance, Lond.), 1951; articles for Encyclopædia Britannica on war finance; papers on finance and economics, etc., in Econ. Journal, Journal of Royal Statistical Society and other scientific journals. *Recreation:* golf, Viceroy's (Lord Hardinge's) Cup, Tollygunge, 1913. *Address:* Trinity College, Dublin; Greystones, Ballater, Aberdeenshire. *Clubs:* East India and Sports; Royal Irish Yacht, Dunlaoghaire (Kingstown); University (Urbana, Illinois). [*Died* 21 *June* 1955.

SHOOSMITH, Major-Gen. Stephen Newton, C.B. 1951; D.S.O. and Bar, 1944; O.B.E. 1943; Principal Staff Officer to Deputy Supreme Allied Commander, Allied Powers, Europe, 1954-56; *b.* 15 Sept. 1900; *s.* of Harry Shoosmith; British; *m.* 1938, Kathleen Mary (*née* Noad); one *s.* one *d.* *Educ.:* Blundell's School; Royal Military Academy. Commissioned with Royal Artillery, 1920; Staff College, Camberley, 1935 and 1936. Served War of 1939-45 (despatches, O.B.E., D.S.O. and Bar): France and Belgium, 1939-40; Asst. Military Secretary, War Cabinet, 1941; N. Africa, 1943; Italy, 1944-45; Greece, 1945; Germany, 1946-48; formerly Commander British Joint Services Mission (Army Staff), U.S.A.; Deputy Chief of Staff, U.N. Command, Japan, 1952-54. Colonel, 1946; Maj.-Gen., 1949. Comdr. U.S. Legion of Merit, 1954. *Recreations:* sailing, fishing, hunting, polo, travelling. *Address:* c/o Lloyds Bank Ltd., 6 Pall Mall, S.W.1. *Club:* Army and Navy. [*Died* 3 *Dec.* 1956.

SHORT, A. H. H.; *see* Hassard-Short.

SHORT, Arthur Rendle, M.D., B.S., B.Sc., F.R.C.S.; Emeritus Professor of Surgery, University of Bristol; Consulting Surgeon, Bristol Royal Infirmary; late Surgeon to Clifton College; Ex-Hunterian Prof., Roy. Coll. of Surgeons; late Mem. Council British Association of Surgeons; *s.* of E. Rendle Short, of Bristol; *m.* Helen, *d.* of late Henry Williams Case; one *s.* two *d.* *Educ.:* Univ. of Bristol; Univ. College, London. 1st Class honours in Geology and Scholarships in Physiology, B.Sc.; Exhibition and Gold Medal in Physiology; Exhibition and Gold Medal in Materia Medica and 1st Class honours in Anatomy, Inter. M.B. London; Scholarship and Gold Medal in Medicine; 1st Class honours in Obstetrics; M.B. London; Gold Medal, M.D. *Publications:* The Causation of Appendicitis; The New Physiology in General and Surgical Practice (5 editions); Editor Index of Prognosis (4 editions); co-Editor, Medical Annual. *Recreation:* naturalizing. *Address:* 69 Pembroke Road, Clifton, Bristol. *T.:* Bristol 33840. [*Died* 14 *Sept.* 1953.

SHORT, Ernest Henry; author; *b.* Melbourne, Australia, 1875; *s.* of Charles Short; *m.* 1906, Agnes Dobrée (*d.* 1956); two *s.*; *m.* 2nd, 1957, Edith Western. *Educ.:* Dulwich College. London Correspondent to Melbourne Argus, 1922-38; General Sec., British Railway Stockholders Union, 1939-48; Hon. Librarian and Sec. Authors' Club, 1940-1952; Managing Director, Hollis & Carter, Ltd. (Publishers), 1942-46; Director, 1946-1953. *Publications:* History of Sculpture, 1907; Mystery of Hope Strange, 2000 dollar prize Chicago Daily News Novel Competition (with A. Compton-Rickett) 1910; Introduction to World History, 1919; Man and Cotton, 1921; Man and Wool, 1921; George Frederick Watts, 1924; William Blake, 1924; House of God, 1925; Book of Revelation, 1926; Hope Strange Mystery; Book of Tobit, 1927; Painter in History, 1929; Brian the Builder (novel), 1932; Waltham St. Lawrence, 1934; Handbook of Geo-Politics, 1935; King George, the Well-beloved, 1936; A History of Religious Architecture, 1936; The Coronation: Its History and Meaning, for National Union of Teachers, 1937; Ring up the Curtain (with A. Compton-Rickett); Railways and the State, The Problem of Nationalization, 1938; Railways, Roads and the Public (with Sir Charles Stuart-Williams); Living with History, four vols., 1939-49; Theatrical Cavalcade, 1942; Fifty Years of Vaudeville, 1946; (ed.) Post-War Church Building, 1947; Man and his Work, 1949; Introducing the Theatre, 1949; Making a Nation (two vols.), 1950; (with H. E. Crawfurd) That's the Way the Money Goes; Sixty Years of Theatre, 1951; History of British Painting, 1953; A Mortal Peril (A Survey of

Economic Crisis), 1956. *Recreation:* chess. *Address:* Tudor Cottage, Graywood, East Hoathly, near Lewes. *T.:* Chiddingly 231. *Club:* Authors'. [*Died* 29 *Aug.* 1959.

SHORT, Lieut.-Colonel Ernest William George, C.B.E. 1919; F.R.I.B.A., F.R.I.C.S.; *b.* 22 Jan. 1877; *m.* Florence Mabel, *d.* of late T. Hickson; two *d.* *Educ.:* R.I.B.A. Student; Silver Medallist in Design; Exhibitor at the Royal Academy of Arts. Architectural practice, 1893-1900; Lieut. 1900; served in England, Ireland, Mauritius, Africa and Singapore; Chief Engineer, South African Military Command, 1916-20; Acting Lt.-Col. 1917; Lt.-Col., 1931; retired pay, 1935; mentioned in communiques for War Service; works include civil and military buildings, fortifications, and defence works. *Publications:* Notes on Military History of the Cape Peninsula; Notes on Preservation Work to the Castle, Cape Town. *Address:* Sherwood, Farnham, Surrey. [*Died* 1 *Nov.* 1953.

SHORT, Rev. Canon F. W. H.; *see* Hassard-Short.

SHORTO, William Alfred Thomas, C.B. 1935; C.B.E. 1920; *b.* 1876; *s.* of late Henry Ralph Shorto; *m.* 1st, 1900, Alice Leonide (*d.* 1934), *d.* of late George Seymour, C.E.; *m.* 2nd, 1948, Eileen Ethel Sarah, *y. d.* of late Major T. Jessop. *Educ.:* Simon Langton School; King's School, Canterbury. Secretary, Department of Controller-General of Merchant Shipbuilding, 1917; Assistant Secretary, Admiralty, 1920-32; Principal Asst. Secretary, and Principal Establishment Officer, Admiralty, 1932-36; Air Ministry, 1939-46. *Address:* Horsell Rise Cottage, Woking, Surrey. *T.:* Woking 623. *Club:* Royal Automobile. [*Died* 27 *Sept.* 1951.

SHRAPNELL-SMITH, Edward Shrapnell, C.B.E. 1918; F.C.S.; M.Inst.T.; M.I.Chem.E.; a pioneer of commercial road motor transport; Director Car and General and Motor Union Insurance, Eastwoods, Ltd., and other Companies; Chairman, R.F.D. Co. Ltd., Phillips Telescopic Taps Co. Ltd., Hurtwood Water Co., Ltd.; Member Road-Rail Appeal Tribunal of the Transport Tribunal (Member Road and Rail Traffic Act, 1933, Appeal Tribunal, 1934-51); Chairman, Petroleum Industry Committee, British Standards Institution, 1934-44; Chairman, National Savings Cttee. of Road Transport Industry, 1941-48; *b.* Liverpool, 10 Feb. 1875; *o. s.* of Edward Charles and Anna Shrapnell-Smith, of Grassendale Park; *m.* 1912, Sarah Rosalie, *y. d.* of Maj.-Gen. R. Temple Godman, Hon. Colonel 5th Dragoon Guards, of Highden Sussex; one *s.* (*er. s.* Ft. Lt., R.A.F., killed on active service, 1939) one *d.* *Educ.:* Liverpool Royal Institution School; Liverpool Univ. Coll. Served apprenticeship Chemical Industry, Widnes; as research chemist was first investigator to obtain crystalline sodium hypochlorite, 1899; organised Lancashire Heavy Motor Trials, 1898, 1899, 1901, and took up motor transport interests; one of four motorists to accompany British troops on Army (Cavalry) manœuvres, 1901; founded, and Gen. Manager and Secretary, Road Carrying Co. Ltd., 1901-3; Editor, The Commercial Motor, 1905-17; Hon. Treasurer, Commercial Motor Users' Association, 1903-18, Chairman, 1918, President, 1920-29; Hon. Secretary and Treasurer, The Commercial Motor Campaign Comforts Fund for the Overseas Mechanical Transport (Army Service Corps), 1914-17; Chairman Standing Joint Committee, Mechanical Road Transport Associations, 1912-29; Commandant, Motor Transport Column, City of London National Gaurd, 1915-19 (retd. as Hon. Major); Chief Economy Officer (unpaid) and a Deputy Director (unpaid) in H.M. Petroleum Executive, 1917-19; Member of Government Committees on Gas Traction, Power Alcohol, Motor Taxation and Regulation, Railways' Claim to conduct Road Transport, Public Service Regulations, and Testing of Motor Vehicle Brakes, 1917-1936; Chairman Empire Motor Fuels Committee of Imperial Motor Transport Council, 1920-30; Member Roads Advisory Committee, Ministry of Transport, 1923-33; an hon. official representative of British Government at International Road Congresses, Milan, 1926, Washington, 1930, and Munich, 1934; Unionist candidate for East Woolwich Parliamentary Division, 1929 and 1931 (By-Election). *Publications:* many papers before learned societies, etc. *Recreations:* motoring, sculling; study of cosmic radiation and nuclear physics. *Address:* Hound House, Shere, Surrey. *T.A.* and *T.:* Shere 15. *Club:* (Founder Life Mem.) Royal Automobile. [*Died* 8 *April* 1952.

SHREEVE, George Harry, C.B.E. 1943; Chairman, St. Ebba's and Belmont Hospital Group; *b.* 6 June 1888; *s.* of late Harry Shreeve; *m.* 1918, Mabel Emily Gilbert; two *s.* one *d.* *Educ.:* Bemrose School, Derby; King's College, London. Civil Service, 1907; Private Secretary to Mr. A. Duff Cooper, Rt. Hon. Douglas Hacking, and Sir Victor Warrender, successive Financial Secretaries to the War Office, 1934-35; Asst. Secretary, War Office, 1939; Command Secretary, Northern Command, 1941-43, Middle East, 1943-44; Principal Assistant Secretary, Ministry of Production, Oct. 1944; Deputy Director-General, British Council, 1947; retired, 1953. *Address:* 4 Buckland Court, Buckland, Betchworth, Surrey. [*Died* 15 *May* 1960.

SHRUBSOLE, Rear-Admiral Percy Joseph, D.S.O. 1919; retired; *b.* 4 Nov. 1875; *s.* of late Charles Baldock Shrubsole, Sheerness, Kent; unmarried. *Educ.:* Sir Joseph Williamson's School, Rochester; Naval College, Keyham. Entered Royal Navy, 1892; service in Somaliland, 1901-3; served as Engineer Officer H.M.S. Glasgow, 1912-16 (despatches of Coronel and Falkland Islands); specially promoted to engineer commander, 1915; served as engineer commander, H.M.S. Calypso, 1916-20 (despatches, D.S.O.); Engineer Captain, 1923; Engineer Rear-Admiral, 1929; Squadron Engineer Officer, Mediterranean Flotillas, 1924-26; Admiralty Engineer Overseer for Scotland, 1927-29; Aide-de-Camp to the King, 1928; retired list, 1929. *Address:* Pauletta, West Mersea, Essex. *Club:* Naval (Portsmouth). [*Died* 28 *Jan.* 1958.

SHUCKBURGH, Sir John Evelyn, K.C.M.G., *cr.* 1922; C.B. 1918; *b.* 18 March 1877; *s.* of late Evelyn Shirley Shuckburgh, Litt.D.; *m.* 1906, Lilian Violet, *er. d.* of late A. G. Peskett, Magdalene College, Cambridge; two *s.* two *d.* *Educ.:* Eton; King's College, Cambridge; B.A. 1899 (1st Class, Classical Tripos); M.A. 1906. Entered India Office, 1900; Secretary, Political Department, India Office, 1917-21; transferred to Colonial Office, 1921; Assistant Under-Secretary of State, 1921-31; Deputy Under-Secretary of State, 1931-42; appointed Governor of Nigeria, 1939, but did not assume office owing to the War; retired, 1942; narrator, historical section, Cabinet Office, 1942-48. *Publication:* An Ideal Voyage and other essays, 1946. *Address:* 37A Connaught Street, W.2. *T.:* Ambassador 1800. *Clubs:* Athenæum, M.C.C. [*Died* 8 *Feb.* 1953.

SHUCKBURGH, Robert Shirley, C.B.E. 1932; *b.* 6 April 1882; *s.* of Evelyn Shirley Shuckburgh, Litt.D., and Frances Mary Pullen; *m.* 1913, Olive Nina, 2nd *d.* of late Sir Henry Fielding Dickens, K.C.; one *s.* one *d.* *Educ.:* Haileybury; Emmanuel College, Cambridge, B.A., 1902; Cape Colony Civil Service, 1903-5; Solicitor, 1908; entered Public Trustee Office, 1908; Principal clerk, 1915; Assistant Public Trustee 1924-48; retired 1948; served European War, R.G.A., 1917-19; Staff Captain G.H.Q. France, 1918 (despatches). *Address:* 8 Mulberry Walk, S.W.3. *T.:* Flaxman 6140. *Clubs:* Garrick, M.C.C. [*Died* 16 *Dec.* 1954.

SHUFFREY, Paul; Owner and Editor of the Church Quarterly Review; *b.* Ealing, 1889; *s.* of Leonard Atkinson Shuffrey, Architect, London and Witney, and Martha, *d.* of William Cary and *g.d.* of James Hardy (kinsman of Adm. Sir Thomas Hardy, Capt. of the Victory); unmarried. *Educ.:* St. Paul's; Lincoln College, Oxford (Scholar, M.A., Litt. Hum.); University College, London (Architecture); under Colonial Office, qualified in Law and African languages. Entered Colonial Service, 1912; Political Officer for Imperri District, Sierra Leone, following serious outbreak of "human leopard" troubles there, 1913; Private Secretary to Sir E. M. Merewether, Governor and C.-in-C., and later to R. J. Wilkinson, holding same office. Served many years in Provincial Administration as District Commissioner and acting Provincial Commissioner; received thanks of Govt. for measures taken during native disaffection of 1919; resigned, 1924, to go into business. Since 1935 much attention to voluntary social services, editing, also, the Social Service Review; Editor of the Guardian, 1939-51. *Publications:* articles in press. *Recreations:* architecture and foreign travel. *Address:* 39 Welbeck St., W.1. *Clubs:* Athenæum, United University, Royal Empire Society; Dublin University (Dublin). [*Died* 22 *March* 1955.

SHURMER, Percy Lionel Edward; M.P. (Lab.) Sparkbrook Div. of Birmingham since 1945; Alderman Birmingham City Council; J.P.; *m.*; one *d.* *Educ.:* British and St. Paul's Schools, Worcester. Apprenticed to Merchant Service; entered Post Office English Department, Birmingham; arrested during General Strike, 1926; dismissed from Civil Service for political offence; entered Birmingham City Council, 1921; J.P. Birmingham. King's Commendation for rescue work in Air Raids, 1941. *Recreation:* social work. *Address:* St. Ives, 140 Belgrave Rd., Birmingham 5. *T.:* Calthorpe 2507. [*Died* 29 *May* 1959.

SHUTE, Geoffrey Gay, C.M.G. 1939; *b.* 1892; *m.* *Educ.:* St. Andrew's School, Eastbourne; Uppingham; Clare College, Cambridge, B.A. Asst. District Officer, Nigeria, 1915. Principal Asst. Sec., Southern Provinces, 1931, later Secretary; formerly Senior Resident, Nigeria; Chief Commissioner Eastern Provinces, Nigeria, 1939. *Address:* 10 Gloucester Walk, W.8; c/o Colonial Service Liaison Officer, Colonial Office, Church House, Great Smith Street, S.W.1. [*Died* 5 *Sept.* 1951.

SHUTE, Nevil; *see* Norway, N. S.

SHUTER, Brig.-General Reginald Gauntlett, D.S.O. 1902; *b.* 11 Jan. 1875; *s.* of late Charles Shuter, Greendale, Victoria; *m.* 1915, Muriel Irene George Ellis (*d.* 1949); two *s.* Commission in Local Military Forces of Victoria, 1894-95; gazetted to Royal Irish Fusiliers, 1895; Lt.-Col. 1921; Col. 1925; served during the South African War with Royal Irish Fusiliers, and Mounted Infantry (despatches twice; Queen's medal with 5 clasps, King's medal with 2 clasps, D.S.O.); European War, 1914-18 (despatches thrice, Bt. Lt.-Col.); Officer in charge of Records, Warwick, 1925-29; retired pay, 1929. *Club:* Army and Navy. [*Died* 3 *Aug.* 1957.

SIBELIUS, Jean Julius Christian; composer; *b.* Tavastehus, Finland, 8 Dec. 1865; *s.* of late D. Christian Sibelius and Maria, *d.* of Provost Gabriel Borg; *m.* 1892, Aino Järnefelt, *d.* of Gen. Alex. Järnefelt and Freiherrin Clodt v. Jürgensburg; five *d.* *Educ.:* Helsinki; Jura. Studied music at Berlin and Vienna; member, Musical Acad. of Stockholm; Gr. Officer Legion of Honour; Grand Cross Order of the White Rose, with brilliants (Helsinki), Dannebrogen (Copenhagen) and Corona d'Italia (Roma); Commander, Cl. I., St. Olaf (Oslo), Vasa (Stockholm); Accademico onorario di Santa Cecilia, Roma, 1916; Hon. Dr. of Music, Yale, 1917, and Oxford, 1947; Hon. Dr. Phil., Helsinki, 1917; Hon. Dr., Heidelberg, 1936; Prof. Lit., Helsinki, 1916; Hon. R.A.M. *Compositions:* music to the tragedy Kuolema (containing the Valse Triste); music to the tragedy King Christian II.; the following orchestral pieces—Carelia Suite, En Saga, Finlandia, Frühlingslied, In Memoriam, Lemminkäinen Suite (containing The Swan of Tuonela), Romance in C; Aallottaret, Tapiola, Scaramouche, Symphony No. 1 in E Minor, No. 2 in D Major, No. 3 in C Major, No. 4 in A Minor, No. 5 in E flat Major, No. 6 in D Minor, No. 7 in C Major; Violin Concerto in D Minor, etc.; many pianoforte pieces, and over one hundred songs, etc. *Address:* Järvenpää, Finland. [*Died* 20 *Sept.* 1957.

SIBLY, William Arthur, M.A.; J.P. (Glos.); President of the Vegetarian Society since 1938; *b.* 14 May 1883; *s.* of George William Sibly and Alice Kate Pillman; unmarried. *Educ.:* Wycliffe College; Lincoln College, Oxford. Headmaster of Wycliffe College, 1912-1947. *Publications:* Register of Old Wycliffians, 1907, 1913, 1926, 1958; Wycliffe and the War, 1923; A Memoir of George William Sibly, founder and first headmaster of Wycliffe College, 1930; Vegetarianism and the Growing Boy, 1914 (4th ed. 1942). *Recreations:* cycling, travel, photography, bee-keeping. *Address:* Pearcroft, Stonehouse, Glos. *T.A.:* Stonehouse, Glos. *T.:* Stonehouse 413. *Club:* Overseas. [*Died* 20 *Sept.* 1959.

SIDGWICK, Prof. Nevil Vincent, C.B.E. 1935; F.R.S. 1922; M.A. Oxon, Sc.D. Tübingen; Hon. D.Sc. Leeds; Hon. LL.D. Liverpool; Fellow and formerly Tutor of Lincoln Coll., Oxford; Hon. Student of Christ Church; *b.* Oxford, 8 May 1873; *s.* of William Carr Sidgwick; unmarried. *Educ.:* Rugby School; Christ Church, Oxford (Scholar. 1st Class Nat. Sci. (Chemistry), 1895; 1st Class Lit. Hum. 1897); Univ. of Tübingen, 1899-1901. Baker Lecturer in Chemistry, Cornell Univ., 1931; Professor of Chemistry, 1933-45; Delegate of the Clarendon Press, 1922-48, and of the Bodleian Library, 1931-48. Member of the Advisory Council of the Department of Scientific and Industrial Research, 1930-35 and Chairman of Chemistry Research Board 1932-35; President of the Faraday Society, 1932-34; President of the Chemical Society, 1935-37; Royal Medal, Royal Society, 1937; Longstaff Medal, Chemical Soc., 1945; Foreign Member, American Academy of Arts and Sciences. *Publications:* Organic Chemistry of Nitrogen, 1910; Electronic Theory of Valency, 1927; The Covalent Link in Chemistry, 1933; The Chemical Elements, 1950; papers in Journal of the Chemical Society, Proc. Roy. Soc., and elsewhere. *Address:* Lincoln Coll., Oxford. *T.:* 2580. *Club:* Athenæum. [*Died* 15 *March* 1952.

SIDMOUTH, 5th Viscount (*cr.* 1805), **Gerald William Addington**; *b.* 19 Aug. 1882; *e. s.* of 4th Viscount and Ethel Mary, *o. d.* of Capt. L. Tonge, R.N.; *S.* father, 1915; *m.* 1915, Mary, *o. d.* of late Sir Donald Campbell Johnstone. *Educ.:* Eton; abroad. Late Capt. 6th Batt. Devon Regt.; served European War in India, Mesopotamia, Aden, and Salonika; J.P. Devon; Church of England; Conservative. *Heir:* *b.* Hon. R. A. Addington. *Address:* Upottery Manor, Honiton, Devon. *T.:* Upottery 202, Exeter group. *Club:* Carlton. [*Died* 4 *April* 1953.

SIEGFRIED, André; Docteur ès lettres; Membre de l'Académie Française depuis 1944; Membre de l'Institut; Professeur à l'Institut d'Études politiques; Professeur honoraire au Collège de France; *b.* Le Havre, 21 April 1875; *s.* of late Jules Siegfried, Minister of Commerce, and Member of the House; *m.* 1907, Paule, *d.* of late M. Hippolyte Laroche, Résident Général, Madagascar, Member of the House; one *d.* *Educ.:* Lycée Condorcet, Paris and Sorbonne. Writer and professor; formerly Chief of the Economic Section of the League of Nations Service at the French Foreign Office; Rumford Medal of Royal Society, 1940; Grand Officier de la Légion d'Honneur, 1955. *Publications:* La Démocratie en Nouvelle-Zélande, 1904; Edward Gibbon Wakefield et la colonisation systématique, 1904; Le Canada, les deux races, 1906; Tableau politique de la France de l'Ouest sous la 3e République, 1913; L'Angleterre d'aujourd'hui, 1924; Les États-Unis d'aujourd'hui, 1927; Tableau des partis en France, 1930; La Crise britannique au XXe siècle, 1931; Impressions of South America, 1933; Europe's Crisis, 1935; Canada, 1937; Suez, Panama et les routes maritimes mondiales, 1940; Vue générale de la Méditerranée, 1943; Quelques Maximes, 1943; La Suisse, démocratie témoin, 1948; Afrique du Sud, notes de voyage, 1949; L'Ame des peuples, 1950; Savoir parler en public, 1950; Géographie humoristique de Paris, 1952; Géographie poétique des cinq continents, 1953; Tableau des Etats-Unis, 1954; America at Mid-Century, 1955; La Fontaine, Machiavel français, 1955; Aspects du XXe siècle, 1955. De la IIIe à la IVe République, 1957; Les Voies d'Israël, 1958. *Recreations:* tennis, skating, swimming. *Address:* 8 rue de Courty, Paris. [*Died* 28 *March* 1959.

SIEVEKING, Albert Forbes, F.S.A., F.R.Hist.S.; *b.* London, 17 July 1857; *y. s.* of late Sir Edward Sieveking, M.D., Physician in Ordinary to Queen Victoria; *m.* Margaret (*d.* 1928), *e. d.* of late Sir George Campbell of Edenwood, K.C.S.I., M.P.; one *d.* *Educ.:* Felstead; Marlborough; abroad. Solicitor, 1881-1913; Librarian, Imperial War Museum, 1917-21; has lectured at London Institution and in provinces on Garden History; organised International Exhibition of Fencing in London, 1899; Secretary Reception Committee International Historical Congress, 1913. *Publications:* The Praise of Gardens, editions 1885 and 1899; edited Worke for Cutlers (acted at Cambridge, 1615), which he revived at Trinity Hall and Gray's Inn, 1904; Sir William Temple and other Carolean Garden Essays (King's Classics, 1908); edited Sir R. Burton's Sentiment of the Sword, 1910; The Origins of Football, 1912; Fencing and Duelling, Horsemanship, Dancing, and Games, in Shakespeare's England, 1916; Duelling and Militarism, (Royal Historical Society); History of the Stirrup, 1917 (Society of Antiquaries); various articles in Reviews and Dict. Nat. Biog. (2nd Suppt.); many articles in Country Life and Field on History of Sports and Games. *Address:* St. Michael's, Liskeard, Cornwall. *Club:* London Fencing. [*Died* 5 *Nov.* 1951.

SIEVWRIGHT, Andrew George Hume, C.B.E. 1934 (M.B.E. 1919); 3rd Class Iraqian Order of the Rafidain, 1935; J.P. Southampton County, 1942; Retired Inspector General of Customs and Excise, Iraq; *b.* 19 Feb. 1885; *s.* of late Captain Charles Frederick Sievwright and late Mary Anne Jane Rooke; *m.* 1924, Mary Lucy Ogilvy, *y. d.* of late Rev. Col. A. D. Seton, of Mounie, Aberdeenshire. Bombay Salt Department, India, 1905-17, serving in Gujerat, Sindh, and the Konkan; acting Captain, I.A.R.O., 1917; Blockade Officer, Baghdad, Local Resources Dept., 1918; Acting Major, 1919; Collector of Customs and Excise, Baghdad, 1919; Basrah, 1920; Director of Customs and Excise, Iraq, 1921-35. *Address:* Ground Floor, Cedar House, Burton, Christchurch, Hants. *T.:* Christchurch 2450. *Club:* East India and Sports. [*Died* 1 *Feb.* 1956.

SIFTON, Sir James David, K.C.S.I., *cr.* 1932 (C.S.I. 1929); K.C.I.E., *cr.* 1931 (C.I.E. 1921); M.A.; late Indian Civil Service; *b.* 17 April 1878; *s.* of Thomas Elgood Sifton; *m.* Harriette May (Kaisar-i-Hind Gold Medal, 1936), *d.* of Thomas William Shettle; one *s.* two *d.* *Educ.:* St. Paul's School; Magdalen College, Oxford. 1st Class Mods., 1st Litt. Hum.; Assistant Magistrate and Collector, Bengal, 1902; Asst. Settlement Officer, Chota Nagpore, 1906; Settlement Officer, Chota Nagpore, 1913; Magistrate and Collector of Shahabad, 1915; Financial Secretary, Government of Bihar and Orissa, 1917; Deputy Commissioner, Ranchi, 1923; Chief Secretary to Government of Bihar and Orissa, 1925; Member of Executive Council, Bihar and Orissa, 1927-31; Acting Governor of Bihar and Orissa, April-Aug. 1929 and June-October, 1930; Governor of Bihar and Orissa, April 1932-March 1936; Governor of Bihar, 1936-37; *Publications:* Settlement Report of Hazaribagh District; Settlement Report of Parganas Barahabhum and Patkum in Manbhum District. *Recreations:* lawn tennis and golf. *Address:* Brownings, Polegate, Sussex. *T.:* Hailsham 433. [*Died* 24 *Jan.* 1952.

SIGRIST, Frederick, M.B.E., A.F.R.Ae.S.; *b.* 1884; *s.* of Edward Sigrist; *m.* 1935, Beatrice Macknight, *d.* of late Capt. J. P. M. Burton, Taverham and Brasted; one *d.*; Founder member Hawker Aircraft Co. Resident of Nassau, Bahamas, since 1939. *Recreations:* yachting, shooting, fishing, etc. *Clubs:* Royal Aero, Royal Thames Yacht; Travellers' (Paris); Metropolitan (New York). [*Died* 10 *Dec.* 1956.

SILBERRAD, Oswald John, Ph.D., F.R.S.A., F.C.S.; Freemason; Scientist; *b.* 1878; third *s.* of Arthur Pouchin du Toict Silberrad, 38th Baron (Franconian *cr.* 1002) of the House of Willigis (von der Silber-Rad) Prince of the Holy Roman Empire; *m.* 1922, Lilian Glendora, *y. d.* of E. George, Knight of the Order of Militia Templi, of Ballinasloe and Oxford; one *s.* *Educ.:* Dean Close Memorial School, Cheltenham; City and Guilds Technical College, Finsbury; University of Würzburg. Superintendent of the Research Department of the Royal Arsenal, Woolwich (which he designed, equipped, manned, and organised), and a Member of the Explosive Committee and Ordinance Research Board, 1901-6; has directed the Silberrad Research Laboratories and practised as a Consulting Research Chemist since 1906, being Hon. Consulting Chemist to the Min. of Munitions, Explosives Supply Dept., during European War, 1914-18. *Discoveries:* Detonation of Lyddite and T.N.T., thus producing the present high explosive shell; Tetryl (introduced into the service in 1903 as Silberrad's Explosive); The method of manufacturing Lyddite in bulk in iron nitrators adopted during both Wars; Dyestuffs from Carbon—also from T.N.T. residues; a new chlorinating agent; method for manufacturing Isoprene; artificial retting of flax; a plastic blasting explosive free from nitroglycerine; a new means of blasting petroleum wells; causes of the rapid deterioration of high-speed ships, propellers, and alloys now universally used on all battleships, destroyers, liners and other high speed ships to withstand this erosion; method of producing flameless artillery powder—for guns up to 4·7″, and howitzers up to 12″. *Publications:* Treatise on the Stability of Nitro-Cellulose, etc.; numerous original scientific papers. *Address:* Dryads' Hall, Loughton, Essex. *T.:* Loughton 444. [*Died* 17 *June* 1960.

SILBERRAD, Una L.; *b.* Buckhurst Hill, Essex, May 1872. *Publications:* The Enchanter, 1897; The Lady of Dreams, 1901; Princess Puck; The Success of Mark Wyngate, 1902; Petronilla Heroven, 1903; The Wedding of the Lady of Lovel, 1905; Curayl, 1906; The Good Comrade, 1907; Desire, 1908; Ordinary People, 1909; Declined with Thanks, 1909; The Affairs of John Bolsover, 1909; Simeon Rideout, Quaker, 1911; Success, 1912; The Real Presence, 1912; Keren of Lowbole, 1913; Cuddy Yarborough's Daughter, 1914; Co-Directors, 1915; The Mystery of Barnard Hanson, 1915; The Inheritance, 1916; The Lyndwood Affair, 1918; Green Pastures, 1919; Jim Robinson, 1920; Rachel and her Relations, 1921; The Honest Man, 1922; The Letters of Jean Armiter, 1923;

Joe: A Simple Soul, 1924; The Vow of Miah Jordan, 1925; Blackstones, 1926; The Book of Sauchia Stapleton, 1927; In the Course of Years, 1929; The Romance of Peter Waine: Timber Merchant, 1931; The Will of James Mark Crane, 1932; The Strange Story in the Falconer Papers, 1934; Saunders, 1935: Sun in November, 1937; The Abundance of Things, 1939; The Escape of Andrew Cole, 1941; The Three Men who went to Ardath, 1944. *Address:* The Wick House, Burnham-on-Crouch, Essex. [*Died* 1 *Sept.* 1955.

SILCOCK, Arnold, F.R.I.B.A., Florence Bursar R.I.B.A., F.R.S.A.; architect and author; *b.* 13 Oct. 1889; 2nd *s.* of late T. B. Silcock, J.P., Bath, and late Mary Frances, *e. d.* of late Rev. Henry Tarrant, Bath. *Educ.:* Bath College; Architectural Association, London. Served European War, 1914-1918, with Infantry and R.A.F.; L/Cpl., Lieut., 1914-19 (wounded). Partner T. B. Silcock and Son, Architects, Bath, 1919-21; organised and lectured at Bristol School of Architecture (now Royal West of England Academy School), 1920-21; China, in practice, and architect to Friends College, Union University, Chêng-tu, Szechwan, and to the Provincial Government, 1921-26; London, in practice; Assist. to Secretary-General, Exhibition of Italian Art, Royal Academy, 1930; Assistant to Secretary-General, and Architect and member Selection Committee, Exhibition of Persian Art, 1931; Official lecturer to these, and the Chinese Exhibition, 1935-36; Art Workers Guild, 1931; Lecture tour Oriental Art, Western States, U.S.A., 1932; served on Schools and Literature Standing Committees and Tite Prize Jury, R.I.B.A.; F.R.S.A., 1935; Architect to Sir Leonard Woolley's British Museum Expedition, Syria, 1937; and Professor Wace's and British School at Athens Expedition, Mycenae, 1939; Florence Bursar R.I.B.A. 1939; Member of Council, Architectural Association, 1920-21, 1938-40 and served as Honorary Liaison Officer and Editor; Exhibitor, Royal Academy. War of 1939-45, R.A.F., Civil and Army service, Ft.-Lieut., Colonel, G.S.O. 2. *Chief Works:* Friends College, Women's College, West China Union University. Architect for the Development of the Isle of Herm, Channel Islands, 1952-. *Publications:* (Joint) Wrought Iron and Its Decorative Use, 1929; Introduction to Chinese Art, 1935; Introduction to Chinese Art and History, 1936; History of Art and the Crafts, Treasury of Knowledge, 1937; Chinese Architecture, 1937; Coming to Life or Perkins Junior, 1950; A Background for Beauty, 1951; Verse and Worse, 1952, etc. *Recreations:* collecting ceramics and collecting and composing comic verse. *Address:* Fairhaven, Letcombe Regis, Wantage, Berks. *Clubs:* Chelsea Arts, Arts. [*Died* 2 *July* 1953.

SILVER, Albert Harlow, C.I.E. 1919; *b.* 1875; *s.* of James Greig Silver; *m.* 1897, Mary (*d.* 1941), *d.* of James Duckworth; one *s.* one *d.* Late Director of Industries, United Provinces, India. Controller of Textiles, Indian Munitions Board, and Manager British India Corporation Ltd. *Address:* Delshangie, Merrow, Surrey. [*Died* 8 *Sept.* 1954.

SILVER, Lt.-Col. John Payzant, C.B.E. 1919; D.S.O. 1917; M.B.; late R.A.M.C.; *b.* 1868; *m.* 1901, Louie Drake Brockman; one *d.* Served N.W. Frontier, India, 1897-98 (medal with 2 clasps); European War, 1914-17 (despatches five times, C.B.E., D.S.O.); retired. 1920. *Address:* 3 Porchester Court, Porchester Gardens, W.2. [*Died* 1 *Nov.* 1957.

SILVESTER, Air Commodore James, C.B.E. 1943; *b.* 5 April 1898; *s.* of Henry Silvester, Oldbury, Worcs; *m.* 1935, Jean, *d.* of Comdr. Coventry Makgill-Crichton-Maitland, Witham Hall, Lincs; two *s.* *Educ.:* privately. Joined Royal Warwickshire Regt. (City of Birmingham Bn.), Sept. 1914, at age of 16½ years. Served European War, 1914-18 (despatches), with Royal Warwickshire Regt., Royal Berkshire Regt., and Royal Flying Corps; with Royal Air Force in France, Germany, Egypt, Iraq (despatches), Turkey, Palestine, and India. Instructed in flying at Central Flying School, 1925-27; on H.Q. Staff, Wessex Bombing Area, 1931-32; specialised in Air Photography, 1928; commanded School of Photography, R.A.F. 1937-38; Chief Test Pilot, R.A.F. Depot, India, 1933-35; commanded No. 60 (B) Squadron, N.W.F., India, 1935-36; No. 51 (B) Squadron, 1939-40; on Directorate of Home Operations and Directorate of Bomber Operations Air Staff, 1940-41; on Staff C.-in-C. Bomber Command, 1941-43, in charge of Organisation Branch (despatches four times); Commanded Royal Air Force Base, Stradishall, 1943; retired, 1946. *Recreations:* golf, squash. *Address:* Witham House, Gerrards Cross, Bucks. *T.:* Gerrards Cross 3482. *Club:* Royal Air Force. [*Died* 5 *Jan.* 1956.

SIM, Brigadier George Edward Herman, D.S.O. 1916; M.C.; late R.E.; *b.* 15 Aug. 1886; *m.* 1915, *d.* of Brodrick Dale, of Apperley Dene, Stockfield, Northumberland; two *d.* 2nd Lieut. R.E. 1906; Captain, 1914; Bt. Major, 1918; Major, 1923; Bt. Lt.-Col., 1929; Lt.-Col. 1930; Col., 1934; served European War, 1914-18 (despatches thrice, D.S.O., M.C.); retired pay, 1942; Order Wen Hu, 5th Class, 1919. *Address:* c/o Lloyds Bank, 6 Pall Mall, S.W.1. [*Died* 5 *March* 1952.

SIMEON, Vice-Admiral Sir Charles Edward Barrington, K.B.E., *cr.* 1945; C.B. 1943; *b.* 24 Dec. 1889; *s.* of late E. A. Simeon, M.R.C.S., L.R.C.P.; *m.* 1918, Gladys, *d.* of late B. Arkle, Spital, Cheshire; two *s.* (and *e. s.* killed in Libya, 1942) three *d.* *Educ.:* Forest School, Wanstead. Entered R.N. 1906; Lieut. 1911; qualified in gunnery, 1915; in H.M.S. Chester at Battle of Jutland, 1916; Comdr. 1924; Capt. 1930; Naval Member of Ordnance Board, 1931-33; commanded H.M.S. Colombo, 1933-35; Director of Naval Ordnance, 1936-39; commanded H.M.S. Renown, 1939-1941; in action with German Fleet off Norway and Italian Fleet off Sardinia (despatches); Rear-Adm. 1941; Deputy Controller, Admiralty, 1941-46; Vice-Adm. retd. 1943. Director of Vickers-Armstrong Ltd., 1946-54. Grand Officer of Order of Orange Nassau, 1946. *Address:* Sunnymead, Little Bushey Lane, Bushey Heath, Herts. *T.:* Bushey Heath 1568. [*Died* 16 *Nov.* 1955.

SIMEON, Sir John (Walter Barrington), 6th Bt., *cr.* 1815; late Capt. 8th Batt. Hampshire Regt.; *b.* 1886; *s.* of 5th Bt. and Laura (*d.* 1949), *d.* of Captain Westropp Dawson, of Charlesfort, Co. Wexford; *S.* father, 1915; *m.* 1909, Adelaide Emily (*d.* 1934), *e. d.* of late Col. Hon. E. A. Holmes-à-Court; one *s.* one *d.* Served European War with R.F.C. Owns about 1000 acres. *Educ.:* Eton; Christ Church, Oxford. *Heir:* *s.* John Edmund Barrington [*b.* 1 March 1911; *m.* 1937, Anne Robina Mary, *er. d.* of Hamilton Dean; one *d.*]. *Address:* Swainston, Newport, Isle of Wight. [*Died* 24 *June* 1957.

SIMMONDS, B(ernard) Sangster, M.S., F.R.C.S.; Consulting Surgeon to West London, Hounslow and Maidenhead Hospitals; *b.* 8 Dec. 1886; *s.* of William and Lucy Sutton Simmonds; *m.* 1914, Elsie Mary Barwell. *Educ.:* Bancroft's School; Middlesex and St. Bartholomew's Hospitals. Capt. R.A.M.C., 1916-20, France and England. Surgeon: to Ministry of Pensions, 1920-25; to West London Hosp., 1921-46; to Hounslow Hosp., 1924-46; to Maidenhead Hosp., 1941-51; Surgical Adviser, Sector Seven, E.M.S., 1940-47. On Court of Drapers' Company (Master, 1950-51 and 1951-52). Member of Council and Estates Cttee. and Convalescent Homes Cttee. of King Edward's Hospital Fund, for London. Member Public

Schools Appointments Bureau G.B.A. *Recreations:* golf, tennis, winter sports. *Address:* Down End, Hindhead, Surrey. *T.:* Hindhead 127. *Clubs:* Savile, Roehampton, Ski Club of Gt. Britain. [*Died* 3 *Sept.* 1953.

SIMMONDS, Hugh Henry Dawes, C.M.G. 1945; *b.* England, 1886; *e. s.* of late W. H. Simmonds, late of London and Hobart, Tasmania; *m.* 1913, Irene, *o. d.* of late A. F. Swayne, Shanklin, I. of Wight; three *s.* *Educ.:* Whitgift School. Studied Art, London; joined B.S.A.P. in London, 1910, proceeding to S. Rhodesia; Dept. of Native Affairs, S. Rhodesia, 1911; Asst. Native Commissioner, 1924; Native Commissioner, 1935; Asst. Chief Native Commissioner, 1936; Chief Native Commissioner and Secretary for Native Affairs, Southern Rhodesia, 1940-46; retired 1946. European War, 1914-1919, Aegean, Western Desert, Palestine; Capt. and Adjt. 1/1 Herts Yeo. *Recreations:* painting, golf. *Address:* Salisbury, S. Rhodesia. *Clubs:* Salisbury, Royal Salisbury Golf (Salisbury, S. Rhodesia). [*Died* 28 *March* 1952.

SIMMONS, Major-General Frank Keith, C.B.E. 1941 (O.B.E. 1937); M.V.O. 1915; M.C.; late Q.O. Cameron Highlanders; *b.* 1888; *s.* of Edward Simmons of The Moorings, Crowthorne, Berks; *m.* 1st, 1922, Amy (whom he divorced, 1926), *d.* of J. A. Fairhurst of Arlington Manor, Newbury: 2nd, 1926, Emily, *d.* of late George Herbert Strutt; three *d.* *Educ.:* Cranbrook School. Served in European War, 1914-1918 (M.V.O., M.C., Croix de Guerre); Military Attaché at Madrid, 1928-31; Commander Southern Brigade, Palestine (temp.), 1936; G.S.O.I. British Forces in Palestine and Transjordan, 1937-39; Commander, Shanghai Area, British Troops in China, 1939-40 (prisoner, released 1945); Maj.-Gen., 1941; retired pay, 1946. *Address:* Appin, Metung, Victoria, Australia. [*Died* 27 *Sept.* 1952.

SIMMONS, Sir Frederick James, Kt., *cr.* 1945; J.P.; Mayor of Londonderry, 1940-45 (5 years), and Ex-Officio Member of N.I. Senate and of Londonderry Harbour Board; Secretary to City of Derry Building Society since 1889, and a Director, 1948; *b.* 14 Feb. 1867; 4th *s.* of Robert George Simmons and Catherine Guilfoyle, Londonderry; *m.* 1897, Annie Olivia (*d.* 1952), 5th *d.* of late Oliver Stewart, Londonderry; three *s.* four *d.* *Educ.:* Mothers private school and National Schools, Athlone and Londonderry. Entered office of late T. S. Magee, J.P., House and Land Agent at age 11 and similar business with late Councillor John Harding Bible, J.P., 1882; entered into partnership with his son, late Alderman Thomas G. Bible, J.P., 1889, and became sole proprietor at his death in 1920, the title of the business remaining still as Bible & Simmons. Member of Council of Londonderry Chamber of Commerce; Past Pres., Londonderry Rotary Club. *Recreations:* bowling, boating, music and elocution as a young man. *Address:* 23 Crawford Square, Londonderry; The Diamond, Londonderry. *T.A.:* Bisims. *T.:* 2034 and 2464. [*Died* 9 *Oct.* 1955.

SIMMONS, George Thomas Wagstaffe; Fellow Institute of Journalists; Editorial Staff of Sporting Life; writer of special articles on Association football, cricket, and general sports; *s.* of late George Simmons, St. Albans; *m.* Marie (*d.* 1921), *d.* of late Sergeant-Major J. Dickerson, 60th Rifles; one *d.* *Educ.:* St. Albans. Articled to journalism on Herts Advertiser; subsequently on staff of Hertfordshire Mercury; editor of Herts Advertiser; chairman and managing director of Herts Standard series of newspapers; played much football and cricket, and for 25 years member of Football Association Council; member of International Selection Committee for 20 years; Vice-President, Herts F.A.; Vice-Chairman Tottenham Hotspur F. C. *Address:* 91 Mount Pleasant Road, Brondesbury Park, N.W.10. *T.A.:* Sporting Life, Inteltube, London. *T.:* Temple Bar 1200, Willesden 1927. [*Died* 1 *Feb.* 1954.

SIMNETT, William Edward, M.B.E.; A.I.C.E.; author, journalist, lecturer, etc.; first editor, later consulting editor Crown Colonist (now New Commonwealth); *b.* City of London, 1880; *y. s.* of Arthur Simnett, Burton-on-Trent, and Mary Donovan, Rosscarberry, County Cork; *m.* 1st, 1909, Margaret Quinn (*d.* 1923), County Longford; 2nd, 1927, Gwendoline Powell, Chippenham, Wilts. Assistant Editor and Librarian Institution of Civil Engineers to 1916; served European War, 1914-18, Royal Engineers; Major, General Staff; attached British Delegation Peace Conference; Director, Ministry of Transport, 1919-21; Secretary, Railways Amalgamation Tribunal, 1921-23; founder and Editor Technical Review of the Foreign Press, 1918-20; projected and first edited Everyman; Member Hendon Council to 1927; Chairman Colonial Empire Union, 1937-38; in 1940 sent by British Govt. to U.S.A. on a Colonial mission; Pres. London Centre, The National Trust; founder and member of various professional and other societies and committees, contributor to journals and reviews. *Publications:* Train Ferries, 1918; Railway Amalgamation in Great Britain, 1923; Books and Reading, 1926 and 1930; (with C. Drury) What Books Shall I Read, (U.S.A.) 1932; Life of Dr. W. H. Maw, 1927; The British Colonial Empire, 1942; American edition, 1943, revised, 1948; Introducing America and Greater Britain, 1942; Leisure, 1946, 1948; Emergent Commonwealth, 1954; many memoirs and papers before Societies, etc. *Recreations:* cycling, travel, social work, and public interests. *Address:* 132 Princes Avenue, W.3. *T.:* Acorn 3736. [*Died* 13 *Aug.* 1958.

SIMON, 1st Viscount, *cr.* 1940, of Stackpole Elidor; **John Allsebrook Simon,** P.C. 1912; G.C.S.I. 1930; G.C.V.O. 1937 (K.C.V.O. 1911); Kt. 1910; O.B.E. 1919; Hon. D.C.L. Oxf.; Hon. LL.D. Edinburgh, Cambridge, St. Andrews, Manchester, Leeds, McGill, Toronto, Columbia and Sheffield Universities; Bencher, Inner Temple, 1910, and Treasurer, 1931; late Standing Counsel to, and now High Steward of, Oxford Univ.; *b.* 28 Feb. 1873; *o. s.* of late Rev. Edwin Simon, Congregational minister, and late Fanny Allsebrook; *m.* 1st, 1899, Ethel Mary Venables (*d.* 1902); one *s.* two *d.*; 2nd, 1917, Kathleen (*see* Viscountess Simon), *d.* of Francis Eugene Harvey, Wexford. *Educ.:* Fettes College, Edinburgh; Wadham Coll., Oxford (Scholar, Hon. Fellow); Fellow of All Souls Coll., Oxford. President Oxford Union Society, 1896; Barstow Law Scholar, 1898; called to Bar, 1899; K.C., 1908; Junior Counsel for British Government in Alaska Boundary Arbitration, 1903; leading Counsel for Newfoundland in Labrador Boundary Reference, 1926; Chm. of Departmental Committee on Street Trading, 1909; Member of Royal Commission on Justices of the Peace, 1910; Member of Royal Commission on Universities of Oxford and Cambridge, 1921; Chairman of Indian Statutory Commission, 1927-30, of R 101 Inquiry, 1931, and of Population Commission 1943, for first two years; M.P. elected as(Lib.) Walthamstow Div., Essex, 1906-18, Spen Valley Div. of Yorks, 1922-31, (L. Nat.) 1931-40; Solicitor-General, 1910-13; Attorney-General with seat in Cabinet, 1913-15; Secretary of State for Home Affairs, 1915-16; Secretary of State for Foreign Affairs, 1931-35; Secretary of State for Home Affairs and Deputy Leader of House of Commons, 1935-1937; Chancellor of the Exchequer, 1937-40; Lord Chancellor, 1940-45, before then Leader of Liberal National Party; Major in Royal Air Force serving in France, 1917-18 (despatches). *Publications:* Three Speeches on the General Strike, 1926; Two Broadcast Talks on India, 1930; Comments and Criticisms, 1930; Portrait of My Mother, 1937; Simon's Income Tax, 5 vols., 1950; Retrospect, 1952. *Recreations:* golf, skating, chess. *Heir: s.* Hon. John Gilbert Simon, C.M.G. *Address:* 84 Marsham Court, S.W.1; Dowding, Tadworth, Surrey. *T.:* Tadworth 3300. *Clubs:* Reform, Royal Automobile. [*Died* 11 *Jan.* 1954.

SIMON, Dowager Viscountess, D.B.E., *cr.* 1933; **Kathleen Simon;** *d.* of Francis Harvey, Kyle, Co. Wexford; *m.* 1st, T. Manning; one *s.* (B. O'D. Manning); 2nd, 1917, 1st Viscount Simon, P.C., G.C.S.I. G.C.V.O.; one *step-s.* (2nd Viscount Simon); two *step-d.* *Educ.:* various schools in Dublin, and privately. Worked as nurse among the London poor; devoted to the cause of freedom everywhere; to Ireland, to Zionism, to assisting backward and oppressed peoples. Chm. Shamrock Club for Irish soldiers in London during War of 1939-45. Joint Pres. Anti-Slavery Soc., D.G.St.J. *Publication:* Slavery, 1929 (also published in French). *Address:* 84 Marsham Court, Westminster, S.W.1. *T.:* Victoria 8181, Ext. 84; Dowding, Tadworth, Surrey. *T.:* Tadworth 3300. [*Died* 27 *March* 1955.

SIMON OF WYTHENSHAWE, 1st Baron, *cr.* 1947, of Didsbury; **Ernest Darwin Simon,** Kt., *cr.* 1932; LL.D.; M.I.C.E., M.I.Mech.E.; Chairman British Broadcasting Corporation, 1947–June 1952; President Simon Engineering Ltd; *b.* Manchester, 1879; *s.* of Henry Simon, M.I.C.E., and Emily Simon; *m.* 1912, Shena, *d.* of John W. and Jane B. Potter, Westminster; two *s.* *Educ.:* Rugby; Cambridge; M.P. (L.), Withington Division, 1923-24, and 1929-31; Parliamentary Sec. Min. of Health, 1931; Mem. Manchester City Council, 1911-25; Chm. Housing Cttee., 1919-23; Lord Mayor of Manchester, 1921; Chairman of Manchester University Council, 1941-57. *Publications:* The Smokeless City; A City Council from Within; How to abolish the Slums; The Anti-Slum Campaign; The Rebuilding of Manchester; Moscow in the Making; The Smaller Democracies; Rebuilding Britain; The B.B.C. from Within. *Recreation:* The Langdale Valley. *Heir: s.* Hon. Roger Simon [*b.* 16 Oct. 1913; *m.* 1951, Anthea Daphne May; one *s.* one *d.*]. *Address:* Broomcroft, Didsbury, Manchester; 116 Marsham Court, S.W.1; Hellsgarth, Langdale, Ambleside. [*Died* 3 *Oct.* 1960.

SIMON, Sir Francis (Eugene), Kt. 1954; C.B.E. 1946; F.R.S. 1941, M.A. (Oxon); Ph.D. (Berlin); Lee Professor of Experimental Philosophy, University of Oxford, and Head of the Clarendon Laboratory, Oxford, since 1956; Fellow of Wadham College, Oxford; *b.* 2 July 1893; *s.* of Ernst Simon and Anna Mendelssohn, Berlin; *m.* 1922, Charlotte Muenchhausen; two *d.* *Educ.:* Gymnasium, Berlin. Universities Munich, Goettingen, Berlin. Privat-Dozent, Berlin, 1924; Prof. Extraord. for Physics, Berlin, 1927; Prof. Ord. and Director Laboratory Physical Chemistry, Breslau, 1931; resigned, 1933; Research position Clarendon Laboratory, Oxford, 1933; Visiting Lecturer, University of California, Berkeley, 1932. Professor of Thermodynamics, University of Oxford, 1945-56. Member of Atomic Energy Project, 1940-46. Student Emeritus of Christ Church. Rumford Medal of Roy. Soc., 1948; Kamerlingh Onnes Medal, 1950; Linde Medal, 1952; Guthrie Lecturer, Physical Soc., 1956; Kelvin Lecturer, Instn. of Electrical Engineers, 1957; For. Hon. Mem. Amer. Acad. of Arts and Sciences. *Publications:* The Neglect of Science, 1951; co-author: Low Temperature Physics, 1952; Atomic Energy, A Survey, 1954; papers in periodicals, chiefly on physics of very low temperatures. *Recreation:* photography. *Address:* 10 Belbroughton Road, Oxford. *Club:* Athenæum. [*Died* 31 *Oct.* 1956.

SIMON, Colonel Maximilian St. Leger, C.B.E. 1920; late R.E.; *b.* Malacca, 28 March 1876; *s.* of late M. F. Simon, M.D., C.M.G.; *m.* 1902, Mabel Louise Lees; one *s.* *Educ.:* Blundell's School, Tiverton; R.M. Academy, Woolwich. Commissioned in R.E., 1895; served in Singapore, Canada, and in France (during war); Militia Dept., Ottawa, 1908-10; War Office, London, 1911-15; Bt. Lt.-Col. 1915; Anti-aircraft Defence Commander of London, 1916-18; Bt. Col. 1918; Anti-aircraft Defence Commander, Ind. Force, R.A.F., France, 1918; Inter-Ser. Mission in Belgium, 1919; General Staff, War Office, 1920-21, for Anti-aircraft duties; Commandant Anti-aircraft School, 1922-24; retired, 1924; Local Chairman National Savings Committee in N. Norfolk area, 1928; Min. of Supply, 1940-41; Royal Obs. Corps, 1932-42. *Publication:* Drawings and Diagrams of Insect Vectors. *Address:* c/o "R" Section, Lloyds Bank, 6 Pall Mall, S.W.1. [*Died* 5 *Jan.* 1951.

SIMON, Oliver, O.B.E. 1953; Typographer; Chairman of the Curwen Press, Editor of Signature; *b.* 29 April 1895; *m.* 1926, Ruth, *d.* of C. H. Ware, Bromyard; one *s.* one *d.* Founder and first Ed. of the Fleuron, a Journal of Typography, 1923; edited Printing of To-day, 1929; edited the Curwen Press Miscellany, 1931; Founder with Hubert Foss of the Double Crown Club (President, 1929), 1924. *Publications:* Introduction to Typography, 1945; Printer and Playground (autobiography), 1956. *Address:* 40 Downshire Hill, Hampstead. *T.:* Hampstead 2125. *Club:* Athenæum. [*Died* 18 *March* 1956.

SIMOND, Charles François, C.B.E. 1920; *m.* 1st, 1898, Lilian Edith, (*d.* 1908) *d.* of F. O. Crump, Q.C.; 2nd, 1909, Adgie (*d.* 1946), *d.* of Hugh Inglis Gray. *Educ.:* London International College; Switzerland. *Club:* East India and Sports. [*Died* 12 *March* 1957.

SIMONDS, Frederick Adolphus; Chairman and Managing Director of H. &. G. Simonds Ltd., Brewers; Director, Saccone & Speed, Ltd., Wine and Spirit Merchants, Gibraltar and London; *b.* 2 Jan. 1881; *e. s.* of late Louis de Luze Simonds, Audleys Wood, Basingstoke; *m.* 1909, Amy FitzGerald (O.B.E. 1929), *d.* of John Sheriff Hill, Hawk's Wick, St. Albans; two *s.* *Educ.:* Eton; Magdalen College, Oxford. High Sheriff of Berkshire, 1928; served South African War, 1900-01 with Service Company, 1st V.B. Royal Berkshire Regiment, attached to 2nd Royal Berkshire Regiment; President Royal Warrant Holders Association 1937 and 1945. *Recreations:* shooting and racing. *Address:* Ashe House, Overton, Hants. *T.:* Overton, Hants, 215. [*Died* 17 *Aug.* 1953.

SIMONSEN, Sir John Lionel, Kt., *cr.* 1949; F.R.S. 1932; F.R.I.C.; D.Sc. (Manch.); Hon. D.Sc. Birm., Malaya; Hon. LL.D. (St. Andrews); *b.* 22 Jan. 1884; *s.* of L. M. Simonsen, merchant, Manchester; *m.* 1913, Jannet Dick Hendrie, M.B., Ch.B., *e. d.* of late R. Hendrie, Nairn, Scotland. *Educ.:* Manchester Grammar School and University. B.Sc. 1st Class Hons. Chemistry, 1904; D.Sc. 1909; Schunck Research Fellow in the University of Manchester, 1906; Assistant Lecturer and Demonstrator, 1907-10; President, Chemistry Section, Indian Science Congress, 1917; Hon. Secretary, Indian Science Congress, 1914-26; President, Indian Science Congress, 1928; Vice-President Chemical Society, 1940-43-1952-55; Sec., Chemical Society, 1945-49; Member Agricultural Research Council, 1944-1949; Pres., Section B, British Assoc., 1947; Vice-President, Royal Society of Arts, 1949-54; Mem. Council, 1954-; Chairman of Board, Pest Infestation Laboratory, 1949-52; Fellow of the Royal Asiatic Society of Bengal; Hon. Member Indian Science Congress; Hon. Fellow Indian Association Cultivation of Science. Kaisar-i-Hind silver medal, 1921; Fritzsche Award, American Chemical Society, 1949; Davy Medal, Royal Society, 1950. Professor of Chemistry, The Presidency College, Madras, 1910-19; Controller of Oils and Chemical Adviser, Indian Munitions Board, 1919; Forest Chemist, Forest Research Institute and College, Dehra Dun, 1919-25; Professor of Organic Chemistry, Indian Institute of Science, Bangalore, 1925-27; Professor of Chemistry, University College of North Wales, Bangor, 1930-42; Director, Colonial Products Research, 1943-1952. *Publications:* The Terpenes, vols. i, ii iii, iv and v; a number of paper in the Proceedings and Transactions of the Chemical Society. *Recreation:* golf. *Address:* 3 Wildcroft Manor, Putney Heath, S.W.15. *T.:* Putney 8959. *Club:* Athenæum. [*Died* 20 *Feb.* 1957.

SIMPSON, Lieut.-Col. Adrian Francis Hugh Sibbald, C.M.G. 1917; O.B.E. 1943; R.E.; *b.* 1880; *s.* of late Surg.-Gen. Sir Benjamin Simpson, K.C.I.E.; *m.* 1929, Wanda, *d.* of Ignace Bychowetz, Councillor of State. *Educ.:* Clifton College; R.M.C., Sandhurst. Entered Army, 1900; Indian Staff Corps, 1901, Hyderabad Contingent; passed military examination for Russian Interpretership, 1906; retired, 1907; studied Electrical Engineering and Wireless Telegraphy; A.M.I.E.E.; European War, Aug. 1914, special mission to Russia; served with Caucasian Cavalry Division and A.D.C. to Grand Duke Michael Alexandrovich in the Galician Campaign, 1914-1915; transferred R.E. 1915; Chevalier of the Order of St. Anne, 2nd degree, 1915; Chevalier of the Order of St. Stanislas, 2nd degree with Crossed Swords, 1916; General Staff, War Office, 1916; Major, 1916; Lieut.-Col. 1919; Director of Wireless Telegraphs to the Government of India, 1919; Deputy Managing Director Marconi's Wireless Telegraph Co., Ltd., 1922-27. War of 1939-45, Special duties, 1939; Intelligence Division General Staff M.E.F., 1940-43; Assistant Director Works Palestine, 1943-44; Press Attaché British Legation, Beirut, Syria and Lebanon, 1944-46. *Recreations:* fishing, shooting. *Address:* 33 Chesham Place, S.W.1. *T.:* Belgravia 3098. *Club:* Turf. [*Died* 2 *Oct.* 1960.

SIMPSON, Rev. Prof. David Capell, M.A., D.D.; Oriel Professor of Interpretation of Holy Scripture, Oxford, 1925-50, Prof. Emeritus from 1950; Residentiary Canon of Rochester Cathedral, 1925-50, Canon Emeritus from 1950; Fellow of Oriel College, 1925-50, Emeritus Fellow from 1950; *b.* 22 May 1883; *o. s.* of late George Simpson, Edgbaston, and Charlotte, *d.* of late David Capell, Edgbaston; *m.* 1919, Alice, 3rd *d.* of late William Stevens Carver, Summertown, Oxford. *Educ.:* Sywell House School, Llandudno; Wadham Coll., Oxford (Hody Hebrew Scholar, 1902). B.A., M.A., B.D., D.D. 1st Class in Final Honour School of Theology, 1905; 1st Class in Final Honour School of Semitic Studies, 1907; Pusey and Ellerton Scholar, 1902; Kennicott Scholar, 1905; Hall Houghton Septuagint Prize, 1903; Syriac Prize, 1908; Denyer and Johnson Scholar, 1906. Deacon, 1907; Priest, 1908; Curate of All Saints, Oxford, 1907-9; Reader in Semitic Languages and Old Testament, Manchester College, Oxford, 1910-49; Examining Chaplain to the Bishop of Southwell, 1913-25, to the Bishop of Rochester, 1925-1950; Hon. Canon of Southwell, 1923-25; Warburtonian Lectr. in Lincoln's Inn, 1927-31; Pres. of the Soc. for Old Testament Study, 1927; Examiner, Final Honour School of Oriental Studies, Oxford, 1918; Examiner, Final Honour School of Theology, Oxford, 1922, 1924, 1925; Examiner, University of London, 1912-25, 1929-1932; Examiner, Univ. of Manchester, 1911-15; Examiner University of Wales, 1930-31; Junior Proctor of University of Oxford, 1923; Tutor of Keble College, Oxford, 1913-25; Lecturer in Theology and Oriental Languages in St. Edmund Hall, 1906-25, and Jesus College, Oxford, 1920-24. *Publications:* Tobit, pp. 174-241 in Apocrypha and Pseudepigrapha of the Old Testament, vol. i. 1913; Pentateuchal Criticism, 1914; Exodus to Ruth in the Study Bible, 1930; (joint) Communion with God, 1911; Editor, The Psalmists, 1926; The Development of the Sabbath Ideal, 1927; 1 and 2 Kings, 1 and 2 Chronicles in Abingdon Bible Commentary, 1929; Assistant General Editor of Westminster Commentary; Contributor to Encyclopædia of Religion and Ethics: Encyclopædia Britannica; The Journal of Egyptian Archæology; The History of Christianity in the Light of Modern Knowledge, 1929. *Address:* 143 Banbury Road Oxford. [*Died* 6 *May* 1955.

SIMPSON, Dame Florence Edith Victoria, D.B.E., *cr.* 1919 (C.B.E. 1918); *b.* 9 Oct. 1874; *d.* of late Col. W. FitzAlan Way; *m.* 1922, Edward Percy Simpson (decd.). Comdt. Cookery Section, Women's Legion, 1915-17; Controller of Inspection, W.A.A.C., 1917-18; Controller-in-Chief, Queen Mary's Army Auxiliary Corps, 1918-20. *Address:* Moyeni Farm, P.O. Box 49, Harrismith, Orange Free State, S. Africa. *Club:* Service Women's. [*Died* 5 *Sept.* 1956.

SIMPSON, James Herbert, M.A.; *b.* 1883; *e.s.* of late J. Herbert Simpson, M.D., Rugby; *m.* 1921, Evelyn (*d.* 1958), *y. d.* of W. Creaser, York; two *d.* *Educ.:* Rugby School; Pembroke College, Cambridge; 2nd Class Classical Tripos and 1st Class History Tripos; Assistant Master at Gresham's School, Holt, Norfolk, 1908-10; Junior Inspector of the Board of Education, 1911-12; Assistant Master at Rugby School, 1913-19; first Headmaster of Rendcomb Coll., Cirencester, 1920-32; Principal College of St. Mark and St. John, Chelsea, 1932-44; Member Consultative Committee of Board of Education, 1933-39; Dean of College of Preceptors, 1942-57. *Publications:* An Adventure in Education, 1917; Howson of Holt, 1925; Sane Schooling, 1936; Schoolmaster's Harvest, 1954. *Address:* Fream's, Painswick, Gloucestershire. [*Died* 28 *Feb.* 1959.

SIMPSON, Sir Maurice George, Kt., *cr.* 1931; C.S.I. 1928; M.I.E.E.; *b.* 1866; 7th *s.* of Thomas Fox Simpson, Tunbridge Wells; *m.* Emma Mina, *d.* of John Connell; one *s.* (and one *s.* decd.). *Educ.:* Tonbridge School; Head boy, 1885. Passed from Coopers Hill Engineering College into the Indian Telegraph Department, 1887; Electrical Engineer-in-Chief, 1906; retired from India, 1914; joined Indo-European Telegraph Department at India Office, 1915; Director-in-Chief, Indo-European Telegraph Department, India Office, S.W.1, 1923-31; retired, 1931. *Address:* c/o Lloyds Bank, Ltd., Tunbridge Wells. [*Died* 2 *July* 1954.

SIMPSON, Robert Gordon, M.C. 1918; Senior Partner of Chiene & Tait, Chartered Accountants, Edinburgh, since 1920; *b.* 14 Feb. 1887; 4th *s.* of late Sir Robert Russell Simpson, Writer to the Signet, Edinburgh. *Educ.:* Edinburgh Academy. Member of Edinburgh Society of Chartered Accountants, 1911; last Pres. of Society before amalgamation with Glasgow Inst. of Chartered Accountants and Aberdeen Soc. of Chartered Accountants; thereafter first Pres. of Inst. of Chartered Accountants of Scotland, 1951. Served in Royal Scots, 1915-18; demobilised as Captain. Mem. of Beveridge Cttee. on Skilled Men in the Forces, 1941-42. Director, subseq. Dep.-Chm., United Molasses Co., Ltd., 1931; Director, subseq. Dep.-Chm., General Accident Fire & Life Assurance Corp. Ltd., 1941; Director several Investment Trust Companies and Industrial Undertakings. O.St.J. 1941. *Recreation:* racing. *Address:* 20 Rothesay Terrace, Edinburgh 3. *T.:* Edinburgh Caledonian 1615. *Clubs:* Bath; New, Scottish Conservative (Edinburgh). [*Died* 29 *Jan.* 1958.

SIMPSON, Samuel, C.M.G. 1926; *b.* Rimington, Yorks, 13 March 1876; 2nd *s.* of late

Henry and Alice Simpson; *m.* 1917, Katharine Nathalie, 2nd *d.* of late Hon. William Broome; three *s.* *Educ.:* Hulme Hall, Owens College, Manchester; University of Edinburgh, B.Sc.; Stevens Scholar; Assistant Secretary and Secretary to the Union; Senior President of the Students' Representative Council; Highland and Agricultural Society's Prizeman; Silver Medallist and Life Member of the Royal Agricultural Society of England; holder of the National Diploma in Agriculture. Joined the Egyptian Civil Service as Senior Lecturer in Agriculture, Ghizeh College of Agriculture, 1903; Cotton Expert to the British Central African Protectorate (Nyasaland), 1905; commissioned to report on the agricultural resources of Angola, 1909, Trinidad, Tobago, British Guiana, and Surinam, 1911; Director of Agriculture, Uganda, 1912-29; Member of both the Executive and Legislative Councils; Commissioner for Uganda at the British Empire Exhibition, 1924. Member of the Rugby Borough Council and Guardians' Cttee., 1932-1947. *Publications:* Report on the Cotton Growing Industry of the British Central Africa Protectorate, 1905; numerous pamphlets on tropical economic products and agricultural education. *Address:* Sunnyside, The Crescent, Rugby. *Club:* Farmers'.
[*Died* 14 *Sept.* 1952.

SIMPSON, Thomas Blantyre, Q.C. (Scot.) 1944; LL.D. Edinburgh University, 1947; F.R.S.E. 1952; Sheriff of Perth and Angus since 1952; *b.* 27 July 1892; *s.* of Sir Robert R. Simpson, W.S., and Helen Dymock Raleigh. *Educ.:* Edinburgh Acad.; Magdalen Coll., Oxford (M.A.). Served European War, 1914-19, Royal Scots (wounded); invalided, 1918. Member Faculty of Advocates, 1921; Treasurer of Faculty, 1937-49; Sec. Royal Commission on Licensing (Scotland), 1929-31; Standing Counsel to Board of Inland Revenue in Scotland, 1931-44; Enemy Aliens Tribunal, Scotland, 1939-40; Price Regulation Committee, S.E. Scotland, 1940-44; Sheriff of Caithness, Sutherland, Orkney, and Zetland, 1944-52; Trustee National Library of Scotland since 1933. *Address:* 13 Moray Place, Edinburgh 3. *T.:* Caledonian 7775. *Clubs:* Oxford and Cambridge; New (Edinburgh); Honourable Company Edinburgh Golfers.
[*Died* 18 *Oct.* 1954.

SIMPSON, Rear-Admiral (E) Thomas Harold, M.V.O. 1934; R.N. retired; Anglo-Iranian Oil Co. since 1948; *b.* 7 July 1896; *s.* of Sir Maurice Simpson, *q.v.*; *m.* 1st, 1920, Bridget Baily (*d.* 1937); 2nd, 1938, Kathleen Newbery; one *s.* one *d.* *Educ.:* R.N. College, Dartmouth. Fleet Engineer Officer to British Pacific Fleet, 1944-46. Rear-Adm. (E) on staff of Flag Officer Scotland and Northern Ireland, 1946-47. *Recreation:* washing up. *Address:* 22 Cunningham Avenue, St. Albans, Herts. *T.:* St. Albans 4964. *Club:* United Service.
[*Died* 5 *Jan.* 1952.

SIMPSON, Rev. W. J. Sparrow, D.D.; Chaplain of St. Mary's Hospital, Ilford, since 1904; Hon. Canon of Chelmsford, 1919; *b.* 1859. *Educ.:* St. Paul's School; Trinity College, Cambridge; M.A. 1886; B.D. 1909; D.D. 1911. Deacon, 1882; Priest, 1883; Vicar of St. Mark's, Regent's Park, 1888-1904. *Publications:* The Catholic Conception of the Church, 1914; Reconciliation and Atonement, 1916; Reconciliation between God and Man, 1917; The Prayer of Consecration, 1917; French Catholics in the Nineteenth Century, 1918; Broad Church Theology, 1919; South Indian Schemes, 1930; The History of the Anglo-Catholic Revival from 1845, 1932; Dispensations, 1936, etc. *Address:* St. Mary's Hospital, Ilford. [*Died* 13 *Feb.* 1952.

SIMPSON, William Marshall, C.B.E. 1928; late Post Office Surveyor, Liverpool District; *b.* Aberdeen, 1868; *m.* 1899, Mary Elizabeth, *e. d.* of late John Jennings; one *s.* *Educ.:* Aberdeen Grammar School and privately. Entered Accountant General's Department, Post Office, 1888, and Surveying Staff, 1892; retired, 1930. *Recreations:* walking, bridge, bowls. *Address:* c/o National Bank of Scotland, 37 Nicholas Lane, E.C.4. *Club:* Overseas.
[*Died* 16 *March* 1951.

SIMS, Brig.-General Reginald Frank Manley, C.M.G. 1917; D.S.O. 1900; late K.R.R.C.; *b.* 2 Aug. 1878; *m.* 1930, May (*d.* 1951), *d.* of Dr Walter Wearne, Helston, Cornwall. Entered Army, 1898; Capt. 1902; served South Africa, 1899-1902 (wounded, despatches, D.S.O., Queen's medal with 5 clasps, King's medal with 2 clasps); European War, Canadian Contingent, 1915-18 (C.M.G.); Agent-General for Ontario, 1918-21. *Clubs:* M.C.C., Overseas.
[*Died* 24 *June* 1951.

SIMSON, Richard Arbuthnot, C.B.E. 1920; Chairman of Imperial Tea Co. Ltd.; *b.* 11 Dec. 1871; *s.* of Herman Simson and Alice Arbuthnot im Thurn; *m.* 1932, Rosannah Grazier. *Educ.:* Marlborough; Cheltenham. After 18 years tea planting in India, joined Metropolitan Special Constabulary, rank of Asst. Commander, 1914; Commander, 1915; Commandant, 1919; retired 1938, after 24 years' service. Special Constabulary Medal with 2 bars; Jubilee Medal, 1935, Coronation Medal, 1937. *Recreation:* racing (horse). *Address:* 45 Clarewood Court, Seymour Place, W.1. *T.:* Paddington 0980. *Club:* Oriental.
[*Died* 28 *Nov.* 1958.

SINCLAIR, 16th Baron (*cr.* 1449), **Archibald James Murray St. Clair,** M.V.O. 1918; Representative Peer for Scotland; Member of Queen's Body Guard for Scotland; *b.* 16 Feb. 1875; *e. s.* of 15th Baron Sinclair and Margaret (*d.* 1935), *d.* of James Murray, Ancoats Hall; *S.* father, 1922; *m.* 1906, Violet (*d.* 1953), *d.* of Col. J. Murray Kennedy, M.V.O.; one *s.* one *d.* Capt. (retd.), Royal Scots Greys, 1896-1911; served S. Africa, 1899-1903; European War 1914-19 in France and Belgium (M.V.O. and Rising Sun of Japan). *Heir:* *s.* Master of Sinclair, M.V.O. *Address:* Knocknalling, Dalry, Castle-Douglas, Kirkcudbrightshire. *Clubs:* United Service, Cavalry; New (Edinburgh); Royal Yacht Squadron.
[*Died* 25 *Nov.* 1957.

SINCLAIR, Hon. Sir Colin Archibald, K.B.E., *cr.* 1953; *b.* 24 Dec. 1876; *s.* of J. Sinclair; *m.* 1916, Edith Grant. *Educ.:* Armidale Gram. Sch.; Univ. of Sydney (B.A., LL.B.). M.L.A. Namoi, 1932-41; Hon. Minister, 1937-38; Min. for Lands, 1938-40. Director: Australian Mercantile Land and Finance Co., 1936-; Union Trustee Co., 1938-; Bank of N.S.W., 1940-; Commercial Union Ass^ce. Soc., 1941-. Pres. R.Agric.Soc. of N.S.W., 1943-. *Address:* 450 Edgecliff Rd., Edgecliff, Sydney, N.S.W.
[*Died* 17 *March* 1956.

SINCLAIR, Rt. Hon. John Maynard, P.C. (N. Ire.) 1943; M.P. N. Ireland since 1938; D.L.; Minister of Finance since 1943; Chairman, Vulcanite Ltd., Director, Eagle Star Insurance Co. Ltd. (local board); *b.* Belfast, 4 Aug. 1896; *s.* of John Sinclair, D.L., Belfast, and Alice Montgomery; *m.* 1922, Marjorie Claridge; no *c.* *Educ.:* Royal Belfast Academical Institution; Germany and Switzerland. The Royal Irish Rifles, 1914-1919; resigned, 1919; Captain R.A.R.O.; Captain, Royal Engineers (T.A.), 1937-41; Chairman, Belfast Savings Bank, 1932-33; Financial Secretary to Ministry of Finance, N. Ireland, 1941-43. *Address:* Springhill, Deramore Park South, Belfast. *T.:* Belfast 65636. *Clubs:* Junior Carlton; Ulster, Ulster Reform (Belfast); Royal Ulster Yacht (Bangor (Down). [*Died* 31 *Jan.* 1953.

SINCLAIR, Lieut.-Col. Malcolm Cecil, O.B.E. 1938; *b.* 25 Sept. 1899; *s.* of Lt.-Col. A. L. Sinclair, I.A. (retd.), Ballyloughan, Bruckless, Co. Donegal, and K. A. Rushton; *m.* 1923, Marjory Mary Fenwick (*d.* 1945);

one *s.* two *d.*; *m.* 1948, Olive Mary Staines (*née* Golding). *Educ.:* Marlborough College. Indian Army, 1918; Indian Political Service, 1920; Consul-General in the French Establishments in India, 1944-46; retired 1948. *Recreations:* fishing, shooting, yachting. *Address:* Old Court, Misterton, Nr. Crewkerne, Somerset. [*Died* 28 *Nov.* 1955.

SINCLAIR, Major Sir Ronald Norman John Charles Udny, 8th Bt., *cr.* 1704; T.D. 1947; 4/5th Seaforth Highlanders T.A.; British Resident, Heide/Holstein, since 1948; *b.* 30 June 1899; *s.* of late Norman A. Sinclair, *g.s.* of 6th Bt., and Edith Lilian, *d.* of Col. R. W. Hamilton; *S.* uncle, 1926; *m.* 1926, Reba Blair, *d.* of Anthony Inglis, M.D.; one *s.* two *d.* *Educ.:* Wellington College; R.M.C. Sandhurst. D.L., J.P., County of Caithness. Kreis Resident Officer, Norderdittumarschen, 1947-48. *Heir:* *s.* John Rollo Norman Blair Sinclair, *b.* 4 Nov. 1928. *Address:* Barrock House, Wick, Caithness; 37a Cavendish Square, W.1. *Club:* Green Room. [*Died* 19 *Oct.* 1952.

SINCLAIR, Rev. Canon Ronald Sutherland Brook, M.A., M.C.; Vicar of St. Peter's, Maidstone, and Hon. Canon of Canterbury Cathedral since 1952; Hon. Chaplain to Forces, 1942; *b.* 5 Sept. 1894; *er. s.* of late John Stewart Sinclair, Archdeacon of Cirencester, and Clara Sophia Birchall; *m.* 1924, Patience Penelope, *yr. d.* of Herbert Chitty, F.S.A.; one *s.* *Educ.:* Rugby School; Cheltenham College; Oriel College, Oxford; Cuddesdon College, Oxford. Served European War as Private in 19th (Public Schools) Royal Fusiliers; then as Capt. in 2/5 Gloucestershire Regt. (wounded, M.C. 1917, Bar, 1918); Diploma in Theology with distinction (Oxford), 1920; Cuddesdon College, 1920-21; Ordained, 1921; Assistant Curate St. Martin-in-the-Fields, 1921-24; East India Docks, 1924-26; All Saints, Maidstone, 1926-1929; Rector of Buckland-in-Dover, 1928-31; Vicar of Ashford, Kent, 1931-37; Canon Residentiary of Chester Cathedral, 1937-44; Provost of Guildford and Rector of Holy Trinity, Guildford, 1944-51; Chaplain to the Forces, 1940-42; formerly Toc H Padre (MK. VII) whilst serving at St. Martin-in-the-Fields; Capt. of Oriel Coll., Oxford, Boat Club, 1919. *Publications:* When We Pray, 1933; Except We Turn, 1935; Confirmed in This Faith, 1937; Victim Victorious, 1940; A Religion for Battledress, 1941; Joking Apart, 1944. *Recreations:* riding, drawing; interested in cricket and rowing. *Address:* St. Peter's Vicarage, Maidstone, Kent. *Clubs:* United University, M.C.C. [*Died* 13 *May* 1953.

SINCLAIR, Lieut.-Col. Sir Walrond Arthur Frank, K.B.E., *cr.* 1918; Life President (formerly Chairman) British Tyre and Rubber Co. Ltd.; Chairman: The India Rubber, GuttaPercha and Telegraph Works Co. Ltd.; Williams Deacon's Bank, Ltd.; Dir. of the Royal Bank of Scotland; Mem., Rubber Control Bd., Min. of Supply, since 1941; *b.* 1880. Was Controller of Registration, Min. of National Service; Director of National Service for the London region, 1917. *Address:* 3 Whitehall Court, S.W.1. *T.:* Whitehall 3160. *Clubs:* Royal Thames Yacht, Oriental. [*Died* 30 *Aug.* 1952.

SINCLAIR, William Angus, O.B.E. 1946; T.D.; M.A.; D.Litt.; F.R.S.E.; Reader in Philosophy in the University of Edinburgh since 1952 (Lecturer from 1932); *b.* 27 Dec. 1905; *e.* and *o. surv. s.* of John Sinclair and Elizabeth, *y. d.* of Murray Campbell; *m.* 1954, Susan Archer, *d.* of T. A. Cameron. *Educ.:* George Watson's; Edinburgh University; Magdalen College, Oxford; Harvard (Commonwealth Fellow, 1930-32); Warden of Cowan House, Univ. of Edinburgh, 1933-37; Lt.-Col. R.A. (T.A.); served War of 1939-45 (O.B.E.); contested E. Edinburgh (U.), 1945; refused invitation to contest by-election, 1945, on disagreement on policy; joined Labour Party, 1951. Visiting Professor of Moral Philosophy, McGill Univ., Montreal, 1952. *Publications:* The Traditional Formal Logic, 1937; The Voice of the Nazi (reprint of broadcast talks), 1940; The Sighting Gear of Field, Medium and Anti-tank Artillery, 1943; An Introduction to Philosophy, 1944; The Conditions of Knowing, 1951; Socialism and the Individual, 1955. *Recreations:* shooting, fishing. *Address:* 5 Great Stuart Street, Edinburgh 3. *T.:* 32966. *Clubs:* Athenæum; New (Edinburgh). [*Died* 21 *Dec.* 1954.

SINCLAIR-LOCKHART, Sir Graeme Duncan Power, of Castlehill, Co. Lanark, 12th Bt., *cr.* 1636; holds Sinclair of Stevenson Baronetcy; *b.* 29 Jan. 1897; *s.* of 11th Bart. and Flora Louisa Jane Beresford, *d.* of late Capt. Edward Power; *S.* father, 1918; *m.* 1932. *Educ.:* Wanganui Collegiate School, Wanganui; Pembroke College, Cambridge. Served New Zealand Mounted Rifles in Egypt and Palestine, 1916-17; Commission in Scottish Horse (Scouts) after War of 1914-18; on reserve as 2nd Lt. R.A., T.A.; served, 1939-40, as Lieut. in Finnish Air Force in Finland; commissioned again in British Army, 1942; Lieut. in Reserve of Intelligence Corps; Baronet of Nova Scotia. *Heir:* *b.* Major John Beresford [*b.* 4 Nov. 1904; *m.* 1949, Winifred Ray Graham]. *Address:* c/o McGrigor, Donald and Co., 172 St. Vincent Street, Glasgow C.2, Scotland. *Clubs:* Royal Automobile, Junior Army and Navy; Royal Scottish Automobile, Royal St. George's Yacht. [*Died* 15 *Feb.* 1959.

SINGER, Charles, D.Litt., M.D., Hon. D.Sc., Oxford; F.R.C.P. Lond.; Professor Emeritus, Univ. of London; Hon. Fellow, Magdalen Coll., Oxford; Fellow, Univ. Coll., London; *b.* Camberwell, 2 Nov. 1876; *s.* of Rev. S. Singer and Charlotte Pyke; *m.* 1910, Dorothea, *d.* of Nathaniel L. Cohen and Julia M. Waley; one *s.* one *d.* *Educ.:* City of London School; University Coll., London; Magdalen Coll., Oxford; St. Mary's Hospital, London; Heidelberg. President, Third International Congress History of Medicine, London, 1922; President Second Internat. Congress of the History of Science and Technology, London, 1931; Visiting Professor, Univ. of California, 1931 and 1932; Pres. British Soc. for the History of Science, 1946-48; Pres. Internat. Acad. for History of Science, 1947-50; Hon. Mem.: Amer. Phil. Soc.; Medieval Acad. of Amer. Dickinson Memorial Medal, Newcomen Soc., 1954; Osler Medal, Oxford, 1956; Sarton Medal, Internat. Soc. for Hist. of Science (jointly with Mrs. Singer), 1956. *Publications:* Greek Biology and Greek Medicine, 1922; History of the Discovery of the Circulation of the Blood, 1922; Studies in History and Method of Science, 1917 and 1920; The Evolution of Anatomy, 1925 (Vol. I reprinted, 1955); (with Edwyn R. Bevan) The Legacy of Israel, 1927, translated into French and Spanish; A Short History of Medicine, 1928 (2nd edn. with E. A. Underwood, 1959); Historical Relations of Religion and Science, 1928; From Magic to Science, 1928, translated into Japanese (2nd edn., 1958); A History of Biology, 1931, translated into French and Spanish (4th edn., 1959); A Short History of Science, 1941; The Christian Failure, 1943; (with C. Rabin) Prelude to Science, 1946; The Earliest Chemical Industry, 1948; (with J. H. G. Grattan) Anglo-Saxon Magic and Medicine, 1952; New Worlds and Old, 1952; Vesalius on the Human Brain, 1952; Galen on Anatomical Procedures, 1955. The Herbal in Antiquity, 1927. (Jt. Ed.) A History of Technology, Vol. I, 1954, Vol. II, 1956, Vol. III, 1957, Vols. IV and V, 1958; Short History of Scientific Ideas, 1959, and other works on history of science, technology and medicine. *Address:* Kilmarth, Par, Cornwall. *T.:* Par 2056. *Club:* Athenæum. [*Died* 10 *June* 1960.

SINGH, Raja Sir Maharaj, Kt., *cr.* 1933; C.I.E. 1915; *b.* 17 May 1878; 2nd *s.* of Hon. Raja Sir Harnam Singh, K.C.I.E., of Kapurthala; *m.* *d.* of late Rai Bahadur Maya Das of Ferozepore, Punjab; two *s.* one *d.* *Educ.:* Harrow; Balliol College, Oxford. B.A. 1900; M.A. 1901; Barrister-at-law, Middle Temple, 1902; entered United Provinces Civil Service in 1904; Officiating Registrar, Co-operative Societies, United Provinces, 1909 and 1910; Assistant Secretary to the Government of India in the Department of Education, 1911; Officiating Joint Secretary to the Government of India, 1914; Senior Assistant Secretary to the Government of India, Department of Education, 1915; Magistrate and Collector of Hamirpur, United Provinces, 1917; Deputy Commissioner of Hardoi, 1918; Judicial and Educational Sec. to the Govt. of the United Provinces, 1919; Deputy Secretary to the Government of India, 1920; Deputy Commissioner, Bahraich; Commissioner, Allahabad, 1927, 1929, 1931; Chief Minister, Jodhpur, 1931-32; Agent General for India in South Africa, 1932-35; Home Member United Provinces Government 1935-37; Vice-Chancellor, Lucknow University, 1941; Prime Minister, Kashmir States 1943; President National Liberal Federation, 1943-44; Pres. Indian Christian Association, 1944; Member U.P. Legislative Assembly, 1937-45; Member, Commonwealth Relation, Conference, 1945. Member Indian Delegation, U.N.O., 1946 and 1947; Mem. U.P. Legislative Council, 1946 and 1947. Governor of Bombay, 1948-52. Commander (Brother), St. John Ambulance Assoc. Hon. LL.D. Allahabad University, 1951. *Publications:* Annual Report on the working of Co-operative Credit Societies in the United Provinces of Agra and Oudh for the year 1908-9; Reports on Indian Emigration to Mauritius and British Guiana, and on Mission to East Africa, 1928 and 1946; Speeches as Governor of Bombay, 1948-52; and various contributions to the newspaper press. *Recreations:* lawn tennis (played in many All India Tennis Tournaments) and travelling; boxed (feather-weight) for Oxford Univ. v. Cambridge Univ. in 1899. *Address:* 10 Mall Avenue, Lucknow. [*Died* 6 *June* 1959.

SINGLETON, Rt. Hon. Sir John Edward, P.C. 1948; Kt., *cr.* 1934; **Rt. Hon. Lord Justice Singleton;** a Lord Justice of Appeal since 1948; *b.* 18 Jan. 1885; 3rd *s.* of late George Singleton, Howick House, nr. Preston; unmarried. *Educ.:* Lancaster; Pembroke College, Cambridge. M.A., LL.B., Hon. Fellow, 1938; called to Bar, Inner Temple, 1906; Bencher, 1929; Treas. 1952; K.C. 1922; Hon. LL.D. Liverpool, 1949. One time Capt., R.F.A.; M.P. (C.) Lancaster Division of County of Lancaster, 1922-23; Recorder of Preston, 1928-34; Judge of Appeal, Isle of Man, 1928-1933; Judge of the King's Bench Div., 1934-1948. *Address:* 2 Crown Office Row, Temple, E.C.4. *T.:* Central 3827. *Clubs:* Oxford and Cambridge, Athenæum, Brooks's. [*Died* 6 *Jan.* 1957.

SINGLETON, William Adam, M.A., Ph.D.; Director of the Institute of Advanced Architectural Studies, Micklegate, York, since 1959; Hoffman Wood Professor of Architecture, Leeds University, since 1959; *b.* 14 Feb. 1916; *s.* of William Singleton and Elizabeth Robb Adam; *m.* 1940, Agnes Edna Davis; two *d.* *Educ.:* Haileybury College; Liverpool University (B.Arch.); M.A. 1945, Ph.D. 1949, Manchester. Commissioned, Royal Engineers, 1939-41. Senior Architectural Assistant with Herbert J. Rowse, Liverpool, 1941-43; Lecturer in Architecture, 1943-53, Senior Lecturer in Architecture, 1954-59, University of Manchester. Private architectural practice in Manchester and York, 1943-59. F.S.A. 1952. *Publications:* Studies in Architectural History, Vol. 1, 1954, Vol. 2 1956. *Recreation:* sailing. *Address:* Sunnyside, Upper Poppleton, York. *T.:* Upper Poppleton 447. *Club:* Yorkshire (York). [*Died* 29 *Feb.* 1960.

SINHA, Sir Rajivaranjan Prashad, Kt., *cr.* 1942; President, Bihar Legislative Council; *b.* 1893; *s.* of late Raja Rajrajeshwari Prasad Sinha, Surajpura, Bihar; *m.* 1912, Shrimati Keshavanandani, *y. d.* of late R. B. Jaiprakash Lal, C.I.E. *Educ.:* St. Xavier's School, Calcutta; Agra College; Patna College; Muir Central College, Allahabad. M.A. 1916. M.L.C. Bihar and Orissa, 1920-; President, 1937-; M.L.A. India, 1927-30. *Address:* Surajpura, Patna, Bihar, India. [*Died* 8 *July* 1948.
[*But death not notified in time for inclusion in Who Was Who* 1941–1950, *first edn.*

SINNOT, Most Rev. Alfred A., D.D., D.C.L., Archbishop (R.C.) of Winnipeg, 1916-1946; *b.* Morell, Prince Edward Island, 22 Feb. 1877; *s.* of late John Sinnot. *Educ.:* St. Dunstan's Coll., Charlottetown, Prince Edward Island; Grand Seminary, Montreal; Canadian Coll., and Appollinare Coll., Rome (D.C.L. 1901). Ordained 1900; on staff of St. Dunstan's Coll., Charlottetown, 1901-03; formerly Secretary to Apostolic Delegate at Ottawa. *Address:* 353 St. Mary's Avenue, Winnipeg, Manitoba, Canada. [*Died* 18 *April* 1954.

SINTON, Lieut.-Col. (Hon. Brig.) John Alexander, V.C. 1916; O.B.E.; F.R.S. 1946; M.D., Hon. (Q.U.B.); D.Sc. (Q.U.B.); M.B., B.Ch., B.A.O. (R.U.I.); D.P.H. Cantab. and Belfast; D.T.M. Liverpool; J.P., D.L., Co. Tyrone; Indian Medical Service, retired; lately Hon. Consultant Malariologist, War Office; Hon. Fellow Ulster Medical Society; Arnott Memorial Medallist, Irish Medical Schools' and Graduates Assoc., 1917; Chalmers Memorial Medallist, Royal Society of Tropical Medicine and Hygiene, 1928; Bisset-Hawkins Medallist, R.C.P., London, 1944; Robert Campbell Memorial Orator and Medallist, Ulster Medical Soc., 1946; Mary Kingsley Medallist, Liverpool Sch. of Trop. Med., 1949; a Pro-Chancellor Queen's Univ., Belfast; late Director, Malaria Survey of India; late Manson Fellow, London School of Hygiene and Tropical Medicine; *b.* 2 Dec. 1884; *m.* 1923, Eadith Seymour Steuart, *o. d.* of late Edwin Steuart Martin, of Azamgarh, India; one *d.* *Educ.:* Queen's Coll., Belfast (First place Honours and Exhibitioner); Liverpool School of Tropical Medicine; Riddell Demonstrator in Pathology, Queen's University; served European War, 1914-18 (V.C., despatches four times, Russian Order of St. George); Transcaspia, 1918-19 (Bt. Majority); Afghanistan, 1919 (despatches); Waziristan, 1919-1920 (O.B.E., despatches); Mahsud, 1920; retired, 1938; re-employed War of 1939-45 (despatches). High Sheriff for Tyrone, N. Ireland, 1953. *Publications:* many papers on Malaria and Entomology in the Indian Journal of Medical Research and the Records of the Malaria Survey of India. *Address:* c/o Lloyds Bank, Ltd., 6 Pall Mall, S.W.1; Slaghtfreedan Lodge, Cookstown, Co. Tyrone, N. Ireland. *Club:* Ulster (Belfast). [*Died* 25 *March* 1956.

SITWELL, Sir Sidney Ashley Hurt, Kt., *cr.* 1925; *b.* 12 June 1871; *s.* of late Isla Ashley Hurt Sitwell; *m.* 1st, 1900, Violet Inez (*d.* 1901), *d.* of Major-General Henry Paterson Cowper, Bengal Cavalry; 2nd, 1903, Rosamond, *d.* of Col. Honorius Sisson Sitwell, R.E.; two *s.* *Educ.:* King Edward VI. School, Bury St. Edmunds. Joined Bank of Bengal, 1894; Secretary and Treasurer, 1921; Managing Governor, Imperial Bank of India, 1923, London Manager, 1924-30. *Recreations:* shooting and fishing. *Address:* c/o State Bank of India, E.C.2. [*Died* 19 *Jan.* 1956.

SIVELL, Robert, R.S.A. 1943 (A.R.S.A. 1936); formerly Principal Teacher of Drawing and Painting, Grays School of

Art, Aberdeen, retired 1954; *b.* Paisley; 16 October 1888; *s.* of Robert Sivell and Agnes Wylie; *m.* 1923, Isobel Sayers; one *d.* *Educ.:* Glasgow School of Art. Served apprenticeship as engineer; spent 2 years in Canada and United States; served as engineer in Merchant Service on South American route during European War, 1914-1918; studied in Paris and Florence; commissioned by War Artists Advisory Cttee. in War of 1939-45; represented in Imperial War Museum, London, Royal Scottish Academy. Municipal collections of Glasgow, Aberdeen, Belfast, Greenock and Paisley; Mural decoration of Students Union Hall, Aberdeen University; now engaged in private work. *Address:* The Hollow, Stell, Kirkcudbright. *Club:* Scottish Arts (Edinburgh). [*Died* 17 *April* 1958.

SKAIFE, Brigadier Sir Eric (Ommanney), Kt. 1956; C.B. 1952; O.B.E. 1919; D.L.; *b.* 18 Oct. 1884; *s.* of Frederic and Josephine Skaife, Chichester; unmarried. *Educ.:* Winchester Coll.; R.M.C. Sandhurst; Staff Coll., Camberley. Royal Welch Fusiliers: 2nd Lieut. 1903; Adjutant 1911; Capt. 1911; Major 1918. Served European War, 1914-18 (wounded, despatches, P.O.W.); G.S.O. 2 and G.S.O. 1, War Office, 1918-19; served in Operations in Waziristan, 1921-23 (despatches); G.S.O. 2, War Office, 1924-28; Lieut.-Col. Roy. Welch Fus., 1929-33; Bt. Col 1933, A.A.G. Eastern Command, 1933-34; Mil. Attaché, Moscow, 1934-37; Comdr. 158 Roy. Welch Inf. Bde., T.A., 1937-39; Brig., Dist. Comdr. and Bde. Comdr., 1940-41; F.O. Research Dept. 1941-44. Cadet Comdt. Merioneth and Montgomeryshire, 1947-50; Hon. Col. 636 Royal Welch L.A.A. Regt., R.A., T.A., 1947-1955; Col. Royal Welch Fusiliers, 1948-52. Mem. Governing Body, Church in Wales, 1945; Mem. Representative Body, Church in Wales, 1949. Mem. Gorsedd Beirdd Ynys Prydain, 1933; Vice-Pres. Urdd Gobaith Cymru (Welsh League of Youth), 1943-55; Chm. Merioneth Conservative and Unionist Assoc., 1950-56. D.L. Merioneth, 1950; Vice-Pres. Hon. Soc. of Cymmrodorion, 1953; High Sheriff of Merioneth, 1956. *Publication:* A Short History of the Royal Welch Fusiliers, 1924. *Address:* Dolserau, Dolgelley, Merionethshire. *T.:* Dolgelley 122. *Clubs:* Naval and Military, Junior Carlton. [*Died* 1 *Oct.* 1956.

SKEATS, Ernest Willington, D.Sc., A.R.C.Sc., F.G.S.; Professor of Geology and Mineralogy, University of Melbourne, 1904-41, Emeritus Professor, 1941; *b.* Southampton, 1875; *s.* of Frank George Skeats; *m.* 1904, Mary de Fraine (*d.* 1932), *d.* of late W. Whitaker, F.R.S., English Geological Survey; *m.* 1940, Mrs. Nancy Sheppard. *Educ.:* Handel College and Hartley College, Southampton; Royal College of Science, South Kensington. Associate in Chemistry, 1896; Geology, 1897; Demonstrator of Geology under Professor Judd, 1897-1904; Doctor of Science degree of London University, 1902; Daniel Pidgeon Fund by the Geological Society, 1903; Excursion Secretary and Member of Council of Geologists' Association, 1904; President Geology Section, Australasian Association for advancement of Science, Brisbane, 1909; Dean of Faculty of Science, Univ. of Melbourne, 1910-15; President Royal Society, Victoria, 1912-14; Pres. Professorial Board, Univ. of Melbourne, 1922-24; President, Australasian Institute of Mining and Metallurgy, 1924-25; Foundation Member Executive Committee Australian National Research Council; Clarke Medal, Royal Society of New South Wales 1929; Mueller Medal for Research, Australian and New Zealand Association for the advancement of Science, 1937. *Publications:* papers in Proc. Royal Society, Victoria, etc. *Recreations:* walking, music, one of founders and first President of Gilbert and Sullivan Society of Victoria, 1935-1940. *Address:* The University, Carlton, Melbourne, N.3. *Club:* Melbourne (Melbourne). [*Died* 19 *Jan.* 1953.

SKELTON, Rt. Rev. Henry Aylmer, D.D., Lambeth, 1942; *b.* 1884; *e. s.* of late Canon Charles Arthur Skelton and Lady Beatrice Skelton; *m.* 1912, Margaret Jermyn, *y. d.* of Rev. A. R. Tomlinson; one *s.* (and one *s.* killed in action, R.N., 1943). *Educ.:* Felsted School; Keble College, Oxford; Bishops' College, Cheshunt. Curate of Chertsey, 1910-13; Vicar of S. Barnabas, Epsom, 1913-16; Vicar of Mentmore and Chaplain to the Earl of Rosebery, 1916-21; Assistant Priest at S. Mary's Cathedral, Auckland, New Zealand, 1921-23, Rector of North Yorke's Peninsular Mission, South Australia, 1923-24; Rector of Toddington, Beds., 1924-27; Sub-Dean of S. Albans, 1927-36; Archdeacon of St. Albans, 1936-1942; Suffragan Bishop of Bedford, 1939-42; Bishop of Lincoln, 1942-46. *Address:* Carwinion Lodge, Mawnan, Falmouth, Cornwall. *Club:* United University. [*Died* 30 *Aug.* 1959.

SKELTON, Engineer Vice-Admiral Sir Reginald William, K.C.B., *cr.* 1931 (C.B. 1919); C.B.E. 1919; D.S.O. 1916; *b.* 3 June 1872; 3rd *s.* of William Skelton of Long Sutton, Lincolnshire; *m.* 1905, Sybil (*d.* 1953), 4th *d.* of William Devenish-Meares, Christchurch, N.Z.; one *s.* two *d.* *Educ.:* Bromsgrove School, Worcestershire; R.N.E. College, Devonport. Served in H.M.S. Centurion, Flagship China, 1894-97; H.M.S. Majestic, Flagship Channel Squadron, 1899-1900; appointed to superintend building of Discovery for National Antarctic Expedition, 1900, and served in that expedition as Chief Engineer under the late Captain R. F. Scott, 1901-4; Submarine Service, 1906-12; H.M.S. Superb, 1912-14; appointed to H.M.S. Agincourt on outbreak of War; Jutland, 31 May 1916; Submarine Service, 1917-18; Engineer Officer on staff of Admiral Sir J. Green, North Russia, Archangel, 1918-19; on staff of Admiral Sir J. de Robeck for duty at Constantinople, 1920-21; Fleet Engineer Officer, Mediterranean Station, 1921-22; Fleet Engineer Officer Atlantic, H.M.S. Queen Elizabeth, 1922-1923; Engineer Rear-Admiral, 1923; on staff of C.-in-C., Portsmouth; Engineer Vice-Admiral, 1928; Engineer-in-Chief of the Fleet, Admiralty, 1928-32; retired list, 1932; Director of J. I. Thornycroft & Co.; Order of St. Stanislas and St. Ann, Russia; F.R.G.S.; M.I.Mech.E., M.I.N.A. *Recreation:* golf. *Address:* Meadow Cottage, Aldingbourne, Chichester. *T.:* Eastergate 110. *Club:* Army and Navy. [*Died* 5 *Sept.* 1956.

SKETCH, Ralph Yeo; Chairman, Phoenix Assurance Co. Ltd. since 1940; *b.* 22 Feb. 1877; *s.* of James Chapel Sketch; *m.* 1st, 1902, Margaret Gladys Martin (*d.* 1936); two *s.*; 2nd, 1939, Amy Lesley Mortleman. *Educ.:* London Orphan School. Insurance at home and abroad; General Manager Norwich Union Fire Office, 1919; General Manager Phoenix Assurance Co., 1920; Managing Director, 1935. *Recreation:* golf. *Address:* 47 Victoria Drive, Wimbledon Park, S.W.19. *T.:* Putney 7870. *Clubs:* Bath, Royal Wimbledon Golf; Sunningdale Golf (Sunningdale). [*Died* 13 *Sept.* 1952.

SKEVINGTON, Sir Joseph Oliver, K.C.V.O., *cr.* 1919; F.R.C.S. (Eng.); *b.* 2 Feb. 1873; *s.* of late J. H. Skevington, J.P. *Educ.:* Oakham; St. Mary's Hospital. Civil Surgeon South African Field Forces, 1900-1; Senior Surgeon No. 2 British Red Cross Hospital, Rouen, 1914-15; Temp. Capt. R.A.M.C. 1918; Surgeon Major Home Guard. *Address:* Belmont, York Rd., Windsor. *T.:* Windsor 119. [*Died* 29 *Feb.* 1952.

SKEY, Rev. Oswald William Laurie; Warden St. John's Hostel, Cape Town, since 1939; *b.* 2 May 1878; *s.* of Rev. F. C. Skey, M.A., for 45 years Vicar of Weare, Somerset; *g.s.* of late Frederick Carpenter Skey, F.R.S.,

Pres. of the Roy. College of Surgeons, England; unmarried. *Educ.:* King's College, London; Theological Student of Grahamstown, S. Africa. Assistant S. African Church Railway Mission; Vicar of St. Peter's Church, Port Elizabeth, S.A.; Vicar of Germiston, Transvaal; Head of St. George's Home, Johannesburg; Archdeacon of Johannesburg, 1924-32; Dean of Salisbury, S. Rhodesia, 1932-39. *Address:* St. John's Hostel, Cape Town. [*Died* 27 *June* 1954.

SKILLICORN, William James Kinlay, C.V.O. 1947; C.B.E. 1944; C.St.J.; M.Inst.T.; *b.* 19 March 1883; *e. s.* of William James and Jane Skillicorn, Liverpool, England; *m.* 1909, Sarah, *d.* of William Henry Merredew, Durban, Natal; two *s.* five *d.* *Educ.:* Liverpool, England. Served with Eng. Rlys. for six years; joined Natal Govt. Rlys., 1903; Chief Rates Officer, 1906; Prin. Clerk (Rates) S. African Rlys., 1913; Asst. Supt., 1919; Rates Asst. to Gen. Manager, 1920 (organised and introduced grain elevator system, member and Sec. of Commission, 1918); Div. Supt., Kimberley, 1925; System Manager: Rlys. and Harbours, S.-W. Africa, 1927; E. Transvaal, 1929; Cape Western System, 1930; Asst. Gen. Manager (Commercial), 1935; Gen. Manager, Rhodesia Rlys., Ltd., 1938-47; Comr. i/c Rhodesia Rlys. Dist., of St. John Ambulance Bde. Chm. Departmental Tariff Enquiries Commission, 1930; Member of Cape Town Foreshore Enquiries Commission; Chm. Moulding Trade Enquiry, 1934. Member, Institute of Transport. *Recreations:* golf and chess. *Address:* Lynford, Mons Avenue, Newlands, Cape Town, S. Africa. *T.:* 6-3677. *Clubs:* Civil Service (Cape Town); Bulawayo, Roy. Cape Golf (Wynberg, C.P.). [*Died* 18 *Sept.* 1955.

SKINNER, Maj.-Gen. Sir Cyriac B.; *see* Skinner, Maj.-Gen. Sir P. C. B.

SKINNER, Professor Herbert Wakefield Banks, F.R.S. 1942; Ph.D.; Lyon Jones Professor of Physics, Liverpool University, since 1949; *b.* 7 Oct. 1900; *s.* of George Herbert and Mabel Elizabeth Skinner; *m.* 1931, Erna Wurmbrand; one *d.* *Educ.:* Rugby School; Trinity College, Cambridge. Research work in Physics at Cavendish Laboratory, Cambridge, 1922-27, and at Wills Physical Lab., Royal Fort, Bristol, 1927-39; Rockefeller Fellow at Massachusetts Institute of Technology, 1932-33; work on Radar at T.R.E., 1940-44; work on Atomic Energy at Berkeley, Calif., 1944-45; Head of General Physics Division, Atomic Energy Research Establishment, Harwell, 1946-50. *Address:* Physics Department, The University, Liverpool. *T.:* Royal 7601. *Club:* Athenæum. [*Died* 20 *Jan.* 1960.

SKINNER, Horace Wilfrid, C.B.E. 1941; Clerk of Peace and Clerk of County Council, Derbyshire, 1930-50; Clerk to the Lieutenancy; *b.* 30 Dec. 1884; *s.* of Frank and Ellen Skinner; *m.* 1912, Mary Amelia Campbell; two *s.* one *d.* *Educ.:* London Univ., LL.B. Solicitor. *Recreation:* cricket. *Address:* Ivy Lodge, Duffield, Derbyshire. *T.:* Duffield 3233. *Club:* County (Derby). [*Died* 30 *Dec.* 1955.

SKINNER, John William, M.A., Ph.D. (Lond.); Headmaster, Culford School, Bury St. Edmunds, 1924-51; *b.* 26 Nov. 1890; *s.* of Thomas Jessup Skinner, Spalding; *m.* 1921, Marjorie Laura Skinner; three *d.* *Educ.:* Grammar Sch., Spalding; Westminster Training Coll.; Univ. of Paris; Univ. College, Lond. Lecturer in French, Westminster Training College, 1914-24; served European War, Lieut. Duke of Cornwall's L.I., Palestine (despatches); External Examiner in French to University of London, 1923-24, 1928-32. *Publications:* Nurseries of Christians; Youth on Fire; Youth at the Helm, 1943; School Stresses, 1949; (with G. S. Edwards) A Rational French Course, 1934. *Recreation:* music. *Address:* Iona, Hardwick Lane, Bury St. Edmunds. [*Died* 1 *April* 1955.

SKINNER, Major-Gen. Sir (Percy) Cyriac Burrell, K.B.E., *cr.* 1922; C.B. 1919; C.M.G. 1918; D.S.O. 1917; Northamptonshire Regt.; *b.* 1871. Served South African War, 1900-2 (Queen's medal and four clasps, King's medal and two clasps); European War, 1914-18 (despatches, C.B., C.M.G., D.S.O., Officer French Legion of Honour, Commandeur Ordre de la Couronne and Croix de Guerre, Belgian); retired pay, 1928. *Address:* The Grange Hotel, Farnham Common, Bucks. *Club:* Army and Navy. [*Died* 24 *May* 1955.

SKINNER, Robert; *b.* 17 Dec. 1877; *s.* of Edward F. Skinner, Silcoorie, Cachar, India; *m.* 1926, Stella, *d.* of Colonel Hon. R. V. Dillon, R.H.A., Clonbrock, Co. Galway; two *s.* one *d.* *Educ.:* Bedford School; Queen's College, Oxford. Secretary's Department, Admiralty 1901-19; Asst. Private Secretary to successive First Lords of the Admiralty (Lord Selborne, Lord Cawdor, Lord Tweedmouth and Reginald McKenna); during the war and until retirement in 1919 Head of the Naval Branch, Secretary's Dept.; High Sheriff of Bedfordshire, 1937. *Address:* Bromham Hall, Bedford. *T.:* Oakley (Beds.) 343. *Club:* Union. [*Died* 23 *May* 1955.

SKINNER, Robert Peet; retired diplomat; *b.* Massillon, Ohio, 24 Feb. 1866; *s.* of Augustus T. Skinner and Cecilia van Rensselaer; *m.* 1897, Helen, *d.* of Hon. Arvine Wales. *Educ.:* public school. American Consul, Marseilles, 1897; Consul-General, 1901; Consul-General, Hamburg, 1908; Berlin, 1913; London, 1914-24; American Consul-General in Paris, 1924-26; Envoy Extraordinary and Minister Plenipotentiary of U.S.A. to Greece, 1926-32; to Estonia, Latvia and Lithuania, 1932-33; United States Ambassador to Turkey, 1933-36; retired, 1936; Commissioner and Plenipotentiary to establish relations between United States and Abyssinia, and conducted first American Mission to that country, 1903; appointed to readjust finances of Republic of Liberia, 1912; American Representative on Nitrates of Soda Executive; Hon. Member of the Society of the Felibrige (organisation of the poets of Provence); Foreign Service Association; Sons of the American Revolution; Member of the Protestant Episcopal Church. *Publication:* Abyssinia of To-day. *Address:* Belfast, Maine, U.S.A. *Clubs:* Pilgrims, American; Metropolitan (New York). [*Died* 1 *July* 1960.

SKIPWITH, Vice-Admiral Harry Louis d'Estoteville, C.M.G. 1919; *b.* 1868; *s.* of Captain Grey Skipwith, R.N.; *g.s.* of Sir Grey Skipwith, Bt., of Newbold Revel, Warwickshire; *m.* 1905, Ethel Maura (*d.* 1946), *d.* of John Henry Sharp, J.P., 21 Palmeira Square, Hove. *Educ.:* H.M.S. Britannia. Retired as Rear-Admiral, 1920; Commanded H.M.S. Carnarvon at Falkland Islands action, afterwards in command of H.M.S. Vernon; Commodore R.N. Barracks, Chatham, 1918-20. *Recreation:* motoring. *Address:* 69 The Drive, Hove, Sussex. *Club:* United Service. [*Died* 13 *March* 1955.

SLACK, Samuel Benjamin, M.A.; formerly Professor of Greek, McGill University; *b.* 26 Dec. 1859; *s.* of Benjamin Slack; *m.* 1925, Lillie Ann, *d.* of late T. G. Levo. *Educ.:* Liverpool College; Balliol College, Oxford (Classical Scholar, Prosser Exhibitioner), 1st Class Classical Moderations, 1879; honourably mentioned Craven Scholarship, 1884. 2nd Master, Sheffield Grammar School, 1884-90; on the Staff of McGill University, Montreal, 1896-1925. *Publications:* Early Christianity, and some translations. *Recreations:* curling, chess. *Address:* 17 Barton Crescent, Dawlish, South Devon. [*Died* 29 *Jan.* 1955.

SLADE, Sir Alfred (Fothringham), 5th Bt., *cr.* 1831; *b.* 17 Jan. 1898; *e. s.* of 4th Bt. and Kathleen, *d.* of Rowland Scovell, Co. Dublin, Ireland; *S.* father, 1908; *m.* 1922, Freda Mary, *yr. d.* of late Sidney Meates and

Mrs. Meates, Whitehall, Maidenhead. Late Lieut. Scots Guards. *Heir: b.* Michael Nial [*b.* 30 July 1900; *m.* 1928, Angela Clare Rosalind (*d.* 1959), *d.* of Orlando Chichester, Barnstaple; one *s.* one *d.* (and one *s.* decd.)]. *Address:* Maunsel, North Petherton, Somerset. *Clubs:* Guards, Pratt's. [*Died* 28 *Oct.* 1960.

SLADE, Mead, C.I.E. 1938; late I.C.S.; *b.* 24 Jan. 1894; *e. s.* of late Sidney Slade, Curry Mallet, Somerset; *m.* 1927, Vera Constance (marriage dissolved 1937), *d.* of Reginald Massey, Hampstead. *Educ.:* Ilminster School; Univ. College, London. Articled 1911 and qualified as a Solicitor (hons.) 1921. Served European War, 1914-1918, with Dorset (Q.V.O.) Yeomanry and Indian Army; Captain, Indian Army, 1910; Joined I.C.S., 1923; posted to Burma; Collector of Customs successively at Calcutta, Rangoon and Bombay, 1930-36; Joint Secretary to Government of India, Dept. of Commerce, 1936, Officiating Secretary, 1938; Member, Central Board of Revenue, Simla, 1938-46; retired 1948. *Recreations:* tennis, golf. *Address:* Perris, Hatch Beauchamp, Somerset. *Club:* East India and Sports. [*Died* 8 *May* 1954.

SLADEN, Joseph Maurice, C.I.E. 1943; *b.* 22 Feb. 1896; *m.* 1924; three *s.* one *d.*; *m.* 1950, Margaret I. Tinn. *Educ.:* Winchester; New Coll., Oxford. Joined Indian Civil Service, 1920; Joint Secretary, Indian Round Table Conference, London, 2nd Session, Sept.-Dec. 1931; Minister Khairpur State, 1932; Collector, 1936; Secretary to Govt. of Bombay, Home Dept., 1938; Chief Secretary to Govt. of Sind, Jan. 1943; retired from I.C.S., 1946. *Address:* St. Cleer's Cottage, Somerton, Somerset. *T.:* Somerton 95. *Club:* East India and Sports. [*Died* 20 *Feb.* 1956.

SLATER, George, D.Sc., D.I.C., A.R.C.S.; *b.* Sharow, nr. Ripon, Yorkshire, 1874; *m.* 1897, Anne, *d.* of Archibald and Louisa Irwin, Tynemouth, Northumberland. *Educ.:* St. John's College, York; Imperial College of Science (Royal College of Science), London. Entered the Teaching Profession; Assistant Master at Haltwhistle, Northumberland, 1895-97; Ipswich, 1897-1918; Demonstrator and Asst. Lecturer in Geology, Imperial College of Science and Technology, 1918-39; Glaciologist to the Oxford University Expedition to Spitsbergen, 1921; B.Sc. (Hon.), M.Sc., D.Sc., of the University of London; Member of the Imperial College (D.I.C.), and A.R.C.S.; awarded the Murchison Fund by the Geological Society of London, 1928 and Foulerton Award of Geologists' Assoc., 1950. *Publications:* papers on the structures developed in disturbed Drift Deposits at home and abroad. *Address:* 8 Porden Road, Brixton, S.W.2. [*Died* 27 *Jan.* 1956.

SLATER, Hon. William; formerly Chief Sec. and Attorney-Gen., Victoria; *b.* N.S.W., 20 May 1890; *m.* 1923, Mary Gordon, M.Sc.; two *s.* *Educ.:* State Schools; University of Melbourne. Served with A.I.F. in France, 1916-17, until wounded; member for Dundas since 1917; Attorney-General and Solicitor-General, 1924; Attorney-General, Solicitor-General, and Minister of Agriculture in the State of Victoria, 1927-28 and 1929-32; Speaker of Legislative Assembly, Victoria, 1940-42; Australian Minister to Russia, 1943. Chief President Australian Native Association, 1926; President, Law Institute of Victoria, 1928-29. *Address:* 28 Hoddle St., Essendon, Victoria, Australia. [*Died* 19 *June* 1960.

SLATTERY, John, C.B.E. 1942 (O.B.E. 1927); *b.* 26 June 1886; *s.* of D. F. Slattery, Solicitor, Dungarvan, Co. Waterford, I.F.S.; *m.* 1915, Mary Franziska, *d.* of Lt.-Col. D. F. Keegan, I.M.S.; one *s.* two *d.* *Educ.:* Rockwell College, Cashel; University College, Blackrock, Dublin, I.F.S. Asst. Supt. of Police in India, 1906; Deputy Inspector-General of Police, Punjab, and offg. Inspector-General of Police, N.W.F. Province; retired from Indian (Imperial) Police, 1937; Chairman, Joint Public Service Commission, Punjab and N.W.F. Province, 1937 to March 1943; and, in addition, Chairman National Service (Labour) Tribunal, Punjab and N.W.F. Province, 1941-42. [*Died* 1 *Aug.* 1958.

SLEEP, Arthur, C.M.G. 1949; *b.* 12 May 1894; *s.* of late John H. Sleep, Dalton-in-Furness, Lancs; *m.* 1918, Constance G. Bell; one *s.* *Educ.:* Ulverston Grammar School; Manchester University (B.Sc.). Served European War, 1914-18, Captain, R.F.C. and King's Own Regt., 1915-18, B.E.F. France. Cadet, Malayan Civil Service, 1920; District Officer, Kuala Selangor, 1926; 2nd Asst. Sec. to Govt., F.M.S., 1931; Asst. Treas., F.M.S., and Registrar of Titles, Selangor, 1934; Dep. Financial Sec., F.M.S., 1938; Fin. Comr., Johore, 1939; Actg. Fin. Sec., S.S., 1941; Resident Comr., Pahang, 1946; British Adviser, Johore, 1948; retired from M.C.S. 1949. Controller of Finance and Accounts, British Administration, Eritrea, 1950-52. *Recreations:* golf, tennis. *Address:* Worden, Spur Hill Avenue, Parkstone, Dorset. [*Died* 11 *Dec.* 1959.

SLESSOR, Alexander Johnston, M.V.O. 1949; Assistant Surgeon, Western General Hospital, Edinburgh, since 1948; *b.* 5 June 1912; *s.* of Thomas Stewart Slessor, late of Inverness, and late Isabella Slessor (*née* Johnston); *m.* 1940, Phyllis Eileen, *d.* of A. A. Davidson, Cults, Aberdeenshire; one *s.* two *d.* *Educ.:* Aberdeen Grammar School; Aberdeen University. M.B., Ch.B. with Honours, Aberdeen, 1935; F.R.C.S. (Edin.), 1938; F.R.C.S. (Eng.), 1941. Major, R.A.M.C., 1943; Lt.-Col., R.A.M.C., 1945. *Publications:* occasional articles in medical press. *Recreation:* squash racquets. *Address:* 94 Liberton Drive, Edinburgh 9. *T.:* 74193. [*Died* 17 *Oct.* 1954.

SLIGO, 8th Marquess of (*cr.* 1800); **Colonel Arthur Howe Browne,** K.B.E., *cr.* 1919; C.B. 1930; F.R.H.S., F.Z.S.; Baron Mount Eagle, 1760; Viscount Westport, 1768; Earl of Altamont, 1771; Earl of Clanricarde, 1543 and 1800 (spec. rem.); Baron Monteagle (U.K.), 1806; retired pay; *b.* 8 May 1867; 3rd *s.* of 5th Marquess; *S.* nephew 1941; *m.* 1919, Lilian Whiteside, *widow* of Major A. F. Mann and *d.* of Charles Chapman, I.C.S. Gazetted S. Staff. Regt., 1887; 1st R. Munster Fusiliers, 1889; Adjutant 2nd R. Munster Fusiliers, 1895-99; A.T.O. Tirah Expeditionary Force; A.T.O. (acting D.A.A.G.) Malakand Field Force and Swat Movable Column, 1898-99; S.S.O. Kimberley District, 1901-2; Assistant D.A.A.G. Instruction, Sirhind District, 1903; Instructor R.M.A. Woolwich, 1905-9; retired as Major, 1909; served Tirah, 1898 (medal and clasp); S. African War, 1899-1902 (Queen's medal 5 clasps); European War, on General Staff, War Office (G.S.O. 1, Intelligence Directorate), 1914-19 (Bt. of Lt.-Col., Col., K.B.E., Legion of Honour, Grand Officer Order of Christ); Principal Assistant Secretary to Imperial War Graves Commission, 1919-30; Director Birmingham Aluminium Castings (1903) Co. and Birmid Industries, 1924-43. *Heir: b.* Lord Terence Morris Browne (*see* 9th Marquess of Sligo). *Address:* Westport House, Co. Mayo. *Club:* Naval and Military. [*Died* 28 *May* 1951.

SLIGO, 9th Marquess of (*cr.* 1800); **Terence Morris Browne;** Baron Mount Eagle, 1760; Viscount Westport, 1768; Earl of Altamont, 1771; Earl of Clanricarde, 1543 and 1800 (special remainder); Baron Monteagle (U.K.), 1806; *b.* 28 Sept. 1873; 4th *s.* of 5th Marquess; *S.* brother 1951. Formerly Superintendent, Bengal Police. *Heir: nephew* Denis Edward Browne. [*Died* 28 *July* 1952.

SLOAN, Hon. Gordon McGregor, Q.C.; LL.D. (Hon.) Univ. of B.C.; Chief Justice of

British Columbia, 1944-57; Forestry Advisor to Govt. of B.C.; *b.* British Columbia, 16 May 1898; *s.* of late Hon. William Sloan, Minister of Mines in the Oliver Government; *m.*; one *s.* one *d.* *Educ.:* private schools at Victoria and Vancouver. Went overseas 1916, serving as a pilot instructor in the Royal Air Force; returning to Victoria was called to Bar, 1921, and joined the firm of Farris, Farris, Stultz and Sloan in Vancouver, retiring in 1933; elected to legislature representing Vancouver, took silk and appointed Attorney-General, 1933; puisne Justice of Court of Appeal, 1937; Member, Newcomen Society. *Publications:* Reports: (1940) Salmon Fishing off Fraser River and Sooke Salmon Traps for Dominion Govt., (1942 and 1952) Workmen's Compensation Law, (1944-56). The Forestry Industry of British Columbia, for Provincial Government. *Address:* Victoria, B.C. *Clubs:* Vancouver (Vancouver); Union, Victoria Golf (Victoria, B.C.). [*Died* 14 *Jan.* 1959.

SMALL, James, D.Sc. (Lond.); F.R.P.S.; M.R.I.A.; F.R.S.E.; Professor of Botany, Queen's University, Belfast, 1920-54; Emeritus Professor, 1954; *b.* Brechin, Angus, 1889; 2nd *s.* of William Small, Brechin; *m.* 1917, Helen, *d.* of David Pattison, Dalmeny; two *s.* one *d.* *Educ.:* Brechin High School; Pharmaceutical Society's School; Birkbeck College, London. Herbarium Medallist and Bell Scholar, Pharmaceutical Society, 1910; Pharmaceutical Chemist, 1912; B.Sc. Lond. 1913; 2nd Lt. Black Watch, 1915; Lecturer in Botany, Armstrong College, Newcastle, 1916; M.Sc. Lond. 1916; Assistant Lecturer in Botany, Bedford College, 1916-20; Lecturer in Botany, Pharmaceutical Society's School, 1917-20; D.Sc. Lond. 1919; awarded the Makdougall Brisbane prize by Royal Society of Edinburgh, for numerous papers on Quantitative Evolution, 1951. *Publications:* Origin and Development of Compositæ; Application of Botany in Utilisation of Medicinal Plants; Textbook of Botany; What Botany Really Means; Hydrogen-ion Concentration in Plant Cells and Tissues; Geheimnisse der Botanik; El Secreto de la Vida de las Plantas; Pocket-Lens Plant Lore; Practical Botany; pH and Plants; Modern Aspects of pH, 1954; pH of Plant Cells, 1955; papers, over 250, in Proc. Royal Society, Edinburgh, Proc. Roy. Irish Acad., etc. *Recreations:* fishing, photography. *Address:* Queen's University, Belfast. [*Died* 28 *Nov.* 1955.

SMART, Henry C., C.B.E. 1926; Director for Propaganda, Australian Government, London; *b.* 8 Sept. 1878; *m.* 1905, Daisy Hope Foster; one *s.* six *d.* *Educ.:* High School, Sydney. Department of Agriculture, New South Wales; Sub-Editor, Hong Kong Telegraph; Editor, Shanghai Free Press; travelled through Japan; represented London Globe in Pekin, 1899; served South African War, 1900-1; Editor, The Regiment; contributor to Punch and leading magazines; Director, Publicity and Intelligence Departments, Australian Government, in London; Deputy Director, Migration for Australia; Manager, Australian Section, British Empire Exhibition; Hon. Captain, Australian Imperial Force; Russia, Siberia and China for Daily Mail, 1927; organised Australian Art Exhibition at Royal Academy; Liaison Officer in London for Australian Government Department of Information, 1940-1944. *Clubs:* Authors', Royal Empire Society. [*Died* 7 *July* 1951.

SMART, Joseph McCaig; *b.* 9 December 1882; *s.* of late David Smart, Schoolmaster, and late Margaret McCaig; *m.* 1920, Margaret Hamilton Scott; one *d.* (two *s.* decd., of whom one was killed, War of 1939-45). *Educ.:* Dumfries Acad.; Glasgow University. Solicitor; Depute Town Clerk, Clydebank; Town Councillor, Magistrate, and Provost of the Burgh of Clydebank. Sheriff Substitute: of Roxburgh, Berwick and Selkirk at Selkirk and at Peebles, 1945-52; retired, 1952; formerly of Ross and Cromarty at Stornoway, Isle of Lewis. *Recreation:* music. *Address:* Nithdale, Bleachfield Road, Selkirk. *T.:* 2276 Selkirk. [*Died* 24 *Aug.* 1953.

SMART, Comdr. Sir Morton, G.C.V.O., *cr.* 1949 (K.C.V.O., *cr.* 1933; C.V.O. 1952); D.S.O. 1917; M.D., M.B., Ch.B.; Extra Manipulative surgeon to the Queen since 1952 (formerly to King George VI); Consultant in Physical Medicine to R.A.F.; Consultant to the London Clinic for Injuries, 21 Grosvenor Square, W.1; late R.N.V.R.; Commendador de la Orden Civil de Alfonso XII., 1931; Chevalier of Order of St. Charles Monaco, 1913; Fellow of Royal Society of Medicine; *b.* Scotland, 1878; 3rd *s.* of late John Smart, R.S.A., R.S.W.; *m.* 1923, Lilian, *d.* of William S. Gibson, London. *Educ.:* privately; Watson's College, Edinburgh; University, Edinburgh. Edinburgh Royal College of Surgeons M.B., Ch.B., 1902; M.D., 1910; served S. African War; European War, 1914-19 (despatches); at Admiralty, North Sea, Chief of Staff to Admiral in command of Gunboats on Belgian Canals, 1914; attached 1st Army, France, 1915; commanded Gunboat Flotilla Dardanelles, 1915-16; in command of all Motor Launches in Ægean, 1916-17; Salonica (despatches, D.S.O., Chevalier of Order of St. Charles of Monaco); Senior Naval Officer, Trinidad, W. Indies, 1918-19; command of H.M. Navy Station, Trinidad, W. Indies, 1918-1919; commanded Flotilla of Motor Launches which made the passage from England to Mudros, Gibraltar, Malta, Mitylene; Vice-President International Motor Yachting Union; Member Empire Rheumatism Council; Member Central War Committee; President British Gladiolus Society. *Publications:* Treatment of Sprains and Allied Injuries to Joints, Practitioners Encyclopædia, 1912; Treatment of Muscular and Joint Injuries by Graduated Contraction, Lancet, 1912; Injuries to Muscles and Joints and their treatment by Graduated Contraction, M.D. Thesis Edinburgh Univ.; Injuries to Muscles and Joints, British Journal of Radiology, 1924; Injured Muscles and Joints and their treatment by Graduated Muscular Contractions, Nelson's Loose Leaf Surgery, 1932; The Principles of Treatment of Muscles and Joints by Graduated Muscular Contractions, 1933; Manipulative Surgery (The Medical Annual, 1936); Physical Medicine and Industry; Muscle action in relation to repair of Joint Tissues; Physical Medicine in War Time. *Recreations:* yachting, motor boating, shooting, fishing. *Address:* (home) Beaulieu Cottage, Cooden Beach, Bexhill-on-Sea. *T.:* Cooden 583; (professional) 21 Grosvenor Square, W.1. *T.:* Mayfair 3763-4. *Club:* Royal Burnham Yacht (Burnham-on-Crouch). [*Died* 16 *March* 1956.

SMETHURST, Rev. Canon Arthur Frederick, Ph.D., M.A.; Canon Residentiary of Salisbury Cathedral since 1949; Treasurer of Salisbury Cathedral since 1956; *b.* 30 March 1904; *s.* of Frederick and Evaline Annie Smethurst; *m.* 1935, Gwynyth Beatrice, *d.* of G. N. Hallett; no *c.* *Educ.:* Marlborough College; Imperial College of Science and Technology, London; Westcott House, Cambridge; St. Catherine's Society, Oxford University. B.Sc. (Lond.) 1925; Ph.D. (Lond.), 1936; M.A. (Oxon) 1942; F.C.S. 1925; A.R.C.S. 1926; F.G.S. 1926; D.I.C. 1936; Deacon, 1929, Priest, 1930; Curate at Petersfield, 1929-30; Senior Curate at Portsmouth Cathedral, 1930-33; scientific research, 1933 - 36; theological study, 1936-38; Rector of Compton Abbas, Shaftesbury, 1938 - 40; Vicar of Market Lavington, 1940-44; Rector of West Dean and East Grimstead, 1944-48; Chancellor of Salisbury Cathedral, 1953-56. Proctor in Convocation, 1941-; Dioc. Sec. for Higher Educ., 1941-52; Exam. Chaplain to Bishop of Salisbury, 1946-; Synodical Sec. of Convocation of Canterbury, 1947- ; Bishop's Ordination Sec., 1946, and Sec. Dioc. Ordination Candidates Council, 1949-. Select Preacher, University of Cambridge, 1949. *Publications:* Convocation of Canterbury; what it is; what it does; how it works, 1949; The New Canons and Obedience to the Book of Common Prayer, 1950; Modern Science and Christian Beliefs, 1955; (Joint Editor) Acts of Convocation, 1921-1946, 1948; (Ed.) The Chronicle of Convocation, 1946-. Scientific papers in Mineralogical Magazine and Quarterly Journal of Geological Society. *Recreations:* motoring, walking; the Arts. *Address:* Hungerford Chantry, 54 The Close, Salisbury. *T.:* Salisbury 2996. *Club:* Royal Societies. [*Died* 15 *Sept.* 1957.

SMILES, Samuel, O.B.E. 1918; F.R.S. 1918; D.Sc.; Hon. D.Sc. (Belfast); Emeritus Professor of Chemistry in the University of London; late Daniell Professor of Chemistry, King's College, London; late Professor of Organic Chemistry at Armstrong College; late Vice-President of Chemical Society; Fellow of University College, London; Fellow of King's College, London; *b.* Belfast, 1877; *s.* of late Samuel Smiles, Beckenham, and *g.s.* of Samuel Smiles, author; *m.* 1920, Minnie, *y. d.* of late G. N. Patterson, Newcastle on Tyne. *Educ.:* Marlborough; Univs. of London, Paris, and Jena. Late Assistant Professor, Organic Chemistry, University College, London. *Publications:* Relations between Physical Properties and Chemical Constitution; various papers in the Transactions of the Chemical Society; Berichte d. Deutsch. Chem. Ges. and Comptes Rendus, chiefly on organic compounds of sulphur. *Address:* c/o Williams Deacon's Bank, Ltd., 9 Pall Mall, S.W.1. [*Died* 6 *May* 1953.

SMILES, Lt.-Col. Sir Walter (Dorling), Kt., *cr.* 1930; C.I.E. 1925; D.S.O. 1916, bar, 1917; M.P. (U.) Co. Down, 1945-50, North Down since 1950; D.L. Co. Down, 1946; Chairman Moran Tea Co. Ltd.; *s.* of W. H. Smiles, Belfast; *g.s.* of Samuel Smiles, author of Self-Help; *m.* Margaret Heighway, Didsbury, Manchester; one *d.* *Educ.:* Rossall School. India, 1904-30; served European War, 1914-18 (D.S.O. and bar, despatches, St. George's Cross, Russia (Officers IV. class), Officer of Crown of Roumania, etc.); member, Legislative Council, Assam, 1922-1930; M.P. (U.) Blackburn, 1931-45. High Sheriff of Down for 1943. *Recreation:* golf. *Address:* Portavo Point, Donaghadee, Co. Down. *Clubs:* Carlton; Ulster (Belfast). [*Died* 31 *Jan.* 1953.

SMIT, Hon. Jacob Hendrik, C.M.G. 1939; former Minister of Finance and Commerce, S. Rhodesia; *b.* 3 Sept. 1881; *s.* of Samuel Marinus Smit and Aleyda Woutera van Wyland; *m.* 1913, Dieta Smilda; one *c.* *Educ.:* Public School, Hilversum, Holland. Merchant; Town Councillor; Mayor of Salisbury, 1927-28. *Recreation:* fishing. *Address:* P.O. Box 128, Salisbury, S. Rhodesia. *Club:* Salisbury. [*Died* 22 *July* 1959.

SMIT, Jacobus Stephanus, D.T.D.; *b.* 9 Oct. 1878; 3rd *s.* of J. S. Smit, Railway Commissioner S.A.R.; *m.* Agnes Cecilia Williams (decd.); one *s.* two *d.* *Educ.:* Pretoria; Leyden; Middle Temple. Private sec. to General Smuts, 1906-7; to General Botha, 1907; to Hon. J. de Viliers, 1907-9; Assistant Magistrate, 1909-10; Magistrate, 1910-15; resigned Magistracy, 1915; Member Legislative Assembly for Klerksdorp, 1920, 1921, and 1924; First Delegate Union of South Africa Meetings League of Nations, Sep. 1925, March 1925, 1926, 1927; Naval Disarmament Conference Geneva, 1927; High Commissioner for the Union of South Africa, 1925-29; Administrator of the Transvaal, 1929-34; Chairman of the Diamond Control Board, 1934-37. *Recreations:* shooting, fishing. *Address:* P.O. Box 12, Malelane, Transvaal, S. Africa. [*Died* 10 *Feb.* 1960.

SMITH, Brigadier Albert, C.B.E. 1951 (O.B.E. 1941); T.D.; retd.; *b.* 2 May 1896; *s.* of Alderman George Smith, M.B.E., Redholm, Doncaster; *m.* 1917, Joyce Elizabeth, *d.* of Alexander Dodds, Portaferry, Co. Down; one *s.* two *d.* *Educ.:* Scarborough College. Served European War, 1914-18, Sherwood Rangers Yeomanry, 6th Battalion Lincolnshire Regiment, and 149 Squadron, Royal Flying Corps. In command 5th Battalion, King's Own Yorkshire Light Infantry, 1936-39; served War of 1939-45, 30 and 553 Light Anti-Aircraft Regiments; Brigadier, 1942; A.D.C. to King George VI, 1948 and subsequently to the Queen until 1958. Retired, 1951. J.P. Doncaster, 1952. *Address:* 31 Avenue Road, Doncaster, Yorks. [*Died* 15 *Nov.* 1959.

SMITH, Lieut.-Col. Alexander Hugh Dickson, M.C. 1917; T.D. 1936, two clasps, 1951; D.L.; M.B.; Hon. Consulting Surgeon and Hon. Consulting Radiologist, Llanelly General Hospital; Pres. South Wales and Mon. Branch, British Medical Association, 1945; *b.* 21 May 1890; *s.* of late William Dickson Smith and Elizabeth Williams; *m.* 1932, Joan Margaret, *d.* of late Dr. Hugh John, Bronygarth, Llangennech, Carmarthenshire; one *d.* *Educ.:* Llandovery College; Univ. of Edinburgh (Grierson Prize Pathology, M.B., Ch.B. (Hons.) 1914). B.E.F. France, Capt. R.A.M.C., 1914-19 (M.C., 1914 Star); served with Guards' Div., 3rd Div., 29 Div. (Certificate of Merit from G.O.C., Passchendale); Lt.-Col. R.A.M.C. Territorial Army, retd.; B.E.F. France, 1939-1940, O.C. Surgical Divisions General Hospitals B.E.F. (1939 Star). Late Hon. Surgeon Llanelly Gen. Hospital; late Hon. Sec. South Wales and Mon. Branch B.M.A. and ex-Chairman South-West Wales Div. B.M.A.; Chm. Carmarthenshire Panel Committee; Chm. 1944-45-46 Carmarthenshire Insurance Cttee.; Ex-Chm. Ministry of Pensions Boards, Swansea and Carmarthen; Ex-Chm. Advisory Committee Llanelly and District under Min. of Labour Disabled Persons Act, 1944; Ex-Chm. Carmarthenshire Executive Health Cttee.; Medical Referee Min. of Labour; Ex-Pres. Carmarthenshire County Cttee. British Legion; High Sheriff of Carmarthenshire, 1944-45; Chm. S.W. Wales Division B.M.A., 1947-1948-49; D.L. Carmarthenshire, 1952; Trustee, Llandovery College; Old Llandoverian; ex-Mem. Carmarthenshire Territorial Association; Pres. Old Contemptibles Assoc., Llanelly and District. *Publications:* Food Poisoning with Delayed Nervous Symptoms (Lancet, 1927); Spontaneous Rupture of Spleen (with Sladden and Morrison) (Lancet, 1936); Preliminary Report of an Outbreak of Gastro-Enteritis (jointly) (B.M.J. 1941), etc. *Recreations:* gardening, cricket, Territorial Army. *Address:* Glan Arthen, Llanelly, Carms. *T.:* Llanelly 281. *Clubs:* English-Speaking Union, M.C.C. [*Died* 31 *Jan.* 1960.

SMITH, Rt. Rev. Alfred William, M.A.; licensed preacher under seal, Derby diocese, 1957; *b.* Benenden, Kent, 21 Aug. 1875; 3rd *s.* of George Smith and Tamar Brignall; *m.* Millicent Coleman (*d.* 1958), *e. d.* of late John Blackwall Evans-Blackwall, J.P., of Blackwall, Kirk Ireton, Derbyshire. *Educ.:* Bethany School, Goudhurst; Church Missionary Coll.; Christ's Coll., Cambridge (Research in Anthropology). Educated for Civil Service; business experience with Borough Accountant of Hastings; after studying at Thurning Rectory, Norfolk, 1898, entered Church Missionary College, London; Deacon, 1902; after short curacy at St. John's, Lowestoft, took charge of Christ Church, Lagos, Nigeria, later, educational and district work; Examining Chaplain to Bishop Tugwell and to late Bishop of Lagos; Sec. of Yoruba and Hausa Missions; Archdeacon of Yoruba Country, 1919; Assistant Bishop in Diocese of Lagos for Northern Nigeria, 1925-42; Examiner in Yoruba for Mission and for Government; Asst. Bishop of Hereford, Preb. of Hereford Cathedral and Vicar of Ford, 1942-47; Rural

Dean of Pontesbury, 1944-47; Chaplain, Addenbrooke's Hospital, Cambridge, 1947-1949. Rector, Kirk Ireton, 1949-57. *Address:* Biggin House, Hulland Ward, Derby. *T.:* Hulland Ward 208. *Club:* Church Imperial. [*Died* 8 *Sept.* 1958.

SMITH, Alic Halford, C.B.E. 1920; Hon. LL.D. St. Andrews, Pennsylvania; Warden of New College, Oxford; Fellow of Winchester College; Hon. Fellow of King's College, Cambridge; Hon. Freeman of the City of Oxford, 1955; *b.* 1883. *Educ.:* Dulwich; New College, Oxford (Scholar). 1st class Classical Moderations, 1904; 1st class Literæ Humaniores, 1906; Scottish Office, 1906-19; Fellow of New College and Tutor in Philosophy, 1919-1944; Vice-Chancellor of the University of Oxford, 1954-57. *Publications:* A Treatise on Knowledge, 1943; Kantian Studies, 1947; H. W. B. Joseph (British Academy Proceedings), 1948; New College and its Buildings, 1952; The Town-Planning of Oxford, 1954. *Address:* New College, Oxford. [*Died* 13 *July* 1958.

SMITH, Sir Allan G. G.; *see* Gordon-Smith.

SMITH, Dame Ann Beadsmore, D.B.E., *cr.* 1925 (C.B.E. 1919); R.R.C.; *d.* of late William Smith, Highbury, N. *Educ.:* Warden Court College, Crickfield. Nursing profession; served with H.M. Forces in Boer War, 1899-1902; as Principal Matron in France and Malta in Queen Alexandra's Imperial Military Nursing Service, 1914-17; at the War Office as Matron-in-Chief of Q.A.I.M.N.S., 1917-1924; Matron-in-Chief Territorial Army Nursing Service 1925-31, Chevalier Légion d'Honneur. *Address:* St. Mary's Convent Guest House, Burlington Lane, Chiswick, W.4. *Club:* United Nursing Services. [*Died* 12 *July* 1960.

SMITH, Sir Anthony P. G.; *see* Grafftey-Smith.

SMITH, Arthur Croxton, O.B.E., F.J.I.; Article writer for leading dailies and weeklies. *b.* 3 Dec. 1865; *s.* of William Croxton Smith; *m.* 1892, Ada Frances, *d.* of late Frederick Stimpson, Northampton; one *s.* one *d. Educ.:* privately. Articled to Northampton Mercury and Daily Reporter; came to London as a young man and appointed Asst. Editor of The Gentlewoman; left in 1909 to take up article writing, and having had a large exhibition kennel of dogs, he soon specialised on this subject; Director of Publicity to the Ministry of Food in European War, 1914-18; served on committees set up by Govt. in connection with all subsequent coal and railway strikes and the General strike; judges many breeds of dogs at all leading shows; put on the Kennel Club Committee in 1901; Vice-Chairman, 1935, Chairman, 1937-48, a Trustee of Club, 1938; one of the first to encourage use of dogs for police work; as Hon. sec. of Association of Bloodhound Breeders organised many man-hunting trials; also writes on country and Dominion subjects; First secretary of Milk Publicity Council; Chairman of Tail-Waggers' Club; for several years Chairman of Guide Dogs for the Blind Assocn. *Publications:* About our Dogs; Tail-Waggers, Sporting Dogs, Dogs since 1900, British Dogs, etc. Edited vol. on Hounds and Dogs in Lonsdale Library; Writer of Tail-Wagger Chats under pseudonym of Philokuon. *Recreations:* as a young man played football for Northamptonshire, ran, rowed, boxed and played lacrosse and lawn tennis, continued to play tennis through most of his life. *Address:* Kipling House, 43 Villiers Street, Strand, W.C.2. *T.:* Trafalgar 6197. *Clubs:* Kennel, National Liberal. [*Died* 27 *Aug.* 1952.

SMITH, Rev. Arthur Edward, M.A.; *b.* 22 March 1871; *s.* of Frederick Smith, Doncaster, and Mary De Pledge; *m.* 1903, Dora Cox Jordan (*d.* 1952); one *s. Educ.:* St. John's Coll., Cambridge. Curate St. Philip's, Dalston, 1895-1903; St. John-at-Hackney, 1903-1907; Vicar of St. Peter's, Hornsey, 1907-25; Vicar of Willesden, 1925-37; Vicar of St. Mary Abbots, Kensington, 1937; Prebendary of St. Paul's, 1935; Examining Chaplain to Bishop of London, 1935, resigned; Rural Dean of Willesden, 1929-37; Joint Editor of Sundays of Man's Life, 1931; Chairman of Campden Trustees, 1937. *Address:* 72 South Terrace, Littlehampton, Sussex. *Club:* Reform. [*Died* 1 *May* 1952.

SMITH, Vice-Admiral Arthur Gordon, C.M.G. 1917; late R.N.; *b.* 30 March 1873; *s.* of H. Arthur Smith, M.A., LL.B., Barrister-at-law; *m.* 1905, Ethel, *d.* of Capt. F. T. Barr, R.N.; one *s.* two *d.* Served as Lieut. in Adm. E. H. Seymour's expedition to Pekin, 1900 (despatches); Commander, 1903; Captain, 1909; lent to Australian Govt., Jan. 1913; Member of Naval Board, 1914-17; President of Australian Munitions Committee, 1915-16; Commanded H.M. Ships Commonwealth and Dominion, 1917-18; Commodore, R.N. Barracks, Portsmouth, 1918-20; Rear-Adm. 1920; retired, 1920; Vice-Adm., retired, 1926. *Publications:* Blue-jackets and Boxers; Jock Scott, Midshipman, his Log. *Recreations:* most games, gardening, painting, music. *Address:* Westbourne House, Emsworth. *T.:* Emsworth 109. [*Died* 10 *Oct.* 1953.

SMITH, Admiral Sir Aubrey Clare Hugh, K.C.V.O., *cr.* 1947 (M.V.O. 1909); K.B.E., *cr.* 1928; C.B. 1921; *b.* 22 Sept. 1872; 4th *s.* of late Hugh Colin Smith and Constance, *d.* of Henry J. Adeane, of Babraham, Cambridge; *m.* 1899, Hon. Elizabeth Emma Beatrice Grosvenor (*d.* 1931), *e. d.* of 1st Baron Stalbridge; one *s.* one *d.* Entered Navy, 1885; Lieut. 1893; Commander, 1903; Captain, 1910; A.D.C. to the King, 1920-21; Rear-Admiral, 1921; Vice-Admiral, 1926; Naval Attaché, Russia, Sweden and Norway, 1908-12; Commodore II. cl. East Coast South America, 1916-19; commanded H.M.S. Ramillies, 1920-21; Head of British Naval Mission to Greece, 1921-1923; British Naval Representative, League of Nations, 1923-27; retired list, 1926; Admiral, retired, 1930. *Address:* Iden Cottage, Rye, Sussex. *T.:* Iden 240. *Club:* Brooks's. [*Died* 6 *Oct.* 1957.

SMITH, Basil T. P.; *see* Parsons-Smith.

SMITH, Sir (Charles) Robert, K.B.E., *cr.* 1947; C.M.G. 1941; *b.* 13 Nov. 1887; *s.* of Capt. C. V. Smith, C.B.E., R.N.; *m.* 1st, 1920, Violet Mure Slight; one *s.* one *d.*; 2nd, 1948, Gwendoline Jessie Holdcroft. *Educ.:* Christ's Hospital. Cadet, North Borneo Civil Service, 1913; Governor and Commander-in-Chief, North Borneo, 1937-46. Interned by Japanese, Jan. 1942-Aug. 1945. Retired Oct. 1946. *Address:* c/o Barclay's Bank, D.C.O., Natal Branch, P.O. Box 965, Durban, S. Africa. [*Died* 4 *Nov.* 1959.

SMITH, Rev. Charles Ryder, B.A., D.D. (Lond.); Methodist Minister (retired); *b.* Mansfield, 10 Jan. 1873; *s.* of John Smith, Wesleyan Minister, and Frances Ryder, both of Selby; *m.* 1899, Charlotte Jane Taylor (*d.* 1954), B.A. (Lond.) Shipley, Yorks, and Aberystwyth College; one *s.* two *d. Educ.*. Kingswood School; Headingley Coll. Entered Wesleyan Methodist Ministry, 1895; Assistant Tutor at Headingley College, 1896-99; between 1900 and 1920 stationed at Leeds, Bombay, Bradford, Wolverhampton, and Newcastle on Tyne; first class Honours at London University, in Philosophy of Religion, 1910; Doctorate in Divinity, 1916; Professor in Theology at Richmond College, 1920-40; Fernley Lecturer, 1927; Principal, Richmond College, 1929-40; President of Wesleyan Conference, 1931; Professor in Theology at London University, 1932-40; Dean of Faculty of Theology, 1938-40. *Publications:* The Bible Doctrine of Society, 1920; The Bible Doctrine of Womanhood, 1923; The Bible Doctrine of Wealth and Work, 1924; The Christian Experience, 1926; The Sacramental Society, 1927;

What is the Old Testament? 1931; The Religion of the Hebrews, 1935; The Bible Doctrine of Salvation, 1941; What do ye? A study in the Social Teaching of the New Testament, 1945; The Bible Doctrine of Man, 1951; The Bible Doctrine of Sin, and of the Ways of God with Sinners, 1953. *Address:* White Stacks, West End Lane, Pinner, Middlesex.
[*Died* 23 *March* 1956.

SMITH, Monsignor Charles William, C.B.E. 1918; D.S.O. 1917; *b.* Oxford, 1873; *s.* of Frederick A. Smith. *Educ.:* Beaumont; Oscott; Collegio Beda, Rome. Ordained, 1909; Privy Chamberlain to His Holiness, 1918; served European War as C.F. (despatches five times, D.S.O.); Assistant Principal Chaplain, 1917-18; A.P.C. 4th Army, 1917-18, and at Western Command, 1918 (C.B.E.): Senior R.C. Chaplain, Mesopotamia, 1921, and Turkey, 1923; Senior R.C. Chaplain, Tientsin, N. China, 1924-25; Malta, 1925-26; retired pay, 1930. *Publications:* Editor of the Music to Milton's Comus; composer of the children's opera, Snowdrop; Mass of St. Wilfred, etc. *Address:* St. Joseph's Nursing Home, Candlemas Lane, Beaconsfield, Bucks. *T.:* 1208.
[*Died* 22 *Dec.* 1954.

SMITH, Chilton L. A.; *see* Addison-Smith.

SMITH, Cicely Fox; *d.* of Richard Smith, B.A., Barrister-at-law, Manchester, and Alice Wilson, *d.* of the Rev. Thomas Wolstencroft, Rector of Moston, Lancs. Travelled in Canada and Africa. *Publications:* Sailortown Days; A Book of Famous Ships; Ship Alley; The Return of the Cutty Sark; There was a Ship; Ocean Racers; Tales of the Clipper Ships; Ancient Mariners; Sea Songs and Ballads; Songs and Shanties; Full Sail; Sailor's Delight; The City of Hope; Singing Sands; Peregrine in Love; A Book of Shanties; A Sea Chest (anthology); The Thames; Anchor Lane, 1933; All the Other Children; A Book of Young Creatures; Adventures and Perils; Peacock Pride (with Madge S. Smith); All the Way Round—Sea Roads to Africa; The Ship Aground; Here and There in England with the Painter Brangwyn: Thames-Side Yesterdays, 1945; Painted Ports; Country Days and Country Ways; Knave-go-By; Ship Models; Seldom Seen (with Madge S. Smith); many contributions to Punch, etc. *Recreations:* travel, the sea and the countryside. *Address:* West Halse, Bow, N. Devon. *T.:* Bow 372.
[*Died* 8 *April* 1954.

SMITH, David; *see* Baird-Smith.

SMITH, David Murray, R.W.S. 1933 (now hon. ret.); landscape painter; *b.* Edinburgh; *e. s.* of late D. Murray Smith, author and journalist. *Educ.:* George Watson's College, Edinburgh. Studied art at the Edinburgh School of Art and the Royal Scottish Academy; came to London, 1893. *Recreation:* music. *Address:* The Bield, Sutton Place, Abinger Hammer, Dorking, Surrey. [*Died* 29 *May* 1952.

SMITH, Dempster, M.B.E., M.Sc.Tech., M.I.Mech.E.; Professor Emeritus in the University of Manchester. *Address:* 6 Maule Terrace, Gullane, East Lothian.
[*Died* 21 *March* 1953.

SMITH, Edward S.; *see* Sharwood-Smith.

SMITH, Edward S. S.; *see* Shrapnell-Smith.

SMITH, Rev. Edwin W., Hon. D.D. (Wesley College, Winnipeg); retd.; Editor of Journal of Royal African Society, 1938-40; Editor of Africa (Jl. of Internat. Af. Inst.), 1944-48; *b.* Aliwal North, Cape Colony, 7 Sept. 1876; *s.* of late Rev. John Smith, sometime Missionary in South Africa and President of the Primitive Methodist Church; *m* 1899, Julia, *d.* of James Fitch of Peasenhall, Suffolk; one *d.* *Educ.:* Elmfield College, York. Served in Africa as a Missionary of the Primitive Methodist Church, 1898-1915; spent the first year in Basutoland, then lived at Aliwal North; in 1902 went to do pioneer work in Northern Rhodesia, where he built the Kasenga Mission, reduced the Ila language to writing; translated first the Gospels, then, with the help of a colleague, the rest of the New Testament, into Ila; was President of the first Conference of N. Rhodesian Missionaries, 1914; returned to England, 1915; became a Chaplain of the Forces, and went at once to France, served twelve months; entered the service of the British and Foreign Bible Society as its Secretary at Rome, 1916; later, Secretary for Western Europe; then Literary Superintendent; Editorial Superintendent, 1933-39; President of Roy. Anthropological Inst., 1933-35; Visiting Prof., Hartford Seminary Foundation, U.S.A., 1939-43. Head of School of African Studies, Fisk Univ., U.S.A., 1943. *Publications:* The Handbook of the Ila language, 1907; Ila made Easy; various educational and religious books in Ila; pamphlets in English and Italian; joint-author (with late Captain A. M. Dale) of the Ila-speaking Peoples of Northern Rhodesia, 1920; The Religion of the Lower Races, 1923; Robert Moffat, one of God's Gardeners, 1925; The Golden Stool, 1926; The Christian Mission in Africa, 1926; The White Fields in Rhodesia, 1928; Aggrey of Africa; The Shrine of a People's Soul; The Secret of the African; Exploration in Africa, an Anthology, 1929; African beliefs and Christian faith, 1936; The Mabilles of Basutoland, 1939; The Life and Times of Daniel Lindley, 1942; Events in African History, 1942; (Ed.) African Ideas of God, 1950; Great Lion of Bechuanaland, 1957. *Recreation:* gardening. *Address:* The Old Watch House, 26 Marina, Deal, Kent. *T.:* Deal 1022.
[*Died* 23 *Dec.* 1957.

SMITH, Sir Eric C.; *see* Conran-Smith.

SMITH, Eric Martin; M.P. (C.) Grantham since 1950; Director of Smith, St. Aubyn & Co. Ltd., and British and Continental Banking Co.; *b.* 28 Dec. 1908; *s.* of Everard Martin Smith and Violet, *d.* of Sir E. Hambro, Hayes Place, Kent; *m.* 1st, 1932, Dorothy Surtees (*d.* 1937); one *d.*; 2nd, 1940, Elizabeth, *d.* of Archibald Morrison, Basildon Park; two *d.* *Educ.:* Eton; Cambridge University. Served War of 1939-45, 4th County of London Yeomanry; invalided out, 1940. *Recreations:* golf (played golf for Cambridge Univ., 1929 and 1930; won British Open Amateur Golf Championship, 1931); shooting. *Address:* Codicote Lodge, Hitchin, Herts. *T.:* Codicote 202. *Club:* White's. [*Died* 13 *Aug.* 1951.

SMITH, His Honour Mr. Justice Ernest Gardiner, LL.B. (Glas.); Advocate. Nigerian Civil Service, 1908-22; Circuit Judge, Ashanti, 1922; Puisne Judge, Gold Coast, 1925; retired, 1931; Chief Justice, Seychelles, 1935-40. *Address:* 14 New High St., Headington, Oxford. *T.:* 61352. [*Died* 17 *Aug.* 1956.

SMITH, Sir Ernest (Woodhouse), Kt., *cr.* 1947; C.B.E. 1930; D.Sc., F.R.I.C., M.Inst. Gas E.; F.Inst.F.; Fuel Consultant (Retd.); *b.* 13 Feb. 1884; *s.* of Rev. H. B. Smith, Unitarian Minister; *m.* Beatrice Arnfield (*d.* 1955), Dolgelley; one *s.* one *d.* *Educ.:* Arnold School, Blackpool; Victoria Univ. of Manchester. Chemist to Gold Dredging Co. in Saskatchewan, 1907-08: Research Chemist to Institution of Gas Engineers, Leeds Univ., 1908-10; Research Chemist in charge of Industrial Gas Laboratories, Birmingham Corporation, Chief Chemist, City of Birmingham Gas Dept., 1912-20; Technical Director of the Woodall Duckham Cos., 1920-44; Technical Adviser to Area Gas Supply Committee of Board of Trade, 1929; Hon. Secretary to World Power Fuel Conference, 1928; on Council of a number of technical institutions; Chairman, Society of British Gas Industries, 1931-32, Pres., 1954. Director-General of Gas Supply, Ministry of Fuel, 1942-43; Pres. Inst. of Fuel, 1943-45; Technical Adviser to District Valuation Boards of Coal Industry (Coke Ovens), 1949-56. Chairman Industrial Coal Consumers Council, 1947-57; formerly Hon. Treas. Smoke Abatement Soc. (Pres. 1954-56); Pres. Fuel Luncheon Club, 1955-57; Pres. Effingham Golf and Cricket Clubs. *Publications:* many technical papers. *Recreation:* golf. *Address:* Higham Cottage, Effingham, Surrey. *T.:* Bookham 529. *Club:* Effingham Golf. [*Died* 7 *Nov.* 1960.

SMITH, E. W.; *see* Whitney-Smith.

SMITH, Frank, M.A., B.Sc., Ph.D.; Professor of Education, Leeds University, 1933 - 47, Pro - Vice - Chancellor 1945 - 47; *b.* Macclesfield, 28 Sept. 1882; *y. s.* of late Matthew Smith; *m.* Evelyn Prichard Moore, A.R.M.C.M., of Langley, Macclesfield; one *d.* *Educ.:* Manchester University; Emmanuel College, Cambridge. Assistant Master at the West Bromwich Secondary School, the Fielden Schools (Manchester University), and Sir John Deane's Grammar School, Northwich; Lecturer in Education, University College of Wales, Aberystwyth; Professor of Education, Armstrong College, Newcastle - upon - Tyne. *Publications:* Life and Work of Sir James Kay-Shuttleworth; The Bilingual Problem (in collaboration); A History of English Elementary Education, 1760-1902; Principles of Class Teaching (joint); many articles and reviews to psychological and educational papers. *Recreations:* walking, skating, golf. *Address:* 76 Moorside, Fenham, Newcastle-upon-Tyne, 4. *T.:* 33996. [*Died* 11 *April* 1951.

SMITH, Ven. Geoffry Bertram; Archdeacon of Surrey since Oct. 1955; *b.* 28 June 1889; 4th *s.* of Charles Smith, M.A., Master of Sidney Sussex College, Cambridge, 1890-1916; *m.* 1917, Chrysogon, *d.* of Henry Blenkarne Beale; two *s.* *Educ.:* Blundell's School. Entered R.N. as Cadet, H.M.S. Britannia, 1904; retired with rank of Capt., 1935. Sec., Guildford New Cathedral and Churches Fund, 1935-37; Westcott House, Cambridge, 1938; deacon, 1938; Asst. Curate of Headley, Hants., 1938-39; priest, 1939; Temp. Chaplain, R.N.V.R., 1939-45; Vicar of Tilford, Surrey, 1945-55; Rural Dean of Farnham, 1954-55. *Publication:* The Christian Faith in Brief, 1942. *Recreations:* gardening and music. *Address:* Kingsbury, 51 Ridgway Road, Farnham, Surrey. *T.:* Farnham 5889. *Clubs:* R.N.V.R.; County (Guildford). [*Died* 23 *July* 1957.

SMITH, George, M.A. (Edin. and Oxon); *b.* Ayr, 15 July 1867; *m.* 1895, *d.* of Rev. Andrew Edgar, D.D.; one *s.* one *d.* (and one *s.* one *d.* decd.). *Educ.:* Ayr Academy; Edinburgh University (1st class Classics, 1888); Trinity College, Oxford (scholar, 1st class Mods. 1889; 1st class Lit. Hum. 1891). Assistant Master at Rugby School, 1892-98; Headmaster, Merchiston Castle, Edinburgh, 1898-1914; Master of Dulwich College, 1914-28; Director of Department of Education, Oxford University, 1928-37. *Address:* 10 Lathbury Road, Oxford. *T.:* 55253. [*Died* 29 *Jan.* 1957.

SMITH, George Frederick Herbert, C.B.E. 1949; M.A., D.Sc., F.R.A.S.; *b.* 26 May 1872; *er. s.* of late Rev. George Smith, M.A., Rector of Hormead, Herts; *m.* 1903, Rosalie Mary Agnes (*d.* 1936), *y. d.* of late John Ellerton, Leamington Spa; one *d.* *Educ.:* Winchester Coll.; New Coll., Oxford (Scholar); University of Munich. 1st class Moderations, Mathematics; 1st class Finals, Mathematics; 1st class Natural Science Finals, Physics: British Museum (Natural History); Assistant, Mineral Department, 1897; Assistant Sec., 1921; Sec., 1931; Keeper of Minerals, 1935-37; Mineralogical Society, Council, 1902-05, 1907-10, 1911-14, 1916-19, 1921-24, 1926-29, 1937-40; Vice-President, 1929-32; Examiner in mineralogy, Natural Sciences Tripos, Cambridge, 1903-4, 1909-10; Principal examiner in gemmology, Gemmological Association of Great Britain, 1913-51, and President since 1942; Hon. Sec. Society for Promotion of Nature Reserves since 1921; Chairman, Wild Plant Conservation Board since 1931; British delegate, International Congress for Protection of Nature, Paris, 1931; British deleg. Internat. Conf. for Protection of Nature, Brunnen, 1947; U.K. delegate and Chm. Juridicial Cttee., Internat. Conference for the establishment of the Internat. Union for the Protection of Nature, Fontainebleau, 1948; Vice-Pres., Internat. Union for Protection of Nature since 1950; Hon. Sec., British Co-ordinating Committee for Nature Conservation since 1949; Chairman U.K. deleg., Gen. Assembly session, Internat. Union for the Protection of Nature, Brussels, 1950; Council of National Trust since 1934; National Forest Park Advisory Committee (England and Wales), 1938; Galapagos Committee of British Association for the Advancement of Science, 1936-39, President of Conf. of Delegates of Corresponding Societies, 1949; Internat. Cttee. for Bird Preservation since 1947; Council of Royal Albert Hall since 1930; Finance Cttee., 1940-1951, Chm., Executive Cttee., 1941-42; Hon. Secretary Conference on Nature Preservation in Post-War Reconstruction, 1941-43 and Nature Reserves Investigation Cttee., 1942-47; Civil Service Sports Council since 1921, Chairman Publicity Cttee. since 1946, Hon. Life Member, 1948; Hon. Sec.-Treas., Civil Service Arts Council, 1924-39; Society of Civil Servants, Joint Hon. Sec., 1918-25; Vice-Pres., 1925-28; Pres., 1928-32; Editor of The Quill, 1923-30, and of Natural History Magazine, 1927-36. *Publications:* Gemstones, 1912; 12th ed. 1952; numerous articles on crystallographical subjects and nature conservation. *Recreations:* reading, music, motoring. *Address:* 9 Ellerton Road, S.W.18. *T.:* Battersea 1100. *Club:* Athenæum. [*Died* 20 *April* 1953.

SMITH, George Geoffrey, M.B.E. 1917; Director of Associated Iliffe Press Ltd., Iliffe and Sons Ltd., Louis Cassier Co. Ltd., and Plastics Press Ltd., Dorset House, Stamford Street, S.E.1; *b.* 4 March 1885; *m.* 1st, 1913, Margaret Cicely Butt (*d.* 1927); two *s.*; 2nd, 1935, Joan Edith Amelia Arnull; one *d.* Joined Iliffe and Sons Ltd., 1904; Edited The Motor Cycle, 1912-15; Inspectind Officer, M.M.G.S., 1915-16; Special letter of thanks by Army Council for honorary war work; R.F.C., 1917; Captain R.A.F., 1918-1919. Served on several Govt. cttees. during War of 1939-45, including Chairmanship of Technical & Trade Press Advisory Panel of Min. of Labour and Nat. Service and Min. of Production. Located in America, 1944-45, at Govt. invitation and attached to British Information Services to disseminate information on British technical achievements. Member of Admiralty, W.O., Air Min. and Press Cttee. Managing Editor of The Autocar, The Motor Cycle, Motor Transport, The Automobile Engineer, Flight, Aircraft Production, Bus and Coach, British Plastics, The Architect, etc.; Freeman of City of London; Liveryman of the Worshipful Company of Coachmakers and Coach Harness Makers of London; Life Governor of The Hospital for Sick Children; Cttee. Royal Automobile Club; Vice-President Auto Cycle Union; Member Newcomen Society; Member of Gas Turbine Co-ordinating Cttee. of the Amer. Soc. of Mech. Engineers; Past Pres. of Circle of Aviation Writers. *Publications:* Gas Turbines and Jet Propulsion (5 edns.); The Modern Diesel (11 edns.); several technical handbooks on automobile and aircraft subjects. *Recreations:* golf, shooting, motor mountaineering, and photography. *Address:* Pembury, The Avenue, Radlett, Herts. *T.:* Radlett 6102. *Clubs:* Royal Automobile; Royal Scottish Automobile (Glasgow); Porters Pk. Golf (Radlett). [*Died* 29 *June* 1951.

SMITH, Colonel Sir Gilbertson, Kt., *cr.* 1946; T.D.; D.L. Essex; Senior Partner Miller & Smiths, 14 Pall Mall, S.W.1; Director and Life Governor (Chairman 1940-1955), Crusader Insurance Co. Ltd.; *b.* 16 Oct. 1867; *s.* of Henry John Smith, Solicitor and Town Clerk, Lambeth; *m.* 1894, Isabel Emily (*d.* 1954), *d.* of Henry Harwyn Tolcher; two *s.* *Educ.:* Dulwich College; Germany. Admitted Solicitor, 1890. Served in 26th Middlesex Cyclist V.R.C., 1888-1908; 25th Cyclist Battalion London Regt., 1908-13; 2/25th Cyclist Battalion, London Regt., 1914-19 (despatches); Col. T.A. 1918. County Council Essex, 1913; Alderman, 1925; Chairman, 1941-46; D.L. Essex, 1929. *Recreation:* cycling. *Address:* Cornwalls, Brentwood, Essex. *T.:* Brentwood 178. *Club:* Junior Carlton. [*Died* 17 *Feb.* 1958.

SMITH, Rt. Rev. Guy Vernon, D.D. Lambeth, 1940; M.C. 1917; *b.* 15 Oct. 1880; *s.* of late Vernon Russell Smith, K.C., and late E. Gertrude, *d.* of late Charles Henry Lovell. *Educ.:* Winchester; New College, Oxford (B.A. 1902, 2nd Class Mod. History; M.A. 1906). Called to Bar, Lincoln's Inn, 1905; Wells Theological College; Deacon, 1906; Priest, 1907; Curate of Romford, 1906-9; Chaplain of Oxford House, Bethnal Green, 1909-11; Resident Chaplain to the Bishop of London, 1911-18; Hon. Chaplain, 1918-29; Secretary of Service Candidates Committee, 1919; Deputy Priest in Ordinary to the King, 1914-16; Priest in Ordinary, 1916-19; Army Chaplain, 1914-18; Rector of Hackney, 1919-25; Archdeacon of Colombo and Incumbent of St. Peter's Church, Colombo, 1925-29; Bishop Suffragan of Willesden, 1929-40; Rector of St. Andrew Undershaft, 1934-40; Bishop of Leicester, 1940-53; Officer's Cross of the Royal Order of the Redeemer, 1918. *Address:* 17 The Close, Salisbury, Wilts. [*Died* 11 *June* 1957.

SMITH, Harold Clifford, M.A., F.S.A.; former Keeper at the Victoria and Albert Museum, South Kensington; *b.* London, 7 July 1876; *e. s.* of late A. Clifford Smith and *g. s.* of Sir William Smith, D.C.L., LL.D., F.S.A.; *m.* 1925, Gladys (*d.* 1957), *d.* of late John Beattie Crozier, LL.D. *Educ.:* Bradfield College; University College, Oxford (B.A. 1898, M.A. 1902); Slade School, University College, London (1899-1900). Assistant National Art Library, Victoria and Albert Museum, 1900; transferred to Department of Woodwork, 1910; Assistant Keeper, 1922; Deputy Keeper, 1934; Keeper, 1935-1936: retired, 1936; Inspector of Furniture and Works of Art at Chequers since 1921; Member of Council, Society of Antiquaries of London, 1913-14; Member of the Board of Governors, and Hon. Historian, Sulgrave Manor, Northants, 1923; Member of the Governing Body, Dr. Johnson's House, Gough Square, E.C., 1929, Trustee, 1940; Member of Executive Committee, National Art-Collections Fund, 1929-32; Member of Executive Committee, Georgian Group, 1937; Member of Council, Kensington Soc., 1953. Lecturer at Victoria and Albert Museum, London County Council, Royal Institution, University College, London, Royal Society of Arts, with the assistance of Her Late Majesty Queen Mary, on the original furniture and equipment of Buckingham Palace, and lecturer, among other subjects on the original equipment of the Royal Pavilion, Brighton. *Publications:* Jewellery, 1908; The Goldsmith and the Young Couple, 1915; Buckingham Palace, its Furniture, Decoration and History, 1931; Sulgrave Manor and the Washingtons, 1933; Marble Hill House, Twickenham, Middlesex, 1939; English Furniture Illustrated (new ed. of Oliver Brackett's Encyc. of English Furniture), 1950; The Mansion House, London, 1956; Official Publications (Victoria and Albert Museum): The Bromley Room, 1914; The Inlaid Room from Sizergh Castle, 1915; Catalogue of English Gothic Furniture, 1923; The Waltham Abbey Room, 1924; Catalogue of Late Tudor and Early Stuart Furniture, 1930; The Haynes Grange Room, 1935. Papers in the Proceedings of the Society of Antiquaries and Antiquaries Journal; contributor to Bryan's Dictionary of Painters and Engravers, The Dictionary of English Furniture, and frequent contributor to periodicals and art magazines including Country Life, The Burlington, The Connoisseur, Apollo and others. *Address:* c/o Westminster Bank, 1 Kensington High Street, W.8. *Club:* Athenæum. [*Died* 14 *Feb.* 1960.

SMITH, Harold Octavius, C.B.E. 1943; Director Imperial Chemical Industries Ltd., 1936-51; *b.* 21 July 1882; 4th *s.* of Sir George Smith, Treliske, Truro, Cornwall; *m.* 1911, Maude Eleanor Mary Martyn; one *s.* *Educ.:* Leys School, Cambridge. Director, Bickford Smith & Co. Ltd., 1915-19; Chairman I.C.I. Metals Ltd., 1930-36; Controller Small Arms Ammunition, Ministry of Supply, 1940-41; Director General Ammunition Production, Ministry of Supply, 1941-42. *Recreation:* golf. *Address:* Mattingley Lodge, Basingstoke. *T.A.* and *T.:* Heckfield 56. *Club:* Bath. [*Died* 17 *May* 1952.

SMITH, Harold Ross, C.B. 1950; Secretary, Department of Health for Scotland since Nov. 1953; *b.* 25 May 1906; *s.* of William Allan Smith, Dunfermline, Fife, and Margaret Ross; *m.* 1935, Mary Margaret Penney; one *s.* *Educ.:* Dunfermline High School; University of Edinburgh. Entered Scottish Office, 1932; Assistant Solicitor, Dept. of Health for Scotland, 1937; Assistant Secretary, 1941-46; Under-Secretary, 1946-1948; Assistant Under-Secretary of State for Scotland, 1948-53. *Recreation:* golf. *Address:* 29 Greenhill Gardens, Edinburgh. *T.:* Edinburgh 57180. *Club:* Caledonian. [*Died* 3 *Feb.* 1956.

SMITH, Major-General Sir Harry Reginald Walter Marriott, K.C.B., *cr.* 1942 (C.B. 1933); C.B.E. 1928; D.S.O. 1916; D.L., J.P.; *b.* Chagford, 1 Aug. 1875; *s.* of late Col. W. W. Marriott Smith, C.B.E.; *m.* 1906, Dorothy Herbert, *d.* of H. Herbert Smith, J.P., of Buckhill, Calne; no *c.* *Educ.:* Elstree; Repton (Exhibitioner 1889, Scholar 1890); Royal Military Acad., Woolwich. 2nd Lt. R.A. 1895; Col. 1921; Maj.-Gen. 1932; served Nile expedition and battle of Omdurman, 1898 (two medals, clasp); S. African War, 1899-1902 (despatches, Queen's medal 3 clasps, King's medal 2 clasps); European War, 1914; battles of the Marne, the Aisne, and the first battle of Ypres, and in the Dardanelles July 1915 to evacuation in Jan. (wounded, D.S.O.); battles of the Somme (wounded) and of Arras; licensed lay reader in the dioceses of Sarum; Deputy-Director of Armaments in India, Sept. 1919-23; Assistant Director of Artillery, War Office, 1924-27; Director of Artillery, War Office, 1927-30; A.D.C. to the King, 1930-32; Vice-President Ordnance Committee, 1930-32; President 1932-34; retired pay, 1934; Governor of Repton School, 1935; Chairman Dorset Territorial Army Assoc., 1937-42; Hon. Col. 94th Field Regiment R.A. 1939-44; Commander Dorset Home Guard to 1942. *Publication:* History of the 13th Battery R.F.A. *Address:* Wareham House, Dorchester. *T.:* Dorchester 202. *Club:* Army and Navy. [*Died* 3 *Nov.* 1955.

SMITH, Harvey Hall; *b.* 12 Sept. 1880; 2nd *s.* of late John Smith, architect, Aberdeen; unmarried. *Educ.:* Robert Gordon's College, Aberdeen. Entered service of North of Scotland Bank, 1895; Secretary, 1920; General Manager, 1922-43. *Address:* Ingleside, West Cults, Aberdeenshire. *Club:* Royal Northern (Aberdeen). [*Died* 5 *Oct.* 1958.

SMITH, Helen Gregory, C.B.E. 1932; R.R.C. 1916; R.G.N. 1922; *d.* of late Henry

G. C. Smith, Edinburgh, and late Camilla Baxter, Edinburgh. *Educ.:* George Watson's Ladies' College, Edinburgh; the Grange Collegiate School, Edinburgh. Trained Western Infirmary of Glasgow, 1896-99; Home Sister and Assistant Matron, Western Infirmary of Glasgow, 1900-4; Lady Superintendent, Dumfries and Galloway Royal Infirmary, 1904-6; Principal Matron, T.A.N.S., 3rd Scottish General Hospital, 1908-33; Matron, The Western Infirmary of Glasgow, 1906-33; Member of Queen Alexandra's Army Nursing Board, 1918-33; Pres., Scottish Matron's Association, 1925-33; President, The Benevolent Fund for Nurses in Scotland, 1925-33; Member of the Council of the College of Nursing, London, 1928-37; Member of the "Nurses' Memorial to King Edward VII" Committees, Edinburgh and Glasgow; Member of the Consultative Council on Medical and Allied Services, Department of Health for Scotland, 1932-38. *Address:* Yondercott, Budleigh Salterton, S. Devon. *T.:* Budleigh 361.
[*Died* 30 *April* 1956.

SMITH, Henry Bompas, M.A. Oxon; M.Ed. Man.; *b.* Hull, 1867; *s.* of Rev. J. Frederick Smith; *m.* 1902, Ethel (*d.* 1949), *d.* of John Grant; one *s.* one *d.* *Educ.:* Jena; Mansfield; Wadham College, Oxford (scholar). Assistant Master at Shrewsbury; Headmaster of Queen Mary's School, Walsall, and King Edward VII. School, Lytham; Professor of Education and Director of the Department of Education, University of Manchester; now Professor Emeritus. *Publications:* Boys and their Management in School; The Nation's Schools, 1926; Growing Minds, 1937. *Address:* Belfield, Hollington Park, St. Leonards on Sea, Sussex.
[*Died* 17 *Sept.* 1953.

SMITH, Sir Henry Moncrieff, Kt., *cr.* 1923; C.I.E.; I.C.S. (retired); *b.* 23 Dec. 1873; one *d.* *Educ.:* Blundell's School, Tiverton; Sidney Sussex College, Cambridge. I.C.S. 1897: posted to U.P. as Assistant Commissioner: District and Sessions Judge, 1908; U.P. Govt. Secretariat, 1914: Deputy Secretary Govt. of India Legislative Dept., 1915; Joint Secretary, 1919; Secretary, 1921; Secretary of the Council of State, 1921-23, and of the Legislative Assembly, 1921-24; President of the Council of State and of the Statute Law Revision Committee, 1924-32; Chairman Indian Red Cross Society and St. John Ambulance Association, and Chief Commissioner for the Empire of India of the St John Ambulance Brigade Overseas; Chairman of the British Empire Leprosy Relief Association (Indian Council), of the Council of the Countess of Dufferin's Fund, and of the Victoria Memorial Scholarship Fund; Deputy Chairman, Indian Round Table Conference Consultative Committee, 1932; Knight of Grace of St. John of Jerusalem. *Address:* Dunmow House, Dunmow Hill, Fleet, Hants.
[*Died* 21 *Nov.* 1951.

SMITH, Herbert; *b.* London, 13 March 1881; *s.* of John Innes Smith and Isa Ewen; *m.* 1910, Agnes Gibson, *d.* of S. Laird, Broughty Ferry; two *s.* *Educ.:* Harris Academy, Dundee; University of St. Andrews (M.A. 1903, Guthrie Scholar); University of Marburg (Ph.D. 1907). English Lektor in Marburg, 1904-7; Lecturer in German, University of Glasgow, 1907-19; William Jacks Professor of Germanic Languages, Univ. of Glasgow, until 1951. *Publications:* New Mozartiana, 1936 (with Dr. H. G. Farmer); articles and reviews in Modern Language Review, and elsewhere. *Recreations:* music, golf, fishing. *Address:* c/o The University, Glasgow.
[*Died* 15 *Feb.* 1953.

SMITH, Brigadier Hubert Clementi, D.S.O. 1915; *b.* 12 Aug. 1878; *m.* 1909, Kathleen Margaret (*d.* 1935), *o. c.* of Sir Harry S. C. Clarke Jervoise, 5th Bt.; one *s.* three *d.* Entered Army, 1898; Capt. 1907; Major, 1914; Lt.-Colonel, 1920; Colonel, 1923; Asst. Director of Army Signals, Aldershot, 1910-11; Instructor Army Signal School, 1913-14; Asst. Director Army Signals, France, 1914-16: Directing Staff, Staff College, 1919-20; General Staff War Office, 1921-25; Headquarters, Aldershot Command, 1925-26; Commandant Signal Training Centre, Catterick Camp, 1926-30; Signal Officer-in-Chief, A.H.Q., India, 1930-34; retired pay, 1934; re-employed, 1939-42; Col. Comdt., Royal Corps of Signals, 1934-44; served South Africa, 1900-2 (Queen's medal 4 clasps; King's medal 2 clasps); European War, 1914-18 (despatches four times, D.S.O., Bt. Lt.-Col., Officier Légion d'Honneur, Croix de Guerre). *Address:* Church Lane Cottage, Houghton, Stockbridge, Hants. *T.:* Kings Somborne 219. *Club:* United Service.
[*Died* 16 *Aug.* 1958.

SMITH, Brig. Hugh G. S.; *see* Seth-Smith.

SMITH, J. Allister; Commissioner of the Salvation Army; retired; Governor of the Hadleigh Land Colony; *b.* Elgin, Scotland, 1866; *m.* Elizabeth Whitfield, Salvation Army Officer; two *s.* three *d.* (and one *s.* decd.). Entered the Salvation Army as an Officer in England, 1887; worked thirty years as a Missionary amongst native tribes of South and East Africa; pioneer of Salvation Army in Zululand and in Kenya; International Travelling Representative, 1922; admitted to Order of the Founder; visited Nigeria and Gold Coast on a special mission for the Salvation Army, 1937; also visited Holland in 1938 as a representative of International Headquarters of Salvation Army. *Publications:* a Missionary Book, Zulu Crusade; A Zulu Apostle, 1953. *Address:* 9 Burnside Road, Tamboer's Kloof, Cape Town, South Africa. [*Died* 26 *July* 1960.

SMITH, Colonel James Aubrey, C.B. 1937; C.M.G. 1919; *b.* 21 Oct. 1877; *s.* of late James Alfred Smith, Swansea; *m.* 1905 Margaret Grace, *d.* of G. H. H. Hunter, Swansea; one *s.* Served European War, 1914-19 (despatches twice, C.M.G., Legion of Honour, Croix de Guerre, Order of Agricultural Merit of France); Inspector of Army Educational Corps, 1921-37; retired pay, 1937. *Club:* Junior Army and Navy. [*Died* 10 *Sept.* 1955.

SMITH, J(ohn) G(uthrie) Spence, R.S.A. 1939 (A.R.S.A. 1930); artist painter; *b.* Perth, 14 Feb. 1880; *s.* of late Joseph Smith, merchant; unmarried. *Educ.:* Dundee; Edinburgh. Received art training at the School of Art, Edinburgh, and the Royal Scottish Academy School, where he took some prizes; has painted in the Highlands of Scotland and North of France; exhibited in R.S.A., Glasgow Royal Institute and Provincial Exhibitions. *Recreations:* billiards and walking. *Address:* 38 Drummond Place, Edinburgh. *Club:* Scottish Arts (Edinburgh).
[*Died* 22 *Oct.* 1951.

SMITH, Sir John James, Kt., *cr.* 1927; Past President Romford Division, Conservative Association; Capt. late 17th Batt. London Regt.; Pres. Essex Agricultural Soc. 1925; *b.* 21 Aug. 1875; *e. s.* of late John Smith, J.P., L.C.C., Dundee and London; *m.* 1904, Margaret Langley (*d.* 1944), 2nd *d.* of late Samuel Hillyard Loake, Romford; *m.* 1946, Maud Mary Hillyard Loake. *Address:* Kendal Court, 19 Hartland Road, Epping, Essex. [*Died* 21 *Oct.* 1957.

SMITH, K. W. A., B.Sc.; *b.* Exeter, 20 Oct. 1899; *s.* of William and Sarah Rayner Smith; *m.* 1927, Edith Winifred Rutt; two *s.* one *d.* *Educ.:* Prince Alfred College and University of Adelaide. Assistant Master at Prince Alfred College for 8 years; Senior Mathematical Master and Sports Master at King's College, 1924; Second Master, 1928; Headmaster, King's College, Adelaide, 1933-42; Senior Master in Mathematics at Prince Alfred College, Adelaide, 1942-50; Member of Mathematical Assoc. (England). *Recreations:*

bowls and reading. *Address:* Prince Alfred College, Adelaide, S.A.; 46 Myall Av. Kensington Gdns., S.A. [*Died* 15 *Aug.* 1951.

SMITH, Sir Keith Macpherson, K.B.E., *cr.* 1919; F.R.G.S. 1921; F.R.Ae.S. 1925; M.Inst.T. 1938; Aviator; joined Aviation Dept. of Vickers, Ltd., 1923; their general representative in Australia since 1924; *b.* Adelaide, South Australia, 20 Dec. 1890; Scottish parents; *m.* 1924, Anita, *d.* of D. H. Smith, Adelaide. *Educ.:* S. Australia and Scotland. Spent early life on a sheep station; served European War 1914-18, with R.F.C. and R.A.F. 1917-19 as a pilot and flying instructor (despatches); accompanied brother on first flight out to Australia, Nov.-Dec. 1919. *Recreation:* golf. *Address:* 247 George Street, Sydney, Australia. *Clubs:* Royal Air Force; Australian (Sydney); Australian (Melbourne). [*Died* 19 *Dec.* 1955.

SMITH, Capt. Sir Lindsey, Kt., *cr.* 1914; J.P.; *b.* 12 Nov. 1870; *s.* of H. J. Smith, Town Clerk of Lambeth, and Mary, *d.* of William Willis of Somerset House; *m.* 1902, Elsie Eveleyn, (*d.* 1948), 2nd *d.* of David Johnson, F.R.G.S., F.C.S.; one *d.* *Educ.:* Dulwich Coll.; Switzerland. Entered Middle Temple, 1889; awarded 2nd class scholarship in Common Law and Criminal Law, 1891; 2nd class scholarship in Real and Personal Law, 1891; and 1st class scholarship in Common Law and Criminal Law, 1892; called to Bar, 1892; became member of Oxford Circuit and Staffordshire and Wolverhampton Sessions; acted as Deputy Recorder for Sandwich, 1899-1901; one of the assistant editors of the Yearly Supreme Court Practice and Stone's Justices' Manual, 1901; Assistant Judge, Zanzibar, and Judge of High Court for East Africa, 1901; Member of Court of Appeal for Eastern Africa, 1902; Acting Judge H.B.M. Court, Zanzibar, April-Oct. 1902; Judge, 1904; President of H.M. Court of Appeal for Eastern Africa, 1904-09; Acting Judge, Supreme Court of China and Korea, 1909; Judge, High Court, Weihaiwai, 1909-10; late Chief Justice of Zanzibar; Hon. Sec. Wounded Allies Relief Committee, 1915-1917; Hon. Capt. attached to General Staff, 1917-19; Judge H.B.M. Supreme Court for the Ottoman Dominions, 1921; Asst. Commissioner for Zanzibar British Empire Exhibition, 1924-25; Member of Departmental Committee on Mental Deficiency Colonies, 1930-31; Chairman Court of Referees (Ministry of Labour), 1930-37; Chairman Italian Hospital, 1930-31; Chairman House Committee West London Hospital, 1927-37; Asst. Chairman Surrey Quarter Sessions, 1933-35, Deputy Chairman, 1935-39; Chairman Surrey Rating Appeal Committee, 1934-39; Trustee and Chairman Board of Governors, Holloway Sanatorium, 1922-48; Member of Executive Council of Federated Superannuation Scheme for Nurses; has Orders of Brilliant Star, Zanzibar, The Crown, Belgium, The Crown, Italy, St. Saba, Serbia, St. John of Jerusalem. *Publication:* Thomas Holloway and his Work. *Address:* 68 Lexham Gardens, W.8. *T.:* Fremantle 2248. [*Died* 8 *March* 1960.

SMITH, Lionel G. H. H.; *see* Horton-Smith.

SMITH, Mary Sybil, M.A. Cambridge, Ph.D., London; Headmistress of King Edward's High School for Girls, Birmingham; *d.* of George Smith, *q.v.* *Educ.:* St. Leonards School, St. Andrews; Girton College, Cambridge. Past Pres. Assoc. of Head Mistresses. *Address:* King Edward's High School for Girls, Edgbaston Park Road, Birmingham 15. [*Died* 16 *Dec.* 1952.

SMITH, Sir Matthew (Arnold Bracy), Kt., *cr.* 1954; C.B.E. 1949; D.Lit. (London), 1956; A.R.C.A. 1951; Artist; Member of London Group; *b.* Halifax, Yorkshire, 1879. *Educ.:* Giggleswick; Manchester School of Art; Slade School. Visited Paris, 1910. Has painted in the South of France. Recently has been living in England, and has a studio in Chelsea. Has given one-man art shows, including one at Tate Gallery, 1953. Works include: Self-portrait, 1909; La Chemise Noire, 1926; Portraits of Augustus John. Has paintings in many public galleries and private collections, including England, Canada, America, Australia, and several paintings in the Tate Gallery. *Address:* c/o The Mayor Gallery, 14 Brook Street, W.1. [*Died* 29 *Sept.* 1959.

SMITH, Norman Kemp, M.A., D.Phil., Hon. LL.D. (St. Andrews and Glasgow); Hon. D.Litt. (Durham); F.B.A.; Professor of Logic and Metaphysics, Univ. of Edinburgh, 1919-1945; *b.* 1872; *m.* 1910, Amy (*d.* 1936), *d.* of Francis Kemp, Manchester; one *d.* *Educ.:* St. Andrews University; studied in Berlin and Paris. Lecturer in Glasgow University, 1897-1906; Professor of Psychology, Princeton University, 1906; M'Cosh Professor of Philosophy, Princeton, 1914; served in the Department of Information, 1916-18; Mills Lecturer, University of California, 1923. *Publications:* Studies in the Cartesian Philosophy; A Commentary to Kant's Critique of Pure Reason; Prolegomena to an Idealist Theory of Knowledge; a translation of Kant's Critique of Pure Reason; Hume's Dialogues concerning Natural Religion; The Philosophy of David Hume; New Studies in the Philosophy of Descartes; a translation of Descarte's Philosophical Writings. *Address:* 14 Kilgraston Road, Edinburgh. *T.:* Edinburgh 41945. [*Died* 3 *Sept.* 1958.

SMITH, Sir Osborne Arkell, K.C.S.I., *cr.* 1937; K.C.I.E., *cr.*1932; Kt., *cr.* 1929; Ex-Managing Governor, Imperial Bank of India; *b.* 26 Dec. 1876; *s.* of Harry Arkell Smith; two *d.* *Educ.:* Sydney Grammar School. Late Governor of Reserve Bank of India; retired. *Recreations:* golf, tennis, cricket. *Address:* Imperial Bank of India, 25 Old Broad Street, E.C.2. *Clubs:* Overseas League; Royal Calcutta Turf (Calcutta). [*Died* 30 *Aug.* 1952.

SMITH, Owen Hugh; 2nd *s.* of Hugh Colin Smith and Constance, *d.* of Henry J. Adeane of Babraham, Cambridge; *m.* Emmeline, *d.* of Eustace Abel Smith, of Longnills, Lincoln; two *d.* *Educ.:* Eton; Trinity Coll., Cambridge. In business. *Recreations:* hunting, fishing, gardening. *Address:* 39 Charles St., W.1. *T.:* Grosvenor 1477; Old Hall, Langham, Oakham, Rutland. *T.:* Langham 23. *Clubs:* Brooks's, Garrick. [*Died* 9 *Jan.* 1958.

SMITH, Owen Maurice, C.B. 1948; *b.* 27 Nov. 1888; *s.* of Harry Smith, Montreal, Canada, and Mary Ann Ethel Smith (*née* Sweet); *m.* 1914, Eleanor, *y. d.* of James Howie and Elizabeth Macfarlane; one *s.* *Educ.:* Christ's Hospital. Entered Civil Service, 1908; first appointment to War Office; transferred to Estate Duty Office, 1910; to National Health Insurance Commission (England), 1912; to Ministry of Health, 1919; to Ministry of National Insurance, as Accountant-General, 1944; Under-Secretary, Ministry of National Insurance, 1946-52. *Address:* Courtland, Embercourt Road, Thames Ditton, Surrey. *T.:* Emberbrook 3243. [*Died* 15 *March* 1957.

SMITH, Maj.-Gen. Richard T. S.; *see* Snowden-Smith.

SMITH, Sir Robert; *see* Smith, Sir C. R.

SMITH, Sir Robert Workman, 1st Bt., *cr.* 1945; Kt., *cr.* 1934; *b.* 7 Dec. 1880; *y. s.* of late George Smith, shipowner, Glasgow; *m.* 1911, Jessie Hill, *y. d.* of late William Workman, Belfast; two *s.* *Educ.:* privately; Trinity Coll., Cambridge. B.A.; Barrister-at-law, Inner Temple; contested Aberdeen and Kincardine Central, 1922-23; M.P. (C.) Aberdeen and Kincardine Central Division, 1924-45; J.P. County of Aberdeen; R.A.S.C., 1917-19. *Recreations:* yachting, shooting, fishing. *Heir: s.* Lt.-Comdr.

William Gordon, R.N.V.R. [*b.* 1916; *m.* 1941, Diana Gundreda, *d.* of late Maj. C. H. Malden, R.M.L.I.]. *Address:* Crowmallie, Pitcaple, Aberdeenshire. *Clubs:* Carlton, Bath, Royal Yacht Squadron, Royal Thames Yacht; New (Edinburgh); Royal Northern (Aberdeen); Royal Northern Yacht. [*Died* 6 *Dec.* 1957.

SMITH, Rt. Rev. Rocksborough Remington, M.A. (Cantab.); B.A. (Lond.); D.D. King's College, Halifax, Nova Scotia, 1925; *b.* Brighton, 30 November 1872; *s.* of Rocksborough Smith, Elm Grove, Brighton; *m.* 1909, Marjorie, *d.* of E. Lipscombe, Teddington; two *s.* *Educ.:* St. Mark's College, Chelsea; Selwyn Coll., Cambridge (Scholar); Salisbury Theological College; B.A. 1899, 1st Class Theological Tripos; 1st Class Part II. 1900; 1st Jeremie Septuagint Prize, 1897; Carus Greek Testament Prize, 1898; Steel University Student, 1899; University Hebrew Prize, 1900. Deacon, 1900; Priest, 1901; Lecturer at Ordsall Hall, Manchester, 1900; Vice-Principal Salisbury Theological College, 1901; M.A. 1902; Principal Clergy House, Wimbledon, 1903; Principal Diocesan High School for Europeans, Rangoon, 1909; Representative of Burma, Govt. of India Education Conference, Simla, 1912; Delhi Durbar Medal, 1912; Captain Rangoon Volunteer Rifles, 1910; Vicar of Broadstone, Dorset, 1914; Harrold Professor, Dean of Divinity, and Vice-Principal, University of Lennoxville, P. Quebec, 1921; Examining Chaplain, Bishop of Quebec, 1924; Bishop of Algoma, 1926-40; Secretary of Church Union, 1940-1943; Rector of Lapford, 1943, resigned, 1952; Assistant Bishop of Exeter, 1947-52. Silver Jubilee Medal, 1935; Coronation Medal, 1937. *Publications:* The Epistle of St. Paul's First Trial, 1899; Christianity in the Home, 1933. *Address:* 34 St. Keyna Avenue, Hove, 3, Sussex. *T.:* Hove 46140. [*Died* 5 *March* 1955.

SMITH, Sir Rudolph H.; *see* Smith, Sir T. R. H.

SMITH, Sheila K.; *see* Kaye-Smith.

SMITH, Sidney Earle, P.C., Q.C. (Can.); M.P.; M.A., LL.D., D.C.L., D.Litt., F.R.S.C.; Secretary of State for External Affairs since 1957; *b.* 9 March 1897; *s.* of John Parker Smith, Port Hood, N.S., and Margaret Jane Smith (*née* Etheridge), Margaree, N.S.; *m.* 1926, Harriet Rand; three *d.* *Educ.:* Port Hood Academy; King's College; Dalhousie University; Harvard University. B.A. 1915, M.A. 1919, King's; LL.B. 1920, Dalhousie. LL.D.: Queen's, 1937; Manitoba, 1945; Ottawa, 1947; Laval, 1947; Dalhousie, 1948; Cambridge, 1948; Western Ontario, 1953; Aberdeen, 1953; McMaster, 1954; Princeton, 1956; British Columbia, 1956; New Brunswick, 1957; Dartmouth, 1957; Columbia, 1958; Brown, 1958; Toronto, 1958; D.C.L.: King's, 1939; Acadia, 1940; Bishop's, 1942; Mount Allison, 1947; McGill, 1948; D.Litt.: Assumption Univ. of Windsor, 1957. Called to the Bar of Nova Scotia, 1921 (K.C. Nova Scotia) 1941); called to the Bar of Manitoba, 1935 (K.C. Manitoba, 1939); called to the Bar of Ontario, 1957. Lecturer, Dalhousie Law School, 1921-22; Assistant Professor, Dalhousie Law School, 1922-25; Lecturer, Osgoode Hall Law Sch., 1925-29; Dean, Dalhousie Law Sch., 1929-34; Pres., Univ. of Manitoba, 1934-44; Principal, Univ. Coll., Univ. of Toronto, 1944-45; President University of Toronto, 1945-57. Served European War with 9th Can. Siege Battery, 1916-18; R.F.C., 1918-19. Member, Board of Governors, Halifax Ladies' College, Can., 1930-34; Sec., Comrs. on Uniformity of Law in Canada, 1929-34; President: Nat. Council of Y.M.C.A.s in Canada, 1939-42; Nat. Film Soc. of Canada, 1937-45; Nat. Conf. of Canadian Univs., 1942-44; Can. Assoc. for Adult Educ., 1941-44; U.N. Soc. in Canada, 1948-50; The Assoc. of Canadian Clubs, 1954-57; World Univ. Service (Can.) 1955-57; Chm. Can. Youth Commn., 1943-45; Chm., S.C.M. Nat. Coun., 1954-57. *Publications:* Cases on Trusts, 1928; (with J. D. Falconbridge, Q.C.) Manual of Canadian Business Law, 1929; (with Prof. H. E. Read) Cases on Equity, 1932. *Recreation:* fishing. *Address:* Department of External Affairs, Ottawa. *Clubs:* York (Toronto); The Century (New York); Rideau (Ottawa). [*Died* 17 *March* 1959.

SMITH, Solomon Charles Kaines, M.B.E. 1919; M.A. Camb. 1901; F.S.A. 1925; Officer, Redeemer (Greece), Military Merit (Greece); Retired in 1953; Lecturer in Art, Gilchrist Educational Trust; Life Trustee, Shakespeare's Birthplace; *s.* of Arthur William Smith, M.D.; *m.*; one *d.* *Educ.:* St. Paul's School; Magdalene College, Cambridge (Scholar); British School of Archæology, Athens. Served during European War, 1914-1918, M.E.F. Salonika and as Ægean Postal Censor and Advisory Officer to the Greek Government (despatches); Major, retired; Director, City Art Gallery, Leeds, 1924-27; Keeper, City Museum and Art Gallery, Birmingham, 1927-41; Official Lecturer National Gallery, 1914-16; Lecturer in Archæology and Art at Magdalene College, Cambridge, 1922-24; Member of Advisory Council of Victoria and Albert Museum, 1933-41; Keeper, Cook Collection, 1941-53, retired. *Publications:* The Elements of Greek Worship, 1906; Greek Art and National Life, 1913; Looking at Pictures, 1921; Wright of Derby, 1922; John Crome, 1924; John Sell Cotman, 1926; An Outline History of Painting, 1928; The Dutch School of Painting, 1929; The Italian Schools of Painting, 1930; Outline of Modern Painting, 1931; Art and Commonsense, 1932; Painters of France, 1932; Painters of England, 1934. *Address:* c/o 9 Lansdowne Place East, Bath. [*Died* 29 *June* 1958.

SMITH, Spence; *see* Smith, J. G. S.

SMITH, Stanley Livingston, C.B.E. 1951; D.Sc. (Eng.), F.C.G.I.; M.I.Mech.E., M.I.N.A., M.I.Mar.E.; Director of Research, British Shipbuilding Research Association, since 1944; *b.* 9 September 1889; *s.* of late Samuel D. Smith and Anne Glover Livingston, Southend-on-Sea; *m.* 1913, Anne Camilla Treadaway; no *c.* *Educ.:* Imperial College of Science and Technology. Practical training with Thames Ironwork Shipbuilding and Engineering Co. Ltd., afterwards an inspecting engineer with Crown Agents for the Colonies; conducted secret experimental research for Royal Society War Committee during European War, 1914-18, and served in R.A.F. as an Engineer Officer; appointed to staff of Mechanical Engineering Dept., City and Guilds (Engineering) College; eventually in 1926 Asst. Professor and in 1931 Reader of Univ. of London in Mechanical Engineering; degrees of M.Sc. and D.Sc. conferred in recognition of research work; appointed by the Univ. as Chief Engineering Inspector of Technical Institutions and for some time represented Imperial College on Surrey County Council Education Committee; Superintendent, Engineering Department, National Physical Laboratory, 1939-44; Vice-President Inst. N.A.; Member of various Govt. Bodies and Committees and during War of 1939-45 was occupied on Engineering problems and researches for the Defence Services. Fellow of Imperial College of Science and Technology, 1958. *Publications:* chiefly on Mechanical Engineering Subjects in Proc. Roy. Soc., Inst. of Mechanical Engineers, and various Technical Journals. *Address:* The Dell, Beech Drive, Kingswood, Sy. *Club:* Athenæum. [*Died* 27 *Oct.* 1958.

SMITH, Stanley Parker, C.B.E. 1942; D.Sc. (Durham); M.I.E.E.; Assoc. M.Inst. C.E.; *b.* Grantham, 23 Feb. 1884; *s.* of

Walter Smith, Grantham; *m.* 1908, Marie A. L. B. Leitz, Heidelberg; one *s.* one *d.* *Educ.:* Grantham Grammar School; Sedgebrook School; Armstrong College, Newcastle on Tyne; Technische Hochschule, Carlsruhe. Awarded 1851 Royal Exhibition Research Scholarship, 1905; Assistant Designer, Siemens, Stafford, 1907; Chief Designer, General Electric Co., 1909; Lecturer and Assistant Professor, City and Guilds (Engineering) Coll., 1912; Prof. of Electrical Engineering, Royal Technical Coll., Glasgow, 1923; Organizer of Staff College at Pitlochry, for North of Scotland Hydro-Electric Board, 1948; Consultant Engineer, Vickers, 1916; Institution of Electrical Engineers, Member of Council, 1926; Chairman, Scottish Centre, 1939-41, Vice-Pres., 1941. *Publications:* Electrical Equipment of Automobiles, 5th ed., 1949; Problems in Electrical Engineering, 5th ed., 1949; Electrical Engineering Laboratory Manuals: Machinery, 1933, Measurements, 1936; Electrical Engineering Design-Class Manual, 1934; numerous original papers in journal of Institution of Electrical Engineers, and of Civil Engineers; works on design of electrical machinery. *Recreations;* walking, motoring. *Address:* Ardshiel, Pitlochry, Perthshire. *T.:* Pitlochry 151. [*Died* 21 *Aug.* 1953.

SMITH, Stanley Wyatt-; *b.* Minchinhampton, Glos., 3 April 1887; *o. s.* of Rev. W. H. Smith and Susannah, *d.* of James Rice, Earl Soham, Suffolk; *m.* 1st, 1913, Clara Mabel (*d.* 1933), *o. c.* of Edward Smyth, Astwick, Beds.; one *s.* one *d.* (and *yr. s.* killed on active service, 1945); 2nd, 1933, Beatrix, *er. d.* of late Sir Francis Metford, K.C.B., O.B.E. *Educ.:* Bedford Modern School. Entered H.B.M. Consular Service in China, 1907; Student Interpreter at Peking, 1907-9; Consular Assistant at Hankow, 1909-12, Shanghai, 1913-14, Swatow, 1914-17; acting Consul at Tsinan, 1917-18, Wuchow, 1918-20; Vice-Consul at Hankow, 1921, Shanghai, 1922-23; Senior District Officer at Wei-hai-wei, 1923-25; Consul at Chinkiang, 1926-27, Tengyeuh, 1927-1931, Changsha, 1931-32, Newchang, 1933, Tsinan, 1933; acting Consul-General at Tsingtao, 1934; Consul at Foochow, 1934-36, Swatow, 1937-38; Consul-General at Manila, 1938-42; interned by Japanese military authorities on occupation of Manila, and repatriated, 1942; Consul-General at Honolulu, 1943-44; retired, 1945. *Publications:* Where China meets Burma (with wife, Beatrix Metford), 1935; articles and stories of life and customs on Burma-China Frontier. *Recreations:* gardening, carpentering. *Address:* The Old House, Burleigh, Stroud, Glos. *T.:* Brimscombe 3258. [*Died* 17 *Nov.* 1958.

SMITH, Sir (Thomas) Rudolph Hampden, 2nd Bt., *cr.* 1897; C.B.E. 1920; M.B., F.R.C.S.; *b.* 24 Jan. 1869; *s.* of 1st Bt. and Ann Eliza (*d.* 1879), *d.* of Frederick Parbury, Lancaster Gate; *S.* father, 1909; *m.* 1897, Ann Ellen (*d.* 1928), *d.* of Joseph William Sharp. *Heir: nephew* Thomas Turner [*b.* 28 June 1903; *m.* 1935, Agnes, *o. d.* of Bernard Page, Wellington, N.Z.; one *s.*]. *Address:* c/o National Provincial Bank, Strand, Torquay, Devon. [*Died* 25 *June* 1958.

SMITH, Tom, C.B.E. 1946; Labour Director of North-Eastern Division Coal Board since 1946; an official of Yorkshire Miners' Association; *b.* Hemingfield, Barnsley, 1886; *m.* 1920, Lily, *d.* of T. Ryder of Sheffield; one *d.* M.P. (Lab.) Pontefract, 1922-24 and 1929-31; Normanton Division of Yorkshire, 1933-46, accepted Chiltern Hundreds, 1946. Parliamentary Private Secretary to Minister for Mines, 1924 and 1929-31; Parliamentary Private Secretary to D. R. Grenfell, Secretary for Mines, 1940-1942; Joint Parliamentary Secretary to Ministry of Fuel and Power, 1942-45; Member of Sheffield Board of Guardians ten years; Empire Parliamentary Association delegate to the South Australia Centenary celebrations, 1936-37; member of British Deleg. to Anglo-American Conf., Bermuda, 1946. *Address:* 16 Marlborough Road, Doncaster. *T.:* Doncaster 3896. [*Died* 27 *Feb.* 1953.

SMITH, Professor Wilfred; John Rankin Professor of Geography, University of Liverpool, since 1950; Dean of the Faculty of Arts, University of Liverpool, since 1953; President, Institute of British Geographers, 1954; *b.* 31 Jan. 1903; *e. s.* of John Smith, Halifax, Yorks; *m.* 1932, Doris Muriel Hampson. *Educ.:* Univ. of Liverpool (Bibby Scholar and University Graduate Scholar). Assistant Lecturer, 1929-32, Lecturer, 1932-45, Senior Lecturer in Geography, 1945-50, University of Liverpool. *Publications:* A Geographical Study of Coal and Iron in China, 1926; Lancashire (The Land of Britain), 1941; The Distribution of Population and the Location of Industry on Merseyside, 1942; Physical Survey of Merseyside, 1946; An Economic Geography of Great Britain, 1949 (2nd ed. 1953); Geography and the Location of Industry, 1952; (ed.) A Scientific Survey of Merseyside, 1953; papers in Geography, British Assoc. Reports, Empire Journ. of Experimental Agriculture, Town Planning Review, etc. *Recreation:* gardening. *Address:* Monks Cottage, Eastham, Cheshire. *T.:* Eastham 1478. [*Died* 27 *Sept.* 1955.

SMITH, Hon. William Forgan, LL.D. University of Queensland, 1935; Chairman of the Queensland Sugar Board since 1944; Chancellor, University of Queensland, 1944; *b.* 15 April 1887; *s.* of George Smith and Mary Forgan; *m.* 1913, Euphemia Margaret, *d.* of Thomas Wilson, Mackay, Queensland; two *s.* *Educ.:* Invergowrie; Queen's Park, Glasgow; Dunoon Grammar School. Painter and decorator by trade; Member for Mackay, Queensland Parliament, 1915-42; Chairman of Committees, Jan. 1920; Member of Executive Council, Dec. 1920, and Minister without Portfolio; Minister for Public Works, 1922; Minister for Agriculture, 1925; and President of the Council of Agriculture; Deputy Premier, 1925; Leader of the Labour Party, and Leader of the Opposition, 1929; Treasurer of Queensland, 1932-38; Premier and Chief Sec. of Queensland and Vice-Pres. of Exec. Council, 1932-42; Chairman, Central Sugar Cane Prices Board, 1942-52; has represented Queensland at a number of interstate Cabinet and Premiers' Conferences; was a member of the Queensland Central Executive of the Australian Labour Party for many years. Freedom of Glasgow, 1936. *Publications:* pamphlets on Unemployment Insurance and Childhood Endowment. *Recreations:* the study of Economics and Philosophy, bowls, golf, reading, gardening, and fishing. *Address:* Airlie, Park Road, Yeronga, Brisbane, Australia. *T.:* JW 1062. *Clubs:* Brisbane Golf, Royal Queensland Golf, Yeronga Bowling (Brisbane). [*Died* 24 *Sept.* 1953.

SMITH, Sir William George Verdon, Kt., *cr.* 1946; C.B.E. 1925; J.P.; member of firm of George White and Co., Stockbrokers, Bristol; Chairman Bristol Aeroplane Co. Ltd. for 27 years until 1955, now Director; *b.* 1876; *m.* 1911, Diana Florence (*d.* 1928), *er. d.* of late M. Anders, Oxton, Cheshire; one *s.* one *d.*; *m.* 1934, Hilda Beatrice, 3rd *d.* of late J. J. Jackson-Barstow, D.L., J.P., Weston-super-Mare. *Address:* Sharcombe, Dinder, Wells, Somerset. *Clubs:* Carlton; Royal Yacht Squadron, Royal Thames Yacht. [*Died* 19 *Feb.* 1957.

SMITH, Major-Gen. William R. R.; *see* Revell-Smith.

SMITH, Sir William Sydney Winwood, 4th Bt., *cr.* 1809; *b.* 1 April 1879; *o. s.* of 2nd *s.* of 3rd Bt. and Caroline, *o. c.* of William Holland of Fitzroy, Queensland; *S.*

grandfather, 1893; *m.* 1905, Caroline, *o. d.* of James Harris, Co. Cork; two *s.* *Heir:* *s.* Christopher Sydney Winwood, *b.* 20 Sept. 1906. [*Died* 27 *June* 1953.

SMITH, Sir William Wright, Kt., *cr.* 1932; F.R.S. 1945; F.L.S.; M.A., D. ès Sc., LL.D.; Queen's Botanist in Scotland; Regius Keeper of Royal Botanic Garden, Edinburgh; Regius Professor of Botany, University of Edinburgh; *b.* Lochmaben, Dumfriesshire, 2 Feb. 1875; *s.* of late James T. Smith, Parkend, Lochmaben; *m.* Emma, *d.* of late Frederick Wiedhofft of Kingston-on-Thames; three *d.* *Educ.:* Dumfries Academy; University of Edinburgh. Lecturer in department of Botany, University of Edinburgh, 1902-07; Curator of Herbarium, Royal Botanic Gardens, Calcutta, 1907-08; Officiating Director, Botanical Survey of India, 1908: explored Vegetation of North West Sikkim and Tibet-Nepalese frontier, 1908; and of Sikkim-Chumbi frontier, 1909; Assistant Keeper Royal Botanic Garden, Edinburgh, 1911-22; Victoria Medal of Honour, Royal Horticultural Society, 1925; Veitch Memorial Medal, Royal Horticultural Society, 1930; Hon. Member American Academy of Arts and Sciences; Hon. Professor of Botany to Royal Horticultural Society, 1938, Vice-Pres., 1944; President Royal Society of Edinburgh, 1944-49; George Robert White Medal, Massachusetts Horticultural Soc., 1952. *Publications:* Botanical, chiefly on the flora of India, Burma, and China. *Address:* Inverleith House, Edinburgh. *Club:* New (Edinburgh). [*Died* 15 *Dec.* 1956.

SMITH-DORRIEN, Lady, D.B.E., *cr.* 1916; **Olive Crofton;** Principal Royal School of Needlework, 1932-50; *d.* of Col. John Schneider, Furness Abbey, Lancashire; *m.* 1902, General Sir Horace Smith-Dorrien, G.C.B., G.C.M.G., D.S.O. (*d.* 1930); one *s.* (and one killed on Active Service in Italy 1944, one killed in bomb outrage on King David's Hotel, Jerusalem, 1946). During European War of 1914-18 provided British and Colonial troops with some five million Hospital Bags for the contents of the men's pockets when wounded, through the medium of her Hospital Bag Fund; reopened Fund, 1940; President Clothing Branch Officers' Families Fund, 1941; Chm. of the Soldiers', Sailors', and Airmen's Families Association Central Clothing Depot; received the gold medal of the Reconnaissance Française from the French Government in recognition of her work for the French horses through her Presidency of the Blue Cross, 1918; Coronation Medal, given for work done in Westminster Abbey, 1937. *Recreations:* lawn tennis, squash racquets and golf. *Address:* 66 Cadogan Square, S.W.1. [*Died* 15 *Sept.* 1951.

SMITHE, Ida Elizabeth, C.B.E. 1918; Officer Order St. John of Jerusalem, Order of Mercy; *d.* of late Captain J. H. Waller, C.V.O.; *m.* Bevil Granville Smithe (*d.* 1937); one *d.* *Address:* Chantry Close, Hastings Road, Bexhill on Sea, Sussex. [*Died* 6 *Jan.* 1951.

SMITHERS, Brig. Leonard Sueton Hirsch, C.B. 1936; Indian Army, retired; *b.* 26 Jan. 1879; *s.* of late Maj.-Gen. Otway Francies Smithers, I.S.C.; *m.* 1915, Grace Margaret, *d.* of W. H. O'Meara, M.B., Carlow, Ireland; one *s.* *Educ.:* Bedford School; R.M.C., Sandhurst. Joined I.A. 1898; Colonel, 1926; Brigadier, 1932; served in Abor Expedition, 1911-12 (despatches); European War, 1914-19 (despatches); Comdt., Kitchener College, India, 1929-31; A.A.G. India, Jan.-Sept. 1932; commanded 11th (Ahmednagar) Inf. Bde., Southern Command, India, 1934-1936; retired, 1936. Order of White Eagle (Serbia). [*Died* 23 *Jan.* 1954.

SMITHERS, Sir Waldron, Kt., *cr.* 1934; M.P. (C.) Orpington Division of Kent since 1945; Member of London Stock Exchange; *b.* 5 Oct. 1880; *e. s.* of late Sir Alfred Smithers, J.P., M.P.; *m.* 1904, Marjory Prudence, *d.* of Rev. F. Page-Roberts, Rector of Strathfieldsaye; one *s.* two *d.* *Educ.:* Charterhouse and in France. M.P. (C.) Chislehurst Division of Kent, 1924-45. Board of Reedham Orphanage; Governor of St. Bartholomew's Hospital; J.P. Kent, 1927. *Address:* Knockholt, Sevenoaks, Kent. *T.:* Knockholt 2121, 2115. [*Died* 9 *Dec.* 1954.

SMOLLETT, Maj.-Gen. A. P. D. T.; *see* Telfer-Smollett.

SMYLY, Sir Philip Crampton, Kt., *cr.* 1905; B.L.; *b.* 28 March 1896; *s.* of late Sir Philip Crampton Smyly and late Hon. Nina, *d.* of 3rd Baron Plunket; *m.* 1905, Aileen Grace (*d.* 1935), *e. d.* of late Sir William J. Smyly; two *s.* one *d.* *Educ.:* Trinity Coll., Dublin; LL.D. Called to the Bar, King's Inns, Dublin, 1888; Gray's Inn, 1902; Queen's Advocate, Sierra Leone, 1895; Attorney-General, 1896-1901; Chief Justice, 1901-11; Chief Justice, Gold Coast Colony, 1911-29; retired, 1929. *Club:* Royal Societies. [*Died* 29 *May* 1953.

SMYTH, James Richard, C.M.G. 1949; Assistant Secretary, Air Ministry, since 1944; *b.* 21 Sept. 1895; *s.* of late Joseph Clarke Smyth; unmarried. Entered Civil Service, 1914. Attached to United Kingdom Mission, British Commonwealth Air Training Conferences, Ottawa, 1939 and 1942. *Recreations:* golf and tennis. *Address:* 12 Colcokes Road, Banstead, Surrey. *T.:* Burgh Heath 768. [*Died* 25 *July* 1953.

SMYTH, Sir Samuel Andrew, K.C.I.E., *cr.* 1931; C.S.I. 1924; I.C.S., retired; *b.* 18 March 1877; *s.* of Rev. James Smyth; *m.* 1906, Mary, *d.* of P. McIlroy, Co. Londonderry; one *s.* *Educ.:* Queen's College, Belfast. Entered Indian Civil Service, 1901; held positions—Officiating Chief Secretary to the Government of Burma, 1918; Commissioner of Irrawaddy, 1921; Commissioner of Mandalay, 1923; Commissioner of Sagaing, 1924; Financial Commissioner, 1925; Member of Executive Council of Governor of Burma, 1928; retired, 1931. *Address:* c/o Grindlays Bank Ltd., 54 Parliament Street, S.W.1. [*Died* 28 *Oct.* 1953.

SNADDEN, Sir William McNair, 1st Bt., *cr.* 1955; J.P.; *b.* 15 Jan. 1896; *y. s.* of late Rev. James Snadden, M.A.; *m.* 1919, Lesley, *e. d.* of late Thomas Henderson, Argaty, Doune, Perthshire; two *d.* *Educ.:* Dollar Academy. Served European War with B.E.F., France, 1915-17; M.P. (U.) Kinross and West Perth, 1938-55; Joint Parliamentary Under Sec. of State for Scotland, 1951-55. Chairman Scottish Food Hygiene Council; formerly Pres. Smithfield Club; Pres. Scottish Unionist Assoc.; *Recreations:* golf, shooting, fishing. *Heir:* none. *Address:* The Coldoch, Blair Drummond, Perthshire. *T.A.:* Doune, Perthshire. *T.:* Doune 221. *Clubs:* Carlton; Royal and Ancient Golf (St. Andrews); New (Edinburgh). [*Died* 23 *Nov.* 1959 (*ext.*).

SNAGGE, Vice-Admiral Arthur Lionel, C.B. 1933; Director of Begwaco Meters Ltd.; *b.* 4 May 1878; 4th and *y. s.* of late Judge Sir Thomas William Snagge, K.C.M.G., D.L.; *m.* 1933, Gladys, *widow* of Percy Lovett, late of Liscombe Park, Bucks, and *d.* of late Charles John Campbell, 69th Regiment. *Educ.:* H.M.S. Britannia. Entered R.N., 1892; Lieutenant, 1901; Comm., 1913; Capt., 1919; Rear-Adm., 1931; Vice-Adm., 1936; served European War in command H.M.S. Humber, 1914-18, off Belgian Coast, Dardanelles, Senussi operations, Southern Section Suez Canal, and as S.N.O., Akaba, in connection with Revolt in Arabia (Order of Nile, Order of El Nahda, despatches); Naval Attaché United States of America, 1918-20 (U.S. Distinguished Service Decoration); commanded British Flotilla up the Danube, 1920-22; H.M.S. Ceres, 1923-25; Director of Training and Staff, Admiralty, 1926; Senior Officer Reserve Fleet, the Nore, 1927; commanded H.M.S. Cumberland,

China, 1928-29; Chief of Staff, China, 1929 (Annamite Order of Kim-Khánh); Commodore Royal Naval Barracks, Chatham, 1929-31; Director of Personal Services, Admiralty, 1932-34; Admiral Superintendent H.M. Dockyard, Devonport, 1935-38; retired list, 1936. *Recreations:* fishing, shooting, golf. *Address:* 6 Kensington Court Gardens, W.8. *T.:* Western 5830. *Clubs:* Army and Navy, Bath; (Service Member) R.Y.S. (Cowes). [*Died* 10 *Feb.* 1955.

SNAGGE, His Honour Sir (Thomas) Mordaunt, Kt., *cr.* 1931; *b.* 1868; *e. s.* of Judge Sir Thomas William Snagge, K.C.M.G., D.L. (*d.* 1914); *m.* 1900, Gwendaline, *y. d.* of late Right Hon. Sir John Colomb, K.C.M.G., M.P., D.L.; three *s.* *Educ.:* Eton; New College, Oxford (M.A., B.C.L. (Honours), Scholarship, Lincoln's Inn); Barrister, Lincoln's Inn, 1893, Oxford Circuit; Prosecuting Counsel, P.O., 1904-19; Recorder of Ludlow, 1915-19; Standing Counsel to Council of Foreign Bondholders, 1901; Chm. Co. of London Profiteering Appeal Tribunal, 1920; Mem. Govt. Rent Restriction Act Committees, 1930, 1937. Judge of County Courts, 1919; Judge of Westminster County Court, 1936-43; J.P. London; formerly Director North London Railway. *Address:* 31 Wildcroft Manor, Putney Heath, S.W.15. *T.:* Putney 3754. *Club:* Oxford and Cambridge. [*Died* 4 *Nov.* 1955.

SNELL, Captain Ivan Edward, M.C.; Metropolitan Police Magistrate, 1925-1948; *b.* 25 April 1884; *s.* of Edward Snell, Durban, Natal; *m.* Marjory Mildred, *d.* of Hon. Sir Francis Villiers; one *s.* one *d.* *Educ.:* Charterhouse; Christ Church, Oxford. Called to Bar, Inner Temple, 1909; Metropolitan Police Magistrate, 1925; served European War, London Scottish and Black Watch, 1914-19 (Brevet Major, M.C., despatches four times). *Address:* 37-38 St. James' Place, W.1. *T.:* Regent 0575; Mengeham House, Hayling Island, Hants. *T.:* Hayling Island 77833. *Club:* Bath. [*Died* 29 *Aug.* 1958.

SNELL, William Thomas; Barrister-at-law; Recorder of Andover, 1928-48; J.P., Dorset, 1934; *s.* of late Thomas Snell, Liskeard, Cornwall; *m.* Agnes Florence, *yr. d.* of late Henry Liddell, of Bodmin, Cornwall. Student at Gray's Inn, 1907-10; called to Bar, Gray's Inn, 1910; joined Western Circuit; Clerk of Assize, Western Circuit, 1934-45. *Publications:* various articles on Common Law. *Recreations:* field sports and fishing. *Address:* Trelawne, Cromer Road, Branksome, Dorset. [*Died* 5 *March* 1951.

SNEYD, Vice-Adm. R. S. W.; *see* Wykes-Sneyd.

SNODGRASS, William Robertson, J.P.; M.A., B.Sc., M.D.; F.R.F.P.S.G.; Visiting Physician, Western Infirmary, Glasgow, since 1941; *b.* 1890; *e. s.* of late William Snodgrass, Physician, and Susan Robertson; *m.* 1918, Agnes Jane Evelyn (*d.* 1955), *er. d.* of late Samuel Black; two *d.* *Educ:* Glasgow Acad.; Morrison's Acad. (Dux); Glasgow Univ. Graduated M.B., Ch.B., 1913; M.D. Hons. and Bellahouston Gold Medal, Glasgow, 1934. Served European War, 1914-19, R.A.M.C. Various grades of medical appointments in Western Infirmary; Lecturer in Clinical Medicine and Examiner in Medicine, Glasgow Univ. Hon. Librarian, Roy. Fac. of Physicians and Surgeons of Glasgow for 20 years, Visitor, 1946, Pres., 1948-50. Sometime Visiting Consultant Physician to Dumfries and Galloway Royal Infirmary, and Glasgow Eye Infirmary; Consultant Physician, Kilmarnock Infirmary and Garrick Hospital, Stranraer; Member Assoc. of Physicians of Great Britain, etc.; many Cttees. connected with Nat. Health Service; Medical member, medical Appeals Tribunal. *Publications:* numerous medical articles, and some official medical papers. *Recreation:* fishing. *Address:* 3 Clairmont Gardens, Glasgow, C.3. *Clubs:* Royal Scottish Automobile, Loch Walton Angling. [*Died* 22 *Nov.* 1955.

SNOW, Ernest Charles, C.B.E. 1938; M.A. Oxford; D.Sc. London; Past Pres., Royal Statistical Soc.; *b.* 12 March 1886; *s.* of Henry and Margaret Snow, Woodford, Essex; *m.* 1913, May, *d.* of Thomas Chettle, Ashby-de-la-Zouche; (one *s.*, Pilot Officer, R.A.F., killed on active service June 1942) two *d.* *Educ.:* Queen's College, Oxford (Scholar). Leather Controller Ministry of Supply, 1939-46. *Publications:* various in Proceedings of Royal Society, Journal of the Royal Statistical Society, Biometrika and elsewhere. *Recreations:* golf, gardening. *Address:* The Old Smithy, Poltimore, Exeter, Devon. *T.:* Broadclyst (Exeter) 330; 17 Barter St., W.C.1. *Club:* Athenæum. [*Died* 28 *Aug.* 1959.

SNOW, Sir Gordon (Keith), Kt., *cr.* 1949; Managing Director, Snows Mens Wear Ltd., Melbourne, Australia, since 1947; *b.* 4 Oct. 1898; *s.* of John and Emily Lark Snow; *m.* 1935, Elizabeth Allingham Hough. *Educ.:* Ballarat College, Ballarat, Victoria. Served overseas with 1st A.I.F., 1916-17. *Address:* 281 Domain Road, South Yarra, Victoria, Australia. *T.:* Windsor 2878. [*Died* 14 *Oct.* 1954.

SNOW, Sir Sydney, K.B.E., *cr.* 1936; Director: General Industries Ltd., Colonial Mutual Life Association (Sydney), etc.; *b.* Ballarat, Australia, 17 Dec. 1887; *s.* of late John and Emily L. Snow; *m.* 1913, Ruby Dent Davies; one *s.* two *d.* *Educ.:* Ballarat College, Ballarat, Australia. *Address:* Kenilworth, Bowral, N.S.W., Australia. *Clubs:* Australian, New South Wales (Sydney); Athenæum (Melbourne). [*Died Nov.* 1958.

SNOWDEN, Viscountess (Ethel Snowden); *b.* Harrogate, 1881; *d.* of Richard Annakin; *m.* 1905, Philip Snowden, (1st Viscount Snowden, P.C.) (*d.* 1937); no *c.* *Educ.:* Edge Hill College, Liverpool. Travelled extensively in Europe, America, and British Dominions, Palestine, etc.; lectured in principal towns of Great Britain, Europe, United States, Canada, and New Zealand; former Member of Executives of the Fabian Society, Labour Party, and Nat. Union of Women's Suffrage Societies; took a prominent part in Women's Suffrage Movement; keen Temperance advocate; Member of the Royal Commission on Food Prices, 1925; Member of Labour Commission of Enquiry to Russia in 1920; reported unfavourably on Bolshevism; Member of the first Board of Governors of the B.B.C., 1927-33; Vice-President of National Education Assoc. *Publications:* The Feminist Movement; Through Bolshevik Russia; A Political Pilgrim in Europe. *Recreations:* music, reading, walking. *Address:* 206 Beatty House, Dolphin Square, S.W.1. *T.:* Victoria 3800. [*Died* 22 *Feb.* 1951.

SNOWDEN-SMITH, Major-General Richard Talbot, C.B. 1942; C.B.E. 1919; M.I.Mech.E.; M.I.A.E.; *b.* 23 April 1887; *s.* of late James Snowden-Smith, Tavistock, Devonshire; unmarried. *Educ.:* Kelly College, Tavistock; Royal Military College, Sandhurst. Commissioned A.S.C., 1906; took up aviation in 1910; Royal Aero Club's Pilot Certificate No. 29; took part in numerous early aviation trials including Brooklands to Brighton Air Race; Staff-Capt., War Office, 1915; Assistant Director Supplies and Transport, 1917; Deputy Director of Supplies and Transport, 1919; Inspector of Mechanical Transport, 1919; served European War, 1914-18 (O.B.E., C.B.E., despatches thrice); Deputy Assistant Director Transport, Simla, 1925; Secretary Mechanical Transport Advisory Committee, India, 1925; Chief Instructor R.A.S.C. Training College, Aldershot, 1926; Deputy Assistant Director of Supplies and Transport, War Office, 1931-33; Officer Commanding R.A.S.C. Depot, Feltham, 1933-34; Assistant Director of Supplies and

Transport, War Office, 1934-37; Inspector of R.A.S.C. War Office, 1937-40; Director of Supplies and Transport, War Office, 1940-43; retired pay, 1943. President R.A.S.C. Regimental Association, 1943-46. *Club:* Junior United Service. [*Died* 14 *Aug.* 1951.

SOAMES, Geoffrey Ewart, C.I.E. 1927; Indian Civil Service, retired; *b.* 11 Jan. 1881; *s.* of late Joseph Soames, Solicitor; *m.* 1915, Una, *d.* of late Rev. Laxon Sweet; no *c.* *Educ.:* Eastbourne College and Merton College, Oxford (Postmastership); First Class in Mods. and Greats. Entered Indian Civil Service, 1905; appointed to the Province of Eastern Bengal and Assam; when the Province was redivided, was allotted to Assam; Chief Secretary, 1925; retired, 1933. *Address:* The Bay House, North Park, Gerrards Cross, Bucks. *T.:* Gerrards Cross 3166.
[*Died* 30 *April* 1952.

SODDY, Frederick, F.R.S. 1910; M.A.; LL.D. (Glasgow); *b.* Eastbourne, 2 Sept. 1877; *m.* 1908, Winifred Moller (*d.* 1936), *d.* of late Sir George Beilby, F.R.S. *Educ.:* Eastbourne College; University College of Wales, Aberystwyth; Merton College, Oxford. Demonstrator in Chemistry, McGill Univ. Montreal, 1900-02; trained in scientific investigation under late Lord Rutherford, Montreal, 1901-03; and late Sir William Ramsay, London, 1903-04; Lecturer in Physical Chemistry and Radioactivity, University of Glasgow, 1904-14; Professor of Chemistry, Aberdeen University, 1914-19; Lee's Professor of Chemistry, University of Oxford, 1919-36, retired; President, Röntgen Society, 1905-6; Science Masters' Association, 1943; awarded Cannizzaro Prize by the Acc. d. Lincei, Rome, 1913; Foreign Member, Swedish, Italian, and Russian Academies of Sciences; Nobel Laureate in Chemistry, 1921; originated, in whole or in part, Theory of Atomic Disintegration and Displacement Law of Radioactivity, Discovery of Isotopes, Virtual Wealth Theory and Application of Laws of Conservation to Economics. Pres. Inst. Atomic Informn. for the Layman. *Publications:* Radioactivity, 1904; The Interpretation of Radium, 1909, revised and enlarged by Section on the Structure of the Atom, 1920; Chemistry of the Radio-Elements, 1912; ditto, Part ii., 1914; Matter and Energy (Home University Library Series), 1912; Science and Life, 1920; Cartesian Economics, 1922; Inversion of Science, 1924; Wealth, Virtual Wealth and Debt, 1926; The Wrecking of a Scientific Age, 1927; Money versus Man, 1931; Interpretation of the Atom, 1932; Rôle of Money, 1934; The Arch-Enemy of Economic Freedom, 1943; The Story of Atomic Energy, 1949, etc. *Relevant publication:* (by Muriel Howorth) Memoirs of Frederick Soddy: Vol. I, Atomic Transmutation, The Greatest Discovery ever made, 1953. *Address:* 39 Overhill Drive, Brighton 6. *T.:* Brighton 56169.
[*Died* 22 *Sept.* 1956.

SOERTSZ, Sir Francis Joseph, Kt., *cr.* 1947; K.C.; LL.B.; Senior Puisne Justice, Supreme Court, Ceylon; *b.* 14 March 1886; *s.* of Francis William and Emily Josephine Soertsz; *m.* 1912, Erin Sophia Daniels; four *s.* three *d.* *Educ.:* St. Joseph's College, Colombo. Joined Law College of Ceylon, 1908; admitted to Bar of Ceylon, 1909; LL.B. (London); called to Bar, Gray's Inn, 1927; acted as Crown Counsel Magistrate and District Judge on many occasions; Commissioner of Assize, Ceylon, 1932; Puisne Justice, Ceylon, 1936; acted as Chief Justice, Ceylon, on several occasions; Pres. Catholic Union of Ceylon; Chm. Police Commission appointed by Governor of Ceylon. *Address:* Erin, Rosmead Place, Colombo, Ceylon.
[*Died* 10 *Jan.* 1951.

SOHEILY, Ali, Persian Order of the Crown, First Class, 1942; Iranian Ambassador to London, 1950-52 and since 1954; *b.* 4 Oct. 1896; *s.* of Zahra and Gholam Ali Soheily; *m.* 1931, Nina; three *s.* *Educ.:* Primary Education; École des Sciences Politiques, Teheran. Member of special Missions: Moscow, for conclusion of a Commercial Treaty and Consular and Postal Conventions, 1923; London, 1924; Head of 2nd Political Department, Min. of Foreign Affairs, 1929; Under-Secretary of State, Min. of Roads and Communications, 1931; President Administrative Council of Iranian-Soviet Soc. of Fisheries, 1932; Under-Secretary of State, Min. of Foreign Affairs, 1934; Iranian Minister to London, 1937; Minister of Foreign Affairs, 1938; Governor of Kerman and Baluchistan, 1939; Ambassador of Iran to Kabul, 1939; Minister of the Interior, 1940; Minister of Foreign Affairs, 1941; Prime Minister, re-elected, 1943; Minister of State, 1947; Ambassador of Iran to Paris, 1948. Knight Commander First Class, Order of the North Star, Sweden; Grand Cross, Order of Leopold II, Belgium; 2nd Class Order of Dannebrog, Denmark; Grand Croix de la Légion d'Honneur, 1950. *Recreations:* reading of history, gardening. *Address:* Iranian Embassy, 26 Princes Gate, S.W.7. *T.:* Kensington 6458. [*Died* 1 *May* 1958.

SOLBERG, Thorvald; United States Register of Copyrights, 1897-1930; *b.* Manitowoc, Wisconsin, 22 April 1852; *s.* of Charles Solberg, Larvik, Norway; *m.* 1880, Mary Adelaide Nourse (*d.* 1920); no *c.* *Educ.:* Common School, Manitowoc. Library of Congress, 1876-89, 1897-1930; Boston Book Company, 1889-97; Hon. Life Fellow of American Library Institute; Hon. Member of Association Littèraire et Artistique Internationale, Paris; United States Official Delegate to International Copyright Conferences, Paris, 1900; Berlin, 1908; Rome, 1928. *Publications:* various works on copyright, and contributions to periodicals, including The Nation, New York for 25 years, and Le Droit d'Auteur, Berne, up to 1940; also some bibliographical works, including Literary Property, 1886; Bibliography of the Balearic Islands, 1929, and Text editions of the Icelandic Eddas; The Development of International Copyright Relations between the United States and Foreign Countries, 1933; Present Copyright Situation; Copyright and Librarians, 1934; Copyright Miscellanies (limited edition), 1939; The Present International Copyright Situation, 1934; Les récentes mesures prises à Washington pour la Revision de la Législation pour le Droit d'Auteur (Berne), 1935; The Long Struggle for Honourable International Copyright Relations, contributed to Geistiges Eigentum, Leiden (Holland), 1937; International Copyright in Congress, 1837-1891; History of the Legal Deposit of Books throughout the British Empire, with Bibliography, Library Quarterly, Oct. 1938; Copyright Reform: Legislation and International Copyright; A Chapter in the Unwritten History of the Library of Congress from Jan. 17 to April 5, 1899: The Appointment of Herbert Putnam as Librarian, Library Quarterly, July 1939; Copyright Reform, Notre Dame Lawyer, May 1939; The New Copyright Bill (S.3043), Notre Dame Lawyer, Jan. 1940; Criticism of the new Copyright Bill (S.3043), Nation, 24 Feb. 1940; The Copyright Bill (S.3043), Saturday Review of Literature, 24 Feb. 1940; The Cathedral at Palma, Majorca, Balearic Islands, with description and Bibliography, 1940. *Recreations:* formerly walking; now auto-driving and foreign travel. *Club:* Cosmos (Washington, D.C.).
[*Died* 15 *July* 1949.
[*But death not notified in time for inclusion in Who Was Who* 1941–1950, *first edn.*

SOLLY-FLOOD, Brig.-Gen. Richard Elles, C.B. 1931; C.M.G. 1918; D.S.O. 1916; Order of the Serbian Eagle, 4th Class, with Swords; Officer Legion of Honour; *b.* 12 Dec. 1877; *y. s.* of late Sir Frederick Solly-Flood, K.C.B.; *m.* 1914, Marguerite, *o. d.* of late Major Connellan, Coolmore, Thomastown; one *s.* one *d.* *Educ.:* Eton. Entered the Rifle Brigade from Eton; served S. African War, 1899-1902 (Queen's medal 5 clasps, King's medal 2 clasps, despatches); European War from landing at Gallipoli, 8 Aug. 1915, to evacuation of Helles, as Brigade-Major and G.S.O.2 (D.S.O., despatches); G.S.O.1 and Brevet Lieut.-Colonel and Col.; Commanded 82nd Brigade, 27th Division, Salonika, Jan. 1918, and 85th Infantry Brigade, 28th Division (despatches, Salonika); commanded 132nd (Middlesex and Sussex) Infantry Brigade, 1924-1927; Rangoon Brigade, 1927-28; 8th (Bareilly) Infantry Brigade, 1928-31; retired pay, 1931. *Recreations:* hunting, shooting. *Address:* Ballyduff, Thomastown, Ireland. *Clubs:* Army and Navy; Kildare Street (Dublin). [*Died* 8 *Oct.* 1954.

SOLOMON, Sir (Aubrey) Kenneth, Kt. *cr.* 1953; C.B.E. 1941; K.C. 1925; President Legislative Council, Bahama Islands, 1946; *b.* 4 April 1884; *s.* of Julius Stafford and Mary Solomon; *m.* 1914, Mercedes Lofthouse; no *c.* *Educ.:* Nassau Grammar School. Called to Bahamas Bar, 1905; Magistrate, 1918-21; acted Attorney-General many occasions; acted Chief Justice, 1920-1921. Speaker of House of Assembly, Bahama Islands, 1942-46; Member of Executive Council, 1926-41; and of House of Assembly, 1908-18 and 1925-46; Legal Adviser House of Assembly, 1923-33. *Publications:* Magistrates' Manual, 1911; A Manual of Evidence, 1911. *Recreations:* tennis, gardening. *Address:* The Ark, Eastern Parade, Nassau, Bahamas. *Clubs:* The Club, Royal Nassau Sailing (Nassau). [*Died* 2 *Nov.* 1954.

SOLOMON, Saul, Q.C.; retired as Judge of Supreme Court of S. Africa, Transvaal Provincial Div. (1927-45); *b.* Cape Town, 9 Apr. 1875; *s.* of Saul Solomon, M.L.A., and Georgiana Margaret Thomson; *m.* 1st, 1903, Gertrude Mary Thompson (*d.* 1904); 2nd, 1910, Wilding Robertson; two *s.* *Educ.:* Bedford Grammar School; Lincoln College, Oxford (Scholar). Called to Bar, Lincoln's Inn, 1900; Admitted to the Cape Bar, 1900; Transvaal Bar, 1902; entered Cuddesdon College, 1906; Deacon, Church of England, 1908; Priest, 1909; received into the Catholic Church, 1916; resumed practice at the Transvaal Bar, 1916; K.C. Union of South Africa, 1919; Q.C. 1952. *Address:* Riviera, Pentrich Road, St. James, Cape Province, South Africa. *Clubs:* Rand, Country (Johannesburg); Civil Service (Cape Town). [*Died* 10 *Dec.* 1960.

SOLTAU, Roger Henry; Professor of Political Science, American University of Beirut, 1930-48 and 1950-52, retd.; *b.* Paris, 31 July 1887; *e. s.* of William Soltau and Louise Monod; *m.* 1914, Irene Constance Whelpton (Honours Theology Oxford, 1912, author of The Freewoman, 1929); one *d.* *Educ.:* Lycée Carnot, Paris; Highgate School; Pembroke College, Oxford (scholar); Sorbonne (Paris). Lothian Prize, Oxford, 1908; 1st class History Schools, 1909; 1st class Modern Languages School, 1910; Beit and Herbert Prizes, 1911; Lecturer, Bristol University, 1911-15; in France with Society of Friends Ambulance and Relief Services, 1915-19; Lecturer, Leeds University, 1919-26; London School of Economics, 1927-30 and 1945-46; University Coll. of Wales, Aberystwyth, 1948-50. On part-time work with censorship and British Security Mission in Beirut, 1941-43; visiting prof., Swarthmore and Bryn Mawr Colls., U.S.A., 1944-45, and Stanford Univ., U.S.A., 1949. *Publications:* The Duke de Choiseul (Lothian Essay), 1908; French Parties and Politics, 1922; Historical Introduction to Victor Hugo's Chatiments, 1925; Pascal, The Man and the Message, 1927; The Economic Functions of the State, 1931; French Political Thought in the Nineteenth Century, 1931; An Outline of European Economic Development, 1935; An Introduction to Politics, 1950; various papers. *Address:* c/o Pembroke College, Oxford. [*Died* 29 *Jan.* 1953.

SOMERHOUGH, Hon. Anthony George; Hon. Mr. Justice Somerhough; O.B.E. 1948 (M.B.E. 1946); Q.C. (Kenya) 1954; Puisne Judge, High Court of Northern Rhodesia, since 1954; Acting Chief Justice, 1958; *b.* 15 December 1906; *o. s.* of Arthur Louis Somerhough; *m.* 1930, Beatrice, *o. d.* of late Robert Baker, O.B.E., H.M. Colonial Service; no *c.* *Educ.:* Dover College; H.M.S. Worcester; Exeter College, Oxford. Entered R.A.F., 1927; Fleet Air Arm, 1928; A.D.C. to Governor of Hong Kong. Called to the Bar, Gray's Inn, 1936; entered Office of Judge Advocate General, 1936; Legal Staff Officer, R.A.F., B.E.F., 1939-40; D.J.A.G., Middle East, 1940-44 (despatches thrice); Officer i/c War Crimes Group, N.W. Europe, 1945-48; entered Colonial Service, 1949; Crown Counsel, Kenya; Deputy Public Prosecutor, Kenya, 1950: Acting Solicitor General, 1953; M.L.C., 1953. C.St.J. 1957 (England). Cruz Vermelha Portuguesa, 1931. *Publication:* A Guide to Air Force Law and Procedure, 1932. *Recreations:* fishing, motoring. *Address:* Mark Oak, Burley, New Forest, Hants. *T.:* Burley 3117; High Court of Northern Rhodesia, Ndola, N. Rhodesia. *Clubs:* Flyfishers', Royal Automobile; Nairobi, Muthaiga (Nairobi). [*Died* 2 *Oct.* 1960.

SOMERLEYTON, 2nd Baron, *cr.* 1916; **Francis Savile Crossley,** Bt., *cr.* 1863; M.C., Major late 9th Lancers; *b.* 1 June 1889; *e. s.* of 1st Baron and late Phyllis, Baroness Somerleyton, C.B.E., *y. d.* of Sir Henry de Bathe, 4th Bt.; *S.* father, 1935; *m.* 1924, Bridget, M.B.E. 1946, 3rd *d.* of William Douro Hoare, C.B.E.; two *s.* one *d.* *Educ.:* Eton. Served European War, 1914-19 (despatches, M.C.); J.P., D.L. Suffolk. Chairman Lowestoft Water Company. *Heir:* *s.* Hon. Savile William Francis Crossley, *b.* 17 Sept. 1928. *Address:* Somerleyton Hall, Lowestoft. *Clubs:* Brooks's, Cavalry. [*Died* 15 *July* 1959.

SOMERS, 7th Baron (*cr.* 1784), **Arthur Percy Somers Cocks;** Bt. 1772; *b.* 23 Nov. 1864; *y. s.* of Arthur Herbert Cocks, C.B., Bengal Civil Service; *S.* nephew, 1944; *m.* 1896, Mary Benita (*d.* 1950), *d.* of Major L. M. Sabin, United States Army; one *s.* two *d.* *Educ.:* Charterhouse. Farmed in North-West Canada, 1883-90, and Colorado, 1893-1900; Resident Agent of Eastnor Estates, 1900-09; farmed in Ontario, 1911-15; served in Canadian Army, 1915-17; Sub-Commissioner, Board of Agriculture, 1917-18. *Heir:* *s.* Hon. John Patrick Somers Cocks [*b.* 1907; *m.* 1935, Barbara Marianne, *d.* of Charles Henry Southall]. *Address:* 3 Eversfield Road, Kew Gardens, Surrey. [*Died* 8 *Feb.* 1953.

SOMERSET, 17th Duke of (*cr.* 1547), **Evelyn Francis Edward Seymour,** D.S.O. 1918; O.B.E. 1919; Col. retired; Lord Lieut. for Wilts. since 1942; J.P., Wilts.; *b.* Ceylon, 1 May 1882; *o. s.* of 16th Duke and Rowena (*d.* 1950), *d.* of George Wall, Ceylon; *S.* father, 1931; *m.* 1906, Edith Mary, *d.* of W. Parker, J.P., Whittington Hall, Derbyshire; one *s.* one *d.* (and two *s.* decd.). *Educ.:* Blundell's School; R.M.C., Sandhurst. Joined Royal Dublin Fusiliers, 1901; served S. African War (Queen's medal with 5 clasps); European War, 1914-18 (despatches, D.S.O., O.B.E.) Adjutant 25th London Regt., 1913-16; commanded 10th Batt. Royal Dublin Fusiliers, 1917-18; served in A.G. Department at War Office, 1919; retired, 1929; late Lieut.-Colonel, commanding a battalion of Devonshire Regiment; late Colonel on General Staff. K.St.J. 1949. *Recreations:* hunting, shooting, golf, cricket, fishing. *Heir:* *s.* Lord Seymour. *Address:* Maiden Bradley, Warminster, Wilts. *Clubs:* Army and Navy, M.C.C., Naval and Military. [*Died* 26 *April* 1954.

SOMERSET, Raglan Horatio Edwyn Henry, Q.C. 1947; J.P. Monmouthshire; Deputy Chairman Monmouthshire Quarter Sessions, 1950; Barrister-at-Law; journalist, translator and literary critic; Recorder of Gloucester since 1937; *b.* 4 Aug. 1885; *s.* of late Raglan Turberville Henry Somerset, J.P., Raglan, Monmouthshire, and Elizabeth Horatia Anne Nelson Ward; *m.* 1915, Adelaide Millicent Blanche Gwendolen, J.P., Monmouthshire, Joint M.F.H. Monmouthshire Fox Hounds, Jr. Comdr., A.T.S., *d.* of A. F. Somerset, Castle Goring, Worthing, Sussex; one *d. Educ.:* Bath Coll.; Queens' Coll., Cambridge (Schol.). B.A. 2nd Class Classical Tripos; Editor of the Granta; travelled abroad; English tutor to H.H. Abdul Medjid of Turkey; called to Bar, 1911; Member of Gray's Inn and Middle Temple; Oxford Circuit; Recorder of Oswestry, 1933-37; commission R.A.S.C., transferred to Intelligence Department, War Office; demobilised with hon. rank of Captain; contested (L.), Erdington Division of Birmingham, 1918; formerly Secretary, third division Anglo-German Mixed Arbitral Tribunal. *Publications:* Twilight and other Verses, 1948; The Chieftain's Ground and other verses, 1953; translations from the German; Manual of Military Law, My Married Life with Ludendorf, Subconscious Europe; From the French: The Calas Case, Revelations from the Secret Service. *Recreations:* shooting, fishing, botanical gardening, amateur philology, verses grave and gay. *Address:* 24 Holbein House, Chelsea. *T.:* Sloane 4039; Hill House, Raglan, Mon. *T.:* Raglan 14. *Club:* Beefsteak. [*Died* 29 *April* 1956.

SOMERVELL OF HARROW, Baron (Life Peer), *cr.* 1954; **Donald Bradley Somervell;** P.C. 1938; Kt. 1933; O.B.E. 1919; *b.* 24 August 1889; *s.* of late Robert Somervell; *m.* 1933, Laelia (*d.* 1945), *d.* of Sir Archibald Buchan-Hepburn, 4th Bt. *Educ.:* Harrow; Magdalen College, Oxford. Fellow of All Souls College, Oxford. Served European War, 1914-19; K.C. 1929; M.P. (U.) Crewe Division, Cheshire, 1931-45; Solicitor-General, 1933-36; Attorney-General 1936-45; Home Secretary, 1945; Recorder of Kingston-upon-Thames, 1940-46; a Lord Justice of Appeal, 1946-54; a Lord of Appeal in Ordinary, 1954-60, retd. Hon. LL.D. St. Andrews, 1947; Hon. D.C.L. Oxford, 1959. *Address:* 1 King's Bench Walk, Temple, E.C.4. *Clubs:* Brooks's, Beefsteak. [*Died* 18 *Nov.* 1960.

SOMERVELL, Sir Arnold (Colin), Kt., *cr.* 1954; O.B.E.; D.L.; J.P.; Chairman Somervell Bros. Ltd., Kendal; Chairman of West Cumberland Industrial Development Company, Ltd.; *b.* 1 Dec. 1883; *e. s.* of Colin Somervell, Kendal; *m.* 1909, Dorothy, 4th *d.* of late J. M. Hay; one *s.* (and one killed in action). *Educ.:* Uppingham; King's College, Cambridge (M.A.). Served European War, 1914-19, Major (despatches twice, O.B.E.); High Sheriff Westmorland, 1936; has been President of most of the National Organisations connected with the Shoe Industry. *Address:* High Borrans, Windermere. *T.:* Windermere 478. *Clubs:* White's, Buck's; Travellers' (Paris). [*Died* 5 *July* 1957.

SOMERVILLE, Col. George Cattell, C.M.G. 1918; D.S.O. 1916; p.s.c.; Secretary to the Royal Agricultural Society of New South Wales, 1924-54; *b.* 13 July 1878; *m.* 1911, Brenda Elsie, *d.* of late Julius Holland; three *d. Educ.:* Brisbane Boys' Grammar School; Sydney University. Diploma in Military Science, Sydney University. Served European War, 1914-18 (severely wounded, despatches thrice, C.M.G., D.S.O.). Belgian Croix de Guerre. *Clubs:* Imperial Service, Union, Royal Sydney Yacht Squadron (Sydney). [*Died May* 1959.

SOMERVILLE, Howard; Member of the International Soc. and of the Royal Soc. of Portrait Painters; Silver Medal Paris Salon, 1928; Hors Concours, 1939; *b.* Dundee, 1873. *Educ.:* private school; studied Science and Engineering at the Technical and University Colleges Dundee; practised Engineering for some time but gave it up because of an earlier and stronger inclination to Art; has lived and worked in Dundee, Glasgow, New York; settled in London, 1899; pictures in the Municipal Galleries of Liverpool, Bradford, Brighton, Oldham, Bournemouth, and Saint Louis, U.S.A.; painted the Rev. H. B. Gray for Bradfield College, and the Rev. J. Estlin Carpenter for Manchester College, Oxford; Dame Bertha Phillpotts, Girton; Prof. John Strong, Leeds Univ.; Dr. J. R. Airey and Mr. Walter Parsons, City of Leeds Training College; Princess Schonburg of Waldenburg; Lady Ashton, Lady Bicester. *Publications:* Etchings. *Address:* c/o Westminster Bank Ltd., 115 Old Brompton Road, S.W.7. *Club:* Chelsea Arts. [*Died* 2 *July* 1952.

SOMERVILLE, Colonel John Arthur Coghill, C.M.G. 1918; C.B.E. 1919; *b.* 26 March 1872; *s.* of Lt.-Col. T. H. Somerville, of Drishane, Co. Cork, and *d.* of Adm. Sir Josiah Coghill, 3rd Bt.; *m.* 1st, 1910, Vera Cooper (*d.* 1937), *d.* of C. W. Aston Key, 52 Cambridge Terrace, W.; 2nd, 1942, Mildred, *y. d.* of Rev. Canon McCheane, Wellbrook, Freshford, Co. Kilkenny. *Educ.:* Bedford Grammar School; R.M.C., Sandhurst. 2nd Lt. Northumberland Fusiliers, 1892; Capt. 1900; Major, 1905; R. Sussex Regt. 1908; Lt.-Col. 1915; Gen. Staff Officer (3rd grade), 1909-11; specially employed War Office, 1914; served South Africa, 1899-1901; Siberia, 1919; Military Attaché, Tokyo and Korea, 1911-14 and 1915-19; Commandant R. Mil. School of Music, 1920-25; retd. pay, 1925; Secretary The Japan Society, 1927-38. *Recreations:* oriental art, music. *Address:* 54 Iverna Court, W.8. *T.:* Western 9048. [*Died* 26 *Dec.* 1955.

SOMERVILLE, Walter Harold, C.B.E. 1944; A.I.A.; Executive Vice-President and Director, Mutual Life Assurance Co. of Canada; Director, Economical Mutual Ins. Co., Waterloo Trust & Savings Co.; *b.* 15 Sept. 1881, Canadian; widower; two *d. Educ.:* Collegiate Institute, London, Ontario. Business life spent in the employ of Mutual Life Assurance Co. of Canada, Associate Society of Acutaries, Institute of Actuaries of Great Britain. Formerly Joint Chairman, National War Savings Committee. *Recreations:* the usual. *Address:* 2 Union St., Waterloo, Ontario. *T.:* 4-4013. *Clubs:* Toronto (Toronto); Westmount Golf and Country, Granite Curling, Kitchener (Ontario). [*Died* 18 *Jan.* 1959.

SOMERVILLE, Lt.-Col. William Arthur Tennison Bellingham, D.S.O. 1915; late the King's Own Royal Regiment (Lancaster); *b.* 8 Aug. 1882; *s.* of late Bellingham Arthur Somerville and Margaret, *y. d.* of late William Clinch; *m.* 1925. Amy Kathleen, *widow* of Alan Campbell Ferguson and *d.* of General Standish Harrison, Castle Harrison, Charleville, Co. Cork. Entered Army, 1901; Captain, 1913; Major, 1916; European War, 1914-18; N. Russia, 1919 (despatches nine times, D.S.O. and bar, Bt. Lt.-Col.); commanding 1st Batt. Loyal Regt., 1927-28; retired pay, 1928. *Address:* Clermont, Rathnew, Co. Wicklow. *Club:* Junior United Service. [*Died* 13 *Feb.* 1951.

SOMMERLAD, Hon. Ernest Christian, C.B.E. 1938; M.L.C. New South Wales; Chm. and Managing Dir. Gotham (Aust.) Pty., Ltd., and Country Press Ltd.; *b.* 30 Jan. 1886; *s.* of late J. H. Sommerlad; *m.* 1913, Mildred Alice Vaughan; two *s.* two *d. Educ.:* Newington College, Sydney; St. Andrews College (Sydney University). Health breakdown compelled retirement from the ministry after six months' missionary service among the Indians in Fiji; took up journalism as a profession; Chairman of the Publicity Committee in connection with Australia's 150th Anniversary Celebrations, also member of Central Council; Member of Special Committee appointed by the Government to report upon secondary education in N.S.W., 1934; Chm. of Methodist Youth Work Commission, 1934-35; Vice-Pres. Council Nat. Roads and Motorists' Assoc.; Trustee N.S.W. Public Library; Chairman, Aust. Country Party (N.S.W.). King's Jubilee and Coronation Medals. *Publications:* Two historical books on development of Northern New South Wales, with place names (1917 and 1922); Mightier than the Sword, a handbook on journalism, advertising, propaganda and broadcasting, 1949. *Recreations:* motoring, bowls, gardening. *Address:* 22 Tryon Road, Lindfield, N.S.W. *Club:* Sydney Rotary (Sydney). [*Died* 6 *Sept.* 1952.

SOPER, Harry Tapley Tapley-; *b.* Stoke Gabriel, Devonshire, 22 Dec. 1875; *m.* 1st, 1906, Clara J. W. Brookes (*d.* 1908); 2nd, 1923, Gwendolyn Edith (*d.* 1950), *d.* of Rev. William Frederick Connor, Rector of Kingsnympton, N. Devon. *Educ.:* Madras House Grammar Sch., Stoke Newington, London. Librarian Univ. Coll., Exeter, 1902-34; and Exeter City Library, 1902-46; Librarian Emeritus, Exeter City Library, 1946; Librarian to Devon and Exeter Law Library Society, 1904-11; Vice-Pres. of the London Devonian Assoc.; Hon. Secretary Devon and Cornwall Record Society and General Editor of its publications; Hon. Sec. Exeter Pictorial Record Society, 1911-33; Local Secretary for Devon of Society of Antiquaries of London; Hon. Member and sometime Chairman of Council of the Devonshire Association, and Recorder of Manuscripts and Records existing in, or relating to, Devonshire; Joint-Editor Devon and Cornwall Notes and Queries, 1910-19; F.S.A., Hon. F.R.Hist.S.; Member of the Society of Genealogists of London; Member of the Royal Archæological Institute of Great Britain and Ireland; Fellow of the Library Association, 1894, Hon. Fellow, 1936, Hon. Treasurer, 1929-1935; Hon. Fellow of the Association of Assistant Librarians; Pupil, Assistant, and Sub-Librarian, Stoke Newington Public Library, 1892-1902. *Publications:* An Official Guide to the City of Exeter, 3rd edition, 1909; Devon Past and Present, 1913; transcribed and edited with Prof. Walter J. Harte and Prof. W. J. Schopp, The Description of the Citie of Excester, by John Vowell, alias Hoker, from a 16th century manuscript in the archives of the city of Exeter, 3 vols., 1919-47; (with O. J. Reichel and F. B. Prideaux) Devon Feet of Fines, vol. 2, 1272-1369, 1939; the Registers of Allhallows, Goldsmith Street, Exeter; St. Pancras, Exeter; St. Paul's, Exeter; Ottery St. Mary, Devonshire; Branscombe, Devonshire; Topsham, Devonshire, etc.; with W. U. Reynell-Upham, The Registers of Exeter Cathedral, etc.; contributor to the Dictionary of National Biography and to the Transactions of Antiquarian and Genealogical Societies and Periodicals. *Recreations:* chess, local archæology and genealogy. *Address:* Wixels, Topsham, Devon. *T.:* Topsham 8259. [*Died* 24 *June* 1951.

SORABJI, Cornelia, B.C.L. Oxford; retired; formerly Barrister-at-law, High Court, Calcutta, and Lecturer in America and Canada on Indian topics; 5th *d.* of late Rev. Sorabji Kharsedji and Franscina Sorabji, pioneer Educationalist of Western India. *Educ.:* Somerville College, Oxford; Lee and Pembertons, Lincoln's Inn Fields, London; Bachelor of Civil Law, Oxford, 1893; obtained special privileges, Lincoln's Inn, London, 1893; conceived the idea of a man of business of her own sex for the secluded women of India; finding the work worth while, she propounded in 1902 a scheme to the India Office for connecting such Lady Counsel with the Provincial Executive Governments of India; in 1904, in pursuance of this scheme, appointed by the Government of Bengal Adviser to the Court of Wards; Legal Adviser to Purdahnishins, Court of Wards, Bengal, Behar and Orissa, and Assam, and Consulting Counsel, 1904-1923; Kaiser-i-Hind Gold Medal, 1909; Bar, First Class, 1922; called to the Bar, Lincoln's Inn, 1923. *Publications:* Love and Life behind the Purdah, 1902; Sun-Babies, 1904; Between the Twilights, 1908; Indian Tales of the Great Ones, 1916; The Purdahnashin, 1917; Shubala: Sun-Babies (second series) illustrated, 1920; Therefore, 1924; Gold Mohur Time, 1930; Life of Susie Sorabji, 1932; India Calling, 1934; India Recalled, 1936; and short stories and articles to English and American magazines and reviews. *Address:* c/o Martin's Bank, Ltd., 68 Lombard Street, E.C.3. [*Died* 6 *July* 1954.

SORINE, Savely; Russian-American Portrait Painter; *b.* Polozk, Govt. of Vitebsk, Russia, 1886; assumed American citizenship, 1936. *Educ.:* Russian Imperial Academy, and was sent abroad with the distinction Prix de Rome; under Repin. *Works:* portraits of The Queen, The Princess Elizabeth, The Duke and Duchess of Kent, Lady Beatty, Chaliapin, Maxime Gorky (San Francisco Museum), Pavlova (Luxembourg Museum), The Maharajah of Baroda, and other portraits in various galleries in Petrograd and Moscow. *Address:* c/o Wildenstein & Co. Ltd., 147 New Bond Street, W.1; 24 W. 59 Street, New York, U.S.A. [*Died* 22 *Nov.* 1953.

SOTHEBY, Lieut.-Colonel Herbert George, D.S.O. 1918; M.V.O. 1914; D.L.; *b.* 9 Nov. 1871; 2nd *s.* of late Admiral Sir Edward Southwell Sotheby, K.C.B., and Lucy Elizabeth, 3rd *d.* of Henry John and Hon. Mrs. Adeane, of Babraham, Cambridgeshire; *m.* 1923, Marjorie, *widow* of Capt. A. Y. Graham Thomson, M.C., Cameron Highlanders, and *o. d.* of A. C. McCorquodale, Cound Hall, Shrewsbury. Served South Africa, 1900-01 (Queen's medal 2 clasps); European War, 1914-19; commanded 10th Batt. Argyll and Sutherland Highlanders, 1916-19 (D.S.O., 1914 Star, French Croix de Guerre); High Sheriff of Northamptonshire, 1943. Lord of the Manor of Ecton. *Recreations:* shooting, golf. *Address:* Ecton Hall, Northampton. *Club:* Boodle's. [*Died* 6 *Dec.* 1954.

SOTHERON-ESTCOURT, Captain Thomas Edmund; *b.* 1881; *s.* of late Rev. Edmund Walter Sotheron-Estcourt; *m.* 1912, Anne Evelyn, 4th *d.* of late F. A. Anson; two *s.* (one killed in action) two *d.* *Educ.:* Harrow; Oxford. Royal Scots Greys, 1904-19; M.P. (U.) Pontefract Division, Yorks, 1931-35; J.P., West Riding, Yorks. *Address:* Estcourt, Tetbury, Glos. *T.:* Tetbury 54. *Clubs:* Cavalry; Royal Yacht Squadron (Cowes). [*Died* 25 *Jan.* 1958.

SOUCHON, Sir (Hippolyte) Louis (Wiehe du Coudray), Kt., *cr.* 1927; C.B.E. 1918; *b.* 1865; *s.* of late Henri Souchon, Mauritius; *m.* 1890, Georgina (*d.* 1928), *d.* of Hyacinthe Rouillard, Mauritius; three *s.* two *d.*; *m.* 1940, Edith, *widow* of Michel Rouillard and *d.* of late Henri Lagesse. Member of Mauritius Council of Government, 1901-12; Representative in London of Mauritius Chamber of Agriculture; retired, 1939. *Address:* Curepipe Road, Mauritius. [*Died* 12 *Dec.* 1957.

SOULBY, Rev. Charles Frederick Hodgkinson, M.A.; Canon Residentiary and Treasurer since 1944, Chaplain of Liverpool Cathedral since 1930; Bishop's Cathedral Chaplain, since 1944; *b.* Coningsby, Lincs, 31 May 1881; *s.* of Frederick Soulby and Ada Hodgkinson, Retford, Notts.; *m.* Mary, *d.* of Randal Podmore, Liverpool; two *s.* *Educ.:* Bromsgrove School; Exeter College, Oxford (Classical Scholar); 1st Class Classical Mod.; 3rd Class Lit. Hum.; Deacon, 1905; Priest,

1906; Curate of Holy Trinity, Warton, 1905-8; All Saints, Stoneycroft, Liverpool, 1908-10; St. Aidan, South Shields, 1910-13; Christ Church, Bishopwearmouth, 1913-14; Rector of Christ Church, Jarrow Grange, 1914-19; Inspector of Schools for Liverpool Diocese, 1919-33; Chaplain of St. Mary's Chapel for the Blind, Liverpool, 1919-27; Diocesan Canon of Liverpool, 1931-1944. *Recreations:* formerly cricket, football, and bicycling. *Address:* Kington, St. Michael's Road, Blundellsands, Liverpool 23. *T.:* Great Crosby 2175. [*Died* 26 *April* 1952.

SOULE, Malcolm H., Sc.D., LL.D.; Professor of Bacteriology, Chairman of the Department of Bacteriology, Director of the Hygienic Laboratory, Medical School, University of Michigan; *b.* 5 Dec. 1896. Medallist, American Medical Association, Detroit, 1930; Member of the Pathological Society of Great Britain and Ireland; Corr. Member: Société de Pathologie Exotique of Paris; La Sociedad Médico-Quirúrgica del Guayas; The Brazalian Leprosy Assoc.; Academy of Tropical Medicine; Consultant on Leprosy, Office of the Coordinator of Inter-American Affairs; Member Medical Advisory Board, Leonard Wood Memorial for the Eradication of Leprosy; National Research Council; Executive Committee and Editorial Board, American Assoc. for Advancement of Science. *Address:* Ann Arbor, Michigan, U.S.A. [*Died* 3 *Aug.* 1951.

SOUTAR, Brigadier John James Macfarlane, C.B.E. 1943; retired; *b.* Edinburgh, 23 Jan. 1889; *s.* of Lawrence Soutar, St. Martins; unmarried. *Educ.:* Royal Grammar School, Newcastle on Tyne; Royal (Dick) Veterinary College, Edinburgh. Lieut. A.V.C. 1910; Capt. R.A.V.C. 1915; Major, 1925; Lt.-Col. (Bt.) 1934; Col. and Temp. Brig. 1940; served ten years seconded to Egyptian Army and Sudan Govt. and three years with Iraqi Army; Senior Instructor R.A.V. School, 1922-26; A.D.V.S. India, 1931-35; Egypt, 1936-37; England, 1938-39; Director of Veterinary Services in India, 1940-44. *Publications:* articles in Professional Journals. *Address:* c/o Glyn Mills & Co., Whitehall, S.W.1; 6 Greyfriars Gardens, St. Andrews, Fife. *Clubs:* Scottish Conservative (Edinburgh); Royal and Ancient (St. Andrews). [*Died* 16 *Dec.* 1956.

SOUTER, Sir Charles Alexander, K.C.I.E. *cr.* 1936; C.S.I. 1933; I.C.S., retired; *b.* 13 June 1877. *Educ.:* Arbroath High School; Edinburgh University; Caius College, Cambridge. Entered I.C.S. 1900; Commissioner of Coorg, 1918-23; Member Board of Revenue, Madras, 1932-35; Member Executive Council, Madras, 1935-37; retd. 1937. *Address:* Little House, Tingewick, Buckingham. [*Died* 9 *Jan.* 1958.

SOUTER, Sir Edward (Matheson), Kt., *cr.* 1944; C.I.E. 1935; Managing Director, Ford & Macdonald Ltd.; *b.* 26 Jan. 1891; *s.* of James Francis Souter and Kate Matheson; *m.* 1916, Dorothy Andreae; two *s.* (and one killed War of 1939-45 on active service). *Educ.:* Inverness Academy. Joined Ford and Macdonald Ltd., Cawnpore, 1908; Managing Director Ford and Macdonald Ltd., Cawnpore, up to 1940; Controller of War Supplies, United Provinces, 1940-44; Member of the Legislature of the United Provinces, 1926-40; President, Development Board, Cawnpore, 1945-48. Chairman, Cawnpore Improvement Trust, 1931-39. *Recreations:* golf, motoring. *Address:* Civil Lines, Cawnpore, U.P., India. *T.A.:* Formac, Cawnpore. *T.:* Cawnpore 2194. *Clubs:* Caledonian; Cawnpore (Cawnpore). [*Died* 17 *June* 1959.

SOUTHAM, Rev. Eric George, M.A.; *b.* 24 May 1884; *s.* of late Frederick Armitage Southam, M.B. Oxon, F.R.C.S. Eng., and Amy Florence, *d.* of Rev. J. B. Hughes, M.A., Vicar of Staverton, Devon; *m.* 1915, Margaret de l'Etang, *d.* of late Sir Francis Champneys, Bt., M.D., F.R.C.P. *Educ.:* Rugby; Christ Church, Oxford; Wells Theological Coll. Curate All Saints, Poplar, 1909-12; Priest in charge S. Nicholas, Blackwall, 1912-15; Vicar S. Paul, Haggerston, E.8, 1915-23; Vicar S. Mark, North End, Portsmouth, 1923-27; Vicar of All Saints, West Southbourne, Bournemouth, 1927-37, with S. Andrew, Boscombe, to 1929 and S. James, Pokesdown, to 1931; Hon. Canon of Winchester, 1936; Provost of Guildford, Canon of Guildford and Rector of Holy Trinity Guildford with St. Mary and St. Luke, 1937-44; Senior Canon Residentiary of Guildford Cathedral and Canon Organiser, 1944-45; Canon Emeritus of Guildford Cathedral, 1945; Proctor in Convocation, 1941; Vicar of Brabourne with Monks Horton and Rector of Bircholt, 1945-47. *Publications:* Teach us to Pray, and The Christian Point of View (Broadcast Addresses). *Recreations:* golf, drama. *Address:* Pinewood, Ferndown, Wimborne, Dorset. [*Died* 20 *June* 1952.

SOUTHAM, Harry Stevenson, C.M.G. 1935; B.A., Hon. LL.D. (Queen's Univ., Kingston); Chairman Board of Trustees of the National Gallery of Canada since 1929; Publisher of Ottawa Citizen since 1920; *b.* London, Ontario; 4th *s.* of late William Southam (Founder of The Southam Newspapers of Canada) and late Wilson Mills; *m.* 1909, Lilias, *o. d.* of late Hon. Thomas Ahearn, Ottawa; two *s.* two *d.* *Educ.:* Upper Canada Coll., Toronto; Univ. of Toronto. Chancellor of Carleton College, Ottawa. Newspaper publisher; joined The Citizen Staff, 1900; Christian Scientist. *Address:* Casa Loma, Rockcliffe Park, Ottawa, Canada. *Clubs:* Rideau, Country, Royal Ottawa Golf (Ottawa). [*Died* 27 *March* 1954.

SOUTHAMPTON, 4th Baron (*cr.* 1780), **Charles Henry Fitzroy,** O.B.E.; Capt. 10th Hussars; retired, 1892; *b.* 11 May 1867; *s.* of 3rd Baron and 2nd wife, Ismay, *d.* of Walter Nugent, and *g.d.* of Sir Charles Jenkinson, Bt.; *S.* father, 1872; *m.* 1892, Lady Hilda Mary Dundas (*d.* 1957), *d.* of 1st Marquess of Zetland; one *s.* three *d.* *Educ.:* Eton; Sandhurst. *Heir:* *s.* Hon. Charles Fitzroy. *Address:* Winkfield Lodge, Windsor. [*Died* 7 *Dec.* 1958.

SOUTHBOROUGH, 2nd Baron, *cr.* 1917; **James Spencer Neill Hopwood,** *b.* 17 Jan. 1889; *e. s.* of 1st Baron Southborough, P.C., G.C.B., G.C.M.G., G.C.V.O., K.C.S.I. and Alice, *d.* of late Captain William James Smith-Neill, R.A., Swindridge Muir and Barnweil, Ayrshire; *S.* father, 1947; *m.* 1923, Dorothy Stewart Leslie, *o.d.* of late Col. Archibald Young Leslie, 14th Laird of Kininvie, Banffshire. *Educ.:* Tonbridge School; St. John's College, Oxford. Served European War, 1914-18, Temp. 2nd Lt. 9th Bn. Q.O. Royal West Kent Regt., 1915-16. Civil Servant, Board of Trade and Ministry of Labour; lent to War Trade Intelligence Dept. and War Trade Dept., 1915-17; retired from Civil Service, 1931. *Heir:* *half-b.* Hon. Sir Francis Hopwood. *Address:* c/o Glyn, Mills & Co. Ltd., 1 Fleet St., E.C.4. [*Died* 25 *Feb.* 1960.

SOUTHORN, Sir (Wilfrid) Thomas, K.C.M.G., *cr.* 1938 (C.M.G. 1927); K.B.E., *cr.* 1933; *b.* 4 Aug. 1879; *s.* of late Josiah Southorn, Leamington Spa; *m.* 1921, Bella, O.B.E. 1935, *widow* of R. H. Lock, Sc.D. and *e. d.* of late Sidney Woolf, Q.C. *Educ.:* Warwick School; Corpus Christi College, Oxford; B.A. 1903; M.A. 1933; Hon. LL.D. Hong Kong University, 1936. Entered Ceylon Civil Service, 1903; Principal Assistant Colonial Secretary, 1920; Principal Collector of Customs and Chairman, Port Commission, 1923; Member, Legislative Council, 1924, and Executive Council, 1925; Colonial Secretary, Hong Kong, 1926-36; administered Government of Hong Kong on various occasions, 1922-32; Governor and Commander-in-Chief of the Gambia, 1936-42; Colonial Service Liaison Officer, 1942-46.

Address: c/o Lloyd's Bank Ltd., Leamington Spa. *Club:* Athenæum. [*Died* 15 *March* 1957.

SOUTHHOUSE-CHEYNEY, Major R. E. P.; *see* Cheyney, Peter.

SOUTHWELL, 6th Viscount (*cr.* 1776), **Robert Arthur William Joseph Southwell,** Bt., 1662; Baron Southwell 1717; Comdr. R.N.; *b.* 5 Sept. 1898; *e. s.* of 5th Visc. Southwell and Dorothy Katharine (*d.* 1952), *d.* of 1st Lord Waleran; *S.* father, 1944; *m.* 1st, 1926, Violet Mary Weldon (who obtained a divorce, 1931; she *m.* 2nd, 1932, Lt.-Comdr. Paul Freeman, R.N.), *o. c.* of Paymaster Captain Francis W. Walshe, M.V.O., O.B.E.; one *d.*; 2nd, 1943, Josephine, *d.* of Denis Joseph de la Mole, and formerly wife of Captain Henry Marryat Hardy. *Educ.:* Osborne; Dartmouth. *Heir:* *nephew* Pyers Anthony Joseph, *b.* 14 Sept. 1930. *Address:* 73 Woodmere Avenue, Croydon, Surrey. *T.:* Addiscombe 1876. [*Died* 18 *Nov.* 1960.

SOWERBY, Arthur de Carle, F.R.G.S., F.Z.S.; Pres., 1936-40, Hon. Life Member, Royal Asiatic Soc. (North China Branch); *b.* Taiyuan Fu, Shansi, China, 8 July 1885; *e. s.* of late Rev. Arthur Sowerby; *m.* 1st, 1909, Mary Ann, *e. d.* of John Mesny; one *s.*; 2nd, 1925, Clarice Sara (*d.* 1944), 2nd *d.* of P. H. Moise; 3rd, 1946, Alice Muriel, 2nd *d.* of Charles Rudolph Cowens. Has travelled extensively in China, S. Mongolia, and Manchuria, collecting zoological specimens for the British Museum (Natural History), Duke of Bedford's Zoological Exploration in Eastern Asia, 1908, Clark Expedition, 1909, and for the United States National Museum, 1910-17 and 1921-31; led the Shensi Relief Expedition during the Chinese Revolution, 1911-12; served in France as Chinese Expert on Headquarters Staff of the Chinese Labour Corps, 1918; One of founders and continuous President of the China Society of Science and Arts 1923-33; Founder, and Editor, 1923-37, of The China Journal; Director Shanghai Museum (R.A.S.), 1925-46; One of Founders and Pres. 1934-40 of Numismatic Society of China. Liberated at Shanghai Sept. 1945. *Publications:* Fur and Feather in North China; A Sportsman's Miscellany; Sport and Science on the Sino-Mongolian Frontier; The Naturalist in Manchuria, vols. i.-v.; A Naturalist's Holiday by the Sea; A Naturalist's Note-Book in China; China and Ivory; China's Natural History, a Guide to the Shanghai Museum (R.A.S.); Nature Notes: a Guide to the Fauna and Flora of a Shanghai Garden; Nature in Chinese Art; Birds Recorded from or Known to Occur in the Shanghai Area; The Sowerby Saga; (with R. S. Clark) Through Shen Kan; numerous zoological and other papers in scientific journals; contributions on Chinese Art and other subjects to newspapers and periodicals, etc. *Address:* c/o Hongkong and Shanghai Banking Corporation, 9 Gracechurch Street, E.C.3; Riggs National Bank, Washington, D.C., U.S.A. *Clubs:* Tientsin (Tientsin); Shanghai (Shanghai). [*Died* 16 *Aug.* 1954.

SPAIN, John Edward; *see* Dixon-Spain.

SPALDING, Henry Norman, M.A.; Hon. D.C.L. (Durham); F.R.S.L.; *b.* Blackheath, S.E., 15 Aug. 1877; *s.* of Henry B. Spalding and Ellen Rebe (*née* Jay); *m.* 1909, Nellie Maud Emma, *d.* of E. and E. Cayford; one *s.* two *d.* *Educ.:* in Switzerland and France; Eastbourne College; New College, Oxford. Civil Servant in Admiralty, 1901-09; Barrister-at-law, Lincoln's Inn, 1906; contested (L.) Northern (East Grinstead) Division of Sussex, Dec. 1910; Prospective Liberal candidate for Reading, 1914; served in Admiralty and Ministry of Munitions (Deputy Director, Welfare Department), 1915-18. Member of Brasenose Coll., Oxford, 1919. With his Wife founded at Oxford a Chair of Eastern Religions and Ethics, a University Lectureship in Eastern Orthodox Culture, an Advisership in Eastern Art, and four temporary Senior Research Fellowships in Indian history and religion at Oriel and Brasenose Colleges; assisted in the gifts of books made by the Univ. of Oxford to those of China, 1939, and to the devastated Univs. of Europe and Asia, 1947; gave Univ. of Oxford a Wild Life Sanctuary on the Cherwell. With his Wife provided a Centre (Holybrook House) in Reading for W.E.A., 1919-39. Was one of founders of Assoc. of British Orientalists, of Museum of Eastern Art at Oxford, and of series of Ethical and Religious Classics of East and West; a Vice-Pres. of World Congress of Faiths; member of Council of Roy. India Soc. and of Oriental Cttee. of Durham Univ. *Publications:* From Youth to Age (verse), 1930; A Poem of Praise, 1950; In Praise of Life (collected poems), 1952; Civilisation in East and West, 1939. *Address:* 9 South Parks Road, Oxford. *T.:* Oxford 3880. *Club:* Athenæum. [*Died* 6 *Sept.* 1953.

SPARKS, Beatrice M., M.A.; Hon. Fellow St. Hugh's College. *Educ.:* St. Hugh's College, Oxford. Headmistress, Wisbech High School, 1905-13; Colston's Girls' School, Bristol, 1914-22; was a member of the Departmental Committee on Scholarships and the Burnham Committee; President, Association of Head Mistresses, 1925-27; Principal of Cheltenham Ladies' College, 1922-36; retired, 1936. *Address:* 13 Vicarage Road, Lillington, Leamington. *T.:* 850. [*Died* 6 *Aug.* 1953.

SPARKS, Sir Frederick (James), Kt., *cr.* 1943; *b.* 1 April 1881; *er. s.* of late James Sparks, Solicitor, Bradford-on-Avon, Wilts; *m.* 1910, Emily Nora, 2nd *d.* of late Frank Henty Elliott, Southampton; no *c.* *Educ.:* privately. Solicitor, 1903; Asst. Solicitor, Southampton, 1906-8; Shoreditch, 1908-9; Portsmouth, 1909-10; Deputy Town Clerk, Portsmouth, 1910-20; Town Clerk, 1920-1946; retired, 1946. J.P. (Portsmouth City) 1946. Member Portsmouth National Safety First Council; Chairman Portsmouth and District Furnished Houses (Rents) Tribunal; Director Southsea Hotels Ltd.; Captain 4th Bn. Wiltshire Regt. 1914-1916, when invalided from India. A.R.P. Controller, Portsmouth, 1939-45. *Recreation:* motoring. *Address:* 21A St. Helen's Parade, Southsea. *T.:* Portsmouth 32030. [*Died* 27 *March* 1953.

SPARKS, Nathaniel, R.E., A.R.C.A. (Lond.); engraver; *b.* Bristol, 18 June 1880. *Educ.:* privately; Bristol Government School of Art; Royal College of Art, London. *Publications:* A long series of Engravings, Drawings and Water Colours of England and Scotland. *Address:* c/o The Westminster Bank, 300 King's Road, S.W.3. [*Died* 29 *Aug.* 1957.

SPARROW, Colonel Richard, C.M.G. 1916; D.S.O. 1918; late commanding 7th (Princess Royal's) Dragoon Guards; retired pay, 1920; *b.* 10 June 1871; *y. s.* of late Basil Sparrow, of Gosfield Place, Halstead, Essex; *m.* 1st, 1918, Cecily Mabel (*d.* 1940), 2nd *d.* of late Major B. C. Garfit of Dalby Hall, Spilsby, and *widow* of Capt. H. P. L. Heyworth, North Stafford Regt.; 2nd, 1941, Dorothea Barbara, *d.* of late W. G. Jackson, and *widow* of Arthur B. Willson. *Educ.:* Wellington College, Sandhurst. Joined 7th Dragoon Guards, 1892; Captain, 1899; Major, 1903; Lt.-Col. 1914; Col. 1918; Remount Dept., S. Africa, 1899-1901; served S. African War, 1899-1902 (despatches, Queen's medal 3 clasps, King's medal 2 clasps); Indian Durbar; served European War (C.M.G., 1914 Star, despatches, D.S.O.); retired, 1920; F.R.G.S., F.Z.S., M.B.O.U. *Recreations:* hunting, shooting, fishing, big-game shooting. *Address:* The Lodge, Colne Engaine, Colchester, Essex. *Club:* Army and Navy. [*Died* 6 *Dec.* 1953.

SPATH, Leonard Frank, D.Sc.; F.R.S. 1940; F.G.S.; Geologist; Palaeontologist in Geology Department of British Museum (Natural History) since 1912; Lecturer in Geology at Birkbeck College (University of London), 1920-51; *b.* 20 Oct. 1882; *m.* 1915, Florence Elizabeth Sweet (*d.* 1942); two *s.* Took B.Sc., M.Sc., and D.Sc. degrees at University of London; Geological explorations in Africa and America before European War; served in France and Belgium, 1916-1919. Lyell Medallist, Geological Soc., 1945. Elected Member of Roy. Danish Acad. of Sciences and Letters, 1951. *Publications:* many memoirs, monographs, etc., on the evolution, morphology, and systematics of fossil Cephalopoda. *Address:* 39 Philbeach Gardens, S.W.5. [*Died* 2 *March* 1957.

SPEARMAN, Sir Alexander Young, 3rd Bt., *cr.* 1840; Consulting Mining Engineer; 2nd *s.* of 2nd Bt. and 1st wife Ethel (*d.* 1909), *d.* of William Leask, 48 Queen's Gate; *b.* 19 June 1881; *S.* father, 1922; *m.* 1909, Dorothy Catherine, *d.* of Thomas Bowyer-Bower-Iwerne, Dorsetshire; two *s.* one *d.* *Educ.:* Stubbington School; Tonbridge. *Recreation:* golf. *Heir:* *s.* Capt. Alexander Bowyer, I.A., retd. [*b.* 15 Feb. 1917; *m.* 1950, Martha Green, Nauwpoort, S. Africa]. *Address:* Oaks Bungalow, Oaks Avenue, Upper Norwood, S.E.19. [*Died* 11 *Feb.* 1959.

SPEED, Harold, R.P. 1896; *b.* London, 1872; *s.* of Edward Speed, A.R.I.B.A.; *m.*; one *d.* *Educ.:* privately. Gold Medal, Nat. Competitions, 1890; Gold Medal and travelling scholarship, Roy. Academy, 1893; gold medal, Anglo-German Exhibition, Crystal Palace, 1906; gold medal, Panama International Exhibition, 1915; painted fresco on wall of Refreshment Room, Royal Academy, 1895; picture The Alcantara, Toledo, bought by Chantrey Bequest for Tate Gallery, 1905; also represented in Walker Art Gallery, Liverpool, and the Municipal Galleries of Manchester, Birmingham, Bristol, Sheffield, Wolverhampton, Leamington, Southampton, Northampton, Blackpool, Burton-on-Trent, Dublin, Melbourne, Australia; Dunedin, Wellington, New Zealand; etc.; painted full length portrait King Edward VII. (exhibited Royal Academy and Paris Salon); King Albert of Belgium, R.A., 1916; had among sitters the Earl of Bessborough, Sir Charles Dilke, Bt., John Burns, John Redmond, Campbell-Bannerman, Lord Carrington, Holman Hunt, The Bishop of Calcutta, Lilian Braithwaite, Lady Alexander, Lord Baden-Powell, Mark Hambourg, Rt. Hon. George Wyndham, Rt. Hon. Sir Frederick Milner, Bart.; Lord Brassey, Viscount Grey of Fallodon, Hensley Henson, Bishop of Durham, etc.; painted frescoes on all walls of chapel of Wesley House, Cambridge; representative exhibition of 70 pictures: Municipal Galleries of Sheffield, Blackpool and 6 other towns; Master of the Art Workers' Guild, 1916; Member of the Société Nationale des Beaux-Arts (Salon, Paris); Member of Royal Society of Portrait Painters (Hon. Treas.), etc. *Publications:* The Science and Practice of Drawing, 1913, Finnish edition, 1923; Spanish edition, 1928; The Science and Practice of Oil Painting, 1924; What is the Good of Art, 1936. *Recreations:* cricket, golf and music (singing). *Address:* 23 Campden Hill Square, W.8. *T.:* Park 9082; Meadow Court, Watlington, Oxfordshire. *T.:* Watlington 63. *Club:* Authors'. [*Died* 20 *March* 1957.

SPEIR, Col. Guy Thomas; *b.* 1875; *e. s.* of late R. T. N. Speir, of Culdees; *m.* Mary Lucy, *d.* of late John Fletcher of Saltoun; three *s.* two *d.* *Educ.:* Eton; Pembroke College, Cambridge (B.A.). Called to Scottish Bar, 1899; Private Secretary to Secretary for Scotland, 1899-1905; Secretary to the Whaling Commission; Chief Conservative Agent for Scotland, 1906-11; A.D.C. Staff of 34th (F.A.) Brigade, 1899-1905; Captain 4th V.B.R.H.; Captain 1/1 H.C. Batt., 1914-16; Lieut.-Colonel commanding 2/6 S. Staffords, 1916-20, with B.E.F., 1917; 1/1 Northern Cyclist Batt., 1918; contested (U.) Buteshire, 1906. *Address:* The Abbey, North Berwick. *T.:* N. Berwick 57. *Club:* Carlton. [*Died* 1 *Sept.* 1951.

SPEIRS, Alexander Archibald Hagart-, J.P., D.L.; *o. s.* of late Capt. Archibald Alexander Speirs of Elderslie, M.P., and Lady Anne, *e. d.* of 4th Earl of Radnor; *b.* and *S.* 1869 [assumed additional name of Hagart, 1911, in accordance with the settlement of his grandmother]; *m.* 1918, Mary Henrietta Elizabeth, *o. d.* of late Henry Darley Livingstone, J.P. of Belclare, Westport, Co. Mayo; late Capt. 4th Batt. Argyll and Sutherland Highlanders; late Major and County Adjutant Renfrewshire Volunteer Regt. Lord-Lieut. of Renfrewshire, 1943-50. *Address:* Houston House, Renfrewshire. *T.:* Johnstone 42; Eastbury Manor, Compton, Guildford, Surrey. *T.:* Puttenham 209. *Clubs:* Brooks's; New (Edinburgh); Western (Glasgow). [*Died* 14 *July* 1958.

SPENCE, Sir James Calvert, Kt., *cr.* 1950; M.C.; M.D.; F.R.C.P.; Hon. D.Sc. (Western Australia); Hon. LL.D. (Cincinnati); Professor of Child Health, University of Durham; Hon. Physician, Royal Victoria Infirmary; Physician to General Hospital, Newcastle on Tyne; Member: University Grants Committee; Medical Research Council, 1944-48; Medical Advisory Committee Nuffield Provincial Hospitals Trust; Central Health Services Council; *b.* 19 March 1892; *s.* of Magnus Spence and Isabella Turnbull; *m.* 1920, Kathleen, *y. d.* of Robert Downie-Leslie, Aberdeen; one *s.* four *d.* *Educ.:* Elmfield, York; Durham Univ. M.B., B.S. (Hons.) 1914, M.D. 1921; served R.A.M.C. 11th Div., European War, 1914-18 (M.C. and bar); House Physician, Great Ormond Street Hospital for Sick Children, 1919; John and Temple Research Fellow, St. Thomas's Hospital, 1920-22; Chemical Pathologist and Medical Registrar, Royal Victoria Infirmary, Newcastle on Tyne, 1922-27; Rockefeller Research Fellow, Johns Hopkins Hospital, U.S.A., 1928; Bradshaw Lecturer R.C.P., 1940; Charles West Lecturer, R.C.P., 1946; Interstate Postgraduate Lecturer, Australia, 1948; Cutter Lecturer, Harvard University, 1949; Blackader Lecturer, Canadian Medical Association, 1949. Dawson Williams Lecturer, B.M.A., 1949; Ingelby Lecturer, Birmingham Univ., 1952. Member: Interdepartmental (Curtis) Cttee. on care of children, 1945-46; Assoc. of Physicians; British Pædiatric Assoc.; Hon. Member: Amer. Pædiatric Soc.; Amer. Acad. of Pædiatrics; and of the Canadian Society for Study of Diseases of Children. *Publications:* scientific papers in Medical Journals and Books. *Address:* 25 Brandling Park, Newcastle on Tyne, 2. *T.:* Jesmond 861. *Club:* Athenæum. [*Died* 26 *May* 1954.

SPENCE, (James) Lewis (Thomas Chalmers); *b.* 25 Nov. 1874; *e. s.* of late J. E. Spence, of Brook Street House, Broughty Ferry, Forfarshire; *m.* 1899, Helen, *d.* of late George Bruce, Edinburgh; one *s.* three *d.* *Educ.:* Collegiate School, Broughty Ferry; privately; Edinburgh University. Contested N. Midlothian as a Nationalist Candidate, Jan. 1929; Sub-editor of The Scotsman, 1899-1904; editor of The Edinburgh Magazine, 1904-05; sub-editor of The British Weekly, 1906-09; Editor The Atlantis Quarterly, 1932; took up the study of mythology, with special reference to that of Mexico and Central America; Fellow Roy. Anthropological Inst. of Great Britain and Ireland; Vice-Pres. Scot. Anthropological and Folklore Soc.; D.Lit. Received Royal Pension for Services to literature, 1951. *Publications:* The Mythologies of Mexico and Peru, 1907; The Popol Vuh, a saga of the Kiche people of Central America, 1908;

A Dictionary of Mythology, 1910; The Civilisation of Ancient Mexico, 1911; Le Roi d'Ys, a volume of verse, 1910; Myths of Mexico and Peru, 1913; A Dictionary of Mediæval Romance and Romance Writers, 1913; Songs, Satanic and Celestial, 1913; The Myths of the North American Indians, 1914; Myths of Ancient Egypt, 1915; Myths and Legends of Babylonia and Assyria, 1916; Mexico of the Mexicans, 1917; Legends and Romances of Brittany, 1917; an Encyclopædia of Occultism, 1920; Legends and Romances of Spain, 1920; An Introduction to Mythology, 1921; The Gods of Mexico, 1923; The Phœnix, verse, 1924; The Problem of Atlantis, 1924; Atlantis in America, 1925; A History of Atlantis, 1926; The Plumes of Time (poems), 1926; Weirds and Vanities, verse, 1927; The Mysteries of Britain, 1928; The Mysteries of Egypt, 1929; The Magic and Mysteries of Mexico; The Problem of Lemuria, 1932; The Archer in the Arras, 1932; Legendary London, 1937; Boadicea, 1937; The Occult Causes of the Present War, 1940; Will Europe follow Atlantis?, 1942; The Occult Sciences in Atlantis, 1943; The Outlines of Mythology 1944; The Religion of Ancient Mexico, 1945; The Magic Arts in Celtic Britain; British Fairy Origins, 1945; Myth and Ritual in Dance, Game and Rhyme, 1946; The Fairy Tradition in Britain, 1947; The Minor Traditions of British Mythology, 1948; The Origins of Druidism, 1949; Second Sight, its History and Origins, 1951; Collected Poems, 1953; Scottish Ghosts and Goblins, 1954. *Recreations:* wandering about Edinburgh and studying types, collecting Edinburgh folklore, verse-writing, listening to music, and collecting books on old America and on the mysterious. *Address:* 34 Howard Place, Edinburgh. *Club:* P.E.N.

[*Died* 3 *March* 1955.

SPENCE, William Robert Locke, C.B.E. 1937; *b.* Bonnyrigg, Parish of Cockpen, Midlothian, 9 Oct. 1875; *s.* of William and Jane Morton Spence; *m.* 1935, Winifred Edith Taylor. *Educ.:* Royal High School, Edinburgh. Went to sea at 15 years of age as apprentice in sail, subsequently as officer in sail and steam; left sea in 1911 to take service with National Union of Seamen; served as an official of that body in various ports in Great Britain until 1928; General Secretary National Union of Seamen, 1928-42. *Address:* 19 Mill Lane, Shoreham by Sea, Sussex.

[*Died* 3 *March* 1954.

SPENCE-COLBY, Colonel Cecil John Herbert, C.M.G. 1919; D.S.O. 1917; T.D.; D.L., J.P.; *o. c.* of late Very Rev. H. D. M. Spence-Jones and Mrs. Spence-Jones of Pantglas, Carmarthenshire; *b.* 1873; *m.* 1908, Aline Margaret, *e. d.* of John Vaughan Colby, D.L., J.P., Ffynone, Pembrokeshire, late Capt. Rifle Brigade; one *d.* (one *s.* decd.). *Educ.:* Harrow. [Assumed by Royal Licence name of Spence-Colby, 1920.] Served S. African War, 1899-1903; Adjt. 1st Mtd. Infantry, and afterwards as A.D.C. to Inspector-General, Mtd. Infantry (despatches); European War; Lt.-Col., 1914; Col., 1918; Commanded Pembroke Yeo.; also 24th Bn. (Pembroke and Glam Yeo.); Welsh Regt. (D.S.O., despatches four times, C.M.G.); D.L. and J.P. for Cos. Pembroke and Carmarthen; High Sheriff of Herefordshire for 1946-47; Lord of the Manor and Patron of the Living of Donnington. *Recreations:* hunting, shooting. *Address:* Donnington Hall, Ledbury, Herefordshire. *T.A.:* Greenway. *T.:* Dymock 234.

[*Died* 18 *Oct.* 1954.

SPENCELAYH, Charles, R.M.S., R.B.S.A. (Hon. Mem.); Vice-Pres. B.W.S.; artist; *b.* Rochester, 27 Oct. 1865; *s.* of Henry Spencelayh, Engineer, Iron and Brass Founder; *m.* 1890; one *s.* *Educ.:* Dr. Burns', Rochester. Student of South Kensington and studied in Paris; portrait painter in oil and miniature, and figure painter, both in oil and water, also etcher; exhibited at the R.A. since 1892, and at Paris Salon, and Provincial Exhibitions for many years. Miniature in Queen's Dolls' House. Two of his oil paintings bought from R.A. by Queen Mary, who commissioned a third. *Address:* St. Mildred, London Road, Bozeat, Northants. *T.:* Bozeat 256.

[*Died* 25 *June* 1958.

SPENCER, George Alfred, D.L. Notts; J.P.; *b.* 1872; President Notts County Cricket Club, 1949-50; late President Nottingham and District Miners' Federated Union and President of the National Federation of Industrial Unions; Member of National Coal Board, and North Midland Regional Coal Board; late President Notts Miners Association; late President Mansfield General Hospital; Vice-President Women's Hospital, Nottingham; served on the Urban District Council and the Education Committee; late checkweighman; M.P. (Lab.) Broxtowe Division of Notts, Dec. 1918-29; has also been a local preacher. *Address:* 139 Gordon Road West, Bridgford, Nottingham. *T.:* 231055.

[*Died Nov.* 1957.

SPENCER, Brig.-Gen. John Almeric Walter, C.M.G. 1919; D.S.O. 1918; late The Rifle Brigade; *b.* 1881; *m.* 1913, Eleanor Georgiana, *y. d.* of William Peel, of Knowlmere Manor, Clitheroe; one *s.* *Educ.:* Harrow; R.M.C., Sandhurst. Served European War, 1914-19 (despatches, C.M.G., D.S.O., Legion of Honour); Assistant Adjutant-General at the War Office, 1927-31; Commander 163rd (Norfolk and Suffolk) Infantry Bde., T.A., 1931-35; retd. pay, 1935. *Address:* Ghyllas, Sedbergh, Yorks.

[*Died* 12 *Feb.* 1952.

SPENCER, Leonard James, C.B.E. 1934; F.R.S. 1925; M.A.; Sc.D. (Camb.); Hon. B.Sc. (Nat. Univ. Ireland); F.G.S.; F.C.S.; F.R.G.S.; Editor Mineralogical Magazine, 1900-55; and Mineralogical Abstracts; President of the Mineralogical Society, 1936-1939; Hon. Life Fellow, Mineralogical Soc. of America (Roebling Gold Medal, 1940); Hon. Member German Mineralogical Society and Royal Geological Society of Cornwall (Bolitho Gold Medal); Special Constable, Metropolitan Police, 1915-18; *b.* Worcester, 7 July 1870; *e. s.* of James Spencer, B.Sc., F.C.S., schoolmaster, and Elizabeth Bonser; *m.* 1899, Edith Mary (*d.* 1954), *e. d.* of Islip J. Close, Mortimer, Berks; one *s.* two *d.* *Educ.:* Keighley Trade and Grammar School; Bradford Technical College; Royal College of Science for Ireland, Dublin (Royal Exhibitioner, Associateship 1st Class in Chemistry, A.R.C.Sc.I.); Sidney Sussex College, Cambridge (Scholar, 1st Class Natural Sciences Tripos, Parts I. and II., Harkness University Scholarship in Geology); University of Munich. Outside work (abridging and indexing) for H.M. Patent Office, 1889; Assistant, Mineral Department, British Museum, 1894; Keeper of Minerals, British Museum of Natural History, 1927-35; Examiner, Natural Sciences Tripos, Cambridge, 1899-1900, 1931-1932; Univ. of Durham, 1907-8, 1912-14; awarded the Wollaston Fund (1902) and Murchison Medal (1937) of the Geological Society (Vice-President, 1945-46); Referee for the Mineralogy Volumes of the International Catalogue of Scientific Literature, 1901-14; in connection with recording the weights of large diamonds, was partly instrumental in the introduction (in 1914) of the metric carat as the legal unit of weight for precious stones; a zinc phosphate and an iron carbide have been named spencerite. *Publicatons:* The World's Minerals, 1911; A Key to Precious Stones, 1936, 2nd and Amer. edns., 1946; numerous mineral articles in Encyclopædia Britannica (11th-14th edits.) and in Thorpe's Dictionary of Applied Chemistry; dictionary lists of new mineral names and biographical notices of mineralogists every three years since 1897; many original papers. *Recreation:* gardening. *Address:* 111 Albert Bridge Road, S.W.11.

[*Died* 14 *April* 1959.

SPENCER, Capt. Richard Austin, Barrister-at-Law; *b.* 8 Aug. 1892; *o. s.* of Thomas William Spencer, shipper, Manchester, and Rachel, *d.* of Abraham Austin; unmarried. *Educ.:* Salford Grammar School; Borough Road College, London. B.A.(Lond.), 1st Class Hons. Modern Languages, 1915; M.A. Mediæval and Modern English, 1924; served European War, Manchester Regiment and R.A.F., Captain (despatches); Senior Lecturer in English, Manchester Training College; French Master, Manchester Central High School; Chairman, Secondary School Teachers Panel, Manchester; Chairman Hale Urban District Council; contested (C.) St. Helens, 1929; M.P. (C.) St. Helens, 1931-1935; called to Bar, Gray's Inn, 1937. Secretary, Royal Society of Teachers, 1936-53. *Publications:* French Composition from French Models, Guirlande de Poésies. and other French text-books; Pointers to Progress, 1935; The Art of Teaching; contributions to Educational Press; Song of Roland, etc. *Address:* Fern Bank, Mobberley, Cheshire. [*Died* 8 *Dec.* 1956.

SPENCER, Sir Stanley, Kt. 1959; C.B.E. 1950; R.A. 1950 (A.R.A. 1932, resigned 1935, re-elected 1950); Member N.E.A.C., 1919-1927; Fellow of University College, London, 1954; Hon. Fellow, Royal College of Art, 1958; Hon. D.Litt. Southampton Univ., 1959; *b.* Cookham, 1891; 7th *s.* of late William Spencer, Professor of Music; *m.* 1st, Hilda Carline; 2nd., Patricia Preece (professional name as artist). *Educ.:* Slade School. *Works:* mural paintings for the oratory of All Souls', Burghclere; Resurrection, Christ bearing the Cross, The Sword of the Lord and of Gideon, Daphne, Terry's Lane, Cookham (Tate Gallery); The Nativity (Univ. of London); Travoys arriving with wounded, Macedonia (Imperial War Museum); Shipbuilding on the Clyde (official War Records). Works in Public Galleries at Aberdeen, Belfast, Birmingham, Bradford, Cambridge, Cardiff, Carlisle, Dublin, Glasgow, Hull, Leamington, Leeds, Liverpool, Manchester, Nottingham, Preston, Rochdale, Sheffield, Southampton; New York, Adelaide, Melbourne, Sydney, Pietermaritzburg, Toronto, Vancouver. *Rel. publ.:* Stanley Spencer, by Gilbert Spencer, 1961. *Address:* c/o Arthur Tooth and Sons, 31 Bruton Street, W.1. [*Died* 14 *Dec.* 1959.

SPENCER, William Kingdon, F.R.S.; M.A., D.Sc. (Oxon.); F.G.S.; H.M. Inspector of Schools (retired); *s.* of John Firth and Mary Spencer, Parkstone, Dorset; *m.* Katherine Violet, *d.* of James Gordon Stewart, Newburgh House, Aberdeenshire; two *d.* *Educ.:* Batley Grammar School; Magdalen College, Oxford; University of Marburg; Demy of Magdalen, Burdett-Coutts University Scholar, Hon. mention Rolleston Memorial Prize. Lecturer and Demonstrator in Department of Geology, Oxford, 1903-4; Chief Examiner in Science. Board of Education; Inspector of Science in Training Colleges; Lyell award, Geological Society. *Publications:* Monographs on Fossil Starfish published by Palæontographical Society; Evolution of Chalk Starfish, Phil. Trans. Royal Society, 1913; other scientific papers. *Recreations:* golf, bridge. *Club:* Authors'. [*Died* 1 *Oct.* 1955.

SPENCER JONES, Sir Harold; *see* Jones.

SPENCER-NAIRN, Major Sir Robert, 1st Bt., *cr.* 1933; Kt. 1928; T.D.; J.P., D.L.; Director of Michael Nairn & Company Ltd., linoleum manufacturers, Kirkcaldy, Fife, N.B.; *b.* 11 July 1880; 2nd *s.* of late Sir Michael Barker Nairn, Bt., of Rankeilour and Dysart House, Fife; *m.* 1906, Clara Kathleen, *d.* of late C. Chaloner Smith, Woodthorpe, Cobham, Surrey; three *s.* three *d.* *Educ.:* Rugby; Trinity Hall, Cambridge. Fife and Forfar Yeomanry (Territorial), rank of Major; served European War. Master, Fife Fox Hounds, 1932-47. *Heir:* *s.* Douglas Leslie Spencer-Nairn, T.D. *Address:* Over Rankeilour, Cupar, Fife. *Clubs:* Carlton Boodle's; New (Edinburgh). [*Died* 20 *Oct.* 1960.

SPENCER-SMITH, Sir Drummond Cospatric Hamilton-, 5th Bt., *cr.* 1804; O.B.E. 1923; *b.* Kingston, Corfe Castle, Dorset, 4 Nov. 1876; *s.* of late Rev. S. C. Hamilton-Spencer-Smith and Mary, *d.* of Adm. Cospatric Baillie-Hamilton; *S.* kinsman, 1947; *m.* 1st, 1915, Roma, *d.* of Arthur Hope, Timaru, N.Z.; one *s.*; 2nd, 1923, Mary Aurora, *widow* of Col. Ridley Boileau, R.E. *Educ.:* Eton; New College, Oxford. Gazetted to Royal Artillery, 1900; R.H.A. as 2nd Lt., Lt., Capt., Maj. and Lt.-Col. Mil. Sec. and Staff Officer, R.A., to G.O.C., N.Z. Forces, 1910-13; served European War, 1914-18, Bde. Major R.A., 4th Div., France, 1916 (despatches); Comdt. R.A. Officers Cadet School, Exeter, 1917-18; commanded 14th R.H.A. Bde., France, 1918-19; served with Military Internat. Commission of Control, H.Q. Berlin, 1920-24. *Recreations:* cricket, golf, hunting, shooting. *Heir:* *s.* Thomas Cospatric Hamilton-Spencer-Smith [later Sir Thomas Hamilton-Spencer-Smith, 6th Bt., *q.v.*]. *Address:* Suttons, Stapleford Tawney, Romford, Essex. *T.:* Stapleford 245. *Clubs:* United Service, M.C.C., Free Foresters, Eton Ramblers. [*Died* 18 *Dec.* 1955.

SPENCER-SMITH, Sir Thomas (Cospatric) Hamilton-, 6th Bt. *cr.* 1804; *b.* 8 Dec. 1917; *s.* of Sir Drummond Cospatric Hamilton-Spencer-Smith, 5th Bt.; *S.* father 1955; *m.* 1944, Lucy Ashton, *d.* of Thomas Ashton Ingram; one *s.* *Educ.:* Eton. R.M.C. Sandhurst, 1936; 2nd Lt. 43rd Light Infantry, 1938; Captain, 1941. *Recreation:* hunting. *Heir:* *s.* John, *b.* 17 March 1947. *Address:* Rotherhill, Fittleworth, Sussex. *Club:* United Service. [*Died* 14 *Oct.* 1959.

SPENDER, Lieutenant-Colonel Sir Wilfrid Bliss, K.C.B. 1929; C.B.E. 1921; D.S.O. 1919; M.C.; Permanent Secretary, Ministry of Finance, and Head of Civil Service, Northern Ireland (1925-44); retired as Member of Joint Exchequer Board (1933-54); *b.* 6 Oct. 1876; *s.* of late Edward Spender; *m.* Lilian Dean; one *d.* *Educ.:* Winchester Coll.; Staff College, Camberley. Entered R.A., 1897; passed Staff College, Royal Naval War Course; served on General Staff and Sub-Committee Imperial Defence; retired on Ulster Question, 1913; H.Q. Staff of Ulster Volunteer Force; served World War on General Staff (G.S.O.1) Ulster and 31st Divisions and G.H.Q. (D.S.O., M.C., despatches four times); selected by Lord Haig to organise Officers' Friend Branch, Ministry of Pensions; Member of his Committee to form British Legion; re-raised and commanded Ulster Volunteer Force (subsequently Special Constabulary, 1920); first Sec. to Cabinet of Northern Ireland (1921-25). Formerly a Director of Western Morning News. One of the founders of the Junior Imperial League. *Recreations:* mountaineering and yachting. *Address:* East Hill Hotel, Liss, Hants. *Club:* United Service. [*Died* 21 *Dec.* 1960.

SPENS, Col. Hugh Baird, C.B.E. 1946; D.S.O. 1918; D.L. Co. Stirling; Ensign, Queen's Body Guard for Scotland, Royal Company or Archers; Director: Bank of Scotland; Scottish Amicable Life Assurance Society, and othef companies; partner in firm of Maclay Murray & Spens, Solicitors, Glasgow; Hon. Sheriff-Substitute of the County of Stirling; Chairman, Local Price Regulation Committee for Glasgow and West of Scotland, 1939-53; *b.* 1 Jan. 1885; 2nd *s.* of late John A. Spens, 25 Park Circus, Glasgow; *m.* 1912, Margaret Emily (*d.* 1950), *d.* of late J. A. Black, Lagarie, Rhu, Dunbartonshire; two *s.* two *d.* *Educ.:* Rugby (Scholar and Head of School); King's College, Cambridge (Scholar), B.A. (Cantab.), LL.B. (Glasgow); served in European War as A.D.C. and A.P.M. 52nd (Lowland) Division (wounded in Gallipoli); commanded 5th Scottish Rifles in France, August 1917 onwards (D.S.O. and bar, despatches five times, French Croix de Guerre, Bt. Maj.); also 1920-24; Col. (T.A.), 1924-43. Commanded Home Guard Bn., 1940-45. Dean of the Faculty of Procurators of Glasgow, 1946-49. Hon. LL.D. Edinburgh, 1957. *Recreation:* golf. *Address:* Braehead House, Barnton, Midlothian. *Clubs:* Boodle's; New (Edinburgh); Western (Glasgow); Royal and Ancient. [*Died* 19 *Feb.* 1958.

SPERRY, Willard Learoyd, B.A., M.A., D.D., Th.D., D.Litt.; Dean of the Harvard Divinity School, 1922-53, and Chairman Board of Preachers to the University, 1929-53; retired 1953; *b.* Peabody, Mass., 5 April 1882; *s.* of Willard Gardner and Henrietta Learoyd Sperry; *m.* 1908, Muriel Laura Bennett; one *d.* *Educ.:* Olivet College, Michigan (A.B.); Queen's College, Oxford (Rhodes Scholar); Yale University (A.M.). A.B. (Olivet), 1903; First Class in Honour Theology (Oxford), 1907; A.M. (Yale), 1908; M.A. (Oxon), 1912. Ordained to Congregational Ministry, 1909; Pastor, First Cong'l. Church, Fall River, Mass., 1907-1914; Pastor Central Cong'l. Church, Boston, Mass., 1914-22. Prof. Andover Theol. Seminary, 1917-22. Dean of Nat. Council on Religion in Higher Educ., 1927-31; Upton Lecturer (Manchester Coll.), 1927; Hibbert Lecturer, 1927; Essex Hall Lecturer, 1927; Haskell Lecturer (Oberlin Coll.), 1930; Lyman Beecher Lecturer (Yale), 1937. F.A.A.S., 1927; Trustee, Vassar Coll., 1943-1946. Preacher at chief American colleges and universities. Hon. Degrees: D.D. Yale, 1922; Amherst, 1923; Brown, 1928; Williams, 1935; D.Litt., Boston Univ., 1942; Th.D. Harvard, 1941. *Publications:* The Disciplines of Liberty, 1921; Reality in Worship, 1925; The Paradox of Religion, 1927; Signs of These Times, 1929; Yes, But, 1931; What You Owe Your Child, 1935; Wordsworth's Anti-Climax, 1935; We Prophesy in Part, 1937; Strangers and Pilgrims, 1938; Summer Yesterdays in Maine, 1941; Religion in America, 1945; Those of the Way, 1946; Jesus, Then and Now, 1949; The Ethical Basis of Medical Practice, 1950. *Recreations:* fishing, bridge, detective stories. *Address:* 984 Memorial Drive, Cambridge 38, Mass., U.S.A. *T.:* Kirkland 6632. [*Died* 15 *May* 1954.

SPICKERNELL, Sir Frank Todd, K.B.E., *cr.* 1927; C.B. 1919; C.V.O. 1954; D.S.O. 1916; Captain (S), R.N. (retired); Extra Gentleman Usher to the Queen since 1954; C.C. Berkshire since 1946; *b.* 21 Dec. 1885; *s.* of late Frank Spickernell, Shipbourne, Kent; *m.* 1925, Amice Delves, *d.* of late Sir Delves Broughton, 10th Bt.; two *d.* Entered Navy, 1903; Secretary to Commander-in-Chief, Grand Fleet, 1916-19; Secretary to 1st Sea Lord of the Admiralty, 1919-27; retired list, 1928; a Gentleman Usher in Ordinary to the Queen, 1952 (to King George VI, 1937-52). *Address:* Deane, Kintbury, Berks. *Club:* Naval and Military. [*Died* 31 *March* 1956.

SPIDLE, Rev. Simeon, B.A., B.D., Ph.D., LL.D.; Professor of Philosophy and Theology, Acadia University, Wolfville, N.S., 1911-38, ret.; *b.* New Cornwall, N.S., 1867; *s.* of Solomon Spidle; *m.* 1891; one *s.* *Educ.:* Acadia University (D.D. 1926); Newton Theological Institution, Mass.; Clark University, Worcester Mass. Successively Pastor at Morien, C.B.; at Worcester, Mass.; at Holden, Mass. *Publication:* The Belief in Immortality. *Address:* Wolfville, N.S. [*Died* 26 *Sept.* 1954.

SPIERS, Harry Ratcliff, C.B.E. 1937; *b.* 1883; *s.* of late H. J. Spiers, M.I.N.A., M.I.M.E.; *m.* 1909, Dorothy May, 3rd *d.* of late William Robert McDonell. *Educ.:* Privately at Southsea; King's College, London. Appointed to the Inland Revenue, 1900; Deputy Accountant and Comptroller General, 1921; Accountant and Comptroller General, 1924-39. *Address:* 95 Ravensbourne Park, S.E.6. *T.:* Forest Hill 1955. [*Died* 4 *March* 1956.

SPINKS, Maj.-Gen. (retd.) Sir Charlton Watson, K.B.E., *cr.* 1927; D.S.O. 1917; late R.A.; late Inspector-General, Egyptian Army; Director for Egypt Auxiliary Defence Service (British) from 1942; *b.* 1877; *s.* of late John Charlton Spinks, Victoria, B.C.; *m.* 1915, Marguerite Stuart, *d.* of late R. H. Coleman, Toronto; three *d.* Served N. Nigeria, 1903, Kano-Sokoto Campaign (despatches, medal with clasp); again 1903-4 operations in the Bassa Province against the Okpotos (despatches, clasp); Sudan, 1912, against Beir and Annak tribes (medal with clasp); European War (Gallipoli and Egypt), 1914-18 (D.S.O., O.B.E.); Darfur, 1916 (despatches); Hedjaz, 1916; Travelling Commissioner, Middle East, War Organisation of the British Red Cross Society and Order of St. John of Jerusalem, 1940-41; Grand Cordon of the Nile; Grand Croix de L'Ordre de Leopold II.; Grand Officier Order of the Crown of Italy; Grand Officier of St. Maurice and St. Lazarus, Italy. *Address:* Garden House, Kyrenia, Cyprus. *Club:* United Service. [*Died* 24 *Oct.* 1959.

SPIRE, Frederick, C.M.G. 1917; *b.* 1863; *s.* of late James Spire; *m.* 1916, Helen Rachel, 3rd *d.* of late F. M. E. Jervoise, of Herriard Park. Water Transport Officer Uganda, 1893; circumnavigated Lake Victoria; Officer in charge Kavirondo, 1894; General Stores, Entebbe, 1895-98; Mumias Station, 1898; organised native transport between Eldama Ravine and Busoga for troops from India in connection with mutiny Uganda; Collector Unyoro and various Nile Stations, 1900-5; First-Class Magistrate; established Gondokoro Station, 1902; Acting Sub-Commissioner and Sessions Judge Nile Provinces, 1906-9; Eastern and Central Africa Medal Unyoro, 1893-94; East and Central Africa medal with clasp, Uganda, 1897-98; British War Medal, 1918; Provincial Commissioner and Sessions Judge, Eastern Province Uganda Protectorate, 1909, retired, Jan. 1919. Late Member of the Cheltenham Guardians Committee; late member of Winchcombe and Cheltenham R.D.C. and Chairman of Woodmancote Parish Council. *Address:* The Slades, Cleeve Hill, Cheltenham. *T.A.:* Cleeve Hill 50. [*Died* 5 *July* 1951.

SPITTA, Harold Robert Dacre, M.V.O. 1914; M.D. (Dur.), M.B., B.S. (Honours), M.R.C.S., L.R.C.P. (Lond.), D.P.H. (Cantab.); Consulting and Hon. Bacteriologist; Bacteriologist to King Edward VII. Hospital and to the Metropolitan Police; Consulting Bacteriologist to General Lying-in Hospital, Grosvenor Hospital for Women, St. Mark's Hospital; Fellow Roy. Sanitary Institute; Capt. R.A.M.C.; *b.* Clapham, 3 Nov. 1877; *s.* of late Dr. Edmund Johnson Spitta; *m.* Sybil Howard, *d.* of late Col. Salusbury Crookenden, 65th Regt. *Educ.:* Durham University; University College, London; St. George's Hospital. Luke Armstrong Scholar in Pathology, 1900; Webb Scholar in Bacteriology, 1898-99, 1900; Proficiency Prizeman, 1898; late Bacteriologist to the Households of King Edward VII., Queen Alexandra, King George V. and Princess Beatrice; formerly Lecturer on Clinical Pathology, Lecturer on Bacteriology, and Lecturer on Public Health and Hygiene, 1913; Curator Pierse-Duncombe Laboratory, St. George's Hospital; and Examiner in Bacteriology and Public Health, Royal Colleges of Surgeons, England, 1907-12. *Publications:* Many specialist articles, including some in Latham's System of Medicine, 1912. *Address:* 46 Lowndes Square, S.W.1. *T.:* Sloane 6316; St. George's Hospital, S.W.1. *T.:* Sloane 7151 (Ext. 10). *T.A.:* Spitta, London; Birchington, Kent. *T.:* Birchington 52. *Club:* Junior Carlton. [*Died* 30 *Sept.* 1954.

SPRAGUE, Oliver Mitchell Wentworth; Professor of Banking and Finance; *b.* Somerville, Mass., 22 April 1873; *s.* of William Wallace Sprague and Miriam Wentworth; *m.* 1905, Fanny Knights Ide, St. Johnsbury, Vermont; one *s.* one *d.* Professor in Economics, Imperial University of Tokyo, 1905-8; Assistant Prof. of Banking and Finance, Harvard, 1908-1913; Edmund Cogswell Converse Professor of Banking and Finance, 1913-31, now Emeritus, Harvard University; Economic and Statistical Adviser to Bank of England, 1930-33; Financial and Executive Assistant to Secretary of the Treasury, U.S., 1933; President American Economic Association, 1937; fellow American Academy of Arts and Sciences; Member of American Philosophical Society. *Publications:* History of Crises under the National Banking System, 1910; Banking Reform in the U.S., 1911; Theory and History of Banking, 1929; Recovery and Common Sense, 1934. *Address:* 13 Follen Street, Cambridge, Mass., U.S.A. *Clubs:* Algonquin, Somerset (Boston). [*Died* 24 *May* 1953.

SPRAWSON, Maj.-Gen. Sir Cuthbert Allan, Kt., *cr.* 1936; C.I.E. 1919; M.D., F.R.C.P. Lond.; I.M.S., retired; *b.* 1 March 1877; *s.* of John Sprawson; widower; one *s.* one *d.* *Educ.:* King's College School and King's College Hospital, London. Professor of Medicine, Allahabad University, 1913-23. Consulting Physician, Mesopotamia E.F.; Major-General 1930; Director-General I.M.S., 1933-37; President, Medical Council of India, 1934-37; K.H.P., 1933-37; retired, 1937; D.Litt. (Hon.) Lucknow University, 1930; O.St.J., 1930. *Publications:* A Guide to the Use of Tuberculin; Moore's Family Medicine for India; Beri-beri in the Mesopotamian Force; several other medical publications. *Address:* 6 Walland's Crescent, Lewes, Sussex. *T.:* Lewes 917. [*Died* 7 *May* 1956.

SPRAWSON, Evelyn Charles, M.C., D.Sc. (Lond.), M.R.C.S. (Eng.), L.R.C.P. (Lond.), F.D.S. (Eng.); *b.* 13 Feb. 1881; 3rd *s.* of late John Sprawson, of Belle Vue, East Finchley; *m.* 1907, Evelyn Jessie, *y. d.* of late John Knox. *Educ.:* King's Coll. School, London; Charing Cross Hospital; London Hospital; Royal Dental Hospital. Walker Scholar; Saunders Scholar and prizes, Dental Surgery, Dental Anatomy, etc., at Royal Dental Hospital; medallist, ophthalmology and midwifery, Charing Cross Hospital; Sir John Tomes prizeman, Royal College of Surgeons of England, 1930; Hon. President, Sec. Histology, International Dental Congress, Paris, 1931; late Professor of Dental Surgery and Pathology, Univ. of London; Consulting Dental Surgeon, Lecturer on Dental Surgery and Pathology, and late Director of Dental Studies to the London Hosp.; Hon. Consulting Dental Surg. to Dr. Barnardo's Homes; Chm. of Bd. of Studies in Dentistry, and Mem. of Faculty of Medicine, Univ. of London; Vice-Pres. and Member of Council, and Member Advisory and Legal Cttee., Medical Protection Society; Hunterian Professor, 1936-37; Sir Charles Tomes lecturer, Royal College of Surgeons of England, 1947; late Member of Home Office Tribunal for Dangerous Drugs Act; Vice-Pres. International Association for Dental Research; President (now hon. mem.) of Odontological Section of Royal Society of Medicine, 1940-41; Deputy Chairman Dental Education Advisory Council; Examiner in Dental Surgery to Royal College of Surgeons of England, and to the Universities of London, Birmingham, Durham, Otago, N.Z., and the Witwatersrand, S.A.; and the Dental Board of the United Kingdom; Fellow of Royal Society of Medicine; Fellow of Zoological Soc.; late Member of Council of Avicultural Soc.; late Member of the Committee for the Investigation of the Causes of Dental Diseases, Medical Research Council. President of Dental Officers' Group of Society of Medical Officers of Health, late Trustee of Odontological Collection at Royal College of Surgeons, and Consulting Dental Surgeon Sectors 1 and 2 Emergency Medical Service; Hon. Vice-Pres. Section of Dental Education XI Internat. Dental Congress, 1952; served in 28th Battalion County of London Artists' Rifles (T.F. efficiency medal); European War: Capt. R.A.M.C. (T.F.) in B.E.F., 1914-1919 (despatches, M.C.). *Publications:* Research Publications before the Royal Society, the Royal Society of Medicine and other Scientific Societies; (with Sir Frank Colyer) Dental Surgery and Pathology, 6th, 7th, 8th and 9th ed.; Chapter, Variations of the Teeth, Bennet's System of Dental Surgery; editor of the British Dental Annual; occasional avicultural articles. *Recreations:* angling, aviculture, numismatics. *Address:* Cranford, Kenley, Surrey. *T.:* Uplands 1688. [*Died* 6 *April* 1955.

SPRIGGE, Cecil Jackson Squire; Member of Editorial Staff of the Guardian; *b.* 1896; *s.* of late Sir Squire Sprigge (for 30 years Editor of the Lancet) and Mab, *d.* of late Chief Justice Sir Charles Moss, Toronto, Canada; *m.* 1st, Katriona Gordon Brown (marriage dissolved); two *s.* one *d.*; 2nd, Sylvia (writer and journalist), *d.* of late George Saunders, of The Times. *Educ.:* Eton College (Newcastle Medallist), abroad. Was Scholar-Elect of King's Coll., Cambridge. Foreign Correspondent, 1923-1929, and then City Editor, 1929-39, of the Manchester Guardian. Reuter's Chief Correspondent in Italy, 1943-46; Chief of British Information Services, etc. in Germany, 1946-1947; Staff Correspondent in Italy of the Economist and other newspapers, 1947-53; translator of some works of Benedetto Croce. *Publications:* Karl Marx, a short biography; The Development of Modern Italy; Benedetto Croce, Man and Thinker; also various historical essays and translations. *Address:* Cherry Cottage, Parkhurst Corner, Abinger Common, Nr. Dorking, Surrey. *T.:* Abinger 397. *Club:* Athenæum. [*Died* 22 *Dec.* 1959.

SPROULE, Brig. James Chambers, C.B.E. 1941 (O.B.E. 1919); late R.A.M.C.; *b.* 28 Aug. 1887; 4th *s.* of Alexander H. R. Sproule, J.P., Fintona, Tyrone; *m.* 1915, Clare Stewart, 2nd *d.* of G. F. Aldous, F.R.C.S.E., Plymouth; one *s.* one *d.* *Educ.:* Royal School, Raphoe; Royal College of Surgeons and Physicians, Ireland. Joined R.A.M.C. as Lieut. 1912; Capt. 1915; Major, 1924; Lt.-Col. 1934; Col. 1940; Temp. Brig. 1942; served France, European War, 1914-18 (O.B.E., French Croix de Guerre with Star in Bronze, despatches twice, 1914-1915 Medal with Star, Victory and General Service Medals); War of 1939-45 (despatches, C.B.E.); retired pay, 1947. County Medical Officer B.R.C.S., Somerset. *Publications:* Notes on Air Conditioning in the Tropics (Conjointly), Journal of R.A.M.C., Oct. 1933; Superchlorination of Water in the Field, Effect on Cercariae, ibid., June 1939. *Recreations:* fishing, shooting. *Address:* Old Bell House, Somerton, Somerset. [*Died* 15 *May* 1955.

SPROULE, Percy Julian; *b.* 4 Dec. 1873; 2nd *s.* of J. H. Sproule, Kandy, Ceylon; *m.* 1902, Alice, O.B.E. 1928, *o. d.* of E. B. Graburn, Horley, Surrey; no *c.* *Educ.:* St. Thomas' Coll., Colombo; private; Pembroke College, Cambridge. B.A. 1894; M.A. 1946; Barrister, Middle Temple, 1895; Straits Settlements C.S., 1895; Solicitor-Gen., 1910; Puisne Judge, 1913; Senior Puisne Judge, 1920; retired, 1932. *Recreation:* golf. *Address:* 6 Church Street, Littlehampton, Sussex. [*Died* 17 *Jan.* 1954.

SPRY, Mrs. Constance, O.B.E. 1953; Chairman of Constance Spry Ltd., and the Constance Spry Flower School; joint-principal of the Cordon Bleu Cookery School and Winkfield Place Ltd., girls' finishing school, near Windsor. Adviser to Ministry of Works on flower decorations for the Coronation, 1953. *Publications:* Flower Decoration; Flowers in House and Garden; A Garden Notebook; Come in to the Garden, Cook!; Winter and Spring Flowers; Summer and Autumn Flowers; How to do the Flowers; A Constance Spry Anthology; The Constance Spry Cookery Book; Simple Flowers; Favourite Flowers. *Address:* Winkfield Place, Winkfield, Windsor, Berks. [*Died* 3 *Jan.* 1960.

SPURGEON, Christopher Edward, C.B.E. 1942; M.I.Mech.E.; Second Class Order of the Nile; *b.* 24 May 1879; *s.* of Rev. J. N. Spurgeon; *m.* 1912, Miss Sinclair (*decd.*); one *d. Educ.:* Aldenham Grammar School; University College, London. On Govt. of India State Railways on North-Western Railway, 1904-34, 8 years of which as Chief Mechanical Engineer; on Egyptian State Railway, Cairo, 1935-, as Chief Mechanical Engineer and Dep. General Manager; Chief Inspecting Engineer, Egyptian Government, London, 1945 - 48. *Clubs:* Junior Carlton, Roehampton. [*Died* 5 *Oct.* 1951.

SQUIRE, Sir Giles Frederick, K.B.E., *cr.* 1946; C.I.E. 1941; *b.* 12 Oct. 1894; 3rd *s.* of late Rev. C. E. Squire, Wootton, Bedford; *m.* 1926, Irene Mary, *d.* of late Dr. E. C. Arnold; three *d. Educ.:* Marlborough; Christ Church, Oxford (M.A.). Captain 7th Glos. Regiment, 1914-19; served Gallipoli, Mesopotamia, N. Persia, South Russia. Indian Civil Service, 1920 (Central Provinces). Indian Political Dept., 1924; Consul-General at Meshed, 1936-41; Counsellor, British Legation, Tehran, 1941-43; Minister, 1943-1948, Ambassador, 1948-49, to Afghanistan. *Recreations:* tennis, golf. *Address:* c/o National Overseas and Grindlays Bank Ltd., 54 Parliament St., S.W.1; P.O. Box 2168, Bulawayo, S. Rhodesia. *Club:* Overseas. [*Died* 11 *April* 1959.

SQUIRE, Sir John Collings, Kt., *cr.* 1933; *b.* Plymouth, 2 Apr. 1884; *s.* of J. Squire and E R. Collings; *m.* 1908, Eileen H. A., *d.* of Rev. A. Anstruther Wilkinson; three *s.* one *d. Educ.:* Blundell's; St. John's College, Cambridge (Historical Scholar, 1903; B.A. 1906; M.A. (1919); Literary Editor, New Statesman, 1913; Acting Editor, 1917-18; Editor London Mercury, 1919-1934, and Chairman London Mercury, Ltd.; contested Cambridge University, 1918; Brentford and Chiswick, 1924; A Governor of the Old Vic, 1922-26; Chairman of the English Association, 1926-29; Hon. Secretary Stonehenge Preservation Society; Member of the Academic Committee, 1921; Hon. Secretary 1922; Chairman of the Architecture Club, 1922-28; President Devonshire Association, 1934; F.S.A.; Hon A.R.I.B.A.; Hon. Member Art Workers' Guild; Hon. F.R.S.L. Editor of the English Men of Letters Series; Joint Editor (with Lord Lee of Fareham) of English Heritage Series. *Publications:* Imaginary Speeches, 1912; Steps to Parnassus, 1913; The Three Hills, and other Poems, 1913; The Survival of the Fittest, 1916; Twelve Poems, 1916; (ed.) The Collected Poems of James Elroy Flecker, 1916; Tricks of the Trade, 1917; The Lily of Malud, 1917; The Gold Tree, 1918; Poems: First Series, 1918; Books in General, 1918; The Birds, and other Poems, 1919; Books in General, second series, 1920; The Moon, a poem, 1920; Life and Letters, 1920; Books in General, third series, 1921; Collected Parodies, 1921; Poems: Second Series, 1922; Essays at Large, 1922; Books Reviewed, 1922; American and other Poems, 1923; Essays on Poetry, 1924; Grub Street Nights, 1924; The Comic Muse, 1925; Poems in One Volume, 1926; Life at the Mermaid, 1927; The Cambridge Book of Lesser Poets, 1927; A London Reverie, 1928; Apes and Parrots, 1928; Sunday Mornings, 1930; (Editor) If it had happened otherwise, 1931; A Face in Candlelight (poems), 1933; Outside Eden, 1933; Reflections and Memories, 1935; Shakespeare as a Dramatist, 1935; Flowers of Speech, 1935; Weepings and Wailings, 1935; The Honeysuckle and the Bee, 1937; Water Music, 1939; Selected Poems, 1948; various anthologies and plays, including three volumes of Selections from Modern Poets and Berkeley Square (with John L. Balderston). *Recreations:* cricket, shooting. [*Died* 20 *Dec.* 1958.

SQUIRE, Rev. John Henry, B.A., B.D.; *b.* Langtree, Devon; *m.* 1st, Mabel A. (*d.* 1926), *d.* of Rev. Samuel Allin; three *s.*; 2nd, 1931, Winifred M. Stringer, Sheringham; one *d. Educ.:* Shebbear College; University of Wales; University of London. Churches in Plymouth and Penzance; Seven Kings, Ilford, 1911-1919; Minister of St. James's United Methodist Church, Forest Hill, 1919; Chairman of United Methodist Churches in London district, 1920-21; President of the Metropolitan Free Church Federation, 1924-25; Member of important Methodist Committees; Associate Editor Methodist Times, 1923-31; Secretary of the Bristol Council of Christian Churches, 1935-1940, and Vice-President of the Council, 1940-1945; President Bristol Methodist Council, 1939; President of Bristol Federation of Free Churches, 1940; Chairman of Bristol District of Methodist Church and Superintendent of Bristol S. Methodist Churches; retired, 1945; Trustee and Governor of Shebbear Boys College, Devon. *Recreations:* motoring and gardening. *Address:* Sunnycliffe, Roundham Crescent, Paignton, Devon. [*Died* 23 *Dec.* 1955.

SQUIRE, Ronald; Actor; *b.* Tiverton, 1886; *s.* of late Lt.-Col. Frederick Squirl, late 93rd Argyll and Sutherland Highlanders, and late Mary, *d.* of Charles O'Toole, Wilfort, County Wicklow; *m.* 1914, Muriel Martin Harvey (marriage dissolved); one *d.*; *m.* 1947, Esyllt Williams, *y. d.* of late Ernest Edwin Williams, barrister-at-law. *Educ.:* Wellington College. Has been an actor since 1910, theatrical manager since 1928; Productions include: By Candle Light, Canaries Sometimes Sing, The Breadwinner, Dr. Pygmalion, Springtime for Henry, Tread Softly; has played in The Last of Mrs. Cheyney, On Approval, Our Betters, Spring Cleaning, Dear Brutus, Bulldog Drummond, A Month in the Country, While the Sun Shines, Jane, The Way Things Go, Ardèle, Aren't We All?, The Iron Duchess, Raising a Riot, Footsteps in the Fog, Josephine and Men, Around the World in Eighty Days, etc. Latest theatrical appearance, A Touch of the Sun. *Recreation:* golf. *Clubs:* Buck's, Boodle's. [*Died* 16 *Nov.* 1958.

SRÁMEK, Monsignor Jan; Doctor of Theology; *b.* 11 Aug. 1870; *s.* of Thomas Šrámek, a farmer. *Educ.:* Olomouc Theological Faculty. Ordained priest, 1892; founded Christian Social Workers' Organisation, 1897; Member Moravian Provincial Parliament, 1906; Member Viennese Parliament, 1907; Member Moravian Provincial Council, 1913; joined Czechoslovak Govt. soon after founding of Republic as leader of People's Party, and remained almost continuously in the Govt., holding various ministerial posts such as Minister of State Railways, Health, Social Welfare, Unification, etc., until time of Munich; several times Deputy Premier, during the illness of Prime Minister led the Govt. in this capacity for approximately one and a half years; after occupation of Czechoslovakia went abroad, and negotiated recognition of Czechoslovak National Committee with the French Govt. in Paris after outbreak of war; after Fall of France became Prime Minister of Czechoslovak Govt. in Great Britain. *Recreations:* collecting antiques and works of art. [*Died* 22 *April* 1956.

SRAWLEY, Rev. James Herbert, D.D.; Canon of Lincoln and Prebendary of Heydour with Walton since 1930; *b.* 1868; *s.* of James Srawley and Anne, *d.* of Eli Stubbs; *m.* 1898, Mary, *d.* of Francis Riddell and Fanny, *d.* of Joseph Stackhouse; one *s.* two *d. Educ.:*

King Edward's School, Birmingham; Gonville and Caius College, Cambridge (Scholar); 1st Class, (Div. II.) Classical Tripos, 1891; Carus Greek Testament Prize (Undergraduates) 1891, and (Bachelors) 1892; 1st Class Theological Tripos, Pt. I., 1893; B.A. 1891; M.A. 1895; B.D. 1903; D.D. 1907. Hon. Fellow, Selwyn College, 1951. Deacon, 1893; Priest, 1894; Curate of St. Matthew's, Walsall, 1893-5; Vice-Principal, Lichfield Theological College, 1895-97; Lecturer at Selwyn College, 1897-1912; Curate, St. Mary the Less, Cambridge, 1898-1906; Examining Chaplain to Bishop of Lichfield, 1905-16; Tutor of Selwyn College, 1907-12; Rector of Weeting, Norfolk, 1912-19; Archdeacon of Wisbech, 1916-23; Vicar of Sutton in the Isle of Ely, 1919-24; Canon residentiary and Chancellor of Lincoln Cathedral, 1923-47; Select Preacher (Cambridge), 1916, 1925, 1930; Proctor in Convocation (Linc), 1924-28. *Publications:* The Epistles of St. Ignatius, Early Church Classics Series, 1900; The Catechetical Oration of Gregory of Nyssa, Cambridge Patristic Texts, 1903; The Early History of the Liturgy (Cambridge Liturgical Handbooks), 1913 and 1947; (Jt. Ed.) Thompson and Srawley, St. Ambrose on the Sacraments and on the Mysteries, 1950; Arts, Antiochene Theology, Cappadocian Theology, Eucharist, Hastings' Dictionary of Religion and Ethics; contributor to Liturgy and Worship, 1932. *Address:* 15 Minster Yard, Lincoln. *T.:* 1591. [*Died* 6 *Jan.* 1954.

SRIVASTAVA, Dr. Sir Jwala Prasad, K.C.S.I., *cr.* 1946: K.B.E., *cr.* 1942; Kt., *cr.* 1934; Hon. D.Sc. and D.Litt. (Agra and Lucknow) 1936, M.Sc. Tech. (Vict.), A.M.S.T. (Manc.), M.L.A.; Governing Director, Sir J. P. Srivastava Group of Industries controlling several large industrial units; *b.* 16 August 1889; *s.* of Janki Prasad Srivastava and Sohni Kuar Srivastava; *m.* 1907, Kailash Sinha; two *s.* five *d.* *Educ.:* Christ Church College, Cawnpore; Muir Central College, Allahabad; Municipal College of Technology, Manchester. Served as Industrial Chemist to U.P. Government, 1912-29; then took to private business, becoming Managing Director Cawnpore Dyeing and Cloth Printing Co. Ltd., Managing Director New Victoria Mills Co. Ltd., Cawnpore, and Managing Agent Indian Turpentine and Rosin Co. Ltd., Cawnpore; Director, Allahabad Bank Ltd. and Western India Match Co. Ltd.; Director and Managing Agent Raza Textiles Ltd., Rampur State, Imperial Bank of India; Dir. and Man. Agent Gwalior Sugar and Agriculture Co. Ltd., Dabra; Bhopal Textiles Ltd., Bhopal; Sadul Textiles Ltd., Sriganganagar; was returned to the U.P. Legislative Assembly by the Upper India Chamber of Commerce Constituency, 1926, 1930, and 1937; Minister of Educn. and Industries to United Provinces Govt., 1931-37; Finance Minister U.P. Govt., April-July 1937; Chairman of the U.P. Simon Committee, 1928-29; Civil Defence Member of Governor-General's Executive Council, 1942-43; Member in charge of Food, 1943-46; Deputy President, Post-war Reconstruction Committee of Council, 1942-43; Member National Defence Council, 1942; Member Constituent Assembly of India, 1947-49; Member First Indian Parliament, 1950-52; elected Member Council of States, Indian Parliament, 1952. *Publications:* speeches and addresses. *Recreations:* shooting and music. *Address:* 5 Scindia House, New Delhi; Kailash, Cawnpore, India. *T.A.:* Jaypee, Cawnpore. *Clubs:* Naini Tal (Nainital); Calcutta (Calcutta); Cricket Club of India (Bombay); Delhi Gymkhana, Roshanara, Chelmsford (Delhi). [*Died* 15 *Dec.* 1954.

STABLE, Emeritus Professor J. Joseph, M.A., LL.D.; J.P.; Darnell Professor of English Language and Literature, University of Queensland, 1923-52; Dean of the Faculty of Arts, 1932-39, and of the Faculty of Commerce, 1932-1938; President, Professorial Board, 1944-50; Member of Senate of Univ. of Queensland, 1944-50; Chairman of Trustees, Queensland National Art Gallery, 1946-48; *b.* Gawler, S. Australia, 14 May 1883; *s.* of Captain Benjamin Penfold Stable; *m.* 1908, Irene Bingham, *y. d.* of Henry Antoine Sheridan, Sydney, N.S.W.; three *s.* *Educ.:* Collège de Geneve; Emmanuel College, Cambridge. Lecturer in English, Commercial Univ. of Cologne, 1905-8; Lecturer in charge of English, French, and German, Univ. of Queensland, 1912; Captain, Australian Field Artillery, 1916-20; Military Censor for Queensland, 1917-19; District Censor, Queensland L. of C. Area, 1939-43. *Publications:* A Book of Queensland Verse, 1924; The Bond of Poetry, 1926; The High Road of Australian Verse, 1929; Gen. Editor Australian Students Shakespeare, 1936. *Address:* Saas Fée, Indooroopilly, Brisbane. *T.A.:* The University, Brisbane. *Clubs:* United Service of Queensland, Royal Automobile of Queensland, Johnsonian (Brisbane). [*Died* 24 *Dec.* 1953.

STABLER, Mrs. Phœbe, F.R.B.S. 1948 (A.R.B.S.); sculptor; *b.* Birmingham; *d.* of James McLeish; *m.* 1906, Harold Stabler (*d.* 1945); no *c.* *Educ.:* University, Liverpool; Royal College of Art, South Kensington. Designed Durban War Memorial, Durban; The Lord Wakefield Speed Trophy, etc. *Address:* 34 Upper Mall, Hammersmith, W.6. *T.:* Riverside 3301. *Clubs:* Forum, Women's Provisional; Faculty of Arts, Royal Glasgow Institute of the Fine Arts (Glasgow). [*Died* 6 *Dec.* 1955.

STACPOOLE, Henry de Vere Stacpoole, J.P. Essex; F.R.G.S.; writer and publicist; *b.* 1863; *s.* of Rev. William Church Stacpoole, D.D., Kingstown, Co. Dublin; *m.* 1st, Margaret (*d.* 1934; author of Practical Hints for V.A.D. Nurses, etc.), *d.* of William Robson of Tynemouth; 2nd, 1938, Florence, *y. d.* of late William Robson, Tynemouth. *Educ.:* Malvern College. After leaving school studied medicine at St. George's and St. Mary's Hospitals; practised for some time as a doctor; first drawn towards literature by the works of Carlyle and the German metaphysicians and poets. President and Founder of the Penguin Club, for the study and protection of sea bird life. *Publications:* Social Comedy: The Bourgeois; Fanny Lambert; The Doctor; The Rapin; Patsy; Garryowen. Romance: Pierrot; Death the Knight and the Lady; Pierrette; The Crimson Azaleas; The Blue Lagoon; The Pools of Silence; The Drums of War; Poems and Ballads, 1910; The Ship of Coral, 1911; The Order of Release, 1912; The Street of the Flute Player, 1912; The Children of the Sea; Bird Cay; The Poems of François Villon, translated into English, 1913; The New Optimism, 1914; The Blue Horizon; Poppyland; The Pearl Fishers, 1915; The North Sea and other Poems, 1915; The Reef of Stars, 1916; The Life of François Villon, 1916; In Blue Waters, 1917; The Starlit Garden, 1918; The Willow Tree (a book of the play); The Man who Lost Himself, 1918; Under Blue Skies; The Beach of Dreams, 1919; The Poems of Sappho translated into English, 1920; Men, Women, and Beasts, 1922; Vanderdecken; The Garden of God, 1923; Golden Ballast, 1924; The Gates of Morning, 1925; The House of Crimson Shadows, 1925; Tales East and West, 1926; Goblin Market, 1927; Roxanne, 1928; Eileen of The Trees, 1929; The Chank Shell, 1930; Pacific Gold, 1931; The Lost Caravan, 1932; The Naked Soul, 1933; The Vengeance of Mynheer Van Lok and other stories, 1934; Green Coral, 1935; The Longshore Girl, 1935; In a Bonchurch Garden (poems), 1937; High-Yaller, 1938; Due East of Friday, 1939; Old Sailors Never Lie, 1939; The Ghost Girl, 1940; An American at Oxford, 1941; Men and Mice, 1942; Oxford goes to War, 1943; More Men and Mice, 1944; The Story of My Village, 1947; The Land of

Little Horses, 1948; books have been translated into French, Italian, Spanish, Dutch, German, and Swedish. *Address:* Cliff Dene, Bonchurch, I. of W. *T.:* Ventnor 77; Rose Cottage, Stebbing, Chelmsford, Essex. *Club:* Authors'. [*Died* 12 *April* 1951.

STAGG, Cecil, M.A.; *m.*; one *s.* one *d.* *Educ.:* Clifton College (Scholar); Caius College (Scholar), Cambridge. Formerly Assistant Master at Marlborough College; Headmaster of Merchiston Castle School, 1914-36. *Address:* 3 Lauderdale St., Edinburgh 9. [*Died* 26 *Nov.* 1955.

STAIG, Sir Bertie Munro, K.C.I.E., *cr.* 1947; Kt., *cr.* 1942; C.S.I. 1936; on staff of U.K. High Commission in Germany; *b.* 14 Aug. 1892; *m.* 1923, Dorothy Powys Stone; one *s.* *Educ.:* St. Andrews; Trinity College, Oxford. Entered Indian Civil Service, 1917; Financial Adviser, Military Finance, Govt. of India, 1935; Financial Comr. Railways, 1937; Auditor-General of India, 1945-48, retired. *Address:* St. Kilda, Goring-on-Thames. *T.:* Goring 55. [*Died* 30 *April* 1952.

STAINES, Donald Victor, C.M.G. 1955; C.B.E. 1950 (O.B.E. 1947; M.B.E. 1946); a Counsellor (Establishment Officer), Foreign Office, retired 1955; *b.* 3 March 1897; *s.* of late A. J. Staines, Bristol; *m.* 1928, Evaline, *d.* of late Dr. G. Macdonald; no *c.* *Educ.:* Fairfield, Bristol. *Address:* Rosehill, Reculver Avenue, Birchington, Kent. [*Died* 25 *March* 1960.

STAINES, Herbert J., J.P.; Chairman of Directors, F. Moody & Co. Ltd., Bath; Director: Sheffield Building Soc.; Painted Fabrics Ltd. Sheffield; Sheffield Telegraph & Star Ltd.; *b.* Bath; *m.* Lilian M., *e. d.* of late F. J. Moody, Bath; one *s.* Director of Press Association, 1934 (Chairman, 1939); Director of Reuters Ltd., 1936. *Address:* 7 Broomgrove Crescent, Sheffield 10. *T.:* 60979. *Club:* Sheffield (Sheffield). [*Died* 12 *Nov.* 1958.

STAINES, Michael; Proprietor of the Central Wholesale Warehouse, Dublin; *b.* Newport, Co. Mayo, 1885; *m.* 1922, Sheila Cullen, Rathmore, Co. Wicklow; four *s.* two *d.* M.P. (S. Fein) St. Michans, Dublin, Dec. 1918-22; Member of Dail for Dublin City, North-West Division, 1921-23; Alderman Dublin Corporation, 1919-52; Senator, Irish Free State, 1930-36. *Address:* 235 N.C. Road, Dublin. *T.:* 2004. [*Died* 26 *Oct.* 1955.

STAINTON, Sir John (Armitage), K.C.B. *cr.* 1953; K.B.E., *cr.* 1939; Q.C. 1947; *b.* 29 February 1888; *e. s.* of late John Prout Stainton; *m.* 1918, Hon. Janet Bertha Dewar, *d.* of 1st Baron Forteviot; two *s.* two *d.* *Educ.:* Winchester; Christ Church, Oxford. Barrister, Lincoln's Inn, 1913; served European War, 1914-19, Capt. Argyll and Sutherland Highlanders; Parliamentary Counsel to Treasury, 1929; Second Parliamentary Counsel to the Treasury, 1937-46; Counsel to Chairman of Committees in House of Lords, 1946-53. *Recreations:* shooting, fishing, golf. *Address:* The Gart, Callender, Perthshire. *Clubs:* Athenæum, Oxford and Cambridge. [*Died* 6 *Sept.* 1957.

STALIN, Generalissimo Joseph Vissarionovich; President of Soviet Council of Ministers since 1946 (late Chairman of the Council of People's Commissars) of the U.S.S.R., head of People's Commissariat of the Armed Forces of the U.S.S.R., 1946-47; Chairman of the State Defence Committee, and People's Commissar for the Defence of the U.S.S.R., 1941-46; member Supreme Soviet of U.S.S.R.; General Secretary, Communist Party of Soviet Union (Bolsheviks); member Political Bureau of C.P.S.U.; *b.* Gori, Tiflis, Georgia, 21 Dec. 1879; *s.* of Vissarion Djugashvili, cobbler; *m.* 1st, 1903, Yekaterina Svanidze (*d.* 1907); one *s.*; 2nd, 1918, Nadejda Sergeyevna Alleluya (*d.* 1932); one *s.* one *d.*; 3rd, Rosa Kaganovich. *Educ.:* Gori Ecclesiastical School, 1888-94; Tiflis Theological School, 1894-99 (expelled for political activity). Joined Tiflis Marxist Social Democratic Organisation, 1898; worked for Tiflis Social Democrats, 1898-1901; organised Batum Social Democrats, 1901; first arrest for political activity, 1902; five arrests for political activity, five escapes, 1902-13; met Lenin at Tammersfors, 1905; at Stockholm Congress, 1906; at London Congress, 1907; founded Pravda, 1911; guided Party press, electoral activities, and work of Bolshevik deputies in Duma in St. Petersburg, 1911-13; arrested and exiled near Arctic circle, 1913-17; edited Pravda, and with Lenin prepared and led October Revolution, 1917; Commissar of Nationalities, 1917; military participation in Civil War (first Order of Red Banner), 1918-20; Commissar for Workers and Peasants Inspection, 1919; member of War Council, 1920-23; elected General Secretary of Central Committee of Communist Party of Soviet Union, 1922; suggested plan of Socialist industrialisation, 1925, and of collectivisation, 1927; second Order of Red Banner for services in construction of Socialism; the Stalin Constitution adopted, 1936; Marshal of the Soviet Union, 1943; Generalissimo of the Soviet Union, 1945; Order of Suvorov 1st Cl. 1943; Order of Victory, 1944. *Publications:* Marxism and the National Question, 1912; Foundations of Leninism, 1924; Questions of Leninism; numerous reports and articles. *Address:* The Kremlin, Moscow, U.S.S.R. [*Died* 5 *March* 1953.

STALLARD, John Prince, senior; M.B., C.M., Edin., 1881; M.D. Edin., 1896; retired 1935; late Hon. Physician St. Mary's Hospital for Women and Children, Manchester; late Examiner for Central Midwives Board; *b.* 17 Nov. 1857; *y. s.* of late Josiah Stallard, D.L., of The Blanquettes, Worcester; *m.* 1st, Nita, *e. d.* of late Rev. Peter Marshall, D.D., first Rector of St. John's Baptist, Hulme; two *s.*; 2nd, 1913, Margaret Ellen, *d.* of late William Dichmont, Accrington. *Educ.:* Rossall School; Edinburgh University; The London Hospital. Formerly House Surgeon Worcester General Infirmary, 1881-83; in practice at Otahuhu, near Auckland, New Zealand, 1883-85; settled in practice in Manchester, 1885; Surgeon to Hulme Dispensary, Manchester; Anæsthetist to Victoria Dental Hospital; to Manchester Southern Hospital for Women and Children; Hon. Physician to Manchester Southern Hospital. *Publications:* Pental as an Anæsthetic, Manchester Odontological Soc. Trans., 1893; Anæsthesia, ibid. vol. i.; Removal of Hæmorrhoids rendered painless by Injection of Cocaine, B.M.J., 1886; Subcutaneous Emphysema Following Labour, B.M.J., 1887. *Recreations:* golf, fly-fishing. *Address:* Penncot, Morin Rd., Paignton, Devon. [*Died* 19 *Jan.* 1952.

STAMPA, George Loraine; artist; *b.* 29 Nov. 1875; *s.* of late G. D. Stampa, Architect; *m.* 1906, Ethel (*d.* 1946), *e. d.* of late Clifford Crowther of Claygate; one *s.* *Educ.:* Heatherleys, and Royal Academy Schools. Painted portraits and some pictures; contributes to Punch and other illustrated papers and magazines; book illustrations and book-covers. *Publications:* Easy French Exercises, book of humorous colour drawings; Ragamuffins, a collection of character drawings from Punch of street urchins; Humours of the Street, drawings of life and character; Anthology, In Praise of Dogs. *Recreations:* change of air and music of others. *Address:* 8 The Ridgeway, N.W.11. *T.:* Speedwell 4015. *Clubs:* Savage, Langham Sketch. [*Died* 26 *May* 1951.

STAMPE, Sir William Leonard, Kt., *cr.* 1935; C.I.E. 1931; Flight-Lieut. R.A.F.V.R.; *b.* 1882; *s.* of late G. Stampe, Tetney, Lincs.; *m.* 1910, Agatha Muriel, *d.* of late Richard Jeff, Hull. Late Chief Engineer and

Secretary to Government P.W.D., Irrigation, United Provinces, India; retired, 1937; Kaisar-i-Hind (gold medal), 1926. *Recreations:* polo and big game shikar. *Club:* East India and Sports. [*Died* 20 *Nov.* 1951.

STANFIELD, Richard, A.R.S.M., M.Inst.C.E., M.I.Mech.E., F.R.S.E.; Professor of Mechanical Engineering, Heriot-Watt College, Edinburgh, 1889-1929; *b.* 23 June 1863; *m.*; one *s.* *Educ.:* Manchester Grammar School; Royal School of Mines, London; Whitworth Scholarship, 1884; National Science Scholarship, 1886. Associate Royal School of Mines, 1889 Consulting Engineer to the Highland and Agricultural Society of Scotland; Fellow and Ex-President, Royal Scottish Society of Arts; Engineer and Secretary, Board of Management, S.E. of Scotland Munitions Committee, 1915-19. *Publications*: Communications and Papers on Technical Subjects to Scientific Societies, etc.; Reports on Trials of Agricultural Machinery, Motors, etc. *Recreations:* angling, bowling. *Address:* 24 Mayfield Gardens, Edinburgh. [*Died* 10 *Oct.* 1950.

[*But death not notified in time for inclusion in Who Was Who 1941–1950, first edn.*

STANHAM, Major-Gen. Sir Reginald George, K.C.B., *cr.* 1948 (C.B. 1946); *b.* 2 Oct. 1893; *s.* of George Graham Stanham; *m.* 1919, Helen Maud, *d.* of late Maj.-Gen. Hon. J. W. Macarthur-Onslow; one *s.* *Educ.:* Lancing College. Commissioned The Buffs, 1914; Private Secretary to Governor of New South Wales, 1918-1919; transferred R.A.P.C., 1920; Major, 1930; Lt.-Col. 1937; Maj.-Gen. 1943; Paymaster-in-Chief, 1943-48; retired pay, 1948. A.C.A. 1920. *Recreations:* shooting, fishing, golf. *Address:* Camden Park, Menangle, New South Wales. *Clubs:* Naval and Military; Woking Golf; Royal St. George's (Sandwich). [*Died* 8 *Oct.* 1957.

STANLEY, Charles S. B. W.; *see* Wentworth-Stanley.

STANLEY, Sir Herbert (James), G.C.M.G., *cr.* 1930 (K.C.M.G., *cr.* 1924; C.M.G. 1913); Knight of Grace of the Order of St. John; Director of De Beers Consolidated Mines Ltd., Anglo-American Corporation of South Africa, Ltd., and other companies; Chief Scout, S. Africa; President, Toc H, Southern Africa; Sub-Prior, O. St. J. in S. Africa; *b.* 25 July 1872; *m.* 1918, Reniera (*d.* 1950), D.B.E., *cr.* 1941, Dame of Grace of Order of St. John, *d.* of late Henry Cloete, C.M.G.; two *s.* two *d.* *Educ.:* Eton; Balliol College, Oxford (M.A.). Private Secretary to H.M. Minister Resident at Dresden and Coburg, and British Vice-Consul at Dresden, 1897-1902; Assistant Private Secretary to the First Lord of the Admiralty, 1906-8; Private Secretary to the Lord President of the Council, 1908-10; Private Secretary to the Governor-General, Union of South Africa, 1910-13; Secretary to the Governor-General, 1913-15; Resident Commissioner, Southern and Northern Rhodesia, 1915-18; Imperial Secretary, South Africa, 1918-24; Governor and Commander-in-Chief, Northern Rhodesia, 1924-27; Governor and Commander-in-Chief, Ceylon, 1927-31; H.M. High Commissioner for South Africa and High Commissioner in the Union of South Africa for H.M. Government in the United Kingdom, 1931-35; Governor and Commander-in-Chief of Southern Rhodesia, 1935-42. *Address:* Alphen Cottage, Alphen, Wynberg, Cape of Good Hope, S. Africa. *Clubs:* Brooks's, Athenæum, Beefsteak, St. James', Bath. [*Died* 5 *June* 1955.

STANLEY, Lieut.-Col. Hon. Oliver Hugh, D.S.O. 1918; Major Reserve of Officers; R.A.; *y. s.* of 4th Baron Sheffield; *b.* 23 Oct. 1879; *m.* 1919, Lady Kathleen Thynne, *e. d.* of 5th Marquess of Bath, K.G., P.C., C.B.; two *s.* Served South African War; European War (D.S.O., Croix de Guerre); D.L., J.P. Anglesey. *Address:* Plas Llanfawr, Holyhead. [*Died* 13 *Feb.* 1952.

STANLEY, Robert Crooks; Chairman The International Nickel Co. of Canada, Ltd., since 1937 (Pres. 1922-49), and a Dir. of assoc. cos.; Chairman The International Nickel Co., Inc., since 1949 (Pres. 1922-49); Dir.: C.P.R. Co.; U.S. Steel Corporation (Mem. Finance Cttee.); Foreign and Examination Cttees. of The Chase National Bank of City of N.Y. (Mem.); Amalgamated Metal Corporation Ltd. and Henry Gardner & Co. Ltd., London; *b.* Little Falls, N.Y., 1 Aug. 1876; *s.* of Thomas Stanley and Ada (*née* Crooks); *m.* 1912, Alma Guyon Timolat; one *s.* one *d.* *Educ.:* Stevens Institute of Technology (mech. eng. degree); Columbia School of Mines, New York (degree of mining eng.). Several hon. degrees. Joined S. S. White Dental Co., Philadelphia, 1901; Asst. Supt. of Camden, N.J., plant of Amer. Nickel Co., 1902; later Supt.; trans. to Bayonne as Asst. Gen. Supt. of Orford Copper Co., 1904; served as a mining engineer, 1904; discovered Monel, an alloy, 1905; Gen. Superintendent, Orford Works, 1912; Director, International Nickel Co., 1917; Vice-Pres. i/c all ops. of International Nickel, 1918; responsible for merger with Mond Nickel Co. Ltd., to form present Internat. Nickel Co. of Canada, Ltd., 1929; member of many industrial boards and assocs. and metallurgical institutes and socs. (awarded several medals). Fellow, Cdn. Geog. Soc.; Member, Newcomen Soc. of Eng. H.M.'s Medal for Service in the Cause of Freedom, 1947; Comdr. Order of Leopold (Belgium). 1937. Many philanthropic activities. *Recreation:* salmon fishing. *Address:* (office) 67 Wall Street, New York 5, N.Y., U.S.A.; (home) Country Club Grounds, Dongan Hills, Staten Is. 4, N.Y. *Clubs:* St. James' (London); (Trustee) City Midday, Mining, Union, New York Yacht, Stevens Metropolitan (New York); (Dir.) Richmond County Country; U.S. Seniors Golf Assoc.; Mount Royal (Montreal); Toronto (Toronto); (member Bd. of Governors) Lucerne-in-Quebec Seigniory; York Fishing (Gaspé, Quebec). [*Died* 12 *Feb.* 1951.

STANMORE, 2nd Baron (*cr.* 1893), **George Arthur Maurice Hamilton-Gordon,** P.C. 1932; K.C.V.O., *cr.* 1930 (C.V.O. 1922); Chairman of Committees and Deputy Speaker, House of Lords, 1944-46; Chief Liberal Whip, House of Lords, 1923-44; *b.* 3 Jan. 1871; *o. s.* of 1st Baron Stanmore and Rachel, *e. d.* of Sir John Shaw Lefevre (*d.* 1879); *S.* father, 1912; Church of England. *Educ.:* Winchester; Trinity College, Cambridge (B.A.). Contested North Dorset (L.), 1900; Lord-in-Waiting to the King, 1914-22; Secretary-General of the Order of St. John of Jerusalem, 1921-22; Treasurer of St. Bartholomew's Hospital, 1921-37. *Heir:* none. *Club:* Brooks's. [*Died* 13 *April* 1957 (*ext.*).

STANNARD, H. Sylvester, R.B.A. 1896; Fellow of the Royal Society of Arts; *e. s.* of late Henry Stannard, R.B.A.; *b.* 1870; *m.* 1st, 1895, Annie, 3rd *d.* of Leslie Clark, M.I.C.E., Lahore; one *d.*; 2nd, 1933, Wilhelmina, *e. d.* of Alec. Fordyce, Ayr; one *s.* *Educ.:* Modern School, Bedford. Founded Northamptonshire Amateur and Professional Art Exhibition, Harpur Art Society, and other sketching clubs, 1895; founded Midland Sketch Society, 1940; silver medallist of Crystal Palace for landscapes in water-colours, 1897; Hon. Fellow of North British Academy of Art; Vice-President South Bedfordshire Art Society; a member of Council of Dudley Art Society; water colours hung in Permanent Art Galleries of Wolverhampton, Kettering, Luton, Bedford, Johannesburg, etc. Member Modern Sketch Club, Norwich Art Circle, and Belfast Art Society; exhibitor Royal Academy, Royal Institute of Painters in Water-Colours, New Gallery, Royal Society of British Artists, Royal Cambrian Academy, Dudley Art Gallery, Manchester, Birmingham, Liverpool, and other exhibitions; inventor of the Sylvester

Stannard Patent Straining Board for Water-colour Painting; made a series of sketches of Queen Alexandra's Wild Gardens, Sandringham Woods, and a special drawing by command of Sandringham Church; contributed a view of Sandringham lake, size of a florin, for the Queen's doll's house; Queen Mary has purchased some of his colour drawings; Duke of Windsor possesses one of his drawings in water-colour. *Recreations:* shooting and music, an imitator of Chevalier's songs, and other comics; member on committee of South Bedfordshire Gun Club; member of Bedford Amateur Operatic Society, and Hon. Musical Director of Bedford Amateur Repertory Co. *Address:* The Studio, Spenser Rd., Bedford; Flitwick, Bedfordshire. *Club:* Overseas. [*Died* 21 *Jan.* 1951.

STANNUS, Hugh Stannus, C.B.E. 1956; M.D., Ph.D.(Lond.); F.R.C.P.(Lond.); M.R.C.S. (Eng.); D.T.M. and H.(Cantab.); Chevalier, Légion d'Honneur; Chevalier de l'Ordre de la Santé Publique; Médaille de la Reconnaissance Française; Consulting Physician French Hospital; Member of the Associate Staff Tropical Diseases Hospital; *b.* 18 June 1877; *o. s.* of late Prof. Hugh Hutton Stannus, F.R.I.B.A.; unmarried. *Educ.:* St. Thomas's Hospital; University of London (Univ. Gold Medallist); Paris. Fellow Royal Society of Medicine; Fellow Royal Society of Tropical Medicine and Hygiene; Fellow of Society of Genealogists and of Nutrition Society; Medical Adviser, Board of Inland Revenue; Consultant to Ministry of Health, Ministry of Pensions; served European War, 1914-19, German East Africa; late Fellow Royal Anthropological Institute of Great Britain; Examiner for Diploma of Tropical Medicine University of Liverpool; Master of the Worshipful Company of Founders of London; Resident appointments at St. Thomas's Hospital, Bethlem Royal Hospital, and the British Hospital, Paris; Colonial Medical Service; Lumleian Lecturer, 1944, Roy. Coll. Phys. *Publications:* Sectional Editor Tropical Diseases Bulletin; Monograph on the Wa-Yao; articles on Anthropological subjects in Biometrika, The Journal of the Royal Anthropological Institute etc.; articles on Tropical Diseases in the Transactions of the Royal Society of Tropical Medicine and Hygiene, etc. *Recreation:* swimming. *Address:* 130 Harley Street, W.1. *T.:* Welbeck 3349. *Club:* International Sportsmen's. [*Died* 27 *Feb.* 1957.

STANSFELD, Miss Margaret, O.B.E. 1939; Founder Bedford Physical Training College, Principal, 1903-45. *Address:* 33 Cedar Road, Berkhamsted, Herts. [*Died* 28 *June* 1951.

STANSFIELD, Herbert, D.Sc. London, A.M.I.E.E.; retired; *b.* Bradford, 1872; *s.* of Frederic and Mary Ellen Stansfield; *m.* 1908, Edith, *d.* of F. E. Grubb, Cahir Abbey, Co. Tipperary, and Berkeley, California; one *s.* *Educ.:* Ackworth School; Bradford Technical College; Royal College of Science, London. Demonstrator in Physical Laboratory, Royal College of Science; Evening Lecturer in Physics at the East London College; Lecturer in Physics and Electrical Engineering, Chelsea Polytechnic; Head of Physics and Electrical Engineering Dept., Municipal Technical School, Blackburn, 1898-1904; Hon. Research Fellow and later Lecturer in Physics, Victoria University of Manchester, 1904-12; Professor of Physics and Electrical Engineering, University College, Southampton, 1912-32. *Publications:* Papers in scientific journals on Soap Films, Echelon Spectroscope, etc. *Address:* Castilla, 49 Plaistow Lane, Bromley, Kent. [*Died* 14 *March* 1960.

STANSGATE, 1st Viscount, *cr.* **1941,** of Stansgate; **William Wedgwood Benn,** P.C. 1929; D.S.O. 1916; D.F.C.; Air Commodore late R.A.F.V.R.; *b.* 10 May 1877; 2nd *s.* of Sir J. Williams Benn, 1st Bart.; *m.* 1920, Margaret Eadie, *d.* of late D. T. Holmes; two *s.* (and one killed on operations 1944). B.A. London, 1898 (1st place in Honours); Fellow, Univ. Coll., London; M.P. (L.) St. George's Division, Tower Hamlets, 1906-18; Leith, 1918-27; (Lab.) North Aberdeen, 1928-31; Gorton Division of Manchester, 1937-42; a Junior Lord of the Treasury, 1910-15; joined Labour Party, 1927; Secretary of State for India, 1929-31; Vice-Pres. Allied Control Commission for Italy, 1943-44; Sec. of State for Air, 1945-1946; Pres. Interparliamentary Union, 1947-1957. Served in Yeomanry and Air Force (1914-15 Star; D.S.O.; Legion of Honour and Croix de Guerre; Italian Bronze Valour Medal; D.F.C.; Italian War Cross); served in R.A.F., 1940-45 (despatches). *Publications:* In the Side Shows; (with wife) Beckoning Horizon, 1935. *Heir:* *s.* Hon. Anthony Wedgwood Benn, M.P. *Address:* 10 North Court, Great Peter St., S.W.1; Stansgate, near Southminster, Essex. *Club:* Athenæum. [*Died* 17 *Nov.* 1960.

STANTON-JONES, Rt. Rev. William, D.D.(hon.); M.A.; *b.* Birkenhead, 1866; *e. s.* of Peter Jones and Helen Martha; *m.* Ada Mary Yapp, Leominster, Herefordshire. *Educ.:* St. Aidan's Theological College; Durham University. Deacon, 1891; Priest, 1892; Curate of Widnes, Lancashire, 1891-97; Vicar of St. Polycarp's, Liverpool, 1898-1905; Vicar of St. Mary's with St. Lawrence, Kirkdale, Liverpool, 1905-12; Rector of Middleton, Lancashire, 1912-19; Rural Dean of Middleton, 1912-19; Hon. Canon of Bradford; Vicar of Bradford, 1919-28; Rural Dean of Bradford, 1919-22; Archdeacon of Bradford, 1921-28; Bishop of Sodor and Man, 1928-42. *Address:* Orleton, Pyrford, near Woking, Surrey. *Club:* Athenæum. [*Died* 13 *Aug.* 1951.

STAPLEDON, Sir (Reginald) George, Kt., *cr.* 1939; C.B.E. 1932; F.R.S. 1939; M.A.; Hon. D.Sc. Nottingham, Wales; Director of Dunns Farm Seeds Ltd.; late Director Grassland Improvement Station, Ministry of Agriculture and Fisheries, Stratford-on-Avon; *b.* 22 September 1882; *y. s.* of Wm. Stapledon, Northam, N. Devon; *m.* 1913, Doris Wood Bourne; no *c.* *Educ.:* United Services College, Westward Ho!; Emmanuel College, Cambridge. Sometime Professor of Agricultural Botany at the Royal Agricultural College, Cirencester; First Director of the Official Seed Testing Station when founded at Food Production Dept. of Ministry of Agriculture during European War, 1914-18; Professor of Agricultural Botany, University College of Wales, Aberystwyth, and Director of the Welsh Plant Breeding Station, 1919-42; President of the Fourth International Grassland Congress, Great Britain, 1937; Foreign Member Royal Swedish Academy of Agriculture; Gold Medallist, Royal Agricultural Society of England; Hon. Life Mem. Royal Highland and Agricultural Soc. of Scotland. *Publications:* A Tour in Australia and New Zealand, 1928; The Land: Now and Tomorrow, 1935; The Way of the Land, 1943; Disraeli and the New Age, 1943; various scientific papers. *Recreation:* primitive gardening. *Address:* Teffont Manor, Teffont, nr. Salisbury, Wilts. *T.:* Teffont 273. *Club:* Farmers'. [*Died* 16 *Sept.* 1960.

STAPLES, Irene E. T.; *see* Warner-Staples.

STAPLETON, Brig. Francis Harry, C.M.G. 1919; late Oxfordshire and Bucks Light Infantry; *b.* 1876; 2nd *s.* of late Rev. E. H. Stapleton and Frances Mary, *d.* of Sir Walter Stirling, Bt.; *m.* 1911, Maud Ellen, *d.* of late Major A. E. Wrottesley; one *s.* *Educ.:* Haileybury; R.M.C., Sandhurst. Served S. African War, 1900-2; European War (Mesopotamia) 1914-19 (despatches seven times, C.M.G.); commanded 10th Infantry Brigade, 1929-32; A.D.C. to the King, 1930-32; retired pay, 1932; has Serbian Order of the White Eagle. *Club:* Naval and Military. [*Died* 13 *Aug.* 1956.

STAPLETON-COTTON, Admiral Richard Greville Arthur Wellington, C.B. 1926; C.B.E. 1919; M.V.O. 1905; *b.* 7 Nov. 1873; *e. surv. s.* of Colonel Hon. R. S. G. Stapleton-Cotton, O.B.E. (*d.* 1925), and Hon. Jane Charlette Methuen (*d.* 1924), *d.* of 2nd Baron Methuen; *m.* 1910, Olive, *y. d.* of late Colonel Sir Edward Cotton-Jodrell. Lieut. 1895; Commander, 1905; Captain, 1913; Rear-Admiral, 1923; Vice-Admiral, 1928; Admiral, retired, 1932; Flag Captain C.-in-C. Portsmouth, 1914-16 (C.B.E.); Rear-Admiral in charge, and Admiral Superintendent, Gibraltar Dockyard, 1925-27; retired list, 1928. Gentleman Usher of the Scarlet Rod of the Order of the Bath, 1928-32; Registrar and Secretary of the Order of the Bath, 1932-48. *Address:* Bryntirion, Corwen, N. Wales. *T.:* Corwen 58. *Club:* Naval and Military.
[*Died* 5 *Jan.* 1953.

STAPLETON-SHAW, Major Peter; *see* Shaw.

STAPYLTON, Colonel Bryan H. C.; *see* Chetwynd-Stapylton.

STARKE, Sir Hayden (Erskine), K.C.M.G., *cr.* 1939; a Justice of the High Court of Australia, 1920-50; *b.* 22 Feb. 1871; *s.* of Anthony George Hayden Starke, M.D.; *m.* 1909, Margaret Mary, *d.* of Hon. John Gavan Duffy; one *s.* one *d.* *Educ.:* Melbourne. Retired, 1950. *Address:* Myoora, Irving Road, Toorak, Victoria, Australia. *Clubs:* Australian (Melbourne); Union (Sydney).
[*Died* 14 *May* 1958.

STARKEY, James Sullivan; *see* O'Sullivan, Seumas.

STATHAM, Reginald Samuel Sherard, O.B.E. 1919; Ch.M., M.D., F.R.C.O.G.; re-joined R.A.M.C. 1940; released as Col. Aug. 1946; appt. to Pensions Appeal Tribunal; late Prof. of Obstetrics, Univ. of Bristol; Hon. Gynæcologist, Bristol Royal Infirmary, 1924; *b.* 11 March 1884; *s.* of Rev. S. P. H. Statham and Meta Gill; *m.* 1916, Nan Maitland Sherwin; one *s.* one *d.* *Educ.:* Bradfield College, Berks (Classical Exhibitioner); Westminster and Bristol Medical Schools (Guthrie Scholar). Qualified, 1909; various Hospital appointments; Obstetric Registrar, Bristol, 1912; Temp. Lieut. R.A.M.C. 10 Aug. 1914; Resigned as Major, 1920 (O.B.E., Mons Star and Bar, despatches); Assistant Gynæcologist at Bristol Royal Infirmary, 1922. *Publications:* An Outline of Practical Obstetrics for Nurses, 1933; Contributions on various Medical subjects. *Recreation:* fly fishing. *Address:* 78 Antrim Mansions, N.W.3. *T.:* Primrose 6434. *Club:* United Service. [*Died* 5 *Oct.* 1959.

STAUNTON, Hugh Geoffrey, C.B.E. 1919; late Commodore of the Orient Steam Navigation Company; *s.* of late General Staunton, C.B., Colonel of the Gordon Highlanders; *b.* 1871; *m.* 1925, Annesta, *d.* of late Frank Villiers-Palmer and Mrs. Cloutte, Canterbury; one *s.* Served European War (despatches, C.B.E.). [*Died* 2 *Feb.* 1951.

STAYNES, Percy Angelo, R.I., R.O.I.; Artist, Designer and Illustrator; *m.* 1919, Emilie Horatia Coote; one *s.* one *d.* *Educ.:* School of Art, Manchester; Royal College of Art, London; Julien's, Paris. *Address:* 3 Bath Road, W.4. *T.:* Chiswick 1884.
[*Died* 14 *April* 1953.

STEAD, Francis Bernard, C.B.E. 1931; M.A.; *b.* 19 Feb. 1873; *s.* of Samuel Stead, formerly Archdeacon of Bombay; *m.* Rachel Elizabeth, *d.* of late Canon G. C. Bell, Master of Marlborough College; two *s.* two *d.* *Educ.:* Clifton College; King's College, Cambridge. Assistant Master, Aldenham School, 1898-1901; Clifton College, 1901-8; Staff Inspector, Board of Education, 1908; Divisional Inspector, 1919; Chief Inspector of Secondary Schools, 1926-33; retired, 1933; Secretary, Prime Minister's Committee on the Teaching of Science, 1916-18. Chairman of the Girls' Public Day School Trust, 1944-48; Deputy Chairman since 1948. *Address:* Fifield, Frensham, Farnham, Surrey. *T.:* Frensham 182. *Clubs:* Athenæum, Alpine.
[*Died* 22 *Dec.* 1954.

STEBBING, Edward Percy, M.A., F.L.S., F.Z.S., F.R.G.S., F.R.S.E., late I.F.S.; Professor of Forestry, University of Edinburgh, 1920, Professor Emeritus, 1952; *b.* 1870; 2nd *s.* of late Edward Charles Stebbing and *g.s.* of late Rev. Henry Stebbing, D.D., F.R.S.; *m.* 1907, Maud Evelyn (*d.* 1950), *o. d.* of late Colonel W. T. Brown, Indian Army, of Warboro' House, South Devonshire; one *s.* *Educ.:* St. Paul's School; Royal Indian Engineering College, Coopers Hill; Prize in Forest Entomology, 1892; Diploma in Forestry, 1893; Assistant Conservator of Forests, Indian Forest Service, 1893; Deputy Conservator, 1900; Forest Entomologist to the Government of India, 1901-2, 1904-6; Acting Superintendent of the Indian Museum, Calcutta, 1903; Forest Zoologist to Govt. of India and Member of Imperial Forest Research Institute and College, 1906-9; Lecturer in Forestry and Head of the Forestry Department, University of Edinburgh, 1910-52; on active service in Macedonia as Transport Officer, 1916; France, University Extension Lecturer—subject, On Macedonian Front, Feb.-Mar. 1917; Mission to Russia, 1917; Visit to West Africa, British and French Colonies, and across the Sahara, 1934; Mission to the Sudan, 1947; F.A.O. Sub-Cttee. Geneva, 1947; Member of 1st World Forestry Congress, Rome, 1926; 2nd, Budapest, 1935; 3rd, Helsinki, 1949. Elected Hon. Mem. of Soc. of American Foresters, 1948; French—Legion of Honour, 1951, Mérite Agricole; Serbian Orders: St. Sava, White Eagle; Editor Indian Forester, 1903-7; first Editor Indian Forest Publications, 1907-9; Silver Medallist, Royal Society of Arts, 1923 and 1926. *Publications:* Injurious Insects of Indian Forests, 1899; Departmental Notes on Forest Insects, 1902-5; Manual of Indian Forest Zoology, 1908; Insect Intruders in Indian Homes, 1909; Jungle By-Ways in India, 1910; Stalks in the Himalaya, 1911; Indian Forest Insects of Economic Importance, 1914; British Forestry, 1916; At the Serbian Front in Macedonia, 1917; From Czar to Bolshevik, 1918; Commercial Forestry in Britain, 1919; The Diary of a Sportsman Naturalist in India, 1920; The Forests of India, vol. i. 1921; vol. ii. 1923; vol. iii. 1926; The Forestry Question in Great Britain, 1928; The Threat of the Sahara, 1937; The Forests of West Africa and the Sahara, 1937; The Man-Made Desert in Africa, 1938; Africa, Its Intermittent Rainfall and rôle of the Savannah Forest, 1938; Cross-Country Riding, 1938; Forests and Erosion, 1941; Erosion and Water Supplies 1945; The Creeping Desert in the Sudan and elsewhere in Africa 15° to 13° Latitude, 1954; Forestry Research in India, Great Britain, the Dominions and the Colonies, 1957; contributions to the press. *Recreations:* hunting, shooting, fishing, travelling in the wilds. *Address:* Romden Castle, Smarden, Kent. *Clubs:* Athenæum, East India and Sports. [*Died* 21 *March* 1960.

STEDMAN, Air Vice-Marshal (retired) Ernest W., C.B. 1944; O.B.E.; Royal Canadian Air Force, 1924-46; formerly Air Member for Research and Development, R.C.A.F.; *b.* 21 July 1888; *s.* of Walter Stedman and Charlotte M. Fremlin; *m.* 1912, Ethel A. Studd; one *s.* *Educ.:* Brunswick House, Maidstone; Royal College of Science, London; City and Guilds Central Technical College, London. Scientific Assist. in Aeronautics at National Physical Laboratory, Teddington, 1913-14; served with Royal Naval Air Service and Royal Air Force, 1914-19; Chief of Technical Staff, Messrs. Handley Page, Ltd., 1919-20; Technical Director Air Board of Canada, 1920-24; Whitworth Scholar; A.R.C.S.;

M.I.C.E.; F.R.Ae.S.; M.E.I.C.; F.I.Ae.S.; Hon. F.C.A.I. *Address:* Tiffany Apartments, Driveway, Ottawa, Canada. [*Died* 27 *March* 1957.

STEED, Henry Wickham; *b.* 10 Oct. 1871; 2nd *s.* of late Joshua George Steed, solicitor, Long Melford, Suffolk; *m.* 1937, Violet Sybille, *e. d.* of late James Francis Mason and Lady Evelyn Mason. *Educ.:* Sudbury Grammar School; Jena, Berlin, and Paris Universities; hon. LL.D. Strasbourg and Cluj Universities. Acting correspondent of The Times at Berlin, 1896; correspondent of The Times at Rome, 1897-1902; at Vienna, 1902-13; Foreign Editor of The Times, 1914-19; Editor of The Times, Feb. 1919-Nov. 1922; Lecturer on Central European History, King's College, Strand, 1925-38; Proprietor and Editor of the Review of Reviews, 1923-30; engaged in propaganda in enemy countries, 1918, and head of special mission to Italy, Mar.-Apr. 1918; Broadcaster on World Affairs in Overseas Service of B.B.C., 1937-47. *Publications:* The Socialist and Labour Movement in England, Germany, and France, Harper's Weekly Magazine, 1894; article on Recent Italian Political History, etc., in Supplement to ninth edition Encyclopædia Britannica; The Hapsburg Monarchy, 1913; 2nd and 3rd editions, 1914; 4th edition, 1918; French edition, 1914; L'Angleterre et la Guerre, 1915; L'Effort Anglais, 1916; La Démocratie Britannique, 1918; Through Thirty Years, 1924; French edition, 1926 and 1927; Journalism, 1928; The Real Stanley Baldwin, 1930; The Antecedents of Post-War Europe, 1932; Hitler: Whence and Whither? 1934, fifth edition, 1937; The Meaning of Hitlerism, 1934; A Way to Social Peace, 1934; Chapter, The Great War, in volume, Great Events, 1934; Vital Peace, A Study of Risks, 1936; The Doom of the Hapsburgs, 1937; The Press, 1938; Our War Aims, 1939; The Fifth Arm, 1940; That Bad Man, 1942; Words on the Air, Vol. I, 1946. *Address:* Holly Bank, Wootton-by-Woodstock, Oxon. *T.:* Tackley 243. *Club:* Athenæum. [*Died* 13 *Jan.* 1956.

STEEL, Gerald, C.B.E. 1956; J.P.; General Managing Director, The United Steel Companies Limited, since 1950; *b.* 15 Feb. 1895; 2nd *s.* of Henry Steel, Skellow Grange, Doncaster; *m.* 1922, Ruth, *o. d.* of Robert Crawshaw, Doncaster; one *s.* two *d.* (and one *s.* killed in action, R.A.F., War of 1939-45). *Educ.:* Charterhouse School; Oriel Coll., Oxford. Served European War, 1914-18, Captain, Roy. Fusiliers and K.A.R. Man. Dir., United Steel Cos. (India) Ltd., 1928; Gen. Manager, Samuel Fox & Co. Ltd., 1932; Joint Man. Dir., United Steel Cos. Ltd., 1944. Director, National Provincial Bank Ltd. 1956-. J.P. West Riding of Yorkshire, 1941-57. *Address:* The Orchards, 47 Copse Hill, S.W.20. *Club:* The Club (Sheffield). [*Died* 14 *Sept.* 1957.

STEEL-MAITLAND, Sir (Arthur) James (Drummond Ramsay-), 2nd Bt., *cr.* 1917; *b.* 27 May 1902; *er. s.* of Rt. Hon. Sir Arthur Steel-Maitland, 1st Bt., and Mary (*d.* 1944), *d.* of Sir James Ramsay-Gibson-Maitland, 4th Bt., of Barnton and Sauchie; *S.* father, 1935; *m.* Matilda Brenda, 3rd *d.* of late Thomas Doughty, Colbbrookdale, Shropshire; one *d.* *Educ.:* Winchester College; Balliol College, Oxford. Price Waterhouse & Co., London; J. P. Morgan & Co., New York; Director: Caledonian Fibreplast Ltd.; Caledonian Tooth Co. Ltd. Served Royal Australian Air Force, 1942-43; Australian Ministry of Munitions (Lend Lease), 1943-44; Historian, 1944-46. *Recreations:* fly-fishing, zoology. *Heir:* *b.* Keith Richard Felix, *b.* 6 May 1912. *Address:* Gogar House, Corstorphine, Edinburgh. *T.:* Corstorphine 1234. [*Died* 1 *March* 1960.

STEELE, Major-General Sir Clive (Selwyn), K.B.E., *cr.* 1953; D.S.O. 1941; M.C. 1918; V.D.; Consulting Engineer since 1923; *b.* 30 Sept. 1892; *s.* of late Herbert S. Steele, Melbourne; *m.* 1917, Amie Osland, *d.* of late F O Bilson, Colac; no *c.* *Educ.:* Scotch College; University of Melbourne (B.C.E.). Served 1st A.I.F., 1915-19, 2nd A.I.F., 1939-46 (despatches twice), Lt. 5th Fld. Coy. Engrs., 1915; Major 1st Fld. Coy. Engrs., 1918; C.R.E. 4th Div. Engrs., 1926-31; C.O. 14th Bn., 1933-39; C.E., A.I.F., 1939-41; E.-in-C., A.M.F., 1942-46. Hon. Col. Corps of R.A.E., 1953. Director: A.M.P. Soc. (V.B.), A.P.M. Ltd.; Brooklands Accessories Ltd.; Commonwealth Oil Refineries Ltd.; Containers Ltd.; Lamson Paragon Ltd.; Regent Motors (Holdings) Ltd.; David Syme & Co. Ltd. Chairman War Nurses Memorial Centre. Kernot Memorial Medal, Univ. of Melbourne, for distinguished engineering achievement, 1944. M.Inst.C.E.; Hon. M.I.E. Aust., 1954; Hon. M.Inst.R.E., 1954. Military Cross (Greece) 1st Class, 1941. *Address:* 4 Ledbury Court, Toorak, Melbourne, Australia. *T.:* UY 5085. *Clubs:* Melbourne, Australian, Naval and Military (Melbourne). [*Died* 5 *Aug.* 1955.

STEELE, Colonel William Lawrence, C.M.G. 1918; R.A.M.C. (retired); *b.* 1878; *s.* of late Lieut.-Colonel W. H. Steele; *m.* Frances Margaret Berthe, *d.* of late Charles Tanner of Yatesbury, Wilts; one *s.* one *d.* *Educ.:* Kelly College; University College Hospital. Served South African War, 1901-2 (Queen's medal and five clasps); European War and War of 1939-45; retired pay, 1932; Commander of the Order of Aviz. *Address:* c/o Glyn, Mills & Co., Holt's Branch, Kirkland House, Whitehall, S.W.1. [*Died* 14 *Dec.* 1958.

STEERE, Sir Ernest A. L.; *see* Lee Steere.

STENNING, John Frederick, C.B. 1916; C.B.E. 1919; M.A.; Hon. Fellow, Wadham College, Oxford; 4th *s.* of late Edward Stenning, Beckenham; *m.* Ethelwyn (*d.* 1957), *e. d.* of W. H. Alexander, Oxton, Cheshire; one *s.* one *d.* *Educ.:* Merchant Taylors' School; Wadham College, Oxford (Exhibitioner). Pusey and Ellerton Scholar, 1887; Junior LXX. Prize, 1888; Junior Kennicott Scholar, 1889; 2nd class Hon. School of Theology, 1889; Houghton Syriac Prize, 1890; 1st class Hon. School of Oriental Languages, 1891; Senior LXX. Prize, 1892; Denyer and Johnson Scholar, 1892; Senior Kennicott Scholar, 1897; Senior Demy of Magdalen College, 1893-97; Fellow of Wadham College, 1898, Warden 1927-38; Senior Proctor 1908-9, 1919-20; formerly Lt.-Col. Commanding O.T.C. (Oxford University); and an Officer Cadet Battalion, 1916-18; Secretary of the University Chest, 1919-27; formerly University Reader in Aramaic. *Publications:* joint editor of Anecdota Oxoniensia, Semitic Series, vol. i. Pt. IX.; various articles in Hastings' Dictionary of the Bible, Encyclopædia Biblica, Encyclopædia Britannica, New Commentary on Holy Scripture; The Targum of Isaiah, Aramaic text (with super linear punctuation), 1949. *Address:* 76 Woodstock Road, Oxford. [*Died* 18 *Nov.* 1959.

STEPHEN, Colonel Charles Merton, C.M.G. 1916; late R.A.O.C.; *b.* 6 Sept. 1874; *s.* of late A. Stephen, Halifax, N.S., Canada; *m.* 1st, 1911, Maud (*d.* 1927), *d.* of late Samuel Bishop, Bathurst, N.B.; 2nd, 1934, Mary, *d.* of Major T. Hibbard, Shepherdswell, Dover. *Educ.:* Royal Military College, Canada. 2nd Lieut. Cheshire Regt. 1896; transferred to R.A.O.C. 1904; served S. Africa, 1902 (Queen's medal 2 clasps); European War, 1914-18 (despatches, C.M.G., Brevet Lt.-Col.); Asst. Dir. Equipment and Ordnance Stores, War Office, 1918-23; retired pay, 1931; War of 1939-1945, temp. Brig. *Address:* Westcourt Cottage, Shepherdswell, Dover. [*Died* 24 *March* 1955.

STEPHEN, Rt. Rev. Reginald, D.D.; M.A. (Honours) Melbourne; Exhibitioner in

Natural Science; Scholar in History and Political Economy; Bromby Prizeman in Greek and Hebrew; *b.* Geelong, Victoria, 1860; *m.* 1905, Elsie (*d.* 1936), *d.* of late Canon Tucker, Melbourne; two *s.* one *d.* Has held parochial charges in Melbourne Diocese; Sub-Warden Trinity College, Melbourne; Canon Melbourne Cathedral; Fellow Australian College of Theology; Warden of St. John's Theological College, Melbourne; Bishop of Tasmania, 1914-19; of Newcastle, N.S.W., 1919-28. *Publication:* Democracy and Character (Moorhouse Lectures, 1898).
[*Died* 5 *July* 1956.

STEPHENS, Herbert John; Managing Editor and Principal Proprietor, The Financial World, 1906-54, also for many years of the Gold Mining Record; *b.* 1 Nov. 1875; 3rd *s.* of Edward B. Stephens, Latchley Central Farm, Calstock, Cornwall. *Educ.:* Privately. *Publication:* Compiled first Oil Investor's Manual, first Nigerian Tin Manual, and first Glossary of Aeronautical Words and Phrases. *Address:* 29 Holly Park Gardens, Finchley, N.3. *T.:* Finchley 3847.
[*Died* 14 *Nov.* 1957.

STEPHENS, Surgeon Rear-Admiral Horace Elliott Rose, O.B.E., M.B., B.S., (Lond.), F.R.C.S. (Eng.), D.P.H.; *b.* Chester, 4 Jan. 1883; *e. s.* of late Rev. Horace Stephens, M.A.; *m.* 1911, Frances Mary Butt; one *s.* one *d.* *Educ.:* Christ College, Brecon; University of Manchester; London Hospital. House Surgeon Manchester Royal Infirmary, 1908; Demonstrator of Anatomy, University of Manchester, 1909; joined R.N. 1910; served in Atlantic Fleet, Mediterranean, China, America and West Indies Station; took up surgery as a speciality; Professor of Hygiene and Director of Medical Studies, Naval Medical School, Royal Naval College, Greenwich, 1935-39; in charge of Royal Naval Auxiliary Hospital, Kingseat, Newmachar, Aberdeenshire, 1939-43; retired, 1943; President United Services Section of Royal Society of Medicine, 1933; during European war served in H.M.S. Eclipse, H.M.S. Lion and R.N. Hospital, Plymouth. *Publications:* surgical papers. *Recreation:* golf. *Address:* Gwynfa, Porth-y-Post, Holyhead. *T.:* Trearddur Bay 46.
[*Died* 18 *Feb.* 1959.

STEPHENS, Engineer Rear-Admiral Lindsay James, C.B.E. 1919; J.P.; Royal Navy (retired); *b.* 23 Sep. 1868; *m.* 1906, Minnie (*d.* 1947), *e. d.* of J. F. Babb, R.N. *Educ.:* Portsmouth Grammar School. Royal Navy, 1883-1922; served in Royal Yachts, 1900-1; served Mudros; Dover Patrol; on staff of Admiral Sir Roger Keyes; Chief Engineer of Gibraltar Dockyard, 1919-22 (C.B.E.). *Address:* 5 Godwyn Gardens, Folkestone. *T.:* Folkestone 3854. [*Died* 25 *Sept.* 1958.

STEPHENS, General Sir Reginald Byng, K.C.B., *cr.* 1919 (C.B. 1918); C.M.G. 1916; late Rifle Brigade; J.P., D.L. Gloucestershire; *b.* 10 Oct. 1869; *s.* of late Capt. F. Stephens, 2nd Life Guards, of Bentworth Lodge, Alton; *m.* 1905, Eleanore Dorothea (*d.* 1950), *d.* of late E. W. Cripps, of Ampney Park, Cirencester; one *s.* two *d.* *Educ.:* Winchester. Served South Africa, 1897; Nile Expedition, 1898 (medals and clasp); S. Africa, 1899-1902 (severely wounded, despatches thrice, Bt. Major, Queen's medal 3 clasps, King's medal 2 clasps); European War, 1914-18 (despatches thrice, Bt. Col., C.M.G., C.B., K.C.B., prom. Maj.-Gen.); Corps Commander, 1918-19; Commandant Royal Military College, 1919-23; Commanded 4th Division, 1923-26; Lieut.-General, 1925; Director-General of the Territorial Army, 1927-31; General, 1930; retired pay, 1931. *Address:* Lechlade, Glos. *T.:* Lechlade 321. *Club:* Naval and Military.
[*Died* 6 *April* 1955.

STEPHENSON, Rev. Henry Spencer, M.A.; Rector and Rural Dean of Gateshead 1914-55, retired 1955; Hon. Canon of Durham since 1922; *b.* 4 Nov. 1871; *s.* of late Lieut.-Col. Sussex Vane Stephenson, Scots Fusilier Guards and late Augusta Melita, *d.* of late Sir Augustus Almeric Spencer, G.C.B. (she *m.* 2nd, late Canon E. M. Young); unmarried. *Educ.:* Sherborne School; Trinity Coll., Cambridge; 3rd Cl. Classical Tripos, 2nd Class Theological Tripos, 1895. Ordained 1895; Curate of Willington, Durham; Rector of Allendale, Northumberland, 1900; Vicar of Christ Church, Gateshead, 1908; interested in Boy Scout Movement (Commissioner) and in Temperance (Chairman, Diocesan Branch, C.E.T.S.), also in social work among the Young and on Central Executive of the C. of E. Children's Society; Proctor in Convocation of York and Member of Church Assembly, 1929-49. Chaplain to the Queen since 1952 (to King George VI, 1938-52); one of eight Chaplains on duty in Westminster Abbey on Coronation Day, 1953. Hon. Freeman of Gateshead, 1946. *Recreation:* reading. *Address:* 8 Greenfield Place, Ryton-on-Tyne, Co. Durham. [*Died* 4 *June* 1957.

STEPHENSON, Sir John (Walker), Kt., *cr.* 1948; C.B.E. 1944; J.P.; Chairman Eastern Area Gas Board, 1949-59. Formerly Adviser to Board of Trade, Ministry of Economic Affairs; Chairman, Building and Civil Engineering Nat. Consultative Committee, Ministry of Works; Chairman, Confed. of Shipbuilding and Engineering Unions; J.P. County of London. *Address:* 603 Beatty House, Dolphin Square, S.W.1. *T.:* Victoria 3800 (Beatty House 603).
[*Died* 15 *May* 1960.

STEPHENSON, Katharine J., C.B.E. 1927; J.P.; 3rd *d.* of Sir Augustus Keppe Stephenson, K.C.B., K.C.; *b.* 1874; unmarried. *Educ.:* at home. Alderman Wilts County Council; serves on Governing Bodies of Godolphin School, Salisbury and S. Wilts Girls' Secondary School (Chairman); Salisbury General Infirmary; Winsley Sanatorium; Hon. Sec. Wilts County Nursing Association. *Address:* Bodenham House, Salisbury. *T.A.:* Bodenham, Wilts. *T.:* Bodenham 235. [*Died* 15 *Jan.* 1953.

STEPHENSON, Lieut.-Colonel Robert, C.B.E. 1919; D.S.O. 1917; Italian War Cross; *b.* 12 Aug. 1876; *s.* of late Robert Stephenson, J.P., The Woodlands, Middlesbrough, Yorkshire; *m.* Ethel, *d.* of A. Staniforth, Sparken Hill, Worksop, Notts; one *d.* (and one *d.* decd.). *Educ.:* The Mount, Northallerton; Uppingham. Served European War, France, and Italy, 1914-19; Major, Northumberland Fusiliers, 1914; Lt.-Col., South Staffordshire Regiment, 1916-19. *Recreations:* shooting, fishing. *Address:* Benwell Lodge, Newcastle upon Tyne. *T.:* 34337 Newcastle. *Club:* Union.
[*Died* 3 *May* 1959.

STERLING, Herbert Harry, C.M.G. 1935; LL.B., J.P., M.Inst.T., F.R.E.S.; Company Director; *b.* 22 April 1886; *s.* of Thomas Sterling and Emmeline Whiting; *m.* 1915; one *d.* *Educ.:* Normal and Richmond primary schools and Boys' High School, Christchurch, N.Z.; Otago University, Dunedin; Victoria University College, Wellington. Joined N.Z. Government Railways as cadet, 1901; trained all branches of railway operation; graduated LL.B. (New Zealand University) and admitted as Barrister-at-Law; Law Officer, New Zealand Government Railways Department, 1919; Assistant General Manager, New Zealand Government Railways, 1924; Member Board of Management, 1925; resigned to take position of General Manager, N.Z. Co-operative Dairy Coy. Ltd. 1926; re-joined N.Z. Govt. Railways as General Manager, 1928-31; Chm. 1931-36. *Address:* P.O.B. 1419, Wellington, New Zealand. *Clubs:* Auckland (Auckland); Wellington (Wellington); Canterbury (Christchurch); Tattersall's, New South Wales (Sydney). [*Died* 5 *Aug.* 1959.

STERLING, Sir Louis Saul, Kt., *cr.* 1937; D.Litt.; Herrburger Brooks, Ltd.; Director, S. G. Warburg & Co. Ltd. *Address:*

7 Avenue Rd., N.W.8. *T.:* Primrose 0884. *Clubs:* Savage, Royal Automobile, Eccentric. [*Died* 2 *June* 1958.

STERNE, Maurice, N.A.; Member Institute of Arts and Letters; Former Member Fine Arts Commission, Washington, D.C.; Painter and Sculptor; *b.* Libau on the Baltic, 12 Aug. 1877; *s.* of Gregory Sterne and Gita Schlossberg; *m.* 1st, 1916, Mabel Dodge; 2nd, 1923, Vera Segal; no *c.* *Educ.:* New York, Paris and Rome. Came to U.S.A. from Moscow, Russia, in 1889, worked at various trades while studying art at Nat. Academy of Design, first made reputation as etcher. Won Moody travelling scholarship in 1904 for 2 years abroad and stayed 12 years, travelling and living in France, Italy and Greece, where became interested in sculpture. Went to Egypt, India and Malaya, stayed in Bali for 2 years, returned to Italy in 1914 and since then lived either in Italy or U.S.A. Represented U.S.A. in third biennial exhibition in Rome, 1925, and invited by Uffizi Gallery, Florence, to paint self-portrait for permanent collection. Rogers Kennedy Memorial, Worcester, Mass. (sculpture), 1930. In 1935 awarded commission for 20 murals for Library of Dept. of Justice, Washington, entitled The Search for Truth. Exhibitions: (one-man shows) Paul Cassirer Gallery, Berlin, Vienna, Prague, Rome; about 6 exhibitions in New York, Boston Art Club, Philadelphia, Chicago Art Institute; also exhibited Paris Salon. Awarded many medals and prizes. Represented at Metropolitan Museum, N.Y., Museum of Modern Art, N.Y., Brooklyn Mus., Boston Mus., Yale Univ., Chicago Art Inst. and other museums and galleries, including Tate Gallery. Hon. Member Internat. Mark Twain Soc. *Publication:* Monograph Valori Plastici, Rome, 1925. *Address:* Byram Lake Rd., Mount Kisco, N.Y. *Club:* Coffee House (N.Y.). [*Died* 23 *July* 1957.

STERRY, Sir Wasey, Kt., *cr.* 1925; C.B.E. 1918; *b.* 26 July 1866; *e. s.* of late Rev. Francis Sterry of Fort Hill, Barnstaple, and Augusta Emily, 3rd *d.* of late Hastings Nathaniel Middleton of Bradford Peverell, Dorset; *m.* 1919, Renée, *e. d.* of late M. Adrien Bonfils, Nice. *Educ.:* Eton (Scholar); Merton College, Oxford (Exhibitioner), 2nd class Mods., 2nd class Lit. Hum. B.A. 1889; M.A. 1892; Barrister of Lincoln's Inn, 1892; first Civil Judge in Sudan, 1901; Chief Judge, 1903; styled Chief Justice 1915; Legal Secretary Sudan Government, 1917-26; Judge of H.B.M.'s Supreme Court for Egypt, 1928-38; Order of Mejidie, 3rd class, 1907; Order of the Nile, 2nd class, 1915. *Publications:* Annals of Eton College, 1898; The Eton College Register (1441-1698), 1943. *Clubs:* Savile, Athenæum. [*Died* 9 *Aug.* 1955.

STEUART, Ethel Mary, M.A., D.Litt. Edinburgh; *o. d.* of late John A. Steuart; *b.* Mumbles, Glam. *Educ.:* North London Collegiate School (Clothworkers' Scholarship); University College, London (Classical Scholarship, Classical Scholar of London); Girton College, Cambridge (Foundation Scholar, Gamble Prize, Research Studentship, and Fellow of the College); Berlin University. Research work in Paris and British School of Archæology, Rome; First Class both parts of Classical Tripos; graduate of London University with first class Honours. Formerly Headmistress, High School for Girls, Bootle, Liverpool, retired; for short time Assistant Lecturer in Latin, University College, Cardiff; Lecturer in Latin, Edinburgh University. *Publications:* The Annals of Quintus Ennius, 1925; contributor to Classical Review, Classical Quarterly, American Journal of Philology. *Recreations:* travelling, especially on Continent of Europe. *Address:* High School for Girls, Bootle, Liverpool. [*Died* 31 *March* 1960.

STEVENS, Air Vice-Marshal Cecil Alfred, C.B. 1947; C.B.E. 1944; M.C. 1917; D.L.; retired; *b.* 31 Oct. 1898; *s.* of late Alfred Stevens, Putney; *m.* 1946, Natalie Pratt (*née* Koltsoff). *Educ.:* Emanuel School; Royal Military College, Sandhurst. Commissioned Duke of Wellington's (West Riding) Regiment, 1916; seconded to R.F.C.; France, 1917-18 (M.C. and Bar); India, 1924-30; Wing Commander, 1936; Group Capt., 1939; Air Commodore, 1941; Senior Air Staff Officer, Aden, 1937-41; A.O.A., Burma, 1944-45; A.O.C., Allied Air Forces, Netherlands East Indies, 1945-46; A.O.C. No. 28 Group, 1947-1949; A.O.C. No. 62 (S) Group, 1949-51; Air Vice-Marshal, 1951; S.A.S.O. Home Command, 1951-54; retired, Nov. 1954. D.L. Sussex, 1957. *Recreation:* golf. *Address:* c/o Westminster Bank, Ltd., St. Leonards Road, Bexhill, Sussex. *Club:* R.A.F. [*Died* 30 *Nov.* 1958.

STEVENS, Clement Henry, C.B.E. 1917; M.I.Mech.E.; M.I.N.A.; Consulting Engineer; *b.* 5 Dec. 1870; 2nd *s.* of late G. J. B. Stevens, M.R.C.S., L.R.C.P.; *m.* 1895, Edith Lutwyche (*d.* 1939), *d.* of G. T. Crook, R.N.; one *s.*; *m.* 1940, Winifred Kate, 3rd *d.* of late Luke Bassham, Wolferton, Norfolk, widow of F. I. Sanderson. *Educ.:* St. Paul's School. Superintendent Engineer to Blandy Bros. & Co., Las Palmas, Grand Canary, 1894-1915; joined Ministry of Munitions, June 1915; Controller of Gun Ammunition, Ministry of Munitions, 1917-18. *Address:* Manor Ho., Diptford, nr. South Brent, Devon. *T.:* Gara Bridge 222. [*Died* 7 *Feb.* 1959.

STEVENS, Brig.-Gen. George Archibald, C.M.G. 1919; D.S.O. 1916; *b.* 1875; *s.* of Col. George Morton Stevens, formerly R.A.; *m.* 1907, Eugenie Macdonald; two *s.* In ranks of Scots Greys, 1894-98; 2nd Lieut. Royal Fusiliers, 1898; Capt., 1904; Major, 1915; Bt. Lt.-Col., 1917; Lt.-Col., 1924; Col., 1928; served Ashanti, 1900 (medal); European War, 1914-19, in France, and Flanders (despatches six times, Bt. Lt.-Col., D.S.O., C.M.G., Belgian Croix de Guerre); operations, Waziristan, 1920; Commanded 2nd Batt. The Royal Fusiliers, 1924-28; Instructor, Senior Officers' School, Sheerness, 1928-30; Inspector-General of West Indian Local Force and Officer Commanding the troops, Jamaica, 1930-32; retired pay, 1932. *Address:* Hesperus, Clarence Road, Southsea. [*Died* 26 *April* 1951.

STEVENS, Lt.-Col. Nathaniel Melhuish Comins, C.M.G. 1915; late 107th Pioneers, Indian army; *b.* 10 Aug. 1868. Entered army, 1888; Captain Indian army, 1899; Major, 1906; Lt.-Col. 1914; Staff Officer, India, 1901-6; served Burma, 1891 (medal with clasp); Chin Hills, 1896 (clasp); Tirah, 1897-8 (medal, two clasps); European War, 1914-16 (despatches, C.M.G.); retired, 1920. *Address:* Fiveways, Church Hill, Camberley, Surrey. [*Died* 2 *Feb.* 1954.

STEVENS, Thomas George, M.D., B.S. (Lond.); F.R.C.S. (Eng.); M.R.C.P. (Lond.); (Retired); Consulting Obstetric Surgeon St. Mary's Hospital; Consulting Surgeon, Queen Charlotte's Lying-in Hospital; Consulting Surgeon, The Hospital for Women, Soho Square; *b.* 25 March 1869; *s.* of Geo. J. B. Stevens, surgeon; *m.* Lizzie Jane (*d.* 1953), *e. d.* of Mrs. James Dunn and late John Reeves of Blackheath; one *s.* *Educ.:* St. Paul's Sch.; Guy's Hosp. Late House Surgeon, Asst. House Surgeon, and Obstetric Resident, Guy's Hospital; Resident Medical Officer, Evelina Hospital and Queen Charlotte's Lying-in Hospital; late Demonstrator of Biology, Guy's Hospital Med. School, and Examiner in Biology to the Conjoint Board of England; late Obstetric Tutor, St. Mary's Hospital; appointed Assistant Surgeon to the Hospital for Women, 1899; Physician to Out-patients, Queen Charlotte's Lying-in Hospital, 1908. *Publications:* Diseases of Women; many papers on Obstetrical and Gynæcological subjects; articles in French's Differential Diagnosis of Main Symptoms, and Latham and English's Dictionary of Treatment; co-Author of Midwifery and of Diseases of Women, by Ten Teachers,

1919. *Recreations:* golf, fishing. *Address:* 6 Dunkeld Road, Bournemouth. *T.:* Bournemouth 3918. [*Died* 10 *Nov.* 1953.

STEVENS, Walter Charles; General Secretary, Electrical Trades Union since 1948; *b.* 26 Sept. 1904; British; *m.* 1926, Olive Vera Edwards; two *s.* two *d.* *Educ.:* County Council School. Work in all phases of the Electrical Industry and Trade Union Movement. *Recreation:* gardening. *Address:* 37 Prince John Road, Eltham, S.E.9. *T.:* Eltham 7439. [*Died* 24 *Oct.* 1954.

STEVENS, William C.; *see* Cleveland-Stevens.

STEVENSON, Alexander Wight, D.Sc., F.Inst.P., F.T.I.; Principal and Professor of Textiles, Scottish Woollen College, 1931-1947; *b.* 1886; *o. s.* of William Stevenson, Melrose; *m.* 1917, Margaret, *d.* of Frank Armstrong, Hawick; one *d.* *Educ.:* Melrose; George Watson's, Edinburgh. Whitworth Exhibitioner, 1909; B.Sc. Edin. 1912. Textile-electric development with Siemens; design and flying at R.A.F.; investigator with Wool Industries Research Association, Leeds; D.Sc. Edin. 1928, for Worsted Spinning Research; *Publications:* papers to British Association, Textile Institute, etc.; Editor Scotch Tweed. *Address:* Meigle View, Galashiels. *T.:* 2765. [*Died* 27 *June* 1954.

STEVENSON, Lieut.-Col. Sir Edward Daymonde, K.C.V.O., *cr.* 1949 (C.V.O. 1935); M.C. 1917; Purse-Bearer to the Lord High Commissioners to the General Assembly of the Church of Scotland since 1930; Ensign, Royal Company of Archers, Queen's Body Guard for Scotland, since 1955 (Brigadier, 1948); Usher of the Green Rod of the Order of the Thistle, 1953; Director: J. Smart & Co. (Contractors) Ltd.; Morgan Lyons & Co., Ltd., Cairnton Trust & Finance Co. Ltd.; The Investment and Property Trust Ltd.; Coca-Cola Bottlers (Scotland) Ltd.; Hunter Robertson & Co. Ltd.; Scottish Television Ltd.; Co-operative Permanent Building Society; Arcadia Nickel Corporation Ltd., Toronto (Representative n Europe); *b.* 1 September 1895; *s.* of George Carew Stevenson and Elizabeth Evans; *m.* 1921, Ela Violet Ethel, *d.* of late Gen. Sir William Eliot Peyton, K.C.B., K.C.V.O., D.S.O.; one *s.* *Educ.:* Clifton College. Seaforth Highlanders, 1914-30, Offices of the War Cabinet, 1940-45; Secretary: National Playing Fields Assoc. (Scotland), 1930-37; Nat. Advisory Council for Scotland on Physical Training and Recreation, 1937-39; National Trust for Scotland, 1931-47. *Address:* 4 Great Stuart Street, Edinburgh, 3; *T.:* Edinburgh 34541 and 30211; Seton House, East Lothian. *T.:* Port Seton 326. *Clubs:* Army and Navy, Boodle's; New (Edinburgh). [*Died* 15 *Dec.* 1958.

STEVENSON, George Hope, M.A. (Oxford and Glasgow); Fellow and Praelector in Ancient History, University College, Oxford, 1906-49, Emeritus Fellow since 1949; *b.* 25 July 1880; *s.* of Hugh F. Stevenson, Merchant, Glasgow; *m.* 1912, Phoebe Wadsworth; one *d.* *Educ.:* Glasgow Academy and University; Balliol College, Oxford (Snell and Jenkyns Exhibitioner). Lecturer in Ancient History, Edinburgh Univ., 1905-6; Univ. Lectr. in Ancient History, 1927-35; Examiner in Litt. Hum., 1919-21, 1931-32, 1934, 1942-44, 1947-48; Pres. Oxford Philological Society, 1935; Lt. (Signalling Officer) Ox. and Bucks. L.I. 1915-1917; Staff-Lt. Intelligence Corps G.H.Q. France, 1918. *Publications:* The Roman Empire, 1930; Roman Provincial Administration, 1939; Contributor to Cambridge Ancient History (vols. 9 and 10), Legacy of Rome, Journal of Roman Studies, Theology, etc. *Recreations:* music, theological reading. *Address:* 10 Chadlington Road, Oxford. *T.:* 5300. [*Died* 5 *Feb.* 1952.

STEVENSON, Colonel George Ingram, C.M.G. 1915; D.S.O. 1918; V.D. 1923; Retired List Australian Military Forces; *b.* Kelvinside, Glasgow, 8 March 1882; *s.* of George Stevenson and Margaret Ann Ingram; *m* 1st, 1923, Frances Clare (*d.* 1931), *y. d.* of late J. W. Dennis, Gonn Station, N.S.W.; one *s.* one *d.*; 2nd, 1936, Hilda Mabel, *d.* of late H. V. M'Kay, Sunshine, Victoria, and *widow* of Cleveland J. Kidd. *Educ.:* Brunswick College, Brunswick; Melbourne, Victoria. Landed in Australia, 1888; served South African War, 1901-2, as trooper in Prince of Wales Light Horse and 4th Batt. Australian Commonwealth Horse (Queen's medal five clasps); Chartered Accountant by profession; joined Australian Imperial Force on 15 Aug. 1914 as Capt. 6th Battery Field Artillery, and landed at Anzac, 25 Apr. 1915 and Cape Helles (Gallipoli), beginning of May 1915; commanded Battery at end of May; Anzac middle of August and commanded 6th Battery there until the evacuation, 1915; returned to Egypt (despatches, C.M.G.); served in France and Belgium, 1916-18 commanding Field Artillery Brigade A.I.F. (despatches, D.S.O.); Hon. A.D.C. to Governor-General of Australia, 1935-40. *Recreations:* formerly amateur rowing, amateur cross-country running. *Address:* 17 St. Georges Road, Toorak, Melbourne, Australia. *Clubs:* Naval and Military, Australian, Melbourne (Melbourne). [*Died* 11 *July* 1958.

STEVENSON, Lieut.-Col. John; Author and Journalist; Associate of Toynbee Hall; F.I.Arb.; *b.* 1895; *s.* of late John Decimus Stevenson, comdg. British Guiana Police; *m.* 1927, Mary, *d.* of Richard Dring, Little Massingham, Norfolk; one *s.* one *d.* *Educ.:* Thetford. Served European War, 1914-19; Capt. Indian Army, 1920; retired, 1922; called to Bar, Gray's Inn, 1924; contested King's Lynn (Lab.), 1923 and 1924; Brentford and Chiswick (Lib.), 1929; Hon. Sec. National Labour Candidates Assoc., 1937-39; Gen. Sec., Incorporated Society of Auctioneers and Landed Property Agents, 1925-45; re-employed on military service, Sept. 1939: Major, 1939; Lt.-Col. 1941; awarded Good Service Certificate, Jan. 1942; served B.L.A. Belgium, Holland, Germany; Senior Prosecutor (C.C.G.), Hamburg and Schleswig-Holstein, 1945-50. *Publications:* Roads East and West (essays), 1922; Estate Agents Commission (with N. E. Mustoe), 1929; How to become an Auctioneer and Estate Agent (Ross's Careers Series), 1944. *Recreations:* cricket, tennis, swimming. *Address:* Kemp's House, Balcombe, Sussex. *T.:* 266. *Club:* National Liberal. [*Died* 31 *July* 1952.

STEVENSON, Rear-Adm. John Bryan, C.M.G. 1925; R.A.N. (retd.); *b.* 1876; *e. s.* of John Stevenson, Lisheen, Little Sutton, Cheshire; *m.* 1914, Olive Brooke Bailey, Hobart; two *c.* *Educ.:* Privately; H.M.S. Britannia. Joined Royal Navy, 1890; Midshipman, 1892; Sub-Lieutenant, 1896; Lieutenant, 1898; Commander, 1910; Acting Captain, 1916; transferred to Royal Australian Navy with rank of Captain, 1919; Commanded H.M.A.S. Berrima and H.M.A.S. Encounter during War, and H.M.A.S. Adelaide in Empire Cruise of Special Service Squadron (C.M.G.); 2nd Naval Member of Commonwealth Naval Board, 1927, 1929; Captain-Supt. of Naval Establishments, Sydney, 1929-31. *Recreations:* cricket, tennis. *Address:* 1 Neringah Avenue, Wahroonga, N.S.W., Australia. *Clubs:* United Service; Union (Sydney, N.S.W.). [*Died* 13 *July* 1957.

STEVENSON, Margaret; *see* Stevenson, Mrs. Sinclair.

STEVENSON, R. Macaulay; Member of the International Society of Sculptors, Painters and Gravers. Formerly resident in Kircudbrightshire and Dunbartonshire. *Address:* 17 Baliol Street, Glasgow. [*Died* 20 *Sept.* 1952.

STEVENSON, Mrs. Sinclair (Margaret), M.A. (Oxon and Dublin); Sc.D. (Dublin); Missionary to India (retired); *d.* of the late H. O. Adams, of Chelmsley House, Sheldon, Warwickshire, and Emily, *d.* of Rev. D. A. Doudney, D.D.; *b.* 26 Dec. 1875; *m.* 1906, Rev. J. Sinclair Stevenson, M.A. (Oxon and Dublin), B.D. (Edin.), author of The Friend of Little Children, etc. (*d.* 1930); one *d.* *Educ.:* The Ladies' College, Jersey; Somerville College, Oxford (Scholar); Trinity College, Dublin; Honour School of Jurisprudence, Oxford, 1899. Went out to India as a Missionary, 1900; M.A. Dublin, 1905; Sc.D. Dublin, 1911; took M.A. Oxford when degrees opened to Women, Oct. 1920. *Publications:* Notes on Modern Jainism, 1910; First Steps in Gujarati, 1913; The Heart of Jainism, 1915; On Some Painters of the Renaissance, 1915; Bridget's Fairies, 1919; Hilary, The Story of a College Girl, 1920; Rites of the Twice Born, 1920; Bridget's History Jingles, 1927; Without the Pale—The Life Story of a Dhed, 1930; Do You Remember Sinclair Stevenson?—A Biography of the Rev. J. Sinclair Stevenson, by his wife, Margaret Stevenson, 1931; contributor on Jain subjects to the Encyclopædia of Religion and Ethics and Chambers's New Encyclopædia. *Recreations:* meeting young people, reading biographies and detective novels, history. *Address:* c/o National Provincial Bank, 7 Water Street, Liverpool, 2. [*Died* 11 *May* 1957.

STEVENSON, Emeritus-Professor William Barron, D.Litt.; D.D. (Edin. and Wales); LL.D.; F.S.A. Scot.; *b.* 12 Aug. 1869; *s.* of late Rev. Robert Stevenson, M.A., parish minister of Forfar and of his second wife, Agnes Barron; *m.* 1907, Margaret Bell, *d.* of late David Kerr, Clonin, King's County; one *s.* *Educ.:* Daniel Stewart's College; Edinburgh University; abroad. Vans Dunlop Scholar in Semitic Languages, 1893; Vice-Chancellor's Essay Prizeman, 1896; professor at Bala Theological College, 1898-1907; professor of Hebrew and Semitic Languages, Glasgow University, 1907-37; on the Admiralty staff, Intelligence department, 1917-19; President of Society for Old Testament Study, 1926, of Glasgow Bibliographical Society, 1932-35, of Glasgow Archæological Society, 1933-36; Schweich Lecturer, 1943. *Publications:* The Crusaders in the East, 1907; Grammar of Palestinian Jewish Aramaic, 1924; The poem of Job, a literary study, with a new translation, 1947; Critical Notes on the Hebrew Text of the Poem of Job, 1951; contributor to the Cambridge Medieval History, etc. *Address:* 31 Mansionhouse Road, Edinburgh, 9. *T.:* 44223. [*Died* 31 *Oct.* 1954.

STEVENSON-HAMILTON, Lieut.-Col. James, F.R.G.S., C.M.Z.S., LL.D. (hon.) Witwatersrand and Capetown Universities; *b.* Dublin, 1867; *e. s.* of Col. James Stevenson, C.B., V.D., and Eliza Hamilton, Fairholm, *e. d.* of James Hamilton; *m.* 1930, Hilda, *e. d.* of R. V. Cholmondeley; one *s.* one *d.* (and one *d.* decd.). *Educ.:* Rugby; Sandhurst. 2nd Lt., 6th (Inniskilling) Dragoons, 1888; Maj., 1902; served Zululand Rebellion, 1888; S.A. War, 1900-2 (Queen's medal with 5 clasps, King's medal with 2 clasps, despatches, Brevet majority); retired 1905; served in Gallipoli and Egypt, 1915-16; Sudan (attached Egyptian Army), 1917-19 (Star, medals and clasps, despatches, Order of the Nile); succeeded to estates of Fairholm and Kirkton, 1888; accompanied Major St. Hill Gibbons on his Cape to Cairo expedition 1898, and exploration of Congo-Zambesi water-shed, 1898-99; Member Royal Company of Archers (Queen's Body Guard for Scotland); Warden of the Transvaal Government Game Reserves, 1902-1926, and of Kruger National Park, 1926-46. Silver Medallist, London Zoological Society and Society for the Preservation of the Fauna of the Empire. *Publications:* Animal Life in Africa (two editions, and one Afrikaans edn.); The Low-Veld, 1929 (two editions); South African Eden, 1937 (three editions); Wild Life in South Africa, 1947 (three editions, and one French edn.). *Recreation:* Natural history. *Address:* White River, Transvaal, South Africa. *Clubs:* Army and Navy; Pretoria (Pretoria, S. Africa). [*Died* 10 *Dec.* 1957.

STEWARD, George Frederick, C.V.O. 1939; C.B.E. 1930 (O.B.E. 1924); *b.* 8 Feb. 1884; *s.* of late J. Steward, Norwich; *m.* 1912, Eva Gertrude, *d.* of late S. Wesley Hanan, Gt. Yarmouth. *Educ.:* Norwich Cathedral School. Entered journalism, 1900, serving articles with Norwich Mercury; later joined London Daily News; employed by Foreign Office and Ministry of Information from 1915 and served in Holland; transferred to Brussels at Armistice and remained as Press Officer at the Embassy till Jan. 1927, when returned to News Department of Foreign Office; Member of United Kingdom delegations to Conferences at the Hague, 1921, Geneva, Brussels, Locarno, Madrid, and Lausanne; to League of Nations Assemblies and Conferences, 1924-30; Inter-Parliamentary Union Conference, London, World Economic Conference, 1930, London Naval Conference, The Hague, 1930, Indian Round Table Conferences, Burma Conference, and Imperial Conference, 1930 and Palestine Conference, 1939; transferred to 10 Downing Street and Treasury, 1931; Chief Press Liaison Officer, H.M. Government, 1937; retired, Oct. 1944. Member of their Majesties Suite on Royal Visit to Canada and U.S.A., May and June 1939; Chevalier de l'Ordre de la Couronne of Belgium, 1923. *Recreations:* sketching and gardening. *Address:* Honeysuckle Lane, Worthing. [*Died* 6 *July* 1952.

STEWARD, Sir Henry (Allan Holden), Kt., *cr.* 1921; T.D.; *b.* 18 May 1865; 2nd *s.* of Walter Holden Steward of Pontrilas, Hereford; *m.* 1890, Georgiana Barbara, *d.* of Joseph Ridgway of Goudhurst, Kent, and Hon. Georgiana Ridgway; one *s.* one *d.* *Educ.:* Charterhouse; New College, Oxford, B.A. Called to Bar, Inner Temple, 1890; Secretary to the Light Railway Commission, 1897; appointed a Commissioner, 1901, and became Chairman, 1918-22; Chairman of the Tramways Charges Advisory Committee, 1920; Clerk of the Railways Amalgamation Tribunal, 1912; Master of the Skinners' Company, 1908-9; a Governor of Tonbridge School, of Skinner's School, Tunbridge Wells, of Judd School, Tonbridge, of Northampton Polytechnic Inst.; Hon. Fell. Imperial College of Science and Technology, 1950; Vice-Pres. City and Guilds of London Institute, 1950; Vice-President Royal Society of Arts, 1938-42; Pres., 1938-43, of Union of Educational Institutions; President, 1939-43, of Association of Technical Institutions; Captain, 8th London Regt.; retired, 1911; rejoined reserve, 1914, and for service abroad, 1915; on the General Staff at advanced G.H.Q. in France, 1916; T.D. *Publications:* Law of Light Railways, 1896; Cromwell's Stuart Descent (Cambridge Antiquarian Society, Vol. 27, 1924-25); Introduction to Records of the Skinners of London, 1933. *Recreations:* formerly most of the usual sports and travelling, now reduced chiefly to newspapers. *Address:* 8 Priory Walk, Kensington, S.W.10. *T.:* Fremantle 3256. *Club:* Travellers'. [*Died* 28 *Aug.* 1954.

STEWART, Sir Alexander (Anderson), Kt., *cr.* 1937; M.I.M.E.; *b.* Aberdeen, 1877; *e. s.* of late Robert Stewart, Aberdeen, Scotland; *m.* 1906, Grace Mary Cuming; two *s.* *Educ.:* Pulteneytown Academy, Wick; Robert Gordon's College, Aberdeen. Settled in Melbourne, Australia, 1906, is proprietor of Consulting Engineering Business carried on under style of Alex. Stewart and Co.; Vice-Pres. Alfred Hospital, Melbourne; Member of the Felton Bequests Committee; Chairman of Trustees Executors and Agency Company Ltd., Australian

Fertilisers Ltd., Broken Hill South, Ltd., Metal Manufactures Ltd., Austral Bronze Co. Pty. Ltd., Dunlop Rubber Australia Ltd., Commonwealth Fertilisers and Chemicals Ltd., Director of Imperial Chemical Industries of Australia and New Zealand Ltd., Commonwealth Industrial Gases Ltd., Emu Bay Railway Co. Ltd., Director of Balm Paints Pty. Ltd., and other companies. Consultant to Electrolytic Zinc Co. *Address:* Collins House, 360 Collins Street, Melbourne, C.1, Victoria, Australia. *Clubs:* Melbourne, Australian (Melbourne); Union (Sydney). [*Died* 6 *May* 1956.

STEWART, Alexander MacKay; Financial Writer; *b.* 25 May 1878; *m.* Katharine, *d.* of late John Brown, J.P., Yelverton. *Educ.:* George Heriot's Hospital School and Heriot-Watt College, Edinburgh. *Address:* 6 Shooters Hill Road, Blackheath, S.E.3. [*Died* 8 *July* 1952.

STEWART, Allan; painter of military and historical subjects, portraits and landscapes; *b.* Edinburgh, 11 Feb. 1865; *yr. s.* of James Stewart, Edinburgh; *m.* Jane, *e. d.* of Thomas Ramsay, Dalry, Galloway; two *d.* *Educ.:* Edinburgh Institution; R.S.A. schools (prizeman). For a number of years on the staff of the Illustrated London News and accompanied King Edward on his cruise in the Mediterranean; has illustrated a number of books on history and travel; has had pictures purchased for Galleries in South Africa, America and the Australian War Museum; served European War Captain Royal Engineers (for some time attached to the Australian and American Forces) (despatches); one of the original founders, and the London Secretary of the Stewart Society since its formation. Engravings after his works include: Major Allan Wilson's Last Stand, Dargai, Charles I. Golfing at Newcastle, King Edward inspecting the Royal Company of Archers at Holyrood (original acquired for Holyrood Palace), The First International Golf Foursome, etc. *Recreations:* fishing, golf, bowls. *Address:* Rose Cottage, Dalry, by Castle Douglas, Kirkcudbrightshire. [*Died* 29 *Jan.* 1951.

STEWART, Captain Arthur Courtenay, C.B.E. 1919; R.N. retd.; *s.* of Charles Patrie Stewart, of Silwood Park, Sunninghill, Berks; *b.* 1871; *m.* 1911, Gwendolyn, *d.* of Waldo Story, Rome; one *s.* one *d.* Entered Navy, 1885; Lieut. 1893; Commander, 1904; Captain, 1913; British Naval Attaché, Rome, Vienna, Constantinople, Athens; Order of Corona d' Italia for services at the earthquake at Messina, 1909. Served European War, 1914-1918 (C.B.E.). *Address:* Ashley Manor, Box, Wiltshire. *T.A.* and *T.:* Box 324. *Club:* Army and Navy. [*Died* 19 *Feb.* 1958.

STEWART, Charles John, C.B. 1942; O.B.E.; F.R.Ae.S.; M.I.M.E.; Chairman and Managing Director Stewart, Broadhurst Limited, Consulting Engineers; *b.* Portsmouth; *o. s.* of Charles Henry Stewart; *m.* 1931, Nora Evelyn, *d.* of Captain H. Broadhurst; no *c.* *Educ.:* Royal College of Science. Entered H.M. Patent Office; joined Board of Education as Inspector of Engineering Education; joined R.E.(T) in 1914 and later R.F.C.; retired 1919 as Squadron Leader R.A.F. and joined Air Ministry on Research Staff; later, Superintendent Technical Development Royal Aircraft Establishment, South Farnborough; Director of Civil Research and Production, Air Ministry, 1938; Deputy Controller of Production, Ministry of Aircraft Production, 1942-45. *Publications:* Aircraft Instruments; Contributor to various scientific and technical journals. *Recreation:* fly fishing. *Address:* 11 Dolphin Court, Southsea, Hants. *T.:* Portsmouth 31397. *Club:* Royal Automobile. [*Died* 7 *May* 1954.

STEWART, Lord Colum C. E.; *see* Crichton-Stewart.

STEWART, Sir Douglas Law, 3rd Bt., *cr.* 1881; late Indian Imperial Police; *b.* 1 July 1878; *s.* of 2nd Bt. and Ada, *d.* of P. Hewitt of Bombay; *S.* father, 1926; *m.* 1903, Lilian Dorothea, *d.* of F. W. Quarry; one *d.* (one *s.* decd.). *Address:* Joydebpur, District Dacca, Bengal, India. *Club:* Bengal United Service (Calcutta). [*Died* 12 *Aug.* 1951 (*ext.*).

STEWART, Sir Findlater; *see* Stewart, Sir S. F.

STEWART, Ven. Henry John; Archdeacon Emeritus of Brecon since 1947; *b.* 2 Mar. 1873; *s.* of John and Margaret Stewart, Silian, Lampeter, Cards.; *m.* 1906, Irene, *d.* of Canon Martin Griffiths, Llansamlet, Glam.; one *d.* *Educ.:* St. David's College, Lampeter; St. Michael's College, Aberdare. B.A., 1894, First Class History Honours; Deacon, 1896; Priest, 1897; Curate of Llandyssul, Cards., 1896-99; Llansamlet, 1899-1906; Vicar of Llangorwen, 1906-7; of St. Peter's, Swansea, 1907-15; of Sketty, Swansea, 1915-41; Canon of Brecon Cathedral, 1923-37; Chancellor of Brecon Cathedral, 1937-41; Archdeacon of Brecon, 1941-47; Vicar of Builth Wells with Alltmawr, 1941-47; retired, 1947; Examining Chaplain to Bishop of Swansea and Brecon; Sec. to Swansea and Brecon Diocesan Conference; Governor of Christ College, Brecon; member of Governing Body, Representative Body and Electoral College of the Church in Wales. Chairman Builth District Education Committee; Governor Builth County School. *Recreations:* golf and fishing. *Address:* 8 Marine Terrace, Aberystwyth, Cards. *T.:* Aberystwyth 7487. [*Died* 2 *May* 1960.

STEWART, James Douglas, B.V.Sc., F.R.C.V.S.; Professor of Veterinary Science, Univ. of Sydney, N.S.W., 1909, now Emeritus; *b.* 18 Aug. 1869; 2nd *s.* of John Stewart; *m.* Edith May, 2nd *d.* of John Forsyth; one *s.* three *d.* *Educ.:* Sydney Grammar School. Articled to an accountant for three years; went to Edinburgh and studied vet. science; M.R.C.V.S. 1893; Lecturer on Elementary Vet. Science, Sydney Technical College, also Hon. Veterinary Officer of N.S.W. Zoological Society, 1896; Veterinary Officer to Stock Department, N.S.W., 1898; Lecturer on Meat Inspection, Sydney Technical College, 1902; Chief Inspector of Stock, N.S.W., 1907; President Veterinary Science Section, Australian Association for Advancement of Science, 1913; Member of Tuberculosis Advisory Board, N.S.W., 1913; Major, Australian Army Veterinary Corps, 1915; Acting Director of Veterinary Services, Central Administration, Melbourne, 1916-17; Member Executive Committee, Bureau of Science and Industry (Federal Government), 1917; President Veterinary Medical Association, N.S.W., 1922 and 1933; Member, Veterinary Surgeons' Board, N.S.W., 1924; Member of Council, Royal Society, N.S.W., 1924-33; President, 1927-28; President Veterinary Science Section, Australasian Association for Advancement of Science, Perth Meeting, 1926; Member N.S.W. State Committee of Council of Scientific and Industrial Research, 1926; President Veterinary Surgeons' Board, N.S.W., 1934; Hon. F.R.C.V.S., 1936. Hon. Life Member Roy. Agric. Soc. N.S.W., 1936; Fellow Aust. Vet. Assoc., 1940; Life Governor Corps of Commissionaires N.S.W., 1940; Life Member Royal Society N.S.W., 1942; Hon. Associate R.C.V.S., 1949; Hon. member Vet. Practitioners' Association, N.S.W., 1950; A.V.A. Gilruth Prize for Meritorious Service to Veterinary Science in Australia, 1953. *Publications:* Repression of Tuberculosis in Dairy Herds; Cattle Tick Fever; Relationship of Veterinary Science to the Prosperity of the State; Application of Science to the Sheep Industry; numerous contributions on veterinary subjects. *Recreations:* riding, golf, and gardening. *Address:* Gladswood House, Gladswood Gardens, Double Bay, N.S.W., Australia. [*Died* 17 *Sept.* 1955.

STEWART, Sir James Watson, 3rd Bt., *cr.* 1920; Partner of J. W. Stewart & Co., C.A.; J.P. County of the City of Glasgow; *b.* 6 Aug. 1889; *s.* of Sir James Watson Stewart, 1st Bt. and Marion Symington, *e. d.* of Rev. Alexander Young, of Darvel, Ayrshire; *S.* brother 1934; *m.* 1921, Janie, *d.* of late James Morton Sim, Glasgow; two *s.* *Educ.:* Kelvinside Academy; Uppingham. Late Lieut. R.G.A.(T.); Major, Home Guard, 1941. *Heir: s.* James Watson, *b.* 8 Nov. 1922. *Address:* 16 Cleveden Gardens, Glasgow, W.2. *T.A.:* Institution, Glasgow. *T.:* Western (Glasgow) 1704. *Clubs:* Conservative, Royal Scottish Automobile (Glasgow). [*Died* 4 *June* 1955.

STEWART, Sir John, Kt. 1956; C.B.E. 1949; Company Director, Scotland; Solicitor, of Wilson, Chalmers and Hendry, Solicitors, Glasgow; Chairman of the Retail Wages Council; Chairman of John Wallace and Sons Ltd.; Director: Alex. Jack and Sons Ltd.; Dalsholm Paper Co. Ltd.; Scottish Board, London and Scottish Assurance Corporation Ltd.; *b.* 1887; *m.* 1919, Isabel Fisher Thompson. *Address:* 46 Hamilton Avenue, Glasgow, S.1; Wilson, Chalmers and Hendry, 33A Gordon Street, Glasgow, C.1. [*Died* 8 *March* 1958.

STEWART, Major-General Sir (John Henry) Keith, K.C.B., *cr.* 1927 (C.B. 1921); D.S.O. 1915; late 39th Garhwal Rifles; *b.* 1872; *e. s.* of late Lt.-Gen. John M. Stewart; *m.* 1898, Frances Jane (*d.* 1952), 2nd *d.* of late Hon. G. A. Hobart Hampden, I.C.S.; one *d.* *Educ.:* Repton; R.M.C., Sandhurst. Entered army, 1892; Captain, 1901; Graduate of the Staff College; Major, 1910; temp. Lieut.-Col. 1915; Bt. Lieut.-Col. 1916; Lieut.-Col. 1916; Bt. Col. 1917; Temp. Brig.-Gen. 1917; Maj.-Gen. 1923; served Tirah Expedition, 1897-8 (medal and 2 clasps); European War, 1914-18 (despatches, D.S.O., Bt. Lt.-Col., Bt. Col., 1914 Star, General Service medal, Victory medal, Croix de Guerre, La Solidaridad (Panama); Iraq, 1918-22 (C.B., medal); commanded 19th Indian Infantry Brigade, 1922-23, and Delhi Independent Brigade Area, 1924-25; G.O.C. and Political Resident, Aden, 1925-28; retired, 1929; D.L. Wigtownshire. *Address:* Duncree, Newton Stewart, Scotland. [*Died* 30 *May* 1955.

STEWART, Professor John McKellar, C.M.G. 1949; M.A., D.Phil. (Edin.); Hughes Professor of Philosophy in the University of Adelaide, 1923-49; Vice-Chancellor, 1944-48; *b.* Ballangeich, Victoria, 4 May 1878; *s.* of Alexander Stewart and Lillias M'Kellar; *m.* Margaret Grace Stuart Bothroyd; three *s.* one *d.* *Educ.:* Ormond College, University of Melbourne; Universities of Edinburgh and Marburg. *Publications:* A Critical Exposition of Bergson's Philosophy; magazine articles. *Address:* Dalkeith, Blackwood, South Australia. [*Died* 25 *April* 1953.

STEWART, Maj.-Gen. Sir Keith; *see* Stewart, Maj.-Gen. Sir J. H. K.

STEWART, Sir Malcolm; *see* Stewart, Sir P. M.

STEWART, Very Rev. Matthew, D.D.; *b.* 1 Jan. 1881; *m.* 1926, Gladys Marriott, *d.* of Sir John W. Kynoch, Keith; three *d.* *Educ.:* Glasgow High School; Glasgow University; Balliol College, Oxford. B.D., D.D., Glasgow Univ.; M.A. Balliol Coll., Oxford; Minister, St. Paul's Parish, Perth, 1912-14; Keith Parish, 1914-26; Hamilton Second Charge, 1926-30; Hamilton First Charge, 1930-48; Moderator of General Assembly of Church of Scotland, 1947-48. *Address:* Otmari, Spey Bay, Moray. *Clubs:* Scottish Conservative (Edinburgh); Royal Scottish Automobile (Glasgow). [*Died* 2 *April* 1952.

STEWART, Matthew John, C.B.E. 1951; Hon. M.D. Melb.; LL.D., Glasgow; F.R.C.P., Lond.; Professor of Pathology, University of Leeds, 1918-50; Hon. Pathologist, Leeds General Infirmary; *b.* Dalmellington, Ayrshire, 4 May 1885; *s.* of William Ritchie Stewart, F.S.A.Scot., and Mary Hunter Mackay; *m.* 1913, Clara, O.B.E., M.B., B.S., London, *e. d.* of E. H. Eglington, Hammerwich, Staffs. *Educ.:* Glasgow Univ., M.B., Ch.B. (Honours and Brunton Memorial Prize), 1907; LL.D., 1938; F.R.C.P., Lond. 1924; F.R.F.P.S., Glasgow, 1932; Hon. Member Faculty of Radiologists. Asst. Pathologist, Glasgow Royal Infirmary, 1909; Clinical Pathologist, Leeds General Infirmary, 1910-18; Hon. Demonstrator in Clinical Pathology, Univ. of Leeds, 1912-18; Capt. R.A.M.C. (T.) 1915-19 (Pathologist, East Leeds War Hospital and 59th General Hospital, B.E.F.); Dean of the Faculty of Medicine, University of Leeds, 1941-48; Academic Sub-Dean, 1923-41; Pro-Vice-Chancellor, 1939-41; Member: General Medical Council, 1942-50; Leeds Regional Hosp. Board and United Leeds Hosps. Bd. of Governors, 1947-50; Trustee of Hunterian Collection, 1941-55; Croonian Lectr., R.C.P., 1931; Macewen Lectr., Univ. of Glasgow, 1953; formerly Examiner in Pathology, Univs. of Oxford, Cambridge, Liverpool, Manchester, Bristol, Aberdeen, Glasgow, Birmingham, Sheffield, Belfast, St. Andrews, Dublin, Wales, and English Conjoint Board, Faculty of Radiologists, and for the Czecho-Slovak Govt.; Editor, Journal of Pathology and Bacteriology, 1934-55; Member of Medical Research Council, 1935-40, and of its Arsenic Cttee. (Chm.); Pres. of Section of Pathology, B.M.A. Annual Meeting, Newcastle on Tyne, 1921; Hon. mem. Leeds and W.R. Medico-Chirurg. Soc. (Pres. 1939-41); Mem., Samuel Pepys Club, Brontë Soc. and Harveian Soc. *Publications:* gastric and duodenal ulcer, 1929 (with Sir Arthur Hurst); various pathological contributions. *Recreations:* walking, topography, mediæval churches, philately. *Address:* The Dutch House, Stoke Wood, Stoke Poges, Bucks. *Club:* Royal Societies. [*Died* 7 *Nov.* 1956.

STEWART, Colonel Patrick Alexander Vansittart, C.B.E. 1919; D.S.O. 1915; D.L. Wigtownshire; late K.O.S.B.; *b.* 29 June 1875; 2nd *s.* of late Lieut.-Gen. J. M. Stewart, Indian Army; *m.* 1911, Mildred Annie Ferrers Young (*d.* 1928), *d.* of late T. Ferrers Guy, and *widow* of Capt. J. F. H. Young, R.A. (*s.* died of wounds received in action in Flanders, 1940); *m.* 1944, Katharine Isabel, *widow* of Charles Skerrett-Rogers and *d.* of late F. H. Hooper, I.C.S. Entered army, 1896; Col., 1926; served N.-W. Frontier, India, 1897-98; S. Africa, 1902; European War, 1914-17 (D.S.O., Bt. Lt.-Col., Belgian Croix de Guerre); retired pay, 1931. *Address:* Little Corsbie, Newton Stewart, Wigtownshire. [*Died* 13 *July* 1960.

STEWART, Sir (Percy) Malcolm, 1st Bt., *cr.* 1937; O.B.E. 1918; D.L. Beds., J.P.; Hon. LL.D., Manchester; *b.* 1872; 2nd *s.* of late Sir Halley Stewart; *m.* 1st, 1896, Cordelia (*d.* 1906), *d.* of late Rt. Hon. Sir Joseph Compton Rickett, D.L., M.P.; one *s.* one *d.*; 2nd, 1907, Beatrice M., 2nd *d.* of late Joseph B. Pratt, Mezzo-tint Engraver; one *s.* one *d.* *Educ.:* Royal High School, Edinburgh; King's School, Rochester. Comr. for Special Areas (England and Wales), 1934-36; Chairman Sir Halley Stewart Trust; Life-Pres. London Brick Co. Ltd. (formerly Chm.); President: Assoc. Portland Cement Manufacturers, Ltd. and British Portland Cement Manufacturers, Ltd.; Cement Makers' Federation: The Cement Statistical and Technical Bureau; National Council of Social Service; Royal Caledonian Schools; Director for Ministry of Munitions of the Government Rolling Mills, Southampton, 1917-19; High Sheriff of Bedfordshire, 1941. *Heir: s.* Ronald Compton Stewart, *b.* 14 Aug. 1903. *Address:* The Lodge, Sandy, Beds. *T.:* Sandy 111. *Clubs:* Boodle's, Garrick, Buck's, Royal Automobile. [*Died* 27 *Feb.* 1951.

STEWART, Robert Strother-; Barrister-at-Law; Colonial Legal Service, retired; one of the Chairmen of the Pensions Appeal Tribunals under the Pensions Tribunals Act, 1943, since 1945; *b.* 1878; *e. s.* of late Rev. Robert Stewart, M.A., Presbyterian Minister, Newcastle on Tyne; *m.* 1913, Ida Lillie, *d.* of G. G. Taylor, Newcastle upon Tyne; two *s.* *Educ.:* privately; Hatfield Hall and Armstrong College, both in Univ. of Durham (M.A. B.Litt., B.C.L.; Gladstone Prizeman; President of the Union); Westminster College, Cambridge. Admitted Solicitor, 1905; Member Newcastle Board of Guardians, 1909-12; Member Newcastle City Council and Education Committee, 1912-24; Commission, Tynemouth R.G.A., T.F., 1913-21; Assistant Competent Military Authority, Tyne Garrison, 1919-20 (mentioned for valuable services); Major (Royal Artillery) Territorial Army Reserve, 1921-28; called to Bar, Inner Temple, 1919; North-Eastern Circuit; contested (L.) Workington Division of Cumberland, 1918; M.P. (L.) Stockton-on-Tees, 1923-1924; Director Newcastle United Football Club, 1915-27; Magistrate, Judge of Petty Civil Court, and Coroner of the County of Victoria, Trinidad, B.W.I., 1927-29; Assistant Legal Adviser (Temporary), Colonial Office, 1929-30; Legal Adviser to the Governor of Malta, 1930-33; Deputy Governor of Malta, July-August, 1932; Member of Nominated and Privy Councils of Malta; Examiner in English Literature and History in the University of Malta; Puisne Judge, Supreme Court, Gold Coast Colony, 1933-42; Member West African Court of Appeal; Acting Chief Justice, Gold Coast Colony, various occasions. *Recreations:* music, acting, stamp collecting. *Address:* 4 Archbold Terrace, Newcastle upon Tyne 2. [*Died* 15 *Nov.* 1954.

STEWART, Sir (Samuel) Findlater, G.C.B., *cr.* 1939 (K.C.B., *cr.* 1932); G.C.I.E., *cr.* 1935 (K.C.I.E., *cr.* 1930; C.I.E. 1919); C.S.I. 1924; U.S.A. Medal of Freedom, with Gold Palm; Chevalier of the Legion of Honour; Hon. LL.D. (Aberdeen), 1931, (Edinburgh) 1945; formerly Chm. British and French Bank; formerly Dir. of Finance Corp. for Industry; *b.* 22 Dec. 1879; *s.* of late Alexander Stewart; *m.* 1st, 1910, Winifred (*d.* 1915), *d.* of late James Tomblin; two *d.*; 2nd, 1940, Stephanie, *o. d.* of late S. Whitmore Robinson, Hampstead. *Educ.:* Edinburgh Univ. Apptd. to India Office, 1903; Jt. Sec. of the Military Department, India Office, 1920; Sec. of the Royal Commission on the Superior Civil Services in India (the Lee Commission), 1923-24; one of the Assistant Under-Secretaries of State for India and Clerk to the Council of India, 1924-30; Secretary to the Indian Statutory Commission (the Simon Commission), 1927-1930; Perm. Under-Secretary of State for India, 1930-42; temp. Director-General of Ministry of Information, Sept.-Nov. 1939; on special duty, May 1940; retired Dec. 1945. *Address:* Fourways, Shroton, Dorset. *T.:* Child Okeford 303. *Club:* Athenæum. [*Died* 11 *April* 1960.

STEWART, Thomas Grainger, M.D. (Edin.), F.R.C.P.; Consulting Physician, National Hospital for the Paralysed and Epileptic, Queen Square; Central London Ophthalmic Hosp.; Consulting Neurologist, West London Hosp.; and Consulting Neurologist to Queen Mary's Hosp., Roehampton, Ministry of Pensions; *s.* of late Sir Thomas Grainger Stewart; *m.* 1922, Lady Playfair, *widow* of Sir Patrick Playfair, C.I.E. *Educ.:* Edinburgh Academy and University; London; Munich. *Publications:* Text-book of Nervous Diseases (with Dr. Aldren Turner); papers on Neurological subjects in Brain, Lancet, Review of Neurology and Psychiatry, etc. *Recreations:* shooting, golf. *Address:* Mayfair House, 14 Carlos Place, W.1. *T.:* Hyde Park 0204; The Smithy, Farnborough, Wantage, Berks. *T.:* Chaddleworth 228. [*Died* 18 *March* 1957.

STEWART, Walter W.; Professor Emeritus, School of Economics and Politics, Institute for Advanced Study, Princeton, New Jersey; *b.* 24 May 1885; *s.* of Albert Alexander Stewart and Ella Winne; *m.* 1912, Helen Wyncoop, St. Louis, Mo.; two *s.* one *d.* *Educ.:* University of Missouri (A.B.); University of Michigan. LL.D. (Hon.) Univ. of Missouri, 1932; Dartmouth Coll., 1933; Amherst Coll., 1944; Columbia Univ., 1951; Litt.D., Princeton Univ., 1951. Instructor, economics, Univ. of Missouri, 1910-11; Univ. of Michigan, 1911-12; asst. prof., economics, Univ. of Missouri, 1913-15; professor, economics, Amherst College, 1916-22; member of price section War Industries Board, 1918; director Division of Research and Statistics, Federal Reserve Board, 1922-25; Vice-Pres. Case, Pomeroy and Co., investment securities, 1926-27; Chairman of Board, 1930-39; economic adviser to Bank of England, 1928-1930; 1931, American member special advisory Committee Bank of International settlements to investigate ability of Germany to resume reparations payments under the Young Plan; Trustee Rockefeller Foundation, General Education Bd., 1931-50; Inst. for Advanced Study, 1933-41; Bennington College, 1932-38; Chairman of the Board, Rockefeller Foundation, 1940-50; General Education Board, 1942-50; Member President's Council of Economic Advisers, Nov. 1953-June 1955; member American Economic Association; American Philosophical Society. Hon. Foreign Member, Political Economy Club (London). Officier, Légion d'Honneur. *Address:* Institute for Advanced Study, Princeton, N.J. *T.A.:* Vanstitute. *T.:* Princeton 4400. [*Died* 6 *March* 1958.

STEWART, William; Secretary Scottish Divisional Council of the Independent Labour Party, 1912-33; retired; *b.* Dunfermline, 8 July 1856, of working-class parents; unmarried. *Educ.:* Elementary Schools. Worked as yarn dresser in linen factories; as a young man began to write to local papers on literary and political subjects; was elected to the first Parish Council of his native city; conducted a local monthly Socialist paper, The Worker, which ceased to exist in 1899, when he went to Glasgow and joined the staff of the Labour Leader, under Keir Hardie; contributed also for six years a weekly article to The Clarion; was for some years a member of the I.L.P. National Administrative Council; regular contrib. to Forward. *Publications:* Fighters for Freedom, 2 eds.; The Nativity of Adam, 2 eds.; Robert Burns and the Common People, 3 eds.; Keir Hardie: a Biography, 2 eds.; War Time and Other Times Impression, 1933; various pamphlets. *Recreations:* reading, smoking, walking, and the theatre and concert room occasionally. *Address:* 136 Crail Street, Glasgow, E. [*Died* 27 *Aug.* 1947.
[*But death not notified in time for inclusion in Who Was Who 1941–1950, first edn.*

STEWART, William Joseph, J.P.; M.P. (Soc.) Houghton-le-Spring Division of Co. Durham, 1935-45. *Address:* The Homestead, Hedworth Villas, Boldon Colliery, Co. Durham. [*Died* 5 *March* 1960.

STEWART-LIBERTY, Capt. Ivor; *see* Liberty.

STINTON, T., M.A.; *b.* 1886; *m.* 1912, Mary, *d.* of late W. A. Tree, Worcester; one *s.* two *d.* *Educ.:* King's School, Worcester; Magdalen College, Oxford (Classical Demy); First Class in Classical Moderations; Second in Greats; was Assistant Master at King Edward's School, Birmingham; served European War, 8th Batt. Worcesters. Regt., 1915-19 (Italian Bronze Medal for Valour); Headmaster of Loughborough Grammar School, 1919-25; Headmaster, The High School, Newcastle, Staffs., 1926-48; retired Aug. 1948; Associate Member Headmasters' Conference. *Address:* 8 Stephenson Terrace, Worcester. [*Died* 25 *Nov.* 1957.

STIRLING, Hon. Grote, P.C.; a Member of H.M.'s Privy Council for Canada; *b.* Tunbridge Wells, 31 July 1875; *s.* of Capt. Charles Stirling, R.N., and S.M. Grote; *m.* 1st, 1903, Mabel Katharine (*d.* 1933), *d.* of Dr. R. W. Brigstocke R.N., Beyrout, Syria; two *s.* two *d.*; 2nd, 1936, Jean Gready, Clifton. *Educ.:* University College School; Crystal Palace Engineering School. A.M.Inst.C.E.; practised as Civil Engineer; came to Canada, 1911; continued practice of profession and also took up fruit growing; M.E.I.C.; Minister of National Defence and Acting Minister of Fisheries, 1934-1935; a Conservative; Church of England. *Address:* Kelowna, B.C. *Club:* Kelowna Golf. [*Died* 18 *Jan.* 1953.

STIRLING, Lieut.-Col. Walter Francis, D.S.O. 1902 and Bar; M.C.; *b.* 31 Jan. 1880; *s.* of Capt. Francis Stirling, R.N., and Mrs. Francis Stirling of Hampton Court Palace; *m.* 1920, Eileen Mary May (Marygold), *er. d.* of Lt.-Col. Mackenzie-Edwards, late Royal Berkshire Regiment; one *d.* *Educ.:* Sandhurst. 2nd Lieut. 1st Royal Dublin Fusiliers, 1899; served with Natal Field Force, S.A., with regiment; with 4th Division Mounted Infantry in Dundonald's Brigade; afterwards appointed Adjt. 14th Batt. M.I. (despatches, Queen's S.A. medal with 5 clasps, King's S.A. medal with 2 clasps, D.S.O.); served with the Egyptian Army, 1906-12; retired, 1912; Observer, R.F.C., 1914; rejoined the 1st Royal Dublin Fusiliers, 29th Division, in Gallipoli, 1915; General Staff, 1916-18 (M.C., bar to D.S.O., 2nd class Order of the Nahda; Order of the Nile; Order of the Crown of Italy; Grand Cordon of the Order of Skanderbeg); Freeman of the City of London; Adviser to Emir Faisal in Damascus; Deputy Chief Political Officer for the Middle East; Acting-Governor of the Sinai Peninsula in the Egyptian Government, and Governor of the Jaffa District in the Palestine Administration, 1920-23; Adviser to the Albanian Government, 1923-1931; Chief Telephone Censor for the Continent, Sept. 1939; was in Near East on special service for 6 years, until retiring in 1946, when commanding Desert and Frontier Areas of Syria under Ninth Army. Settled in Damascus; became Times correspondent for Syria. After his attempted assassination, Damascus, 1949, lived in Egypt until expelled by the Egyptian Government in 1951; now settled in Tangier. *Publications:* Safety Last, 1953; various articles. *Address:* Tel el Bahr, Calle Estrecho, Tangier, Morocco. *Club:* United Service. [*Died* 22 *Feb.* 1958.

STIRLING-MAXWELL, Sir John M.; *see* Maxwell.

STOBART, Lieut.-Colonel Hugh Morton, C.B.E. 1919; D.S.O. 1918; D.L. Co. Durham; Chairman of Wearmouth Coal Co. Ltd., France Fenwick Tyne and Wear Co. Ltd.; Director, Yorkshire Amalgamated Collieries, Ltd., and several other companies; *b.* 14 Feb. 1883; *s.* of late Frank Stobart, D.L., J.P.; *m.* 1st, 1910, Esmée (from whom he obtained a divorce, 1940), *d.* of late Alfred Bethell, J.P.; two *s.* (and one "missing believed killed" since 1942); 2nd, 1941, Rosalie, *d.* of Benjamin Dodsworth, J.P.; one *s.* *Educ.:* Eton; Magdalen College, Oxford, B.A. Late Deputy Controller Cultivation Department, Food Production Department. *Recreations:* shooting, fishing, racing. *Address:* Headlam Hall, Gainford, near Darlington. *T.:* Gainford 238. *Club:* White's. [*Died* 14 *Sept.* 1952.

STOBART, Mrs. St. Clair (Mrs. Stobart Greenhalgh); *d.* of late Sir Samuel Boulton, 1st Bart.; *m.* 1st, St. Clair Stobart, late of Mount Bagnal, Co. Down, Ireland; 2nd, John Stobart Greenhalgh (*d.* 1928), Barrister. Founder of the Women's Sick and Wounded Convoy Corps; in command of detachment of corps with Bulgarian army in Thrace in Balkan War, 1912-13 (Bulgarian Red Cross); in European War, Aug. 1914, organised Hospitals (Women's Units) in Belgium and France (for St. John's Ambulance Assoc.); was taken prisoner by Germans; imprisoned at Aachen, and condemned to be shot as spy; in 1915 took Unit to Serbia (for Serbian Relief Fund); in Sept. 1915 was appointed Commander of Column, First Serbian English Field Hospital (Order of St. John of Jerusalem, 1914 Star, Serbian Orders of White Eagle, St. Sava, and Red Cross); lectured for Ministry of Information in Canada and U.S., Oct. 1917-May 1918, and in Ireland, Sept.-Nov. 1918; candidate (Progressive) for Westminster at London County Council Election, 1913; Part Founder and Vice-Chairman of S.O.S. Society; Chairman of and Leader of the Spiritualist Community, 1924-41. Member of Council of World Congress of Faiths. *Publications:* War and Women; The Flaming Sword—in Serbia and Elsewhere; Ancient Lights; Torch-bearers of Spiritualism; The Either—Or of Spiritualism; The Apocrypha Reviewed; Psychic Bible Stories; Spiritual Songs for Congregational Singing; The Open Secret; The Prayer Book X-rayed; A Ladder to Heaven; Miracles and Adventures, 1936; translated Björnson's Captain Mansana; contributor to Fortnightly, Contemporary, etc.; playwright. *Address:* Knapwynd, Studland, Dorset. [*Died* 7 *Dec.* 1954.

STOBIE, William, O.B.E., J.P., M.A. (Oxon), M.D. (Edin.), F.R.C.P. (Lond.); Honorary Physician United Oxford Hospitals; Hon. Physician, Osler Pavilion for diseases of the chest, Radcliffe Infirmary, Oxford, and Oxford Eye Hospital; Consultant Physician E.M.S.; Cardiologist and Medical Specialist Ministry of Pensions, Oxford Area; Consultant for Tuberculosis, Oxford County Borough Council, and Oxfordshire County Council; *b.* 2 May 1886; *s.* of William Stobie, Edinburgh, and Gloranna Kerr; *m.* 1914, Irene Beatrice, *d.* of Montague Taylor, Shelsley Walsh, Worcs; two *s.* one *d.* *Educ.:* George Watson's College, Edinburgh; Edinburgh University. M.B., Ch.B. 1908, M.D. 1921 (Edin. Univ.), M.R.C.P. (Lond.), 1922; F.R.C.P. (Lond.), 1934; Major R.A.M.C., Lieut.-Colonel Defence Force (despatches twice, O.B.E.); France, etc.; Mayor, Oxford County Borough, 1930-31; Alderman, 1930; President Tuberculosis Section British Medical Association Annual Meeting, Oxford, 1936. President Oxfordshire Rugby Football Union. *Publications:* various medical papers. *Recreation:* golf (Edinburgh Univ., 1908). *Address:* 9 Bertie Road, Cumnor, Oxford. *T.:* Cumnor 122. [*Died* 2 *March* 1957.

STOCKDALE, Brig.-General Herbert Edward, C.B. 1919; C.M.G. 1916; D.S.O. 1915; late R.F.A.; *b.* 22 June 1867; 4th *s.* of late H. Minshull Stockdale of Mears Ashby Hall, and Sarah Emily, *d.* of late Rev. R. H. Knight; *m.* 1909, Margaret Frances, *d.* of Canon J. T. Bartlet; one *d.* *Educ.:* Temple Grove: Wellington College; R.M. Academy. Entered R.A. 1886; Captain, 1896; Major, 1901; Lt.-Col. 1913; Col. 1917; retired with hon. rank of Brig.-Gen. 1919; served S. African War, 1899-1901 (despatches, Queen's medal 6 clasps); European War, 1914-19 (despatches five times, C.B., C.M.G., D.S.O.). *Address:* The Old House, Little Houghton, Northampton. [*Died* 28 *Dec.* 1953.

STOCKDALE, Herbert Fitton, LL.D., F.R.S.E.; Secretary, 1899-1929, and Director, 1904-33, the Royal Technical College, Glasgow; *b.* 13 Jan. 1868; *m.* 1894, Helen, *d.* of Andrew Steven, Newcastle-on-Tyne; two *s.* one *d.* *Educ.:* The Boothroyd School, Yorks. Assistant Secretary, 1889-90, Secretary, 1891-99, of University of Durham College of Science, Newcastle-on-Tyne. *Publications:* magazine and newspaper articles on educational questions. *Recreation:* Braille! *Address:* Clairinch, Helensburgh, Dumbartonshire. *T.:* 189. [*Died* 28 *Dec.* 1951.

STOCKENSTRÖM, Sir Anders Johan Booysen, 4th Bt., *cr.* 1840; *b.* 13 March 1908; *s.* of 3rd Bt. and Mabel, *d.* of J. H. Booysen of Klip Drift, Graaf Reinet, S. Africa; *S.* father, 1922; *m.* 1937, Elaine Constance Brunette-Smith; one *d.* *Educ.:* St. Andrew's College, Grahamstown. *Heir:* none. *Address:* Maaström, Bedford, Cape Province, S. Africa. [*Died* 20 *June* 1957 (*ext.*).

STOCKER, Edgar Percy, C.B.E. 1937; *b.* Exeter, Devon, 6 March 1888; *s.* of George Stocker and Emma Sophia Luxmoore; *m.* 1916, Emily Gertrude, *d.* of William Royle, Rusholme, Manchester. *Educ.:* Mount Radford School, Exeter. Joined Lloyds Bank Ltd. 1904; Bank of Madras (now State Bank of India), 1910; Deputy Managing Director Imperial Bank of India, 1935-38. *Address:* c/o State Bank of India, 25 Old Broad Street, E.C.2. [*Died* 29 *June* 1959.

STOCKLEY, Lieut.-Col. Charles Hugh, D.S.O. 1919; O.B.E., M.C.; late Commanding 3/14th Punjab Regt.; *b.* Stonehouse, Plymouth, 12 Feb. 1882; *s.* of Colonel J. C. Stockley; *m.* 1930, Veronica (marriage dissolved, 1946), *o. d.* of H. Percy E. Harding, Backlane Farm, Waldron, Sussex. *Educ.:* Haileybury; Sandhurst. Commissioned Indian Army, 1901; War, served Somaliland, 1908-10 (Mounted Infantry); European War, Mesopotamia, 1915-16, Defence of Kut, prisoner of war (D.S.O., M.C.); 3rd Afghan War and N.W. Frontier of India, 1919, 1922, 1924; Intelligence Officer to R.A.F. (O.B.E.) despatches seven times; Shanghai Defence Force, 1927; retired, 1932. Travelled much in S. Asia, including 17 Himalayan journeys and four crossings of the country between Bangkok and Moulmein. Collects for Natural History Museum, and worked on Mammal Survey of India. *Publications:* A Shikari's Pocket Book; Big Game Shooting in the Indian Empire; Shikar; Stalking in the Himalayas and Northern India; African Camera Hunts. A regular contributor to illustrated weeklies and monthly magazines in England, India, and Africa. *Recreations:* field sports, photography and gardening. *Address:* c/o Standard Bank of S. Africa, Nairobi, Kenya. *Club:* Himalayan (Calcutta). [*Died* 30 *April* 1955.

STOCKLEY, Major Sir Harry (Hudson Fraser), K.C.V.O., *cr.* 1943 (C.V.O. 1936; M.V.O. 1923); O.B.E. 1920; Major, Royal Marines (retired); Deputy Secretary, Order of the Bath, since 1925; C.St.J.; *b.* 30 Oct. 1878; *s.* of late Colonel George Watts Stockley, J.P., R.E., of West Malling, Kent; *m.* 1908, Ismay Madeleine, *d.* of Dacre M. A. Hamilton, J.P., D.L., of Cornacassa, Monaghan; no *c.* *Educ.:* Haileybury. 2nd Lieut. R.M.L.I. 1897; awarded Sword of Honour, Royal Naval College, Greenwich, 1897; Lieut. R.M.L.I., 1898; H.M.S. Niobe during South African War. H.M.S. Ophir during tour of the Duke and Duchess of Cornwall and York, 1901; Captain R.M.L.I., 1903; A.D.C. to the Governor of Straits Settlements, 1904-10; served European War with Portsmouth Battalion R.M.L.I., France and Flanders, 1914; Gallipoli, 1915 (despatches, severely wounded); Major, 1916; entered Lord Chamberlain's Department, 1916; Secretary, Central Chancery of the Orders of Knighthood, 1936-46; Sergeant-at-Arms in Ordinary to H.M., 1931-46. *Address:* 4 St. Martin's Avenue, Canterbury, Kent. *T.:* Canterbury 3954. *Club:* Naval and Military. [*Died* 30 *July* 1951.

STOCKS, Harold Carpenter Lumb, Mus.D. Dublin; Mus.B. Oxon.; F.R.C.O.; Organist and Choirmaster of St. Asaph Cathedral since 1917; Hon. Secy. Cathedral Organists' Association; *b.* Essendon, Herts, 21 Oct. 1884; *o. s.* of late Walter Fryer Stocks, and *g.s.* of late Lumb Stocks, R.A.; *m.* 1923, Elisabeth, *e. d.* of late William Price Smith, Bangor; two *s.* one *d.* *Educ.:* St. Asaph Grammar School. Studied music under Dr. A. W. Wilson and others; Organist of Littleport Parish Church, 1902; St.Mary's, Ely, 1906; Assistant Organist of Ely Cathedral, 1906; Organist of Parish Church and conductor Choral Society, Yeovil, 1909, and Ludlow, 1911; invalided from Army after R.A.M.C. service in Salonika, 1916. *Publications:* Communion Service in E flat; Missa Sancti Asaph; Missa Cambrensis; Evening Services in E minor, D major, and D minor; Welsh Communion Service in E minor; anthems, As now the Sun's Declining Rays, Thus saith the Lord, Let Saints on earth, Breathe on me, Breath of God, Lord of All Being, O Gladsome Light, and Grant, we beseech thee; service book for use in Choral Festivals; songs; part-songs, O breathe not his name, and I arise from dreams of thee; Barbara Allen (arr. for Soprano, Alto, Tenor and Bass); chamber-music, A Wessex Pastorale for Clarinet and Piano; seventeen duets with five-finger-exercise basses; Variations for Organ on Y Delyn Aur; ed. Bach's Pastorale, Jig, and Corelli Fugues. Books: The Training of Boy Choristers; British Cathedral Organists; A Beginner's Book on Counterpoint. *Recreation:* crosswords. *Address:* The Chantry, St. Asaph, Flintshire. *T.:* St. Asaph 3137. [*Died* 10 *Feb.* 1956.

STOCKWELL, Brig.-Gen. Clifton Inglis, C.B. 1919; C.M.G. 1918; D.S.O. 1915; Royal Welch Fusiliers (retired 1932, Reserve of Officers); *b.* 1879; *e. s.* of late Colonel C. de N. O. Stockwell, Lincolnshire Regiment; *m.* 1st, 1908, Hilda Rose (*d.* 1927), *d.* of Colonel Westmorland, R.E.; one *s.* two *d.*; 2nd, 1944, Madeline, *widow* of Lt.-Col. W. C. Critchley-Salmonson. *Educ.:* Haileybury; R.M.C., Sandhurst. Gazetted to Royal Welch Fusiliers, 1899; Brig.-General, 1916; 164th Infantry Brigade until 1919; p.s.c. 1919; Bt. Col. 1923; Lt.-Col. 1924; Col. 1927; served European War, 1914-1918 (despatches nine times, C.B., C.M.G., D.S.O.); Commandant Senior Officers' School, Belgaum, 1928-30; Commander 11th Indian Infantry Brigade, Ahmednagar, 1930-31; retired pay, 1932. *Recreations:* hunting and tennis. *Club:* Naval and Military. [*Died* 4 *Dec.* 1953.

STOCKWOOD, Ven. Charles Vincent; Archdeacon of Man since 1938; Vicar of St. Johns, I.o.M., since 1948; *b.* 29 June 1885; *s.* of John Stockwood, Cowbridge, Glam.; *m.* 1912, Edith Mary, *d.* of Alderman J. Llewellyn, Cowbridge, Glam.; one *d.* *Educ.:* Cowbridge Grammar School; St. Catherine's Society, Oxford. B.A. 2nd, Cl. Th., 1907; M.A. 1911; Deacon, 1909; Priest, 1910; Curate, of All Saints, Camberwell, 1909-14; Assoc. Sec. Church Pastoral Society, 1914-18; Vicar of St. Olave's Ramsay, I. o. M., 1918-1927; Lecturer Bishop Wilson's Theological College, 1918-27; Rural Dean of Douglas, 1931-38; Examining Chaplain to Bishop of Sodor and Man since 1932; Vicar of St. George's, Douglas, I.o.M., 1927-48. *Address:* The Vicarage, St. Johns, I. o. M. *T.:* St. Johns 256. [*Died* 28 *March* 1958.

STODART, James Carlyle; *b.* 18 Feb. 1880; *s.* of Thomas Alexander and Melissa Stodart; *m.* 1904, Anna Maud Campbell; two *s.* one *d.* *Educ.:* Campbell College, Belfast; Brasenose College, Oxford; Trinity College, Dublin. Entered Indian Civil Service, 1903; Joined at Madras, 1904; Served in Madras Presidency as Assistant Collector and Sub-Collector, 1904-18; Collector, 1918; District Judge, 1919-3; Member, Legislative Assembly, 1930; Acting Judge of the High Court Madras, 1935; Judge of the High Court of Judicature, Madras, 1936-40. *Address:* 12 Fore St., Hatfield, Herts. *T.:* Hatfield, Herts 2126. *Club:* Madras (Madras). [*Died* 2 *Aug.* 1956.

STOGDON, Rev. Edgar; *b.* 30 July 1870; *s.* of John Stogdon, Fellow of Clare College, Cambridge; *m.* 1914, Louise Dalrymple (*d.* 1940), *d.* of late Henry Dundas and Catherine, *d.* of 1st Baron Napier of Magdala; one *s.* one *d.* *Educ.:* Harrow (entrance and leaving scholar); Clare College, Cambridge (Scholar). Athletic Blue (Mile) 1892, 1893; played for the University against Surrey and Yorkshire; chosen for the Arsenal in 1890; Assistant Master at Harrow School, 1902; Housemaster to Headmaster; Major commanding 27th Middlesex (Harrow School) Volunteer Rifle Corps, p.s. (Field Officer's Certificate); Member of first Committee for starting the O.T.C. in 1907, and of the Harrow Association; Vicar, Holy Trinity, Latimer Road (Harrow Mission), 1908; Chairman of Managers of Hammersmith Council Schools, and of local Association of Care Committees; Vicar of Aldenham, 1914; Y.M.C.A. France war zone, 1917-18; Vicar and Rural Dean of Harrow, 1923; Chairman Harrow Education Committee; writer of articles on Harrow Athletics in Fifty Years of Sport; Booklet of Letters to the Times; Member the Hellenic Society. *Recreations:* riding, picture galleries, museums, reading Æschylus. *Address:* Edgcumbe, Northwood. *Clubs:* M.C.C., Quidnuncs. [*Died* 30 *June* 1951.

STOKES, Rev. Anson Phelps, D.D. Gettysburg, Princeton; LL.D., Yale, Illinois S.T.D., Kenyon; D.Can.L., Berkeley Divinity School; President-emeritus of Phelps-Stokes Fund; Canon of Washington (resigned, 1939); *b.* 13 April 1874; *s.* of Anson Phelps Stokes (banker), and Helen Louisa Phelps; *m.* 1903, Carol Green Mitchell; two *s.* one *d.* *Educ.:* Yale University (B.A., M.A.); Episcopal Theological School (B.D.), Cambridge, Mass.; Oxford; University of Berlin. Secretary of Yale University, 1899-1921; former Member of Rockefeller Foundation, General Education and International Education Boards and Institute of International Education; one of founders of Yale in China and long President of its Board of Trustees; Organiser and first President, American University Union in Europe; Organiser, Army Educational Commission, A.E.F. (during war of 1914-1918); Chevalier of Legion of Honour; Visiting Carnegie Lecturer to Universities of Union of South Africa, 1932; Chairman of the Washington Housing Association, 1937-1939; Chm. Department of Social Welfare, Diocese of Washington, 1938-39; Associate Fellow, Trumbull College, Yale University; Organiser of Committee on Religious Life in Nation's Capital; Organiser and Chairman of Committee on Negro Americans in Defense Industry, 1941, and of Committee on Africa, the War and Peace Aims, which published The Atlantic Charter, and Africa from an American Standpoint, 1942. Churchman of the Year Award for 1951; Archbishop Ireland Lectr., College of St. Thomas, St. Paul, 1951. Yale Medal, 1952. Hon. D.D. Princeton University, 1956. *Publications:* What Jesus Christ Thought of Himself; Memorials of Eminent Yale Men; Educational Plans for the American Army Abroad; Tuskegee Institute — The First Fifty Years; Introductions to Reports on Education in Africa and Education in East Africa and Twenty Years' Report of Phelps-Stokes Fund; Report on Education, Native Welfare and Race Relations in East and South Africa (Carnegie Corporation); A Brief Biography of Booker Washington; Art and the Color Line; The Two Fronts of Freedom, etc.; Church and State in the U.S. (3 vols.), 1950; The "Happy Mean" of the Book of Common Prayer, 1952; Chm. of Encyclopedia of the Negro, Inc., and Editor of its Preparatory Volume, 1944; Thirty-five Year Report of Phelps-Stokes Fund, on Changes in Negro Status and Race Relations, 1948. *Recreations:* extensive travel; collecting Americana, historical Bibles and University History; walking. *Address:* Lenox, Mass.; (office) c/o Phelps-Stokes Fund, 101 Park Avenue, N.Y. City. *T.A.:* Stokes, Lenox, Massachusetts. *Club:* Century (New York). [*Died* 13 *Aug.* 1958.

STOKES, George Vernon, R.B.A. 1929; *e. s.* of George Edward Stokes, Porchester Gardens, W.; *b.* 1 Jan. 1873. *Educ.:* privately. Painter and etcher of animals; works bought for Corporation Gallery at Carlisle; a member Royal Society of British Artists, etc. *Publications:* Colour Etchings in Two Printings; How to Draw and Paint Dogs. *Recreation:* gardening. *Address:* Byways, Great Mongeham, nr. Deal, Kent. [*Died* 4 *Jan.* 1954.

STOKES, Sir Hopetoun Gabriel, K.C.I.E., *cr.* 1934 (C.I.E. 1911); C.S.I. 1928; B.A.; *s.* of Sir H. E. Stokes, K.C.S.I.; *b.* 1873; *m.* 1922, Alice Henrietta, Kaisar-i-Hind Gold Medal, 1935, 2nd *d.* of Sir Henry Hayes Lawrence, of Belgard, Co. Dublin, and Mrs. Berkeley Bristow, 10 Portsea Place, W.2. *Educ.:* Clifton; Oriel College, Oxford. Entered I.C.S. 1896; served in Govt. of India (Home and Finance Depts.), 1909-14; Private Secretary to H.E. Lord Pentland, Governor of Madras, 1915; Secretary to the Government of Madras, 1918-19; Administrative Adviser, Klagenfurt Plebiscite Commission, 1920; Member, Board of Revenue and Chief Secretary to Government, Madras, 1922-29; Member Executive Council, Madras, 1930-35. *Address:* 4 Holly Terrace, West Hill, Highgate. *Club:* East India and Sports. [*Died* 10 *Nov.* 1951.

STOKES, Rt. Hon. Richard Rapier, P.C. 1950; M.P. (Lab.) Ipswich, since 1938; Chairman and Managing Director Ransomes and Rapier Ltd.; Managing Director Cochran and Co., Annan Ltd.; *b.* 27 Jan. 1897; 2nd *s.* of Phillip Folliot Stokes, Barrister-at-law, and Mary Fenwick Rapier. *Educ.:* Downside; Trinity College, Cambridge. Entered Royal Military Academy, Woolwich, 1915; served in R.A., during European War, in France, 1916-18, Major, 1917 (M.C. and bar, French Croix de Guerre); contested Glasgow Central, 1935. Minister of Works, 1950-51; Lord Privy Seal, April-Oct. 1951, and Minister of Materials, July-Oct. 1951. Commander Order of the Nile. *Address:* 29 Palace Street, S.W.1. *Clubs:* White's, Garrick. [*Died* 3 *Aug.* 1957.

STONE, Henry Walter James; *b.* London, 12 Feb. 1877; *s.* of late Henry Stone, Framfield, Sx.; *m.* 1907, Lucy Marion, 6th *d.* of late C. Sutton Chantler, Banstead; one *s.* *Educ.:* St. Olave's Grammar School, London, and London School of Economics. Organising Officer, Metropolitan Employment Exchanges, 1906-08; in charge of Literature Department, Budget Protest League, 1909; Political and Private Secretary to Col. Right Hon. George Gibbs, M.P. (1st Lord Wraxall), 1909-31; Founder, Hon. Sec. and Treasurer, The Parliamentary Science Committee, 1933-45; Editor of Science in Parliament, 1933-45; Lieutenant, Royal Air Force, during War, 1914-1918. *Publications:* articles in various periodicals and newspapers. *Recreation:* billiards. *Address:* Framfield, Sutton Valence, Maidstone, Kent. *T.:* Sutton Valence 2185. *Club:* Authors'. [*Died* 17 *Jan.* 1954.

STONE, Brig.-Gen. Percy Vere Powys, C.M.G. 1918; D.S.O. 1917; *b.* 29 Sept. 1883; *s.* of Percy Goddard Stone and Fanny M. Belden Powys. *Educ.:* Blundell's; Sandhurst. Served S. African War 1902 (medal); in N. Nigeria 1905-10 (medal); European War 1914-18 (wounded thrice, despatches 7 times, Brevet Major, Brevet Lieut.-Colonel, D.S.O., C.M.G., Legion of Honour); formerly Major and Bt. Lt.-Col. Norfolk Regt.; retired as Hon. Brig.-Gen., 1920; Secretary Norfolk Territorial Army Association, 1922-23. *Address:* Meadowside, Wroxall, I. of Wight. [*Died* 20 *Oct.* 1959.

STONE, William, M.A. (Camb.); F.L.S., F.C.S., F.R.G.S., F.Z.S.; *b.* 14 Jan. 1857; *s.* of late John Stone, Royal Crescent, Bath; unmarried. *Educ.:* Clifton College; Peterhouse,

Cambridge (Scholar and Prizeman). First-class Honours Natural Sciences Tripos, 1878; some time lecturer on Botany at Newnham College, Cambridge; late Captain Cambridge University Rifle Corps; contested (C.) Northern Division of Wilts., 1885; present at the Coronation of Czar Nicholas II in the Kremlin, Moscow, 1896; a former manager of the Royal Institution of Great Britain; Senior Trustee (Chairman, 1909-41) of the Board of Trustees, Albany, Piccadilly, W.1.; A Governor of the Royal Mineral Water Hospital, Bath; travelled extensively (first visited Khartoum and the White Nile in 1882). *Publications:* Shall we Annex Egypt?; The Squire of Piccadilly, 1951 (relevant, by H. Baerlein). *Recreations:* riding, foreign travel. *Address:* A.1, Albany, Piccadilly, W.1. *Clubs:* Athenæum, Oxford and Cambridge, Garrick, United University, Reform, Hurlingham. [*Died* 25 *Oct.* 1958.

STONEMAN, Walter E., M.B.E. 1948; F.R.P.S., F.R.G.S.; portrait photographer and lecturer; Chairman of J. Russell & Sons, Ltd.; *b.* 6 April 1876; *y. s.* of late E. W. Stoneman, Plymouth; *m.* 1915, Kathleen Irene, *e. d.* of late G. H. Stoneman, Ealing; one *s.* *Educ.:* Plymouth Coll. Photographer for the National Portrait Gallery Record; has photographed over 6000 men of note and completed 60 years as a portrait photographer; Vice-President London Devonian Association. *Recreation:* studying human nature. *Address:* 11 Thayer Street, W.1. *T.:* Welbeck 1232. [*Died* 14 *May* 1958.

STOPES, Marie Carmichael, D.Sc., Ph.D., F.L.S., F.G.S. F.R.S.L.; Pres., Society for Constructive Birth Control and Racial Progress; Fellow and sometime Lecturer in Palæobotany at University College, London University; alsc Lecturer in Palæobotany at the University, Manchester; *e. d.* of late Henry Stopes, Anthropologist, and late C. C. Stopes; *m.* 1918, Humphrey Verdon Roe (*d.* 1949); two *s.*; retained Stopes as legal name. (At her suit, marriage with R. R. Gates annulled, 1916). *Educ.:* St. George's, Edinburgh; North London Collegiate School; University of London. 1st Class Honours Degree, Gold Medallist of University College, London; graduated Ph.D. at Munich under Goebel and Radelkofer; the first woman to be appointed to the Science Staff of the University of Manchester in 1904; went to Japan on a Scientific Mission in 1907; spent a year and a half at the Imperial University, Tokio, and explored the country for fossils; specialises on Coal Mines and Fossil Plants; jointly with H. V. Roe, founded Mothers' Clinic for Constructive Birth-Control, 1921 (the first birth control clinic in the world). *Publications:* The Study of Plant Life for Young People; Ancient Plants; A Journal from Japan; Botany, the Modern Study of Plants; Catalogue of the Cretaceous Plants in the British Museum, vols. i. and ii.; with Professor Sakurai, Plays of Old Japan, The Nō, 1913; Man, Other Poems and a Preface, 1914; Catalogue of the Cretaceous Plants in the British Museum, vol. ii.; The Lower Greensand (Aptian) Plants of Great Britain, 1915; Conquest, Gold in the Wood, and The Race (three plays); Married Love, and Wise Parenthood, 1918; The Constitution of Coal, with Dr. R. V. Wheeler, 1918; Radiant Motherhood, 1920; A New Gospel to All Peoples, 1921; Contraception: its Theory, History and Practice, 1923; The First Five Thousand, 1925; Sex and the Young; The Human Body, 1926; scientific papers in the Trans. Roy. Soc. and elsewhere; Enduring Passion, 1928; Our Ostriches, a three-act play, 1923; A Banned Play and a Preface on the Censorship, 1926; first novel, Love's Creation as by Marie Carmichael, 1928; Sex and Religion, 1929; Mother England, 1929; Ten Thousand Birth Control Cases, 1930; Contraception, enlarged and rewritten, 1931; Roman Catholic Methods of Birth Control, 1933; Birth Control To-day, 1934; Marriage in My Time, 1935; Change of Life in Men and Women, 1936; Poems: Love Songs for Young Lovers, 1939; Oriri, 1940; Instead of Tears, 1943; War-time Harvest, 1944; The Bathe, 1946; Selected Poems: We Burn (illustr. Gregorio Prieto), 1949; Joy and Verity, 1952; Sleep, 1956. *Recreations:* travelling, particularly tramping in little-known parts, gardening, needlework. *Address:* Norbury Park, near Dorking, Surrey. *Clubs:* Arts Theatre, Overseas. [*Died* 2 *Oct.* 1958.

STOPFORD, Vice-Admiral Hon. Arthur, C.M.G. 1918; *b.* 29 April 1879; 2nd *s.* of 6th Earl of Courtown; *m.* 1st, 1908, Mary Augusta Grace (who obtained a divorce, 1924), *e. d.* of Godfrey C. Chester-Master, Rangeworthy Court, Yate, Glos.; one *s.* one *d.*; 2nd, 1932, Mrs. Elsa Von Wendt, Helsingfors. *Educ.:* Stubbington House; H.M.S. Britannia. Lieut. 1901; Commander, 1912; Capt. 1917; Rear-Adm., 1929; served in South African War and Grand Fleet in European War; appointed to R.N.A.S., 1917; Col. R.A.F. 1918; returned to Navy, 1919; Naval Attaché to U.S.A., 1925-28; retired list, 1929; Vice-Adm., retired, 1934. *Recreations:* shooting and fishing. *Address:* 57 Whitecroft Way, Beckenham, Kent. *T.:* 1284. *Club:* United Service. [*Died* 25 *May* 1955.

STOPFORD, Captain Hon. Guy, R.N., retired; D.L.; *b.* 1884; 3rd *s.* of 6th Earl of Courtown; *m.* 1923, Rosalinde Cecil, M.B.E., *d.* of late Rev. C. F. Townley, C.B.E. Lieutenant, 1905; Lieut.-Commander, 1913; Commander, 1918; served European War, 1914-18; Chief of the Staff and War Staff Officer at Rosyth, 1927-1930; retired with rank of Captain, 1930. D.L. Co. Durham, 1948. *Address:* Sherburn House, Co. Durham. *Club:* United Service. [*Died* 10 *June* 1954.

STOREY, Sir John Stanley, Kt., *cr.* 1950; Chairman: Repco Ltd.; Overseas Corporation (Aust.) Ltd.; Bristol Aeroplane Co. (Aust.) Pty. Ltd.; National Motor Springs Pty. Ltd.; Kirkstall-Repco Ltd.; Dep.-Chm., Allied Ironfounders (Aust.) Pty. Ltd.; Director, Royal Insurance Co. Ltd. (Aust.) and a number of industrial companies; *b.* 1 Nov. 1896; *s.* of John and Elizabeth Storey; *m.* 1923, A. Leddin; one *s.* two *d.* (and one *s.* decd.). *Educ.:* Fort St. High School; Sydney University (B.Sc.). Director of Production, General Motors-Holdens Ltd., 1934-40; member Aircraft Production Commission and Aeronautical Advisory Committee, 1940; Vice-Pres. New South Wales Chamber of Manufactures, 1928-1932; Vice-President, Melbourne Technical College; Past Pres.: Australian Institute of Management; Inst. of Prod. Engineers (Austr. Sub-Council); Director Department of Aircraft Production, Australia, 1942-46; Member Australian Council of Aeronautics, 1942-47. Chairman: Joint War Production Committee, Dept. of Defence, Australia; Immigration Planning Council, Australia. *Recreation:* golf. *Address:* 402 Wattletree Road, East Malvern, S.E.5., Melbourne. *Clubs:* Athenæum, Australian (Melbourne), Peninsula (Frankston). [*Died* 3 *July* 1955.

STOREY, Robert Holme; *s.* of late Sir Thomas Storey, D.L.; *m.* 1907, Beatrice Maud, *d.* of late Sir W. H. Tate, Bt., D.L.; (one *s.* killed, serving R.A.F. 1939, and one killed, 1944, serving in K.S.L.I.). *Educ.:* Fettes College, Edinburgh; Clare College, Cambridge. M.A. Cantab. 1895; Barrister, Inner Temple, 1893; J.P. Denbighshire, 1904; County Councillor, Denbighshire, 1907; J.P. Herefordshire, 1920; High Sheriff of Herefordshire, 1938. *Recreations:* shooting, fishing. *Address:* The Home Farm, Bishopswood, Ross-on-Wye. *T.:* Ross-on-Wye 205. *Club:* Royal Automobile. [*Died* 15 *Jan.* 1956.

STORRS, Sir Ronald, K.C.M.G., *cr.* 1929 (C.M.G. 1916); Kt., *cr.* 1924; C.B.E. 1919; Knight of Justice of the Order of St. John of Jerusalem; Commander of the Crown of Italy and St. Saviour of Greece; Hon. LL.D. (Aberdeen and Trinity College Dublin); *b.* 19 Nov. 1881; *s.* of late Very Rev. J. Storrs and Hon. Lucy Cust; *m.* 1923, Mrs. Louisa Lucy Clowes, *widow* of Lt.-Col. H. Clowes, and *d.* of late Rear-Adm. Hon. Algernon Littleton and Lady Margaret Littleton, *sister* of late Earl of Kilmorey. *Educ.:* Temple Grove; Classical Scholarship, Charterhouse and Pembroke College, Cambridge; 1st Class Classical Tripos, 1903. Egyptian Govt., Ministry of Finance, 1904; several branches of administration until 1909; Oriental Secretary to British Agency, Egypt; Assistant Political Officer to Anglo-French Political Mission, E.E.F., 1917 (despatches); Liaison Officer for the Mission in Baghdad and Mesopotamia (despatches); Secretariat of War Cabinet, autumn 1917; Military Governor of Jerusalem (despatches), 1917-20; Civil Governor Jerusalem and Judaea, 1920-26; Governor and C.-in-C., Cyprus, 1926-32; Northern Rhodesia, 1932-34; invalided from tropical service, 1934. Mem. L.C.C., E. Islington, 1937-45; D.L., Essex; Pres. E.S.U., Essex, 1942-53; Chm. Council St. J. of J., Essex; Mem. Comité Conservation des Monuments Arabes, Cairo; Cttee. Palestine Exploration Fund; Mem., Church of England Council of Foreign Relations: Chm., Lesser Eastern Churches Cttee.; Chm. Nikaean Club; F.R.S.L.; Chm. English Assoc., 1949-51 and Vice-Pres.; Trustee, Royal Philharmonic Soc.; Pres., London Choral Soc.; a Vice-Pres., Trinity College of Music: a Governor, Shakespeare Memorial Theatre; Crown Rep., Council British School in Rome, 1951-; Member Anglo-Egyptian Chamber of Commerce, London. Ministry of Information: Lectures, Broadcasts, War Articles, 1940-45; Lecturer for British Council and Special Correspondent Sunday Times from Portugal to Persia, 1942-43. *Publications:* Orientations, 1937, Final Definitive ed. reprinted 1949; A Quarterly Record of the War, The First and Second Quarters, 1940; Drawing the R.A.F., 1942; Dunlop in War and Peace, 1946. *Recreations:* music, Eastern travel, chess. *Address:* 15 Alexander Square, S.W.3. *T.:* Kensington 3724. *Clubs:* Travellers', Beefsteak.

[*Died* 1 *Nov.* 1955.

STOTT, Sir Arnold Walmsley, K.B.E., *cr.* 1946; M.A., B.Chir., Camb.; F.R.C.P., Lond.; Hon. Maj.-Gen.; Extra Physician to H.M. Household; Hon. Consulting Physician, Westminster Hospital; late Hon. Consulting Physician to Army; Consulting Physician, Royal Chest Hospital; 2nd *s.* of late John Robert Stott, Bardsley, Lancs.; *m.* 1911, Lily, *e. d.* of late Alfred Robert Holland, Hampstead; one *s.* two *d.* *Educ.:* Rugby School; Trinity College, Cambridge; St. Bartholomew's Hospital. Formerly Examiner in Medicine, University of Cambridge, Birmingham, and R.C.P.; House Physician St. Bartholomew's and Royal Chest Hospital; Hon. Physician, Western General Dispensary; Chief Assistant, Electrocardiographic Dept.; Demonstrator of Pathology and Chief Assistant, Children's Department, St. Bartholomew's Hospital. *Recreation:* fly fishing. *Address:* Bullens Hill Farm, Stringers Common, Guildford, Surrey. *T.:* Guildford 4029.

[*Died* 15 *June* 1958.

STOTT, Sir George Edward, 2nd Bart., *cr.* 1920; F.I.A.A. & S.; L.R.I.B.A.; Capt. (retired) late 10th Bn. The Manchester Regt., T.A.; late Pilot Officer, Administrative and Special Duties Branch, R.A.F.V.R.; a registered archt.; *b.* 20 May 1887; *er. s.* of Sir Philip Sidney Stott, 1st Bt., and Hannah (*d.* 1935), *d.* of James Nicholson, Oldham; *S.* father 1937; *m.* 1912, Kate (*d.* 1955), *o. d.* of late George Swailes, J.P., Oldham; three *s.* *Educ.:* Rossall and abroad. Joined father in practice at Oldham, 1907; took over practice, 1921; retired 1935; High Sheriff of Gloucestershire, 1947-48. Commissioned in T.A., 1909; served European War, 1914-18, Egypt, Sinai, Gallipoli and France; also War of 1939-45. *Recreations:* golf, philately, amateur cinematography. *Heir:* *s.* Philip Sidney [*b.* 1914; *m.* 1947, Mrs. Cicely Florence Trowbridge, *o. d.* of Bertram Ellingham, Ely House, Hertford; two *s.*]. *Address:* Sandy Knowe, Compton, nr. Guildford, Sy. *T.:* Puttenham 286.

[*Died* 11 *July* 1957.

STOW, Sir Elliot Philipson Philipson-, 2nd Bt., *cr.* 1907; *b.* 12 July 1876; *e. s.* of 1st Bt., and Florence Henchman, *d.* of late Henry Hewitt, Cape Town; *S.* father, 1908; *m.* 1904, Edith (*d.* 1943), *y. d.* of late E. H. Pery-Knox-Gore, D.L., J.P., of Coolcronan, Ballina, Co. Mayo; two *s.* two *d.* Lieut. 14th Hussars, 1897-1903. *Heir:* *s.* Frederic Lawrence [*b.* 19 Sept. 1905; *m.* 1st, 1932, Daphne Morriss, *e. d.* of late W. G. Daffarn (marriage dissolved); 2nd, 1951, Cynthia Yvette, *d.* of late W. R. Jecks, Johannesburg]. *Address:* Frobury, Kingsclere, Newbury, Berks. *T.:* Kingsclere 259.

[*Died* 23 *Sept.* 1954.

STRABOLGI, 10th Baron of England, *cr.* 1318; **Lieut.-Comm. Joseph Montague Kenworthy;** R.N. retired; *b.* 7 Mar. 1886; *e. s.* of 9th Baron and Elizabeth Florence, 5th *d.* of George Buchanan Coupar and Elizabeth, *d.* and *co-heiress* of Jean Beverley Mackenzie, of Braemar, Scotland; *S.* father, 1934; *m.* 1st, 1913, Doris (marriage dissolved, 1941), *o. c.* of late Sir Frederick W. Whitley-Thomson; three *s.* one *d.*; 2nd, 1941, Geraldine Mary Hamilton, *o. d.* of late Maurice Francis; one *d.* *Educ.:* Royal Naval Academy, Northwood Park, Winchester; H.M.S. Britannia. Entered Royal Navy, 1902; Sub-Lieut. 1907; Lt. 1908; Lt.-Commander, 1916; retired, 1920; served European War, Commander H.M.S. Bullfinch, H.M.S. Commonwealth; Admiralty War Staff, 1917; Asst. Chief of Staff, Gibraltar, 1918; M.P. (L.) Central Hull, 1919-26; (Lab.), 1926-1931; Pres. United Kingdom Pilots Assoc., 1922-25; Chairman British Branch of Inter-Parliamentary Union, 1929-31; Chairman Advisory Committee on Sea Fisheries, 1926-1932; Vice-Pres. Hull Branch British Legion; Pres. Hull Navy League Cadet Corps; Vice-President Air League of British Empire. Opposition Chief Whip, House of Lords, 1938-1942; Lieut. Home Guard, 1940-46. Member of Advisory Committees on Civil Aviation, Shipping, sea fisheries, and iron and steel. *Publications:* Will Civilization Crash?, 1927; Freedom of the Seas (with Sir George Young), 1928; New Wars, New Weapons, 1930; India: A Warning, 1931; The Real Navy, 1932; Our Daily Pay; The Economics of Plenty, 1932; Sailors, Statesmen and Others, an Autobiography, 1933; The Battle of the River Plate, 1940; Narvik and After: A Study of the Scandinavian Campaign, 1940; The Campaign in the Low Countries, 1940; From Gibraltar to Suez, 1941; Singapore and After, 1942; Sea Power in the Second World War, 1943; Conquest of Italy, 1944. *Recreations:* shooting, fishing, tennis, golf. *Heir:* *s.* Hon. David Montague de Burgh Kenworthy. *Address:* 20B Collingham Gardens, S.W.5. *T.:* Fremantle 6897; Burwood House, Caxton Street, S.W.1. *T.:* Abbey 5276. *Clubs:* Reform, Royal Automobile. [*Died* 8 *Oct.* 1953.

STRACHAN, Rev. Robert Harvey, M.A. (Aberd. and Cantab.), D.D. (Aberd.); Emeritus Prof. of N.T. Language and Literature, Westminster College, Cambridge; *b.* 1873; *s.* of Robert Harvey Strachan, merchant, and Mary Anderson; *m.* Emily Rannie, (*d.* 1951), *d.* of George Mackenzie, W.S., Perth; one *s.* one *d.* *Educ.:* Walker's Academy and Robert Gordon's College, Aberdeen; Univ. of Aberdeen; New College, Edinburgh; Christ's College, Cambridge. Ordained, 1901; held charges in East Wemyss, Elie (Fife), Cambridge, Glasgow Edinburgh; Carew Lecturer, Hartford, U.S.A. 1927; Alexander Robertson Lecturer, Glasgow

University, 1927-28; Cunningham Lecturer, New Coll., Edinburgh, 1928-30; Armstrong Lecturer, Victoria Univ., Toronto, 1952. Moderator of the Presbyterian Church of England, 1940. *Publications:* The Fourth Gospel: its Significance and Environment, 1914, Third Edition, revised and re-written, 1941; The Individuality of St. Paul, 1916; The Fourth Evangelist: Dramatist or Historian? 1925; The Soul of Modern Poetry, 1924; The Authority of Christian Experience, 1928; The Historic Jesus in the New Testament, 1930; Commentary on II Corinthians, 1935. *Address:* Up Hall, Cherry Hinton, Cambridge. *Club:* Authors'. [*Died* 7 *Dec.* 1958.

STRACHEY, Joan Pernel; *b.* 1876; *d.* of late Lieutenant-General Sir Richard Strachey, G.C.S.I., F.R.S., and late Lady Strachey. *Educ.:* Allenswood; Newnham; Paris. Was Tutor, Director, and Lecturer in Modern Languages; Principal, Newnham College, Cambridge, 1923-41. *Address:* 51 Gordon Square, W.C.1. [*Died* 19 *Dec.* 1951.

STRACHEY, Oliver, C.B.E. 1943; retired; *b.* 3 Nov. 1874; *s.* of Sir Richard Strachey, G.C.S.I., F.R.S., and Jane Maria Grant of Rothiemurchus; *m.* 1st, Ruby Julia Mayer; one *d.*; 2nd, Rachel Conn Costelloe; one *s.* one *d.* *Educ.:* Eton. Has been engaged in work on East Indian Railway, on Historical Research, and in the Foreign Office. ***Publication:*** Keigwin's Rebellion, 1916. ***Recreations:*** music and reading. *Club:* Oriental. [*Died* 14 *May* 1960.

STRADLING, Sir Reginald Edward, Kt., *cr.* 1945; C.B. 1934; M.C.; F.R.S. 1943; D.Sc.; Ph.D.; M.Inst.C.E.; Hon. A.R.I.B.A.; Dean of the Military College of Science since 1949. *Educ.:* Bristol Grammar School; Bristol Univ. Temporary Commission, Royal Engineers, 1914-18; Captain R.E. (despatches twice, M.C.). Lecturer in Civil Engineering, Birmingham Univ., 1918-22; Head of Civil Eng., Architecture and Building Dept., Bradford Technical Coll., 1922-24; Director of Building Research, 1924-39; Chief Adviser, Research and Experiments, Ministry of Home Security, 1939-45; Civil Defence Department Home Office (part-time), 1945-48; Chief Scientific Adviser, Ministry of Works, 1944-49. Medal of Merit (U.S.A.), 1947; James Alfred Ewing Medal (Inst. of Civil Engs.). *Publications:* various scientific papers. *Address:* Military College of Science, Shrivenham, nr. Swindon, Wilts. [*Died* 26 *Jan.* 1952.

STRAFFORD, 6th Earl of, *cr.* 1847; **Edmund Henry Byng,** Baron Strafford (U.K.), 1835; Viscount Enfield, 1847; A.M.I.C.E.; D.L., J.P. Middlesex; J.P. Hertfordshire; County Alderman for Hertfordshire since 1901 and Middlesex, 1901-46; *b.* 27 Jan. 1862; *e. s.* of 5th Earl of Strafford and Florence, *d.* of late Sir W. Miles, 1st Bt. (*d.* 1862); *S.* father 1918; *m.* 1894, Mary Elizabeth (*d.* 1951), *y. d.* of Sir Thomas Edward Colebrooke, 4th Bt.; two *d.* *Educ.:* Eton; abroad. Civil Engineer, 1881-87; Member of London Stock Exchange, 1889-1919; Chm. Finance Cttee., Middlesex C.C., 1922-25; Almoner St. Bartholomew's Hospital, 1929-46. *Heir: nephew,* Robert Cecil Byng [*b.* 29 July 1904; *m.* 1934, Maria Magdalena Elizabeth, *d.* of late Henry Cloete, C.M.G., Alphen, S. Africa; two *s.*]. *Address:* 5 St. James's Square, S.W.1; Wrotham Park, Barnet, Herts. *T.:* Whitehall 2635; Barnet 0034. *Clubs:* Garrick, Brooks's, Royal Automobile. [*Died* 24 *Dec.* 1951.

STRAIN, Lieut.-Colonel Laurence Hugh, O.B.E., D.S.C.; *b.* 1876; *s.* of John Strain, M.I.C.E.; *m.* Margaret Ellen, *d.* of A. H. Howard, Providence, New England. *Educ.:* Uppingham; Clare Coll., Cambridge, B.A., LL.B. Scots Advocate, 1900; K.C. 1919. Conservative Candidate, Inverness-shire, 1906; Caithness, 1910; Air pilot No. 476, 1913; War Service, 1914-19, with R.N.A.S., Dardanelles, Gallipoli, Salonika, latterly G.S.O.I. in charge of Air Operations E.M.S.; Deputy Director Air Division Admiralty for Anti-Submarine Air operations, 1918 (despatches 4 times, D.S.C., O.B.E., Commander Greek Order of Redeemer); Staff Officer, Coastal Command, R.A.F., 1940-42; retired, 1942. *Recreations:* fishing, shooting, golf. *Address:* Cassillis House, Maybole. *T.:* Dalrymple 254; Drummore, Hoeys Bridge, Kenya. *Club:* County (Ayr). [*Died* 8 *April* 1952.

STRANG, Ian, R.E.; Member of Faculty of Engraving, British School at Rome; *b.* 1886; *e. s.* of William Strang, R.A., LL.D., and Agnes McSymon Rogerson; *m.* 1933, Frances Hookham. *Educ.:* Merchant Taylors' School; Slade School, London; Académie Julian, Paris. Travelled and studied in France, Belgium, Italy, Sicily, and Spain; enlisted, 1914, Middlesex Regt.; Commission, 1915, Royal Berkshire Regt.; Western Front, 1915-18; Demobilised, 1919 (Captain); has held one-man exhibitions at the Goupil, Chenil, Lefevre and Leicester Galleries; Represented by works in the permanent collections of Tate Gallery, British Museum, Imperial War Museum, Victoria and Albert Museum, and numerous other galleries and museums in England, Australia, Canada, Italy, and Moscow. *Publications:* The Students Book of Etching, 1937; Illustrations to Town and Country in Southern France by Frances Strang, 1937. *Address:* The Old Manor, Wavendon, Bletchley, Bucks. *T.:* Woburn Sands 3187. [*Died* 23 *March* 1952.

STRATEGICUS; *see* O'Neill, H. C.

STRATFORD, Rt. Hon. James, P.C. 1938; *b.* The Dene, Port Elizabeth, 1869; *s.* of James Stratford, late of Uitenhage; *m.* Louise Mary, *d.* of late Count Wilmot, Wynberg; one *s.* *Educ.:* St. Aidans College, Grahamstown; Exeter College, Oxford. M.A. and B.C.L.; called to Bar, Inner Temple, 1898; read with Earl Cave, then a junior at Chancery Bar; returned to S. Africa, 1901; large practice Johannesburg; K.C. 1912; Judgeship, 1921; Judge of Appeal (Appellate Division Supreme Court of S. Africa), 1927-38; Chief Justice of Union of S. Africa, 1938-39; retired, 1939. *Recreation:* golf. *Address:* Robinrise, Kalk Bay, Cape Peninsula. *Clubs:* Brooks's Rand (Johannesburg); Civil Service (Cape Town). [*Died* 17 *Jan.* 1952.

STRATHCONA and MOUNT ROYAL, Baron, 3rd in line, *cr.* 1900, **Donald Sterling Palmer Howard;** Lt.-Col. late The London Scottish; *b.* 14 June 1891; *s.* of late R. J. B. Howard, F.R.C.S., and the Baroness Strathcona and Mount Royal; *S.* mother, 1926; *m.* 1922, Diana Evelyn, twin *d.* of 1st Baron Wakehurst; three *s.* one *d.* *Educ.:* Eton; Trinity College, Cambridge; B.A. Honours Historical Tripos. Joined Regular Army, 3rd Hussars, Aug. 1913; served European War with above regiment, 1914-19 (Belgian Croix de Guerre); retired as Captain, 1919; M.P. (U.) North Cumberland, 1922-26; Parliamentary Private Secretary to First Lord of the Admiralty (Rt. Hon. W. Bridgeman), 1925-26; Member of the Indian Statutory Commission, 1928-30; Captain of the King's Body Guard of the Yeomen of the Guard, 1931-34; Parliamentary Under-Secretary of State for War, 1934-39. Served War of 1939-45 as Major, 2nd Bn. London Scottish, and on various Staff appts., including period 1943-44 as M.L.O. on C.M.A.B. at Washington. (U.S. Legion of Merit and Bronze Star); retired as Lt.-Col., 1945. *Recreations:* all sports, shooting, etc. *Heir: s.* Hon. Donald Euan Howard [*b.* 1923; *m.* 1954, Lady Jane Mary Waldegrave, 2nd *d.* of Earl Waldegrave; one *d.*]. *Address:* 2 Curzon Place, W.1. *T.:* Grosvenor 1594; Colonsay, Argyllshire. *Clubs:* Carlton, Buck's, Cavalry. [*Died* 22 *Feb.* 1959.

STRATHEDEN and CAMPBELL, Lady, (Jean Helen), C.B.E. 1954; Chief Commissioner, 1949-56, Chairman since 1951, of Girl Guides Association; *d.* of late Colonel William Anstruther-Gray, Kilmany, Fife; *m.*

1923, 4th Baron Stratheden and Campbell; three *d.* Commandant and Chairman Scottish Girls' Training Corps, 1942-46; Commissioner British Girl Guides in Germany, 1947. *Address:* Hunthill, Jedburgh, Scotland; Girl Guides Association, 17 Buckingham Palace Road, S.W.1. [*Died* 9 *Aug.* 1956.

STRATHIE, Sir (David) Norman, K.C.I.E., *cr.* 1944 (C.I.E. 1939); Chairman, of the Management Committee of Dr. Barnardo's Homes; *b.* 31 October 1886; *s.* of David Strathie, C.A., Glasgow; *m.* 1st, 1912, Williemina Sadler Bain (*d.* 1949); 2nd, 1951, Mrs. Joyce Parfett, *d.* of Mrs. C. E. Robjant, Hampstead; (one *s.* decd.). *Educ.:* Glasgow Acad. and Univ.; Balliol Coll., Oxford. I.C.S., 1911; Under-Sec., Revenue Judicial and Public Departments, Madras, 1915-18; Under-Sec. Commerce Dept., Govt. of India; Sec. to Board of Revenue, Madras; Commissioner of Income Tax; Registrar of Co-operative Societies; Collector; Inspector of Local Boards; Labour Commissioner; Commissioner of Income Tax, Palestine; Chief Civil Representative with Southern Army, India; Financial Secretary, Jamaica, retd. *Recreations:* golf, music. *Address:* 281 Petersham Road, Petersham, Surrey. *T.:* Richmond 4160. [*Died* 3 *Aug.* 1959.

STRATTON, Arthur, F.S.A., F.R.I.B.A. (retired). *Educ.:* King's College School. Reader in Architecture, University College, University of London, 1920-30. *Publications:* Life, Work and Influence of Sir Christopher Wren, 1897; The Domestic Architecture of England during the Tudor Period, 1911; second edition, 1928; The English Interior, 1920; Abraham Swan and his Work, 1923; Elements of Form and Design in Classical Architecture, 1925; The Architecture of the Renaissance in Italy, fifth edition, 1928; Introductory Handbook to the Styles of English Architecture, Part I. Mediæval, 1928, Part II. Renaissance, 1929; The Orders of Architecture, 1931; numerous others. *Address:* Greenford, Mare Hill, Pulborough, Sussex. *T.:* Pulborough 27. [*Died* 9 *April* 1955.

STRATTON, Frederick John Marrian, D.S.O. 1917; O.B.E. 1929; T.D. 1924; F.R.S. 1947; M.A. (Cantab); Hon. LL.D. (Glasgow); D.Phil. (Copenhagen); D.L. Cambs. 1924; V.L., 1945-57; Professor of Astrophysics, Cambridge Univ., and Director of the Solar Physics Observatory, 1928-47; *b.* Birmingham, 16 Oct. 1881; *s.* of late Stephen Samuel Stratton and Mary Jane, *d.* of John Marrian. *Educ.:* King Edward's Grammar School, Five Ways, and Mason University College, Birmingham; Gonville and Caius College, Cambridge. 3rd Wrangler, 1904; Isaac Newton Student, 1905; Smith's Prizeman, 1906; formerly Lecturer in Mathematics and Tutor Gonville and Caius College, Camb.; President of Gonville and Caius College, 1946-48. Halley Lecturer, Oxford, 1927; Secretary International Astronomical Union, 1925-35; General Secretary British Assoc., 1930-35; Pres. Roy. Astronomical Soc., 1933-35; Pres., Cambridge Philosophical Soc., 1930-31; Gen. Sec. Internat. Council of Scientific Unions, 1937-52; Pres. Soc. for Psychical Research, 1953-55. Signal Service, R.E., 1914-19 (D.S.O., Legion of Honour, Bt. Lt.-Col.); Royal Corps of Signals, 1940-45; Dep. Scientific Adviser to the Army Council, 1948-50; Prix J. Janssen, Société Astronomique de France; Correspondant de l'Académie des Sciences et du Bureau des Longitudes, Paris; Fellow of the Institute of Coimbra; Corresp. Nat. Acad. of Science, Lima; Hon. mem. Royal Astronomical Society of Canada, Royal Signals Instn. Japanese Order of the Sacred Treasure. *Publications:* Astronomical Physics, 1925; papers in the Monthly Notices and Memoirs of the Royal Astronomical Society. *Address:* Gonville and Caius College, Cambridge. *T.:* Cambridge 3275. *Club:* Savile. [*Died* 2 *Sept.* 1960.

STRAUS, Oscar, composer; *b.* Vienna, 6 March 1870; *m.*; three *s.* one *d.* *Educ.:* Vienna. Conductor in several theatres, 1885-1900; conductor and composer, Wolzogenschen Überbrettel, in Berlin, 1900; afterwards only living for composition. *Publications:* A Waltz Dream; The Last Waltz; Teresina; Chocolate Soldier; Die Lustigen Nibelungen, Hugdietrichs Brautfahrt; Rund um die Liebe, Die schöne Unbekannte, Die törichte Jungfrau, Naughty Riquette, Die Königin, Cleopatra, Mariette (Paris-London-Berlin-Vienna), 1929; Zwei lachende Augen; Liebelei; Walzerparadies; Three Waltzes, etc. *Address:* Zürichverlag A.G., Utoquai 41, Zürich, Switzerland. [*Died* 11 *Jan.* 1954.

STREATFEILD, Brigadier Richard John, D.S.O. 1945; Royal Artillery; Extra Equerry to the King since 1937; Commander 1st A.A. Brigade; Chairman Kent T.A. and A.F. Association; *b.* 18 Dec. 1903; *s.* of late Mervyn and Madeleine Streatfeild, Chested, Chiddingstone, Kent; *m.* 1937, Jane Eglantine, *o. d.* of late Sir Guy Stephenson; three *s.* three *d.* *Educ.:* Wellington; R.M.A., Woolwich. Joined R.A. 1924; A.D.C. to Governor-General of Canada, 1929-31; A.D.C. to Viceroy of India, 1931-33; Groom in Waiting, and also Private Secretary to the Queen, 1937-46; C.R.A. 44 (Home Counties) Inf. Div. T.A., 1947-50. Hon. Col. 458 (Kent) H.A.A. (M.) Regt., R.A.T.A. Asst. County Comr. for Kent, Boy Scouts Assoc., 1947-50; D.L. Kent, 1949. *Address:* Hoath House, Chiddingstone, Kent. *T.:* Cowden 3162. *Club:* Army and Navy. [*Died* 17 *July* 1952.

STREET, Sir Arthur William, G.C.B., *cr.* 1946 (K.C.B., *cr.* 1941; C.B. 1935); K.B.E., *cr.* 1938; C.M.G. 1933; C.I.E. 1924; M.C.; J.P.; Deputy Chairman, National Coal Board, since 1946; *b.* 1892; *s.* of late William Charles Street, Cowes; *m.*; two *s.* (and one killed on active service, R.A.F., 1944) one *d.* *Educ.:* County School, Sandown; King's College, London. Served European War, Inns of Court Regiment, Hampshire Regiment and Machine Gun Corps, Egypt, Sinai and Palestine (wounded, despatches, M.C.); Principal Private Secretary to Minister of Agriculture and Fisheries, and to First Lord of the Admiralty, 1919-22; Principal, 1922, Assistant Secretary, 1929, Principal Assistant Secretary, 1932, and Second Secretary, Ministry of Agriculture and Fisheries, 1936-38; Deputy Under-Secretary of State for Air, 1938-39; Permanent Under-Secretary of State for Air and Member and Secretary of the Air Council, 1939-45; Permanent Secretary, Control Office for Germany and Austria, 1945-46. Attached to British Empire Delegation, Washington Disarmament Conference, 1921-22; accompanied First Lord to Constantinople (Chanak crisis), 1922; Secretary to Royal Commission on Superior Civil Services in India, 1923-24, and to Linlithgow Committee on Distribution and Prices of Agricultural Produce, 1922-24; attached to United Kingdom Delegation, Imperial Economic Conference, Ottawa, 1932, and other Imperial Conferences, also World Monetary and Economic Conference, London, 1933; Chairman, Anglo-French Co-ordinating Committee for Aircraft Production and Supply, 1939-40; led U.K. Delegation at Commonwealth Air Conversations, Montreal, Oct. 1944; Member of U.K. Delegation at International Civil Aviation Conference, Chicago, Nov.-Dec. 1944; Member, Industrial and Domestic Coal Consumers' Councils since 1947. Commander of the Legion of Honour; Grand Officer of the Order of Orange Nassau of the Netherlands; Order of the White Lion of Czechoslovakia (First Class). *Address:* Engel Park, Mill Hill, N.W.7. *T.:* Finchley 0216. *Club:* Oriental. [*Died* 24 *Feb.* 1951.

STREET, Robert William; late Joint General Manager, Barclays Bank, Ltd.; *b.* 30

June 1860; *s.* of late George Street; *m.* 1901, Ethel, 2nd *d.* of late George Eaton Goldsmith of Bury St. Edmunds; no *c.* *Educ.:* St. John's School, King's Lynn. Entered the bank of Jarvis & Jarvis, 1878; Gurney's, 1888; Barclays, 1896. *Address:* Broom Heath, Woodbridge. *T.:* 178. [*Died* 27 *April* 1954.

STRETTELL, Major-General Sir C. B. Dashwood, K.C.I.E., *cr.* 1940; C.B. 1935; a Governor of Wellington College, Berks, 1947-56; *b.* 6 August 1881; *s.* of Lieutenant-Colonel A. D. Strettell and Harriett Batho; *m.* 1922, Margery Gillian de Hane Brown; one *s.* *Educ.:* Wellington College; R.M.C. Sandhurst. Joined Indian Army, 1900; 13th Rajputs, 1901; 3rd Punjab Cavalry, Punjab Frontier Force, 1902; served Waziristan, 1901-02 (Medal and clasp); Nmai-Hka Expedition, 1912-13 (King's Police Medal and letters of appreciation from Governments of India and Burma); European War, 1914-19; raised service squadron 6 Innis. Dgns.; Mesopotamia, with Regt., Bde. Maj. 7th Ind. Cav. Bde., 1916-19 (General Service and Victory Medal, despatches thrice, Brevet Lt.-Colonel); Commandant P.A.V.O., Cavalry Frontier Force, 1924-28; Colonel, 1923; A.A.G. Northern Command, India, 1928; Commander 3. Meerut Cavalry Brigade, 1929-32; B.G.S. Southern Command, India, 1932-34; Offg. Deputy Quartermaster General A.H.Q., India, 1934; Deputy Quartermaster General, 1935-36; Deputy Adj., General and Director of Organisation, 1936; Commander, Peshawar District India, 1936; retired, 1940; re-employed as Group Commandant, Prisoners of War Camps, 1941; Director of Demobilisation and Reconstruction, G.H.Q., India, Oct. 1941-Oct. 1943; Colonel P.A.V.O. Cavalry F.F. Sept. 1943; finally retired 1944; on Council, Central Asian Soc., 1945-52; Governor Wellington College, 1947-; Chm. Punjab Frontier Force Exec. Committee, 1951-54; Vice-Patron P.F.F. Officers' Assoc., 1954. *Publications:* contributions to magazines, professional and others. *Recreation:* golf. *Address:* c/o Lloyds Bank, 6 Pall Mall, S.W.1. *Club:* Royal Empire Society. [*Died* 27 *Jan.* 1958.

STRICKLAND, Rear-Admiral Sir Arthur Foster, K.C.B., *cr.* 1938 (C.B. 1937); O.B.E. 1929; *b.* 12 Apr. 1882; *s.* of M. P. Strickland, Torquay; *m.* 1908, Helen, *d.* of C. Moorshead; one *d.*; Paymaster Director-General, R.N., 1936-39; retired list, 1939; Divisional Food Officer, S.W. England, 1940; Chief Divisional Food Officer, Southern Command Area, 1941-43. *Address:* Troy, St. Margarets Bay, Kent. [*Died* 19 *Oct.* 1955.

STRICKLAND, General Sir (Edward) Peter, K.C.B., *cr.* 1919 (C.B. 1917); K.B.E., *cr.* 1923; C.M.G. 1913; D.S.O. 1899; *b.* Snitterfield, Warwickshire, 3 Aug. 1869; 3rd *s.* of Major F. W. Strickland; *m.* 1918, Barbara, D.B.E., *cr.* 1923, *d.* of late Martin W. B. ffolkes and *widow* of Capt. F. J Cresswell, Norfolk Regiment; one *d.* *Educ.:* Warwick School. Joined Norfolk Regt. 1888; served in Upper Burma, 1887-89 (medal and clasp); served with Egyptian Army; Dongola Expedition, 1896 (despatches, medal, 2 clasps); operations Sudan, 1897 (despatches, clasp); Atbara Campaign, 1898 (despatches, clasp); Khartoum Campaign, 1898 (despatches, Brevet-Majority, English medal, clasp to Khedive's medal); operations against Ahmed Fedil, 1899 (despatches, D.S.O., 3rd class Medjidie); operations, N. Nigeria, 1906 (medal and clasp); temp. Lt.-Col. 1906; temp. Col. Northern Nigeria Regiment, 1909; European War, 1914-18 (despatches eight times, Bt.-Colonel, promoted Maj.-Gen., K.C.B., Order of Leopold of Belgium, Croix de Guerre of France and Belgium); promoted Lt.-Col. to Manchester Regt. 1914; Brig.-Gen. 1915; temp. Major-General, 1916; commanded 6th Division, Ireland, 1919-22; temp. Lieut.-Gen. 1921-22; commanding 2nd Division, 1923-26; Lieut.-Gen. 1926; G.O.C. the British Troops in Egypt, 1927-31; General, 1931; retired pay, 1931. *Address:* Old Hall, Snettisham, Norfolk. [*Died* 24 *June* 1951.

STRICKLAND, Captain William Frederick; Past Chm.: Cornercroft Ltd.; Thomas Mouget & Co. Ltd., Mouget & Co. Ltd.; Dep. Chm. Thames Plywood Manufacturers Ltd.; Director E. & H. P. Smith, Ltd., Strickland's (Northampton) Ltd.; Vice-Pres. Coventry Conservative Association; *b.* 1880; *m.* 1907, Anne Lucretia, *d.* of late George Storton, Northants; two *s.* *Educ.:* privately; Waterloo College, Northampton. Served European War, 1914-19, 4th Bn. Northamptonshire Regt. and Imperial Camel Corps, Egypt; Military Prosecutor, Wasta Area, Egypt, 1919. M.P. (U.) Coventry, 1931-45; Governor Coventry and Warwickshire Hospital, 1935-48; Member of the House of Laity, 1934-45. Director John Morton & Son Ltd., 1933-48. *Address:* 11 Lenton Avenue, The Park, Nottingham. *T.:* Nottingham 43995. *Club:* Constitutional. [*Died* 29 *Nov.* 1954.

STRIJDOM, Hon. Johannes Gerhardus; Prime Minister of the Union of South Africa and Leader in Chief of the National Party of South Africa since 1954; Minister of Lands and of Irrigation since 1948; M.P. (Nat.) Waterberg, Transvaal, since 1929; *b.* Willowmore, C.P., 14 July 1893; *s.* of P. G. Strijdom; *m.* 1931, Susanna, *d.* of late Rev. J. de Klerk; one *s.* one *d.* *Educ.:* Willowmore; French Hoek; Stellenbosch and Pretoria Universities (B.A., LL.B.). Farmed in Willowmore district since 1912, then entered Civil Service of S.A., 1914. Joined a Pretoria firm of Attorneys, 1917; admitted as Advocate, Supreme Court, 1918; in practice as Attorney, Nylstroom, until 1934; has farmed in that district since 1923; Pres. Waterberg Agric. Assoc., 1923-29. Chm. Bd. of Directors: Die Voortrekker Pers Bpk, Dagbreek Trust Bpk. Leader of National Party in Transvaal, 1934. Ph.D. (*h.c.*) Pretoria University. *Address:* Union Buildings, Pretoria, South Africa. [*Died* 24 *Aug.* 1958.

STRITCH, His Eminence Cardinal Samuel Alphonsus; Archbishop of Chicago from Dec. 1939; appointed Pro-Prefect of the Congregation for the Propagation of the Faith, Vatican, 1958; *b.* 17 Aug. 1887; *s.* of Garrett Stritch and Catherine Malley. *Educ.:* North American College, Rome, Italy. Priest, 1910; Chancellor, Diocese of Nashville, Tenn., 1917; Domestic Prelate, 1921; Bishop of Toledo, Ohio, 1921; Archbishop of Milwaukee, Wis., 1930. Cardinal, 1946. *Address:* 719 North Wabash Av., Chicago 11, Ill., U.S.A. *T.:* Superior 7-2315. [*Died* 27 *May* 1958.

STRODE, Edward D. C.; *see* Chetham-Strode.

STRONG, Austin; Dramatist; Mem. Executive Cttee. of Pilgrims of the United States; *b.* San Francisco, 18 April 1881; *s.* of Joseph Dwight Strong, and Isobel Stuart Osbourne; *m.* 1906, Mary Holbrook Wilson, Providence, R.I. *Educ.:* Vailima; Wellington College, New Zealand. Studied landscape architecture in Philadelphia; work included laying out Cornwall Park, Auckland, N.Z.; since then has written plays. Ex-Vice-Pres. Nat. Inst. of Arts and Letters. Plays produced:—The Exile (written with Lloyd Osbourne), London, 1903; The Little Father of the Wilderness (with same), London and New York, 1905; The Drums of Oude, London, 1906; The Toymaker of Nüremburg, New York and London, 1907-8; Rip Van Winkle (new version), London, 1911; Adaptation of Le Bon Petit Diable, New York, 1913; Bunny, 1916; Three Wise Fools, New York and London, 1918-19; Seventh Heaven, New York, 1922. London, 1927. Contributor to Atlantic Monthly, Saturday Evening Post, etc. *Recreations:* friends, conversation, sailing. *Address:* 7 W. 43rd Street, New York

City. *T.A.:* Astrong, Nantucket, Mass. *Clubs:* Garrick; Century (New York); Nantucket Yacht (Nantucket). [*Died* 18 *Sept.* 1952.

STRONG, Leonard Alfred George; Author and Journalist; Director of Methuen Ltd., 1938-58; *b.* 1896; *o. s.* of Leonard Ernest Strong, and Marion Jane Mongan; *m.* 1926, Dorothea Sylvia Tryce, 2nd *d.* of Hubert and Dorothea Brinton, Eton; one *s.* *Educ.:* Brighton College; Wadham College, Oxford (Open Classical Scholar); M.A.; Member Irish Academy of Letters; F.R.S.L. For twelve years Assistant Master at Summer Fields, Oxford; Visiting Tutor, Central School of Speech and Drama. *Publications: verse:* Dublin Days; The Lowery Road, Difficult Love; Northern Light; Call to The Swan; The Body's Imperfection; *fiction:* Dewer Rides; The English Captain; The Jealous Ghost; The Garden; The Brothers; Don Juan and the Wheelbarrow; Sea Wall; Corporal Tune; The Seven Arms; Mr. Sheridan's Umbrella; Tuesday Afternoon; The Last Enemy; The Swift Shadow; The Open Sky; Sun on the Water; The Bay; The Unpractised Heart; All Fall Down; The Director; Othello's Occupation; Travellers, 1945 (James Tait Black memorial prize); Trevannion; Darling Tom; The Hill of Howth; Deliverance; Treason in the Egg; Light above the Lake (posthumous); *belles lettres:* Common Sense about Poetry; A Letter to W. B. Yeats; (with M. Redlich) Life in English Literature; The Hansom Cab and The Pigeons; The Minstrel Boy; The Man who asked Questions; Shake Hands and Come out Fighting; John McCormack: The Story of a Singer; English for Pleasure; A Tongue in your Head; The Sacred River; Maud Cherrill; Personal Remarks; The Writer's Trade; Dr. Quicksilver; Flying Angel; The Rolling Road; Green Memory (*autobiography*, posth., 1961). *Recreations:* music, walking in the country, swimming, and talking dialect. *Address:* Dromore, Old Frensham Road, Lower Bourne, Farnham, Surrey. *Clubs:* Pen, Savile, Writers' and Artists', I.M.A. [*Died* 17 *Aug.* 1958.

STRONG, Brig.-General William, C.B. 1917; C.M.G. 1918; R.A.; *b.* 1 Jan. 1870; *s.* of late Charles Isham Strong of Thorpe Hall, Peterborough; *m.* 1900, Katharine Mary (*d.* 1940), *d.* of Colonel P. W. Powlett, C.B., C.S.I.; one *d.* *Educ.:* Harrow; R.M. Academy, Woolwich. 2nd Lieut. R.A. 1888; Capt. 1898; Major, 1904; Lt.-Col. 1914; served European War, 1914-19 (despatches, C.B., C.M.G., Bt. Col.); retired from the Army, 14 June 1919. D.L. Northants; Pres. Soke of Peterborough Boy Scouts Assoc., 1919-. *Recreation:* shooting. *Address:* Lady Anne's House, Stamford. *T.:* Stamford 2170. *Club:* Army and Navy. [*Died* 17 *March* 1956.

STROTHER-STEWART, Robert; *see* Stewart.

STRUDWICK, Ethel, C.B.E. 1948 (O.B.E. 1936); M.A. (Lond.); High Mistress of St. Paul's Girls' School, 1927-48; *b.* London, 1880; *o. c.* of late J. M. Strudwick, artist. *Educ.:* Queen Elizabeth School, West Kensington; Bedford College, University of London (Reid Trustees Scholar). Honours in Classics in the B.A. Examination of the University of London, 1900; Classical Mistress, the Laurels, Rugby, 1901-2; Assistant in Greek, Bedford College, 1902-6; M.A. in Classics with special distinction, University of London, 1904; Assistant Lecturer in Classics, Bedford College, 1906-9; Lecturer and Head of the Department in Latin, Bedford College, 1909-13; Headmistress City of London School for Girls, 1913-27; President of Association of Head Mistresses, 1931-33; Member of the Senate of the University of London, 1921-52; Member of the Council of Westfield Coll., 1930-50; Member of Committee of Management Dartford College of Physical Education; Member of Council of Harrogate College and of The Girls' Public Day School Trust. *Recreations:* novels, plays, boating, and country walks. *Address:* 15 Leinster Avenue, East Sheen, S.W.14. [*Died* 15 *Aug.* 1954.

STRUTHER, Jan; (Pen-name of Mrs. A. K. Placzek; *née* Joyce Anstruther); *b.* 6 June 1901; *d.* of late Henry Torrens Anstruther, J.P. and late Hon. Dame Eva Anstruther, D.B.E.; *m.* 1st, 1923, Anthony, *e. s.* of late James Maxtone Graham; two *s.* one *d.*; 2nd, 1948, A. K. Placzek, of Columbia University. *Educ.:* London, privately. Has been contributing, since 1917, poems, articles and short stories to various periodicals, including Punch, the Spectator, the New Statesman, the London Mercury, and the Times. *Publications:* Betsinda Dances and Other Poems, 1931; Sycamore Square and Other Verses, 1932; The Modern Struwwelpeter, 1936; Try Anything Twice, 1938; Mrs. Miniver, 1939; The Glassblower and other poems, 1940; Letters from Women of Britain (pub. U.S.A.), 1941; A Pocketful of Pebbles, 1945. *Address:* 17 Alexander Place, S.W.7. [*Died* 20 *July* 1953.

STUART, Colonel (Hon. Brig.-Gen.) Burleigh Francis Brownlow, C.B. 1915; C.M.G. 1919; late Worcestershire Regiment; *b.* 1 Nov. 1868; 2nd *s.* of late Major Burleigh Stuart, Dergmony, Co. Tyrone; *m.* 1916, Evelyn Margaret, *o. d.* of late Lt.-Col. Sir Edward H. St. Lawrence Clarke, 4th Bt., C.M.G., D.S.O.; two *s.* *Educ.:* Cheltenham College. Entered army, 1889; Captain, 1899; Major, 1904; Lt.-Col. 1912; Col. 1916; served South African War, 1900-2 (despatches, Bt. Major, Queen's medal 2 clasps, King's medal 2 clasps); European War, 1914-18 (despatches, C.B., C.M.G.). *Address:* Letton, Blandford. *T.:* 110. [*Died* 8 *March* 1952.

STUART, Major-General Douglas, C.B. 1946; C.I.E. 1943; O.B.E. 1933; late I.A.; *b.* 20 July 1894; *m.* 1916, Muriel, *d.* of E. J. Gibbs. Served European War, 1916-17, France and Belgium, with Canadian Forces; Afghanistan, 1919 (despatches), Waziristan, 1919-20 (despatches); War of 1939-45 (Comdr. U.S. Legion of Merit). Retired, 1949. *Address:* Comforts Farm, Hurst Green, Oxted, Surrey. *Club:* United Hunts. [*Died* 9 *May* 1955.

STUART, Major Godfrey Richard Conyngham, C.B. 1918; formerly Major E. Lancs. Regt.; *e. s.* of Major Burleigh W. H. F. Stuart, of Dergmony, Co. Tyrone; *b.* 1866; *m.* 1899, Alice (*d.* 1936), *d.* of J. A. Smyth of Ardmore, Londonderry; three *s.* Served Chitral, 1895; N.W. Frontier, India, 1897-98; Tirah, 1898. D.L. Suffolk. *Address:* Glenroy, Gadshill Road, Charlton Kings, Cheltenham. [*Died* 9 *Jan.* 1955.

STUART, Sir Houlton John, 8th Bt., *cr.* 1660; *b.* 30 Dec. 1863; *s.* of Lieut.-Col. Charles Robert William Stuart, 2nd *s.* of 5th Bt.; *S.* cousin, 1939. *Heir: nephew* Phillip Luttrell Stuart, *b.* 7 Sept. 1937. [*Died* 3 *May* 1959.

STUART, Col. John P. V.; *see* Villiers-Stuart.

STUART, Gen. Sir John T. B.; *see* Burnett-Stuart.

STUART, Brig. Lionel Arthur, C.I.E. 1944; M.C.; late Indian Army; *b.* 22 Apr. 1892; *s.* of Henry Stuart and Lilian Buchanan, Cloonaquin, Manorhamilton, County Leitrim, Eire; *m.* 1915, Mary Gerard, *d.* of Joseph Gerard Bolger, Dublin; one *d.* *Educ.:* privately; R.M.C. Sandhurst. Served European War, 1914-18, Palestine and on N.W.F. (despatches); Staff College, 1924-25. Late Col. 4 Rajputana Rifles. Retired, 1947 (Hon. Brig.). [*Died* 13 *Feb.* 1959.

STUART, Captain Ronald Niel, V.C.; D.S.O. 1917; R.D., R.N.R., retired from Canadian Pacific Steamships (General Superintendent Steamships 1936-38, General Manager, U.K., 1938-51); *b.* 26 Aug. 1886; *s.* of Niel Stuart, Prince Edward Island; *m.* 1919, Evelyn (decd.), *d.* of W. Wright; three *s.* two *d.* *Educ.:* Liverpool College. Commenced career at sea in sailing vessel, 1901; joined Allan Line, 1913; Extra Master (square rig), 1913; served in Royal Navy as Lieutenant, R.N.R., 1914-19 (V.C., D.S.O., despatches, United States Navy Cross); in Command of Q boat and Destroyers; A.D.C. to the King, 1941. *Address:* Beryl Lodge, Charing, Kent. *T.:* Charing 232. [*Died* 8 *Feb.* 1954.

STUART-MENTETH, Sir W. F.; *see* Menteth.

STUART-WILLIAMS, Sir (Sydney) Charles, Kt., *cr.* 1929; *b.* May 1876; *s.* of Rev. W. Charles Williams; *m.* 1st, 1903, Elizabeth Mary (*d.* 1941), *d.* of John Stuart; two *s.* (and one *s.* decd.); 2nd, 1944, Mrs. N. R. Wyatt-Symonds, *d.* of late H. J. Reynolds, of Pelham Place, S.W.1. *Educ.:* Kingswood School, Bath; University College, Aberystwyth; Trinity College, Cambridge; B.A. London and Wales, 1897; M.A. Cambridge. In service of East Indian Railway, 1900-14; joined Calcutta Port Commissioners as Secretary, 1914; Vice-Chairman and Deputy Chairman, 1916-22; Chairman, 1922-30; Member, Indian States Enquiry Committee, 1932. *Publications:* Economics of Railway Transport; History of Port of Calcutta, 1870-1920; (with E. H. Short) Railways, Roads and the Public, 1939. *Address:* 2 Melina Place, St. John's Wood, N.W.8. [*Died* 9 *Dec.* 1960.

STUART WORTLEY, Hon. Mrs., C.B.E. 1918; J.P.; **(Violet),** *widow* of Major-General Hon. E. Stuart Wortley, C.B., C.M.G., D.S.O., M.V.O. (*d.* 1934); two *d.*; *d.* of James Guthrie of Craigie and Elinor Stirling. *Publications:* A Prime Minister and His Son; Highcliffe and the Stuarts; The Palaces of Paris; Sophy, the Winkle-Picker, 1941; Magic in the Distance, 1949; Grow Old Along with Me, 1952. *Address:* Highcliffe, Hants. [*Died* 11 *Feb.* 1953.

STUBBS, Lawrence Morley, C.S.I. 1931; C.I.E. 1922; I.C.S., retired; *b.* 23 March 1874; *e. surv. s.* of William, 33rd Bishop of Oxford; *m.* 1900, Helen Christina, M.B.E. 1925, K.I.H. medal, 1932, *d.* of Frederick Malcomson, Clodiagh, Portlaw, Co. Waterford; three *s.* one *d.* *Educ.:* Winchester; New College, Oxford. B.A. 1897; 1st class History; M.A. 1900; I.C.S. 1898; Commissioner of Fyzabad, Rohilkhand and the last Commissioner of Kumaon. *Address:* Paddock House, Benson, Oxon. *T.:* Benson 337. [*Died* 9 *Aug.* 1958.

STUBBS, Roy; Director, Joseph Stubbs, Limited, Ancoats and Openshaw, Manchester, Machine Makers and Ironfounders, since 1928; *b.* 14 June 1897; *s.* of John Stubbs and Mary Louise Wayne; *m.* 1931, Ethel May Brotherton. *Educ.:* Victoria Park School; Manchester Grammar School. Joined firm of Joseph Stubbs, Ltd., as apprentice; went through all departments in the Foundry; joined H.M.'s Forces in the R.F.A.; Demobilised, took up executive position on Foundry side of business; President Institute of British Foundrymen, 1934. President Cheadle Rovers R.F.C. *Recreations:* gardening and golf. *Address:* Joseph Stubbs Ltd., Mill Street Works, Ancoats, Manchester 4. *Club:* Gatley Golf (Gatley). [*Died March* 1951.

STUBBS, Sydney, C.M.G. 1947; J.P. for State of W. Australia; retired M.P.; *b.* 19 July 1861; *s.* of William and Agnes Stubbs; *m.* 1891, Martha Jeffrey; one *s.* four *d.* *Educ.:* Warrnambool and Melbourne. Many years Intercolonial Traveller for John Danks & Son, Melbourne; thirty-nine years M.P. in W. Australia. Mayor of City of Perth, 1905-6. Mayor of Claremont, 1899-1903. *Address:* 47 Hensman Road, Subiaco, Western Australia. *Clubs:* Masonic, West Australian, Commercial Travellers' (Perth). [*Died* 30 *July* 1953.

STUCLEY, Sir Hugh Nicholas Granville, 4th Bt., *cr.* 1859; *b.* 22 June 1873; *s.* of 1st Bt. and 2nd wife, Louisa, *d.* of Bernard Granville, Wellesbourne Hall, Warwicks.; *S.* half-brother, 1927; *m.* 1902, Gladys (*d.* 1950), *d.* of W. A. Bankes of Wolfeton House, Dorchester; three *s.* two *d.* *Heir:* *s.* Dennis Frederick Bankes Stucley, D.L., J.P., C.A., Devon, Major North Devon Yeomanry Artillery [*b.* 29 Oct. 1907; *m.* 1932, Hon. Sheila Margaret Warwick Bampfylde, *o. d.* of 4th Baron Poltimore; one *s.* four *d.*]. *Address:* Moreton, Bideford, Devon. [*Died* 25 *Oct.* 1956.

STURDY, William Arthur, C.B.E. 1928; *b.* 1877; *s.* of late J. Sturdy; *m.* 1905, Beatrice Maude (*d.* 1951), *d.* of William Oglesby; two *s.* *Educ.:* Leeds Grammar School. Entered India Audit Office, 1894; Senior Clerk, 1913; Assistant Auditor, 1915; Auditor of Indian Home Accounts, 1921-34; retd., 1934. *Address:* Envilles, Felsted, Dunmow, Essex. [*Died* 19 *Aug.* 1958.

STURGES, His Honour Hugh (Murray), J.P. Lancs and Herts; *b.* 26 Aug. 1863; 2nd *s.* of Canon Sturges, Rector of Wokingham, Berks, and Jane, *d.* of William Murray, M.P.; unmarried. *Educ.:* Winchester; Keble Coll., Oxford. Called to Bar, 1889; K.C. 1912. Practised in London and the Oxford Circuit; Bencher of Lincoln's Inn, 1926; Treasurer, 1945; Recorder of Tewkesbury, March 1912; Windsor, Oct. 1912-May 1945; County Court Judge, Circuit No. 4 (North Lancs), 1913-21; Circuit No. 37, etc. (West London), 1921-28; retired, 1928; Deputy Chairman Quarter Sessions, Herts, 1924; Chm., 1932-46. *Address:* 105 Pall Mall, S.W.1. *T.:* Whitehall 9374. *Clubs:* Brooks's, Reform, Oxford and Cambridge. [*Died* 12 *Oct.* 1952.

STURROCK, Alick Riddell, R.S.A. 1937; landscape painter; *b.* 1885; *s.* of late Alex. Sturrock and Katherine Riddell; *m.* Mary, *d.* of F. H. Newbery. *Educ.:* George Watson's College, Edinburgh; Edinburgh School of Art; Royal Scottish Academy Life Class; Travelling Scholarship, Paris, Italy, Munich, Holland. Served European War as Captain The Royal Scots. *Recreations:* fishing, golf, gardening. *Address:* 13 South Gray Street, Edinburgh. *Club:* Scottish Arts (Edinburgh). [*Died* 16 *May* 1953.

STURROCK, Hon. (Frederick) Claud, M.I.Mech.E.; M.Inst.T.; F.R.S.A.; Hon. Commodore South African Navy since 1941; *b.* 25 May 1882; *s.* of James Sturrock, Dundee, Scotland and Eva Leng, Newport, Fife; *m.* 1912, Elizabeth Isobel Robertson, Newport, Fife; three *s.* *Educ.:* High School, Dundee; Technical Coll. Apprentice Engineer; James Carmichael and Sons, Ward Foundry, Dundee; Construction Supt., J. G. White and Co., London; established business in South Africa, 1907; Member of Education Administration Commission, 1923; Port Elizabeth Harbour Commission, 1926; Main Reef Road Commission, 1927; Provincial Finance Commission, 1934; M.P. for Turffontein Division of Johannesburg, 1929-50, retired; Minister without Portfolio, 1936-38; Minister of Transport, 1939-48; Minister of Finance, 1948. *Recreations:* tennis and yachting. *Address:* Earnholme, The Valley Road, Parktown, Johannesburg; The River House, Eastford, Knysna, C.P. *T.A.:* Delta Johannesburg and Capetown. *Clubs:* Caledonian; Rand, Country, Wanderers, Turf (Johannesburg); Civil Service, City, Royal Cape Yacht (Capetown); Pretoria (Pretoria). [*Died* 4 *Aug.* 1958.

SUDMERSEN, Frederick William, C.I.E. 1926; late Indian Educational Service; *m.* Eugénie Onillon; one *s.* two *d.* London University (B.A. 1894); Principal, Cotton College, Gauhati, Assam, India, 1901-26. *Address:* Woodcock Farm, Nutley, Sx. *T.:* Nutley 58. [*Died* 8 *Feb.* 1953.

SUETER, Rear-Admiral Sir Murray F(raser), Kt., *cr.* 1934; C.B. 1914; *b.* 1872; *s.* of J. T. Sueter, Fleet Paymaster, R.N.; *m.* 1903, Elinor Mary de Winton (*d.* 1948), *o. c.* of Lt.-Gen. Hon. Sir Andrew Clarke, G.C.M.G., R.E.; two *d.* Entered Navy, 1886; Lieut., 1894; in 1898 gave the first lecture on Wireless Telegraphy ever given in the Naval Torpedo School Ship, Vernon; Comm., 1903; Capt., 1909; Commodore, 1st class, 1915; Rear-Admiral, 1920; assisted Captain Bacon in introducing submarines into British Navy, 1902-3; commended by Lords of Admiralty for saving life in a hydrogen gas explosion in A1 Submarine; Assistant to Director of Naval Ordnance at Admiralty, 1903-1905; Command of Cruiser Barham, 1906-8; a pioneer of British Aviation; Inspecting Captain of Airships, 1908-11; delegate to International Conference on Aerial Navigation held at Paris, 1910; created the Royal Naval Air Service; Director of Air Department, 1911-15; in 1912 sent on a Government Mission with Col. Mervyn O'Gorman, C.B., to report on European aeronautics; Superintendent of Aircraft Construction, 1915-17; Member of First War Air Committee; in command of R.N.A.S. units in Southern Italy, 1917-18; Member of Advisory Committee on Aeronautics, 1908-17; created the first Anti-aircraft Corps for London and the Armoured Car Force; received thanks of Army Council for his contribution to evolution of the Tank; M.P. (C.) Hertford Div., 1921-45; Member, Post Office Advisory Council, 1934-45; received the thanks of three Postmaster-Generals for valuable assistance in connection with developing Empire airmail services, 1935-39; Commander of Legion of Honour and Saviour of Greece; Order of Rising Sun, 3rd Class; Order of St. Vladimir; despatches; joint inventor with the late Lieut.-Commander Douglas Hyde-Thomson of the torpedo aeroplane and seaplane; received official appreciation from Lords of Admiralty for promoting use of torpedo-carrying aircraft, 1942. *Publications:* Evolution of the Submarine, Mine, and Torpedo; The Evolution of the Tank, 1937; hon. mentioned R.U.S.I. prize essay, 1904; Lectures on Submarines; Technical Papers on Air Subjects; Airmen or Noahs, etc. *Recreations:* boxing, football, fishing, shooting. *Address:* The Howe, Howe Hill, Watlington, Oxon. *Club:* Royal Aero. [*Died* 3 *Feb.* 1960.

SUFFIELD, 10th Baron (*cr.* 1786), **Admiral Richard Morden Harbord-Hamond,** Bt., *cr.* 1745; (retired); D.L.; Norfolk; Lord of the Manor of Swaffham; Officer of the Legion of Honour; *b.* 24 Aug. 1865; 4th *s.* of late Rev. Hon. John Harbord and Caroline Penelope, 4th *d.* of late Anthony Hamond of Westacre, Norfolk; assumed the additional name of Hamond, 1917; *S.* cousin 1946; *m.* 1913, Nina Annette Mary Crawfuird, *e. d.* of late John Hutchison of Lawrieston, Stewartry of Kirkcudbright; one *s.* two *d.* *Educ.:* H.M.S. Britannia. Served in Egyptian War, Midshipman H.M.S. Superb, at bombardment of Alexandria; in command of H.M. Battleships Mars and Zealandia, Grand Fleet, also Commodore in charge at Portland during War, 1914-17; Rear-Admiral, 1917; retired, 1917; Admiral (retired), 1927. *Recreations:* usual. *Heir:* *s.* Hon. Anthony Philip Harbord-Hamond, *b.* 19 June, 1922. *Address:* Manor House, Swaffham, Norfolk. *T.A.* and *T.:* Swaffham 206. *Club:* United Service. [*Died* 2 *Feb.* 1951.

SUGDEN, Alan Victor, J.P.., F.R.S.A.; Liveryman—Worshipful Company of Stationers and Newspaper Makers; *b.* 11 Oct. 1877; *s.* of William Sugden and Agnes Ellen Lightbown; *m.* 1904; one *d.* *Educ.:* Tettenhall; Dresden. *Publications:* A History of English Wallpaper, (with J. L. Edmondson); Potters of Darwen; The Crace Papers (with E. A. Entwisle). *Address:* Longmynd, Alderley Edge, Cheshire. *T.:* Alderley Edge 2171. *Clubs:* Union, Reform (Manchester). [*Died* 27 *Feb.* 1956.

SUGDEN, Sir Bernard, Kt., *cr.* 1939; J.P.; Chairman of: Wm. Sugden and Sons, Ltd., A. Holroyd and Co., Ltd.. Hawksclough Mill Co. Ltd.; *b.* 1877; 2nd *s.* of William Sugden, Cleckheaton; *m.* 1900, Lily (*d.* 1949), *d.* of Enos Smith, J.P., Pyenot Hall, Cleckheaton; one *s.* two *d.* *Educ.:* Cleckheaton; Bradford. Travelled extensively throughout the world: President Bradford Equitable Building Soc.; Vice-President, Federation of Chambers of Commerce of the British Empire; Past President, Spen Valley Incorporated Chamber of Commerce; Hon. Treasurer and Past President, Shirt Collar and Tie Manufacturers Federation of Great Britain; Governor, United College, Bradford. *Recreation:* foreign travel. *Address:* Hill Top House, Gomersal, nr. Leeds. *T.:* Cleckheaton 299. [*Died* 17 *Nov.* 1954.

SUGDEN, Brig.-General Richard Edgar, C.B. 1926; C.M.G. 1919; D.S.O. 1916; late T.A.; *b.* Aug. 1871; *s.* of R. Sugden, Ye Farre Close, Brighouse, Yorks; *m.* Norah, *d.* of W. H. Wayman, South Field, Halifax; one *s.* one *d.* (one *s.* died on active service, 1943). *Educ.:* Marlborough College. Served South African War with the Imperial Yeomanry, 1900-2; played football for Yorkshire, 1895-96; two years President of the Brighouse Chamber of Commerce; European War, 1914-18 (despatches six times, C.M.G., D.S.O. and bar, Bt. Lt.-Col.); Brig.-Gen. 1918; retired from T.A. 1929; D.L., J.P., West Riding. *Address:* The Newlands, Brighouse, Yorkshire. *T.:* 153. [*Died* 9 *May* 1951.

SUGDEN, Sir Wilfrid Hart, Kt., *cr.* 1922; late R.E.; Barrister-at-law; Member of the Middle Temple and Gray's Inn; late Hon. Secretary Lancashire Members of Parliament; constructional engineer; *b.* Bolton, Lancs; *s.* of William Arthur and Isabella Sugden; unmarried. *Educ.:* Waterloo School; London University. M.P. (U.) Royton Div. of Lancashire, Dec. 1918-23; The Hartlepools, 1924-29; Leyton West, 1931-35; Parliamentary Private Secretary to the last Chief Secretary for Ireland, 1921-22; Member, Oldham Town Council, 1912-18; called to Bar, 1928: Member of Oldham Education Committees, Special Schools Committees, Higher Education Committee; Governor, Waterloo School; Governor, Municipal Technical Schools; Member of Electricity Committee; travelled for purposes of education and commerce in many European countries and in Africa; has done much social work in Lancashire. *Recreations:* swimming (long distance), tennis, music. *Address:* 206 Waterloo Street, Oldham, Lancashire. *Club:* Carlton. [*Died* 27 *April* 1960.

SUKUNA, Sir Joseva Lalabalavu Vanaaliali, K.C.M.G., *cr.* 1953; K.B.E., *cr.* 1946 (C.B.E. 1939); Speaker of Legislative Council, Fiji, 1954-58. *Educ.:* Wanganui, New Zealand; Wadham College, Oxford (B.A.). Called to Bar, Middle Temple, 1921. Assistant Commissioner for Fiji, British Empire Exhibition, 1924; Secretary, Fijian Affairs, Fiji, 1943-53. Served European War, 1914-18 in France; French Military Medal; served War of 1939-45: Col. of Fiji Military Forces Staff; led Fijian contingent in victory march, London, 1946; Hon. Col. 2nd Bn., Fiji Infantry; Lt.-Col., Fiji Defence Force. *Address:* Suva, Fiji. [*Died* 29 *May* 1958.

SULLIVAN, Alexander Martin, Q.C. (Ire.) 1919; Barrister-at-law; *b.* 1871; 2nd *s.* of late A. M. Sullivan, M.P.; *m.* 1900, Helen (*d.* 1952), *e. d.* of late Major John D. Keiley, Brooklyn, N.Y. Journalist on the Nation, Weekly News, and Evening Press, and contributor to various periodicals prior to call to the Bar in 1892; K.C. Ire. 1908;

called English Bar, 1899; H.M. Serjeant-at-law, 1920. *Publications:* Old Ireland, 1927; The Last Serjeant, 1952. *Address:* 9 The Avenue, Beckenham, Kent. *T.:* 3242. [*Died* 9 *Jan.* 1959.

SULLIVAN, Bernard Ponsonby, M.B.E. 1923; *b.* 8 May 1891; 2nd *s.* of late Rev. Ponsonby Augustus Moore Sullivan and late Emma Elizabeth Adey, Wotton-under-Edge; *m.* 1918, Dorothy Evelyn, M.B.E., *d.* of late I. A. Hattersley; one *s.* *Educ.:* Exeter School; in France and Germany. Employed in Consulate-General at Hamburg, 1910-11; in Consulate at Danzig, May-Dec. 1912; passed competitive Consular examination July and War Office tests for interpretership in French and German on active service September, joined Inns of Court O.T.C. November 1914, demobilised and appointed a Vice-Consul in Consular Service, January 1915; in F.O. 1915-18 and in Dept. of Overseas Trade, Aug.-Dec. 1918; Vice-Consul at Ghent 1917; Commercial Secretary (Grade III), Brussels, 1920; reverted to Consular Service as Vice-Consul at Budapest, 1922; in Foreign Office, 1924; promoted Consul and transferred to Rome, 1925; left Rome, 1940; seconded to Home Office, Oct. 1940; a member of Home Office Advisory Committee (Isle of Man), 1940-41; seconded to Dominions Office; Foreign Office member on staff of U.K. High Commissioner in South Africa, 1942-44; H.M. Consul-General at Boston, 1944-47; Minister to Costa Rica (appointed Special Ambassador at inauguration of President of Costa Rica, Nov. 1949), 1948-51. Chevalier of Belgian Order of Leopold. *Recreations:* painting, gardening. *Address:* 15 Sands Road, Paignton, Devon. [*Died* 19 *Nov.* 1958.

SULLIVAN, Francis Loftus; Stage and Film Actor; *b.* London, England, 6 Jan. 1903; *s.* of Michael Sullivan and Gertrude Wilson; *m.* 1935, Frances Joan, *d.* of Arthur T. Perkins, Solicitor, Leeds, Yorkshire; no *c.* *Educ.:* Neuchâtel, Switzerland; Stonyhurst College, Lancs. First appeared on stage, Old Vic, 1921; toured for some years with Matheson Lang, and in Shakespeare and Shaw. Appeared for first time on New York stage as Stanley Rosel in Many Waters, Maxime Elliott Theatre, 1929; success as Hercule Poirot in Agatha Christie's Black Coffee, St. Martin's Theatre, W.C.2, 1931; other West End successes include: Canon Ronder in Hugh Walpole's The Cathedral, 1932; Gorotchenko in Tovaritch, 1935; Claudius in Hamlet, Old Vic, 1937; Oscar Wilde, 1938; Bottom in Midsummer Night's Dream, 1940; Hercule Poirot again, in Peril at End House, 1940; Mr. Crispin in The Man with Red Hair, 1942. Reappeared in New York in Duet for Two Hands, 1947; and in Cæsar and Cleopatra, 1950. Became an American citizen, 1954; made first appearance in films in 1931 and has since appeared in many pictures in England and America, including: Jew Süss, Pimpernel Smith, The Ware Case, Action for Slander, Great Expectations, Joan of Arc, Christopher Columbus, Oliver Twist, Night in the City, My Favourite Spy, Caribbean, Plunder of the Sun, Sangaree, Drums of Tahiti, The Prodigal, Hell's Island. Has frequently appeared in radio and television plays in London and New York. *Recreation:* swimming. *Address:* c/o J. F. Sullivan, 29 The Chase, Clapham Common, S.W.4. [*Died* 19 *Nov.* 1956.

SULLIVAN, Rev. Sir Frederick, 7th Bt., *cr.* 1804; *b.* 28 April 1865; *s.* of 6th Bt. and Agnes, *d.* of late Sir Sidney S. Bell; *S.* father, 1906; *m.* 1st, 1901, Hon. Judith Harbord (*d.* 1942), 5th *d.* of 5th Lord Suffield; 2nd, 1943, Mrs. Logan-Home (*d.* 1952). *Educ.:* Wellington Coll.; Exeter Coll., Oxford. Ordained, 1891; Curate of Penistone, Yorks, 1891-93; Cumberworth, 1894; Kimpton, Welwyn, 1895-1901; Rector of Southrepps, Norwich, 1901-21. *Heir:* *n.* Richard Benjamin Magniac, *b.* 1906. *Address:* 29 Adelaide Crescent, Hove. *Club:* Union (Brighton). [*Died* 24 *July* 1954.

SUMMERS, Captain Joseph J., C.B.E. 1953 (O.B.E. 1946); Consultant and Company Director; *m.* 1921, Dulcie, *d.* of Harry Belcher, Gloucester; one *s,* two *d.* Chief Test Pilot, Vickers-Armstrongs Ltd., Weybridge, 1929-51; Chief Liaison Officer, Weybridge Division of Vickers-Armstrongs Ltd., 1951-52. British Silver Medal for practical achievement in Aeronautics, 1950. *Club:* Royal Aero. [*Died* 16 *March* 1954.

SUMNER, Benedict Humphrey, M.A.; F.B.A.; F.R.Hist.S.; Warden of All Souls College, Oxford, since 1945; *b.* 8 Aug. 1893; *s.* of Heywood Sumner and Agnes Mary Benson. *Educ.:* Winchester; Balliol College, Oxford. Served in the K.R.R.C. in England and France, in War Office (Military Intelligence), and on British Delegation to Peace Conference; Fellow of All Souls, 1919-25; Member of the staff of the International Labour Office, Geneva, 1920-22; Fellow and Tutor in Modern History at Balliol, 1925-44; Lecturer at Aberystwyth University College, 1928; Lecturer at Harvard, 1930; attached to Foreign Office, 1939-42; Professor of History, Edinburgh University, 1944-45; Visiting Member, Institute for Advanced Study, Princeton, 1948. Member of University Grants Committee. *Publications:* Russia and the Balkans, 1870-1880; Survey of Russian History; articles in historical reviews. *Club:* United University. [*Died* 25 *April* 1951.

SUMNER, James Batcheller, A.B., A.M., Ph.D., Harvard; Professor of Biochemistry and Director of Enzyme Research Laboratory, Cornell University, Ithaca, New York; *b.* Canton, Mass., 19 Nov. 1887; *s.* of Charles Sumner and Elizabeth Rand Kelly; *m.* 1st, 1915; two *s.* two *d.* (and one *s.* decd.); 2nd, 1931; 3rd, 1943, Mary Morrison Beyer; one *s.* (and one *s.* decd.). *Educ.:* Roxbury Latin School; Harvard University. Left arm amputated, 1904, after a hunting accident; taught at Mt. Allison Coll., Sackville, N.B., Canada; Worcester Polytechnic Institute, Worcester, Mass.; Cornell Univ., 1914-. Studied at Univ. of Grenoble, Brussels, Stockholm, Upsala; Scheele Medal, Stockholm, 1937; Nobel Prize in Chemistry, 1946. *Publications:* (with G. Fred Somers) Enzymes, 3rd ed., 1952, also Laboratory Methods of Biochemistry; Ed. (with Prof. Karl Myrbäck) The Enzymes, 4 vols.; about 100 research and review articles dealing principally with enzyme chemistry and analytical methods. *Recreations:* nearly all sports, but especially tennis and ski-ing. *Address:* Savage Hall, Cornell Campus, Ithaca, New York, U.S.A. [*Died* 12 *Aug.* 1955.

SUNDERLAND, Earl of; John David Ivor Spencer-Churchill; *b.* 17 Nov. 1952; *s.* and *heir* of Marquess of Blandford. [*Died* 14 *May* 1955.

SUNDERLAND, J. E., A.R.C.A. (Lond.); retired; *b.* 6 Mar. 1885; *s.* of late J. Sunderland, Oakworth, Keighley; *m.* Maria, *d.* of late D. Wright, Morecambe. *Educ.:* Keighley Boys' Grammar School; Keighley School of Art; Royal College of Art. Design Master, Shipley School of Art, 1908; Headmaster, 1912-19; Principal of Keighley School of Art and Crafts, 1919-27; of Medway School of Art and Crafts, 1927-28; of Sheffield College of Arts and Crafts, 1929-44; Lieut., Royal Garrison Artillery, 1916-19. *Address:* 46 Tom Lane, Fulwood, Sheffield, 10. *T.:* 32337. [*Died* 23 *Dec.* 1956.

SUPOMO, Professor Raden, LL.D.; Indonesian Statesman; *b.* 22 Jan. 1903; *m.* 1929, Bandoro Raden Adjung Kushartati; two *d.* *Educ.:* Universities of Leyden and Djakarta. Presiding Judge, dist. court, Purworedjo, Central Java, 1933-38; Chairman: Cttee. to draft Constitution of Republic of Indonesia, 1945, of Republic of the United States of Indonesia, 1949; Cttee., drafting Provisional Constn. of Republic of (unitarian) Indonesia, 1950; Delegate to numerous confs., 1949-; Chief Delegate with rank of Ambassador to Dutch-Indonesia Conf., The Hague, 1952; Professor of Adat Law: Univ. of Djakarta, 1940-; Gadja Madha Univ., 1947; Minister of Justice, 1945 and 1950; Pres. Univ. of Indonesia, 1951-54; Ambassador to the United Kingdom, 1954-56. Chm. Indonesian Inst. of World Affairs, 1953-54; corresp. mem., Internat. Commn. for Scientific and Cultural History of Mankind, 1952-54; Vice-Pres., Internat. Inst. of Differing Civilisations, 1952-55. Editor, Mimbar Indonesia, 1947-54. Delegate to Dutch-Indonesian Conf., The Hague, 1954; Delegate to Gen. Assembly, U.N., 1950-54. *Publications:* The Reorganisation of the Agrarian System in Central Java, 1927; Adat Law in West Java, 1933; The Relation between the Individual and the Community according to Adat Law, 1941; An Explanation of the Provisional Constitution of the Republic of Indonesia, 1950; An Explanation of the Statute of the Indonesian-Netherlands Union, 1950; The Law System in Indonesia before World War II, 1953; The Law of Civil Procedure in Indonesia, 1958. Articles in various magazines on government, law, culture, politics and international relations. *Recreations:* tennis, swimming and golf. *Address:* c/o Djalan Diponegoro 9, Jakarta, Indonesia. [*Died* 11 *Sept.* 1958.

SURTEES, Major (Henry) Siward (Balliol), J.P., D.L.; *e. s.* of late Henry Edward Surtees and 2nd wife Isabel Mary, *y. d.* of late Francis Adams of Cotswold Grange, Gloucestershire; *b.* 1873; *m.* 1st, 1898, Helen Winifred Muriel (from whom he obtained a divorce, 1928), *o. surv. c.* of late John James Thomson; one *s.* one *d.*; 2nd, 1932, Veronica, *d.* of Capt. Cunliffe, Petton Park, Shropshire, and *widow* of Lt.-Col. Stone, Bedfords, Essex. *Educ.:* Eton. Formerly Capt. 2nd Life Guards; retired Major; High Sheriff of Durham, 1929-1930. *Address:* Redworth Hall, Heighington, Darlington. *Club:* Army and Navy. [*Died* 9 *Feb.* 1955.

SURTEES, Right Rev. William F.; Assistant Bishop, Diocese of Exeter; Canon Residentiary and Precentor of Exeter Cathedral; Suffragan Bishop of Crediton, 1930-54; *b.* 1871; 3rd *s.* of late A. W. Surtees, Dinsdale-on-Tees, Co. Durham; unmarried. *Educ.:* Bedford Grammar School; King's College, Cambridge. Deacon, 1899; Priest, 1900; Assistant Curate, Lythe, 1899-1901; All Saints', Leeds, 1901-06; Rector of Sampford Courtenay, 1906-12; Vicar of S. Simon's, Plymouth, 1912-25; Archdeacon of Exeter, 1925-30. *Address:* 52 Wonford Road, Exeter. [*Died* 23 *March* 1956.

SURVEYER, Hon. Edouard-Fabre; *b.* Montreal, 24 March 1875; *s.* of L. J. A. Surveyer and Hectorine Fabre; *m.* 1906, Elodie (*d.* 1953), *d.* of Edmund Barnard, Q.C.; one *s.* two *d.* *Educ.:* Coll. Sainte-Marie, Montreal; Laval Univ.; McGill Univ. Admitted to Bar, 1896; K.C. 1909; Lecturer, McGill University, 1905-16; Prof. McGill University, 1916-40; Judge of the Superior Court, 1920-55; retired 1955. Lecturer before Academy of International Law in the Peace Palace, The Hague, 1935; Representative of the Province of Quebec on the Commission of Sites and Monuments of Canada since 1933. Officier d'Académie, 1909; Officier d'Instruction publique, 1914; Chevalier of the Legion of Honour, 1928; Knight of the Crown of Italy, 1938; Hon. Doctor of Laws, University of Louisiana, 1938, Univ. of Montreal, 1954. F.R.S.C. 1930. *Publications:* Les Députés au Premier Parlement du Bas-Canada (with F. J. Audet), 1946; Le Centenaire du Barreau de Montréal (with Pierre Beullac, Q.C.), 1949; many law works, addresses, pamphlets on historical and literary subjects, in English and French. *Address:* 128 Maplewood Avenue, Outremont, Montreal, Canada. *Clubs:* Canadian, University, Montreal, Pen and Pencil, P.E.N., Universitaire (Montreal); Union Inter-Alliée (Paris). [*Died* 20 *May* 1957.

SUTCLIFFE, Sir Harold, Kt. *cr.* 1953; *b.* December 1897; *e. s.* of late William Henry Sutcliffe, Solicitor, Brearley House, Luddenden Foot, and Hebden Bridge, Yorks; *m.* 1926, Theodora (from whom he obt. a div., 1947), *o. d.* of late Canon Cochrane, Yardley, Warwicks.; one *s.* three *d.*; *m.* 1948, Eileen, *d.* of late Lt.-Col. J. T. Field, The 24th Regt. *Educ.:* Harrow; Oriel Coll., Oxford, M.A. Served European War with R.F.A., 1917-18; called to Bar, Inner Temple, 1925; North Eastern Circuit. M.P. (C.) Royton Division of Lancaster, 1931-1950, Heywood and Royton Division, 1950-55; Parl. Private Sec. to William Mabane, when Parl. Sec. to Ministry of Home Security, Dec. 1939 to June 1942, and to Osbert Peake, when Parl. Under-Sec., Home Office, 1940-44; when Finl. Sec. Treasury, 1944-45; and when Minister of Nat. Insurance (now Min. of Pensions and Nat. Insurance), 1951-55; Mem. Bd. of Governors, Roy. Nat. Orthop. Hosp. Jt. Hon. Treas. Yorkshire Council of British Empire Cancer Campaign. *Recreation:* golf. *Address:* Great Fosters, Egham, Surrey; May Royd, Hebden Bridge, Yorks; 3 Hare Court, Temple, E.C. *T.:* Central 3344. *Clubs:* Carlton, Bath, International Sportsmen's. [*Died* 20 *Jan.* 1958.

SUTER, Captain Roy Neville, C.B.E. 1944; D.S.O. 1918; R.N., retired; *b.* 1884; *s.* of late Arthur Suter; *m.* 1922, Edith Godwin, *d.* of late Walter Edwin Birchenough; one *s.* Served S. Africa, 1900-1; Persian Gulf 1912; European War, 1914-18 (despatches, D.S.O.); S. Russia, 1920-21; retired list, 1930; War of 1939-45, Commodore 2nd Cl. 1944-46. *Club:* United Service. [*Died* 10 *June* 1958.

SUTHERLAND, Millicent, Duchess of, (Lady Millicent Fanny St. Clair-Erskine); *e. d.* of 4th Earl of Rosslyn; *m.* 1st, 4th Duke of Sutherland (*d.* 1913); one *s.*; 2nd, 1914, Maj. P. D. FitzGerald, D.S.O. (marriage dissolved 1919; he died 1933); 3rd, 1919, Lt.-Col. G. E. Hawes, D.S.O. (*d.* 1945). Widely travelled; visited U.S.A. 7 times. Ex-President, Potteries Cripples' Guild and Scottish Home Industries Assoc.; President Nicholson Institute, Leek, 1897. Directed a Red Cross front-line ambulance, 1914-18; subsequently made her home in France. French Croix de Guerre; Belgian 1st Class Red Cross; Silver Medal from Société Botanique et d'Acclimatation, Paris, for her interest in, and contribution of, plants, 1950. *Publications:* How I Spent my Twentieth Year, 1889; One Hour and the Next, 1899; The Winds of the World; Seven Love Stories, 1902; The Conqueror (play), 1905; Six Weeks at the War, 1914; That Fool of a Woman, 1925; many articles and short stories. *Address:* 55 rue Geoffroy, St. Hilaire, Paris V^e^. [*Died* 20 *Aug.* 1955.

SUTHERLAND, Sir Arthur Munro, 1st Bt., *cr.* 1921; K.B.E., *cr.* 1920; D.C.L. 1932; D.L. Northumberland; J.P. Newcastle on Tyne; Chairman Newcastle Commercial Exchange; *b.* 2 Oct. 1867; 3rd *s.* of Benjamin John Sutherland, Newcastle on Tyne; *m.* 1st, 1893, Fanny Linda (*d.* 1937), 2nd *d.* of Robert Hood Haggie; two *s.* one *d.* (and *e. s.* decd.); 2nd, 1938, Ella Bertha Louise (*d.* 1940), *widow* of W. R. Heatley. *Educ.:* Newcastle Royal Grammar School. Shipowner and coal exporter; Chairman of Sutherland Steamship Co. Ltd., Donkin & Co. Ltd., Barnett Bros. Ltd.; Director, John Bowes and Partners Ltd., President: Chamber of Shipping, 1930; Shipping Federation Ltd., 1938-50; Newcastle and Gateshead Chamber of Commerce, 1932; Chairman Tyne Improvement Commis-

sion; Member, Feltmakers and Shipwright Companies; Member of Committee of Lloyd's Register of Shipping; Deputy Lord Mayor of Newcastle, 1916; Sheriff of Newcastle, 1917; Lord Mayor of Newcastle on Tyne, 1919; High Sheriff of Northumberland, 1943; Knight Commander with star of the order of St. Olaf (Norway). *Recreations:* motoring, fishing, golf. *Heir:* *s.* Benjamin Ivan [*b.* 1901; *m.* 1st, 1927, Marjorie Constance Daniel (divorced 1944), *d.* of Frederic William Brewer, O.B.E., Newcastle on Tyne; two *s.*; 2nd, 1944, Margaret Owen; three *s.*]. *Address:* Thurso House, Newcastle on Tyne. *T.A.:* Sutherland, Newcastle. *T.:* Jesmond 863, Newcastle; Hethpool, Northumberland. *Clubs:* Bath; Union (Newcastle).
[*Died* 29 *March* 1953.

SUTHERLAND, D. M.; late Secretary and Director of Propaganda, Anti-Socialist and Anti-Communist Union; *b.* Edinburgh; *m.* Dorothy, *d.* of H. E. Dehane; one *d.* *Educ.:* George Watson's College and Edinburgh Univ. London Editor, Manchester Daily Dispatch; Editor-in-Chief, Sheffield Daily Telegraph and allied publications; Editor of the Pall Mall Gazette, 1915-23; Editor Evening Standard, 1914-15. *Address:* 5 Springfield Road, St. John's Wood, N.W.8. *Club:* Constitutional. [*Died* 13 *Dec.* 1951.

SUTHERLAND, Halliday Gibson; Hon. Physician and Member of Council, Queen Alexandra Sanatorium Fund; Mem., Tuberculosis Assoc. and Past Pres. Tuberculosis Soc. of Great Britain; Hon. Fellow Mark Twain Society of America; Chairman Anglo-Spanish League of Friendship; Member of Council Guild of St. Luke; F.R.S.L.; *b.* Glasgow, 24 June 1882; *e. s.* of late J. F. Sutherland, M.D., of Board of Control for Scotland, and Jane, *d.* of Rev. John Mackay, Free Church Manse, Lybster, Caithness; *m.* 1920, Muriel, *d.* of late J. F. Fitzpatrick, Highgate; four *s.* one *d.* (and one *s.* killed in War of 1939-45, R.A.F.). *Educ.:* Glasgow High School, and Merchiston Castle School, Edinburgh (essay prizes, including Sir Walter Scott Prize open to all Edin. schools); Universities of Aberdeen, Dublin and Edinburgh. Graduated M.B., Ch.B., 1906; M.D. (with Honours) Edin., 1908; Bacteriologist, Liverpool Hospital for Diseases of the Chest, 1906; Assistant in British Clinic, Huelva, Spain, 1907; Clinical Assistant, Royal Edinburgh Asylum, 1908; Resident Physician, Royal Victoria Hospital, Edinburgh, 1909; Medical Superintendent, Westmorland Sanatorium, 1910; Medical Officer, St. Marylebone Tuberculosis Dispensary, 1911-14; Temporary Surgeon, R.N., and Captain, R.A.F., 1914-18; Assistant Physician, Royal Chest Hospital, and Physician, St. Marylebone Hospital, 1919; Deputy Commissioner of Medical Services (Tuberculosis) for South-Western England and Wales, 1920-25; Assistant Medical Officer, L.C.C., 1926; Asst. M.O.H., Coventry, 1941; Executive Medical Officer, Mass Radiography, Birmingham, 1943; Medical Director, Mass Radiography Centre, Birmingham, and Consultant, National Health Service, 1948-51; Lectr., B.M.A., 1952; founded Regent's Park Bandstand School, the first open-air school in a London park, 1912; discovered Etiology of cerebro-spinal fever, 1915; wrote and directed the first anti-tuberculosis silent film, The Story of John McNeil, 1918. Lecture tour, Australia and N.Z., 1939-40. Contested (Lab.) Scottish Universities, General Election, 1945. Guest of Spanish Govt. for three months, 1946. Knight-Commander of the Order of Isabel the Catholic, 1954; Pope John XXI Medallist, 1955. *Publications: Medical:* Control and Eradication of Tuberculosis, 1912; Pulmonary Tuberculosis in General Practice, 1916; The Tuberculin Handbook, 1935; Ed. J. F. Sutherland's First Aid to Injured and Sick, 46th Edition, 1957; many contributions to medical press, Great Britain and America. The Arches of the Years (autobiography to end of Great War), 1932 (35 English editions; trans. into 8 European langs.); A Time to Keep (further autobiography), 1934; Laws of Life, 1935; In My Path, 1936; Lapland Journey, 1938; Hebridean Journey, 1939; Southward Journey, 1942; Control of Life, 1944; Spanish Journey, 1948; Irish Journey, 1956; Introduction to Religio Medici (Dents Everyman Series), 1956. *Recreations:* fishing, shooting, sailing and travel. *Address:* 5 Stafford Terrace, W.8. *T.:* Western 7040. [*Died* 19 *April* 1960.

SUTHERLAND, Sir John Donald, Kt., *cr.* 1935; C.B.E. 1919; LL.D., F.R.S.E.; Chevalier of the Legion of Honour; Officer of Order of Leopold; *b.* Inverness, 10 Nov. 1865; *s.* of John Sutherland, County Assessor for Ross-shire, and Mary Hildyard Murray Hosack; *m.* 1892, Kate, *d.* of Rev. Andrew Holmes Belcher, Rector of Fasque. *Educ.:* Inverness Acad.; Edinburgh Univ. Qualified in law, 1892; Notary Public, 1894; Member Scottish Advisory Committee on Forestry; also Reconstruction Sub-Committee on Afforestation; Assist. Forestry Commissioner for Scotland, 1919-34; Forestry Commissioner, 1934-43; Col., Royal Engineers, 1917-19 (despatches twice); Assist. Director of Forestry in France, 1917-19; Member of Board of Agriculture for Scotland, 1912-20; Small Holdings Commissioner, 1912-17. *Publications:* various on afforestation, agriculture and rural industries. *Recreation:* golf. *Address:* 3 Eglinton Crescent, Edinburgh. *Club:* University (Edinburgh). [*Died Aug.* 1952.

SUTTON, Ralph, O.B.E.; Q.C. 1935; Reader in Common Law to the Council of Legal Education; Wales and Chester Circuit; *b.* 1881. *Educ.:* Shrewsbury; Oriel College, Oxford. Called to Bar, Lincoln's Inn, 1905; Bencher, 1938. Judge of the Admiralty. Court of the Cinque Ports. *Address:* Carylls, Faygate, Horsham, Sussex.
[*Died* 8 *Oct.* 1960.

SWABEY, Vice-Admiral Sir George Thomas Carlisle Parker, K.B.E., *cr.* 1946; C.B. 1930; D.S.O. 1916; *b.* 1881; *s.* of late Thomas Swabey, of Woodcote, Woburn Sands; *m.* Lois Mary Elsa, *d.* of late Samuel Forde Ridley; one *s.* (and one killed in action) one *d.* Entered R.N. 1894; Lieutenant, 1901; Commander, 1913; Capt. 1918; served in Dardanelles, 1915-16, as Naval Observation Officer (despatches, D.S.O., Legion of Honour); Captain, Royal Naval College, Greenwich; First Naval Member Royal New Zealand Naval Board, 1926-29; Naval A.D.C. to the King, 1929; Rear-Adm. and retired list, 1929; Vice-Adm., retired, 1935. Served in War of 1939-45 as Commodore of Convoy, 1940-41; as Flag-Officer-in-charge, Portland, 1942-44; as Naval Officer-in-Charge, Leith, 1945. United States Legion of Merit, 1946. *Address:* Home Farm House, Eartham, Chichester. *T.:* Slindon 208.
[*Died* 9 *Feb.* 1952.

SWAIN, Very Rev. George Lill, M.A., Dean of Limerick, 1929-53; *b.* 1870; *m.* 1904, Isobel, *y. d.* of Ven. F. C. Hamilton, M.A., Archdeacon of Limerick; two *s.* two *d.* *Educ.:* Arlington House School; Trinity College, Dublin. [*Died* 26 *April* 1955.

SWAIN, Professor James, C.B. 1917; C.B.E. 1919; J.P. Co. Somerset; M.S.; M.D. Lond.; F.R.C.S. Eng.; Emeritus Professor of Surgery, University of Bristol; Honorary Consulting Surgeon to Bristol Royal Infirmary since 1922; Hon. Member, Bristol Medico-Chirurgical Society (President, 1909-10); Colonel R.A.M.C., T. (ret.); *s.* of late George Swain; *m.* 1899, Hilda May, 6th *d.* of A. J. Harrison, J.P., M.B., Lond.; one *s.* one *d.* *Educ.:* Westminster Hospital Medical School. Graduated M.B. Lond. (Honours), 1885; Assistant-Surgeon, Bristol Royal Infirmary, 1892-1902; Surgeon, 1902-22; Professor of Surgery in University College, Bristol, 1897-1909, and in the University of Bristol, 1909-20; served as Consultant Surgeon to British Forces in France, European War (despatches); Consultant Surgeon to the Troops serving in the Southern Command, 1914-19 (Colonel, Army Medical Service); one of the British delegates to Inter-Allies Congress on treatment of wounds in War, held in Paris, 1917-19. *Publications:* Associate-Editor Bristol Medico-Chirurgical Journal, 1897-1924; Editor 6th ed. of Greig Smith's Abdominal Surgery (2 vols.); various articles on surgical subjects in Encyclopædia Medica and other publications. *Address:* Wyndham House, Easton-in-Gordano, Somerset. *T.:* Pill 31238. [*Died* 6 *Jan.* 1951.

SWALES, A. B.; late Executive Councilman to the Amalgamated Engineering Union; Vice-Chairman of the General Council of the T.U.C. *Address:* 110 Peckham Road, S.E.15. [*Died* 26 *Sept.* 1952.

SWALES, John Kirby, C.B.E. 1942; M.C., M.Inst.C.E.; formerly General Manager and Engineer of the Sheffield Corporation Waterworks; *b.* 31 July 1879; *m.* 1910, Emily Florence Marr; one *s.* *Educ.:* Leeds Boys' Modern School; Leeds University. Articled to late Thos. Hewson, M.Inst.C.E., then City and Water Engineer, Leeds; Resident Engineer on Ure Valley Scheme of water supply for Leeds; Water Eng. and Manager, Bolton Corp., 1919-30. *Address:* 19 Stepney Drive, Scarborough. *T.:* 77. [*Died* 20 *Oct.* 1956.

SWAN, Capt. Donald C.; *see* Cameron-Swan.

SWAN, Rear-Admiral (S) Edgar Bocquet, C.B.E. 1925; R.N. (retired); *b.* 1874; *s.* of late Edgar A. Swan, Barrister, London; *m.* 1914, Edith Ellen, *d.* of late Rev. Canon Francis Huyshe of Clysthydon. Served European War, 1914-19. *Address:* Surf, Saunton, Braunton, N. Devon. [*Died* 16 *Jan.* 1951.

SWAN, John Edmund; *b.* 1877; *m.* 1902, Alice, *d.* of Henry Beatham Dipton; miner and check-weighman; Miners' Agent; General Secretary Durham Miners' Assoc., retired 31 Dec. 1945; M.P. (Lab.) Barnard Castle Division of Durham, Dec. 1918-22. *Publications:* The Mad Miner; People of the Night, 1937; play, On the Minimum, 1939. *Address:* 12 St. Cuthbert's Avenue, Blackhill, Co. Durham. [*Died* 9 *Feb.* 1956.

SWANSTON, John Francis Alexander; Chairman of the English Association of American Bond and Share Holders Ltd. Member of London Stock Exchange; Senior Partner, Smithers & Co.; *b.* 9 May 1877; 3rd *s.* of John Alexander Swanston, Marshall Meadows, Berwick-on-Tweed; *m.* 1906, Florence, *er. d.* of Sir Alfred Smithers. *Educ.:* Loretto School; Trinity College, Oxford. Served European War, 1914-18, Major i/c 262 Machine Gun Company. *Recreations:* formerly Rugby football (Capt. Oxf. Rugby XV, Dec. 1900), cricket, golf. *Address:* Letts Green, Knockholt, Kent. *T.:* Knockholt 2134. *Clubs:* Carlton, City of London; Hon. Co. of Edinburgh Golfers; Royal St. George's Golf (Sandwich). [*Died* 4 *Feb.* 1958.

SWENY, Captain William Halpin Paterson, C.B.E. 1918; R.D.; R.N.R. (retd.); *b.* 1871; *s.* of late Rev. Eugene Sweny; *m.* 1st, 1895, Adèle Mabel Annie (*d.* 1921), *d.* of F. Pearson; 2nd, 1923, Nora, *d.* of late Capt. Charles Cottew, R.N. Marine Superintendent P. and O. Company; retired, 1943. *Address:* 57 Old Road East, Gravesend. [*Died* 7 *Aug.* 1951.

SWIFT, Herbert Walker, M.A., D.Sc. (Eng.); M.I.Mech.E.; formerly Professor of Engineering in University of Sheffield: retired, 1955; *b.* 15 Dec. 1894; *m.* 1924, Maisie Hobbins; two *d.* *Educ.:* Christ's Hospital; St. John's College, Cambridge. Commissioned active service, 1915-18 (wounded, despatches); Chief engineer to Wm. Hollins and Co., 1920-22; Demonstrator and Lecturer, Leeds University, 1922-26; Head of Department of Mechanical Engineering, Bradford Technical College, 1926-1936; Thomas Hawksley Medallist, I.Mech.E.; Clayton Prizeman, 1953. *Publications:* Technical papers on mechanical engineering subjects, etc. [*Died* 14 *Oct.* 1960.

SWINBURNE, Sir James, 9th Bt., *cr.* 1660; F.R.S.; M.Inst.C.E.; consulting engineer; *b.* Inverness, 28 Feb. 1858; 3rd *s.* of late Capt. T. A. Swinburne, R.N., of Eilean Shona, Inverness-shire; *S.* kinsman, 1934; *m.* 1st, 1886, Ellen (*d.* 1893), *d.* of R. H. Wilson, M.D., Gateshead; one *s.* (and one *s.* decd.); 2nd, 1898, Lilian, *d.* of Sir Godfrey Carey, Guernsey; one *d.* (and one *d.* decd.). *Educ.:* Clifton College. Trained as engineer, Tyneside, 1874-81; did purely electrical work, 1881-94, since then practised as consulting engineer; President of Institution of Electrical Engineers, 1902-1903; Past President Faraday Society. *Publications:* Population and the Social Problem; books, papers before Societies, and articles in technical journals. *Recreations:* music, sociology. *Heir:* *s.* Spearman Charles Swinburne, M.R.C.S., L.R.C.P.; [*b.* 8 Jan. 1893; *m.* 1st, 1913, Irene Gertrude (*d.* 1935), *d.* of G. Travers; 2nd, 1935, Millicent Agnes, *d.* of late Lt.-Col. E. H. Montrésor, Roy. Sussex Regt., and *widow* of G. R. Fenton. *Educ.:* Tonbridge; Edinburgh University. Maj. R.A.M.C. (T.A. Reserve). Served European War, 1915-17; War of 1939-45]. *Address:* Balholm Grange, Branksome Park, Bournemouth. [*Died* 30 *March* 1958.

SWINSTEAD, Felix Gerald, F.R.A.M.; formerly Professor of Pianoforte, Royal Academy of Music, retired 1955; *b.* 25 June 1880; *s.* of Alfred H. Swinstead; *m.* 1912, Evelyn Dawkin (*d.* 1954); two *s.* one *d.* *Educ.:* Private. Thalberg Scholarship, 1898, and studied with Matthay and Corder; gave many recitals in London and Provinces; examined in Canada, S. Africa, Australia, W. Indies, etc.; toured Australia and New Zealand, 1938. *Publications:* Sonata for Violin and Piano, Suite for Piano and Strings (Scarlatti); Technique with a Purpose; about 200 pianoforte pieces. *Recreations:* bridge, tennis, motoring. *Address:* 2 Loudoun Road, St. John's Wood, N.W.8. *T.:* Primrose 2488. [*Died* 14 *Aug.* 1959.

SWINTON, Major-General Sir Ernest (Dunlop), K.B.E., *cr.* 1923; C.B. 1917; D.S.O. 1900; R.E.; M.A.; Chichele Professor of Military History, Oxford University, 1925-1939; *b.* 21 Oct. 1868; *m.* 1897, Grace Louisa, 2nd *d.* of late Major Sir Edward G. Clayton; two *s.* *Educ.:* Rugby; Cheltenham. Entered Army, 1888; Captain, 1899; Major, 1906; Lt.-Col. 1915; served South Africa, 1899-1902 (despatches, Queen's medal 3 clasps, King's medal 2 clasps, D.S.O.); European War, 1914-1917 (despatches thrice, Commander Legion of Honour, Bt. Col.); Assistant Secretary Committee of Imperial Defence and War Cabinet; journey through the United States, speaking about the War, 1918; late Controller of Information Department of Civil Aviation; originated the Tanks and raised the Heavy Section M.G.C., 1916; Col. Comdt., Royal Tanks Corps, 1934-38. *Publications:* The Study of War, 1926; Eye-Witness, 1932; under the pseudonym of Backsight-Forethought, The Defence of Duffer's Drift, 1904; under the pseudonym Ole-Luk-Oie, The Green Curve, 1909; The Great Tab Dope, 1915: A Year Ago, 1916; transl. of Galet's Albert, King of the Belgians in the Great War, 1931; of Le Fèvre's An Eastern Odyssey, 1935. *Address:* All Souls College, Oxford. *Club:* United Service. [*Died* 15 *Jan.* 1951.

SWITHINBANK, Bernard Winthrop, C.B.E. 1938; *b.* Denmark Park, 4 Oct. 1884; *er. s.* of Rev. H. S. Swithinbank and Amy, *d.* of Admiral G. T. S. Winthrop; *m.* 1917, Dorothea, *d.* of Rev. E. H. Molesworth; one *s.* one *d.* *Educ.:* Aysgarth

School, Newton-le-Willows; Eton; Balliol College, Oxford. Appointed to Indian Civil Service (Burma), Oct. 1909; Commissioner, Pegu Division, 1933-42; Adviser to the Secretary of State for Burma, 1942; retired, 1946. *Address:* Four Acres, Caring Lane, Bearsted, Kent. *Club:* Athenæum.

[*Died* 25 *July* 1958.

SYDENHAM, Engineer-Rear-Admiral Ernest Dickerson, C.B.E. 1927; Royal Navy, retired; *b.* Plymouth, 1875; *s.* of Lewis John Sydenham and Lavinia Goldsworthy Sydenham; *m.* Edith Steele, *d.* of Thomas Bailie, J.P., Westport, N.Z.; no *c.* *Educ.:* Royal Naval Engineering College Keyham; R. Naval College, Greenwich. Admiralty Representative for Coal Supply, Cardiff, 1902-5; Australasia, 1909-13; H.M.S. Highflyer, 1913-17; Director of Engineering, Naval Board of the Commonwealth of Australia, 1923-31; retired list, 1931. *Publications:* contributions on Naval Life to Melbourne Argus, 1925-27, under pen-name of Trident. *Recreation:* golf. *Address:* Westport, New Zealand.

[*Died* 13 *June* 1952.

SYDNOR, Charles Sackett, M.A. (Oxon.); Dean of Graduate School of Arts and Sciences, Duke University, since 1952; *b.* Augusta, Georgia, 21 July 1898; *e. s.* of Giles Granville Sydnor, and Evelyn Aiken Sackett; *m.* 1924, Betty Brown; two *s.* *Educ.:* Darlington School; Hampden-Sydney College (A.B., 1918); Johns Hopkins University (Ph.D., 1923); Litt.D. (hon.), Washington and Lee Univ., 1948, Princeton Univ., 1953; LL.D. (hon.), Davidson Coll., 1953; Professor of History and Political Science, Hampden-Sydney Coll., 1923-25; Professor of history, Univ. of Mississippi, 1925-36; Associate Professor of History, Duke Univ., 1936-38; Professor since 1938, and Chairman of Department of History since 1952; Harold Vyvyan Harmsworth Professor of American History, Univ. of Oxford, and Fellow of Queen's College, 1950-51. President Southern Historical Assoc., 1939; President N. Carolina Literary and Historical Assoc., 1949-50. Member: advisory cttee., Historical Division, Dept. of the Army, U.S.A.; of Council, Inst. of Early American History and Culture. Lecturer, Salzburg Seminar in American Studies, 1951; member editorial boards, Jl. of Southern History and South Atlantic Quarterly. *Publications:* Slavery in Mississippi, 1933; A Gentleman of the Old Natchez Region: Benjamin L. C. Wailes, 1938; The Development of Southern Sectionalism, 1819-1848, 1948; Gentlemen Freeholders: Political Practices in Washington's Virginia, 1952; contrib. to Dictionary of American Biography, and to historical jls. *Address:* 116 Pinecrest Road, Durham, N.C., U.S.A.

[*Died* 2 *March* 1954.

SYKES, Ernest, B.A.; late Secretary to Committee of London Clearing Bankers, of the British Bankers Association and of the Foreign Exchange Committee; Secretary of the Institute of Bankers, 1905-35; *b.* 13 Sept. 1870; *e. s.* of late George Cawthorne Sykes, Banbury; *m.* 1899, Amy Elizabeth (*d.* 1952), *d.* of late Joseph Eagleston, M.A., Oxford; one *d.* *Educ.:* Owen's School, Islington; Oxford University. *Publications:* various contributions to periodicals on banking and economic subjects. *Address:* Barramore, Solsbro Road, Torquay.

[*Died* 4 *May* 1958.

SYKES, Major-General Rt. Hon. Sir Frederick (Hugh), P.C., 1928; G.C.S.I., *cr.* 1934; G.C.I.E., *cr.* 1928; G.B.E., *cr.* 1919; K.C.B., *cr.* 1919; C.M.G. 1916; K.J.St.J. 1936; *m.* 1920, Isabel (Kaisar-i-Hind Medal of the First Class, 1934), *d.* of late Right Hon. A. Bonar Law; one *s.* 15th (The King's) Hussars; 2nd Lieut. 1901; Lieut. 1903; Capt. 1908; Bt. Major, 1913; Bt. Lt.-Col. 1915; Bt. Col. 1918; Maj.-General 1918; employed with West African Regt., 1903-04; Intelligence Br. India, 1905-06; Attaché German manœuvres, 1907; p.s.c. 1908-09; G.S.O. War Office, 1911-12; Comdr. R.F.C., Military Wing, 1912, which he raised and commanded till 1914; G.S.O. 1st Grade, France, 1914; sometime commanding R.F.C. France, 1914-1915; temp. Colonel (2nd Commandant) Royal Marines; and Wing Captain R.F.C. (Naval Wing) whilst commanding Royal Naval Air Service in E. Mediterranean, 1915-1916; A.A. and Q.M.G., 4th Mounted Division, 1916; A.A.G. War Office, 1916; Brig.-Gen. and Deputy Director, War Office, 1917; Brig.-Gen. General Staff, Supreme War Council, Versailles, 1917-18; Maj.-Gen. and Chief of the Air Staff, 1918-19; Chief of British Air Section of the Peace Conf., Paris; First Controller-General of Civil Aviation, 1919-22; M.P. (U.) Hallam Division of Sheffield, 1922-28; Governor of Bombay, 1928-33; M.P. (U.) Central Div. of Nottingham, 1940-45; served as scout Imperial Yeomanry Scouts, and Lieut. C.-in-C.'s Bodyguard in South African War, 1900-01 (severely wounded, Queen's medal with 4 clasps); European War, 1914-18 (despatches five times, Bt. Lt.-Col., Bt. Col., Maj.-Gen., C.M.G., K.C.B.); Member of Imperial War Cabinet; Ritter Kreuz, Germany, 1902; Croix de Comdr. de la Légion d'Honneur; Croix de Comdr. de l'Ordre de Leopold, Belgium; Vladimir of Russia; D.S.M. (U.S.A.); Order of the Rising Sun, Japan; Grand Cross of the Order of the Lion, Persia; obtained ballooning certificate, 1904; learnt to fly, 1910, and obtained pilot's certificate (No. 95), 1911; Lees-Knowles Lecturer at Cambridge Univ., 1921; Chairman of Government Committees on Meteorological Service, 1920-22, Wireless Communications and on Broadcasting, 1923; Chairman of Government Broadcasting Board, 1923-27; Chairman, Miners Welfare Commission, 1934-1946; Member, Post Office Advisory Council, since 1934; Hon. Treasurer, British Sailors Society, since 1934; Chairman, Royal Empire Society, 1938-41; Member of Government Licensing Board for Air Transport, 1938-39; Vice-Pres. Royal Empire Society since 1941; Pres. East India Assoc.; Vice-Pres. Royal India Soc.; Chairman, Vice-Chairman or member of other Govt. Committees; Chairman or Director of various companies. *Publications:* Aviation in Peace and War, 1922; From Many Angles (Autobiography), 1942; Roads to Recovery, 1944; articles on politics, communications, defence, transport, mining, air and other subjects in various Reviews, etc. *Address:* 1 York House, Chelsea, S.W.3; Conock Manor, nr. Devizes, Wilts. *Club:* United Service.

[*Died* 30 *Sept.* 1954.

SYKES, Rev. Sir Frederic John, 8th Bt., *cr.*1781; *b.* 10 Nov. 1876; *s.* of Rev. E. J. Sykes, *g.-g.s.* of 2nd Bt. and Constance Mary, *d.* of Edward Brown; *S.* brother, 1934. *Educ.:* Chichester Theological College. Deacon, 1902; priest, 1904; Rector of Butterleigh, 1927-36; Vicar of Stoke Canon, near Exeter, Devon, 1936-46. *Heir: cousin*, Francis Godfrey [*b.* 27 Aug. 1907; *m.* 1934, Eira Betty (*née* Badcock); one *s.* one *d.*]. *Address:* Hoopers House, Days Lane, Exminster, Devon.

[*Died* 17 *March* 1956.

SYKES, Sir John Charles Gabriel, K.C.B., *cr.* 1919 (C.B. 1908); Member of Council for State Management Districts under the Licensing Act 1921, since 1921; J.P. County of London, and Chairman St. Margaret's Division, 1925-50; *b.* 3 Aug. 1869; *s.* of late John Sykes, of the Education Department; *m.* 1st, 1898, Maud (*d.* 1914), *d.* of C. Faulkner Dobell, of Whittington Court, Glos.; 2nd, 1916, Ethel Mary (*d.* 1935), *widow* of Walter D. Dobell; 3rd, 1946, Nancy, *widow* of Rev. Percy Dearmer, D.D., Canon of Westminster. *Educ.:* Winchester; New College, Oxford. Entered Education Department, 1893; Assist. Secretary to Board of Education, 1904; Secretary of Departmental

Committee on future organisation of Royal College of Science, Royal School of Mines, etc., 1904-6; Member of Governing Body of Imperial College of Science and Technology, 1907-17; Secretary to the Central Control Board (Liquor Traffic), 1915-21; joint editor of the Law of Public Education in England and Wales. *Address:* 46 Warwick Square, S.W.1. *T.:* Victoria 4114. *Clubs:* Athenæum; Royal and Ancient Golf (St. Andrews).
[*Died* 23 *April* 1952.

SYLVAINE, Vernon; *b.* 9 Aug. 1897; *s.* of Dr. John Conrad Scotchburn and Rhoda Sophia Winter; *m.* 1924, Marion Barlow; one *d.* *Educ.:* College of St. Francis Xavier, Mayfield, Sussex. European War, 1914-1918, joined Queen's Westminster Rifles, 1914; commissioned, 1915, and served, Belgium, Lieut. Somerset L.I.; invalided from service, 1917. Stage career, as actor, playwright and producer, in London and New York, 1917-. *Author of plays:* The Phantom Fear, His Majesty's, 1928; The Road of Poplars, London Coliseum, 1930; And A Woman Passed By, Duke of York's, 1935; Aren't Men Beasts, Strand, 1936; A Spot of Bother, Strand, 1937; Worth A Million, Saville, 1939; Nap Hand, Aldwych, 1940; Women Aren't Angels, Strand, 1940; Warn That Man, Garrick, 1941; Murder for a Valentine, Lyric, 1944; Madame Louise, Garrick, 1945; The Anonymous Lover, Duke of York's, 1947; Quiet in the Forest, Q, 1947; One Wild Oat, Garrick, 1948; I Married Two Men (Repertory Players), Strand, 1950; Will Any Gentleman?, Strand, 1950; There's Something in the Cellar!, tour, 1951; As Long As They're Happy, Garrick, 1953; Three Times a Day, tour prior to London, 1955. *Recreation:* deep-sea fishing. *Club:* Savage.
[*Died* 22 *Nov.* 1957.

SYMES, John Odery, M.D., D.P.H., M.R.C.S., L.R.C.P.; retired; Consulting Physician to the Bristol General Hospital and Cossham Memorial Hospital; Ex-President Bristol Medical Chirurgical Society and Bath and Bristol branch of the British Medical Association; Major R.A.M.C. Territorial, retired; *b.* 1867; *s.* of late Robert Symes of Taunton; *m.* Martha Ramsay, *d.* of J. Dunnachie, J.P., Glenboig, Scotland; three *d.* *Educ.:* University College, London; St. Mary's Hospital. Late House Surgeon and House Physician St. Mary's Hospital, London; resident medical officer to the London Fever Hospital; late Physician to Clifton College and Lecturer in Clinical Medicine, University of Bristol. *Publications:* The Rheumatic Diseases; a short history of the Bristol General Hospital; Erythema Nodosum. *Recreations:* golf and fishing. *Address:* 6 Pembroke Vale, Clifton, Bristol. *T.:* Bristol 33507.
[*Died* 25 *March* 1951.

SYMES-THOMPSON, Henry Edmund; Consulting Physician to the Royal Chest Hospital, London; F.R.S.M.; *s.* of late Edmund Symes-Thompson, M.D., F.R.C.P.; *m.* Caroline, *d.* of Rev. R. J. Tacon, M.A., J.P.; one *s.* one *d.* *Educ.:* Winchester; Christ's College, Cambridge. M.A. 1898; M.D. 1903; M.R.C.P. 1903; late Physician to: the Royal National Hospital for Consumption, Ventnor; the Royal Northern Hospital; S.P.G.; and the Artists' Annuity and Benevolent Funds. *Publications:* medical. *Address:* Finmere House, Oxon. *T.:* Finmere 268. *Club:* Athenæum. [*Died* 18 *Jan.* 1952.

SYMON, Colonel Frank, C.B. 1935; C.M.G. 1916; D.S.O. 1917; late Royal N.Z. Artillery; *b.* 1879; *s.* of Robert Blair Symon, Auckland, N.Z., and Fifeshire, Scotland; *m.* 1912, Mary, *d.* of late George Flux, Wellington, N.Z. Served European War, 1914-18, Gallipoli, Egypt, France and Belgium, 1915-1918 (despatches twice, C.M.G., D.S.O., 1914-1915 Star, two medals); was Hon. A.D.C. to Governor-General of N.Z., 1925-30; A.D.C. (additional) to the King, 1931-36. *Address:* 343 Muritai Rd., Eastbourne, New Zealand. [*Died* 11 *May* 1956.

SYMONDS, (Arthur) Leslie, O.B.E. 1959 (M.B.E. 1945); M.A.; J.P.; *b.* 2 October 1910; *s.* of John Frederick Symonds and Ethel Daisy Symonds of Cambridge; *m.* 1946, Barbara Mary, *d.* of Alfred Pryer and Laura Draycon, Ramsgate; three *s.* two *d.* *Educ.:* Perse and Jesus College, Cambridge. Assistant Master, St. Austell County School for Boys, 1933-40; served with H.M. Forces, 1940-45 (despatches twice, M.B.E.); M.P. (Lab.) Borough of Cambridge, 1945-50. J.P. Cambridge 1957. *Address:* 66 St. Barnabas Rd., Cambridge. *T.:* Cambridge 56352. [*Died* 25 *Feb.* 1960.

SYMONDS, Vice-Admiral Frederick Parland Loder-, C.M.G. 1917; J.P. City of Hereford; D.L. Herefordshire, 1948; R.N. (retired); *b.* May 1876; *o. surv. s.* of late Captain F. C. Loder-Symonds; *m.* 1907, Marion Theresa (*d.* 1940), *o. d.* of late Col. J. G. Y. Wilson, C.B.E.; *m.* 1945, Anne Lilian, *widow* of Brigadier Robert H. Anderson, C.B., C.I.E. Commanded H.M.S. Cleopatra and H.M.S. Dauntless, 1915-18; Director of Navigation, Admiralty, 1921-23; Commanded H.M.S. Emperor of India, 1924; A.D.C. to the King, 1924; Rear-Admiral, 1926; Retired List, 1926; Vice-Adm., retd., 1930. High Sheriff of Herefordshire, 1945-1946. *Address:* Waldrist, Hereford. *Club:* Junior United Service. [*Died* 24 *Nov.* 1952.

SYMONDS, Rev. Henry Herbert; Vice-Pres. Friends of Lake District; lately Drafting Sec., Standing Committee on National Parks and member of Lake District Planning Board; and of National Parks Commission; Chairman, North Wales (Hydro-Electricity) Protection Committee; Vice-President Ramblers' Association and Merseyside Youth Hostels Association; *b.* 1885; *m.* 1st, 1911, C. Gwendolen W. Watson (*d.* 1937); one *s.* two *d.*; 2nd, 1938, Ruth B. W. Williams. *Educ.:* Rugby (Senior Exhibitioner); Oriel College, Oxford (Classical Scholar); 1st Class Classical Mods.; 1st Class Greats; Assistant Master, Clifton College, 1909-12; Form Master, Rugby Classical Sixth (Upper Bench), to 1922; Headmaster of the King's School, Chester, to 1924; Headmaster of Liverpool Institute School, Liverpool, 1924-35; sometime Mem. Council Modern Churchmen's Union. *Publications:* Walking in the Lake District, 1933; Afforestation in the Lake District, 1937. *Recreation:* rescuing scraps of natural beauty. *Address:* The Flags, Cartmel, Grange-over-Sands, Lancs. *T.:* Cartmel 272.
[*Died* 28 *Dec.* 1958.

SYMONDS, Leslie; *see* Symonds, A. L.

SYMONDS, Robert Wemyss, F.R.I.B.A.; F.S.A.; Architect; *b.* 31 Dec. 1889; *s.* of W. R. Symonds, artist, and Margaret Swan; *m.* 1st, 1921, Daphne Loveland (*d.* 1948); two *d.*; 2nd, 1949, Monica Sheila Harrington (she *m.* 1925, Edward Charles Fitz-Clarence, from whom she obtained a divorce, 1930), *d.* of Lt.-Col. Sir Henry Mulleneux Grayson, 1st Bt., K.B.E. *Educ.:* St. Paul's School. Consultant architect for rebuilding of Middlesex Hosp., 1931-34; St. Swithin's House (on site of Salters' Hall), E.C.4, 1950-51. Adviser on Furniture to Colonial Williamsburg, Va., U.S.A., 1955-. *Publications:* Present State of Old English Furniture, 1921; Old English Walnut and Lacquer Furniture, 1922; English Furniture from Charles II. to George II., 1929; Masterpieces of English Furniture and Clocks, 1940; History of English Clocks, 1946 (King Penguin); Veneered Walnut Furniture, 1946; Chippendale Furniture Designs, 1948; The Ornamental Designs of Chippendale, 1949; Thomas Tompion, his life and work, 1951; Furniture-Making in 17th and 18th Century England, 1954. Contributions to English and American periodicals on architectural and antiquarian subjects; chapter in The London Furniture Makers, by Sir Ambrose Heal, 1953. *Address:* 8 Shelley Court, Tite Street, Chelsea, S.W.3; The Ancient House, Peasenhall, Suffolk. *Clubs:* Arts, Chelsea Arts. [*Died* 5 *Sept.* 1958.

SYMONS, Brig.-Gen. Adolphe, C.M.G. 1916; late commanding 13th Hussars; *b.* 9 June 1872; *m.* 1901, Beryl Mary Elizabeth, *e. d.* of Francis Goldie Taubman; two *d.* (one *s.* died of wounds). *Educ.:* Clifton College. Served S. Africa, 1899-1900 (despatches, Queen's medal 4 clasps); European War, 1914-18 (despatches thrice, C.M.G., Bt. Col.); 2nd in command Home Guard, London District, 1940-42. *Address:* c/o Lloyds Bank, Ltd., 6 Pall Mall, S.W.1. [*Died* 4 *Aug.* 1954.

SYRETT, Herbert Sutton, C.B.E. 1919; LL.B., C.C.; Solicitor; member of the firm of Syrett & Sons, 2 John Street, Bedford Row, W.C.1; 2nd *s.* of late Alfred Syrett, J.P., Oaklands, Sydenham, S.E.; *m.* 1910, Rosina Alice (*d.* 1943), *d.* of John Jenkins; one *s.* (and one killed in France, 1944). *Educ.:* privately; Univ. College, London. Solicitor of the Supreme Court, 1901; graduated in Laws at the London University (Honours—Jurisprudence and Roman Law); a representative of the L.C.C. on the Metropolitan Water Board, 1913; Member of the City Corporation, 1924; Chief Commoner of the City, 1941; D.L. City of London, 1949; Private Secretary to Mr. Lloyd George at the Ministry of Munitions, 1915-16; to Mr. Clynes when Food Controller, 1917-19; Secretary, Consumers Council, Ministry of Food; Member of Committee on Trusts; Member Executive Committee of the United Nations Association; Director Beacon Insurance Co. Ltd.; Officer of the Crown of Rumania; Chevalier of the Order of the Star of Rumania. *Recreations:* riding and golfing. *Address:* Fir Crest, Westcott, Surrey; 2 John Street, Bedford Row, W.C.1. *Club:* Royal Automobile. [*Died* 21 *June* 1959.

SYSONBY, 2nd Baron, *cr.* 1935, of Wonersh. **Edward Gaspard Ponsonby,** D.S.O. 1940; Lt.-Col., The Queen's Regt., T.A.; *b.* 7 June 1903; *s.* of 1st Baron and Ria (*d.* 1955), *d.* of Colonel Hegan Kennard; *S.* father, 1935; *m.* 1936, Sallie Monkland, *d.* of Dr. Leonard Sanford, New York; one *s.* one *d.* *Educ.:* Eton. *Heir:* *s.* Hon. John Frederick Ponsonby, *b.* 5 Aug. 1945. *Clubs:* White's, Turf, Alpine. [*Died* 21 *Jan.* 1956.

T

TABOR, Margaret Emma; formerly Warden, Univ. Hall, Liverpool; *d.* of late Henry S. Tabor of Bocking, Essex. *Educ.:* Notting Hill High School, G.P.D.S.C.; Newnham College, Cambridge (Mathematical Tripos); M.A.; J.P. Essex. *Publications:* The Saints in Art; The City Churches; The National Gallery for the Young; The Other London Galleries; Pioneer Women; Round the British Museum. *Address:* 9 Park Terrace, Cambridge. [*Died* 4 *Feb.* 1954.

TABOR, Richard John, B.Sc.; retired Assistant Professor of Botany, Imperial College of Science and Technology, S. Kensington, S.W.7; *m.* 1st, Lilian M. (*d.* 1947), *d.* of P. L. Sheaff, Dover; one *s.*; 2nd, Kate Barratt, C.B.E., D.Sc., *d.* of C. I. Barratt, Clapham. *Educ.:* Horticultural College, Swanley; Royal College of Science, London. Formerly Lecturer in Botany at the Horticultural College, Swanley. *Address:* The Knoll, 32 Military Road, Rye, Sussex. *T.:* Rye 2131. [*Died* 6 *Sept.* 1958.

TAFT, Robert A.; Senator, United States, from 1939; Republican Floor Leader, 1953; *b.* 8 Sept. 1889; *e. s.* of William Howard Taft, Cincinnati, Ohio; *m.* 1914, Martha Wheaton Bowers; four *s.* *Educ.:* Cincinnati and Manila public schools; Taft School, Watertown, Connecticut; Yale College; Harvard Law School. Practised law in Cincinnati with firm of Maxwell and Ramsey, 1913-17; served European War as Asst. Counsel of Food Administration, 1917-18; served as Counsel of American Relief Administration in Europe, 1918-19. Served in Ohio House of Representatives, where he became Republican Floor Leader and Speaker of the House, 1921-26. Practised law in Cincinnati; member law firm of Taft, Stettinius, and Hollister, 1920-38. Served in Ohio Senate, 1931-33; first term in Senate of U.S., 1939-44; re-elected to U.S. Senate, 1944 and 1950. *Publication:* A Foreign Policy for Americans, 1951. *Recreations:* golf, fishing. *Address:* Station M, R.R. 1, Cincinnati, Ohio. *T.:* Locust 8124. *Clubs:* Queen City, Camargo (Cincinnati); Burning Tree (Washington, D.C.). [*Died* 31 *July* 1953.

TAGART, Edward Samuel Bourn, C.B.E. 1927; B.A.(Cantab.).; Barrister-at-law late Secretary for Native Affairs to Government of Northern Rhodesia; *b.* Bath, 8 Oct. 1877; *s.* of William Henry Tagart and Anna Maria Peters; *m.* 1st, 1918, Lilian Edith, *d.* of late Sir Herbert Sloley, K.C.M.G.; one *s.*; 2nd, 1931, Elizabeth, *d.* of Dr. A. S. Boyd. *Educ.:* Bath Coll.; Christ's College, Cambridge. Entered service of British South Africa Company as Assistant Collector in North-Eastern Rhodesia, 1901; served as Assistant Native Commissioner, Native Commissioner, Magistrate, Assistant Legal Adviser, Acting Judge of the High Court of Northern Rhodesia, etc.; Secretary for Native Affairs on assumption of Government of Northern Rhodesia by the Crown, 1924; Special Commissioner to Bechuanaland, 1931; called to Bar, Lincoln's Inn, 1912. *Recreations:* shooting, golf, tennis. *Address:* 11 Bolus Av., Kenilworth, C.P., S. Africa. [*Died* 15 *Aug.* 1956.

TAGORE, Abanindra Nath, C.I.E.; Zemindar of Shazädpur, Bengal; *b.* 1871; *s.* of Goonendra Nath Tagore; *m. g.-g.d.* of Prasanno Coomar Tagore; two *s.* three *d.* *Educ.:* Sanskrit Coll., Calcutta; at home. Professor of Fine Art, Calcutta Univ.; Designed the Memorial Address to Lady Curzon; the Casket presented to His Majesty by Corporation of Calcutta, 1911; panels for decoration of paudal on that occasion; Lord Carmichael's medal; illustrated in colour Omar Khayyam, Rabindranath Tagore's Crescent-Moon, and Sister Nivedita's Myths and Legends of India; principal work consists in reviving the School of Indian Art; painted about 200 pictures; painted water-colour picture of Queen of Asoka for the Queen; has many successful disciples; exhibited works at Simla, Bombay, Calcutta, and at Lord Curzon's Delhi Durbar Exhibition; holder of many medals and first prizes; Ex-President and Founder-Member of the Indian Society of Oriental Arts; Member of Sahibya Parisad, Bengal; Founder-Member of Allied Artists' Association, London; ex-Vice-President and Life-Member of India Society, London. *Publications:* Original Writings, Art Lectures, Short Stories from Sanskrit Literature, from Annals of Ragasthan and Indian Classics; contributions to monthly magazines. *Recreations:* gardening and keeping birds. *Address:* 5 Dwarkanath Tagore's Lane, Calcutta, India. *Club:* The Indian Society of Oriental Art. [*Died* 5 *Dec.* 1951.

TAINSH, Lieut.-Col. Joseph Ramsay, C.B.E. 1924; V.D.; *b.* 30 Jan. 1874; *s.* of late John Tainsh, Hamilton; *m.* 1901, Rose Cameron (*d.* 1944), 2nd *d.* of Archibald Brown, Stransaule, Tobermory; two *s.* two *d.* *Educ.:* Academy and St. John's, Hamilton; West of Scotland Technical College. Railway Engineer, India, 1905-16; served in Indian Volunteers; Major, 1915; with B.E.F., Mesopotamia, 1917-19; Lt.-Colonel R.E.; Assistant Director, 1917; Deputy Director Railways, 1919 (despatches twice);

Director, Iraq State Railways, 1921-36; retired, 1936. *Club:* East India and Sports. [*Died* 16 *Feb.* 1954.

TAIT, Hugh Nimmo, C.M.G. 1937; *b.* 1888; *s.* of late T. S. Tait, formerly of Baroda College, India, and Harrogate; *m.* 1917, Alice L. Barnes (*d.* 1939); two *s.* one *d.* *Educ.:* Clifton; St. John's College, Cambridge. Wrangler, 1910; Home Civil Service, 1911; Chief Secretary's Office, Dublin Castle, 1911-12; Colonial Office, 1912-25; Dominions Office from 1925; lately Assistant Secretary, Commonwealth Relations Office, retired 1949. Visited Southern Rhodesia as Secretary to the Southern Rhodesian Commission, 1919; on military service in 1918. *Address:* Bankside, Wolsey Road, Moor Park, Herts. *T.:* Northwood 1096. [*Died* 10 *May* 1960.

TAIT, Lieut.-Col. John Spottiswood, C.B.E. 1919; V.D.; *b.* 1875. Served European War, 1914-19 (despatches, C.B.E.). *Address:* 1531 Beach Avenue, Vancouver, B.C. [*Died* 17 *July* 1951.

TAIT, Thomas Smith, F.R.I.B.A.; F.R.I.A.S.; F.R.S.A.; Senior Partner in the Firm of Sir John Burnet, Tait & Partners; *b.* 1882; *m.*; three *s.* *Educ.:* Paisley and Glasgow Schools of Art; Royal Academy, London. Director of Standardisation, Min. of Works and Buildings, 1940-42. R.I.B.A. Medallist for Lloyds Bank and Royal Masonic Hospital. Other principal works: New Government Building, Edinburgh; Empire Exhibition, Scotland, 1938; Adelaide House, London Bridge; Unilever House, Blackfriars; Daily Telegraph, Fleet Street; Eastman Dental Clinic, Royal Free Hospital; Burlington School, Hammersmith; I.D. Hospital, Paisley; New Colonial Office, Westminster. *Address:* Scotrea, Strathtay, Perthshire; (business) 10 Bedford Square, W.C.1; 44 Charlotte Square, Edinburgh. *Clubs:* Caledonian, Arts; Scottish Arts, Scottish Conservative; Royal Scottish Automobile, Art (Glasgow). [*Died* 18 *July* 1954.

TALBOT, Vice-Admiral Arthur George, C.B. 1945; D.S.O. 1939; *b.* 31 March 1892; *s.* of G. P. Talbot, Wentworth, Yorks; *m.* 1918, Doris, *d.* of C. F. Branson; one *d.* *Educ.:* R.N. Colleges, Osborne and Dartmouth. Entered R.N. College, Osborne, 1905; Midshipman, 1910; Lieut. 1914; Lt.-Comdr. 1922; Comdr. 1927; Capt. 1934; A.D.C. to the King, 1943; Rear-Adm. 1943; Vice-Adm. 1948. Served European War, 1914-18; Directing Staff of R.N. War College, 1934; commanded Third Destroyer Flotilla, 1937-39 (D.S.O.); Director of Anti-Submarine Warfare Division, Admiralty, 1940; commanded H.M.S. Furious, 1941 (despatches); H.M.S. Illustrious, 1942 (despatches); H.M.S. Formidable, 1943 (despatches); Naval Commander of Eastern Assault Force at Invasion of Normandy, 1944 (Bar to D.S.O., Comdr. U.S. Legion of Merit, Officer of Legion of Honour, Croix de Guerre); Pacific, 1945; Head of British Naval Mission to Greece, 1946-48; retired list, 1948. Now a pig-breeder. Officer of Redeemer of Greece. *Address:* Northbrook, Broadstone, Dorset. *Club:* White's. [*Died* 15 *Oct.* 1960.

TALBOT, Matilda Theresa, C.B.E. 1947 (M.B.E. 1919); Occupier of Lacock Abbey, Chippenham, Wilts (which she presented to National Trust, 1944); *b.* 15 July 1871; *d.* of John Gilchrist Clark (Advocate at Scottish Bar), Speddoch, Dumfriesshire, and Matilda Caroline Talbot, *d.* of William Henry Fox Talbot, Lacock Abbey; after inheriting Lacock from uncle, Charles Henry Talbot, assumed name of Talbot by deed poll. *Educ.:* Kensington High School; Francis Holland High School. After leaving school, trained as teacher of cookery at National Training Coll. of Domestic Subjects, Buckingham Palace Road; taught at various schools, including 2½ years at Roan Girls. School, Greenwich; studied at Cordon Bleu Cookery School, Faubourg St. Honore, Paris. Served European War, 1914-18, commanding W.R.N.S., Cranwell; served with the French Red Cross, La Courneuve, 1916, and Bussang, 1917; has done some translations from Danish and Norwegian; War of 1939-45, received billetees at Lacock Abbey; also received a London Elementary School for 6 years in the house, and numerous units of troops over same period. Presented Lacock Abbey copy of Henry III's confirmation of Magna Carta to British Museum, 1945. *Publication:* My Life and Lacock Abbey, 1956. *Recreations:* skating, dancing, sea and land travel under simple conditions, staying with foreign friends in their homes. *Address:* Lacock Abbey, Chippenham, Wilts. *T.:* Lacock 227. *Club:* Cowdray. [*Died* 25 *March* 1958.

TALBOT, Dame Meriel, D.B.E., *cr.* 1920 (C.B.E. 1918; O.B.E. 1917); accompanied the Headmistresses Tour to Canada, 1931; Member of Royal Commission on Police Powers and Procedure, 1929; 5th *c.* of late Rt. Hon. J. G. Talbot and Hon. Mrs. Talbot (*née* Lyttelton). *Educ.:* Kensington High School. Was Hon. Sec. of the Lambeth Charity Organisation Society for a short time; Member of Advisory Committee for Repatriation of Enemy Aliens, 1915; Secretary The Victoria League, 1901-16; Director Women's Branch, Food Production Dept. Board of Agriculture, 1917-20; Woman Adviser to the Ministry of Agriculture, 1920-21; travelled to Australia, N.Z., and Canada, as a representative of the Victoria League, 1909-10; to South Africa, 1910-11. *Address:* The Lodge, Newtimber Place, Hassocks. *T.:* Hurstpierpoint 3173. *Club:* Ladies' Empire. [*Died* 15 *Dec.* 1956.

TALLENTS, Sir Stephen (George), K.C.M.G., *cr.* 1932 (C.M.G. 1929); C.B. 1918; C.B.E. 1920; Chairman, Group 1 Ltd. since 1949; *b.* 20 Oct. 1884; *e. s.* of G. W. and Hon. Mrs. Tallents; *m.* 1914, Bridget, *d.* of late S. H. F. Hole; two *s.* two *d.* *Educ.:* Harrow; Balliol College, Oxford. Entered Board of Trade, 1909; served with Irish Guards (S.R.), 1914-15 (wounded); Ministry of Munitions, 1915-16; a Principal Assistant Secretary Ministry of Food and Member of Food Council, 1918; Chief British Delegate for Relief and Supply of Poland, 1919; British Commissioner for the Baltic Provinces 1919-20; Private Secretary to Viscount Fitz-Alan, Lord-Lieutenant of Ireland, 1921-22; Imperial Secretary, Northern Ireland, 1922-1926; Secretary to Empire Marketing Board, 1926-33; Public Relations Officer, General Post Office, 1933-35; Controller (Public Relations) B.B.C., 1935-40, (Overseas Services), 1940-41; Principal Assistant Secretary, Min. of Town and Country Planning, 1943-46; First Pres. (1947-49 and 1953) and Fellow of Institute of Public Relations. Awarded Cup of Publicity Club of London, 1935. Hon. A.R.I.B.A., 1946; Hon. F.S.I.A., 1949; Mem. Council R.S.A., 1953; Pres. Design and Industries Assoc., 1955-56. *Publications:* The Starry Pool, and other Tales, 1918; The Dancer, and other Tales, 1922; The Projection of England, 1932; Man and Boy, 1943; Green Thoughts, 1952. *Address:* St. John's Jerusalem, Sutton-at-Hone, Dartford, Kent. *T.:* Farningham 3380. *Club:* Athenæum. [*Died* 11 *Sept.* 1958.

TAN, Dato Sir Cheng-lock, K.B.E., *cr.* 1952 (C.B.E. 1933); D.P.M.J. (an Order of Crown of Johore), 1949; J.P. Malacca, 1912; Rubber Estate and Landed Proprietor; Chm. and Man. Dir. Unitac Ltd.; Chm.: Malaka Pinda Rubber Estates Ltd.; United Malacca Rubber Estates Ltd.; *b.* Malacca, 5 April 1883; *s.* of Tan Keong Ann and Lee Seck Bin; *m.* 1913, Yeo Yeok Neo, *d.* of Yeo Tin Hye. Patron of the Malacca Chinese Hokkien Community; one *s.* four *d.* *Educ.:* High School, Malacca; Raffles Institution, Singapore. A Schoolmaster at Raffles Institution, Singapore, 1902-8; Member Anglo-Chinese Coll. Council, 1918, formed by

Methodist Mission to establish Institution for Higher Educ. in Malaya, led to founding of Raffles Coll., Singapore, 1928; Assistant Manager, Bukit Kajang Rubber Estates Ltd., 1908-9; floated Rubber Cos. and Estates, 1909-10; Visiting Agent, Nyalas Rubber Estates Ltd., 1912-35, Chairman and Resident Director since 1935; travelled with family to Europe, 1935-39; lived in India, 1942-46; Director Oversea Chinese Banking Corp. Ltd., Sime Darby & Co. Ltd. and of various industrial companies; Trustee of Reserved Trust Estate of grandfather, late Tan Choon Bock; active in public life since 1912; Municipal Commissioner, Malacca, 1912-22; ex-Pres. of Malacca Chiang Chew Hoo Assoc.; ex-President Malacca Chinese Chamber of Commerce; Trustee, Cheng Hoon Teng Temple; served on a number of Govt. Committees and Commissions, 1923-1935; an official Representative of S.S. at Coronation, 1937; nominated unofficial member Straits Settlements Legislative Council 4 terms, 1923-34; Unofficial Member Governor's Executive Council, 1933-35. Served as a Volunteer in Chinese Volunteer Company, Malacca, 1915-19, after he had helped to revive it in 1914. Chm. All-Malaya Council of Joint Action, 1946-48, and has taken active part in movement to attain self-govt. for Malaya; President of lately-formed Malayan Chinese political organisation, viz. the Malayan Chinese Assoc., 1949, re-elected Pres. 1951, 1953-58; member of: Malayan Communities Liaison Cttee., 1948 (helped, in 1952, to form Alliance between United Malays Nat. Organization and Malayan Chinese Assoc.); Emergency Chinese Advisory Committee, 1949; Council of University of Malaya, 1949-52; Federal War Council, 1951-52. *Publication:* Malayan Problems, 1947. *Recreations:* reading and literature. *Address:* 111 Heeren Street, and 1771 Klebang Besar, Malacca; (office) 96 First Cross Street, Malacca, Malaya.
[*Died* 13 *Dec.* 1960.

TANDY, Brig.-Gen. Ernest Napper, C.M.G. 1918; D.S.O. 1917; late R.A.; Director of Abdulla and Co. Ltd. since 1921; Chairman since 1933; *b.* 1879; 3rd *s.* of late Surg.-Col. E. O. Tandy; *m.* 1904, Brenda Moncrieff, *d.* of late A. Laing, J.P.; one *s.* (and one *s.* one *d.* decd.). *Educ.:* Wellington Coll.; R.M.A. Woolwich. Entered Royal Artillery, 1898; served S. Africa, 1899-1902 (despatches, Queen's medal with four clasps, King's medal with two clasps); passed Staff College, Camberley, 1913; European War, 1914-18 (despatches, Officer Legion of Honour, Croix de Guerre, C.M.G., D.S.O., Officer Order of Leopold and Belgian Croix de Guerre); Col. 1920; Brig.-Gen., retired pay, 1921. *Address:* 43 Edwardes Square, W.8. *T.:* Western 4589. *Club:* Army and Navy. [*Died* 6 *May* 1953.

TANGYE, Claude Edward, C.B.E. 1944; M.D. Lond. 1907; retd.; late County Medical Officer for Wiltshire; *b.* 1877; *s.* of Edward and Ann Tangye; *m.* 1910, Eva Bertha Oakden (*d.* 1948); no *c.* *Educ.:* Blundell's School; Birmingham Medical School. M.O.H. Mid-Warwickshire, 1909-1919; with R.A.M.C. 1916-19. *Address:* Andennis, St. Mawes, Cornwall. *T.:* 347.
[*Died* 20 *Aug.* 1952.

TANNER, Dame Emmeline Mary, D.B.E., *cr.* 1947; M.A. (Lond.); *b.* Bath, Dec. 1876; *e. d.* of S. T. Tanner, J.P. *Educ.:* privately. Asst. Mistress, Sherborne School for Girls, 1905-9; First Headmistress, Nuneaton High School, 1910-20; Headmistress, Bedford High School, 1920-24; Headmistress of Roedean School, 1924-47; Chm. of Cttee., 1923-25, Pres. 1937-39, Association of Headmistresses; Chairman Joint Committee of Four Secondary Associations, 1940-42; Member of Consultative Committee of Board of Education, 1920-30; Member of Board of Education Committee on Public Schools, 1942-44. *Publication:* The Renaissance and the Reformation, 1908. *Address:* Lilbourne, Barnfield, Marlborough, Wilts. *T.:* Marlborough 683. *Clubs:* Forum, University Women's, English-Speaking Union.
[*Died* 7 *Jan.* 1955.

TANNER, Col. Sir Gilbert, Kt., *cr.* 1937; D.S.O. 1918; T.D., D.L. West Riding and City of York; J.P.; Ex-Governor of Oldham Royal Infirmary; Trustee Henshaw Blue Coat School, Oldham; *b.* 22 Oct. 1877; *s.* of James William and Mary Buckley Tanner; *m.* 1st, 1906, Eliza Bertha Mallalieu (*d.* 1923); two *s.*; 2nd, 1927, Edith Elizabeth Ogden. *Educ.:* University School, Southport; Leeds University. Founded the firm of Tanner Bros. (Greenfield) Ltd., Saddleworth, Yorkshire, making special cotton goods; joined the 2nd Volunteer Battalion Duke of Wellington Regt. 1901; commanded the 2nd West Riding Brigade detachment at King George V's Coronation; served European war 1914-19 (despatches, Allied Victory Medal, Territorial Army Medal, British War Medal Laurel Wreath, D.S.O.); reformed 7th Duke of Wellington Regt., 1920; commanded as Lieut.-Col. till 1924 and retired with rank of Brevet Colonel; King George V Coronation Medal. Special constabulary, retired. *Recreations:* Antiquarian; visiting various manufacturing concerns and studying their methods. *Address:* Fernhill, Greenfield, nr. Oldham, Yorks. *T.A.:* Colonel Tanner, Greenfield, Oldham. *T.:* Saddleworth 86. *Clubs:* Albion (Oldham); Huddersfield Conservative (Huddersfield). [*Died* 30 *May* 1953.

TANNER, William Edward, M.S., F.R.C.S., M.B., L.R.C.P.; Surgeon, Prince of Wales's Hospital, Tottenham, and Evelina Hospital for Children; Consulting Surgeon, St. Nicholas Hackney, St. Leonard's, Edenbridge, Horsham and Waltham Abbey War Memorial Hospitals; Hon. Editor, Medical Soc. of London; Chm. of Executive Council, and Finance Com., R.I.P.H.H.; *b.* London, 1889; *m.* Marie Louise Humphries; three *d.* *Educ.:* Roan School; Birkbeck College; Royal College of Science; Guy's Hospital and Medical School; Berlin. Michael Harris Prize in Anatomy, Wooldridge Certificate in Physiology, First Prize for Junior Proficiency, Honours M.B. (London); Physiological Society's Prize, Physical Society's Prize, Proxime-Accessit Golding-Bird Medal and Scholarship in Bacteriology, Editor Guy's Hospital Gazette; Hon. Secretary Guy's Hospital Pupils' Physical Soc., and Medical Soc. of London; Past Pres. Hunterian Society and Medical Society of London; Prosector Royal College of Surgeons; Resident Surgical Officer, Surgical Registrar and Tutor, Demonstrator of Anatomy; Surgical Assistant and Operator, Anæsthetist, Guy's Hospital; Captain, R.A.M.C., Surgical Specialist; Surgical Specialist, Ministry of Pensions; Lecturer on Surgery, North-East London Post-Graduate College and N. London Post-Graduate Medical Institute. *Publications:* Arbuthnot Lane, His Life and Work; articles on The Surgery of the Neck, Carson's Modern Operative Surgery, Diseases of the Lips, Mouth, Jaws, Tongue, and Salivary Glands, Walton's Text Book of Surgical Diagnosis; articles in Med. Press. *Address:* 38 Queen Anne St., Cavendish Square, W.1. *T.:* Langham 3802; Summerholme, Frinton-on-Sea, Essex. *T.:* Frinton-on-Sea 360.
[*Died* 5 *July* 1951.

TANQUERAY, Rev. Truman, M.A.; *b.* 2 Aug. 1888; *s.* of Frederic Thomas Tanqueray; *m.* 1925, Cicely Alice Curtis Green; one *s.* four *d.* *Educ.:* Tonbridge School; Magdalene College, Cambridge. Assist. Master, Eastbourne College, 1911-14; served on Special Reserve of Officers, The Queen's Royal West Surrey Regt.; wounded at Gheluvelt, 1914; commanded a company of No. 13 Officer Cadet Battalion, for which received mention; returned to Eastbourne College as Assistant and Housemaster, 1919; took over command of O.T.C. and retired with the rank of Major, 1930; Headmaster,

Ipswich School, 1933-50; resigned, 1950. Deacon, 1949; Priest, 1950; Curate in charge of parish of Hintlesham, 1950; Rector of parish of Hintlesham with Chattisham, 1951-56. *Publications:* (Part) Western Europe; and Australia, New Zealand and Pacific Islands. *Recreations:* golf, tennis, archæology. *Address:* Hillside, Peaslake, Surrey. [*Died* 12 *Dec.* 1960.

TANSLEY, Sir Arthur George, Kt., *cr.* 1950; F.R.S. 1915; M.A.; Hon. Fellow Trinity College, Cambridge, since 1944; *b.* 1871; *s.* of late George Tansley, M.A., of the Working Men's College, London; *m.* 1903, Edith Chick; three *d.* *Educ.:* Highgate School; University College, London; Trinity College, Cambridge. Demonstrator and later Assist. Prof. of Botany, Univ. College, London, 1893-1906; University Lecturer in Botany, Cambridge, 1906-23; Pres. Botanical Section, Brit. Assoc., 1923; Fellow of Magdalen Coll. and Sherardian Prof. of Botany, Oxford, 1927-37, retired as Professor Emeritus; Linnean Gold Medal, 1941; founder, 1902, and editor for 30 years, New Phytologist; editor for 21 years, Journal of Ecology; Pres. British Ecological Soc., 1913-15 and 1938-40; Chm., The Nature Conservancy, 1949-53. Pres. Council for Promotion of Field Studies, 1947-3. *Publications:* Evolution of the Filicinean Vascular System, 1908; Types of British Vegetation, 1911; The New Psychology, 1920; Elements of Plant Biology, 1922; Practical Plant Ecology, 1923; co-editor of Aims and Methods in the Study of Vegetation, 1926; The British Islands and their Vegetation, 1939; The Values of Science to Humanity, 1942; Our Heritage of Wild Nature, 1945; Plant Ecology and the School (with E. Price Evans), 1946; Introduction to Plant Ecology, 1946; Britain's Green Mantle, 1949; Oaks and Oakwoods, 192; Mind and Life, An Essay in Simplification, 1952; contributions to botanical, ecological and psychological journals. *Address:* Grantchester, Cambridge. *Club:* Athenæum. [*Died* 25 *Nov.* 1955.

TAPLEY, Major-General James John Bonifant, C.B. 1935; D.S.O. 1915; late Royal Army Veterinary Corps; *b.* 14 Nov. 1877; *s.* of Samuel Gover Tapley, Torrington, Devon. Entered Army, 1903; Captain, 1908; Major, 1915; Lieut.-Col., 1928; Col., 1929; Maj.-Gen., 1933; with Egyptian army, 1911-14 and 1915-22; served South Africa, 1901-2 (Queen's medal 4 clasps); European War, 1914-15, in France and Belgium (despatches twice, D.S.O.); Darfur operations (despatches, Bt. Lt.-Col., Soudan medal with clasp); Director-General Army Veterinary Services, War Office, 1933-37; retired pay, 1937. [*Died* 17 *July* 1958.

TAPLEY-SOPER, Harry T.; *see* Soper.

TAPPS-GERVIS-MEYRICK, Sir G. L.; *see* Meyrick.

TARN, Sir William (Woodthorpe), Kt., *cr.* 1952; Litt.D. (Camb.); Hon. LL.D. (Edin.); F.B.A.; Hon. Fellow of Trinity College, Cambridge; *b.* 1869; *s.* of William Tarn; *m.* 1896, Flora Macdonald (*d.* 1937), 3rd *d.* of John Robertson, Orbost, Skye; one *d.* *Educ.:* Eton; Trinity College, Cambridge. Member of Inner Temple. *Publications:* Antigonos Gonatas, 1913; The Treasure of the Isle of Mist, 1920 (later edns., U.S.A., 1934; England, 1950); Hellenistic Civilisation, 1928 (3rd rev. ed., 1951); Hellenistic Military and Naval Developments, 1930; Chapters in Cambridge Ancient History, vols. VI, VII, IX, X; The Greeks in Bactria and India, 1938, 2nd ed., 1951; Alexander the Great, 2 vols., 1948; Greece and Rome, in The European Inheritance, Vol. I, 1954; articles and studies. *Address:* Muirtown House, Inverness. *T.A.:* Muirtown, Inverness. *T.:* Inverness 72. [*Died* 7 *Nov.* 1957.

TARVER, Major-Gen. William Knapp, C.B. 1918; C.M.G. 1919; *b.* 2 Nov. 1872; *s.* of Rev. Joseph Tarver, Filgrave Rectory, Newport Pagnell; *m.* 1902, Kathleen Gladys (*d.* 1947), *e. d.* of late Sir Henry Pipon-Schooles; one *d.* *Educ.:* Warwick School; Sandhurst. Joined Cheshire Regt. 1892; transferred to R.A.S.C. 1896; Assist. Director of Supplies, W.O., 1922; Maj.-Gen. 1925; Inspector of the Royal Army Service Corps, 1925-29; retired pay, 1929; Col. Comdt. R.A.S.C., 1935-42. *Recreations:* cricket, lawn tennis, golf. *Club:* United Service. [*Died* 8 *April* 1952.

TASCHEREAU, Hon. Louis Alexandre; *b.* 5 Mar. 1867; *s.* of Judge Jean Thomas Taschereau; *m.* 1891, Adine, *d.* of late Elisée Dionne; three *s.* two *d.* *Educ.:* Quebec Seminary; Laval University. Advocate, 1889; called to Quebec Bar, 1889; partner with Sir Charles FitzPatrick; subsequently Syndic and Batonnier Quebec Bar; Alderman, 1906-08; M.P. Montmorency since 1900; Minister of Public Works and Labour, Quebec, 1907-19; Attorney-General of the Province of Quebec, 1919-20; Prime Minister of Quebec, 1920-36. *Address:* 187 Grande Allée, Quebec. *Clubs:* Garrison, Canadian, Mount Royal, Reform (Quebec). [*Died* 6 *July* 1952.

TASKER, Major Sir Robert Inigo, Kt., *cr.* 1931; retired; T.D.; D.L.; J.P. County of London, 1910; *b.* 1868; 6th *s.* of Geo. Richard Tasker, The Firs, Shilingstone, Dorset; *m.* 1900; one *s.* one *d.* (and one *s.* died on active service, War of 1939-45). *Educ.:* Ardingly College. Articled to father; partner, 1892; senior partner, 1916; M.P. (U.) East Islington, 1924-29; M.P. (U.) Holborn, 1935-45; Member L.C.C., 1910-1937; Chairman, 1930-31; Chairman, Building Acts Committee, 1924-30; Chairman L.C.C. Advisory Committee New Building Act for London, 1931-35; Chairman London Old Age Pensions Committee, 1922-37; Chairman Royal Maternity Charity, 1911-50; a member of Paviors, Fan-makers, and Gardeners Company; Master, 1908-9 and 1939-40; elected Fellow R.S.L., 1897, member of Council for many years; served in Volunteers and Territorial Forces, 1885-1920; raised and commanded 3/11th Battalion London Regt. 1915; Member T.A. Assoc., 1910-45; Hon. Surveyor to many charitable institutions; Fellow of the Incorporated Association of Architects and Surveyors; President, 1927-29; M.I.Struct.E.; F.I.Arb.; Member Institute of Registered Architects; Member of Council of Architects Registration Council of United Kingdom, 1931-45. *Recreations:* fishing, golf. *Address:* 3 Field Court, Gray's Inn, W.C.1. *T.:* Chancery 5957; 3 Metropole Court, Folkestone. *T.:* Folkestone 2614. *Club:* Devonshire. [*Died* 28 *Feb.* 1959.

TATE, Charles James Gerrard, C.B.E. 1934; Director Danish Punchcard System A/S Copenhagen; lately in charge of administration of the Control of Civil Building at Ministry of Works; *b.* 15 Aug. 1880; *s.* of Charles James and Emily Tate; *m.* 1907, Rene Augusta Hamilton de la Poer; two *s.* *Educ.:* Privately; King's College, London. Customs and Excise, 1900-19; Controller Pension Issue Office, 1920-28; Assistant Secretary Ministry of Pensions, 1928-39; Principal Assistant Secretary and Director of Establishments, Ministry of Pensions, 1939-41; Chief Administrator, War Service Grants, 1939-40. *Address:* Carrington House, Hertford Street, W.1. *T.:* Mayfair 2400; Coombe Grange, Sunninghill, Ascot. *T.:* Ascot 1214. *Club:* Reform. [*Died* 7 *Sept.* 1951.

TATE, George Vernon, M.C. 1918; President Tate & Lyle Ltd. since 1954; *b.* 21 April 1890; *m.* 1922, Evelyn Victoria Ann Stock; two *d.* *Educ.:* Winchester College; Trinity College, Oxford. Chairman of Tate & Lyle Ltd., 1936. *Address:* 7 Princes Gate, S.W.7. *Club:* Bath. [*Died* 30 *Sept.* 1955.

TATE, Professor Jonathan Professor of Greek, University of Sheffield, since 1945;

b. 9 March 1899; *s.* of Jonathan Tate and Sarah (*née* Cobain), Belfast; *m.* 1932, Anna Anderson Blues; two *d.* *Educ.:* Royal Belfast Academical Institution; Trinity College, Dublin. Schol. 1918, Sen. Moderator in Classics and Philosophy, 1921, M.A. 1925, Litt.D. 1938. Asst., later Lectr., in Latin, Queen's Univ., Belfast, 1923-29; Lectr. in Greek, Univ. of St. Andrews, 1929-45. External Examiner: Sheffield, 1937-39; Leeds, 1946-49; St. Andrews, 1946-50; London, 1948-52; Durham, 1952-54; Wales, 1952-54. Dean of the Faculty of Arts, Sheffield, 1948-51. Hon. Vice-President Newman Association, 1945-55; Member Council Classical Association, 1948-51. Mem. Edit. Bd. Journal of Hellenic Studies, 1952-. *Publications:* The Satires of A. Persius Flaccus rendered into English Verse with an introduction and notes, 1930; Chaos or Catholicism (in part), 1937; Grammarian's Progress, 1947; contrib. to Oxford Classical Dictionary, Chambers's Encyclopædia, and Brit. Amer. and continental classical and philosophical jls., 1925-. *Address:* 16 Wellesley Road, Sheffield 10. *T.:* Sheffield 62812. [*Died* 1 *Jan.* 1958.

TATE, Major Sir Robert William, K.B.E., *cr.* 1920 (C.B.E. 1919); Litt.D. 1943; M.A.; Senior Fellow of Trinity College, Dublin, since 1941; Fellow, 1908; Public Orator in the University of Dublin since 1914; President of the College Historical Society, 1950; Hon. Fellow of St. John's Coll., Cambridge, 1948; Officier de l'Instruction Publique, 1927; Cavaliere della Corona d'Italia, 1929; Chevalier de la Légion d'Honneur, 1934, Officier, 1950; *b.* 27 Aug. 1872; *o. s.* of late Rev. Richard Tate, Rector of Rossinver, Co. Leitrim, and Elizabeth, *y. d.* of late Rev. William Ashe; *m.* 1917, Raby Georgina (*d.* 1939), *d.* of late William Clarke, Dublin, and *widow* of C. J. Lowry; no *c.* *Educ.:* Shrewsbury School (First Open Scholarship, 1887); St. John's College, Cambridge (Open Scholarship in Classics). Wright's Prizeman, 1892; First Class (Div. 2) in the Classical Tripos Part I, 1894; First Class (Sec. A.) in the Classical Tripos Part II, 1895; Senior Classical Master, St. Columba's College, Rathfarnham, Co. Dublin, 1896-1903; M.A. Cambridge, 1898; M.A. (ad eundem) Dublin, 1903; The Madden Prize, Trinity College, Dublin, 1907; founded Dublin Univ. Contingent O.T.C. 1910 and commanded it until its disbandment, 1922; 2nd Lieut. T.F. (unattached list), 1910; Major, 1912; First Class Military Interpreter in French, Jan. 1913; in German, Jan. 1914. O.St.J. 1927. *Publications:* Orationes et Epistolae Dublinenses, 1941; Carmina Dublinensia, 1943. *Address:* 40 Trinity College, Dublin; Old Vienna House, Lower Hatch Street, Dublin. *Club:* Royal Irish (Kingstown). [*Died* 22 *Jan.* 1952.

TATE, Thomas Bailey, C.S.I. 1937; A.M.I.C.E., A.C.H.; *b.* 11 Dec. 1882; *s.* of Thomas Tate, J.P., Bank House, Acklington, Northumberland; *m.* 1914, Decima Trotter; (*s.* killed in action, 1941) one *d.* *Educ.:* Malvern College; Royal Indian Engineering College, Coopers Hill. Indian Service of Engineers, Punjab and N.W. Frontier Province, P.W. Dept., Irrigation Branch, 1904. Served European War with Guides Cavalry and as Recruiting Officer for Pathans, 1916-18; Chief Engineer and Secretary to Government, Punjab P.W. Dept., Irrigation Branch, 1932; President, Central Board of Irrigation, India, 1936; retired, 1937; Home Office, A.R.P. Department, 1939-44. *Address:* Sea View, Alnmouth, Northumberland. *T.:* Alnmouth 346. *Clubs:* East India and Sports; Northern Counties (Newcastle upon Tyne). [*Died* 4 *June* 1957.

TATLOCK, Robert Rattray, F.S.A.; *b.* Glasgow, 25 Jan. 1889; 2nd *s.* of John Tatlock, scientist, Glasgow, D.B.O.A. (Lond.), 1911; *m.* 1924, Cicely, 2nd *d.* of Dr. H. Darwin Hey. *Educ.:* The Glasgow Academy; The Glasgow School of Art; the Royal Glasgow Technical College. British Red Cross, France and Russia; British Adriatic Mission (F.O.), 1917; Editor, the Burlington Magazine, 1920-33; Art Critic, the Daily Telegraph, 1924-34. *Publications:* Matteo Falcone (B.B.C.); Catalogue of Pictures in the Lady Lever Art Gallery, Port-Sunlight; articles on art and archæology in the New Statesman, etc.; edited Chinese Art, Spanish Art, Georgian Art, French Art, History of Art (with Dr. A. Blum), Contemporary Review, American journals. *Recreation:* horticulture. *Address:* Arkesden, Saffron Walden, Essex. [*Died* 29 *June* 1954.

TATLOW, Rev. Canon Tissington, M.A.; Hon. D.D. Edin. 1925; Rector of St. Edmund the King and St. Nicholas Acons, with All Hallows, Lombard Street, St. Benet, Gracechurch, St. Leonard, Eastcheap, and St. Dionis, Backchurch, since 1937; Hon. Chaplain of the Student Christian Movement of Great Britain and Ireland; Hon. Canon of Canterbury Cathedral, 1926; Chairman, S.C.M. Press Ltd., 1929; Hon. Director Institute of Christian Education at Home and Overseas, 1936; Fellow of Sion College, 1927, Hon. Treas. 1937-40, Pres. 1940-41; Dep. Chm. St. Catharine's, Cumberland Lodge, Windsor Great Park, 1947; *b.* 11 Jan. 1876; *e. s.* of late Tissington W. G. Tatlow, Co. Cavan; *m.* 1903, Emily, *d.* of late Richard Scott, Co. Clare; two *d.* (and one *d.* decd.). *Educ.:* St. Columba's Coll., Rathfarnham; private school, Dublin; Trinity Coll., Dublin. B.A. 1897; M.A. 1900; Travelling Secretary, Student Volunteer Missionary Union, 1897-1898; General Secretary, Student Christian Movement, 1898-1900; Editor, The Student Movement, and Educational Secretary, Student Volunteer Missionary Union, 1900-03; returned Divinity School, Trinity College, Dublin, 1900-02; Downes Prize, 1901; Divinity Testimonium, 2nd class, 1902; Curate of St. Barnabas, Kensington, 1902-03; General Secretary, Student Christian Movement, 1903-29, Chairman 1929-33; preaching curacy, St. Peter's, Bayswater, 1904-09; Hon. Sec. Archbishops of Canterbury and York's Committee, World Conference on Faith and Order, 1913-27; founder and first Secretary of the Anglican Fellowship, 1912, Chairman, 1913-17; Select Preacher, Cambridge Univ., 1915, Oxford Univ., 1934-36; Chm. of The Challenge newspaper, 1915-22; Hon. Sec., Army and Religion Enquiry, 1917-18; Vice-Chairman, World's Student Christian Federation, 1922-28; Chairman International Student Service, 1926-37; Rector of All Hallows, Lombard Street, E.C., 1926-37; has travelled widely among universities and taken part in student conferences, U.S.A., Canada, and Europe; Order of St. Sava (5th class) 1919, (3rd class) 1935. *Publications:* Missionary Studies on Japan, India, S. America, Mohammedanism, etc.; Life of Martyn Trafford; Editor of The Student Movement, 1903-33; The Story of the Student Christian Movement, 1933; Sub-Editor, A Christian Year Book, 1941-50. *Recreations:* reading, motoring, travelling. *Address:* 46 Gordon Square, W.C.1. *T.:* Euston 4730; 31 Templars Avenue, N.W.11. *Club:* Royal Societies. [*Died* 3 *Oct.* 1957.

TATTERSALL, Creassey Edward Cecil, B.A.; Keeper of the Department of Textiles, Victoria and Albert Museum (retired); *b.* London, 1877; *s.* of Edward Tattersall; unmarried. *Educ.:* City of London School; Trinity College, Cambridge. Textiles Department, Victoria and Albert Museum, from 1915. *Publications:* 1000 End Games (Chess); Hand-Woven Carpets, Oriental and European; Fine Carpets at the V. and A. Museum; The Carpets of Persia; History of British Carpets; Notes on Carpet Knotting and Weaving; contrib. to Art and Chess Journals. *Recreations:* painting, chess. *Address:* Sorrento, Lyme Regis. [*Died* 26 *Oct.* 1957.

TAUNTON, Sir Ivon (Hope), K.C.I.E., *cr.* 1947 (C.I.E. 1941); Kt., *cr.* 1946; Grand Secretary, United Scottish Freemasonry of India and Ceylon, 1952; *b.* 19 Nov. 1890; *er. s.* of Major H. Percy Taunton, J.P., of Redlynch, nr. Salisbury, Wilts; unmarried. *Educ.:* Uppingham; Clare College, Cambridge. Entered Indian Civil Service, 1914; served in Sind, 1914-16 and 1919-26; military duty, 1917; assistant political officer in Mesopotamia, 1918; Minister Khairpur State, 1927-32; Municipal Commissioner, Bombay, 1934-38; Chief Secretary to Government of Sind, 1939; Revenue Commissioner of Sind, 1940-41; Adviser to Governor of Bombay, 1942-46, Chief Sec. 1946-48. Grand Master of All Scottish Freemasonry in India, 1945-47, in India and Pakistan, 1947-50; Pres.: Bombay Presidency Adult Educ. Assoc. O.St.J. *Recreations:* cycling, music. *Address:* Taj Mahal Hotel, Bombay, India. *Club:* East India and Sports. [*Died* 3 *Dec.* 1957.

TAVERNER, William Burgoyne, O.B.E. 1953; *b.* 16 Aug. 1879. Mayor of Dunedin, 1927-29; M.P. Dunedin South, 1928-31; Minister of Railways, Minister of Customs and Commissioner of State Forests, New Zealand, 1929; Minister of Transport, 1930-1931; Minister of Public Works, 1930-31. *Address:* 221 Elgin Rd., Dunedin, W.1, N.Z. [*Died* 18 *July* 1958.

TAWSE, Col. Harry Storey, C.B. 1946; T.D.; D.L.; J.P.; senior partner in firm of Tawse & Allan, Civil Engrs. and Architects, Aberdeen; *b.* 18 April 1889; *m.* Isabelle Livingstone McCallum; two *s.* one *d.* *Educ.:* Universities of Aberdeen and Glasgow; Royal Technical College of Glasgow (Associate in Civil Engineering). European War, 1914-19; also 1940-42; Active Service List T.A., 1919-1948. Assoc. Member Inst. Water Engrs.; Fellow Royal Incorporation Architects in Scotland. *Address:* 74 Beaconsfield Place, Aberdeen. *T.A.:* Alta Aberdeen. *T.:* Aberdeen 23050. *Club:* University (Aberdeen). [*Died* 24 *Dec.* 1959.

TAYLOR; *see* Worsley-Taylor.

TAYLOR, Sir Alexander Thomson, K.B.E., *cr.* 1938 (O.B.E. 1919); J.P., D.L.; *b.* 1873; *s.* of John Taylor, Glasgow; *m.* 1897, Jessie Smith (*d.* 1946), *d.* of William Roxburgh, Glasgow. President of Scottish Unionist Association, 1937; Convener, Renfrewshire County Council, 1944-49; contested Western Division of Renfrewshire (U.), Dec. 1923 and May 1929. *Address:* The Grange, Kilmacolm, Renfrewshire. [*Died* 1 *July* 1953.

TAYLOR, Lieut.-Col. Arthur James, C.M.G. 1918; D.S.O. 1917; M.C.; Lieut.-Col. retd.; South African Staff Corps; Past Member of Legislative Assembly, Southern Rhodesia; *b.* 1876; *y. s.* of R. Taylor; *m.* Edith Ruby, *e. d.* of C. Klemsmith, M.L.A., Midlands, S. Rhodesia. Served Boer War, 1899-1902; European War, 1914-19 in German South-West and East Africa (despatches twice, M.C., D.S.O., C.M.G.). [*Died* 26 *March* 1949.
[*But death not notified in time for inclusion in Who Was Who 1941–1950, first edn.*

TAYLOR, Captain Arthur Trevelyan, C.B.E. 1919; R.N.; retired; *b.* 8 Aug. 1864; *s.* of late George Noble Taylor, Indian C.S.; Member of Council; J.P. Berks; *m.* 1897, Geraldine de Courcy Barton; one *s.* one *d.* Entered Royal Navy, 1877; retired Captain, 1910; served West Africa, 1887-88 (medal and clasp); Naval Intelligence Officer and H.M. Consul in Cape Verde Islands, 1914-19; H.M. Consul at Rhodes, Feb.-Oct. 1921. *Address:* c/o Glyn, Mills & Co., Holt's Branch, Kirkland House, Whitehall, S.W.1. *Club:* United Service. [*Died* 16 *June* 1956.

TAYLOR, Austin; 2nd *s.* of late Archdeacon Taylor, D.D.; *m.* 1st, 1886, Lucia (*d.* 1906), *d.* of Edward Whitaker, Liverpool; two *d.* (and one *s.* decd.); 2nd, 1909, Gertrude Adeline (*d.* 1944), *d.* of late Pennington Evans. *Educ.:* Liverpool College; Corpus Christi College, Cambridge; M.A. 1910. Shipowner (retired, 1912); entered City Council of Liverpool, 1892; retired, 1895; again elected 1900, and was Chairman of Housing Committee, 1901-3; M.P. for East Toxteth Division of Liverpool, 1902-10; Chairman, Westminster Hospital, 1925-28. *Publications:* Addresses on Edmund Burke, Ibsen, Capt. Mahan, French Revolution; Sidelights on Protection. *Address:* Avenue Lodge, Llandrindod Wells. [*Died* 27 *April* 1955.

TAYLOR, Charles William, R.E.; Wood and Copper Plate Engraver; *b.* 1878; *s.* of Thomas Taylor, Wolverhampton; *m.* 1902, Maud Lillian Parr (*d.* 1960). *Educ.:* Wolverhampton School of Art; The Royal College of Art (Royal Exhibitioner). Was previously apprenticed to Wood and Copper Plate Engravers; Teacher of Life Drawing and Engraving at Dover, and Southend, Essex; Exhibited in the Royal Academy and in Canada, America, France and Sweden; works acquired by British Museum, South Kensington Museum, several British Cities, and by Galleries abroad. *Recreations:* motoring and gardening. *Address:* Retreat, Steep Lane, Findon, Sussex. [*Died* 2 *March* 1960.

TAYLOR, Claude, C.V.O. 1933; O.B.E.; *b.* 28 Sept. 1877; *o. s.* of late Alfred Claude Taylor, M.D., F.R.C.S., Nottingham. *Educ.:* Blundell's, Tiverton; Trinity College, Cambridge. Natural Science Tripos 1900; News Editor, Daily Mirror 1904; Evening News 1905; Editor, Weekly Dispatch 1906-10; Joined Exhibitions Branch of the Board of Trade 1912; Organizing Secretary British Industries Fair 1914; Director, Exhibitions Division, Department of Overseas Trade, and Director of the British Industries Fair, 1932-37; Controller Government Pavilion, British Empire Exhibition (Wembley), 1924 and 1925; British Commissioner-General Adjoint, French Colonial Exhibition, 1931; British Commissioner-General Brussels International Exhibition, 1935; Commissioner-General for United Kingdom participation at Empire Exhibition, South Africa, 1936; British Commissioner-General, Paris International Exhibition, 1937. *Clubs:* Union; Metropolitan (New York). [*Died July* 1957.

TAYLOR, Francis Henry; Director, Worcester Art Museum, since 1955; Director Emeritus, Special Consultant and Member Board of Trustees of The Metropolitan Museum of Art, New York City (Director 1940-55); *b.* Philadelphia, Pa., 23 April 1903; *s.* of Dr. William Johnson Taylor and Emily Buckley Newbold; *m.* 1928, Pamela Coyne; one *s.* three *d.* *Educ.:* Kent (Conn.) School; Univ. of Pennsylvania (A.B.) D.Litt. Clark, L.H.D. Tufts, Rollins, Hamilton, Amherst Columbia Univ.; Hon. Doctor of Fine Arts, Univ. of Pennsylvania, and Yale; Doctor of Arts, Harvard Univ., Princeton Univ., New York Univ., Holy Cross Coll.; Doctor of Laws, Miami Univ. (Ohio); graduate study at Universities of Paris, Rome. Florence and Barcelona; Visiting Fellow Am. Acad. in Rome, Carnegie Fellow, Graduate Coll., Princeton Univ., 1924-27; Asst. Curator, Phila. Museum of Art, 1927-1928, Curator of Medieval Art, 1928-31; Dir. Worcester (Mass.) Art Museum, 1931-1940; Chm. Advisory Com. Walters Art Gallery, Baltimore, 1934-44; Regional Dir. for New Eng. States, Federal Art Projects, 1933-34; Chm. Nat. Council for Art Week, 1940; Member Advisory Com. on Art, Dept. of State, visiting and lecturing in Latin American Countries, 1942; Member Am. Commission for Protection and Salvage of Artistic and Historic Monuments in War Areas (Roberts Commission), 1943-46, serving in London and Paris July-Sept. 1944. Mem. Bd., Sch. of Fine Arts; Trustee: Metropolitan Museum of Art; Amer. Acad. in Rome; former Trustee: Archeol. Inst. of Amer.; Amer. Fedn. of Arts; Museum of City of New York; Univ. of Pennsylvania; Former Mem. Visiting Cttee. Dept. Art and Archeology, Princeton and Amherst Coll.; Member: Dumbarton Oaks Coll. and Library and Fogg Art Museum and Dept. Fine Arts Harvard; Inst. of Internat. Education, etc.; Member-at-large, Amer. Council of Learned Societies; Mem. Amer. Philos. Soc., Philadelphia; Fellow: Amer. Acad. Arts and Sciences (Boston); Amer. Antiquarian Soc., etc.; Hon. Mem.: Amer. Inst. of Architects; Mem. Amer. Assoc. Museums (Mem. of Council; ex-Vice-Pres.); Assoc. Art Museum Directors. Received Award for Distinguished Service in the Arts of the American Acad. of Arts and Letters, 1957. Commander of Royal Order of Vasa (Sweden); Chevalier Order of the Crown (Belgium); Commander Order of Merit (Ecuador); Officer Legion of Honour (France); Commander of the Order of Orange-Nassau (Netherlands); Commander Order of Merit (Italy). *Publications:* The Taste of Angels—A History of Art Collecting from Rameses to Napoleon, 1948; Fifty Centuries of Art, 1954; Editor-at-large, Saturday Review of Literature; numerous monographs and articles on art and archæological subjects. *Address:* Worcester Art Museum, Worcester, Mass., U.S.A. *Clubs:* Century (New York); Odd Volumes (Boston). [*Died* 22 *Nov.* 1957.

TAYLOR, Francis M. G. Du-Plat; *see* Du-Plat-Taylor.

TAYLOR, Frank Alwyn, M.A.; Student and Librarian of Christ Church, Oxford; *b.* Auckland, N.Z., 1 March 1890; *s.* of late Francis Collingwood Taylor; *m.* 1930, Kathleen Eleanor Buttle, *e. d.* of late Charles Byass, Bainton Balk, E. Yorks; two *s.* *Educ.:* Auckland Grammar School and University College, University of New Zealand (Senior Scholar, M.A.). Served European War, 1915-17 in Egypt, France and Belgium; Captain, 2nd A.I.R., N.Z. Expeditionary Force; Exeter College, Oxford, 1918-21; 1921 First Class Honours in Final School of Mediæval and Modern Languages; Heath Harrison Travelling Scholar in Italian; M.A. 1923; Censor of Christ Church, Oxford, 1924-29; Rhodes Travelling Fellow, 1930. Chevalier de la Légion d'Honneur, France, 1953. *Publications:* The Theatre of Alexandre Dumas fils, 1937; A Critical Edition of Voltaire's Lettres Philosophiques, 1943; articles in Chambers's Encyclopædia, etc. *Recreation:* foreign travel. *Address:* Home Farm House, Elsfield, Oxford. *T.:* Stanton St. John 237. [*Died* 25 *June* 1960.

TAYLOR, F(rank) Sherwood; Director of the Science Museum, South Kensington, since 1950; *b.* 26 Nov. 1897; *s.* of Seaton Frank and Helen Sennerth Taylor. *Educ.:* Sherborne School; Lincoln College, Oxford; University College, London. Chemistry master at various schools including Gresham's School and Repton, 1921-33; Assistant Lecturer in Inorganic Chemistry, Queen Mary College, Univ. of London, 1933-38; Curator of Museum of the History of Science, Oxford, 1940-50 Hon. Editor Ambix, Journal of Soc. for study of Alchemy and Early Chemistry, since 1937; Consulting Editor of Chymia; Governor of Imperial College of Science and Technology. *Publications: Chemistry:* Inorganic and theoretical Chemistry; Organic Chemistry, 1933; Modern Elementary Chemistry, 1936; *Science:* The World of Science, 1936; General Science for Schools, 1939; *History of Science:* Galileo and the Freedom of Thought, 1938; The Century of Science, 1840-1940; Science Past and Present, 1945 (published in U.S.A. as a Short History of Science and Scientific Thought, 1949); The Alchemists, 1952 (U.S.A.) 1949; Illustrated History of Science, 1955; History of Industrial Chemistry, 1955; *Religion:* The Fourfold Vision, a study of the relations of Science and Religion, 1945; Two Ways of Life, Christian and Materialist, 1947; numerous contributions to Annals of Science. Ambix. Philosophical Magazine, Jl. of Hellenic Studies. *Recreation:* bee-keeping. *Address:* St. Denis, Crowthorne, Berks. *Clubs:* Athenæum, United University. [*Died* 5 *Jan.* 1956.

TAYLOR, Ven. Frederic Norman; Archdeacon Emeritus; *b.* 31 Oct. 1871; *s.* of Joseph and Catherine Mary Taylor; *m.* 1908, Dorothy Warburton; three *s.* five *d.* *Educ.:* St. Olave's Grammar School, Southwark; Jesus College, Oxford. Ordained 1896; Assistant Curate All Saints', Small Heath, Birmingham; Organising Secretary, Society for Promoting Christian Knowledge, 1903-10; Assistant Curate Stratfield Mortimer, Berks, 1910-13; Vicar of St. Luke's, Christchurch, N.Z., 1913-36; Archdeacon of Akaroa, 1922-33, Emer., 1942; Vicar of Amberley, N.Z., 1936-39; Priest-in-charge of St. Michael's, Christchurch, N.Z., 1942-45. *Address:* 7 Clare Road, Christchurch, N.1, N.Z. [*Died* 30 *Sept.* 1960.

TAYLOR, Sir Gordon G.; *see* Gordon-Taylor.

TAYLOR, H. Stanley; *b.* 1871; *e. s.* of James D. and Hester Anna Taylor; *m.* 1897, Edith Maud Godfrey, 3rd *d.* of James Stone; no *c.* *Educ.:* Preparatory School, Reading; Blundell's School, Tiverton. On leaving school, entered his father's office, an old established malting business; Partner 1897 (James D. Taylor and Sons), and later, when the firm was formed into a company (James D. Taylor and Sons, Ltd.); was Chairman of the Company for some years; during European War was Hon. Secretary of Malt Clearing House Committee; was in charge of Malt Section of Ministry of Food; Board's representative (Bath area) Assistance Board; Member of Institute of Brewing; Vice-Chairman, Somerset Automobile Club; Member of Management Committee, Bath Southern Dispensary; Past Pres., British Commercial Gas Association, 1935-36; last Chm. of Bath Gas Co., founded 1818; late Chm. Bristol Brewery Georges and Co., Ltd., Bristol, and Crocker Brothers Ltd., Bristol. *Recreations:* tennis, hunting. *Address:* Bewdley House, Widcombe, Bath, Somerset. *T.A.* and *T.:* Bath 2554. *Clubs:* Farmers'; Bath and County (Bath). [*Died* 2 *June* 1959.

TAYLOR, Major-General Sir John, Kt., *cr.* 1942; C.I.E. 1937; D.S.O. 1915; M.D.; LL.D.; D.P.H.; Indian Medical Service, retired; late Director Central Research Inst., Kasauli, Punjab; *b.* 14 Feb. 1884; *m.* Katherine (*d.* 1954), *e. d.* of late Alexander Monro, C.I.E.; two *d.* Entered I.M.S. 1906; Capt., 1909; Major, 1918; Lt.-Col., 1926; Col., 1936; Acting Maj.-Gen., 1941; served N.W. Frontier, India, 1908 (medal with clasp); European War, 1914-19 (despatches twice, D.S.O.). *Address:* 88 Onslow Gardens, S.W.7. *Club:* Flyfishers'. [*Died* 7 *Feb.* 1959.

TAYLOR, Sir Joshua R.; *see* Ross-Taylor.

TAYLOR, General Sir Maurice Grove, K.C.B., *cr.* 1938 (C.B. 1932); C.M.G. 1919; D.S.O. 1916; late Col. Comdt. R.E.; *b.* 31 May 1881; *s.* of Franklin Taylor; *m.* Winifred Anderson (*d.* 1955), *d.* of S. J. Thacker; one *s.* *Educ.:* St. Mark's, Windsor; Woolwich. Joined Royal Engineers, 1900; Capt. 1910; Bt. Major, 1916; Major, 1917; Bt. Lt.-Col. 1917; Bt. Col. 1919; Col. 1920; Maj.-Gen. 1930; Lt.-Gen. 1937; General, 1940; served in Gibraltar and Malta, and was Adjutant Scottish Command Telegraph Companies R.E. Territorial Force, 1907-12; entered the Staff College, Camberley, 1914; served European War, 1914-18 (despatches seven times, Bt. Maj., D.S.O., Lieut.-Col., and Col. C.M.G.); Deputy Director of Movements, War Office, 1919-21; Senior Instructor, Staff College, Camberley, 1921-25; Assistant Quartermaster-General, Eastern Command, 1925-27; Commander 166th South

Lancs and Cheshire Infantry Brigade, T.A., 1927-31; Commander 46th (North Midland) Division, T.A., 1932-34; Maj.-Gen. in charge of Administration, Aldershot Command, 1934-1937; Deputy Master-General of the Ordnance, War Office, 1938-39; Senior Military Adviser to the Minister of Supply, 1939-41; retired pay, 1941. *Recreations:* music, and all sports. *Address:* Asphodel, Rock, Cornwall. *Club:* East India and Sports. [*Died* 6 *April* 1960.

TAYLOR, Myron C.; lawyer, industrialist, diplomat (now retired), United States; *b.* Lyons, N.Y., 18 Jan. 1874; *s.* of William Taylor and Mary Morgan Underhill; *m.* 1906, Anabel Stuart Mack, New York; no *c.* *Educ.:* Cornell University, LL.B., 1894. Chairman Finance Committee United States Steel Corp. 1927-34, Chairman Board and Chief Executive Officer, 1932-38, Dir., 1925-1956; Director Amer. Telephone & Telegraph Co., 1929-58. Participant numerous civic activities, 1920-, including nat. and internat. Red Cross, local and nat. relief work. Trustee: Community Service Soc., N.Y., Lycée Français de N.Y., Wells Coll.; Trustee Emeritus: Amer. Acad. in Rome, Cornell Univ.; Hon. Trustee: Met. Museum of Art (Fellow), Met. Opera Assoc., N.Y. Public Library, St. Luke's Hospital. Mem. and past official numerous professional, scientific and genealogical socs. Mem. Ancient and Hon. Artillery Co. of Mass., R.S.A. (Lond.), Ct. of Worshipful Co. of Goldsmiths (Lond.), Bd. of Governors, Shakespeare Memorial Theatre (Stratford-upon-Avon). Special Ambassador of the United States, Chm. of Evian Conf. on Political Refugees, 1938, and Vice-Chm. of Inter-governmental Cttee. on Political Refugees; Personal Rep. of President of U.S.A. to the Pope at the Vatican, 1939-50; Consultant U.S. Department of State; Chairman of its Committee on Post-War Foreign Economic Policy, Member of its Post-War Planning Committee and Advisory Council on Post-War Foreign Policy and of President's Advisory Committee on Post-War Foreign Policy, 1942-44. Holds Hon. Doctorates various Univs. Medal of Merit (U.S.), 1948, and several foreign decorations. *Recreations:* tennis, the fine arts, travel, yachting. *Address:* Killingworth, Locust Valley, L.I., N.Y.; 16 East 70th Street, New York City; Palm Beach, Florida; (office) 575 Madison Ave., N.Y.C. 22. *Clubs:* Bankers, Cedar Creek, Cornell, Knickerbocker, N.Y. Athletic, N.Y. Yacht, Pilgrims, Piping Rock, Turf and Field, Union, University (N.Y.C.); Metropolitan (Washington); Everglades (Florida); International Sportsmen's, Royal Automobile (England); Travellers' (Paris). [*Died* 6 *May* 1959.

TAYLOR, Rachel Annand; Author and Journalist; *b.* 1876; *d.* of late John Wilson Annand and late Clarinda Dinnie Annand, Aberdeen; *m.* 1901, late Alexander Cameron Taylor. *Educ.:* Aberdeen schools and University. LL.D. Aberdeen Univ. 1943. *Publications:* Poems, 1904; Rose and Vine, 1908; Hours of Fiammetta, 1909; Aspects of the Italian Renaissance, 1923; End of Fiammetta, 1923; Leonardo the Florentine, 1927; Dunbar and his Period, 1931; Renaissance France, 1949. *Recreations:* novel-reading and conversation. *Address:* 17 Jenner House, Hunter Street, W.C.1. [*Died* 15 *Aug.* 1960.

TAYLOR, Robert Bruce, M.A., D.D., LL.D.; *b.* Cardross, Scotland, 22 Oct. 1869; *s.* of Robert Taylor, surveyor, Glasgow, and Margaret McNab; *m.* 1st, 1896, Harriet (*d.* 1925), *d.* of late J. G. McKendrick, M.D., F.R.S.; one *s.* four *d.*; 2nd, 1927, Muriel, *d.* of Arthur Bray, Hastings. *Educ.:* Sherborne School; Glasgow University; Marburg; Göttingen. Graduated M.A. in Glasgow, 1890; studied Law; lectured on Economics and acted as Examiner in Economics in Glasgow and Aberdeen Universities; studied Theology, specialising in Semitic languages; assisted Sir George Adam Smith in teaching of Hebrew; Presbyterian Minister successively in Loudoun, Aberdeen, London, and Montreal; Principal of Queen's University, Kingston, Ontario, Canada, 1917-30; Chaplain, Church of Scotland, Rome, 1935; served in France and Belgium as Chaplain and Major in the 42nd Battalion Royal Highlanders of Canada; D.D. Glasgow, Queen's, Canada; LL.D. McGill, Toronto, Lafayette. *Publications:* Ancient Hebrew Literature, 4 vols.; has contributed largely to current theological and economic publications. *Recreations:* sailing, golf. *Address:* Le Rucher, Auribeau, France, A.M. *Clubs:* Century Association (New York); Union (Victoria, B.C.). [*Died* 30 *May* 1954.

TAYLOR, Rt. Hon. Robert John, P.C. 1951, C.B.E. 1949; M.P. (Lab.) Morpeth Division of Northumberland since 1935; *b.* 1881. Miner, checkweighman. J.P. Northumberland. Chairman Morpeth Division of Labour Party. A Lord Commissioner, H.M. Treasury and Deputy Chief Whip, 1945-51; has been member Northumberland County Council and Blyth Borough Council. *Address:* Crow Ash, Marine Terrace, Blyth, Northumberland. [*Died* 19 *July* 1954.

TAYLOR, Sidney Berald, B.Com. (Lond.); F.C.I.S.; M. Inst.T.; Chief Secretary, British Transport Commission, since 1951; *b.* 19 Sept. 1900; *s.* of George Taylor, Fochabers, Morayshire, and Mary Margaret Stuart Johnston, Aberdeen; *m.* 1929, Evelyn Mary, *d.* of Edmund Burke Nagle, Ottawa; one *s.* one *d.* *Educ.:* London School of Economics (Cassel Travelling Schol., Univ. of London); Columbia University, N.Y.C. Entered service of Great Western Railway Co., 1915; Acting Secretary, G.W.R. Co., 1947; Deputy Secretary, British Transport Commission, 1947; Treas., Inst. of Transport, 1953-56. Member of Council: Chartered Institute of Secretaries; Royal Inst. of Public Administration. *Recreations:* golf, fishing. *Address:* 146 Westwood Road, Tilehurst, Berkshire. *T.:* Reading 67382. *Club:* Transportation. [*Died* 3 *June* 1960.

TAYLOR, Theodore Cooke, J.P.; Head of J., T. & J. Taylor, Ltd., woollen manufacturers, Batley; *b.* 1850; *e. s.* of Joshua Taylor, woollen manufacturer; *m.* 1st, 1874, Sara Jane (*d.* 1919), *d.* of W. J. P. Ingraham of Philadelphia, U.S.; one *d.* (one *s.* and one *d.* decd.); 2nd, 1920, Mary Isabella, *d.* of Colin A. McVean, Kilfinichen, Isle of Mull. *Educ.:* Batley Grammar School; Northern Congregational School, Silcoates. M.P. (L.) South-East (Radcliffe-cum-Farnworth) Division of Lancs, 1900-18; was prominent in anti-opium movement, in the interest of which he visited China; in 1892 commenced a scheme of profit-sharing with all his employees in the cloth making business, among whom he has thus distributed over £2,240,000 in addition to standard rates of wages; active advocate and pioneer of this principle. J.P. Batley. *Publications:* Pamphlets and articles on economic questions. *Recreations:* travel and nature study. *Address:* The Moraine, Grassington, Skipton, Yorks. *T.:* Grassington 54. *T.A.:* Theodore Taylor, Grassington. *Club:* National Liberal. [*Died* 19 *Oct.* 1952.

TAYLOR, Sir Thomas (Weston Johns), Kt., *cr.* 1952; C.B.E. 1946; M.A., D.Sc. (Oxon.); Principal of the University College of the South-West of England, Exeter, since 1952; *b.* 1895; *o. s.* of Thomas George Taylor; *m.* 1922, Rosamond Georgina, Junior Comdr. A.T.S., *yr. d.* of Col. T. E. J. Lloyd, C.B., D.L., of Plâs Tregayan, Anglesey. *Educ.:* the City of London School; Brasenose College, Oxford. Served European War, 1914-18, with the Essex Regiment in Gallipoli and France (twice wounded); 1st class Final School of Natural Science, Oxford, 1920;

Fellow of Brasenose College, Oxford, 1920-46; Lecturer in Organic Chemistry, University of Oxford, 1927-46; Rhodes Travelling Fellow, 1931; Member of Council, Chemical Society, 1936-39; Royal Engineers, 1940-43; Capt., then Major; Middle East, 1940-42 (despatches); Secretary, then Director of British Central Scientific Office, Washington, D.C., 1943-44; Head of Operational Research Division, H.Q. Supreme Allied Commander, S.E. Asia, 1944-45; Principal of the University College of the West Indies, 1946-1952. *Publications:* new edition of Sidgwick's Organic Chemistry of Nitrogen (with W. Baker), 1937; various papers in the Journal of the Chemical Society, etc.; editor of Richter-Anschutz Organic Chemistry, Vol. II, 1939. *Recreations:* music, travel, etc. *Address:* University College of the South-West of England, Exeter. *Club:* Athenæum. [*Died* 29 *Aug.* 1953.

TAYLOR, Tom Lancelot; Chairman of Yorkshire Conservative Newspaper Co.; *b.* May 1878; *s.* of late T. A. O. Taylor; *m.* Ethelwynne Rose, *e. d.* of late Howard Childs Parkes; three *d.* *Educ.:* Uppingham; Trinity Coll., Cambridge. *Address:* Hawkhills, Chapel Allerton, Leeds. *T.:* Chapeltown 42002. [*Died* 16 *March* 1960.

TAYLOR, Walter R.; *see* Ross Taylor.

TAYLOR, Lt.-Col. William Herbert, J.P.; Vice-Lieutenant of Worcestershire since 1957; *b.* 23 June 1885; *s.* of William and Hannah Taylor, Devon Villas, Sale, Cheshire; *m.* 1911, Harriet, 2nd *d.* of late Charles Whitaker, J.P., Caldewell, Pershore, Worcestershire; one *s.* one *d.* *Educ.:* privately; Manchester University. Served European War, 1914-18, with Royal Field Artillery (despatches); Major, 1916. Joint Master, Croome Foxhounds, 1926-32; Captain of Worcestershire Cricket Club, 1914 and 1919-20. J.P. Worcs. 1936; D.L. 1941; C.A. Worcs. 1948 (since resigned C.C.); High Sheriff of Worcs., 1949. *Recreations:* hunting, cricket. *Address:* The Moors, Birlingham, Pershore, Worcs. *T.:* Eckington 211. *Club:* Worcestershire County (Worcester). [*Died* 27 *May* 1959.

TEALE, Sir Francis Hugo, K.C.V.O., *cr.* 1951 (C.V.O. 1944); M.D. (Lond.); B.Sc.; F.R.C.P.; Lecturer on Bacteriology, etc., and Lecturer on immunotherapy, University College Hospital Medical School; Hon. Officer i/c immunotherapy Department, University College Hospital; Hon. Bacteriologist Radium Beam Research Institute; Fellow of University College (London); *m.* Dorothea (*née* Felsen). *Educ.:* University College, London. Dobell Lecturer (R.C.P.), 1918; S. Ringer Lecturer (U.C.L.), 1919. Chev. (1st Class) Royal Order St. Olaf. *Publications:* articles in medical journals. *Address:* 32 Harley House, N.W.1. *T.:* Welbeck 2600. [*Died* 22 *Aug.* 1959.

TEARLE, Sir Godfrey (Seymour), Kt., *cr.* 1951; Actor; First President British Actors' Equity Assoc.; *b.* New York, 12 Oct. 1884; *s.* of late Marianne Conway and Osmond Tearle. *Educ.:* privately. First appearance 1893; parts include: Waverley Ango in The Faithful Heart (by Monckton Hoffe), Comedy, 1931; Saul in The Boy David (by J. M. Barrie), His Majesty's, 1936; Maddoc Thomas in The Light of Heart (by Emlyn Williams), Apollo, 1940; Antony in Antony and Cleopatra, Piccadilly, 1947, Martin Beck, New York, 1948; Othello and Macbeth, Stratford, 1948-49; Dr. Sloper in The Heiress, Haymarket, 1950; Hilary Jesson in His House in Order, New, 1951; name part in Hanging Judge, New, 1952; Prod. as actor manager: The Flashing Stream by Charles Morgan, Lyric; The Fake by Fredk. Lonsdale, Apollo. *Club:* Garrick. [*Died* 8 *June* 1953.

TEE, Lieutenant-Colonel James Henry Stanley, C.B.E. 1919; T.D.; *s.* of James Henry Tee; *b.* 1876; *m.* Agnes, *d.* of John Carr, Tatham Fells. Served S. Africa, 1900-1 (Queen's medal with seven clasps); European War, 1914-19 (despatches, C.B.E.). *Address:* Winfield, Eastbourne Road, Lower Willingdon, Sussex. [*Died* 17 *Jan.* 1951.

TEEVAN, Thomas Leslie; Barrister-at-Law; *b.* July 1927; *s.* of R. Teevan, Limavady. *Educ.:* Limavady Academy; Queen's University, Belfast (B.A., LL.B.). Formerly Lecturer in the Faculty of Law, Queen's Univ., Belfast. M.P. (U.U.) Belfast West, November 1950-October 1951; called to the Bar, 1952; formerly Chairman of Limavady Urban District Council, N. Ire.; Chairman of Limavady Unionist Association; Vice-President of North Derry Unionist Association; Member of the Standing Committee of the Ulster Unionist Council. *Address:* Portstewart, Co. Londonderry. [*Died* 11 *Oct.* 1954.

TEHRI-GARHWAL, Lieut.-Col. H.H. Sir Narendra Shah Sahab Bahadur, Retired Maharaja of, K.C.S.I., *cr.* 1932 (C.S.I. 1922); LL.D. Benares; *b.* 3 Aug. 1898; *s.* of late Raja H.H. Sir Kirti Shah Bahadur, K.C.S.I., and *e. d.* of H.H. General Rana Padam Jung, Saheb Bahadur of Nepal; *m.*; three *s.* three *d.* Succeeded to the throne, 1913; abdicated, for health reasons, in favour of his son, 1946. *Educ.:* Mayo College, Ajmere, Rajputana. *Address:* Narendranagar, Tehri-Garhwal State, U.P. Agra and Oudh, India. *T.A.:* Vishalesh, Narendauagar [*Died* 22 *Sept.* 1950.

[*But death not notified in time for inclusion in Who Was Who 1941–1950, first edn.*

TEICHMAN, Major Oskar, D.S.O. 1918; M.B.E. 1944; M.C. 1917; T.D.; late R.A.M.C.; Founder of the Teichman Scholarships; *b.* Eltham, Kent, 1 Nov. 1880; *s.* of late E. Teichman; *m.* 1909, Edith Henrietta, *d.* of late William Harbord, Stamford, Lincs. Endowed (1945) four scholarships at Caius Coll. and one at Inner Temple in memory of his sons Major Philip Raymond Teichman, M.A., and Major Dennis Patrick Teichman, M.C., M.A., killed in action, North Africa, 1942, and Normandy, 1944. *Educ.:* Aldenham; Repton; Caius Coll., Cambridge. M.A.; M.R.C.S. (Eng.); L.R.C.P. (Lond.); F.R.Hist.S.; F.R.G.S.; Member Society Army Historical Research and Royal United Service Institution; joined R.A.M.C. (T.), 1911; attached to Worcestershire Yeomanry; served European War, 1914-19, with Worcestershire Yeomanry—Egypt, Gallipoli, Sinai, and Palestine; with 7th Division — Italy (wounded severely twice, despatches thrice, D.S.O., M.C., Croix de Guerre with palm, Croce di Guerra, Italy, 1914-15 Star, T.D.); D.A.D.M.S. 2nd Lond. Div. 1920-22; Assistant Medical Dir. Radium Institute, 1922-1927; Army Welfare Officer, Wilts, 1939-47. *Publications:* Contributions to R.A.M.C. Journal, Cavalry Journal, R.A. Journal, Army Hist. Res. Journal, Army Quarterly, etc.; The Diary of a Yeomanry M.O., 1921; The Cambridge Undergraduate 100 Years Ago, 1926; Pandour Trenck, 1710-1749, 1927; Black Horse Nemo, 1957. *Recreation:* military history. *Address:* Highbury, Warminster, Wilts. *T.:* Warminster 3074. *Club:* United University. [*Died* 21 *April* 1959.

TELFER-SMOLLETT, Major-General Alexander Patrick Drummond, of Bonhill, Dunbartonshire, C.B. 1938; C.B.E. 1947; D.S.O. 1919; M.C.; Lord Lieutenant Co. of Dunbarton, since 1948; Keeper of Dunbarton Castle, 1949; Member Royal Company of Archers (Queen's Body Guard for Scotland); *b.* 1884; *s.* of Colonel Charles Edward Drummond Telfer-Smollett of Bonhill; *m.* 1913, Lucy (*d.* 1940), *d.* of late Herbert Strutt, Belper, Derbyshire; two *s.* *Educ.:* Sandhurst. Joined Army,

1904; served European War, 1914-18 (D.S.O., M.C., French Croix-de-Guerre, Brevet Majority and Lt.-Col.); Commander British Troops, Shanghai, 1936-39; Lieutenant-Governor of Guernsey, 1939-40; District Commander, 1940; retired pay, 1942; Commissioner British Red Cross, S.E.A.C., 1944-46; Colonel, The Highland Light Infantry, 1946-54. K.St.J. *Recreations:* shooting, fishing, golf. *Address:* Cameron House, Dunbartonshire. *Clubs:* Caledonian, Junior Carlton. [*Died* 9 *Oct.* 1954.

TELLIER, Hon. Sir Joseph Mathias, Kt., *cr.* 1934; *b.* 1861; *s.* of Zephirin Tellier, Joliette, Province of Quebec; *m.* 1885, Maria, *d.* of Joseph Octave Desilets, Protonotary of Superior Court, District of Joliette. Appointed a Puisne Judge, of Superior Court, Montreal, 1916, of King's Bench, 1920; Chief Justice of Province of Quebec, 1932; retired, 1942. *Address:* Joliette, Quebec, Canada. [*Died* 18 *Oct.* 1952.

TEMPANY, Sir Harold Augustin, Kt., *cr.* 1946; C.M.G. 1941; C.B.E. 1933; D.Sc., F.R.I.C.; Editor World Crops, 1949; *b.* 23 July 1881; *s.* of Thomas William Tempany and Emily Anne Palmer; *m.* 1st, 1911, Annie Frances Agnes (*d.* 1945), *e. d.* of Robert Goodwin, Antigua; one *s.* decd.; 2nd, 1946, Kate, *y. d.* of William Welfare. *Educ.:* The County School, Richmond, Surrey; University College, London. Assistant Agricultural Chemist, Leeward Islands, 1903; Govt. Agricultural Chemist and Superintendent of Agriculture, 1909; Director of Agriculture and Registrar Co-operative Credit-Societies, Mauritius, 1917; Member of Mauritius Council of Govt., 1917; First Principal, Mauritius College of Agriculture, in addition to other duties, 1924; Director of Agriculture, Strait Settlements and Federated Malay States, 1929-36; Member: Federal Council, F.M.S., 1934-36; Assistant Agricultural Adviser to the Secretary of State for the Colonies, 1936-40; Agricultural Adviser to the Secretary of State for the Colonies, 1940-46; Colonial Advisory Council on Agriculture, 1937-46; Vice-Chairman, 1940-43; Member Board of Governors, Imperial Institute, 1942; Member, Imperial Institute Council of Plant and Animal Products, 1937, Chairman, 1940; Member Governing Body Imperial College of Tropical Agriculture, 1941-46; Chemical Council, 1940-43; Council Royal Institute of Chemistry, 1937-40, Vice-President, 1940-43; Chairman Commission of Enquiry Uganda Cotton Industry, 1938; Chm. Agriculture Group and Mem. Council, Society Chemical Industry, 1950-. King's Jubilee Medal, 1935; Coronation Medal, 1937; Silver Medal, Royal Soc. of Arts, 1950. *Publications:* (with G. E. Mann) Principles of Tropical Agriculture; Agriculture in the West Indies; Soil Conservation Practice in the Colonial Empire; numerous technical and administrative papers and reports on Tropical Agriculture. *Address:* 7 North End House, W.14. *T.:* Fulham 5701, Euston 5911. *Clubs:* Royal Empire Society, Farmers'. [*Died* 2 *July* 1955.

TEMPLE, Frederick Charles, C.I.E. 1931; C.B.E. 1949; V.D.; L.R.I.B.A.; Chartered Civil and Consulting Engineer; *b.* Exeter, 25 June 1879; *s.* of late Frederick Temple, Archbishop of Canterbury, and Beatrice Blanche, *d.* of Rt. Hon. William Sebright Lascelles; *m.* 1907, Frances Mary, *d.* of late Reginald Stephen Copleston, Bishop of Calcutta; one *s.* four *d.* *Educ.:* Rugby School; Balliol College, Oxford. Apprenticeship under late James Mansergh, F.R.S., 1901-3; Engineer, Birmingham Elan Valley Waterworks, 1903-1905; Military Works Services, India, 1905-1907; various appointments P.W.D. India, 1907-19; Chief Town Engineer 1919 and Administrator 1924-32, Jamshedpur; District Grand Secretary, District Grand Lodge of Bengal, 1932-34; Relief Eng. and Supply Officer, Government of Bihar and Orissa, 1934-35; served in Indian Volunteer Force, Bihar Light Horse, Indian Defence Force, Auxiliary Force (India), Chota Nagpur Regiment, 1908-28; Lt.-Col. (Hon. Col.) commanding, 1928-33; Hon. A.D.C. to the Viceroy, 1931-36; Lieut.-Col Comdg. Home Defence Bn. 1940-41; served in Min. of Home Security, 1941-42; Regional Controller Ministry of Fuel and Power, 1942-1946; Director of Opencast Coal Production, 1947-49. Councillor Lewes Borough, 1954. M.Inst.C.E., M.I.Mech.E. *Address:* Dale House, 18 Keere St., Lewes, Sussex. *T.:* Lewes 257. *Clubs:* Victory; Bengal United Service (Calcutta). [*Died* 26 *March* 1957.

TEMPLE, Lt.-Gen. Reginald Cecil, C.B. 1923; O.B.E.; retd.; *b.* 1877; *s.* of Lt.-Col. W. Temple, V.C.; *m.* 1920, Zillah Edith, *d.* of Vere D. U. Hunt; two *s.* *Educ.:* Dulwich College. Entered Royal Marine Artillery, 1895; Assistant Adjutant-General, Royal Marines, 1921-25; Colonel Commandant Depot R.M., Deal, 1925-27; Maj.-Gen., 1927; Lt.-Gen. 1929; A.D.C. to the King, 1926; retired list, 1930. Awarded pension for good and meritorious service, 1943. *Address:* Carnahalla, Catisfield, Fareham, Hants. [*Died* 30 *May* 1959.

TEMPLE BELL, Eric; *see* Bell.

TEMPLEMORE, 4th Baron (*cr.* 1831), **Arthur Claud Spencer Chichester,** P.C. 1943; K.C.V.O., *cr.* 1938; D.S.O. 1918; O.B.E. 1919; High Steward of Winchester, 1942-1951; Col. late T.A., late Lt.-Col. comdg. 5/7 Bn. Hants Regiment, T.A.; Major late Irish Guards; late Captain Royal Fusiliers; late C.C. (M.R.) for Tower Hamlets (Stepney); late C.C., D.L. Hants.; *b.* 12 Sept. 1880; *e. s.* of 3rd Baron Templemore and Evelyn (*d.* 1883), *d.* of late Rev. W. J. Stracey-Clitherow; *heir-pres.* to 6th Marquess of Donegall; *S.* father, 1924; *m.* 1911, Hon. Clare Meriel Wingfield, 2nd *d.* of 7th Viscount Powerscourt; two *s.* (and one *s.* killed on active service, N. Africa, 1943). *Educ.:* Harrow; Sandhurst. Served South Africa, 1902 (Queen's medal 4 clasps); Tibet, 1904, including march to Lhassa (medal and clasp); European War (D.S.O., O.B.E., Italian Croce di Guerra, 1914-15 Star, G.S. and Victory Medals, despatches 3 times); retired pay, 1924; Parliamentary Private Secretary to Earl of Onslow, Under-Secretary of State for War, 1927-29; Lord-in-Waiting to H.M. Feb.-May 1929 and 1931-34; Capt. of the Yeomen of the Guard, 1934-45; Governor of Harrow School, 1943-48; has 4th class Belgian Order of Leopold and 4th class Order of the Rising Sun of Japan, 1921; 2nd Class Order of Al Rafidain of Iraq, 1933; D.L. Co. Wexford. *Heir: s.* Major Hon. Dermot Richard Claud Chichester, late 7th Q. O. Hussars [*b.* 18 April 1916; *m.* 1946, Lady Josceline Gabrielle Legge, *y. d.* of 7th Earl of Dartmouth, *q.v.*; one *s.* one *d.*]. *Address:* Askefield, Bray, Co. Wicklow, Ireland. *Clubs:* Carlton, Turf; Kildare Street (Dublin). [*Died* 2 *Oct.* 1953.

TEMPLEWOOD, 1st Viscount, *cr.* 1944, of Chelsea; **Samuel John Gurney Hoare,** 2nd Bt., *cr.* 1899; P.C. 1922; G.C.S.I., *cr.* 1934; G.B.E., *cr.* 1927, for 1st civil flight to India; C.M.G. 1917; D.C.L. (Oxford); LL.D. (Cambridge, Reading, Nottingham); Hon. Air Commodore; D.L., J.P.; Chancellor of Reading University since 1937; Hon. Air Commodore 3604 Squadron R.Aux.A.F.; An Elder Brother of Trinity House since 1936; Chm. of Magistrates Assoc., 1947-52; *b.* 24 Feb. 1880; *e. s.* of 1st Bart. and Katharine Louisa Hart (*d.* 1931), *d.* of R. Vaughan Davis, one of H.M.'s Commissioners of Audit; *S.* to father's Baronetcy, 1915; *m.* 1909, Lady Maud Lygon, D.B.E., *cr.* 1927, *d.* of 6th Earl Beauchamp. *Educ.:* Harrow; New College, Oxford. 1st Class Mods.; 1st Class History; Asst. Private Sec. to Rt. Hon. A. Lyttelton, Colonial Secretary, 1905; M.P. (C.) Chelsea, 1910-44; Secretary of State for Air, 1922-24 and Nov. 1924-June 1929; with seat in Cabinet, 1923-24 and 1924-29; Secretary of State for India, 1931-35; Secretary of State for Foreign Affairs, 1935; First Lord of the Admiralty, 1936-37; Secretary of State for Home Affairs, 1937-39; Lord Privy Seal, 1939-40; Secretary of State for Air, 1940; Ambassador to Spain on Special Mission, 1940-44. Contested Ipswich, 1906; Treasurer of Conservative Party Organisation, 1930-31; Member of Royal Commission on Civil Service; L.C.C. Brixton, 1907-10; Chairman London Fire Brigade Committee, 1908; Member of Royal Commission on Honours; Member of Ullswater Conference on Electoral Reform and Indian Round Table Conference; Deputy High Commissioner of the League of Nations for care of Russian Refugees, 1921; formerly member of House of Laymen; Lt.-Col. G.S.O.1. 1917 (despatches twice). President of the Lawn Tennis Association, 1932-58; President National Skating Association, 1945-57. Commander of Orders of St. Anne and St. Stanislaus, Officer of the Order of St. Maurice and Lazarus, Czecho-Slovak Croix de Guerre, Grand Cross Northern Star, White Lion, Dannebrog and Orange Nassau (despatches twice). *Publications:* A Flying Visit: India by Air, 1927; The Fourth Seal, 1930; The Balanced Life; Ambassador on Special Mission, 1946; Crime and Punishment; The Unbroken Thread, 1949; The Shadow of the Gallows, 1951; Nine Troubled Years, 1954; Empire of the Air, 1957. *Recreations:* represented Oxford at racquets and tennis, skating (silver medallist). *Heir:* none. *Address:* Templewood, Northrepps, Cromer. *T.:* Overstrand 243; 12A Eaton Mansions, S.W.1. *T.:* Sloane 6468. *Clubs:* Carlton, Turf. [*Died* 7 *May* 1959 (*ext.*).

TENNANT, Rev. Frederick Robert, F.B.A., D.D. (Cantab.); B.Sc. (Lond.); Hon. D.D. (Oxon); Fellow of Trinity Coll., Camb., since 1913; *b.* Burslem, Staffs., 1866; *m.* 1891, Constance Yates; no *c.* *Educ.:* Newcastle-under-Lyme High School; Caius College, Cambridge. 1st class Natural Science Tripos, Part I. 1887, Part II. (Chemistry) 1889; Senior Science Master, Newcastle-under-Lyme High School, 1891-94; Curate of St. Matthew's, Walsall, 1894-97; Chaplain of Caius College, Cambridge, 1897; Curate of St. Mary the Great, Cambridge, 1899; Hulsean Lecturer in the University of Cambridge, 1901; Rector of Hockwold and Vicar of Wilton, 1903; University Lecturer in Philosophy of Religion, 1907; Lecturer in Theology, 1913-31; Tarner Lecturer, 1931. *Publications:* The Origin and Propagation of Sin; Sources of the Doctrine of the Fall and Original Sin; The Being of God in the Light of Physical Science; The Concept of Sin; The Aim and Scope of Philosophy of Religion; Miracle and its Philosophical Presuppositions; Philosophical Theology, Vol. I. The Soul and its Faculties; Vol. II. The World, The Soul and God; The Philosophy of the Sciences; The Nature of Belief. *Address:* The Knott, Lady Margaret Road, Cambridge. [*Died* 9 *Sept.* 1957.

TENNYSON, 3rd Baron (*cr.* 1884), **Lionel Hallam Tennyson;** late Rifle Brigade; late Coldstream Guards; Colonel 51st (London) Anti-Aircraft Brigade Territorial Artillery; *b.* 7 Nov. 1889; *e. s.* of 2nd Baron; *S.* father 1928; *m.* 1st, 1918, Hon. Clarissa Tennant (whom he divorced, 1928; she *m.* 3rd, 1928, James Montgomery Beck), *o. d.* of 1st Baron Glenconner; two *s.*; 2nd, 1934, Mrs. Joseph William Donner (from whom he obtained a divorce, 1943), *widow* of Joseph Donner, Buffalo, U.S.A., and *d.* of Howard Elting, Chicago. *Educ.:* Eton; Trinity College, Cambridge. Served European War, 1914-18 (wounded thrice, despatches twice, Mons medal), 1940, re-employed with Royal Naval Air Arm. *Publications:* From Verse to Worse, 1933; Sticky Wickets, 1950. *Recreations:* cricket (played for Eton, 1907 and 1908, for England in S. Africa, 1913, 1914, 1924-25, captain Hampshire Cricket XI., Captained England versus Australia in England, 1921), golf, hunting, shooting, tennis. *Heir:* *s.* Hon. Harold Christopher Tennyson, *b.* 25 March 1919. *Address:* Farringford, Freshwater, Isle of Wight. *Clubs:* White's, M.C.C. [*Died* 6 *June* 1951.

TENNYSON-D'EYNCOURT, Sir Eustace (Henry William), 1st Bt., *cr.* 1930; K.C.B., *cr.* 1917 (C.B. 1915); F.R.S. 1921; M.I.C.E.; Hon. D.Sc. Durham; LL.D. Cambridge; Consulting Naval Architect and Engineer; Director of Parsons Marine Steam Turbine Co., 1928-48; Adviser to Vickers Armstrongs; Member of the Association Technique Maritime, Paris; 3rd *s.* of late Louis C. Tennyson-D'Eyncourt of Bayons Manor; *b.* 1 April 1868; *m.* 1898, Janet (*d.* 1909), *widow* of late John Burns, *e. d.* of Mathew Finlay of Langside, Glasgow; one *s.* one *d.* *Educ.:* Charterhouse; Royal Naval College, Greenwich. Served apprenticeship at Elswick; went to Fairfield as Naval Architect, 1898-1902; returned to Elswick as Naval Architect, till appointment at Admiralty; Director of Naval Construction and Chief Technical Adviser to Admiralty, 1912-23; Managing Director of Armstrong Whitworth & Co.'s shipyards at Newcastle, 1924; Pres. of Junior Institution of Engineers, 1920; Vice-Pres. of Institution Naval Architects; 3rd Class Medjidieh for reporting upon Ships of Turkish Fleet in 1900; was head of the Admiralty Committee which produced the first Tank; Vice-President of Tank Board, 1918; on Advisory Committee for Aeronautics during the War; Member of War Office Tank Committee after Armistice; Commander of the Legion of Honour, 1918; D.S.M., U.S.A.; on Grand Council of Federation of British Industries; on Executive Committee of National Physical Laboratory; Chm. Advisory Committee for the William Froude Laboratory, N.P.L. *Publication:* A Shipbuilder's Yarn, 1948. *Recreations:* reading and outdoor exercise. *Heir:* *s.* Eustace Gervais [*b.* 19 Jan. 1902; *m.* 1926, Pamela, *d.* of late W. B. Gladstone; two *s.* one *d.*]. *Address:* 168 Ashley Gardens, S.W.1. *T.:* Victoria 3347; Carter's Corner Farm, Hailsham, Sussex. *Clubs:* Athenæum; Northern Counties (Newcastle-on-Tyne). [*Died* 1 *Feb.* 1951.

TERRELL, Arthur Koberwein a Beckett; *b.* 8 Dec. 1881; *o. surv. s.* of late Arthur à Beckett Terrell, Barrister-at-Law of Lincoln's Inn; *m.* 1924, Aleyne Helen Mary, *e. d.* of A. W. B. Hamilton; one *s.* two *d.* *Educ.:* Banstead School; Tonbridge School (open scholarship); Exeter College, Oxford (open Classical Exhibitioner). 2nd cl. Lit. Hum., M.A.; called to Bar, Lincoln's Inn, 1906; Advocate and Solicitor of the S.S. 1910 and of the F.M.S. 1911; served European War, 1914-1918, Western Front; demobilised 1919 with rank of Captain in the R.F.A.; practised at the S.S. Bar in Penang, 1919-30; Puisne Judge, Straits Settlements and Federated Malay States, 1931; Judge of Appeal, Malaya, 1939-1942; acting Chief Justice Federated Malay States, 1933, 1936, 1938 and 1941, and of the Straits Settlements, 1937 and 1940. Chairman of a Pensions Appeal Tribunal, 1945-55. *Publication:* Malayan Legislation and its Future, 1932. *Recreation:* forestry. *Address:* 44 Addison Road, W.14. *T.:* Western 4139; Chapel Cottage, Ashmansworth, Newbury, Berks. *T.:* Crux Easton 58. *Clubs:* Brooks's, Arts. [*Died* 29 *Jan.* 1956.

TERRELL, George; *b.* 1862; *s.* of late Judge Terrell; *m.* Grace (*d.* 1939), *d.* of late J. J. Hawkins; two *s.* *Educ.:* privately. Early years at sea; subsequently in the law. President, National Union of Manufacturers, 1916-32; M.P. (U.) North-West Wilts, 1910-22; Superintendent in charge of the tenders to the ambulance ships on the Thames, 1940-42; Hon. Treasurer of the

National League for Freedom. *Recreations:* golf, yachting, shooting. *Address:* 64 Highland Heath, Putney, S.W.15. *T.:* Putney 8020. *Club:* Carlton. [*Died* 7 *Nov.* 1952.

TERREY, Henry; Special Lecturer on Chemistry, University College, London; *m.* 1919, Dorothy May Adams; two *d.* *Educ.:* Peter Symonds School, Winchester; University College, London. Professor of Chemistry, University College, London, 1952-54. Governor, Woolwich Polytechnic, London, and College of St. Mark and St. John. *Publications:* numerous scientific papers in Jl. of Chemical Soc., Trans. of Faraday Soc., etc. *Recreations:* cricket and gardening. *Address:* 103 Blackheath Park, S.E.3. *T.:* Lee Green 2554. [*Died* 24 *Dec.* 1954.

TERRY, Sir Francis (William), Kt., *cr.* 1936; Director Joseph Terry and Sons, Limited, York; *b.* 29 Nov. 1877; *s.* of Sir Joseph Terry, Hawthorne Villa, York; *m.* 1908, Sophia Maud, *d.* of Robins Cook, Bowthorpe Hall, Norfolk; one *s.* one *d.* *Educ.:* Uppingham. Late Director Yorkshire Insurance Co. Ltd. (retd.); Pres. York County Savings Bank; entered York City Council, 1924; Alderman, 1934; retired, 1937; High Sheriff for Yorkshire, 1945-46; Vice-Pres. Yorkshire Agricultural Society; Pres. York County Hospital, 1939-41. *Recreation:* shooting. *Address:* Middlethorpe Manor, York. *T.:* York 23573. *Club:* Yorkshire (York). [*Died* 29 *May* 1960.

TERRY, Mrs. Fred; *see* Neilson, Julia.

TERRY, Joseph Pitches, C.B.E. 1949; J.P.; Chairman of Gloucestershire Agricultural Executive Committee, 1942; *b.* 20 Nov. 1880; *m.* 1924, Ellen Mabel Ellis. *Educ.:* Wellingborough Grammar School. Farmer, retired in 1939. J.P. County of Gloster; Councillor for Gloucester, 1925, County Alderman, 1934. *Recreation:* chiefly fox-hunting. *Address:* Denbury, Highnam, Gloucester. *T.:* Gloucester 24237. [*Died* 7 *May* 1955.

TEW, Thomas Percy, J.P.; *b.* 1876; *s.* of late Percy Tew of Heath, Yorks and Brightling Park, Sussex, D.L., J.P.; *m.* 1901, Constance M. (*d.* 1940), 2nd *d.* of late Rev. Canon Thomas Greenall, Grappenhall, Cheshire; (one *s.* killed on active service) two *d.* *Educ.:* Eton. High Sheriff of Sussex, 1934-35. *Address:* Brightling Park, Sussex. *T.:* Brightling 207. *Club:* Boodle's. [*Died* 2 *Dec.* 1953.

TEY, Josephine; *see* Daviot, Gordon.

THACKER, Maj.-Gen. Herbert Cyril, C.B. 1919; C.M.G. 1916; D.S.O. 1918; *b.* 16 Sept. 1870; *s.* of late Maj.-Gen. J. Thacker, Bombay Staff Corps. *Educ.:* Upper Canada College; Royal Military College of Canada. Served S. Africa, 1899-1900 (Queen's medal 3 clasps); Russo-Japanese War, 1904-5, attached to Japanese Army in Manchuria (Japanese War Medal, Order Sacred Treasure, 4th Class); European War, 1914-18 (C.B., C.M.G., D.S.O.); Chief of General Staff, Canadian Militia, 1927-28. *Address:* Victoria, B.C., Canada. *Club:* East India and Sports. [*Died* 2 *June* 1953.

THACKERAY, Colonel Edward Francis, C.M.G. 1916; D.S.O. 1916; late Permanent Force, Union of South African Defence Forces; *b.* 1870; *s.* of late Col. Sir E. T. Thackeray, V.C., K.C.B.; *m.* Linda, *d.* of late Baron von Wurtzburg; two *d.* Served Chitral, 1895; Matabeleland Rebellion, 1896; S. African War, 1899-1902; European War, 1914-16 (C.M.G., D.S.O., Croix de Guerre with Palms), War of 1939-45. *Address:* Larkbeare, 28 Sussex Road, Parkwood, Johannesburg. [*Died* 9 *Nov.* 1956.

THACKERAY, Brig.-General Frank Staniford, D.S.O. 1917, M.C.; *b.* 25 Feb. 1880; *e. s.* of late Alexander Thackeray, J.P., of Glan Ely, St. Fagans; *m.* 1st, 1918, Leila May (*d.* 1941), *e. d.* of Oliver Warner, Colonial Civil Service; 2nd; 1952, Barbara Gertrude, *y. d.* of John St. Foyne Fair, Winchester. *Educ.:* Charterhouse; Oriel College, Oxford. Gazetted to Highland Light Infantry, 1901; European Wa 1914-18 (M.C., D.S.O., slightly wounded twice, despatches five times, Bt. Lt.-Col.); Commanded 1st Batt. Lincolnshire Regt. 1927-1931; Commander 138th (Lincolnshire and Leicestershire) Infantry Brigade, T.A., 1932-1933; Commander Shanghai Area the British Troops in China, 1933-36; A.D.C. to the King, 1935-36; retired pay, 1936. *Recreations:* golf, fishing, ski-ing. *Address:* Melrose, Bereweeke Road, Winchester. *T.:* Winchester 4935; c/o Glyn, Mills & Co., Kirkland House, Whitehall, S.W.1. *Clubs:* Royal Automobile, English-Speaking Union. [*Died* 18 *Aug.* 1960.

THAKORRAM KAPILRAM, Diwan Bahadur, C.I.E. 1927; B.A., LL.B.; Advocate O.S.; *b.* 16 Apr. 1868; *m.* 1888, Ratangavri, *d.* of Keshavrai A. Raiji, at one time private secretary to Ardeshir Kotwal of Surat; one *s.* two *d.* *Educ.:* Primary and secondary education at Bhavnagar; Collegiate education at Elphinstone College, Bombay. Began to practise, 1894; The District Government Pleader and Public Prosecutor, Surat, 1921-1938; a member of the Local Self-Government Committee appointed in 1918 by the Government of Bombay; selected as a witness before the Royal Commission of Reforms in both sections; Rao Bahadur, 1917; Diwan Bahadur, 1923; Secretary Home for the Destitute Children, 1905, President since 1921; one of the Joint Secretaries of the Provincial Conference at Surat in 1907 and of the Congress of 1907, and member of the Convention of 1908; Member of All-India Congress Committee, 1914-16; Secretary of the District Congress Committee, and also its President up to 1917; the Chairman of the Executive Committee of the Surat District Scout Association since 1923 and the District Commissioner since 1925 (Medal of Merit, 1936); on the Raichand Dipchand Schools Managing Committee since 1906, Pres. since 1929; Pres. of the Surat People's Co-operative Bank, 1929-31; Chairman Supervising Union Co-operative Societies, 1929-32; Silver Jubilee Medal, 1935; Coronation Medal, 1937. *Publications:* prepared catalogues of the Andrews Library with Rev. Dr. J. Shillidy and Rev. Dr. H. R. Scott; Tables of Pedigrees, etc., of Surat Vadnagra Nagirs; Account of Dahyabhai Manchharam Hatkeshwar Trust. *Recreations:* nothing special, morning walks. *Address:* Athwa Lines, Surat, Bombay Presidency, India; Shanti Nivas, Kentish Road, Athwa, Surat, Bombay Presidency, India. [*Deceased.*

THARP, Philip Anthony, M.A.; Hon. Assistant Tutor, Ripon Hall, Oxford, since 1956; *b.* 5 July 1890; *s.* of late William Anthony Tharp and late Rose Leontine Swinburn Beadnell; *m.* 1921, Evelyn Nellie Inkster (*d.* 1950); no *c.* *Educ.:* Colet Court; St. Paul's School; Queens' Coll., Camb. (Classical Exhibitioner, later Scholar); Ridley Hall, Camb. Classical Tripos Cl. II. Div. 2, Theological Tripos Cl. II. Gazetted 5th Bn. Royal West Kent Regiment, 1914; served in Gallipoli with 2/4th Bn. and in France with 6th Bn. (wounded); demobilised as Capt. 1919; 2nd Master and House Master, Cranbrook School, Kent, 1919-24; Assistant Master, Wellington College, 1925-26; Headmaster, Collyer's School, Horsham, 1926-56; Freeman of the City of London; Liveryman of the Gardeners' Company of the City of London. Diocesan Lay Reader. *Address:* Hembury, Heathfield, Royston, Herts. *T.:* 3136. [*Died* 17 *Nov.* 1958.

THATCHER, Sir Reginald (Sparshatt), Kt., *cr.* 1952; O.B.E. 1919; M.C.; M.A.; Mus.Doc. (Oxon), F.R.C.O.; Hon. R.A.M.; F.R.C.M.; F.T.C.L. (Hon.); Hon. Fellow of Worcester College, Oxford; *b.* 1888; *m.* 1915, Ruth, *y. d.* of late William Trethowan, Salisbury; one *d.* (one *s.* killed in action, 1942). *Educ.:* privately; Royal College of Music (Open Organ Scholarship); Worcester College, Oxford (Organ Scholar). Assistant Music-Master at Clifton College, 1911; Director of Music, Royal Naval College, Osborne, 1914; Director of Music at Charterhouse School, 1919; at Harrow School, 1928-36; Deputy Director of Music, B.B.C., 1937-44; Principal of the Royal Academy of Music (Vice-Principal, 1945-49), 1949-55; retired, 1955. Pres. Roy. Coll. of Organists, 1954-56; Pres. Incorporated Soc. of Musicians, 1956. *Address:* Barnvale, The Common, Cranleigh, Surrey. [*Died* 6 *May* 1957.

THEAK, Air Vice-Marshal William Edward, C.B. 1948; C.B.E. 1944; Royal Air Force, retired; *b.* 22 Aug. 1898; *s.* of Frank Theak, Ewell, Surrey; *m.* 1922, Florence Alice Easton; two *d. Educ.:* Forest School. Commissioned R.F.C. 1917; Service, France, 1917-18; Egypt, Iraq, India, 1920-24; Malta, 1932-35; France, 1939-40; Chief Signals Officer, Bomber Command, 1940-44; A.O.C. No. 60 Group, 1944-45 (despatches thrice); Director-General of Signals, Air Ministry, 1945-49. Air Officer Administration, Middle East Air Force, 1949-51; A.O.C. No. 90 Group, 1951-1954; retired, 1954. *Address:* The Cottage, Kettleburgh, nr. Woodbridge, Suffolk. *T.:* Framlingham 2071; c/o Lloyds Bank Ltd., 6 Pall Mall, S.W.1. *Club:* United Service. [*Died* 28 *Jan.* 1955.

THEAKER, Harry G., R.B.A., A.R.C.A.; late Headmaster Polytechnic School of Art, Regent Street, W.1; *b.* Wolstanton, Staffs, 1873; *s.* of George Theaker; *m.* Beatrice Winifred, *d.* of James Hawker; two *d. Educ.:* Burslem Endowed School Royal College of Art (Travelling Scholarship and Gold Medal for Design). Decorative artist and water colour painter; executed many works in pottery, stained glass, etc., also book illustrations; frequent exhibitor at principal galleries; member Art Workers' Guild. *Address:* 1 Blenheim Road, Bedford Park, W.4. *T.:* Chiswick 4988. [*Died* 23 *Jan.* 1954.

THOMAS, Reverend Canon Alfred, M.A., F.R.S.L.; Vicar of St. Barnabas', Jesmond, Newcastle upon Tyne; Hon. Canon of Newcastle upon Tyne Cathedral since 1947; *er. s.* of late B. Thomas, Swansea; *m.* 1901, Jessie Adams-Daniells; two *s.* one *d.*; *m.* 1937, Helen Robson. *Educ.:* The London Coll. of Divinity (London Univ.); Univ. College, Durham. Member Honourable Society of Cymmrodorion (London), 1935; admitted in 1925 as a Druid of the Gorsedd of the Isle of Britain under the name "Alfred Gwalia"; Senior Curate of Jesmond Parish Church, 1903-09; Vicar of St. Barnabas', 1909; Chaplain of the Northern Cyclist Batt. T.F., 1914-21; Chaplain to Territorial Res. Force, 1923; President of the Home Teaching Society for the Blind for Newcastle and Gateshead; Vice-President and Governor of the Newcastle Poor Children's Holiday Association; Pres. of the Newcastle and Gateshead Brotherhood Federation, 1928. *Publications:* The Legacies of Christ; Modern Messages to Men; In Christ's Footsteps; Passion Personalities; Spiritual Stepping Stones; Great Prayers of the Bible; also a number of other volumes, pamphlets and sermons. *Recreations:* Rugby football and tennis. *Address:* St. Barnabas' Vicarage, Jesmond, Newcastle upon Tyne. *T.:* 27837. [*Died* 5 *Jan.* 1957.

THOMAS, Rt. Rev. Arthur Nutter; *b.* Hackney, 11 Dec. 1869; *s.* of Charles James Thomas, merchant, member of the Common Council of City of London, and Mary Matilda, *d.* of John Nutter; *m.* 1904, Mary Theodora (*d.* 1941), 4th *d.* of Rev. W. A. H. Lewis, Vicar of Upper Gornal; one *s.* two *d. Educ.:* St. John-at-Hackney Gram. School; Sutherland House School, Folkestone; Oundle School; Pembroke College, Cambridge (Scholar); B.A. (1st class Classical Trip.), 1891; Jeremie Septuagint Prize, 1892; Carus Greek Testament Prize and 2nd cl. Theol. Trip. Pt. ii. 1893; M.A. 1895; D.D. 1906; Wells' Theological Coll., 1893-94; Deacon, 1894; Priest, 1895; Curate of Wakefield Cathedral, 1894-95; Domestic Chaplain to Archbishop of York, 1895-99; Curate of Leeds, 1899-1901; Rector of Guisborough, 1901-06; Chaplain to Archbishop of York, 1905-06; Bishop of Adelaide, 1906-40. *Recreations:* music, gardening. *Address:* 82 Hill Street, N. Adelaide. [*Died* 10 *April* 1954.

THOMAS, His Honour (Aubrey) Ralph, B.C.L., M.A. Oxon; a Judge of the Mayor's and City of London Court, 1936-54; retired; *b.* London, 11 Feb. 1879; *s.* of late Ralph Thomas, Solicitor; *m.* 1913, Beatrice, *y. d.* of late Richard Porter; no *c.* Called to bar, Middle Temple, 1902; Bencher, 1934; Treasurer, 1951; Oxford Circuit; on the instructional staff of the School of Musketry, Bisley, 1916-18; Recorder of Gloucester, 1932-37; Hon. Junior Counsel to Officers' Association, 1928-36. *Address:* Forton, The Heath, Weybridge. *T.:* Weybridge 579. [*Died* 31 *May* 1957.

THOMAS, David Emlyn; M.P. (Lab.) Aberdare Division since December 1946; *b.* 16 Sept. 1892; *m.* Bessie Thomas (*d.* 1953), schoolmistress; one *s.* two *d. Educ.:* Elementary Schools. Attended evening classes in Mining and Mine Surveying. Employed at Collieries from age of 14 years until 1919 when became full time official of South Wales Miners' Federation. Miners' Agent of Merthyr and Aberdare Valleys and Advisory Member of Executive of National Union of Mineworkers, South Wales Area, 1936-46. *Address:* 65 Broniestyn, Aberdare, Glam. *T.:* 295; House of Commons, S.W.1. [*Died* 20 *June* 1954.

THOMAS, David Rowland, Q.C. 1931; a Metropolitan Police Magistrate, 1941-54; Called to Bar, Middle Temple, 1909; joined the South Wales and Chester Division of the North and South Wales and Chester Circuit. Recorder of Carmarthen, 1935-41. Bencher of Hon. Society of Middle Temple. *Club:* Reform. [*Died* 25 *Feb.* 1955.

THOMAS, Venerable David William, M.A.; Archdeacon; retired; *s.* of Richard Thomas, Taliaris, Carmarthenshire; *m.* 1914, Maud, *o. d.* of Alfred Noyes, Burland House, Devonshire; one *s. Educ.:* St. David's College School, Lampeter; St. David's College, Lampeter; Jesus College, Oxford. Curate of Llanelly, Carmarthenshire, 1896-1903; Assistant Missioner in the Diocese of St. David's, 1903-8; Minor Canon of St. David's Cathedral and Senior Diocesan Inspector of Schools in the Diocese of St. David's, 1908-12; Vicar of Llandebie, Carmarthenshire, 1912-28; Rural Dean of Llandilo, 1920-28; Vicar of Lampeter, 1928-1946; Rural Dean of Lampeter, 1929-36; Canon of St. David's Cathedral, 1924-36; Archdeacon of Cardigan, 1936-44; Vicar of Skenfrith, Mon., 1946-48. *Address:* Bryn Hawk, New Road, New Quay, Cards. [*Died* 5 *March* 1951.

THOMAS, Dylan Marlais; poet, story-writer, broadcaster; *b.* Oct. 1914; *m.* 1936, Caitlin Macnamara; two *s.* one *d. Publications:* Eighteen Poems, 1934; Twenty-five Poems, 1936; The Map of Love, 1939; Portrait of the Artist as a Young Dog, 1940; The World I Breathe (in America), 1940; Deaths and Entrances, 1946; Collected Poems, 1952; The Doctor and the Devils, 1953 (his only screen play; it was not filmed, but was adapted for stage for R.A.D.A. Vanbrugh Theatre, 1961); In Country Sleep (publ. U.S.A.); (posthumous): Under Milk Wood (radio play, and later stage play), 1954; Quite Early One Morning (broadcast talks), 1954; Adventure in the Skin Trade, 1955; Letters to Vernon Watkins (Ed. Vernon Watkins), 1957. *Relevant publication:* Leftover Life to Kill (by his wife Caitlin Thomas), 1957. *Address:* Boat House, Laugharne, Carmarthenshire. *Club:* Savage. [*Died* 9 *Nov.* 1953.

THOMAS, Edward Francis, C.S.I. 1935; C.I.E. 1922; Indian Civil Service, retired; *b.* 30 June 1880; *s.* of Maj. E. C. Thomas; *m.* 1919, Honor, 2nd *d.* of late Lionel Johnstone Bigge; no *c.* *Educ.:* St. Paul's School; Trinity College, Oxford (Scholar). Took degree 1903; I.C.S. examination, 1903; arrived Madras, 1904; passed through the usual stages of Assistant Collector and Magistrate; was temporarily attached to the Indian Police; Secretary, Board of Revenue, Madras, 1915; joined Indian Army Reserve and was attached to Army H.Q., India, 1917; Collector and District Magistrate, Malabar, 1919, and held this position when the Mopla rebellion broke out 21 ug. 1921; A Director of Industries, Madras, 1922-26; Board of Revenue, 1931; First Member Board of Revenue, 1935-38 retired, 1938. *Address:* c/o Lloyds Bank, Ltd. 6 Pall Mall, S.W.1; 2 Winston House, Glenwood, Durban, S. Africa. [*Died* 10 *Aug.* 1954.

THOMAS, Elbert Duncan, A.B., Ph.D., LL.D., Litt.D.; High Commissioner for the Trust Territory of the Pacific Islands (with personal rank of Ambassador), since 1951; United States Senator from Utah, 1933-50; *b.* Salt Lake City, 17 June 1883, English parentage; *s.* of Richard Kendall Thomas and Caroline Stockdale; *m.* 1907, Edna Harker (*d.* 1942); three *d.*; *m.* 1946, Ethel Evans. *Educ.:* Common schools; University of Utah, A.B.; University of California, Ph.D.; University of Southern California, LL.D.; University of Hawaii; National University, Litt.D.; Student traveller Europe, 1912-13. Missionary in Japan and President of the Japan Mission, Church of Jesus Christ of Latter-day Saints, 1907-12; Instructor in Latin and Greek, 1913-15; Secretary-Registrar, 1915-22; President, Utah Alumni Association, 1913-14; Chairman, Military Committee, 1916-22; Professor, Political Science, University of Utah, 1922-33; Major, Inspector-General's Department, U.S.R., 1918-24; Democratic nominee for Secretary of State, 1920; Fellow in Political Science, University of California, 1922-24; Guest Professor, 1935; Member of the Carnegie European Conference of American Professors, 1926; Member of the Second, Third and Fourth Conferences of Teachers of International Law, Washington, 1925, 1928 and 1933; Amer. mem. Internat. Commn. for Adjustment of Disputes between S. Africa and U.S., 1935; Assoc. Moderator of President's 1941 Industry-Labor Conf. which recommended War Labor Bd.; Chairman: U.S. Senate Education and Labor Committee, 1937-44; Military Affairs Cttee., 1944-46; U.S. Senate Labor and Public Welfare Committee, 1949-50; Member Civil Liberties Committee, 1934-39; Member Committee on Reorganization of Congress, 1945-46. Chairman, Thomas Jefferson National Memorial Commission; Hon. Vice-Pres. American Society of International Law; Vice-President American Political Science Association, 1940; granted Oberlaender Award for study in Germany, in 1934; represented U.S. Senate at Inter-Parliamentary Union, Budapest, 1936, and Paris, 1937; represented U.S. at International Labor Organization Conference, Philadelphia, 1944, Paris 1945, Montreal, 1946, Geneva, 1947, San Francisco, California, 1948; U.S. Delegate to Commonwealth Parl. Assoc., Bermuda, 1948; Mem. of Council of American Learned Societies, 1938-46. Member of several other learned societies. *Publications:* Sukui No Michi (in Japanese), 1911; Chinese Political Thought, 1927; World Unity Through Study of History, 1933; Thomas Jefferson—World Citizen, 1941; The Four Fears, 1944; This Nation Under God, 1950. *Address:* (Pres.) 4758 Aukai Ave., Honolulu 15, Hawaii; (permanent) 137 North West Temple, Salt Lake City, Utah, U.S.A. *Clubs:* (Hon.) Pacific, (Hon.) Chamber of Commerce (Honolulu). [*Died* 12 *Feb.* 1953

THOMAS, Sir Eustace, Bt.; *see* Thomas, Sir W. E. R.

THOMAS, Rev. Evan Lorimer, M.A.; Archdeacon of Montgomery and Vicar of Llansantffraid, 1938-44; Canon of St. Asaph, 1926, now Canon Emeritus; Professor of Welsh at St. David's College, Lampeter; Examining Chaplain to Bishop of St. Asaph; *b.* 21 Feb. 1872; *s.* of Rev. D. Walter Thomas, Canon Residentiary of Bangor Cathedral and Vicar of Holyhead, and Mrs. A. Walter Thomas (Morfudd Eryri); *m.* 1903, Mary Rice-Williams, Holyhead; one *s.* *Educ.:* Westminster School; Jesus College, Oxford (Scholar and Exhibitioner); Leeds Clergy School. Curate of St. Mary's, Bangor, 1897-98; Wrexham, 1898-1900; Cuddesdon, 1901-2; Colwyn Bay, 1902-3. *Recreations:* any games and fishing, ornithology. *Address:* Roselea, Llanfairfechan, N. Wales. [*Died* 9 *April* 1953.

THOMAS, Frederick William, C.I.E. 1928; M.A.; late Fellow of Balliol College; Fellow (Member of Council and Chairman of Section IV., Oriental Studies, 1935-41) of the British Academy; Hon. Fellow of School of Oriental and African Studies in University of London; Hon. Ph.D. Munich; Hon. D.Litt. (Allahabad), 1937; Hon. D.Litt. (Birmingham), 1949; Foreign, Corresponding or Hon. Member of various foreign academies, Institut de France (Académie des Inscriptions et Belles-Lettres), oriental societies, etc.; Member (appointed by the British Academy) of the Governing Body of the School of Oriental Studies; Vice-President Royal India Society; *b.* 21 Mar. 1867; *m.* 1908, Eleanor Grace, *e. d.* of Walter Hammond of the Grange, Knockholt; one *s.* one *d.* *Educ.:* King Edward's School, Birmingham; Trinity College, Cambridge (Fellow, 1892-98). Headmaster's Assistant, King Edward's School, Birmingham, 1891-1898. Asst. Librarian, India Office, 1898-1903; Librarian, 1903-27; Boden Professor of Sanskrit in Univ. of Oxford, 1927-37; Lecturer in Comparative Philology, Univ. Coll., London, 1908-35; Reader in Tibetan, London Univ., 1909-37; Temp. Lecturer Post-Grad. Dept., Univ. of Calcutta, 1938; Pres. Ninth All-India Oriental Conf., 1937. Hon. Sec. (Director, 1921-1922) of Royal Asiatic Soc., 1920-27; Hon. Treas. Aristotelian Soc., 1923-28; Hon. Correspondent Govt. of India, Archæologica Dept.; has received the title of Vidyāvāridhi from the Sri Bharat Dharma Mahamandal of all India and that of Jnānabandhu from the Sanskrit College, Calcutta; and a medal for Buddhist studies awarded at celebration in Tokyo, 1934, of 2000th anniversary of Buddha's birth; Triennial Gold Medal (1941) of Royal Asiatic Society; Campbell Memorial Medal of Bombay Branch of Royal Asiatic Society, 1947; has examined in Comparative Philology, Sanskrit, Pali, Zend and Tibetan for univs. in England and India; Ed. Epigraphia India (1916-22); Vice-Pres., International Congress of Linguists, 1952; Pres. Philological Soc., 1926-29. *Publications:* Translation of the Sanskrit Harsa-Carita of Bāna (with the late Professor E. B. Cowell), 1897; British Education in India, 1891; Mutual Influence of Muhammadans and Hindus in India, 1892; The *D*-Suffix, 1900; Catalogues of certain Sanskrit MSS. belonging to Royal Asiatic Society and the India Office Library, 1902, 1903, 1908, 1935; Tibetan Literary Texts and Documents concerning Chinese Turkestan, Vol. I., 1935, Vol. II, 1951, Vol. III, 1954; Indianism and its Expansion, 1942; The Nam Language, 1948; editor Sanskrit Kavīndravacanasamuccaya, 1912; translator (with Miss L. A. Thomas) of M. A. Foucher's The Beginnings of Buddhist Art and other Essays in Indian and Central-Asian Archæology, 1914; edited Outlines of Jainism, by J. L. Jaini, The Vaisesika Philosophy, by H. Ui, the Pravacanasara of Kundakunda, by B. Faddegon, 1934, and Antiquities of Indian Tibet, by A. H. Francke. vol. ii.; many papers to the Journal of the Royal Asiatic Society, Journal of Theological Studies, Hibbert Journal, and Proceedings of the Aristotelian Society, etc. *Address:* Limen, Bodicote, nr. Banbury. [*Died* 6 *May* 1956.

THOMAS, George Ross, C.M.G. 1938; Under-Secretary and Director, Department of Public Instruction, New South Wales, 1930-40; *b.* 1876; *s.* of Henry Thomas; *m.* 1907, Amy Edith Devey. *Educ.:* Sydney University, B.A. Inspector of Schools, New South Wales, 1918; Chief Inspector, 1929. *Address:* c/o Dept. of Public Instruction, Sydney, New South Wales. [*Died* 6 *Sept.* 1955.

THOMAS, His Honour Judge Gerwyn Pascal; County Court Judge since 1953; Circuit 30, Glamorganshire, etc., since Oct. 1955 (formerly of County Court Circuit No. 24, Cardiff, etc., 1953-55); *b.* 15 April 1895; *s.* of William and Maria Jane Thomas; *m.* 1928, Dorothy Jones; one *d. Educ.:* Llandilo Grammar School; Downing College, Cambridge. Called to Bar, 1922. Referee, South Wales and Monmouthshire Coalfield, 1948; Vice-Chm. Carmarthenshire Quarter Sessions, 1951; formerly Chairman Medical Appeals for Wales, 1951. *Recreation:* golf. *Address:* Coedsaeson, Parc Wern Road, Swansea. *T.:* 22220. [*Died* 9 *April* 1956.

THOMAS, Gwilym E. A.; *see* Aeron-Thomas.

THOMAS, Rt. Rev. Harry; Suffragan Bishop of Taunton since 1945; *b.* 1897; *s.* of Theo J. Thomas; *m.* Léonie Tod; one *s. Educ.:* St. David's Coll., Lampeter (B.A. 1923); Oriel Coll., Oxford (B.A. 1929, M.A. 1932). Deacon, 1923; Priest, 1924; Vice-Principal Ely Theological College, 1930-36; Principal St. Francis College, Milton, Diocese of Brisbane, 1936; Canon Res. of St. John's Cathedral, Brisbane, and Archdeacon of Brisbane, 1938-44; Chap. A.M.F. 1939. *Address:* East Liberty, Wells, Somerset. [*Died* 8 *July* 1955.

THOMAS, Sir Henry, Kt., *cr.* 1946; F.B.A. 1936; F.S.A.; D.Litt., Hon. LL.D. (Birm.), D.Lit. (Lond.); Principal Keeper of Printed Books, Br. Museum, 1946-47; Keeper, 1943-45; Dep. Keeper, 1924-43; *b.* Eynsham, Oxon, 1878; 2nd *s.* of late Alfred Charles Thomas of Birmingham and Coventry. *Educ.:* King Edward's School, Aston, Birmingham; University of Birmingham. Research scholar in Classics; Constance Naden Gold Medallist; Associate of Mason Univ. College; Norman MacColl Lecturer, Cambridge, 1916; Taylorian Lecturer, Oxford, 1922; Corr. or Hon. Member of Spanish, Portuguese, and American Academies, etc.; Hon. For. Corr. Member, Grolier Club, New York; President Anglo-Spanish Soc., 1931-47; Pres. Bibliographical Soc., 1936-38; Vice-Pres.: Library Assoc., 1948; Hispanic and Luso-Brazilian Councils; Hon. Councillor, Spanish Higher Council for Scientific Research; Trustee National Central Library. *Publications:* Dos Romances Anónimos del Siglo XVI., Madrid, 1917; Spanish and Portuguese Romances of Chivalry, 1920 (awarded Bonsoms prize and gold medal, Institut d'Estudis Catalans, 1921); Short-title Catalogue of Spanish Books printed before 1601 now in the British Museum, 1921; of Portuguese and Spanish-American Books, 1926; of Portuguese Books, 1940; and of Spanish-American Books, 1944; Shakespeare and Spain, 1922; Spanish Sixteenth-Century Printing, 1926; Andrés Brun, Calligrapher of Saragossa (with Stanley Morison), 1929; Monster and Miracle, 1935; The Discovery of Abyssinia by the Portuguese in 1520 (with Dr. A. Cortesão), 1938; Early Spanish Bookbindings, 1939, Anti-English Propaganda in the time of Queen Elizabeth, 1946; Shakespeare in Spain (Br. Acad. annual Shakespeare lecture), 1949, and other works; verse trans. of La Estrella de Sevilla, 1935, 2nd edn. 1950, and of J. E. Hartzenbusch's Los Amantes de Teruel, 1938, 2nd. edn. 1950; edited La Estrella de Sevilla, 1923, 2nd ed. 1930; British Museum Catalogue of French Books (1470-1600), 1924; Early Spanish Ballads in the British Museum, 1927; Thirteen Spanish Ballads, 1931; Coplas de Ambrosio Montesino, 1936; Coplas del Comendador Román, 1936; Carta das novas do descobrimento do Preste João (with A. Cortesão), Lisboa, 1938; Guevara's Praise of the Countrie Life, 1938; G. Sulpizio's Doctrina mensae, with Eng. trans., 1949; contributions to reviews, etc. *Address:* Lancaster Lodge, Bolingbroke Grove, S.W.11; Arden, Manor Rd. North, Edgbaston, Birmingham 16. *T.:* Edgbaston 3269. [*Died* 21 *July* 1952.

THOMAS, Herbert James; *b.* 29 January 1882; *s.* of late Herbert Thomas, Bristol; *m.* 1909, Charis, *d.* of L. C. B. Muirhead, Haseley Court, Oxford; two *s.* one *d. Educ.:* Clifton College; Magdalen College, Oxford. Barrister, Inner Temple, 1907. Served European War, 1914-1918, Oxfordshire Yeomanry and 2nd Life Guards (Lieut.). Berkshire County Council, 1938, Alderman, 1944, Chairman, 1947-54. High Sheriff of Berkshire, 1946. *Address:* Longleys House, Cumnor, nr. Oxford. *T.:* Cumnor 87. *Clubs:* Savile; Berkshire (Reading). [*Died* 16 *Feb.* 1960.

THOMAS, Hugh Whitelegge, C.M.G. 1941; Liaison Officer in Accra for the African Manganese Company; *s.* of late Rev. T. W. and late Charlotte Susanna Thomas; *m.* 1929, Margery Angelo Augusta Swynnerton; one *s. Educ.:* Dean Close School, Cheltenham; Choral Scholar, Jesus College, Cambridge. B.A. Cantab.; First master at Cheam School, Surrey, afterwards Aysgarth School, Yorks; Assistant District Commissioner, 1913, District Commissioner, 1917, Provincial Commr., 1928, Sec. for Native Affairs, 1931-44, Gold Coast. Acting Colonial Sec., Gold Coast, in 1932 and 1934, and on occasion Governor's Deputy. Acting Chief Commissioner, Ashanti, 1932; accredited representative of H.M. Govt. to League of Nations in 1931 and 1934 in respect of the Report on the Mandated Territory of Togoland. *Recreations:* cricket, tennis, golf. *Address:* P.O. Box 277, Accra, Ghana; Queen's Rd., Belmont, Surrey. *Clubs:* United University, Public Schools. [*Died* 1 *Feb.* 1960.

THOMAS, Sir Ivor Broadbent, Kt., *cr.* 1938; J. P.; D.L. (Glamorgan); *b.* Cardiff, 1890; *s.* of late Sir Thomas Powell Thomas, J.P. and Mrs. Lillie Thomas, O.B.E.; *m.* 1912, Jean Erskine McColl; one s. one *d. Educ.:* Llandaff Cathedral School; Malvern College. Member Glamorgan County Council since 1930; Member Cardiff Rural District Council since 1923; President Barry Conservative and Unionist Association; Pres. Internat. Bowling Board, 1939-53; Vice-Chm. United Cardiff Hosps., since 1948; Vice-Chm. Glamorgan County Council, 1955-56, Business, Coal Exporter (retired 1929); European War, 1914-19, Captain, Headquarters Staff for Embarkation Duties 5th Welsh Supy. Batt. and Royal Defence Corps; rejoined Army, 1940 (Major, Gen. List Movement Control); resigned commission, 1943. *Recreations:* golf, bowls. *Address:* Kenmore, Dinas Powis, Glam. *T.:* Dinas Powis 3170. *Clubs:* Constitutional; Cardiff and County (Cardiff). [*Died* 22 *Nov.* 1955.

THOMAS, John Herbert, C.I.E. 1943; Civil Servant, retired; *b* 21 Feb. 1895; *y. s.* of late W. M. Thomas, Cardiff. *Educ.:* Cardiff High School; F.I.A. 1923. Actuary in Govt. Actuary's Dept., London, 1938-55; retired 1955. Seconded from U.K. Civil Service to India as first Superintendent of Insurance with Govt. of India under (Indian) Insurance Act, 1938, and to Govt. of Pakistan, 1948. *Club:* East India and Sports. [*Died* 7 *May* 1960.

THOMAS, Ven. Lawrence, D.D.; Archdeacon of Margam since 1948; Canon of Llandaff Cathedral since 1944; *b.* 19 Aug.

1889; *s.* of David and Elizabeth Thomas; *m.* 1923, Beatrice Lilian Williams, Crickhowell, Brecs.; one *d.* *Educ.:* Lewis's Sch., Pengam; St. David's Coll., Lampeter; St. John's College, Oxford; Trinity Coll., Dublin; St. Michael's Coll., Llandaff. B.A. Lampeter, 1911; B.A. Oxon, 1916; M.A. Oxon, 1920; B.Litt. Oxon., 1925; B.D., T.C.D., 1926; D.D. T.C.D., 1930. Curate, St. John's Canton, Cardiff, 1912-13; Curate, Headington Quarry, Oxford, 1913-16; Curate, St. John Baptist, Cardiff, 1916-24; Vicar, Briton Ferry, 1924-42; Vicar of Bargoed, 1942-46; Vicar of Aberavon, 1946-58. Treasurer of Llandaff Cathedral, 1948-. *Publications:* The Reformation in the Old Diocese of Llandaff; Life of Griffith Jones, Llanddowror. Contributor to Dictionary of Welsh National Biography. *Recreation:* antiquarian and ecclesiastical architecture. *Address:* Twynyderi, 20 Dinas Baglan Rd., Port Talbot, Glam. *T.:* Port Talbot 3829. [*Died* 19 *Oct.* 1960.

THOMAS, Percy Goronwy, M.A. (Cantab.); Litt.D. (Liv.); Emeritus Prof. of English Language and Medieval Literature at Bedford College, Univ. of London; *b.* 1875; *s.* of late Josiah Thomas, J.P. (Liverpool), and *g.s.* of Rev. John Thomas, D.D.; *m.* 1918, Mary, *e. d.* of late John Ivor Jones of Llangollen and Colombia, S. America; two *s.* *Educ.:* University of Liverpool; Caius College, Cambridge. Assistant Lecturer in English at the University College of North Wales, 1903-6; Lecturer in English Language at King's College, University of London, 1908-23; External Examiner to the University of Wales, 1927-30; External Examiner to the University of London, 1930-33. *Publications:* Glossary of the Mercian Hymns (with H. C. Wyld), 1903; Alfred and the Prose of his Reign (Camb. Hist. Lit., vol. i.), 1907; Greene's Pandosto (Shakespeare Classics), 1907; Introduction to the History of the English Language, 1920; Middle English Section in The Year's Work in English Studies (English Association), 1923 and 1924; English Literature before Chaucer, 1924; Aspects of Literary Theory and Practice, 1931; Notes on The Pearl (London Mediaeval Studies), 1938; articles in Modern Language Review, etc. *Recreation:* golf. *Address:* Winfrith, 26 Forty Avenue, Wembley Park, Middlesex. *T.:* Arnold 3221. *Club:* Sudbury Golf (Wembley). [*Died* 28 *May* 1954.

THOMAS, Major Peter David, C.B.E. 1920; M.V.O. 1919; Solicitor; Director of Mark Oldroyd Ltd., Dewsbury, and of several other companies; *b.* Neath, S. Wales, 1873; *s.* of Nicholas Howell Thomas, Bridge House, Neath, and Mary David; *m.* Ada (*d.* 1950), *d.* of David Isaac, Heathfield, Swansea; one *s.* *Educ.:* Neath Grammar School. Admitted Solicitor, 1894; Clifford's Inn Prizeman; Partner Simpson Thomas & Co., Leeds, 1902-13; Lieut. Army Motor Reserve, 1907-13; Lieutenant 6th Welsh Battalion, Aug. 1914; Captain, 1915; service in France as Machine-Gun Officer, Oct. 1914-May 1915; Organising Secretary, Yorkshire Area Ministry of Munitions, July 1915 - Jan. 1919 (despatches twice, Brevet Major, M.V.O., Cavaliere Crown of Italy, C.B.E.). Member Poor Persons Cttee. of Law Society. *Publications:* various Pamphlets and Journalistic Articles on Labour, Educational, and Social Subjects. *Recreations:* motoring, shooting, and golf. *Address:* Invercairn, Charlton Kings, Cheltenham. *Clubs:* Constitutional, Royal Automobile. [*Died* 19 *June* 1952.

THOMAS, His Honour Ralph; *see* Thomas, His Honour A. R.

THOMAS, Rt. Rev. Richard, D.D.; Bishop of Willochra since 1926; *b.* 24 Oct. 1881; *s.* of Daniel Thomas, Llantrisant, Glamorganshire, S. Wales. *Educ.:* Monmouth Grammar School. Deacon, 1908; Priest, 1909; Curate of St. John Baptist, Coventry, 1908-14; Member of the Bush Brotherhood of St. Barnabas in North Queensland, 1914-1922; Archdeacon of North Queensland, 1923-25. *Recreations:* horse riding, tennis, walking. *Address:* Bishop's House, Gladstone, South Australia. *T.:* 7. [*Died* 17 *April* 1958.

THOMAS, Sir Robert John, 1st Bt., *cr.* 1918; *b.* 23 Apr. 1873; *m.* 1905, Marie Rose (*d.* 1948), *d.* of Arthur Burrows; two *s.* one *d.* *Educ.:* Bootle College; Liverpool Institute; Tettenhall College. M.P. (Coal. L.) Wrexham Division of Denbighshire, Dec. 1918-22; M.P. (L.) Anglesey, 1923-29; ex-High Sheriff of Anglesey; founded Welsh Heroes Memorial Fund. *Heir:* *s.* William Eustace Rhyddlad (*see* Sir W. Eustace R. Thomas, 2nd Bt.). *Address:* Garreglwyd, Holyhead, Anglesey. [*Died* 27 *Sept.* 1951.

THOMAS, Sir Roger, Kt., *cr.* 1947; C.I.E. 1942; B.Sc. (Honours); F.R.G.S.; Managing Director Sind Land Development, Ltd., since 1932; *b.* 4 May 1886; *s.* of late Lewis and Sophia Thomas, of Great Vaynor and Penrardd, Clynderwen, Pem.; *m.* 1939, Margaret Ethelwynne Roberts; one *d.* *Educ.:* Narberth County School; Univ. Coll. Wales, Aberystwyth. Deputy Director of Agriculture, Indian Agricultural Service, Madras, 1913; Member of Mesopotamia Expeditionary Force, 1917; retired with military rank of Captain; Cotton Expert, Mesopotamia, 1917; Director of Agriculture, Mesopotamia, 1921; retired from Govt. Service, 1926; Manager, British Cotton Growing Association, Punjab, 1928. Ex-Mem. Viceroy's Reconstruction (Policy) Committee, Imperial Council of Agricultural Research (India) and of Indian Central Cotton Committee. Cabinet Minister to Govt. of Sind 1944, relinquished appt. same year to serve as Hon. Adviser to Govt. of Sind in Agriculture and Post-War Development; Chm. Farm Tenancy Legislation Cttee. (Sind), 1947. Member Lord Boyd-Orr Agricultural Enquiry Cttee., Pakistan, 1951; Member Pakistan Council of Agriculture and Central Cotton Cttee. since partition of India; Chm. Pakistan Flower Show, 1951-57, and Pakistan Poultry Show, 1952; Vice-Pres. Pakistan Horticultural Soc., 1953-. *Publications:* various press articles on agricultural economics. *Recreations:* riding, fishing and gardening. *Address:* 66 Clifton, Karachi, Pakistan. *T.A.:* Sindlandco, Mirpurkhas. *T.:* Mirpurkhas 04. *Clubs:* Royal Societies; Sind (Karachi). [*Died* 19 *Sept.* 1960.

THOMAS, Sir Samuel Joyce, Kt., *cr.* 1935; Chief Justice, Federated Malay States, 1933-37; *s.* of Edmund Thomas, Barr.-at-law; *g.s.* of Ralph Thomas, Serjeant-at-law. *Educ.:* King's College, London; Inglis Scholar and Early English Text Society Prizeman; Associate (with distinction) King's College, London, 1897; B.A. London, 1897. Called to Bar, Middle Temple, 1898; Chairman, Tatsfield Parish Council, 1906-16; member L.C.C., 1913-19; contested Stoke-upon-Trent, 1910; prospective Unionist candidate, 1910-14; W.M. Midland and Oxford Circuit Bar Lodge, 1914; enlisted, 1915; commissioned in A.S.C. (M.T.), and attached to R.G.A. (145th Siege Battery), France, Flanders, Italy; invalided out of Army, 1919; Chief Justice, St. Vincent, 1919; acting Administrator, St. Vincent, 1920; Second Puisne Judge of Trinidad and Tobago, 1923-29; Chairman, Oil and Water Board (unpaid), Trinidad and Tobago, 1923-29; Puisne Judge, Kenya, 1929-33. *Publications:* The Colclough Chronicle; Red Roses, 1915; Evelyn, 1947; Albert; Aunt Kate; Memoirs of Georgiana Dowager Countess Mere. Law Relating to Clubs, 1902. *Recreation:* general. *Clubs:* Constitutional, Carlton. [*Died* 19 *Jan.* 1952.

THOMAS, Sir Theodore Eastaway, Kt., *cr.* 1946; C.B.E. 1941; Director: Lancashire United Transport Ltd.; South Lancashire Transport Co.; *b.* 9 Feb. 1882; *s.* of Philip Henry and Mary Elizabeth Thomas; *m.* 1924, Elsie, *d.* of Thomas Brown, J.P.; two *s.* *Educ.:* Battersea Grammar School, Technical experience with London United Tramways Ltd., 1899-1902; District Engineer, 1909; Commercial Superintendent, Underground Railway Group and London General Omnibus Company; Traffic Manager, London County Council Tramways, 1925; General Manager, 1930; General Manager, Operation, 1936-43, L.P.T.B.; General Manager, L.P.T.B., 1943-45; President, Institute of Transport, 1939-41. *Recreations:* walking and nature study. *Address:* 5 Kepplestone, Eastbourne. *Club:* Athenæum. [*Died* 3 *July* 1951.

THOMAS, Rt. Rev. Wilfrid William Henry, D.D. (St. John's College, Manitoba); Curate of Cathedral, Hamilton, Ont., 1898; Rector of St. Luke, Winnipeg, 1899-1901; Selkirk, 1901-13; Archdeacon of East Manitoba, 1916-24; Hon. Fellow, St. Augustine's College, Canterbury, 1924; Bishop of Brandon, 1924-50; retired, 1950. *Address:* Brandon, Manitoba, Canada. [*Died* 2 *July* 1953.

THOMAS, William, C.B. 1953; *b.* 27 Nov. 1891; *o. s.* of late Catherine and James Thomas, Cymmer, Porth, Rhondda; *m.* 1925, Mary Olwen, *d.* of late Rev. E. Caleb Davies, Ynyshir, Rhondda. *Educ.:* Porth Secondary School; University College, Cardiff (B.Sc. 1911). Inns of Court O.T.C.; gazetted to S. Lancashire Regt.; served European War, 1914-18; attached G.S.I. Egyptian Expeditionary Force. Called to the Bar, Inner Temple, 1928; Member of Welsh Board of Health until 1951; Under-Secretary, Welsh Office, Ministry of Housing and Local Government, 1951-54. *Address:* 27 Maesycoed Rd., The Heath, Cardiff. *T.:* Rhiwbina 1185. [*Died* 20 *April* 1958.

THOMAS, Sir William Beach, K.B.E., *cr.* 1920; *s.* of Rev. D. G. Thomas, Rector of Hamerton, Hunts; *b.* 1868; *m.* 1900, Helen Dorothea, *d.* of late Augustus George Vernon Harcourt; one *s.* one *d.* *Educ.:* Shrewsbury; Christ Church, Oxford. Was President Oxford University Athletic Club; War Correspondent, Daily Mail; regular contributor to the Observer and Spectator. *Publications:* The English Year; With the British on the Somme; The Happy Village; A Letter to my Dog; The Yeoman's England, 1934; Village England, 1935; A Countryman's Anthology, 1936; The Way of a Countryman, 1944; The Poems of a Countryman, 1946; A Countryman's Creed, 1946; The Way of a Dog, 1948; Hertfordshire (County Books Series), 1950; Gardens (Pleasures of Life Series), 1952. *Address:* Wheathampstead, Herts. *T.:* 3100. *Club:* Authors'. [*Died* 12 *May* 1957.

THOMAS, Sir William Bruce, Kt., *cr.* 1941; Q.C. 1928; President of the Railway Rates Tribunal (later Transport Tribunal), 1932-50; Chairman of the Charges (Railway Control) Consultative Committee, 1940 and the Charges Consultative Committee, 1946; *b.* June 1878; *s.* of late Jabez Thomas, F.R.C.S., Swansea; *m.* Ida, *d.* of late Arthur D. Hughes. *Educ.:* Christ College, Brecon. Solicitor till 1911; called to Bar, Middle Temple, 1912; Bencher, Middle Temple, 1936. *Publication:* (with E. F. M. Maxwell) Railways and Canals in Halsbury's Laws of England, 2nd Edition. *Recreation:* gardening. *Address:* 3 Paper Buildings, Temple, E.C.4; Dye House, Thursley, Surrey. *T.:* Elstead 2217. [*Died* 5 *Sept.* 1952.

THOMAS, Sir (William) Eustace (Rhyddlad), 2nd Bt., *cr.* 1918; M.B.E. 1945; *b.* 19 June 1909; *s.* of Sir Robert John Thomas, 1st Bt., and Marie Rose (*d.* 1948), *d.* of Arthur Burrows; *S:* father, 1951; *m.* 1st, 1929, Enid Helena (marriage dissolved, 1946), *d.* of Ernest Marsh, Rawdon, Leeds; one *s.*: 2nd, 1947, Molly (marriage dissolved, 1951), *d.* of late John McGeachin, Eastbourne; 3rd, 1957, Mrs. Patricia Larkins. Served War of 1939-45 as Major, Royal Artillery (M.B.E.). *Heir:* *s.* William Michael Marsh, *b.* 4 Dec. 1930. *Address:* Garreglwyd, Holyhead, Anglesey. [*Died* 27 *Dec.* 1957.

THOMAS, William Norman, C.B.E. 1946; M.A., D.Phil. (Oxon); M.Sc. (B'ham.), B.Sc. (Lond.), M.Inst.C.E., F.R.I.B.A., M.I.Mech.E., (ret.); *b.* 11 March 1885; *s.* of Josiah Thomas, M.A., late H.M.I. *Educ.:* Sandbach School, Cheshire. Pupil, 1900-04; and Engineering Assistant (1904-10) to Borough Engineer, Crewe; Lecturer in Engineering at Nottingham University College, 1910-13, and at Birmingham University, 1913-20; Lieut. R.E. 1915-18; Brasenose College, Senior Assistant to Prof. of Engineering University of Oxford, 1920-25; Principal Assistant H.M. Building Research Station, 1925-28; Professor of Engineering, Univ. Coll., Cardiff, 1928-50; Member Civil Defence Research Committee, 1939-48. Scientific Adviser (1939-45) and Deputy Chief Adviser, Research and Expt. Department, Ministry of Home Security; Senior Scientific Adviser for Wales on Civil Defence, 1952-59. Medal of Freedom (U.S.A.). *Publications:* Surveying; various papers in Building Research Board, and Aero. Res. Comm. Reports; in Proceedings and Journals of Professional Institutions; and in the technical press. *Recreation:* philately. *Address:* 1 St. John's Crescent, Whitchurch, Glam. [*Died* 17 *Nov.* 1960.

THOMAS, William Stanley Russell; *b.* 5 Feb. 1896; *s.* of late David and Mary Ann Abigail Thomas, Talgarth, Breconshire; *m.* 1922, Kathleen Maud, *d.* of late Raymond Christmas and Alice Mary Bennett (*née* Vidler). *Educ.:* Christ's College, Brecon; Queens' College, Cambridge; Guy's Hospital (Treasurer's Gold Medallist in Clinical Medicine). Called to Bar, Lincoln's Inn, 1930; M.A., M.B., B.Ch. (Cantab.); M.R.C.S., L.R.C.P.; a Vice-Pres. of National Federation of Property Owners, 1944-; Member of Council, R.S.P.C.A., 1943-54, Chm., 1951-52; Mem. Council, Liberal National Party, 1937-1940; Dep. Chm. London Liberal National Party, 1937-45; Prospective Liberal Candidate East Ham (N.) 1931; contested (L.) Ilford, 1931; Central Aberdeenshire and Kincardine, 1935, Ross and Cromarty, 1936; Prospective L.Nat. Candidate, Hillsborough Division of Sheffield, 1937-40; M.P. (L.Nat.) County Borough of Southampton, 1940-45; Member: London Advisory Cttee. to Min. of Information, 1940; Select Cttee. on National Expenditure (and Building Industry Sub-Cttee.), 1944; Select Cttee. on Public Petitions, 1942-44; Exec. Cttee. of British-American Parliamentary Committee, 1942-1945; contested (L.Nat.) Southampton, 1945, (L.) Middlesbrough East, 1950; contested (L.) Brecon and Radnor, 1955. Member of Court of Governors, Southampton University College, 1941-45; Caterham and Warlingham Urban District Council, 1926-32. Served War of 1914-1918, as Surgeon Sub. Lieutenant, in Royal Naval Volunteers, Northern Patrol. *Recreations:* gardening, European travel. *Address:* Bramley House, Warlingham, Surrey. *T.:* Upper Warlingham 12. [*Died* 21 *March* 1957.

THOMPSON, Alexander Hamilton, C.B.E. 1938; M.A., Cantab.; Hon. D.Litt. Oxford and Durham; Hon. LL.D. Leeds; F.B.A., F.S.A. (Vice-Pres., 1933-37); Hon. A.R.I.B.A.; Member of Royal Commission on Historical Monuments since 1933 and of Ancient Monuments Board for England since 1935; *b.* Clifton, 7 Nov. 1873; *e. s.* of Rev. John Thompson, Vicar of St. Gabriel's, Bristol, and Annie Hastings, *e. d.* of Rev. D. Cooper, Hon. Canon of Bristol Cathedral; *m.* 1903, Amy (*d.* 1945), *d.* of Alfred Gosling; two *d.* *Educ.:* Clifton College; St. John's College, Cambridge (B.A. 1895; M.A.

1903; Hon. Fellow, 1938). Lecturer for Cambridge Local Lectures Syndicate, 1897; Lecturer in English, Armstrong College, University of Durham, 1919-21; Reader in Medieval History and Archæology, Armstrong College, 1921-22; Reader in Medieval History, Univ. of Leeds, 1922-24, and Professor, 1924-27; Professor of History, 1927-39; Member of the Cathedrals Commission, 1925-28; one of the Cathedral Commissioners for England, 1932-42; Member of the Archbishops' Commission on Canon Law, 1943; Ford's Lecturer in the University of Oxford, 1932-33; Birkbeck Lecturer in Ecclesiastical History, Trinity College, Cambridge, 1933-35; Pres. Royal Archæological Institute, 1939-45; has been Vice-Pres. and Pres. numerous archæological and historical societies, etc.; Sec. of Surtees Soc. since 1919; Member of Central Council for care of Churches, and of several Diocesan Advisory Committees. *Publications:* Cambridge and its Colleges, 1st ed. 1898; The Ground Plan of the English Parish Church, 1911; Historical Growth of the English Parish Church, 1911; Military Architecture in England in the Middle Ages, 1912; English Monasteries, 1913; Students' History of English Literature, 1903; Visitations of Religious Houses in the Diocese of Lincoln, 3 vols., 1914-28; Northumberland Pleas, 1922; The Cathedral Churches of England, 1925; History and Architectural Description of Bolton Priory, 1928; The Statutes of the Cathedral Church of Durham, 1930; Records of Wyggeston's Hospital, Leicester, 1933; (editor) Bede, 1935; The Hospital and College of the Newarke, Leicester, 1937; The Premonstratensian Abbey of Welbeck, 1938; Visitations in the Diocese of Lincoln, 1518-1531, 3 vols., 1940-47; The English Clergy and their Organization in the later Middle Ages, 1947; Leicester Abbey, 1949; Contributions to Cambridge Medieval History and Cambridge History of English Literature, Enciclopedia Italiana, and to numerous historical and antiquarian periodicals; Editor of various English Classics. *Address:* Alton Cottage, Budleigh Salterton, South Devon. *Club:* Athenæum.
[*Died* 4 *Sept.* 1952.

THOMPSON, Ven. Arthur Huxley; Archdeacon and Canon Residentiary of Exeter since 1930; Treasurer since 1939; *b.* 8 July 1872; *s.* of John David Thompson, Henwick, Worcester; *m.* Mary Ellen (*d.* 1948), *d.* of Rev. T. Flavell, Vicar of Christow, Devon. *Educ.:* Malvern Coll.; Jesus College, Oxford. Vicar of Ide, Devon, 1906; Rector of St. Paul's, Exeter, 1918; Vicar of Ashburton, 1923; Prebendary of Exeter, 1922; sub-Dean, 1927. *Publications:* The Story of Exeter Cathedral, 1933; The Patience of God, 1937. *Address:* 10 The Close Exeter. *T.:* 3509.
[*Died* 17 *April* 1951.

THOMPSON, Edward, O.B.E.; B.A., F.R.G.S., M.I.Mech.E.; *b.* 25 June 1881; *o. s.* of late F. E. Thompson, M.A., Oxford, formerly assistant Master and subsequently Governor of Marlborough Coll.; *m.* 1913, Edith Guendolen (*d.* 1938), *yr. d.* of late Sir Vincent Raven, K.B.E.; no *c.* *Educ.:* St. David's, Reigate; Marlborough; Pembroke College, Cambridge, B.A. 1902. Served in war of 1914-18 (despatches twice, O.B.E.); Lt.-Col. R.E.; Chief Mechanical Engineer L.N.E.R., 1941; retired, 1946. *Recreation:* golf. *Address:* 61 Westgate Bay Avenue, Westgate-on-Sea, Kent. *Club:* Oxford and Cambridge.
[*Died* 15 *July* 1954.

THOMPSON, Fred; Director; *b.* 24 March 1883; *s.* of James and Mary Thompson; *m.* 1916, Lily, *d.* of Rev. George Wedgwood; two *s.* two *d.* *Educ.:* Belmont National School; Greenwood College. Entered Belfast Corporation, 1929, for Ormeau Ward, retired 1938; M.P. (U.) Northern Ireland Parliament, Ballynafeigh Division, 1937-49; first Chairman of General Health Services Board, Northern Ireland, 1948; retired from all public work, 1949. Governor of Edge Hill Theological College. *Address:* Innisfallen, Annadale Avenue, Belfast. *T.:* Belfast 41054. *Club:* Reform.
[*Died* 5 *Sept.* 1951.

THOMPSON, George Henry Main; Admiralty Registrar, Royal Courts of Justice, London, Jan. 1948 to Oct. 1957; *b.* 18 Oct. 1882; *e. s.* of William and Jane Ann Thompson, Newport, Mon., and Ealing; *m.* 1915, Margaret Angela Haughey, Ferbane, Offaly, Eire; one *s.* *Educ.:* Newport High School; Univ. Coll., Cardiff (B.A.); Christ's Coll., Cambridge (M.A.). Schoolmaster for some years; M.R.S.T. Served European War, 1914-18. Called to the Bar, Gray's Inn, 1919, and practised at Admiralty Bar; Lecturer in Law of Shipping at Law Society's School of Law, 1936-39; Assistant Admiralty Registrar, 1939. *Publication:* contributed several articles on the Law of Shipping and Navigation to Hailsham edition of Halsbury's Laws of England. *Address:* Glenmorven, 39 Birchwood Rd., Petts Wood, Kent. *T.:* Orpington 21934. *Club:* Athenæum.
[*Died* 15 *Dec.* 1957.

THOMPSON, Henry E. S.; *see* Symes-Thompson.

THOMPSON, Hubert C. M.; *see* Meysey-Thompson.

THOMPSON, Rev. James Matthew, F.B.A. 1947; *b.* Iron Acton Rectory, Gloucestershire, 27 Sept. 1878; *s.* of late Rev. H. L. Thompson, Rector of Iron Acton, previously Student and Censor of Christ Church Oxford, and afterwards Warden of Radley, and Vicar of St. Mary's, Oxford, and Catharine, *e. d.* of Sir James Paget, 1st Bt.; *m.* 1913, Mari Meredyth, *d.* of Rev. David Jones, Vicar of Penmaenmawr; one *s.* *Educ.:* Winchester (Scholar); Christ Church, Oxford (Junior Student). 2nd in Mods., 1st in Greats; 2nd in Theology; Liddon Student; Curate at St. Frideswide's, Poplar (the Christ Church Mission), 1903; Fellow of Magdalen, 1904-38; Dean of Divinity, 1906-15; Home Bursar, 1920-27; Vice-President, 1935-37; Hon. Fellow, 1944; Examining Chaplain to the Bishop of Gloucester, 1905-10; Senior Proctor, 1916-17; temporary Master at Eton Coll., 1917-19; Examiner, School of Mod. Hist. Oxford, 1929-31, 1938, 1945-46; Univ. Lecturer in Mod. French Hist., 1931-39; Examiner. Mod. Hist. Tripos (Part II), Cambridge, 1936, 1937; F.R.Hist S.; Trustee, Oxford Preservation Trust, 1938-; Lecturer in History, Univ.-Coll., 1942-45; Editor Oxford Magazine, 1945-47. *Publications:* An Annotated Psalter; Jesus According to St. Mark; The Synoptic Gospels; Miracles in the New Testament; Through Facts to Faith; Lectures on Foreign History; Leaders of the French Revolution; Historical Geography of Europe; French Revolution: Documents, 1789-94 (editor); Letters of Napoleon; Robespierre; English Witnesses of the French Revolution; The French Revolution; Collected Verse, 1939-46; The Spider's Web; Napoleon Bonaparte; Robespierre and the French Revolution; Louis Napoleon and the Second Empire. *Address:* 5 Chadlington Road, Oxford. *T.:* 55224.
[*Died* 8 *Oct.* 1956.

THOMPSON, John William Howard; Solicitor: *m.* Antoinette Ebden (*d.* 1940), *d.* of Theophilus Joseph Keene, Crewkerne, Somerset; two *d.* *Educ.:* Carshalton; Whitgift, Croydon. Captain in the Devons 11th Service Batt. 1915; Major London Regt. 1916; M.P. (L.) East Somerset, 1906-1910. *Address:* Devereux Chambers, Strand, W.C.; Prior's Field, Chipstead, Surrey. *Clubs:* Boodle's, Eighty, Cobden.
[*Died* 17 *Oct.* 1959.

THOMPSON, Sir Matthew William, 3rd Bt., *cr.* 1890; painter artist; F.R.A.S.; *b.* 28 June 1872; *e. s.* of 2nd Bt. and Jessie, *d.* of Joseph Beaumont, Huddersfield; *S.* father, 1918; *m.* 1909, Harriet Kathleen, *o. d.* of late Col. S. Hamilton-Grace. *Educ.:* Trinity College, Cambridge. Hon. Life Mem-

ber National Rifle Association, North London Rifle Club, Bisley Camp. *Heir:* *b.* Peile Beaumont [*b.* 4 Feb. 1874; *m.* 1908, Stella, *d.* of Arthur Harris, Heaton Grove, Bradford; one *s.* one *d.* *Educ.:* Trinity College, Cambridge]. *Address:* 39 Steeles Road, N.W.3. *T.:* Primrose 2639. *Clubs:* Royal Thames Yacht; Royal Empire Society.
[*Died* 25 *Nov.* 1956.

THOMPSON, His Honour Owen, Q.C. 1919; County Court Judge, Circuit No. 46, 1928, Circuit No. 40, Oct. 1928-40, retd.; *b.* Colchester, 17 March 1868; *s.* of Henry Thompson, Colchester, and Mary Jane Deed; *m.*; one *s.* two *d.* (and two *s.* decd.) *Educ.:* Univ. Coll. Sch., Lond.; Trin. Coll., Camb. (Major Scholar); Chancellor's English Medallist, 1888, 1st Class Classical Tripos, Part I. 1889, Part II. 1890. Bencher of Lincoln's Inn; called to Bar, 1893; practised as Conveyancer and Equity Draftsman and in Chancery Division. *Recreation:* music. *Address:* The Sheiling, Burnham-on-Crouch, Essex. *T.:* Burnham-on-Crouch 3100.
[*Died* 16 *Jan.* 1958.

THOMPSON, Rev. Reginald William, M.A.; B.D. (London); *m.* 1st, 1907, Dorothy Mabel Holmes; 2nd, 1915, Elsie May Adams; three *d.* *Educ.:* Cardiff Higher Grade Sch.; New College, University of London. Civil Service five years, 1896-1901; Congregational Minister, Basingstoke, Wolverhampton, Bolton; Leader of Bolton Group Churches, 1917-30: Chairman Congregational Union of England and Wales, 1938-39; Congregational Minister Redland Park Church, Bristol, 1930-1948. Y.M.C.A. Belgium and France, 1916. Secretary Bristol Congregational Council, 1941. *Publications:* Text books; Our Empire and the Faith; Fit for Life. *Recreation:* golf. *Address:* 2 Westdene, Westbury-on-Trym, Bristol. *T.:* Stoke Bishop, Bristol, 81672. *Club:* Rotary.
[*Died* 23 *March* 1953.

THOMPSON, Major-Gen. Richard Lovell Brereton, C.B. 1929; C.M.G. 1918; D.S.O. 1917; Colonel Commandant R.E., 1939-44; *b.* 23 Nov. 1874; *s.* of late Colonel R. Thompson, C.B., R.E., *m.* 1898, Louise (*d.* 1956), *d.* of late P. P. Vassallo, Collector of Customs at Malta; one *s.* one *d.* *Educ.:* Mannamead School, Plymouth; R.M. Academy, Woolwich. 2nd Lt. R.E. 1893; Lt. 1896; Capt., 1904; Major, 1913; served European War (Bt. Lieut.-Colonel, despatches thrice, D.S.O., C.M.G.); Assistant Instructor in Fortification, S.M.E., Chatham, 1902-6; Staff-Captain, Headquarters of Army, 1910-15; on Staff, British Expeditionary Force, 1916-19; Deputy Assistant Director of Fortifications and Works, 1919-20; Lieut.-Col. R.E. 1920-24; Col. 1924; Assistant Director of Fortifications and Works, War Office, 1925-28; Chief Engineer, Headquarters, Western Command, Chester, 1929-30; Maj.-Gen. 1930; Director of Works, War Office, 1931-35; retired pay, 1935. *Recreations:* shooting, fishing, golf. *Address:* c/o Lloyds Bank, Ltd., Cox's and King's Branch, 6 Pall Mall, S.W.1. [*Died* 11 *May* 1957.

THOMPSON, Robert John, C.B. 1923; O.B.E. 1918; Assistant Secretary, Ministry of Agriculture, retired, 1929; *b.* 1867; *s.* of late Samuel James Thompson, Stroud Green; *m.* 1899, Mabel Persis Jones; two *d.* Representative of British Government and Governments of Canada, India, Australia and New Zealand on Permanent Committee of International Institute of Agriculture, Rome, 1925-1930; Member of Committee on Prices of Agricultural Products (the Linlithgow Committee), 1922; President, Agricultural Economics Society, 1929-30. *Publications:* papers and notes in Journal of Royal Statistical Society. *Address:* Merlewood, Tarn Road, Hindhead, Surrey. *T.:* Hindhead 485.
[*Died* 10 *Feb.* 1951.

THOMPSON, Sir Robert Norman, Kt., *cr.* 1946; Chairman Joseph L. Thompson & Sons Ltd.; Director of Sir James Laing & Sons Ltd. and other associated companies; *b.* 2 July 1878; *s.* of Robert and Georgiana Thompson, Over Dinsdale Hall, Darlington; *m.* 1906, Helena Victoria, *d.* of J. Y. Short; two *s.* one *d.* *Educ.:* Leys School, Cambridge. Liveryman of Co. of Shipwrights. *Address:* Belford House, Sunderland. *T.:* Sunderland 4237.
[*Died* 2 *Oct.* 1951.

THOMPSON, Lt.-Col. Rt. Hon. S. H.; *see* Hall-Thompson.

THOMPSON, Major Stephen John, D.S.O. 1916; Governing Director of John Thompson, Limited, Wolverhampton; *b.* Wolverhampton, 1875; *s.* of John Thompson, founder of firm John Thompson, Ltd., Engineers, Wolverhampton; *m.*; three *s.* *Educ.:* Wolverhampton Grammar School. Joined Territorial Force, 1907; served European War as R.A. Battery Commander; High Sheriff of Staffordshire, 1938-39; Past Pres. I.Mech.E. *Publications:* various papers before Engineering Societies. *Recreation:* hunting. *Address:* Stanley Hall, Bridgnorth, Shropshire. *T.:* Bridgnorth 3231.
[*Died* 30 *April* 1955.

THOMPSON, Sir Walter, Kt., *cr.* 1947; D.C.L., J.P.; Managing Director, W. J. Ward & Co. Ltd., Clothiers and Outfitters; *b.* 16 Aug. 1875; *s.* of John and Mary Ann Thompson; one *d.* *Educ.:* elementary. Newcastle-upon-Tyne City Council, 1921; Alderman, 1938; Sheriff, 1940; Lord Mayor, 1942. Chairman of Newcastle-upon-Tyne Regional Hospital Board, 1947; Member Council King's College, Newcastle-upon-Tyne. *Address:* 120 Severus Road, Newcastle-upon-Tyne. *T.:* Newcastle 33091.
[*Died* 15 *Nov.* 1951.

THOMPSON, William George; Senator of the Australian Commonwealth Parliament, 1922-32; Brig.-General Australian Military Force (retired list); Chevalier (1st Class) Royal Order of Vasa (Sweden); *b.* Lurgan, Co. Armagh, 2 March 1863; *m.* 1901, Nellie Bancroft; one *d.* *Educ.:* State School, North Rockhampton. Was principal of a firm of merchants in Rockhampton till Dec. 1925; Pres. Chamber of Commerce, 1905-8, 1917, and 1933-43; Pres. Employers' Association of Central Queensland 1917-23; Chairman; Central District Coal Board, 1936-48; Director Mt. Morgan Gold Mining Co. Ltd., 1912-27, and of Bluff Colliery Co. Ltd., 1905-48; Vice-Consul for Sweden at Rockhampton since 1914; joined Queensland Mounted Infantry as a private, 1889; retired, 1922; served in S. African War, 1900-1, Second-in-command and later commanding Queensland Second Contingent (despatches, Queen's medal with three clasps); appointed by Lord Roberts one of the three Magistrates of the High Court of Pretoria, administering martial law; Colonel A.I.F. (Sea Transport), European War, 1916-17; served on Public Accounts Committee and on Select Committees regarding Central Reserve Bank and Electoral Law and Procedure. Has taken leading part in Red Cross Society work since 1939. *Recreation:* bowls. *Clubs:* Rockhampton, Anzac (Rockhampton).
[*Died* 7 *March* 1953.

THOMPSON, William John; *b.* 1871; *s.* of John Thompson, Penn, Staffs; *m.* 1st, 1899, Frances Mary Williams; 2nd, 1928, Enid Marie Fergusson; one *d.*; 3rd, 1953, Dorothy Mary Bowerman Bulley. J.P. Worcs., 1908; High Sheriff of Worcestershire, 1941. *Address:* All Stretton Hall, Church Stretton, Salop. *T.:* Church Stretton 298. [*Died* 29 *Sept.* 1959.

THOMS, Lieut.-Colonel Nathaniel William Benjamin Butler, C.B.E. 1934; D.S.O. 1917; M.C.; New Zealand Staff Corps (retired); *b.* 5 Apr. 1880; *s.* of late John Alexander Thoms, London; *m.* 1st, 1908, Frances Beatrice Elizabeth (*d.* 1952), *d.* of James Apted; one *s.*; 2nd, 1954, Mrs. R. Sylvia Forbes, *d.* of late

Rev. J. G. Clark, formerly of Anglesey Abbey, Cambridge. Served S. Africa, 1900-1902 (Queen's medal with four clasps); European War, 1914-17 (despatches thrice, M.C., D.S.O., 1914-15 star, two medals); Commandant of the Shanghai Volunteer Corps, 1931-34. R.A.F. Regiment, 1940-43 (Wing Commander). *Address:* P.O. Box 504, Kitale, Kenya Colony. [*Died* 24 *May* 1957.

THOMSON, 1st Baron; *see* Courtauld-Thomson.

THOMSON, Brigadier Alan Fortescue, D.S.O. 1916; *b.* Nelson, N.Z., 7 Sept. 1880; *s.* of late Henry Thomson of Boynsmill, Aberdeenshire; *m.* 1905, Edythe Mary, *er. d.* of late J. Owen Unwin of 40A Hyde Park Gate, S.W.7; two *d.* *Educ.:* Cheltenham College; Royal Military Academy, Woolwich. Joined Royal Artillery, 1898; served European War, 1914-18, Gallipoli, Egypt, France and Flanders (Brevet Lt.-Col., despatches six times, D.S.O.); Colonel, 1922; Military Inter-Allied Commission of Control, Berlin, 1920-24; commanded 26th London Air Defence Brigade, T.A., 1926-29; Commandant, School of Anti-Aircraft Defence, 1929-31; Commander 1st Air Defence Brigade, 1931-35; retired pay, 1935. *Address:* Clashnadarroch Lodge, Huntly, Aberdeenshire. *T.:* Gartly 215. *Club:* Army and Navy. [*Died* 6 *Aug.* 1957.

THOMSON, Lieutenant-Colonel Alexander Guthrie, C.M.G. 1919; D.S.O. 1915; 58th Vaughan's Rifles (Frontier Force), I.A., retired; *b.* 11 Feb. 1873; *s.* of late J. W. Thomson, M.D., Brechin, Angus; *m.* 1907, Annie Wilhelmina (*d.* 1951), *d.* of W. A. Finlay, M.D., F.R.C.S., Edinburgh; one *s.* three *d.* *Educ.:* Cargilfield and Fettes College, Edinburgh; Sandhurst. Entered army, 1893; Captain Indian Army, 1902; Major, 1911; Bt. Lt.-Col. 1918; retired, 1920; Staff Captain, India, 1909-10; General Staff Officer, 3rd Grade, India, 1910-1911; 2nd Grade, 1911-13; served N.-W. Frontier, India, 1902; European War, 1914-18 (C.M.G., D.S.O., despatches four times, Bt. Lt.-Col., Croix de Guerre avec Palme, Belgian Croix de Guerre). Director of Industrial Training, Ministry of Labour, North-Western Division, 1919-22; Sec. and Man. Director, Hampstead Garden Suburb Trust Ltd., 1923-49, Director until 1952. *Address:* 39 Pattison Road, N.W.2. [*Died* 10 *Feb.* 1953.

THOMSON, Rev. Canon Clement R., B.A. Lond., M.A. Oxon and Cape University; Canon, 1926-38, Chancellor of St. Asaph Cathedral, 1938-39, Canon Emeritus, 1939; *b.* Tunbridge Wells, July 1870; *s.* of Rev. Prof. J. Radford Thomson, M.A. Lond.; *m.* 1921, Agnes Jean, *d.* of late Joseph Chamberlain Stone, Leicester; no *c.* *Educ.:* Mill Hill School; King's College, London; Trinity Coll., Oxford, Honours in Classical Moderations 1891, and in Classical Greats, 1893; University of London B.A. 1893; University of Cape M.A. (ad eund.) 1907. Ordained, 1894; Curate of Wrexham, Denbighshire, 1894-97; Licensed Preacher Diocese of Wakefield, 1897-1902; Diocese of London, 1898-1903; Diocese of Pretoria, 1903-20; Assistant Master St. John's (Diocesan) College, Johannesburg, 1904-1917; Headmaster, 1917-21; Vicar of Ruabon-with-Penylan, Denbighshire, 1921-26; of Colwyn Bay, 1926-39; of Norton, Radnorshire, 1939-50; Chaplain to High Sheriff of Denbighshire, 1923, Radnorshire, 1940; Chaplain to Mayor, Colwyn Bay, 1938-39. O.C.F. 1942-45. *Recreation:* walking. *Address:* 1 Grimston Gardens, Folkestone, Kent. [*Died* 23 *June* 1953.

THOMSON, David Couper, D.L., J.P.; newspaper proprietor and shipowner; 2nd *s.* of William Thomson, founder of Thomson Line of Steamships to Canada; *b.* Dundee, 1861; *m.* Margaret (*d.* 1952), 2nd *d.* of John M'Culloch, Ballantrae, Ayrshire; three *d.* Managing Director of Dundee Courier and Advertiser, Evening Telegraph and Post, Weekly News, Weekly Welcome, Red Letter, Sunday Post, etc.. *Recreations:* travelling, motoring, photographing, books. *Address:* Inveravon, Broughty Ferry, Dundee. *Clubs:* Press; Royal Scottish Automobile (Glasgow); Eastern (Dundee). [*Died* 12 *Oct.* 1954.

THOMSON, Sir (Francis) Vernon, 1st Bt., *cr.* 1938; G.B.E., *cr.* 1946 (K.B.E., *cr.* 1921); of Dodd, Thomson & Co., Ltd., Chairman of the King Line, Ltd., London; Chm. and Managing Director of Union-Castle Mail S.S. Co., Ltd.; Chairman of Bullard, King & Co., Ltd.; Chm. of London and Thames Haven Oil Wharves, Ltd.; Principal Shipping Adviser and Controller of Commercial Shipping, Ministry of Shipping, subsequently Ministry of War Transport, 1939-1946; Chm. of Tramp Shipping Subsidy Committee, 1935, 1936 and 1937; Chairman of Tramp Shipping Administrative Committee, 1935-37; President of the Chamber of Shipping of the United Kingdom, 1936-37; (Hon.) Assistant Director of Ship Management Branch, Ministry of Shipping, 1918-21; and Vice-Chairman of Ship Licensing Committee, 1919-20; Chairman of London General Shipowners' Society, 1928-1929; Chairman of Baltic Mercantile and Shipping Exchange, 1931-33; Chairman of Documentary Committee of the Chamber of Shipping of the United Kingdom, 1923-35; Member of the Committee of Lloyd's Register of Shipping since 1927; Member of Council of King George's Fund for Sailors since 1938; Hon. Life-Governor of Royal National Lifeboat Institution, 1938; Hon. Treasurer, Royal Alfred Merchant Seamen's Society; Mem. of Cttee. of Management of H.M.S. Worcester; *b.* 10 Feb. 1881. *Heir:* none. *Address:* Hawthornden, Hadley Common, Barnet, Herts. *T.:* Barnet 0272. *Clubs:* Reform, City of London; Pretoria (Pretoria); City (Capetown). [*Died* 8 *Feb.* 1953 (*ext.*).

THOMSON, Rev. George Thomas, M.A. (Edin.); M.A. (Oxon.); B.D., Hon. D.D. (Edin.); *b.* 1887; *s.* of late James Thomson, C.E., Edinburgh, and of Jane Haswell Smith; *m.* 1st, Christian Isabel (*d.* 1937), *d.* of late Very Rev. Thomas Martin, D.D.; one *s.*; 2nd, 1938, Alice, *d.* of late Alexander Davidson, Perth; one *s.* *Educ.:* Daniel Stewart's College and University, Edinburgh; Christ Church, Oxford; Berlin. Served 8th Royal Scots T.F., Intelligence Corps, 1914-19; A. and S., Tain, 1920-24; Minister of St. Boswells, 1924-28; Professor of Systematic Theology, Aberdeen University, 1928-36; Professor of Christian Dogmatics, University of Edinburgh, 1936-52; retired 1952. Translator of Karl Barth's Dogmatik, The Doctrine of the Word of God, 1935; Dogmatics in Outline; Heppe's Reformierte Dogmatik. *Recreations:* golf, piping. *Address:* 28 India Street, Edinburgh 3. [*Died* 5 *March* 1958.

THOMSON, Sir Godfrey (Hilton), Kt., *cr.* 1949; D.C.L., D.Sc. (Dunelm.), Ph.D. (Strasburg); Order of Polonia Restituta (third class); *b.* 27 Mar. 1881; *m.* 1912, Jane, *d.* of late Thomas Hutchinson, of Newcastle and Bardon Mill; one *s.* *Educ.:* Rutherford Coll., Newcastle; Univs. of Durham and Strasburg. Open Exhibitioner, Junior Pemberton Scholar, and Charles Mather Scholar, Armstrong College; Pemberton Fellow of the University of Durham, 1903-6; B.Sc. (distinction in mathematics and physics) 1903; M.Sc. 1906; D.Sc. in psychology, 1913; Ph.D. *summa cum laude*, Strasburg, 1906; Hon. D.C.L. (Dunelm.) 1939; F.R.S.E. 1926; Hon. F.E.I.S. 1947; Visiting Professor of Education, Columbia University, 1923-24; Lecturer in Education, Armstrong College, 1906, Professor 1920; Professor of Education, University of Edinburgh, and Director of Studies at the Edinburgh Training Centre, 1925-51; retired, 1951. Nineteen years' service in Volunteer and Territorial Forces; acting Adjutant of the Durham Univ. O.T.C. 1915-19; in command, 1921-23. Member: Population Investigation Committee; Scottish Mental Survey Committee; National Foundation for Educational Research; International Statistical Institute; Foreign Assoc. U.S. Nat. Acad. Sc., 1951; Foreign Hon. Mem. Am. Acad. of Arts and Sciences, 1947; Fellow, Am. Ass. Adv. Sc.; Hon. Fellow Swedish Psychol. Soc., and Brit. Psychol. Soc.; Pres. British Psychological Society, 1945-46; Pres. Section J. British Assoc., 1949; Vice-Pres., Roy. Soc. Edin. *Publications:* The Essentials of Mental Measurement (with late Dr. William Brown); Instinct, Intelligence and Character, an Educational Psychology; A Modern Philosophy of Education; the Factorial Analysis of Human Ability (French edn., 1950); The Geometry of Mental Measurement; The Northumberland Mental Tests; The Moray House Tests; articles in psychological journals in Britain and America. *Address:* 5 Ravelston Dykes, Edinburgh 4. [*Died* 9 *Feb.* 1955.

THOMSON, Major-General James, C.B. 1917; C.M.G. 1919; K.G.St.J.; M.B., A.M.S. (retired); *b.* 15 July 1862. Captain R.A.M.C. 1887; Major, 1899; Lt.-Col. 1911; Col. 1915; Maj.-Gen. 1919; Deputy Director-General Medical Services, British Armies in France, 1918-19; served Nile Expedition, 1898 (British medal, Khedive's medal with clasp); European War, 1914-18 (despatches, C.B., C.M.G., Grand Officier Order of Crown of Rumania); retd. 1920. *Address:* 23 Carden Pl., Aberdeen. [*Died* 17 *April* 1953.

THOMSON, James, C.M.G. 1953; O.B.E. 1943; M.M. 1917 and Bar 1918; U.K. Information Officer, Alberta, since 1958; *b.* 1 Apr. 1895; *s.* of John and Ellen Thomson, Edinburgh; *m.* 1922, Ivy Fisher, Glasgow; one *s.* one *d.* *Educ.:* Edinburgh. Appointed General Post Office, 1914. Served European War 1915-19, with 2nd and 4th Canadian Divisions. Appointed India Office, 1927; Information Officer, India Office, 1936-37; visited India and Burma, 1945; Delegate to Commonwealth Consultative Cttee. meetings in Sydney, Australia and Colombo, 1950. Deputy High Commissioner for the U.K. in Canada, 1951-54, 1957-58, retd. Officer of Order of Orange Nassau, 1948. *Recreations:* gardening, swimming, fishing, photography. *Address:* Imperial Bank Building, Jasper Ave., Edmonton, Alberta, Canada. *Clubs:* Rideau (Ottawa); Edmonton, Glengarry (Edmonton). [*Died* 17 *Dec.* 1959.

THOMSON, James Alexander Kerr, M.A. (Aberdeen); B.A. (Oxford); Professor Emeritus of Classics, University of London, King's College, since 1945; *b.* Stonehaven, Kincardineshire, 1879; *s.* of J. C. Thomson; unmarried. Lecturer in Universities of Aberdeen, St. Andrews, Harvard, and at Bryn Mawr College, U.S.A. *Publications:* Studies in the Odyssey, 1914; The Greek Tradition, 1916; Greeks and Barbarians, 1921; Desiderius Erasmus, in Social and Political Ideas of the Renaissance, 1925; Irony, 1926; Erasmus in England, in Vorträge, Bibliothek Warburg, 1930-31; The Art of the Logos, 1935; The Classical Background of English Literature, 1948; Classical Influences on English Poetry, 1951; Shakespeare and the Classics, 1952; The Ethics of Aristotle, 1953; Classical Influences on English Prose, 1955; Gilbert Murray, from Proceedings of British Academy, vol. XLIII, 1958. *Address:* Balvenie, Newtonmore, Inverness-shire. *T.:* Newtonmore 296. [*Died* 6 *Feb.* 1959.

THOMSON, James Moffat, C.B.E. 1932; Colonial Administrative Officer, retired 1934; *b.* Edinburgh; *m.* Mabel Evelyn, *y. d.* of late Edward Dunsterville, Woodlands, Walton-on-Thames. *Educ.:* George Watson's College, Edinburgh. District Administration, North Eastern Rhodesia, 1903; Native Commissioner, 1907; Magistrate, Northern Rhodesia, 1923; Secretary for Native Affairs, Northern Rhodesia, 1929-34; Chairman, Native Reserve Commission, 1927; Chairman, Advisory Board on Native Education, 1929; M.E.C. and M.L.C., 1929-36. *Recreation:* golf. *Address:* Fairway, Riverton Road, Rondebosch, Cape Town, S. Africa. *Club:* Civil Service (Cape Town). [*Died* 26 *Aug.* 1953.

THOMSON, Brig.-Gen. Noel (Arbuthnot), C.M.G. 1918; D.S.O. 1916; *b.* 1 April 1872; *s.* of Col. C. W. Thomson of Broomhill, Woodbridge, Suffolk; *m.* 1903, Mary Augusta (*d.* 1948), *d.* of Stephen Moore, D.L., of Barne Park, Clonmel; one *s.* one *d.* *Educ.:* Wellington College. Served occupation of Crete; 1897; Nile Expedition, 1898 (wounded); South African War, 1899-1902 (despatches, Queen's medal and three clasps, King's medal and two clasps); European War, 1914-18, in command of 8th Batt. Seaforth Highlanders, 102nd (Tyneside Scottish) Infantry Brigade, and 44th (Highland) Infantry Brigade (twice wounded, despatches eight times, C.M.G., D.S.O., Bt. Lt.-Col., Officer Legion of Honour); retired pay, 1923. *Address:* Mansfield, Kokstad, East Griqualand, S. Africa. *Club:* Army and Navy. [*Died* 15 *Oct.* 1959.

THOMSON, The Very Rev. P. D., M.A., D.D., H.C.F.; *b.* 8 Jan. 1872; *s.* of James M. Thomson and Margaret McDougall; *m.* 1901, Marian Helen Scott; one *s.* three *d.* *Educ.:* Hermitage School, Helensburgh; Glasgow University; Glasgow Free Church College (now Trinity College). Freeland Tutor in Hebrew, Trinity Coll., Glasgow 1895-96; Joshua Paterson Scholar 1896: Assistant in South Free Church, Aberdeen, 1896-97; Minister of Peterculter Free Church, Deeside, 1897-1900; Minister of St. Brycedale Church, Kirkcaldy, 1901-7; Minister of the Church of Scotland at Kelvinside Church (Botanic Gardens), Glasgow, 1907-42; Chaplain to the Forces, and Senior Chaplain of the Highland Division, 1914-16, 1918-19; Moderator of the General Assembly of the Church of Scotland, 1934-35. *Publications:* Parish and Parish Church: Their Place and Influence in History; The Gordon Highlanders: Being a Short Record of the Services of the Regiment; The Living Word: Other Sermons and Addresses. *Recreations:* reading, golf, contract bridge. *Address:* 6 Hughenden Terrace, Glasgow, W.2. *T.:* Kelvin 1530. [*Died* 14 *April* 1955.

THOMSON, Sir Vernon, Bt.; *see* Thomson, Sir F. V.

THORBURN, Lt.-Col. William, D.S.O. 1919; T.D.; Chairman, Lowe, Donald & Co. Ltd., Peebles; Member Royal Company of Archers (Queen's Body Guard for Scotland); *b.* 1881; *e. s.* of late Wm. Thorburn, Craigerne, Peebles; *m.* 1909, Winifred Alison Hopkins; (only son killed Burma, 1944) three *d.* *Educ.:* Blairlodge; Paris; Bonn. Entered family business, Lowe, Donald & Co. Ltd., Peebles and London, Woollen Merchants and Exporters, in 1900, and succeeded father as Chm. of the Coy. in 1926. Joined 6th V.B. Royal Scots, 1901; served with 8th and 9th Bns. Royal Scots, France, cmd. 8th Bn. 1918 (D.S.O.); cmd. Peeblesshire Bn. H.G., 1940-44. J.P. and D.L. County of Peebles, Lord-Lieutenant, 1945-56; Hon. Col. 8th Bn., The Royal Scots, 1946-57. *Recreations:* cricket, golf, shooting. *Address:* 5 Belgrave Cres., Edinburgh. *Clubs:* Oriental; New (Edinburgh). [*Died* 17 *Oct.* 1959.

THORNE, Alfred Charles; *b.* 23 Dec. 1870; *s.* of James Thorne, F.S.A.; *m.* 1938, Gladys Dorothea, *widow* of Henry Cameron Hind. *Educ.:* City of London School; Switzerland. Fellow of the Institute of Actuaries, 1893; Vice-President, 1923-26; Joint Librarian Inst. of Actuaries, 1924-35; late Manager and Secretary, Equity and Law Life Assurance Society; Actuary, Law Reversionary Interest Society; Manager, Equity and Law Investment Trust Ltd. *Recreation:* golf. *Address:* 44 Berkeley Court, Baker Street

N.W.1. *T.:* Welbeck 8625. *Clubs:* Union, Royal Automobile. [*Died* 28 *Oct.* 1952.

THORNE, Air Vice-Marshal Walter, C.B. 1946; C.B.E. 1940; *b.* 20 Feb. 1890; *s.* of Walter Thorne and Alice Skull; *m.* 1920, Gertrude, *d.* of J. W. Rowe; two *d.* *Educ.:* Harrow Green School. Enlisted Oxf. and Bucks Light Infantry, 1907; transferred to Royal Flying Corps, 1912; commissioned, 1916; served European War, 1914-18, with R.F.C.; served: Bomber Command, 1939-1942; Maintenance Command, 1942-47; Group Capt. 1939; Air Commodore, 1942; Air Vice-Marshal, 1946; retired, 1947. *Recreations:* cricket, gardening. *Address:* Combe Edge, 23 Barlow Rd., Eastbourne. *T.:* 1189. [*Died* 5 *Oct.* 1960.

THORNE, William Huxtable; late Judge, Johore, Johore Bahru; *b.* 5 Sept. 1882; *s.* of Arnold Thorne, Barnstaple, N. Devon; *m.* 1908; two *s.* one *d.* *Educ.:* privately. English Solicitor, 1903; practised in Lincolnshire, 1903-1906; called to local bar of the Colony of the S.S., 1907, and of the F.M.S., 1908; practised in Penang, 1907-26; Member of the Legislative Council of the Colony of the S.S., 1920-26; Judge of the Supreme Court of the Colony of the Straits Settlements and of the F.M.S., 1926. *Recreations:* riding, golf, swimming, etc. *Address:* Rossyln, Falmouth Road, Helston, Cornwall. [*Died* 13 *Sept.* 1951.

THORNELY, Sir Arnold, Kt., *cr.* 1933; retired Architect; *b.* 1870; *s.* of James Thornely, Godley, Cheshire, and Mary Harris; *m.* Caroline, *d.* of Frederick Thornely, Helsby, Cheshire; one *s.* one *d.* *Educ.:* privately. Architect to the following buildings: Parliament Building, Northern Government of Ireland; Head Offices, Mersey Docks and Harbour Board, Town Hall, Wallasey; Municipal Buildings, Barnsley and Preston; Geology Building, Liverpool University; numerous other public and private buildings. *Address:* Greystones, Eaton Park Road, Fairmile, Cobham, Surrey. *T.:* Cobham Surrey 2656. [*Died* 1 *Oct.* 1953.

THORNEYCROFT, Harry; *b.* 21 Feb. 1892. *Educ.:* Elementary, Manchester. Army, 1914-19; elected Manchester City Council, 1923; J.P. 1933; contested Blackpool Div., 1935; Alderman Manchester City Council, 1939. M.P. (Lab.) Clayton Div. of Manchester, 1942-55; Private Parliamentary Secretary, Air Ministry, 1950-51. *Recreations:* fishing, cycling. *Address:* 140 Droylsden Road, Manchester 10. *T.:* Failsworth 1637. [*Died* 7 *March* 1956.

THORNEYCROFT, Wallace, J.P.; F.R.S.E.; M.I.M.E. (Past Pres.); Mining Engineer (retired); *b.* 24 Feb. 1864; *s.* of Col. Thorneycroft, Tettenhall, Wolverhampton; *m.* Margaret, *d.* of J. A. Campbell, Dremore Lodge, County Down; three *s.* three *d.* *Educ.:* Charterhouse; Owens College, Manchester. Well known in coal, iron, and steel trades, 1910-28; contested (C.) the Cannock Division of Staffordshire, 1923 and 1924. *Address:* Chalmington, Dorchester. *T.:* Maiden Newton 263. *Club:* Bath. [*Died* 26 *April* 1954.

THORNHILL, Colonel Cudbert John Massy, C.M.G. 1920; D.S.O. 1918; *b.* 1883; *s.* of late Lt.-Col. Sir Henry Beaufoy Thornhill, K.C.I.E., C.M.G.; *m.* 1939, Dame Rachel Eleanor Crowdy, D.B.E. *Educ.:* Bradfield; R.M.C., Sandhurst. Served European War, 1914-19; Military Attaché, Petrograd, 1916-18, Brevet Major, 1917; North Russian Expeditionary Force, 1918-19 (despatches, D.S.O. with bar, Brevet Lieut.-Col., Officer Legion of Honour); served Political Intelligence Dept. of Foreign Office, India and Egypt, 1940-46. Order of St. Vladimir, 3rd class (Russia); Order of St. Stanislas, 2nd class (Russia); Order of St. Anne, 3rd class (Russia); Order of White Eagle, 4th class (Serbia). *Address:* 100 Beaufort St., Chelsea, S.W.3. *T.:* Flaxman 7076; Sheppards, Outwood, Surrey. *T.:* Smallfield 5. *Clubs:* Bath, United Service. [*Died* 12 *Aug.* 1952.

THORNHILL, Col. George B.; *see* Badham-Thornhill.

THORNHILL, Noel, M.C.; M.A.; J.P. Co. Huntingdon; *b.* 18 Dec. 1881; *er. s.* of Rev. Francis Herbert William Thornhill; *m.* 1916, Margaret Octavia (*d.* 1917), *y. d.* of Col. T. W. C. Chester-Master, The Abbey, Cirencester; no *c.* *Educ.:* Eton; King's College, Cambridge. B.A. 1904; Grenadier Guards, Spec. Res., 1916-19, Lieut.; previously Lieut. Beds. Yeomanry; Jt. Master Cambridgeshire Foxhounds, 1932-35; High Sheriff Counties Cambridge and Huntingdon, 1941-42. *Address:* Diddington Hall, Buckden, Hunts. *T.A.:* Buckden, Hunts. *T.:* Buckden 349. *Club:* Junior Carlton. [*Died* 13 *Jan.* 1955.

THORNTON, Sir Ernest Hugh, Kt., *cr.* 1944; R.D.; R.N.R.; *b.* 31 Jan. 1884; *s.* of James Thornton, Oxford; *m.* 1912, Jean Gordon Sparke, Sydney, N.S.W.; two *d.* *Educ.:* Avenue House School, Sevenoaks. Late Commodore Commander of Union-Castle Mail Steamship Co. Ltd.; retired, 1947. *Recreations:* golf and gardening. *Address:* Box 4967, Ngong, Kenya. [*Died* 24 *Nov.* 1951.

THORNTON, George Lestock, C.B.E. 1939; M.C.; T.D.; M.A. Cantab.; M.R.C.P. Lond.; M.R.C.S.; Colonel (late R.A.M.C.) T.A.; Retired List; late Hon. Col. R.A.M.C. Wessex Division; *b.* Feb. 1872; *s.* of late Rev. John Thornton, Betchworth, Surrey, and formerly Vicar of Ewell, Surrey; *m.* 1898, Leta Anna (*d.* 1943), *d.* of late R. A. Cordner, M.I.C.E., Public Works Department, N.W.P. India; three *s.* one *d.* *Educ.:* Rossall School; Trinity College, Cambridge; St. George's Hospital. In medical practice pre-European War and subsequently served in Ministry of Pensions as Dep. Comm. of Medical Services Exeter Area; retired, 1937; recalled (temp.) as Commissioner Medical Services, S.W. Region, 1941-45; in European war served in R.A.M.C. in France, Macedonia and Palestine (M.C. and Bar); post-war, served in Territorial Army in Command of Wessex Field Ambulance, and subsequently as A.D.M.S. 43rd Wessex Division; late Hon. Physician to King George V, 1930-34; late Member of Devon County Council, retd. 1951; President British Legion, Exmouth Branch. *Publications:* various contributions to medical journals. *Recreations:* golf, walking. *Address:* c/o Lloyds Bank, Exmouth. [*Died* 4 *Dec.* 1951.

THORNTON, Rev. Lionel Spencer; Member Community of the Resurrection, House of the Resurrection, Mirfield, Yorks, since 1915; *b.* High Cross Vicarage, Herts, 27 June 1884; *s.* of Rev. Claude Cecil Thornton and Alice Henrietta (*née* Puller). *Educ.:* Tyttenhanger Lodge, St. Albans; Malvern College; Emmanuel College, Cambridge; Westcott House, Cambridge. House Scholar of Malvern; Foundation Scholar of Emmanuel Coll.; B.A. (first class Hons. in Theology), 1907; Carus Prize, 1907; M.A. 1911; Norrisian Prize, 1913; B.D. 1929; D.D. 1943; Hon. D.D., Durham, 1944; deacon, 1908; priest, 1909. Curate of: St. Paul's, Lorrimore Square, 1908-09; Lingfield, 1909-13. Joined Community of the Resurrection, 1913; professed member, 1915; Lecturer in Theology, College of the Resurrection, Mirfield, 1914-44, resident in Community's London House (Priory of St. Paul, 8 Holland Park, W.11), 1944-58. Member of Archbishops' Commission on Christian Doctrine, 1923-38; Select Preacher, Cambridge, 1927, 1932, 1938, 1945; Oxford, 1928-30. *Publications:* Conduct and the Supernatural, 2nd edn., 1916; Richard Hooker, A Study of his Theology, 1924; The Incarnate Lord, 1928; The Doctrine of the Atonement, 1937; The Common Life in the

Body of Christ, 4th edn., 1950; Revelation and the Modern World, 1950; The Dominion of Christ, 1952; Confirmation—Its place in the Baptismal Mystery, 1954; Christ and the Church, 1956. Contributor to: Essays Catholic and Critical, 3rd edn., 1929; Jl. of Theological Studies, 1945, 1954; The Apostolic Ministry, 2nd edn., 1947. *Recreations:* reading and walking. *Address:* House of the Resurrection, Mirfield, Yorkshire. [*Died* 19 *July* 1960.

THORNYCROFT, Sir John Edward, K.B.E., *cr.* 1918; President and Director of J. I. Thornycroft & Co. Ltd.; Past President Inst.C.E.; Vice-President Royal Inst. Naval Architects; *b.* 5 Sept. 1872; *s.* of late Sir J. I. Thornycroft, LL.D., F.R.S.; *m.* 1896, Isabel, *o. d.* of A. B. Ward; two *s.* two *d.* *Address:* Thornycroft House, Smith Square, Westminster, S.W.1; Steyne, Bembridge, Isle of Wight. *Clubs:* Athenæum, Junior Carlton; Bembridge Sailing (Bembridge). [*Died* 21 *Nov.* 1960.

THORNYCROFT, Oliver, C.B. 1948; O.B.E. 1920; M.A., F.R.Ae.S., M.I.Mech.E.; Consulting Engineer; *b.* 19 April 1885; *s.* of Sir Hamo Thornycroft, R.A., and Agatha, *d.* of Homersham Cox; *m.* 1911, Dorothy, *d.* of Edward Rose (Playwright); two *s.* three *d.* *Educ.:* Bedales School; Clare College, Cambridge. Engaged in Engineering (Electrical and Mechanical). Served European War, 1914-18, R.N.V.R. attached to R.N.A.S.; Chief Engineer and Works Manager to Messrs. Ricardo & Co. Ltd., 1919-39. War of 1939-45, Admiralty department engaged on mine and anti-submarine weapon design. Director Aeronautical and Engineering Research, Admiralty, 1946-50. *Publications:* various on engineering in technical journals. *Recreation:* mountaineering. *Address:* 82 Corringham Road, N.W.11. *T.:* Speedwell 7218. *Clubs:* United University, Alpine, Climbers'. [*Died* 24 *Aug.* 1956.

THOROGOOD, Stanley, A.R.C.A.; *b.* 1873; *s.* of Edward Thorogood; *m.* 1900, Edith A. Gibbs; two *d.* *Educ.:* private school. Studied at the Brighton School of Art, won Royal Exhibition Scholarship; later at the Royal College of Art, South Kensington, won the Gold Medal Travelling Scholarship of the College; studied in Italy and France; for many years was Head of the Burslem School of Art, and later of the five Schools of the Federated Borough; Principal of the L.C.C. Camberwell School of Arts and Crafts, 1920-38; specialised in Pottery Figure Work, and one of the early exhibitors of this class of work at the Royal Academy, Salon, and other Galleries. *Publication:* Manipulation of the Brush. *Recreation:* gardening. *Address:* The Garth, Cornwall Gardens, Brighton. [*Died* 7 *Nov.* 1953.

THOROLD, Sir John George, 13th Bt., *cr.* 1642; *b.* 2 Oct. 1870; *e. s.* of 12th Bt. and Hon. Henrietta Alexandrina Matilda Willoughby, *e. d.* of 8th Baron Middleton; S. father, 1922; unmarried. *Educ.:* Eton. Major (retired) 3rd Bn. (Special Reserve) Lincolnshire Regt. Owns about 1000 acres. *Heir:* *b.* James Ernest, *b.* 27 Jan. 1877. *Address:* Green Cottage, Dawlish, S. Devon. [*Died* 25 *Dec.* 1951.

THOROLD, William James; Director British and General Debenture Trust, Ltd.; Federal Debenture Company Incorporated; Federated Capital Corporation; *b.* Toronto, 7 Oct. 1871; *s.* of W. H. Thorold, of Thorold, Canada, and Toronto; *m.* 1906, Muriel (*d.* 1931), *twin d.* of Joseph C. Mappin, of London, S.W. *Educ.:* Parkdale Collegiate Institute, Toronto; McMaster Univ. of Toronto (B.A.). *Address:* 60 Wall Street Tower (54th floor), New York. *Clubs:* Royal Automobile; Bankers (New York); Royal Canadian Yacht (Toronto); Lido Country, Long Beach (N.Y.). [*Died* 1942.
[*But death not notified in time for inclusion in Who Was Who 1941–1950, first edn.*

THORP, Lt.-Col. Arthur Hugh, C.M.G. 1919; D.S.O. 1918; *b.* 1869; *m.* 1920, Ethel Mary Muriel, *o. d.* of W. Benton, Texas, U.S.A. *Educ.:* Bath College; Royal Military Academy, Woolwich. Commissioned into R.A., 1888; served in Malta and Jamaica; at latter station for five years taking great interest in local affairs; served for many years in the Royal Arsenal, Woolwich, in the scientific instruments department, during which time he invented, designed, and improved some fifty different instruments used in H.M. Service; served European War (despatches four times, C.M.G., D.S.O.); after the Armistice served in Army of Occupation, Rhine; went on half-pay upon marriage and retired six months later. *Address:* Elmsleigh, Send, Woking. [*Died* 2 *Feb.* 1955.

THORP, Admiral Charles Frederick, C.B.E. 1919; Royal Navy (retired); *b.* 1869; *s.* of Rev. Frederick Thorp, of Burton Overy, Leicestershire; *m.* 1910, Annie Ethel, *d.* of Geo. Handford; no *c.* Entered Royal Navy as Naval Cadet on board H.M.S. Britannia, 1882; Sub-Lieut., 1888; Lieut., 1889; Comdr., 1901; Capt., 1906; Rear-Admiral, 1917; retired as R.A., 1917; Vice-Admiral, 1922, Admiral, 1927, retired. Served European War, 1914-19; S.N.O. Harwich, 1919. *Address:* Spring Lodge, Prestbury Rd., Cheltenham. [*Died* 31 *Oct.* 1954.

THORPE, A(rthur) Winton, O.B.E.; journalist; *b.* 19 Feb. 1865; *s.* of late Thomas Miller Thorpe, Winchester; *m.* 1897, Alice (*d.* 1934), *d.* of late Benjamin Wheeler, Northampton; one *s.* Assistant Editor, Nottingham Daily Express, 1892; Editor, the Galignani Messenger (Paris), 1893; Managing Director, London News Agency, Ltd., 1898-1919; Director of Publicity, Ministry of Food, 1917-18. *Club:* Junior Carlton. [*Died* 29 *April* 1952.

THORVARDSSON, Stefan; Icelandic, Minister to the Court of St. James, 1944-1951, and to the Netherlands, 1950-51; *b.* 26 November 1900; *s.* of Rev. Thorvardur Brynjólfsson; *m.* 1934, Gudrún, *d.* of Professor Jón Hj. Sigurdsson; one *s.* two *d.* *Educ.:* Reykjavik; Copenhagen; Montreal. Danish Foreign Service, 1925-29; Permanent Secretary in the Icelandic Dept. of External Affairs, 1929-38; Permanent Under-Secretary of the Ministry for External Affairs, 1938-1944. Delegate Member of several Trade Negotiation Missions, 1932-38. *Recreations:* salmon fishing, ski-ing. [*Died* 21 *Aug.* 1951.

THOSEBY, William Martin; Headmaster, St. Edmund's School, Canterbury, since 1945; *b.* 3 Feb. 1901; *s.* of A. E. Thoseby, Headmaster, The Grammar School, Harrogate; *m.* 1st, 1926, Mary Joyce Brown (*d.* 1952); one *d.*; 2nd, 1953, Joan Sherwood Dodd, M.B.E., *d.* of late Sir Robert Dodd, C.S.I. *Educ.:* Bradford Grammar School; Queen's College, Oxford. Senior English Master and Housemaster, Blundell's School, Tiverton, Devon, 1924-45. *Recreations:* cricket—Devon County and Oxford Univ. Authentic C.C.; golf. *Address:* St. Edmund's School, Canterbury. *T.:* 4496. [*Died* 4 *July* 1959.

THRELFORD, Sir W. Lacon, Kt., *cr.* 1933; M.B.E.; R.D.; F.C.A.; Commander Order of Al Rafidan; Commander Order of Leopold II. Served European War, 1914-19, Commander R.N.R. (retd.); a Lieutenant of the City of London; Past Second Master and Hon. Treasurer of Company of Shipwrights; Past Master Company of: Parish Clerks, Needlemakers and Glaziers; member Court of Companies of Gold and Silver Wyre Drawers, and Basketmakers; Liveryman of Companies of Carmen, Feltmakers, Gardeners, Loriners and Woolmen; Sheriff of City of London, 1932-33; Chm. of the Machinery Users Association of Great Britain; Pres. of the Institute of Linguists; Hon. Vice-President Cercle Belge; Vice-President Anglo-Belgian Union; Member of the Committee of Honour, International Handicrafts and Hobbies

Exhibition; Chairman Westbourne Park Building Society. *Address:* 11 Chelsea Embankment, S.W.3; Cosy Nook, Broadstairs, Kent. *Clubs:* Carlton, Royal Automobile, City Livery, Royal Motor Yacht, Anglo-Belgian (Chm.). [*Died* 28 *April* 1958.

THUILLIER, Maj.-Gen. Sir Henry Fleetwood, K.C.B., *cr.* 1930 (C.B. 1916); C.M.G. 1916; D.L. for Glos., 1936; *b.* Meerut, India, 30 Mar. 1868; *e. s.* of late Col. Sir Henry Ravenshaw Thuillier, K.C.I.E.; *m.* 1894, Helen (*d.* 1923), *e. d.* of Maj.-Gen. G. R. Shakespear, I.S.C.; one *s.* (and two *s.* decd.). *Educ.:* Wimbledon School; R.M.A., Woolwich. Entered Royal Engineers as 2nd Lieut., 1887; Lieutenant, 1890; Captain, 1898; Major, 1906; Lt.-Col. 1914; Brig.-Gen. 1915; Maj.-Gen. 1919; served Chitral Relief Expedition, 1895; European War, 1914-18, in which held following appointments: Command 2nd Infantry Brigade; Director Gas Services, G.H.Q.; Command 15th (Scottish) Division; Controller Chemical Warfare, Ministry of Munitions; Command 23rd Division (despatches five times, C.M.G., C.B., Bt. Col., Maj.-Gen.); Commandant School of Military Engineering, and G.O.C. Thames and Medway Area, 1919-23; Director of Fortifications and Works, War Office, 1924-27; G.O.C. 52nd (Lowland) Div. Territorial Army, Glasgow, 1927-30; retired, 1930; Col. Comdt. R.E. 1935-1940; re-employed under Ministry of Supply in rank of Major, 1940-45. *Publications:* The Principles of Land Defence, 1902; Gas in the Next War, 1939. *Address:* Bretforton, Moorend Park Road, Cheltenham. *T.:* Cheltenham 3696. *Club:* United Service. [*Died* 11 *June* 1953.

THURLOW, 6th Baron, *cr.* 1792; **Rev. Charles Edward Hovell-Thurlow-Cumming-Bruce;** *b.* 6 Oct. 1869; *s.* of 5th Baron Thurlow and Lady Elma Bruce, *o. d.* of 8th Earl of Elgin and Kincardine; *S.* father, 1916; *m.* 1909, Grace Catherine (J.P. 1935), *d.* of Canon Trotter of Christ Church, Barnet; four *s. Educ.:* Eton; Trinity College, Cambridge; M.A. Ordained 1898; has served at Portland, Oregon; Valparaiso, and West Coast South America, and as a Superintendent of the Missions to Seamen; Vicar of St. Andrew's, Bishop Auckland, Rural Dean of Auckland, 1913-21; Chaplain Superintendent Mersey Missions to Seamen, Liverpool, 1921-30; Rector of Sedgfield, Co. Durham, 1930-39; Rural Dean of Liverpool N., 1925-30. Chaplain, Hon. Company of Master Mariners, 1928-30. *Heir: s.* Bt. Lt.-Col. Hon. Henry Charles Cumming-Bruce, D.S.O. *Address:* Ardleigh Court, Colchester. *T.:* Ardleigh 338. [*Died* 23 *April* 1952.

THURSFIELD, Captain (S) Raymond Spencer, C.M.G. 1919; Royal Navy, retired; *b.* 27 March 1882; *s.* of late Major Alfred Spencer Thursfield, J.P., V.D., Malvern; *m.* 1918, Evelyn Mary, *d.* of late Colonel C. H. Beck, C.B., Upton Priory, Macclesfield; two *s. Educ.:* Royal Academy, Gosport. Entered Royal Navy, 1899; served European War, 1914-1918 (C.M.G., Order of St. Anne (Russia) 3rd class with swords): retired list, 1932. Bursar of St. Edward's School, Oxford, 1932-46. *Address:* 200 Woodstock Road, Oxford. *T.:* 55102. [*Died* 24 *Jan.* 1953.

THURSTON, Frederick John, C.B.E. 1952; Professor of Clarinet at Royal College of Music; also soloist; *b.* 1901; *s.* of Frederick Thurston; *m.* 1st, 1927, Eileen (*d.* 1947), *d.* of Dr. A. C. King-Turner, Fairford; one *d.*; *m.* 1953, Thea, *d.* of H. W. M. King, M.B.E., Hitchin. *Educ.:* St. Mary and St. John's School, Oxford; Royal College of Music. Soloist at Edinburgh Festivals; International Music Festivals; toured Europe, Jugoslavia and Bulgaria, 1949. Made gramophone records for Decca. Examiner for Royal Schools of Music. Has given first performances of important works for clarinet. *Publications:* A Comprehensive Tutor for the Clarinet, 1939; 3 volumes of passage studies, 1947; Clarinet Technique, 1953. *Recreation:* golf. *Address:* 38 Cheyne Walk, Chelsea, S.W.3. *T.:* Flaxman 5381. *Club:* Savage. [*Died* 12 *Dec.* 1953.

THURTLE, Ernest; M.P. (Lab.) Shoreditch, 1923-31 and 1935-50, Shoreditch and Finsbury since 1950; Capt. Pioneer Corps; *b.* New York State, U.S.A., 11 Nov. 1884; *s.* of Philip Thurtle, Norfolk; *m.* 1912, Dorothy, *d.* of late Rt. Hon. George Lansbury, M.P.; one *s.* one *d. Educ.:* Elementary School; private study. An accountant and salesman; served European War, first in the ranks and then commissioned; severely wounded at Cambrai; actively identified with Ex-Service Men's movement, 1919-21, and connected with the United Services Fund, forming one of the first Council of management of this; contested S.W. Bethnal Green, Dec. 1918, and Shoreditch, Nov. 1922; Parl. Priv. Secretary to the Minister of Pensions, Labour Government, 1924; Junior Lord of the Treasury, 1930-31; Parliamentary Secretary, Ministry of Information, 1941-45. *Publications:* Military Discipline and Democracy; Time's Winged Chariot; pamphlet—Shootings at Dawn, and several Labour pamphlets. *Recreations:* cricket, tennis. *Address:* 77 Moreland Court, Finchley Road, N.W.2. *T.:* Hampstead 5850; 2 Paper Bldgs., E.C.4. *T.:* Central 2569; 8 St. Margaret's, Rottingdean, Sussex. *T.:* 3130. [*Died* 22 *Aug.* 1954.

THWAITES, Lieutenant-Colonel Norman Graham, C.B.E. 1919; M.V.O. 1919; M.C.; late London Representative of Bahamas Government; late Secretary Air League and Editor of Air; former Hon. Secretary English-Speaking Union; *b.* 24 June 1872; 2nd *s.* of Rev. H. Graham Thwaites and Clara Hepworth, of Cambridge Park, Redland, Bristol; *m.* 1919, Eleanor (*d.* 1951), *d.* of Fredk. W. Whitridge, New York; one *s.* (and one killed in action, 1944, in Italy) two *d. Educ.:* S. Lawrence College, Kent; abroad. Read for the Bar, but not called; served Boer War, 1899-1901; South African Light Horse (Queen's medal 4 clasps); joined 2nd Co. of London Yeomanry (Westminster Dragoons), 1902; secretary to the late Joseph Pulitzer, proprietor New York World, for ten years; then represented World at most of the European capitals; Asst. Foreign Editor in New York; appointed 1914 to 4th Royal Irish Dragoon Guards; served in France and Belgium (severely wounded, despatches, M.C.); sent on special mission to United States, 1916; promoted temp. Major; P.M. New York with rank of Lt.-Col.; Director British Mission, 1918; temporarily attached staff of Prince of Wales during his visit to Canada and U.S.A.; contested (C.) Hillsboro' Division (Sheffield), 1924. *Publications:* Velvet and Vinegar, a volume of memoirs; The World's Mine Oyster, further memoirs; Prankman, being family Chronicles. *Recreations:* polo, cricket, tennis, Alpine sports. *Clubs:* Bath, Beefsteak. [*Died* 24 *Jan.* 1956.

THYNNE, Captain Denis Granville, C.M.G. 1919; R.N. retd.; *b.* 1875; *s.* of Rev. A. C. Thynne; *m.* 1921, May, *widow* of Admiral Noel Grant, C.B. Served European War, 1914-1919 (C.M.G.); Retired List, 1922; Temp. Lieutenant R.N.V.R. (unpaid), 1940. *Address:* 9 Poughill Road, Bude, N. Cornwall. [*Died* 18 *Dec.* 1955.

THYNNE, Colonel Ulric Oliver, C.M.G. 1918; C.V.O. 1946; D.S.O. 1901; T.D. 1917; *b.* 6 July 1871; 4th and *o. surv. s.* of Rt. Hon. Lord Henry Frederick Thynne and Lady Ulrica Frederica Jane St. Maur, *d.* of 12th Duke of Somerset; *m.* 1st, 1899, Marjory (*d.* 1950), *d.* of Edward Wormald; two *s.* one *d.*; 2nd, 1951 Elspeth (*d.* 1955), *e. d.* of David Tullis, Glencairn, Rutherglen, and *widow* of 1st and last Baron Invernairn. *Educ.:* Charterhouse; R.M.C., Sandhurst. Served Chitral Campaign, 1895 (medal with clasp); South Africa, 1900 (despatches, medal 3 clasps, D.S.O.); European War, 1914-

1918 (despatches, C.M.G., promoted Colonel); served 60th Rifles, 1891-1900; Royal Wiltshire Yeomanry, 1900-1920, Lt.-Col. commanding 1914-20, Hon. Col. 1938-46; His Majesty's Body Guard (Hon. Corps of Gentlemen-at-Arms), 1922-46, Standard Bearer, 1945-46. *Recreations:* hunting, shooting, polo. *Address:* Muntham Court, Findon, Sussex. *Club:* Turf. [*Died* 30 *Sept.* 1957.

TIARKS, Frank Cyril, O.B.E.; banker; partner in J. Henry Schroder & Co. since 1902; Lieutenant of the City of London; *b.* 9 July 1874; *e. surv. s.* of Henry Frederic Tiarks, Foxbury, Chislehurst, Kent; *m.* Emmy Maria Franziska (*d.* 1943), 2nd *d.* of Edward M. Broedermann of Hamburg; two *s.* two *d.* *Educ.:* H.M.S. Britannia. Royal Navy, 1887-94. Director of Bank of England, 1912-45. Director of The Anglo-Iranian Oil Co. Ltd., 1917-48. High Sheriff of Kent, 1927. *Address:* North Lodge, Loxton, Axbridge, Somerset. *T.:* Edingworth 257. *Clubs:* Carlton, Royal Thames Yacht. [*Died* 7 *April* 1952.

TIBBLES, Sydney Granville, L.R.C.S., L.R.C.P. Edin.; L.F.P. and S. Glasg. 1909; 1st Class Honours, Diseases of the Eye; Mem. B.M.A.; Lecturer and Examiner, L.C.C.; *b.* Nottingham, 1884; *s.* of late Dr. William Tibbles, LL.D. (hon.) Chicago, D.C.L. (hon.) Washington; *m.* 1st, Lillie Wilson Ker (*d.* 1923); two *d.*; 2nd, Sara Galliaerdt (*née* Colmans, of Antwerp). *Educ.:* High School, Nottingham; University of Edinburgh. Hon. Eye Surgeon War Office, 1914-15; Ministry of Labour and National Service; Ministry of Pensions; Specialist in Ophthalmology, Devonport Military Hospital and to Hospitals 24 and 10 B.E.F.; late Eye Surgeon L.C.C. Clinics at Hammersmith, and to Kent County Council for Clinics at Beckenham and West Wickham; Hon. Eye Surgeon Officers' Families Fund; Clinical Asst., Eye Department, Royal Infirmary, Edinburgh, Nottingham and Midland Eye Infirmary; R.M.O., Roy. I.O.W. County Hosp.; Anæsthetist Roy. Dental Hosp. and St. George's Clinic, Blackfriars, S.E.; Clin. Asst., Roy. Westminster Ophth. Hosp., Miller Gen. Hosp.; Sen. House Surg., Western Ophth. Hosp.; Hon. Ophth. Surg., Western Gen. Dispensary and St. Pancras Dispensary, and to Ex-Service's Welfare Assoc.; attached 2nd North Midland Field Ambulance and 4th King's Liverpools. *Publications:* Light and Sight; The Sight of School Children, and papers on Sight, in Lancet, British Medical Journal, Medical World, Evening Standard, Locomotive Journal. *Recreations:* travel and music. *Address:* 91 The White House, N.W.1. *T.:* Euston 1200. [*Died* 4 *April* 1960.

TIDBURY-BEER, Sir Frederick (Tidbury), Kt., *cr.* 1947; *b.* 16 Jan. 1892; 3rd and *y. s.* of George Jeffrey Beer and Elizabeth Tidbury; *m.* 1930, Mabel Constance, *yr. d.* of Robert L. and Sarah Johnson, Butterton Hall, Newcastle, Staffs; one *d.* *Educ.:* Temple Grove, Mercers' and King's College Schools. Commenced business life at age of 13 as office boy in stockbroking firm; entered Stock Exchange as Clerk, 1911; Member since 1922. Served with Anglo-French Red Cross, attached to French Army Medical Service, as Radiologist and Pharmacist, 1915-18 (Médaille d'Honneur); Technical Officer, Royal Air Force, 1918-19. Master of Co. of Gold & Silver Wyre Drawers, 1947-48; Member Court of Assistants Co. of Innholders. Freeman of the Co. of Fan Makers (*h.c.*) and Master Co. of Parish Clerks. Member of Council City Livery Club since 1933, President, 1944-45, Master of Guild of Freeman, 1950-51; Guild Master of Civic Guild of Old Mercers, 1948-49; Member: U.D.C. of Welwyn Garden City, 1929-30; Court of Common Council, 1940-1954; Member (Chm. 1945-46) Improvements and Town Planning Cttee. dealing with reconstruction of City of London; Member Advisory Committee London Regional Planning, 1945-46; Member of County of London Licensing Planning Committee, 1948-54, and Chairman of City of London Licensing Planning Committee, 1952-54; Vice-President London Trustee Savings Bank; Governor of Christ's Hosp., and Bridewell Royal Hosp. (King Edward's School, Witley), 1946-54; Vice-Chm. Central Foundation Schools of London, 1949-51. Governor, Bishopsgate Foundation, 1941-53 (Chm. 1944-47); Churchwarden St. Botolph Without Bishopsgate, 1944-53; Sheriff of City of London, 1945-46; Alderman of the Ward of Cheap, one of H.M.'s Lieutenants of the City of London, and Pres. Ward of Cheap Club, 1946-54; President Bishopsgate Ward Club, 1947; Vice-Pres. of Cecil Houses (Chm. of Council, 1949-54); Governor of St. Bartholomew's Hospital, 1944-55; Past Life Governor of several other hospitals; Trustee Sheriffs' Fund Soc. (Chm. 1948-51); Member Court of Assistants of the Hon. the Irish Soc., 1944-48; Vice-Pres. London and Middlesex Archæological Society, and Roman and Mediæval London Excavation Council; Mem. Council, London Soc.; Hon. Associate Town Planning Inst.; F.R.S.A. *Recreations:* history and topography of Old London; architecture; town-planning; archæology. *Address:* Heath Lane House, Godalming, Surrey. *T.:* Godalming 1407. *Clubs:* City Livery, Old Mercers', United Wards. [*Died* 7 *Feb.* 1959.

TIDY, Sir Henry Letheby, K.B.E., *cr.* 1943; M.A., M.D. (Oxon), F.R.C.P.; Extra Physician to the Queen since 1952 (formerly to King George VI); Consulting Physician to the Royal Military Hospital, Millbank, and to St. Thomas's Hospital; Maj.-Gen. A.M.S.; Examiner in Medicine, Universities of Glasgow, Manchester, Belfast, Newcastle; Former Censor, Royal College of Physicians; *b.* 1877; *o. s.* of late Dr. C. M. Tidy; *m.* Elizabeth Catherine, *d.* of late Sir William Ramsay; two *s.* one *d.* *Educ.:* Winchester; New College, Oxford; London Hospital; Freiburg; Berlin. Formerly Consulting Physician to the Army. Visiting Professor of Medicine, University of Cairo, 1946-51. Ex-President: Roy. Soc. of Med.; Assoc. of Physicians of Great Britain; British Soc. of Gastro-enterology; Hon. LL.D. Belfast University, 1948. Legion of Merit (Commander) United States, 1946; Order of the White Lion (Czechoslovakia), 1946; Order of Orange-Nassau, Netherlands, 1947; Order of the Crown of Belgium, 1951. *Publications:* Synopsis of Medicine (10th Ed., 1954); articles on medical and pathological subjects. *Address:* 80 Campden Hill Court, Kensington, W.8. *T.:* Western 6536. *Clubs:* Athenæum, United University. [*Died* 3 *June* 1960.

TIEGS, Oscar Werner, F.R.S. 1944; Professor of Zoology, University of Melbourne; *b.* 12 March 1897; *s.* of O. Tiegs, Brisbane, Queensland; *m.* 1926, Ethel Hamilton. *Educ.:* Brisbane Grammar School. D.Sc. Adelaide. *Publications:* Papers on various biological subjects. [*Died* 5 *Nov.* 1956.

TIFFIN, Arthur Ernest, O.B.E. 1951; General Secretary, Transport and General Workers Union, since 1955; *b.* Carlisle, 11 Feb. 1896; *m.* 1st, 1920, Ethel Hart (*d.* 1947); two *s.*; 2nd, 1952, Joyce Robinson. *Educ.:* Fawcett's Higher Grade School; Bishop Creighton School. Permanent officer, Passenger Section Union, 1932; London and Home Counties Organiser, 1940; Asst. Gen.-Sec. Transport and General Workers Union, 1948. Chairman London Trades Council (7 years). Member of General Council of T.U.C. 1955-. *Recreations:* reading, walking. *Address:* Transport House, Smith Square, S.W.1. *Club:* Victory Ex-Servicemen's (Hon. Life Member). [*Died* 27 *Dec.* 1955.

TILDEN, Philip Armstrong, F.R.S.A.; F.R.I.B.A., practising alone; a Fellow of the Devon and Cornwall Architectural Society; *b.* 31 May 1887; *o. s.* of late Sir William Augustus Tilden, F.R.S., and his first wife Charlotte Bush; *m.* 1914, Caroline Brodin. *Educ.:* Bedales; Rugby; Architectural Association. Articled to T. E. Collcutt, past President R.I.B.A.; has built many country houses, amongst them work at Port Lympne, Kent, for Sir Philip Sassoon, at 25 Park Lane; rebuilding of Easton Lodge for Lady Warwick; 96 Cheyne Walk for Viscount Ednam; Brony-de, Churt, for Rt. Hon. D. Lloyd-George; Chartwell Manor for Rt. Hon. Winston S. Churchill; Flats in Portland Place; Blackhall, Eire; also work in numerous country houses; rebuilding and reconstruction of Allington Castle for Lord Conway, and Great Audience Chamber, Saltwood Castle; First Church of St. John Bosco, Shrigley, near Macclesfield; also conversion and adaptation of many historic houses including Antony, North Mymms Park and Cortachy Castle, Luton Hoo, Whitfield (Hereford), Rockingham (Boyle, Eire) and Knebworth House; a great deal of mural decoration; exhibited at R.A. for some years; interested in Black-and-White drawing, and has made Bookplates for many people, including Prince of Wales and Princess Royal; for 5 years Consulting Architect to J. S. Fry, Bristol; Governor of Old Vic Theatre, and Sadlers Wells. Pres. of the Devon and Cornwall Architectural Soc., 1944-46. *Publications:* has contributed many articles to the papers on Architecture; also a novel—Noah, 1932, and a volume of reminiscences, True Remembrances. *Address:* Dunsland House, Holsworthy, Devon. *T.:* Shebbear 264. [*Died* 25 *Feb.* 1956.

TILDEN, William Tatem; publisher and editor of Racquet Magazine; *b.* Germantown, Philadelphia, 10 Feb. 1893; *s.* of William Tatem Tilden and Selina Hey; unmarried. *Educ.:* Germantown Academy; University of Pennsylvania. Journalist and author, also actor; three times World Champion of Tennis; seven times U.S.A. Champion; ten years Davis Cup Star; eleven years U.S.A. No. 1 in Tennis, all Amateur; now U.S.A. Professional Tennis Player (U.S.A. Champion, 1931); won World Championship from Kozeluh in nine consecutive matches. *Publications:* Art of Lawn Tennis; Doubles and Singles; Handbooks on Tennis; Match Play and Spin of the Ball; Common Sense of Tennis; Me—The Handicap; The Phantom Drive; The Pinch Quitter—All in the Game; Aces, Places and Faults; Glory's Net (novel). *Recreations:* tennis, skating, squash racquets. *Address:* 1475 Broadway, New York. *Clubs:* All England Tennis; Germantown Cricket; Penn. Athletic. [*Died* 6 *June* 1953.

TILLARD, Rear-Admiral Sir Aubrey Thomas, K.B.E., *cr.* 1944; D.S.O. 1920; R.N. (retired); *b.* 1881; 2nd *s.* of late Rev. R. M. Tillard; *m.* 1924, Margery Gillian Crothers, *d.* of late Robert Michell (India Office); one *s.* one *d.* *Educ.:* Marlborough College; H.M.S. Britannia. Served China, 1900 (medal); European War, 1914-19 (despatches, D.S.O.); Captain in charge of the Naval Establishments at Bermuda, 1924-26; Captain of the Dockyard and King's Harbour Master, Chatham, 1931-32; A.D.C. 1932; Rear-Admiral and retired list, 1932; Commodore R.N.R., 1942 (despatches). *Address:* Lamorna, Penzance, Cornwall. [*Died* 12 *Dec.* 1952.

TILLEY, Rt. Hon. Sir John Anthony Cecil, P.C. 1920; G.C.M.G., *cr.* 1927 (K.C.M.G., *cr.* 1919); G.C.V.O., *cr.* 1929; C.B. 1916; *b.* 21 Jan. 1869; *s.* of late Sir John Tilley, K.C.B., and *d.* of William Eglinton Montgomerie (nephew of 12th Earl of Eglinton); *m.* 1901, Edith Honoria (*d.* 1949), *e. d.* of Sir William Montgomery Cuninghame, 9th Bt., V.C.; one *s.* two *d.* *Educ.:* Eton; King's College, Cambridge (Class. Honours, M.A.). Entered Foreign Office, 1893; Second Sec. in Diplomatic Service, and Secretary to British Agent for Venezuela Arbitration at Paris, 1899; Secretary to Committee on Consular Service, 1902; Secretary to Imperial Defence Committee, 1903-4; First Secretary to Embassy at Constantinople, 1906-8; British Plenipotentiary at Brussels Arms Conference, 1909; Delegate at Conference respecting Frontiers between Uganda, German East Africa, and Congo, Brussels, 1910; Plenipotentiary at African Liquor Conference, Brussels, 1912; Chief Clerk of Foreign Office, 1913; Assistant Secretary, 1919-20; British Ambassador to Brazil, 1921-25; to Japan, 1926-31; has Grand Cordon of Rising Sun of Japan; J.P. Suffolk; Vice-President of Overseas League. *Publications:* London to Tokyo, 1942; (with Stephen Gaselee) The Foreign Office, 1933. *Address:* Felsham House, Bury St. Edmunds. *Club:* Athenæum. [*Died* 5 *April* 1952.

TILLEY, Vesta (Lady de Frece); Matilda Alice; actress and male impersonator; *b.* 13 May 1864; *d.* of William Henry Powles, Worcester; *m.* 1890, Sir Walter de Frece (*d.* 1935). First appeared on stage at age of four at Nottingham, 1868, in London 1878; retired, 1920. *Publication:* Recollections of Vesta Tilley, 1934. *Address:* Arlington House, Arlington Street, S.W.1. [*Died* 16 *Sept.* 1952.

TILNEY, Frederick Colin, F.R.P.S.; Editor (also Founder and Proprietor) of Art and Reason, a monthly magazine (discontinued after 14 years but followed by Supplements to Art and Reason); privately, painter and press critic in art matters; *b.* 28 Dec. 1870; *s.* of Wm. Walden Tilney and Catherine Ellen; *m.* Una Constance, *d.* of Rev. J. S. Mummery; one *s.* *Educ.:* Birkbeck College. Painter and Designer; 12 years Art Director for W. Swan Sonnenschein and Co.; 12 years a master at Hornsey School of Art; for 30 years critical articles to Photographic Press; designing for The Munich Lionbrew Co., pictorial interior decorations of restaurants; designer of well-known Shakespearean Playing Cards; organiser of many campaigns for War Savings Committee, 1914-18; designer of Ruined Village, Trafalgar Sq., 1918; in later years, painting only, exhibiting at Royal Academy and other London Galleries; "Brother" of Art Workers' Guild. *Publications:* Wagner's Lohengrin (trans. and illustr.), 1906; Ruskin's Poetry of Architecture, (edited) 1907; Tales from Many Lands, (edited) 1915; Robin Hood, 1915; La Fontaine's Fables (trans. and illustr.), 1915; The Appeal of the Picture, 1915; The Art of Life; Appreciation of the Fine Arts: Correspondence Courses, 1921; The Principles of Photographic Pictorialism, 1930; The Lure of the Fine Arts, 1931. *Recreations:* In early years, rowing and sculling, later musical composition, acting, and singing (Beecham Tours and Carl Rosa Co. Played in Siegfried at Covent Garden). *Address:* 1 Lumley Road, Cheam, Surrey. *T.:* Fairlands 8560. [*Died* 4 *May* 1951.

TILSLEY, Frank; Author; Novelist and broadcaster; *b.* 5 May 1904; *s.* of William Berry Tilsley, tailor, and Emily Louise Bennett; *m.* 1926, Clarice Holding; one *s.* one *d.* *Educ.:* Chapel Street Council School, Levenshulme, Manchester. Has worked at a wide variety of jobs including accountancy, shopkeeping, school-teaching, journalism. Served in R.A.F., 1940-45, attaining rank of Squadron-Leader. *Publications:* The Plebeian's Progress, 1933; I'd Do It Again, 1936; Devil Take the Hindmost, 1937; I'd Hate to be Dead, 1938; She was There Too, 1938; Little Tin God, 1939; Love Story of Gilbert Bright, 1940; The Wonderful Journey, 1940; The Lady in the Fur Coat, 1941; What's in it for Walter, 1942; Pleasure Beach, 1944; Jim Comes Home, 1945; Peggy Windsor and the American Soldier, 1946; Champion Road, 1948; Icedrome,

1949; The Jungle of Your Heart, 1950; Heaven and Herbert Common, 1953; Voice of the Crowd, 1954; Brother Nap, 1954; Thicker Than Water, 1955 (all novels); Boys of Coastal (short stories), 1944. First Things First, 1938; We Live and Learn, 1939; Mutiny (posthumous), 1958. Television play cycle (with Vincent Tilsley) The Makepeace Story, 1955. *Recreations:* gardening, walking, reading, history. *Address:* 10 Whitecroft Way, Park Langley, Beckenham, Kent. *T.:* Beckenham 5653. *Clubs:* Press, R.A.F. [*Died* 16 *March* 1957.

TIMMIS, Shirley Sutton; *b.* 17 Aug. 1875; *y. s.* of late T. Sutton Timmis, Liverpool; *m.* 1904, Avis Brenda Hughes; no *c. Educ.:* Clifton College. Commissioned to Duke of Lancaster's Own Yeomanry, 1900; retired, 1906; rejoined Aug. 1914; retired with rank of Capt., 1919; in business, 1894-1914; J.P., County of Lancaster; Sheriff of Buckinghamshire, 1941-42. *Address:* Grove House, Grove Road, Beaconsfield. *T.:* Beaconsfield 358. *Club:* Bath. [*Died* 29 *March* 1957.

TIMS, Henry William Marett, O.B.E. M.A. (Cantab.); M.D., M.Ch. (Edin.); Order of St. Sava of Serbia; Lieut.-Col. late R.A.M.C.; retired; Lecturer on Comparative Dental Anatomy and Physiology, Royal Dental Hospital, London; *b.* Calcutta, 1863; *s.* of Dr. T. Lamb Tims and Sophia Ann Marett; *m.* 1888, Alice Maud Mary (*d.* 1950), *d.* of Col. Alex. Findlay 3rd W.I. Regt.; one *s.* one *d. Educ.:* Reading School; Edinburgh and Cambridge Univs.; St. Thomas's Hospital; Strassburg. M.B., M.Ch. (Edinburgh) 1887; M.D. (Commendation) 1890; B.A. (Research) King's College, Cambridge, 1901; M.A. 1905; late Assistant Demonstrator in Anatomy and Physiology, Edinburgh University; Clinical Assistant, Great Ormond Street Hospital for Children; Blackfriars Hospital for Skin Diseases, and Electrotherapeutic Dept. St. Mary's Hospital, Paddington; Lecturer on Biology and Comparative Anatomy, and Senior Demonstrator of Human Anatomy. Westminster Hospital Medical School; Lecturer on Biology and Comparative Anatomy. Charing Cross Hospital Medical School; Prof. of Biology, Royal Veterinary College, London; Reader in Zoology and Comp. Anatomy, Bedford College, University of London, Univ. Demonstrator of Human Morphology, Cambridge Univ.; late Recorder and V.P. Section D, British Association Advancement of Science; Member of Faculties of Science and Medicine, London University; Examiner, London University; Conjoint Board R.C.P. London and R.C.S. England; Society of Apothecaries, London. *Publications:* numerous scientific papers; Editor, 7th and 8th editions, Tomes' Dental Anatomy. *Recreations:* travelling and gardening. *Address:* Helion's Bumpstead, Essex. [*Died* 4 *March* 1954.

TINDALL, Christian, C.I.E. 1919; *s.* of John Tindall, of Sidmouth; *b.* 1878; *m.* 1906, Elsie Kate (*d.* 1943), *d.* of John Henry Toogood; one *s.* one *d. Educ.:* Malvern College; Corpus Christi College, Oxford. Entered I.C.S. 1901; Under-Sec. to Govt., Revenue Depart., E. Bengal and Assam, 1906; District and Sessions Judge, 1915; Sec. 1916; Sec. to Govt. of Bengal; retired 1926; Kaisar-i-Hind medal. *Address:* Daneway, Elwyn Road, Exmouth. [*Died* 13 *April* 1951.

TINKER, John Joseph; miners' agent; *b.* 1875. Member of St. Helens Town Council; M.P. (Lab.), Leigh, 1923-45; Parliamentary Private Secretary to Secretary of State for War, 1924. *Address:* 4 Hartington Road, St. Helens, Lancs. [*Died* 30 *July* 1957.

TINKLER, Charles Kenneth, D.Sc.; F.R.I.C.; *b.* Shrewsbury, 6 Nov. 1881; 4th *s.* of late Rev. F. Tinkler; *m.* 1907, Winifred, *y. d.* of Charles Davis, Halifax; one *s. Educ.:* Caterham School; University College, Bangor; University of Edinburgh. Lecturer in Chemistry, University of Birmingham, 1904-15; Head of the Chemistry Department King's College of Household and Social Science, Kensington, 1915-47; late Professor of Chemistry in the University of London; retired, 1947. *Publications:* various papers in the Journal of the Chemical Society and Biochemical Journal; (joint) The Chemistry of Petroleum, 1915; and Applied Chemistry, 1920. *Address:* The Paddock, Ducks Hill Road, Northwood, Middlesex. *T.:* Northwood 317. [*Died* 25 *Oct.* 1951.

TIREMAN, Henry Stainton, C.I.E. 1925; *b.* 2 Oct. 1871; *s.* of Rev. F. S. Tireman of Kirk Sandall, near Doncaster; *m.* 1906, Mary Edith Louisa, *d.* of A. G. Barton, 90 Lower Thames Street, E.C.; one *d. Educ.:* Malvern College; Royal Indian Engineering Coll., Coopers Hill. Appointed to Indian Forest Service, 1893; Chief Conservator of Forests, Madras, 1922; Member Council of State, 1926; Officiating Inspector-General of Forests to Government of India, 1927; Timber Adviser to High Commissioner for India, 1929-32. *Address:* 130 Old Bath Road, Cheltenham. *T.:* Cheltenham 3162. [*Died* 11 *Jan.* 1951.

TITTA, Commendatore Ruffo (Colonel by Military order of Spanish Army); grand opera artist; baritone (Titta Ruffo); *b.* Pisa, Italy, 9 June 1877; *s.* of Oreste Titta and Amabilia Siguenza; *m.* Lea Fontana; one *s.* one *d. Educ.:* Rome. Studied designing of wrought iron at Academy of Rome; among his best works are his iron wreath on Pres. Carnot's tomb at the Panthéon in Paris; aspired to become an opera singer, however, and made his début in Lohengrin, in Rome at the age of twenty; won almost immediate fame, and was decorated by almost every European court before the age of thirty; inaugurated the Teatro Colon, Buenos Aires, Teatro Municipale, S. Paolo, Brazil, Teatro National, Havana, Cuba. *Recreations:* collection of modern painters and stamps (filatelica). *Address:* c/o Academy of Rome, Italy. [*Died* 6 *July* 1953.

TITTERTON, Frank; tenor; *b.* Birmingham, 31 Dec. 1882. Studied under Ernesto Beraldi and Charles Victor. Was an early Member of Barry Jackson's dramatic society. Has sung at all leading Festivals. Sang "Gerontius" with Sir Edward Elgar, 4 years running, at 3 Choirs Festivals. Opera, Oratorio, Ballads. Broadcasts England and abroad. Specialist in Voice Production. Served in Army, 1914-18. *Address:* 14 Wedderburn Rd., Hampstead, N.W.3. *T.:* 3060 Hampstead. [*Died* 24 *Nov.* 1956.

TITZELL, Mrs. Josiah; *see* Parrish, Anne.

TIZARD, Sir Henry Thomas, G.C.B. *cr.* 1949 (K.C.B., *cr.* 1937; C.B. 1927); A.F.C.; F.R.S. 1926; Hon. D.C.L. (Durham); Hon. LL.D. (Queensland, Edinburgh and Sheffield); Hon. D.Sc. (Leeds, Belfast, Manchester, Reading and London); Hon. Sc.D. (Cambridge); Hon. F.R.Ae.S.; Hon. Mem. Inst. of Mining and Metallurgy; Hon. Fell. Roy. Inst. Chem.; Hon. Foreign Fellow Inst. Aeronautical Sciences; Trustee of British Museum, 1937-59; Honorary Fellow: Oriel College and Magdalen College, Oxford; Imperial College and University College, London; *b.* 23 August 1885; *s.* of late Captain T. H. Tizard, C.B., R.N., F.R.S.; *m.* 1915, Kathleen Eleanor Wilson, *d.* of Arthur Prangley Wilson; three *s. Educ.:* Westminster School; Magdalen College, Oxford. Fellow of Oriel College, Oxford, and Lecturer Natural Science, 1911-21; joined R.G.A. 1914; transferred to R.F.C. 1915; Lieut.-Colonel and Assistant Controller Experiments and Research, Royal Air Force, 1918-1919; Permanent Secretary, Department of Scientific and Industrial Research, 1927-29; Rector of Imperial College of Science and Technology, 1929-1942; President of Magdalen College, Oxford, 1942-46; Chairman, Aeronautical Research Committee, 1933-43; Member of

Council of Minister of Aircraft Production; an additional Member of the Air Council, 1941-43; a Development Commissioner, 1934-45; Chairman, Advisory Council on Scientific Policy and Defence Research Policy Committee, 1946-52; President British Association for 1948. Albert Gold Medal, R.S.A., 1944; Gold Medal, Franklin Society of Phila., 1946; Messel Medallist, Soc. Chem. Ind., 1952. *Publications:* various in scientific and other jls. *Address:* Keston, Hill Head, Fareham, Hants. *Club:* Athenæum. [*Died* 9 *Oct.* 1959.

TOBIN, Maurice J.; Secretary of Labor, U.S., 1948-53; *b.* 22 May 1901; *s.* of James Tobin and Margaret Tobin (*née* Daly); *m.* 1932, Helen Noonan; one *s.* two *d.* *Educ.:* High School of Commerce, Boston; Boston College. Mass. House of Representatives, 1927-28; Boston School Cttee., 1931-1937; Mayor of Boston, 1938-41, 1942-44; Governor of Mass., 1945-46; Member of Guam-Samoa Commission, 1947. Delegate to Democratic National Conventions, 1928-1936, 1940, 1944, 1948. Many American hon. degrees. *Recreation:* golf. *Address:* 30 Hopkins Road, Jamaica Plains, U.S.A. *Clubs:* Commonwealth Country (Newton); Clover, Charitable Irish (Boston). [*Died* 19 *July* 1953.

TODD, Colonel Arthur George, C.B.E. 1919; D.S.O. 1916; Retired; *e. s.* of late G. A. Todd, Darlington; *m.* Hilda, *y. d.* of late J. W. Smithies, J.P. Halifax, Yorks; one *s.* *Educ.:* Queen Elizabeth Grammar School, Darlington; New Veterinary College, Edinburgh. Entered Army Veterinary Dept., 1898; S.V.O., 11 Division (medal with 7 clasps, King's medal with 2 clasps); Captain, 1903; Brevet-Major, 1911; Major, 1913; Lt.-Col., 1921; Brevet-Col., 1921; Colonel, 1925; Retired, 1928; Assistant Professor, Army Veterinary School, 1906-10; Deputy Assistant Director General, Army Veterinary Service, War Office, 1912; Commandant, Army Veterinary School, 1912-14; Assistant Director General, Army Veterinary Service, War Office, 1914-15; Deputy Director of Veterinary Services Levant Base, 1915-16; E.E.F., 1916-19 (despatches thrice); Assistant Director of Veterinary Services, Curragh, 1921; Deputy Director of Veterinary Services, Eastern Command, 1921-1924; Commandant, Royal Army Veterinary School, 1924-25; Deputy Director of Veterinary Services, Southern Command, 1925-28. *Publications:* History of the War Veterinary Services, E.E.F.; History of the Royal Army Veterinary School; various professional papers. *Recreation:* golf. *Address:* Amulree, Fleet, Hants. *Clubs:* Naval and Military; N. Hants Golf (Fleet). [*Died* 17 *Oct.* 1954.

TODD, Charles, O.B.E.; F.R.S. 1930; M.A., M.D. (Cambridge); *b.* 17 Sept. 1869; *s.* of late J. Todd, Harraby, Carlisle. *Educ.:* Carlisle Gram. Sch.; Clare College, Cambridge (open scholar). St. Bartholomew's Hospital (open scholar). First Class Nat. Sci. Tripos, 1891; House Surg. Addenbrooke's Hospital, Cambridge; Assistant Bacteriologist, Lister Institute; Director Serum Institute, Abbassia, Cairo; Director Public Health Laboratories, Cairo; Consultant Public Health Department, Egyptian Government; Attached worker, National Institute for Medical Research, Hampstead, 1926-40. Member Egyptian Cattle Plague Commission, 1912; Egyptian Public Health Commission, 1918; Colonial Medical Research Committee, 1927; Foot and Mouth Research Committee; Research Advisory Committee of Empire Rheumatism Council; 2nd Class Order of the Nile; Third Class Order of the Medjidieh. *Publications:* Numerous articles, mainly dealing with immunity, in Proc. Roy. Soc., etc.; articles in A System of Bacteriology (M.R.C.). *Address:* 8 Mayfield Road, Sutton, Surrey. [*Died* 23 *Sept.* 1957.

TODD, Colonel Charles Campbell, C.M.G. 1917; C.B.E. 1930; late R.A.P.C.; *b.* 6 May 1870; *m.* 1911, Sylvia Mary Elizabeth Patricia Buckley; two *d.* 2nd Lieutenant R. Dublin Fusiliers, 1892; Captain, 1898; Major, 1908; Lieut.-Colonel, 1913; Temp. Col. 1914; Col. 1920; Inspector of Army Pay Offices, 1919-20; served S. Africa, 1899-1900 (Queen's medal 5 clasps); European War, 1914-1918 (C.M.G., despatches); retired pay, 1930. *Publications:* Gentlemen—the King; and other plays. *Address:* Lennox Tower, Southsea, Hants. *Club:* Royal Albert Yacht (Southsea). [*Died* 27 *Dec.* 1956.

TODD, Guy M., C.B.E. 1919; Chairman, Dominick Corporation of Canada, Montreal, since 1929; *b.* 10 Nov. 1883, Canadian Parentage; *m.* Donalda Coates, Montreal; two *d.* *Educ.:* Montreal. Deputy Paymaster-General, Canadian Overseas Forces, during war; retired as Assistant Manager, Royal Bank of Canada, Montreal, 1929; Lt.-Col. Reserve Can. Grenadier Guards. *Address:* Senneville, Que., Canada. *Club:* St. James's (Montreal). [*Died* 17 *Dec.* 1958.

TODD, John Aiton, M.A. (Oxon); B.L. (Glasgow); *b.* Glasgow, 5 July 1875; *m.*; two *s.* one *d.* *Educ:* Hutchesons' Grammar School, Glasgow; Glasgow University. Solicitor in Glasgow, 1896-1907; Lecturer on Economics and Public Finance in the Khedivial School of Law, Cairo, 1907-12; Imperial Ottoman Order of the Medjidieh (Third Class), 1912; Professor of Economics, University College, Nottingham, 1912-19; Special Lecturer on Economics, University of the Panjab, Lahore, 1915-16; Silver Medal, Royal Society of Arts, 1917; Secretary of the Empire Cotton-Growing Committee, Board of Trade, 1917-19; Fellow of the Royal Economic Society; Lecturer in Economics, Balliol College, Oxford, 1918-23; Principal of the City School of Commerce, Liverpool, 1923-40; formerly Special Officer (Jute), Government of Bengal. *Publications:* Political Economy for Egyptian Students, 1910; The Banks of the Nile, 1913; The World's Cotton Crops, 1915; The Mechanism of Exchange, 1917; The Science of Prices, 1925; The Cotton World, 1927; The Shipping World, 1929; The Fall of Prices, 1931; The Marketing of Cotton, 1933. *Recreation:* travel. *Club:* Bengal (Calcutta). [*Died* *July* 1954.

TODD, John William, C.B. 1936; C.B.E. 1927; Director of Hostels Corporation Limited; *b.* Bradford, 31 Jan. 1882; *s.* of William Todd, cloth merchant; *m.* 1906, Louisa, *d.* of John Wm. Brown; one *s.* one *d.* *Educ.:* Bradford Municipal Coll.; The Salt Schools, Shipley. Incorporated Accountant, 1910; Accountant to the Shipley U.D. Council to 1912; Auditor, National Insurance Audit Dept., 1912; Inspector of Audit, 1917; Assistant Accountant-General, Ministry of Labour and National Service, 1920; Deputy Accountant-General, 1922-1933; Accountant-General, 1933-43. *Address:* Appleby, 11 Lancaster Road, West Worthing, Sussex. [*Died* 7 *Dec.* 1957.

TOLERTON, Sir Robert Hill, Kt., *cr.* 1947; C.B. 1941; C.B.E. 1937; D.S.O. 1919; M.C.; *b.* 1887; *o. surv. s.* of late S. Tolerton, Stangmore, Tyrone; *m.* 1931, Sarah Elizabeth, O.B.E., *er. d.* of late J. E. H. Burnet, Bare, Lancs; no *c.* *Educ.:* Trinity College, Dublin. Entered Board of Trade, 1910. Served European War, 1914-19 (twice wounded, despatches, D.S.O., M.C., Lt.-Col.). Transferred to Ministry of Transport, 1919; principal private sec. to Sir Eric Geddes and other Ministers; Sec. Roy. Commission on Transport, 1928-30; Asst. Sec., 1929; Principal Asst. Sec., 1934; Asst. Director-General, Ministry of War Transport, 1942-46; Under-Secretary, Ministry of Transport, 1946; seconded for duties abroad, 1946-48; retired, 1948. *Address:* 23 The Avenue, Cheam, Surrey. *Club:* Union. [*Died* 14 *Dec.* 1956.

TOLLEMACHE, 3rd Baron (*cr.* 1876), **Bentley Lyonel John Tollemache;** Lieut.-Comdr. R.N.V.R. 1915; *b.* 7 March 1883; *e. s.* of Hon. Lyonel Tollemache (*s.* of 2nd Baron) and Lady Blanche Sybil, *d.* of 7th Earl of Kingston (she *m.* 2nd, Granville L. Findlay); *m.* 1st, 1902, Wynford Rose (*d.* 1926), *o. c.* of late Gen. Sir Arnold Kemball, K.C.B., K.C.S.I., K.C.I.E.; two *d.*; 2nd, 1928, Lynette, M.B.E. 1944, *d.* of A. V. Pawson, Nynehead Court, Somerset; one *d.* *S.* grandfather, 1904. Owns about 35,800 acres. *Heir: kinsman,* John Edward Hamilton Tollemache, M.C. [*b.* 24 April 1910; *m.* 1939, Dinah Susan, *d.* of Sir Archibald A. Jamieson, *q.v.*; four *s.*]. *Address:* Clover Cottage, South Cliff, Eastbourne. *T.:* 1284; Peckforton Castle, Tarporley, Cheshire. *T.:* Bunbury 315. *Clubs:* Lansdowne, Hurlingham. [*Died* 13 *Jan.* 1955.

TOLLEMACHE, Sir Lyonel Felix Carteret Eugene, 4th Bt., *cr.* 1793; a Governor, Star and Garter Home, Richmond; *b.* 15 Jan. 1854; *s.* of late Rev. Ralph William Lionel Tollemache and Caroline, *o. d.* of late Hon. Felix Thomas Tollemache; and *g. s.* of late Rev. the Hon. Hugh Francis Tollemache; *S.* to baronetcy of 9th Earl of Dysart, 1935; *m.* 1881, Hersilia Henrietta Diana, *d.* of late Joseph Collingwood; two *s.* two *d.* (and one *s.* killed in European War, *e. d.* decd.). *Educ.:* Jesus College, Cambridge, B.A. *Heir: s.* Cecil Lyonel Newcomen, *b.* 14 March 1886. *Address:* Langham House, Ham Common, Richmond, Surrey. [*Died* 4 *March* 1952.

TOLLEY, Louis; *m.*; one *d.* *Educ.:* Sacht Younger School, Kidderminster. A former Mayor of Kidderminster; 26 years a member of the Kidderminster Town Council; President of the Kidderminster National Savings Cttee. M.P. (Lab.) Kidderminster Division of Worcestershire, 1945-50. *Recreations:* horticulture; bowls and fishing. *Address:* Stanislaus, Larches Road, Kidderminster. *T.:* Kidderminster 2056. *Club:* Kidderminster Trades and Labour. [*Died* 30 *April* 1959.

TOMKINS, William Douglas, C.I.E. 1941; O.B.E. 1937; *b.* 29 July 1882; *m.* 1911, Lizzie Alice Mathers; no *c.* *Educ.:* University College School. Appointed to India Office, 1902; Private Secretary to Parliamentary Under-Secretary of State, 1924-27; Secretary to Indian Delegation to numerous International Conferences, 1921-1939; Secretary, Ministry of Supply Mission to India, 1940-41; Secretary, Economic and Overseas Dept., India Office, 1940-46. *Address:* No. 3 The Orchards, Pelling Bridge, Scaynes Hill, Sussex. *T.:* Lindfield 3191. [*Died* 6 *April* 1959.

TOMLEY, John Edward, C.B.E. 1920; Solicitor, member of the firm of Pryce, Tomley & Pryce, Montgomery; *b.* Montgomery, 3 Feb. 1874; *o. s.* of Robert Tomley and Esther Weaver; *m.* 1902, Edith Florence, *o. d.* of Thomas Soley, J.P., Montgomery; one *s.* two *d.* *Educ.:* Montgomery; Shrewsbury. Articled to Charles S. Pryce, former Town Clerk of Montgomery and obtained Honours in the Solicitors' Final examination, 1901; since appointed as Clerk to various public administrative bodies in Montgomeryshire and Shropshire; one of the Governing Body of the Church in Wales; Member of the Governors, Council and various Committees of the Welsh National Memorial Association (now merged in National Health Service); Past President of the Association of Welsh Insurance Committees. *Publications:* Place Names; Forms of Religious Worship; The Old Age Pensions Act; The Castle of Montgomery; The Derating Act, and various statistical articles. *Recreations:* cricket, golf, bowls. *Address:* The Hollies, Montgomery. *T.A.:* Tomley, Montgomery. *T.:* Montgomery 8. [*Died* 14 *June* 1951.

TOMLIN, Rev. James William Sackett; Canon Emeritus, Canterbury, 1958; Hon. Canon of Canterbury, 1941; *b.* Canterbury, 18 July 1871; *s.* of G. T. Tomlin, Barrister-at-law, and 7th *d.* of Canon Chesshyre of Canterbury; *m.* 1906, D. E., *y. d.* of Canon Meyrick of Blickling, Norfolk; one *d.* *Educ.:* Harrow; New College, Oxford, 2nd Class Hon. Mods., 1st Class Hon. History; Wells Theological College. Deacon, 1896; Priest, 1897; worked for two years at St. Matthew's, Bethnal Green, under the late Bishop of London and Rev. Bernard Wilson; went to Australia, 1899, and held posts of Mission Chaplain, 1899; Curate in charge of Milton, 1900-3; Rector, 1903-5; Principal of Theological College for Province of Queensland, 1906-10; came home to England, 1911; Rector of Farmington, Glos., 1911-14; Principal of St. Boniface Missionary College, Warminster, 1914-29; served as Chaplain in France, 1916; Rector of Bishopstrow, Wilts, 1921-24; Prebendary of Salisbury, 1928-29; Warden, St. Augustine's Coll., Canterbury, 1929-40; Rector of Kingston, Canterbury, 1939-45, retd. *Publications:* Australia's Greatest Need; Hollyhocks from the Holy Land; The Story of the Bush Brotherhoods, 1949; Awakening (A History of the New Guinea Mission), 1951; Halford's Challenge, 1952. *Recreation:* gardening. *Address:* Seatonden, Ickham, nr. Canterbury, Kent. *T.:* Littlebourne 247. [*Died* 3 *Nov.* 1959.

TOMLIN, Lieut.-Colonel Julian Latham, C.B.E. 1920; D.S.O. 1918; late Royal Corps of Signals; *b.* 23 Apr. 1886; *s.* of late Captain Bankes Tomlin, King's Dragoon Guards; *m.* 1920, Gertrude Faulkner (*d.* 1937); two *d.* *Educ.:* King's School, Canterbury; R.M.A., Woolwich. Commissioned in Royal Engineers, 1906; Signal Service, 1914-18; attached Supreme Council of Food and Relief, Paris, 1919; Director, Post and Telegraphs, Sudan, 1931-1939; Adviser Post and Telegraphs, Ethiopian Govt., 1942-43; representative Intergovernmental Cttee. for Refugees in Italy, 1945-47. *Address:* c/o Barclays Bank, 19 Fleet Street, E.C.2. [*Died* 29 *Aug.* 1960.

TOMLINSON, Rt. Hon. George, P.C. 1950; M.P. (Lab.) Farnworth division of Lancs. since 1938; J.P. County of Lancaster; Secretary Rishton Weavers Association since 1935; *b.* Rishton, Lancs, 21 March 1890; *s.* of John Wesley and Alice Tomlinson; *m.* 1914, Ethel, *d.* of Humphrey and Jane Pursell. *Educ.:* Rishton Wesleyan Day School. Member Lancs County Council since 1931; Cotton Weaver from 12 years of age to 25; in business, 1915-35; Parliamentary Secretary, Ministry of Labour, 1941-45; Minister of Works, 1945-47; Minister of Education, 1947-51. *Recreations:* cricket and reading. *Address:* House of Commons, S.W.1. [*Died* 22 *Sept.* 1952.

TOMLINSON, H. M., Hon. LL.D. (Aberdeen); Hon. mem. Amer. Acad. of Arts and Letters; Officer Brazilian Order of Southern Cross; *b.* 1873; *m.* 1899, Florence Margaret Hammond; one *s.* two *d.* Joined the staff of the Morning Leader, 1904, and the Daily News when the two papers amalgamated; War Correspondent in Belgium and France from Aug. 1914, and an Official Correspondent at General Headquarters of the British Armies in France, 1915-17; Literary Editor, Nation and Athenæum, 1917-23. *Publications:* The Sea and the Jungle, 1912; Old Junk, 1918; London River, 1921 (new illustrated edition, 1951); Waiting for Daylight, 1922; Tidemarks, 1924; Under the Red Ensign, 1926; Gifts of Fortune, 1926; Gallions Reach, 1927 (awarded Femina-Vie Heureuse Prize); Between the Lines, 1928; All our Yesterdays, 1930; Out of Soundings; Norman Douglas, 1931; The Snows of Helicon, 1933; South to Cadiz, 1934; Below London Bridge (with H. Chas. Tomlinson), 1934; Mars His Idiot, 1935; All Hands, 1937; The Day Before, 1940; The Wind is Rising, 1941; The Turn of the Tide, 1945; Morning Light, 1946; The Face of the Earth, 1950; Malay Waters, 1950; The Haunted Forest, 1951; A Mingled Yarn, 1953; The Trumpet Shall Sound, 1957. *Address:* 1 St. Peter's Sq., W.6. [*Died* 5 *Feb.* 1958.

TOMLINSON, Major-General Sir Percy Stanley, K.B.E., *cr.* 1943; C.B. 1941; D.S.O. 1919; F.R.C.P. 1943; *b.* 11 November 1884; *s.* of late Lieut.-Colonel W. W. Tomlinson, R.A.M.C. (retd.), and late Anne Maud Mary Druitt; *m.* 1920, Gertrude Muriel Barr; (one *s.* killed on active service) one *d.* *Educ.:* Clifton College and University College, Bristol. M.R.C.S., L.R.C.P. (London) 1908; M.R.C.P. (London) 1931; F.R.C.P. (London), 1943; Hon. F.R.C.P. (Edin.) 1946; R.A.M.C. 1909; Director Medical Services, M.E.F., 1940-1943; D.M.S. 21 Army Group, Sept. 1943-Nov. 1944; Hon. Physician to the King, 1941-44; retired pay, Nov. 1944; Col. Comdt. R.A.M.C., 1945-50, Rep. Col. Comdt., 1947. Member of B.M.A. Council, 1948-50. Fellow Royal Society of Medicine; Fellow Royal Society of Tropical Medicine and Hygiene. Officer, Legion of Honour, (French) Croix de Guerre (avec palme), Commander Order of St. John of Jerusalem; American Order of Merit (Officer). *Address:* c/o Glyn, Mills & Co., Whitehall, S.W.1.
[*Died* 6 *March* 1951.

TOMLINSON, Sir Thomas, Kt., *cr.* 1954; B.E.M. 1945; J.P.; Chairman of West Riding County Council, 1946-49 and 1952-55 (Vice-Chm.. 1950-51); *b.* 27 Jan. 1877; *s.* of William and Ruth Elizabeth Tomlinson; *m.* 1899, Alice Tomlinson (*née* Hirst); one *s.* one *d.* *Educ.:* Elsecar, Nr. Barnsley, Church of England School. Commenced work at Cortonwood Colliery, 1889; Lidgett Colliery, 1892-1906; Earl Fitzwilliam's Homingfield Colliery, 1906-13; Colliery Checkweighman, 1913-52 (resigned). Member: Hoyland Urban Dist. Council, 1912-40 (Chm. 1921-1923 and 1933-35); Miners' Branch Cttee. (Sec., 1910-44); Miners' Welfare Cttee., 1922-47; Convalescent Homes Cttee.; Mining Examination Bd., London, 1943. Magistrate, 1919; Chm. Local Education Cttee., Hoyland, 1920-45; National Pres., Wesleyan Reform Union of Churches, 1945-46; West Riding County Council: Member, 1921; rep. to C.C. Assoc., 1924-46. *Address:* 20 Fitzwilliam St., Elsecar, Nr. Barnsley, Yorks. *T.:* Hoyland 2221.
[*Died* 11 *Feb.* 1957.

TONGE, George Edward, F.R.I.B.A.; F.I.A.A.; F.R.S.A.; retired Architect; *b.* 8 Dec. 1876; *s.* of James Tonge, C.E., F.G.S., and Elizabeth Tonge; *m.* 1903, Evelyn, *d.* of William Cross Travers; one *s.* two *d.* *Educ.:* Bolton High School; Manchester School of Art. Articled to W. R. Haworth of Bolton in 1891. Commenced practice in Southport in 1900. Architect to the Hulton Park Estate. Works include: first "United" Methodist Church and Schools, Manchester; Garrick Theatre and Palladium Music Hall, Southport; Theatre Model for Royal Theatrical Charities Trust; Westhoughton Housing Estate of 350 houses; Roy. Birkdale Golf Club, 1936. Cinemas: Southport, Manchester, Liverpool, Oldham, Chester, Preston, Mold, Ilfracombe, Sleaford and other towns. *Recreation:* sketching. *Address:* Hesketh Lodge, Roe Lane, Southport, Lancs. *T.A.:* Tonge, Southport. *T.:* Southport 88261. *Clubs:* Savage; West Lancashire Yacht (Southport).
[*Died* 12 *March* 1956.

TONKS, Ven. Charles Frederick, M.B.E. 1929; Archdeacon and Vicar of Croydon since 1948; Rural Dean of Croydon since 1949; Hon. Canon of Canterbury since 1928; Surrogate since 1936; *b.* 28 Sept. 1881; *s.* of Charles and Jane S. Tonks, Harborne, Staffs, and Bournemouth; *m.* 1908, *d.* of John and Lydia Cabell, Bournemouth; one *s.* *Educ.:* Breydon House, Bournemouth; King's College, London. A.K.C. 1st class, 1908; Leitner, Philosophy and Homiletic Prizes, 1908. Deacon, 1908; Priest, 1909; Curate of St. Luke, Hackney, 1908-12; Secretary Church of England Temperance Society, 1920-21; Dioceses of Canterbury and Rochester, 1912-28; Rector of St. George with St. Mary Magdalene, Canterbury, 1917-28; Rural Dean of Canterbury, 1926-28; Editor Canterbury Diocesan Gazette, 1923-35; Vicar of Walmer, 1928-1947. Rural Dean of Sandwich, Kent, 1947. Officiating Chaplain to the Forces, 1941-46; Officiating Chaplain to the R.A.F., 1943-46. Chaplain to Whitgift Foundation, 1948-; Chaplain to Croydon Gen. Hosp., 1948-. *Address:* 22 Bramley Hill, South Croydon, Surrey. *T.:* Croydon 1387.
[*Died* 27 *March* 1957.

TONKS, Rt. Rev. Horace Norman Vincent; Rector of Castries, St. Lucia, diocese of the Windward Islands, since 1956; Canon of St. Augustine in St. George's Cathedral, St. Vincent, since 1959; *b.* Walsall, 29 January 1891; *s.* of Henry and Emily Tonks, Walsall; *m.* 1921, Alice, *d.* of Joseph and Alice Underwood, Danby, Yorks; three *s.* two *d.* (and one *s.* decd.). *Educ.:* Walsall Grammar School; Lichfield Theological College. Deacon, 1916; Priest, 1918; Curate of Fenton, 1916-19; served European War, Belgium; Curate of S. Saviours, Scarborough, 1919-20; Priest-in-charge of Holy Cross, Airedale, 1923-26; York Diocesan Organising Sec. for English Church Union, 1925-35; Vicar of S. Sampson with Holy Trinity, King's Court, York, 1926-35; Northern Area Secretary of the Anglo-Catholic Congress, 1926-35; Secretary of the Overseas Association of the Anglo-Catholic Congress and the Church Union, 1929-35; Commissary for the Diocese of the Windward Islands, 1931-35; Archdeacon of Grenada, B.W.I., Canon of S. Anselm in S. George's Cathedral, S. Vincent, and Rector of S. George's, Grenada, 1935-36; Bishop of Windward Islands, 1936-49; Commissary for Dioceses of the Windward Islands, 1949-56, and Antigua, 1949-52; Rector of Leybourne, Malling, Kent, 1949-56. Coronation Medal, 1937. *Recreation:* autograph-collecting. *Address:* Castries, St. Lucia, Windward Is.
[*Died* 25 *Nov.* 1959.

TOOMER, Air Vice-Marshal Sydney Edward, C.B. 1946; C.B.E. 1945; D.F.C. 1918; R.A.F. (retd.); *b.* Jan. 1895; *s.* of late John G. Toomer; *m.* 1917, Poppe, *o. d.* of Samuel Mountjoy Smith; one *d.* *Educ.:* Dean Close School, Cheltenham. Served European War, 1914-18, in R.A., R.F.C. and R.A.F., Gallipoli and France (despatches, D.F.C.); R.A.F. Staff College, 1925-26; Army Staff College, Camberley, 1932-34; seconded R.A.A.F. Melbourne, 1936-38; R.A.F. Instructor, Staff College, Camberley, 1939; Fighter Command, 1940-42; Director of Fighter Operations, Air Ministry, 1942-43; S.A.S.O. Middle East H.Q. and then A.O.C. Eastern Mediterranean, Nos. 219 and 205 Gps., 1943-47; Air officer in charge of Administration, Technical Training Command, 1947. Retired, 1948. *Recreations:* golf, shooting, riding. *Address:* 188 Latymer Court, W. 6. *Club:* Royal Air Force.
[*Died* 22 *March* 1954.

TOOTH, Sir Edwin Marsden, Kt. 1957; M.C. 1918; Managing Director, Austral Motors Pty. Ltd. (1923) and Stradbroke Motors Pty. Ltd. (1928); Chairman: Farsley Motors Pty. Ltd. (1952); British Tractor and Implements Pty. Ltd. (1948); *b.* 9 Oct. 1886; *s.* of Sidney Herbert and Emily Isabel Tooth; *m.* 1935, Elsie Marguerite Fuller. *Educ.:* Normal School, Brisbane. Motor Industry 52 years. War Service, 1915-18, Captain Australian Mining Corps. *Recreations:* fishing, shooting, golf. *Address:* Farsley, Eldernell Avenue, Hamilton, Brisbane, Queensland. *T.:* M. 1218. *Clubs:* Brisbane, United Service, Tattersalls (all in Brisbane). [*Died* 27 *May* 1957.

TOOVEY, Major-Gen. Cecil Wotton, C.B. 1943; C.B.E. 1941; M.C. 1920; *b.* 17 Apr. 1891; *s.* of John and Blanche Maude Toovey

Berkhampstead, Herts; *m.* 1923, Phyllis Mary Stuart, *d.* of Lt.-Col. R. W. Burton, I.A.; one *s.* two *d.* *Educ.:* Malvern Coll. Indian Army, 1st Punjab Regt.; served European War, 1914-18, in Mesopotamia; Afghan Mahsud and Waziristan Campaigns (M.C.); N.W. Frontier 1930 (Bar to M.C.) and 1937 Campaigns; Comdt. 3rd Bn. 1st Punjab Regt.; G.S.O. 1 Liaison Middle East, 1940-41; Brig. i/c L. of C. Eritrea, 1941; Deputy Adj. General G.H.Q. India, 1941-43; G.O.C. Rawalpindi Dist., 1943-46; retired, 1947. Graduate of Staff College, Quetta; despatches 4 times. Member of Governing Body and Chairman Executive Cttees. of Dockland Settlements, 1946. Governor of Malvern College. Commissioner St. John Ambulance Brigade for the County of Surrey, 1951; O.St.J. *Recreations:* golf, drawing, and painting. *Address:* Frith Hatch, Chalk Road, Godalming. *T.:* 587. *Club:* United Service. [*Died* 23 *Feb.* 1954.

TOPHAM, His Honour Alfred Frank, K.C. 1922; *b.* 1874; *e. s.* of late Frank W. W. Topham, R.I.; *m.* 1903, Alice Charlotte, *d.* of Maj.-Gen. A. Clark Kennedy; one *s.* two *d.* *Educ.:* Highgate; Queens' College, Cambridge. Called to Bar, 1900; late Editor of the Law Reports; County Court Judge, Circuit 51 (Hampshire), 1938-48. *Publications:* Books on Company Law and Real Property. *Recreations:* various. *Address:* Cracknells, Yarmouth, Isle of Wight. *T.:* Yarmouth 240. [*Died* 18 *Jan.* 1952.

TOPHAM, Rev. John; Canon and Prebendary of York since 1917; *b.* 1863; *m.* Lilian Henrietta, *y. d.* of Major H. A. Graham, Trevallyn, Sandown, I.O.W. Curate, Armley Hall, St. Peter's, Leeds; Chaplain to Farnley Iron Co.; Holy Trinity, Tunbridge Wells; Rector, St. Paul's, York, 1901-1915; Rector of Bridlington and Vicar of Bessingby, 1915-44; Hon. T.C.F., 1916-19; Rural Dean of Bridlington, 1928-37. *Address:* High Bank, Cromwell Road, Scarborough. *T.:* 176 Scarborough. [*Died* 14 *Dec.* 1955.

TOPPING, Andrew, C.M.G. 1954; T.D.; M.D.; Dean of the London School of Hygiene and Tropical Medicine since 1950; *b.* 20 December 1890; *s.* of Robert Topping, M.A., H.M.I.S. Scottish Education Dept., and Robina Bayne; *m.* Freda Wood; one *s.* one *d.* *Educ.:* Robert Gordon's College, Aberdeen University, Aberdeen. R.A.M.C. 1914-19, France, Gallipoli, Mesopotamia, Officer in charge Medical Section No. 3 British Hospital (despatches); O.C. 5th London General Hospital. M.A., M.B., Ch.B., M.D., D.P.H. (Aberdeen), F.R.S.Ed., F.R.C.P. (London); F.R.San. Inst. member of Council; Senior M.O. A.P.O.C. Abadan, Persia; Asst. M.O.H. Woolwich and Lancs; M.O.H. Rochdale; M.S. Southern Fever Hosp. L.C.C.; Deputy M.O.H. L.C.C.; Director London Ambulance Service; Lecturer Public Health, Charing Cross Hospital Med. School; Examiner D.P.H. Conjoint Board; Examiner in Hygiene, Univ. of London; Examiner in Public Health, Aberdeen, Durham, Belfast; Member: Colonial Medical Advisory Cttee., and Senate Cttee. on Higher Education in the Colonies; Army Health Advisory Cttee.; Chm., Archway Group Hosp. Management Cttee.; Deputy Chief Relief Services U.N.R.R.A.; Director of Health (European Division), U.N.R.R.A.; Pres. Soc. of Medical Officers of Health, 1952-53; late Professor of Social and Preventive Medicine, Manchester University. *Publications:* articles on fevers, maternal mortality, hospital administration, international health, etc. to professional journals. Report on survey of hospitals of London and surrounding counties (jointly), 1944. *Address:* London School of Hygiene and Tropical Medicine, Keppel St., W.C.1. *Club:* Athenæum. [*Died* 28 *Aug.* 1955.

TOPPING, Sir (Hugh) Robert, Kt., *cr.* 1934; *b.* Dublin, 2 May 1877; *m.* 1919, Ethel M. Withycombe (*d.* 1936); one *s.* General Secretary, City of Dublin Unionist Association, 1904-11; Secretary and Agent, South Glamorgan Conservative and Unionist Association, 1911-18; City of Cardiff, 1918-23; Llandaff and Barry, 1918-23; Northwich, 1923-24; Secretary, Glamorgan Provincial Division, National Unionist Association, 1913-23: Conservative Central Office Agent for Lancashire and Cheshire, 1924-28; General Director of the Conservative and Unionist Central Office and Principal Agent of the Party and Hon. Secretary of National Union of Conservative and Unionist Associations, 1927-45. *Address:* 85 Twickenham Road, Teddington, Middlesex. *T.:* Kingston 9111. *Clubs:* Carlton, Constitutional. [*Died* 27 *Dec.* 1952.

TORRENS, Jas. Aubrey, M.D., F.R.C.P.; Consulting Physician to St. George's Hospital, S.W.; Consulting Physician to W. Middlesex Hosp.; *b.* Sept. 1881; *s.* of Henry C. Torrens and Juliet, *d.* of late James Riley, M.R.C.S.; *g.s.* of late Wm. McCullagh Torrens, M.P.; *m.* 1910, Hilda (*d.* 1944), *o. d.* of Rev. Wm. Martin, B.D., Gt. Brington, Northants; one *d.*; *m.* 1945, Elizabeth, *d.* of W. Chapman. *Educ.:* St. Paul's School (Entrance Scholarship, Senior Scholarship, and leaving Exhibition in Science); St. George's Hospital (Entrance Scholarship in Arts; Anatomy and Physiology Prizeman, Brodie Prizeman in Surgery); University of London. House Physician, House Surgeon, Assistant Curator of Museum, Medical Registrar and Physician, St. George's Hospital; Physician to Chelsea Hospital for Women; Physician to out-patients, Paddington Green Children's Hosp.; Consulting Physician, Harrow Hosp.; Pathologist Hampstead General Hospital; Examiner in Medicine to the Conjoint Board of the Royal Colleges of Physicians and Surgeons, and to the University of Oxford, etc.; Major R.A.M.C. (T.), 1914-19; service in France and Mesopotamia. *Recreations:* racing, bridge. *Address:* 8 Halfmoon Hill, Haslemere, Surrey. *T.:* Hindhead 789. *Club:* Three Counties (Haslemere). [*Died* 23 *Aug.* 1954.

TORREY, Charles Cutler, Ph.D., D.D., Litt.D.; Professor of Semitic Languages, Yale University, 1900, Emeritus, 1932; *b.* East Hardwick, Vermont, 20 Dec. 1863; *s.* of Rev. Joseph Torrey, D.D.; *m.* 1911, Marian Edwards Richards, *d.* of Professor Charles B. Richards; one *d.* *Educ.:* Bowdoin College. Tutor in Latin, Bowdoin College, 1885-86; studied at Andover Theol. Sem., 1886-89; Univ. of Strassburg, 1889-92 (Ph.D.); instructor in Semitic Languages, Andover Theol. Sem., 1892-1900; D.D., Bowd. Coll., 1900; Litt.D., Bowdoin Coll. and Yale Univ. 1934; D.H.L. Jewish Institute of Religion, 1934, Jewish Theological Seminary of America, 1935, Chicago College of Jewish Studies, 1954; Director Am. School of Orient. Research in Palestine, 1900-1901; Editor Journal American Oriental Society, 1900-7, and 1911-16; President of the Society, 1917-18; F.A.A.S.; member various learned societies. *Publications:* The Commercial-Theol. Terms in the Koran, 1892; Composition and Historical Value of Ezra-Nehemiah, 1896; The Mohammedan Conquest of Egypt and North Africa (trans. from the Arabic of Ibn 'Abd al-Hakam), 1901; Selections from the Sahih of al-Bokhari, 1906; Notes on the Aramaic Part of Daniel, 1909; Ezra Studies, 1910; The Composition and Date of Acts, 1916; The Futuh Misr of Ibn Abd-al-Hakam, Arabic Text, 1922; The Second Isaiah, 1928; Pseudo-Ezekiel and the Original Prophecy, 1930; The Jewish Foundation of Islam, 1933; The Four Gospels: a New Translation, 1933; Our Translated Gospels: Some of the Evidence, 1936; Aramaic Graffiti on Coins of the Demanhur Hoard, 1937; Documents of the Primitive Church, 1941; The Apocryphal Literature, a Brief Introduction, 1945; The Lives of the Prophets,

1946; The Four Gospels (rev. ed.), 1947; Gold Coins of Khokand and Bukhara, 1950; The Chronicler's History of Israel, Chronicles-Ezra-Nehemiah, restored to its original form, 1954. *Address:* 5235 S. University Ave., Chicago 15. [*Died* 12 *Nov.* 1956.

TORTISE, Colonel Herbert James, D.S.O. 1918; O.B.E. 1945; T.D. 1943; (T.A.); *m.* 1929, Margaret Elizabeth, *e. d.* of Brig. P. W. L. Broke-Smith, C.I.E., D.S.O., O.B.E.; one *s.* one *d.* Served European War, 1914-18 (despatches thrice, D.S.O. and bar); War of 1939-45. *Address:* c/o Cox's & King's Branch, Lloyds Bank Ltd., 6 Pall Mall, S.W.1. [*Died* 13 *Feb.* 1954.

TOSCANINI, Arturo; *b.* Parma, Italy, 25 Mar. 1867; *s.* of Claudio and Paola Montani; *m.* Carla De Martini (*d.* 1951); one *s.* two *d.* *Educ.:* Parma Conservatory of Music. Started musical career as 'cellist in various touring opera companies. First conducted in Rio de Janeiro in 1886. Conducted world première of I Pagliacci, Milan, 1892, of La Bohème, Turin, 1896. Owing to shortsightedness was forced to memorize scores. Conductor at La Scala Opera House, Milan, 1898-1903, 1906-1908 and 1920-29; the Metropolitan Opera House, New York, 1908-15; the Philharmonic Symphony Society of New York, 1926-36; Guest Conductor of the Wagner's Festspielhaus in Bayreuth, 1930-31; and of Salzburg Festival, 1934-37; Guest Conductor of Philharmonic Orchestra of Vienna, 1933-36; Staram Orchestra of Paris, 1933-35; B.B.C. Orchestra, London, 1935-37; the Israeli Philharmonic Orchestra, Tel-Aviv, 1936-37; Conductor, N.B.C. Symphony Orchestra of N.Y., 1937-53; conducted Philharmonia Orchestra, twice, Festival Hall, London, 1952; retired, 1954. Dr. of Music of Acad. of Music of Georgetown Univ., U.S.A. (1930); Comd. Legion of Honour, 1932. *Recreation:* watching prize fighting and wrestling on Television. *Address:* c/o La Scala, Milan, Italy. [*Died* 16 *Jan.* 1957.

TOSTEVIN, Engineer-Captain Harold Bertram, D.S.O. 1916; R.N., retd.; *b.* 1884; *s.* of P. Tostevin, Gosport, Hants; *m.* 1912, Eva Grace, *d.* of W. T. Lewis, of Goodmayes, Essex; one *s.* Served Battle of Jutland, 1916 (despatches, D.S.O.); Gold Medallist, Institution of Naval Architects, for paper on Warship Reduction Gearing, 1920; Superintendent, Admiralty Engineering Laboratory, 1922-25; Professor of Marine Engineering, R.N. College, Greenwich, 1927-33; retired list, 1933; Chief Engineer Marine Department, Vacuum Oil Co. 1933-39; Admiralty Engineer Overseer, Cammell Laird & Co., Ltd., Birkenhead, 1939-46; Engineer-in-Chief's Department, Admiralty, Bath, 1946-47. *Address:* 28 Peel Rd., Gosport, Hants. *T.:* Gosport 88955. [*Died* 6 *Dec.* 1956.

TOTTERDELL, Sir Joseph, Kt., *cr.* 1953; sometime Lord Mayor of City of Perth, Western Australia; *b.* 10 August 1885; *s.* of Charles and Mary Totterdell; *m.* 1910, Florence Watson; one *d.* (one *s.* killed, War of 1939-45). *Educ.:* State School, Manchester. Master Builder. *Recreations:* golf, billiards. *Address:* 12 Nicholson Rd., Subiaco, W. Australia. *T.:* W. 2108. *Clubs:* Commercial Travellers (W.A.), Mount Yokine Golf Links. [*Died* 26 *Dec.* 1959.

TOWLE, Lieut.-Colonel Sir Francis William, Kt., *cr.* 1919; C.B.E. 1918; M.A.; Hon. Lieut.-Colonel in Army; *b.* 18 April 1876; *s.* of late Sir William Towle; *m.* 1901, Emma Annette (*d.* 1951), *widow* of Capt. and Adjt. D. A. M. Lomax, 1st Welsh Regt.; one *d.* *Educ.:* Marlborough; Trinity College, Cambridge. Formerly Lieut.-Col. R.A.S.C. and Controller of Navy and Army Canteen Board, 1916-19; Managing Director Gordon Hotels, Ltd., 1921-36; President International Hotel Alliance, 1935-38; President International Hotel Association, 1946-. *Recreations:* golf, tennis. *Address:* Kensington Close, W.8. *T.:* Western 8170; Church Cottage, Winkfield, Windsor Forest, Berks. *T.:* Winkfield Row 289. *Club:* Bath. [*Died* 19 *Dec.* 1951.

TOWNSEND, Crewe Armand Hamilton, C.I.E. 1924; I.C.S., retired; *s.* of late H. H. Townsend, J.P., of Cordangan Manor, Tipperary; *m.* 1906, Rhoda Mary Whitmore, *d.* of late T. J. Franks, J.P., of Ballyscadane, Co. Limerick; two *s.* one *d.* *Educ.:* Shrewsbury School; St. John's College, Cambridge. Entered I.C.S. 1898; held various posts as District Officer, Settlement Officer, 1906; Director of Agriculture, 1914; Financial Comr., Punjab, 1928-31; Member of Legislative Assembly, 1921, 1923, and 1925; Public Works and Revenue Minister Bahawalpur State, 1931-39. *Recreations:* tennis, riding. *Address:* Red House, Castle Townshend, Co. Cork. *Club:* County (Cork). [*Died* 25 *Feb.* 1954.

TOWNSEND, Rev. Henry, M.A., D.D. (Lond.); Principal and Professor of Philosophy of Religion and Theology at the Manchester Baptist College, 1919-49; President Baptist Union, 1936; Dean of Faculty of Theology, Manchester University, 1926-28; Moderator of National Federal Free Church Council of England and Wales, 1944. Governor John Rylands Library; Lecturer in History of Doctrine and Philosophy of Religion for Manchester Univ. B.D. degree. *Publications:* Doctrine of Grace in the Synoptic Gospels; The Freedom of God; Religion, Revolution and Democracy; The Claims of the Free Churches; Life of R. Wilson Black. *Address:* 22 Crichton Road, Carshalton Beeches, Surrey. *T.:* Wallington 1239. [*Died* 2 *July* 1955.

TOWNSEND, Sir John Sealy Edward, Kt., *cr.* 1941; M.A. Dublin; Hon.D.Sc. Paris; F.R.S. 1903; Hon. Fellow of New College, Oxford; *b.* Galway, 7 June 1868; 2nd *s.* of Prof. Edward Townsend; *m.* 1911, Mary Georgiana, O.B.E. 1957, *d.* of P. F. Lambert, Co. Galway; two *s.* *Educ.:* Trinity Coll., Dublin. Formerly Demonstrator Cavendish Laboratory, Cambridge, Fell. of Trinity Coll., Cambridge, Wykeham Professor of Physics, Oxford. Chevalier de la Légion d'Honneur; Member: Institute of France, Academy of Science; Franklin Institute. *Publications:* contribs. to Scientific Journals and Societies on Electrical subjects; Treatises on: Theory of Ionisation of Gases by Collision; Electricity in Gases; Electricity and Radio Transmission; Electrons in Gases; Electromagnetic Waves. *Address:* 55 Banbury Road, Oxford. [*Died* 16 *Feb.* 1957.

TOYE, Brig. Alfred Maurice, V.C.; M.C.; p.s.c.; late Oxfordshire and Buckinghamshire Light Infantry; Commandant Home Office Civil Defence School, Falfield, Glos., 1948; *b.* 7 April 1897; *m.* Flora Robertson; two *d.* Granted regular commission in Middlesex Regiment, from R.E., 15 Feb. 1917; served European war in France, 1915-18 (thrice wounded, M.C. 1917, V.C. 1918); Second-in-Command 2nd Middx. Regt., 1918-19; General Staff, North Russia, 1919 (despatches); General Staff, 54th East Anglian Division, 1921; Special Appointment, Rhine Army, 1922-1924; transferred to Oxfordshire and Buckinghamshire Light Infantry on promotion, 1924; Chief Instructor, Royal Egyptian Military College, 1925-35; Order of the Nile (Commander); Comdt. War Office Schools of Chemical Warfare, 1940-42; Staff College, Camberley, 1943; 6th Airborne Div., 1943-44; G.H.Q. M.E.L.F., 1945-48; retired pay, 1949. *Address:* Eastwood Park, Falfield, Glos. *T.:* Falfield 207. *Club:* Army and Navy. [*Died* 6 *Sept.* 1955.

TOZER, Mrs. Basil; *see* Langley, Beatrice.

TRACEY, Herbert Trevor, C.B.E. 1950; on headquarters staff of Labour Party and T.U.C., 1917-50; T.U.C. Publicity Officer, and Editor of Labour, Industrial News, 1926-50; *b.* 13 March 1884; 3rd *s.* of James Tracey, Cardiff; *m.* Margaret, *d.* of

William Moore, Cardiff; one *d.* *Educ.:* village school for four years; otherwise self-educated. Began as errand boy, office boy, deputy-foreman in flourmill: studied for Methodist ministry and served for six years as pastor of churches in Welsh mining valleys; turned to journalism in 26th year; Assistant Editor, Christian Commonwealth, 1911-17; organised and directed Labour Party Press Bureau, 1917-20; visited Canada and U.S. in 1921 for journalism and lecturing; returned to Labour headquarters as Industrial Correspondent, 1922; organised and took charge of Trades Union Congress Publicity Department, 1926, having control of T.U.C. publicity arrangements, including The British Worker, in General Strike; edited Brotherhood Outlook, 1920-25; associated with editorial department, Labour Magazine, since its foundation; special correspondent, English and Foreign newspapers and news agencies at various periods since 1918. *Publications:* Coal War in Britain (American edition); J. Ramsay MacDonald: A Biographical Essay; The Book of the Labour Party (3 vols.); Sixty Years of Trade Unionism; The British Press: A Survey; A Century of Vehicle-building; Trade Unions Fight—For What? 1940; The British Labour Party (3 vols.); numerous pamphlets; extensive contributions to Trade, Socialist, and Labour journals. *Recreations:* reading novels, writing, and sitting about. *Address:* 16 Church Grove, Hampton Wick, Kingston-on-Thames. *Club:* Savage. [*Died* 28 *June* 1955.

TRACY, Frederick, B.A., Ph.D., LL.D.; *b.* Claremont, Ontario, 18 May 1862; *s.* of Alfred Tracy and Eliza Gostick; *m.* 1893, Charlotte Haines; three *s.* *Educ.:* Pickering College; University of Toronto; Clark University. Public School teacher; master in Pickering College; Fellow in Philosophy in University of Toronto, 1889-92; Fellow in Psychology in Clark University, 1892-93; Lecturer in Philosophy, University of Toronto, 1893-1905; Associate Professor, 1905-16; Professor of Ethics, University College, Toronto, 1916-32; Professor Emeritus, 1932; Baptist. *Publications:* Psychology of Childhood (7th ed.); Psychologie der Kindheit (4th ed.); The Teacher and the School; Introductory Educational Psychology (with S. B. Sinclair); Kinderpsychologie in England und Nordamerika; Broken Lights; The Psychology of Adolescence; many articles. *Recreations:* music, gardening, boating. *Address:* 260 Johnson St., Kingston, Ont., Canada.
[*Died* 10 *June* 1951.

TRAFFORD, M. A. J. de L.; *see* de Lavis-Trafford.

TRAHAN, The Hon. Arthur, B.Sc., Q.C., formerly M.L.A., P.Q., Canada; *b.* Nicolet, P.Q., 26 May 1877; *s.* of Narcisse Trahan, Collector of Customs, J.P., and Rebecca Rousseau, both French-Canadians; *m.* 1st, 1902, Josephine R., *d.* of H. R. Dufresne, N.P. of Nicolet; four *s.* two *d.*; 2nd, 1924, Diane, *d.* of Charles Le Duc, Hull; one *s.* *Educ.:* The Nicolet Seminary. Admitted to Bar, 1901; K.C. 1912; Secretary of the Commission charged with the revision, consolidation, and modification of the Municipal Code of the Province of Quebec, 1910-12; Alderman of town of Nicolet, 1911-19; M.L.A., Nicolet, 1913-17, M.P., 1917-23. Judge of the Superior Court for Province of Quebec from 1923. Batonnier of the Bar, Dist. of Trois Rivières, 1916-17. Chm. of Mobilisation Bd., Montreal, 1941-46. Roman Catholic.
[*Died* 23 *Sept.* 1950.
[*But death not notified in time for inclusion in Who Was Who 1941–1950, first edn.*

TRAILL, Lieut.-Col. William Henry, C.M.G. 1919; D.S.O. 1917; late J.P. Shropshire; late East Lancashire Regt.; *b.* 1871; *m.*; two *d.* Served Tirah Expedition, 1897-98 (medal and clasp); European War, 1914-18 (despatches, C.M.G., D.S.O.; Chevalier Légion d'Honneur; Bt. Lt.-Col.); retired pay, 1921. *Address:* The Hurdles, Chestfield, Whitstable, Kent.
[*Died* 1 *Feb.* 1951.

TRAILL, Lieut.-Colonel William Stewart, D.S.O. 1916; D.L., J.P. Co. Antrim; High Sheriff, 1929; Royal Engineers; *b.* 28 Mar. 1868; *s.* of Anthony Traill, Provost of Trinity College, Dublin; *m.* 1896, Selena Margaret, *y. d.* of Charles Frizell, Castlekevin, Co. Wicklow; three *s.* *Educ.:* Birney's, Gosport; Trinity College, Dublin. Entered Army, 1900; served Waziristan, N.W. Frontier of India, 1894-95 (medal and clasp); Tirah, N.W. Frontier, 1897-98 (medal and 3 clasps); lent to Government of Mysore P.W.D. in connection with Cauvery Power Scheme as Deputy Chief Engineer and Superintending Engineer, 1902-7; lent to Government of Indore as Chief Engineer, 1910-12; served European War, 1915 (despatches thrice, D.S.O., Croix de Guerre); retired, 1919. *Recreations:* shooting, fishing. *Address:* Ballylough, Bushmills, Co. Antrim. [*Died* 20 *Aug.* 1959.

TRANSJORDAN, King of, since 1946; **H.H. Abdullah Ibn Hussein;** Hon. G.C.M.G. 1935; G.B.E., K.C.M.G. 1927; Air Commodore, R.A.F.; Member of the Hashemite family. During European War, 1914-18, he led the Arab Revolt against Turkey. Emir of Transjordan, 1921-46, when became King of Jordan (formerly Transjordan). Supported British policies and wished for a United Arabia under Hashemite rule; was assassinated. *Address:* Amman, Transjordania. [*Died* 20 *July* 1951.

TRANT, John Philip; *b.* Thurles, Co. Tipperary, Ireland, 23 Dec. 1889; 2nd *s.* of Col. Fitzgibbon Trant, J.P., D.L., Dovea, Thurles; *m.* 1923, Sophia Irene Kelley; twin *s.* one *d.* *Educ.:* Haileybury; Trinity Coll., Dublin. Consul at Teneriffe, 1928; Riga, 1932; Consul-General at Rio de Janeiro, 1937; First Secretary, British Embassy, Moscow, 1939; Chargé d'Affaires, Monrovia, Liberia, 1943; H.M. Consul-General at Antananarivo, 1945; retired, 1947. *Address:* 24 Queensberry Place, South Kensington, S.W.7. *Club:* Royal Empire Society, Royal Geographical Society.
[*Died* 14 *Dec.* 1953.

TRAQUAIR, Harry Moss, M.B., C.M., M.D., D.P.H., F.R.C.S.Ed.; Retired; Cons. Ophthalmic Surgeon, Royal Infirmary, Edin.; Mem. Soc. Franc. d'Ophth.; Hon. Member: Ophth. Soc. of the U.K.; Amer. Ophth. Soc.; Copenhagen Ophth. Soc.; Council Faculty of Ophthalmologists; *b.* Edinburgh, 1875; *y. s.* of late R. H. Traquair, F.R.S., and Phoebe Anna Moss; *m.* 1906, Beatrix, *y. d.* of late John Nairn and Susan Wright; one *s.* one *d.* *Educ.:* Edinburgh Academy; Universities, Edinburgh (M.B., C.M., 1st class honours, 1901) and Halle. Awarded Middlemore Prize, Nettleship, Doyne and Mackenzie medals. Pres. R.C.S.Ed., 1939-41; Pres. Ophthalmological Society of the U.K., 1943-44. *Publications:* An Introduction to Clinical Perimetry, 6th Ed. 1949; Clinical Opthalmology for Practitioners and Students, 1948; and contributions to ophthalmic literature. *Recreation:* fishing. *Address:* 7 Lansdowne Crescent, Edinburgh, 12. *T.:* Caledonian 7746. [*Died* 14 *Nov.* 1954.

TRAQUAIR, Ramsay, M.A. (Hon.), D. ès L., F.R.I.B.A.; F.R.A.I.C.; *b.* Edinburgh, 29 March 1874; unmarried. *Educ.:* Edinburgh Academy; Edin. Coll. of Art. A.R.I.B.A. 1900; Lecturer on Architecture, Edinburgh College of Art, 1904; in practice as an Architect in Edinburgh, 1905-13; Macdonald Professor of Architecture, McGill University, Montreal, 1914; retired, 1939; Student of the British School of Archæology at Athens, 1905 and 1909. *Publications:* Old Architecture of Quebec; Old Silver of Quebec; Byzantine Churches of Constantinople (with Professor A. van Millingen); numerous papers on Byzantine Architecture, French Canadian Architecture, Education, and social subjects. *Recreations:* fishing and gardening. *Address:* Guysborough, Nova Scotia, Canada. *Club:* McGill University Faculty (Montreal). [*Died* 26 *Aug.* 1952.

TRATMAN, David William, C.M.G. 1930; *s.* of J. F. W. Tratman, Bristol; *m.* R. E. Malory Farmer. *Educ.:* Clifton; University College, Oxford, B.A. Hong Kong Civil Service, 1904; retired, 1936. *Recreations:* shooting, fishing. *Address:* Bydown, Swimbridge, Devon. *Club:* Junior Carlton. [*Died* 13 *Sept.* 1953.

TRAVERS, Captain Francis Eaton, C.M.G. 1917; R.N. retired; *m.* Lieut. 1886; Commander, 1899. Midshipman of Minotaur during Egyptian War, 1882 (medal, bronze star); Legion of Honour. *Club:* Army and Navy. [*Died* 16 *Dec.* 1953.

TRAVERS, Colonel Henry Cecil, C.B.E. 1919; D.S.O. 1916; *s.* of late Wm. Travers, M.D., F.R.C.S., London *m.* 1904, Julia Elizabeth (*d.* 1948), *d.* of late J. Robson, Liverpool; two *s.* two *d.* *Educ.:* Blundell's School, Tiverton; University College, London. Lieutenant, Royal Artillery, 1900; Captain, Army Ordnance Dept., 1909; Major, 1914; Act. Lt.-Col., 1915; Act. Colonel, 1917; Lt.-Col., Royal Army Ordnance Corps, 1923; Col. 1929; served European War, Mediterranean Expeditionary Force, Egyptian Expeditionary Force (despatches 5 times, 1914-15 Star, British War Medal, Victory Medal, C.B.E., D.S.O., White Eagle 4th class with swords); retired pay, 1933; late Lt. Home Guard; late R.A.O.C. *Address:* Marinstow, Bourne Avenue, Salisbury, Wilts. [*Died* 28 *June* 1958.

TRAVIS, Commander Sir Edward Wilfrid Harry, K.C.M.G., *cr.* 1944; C.B.E. 1936; R.N.; Director of a Department in the Foreign Office; *b.* 1888; *s.* of late H. Travis, C.B.E., I.S.O., and Emmeline Hamlyn; *m.* 1913, Muriel Irene, *d.* of late Lt.-Col. W. H. Fry; two *d.* *Educ.:* Blackheath. Joined Navy, 1906; served on Staff of Admiral Sir John Jellicoe, 1914-16; Signal Division of the Naval Staff Admiralty, 1916-18; Vice-Chairman International Code of Signal Committee, 1928-30; Chevalier of Legion of Honour; Officer of the Crown of Italy; U.S.A. Medal for Merit. *Address:* Burners', Pirbright, Surrey. *T.:* Brookwood 2183. [*Died* 18 *April* 1956.

TREDEGAR, 5th Baron, *cr.* 1859; **Frederic George Morgan,** Bt., *cr.* 1792; J.P.; *b.* 22 Nov. 1873; 2nd *s.* of Hon. Frederick Courtenay Morgan, M.P. (*d.* 1909; *b.* of 1st and last Viscount Tredegar), and Charlotte Anne (*d.* 1891), *d.* of Charles Alexander Williamson, Balgray, Co. Dumfries; *b.* of 1st Viscount Tredegar (2nd creation); *S.* to barony and baronetcy of nephew (2nd Viscount), 1949; *m.* 1898, Dorothy Syssylt (from whom he obtained a divorce, 1921; she *died* 1929), *d.* of Ralph Thurston Bassett, formerly of Crossways, Glam; one *s.* one *d.* *Educ.:* Eton; Oxford. J.P. Brecon and Radnor, 1909 (now of supp. list). *Heir:* *s.* Hon. Frederic Charles John Morgan, 2nd Lieut. 24th London Regt. (T.A.) [*b.* 26 Oct. 1908. *Educ.:* Eton]. *Address:* 42 Upper Brook St., W.1. *Club:* Boodle's. [*Died* 21 *Aug.* 1954.

TREDGOLD, Alfred Frank, M.D. Durh., F.R.C.P. Lond., M.R.C.S. Eng., F.R.S. Edin.: Consulting Physician to University College Hospital, London; National Assoc. for Feeble-Minded; Physician in Neurology Royal Surrey County Hospital; Lecturer at London Univ.; Fellow Royal Society of Medicine (ex-Pres. Section of Psychiatry); Member Royal Medico-Psychol. Assoc.; Hon. Fellow American Assoc. on Mental Deficiency; *b.* 5 Nov. 1870; *m.* 1899, Zoë B. T. (*d.* 1947), *d.* of F. A. Hanbury, Barrister-at-law; one *s.* two *d.* *Educ.:* Durham University; London Hospital (Scholarships in Anatomy, Biology, Physiology, Medicine, and Pathology). Appointed by London County Council to Research Scholarship, 1899, and for two years conducted researches into Mental Defect at Pathological Laboratory, Claybury Asylum; Medical Expert to Royal Commission on Feeble-Minded, 1905; Member of Board of Education Mental Deficiency Committee; Member of Ministry of Health Committee on Sterilization; took an active part in promoting passage of Mental Deficiency Act of 1913; Major, 5th Batt. The Queen's Regiment, (retired); T.D.; served as Adjutant 2/4th Batt. in Gallipoli Campaign (Suvla Bay landing), 1915; western frontier of Egypt and Sinai Peninsula, 1916. *Publications:* A Text-book on Mental Deficiency, 8th edit. 1952; Manual of Psychological Medicine, 3rd Ed. 1953; numerous articles. *Address:* St. Martin's, Guildford, Surrey. *T.:* Guildford 5112. [*Died* 17 *Sept.* 1952.

TREFGARNE, 1st Baron, *cr.* 1947, of Cleddau; **George Morgan Trefgarne** (formerly **Garro Jones**); Barrister-at-law; Chairman, W. E. Sykes Ltd., and associated companies; *b.* 1894; *o. s.* of late Rev. D. Garro-Jones, Congregational minister; surname changed to Trefgarne by Deed Poll, 1954; *m.* 1940, Elizabeth, *d.* of C. E. Churchill; three *s.* one *d.* *Educ.:* Caterham School. Served in Denbighshire Yeomanry, 1914; France, in S.W.B. and Royal Flying Corps, 1915-17; Advisory Officer to U.S. Air Service, 1918; Hon. Capt. Royal Air Force: Private Secretary to Sir Hamar Greenwood (Lord Greenwood) while at Home Office, at Department of Overseas Trade, and while Chief Secretary for Ireland; contested Bethnal Green, 1922, and South Hackney, 1923; M.P. (L.) South Hackney, 1924-29; M.P. (Lab.) Aberdeen, 1935-45; Parliamentary Secretary to Ministry of Production, 1942-45; Member of Empire Parliamentary delegation to Nigeria, 1928; Member of Departmental Committee on Electoral Machinery, 1942; Deputy Chairman Radio Board, 1942-45; Chairman Television Advisory Committee, 1946-49; Founder Chairman of Colonial Development Corporation, 1947-50. *Heir:* *s.* Hon. David, *b.* 31 March 1941. *Address:* Pembroke House, Valley End, Chobham, Sy. *Club:* Royal Air Force. [*Died* 27 *Sept.* 1960.

TREHEARNE, Frank William; Master of the Supreme Court of Judicature (Chancery Division) 1938, retired 1954; *b.* 21 Dec. 1881; *y. s.* of late W. J. and Elizabeth Trehearne, The Grange, Gunnersbury, Middlesex; *m.* 1915; Margaret Evelyn, *d.* of late R. A. Walker; one *s.* one *d.* (and one *d.* killed by enemy action). *Educ.:* St. Paul's School. Admitted a Solicitor, 1904; served with R.H.A., 1915-19. *Recreations:* fishing and gardening. *Address:* 4 Chyngton Gardens, Seaford, Sussex. *T.:* Seaford 2112. [*Died* 16 *April* 1956.

TREHERNE, Major-Gen. Sir Francis Harper, K.C.M.G., *cr.* 1917 (C.M.G. 1915); F.R.C.S., L.R.C.P. (Edin.); D.P.H. (Camb.); A.M.S.; *b.* 15 April 1858; *s.* of late H. Treherne; *m.* 1st, 1884, Meliora Alianor Cotgrave (*d.* 1891), *d.* of late Maj.-Gen. W. R. Farmar; two *s.*; 2nd, 1900, Nona Thérèse Burne, *d.* of late Gen. Sir Frank Turner, K.C.B.; one *d.* *Educ.:* Godolphin School; St. Bartholomew's Hospital. Major, R.A.M.C. 1894; Surgeon to Commander-in-Chief in India, 1893-1898; Lt.-Col. 1902; Colonel, A.M.S. 1911; Hon. Surgeon to Viceroy of India, 1912; Surg.-Gen. 1915; Maj.-Gen. 1918; A.D.M.S. India, 1911-14; D.D.M.S., B.E.F. 1914; D.M.S. 3rd Army, B.E.F. 1915-16; D.M.S. Mesopotamia, 1916-17; D.D.M.S. London District, 1917-18; Inspector Medical Services, 1918-19; served Egypt, 1882 (despatches, medal with clasp, bronze star); Sudan, 1884 (2 clasps); Nile, 1884-5 (2 clasps); S. African War, 1899-1901 (despatches, Queen's medal 3 clasps); N.W. Frontier, India, 1908 (medal with clasp); European War, 1914-16 (despatches three times, C.M.G., Order of White Eagle, 2nd Class); Mesopotamian Expedition, 1916-17, Actions at Kut, Diala, and capture of Baghdad (despatches twice, K.C.M.G.). *Address:* The Red House, Woodbridge, Suffolk. *T.:* Woodbridge 201. [*Died* 30 *Jan.* 1955.

TRELAWNY, Sir John William Robin Maurice Salusbury-, 12th Bt., *cr.* 1628; Flight Lieut. R.A.F.V.R.; *b.* 16 Jan. 1908; *s.* of Sir John Salusbury-Trelawny, 11th Bt., and Catherine Penelope, *d.* of late Ambrose Sneyd Cave-Browne-Cave; *S.* father, 1944; *m.* 1st, 1932, Glenys Mary Kynoch (who obtained a divorce, 1935); one *s.*; 2nd, 1937, Rosamund Helen Ropes; one *s.* one *d.* *Educ.:* privately. *Recreations:* golf, ski-ing, flying, carpentry. *Heir:* *s.* John Barry, *b.* 4 Sept. 1934. *Address:* Jersey House, Cowfold, Sussex. *Club:* Royal Automobile. [*Died* 28 *Nov.* 1956.

TREMAYNE, Arthur; Governing Director N.A.G. Press Ltd.; Editor of Goldsmiths' Journal, Horological Journal, Gemmologist and Industrial Diamond Review; *b.* 12 Nov. 1879; *m.* 1900, Ada Cross; no *c.* *Educ.:* Coopers' Company School. After experience in many branches of the jewellery industry, studied advertising and specialised in publicity for jewellery and allied trades; elected to Council of Incorporated Society of Advertisement Consultants, 1914; Hon. Treas., 1916; Vice-President, 1917-20; has travelled largely in centres concerned with production of jewellers' merchandise; suggested the Jubilee Mark for Silver which the trade agreed to use to commemorate the Royal Silver Jubilee, 1935. Liveryman, Clockmakers' Company, 1945. *Recreations:* travel and motoring. *Address:* 226 Latymer Court, Hammersmith, W.6. *T.:* Riverside 2143. *Club:* Royal Automobile. [*Died* 20 *March* 1954.

TREMBLAY, Major-Gen. Thomas Louis, C.B. 1944; C.M.G. 1917; D.S.O. 1916; E.D.; Hon. A.D.C. to the Governor-General of Canada; Inspector-General (Army); *b.* 1886; *m.* 1922, Marie Hamel; two *s.* (one *d.* decd.). Served European War, 1914-18 (despatches, C.M.G., D.S.O., Legion of Honour); Graduate Roy. Mil. Coll., Kingston, 1907. *Address:* 131 Belvedere Road, Quebec, Canada. *Clubs:* Royal Quebec Golf, Quebec Garrison (Quebec); Laurentide Fishing. [*Died* 28 *March* 1951.

TRENCH; *see* Chenevix-Trench.

TRENCH, Ernest Frederic Crosbie, C.B.E.; T.D.; M.I.C.E.; M.A.; Chartered Civil Engineer; *b.* Ardfert Abbey, Co. Kerry, 1869; *s.* of George F. Trench, J.P.; *m.* 1895, Netta (*d.* 1950), *d.* of Herbert Wilbraham Taylor, J.P., Monken Hadley; three *s.* one *d.* *Educ.:* Switzerland; Trinity Coll., Dublin. Formerly Chief Engineer of the London and N.-W. Railway 1909; of the London, Midland and Scottish Railway, 1924; is Past President of the Institution of Civil Engineers. *Recreations:* shooting, fishing. *Address:* Furze Coppice, Savernake Forest, Marlborough. *T.:* Marlborough 73. *Club:* Athenæum. [*Died* 15 *Sept.* 1960.

TRENCHARD, 1st Viscount, *cr.* 1936; of Wolfeton; **Marshal of the R.A.F. Hugh Montague Trenchard,** Baron, *cr.* 1930, Bt., *cr.* 1919; G.C.B., *cr.* 1924 (K.C.B., *cr.* 1918; C.B. 1914); O.M. 1951; G.C.V.O., *cr.* 1935; D.S.O. 1906; Chm. The United Africa Co. since 1936; Director Goodyear Tyre and Rubber Co. (Great Britain) Ltd.; *b.* 3 Feb. 1873; *m.* 1920, Katherine, 2nd *d.* of late Edward Salvin Bowlby, Gilston Park, Herts, and Knoydart, Inverness-shire, and of Mrs Salvin Bowlby, 56 Lowndes Square, and *widow* of Captain Hon. James Boyle, Royal Scots Fusiliers; one *s.* (and *er. s.* killed in action, 1943) one *step d.* (and two *step s.* both killed in action, 1938 and 1944). Entered Army, 1893; Captain, 1900; Bt. Major, 1902; Bt. Lieut.-Colonel, 1915; Bt. Colonel, 1915; Major-General, 1916; Air-Marshal, 1919; Air Chief Marshal, 1922; Marshal of the Royal Air Force 1927; served with Imperial Yeomanry, Bushmen Corps, South Africa, 1899-1902, and afterwards with Canadian Scouts (dangerously wounded, Brevet Major, Queen's medal 3 clasps, King's medal 2 clasps); West African Frontier Force, Commandant of S. Nigeria Regt., West African Frontier Force, 1903-10; European War, 1914-1918 (despatches eight times, prom. Maj.-Gen. K.C.B., 1914 Star); A.D.C. (extra) to the King, 1915; Assist. Commandant, Central Flying School, 1913-14; G.O.C. R.F.C. in the Field, 1915-17; Chief of Air Staff, 1918-29; Principal Air A.D.C. to the King, 1921-25; Commissioner Metropolitan Police, 1931-35; Trustee of Imperial War Museum, 1937-45; Comdt. of the Legion of Honour; Order of St. Anne (3rd class with swords); Order of King Leopold; American Distinguished Service Medal; Order de la Couronne, Italy; Order of the Sacred Treasure of Japan. Hon. LL.D. Cambridge; D.C.L. Oxford, 1926. *Heir:* *s.* Capt. Hon. Thomas Trenchard, M.C. 1945, K.R.R.C. [*b.* 1923; *m.* 1948, Patricia S., *d.* of late Admiral Sir Sidney Bailey; two *s.*]. *Address:* The King's House, Burhill, Walton-on-Thames, Surrey. *T.:* Walton-on-Thames 1887. *Clubs:* Army and Navy, Brooks's, R.A.F. [*Died* 10 *Feb.* 1956.

TREND, John Brande, M.A., Litt.D.; Fellow of Christ's College, Cambridge; Emeritus Professor of Spanish; *b.* Southampton, 17 Dec. 1887; *s.* of late Theophilus William Trend, M.D., J.P., and Frances, 2nd *d.* of R. G. Stevens. *Educ.:* Charterhouse; Christ's College, Cambridge (Exhibitioner); Germany, Italy. Served European War (Flanders); correspondent of the Athenæum in Spain, 1919-1920; travels in Spain, Portugal, Morocco and Mexico; worked at Spanish at the Residencia de Estudiantes in Madrid; Arabic at the School of Oriental Studies, London; Comendador, Order of the Republic (Spain); Officer, Order of Liberators (Venezuela); member and medallist, Hispanic Soc. of America. *Publications:* A Picture of Modern Spain, 1921; Luis Milan, 1925; Spanish Madrigals, 1925; The Music of Spanish History, 1925; Alfonso the Sage, 1925; Escenografia Madrileña en el siglo XVII, 1926; Catalogue of the Music in the Biblioteca Medinaceli, 1927; Spain from the South, 1928; Manuel de Falla, 1929; The Origins of Modern Spain, 1934; Mexico, 1940; South America (The World To-day), 1941; The Civilization of Spain (Home Univ. Library), 1944; Bolívar and the independence of Spanish America, 1946; Juan Ramón Jiménez, 1950; Antonio Machado, 1953; The Language and History of Spain, 1953; Lorca and the Spanish poetic tradition, 1956; Portugal (Nations of the Modern World), 1957; Spain, in The Legacy of Islam, 1931; Calderón and the Spanish religious theatre, in 17th century studies presented to Sir Herbert Grierson, 1938; edited Isaac Abravanel (with H. M. J. Loewe), Unamuno (with J. L. Gili), Prosa diversa, 1938; Santillana Prose and Verse, 1940; Oxford Book of Spanish Verse, 2nd edition 1940; translated (with Frank Birch) Calderón's Life's a Dream, 1925. *Recreation:* bathing. *Club:* Oxford and Cambridge. [*Died* 20 *April* 1958.

TRENT, 2nd Baron, *cr.* 1929, of Nottingham, **John Campbell Boot;** Bt., *cr.* 1916; K.B.E., *cr.* 1954; *b.* 19 Jan. 1889; *o. s.* of 1st Baron Trent and Florence (*d.* 1952), *d.* of William Rowe, Jersey; *S.* father 1931; *m.* 1914, Margaret Joyce Pyman; four *d.* *Educ.:* Leys School, Cambridge; Jesus College, Cambridge. Served European War, 1914-18; Sherwood Foresters, 1914-19; Regional Commissioner for Civil Defence, North Midland Region, 1939-45; Chairman, Council of Industrial Welfare Society, 1945-1952; Chancellor, Nottingham University, 1948-54. Chairman and Managing Director Boots Pure Drug Co. Ltd., and associated companies, 1926-54. Hon. Fellow Jesus College, Cambridge. Past President Nottingham Chamber of Commerce; D.L. 1941-54; J.P. 1924-53. Hon. LL.D., Nottingham University. *Address:* The Grove, St. Lawrence, Jersey, Channel Islands. [*Died* 8 *March* 1956 (*ext.*).

TRENT, Newbury Abbot, R.B.S.; sculptor; *b.* 14 Oct. 1885; *m.* 1911, Phyllis Hilda

Ledward; two *d.* Studied at South Kensington and Royal Academy. *Works:* King Edward VII Memorial at Brighton and Hove; King Edward VII Memorial at Bath; Dean Pigou, recumbent effigy Memorial in Bristol Cathedral; War Memorials at New Barnet, Beckenham, Wanstead, and Ilford. *Address:* 1 Beaufort St., Chelsea, S.W.3. *Club:* Chelsea Arts.

[*Died* 2 *Aug.* 1953.

TRESTON, Hubert Joseph, M.A., D.Litt.; retired as Professor of Ancient Classics (1915-Dec. 1958) and Dean of the Faculty of Arts (1920-Dec. 1958) in University College, Cork; *b.* Ballyhaunis, Co. Mayo, 1 December 1888; *e. s.* of James Michael Treston and Mary Agnes Heavey; *m.* 1925, Cynthia, *y. d.* of late George Edward Rudd, M.A. (Oxon), of Stoneygate, Leicester; one *s. Educ.:* Tuam; Maynooth College (R.U.I.); London. Intermediate: medal for first place in Ireland in Greek, and Classical Exhibition, Junior Grade, 1904; medal for first place in Latin, Exhibition, 1905 (middle); medal for first place in Greek, Exhibition, 1906 (senior); University: B.A. Honours (with Exhibition) Royal University of Ireland, 1909; M.A. Degree (R.U.I.) 1911; D.Litt. Degree, for published work, National University of Ireland, 1925. *Publication:* Poine, a Study in Ancient Greek Blood-Vengeance, 1923. *Recreations:* bridge, motoring, golf, foreign travel. *Address:* c/o University College, Cork.

[*Died* 5 *Feb.* 1959.

TREVAN, John William, F.R.S. 1946; M.B., B.S., B.Sc.; F.R.C.P.; Consultant, Wellcome Foundation Ltd.; Director Wellcome Research Laboratories, Beckenham, 1940-53; Hon. Lecturer, University College, London; Deacon of S. Aubyns Congregational Church, Norwood; Member Board of Studies Pharmacology, University, London; *b.* Bodmin, Cornwall, 23 July 1887; *s.* of J. W. S. Trevan, Plymouth; *m.* 1st, Ida Kathleen (*d.* 1937), *d.* of Rev. J. L. Keys; three *s.* two *d.*; 2nd, Margaret, *d.* of Sir Hubert Llewellyn Smith; one *s.* two *d. Educ.:* Plymouth Council and Technical Schools; St. Bartholomew's Hospital, London. Demonstrator of Physiology, 1914-20; Casualty Physician, 1914-1920, at S. Bartholomew's; Capt. R.A.M.C., 1917-19. Pharmacologist, the Wellcome Physiological Research Laboratories, Beckenham, 1920-40. President Section of Therapeutics, Royal Society Medicine, 1937-1938. *Publications:* papers on Pharmacology and Physiology in technical journals. *Recreations:* music, sailing. *Address:* Woodside Cottage, 169 Woodside Green, S.E. 25. *T.:* Addiscombe 5798. [*Died* 13 *Oct.* 1956.

TREVELYAN, Rt. Hon. Sir Charles Philips, P.C. 1924; 3rd Bt., *cr.* 1874; *b.* Park Lane, W., 28 Oct. 1870; *e. s.* of Rt. Hon. Sir G. O. Trevelyan, 2nd Bt., O.M.; *S.* father, 1928; *m.* 1904, Mary Katharine, *y. d.* of Sir Hugh Bell, 2nd Bt.; two *s.* four *d. Educ.:* Harrow; Trinity College, Cambridge; M.A.; 2nd class Historical Tripos, 1892. Secretary to Lord Crewe when Lord Lieutenant of Ireland, 1892-93; contested N. Lambeth, 1895, Central Newcastle, 1931; Member of London School Board, 1896-97; Parliamentary Charity Commissioner, 1906-1908; M.P. (L.) Elland Division West Riding Yorks, 1899-1918; M.P. (Labour) Central Newcastle, 1922-31; Parliamentary Secretary, Board of Education, 1908-14; President Board of Education, 1924 and 1929-31; Member M.R.C., 1928-29; H.M. Lieutenant for County of Northumberland, 1930-49. *Heir:* *s.* George Lowthian [*b.* 1906; *m.* 1940, Helen, *d.* of Col. J. Lindsay Smith, C.B.E.]. *Recreations:* shooting, walking. *Address:* Wallington, Cambo, Morpeth, Northumberland. *Club:* Athenæum.

[*Died* 24 *Jan.* 1958.

TREVELYAN, Hilda; *m.* Sydney Blow. Associated mostly with Sir J. M. Barrie's plays; the original Wendy in Peter Pan, Maggie Wylie in What Every Woman Knows, Cinders in A Kiss for Cinderella, and others; has also appeared in The Great Adventure, Mary Rose, and Quality Street at the Haymarket Theatre; also Housemaster, The Admirable Crichton, Trelawny of the Wells, and many other plays. *Address:* Janes, Witheridge Hill, Henley-on-Thames. [*Died* 10 *Nov.* 1959.

TREVELYAN, Janet Penrose, C.H. 1936; *b.* 6 Nov. 1879; *d.* of Humphry and Mary Ward; *m.* 1904, George Macaulay Trevelyan, O.M., C.B.E., F.R.S.; one *s.* one *d. Educ.:* Private. Succeeded her mother in conducting the Play Centre movement for London Children, 1920-41, when she handed over 50 Play Centres to the London County Council. Organised the Appeal to "Save the Foundling Site" as a playground and welfare centre for children, 1931-35, and with the help of Viscount Rothermere, the Governors of the Foundling Hospital and the London County Council was successful in raising the large sum required for the purchase. Now Deputy-Chairman, Council of Coram's Fields; Hon. Secretary British Institute of Florence (Royal Charter), 1920-46. *Publications:* Trans. Jülicher's Introduction to the New Testament, 1904; Evening Play Centres for Children, 1920; A Short History of the Italian People, 1920; The Life of Mrs. Humphry Ward, 1923; Two Stories, 1954. *Recreation:* watching birds. *Address:* 23 West Road, Cambridge. *T.:* Cambridge 56704; Hallington Hall, Newcastle upon Tyne. *Club:* University Women's. [*Died* 7 *Sept.* 1956.

TREVELYAN, Robert Calverley; author; *b.* 28 June 1872; 2nd *s.* of Rt. Hon. Sir G. O. Trevelyan, 2nd Bt., O.M.; *m.* 1900, Elizabeth des Amorie van der Hoeven; one *s. Educ.:* Harrow; Trinity College, Cambridge. *Publications:* Poetry: Mallow and Asphodel, 1898; Polyphemus, 1901; Cecilia Gonzaga, 1903; The Birth of Parsival, 1905; Sisyphus, 1908; The Bride of Dionysus, 1912; The New Parsifal, 1914; The Foolishness of Solomon, 1915; The Pterodamozels, 1917; The Pearl Tree (in An Annual of New Poetry), 1917; The Death of Man, 1919; Poems and Fables, 1925; The Deluge, 1926; Meleager, 1927; Cheiron, 1928; Three Plays, 1931; Rimeless Numbers, 1932; Beelzebub, 1935; Collected Works (vol. I. Poems, vol. II. Plays), 1939; Aftermath, 1942; From the Shiffolds, 1947; Verse translations; The Oresteia and Prometheus of Aeschylus; The Ajax and Antigone of Sophocles; The Medea of Euripides; Theocritus; Lucretius De Rerum Natura; Translations from Horace; Translations from Leopardi; Virgil's Georgics; Sophocles' Oedipus at Colonus. Prose: Thamyris or the Future of Poetry, 1925; Windfalls, 1944. *Address:* The Shiffolds, Holmbury St. Mary, Dorking. *T.A.* and *T.:* Forest Green 215.

[*Died* 21 *March* 1951.

TREVETHIN, 2nd Baron, *cr.* 1921, of Blaengawney; **Charles Trevor Lawrence,** D.S.O. 1918; D.L.; late Royal Horse and Field Artillery; *b.* 1879; *e. surv. s.* of 1st Baron and Jessie Elizabeth (*d.* 1931), *d.* of George Lawrence; *S.* father 1936. *Educ.:* Haileybury; New Coll., Oxford. Served European War, 1914-18; North Russia, 1918-19 (D.S.O., despatches thrice, St. Anne of Russia, 2nd class, with swords); Lieut.-Col. 1929; retired pay, 1932. D.L. Breconshire. *Heir:* *b.* 1st Baron Oaksey, D.S.O., T.D., K.C. *Address:* Abernant, Builth, Breconshire. *Club:* Army and Navy.

[*Died* 25 *June* 1959.

TREVOR, Sir (Charles) Gerald, Kt., *cr.* 1937; C.I.E. 1933; J.P. Co. Montgomery; *b.* 28 December 1882; *s.* of Sir Francis Trevor, K.C.S.I., C.B., and Mary Helen Mytton; *m.* 1912, Enid Carroll Beadon; three *d. Educ.:* Wellington College; R.I.E.C. Coopers Hill. Joined the Indian Forest Service as Assistant Conservator, 1903, posted to Punjab; Conservator of Forests, United Provinces, 1920; Vice-President and Professor of Forestry, Forest Research Institute, Dehra Dun, 1926; Chief Conservator of Forests, Punjab and N.W.F. Province, 1930-33; Inspector General of Forests to the Government of India, 1933-37; retired, 1937; represented India at Imperial Forestry Conferences in Canada, 1923, Australia and New Zealand, 1928, S. Africa, 1935; High Sheriff, Co. Montgomery, 1941. *Publications:* Manual of Indian Silviculture; Practical Forest Management. *Address:* Trawscoed Hall, Welshpool, Montgomeryshire. *Club:* East India and Sports. [*Died* 20 *May* 1959.

TREWBY, Vice-Admiral George, C.M.G. 1919; D.S.O. 1915; *b.* 19 October 1874; *e. s.* of late G. C. Trewby; *m.* 1916, Dorothea, *o. d.* of late Dr. A. de W. Allan, Port Nolloth, Namaqualand; two *s.* Served European War, 1914-17 (D.S.O.), as Flag-Captain and Chief of Staff to Rear-Admiral commanding 10th Cruiser Squadron; Rear-Admiral and retired at own request, 1923; Vice-Admiral retired, 1928. *Address:* 94 Richmond Hill Court, Richmond, Surrey. [*Died* 23 *April* 1953.

TRIBE, Sir Frank Newton, K.C.B., *cr.* 1945 (C.B. 1938); K.B.E., *cr.* 1941 (C.B.E. 1930; O.B.E. 1919); Comptroller and Auditor General, Exchequer and Audit Department, since 1946; Member Joint Panel of External Auditors of United Nations since 1950 (Chairman, 1954-); External Auditor of U.N.E.S.C.O. since 1950, of F.A.O. since 1951 and of World Meteorological Organisation since 1952; *b.* 15 July 1893; *o. s.* of late Frank N. Tribe, J.P., Bristol; *m.* 1923, Eileen Mary (*d.* 1952), *e. d.* of late Dr. Henry Layng, Swatow, China; one *s.* two *d.* *Educ.:* Clifton Coll.; Trinity Coll., Oxford (Foundation Scholar); Gaisford Greek Verse Prizeman, Oxford, 1914, M.A. Served European War, 1914-19 (despatches, O.B.E.); Staff Captain, 1918-19; appointed to Ministry of Labour, 1920; Principal Private Sec. to three Ministers of Labour, 1923-28; Secretary of the National Advisory Council for Juvenile Employment (England and Wales), 1928-34; Secretary to Commissioner for Special Areas (England and Wales), 1934-38; Principal Assistant Secretary, H.M. Treasury, 1938-40; Deputy Sec., Ministry of Labour and National Service, 1940-42; Secretary, Office of the Minister of Production, 1942; Permanent Sec., Min. of Fuel and Power, 1942-45; Permanent Sec. Ministry of Aircraft Production, 1945; Permanent Secretary, Ministry of Food, 1945-46. Member of Council of Clifton College, 1944- (Chairman, 1951-); Member of Council of Wycombe Abbey School 1953- (Chairman 1956-). *Address:* 24 Rutland Court, Knightsbridge, S.W.7. *T.:* Kensington 1789. *Club:* Oxford and Cambridge. [*Died* 20 *June* 1958.

TRIMINGHAM, Sir Eldon Harvey, Kt., *cr.* 1950; C.B.E. 1941; *b.* 1889; *s.* of Thomas Darrell Trimingham; *m.* 1929, Esther Arabel, *d.* of Dr. Eldon Harvey. Member of the Legislative Council, Bermuda. *Address:* Hamilton, Bermuda. [*Died* 12 *Dec.* 1959.

TRIMNELL, Colonel William Duncan Conabeare, C.B. 1918; C.M.G. 1916; late R.A.O.C.; *b.* 9 Aug. 1874; married; one *d.* *Educ.:* Clifton College. Served European War, 1914-18 (despatches, C.M.G., C.B., French and Belgian Croix de Guerre); retired pay, 1928; Officier du Légion d'Honneur, de l'Ordre de Leopold, and of the Order of Aviz. *Address:* But-and-ben, Ewell Minnis, Dover. [*Died* 14 *Sept.* 1953.

TRINE, Ralph Waldo; author and fruit-raiser; *b.* Mt. Morris, Illinois, 9 Sept. 1866. *Educ.:* Carthage College, Academy; Knox College, Illinois; University of Wisconsin; Johns Hopkins University, Baltimore. *Publications:* In Tune with the Infinite; What all the World's A-Seeking; This Mystical Life of Ours; The Land of Living Men; The New Alinement of Life; The Wayfarer on the Open Road; The Greatest Thing Ever Known; Every Living Creature; Character-Building; Thought Power; The Winning of the Best Thoughts I Met on the Highway; In the Hollow of His Hand; The Higher Powers of Mind and Spirit; My Philosophy and My Religion; The Power that Wins. *Address:* 620 W. 8th St., Pilgrim Place, Claremont, Calif. [*Died* 22 *Feb.* 1958.

TRIPP, Sir (Herbert) Alker, Kt., *cr.* 1945; C.B.E. 1935; Assistant Commissioner of Police of the Metropolis, 1932-47; *b.* 23 Aug. 1883; *s.* of late George H. Tripp, C.B.; *m.* 1910, Abigail (*d.* 1951), *d.* of John Powell, Dublin; one *s.* one *d.* Appointed Officer of Staff, New Scotland Yard, by nomination of the Home Secretary, 1902; Chairman of Police Recruiting Board, 1920-25; Member of Standing Committee on Aliens and Nationality, 1925-29; Member of Advisory Committee on Homeless Poor of London, 1927-32; Member of the Road Safety Committee, 1934-35; Chairman of Public Carriage Drivers, etc., Licensing Committee (Metropolitan Area) since 1932; British Delegate at the International Road Congress, Munich, 1934 and The Hague, 1938; Member: London and Home Counties Traffic Advisory Cttee., 1932-47; Royal Academy Planning Cttee., 1942-49; Committee on Road Safety, 1944; Road Research Board, 1946-49. *Publications:* Shoalwater and Fairway, 1924; Suffolk Sea-Borders, 1926; The Solent and the Southern Waters, 1928; Road Traffic and its Control, 1938, 1950; Town Planning and Road Traffic, 1942; Under the Cabin Lamp, 1950; Papers: The Design of Streets for Traffic Requirements, 1933; Contributions to Nineteenth Century, Encyclopædia Britannica, and numerous articles in the Yachting Magazines of England and America; Pictures: in Royal Academy and other leading Exhibitions. *Recreations:* yachting, painting, writing. *Address:* Lee Cottage, Thames Ditton. *T.:* Emberbrook 1876. *Clubs:* Athenæum, Royal Cruising. [*Died* 12 *Dec.* 1954.

TRIPP, Lieut.-Gen. William Henry Lainson, C.B. 1934; D.S.O. 1917; M.C.; *b.* 6 July 1881; *s.* of George William and Caroline Ada Tripp; unmarried. *Educ.:* King's School, Canterbury. Joined Royal Marine Artillery, 1899; served in German South West Africa, 1914-15 with South African Heavy Artillery and afterwards in France 1916 till the end of the war, with the rank of Lt.-Col. (D.S.O., M.C., despatches four times); retired list, 1939; Naval adviser M.O.I., 1939-45. *Address:* c/o Standard Bank, Claremont, C.P., S. Africa. *Clubs:* United Service; Civil Service (Cape Town). [*Died* 15 *Feb.* 1959.

TRISTRAM, Ernest William, Hon. D.Litt., Oxford, 1931, Birmingham, 1946; A.R.C.A.; Hon. A.R.I.B.A.; Prof. Emeritus Royal Coll. of Art; *b.* 27 Dec. 1882; *s.* of F. W. Tristram; *m.* Eileen, *d.* of late Lt.-Col. H. C. B. Dann, I.A.; two *d.* Work executed on preservation of mediæval paintings and monuments throughout the country, notably at:—Westminster Abbey, Canterbury Cathedral, Norwich Cathedral, Exeter Cathedral, Winchester Cathedral, St. George's Chapel, Windsor, St. John's College Gateway, Cambridge, Christ Church Cathedral, Oxford, Christchurch Priory, Hants. Restoration of the Pre-Raphaelite paintings in the Oxford Union Library. Reconstructions of mediæval paintings at the Houses of Parliament, Westminster Abbey, Eton College Chapel, Canterbury, Exeter and Winchester Cathedrals, Oriel College, Oxford, and other places. Large collection of drawings of ancient wall-paintings at the Victoria and Albert Museum, South Kensington. *Original Work:* Paintings in York Cathedral, St. Elizabeth's Church, Eastbourne, St. Fin Barre's Cathedral, Cork, Ireland, and other churches. *Publications:* English Mediæval Painting (with T. Borenius);

The Cloister Bosses of Norwich Cathedral (with Dr. D. H. S. Cranage); English Mediæval Wallpainting, vol. 1, 12th century, 1945; vol. 2, 13th century, 1950; articles on Ancient Painting in various magazines; illustrator: The Lakes, An Anthology of Lakeland Life and Landscape by G. S. Sandilands, 1947. *Address:* Chase Cottage, Chase Lane, Haslemere, Surrey. [*Died* 11 *Jan.* 1952.

TRISTRAM, Rev. Henry; Priest of Birmingham Oratory; on staff of the Oratory School, Caversham, Reading, 1922-41, sometime Warden and Headmaster; *b.* Carmarthen, 1881. *Educ.:* Jesus College, Oxford, B.Litt., M.A. Priest of the Congregation of the Oratory, ordained, 1911; has done parochial work in Birmingham, and served on the staff of the Oratory School; has made Cardinal Newman's works his special study; President of the Catholic Headmasters' Conference, 1929-30; Member of the Hellenic Society and Classical Association. *Publications:* Newman and His Friends, 1933; The Living Thoughts of Cardinal Newman, 1949; articles to the Cornhill, Dublin Review, and other periodicals. *Address:* The Oratory, Edgbaston, Birmingham 16. [*Died* 8 *Feb.* 1955.

TROLLOPE, Fabian George, C.B.E. 1920; *e. s.* of late Col. G. H. Trollope, V.D., D.L., J.P., Hammershott, Liphook; *b.* 1872; *m.* 1900, Violet, *d.* of late William Tebbutt. *Educ.:* Radley. *Address:* 13 Greville Place, N.W.6. *Club:* Junior Carlton. [*Died* 17 *May* 1960.

TROLLOPE, Sir Frederic Farrand, 14th Bart., *cr.* 1642; Manager of the Legal and Security Dept. of the Commercial Banking Co. of Sydney Ltd., Sydney; *b.* 20 Sept. 1875; *s.* of Frederic James Anthony Trollope; *S.* kinsman, 1937; unmarried. *Educ.:* Collegiate School, Croydon, N.S.W.; Grammar School, Grafton, N.S.W. *Heir: b.* Gordon Clavering (*see* Sir Gordon Clavering Trollope, 15th Bt.). *Address:* Clavering, 108 Beaconsfield Rd., Chatswood, N.S.W. [*Died* 9 *Nov.* 1957.

TROLLOPE, Sir Gordon Clavering, 15th Bt., *cr.* 1642; *b.* 1885; 6th *s.* of late Frederic James Anthony Trollope and Susanna Farrand; *S.* brother 1957; *m.* 1913, Mary Isabel, *y. d.* of Owen Blacket, Lindfield, Sydney, N.S.W.; two *s.* one *d. Heir: s.* Anthony Owen Clavering Trollope [*b.* 15 Jan. 1917; *m.* 1942, Joan Mary Alexis, *d.* of Alexis Robert Gibbes, Manly, N.S.W.; two *s.*]. *Address:* Glencourse, Oaklands Road, Hazelbrook, N.S.W. [*Died* 18 *Oct.* 1958.

TROLLOPE, Brig. Hugh Charles Napier, C.B.E. 1944; D.S.O. 1919; M.C. 1916; D.L. Essex; Suffolk Regiment (R. of O.); Member T.A. and A.F. County of Essex; *b.* 1895; *s.* of C. G. N. Trollope, Beccles, Suffolk; *m.* 1930, Lorna Jarvis, *d.* of late Capt. N. F. J. Wilson, C.M.G., C.B.E.; one *s.* one *d.* Served European War, 1914-19 (twice wounded, despatches thrice, M.C., D.S.O., 1914-15 Star, two medals); commanded 5th Bn. Essex Regt., 1938; War of 1939-45 (C.B.E.); ceased to be employed, 1945. *Address:* The Mount, Coggeshall, Essex. [*Died* 16 *April* 1953.

TROTT, Alan Charles, C.M.G. 1948; O.B.E. 1941; *b.* 26 Mar. 1895; *s.* of late John Trott; *m.* 1927, Hester Dorothy Richardson; two *s.* one *d. Educ.:* Exeter School, Exeter; St. John's College, Cambridge (Scholar). Served European War, 1914-1918 (despatches). Barrister-at-law, Gray's Inn, 1925. Served in various posts in Levant Consular Service from 1920: including Tehran, Resht, Ispahan, Casablanca, Shiraz and Jedda (where he was Chargé d'Affaires in 1937, 1938 and 1939); Consul-General at Ahwaz, Persia, 1945-47; Ambassador to Saudi Arabia, 1947-51; resigned, Dec. 1951. Director, Middle East Centre for Arab Studies, Shemlan, the Lebanon, 1953-57. *Recreations:* birds and flowers. *Address:* Avonmore, Portmore Park Road, Weybridge. *T.:* Weybridge 4001. *Club:* Athenæum. [*Died* 6 *July* 1959.

TROTTER, Reginald George, A.M., Ph.D.; Hon. D.C.L. Acadia, 1938; F.R.S.C.; Douglas Professor of Canadian and Colonial History, Queen's University, from 1934 and Head of the Department of History from 1935; Associate Professor of History, 1924-1934; *b.* Woodstock, Ontario, 14 July 1888; *e. s.* of Thomas Trotter, D.D., LL.D., and Ellen Maud, *d.* of Rev. David Freeman, M.A.; *m.* 1923, Prudence Hale Fisher; two *s. Educ.:* Horton Collegiate Academy, Wolfville, Nova Scotia; Acadia Univ.; McMaster Univ.; Yale Univ. (B.A.); Harvard Univ. (A.M., Ph.D.). Master, Thacher School, Ojai, California, 1908-9, 1911-14; during post-graduate studies successively Travelling Fellow, Teaching Fellow, and Instructor in History, Harvard Univ. and Lecturer, Boston Univ. and Northeastern College; Assist. Prof. of History, Stanford Univ. California, 1919-24; Visiting Prof., Univ. of British Columbia, Summer Session, 1936; Pres. Canadian Historical Assoc., 1938-39; Chm. Canadian Social Science Research Council, 1940-41; Mem. of Delegation of Canadian Inst. of International Affairs to Inst. of Pacific Relations Conference at Mont Tremblant, 1942, and British Commonwealth Relations Con fs. in London, 194, and at Bigwin, 1949. Member Canada-U.S. Cttee. on Education, 1944-. *Publications:* Canadian Federation: Its Origins and Achievement, 1924; Canadian History: A Syllabus and Guide to Reading, 1926; new and enlarged edition, 1934; contributor to the Cambridge History of the British Empire, Vol. VI, Canada and Newfoundland, 1930; The British Empire-Commonwealth, 1932; joint editor of Conferences on Canadian-American Affairs, 1935-1937, 1939, and 1941; North America and the War: A Canadian View, 1940; Commonwealth: Pattern for Peace?, 1944; Modern History (in collab.), 1946; Charters of Our Freedom, 1946; contrib. of U.S. and Canada to W. B. Wilcox and R. B. Hall's The United States in the Post-war World, 1947; Canada in World Affairs, Vol. III, September 1941-May 1944 (in collab.), 190; articles in current journals. *Recreations:* country, sketching. *Address:* 320 King St. W., Kingston, Ontario, Canada. *Club:* Royal Empire Society. [*Died* 7 *April* 1951.

TROUNCER, Cecil; actor (stage, films and radio); *b.* Southport, 5 Apr. 1898; *s.* of Ernest Stallard Trouncer and Edith Dennett; *m.* Queenie Russell; one *d. Educ.:* St. Wilfrid's, Bexhill-on-Sea; Clifton College. Served European War, 1914-18, 3rd Bn. Dorsetshire Regt. First London appearance, Haymarket, 1921; toured in South Africa with Macdona Players in Bernard Shaw repertory, 1925; toured in Egypt in Robert Atkins's company, playing Brutus, Hotspur, Joseph Surface, etc.; various leading parts in West End and in repertory companies, 1929-32; appeared in revue, Fanfare; with Croydon Repertory Co., 1932-34; The Man with the Bowler Hat in Emil and the Detectives, Vaudeville, 1934; at Old Vic, Sept. 1934-Feb. 1936, playing Leonato in Much Ado About Nothing, de Beaudricourt and the Inquisitor in Saint Joan, the Duke in Othello, Andrew in Major Barbara, Julius Caesar, Ivan in The Three Sisters, Sir Peter Teazle in The School for Scandal, Buckingham in Richard III, Sir Hudson Lowe in St. Helena, etc.; subsequent London successes included Ignati in A Month in the Country, Old Ekdal in The Wild Duck, Michail Astrov in Uncle Vanya, Captain Shotover in Heartbreak House, Polonius in Hamlet, Bombardone in Geneva. Malvern Festival, 1939; joined B.B.C. Drama Repertory Company, 1939; Sir Sampson Legend in Love for Love, Phoenix, 1943-44; played leading parts with John Gielgud in repertory season, Haymarket,

1944-45; toured Germany for E.N.S.A., in the Circle, 1945; played Lloyd Hartley in The Guinea Pig, Criterion, 1946; Messerschmann in Ring Round the Moon, 1950-51; Mr. Vanhatten in The Apple Cart, Haymarket, 1953. Films include: Pygmalion, While the Sun Shines, Saraband for Dead Lovers, The Guinea Pig, London Belongs to Me, The Lady With The Lamp, The Pickwick Papers. *Address:* 1 Avenue House, 191 Fulham Road, S.W.3. [*Died* 15 *Dec.* 1953.

TROY, Hon. Michael Francis; *b.* 15 Sept. 1877; 6th *s.* of late Patrick and Ellen Troy; *m.* Flora Brown, *d.* of Lauchlan and Margaret Mackinnon, Perth, Western Australia; no *c.* *Educ.:* Public School, Wardell, N.S.W. Started career as a State School Teacher, New South Wales attracted to Western Australia by gold mining boom; for some years followed mining; elected to Parliament, 1904, as the representative Mount Magnet electorate, Western Australian Parliament; re-elected 1905, 1908, and 1911; Speaker, Legislative Assembly, Western Australia, 1911-1916, Member, 1911-1939; Minister for Mines and Agriculture, West Australia, 1924-30, and of Lands and Immigration, 1927-30, and 1933-39; Agent-General for W.A. in London, 1939-46. *Recreations:* bowls and amateur carpentry. *Address:* 27 Park Rd., Mt. Lawley, Perth, W.A. *T.:* 106. [*Died* 7 *Jan.* 1953.

TRUBSHAW, Dame Gwendoline Joyce, D.B.E., *cr.* 1938 (C.B.E. 1920); J.P. Carmarthenshire; Alderman Carmarthenshire County Council, Chairman 1937-38; *d.* of late E. Trubshaw, D.L., J.P. Chairman South West Wales War Pensions Committee; Hon. County Sec. S.S.A.F.A. since 1917; County Organiser W.V.S., 1939. Member Central Health Services Council, 1951. *Address:* Caerdelyn, Llanelly. *T.:* 131. *Club:* Forum. [*Died* 8 *Nov.* 1954.

TRUEMAN, Sir Arthur Elijah, K.B.E., *cr.* 1951; F.R.S. 1942; D.Sc.Lond.; Hon. LL.D. (Rhodes, Glasgow, Leeds, Wales); *b.* 26 April 1894; *s.* of Elijah Trueman and Thirza Cottee; *m.* 1920, Florence Kate Offler; one *s.* *Educ.:* High Pavement, Nottingham; University College, Nottingham. Lectr. in Geology at Univ. Coll., Cardiff, 1917-20; Head of Department of Geology and Geography, and Professor of Geology at University College of Swansea, 1920-33; Chaning Wills Professor of Geology in the University of Bristol, 1933-37; Professor of Geology, Glasgow University, 1937-1946; Chairman of the Univ. Grants Committee, 1949-53 (Deputy Chm., 1946-49); Chairman of the Geological Survey Board, 1943-54; Member of Elliot Commission on Higher Education in West Africa, 1943-1944; President of Geological Society, 1945-1947; President, Section C, British Association, 1948; Bigsby Medal, Geological Society, 1939; Wollaston Medal, Geological Soc., 1955. *Publications:* The Scenery of England and Wales, 1938; an Introduction to Geology, 1938; (ed.) The Coalfields of Great Britain, 1954; books and papers on Geological and Palæontological subjects, particularly relating to British coalfields. *Address:* 21 Audley Road, Ealing, W.5. *T.:* Perivale 5029. *Club:* Athenæum. [*Died* 5 *Jan.* 1956.

TRUMBLE, Thomas, C.M.G. 1923; C.B.E. 1918; *b.* Ararat, Victoria, 9 Apr. 1872; *y. s.* of late William Trumble; *m.* 1899, Katherine Ellen Hutchinson; one *d.* *Educ.:* Wesley College, Melbourne. Joined the Public Service of Victoria, 1888, and Commonwealth of Australia, 1901; Acting Secretary, Nov. 1914; Secretary to Department of Defence, Commonwealth of Australia, 1918-27; Official Secretary in London Commonwealth of Australia, 1927; Defence Liaison Officer, 1931-32; retired, 1932; Director of Voluntary Services, Dept. of Defence Co-ordination, 1940-43. *Recreation:* golf. *Address:* 30 Belgrave Rd., E. Malvern, Vic., Aust. [*Died* 2 *July* 1954.

TRUST, Mrs. Helen; soprano vocalist; A.R.A.M., F.G.S.M.; *b.* Norwich; *e. d.* of Michael John Stark, *g.-niece* of James Stark the landscape painter; *m.* Henry T. Trust, professor of violoncello. *Educ.:* Norwich; Paris; Royal Academy of Music, London; pupil of Signor Tramezzani. Has sung at Leeds and Norwich Festivals, Monday Popular Concerts, Ballad concerts, and all provincial towns of note. *Publications:* Arrangements of Songs by Giordani, James Hook, etc. *Recreations:* needlework and reading. *Address:* 7 Hilgrove Road, Swiss Cottage, N.W.6. *T.:* Primrose 4536. [*Died* 3 *Aug.* 1953.

TRYE, Captain John Henry, C.B.E. 1918; D.L. Glos.; R.N., retired; 3rd *s.* of late Henry Norwood Trye, J.P., of Hartshill, Co. Warwick, and formerly of Leckhampton Court, Co. Gloucester; *b.* 1 June 1875; *m.* 1st, Elsie Marguerite, *d.* of Richard Hewitt, London; 2nd, Elizabeth Martinet, *d.* of Robert Hewitt, Ardsley-on-Hudson, New York; two *d.* (one *s.* decd.). *Educ.:* H.M.S. Britannia. Retired, 1912; Member of the Reading Borough Council, 1912-1920; Assistant to the Naval Representative of the Commonwealth of Australia in London, 1912; Admiralty Representative on the Cable Censorship, 1914-17; Liaison Officer with the United States Cable Censorship in Washington, 1917-19; Member of the Cheltenham Borough Council since 1920; Alderman, 1934; Mayor, 1932-33 and 1937-38; Member of the Gloucs. C.C., 1921-49, and Alderman 1931. Hon. Freeman of Borough of Cheltenham, 1958. U.S. Navy Cross, 1919. *Address:* Laracor, 117 Old Bath Rd., Cheltenham. *T.:* Cheltenham 4102. *Club:* Royal Automobile. [*Died* 5 *Dec.* 1959.

TSCHIFFELY, Aimé Felix; author and traveller; *b.* Switzerland, 1895; *m.* 1933, Violet Theodora Hume (Violet Marquesita). Formerly Schoolmaster; taught Park Hill, Lyndhurst, The Priory Malvern, St. George's College, Buenos Aires; Temp. Head Master Buenos Aires English High School; accomplished ride of over 10,000 miles through three Americas, from Buenos Aires to Washington, D.C.; took up writing in 1929; first articles in National Geographic Magazine (U.S.A.), followed by publications (English and Spanish) in Argentine, English, and American newspapers, magazines, and periodicals. *Publications:* From Southern Cross to Pole Star, 1933; Tschiffely's Ride; The Tale of Two Horses; Bridle Paths, 1936; Don Roberto, 1937; This Way Southward, 1940; Coricancha (Garden of Gold), 1943; Ming and Ping, 1947; Bohemia Junction, 1950; Round and About Spain, 1952; The Man from Woodpecker Creek, 1953. *Club:* Savage. [*Died* 5 *Jan.* 1954.

TSEN, Rt. Rev. P(hilip) Lindel. *Educ.:* Boone College and Divinity School, Wuchang, China, B.A., 1908; Philadelphia Divinity School, U.S.A., S.T.B., 1925; University of Pennsylvania, U.S.A., M.A., 1926. Hon. Degrees: S.T.D., Philadelphia Divinity School, 1929; D.D., Wycliffe College, Canada, 1929, Virginia Theological Seminary, U.S.A., 1929, St. John's University, Shanghai, China, 1929, Trinity College, Canada, 1930, King's College, Halifax, N.S. and Huron College, London, Ont. Dean of Cathedral Anking, China, 1926-28; Assistant Bishop of Honan, 1929-35; Bishop of Honan, 1935-49; retired, 1949. Chairman of House of Bishops, Chung Hua Sheng King Hui (Anglican Communion in China), 1947-49. Returned from Canada to China, 1951. *Address:* c/o Church House, 604 Jarvis Street, Toronto, Canada. [*Died* 6 *June* 1954.

TUCK, Colonel Charles Harold Amys, C.I.E. 1921; late 3rd Q.A.O. Gurkha Rifles (Indian Army); retired, 1928; *b.* 6 Dec. 1880; *s.* of Albert Hustler Tuck and H. Lumb; *g.s.* of C. E. Tuck, J.P., of Blofield, Norfolk; *m.* 1910, Sybil Marguerite, *d.* of John Julius Dare, member of Council, Georgetown, Demerara; one *s.* one *d.* *Educ.:* Wellington College. Gazetted to 3rd Norfolk Regt., 1900; served S. Africa 1900-1 (Queen's medal and 3 clasps); gazetted to 1st Norfolk Regt., 1901; 1/3rd Gurkhas, 1904; Captain, 1909; Major, 1917; Lt.-Col., 1924; Col., 1925; served European War, Mesopotamia (despatches); S. Kurdistan (despatches, Brevet Lt.-Col.); Iraq, 1920 (despatches, C.I.E.); War of 1939-1945, in R.O.C. and Home Guard, 1940-44. *Address:* Brook House, Rickinghall, Diss. *T.:* Botesdale 47. [*Died* 5 *Nov.* 1951.

TUCK, Major Sir (William) Reginald, 2nd Bt., *cr.* 1910; late 3rd County of London Yeomanry (Sharpshooters); late Joint Managing Director Raphael Tuck & Sons, Ltd., art publishers; *b.* 8 July 1883; *s.* of 1st Bt. and Jeanetta (*d.* 1948), *d.* of late William Flatau of Lusan House, Highbury; *S.* father, 1926; *m.* 1917, Gladys, 2nd *d.* of late N. Alfred Nathan of Wickford, Auckland, N.Z., and *widow* of Desmond Fosberry Kettle, Lieut. Auckland Mounted Rifles; one *s.* two *d.* *Educ.:* Clifton. Served War of 1914-18 with 3rd County of London Yeomanry (Sharpshooters); Major, 1916; Royal Humane Society's Silver Medal for life saving (New Zealand Branch). *Heir:* *s.* Bruce Adolph Reginald, *b.* 29 June 1926. *Address:* 321 Rodney House, Dolphin Square, S.W.1. *Club:* Junior Carlton. [*Died* 12 *May* 1954.

TUCKER, Rev. John Savile, M.A.; *b.* 1 March 1866; *s.* of J. H. Tucker, Bank of England, Bristol; *m.* 1896, H. Grace Darley (*d.* 1932); one *s.* one *d.* *Educ.:* Bristol Grammar School; Balliol College, Oxford. Open Scholarship, 1885; Junior University Mathematical Exhibition, 1887; 1st Class Hons. Mathematical Moderations, 1887; Junior University Mathematical Scholarship, 1888; 1st Class Honours Final School of Mathematics and Physics, 1889; Senior University Mathematical Scholarship, 1890; Assistant Master at Rugby School, 1889; Assistant Master at Wellington College, 1890-95; Headmaster of Trent College, 1895-1927; Vicar of Christ Church, Great Malvern, 1928-35; retired 1935; elected on the Headmasters' Conference, 1899; Examining Chaplain to the Bishop of Liverpool, 1900. *Publications:* Trent College Hymn Book; Supplementary Prayer Book; Officer Training Corps Service Book. *Address:* The Midland Bank, Bath. [*Died* 24 *Jan.* 1954.

TUCKER, Lieut.-Colonel William Kington, C.B.E. 1919; T.D.; Officer Belgian Ordre de la Couronne; King's Jubilee Medal, 1935; Coronation Medal, 1937; Managing Director East African Estates, Ltd., and their associated company; Member Joint East African Board; *b.* 23 July 1877; *s.* of late W. Lambly Tucker, Calne, Wiltshire; *m.* 1934, Mildred, 2nd *d.* of H. W. J. Lavers, 40 Carlton Hill, St. John's Wood, N.W.8. *Educ.:* privately. Joined 4th V.B. Wilts Regt. 1900; transferred R.A.S.C. (T.) 1908; Brigade Supply Officer, 2nd S.W. Mounted Brigade; Assistant Director Supplies, War Office, with rank of Lt.-Col. 1917; Manager and Secretary, C. and T. Harris & Co. Ltd., Calne, Wilts, prior to European War, at termination of which accepted appointment in British E. Africa (now Kenya). *Recreation:* golf. *Address:* Crabtrees, Pembury Grange, Tunbridge Wells. *T.:* Pembury 223. [*Died* 4 *Oct.* 1956.

TUCKWELL, Gertrude Mary, C.H. 1930; J.P.; *b.* 1861; *d.* of Rev. William Tuckwell. *Educ.:* at home. Member of Advisory Committee to the Lord Chancellor for Women Justices of the Peace; Member of Women's Central Committee on Women's Training and Employment; J.P. St. George's, Hanover Square; Elementary Schoolmistress under London Board, 1885-92; Secretary to her aunt, Lady Dilke, and Hon. Secretary to Women's Trade Union League, 1892-1904; Ex-President of Women's Trade Union League. Served on various Committees for Ministry of Reconstruction, and on Advisory Committee to Ministry of Health, 1905-23; Member of Advisory Committee appointed to report to Lord Chancellor on List of suitable women for Justices of Peace, 1921-22; Member of Royal Commission National Health Insurance, 1924-1926; Ex-Pres. Women Public Health Officers Assoc.; Ex-Chairman National Assoc. of Probation Officers. *Publications:* completed and edited the Life of Sir Charles Dilke; has prepared a short Life of Sir Charles W. Dilke for W.E.A.; The State and its Children; Workers Handbook; articles on industrial questions in numerous journals. *Address:* Little Woodlands, Wormley, Godalming. [*Died* 5 *Aug.* 1951.

TUDHOPE, George Ranken, M.B., Ch.B., Ph.D., D.P.H., M.D. (Honours) (St. Andrews); F.R.S.E.; Senior Lecturer in Pathology, University of St. Andrews; Pathologist, Dundee Royal Infirmary; Warden, Airlie Hall, Queen's Coll., Dundee; Past Pres., Association of University Teachers, 1953-54; *b.* Newport, Fife, 7 July 1893; *e. s.* of late George Tudhope; *m.* 1st, 1922, Elizabeth Florence (*d.* 1946), *d.* of late James McCombe, Dundee; one *s.*; 2nd, 1949, Christian Johnston, M.A., LL.B., J.P., *d.* of late Christopher J. Bisset, O.B.E. *Educ.:* High Sch. of Dundee; University of St. Andrews (Rutherford Gold Medal, 1937). F.R.I.P.H.H.; Hon. Treasurer, Students Charities Campaigns, Dundee, 1925-1945; House Surgeon and House Physician, Dundee Royal Infirmary; Assistant in Anatomy, University College, Dundee; President Students' Union, 1916-17, 1917-18; Assistant in Pathology, Univ. of St. Andrews. *Publications:* papers to med. journals. *Address:* Warden's House, Airlie Hall, 1 Airlie Place, Dundee. *T.:* 3396. [*Died* 12 *Dec.* 1955.

TUFNELL, Lt.-Commander Richard Lionel; Royal Navy (retd.); M.A.; *b.* 10 Dec. 1896; *s.* of Lieut.-Col. Edward Tufnell, late Conservative M.P. for S.E. Essex, and Ellen Bertha Gubbins; *m.* 1922, Eleanor Dorothy Falconer; one *s.* *Educ.:* Osborne and Dartmouth; Navy; Trinity College, Cambridge. Served with the Royal Navy during European War; M.P. (National Conservative) Cambridge Borough, 1934-45; Member of the Board of Guardians and Public Assistance Committee for St. George's, 1928-31. *Recreations:* shooting, tennis, painting. *Address:* 46 Boscobel Place, Eaton Square, S.W.1. *T.:* Sloane 3605; Manor House, Calmsden, Cirencester. *T.:* North Cerney 247. *Clubs:* Carlton, United Service, 1900. [*Died* 1 *Oct.* 1956.

TUKE, Colonel John Melville, C.B.E. 1938 (O.B.E. 1931); Retired Pay, Royal Marines; *b.* 19 July 1885; *s.* of late Commander F. M; and Mrs. C. E. Tuke; *m.* 1924, Gwladys Ruth; 2nd *d.* of late Dr. E. J. Lewis. *Educ.:* King's School, Canterbury. 2nd Lt., Royal Marine Artillery 1903; Captain, 1914; Major, 1924; Brevet Lieut.-Colonel, 1932; Lieut.-Colonel, 1933; Colonel 2nd Commandant, 1936; Retired, 1938. *Recreation:* fishing. *Address:* Meridian Lodge, Robertsbridge, Sussex. [*Died* 9 *Oct.* 1958.

TUN, Hon. Sir Paw, Kt., *cr.* 1938; A.T.M., Barrister-at-Law; Home and Judicial Minister and Member of Executive Council, Burma, since 1945; *s.* of U. Rai Phaw of Akyab, Burma; *m.* Sarah Elesabeth, *d.* of Dr. E. H. Jewitt, Cleveland, Ohio, U.S.A.; one *d.* Minister of Home and Judicial Affairs, Burma, 1937-38; also acting Chief Minister in 1937; Minister of Lands and Revenue, 1939-41; Acting Premier, 1941-42; Prime Minister of Burma, 1942. *Address:* Rangoon, Burma. [*Died* 28 *Feb.* 1953.

TUPPER, Sir Charles (Stewart), 2nd Bt., *cr.* 1888; barrister; Captain, 79th Cameron Highlanders of Canada; *b.* 8 Aug. 1884; *s.* of late James Stewart Tupper, K.C. (*e. s.* of Sir Charles Tupper, 1st Bt.) and Ada Campbell, *d.* of late Sir Thomas Galt, Toronto; *S.* grandfather, 1915; *m.* 1910, Margaret Peters, *d.* of Charles Morse, K.C., Ottawa; one *d.* *Educ.:* Upper Canada College, Toronto; Harrow

School; McGill University, Montreal (B.A., 1905). Called to Manitoba Bar, 1908; Q.C. 1929; Member of legal firm of Tupper, Tupper, Adams, and McDonald, Winnipeg; served European War, 1915-19. *Recreation:* shooting. *Heir:* c. Charles Tupper, *b.* 1880. *Address:* 2 Rosslyn Place, Winnipeg, Canada. *T.A.:* Tupper, Winnipeg. *Clubs:* Manitoba, Adanac, Hunt, St. Charles Country (Winnipeg). [*Died* 16 *July* 1960.

TURBERVILL, Edith P.; *see* Picton-Turbervill.

TURING, Alan Mathison, O.B.E. 1946; F.R.S. 1951; Reader in Mathematics, Manchester University, since 1948; *b.* 23 June 1912; *s.* of Julius Mathison Turing and Ethel Sara Turing (*née* Stoney); unmarried. *Educ.:* Sherborne; King's College, Cambridge. Fellow, King's College, Cambridge, 1935; Foreign Office, 1939-45; National Physical Laboratory, 1945-48. *Publications:* papers in mathematical and other journals. *Recreations:* long distance running, chess, gardening. *Address:* Hollymeade, Adlington Rd., Wilmslow, Cheshire. [*Died* 7 *June* 1954.

TURNBULL, Col. Bruce, C.B.E. 1937; T.D. 1950; D.L. Edinburgh; I.A. (retd.); p.s.c.; *b.* 4 Nov. 1880; 2nd *s.* of late Major-General P. S. Turnbull, Hon. Surgeon to the King, and late Mary Oliver, Borthaugh, Hawick; *m.* Jessie Barbara Allan, *d.* of late Thomas Ker, Edinburgh; two *s.* two *d.* *Educ.:* Merchiston Castle School; Royal Military College, Sandhurst. Joined Indian Army, 1900, 23 Sikh Pioneers; served in N.W.F., Waziristan, 1901-2 (medal and clasp); Tibet, 1903-4 (medal and clasp); N.W.F. Zakha Khel, 1908 (medal and clasp); European War, 1914-18 (despatches, brevet Lt.-Colonel); N.W.F., Afghanistan, 1919 (clasp); Staff College, Camberley, 1921; Colonel, 1923; Inspector of Physical Training (India), 1922-26; Commanded 155 (East Scottish) Infantry Bde. (T.A.), 1932-36; Member Edinburgh Education Authority, 1928-30; President Scottish Hockey Assoc., 1935-37; Member Edinburgh Town Council since 1938, Bailie 1944-47, Senior Bailie, 1947; Senior Military Liaison Officer, Scottish Region, 1939-41; Deputy Commissioner, S.E. District, Scottish Region, 1941-1944; White Eagle (Serbia). *Recreations:* golf, gardening, philately, etc. *Address:* 13 Albert Terrace, Edinburgh. *T.:* 51447. *Clubs:* Junior United Service; New (Edinburgh). [*Died* 21 *Jan.* 1952.

TURNBULL, Hubert Maitland, F.R.S. 1939; Hon. D.Sc. (Oxon) 1945; M.A., D.M. (Oxon), F.R.C.P.; Consulting Morbid Anatomist, at the London Hospital, 1946; *b.* 3 March 1875; 2nd *s.* of late Andrew H. Turnbull, Edinburgh, and Margaret Lothian, *d.* of Adam Black, M.P. for City of Edinburgh; *m.* 1916, Catherine Nairne Arnold (*d.* 1933), *d.* of late F. Arnold Baker; three *s.* one *d.* *Educ.:* St. Ninian's, Moffat; Charterhouse; Magdalen College, Oxford; London Hospital; Copenhagen; Dresden, voluntary assistant to Prof. Schmorl, 1905-06. Director of Pathological Institute (Bernhard Baron Institute of Pathology, 1927) of London Hospital, 1906-46; Prof. of Morbid Anatomy, in London Univ., Emeritus 1947. Hons. (2nd class) Classical Moderations, 1896, and Physiology, 1898; James Welch University Prize, Oxford, 1899; Price Scholarship, 1900, and Anderson Prize, London Hospital, 1900; Radcliffe Travelling Fellow, Univ. Coll. Oxford, 1904-06; Examiner in Radcliffe Prize, Oxford, 1913; Examiner in Pathology, Oxford, 1913-16. Hon. Member of Pathological Society of Great Britain and Ireland, Association of Clinical Pathologists and Pathological Section of Royal Society of Medicine. *Publications:* Bilateral loss of post-central cortex, Brain, 1904; editor of and contributor to Archives of Pathological Institute, London Hospital, 1908; papers on morbid anatomy; The Scales of Salmon, Field, 1909-10. *Recreations:* golf, fishing, ornithology, geology; played for Oxford *v.* Cambridge, and United Universities *v.* London, Association football, 1897. *Address:* Balgarvie, St. John's, Woking. [*Died* 29 *Sept.* 1955.

TURNBULL, Jane Holland, C.B.E.; M.D., B.S. Lond.; retired; *d.* of late Lt.-Col. Archibald Turnbull, Vet. Service, Indian Army. *Educ.:* Edinburgh; Reading; Lond. Roy. Free Hospital School of Medicine for Women. Lately on Honorary Medical Staff of Elizabeth Garrett Anderson Hospital and South London Hospital for Women; War Service: Controller of Medical Services, Queen Mary's Army Auxiliary Corps; Medical Officer Ministry of Health, 1919-36. *Address:* c/o Westminster Bank Ltd., 133 Baker St., W.1. [*Died* 15 *Oct.* 1958.

TURNBULL, Sir Roland (Evelyn), K.C.M.G. 1956 (C.M.G. 1946); retired as Governor and Commander-in-Chief, North Borneo (1954-60); *b.* 9 June 1905; *s.* of late George Turnbull, Berwick-on-Tweed; *m.* 1948, Sylvia, *d.* of Sir (Richard) Woodman Burbidge, 2nd Bt. *Educ.:* King's College, London; St. John's College, Oxford. Malayan Civil Service, 1929; served in Federated Malay States, Trengganu; acted as Secretary to High Commissioner for Unfederated Malay States; British Resident, Brunei, 1934; seconded to Colonial Office, 1937; Controller of Foreign Exchange, Malaya, 1939; Colonial Secretary, British Honduras, 1940-43; Colonel (C.A.), War Office, 1943-45; Colonial Secretary, Cyprus, 1945-50; Chief Secretary, High Commission Territories, South Africa, 1950-53. *Club:* East India and Sports. [*Died* 23 *Dec.* 1960.

TURNER, Brig.-Gen. Arthur Jervois, C.B. 1920; C.M.G. 1918; D.S.O. 1915; late R.A.; *b.* 10 June 1878; *m.* 1912, Maud (*d.* 1913), *o. c.* of late Michael Walton. *Educ.:* R. Mil. Academy (Sword of Honour). Entered army, 1897; Captain, 1905; Major, 1914; with West African Frontier Force, 1903-4; General Staff Officer, 3rd Grade, Aldershot Command, 1911-1913; p.s.c.; served South Africa, 1899-1900 and 1902 (severely wounded; despatches, Bt. Major; Queen's medal 5 clasps, King's medal 1 clasp); West Africa, 1904 (medal with clasp); European War (Cameroons and France), 1914-18 (despatches, D.S.O., Bt. Lt.-Col., Brevet Col., C.M.G.); Operations in N. Russia (despatches, C.B.); G.S.O.1. Kohat District, 1921-25; Operations in Waziristan, 1923 (medal and clasp, despatches); B.G.G.S. Egypt, 1925-29; retired pay, 1930. *Address:* Malt House, Graffham, Sussex. *Clubs:* Junior United Service, Army and Navy. [*Died* 8 *Sept.* 1952.

TURNER, Major Charles Cyril, late R.A.F.; F.R.Ae.S.; *b.* 30 April 1870; *y. s.* of late Frederick Turner; *m.* 1898, Agnes Maude, *e. d.* of late William Henry Nash, Brighton; one *s.* Writer; much flying and ballooning; Aviator's Certificate, No. 70, Royal Aero Club; also balloon pilot; was in the late A. E. Gaudron's balloon on record (British) voyage from London to Mateki Derevni, Russia, 1117 miles, Nov. 1908; also London-Sweden, Oct. 1907, when world oversea record was made; on Cairo-Cape aeroplane attempt (pilot, Major Brackley); machine wrecked 70 miles N. of Atbara, Feb. 1920; on outbreak of war, 1914, was granted commission, and attached R.N.A.S.; throughout war engaged in instructional and experimental work; one brief visit France (despatches); Chief Instructor School Military Aeronautics, Oxford. *Publications:* Cantor Lectures on Aeronautics, Royal Society of Arts, 1909; Aerial Navigation of To-day, 1909; Flying: some Practical Experiences (with Hamel), 1914; The Struggle in the Air, 1914-1918, 1919; The Old Flying Days, 1927; Britain's Air Peril, 1933; My Flying Scrap Book, 1946, etc.; many contributions on aeronautics in Field,

Daily Telegraph, Aeronautical Journal, etc.; novels, Dusk and Dawn; Unlawful; The Secret of the Desert. *Address:* 21 Lanercost Road, Tulse Hill, S.W.2. *T.:* Tulse Hill 1973. *Club:* Royal Aero. [*Died* 7 *Dec.* 1952.

TURNER, Vice-Adm. Charles W. R.; *see* Round-Turner.

TURNER, Maj. Clarence Roy, C.M.G. 1947; E.D.; A.M.I.Mech.E.; late Gen. Manager and Harbour Authority, Gold Coast Govt. Railways; *b.* 4 Sept. 1891; Australian. *Educ.:* Brompton Public School; School of Mines, Adelaide. Served European War, 1914-18, with Australian Forces; Great Southern of Spain Rly, 1919-22; Colonial Service, 1923-47. *Address:* c/o Barclay's Bank, 137 North End Rd., W.14. *Club:* Royal Automobile. [*Died* 9 *Jan.* 1957.

TURNER, Dudley Charles, C.M.G. 1951; F.C.I.S.; *b.* Gundagai, N.S.W., 1 Nov. 1885; *s.* of late M. W. Macartney Turner; *m.* 1913, Kathleen Maud, *d.* of late A. Ernest Ayers, Adelaide, S.A.; one *d.* *Educ.:* Sydney Grammar School. Royal Australian Naval Radio Service, 1918. Member: Bd. Management (and Hon. Treas.) Adelaide Children's Hosp., 1930-47; Gen. Cttee. Exec. and Finance, St. Mark's Coll. (Univ. of Adelaide), 1923- (Chm. Fin. 1927-), Hon. Fellow, 1947, Chairman Council, 1954. Gen. Cttee. Roy. Automobile Assoc. of S.A., 1931- (Chm. 1946, Pres. and Chm. 1951); Vice-Chm. of Australian Red Cross and Comr. at Land Headquarters, Melbourne, 1940-42, Chm. 1942-44. Liberal and Country League of S.A.: Deputy Chm. and Chm. Finance Cttee., 1932-40; Pres. 1947, and 1950-53. O.St.J. 1947. *Recreation:* golf. *Address:* 256 Stanley Street, North Adelaide, South Australia; Thorpe, Crafers, S.A. *Clubs:* Bath; Adelaide (Adelaide); Union (Sydney). [*Died* 3 *March* 1958.

TURNER, Ethel, (Mrs. H. R. Curlewis); novelist; *b.* Yorkshire, 24 Jan. 1872; father a manufacturer; *m.* 1896, H. R. Curlewis, B.A., LL.B. (*d.* 1942), barrister-at-law (Judge Curlewis); one *s.* (one *d.* decd.). *Educ.:* The Girls' High School, Sydney, N.S.W. *Publications:* Seven Little Australians, 1894; The Family at Misrule, 1895; The Story of a Baby; The Little Duchess; The Little Larrikin, 1896; Miss Bobbie, 1897; The Camp at Wandinong, 1898; Three Little Maids, 1900; The Wonder Child, 1901; Betty and Co., 1902; Little Mother Meg, 1904; White Roof Tree, 1905; In the Mist of the Mountains, 1906; The Stolen Voyage, 1907; That Girl, 1908; Fugitives from Fortune, 1909; Fair Ines, 1910; The Apple of Happiness, 1911; Ports and Happy Havens, 1912; The Secret of the Sea, 1913; Flower o' the Pine, 1914; The Cub, 1915; John of Daunt, 1916; Captain Cub, 1917; St. Tom and the Dragon, 1918; Brigid and the Cub, 1919; Laughing Water, 1920; King Anne, 1921; Jennifer J., 1922; Nicola Silver, 1924; The Ungardeners, 1925; Funny, 1926; Judy and Punch, 1929; Seven Little Australians, produced at Australian theatres, 1915, produced as a film, 1939. First Australian book televised by B.B.C. as a serial, 1953; broadcast as a serial in Australia and S. Africa, 1953. *Address:* Avenel, 17 Warringah Road, Mosman, Sydney, N.S.W. [*Died* 8 *April* 1958.

TURNER, Frank Douglas, C.B.E. 1942; M.B. (Lond.), etc.; retired; late Medical Supt., Royal Eastern Counties' Institution for Mental Defectives; *b.* 8 Oct. 1871; *s.* of John J. C. Turner, Essex Hall, Colchester; *m.* 1900, Louisa Caroline Dalby; no *c.* *Educ.:* Neuwied, Germany; Guy's Hospital. Asst. Demonstrator and House Surgeon, Guy's Hosp.; General Practice, Huddersfield; Med. Officer, and in 1914 Med. Supt., Royal Institution, Colchester; Past Pres. R.M.P.A.; Hon. Mem. and Past Chm. Mental Deficiency Committee; Vice-Pres. and late Chm. Executive Council C.A.M.W.; Past-Pres. Assoc. of Institutions previously under Idiots Act; Vice-Pres. Nat. Assoc. Mental Health; Past-Chm., S.E. Division Mental Health Workers' Assoc. Served on two Departmental Committees. Hon. Mem. American Assoc. for Mental Deficiency. *Recreations:* climbing and Masonry. *Address:* 8A Beverley Road, Colchester, Essex. *T.:* Colchester 4831. [*Died* 1 *Nov.* 1957.

TURNER, George Grey, LL.D. Glas. (Hon.); D.Ch. Dunelm (Hon.); M.S. Dunelm; F.R.C.S. Eng.; F.R.C.S.Ed. (Hon.); F.A.C.S. (Hon.); F.R.A.C.S. (Hon.); Emeritus Professor of Surgery in the Universities of Durham and London; Director of Dept. of Surgery at the British Postgraduate Hospital and Medical School, 1934-1946; Consulting Surgeon Royal Infirmary, Newcastle-upon-Tyne; Hon. Consulting Surgeon, King Edward VII Hospital, Windsor and Tynemouth Infirmary; Member of Council, 1926-50 (Vice-Pres. 1937-39) Royal College of Surgeons of England; a trustee of the Hunterian Collection, R.C.S.; Hunterian Prof. R.C.S.; Bradshaw Lecturer, 1935; Hunterian Orator, 1945; Perpetual Student, St. Bartholemew's Medical College; Major, R.A.M.C. (T.); *b.* 8 Sept. 1877; *s.* of James Grey Turner; *m.* 1908, Alice Grey, B.Sc., *d.* of late F. E. Schofield, J.P., Morpeth; one *s.* three *d.* *Educ.:* University of Durham; King's College; Vienna. Served European War, 1914-19, at home and overseas; late Acting Consulting Surgeon, Amara; District Consulting Surgeon and Specialist in Chest Surgery, Northern Command; Fellow Assoc. Surgeons, Pres. 1928; F.R.S.M., Pres. Clinical Section and past Pres. Section of Surgery, and sub-Section Proctology; Pres. Med. Soc. of London, 1943-44; Orator, 1929, Lettsomian Lecturer, 1939; past Vice-Pres. and Pres. Section of Surgery B.M.A.; Membre d'Honneur, Internat. Soc. of Surgery and Pres. XIIIth Congress, New Orleans, 1949. Hon. Fellow American Surgical Association; Hon. and Corresponding Member numerous other medical and surgical societies in England, Europe and America; delivered John B. Murphy Oration at Clinical Congress, American Coll. of Surgeons in Philadelphia, 1930; H. J. Bigelow medal conferred in Boston, 1931, and delivered Bigelow Oration; Macewen Memorial Lecturer, 1939; Prosser White Oration, 1939; Donald Balfour Lecture Univ. Tononto, 1939; George Halliburton Hume Memorial Lectures, 1943; Moynihan Memorial Lecture, 1949; Mem. Barbers Company and Freeman, City of London; Liveryman Society of Apothecaries. *Publications:* Encouragements in Cancer Surgery; (with W. D. Arnison) The Newcastle-upon-Tyne School of Medicine; The Paget Tradition; Injuries and Diseases of the Oesophagus; contributor to Choyce's System of Surgery, and Editor Modern Operative Surgery; consulting Editor: for Surgery, The British Encyclopædia of Medical Practice, British Surgical Practice; Medical and Surgical Notes from Mesopotamia; Notes on Visits to some American Hospitals, and numerous contributions to surgical literature. *Recreations:* travelling and archæology. *Address:* Huntercombe Manor, Taplow, Bucks. *T.:* Burnham 403. [*Died* 24 *Aug.* 1951.

TURNER, Ven. John Carpenter, M.A. Cantab.; Hon. Canon of Winchester, 1920; *b.* 12 Nov. 1867; *m.*; two *s.* one *d.* Deacon, 1890; Priest, 1891; Vicar of Whitchurch, 1899-1910; Rector of Overton, Hants, 1910-1934; Archdeacon of Basingstoke, 1927-47. *Address:* Abbey Hill Hotel, Winchester. [*Died* 9 *Feb.* 1952.

TURNER, Colonel John Eamer, C.M.G. 1919; D.S.O. 1917; Scottish Rifles; retd. pay; *b.* 1880; *o. s.* of late H. J. C. Turner, Calcutta; *m.* 1908, Una Gertrude (*d.* 1951), *d.* of Tom Nickalls, Patteson Court, Nutfield, Sy.; two *s.* two *d.* *Educ.:* Cheltenham; Sandhurst; Staff College, Camberley; Hon. M.A.

Oxon. Served S. African War, 1899-1902 (Queen's medal with two clasps, King's medal with two clasps); European War, 1914-19 (despatches, D.S.O., Legion of Honour, Brevet Lieut.-Col., Belgian Croix de Guerre, Italian Order St. Maurice and Lazarus, Italian Croce di Guerra, C.M.G.); War of 1939-45 (Defence medal, War medal). *Address:* Newdigate House, Knole Rd., Bexhill-on-Sea, Sussex. *T.:* Bexhill 2578. [*Died* 25 *Nov.* 1955.

TURNER, Colonel Sir John Fisher, Kt., *cr.* 1941; C.B. 1936; D.S.O. 1918; *b.* 24 Apr. 1881; *s.* of late Alweyne Turner, barrister-at-law, and Violet, 4th *d.* of late Surgeon-General Thorpe; unmarried. *Educ.:* Rugby; R.M.A., Woolwich. Commissioned in Royal Engineers, 1900; retired, 1931; served N.W. Frontier, 1908 (medal and clasp); European War (despatches 5 times, D.S.O., Legion of Honour, Bt. Lieut.-Col.); Chief Engineer, Royal Air Force, India, 1928-31; Director of Works and Buildings, Air Ministry, 1931-39. *Recreations:* aviation, shooting. *Address:* 73 St. James's Street, S.W. *T.:* Hyde Park 6242. *Clubs:* United Service, Royal Automobile. [*Died* 21 *May* 1958.

TURNER, John Hastings; dramatic author; *b.* London, 16 Dec. 1892; *s.* of Augustus Turner and Annie Hockley; *m.* Laura Cowie. *Educ.:* Rugby School; St. John's College, Oxford. *Publications:* The Affairs of Men (novel), 1932; Simple Souls; A Place in the World; The Cloak of Gold, (Novels); Bear, Mouse and Waterbeetle, 1938. *Plays and Revues:* Account Rendered, 1913; Havoc, 1913; Iris Intervenes, 1915, Nothing New, 1916; Bubbly, 1917; A Breath of Fresh Air, 1917; Tails Up, 1918; Hullo, America, 1918; Ladies and Gentlemen, 1919; Back Again, 1919; Everywoman's Privilege, 1920; The Naughty Princess (from the French), 1920; Jumble Sale, 1920; The Lilies of the Field, 1923; The Sea Urchin, 1925; The Scarlet Lady, 1926; The Spot on the Sun, 1927; The Lord of the Manor, 1928; Wake Up and Dream, 1929; To Account Rendered, 1931; Punchinello, 1932; (with Roland Pertwee) This Inconstancy, 1933; For the Defence, 1935; Mother's Gone A Hunting, 1938. *Recreations:* golf and fishing. *Address:* Blue Tile Farm, Brancaster, King's Lynn, Norfolk. *T.:* Brancaster 66. *Clubs:* Garrick, Dramatists'. [*Died* 29 *Feb.* 1956.

TURNER, His Honour Judge Maxwell Joseph Hall; an additional Judge of Mayor's and City of London Court, 1959; *b.* 10 May 1907; *s.* of Augustus Turner and Annie Margaret Hockley; *m.* 1938, Fabia Drake; one *d.* *Educ.:* Rugby School; Trinity College, Oxford. Called to Bar, Inner Temple, 1930; Bencher, 1959. Prosecuting Counsel to P.O. on South-Eastern Circuit, 1935; Military Asst., Office of Judge Advocate Gen., 1939-45. Served War of 1939-45; Captain 1939, Major 1941, Lieut.-Col., 1943. Counsel to Director of Public Prosecutions in certain Appeals, 1945; Third Junior Counsel to the Crown at the Central Criminal Court, 1950, Second Junior Prosecuting Counsel, 1950, First Junior Prosecuting Counsel, 1953; Third Senior Prosecuting Counsel to the Crown at the Central Criminal Court, 1954-58; Second Senior Prosecuting Counsel, 1958; First Senior Prosecuting Counsel to the Crown at the Central Criminal Court, 1959; Recorder of Great Yarmouth, 1953-1958; Dep. Chm., East Kent Quarter Sessions, 1957-60; Recorder of Hastings, 1958-59. *Publications:* (Joint Editor) Archbold's Criminal Pleading, 30th edn. *Address:* 2 Royal Avenue, Chelsea, S.W.3. *T.:* Sloane 5316; Deudraeth Castle, Penrhyndeudraeth, Merioneth. *T.:* Penrhyndeudraeth 360. *Club:* Garrick. [*Died* 10 *Dec.* 1960.

TURNER, Philip, M.B., M.S., B.Sc. (Lond.), F.R.C.S.(Eng.); Consulting Surgeon to Guy's Hospital; Major R.A.M.C. (T.C.) retired; formerly Senior Surgeon Joyce Green Hospital and the E.M.S.; *b.* 27 December 1873; *s.* of Arthur James Turner, Kensington; *m.* 1908, Helen B. Lambert, O.B.E. (*d.* 1932). *Educ.:* King's College, University College and Guy's Hospital. Fellow Royal Soc. of Medicine and of Assoc. of Surgeons; formerly Lecturer on Surgery and Teacher of Operative Surgery, Guy's Hospital and Medical School; Civil Examiner in Surgery to the Admiralty; Examiner in Surgery to Society of Apothecaries. *Publications:* The Operations of Surgery (Joint), 8th edition 1936; Papers and reports of cases to Proc. Roy. Soc. Med., Brit. Journ. of Surgery and other medical journals. *Address:* Overseas League, St. James's, S.W.1; 129 Old Church Street, Chelsea, S.W.3. [*Died* 16 *Feb.* 1955.

TURNER, Lt.-Col. Reginald, D.S.O. 1900; *b.* 1870; *s.* of F. Turner, surgeon. *Educ.:* St. John's College, Cambridge. Served S. Africa, Lt. South African Light Horse, 1899-1901 (despatches three times, medal, six bars, D.S.O.); European War, 1914-19, Capt. Special Reserve 3rd Dragoon Guards, Major Royal Fusiliers, Lt.-Col. 1917, Comd. 6th Bn. Northamptonshire Regt. (wounded, despatches, bar to D.S.O.); in War of 1939-45: Capt. from 1939, P.O.W. *Clubs:* Carlton, Boodle's. [*Died* 9 *Oct.* 1953.

TURNER, Colonel Reginald George, C.M.G. 1918; D.S.O. 1917; F.R.C.S., I.M.S. retired; *b.* 1870; *s.* of Surgeon Major A. F. Turner, A.M.S.; *m.* 1907, Beatrice Maria (*d.* 1935), *d.* of W. H. Marks and *widow* of Rev. W. F. Ommanney; *m.* 1946, Amy Janet *d.* of E. Colston Hiles and *widow* of W. Richard Musgrave, Cape Mounted Rifles. Served Waziristan Expedition, 1894-95 (medal and clasp); Uganda, 1897-98 (despatches, medal and two clasps); China, 1900 (medal); European War, 1914-18 (despatches, C.M.G., D.S.O.); retired 1923. *Address:* Dene Hollow, 11 Ardmore Road, Parkstone, Dorset. *Club:* East India and Sports. [*Died* 9 *Feb.* 1953.

TURNER, Sir Samuel, Kt., *cr.* 1938; Hon. LL.D. (Manchester); J.P.; High Sheriff of Lancashire, 1930; Freeman of Rochdale, 1937; Deputy Chairman of Turner & Newall, Ltd. (Chm., 1929-46), Director of Subsidiary Companies of Turner & Newall, Ltd.; *b.* 18 Feb. 1878; *s.* of Robert Turner, Rochdale; *m.* 1902, Jane Fielden; one *s.* one *d.* *Educ.:* Schools in England, Germany, and Switzerland. President, Devonshire Royal Hospital, Buxton, 1938-1939. Vice-Chairman of the District Bank, 1942-49. Formerly Member of Court of Governors of Victoria University of Manchester. *Publications:* (with late H. B. Gray) Eclipse or Empire, 1916; From War to Work, 1918. *Recreations:* travel, yachting, golf. *Address:* North Dean, Hughenden, High Wycombe, Bucks. [*Died* 23 *Dec.* 1955.

TURNER, Thomas, M.Sc., A.R.S.M., F.R.I.C.; Prof. Emeritus of Metallurgy, University, Birmingham; *b.* 1861; *s.* of H. Turner, of Ladywood, Birmingham; *m.* 1887, Christian, *y. d.* of C. F. Smith, of Edinburgh; two *s.* two *d.* *Educ.:* Edgbaston; Royal School of Mines, London; De la Beche Medallist. Demonstrator of Chemistry, Mason College, 1883; Lecturer in Metallurgy, 1887; Director of Technical Instruction to the Staffordshire County Council, 1894-1902; Professor of Metallurgy, University of Birmingham, 1902-26; Past President Institute of Metals; Member of Advisory Committee, Imperial Institute; Councils of British Cast Iron, and Non-Ferrous Research Associations; Bessemer Gold Medallist and Hon. Vice-Pres. Iron and Steel Institute; Seaman Gold Medallist, Amer. Foundrymen's Assoc.; Fox Gold Medallist, Inst. of British Foundrymen; Life Governor Univ. of Birmingham; Hon. Fellow Imperial College; Examiner in Metallurgy Univs. of London, Edinburgh, Glasgow,

Manchester, Birmingham and Wales; conducted researches on the influence of silicon and other elements on iron and steel, results of which have been largely applied in iron foundries throughout the world. Has travelled extensively. *Publications:* Metallurgy of Iron, 1895 (5th ed. 1918); Lectures on Iron Founding (2nd ed. 1910); Practical Metallurgy (2nd ed. 1919); and many papers on Metallurgical and Educational subjects. *Recreations:* gardening, motoring, and travel. *Address:* Netheridge, Elm Drive, Leatherhead. *T.:* Leatherhead 2348. [*Died* 31 *Jan.* 1951.

TURNER - SAMUELS, Moss, Q.C. 1946; Barrister-at-law; M.P. (Lab.) for Gloucester since 1945; Recorder of Halifax since 1948; Legal and Political Writer; *b.* Newcastle on Tyne; *m.* 1917, Gladys Rosemount, *d.* of late D. Belcher; two *s.* one *d.* *Educ.:* Newcastle on Tyne Grammar School. Honoursman Solicitor and Bar Final Exams.; Solicitor, 1914-21; called to Bar, Middle Temple, 1922; C.C. Newcastle, 1921; M.P. (Lab.) Barnard Castle, 1923-24; Parl. Lab. Candidate for Sowerby Div. of Yorks. 1925-28, and Leeds Central, 1931; Gloucester, 1935; High Sheriff of Gloucester, 1945-46. *Publications:* British Trade Unions; Industrial Negotiation and Arbitration; The Law Relating to Married Women. *Address:* 48 Pont Street, S.W.1. *T.:* Kensington 4816; Portway, Upton St. Leonards, Gloucestershire. [*Died* 6 *June* 1957.

TUSON, Brig.-Gen. Harry Denison, C.M.G. 1916; p.s.c.; *b.* 1866; *s.* of late Gen. Sir H. B. Tuson and Anne Frances, *d.* of late Major J. Bates; *m.* 1896, Emilie Gertrude, *y. d.* of J. A. Mullens; two *d.* *Educ.:* Royal Military College, Sandhurst. Egyptian Army, 1892-94; Served S. Africa, 1899-1900 (Queen's medal 5 clasps); A.G. and Q.M.G. New Zealand Defence Force, 1907-10; commanded 2 D.C.L.I., 1912-16; European War, 1914-16 (despatches twice, C.M.G.); retired pay, 1919. *Address:* c/o Lloyds Bank Ltd. Cox's branch, 6 Pall Mall, S.W.1. [*Died* 19 *June* 1958.

TWEEDIE, Adm. Sir Hugh Justin, K.C.B., *cr.* 1933 (C.B. 1919); J.P., D.L., C.C. Somerset; *b.* 5 April 1877; *s.* of Gen. Michael Tweedie, R.A., who served in Crimea and Mutiny; *m.* 1907, Constance Marion Crossman; two *s.* four *d.* *Educ.:* Britannia. Served in Mediterranean, Cape, China, West Indies and N. America; Mexico, under Admiral Cradock; present at Tampico and Vera Cruz during American landing; carried despatches to British and Foreign Embassies in Mexico City, railway and telegraphic communications being interrupted; returned with over 100 American refugees, women and children, from Solidad and district; outbreak of war served in West Indies; afterwards in command of Marshal Ney Monitor on Belgian Coast, S.N.O. Ismailia, Suez Canal, Dardanelles Patrol, Struma River operations against Bulgars and Turks, Adriatic, Venice; Command of 13th Flotilla Battle Cruiser Force; Commodore Commanding Flotillas with Grand Fleet (West African medal, Sierra Leone Clasp, C.B., Japanese Order of Rising Sun, Officier Légion d'honneur); Director of Training and Staff Duties, Admiralty, 1923-25; a Naval A.D.C. to the King, 1925; Rear-Adm. 1926; Rear-Adm. and Senior Naval Officer, Yangtze, 1927-29; Vice-Adm. 1930; Commander-in-Chief, Africa Station, 1931-33; Commander-in-Chief, The Nore, 1933-35; Admiral, 1935; retired list, 1936; Younger Brother, Trinity House. *Publication:* The Story of a Naval Life, 1939. *Address:* c/o Westminster Bank, 26 Haymarket, S.W.1. *Club:* Army and Navy. [*Died* 20 *Aug.* 1951.

TWENTYMAN-JONES, Hon. Percy Sydney, Q.C., 1924; B.A., LL.B., Judge of the Supreme Court of South Africa, 1926; Judge-President, Jan. 1946; since retired; Chairman of Women's Legal Disabilities Commission; *b.* Beaufort West, S.A., 13 Sept. 1876; 4th *s.* of late A. G. Twentyman-Jones and Eliza Elizabeth Jones; *m.* 1st, 1901, Martha Bertholda, *y. d.* of late Charles Torriano Vos; one *d.*; 2nd, 1935, Gwynnyth Constance Dorothy Wilkinson, *d.* of R. R. V. Jeffreys, Bulawayo. *Educ.:* Diocesan College, Rondebosch. Called to Bar, Supreme Court of South Africa, 1898; Law Lecturer to the Diocesan College for some years; later Examiner in Law to the Cape University; now Moderator in Roman Dutch Law for University of South Africa; external Examiner for final LL.B. at Univ. of Cape Town; represented S. Africa at Rugby, 1896, at cricket, 1896 and 1902; Life Member Western Province Rugby Football Union since 1928 (Pres. for ten years). *Publications:* The Liquor Law of the Cape Colony, 1908; The Civil Practice of the Magistrates' Courts of South Africa, 1918, 2nd edn., 1924, 3rd edn. 1931, 4th edn. 1945, 5th edn. 1946; The Transkeian Magistrates' Court Practice, 1925. *Recreations:* tennis, golf, fishing, and sport generally. *Address:* Ludlow, Lover's Walk, Kenilworth, Cape, S. Africa. *T.:* 74934. [*Died* 8 *March* 1954.

TWIGG, Brig.-Gen. Robert Henry, C.B. 1913; *b.* 4 April 1860; *s.* of late Canon Thos. Twigg, M.A. Entered Army 1879; Captain, I.S.C. 1890; Major, Indian Army, 1899; Lt.-Col. 1905; Colonel, 1909; served Akha Expedition, 1883-84; Burmese Expedition, 1886-87 (medal with clasp); Hunza-Nagas Expedition, 1891-92 (despatches, brevet Major, clasp); N.W. Frontier, India, 1897-98 (medal two clasps); Tirah, 1897-98 (clasp); Commanded Brigade in European War, 1914-16 (medals and star). *Address:* Greenwood, Malahide, Co. Dublin. [*Died* 16 *March* 1956.

TWISS, Brig.-Gen. Francis Arthur, C.M.G. 1919; D.S.O. 1917; M.V.O. 1905; *b.* 5 May 1871; *m.* 1903, Bessie Clayton, *e. d.* of Hugh Clayton Armstrong; two *d.* Entered R.A. 1891; Capt. 1899; Major, 1911; Col. 1921; Adjutant Militia, 1901-06; served N.W. Frontier, India, 1897-98 (medal 2 clasps); Tirah, 1897-98 (clasp); S. Africa, 1901-02 (Queen's medal 5 clasps); European War, 1914-18 (D.S.O., C.M.G.); ret., 1921. *Address:* Lydbrook, Farnham, Sy. [*Died* 14 *Nov.* 1952.

TWYMAN, Frank, F.R.S.; F.R.A.S.; F. Inst. Phys.; F.C.G.I.; Hon. Assoc., Manchester College of Technology; Technical Adviser to Hilger & Watts Ltd., 1948; Managing Director of Adam Hilger, Ltd., 1904-46; Pres. of the Optical Society, 1930 and 1931; *s.* of George Edmund Twyman and Jane Lefevre; *m.* 1906, Elizabeth K. P. Hilger; three *d.* (one *s.* decd.). *Educ.:* Simon Langton School, Canterbury; Finsbury Technical Coll., and City and Guilds Central Technical College (Siemens Scholar). Went to Otto Hilger (then the owner of the firm of Adam Hilger) as scientific assistant, 1898; Manager on the death of Otto Hilger, 1902; has invented many scientific instruments widely used in physical and chemical researches. Traill-Taylor Memorial Lecture, 1918; Grant by Franklin Institute, U.S.A., of the John Price Wetherell Medal, 1926; Duddell Medallist, 1926; all for developments of optical instruments. *Publications:* The Spectrochemical Analysis of Metals and Alloys; Metal Spectroscopy; Prism and Lens Making, 1st and 2nd edns.; Apprenticeship for a Skilled Trade; Optical Glassworking; An East Kent Family; and other books; lectures and papers on optical instruments, properties of glass and spectroscopy. *Recreations:* violin, gardening, walking. *Address:* 98 St. Pancras Way, N.W.1. *T.:* Gulliver 5636. *Club:* Athenæum. [*Died* 6 *March* 1959.

TYLOR, His Honour Judge Alfred; Judge of Circuit No. 51 (Hampshire) since 1948; Judge of Bow County Court, 1947; *b.* 1888; *s.* of Joseph John Tylor, Mayfield, Sussex; *m.* 1st, 1928, Ethne, *d.* of P. J. Henan, Derby; three *s.*; 2nd, 1950, Mrs.

Barbara Wakefield. *Educ.:* Marlborough; University College, Oxford. Called to Bar, Middle Temple, 1913; K.C. 1943; Q.C. 1952. Legal Adviser Ministry of Food, 1939-46. *Address:* 3 Paper Buildings, Temple, E.C.4; Brooklyn, Timsbury, Romsey, Hants. [*Died* 20 *May* 1958.

TYNDALE-BISCOE, Brig.-Gen. Julian Dallas Tyndale, C.B. 1916; *b.* 25 July 1867; 5th *s.* of William Earle Biscoe of Holton Park, Oxford; *m.* Agnes Dorothy, *e. d* of Ellis Frederick Dudgeon of Gogar Bank, Midlothian; one *s.* one *d.* (and one *s.* killed on active service). *Educ.:* Bradfield College, Berks. Gazetted to 11th Hussars from 4th Batt. Oxfordshire Light Infantry, 1887; Capt., 1894; Major, 1903; Lt.-Colonel, 1908; Colonel, 1912; temp. Brig.-General, 1914; commanded Highland Mounted Brigade, 1913-14; served in N.W. Frontier Campaign, 1897-98; S. Africa, 1901-2; France, 1914-15 (despatches); operations, Suez Canal, Egypt, and Gallipoli, 1915; commanded Mounted Troops W. Frontier Force; Egypt in operations against the Senoussi (despatches, C.B.); British Salonika Force, 1916-19 (despatches 5 times); Army of the Black Sea, 1919; retired with the hon. rank of Brig.-Gen. 17 Oct. 1919; Special Constabulary Long Service Medal 1930, and Bar. *Address:* Brookdale Farm, Broadstone, Dorset. [*Died* 17 *Feb.* 1960.

TYNER, Rt. Rev. Richard, M.A., D.D., Bishop of Clogher since 1943. *Educ.:* Trinity College, Dublin. B.A. 1907, M.A. 1919, B.D. 1920, D.D. 1943; Deacon, 1909; Priest, 1910; Incumbent of Clontibret, 1914-1924; Ematris and Rockcorry, 1924-37; Rector of Fivemiletown, 1937-43; Canon of Clogher, 1936-43. *Address:* Clonboy House, Clones, Co. Monaghan, Ireland. [*Died* 6 *April* 1958.

TYRRELL, Lt.-Col. Jasper Robert Joly, C.I.E. 1931; I.M.S., retired; 2nd *s.* of late Garrett Charles Tyrrell; *m.* Doris May Southerland; one *s.* one *d.* *Educ.:* Galway Grammar School; Trinity College, Dublin. Joined the Indian Medical Service, 1902; retired, 1931; served in various parts of India and in European War; joined Foreign and Political Dept., Govt. of India, 1906; recalled to Military during European War; Chief Medical Officer in Central India and Residency Surgeon, Indore, C.I.; retired 1931; Inspector General Hospitals and Director Public Health, Holkar State, 1931-36; Kaisar-i-Hind, 1st Class, 1912. *Publications:* various articles on medical subjects. *Recreations:* outdoor sports. *Address:* Ballinacoola, Glenealy, Co. Wicklow, Ireland. [*Died* 26 *Aug.* 1951.

TYRWHITT, Admiral of the Fleet Sir Reginald Yorke, 1st Bt., *cr.* 1919; G.C.B., *cr.* 1929 (K.C.B., *cr.* 1917; C.B. 1914); D.S.O. 1916; *b.* 10 May 1870; *s.* of late Rev. Richard St. John Tyrwhitt; *m.* 1903, Angela, *d.* of late Matthew Corbally, J.P., Rathbeale Hall, Swords; one *s.* two *d.* Lieut. of H.M.S. Cleopatra, with landing party at Nicaragua, 1894; Commodore, 1st Class, in command of Destroyer Flotillas of First Fleet, 1913; served European War; commanded Destroyer Flotillas in actions in Heligoland Bight, Aug. and Dec. 1914; also in action off Dogger Bank, 1915 (despatches, D.S.O., C.B., thanks of Admiralty); 1916-17 (K.C.B.), Commander, Legion of Honour; Acting Rear-Admiral, 1918; promoted Rear-Admiral, Dec. 1919; Vice-Adm. 1925; commanded the Third Light Cruiser Squadron, Mediterranean, 1921-22; Commanding Officer, Coast of Scotland, 1923-25; Commander-in-Chief, China Station, 1927-29; Admiral, 1929; Com.-in-Chf., The Nore, 1930-33; First and Principal Naval A.D.C. to the King, 1932-34; Admiral of the Fleet, 1934; retired list, 1939; restored to active list, 1940; Officer of the Military Order of Savoy, 1917; Order of the Sacred Treasure 1st Class (Japanese); Hon. D.C.L. Oxon, 1919. *Recreations:* fishing and carpentering. *Heir:* *s.* Capt. St. John Reginald Tyrwhitt, D.S.O., D.S.C. and Bar, R.N. [*b.* 18 April 1905; *m.* 1944, Nancy Veronica, *o. c.* of Capt. Charles Newman Gilbey, Gibsons, Hatfield Heath, Essex; one *d.*]. *Address:* Ellerslie House, Hawkhurst, Kent. *T.:* Hawkhurst 161. *Clubs:* United Service, Naval and Military, Eccentric. [*Died* 30 *May* 1951.

TYSSEN, Air Vice-Marshal John Hugh Samuel, C.B. 1941; *b.* 20 June 1889; *s.* of late Hugh S. Tyssen, Hylsbroke, Langford, nr. Bristol; *m.* 1914, *d.* of P. O. Gill, Exmouth; one *s.* *Educ.:* Wellington College, Berks. Went to France, 1914, with North Somerset Yeomanry; transferred to R.F.C. 1915, serving in France during the war (M.C.); Major in Royal Air Force, 1919; No. 20 Squadron, India, 1920-23; Wing Commander, 1923; S.A.F.O., H.M.S. Argus, 1928-30; Group Captain, 1931; Gosport, 1931-35; S.A.S.O. H.Q. Fighting Area, 1935-1936; Air Commodore, 1935; A.O.C. No. 12 Group, 1937; Iraq A.O.A. 1937; Air Vice-Marshal, 1938; A.O.C. British Forces in Iraq, 1938-39; A.O.C. No. 16 Group R.A.F., Chatham, 1940-41; retired, 1942; R.A.L.O. N.E. Civil Defence Region, 1942-45. *Recreations:* tennis, golf. *Address:* Petertavy Lodge, nr. Tavistock, Devon. *Club:* Royal Air Force. [*Died* 4 *Jan.* 1953.

TYTLER, Dr. William Howard; *b.* 2 Nov. 1885; *s.* of William Tytler and Martha Catherine Harrison; *m.* 1945, Eileen Mary Agnes Sellar. *Educ.:* University of Toronto. B.A. 1906; M.B. 1909. Royal Victoria Hospital, Montreal, 1909-10; Pathologist, Hamilton City Hospital, Canada, 1910-11; Rockefeller Inst. for Med. Research, New York, 1911-12; Cornell Univ. Med. College, New York, and Asst. Pathologist, New York Hospital, 1912-14. Served War in Canadian Army Medical Corps, B.E.F., France and Belgium, 1914-19. Medical Research Council, Nat. Inst. for Med. Research, Hampstead, 1919-22; Rockefeller Foundation, 1st Yellow Fever Commission, W. Africa, 1920; Bacteriologist, Welsh Nat. Memorial Assoc., 1922-38; David Davies Prof. of Tuberculosis, Welsh Nat. School of Medicine, 1938-49; World Health Organization, Consultant on Tuberculosis Laboratories, 1949-52; retired, 1952. *Publications:* reports and articles on experimental tumours and on tuberculosis. *Address:* Hillcroft, Banchory, Kincardineshire. [*Died* 6 *May* 1957.

U

UDAIPUR, H.H. Sir Bhupal Singh, Maharana of; G.C.S.I., *cr.* 1931; K.C.I.E., *cr.* 1919; Chairman of Union of Rajputana States since 1947; Hon. Major-General in British Army; *b.* 22 Feb. 1884; *o. s.* of Maharajah-dhiraja Maharana Sir Fateh Singh, G.C.S.I., G.C.I.E., G.C.V.O.; *S.* father, 1930. *Address:* Udaipur, Mewar, Rajputana. [*Died* 4 *July* 1955.

UNDERDOWN, Thos. H. J., M.A. (Camb.); M.R.S.T.; J.P.; *b.* Sittingbourne, 2 June 1872; *s.* of former Headmaster Greenwich British and other schools; *m.* Florence V. Ludwell, Hambrook, Bristol; two *s.* *Educ.:* Winterbourne School, Bristol; St. Luke's College, Exeter. Formerly Lecturer Bristol P.T. Centre in Mathematics, History, etc.; Assistant Master Bristol Council Schools; Headmaster of Police School; Principal of Merrywood Commercial, Technical, and Art Institute, Bristol; Headmaster South Street Senior School, Bristol; Member of Departmental Committee on Salaries of Teachers' Board of Education; Member of Committee on Non-Vocational Education of Adults, Ministry of Reconstruction; Pres. N.U.T. 1917-18; hon. M.A. Cantab.

1918; Member Bristol City Council, 1920-1929 and since 1932, and Education Authority since 1920; Alderman of City and County of Bristol since 1938; Lord Mayor of Bristol, 1940-41; contested Totnes Division of Devonshire, 1922; Chairman, Bristol South Divisional Liberal Assoc., 1928-33; Divisional Secretary, N.U.T., until 1937; Chairman of Bristol Royal School of Industry for the Blind, 1942-. *Publication:* Bristol under Blitz, 1942. *Address:* 4 Greville Road, Bristol. *T.:* Bristol 63826.

[*Died* 9 *July* 1953.

UNDERWOOD, Eric Gordon; Publicist, Author, Lecturer; 2nd *s.* of late William Arthur Underwood, *g.s.* of George Underwood, Sywell Hall, Northants. and late Emily Isabel, *d.* of Alexander Ogilvy Webster, Kirriemuir, Scotland; *m.* Kathleen Aimée, 3rd *d.* of late Thomas Thurlow, of Bloomville Hall, Suffolk; one *s.* one *d.* *Educ.:* Universities of Bonn and Paris; Christ Church, Oxford. 1st Class Honours, Mediæval and Modern Languages and Literature; Founder and President Oxford University Co-operative Society; Founder and Pres. Oxford Univ. French Club; Founder (with Gilbert Murray) and Vice-Pres. Oxford Univ. War and Peace Soc.; tutor to the Crown Prince of the Belgians (now King Leopold III.); introduced the Study of Russian at Eton College; Driver, Honourable Artillery Company; 2nd Lieut. Rifle Brigade; Hon. Lt.-Col. and A.D.C. (U.S.A.); Barrister-at-Law, Inner Temple; a principal officer Admiralty and War Office; Dir. in Labour Supply Dept., Min. of Munitions; a Founder Deleg. of Internat. Chamber of Commerce; voted privileges of floor by Senate of Georgia, U.S.A.; Founder: American and British Commonwealth Assoc. (U.S.A.); English-Speaking Union in Georgia, N. and S. Carolina, and Tennessee; travelled 250,000 miles broadcasting and lecturing to universities, clubs, etc., in U.S.A., 1937-51. Hon. member Virginia Soc.; Hon. Trustee of Public Reservations, Massachusetts. Presented statue of the Founder of Georgia to the City of Atlanta; bust of A. H. Clough to the City of Charleston, South Carolina; relics from the House of Commons to U.S. Congress and each of 48 states of U.S.A. Many years Mem. Council Overseas League, English-Speaking Union, National Trust; raised funds to save Stonehenge for nation. *Publications:* A Russian Grammar; Russian Accentuation; A Short History of French Painting; A Short History of English Painting; A Short History of English Sculpture; The British Commonwealth of Nations; (with John Underwood) America in England; articles in about 500 newspapers and reviews in the U.S.A.; articles on 7 occasions read in U.S. Senate and House of Representatives and unanimously ordered to be reprinted in Congressional Record. Contributor as Peter Simple, Way of the World to Morning Post; formerly Editor: World-wide Listener, Modern Languages; Editor London News Letter. *Recreations:* the promotion of Anglo-American understanding; the preservation of the countryside and historic buildings; travel, gardening. *Address:* c/o Child & Co., 1 Fleet Street, E.C.4. *Club:* Athenæum.

[*Died* 10 *June* 1952.

UNDERWOOD, John Ernest Alfred, C.B.E. 1948; B.Sc., M.B., B.S., D.P.H.; *b.* 25 December 1886; *s.* of late Ernest Underwood, Blackheath, and late Lucy Underwood; *m.* 1923, Katherine German. *Educ.:* Blackheath School; University College, London (President Union Society, 1912-13); University College Hospital. B.Sc. 1910; M.R.C.S., L.R.C.P., 1915; R.A.M.C., 1915-19; served in France and India; M.B., B.S. (Lond.), 1920; D.P.H. 1921; Assistant M.O.H. and School Medical Officer, Willesden, 1921-25; Medical Officer to Board of Education, 1925-41; Principal Medical Officer, Ministry of Education, 1941-51; retired, 1951. Government Delegate to International Conference on Blind Welfare, New York, 1931; Secretary to Committee on Partially Sighted Children, 1932-34; Vice-Chairman, Committee on Children with Defective Hearing, 1934-38. Chairman, Cttee. on Maladjusted Children, Ministry of Education, 1950. Mem. Mid-Sussex Hosp. Management Cttee., 1957-. *Publications:* Official Publications, 1926 onwards. *Recreations:* golf, music, motoring. *Address:* Rossmore, Copsale, Nr. Horsham, Sussex. *T.:* Southwater 352.

[*Died* 1 *Jan.* 1960.

UNDERWOOD, Brigadier John Percy Delabene, D.S.O. 1916; *b.* 1882; *s.* of late C. F. W. Underwood, Somerby Hall, Brigg; *m.* 1920, Rosina, *d.* of late R. C. Watts, Weymouth. Served South Africa, 1900-2 (Queen's medal with three clasps, King's medal with two clasps); European War, 1914-16 (despatches, D.S.O.); Commanded 3rd Battalion Nigeria Regiment, West African Frontier Force, 1927-1929; commanded 2nd Battalion The Loyal Regiment, 1931-35; Commander 150th (York and Durham) Infantry Brigade, 1935-39; retired pay, 1939. Colonel The Loyal Regiment, 1945-1949. *Address:* Ashley, Winchfield, Hants. *T.:* Hartley Wintney 299. *Club:* Naval and Military.

[*Died* 7 *Dec.* 1958.

UPCHER, Sir Henry Edward Sparke, Kt., *cr.* 1942; Director of Norfolk and Norwich Agricultural Hall Company, Ltd., Norfolk Properties Trust, Ltd. and Industrial Finance Ltd.; *b.* 1870; *m.* 1904, Fanny (*d.* 1941), *yr. d.* of late T. G. Simpson; one *s.*; *m.* 1942, Harriet Mary Susan, *d.* of late J. R. C. Deverell. Late Chairman Norfolk C.C., and Norfolk Agricultural Executive Committee, retired. Director Lloyds Bank Ltd. *Address:* Sheringham Hall, Upper Sheringham, Norfolk. *Clubs:* Oxford and Cambridge; Norfolk (Norwich).

[*Died* 23 *Sept.* 1954.

URBAN, Wilbur Marshall, A.M., Ph.D., L.H.D.; Professor of Philosophy, Yale, 1931, Emeritus since 1941; *b.* Mt. Joy, Pa., 27 March 1873; *s.* of Rev. Abram L. Urban (Protestant Episcopal Church) and Emma Louisa Trexler; *m.* 1896, Elizabeth Newell Wakelin; two *d.* *Educ.:* William Penn Charter School, Philadelphia; Princeton University; Jena and Leipzig (Ph.D. Leipzig, 1897). Chancellor Green Fellow in Mental Science, Princeton University, Reader in Philosophy, Princeton University; Professor of Philosophy, Ursinus College, 1898-1902; Professor of Philosophy, Trinity College, Hartford, 1902-20; Stone Professor of Philosophy, Dartmouth College, 1920-31; Visiting Professor, Harvard University, 1918; Visiting Lecturer (Mills Foundation), University of California, 1930. *Publications:* Valuation, Its Nature and Laws, 1908; The Intelligible World, Metaphysics and Value, 1929; Fundamentals of Ethics, 1930; Language and Reality; also sundry articles in philosophical and psychological journals, and articles on Value in Dictionary of Philosophy and Psychology and Encyclopædia Britannica. *Recreations:* gardening, golf, and winter sports. *Address:* c/o Yale University, New Haven, Conn., U.S.A.

[*Died* 15 *Oct.* 1952.

URIBURU, Jose Evaristo, G.B.E., *cr.* 1922; LL.D.(Hon.) Cambridge Univ.; *s.* of late Dr. Don José Evaristo Uriburu, statesman and President of the Republic, and Leonor de T. Pinto; *m.* Agustina, *d.* of Lieut.-General Julio A. Roca; four *s.* two *d.* Lieut.-Colonel in the Army Reserve; in 1916 the Argentine Government, with the approval of the National Senate, appointed him as a Municipal Commissioner for the Federal capital; with the sanction of the Senate, a Director of the Bank of the Nation, 1919; Envoy Extraordinary and Minister Plenipotentiary at the Court of St. James, 1921-27; Ambassador Extraordinary and Plenipotentiary of the Argentine Republic at the Court of St. James, 1927-31; Vice-Pres.

of the Central Bank of the Argentine 1935-1945. Academician of the National Historical Academy and the Academy of Politic and Moral Science; Corr. Academician and Corr. Member various historical academies and societies. *Publications:* El General Arenales en la Epoca Colonial, 1915; The History of General Arenales, 1924-27; Memories of Don Damaso de Uriburu, 1935; General Report on the River Plate Countries' Conference, 1941; La República Argentina A Través de las Obras de los Escritores Ingleses, 1949; monographs and articles on historical subjects. *Address:* Parera 78, Buenos Aires, Argentina. *Clubs:* Turf, Travellers', Argentine, Bath, Royal Automobile, United Service.
[*Died* 29 *July* 1956.

URQUHART, George A.; Mr. Justice Urquhart; Judge of High Court of Justice, Ontario, since 1938; *b.* Toronto, Ont., 19 March 1888; *s.* of Daniel Urquhart, K.C., and Mary Ellen Spence; *m.* 1916, Eileen Alma Taylor, Windsor, Ont.; one *s.* one *d.* *Educ.:* University of Toronto (Gold Medal in Political Science); Osgoode Hall Law School (Silver Medal). Asst. Corporation Counsel, City of Toronto, 1911-12; with Bartlet, Bartlet and Urquhart, Windsor, 1913-20; Crown Attorney, Windsor, Ont., 1921-1925; with firm of Urquhart and Urquhart, Barristers, Toronto, 1925-38; President County of York Law Assoc., 1932; Bencher Law Society of Upper Canada, 1933-38; Past President International Legal Fraternity of Phi Delta Phi. *Recreations:* golf (summer), curling (winter). *Address:* Osgoode Hall, Toronto, Ont. *T.:* AD 4101. *Clubs:* Arts and Letters, Toronto Golf, Toronto Curling (Toronto).
[*Died* 8 *Oct.* 1951.

USBORNE, Vice-Admiral Cecil Vivian, C.B. 1930; C.M.G. 1918; R.N., retired; rejoined Navy, 1941; retired, 1945; Chairman of Tungum Sales Co.; an underwriting member of Lloyd's since 1934; *b.* Queenstown, Ireland, 17 May 1880; 2nd *s.* of late Captain George Usborne, R.N.; *m.* Ellin Mary Caryll, *o. d.* of J. W. Sharpe, M.A., late Senior Fellow of Gonville and Caius College, Cambridge, of Birch Hall, Windlesham, Surrey; one *d.* *Educ.:* The Philberds, Maidenhead; H.M.S. Britannia, Dartmouth. Obtained five firsts and promotion marks; Beaufort Testimonial, Goodenough Medal, Ryder Prize; Gunnery-Lieut. 1903-4; Commander of H.M.S. Colossus, 1913; invented apparatus which led to introduction of Paravane Mine protection, 1915; commanded H.M.S. Latona, a mine-layer in Eastern Mediterranean, 1916; engaged in mining operations off Dardanelles, blockade work off Asia Minor, etc.; Captain, 1917; Senior British Naval Officer, Salonica, 1917, Corfu, 1918; commanded Naval Brigade on Danube, 1918-19; Deputy Director of Naval Ordnance, 1919; in command H.M.S. Dragon, 1921; Deputy Director Gunnery Division Naval Staff, 1922; Vice-President Chemical Warfare Committee, 1923; Director Tactical School, 1925; Captain, H.M.S. Malaya, 1927; Captain, H.M.S. Resolution, 1928; Rear-Admiral, 1928; Director of Naval Intelligence Division, 1930-32; retired, 1933; Director of Censorship Division of Press and Censorship Bureau, 1939-40; Special service, Admiralty, 1941-45. Chief Organizer of the India Defence League. Officer of Order of Redeemer, Greece; Order of Serbian Eagle with crossed swords; Officer of Legion of Honour. *Publications:* Smoke on the Horizon, 1933; Blast and Counterblast, 1935; The Conquest of Morocco, 1936; Fiction: Malta Fever; Virgin of Atlas, 1941; Blue Tally-ho. *Address:* 97 Cadogan Gardens, S.W.3. *Club:* United Service.
[*Died* 31 *Jan.* 1951.

USHER, Col. Sir John Turnbull, 3rd Bt., *cr.* 1899; O.B.E. 1945; of Norton, Midlothian, and Wells, Roxburgh; retired, 9th Lancers; served War of 1939-45, Lieut.-Col. Pioneer Corps (O.B.E.); *b.* 2 June 1891; *e. s.* of late Sir Robert Usher, 2nd Bt., and late Katharine Scott, *d.* of James Turnbull, of Edinburgh; *S.* father, 1933; *m.* 1918, Jean Elspeth (*d.* 1950), 2nd *d.* of H. L. Usher, Summerfield, Dunbar; two *d.* *Educ.:* Uppingham. 18 years' service; Inniskilling Dragoons, European War, 1914-1918; commanded Lanarkshire Yeomanry, 1933-37. *Heir:* *b.* Robert Stuart [*b.* 19 Apr. 1898; *m.* 1930, Gertrude Martha, *d.* of Capt. Sampson Tresmontes, Argentina; two *s.* *Educ.:* R.M.C., Sandhurst]. *Address:* Norton, Newbridge, Midlothian. *T.:* Ratho 75. *Clubs:* Cavalry; New (Edinburgh).
[*Died* 5 *May* 1951.

USMAN, Sir Mahomed, K.C.S.I., *cr.* 1945; K.C.I.E., *cr.* 1933; Kt., *cr.* 1928; B.A.; *b.* 1884; *s.* of Mahomed Yakub Sahib Bahadur, Madras; *m.* 1915, Shahzady Begam, *d.* of Shifaulmulk Zynulabudeen Sahib Bahadur of Madras. *Educ.:* Madras Christian College, Madras. Honorary Presidency Magistrate, Madras, 1916-20; Member of the Senate of the University of Madras, 1922-34, and Chancellor of the Madras Univ., the Andhra University and the Annamalai University in 1934; Municipal Councillor, Madras, 1913-25; Sheriff of Madras, 1924; President, Corporation of Madras, 1924-25; Member Madras Legislative Council, 1921-23; Member of the Executive Council of the Gov. of Madras, 1925-34; Vice-Pres. of the Executive Council, 1929-34; acting Governor of Madras, 1934; Vice-Chancellor, Univ. of Madras, 1940-42; Member for Posts and Air, Governor-General's Executive Council, India, 1942-46; also Defence Member, 1944 and 1945; Member Nat. Def. Council, 1941-42; Khan Sahib, 1920; Khan Bahadur, 1921; Kaisar-i-Hind medal, 2nd class, 1923. *Address:* Teynampet Gardens, Teynampet, Madras. *Club:* Cosmopolitan (Madras).
[*Died* 1 *Jan.* 1960.

UTHWATT, Ven. William Andrewes; Archdeacon of Huntingdon, 1943-47, Archdeacon Emeritus since 1947; Vicar of Diddington, Huntingdon, since 1945; *s.* of Thomas Andrewes Uthwatt, Bucks; *b.* Ballarat; *m.* Elsie Mary (*d.* 1932), *d.* of late J. C. Small. *Educ.:* Trinity College, Cambridge; Wells Theological College. Ordained, 1904; Curate of St. Mary, Portsea, 1904-10; Archdeacon of Solomon Islands, 1910-15; T.C.F. 1915-19; Curate of Southwell Minster, 1919-20; Vicar of St. Luke's, Derby, 1920-26; Vicar of Bottisham, Cambridge, 1926-37; Rector of Brampton, 1937-1945. *Address:* Diddington Vicarage, Huntingdon. *T.:* Buckden 215.
[*Died* 23 *June* 1952.

UTRILLO, Maurice; (Maurice Valadon); Officer Legion of Honour, 1951 (Chevalier, 1928); French Painter; *b.* Paris, Dec. 1883; *s.* of painter, Suzanne Valadon; *m.* 1935, Mme. Lucie Pauwels. *Educ.:* Collège Rollin, Paris. First exhibited in 1909 at the Salon d'Automne. Exhibitor at many French and foreign exhibitions; 8 exhibitions since 1934 at Galerie Paul Pétridès, and has had several one-man shows, including 20 paintings at the Marlborough Gallery, 18 Old Bond St., 1951. Is represented in collections all over the world. Signs work Maurice Utrillo V. *Publications:* numerous books on art, and articles in the press. *Relevant publication:* Man of Montmartre, by Stephen and Ethel Longstreet, 1959. *Address:* c/o Paul Pétridès, 53 Rue La Boétie, Paris VIII; 27 Rue Jean Mermoz, Paris VIII; Villa La Bonne Lucie, Vésinet (S. & O.), near Paris. [*Died* 5 *Nov.* 1955.

UTTLEY, George Harry, C.M.G. 1947; M.A., D.Sc., F.G.S.; retired; *b.* 9 Oct. 1879; *s.* of W. H. Uttley, Dunedin, N.Z.; *m.*; two *s.* *Educ.:* Otago Boys' High School and University of Otago, Dunedin, N.Z. Science Prizeman, N.Z. Education Department's Examinations, 1901; M.A. (Hons.), 1902; D.Sc. 1922. Asst. Master, Senior House Master, Senior Science Master, Waitaki Boys'

High School, 1903-13; Senior Science and Mathematical Master, Presbyterian Ladies' Coll., Melb., 1914-15; Principal Scots Coll., 1916-22; Principal Wairarapa High School, 1923-29; Lecturer Geology, W.E.A., Victoria Univ. Coll., 1929; Rector Southland Boys' High School, 1930-45. Fellow Geological Soc. London, 1913; Pres. Geol. Section and Member Council, Wellington Philosophical Inst., 1920; Pres. N.Z. Secondary Teachers' Assoc., 1926-27; Pres. Masterton Rotary Club, 1926-27; Pres. Invercargill Rotary Club, 1932-33; Mem. of Council and Vice-Pres., Roy. Soc. of N.Z. (Canterbury Branch), 1949-50; Pres.-Elect, 1951. *Publications:* various on geology, 1913-20. *Recreations:* still greatly interested in football and cricket (Otago Rugby rep., 1901; Capt. Univ. of Otago Rugby XV, 1902; North Otago Rugby rep. 1903-7; cricket rep. and Capt., 1903-13) and science work, particularly in geology which is now his main activity in retirement. *Address:* 292 Karori Road, Wellington, N.Z. [*Died* 14 *Jan.* 1960.

V

VACHELL, Horace Annesley, F.R.S.L.; Ex-President of Dickens Fellowship; *b.* 30 Oct. 1861; *e. s.* of Richard Tanfield Vachell, late of Coptfold Hall, Essex, and Georgina, *d.* of Arthur Lyttelton Annesley, late of Arley Castle, Staffordshire; *m.* Lydie (*d.* 1895), *d.* of C. H. Phillips of San Luis Obispo, California (one *s.* killed on active service, European War, 1914-1918; one *d.* decd.). *Educ.:* Harrow; Royal Military Coll., Sandhurst. Lieut. Rifle Brigade, 1883. *Publications:* Romance of Judge Ketchum, 1894; Model of Christian Gay, 1895; Quicksands of Pactolus, 1896; An Impending Sword, 1896; A Drama in Sunshine, 1897; The Procession of Life, 1899; John Charity, 1900; Life and Sport on the Pacific Slope, 1900; The Shadowy Third, 1902; The Pinch of Prosperity, 1903; Brothers, 1904; The Hill, 1905; The Face of Clay, 1906; Her Son, play in four acts; Her Son, novel, 1907; The Waters of Jordan, 1908; The Paladin, 1909; The Other Side, 1910; John Verney, 1911; Jelf's, a comedy in four acts; Blinds Down; Bunch Grass, 1912; Loot, 1914; Quinney's, 1914; Spragge's Canyon, 1914; Searchlights, play in three acts, 1915; Quinney's, comedy in four acts, 1915; The Case of Lady Camber, play, 1915; Who is He? play, 1915; The Triumph of Tim, 1916; Fishpingle, play, 1916; Fishpingle, a novel, 1917; Humpty Dumpty, a comedy in four acts, 1917; Mrs. Pomeroy's Reputation, play (with Thomas Cobb); The Soul of Susan Yellam, 1918; The House of Peril, play, 1919; Whitewash (novel); The Fourth Dimension, 1920; Count X (play); Blinkers, 1921; Change Partners, 1923; The Yard, 1923; Plus Fours (play), 1923; Fellow Travellers, 1923; Quinney's Adventures, 1924; Leaves from Arcadia, 1924; Watlings for Worth; Mr. Allen 1926; A Woman in Exile, 1926; Miss Torrobin's Experiment, 1927; The Actor, 1928; The Enchanted Garden, 1929; Virgin, 1929; The Best of England, 1930; Into the Land of Nod, 1931; At the Sign of the Grid, 1931; The Fifth Commandment, 1932; Experiences of a Bond Street Jeweller, 1932; Vicars' Walk, 1933; This was England, 1933; The Disappearance of Martha Penny, 1934; The Old Guard Surrenders, 1934; Moonhills, 1935; Arising Out of That, 1935; When Sorrows Come, 1935; My Vagabondage, 1936; Joe Quinney's Jodie, 1936; Distant Fields, A Writer's Autobiography, 1937; The Golden House, 1937; Lord Samarkand, 1938; Quinneys for Quality, 1938; Where Fancy Beckons, 1938; Phoebe's Guest House, 1939; Great Chameleon, 1940; Little Tyrannies, 1941; Black Squire, 1941; Gift from God, 1942, The Wheel Stood Still, 1943; Hilary Trent; 1944; Averil, 1945; Farewell Yesterday, 1945; Now Came Still Evening On, 1946; Rebels, 1946; Eve's Apples, 1946; Quiet Corner, 1947; Twilight Grey, 1948; Children of the Soil, 1948; In Sober Livery, 1949; Methuselah's Diary, 1950; More from Methuselah, 1951; Quests, 1954. *Address:* The Priory House, Sherborne, Dorset; The Manor Farm, Widcombe, Bath. *Club:* Authors'.
[*Died* 10 *Jan.* 1955.

VACHON, Most Rev. Mgr. Alexandre, Ph.M., S.T.D., D.U.J., D.Sc., LL.D., M.A., F.C.I.C., F.R.S.C.; Roman Catholic Archbishop of Ottawa since 1940; former Rector of Laval Univ.; Assistant at Pontifical Throne and Roman Count; former Vicar-General of Archdiocese of Quebec; Emeritus Professor of Analytical Chemistry in Laval University, Quebec; former Director of the École Superieure de Chimie, Laval University; former Dean of the Faculty of Science; *b.* 16 Aug. 1885; 9th *s.* of J. Alexander Vachon and Mary Davidson, St. Raymond, P.Q. *Educ.:* Quebec Seminary; Laval University; Harvard University; Massachusetts Institute of Technology. Priest, 1910; former Governor of the Canadian Broadcasting Corporation; Member of the National Research Council of Canada; former Director of Station Biologique du St. Laurent à Trois-Pistoles, Université Laval; Past President of Canadian Chemical Assoc. and of Canadian Institute of Chemistry; F.R.S.C.; Chm. of Canadian Catholic Conf.; Pres. of Permanent Cttee. of Internat. Eucharistic Congresses. Major-Chaplain of the 5th Div. S.C.C.S.; State Chaplain of Knights of Columbus; Officer of the Légion d'Honneur (France). Roman Count; Assistant to the Pontifical Throne. Travelled extensively. *Publications:* Traité élémentaire de Chimie; Minéralogie, Géologie, Botanique; L'Étoile de mer: son utilité comme engrais; Hydrography of Passamaquoddy Bay; many articles in Canada-Français, Le Naturaliste Canadien, etc. *Recreation:* bridge. *Address:* Archbishop's Palace, 145 St. Patrick's Street, Ottawa. [*Died* 30 *March* 1953.

VALADON, Maurice; *see* Utrillo, Maurice.

VALENTIA, (*de jure*), 13th Viscount (*cr.* 1621) (died without proving succession; Viscountcy dormant, 1844-1958); **Rev. William Monckton Annesley,** Bt. 1620; Baron Mountnorris, 1628; Premier Baronet of Ireland; Vicar of Brewham-cum-Redlynch since 1920; Hon. Chaplain to the Forces; Cottonian Family Trustee of British Museum; *b.* 23 Jan. 1875; *s.* of Rev. Henry Arthur Annesley and Anna Maria, *d.* of William Monckton; *S.* kinsman, 1949 (to Irish viscountcy only); *m.* 1938, Gladys May Kathleen, *d.* of late Uriah Fowler. *Educ.:* Peterhouse College, Cambridge (M.A.). Curate of St. Margaret's, Ipswich, 1905-08; St. Peter's, Palgrave, 1908-12; St. John Baptist, Woking, 1912-1916; St. John Evangelist, Wimborne, 1916-19; St. Andrew's, Bournemouth, 1919-1920. Served European War, 1914-18, Chaplain to the Forces, 1917-19. *Heir: kinsman* Francis Dighton Annesley, M.C., Brig. R.A.M.C. [*b.* 12 Aug. 1888; *m.* 1925, Joan Elizabeth, *d.* of John J. Curtis, Sunnybrook, Sandhurst; one *s.* three *d.*]. *Address:* Wassall House, Wincanton, Somerset.
[*Died* 2 *Feb.* 1951.

VALENTINE, William Alexander, C.B.E. 1926; *b.* 1869; *s.* of William Valentine, Stirling; *m.* 1905, Edith Jane, *e. d.* of Peter Wright, Windermere. *Educ.:* Craigs School, Stirling. District Manager, Telephone Service, Manchester, 1893-98; Glasgow, 1898-1912; Provincial Superintendent, London, 1912-16; Deputy Controller, London, 1916-23; Controller, 1923-29, retd. *Address:* 11 Cambridge Road, Talbot Woods, Bournemouth. *T.:* Winton 3726.
[*Died* 17 *July* 1959.

VALLANCE, Lieut.-Col. Aylmer; (George Alexander Gerald Vallance);

journalist and author; Assistant Editor, New Statesman; *b.* 4 July 1892; *s.* of George Henry Vallance and Agnes Felton; *m.* 1950, Ute Fischinger. *Educ.:* Fettes College, Edinburgh; Balliol College, Oxford. 5th Somerset L.I. and General Staff, Indian Army, 1914-19; Assistant Editor, The Economist, 1930-33; Director, Daily News Ltd., 1933-36; Editor, News Chronicle, 1933-36; Financial Editor, New Statesman, 1937-39; General Staff, War Office 1930-45. *Publications:* The Centre of the World; Those Foreigners (with R. W. Postgate); Hire Purchase; The Press; This Dollar Question; Troubled Waters (Bureau of Current Affairs); Very Private Enterprise; The Summer King. *Recreations:* walking, fishing. *Address:* 2 Primrose Hill Road, N.W.3. [*Died* 24 *Nov.* 1955.

VALTORTA, Rt. Rev. Mgr. Henry Paschal; first R.C., Residential Bishop of Hong Kong since 1946; *b.* Carate Brianza, Milan, Italy, 14 May 1883. Went as missionary to Hong Kong, 1907; engaged in missionary and educational work in Kwangtung and Hong Kong, 1907-26; Catholic Bishop of Leros and Vicar-Apostolic of Hong Kong, 1926-46. *Address:* 16 Caine Road, Hong Kong. *T.:* 22674. [*Died* 3 *Sept.* 1951.

VAN BEINUM, Eduard; Grand Officer of the Order of Orange-Nassau; Chevalier of the Order of the Netherlands Lion; Music Director of the Los Angeles Philharmonic Orchestra since 1957; *b.* 3 September 1900; Dutch; *m.* 1927, Sepha Jansen; two *s.* *Educ.:* Arnhem Hoogere Burgerschool; Amsterdam Conservatorium Musick. Conductor Orchestra in Haarlem, 1927-31, and choir in Zutfen and Haarlem, 1927-31; second conductor Concertgebouw Orch., 1931-37; principal conductor Concertgebouw Orchestra, 1937-43, with Mengelberg; after 1943, alone. Has been guest conconductor in all the countries of Europe; guest conductor London Philharmonic Orchestra. Officer of the Acad., France; Order of the Star of the North, Sweden; Order of the Dannebrog, Denmark; Chevalier of the Legion of Honour, France; Commander of Order of Leopold II, Belgium; Commander of Lodewyk Nassau, Luxembourg, etc. *Recreations:* horse riding, hunting, reading history, books of travel. *Address:* Job. Verhulststraat 37, Amsterdam, Holland. *T.:* 93701. *Club:* Dutch. [*Died* 13 *April* 1959.

van BROEKHUIZEN, Herman Dirk; *b.* Ryssen, Holland, 17 June 1872; *s.* of Rev. Herman van Broekhuizen, Clergyman, Winburg, Ficksburg, O.F.S. and Johanna van Andel; *m.* 1903, Elsie Francina Eloff; one *s.* two *d.* *Educ.:* School Ficksburg; Grey College, Bloemfontein; University of Stellenbosch, Cape; Utrecht; Leiden, Holland. Minister of the Gospel, Pretoria; Member of Parliament, 1923-32; Envoy Extraordinary and Minister Plenipotentiary of the Union of South Africa, to the Netherland Govt., 1933-41, and Belgian Govt. 1934-41. Member of National Party; Member of Head Committee, 1916-32; Member of Federal Council, National Party, 1916-32; Delegate to Geneva, 1934. Represented South Africa, League of Nations, 1936. Groot Kruis van Oranje Nassau, Holland, 1941. *Publications:* Wij zullen handhaven; Die wordingsgeskiedenis van die Holl. Kerke in Suid-Afrika. *Recreations:* tennis, cricket, golf, formerly Rugby, (represent. Stellenbosch, 1890-97, W.P. 1894-97, South Africa 1896). *Clubs:* Pretoria; De Witte (Hague). [*Died* 4 *Aug.* 1953.

VANDELEUR, Brigadier Henry Martley, C.B.E. 1919; retired; late R.A.; *b.* 12 Dec. 1875; *y. s.* of late Rev. Gerald Ormsby Vandeleur of Ballinamona, Co. Limerick; *m.* 1st, 1918, Theodosia Agnes (*d.* 1933), *d.* of late W. H. Sinclair, of Moreton Manor, Brading, Isle of Wight; 2nd, 1934, Jane Wilhelmina (*d.* 1945), *widow* of Lieut.-Col. Sir John Mansell, K.B.E. *Educ.:* Bedford School; R.M.A., Woolwich. Staff Captain to Inspector of Royal Garrison Artillery, 1906-10; Director of Inspection of Guns, 1916-19; Chief Inspector of Armaments, 1921-25; Member of the Ordnance Committee, 1919-21 and 1925-29; Superintendent of Design Department, Royal Arsenal, 1929-30; Commandant, Military Coll. of Science, 1930-32; retired pay, 1932. *Address:* c/o Lloyds Bank, Ltd., Cox's and King's Branch, 6 Pall Mall, S.W.1. *Club:* Army and Navy. [*Died* 9 *May* 1951.

VANDELEUR, Brig.-Gen. Robt. Seymour, C.B. 1919; C.M.G. 1915; late 2nd Batt. Seaforth Highlanders (Ross-shire Buffs, the Duke of Albany's); *b.* 6 June 1869; 2nd *s.* of late Crofton Toler Vandeleur; *m.* 1900, Hester Caroline, (*d.* 1940), *d.* of Maj.-Gen. George de la Poer Beresford; one *d.* Entered Army, 1889; Capt., 1898; Maj., 1905; Lt.-Col. 1908; served Nile expedition, 1898 (despatches); N.W. Frontier, India, 1908 (despatches, Bt. Lt.-Col., medal with clasp); European War (France, Gallipoli, Macedonia, Palestine), 1914-18 (despatches six times, C.M.G., C.B., Bt, Col.); temp. Brig.-Gen. Aug. 1915; retired pay, 1922. *Address:* The Hive, Canford Cliffs, Bournemouth. *Club:* United Service. [*Died* 20 *June* 1956.

VANDENBERG, Arthur Hendrick; Senator, U.S., since 1928; *b.* Grand Rapids, Michigan, 22 March 1884; *s.* of Aaron Vandenberg and Alpha Hendrick; *m.* 1918, Hazel H. Whitaker (*d.* 1950); one *s.* two *d.* *Educ.:* Grand Rapids High School; Univ. of Michigan. Editor Grand Rapids Herald, 1906-28. U.S. Rep. to Gen. Assembly, United Nations, 1945. Holds several honorary degrees. *Address:* 316 Morris Avenue, Grand Rapids, Mich., U.S.A. [*Died* 18 *April* 1951.

VAN DEN BERG, Frederick, Q.C. 1931; Barrister-at-law; *b.* Johannesburg, 1893; *o. s.* of late N. Van Den Berg, Chief Magistrate of Johannesburg; unmarried. *Educ.:* St. John's College, Johannesburg. Called to Bar, Middle Temple, 1916; Contested Holland with Boston, Lincs (C.) 1929. *Recreation:* golf. *Address:* c/o The Standard Bank of South Africa Ltd., Adderley Street, Cape Town. [*Died* 27 *Jan.* 1957.

VAN DEN HEEVER, C. M., M.A., D.Litt. (S.A.), Litt. Docts. (Utrecht); Prof. of Afrikaans, University of the Witwatersrand, Johannesburg, since 1933; *b.* 27 February 1902; *s.* of late C. M. van den Heever and Maria Oberholzer; *m.* 1927, Martha Maria Klopper; one *s.* two *d.* *Educ.:* Grey College School, Bloemfontein, O.F.S.; Grey University College, Bloemfontein, O.F.S. (scholarship for oversea study); Univ. of Utrecht, Holland. Journalist, 1924-27; lecturer in Afrikaans and High Dutch, Univ. College, London; lecturer, Grey University College, Bloemfontein, 1930-32. *Publications: novels in Afrikaans:* Langs die Grootpad; Droogte; Groei; Somer; Kromburg; Laat Vrugte; Gister; Van Aangesig tot Aangesig; Anderkant die Berge; Woestynsand dek die Spore; Die Held, Marthinus se Roem; Jeug; Vannag kom die Ryp; Dirk se Oorwinning; *poems in Afrikaans:* Versamelde Gedigte; *essays:* Die Stryd om Ewewig; Mens en Woord; *biography:* General J. B. M. Hertzog. *Recreation:* golf. *Address:* University of the Witwatersrand, Johannesburg. [*Died* 8 *July* 1957.

VAN DER BYL, Brigadier John, D.S.O. 1917; *b.* 11 Oct. 1878; *s.* of late P. G. Van der Byl; *m.* 1936, Mary, *d.* of late W J. H. Whittall and *widow* of Captain G. A. Atkinson-Willes. *Educ.:* Wellington College; R.M.C. Sandhurst. Joined 8th Hussars, 1898; served South Africa, 1899-1902 (Queen's medal and five clasps, King's medal and two clasps); European War, 1914-18 (wounded, despatches, D.S.O.); Commander 1st (Risalpur) Cavalry Brigade, 1927-31; retired pay

1931; Colonel 8th Hussars, 1930-47. *Address:* Elsenwood, Camberley. *T.:* Camberley 158. *Club:* Cavalry. [*Died* 15 *Aug.* 1953.

VAN DER HOEVE, Jan, M.D., LL.D.h.c.; Prof. of Ophthalmology; *b.* Santpoort, Holland, 13 Apr. 1878; *m.* Elizabeth Adriana Laurillard; one *d.* *Educ.:* University of Leiden. Med. Doct. at the University of Bern, 1902; Assistant at the University Ophthalmic Clinic in Leiden, 1900-5; Professor of Ophthalmology in Groningen, 1913; Leiden, 1919; Pres. of the Royal Netherlands Academy of Science in Amsterdam, 1931-4y. LL.D. Hon. (Edin.); M.D. Hon. (Heidelberg); Member and Hon. Fellow of many Dutch, British, and foreign scientific societies. *Publications:* many publications in ophthalmological journals of different nations. *Address:* Leiden, Holland. [*Died* 26 *April* 1952.

VANDERPANT, Sir Harry Sheil Elster, Kt., *cr.* 1939; D.L. Co. of London; *b.* 20 Oct. 1866; *s.* of Henry George Vanderpant, of Maddox Street, W.; unmarried. *Educ.:* privately. Barrister, Gray's Inn, 1919; Westminster City Council, 1929; Mayor of City of Westminster, 1937-38; Chairman of London and Home Counties Traffic Advisory Committee, 1937-48; Almoner and Governor, Christ's Hosp. and Mem. Board of Governors, Westminster Hosp. *Address:* c/o Westminster Bank, 63 Piccadilly, W.1. *Club:* Athenæum. [*Died* 20 *March* 1955.

VANDERVELL, Harry, C.B.E. 1946; *b.* 1870; *m.* 1907, Beatrice Muriel, *d.* of late Thos. White Waldron, Ramsbury, Wilts; three *d.* *Educ.:* University College School, London. Member, London Stock Exchange, 1898; received a Commission as Lieut. R.N.V.R. for service in motor boats, Aug. 1914; appointed for Special Service in Auxiliary Patrol Admiralty under the Fourth Sea Lord, Feb. 1918; promoted to Commander, May 1918; founder and President of R.N.V.R. (Auxiliary Patrol) Club, 1919; Vice-President Royal Naval Association; Vice-Patron R.N.V.R. Club; Vice-Pres. Soc. of Marine Artists; Mem. Society of Nautical Research. *Publications:* A Shuttle of an Empire's Loom; articles on seafaring matters. *Address:* 20 Copthall Avenue, E.C.2. *T.:* National 0441. *Clubs:* Royal Thames Yacht, Royal Naval Sailing Association, Royal Corinthian Yacht, Pilgrims, R.N.V.R., etc. [*Died* 6 *Sept.* 1956.

VAN DRUTEN, John William; author; *b.* London, 1 June 1901; 2nd *s.* of late Wilhelmus and Eva van Druten; unmarried; naturalised American citizen, 1944. *Educ.:* University College School. LL.B., London University, 1922; qualified as Solicitor of the Supreme Court of Judicature, 1923; lecturer in English Law at University College of Wales, Aberystwyth, 1923-26. Directed all own plays, 1942-; also The King and I (by Rodgers and Hammerstein), 1950. *Publications: plays:* Young Woodley, 1928; The Return of the Soldier (adapted from Rebecca West's novel), 1928; Diversion, 1928; After All, 1929; London Wall, 1931; There's Always Juliet, 1931; (with Benn W. Levy) Hollywood Holiday, 1931; Somebody Knows, 1932; Behold We Live, 1932; The Distaff Side, 1933; Flowers of the Forest, 1934; Most of the Game, 1935; Gertie Maude, 1937; Leave Her to Heaven 1940; Old Acquaintance, 1940; Solitaire (adapted from Edwin Corle's novel), 1941; The Damask Cheek (with Lloyd Morris), 1942; The Voice of the Turtle, 1943; I Remember Mama (from Kathryn Forbes' book: Mama's Bank Account), 1944; The Mermaids Singing, 1945; The Druid Circle, 1947; Make Way for Lucia (adapted from E. F. Benson), 1948; Bell, Book and Candle, 1950; I am a Camera (from Christopher Isherwood's Stories), 1951; I've Got Sixpence, 1952; *novels:* Young Woodley, 1929; A Woman on Her Way, 1930; And Then You Wish, 1936; The Vicarious Years, 1955; *autobiography:* The Way to the Present, 1938; *belles lettres:* Playwright at Work, 1953; The Widening Circle, 1957. *Address:* c/o Monica McCall, 667 Madison Avenue, New York. [*Died* 19 *Dec.* 1957.

VANSITTART, 1st Baron, *cr.* 1941, of Denham; **Robert Gilbert Vansittart,** P.C. 1940; G.C.B., *cr.* 1938 (K.C.B., *cr.* 1929; C.B. 1927); G.C.M.G., *cr.* 1931 (C.M.G. 1920); M.V.O. 1906; Hon. D. Litt. (Reading); Hon. LL.D. (Aberdeen); Membre de l'Académie des Sciences Morales et Politiques (Institut de France); *b.* 25 June 1881; *e. s.* of late R. A. Vansittart; *m.* 1st, 1921, Gladys (*d.* 1928), *o. d.* of General William C. Heppenheimer, U.S.A.; one *d.*; 2nd, 1931, Sarita Enriqueta, *d.* of Herbert Ward and *widow* of Sir Colville Barclay, K.C.M.G., C.B., late H.M. Ambassador at Lisbon. *Educ.:* Eton. Attaché, 1902; 3rd Secretary, 1905; 2nd Sec., 1908; Assistant Clerk, Foreign Office, 1914; 1st Sec., 1919; Paris, 1903; Teheran, 1907; Cairo, 1909; Stockholm, 1915; Paris, 1919; Counsellor in H.M. Diplomatic Service, 1920; Secy. to Earl Curzon, Secretary of State for Foreign Affairs, 1920-24; Assistant Under-Secretary of State for Foreign Affairs and Principal Private Secretary to the Prime Minister, 1928-30; Permanent Under-Secretary of State for Foreign Affairs, 1930-38; Chief Diplomatic Adviser to Foreign Secretary, 1938-41. *Publications:* The Gates; John Stuart; Songs and Satires; The Singing Caravan; Foolery; Dusk; Pity's Kin; Tribute; Black Record; Roots of the Trouble; Lessons of My Life; Green and Grey; Bones of Contention; Events and Shadows; Even Now. Theatre: Les Pariahs; The Cap and Bells; People Like Ourselves; Class; Dead Heat Sweet William; The Mist Procession (posthumous). *Address:* Denham Place, Denham, Bucks. *T.:* Denham 2015. *Clubs:* St. James', Athenæum. [*Died* 14 *Feb.* 1957 (*ext.*).

van STRAUBENZEE, Maj.-Gen. Sir Casimir Cartwright, K.B.E., *cr.* 1928; C.B. 1918; C.M.G. 1917; R.A.; *b.* 11 Nov. 1867. Lieutenant R.A. 1886; Captain 1897; Major 1902; Lt.-Col. 1914; Professor R.M.C., Canada, 1898-1903; Instructor, School of Gunnery, 1909-1912; Chief Instructor R.H. and R.F.A., 1914-15; Inspector General of R.A., 1917-18; Maj.-Gen. R.A., 5th Army in France, 1918-1919; served Ashanti, 1895-96 (star); European War, 1914-18 (despatches four times, Bt. Col., promoted Major-General, C.M.G., C.B.); G.O.C. 46th (North Midland) Division, T.A., 1923-27; Commanded the Troops, Malaya, 1927-29; retired pay, 1929; Col. Comdt. R.A., 1932-37. *Club:* Army and Navy. [*Died* 28 *March* 1956.

VAN SWINDEREN, Jonkheer Rene de Marees-, G.C.V.O.; *b.* 6 Oct. 1860; *m.* Elizabeth Linsey (*d.* 1950), *d.* of late Charles C. Glover; one *d.* *Educ.:* Groningen. Entered Foreign Office at the Hague, 1886; attached to the Netherland Legation at Berlin and Washington as attaché, at Rome, Vienna, St. Petersburg, and Paris, as Secretary and Counsellor of Legation; Minister Plenipotentiary at Bucharest, Belgrade and Washington; Minister of Foreign Affairs at the Hague, 1908-13; Envoy Extraordinary and Minister Plenipotentiary of the Netherlands, London, 1913-37. *Publication:* The Suez Canal. *Address:* 83 Eaton Square, S.W.1. *T.:* Sloane 7675. [*Died* 17 *Jan.* 1955.

van VERDUYNEN, Dr. (Edgar) Michiels; Grand Cross, Order of Orange Nassau, 1949; Ambassador of the Netherlands to the Court of St. James since 1939; *b.* 2 Dec. 1885; *m.* 1917, Henriette Jochems. *Educ.:* Leiden University. Under Secretary, Netherlands Foreign Office; Minister in Prague; Chief Section Political Affairs, Foreign Office; Minister without portfolio, 1942-45. *Recreations:* golf, shooting, racing. *Address:* 21 Portman Square, W.1. *T.:* Welbeck 6787. *Clubs:* Turf, Buck's, St. James'. [*Died* 13 *May* 1952.

VAN ZYL, Rt. Hon. Gideon Brand, P.C. 1945; LL.D.; Attorney-at-Law; *b.* Sea Point, 3 June 1873; *e. s.* of late Dr. Casper Hendrik van Zyl: *m.* 1900. Marie Elizabeth, *d.* of late Sir (John) George Fraser. *Educ.:* Normal College; South African College, Cape Town. Hon. LL.D. (Cape Town), 1948. Admitted an Attorney-at-law and Notary Public, 1898; Conveyancer, 1897; apptd. Asst. Dir. of War Recruiting, Feb., 1918; at end of war was Dep. Comr. for Returned Soldiers; for over 20 years mem. Cape Town Univ. Council; for many years Chm. Kennel Union. Chm. Nat. Mutual Life Assoc. of Australasia; Nat. Pres. Y.M.C.A. and Pres. Sunday School Union; Pres. several sporting bodies. Ex-M.P. for Sea Point; Dep.-Chm. Cttees., 1921-24; apptd. Dep.-Speaker and Chm. Cttees., Union Parl., 1934; during Mr. Speaker's illness apptd. Actg. Speaker; Chm. S.A. Deleg. to Int. Parl. Coml. Conf., 1935; represented Union Parl. at Coronation of King George and Queen Elizabeth, 1937; also Dep. Leader S.A. Deleg. to Empire Parl. Assoc. Meeting, London; administrator of Cape Province, 1942-45; Governor-General Union of S. Africa, 1945-Dec. 1950; first South African-born Governor-General. K.St.J., Prior of the Priory in Southern Africa of the Order of St. John of Jerusalem. *Recreations:* gardening; keen sportsman. *Address:* Cape Town, South Africa. [*Died* 1 *Nov.* 1956.

VASSAL, Gabrielle M.; Chevalier de la Légion d'Honneur, 1931; *b.* Uppingham, Rutland; *d.* of Howard Candler, M.A., Head Mathematical Master of Uppingham School, 1861-1900; *m.* Doctor Vassal, J.J.M., Médecin Colonel des Troupes Coloniales, Officier de la Légion d'Honneur. Journalist. *Educ.:* Solothurn, Switzerland; Ladies' Coll., Cheltenham. Prix de l'Alliance Française; Prix Boutroue and Prix Milne-Edwards de la Société de Géographie; Prix Montyon de l'Académie Française. Accompanied her husband on French Government Service to many parts of the world; lectured on French Indo-China, Philippines, French Congo, Yunnan, Andorra, and Majorca to geographical and other societies in England, Scotland, and on the Continent, also to English public schools; broadcasts B.B.C. and Radio-Paris. In the French Resistance movements from 1943 till the Liberation (diplomas from British Commonwealth and United States for helping escape of Allied airmen, 1946). *Publications:* Mes Trois Ans d'Annam, 1911; On and Off Duty in Annam, 1910; Uncensored Letters from the Dardanelles, 1916; A Romance of the Western Front, 1918; In and Round Yunnanfou, 1922; Mon Séjour au Congo français, 1925; Life in French Congo, 1925; Mon Séjour au Tonkin et au Yunnan, 1927; Français, Belges, et Portugals en Afrique Equatoriale, 1931: mem. French foreign press; Paris correspondent of British Columbian, Canada. *Recreations:* tennis; handicapped +15 in Official Classification of French women players. *Address:* 2 Avenue de Lamballe, Paris 16e. *T.:* Jasmin 09.47. *Club:* Racing Club de France. [*Died* 31 *May* 1959.

VAUGHAN, Brig.-General Edward, C.M.G. 1919; D.S.O. 1917; D.L., J.P., Cardiganshire; *b.* 1866; *s.* of late Capt. Vaughan; *m.* 1924, May, *er. d.* of late Edwin Bennett. *Educ.:* Cheltenham College. Joined The Manchester Regiment; served S. Africa, 1899-1902 (Queen's medal with five clasps, King's medal with two clasps); European War, commanded a Brigade in France, 1914-19 (despatches, D.S.O., C.M.G., Légion d'Honneur, Croix de Guerre); retired, 1923. *Address:* Kingsway Hotel, Hove, Sussex. *Club:* Army and Navy. [*Died* 12 *Feb.* 1956.

VAUGHAN, Brig.-General Edward James Forrester, C.M.G. 1918; D.S.O. 1916; D.L.; *b.* 1875; *s.* of Lt.-Col. E. H. Vaughan, late Devonshire Regt.; *m.* 1924, Ethel Winifred, *widow* of Lt.-Col. J. A. C. Forsyth, C.M.G., D.S.O., R.F.A. *Educ.:* Winchester. Joined Devonshire Regt. from the Militia, 1896; served S. African War (despatches, Queen's medal 5 clasps, King's medal 2 clasps); with Egyptian Army on Staff of Governor-General of the Sudan, 1902-11 (Sudan medal and clasp, 3rd Class Osmanieh, 4th Class Medijieh); served European War as Adjutant Special Reserve Batt. Devonshire Regt., 1914; then D.A.A. and Q.M.G. Base, Egypt; commanded 2/4th R.W. Kent Regt. at Gallipoli (despatches, D.S.O.); A.A. and Q.M.G. 27th Div. B.S.F. (despatches, Bt. Lt.-Col., Croix de Guerre), A.Q.M.G. 12th Corps, B.S.F.; D.A. and Q.M.G. 12th Corps with temp. rank of Brig.-Gen. (despatches, Brevet Col., Order of White Eagle 3rd Class); D.A. and Q.M.G. Allied Forces, Constantinople, with temp. rank of Brig.-Gen.; retired pay, 1921. *Recreations:* hunting, golf. *Address:* Platte Rocque, La Rocque, Jersey, C.I. *T.:* Gorey 498. *Club:* Army and Navy. [*Died* 9 *June* 1957.

VAUGHAN, Brigadier Edward William Drummond, C.B. 1947; D.S.O. 1941; M.C. 1918; A.D.C.; retired; late 2nd Royal Lancers Indian Army; *b.* 12 Mar. 1894; *s.* of late Major-General R. E. Vaughan, C.B.; *m.* 1920, Florence Marjorie Fletcher; one *d.* *Educ.:* Malvern College; R.M.C., Sandhurst. Served European War, 1914-18, France, Palestine (severely wounded); Da Solidaridad of Panamainian Republic, 1918. War of 1939-45; commanded 3rd Indian Motor Brigade, Mechili, N. Africa (prisoner of war, 1941; escaped from Italy, 1944); commanded Delhi Area and District, 1944-47. A.D.C. to The King, 1945-; retired, 1948, with Hon. rank of Brigadier. *Recreations:* shooting, fishing. *Club:* Cavalry. [*Died* 10 *Feb.* 1953.

VAUGHAN, Maj.-Gen. John, C.B. 1915; C.M.G. 1919; D.S.O. 1902; J.P.; *b.* 31 July 1871; *s.* of John Vaughan, Nannau, Dolgelly; *m.* 1913, Louisa Evelyn, *d.* of late Capt. Stewart, Alltyrodyn, Cardigans, and *widow* of Harold P. Wardell, Brynwern, Newbridge-on-Wye. *Educ.:* Eton; Sandhurst. Joined 7th Hussars, 1891; Major 10th Hussars, 1904; served Matabele relief expedition, 1896; Mashonaland, 1897; Soudan Campaign, 1898; South African War, 1899-1901 (wounded) (despatches thrice, Brevet of Major, Queen's medal 6 clasps, King's medal 2 clasps, D.S.O.); European War, 1914-18 (despatches, C.B., C.M.G., Commandeur Légion d'Honneur); Commandant, Cavalry School, Netheravon, 1911-14; Vice-Lieut. County of Merioneth, 1943. *Publication:* Cavalry and Sporting Memories, 1955. *Recreation:* fishing. *Address:* Nannau, Dolgelley, Merioneth. *T.:* 255872. *Clubs:* Cavalry, Roehampton. [*Died* 21 *Jan.* 1956.

VAUGHAN, John Howard, C.B.E. 1932; LL.B.; *b.* Norwood, South Australia, 14 Nov. 1879; *s.* of Alfred and Louisa Vaughan; *m.* Helene, *d.* of late James Fry; no c. *Educ.:* Norwood State School (Government Bursary); Prince Alfred College. LL.B. University of Adelaide, 1900; Roby Fletcher Scholar in Logic and Psychology, 1898; admitted to Bar, 1901; Member for Central District Legislative Council, 1912-18; Attorney-General, S. Australia, 1915-1917; Consul for Czechoslovakia, 1929-36; Order of the White Lion (Officer Class), Czechoslovakia, 1937. *Recreation:* golf. *Address:* Mt. Osmond, South Australia. [*Died* 21 *Aug.* 1955.

VAUGHAN, Reginald Charles, O.B.E. 1945; M.C. 1915; Q.C. 1947; Recorder of Birmingham since 1954; Deputy Chairman of Quarter Sessions, Liberty of Peterborough, since 1948; Chairman, London Medical Appeal Tribunal, since 1957; *b.* 10 Feb. 1896; *o. surv. s.* of late Rev. E. J. Vaughan, R.N.; *m.* 1945, Kathleen Ramsay; two *s.* *Educ.:* Victoria Coll., Jersey. Served European War, 1914-18, 4th Dragoon Guards, K.S.L.I. and

R.F.C., later R.A.F.; called to Bar, Gray's Inn, 1918; member of Middle Temple; Bencher, Gray's Inn, 1952; practising London and Midland Circuit; Recorder of Lincoln, 1941-54. Commissioned R.A.F.V.R. as Pilot Officer, June 1939; called up August 1939; served War of 1930-45; acting Group Captain, 1943 to release. J.P. Birmingham and Peterborough. *Address:* 2 Crown Office Row, Temple, E.C.4. *T.:* Central 1365; Park Lodge, Gloucester Road, Redhill, Surrey. *T.:* Redhill 4942. *Club:* Devonshire. [*Died* 16 *May* 1960.

VAUGHAN, William Hubert, C.B.E. 1958 (O.B.E. 1949); D.L.; J.P.; Chairman, Welsh Land Settlement Society Ltd., since 1953; *b.* 21 March 1894; *s.* of Henry Charles Vaughan and Catherine Vaughan; *m.* 1921, May Bishop; one *d.* *Educ.:* Eastern School, Port Talbot. Member of Forestry Commission, 1945-; Member of National Parks Commission, 1952-; Member of National Council of Domestic Food Production, 1950-. Member of Port Talbot Borough Council, 1927-48, Mayor of Port Talbot, 1941-42; Deputy-Chairman of Glamorgan Agricultural Executive, 1939-; General Secretary of Aberavon Constituency Labour Party, 1934-; Member of Milford Haven Conservancy Board, 1958; Member of Glamorgan River Board. J.P. 1949, D.L. 1957, Glamorgan. 1914-18 Star, G.S. and Victory medals; Civil Defence Medal, 1939-1945; Coronation Medal, 1953. *Recreations:* boxing and Rugby football. *Address:* Groeswen Ganol, Groeswen, Port Talbot, Glamorganshire. *T.:* Port Talbot 3354. [*Died* 17 *April* 1959.

VAUGHAN-RUSSELL, John Francis Robert, C.B.E. 1951; *b.* 22 Oct. 1895; *s.* of late John Stanley and Annette Vaughan-Russell; *m.* 1926, Charlotte Collyer, *e. d.* of late William Kirkaldy-Willis, J.P., of Richmond, Surrey, and of Mrs. C. Kirkaldy-Willis, Blacket Place, Edinburgh; one *s.* one *d.* *Educ.:* privately; Queens' College, Cambridge. Served European War 1914-1918; in France, 1918; 2nd Lt. 7th London Regt., T.F. Entered Foreign Service, Oct. 1919; served in Constantinople, 1920-22; Vice-Consul: Beirut, 1922-23; Aleppo, 1923-1924; Damascus, 1924-26; Durazzo, 1927; Marrakesh, 1928-30; Patras, 1930-33; Consul: Marrakesh, 1933-36; Kermanshah, 1936-42; Tehran, 1942-43; Jibuti, 1943-44; Aleppo, 1945-47; Consul-General Buenos Aires, 1947-52; Consul-General, Cairo, 1952-1955, retired. *Recreations:* tennis, philately. *Address:* Tretower, Merrow Street, Merrow, Guildford, Surrey. *Club:* Royal Automobile. [*Died* 17 *Jan.* 1958.

VAUGHAN WILLIAMS, Ralph, O.M. 1935; *b.* 12 Oct. 1872; *s.* of late Rev. Arthur Vaughan Williams; *m.* 1st, 1897, Adeline (*d.* 1951), *d.* of late Herbert W. Fisher, Brockenhurst, Hants; 2nd, 1953, Ursula (author of No Other Choice, Fall of Leaf, Need for Speech, Wandering Pilgrimage), *d.* of late Maj.-Gen. Sir Robert Lock, and *widow* of Lt.-Col. J. M. J. Forrester Wood, R.A. *Educ.:* Charterhouse; Trinity College, Cambridge; Mus. Bac. 1894; Mus. Doc. 1901; D.Mus. (honoris causa), Oxford, 1919; Royal College of Music; Berlin; Paris. Gold Albert Medal, Roy. Soc. of Arts, 1955. *Works:* Toward the Unknown Region, 1907; London Symphony; Sea Symphony; Hugh the Drover, 1924; Flos Campi, 1925; Sir John in Love, 1929, The Poisoned Kiss; Dona Nobis Pacem, 1936; Five Variants on Dives and Lazarus, 1939; Sixth Symphony, 1947; Partita for Strings, 1948; The Pilgrim's Progress, 1951; Sinfonia Antartica, 1953; Eighth Symphony, 1956; Epithalamion, 1957; Ninth Symphony, 1958. *Publications:* National Music, 1935; Some Thoughts on Beethoven's Choral Symphony, with Writings on other Musical Subjects, 1953; The Making of Music, 1955. *Address:* 10 Hanover Terrace, N.W.1. *T.:* Ambassador 8200. [*Died* 26 *Aug.* 1958.

VAUX of Harrowden, 8th Baroness, *cr.* 1523; **Grace Mary Eleanor Gilbey;** *b.* 22 May 1887; *e. d.* of 7th Baron Vaux of Harrowden (*d.* 1935); Barony called out of abeyance, 1938; *m.* 1911, William Gordon Gilbey; two *s.* one *d.* *Heir:* *s.* Rev. Hon. Peter Hubert Gordon Gilbey, O.S.B. [*b.* 28 June 1914. *Educ.:* Ampleforth College; St. Benet's Hall, Oxford. B.A., 1939]. *Address:* Harrowden Hall, Wellingborough, Northants. *T.:* Wellingborough 2065 [*Died* 11 *May* 1958.

VAUX, Lt.-Col. Henry George, C.S.I. 1928; C.I.E. 1921; M.V.O. 1921; *b.* 25 Jan. 1883; *m.* 1915, Baroness Edna von Stockhausen (*d.* 1949) (American); no *c.* *Educ.:* private. Joined 3rd Essex Regt., 1900; gazetted to the Duke of Cornwall's Light Infantry, 1905; Aide-de-Camp to Lord Carmichael, Governor of Victoria, 1908-11; to Governor of Madras, 1911-12; to Governor of Bengal, 1912-1914; Military Secretary to Lord Carmichael, 1914-17, to Earl of Ronaldshay, 1917-22, to Earl of Lytton, 1922; to Sir George Lloyd, 1922-23; to Sir Leslie Wilson, 1923-28; to Sir Frederick Sykes, 1928-33; to Lord Brabourne, 1933-35; A.A.G. War Office, 1939-43; Commandeur de l'Ordre de la Couronne, 1926. *Address:* The Look Out, Dovercourt, Essex. [*Died* 12 *May* 1957.

VEBLEN, Oswald, Ph.D., Hon. Ph.D., Oslo and Hamburg; Hon. D.Sc.: Oxford, Chicago, Princeton; Hon. LL.D. Glas.; Prof. of Mathematics, Institute for Advanced Study, Princeton, N.J., 1932-50; Emeritus Professor since 1950; *s.* of Andrew A. Veblen and Kirsti Hougen; *b.* Decorah, Iowa, 24 June 1880; *m.* 1908, Elizabeth Mary Dixon Richardson, Askern, Yorkshire; no *c.* *Educ.:* University of Iowa (A.B. 1898); Harvard (A.B. 1900); University of Chicago (Ph.D. 1903). Associate in Mathematics University of Chicago, 1903-5; Preceptor in Mathematics, Princeton University, 1905-10; Professor, 1910-26; Henry B. Fine Professor of Mathematics, Princeton University, 1926-32; Deputy for the Savilian Professor of Geometry, Oxford, 1928-9; Captain and Major, U.S. Army, 1917-19; Member various learned societies, including American Mathematical Society (President 1923-24). *Publications:* Infinitesimal Analysis (with N. J. Lennes), 1907; Projective Geometry (with J. W. Young), vol. I., 1910; vol. II., 1918; Analysis Situs, 1922; Invariants of Quadratic Differential Forms, 1927; The Foundations of Differential Geometry (with J. H. C. Whitehead), 1932; Projektive Relativitätstheorie, 1933; Geometry of Complex Domains (with Wallace Givens), 1936. *Address:* Princeton, New Jersey, U.S.A. *T.:* WALnut 4-0958. [*Died* 10 *Aug.* 1960.

VELLACOTT, Paul Cairn, C.B.E. 1946; D.S.O. 1917; M.A.; Master of Peterhouse, Cambridge, since 1939; *b.* 24 May 1891; *s.* of late W. E. Vellacott, F.C.A.; *m.* 1929, Hilda Francesca, *d.* of late Sir Nevile Lubbock, K.C.M.G. *Educ.:* Marlborough; Peterhouse, Cambridge, (Scholar). B.A. (1st Class Honours Historical Tripos, part ii.), 1913; Cambridge University Hockey XI. 1914; served European War, France, 1914-18; Major, South Lancashire Regiment; Brigade-Major, General Staff (despatches, D.S.O.); Fellow of Peterhouse, 1919; Tutor and History Lecturer, 1920-34; Head Master of Harrow School, 1934-39; Home Guard Directorate, War Office, Jan. 1941; Inspector of Administration, Home Guard, (Lt.-Col.), 1941-42; Director of Political Warfare, Middle East, 1942-44. *Address:* Peterhouse, Cambridge. *Club:* Brooks's. [*Died* 15 *Nov.* 1954.

VENABLES, Rev. Canon E(dward) Malcolm; Canon of St. George's, Windsor, since 1948, Precentor since 1949; *b.* 27 Oct. 1884; *e. s.* of E. G. Venables, Oatlands, Weybridge; *m.* 1913, Florence Mary, *e. d.* of W. M. Ogilvie, The Glade, Harrow Weald; two *s.* three *d.* (and one *d.* decd.). *Educ.:* Magdalen College School (Choral Scholar); Magdalen College, Oxford; Cuddesdon Coll. M.A. Oxon., Hons. Classics and History; Oxford Univ. Hockey XI, 1906-07; B.D. Oxon, 1924. Assistant Master: Packwood Haugh, 1907-11; Felsted School; O.T.C. 1912-17; Harrow School, 1917, Housemaster, 1922-42; Chaplain, 1926-32. Rector of Wootton Courtenay, Somerset, 1943-45. *Publications:* Prayers for my Son; Sons of God; Sweet Tones Remembered. *Recreations:* poetry, bird-watching, fishing, painting. *Address:* 4 The Cloisters, Windsor Castle. [*Died* 28 *Sept.* 1957.

VENABLES, Oswald Eric; Malayan Civil Service (retd.); *b.* 1 July 1891; *y. s.* of W. J. Venables, solicitor; *m.* Carol (*d.* 1947), *e. d.* of G. H. Frend, Elmington House, Canterbury; no *c.* *Educ.:* Campbell College, Belfast; Trinity College, Dublin. Appointed, 1914; attached Colonial Secretariat, Singapore; War service, 1917-19; District Officer, Jasin, 1919; District Officer, Dindings, 1922; Second Magistrate, Singapore, 1923; Colonial Secretariat, Singapore, 1924; British Resident, Brunei, 1926; Magistrate, Seremban, N.S., 1927; District Officer, Upper Perak, 1929; Collector of Land Revenue, Kuala Lumpur, 1931; British Adviser, Perlis, 1932; District Officer, Kuala Kangsar, 1936; Acting Under Secretary to Government, F.M.S., 1938; Commissioner of Lands and Mines, Johore, 1939; interned Singapore, 1942-45; Resident Commissioner, Kedah, 1946; retired 1948. *Recreation:* golf. *Address:* c/o Lloyds Bank, St. Helier, Jersey, Channel Islands. [*Died* 12 *July* 1960.

VENABLES-LLEWELYN, Sir Charles Leyshon Dillwyn-, 2nd Bt., *cr.* 1890; C.B. 1946; J.P., D.L.; *b.* 29 June 1870; *o. surv. s.* of Sir John Talbot Dillwyn-Llewelyn, 1st Bart., and Julia (*d.* 1917), *d.* of Sir M. Hicks-Beach, 8th Bt.; *S.* father, 1927; *m.* 1893, Katharine Minna, *e. d.* and *co-heiress* of Rev. Richard Lister-Venables of Llysdinam Hall, Radnorshire; one *s.* (and two killed in action) one *d.* *Educ.:* Eton; New College, Oxford. Assumed additional name of Venables, 1893; Lieut.-Col. commanding Glamorgan Yeomanry, 1908-18; Col. 1918; served European War in France, 1916-18; M.P. (C.) Radnors, 1910; Lord Lieut., Radnorshire, 1929-49. *Recreations:* shooting, fishing. *Heir: s.* Brigadier Charles Michael Dillwyn-Venables-Llewelyn. *Address:* Llysdinam, Newbridge-on-Wye, Radnors. [*Died* 24 *June* 1951.

VENKATANARAYANA NAYUDU, Diwan Bahadur J., C.I.E. 1930; B.A., B.L.; *b.* 9 Nov. 1875, Telaga Nayudu Community; *m.*; five *s.* two *d.* *Educ.:* Ellore, Mission High School; Noble College, Masulipatam; Law College, Madras. Tahsildar, 1903; Land Records Superintendent, 1908; Revenue Officer, Record of Rights, 1910; Deputy Collector, 1913; Special Settlement Officer, 1917; Director of Land Records, 1919; Rao Sahib, 1920; Acting Collector and District Magistrate, 1921; Diwan Bahadur, 1923; Inspector-General of Registration, 1922-25; Commissioner, Corporation of Madras, 1925-28; Permanent Collector and District Magistrate, 1926; Secretary to the Government of Madras, Law and Education Department, 1928-30; President: The Indian Fine Arts Society, Suguna Vilasa Sabha, Madras; Cardiology Fund, Madras, etc. *Publications:* Students' Manual of the History of England; Chain Survey Manual for Revenue Subordinates; The Adoration of the Supreme Being; The Essential Teachings and Sadhanas of the Bhagavadgita; The Hinduism of the Upanishads. *Address:* 2/11 Venkata Vilas, Ormes Road, Kilpauk, Madras. [*Died* 29 *May* 1958.

VENN, John Archibald, C.M.G. 1956; Litt.D., F.S.A.; J.P.; President of Queens' College, Cambridge, since 1932; Vice-Chancellor, 1941-43; University (Gilbey) Lecturer in the History and Economics of Agriculture, 1921-49; University Archivist, 1949; *b.* 10 November 1883; *o. c.* of late John Venn, Sc.D., F.R.S., Senior Fellow of Gonville and Caius College; *m.* 1906, Lucy Marion, *o. c.* of the late Professor Sir William Ridgeway, Kt., F.B.A. *Educ.:* Eastbourne College; Trinity College, Cambridge. Captain, Cambs. Regt., 1915-17; Statistician to the Food Production Department 1917-19, and afterwards at the Ministry of Agriculture; Advisory Officer in Agricultural Economics, 1923-32; Fellow of Queens' College, 1927. Member of the Council of the British Association for the Advancement of Science, 1934-39; Pres. Section M. 1935; Member of Scientific Council of the International Agricultural Institute, Rome, and of various Departmental Committees of the Ministry of Agriculture, Colonial Office, and Empire Marketing Board. President, Agricultural Economics Society, 1933-1934; Chairman, Cambridgeshire and Isle of Ely Agricultural Wages Board; Senior Proctor, Cambridge University, 1930-31; Member of the Council of the Senate of Cambridge University, 1934-43; Governor and Perpetual Student of the Medical Coll. of St. Bartholomew's Hospital, 1940. Member, Commission on Higher Education in the Colonies, 1944-45; and of Hong-Kong University Advisory Cttee., 1945-46; Chairman of the Commission on the sugar industry in British Guiana, 1948-49. Finlay Lecturer, University Coll., Dublin, 1946. Coronation medal, 1953. *Publications:* The Book of Matriculations and Degrees, 1544-1659; Alumni Cantabrigienses; Foundations of Agricultural Economics (2nd edn. 1933); numerous contributions to the Economic Journal and other periodicals. *Recreations:* formerly lawn tennis (County Colours, Secretary of the Cambs. L.T.A., 1908-14); archæology, ornithology, motoring. *Address:* The President's Lodge, Queens' College, Cambridge. *T.:* 4653, 4425. [*Died* 15 *March* 1958.

VENNER, Sir Edwin John, Kt., *cr.* 1951; Chartered Accountant; Director Wenlock Brewery Co. Ltd. and other Companies; Council, State Management, Carlisle; *b.* 12 July 1871; *m.* 1895, Ethel Mary Moore (*d.* 1925); two *s.* one *d.* *Address:* 37 Kingston House, Prince's Gate, S.W.7. *T.:* Kensington 2978. *Clubs:* Constitutional, Royal Automobile. [*Died* 9 *March* 1955.

VENNER, John Franklyn, C.M.G. 1945; Group Capt. R.A.F.; F.C.A. 1936; Partner in Firm of Edward Moore & Sons, Chartered Accountants, London, E.C.4, since 1926; *b.* 20 October 1902; *s.* of Sir Edwin John Venner, *q.v.*; *m.* 1926, Margaret Peech; two *s.* one *d.* *Educ.:* Rugby. Articled to Edward Moore & Sons, Chartered Accountants, London, 1920; qualified, 1924. Commissioned A.A.F. May 1939; Group Capt. 1943. Officer of the Order of Leopold (Belgium). *Recreations:* general. *Address:* Frith Manor, nr. East Grinstead, Sussex. *T.:* Dormans Park 332. *Club:* Royal Automobile. [*Died* 31 *May* 1955.

VERDON-ROE, Sir Alliott; *see* Roe.

VERNE, Adela; pianist; *b.* Southampton. *Educ.:* The Convent, Southampton. First appeared in London, 1898; has toured all the world. [*Died* 4 *Feb.* 1952.

VERNEUIL, Louis; playwright, actor, producer and director; *b.* Paris (France), 14 May 1893; *m.* 1921, Lysiane Bernhardt, *g.d.* of Sarah Bernhardt; divorced in 1923; *m.* 1937, Germaine (*d.* 1940), *d.* of Georges Feydeau, the French dramatist. *Educ.:* Paris. Started as newspaperman at Excelsior, 1911; then assistant to manager of Theatre Femina, 1912. Had first some ten one-act comedies and music-hall reviews produced in Paris from 1911 to 1914. His first three-act comedy was La Charrette anglaise

(Gymnase, 1916). Then he gave Mon Œuvre and Mr. Beverley (both in 1917). Made his debut as an actor on 30 April 1917 in La Jeune fille au bain, a one-act play of his. From then on he played the lead in practically all his plays, the most important of which are: Le Traité d'Auteuil, Pour avoir Adrienne (The Love Habit), Mademoiselle ma mère (Oh, Mama), L'Inconnu (Her Destiny), L'Amant de cœur, La Dame en rose (The Pink Lady), La Maison du Passeur, Un jeune ménage, La Pomme, La maîtresse de Bridge, Le Fauteuil 47 (Mother of Pearl), Ma Cousine de Varsovie, Lison, Pile ou Face (First Love), En Famille, La Joie d'Aimer, Le Mariage de Maman (This Time it's Love), Azais (Fifty-Fifty), Maître Bolbec et son mari (The Lady in Law), Tu m'épouseras (He's Mine), Melle Flûte, Satan, Monsieur Lamberthier (Jealousy, then Obsession), L'honnête Mrs. Cheyney (adaptation of Lonsdale's The Last of Mrs. Cheyney), L'Amant de Mme. Vidal, Ma Sœur et moi (Meet my Sister), La Course à l'Étoile, Boulard et ses filles, Guignol (No Ordinary Lady), Miss France, La Banque Némo, Avril, Une femme ravie (Doctor's Orders), L'École des contribuables, Parlez-moi d'amour, Le mari que j'ai voulu, Mon Crime, La belle Isabelle, Vive le Roi, Les fontaines lumineuses, Une femme d'un autre âge, Le Rosier de Mme. Husson, Le Train pour Venise, Léonidas, La femme de ma vie, Le Coffre-fort vivant, Fascicule Noir, etc. In 1940 he had more than 60 three- or four-act plays produced in Paris, most of them translated in some ten languages and played throughout the world. Among them are Daniel (1920) and Régine Armand (1922), the two last dramas Sarah Bernhardt appeared in. Moreover, he introduced to the stage Yvonne Printemps (1915), Gaby Morlay (1918), and Elvire Popesco (1923); for the latter he wrote more than ten plays and was, for 15 years, her exclusive author and partner. In June 1940, three days before the Germans entered Paris, he sailed for the U.S. He first lived in New York, then in Los Angeles where he definitely settled in 1943. He wrote there The Fabulous Life of Sarah Bernhardt (Harper and Bros), Curtain at Nine, a book of his theatrical recollections, and numerous films; in 1950 wrote and directed Affairs of State, his first play in English, which ran for over 600 performances in New York. *Address:* 474 North Faring Road, Holmby Hills, Los Angeles 24, Calif. [*Died* 3 *Nov.* 1952.

VERNEY, Frank Arthur, C.B.E. 1932; F.R.C.V.S.; Principal Veterinary and Agricultural Officer, Basutoland; *b.* 1874; *s.* of Richard Grainger Verney; *m.* Malvina, *d.* of late Edward Way, Bosch Hoek, Natal; three *s.* two *d.* *Educ.:* King Edward VI. Grammar School, Stratford-on-Avon; Royal Veterinary College, London (five silver, three Bronze Medals, and Fitzwygram prize). Government Veterinary Officer to Natal Government, 1896-1908; joined the Basutoland Government Service, 1908; Lieutenant in the Natal Carbineers, Anglo-Boer War (despatches, Queen's medal with three clasps). *Publications:* numerous contributions to the serious epizootics affecting South Africa. *Recreations:* golf, riding, horsebreeding. *Address:* Mountain View, Kokstad, S. Africa. *Club:* Durban Country. [*Died* 16 *March* 1952.

VERNEY, Maj.-Gen. Gerald Lloyd, D.S.O. 1945; M.V.O. 1937; retd.; *b.* 10 July 1900; *e. s.* of late Sir Harry Lloyd-Verney, G.C.V.O., and Lady Joan Verney (*née* Cuffe); *m.* 1926, Joyce Sybil Vivian, 3rd *d.* of 1st Baron Bicester; one *s.* one *d.* *Educ.:* Eton; R.M.C., Camberley. Page to King George V, 1914-17. Grenadier Guards, 1919; Capt., 1929; Maj., 1937; p.s.c.; transf. to Irish Guards, 1939; served in France, 1940; Instructor, Staff Coll., 1940; Lt.-Col. Comdg. 2 Bn. Irish Guards, 1940-42; Brig. 1942; Maj.-Gen. 1944; Comdr.: 1st Guards Bde. 6th Guards Tank Bde., 32nd Guards Bde., 7th Armoured Div., 56th (London) Armoured Div., T.A., Italy and N.W. Europe (despatches twice); Comd. Vienna, 1945-46; retd., 1948. O.St.J. 1936. *Publications:* The Desert Rats, 1954; History of the Guards Armoured Division, 1955; The Devil's Wind, 1956; articles in mil. and sporting press; book reviews. *Recreations:* shooting, fishing. *Address:* Knockmore, Enniskerry, Co. Wicklow. *T.:* Enniskerry 27. *Clubs:* Guards; Kildare Street (Dublin). [*Died* 3 *April* 1957.

VERNEY, Lt.-Col. Sir Ralph, 1st Bt., *cr.* 1946; Kt., *cr.* 1928; C.B. 1934; C.I.E. 1920; C.V.O. 1921; Secretary to the Speaker of the House of Commons, 1921-55; Examiner of Private Bills and Taxing Officer, House of Commons, 1927-44; *b.* 25 May 1879; *o. s.* of late Frederick Verney, M.P., North Bucks, and Maude Sarah, *d.* of Sir John and Lady Sarah Hay-Williams, and *g.s.* of late Rt. Hon. Sir Harry Verney, 2nd Bart.; *m.* 1909, Janette, *d.* of Hon. J. T. Walker, Sydney, N.S. Wales; two *s.* one *d.* *Educ.:* Harrow; Christ Church, Oxford. Joined Rifle Brigade, 1900; served South African War for 2½ years, also in Egypt and India; joined the Staff of Lord Chelmsford, Governor of Queensland, as A.D.C., 1907; served on his Staff as Private Secretary in N.S.W. till 1912; Military Secretary to Lord Chelmsford, Viceroy of India, 1916-21; served with the Rifle Brigade in France, 1914-15. *Recreation:* motoring. *Heir:* *s.* John [*b.* 30 Sept. 1913; *m.* 1939, Jeannie Lucinda, *d.* of late Major Herbert Musgrave; one *s.* five *d.*]. *Address:* 73 Eaton Square, S.W.1. *Clubs:* Travellers', St. James'. [*Died* 22 *Feb.* 1959.

VERNON, Ambrose White, D.D., LL.D., Litt.D.; *b.* New York City, 13 Oct. 1870; *s.* of William Vernon, Newport, R.I., and Rebecca Peace White, Philadelphia; *m.* 1896, Katharine Tappe (*d.* 1932), Wernigerode, Germany; no *c.* *Educ.:* Morris Academy; Princeton University; Union Seminary; Berlin University. Pastor First Congregational Church, Hiawatha, Kansas, 1896-99; First Congregational Church, East Orange, N.J., 1899-1904; Professor of Biblical Literature and Pastor of the College Church at Dartmouth College, 1904-7; Professor of Practical Theology at Yale University, 1907-9; Pastor of Harvard Church, Brookline, 1909-18; Professor of Biography in Carleton College, 1919-1924; at Dartmouth College, 1924-31. *Publications:* The Religious Value of the Old Testament; Turning Points in Church History; Pivotal Figures of History. *Recreation:* tennis. *Address:* Dartmouth College, Hanover, New Hampshire, U.S.A.; (winter) 699 Osceola Ave., Winter Park, Florida. [*Died* 24 *Aug.* 1951.

VERNON, Horace Middleton, M.A., M.D.; *b.* 3 Oct. 1870; 2nd *s.* of Thomas Heygate Vernon; *m.* Katharine Dorothea, *e. d.* of late Rev. William Ewart, Bishops Cannings, Wilts; one *s.* three *d.* *Educ.:* Dulwich College; Merton College, Oxford (Scholar); St. George's Hospital, London. 1st class Honours at Oxford in Chemistry, 1891, and in Physiology, 1893; Naples Biological Scholar, 1894; Rolleston Memorial Prizeman, 1896; George Henry Lewes Student, 1896; Radcliffe Travelling Fellow, 1897; late University Lecturer in Chemical Physiology at Oxford; Fellow of Magdalen College, Oxford, 1898-1920; Investigator for the Industrial Health Research Board, 1919-32. *Publications:* Variation in Animals and Plants, 1903; Intracellular Enzymes, 1908; Industrial Fatigue and Efficiency, 1921; The Alcohol Problem, 1928; The Principles of Heating and Ventilation, 1934; The Shorter Working Week, 1934; Accidents and their Prevention, 1936; Health in Relation to Occupation, 1939; The Health and Efficiency of Munition Workers, 1940; numerous scientific papers published in the Journal of Physiology, and elsewhere. Memos. on the conditions of Industrial Efficiency and Fatigue in Munition Workers, 1915-18; reports for Industrial Health Research Board. *Address:* 34 York Mansions, S.W.11. *T.:* Macaulay 5371. [*Died* 11 *Feb.* 1951.

VERNON-JONES, Vernon Stanley; Rudyard Kipling Fellow of Magdalene College, Cambridge; *b.* Ystradmeurig, Cardiganshire, 6 Aug. 1875; *s.* of Rev. John Jones, M.A., and Mary Davies; *m.* 1906, Gertrude Cobham (*d.* 1949), *d.* of F. W. and Frances Payne, of Water Hall, Whixoe, Essex; one *s.* one *d.* *Educ.:* Eton; King's College, Cambridge. *Recreations:* fishing, gardening. *Address:* Orchard Cottage, Commercial End, Swaffham Bulbeck, Cambs.

[*Died* 4 *Dec.* 1955.

VERNON SMITH, Rt. Rev. Guy; *see* Smith.

VERNON-WENTWORTH, Capt. Bruce Canning, J.P.; late Grenadier Guards; *b.* 14 Dec. 1862; *e. s.* of late Thomas F. C. Vernon-Wentworth of Wentworth Castle, York, Aldebrough, Black Heath, Suffolk, and Dal, Rannoch, N.B., and late Lady Harriet Augusta Canning, *d.* of 1st Marquis of Clanricarde, and *g. d.* of Canning. *Educ.:* Harrow; Sandhurst. Contested Barnsley thrice; M.P. (C.) Brighton, 1893-1906. *Address:* Wentworth Castle, Barnsley. *Clubs:* Guards, Carlton.

[*Died* 12 *Nov.* 1951.

VERRALL, Paul Jenner, M.B., B.C. (Cantab.), F.R.C.S. (Eng.); Consulting Orthopædic Surgeon, Royal Free Hospital, London; Surgical Specialist London Region, Ministry of Pensions; *b.* 9 Feb. 1883; *s.* of late Sir Thomas Jenner Verrall; *m.* 1908, Edmée, *d.* of Comte Lostie de Kerhor de St. Hippolyte; one *d.* *Educ.:* Winchester College; Trinity College, Cambridge; St. Bartholomew's Hospital, London. Chief Assistant, Orthopædic Dept., St. Bartholomew's Hospital, 1910-26; Surgeon, Military Orthopædic Hospital, Shepherd's Bush, 1917-24; Orthopædic Surgeon, Queen Mary's (Roehampton) Hospital, 1924-41; Orthopædic Surgeon, Royal Free Hospital, London; Lecturer in Orthopædic Surgery, London School of Medicine for Women, 1927-45; Member War Wounds Committee Medical Research Council, 1940-41 F.R.S.M. *Publications:* Operations on the Joints (Modern Operative Surgery); B.M.A. lectures, and many other articles on orthopædic surgery. *Address:* 48 Carlton Hill, N.W.8. *T.:* Maida Vale 6862. *Club:* Savage.

[*Died* 22 *April* 1951.

VERRILL, Alpheus Hyatt; author, artist, ethnologist, archæologist, explorer; *b.* New Haven, Conn., U.S.A., 23 July 1871; *s.* of Professor Addison E. Verrill, and Flora L. Smith; *m.* 1st, 1892, Kathryn L. McCarthy; three *c.*; 2nd, 1944, Lida Ruth Shaw. *Educ.:* Yale University. Scientific expeditions to West Indies, Central and S. America, 1889-1913; discovered supposedly extinct Solenodon Paradoxus, Santo Domingo, 1907; ethnological explorations S. and C. America, 1920-23; discovered and excavated remains of hitherto unknown ancient civilization in Panama, 1924-25; in charge of expedition in search of Mayan treasures in Campeche, 1931; in charge of expeditions to recover treasure in sunken Spanish galleons in West Indies; found and partly salvaged three centuries old galleon, 1933-34; archæological researches, Panama, Peru, Chile, Bolivia, 1924-29; in 1945 established wholesale and retail shell business, Lake Worth, Fla.; Conchological exped. to B.W.I., 1948. Exped. to Southern Mexico, 1951, obtained living specimen of unknown mammal believed to be the supposedly long-extinct sacred Warri-Willki of the Aztecs, Mayas, and Incans. *Publications:* Cuba of To-day; West Indies of To-day; Jamaica of To-day; Panama of To-day; In the Wake of the Buccaneers; Under Peruvian Skies; An American Crusoe; Getting Together with Latin America; Marooned in the Forest; The Ocean and its Mysteries; Rivers and their Mysteries; Islands; Smugglers and Smuggling; Jungle Chums; Uncle Abner's Legacy; Real Story of the Whaler; Real Story of the Pirate; Great Conquerors; The American Indian; Old Civilizations of the New World; Lost Treasures; Secret Treasures; The Inquisition; Barton's Mills; Romantic and Historic Maine; Romantic and Historic Florida; Romantic and Historic Virginia; Before the Conquerors; Our Indians; They Found Gold; The Heart of Old New England; Along New England Shores; Strange Shells and their Stories; Strange Insects and their Stories; Strange Birds and Their Stories; Strange Reptiles and Their Stories; Strange Monsters and Their Stories; Strange Fish and Their Stories; Strange Animals and Their Stories; Strange Customs of Strange People; My Jungle Trails; Foods America Gave the World; The Treasure of Bloody Gut; Wonder Plants and Plant Wonders; Wonder Creatures of the Sea; Shell Collector's Handbook; Story the Earth has told; Bridge of Light; America's Ancient Civilizations; The Real Americans, etc. Many boys' books; scientific reports and monographs; contributor to leading periodicals in U.S.A. and Great Britain; described numerous new species of marine shells. *Recreations:* gardening, color photography. *Address:* Chiefland, Fla., U.S.A.

[*Died* 14 *Nov.* 1954.

VERULAM, 5th Earl of, James Brabazon Grimston; Baronet, 1628; Baron Forrester (Scotland), 1633; Baron Dunboyne and Viscount Grimston (Ireland), 1719; Baron Verulam (Great Britain), 1790; Viscount Grimston and Earl of Verulam (United Kingdom), 1815; M.A. (Oxon.), Comp.I.E.E., F.R.G.S., F.B.I.M., F.S.A., Hon. M.I.H.V.E., J.P.; Chairman, Enfield Rolling Mills, Ltd., since 1949; Director: District Bank Ltd.; Chairman: Engineering & Lighting Equipment Co. Ltd., Sternol Ltd., Sterns Ltd.; Droitwich Medical Trust; National Baby Welfare Council; British Council for Rehabilitation (Executive); Ancient Monuments Society; National Advisory Council on the Employment of the Disabled; Pres. St. Mary's Medical School; Chairman: Bryanston School; Cranborne Chase School; Member Councils of: Anglo-Swedish Society; Society of Antiquaries; Industrial Welfare Society; Member: North Thames Gas Board; Church Assembly; *b.* 11 Oct. 1910; *e. s.* of 4th Earl and Lady Violet Brabazon, *y. d.* of 12th Earl of Meath; *S.* father 1949. *Educ.:* Eton (rowed in Eight, winner of School Steeplechase, 1929, 4 times winner Jelf Latin Verse Prize); Christ Church, Oxford (read Zoology). Firma Fried. von Neuman, Marktl, Austria, 1932-33; Managing Director, Enfield Zinc Products, Ltd., 1933-36; Area Organiser, Subsistence Production Society of the Eastern Valley of Monmouthshire, 1935-39; Director, Enfield Cables, Ltd., 1936-54 (Man. Dir. 1943-53); Mayor of St. Albans, 1956; President Cremation Society, 1955-58. *Publications:* many articles and pamphlets on industrial subjects: Industries of Enfield; Works Lavatories; St. Albans City Guide; Factory Gardens. *Recreations:* swimming, languages, farming, photography. *Heir:* *b.* Hon. John Grimston. *Address:* Gorhambury, St. Albans. *Clubs:* Athenæum, Bath.

[*Died* 13 *Oct.* 1960.

VESEY, Lieut.-Col. Hon. Sir Osbert (Eustace), K.C.V.O. 1956 (C.V.O. 1953); C.M.G. 1950; C.B.E. 1919 (O.B.E. 1918); late R. of O., 9th Lancers; one of H.M.'s Hon. Corps of Gentlemen-at-Arms, 1922-56 (Clerk of the Cheque and Adjt., 1948-53; Standard Bearer, 1953-55; Lt., 1955-56); *b.* and *heir-pres.* of 5th Viscount De Vesci; *b.* 20 Feb. 1884; *m.* 1910, Dorothy, *y. d.* of late William Morison Strachan, of Strood Park, Horsham; two *d.* *Educ.:* Eton; Sandhurst. Private Sec. to Under-Sec. of State for Air, 1919-21; served European War, 1914-18 (despatches thrice, O.B.E., C.B.E., Chevalier Légion d'Honneur); re-employed, 1940-46; A.M.S. War Office, 1943-46. *Address:* 11 Sloane Gardens, S.W.1. *T.:* Sloane 3503. *Club:* Boodle's.

[*Died* 20 *July* 1957.

VESEY-FITZGERALD, Seymour Gonne, Q.C. 1950; M.A. (Oxon), LL.D. (London); Barrister-at-Law (Gray's Inn, 1921); Hon. Fellow of the School of Oriental and African Studies, University of London; Lecturer in Hindu and Mohammedan Law at the Inns of Court, 1927; *b.* 30 May 1884; *e. s.* of late P. S. Vesey-FitzGerald, C.S.I., and Catherine, *d.* of Rev. Brymer Belcher; *m.* 1920, Dulce Laura, *e. d.* of late Captain W. H. Forbes Montanaro, R.N.; no *c. Educ.:* Charterhouse; Keble College, Oxford (open scholar 2nd cl. Classical Mods., 1st class, Modern History). Indian Civil Service, 1907-1923; held posts in the Central Provinces as Registrar, Judicial Commissioner's Court, District and Sessions Judge, Legal Remembrancer, Legal Secretary and Secretary to the Legislative Council; Indian Army Reserve of Officers, 1918-19; held posts at Oxford, 1923-32, and in London, 1929-, in connection with Oriental Laws and training of Indian and Colonial Civil Service probationers; Supervisor of I.C.S. Probationers, 1935; Reader in Indian Law, 1937; Head of the Department of the languages and cultures of India and Ceylon, School of Oriental and African Studies, 1946-48; Professor of Oriental Laws in the University of London, 1946-51; Head of the Department of Law, School of Oriental and African Studies, 1948-1951; Dean of the Faculty of Laws, University of London, 1948-51; Chairman, Cttee. of Management, Holloway Sanatorium, 1946-1951. *Publications:* Amraoti District Gazetteer (with Sir A. E. Nelson), 1910; Muhammadan Law, an Abridgement, 1931; articles in various law journals, etc. *Address:* 10 King's Bench Walk, Temple, E.C.4. *T.:* Central 1365; 30 Browning Avenue, Boscombe, Bournemouth. *T.:* Boscombe 36493. [*Died* 28 *Sept.* 1954.

VESTEY, 2nd Baron, *cr.* 1922, of Kingswood; **Samuel Vestey,** Bt., *cr.* 1913; *b.* 25 Dec. 1882; *e. s.* of 1st Baron and Sarah (*d.* 1923), *d.* of George Ellis, Birkenhead, Cheshire; *S.* father 1940; *m.* 1908, Frances, *e. d.* of John Richard Howarth, Freshfield, Lancs; two *d. Educ.:* Merton College, Oxford. Sheriff of Gloucestershire, 1933. *Heir: g.s.* Samuel George Armstrong Vestey [*b.* 1941; *er. s.* of Hon. William Howarth Vestey (killed in action in Italy, June 1944)]. *Address:* Stowell Park, Glos. *T.:* Fossebridge 308; 6 Manchester Square, W.1. *T.:* Welbeck 1251. [*Died* 4 *May* 1954.

VESTEY, Sir Edmund (Hoyle), 1st Bt., *cr.* 1921; Chairman of the Union International Company Ltd., and affiliated companies; Joint Head of Blue Star Line; *b.* 3 Feb. 1866; *s.* of Samuel Vestey, Liverpool; *m.* 1st, 1887, Sarah, *d.* of Joseph Barker, Formby, Lancashire; two *s.* two *d.*; 2nd, 1926, Ellen, *d.* of Arthur Franklin Soward, Sutton, Surrey. *Educ.:* Liverpool Institute. *Heir: g.s.* John Derek Vestey [*b.* 4 June 1914; *s.* of late J. J. Vestey and Dorothy Mary, *d.* of John Henry Beaver, Oxenhope, Yorks; *m.* 1938, Phyllis Irene, *o. d.* of H. Brewer, Banstead; one *s.* one *d.*]. *Address:* Thanet Place, North Foreland, Kent; Woodberry, West Overcliff Drive, Bournemouth. [*Died* 18 *Nov.* 1953.

VIBART, Captain John Fleming, C.B.E. 1919; retired from Royal Indian Navy; *b.* 10 Aug. 1877; *o. s.* of Captain John Vibart, late R.A.; *m.* 1911, Edyth Gladys, *o. d.* of Col. H. J. Bremner, Indian Army, retired; no *c. Educ.:* Bath; H.M.S. Worcester. Went to sea in the sailing ship Hesperus, 1893, where served his time; did two voyages to Australia as second mate; appointed to the Royal Indian Marine, 1899; took part in S. African War (Queen's medal); China, 1900 (medal); Somaliland, 1902-4 (medal); European War, 1914-19 (despatches, C.B.E., Order of the Nile and Greek Military Cross); retired, 1929. War of 1939-45, rejoined for active service, 1940 (1939-45 Star, Burma Star, Defence Medal, War Medal). *Recreations:* shooting, fishing, golf, tennis. *Address:* c/o Grindlay's Bank Ltd., 54 Parliament St., S.W.1. *Club:* Naval and Military. [*Died* 9 *Dec.* 1948.
[*But death not notified in time for inclusion in Who Was Who 1941-1950, first edn.*

VICK, His Honour Judge Sir Godfrey Russell, Kt. 1950; Q.C. 1935; M.A., LL.B.; one of H.M. Judges of County Courts since October 1956; Barrister-at-Law; Bencher of the Inner Temple; *b.* 24 Dec. 1892; *y. s.* of Richard William Vick, J.P., and Emily Oughtred, West Hartlepool, Durham; *m.* Marjorie Hester, *y. d.* of late John Albert Compston, K.C.; two *s.* two *d. Educ.:* The Leys School, Cambridge; Jesus Coll., Cambridge. Capt. Durham Light Infantry; General Staff (1st Army), 1914-1918; called to Bar, Inner Temple, 1917; Recorder of Richmond, Yorkshire, 1930-31; of Halifax, 1931-39; Recorder of Newcastle upon Tyne, 1939-56. Master the Worshipful Company of Curriers, 1947-48; Co-President of the International Bar Assoc., 1950; Chairman of the General Council of the Bar, 1948-1952. *Recreations:* hunting and golf. *Address:* 3 Hare Court, Temple, E.C.4. *T.A.:* 6 Temple. *T.:* Central 3344; Little Hermitage, Seal, Sevenoaks. *Clubs:* M.C.C., Royal Thames Yacht. [*Died* 27 *Sept.* 1958.

VICKERS, Kenneth Hotham, M.A.; Professor Emeritus, University of Southampton; *b.* 22 May 1881; *s.* of late Rev. Randall W. Vickers, Vicar of Naburn, Yorkshire; *m.* 1911, Alice Margretha (*d.* 1948), *y. d.* of late Dr. Edward Crossman, Hambrook, Gloucestershire; one *s. Educ.:* Oundle; Exeter College, Oxford. Lecturer in History, University College, Bristol, 1905-08; Organiser and Lecturer in London History for the London County Council, 1907-09; Tutor to Univ. of London Joint Committee for Tutorial Classes, 1908-13; Professor of Modern History in the University of Durham (Armstrong College), 1913-22; Secretary Univ. of Durham Schools Examinations, 1919-22. Principal, Univ. Coll., Southampton, 1922-46. Dr. of Laws (*h.c.*). *Publications:* Humphrey Duke of Gloucester, a Biography, 1907; England in the Later Middle Ages (1272-1485), 1913; A Short History of London, 1913; Vol. XI. Northumberland County History, 1921, etc. *Address:* Westcliffe, 156 Regent's Park Rd., Millbrook, Southampton. [*Died* 5 *Sept.* 1957

VICKERY, Col. Charles Edwin, C.M.G. 1919; D.S.O. 1902; J.P., D.L., Durham; late R.A.; *b.* 6 July 1881; *m.* 1930, Elizabeth, *d.* of Dr. E. J. Burnett, M.B.E., J.P.; one *d. Educ.:* Felsted School, Essex; Aerzen, nr. Hanover, Germany. Obtained first commission in R.F.A., 1900; Major, 1914; Lt.-Col., 1925; Col. 1929; served with 42nd Battery in South Africa (despatches, Queen's and King's medals 5 clasps, D.S.O.); with S. Nigerian Regt. in operations in West Africa, 1903-6; (wounded, despatches twice, medal and 4 clasps); served with Egyptian army, 1907-12; present at the operations in South Kordofan (Nyima), 1908 (Egyptian medal and clasp); the operations in South Kordofan, 1910 (Sudan medal and clasp, 4th class Medjedieh); operations in the Sudan, 1914 (clasp, 4th class Order of the Nile); served in Gallipoli (including evacuation) and Egypt, 1915; France, 1916; special mission to the King of the Hedjaz, Dec. 1916–March 1917; France, 1917-19 (wounded, despatches seven times, Bt. Lt.-Col., C.M.G., bar to D.S.O., Croix de Guerre); 1st Class Order of Nahda; British Agent at Jeddah to King of Hedjaz, 1919-20; Col. R.A. Northern Command, York, 1933-35; retired pay, 1935; B.E.F. France, 1939-40 (despatches); contested Blaydon-on-Tyne, 1935; J.P. 1936; D.L. 1937; C.C. Durham, 1937; High Sheriff of Durham, 1945-46. *Address:* Whorlton Grange, Whorlton, Co. Durham. [*Died* 11 *March* 1951.

VIDAL, Colonel Francis Peter, C.B.E, 1939 (O.B.E. 1918); *b.* 22 Feb. 1879; *s.* of

Captain J. H. Vidal, R.N.; *m.* 1906, Mary Hepburn; one *s.* *Educ.:* Stonehouse; Bede College. Bank Manager until 1914; joined Army as private, transferred to Reserve for service as civilian Acting Paymaster; Commissioned, 1916; Secretary, War Office demobilisation sub-committee, 1916-17, and Assistant Inspector of Army Pay Offices, 1916-17; Major and Staff-Paymaster, 1924; Lieutenant-Colonel, 1925; Colonel and Chief Paymaster, 1936; retired, 1939; re-employed 1939-43 as D.A.A.G., H.Q. Southern Command; Hon. Sec. S.S. & A.F.A., County of Shropshire, 1943-51; County Military Army Welfare Officer, 1945-51. *Address:* c/o Midland Bank, Salisbury, Wilts. [*Died* 14 *Sept.* 1952.

VILLIERS, Lt.-Col. Evelyn Fountaine, C.M.G. 1916; D.S.O. 1900; late Royal Sussex Regt.; *b.* 4 May 1875; *y. s.* of late Rev. Charles Villiers, Rector of Croft, Yorks; *m.* 1st, 1901, Muriel (*d.* 1941), 3rd *d.* of Col. Wisden of the Warren, Broadwater, near Worthing; one *s.* three *d.*; 2nd, 1949, Edith Ellen, *yr. d.* of late Richard Scoffin, Grantham. *Educ.:* Winchester College. Entered army, 1895; Capt. 1903; Major, 1915; served S. Africa, 1900-1901 (despatches, Queen's medal 5 clasps, D.S.O.); European War, 1914-16 (despatches five times, wounded, C.M.G.); Siberia on Military Mission, 1918-19; Inter-Allied Commission of Control in Upper Silesia, as District Controller, 1921-22; retired pay, 1924. *Address:* c/o Lloyds Bank, 6 Pall Mall, S.W.1. [*Died* 3 *Jan.* 1955.

VILLIERS, Gerald Hyde, C.M.G. 1923; Assistant Secretary, Foreign Office; *b.* 31 Aug. 1882; *yr. s.* of late Rt. Hon. Sir Francis Hyde Villiers, G.C.M.G.; unmarried. *Educ.:* Harrow. Passed a competitive examination and appointed a clerk in the Foreign Office, 1903; an Active 3rd Secretary in the Diplomatic Service, 1907; Secretary to the Earl of Granard's Special Embassy to the Courts at Brussels, Copenhagen, Christiania, Stockholm, The Hague, Madrid, and Lisbon to announce the Accession of King George V., 1910; in attendance on the Representative of Peru at the Coronation of King George V., 1911 (Coronation medal); Private Secretary to late Right Hon. F. D. Acland, M.P., Parliamentary Under-Secretary of State for Foreign Affairs, 15 March-31 Oct. 1913; an Assistant Clerk, 1913; an Assistant Secretary in the Foreign Office, 1921; Second British Plenipotentiary at the Tangier Conference, Paris, 1923; resigned, 1929; Ministry of Economic Warfare, Sept. 1939-45. *Recreations:* travelling and music. *Address:* 21A Prince Edward Mansions, Pembridge Square, W.2. *T.:* Bayswater 7397. *Club:* Brooks's. [*Died* 10 *Feb.* 1953.

VILLIERS, Sir Thomas Lister, Kt., *cr.* 1933; *b.* 31 Oct. 1869; *s.* of Prebendary Henry Montagu Villiers and Lady Victoria Russell; *m.* 1st, 1896, Evelyn Hope (*d.* 1938), *d.* of William Higgin Walker; one *s.*; 2nd, 1953, Marjorie Keyt, *d.* of late Edwin Keyt, Colombo, Ceylon. *Educ.:* Sherborne. Planter in Ceylon, 1887-1906; Merchant, Colombo, since 1906; Member Municipal Council of Colombo, 1907-8 and 1911-20; Member Legislative Council of Ceylon, 1924-1931; Member State Council of Ceylon, 1931-32; retired, 1932. *Recreation:* fishing. *Address:* 26 Lowndes Street, S.W.1. *T.:* Belgravia 3413. *Club:* Oriental. [*Died* 21 *Dec.* 1959.

VILLIERS-STUART, Colonel John Patrick, C.B. 1924; D.S.O. 1915; O.B.E. 1920; late Coke's Rifles, Panjab Frontier Force; *b.* 1 March 1879; *y. s.* of late Lt.-Col. Villiers-Stuart, sometime of Castletown, Co. Kilkenny; *m.* 1st, 1914, Phyllis Mary (*d.* 1933), *d.* of late James Read; one *s.* two *d.*; 2nd, 1933, Eileen Nora, *d.* of late Col. A. J. M. MacLaughlin, C.I.E. *Address:* Old Acres, Battle, Sussex. [*Died* 22 *Oct.* 1958.

VINALL, Joseph William Topham, A.R.C.A.; S.M.A.; F.R.S.A., F.R.S.T., U.S.O.A.; painter, pastellist, etcher, and illustrator of English classics; *b.* Liverpool, 11 June 1873; *s.* of N. Vinall, Liverpool, and Elizabeth Topham, Birmingham; *m.* 1901, Kate Adelina Chocqueel; two *d.* *Educ.:* Royal Coll. of Art. First public appointments were in art organising and lecturing in London, and as an art examiner to various bodies, retired L.C.C. Service, 1938; served as British Representative and Chairman of Committees of several International Art Congresses; exhibited at the Paris Salon, the R.A., R.I., R.O.I., R.P.S., L.P.S., and other leading London and Provincial Art Galleries, including the R.S.A., and the R.H.S., W.G., Laing A.G., I.War M.; held various exhibitions in London, including Exhibition of Pastels (96 works) entitled, In and Around Westminster, 1927, of which 32 have been permanently placed by Australian Government in Federal Parliament House at Canberra, 1940. Leading Works: King Albert on the Dunes, 1914 (Belgian Embassy); Capt. H. Duggan, M.P.; Western Sea, Barque of Fancy; The Discovery; Embankment Gardens (Whitechapel Art Gallery); Under the Dome (Hull); Nave of St. Paul's (Walker Gallery, Liverpool); The Bloomsbury Site—1931 (University of London); The Amateur (Glasgow Art Gallery); Liverpool and the Royal Iris (Newcastle upon Tyne); Last of the Thetis Zeebrugge; Liverpool Horse Parade (Liverpool Corporation); Gate of London; Evensong Westminster (York); St. Paul's, St. Stephen's Walbrook (Corporation of London Guildhall Art Gallery); King's College Chapel, Cambridge and Cambridge Backs (C.I.A.D.); Water-colour drawings of Vanished London, acquired by British Museum, 1938; Drawings in the Victoria and Albert Museum, 1941. 2 Works of School Subjects (School Prayers, First Empire Day, 1910; The Art Class, 1912), L.C.C. County Hall, 1944; 150 Works Hammersmith Town Hall, 1946; The Empire's Capital. Portrait of Young Girl, Paris Salon, 1940, survived German occupation 1945, returned by War Office 1946, exhibited London and on tour, 1946-47; 40 exhibited works of Interiors of Chiswick House and Grounds, and Gunnersbury Mansion, 1951. *Publications:* many Art Textbooks and articles; also Plays on Great Artists:—The Masterbuilders of the Dome (Wren); Romney; Farrago of Moonshine (comedy); A Sculptor of Dreams (Stevens), The Man from Leicester Fields (Hogarth), and others (1941-43). *Recreations:* walking, rowing. *Address:* 8 Devonshire Gardens, Grove Park, Chiswick, W.4. [*Died* 21 *March* 1953.

VINCENT, Arthur Rose, C.B.E. 1919; D.L.; late of Muckross, Killarney, which he presented to the Irish Free State as a National Park in 1933; *b.* 9 June 1876; 2nd *s.* of late Col. A. H. Vincent of Summerhill House, Co. Clare; *m.* 1st, 1910, Maud (*d.* 1929), *d.* of William Bowers Bourn of Filoli House, San Mateo, California; one *s.* one *d.*; 2nd, 1933, Mrs. Dorothy Sands, *d.* of John Crouteau, Southampton. *Educ.:* Wellington College; Trinity College, Dublin. Called to Irish Bar; in the Foreign Office Judicial Service, 1903; retired, 1910; High Sheriff for Co. Kerry, 1916; Senator, Irish Free State, 1931-34. *Clubs:* White's; Kildare Street (Dublin); Travellers' (Paris). [*Died* 24 *Sept.* 1956.

VINCENT, Lady (Ethel Gwendoline); *widow* of Col. Sir C. E. Howard Vincent; *b.* 14 Feb. 1861; *d.* and *co-heiress* of late George Moffatt, M.P., Goodrich Court, Herefordshire; *m.* 1882; one *d.* Has travelled much. *Publications:* 40,000 Miles over Land and Water, 1885; Newfoundland to Cochin China, 1892; China to Peru, over the Andes, 1894; and various records of travel. *Address:* 42 Belgrave Square, S.W.1. *T.:* Sloane 2622. [*Died* 14 *Feb.* 1952.

VINCENT, Sir Harry, Kt., cr. 1939; Hon. LL.D. Birmingham; Governing Director, Harry Vincent Limited; *b.* 25 Oct. 1874; *s.* of John Gray Vincent, Evesham, Worcs.; *m.* 1896, Effie Mary Ann (*d.* 1948), *d.* of Henry Lobb; one *s.* five *d.* High Sheriff of Warwickshire, 1945-1946; Hon. Treasurer, Birmingham Hospitals Centre, 1930-43; Life Governor, University of Birmingham; Vice-Pres., Birmingham United Hospital; Past President, and Life Governor of Midland Nerve Hospital; Member Board of Management of Children's Hospital; Life Governor, Royal Cripples Hospital; O.St.J.; Gold Medal of Birmingham Civic Society in 1936. *Recreation:* yachting. *Address:* Priory Dene, Priory Road, Edgbaston, Birmingham. *T.:* Calthorpe 2216. [*Died* 22 *Oct.* 1952.

VINCENT, Rt. Rev. John Dacre, M.C. 1916, Bar 1917; Bishop of Damaraland since 1952; *b.* 1 January 1894; *s.* of Rev. Prebendary G. H. Vincent; *m.* 1927, Daphne Clark, Coerney, Port Elizabeth, S. Africa; two *s.* *Educ.:* Marlborough College, Wilts.; St. John's College, Oxford (M.A.); Ely Theological College. Served European War, 1914-1918, Lieut. Devon Regt. (attached R.E. Signals), 1914-19. Priest, 1921; Asst. Curate: Gillingham, Dorset, 1920-25; Bloemfontein Cathedral, 1925-28; Vicar of Longbridge Deverill, Wilts., 1929-37; Archdeacon of Bloemfontein, 1937-52; Rector of St. Margaret's, Bloemfontein, 1937-41. Senior Chaplain to the Forces (S.A.), 1941-46. *Address:* Bishop's House, Box 57, Windhoek, S.W. Africa. *T.:* Windhoek 3607. [*Died* 19 *May* 1960.

VINCENT, William James Nathaniel, C.B.E. 1919; M.D.; late Medical Superintendent, South Yorkshire Mental Hospital, Wadsley, Sheffield; *b.* 1867; 2nd *s.* of late H. J. Vincent; *m.* 1917 Kate Helen, *d.* of Major Claude Barker, Sheffield; two *s.* two *d.* *Educ.:* University of Durham; London Hospital. Formerly Lecturer in Mental Diseases, University of Sheffield; Temp. Lieut.-Colonel, R.A.M.C., Officer in charge, Wharncliffe War Hospital, Sheffield, 1915-20, and of Ministry of Pensions Hospital, Wadsley, Sheffield. *Recreation:* Life Member British Section, Swiss Alpine Club. *Address:* 37 Westbourne Road, Sheffield. [*Died* 15 *March* 1953.

VINE, Laurence Arthur; a Deputy Chairman of London Sessions since 1947; Barrister at Law; *b.* 18 Dec. 1885; 3rd *s.* of late Frederick William and Catherine Vine; *m.* 1915, Nellie Florence Ashley (*d.* 1951); one *s.* *Educ.:* Univ. of London. Started life as journalist; reporter or sub-Editor on various provincial and London newspapers. Called to Bar, Gray's Inn, 1924; practised South-Eastern Circuit. Recorder of Colchester, 1947. *Recreation:* golf. *Address:* Sessions House, Newington Causeway, S.E.1; Oakwood, Warnham, Sx. [*Died* 14 *Jan.* 1954.

VINING, Most Rev. Leslie Gordon, C.B.E. 1946; D.D. (Lambeth) 1951; M.A. (Cantab.); Archbishop of West Africa since 1951; Bishop of Lagos, since 1940; *b.* 5 Feb. 1885; unmarried. *Educ.:* Privately; Emmanuel College, Cambridge (M.A.); Ridley Hall. Curate at St. Gabriel's, Sunderland, 1911-14; Private Secretary and Domestic Chaplain to Bishop of Bristol, 1914-15; Chaplain to the Forces, 1915-18 (despatches twice); Vicar of S. Albans, Westbury Park, 1918-38; Assistant Bishop on the Niger, 1938-40. *Address:* Bishopscourt, Lagos. *Club:* Royal Empire Society. [*Died* 4 *March* 1955.

VINSON, Frederick Moore; Chief Justice of the United States since 1946; *b.* Louisa, Kentucky, 22 Jan. 1890; *s.* of James Vinson and Virginia Ferguson; *m.* 1923, Roberta Dixon; two *s.* *Educ.:* Kentucky Normal College; Centre College, Kentucky (A.B. 1909, LL.B. 1911, LL.D. 1938). Hon. LL.D. University of Kentucky, Mercer Univ., Washington and Lee Univ., Bethany Coll., Princeton Univ. and Univ. of Louisville, and also Dickinson College. Law practice at Louisa, 1911; City Attorney, Louisa, 1913; Commonwealth Attorney, 32nd Judicial District, Kentucky, 1921-24; member of Congress, 1923-29 and 1931-38; Associate Justice, U.S. Court of Appeals for D.C., 1938-43; Chief Judge U.S. Emergency Court of Appeal, 1942-43; Director Office of Economic Stabilization, 1943-45; Vice-Chm., U.S. deleg. to U.N. Monetary and Financial Conf., Bretton Woods, 1944; Federal Loan Administrator, March 1945; Director Office of War Mobilization and Reconversion, April 1945; Secretary of the Treasury, 1945-46. Chm. Nat. Advisory Council; 1st Chm. Bd. of Governors Internat. Monetary Fund, and of Internat. Bank for Reconstruction and Development. D.S.M. of American Legion, 1947; Presidential Medal for Merit, 1947. *Address:* Ashland, Kentucky, U.S.A. [*Died* 8 *Sept.* 1953.

VIRGO, John James, C.B.E. 1918; retired; *b.* 22 April 1865; *s.* of Caleb and Mary Virgo, Glenelg, South Australia; *m.* 1st, Lucy Stapleton (*d.* 1915), *d.* of Dr. Crabb, Adelaide; three *s.* one *d.*; 2nd, 1920, E. Dorothy, *d.* of Rev. F. Aston. *Educ.:* Glenelg Grammar School. Chose Y.M.C.A. as life-work, 1886; held various secretarial appointments in Australia and London for over 60 years; made eleven world tours in connection with Association work; Vice-President Y.M.C.A. National Council: Chairman Y.M.C.A. British Commonwealth Union; National Field Secretary Young Men's Christian Association, 1915-25; retired. *Publications:* 50 Years with the Y.M.C.A.; Associational topics; 50 Years Fishing for Men, 1939. *Recreations:* cricket, football, sailing, tennis; singing and elocution; soloist in oratorios. *Address:* 11 Woodside Road, Parkstone, Dorset. *T.:* Parkstone 1025. *Club:* Royal Empire Society. [*Died* 2 *Aug.* 1956.

VIVIAN, Adm. Algernon W. H.; *see* Walker-Heneage-Vivian.

VIVIAN, Sir Sylvanus (Percival), Kt., cr. 1937; C.B. 1925; *b.* 1 Oct. 1880; 2nd *s.* of late Thomas Comley Vivian of Kensington; *m.* 1906, Mary Elizabeth, 2nd *d.* of W. J. Barnett; one *d.* *Educ.:* St. Paul's School; St. John's College, Oxford. Inland Revenue Department, 1903; Assistant Secretary, National Health Insurance Commission (England), 1913; Ministry of Food and Ministry of National Service (on loan), 1917-18; Deputy Registrar-General, 1919; Registrar-General, 1921-45; National Registration from 1938; Chairman, Electoral Machinery Committee, 1942; Member, Boundary Commission (Redistribution of Parliamentary Seats), 1944; wrote (by 1948) Section of War History. *Publications:* Campion's Works, 1909; Manor of Etchingham cum Salehurst, 1953; contributions, Encyclopædia Britannica; Cambridge History of English Literature; Dictionary of Literary Terms. *Address:* One Oak, Wishing Tree Road, St. Leonards-on-Sea, Sussex. [*Died* 28 *March* 1958.

VODDEN, Rt. Rev. Henry Townsend, M.A.; *b.* 10 June 1887; *s.* of late Rev. Harry Vodden; *m.* 1915, Violet Agnes, *d.* of Sir Matthew Smith Dodsworth, 6th Bart.; two *s.* *Educ.:* Exeter School; Exeter College, Oxford; Ridley Hall, Cambridge. Ordained 1910; a Missionary in India, 1914-20; Departmental Secretary, C.M.S., 1924-27; Assistant Home Secretary (Education), 1927-1933; Secretary for Persia, India and Ceylon, 1933-34. Suffragan Bishop of Hull, 1934-57; Archdeacon of East Riding of Yorkshire, 1934-57. *Address:* Old Rectory, Dalton Holme, Beverley. *T.:* Dalton Holme 251. [*Died* 24 *Aug.* 1960.

VOELCKER, Francis William, C.B.E. 1949; D.S.O. 1944; M.C. 1919; United Nations Korean Reconstruction Agency since 1951; *b.* 9 Oct. 1896; *s.* of Edward

William Voelcker and Jessie McCaskie Beattie; *m.* 1924, Norah Hodgson; two *d.* *Educ.:* Shrewsbury; R.M.C., Sandhurst. Commissioned King's Shropshire Light Inf., 1914; served Ypres, 1915 (wounded, prisoner); with 1st K.S.L.I., Aden, 1919-20, India, 1920-27; retired, 1928, and emigrated to New Zealand; fruit farmer, 1928-39. War of 1939-45, joined N.Z. Forces as Capt., 1939; Major, 1940; Lt.-Col., 1940; comd. 34th Bn. in Fiji; transferred to Fiji Military Forces, 1942, comdg. 3rd Bn. Fiji Infantry; took part in fighting on Bougainville, Solomon Islands, 1944. Administrator, Western Samoa, 1945; First High Commissioner, Western Samoa, 1948; New Zealand Commissioner, South Pacific Commission, 1949-50. American Bronze Star, 1944. *Recreation:* fishing. *Address:* Godley Road, Titirangi, Auckland, N.Z. [*Died* 22 *May* 1954.

VOIGT, F. A.; Author; Editor, Nineteenth Century and After, 1938-46; *b.* 9 May 1892. *Educ.:* Haberdashers' Aske's Hampstead School; University of London (B.A.). *Publications:* Combed Out; Hindenburg (with Margaret Goldsmith); Unto Cæsar; Pax Britannica; The Greek Sedition. *Address:* St. Gabriel's, Bramley, Surrey. *Club:* Reform. [*Died* 7 *Jan.* 1957.

VON BIBRA, Major Sir Eric (Ernest), Kt., *cr.* 1953; O.B.E. 1938; Agent General for Tasmania in London since 1950; *b.* 2 Sept. 1895; *s.* of Ernest W. von Bibra, Launceston, Tasmania; *m.* 1928, Dulcie Buchan Shields; three *s.* *Educ.:* Launceston Church of England Grammar School, Tasmania. Enlisted Aug. 1914, 1st A.I.F.; landed at Anzac, 3rd Australian Brigade; commissioned, field, Gallipoli, 1915; served in France, 1916; commanded 13th Lt. Trench Mortar Battery, Capt. (severely wounded and invalided to Australia); discharged, medically unfit, 1918. Mayor Launceston, 1935-1936 (Alderman 9 years). Called up from R. of O. Sept. 1939, and served on a Mil. Dist. H.Q. Staff, Major, 1944-50. State Secretary Returned Servicemen's League. *Recreations:* bowls, gardening. *Address:* 457 Strand, W.C.2. *Clubs:* Royal Automobile, Constitutional, Hurlingham; Naval, Military, Air Force (Hobart), C.T.A. (Hobart). [*Died* 27 *Feb.* 1958.

VON LAUE, Professor Max (Theodor Felix); Scientific Member of the Fritz Haber Institute of the Max Planck Society (formerly Kaiser Wilhelm Institute for Physical and Electrical Chemistry), Berlin-Dahlem, since 1959 (Director, 1951-59); *b.* 9 Oct. 1879; *s.* of Julius Laue and Minna Laue (*née* Zerrenner); *m.* 1910; one *s.* one *d.* *Educ.:* Univs. of Strassburg, Els., Göttingen, Munich, Berlin. Dr.phl. Univ. of Berlin, 1903; Lecturer, University of Berlin, 1906, Univ. of Munich, 1909; Asst. Prof. Univ. of Zürich, 1912; Prof. Univ. of Frankfurt, 1914, Univ. of Berlin, 1919; resigned 1943. Kaiser-Wilhelm-Institut für Physik, Hechingen, Hohenzollern, 1944-45; Hon. Prof. Univ. of Göttingen, 1946-. Nobel Prize for Physics, 1914; Max Planck-Médaille, 1932. For. Mem. Royal Society, 1949. Dr.Ing.E.h.; Dr.med. (*h.c.*); Dr. rer.nat. (*h.c.*). Hon. Doctor of Science; Manchester, 1936; Chicago, 1948. *Publications:* Relativitätstheorie, Vol. I, 1911, Vol. II, 1921; Röntgenstrahlinterferenzen, 1941; Materiewellen u. ihre Interferenzen, 1943; Geschichte der Physik, 1946 (Eng. trans., 1950); Theorie der Supraleitung, 1947; Annalen der Physik, Zeitschrift für Physik. *Address:* Berlin-Dahlem, Faradayweg 8, Germany (West-Berlin). *T.:* 76 45 86. [*Died* 24 *April* 1960.

von NEUMANN, John; Member, U.S. Atomic Energy Commission, Washington, D.C. (Presidential Appointment), since 1955; Director of Electronic Computer Project (1945-55) and Professor of Mathematics, 1933-55, Institute for Advanced Study, Princeton, N.J. (on leave of absence since March 1955); *b.* Budapest, Hungary, 28 Dec. 1903; *s.* of Max von Neumann and Margaret (*née* Kann); *m.* 1930, Mariette Kovesi (marriage dissolved); one *d.*; *m.* 1938, Klara Dan. *Educ.:* University of Berlin; Federal Institute of Technology, Zürich, Switzerland; Univ. of Budapest (Hungary). Asst. Prof., Univ. of Berlin, 1926-29; Asst. Prof., Univ. of Hamburg, 1929-30. Visiting Lecturer, 1930, Princeton Univ., U.S.A. Holds several hon. doctorates at Univs. and Institutes in America and Europe. Awards include: Rockefeller Fellowship, 1926; Medal for Merit (U.S.), 1947; Medal of Freedom (U.S.), 1956; Enrico Fermi Award, U.S. Atomic Energy Commission, 1956. *Publications:* Mathematical Foundations of Quantum Mechanics (German), Berlin, 1932, New York, 1942, (Spanish trans.) Madrid, 1949, (English) Princeton, N.J., 1955; Theory of Games and Economic Behavior (with O. Morgenstern), Princeton, N.J., 1944 (several edns.). Numerous papers on subjects in mathematics. *Address:* The Woodner, Apt. B-1037, 3636-16th Street, N.W., Washington 25, D.C., U.S.A. *T.:* DU-7-8556. [*Died* 8 *Feb.* 1957.

VON NEURATH, Freiherr Constantin; *b.* 2 Feb. 1873; *s.* of Freiherr Constantin von Neurath, Lord Chamberlain to the late King of Württemberg, and Mathilde, Frein von Gemmingen-Hornberg; *m.* 1901, Marie Moser von Filseck; one *s.* one *d.* *Educ.:* Stüttgart; Tübingen; Berlin. Vice-Consul in London, 1903; Foreign Office; Councillor of the Embassy in Constantinople; Private Secretary to the King of Württemberg; Minister in Copenhagen; Ambassador to the Quirinal, 1922; to the Court of St. James, 1930-32; Minister for Foreign Affairs, Germany, 1932-38; President of the Privy Council of the Cabinet, Germany, 1938; Reich Protector for Bohemia and Moravia, 1939-41. Senior S.S. Group Leader, 1943. Released, Nov. 1954, after serving 8 yrs. of a 15 yr. political sentence passed by International Military Tribunal in Oct. 1946. *Recreations:* formerly shooting, mountaineering. *Address:* Stuttgart, Germany. [*Died* 15 *Aug.* 1956.

VONNOH, Bessie Potter, N.A.; artist, sculptor; *b.* St. Louis, 17 Aug. 1872; *d.* of Alexander C. and Mary McKenney Potter; *m.* 1899, Robert Vonnoh (*decd.*); *m.* 1948, Dr Edward L. Keyes. *Educ.:* Art Institute of Chicago Bronze medal, Paris Exhibition, 1900; gold medal, St. Louis Exhibition, 1904; Member of National Institute of Arts and Letters; represented in Metropolitan Museum of Art, Art Institute, Chicago, Corcoran Art Gallery, Washington, Brooklyn Museum; Roosevelt Memorial Bird fountain Oyster Bay, L.I., 1927; Children's Garden fountain; Frances Hodgson Burnett Memorial in Central Park, N.Y. City. *Address:* 33 W. 67th St., New York. [*Died* 7 *March* 1955.

VON STROHEIM, Erich; (Oswald Hans Carl Maria von Nordenwall); film actor and director; *b.* Vienna, 22 September 1885; *m.* Marguerite Knox (*decd.*); *m.* May Jones; one *s.*; *m.* Valerie Marguerite Germonprez; one *s.*; *m.* Denise Vernac. *Educ.:* Imperial and Royal Military Academy, Wiener-Neustadt, Austria. Served in Imperial and Royal Austrian Army; went to U.S.A. 1909; served in American Army; became a naturalized citizen, 1926. Made début, Hollywood, 1914; has since written, directed and acted in many films in U.S.A., France and England. Played Rommel in Five Graves to Cairo, 1943; other important films include: North Star, Sunset Boulevard, La Grande Illusion, I Was an Adventuress, So Ends Our Night. Films personally directed: Blind Husbands, Foolish Wives, Devil's Passkey, Merry-go-Round, Greed, The Wedding March, Queen Kelly, Walk-

ing Down Broadway. Elected best director by All American Critics, 1926. Member: Academy of Motion Picture Arts and Sciences; Actors' Guild; Writers' Guild; Directors' Guild. *Publications:* Paprika, 1935; Feux de la St. Jean, 1951. *Address:* c/o Jean London, 65 Champs Elysées, Paris; Château de Maurepas (S.-et-O.), France.
[*Died* 12 *May* 1957.

VORA, Sir Manmohandas Ramji, Kt., *cr.* 1927; Member of Council of State, 1925-30; *b.* 19 Aug. 1857; *s.* of Ramji Purshottam Vora; *m.* 1872; three *s.* three *d.* *Educ.:* Bombay High School. Founder of the Indian Merchants' Chamber, Bombay; President, 1907-13, 1924 and 1933; Member of the Committee of the Chamber, 1907-28; Pres. of the Bombay Native Piece Goods Merchants' Assoc. for more than thirty years; Member of the Board of Trustees of the Victoria Jubilee Technical Institute; Member Advisory Committee B.B. and C.I. Railway; Member old Bombay Legislative Council representing Indian commercial community, 1910-20; Member Indian Legislative Assembly representing Indian Merchants' Chamber, Bombay, 1921-23; Member of the Bombay Municipal Corporation for eighteen years, and President, 1912-13; Member Advisory Committee to the Director of Industries. *Recreation:* reading. *Address:* The Ridge, Ridge Road, Malabar Hill, Bombay, India. *T.A.:* Ghorupdeo, Bombay. *T.:* 20181. [*Died* 13 *Aug.* 1934.
[*But death not notified in time for inclusion in Who Was Who 1929–1940.*

VORLEY, Lt.-Col. John Stuart, C.B.E. 1942; Director of National Parks, S. Rhodesia; *b.* 19 Dec. 1898; *s.* of H. A. Vorley and E. G. Fordham; *m.* 1926, Helen Marion, *d.* of late Sir William Dring, K.C.I.E.; one *s.* *Educ.:* Whitgift Grammar School, Croydon; Emmanuel College, Cambridge. Joined Inns of Court, O.T.C., 1915; Commissioned Royal Irish Fusiliers, 1915; France, 1916-17; West African Frontier Force (2nd Nigeria Regt.), 1918-20; Indian Forest Service (Burma), 1922; Commissioner Civil Evacuation (Burma), 1941-42; Deputy Director, Civil Defence Dept., Govt. of India, 1942-43. *Recreations:* riding, golf. *Address:* c/o Grindlay's Bank Ltd., 54 Parliament St., S.W.1; P.O. Box 89, Causeway, Salisbury, S. Rhodesia. [*Died* 2 *Jan.* 1953.

VORONOFF, Doctor Serge; Director of Experimental Surgery of Station Physiologique du Collège de France; *b.* Russia, 10 July 1866; naturalized French citizen, 1897; *m.* 1934, Fraulein Schwetz, Vienna. *Educ.:* Paris. Doctor in Medicine of Faculté de Paris; Surgeon-in-chief Russian Hospital, Paris; Surgeon-in-chief Military Hospital, 197; Director of the Laboratory of Biology à l'école des Hautes Etudes. Officer of the Legion of Honour, 1933. *Publications:* Treatise on Surgery; Treatise on Gynæcology; Treatise on Bone Grafting; Treatise on Articulation Graft; Treatise on Ovarian Grafting; Treatise on Thyroid Grafting; Grafting of Interstitial Glands; Skin Grafting; Life; The Conquest of Life. *Address:* Château Grimaldi, Menton, A.M., France. [*Died* 2 *Sept.* 1951.

VOULES, Arthur Blennerhassett; late Dir. Kepong (Malay) Rubber Estates, Ltd.; late Resident Councillor, Penang; *yr. s.* of late Sir Gordon B. Voules; *b.* 15 Sep. 1870; *m.* 1921, Grace Geraldine, *d.* of late Lt.-Col. F. West. *Educ.:* Dulwich College; Sidney Sussex College, Cambridge. Barrister-at-law, Inner Temple; Malayan Civil Service; retired, 1925. *Address:* 95 Bath Hill Court, Bournemouth. *Clubs:* East India and Sports, M.C.C.
[*Died* 21 *May* 1954.

VULLIAMY, Grace, C.B.E. 1919; Vice-President, Save the Children Fund; *b.* Ipswich, 12 Sept. 1878; *d.* of Arthur Frederick Vulliamy and Anna Marie Vulliamy. *Educ.:* Ipswich; abroad. *Address:* Princess Vlei, Retreat, Cape, South Africa.
[*Died* 10 *April* 1957.

VYSHINSKY, Andrei Yanuarievich; Order of Lenin (4 times); U.S.S.R. Permanent Delegate to U.N. since 1953; First Deputy Foreign Minister, U.S.S.R., since 1953 (Minister, 1949-53); *b.* Odessa, 1883. *Educ.:* Kiev University; LL.D. 1913; Dr. of State and Social Sciences, 1935. Joined revolutionary movement, 1905; worked in Caucasus, becoming Sec. of Baku Soviet; imprisoned several times for political reasons, 1907; literary work and teaching, 1913-17; lecturer, Moscow Univ., 1921-22; Prof. of Criminal Law Procedure, Moscow Univ., 1923-25; Rector Moscow State Univ., 1925-1928; Dep. Public Prosecutor and Public Prosecutor, 1931-38; prosecutor in many prominent trials. Director U.S.S.R. Acad. of Sciences Law Inst., 1937-41; Member: Central Exec. Cttee., U.S.S.R., 1935-37; Supreme Soviet of U.S.S.R., 1947-; Central Cttee., Communist Party of Soviet Union; Dep. Minister for Foreign Affairs, 1940-49. Soviet Rep. Allied Mediterranean Commn., 1943-45; Mem. Soviet deleg. to Potsdam Conf., 1945; Mem. Paris Peace Conf., 1946; Mem. Council Foreign Ministers (N.Y. City, Moscow, London, Paris); head Soviet deleg. to U.N. Gen. Assembly (London, N.Y. City, Paris). *Publications:* Outlines of the History of Communism, The Legal Structure of the U.S.S.R., etc.; several publs. in Russian language. *Address:* The Kremlin, Moscow, U.S.S.R.; c/ U.N., 610 Fifth Av., N.Y. City. [*Died* 22 *Nov.* 1954.

W

WACE, Alan John Bayard, M.A., Litt.D.; Hon. D.Litt., Amsterdam, Pennsylvania; Hon. LL.D., Liverpool; F.B.A.; F.S.A.; Member Institute for Advanced Study, Princeton, 1948, 1951, 1952-55; *b.* 1879; 2nd *s.* of F. C. Wace, M.A., J.P., D.L.; *m.* 1925, Helen, *d.* of Prof. W. D. Pence, Evanston, Ill., U.S.A.; one *d.* *Educ.:* Shrewsbury School; Pembroke Coll., Camb. (Scholar, Fellow, 1904-13, 1934-44, Hon. Fellow, 1951-). Univ. Prendergast Student 1902, 1904, Craven Student 1903; Student Brit. School at Athens, 1902-12, Dir., 1914-23; Librarian Brit. School at Rome, 1905-6; excavated Sparta, Mycenæ, Troy, Thessaly, Corinth, Alexandria, etc.; travelled Greece, Archipelago, Asia Minor, Balkans, Palestine, Egypt, Cyrene; Lecturer, Ancient History and Archæology, St. Andrews, 1912-14; Vanuxem Lecturer, Princeton, 1923; Norton Lecturer, American Arch. Institute, 1923-24; Deputy Keeper, Victoria and Albert Museum, 1924-34; Armstrong Lecturer, Toronto, 1939; Laurence Professor Classical Archæology, Cambridge, 1934-44; served British Legation, Athens, 1915-19; Athens, G.H.Q. Cairo, 1939-43; Professor of Classics and Archæology, Farouk I Univ., Alexandria, 1943-52. Foreign Member Royal Swedish Academy, Member American Philosophical Society, German Arch. Institute, Hon. Member American Arch. Institute, Royal Northern Antiquaries, Greek Arch. Soc., and other foreign arch. societies. *Publications:* Catalogue of Sparta Museum; Prehistoric Thessaly; Nomads of the Balkans; Excavations at Mycenæ; Chamber Tombs at Mycenæ; Cretan Statuette in Fitzwilliam Museum; Catalogue Algerian Embroideries; Sheldon Tapestries; Near Eastern and Mediterranean Embroideries; Approach to Greek Sculpture; Mycenæ, an Archæological History; many papers in arch. books and periodicals (English and Foreign), etc. *Address:* c/o British School of Archæology, 52 Odos Souedias, Athens; (residence) 27 Voukourestiou, Athens. [*Died* 9 *Nov.* 1957.

WADDINGTON, Sir (Eubule) John, G.B.E., *cr.* 1948 (O.B.E. 1919); K.C.M.G., *cr.* 1939 (C.M.G. 1935); K.C.V.O., *cr.* 1947; *b.* 9 April 1890; *s.* of late Thomas Waddington; *m.* 1923, Edith, *d.* of late George Galloway; two *s.* *Educ.:* Dulwich College; Merton College, Oxford. Entered Colonial Service, 1913; Kenya, 1913-32; Colonial Sec., Bermuda, 1932-35; British Guiana, 1935-38; Governor and C.-in-C., Barbados, 1938-41; Northern Rhodesia, 1941-47. *Recreations:* golf, tennis. *Address:* The Holt, Lindfield, Sussex. *T.:* Lindfield 34. *Club:* East India and Sports. [*Died* 18 *Jan.* 1957.

WADDINGTON, Brig. Thomas Thelwall, C.B.E. 1942; M.C.; *b.* 4 Dec. 1888; *s.* of Thomas Waddington, B.A.; *m.* 1922, Norah, *d.* of late Leonard Brooke; one *s.* one *d.* *Educ.:* Dulwich College; Exeter College, Oxford. Comd. 132 Inf. Bde., 1938-39; West Lancashire area, 1940; Mersey Garrison, 1941-44; Chief Norway Mission, U.N.R.R.A., 1945; Chief Middle East, U.N.R.R.A., 1945-47. *Address:* c/o Westminster Bank, 65 Piccadilly, W.1. *Club:* East India and Sports. [*Died* 26 *Oct.* 1958.

WADDY, Bentley Herbert, M.C.; Q.C. 1951; *b.* 9 December 1893; *s.* of Harry Waddy (Mem. of London Stock Exchange) and Fanny Millicent Woodley; *m.* 1st, 1916, Olive Mary Crook (*d.* 1947); one *s.* two *d.*; *m.* 2nd, 1947, Dorothy Knight Dix, Q.C.; one adopted *d.* *Educ.:* Cheltenham College; Worcester College, Oxford (B.A.). Supplementary List, Gloucestershire Regiment, 1913-19; European War, France and Italy (M.C.). Called to Bar, 1920; South Eastern Circuit; Kent Sessions; Recorder of Borough of Margate, Kent, 1944-53. Director, Sussex Brick Ltd. Master of the Curriers Company, 1941-42. *Recreations:* gardening, photography. *Address:* Gloucester House, 5 Bickley Rd., Bickley, Kent; Goldsmith Building, Temple, E.C.4. *T.:* Imperial 1174, Central 3399, Central 4622. [*Died* 2 *Nov.* 1956.

WADE, Sir Henry, Kt., *cr.* 1946; C.M.G. 1919; D.S.O. 1918; M.D., Ch.B., F.R.C.S.Ed.; F.R.S.E., F.R.C.S. (Hon.), F.A.C.S. (Hon.); F.R.A.C.S. (Hon.); F.R.C.S.I. (Hon.).; Hon. Col. A.M.S.; Consulting Surgeon Royal Infirmary, Edinburgh; *b.* 1877; *s.* of Rev. George Wade, Falkirk; *m.* 1924, Marjorie (*d.* 1929), *o. d.* of late James William Fraser-Tytler of Woodhouselee, Midlothian, and Mrs. Fraser-Tytler, Sen., Sunlaws, Roxburghshire. *Educ.:* Royal High School, Edinburgh; Edinburgh University. M.B., Ch.B. (Hons.) Edinburgh University, 1898; F.R.C.S.Ed., 1903; M.D. (Gold Medal) Edin. Univ., 1907; served S. Africa, 1899-1901 (Queen's medal with 4 clasps); Conservator, Museum R.C.S., Edinburgh, 1903-20; Consulting Surgeon to Leith Hosp.; Hon. Fellow or member various American and other surgical societies; Past Pres., R.C.S., Edinburgh; Lecturer in Surgery in the School of Medicine of the Royal Colleges, Edinburgh, 1906-23; European War, 1914-1919, Captain, Scottish Horse Mounted Brigade Field Ambulance, 1914-16, Consulting Surgeon, Egyptian Expeditionary Force, 1916-19 (despatches twice, D.S.O., C.M.G., Order of White Eagle of Serbia). *Publications:* various medical publications dealing mainly with renal and vesical disease. *Recreation:* amateur farming. *Address:* 6 Manor Place, Edinburgh. *T.:* 20640; Pilmuir, Haddington. *T.:* Pencaitland 213; The Private Clinic, 35 Drumsheugh Gardens, Edinburgh. *T.:* 20553. *Clubs:* Athenæum; New (Edinburgh). [*Died* 21 *Feb.* 1955.

WADE, Sir Robert Blakeway, Kt., *cr.* 1938; M.D., Ch.M. (Syd.); F.R.C.S. Eng. (Hon.); F.R.A.C.S.; President (1932-44) and Hon. Consulting Surgeon since 1932, Royal Alexandra Hospital for Children; Chm. of Infantile Paralysis Cttee., New South Wales; Chm., New South Wales Institute of Almoners; Foundation Fellow, Member of Council, Member of Board of Censors and President (1935-37), Royal Australasian College of Surgeons; Vice-President The Prince Henry Hospital, Hon. Surgeon since 1933; *b.* 27 Jan. 1874; *s.* of late W. Burton Wade, M.I.C.E.; *m.* M. M. Furber (*d.* 1943); two *d.* *Educ.:* Sydney Grammar School. Surgical Tutor, University of Sydney, 1908-16, Lecturer in Surgical Diseases of Children, 1926-32; Hon. Surgeon, South Sydney Hospital, 1913-32, Hon. Consulting Surgeon since 1932; President, New South Wales Branch of B.M.A., 1925-26; President, Medical Board of New South Wales, 1932-44; President, Section of Diseases of Children, 1933; Vice-President, Section Orthopaedic Surgery, B.M.A., Annual Meeting, 1932. *Address:* c/o Dr. S. L. Cameron, Blair Athol, Bathurst, N.S.W., Australia. *Club:* Royal Sydney Golf (Sydney, N.S.W.). [*Died* 13 *May* 1954.

WADE, Squadron Leader Trevor Sidney, D.F.C. 1941; A.F.C. 1944; Chief Test Pilot, Hawker Aircraft Ltd., since 1948; *b.* 24 Jan. 1920; *m.* 1941, Josephine Clow; two *s.* one *d.* *Educ.:* Tonbridge. Law student, 1937 to outbreak of war; joined R.A.F.V.R., 1938; Member 92 Squadron (Battle of Britain, etc.); O.C. Flying Air Fighting Development Unit, 1943-45; Test Pilot for The Aeroplane, 1946-47. Polonia Restituta, 1945. *Address:* Newland Cottage, Esher Avenue, Walton-on-Thames, Surrey. *T.:* 4695. *Club:* Royal Aero. [*Died* 3 *April* 1951.

WADIA, Sir Ness Nowrosjee, K.B.E., *cr.* 1926; C.I.E. 1918; M.I.M.E.; J.P.; millowner; *b.* 30 May 1873; *s.* of Hon. Nowrosjee Nusserwanjee Wadia, C.I.E.; *m.* 1906, Evelyne Clara Powell (*d.* 1946); one *s.* two *d.* *Educ.:* St. Xavier's College, Bombay. *Address:* Bella Vista, Peddar Road, Bombay. *Clubs:* Constitutional; Willingdon, Orient (Bombay). [*Died* 22 *April* 1952.

WADSLEY, Olive; authoress; *y. d.* of George and late Mary Wadsley. *Educ.:* Haus Sonderburg-Glücksburg, Germany; Château d'Aire, Geneva. Won Evening News Serial prize; wrote short sketches for the Tatler; first novel sent to Cassells immediately accepted; novels filmed by World Film Co.; Hepworths Stoll Company; travelled extensively in Europe. *Publications:* The Flame; Reality; Conquest; Possession; Frailty; Nevertheless; Instead; Belonging; Almond-Blossom; Flood-Tide; Wait for Me; various newspaper serials; magazine stories. *Recreations:* motoring; languages. *Address:* 40 Montpelier Street, S.W.7. [*Died* 4 *March* 1959.

WADSWORTH, Alfred Powell; Editor Emeritus Manchester Guardian (Editor 1944-56); Director Manchester Guardian and Evening News Ltd.; *b.* Rochdale, 26 May 1891; *m.* 1922, Alice Lillian Ormerod (*d.* 1955); one *d.* Trained as journalist on Rochdale Observer; joined Manchester Guardian 1917, successively special correspondent, Labour correspondent, leader-writer and Asst. Editor. Hon. M.A. Manchester Univ., 1932. Gov. of John Rylands Library; Visiting Fellow, Nuffield Coll., Oxford. Hon. LL.D. Manchester, 1955. *Publication:* (with Julia de Lacy Mann) The Cotton Trade and Industrial Lancashire 1600-1780, 1931. *Address:* Guardian Office, Manchester. *Clubs:* Reform, National Liberal; Reform (Manchester). [*Died* 4 *Nov.* 1956.

WAGSTAFF, Lieut.-Col. Lewis Cecil, C.I.E. 1917; O.B.E., 1919; Indian Army, retired; late 7th Rajput Regt.; *b.* 1882; *m.* Beatrice; one *d.* Served South African War, 1902 (Queen's medal and four clasps); European War, 1914-19 (despatches, C.I.E., O.B.E.); Lt.-Col., 1928; retired, 1932. [*Died* 24 *Jan.* 1951.

WADDELL, Hon. Sir (Charles) Graham, K.B.E. See page xxxi.

WAINWRIGHT, Sir Gilbert Cochrane, Kt., *cr.* 1942; O.B.E. 1936; retired Banker; *b.* 16 Dec. 1871; *s.* of Willis R. Stowe Wainwright and Harriet Isabel Cochrane, Halifax, N.S., Canada; *m.* 1916, Alice, *d.* of Robert Woon, Oshawa, Canada; no *c.* *Educ.:* Ottawa, Canada. Entered Bank of Ottawa, Ottawa, Can., 1889, Manager of branches in several cities (Bank of Ottawa amalgamated with Bank of Nova Scotia, 1919); came to Jamaica 1923 as Manager (Bank of Nova Scotia), Kingston; retired, 1932; Member of Legislative Council of Jamaica, 1932-42; Chairman Banana Industry Aid Board; Member of several Govt. Boards. *Address:* Acadia House, Constant Spring, Jamaica, B.W.I. *Clubs:* Royal Empire Society; Royal Ottawa Golf. [*Died* 21 *Aug.* 1954.

WAISTELL, Admiral Sir Arthur Kipling, K.C.B., *cr.* 1929 (C.B. 1916); *b.* 30 March 1873. Commanded Destroyer Flotillas, Atlantic Fleet, 1922-23; a Lord Commissioner of the Admiralty and Assistant Chief of Naval Staff, 1923-24. Served European War, 1914-18 (despatches, C.B.); Commanded First Cruiser Squadron, 1924-26; Commander-in-Chief China Station, 1929-30; Commander-in-Chief, Portsmouth, 1931-34; retired list, 1934. *Address:* Old Mead, Freshwater, I. of W. [*Died* 26 *Oct.* 1953.

WAITE, Col. Hon. Fred, C.M.G. 1946; D.S.O. 1915; O.B.E. 1944; V.D.; farmer; Chairman of Directors of Co-operative Dairy Co., Otago; Dominion Vice-President, N.Z. Farmers' Union; President, Balclutha Returned Soldiers' Association; Chairman Mortgagors Adjustment Commission, 1933; Member of Legislative Council, 1934-50; *b.* 20 Aug. 1885; *m.* 1912, Ada Philipson, *d.* of F. W. Taylor, Manchester. Served European War, in Egypt and Dardanelles, 1914-18 (despatches twice, D.S.O., 1914-15 Star, British War Medal, Victory Medal); Adjutant N.Z. Engineers, A.N.Z.A.C. Division, 1915-16; Chief Instructor of Engineers, N.Z.E.F. Training Camps, 1917-18; Member for Clutha, N.Z. Parliament, 1925-31; Member N.Z. Patriotic Council, 1939-40; Overseas Commissioner N.Z. Patriotic Fund, 1940-46, attached 2nd N.Z.E.F. *Publications:* The New Zealanders at Gallipoli (official history); Port Molyneux: A History of Pakeha and Maori in South Otago (centennial history); Pioneering in S. Otago (official Otago Centennial History). *Address:* Balclutha, N.Z. [*Died* 29 *Aug.* 1952.

WAKE, Vice-Admiral Sir St. Aubyn Baldwin, K.B.E., *cr.* 1944; C.B. 1935; *b.* 1 Nov. 1882; *s.* of Sir Herewald Wake, 12th Bart. *Educ.:* H.M.S. Britannia; R.N. College, Greenwich. Lieut., 1902; Commander, 1915; Capt., 1921; Rear-Adm., 1933; Vice-Adm. 1937; served China, 1900 (medal); European War, 1914; Naval Attaché, Buenos Aires, 1927; A.D.C. to the King, 1933; Director of Naval Equipment, Admiralty, 1934-36; retired list, 1937; Adm. Supt. of Contract-Built Ships, 1937-44. *Club:* United Service. [*Died* 1 *Oct.* 1951.

WAKELY, Major-Gen. Arthur Victor Trocke, C.B. 1942; D.S.O. 1934; M.C.; *b.* 28 Nov. 1886; *s.* of Rev. J. M. Robinson; assumed name of Wakely by deed poll, 1919; *m.* 1913, Raby Clare Jellett (*d.* 1958), *d.* of late Judge John Wakely; two *s.* *Educ.:* Campbell College, Belfast; Royal Military Academy, Woolwich; Staff College, Camberley. 2nd Lt. R.E., 1906; Capt., 1914; Bt. Maj., 1918; Major, 1924; Lt.-Col., 1930; Colonel, 1934; Maj.-Gen., 1940; retired, 1945. Served European War, 1914-1918, France and Belgium (despatches twice, Bt. Maj., M.C.); North-West Frontier, India (Mohmand), 1933 (despatches, D.S.O.); War of 1939-45 (despatches twice, C.B.). *Address:* Skehana House, Templemore, Co. Tipperary, Eire. [*Died* 29 *April* 1959.

WALDE, Ernest Herman Stewart, M.A. (Oxon); *b.* 22 Feb. 1874; *m.* 1905, Ethel Mary, *e. d.* of Richard Garnett Janion; four *s.* one *d.* *Educ.:* Charterhouse; Hertford College, Oxford (Scholar). Senior Classical Master and Headmaster's Assistant, Berkhamsted School, 1902-12; Headmaster, Chigwell School, Essex, 1912-39. *Recreations:* scrambling, sea-fishing, second-hand books. *Address:* Norton Manor, Blackmore, Essex; Bwlch, Morfa Nevin, N. Wales. *T.:* Blackmore 261. [*Died* 21 *Sept.* 1958.

WALDRON, Col. Sir William James, Kt., *cr.* 1936; J.P., Sheriff of City of London, 1935-36; Mayor of Fulham, 1923-24, 1925-1926, 1926-27, 1927-28, 1930-31, 1931-32; Hon. Freeman Borough of Fulham; *b.* Chelsea, 2 Jan. 1876; *y. s.* of late William Waldron, Chelsea; *m.* 1905, Leila (*d.* 1946), *e. d.* of Richard Lock; one *s.* decd., one *d.* decd. *Educ.:* Chelsea. Member Fulham Borough Council, 1906-19 and 1923-34; twice co-opted from outside Council to the Mayoralty; Alderman, 1925-37; F.R.G.S.; Pres. Metropolitan Mayors' Assoc. Contested E. Fulham (C.), 1933; a Vice-Pres. British Legion (Metropolitan Area), 1927-30; Sheriff of City of London, 1936; Hon. Colonel 1st Anti-Aircraft Divisional R.A.S.C. (T.A.). 1934-39; Past Master of the Worshipful Company of Glaziers (1947); President Royal Forest Agricultural Association. *Recreations:* racehorse owner, thoroughbred breeder, motoring, swimming, farming. *Address:* Ascot Cottage Estate, Winkfield, Berks; 77 Cromwell Road, S.W.7. *T.A.:* Waldron, Winkfield, Berks. *T.:* Winkfield Row 26; Frobisher 4581. *Club:* Royal Automobile. [*Died* 15 *Oct.* 1957.

WALEY, Alfred Joseph; *b.* London, 10 June 1861; 2nd *s.* of Simon Waley Waley, 22 Devonshire Place, W.1, and Anna Hendelah (*née* Salomons); *m.* 1887, Laura Landauer, Vienna; one *s.* one *d.* (and two *s.* decd.). *Educ.:* University College School, London. Served in ranks of Victoria Rifles, 1878-82; Officer, Tower Hamlets R.E. (Volunteers), 1883-88, retired with rank of Capt. Stock Exchange, 1882- (now Father of the House); served on Committee for General Purposes, 1900-09; Trustee and Manager, 1910; resigned, 1941, on reaching age of 80; witness for Stock Exchange before House of Commons Cttee. on Foreign Debts, 1917; rep. of Stock Exchange on Lord Chancellor's Cttee. to enquire into Public Trustees Office. Member Court of Worshipful Company of Musicians (Master, 1937); Hon. Treas. Roads Beautifying Assoc. Formerly Cttee. Paddington Green Children's Hosp.; Vice-Chm. Reigate Cottage Hosp. (now E. Surrey Hosp.); was a member of Council, Royal National Pension Fund for Nurses, until 1931; Cttee. of Management (now a Pres.) London Orphans' Asylum (now Reed's School); Pres. Reigate Constitutional Club, 1910-19. Became associated with firm of Joseph Sebag & Co., 1881; partner, 1887; retd., as sen. partner, 1935, after 54 years' association with the firm. Elected member Cttee. of Management Royal Academy of Music, 1914, Treas., 1924-46; Hon. Fellow, 1939; Vice-Pres., 1942; Chm. Cttee. of Management, 1946. *Recreations:* constant attendance at concerts and rehearsals of R.A.M.; football (Harlequin and Richmond F.C. till 1883), golf, gardening (Medals Chelsea Show). *Address:* 92 Mount St., W.1. *T.:* Grosvenor 3788. *Club:* Athenæum. [*Died* 8 *March* 1953.

WALKDEN, 1st Baron, *cr.* 1945; **Alexander George Walkden;** *b.* London, 11 May, 1873; 2nd *s.* of Charles Henry Scrivener Walkden; *m.* 1898, Jennie (*d.* 1934), *d.* of Jesse Wilson, Market Rasen, Lincs; three *d.* *Educ.:* The Merchant Taylors' School, Ashwell, Herts. Started as a clerk on the Great Northern Railway, 1889; Goods Traffic Representative at Nottingham, then Agent at Peterborough; left the railway service, 1906; General Secretary of the Railway Clerks' Association of Great Britain and Ireland, 1906-36; M.P. (Lab.) South Bristol, 1929-31 and 1935-45; acted as Parliamentary Secretary to the R.C.A.; Member of General Council of the Trades Union Congress, 1921-36, Chairman, 1932-33. Joined the Administrative Committee of the Parliamentary Labour Party, 1943-45; Captain of the King's Bodyguard of Yeoman of the Guard, 1945-49. *Publications:* various articles on Railway Nationalisation and kindred subjects. *Recreations:* gardening and the theatre. *Address:* Meadowside, Great Bookham, Surrey. *T.:* Bookham 215. [*Died* 25 *April* 1951 (*ext.*).

WALKER, Charles Edward, D.Sc., L.R.C.P., M.R.C.S. Eng.; late Associate Prof. of Cytology, University of Liverpool; *e. s.* of Col. Edward Walker, Woodnorton, Mayfield, Sussex; *m.* 1906, Eleanor (*d.* 1952), *d.* of Godfrey F. Meynell, Meynell Langley, Derbyshire, and *widow* of Capt. A. T. England, Sherwood Foresters; one *s.* one *d.* *Educ.:* St. George's College, Weybridge. Assistant Medical Registrar at St. George's Hospital; Editor of Shooting and Fishing of Land and Water, 1897-1903; Demonstrator in Zoology, R.C. Science, London; late Assistant Director of Cancer Research, Liverpool University; Hon. Lecturer in Cytology, Liverpool School of Tropical Medicine; Director of Cancer Research, Royal Cancer Hospital, Glasgow; served France 1914, Gallipoli, Palestine and Egypt, 1915-19. *Publications:* Shooting on a Small Income; Self-Defence (with R. G. Allanson-Winn); Essentials of Cytology, 1907; Hereditary Characters, 1910; Old Flies in New Dresses, 1898; Theories and Problems of Cancer; Evolution and Heredity, 1936; numerous communications to the Proceedings of the Royal Society and other scientific publications, mainly on Cytology. *Recreations:* skating, shooting, fishing, fencing, sailing; sometime owner of sailing yacht Thebe; with her won Challenge Cup of Royal Cruising Club. *Address:* 2 Belgrave Place, Kemp Town, Brighton. *T.:* Brighton 2658. *Clubs:* Savile, Royal Cruising; University (Liverpool). [*Died* 6 *June* 1953.

WALKER, Cyril Hutchinson; Retd. Consulting Surgeon to Bristol Eye Hospital and Consulting Ophthalmic Surgeon to Bristol General Hospital; late Major R.A.M.C. (T.); *b.* 1861; *s.* of Rev. John Walker, Rector of Bradwell, Gt. Yarmouth; *m.* Theodosia Caroline (*d.* 1953), *d.* of Rev. J. H. B. Green, Rector of Normanton-le-Heath, Leicestershire; two *s.* three *d.* *Educ.:* Haileybury College; Jesus College, Cambridge; London Hospital. B.A., M.B. Camb.; F.R.C.S.Eng.; late President of the Section of Ophthalmology of R.S.M.; late Master, Oxford Ophthalmological Congress. *Publications:* contributions to the Transactions of the Ophthalmological Society, etc. *Address:* 50 St. John's Road, Clifton, Bristol 8. *T.:* Bristol 37326. [*Died* 29 *Sept.* 1955.

WALKER, Ernest William A.; *see* Ainley-Walker.

WALKER, Dame Ethel, D.B.E., *cr.* 1943 (C.B.E. 1938); A.R.A. 1940; R.B.A. 1932; R.P. 1933; Member of New English Art Club; Society of mural painters; *b.* Edinburgh, 9 June 1861. *Educ.:* Westminster and Slade Schools of Art (under Prof. Frederick Brown). Exhibited regularly at the New English Art Club, the Royal Academy, The Roy. Soc. of British Artists, The Soc. of Women Artists, and the London Group. Rep. in Tate Gallery by 10 works: four portraits, one seascape, two figure studies, Nausicaa, The Zone of Love, The Zone of Hate (last two presented by herself, 1946). *Address:* 127 Cheyne Walk, Chelsea, S.W.10. [*Died* 2 *March* 1951.

WALKER, Lieut.-Col. Frederic William, O.B.E. 1919; Member of Staff, Royal Tournament, 1914-51, for raising funds for Service Charities; Emergency work as recruiter, adviser to civil formations, women's companies and boys' units; accredited to Supreme Allied Headquarters, 1944; Broadcaster, 1942-3; Mem. R.U.S.I.; F.J.I.; Life Member, N.R.A.; Member, Mechanised Transport Corps and British National Cadet Assoc. to 1943; Hon. Col. 4th C.B. Hampshire Regt., 1921-27; Cadet Comdt., 1923-29; a Director of the Army and Navy Gazette Company and Editor, 1922-27; a Times Military Writer, 1925-40; Associated with Sir J. Walker's Indian journals, 1904-1932; *b.* 21 Feb. 1870; *s.* of Edward Walker, Newcastle on Tyne; *m.* 1901, Rose (*d.* 1951), *y. d.* of Major J. H. King, Royal Scots Greys; no *c.* *Educ.:* privately. 6th Northumberland Fusiliers, 1892; War Correspondent, Daily Mail and Daily Express, 1899-1902 (Queen's medal); Sir Arthur Pearson's Military Correspondent for his newspaper group, including Standard, 1902-11; and Morning Post, 1911-14; with 1st Army Staff, Central Force, 1915-16; an acting H.Q. Commandant, 1916; Army H.Q., War Office, 1917-21; Staff-Captain to Maj.-Gen. Earl of Scarbrough in the Territorial Directorate for formation of Home Defence Force; Staff Officer to General Sir Noel Birch, and in charge of Cadet Branch (despatches twice, O.B.E.); Lieut.-Col. 1921; raised and commanded a Cadet Battalion; Liaison Officer, Overseas Trade Dept. for British Empire Exhibition work; Editorial, 1924; Tattoo, 1925. *Publications:* Histories of The Black Watch, Seaforth Highlanders, and Coldstream Guards. *Recreation:* rifle-shooting. *Address:* Barnsley House, Teignmouth, S. Devon. *T.:* Teignmouth 599. [*Died* 22 *Aug.* 1954.

WALKER, Sir G. Bernard L.; *see* Lomas-Walker.

WALKER, George Abram, Q.C. (Can.); D.C.L.; Director and Member of Executive Committee, Canadian Pacific Railway Co. since 1947 (Chairman, 1948-55); *b.* Toronto, Ont., 8 Oct. 1879; *s.* of William Walker and Mary Martin; *m.* 1928, Gladys Graves; one *d.* *Educ.:* Wellesley School and Osgoode Hall, Toronto. Grad. in law, 1906; K.C., Alberta, 1916. Career, all with Canadian Pacific; Solicitor, Toronto, Ont., 1906-11; Solicitor, Calgary, Alta., 1911-34; Asst. General Solicitor, Montreal, Que., 1934-36; Gen. Solicitor, 1936-45; Vice-Pres. and Gen. Counsel, Montreal, 1945-47; Senior Vice-Pres., Montreal, 1947-48. *Address:* 3940 Côte des Neiges Rd., Montreal, Quebec, Canada. *Club:* Ranchmen's (Calgary). [*Died* 7 *June* 1959.

WALKER, Major George Goold, D.S.O. 1918; M.C.; F.S.A.; F.R.Hist.S.; late R.A.; Sec. to the Honourable Artillery Company, 1922-47; *m.* 1911, Lilian Sophie, *d.* of late F. C. P. Clarke, Runnymede, St. Helier, Jersey; (one *s.* died of wounds 1945) one *d.* Served European War, 1914-18 (despatches thrice, M.C., D.S.O.); re-commissioned in Royal Artillery, Sept. 1939; Lt.-Col. City of London A.A., Home Guard, 1942-43. *Publications:* The Honourable Artillery Company; The H.A.C. in the Great War; The Trained Bands of London. *Address:* Blanche Maison, L'Etacq, Jersey, C.I. *Club:* United Service. [*Died* 24 *Dec.* 1955.

WALKER, George Henry, J.P.; retired; *b.* 1874; *m.* 1897; one *d.* *Educ.:* Kendal British School. M.P. (Lab.) Rossendale, 1945-50. C.C., 1937-49. *Recreations:* camping and motoring. *Address:* 50 Oxenholme Road, Kendal. [*Died* 24 *Jan.* 1954.

WALKER, Sir Gilbert Thomas, Kt., *cr.* 1924; C.S.I. 1911; F.R.S. 1904; F.R.A.S., Sc.D.; M.A.; *b.* 1868; *m.* 1908, May Constance (*d.* 1955), *d.* of Charles Stephens Carter; one *s.* one *d.* *Educ.:* St. Paul's

School; Trinity College, Cambridge. Fellow, 1891; Mathematical Lecturer, 1895-1904; Director-General of Indian Observatories, 1904-24; Professor of Meteorology, Imperial College of Science and Technology, 1924-34; Hon. Fellow Imperial College, 1946; Symons Gold Medal of Royal Meteorological Society, 1934. *Publications:* Aberration; The Theory of Electro-magnetism; various papers on Mathematical Physics, Meteorology and the Flight of Birds. *Address:* Woodcote Grove House, Coulsdon, Surrey. *T.:* Uplands 3610. [*Died* 4 *Nov.* 1958.

WALKER, Sir Henry, Kt., *cr.* 1928; C.B.E. 1920; LL.D.; *b.* 1873; 2nd *s.* of late William Walker of Hinderwell, Yorks; *m.* 1909, Susan (*d.* 1954), *d.* of William Carson, Chester; two *s.* *Educ.:* Durham School. Chief Inspector of Mines, 1924-38. *Address:* The Mount, Worplesdon, Surrey. *T.:* Worplesdon 125. [*Died* 3 *Aug.* 1954.

WALKER, Brigadier-General Henry Alexander, C.B. 1921; C.M.G. 1918; D.S.O. 1915; *b.* 20 Oct. 1874. Entered Army, Royal Fusiliers, 1894; Captain, 1900; Bt. Maj., 1906; Major, 1910; Lieut.-Colonel, 1920; Colonel, 1924; with Central and King's African Rifles, 1901-1910; served Somaliland, 1902-4 (medal 3 clasps); Nandi, 1905-6 (despatches, Brevet Major, clasp); Somaliland, 1908-10 (despatches, clasp); European War, 1914-19 (despatches eight times, 1914 Star and clasp, British War Medal and Victory Medal, D.S.O., C.M.G., Order of St. Stanislaus 3rd class with swords, Bt. Lt.-Col.); Insurrection in Mesopotamia, 1920 (despatches, medal and clasp, C.B.); commanded 165th (Liverpool) Infantry Brigade, T.A., 1925-1927; Inspector-General of King's African Rifles, 1927-31; retired pay, 1931. *Address:* Manor House, Lower Woodford, Salisbury. *Club:* Army and Navy. [*Died* 1 *May* 1953.

WALKER, Hirst, R.B.A.; *b.* 24 Nov. 1868; *y. s.* of Hirst Walker, The Elms, Malton, Yorkshire, and Emily Walker; unmarried. *Educ.:* King's College School, London. Landscape Painter in water colours; his work generally suggests an interest in pattern and design rather than in colour. *Works:* Xavier: Pools of The Holy Family, and a sketch book, Victoria and Albert Museum, London; two drawings, British Museum Print Room; other works in permanent collections at the Leeds, Hull, Sheffield, Bradford, York, Scarborough and Whitby Art Galleries, also by invitation in The Queen's Doll's House; first exhibited Royal Academy, 1907 (during succeeding years, 19 works in all). *Address:* c/o Midland Bank Ltd., Leyburn, Yorkshire. [*Died* 1 *Jan.* 1957.

WALKER, James Atkinson; Leader-writer and Assistant Editor, Western Mail and South Wales News; *b.* Otley, Yorkshire, 14 Nov. 1878; *m.* Mary, *e. d.* of Richard Burley, Otley; three *s.* two *d.* *Educ.:* privately. First engaged on the Leeds Mercury, and then successively on daily or evening newspapers in Birmingham, Glasgow, London, and Cardiff; Editor, Bristol Times and Mirror, 1928-32. *Publications:* The Way of Truth; State Morality and the League of Nations. *Recreation:* fishing. *Address:* 23 Ovington Terrace, Cardiff. *T.:* 21183. [*Died* 5 *May* 1954.

WALKER, Col. John N. N.; *see* Norman-Walker.

WALKER, Norman Marshall; J.P. Reigate; *b.* 16 Aug. 1882; 2nd *s.* of Henry Claude Walker; *m.* 1923, Winifred Mary Whitton; two *s.* one *d.* *Educ.:* New College, Eastbourne. Founder and Managing Director, British General Insurance Co. Ltd., 1904-40; President of Insurance Institute of London, 1932-33; President Insurance Orphanage and Insurance Benevolent Fund, 1937; President Chartered Insurance Institute, 1939-41; Chairman, E. Surrey Hosp.; Vice-Chairman Redhill Group Hosp. Management Cttee. Member Surrey County Council. Freeman of the City of London; Liveryman, Worshipful Company of Leather-sellers. *Recreations:* billiards, fishing, gardening. *Address:* Oakwood, Merstham, Surrey. *T.:* Merstham 2571. [*Died* 20 *Feb.* 1956.

WALKER, Paymaster Captain Reginald Phelps, C.M.G. 1919; R.N. (retired); *b.* 8 July 1871; *s.* of late Rev. St. George Walker, M.A.,; *m.* 1913, Adeline Mary Walker; three *s.* one *d.* *Educ.:* privately. Entered R.N., 1888; served European War; present at Battle of Jutland on board H.M.S. Warrior; retired, 1923; Russian Order of St. Stanislas, 2nd class, with swords, 1917. *Address:* Moray House, Monckton Road, Alverstoke, Hants. *T.:* Gosport 8336. [*Died* 9 *March* 1958.

WALKER, Sir Robert Bryce, Kt., *cr.* 1942; C.B.E. 1938; J.P., D.L.; LL.D.; Member: Scottish Tribunal for Conscientious Objectors, 1939; General Board of Control for Scotland, 1940; Chm. Scottish N.F.S. Commission, 1941; *b.* 26 July 1873; *s.* of late William Walker, M.D., L.R.C.S.E., Physician, Pollokshaws; *m.* 1906, Jean Sheddan (*d.* 1938), *d.* of Hugh McTaggart, Meadowhead, Maxwell Park, Glasgow; two *s.* two *d.* *Educ.:* High School of Glasgow; University of Glasgow. M.A. 1893; LL.B. 1896; LL.D. 1950; Solicitor, 1896; Town Clerk of Burgh of Pollokshaws, 1902-12; Legal Assist. to Lanarkshire County, 1912-23; County Clerk, 1923-38; Commissioner for Special Areas in Scotland, 1939-45. *Address:* 51 Fotheringay Road, Glasgow, S.1. *T.:* Pollok 1348; The Haven, Dunoon, Argyllshire. *T.:* Innellan 272. *Club:* Royal Scottish Automobile (Glasgow). [*Died* 14 *June* 1956.

WALKER, Lt.-Col. Thomas Henry, D.S.O. 1919; B.A. Oxon; late R.A.; *b.* 15 March 1877; 4th *s.* of late Thomas James Walker, M.D., F.R.C.S., V.D., J.P., Peterborough; *m.* 1926, Joan (*d.* 1948), *yr. d.* of Sir Charles Hulbert; one *s.* *Educ.:* Haileybury; Merton College, Oxford. Served South African War, 1901-02 (medal and 5 clasps); practised as solicitor, 1904-15, 1925-32; a Taxing Master of Supreme Court of Judicature, 1932-50; served European War in France, Egypt and Palestine on Staff and in command of Field Artillery Brigade (D.S.O., despatches); granted permanent Regular Commission as Major in Royal Artillery, 1915; retired, 1922. *Address:* 99 Eaton Place, S.W.1. *T.:* Sloane 0520. [*Died* 27 *Jan.* 1955.

WALKER, William James Stirling, Ph.D., A.H.W.C., F.R.I.C., F.I.L., F.R.S.E.; Research Chemist, Technologist and Linguist, engaged in private practice; *b.* North Berwick, E. Lothian, 8 Mar. 1897; *s.* of late John Dalling (MacDonald) Walker, Peebles and Edinburgh, and Margaret Vera (Murray) Russell, Chirnside; *m.* *Educ.:* James Gillespie's School; various Board Schools in Scotland; Heriot-Watt Technical Coll.; Edinburgh University. Bronze Medal in Non-Ferrous Metallurgy, City and Guilds of London Institute, 1923. Served European War in R.F.A., 1914-19, in France and Belgium consecutively with the 1st Lowland Brigade, the 51st (Highland) Div., the 232nd (Flying Column) Bde., and the 286th Bde. (invalided home from the Somme, 1916, wounded 1918, 1914-15 Star, etc.); Analytical and Research Chemist, W. Hunter and Sons, Consulting Engineers, Edinburgh, 1923-29; Research Chemist, Fuel Research Station (D.S.I.R.), 1929-58, retd. Member: Council, Inst. of Linguists, 1951; Governing Body: Princeton Coll. of Languages and Commerce, 1957; Holborn Coll. of Law, Languages and Commerce, 1958. *Recreations:* travel, photography. *Address:* 13 The Lawns, Lee Terr., Blackheath, S.E.3. *Club:* St. Andrews. [*Died* 20 *Nov.* 1958.

WALKER - HENEAGE - VIVIAN, Admiral Algernon, C.B. 1916; M.V.O.

1904; J.P., D.L., Glamorgan; High Sheriff of Glamorganshire, 1926; Chairman of Vivian & Sons, Ltd.; Chairman South West Wales Savings Bank; *b.* 4 Feb. 1871; 3rd *s.* of late Maj. C. Walker Heneage, V.C., 8th Hussars, and Henrietta Letitia Victoria, *d.* of late John H. Vivian, of Singleton, Swansea; *m.* 1st, 1912, Helen Mary, *d.* of Capt. E. de V. du Boulay, late R.H.A.; three *d.*; 2nd, 1931, Beryl, *d.* of late T. Stanley, Cardiff. *Educ.:* Evelyn's; Stubbington. Assumed name of Walker-Heneage-Vivian by Royal Licence, 1921. Entered Royal Navy, 1886; served South Africa, 2nd in command Naval Contingent in defence of Ladysmith (despatches); Commanded the First Squadron of Mine-layers, and at commencement of war H.M.S. Albion in South Atlantic and Dardanelles (despatches twice); Commodore commanding small vessels in the Eastern Mediterranean, 1915-16; Commodore, 1st class, commanding the allied barrage in the Straits of Otranto, 1917; Senior British Naval Officer in Italy; Rear-Admiral, 1918; retired, 1920; Vice-Adm., 1923; Adm., 1927; Officer of Legion of Honour; 2nd class Rising Sun of Japan, Grand Officer of the Crown of Italy. *Address:* Clyne Castle, Blackpyl, Swansea; Parc-le-Breos, Penmaen, Swansea. *T.* and *T.A.:* Swansea 88128; 8 Hyde Park Gardens, W.2. *Clubs:* United Service; Royal Naval (Portsmouth); Garden Society; Rhododendron Society. [*Died* 26 *Feb.* 1952.

WALKEY, Rev. James Rowland, C.B.E. 1937; M.A.; retired as Rector of Moreton (1951-59); *b.* 10 April 1880; *s.* of Col. Rowland Walkey, late R.A. and Lucy Bazalgette (*née* Chamberlin); *m.* 1906, Bijou Frances, *d.* of Col. H. J. Paske, Sherwood Foresters, and Amy Paske; four *d.* (and one *d.* decd.). *Educ.:* Plymouth; Mannamead College; Christ's College, Cambridge; Rdliey Hall, Cambridge. Rowed in College boat three years, 1st XV. two years, Athletic team, Blue for Rugby football, 1902. Curate St. Cuthbert's, Bedford; Army Chaplain, 1905-06; Army sprint champion, 1906; Curacies Plumstead and Blackheath, 1907-11; Army Chaplain Woolwich, 1911-1914; served European war, Flanders and France, 1914-18 (despatches); granted special promotion June 1915; Senior Chaplain 19th Division 1915-16; Deputy Assistant Chaplain General VII. Corps, 1916-18; Deputy Chaplain-in-Chief, Royal Air Force, 1918-19; Chaplain Uxbridge, 1919-22; Fenced for Royal Air Forcer 1920-1922; Senior Chaplain in Iraq, 1922-24 (Ku, distan medal, 1924); Senior Chaplain R.A.F. Middle East, 1924-26; Home Service, 1927; Chaplain, in-Chief, R.A.F., 1933-40; K.H.C. 1933-40; retired list, 1940; Vicar of Wateringbury, 1940-1943; Rector of Worting, 1943-46; of Angmering, 1946-49; of Haversham, 1949-50. *Recreations:* walking, shooting, swimming. *Address:* The Lodge Cottage, Craddock, Ashill, Nr. Cullompton, Devon. [*Died* 8 *Jan.* 1960.

WALL, Colonel Edward Watkin, C.M.G. 1917; Indian Army, retired; *b.* 20 Dec. 1866; *s.* of late George Wall, Colombo; unmarried. *Educ.:* Sandhurst. Lieut. Devons. Regt. 1886; Capt. Indian Army, 1897; Major, 1901; Lieut.-Col. 1912; Col. 1917; retired, 1920; Served European War, France and Flanders, 1914-16; Bushire Field Force, Persian Gulf, 1918-19 (despatches thrice, C.M.G.). *Recreations:* shooting, fishing. *Address:* Peplow, Private Bag J.185, Umtali, Southern Rhodesia. *Club:* East India and Sports. [*Died* 2 *Feb.* 1954.

WALLACE, Sir David, K.B.E., *cr.* 1920 (C.B.E. 1918); C.M.G. 1900; LL.D., M.B., C.M., F.R.C.S.E.; Bt. Lt.-Col. R.A.M.C. (T.F.), retired; D.L. City of Edinburgh; *b.* July 1862; *s.* of David Wallace of Balgrummo, Fife; *m.* 1905, Augusta Maud, C.B.E. 1946, *o. d.* of late Sir Thomas Clouston, M.D.; two *s.* *Educ.:* Dollar Academy; Edinburgh University. Served S. Africa (despatches, medal and clasp); European War, 1914-19. *Publications:* numerous surgical articles. *Address:* 6 Eton Terrace, Edinburgh. *Club:* University (Edinburgh). [*Died* 21 *April* 1952.

WALLACE, Denis B. J.; *see* Johnstone-Wallace.

WALLACE, Colonel George Smith, O.B.E.; M.B., Ch.B., D.P.H.; late Professor of Hygiene, Royal Army Medical College; *b.* 18 Aug. 1878; *s.* of M. Wallace and A. Smith; *m.* 1911, Belle Hentz; two *s.* *Educ.:* Kilmarnock Academy; Glasgow University. Civil Surgeon, South Africa, 1901-02; Lieut. R.A.M.C. 1905; Capt. 1908; Maj. 1915; Lt.-Col. 1928; Brevet Colonel, 1932; Colonel, 1934; Health Officer, Secunderabad, 1916-17; D.A.D.M.S. 9th Divn. India, 1917-18; D.A.D.M.S., S. Persia, 1919; D.A.D.M.S. Waziristan, 1919-20; A.D.H. South Command, India, 1923-28; Commandant Army School of Hygiene, Aldershot, 1929-33. *Address:* Belgrave House, Palace Road, East Molesey, Surrey. *T.:* Molesey 1345. [*Died* 26 *April* 1951.

WALLACE, George Williamson, C.B. 1929; *b.* 1862; *y. s.* of late James Wallace, M.D., Greenock; *m.* Alice, *d.* of late John Walker, of Bolling, Bradford; one *s.* (and one died on service, 1943) one *d.* *Educ.:* Fettes College, Edinburgh; Corpus Christi College, Oxford. Called to Bar, Inner Temple, 1889; Assistant Commissioner, Charity Commission, 1893; Commissioner, 1921; Chief Charity Commissioner for England and Wales, 1924-32. *Address:* Waterfall Cottage, Kearsney, Dover. *T.:* Kearsney 105. *Club:* Oxford and Cambridge. [*Died* 28 *Nov.* 1952.

WALLACE, James Sim, M.D., D.Sc., F.D.S.R.C.S.; F.A.C.D., Hon. Fellow of Soc. of Medical Officers of Health; Hon. Member of British Dental Assoc., British Soc. for the Study of Orthodontics, and a number of other Dental Societies at home and abroad; Hon. President Sixteenth International Medical Congress, section Stomatology; President British Society for Study of Orthodontics, 1910; Vice-President Food Education Soc.; *b.* 29 June 1869; *y. s.* of James Wallace, Braehead, Renfrewshire; *m.* Anne, *d.* of late Chas. J. Alexander of Hawick; one *s.* (and one *s.* decd.). *Educ.:* Langside Acad.; Glasgow University; Glasgow Dental Hospital; National and Royal Dental Hospitals. Awarded the John Tomes prize for work on the prevention of dental caries, the Cartwright Medal and Prize, 1920-25, by R.C.S.; Neech Prize by the Society of M.O.H.; lectured in 23 of the principal cities of the U.S. and Canada; formerly Lecturer on Dental Surgery and Pathology, London Hospital and on Preventive Dentistry, King's College Hospital. *Publications:* The Cause and Prevention of Decay in Teeth, 1900; The Irregularities of the Teeth, 1904; The Rôle of Modern Dietetics in the Causation of Disease, 1905; Supplementary Essays on the Cause and Prevention of Dental Caries, 1906; The Prevention of Dental Caries, 2nd ed. 1912 (Swedish translation); The Prevention of Common Diseases in Childhood, 1912; Dental Diseases in relation to Public Health, 1914; Child Welfare, 1919; Oral Hygiene, 1923, 2nd ed. 1929; The Teeth and Health, 1926; Variations in the Form of the Jaws, with special reference to their Etiology and their relation to the occlusion of the Dental Arches (Cartwright Prize Essay), 1926. *Address:* 14 Church Grove, Hampton Wick. *T.:* Kingston 2300. [*Died* 13 *July* 1951.

WALLACE, John Henry; C.M.G. 1955; Commissioner for Northern Rhodesia in London since 1953; *b.* 24 Oct. 1903; 2nd *s.* of late Octavius and Helena Wallace, Dublin; *m.* 1st, 1932, Zaidee Frances Morton; one *s.* one *d.*; 2nd, 1949, Joy Mary Nicholson. *Educ.:* St. Andrew's College; Trinity College, Dublin. Colonial Administrative Service, 1927-51; seconded to Colonial Office, 1932-34 and 1947-50; Dist. Comr., N. Rhodesia, 1936; Asst. Chief Sec., 1940; Comr. for Native Development,

1944; Admin. Sec., 1945; acting Chief Sec., 1946. M.E.C., M.L.C. Mem. Commn. on Disposal Ex-Enemy Sisal Estates, Tanganyika, 1951; Sec. London Cttee. United Central Africa Assoc., 1952. *Recreations:* tennis, swimming. *Address:* Northern Rhodesia House, 57 Haymarket, S.W.1. *T.:* Whitehall 5858; The Chalfonts, White Rose Lane, Woking, Surrey. *T.:* Woking 1988. *Club:* East India and Sports. [*Died* 6 *Dec.* 1960.

WALLACE, Malcolm William; Prof. of English Literature, Univ. Coll., Toronto, 1916-44, Prof. Emeritus since 1944; Principal 1928-44, Principal Emeritus since 1944; *b.* Essex Co., Ont., 1 May 1873; *e. s.* of William and Elizabeth Wallace; *m.* 1902, May Pitkin of Oak Park, Ill.; one *s.* one *d.* Windsor High School; the University of Toronto, B.A.; University of Chicago, Fellow in English, 1897-99; University of Chicago Ph.D.; Professor of English, Beloit College, 1899-1904; Lecturer in English, University College, Toronto, 1904; Registrar, 1906; Associate Professor of English, 1909; Second in Command of the University of Toronto Overseas Training Company, March 1916. *Publications:* The Birthe of Hercules, 1902, and Abraham's Sacrifice, 1907—hitherto unpublished Elizabethan plays; The Life of Sir Philip Sidney, 1915; Milton's Prose Works (World's Classics), 1925; The English Literary Tradition (The Alexander Lectures), 1952. *Address:* 91 Walmer Road, Toronto. *Clubs:* Arts and Letters, York (Toronto). [*Died* 7 *April* 1960.

WALLACE, Robert Charles, C.M.G. 1944; M.A., Ph.D., D.Sc., F.G.S.; LL.D. (Manitoba, Queen's, Toronto, Sask., McMaster, McGill, Western, Temple, St. Lawrence, Harvard, Buffalo, Edin., Ottawa, N.B., Alberta); D.C.L. (Bishops, Oxford); Hon. D.Sc. (Mich. School of Mines, Q.U.B., Laval); Principal Queen's University, Kingston, Ontario, 1936-51; Executive Director Arctic Institute of North America since 1952; Consultant, Ontario Department of Education; *b.* Orkney, 15 June 1881; *s.* of James Wallace and Mary Swanney; *m.* 1912, Elizabeth Harcus (M.A. Edin.), *d.* of Charles Smith, Kirkwall; three *d.* *Educ.:* Edinburgh University (M.A. 1901, B.Sc. 1907, D.Sc. 1912); Göttingen (Ph.D., 1909). F.G.S., 1912; M. Can. Min. Inst., 1913; F.R.S.C., 1921. Neil Arnott Scholar in Physics, 1900; Hope Prize Scholar in Chemistry, 1901; Science Master in Secondary Schools, 1901-04; Carnegie Scholar, 1907-08; 1851 Royal Exhibition Scholar from Edinburgh University, 1908-10 (re-awarded for 3rd year); Carnegie Fellow, 1910; Research Scholar in Crystallography and Demonstrator, St. Andrews University, 1910; Lecturer in charge of Department of Geology and Mineralogy, University of Manitoba, 1910-12; Professor of Geology and Mineralogy, University of Manitoba, Winnipeg, 1912-28; President of University of Alberta, 1928-36; Commissioner of Mines and Natural Resources for Manitoba, 1926-28; Commissioner for Northern Manitoba, with headquarters at The Pas, Manitoba, 1918-21; President Can. Inst. Min. Metall., 1924-25; President Manitoba Educational Association, 1925-26; Pres. Association of Canadian Clubs, 1930-32; Pres. Royal Society of Canada, 1940-41; Chairman Ontario Research Commission, 1945-48; Pres. Research Council of Ontario, 1948-51; Pres., Canadian Assoc. for Adult Education, 1952-; Canadian Advisory Editor, Encyclopedia Americana, 1950-; specialised in physical chemistry of rock magmas, in petrology, and in crystallography. *Publications:* The Burwash Lectures, 1932; A Liberal Education in a Modern World; Religion, Science and the Modern World; various papers in mineral statics, economic geology, natural resources, and educational subjects. *Address:* 4 Centre Street, Kingston, Ontario, Canada. [*Died* 29 *Jan.* 1955.

WALLACE, Thomas Brown; Chief Clerk in Chancery and Registrar in Lunacy, High Court of Justice of Northern Ireland, 1922-1950. M.P. (U.) West Down, 1921-22; *b.* 1865; *s.* of Robert S. Wallace, of Dromore. Admitted a Solicitor, 1887. *Address:* Regent House, Dromore, Down, N.I. [*Died* 28 *April* 1951.

WALLER, Very Rev. Charles Kempson; Provost and Rector of the Cathedral Church of St. Mary, Chelmsford, since 1949; *b.* 22 Sept. 1891; *s.* of Theodore Harry and Maud Waller; *m.* 1918, Marion Ruth, *d.* of Rev. John Warmington Eisdell and Ruth Mary Eisdell; two *s.* one *d.* *Educ.:* Felsted School; St. John's College, Oxford (M.A.); Wells Theological College. Deacon, 1914, Priest, 1915; Curate, Barking, 1914-18; Holy Trinity, Latimer Road, 1918-19; All Saints, Fleet, 1919-25; in charge St. Martin's, Dagenham, 1925-27; Vicar, 1927-29; Rector St. Andrew, Romford, 1929-30; Chap. and Vicar Temporal, Hornchurch, 1930-41. R.D. of Chafford, otherwise Romford, 1940-41. Rector of Wanstead, 1941-49; Hon. Canon of Chelmsford, 1946-49. Surrogate. *Address:* Guy Harlings, Chelmsford, Essex. *T.:* Chelmsford 3514. [*Died* 16 *Jan.* 1951.

WALLER, Sir Edmund, 6th Bt., *cr.* 1815; *b.* 24 Oct. 1871; *s.* of late Rev. Ernest Alured Waller; *S.* cousin, 1947; *m.* 1906, Hon. Muriel Grace, *d.* of 5th Baron Norton. *Educ.:* Marlborough; University College, Oxford (B.A.). *Heir:* *c.* John Stanier Waller, *b.* 27 July 1917. *Address:* Goffies Park, Marhamchurch, nr. Bude, Cornwall. [*Died* 7 *Aug.* 1954.

WALLER, Sir Roland Edgar, 8th Bt., *cr.* 1780, of Newport, Tipperary; Merchant; *b.* 11 Jan. 1892; *s.* of Sir William Edgar Waller, 7th Bt., and Mary Augusta Meyers; *S.* father, 1943; *m.* 1919, Helen Madeline Radl; one *s.* two *d.* *Educ.:* Peekskill Military Academy; Cornell University. Served European War, 1917-18; Ensign U.S.N. (Aviation), 1920-23; Member American Legion; Catholic War Veterans; Phi Sigma Kappa Fraternity. *Heir:* *s.* Robert William, *b.* 16 June 1934. *Address:* 156 Patterson Avenue, Hasbrouck Heights, N.J., U.S.A. [*Died* 20 *May* 1958.

WALLIS, Rev. Charles Steel, M.A.; Principal St. John's College, Durham, 1919-45, and Rector of St. Mary-le-Bow Church, Durham, 1930-49; Hon. Canon of Durham Cathedral since 1937; *b.* 1875; *s.* of late William Wallis, solicitor, and Mary Wallis, Newark-on-Trent. *Educ.:* Hatton House School, Newark; private tuition; Durham University; London College of Divinity. Universities Prelim. Theological Examination (1st class), 1902; Deacon, 1902; Priest, 1903; Associate in Music, Trinity Coll., London, 1903; Assistant Chaplain, London College of Divinity, 1902; Tutor, 1903; Dean, 1904-12; Vice-Principal St. John's College, Durham, 1912-19; temporary Chaplain to the Forces (served with the Mediterranean Expeditionary Force) 1915-19; Examining Chaplain to Bishop Moule of Durham, 1914-20, to Bishop Hensley Henson of Durham, 1927-39; Lecturer in Ecclesiastical History, University of Durham, 1920-31; Lecturer in Logic, University of Durham, 1931-45; Member of Senate, Durham University, 1921; Sub-Warden of the Durham Colleges in University of Durham, 1940-45; Hon. C.F., 1921; Proctor in Convocation for Archdeaconry of Durham, 1922-45; Examining Chaplain to the Bishop of Durham, 1939-1952; and to the Bishop of Sodor and Man, 1928-42; Commissary and Examining Chaplain to the Bishop of Sierra Leone, 1936-57; Commissary to the Bishop of Shensi, 1946-47. *Publications:* Fifty Thousand Miles in a Hospital Ship; Co-editor of Bedæ, Historiæ Ecclesiasticæ, Bk. III.; Editor of Augustini, De Cathechizandis Rudibus; contributor to the Tutorial Prayer-book. *Recreations:*

travel and music. *Address:* 16 South Bailey, Durham. *T.:* Durham 2624.
[*Died* 6 *June* 1959.

WALLIS, Harry Bernard, C.B. 1944; formerly Principal Assistant Secretary, Technical Branch, Ministry of Education; *b.* 1882; *s.* of Charles Wallis, J.P., and Mary Wallis, Edgbaston, Birmingham. *Educ.:* King Edward's School, Birmingham; Balliol College, Oxford (Brackenbury Scholar). 1st class Lit. Hum. 1905; Lecturer in Philosophy, Univ. of Manchester, 1906-9; joined Board of Education, 1909; retired, 1945. Served European War, 1914-18. *Recreations:* golf, painting. *Address:* 29 Sheffield Terrace, Kensington, W.8. *T.:* Park 6460. *Clubs:* Savile; Rye Golf.
[*Died* 13 *Nov.* 1956.

WALLIS, Rev. Canon John Eyre Winstanley; Canon Residentiary and Chancellor of Lichfield Cathedral, and Examining Chaplain to the Bishop of Lichfield, since 1945; *b.* 16 June 1886; *e. s.* of Chas. W. G. R. and Edith Eyre Wallis; *m.* Violet, *d.* of Rev. Dr. Sherard M. Statham, LL.D., Rector of Cottisford cum Hardwick, Oxon; two *s.* two *d.* (and one *s.* killed in action, 1940). *Educ.:* Christ's Hospital; Brasenose College, Oxford (M.A.). Deacon, 1912; Priest, 1913; Assistant Chaplain Christ's Hospital, 1912-15; Vicar of Habergham Eaves, 1915-1918; Surrogate, 1915; Vicar of Whalley, 1918-33; Examining Chaplain to Bishop of Blackburn, 1928-45; Rural Dean of Whalley, 1928-33; Vicar of Preston, 1933-45; Rural Dean of Preston, 1941-45; Warden of the Young Clergy, diocese of Lichfield, 1945-56; Proctor in Convocation, 1945-54. *Publications:* The Welding of the Race, 1913; First English Grammar, 1914; The Sword of Justice, 1919; English Regnal Years and Titles, 1920; Whalley Church, 1921; The Church in Clitheroe, 1922; The Church in Burnley, 1922; Whalley Abbey, 1923; Church Vestments, 1924; The Church in Blackburnshire, 1926; Lichfield Cathedral, 1956. *Recreations:* textile printing. *Address:* 15 The Close, Lichfield. *T.:* Lichfield 2348. *Club:* Athenæum.
[*Died* 2 *Sept.* 1957.

WALLOP, Hon. Frederick (Henry Arthur); *b.* 16 Feb. 1870; 6th *s.* of 5th Earl of Portsmouth. A Trustee of the National Portrait Gallery, 1918-48; late Assistant Private Secretary to President of Board of Agriculture. *Club:* St. James. [*Died* 9 *Aug.* 1953.

WALMSLEY, Thomas; Professor of Anatomy, Queen's University, Belfast; *s.* of late Thomas Walmsley, Royal Indian Navy; *m.* Denzil, *d.* of T. S. Kirk, Belfast; one *s.* one *d.* *Educ.:* High School, Greenock; Glasgow Univ.; London, Paris, Bonn. *Publications:* Manual of Practical Anatomy; Quain's Anatomy (11th ed.); The Heart, etc. *Recreations:* golf, gardening, stamps. *Address:* Ardmore, Armagh, N. Ireland. *T.:* Armagh 426. *Clubs:* Ulster (Belfast); University (Dublin).
[*Died* 12 *Nov.* 1951.

WALSH, Hon. Sir Albert Joseph, Kt., *cr.* 1949; Q.C.; Chief Justice of the Newfoundland Supreme Court since 1949. Asst. Sec. for Justice, 1940; Labour Relations Officer, Dept. of Public Works Division of Labour, 1942-44; Commissioner for Home Affairs and Education, Newfoundland, 1944. Commissioner for Justice and Attorney General, 1947. Lieutenant-Governor of Newfoundland, 1949. *Address:* St. John's, Newfoundland. [*Died Dec.* 1958.

WALSH, Ernest Herbert Cooper, C.S.I. 1911; M.A. Oxon.; late Indian Civil Service; *b.* 7 March 1865; *s.* of late Rev. Thomas Harris Walsh, Riddings Vicarage, Derbyshire; *m.* 1892, Beatrice Ivy (*d.* 1943), *d.* of Rev. Henry Huntington, British Government Chaplain at Leghorn, Marseilles, and Malaga; two *d.* *Educ.:* Trent; University College, London; Middle Temple. Assistant Magistrate and Collector, Bengal, 1884; served as Settlement Officer, Jalpaiguri Duars, 1889; and on Orissa Settlement, 1891; Magistrate and Collector, 1895; Junior Secretary, Board of Revenue, 1895; Deputy Commissioner, Darjeeling, 1901; Senior Secretary, Board of Revenue, 1903; Assistant Commissioner on the British Mission to Tibet, 1903-4; Commissioner of the Burdwan Division, 1904; Bhagalpur Division, 1907; Officiating Member, Board of Revenue, Behar and Orissa, 1912, 1913, and 1914; Member Viceroy's Legislative Council, 1912, 1914, 1917 and 1918; Commissioner Chota Nagpur Division, 1912; Member, Board of Revenue, Bihar and Orissa, 1916; retired, 1919; temporarily re-employed, India Office, May-Oct. 1920; Lecturer in Tibetan, School of Oriental Studies, London, 1920; Lecturer in Bengali, Oxford Univ., 1920-22. *Publications:* A Vocabulary of the Tromowa Dialect of Tibetan; Examples of Tibetan Letters; and papers in journals. *Address:* c/o Lloyds Bank Ltd., Cox's and King's Branch, 6 Pall Mall, S.W.1.
[*Died* 30 *April* 1952.

WALSH, Air Vice-Marshal George Victor, C.B. 1946; C.B.E. 1944 (M.B.E. 1919); late R.C.A.F.; *b.* 27 May 1893; *s.* of late Comdr. J. T. Walsh, R.N.R., and Florence Woods. *Educ.:* Loyola College, Montreal. European War, 1915-19 with Victoria Rifles, Canada, later with R.A.F. Served with R.C.A.F. since formation, in various staff and command appointments; Graduate R.A.F. Staff College, 1927; Commanded R.C.A.F. Overseas Hqrs. 1940 and No. 3 Training Command, Montreal, 1941; Air Attaché, Washington, U.S.A., 1942; Air Member Canadian Joint Staff Mission, Washington, 1942-45; employed 1946 on special duties R.C.A.F. H.Q., Ottawa; retired Oct. 1946. Comdr. U.S. Legion of Merit, 1946. *Recreations:* sailing, fishing. *Address:* 150 Argyle St., Ottawa, Ontario, Canada. *Club:* United Services (Montreal).
[*Died* 4 *June* 1960.

WALSH, Sir Hunt Henry Allen Johnson-, 5th Bt., *cr.* 1775; J.P., D.L.; late Capt. 60th Rifles (retired, 1897); *b.* Ireland, 18 Jan. 1864; *e. s.* of 4th Bt. and Harriett, *d.* of Rev. W. B. Forde, Seaforde, Co. Down; *S.* father, 1893; *m.* 1910, Grace (*d* 1941), *y. d.* of Right. Hon. Henry Bruen; one *d.* *Educ.:* Eton; R.M.C., Sandhurst. Joined 60th Rifles, 1884; served in Manipur Expedition, 1891 (medal and clasp); orderly officer to Maj.-Gen. Sir T. Graham in Expedition to the Chin Hills, 1892. *Recreations:* hunting, shooting, fishing. *Heir:* none. *Address:* Ballykilcavan, Stradbally, Queen's Co. [*Died* 3 *Sept.* 1953 (*ext.*).

WALSH, James Morgan, author; *b.* Geelong, Victoria, Australia, 1897; *m.* Louisa Mary Murphy; one *s.* one *d.* *Educ.:* Xavier College, Melbourne. *Publications:* The White Mask; The Images of Han; The Silver Greyhound; The Crimes of Cleopatra's Needle; Spies in Spain; Black Dragon; Dial 999, 1938; Bullets for Breakfast, 1939; The Tempania Mystery; Lady Incognito; Vandals of the Void; Spies are Abroad; The Secret Service Girl; King's Messenger; Spies in Pursuit; Island of Spies; The Man from Whitehall; Chalk-Face; Spies Never Return; Tiger of the Night; The Silent Man; The Half Ace; Spies' Vendetta; King's Enemies, 1939; Secret Weapons, 1940; Spies from the Skies, 1940 (75th book); Death at his Elbow, 1941; Danger Zone, 1942; Island Alert, 1943; Face Value, 1944; Whispers in the Dark, 1945; Express Delivery, 1946; Once in Tiger Bay 1947; Walking Shadow, 1948; Time to Kill, 1949; Return to Tiger Bay, 1950; Next, Please, 1951; *Address:* 78 Bristol Road, Weston-super-Mare, Somerset. *Club:* Weston-super-Mare and District Constitutional.
[*Died* 29 *Aug.* 1952.

WALSH, Brig.-Gen. Richard Knox, C.B. 1919; C.M.G. 1918; D.S.O. 1916; late Royal Scots Fusiliers; *b.* 25 Dec. 1878; *s.* of late Surg., Gen. Thomas Walsh, A.M.S., and Mary Letitia, *d.* of Lt.-Gen. Richard Knox of Grace Dieu, Co. Dublin. *Educ.:* Beaumont; R.M.C., Sandhurst. Served S. African War, 1901-2 (Queen's medal 4 clasps); European War, 1914-18 (despatches, C.B., C.M.G., D.S.O.); retired pay, 1924. *Address:* Hilgay Lodge, The Park, Cheltenham. [*Died* 20 *March* 1960.

WALSHE, Lt.-Col. Sarsfield James Ambrose Hall, D.S.O. 1915; M.B., Ch.B. Edin.; late R.A.M.C.; *b.* 1881; *s.* of late T. B. Walshe, M.D., Mallow; *m.* May (*d.* 1943), *d.* of late Archibald McWilliams, Dublin; two *s.* one *d.* *Educ.:* Edinburgh University and Royal College of Surgeons. Late House Surgeon, Torbay Hospital; Captain, R.A.M.C.; Major, 1926; Lt.-Col. 1936; served European War, 1914-18 (despatches thrice, D.S.O.); retired pay, 1936. *Publications:* Effect on Mental State of Minor and Major Attacks in Epileptic Insanity, 1912; Six Months with Bearer Division of a Field Ambulance at the Front, Practitioner, March 1915. *Recreations:* racing, hunting. *Address:* Sanci, Minster, Sheerness. *Club:* Mallow (Mallow, Cork). [*Died* 11 *July* 1959.

WALTER, Lieutenant-Colonel Edmund, C.I.E. 1917; J.P. Surrey; *b.* 29 Jan. 1881; 3rd *s.* of late Major F. E. Walter, M.V.O.; *m.* 1906, Helen Brooke Cunliffe; one *s.* three *d.* *Educ.:* Dulwich College; R.M.A., Woolwich. 2nd Lt. Royal Artillery, 1900; A.D.C. to G.O.C., Ceylon, till 1901; No. 1 Mountain Battery till 1906; transferred to Indian Army, 1909; Japan, 1910-12; Deputy Assistant Director of Transport, A.H.Q., India, 1913-16; as D.A.Q.M.G. Basra, 1916, invalided to India; Deputy Controller of Contracts, A.H.Q., India, 1918-20; retired, 1921. Commandant, Corps of Commissionaires, 1931-50. *Address:* Orford Lodge, Cumberland Road, Kew. *Club:* Junior United Service. [*Died* 12 *April* 1951.

WALTER, Maj.-Gen. John McNeill, C.B. 1916; C.S.I. 1918; D.S.O. 1902; *b.* Meerut, E. India, 10 June 1861; *s.* of late General John McNeill Walter, C.B., Col. Royal Sussex Regiment; *m.* Annie, *d.* of late Alfred Chenery of Loyola and Delatite, Victoria, Australia. *Educ.:* Cheltenham College; R.M.C., Sandhurst. Entered Army, 1880; served D.A.A.G., 2nd Brigade Toch, Field Force, 1897-98 (despatches, clasp); served South African war, 1899-1902 (despatches twice, D.S.O.); European War, India (despatches, C.S.I.); commanded 1st Batt. The Devonshire Regt., 1906-10; Assist. Adjut.-Gen., India, 1910-13; Deputy Adjut.-Gen. India, 1913-15; Adjut.-Gen. India, 1915-17; M.G.A., Northern Army, India, 1917-20; retired, 1920. [*Died* 17 *Aug.* 1951.

WALTER, Madison Melville; Chairman and President, The Royal Bank of Canada, since 1960; *b.* 1 Feb. 1897; *s.* of Orma Madison Walter and Maud B. Walter (*née* Annis); *m.* 1927, Margaret Elizabeth McCullough; one *d.* *Educ.:* Oshawa, Ont., Canada. Joined Royal Bank of Canada, Oshawa, 1912; subs. served at various W. Ontario branches; transferred to Supervisor's Dept., Toronto, 1924; to Head Office, Montreal, 1928; Asst. Manager, Montreal Branch, 1928, Manager, 1938; Asst. Gen. Man., 1944; Vice-Pres. and Director, 1955. Vice-Pres. Montreal Trust Co.; Director: Capital Investment Corp. of Montreal Ltd.; J. & P. Coats (Canada) Ltd.; Consolidated Paper Corp. Ltd.; Elican Development Co. Ltd.; National Drug & Chemical Co. of Canada Ltd.; Power Corp. of Canada Ltd.; Sogemines Ltd.; Sun Life Assurance Co. of Canada; Westcoast Transmission Co. Ltd. Governor, Royal Victoria Hosp.; Hon. Treas., Verdun Protestant Hosp. *Recreations:* golf, skiing. *Address:* The Royal Bank of Canada, 360 St. James St. West, Montreal, P.Q., Canada. *T.:* VI-2-6123. *Clubs:* Mount Royal, Forest and Stream, St. James's, Montreal (Montreal); Royal Montreal Golf; Mount Bruno Golf and Country; York (Toronto); Royal Montreal Curling. [*Died* 9 *Dec.* 1960.

WALTER, Robert, C.M.G. 1918; 2nd *s.* of late Major F. E. Walter, M.V.O., and *g.s.* of late John Walter, M.P., of Bearwood, Berks; *m.* Alice Mary Le Hunte (*d.* 1955), 2nd *d.* of late Admiral T. Le Hunte Ward, C.B.; two *s.* one *d.* *Educ.:* Marlborough; Worcester Coll., Oxford; 1st Class Classical Moderations, 1894; 3rd Class Greats, 1896; Cadet in Colonial Service, 1896; Secretary to Government, Wei-hai-wei, 1902-13; Colonial Secretary British Honduras, 1914-20; Administrator Dominica, 1920-23; Administrator St. Vincent, 1923; retired, 1929; gold medallist Poetry Society, 1932. *Recreations:* walking, reading, learning and speaking poetry. *Address:* Minster House, Sturminster Newton, Dorset. *T.:* Sturminster Newton 69. [*Died* 21 *March* 1959.

WALTERS, Rev. Harold Crawford; Chairman, North Lancashire District of the Methodist Church 1950-57; President of the Methodist Conference, July 1956-57; *s.* of late Rev. W. D. Walters; *m.* 1951, Enid Newstead Goad. *Educ.:* The Grove School, Highgate; Richmond College. Missionary in Burma, 1910-30; Chairman of Burma Methodist District, 1925-30; Chairman of Bradford Methodist District, 1939-46; Chairman of Ceylon and Burma Provincial Synod, 1929. Member of Lancashire Education Cttee., 1952. Hon. D.D. Lycoming Univ., U.S.A. *Recreations:* walking and gardening. *Address:* 10 Mill Gap Road, Eastbourne. [*Died* 24 *Feb.* 1958.

WALTHEW, Richard Henry; late Music Professor Guildhall School of Music and Queen's College, Harley Street; *b.* 1872; *m.* 1901; one *s.* one *d.* *Educ.:* Islington High School; Royal College of Music (Open Scholarship for Composition). Examiner to the Associated Board of the Royal Schools of Music; works performed on various occasions at Monday Popular Concerts, Crystal Palace Saturday Concerts, Handel Society, Promenade Concerts, &c. *Publications:* Choral works—The Pied Piper; Ode to a Nightingale; Chamber music—a quintet, two trios, suites for clarinet, pianoforte, &c.; about 100 songs and pianoforte pieces. *Recreation:* writing music. *Address:* 1 Clarence Drive, East Preston, Sussex. *T.:* Rustington 935. [*Died* 14 *Nov.* 1951.

WALTON, Cecil Simpson, M.A.; Headmaster University College School, Hampstead, since 1936; *b.* 1905; *o. s.* of Rev. S. S. Walton. *Educ.:* Rugby (scholar); Balliol College, Oxford (scholar). First class in Classical Honour Moderations; first class in Lit. Hum. Seventh Form Classical Master at Westminster School, 1930-36. *Address:* University College School, N.W.3. [*Died* 21 *Dec.* 1955.

WALTON, Rev. Herbert Arthur; *s.* of late G. E. Walton, Handsworth, Staffs; *m.* 1906, Gladys Amy, *d.* of Very Rev. Dean Shepherd of Antigua; two *s.* *Educ.:* King Edward's High School, Birmingham; St. Boniface College, Warminster. Deacon, 1903; Priest, 1905; Curate of St. John's Cathedral, Antigua, 1903; Rector of St. George's, Dominica, 1905; Archdeacon of Grenada, 1915-22; Rector of St. George's, Grenada, 1911-22; and Canon of St. Vincent; Organising Secretary S.P.G. for Midlands, 1922-24; Rector of Avon Dassett, Warwickshire, 1924-1927; Home Secretary, S.P.G., 1927-33; Rector of Ascot, 1933-46. Rector of Brightwell, 1946-54. *Address:* College of St. Mark, Saffron Walden, Essex. [*Died* 15 *April* 1955.

WALTON, Sir James, K.C.V.O., *cr.* 1935; M.S., F.R.C.S., M.B., B.Sc., L.R.C.P.; F.A.C.S. (Hon.); F.G.A.; Officier de la Légion d'Honneur; Extra Surgeon to the

Queen since 1952 (formerly to King George VI); Extra Surgeon to Queen Mary; late Vice-Pres. and Member of Council, R.C.S.; Consulting Surgeon, London Hospital and Victoria Hospital, Kingston; Brig. A.M.D.; late President Association of Surgeons; President Med. Society of London; F.R.S.M. (late President surgical section) and member of several medical societies; *b.* London, 1881; *m.* 1st, Nancy Mary Trevett (*d.* 1953); one *s.* one *d.*; 2nd, 1953, Renée Carrington. *Educ.:* Framlingham Coll.; London Hosp. Medical College. M.R.C.S., L.R.C.P. (Lond.) 1905; B.Sc. (London University), Honours Anatomy and Morphology, 1906; M.B., B.S. (Lond. Univ.), Honours Pathology, Midwifery and Gynæcology, 1908; F.R.C.S. (England), 1907; M.S. (London), 1909; F.G.A. (with distinction) 1945. Scholarships at London Hospital: Obstetric, Duckworth-Nelson Clin. Med. and Pathology, Andrew-Clark (Pathology), Sutton (Clin. Medicine and Surgery), The Medical Scholarship, The Surgical Scholarship, Scholarship (Anatomy) Intermediate M.B. 1905; Emergency Officer, London Hospital, House Physician, Receiving-Room Officer and Resident Anæs., House Surgeon, Assistant Director Pathological Institute, Surgical Registrar, Demonstrator of Anatomy, Assistant Surgeon to London Hospital; Surgeon to London Hospital; to Poplar Hospital for Accidents; to Evelina Hospital for Children, and to Seamen's Hospital, Greenwich; late Surgeon to King George V, to King Edward VIII and to King George VI; Surgeon to H.M.'s Household, 1930-36; late Hunterian Professor of Surgery; late Capt. R.A.M.C. 2nd London General Hospital; Endsleigh Hospital for Officers, Empire Hospital for Diseases of Brain and Spinal Cord, Palace Green Hospital for Officers. *Publications:* Fractures and Separated Epiphyses; A Text-Book of the Surgical Dyspepsias; Physical Gemmology; Editor: A Text-Book of Surgical Diagnosis; author of many articles in text-books and the medical press mainly devoted to the surgery of the upper abdomen, the thyroid gland, and the central nervous system. *Recreations:* fishing, tennis, badminton. *Address:* Spey House, Mayfield, Sussex. *T.:* Mayfield 3162.
[*Died* 27 *Aug.* 1955.

WALTON, Sir John Charles, K.C.I.E., *cr.* 1942; C.B. 1930, M.C.; *s.* of Charles Walton, Tunbridge Wells; *b.* 14 March 1885; *m.* 1923, Nelly Margaret, *d.* of Professor W. R. Scott, F.B.A.; one *s.* two *d.* *Educ.:* Tonbridge School; Brasenose College, Oxford, 1st Cl. Mods., 1906, and Lit. Hum., 1908; Arnold Historical Essay Prize, 1909. Entered Admiralty, 1908; transferred to India Office, 1909; Secretary, Political Department, 1930; Asst. Under-Sec. of State for India, 1936; Deputy Under-Secretary of State for Burma, 1942; retired, 1946; Military Service with R.A., 1916-18. *Address:* 37 Clifton Hill, St. John's Wood, N.W.8. *T.:* Maida Vale 2946. *Club:* Athenæum. [*Died* 1 *Aug.* 1957.

WALTON, Leslie Bannister, M.A., B.Litt.; Forbes Reader in Spanish, and Head of Department of Hispanic Studies, University of Edinburgh, since 1920; *b.* 11 Oct. 1895; *e. s.* of William Arthur Walton, of Sunderland, and Elizabeth Ann, *d.* of late Duke Bannister of Slaidburn, Yorks; *m.* 1920, Mona (marriage dissolved, 1938), *o. d.* of J. R. Johnson of Streatham. *Educ.:* Queen's College, Taunton, and mainly privately; Univ. College, London; Jesus College, Oxford (Open Scholar). B.A. (Lond.), 2nd Class Hons., Final School of Mediæval and Modern Languages (French), 1918; B.A. (Oxon), 1st Class Hons., Final School of Mediæval and Modern Languages (Spanish), with distinction, 1920; M.A. (Oxon), 1924; B.Litt. 1926; Examiner in Spanish in the Univ. of Durham, 1921-23; University of Manchester, 1922-24; Queen's University, Belfast, 1923-25; University of Sheffield, 1924; University of Aberdeen, 1923-26; University of Birmingham, 1926; Trinity College, Dublin, 1934; University of Cambridge, 1937; University of Leeds, 1939; Visiting Professor of English Literature, University of Madrid, summer term, 1931; lectured for M.O.I., 1940; Lecturer under Central Advisory Council for Adult Education in H.M. Forces, 1942-43; broadcasts in Foreign Service of B.B.C., 1942; lectured for British Council, etc., in South America, 1946; delegate to Cervantes Congress in Spain, 1948; lectured for British Council in Spain, 1949 and 1950; delegate to Internat. Congress organised by Spanish Council for Higher Research, Madrid, 1950; Lectured in Venezuela, on invitation of Venezuelan Ministry of Education, 1951. General Editor Bell's Spanish Classics. *Publications:* Edition of Moratin's El Viejo y La Niña (with Critical Introduction); edition of José Cadalso's Cartas Marruecas; English translation of Enrique Larreta's La Gloria De Don Ramiro; Pérez Galdós and the Spanish Novel of the Nineteenth Century, a critical Study; The Living Thought of Cervantes; A Spanish Reader for Adult Beginners and Others; English trans. El Oráculo of Baltasar Gracián (with Critical Introduction); new edition, Motteux's trans. of Don Quixote; articles in reviews, etc. *Recreations:* reading and talking. *Address:* Minto House, Chambers St., University, Edinburgh. *Clubs:* P.E.N.; New, Scottish Arts, International (Edinburgh). [*Died* 9 *Sept.* 1960.

WALTZ, Jacques; *see* Hansi.

WALWYN, Vice-Admiral Sir Humphrey Thomas, K.C.S.I., *cr.* 1933; K.C.M.G., *cr.* 1939; C.B. 1928; D.S.O. 1916; R.N. retired; Governor of Newfoundland, 1936-46; *b.* 25 Jan. 1879; 2nd *s.* of late Colonel J. Walwyn; *m.* 1912, Eileen Mary (D.B.E. 1947), *d.* of Major-General T. van Straubenzee; one *s.* *Educ.:* H.M.S. Britannia, Dartmouth. Went to sea in H.M.S. Camperdown, Jan. 1895; qualified as Gunnery Lieut. 1904 and obtained the Egteron Memorial Prize; Gunnery Lieut. of H.M.S. Drake, H.M.S. Superb, Neptune; Comdr, 1912; H.M.S. Warspite, 1915-17 (D.S.O.); Captain, 1916; in command destroyer flotillas and Senior Officer Mediterranean Destroyers, 1923; Director of Gunnery Division, Naval Staff, Admiralty, 1924-26; commanded H.M.S. Valiant, 1926; Flag Officer commanding the Royal Indian Navy, 1928-34; Rear-Admiral, 1928; Vice-Admiral, 1932; retired list, 1934. *Address:* Lower Wraxall House, Maiden Newton, Dorchester. *Clubs:* United Service; Royal Dorset Yacht (Weymouth). [*Died* 28 *Dec.* 1957.

WANKANER, Capt. H.H. Maharana Shri, Sir Amarsinhji, Maharana Raj Saheb of, K.C.S.I., *cr.* 1936; K.C.I.E., *cr.* 1912; represents senior branch of Zala Rajputs; *b.* 4 Jan. 1879; *S.* 1881; three *s.* three *d.* *Educ.:* Rajkumar College. Has travelled in India, England, and America. The State has an area of 417 sq. miles, and a population of 54,966. Salute, 11 guns. *Heir:* Yuvraj Shri Pratapsinhji. *Address:* Wankaner, Kathiawar.
[*Died* 28 *June* 1954.

WARBURTON, Lieut.-Col. William Melvill, C.M.G. 1919; D.S.O. 1917; *b.* 7 June 1877; *s.* of late Col. William Pleace Warburton, C.S.I.; *m.* 1st, 1906, Yda Frances (*d.* 1907), *d.* of late Col. Jacob Peter Deneys Vanrenen; 2nd, 1912, Muriel Frances, *d.* of late William James Henderson; two *d.* *Educ.:* Wellington College; R.M.A., Woolwich. Commission in R.A. 1897; 1st Lieut. 1900; Captain, 1902; Major, 1914; Lieut.-Col. 1917; served European War, 1914-18 (despatches 4 times, D.S.O., C.M.G., Croix d'Officier of the Légion of Honneur, and Croix de Guerre with Palme); retired pay, 1922. *Address:* Lower Dairy House, Nayland, nr. Colchester. *T.:* Nayland 220.
[*Died* 20 *July* 1952.

WALTON, Lt.-Col. Robert Henry C.B.E., M.D., F.R.C.S. See page xxxi.

WARD, Col. Sir (Albert) Lambert, 1st Bt., *cr.* 1929; C.V.O. 1937; D.S.O. 1915; T.D.; D.L. County of London; *b.* 7 Nov. 1875; *o. s.* of A. B. Ward, J.P.; *m.* 1920; Constance, *o. d.* of J. B. Tidmas, J.P., Normanton-on-Soar and Sutton Bonnington; one *d. Educ.:* St. Paul's School; Paris; Darmstadt. Com. in H.A.C. 1902; Lt. 1904; Capt. 1912; Maj. 1914; Lt.-Col. 1916; Bt. Col. 1926; 2nd in Command, 1915; served with Expeditionary Force in Flanders, 1914-15 (wounded twice, despatches twice, and D.S.O.); commanded 2nd Batt. H.A.C. during operations on the Ancre and during the advance of 1917 (wounded, despatches); contested (C.) West Hull Dec. 1910; Conservative candidate, Burnley, 1912-13; M.P. (U.) North-West Kingston-on-Hull, 1918-45; Parliamentary Private Sec. to the Home Sec. (Mr. Bridgeman), 1922-23; Parliamentary Private Sec. to First Lord of the Admiralty, 1924-25; to Sec. of State for War (Sir L. Worthington Evans), 1927-28; Lord Commissioner of H.M. Treasury, 1931-35; Vice-Chamberlain of H.M. Household, 1935; Comptroller of H.M. Household, 1936-37; Treasurer of H.M. Household, 1937; introduced as a Private Member's Bill in 1924 and secured the passing into law the legislation making permanent the principle of Summer Time; raised H Zone of the Home Guard and commanded it, 1940-42. *Publication:* (Joint author) H.A.C. History of European War, 1914 - 18. *Recreations:* shooting, rifle shooting (English XX, 1907-8-9), stalking, swimming, and golf. *Address:* 12A Collingham Gdns., S.W.5. *T.:* Frobisher 3030. *Club:* Carlton. [*Died* 21 *Oct.* 1956 (*ext.*).

WARD, Arthur Samuel, K.C. 1943; Recorder of Coventry since 1943. Called to Bar, Lincoln's Inn, 1906; Recorder of Newark on Trent, 1935-43. *Address:* 2 Garden Court, Temple, E.C.4; Library Chambers, 8 Temple Street, Birmingham. [*Died* 6 *Feb.* 1952.

WARD, Sir Ashley (Skelton), LL.D.; President of Thos. W. Ward Ltd., Albion Works, Sheffield, since 1950; Chairman, Park Gate Iron and Steel Co. Ltd.; Dep.-Chm. Laycock Engineering Co. Ltd.; Director: Liverpool & London & Globe Insurance Co. Ltd. (Local); National Provincial Bank Ltd. (Local); *b.* 8 Oct. 1877; *m.* 1st, 1905, Hilda Lewis (*d.* 1942); one *d.* (one *s.* decd.); 2nd, 1958, Lady (Edith) Dunbar. Master Cutler, 1939-40. President for some years of the Federated Associations of Scrap, Iron, Steel Metals and Machinery Merchants of Gt. Britain, and took an active part in formation of Central Scrap Agency of Brit. Iron and Steel Fedn. Hon. LL.D. Sheffield Univ., 1955. *Recreation:* golf. *Address:* Ran Farm, 10 Ranmoor Crescent, Sheffield 10. *T.:* Sheffield 33055. *Club:* Sheffield (Sheffield). [*Died* 26 *March* 1959.

WARD, Rear-Admiral (S) Cecil Arthur, C.M.G. 1919; R.N. retired; *b.* 1881; *s.* of Rev. James Rimington Ward, Richmond, Natal; *m.* 1908, Barbara, *d.* of F. H. Heathcote. Secretary to Vice-Adm. Commanding Battle Cruisers during European War (C.M.G.).; retired, 1936. *Address:* Little House, Sidford Road, Sidmouth, Devon. *T.:* Sidmouth 1460. [*Died* 3 *July* 1954.

WARD, Dudley, C.B.E. 1922; London representative of United Nations International Children's Emergency Fund; *b.* 23 Sept. 1885; *s.* of F. W. Ward and Edith Welch Bardill; *m.* 1912, Anne-marie Elisabeth Clothilde, *d.* of Hans Edler von der Planitz; one *s.* two *d. Educ.:* Derby School; St. John's College, Cambridge (Fellow). Assistant Editor Economist, 1910-12; Research work in Germany, 1913-14; Treasury, 1914-19; Representative of Treasury at Peace Conference, 1919, and at Brussels Conference, 1921; British Representative under Dawes Scheme for Reparation Commission on Bank für deutsche Industrie Obligationen. Dir. British Overseas Bank, Ltd., and of other companies; General Counsel, European Office of U.N.R.R.A., 1944-48. *Address:* 7 King's Bench Walk, Temple, E.C.4; The Old Vicarage, Grantchester, Cambs. *T.:* Central 1231. *Club:* United University. [*Died* 8 *Feb.* 1957.

WARD, F. K.; *see* Kingdon-Ward.

WARD, George, J.P.; *s.* of late William Ward, Barwell; *b.* 1878; *m.* 1906, Emily J. Haydon. *Educ.:* Barwell National School. Boot manufacturer; M.P.(L.) Bosworth 1923-24. *Address:* Rosslyn, Barwell, nr. Leicester. [*Died* 3 *Dec.* 1951.

WARD, John Frederick, O.B.E. 1948; M.A.; *b.* 20 July 1883; *s.* of John Ward and Mary Anne Russel; *m.* 1912, Florence Winnifred Braddock; one *s.* two *d.* (and one *s.* decd.). *Educ.:* Prince Alfred Coll. and Univ. of Adelaide, S.A. First H.M. of 2 new Church boarding schools, one in North Queensland and one in Perth, W.A.; Headmaster, Prince Alfred Coll., Kent Town, S. Austr., 1930-48; retd. 1948. *Publication:* Prince Alfred College, "The first eighty years," 1867-1948, 1951. *Address:* c/o Prince Alfred College, Kent Town, S. Australia. [*Died* 18 *Aug.* 1954.

WARD, Captain John Richard Le Hunte, C.B.E. 1919; R.N., retd.; *b.* 1870; *e. s.* of late Admiral Thomas Le Hunte Ward, C.B.; *m.* 1905, Violet Ella Mary, *d.* of late Lt.-Col. B. E. Ward; two *s.* Captain Supt. Humber Dist., 1914-20; retd., 1920. *Address:* Sarnia, Westella Rd., Yelverton, South Devon. *T.:* 219. [*Died* 13 *Feb.* 1953.

WARD, Col. Sir Lambert; *see* Ward, Col. Sir A. L.

WARD, Sir Lancelot E. B.; *see* Barrington-Ward.

WARD, Brig.-Gen. Walter Reginald, C.B.E. 1919; Military Forces of Canada (retired); *b.* Saltash, Cornwall, 24 Oct. 1869; *y. s.* of Commander Henry Purcell Ward, R.N.; *m.* 1896, Irene Silver, *d.* of John Y. Payzant, Halifax, Nova Scotia; one *s.* one *d. Educ.:* Christ's Hospital. Entered Royal Navy 1886; resigned 1904 and joined Canadian Permanent Force; organised and administered the Canadian Army Pay Corps on its establishment in 1906, and appointed Assistant Paymaster-General at Militia Headquarters, Ottawa; proceeded to England with 1st Canadian contingent on outbreak of war in 1914 in charge of financial services and Records of the Force; subsequently appointed Accountant Gen. and actg. Dep. Minister for Overseas Forces. *Address:* Summerleas, Newton Ferrers, Devon. *T.:* Newton Ferrers 288. [*Died* 25 *Sept.* 1952.

WARDALE, Professor John Dobson; late Prof. of Ophthalmology, College of Medicine, Durham University; Ophthalmological Surgeon, Royal Victoria Infirmary, Newcastle; *b.* Newcastle. *Educ.:* Durham University; Royal London Ophthalmological Hospital. *Address:* Brokenheugh, Haydon Bridge, Northumberland. *T.:* Haydon Bridge 206. [*Died* 7 *Dec.* 1958.

WARDE, Engineer Rear-Admiral Thomas Herbert, C.B. 1939; *b.* 1882; *m.* 1912, Lilian Mary Dorothy, *d.* of Capt. W. R. Lugar; (one *d.* decd.). Joined Royal Navy, 1899; Engineer Captain, 1930; Engineer Rear-Admiral, 1936; retired list 1942, but served at Admiralty until 1945. *Address:* 41 Berwyn Road, Richmond, Surrey. *T.:* Prospect 1931. *Club:* Army and Navy. [*Died* 5 *May* 1960.

WARDE-ALDAM, Colonel William St. Andrew, D.S.O. 1917; *b.* 1882; *e. s.* of late William Wright Warde-Aldam, of Frickley Hall, Yorkshire, Healey Hall, Northumberland, and Ederline, Argyllshire, and late Sarah Julia, *d.* and *co-heiress* of Rev. William Warde of Hooton Pagnell; *m.* 1908, Clara (*d.* 1952), *d.* of late George Macavoy, of Hauxton, Cambridgeshire; one *s.* one *d.*

(one *s.* killed in action, 1943, and one *s.* decd., 1957). *Educ.:* Eton; Trinity College, Cambridge; B.A. Served Coldstream Guards, 1904-25; commanded 2/20 London Regiment, 1916-19; 3rd Batt. Coldstream Guards, 1921-25; Commander, 149th (Northumberland) Infantry Brigade, T.A., 1927-31; European War, 1914-18 (despatches, D.S.O., Brevets Major and Lt.-Col., Legion of Honour); retired pay, 1933; Hon. Col.: 5th K.O.Y.L.I., 1938-39; 53rd L.A.A. Regt. 1939-45, 553rd (K.O.Y.L.I.) L.A.A. Regt., 1941-53; 57th L.A.A. Regt., 1939-45; 557th (K.O.Y.L.I) H.A.A. Regt., 1945-53; Zone Commander Home Guard, 1941-44; contested (C.) Doncaster, 1923; President, Royal English Forestry Society, 1934-36; President Yorkshire Agricultural Society, 1937-38; High Sheriff of Yorkshire, 1940; D.L. Northumberland; D.L., J.P., W.R. Yorkshire. *Address:* Hooton Pagnell Hall, Doncaster; Healey Hall, Riding Mill on Tyne. *Clubs:* Oxford and Cambridge; Northern Counties (Newcastle upon Tyne). [*Died* 14 *Sept.* 1958.

WARDELL, John Henry, M.A.; *b.* 1878. *Educ.:* Wellington; Trinity College, Dublin. Lecturer I.C.S. 1901; Professor of Jurisprudence and Economics at the Queen's College, Galway, 1903-8; Professor of Modern History in the University of Dublin, 1904-11; Reader, 1902, in succession to Prof. Bury; Director Military Studies, Dublin University, 1904; Life Member Senate, 1903; Lecturer at Alexandra College; Barrington Lecturer (Elect), 1903; Member Royal United Service Institution, and many foreign and British Societies. *Publications:* contributions to Reviews; With the 32nd in the Peninsula and other Campaigns. *Recreations:* pedigrees, languages. *Address:* The Abbey, Shanagolden, Co. Limerick. [*Died Aug.* 1957.

WARDLAW, Sir Henry, 19th Bt. of Pitreavie, *cr.* 1631; *b.* 8 Feb. 1867; 2nd *s.* of 18th Bt. and Christina, 3rd *d.* of James Paton; *S.* father, 1897; *m.* 1892, Janet Montgomerie, *d.* of James Wylie; one *s.* two *d.* *Educ.:* Dollar Institution. Went out to Australia, 1926. *Recreations:* golf, curling, cricket. *Heir:* *s.* Henry [*b.* 30 Aug. 1894; *m.* 1929, Ellen, *d.* of John Francis Brady; four *s.* one *d.*]. *Address:* Lammas Cottage, Station Rd., Thames Ditton, Surrey. [*Died* 4 *Feb.* 1954.

WARDLAW, William, C.B.E. 1949; D.Sc., F.R.I.C.; Professor Emeritus of Physical Chemistry in Univ. of London, Birkbeck College; *b.* 29 Mar. 1892; *m.* Doris Whitfield, B.Sc.; one *d.* *Educ.:* Rutherford College, Newcastle on Tyne; University of Durham, Armstrong College. Formerly Senior Lecturer in Inorganic Chemistry in University of Birmingham; Jt. Sec. War Cabinet Scientific Advisory Cttee., 1941-45; Scientific Adviser Appointments Dept., Min. of Labour and National Service; Professor of Physical Chemistry, Univ. of London, 1937-1957; Hon. Secretary of the Chemical Society, 1940-48; President Chemical Society, 1954-56; President Royal Institute of Chemistry, 1957-. Council of Royal Institute of Chemistry, 1929-32, 1933-36; President of Section B, British Association, Belfast, 1952; General Secretary, British Assoc. 1955-; sometime Examiner Final Honour Chemistry School at Oxford; lately External Examiner Univs. of London, Durham, Sheffield, Wales, Cambridge, Birmingham, Leeds, Glasgow, St. Andrews, Alexandria, Cairo. *Publications:* scientific papers mainly in Journal of Chemical Society. *Address:* Royal Institute of Chemistry, 30 Russell Square, W.C.1. *Club:* Savage. [*Died* 19 *Dec.* 1958.

WARDLAW, Rear-Adm. William P. M.; *see* Mark-Wardlaw.

WAREING, Eustace Bernard Foley; writer; formerly foreign correspondent; *b.* 12 Jan. 1890; 2nd *s.* of Bernard Wareing, Edgbaston, Birmingham, and of Mary, *yr. d.* of Charles Faulkner, Barnt Green, Worcs.; *m.* 1920, Jane, *o. d.* of Joseph Duquenne, Charleroy, Belgium. *Educ.:* privately; Bishop Vesey's School, Sutton Coldfield; Birmingham Univ. (B.Com.); Munich Univ.; Lector and Times Correspondent, Munich, 1912-14; R.G.A. and G.S. Intelligence, France, 1915-18; Inter-Allied Rhineland High Commission (Secretary-General, 1928), Coblenz, 1918-29; Daily Telegraph Correspondent at Rome and Vatican City, 1929-33; Berlin, 1933-38; Paris, 1938-40; special Correspondent for French Affairs and Joint Diplomatic Correspondent of Daily Telegraph, 1940-43; Special Correspondent Algiers, 1943; Washington, Ottawa with Gen. de Gaulle, 1944; again Paris Correspondent of Daily Telegraph until 1948; temp. civil servant, C.C.G., Bonn, until 1953. Mem. Roy. Inst. Internat. Affairs. *Publications:* Translations from French and German of works on history, psychology, science and music; contributory suggestions acknowledged in Concise Oxford Dictionary; numerous reviews in Spectator, International Affairs, and learned journals. *Recreation:* travel. *Address:* (temp.) c/o Lloyds Bank, 6 Pall Mall, S.W.1. *Club:* Savile. [*Died* 18 *Sept.* 1958.

WARING, Sir Holburt Jacob, 1st Bt., *cr.* 1935; Kt., *cr.* 1925; C.B.E. 1919; M.S., Lond. and Egypt, B.Sc., F.R.C.S.; F.R.A.C.S., LL.D., D.C.L.; Officier de la Légion d'Honneur; Consulting Surgeon, St. Bartholomew's Hospital, Metropolitan Hospital and Royal Dental Hospital; Consultant Surgeon, Ministry of Pensions; Treasurer Imperial Cancer Research Fund; Hunterian Trustee Royal Coll. of Surgeons; Governor of Imperial College, 1930-47; Vice-Chancellor, 1922-24, and late Dean of Faculty of Medicine, Univ. of London; late Examiner in Surgery, Universities of London, Oxford, and Manchester, and Royal College of Surgeons; Bt. Col. R.A.M.C. (T.), retired; late Member and Treasurer of General Medical Council, 1917-32; late Member and Treas. of Dental Board of U.K., 1921-1932; Member (late Chm.) of Court of Governors, 1921-47, Member (late Chairman) of Board of Management and Treasurer, London School of Hygiene and Tropical Medicine; President, Medical Society of London, 1925-26; Pres. Section of Surgery (Royal Society of Medicine), 1928-30; Pres., R.C.S. of England, 1932-35; Governor of St. Bart's Hosp. and member of Council of Med. Coll.; *b.* 1866; *e. s.* of I. Waring, Southport; *m.* 1900, Annie Cassandra (*d.* 1948), *d.* of Charles Johnston Hill of Holland Pk., W.; one *s.* *Educ.:* Owens Coll., Manchester; St. Bartholomew's Hospital Med. College. *Publications:* Surgical Diseases of Liver, Gall Bladder, and Biliary System, 1897; Manual of Operative Surgery, 6th edit., 1927; Surgical Treatment of Malignant Diseases, 1928; (with Sir D'Arcy Power), A Short History of St. Bartholomew's Hospital, 1923; etc. *Recreations:* shooting, fishing, travel. *Heir:* *s.* Alfred Harold [*b.* 14 Feb. 1902; *m.* 1930, Winifred, *d.* of Albert Boston, Stockton-on-Tees; one *s.* two *d.*]. *Address:* Pen-Moel, Tidenham, Gloucestershire. *T.:* Chepstow 448. *Club:* Athenæum. [*Died* 10 *Feb.* 1953.

WARMAN, Rt. Rev. (Frederic Sumpter) Guy, M.A., D.D., Hon. LL.D. Manchester; *b.* 5 Nov. 1872; *s.* of Frederick Warman, Highbury, London, and Caroline Ash; *m.* 1899, Gertrude, *d.* of late Norwood Earle, Dover; two *s.* *Educ.:* Merchant Taylors' School, London; Pembroke College, Oxford. Classical scholar; 2nd class Hon. Classical Mods.; 2nd class Theol. Schol.; Hall Houghton University prizeman; M.A. Durham, 1908; B.D. Oxon, 1907; D.D. Oxon, 1911; Curate of Leyton, 1895-99; St. Mary's, Hastings, 1899-1901; Vice-Principal of St. Aidan's, 1901-2; Vicar of Birkenhead and Surrogate, 1902-8; Chairman, Birkenhead Board of Guardians, 1908; Principal, St. Aidan's Theological College, Birkenhead, 1907-16; Vicar of Bradford, 1916-19; Bishop of Truro, 1919-23; Bishop of Chelmsford, 1923-29; Bishop of Manchester, 1929-47; Select Preacher, University of Oxford, 1929-1931; Hon. Fellow of Pembroke College, Oxford; teacher in Hellenistic Greek in University of Liverpool; Chairman Birkenhead Distress Committee; Chairman Birkenhead War Pensions Committee, 1916; Commissary to the Archbishop of Sydney; Examining Chaplain to the Bishop of Chelmsford and to the Bishop of Manchester; Member of Archbishop's Committee on Church and State, also Prayer Book Revision Committee; Chairman of Central Advisory Council of Training for the Ministry and Chairman of Council of Deaconesses since 1926. *Clubs:* Authors'; Union (Manchester). [*Died* 12 *Feb.* 1953.

WARNER, Sir Christopher Frederick Ashton, G.B.E. 1956; K.C.M.G. 1951 (C.M.G. 1943); Director, Imperial Continental Gas Association, and Société Internationale d'Energie Hydro-electrique (Sidro), 1955; *b.* 17 January 1895; *s.* of Frederick Ashton Warner, F.R.C.S.E., L.R.C.P. *Educ.:* Winchester Coll.; Magdalen Coll., Oxford. Served European War, 1914-18, Royal Fusiliers (Capt.); Foreign Office, 1920-23 and 1928-51; H.M. Embassy, Constantinople, 1923-25; H.M. Legation, Tehran, 1925-28; H.M. Ambassador to Belgium, 1951-55, retired from H.M. Foreign Service, 1955. *Address:* 33 Moore St., Cadogan Sq., S.W.3. *T.:* Kensington 6816. *Clubs:* Oxford and Cambridge University, M.C.C.; Vincent's (Oxford). [*Died* 13 *Jan.* 1957.

WARNER, Col. Sir Edward Courtenay Thomas, 2nd Bt., *cr.* 1910; D.S.O. 1917; M.C.; D.L., J.P., Suffolk; *b.* 4 Jan. 1886; *e. s.* of Sir Courtenay Warner, 1st Bt., and Lady Leucha Diana Maude (*d.* 1947), D.G.St.J., 6th *d.* of 1st Earl de Montalt; *S.* father, 1934; *m.* 1920, Hon. Nesta Douglas-Pennant, *yr. d.* of 2nd Baron Penrhyn; one *s.* two *d. Educ.:* Eton; Christ Church, Oxford. 2nd Lt. Scots Guards, 1905; Capt. 1915; Bt. Major, 1918; Major, 1920; Lt.-Colonel, 1928; Bt. Col. 1931; Colonel, 1932; A.D.C. to the Lord Lieutenant of Ireland, 1910-14; Brigade-Major, Brigade of Guards, 1920; served European War, 1914-18 (D.S.O., M.C., despatches six times, 1914 Bronze Star, Croix de Guerre, Order of Danilo (Montenegro), St. Avis (Portuguese); Brigade-Major 1st (Guards') Brigade, 1925-1927; commanded 2nd Batt. Scots Guards, 1928-31; Officer-Commanding Scots Guards and Regimental District, 1931-34 and Commander 4th Guards Brigade 1933-34; General Staff Officer, 1st Grade, 3rd Division, 1934-1937; retired pay, 1938; G.S.O. 1st Grade, 54th Division, 1939, and to B.E.F. 1940 (1939 Star); Commander Maidstone Sub-Area, 1941; Senior Regional Officer, London Civil Defence Region, 1942-45; Chairman Warner Estate Ltd.; Vice-Chairman Law Land Co. Ltd.; High Sheriff Suffolk, 1947-1948; Co-Director, B.R.C.S., 1946-53. *Heir: s.* Edward Courtenay Henry, Lt., Scots Guards [*b.* 3 Aug. 1922; *m.* 1949, Jocelyn Mary, *d.* of Comdr. Sir Thomas Beevor, 6th Bt., R.N., Hargham Hall, Norfolk, and of Mrs. Robert Currie, and *sister* of Sir Thomas Beevor. Served War of 1939-45 (wounded)].) *Address:* Brettenham Park, Suffolk. *T.A.:* Brettenham. *T.:* Bildeston 252; 5 Culford Mansions, Culford Gardens, S.W.3. *Clubs:* Guards, Leander. [*Died* 2 *Oct.* 1955.

WARNER, Leonard William, F.R.Ae.S.; Director Ratcliffe Tool Co. Ltd. Aeronautical Inspection Directorate, Air Ministry, 1914-1938; Ministry of Aircraft Production: Deputy Director, 1938-41; Director, 1941-1943; Deputy Director-General, 1944; Director-General, 1945. *Address:* Ratcliffe Tool Co. Ltd., 21 Gorst Rd., Park Royal, N.W.10. *T.:* Elgar 6693; 29 Puckle Lane, Canterbury. *T.:* Canterbury 3866. *Club:* Royal Automobile. [*Died* 20 *March* 1959.

WARNER, Sir Lionel Ashton Piers, Kt., *cr.* 1936; C.B.E.; *b.* Bedford, 30 Apr. 1875; *s.* of late Major Ashton C. Warner, XX Hussars; *m.* 1st, 1904, Nina Mary (*d.* 1943), *e. d.* of Capt. Liddon, 8th the King's; one *s.* one *d.*; 2nd, 1945, Margaret Elizabeth, *widow* of S. Bryce, Newbery, Minehead. *Educ.:* Marlborough College. L. and N.W. Railway, 1893-1914; General Manager and Secretary, Mersey Docks and Harbour, 1920-41; Ministry of Shipping, 1917-19. J.P. Liverpool, 1936-42; Hon. Col. R.A. T.A., 1940-49. *Address:* Farleigh, Beacon Road, Minehead. *T.:* Minehead 38. [*Died* 22 *Nov.* 1953.

WARNER-STAPLES, Irene E. Toye; *b.* Bristol; *o. c.* of Wiclif and Annie Warner; *m.* 1920, *cousin*, Albert Warner-Staples (*d.* 1927) of Staplehurst Manor, Springfontein, S. Africa. *Educ.:* Royal School for Daughters of Officers, Bath; private tuition. Became interested in literature and astronomy at an early age; member several astronomical societies; interested in Broadcasting, all forms of spiritual healing, and all occult and psychic subjects. Has been resident in South Africa for many years. *Publications:* Critics of the Christ—Answered by Spiritualism; Volume of Verse: In Light and Darkness—Hope; Through the Cape by Caravan and Car; The Uttermost Farthing (novel); My Telepathic Experiments; numerous astronomical, psychic science, and other articles. *Recreations:* travelling in S. Africa and Europe, broadcasting, motoring, reading, scientific and literary research. *Address:* c/o C. H. Tucker and Co., 11 Small St., Bristol 1. [*Died* 31 *Dec.* 1954.

WARRE, Fel x Walter, O.B.E., M.C.; formerly Director and Chairman of Sotheby and Co., Auctioneers, 34 and 35 New Bond Street, W.1 (retired 1947); *b.* 5 May 1879; 5th *s.* of Rev. E. Warre, C.B., C.V.O., D.D., late Provost of Eton, and Florence Dora, *d.* of Lt.-Col. C. St. Lo Malet; *m.* 1915, Marjorie Monteith, *d.* of Vereker M. Hamilton; one *s.* three *d.* (and one *s.* decd.). *Educ.:* Eton; Balliol College, Oxford. Eton VIII 1896, 1897; Oxford VIII 1898, 1899, 1901; President, O.U.B.C., 1900 and 1901; Leander Crews, 1900, 1902, 1903; Gilman and Co., Merchants, Hong Kong, 1903; Partner in Sotheby's, 1909; K.R.R.C. XIth Batt. XXth Divn. France, 1915 (wounded, M.C.); Capt. 1916; G.S.O.3, I., G.H.Q. France, 1917-18 (despatches twice, O.B.E.); retired major, 1919. *Recreations:* rowing, shooting. *Address:* Wytherston, Powerstock, Bridport, Dorset. *T.:* Powerstock 227. *Clubs:* Brooks's, Leander. [*Died* 17 *Sept.* 1953.

WARRE, Captain George Francis, C.B.E. 1919; *b.* 1876; *s.* of late George Acheson Warre, Twyford House, Winchester; *m.* 1912, Norah Mossom, *d.* of Henry Merryweather and *widow* of Emerson Bainbridge; one *d. Educ.:* Eton. Dir. Motor Boat and Hosp. Ship Dept., B.R.C.S., European War; Capt. R.A.S.C., served France and Italy. *Address:* Villa Roquebrune, Cap Martin, A.M., France. *Club:* Brooks's. [*Died* 14 *June* 1957.

WARREN, Sir (Augustus George) Digby, 7th Bt., *cr.* 1784; M.B.E. 1945; Temp. Major 17th/21st Lancers; *b.* 23 Oct. 1898; *s.* of 6th Bt. and Agnes Georgina, *d.* of late George M. Ievers of Inchera, Co. Cork; *S.* father, 1914. *Educ.:* Harrow; R.M.C., Sandhurst. Served War of 1939-45 (M.B.E.). *Heir: kinsman* Col. T. R. P. Warren, C.B.E. *Address:* Ballylickey, Bantry, Co. Cork, Eire. [*Died* 20 *Jan.* 1958.

WARREN, Charles; Lawyer, practising in Washington, D.C.; *b.* Boston, Massachusetts, 9 March 1868; *s.* of Winslow and Mary Lincoln (Tinkham) Warren; *m.* 1904, Annielouise, *d.* of William Henry Bliss. *Educ.:* Harvard Univ. (A.M.); LL.D. (Hon.)

Columbia Univ., 1933. Admitted to bar, 1892, and practised at Boston; assoc. in practice with Moorfield Storey, 1892-93; priv. sec. to Gov. William E. Russell, 1893; Assoc. in law practice with Gov. Russell until death of latter, 1896; sr. mem. Warren & Perry, Boston, 1897-1914. Chm. Mass. Civil Service Commn., 1905-11; Asst. Atty. Gen. of U.S., Washington, 1914-Apr. 1918; now practising law; apptd. Special Master by Supreme Court of U.S. in case of New Mexico *v.* Texas, 1924; U.S. *v.* Utah, 1929 and Texas *v.* New Mexico, 1936. Apptd. by President Roosevelt as Amer. Mem., Trail Smelter Arbitral Tribunal constituted under Convention of 1935 betw. U.S. and Canada, 1937 (final decision filed, 1941); Amer. mem., Conciliation Internat. Cttee., under Treaty betw. U.S. and Hungary; mem. President's War Relief Control Bd., 1943-46. Stafford Little lecturer, Princeton Univ., 1924; Cutler lecturer on Constitution, Univ. of Rochester, 1927; Bacon lecturer on same, Boston Univ. Law Sch., 1928; James Schouler lecturer on history, Johns Hopkins Univ., 1928; William H. White lecturer on jurisprudence, Univ. of Virginia, 1932; Julius Rosenthal Foundation lecturer on law, Northwestern Univ. Law Sch., 1934; Norman Wait Harris lecturer on neutrality, Univ. of Chicago. 1936; Frank Irvine lecturer, Cornell Univ., 1937; Cutler lecturer on Constitution, Coll. of William and Mary, 1940. Mem. Bd. of Overseers, Harvard Coll., 1934-40; Pres., Harvard Alumni Assoc., 1941-42; Trustee, New England Conservatory of Music, 1905-; Trustee, Nat. Trg. Sch. for Boys, 1934-37; Mem., Mass. Hist. Soc.; Amer. Soc. of Internat. Law (Hon. Vice-Pres.); Nat. Inst. of Arts and Letters, 1925; Amer. Acad. of Arts and Letters, 1937; Amer. Philos. Soc., 1939; mem. cttee. management, Dictionary of Amer. Biog. *Publications:* The Girl and The Governor, 1902; History of the Harvard Law School and Early Legal Conditions in America (3 vols.), 1909; History of the American Bar, Colonial and Federal, to 1860, 1911; The Supreme Court in United States History (3 vols.), 1922, awarded Pulitzer Prize ($2,000), 1923, for best book on American history publ. in 1922; new ed., 2 vols., 1926; The Supreme Court and Sovereign States, 1924; Congress, the Constitution and the Supreme Court, 1925, enlarged ed., 1935; The Making of the Constitution, 1928, 2nd ed. 1937; Jacobin and Junto, 1931; Congress as Santa Claus—The General Welfare Clause, 1932; Bankruptcy in United States History, 1935; Odd Byways in American History, 1942. *Address:* 1527 18th St., N.W., Washington, D.C.; (office) Mills Building, Washington, D.C. *Clubs:* Metropolitan, Cosmos (Washington, D.C.); Harvard, Saint Botolph (Boston); Century, Harvard (New York). [*Died* 16 *Aug.* 1954.

WARREN, Cuthbert L.; *see* Leicester-Warren.

WARREN, Sir Digby; *see* Warren, Sir A. G. D.

WARREN, Frederick Samuel Edward Wright, C.B.E. 1921, President of Canadian Chamber of Commerce in Great Britain (Inc.), 1948; Managing Director J. & J. Lonsdale & Co. Ltd. since 1922, Chm. since 1936; Chm. of Pollock & Co. Ltd., and H. P. Bloomer & Co. Ltd.; *b.* Keyworth, Notts, 17 June 1878; *m.* 1904, Annie E., *e. d.* of Frederick E. Hodgett, Keyworth; two *s.* *Educ.:* Keyworth, Notts. Eight years with W. & G. King, and G. King & Sons, Nottingham; fifteen years with founder of Pollock & Co., Ltd. (J. H. Pollock); Director of Butter and Cheese Supplies, Ministry of Food (voluntary), 1917 to close of Ministry; served on numerous other British and Allied Committees at home and abroad. *Recreation:* golf. *Address:* 30 Avenue Mansions, Finchley Road, N.W.3. *T.:* Hampstead 4617. *Clubs:* National Liberal, Royal Automobile. [*Died* 24 *May* 1952.

WARREN, John Herbert, O.B.E. 1954; M.A., D.P.A.; solicitor; General Secretary, National and Local Government Officers Association, and ancillaries Nalgo Building Soc., Provident Soc., Mutual Insurance Assoc., 1946-57, retired; *b.* 2 Sept. 1895; *s.* of George William Warren and Alice Maud Cass; *m.* 1924, Iris Mary Wilson; one *s.* three *d.* *Educ.:* secondary school; Liverpool Univ. Admin. Assistant to Town Clerk of Birkenhead, 1924; Asst. Solicitor, Birkenhead Corp., 1933; Clerk to Newton U.D.C., 1935; Town Clerk, Slough, 1939; J.P. for Wallasey, 1926-37; external Lecturer in Public Administration, Liverpool Univ., 1933-45; Member National Executive Council of Nalgo, 1935-46; Member Council of Inst. of Public Administration, 1942-47; Member Permanent Bureau of Internat. Union of Local Authorities, 1946-49; Member Sec. of State for Colonies' Advisory Panel on Colonial Local Govt., 1948-. Joint Secretary, National Joint (Whitley) Council for Local Authorities Administrative, Professional, Technical and Clerical Services, 1950-57; Member: Local Govt. Exams. Bd., 1950-; Court of Inquiry into manning of Britannia aircraft, Feb. 1957; London Electricity Bd., 1958-. *Publications:* Municipal Trading, 1923; The English Local Government System, 1946 (with translations in German and Hindi); Municipal Administration, 1948; The Local Government Service, 1952. Editor-in-Chief: Town and County Hall Series and National Board Series. Contrib. to Chambers's Encyclopædia (1950), to British Government since 1918 (symposium), 1950, to the British Party System (symposium), 1952, and to a variety of journals in field of public administration. *Recreations:* music, reading and travel. *Address:* 5 Bradby House, Carlton Hill, N.W.8. *T.:* Maida Vale 9743. [*Died* 11 *July* 1960.

WARREN, Colonel John Raymond, O.B.E.; M.C.; T.D.; *b.* 1888; *s.* of late T. P. Warren, and of late Lily Warren, Handcross Park, Sussex; *m.* 1926, Eveline, *y. d.* of late Lt.-Col. Lionel Bosanquet, Sherwood Foresters; one *s.* one *d.* *Educ.:* Harrow; Magdalen College, Oxford. Joined 4th Battn. The Royal Sussex Regt., 1907; served European War, 1914-19; Commanded the Battn., 1928-32; Barrister, Inner Temple, 1921; D.L. (Sussex), 1932; J.P. Sussex, 1922; Chairman, East Sussex County Council, 1940; High Sheriff of Sussex, 1938; President, East Grinstead Conservative Assoc., 1947. *Address:* The Hyde, Handcross, Sussex. *T.:* Handcross 231. *Clubs:* Carlton, Lansdowne. [*Died* 8 *June* 1956.

WARREN, Colonel Peter, C.M.G. 1916; C.B.E. 1919; Order of the Nile, Egypt, 1917; R.E. (S.R.); *b.* Paignton, Devon 1866; *s.* of William Ellis Warren; *m.* 1896, Helen Marian, *d.* of James Squire Steele, Upper George Street, Bryanston Square, W.; one *d.* Served S. African War in Army Postal Corps (Queen's medal 5 clasps); Deputy Director Army Postal Services, B.E.F., France, 5 Aug. 1914 (despatches thrice, 1914 Star); Director Army Postal Services, Egyptian Expeditionary Force, 1916-20; and Director of Civil Postal and Telegraph Services in the occupied enemy territories of Palestine, Syria and Cilicia (despatches thrice); Sheriff of York, 1932-33. *Address:* 6 Marlborough Grove, York. [*Died* 17 *Jan.* 1952.

WARREN, Richard, M.D., M.Ch. (Oxon); F.R.C.S. Eng.; late Surgeon to the London Hospital; late Senior Surgeon Shadwell Children's Hospital; late Surgeon to: Brompton Hospital for Chest; late Weston-super-Mare Hospital; Consulting Surgeon, The War Memorial, Burnham-on-Sea; *b.* 17 Feb. 1876; *s.* of late General Sir Charles Warren, G.C.M.G., K.C.B.; *m.* 1912, Violet Irene (*d.* 1941), *d.* of A. C. Jenkin of Heamoor, Cornwall; two *s.* one *d.* *Educ.:* Charterhouse (Scholar);

New Coll., Oxon (Scholar); London Hospital (Scholar); 1st Class Honours Natural Science, B.A. degree, 1897; Radcliffe Travelling Fellow, 1901-3; Surgeon, Shadwell Hospital, 1907; London Hospital, 1909; late Maj. R.A.M.C. (T.), B.E.F.; Chairman Bristol Division, B.M.A., 1928-29; Consulting Surgeon West of England Sanatorium, Weston-super-Mare; President, Bath and Bristol and Somerset Branch, B.M.A., 1935. *Publications:* Text Book of Surgery, 1916; contributions to Lancet, London Hospital Gazette, etc. *Recreations:* fishing, shooting, boxing, ski-ing. *Address:* 56 Stanhope Rd., Weston-super-Mare. [*Died* 31 *Oct.* 1957.

WARREN, Sir Victor Dunn, Kt., *cr.* 1951; M.B.E. 1939; T.D. 1941; D.L.; J.P.; *b.* 21 May 1903; *s.* of David Dunn Warren and Jean C. McCaull; *m.* 1927, Mary Winifred Wishart; one *s.* *Educ.:* Kelvinside Academy; Warriston; Rossall. Chairman, Hunter & Warren Ltd., 1929; Regional Manager, Scotland & Northern Ireland, Imperial Chemical Industries Ltd., 1949. Entered Corporation of Glasgow, 1931; Magistrate, 1935-38; Chairman Glasgow Corporation Progressive Party, 1946; Member, T. and A.F.A. of County of City of Glasgow, 1934-37 and 1946-49; Lord Provost of Glasgow, 1949-52; Member, Clyde Navigation Trust, 1949; H.M. Lieutenant of the County of the City of Glasgow, 1949-52; D.L. 1952. War of 1939-45; commanded 15th Scottish Div. Signals and 82nd W. African Div. Signals, serving in W. Africa, French Equatorial Africa and the Belgian Congo. Formerly: Deacon, Incorp. of Gardeners', Preses Weavers Soc. of Anderston. Associate Institute of Mining Engineers; Associate Institute of Quarrying; Member Scottish Tourist Board. Hon. LL.D. Glasgow, 1951. Comdr. of Order of St. John, 1949. Royal Humane Society's Bronze Medal for Saving Life, 1949. *Recreations:* fishing, golf and shooting. *Address:* 5 Bute Gardens, Glasgow. *T.:* Western 5766. *Clubs:* Junior United Service; Conservative (Glasgow). [*Died* 3 *March* 1953.

WARWICK, Rev. William Geoffrey; *b.* 1898. *Educ.:* Probus School; King's College, London; Bishops' College, Cheshunt. Served European War, 1916-19; Artists' Rifles; Lieut. Devonshire Regt., B.E.F., R.F.C. and R.A.F. as pilot. Rector of Cheveley, 1930-34; Vicar of St. Peter's, Walthamstow, 1934-39; Rector of Bloomsbury, 1939-; Chaplain R.A.F.V.R., 1943-47. Home Guard (London H.Q.), 1941-43. Vice-President and Chairman of Society for Improving the Condition of the Labouring Classes, 1948. *Address:* 7 Little Russell St., W.C.1. *Club:* Garrick. [*Died* 19 *Nov.* 1955.

WASHBOURN, William, C.B.E. 1920; L.R.C.P., M.R.C.S.; Consulting Surgeon, Royal Infirmary, Gloucester; *b.* 1862; *s.* of William Washbourn, Blackfriars, Gloucester; *m.* 1910, Mabel Woods, *d.* of late W. W. Collins. *Address:* Blackfriars, Gloucester. *T.:* Gloucester 22454. [*Died* 4 *Feb.* 1959.

WATCHORN, Colonel Edwin Thomas, C.B. 1902; V.D.; retired; *b.* 13 Aug. 1856; *s.* of Hon. John Watchorn, M.L.C.; *m.* 1896, Ethel Maude, *d.* of William James Baynton, Huntingfield, Kingston; two *s.* one *d.* *Educ.:* City School, Hobart, Tas. Was connected with the military service of the State for over forty years; late in command of the Hobart Defence; commanded 2nd Tasmanian Imperial Bushmen, 1901-2 (despatches); represented Tasmania at Wimbledon shooting for Kolapore Cup, 1886. *Recreation:* rifle shooting (holder of the Champion Medal of the State of Tasmania, 1885, 1886, 1887). *Club:* Naval and Military (Hobart). [*Died* 15 *March* 1940.
[*But death not notified in time for inclusion in Who Was Who 1929–1940.*

WATERFALL, Sir Charles Francis, Kt., *cr.* 1946; C.S.I. 1937; C.I.E. 1935; *b.* Bridgnorth, Shropshire, 24 Feb. 1888; *s.* of Charles and Louisa Waterfall; *m.* 1915, Ada Duckworth; one *s.* four *d.* *Educ.:* Manchester Grammar School; Queens' College, Cambridge. B.A. (Camb.), 1909; apptd. to I.C.S. after exam. of 1910; arrived in India, 1911; served in the Central Provinces and Berar as Assistant Commissioner, Deputy Commissioner, Settlement Officer, Director of Land Records, Excise Commissioner, Financial Secretary, Chief Secretary and Commissioner; Member of Central Provinces Legislative Council, 1928, 1930-33; Chief Commissioner Andaman and Nicobar Islands, 1938-42; interned by Japanese, 1942-45; retired, 1948. *Address:* Brookfield House, Colyton, Devon. [*Died* 23 *Oct.* 1954.

WATERHOUSE, Rupert, M.D. (Lond.), F.R.C.P.; retired; formerly Consulting Physician and Vice-President, Royal Mineral Water Hospital; Consulting Physician, Royal United Hospital, Bath, Victoria Hospital, Frome, Chippenham Cottage Hospital, and Trowbridge and District Hospital; *b.* Sheffield, 15 Jan. 1873; *y. s.* of J. H. Waterhouse, M.D.; *m.* 1919, Mabel Dorothy Connor; one *s.* one *d.* *Educ.:* Collegiate School, Sheffield; Wesley College, Sheffield; St. Bartholomew's Hospital, London; Ex-President Bath Clinical Society; Ex-President Bath and Bristol Branch, British Medical Association; Col. R.A.M.C. (T.F.), served on East Coast, 1914, Gallipoli, 1915; Egypt, 1916; Palestine, 1917; France, 1918; O.C. 2nd South Western Mounted Brigade Field Ambulance, 1915-17; gazetted to command of 4th Southern General Hospital, 1920. *Publications:* numerous papers in the medical journals, etc. *Recreations:* bridge and golf. *Address:* 12 Marlborough Buildings, Bath. *T.:* 2769. [*Died* 1 *Sept.* 1958.

WATERLOW, Sir Edgar Lutwyche, 3rd Bt., *cr.* 1873; Joint Managing Director of Waterlow & Sons, Ltd., 1914-45, and Chairman, 1927-40 (resigned); *b.* 15 June 1870; *e. s.* of 2nd Bt. and 1st wife, Amy Grace (*d.* 1897), *d.* of late Edgar Lutwyche, Streatham; *S.* father, 1931; *m.* 1st, 1896, Martha, *d.* of late Robert Carter; two *s.*; 2nd, 1913, Harriet Victoria, *y. d.* of late Joseph Gecks; one *s.* one *d.* (and one *s.* decd.). *Educ.:* Harrow; Heidelberg University; Trinity Hall, Cambridge (M.A.). President of Printers Pension Corp. Festival, 1938. On House Cttee. of Royal Sea Bathing Hosp.; Governor of Christ's Hospital. Director of French Hosp., Compton Lea, Roffey, Sussex, since 1898, and on committee. *Recreations:* sea fishing, billiards, philately and crossword puzzles. *Heir:* *s.* Philip Alexander [*b.* 17 Mar. 1897; *m.* 1st, 1923, Gwendoline Iris, *d.* of late Charles R. Butler; one *s.*; 2nd, 1937, Nan Tee, *er. d.* of late John Hay]. *Address:* Winscombe, The Beacon, Crowborough, Sussex. *Clubs:* Junior Carlton, Leander, London Rowing. [*Died* 12 *Jan.* 1954.

WATERMEYER, Rt. Hon. Ernest Frederick, P.C. 1943; Hon. LL.D. Cape Town University; *b.* 12 Oct. 1880; *s.* of late C. J. Watermeyer, Colonies Plaats, Graaff Reinet; *m.* 1908, Petronella Hester Wege; two *s.* one *d.* *Educ.:* Graaff Reinet College; Stellenbosch Boys' School; Bath College; Caius College, Cambridge (Mathematical Scholar, B.A., LL.B.). Called to Bar, Inner Temple, 1904; practised at bar in Cape Town from 1905; President Income Tax Court, 1920; Q.C. 1921; Puisne Judge of Supreme Court, 1922; Judge of Appeal, 1937; Chief Justice of South Africa, 1943-1950; acted as Officer Administering the Government of the Union of S. Africa, 1950. During European War, Captain in Cape Garrison Artillery. Trustee Kirstenbosch National Botanic Gardens. *Publication:* Chapter on Roman Dutch Law in Cambridge History of British Empire. *Recreations:* golf, lawn tennis, gardening, sea angling, and trout fishing. *Address:* Cranborne House, Hermanus, Cape. *Clubs:* Civil Service, City (Cape Town); Bloemfontein. [*Died* 18 *Jan.* 1958.

WATERS, Arthur George; Editor News of the World since 1947; *b.* 27 Feb. 1888; *s.* of George Edward and Emma Waters; *m.* 1919, Priscilla Maude Evans. *Educ.:* Barry, Glamorgan. Articled Barry Dock News, Sub-Editor Western Mail and Evening Express, Cardiff; joined News of the World editorial staff, 1914. *Recreation:* journalism. *Address:* Lavender Cottage, Hillside Gardens, Brockham, Surrey. *T.:* Betchworth 3131. [*Died* 17 *Nov.* 1953.

WATERS, Frank Henry; Managing Director: News Chronicle, Star, Daily News Ltd. since 1951; *b.* 2 Dec. 1908; *s.* of Joseph Bow Waters and Louie Melville Kerr; *m.* 1933, Joan Nancy Maude; one *d.* *Educ.:* Loretto School; Pembroke College, Cambridge. Joined Daily Express, 1929; General Manager: Scottish Daily Express, Evening Citizen, Glasgow, 1934-42. Served War of 1939-45, Royal Marines, 1942-45, Lt.-Col. Assistant Manager, The Times, 1945-50. Assistant Managing Director, News-Chronicle and Star, 1950. *Recreations:* walking, reading, etc. *Address:* 1 Robert St., Adelphi, W.C.2. *T.:* Trafalgar 3874. *Clubs:* Garrick, Royal Automobile. [*Died* 18 *Oct.* 1954.

WATERSON, David, R.E.; F.S.A. (Scot.); artist, painter, etcher, mezzotint engraver; *b.* 1870; *m.* 1924, Ann, *d.* of James Wallis, Beverley. Freedom of City and Royal Burgh of Brechin, Angus, 1954. *Address:* Bridgend House, Brechin, Angus. [*Died* 12 *April* 1954.

WATES, George Leslie, Comp. I.E.E.; Solicitor; *b.* 12 July 1884; *o. s.* of George Frederick Wates; *m.* 1910, Lucy Winifred, *d.* of William John Ainsworth, Swindon; two *s.* two *d.* *Educ.:* Haberdashers' Aske's School, Hatcham. Admitted Solicitor, 1905; Partner: Whale & Wates, Solicitors, 1910-1920, J. D. Langton & Passmore, Solicitors, 1920-51. J.P. 1928, Hon. Pres., Johnson & Phillips Ltd.; Director Woolwich Equitable Building Society; Governor Woolwich Cottage Hospital and Woolwich War Memorial Hosp., 1908-48; Member Executive Cttee. Roffey Park Rehabilitation Centre, 1943-48; Member of Roffey Park Hospital Management Cttee., 1950; Governor Woolwich Polytechnic, 1939-57 (Vice-Chm. 1942-44, Chm. 1944-47, Chm. Educ. Cttee. 1946 and 1947, Pres. Union, 1948-50); Chairman Cable Makers' Assoc., 1946 and 1947; Chairman British Electrical and Allied Manufacturers' Assoc., 1950-1951; Mem. Council, Instn. of Electrical Engineers, 1955-56-57-58. Served European War, 1914-18, Anti-Aircraft Corps, R.N.V.R. (General Service Medal). *Address:* Rowhill Grange, Wilmington, nr. Dartford, Kent. *T.:* Swanley Junction 83. *Club:* Devonshire. [*Died* 22 *Jan.* 1958.

WATHEN, Gerald Anstruther, C.I.E. 1922; M.A.; Headmaster, The Hall School, Hampstead, 1924-55, retired 1955; *b.* Bexley, Kent, 28 December 1878; *s.* of late W. H. Wathen, Westerham, Kent; *m.* 1909, Melicent, *d.* of C. L. Buxton, of Marsham, Norfolk; two *s.* one *d.* (and one *s.* decd.). *Educ.:* St. Paul's School; Peterhouse, Cambridge; Bonn; Paris. Travelled in the Balkans and Anatolia on palæographic and archæological research, 1899-1902; Asst. Master, Tonbridge School, 1903; Indian Educational Service, 1905; Professor of English at Government College, Lahore, India, 1905-14; Inspector of Schools, Jullundur Division, Punjab, 1914; Principal, Khalsa College, Amritsar, 1915-24; Master, Mercers' Company, 1933-34. *Clubs:* Bath, M.C.C. [*Died* 9 *Aug.* 1958.

WATKIN, Ernest Lucas, M.A.; Professor Emeritus, 1943, University College, Southampton; *b.* Wellingborough, 1876; unmarried. *Educ.:* Wellingborough Grammar School; S. John's College, Cambridge (scholar). 7th Wrangler, Math. Tripos, 1898; 2nd Class Math. Tripos Pt. II. 1899; lecturer in Mathematics, University College, Bristol, 1900-4; Professor of Mathematics, University College, Southampton, 1904-31; Assistant Inspector, Ministry of Munitions, 1918. *Recreations:* gardening, mechanics. *Address:* 2 Carlton Rd., S. Croydon, Surrey. [*Died* 4 *July* 1951.

WATKIN-JONES, Rev. Howard, M.A., D.D. (Cantab.); Banks - Crossfield Tutor in Church History and History of Doctrine, Wesley Coll., Headingley, since 1930; Principal since 1953; *b.* Ironbridge, Salop, 13 Aug. 1888; *s.* of Rev. Robert and Elizabeth Mary Watkin-Jones; *m.* 1916, Dorothy Gwendoline, *d.* of late Joseph Banks, Hallow Park; two *s.* one *d.* *Educ.:* Kingswood School, Bath; Gonville and Caius College, Cambridge (B.A. Historical Tripos, 1910; M.A. 1914; B.D. 1923; D.D. 1929); Didsbury Methodist College; Manchester Univ. Precentor of the Wesleyan Methodist Conference, 1918-29; held pastorates in Cambridge, Hull, London, Southport, Edinburgh, Birmingham, Leeds; Delegate to World Conferences on Faith and Order (Edinburgh), 1937 (member of its Continuation Committee), and Lund, 1952 (member of its Theological Commission); Moderator Leeds Free Church Federal Council, 1943-44; Chairman Leeds District of Methodist Church, 1942-46; Member British Council of Churches; Delegate to World Council of Churches (Amsterdam), 1948; Mem. Exec. World Methodist Council; Fernley-Hartley Lecturer, 1949; President Methodist Conference, 1951; Moderator of Free Church Fed. Council of England and Wales, 1954-. Select Preacher, Cambridge University, 1952-53. *Publications:* The Holy Spirit in the Mediæval Church, 1922; The Holy Spirit from Arminius to Wesley, 1929; Lecture iii. in The Doctrine of the Holy Spirit (Headingley Lectures, 1937); Methodist Churchmanship and its Implications, 1946; (with W. M. F. Scott) The Creed of a Christian, 1947; (with others) One Catholic and Apostolic Church, 1949; Articles in The Hibbert Journal. *Address:* Redcliffe, North Grange Road, Headingley, Leeds 6. *T.:* Leeds 52440. *Club:* Rotary (Leeds). [*Died* 23 *Oct.* 1953.

WATKIN-WILLIAMS, Robert Thesiger, J.P. Devon; *b.* 7 Jan. 1867; *e. s.* of late Hon. Mr. Justice Watkin-Williams; *m.* 1897, Mary, *d.* of late George T. Skilbeck, J.P.; one *s.* two *d.* *Educ.:* Westminster School; privately. Admitted a solicitor, 1889; a Master of the Supreme Court in Chancery, 1910-32; retired, 1933. *Address:* The White House, Stockland, near Honiton, Devon. *T.:* Stockland 230. [*Died* 1 *March* 1953.

WATKINS, Frederick Charles; *b.* 24 Feb. 1883; *m.* 1908, Enid, *d.* of William Hall, Rochester; two *d.* M.P. (Lab.) Central Hackney, 1929-31 and 1935-45; Parliamentary Private Secretary to Mr. Herbert Morrison, 1942-45. *Address:* 71 King Street, Aldeburgh, Suffolk. [*Died* 31 *Jan.* 1954.

WATKINS, Rt. Rev. Ivor Stanley; Bishop of Guildford since 1956; *b.* 10 Nov. 1896; *s.* of Herbert and Nellie Watkins, Ross-on-Wye; *m.* 1925, Evelyn Maud France, Birmingham; one *d.* *Educ.:* Hereford Cathedral School; Trinity Hall, Cambridge; Cuddesdon Theological College. Deacon, 1924; Priest, 1924; Curate of St. John, Bedminster, 1924-28; Curate-in-Charge, St. Gregory, Horfield, 1928-30; first Vicar of St. Gregory, Horfield, 1930-41; Rural Dean of Clifton, 1936-41; Chaplain H.M. Prison, 1932-41; Archdeacon of Bristol, 1941-50; Suffragan Bishop of Malmesbury, 1946-56. Canon Residentiary in Bristol

Cathedral, 1943-55; Diocesan Missioner, 1950. *Publications:* First Days in the Ministry, 1934; The Church and the Young Offender, 1936; There is a Lad Here, 1937. *Recreations:* tennis, golf, swimming. *Address:* Willow Grange, Stringer's Common, Guildford, Surrey. *T.:* Guildford 3922. *Club:* United University.

[*Died* 24 *Oct.* 1960.

WATKINS, James William, C.V.O. 1951; D.S.O. 1918; M.C. 1918; M.Inst.T.; Member (full-time), British Transport Commission, since 1956; *b.* 4 Sept. 1890; *s.* of William and Mary Watkins; *m.* 1918, Ethel Mary Price (*d.* 1953); three *d.* *Educ.:* Tewkesbury Grammar School. Joined Midland Rly. Co., 1905; successively L.M.S. Rly. Co. and British Rlys.; General Manager, London Midland Region, British Railways, 1953-56. Served European War in Army, 1914-19: joined 5th Battalion Gloucestershire Regiment as Private, 1914; commissioned on Field to 2nd Bn. Lancashire Fusiliers; commanded 2nd Bn. Lancashire Fusiliers; retired with rank of Lt.-Col. *Recreation:* gardening. *Address:* Allways, Shepherds Rd., Watford, Herts. *T.:* 7879.

[*Died* 12 *Jan.* 1959.

WATKINS, Rev. Owen Spencer, C.M.G. 1916; C.B.E. 1919; Hon. Padre Toc H; *b.* Portsmouth, 28 Feb. 1878; *s.* of Rev. Owen Watkins; *m.* 1st, 1901, Sadie Soule, *o. d.* of William Mathias, H.M. Dockyard, Malta (*d.* 1910); 2nd, 1918, Ethel Elizabeth, *e. d.* of G. George, Llandilo. *Educ.:* Kingswood School, Bath; Richmond College. Entered Wesleyan ministry, 1896; served with International Force of Occupation, Crete, 1897, 1898-99; Nile Expedition, 1898; Battle of Omdurman; one of four Chaplains who conducted the Memorial Service to General Gordon at Khartoum (despatches, Queen's medal, Egyptian medal with clasp); South African War, 1899-1900 (despatches four times, Queen's medal with five clasps); Senior Wesleyan Chaplain, B.E.F. in France and Flanders (despatches four times, C.M.G.); Assistant Principal Chaplain Third Army, 1917-18; Principal Chaplain Italian E.F., 1918-19; Battle of Piave, etc. (despatches, C.B.E.); Chaplain to the Forces, 1st Class, 1920; Representative to Œcumenical Conference, Toronto, 1911; London, 1921; Atalanta, 1931; Commander Italian Order of St. Maurice and St. Lazarus, 1923; Asst. Chaplain-General Eastern Command, 1920-24; Deputy Chaplain-General, 1925-29; Hon. Chaplain to the King, 1925; Principal Chaplain (retired), 1929; Assistant Grand Chaplain of England, 1932; Grand Standard Bearer of Royal Arch Freemasons of England, 1932. *Publications:* With Kitchener's Army; Chaplains at the Front; Soldiers and Preachers Too; Ahmed of the Camels; With French in France and Flanders; Spud Murphy, etc. *Address:* Brooms, Bucklebury Common, Berks. *T.:* Thatcham 2260. *Club:* Junior Army and Navy.

[*Died* 9 *Jan.* 1957.

WATKINS-PITCHFORD, Lt.-Col. Herbert, C.M.G. 1918; F.R.C.V.S.; F.R.S.E., etc.; retired H.M. Service: *s.* of Rev. J. Watkins Pitchford, M.A., Vicar St. Jude's, S.E.; *m.* May, *d.* of Henry Willson, M.D. etc.; three *s.* one *d.* *Educ:* Queen Elizabeth's Grammar School; Private tuition. Principal Veterinary Surgeon, Natal, 1896; Director Veterinary Department, 1902; Government Bacteriologist, 1901; Director of Veterinary and Remount Staff Officer, 1903; Commandant, Army Veterinary School, Aldershot, 1918-22. Was the originator of modern treatment of disease Rinderpest; showed cause and manner of prevention of African horse sickness, also of pneumonia amongst British horses in the Great War, etc. *Publications:* Some of more recent observations include: The Efficacy of various Disinfectants; Natal Snake Venoms and their Action; Observations on the Mark VI. Service Bullet; Copper and its Salts in the Purification of Water; Observations on the Bacteriology of Bubonic Plague; the South African Disease of Sheep known as Blue Tongue; observations on the Mark V. and Sundry Patent Bullets; An Inquiry into the Efficacy of Cattle Dips, etc.; a Report on Dipping and Tick Destruction; The Conformation of the South African Remount; The Saddle from the Horse's Point of View; South African Defence Problems; etc. *Address:* St. Winifred's, South Coast, Natal, S. Africa.

[*Died* 25 *June* 1951.

WATKINSON, Arnold Edwards, C.B.E. 1945; H.M. Foreign Service (retired); *b.* 2 Dec. 1893; *s.* of Thomas Edwards Watkinson; *m.* 1951, Barbara Todd, Kaisar-i-Hind. Served in European War, 1914-19, with East Yorkshire Regt., Royal Flying Corps and Royal Air Force. Consul-General at Naples, 1947-52. *Address:* 20 Taylor Avenue, Kew Gardens, Richmond, Surrey. *T.:* Prospect 6082. *Club:* Royal Automobile.

[*Died* 14 *Feb.* 1953.

WATLING, Colonel Francis Wyatt, C.B.E. 1919; D.S.O. 1917; R.E. (retired); *b.* 9 July 1869; *s.* of late Colonel J. T. Watling, Bombay Staff Corps and late Marian Eliza Watling; *m.* 1905, Helen Caroline Fuller (*d.* 1939); one *d.* *Educ.:* Cheltenham College; Woolwich. Served N. W. Frontier of India, 1897 (wounded, despatches, medal with two clasps); European War, 1914-19 (despatches, D.S.O., C.B.E.). *Address:* c/o Lloyds Bank Ltd., Cox's and King's Branch, 6 Pall Mall, S.W.1. *Club:* United Service. [*Died* 14 *May* 1953.

WATNEY, Colonel Charles Norman, C.I.E. 1919; Hon. Col. 4th Bn. Queen's Own R.W. Kent Regt., 1926-39; late Lt.-Col. commanding; T.D.. 1911; *b.* 26 July 1868; *e. s.* of late Norman Watney, J.P.. D.L., Kent; *m.* 1911, Ada Winifred, (*d.* 1953), 2nd *d.* of late E. G. Crew, Bristol; two *s.* one *d.* *Educ.:* Eton; Trinity College, Cambridge, M.A. Served South Africa, 1900-1 (Queen's medal and 4 clasps); European War, 1914-18. *Address:* Bishops Caundle House, Sherborne. *T.:* Bishops Caundle 205. [*Died* 22 *Nov.* 1956.

WATNEY, Dendy; *b.* 20 Nov. 1865; *e. s.* of Daniel Watney, P.P.S.I.; *m.* 1890, Ethel, *d.* of Ambrose Boyson; one *s.* two *d.* *Educ.:* Winchester. President of the Surveyors' Institution, 1926; Surveyor to the Mercers' Company; retired, 1936. *Recreations:* fishing, shooting, and golf. *Address:* c/o The Charterhouse, Charterhouse Square, E.C.1.

[*Died* 29 *Sept.* 1955.

WATSON, Sir Arthur, Kt., *cr.* 1924; C.B.E. 1917; LL.D.; J.P. Devon, 1938; F.R.S.A., 1938; *b.* Manchester, 18 Sept., 1873; 2nd *s.* of late Daniel Watson, merchant shipper, Manchester; *m.* 1902, Grace Ethel (*d.* 1946), 2nd *d.* of late James Barton, merchant, Manchester; two *d.* *Educ.:* Manchester Grammar School; Victoria University, Manchester. A Civil Engineer by profession; Chief Assist. Engineer to the Lancashire and Yorkshire Railway Company, 1905-10; Superintendent of the Line, 1910-18; Chairman of the Superintendents' Conference at the Railway Clearing House, London, 1915-1918; Assistant General Manager, 1918-19; General Manager, 1919-20; General Manager London and North-Western Railway, 1921-1923; First General Manager of the L.M.S., 1923-24; Lt.-Col. Railway Engineer and Staff Corps (R.E.); Member Advisory Council of Board of Trade, 1921; Member of the Permanent Commission of the International Railway Association, 1922; M.Inst.C.E.; Founder Member of Institute of Transport; Chairman Royal Victoria and West Hampshire Hospitals, Bournemouth, 1941-48, and Chairman of Hants and Dorset Area of British Hospitals Assoc., 1945-48; Member Exec. Committee of British Hospitals Assoc., 1946-48; first Chairman South Midlands Provincial Council for Staff of Hospitals and Allied Institutions, 1946; Member South-West Metropolitan

Regional Hosp. Board, 1947-49; O.St.J., 1935 (Member Dorset Council, 1947-49); Commander of Domestic Order of Orange (Netherlands), 1924. *Address:* Thornwood, Tedburn St. Mary, Exeter, Devon. *T.:* Tedburn St. Mary 352. *Clubs:* Overseas, Royal Motor Yacht. [*Died* 13 *April* 1954.

WATSON, Ven. Arthur Herbert, M.A., Rural Dean of Keswick since 1942; Examining Chaplain to the Bishop of Ripon, 1927; *b.* 15 May 1864; *s.* of Rev. Shepley Watson Watson, Rector of Bootle, Cumberland; *m.* 1900, Louisa Caroline, *d.* of Edward Yorke, Bewerley Hall, Pateley Bridge; three *s.* two *d.* *Educ.:* Marlborough; Queen's Coll., Oxford (Exhibitioner), 3rd Class Moderations. Ordained, 1890; Curate of Beeston Hill, Leeds, 1890-96, Chaplain to the Forces (Natal), 1896-98; Vicar of St. Peter's, Maritzburg, 1899; Ovingham-on-Tyne, 1900; Long Preston, 1904; Rector of Kirkby Wiske, 1911; S.C.F., 1916-17; Diocesan Inspector of Schools, 1918; Archdeacon of Richmond, 1921-1937, Archdeacon Emeritus since 1938; Canon Residentiary of Ripon Cathedral, 1922-37; Proctor in Convocation; Provost Woodard Corporation, Northern Division, 1937-45. *Recreation:* gardening. *Address:* Lyzzick House, Keswick, Cumberland. [*Died* 13 *July* 1952.

WATSON, Most Rev. Campbell W. W.; *see* West-Watson.

WATSON, Hon. David John, Q.C. (Scot.) 1952; *b.* 29 July 1911; *s.* of late Baron Thankerton, P.C. (Lord of Appeal in Ordinary) and late Sophia Marjorie, Lady Thankerton (*née* Cowan); unmarried. *Educ.:* Cargilfield; Winchester; Trinity College, Cambridge. Barrister (Gray's Inn), 1934; Advocate, Scotland, 1944. Member: Law Reform (Scotland) Committee; Board of Management, Edinburgh Central Hospitals; Committee of Management, Chalmers Hospital, Edinburgh; Committee of Management, Edinburgh Orthopædic Clinic; Publicity Committee National Trust for Scotland; Council Association for Preservation of Rural Scotland; Council, Edinburgh Gateway Company Ltd. (Gateway Theatre). *Recreation:* life. *Address:* 45 Northumberland Street, Edinburgh 3. *T.:* Waverley 2291. *Clubs:* Caledonian; New (Edinburgh). [*Died* 27 *Nov.* 1959.

WATSON, Sir Duncan, Kt., *cr.* 1927; J.P.; M.I.E.E.; Founder Duncan Watson Electrical Engineers Ltd.; Director of Perak River Hydro-Electric Power Co. Ltd., Chairman: Harley-Davidson Motor Co. Ltd.; *b.* 1873; *s.* of late Joseph Watson; *m.* 1900, Ella Mary Orchard (*d.* 1946); one *s.* two *d.* *Educ.:* Hutchison's Grammar School, Glasgow; Glasgow and West of Scotland Technical Coll.; King's Coll., London. Mayor of St. Marylebone, 1919-20; J.P. County of London; Vice-President of International Association for Promotion and Protection of Trade; Member of the Central Electricity Board from its inception, Feb. 1927, until transferred to British Electricity Board, 1948, and of the North of Scotland Hydro Electric Board until Apr. 1948. Governor, Regent Street Polytechnic, 1931-53, on retiring founded scholarships for electrical engineers. *Address:* Scamells Corner, Blackbrook, nr. Dorking. *T.:* Dorking 73125. *Club:* Constitutional. [*Died* 27 *Sept.* 1959.

WATSON, Edith Margaret, C.V.O. 1937; C.B.E. 1919; *d.* of late David G. Watson, Dulwich. 1916-45, Private Secretary to:—Secretary of State for Colonies (Mr. Bonar Law), Chancellor of Exchequer and Leader of House of Commons (Mr. Bonar Law), Lord Privy Seal (Mr. Bonar Law, Mr. Austen Chamberlain, Mr. Clynes), Prime Minister (Mr. Bonar Law, Mr. Baldwin (twice), Mr. J. Ramsay Macdonald, Mr. Neville Chamberlain) and Mr. Winston Churchill. *Address:* The Cottage, Salvington Hill, High Salvington, Worthing. [*Died* 13 *Oct.* 1953.

WATSON, Rear-Admiral Fischer Burges, C.B.E. 1943; D.S.O. 1917; *b.* Sept. 1884; *e. s.* of late Rear-Admiral Burges Watson and Marie Thérèse Fischer, Sydney, N.S. Wales; *m.* 1st, 1909, Sybil Mona Caroline (*d.* 1926), *o. d.* of late Major Harry Holden of Bramcote Hills, Notts; three *d.*; 2nd, 1931, Mabel Harford, 3rd *d.* of late Captain P. C. Underwood, R.N. *Educ.:* private school (Ashdown House, Forest Row); H.M.S. Britannia. Midshipman, 1900; retired list, 1935; Convoy Service, 1939-42 (despatches); Captain Landingship Flotilla, Med., 1943-44 (despatches, C.B.E., bar to D.S.O.). *Recreations:* games, shooting, fishing. *Address:* Monks Horton, Bosham, Sussex. [*Died* 14 *Aug.* 1960.

WATSON, Lt.-Col. Forrester Colvin, O.B.E., M.C., D.L.; J.P.; commanding 15th Bn. Essex Home Guard up to 1944; *b.* 26 July 1878; *s.* of late William Farnell Watson; *m.* 1904, Cecilia, *d.* of Walter Grimston, Earls Colne, Essex; one *s.* two *d.* *Educ.* Rugby. Joined 7th Dragoon Guards and served throughout S. African War; returned with the Regiment to England; exchanged into 3rd (K.O.) Hussars, 1913; served European War 1914-18 with Regiment, Staff Captain 1st Divisional Artillery and D.A.Q.M.G. III Corps; Retired 1919; High Sheriff of Essex 1937-38; ten years Hon. Secretary Essex Hunt and acted Master for the last 3 years of that time. *Recreations:* hunting and shooting. *Address:* 217 Ashley Gardens, S.W.1. *Club:* Cavalry. [*Died* 8 *Feb.* 1951.

WATSON, Rev. Frederick Vincent, M.A.; Canon Emeritus of Ely Cathedral and Permission to officiate Diocese of Salisbury since 1952; *b.* 1869; *e. s.* of late Lt.-Gen. George Vincent Watson. *Educ.:* Cheltenham College; Pembroke College, Cambridge; Clergy School, Cambridge. Deacon, 1894; Priest, 1895; Curate of Westbury-on-Trym, Bristol, 1894-96; St. Matthias, Plymouth, 1897-98; Chaplain of S. Devon and E. Cornwall Hospital, Plymouth, 1898-1900; Assistant Diocesan Missioner, Diocese of Exeter, 1896-1902; Sub-Warden of Society of Mission Clergy, Diocese of Exeter, 1902-4; Diocesan Missioner and Sub-Warden of Society of Mission Clergy, Diocese of Winchester, 1904-12; Diocesan Tait Missioner in Diocese of Canterbury, 1912-25; Six-Preacher in Canterbury Cathedral, 1916-19; Hon. Canon of Canterbury Cathedral, 1919-1925; Canon Residentiary of Ely and Diocesan Missioner, 1925-52; Examining Chaplain to Bishop of Ely, 1926-52; Treasurer of Ely Cathedral, 1931-51; Vice-Dean, 1941-52; Select Preacher, Cambridge, 1943. *Recreation:* golf. *Address:* Wren House, Warminster, Wilts. *Club:* Oxford and Cambridge. [*Died* 11 *Dec.* 1954.

WATSON, Sir Geoffrey Lewin, 3rd Bt., *cr.* 1918; *b.* 19 July 1879; *s.* of 1st Bt. and Mary Elizabeth, *e. d.* of late Thomas Harrison and Sarah Jane Lewin, Scarborough; *S. bro.* 1922; *m.* 1906, Gertrude Margaret, *d.* of late James Mountain, Leeds; one *d.* *Heir:* none. *Address:* Forsyte Shades, Canford Cliffs, Dorset. [*Died* 15 *Dec.* 1959 (*ext.*).

WATSON, George William, M.D. (Lond.), F.R.C.P. (London); Hon. Consulting Physician, The General Infirmary at Leeds, St. James' Hospital, Leeds, Dewsbury Infirmary; late Regional Consultant Adviser in Medicine E.M.S.; *b.* Cowling, nr. Keighley, Yorks, 9 Aug. 1877; *s.* of Thomas and Mary Watson; *m.* 1919, May Isabel Armstrong Nicholson; two *s.* *Educ.:* Keighley Grammar School; University of Leeds; Middlesex Hospital; Vienna. West Riding County Scholar, 1894; Hon. Assistant Physician General Infirmary at Leeds, 1912, Hon. Physician. 1919; Prof. Clinical Medicine, Univ. of Leeds, 1924; Prof. of Medicine, Univ. of Leeds, 1933, Emeritus, Prof. 1938; Major R.A.M.C.(T); Bt. Lt.-Colonel R.A.M.C. (T), 1917; Registrar 2nd Northern General Hospital, 1915-18; late Member of Council, Royal College of Physicians,

London; Examiner in Medicine, Conjoint Board, London; Member of Council of Empire Rheumatism Research. *Publications:* various medical. *Recreations:* music, golf. *Address:* Adel Willows, Adel, Leeds. *T.:* Adel, Leeds 73100; 42 Park Square, Leeds. *T.:* Leeds 22384; *Club:* National Liberal. [*Died* 11 *Dec.* 1956.

WATSON, Harold Argyle, C.I.E. 1932; I.C.S. (retired); *b.* 6 Dec. 1884; *s.* of William Watson, Bulwell, Nottingham; *m.* Edith Lily, *d.* of John Davenport, Condover, Shropshire; two *s.* one *d.* *Educ.:* Nottingham High School; Queens' College, Cambridge (Senior Foundation Scholar); 7th Wrangler, 1906; passed into Indian Civil Service, 1907, and went to Madras, 1908; Under-Secretary to Govt. of Madras, Revenue Dept., 1913-14; Special Settlement Officer, 1914-19; Director of Land Records, 1920-21; Deputy Secretary to Govt. of Madras, Finance Dept., 1922-23; Estate Collector, Sivaganga Estate, 1923-26; Secretary to Govt. of Madras, Finance Dept., 1927-31. *Address:* Coombe Lea, 18 Grove Road, Coombe Dingle, Bristol 9. *T.:* 681270. [*Died* 23 *July* 1959.

WATSON, Henry Angus, C.B.E. 1918; M.V.O. 1924; Railway Consultant; *b.* 1863; *y. s.* of late Rev. William Watson, M.A., Forres, Scotland; *m.* 1917, Dorothy Bannerman, *d.* of late James Ramsay, M.D., York; two *s.* *Educ.:* Aberdeen and Edinburgh Universities. In service of Highland Railway, 1884-90; North British Railway, 1891-93; joined North-Eastern Railway, 1893; General Superintendent, 1901-1924, retd. 1923; Hon. Serving Brother of the Order of St. John of Jerusalem, 1917; Major Engineer and Railway Staff Corps, 1910; Director Charles Roberts and Co. Ltd., S. J. Claye's Coke Co. Ltd., Yorkshire Lubricator Co. Ltd., and Derwent Valley Light Railway Co.; Chairman Association of Minor Railway Cos. *Recreations:* motoring and golf. *Address:* Deighton House, Escrick, York. *T.:* Escrick 57. *Clubs:* Royal Empire Society; Yorkshire (York). [*Died* 16 *Nov.* 1952.

WATSON, Henry C.; *see* Cradock-Watson.

WATSON, Admiral Sir Hugh Dudley Richards, K.C.B., *cr.* 1928 (C.B. 1914); C.V.O. 1922 (M.V.O. 1913); C.B.E. 1919; *b.* 20 April 1872; *s.* of late Rev. W. R. Watson of Saltfleetby St. Peter's, Lincolnshire; *m.* 1903, Janie Amina (*d.* 1950), *d.* of George Pearson, of Brickendonbury, Herts., and *sister* of 1st Viscount Cowdray of Midhurst; three *d.* *Educ.:* Llandaff Cathedral School; H.M.S. Britannia. Entered Royal Navy, 1885; Lieut. 1894; Comdr. 1903; Capt. 1909; Vice-Adm. 1925; Adm. 1929; served in slave cruising and blockade operations, East Coast of Africa, 1888-1890; and in Vitu Expedition, 1890 (medal with clasp); commanded first expedition of gunboats over Yangtse River Rapids to Szechuan, 1898-1901; China medal, 1900; Naval Attaché at Berlin, The Hague, and Copenhagen, 1910-1913; European War, commanded H.M.S. Essex, Bellerophon and Canada (C.B.E.); Naval Secretary to First Lord of the Admiralty, 1921-1923; Rear-Admiral in Fourth Battle Squadron, 1923; Third Battle Squadron, and Second in Command, Mediterranean Fleet, 1924-25; Vice-Admiral commanding Reserve Fleet, 1926-1928; retired list, 1930; Chevalier Order of the Sword of Sweden. *Recreations:* cricket, golf, shooting. *Club:* Naval and Military. [*Died* 22 *May* 1954.

WATSON, Sir Hugh (Wesley Allen), Kt., *cr.* 1930; *b.* 1875; *s.* of late Hugh Watson, Lurgan, N. Ireland; *m.* 1908, Letitia (*d.* 1951), *d.* of late Wm. Scott, M.D., J.P.; one *s.* one *d.* *Educ.:* Lurgan College; R.I.E. College, Coopers Hill. Joined Indian Forest Service, 1897; Chief Conservator of Forests, Burma, 1924-30; retired, 1930; Timber Adviser to the High Commissioner for India, 1932-42. *Address:* c/o Grindlay's Bank, Ltd., 54 Parliament Street, S.W.1. [*Died* 25 *May* 1953.

WATSON, James Murray, D.L. County of City of Edinburgh, 1951; M.A.; F.J.I. (Pres. 1948); *b.* Kirkcudbright, 26 Aug. 1888; *e. s.* of late Robert Watson, M.A., Rector, Kirkcudbright Academy; *m.* 1935, Eleanor, *d.* of late Thomas Foxley, R.N., Tiptree, Essex. *Educ.:* George Watson's College, Edinburgh; Edinburgh University (M.A., First Class Honours in English, 1911). Barrister, Lincoln's Inn, 1915; Editorial Assistant Thomas Nelson & Sons, Ltd., 1911; entered journalism 1912 on Weekly Scotsman; Assistant Editor Edinburgh Evening Dispatch, 1912-16; Chief Assistant Editor the Scotsman, 1924; Editor of the Scotsman, 1944-55. Member U.K. delegation to U.N. Conf. on Freedom of Information, Geneva, 1948; Member Scottish Tourist Board, 1950. Executive member International Press Institute, Zürich, 1951-54. Chevalier de la Légion d'Honneur, 1954. *Address:* 9 Polwarth Terrace, Edinburgh. *T.:* Fountainbridge 7019. [*Died* 2 *Nov.* 1955.

WATSON, Sir John (Ballingall) Forbes, K.C.M.G., *cr.* 1947; Kt., *cr.* 1939; M.A., LL.B.; Barrister (Middle Temple) and Advocate (Scottish Bar); Director British Employers' Confederation since 1921; *b.* 10 Oct. 1879; *yr. s.* of late John Watson, Milnathort, Kinross-shire; *m.* Alexandra Mary Georgie, *o. d.* of late Rev. Canon J. N. Dalton, K.C.V.O., C.M.G., The Cloisters, Windsor Castle; two *s.* one *d.* *Educ.:* Dollar Academy; Universities of Edinburgh, Paris, Göttingen and Heidelberg. Served in R.F.C. and R.A.F. 1915-19. Member: Nat. Jt. Advisory Council to Minister of Labour and Nat. Service; Nat. Production Advisory Council to Treasury on Industry and Labour Advisory Cttee. to Sec. of State for Colonies; rep. British Employers: on Anglo-American Council on Productivity; as Chief Deleg., Internat. Lab. Confs., 1929-32 and 1936-51 (Vice-Pres. of Conf., 1941-47); Employers' Member of Governing Body of I.L.O. since 1928 (Vice-Chairman, 1941-45, and since 1948); Pres. Internat. Organisation of Employers, 1932-1933, and Chm. Exec. Cttee., 1949-; attended Ottawa Conf., 1932, and rep. I.L.O. at World Economic Conf., 1933. During War of 1939-45 was member of Advisory Committees to Ministers of Labour and National Service, Home Security and Reconstruction, and to Production Executive of War Cabinet; Rep. I.L.O. at drafting of Charter of U.N. at San Francisco 1945, and appointed Advisory Member British Govt. Delegs. to Gen. Assembly of U.N. and to Paris Peace Conf. 1946. *Recreation:* golf. *Address:* 10 York House, Kensington Church St., W.8. *T.:* Western 0060. *Club:* Bath. [*Died* 25 *Aug.* 1952.

WATSON, Brig.-Gen. John Edward, C.B. 1911; retired pay; *b.* 2 March 1859; *y. s.* of Lt.-Colonel E. J. Watson, H.E.I.C.S., Bucksbridge House, Wendover, Bucks; *m.* 1906, Charlotte J. (*d.* 1950), *d.* of Maj. R. Nicolls; one *s.* one *d.* *Educ.:* Bradfield; R.M.C., Sandhurst. 96th Regiment, 1878; commanded 2nd Batt. The Manchester Regt.; served in Egypt Expedition, 1882; Miranzai, Indian frontier, 1891; South African War, 1899-1902 (despatches thrice); European War, 1914-18; commanded No. 5 District N.C., 1911-15; commanded 116th Brigade, 1915-16; commanded West Riding T.F. Reserve Brigade. 1916-18; retired pay, 1918, with rank of Brigadier-General. *Address:* Garth House, Mortimer, Berks. *Club:* Naval and Military. [*Died* 16 *June* 1951.

WATSON, Sir Malcolm, Kt., *cr.* 1924; M.B., C.M., with commend., 1895; M.D. with commend., 1903, Glas.; D.P.H; Cantab. 1900; F.G.S.; Hon. Consultant (Director, 1933-42), The Ross Institute of Tropical Hygiene, London School of Hygiene and Tropical Medicine. London University; *b.* 24 Aug. 1873; *s.* of late George Watson, Eastfield, Bridge of Allan; *m.* 1st, 1900, Jean Alice (*d.* 1935), *e. d.* of late David Gray,

Glasgow; three *s.*; 2nd, Constance Evelyn, *e. d.* of late Lt.-Col. W. L. Loring, Royal Warwickshire Regt.; one *d.* *Educ.:* High School and Univ., Glas.; Univ. Coll., Lond.; Hon. LL.D. Glas., 1924; Hon. Fellow Incorp. Soc. Planters, Malaya, 1925; Dipl. (Hon.) Singapore, 1926; Hon. F.R.F.P. & S. 1933; Corr. Mem. Soc. Path. Exotique, Paris, 1936; Hon. Gold Medal, Rubber Growers' Assoc., 1914; Stewart Prize, B.M.A., 1927; Sir William Jones Gold Medal of Asiatic Soc. of Bengal, 1928; Mary Kingsley Medal, Liverpool School Trop. Med., 1934; Albert Medal, Roy. Soc. Arts, 1939; formerly H.S., H.P., Glas. Roy. Infirmary; R.M.O. Smithston Asylum, Greenock; Malayan Med. Service, 1900-8; private and consultant practice, Malaya, 1900-28; Principal, Malaria Dept. and Director of Ross Institute, Putney, 1928-1933; Mem. Council, B.M.A., 1928-34; Pres. Assoc. British Malaya, Lond., 1933-34; Finlayson Memorial Lecture, 1934; Stephen Paget Mem. Lect., 1936; Bacot Mem. Lect., 1937; Ronald Ross Oration, Washington, D.C., 1948. Chm. Kundong Rubber Co. and Jas. Craig Ltd., Engineers, in Malaya; began Anti-malaria work at Klang, F.M.S., in 1901; extended to rural area, 1904; to Netherland East Indies, 1911; India, 1923; Africa, 1929; Balkans, 1930; Mem. Malaria Board, F.M.S., 1911-28; organised anti-malarial work in Singapore City from 1911; has advised Govts. of Nepal, Hyderabad (Deccan), Baroda, Patiala, Bengal, Southern Rhodesia, and rubber, tea, engineering companies, etc.; visited North, Central, and South America to study. Discovered origin of the Crescent (M.T.) malaria, 1901, Quartan malaria and Nephritis, 1904; originated control of malaria by Species Sanitation and Naturalistic Methods, Anti-malarial Sub-Drainage of Ravines, 1909; Larvicide for mosquitoes in running water, 1914; Inventor of Watson's Patent Process for Rubber Tapping; inventor (with Lady Watson) Patent Process for control of dust in mines and prevention of silicosis and explosions in coal mines, 1948, patented in association with Shell; Hon. Pres. Fourth Internat. Congress Tropical Medicine and Malaria, Washington D.C., 1948. *Publications:* Rural Sanitation in the Tropics, 1915; Prevention of Malaria in the Federated Malay States, 2nd ed., 1921; African Highway, 1952. Sect. Malariology, by Mark Boyd, et al., 1949. Official reports, and articles in scientific and other journals. *Recreations:* yachting, riding, golf. *Address:* Hillside, Peaslake, Surrey. *T.:* Abinger 186. [*Died* 28 *Dec.* 1955.

WATSON, Robert W. S.; *see* Seton-Watson.

WATSON, Thomas William, M.A.; Headmaster, King Edward VI. School, Stourbridge, 1934-51; retired; *b.* 18 March 1889; *s.* of Thomas Watson and Sarah Bonnington; *m.* 1915, Mildred Cunningham, *d.* of F. Cunningham Woods, M.A., Mus.Bac., F.R.C.O.; two *d.* *Educ.:* King Edward VI. School, Stourbridge; St. John's College, Cambridge (Scholar). 1st Class Pt. I., 1st Class (b) Pt. II. Mathematical Tripos, 2nd Class Pt. I., Natural Sciences Tripos; Assistant Master at Merchant Taylors' School, E.C., and Highgate School, N.6, 1912-14; served Artists' Rifles, Sep. 1914-March 1915; R.F.A. (T.F.), March 1915-May 1919; a/Major, service overseas in France and Belgium (M.C., despatches); served in Ministry of Munitions, 1918-22; Senior Maths. and Physics Master and House Master, Pocklington School, Yorks, 1922-25; Headmaster, King Edward's School, Camp Hill, Birmingham, 1925-30; Headmaster, Dudley Grammar School, Worcs., 1931-34. *Recreation:* golf. *Address:* Longlands, Links Rd., Uphill, Weston-super-Mare. *T.:* Weston-super-Mare 6757. [*Died* 18 *Jan.* 1957.

WATSON, William Law, C.B.E. 1942 (M.B.E. 1919); A.M.I.C.E.; M.I.Loco.E.; Engineer-in-Chief, Crown Agents for the Colonies, retired 1949; (Acting Engineer-in-Chief, 1949-50); *b.* 25 February 1883; *s.* of Robert Caird Watson, Head Schoolmaster, Aberdeen; *m.* 1924, Eleanor Lloyd (*d.* 1949), Chester; one *s.* one *d.* *Educ.:* Grammar Sch. and Robert Gordon's Coll., Aberdeen. Locomotive Works, Great North of Scotland Rly., Kittybrewster and Inverurie; Locomotive Works G.W.R., Swindon, 1905; Technical Staff Crown Agents for the Colonies, 1912; seconded to Raw Materials Dept., Ministry of Munitions, 1915-18. Council Institution of Locomotive Engineers. *Recreation:* golf. *Address:* 10 Bigwood Road, Golders Green, N.W.11. *T.:* Speedwell 9329. [*Died* 3 *July* 1958.

WATT, Lt.-Col. Alexander Fitzgerald, D.S.O. 1915; late Yorkshire Hussars; Chevalier Légion d'Honneur; *b.* 1871; *e. s.* of late Alexander Y. Watt and Georgina Watt of Cadogan Gardens, S.W.; *m.* 1903, Georgina, *o. c.* of late Augustine Robert Whiteway, Barrister-at-law, of Hemingford Grey, Hunts; one *d.* *Educ.:* privately; Jesus College, Cambridge. Served S. African War (Queen's medal 8 clasps); A.D.C. to Inspector-General of the Forces, 1907-12; Private Secretary to Chief of the Imperial General Staff, 1912-14; served European War, 1914-15 (despatches twice, D.S.O., Bt. Lt.-Col., Legion d'Honneur); A.D.C. to Com.-in-Chief British army in France, 1914-15; A.D.C. to Com.-in-Chief Home Forces, 1916-1918; Comptroller of the Household Vice-Regal Lodge, Dublin, 1918-19; Hon. Attaché British Legation, Vienna, 1920; a Gold Staff Officer at the Coronation, 1937. Formerly Director, Pyrene Co. Ltd., Yorkshire Insurance Co. Ltd. (Chairman West End Branch), and Belvoir Estates Ltd.; patron one living. *Recreations:* yachting, shooting, fishing, motoring. *Address:* Hemingford Grey House, Huntingdonshire. *T.:* St. Ives (Hunts) 2112. *Clubs:* Turf; Royal Yacht Squadron (Cowes). [*Died* 10 *March* 1957.

WATT, Lt.-Col. Edward William, T.D.; D.L., J.P.; LL.D.; Director, Aberdeen University Press, Ltd.; William Jackson (Aberdeen), Ltd.; John Avery & Co. Ltd.; *b.* 1877; *e. s.* of William Watt of The Aberdeen Free Press; *m.* 1909, Alice Isabella (*d.* 1948), J.P. 1938, City of Aberdeen, *d.* of George Murray, Aberdeen; one *s.* three *d.* *Educ.:* Aberdeen Grammar School; Aberdeen University (M.A.). Journalist, 1898-25 on The Aberdeen Free Press, Evening Gazette, and Aberdeen Press and Journal; in Parliamentary Press Gallery, 1902-04. The Gordon Highlanders: commissioned in 1st Vol. Bn., 1901; commanded Aberdeen Univ. Company of that Bn. as Capt. in 4th Bn.; served European War, 1914-19, commanding at home 4th (Reserve) Bn. and later serving with 4th Bn. on Western front; Lt.-Col. 1915; retd. 1921; Member City of Aberdeen T.A. Assoc., 1915-38; T.D. 1920. Member Aberd. Town Council, 1927-38; Lord Provost and Lord Lieut. of County of City of Aberdeen, 1935-38; Mem. Aberd. Univ. Court, 1928-38; Dir. and then Chm. Macaulay Inst. for Soil Research, 1939-45; Mem., 1940-50, Extra-Parl. Panel in terms of Private Legislation Procedure (Scotland) Act, 1936; Mem. Morgan Cttee. at Min. of Labour, 1939; Pres. Congregational Union of Scotland, 1940-41; Comr. Gen. Bd. of Control for Scotland, 1941-52; Mem. Scottish Central Probation Council, 1932-51; first Chm. Aberdeen Juvenile Court; Chm. various cttees. J.P. 1929, D.L. 1939. Hon. LL.D. Aberdeen, 1939. *Publications:* newspaper leaders and articles; several pamphlets. *Address:* Glenburnie Park, Rubislaw Den North, Aberdeen. *T.:* Aberdeen 37610. *Clubs:* National Liberal; Royal Scottish Automobile (Glasgow); University (Aberdeen). [*Died* 19 *April* 1955.

WATT, George Fiddes, R.S.A. 1924, non-resident 1930; R.P.; LL.D.; *b.* Aberdeen, 15 Feb. 1873; *o. s.* of George Watt and J.

Frost; *m.* 1903, Jean (*d.* 1956), *yr. d.* of William Willox, Park, Lonmay; two *s.* one *d.* Studied at Royal Scottish Academy, gaining Chalmers' Bursary for painting; extra painting prize and MacLean Watters medal. Exhibited in R.S.A. and R.A., etc., portraits of Viscount Haldane for Lincoln's Inn; Rt. Hon. H. H. Asquith and Lord Loreburn for Balliol Coll., Oxford; Archbishop of York for All Souls College, Oxford; Earl Grey, Lord Balfour of Burleigh, Hon. A. J. Balfour; The Artist's Mother, painting bought by Chantrey Bequest for Tate Gallery. Hon. LL.D. Aberdeen, 1955. *Recreations:* fishing, motoring. *Address:* 73 Cranford Road, Aberdeen. *T.:* 34375. [*Died* 22 *Nov.* 1960.

WATT, Langmuir; *see* Watt, W. L.

WATT, Very Rev. Lauchlan MacLean; Minister of Glasgow Cathedral, 1923–1934, retired, 1934; Moderator, Church of Scotland, 1933; *m.* 1897, Jennie Hall Reid (*d.* 1927), New Kelso, Ross-shire. *Educ.:* Edinburgh Univ.; M.A.; B.D.; D.D.; LL.D.; J.P., F.R.S.E., F.S.A. (Scot.). Accompanied King of Denmark in Iceland as correspondent of Times, Scotsman, and Manchester Guardian, 1907; in France with the Expeditionary Force, 1914-15; Chaplain to the Forces, France and Flanders, 1916-17; in United States and Canada on War Propaganda, 1918; Murtle Lecturer, Aberdeen University; Warrack Lecturer, St. Andrews and Edinburgh Universities; Frazer Lecturer, Glasgow University; President of the Pan-Celtic Congress, London, 1930; in Australia as Turnbull Trust Preacher, Melbourne, and visiting the Churches and Colleges in Victoria, New South Wales, and New Zealand, 1932. *Publications:* God's Altar Stairs, Lectures on the Lord's Prayer, 1899; In Love's Garden, 1901; Alloa and Tullibody, a historic sketch; The Grey Mother and Songs of Empire; The Communion Table, 1903; By Still Waters, 1904; Metrical Psalms and Paraphrases, selected and edited, 1906; The Tryst (poems); Edragil, 1745, a story of the Jacobite rising; edited Smith's Summer in Skye; edited Mrs. Stowe's Dred, 1907; Attic and Elizabethan Tragedy, 1908; Moran of Kildally, 1909; In Poets' Corner; Oscar, 1910; Carlyle; Literature and Life; History of Britain from Accession of George I.; Ministers' Manual; Scottish Life and Poetry, 1912; The House of Sands; Burns, 1913; Hills of Home; Gates of Prayer, 1915; In the Land of War, three editions; The Soldiers' Friend, eight editions, 1916; In France and Flanders with the Fighting Men; The Heart of a Soldier; The Land of Memory; Gawain Douglas's Æneid; The Scottish Ballads and Ballad Writing; The Book of the Beloved; Prayers for Public Worship; Life and Religion; The Advocate's Wig; The Minister's Life and Work, 1932; While the Candle Burns, 1933; contributions to various magazines; Welsh Bardic Title—Gwylan yr Ynys. *Recreations:* Gaelic antiquities, history and folklore. *Address:* Kinloch, Lochcarron. [*Died* 11 *Sept.* 1957.

WATT, Sir Thomas, Kt., *cr.* 1943; D.L., J.P.; Income Tax Commissioner; *b.* 29 Nov. 1882; *s.* of John Watt, J.P., Drumgray, Lanarkshire, and Jean Wotherspoon Waddell; *m.* 1935, Margaret Cameron Mitchell; no *c.* *Educ.:* Glasgow Academy. Shipowner till 1914; served 1914-19, Cameronians (wounded), retired rank of Capt.; Convener of Lanarkshire, 1935-42. *Recreation:* shooting. *Address:* Viewbank, Airdrie, Lanarkshire. *T.:* Airdrie 2311. *Clubs:* Conservative, Royal Scottish Automobile (Glasgow). [*Died* 16 *May* 1955.

WATT, (Walter) Langmuir, C.M.G. 1918; V.D.; M.A., M.D., C.M.; L.R.C.P. and S. Edin.; Colonel C.A.M.C.; late Surgeon Deep Therapy Department, Guy's Hospital; Director Sanitas Trust, Ltd.; *b.* Walkerton, Ontario, Canada, 12 July 1876; *m.* 1916, Violet, *d.* of John Clarke; two *c.* *Educ.:* Manitoba University (Medallist Arts and Medicine). In charge X-Ray and Electro-Therapeutics, Winnipeg General Hospital, to Aug. 1914; Lieutenant C.A.M.C. 1902; Officer Commanding No. 19 Cavalry Field Ambulance many years; European War, 1914-19 (despatches, C.M.G.). *Address:* c/o Westminster Bank Ltd., Cavendish Square Branch, W.1. *Clubs:* City Livery; Union (Brighton). [*Died* 14 *Aug.* 1953.

WATTS, Rev. Arthur Herbert, M.A., Ph.D.; retired as Rector of Cherington, Glos. (1948-58); *b.* 1886; *m.* 1913, Dorothy Pritchard; one *s.* *Educ.:* Hereford Cathedral School; University of London; Bishop's College, Cheshunt. Assistant Master various preparatory schools; 2nd master, bursar, senior Classics and English, O.C. of O.T.C., Solihull School, Warwickshire; Director of English Studies, Nottingham High School; 2nd Master St. George's School, Harpenden; Headmaster, 1936-47. Commission in T.F., 1912; retired 1920. *Publications:* theses on Classical Archæology. *Address:* 2 Carisbrooke Rd., Harpenden, Herts. *Club:* Authors'. [*Died* 27 *May* 1960.

WATTS, Rt. Rev. Christopher Charles, M.A.; *b.* Kensworth, Herts; *s.* of Rev. G. E. Watts, M.A. *Educ.:* Shrewsbury School; Corpus Christi College, Cambridge; Cuddesdon Theological College. Curate St. Mark's, Noel Park, 1900-7; Headmaster St. Mark's European School, Swaziland, 1909-20; Principal, St. Mark's Coloured School, 1920-27; formerly Canon of St. Peter's, Vryheid, Archdeacon of Swaziland, S. Africa, 1927; Vicar of St. Mark's, Noel Park, 1927-30; Warden of Zonnebloem College, Cape Town, 1930-31; Bishop of St. Helena, 1931-35; Bishop of Damaraland, 1935-39; Vicar of Victoria West; C.P., 1939. *Publications:* Dawn in Swaziland, In Mid-Atlantic; Kensworth Church. *Address:* c/o The Ridge, Haywards Heath, Sussex. [*Died* 2[illegible] *July* 1958.

WATTS, Rt. Rev. Horace Godfrey, D.D.; Bishop of Caledonia, since 1953; *b.* 29 May 1901; *s.* of William and Harriet Watts; *m.* 1927, Ruth Lampman Jenkins; two *s.* two *d.* (and one *d.* decd.). *Educ.:* Ryde House School; University of Saskatchewan; University Emmanuel College, Saskatoon. B.A. (Saskatchewan), 1926; L.Th. (Emmanuel College), 1926; B.D. (General Synod Church of England in Canada), 1932; Missionary Priest: Honan China, 1926; Diocese of Mid-Japan, 1927; Secretary Treasurer, Diocese Mid-Japan, 1940; Field Secretary of Missionary Society of the Church of England in Canada, 1941-52; Canadian Representative, Archbishop of Canterbury's Commission to Japan, 1946. Episcopal Commissary of Diocese of Cariboo, 1955-57. Hon. D.D. (Emmanuel Coll.), 1947. F.R.G.S., 1930. *Recreations:* fishing, photography, geography. *Address:* Bishop's Lodge, Prince Rupert, B.C., Canada. *T.:* Prince Rupert 6013. [*Died* 5 *April* 1959.

WATTS, Sir Hugh (Edmund), Kt., *cr.* 1955; C.B. 1951; M.B.E. 1920; G.M. 1948; *b.* 5 Dec. 1888; *s.* of T. W. Watts; *m.* 1928, Adelaide Irene Woods; one *s.* one *d.* *Educ.:* Mercers' School; Univs. of London and Zürich. B.Sc. (London), 1909; Ph.D. (Zürich), 1912; F.R.I.C. 1917. H.M. Chief Inspector of Explosives Home Office, 1946-54, retired. Consulting Chemist, 2 Norfolk Street, W.C.2. *Publications:* Ueber Kobaltiake mit Assymetrischen Kohlenstoffatomen, 1912; Storage of Petroleum Spirit, 1951; The Law Relating to Explosives, 1954; The Law Relating to Petroleum Mixtures, Acetylene, Calcium Carbide, and to the transport of Carbon Disulphide and certain compressed gases, 1956. *Recreation:* philately. *Address:* Courtfield, The Ridgeway, Fetcham, Leatherhead. [*Died* 16 *Oct.* 1958.

WATTS, Leonard, R.B.A.; a School Manager of Findon Church School; *b.* 1871; *m.* 1st, 1894; 2nd, 1926, Dorothy, *widow* of

Rev. L. D. Rutherford. *Educ.:* St. John's Wood and Royal Academy Schools. Landseer and British Institution Scholarships, and silver medal and other prizes of the Royal Academy. Began to paint at a very early age; 8 years' study in the schools; has painted the portraits of several well-known men, amongst others, Sir Arthur Arnold, L.C.C., and Sir John Hutton and T. Brock, R.A.; the portrait of James Stuart, M.P., was unveiled at Hoxton; for several years Hon. Representative of Associated Board of Royal Schools of Music, London. *Address:* The Chestnuts, Westbrooke, Worthing. *T.:* 2048. [*Died* 20 *Feb.* 1951.

WATTS, Sir Thomas, Kt., *cr.* 1928; M.D., M.B., B.S. (Durham), B.Sc. (Manchester), M.R.C.S. (Eng.), L.R.C.P. (London); Physician; *b.* Hyde, Cheshire, 1 July 1868; *s.* of late John Taylor Watts, J.P.; *m.* 1922, Dorothy Dudley, *y. d.* of Alfred Ryder, Durban, Natal; one *s.* one *d.* *Educ.:* Owens College, Manchester; University of Durham. Practised at Hyde, Cheshire, for twenty-nine years; for twenty-five years certifying factory surgeon; M.P. (C.) Withington Division of Manchester, 1922-23, and 1924-29; Ex-President, Ashton-under-Lyme Division of B.M.A., and of the Association of Certifying Factory Surgeons; ex-Vice-Pres. Lancs. and Cheshire Branch of B.M.A.; Member of Cheshire Insurance Committee, 1913-21. *Publication:* Paper on Shuttle Kissing as a Source of Infection, British Medical Association. *Recreations:* golf, travelling. *Address:* 19 Cambridge Road, Southport, Lancs. [*Died* 3 *June* 1951.

WAUCHOPE, Sir John Douglas Don-, 9th Bt., *cr.* 1667; Lieut. 3rd Batt. Royal Scots, retired; *b.* 15 Sept. 1859; *e. s.* of 8th Bt. and Bethia Hamilton, *d.* of Andrew Buchanan; *S.* father, 1893. *Educ.:* Trin. Coll. Camb. (B.A.). *Heir:* *nephew* Patrick George [*b.* 7 May 1898; *m.* 1936, Ismay Lilian Ursula, *d.* of Sidney Hodges, Edendale, S. Africa; two *s.*] *Address:* 10 Grosvenor Crescent, Edinburgh. [*Died* 28 *April* 1951.

WAUTON, Edric Brenton; *b.* 25 July 1883; *er. s.* of late Edward Wauton, Uppingham School; *m.* 1911, Mary, *y. d.* of late G. Carew Searle, West Dulwich; one *s.* one *d.* *Educ.;* Uppingham. Major, Royal Monmouth R.E. (retired); served Boer War, 1901-2 (Queen's Medal); Zulu Rebellion, 1906 (Medal); attached to Nigeria Regiment, R.W.A.F.F., 1914; served with Cameroons Expeditionary Force (1914 Star, General Service Medal and Allied Star); Assistant District Commissioner, Southern Nigeria, 1909; District Officer, 1917; Acting Resident, Ondo Province, 1926; Benin Province, 1927; Resident, 1928; in charge of Benin Province, 1928-29; Onitsha Province, 1930; Ogoja Province, 1931; retired, 1932; Director Society of Herbalists, 21 Bruton Street, W.1. since 1936. *Recreations:* cricket, golf, tennis. *Address:* Heathcote, Little Common Road, Bexhill-on-Sea. *T.:* Bexhill 1066. *Clubs:* Public Schools; New (Bexhill); Cooden Beach Golf. [*Died* 8 *Nov.* 1957.

WAVELL, 2nd Earl, *cr.* 1947; **Archibald John Arthur Wavell,** M.C. 1947; Viscount Wavell of Cyrenaica and of Winchester, 1943; Viscount Keren of Eritrea and Winchester, 1947; Major, The Black Watch (R.H.R.); *b.* 11 May 1916; *o. s.* of 1st Earl Wavell, P.C., G.C.B., G.C.S.I., G.C.I.E., C.M.G., M.C., and Eugenie Marie, C.I. 1943, *o. c.* of late Col. Owen Quirk, C.B., D.S.O.; *S.* father 1950. *Educ.:* Winchester College. Palestine, 1936-39 (Medal with clasp); served War of 1939-45. *Recreations:* hill-walking, golf. *Heir:* none. *Address:* 51 South St., W.1. *T.:* Grosvenor 1920; c/o Glyn, Mills and Co., Kirkland House, Whitehall, S.W.1. [*Died* 24 *Dec.* 1953 (*ext.*).

WAVERLEY, 1st Viscount, *cr.* 1952, of Westdean; **John Anderson;** P.C. 1938 (P.C. Ire. 1920); G.C.B. 1923 (K.C.B. 1919; C.B. 1918); O.M. 1957; G.C.S.I. 1937; G.C.I.E., 1932; F.R.S. 1945; Hon. D.C.L. Oxon. 1957. Chairman of the Port of London Authority since 1946; Chairman of Directors of Royal Opera House, Covent Garden; Chairman, the Royal Ballet; Chairman, British Postgraduate Medical Federation; Visitor of Bedford College; Chairman Council of Toynbee Hall; Member B.B.C. General Advisory Council; *b.* 8 July 1882; *o. s.* of D. A. P. Anderson of Westland House, Eskbank, Midlothian; *m.* 1st, 1907, Christina (*d.* 1920), *d.* of late Andrew Mackenzie, Edinburgh; one *s.* one *d.*; 2nd, 1941, Ava, *d.* of late J. E. C. Bodley and *widow* of Ralph Wigram, C.M.G. *Educ.:* George Watson's College, Edinburgh; Edinburgh and Leipzig Universities (M.A., B.Sc.); Hon. LL.D. (Aberdeen, Cambridge, St. Andrews, Edinburgh, Liverpool, Leeds, Sheffield, London); Hon. D.Sc. (McGill and Reading); Hon. Fellow, Gonville and Caius College, Cambridge. Entered Colonial Office, 1905; Secretary N. Nigeria Lands Committee, 1909; Secretary West African Currency Committee, 1911; Prin. Clerk in office of Insurance Commissioners, 1912; Secretary to Insurance Commissioners, 1913; Secretary Ministry of Shipping, 1917-19; additional Sec. to Local Government Board, April 1919; Second Secretary, Ministry of Health, 1919; Chairman of Board of Inland Revenue, 1919-22; joint Under Sec. to Lord Lieut. of Ireland, 1920; Permanent Under-Secretary of State, Home Office, 1922-32; Governor of Bengal, 1932-1937; M.P. (Nat.) Scottish Universities, 1938-50; Lord Privy Seal, 1938-39; Home Secretary and Minister of Home Security, 1939-40; Lord President of the Council, 1940-43; Chancellor of the Exchequer, 1943-45. K.St.J. 1936; Grand Officer Legion of Honour; Order of St. Anne; Commander of the Crown of Italy; Knight Grand Cross: Order of St. Olaf; Royal Order of North Star; Military Order of Christ; Order of Dannebrog. *Heir:* *s.* Hon. Alastair Anderson [*b.* 18 Feb. 1911; *m.* 1948, Myrtle, *d.* of Lt.-Col. Ledgerwood; one *s.* two *d.*]. *Address:* 4 Lord North Street, Westminster, S.W.1; Westdean Manor, Seaford, Sussex. *Clubs:* Athenæum, Brooks's. [*Died* 4 *Jan.* 1958.

WAVERTREE, Lady, (Sophie Florence Lothrop), C.B.E.; **(Mrs. F. M. B. Fisher);** Dame of Grace, St. John of Jerusalem; *y. d.* of late A. Brinsley Sheridan, J.P., of Frampton, Dorset, *g.-g.-g.d.* of Richard Brinsley Sheridan, M.P., Orator and Dramatist, and *g. d.* of John Lothrop Motley, Historian and American Ambassador; *m.* 1st, 1896, 1st Baron Wavertree of Delamere (*d.* 1933); no *c.*; 2nd, 1947, Francis Marion Bates Fisher, *q.v.* *Educ.:* England; abroad. Was Matron of Sussex Lodge Hospital for duration of War; equipped own house for wounded officers; started Trust Fund for Wallingford Home for Invalid Children. *Publications:* articles on tennis for newspapers. *Recreations:* tennis, golf. *Address:* Makona, Ngongotaha, Rotorua, N.Z. [*Died* 27 *Nov.* 1952.

WAYMAN, Lieut.-Col. Sir Myers, K.B.E., *cr.* 1951 (O.B.E. 1918); Kt., *cr.* 1945; J.P.; D.L.; Chairman of Sunderland Magistrates Courts Cttee.; Sunderland Licensing Planning Cttee.; Sunderland Disablement Advisory Cttee.; Past President Sunderland Chamber of Commerce; Vice-Chairman National Savings Cttee.; Commissioner for Durham County St. John Ambulance Brigade; *b.* 29 November 1890; *s.* of late Myers and Jane Wayman; *m.* 1911, Margaret Winifred Bland (C.St.J.); three *d.* (one *s.* killed in action 1943). *Educ.:* Argyle House Sch., Sunderland; Christ's Coll., Cambridge. Served in Durham L.I. 1914-19 (seriously wounded). World traveller, 1922-

1933; Member Sunderland Borough Council, 1936-45; Mayor of Sunderland, 1938-43 (5 times); Deputy Mayor, 1943-45; Chairman Sunderland War Emergency Cttee., 1939-45: of Food Control Cttee., 1939-45, etc. Chairman Sunderland Industrial Development Board, 1938-43. D.L. Durham County, 1955. F.S.S.; C.St.J. 1952. *Address:* Coanwood, Sunderland. *T.:* Whitburn 3332. [*Died* 11 *Sept.* 1959.

WAYNE, Richard St. John Ormerod, M.A.; *b.* 27 Aug. 1904; *s.* of late Canon St. John Wayne and Dorothy Ann Williams, Conington Rectory, Peterborough. *Educ.:* Eton; Trinity College, Cambridge. Assistant Secretary, Cyprus, 1927; Commissioner Famagusta, 1935, Paphos, 1937, Government of Cyprus Information Office, London, 1940; Commissioner of Labour, Cyprus, 1941-47; Administrator, Antigua, 1947-54. Retired, 1954; resumed administrative work, Cyprus, 1956. *Recreations:* fishing, walking, gramophone, tree-planting, shooting. *Address:* Commissioner Troodos, Platres, Cyprus. *Club:* Bath. [*Died* 5 *Jan.* 1959.

WAZIR HASAN, Hon. Sir Saiyid, Kt., *cr.* 1932; B.A., LL.B.; *b.* 14 May 1874. Joined the Lucknow Bar, 1903; Secretary, All India Moslem League, 1912-19; was instrumental in bringing about Hindu-Moslem Pact of 1916; Additional Judicial Commissioner of Oudh, 1920; Judge of the Chief Court of Oudh, 1925; Chief Judge, 1930; retired 1934. *Address:* Wazir Hasan Road, Lucknow, India. *Club:* United Service (Lucknow).
[*Died* 31 *Aug.* 1947.
[*But death not notified in time for inclusion in Who Was Who 1941–1950, first edn.*

WEATHERHEAD, Arthur Evelyn, C.M.G. 1934; M.B.E. 1943; Colonial Administrative Service (retired); *b.* 10 Feb. 1880; *s.* of Rev. Canon R. J. Weatherhead, M.A., and Anna Bagot Steele; *m.* 1916, Helen Dorothea Wilcox; two *s.* one *d.* *Educ.:* Monmouth School. Enlisted South African Constabulary, 1900; Commission, 1902; resigned 1907; District Superintendent Uganda Police, 1908; Assistant District Commissioner Uganda, 1911; District Commissioner, 1916; Director of Labour, 1925; Provincial Commissioner, 1926; Acting Chief Secretary to the Government, 1932-33; Governor's Deputy on various occasions; Acting Governor, 1935; appointed to Executive Council, 1934; Acting Governor, Seychelles, 1935-36; J.P. Somerset. *Recreations:* tennis, golf, cricket. *Address:* Washingpool, Wells. *Club:* Royal Empire Society.
[*Died* 19 *Oct.* 1956.

WEBB, Augustus D., C.B.E. 1933; late Chief of Intelligence Branch, H.M. Customs and Excise; *b.* 13 Nov. 1880; *s.* of James Webb and Helen Gibbs; widower. *Educ.:* Thornhill Road; London University; B.Sc. (Econ.). Fellow of Royal Statistical Society, and of Royal Economic Society. *Publications:* New Dictionary of Statistics, 1911; also Articles and Reviews in Economic Journal and Statistical Journal. *Recreations:* gardening, music, reading. *Address:* 47 Northway, N.W.11. [*Died* 27 *Jan.* 1953.

WEBB, Clement Charles Julian, M.A.; D.Litt.; F.B.A. 1927; Hon. Fellow of Oriel College, Oxford, 1930, and of Magdalen College, Oxford, 1938; Hon. Student of Christ Church, Oxford, 1953; *b.* London, 25 June 1865; *y. s.* of Rev. Benjamin Webb, Vicar of St. Andrew's, Wells Street, London, and Prebendary of St. Paul's, and Maria Elphinstone, *d.* of W. H. Mill, D.D., Canon of Ely and Regius Professor of Hebrew at Cambridge; *m.* 1905, Eleanor Theodora (*d.* 1942), *d.* of Alexander Joseph, Hon. Canon of Rochester. *Educ.:* Westminster; Christ Church, Oxford; B.A. (1st Lit. Hum.) 1888. Fellow and Tutor of Magdalen College, 1889-1922; Senior Proctor, 1905-6; member of the Governing Body of St. Peter's College, Westminster, since 1905; a Governor of the Grammar School, Aylesbury, since 1938; Examiner in Lit. Hum. 1906-9; Tutor in Philosophy to the non-collegiate students, Oxford, 1907-20; Wilde Lecturer on Natural and Comparative Religion, Oxford, 1911-14; Gifford Lecturer, Aberdeen, 1918-19; First Oriel Professor of the Philosophy of the Christian Religion, 1920-30; Fellow of Oriel College, Oxford, 1922-30; Stephanos Nirmalendu Ghosh Lecturer, Calcutta, 1930-31; Olaus Petri Lecturer, Upsala, 1932; Forwood Lecturer in the Philosophy of Religion, Liverpool, 1933; Lewis Fry Lecturer, Bristol, 1934; Hon. LL.D., St. Andrews, 1921; Hon. D.Theol. Upsala, 1932; Hon. D.D., Glasgow, 1937. *Publications:* Devotions of St. Anselm, 1903; Joannis Saresberiensis Policraticus, 1909; Metalogicon, 1929; Problems in the Relations of God and Man, 1911 and 1915; Natural and Comparative Religion (Inaugural Lecture), 1911; History of Philosophy (Home Univ. Library), 1915 and 1944; Studies in the History of Natural Theology, 1915; Group Theories of Religion and the Individual, 1916; In Time of War, 1918; God and Personality, 1919; Divine Personality and Human Life, 1920; Philosophy and the Christian Religion (Inaugural Lecture) 1920; A Century of Anglican Theology and other Lectures, 1923; Kant's Philosophy of Religion, 1926; Religious Thought in the Oxford Movement, 1928; Religion and the Thought of To-day (Riddell Lectures), 1929; Pascal's Philosophy of Religion, 1929; Our Knowledge of One Another (Herz Lecture), 1930; John of Salisbury, 1932; The Contribution of Christianity to Ethics (Stephanos Nirmalendu Ghosh Lectures), 1932; Religious Thought in England from 1850, 1933; Religion and Theism, 1934; The Historical Element in Religion, 1935; Religious Experience with Bibliography, 1945; also contributions to religious and philosophical works. *Address:* Old Rectory, Pitchcott, nr. Aylesbury. *T.:* North Marston 209.
[*Died* 5 *Oct.* 1954.

WEBB, John, C.M.G. 1944; C.B.E. 1941; M.C. 1918; M.I.E.E.; Inspector-General of Egyptian State Telegraphs and Telephones since 1931; *b.* 1885; *s.* of late John Webb; *m.* 1906, Florence, *d.* of Jason Giles, Coventry; one *s.* one *d.* S. Africa, 1899-1902, with Imperial Yeo.; European War, 1914-19, as Lieut. R.E. (M.C.); Tadj. D'Iran, 1939; Grand Officer Order of Nile, 1941. *Address:* Egyptian State Telegraphs and Telephones, Cairo. *Clubs:* Turf, Gezira (Cairo); Union, Smouha (Alexandria). [*Died* 12 *Sept.* 1954.

WEBB, Katharine; *b.* Bracknell, Berks, 1862; 2nd *d.* of Rev. William Fulford Adams; *m.* Edmund J. Webb. Pupil of Miss S. T. Prideaux. Worked as a bookbinder for many years at Eadburgha Bindery, Broadway, Worcestershire; is a member of the Arts and Crafts Exhibition Society, London, and the Women's Guild of Arts (Hon. Pres. since 1939); F.R.S.A. 1938; exhibits under the name of Katharine Adams, and has shown work at St. Louis, 1904; Brussels, 1910 (gold medal); Ghent, 1913; Paris, 1914; Paris, 1925 (silver medal), etc. *Address:* Cherries, St. Briavels, Glos. *T.A.:* Cherries St. Briavels. *T.:* St. Briavels 236.
[*Died* 15 *Oct.* 1952.

WEBB, Rt. Hon. Maurice, P.C. 1950; political journalist and broadcaster; *b.* 26 Sept. 1904; *s.* of George and Annie Webb, Lancaster; *m.* 1931, Mabel Hughes, Lancaster; (one *s.* decd.). *Educ.:* Christ Church Schl., Lancaster. Political Agent for Labour Party in Skipton, 1927-29; Propaganda Officer for Labour Party Headquarters, 1929-35; Daily Herald staff, 1935-44; Sunday Express staff, 1944-45. M.P. (Lab.) for Central Bradford, 1945-55; Chairman Parliamentary Labour Party, 1946-50; Ministry of Food, 1950-1951. Contested (Lab.) North Bradford, 1955. Has done considerable home and overseas broadcasting for B.B.C. Has served as Chairman of Parliamentary Lobby Journalists and on Press Gallery Committee. *Publications;* Britain's Industrial Front, 1943; various political pamphlets. *Recreation:* painting. *Address:* Willow Cottage, Pinner Hill, Pinner, Middx. *Club;* Savage. [*Died* 10 *June* 1956.

WEBB, Wilfred Mark, O.B.E. 1943; F.L.S., F.R.M.S.; lecturer and writer; Sec. of Selborne Society; Chairman Brent Valley Bird Sanctuary Committee; *b.* Primrose Hill, 28 May 1868; *o. s.* of late William James Webb ("Eastern Webb"), artist, and Bessie, *o. d.* of late William Weighill; *m.* 1st, 1896, Mathilda Elizabeth (*d.* 1931), *o. d.* of John Hunter Davie; one *s.*; 2nd, 1933, Daphne Margot Dudley, *o. d.* of Cecil Dudley Lewis. *Educ.:* St. John's Wood School; University and King's Colleges, London; privately. Engaged in tuition, 1889-92; original member of the Malacological Soc., 1893; Senior Assist. Lecturer on Biology, Essex County Council, 1893-98; editor of the Journal of Malacology, 1895-97; has actively promoted the Nature Study Movement; Lecturer on Biology and Nature Study, Surrey County Council, 1901-8; Editor of the Country Home, 1907-12; of Knowledge, 1910-17; of Selborne Magazine, 1911-25; Sec., Corresponding Societies Committee, British Association, 1914-22; at work for the War Office, 1915-19; Assist. (Postal) Censor, 1918-19, 1938-41; Censor in Charge, 1941-46; Examiner of Questioned Documents to the Home Office, 1920-21; member of Council, National Trust, etc.; British War Medal. *Publications:* The Eton Nature Study Note-Book, 1903; Eton Nature Study and Observational Lessons (with Matthew Davenport Hill), part i. 1903, part ii. 1904; The British Woodlice (with Charles Sillem), 1906; The Principles of Horticulture, 1907; The Heritage of Dress, 1908; Gilbert White's Nature Calendar (for 1766), 1911; The Microscope and its Uses, 1914. *Recreations:* field natural history, archæology, photography. *Address:* The Hermitage, Hanwell, W.7. *T.:* Ealing 0642. [*Died* 7 *Jan.* 1952.

WEBB-BOWEN, Colonel Hildred Edward, C.M.G. 1919; D.S.O. 1918; T.D.; D.L. Staffordshire; A.M.I.E.E.; Engineer British Aluminium Co., Ltd.; retd. 1947; *b.* 1882; *s.* of late B. Ince Webb-Bowen; *m.* 1920, Gladys, *e. d.* of W. J. Crampton, Southsea; one *s.* *Educ.:* St. Paul's School; City and Guilds of London Technical College; served with London Electrical Engineers (V.) in South Africa, 1901-2 (S.A. medal, five bars); served apprenticeship Elswick Works, Newcastle on Tyne (Sir W. Armstrong Whitworth, Ltd.); joined Staff of British Aluminium Company, Ltd., 1906; served in London Electrical Engineers (T.), 1914-16; Salonica, 1916-19 (Serbian White Eagle with cross swords, T.D.). *Address:* The Firs, Robinson Road, Trentham, Stoke-on-Trent, Staffs. *T.:* Stoke-on-Trent 49511. *Clubs:* Junior Army and Navy, M.C.C. [*Died* 10 *April* 1958.

WEBB-BOWEN, Air Vice-Marshal Sir Tom Ince, K.C.B., *cr.* 1932 (C.B. 1919); C.M.G. 1918; late R.A.F.; late Bedfordshire Regiment; re-employed with R.A.F., 1939-44; *b.* 1879; *m.* 1919, Violet Louise, *e. d.* of C. A. Hadley, Johannesburg; two *s.* one *d.* Served N.W. Frontier of India, 1902; European War, 1914-18 (despatches, C.M.G., Bt. Lieutenant-Colonel, Legion of Honour, Military Order of Savoy, Order of St. Anne of Russia); commanded R.A.F., India, 1919-21, Inland Area, 1924-26; commanded Royal Air Force in Middle East, 1926-29; Air Member for Personnel on Air Council, 1930-31; Air Officer Commanding Wessex Bombing Area, 1931-33; retired list, 1933. High Sheriff of Pembrokeshire, 1949-50, D.L., 1949. *Address:* Hillborough House, Haverfordwest, Pembs. [*Died* 29 *Oct.* 1956.

WEBB-JOHNSON, 1st Baron, *cr.* 1948, of Stoke-on-Trent; **Alfred Edward Webb-Johnson,** 1st Bt., *cr.* 1945; G.C.V.O., *cr.* 1954; (K.C.V.O., *cr.* 1942); Kt., *cr.* 1936; C.B.E. 1919; D.S.O. 1916; T.D.; Honours M.B., Ch.B. Victoria University of Manchester; F.R.C.S. Eng.; Hon. F.A.C.S.; Hon. F.R.A.C.S.; Hon. F.R.C.S. (Edin.); Hon. F.R.F.P.S. (Glas.); Hon. F.R.C.S. (Ireland); Hon. F.R.C.S. (Can.); Hon. LL.D. (Liverpool and Toronto); Grand Cordon Order of the Nile; Surgeon to H.M. Queen Mary, 1936-53; Pres. Roy. Soc. Med. 1952-54; Chm., Army Med. Advisory Bd., 1946-1957; Hunterian Prof. of Surgery and Pathology Royal Coll. of Surgeons of England, 1917; Hon. Medallist, Pres. 1941-49, and Mem. of Court of Examiners, Roy. Coll. of Surgeons of England; Vice-Pres. and Cons. Surgeon to the Middlesex Hosp.; late Dean of the Medical School. Consulting Surgeon, Queen Alexandra's Military Hospital, London, and the Royal Hospital, Chelsea; late Examiner in Surgery Univ. of Cambridge; Hon. Col., A.M.S.; Vice-Pres. Royal Hospital, Wolverhampton, Royal Eye Hosp., and Marie Curie Hosp.; late Consulting Surg., B.E.F., France; served European War, 1914-19 (despatches three times, C.B.E., D.S.O.); Member: International Society of Surgery; International Assoc. of Urology; Corresp. Etranger de l'Académie de Médicine de France; Assoc. Etranger de l'Académie de Chirurgie de Paris; Hon. Fellow Greek Surgical Soc.; Hon. Member American Surgical Assoc.; President Royal Medical Benevolent Fund; F.Z.S.; Pres. Epsom Coll., 1951; ex-Dir., Savoy Theatre; Hon. Freeman of Barbers' Company, 1949; *b.* 1880; *s.* of late Samuel Johnson, M.D., M.O.H., Stoke-on-Trent, and Julia (*d.* 1931), *d.* of late James Webb; *m.* Cecilia Flora, (D.J.St.J.), *d.* of late D. G. MacRae of Norbiton, Surrey. *Educ.:* Manchester Univ.; London. Dumville Surgical Prizeman and Tom Jones Surgical Scholar; late Demonstrator of Operative Surgery, Univ. of Manchester; Surgical Registrar, Manchester Royal Infirmary; Resident Medical Officer, the Middlesex Hosp. G.C.St.J. 1955, late hospitaller. D.L. County of London; Lord High Steward of Newcastle-under-Lyme. *Publications:* Surgical Aspects of Typhoid and Paratyphoid Fevers, 1919; Notes on a Tour of the Principal Hospitals and Medical Schools of the United States and Canada, 1923; Syme Oration, Surgery in England in the Making; The Bradshaw Lecture: Pride and Prejudice in the Treatment of Cancer, 1940; numerous contributions to medical press and Proc. R.S.M. *Heir:* none. *Address:* 70 Portland Place, W.1. *T.:* Langham 1683, 1684. *Clubs:* Athenæum, Bath, Garrick. [*Died* 28 *May* 1958 (*ext.*).

WEBBER, Sir Arthur Frederick Clarence, Kt., *cr.* 1936; B.A.; *b.* British Guiana; 1873; *s.* of Arthur and Magdalen Weber; *m.* Kathleen Mary, *d.* of late David Kennard, Linton, Kent; three *s.* two *d.* *Educ.:* Queen's Coll., British Guiana; Merton Coll., Oxford. Graduated at Oxford, 1896; called to Bar, Inner Temple, 1896; practised at the Bar in British Guiana; Stipendiary Magistrate in British Guiana, 1900-9; Judge of the Supreme Court of Nigeria, 1909-33; Chief Justice, Sierra Leone, 1933-37; Chairman Yorkshire Regional Valuation Board under Coal Commission, 1939. *Publications:* The Justice of the Peace in British Guiana; Local Government Board under the Local Government Board Ordinance of British Guiana. *Address:* Seven Chimneys, Henfield, Sussex. *T.:* 135. [*Died* 19 *Dec.* 1952.

WEBBER, Harold Norris, M.A., B.Chir. Cantab.; Consulting Anæsthetist, University College Hospital; *b.* 1881; *e. s.* of W. H. Webber, Brighton; *m.* Madeleine Mary, *d.* of Major J. J. Ryder, late 2nd Worcs. Regt. *Educ.:* Brighton Grammar School; St. John's College, Cambridge; University College Hospital. Resident Medical Officer, West London Hospital and University College Hospital; served in E.E.F., 1917-20, with rank of Major. *Publications:* (with late W. H. R. Rivers) papers on the action of caffeine and alcohol on the capacity for muscular work; (with late F. S. Rood) a small textbook of anæsthetics. *Address:* Hawthorns, 14 The Meads, Bricket Wood, Herts. [*Died* 24 *Dec.* 1954.

WEBSTER, Adam Blyth, M.A. (Edin.); LL.D. (St. Andrews, Calif.); J.P.; Berry Professor of English Literature, University of St. Andrews, 1920-55; Emeritus Professor, 1955; *b.* Girvan, Ayrshire, 1882; 2nd *s.* of late Rev. Gordon Webster, M.A.; *m.* 1906, *e. d.* of late Cossar Mackenzie, Edinburgh. *Educ.:* Boys' High School, Christchurch, Canterbury, N.Z.; University of Edinburgh. Lecturer in English Language and Literature, University of Edinburgh, 1905-16; Lecturer in English, Edinburgh Provincial Training College for Teachers, 1909-16; served European War, R.G.A. and I.B. (Despatches); Senior Lecturer in English, University of Edinburgh, 1919-20; General Editor of Scottish Text Society, 1905-16; Visiting Professor, Univ. of California, 1926, 1929, 1931 and 1939; Dean of Faculty of Arts, St. Andrews, 1921-36; Andrew Lang Lecturer, St. Andrews, 1937. *Publications:* On the Runic Inscriptions on the Ruthwell and Bewcastle Crosses, in Baldwin Brown's Arts in Early England, vol. v., 1921; George Saintsbury, 1933; Andrew Lang's Poetry, 1938; Concerning Andrew Lang, 1949. *Address:* University, St. Andrews. *Club:* New (Edinburgh). [*Died* 19 *March* 1956.

WEBSTER, George Frederick, C.M.G. 1942; *b.* 27 Sept. 1889; *s.* of late Dr. G. L. Webster, Croydon. *Educ.:* Whitgift School; privately. Lieut. Baganda Rifles, G.E.A. campaign, 1915-16; Asst. Political Officer, German East Africa provisional administration, 1916; Administrative Officer, Tanganyika Territory, 1922; Deputy Provincial Commissioner, 1926; M.L.C. 1926, 1927, 1935, and 1936; M.E.C. Jan.-Apr. 1927; Provincial Commissioner, 1929; Senior Provincial Commissioner, 1934; retired, 1946; Member for Tanganyika Territory of Makerere College Council (Uganda), 1939-45. *Recreations:* golf, billiards. *Address:* 3 The Rock, Reigate Hill, Surrey. [*Died* 13 *Oct.* 1959.

WEBSTER, George Henry, C.M.G. 1942; O.B.E. 1937; Colonies Representative, Commonwealth Telecommunications Board, 1948; *b.* 14 Aug. 1887; *s.* of Joseph Webster, Ivy Farm, Litherland, Lancs; *m.* 1918, Annie, *d.* of William Bond, Master Mariner, Cunard Line; one *s.* *Educ.:* St. Philip's School, Litherland, and privately. British Post Office, 1905; Royal Engineers (S.R.,) Dardanelles, Palestine, Egypt, 1914-20 (despatches twice, Médaille d'Honneur, Français, avec glaives, en vermeil); Asst. Director Post and Telegraphs, Palestine, 1920; Deputy Postmaster-General, Palestine, 1935; Postmaster-General, Palestine, 1937; Chairman, Municipal Commission, Jerusalem, 1945. *Address:* Willowbrook, Rayleigh Rd., Thundersley, Essex. [*Died* 24 *May* 1955.

WEBSTER, Rt. Rev. Hedley, D.D.; *b.* 21 July 1880; *s.* of George Webster, Bandon; *m.* 1913, Annie Irene Mary, *d.* of Charles E. O. Wagentreiber, Gabroo, Assam; two *d.* *Educ.:* Trinity College, Dublin. B.A. 1900; B.D. 1906; D.D. 1945. Deacon, 1903; Priest, 1904; Curate St. Luke's, Cork, 1903-7; Curate Holy Trinity, Cork, 1907-13; Rector of Kinneigh, 1913-16; of Holy Trinity, Cork, 1916-26; of Blackrock, Cork, 1926-45. Examining Chap. 1933-45; Archdeacon of Cork, 1938-45; Bishop of Killaloe, Kilfenora, Clonfert and Kilmacduagh, 1945-Oct. 1953, retired. *Address:* Clarisford, Killaloe, Co. Clare. *Club:* University (Dublin). [*Died* 28 *June* 1954.

WEBSTER, Walter Ernest, V.P.R.I.; R.O.I., R.P.; artist (portrait and genre); *b.* Manchester, 1878; *m.* Susan Beatrice Pearse. *Educ.:* Royal Academy Schools. Exhibited R.A. since 1904; gold medal, Salon, 1931. *Address:* Broom Villa, Broomhouse Road, Hurlingham, S.W.6. *T.:* Renown 2546. *Clubs:* Arts, Chelsea Arts. [*Died* 30 *April* 1959.

WEBSTER, William, C.B.E. 1918; J.P.; late Gen. Sec., Scottish Liberal Federation; retd. 1934; reappointed Acting Secretary for duration of war, 1940; retired, April 1946; *b.* 1866; *s.* of William Webster, Glasgow; *m.* 1899, Mary, *d.* of W. Hughes; two *d.* Was a Member of National War Aims, Central Recruiting (Scotland); first Scottish War Savings Committees, and National Service Department (Agricultural Section) during European War. *Address:* 8 Cairnmuir Road, Corstorphine, Edinburgh 12. [*Died* 20 *Oct.* 1953.

WEDDERBURN, Sir Ernest Maclagan, Kt., *cr.* 1942; O.B.E.; D.L.; D.Sc., LL.B.; LL.D. (Edin.); W.S.; *b.* 3 Feb. 1884; *s.* of Alexander Stormonth Maclagan Wedderburn, M.D., Pearsie, Angus, and Anne Ogilvie; *m.* 1911, Mary, *d.* of Rev. T. S. Goldie, Granton; two *s.* one *d.* (and one *s.* killed on active service). *Educ.:* George Watson's College, Edinburgh; Edinburgh University. Professor of Conveyancing in University of Edinburgh, 1922-35. Deputy Keeper of H.M. Signet, 1935-54. Chairman of General Council of Solicitors in Scotland, 1936-49, and of Law Society of Scotland, 1949-50; Chairman of Solicitors (Scotland) Discipline Committee, 1943-53; Vice-President Royal Society of Edinburgh, 1946-50; Vice-President of Royal Meteorological Society, 1950-52 and 1955-56; Rector's Assessor, University of Edinburgh, 1938-52. *Address:* 6 Succoth Gardens, Edinburgh. *T.A.:* Equitable Edinburgh. *T.:* Edinburgh 61341. *Clubs:* New, Caledonian United Service (Edinburgh). [*Died* 3 *June* 1958.

WEDDERBURN, Sir J. A. O.; *see* Ogilvy-Wedderburn.

WEDDERBURN, Sir Maxwell MacLagan, K.B.E., *cr.* 1941; C.M.G. 1935; Ceylon Civil Service (retired); *b.* 25 March 1883; *s.* of Laurence Craigie MacLagan Wedderburn and Gertrude Elizabeth Maxwell; *m.* 1909, Dorothy Ellen Mary Viner; three *d.* *Educ.:* Morrison's Academy, Crieff; George Watson's College, Edinburgh; Edinburgh University (M.A.). Passed into the Ceylon Civil Service, 1906; Chief Secretary, Ceylon, 1937-40. *Address:* Sussex Lodge, Beacon Rd., Crowborough, Sussex. [*Died* 30 *June* 1953.

WEDGWOOD, 2nd Baron, *cr.* 1942, of Barlaston; **Francis Charles Bowen Wedgwood;** Artist; *b.* 20 Jan. 1898; *s.* of 1st Baron Wedgwood, P.C., D.S.O., and Hon. Ethel Kate Bowen (*d.* 1952), *d.* of Charles, Lord Bowen; *S.* father, 1943; *m.* 1920, Edith May, *d.* of William Telfer, Glasgow; one *s.* *Educ.:* Bedales School. Studied Burslem School of Art, 1920-22; Slade School, London Univ., 1922-25. Served European War, R.N.V.R. and R.F.C., 1914-19 (wounded). Exhibited N.E.A.C., 1927-30 and R.A. 1931-39. *Heir:* *s.* Hon. Hugh Everard Wedgwood [*b.* 20 Apr. 1921; *m.* 1945, Heather, *o. c.* of Mr. Leake, Bournemouth]. *Address:* c/o Barclay's Bank, Pritchard Street, Johannesburg, S. Africa. [*Died* 22 *April* 1959.

WEDGWOOD, Hon. Camilla Hildegarde; Lecturer in the Australian School of Pacific Administration; *b.* 25 March 1901; *d.* of 1st Baron Wedgwood and Hon. Ethel Kate Bowen. *Educ.:* The Orme Girls' School, Newcastle, Staffs; Bedford College, London; Newnham Coll., Cambridge. B.A. (Cantab.), 1923; M.A. 1927; Lecturer in Anthropology, Sydney Univ., 1928-30; Temp. Lecturer, Dept. of African Life and Languages, Univ. of Cape Town, 1930. Member of Council of Royal Anthropological Institute, 1932; Research Fellow of Australian National Research Council for work in New Guinea, 1932-34; Anthropological Fieldwork in Nauru, 1935; Principal of Women's College, University of Sydney, 1935-44. Served with rank of Temp. Lt.-Col. with the Australian Women's Services, 1944-46. *Publications:* Articles in Encyclopædia Britannica, 1928; (Edited) Malekula (by A. B. Deacon), 1933. Articles in Oceania, etc. *Recreation;* reading. *Address:* Australian School of Pacific Administration, Mosman, N.S.W. *Club:* University Women's. [*Died* 17 *May* 1955.

WEDGWOOD, Sir Ralph Lewis, 1st Bt., *cr.* 1942; Kt., *cr.* 1924; C.B. 1918; C.M.G. 1917; *b.* 2 Mar. 1874; 3rd *s.* of Clement Francis Wedgwood, of Barlaston Lea, Stoke-on-Trent; *m.* 1906, Iris Veronica (author of The Iron Age; The Livelong Day; Perilous Seas; The Fairway; Northumberland and Durham; Fenland Rivers), *d.* of Albert H. Pawson, of Farnley, Leeds; one *s.* one *d.* *Educ.:* Clifton; Trinity College, Cambridge. Director of Docks, G.H.Q., France (Hon. Brigadier-General), 1916-19; Deputy General Manager, North-Eastern Railway, 1919-21; General Manager, North-Eastern Railway, 1922; Chief General Manager, London and North-Eastern Railway, 1923-39; Chairman, Railway Executive Committee, 1939-41; Brig.-Gen. late Engineer and Railway Staff Corps, R.E. (T.A.); President, National Confederation of Employers' Organisations, 1929-30; Member of Weir Committee on Main Line Electrification, 1930-31; Member of Central Electricity Board, 1931-46; Member of Chinese Government Purchasing Commission 1932-51; Chairman, Indian Railway Inquiry Committee, 1936-37; Member King's College Delegacy since 1939, Chairman, 1945-50; Member Council of Royal Society of Arts, 1939-40. *Recreation:* walking. *Heir:* *s.* Major J. H. Wedgwood. *Address:* Leith Hill Place, Dorking. *T.:* Dorking 73236. *Club:* Reform. [*Died* 5 *Sept.* 1956.

WEDLAKE, John, C.B. 1952; M.B.E. 1920; Director of Armament Supply, Admiralty, since 1950; *b.* 14 Feb. 1892; *s.* of late Anthony Manning Wedlake and Martha Wedlake; *m.* 1918, Charlotte Palmyre, *d.* of late Col. André Hack (French); one *d.* (one *s.* decd.). *Educ.:* Dr. Morgan's School, Bridgwater. Entered Admiralty Service, 1910; at home establishments, 1910-22, in various ranks; Hong Kong, 1922-27; Admiralty, 1927-30; Malta and Trincomalee, 1930-32, as Naval Armament Supply Officer; Plymouth, Mediterranean, Admiralty and Portsmouth, as Superintending Armament Supply Officer, 1932-42; on staff of Commander-in-Chiefs, Eastern Fleet and British Pacific Fleet, 1942-45, as Dep. Dir. of Armament Supply; Sen. Dep. Dir. of Armament Supply, Admiralty, 1945-50. *Address:* Ordnance House, Simonstown, Cape Province, S. Africa. *Club:* Overseas. [*Died* 11 *Sept.* 1958.

WEDMORE, Edmund Basil, C.B.E. 1938; M.I.E.E., F.Inst.P., etc.; Director of E.R.A. Patents Ltd., The Bee Research Association and of Bee Craft; *b.* Bristol, 24 Jan. 1876; *s.* of Edmund Tolson and Anne Grace Wedmore; *m.* 1st, Elsie Hilda Brison; one *s.* two *d.*; 2nd, Winifred A. M. Parry; one *s.* one *d.* *Educ.:* Privately; University College, Bristol. Lecturer and Demonstrator, Finsbury Technical College, 1895-99; Designing Engineer, British Thomson-Houston Co. Ltd., 1899-1919; Technical Officer, Electrical Research Committee, 1919-21; Director and Secretary British Electrical and Allied Industries Research Association, 1921-44. *Publications:* Switchgear for Electric Power Control, 1924; A Manual of Bee-Keeping, 1932 and 1945; The Ventilation of Beehives, 1947; Successful Bee-keeping, 1948; many contributions to technical journals. *Recreation:* bee-keeping. *Address:* 47 Culmington Road, Ealing, W.13. *T.:* Ealing 0986. [*Died* 16 *June* 1956.

WEEKES, Rev. George Arthur, M.A.; Fellow of Sidney Sussex College, Cambridge, Master, 1918-45; Hon. Canon of Ely since 1935; *b.* 5 Sept. 1869; 2nd *s.* of late Arthur Weekes, M.A., Clifton, Bristol, and Mary Anne, *d.* of late George Haye, Captain R.N.; *m.* 1899, Catherine (*d.* 1940), *y. d.* of late Llewelyn David of Margam, S. Wales; no. *c.* *Educ.:* Bristol Grammar School; Sidney Sussex College, Cambridge (Classical Scholar). 1st class Classical Tripos, Part I., 1891; 1st class Classical Tripos, Part II., 1892; 3rd class Theological Tripos, Part II., 1893; Deacon, 1893; Priest, 1894; Chaplain of Sidney Sussex College, 1893; Fellow and Dean, 1894; Praelector, 1896; Tutor, 1905; Senior Proctor of Univ., 1906-7 and 1916-17; Vice-Chancellor of University, 1926 and 1927; Select Preacher, University of Oxford, 1926, 1929, 1934. *Address:* 56 Lensfield Road, Cambridge. [*Died* 23 *June* 1953.

WEEKLEY, Ernest, M.A., D.Litt.; Professor Emeritus of the University of Nottingham. *Educ.:* Universities of Berne, Cambridge, Paris, Freiburg im Breisgau. *Publications:* The Romance of Words; The Romance of Names; Surnames; papers published in Transactions of the Philological Society; An Etymological Dictionary of Modern English, 1921; A Concise Etymological Dictionary, 1924, revised edn. 1952; Words Ancient and Modern, 1926; More Words Ancient and Modern, 1927; The English Language, 1928, 2nd edn. 1953; Adjectives and other Words, 1930; Saxo Grammaticus or First Aid for the Best seller, 1930; Words and Names, 1932; Something About Words, 1935; Jack and Jill, a Study of our Christian Names, 1939. *Address:* 446 Upper Richmond Road, Putney, S.W.15. *T.:* Prospect 6343. [*Died* 7 *May* 1954.

WEEKS, 1st Baron, *cr.* 1956, of Ryton, Co. Durham; **Ronald Morce Weeks,** K.C.B. 1943; C.B.E. 1939; D.S.O. 1918; M.C.; T.D.; Hon. Fellow of Caius College, Cambridge, 1946; H.M. Government Representative on Board of British Petroleum Co. Ltd. since Dec. 1956; Chairman: Finance Corporation for Industry; Vickers Nuclear Engineering Ltd.; Director: Vickers Ltd. (Chairman, 1948-56); Massey-Ferguson Organisation (U.K.); Pilkington Brothers, Ltd.; Public Schools Appointments Bureau; Oldings (Hatfield) Ltd.; Associated Electrical Industries Ltd.; Royal Exchange Assurance; Hudson's Bay Co.; Vice-Chm. King George's Jubilee Trust; *b.* Durham, 13 November 1890; *s.* of late Richard Llewellyn Weeks, Broomhough, Riding Mill, Northumberland, and Susan Helen Walker Weeks; *m.* 1st, 1922, Evelyn Elsie (decd.), *d.* of Henry Haynes; 2nd, 1931, Cynthia Mary Cumming, *d.* of late John Wood Irvine, Liverpool; two *d.* *Educ.:* Charterhouse; Gonville and Caius Coll., Cambridge. B.A.; Capt. Camb. Univ. Association Football XI, 1912. Joined Pilkington Bros. Ltd., 1912. Served European War, 1914-18; commission Prince of Wales Vols. T.F. and Rifle Brigade (despatches thrice, D.S.O., M.C. and Bar, Brevet Major, Croix de Guerre). Retired from Army, 1919, and rejoined Pilkington Bros.; Director, 1926. Comd. 5th Bn. S. Lancs. Regt. T.A., 1934-38. Chairman, Exec. Bd., Pilkington Bros., 1939. War of 1939-45: Chief of Staff, Territorial Div., 1939; B.G.S. Home Forces, 1940; Maj.-Gen., Dir.-Gen. of Army Equipment, 1941; Lieut.-Gen., D.C.I.G.S., 1942-45. Dep. Military Governor and Chief of Staff, British Zone. C.C.G., June-Aug. 1945; retired from Army, 1945. Hon. Col. 596 L.A.A. Regt. (S. Lancs) T.A., 1946-55. Chairman: Brit. Scientific Instrument Research Assoc., 1946-1951; Nat. Advisory Council on Education for Industry and Commerce, 1948-56. Hon. LL.D. Liverpool, 1946; Hon. Doctor of Tech. Science, Sheffield, 1951; Hon. LL.D. Leeds, 1957; Hon. Assoc. Manchester Coll. of Technology, 1951, Coll. of Tech., Birmingham, 1955; Hon. F.R.C.O.G., 1956. Comdr. Legion of Merit (U.S.A.), 1947. *Recreations:* golf, shooting. *Heir:* none. *Address:* (business) Vickers House, Broadway, S.W.1. *T.:* Abbey 7777; (home) 43 Lowndes Square, S.W.1. *T.:* Belgravia 3738. *Clubs:* Athenæum, Naval and Military. [*Died* 19 *Aug.* 1960 (*ext.*).

WEEKS, Engr. Rear-Adm. Edward John, C.B. 1919; R.N. retired list; *s.* of late John C. Weeks, Chief Insp. of Machinery, R.N.; *b.* 26 March 1868; *m.* 1897, Gladys L., *d.* of late John Priston of Exeter; one *s.* two *d.* *Educ.:* H.M.S. Marlborough. Specialised in gun mountings; served in European War, Heligoland Bight and Falklands Battle in H.M.S. Invincible (despatches, C.B.) and 9th Cruiser Squadron. *Address:* c/o Lloyds Bank, Southsea, Hants. *Club:* Hamble Yacht. [*Died* 8 *April* 1954.

WEIGALL, Lt.-Col. Sir Archibald; *see* Weigall, Lt.-Col. Sir W. E. G. A.

WEIGALL, Cecil Edward, Q.C. 1925; *b.* 28 March 1870; *e. s.* of Albert Bythesea Weigall, C.M.G.; *m.* 1912, Maud Lyman Sise, Dunedin, New Zealand; two *d.* *Educ.:* Sydney Grammar School; Corpus Christi College, Oxford, B.A. Admitted to the New South Wales Bar, 1896; King's Jubilee Medal, 1935; Coronation Medal, 1937. *Recreation:* golf. *Address:* Darling Point, Sydney, New South Wales. *T.:* F.B. 2165. *Clubs:* Union, Royal Sydney Golf (Sydney). [*Died* 12 *June* 1955.

WEIGALL, Lt.-Colonel Sir (William Ernest George) Archibald, 1st Bt., *cr.* 1938; K.C.M.G., *cr.* 1920; J.P., Kent, Lincs, and Berks; D.L. Lincs. (High Sheriff, 1926); D.L. Berks; High Sheriff of Berkshire, 1944; King of Arms, Order of St. Michael and St. George, since 1938; *b.* 8 Dec. 1874; 5th *s.* of late Henry Weigall and Lady Rose, 2nd *d.* of 11th Earl of Westmorland; *m.* 1910, Baroness von Eckhardstein, Grace Emily (*d.* 1950), *o. c.* of Sir Blundell Maple, 1st and last Bart.; one *d.* *Educ.:* Wellington College; Royal Agricultural College (Gold Medallist). (Major retired) 3rd Batt. Northants Regiment; served South Africa, 1902; M.P. (U.) Horncastle Division Lincs, 1911-20; Captain Lincolnshire Yeomanry, and Lt.-Col. and Inspector Q.M.G. Services, Northern Command, 1914-Aug. 1917. Surveyor Food Consumption, Public Services, and Chairman Food Survey Board, Ministry of Food; Member of National Salvage Council; Deputy Chairman Surplus Govt. Property Disposal Board; Member of Select Committee on National Expenditure; Member (Representative) National Agricultural Council; Pres. Agricultural Organisation Society, 1919; Governor Royal Agricultural College; Deputy Chairman Federation of County Agricultural Committees; Governor of South Australia, 1920-22; Territorial Army Reserve, General List Yeomanry; President Royal Agricultural Society, 1946; Chairman of the Royal Empire Society, 1932-38; Pres. Land Agents' Society, 1934; Governor Wellington College; Chairman Royal Veterinary College. *Recreations:* hunting, shooting, cricket. *Address:* West Lodge, Twatley, Malmesbury, Wilts. *T.:* 3189; Englemere, Ascot, Berks. *T.:* Ascot 179. *Clubs:* Carlton, Cavalry. [*Died* 3 *June* 1952 (*ext.*).

WEILL, David D.; *see* David-Weill.

WEIR, 1st Viscount, *cr.* 1938, of Eastwood, Renfrewshire; **William Douglas Weir;** Baron of U.K., *cr.* 1918; P.C. 1918; G.C.B., *cr.* 1934; Kt., *cr.* 1917; D.L.; Hon. President and Director of G. & J. Weir, Ltd., Glasgow; *b.* 12 May 1877; *s.* of late James Weir, of Over Courance, Dumfriesshire, and Mary Douglas; *m.* 1904, Alice Blanche, *d.* of John MacConnachie of Glasgow; one *s.* one *d.* (and one *s.* decd.). Scottish Director of Munitions, 1915-16; Controller of Aeronautical Supplies and a Member of Air Board, 1917-18; Director General of Aircraft Production, Ministry of Munitions (also a Member of Council thereof), 1918; Secretary of State and President of Air Council, Apl.-Dec. 1918; Chairman of Advisory Committee Civil Aviation, 1919; Director-General of Explosives, Ministry of Supply, 1939; Chairman of Tank Board, 1942; LL.D., Glasgow Univ.; Pres. of Royal Scottish Automobile Club; Hon. Pres British Employers Confederation. Freedom of City of London, 1957. Order of Crown of Italy; American D.S.M.; Commander of Legion of Honour. *Heir: s.* Hon. James Kenneth Weir, C.B.E. *Address:* Eastwood Park, Giffnock, Renfrewshire. *Clubs:* Athenæum, Carlton; Royal Scottish Automobile (Glasgow). [*Died* 2 *July* 1959.

WEIR, Sir Cecil McAlpine, K.C.M.G., *cr.* 1952; K.B.E., *cr.* 1938; M.C.; D.L.; U.S. Medal of Freedom; Chairman, International Computers and Tabulators Ltd. Mem. (part-time) British Transport Commission; *b.* 5 July 1890; *y. s.* of Alexander Cunningham Weir; *m.* 1915, Jenny Paton Maclay (*d.* 1958); one *s.* one *d.* *Educ.:* Morrison's Acad., Crieff; Switzerland; Germany. Business Member of Industrial and Export Council, Board of Trade, 1940-46; Civil Defence Commissioner for Western District of Scotland, August 1939 to March 1940; Controller-Gen. of Factory and Storage Premises, 1941-42; Director-General of Equipment and Stores (Ministry of Supply), 1942-46; Economic Adviser, Control Commission for Germany, 1946-49; Chm. Dollar Exports Board, 1949-1951; Head of U.K. Delegation to High Authority of European Coal and Steel Community, 1952-55. Former Pres., Glasgow Chamber of Commerce; Chm., Admin. Cttee. Empire Exhibition, Scotland, 1938. *Publication:* Civilian Assignment, 1953. *Address:* 19 Thorney Court, Palace Gate, W.8. *Clubs:* National Liberal, English-Speaking Union, R.A.F.; Caledonian; New (Glasgow). [*Died* 30 *Oct.* 1960.

WEIR, General Sir George (Alexander), K.C.B., *cr.* 1934 (C.B. 1923); C.M.G. 1919; D.S.O. 1915; late Col. 3rd D. G.; late Colonel 3rd Carabiniers; Hon. Col. 8th Bn. Worcestershire Regt.; D.L. Worcestershire; *b.* 1 Dec. 1876; *s.* of late Archibald Weir, M.D., of Malvern; *m.* 1917, Margaret Irene, *d.* of Robert More, Woodsgate Place, Bexhill; one *s.* one *d.* *Educ.:* Harrow; Trinity College; Camb. Capt. 1902; Maj. 1912; Brig.-Gen. 1915; Maj.-Gen. 1927; Lt.-Gen. 1933; Gen. 1937; Comdt. Equitation School and Inspector of Cavalry, 1922-26; G.O.C. Bombay District, 1927-31; Commander 55th (West Lancs) Division, T.A., 1932-33; General Officer Commanding the British Troops in Egypt, 1934-38 (G.O.C. in C., 1936); retired, 1938; served S. Africa, 1899-1901 (despatches twice; Queen's medal 4 clasps); European War, 1914-18 (wounded, despatches, D.S.O., Bt. Lt.-Col. and Col.); Officer of St. Maurice and St. Lazarus; Croix de Guerre avec palmes. *Address:* Link Lodge, Malvern Link, Worcs. *T.:* Malvern 1801. *Club:* Army and Navy. [*Died* 15 *Nov.* 1951.

WEISS, Frederick Ernest, F.R.S. 1917; D.Sc. (London); Hon. LL.D. Manchester, 1931; F.L.S.; *b.* Huddersfield, 2 Nov. 1865; *s.* of Charles Weiss, merchant, of Huddersfield; *m.* 1898, Evelyn, *d.* of Dr. R. Spence Watson, of Newcastle on Tyne; three *d.* *Educ.:* The Gymnasia of Heidelberg and Neuchatel; the International Coll., Isleworth; Univ. Coll., London. Assistant Professor in Botany at University College, London; Professor of Botany in the University of Manchester, 1892-1930, now Emeritus Professor; President of Manchester Literary and Philosophical Society, 1911-13; Vice-Chancellor of the University of Manchester, 1913-15; President of the Linnean Society of London, 1931-34; Council of Royal Horticultural Society, 1935-40 and 1941-46; R.H.S. Victoria Medal of Honour, 1947; Linnean Medal, 1949. *Publications:* contributions to several botanical periodicals. *Recreation:*

gardening. *Address:* Norbury Lodge Hotel, 2 Fox Hill, S.E.19. [*Died* 7 *Jan.* 1953.

WEIZMANN, Chaim, D.Sc., Sc.D., LL.D.; President of the State of Israel since 1949 (of Provisional Council, 1948-1949); Director of Daniel Sieff Research Institute and Weizmann Institute of Science in Rehovoth, Israel; Chairman, Board of Governors of the Hebrew University in Jerusalem, 1932-50; President: World Zionist Organisation and Jewish Agency for Palestine, 1921-31 and 1935-46; *b.* Motol (Province of Grodno, Russia), 27 Nov. 1874; *m.* 1906, Dr. Vera Chatzmann; two *s.* (one of whom, F./Lt. Michael Weizmann, was reported missing in Feb. 1942). *Educ.:* Pinsk; Universities of Berlin and Freiburg. Lecturer in Chemistry in Geneva; Reader in Biochemistry, Univ. of Manchester; Director of Admiralty of Manchester; Dir. of Admiralty Labs., 1916-19; Hon. Adviser to British Ministry of Supply, 1939-45. *Publications:* Trial and Error, 1949; series of scientific publications in various chemical journals. *Address:* Rehovoth, Israel. [*Died* 9 *Nov.* 1952.

WELBY, Charles C. A. P.; *see* Pelham Welby.

WELBY-EVERARD, Edward Everard Earle, J.P., D.L.; *b.* 22 Dec. 1870; *s.* of Edward Montague Earle Welby and Sarah Elizabeth Everard; *m.* 1899, Gwladys Muriel Petra (*d.* 1946), *y. d.* of late Rev. G. W. Herbert; two *s.* one *d.* *Educ.:* Eton Coll.; Corpus Christi Coll., Oxford. M.A. 1st Class Hons. School of Jurisprudence; called to Bar, Inner Temple, 1896; assumed by Royal licence additional surname and arms of Everard under will of great-uncle late Henry Everard, 1894; Assist. to Sec. Light Railway Commission, to Solicitor Min. of Transport, and to Treasury Solicitor, successively, 1902-28; Chairman Holland Quarter Sessions, 1939-42 (Vice-Chairman, 1930-39); High Sheriff Lincs, 1935; Chairman River Welland Catchment Board, 1930-46; Member Church Assembly (House of Laity), 1930-50. *Address:* Gosberton House, nr. Spalding, Lincs. *T.:* Gosberton 250. *Club:* United University. [*Died* 20 *July* 1951.

WELCH; *see* Kemp-Welch.

WELCH, Sir (Henry George) Gordon, Kt., *cr.* 1954; C.B.E. 1946; *b.* 13 June 1890; *er. s.* of late Rev. E. J. Welch, Rector of Farnborough, Kent; *m.* 1916, Winifred Emily, *d.* of late S. B. Bowles; two *d.* *Educ.:* Merchant Taylors' School; St. John's College, Oxford (B.A. 1913). General Post Office Headquarters, 1913-17 and 1919-39; Commission Internationale de Ravitaillement, 1917-18 (Chevalier, Crown of Italy); Ministry of Information, 1939-46; Deputy Controller, H.M. Stationery Office, 1946-49; Controller, H.M. Stationery Office (also Queen's Printer of Acts of Parliament, holder of Crown copyright and Member of Statute Law Cttee.), 1949-53. *Address:* 9 Smitham Downs Road, Purley, Surrey. *T.:* Uplands 1917. [*Died* 12 *May* 1960.

WELCH, Henry John; Vice-President National Institute of Industrial Psychology; Past Chairman and Director of Malayalam Plantations Ltd., Lunuva (Ceylon) Tea and Rubber Estates Ltd., London, Asiatic Rubber and Produce Co. Ltd., and other Companies; Hon. Member of Council Rubber Growers' Assoc. Past Member of Ceylon Assoc. in London, South Indian Assoc. in London; *b.* London, 8 Feb. 1872; *s.* of A. and E. F. Welch; *m.* 1st, 1893, Laura Annie Tonkin (*d.* 1928); one *s.* (and one *s.* decd.); 2nd, 1939, Joyce Marjorie, *d.* of T. E. Hitchcock, Beckenham, Kent. *Educ.:* privately; Birkbeck College. Honourman, Solicitors' Final Examination; retired from active practice as Solicitor, 1917, to join firm as Director of Harrisons and Crosfield Ltd., Eastern Merchants; retired from business, 1924. *Publications:* Ten Years of Industrial Psychology (with Dr. C. S. Myers), 1932; Industrial Psychology in Practice (with Dr. G. H. Miles), 1932; Money, Foreign Trade and Exchange, 1934. *Address:* Blackdog Hill, Westmeston, Hassocks, Sussex. *T.:* Hassocks 586; 1-4 Great Tower Street, E.C.3. *T.A.:* c/o Harricros, London. *T.:* Mansion House 4333. [*Died* 28 *March* 1958.

WELCHMAN, Ven. William, M.A.; Archdeacon of Bristol, 1927-38, Archdeacon Emeritus since 1938; *b.* 1866; *s.* of late George Welchman, of Cullompton, Devon; *m.* 1902, Elizabeth Marshall (*d.* 1936), *d.* of late Rev. E. M. Griffith, B.A. Cambridge; one *s.* one *d.* *Educ.:* Queens' College and Ridley Hall, Cambridge. Curate of St. Paul's, Leamington, 1890-92; Missionary in Ceylon, 1892-99; Vicar of Fishponds, Bristol, 1901-7; Vicar of The Temple, Bristol, 1907-41; Rural Dean of Bedminster, 1920-27; Examining Chaplain to Lord Bishop of Bristol, 1921; Hon. Canon, Bristol Cathedral, 1915-27; Proctor in Convocation, 1919-24 and 1925-27; Chaplain Territorial Forces. *Address:* Widbrook House, Bradford-on-Avon, Wilts. [*Died* 7 *March* 1954.

WELD, Francis Joseph; *b.* 16 Oct. 1873; *s.* of Walter Weld (Leagram) and Frances Elizabeth, *d.* of Herman Walmesley, Gidlow, Wigan. *Educ.:* Stonyhurst. Solicitor, 1897; Knight of the Sovereign Order of Malta; Under-Sheriff for Cheshire, 1920-21 and 1923-24; Pres. Liverpool Law Society, 1925-26; Pres. Stonyhurst Assoc., 1930; J.P. County Borough of Southport; High Sheriff for Lancashire, 1942-43; Governor St. Francis Xavier's College, Liverpool, 1902-47. Pres. Southport Conservative Assoc. *Address:* 32 Weld Road, Birkdale, Lancs. *T.:* Southport 68246. *Clubs:* Boodle's, Bath; Athenæum (Liverpool); (Pres.) Conservative (Birkdale). [*Died* 30 *April* 1958.

WELD, Rt. Rev. George, C.B.E. 1954; S.J.; Titular Bishop of Mallo and Vicar Apostolic of British Guiana and Barbados, 1932-54; retired, 1954; *b.* 13 Sept. 1883; *s.* of Walter Weld, Leagram, and Frances, *d.* of Herman Walmesley, Gidlow Hall, Wigan. *Educ.:* Stonyhurst College; Oxford. Entered Society of Jesus, 1901; studied Philosophy at Stonyhurst, 1904-07; Lit. Hum. at Pope's Hall (now Campion Hall), Oxford, 1907-11; Hon. B.A., M.A.; taught Stonyhurst and Beaumont, 1911-14; studied Theology, St. Beuno's, N. Wales, 1914-18; ordained 1917; taught St. Francis Xavier, Liverpool, 1918-20; Stonyhurst, 1921-22; Principal, St. Stanislaus College, Georgetown, British Guiana, 1923-32; King's Jubilee Medal, 1935. *Address:* Brickdam Presbytery, Georgetown, British Guiana. [*Died* 2 *Feb.* 1959.

WELDON, Surgeon-Rear-Admiral (Samuel) Gerald, C.B.E. 1953; Q.H.P. 1956; Medical Officer in charge R.N. Hospital, Malta, Command Medical Officer, Mediterranean Station, and Medical Adviser to C.-in-C. Allied Forces, Mediterranean, since 1956; *b.* 3 Feb. 1900; *s.* of Samuel Baker Weldon, Linziestown House, Co. Wexford, Eire; *m.* 1931, Isabel Elizabeth, *d.* of Surgeon Capt. J. McA. Holmes, F.R.C.S., R.N.; one *s.* one *d.* *Educ.* St. Bees School; Trinity College, Dublin University (B.A.). M.B., B.Ch., B.A.O., 1922; D.P.H., 1923. Joined R.N., 1923; H.M.S. Marlborough, 1923, Mediterranean; R.N. Hosp. Plymouth, 1926; H.M.S. Veronica, 1928, N.Z. and Pacific; R.N. Hosp., Plymouth, 1931, Pathologist; Naval M.O.H., Mediterranean, 1934; R.N. Hosp., Haslar, 1937, Pathologist; H.M.S. Medway, 1939, Far East and Mediterranean; R.N. Hosp., Haslar, 1942, Medical Specialist; Naval M.O.H., Mediterranean, 1946; Naval M.O.H., Plymouth Command, 1949. *Recreations:* shooting, sailing, fishing. *Address:* Furzetor, Horrabridge, Devon. *T.:* Sampford Spiney 35. [*Died* 11 *Jan.* 1958.

WELDON, Thomas Dewar, M.C. and Bar 1918; Fellow and Tutor, Magdalen College, since 1923; *b.* 5 Dec. 1896; unmarried. *Educ.:* Tonbridge School; Magdalen College. Served European War, 1915-1918, R.F.A., France. Rhodes Travelling Fellow, 1930; University Lecturer in Philosophy; Temporary Civil Servant Air Ministry, 1940-42; Wing Comdr. R.A.F., H.Q. Bomber Command, 1942-44. *Publications:* Kant's "Critique of Pure Reason", 1945; States and Morals, 1946; The Vocabulary of Politics, 1953. *Address:* Magdalen College, Oxford. *T.:* Oxford 3151. *Club:* United University. [*Died* 13 *May* 1958.

WELLESLEY, Sir Victor (Alexander Augustus Henry), K.C.M.G., *cr.* 1926; C.B. 1919; *b.* 1 March 1876; *s.* of late Col. Hon. Frederick Wellesley; *m.* 1909, Alice Muriel (*d.* 1949), *e. d.* of O. Leslie Stephen; one *d.* Godson to Queen Victoria and Page of Honour, 1887-92; Clerk in the Foreign Office, 1899; Acting 2nd Secretary in the Diplomatic Service, 1905; attached to the Embassy at Rome, 1905-1906; Secretary to the British Delegates to the Labour Conference at Berne, 1906; Commercial Attaché, 1908; Assistant Clerk in the Foreign Office, 1910; Assistant Under-Secretary, 1924-1925; received the Coronation Medal and Silver Jubilee Medal; Senior Clerk, 1913; Controller of Commercial and Consular Affairs, 1916; Deputy Under-Secretary of State, Foreign Office, 1925-36; retired, 1936; has exhibited pictures at the Royal Acad., Roy. West of England Acad., R.O.I., R.B.A., and other exhibitions. *Publications:* (with Robert Sencourt) Conversations with Napoleon III, 1934; Diplomacy in Fetters, 1944; Recollections of a Soldier-Diplomat, 1947. *Address:* 12 Ranelagh Grove, Ebury Bridge, S.W.1. *T.:* Sloane 5084. *Club:* Royal Automobile. [*Died* 20 *Feb.* 1954.

WELLS; *see* Sanderson-Wells.

WELLS, Arthur Quinton, M.A., D.M., B.Ch. Oxon; Member of Scientific Staff, Medical Research Council, since 1937; *b.* 22 June 1896; 5th *s.* of Arthur Poulett Lethbridge and Anna Maria Wells; *m.* 1925, Rhona Margaret Alice, 2nd *d.* of James Francis and Lady Evelyn Mason; four *s.* one *d.* *Educ.:* Peterborough Lodge School; University College School; St. John's College, Oxford; St. Bartholomew's Hospital. Surgeon Sub-Lt., R.N.V.R., 1915-1918; General Medical Practice, Eyam, Derbyshire, 1923-25; Research Student, Dept. of Pathology, Univ. of Cambridge, 1926-30; Lecturer in Bacteriology and Asst. Bacteriologist, St. Bartholomew's Hosp., 1930-36; Cattlin Research Fellow, 1935-36; Pathologist, Bureau of Animal Population, Oxford, 1937-39; Emergency Public Health Laboratory Service, 1939-45. C.C., Oxon., 1938-45; Chairman: Oxford Regional Hosp. Bd., 1947-50; Public Health Cttee.; Trustee Nuffield Provincial Hosps. Trust, 1938-; Member: Committees of Medical Research Council and Agricultural Research Council. High Sheriff, Oxfordshire, 1953. *Publications:* many scientific papers in journals, mostly relating to tuberculosis. *Recreations:* collection and growing of alpine flora; shooting, golf. *Address:* Shipton Manor, Kidlington, Oxford. *T.:* Kidlington 2128. *Club:* United University. [*Died* 9 *Oct.* 1956.

WELLS, (Grant) Carveth, A.M.I.C.E., F.R.G.S.; F.A.G.S.; Author and Civil Engineer; *s.* of Thomas Grant Wells; *m.* Zetta Robart, Norfolk, Virginia, U.S.A.; one *s.* one *d.* *Educ.:* St. Paul's School; Central Technical College, London University. Survey Grand Trunk Pacific Railway, Canada; Assistant Professor Civil Engineering at Central Technical College, London University; Survey Federated Malay States Railway; spent 6 years in the Malayan jungle; Leader of expeditions to Lapland for American Museum of Natural History; to Ruwenzoir, Uganda, for Geographic Society of Chicago; to Caucasus Mountains and Mount Ararat also Mexico, Mount Popocatapetl, also Panama for Geographic Society of Chicago and Pakistan, Kashmir, Thailand; Formosa, for the American Museum of Natural History, 1955; producer of Travel Motion Picture Films; lectured extensively in America and England; Pioneer in Radio Broadcasting and Television. *Publications:* Field Engineers' Handbook; Six Years in the Malay Jungle; The Jungleman and his Animals; Let's do the Mediterranean; In Coldest Africa; Light on the Dark Continent; Adventure; Kapoot; Exploring the World; Bermuda in Three Colors; Panamexico; North of Singapore; Round the World with Bobby and Betty; Raff, the Jungle Bird; Introducing Africa; Raffles, the Bird who Thinks he's a Person; The Road to Shalimar. *Recreations:* photography, gardening. *Address:* Suite 206, 9533 Brighton Way, Beverly Hills, California, U.S.A.; Mandalay, Southampton, Bermuda. *Cable Address:* Suite 206, 9533 Brighton Way, Beverly Hills, California. *Clubs:* Explorers', Adventurers', Circumnavigators', Dutch Treat, Authors', National Arts (New York). [*Died* 16 *Feb.* 1957.

WELLS, Air Commodore Hardy Vesey, C.B.E. 1919; Royal Air Force, Medical Service, retd.; *b.* 1877; *s.* of late George Wells, J.P., Bedford; *m.* 1912, *o. d.* of late Major Philip Justice, Freshwater, I.W.; one *d.* *Educ.:* Bedford School; St. Mary's Hospital, London. Entered Royal Navy as Medical Officer, 1900; appointed to Naval Wing of R.F.C., 1912; qualified pilot, 1913; served European War; transferred to Royal Air Force on formation; P.M.O. British Forces, Iraq, 1924-26; P.M.O. Inland Area, 1927-32; Principal Medical Officer, Air Defence of Great Britain, 1932-34; K.H.P., 1925-34; retired list, 1934. *Publications:* contributions to medical journals. *Recreations:* tennis, golf. *Address:* 50 Leeson Road, Queen's Park, Bournemouth, Hants. [*Died* 30 *Dec.* 1956.

WELLS, Brig.-Gen. John Bayford, C.M.G. 1918; C.B.E. 1941; D.S.O. 1902; Col. of The Loyal Regiment (North Lancashire), 1931-45; *b.* 12 April 1881; *s.* of late Charles A. E. Wells, Heathfield, Albury, Guildford, Sy.; *m.* 1916, Arabella (*d.* 1950), *d.* of William Walter Wright; one *d.* (one *s.* killed in action, North Africa, 1943). *Educ.:* Westminster. Entered army, Loyal North Lancs Regiment, 1899; passed Staff College, Camberley, 1911; Colonel, 1919; served South Africa, 1899-1902 (despatches twice, Queen's and King's medals 6 clasps, D.S.O.); Adjutant, 1906-9; Staff Captain, War Office, 1912; served European War, 1914-18 (despatches twice, C.M.G., Bt. Major, Lt.-Col., and Col.); Colonel on Staff in charge of Administration, H.Q. British Troops in Egypt, Cairo, 1923-27; retired pay, 1929. *Address:* The Cedars, Nightingale Road, Guildford, Surrey. *T.:* Guildford 66442. [*Died* 6 *April* 1952.

WELLS, Madeline, R.B.A.; artist; *d.* of William Henn Holmes, I.C.S.; *m.* R. Douglas Wells, M.A. *Educ.:* Westminster and London Schools of Art. Brangwyn medal for composition at London School, 1908; Member Society of Mural Decorators and Painters in Tempera, Société Nationale des Beaux Arts, Paris, Society of Women Artists, retd. Exhibitor at R.A., R.O.I., R.I., International Society of Sculptors, Painters, and Gravers, Goupil Gallery, Salon, Ghent Exhibition of 1931, Canada, America, and many provincial galleries. *Principal Works:* decoration for Church of Saint Elizabeth, Marloes Road, Kensington, and for S. Mary's Hall, Putney, also the Pergola Builders, decoration purchased by Lady Hamilton; represented in Russell-Cotes Art Gallery, Bournemouth and Rotherham Art Gallery. *Recreations:*

reading and travelling. *Address:* 30 Palace Gardens Terrace, Kensington, W.8. [*Died 7 Dec.* 1959.

WELLS, Reginald F.; Sculptor; *b.* 1877; Member of Internat. Soc. of Sculptors, Painters, and Gravers; Designer of Col'drum and Soon pottery. *Recreations:* aeronautics and boat-building; architecture and building. *Address:* Roundabout, Pulborough, Sussex. [*Died July* 1951.

WELLS, Sir (Sydney) Richard, 1st Bt., *cr.* 1944; Kt., *cr.* 1938; D.L.; *b.* 1879; *m.* 1907, Mary Dorothy Maltby (*d.* 1956); four *s.* (and three killed in action) two *d.* *Educ.:* Bedford School. M.P. (U.) Bedford, 1922-45. Vice-Chairman, 1928-46, Chancellor, 1946-48, Primrose League; Chairman Brewers' Society, 1940-42. *Recreations:* yachting, shooting. *Heir:* *s.* Charles Maltby, Col. [*b.* 24 July 1908; *m.* 1935, Katherine Boulton, *d.* of F. B. Kenrick, Toronto; two *s.*]. *Address:* Felmersham Grange, Beds. *T.:* Sharnbrook 217. *Clubs:* Carlton, Constitutional, Royal Thames Yacht. [*Died* 26 *Nov.* 1956.

WELSH, Hon. Sir Allan Ross, Kt., *cr.* 1943; C.M.G. 1952; J.P.; Speaker of Legislative Assembly, Southern Rhodesia, 1935-52; *b.* 8 July 1875; *s.* of Alexander Robert Welsh; *m.* 1901, Maude Marianne Smit; three *d.* *Educ.:* Dale College, Kingwilliamstown, S. Africa. Attorney and Notary, Cape Colony, 1896; admitted as an Attorney in S. African Republic, 1897, and practised in Johannesburg until 1899; admitted Attorney, Notary and Conveyancer, Southern Rhodesia, 1899, and has practised in Bulawayo since then; M.P., S. Rhod. Parl. for Bulawayo North, 1927-39; previously partner in legal firm of Coghlan & Welsh with Sir Charles Coghlan; now partner with C. I. Jacobs, J. A. Stirling, and F. Walsh under same style of Coghlan & Welsh; elected Speaker, Legislative Assembly, Southern Rhodesia, 1935; re-elected as Speaker 1939, 1946 and 1948 without being M.P.; resigned owing to ill-health, March 1952. J.P. Bulawayo. Cross, Grand Commander of Royal Order of the Phœnix, 1950; Legion of Honour, France, 1953. *Address:* Grand Hotel, Bulawayo. [*Died* 6 *Sept.* 1957.

WELSH, James C.; *b.* 1880. M.P. (Lab.) Coatbridge, 1922-31, Bothwell Division of Lanarkshire, 1935-45; formerly an official of the Lanarkshire Miners' Association. *Publications:* The Underworld; Songs of a Miner; The King and the Miner; The Morlocks. *Address:* c/o Gilfillan, Douglas Water, Lanarkshire; c/o National Union of Mineworkers (Scottish Area), 5 Hillside Crescent, Edinburgh 7. [*Died* 4 *Nov.* 1954.

WEMYSS, General Sir Colville; *see* Wemyss, Gen. Sir H. C. B.

WEMYSS, Sir Francis; *see* Colchester-Wemyss.

WEMYSS, General Sir (Henry) Colville (Barclay), K.C.B., *cr.* 1945 (C.B. 1940); K.B.E., *cr.* 1941; D.S.O. 1914; M.C. 1916; late Roy. Corps of Signals; *b.* 26 April 1891; 2nd *s.* of late Alexander Wemyss; *m.* 1919, Vera, *y. d.* of late Alfred Mozley and Mrs. Russell, of Ridgmont, Bedfordshire; one *s.* one *d.* *Educ.:* Bedford; R.M.A., Woolwich. Entered Royal Engineers, 1910; Bt. Major, 1918; Major and Bt. Lt.-Col. 1926; Lt.-Col. 1933; Col. 1935; Maj.-Gen. 1939; Acting Lt.-Gen. 1940; Lt.-Gen. 1941; General, 1945; served European War, 1914-18 (despatches five times, D.S.O., M.C.); Assistant Adjutant-General, War Office, 1935-37; Imperial Defence College, 1938; Director of Mobilisation, War Office, 1939; Adjutant-General to the Forces, 1940-1941; Head of British Army Staff in Washington, 1941-42; Military Secretary to the Secretary of State for War, 1942-46; retired, 1946: Col. Comdt. Royal Corps of Signals, 1944-48. Director, Brewers' Society, 1947-1957. *Address:* Brook House, Warsash, Hants. *T.:* Locks Heath 2175. *Club:* United Service. [*Died* 2 *April* 1959.

WENGER, Adolph Henry Charles; J.P. for the City of Stoke-on-Trent; *b.* 1877; *s.* of Albert Francis Wenger, Newcastle-under-Lyme; *m.* 1902, Isabelle, *d.* of James Lovatt, J.P.; two *s.* two *d.* *Educ.:* Newcastle-under-Lyme High School; on the Continent. Managing Director of Wengers Ltd., Ceramic Colour and Chemical Manufacturers, Etruria, Stoke-on-Trent; Chairman of Keates Ltd., Manufacturing Stationers, Hanley; Vice-President of the North Staffordshire Chamber of Commerce; Pres. Trentham Branch Stoke South Conservative Assoc.; a Life Governor of North Staffordshire Royal Infirmary, 1936-48. High Sheriff for the County of Staffordshire, 1935-1936; served ten years on the Newcastle-under-Lyme Town Council; F.R.S.A. Vice-Pres. North Staffs Motor Club. *Recreations:* foxhunting and farming. *Address:* Trentham Priory, Stoke-on-Trent. *T.A.:* Wenger, Trentham. *T.:* Trentham 49063. *Club:* Royal Automobile. [*Died* 26 *July* 1954.

WENHAM, Edward Gordon; *b.* 1884; *m.* 1931, Eleanor Joyce (*d.* 1956), F.R.C.S., L.R.C.P., *d.* of late Leonard Partridge, Nymett Rowland, Devon; one *d.* *Educ.:* Ware; King's College, London. Served in S. African Constabulary; resided in U.S., 1907-31; Editor, The Antiquarian (New York), 1926-29; Editor, Arts and Decoration Quarterly (New York), 1929; Managing Editor, Arts and Decoration (New York), 1929; Editor, The Connoisseur, 1934-35; Contributor to numerous art and sporting journals, etc. *Publications:* The Collector's Guide to Furniture Design, 1928; Domestic Silver of Great Britain and Ireland, 1931; English Silver 1675-1825, 1937; Old Furniture in Modern Rooms, 1939; The Practical Book of American Silver, 1950; Old Silver in Modern Setting, 1949; Old Clocks for Modern Use, 1951; Antiques A to Z, 1954; Old Sheffield Plate—Its Romantic Discovery and Brief Existence, 1955. *Recreations:* golf, riding. *Address:* Lympstone, Devon. [*Died* 23 *July* 1956.

WENTWORTH, 16th Baroness, *cr.* 1529; **Judith Anne Dorothea Blunt-Lytton** (assumed surname of Blunt-Lytton by deed poll, 1904); *g.d.* of 1st Earl of Lovelace and *d.* of late Baroness Wentworth and late Wilfrid S. Blunt; *S.* mother, 1917; *m.* 1899, Hon. N. S. Lytton (who *S.* as 3rd Earl of Lytton, divorced 1923); one *s.* two *d.* *Publications:* Love in a Mist; Toy Dogs and their Ancestors; The Flame of Life; Thoroughbred Racing Stock and its Ancestors, 1939; War Nonsense, 1943 and 1944; Horses of Britain, 1944; The Authentic Arabian Horse and his Descendants, 1945; The World's Best Horse; The Swift Runner; Horses in the Making; Drift of the Storm, 1951; Passing Hours; Sport for the Million; contributor to the Veterinary Journal and several Encyclopædias. *Recreations:* world's lady tennis champion, riding, horse-breeding (owner of Crabbet Park Stud Farm, Burton Park Stud Farm, White Mountain Pony Stud Farm). *Heir:* *s.* 4th Earl of Lytton, O.B.E. *Address:* Crabbet Park, Poundhill, Sussex. *T.:* Poundhill 2122. *T.A.:* Wentworth, Poundhill, Sussex. [*Died* 8 *Aug.* 1957.

WENTWORTH, Capt. Bruce C. V.; *see* Vernon-Wentworth.

WENTWORTH-SHEILDS, Francis Ernest, O.B.E., M.I.C.E.; Docks Engineer, Southern Railway, retired; Past Pres., Inst. C.E.; *b.* 16 Nov. 1869; *s.* of F. W. Wentworth-Sheilds, M.Inst.C.E., and Adelaide Baker; *m.* 1906, Mary (*d.* 1956), *d.* of Rt. Rev. Bishop Boyd Carpenter, K.C.V.O., D.D.; no *c.* *Educ.:* St. Paul's School. Past President, Inst. Struct. E.;

George Stephenson Gold Medal, Inst. C.E., 1914; Vernon-Harcourt Lectures, 1921. *Publications:* Reinforced Concrete Piling (with W. S. Gray, B.A.I.); various technical papers in Proceedings of Inst. C.E. and technical journals. *Recreation:* golf. *Address:* Northlands Hotel, Northlands Road, Southampton. *T.:* 22871.
[*Died* 10 *May* 1959.

WENTWORTH-STANLEY, Charles Sidney Bowen, C.B.E. 1958; M.A.; *b.* 20 Jan. 1892; *o. s.* of late Maj. Sir Charles Wentworth-Stanley, D.L., J.P., M.A.; *m.* 1st, 1915, Edith Katherine Brocklebank, J.P. (*d.* 1948); three *s.* one *d.*; 2nd, 1951, Charlotte Catherine McBain. *Educ.:* Eton; Trinity College, Cambridge. Served European War, 1915-19, Captain 1/1 West Kent Yeo., Gallipoli, Palestine, France. E.I. Merchant Banker, Karachi and London, 1919-48; Hon. Sec. Lady Dufferin Hosp., Karachi, 1919-29; Chairman of Governors, Y.W.C.A. Central Club, London, 1933-48; Founder and Chairman Assoc. of Special Hosps., England and Wales, 1934-48; Member Rushcliffe Midwives Salaries Cttee., 1942-48; Member N.E. Metropolitan Regional Hosp. Bd., 1947- (Chm. Mental Health Cttee.); Member of Council, King Edward's Hospital Fund and Chairman Distribution Cttee. Mental Hospital Grants; Governor, The London Hospital; Member Hospital Management Cttees., Harperbury and Cell Barnes Hosps., Claybury Hosp.; Chm. Whipps Cross and Langthorne Hosp. Gp., 1952-58; Chm. Bow Hosp. Gp., 1958-; Vice-Chm. Whitley Medical Council; Chm. Appeal and Building Cttee., Roy. Coll. of Midwives; Chm. Hertford Div. Conservative Assoc., 1944-49; Dep. Pres. East Herts. Conservative Assoc., 1949-57; Vice-Pres. Royal College of Midwives; Vice-Pres. Herts. Boy Scouts Association. High Sheriff of Hertfordshire, 1947; Alderman, Herts. County Council, 1954. *Address:* High Wych Grange, Sawbridgeworth, Herts. *T.:* Sawbridgeworth 2374.
[*Died* 13 *Feb.* 1960.

WERNER, Professor E. A.; Professor of Applied Chemistry, Trinity College, Dublin University, retired. *Address:* 1 Fairfield Park, Highfield Road, Rathgar, Ireland.
[*Died* 18 *March* 1951.

WERNER, Edward Theodore Chalmers; H.B.M. Consul, Foochow (retired); Barrister-at-law; author; *b.* Dunedin, N.Z., 12 Nov. 1864; *s.* of late Joseph Werner and Harriet Taylor; *m.* 1911, Gladys Nina (*d.* 1922), 2nd, *d.* of Lt.-Col. C. W. Ravenshaw, Indian Army and British Resident, Nepal (retired). *Educ.:* Tonbridge School. Studied in London for China Consular Service, 1882-84; entered H.B.M. Consular Service, China, 1884; stationed at Peking, 1884-89; Canton, 1890-91; Tientsin, 1892-94; Macao, 1894-96; Hangchow, 1898-1899; Pagoda Anchorage, 1899-1900; Kiungchow, 1900-01; Kiungchow and Pakhoi jointly, 1901-04; Kongmoon, 1904; Kiukiang, 1905-09; Foochow, 1910-13; called to Bar, Middle Temple, 1905; was sent on a mission in H.M.S. Snipe to investigate and settle massacre of missionaries at Nanch'ang, 1905; Coronation medal, 1911; retired on a pension, 1914; Member Chinese Government Historiographical Bureau; President Chinese Historical Association. A life-long keen Individualist; an original member Individualist Club (now the Society of Individualists and League of Freedom). Returned to Peking, 1914-43, to study early Chinese Sociology; Prisoner of War in Japanese camp at Wei Hsion, 1943-45. F. R. Philharmonic Society London, 1947. *Publications:* Descriptive Sociology—Chinese (Pt. IX. of Herbert Spencer's series, Descriptive Sociology); Herbert Spencer and Bergson; The Great Wall of China; A Journey North and East of Peking [in 1887]; An Index to Consular and Marriage Fee Tables; China of the Chinese; Myths and Legends of China; Chinese Ditties; revision of Dyer Ball's Things Chinese (5th ed.); Autumn Leaves; A Dictionary of Chinese Mythology; The Mischief-working Metric System; Chinese Weapons; The Chinese Idea of the Second Self; The Origin of the Chinese Priesthood; A History of Chinese Civilization, Vol. I; Social Life in Ancient China; Memorigrams; More Memorigrams; Suggestion for an Alphabetical Chinese-English Dictionary, etc.; numerous essays and reviews and several vols. of translations. *Recreations:* formerly tennis, riding, rugger, skating; now motoring, walking. *Club:* Athenæum.
[*Died* 7 *Feb.* 1954.

WEST, Brigadier Alexander Henry Delap, D.S.O. 1917; late R.H.A.; *b.* Longford, Ireland, 27 Dec. 1877; *o. surv. s.* of late Rev. H. M. West, M.A.; *m.* 1915, Harriet Laura, *e. d.* of late Canon Edward Chichester and Hon. Mrs. Chichester, Dorking. *Educ.:* Haileybury College; Royal Military Academy, Woolwich. Entered Army, 1898; served South African Campaign, 1900-2 (severely wounded, despatches, King's and Queen's medals); European War, 1914-18 (despatches four times, D.S.O. and bar, Bt. Lt.-Col.); Commanded R.A. 53rd (Welsh) Division T.A., 1925-28; Brig. R.A., Eastern Command, India, 1928-32; retired pay, 1932; holds Royal Humane Society's silver medal. *Address:* Broomdown, Chieveley, Newbury, Berks. *Club:* Naval and Military.
[*Died* 10 *March* 1959.

WEST, Rev. Arthur George Bainbridge, M.A. Oxon and Adelaide; Master-Parson St. Dunstan's in the East, E.C. since 1908; Governor St. Dunstan's Educational Foundation; *b.* 28 Jan. 1864; *s.* of John West, Dunholme Lodge, Lincoln; *m.* 1893, Annie Elise Florence, *d.* of Col. Edwards, Ness Strange, Salop; two *s.* five *d.* *Educ.:* Grey Friars, Lincoln; Tonbridge School; New Coll., Oxford; Auckland Castle, Durham. Deacon, 1891; Priest, 1892; Curacy St. Mary's, South Shields; Curate, St. Paul's, West Hartlepool, 1893 Curate and Rector, St. Augustine's, Unley, South Australia, 1896-1905; Vicar, St. Thomas, Essendon, Victoria, and Rural Dean of Melbourne, 1905-8; Hon. Sec. Bishop of London's Evangelistic Council, Royal Naval Ports Church Building Fund; T.C.F. 1915-20; Hon. Chaplain, Royal Society of St. George, etc.; Commissary to Bishop of Wangaratta; Hon. Acting Treasurer, Fairbridge Farm Schools; Chairman Church Emigration Society. *Publications:* Articles in Treasury, Edinburgh Review, Nineteenth Century, Quarterly; Sermons, The Gospel of Joy and Strength; History, *a.* Parish of St. Dunstan in the East; *b.* History of Education in a City Parish; Memories of Brooke Foss Westcott; Memoir of Cecil Henry Boutflower, Bishop; Memoir of Rance Woodhouse. *Address:* St. Dunstan in the East, E.C.3; Mill House, Shorne, Kent. *T.:* Shorne 350.
[*Died* 29 *Jan.* 1952.

WEST, Cecil McLaren, M.C., M.B., B.Ch., B.A.O.; Sc.D.; Prof. of Anatomy, University College, Cardiff; *b.* Chorlton-cum-Hardy, Lancashire, 8 Feb. 1893; *s.* of Arthur Birt West; *m.* Lucy Mary, M.B., *d.* of late Charles Joly, F.R.S., Royal Astronomer of Ireland; one *s.* two *d.* *Educ.:* Blundell's School, Tiverton; Trinity College, Dublin. M.B. 1915; D.Sc. 1926; T.C.D.; Captain R.A.M.C. 1916 (M.C.); Senior House Surgeon, West Kent General Hospital, Maidstone, 1919-20; Chief Demonstrator of Anatomy, 1920-27, and University Anatomist, 1922-27, Trinity College, Dublin. *Publications:* contributions to medical journals, etc. *Address:* Department of Anatomy, University College, Cardiff. *T.:* 654.
[*Died* 23 *July* 1951.

WEST, Charles Ernest, F.R.C.S. Eng.; retired; Consultant Aural Surgeon to St. Bartholomew's Hospital. *Educ.:* University of Oxford; St. Bartholomew's Hospital. B.A. Oxon; M.R.C.S. Eng., L.R.C.P. Lond.,

1900; F.R.C.S. Eng., 1902. Formerly Head of Aural Department, St. Bartholomew's Hospital. Specialized in surgery of the labyrinth, meningitis, brain abscess, sinus thrombosis, and the treatment of malignant disease of the ear. *Publications:* (with Sydney Scott) Operations of Aural Surgery, 1908; etc. *Address:* Broadpark, Moor Lane, Budleigh Salterton, Devon. *T.:* 157.
[*Died* 1 *Jan.* 1951.

WEST, Sir Frederick Joseph, G.B.E., *cr.* 1947 (K.B.E., *cr.* 1943; C.B.E. 1920); Kt., *cr.* 1936; J.P., M.Inst.C.E., M.I.Mech.E.; LL.D.; Director of West's Gas Improvement Co. Ltd., Engineers, Miles Platting, Manchester. Past President: Institution of Gas Engineers; Society of British Gas Industries; Dock and Harbour Authorities Assoc.; Manchester Assoc. of Engineers; Manchester Engineering Employers' Association (twice Pres.); Manchester Engineering Council. Lord Mayor of Manchester, 1925. Formerly Hon. Col. Signals 42nd Div. Territorials (E. Lancs.). Hon. LL.D. (Manchester), 1955. *Address:* Albion Works, Miles Platting, Manchester. [*Died* 14 *Nov.* 1959.

WEST, Major G. F. M. C.; *see* Cornwallis-West.

WEST, Sir James Grey, Kt., *cr.* 1936; O.B.E. 1930; F.R.I.B.A. (retd.); *b.* Cardiff, 1885; *s.* of William Henry West; *m.* 1st, 1911, Margaret, *d.* of Thomas Wathen; one *s.* two *d.*; 2nd, 1934, Ivy, *d.* of Farrant Good. *Educ.:* High School, Cardiff. Entered H.M. Office of Works, 1904; Chief Architect, 1934-40. Retired from post of Chief Architectural Adviser, Ministry of Works, 1945. Designer of R.A.F. College, Cranwell; Royal Courts of Justice, Belfast; Ministry of Pensions Offices, Acton; Consulate General, Alexandria; the Catafalque at Westminster Hall for the lying-in-state of King George V.; annexe to Westminster Abbey for Coronation of King George VI. and Queen Elizabeth, etc. Member British Building Mission to U.S.A., 1943. *Recreation:* photography. *Address:* Rosewarne, Beer, Seaton, Devon. *T.:* Seaton 138. [*Died* 15 *June* 1951.

WEST, Sir Walter Wooll, Kt., *cr.* 1928; *b.* 1861; *m.* 1890, Sarah Grace (*d.* 1941), *d.* of Stephen Wright Hawks, Tynemouth; one *s.* one *d.*; *m.* 1945, Phyllis, *d.* of M. J. B. Driver, Tetbury. Sheriff of Cambridgeshire and Huntingdonshire, 1910; Chairman of County Council for six years; Custos Rotulorum for the Isle of Ely, 1935-50. *Address:* Little Needham, Wisbech. *T.:* 1575.
[*Died* 13 *Oct.* 1952.

WEST, William Frederick, C.I.E. 1946; *b.* 13 June 1882; *e. s.* of W. F. West; *m.* 1916, Elsie Williams, *d.* of Arthur Williams Gunnell; one *d.* *Educ.:* Latymer Upper School, Hammersmith. Appointed to India Office, 1900; Director General, India Store Department, 1941-43 and 1945-48. Governor of Latymer Upper School, Hammersmith, since 1923. *Recreation:* golf. *Address:* 35 Ashworth Mansions, W.9. *T.:* Cunningham 4177. [*Died* 18 *Aug.* 1954.

WEST-WATSON, Most Rev. Campbell West, C.M.G. 1952; *b.* 23 April 1877; *s.* of Adam West Watson, merchant, of Liverpool, and Caroline, *d.* of late Theophilus Campbell, Dean of Dromore; *m.* 1905, Emily Mabel Monsarrat (*d.* 1936); two *s.* three *d.* *Educ.:* Birkenhead School; Emmanuel Coll., Camb. (Scholar; 1st Class Div. 2 Class Tripos, 1899, B.A.; 1st Class Theol. Tripos, 1901; Carus Greek Test. Prize and Crosse Theological Scholarship; M.A. 1903; Hon. D.D. 1910). Ridley Hall, Camb., 1901; Ordained Deacon, 1902; Priest, 1903, Ely. Bursar and Lecturer of Ridley Hall, 1902-03; Fellow and Theological Lecturer of Emmanuel College, 1903-09; Chaplain, 1903-07; Dean, 1907-09; Examining Chaplain to Bishop of Carlisle, 1905-20; Junior Proctor, Cambridge University, 1907-08; Canon of Carlisle, 1909-21; Bishop Suffragan of Barrow-in-Furness, 1909-26; Archdeacon of Westmorland, 1915-1923; Archdeacon of Furness, 1923-26; Rector of Aldingham, Diocese of Carlisle, 1921-26; Proctor in Convocation, 1912-26; Bishop of Christchurch, N.Z., 1926-51; Primate and Archbishop of New Zealand, 1940-51; retd. 1951; T.C.F. 1918; Hon. C.F. 1919; Chaplain, Order of St. John (and Sub-Prelate) 1938. *Publications:* School Commentary on English Acts of Apostles, Revised Version, 1908. *Address:* Stoke, Nelson, New Zealand. [*Died* 19 *May* 1953.

WESTCAR, Lt. Col. Sir William V. L. P.; *see* Prescott-Westcar.

WESTERMAN, Percy F.; *b.* 1876. *Publications:* well over 150 boys' books, from A Lad of Grit, 1908; The Winning of the Golden Spurs, 1909 . . . to Standish Holds On, 1938; The Eagle's Talons, 1938; In Dangerous Waters, 1938; "Sea Scouts, Alert!", 1938; Standish Pulls It Off, 1939; At Grips with the Swastika, 1940; The War and Alan Carr, 1940; When the Allies Swept the Seas, 1940; Sea Scouts at Dunkirk, 1940; Fighting for Freedom, 1941; War Cargo, 1941; On Guard for England, 1941; Destroyer's Luck, 1942; Alan Carr in the Arctic, 1942; Sub-Lieutenant John Cloche, R.N.V.R., 1943; With the Commandos, 1943; Secret Convoy, 1943; Combined Operations, 1943; "Engage the Enemy Closely," 1944; Alan Carr in Command, 1944; "Operations Successfully Executed," 1944; One of the Many, 1945; By Luck and by Pluck, 1945; "Return to Base," 1945; Squadron Leader, 1946; Mystery of the Key, 1947; First Over, 1947; The Golden Gleaner, 1947; Contraband, 1948; Beyond the Burma Road, 1948; Missing, believed Lost, 1948; Sabarinda Island, 1949; The Mystery of Nix Hall, 1949; Desolation Island, 1949; Held to Ransom, 1950; Working Their Passage, 1950; The Isle of Mystery, 1950; Round the World in the Golden Gleaner; Sabotage!; Dangerous Cargo, 1951; The Missing Diplomat; Rolling Down to Rio, 1952; Bob Strickland's Log, 1953; A Midshipman of the Fleet, 1953; Lure of the Lagoon, 1954; Daventry's Quest, 1954; Sea Scouts: Alert!, 1954; Held in The Frozen North, 1955; Mystery of the Sempione, 1956, etc. Translations into French, Dutch, Danish, Norwegian, Swedish, Finnish, Polish and Hungarian. *Address:* Eastcote, Bestwall, Wareham, Dorset. [*Died* 22 *Feb.* 1959.

WESTERMANN, Diedrich H.; Professor of African Languages, University of Berlin, since 1920 (now Emeritus); Director of the Institut für Phonetik an der Universität, Berlin since 1934; Member of Deutsche Akademie der Wissenschaften since 1938; *b.* Baden (Hannover), 24 June 1875; *s.* of Johann Westermann and Christine Mindermann; *m.* 1905, Katharine Claus; one *s.* three *d.* *Educ.:* Basel; Tübingen. Missionary in West Africa, 1901-8; Lecturer in African Languages at the Seminar für Oriental-Sprachen, Berlin, since 1909; lately travelled extensively in Africa. *Publications:* Grammatik der Ewe-Sprache, 1906; The Shilluk People, 1912; Die Kpelle, ein Negerstamm in Liberia, 1921; Die westlichen Sudansprachen, 1927; Ewe-English Dictionary, 1928; (with I. C. Ward) Practical Phonetics for Students of African Languages, 1933, 2nd edn., 1948; The African To-Day, 1934 (also a French and a German edition); Die Glidyi-Ewe, Züge aus ihrem Gesellschaftsleben, 1935; Africa and Christianity, 1937; Afrikaner erzählen ihr Leben, 1938; The African To-day and To-morrow, 1939, 3rd edn., 1949; Völker-kunde von Afrika (with H. Baumann and R. Thurnwald), 1940; Die heutigen Naturvölker im Ausgleich mit der neuen Zeit (editor), 1940; Wörterbuch der Ewe-Sprache, 1954. *Address:* Baden/Bremen, Germany.
[*Died* 31 *May* 1956.

WESTERN, Rt. Rev. Frederick James, M.A.; *b.* 24 Feb. 1880; *s.* of E. Y.

Western, Solicitor, 35 Essex Street, Strand; *m.* 1934, Mabel Grace (*d.* 1935), *d.* of Rev. Walter New, Stathern, Melton Mowbray. *Educ.:* Windlesham House, Brighton; Marlborough College; Trinity College, Cambridge (Exhibitioner), Mathematical Tripos (Senior Optime), 1901. Joined Cambridge Mission, Delhi, 1904; Deacon and Priest, 1916; became Head of S.P.G. and Cambridge Mission, Delhi, 1918; Canon of Lahore Cathedral, 1923-29; Bishop of Tinnevelly, 1929-38. *Address:* 85 New Road, Ware, Herts. [*Died* 24 *Nov.* 1951.

WESTHOVEN, Joseph Charles, C.M.G. 1939; A.I.C.A.; *b.* Stanthorpe, Queensland, 14 April 1876; *s.* of Charles G. and Kate Westhoven, of Stanthorpe, Brisbane and Perth; *m.* 1910, Sarah Ann Cruice, *d.* of J. J. and R. V. Davies, Perth; one *d.* *Educ.:* Brisbane; Perth. Entered W.A. State Railway Service, Finance Branch, 1896; Auditor of Disbursements, 1910-12; transferred, 1912, to Commonwealth Public Service, P.M.G.'s Dept., Inspector of Accounts, Central Administration; Accountant, P.M.G.'s Dept., Victoria, 1915; Acting Chief Accountant, 1917-19; Accountant, P.M.G.'s Dept., New South Wales, 1923; Public Service Inspector, Central Administration Public Service Board, 1923-25; Deputy P.M.G. Victoria, 1925-31; Commonwealth Public Service Arbitrator, 1931-39; retired, 1939; Special Wartime Service: Member Commonwealth War Workers Housing Trust; Controller of Liquidations (surplus property) Ministry of Munitions; Chief Executive Officer, Office Accommodation, etc. for all Commonwealth Requirements; retired, 1947. Chm. Commonwealth Electoral Redistribution Commission, State of Victoria, 1930; Pres. Institute of Public Administration, Victorian Regional Group, 1931 and 1932; Chairman, Appeal for £50,000 St. Vincent's Hospital; Past Pres., Central Catholic Library; Chm. Aberfoyle Tin Mine, Tasmania; Chm. Western Titanium, Western Australia; Member Special Cttee. to advise Government on Parliamentary Salaries and Allowances, State of Victoria, 1954. *Recreations:* racing and literature. *Address:* 55 Studley Park Road, Kew, E.4, Victoria. *Clubs:* Victoria Racing; Mooney Valley Racing. [*Died* 9 *Dec.* 1957.

WESTLEY, Lieut.-Col. Joseph Harold Stops, C.M.G. 1919; D.S.O. 1916; D.L.; J.P.; late Green Howards; *b.* 10 Sep. 1882; *s.* of late S. Westley, Dunthorpe, Harrogate; *m.* 1913, Marion (*d.* 1953), *d.* of Charles Bennion, Thurnby Grange, nr. Leicester; one *d.* *Educ.:* Marlborough; R.M.C. Sandhurst. Served S. African War, 1902 (Queen's medal 4 clasps); European War, 1914-18 (despatches, D.S.O., C.M.G.). *Address:* Ryton Grove, Dorrington, Shropshire. [*Died* 22 *Dec.* 1959.

WESTMINSTER, 2nd Duke of (*cr.* 1874), **Hugh Richard Arthur Grosvenor;** Bt. 1662; G.C.V.O., *cr.* 1907; D.S.O. 1916; Commandeur de la Légion d'Honneur, 1934; Baron Grosvenor, 1761; Earl Grosvenor and Viscount Belgrave, 1764; Marquess of Westminster, 1831; late Personal Assistant to Controller of Mechanical Department, Ministry of Munitions; late 2nd Lieut. Royal Horse Guards; Major, Cheshire Yoemanry; *b.* 19 March 1879; *s.* of Victor Alexander, Earl Grosvenor, and Lady Sibell Mary Lumley (who married 2nd, 1887, late Rt. Hon. George Wyndham, and *d.* 1929); grandson of 1st Duke; *S.* grandfather, 1899; *m.* 1st, 1901, Constance Edwina, C.B.E., *y. d.* of late W. C. Cornwallis-West (marriage dissolved, 1919; she *m.* 2nd, 1920, Wing Commander James Fitzpatrick Lewis, late R.A.F.); two *d.* (one *s.* decd.); 2nd, 1920, Violet Mary Geraldine Rowley, *d.* of Sir William Nelson, 1st Bt. (marriage dissolved, 1926; she *m.* 2nd, 1927, Hon. Frederick H. Cripps); 3rd, 1930, Loelia Mary, *o. d.* of 1st Baron Sysonby (marriage dissolved, 1947); 4th, 1947, Anne, *o. d.* of Brig.-Gen. E. L. Sullivan. *Educ.:* Eton. Late A.D.C. to Viscount Milner; served S. Africa as A.D.C. to Lord Roberts, 1899-1900 (despatches, Queen's medal 5 clasps); European War, 1914-18; led successful attack of light armoured car battery against Senussi (despatches, D.S.O.). Owns about 30,000 acres in Cheshire and Flintshire, besides an estate in Scotland, and 600 acres in London. *Heir: cousin* William Grosvenor. *Address:* Bourdon House, Davies Street, W.1. *T.:* Mayfair 1616; Eaton Hall, Chester. *T.:* Chester 53. [*Died* 19 *July* 1953.

WESTON, George, J.P.; Auctioneer and Estate Agent; *b.* 9 March 1878; *y. s.* of John Wilsley Weston, late of Cranbrook, Kent; *m.* 1912, Agnes Maud (*née* Shaw); one *s.* two *d.* *Educ.:* Philological School (now St. Marylebone Grammar School). Joined brother W. R. Weston, auctioneer, in 1897; Associate of Auctioneer's Institute, 1906, Fellow, 1921; member Incorporated Association of Surveyors, 1929; Fellow Institute of Arbitrators. J.P. 1942; High Sheriff, County of Middlesex, 1949-50. *Recreation:* golfing. *Address:* 14 Cropthorne Court, Maida Vale. *T.:* Cunningham 6570. *Club:* United Wards. [*Died* 5 *Nov.* 1956.

WESTROPP, Col. John M.; *see* Massy-Westropp.

WESTWOOD, 1st Baron, *cr.* 1944, of Gosforth, **William Westwood,** O.B.E. 1920; J.P. Northumberland; F.R.S.A.; F.R.E.S.; Director of: Olympia Ltd.; Covent Garden Properties Ltd.; Investment Registry Ltd.; also Chairman and Director of several private and public companies; Chairman Mineral Development Cttee. under Min. of Fuel and Power, 1946; Chm. Newcastle Exec. Council under Nat. Health Service Act, 1946; Vice-Pres. Building Socs. Assoc.; *b.* Dundee, 28 Aug. 1880; *s.* of late William Westwood and Elizabeth Shaw; *m.* 1st, 1905, Margaret Taylor Young (*d.* 1916); three *s.* two *d.*; 2nd, 1918, Agnes Helen Flockhart Downie (*d.* 1952); no *c.* *Educ.:* Elementary School, Dundee. Started work in jute mills at ten years of age; served apprenticeship to shipbuilding at Dundee; Sec. Dundee Labour Representation Committee and Political Agent (Labour) for many years; Chm. of Scottish Labour Advisory Council, 1918-19; Supervisor of Shipconstructors' and Shipwrights' Assoc. 1913-29, General Secretary, 1929-45; Principal Labour Adviser to the Board of Admiralty, 1940, and Director of Contract Labour, Admiralty, 1941-42; Chief Industrial Adviser to Board of Admiralty, 1942-45; a Lord-in-Waiting to the King, 1945-47. Member of Northumberland County Council, 1937-46; contested Perth (Lab.), 1922, Sutton Division of Plymouth, (Lab.) 1929; President of Engineering and Shipbuilding Trades Federation, 1933-36; President of Confederation of Shipbuilding and Engineering Unions, 1936-39; Liveryman and Freeman of Worshipful Company of Shipwrights; Freeman of City of London, 1942. *Heir: s.* Hon. William Westwood, *b.* 25 Dec. 1907. *Address:* 7 Kensington Terrace, Newcastle on Tyne 2. *T.:* Gosforth 52455. *Clubs:* Royal Automobile, City Livery, Albany. [*Died* 13 *Sept.* 1953.

WETHERED, Brigadier Herbert Lawrence, C.M.G. 1919; D.S.O. 1917; R.A.O.C.; *b.* 10 Nov. 1877; *s.* of late Rev. F. T. Wethered, Vicar of Hurley; *m.* 1907, Eileen (*d.* 1945), *e. d.* of Col. Dominick Browne, D.L., Co. Mayo; one *s.*; *m.* 1948, Dorothy Phyllis, *o. c.* of late Sir Henry Moncrieff Smith, C.I.E. S. African War, 1899-1902, on staff (Queen's medal with four clasps, King's medal with two clasps); European War, 1914-19 (despatches, D.S.O., C.M.G.); Assistant Director of Ordnance Services, War Office, 1930-31; Inspector of Army Ordnance Services, War Office, 1932; retired pay. 1934. *Address:* Winterstoke, Fleet, Hants. [*Died* 2 *Jan.* 1953.

WETHERED, Vernon; Member New English Art Club; Director of public companies, retired; *b.* Clifton, Bristol, 13 April 1865; *m.* 1896, Mary Geraldine Dingwall; one *s.* two *d.* *Educ.:* Clifton College (Head of School); Oriel College, Oxford (Scholar). Trained for the Law; studied Art at Slade School under Prof. Brown; after marriage retired to country for twelve years to paint landscape. *Address:* 2 Kidderpore Gardens, Hampstead, N.W.3. [*Died* 6 *June* 1952.

WETHERELL, Colonel Robert May, C.M.G. 1918; Duke of Cornwall's L.I.; *b.* 1874; 2nd *s.* of Colonel R. W. M. Wetherell; *m.* 1897, Eileen Mary (*d.* 1948), *d.* of J. Macdonough, M.D.; one *s.* two *d.* *Educ.:* Cheltenham College. Served South African War, 1899-1902; European War, 1914-18; A.A.G., Egypt, 1924-27; Officer in charge of Record Office, Exeter, 1927-31; retired pay, 1931. *Address:* Malvern House, Thame, Oxon. [*Died* 21 *Feb.* 1960.

WETHERILL, Henry Buswell, C.I.E. 1931; M.A.; *b.* 21 Nov. 1876; *s.* of late J. E. Wetherill, Worthing, Sussex; *m.* Rhoda, *o. d.* of late F. W. Hindley, Bushey, Herts; one *s.* one *d.* *Educ.:* King's College, Taunton; St. John's College, Oxford. Entered Indian Educational Service, 1913; Head Master, Govt. High School, Allahabad, 1914-16; Inspector of Schools, Fyzabad, 1916-20; Bareilly, 1921-26; Lucknow, 1926-31; retired, 1931. *Publications:* The World and its Discovery; several educational works. *Recreations:* gardening, wood-carving. *Address:* 3 Woodlands Road, Surbiton, Surrey. [*Died* 13 *Oct.* 1959.

WHARNCLIFFE, 3rd Earl of (*cr.* 1876), **Archibald Ralph Montagu-Stuart-Wortley-Mackenzie;** Viscount Carlton, 1876; Baron Wharncliffe, 1826; *b.* 17 April 1892; *e. s.* of 2nd Earl and Ellen (*d.* 1922), 2nd *d.* of late Lieut.-Gen. Sir T. L. Gallwey, R.E.; *S.* father, 1926; *m.* 1918, Lady Elfrida Wentworth Fitzwilliam, *d.* of 7th Earl Fitzwilliam; one *s.* four *d.* *Educ.:* Eton. Late Capt. 2nd Life Guards; was A.D.C. to Viscount Buxton, Governor-General, South Africa whilst invalided from France, 1915. *Heir: s.* Viscount Carlton, *Address: T.A.:* Carlton House, Wortley, Sheffield. Wortley, Sheffield. *T.:* Stocksbridge 2157. *Club:* St. James'. [*Died* 16 *May* 1953.

WHAYMAN, Engineer Rear-Admiral William Matthias, C.B. 1924; C.B.E. 1919; retired Naval Engineer Officer; Director Alfol Insulation, Ltd.; *b.* 13 Aug. 1871; *s.* of George and O. H. Whayman, Rainham, Kent; *m.* 1902, Bertha (*d.* 1950), *d.* of William Acworth, Gravesend, Kent; one *s.* one *d.* *Educ.:* Sir Joseph Williamson's Mathematical School, Rochester. Engineer student at R.N. College, Devonport, 1886-91; advanced engineering course R.N. College, Greenwich, 1891-94; various ships and shore appointments at Admiralty and Dockyard till beginning of War; H.M.S. St. Vincent, 1914-1915; First Assistant to Engineer Manager, H.M. Dockyard, Chatham, 1915-17; Chief Engineer, H.M. Dockyard, Pembroke Dock, 1917-18; Engineer Manager H.M. Dockyard, Rosyth, 1918-20; Assistant Engineer-in-Chief, Admiralty, 1920-22; Deputy Engineer-in-Chief, Admiralty, 1922-27; Marine Engineer with Babcock and Wilcox, 1927-35. *Address:* 26 Colebrook Close, West Hill, Putney, S.W.15. *T.:* Putney 6384. [*Died* 21 *March* 1955.

WHEATLEY, Frederick William, C.B.E. 1932; B.Sc. (Oxon.); B.A., D.Sc. (Adelaide); Associate in Metallurgy, S. Australian School of Mines, retd.; late Sec. Roy. Empire Soc.; *b.* Kapunda, South Australia, 7 June 1871; *e. s.* of James E. Wheatley, Lewes, Sussex; *m.* Alice Ruth, *d.* of Charles Kimber, Clare, South Australia; one *s.* one *d.* *Educ.:* Prince Alfred College and University, Adelaide; Lincoln College, Oxford. Second Master, Way College, Adelaide, 1890-1901; Mathematical Master, Prince Alfred College, Adelaide, 1901-4; Second Master, King's College, Goulburn, 1905; Head Master, Rockhampton Grammar School, Queensland, 1906-12; engaged in research work on Ionization of Gases with Professor Townsend at Oxford, 1912-14; Senior Naval Instructor, 1914-19, and Head Master, 1920-31, Royal Australian Naval College, Jervis Bay; seconded to Intelligence Branch of the War Staff at Navy Office, Melbourne, 1914-15. *Publications:* Papers on the Ionization of Gases in the Philosophical Magazine. *Recreations:* tennis and golf. *Address:* 11 Wollombi Road, Avalon Beach, N.S.W., Australia. [*Died* 14 *Nov.* 1955.

WHEATLEY, John, A.R.A. 1945; R.W.S. 1947 (A.R.W.S. 1943); painter and engraver; *b.* Abergavenny, 1892; *o. s.* of Sir Zacariah Wheatley; *m.* Edith Grace (Grace Wheatley, R.P., R.W.S.), 4th *d.* of James Wolfe; one *d.* *Educ.:* studied under Stanhope Forbes, R.A., Walter Sickert, and at The Slade. Assistant Teacher of The Slade, 1920-25; Michaelis Professor of Fine Art, University of Cape Town, South Africa, 1925-37; Director and Trustee of National Gallery of S. Africa; Director of Sheffield Art Galleries, 1938-47; Mem. Roy. Fine Art Commn., 1946-52; Works in British Museum, Tate Gallery, Manchester Art Gallery, National Gallery of Wales, National Gallery of S. Africa. *Address:* Heathfield House, Windmill Road, Wimbledon Parkside, S.W.19. *Clubs:* Arts, Athenæum. [*Died* 17 *Nov.* 1955.

WHEATLEY, Brig.-Gen. Leonard Lane, C.M.G. 1918; D.S.O. 1898; late Argyll and Sutherland Highlanders; Honourable Corps of Gentlemen-at-Arms, 1926-52; *b.* 18 June 1876; *e. s.* of late Lieut.-Col. Charles R. E. Wheatley, R.A.; *m.* 1917, Esther, *e. d.* of Charles Fairbairn, Banongill, Australia; one *s.* one *d.* *Educ.:* Wellington College; Royal Military College, Sandhurst. Entered Army, 1896; Captain, 1905; Major, 1915; Bt. Lt.-Col. 1917; Brigade Commander, 1918; retired 1920; served on N.W. Frontier of India (defence of Chakdarra Fort, despatches, D.S.O.); Malakand Field Force (medal and 2 clasps); Mahsud Waziri Blockade, 1901-2 (despatches, clasp); N.W. Frontier of India, 1908 (medal and clasp); A.D.C. to Governor of Victoria, 1911-13; Instructor at Royal Military College, Sandhurst, 1913-14; European War, 1914-18 (despatches 5 times, Bt. Lt.-Col., C.M.G., bar to D.S.O., Croix de Guerre); Military Secretary to Governor-General of Australia, 1920-1921; Board of Governors United Westminster Schools, 1928; Territorial Army Assoc., Kent, 1933-47; War Department Constabulary, 1939-46. J.P., Kent. *Address:* Chart Place, Sutton Valence, Kent. *T.:* Sutton Valence 2236. *Clubs:* Naval and Military, M.C.C. [*Died* 7 *June* 1954.

WHEATLEY, Robert Albert, M.A., B.C.L.; Solicitor; Commissioner for Oaths; D.L. County of Pembroke; J.P. Haverfordwest; *b.* 27 March 1873; *s.* of Joseph Larke Wheatley and Maria Young; *m.* 1940, Catherine Gwenllian, *d.* of William Andrew, Swansea; one *s.* one *d.* *Educ.:* Rugby; Exeter College, Oxford. Deputy Clerk of the Peace, Cardiff, 1896-98; Deputy Clerk of the Peace and Deputy Town Clerk, Burnley, 1898-1901; Assistant Solicitor to Swansea County Borough Council, and Deputy Clerk of the Peace, 1901-05; Assistant Clerk of the Peace of the County Council of Durham, 1905-06; Deputy Clerk of the Peace and of Durham County Council, 1906-11; Clerk of the Peace for County of Pembroke, Clerk of Pembrokeshire County Council, 1911-39; Clerk of Pembrokeshire Insurance Committee, 1912-39; Clerk of Pembrokeshire Assessment Committee, 1919-39; High Sheriff of Pembrokeshire, 1940-41; Clerk of the Peace Haverfordwest, 1913-39. *Recreations:* yachting, shooting, and fishing. *Address:* Highclere, Crowhill, Haverfordwest, Pembs. *T.:* Haverfordwest 159. *Club:* Pembrokeshire County (Haverfordwest). [*Died* 6 *May* 1954.

WHEELDON, William Edwin; M.P. (Lab. and Co-op.) Small Heath Div. of Birmingham since Nov. 1952; *b.* 1898; *s.* of William Wakefield Wheeldon; *m.* 1922, Annie, *d.* of Robert Davies, Crewe. *Educ.:* Elementary Schools. Member of Birmingham City Council, 1927; Alderman, 1945-53; Chairman Finance Committee, 1946-49, 1952-53. *Address:* House of Commons, S.W.1; 83 Aubrey Road, Small Heath, Birmingham 10. [*Died* 7 *Oct.* 1960.

WHEELWRIGHT, Charles Apthorpe, C.M.G. 1901; Magistrate of Malabatini, Zululand; *b.* 1 Oct. 1873; *s.* of William Douglas Wheelwright. *Educ.:* Pietermaritzburg College. Clerk and Interpreter, Eshowe Magistracy, 1890; Lower Umfolozi, 1892; in Resident Commissioner's and Chief Magistrate's department, 1894; Registrar and Master, Chief Magistrate's and High Court of Zululand, 1894; Magistrate, Ingwavuma district, 1897; Malabatini, 1898. *Club:* Victoria (Pietermaritzburg). [*Died* 6 *Sept.* 1954.

WHEELWRIGHT, Rowland, R.B.A.; *b.* Ipswich, Queensland, Australia, 1870; *m.* 1908, Janie, *d.* of Stair Stewart. *Educ.:* Tonbridge Grammar School. Working as an Artist at Bushey, Herts. *Recreations:* tennis, etc. *Address:* Meadowbrook, Chiltern Avenue, Bushey, Herts. *T.:* Bushey Heath 45. [*Died* 20 *May* 1955.

WHELAN, Leo, R.H.A. 1923 (A.R.H.A. 1920), F.R.S.A.; *b.* Dublin 1892, of Irish parents from Co. Kerry. *Educ.:* Belvedere College, Dublin. Studied Art under Sir William Orpen, R.A., at the Metropolitan School of Art, Dublin; won the Taylor Art Scholarship, Royal Dublin Society, 1916. Exhibited R.A., Roy. Soc. of Portrait Painters, R.I. Gallery; portraits in Royal Institution of Surveyors, London; Nat. Gallery of Ireland; Municipal Gall. of Modern Art, Dublin; Royal Dublin Society; Trinity Coll., Dublin; Nat. University of Ireland; Alexandra Coll., Dublin; St. Columba's, Dublin, etc. *Address:* 65 Eccles Street, Dublin. *T.:* Dublin 76928; Studio 7 Lower Baggot Street, Dublin. *T.:* 61257. *Clubs:* Chelsea Arts; Stephens Green, United Arts (Dublin). [*Died* 6 *Nov.* 1956.

WHELDON, Professor Robert William, D.Sc. (Durham), F.R.S.E.; Professor of Agriculture and Rural Economy and Dean of Agriculture, King's College, University of Durham, since 1947; *b.* 17 Jan. 1893; *m.* 1920, Edith Marjorie, *d.* of Peter Grant Tulloh; three *s.* *Educ.:* Rutherford College, Newcastle on Tyne; Armstrong College, Univ. of Durham. Lecturer, Armstrong Coll., 1915; Prof. of Agriculture, King's Coll., Univ. of Durham, 1943. Farmer and Breeder of Jersey cattle; President English Jersey Cattle Soc., 1945; Member Durham Agricultural Exec. Cttee.; Hill Sheep Farming Cttee. for England and Wales, 1941-44. *Publications:* bulletins, reports and papers dealing with agricultural subjects. *Address:* Middle Herrington, Co. Durham. *T.:* East Herrington 2265. [*Died* 15 *Jan.* 1954.

WHEWELL, Herbert, R.I., R.C.A.; landscape painter; *b.* Bolton, Lancashire, 1863; *s.* of Henry Whewell; unmarried. *Educ.:* Bolton Grammar School. Entered on a business career with his father, which lasted until the latter's death, 1899; exhibits at some of the principal exhibitions, including the Royal Academy, and Royal Institute of Painters in Water Colours. *Address:* Southbrook Copse, Gomshall, Surrey. *T.:* Shere 119. *Club:* Arts. [*Died* 20 *Oct.* 1951.

WHIDDEN, Howard Primrose, B.A., D.D., LL.D., D.C.L.; F.R.S.C. 1934; *b.* Antigonish, N.S., 12 July 1871; *s.* of Charles Blanchard Whidden and Eunice Graham, both Canadians; *m.* 1894, Katherine Louise, *d.* of James H. Ganong, manufacturer, St. Stephen, N.B.; five *s.* one *d.* *Educ.:* Acadia and McMaster Universities; post-graduate at University of Chicago. A Baptist Clergyman; Home Mission Pastorate, Morden, Manitoba, 1894-96; Pastorate in Galt, Ontario, 1897-1900; Lecturer in McMaster University, 1898-1900; Professor in Brandon College, 1900-3; Pastor, First Baptist Church, Dayton, Ohio, 1904-12; President, Brandon College, 1912-23; Chancellor, McMaster University, Hamilton, Ontario, 1923-41; elected (U.) to House of Commons for Brandon, Manitoba, 1917. Retired. *Address:* 95 Snowdon Ave., Toronto 12, Ontario, Canada. [*Died* 30 *March* 1952.

WHILLIS, Professor James; Professor of Anatomy, University of London, Guy's Hospital Medical School, since 1948; *b.* 8 Sept. 1900; *s.* of C. Whillis, Newcastle on Tyne; *m.* 1926, Dorothy Margaret Lee; one *s.* *Educ.:* Carlisle Grammar School; University of Durham. M.B., B.S. Durham, 1922, with 1st Cl. Hons.; M.D., M.S. Durham; F.R.C.S. Demonstrator and Lecturer in Anatomy Univ. of Durham, 1922-35; Univ. Reader in Anatomy, Guy's Hosp., 1935-48. Chairman of Council of Chartered Society of Physiotherapy, 1950-54. *Publications:* Elementary Anatomy and Physiology, 1938 and 1944; co-Editor (with Prof. T. B. Johnston) Gray's Anatomy, 28th, 29th, and 30th edns.; (with Prof. Lucas Keene) Anatomy for Dental Students, 1950; papers in Lancet, Journal of Anatomy and Guy's Hosp. Reports. *Recreation:* golf. *Address:* Guy's Hospital, London Bridge, S.E.1; St. Denis, Seal, Sevenoaks. *T.:* Sevenoaks 61324. *Club:* Savage. [*Died* 27 *Jan.* 1955.

WHIPPLE, Robert Stewart; retired; *b.* 1 Aug. 1871; *e. s.* of G. M. Whipple, Superintendent of the Kew Observatory; *m.* 1903, Helen, *d.* of Allan Muir; one *s.* one *d.* (and one *d.* decd.). *Educ.:* King's College School, London. Asst., Kew Observatory, 1888; Asst.-Manager to L. P. Casella, 1896; Manager and Sec., 1898, Jt. Manager-Director, 1909-35, Chm., 1939-49, Cambridge Instrument Co. President: Scientific Instrument Manufacturers' Assoc., 1926-28, 1932-37; Optical Soc., 1920-22; Treas. Physical Soc., 1925-35; Pres., Section A British Assoc., Dundee, 1939; Bd. of Inst. of Physics for 21 years; Pres. Highgate Literary and Scientific Inst., 1938-. Presented collection of historic scientific instruments and books to Cambridge University, 1944, forming nucleus of Whipple Museum of the History of Science (inaugurated 1951). *Publications:* several papers on design and use of scientific instruments and also on old Instrument Makers. *Address:* 6 The Old Hall, Highgate, N.6. *T.:* Mountview 3540. *Club:* Athenæum. [*Died* 13 *Dec.* 1953.

WHISKARD, Sir Geoffrey (Granville), K.C.B., *cr.* 1943 (C.B. 1923); K.C.M.G., *cr.* 1933 (C.M.G. 1931); M.A., Oxford; Doctor of Laws (Hon.), Melbourne; A.R.I.B.A. (Hon.); *b.* 1886; *o. s.* of late Ernest Whiskard of Mildenhall, Suffolk; *m.* 1st, 1915, Cynthia Salome Caroline (*d.* 1940), *y. d.* of Edmund Whitelock Reeves; one *s.* one *d*; 2nd, 1946, Eileen Margaret, *d.* of late E. W. Voelcker. *Educ.:* St. Paul's School; Wadham College, Oxford (Hon. Fellow, 1935); First Class Mods. 1907; First Class Lit. Hum. 1909. Entered Home Office, 1911; Assistant Secretary, Chief Secretary's Office, Dublin Castle, 1920-1922: Colonial Office, 1922-25; Dominions Office, 1925-29; Assistant Under-Secretary of State, Dominions Office, S.W.1., 1930-35; High Commissioner for United Kingdom in Commonwealth of Australia, 1936-41; Permanent Secretary: Ministry of Works and Buildings (subs. Ministry of Works and Planning), 1941-43; Ministry of Town and

Country Planning, 1943-46. *Address:* Mildenhall, Suffolk. *T.:* Mildenhall 2288. [*Died* 19 *May* 1957.

WHITAKER, Major George Cecil; retired Major Guards M.G. Regiment; Captain (retired) Coldstream Guards; *b.* Lymington, Hants, Oct. 1880; *s.* of William Ingham Whitaker and Margaret, *d.* of Admiral Sir George Sartorius, G.C.B.; *m.* 1912, Margaret Maitland (O.B.E. 1946); one *s.* three *d.* *Educ.:* Eton; Trinity College, Oxford. Entered Coldstream Guards, 1902; served till 1906; then on Reserve of Officers till 1916, when rejoined Coldstream Guards from Sussex Yeomanry, and proceeded to France; seconded to Guards Machine-Gun Regt. 1917; J.P. Oxford County; Sheriff of Oxfordshire, 1941. *Recreations:* big-game shooting, yachting. *Address:* Britwell House, near Watlington, Oxon. *T.:* Watlington 14. *Clubs:* Carlton; Royal Yacht Squadron. [*Died* 31 *Aug.* 1959.

WHITAKER, Major-General Sir John Albert Charles, 2nd Bt., *cr.* 1936; C.B. 1944; C.B.E. 1942; *b.* 5 March 1897; *s.* of Sir Albert E. Whitaker, 1st Bt., and Eileen (*d.* 1947), M.B.E., *d.* of Col. J. Croker; *S.* father, 1945; *m.* 1923, Pamela (*d.* 1945), *d.* of late H. G. Snowden; three *s.* *Educ.:* Eton; R.M.C., Sandhurst. Joined Coldstream Guards, May 1915; wounded, 1916; commanded 3rd Bn. Coldstream Guards, 1936-38; commanded Coldstream Guards, 1938-39; commanded 7th Guards Brigade, France and Belgium, 1939-40; Brigadier General Staff, 1940-42; Director of Military Training, War Office, 1942-45; retired pay, 1946. High Sheriff of Notts, 1950-51; Lord High Steward of Retford, 1952. *Heir:* *s.* Captain James Herbert Ingham [*b.* 27 July 1925; *m.* 1948, Marybeth, *widow* of Capt. David Urling Clark, M.C., and *d.* of Ernest Johnston, Cockshut, Reigate; one *s.* one *d.*]. *Address:* Babworth Hall, Retford, Notts; Auchnafree, Dunkeld. *Club:* Guards. [*Died* 5 *Oct.* 1957.

WHITBY, Sir Lionel Ernest Howard, Kt., *cr.* 1945; C.V.O. 1929; T.D.; Regius Professor of Physic at Cambridge University since 1945, Master of Downing College since 1947; Hon. Physician Addenbrooke's Hospital; Emeritus Lecturer in Bacteriology, The Middlesex Hospital; Consultant in Haematology to the Army and Ministry of Supply; Chairman R.A.F. Educational Advisory Committee; *b.* 1895; 2nd *s.* of late Benjamin and Jane Elizabeth Whitby, Yeovil, Somerset; *m.* 1922, Ethel Whitby, M.A. (Cantab.), M.R.C.S., L.R.C.P., 2nd *d.* of late James Murgatroyd, Carr Wood House, Shelf, Yorks; three *s.* one *d.* *Educ.:* Bromsgrove School; Downing College, Cambridge (sen. open scholar); The Middlesex Hospital (Freeman Scholar and Leopold Hudson prizeman, Hetley Clinical prizeman, M.R.C.S., L.R.C.P.). Served European War, 1914-18; Maj. Royal West Kent Regt. (M.C.); M.B., B.Ch. 1923; D.P.H. 1924; M.A. and M.D. (Camb.) 1927; M.R.C.P. 1927; F.R.C.P. 1933; Hon. D.Sc. Toronto; Hon. LL.D., Glasgow; Hon. M.D. Louvain, 1956; Hon. Fellow Lincoln College, Oxford. F.R.S.M.; Member Assoc. Physicians Great Britain and Ireland; Bradshaw Lectr., R.C.P., 1938; Harben Lecturer, 1948; Thomas Huxley Memorial Lectr, 1954. Thomas Addison Lectr., 1955; Arthur Sims Travelling Professor, Australia and New Zealand, 1956; John Hunter Medallist R.C.S., 1939; Gold Medallist, R.S.M., 1945; Gold Medal Society of Apothecaries, 1948; Visiting Professor of Medicine, Cutter Lectr., Harvard Univ., 1946; Visiting Prof., State Univ. of New York, 1955; President: B.M.A. 1948; Internat. Soc. of Hæmatology, 1950; Assoc. Clinical Pathologists, 1951. Vice-Chancellor, Univ. of Cambridge, 1951-53. Hon. member: New York Academy Medicine, Assoc. Amer. Physicians, Amer. Soc. Clinical Pathologists, Med. Society of Nova Scotia, Med. Society of Finland, Med. Soc. of Turkey. Late Bacteriologist, Middlesex Hosp., late Pathologist, Hampstead Hospital for Children. Served War of 1939-45; Brigadier R.A.M.C. (T.A.), late O/C Army Blood Transfusion Service, and Consulting Physician in Blood Transfusion to the Army. Commander American Legion of Merit. Chevalier Légion d'Honneur. *Publications:* The Laboratory in Surgical Practice (with E. C. Dodds), 1931; Medical Bacteriology, 5th edition, 1950; The Nurse's Handbook of Hygiene, 8th edition, 1944; Disorders of the Blood, 8th edition, 1957; contributions to medical literature on haematological and bacteriological subjects. *Recreations:* gardening, fishing, philately. *Address:* The Master's Lodge, Downing College, Cambridge. *T.:* Cambridge 56338. *Club:* Athenæum. [*Died* 24 *Nov.* 1956.

WHITE, Charles Frederick, C.B.E. 1951; J.P.; C.A., Derbyshire; *b.* 23 Jan. 1891; *s.* of Charles Frederick and Alice White; *m.* 1915, Alice, *d.* of George Harrison and Rose Moore; no *c.* *Educ.:* Cromford Elementary School; Wirksworth Grammar School. Carpenters' apprentice until 19 years of age. Since held political appointments in many parts of the country. Held positions on local authorities since 1911, including membership of Derbyshire County Council since 1928; Chairman Derbyshire C.C., 1946. M.P. (Ind. Lab.), 1944-45, (Lab.), 1945-50, for West Derbyshire. *Address:* Tansley House, Tansley, Matlock, Derbys. *T.A.* and *T.:* Matlock 521. [*Died* 27 *Nov.* 1956.

WHITE, Major Charles J. B.; *see* Brooman-White.

WHITE, Claude G.; *see* Grahame-White.

WHITE, Clifford, M.D., B.S., F.R.C.P., F.R.C.S., F.R.C.O.G.; Consulting Obstetrical Surgeon, University College Hospital; Surgeon, Samaritan Hospital for Women; Lecturer, University College Hospital Medical School; *b.* 1881; 2nd *s.* of late Charles Stewart White, Hampstead; *m.* 1911, Elaine, *o. d.* of late Francis Walford Mawe, Charterstowers, Queensland; one *s.* one *d.* *Educ.:* University College. Graduated, 1904; Obstetrical Registrar, University College Hospital, 1910-12; Surgeon, Queen Charlotte's Hospital, 1912-23; Surgeon, Belgian Army, 1914-15, (medal); Examiner to the Universities of Cambridge, London, Liverpool, Durham, Cairo and Alexandria, and to the Royal College of Physicians and Surgeons; Past President, Obstetrical and Gynæcological section of Royal Society of Medicine; Consulting Surgeon, Metropolitan Hospital and St. Mary's Hospital for Women; Fellow of University College; Councillor Royal College of Physicians. *Publications:* Various papers and articles in professional journals and text-books. *Recreations:* foreign travel, swimming. *Address:* 48 Circus Road, N.W.8. [*Died* 24 *Oct.* 1957.

WHITE, Edward; landscape architect and expert in horticulture; President, Institute of Landscape Architects, 1931-32 and 1932-33; Victorian medal of Horticulture; Hon. Managing Director of Royal International Horticultural Exhibition, 1912; Consultant Landscape Architect to British Empire Exhibition, 1924; Diplôme de Grand Prix Brussels Exposition, 1935; *b.* Worthing; *s.* of James White; *m.* 1st, Winifred Blair (*d.* 1926), *e. d.* of H. E. Milner, C.E.; two *s.* one *d.*; 2nd, 1930, Editha Whitney, Rudderow, California. *Address:* (Milner White & Son) 7 Victoria Street, S.W.1. *T.:* Abbey 5271. [*Died* 6 *Jan.* 1952.

WHITE, Major-General Geoffrey Herbert Anthony, C.B. 1919; C.M.G. 1918; D.S.O. 1916; *b.* 3 Nov. 1870; *s.* of late F. A. White, Trevor House, Belgrave Place, S.W.1; *m.* 1918, Beatrice (*d.* 1953), *d.* of Dudley Raikes de Chair. *Educ.:* Eton; Royal Military Academy, Woolwich. First commissioned in R.A. 1890; R.H.A. 1895-1916; Capt. 1900; Major, 1908; served South African War, 1899-

1900 (Queen's medal 4 clasps); Superintendent Riding Establishment, R.A., 1910-13; European War, 1914-18, with 7th Cavalry Brig. (3rd Cavalry Division) in command of K Battery, R.H.A. (prom. Lt.-Col. 1915, despatches six times, D.S.O., C.M.G.); temp. Brig.-Gen. and C.R.A. 30th Division, 1916; Bt. Col. Jan. 1917; Subst. Col. 1919; Commandant R.M. Academy, Woolwich, with temp. rank of Maj.-Gen., 1918-1920; Comdt. Woolwich Sub-Area, 1920-23; Maj.-Gen. 1923; Director of Remounts, War Office, 1925-29; retired pay, 1929; Colonel Commandant R.A., 1934-40, R.H.A., 1939-40. *Address:* 19 Chesham Street, S.W.1. *T.:* Sloane 5543. *Clubs:* Army and Navy, Royal Automobile. [*Died* 15 *Dec.* 1959.

WHITE, Brigadier George Frederick Charles, D.S.O. 1917; *b.* 4 Aug. 1882; *s.* of late G. F. White; *m.* 1913, Violet, *y. d.* of late Captain N. P. Stewart, J.P., Bangor, N. Wales; one *s.* *Educ.:* Giggleswick; R.M.A., Woolwich. Commissioned in R.G.A. 1900; Captain, 1913; Major, 1915; Lt.-Col., 1929; Col. 1933; served European War, 1914-17 (despatches, D.S.O., Order of Crown of Belgium, Belgian Croix de Guerre); Comdr. R.A., Gibraltar, 1934-38; retired pay, 1938. [*Died* 4 *Nov.* 1953.

WHITE, Lt.-Col. Sir Godfrey D. D.; *see* Dalrymple-White.

WHITE, Herbert Arthur; formerly Editor, War Correspondent, Company Director, etc.; *b.* Tisbury, Wiltshire, 1876; *y. s.* of late Rev. J. Metcalfe White; *m.* May, *d.* of late Henry Barnard, Mentone. *Educ.:* Caterham School; Universities of Wales, Aberystwyth, Heidelberg, and Berlin. War Correspondent of the New York World in the Turco-Greek campaign of 1897; represented the Morning Post and United Press of America in Vienna, 1898-1902; Berlin Correspondent of the United Press of America, 1903-10, and of the Standard, 1904-10; travelled extensively as war correspondent and special correspondent, 1900-1910; Editor-in-Chief of the Standard, 1911-15; was employed on official political missions abroad, 1916-18; negotiated for British companies a series of concessions and contracts with Governments and other public authorities in Central and East Europe, 1919-1923; Chairman and Managing Director of Mid-European Concessions, Ltd., 1920-23; founded Swiss Marconi Co., 1921, and Austrian Marconi Co., 1923; Managing Director Austrian Marconi Co., Vienna, 1923-27; Co-President of British-Hungarian Bank, Budapest, and Chairman of Group Executive of its eighteen manufacturing and trading subsidiary companies, 1924-27; Vice-President of British-Austrian Bank, Vienna, 1925-30, and of Bank of Timisoara, Rumania, 1925-33; General Manager, 1927-32, and Managing Director, 1933-37, of Marconi Wireless Telegraph Co. Ltd.; Adviser to, and a Director of, Cable and Wireless (Holding) Ltd., 1933-40; Chairman and Managing Director Marconi Wireless Telegraph Co. Ltd., 1937-40, and of Marconi Marine Co. Ltd., and Marconi Sounding Device Co. Ltd., 1937-41; Managing Director Radio Communications Co. Ltd., 1937-41, and a Director of Cable & Wireless (operating) Ltd., 1933-41; President Polskie Zaklady Marconi Ltd. (Warsaw), and of Hungarian Marconi Co., Budapest, 1930-45; Vice-President, Radio-Slavia, Ltd., Prague, and of Radio-Austria, Ltd., Vienna, 1927-38; a Director of sixteen other companies of the Marconi group between 1922 and 1945, and of thirteen other companies of the Cable and Wireless group between 1933 and 1941; political adviser to United Nations government departments, 1941-45. *Address:* c/o Westminster Bank, 1 St. James's Square, S.W.1; Ballantrae Manor, R.R.2, Stouffville, Ontario, Canada. [*Died* 20 *July* 1958.

WHITE, J(ames) Dundas, M.A., LL.D.; Barrister-at-law (Inner Temple); *b.* 10 July 1866; *e. s.* of late John Orr White of Sunnyside, Kingswood Road, Upper Norwood; *m.* 1894, Lydia Grace (*d.* 1923), *d.* of late Rev. R. Haythornthwaite, Vicar of Cleator Moor, Cumberland. *Educ.:* Rugby; Trinity College, Cambridge. M.P. (L.) Dumbartonshire, 1906-10, and Jan.-Dec. 1910; Tradeston Division of Glasgow, 1911-18; Parliamentary Private Secretary to Lord Pentland (Secretary for Scotland), 1910-12; to Rt. Hon. T. M'Kinnon Wood, M.P. (Secretary for Scotland and afterwards Secretary to the Treasury and Chancellor of the Duchy of Lancaster), 1912-18; Chairman of one and member of several other Departmental Committees during European War; Joined I.L.P., 1919; contested (Lab.) West Middlesbrough, 1923; Central Glasgow, 1924. Now non-party. *Publications:* works on the Merchant Shipping Acts, 1st ed. 1894, 4th ed. 1908; and on the Marine Insurance Act, 1906; Economic Ideals, 1903; Island Economy, 1903; The Truth about Tariffs, 1904; Land and Labour, 1st ed. 1904, 2nd ed. 1905; Land Reform in Theory and Practice, 1910; The A B C of the Land Question, 1911; Land Values in a Nutshell, 1913; A Scheme for Land-value Taxation, 1916; Land-value Taxation and Feu-duties, 1916; Steering by the Stars for Night-flying, Night-marching, etc., 1916; Land Value Problems, 1918; Economic Justice, 1918, reprinted 1919; Land Value Policy, 1924; "Our" Land and How to Make it So, 1926; Our Natural Inheritance, 1927: The A B C of Plenty Employment, 1929; Nature's Budget of Land-Rent for the People, with Improvements and Food and Industry Tax-Free, 1936; A Correlation of Longitude, Hour Angle, and G.M.T., 1947; Land Value Reform in Theory and Practice, 1948; and numerous articles and papers on economic, legal, and nautical subjects. *Recreations:* walking, sailing, lawn tennis, chess. *Address:* 39 Burton Court, Chelsea, S.W.3. *T.:* Sloane 7976. *Club:* Reform. [*Died* 30 *April* 1951.

WHITE, Jessie, D.Sc. (Lond.); B.A. (B'ham); Moral Sciences Tripos, Cambridge; Psychological pedagogist; lecturer and writer; Hon. Directress Auto-Education Institute, London; *b.* 1865; *e. d.* of Andrew Charles, Birmingham; *m.* Robert White, editor Yorkshire Herald (*d.* 1914). *Educ.:* private school; Mason, Bedford, and Newnham Colleges (Marion Kennedy Student); Breslau and Leipzig Universities. Voluntary Social Worker, 1898; lecturer at the Ladies' College, Cheltenham; Head of the Home and Colonial K.G. Training College, science and maths. teacher; since 1912, has concentrated on the testing and promotion of the Montessori Method, visiting Italy, 1913; formerly Directress, Children's House of St. Bartholomew; formerly Member, Teachers' Guild; Hon. Treasurer and Organiser of the Montessori Society, 1914-20. F.B.Ps.S. *Publications:* The Educational Ideas of Froebel; various pamphlets on the Montessori Method. *Address:* 86 Monument Lane, Rednal, Birmingham. *T.:* Rubery 336. *Club:* Crosby Hall. [*Died* 7 *April* 1958.

WHITE, The Right Rev. John, C.H. 1935; D.D., LL.D.; first Moderator of United Church of Scotland, 1929; Moderator of the General Assembly of the Church of Scotland, 1925; Chaplain in Ordinary to the King; Minister of the Barony of Glasgow; Hon. T.C.L. Trinity College of Music, London, and Vice-President; *b.* Sandyford, Glasgow, 16 Dec. 1867; *s.* of Matthew White, grain merchant and flour miller, Glasgow and Kilwinning; *m.* 1893, Margaret (*d.* 1942), *e. d.* of John Gardner, Muirpark, Partick; two *s.* one *d.*; *m.* 1945, Anne May Calderwood, *o. d.* of late Rev. David Woodside, D.D., Glasgow. *Educ.:* Kilwinning; Irvine Royal Academy Glasgow University. Minister of Shettleston parish; Minister of South Leith; Convener of General Assembly's Home Board; Convener of National Church Extension Committee; Convener of War Damage Committee; Church and National Service; served in France, 1915-1917; Freedom of City of Edinburgh. *Address:* The Barony, 61 Partickhill Road, Glasgow. *T.:* Western 3960. *Clubs:* Conservative, Royal Scottish Automobile (Glasgow); Conservative (Edinburgh). [*Died* 20 *Aug.* 1951.

WHITE, Robert, C.B.E. 1920; Chairman and Managing Director, Gibson and Lumgair, Ltd., Selkirk, Scotland; Past President National Association of Scottish Woollen Manufacturers; *b.* 31 Aug. 1872. Assistant Director, Wool Textile Production, War Office, during European War; same post under Wool Control, Ministry of Supply, during War of 1939-45. Member of National Wool Textile Export Corporation, and various committees connected with Woollen Trade. *Address:* Kinnaird, Melrose, Roxburghshire. *T.:* 49. *Clubs:* Junior Carlton; Scottish Conservative (Edin). [*Died* 17 *Feb.* 1959.

WHITE, Captain Samuel Albert; Corresp.M.B.O.U.; Corresp. Fellow American Ornithologist Union; *b.* Adelaide, 20 Dec. 1870; *s.* of Samuel White and Martha Taylor; *m.* 1st, 1906, Ethel Rosina (*d.* 1926), *d.* of late Samuel Toms; no *c.*; 2nd, 1927, Muriel Beatrice, *d.* of George G. Fisher, Back-Te-Nandra Station, New South Wales; one *s.* one *d.* *Educ.:* Christian Brothers College and St. Peter's College, Adelaide. First scientific expedition up the Murray River, 1887; led an expedition into West Australia, 1888; returned in 1889 and went to Eyre's Peninsula, 1891; undertook an expedition into N. Queensland; for next ten years raced horses, etc.; served S. Africa, 1900-2 (Captaincy on the field, Queen's medal 3 bars, King's medal 2 bars); Central and E. Africa big-game shooting and scientific work, 1903; fitted out at own expense and led an expedition into the interior of Australia, 1913; accompanied the Government Exploration party to the N.W. of S.A. as scientist, 1914; went into the Cooper Creek country with the S.A. Museum Expedition, 1917. *Publications:* Scientific Notes on an Expedition into the interior of Australia, 1914; Scientific Notes of an Expedition into the North-Western Region of South Australia, 1915; Ornithologists at Warunda Creek; Into the Dead Heart; Into the Far North-West; The Cruise of the Avocet; Into the Far North-East; Ooldea on the East-West Railway; The Life of Samuel White. *Recreation:* life's work, ornithology. *Address:* Wetunga, Fulham, South Australia. *T.A.:* Henley Beach. *T.:* Henley 8726. [*Died* 19 *Jan.* 1954.

WHITE, Stuart Arthur Frank, M.A. Oxford; Emeritus Professor of Mathematics, King's College, London; late Scholar of Wadham College, Oxford. *Address:* 47 Kensington Mansions, S.W.5. [*Died* 10 *Jan.* 1951.

WHITE, Sir Sydney (Arthur), K.C.V.O., *cr.* 1952 (M.V.O. 1938); Grand Secretary, United Grand Lodge of England, since 1937; *b.* 19 Oct. 1884; *s.* of late Charles William White, Blisworth, Northamptonshire; *m.* 1909, Grace Mary Ward, *d.* of late Edward William James, Brockley, Kent; one *s.* *Educ.:* privately. Associate, Institute of Chartered Accountants, 1913. Chev. Order of St. Olav (Norway), 1945; Officer, Order of George I (Greece), 1946; Chev., First Class, Order of Vasa (Sweden), 1950. *Recreations:* gardening, motoring. *Address:* Freemasons' Hall, Gt. Queen St., W.C.2; Pelham Lodge, Pines Road, Bickley, Kent. *T.:* Imperial 4343. [*Died* 9 *March* 1958.

WHITE, Rt. Hon. Sir Thomas; *see* White, Rt. Hon. Sir W. T.

WHITE, Group Capt. (formerly Lt.-Col.) Hon. Sir Thomas Walter, K.B.E. *cr.* 1952; D.F.C., V.D., F.R.G.S.; High Commissioner for Australia, in London, 1951-56; *b.* Melbourne, 26 April 1888; *s.* of late Charles and Emily White; *m.* 1920, Vera, *y. d.* of late Hon. Alfred Deakin, formerly Prime Minister of Australia; four *d.* Commanded 6th Battalion Royal Melbourne Regt., 1926-31; served first Australian Flying Unit overseas; attached 6th Division in Mesopotamia; taken prisoner by Turks near Baghdad, Nov. 1915; escaped from Constantinople, Aug. 1918 (Distinguished Flying Cross, despatches twice, Victoria Decoration); War of 1939-45 served with R.A.A.F. in Australia and Britain, 1940-44; was C.O. R.A.F. Station, Brighton, Eng. M.H.R. for Balaclava, 1929-51; Minister for Trade and Customs, Australia, 1933-38; Minister for Air and Civil Aviation, Australia, 1949-51; Represented Australia at Trade Conferences: N.Z., 1937; U.K., 1938; Internat. Civil Aviation Organization Convention, 1950; also Evian Refugee Conference, 1938; Founder Australian Aero Club, also Past President; President Royal Life Saving Society Australia, 1934-51, and Federal President. Whilst High Commissioner was: Chm. Empire Council, Brit. Empire Service League; Deputy Pres. Roy. Life Saving Soc.; Mem. Executive Imperial Institute. Past Pres. and Founder Australian Musical Assoc.; Founder Patron Australian Artists' Assoc.; Founder Patron Soc. of Australian Writers. Director: AEI. Ltd.; Capel Court Investment Companies; Rootes (Australia) Ltd. *Publications:* Guests of the Unspeakable; Sky Saga; The R.A.A.F. (encyclopedia). *Recreation:* golf. *Address:* 32 Kensington Road, South Yarra, Melbourne, Australia. *T.:* BJ 5945. *Clubs:* Escaping Society, Army and Navy; Royal Empire Society (Pres.), Melbourne (Melbourne). [*Died* 13 *Oct.* 1957.

WHITE, Rt. Rev. William Charles, B.D., D.D. (hon.); F.R.S.C. 1942; F.R.G.S.; Professor of Chinese Studies, Univ. of Toronto, 1934-48, Director, School of Chinese Studies, 1941-48. Keeper East Asiatic Collection, and Assist. Dir., of the Royal Ontario Museum, 1934-48, Emeritus Keeper, 1948; Member Lambeth Conference, 1920, 1948; *b.* Devon, 22 Aug. 1873; *m.* 1st, 1897, one *s.* one *d*; 2nd, 1935, Annie Daisy Masters. *Educ.:* Toronto. Assistant Minister of Trinity Church, Toronto, for one year Canadian Church Missionary to Fuhkien, China, 1897-1909; first Bishop of Honan, 1909-34; Assistant Bishop of Honan, 1946-49; Hon. Assistant Bishop of Niagara, 1949; Adviser in Canada of the China International Famine Relief Commission, 1934; Adviser to Director-General of C.N.R.R.A. for the North China area, 1946; C.F. (Canadian Expeditionary Force), 1916; Order of Excellent Crop, China, Third Class, 1915; Second Class, 1919; Grand Cordon, 1921; Order of Brilliant Rays, 2nd Class, 1922; Order of Striped Tiger, 4th Class, 1920; Order of Rhinoceros, 1st Class, 1925; Order of the Tsou Yü, 1st Cl. (Diplomatic), 1925; Gold Medal of the Red Cross Society of China, 1923. *Publications:* Chinese-English Dictionary of the Kienning Dialect; Without the Gate, a small book on work amongst Lepers in China; Tombs of Old Lo-yang, 1934; Tomb Tile Pictures of Ancient China, 1938; An Album of Chinese Bamboos, 1939; Chinese Temple Frescoes, 1940; Chinese Jews, 1942; Bone Culture of Ancient China, 1945; Canon Cody of St. Paul's (Toronto), 1952; Bronze Culture of Ancient China, 1955. *Address:* Church House, 604 Jarvis St., Toronto, Canada; (home) 157 Roxborough St. W., Toronto 5, Ontario, Canada. [*Died* 24 *Jan.* 1960.

WHITE, Brigadier William Nicholas, C.B. 1936; D.S.O. 1916; late Royal Army Service Corps; *b.* 10 Sept. 1879; *s.* of William Nicholas White; *m.* 1906, Evelyn Laura, *y. d.* of late Sir Gilbert Gilbert-Carter, K.C.M.G.; two *s.* *Educ.:* Malvern College. Joined 4th Sherwood Foresters, 1900; transferred to Army Service Corps, 1901; commanded A.S.C. depôt, Aldershot, 1906-12; Adjutant to a Territorial unit in Yorkshire, 1912-14; served South African War (Queen's medal 4 clasps); European War,

1914-19 (despatches thrice, Bt. Lt.-Col., D.S.O.); Commandant R.A.S.C. Training College, Aldershot, 1930-33; Inspector of R.A.S.C., War Office, 1933-36; retired pay, 1936; King George's Coronation Medal. *Recreations:* Hampshire County cricket team, 1907-14; Army team for four years; captained Army Association football team, 1901-2. *Address:* The Mount, Portland Avenue, Exmouth. *Club:* Army and Navy. [*Died* 27 *Dec.* 1951.

WHITE, Rt. Hon. Sir (William) Thomas, P.C. 1920; G.C.M.G. *cr.* 1935 (K.C.M.G., *cr.* 1916); formerly Director, Canadian Bank of Commerce, and other Canadian Companies; *b.* Halton County, Ontario, 13 Nov. 1866; *s.* of James White, who came to Canada in 1860 from Omagh, County Tyrone, Ireland; *m.* 1890, Annie Silverthorne; no *c.* *Educ.:* Public and High School, Province of Ontario; University of Toronto. Graduate University of Toronto. Graduate (with gold medal) Law Society of Upper Canada; called to Bar of Ontario, 1899; Vice-President and General Manager National Trust Company, Limited, of Toronto, Montreal, and Winnipeg; took active part in Dominion Elections, 1911, on Reciprocity issue; Member for Leeds, Ontario, 1911-21, and Minister of Finance, 1911-19. *Recreation:* golf. *Clubs:* Toronto, York (Toronto); National, Rideau (Ottawa). [*Died* 11 *Feb.* 1955.

WHITEHEAD, Vice-Admiral Frederic Aubrey, C.B. 1919; J.P. West Lothian; *b.* 29 Aug. 1874; 8th *c.* of George Whitehead, of Deighton Grove, York; *m.* 1916, Elizabeth, *d.* of Patrick T. Caird, Belleaire, Greenock; two *s.* one *d.* *Educ.:* H.M.S. Britannia. Midshipman, 1889; Lieut. 1893; Commander, 1904; Capt. 1910; Rear-Adm. 1921; during European War commanded H.M. ships Magnificent, Royal Arthur, Roxburgh; Director of Mercantile Movements, Sept. 1917; Retired List, 1923; Vice-Adm. retired, 1926. *Address:* Ashburnham, South Queensferry, West Lothian. *T.:* South Queensferry 320. [*Died* 30 *April* 1958.

WHITEHEAD, Brig. James, C.B. 1940; C.M.G. 1920; C.B.E. 1937; D.S.O. 1916; Indian Army, retd.; *b.* 1880; *s.* of late Lt.-Col. Edmund Whitehead, late Black Watch; *m.* 1907, *y. d.* of late Sir Arthur Fell; four *s.* one *d.* *Educ.:* Royal Military College, Sandhurst; Staff College, 1911-12. Served European War, 1914-19 (D.S.O., C.M.G., Legion of Honour); Dir. of Organisation, Simla, 1921-25; comd. Abbottabad Bde., 1925-27; A.D.C. to King George V; retired, 1927; a Chief Constable, Metropolitan Police, 1927-33; Deputy Assistant Commissioner, 1933; Assistant Commissioner, Metropolitan Police, 1933-38; Deputy Adjutant General, B.E.F., France, Sept. 1939-40; Commander, Home Guard, London District, since 1940. *Address:* 16 Malcolm Road, Wimbledon, S.W.19. *T.:* Wimbledon 1004. [*Died* 1 *Dec.* 1955.

WHITEHEAD, John Henry Constantine, F.R.S. 1944; Waynflete Professor of Pure Mathematics and Fellow of Magdalen College, Oxford, since 1947; Pres. London Mathematical Soc., 1953-55. *b.* 11 Nov. 1904; *s.* of late Rt. Rev. Henry Whitehead, D.D., Bishop of Madras, 1899-1922; *m.* 1934, Barbara Sheila Carew Smyth; two *s.* *Educ.:* Eton; Balliol College, Oxford. Commonwealth Fund Research Fellow in mathematics at Princeton University, U.S.A., 1929-32; Fellow and Tutor of Balliol College, Oxford, 1933-46 (war service with Admiralty and Foreign Office, 1941-45). *Publications:* The Foundations of Differential Geometry (with Prof. O. Veblen), 1932; various papers on mathematics. *Recreations:* cricket, skiing, farming. *Address:* Manor Farm, Noke, Oxford. *T.:* Kidlington 3142. [*Died* 8 *May* 1960.

WHITEHEAD, Major Sir Philip Henry Rathbone, 4th Bt., *cr.* 1889; *b.* 24 July 1897; *er. s.* of Sir Rowland Whitehead, K.C., 3rd Bt., and Ethel M. L. (*d.* 1945), *d.* of Philip H. Rathbone, Liverpool; *S.* father, 1942; *m.* 1st, 1929, Gertrude (whom he divorced, 1938), *d.* of J. C. Palmer, West Va. U.S.A.; twin *s.*; 2nd, 1946, Margery, *d.* of late E. W. Hickes, and of Mrs. Hickes, Brasted Hall, Kent. *Educ.:* Clifton College; Royal Military College, Sandhurst. Served European War, Oxford and Bucks Lt. Inf., 1915-19 (wounded); retd., 1922. War of 1939-45, 1940-45, Oxford and Bucks Lt. Inf. and Intelligence Corps. Trustee Rowland Hill Benevolent Fund, G.P.O.; Member of Fruiterers Company. Governor Appleby Gr. School. *Heir:* *s.* Rowland John Rathbone, *b.* 24 June 1930. *Address:* Culham Home Farm, Abingdon, Berks; Sotik, Kenya Colony. *Clubs:* National Liberal, M.C.C. [*Died* 31 *Dec.* 1953.

WHITEHEAD, Thomas Alec, C.I.E. 1938; *b.* 8 May 1886; *m.* 1926, Dorothy F. Lunn; no *c.* *Educ.:* Bowdon College; Cooper's Hill R.I.E. College; New College, Oxford. Assistant Conservator of Forests, Madras Presidency, 1907; Deputy Conservator of Forests, 1911; Conservator of Forests in 1923; Chief Conservator of Forests, 1935-40; retired, 1940. *Address:* c/o Westminster Bank Ltd., 1 York Street, Manchester 2. [*Died* 16 *Feb.* 1959.

WHITEHOUSE, John Howard, Hon. M.A., Oxford; F.R.G.S., F.R.S.A., Knight of the First Class of the Order of St. Olav; Warden of Bembridge School (Headmaster, 1919-54); *b.* 1873. *Educ.:* Mason College and Midland Institute. First Secretary to the Carnegie Dunfermline Trust, 1903-4; Sec. of Toynbee Hall, London, 1905-8; Sub-Warden, St. George's School, Harpenden, 1908; Warden, Manchester University Settlement, 1909-10; Member of Home Office Departmental Committee on Employment of Children Act, 1909; Manager of East London Schools, 1906-8; Editor, Toynbee Record, 1906-8; M.P. (L.) Mid-Lanark, 1910-18; Parliamentary Private Secretary to Under-Secretary of State, Home Office, 1910-13; and to the Chancellor of the Exchequer, 1913-1915; Member of the Departmental Committee on Night Work for Young Persons, 1911; Member of Departmental Committee on Reformatory Schools, 1912; Relief Commissioner in the Balkans, 1912; Commissioner for Belgian Refugees, 1914; in America visiting educational institutions, 1916-17; founded Bembridge School, 1919; Chairman of Society for Research in Education, 1920; Trustee and Companion of the Guild of Saint George since 1918; a Governor of the Sulgrave Institution since 1922; Chairman of the Fram Preservation Committee, 1929; President of the Ruskin Society, 1932; President of the Froebel Society, 1932; acquired Ruskin's old home, Brantwood, 1933; President of the Friends of Brantwood since 1935; organised lectures on America in English Schools, 1938. *Publications:* Problems of a Scottish Provincial Town, 1905; The Boys' Club: It's Place in Social Progress, 1906; Problems of Boy Life, 1911; An Enquiry into Working Boys' Homes in London, 1908 (part author); Camping for Boys, 1911; Song and Hymns for Boys (edited), 1912; A National System of Education, 1913; Essays on Social and Political Questions, 1914; Belgium in War, 1915; Educatioanl and Social Experiments, 1917; The English Public School System, 1919; Ruskin Centenary Addresses and Ruskin Centenary Letters, 1919; Ruskin the Prophet, 1920: Wider Aspects of Education (with Dr. G. P. Gooch), 1923; To-Day: Stories, Biographies, Addresses, 1925; Holiday Occupations for Boys, 1926; Creative Education. 1928; The Craftsmanship of Books, 1928; The Solitary Warrior, 1928; A Visit to Nansen, 1928; Tintoretto's Paradise, 1930; Nansen, a Book of Homage, 1930; Scott Holland's St. Paul's Cathedral (edited

with introduction), 1930; To My Boys, 1932; A Boys' Symposium, 1932; Three Bembridge Fables, 1932; The Road to Bethlehem: a Nativity Play (with J. C. R. Cook), 1933; The Boy of To-day, a Defence, 1933; Thy Youth and Cause, 1934; The Master: a study of Michelangelo (with Colin Rocke), 1934; The Mystic Spring, a Nativity Play (with Donald Sutcliffe), 1935; Education in My Time, 1935; Broadcasting and Education, 1936; The Inn at the End of the World and other plays of the Nativity, 1936; Ruskin and Brantwood, 1937; The Unknown, a Nativity Play, 1937; Youth and other Poems, 1937; Ruskin the Painter, 1938; America in Our Schools, 1938; The School Base, 1943; A Memory of Patrick Geddes and His Son Alastair, 1947; Vindication of Ruskin, 1950; The Boys of Shakespeare, 1952, etc. *Recreations:* literature, travel. *Address:* Yellowsands, Bembridge, Isle of Wight. *T.:* Bembridge 77. *Clubs:* National Liberal, Reform, Authors'.
[*Died* 28 *Sept.* 1955.

WHITELEY, Sir Gerald Charles, Kt., *cr.* 1944; C.M.G. 1937; temporarily employed in Colonial Office; *b.* 1891; *s.* of Charles James Whiteley, Manningham, Yorks.; *m.* 1918, Elsie Evelyn, *y. d.* of Rev. W. P. L. Davies, Rector of Kinton, Ipswich. *Educ.:* Bradford; Jesus Coll., Oxford. B.A. Deputy Chief Secretary, Nigeria, 1934-39; Chief Commissioner, Western Provinces, Nigeria, 1939-47; retired 1947. *Address:* c/o Colonial Office, Great Smith St., S.W.1.
[*Died* 28 *Feb.* 1958.

WHITELEY, Martha Annie, O.B.E.; Hon. Fellow Imperial College of Science and Technology; D.Sc.; F.R.I.C.; A.R.C.S.; Editor of Thorpe's Dictionary of Applied Chemistry, 4th Edition (revised and enlarged); *b.* 11 Nov. 1866; 2nd *d.* of late William Sedgwick Whiteley; unmarried. *Educ.:* Kensington High School; Royal Holloway College, 1887-91 (B.Sc.Lond., Math. Mods. Oxford); Royal College of Science, London, 1898-1902 (D.Sc.Lond.) Science Mistress, Wimbledon High School, 1891-1900; Science Lecturer, St. Gabriel's Training Coll., 1900-2; Asst. in Chemical Dept., R.C.S., 1904; Demonstrator in the R.C.S., Imperial College of Science and Technology, 1907; Lecturer, 1913; Assistant Professor, 1920-34. *Publications:* A Student's Manual of Organic Chemical Analysis; numerous articles in Thorpe's Dictionary of Applied Chemistry; contributions to the Proc. Roy. Soc. and Trans. Chem. Soc. *Recreations:* domestic and social duties. *Address:* Flat II, 4 Roland Gardens, South Kensington, S.W.7.
[*Died* 24 *May* 1956.

WHITELEY, Rt. Hon. William, P.C. 1943; C.H. 1948; D.L.; M.P. (Lab.) Blaydon Division of Durham, 1922-31, and since 1935; Labour Chief Whip, 1942-55; an official of the Durham Miners' Association; President Durham Aged Mineworkers' Assoc.; Pres. Durham Miners' Approved Soc.; Treas. Northern Dist., W.E.A., 1937-46; *b.* 3 Oct. 1882; *s.* of late Samuel Whiteley, Elland; *m.* 1901. Elizabeth Swordy Jackson; one *s.* one *d.* Labour Whip, 1927; Junior Lord of the Treasury, 1929-31; Comptroller of H.M. Household, 1940-42; Joint Parliamentary Secretary to Treasury, 1942-45; Parliamentary Secretary to the Treasury, 1945-51. D.L. Durham. *Address:* Long Garth, White Smocks, Durham City. *T.:* Durham 782. *Club:* Labour.
[*Died* 3 *Nov.* 1955.

WHITEWAY, Ronald Harry Clift, J.P.; Managing Director of Whiteways Cyder Co. Ltd.; *b.* 17 June 1885; *s.* of Henry and Edith Whiteway; *m.* 1913, Alice May de Witt, Nova Scotia; no *c.* *Educ.:* West Buckland, Devon; Exeter School, Exeter. Developing the cyder apple-growing and cyder-making industries in Devon; President of National Association of Cider Makers, 1934-35; J.P. for Ottery, Devon. *Recreation:* cricket. *Address:* Alexandra House, Exeter. *T.A.:* Whiteway Whimple. *T.:* Whimple 332.
[*Died* 2 *Jan.* 1951.

WHITHAM, Lieut.-Gen. John Lawrence, C.M.G. 1916; D.S.O. 1918; p.s.c.; Retired List, Australian Military Forces; *b.* 7 Oct. 1881; *m.* 1920, Olive, *widow* of Edward Doveton Carder Young. Cape Town, and *d.* of George Renatus Le Pays, London. Australian Permanent Forces (Staff Corps), 1910-40; also served in Tasmanian Infantry Regt., 1899-1902; Australian Commonwealth Horse (S. African War), 1902; S. African Constabulary, 1902-3; European War, 1914-18 with Aust. Imp. Force (Gallipoli, Egypt, France); 12th Battalion, Sept. 1914-Jan. 1916; Headquarters 2nd Division, Feb.-Sept. 1916; Headquarters A.I.F., Oct. 1916-June 1917; 52nd Battalion, July 1917-May 1918; 49th Battalion, June-Dec. 1918; Repatriation and Demobilisation Staff, A.I.F., 1919; Staff College, Camberley, 1920; Staff appointments, Victoria Military District and Army H.Q. 1921-33; Comdr. Field Troops and Base Commandant, Tasmania, 1933-35; Commander, 11th Mixed Brigade and Base Commandant, Queensland, 1935-37; Commander 4th Division and District Base Commandant, Victoria, 1937-40; Commanded Southern Command (Australia), 1940 with temp. rank of Lt.-General. Comdr. Volunteer Defence Corps (Home Guard), Victoria, 1942-45. *Address:* White Cottage, Lucinda Avenue, Wahroonga, Sydney, N.S.W. *Club:* Imperial Service (Sydney).
[*Died* 12 *May* 1952.

WHITING, Rev. Charles Edwin; Vicar of Hickleton, Doncaster, since 1939; Hon. Canon of Durham Cathedral, since 1939; *b.* 1871; *s.* of Edwin John Whiting; unmarried. *Educ.:* Hatfield College, Durham. Theological Scholar, 1898, Theological Exhibitioner, Barry Scholar and L.Th. (2nd Class Hons.), 1899; Gabbett Philosophy Prize, 1899, 1901, 1902; Gibson Archæology Prize, 1901; B.A. 3rd Class Classics, 1902; M.A. 1905; B.D. 1911; B.C.L. 1915; D.D. 1927; Hon. D.Litt. 1946; Deacon, 1899; Priest, 1900; Curate of St. James's, Gateshead, 1899-1906; Vice-Principal St. Chad's Hostel, Hooton Pagnell, 1906-1916; Vice-Principal, St. Chad's College, Durham, 1916-39, Senior Fellow, 1934-39; Lecturer in Ecclesiastical History, Univ. of Durham, 1918-22; Reader in History, 1922-1931; Professor of History, 1931-39; Emeritus Professor, 1939; Member of Senate, 1920-39; Member of Council of Durham Colleges, 1919-39; Dean of Faculty of Arts, 1925-26; Examiner Jt. Board for Training Colleges, 1940-43 and 1948-49; Examiner in History, Univ. of Leeds, 1928-31; in Ecclesiastical History, 1939-42 and 1947-49; Chaplain to the High Sheriff of York, Capt. C. Grant-Dalton, 1942-43; Officiating C.F., 1942; F.R.Hist.S.; F.S.A.; Hon. Corr. Member and Great Silver Medallist, Institut Historique et Héraldique, France; President Durham and Northumberland Archæological Society since 1933; President Yorkshire Archæological Society, 1948; Vice-President Surtees Society; Member numerous Historical and Archæological Societies. *Publications:* Studies in Restoration Puritanism, 1931; The University of Durham, 1832-1932; Nathaniel, Lord Crewe, Bishop of Durham (1674-1721), and His Diocese, 1940; The Autobiography and Letters of Thomas Comber, Vol. I. 1946, Vol. II., 1948; Editor of The Registers of Hooton Pagnell, 1929, The Registers of Frickleywith Clayton, 1933, The Registers of Brodsworth, 1937, The Registers of Hickleton, Yorks, 1940, The Registers of Cantley, Yorks, 1941; The Registers of Burghwallis, Yorks, 1945; Rillington, Yorks, 1938; The University of Durham, 1937; The Accounts of the Churchwardens, Constables and Overseers of Hooton Pagnell, 1938; Durham Civic Papers 16th Century, 1952; Two Yorkshire Diaries of the 18th Century, 1952; Transactions of Durham and Northumberland Archæological Society since 1934; Durham Univ. Journal, 1918-39; Contrib. Archæological Journals, etc. *Address:* Hickleton Vicarage, Doncaster. [*Died* 24 *March* 1953.

WHITLEY, Sir Michael Henry, Kt., *cr.* 1929; J.P. Hampshire; *b.* 26 Sept. 1872; *s.* of late George Whitley, of Weybridge; *m.* 1920, Ethel, *d.* of late John Keegan, J.P., of Holywood, Co. Down; one *d. Educ.:* Blundell's School, Tiverton; King's College, London. Joined Civil Service of Federated Malay States, 1896; a Puisne Judge of the Straits Settlements, 1918-25; Attorney-General of the Straits Settlements, 1925-29; retired, 1929. *Address:* Thornhill Court, Passfield, Hants. [*Died* 14 *Oct.* 1959.

WHITLEY, Sir Norman Henry Pownall, Kt., *cr.* 1941; M.C.; Chairman Uganda Cotton Industry Commission, 1948; Chief Justice, Uganda, 1937-47; *b.* Manchester, 29 June 1883; *s.* of Henry Charles Whitley; *m.* 1922, Florence May (from whom he obtained a divorce, 1941), *d.* of Arthur Erskine, Manchester; one *s. Educ.:* Manchester; Emmanuel College, Cambridge, B.A. Called to Bar, Inner Temple, 1907; practised Northern Circuit till 1921; enlisted as private 7th Manchester Regt., Aug. 1914; served in Egypt, Gallipoli, Palestine, and Arabia; demobilized, 1920 with rank of Major (M.C., French Croix de Guerre, Order of Crown of Italy, Order of Nahdar (Hedjaz); Deputy Public Prosecutor, Penang, 1921; Deputy Public Prosecutor, Singapore, 1922; Puisne Judge, Straits Settlements, and Judge, Federated Malay States, 1929-37; Acting Chief Justice Straits Settlements, 1936; Acting Chief Justice Federated Malay States, 1937. *Recreations:* Lacrosse (captained England and played for U.K. in Olympic Games), cricket, lawn tennis, golf. *Address:* c/o Barclays Bank, Kampala, Uganda. [*Died* 12 *April* 1957.

WHITMEE, His Honour Judge Harold James Conder, B.A.; Judge of County Courts, Circuit No. 33 (Essex and Suffolk), since 1947; *b.* 4 Oct. 1901; *er. s.* of late Andrew Conder and Clara Whitmee; *m.* 1928, Margaret Ann Ewen Bisset; one *s.* one *d. Educ.:* Mill Hill; Clare College, Cambridge (graduated in law and economics). Called to Bar, Gray's Inn, 1925. Practised in London and on South Eastern Circuit until 1940 when volunteered for and was commissioned in R.A.F.V.R. Served as Squadron Leader till released Oct. 1943 to be Legal Chm. of a Pensions Appeal Tribunal, 1943-45; returned to practise at the Bar, 1945; Judge of Circuit No. 25 (Wolverhampton, etc.), 1946; Circuit No. 38 (Edmonton, etc.), 1947. J.P. Suffolk. *Recreations:* golf, gardening. *Address:* Eyke House, nr. Woodbridge, Suffolk. *T.:* Eyke 92. *Clubs:* Oxford and Cambridge; County (Ipswich). [*Died* 6 *March* 1954.

WHITNEY, Sir Cecil Arthur, Kt., *cr.* 1946; J.P.; Director of the Colonial Ammunition Company Limited, Auckland, New Zealand; *b.* 13 Aug. 1862; 2nd *s.* of Major John Whitney and Harriett Chaworth Musters; *m.* 1891, Mary Ellen, *d.* of Joseph Liston Wilson; two *s.* one *d. Educ.:* Borgue Public School, Kirkcudbrightshire, Scotland. Joined father's firm of Whitney & Sons, 1885. Firm became The Colonial Ammunition Co. Ltd., 1888, and a branch factory was erected in Footscray, Melbourne, 1889; Managing Director of the N.Z. Company, 1920, and later succeeded his father as Chairman of Directors; retired from the Chairmanship, 1944, in favour of his son John Cecil Whitney; took an active interest in acclimatisation work, shooting, fishing, yachting and various societies for the welfare of the community. *Recreations:* shooting and fishing, golf, tennis and bowls. *Address:* Remuera, Auckland, N.Z. *Clubs:* Northern, Rotary (Auckland, N.Z.). [*Died* 7 *Feb.* 1956.

WHITNEY-SMITH, E., F.R.B.S.; portrait sculptor; *b.* 2 Aug. 1880; *m.* 1911, Rachel Pitt (*d.* 1950), Clifton, Bristol; one *s.* *Address:* 41 Priory Road, N.W.6. *T:* Maida Vale 7457. [*Died* 8 *Jan.* 1952.

WHITTAKER, Sir Edmund Taylor, Kt., *cr.* 1945; F.R.S. 1905; Hon. LL.D. St. Andrews and Univ. of California; Hon. Sc.D. Dublin; Hon. D.Sc.: London, Manchester, Birmingham, N.U.I.; Hon. Fellow of Trinity College, Camb.; Hon. Fellow Faculty of Actuaries in Scotland; Foreign Member of the R. Accademia dei Lincei and other foreign learned societies; *b.* 24 Oct. 1873; *s.* of John Whittaker, Birkdale; *m.* 1901, Mary, *d.* of Rev. Thos. Boyd; three *s.* two *d. Educ.:* Manchester Grammar School; Trinity Coll., Camb.; Second Wrangler and First Smith's Prizeman; Fellow of Trinity College, Camb., 1896-1907; Royal Astronomer of Ireland, 1906-12; Pres. Mathematical Association, 1920-21; Rouse Ball Lecturer, Cambridge Univ., 1926; Pres. of Section A of the British Assoc., 1927; Sylvester Medallist of the Royal Society, 1931; Hitchcock Professor, University of California, 1934; President, 1928-29, De Morgan Medallist, 1935, of London Mathematical Soc.; President of Royal Society of Edinburgh, 1939-44; Riddell Lecturer, Univ. of Durham, 1941; Guthrie Lecturer, Physical Soc., 1943; Donnellan Lecturer, Univ. of Dublin, 1946; Prof. of Mathematics, Edin. Univ., 1912-46; Tarner Lecturer, Camb., 1947; Herbert Spencer Lecturer, Oxford, 1948; Larmor Lectr., Roy. Irish Acad., 1948; Eddington Lecturer, 1951; Copley Medallist of the Royal Society, 1954. Cross pro Ecclesia et Pontifice, 1935. *Publications:* Modern Analysis; Treatise on Analytical Dynamics; Theory of Optical Instruments; History of the Theories of Æther and Electricity (2 vols.); The Calculus of Observations; The Beginning and End of the World (Riddell lectures); Space and Spirit (Donnellan lectures); The modern approach to Descartes' problem; From Euclid to Eddington (Tarner lectures); Eddington's Principle in the Philosophy of Science (Eddington Memorial Lecture); and various memoirs. *Address:* 48 George Sq., Edinburgh. *T.:* Edinburgh 43490. [*Died* 24 *March* 1956.

WHITTING, Brigadier Everard Le Grice, D.S.O. 1918; M.C.; *b.* 5 Sept. 1881; *s.* of late Rev. William Henry Whitting, M.A.; Rector of Stower Provost and Todber, Dorset, and formerly Fellow of King's College, Cambridge; *m.* Doris, *d.* of late J. Macpherson Lawrie, M.D., J.P., D.L., of Greenhill, Weymouth; one *s.* and one adopted *s.* (and one *s.* killed in action, 1942). *Educ.:* King's Choir School, Cambridge; Aldenham School. 2nd Lieutenant R.G.A. 1900; served in India, 1900-14 and 1921-28; N.W. Frontier of India (Mohmand) 1908 (medal with clasp); Egypt (Suez Canal), 1915 (despatches); Gallipoli, 1915 (despatches twice, M.C.); France, 1914-1918 (despatches twice, D.S.O.); N.W.F. (Waziristan), 1921-22; Military Adviser, Indian States Artillery, 1925-28; Commander Royal Artillery, Malta, 1934-38; retired, 1938; G.S.O. (I) Scottish Command, 1939-40. *Address:* Hunter's Spinney, North Road, Bath. *T.:* Bath 4981; c/o Lloyds Bank, 6 Pall Mall, S.W.1. *Club:* Naval and Military. [*Died* 10 *May* 1953.

WHITTINGSTALL, W. A. F.; *see* Fearnley-Whittingstall.

WHITTY, Sir Reginald (Ramson), K.B.E. 1948 (C.B.E. 1944); retired; *b.* 18 Sept. 1891; Director of M. E. C. Holdings Ltd.; *s.* of late Thomas Ramson Whitty, Solicitor, Norwich and Bath, and Charlotte Frances Smit, Grahamstown, S. Africa; *m.* 1915, Dorothy Mary, *d.* of John Abel Martin, Lewes, Sussex; no *c. Educ.:* Bracondale School, Norwich; King's College, London. Admitted a Solicitor, 1913, Clements Inn and Daniel Reardon Prizeman; LL.B. (London), 1920. Entered Public Trustee

Office, Jan. 1914. Served European War, 1914-19; Captain and Qr.-Mr. 4th London Field Ambulance and Railway Transport Officer, Boulogne. Deputy Public Trustee at Manchester, 1938-44; Custodian of Enemy Property for England, 1945-48; Public Trustee, 1945-49. Retired, 1949. *Recreations:* books, walking, travel. *Address:* Alderley, Chipping Campden, Glos. *T.:* Campden 369. [*Died* 6 *Jan.* 1960.

WHITWORTH, Geoffrey Arundel, C.B.E. 1947; F.R.S.L.; Chairman of British Drama League; *b.* 1883; 3rd *s.* of William Whitworth, J.P., Barrister-at-Law, Ouse Manor, Sharnbrook, Beds.; *m.* 1910, Phyllis, *d.* of Rev. G. E. Bell, Vicar of Henley-in-Arden, Warwickshire; one *s.* one *d.* *Educ.:* privately; New College, Oxford. Joined editorial staff of Burlington Magazine, 1906; Art Editor to Chatto and Windus, 1907; founded (1918) British Drama League, of which he was Director till 1948; organised Theatre Section Brit. Empire Exhib., 1924-25; Mem. of Carnegie Cttee. for Music and Drama, 1945-48; Chm. British Section Universal Soc. of the Theatre, 1927; Governor and Member Executive Committee of Stratford Memorial Theatre; Hon. Sec. Shakespeare Memorial National Theatre Committee, 1931; Member of the Joint Council of the National Theatre and the Old Vic; Member British Council. Member U.N.E.S.C.O. National Co-operating Body for the Arts and of Committee for the British Centre of International Theatre Institute. *Publications:* A Book of Whimsies (with Keith Henderson), 1909; The Art of Nijinsky, 1913; English version of de Coster's Tyl Ulenspiegel, 1918; The Bells of Paradise, 1918; Father Noah, 1918; The Theatre of My Heart, 1930; Haunted Houses, 1935; Theatre in Action, 1938; The Great Refusal, 1942; contributor to Encyclopædia Britannica and to various periodicals. *Recreation:* music. *Address:* 24 Old Court Mansions, W.8; Foxcombe Field, Boars Hill, Oxford. *Clubs:* Athenæum, Garrick. [*Died* 9 *Sept.* 1951.

WHITWORTH, William Hervey Allen, M.C.; *e. s.* of late Rev. Prebendary Allen Whitworth, Vicar of All Saints, Margaret Street, W.; *m.* 1929, Vanessa Van Homrigh; one *d.* *Educ.:* Westminster School (Queen's Scholar); Trinity Coll., Cambridge. Bracketed 1st Senior Optime Mathematical Tripos, 1908; Assistant Master Gresham's School, Holt, 1909-11; Headmaster of Central High School, Coorg, S. India (I.E.S.), 1911-13; Asst. Master, Lancing Coll., 1913-29; Headmaster Framlingham College, 1929-40; served European War, in Dorset Regt. and a pilot in the Royal Air Force (M.C., wounded); in War of 1939-45, Skipper in Small Vessels Pool, Admiralty. *Publications:* Rocks and Tides; various yachting articles in sporting journals. *Address:* Rendham, Saxmundham, Suffolk. *T.:* Rendham 462. [*Died* 9 *June* 1960.

WHYTE, Ian, O.B.E. 1952; Conductor (B.B.C. Scottish Orchestra); Composer *b.* 13 Aug. 1901; Scottish; *m.* 1924, Agnes Mary McWhannell; one *s.* *Educ.:* Dunfermline High Sch.; Roy. Coll. of Music, London. Left Roy. Coll., 1923; Music Director to B.B.C. in Scotland, 1931; with Lord Glentanar in intervening years in music-making (opera, etc.) in Aberdeenshire. Helped to found B.B.C. Scottish Orchestra in 1935, and in 1946 resigned music-directorship in order to gain more time for composition and conducting the same orchestra, and to be able to conduct abroad. Hon. Member, Glasgow Society of Musicians. Unpublished works: Symphony, Piano Concerto, Violin Concerto, Ballet, Symphonic Poems, Choral-orchestral works, Choral works, Pianoforte music, Songs. Hon. D.Mus. (Edinburgh) 1958. *Recreation:* fishing for trout. *Address:* 72 Clouston St., Glasgow, N.W. *T.:* Maryhill 1559. [*Died* 27 *March* 1960.

WHYTE, Jardine Bell, J.P., M.I.Mech.E.; *b.* 1880; *s.* of late Robert Whyte, 111 St. Vincent Street, Glasgow, and Lauchope House, Lanarkshire, Consulting Engineer and Naval Architect. *Educ.:* Royal High School, and University, Edinburgh. Served European War, 2½ years at sea, 1 year Admiralty as personal assistant to D.A.S.E.; technical adviser and director British Ministry of Shipping in U.S.A. and Canada, 1918-21; M.P. (U.) North East Derbyshire, 1931-35. *Club:* Whitehall (New York). [*Died* 8 *July* 1954.

WHYTEHEAD, Rev. Canon Ralph Layard; Hon. Chaplain to the Queen since 1952 (to King George VI, 1949-52); *b.* 1883; 4th *s.* of Canon H. R. Whytehead; *m.* 1911, Catherine Margaret, *d.* of Sir David M. Barbour, K.C.M.G., K.C.S.I.; four *d.* *Educ.:* Marlborough College; Warminster Grammar School; Cuddesdon Theological Coll.; St. John's Coll., Oxford. Rector of Diss, Norfolk, 1922; Vicar of Eaton, Norwich, 1930; Rector of Lowestoft, Suffolk, 1938; Vicar of St. Margaret's with St. Nicholas, King's Lynn, 1949-Nov. 1953. Chaplain to Forces, 1915-18; Proctor in Convocation, 1931-55; Hon. Canon of Norwich, 1939; Rural Dean of Lothingland, 1939-48; Vice-Chairman, House of Clergy, Church Assembly, 1945-50; Pro-prolocutor, Lower House, Canterbury Convocation, 1945-50. Prolocutor, 1950-55; Church Commissioner, 1948, re-elected, 1953. *Publication:* Let the People Praise Thee, 1934. *Recreation:* golf. *Address:* 21 The Close, Norwich. *T.:* Norwich 25179. *Club:* Church Imperial. [*Died* 15 *Nov.* 1956.

WHYTLAW-GRAY, Robert Whytlaw, O.B.E.; F.R.S. 1928; Ph.D.; Hon. D.Sc.; F.R.I.C.; Fellow of University College, London; Consultant, Imperial Chemical Industries; *b.* 1877; *m.* 1911, Doris Fortescue, *d.* of Arthur Fortescue Carr; two *d.* *Educ.:* St. Paul's School; Glasgow University; University Coll., London; University of Bonn, Germany. Worked under late Sir William Ramsay on the determination of the atomic weight of radium emanation by means of a micro-balance; re-determined atomic weight of nitrogen, 1906; on chemistry staff of University College, London, 1906; Assistant Professor, 1908; Science Master at Eton College, 1914-23; during 1914-18 war civilian chemical adviser to the Chemical Warfare Committee; British representative on committee on atomic weights of international union of Chemistry, 1940-. Professor of Chemistry, University of Leeds, 1923-45, Emeritus Professor, 1945. *Publications:* (with collaborators) papers on atomic weights of radium, chlorine, xenon, carbon, fluorine, sulphur and silicon. Has also specialised in the scientific study of disperse systems in gases, smoke, dust and atmospheric pollution and published a number of papers in this field. *Address:* 34 Valley Road, Welwyn Garden City, Herts. *Club:* Athenæum. [*Died* 21 *Jan.* 1958.

WICKHAM, Lt.-Col. Edward Thomas Ruscombe, M.V.O. 1928; Indian Army, retired; late Political Dept.; *b.* 4 May 1890; *s.* of late Col. W. J. R. Wickham, C.B.; *m.* 1929, Rache Marguerite Alexander Keeble (*d.* 1955), *o. c.* of late William Geoffrey Alexander of Boldre Hill, Hants; one *s.* M.P. (U.) Taunton division of Somerset, 1935-45; Secretary Parliamentary Conservative Agricultural Committee, 1942; Leader Parliamentary Delegation to Australia and New Zealand, 1944. Vice-Chm. British Van Heusen Co. Ltd.; Director J. & J. Ashton Ltd. *Address:* Rake House, Rake, Liss, Hants. *T.:* Liss 2241. *Clubs:* Carlton, East India and Sports. [*Died* 25 *Aug.* 1957.

WICKHAM, William Reginald Lamplugh, O.B.E. 1945; M.A.; Controller, European Division, The British Council, since 1954; *b.* Royds Hall, Low Moor, Yorkshire, 22 June 1908; *o. s.* of R. W. Wickham, J.P.; *m.* 1944, Ena, *o. c.* of P. Galea Holzer,

Sliema, Malta; one *s.* one *d.* *Educ.:* Harrow; New College, Oxford. Senior History Master, Bedford School; Lecturer in English, Fuad-el-Awal University, Cairo; Protection Officer, Lija, Malta, 1940; Regional Protection Officer, The Three Villages Region, Malta, 1941; Director, British Institute in Malta, 1938; Deputy Director, Foreign Division, The British Council, 1944; Rep. in Brazil, 1945, in India, 1948, in Austria, 1949-54. *Recreation:* travel. *Address:* 11 The Avenue, Beckenham, Kent. *T.:* Beckenham 1980. *Club:* M.C.C. [*Died* 17 *Sept.* 1956.

WICKS, Pembroke, C.B.E. 1922; Registrar, Architects Registration Council (under the Act of Parliament of 1931) since 1936; *b.* 1882; *y. s.* of late Frederick Wicks, author, of Halfway Lodge, Esher; *m.* Kathleen Elizabeth Breffney, *d.* of Lt.-Col. H. Breffney Ternan, late of the Indian Army; two *d.* *Educ.:* King's College School; LL.B. London University, 1907. Private Secretary to Sir William Ward, 1901-2; called to Bar, Middle Temple, 1908; First-Class Honours Bar Final Examination; Private Secretary to late Lord Carson, 1911-1918; an Assistant Secretary to the Cabinet Office, 1918, during which period was seconded as personal assistant to Lord Beaverbrook and later as private secretary to Mr. Austen Chamberlain; Private Secretary (Parliamentary) to the Marquess Curzon of Kedleston, 1923; Principal Assist. Sec. Policy Secretariat, Unionist Party, 1924; Political Secretary Unionist Central Office, 1925-31. *Recreation:* fly-fishing. *Address:* Mole Bridge House, Esher Rd., Walton-on-Thames. *T.:* Esher 501. [*Died* 27 *Feb.* 1957.

WIDDICOMBE, Lt.-Col. George Templer, C.B. 1915; late 9th Gurkha Rifles, Indian Army; *b.* 13 Oct. 1867; *y. s.* of late Colonel W. Widdicombe, Judge of Karachi; *m.* Lydia Constance (*d.* 1944), *twin d.* of late Lieut.-Col. A. Baird; two *s.* one *d.* *Educ.:* Wellington College. Entered Army, 1886; Captain Indian army, 1897; Major, 1904; Lieut.-Col. 1912; served Lushai expedition, 1889 (medal with clasp; Chin-Lushai, 1889-90 (clasp); Hunza-Nagar expedition, 1901-2 (despatches, clasp); N.W. Frontier, India, 1897-98 (medal with clasp); Tirah, 1897-98 (clasp); European War, 1914-17 (despatches, C.B.), France, 1914-16, Mesopotamia, 1916-17. *Address:* c/o The Westminster Bank, 21 Clarendon Road, Southsea, Hants. [*Died* 19 *March* 1952.

WIDDOWSON, Thomas William, F.D.S. R.C.S. Eng.; Hon. Consulting Dental Surgeon, Member of the Dental Council, King's College Hospital; Referee for recognition of teachers in dental subjects, University of London; Emeritus lecturer in Dental Surgery, King's College Hospital; Lectr. in Special Anatomy and Physiology, King's Coll., London Univ.; British Dental Assoc.; Soc. of Authors; *b.* 18 June 1877; *s.* of John James and Charlotte Widdowson, Liverpool; *m.* 1905, Ethel, *d.* of George and Annie Bryan, Liverpool; two *s.* one *d.* *Educ.:* Liverpool College; Liverpool University; late Member: Board of Studies in Dentistry, London University; Board of Examiners in Dental Surgery, Royal College of Surgeons, England; late Deputy Director of Dental Studies and Chairman of Dental Committee, King's College Hospital, late House Dental Surgeon, Liverpool Dental Hospital; late external examiner in Dental Subjects to Liverpool University; Late Examiner in Special Anatomy, London Univ.; Late Pres. of Dental Soc., King's Coll. Hospital; Late Contributing editor to Oral Health, and Dental Practice, Toronto, Canada; Assistant Dental Surgeon and Dental Surgeon, King's College Hospital. *Publications:* Care and Regulation of Children's Teeth; Dental Surgery and Pathology, 3rd Edn., 1937; 4th Edn., 1950; Special Anatomy and Physiology and Dental Histology, reprint 1948, 8th Edn., 1952. *Recreations:* walking, histology, anthropology. *Address:* 85 Harley Street, W.1; 10 Newton Grove, Bedford Park, W.4. *T.:* Welbeck 5382, Chiswick 4864. [*Died* 27 *Dec.* 1956.

WIELAND, Dr. Heinrich; Professor, Munich University, retired, 1952; *b.* 4 June 1877; *m.*; three *s.* one *d.* *Educ.:* Pforzheim, Dr. Phil., Munich Univ., 1901; habilitation, 1904; a.o. Professor, 1909; Professor, Technische Hochschule, Munich, 1917; Professor, Univ. of Freiburg i. B. 1921; succeeded Willstätter in Munich, 1924. *Publications:* Arbeiten auf vielen Gebieten der organischen Chemie und der Biochemie; publiciert in Berichte der Deutschen Chemischen Gesellschaft, Liebig's Annalen der Chemie, Hoppe-Seyler's Zeitschrift für Physiolog. Chemie. *Address:* Starnberg, Oberbayern, Germany. [*Died* 5 *Aug.* 1957.

WIGAN, Brig.-General John Tyson, C.B.; 1919; C.M.G. 1918; D.S.O. 1916; T.D.; D.L. *b.* 31 July 1877; *o. s.* of late M. C. Wigan; *m.* 1911, Aline, *e. d.* of H. W. Henderson, West Woodhay House, Newbury; two *s.* one *d.* *Educ.:* Rugby. Served South African War with 13th Hussars (severely wounded, King and Queen's medals with 4 clasps); Adjutant of the Berks Yeomanry for 5 years; served European War in command of Berks Yeomanry in Gallipoli (wounded at Suvla Bay); commanded Mounted Composite Regiment, 1915, and later, Berks Yeomanry on the Western Frontier of Egypt (D.S.O., C.M.G.); wounded at Gaza when commanding the Berks Yeomanry in Palestine, 19 April 1917; Brig.-Gen., 1 July 1917; wounded, 28 Nov. 1917, during capture of Jerusalem; M.P. (C.U.) Abingdon Division of Berks, Dec. 1918-21; Hon. Col. (1/4th) Batt. Essex Regt., 1922-45; High Sheriff, Essex, 1930; J.P., Essex, 1923-46. Partner in firm of Wigan Richardson Co., Hop Merchants; Director: Phœnix Assurance Co., Ltd.; G. Nott & Co., Ltd., Hop Growers. *Recreation:* shooting. *Address:* Bolney Lodge, Bolney, Sussex. *T.:* Bolney 289. *Clubs:* Carlton, Royal Automobile; Union (Brighton). [*Died* 23 *Nov.* 1952.

WIGAN, Sir Roderick Grey, 3rd Bt., *cr.* 1898; *b.* 11 Nov. 1886; *e. s.* of 2nd Bt. and Elizabeth Adair, *e. d.* of Lt.-Col. F. D. Grey; *S.* father, 1907; *m.* 1909, Ina, *o. c.* of late Lewis D. Wigan, The Cairnies, Glenalmond, Perthshire; two *s.* one *d.* *Educ.:* Eton College; Magdalen College, Oxford. *Heir:* *s.* Frederick Adair, *b.* 13 April 1911. *Address:* Borrobol, Kinbrace, Sutherland. *Club:* Bath. [*Died* 15 *Jan.* 1954.

WIGGIN, Lieut.-Colonel (Bt. Col.) Sir William Henry, K.C.B., *cr.* 1948 (C.B. 1944); D.S.O.; T.D.; D.L., J.P. Worcs.; Chairman Territorial Army Assoc. of the County of Worcester; Director Barclays Bank Ltd., W. T. Avery Ltd., and other companies; *b.* 1888; *m.* 1935, Elizabeth Ethelston, *o. d.* of late J. Danvers Power, M.V.O.; two *s.* *Educ.:* Eton; Trinity College, Cambridge (B.A.). *Address:* St. Cloud, Callow End, nr. Worcester. *T.:* Powick 48. *Club:* Boodle's. [*Died* 11 *Sept.* 1951.

WIGHAM, Joseph Theodore, M.D., D.P.H., F.R.C.P.I.; Professor of Pathology, University of Dublin, 1924-45; *b.* 11 Dec. 1874; *s.* of John Richardson Wigham and Mary Pim of Albany House, Monkstown, Co. Dublin; *m.* 1916, Elsie Mary, *d.* of Maurice Smith, of Hoddesdon, Herts; one *s.* one *d.* *Educ.:* Bootham School, York; Trinity College, Dublin; B.A. (Mod. in Experimental Science), 1895; M.B., B.Ch., B.A.O. 1898; House Surgeon, Sir P. Dun's Hospital, 1899; M.D. 1900; Assistant to the Prof. of Pathology, 1901; travelled extensively studying tropical diseases, 1911-12; served as Red Cross surgeon under the Friends Ambulance Unit in France and Flanders during the War, chiefly in 1915; Acting Professor, 1916-17; Council Member of League of Nations Society of Ireland since 1919 and President, 1935-42; Representative of Society of Friends in Ireland on World Conferences on Faith and Order at Lausanne, 1927 and Edinburgh, 1937. *Recreations:* yacht and sailing-boat racing, and cruising; President The Water Wags, 1939; Commodore Dublin Bay Sailing Club, 1944. *Address:* Edenvale, Conyngham Road, Dublin. *T.:* Dublin 71005. *Club:* Royal Irish Yacht (Dun Laoghaire, Kingstown). [*Died* 22 *March* 1951.

WIGLEY, Sir Wilfrid Murray, Kt., *cr.* 1941; O.B.E. 1931; *b.* 9 Nov. 1876; *s.* of Francis Spencer Wigley, Frigate Bay, St. Kitts; *m.* 1906, Marjorie, *d.* of William W. Reid, West Farm, St. Kitts; three *s.* two *d.* *Educ.:* Derby School. Called to Bar, Middle Temple, 1901; Crown Attorney, St. Kitts-Nevis, 1918; 1st puisne judge, Leeward Islands, 1935; Chief Justice, 1937. Admin. Govt., St. Kitts-Nevis, on many occasions; retired 1941. *Address:* Frigate Bay, St. Kitts, W.I. [*Died* 19 *Dec.* 1959.

WIGRAM, 1st Baron, *cr.* 1935, of Clewer; **Clive Wigram,** P.C. 1932; G.C.B., *cr.* 1933 (K.C.B., *cr.* 1931; C.B. 1918); G.C.V.O., *cr.* 1932 (K.C.V.O., *cr.* 1928; C.V.O. 1915; M.V.O. 1903); Royal Victorian Chain, 1937; C.S.I. 1911; late 18th (K.G.O.) Lancers; Col. 19th (K.G.O.) Lancers, Indian Army, 1932-45; Permanent Lord in Waiting and Extra Equerry to the Queen since 1952 (Permanent Lord in Waiting and Extra Equerry to King George VI, 1936-52); *b.* 1873; *s.* of late Herbert Wigram, Madras Civil Service; *m.* 1912, Nora (*d.* 1956), *o. d.* of late Sir Neville Chamberlain, K.C.B., K.C.V.O.; one *s.* (second son Capt. Hon. Francis, Grenadier Guards, killed in action 1943; one *d.* decd.). *Educ.:* Winchester. First Commn. in R.A., 1893; A.D.C. to Lord Elgin, Viceroy of India, 1895; exchanged to 18th Lancers, Indian Army, 1897; served N.W. Frontier of India, 1897-98 (medal with 3 clasps); A.D.C. to Lord Curzon, Viceroy of India, 1899-1904; served in S. Africa (despatches, medal with 6 clasps); Assistant to the Chief of the Staff during H.R.H. the Prince of Wales' visit to India, 1905-6; Brevet-Majority, 1906; Brevet Lt.-Col. 1915; Brevet Col. 1919; Indian Staff College, 1906-8; Military Secretary to G.O.C. in C., Aldershot Command, 1908-1910; Assistant Private Secretary and Equerry to the King, 1910-31; Private Secretary and Extra Equerry to the King, 1931-35, and Private Secretary and Keeper of H.M. Privy Purse, 1935-36; late Deputy Constable and Lieut.-Governor, Windsor Castle and Keeper of the King's Archives; former Fellow of Winchester Coll.; former Governor: Wellington College; and of Haileybury and Imperial Service Coll. Junior School; Vice-Pres. King Edward VII Sanatorium, Midhurst; Vice-Pres. Windsor Hosp.; Council King Edward's Hosp. Fund for London; Pres. Westminster Hosp., 1936-48; Vice-Pres. National Association Boys Clubs; Member Central Council Physical Recreation; Governor of The Corps of Commissioners; Council of King George's Jubilee Trust; Member Royal Commission for the Exhibition of 1851. *Heir:* *s.* Hon. (George) Neville (Clive) Wigram, M.C. 1945; Lieut.-Col. Grenadier Guards [*b.* 2 Aug. 1915; *m.* 1941, Margaret Helen, *yr. d.* of General Sir Andrew Thorne, K.C.B., C.M.G., D.S.O.; one *s.* (*b.* 18 March 1949) two *d.*]. *Address:* 62 Avenue Rd., Regent's Park, N.W.8. *T.:* Primrose 3202. *Clubs:* Cavalry, Bath. [*Died* 3 *Sept.* 1960.

WIGRAM, Rev. William Ainger, B.D. Camb., D.D. Lambeth; *b.* Furneaux Pelham, Herts, 16 May 1872; 3rd *s.* of late Rev. Woolmore Wigram, Canon of St. Albans; unmarried. *Educ.:* King's School, Canterbury; Trinity Hall, Cambridge; Bishop Auckland Theological College. Formerly Hon. Chaplain to the Archbishop of Canterbury; Head of the Archbishop of Canterbury's Mission to the Assyrian Christians, in which he worked for ten years at Urmi (Persia), and Van and Amadia in Eastern Turkish Kurdistan; Assyrian repatriation, Mesopotamia; Chaplain to British Legation, Athens, 1922-26; Canon of St. Paul's, Malta, 1928-36. *Publications:* History of the Assyrian Church; The Separation of the Monophysites; The Cradle of Mankind; Assyrians and their Neighbours; Hellenic Travel; various articles in reviews and magazines. *Recreation:* travelling. *Address:* Green Acres, Wells, Som. *T.:* 2162. [*Died* 16 *Jan.* 1953.

WIJEYEKOON, Sir Gerard, Kt., *cr.* 1941; Barrister-at-Law, Gray's Inn, London; President of Ceylon Senate since 1947; Director Ceylon State Mortgage Bank; *b.* 5 May 1878; *o. s.* of Abraham Andrew Stephen Wijeyekoon and Josephine Maria de Silva Jayewardene; *m.* 1909, Florinda Beatrice Mary Silva; two *s.* two *d.* *Educ.:* Royal and Wesley Colleges, Colombo. Held various judicial appointments, 1904-10; member of Legislative Council, Ceylon, representing the Central Province, 1921-32; member of Governor's Executive Council, 1924-32; served on several commissions and committees and Selection Boards, including the University Commission and the Retrenchment Commission of 1922; member of Local Government Board, 1925-32; Commissioner under Land Settlement Appeal Board and a member of Tea and Rubber Appeal Boards and Advisory Committee under the Emergency Powers Act of 1939; Chairman Ceylon Branch of Navy League. *Recreation:* walking. *Address:* Sudassana, Turret Road, Colombo, Ceylon. *T.:* Colombo 2631. *Clubs:* National Liberal; Orient (Colombo). [*Died* 17 *Sept.* 1952.

WILBERFORCE, Brig.-General Sir Herbert William, K.B.E., *cr.* 1919; C.B. 1915; C.M.G. 1918; late Queen's Bays; *b.* 4 July 1866; *s.* of Ven. A. B. O. Wilberforce; *m.* 1905, Eleanor, *o. d.* of late Major-Gen. E. Micklem. *Educ:* Eton; R.M.C. Sandhurst. Entered Army, 1886; Capt., 1896; Major, 1900; Lt.-Col., 1911; Col., 1914; A.D.C. to Governor-General, Canada, 1895-8; employed with S. African Constabulary, 1900-3; served Hazara Expedition, 1891 (despatches, medal and clasp); S. African War, 1899-1902 (Queen's medal 4 clasps, King's medal 2 clasps); European War, 1914-18 (despatches 5 times, K.B.E., C.B., C.M.G., K.G.St.J., 1920; Grand Officer Military Order of Aviz, 1918; Portuguese Red Cross Medal, Benemerencia, 1920; Croix de Commandeur, Legion of Honour, 1919); retired 1920. *Address:* 3 Eaton Gardens, Hove 3, Sussex. *T.:* Hove 1667. [*Died* 28 *April* 1952.

WILBERFORCE, Samuel; Examiner in Hindu and Mahomedan Law at Inns of Court since 1928; *b.* 1874; *s.* of R. G. Wilberforce of Lavington Park, Sussex; *m.* 1906, Katherine, *d.* of late Rt. Rev. John Sheepshanks, Bishop of Norwich; one *s.* one *d.* *Educ.:* Malvern College; Pembroke College, Cambridge. Entered Indian Civil Service, 1896; posted to the Punjab; served the greater part of his career in the Judicial Branch, and acted as Judge of the High Court, Lahore, 1918; Puisne Judge of the Lahore High Court, 1921-23; retired, 1923; introduced the co-operative credit movement in the Punjab, 1904-9; deputed by the Government of India, at request of Colonial Office, to introduce the same movement into Mauritius, 1903. *Recreations:* polo, golf, shooting. *Address:* Lavington, Walton-on-the-Hill, Surrey. [*Died* 10 *Dec.* 1954.

WILBERFORCE-BELL, Lt.-Col. Sir Harold, K.C.I.E., *cr.* 1938 (C.I.E. 1931); lately of H.M. Indian Political Service; D.L., J.P. East Riding of Yorkshire; *b.* 17 Nov. 1885; *e. s.* of late Capt. H. Wilberforce-Bell, a Military Knight of Windsor, and Lucy, *d.* of Rev. Frederick Wilson, D.D., Vicar of Sledmere, and *g.s.* of William Henry Bell, of Portington Hall, E. Yorks, and of Jane Wilberfosse; *m.* 1912, Margaret, *d.* of late

Captain Michael Festing, formerly 20th Regt.; no *c*. *Educ.:* Ellesmere College; Pembroke College, Oxford. Gazetted to The Connaught Rangers, 1905; transferred to the Indian Army, 1908; entered the Indian Political Service, 1909; reverted to military employ, 1914, and served in France, 1915, with 1st (King George's Own) Gurkha Rifles; Gen. Staff, Northern Army, India, 1917; Asst. Military Sec. to C.-in-C. in India, 1918; served in political appointments in Aden, Western India, Panjab, and Central India; Deputy Political Sec., Govt. of India, 1928; Political Sec. to the Govt. of India, 1930; Agent to the Governor-General for the Deccan States and Resident at Kolhapur, 1933; Resident for the Panjab States, 1934-39; retired, 1940. Life Governor, University of Hull; Vice-Pres. S.S. and A.F.A., East Riding; Vice-Pres. B.R.C.S., East Yorks; Vice-Pres. East Riding Playing Fields Assoc.; Vice-Pres. Royal Soc. of St. George, Yorkshire Br.; Chm. No. 7 Hospl. Management Cttee.; Chm., Hull Borstal Inst. *Publications:* The History of Kathiawad, 1916; Some Translations from the Marathi Poets, 1912, etc. *Address:* Portington Hall, Howden, East Yorks. *T.:* Eastrington 212. *Clubs:* Athenæum; Yorkshire (York). [*Died* 24 *Jan.* 1956.

WILBRAHAM, Sir Philip Wilbraham Baker, 6th Bt., *cr.* 1776; K.B.E., *cr.* 1954; D.C.L.; First Church Estates Commissioner, 1939-54; Vicar-General of the Province of Canterbury, 1934-55; formerly: Dean of the Arches; Auditor of the Chancery Court of York; Master of the Faculties; *b.* 17 Sept. 1875; *s.* of 5th Bt. and Katharine Frances, *o. c.* of Lt.-Gen. Sir Richard Wilbraham, K.C.B.; *S.* father, 1912; *m.* 1901, Joyce Christabel, *y. d.* of Sir John H. Kennaway, 3rd Bt.; one *s.* three *d.* *Educ.:* Harrow; Balliol, Oxford; Fellow of All Souls, Oxford, 1899. Called to bar, Lincoln's Inn, 1901; Bencher, 1943; Chancellor, Diocese of Chester, 1913-34; Chancellor and Vicar-General, Diocese and Province of York, 1915-1934; Chancellor, Diocese of Truro, 1923-1934; of Chelmsford, 1928-34; of Durham, 1929-34; Secretary of National Assembly of the Church of England, 1920-39. *Heir:* *s.* Randle John Baker Wilbraham. *Address:* Rode Hall, Scholar Green, Cheshire. *Club:* Athenæum. [*Died* 11 *Oct.* 1957.

WILCOCK, Dr. Alfred William, F.R.C.O., F.R.M.C.M., Hon. R.C.M.; L.R.A.M.; organist and Master of the Choristers at Exeter Cathedral, 1933-52; retired 1952. Late organist at Derby Cathedral and Professor of Harmony and Composition in Royal Manchester College of Music, 1918-33. *Address:* 9 Beach Bank, Waterloo, Liverpool. [*Died* 26 *Oct.* 1953.

WILCOCK, John Stewart, C.I.E. 1948; O.B.E. 1939; I.C.S. retd.; *b.* 6 Feb. 1905; *s.* of George and Edith Gwenllian Wilcock; *m.* 1940, Mary Gwendoline Warden Wilcock (*née* Crooks); two *s.* two *d.* *Educ.:* Manchester Grammar School; Pembroke College, Cambridge. Appointed to Indian Civil Service, 1928, Private Secretary, 1936, Secretary, 1937, to Governor of Orissa; Secretary to Bihar Government, Revenue Department, 1944; Secretary to Bihar Government, Development Department, 1946-1949. *Address:* Westfield, Sidmonton Rd., Bray, Eire. *T:* Bray 378. *Club:* University (Dublin). [*Died* 1 *Feb.* 1951.

WILCOX, Rev. Arthur John, C.B.E. 1941; M.A.; *b.* 28 Mar. 1889; *s.* of late F. H. Wilcox, Cheltenham, Glos.; *m.* Esmé, *y. d.* of late W. H. T. Dawe, Crownhill, Plymouth; one *d.* (and one *d.* decd.). *Educ.:* Dean Close; Emmanuel College, Cambridge; Ridley Hall, Cambridge. Curate of Emmanuel Church, Compton Gifford, 1913; Chaplain to the Forces, 1915; Captured by the Turks at battle of Ograhtina, Sinai Desert, 1916; released, 1918; Catterick Camp, 1919; Egypt, 1919-24; Warley, 1924-26; Guards Depot, Caterham, 1926-28; 3rd class C.F. 1927; Bulford, 1928-32; Guards Depot, 1932-34; Chaplain to Brigade of Guards, Wellington Barracks, 1934-38; 2nd class C.F. 1935; 1st class and A.C.G. 1938; Assistant Chaplain-General, Egypt, 1938; Deputy Chaplain-General, Middle East Force, 1939-44 (despatches twice); K.H.C. 1945; retired pay, 1945. Assistant Priest at St. Margaret's, Westminster, 1945-55. *Recreations:* rowing and golf. *Address:* 5 Artillery Mansions, 75 Victoria Street, S.W.1. *Club:* United Service. [*Died* 6 *June* 1960.

WILD, Brig.-Gen. R. K. B.; *see* Bagnall-Wild.

WILD, Lieut.-Colonel Wilfrid Hubert, D.S.O. 1916; O.B.E. 1942; J.P., D.L. Herts.; *b.* 1874; *s.* of late Rev. Robert Louis Wild, Rector of Hurstmonceux; *m.* 1906, Violet Grace, *d.* of late Alfred Harmsworth, Barrister-at-law, Middle Temple; two *s.* three *d.* *Educ.:* Charterhouse School. Entered Northumberland Fusiliers, 1895; Major, 1915; Brevet Lieut.-Col., 1919; retired, 1920; served European War, 1914-18; commanded a battalion of his regiment (despatches, D.S.O., and Brevet Lieut.-Col.); High Sheriff of Herts, 1935. *Address:* Shenley Hill, St. Albans, Herts. *T.A.:* Shenley Hill, Shenley, Herts. *T.:* Radlett 6694. *Club:* United Service. [*Died* 3 *Jan.* 1953.

WILDING, Brig.-General Charles Arthur, C.M.G. 1915; J.P. Montgomeryshire, 1908; *b.* 13 June 1868. *Educ.:* Marlborough; Sandhurst. Entered army, 1887; Captain, 1897; Major, 1905; Lt.-Col. 1914; Brig.-Gen. 1916; served Burma, 1889-92 (medal); Nigeria, 1893-94 (medal); European War, 1914-16 (C.M.G., despatches thrice); retired pay, 1918. *Club:* Army and Navy. [*Died* 9 *July* 1953.

WILES, Rt. Hon. Thomas, P.C. 1916; *b.* St. Albans, Herts, *y. s.* of late Joseph Wiles of St. Albans; *m.* 1890, Winifred Alice, *y. d.* of Rev. Harris Crassweller of Highbury; one *s.* two *d.* *Educ.:* Amersham Hall School. Life Governor of Joseph Wiles & Son, Ltd., merchants, of Mark Lane, E.C.; late Chairman Port of London Authority; Chairman of Corn Exchange; Chairman Anglo-Portuguese Colonial and Overseas Bank, Ltd.; Chairman Royal Surgical Aid Society; L.C.C. for South-West Bethnal Green, 1899; for some years Whip to Progressive party at Spring Gardens; M.P. (L.) South Islington, 1906-18; Parliamentary Secretary to Mr. T. M'Kinnon Wood, M.P., Under-Secretary for Foreign Affairs. *Address:* Stoke Court, Stoke Poges, Bucks. *Clubs:* Reform, City of London, Hurlingham. [*Died* 18 *May* 1951.

WILFORD, Canon John Russell, B.D.; Principal of Christ's College Collegiate Department, 1913-33; Canon of Christchurch Cathedral and Examiner in Hebrew for Canterbury University College, New Zealand; Watts-Russell Professor of Divinity and Hulsean-Chichele Professor of History, 1913-33; *b.* Welney Rectory, Wisbech, 1877; *s.* of Rev. Edward Russell Wilford, M.A.; *m.* 1901, Dorothy, *d.* of Rev. James Smart, M.A.; two *s.* *Educ.:* Oundle; Christ's College, Cambridge; Carus Greek Testament Prize. Curate Denver, Norfolk, 1900-4; Vicar of Waikari, N.Z., 1904-7; Vicar of Prebbleton, N.Z., and Examiner for the N.Z. Board of Theological Studies, 1907-13; Preacher-in-Ordinary at Christchurch Cathedral and Examining Chaplain to the Bishop of Christchurch; founder of S. George's Hospital, 1928; founder N.Z. Educ. Soc., the Assoc. of the Love of God. The Friends of Montana, 1939. *Publications:* Faith Moves Mountains; The Story of St. George's Hospital; Southern Cross and Evening Star; A Jersey Country Parish during the Time of Occupation; Steps to Heaven; A Father at Home with his Children. Ed. Report of first N.Z. Church Congress; papers dealing with educ. and the Church's work amongst the sick. *Recreations:* cricket, tennis, and gardening. *Address:* Petit Coin, St.

Martins, Jersey, C.I. *T.A.:* Jersey. *T.:* Five Oaks 201. [*Died* 9 *April* 1954.

WILGRESS, Rev. George Frederick; Warden of Browne's Hospital, Stamford, since 1933; *b.* 1868; *s.* of late Rev. George Frederick Wilgress; *m.* 1910, Alice Mildred W. (*d.* 1929), *y. d.* of late T. W. Mills, Eltham. *Educ.:* Lancing College; Keble College, Oxford; Cuddesdon College; B.A. 1890; M.A. 1894; Curate of St. James, Grimsby, 1891-94; Domestic Chaplain to Bishop King, 1894-1910; Rector of Kettlethorpe, 1910-12; Prebendary of Lincoln Cathedral, 1906; Organising Sec. for Preventive and Rescue Work in diocese of Winchester, 1912-1913; Assistant Curate at St. Thomas', Winchester, 1913-15; St. Cross, Winchester, 1915; Rector of Great Elm, 1917-24; Warden of St. Anne's Bede Houses, Lincoln, 1926-33. *Address:* Browne's Hospital, Stamford, Lincs. [*Died* 21 *Sept.* 1953.

WILKIE, Rev. Arthur West, C.B.E. 1926; D.D.; *b.* Liscard, Cheshire, 9 Nov. 1875; *s.* of late Rev. James Mougach Wilkie and late Jessie Thomson; *m.* 1903, Marian Boyd, *d.* of late Rev. George Robson, D.D. *Educ.:* Liverpool University; Glasgow University; United Presbyterian Theological Hall, Edinburgh. Missionary, United Free Church of Scotland, Calabar, 1901-18; on exclusion of Basel and Bremen Missions took over control of these former Germanic Missions, 1918-27; represented British Missionary Societies on first Phelps-Stokes Commission on Education to West Africa, 1920; Secretary Scottish Mission, Gold Coast Colony; Principal, Lovedale, South Africa, 1932-42; retired, 1942. *Address:* Cheylesmore Lodge, Dirleton Avenue, North Berwick. [*Died* 19 *April* 1958.

WILKIE, James, M.C.; Slade School of Fine Art, University College, London; *b.* 28 May 1890; *s.* of late James Wilkie, Birmingham; unmarried. Came to London, 1910; studied Art at the Slade School, University College, W.C.; joined Artists' Rifles O.T.C.; went to France, 1916; commissioned Loyal North Lancashire Regt. attached East Lancs (M.C.); returned after War to Slade School, Prize Winner; joined the Staff under late Prof. Tonks; Member of New English Art Club. *Recreations:* Football with Dulwich Hamlet, Chelsea, Luton Town, ice figure skater (Silver Medallist), golf. *Address:* 20 Gunter Grove, Chelsea, S.W.10. *T.:* Flaxman 3477. *Club:* Chelsea Arts. [*Died* 18 *Dec.* 1957.

WILKINS, Sir (George) Hubert, Kt., *cr.* 1928; M.C.; F.R.G.S., F. R. Met. Soc., M.B.O.U.; *b.* Mt. Bryan East, South Australia, 31 Oct. 1888; *s.* of late H. Wilkins, of Netfield, South Australia; *m.* 1929, Suzanne Bennett. *Educ.:* State School and Adelaide School of Mines. Photographic Correspondent with Turkish troops in Balkan War, 1912-13; Second in command of Stefansson's Party Canadian Arctic Expedition, 1913-17; granted commission Australian Flying Corps, A.I.F., May 1917; seconded to Military History Department as Official Photographer, 1917 to close of War (despatches twice, M.C., bar to M.C.); Navigator Blackburn Kangaroo Aeroplane, England-Australia Flight, 1919; Second-in-Command British Imperial Antarctic Expedition, 1920-21; Naturalist with Shackleton-Rowett Quest Expedition, 1921-22; Leader, Wilkins Australia and Islands Expedition for British Museum (Natural History), 1923-25; Commander Detroit Arctic Expedition, 1926-27; Commander Wilkins Detroit-News Arctic Expedition, 1928; Commander Wilkins Hearst Antarctic Expedition, 1928-29; Commander Nautilus Arctic Submarine Expedition, 1931; Manager, Ellsworth Trans-Antarctic Expeditions, 1933-39; Consultant, U.S. Army Military Planning Division, 1942-52; Geographer: Research and Development Command, Dept. of Defense, U.S.A., 1953-. Awarded Patron's Medal, 1928, by R.G.S. and numerous medals by English and foreign geog. and aeronautical socs. Hon. Member various geog. socs., etc.; Companion Order of St. Maurice and Lazarus, 1932. *Publications:* Flying the Arctic, 1928; Undiscovered Australia, 1928; Under the North Pole, 1931; Thoughts Through Space, 1952; Naturalist's Reports, Proceedings of Linnean Society, and Ibis; contrib. to public press and magazines. *Address:* City Club, 45 Park Av., New York. *Clubs:* Royal Societies; Explorers' (New York). [*Died* 1 *Dec.* 1958.

WILKINS, William Vaughan; author; *b.* London, 6 Mar. 1890; *s.* of Rev. W. H. and Lena Charlotte Wilkins; *m.* 1930, Mary Isabel Stanistreet, *e. d.* of Lt.-Col. J. E. Powell, D.S.O.; two *s.* *Educ.:* Merchant Taylors' School. Foreign editor, The Standard; editor, Daily Call; news-editor, Central Council for Economic Information; assistant-editor, Sunday Referee; assistant-editor, Daily Express; assistant-editor, News Chronicle; served European War, 1914-18, Egypt, Palestine, and France. *Publications:* Once Upon a Time—; Being Met Together; Seven Tempest; And So—Victoria; Endless Prelude; Sidelights on Industrial Evolution; Hermsprong (ed.); The City of Frozen Fire; Crown Without Sceptre; A King Reluctant; Fanfare for a Witch; Lady of Paris; Valley Beyond Time; Husband for Victoria; After Bath (for children). *Recreation:* idling. *Address:* Instead, Duxmere, Ross-on-Wye, Herefordshire. *T.:* Ross-on-Wye 2813. [*Died* 8 *Feb.* 1959.

WILKINSON, Colonel Charles William, C.M.G. 1918; D.S.O. 1917; late R.E.; *b.* 1868; *m.* 1899; three *d.*; *m.* 1910 (wife *d.* 1952); one *s.* *Educ.:* Haileybury; Woolwich. Served N.W. Frontier of India, 1897-1898 (medal and clasp); European War, 1914-18 (despatches, C.M.G., D.S.O.); retd. 1924. *Address:* c/o Lloyds Bank, 6 Pall Mall, S.W.1. [*Died* 6 *Feb.* 1954.

WILKINSON, Clennell F. M.; *see* Drew-Wilkinson.

WILKINSON, Cyril Hackett, O.B.E., M.C.; T.D.; Hon. Fellow of Worcester College, Oxford, 1958, formerly Dean and Vice-Provost; *b.* 16 November 1888; 2nd *s.* of Rev. H. M. Wilkinson, Vicar of Milford-on-Sea, Hants, and Florence Amy, *d.* of John Kemp-Welch of Sopley Park, Christchurch. *Educ.:* Eton; Oxford. Assistant Master, Eton College, 1912-14; served in France with 2nd Batt. Coldstream Guards and as G.S.O.3 with 2nd Army Staff, April 1915-Nov. 1917; in Italy as G.S.O.2 on the staffs of Sir Herbert Plumer and Lord Cavan, Nov. 1917-Dec. 1918 (M.C., Croix de Guerre, Croce di Guerra); Lt.-Col. O.U.O.T.C. 1919-31; Brevet Colonel, 1931; commanded, O.U.S.T. Corps, 1939-45 (O.B.E., T.D.). *Publications:* Worcester College Library; edited the Poems of Richard Lovelace, The King of the Beggars, Diversions, and More Diversions; Goddords Neaste of Wasps; Saltonstall's Picturae Loquentes, A Challenge from Sir Thomas Urquhart; Chaloner's Moses his Tombe. *Address:* Worcester College, Oxford; Salt Grass, Keyhaven, Hants. [*Died* 19 *Jan.* 1960.

WILKINSON, Fanny Rollo; Principal of the Horticultural College, Swanley, 1902-16, 1921-22; *e. d.* of late M. A. Eason Wilkinson, M.D., F.R.C.P., Pres. of the British Medical Association. *Educ.:* privately; Crystal Palace School of Gardening. Formerly landscape gardener to the Metropolitan Public Gardens Association and to the Kyrle Society. *Recreations:* travelling, gardening. *Address:* 54 Tadcaster Road, York. [*Died* 22 *Jan.* 1951.

WILKINSON, George; Consulting Aural Surgeon Chesterfield Royal Hospital; *b.* Hull, 1867; *s.* of John Wilkinson, surgeon; *m.* 1895, Alice Foster (*d.* 1948), The Pillars, Hornsea; one *s.* three *d.* *Educ.:* Emmanuel Coll., Camb. (scholar); St. Mary's Hosp., Lond. (Univ. scholar). B.A.; 1st class Natural Science Tripos, Camb. 1888; L.S.A. 1890; M.B., B.C. Cantab. 1891; M.R.C.S. England; L.R.C.P. London, 1894; F.R.C.S.

England, 1894; Consulting Aural Surgeon, late Hon. Surgeon, Sheffield Royal Hospital; Lecturer on the History of Medicine at the University of Sheffield. *Publications:* The Mechanism of the Cochlea (Wilkinson and Gray); article—Hearing, in Ency. Brit. *Address:* 6 Claremont Place, Sheffield 10. [*Died 5 Dec.* 1956.

WILKINSON, Kenneth Douglas, O.B.E. 1918; Physician to the Birmingham United Hospital since 1925 and Consulting Physician to Children's Hospital, Birmingham; Professor of Therapeutics in the University of Birmingham, 1929-46; Emeritus Professor since 1946; Examiner Pharmacology and Therapeutics, University of Cambridge and Royal College of Physicians; Examiner in Medicine, University of Birmingham and University of Manchester; *b.* High Legh, Cheshire, 17 April 1886; *s.* of late Rev. H. C. Wilkinson; *m.* 1916, Phebe Helena (*d.* 1940), *d.* of late Capt. C. H. Homewood, Wallasey, Cheshire; three *s.* one *d.*; *m.* 1941, Agnes Hallimond Crozier, M.B., Birmingham, M.R.C.P. Lond.; one *s.* two *d.* *Educ.:* Berkhamsted; Birmingham Univ. M.B., Ch.B. 1909; M.D. 1912; M.R.C.P. 1914; F.R.C.P. 1929. Assistant Physician to the Children's Hospital, 1913; Assistant Physician to the General Hospital, 1914. Major, retired, R.A.M.C. (despatches, O.B.E.) Group Officer, Birmingham; Regional Consultant of Medicine, No. 9 Region; Clinical Gas Expert, No. 9 Region, Ministry of Health, 1940-45. *Publications:* The History of the Birmingham Medical School, 1925; Dr. William Withering of Birmingham, 1950; Congenital Diseases of the Heart in Diseases of Infancy and Childhood, Parsons and Barling; various articles in professional journals. *Recreations:* golf, bridge, photography. *Address:* 89 Harborne Road, Edgbaston. *T.:* Edgbaston 0328. *Clubs:* Graduates, Edgbaston Golf (Birmingham). [*Died* 12 *April* 1951.

WILKINSON, Major-Gen. Sir Percival Spearman, K.C.M.G., *cr.* 1917 (C.M.G. 1914); C.B. 1914; Secretary - General, Order of St. John, 1923 - 43; *b.* 5 July 1865; *e. s.* of late Percival Wilkinson of Mt. Oswald, Durham; *m.* 1910, Cicely, D.G.St.J., *d.* of late Maj.-Gen. W. C. Hunter-Blair, C.B., C.M.G.; two *d.* *Educ.:* Uppingham. Inspector-General West African Force, 1909-13; served with Niger expedition, 1897-98 (despatches, Bt. of Major, medal with clasp); Ashanti, 1900 (despatches, Bt. Lt.-Col., medal with clasp, wounded); European War, 1914-18 (despatches, wounded, K.C.M.G.); Inspector of Musketry, 1918 - 19; Commanding No. 1 Area, 1919 - 23; Colonel Northumberland Fusiliers, 1915-35; retired pay, 1923; K.G.St.J. *Recreations:* shooting, fishing. *Address:* Rosebery House, Gorebridge, Midlothian. *Club:* United Service. [*Died* 4 *Nov.* 1953.

WILLAN, Brig.-Gen. Frank Godfrey, C.M.G. 1919; D.S.O. 1915; *b.* 16 Sept. 1878; *s.* of late Col. Frank Willan; *m.* 1945, Maud Valerie, *widow* of Brig. - Gen. H. A. Vernon. *Educ.:* Eton. Joined 4th Oxfordshire Light Infantry, 1896; King's Royal Rifle Corps, 1899; Capt. 1906; Major, 1915; temp. Brig.-Gen., 1917; Lt.-Col. 1924; Col. 1928; served South Africa, 1899 - 1900 (Queen's medal 3 clasps); European War, 1914-18 (despatches six times, D.S.O., C.M.G., Bt. Lieut.-Col.); retired pay, 1933. *Address:* The Close, Winchester, Hants. *Club:* Army and Navy. [*Died* 2 *June* 1957.

WILLAN, Colonel (Hon. Brig.) Robert Hugh, D.S.O. 1916; M.C.; *b.* 6 Sept. 1882; 2nd *s.* of Colonel Frank Willan; *m.* Violet (*d.* 1951), *d.* of Brig.-Gen. Eyre Crabbe, C.B., Grenadier Guards; one *s.* (and one killed in action, 1940). *Educ.:* Eton. Joined 4th Oxfordshire Light Infantry, 1899; King's Royal Rifle Corps, 1902; Royal Corps of Signals, 1920; Chief Signal Officer Southern Command, 1929-31; General Staff Officer 1st grade, War Office, 1931-33; half pay, 1933; Commanded 10th Infantry Brigade, 1934-38; A.D.C. to the King, 1934-38; Col. Comdt., Royal Corps of Signals, 1934-44; retired pay, 1938; served European War, 1914-18 (Military Cross, D.S.O., Croix de Guerre, Bt. Lt.-Col.); Inspector Royal Signals, Sept. 1939-Apr. 1942. *Address:* Bridges, Teffont, nr. Salisbury. *T.:* Teffont 230. *Club:* Army and Navy. [*Died* 4 *May* 1960.

WILLAN, Robert Joseph, C.B.E. 1946 (O.B.E. 1919); M.V.O. 1915; V(R)D.; M.B., M.S., F.R.C.S. England; Emeritus Prof. of Surgery, Durham University; Hon. Consulting Surgeon, late Senior Hon. Surgeon, Royal Victoria Infirmary, Newcastle upon Tyne, also Hon. Life Governor Ingham Infirmary, South Shields, and to Newcastle upon Tyne Dental Hospital; Surgical Adviser to No. 1 Region, Ministry of Health; Surgeon to Ministry of Pensions Hospital, Dunston Hill; Surgeon Rear-Admiral and R.N. Consultant in Surgery for Scotland, 1943-46; late Member of Council of Royal College of Surgeons of England; *b.* 10 Jan. 1878; 2nd *s.* of John Willan, J.P., Durham; *m.* 1910, Dorothy Eleanor (*d.* 1949), 2nd *d.* of J. B. Shawyer, Carlisle; one *s.* two *d.* *Educ.:* Durham School; Durham University. F.R.Soc.Med.; K.H.S. 1930-33. *Publications:* Clinical Hat-pegs for Students and Graduates, and numerous monographs in medical journals. *Address:* 75 Harley House, N.W.1. *T.:* Welbeck 3858; Shincliffe, Thurlestone, S. Devon. *T.:* Thurlestone 255. *Club:* Athenæum. [*Died* 12 *Jan.* 1955.

WILLCOCK, Hon. John Collings, M.L.A. retired, of Western Australia (1917-1947); *b.* Frogmoor, N.S.W., 9 Aug. 1879; *s.* of late Joseph Willcock and Ellen Webb; *m.* 1907; one *s.* three *d.* *Educ.:* Sydney. Minister for Railways and Justice, 1924 - 30, and 1933-36; Minister for Forests, 1936-43; Premier and Treasurer, W.A., 1936-45. *Address:* 45 Rookwood St., Mt. Lawley, W. Australia. [*Died* 7 *June* 1956.

WILLES, Lieut.-Col. Charles Edward, C.M.G. 1919; *b.* 1870; *e. s.* of Capt. H. C. Willes; *m.* 1st, 1898, Wilhelmina Susan (*d.* 1911), *d.* of Sir Robert Keith Alexander Dick-Cunyngham, 7th Bt.; 2nd, 1915, Madeleine, *widow* of Capt. Harold Whitaker; two *d.* *Educ.:* Malvern; R.M.C. Sandhurst. Served Hazara Expedition, 1891; European War, 1914-19 (despatches, C.M.G.). *Clubs:* M.C.C., Free Foresters. [*Died* 4 *Nov.* 1952.

WILLEY, Octavius George, C.B.E. 1951; M.P. (Lab.) Cleveland Div., N. Riding, Yorkshire, since 1945; *b.* 12 Jan. 1886; *s.* of Octavius Dalby Willey and Elizabeth Anne Jackson; *m.* 1916, Fannie Grunwell, Bramley, Leeds; no *c.* *Educ.:* Sherbrooke Higher Grade School, Fulham. Office ten years; with R. J. Campbell's Progressive League as Organiser two years; Swarthmore Settlement, Leeds, eight years; Lecturer History and Social Economics. With Labour Party twenty years, agent, organiser and speaker. Contested (Lab.) Skipton, Yorkshire, 1923 and 1924, West Birmingham 1929, 1931 and 1935. Outside Meetings Officer, Ministry of Information, 1940-41. Deputy Regional Commissioner for Civil Defence, N.E. Region, 1941-45. *Recreation:* reading. *Address:* House of Commons, S.W.1. [*Died* 12 *July* 1952.

WILLIAMS, Alice Helena Alexandra, C.B.E. 1937; *b.* Castle Deudraeth, Merionethshire, 12 March 1863; *y. d.* of David Williams, M.P. Worked during the War for the French Wounded Emergency Fund and other organisations (Médaille de la Reconnaissance Française); was Vice-Chairman of the Merioneth Women's War Agricultural Committee; gave the ground and raised the funds for building the first Women's Institute Hall in Britain, at Penrhyn-

deudraeth, Merionethshire; first Hon. Secretary and Treasurer of the National Federation of Women's Institutes, London, 1917; founded the N.F.W. Institutes' Journal, "Home and Country"; originated and organised the first two exhibitions of Women's Institute Work; has been a member of the Union des Femmes Peintres et Sculpteurs, Paris, and of the Union Internationale des Aquarellistes, Paris; one of the founders of the Forum Club 1919, of which she was first Chairman, and again 1928-35; one of the three first women elected on the House Committee of St. George's Hospital. *Publications:* Aunt Mollie's Story, 1913; Liz, 1915; Britannia, 1917, for which she was created a Bard the same year, Bardic name Alys Meirion; Life's a Game o' See-Saw; Britain Awake: an Empire Pageant Play, 1932; Caught, 1934; Gossip, 1935. *Address:* Forum Club, 42 Belgrave Square, S.W.1.
[*Died* 15 *Aug.* 1957.

WILLIAMS, Arnold, F.R.Econ.S.; Managing Director of National Screen Service, Ltd.; *b.* 30 Sept. 1890; *s.* of late S. W. Williams, chartered accountant, Manchester, and Alice Collins; *m.* 1915, Bessie Clarke, *d.* of late J. R. Morland, Manchester; one *s.* one *d.* *Educ.:* privately; Victoria University, Manchester. M.P. (L.) for Sowerby Division, W. Yorks, 1923-24. *Address:* Nascreno House, Soho Square, W.1. *T.:* Gerrard 4851. *Clubs:* Royal Automobile, Wardroom, Empress, Screen Writers'.
[*Died* 1 *Jan.* 1958.

WILLIAMS, Rt. Hon. Charles, P.C. 1952; late Lieut.-Commander R.N.V.R.; M.P. (C.) Torquay Division since 1924; *b.* 21 April 1886; *e. s.* of late John Charles Williams; *m.* 1915, Mary Frances, *d.* of late T. B. Bolitho, Trewidden, Penzance. *Educ.:* Eton; Trinity College, Cambridge. Served Antwerp in Naval Division and Gallipoli; contested as Unionist Northwich and Truro and Torquay; M.P. (Coal. U.) Tavistock Division of Devon, Dec. 1918-22. Deputy Chairman of Ways and Means, 1943-45; Chairman of Ways and Means and Deputy Speaker, May 1945. *Recreations:* gardening and country pursuits. *Address:* Caerhays Castle, Gorran, St. Austell, Cornwall; Rozel, Middle Lincombe Road, Torquay. *T.:* Torquay 3365. *Club:* Carlton. [*Died* 28 *Oct.* 1955.

WILLIAMS, Major Charles Edward, C.B.E. 1933 (O.B.E. 1918); M.I.Mech.E.; *b.* 1873; *s.* of David Edwardes and Hannah Sophia Williams; *m.* 1901, Ethel Smith; one *d.* *Educ.:* Llandovery College. Assistant Works Manager Vulcan Loco Works, Lancs; Inspector for New Zealand Railways 1898; Assistant Manager Robt. Stephenson, Darlington, 1901; Deputy Chief Inspecting Engineer Crown Agents 1904; Chief Inspecting Engineer Crown Agents for the Colonies 1922-34; Staff Captain W.O. 1914; Major R.E., D.A.D., W.O. 1918; Visited Nigeria and Sierra Leone 1920; Palestine and Cyprus 1921; Railways Engineer United Steel Cos. 1934-37; General Manager, C.W. Railway Eng. Works, Biddulph, 1943-46; retired. Freeman of the Borough of Carmarthen; Past President of the Institution of Locomotive Engineers. *Publication:* Colonial Railways. *Address:* Bonaventure, Caledon Road, Parkstone, Dorset. *T.:* Parkstone 972.
[*Died* 8 *Nov.* 1955.

WILLIAMS, Charles Wodehouse, C.M.G. 1949; M.B.E. 1928; Secretary, Jerusalem and the East Mission since 1950; *b.* Wadhurst, Sx., 12 Feb. 1899; *s.* of John Wodehouse Williams; *m.* 1928, Sheila McNeil, *d.* of late William Wallace, C.B.E., Oban, Argyll; one *s.* one *d.* *Educ.:* Wellington College; Oriel College, Oxford. Served European War, 2nd Lieut. Coldstream Guards, 1918-19 (wounded). Tutor, Gordon Memorial College, Khartoum, 1920-24; Senior Tutor, 1924-28; Inspector of Education, Sudan Govt., 1928-30; Warden, Gordon Memorial College, 1930-37; Asst. Director of Education, 1937-44, Director of Education, 1944-49. Member: Governor-General's Council, 1944-49; Gordon Memorial College Council, 1944-49, etc. Retired, 1950. *Recreations:* tennis, swimming, reading. *Address:* 12 Warwick Square, S.W.1. *T.:* Victoria 3232. *Club:* Royal Empire Society. [*Died* 20 *Feb.* 1957.

WILLIAMS, E. G. Harcourt; Actor and Producer; *b.* Croydon, 30 March 1880; *s.* of John Williams; *m.* 1908, Jean Sterling Mackinlay, *q.v.*; one *s.* (one *d.* decd.). *Educ.:* The Abbey, Beckenham; The Whitgift, Croydon. Began stage career at the age of seventeen with Sir Frank Benson; played important parts with Ellen Terry, Sir George Alexander, Sir Herbert Tree, H. B. Irving, Sir John Gielgud, Sir Ralph Richardson, Sir Laurence Olivier; has acted in plays by Shakespeare, Sheridan, Goldsmith, Ibsen, Tchechov, Zangwill. Shaw, Granville Barker, Masefield, Drinkwater, Chesterton, Priestley, Fry; four years producer at Old Vic Theatre, 1929-33; other productions, Pompey the Great, Thunder on the Left, Magic, etc.; has Broadcast and Televised frequently, and made many films; produced and acted in The Zeal of Thy House, by Dorothy L. Sayers, Old Vic Theatre Co., 1944-46; played The Waiter in longest run of Shaw's You Never Can Tell, Wyndham's, 1947-48; has since played in four London successes. *Publications:* Four Years at the Old Vic; Tales from Ebony; Short Stories; Old Vic Saga. *Recreations:* "Living" in the country, swimming. *Address:* 310 Clive Court, W.9. *T.:* Cunningham 0758; Ebony Cottage, near Tenterden, Kent. *T.:* Appledore 255.
[*Died* 13 *Dec.* 1957.

WILLIAMS, Sir Evan, 1st Bt., *cr.* 1935; President, Mining Association of Great Britain, 1919-44, and Hon. Life President; Vice-President Federation of British Industries; Director: Lloyds Bank, Ltd. (retd. 1951), Steel Co. of Wales Ltd. and other industrial cos. Chairman: Thos. Williams & Sons, Ltd., Lime Firms, Ltd., Llanelly Associated Tinplate Co. Ltd., South Wales Cttee., Lloyds Bank, and other companies; *b.* 2 July 1871; *er. s.* of late Thos. Williams, of Llwyn Gwern, Pontardulais; *m.* 1903, Charlotte Mary, *y. d.* of David Lackie, J.P.; no *c.* *Educ.:* Christ College, Brecon; Clare College, Cambridge, M.A. Chairman of Central Council under Coal Mines Act, 1930-1938; President National Confederation of Employers' Organisations, 1925-26; President of Conciliation Board for Coal Trade of South Wales since 1918; Pres. British Colliery Owners' Research Assoc.; Pres. of Coal Utilisation Joint Council; Pres. Coal Utilisation Research Assoc.; President of National Board for Coal Mining Industry, 1921-25; Chairman Joint Standing Consultative Committee for Coal Mining Industry, 1926-44; Seneschal of Priory for Wales of the Order of St. John of Jerusalem and Kt. of the Order; D.L., J.P. Carmarthenshire; High Sheriff of Carmarthenshire, 1922-23; Chairman, Monmouth and South Wales Coal-owners Association, 1913; Hon. LL.D. (Birmingham). *Heir:* none. *Address:* Glyndwr, Pontardulais, Carmarthenshire. *Clubs:* Oxford and Cambridge, Carlton.
[*Died* 3 *Feb.* 1959 (*ext.*).

WILLIAMS, Ven. (Evan Daniel) Aldred, B.A.; Vicar of Llanddewi Aberarth since 1940; Archdeacon of Cardigan since 1944; *b.* 20 Aug. 1879; *s.* of David and Martha Williams, Llansawel, Carmarthenshire; *m.* 1918, Alice, *d.* of Rev. E. A. Davies, Vicar of Garnant, Carms. *Educ.:* Llandovery College; St. David's College, Lampeter; St. Michael's College, Llandaff. Curate of St. Thomas, Swansea, 1903-6; Curate of St. Peter's, Carmarthen, 1906-14; Vicar of Golden Grove, 1914-20; of Llansamlet, 1920-1930; of Dafen, Llanelly, 1930-40. *Address:*

WILLIAMS, David Davey, J.P. See page xxxi.

Llanddewi Aberarth Vicarage, Aberayron, Cards. *T.:* Aberayron 275. [*Died* 25 *Jan.* 1951.

WILLIAMS, Rev. Frederick Farewell Sanigear; *b.* Spofforth, Yorks, 16 Mar. 1870; *s.* of late Rev. Frederick Williams, of Chignal St. James, Chelmsford; *m.* 1908, Muriel Hayes, *o. d.* of E. H. Oxley, The Thorpe, Eastbourne, and Hankow, China; one *s.* *Educ.:* King William's Coll., Isle of Man; Jesus College, Cambridge (scholar). 1st class, Classical Tripos, 1892; Bell University Scholar, 1890. Master at King's School, Canterbury, 1892-99; Rugby School, 1899-1905; Headmaster of Eastbourne College, 1906-24; English Chaplain at Algiers, 1924-25; British Embassy Church, Paris, 1925-26; Chaplain to British Embassy, Madrid, 1927-31; Holy Trinity, Florence, 1931-32; Vicar of Coleman's Hatch, Sussex, 1932-36; Headmaster St. Edmund's School, Canterbury, 1941-45. *Address:* 69 Onslow Square, S.W.7. *T.:* Kensington 6693. [*Died* 7 *April* 1956.

WILLIAMS, Very Rev. Garfield Hodder, O.B.E. 1919; LL.D.; M.B., B.S., M.R.C.S. L.R.C.P.; Dean Emeritus of Manchester since 1948; Canon to the Ordinary in the Diocese of Central New York, U.S.A., since 1950; *b.* Bromley, Kent, 21 Nov. 1881; *m.* Myfanwy, *d.* of Rev. Thomas Nicholson; one *s.* two *d.* *Educ.:* City of London School; St. Bartholomew's Hosp., Univ. of London. London Secretary, Student Christian Movement, 1907; Calcutta, 1908-10; Vice-Principal and Superintendent of Science Department of St. John's College, Agra, 1910-1914; ordained, 1914; Principal of St. Andrew's College, Gorakhpur, 1914-18; Fellow of Allahabad University, 1917; special work under the War Board of the United Provinces Government, 1918-20; Assistant-Master, Rugby School, 1920-21; Foreign Secretary of the Church Missionary Society in charge of Education, 1921-24; Secretary of the Missionary Council of the National Church Assembly, 1924-29; Hon. Canon of St. Albans, 1926; Dean of Llandaff, 1929-31; Dean of Manchester, 1931-48. *Publications:* Several reports on Educational and Missionary Problems in India and Africa; contributions to various symposia; general editor of The World Call Reports issued by the Missionary Council of the Church Assembly; What if He Came, a meditation on the gospel of St. Mark; Personal Questionings. *Recreations:* walking and gardening. *Address:* Vicary's Close, Bishops Nympton, S. Molton, N. Devon. [*Died* 8 *Aug.* 1960.

WILLIAMS, Geoffrey Sydney; *b.* 1 May 1871; *s.* of E. Sydney Williams and Nora S. (sister of Sydney Dobell); *m.* K. S. Mary (*d.* 1931), *d.* of late C. J. A. Dick of Fornebo, nr. Christiania; one *s.* one *d.* *Educ.:* Dulwich College; Germany. Until 1923 senior partner in Williams & Norgate, publishers; president of Publishers' Association of Great Britain and Ireland, 1921-1923; Vice-President, 1923-27; Hon. Attaché Christiania, 7 Aug. 1914-Nov. 1915; Editor of the Publisher and Bookseller, 1928-33; Officer of the Order of the Crown (Belgium). *Publications:* edited Foster, 1700 miles in Open Boats; contributions to Der Buchhandel der Welt and periodicals. *Recreation:* gardening. *Address:* The Gables, Wareham, Dorset. *T.:* Wareham 117. [*Died* 9 *July* 1952.

WILLIAMS, George, C.B.E. 1938; *b.* 2 Dec. 1879; *s.* of Frederick Williams, Haverfordwest, Pem.; *m.* 1904, Margaret, *d.* of Thomas Jones, Caerphilly, Glam.; two *s.* two *d.* *Educ.:* Haverfordwest Grammar School. Director of several companies; Chairman of National Industrial Development Council of Wales and Monmouthshire; Director of South Wales Trading Estates, Ltd.; Chairman City of Cardiff Airport Committee; Chairman Development and Estates Committees City of Cardiff; of Advice and Information Committee; Deputy Lord Mayor of Cardiff for 1940; Lord Mayor, City of Cardiff, May 1950-May 1951; Member of Council for Wales and Monmouthshire. *Publications:* numerous press articles on economic affairs of Wales and Monmouthshire. *Recreations:* various: golf, etc. *Address:* 42 Bettws y Coed Road, Cardiff. [*Died* 7 *Oct.* 1951.

WILLIAMS, His Honour Sir George Clark, 1st Bt., *cr.* 1955; Q.C. 1934; J.P. Swansea County Borough and Carmarthenshire; Life Governor, University College of Wales, Aberystwyth; Vice-President, University College of Swansea; Member, Court of Governors, University of Wales; *b.* 2 Nov. 1878; *s.* of Samuel and Martha Williams, Llanelly. *Educ.:* Bishop's Stortford; Univ. Coll. of Wales, Aberystwyth. B.A., London Univ., 1898; Solicitor, 1902; Partner, Roderick, Richards and Williams, solicitors, Llanelly, 1902-8; Called to Bar, Inner Temple, 1909; joined South Wales Circuit, 1909; Judge of County Courts on Circuit 30 (Glamorgan), 1935-48; Deputy National Insurance Commissioner, 1948-50; served European War, 1914-19, with 4th Bn. (T.F.) and (in France) with 14th Bn. Welch Regt.; retd. with rank of Captain. Lord Lieutenant of Carmarthenshire, 1949-53. LL.D. (hon.) Univ. of Wales, 1956. C.St.J. 1951. *Heir:* none. *Address:* Llwyn Helyg, Swansea. *Clubs:* Reform, National Liberal. [*Died* 15 *Oct.* 1958 (*ext.*).

WILLIAMS, Godfrey Herbert; *b.* 5 Jan. 1875; *s.* of late Morgan Stuart Williams and Josephine, *d.* of W. Herbert, of Clytha, Monmouthshire; *m.* 1901, Hon. Miriam Isabel (who obtained a divorce, 1923), *d.* of 5th Lord Rendlesham; four *d.* *Educ.:* Eton. *Recreations:* yachting and travelling. *Clubs:* Carlton, White's, Royal Thames Yacht; R.Y.S. (Cowes). [*Died* 7 *April* 1956.

WILLIAMS, Gen. Sir Guy Charles, K.C.B., *cr.* 1939 (C.B. 1935); C.M.G. 1919; D.S.O. 1915; p.s.c. late R.E. (retd.); Resettlement Officer, B.B.C., since 1944; Col. Commandant, R.E., 1940-51; Chief Royal Engineer, 1946-51; *b.* Bangalore, 10 Sept. 1881; *e. s.* of late Col. R. F. Williams, R.A.; *m.* 1912, Ruth Eleanor (*d.* 1948), *e. d.* of late Rev. Athelstan Coode; two *s.* *Educ.:* Sherborne School. Entered Army, 1900; Captain, 1910; temporary Lieut.-Colonel, 1915; Brigadier-General, 1918; Col. 1923; Maj.-Gen. 1934; Lt.-Gen. 1938; General, 1941; Bermuda, 1901-4; Colchester, 1904-8; Surveys East Africa Protectorate, 1909-14; European War, 1914-18 (despatches seven times, Bt. Major, D.S.O., Bt. Lt.-Col., C.M.G.); Order of S. Stanislaus, 3rd class, with sword; Staff College, Camberley, 1919; G.S.O. 1, U.P. District, India, 1920; G.S.O.1 Staff College, Quetta, 1922-23; Deputy Military Secretary, War Office, 1923-1927; commanded 8th Bareilly Infantry Brigade, 1927-28; Army Instructor, Imperial Defence College, 1928-32; Chief Engineer, Aldershot Command, 1932-34; Commandant Staff College, Quetta, 1934-37; Commander 5th Division, 1937-38; General Officer Commanding-in-Chief, Eastern Command, 1938-41; Military Adviser to N.Z. Government, May-Nov. 1941; retired pay, 1941. *Address:* 27 Queens Grove, N.W.8. [*Died* 2 *Feb.* 1959.

WILLIAMS, Gwyn, D.Sc. (Wales); Ph.D. (Cantab.); Professor of Chemistry in University of London, at Royal Holloway College, since 1946; *b.* London, 27 Nov. 1904; *s.* of late W. J. Williams, J.P., and late Mary Williams. *Educ.:* University College School, London; University College of North Wales, Bangor; St. John's College, Cambridge (Strathcona Research Student, 1927-29). Fellow of the University of Wales, 1929-31; research worker in Department of Colloid Science, Cambridge, 1931-35, and in Research Laboratory of Eastman Kodak Company,

Rochester, New York, 1936-37; Assistant Lecturer and Lecturer in Chemistry, University of London, King's College, 1939-46. Hon. Treasurer of Coleg Harlech; Member of Senate, Univ. of London. *Publications:* chemical papers in scientific periodicals since 1928. *Address:* Royal Holloway College, Englefield Green, Surrey; Cae Ffynnon, Llandudno Junction, North Wales. *Clubs:* Athenæum, Alpine.
[*Died* 6 *April* 1955.

WILLIAMS, Gwynne Evan Owen, M.S. Lond., F.R.C.S. Eng.; Consulting Surgeon, University College Hospital; *s.* of H. O. Williams, Luton; *m.* Cecily Innes, Inverness; three *s.* *Educ.:* Bedford Grammar School; University College Hospital. *Address:* The Old Cottage, Kimpton, Hitchin, Herts. *T.:* Kimpton 267.
[*Died* 3 *Feb.* 1958.

WILLIAMS, Sir Herbert (Geraint), 1st Bt. *cr.* 1953; Kt., *cr.* 1939; M.P. (C.) Croydon East since 1950; M.Sc., M.Eng., Assoc. M.Inst.C.E.; Hon. Sec., Empire Economic Union; *b.* 2 Dec. 1884; *s.* of Thomas Williams, M.A., LL.D. (Cantab.), Schoolmaster of Hooton, Cheshire; *m.* 1916, Dorothy Frances, *d.* of Barton Jones; one *s.* one *d.* *Educ.:* privately; University of Liverpool. Rathbone Scholar, B.Eng. (1st Honours) 1906; University Scholar and Medallist, B.Sc. (2nd Hons. in Maths.) 1907; M.Sc. 1908; M.Eng. 1911. President British University Students Congress, 1907; apprentice Siemens Bros. Dynamo Works, Stafford; marine engineer, assistant to L. A. Smart, M.I.Mech.E. (consulting engineer); electrical engineer with Sir John Norton Griffiths, Bart., on contract work; candidate L.C.C. Bow and Bromley, 1919; candidate for combined English Universities, 1918 and 1931; Wednesbury, 1922 and 1923; Reading, 1929; South Croydon, 1945; Alderman, L.C.C., 1940-44; M.P. (C.) Reading, 1924-29; M.P. (C.) S. Croydon, 1932-45; Parliamentary Secretary Board of Trade, 1928-29; Member of Select Committee of House of Commons on National Expenditure, 1939-44; acted as Joint Secretary of the Engineering and Shipbuilding Hours of Labour Investigation Committee, 1920-22; Secretary and Manager, Machine Tool Trades Association, Incorporated, 1911-28; Director, Empire Industries Association, 1926-28 and 1931-41; late Executive Director Incorporated Assoc. of Electric Power Companies; Chairman of Executive, London Conservative Union, 1939-48; Chairman National Union of Conservative and Unionist Assoc., 1948; Grand Council of Primrose League; Chairman of Conservative Conference at Llandudno, 1948. Sgt. Special Constabulary, 1914; Secretary Machine Tool Dept., Ministry of Munitions; Lt. Royal Army Ordnance Corps. *Publications:* Politics and Economics; Through Tariffs to Prosperity; The Nations' Income; Britain's Economic and Financial Position; What is Socialism?; Elementary Principles of Political Economy; Politics, Grave and Gay; and numerous articles. *Heir:* *s.* Robin Philip, *b.* 27 May 1928. *Address:* 80 Ashley Gardens, S.W.1. *T.:* Victoria 3460; 145 Abbey House, Victoria Street, S.W.1. *T.:* Abbey 7106. *Clubs:* Constitutional, 1900; Ham Manor Golf (Angmering).
[*Died* 25 *July* 1954.

WILLIAMS, Ven. James Evan, M.A.; *y. s.* of late Rev. Evan Williams, Vicar of Nantcwnlle, Cardiganshire; *m.* Constance Emily Kerr, 3rd *d.* of late Admiral Robert Mark Pechell; one *s.* one *d.* *Educ.:* St. John's Foundation School, Leatherhead; St. David's College School, Lampeter; Christ's College, Cambridge. Deacon, 1891; Priest, 1892; Curate of Carnarvon, 1891-94; Diocesan Curate, Bangor, 1894-97; Vicar of Caerdeon w. Bontddu, 1897-1902; Vicar of Ynyscynhaiarn w. Portmadoc, 1902-9; Vicar of Portmadoc, 1909-16; Vicar of Gresford, 1916-32; Rural Dean of Wrexham, 1925-30; Archdeacon of Wrexham, 1930-47; Canon St. Asaph Cathedral, 1927; retired 1947. Hon. Secretary Bangor Diocesan Conference, 1894-1916; Rural Dean Eifionydd, 1906-16. *Recreation:* motoring. *Address:* Bryn Eglwys, Chirk, Denbighshire.
[*Died* 12 *Feb.* 1953.

WILLIAMS, James Howard, O.B.E. 1945; retired; Author and Farmer; *b.* 15 Nov. 1897; *s.* of late N. T. and Madge Williams; *m.* 1932, Susan Margaret Williams (*née* Rowland); one *s.* one *d.* (one *s.* decd.). *Educ.:* Queen's College, Taunton. Served European War, 1914-18, Devonshire Regiment; Forestry with Bombay Burmah Trading Corp., 1920-42; served War of 1939-45, XIVth Army, 1942-46 (O.B.E., despatches thrice). *Publications:* Elephant Bill, 1950; Bandoola, 1953; The Spotted Deer, 1957. *Address:* Menwinnion, St. Buryan, Cornwall. *T.:* St. Buryan 233. *Club:* Oriental.
[*Died* 30 *July* 1958.

WILLIAMS, John; *b.* London; *m.* Laurie Elizabeth Clayden; one *s.* one *d.* *Educ.:* S. Thomas, Charterhouse; Birkbeck and Westminster Schools of Art, etc. Studied art in London and abroad; Member of the School of Handicraft, Toynbee Hall and Essex House, London, 1888-90; Organiser of Arts and Craft Classes, Surrey Education Committee, 1890-96; Head of Artistic Crafts School, Northampton Polytechnic, 1896-1916; Principal, London County Council, Hammersmith School of Arts and Crafts, W.12, 1916-30; Examiner in Art and Crafts subjects to H.M. Civil Service Commission, London, Surrey, Cambridge, Hastings, and other educational authorities; Member of Art Workers' Guild, etc. *Publications:* Articles on Artistic Crafts in educational publications, encyclopedia, etc. *Recreations:* architecture, rambling, and sketching. *Address:* 103 Bouverie Road West, Folkestone.
[*Died* 17 *March* 1951.

WILLIAMS, John Basil, C.M.G. 1949; Assistant Under Secretary of State, Colonial Office, since 1949; *b.* 1 Nov. 1906; *s.* of late Basil Williams, F.B.A.; *m.* 1942, Morag Elizabeth Anning, *d.* of W. E. Forster; no *c.* *Educ.:* Marlborough; McGill University, Montreal; Trinity College, Cambridge (Colonial Exhibitioner). M.A. (Nat. Sci. Tripos). Assistant Principal, Dominions Office, 1929; transferred to Colonial Office, 1930; Sec. of Colonial Development Advisory Cttee., 1934; seconded to Government of Northern Rhodesia, 1935-36; Colonial Adviser, Eastern Group Supply Council, New Delhi, 1941; seconded to Ministry of Supply, 1942; Assistant Secretary, Colonial Office, 1943. Commonwealth Fund Fellow (U.S.A.), 1947-48. *Address:* 67 Albany Mansions, S.W.11; Burnt House, Holtye Common, Cowden, Kent. *Clubs:* Athenæum, Ski Club of Great Britain.
[*Died* 15 *Feb.* 1953.

WILLIAMS, Prof. John Williams, M.A., B.Litt., LL.D.; Professor of History, University of St. Andrews, 1929-55; *b.* 28 May 1885; 3rd *s.* of late John Williams, Dunmurry House, Dunmurry, Co. Antrim; *m.* 1st, 1912, Helen Marjorie (*d.* 1952), *d.* of John W. Burton, The Red House, Leatherhead; two *s.*; 2nd, 1953, Marjory, *widow* of Thomas H. Burton, Sutton, Surrey. *Educ.:* Campbell College, Belfast; Exeter Coll., Oxf. (Schol.), B.A., First Class Hons. Sch. of History, 1906; M.A., 1910; B.Litt. 1910. Lecturer in Sociology, St. Andrews, 1913; Lecturer in Mediæval History, 1921; Reader in Modern History, 1927. *Publications:* Great Britain in the Seventeenth Century (Cassell's History of the British People, Vol. IV, 1923); Readings from the Great Historians, The Seventeenth Century, 1924; Articles and Reviews. *Recreations:* golf, book collecting. *Address:* 14B The Links, St. Andrews, Fife. *T.:* St. Andrews 294. *Club:* Royal and Ancient.
[*Died* 25 *Nov.* 1957.

WILLIAMS, L. Gwendolen; sculptor and painter; Welsh family from Gwysaney and Highfield Hall, Flintshire; *d.* of late Rev. H. L. Williams, Vicar of Bleasby, Notts, and Rural Dean. Studied at Wimbledon Art College, where Mr. A. Drury R.A., was modelling master, and at the Royal College of Art under Mons. Lantèri. Exhibits the Royal Academy, Paris Salon, Internationals, and in New York; chiefly portrait busts, heads of children, and bronze statuettes; two of the latter bought by Leeds, one by Liverpool for their Permanent Collections, and three for the National Gallery of Wales at Cardiff, one by Queen Margherita of Italy, and six by Queen Alexandra; Franco-British, Welsh Eisteddfod, silver medals and Santiago bronze; one-man show of bronzes and water-colours at Brook St. Gallery, Sept. 1935. Fellow of Brighton and Hove Theosophical Society. *Works:* Sappho; Pandora; Chasing the Butterfly; Mary and Her Babe; Beggar Maid of King Cophetua; The Lorelei; The Green Beetle; Faded Flower; Queen of Dreams; Bust of Robert Owen for his Memorial Room at Newtown, N. Wales. *Recreation:* gardening. *Address:* c/o Miss L. Thomson, 12 Glebe Place, Chelsea, S.W.3. [*Died* 11 *Feb.* 1955.

WILLIAMS, Rt. Rev. Lennox Waldron, M.A., D.D. Oxon; D.D., D.C.L., Lennoxville; *b.* 12 Nov. 1859; *s.* of Rt. Rev. James William Williams, D.D., former Bishop of Quebec, and Anna Maria Waldron; *m.* Caroline Anne, *d.* of Colonel William Rhodes; one *s.* (and one killed in War) two *d.* *Educ.:* Bishop's College School, Lennoxville; St. John's College, Oxford; Leeds Clergy School. Ordained, 1885; Curate St. Matthew, Quebec, 1885-87; Rector, 1887-99; Rural Dean, Quebec, 1896; Dean of Quebec, 1899-1915; Bishop of Quebec, 1915-35. *Address:* 15 Grenville Av., Westmount, P.Q., Can. *Club:* Royal Quebec Golf. [*Died* 8 *July* 1958.

WILLIAMS, Margaret Lindsay, R.C.A. (A.R.C.A. 1926); artist; *b.* Cardiff; *d.* of Samuel A. Williams, shipbroker, Barry Dock, and Martha Margaret Lindsay. *Educ.:* privately; Cardiff Technical Coll.; Pelham Street School of Painting, Kensington, under Sir Arthur S. Cope, R.A., Geo. Clausen, R.A., and J. Watson Nicholl; Royal Academy of Arts, London (R.A. Gold Medal and Travelling Scholarship, four Silver Medals and the Creswick Prize); France, Italy and Holland; Gold Medal in Art of the Cardiff Technical College. Painted many presentation and other portraits, including:—King George V, Queen Mary, Queen Elizabeth the Queen Mother; five portraits of Queen Elizabeth II, Prince Charles, Duke of Cornwall and Princess Anne, 1952; Princess Margaret Rose; late Warren G. Harding, President of the United States of America, 1920-23 (presented to the English-Speaking Union, London); King Edward VII (Cardiff City Memorial Picture); Queen Alexandra; The Prince of Wales (in possession of late Queen Mary); Lord Leathers; late Lord Ebbisham, H.E. The Nepalese Ambassador; Rt. Hon. G. Lloyd George; Mr. Maisky; late Duke of Devonshire (4 times); Field Marshal Sir William Slim; late Mr. Henry Ford. Exhibited at The Royal Academy of Arts and numerous other galleries in the British Isles and U.S.A., also Paris Salon. Hon. Life Member British Red Cross Society for services rendered, 1941; Member Hon. Society of Cymmrodorion; Member English-Speaking Union; Fellow Ancient Monuments Society; F.R.S.A. *Publications:* Pictures published include Princess Elizabeth and Princess Margaret, 1937; Princess Elizabeth, 1947; H.M. Queen Elizabeth II, 1952 and 1953; Prince Charles and Princess Anne, 1953; The Devil's Daughter, 1919; The Triumph, 1919; The Rt. Hon. Earl Lloyd George, Prime Minister, unveiling the National Statuary at Cardiff, 1919; The National Welsh War Service in Westminster Abbey, 1924; invited by late G. A. Story, R.A., to assist him with the illustrations of his book—The Theory and Practice of Perspective, 1910; illustrated in colour, Llyn y fan, 1917. *Address:* 108 Hamilton Terrace, N.W.8. [*Died* 4 *June* 1960.

WILLIAMS, Brig.-Gen. Oliver de Lancey, C.M.G. 1917; D.S.O. 1915; late 2nd Batt. R. Welsh Fusiliers; *b.* 5 Nov. 1875; *s.* of late Lieut.-Gen. Sir W. G. Williams, K.C.B.; *m.* 1924, Mildred Lota Ramsay-Hill, Oberland, Guernsey, *d.* of A. H. Baines, Bournemouth and Rosario. *Educ.:* Oxford Military College; R.M.C., Sandhurst. Entered army, 1894; Captain, 1903; Major, 1913; served South African War, 1899-1900 (Queen's medal 5 clasps); European War, 1914-17 (wounded, despatches, D.S.O., C.M.G., brevets Lt.-Col. and Col.); retired, 1921. *Address:* Grange, Guernsey. [*Died* 27 *Nov.* 1959.

WILLIAMS, Owen Gwyn Revell, C.M.G. 1935; *b.* 6 Nov. 1886; *s.* of Owen Evan Williams and Ethel Henrietta Augusta Bernard. *Educ.:* Lancing College; Hertford College, Oxford. Entered Civil Service, Department of Inland Revenue, 1910; transferred to Colonial Office, 1911; Assistant Secretary, Colonial Office, 1926-46; retired, 1946. *Address:* Corneil, Albany Road, Douglas, Isle of Man. [*Died* 27 *Oct.* 1954.

WILLIAMS, Sir Philip (Francis Cunningham), 2nd Bt., *cr.* 1915; *b.* 6 July 1884; *s.* of Col. Sir Robert Williams, 1st Bt., and Rosa Walker Simes; *S.* father, 1943; *m.* 1908, Margaret (*d.* 1948), *d.* of late Sir Cuthbert and Hon. Lady Peek; three *s.* six *d.* *Educ.:* Eton; Trinity College, Oxford. Director: Fine Castings, Ltd., Western Gazette Co. Ltd.; Chm. Salisbury Diocesan Bd. of Finance; a Church Comr.; Chairman Church of England Pensions Board; High Sheriff of Dorsetshire, 1949. *Heir:* *s.* David Philip [*b.* 5 Oct. 1909; *m.* 1948, Elizabeth Mary Garneys, *o. d.* of Ralph Bond, Moigne Combe, Dorchester]. *Address:* Bridehead, Dorchester, Dorset. *T.A.:* Little Bredy. *T.:* Long Bredy 232. *Club:* Travellers'. [*Died* 6 *May* 1958.

WILLIAMS, Ralph V.; *see* Vaughan-Williams.

WILLIAMS, Lieut.-Col. Sir Rhys Rhys-, 1st Bt., *cr.* 1918; D.S.O. 1915; Q.C. 1913; Lieut-Col. late Welsh Guards; *b.* 20 Oct. 1865; *s.* of His Honour Judge Gwilym Williams, Miskin Manor, Glamorgan; *m.* 1921, Juliet Evangeline (Lady (Juliet Evangeline) Rhys-Williams, D.B.E. 1937, D.G.St.J. 1942), *yr. d.* of late Clayton Glyn, Durrington House, Harlow, and late Elinor Glyn; one *s.* two *d.* *Educ.:* Eton; Oriel Coll., Oxford. Called to Bar, Inner Temple, 1890; South Wales Circuit. Served European War (despatches twice, D.S.O.); Acting Military Attaché, British Legation, Tehran, Dec. 1915-Dec. 1916; Assistant Director-General Movements and Railways, War Office, July 1917-Feb. 1918; Deputy Director, Staff Duties, Admiralty, Feb. 1918-Dec. 1918; M.P. (Co. L.), Oxford (Banbury Div.), 1918-22; Parliamentary Secretary to Ministry of Transport, 1919; Recorder of Cardiff, 1922-30; Chairman of Quarter Sessions, Glamorgan. *Heir:* *s.* Brandon Meredith, *b.* 14 Nov. 1927. *Address:* Miskin Manor, Pontyclun, Glamorgan; 47 Eaton Place, S.W.1. *T.:* Sloane 5268. *Clubs:* Brooks's, White's. [*Died* 29 *Jan.* 1955.

WILLIAMS, Robert Allan, M.A. (Cambridge), Ph.D. (Leipsic), Lit.D. (Dublin and Belfast); late Schröder Professor of German, Cambridge University; since 1941, Emeritus Professor of German, Cambridge University. Formerly Professor, University of Dublin; Professor of German and Teutonic Philology, Queen's University, Belfast, 1915-1932. *Publications:* The Finn Episode in Beowulf; articles and reviews in English and German learned journals. *Address:* 6 Wordsworth Grove, Cambridge. [*Died* 27 *Jan.* 1951.

WILLIAMS, Robert J. P.; *see* Probyn-Williams.

WILLIAMS, Robert P. H.; *see* Hodder-Williams.

WILLIAMS, Robert T. W.; *see* Watkin-Williams.

WILLIAMS, Ronald Watkins; M.P. (Lab.) Wigan Div. since March 1948; Solicitor; Legal Adviser to National Union of Mineworkers since 1948; *b.* 18 July 1907; *s.* of Thomas Jenkin Watkins (Miner); *adopted s.* of Isaac Williams (Tobacconist); *m.* 1934, Olive May Bazzard, *d.* of Ivor N. Bazzard; no *c.* *Educ.:* Council School; Commercial School. Solicitor, in partnership, in Swansea and Briton Ferry, 1930-36; full-time Solicitor to Durham Miners' Assoc., 1936-45; full-time Solicitor to National Union of Mineworkers, 1945-48. Member of Commission of Enquiry into Disorders in Nigeria, 1949-50; Inter Parliamentary Union Delegation Nice, 1949, Stockholm, 1949; Commonwealth Parl. Deleg., Malaya, 1950; Council of Europe, Strasbourg, 1951. Admitted North Rhodesian Bar, 1953; Parliamentary Delegation to Kenya, 1954; Commonwealth Parliamentary Assoc. Delegation to Kenya, 1956. *Address:* 5 Briton Close, Sanderstead, Sy. *T.:* 4511. [*Died* 14 *March* 1958.

WILLIAMS, Ven. Thomas John, M.C. 1918; V.D. 1927; Archdeacon of Craven since 1949; Vicar of Otley since 1937; Hon. Canon of Bradford since 1939; *b.* 9 May 1889; *s.* of Joseph and Elizabeth Ann Williams; *m.* 1917, Ethel Marion (*née* Roberts); one *s.* *Educ.:* Durham University; Westcott House, Cambridge; Serampore University, Bengal. L.Th. 1913, B.A. 1918, M.A. 1920, Durham Univ.; B.D. Serampore Univ., 1926; deacon, 1914, priest, 1915, Diocese of Ripon; Proctor in Convocation, 1937-45. Served European War, 1914-1918, as Chaplain to Forces, 1916-19; War of 1939-45, Senior Chaplain to the Forces, 1939-1942. *Address:* The Vicarage, Otley, Yorks. *T.:* Otley 2240. *Clubs:* Manor (Otley); Union (Bradford). [*Died* 4 *July* 1956.

WILLIAMS, Air Marshal Sir Thomas Melling, K.C.B., *cr.* 1950 (C.B. 1944); O.B.E. 1941; M.C., D.F.C., M.A.; J.P.; R.A.F. retired; *b.* 27 Sept. 1899; *s.* of late Thomas Henry Williams and Sarah Isobel Melling; *m.* 1938, Patricia Joan, *e. d.* of late Wing Commander E. Osmond, C.B.E.; one *s.* two *d.* *Educ.:* Germiston, S. Africa. Served with 12th S.A. Infantry, German East Africa, 1916-17; with R.F.C. and R.A.F. in England, France, and Russia, 1917-19; Fleet Air Arm, 1919-26; Malta, 1926-31; Cambridge University Air Squadron, 1931-34; R.A.F. Staff College, 1935; Air Ministry, 1936-37; C.O. Andover, Jan. - Oct. 1938; H.Q. 1 Group, 1938-39; France, Advanced Air Striking Force, Sept. 1939-June 1940; C.O. R.A.F. Station, Watton, July 1940-June 1941; S.A.S.O. No. 2 Group, July-Oct. 1941; D./S.A.S.O. Bomber Command, 1941-42; Java, S.A.S.O. to Air Marshal Peirce, Jan.-Feb. 1942; India, S.A.S.O. to Air Forces in India, March-Dec. 1942; A.O.C. Bengal Command, R.A.F., India, 1943; Deputy Commander, H.Q. Eastern Air Command (Air Command South-East Asia), 1944; Assistant Chief of Air Staff (Operations), 1944-47; Commandant R.A.F. Staff College, Bracknell, 1947-48; A.O.C.-in-C. B.A.F.O., Germany, 1948-51; Inspector General of the R.A.F., 1951-52; retired 1953. *Recreations:* squash, golf, tennis. *Address:* Glovers, Kennington, Kent. *Club:* Army and Navy. [*Died* 10 *June* 1956.

WILLIAMS, V. E. N.; *see* Nash-Williams.

WILLIAMS, Engineer - Captain William Arthur, C.I.E. 1932; R. Indian Navy, retired; *b.* 1882; *s.* of late W. J. and Rose Williams; *m.* 1917, Muriel May, *d.* of late Robert Charles and Helena Emma Lees; two *s.* one *d.* Assistant Engineer, R.I.M., 1902; Engineer, 1908; Engineer-Lieut.-Commander, 1916; Engineer-Commander, 1923; Engineer-Captain, 1927; served European War (thanks of Government of India, despatches twice); acted Superintending Engineer, Govt. of Burma, 1915; Principal Engineer and Ship Surveyor, Govt. of Bengal, 1924-27; Engineer-Manager, Govt. Dockyard, Bombay, 1927-31; retired, 1932; Temp. Comdr. (E) R.N.R., 1940; served at Admiralty in above rank of Eng.-Capt. R.I.N.; retired, 1947. *Address:* 11c Gledhow Gardens, S.W.5. *T.:* Fremantle 1886. [*Died* 25 *May* 1953.

WILLIAMS, William John, Hon. LL.D. (Wales); Director of Council of Social Service for Wales and Monmouthshire since 1945; *b.* 1878; 4th *s.* of Richard and Anne Williams, Hafod, Swansea; *m.* 1906, Maud, *d.* of David Owen, J.P., and Anne Owen, Morriston, Swansea; one *s.* *Educ.:* Swansea; University College of Wales, Aberystwyth (M.A.). Master at Gowerton County School, Bootle Intermediate School, Newport High School; called to the Bar, Middle Temple, 1912; H.M. Inspector, Board of Education (Welsh Dept.), 1915; H.M. Chief Inspector, 1933-45, retired. Member: Arts Council of Great Britain (Welsh Cttee.); British Council (Welsh Cttee.); Rural Industries Bureau Council; Survey Council of Rural Wales; B.B.C. Appeals Cttee. (Wales); Welsh Nat. Opera Co. (Director); Coleg Harlech (Vice-Pres.); U.N.E.S.C.O. (Welsh Cttee.). *Address:* 4 North Road, Cardiff, Glam. *T.:* Cardiff 5707. *Club:* Authors'. [*Died* 23 *Jan.* 1952.

WILLIAMS, Sir William Law, 8th Bt., *cr.* 1866; late Captain Royal Welch Fusiliers; *b.* 1 May 1907; *s.* of 7th Bt. and Emily, *d.* of William Reid, Downpatrick; *S.* father, 1921; *m.* 1950, Betty Kathleen Taylor, *d.* of Mrs. J. Nowell Philip, The Haven, Torquay. *Educ.:* Sherborne; St. John's College, Cambridge (B.A. 1930). *Heir:* *kinsman* Robert Ernest [*b.* 6 June 1924; *m.* 1948, Ruth Margaret, *d.* of C. Butcher; three *s.* one *d.*]. *Address:* Upcott House, Barnstaple, North Devon. *T.:* Barnstaple 2498. *Club:* Naval and Military. [*Died* 1 *July* 1960.

WILLIAMS-WYNN, Col. Sir Robert William Herbert Watkin, 9th Bt., *cr.* 1688; K.C.B., *cr.* 1938 (C.B. 1923); D.S.O. 1902; T.D. 1909; Lord Lieutenant of Denbighshire since 1928; K.St.J.; *b.* 3 June 1862; *y. s.* of late Col. Herbert Watkin Williams-Wynn, M.P., and Anna, *d.* and *heiress* of Edward Lloyd, Cefn, Co. Denbigh; *S.* nephew, 1949; *m.* 1904, Elizabeth Ida, M.B.E. 1918, 2nd *d.* of late George W. Lowther, Swillington, Yorks; two *s.* two *d.* *Educ.:* Wellington; Christ Church, Oxford. Served South Africa, Imp. Yeo., 1900-01 (despatches, D.S.O.); Hon. Captain in Army, 1900; served European War, 1914-18 (despatches thrice); Lt.-Col. Comdg. (Brevet Col. 1913) Montgomeryshire Yeomanry, in Egypt, 1916; Comdg. Southern Section (Egypt), 1917-19; Chairman and President Denbigh Territorial Assoc.; Master of Flint and Denbigh Fox Hounds, 1888-1946; J.P. Denbighshire and Flintshire (V.L. 1927). Contested (C.) Montgomeryshire, 1894, 1895, 1900. *Heir:* *s.* Lt.-Col. Owen Watkin Williams-Wynn. *Address:* Plâs-yn-Cefn, St. Asaph, Denbighshire. *T.:* Trefnant 321. *Club:* Junior Carlton. [*Died* 23 *Nov.* 1951.

WILLIAMSON, David; Editor of the Daily Mail Year Book, 1912-53; *b.* Guildford, 16 Nov. 1868; 5th *s.* of late D. Williamson, J.P., Guildford, a founder of the National Deposit Friendly Society; *m. d.* of John Allan (she *d.* 1950); two *s.* one *d.* (and one *d.* decd.). *Educ.:* privately. Edited Hazell's Annual; editorial staff Illustrated London News, 1892; asst. editor, 1895; editor Windsor Magazine,

1895-98; Temple Magazine, 1898-99; Cassell's Magazine and The Quiver, 1905-09; contested (L.) Dulwich, 1906, and by-election, 1906. Vice-President of Reedham Orphanage. *Publications:* Victoria, R. and I., 1897; William Ewart Gladstone: Statesman and Scholar, 1898; Gladstone: the Man, 1898; Parliament's Tribute to Gladstone, 1898; The Life of D. L. Moody, 1900; President McKinley, 1901; From Boyhood to Manhood, 1910; The Life of Dr. Alexander Maclaren, 1910; Our King and Queen, 1911; The Life of the Prince of Wales, 1916; Queen Alexandra, 1919; Life of Sir John Kirk, 1922; Lord Shaftesbury's Legacy; Before I Forget, a vol. of reminiscences, 1932; Ninety—Not Out, a history of the Shaftesbury Society, 1934; Forty-Five Years in India, a Memoir of Principal Mackichan, 1934; Twenty-five Years' Reign, 1935; Our Three Great Queens: Victoria, Alexandra and Mary, 1935; Religion in the King's Reign, 1935; Our King, 1936; King George VI and his Queen, 1937; Gathered Harvest, 1938; various books on war topics. *Club:* National Liberal. [*Died* 30 *March* 1955.

WILLIAMSON, Rt. Rev. Edward William, D.D. (Lambeth), M.A., F.S.A.; Bishop of Swansea and Brecon since 1939; *b.* 22 April 1892; *s.* of Edward Williamson and Florence Frances Tipton. *Educ.:* Llandaff Cathedral School; Westminster School; Christ Church, Oxford; Wells Theological College. Curate of St. Martin's, Leeds, 1915-17; of Lambeth, 1917-22; Lecturer, 1922, and Fellow 1923-26, of St. Augustine's College, Canterbury; Hon. Fellow, 1936; Warden of St. Michael's Theological College, Llandaff, 1926-39. Canon, 1930-39, and Chancellor, 1937-39, of Llandaff Cathedral. Select Preacher, Oxford, 1944-46, Cambridge, 1951. *Publications:* The Letters of Osbert of Clare, 1929; An Anatomy of Christian Joy, 1946; and other minor works, mostly antiquarian. *Address:* Ely Tower, Brecon. [*Died* 23 *Sept.* 1953.

WILLIAMSON, George Watkins; *b.* 9 July 1875; *e. surv. s.* of late George Williamson of Lincoln's Inn, Barrister-at-law, and Emily, *d.* of late Rev. C. F. Watkins, Vicar of Brixworth, Northants; *m.* Marguerite Joie, *o. d.* of Alfred Cronin Fleuret; one *d. Educ.:* Cheltenham College. Called to Bar, Lincoln's Inn, 1896; Land Registry, London, 1901-06; Judge of the High Court and Registrar-General of Lands, Sudan, 1906. *Recreations:* golf, lawn tennis. [*Died* 23 *Dec.* 1957.

WILLIAMSON, Sir James, Kt., *cr.* 1935; V.D.; M.I.E. (I.); Col. A.F.I.; *b.* Cupar, Scotland, 24 Feb. 1877; *s.* of William Williamson; *m.* Jennie Geddes Black (*d.* 1952); four *d. Educ.:* Madras Academy; Bell-Baxter, Cupar, Fifeshire; and as Civil Engineer, Engaged Indian Railways, Bengal Dooars Constructions, 1898-1903; Bengal and North Western Railway, 1903-36; President Indian Railway Conference Association, 1934-35; Chairman Hardinge Bridge Committee, 1934-1936; Managing Director Bengal and North Western and Rohilkund and Kumaon Railways until 1943; commanded United Provinces Horse (A.F.I.) until 1929. *Recreations:* riding, fishing. *Address:* c/o National Overseas and Grindlay's Bank Ltd., 54 Parliament Street, S.W.1. *Club:* Caledonian United Service (Edinburgh). [*Died* 21 *March* 1959.

WILLIAMSON, John Thoburn, B.A., M.Sc., Ph.D., Hon. D.Sc. (all McGill); Governing and Sole Director Williamson Diamonds Ltd. since 1942; Managing Director Buhemba Mines Ltd. since 1946; *b.* 10 Feb. 1907; Canadian; *s.* of Bertie J. Williamson and Rose C. Boyd; unmarried. *Educ.:* MacDonald High School; McGill University. Bursary, National Research Council, 1930-31; McGill Univ.: Leroy Memorial Fellowship, 1929-30; Demonstrator, in Mineralogy, 1931-32, in Geology, 1932-33. Mining and Geological experience in Canada, Newfoundland, Rhodesia and East Africa. Discovered Mwadui Diamond Field, 1940. *Recreations:* music and literature. *Address:* Williamson Diamonds Ltd., P.O. Mwadui, Shinyanga District, Tanganyika Territory, East Africa. *Clubs:* University (Montreal); Dar es Salaam (Dar es Salaam); Nairobi (Nairobi). [*Died* 7 *Jan.* 1958.

WILLIAMSON, Kenneth Bertram; *b.* Monghyr, India, 1875; 4th *s.* of late James Franklin Williamson, Executive Engineer, P.W.D. Irrigation, and Margaret Elizabeth (*née* Cowen); *m.* 1920, Emilia Stuart (decd.), *d.* of late Rev. Robert and Mrs. Lorimer (*née* Robertson), of Mains and Strathmartine. *Educ.:* Bristol Grammar School; St. Paul's School, London (Foundation Schol. and Exhibitioner); St. John's College, Cambridge (Minor Scholar); Imperial Coll., London; Teachers' Training Coll., Cambridge. M.A. (2nd Cl. Nat. Sci. Tripos, 1896; Junior Demonstrator, Univ. Biol. Laboratory, 1897), Dip. Agric. (Cantab.); D.I.C. (Res. in Med. Entomology). Taught in the following Schools; St. Paul's, Kings Lynn; Sheffield Grammar and Perse, Cambridge. Lecturer in Bacteriology, King's College for Women, London University; Principal and Professor, Jubbulpore College, C.P. India; Professor of Biology, King Edward VII Medical College, Singapore; Inspector of Schools, Indian Educ. Service; Malaria Research Officer, F.M.S. Served European War 1915-19 (despatches twice). Post War Chief Instructor in Agric. to E.E.F. *Publications:* Cambridge, and Indian and Other Verses, 1908; contribs. on Malarial Science to Scientific Jls., League of Nations, etc.; sometime Editor of The Malayan Naturalist. *Recreation:* natural history. *Address:* c/o National and Grindlay's Bank Ltd., 54 Parliament Street, S.W.1. [*Died* 27 *Dec.* 1959.

WILLIAMSON, Lawrence Collingwood, C.B. 1946; Royal Corps of Naval Constructors (retd.); *b.* 1886; *s.* of Captain J. C. Williamson, Master Mariner. Late Deputy Director of Naval Construction, Admiralty. Retired, 1947. *Address:* Pendragon, Newmill, Penzance, Cornwall. [*Died* 7 *Feb.* 1955.

WILLIAMSON, Sir Walter James Franklin, Kt., *cr.* 1927; C.M.G. 1919; F.Z.S.; *b.* 16 April 1867; *s.* of late James Franklin Williamson, Indian Public Works Department; *m.* 1894, Marion (*d.* 1945), *d.* of Lancelot Crozier. *Educ.:* City of London School; Winder's, Eastbourne. Entered Indian Financial Department, 1890; Assistant Accountant-General, United Provinces, Bengal, and Madras, 1891-1900; services lent to Siamese Government, 1900; Director of Paper Currency and Assistant Financial Adviser, 1900-04; Financial Adviser to the Government of Thailand, 1904-25; Financial Adviser to Estonian Govt. and Bank of Estonia, 1926-30; Grand Cross of the Crown of Siam, 1913; Grand Cross of the White Elephant of Siam, 1916. *Recreations:* natural history and angling. *Address:* c/o Lloyds Bank, 6 Pall Mall, S.W.1. [*Died* 19 *Nov.* 1954.

WILLINGDON, Marie, Marchioness of, C.I. 1917; G.B.E., *cr.* 1924 (D.B.E., *cr.* 1918); **Marie Adelaide Freeman-Thomas;** *b.* 1875; *d.* of 1st and last Earl Brassey, G.C.B.; *m.* 1892, 1st Marquess of Willingdon, P.C., G.C.S.I., G.C.M.G., G.C.I.E., G.B.E. (*d.* 1941); one *s.* Received Freedom of Edinburgh, 1934; Hon. LL.D. Edin. 1934; Dame of Grace, Order of St. John of Jerusalem; 1st class Kaisar-i-Hind Gold Medal; Order of Mercy. *Address:* 5 Lygon Place, Grosvenor Gdns., S.W.1. *T.:* Sloane 1851. [*Died* 30 *Jan.* 1960.

WILLIS, Sir Addington; *see* Willis, Sir W. A.

WILLIS, Hon. Albert Charles, J.P.; *b.* Tonyrefail, Wales, 24 May 1876;

m. Alice Maud Parker; one *s.* two *d.* *Educ.:* Brynmaur Board School; King's College, London; Ruskin College, Oxford. Went to Australia, 1911; President, Illawarra Miners' Association, New South Wales, 1913; 1st General Secretary, Australasian Coal and Shale Employees' Federation, 1916-25; Founder and Managing Director, Labor Daily newspaper, Sydney, 1923; President, Australian Labor Party (N.S.W.), 1923-25; Member of Legislative Council of New South Wales, 1925-33; Vice-President of the Executive Council and Representative of Government in Legislative Council, 1925-27 and 1930-31; Agent-General for N.S.W. 1931-32; Central Coal Authority, 1943; Commonwealth Conciliation Commissioner and Central Industrial Authority under Coal Production (wartime) Act 1944, 1944-47; retd. 1947. Vice-Pres., British Empire Producers' Organisation. *Recreations:* boating, motoring, and gardening. *Address:* Bryn-Eirw, Gannon's Road, Burraneer Bay, N.S.W. [*Died* 22 *April* 1954.

WILLIS, Arthur d'Anyers; *b.* 19 April 1879; *s.* of late Rev. Canon F. W. Willis and late Gertrude Gray; *m.* 1st, Dorothea Lister-Kaye; two *s.* one *d.*; 2nd, Katherine Moore; one *d.* *Educ.:* Bradfield College. Director of: Chartered Bank of India, Australia, and China; Atlas Assurance Co., Ltd.; India General Navigation and Railway Co., Ltd.; Westminster Bank Ltd.; Ashanti Goldfields Corporation, Ltd.; Perham Investment Trust Co., Ltd.; Kolar Power Company Ltd.; Bibiani (1927) Ltd.; Nundydroog Mines Ltd.; Chairman of: Dooars Tea Co., Ltd.; Empire of India and Ceylon Tea Co., Ltd.; Singlo Tea Co., Ltd. Champion Reef Gold Mines of India Ltd. *Recreations:* shooting, golf. *Address:* Chipstead, Fleet, Hants. *Club:* Oriental. [*Died* 23 *Aug.* 1953.

WILLIS, John Christopher, F.R.S.; M.A., Sc.D. (Cantab.); Hon. S.D. (Harvard); Correspondent, Botanic Gardens, Rio de Janeiro; late Editor of the Empire Cotton Growing Review; *b.* Birkenhead, 20 Feb. 1868; father American, cousin to N. P. Willis, the poet; mother Scotch; *m.* 1897, Minnie (*d.* 1931), *e. d.* of T. Baldwin, of Barnsley; one *d.* (and two *d.* decd.). *Educ.:* Birkenhead School; Univ. Coll., Liverpool; Gonville and Caius Coll., Cambridge. Frank Smart Student for Botanical Research, 1890-93; Senior Assistant in Botany, Glasgow University, 1894-96; Director, Royal Botanic Gardens, Ceylon, 1896-1911; organised them into a large agricultural department; Director, Botanic Gardens, Rio de Janeiro, on contract, 1912-15; retired; reported on agriculture in the Malay States, 1904; late editor of Tropical Agriculturist, and other journals; elected Corresponding Member of the German Botanical Society, 1907; lectured on tropical agriculture before the University of Harvard, 1909, and received hon. doctorate of science, etc. *Publications:* Rubber in the East; Ceylon, a Handbook for the Resident and the Traveller; Agriculture in the Tropics, 3rd ed. 1922; Age and Area; The Course of Evolution; The Tube-Bus Guide to London, 3rd ed., 1932; A Manual and Dictionary of the Flowering Plants and Ferns, 7th ed. 1948; The Birth and Spread of Plants, 1949; many botanical papers. *Recreation:* travel. *Address:* Les Terrages, Avenue des Alpes, Montreux, Switzerland. [*Died* 21 *March* 1958.

WILLIS, Rt. Rev. John Jamieson, C.B.E. 1934 (O.B.E. 1919); D.D.; *b.* 8 Nov. 1872; *s.* of Sir William Willis; *m.* 1924, Beatrix Maud, (*d.* 1953) *o. d.* of Lt.-Gen. F. H. Tyrrell. *Educ.:* Haileybury Coll.; Pembroke Coll. and Ridley Hall, Cambridge. Curate of Great Yarmouth, 1895-1900; C.M.S. Missionary in Ankole, 1900-02; Entebbe, 1902-05; Kavirondo, 1905-11; Archdeacon of Kavirondo and Chaplain to Bishop of Uganda, 1909-11; Bishop of Uganda, 1912-34; Asst. Bishop to Bishop of Leicester, 1935-49; retired, 1949. *Address:* White Court, Dawlish Road, Teignmouth, Devon. [*Died* 12 *Nov.* 1954.

WILLIS, Colonel Richard ffolliott, C.B. 1919; R.M.L.I.; retired; *b.* 16 Nov. 1875; *o. s.* of late Major William Wynch G. B. Willis, R.M.L.I.; *m.* 1st, 1903, Kate Annie (*d.* 1928), *d.* of Arthur Lewis, Lieut. and Adj. 65th Regt., Violetstown, Mullingar; 2nd, 1949, Irene Mary Anna Legh, *d.* of Legh Richmond Powell, Bexhill, Sussex. *Educ.:* Cheltenham College. 2nd Lieut. R.M.L.I. 1894; Chief Ordnance Officer, Barbados, 1901-05; in charge of Cleethorpes Wireless Telegraph Station, 1908-12; Wireless Stations at Gibraltar, 1912-19, and in Ireland, 1921-22; retired pay, 1923. M.I.E.E.; Mem. Brit. Inst. of Radiology. *Address:* Atherfield, Woldingham, Surrey. *T.:* Woldingham 2152. *Club:* United Service. [*Died* 18 *July* 1960.

WILLIS, Sir (Walter) Addington, Kt., *cr.* 1947; C.B.E. 1924; Barrister-at-law; *b.* 30 Oct. 1862; 4th *s.* of Rev. Joseph Willis; *m.* Mary Morris (*d.* 1951), *d.* of E. Morris Gibson, Sutton, Surrey; one *s.* *Educ.:* Kingswood School, Bath. LL.B. London Univ. (first class Hons. in Jurisprudence and Roman Law). Called to Bar, Inner Temple, 1889; joined North-Eastern Circuit; arbitrator and conciliator in industrial disputes, 1915-37; Member of the Panel of Chairmen for Boards of Arbitration under the Industrial Courts Act, 1919; Member and Chairman of Trade Boards, 1919-45; Deputy Umpire of Unemployment Insurance, 1924-45 and of Reinstatement in Civil Employment, Sept. 1944-May 1945; Umpire of Unemployment Insurance and of Reinstatement in Civil Employment, 1945-47, retired Nov. 1947; Chadwick Trustee, 1915-45; has acted as arbitrator or conciliator in numerous industrial disputes; Chairman of the National Conference of the Boot and Shoe Manufacturing Industry, 1922-37; was Chairman of the Conciliation Committee of the National Joint Industrial Council for the Electricity Supply Industry and of the special tribunal subsequently appointed to investigate the dispute of 1924. *Publications:* Workmen's Compensation (36th Edition, 1944); Approved Societies; Trade Boards; Law relating to Sewers and Drains; Law of Housing; articles on Local Government Law. *Address:* 41 Mill Street, Ludlow, Salop. *T.:* Ludlow 25. [*Died* 18 *July* 1953.

WILLIS-O'CONNOR, Col. H.; *see* O'Connor.

WILLOCK, Brig.-General Frederick George, C.B.E. 1919; D.S.O. 1918; late R.F.A. and R.A.F.; late of Turnberry, Ayrshire; *o. c.* of Hugh Douglas Willock, J.P., Hon. Sheriff of Ayrshire, and Elizabeth, *o. c.* of David Craig of Gleniffer; *m.* Louise Margaret, *er. d.* of late William George Warner, Montreal. Major, 1908; Lt.-Col. 1914; acting C.R.A. 1917; Brig. Gen. 1918; G.O.C. Blandford and Halton, 1918-20 (25,000 men). Served European War, 1914-18; commanded Brigade of Artillery in France and Belgium (despatches thrice, D.S.O., C.B.E.). *Recreations:* riding, swimming, fishing, golf. *Club:* Union (Victoria, B.C.). [*Died* 23 *Sept.* 1955.

WILLOUGHBY LYLE, Herbert; *see* Lyle, H. W.

WILLS, Cecil Upton, C.I.E. 1927; Indian Civil Service (retired); *s.* of late Lt.-Col. C. S. Wills, C.B., R.A.M.C., Lunecliffe, Lancaster; *m.* 1922, Honor, *d.* of A. H. Gordon of Delamont, Killyleagh, Co. Down; three *d.* *Educ.:* Blundell's School, Tiverton; Balliol College, Oxford, B.A., 1899. Indian Civil Service, 1900; Assistant Commissioner in the Central Provinces, India, 1901; Settlement Officer, 1906; Deputy Commissioner, 1915; Commissioner, 1925; retired, 1927; employed in Indore and Jaipur States, 1929-35. *Publications:* The Raj-Gond Maharajas, 1923; Nagpur in the Eighteenth Century, 1926; The Land-System of the Holkar State, 1931. *Address:* Woodend, Knotty Green, Beaconsfield. [*Died* 15 *Nov.* 1954.

WILLS, Sir Ernest (Salter), 3rd Bt., *cr.* 1904; C.St.J.; J.P.; lately Director of the Imperial Tobacco Co. and of Portishead District Water Co.; H.M. Lieutenant in County of Wilts, 1930-42; Jubilee and Coronation Medals; *b.* 30 Nov. 1869; *s.* of 1st Bt. and Mary Ann, *e. d.* of J. Chaning Pearce, F.G.S., Montagu House, Bath; *S.* brother, 1921; *m.* 1894, Caroline Fanny Maud, D.St.J. (*d.* 1953), *d.* of William Augustine de Winton, Westbury Lodge, Durdham Down, Bristol; two *s.* three *d.* *Heir: s.* Ernest Edward de Winton Wills, Lt.-Col. Scots Guards [*b.* 8 Dec. 1903; *m.* 1926, Sylvia Margaret (*d.* 1946), *d.* of late W. B. Ogden and Mrs. Gordon Moore, 90 Knightsbridge, S.W.; two *d.*; *m.* 1949, Juliet, *yr. d.* of Capt. J. E. H. Graham-Clarke, Frocester Manor, Gloucs.]. *Address:* Littlecote, nr. Hungerford, Wilts; Meggernie Castle, Glenlyon, Perthshire. *Club:* Junior Carlton. [*Died* 14 *Jan.* 1958.

WILLS, Wilfrid Dewhurst; *b.* Bromley, Kent, 15 Oct. 1898; *s.* of late Arthur Stanley Wills, 14 Royal Crescent, Bath; unmarried. *Educ.:* Cheltenham College; R.M.C., Sandhurst. Served in 5th Dragoon Guards, 1916-19; M.P. (Nat. C.) Batley and Morley, 1931-35; Lieutenant-Commander, Royal Naval Volunteer (Wireless) Reserve. *Recreation:* yachting. *Address:* Hamswell House, Bath. *Clubs:* Cavalry, Carlton, Royal Thames Yacht. [*Died* 20 *April* 1954.

WILLSON, Preb. Archdall Beaumont Wynne; Prebendary of Moreton Magna in Hereford Cathedral, 1917-38, now Prebendary Emeritus; *s.* of Rev. William Wynne Willson and Mary Ann, *d.* of First Anglican Bishop in Jerusalem; *m.* Andrina (*d.* 1955), *d.* of John Jardine, Derby House, Liverpool; three *c.* *Educ.:* Marlborough Coll.; London Univ. (Honours); Wycliffe Coll., Oxford. Tutor in Germany, 1885-88; Assistant-Master and Chaplain Berkhamsted School, 1888-97; Ordained, 1895; Domestic Chaplain to the Bishops of Hereford, 1897-1901, 1919-20; Assistant-Curate, Fairfield, Liverpool, 1901-03; Vicar of Kimbolton, 1903-08; Rural Dean of Hereford, 1909-20; Rector of S. Nicholas, Hereford, 1908-23; Rector of Bishop Wearmouth, Sunderland, 1923-34; Rural Dean of Wearmouth, 1923-33; Examining Chaplain to Bishop of Durham, 1920-34; Hon. Chaplain to Bishop of Durham, 1934-39. *Publications:* formerly Editor of Liverpool Diocesan Magazine and of Hereford Diocesan Messenger; (joint) Beginnings of Divine Society. *Address:* The Mount, Long Ashton, Bristol. *T.:* Long Ashton 3142. [*Died* 12 *May* 1958.

WILLSON, Sir Walter Stuart James, Kt., *cr.* 1926; *b.* Dublin, 16 Nov. 1876; *e. s.* of Albert and Mary Elizabeth Willson; *m.* 1919, Ethel Winifred, *e. d.* of late J. J. Morris; two *s.* three *d.* *Educ.:* St. Paul's School, Director, Waldegrave Co., Ltd., since 1923; Turner, Morrison & Co. Ltd., India, 1913-22; Member of Legislative Council, Behar and Orissa, 1920; Legislative Assembly for the Bengal European Constituency, 1922-1923; Member of the Legislative Assembly, First Member for the Associated Chambers of Commerce of India and Burma, 1924-28; Member of various Standing Committees; including Commerce and Industry Advisory, and Railway Advisory; Municipal Commissioner representing Bengal Chamber of Commerce, 1920-24; Municipal Councillor nominated by Government, 1924-25; Vice-President, Indian Mining Association, 1920-21; Committee, Indian Lac, 1917-18; Indian Engineering Association, 1912-15-17; Governor, Mayo Hospital, 1921-26; Trustee, Marwari Hindu Hospital, 1917-21; Councillor Tunbridge Wells Corporation, 1932-35 and 1941-49; Group Hospitals House Cttee., 1948. *Address:* Kenward, Tonbridge. *T.:* Pembury 29. *Clubs:* Oriental; Royal Calcutta Turf, Tollygunge (Calcutta). [*Died* 16 *April* 1952.

WILLSON, William T. C.; *see* Curtis-Willson.

WILMER, Brig. Eric Randal Gordon, D.S.O. 1915; *b.* 24 May 1882; *s.* of Col. J. R. Wilmer, I.A., Survey of India; *m.* 1910, Marjory Louisa (*d.* 1947), *y. d.* of Major-General Worsley, I.A.; two *s.* one *d.*; *m.* 1953, Marjorie Monoux (*née* Payne), *widow* of Harold Pemberton, D.S.O. *Educ.:* St. Paul's School; R.M. Academy, Woolwich. Entered Army, 1900; Captain, 1911; Adjutant, 1913; Major, 1914; Lt.-Col., 1928; Col., 1929; Adjutant T.F., 1909-12; served European War, 1914-18 (D.S.O., wounded, Bt. Lt.-Col., Légion d'Honneur); commanded 23rd Field Brigade R.A. Jubbulpore, India, 1929; Commandant, School of Artillery, Kakul, India, 1929-31; Brig., R.A., Southern Command, India, 1931-35; retired pay, 1935; recalled A.M.S. War Office, 1939; School of Artillery, 1940; retired pay, 1942. *Address:* 66 Broadway East, Paris, Ontario, Canada. [*Died* 25 *May* 1958.

WILMOT, Chester, (Reginald William Winchester Wilmot); Author and Broadcaster; *b.* 21 June 1911; *s.* of late R. W. E. Wilmot, Melbourne, Australia; *m.* 1942, Edith French, *d.* of late Rev. W. H. Irwin, St. Peter's College, Adelaide, S.A.; one *s.* two *d.* *Educ.:* Melbourne Grammar School; Trinity College, University of Melbourne. B.A., LL.B. Toured Far East, U.S.A., Canada, Gt. Britain, Europe as Leader of Melbourne Univ. Debating Team, 1937-39; War Corresp. for Australian Broadcasting Commn. in Middle East and New Guinea, 1940-42; editor and narrator of documentary film Sons of the Anzacs produced for Commonwealth Govt., 1943; War Corresp. for B.B.C. in Western Europe, 1944-45; special corresp. for B.B.C. at Nuremberg Trial of German War Criminals, 1945-46; contrib. talks and feature programmes to B.B.C. for radio and television; television commentator for Coronation, 1953; commissioned to write Tobruk-Alamein Vol. of Australian Official History of Second World War, 1947; Military Corresp., The Observer, 1952. *Publications:* Tobruk, 1944; The Struggle for Europe, 1952. *Recreations:* tennis, cricket. *Clubs:* Savile; Yorick (Melbourne); University (Sydney). [*Died* 10 *Jan.* 1954.

WILSON, Adam, C.B.E. 1942; J.P. Ayrshire; M.I.Chem.E.; Member of Scottish Savings Committee; *b.* 13 Aug. 1882; *s.* of late David Wilson and late Mary Conn; *m.* 1909, Bessie McIntosh; one *d.* *Educ.:* Stevenston Public School. Has been in Explosives Industry with Nobel's Explosives Co., and later Imperial Chemical Industries Ltd. for 51 years; joined Nobel's Explosives Co., Ardeer, as apprentice in engineering div., 1894; Chairman, Explosives Div., Imperial Chemical Industries Ltd., 1942-45; supervised design and erection of factories in var[illegible]s parts of world, including large explosives factory for Ministry of Munitions during war of 1914-18. Travelled extensively on business in Central Europe, Balkans, America, Japan, and Manchuria; formerly Delegate Director I.C.I. (Explosives) Ltd. and I.C.I. (Metals) Ltd.; a Director of Czechoslovak Explosives Ltd., Prague; Synthesia Chemical Works Ltd., Prague; seconded for special services Portland Glass Co.; Irvine Harbour Co.; and constructed seven large Explosives Factories for the Ministry of Supply and Ministry of Aircraft Production, 1939-42. *Recreations:* golf, gardening. *Club:* Royal Scottish Automobile (Glasgow). [*Died* 15 *Feb.* 1951.

WILSON, Alan, C.B. 1952; Chief Inspector of Audit, Ministry of Housing and Local Government, 1947-58, retd.; *b.* 2 June 1896; *s.* of J. P. Wilson, B.A., Highgate Village, London; *m.* 1928, Madge, *d.* of J. Dearnaley, Buxton, Derbyshire; one *s.* *Educ.:* Stationers' Company's School. Barrister-at-Law. Entered Civil Service, 1914. Served European War, Wiltshire Regt., 1914-19; retired as Captain. Asst. District Auditor, Ministry of Health, 1921; passed through various grades of audit service to appointment as District Auditor (Newcastle), 1938; Deputy Chief Inspector of Audit, 1942. *Recreations:* golf and gardening. *Address:* The Homestead, Rogate, Sussex. [*Died* 3 *Nov.* 1959.

WILSON, Albert Edward; journalist; dramatic critic of The Star, 1920-54, retired; Hon. Sec. Nat. Soc. for the Abolition of Cruel Sports since 1957; *m.* 1924, Maude Cox; two *s.* Apprenticed Thanet Times, Margate; subsequently on staff of Bristol Daily Mercury, Daily Dispatch (Manchester), Daily Sketch (London), joined editorial staff The Star, 1914; Foundation, Life and Hon. Mem. of the Nat. Union of Journalists; President, Critics Circle, 1941-42, Hon. Treasurer, 1943. *Publications:* Penny Plain, Twopence Coloured, 1932; Christmas Pantomime, 1934; Theatre Guyed, 1935; part-author Playtime in Russia, 1935; editor definitive edition Plays of J. M. Barrie, 1942; Pantomime Pageant; Playwrights in Aspic, 1946; Playgoer's Pilgrimage, 1948; Post-War Theatre; Story of Pantomime, 1949; Half a Century of Entertainment, Edwardian Theatre, 1951; The Lyceum, 1952; East End Entertainment, 1954; Prime Minister of Mirth, 1956, etc. *Recreations:* gardening, travel and listening to music. *Address:* 99 Streathbourne Road, S. W.17. *T.:* Balham 6150. [*Died* 22 *Jan.* 1960.

WILSON, Archibald Wayet, M.A. (Oxon); Mus.Doc. (Oxon); F.R.C.O.; Organist Emeritus of Manchester Cathedral; 5th *s.* of Rev. P. S. Wilson, late Vicar of Horbling, Lincolnshire. *Educ.:* Rossall School; Royal College of Music; Keble College, Oxford (Organ Scholar). Organist, St. John's, Upper St. Leonard's, and St. Asaph Cathedral; Organist and Magister Choristarum of Ely Cathedral. *Publications:* Morning, Communion, and Evening Service in E for S.A.T.B.; Evening Service in E♭ for Men's Voices; Communion Service in D for Parish Church Choirs; Anthems and Part-Songs; Ballad for Chorus and Orchestra; The Organs and Organists of Ely Cathedral; The Chorales: their Origin and Influence. *Address:* S. Audrey, Sedgley Park Road, Prestwich, Manchester. [*Died* 1950.
[*But death not notified in time for inclusion in Who Was Who 1941–1950, first edn.*

WILSON, Col. Arthur H.; *see* Hutton-Wilson.

WILSON, Beryl Charlotte Mary, C.B.E. 1920; J.P. London; *e. d.* of David Sinclair Smith, Aberdeenshire; *m.* 1907, Samuel Barrow (decd.), *yr. s.* of Walter Hebden Wilson, Liverpool; one *s.* *Educ.:* Crofts. Qr.-Master Belgian Refugees, Victoria Station, 1914; Hon. organiser, Anzac Buffet, 1915; Lady Superintendent, Waterloo Free Buffet for Sailors and Soldiers, 1915-20; Hon. Treasurer, South Kensington Conservative and Unionist Association, Women's Branch, 1924-35; Vice-Chairman, 1935; Chairman, 1936; President, 1947; Member of Council of Royal Boro, Kensington, 1928-49, retd.; Vice-Chm. National Society for Epileptics, Chalfont; Vice-Chairman Kensington District Nursing Association; Vice-President Kensington Nursing Division St. John's; St. Mary Abbots Hospital, Kensington. *Recreation:* sociology. *Address:* 38 Pembroke Road, W.8. *T.:* Western 4280. *Club:* Ladies' Carlton. [*Died* 13 *April* 1951.

WILSON, Captain Charles Benjamin, M.C.; late 10th Royal Hussars and R.F.C.; Officer in Home Guard; *b.* 28 Dec. 1885; *s.* of Colonel Hubert M. Wilson; *m.* 1919, Janet (*d.* 1946), *d.* of John Mackinnon; no *c.* (*o. s.*, 2nd Lt. 10th R. Hussars, killed in action, Libya, 1942); *m.* 1948, Phyllis Marija, *d.* of late Karl N. Briggs, Bendigo, Victoria, Australia. *Educ.:* Eton. 3rd Bn. K.O.Y.L.I., 1903-5; 10th Royal Hussars, 1905-12; 10th Royal Hussars and Royal Flying Corps, 1914-18 (M.C., despatches, 1914 Star, Victory and Allied medals); High Sheriff of Norfolk, 1942. *Recreations:* sailing and travelling. *Address:* Irstead Lodge, Neatishead, Norfolk. *T.:* Horning 234. *Clubs:* Cavalry, White's, Buck's, Royal Automobile, Royal Aero, R.A.F.; Norfolk (Norwich); Royal Norfolk and Suffolk Yacht (Lowestoft). [*Died* 9 *Aug.* 1957.

WILSON, Rev. Charles Edward; Sec. of the Baptist Missionary Soc. 1905-39, retired; Chm. 1942; *b.* London, 1871; *m.* 1897, Amy Pike; four *d.* *Educ.:* St. Olave's School, Southwark; Regent's Park College; London University (B.A.). Missionary, B.M.S. Bengal, Jessore, 1894; Serampore, 1895-1904; acted as Principal of Serampore College; B.M.S. deputation to China Mission Stations, 1907-8; deputation to Jamaica, 1909; deputation to Ceylon and India, 1913-14; deputation to the Congo, 1919; deputation to China, 1929; Deputation to Ceylon and India, 1931-32. Hon. D.D. Acadia, N.S. F.R.G.S. *Address:* Furnival, Belgrave Road, Seaford, Sussex. *T.:* Seaford 2806. [*Died* 9 *Dec.* 1956.

WILSON, Charles Thomson Rees, C.H. 1937; F.R.S.; M.A. (Cantab.), Hon. LL.D. (Aberdeen and Glasgow), Hon. D.Sc. (Manchester, Liverpool, London and Cambridge); Fellow of Sidney Sussex College; Jacksonian Prof. of Natural Philosophy, Cambridge, 1925-34; *b.* Glencorse, Midlothian, 14 Feb. 1869; *s.* of late John Wilson, farmer, Crosshouse, Glencorse; *m.* 1908, Jessie Fraser, *o. d.* of late Rev. G. Hill Dick, Glasgow; one *s.* two *d.* *Educ.:* Owens College, Manchester; Sidney Sussex College, Cambridge. Engaged in research since 1895 on condensation nuclei, ions, and atmospheric electricity; Nobel Physics Prize, 1927 (with Professor Arthur Compton); Copley Medal of Royal Society, 1935. *Address:* The Cottage, Carlops, Peebles-shire. [*Died* 15 *Nov.* 1959.

WILSON, Christopher James, C.M.G. 1939; M.C.; M.A., M.D., B.Ch. (Cantab.); retired, farming in Kenya Colony; *b.* 29 Mar. 1879; *s.* of James Pillans Wilson; *m.* 1919, Grace Sinclair; no *c.* *Educ.:* St. Paul's School; Christ's College, Cambridge; London Hospital. Resident appointments, Royal Portsmouth Hospital, 1906; Ship's Surgeon, Royal Mail Steam Packet Co., 1907; Medical Officer Trans-Andine Tunnel Construction, S. America, 1909; Medical Officer, Colonial Medical Service, British East Africa, 1911; Captain, East African Medical Service, 1914-1919 (M.C., despatches twice); Deputy P.M.O., Kenya Colony, 1923; P.M.O., F.M.S., 1928; Director of Medical Services, Straits Settlements, 1931. *Publications:* The Story of the East African Mounted Rifles, 1938; Before the Dawn in Kenya, 1952; Kenya's Warning, 1954. *Address:* Kikuyu, Kenya. [*Died* 8 *Feb.* 1956.

WILSON, Very Rev David Frederick Ruddell, M.A., T.C.D.; *b.* 1871; *s.* of Rev. James Wilson, Rector of Tyholland, Monaghan, and Laetitia Ferris; *m.* 1912, Maria Percy, *d.* of Rev. Dr. Jordan, Treasurer of St. Patrick's, Armagh, and Rector of Magherafelt; no *c.* *Educ.:* Monaghan Collegiate School; Trinity College, Dublin. Ordained, 1895; Curate of Belfast (St. Anns), 1898-99; Succentor of St. Patrick's Cathedral, and Warden of the Cathedral Grammar School, 1899; Treasurer's Vicar, 1914, and Minor Canon Treasurer, 1918; Precentor, 1924; Rector of Drumcondra, with North Strand, Dublin, 1914; Rector of Donnybrook, 1917; Chaplain to the Lord-Lieutenant, 1919-21; Dean of St. Patrick's, Dublin, 1935-50, retired; Select Preacher before the University of Dublin, 1922, 1924, 1938. *Publications:* General Editor of the Irish Church Hymnal, 1911-17, and of the Irish Chant Book, 1925.

Recreation: yachting, owner and skipper of yacht Esterel. *Address:* Pembroke Lodge, Sydney Parade, Dublin. *T.:* Dublin 64251. *Club:* Royal Irish Yacht (Kingstown). [*Died* 24 *Nov.* 1957.

WILSON, Major-General Francis Adrian, C.B. 1927; C.M.G. 1917; D.S.O. 1900; Officier Légion d'Honneur; *b.* 12 Oct. 1874; *s.* of late Gen. Sir C. W. Wilson; *m.* 1903, Mabel, *d.* of Edward Wilson Crosfield; one *s.* one *d.* Entered R.A. 1894; Captain, 1901; Major, 1910; Maj.-Gen. 1929; served South Africa, 1899-1902 (despatches twice, Queen's medal 6 clasps, King's medal 2 clasps, D.S.O.); European War, 1914-19 (despatches five times, wounded, Bt. Lt.-Col., Bt. Col., C.M.G.); Brig. R.A. Eastern Command, 1925-29; Inspector of the Royal Artillery, War Office, 1929-33; retired pay, 1933; Col. Comdt. R.A., 1940-44. *Address:* The Beeches, Lower Bourne, Farnham, Surrey. [*Died* 6 *May* 1954.

WILSON, Colonel Frank Walter, C.B. 1926; C.M.G. 1917; F.R.C.V.S. (retired); *b.* 28 June 1869; *s.* of W. Wilson, F.R.C.V.S., Berkhamstead; *m.* 1st, Elsie (*d.* 1935), *d.* of late Hugh Brown; one *d.*; 2nd, 1939, Norah, *d.* of late William Bingley. *Educ.:* King Edward VI Grammar School, Berkhamstead; R.V. College, London; House Surgeon, 1891-1892; Lecturer, Durham College of Science, 1893-94. Capt. A.V. Dept. 1900; Major A.V.C. 1906; Lt.-Col. 1915; Col. 1921; Senior Veterinary Officer, Meerut Division, 1906-11; Commanded Station Veterinary Hospital, Aldershot, 1912; served N.W. Frontier, India, 1897-98 (medal 2 clasps); S. Africa, 1899-1902 (despatches, Capt., 2 medals 7 clasps); European War, 1914-17 (despatches four times, Bt. Lt.-Col., C.M.G.); Officier Order of St. Maurice and St. Lazarus; retired pay, 1926. *Address:* c/o Glyn, Mills and Co. (Holt's Branch), Kirkland House, Whitehall, S.W.1. [*Died* 18 *Dec.* 1953.

WILSON, Major-General Frederick Maurice, C.B. 1915; C.M.G. 1918; late R.A.S.C.; *b.* 19 Nov. 1868; *m.* 1897, Lorna Sophia Glynn, *d.* of late Rev. W. Baker, Batcombe; one *s.* two *d.* Entered Army, 1890; Captain, 1897; Major, 1903; Lt.-Colonel, 1911; Major-General, 1921; Comdt. A.S.C. Training Establishment, 1913-14; Assistant Director of Supplies, 1914; Director S. and T., Cologne, 1919-1920; India, 1921-2; served Ashanti, 1895-96 (star); European War, 1914-18 (despatches, C.B., Bt. Col., C.M.G.); retired pay, 1925. *Address:* Lloyds Bank, 6 Pall Mall, S.W.1. [*Died* 16 *Aug.* 1956.

WILSON, George Bailey; *b.* 1868; *s.* of Isaac Whitwell Wilson, J.P., and Annie, *d.* of Jonathan Bagster, Bible Publisher; *m.* 1904, Margaret Whitridge (*d.* 1947), *d.* of John Whitridge Davies, Oswestry, Salop; two *s.* one *d.* *Educ.:* Friends' School, Kendal; Oliver's Mount School, Scarborough; B.A., Ph.D. London University; Clifford's Inn and Daniel Reardon prizeman. Solicitor's Final Examination, 1887; Secretary of the United Kingdom Alliance, 1909-32; Consulting Secretary, 1932-1943. Howard medallist of Royal Statistical Society, 1911; Author of Alcohol and The Nation (degree Thesis for London University); Editor of Alliance Year Book; Life of Lord Rhayader; prepared Annual Letter, containing Estimate of National Drink Bill, 1910-40. *Address:* 28 Wilton Crescent, S.W.1. [*Died* 7 *June* 1952.

WILSON, Rev. Canon George Herbert, M.A.; *b.* Alfreton, Derbyshire, 13 May 1870; *s.* of J. G. Wilson. *Educ.:* Cheltenham College; St. John's College, Oxford; Wells Theological College. Deacon, 1894; Priest, 1895; Curate of Aughton, 1894-96; of Wincanton, 1897-1904; joined the Universities Mission to Central Africa, 1905; Archdeacon of Shiré, 1921-32; Canon of Likoma, 1922-32; Priest-in-Charge, Mponda's, British Nyasaland, 1913-32; Vicar of Pattishall, 1933-1946; Rural Dean, 1939-44. *Publications:* A Missionary's Life in Nyasaland; The History of the Universities' Mission to Central Africa. *Address:* The White House, Bruton, Somerset. *T.:* Bruton 2184. [*Died* 24 *Sept.* 1952.

WILSON, George Heron, C.B.E. 1920; *b.* Jan. 1868; *s.* of Charles John Wilson, Deanfield, Hawick; *m.* Julia Baker, *d.* of Andrew Tod, Elmpark, Edinburgh. *Educ.:* George Watson's College, Edinburgh; abroad. Member of East Sussex Education Committee, 1926-46; Chairman Roxburghshire National Insurance Committee; Vice-Chairman Roxburghshire Education Authority; Provost of Hawick; Deputy Controller Priority Dept., Ministry of Munitions; Member of the Interim Court of Arbitration, Ministry of Labour; J.P. Roxburghshire, 1912, and East Sussex, 1929. *Address:* The Old Vicarage, Iford, nr. Lewes. *Club:* Caledonian. [*Died* 25 *April* 1959.

WILSON, Lieut.-Col. George Robert Stewart, C.B.E. 1953; late R.E.; Chief Inspecting Officer of Railways, Ministry of Transport, since 1949; *b.* 17 April 1896; *s.* of George Prangley Wilson, Wedhampton Cottage, Devizes, Wilts, and Frances Elizabeth, *yr. d.* of Robert Stewart, Kinlochmoidart, Inverness-shire; and *g.s.* of George Wilson, Banner Cross, Sheffield; *m.* 1923, Marion Isabel, *yr. d.* of William Barry, Buttevant, County Cork, Ireland; one *s.* one *d.* *Educ.:* Marlborough; Royal Military Acad., Woolwich. Served European War, in France, Flanders, and Macedonia, 1915-18; 2nd Lt., Royal Engineers, 1914; Lt., 1916; Captain, 1917; seconded to Colonial Office, 1921, for survey work of Syria-Palestine Boundary Commission; Major, R.E., 1930; retired from Army, 1935; Inspecting Officer of Railways, Ministry of Transport, 1935; recalled to active list, 1939; served with B.E.F., France, till 1940; returned to Ministry of Transport as Inspecting Officer of Railways, 1940. *Recreations:* sailing, fishing. *Address:* St. Catherine's Cottage, Guildford, Surrey. *Club:* United Service. [*Died* 20 *March* 1958.

WILSON, Gerald Sidney, C.S.I. 1931; *b.* 1880; *s.* of Sidney Wilson, late of H.E.I.C.'s Navy; *m.* 1915, Ellinor, *d.* of John Cunningham Thomson; one *s.* two *d.* *Educ.:* Tonbridge School; abroad. Passed into Indian Police Service, 1901; posted to the Bombay Presidency and held appointments of Assistant and District Superintendent of Police up to 1912; Personal Assistant to Inspector-General of Police, 1912-14; Deputy Commissioner of Police, Bombay City, 1914-18; Principal, Police Training School, 1920-21; Deputy Inspector-General of Police, 1921-28; Officiating Inspector-General of Police, Bombay Presidency, 1928-29; Commissioner of Police, Bombay City, 1930-32; Inspector-General of Police, Bombay Presidency, 1932-34; retired, 1934; civilian attached General Staff, War Office, Sept. 1939-43; Asst. Divnl. Food Officer (Enforcement) N.W. Divn., 1943-44; holds King's Police Medal. *Address:* Jordans, Four Throws, Hawkhurst, Kent. *T.:* Hawkhurst 3189. [*Died* 5 *Feb.* 1960.

WILSON, Godfrey Harold Alfred, O.B.E.; Master of Clare College, Cambridge, 1929-39; Vice-Chancellor, 1935-36, and 1936-1937, late Treasurer of the University of Cambridge; *b.* 29 Oct. 1871; *s.* of late Daniel Wilson, Melbourne; *m.* Margaret Mabel, *d.* of late Rev. J. E. P. Bartlett, of Barnham Broom Rectory, Norfolk; no *c.* *Educ.:* Melbourne Grammar School; Trinity College, Univ. of Melbourne; Clare College, Cambridge; Fellow: 1897; M.P. (U.) Cambridge University, 1929-1935; Hon. D. C. L. Durham, 1937. *Address:* Hemingford Grey, Huntingdon. *T.:* St. Ives 3121. [*Died* 13 *July* 1958.

WILSON, Grace Margaret (Mrs. Bruce Campbell), C.B.E., R.R.C., Florence Nightingale Medal; *b.* Brisbane; *d.* of J. P. Wilson, Brisbane. *Educ.:* Brisbane Gram. School. Trained Brisbane Hosp. and Queen Charlotte Hosp., London; Sister, Albany Memorial

Hosp., Queen's Square, London; Matron, Brisbane Hosp.; P/Matron A.A.N.S. 1st Military District; P/Matron No. 3 Aust. Gen. Hosp. A.I.F.; Temp. Matron-in-Chief A.I.F; Matron, Rosemount Military Hospital, Brisbane; Matron, Children's Hospital, Melbourne; Sister-in-Charge, Somerset House Private Hospital, Melbourne; Matron of Alfred Hospital, Melbourne; on active service five years (despatches five times); on service again as Matron-in-Chief on outbreak of war, 1939; on service abroad, 1940-41, when discharged as medically unfit. *Recreation:* golf. *Address:* c/o Bank of N.S. Wales, 325 Collins Street, Melbourne, Victoria, Australia. *Clubs:* Lyceum; Returned Nurses' (Melbourne). [*Died* 12 *Jan.* 1957.

WILSON, Gregg, O.B.E., M.A., D.Sc., Ph.D., M.R.I.A.; Emeritus Professor and Pro-Chancellor, Queen's University, Belfast; *b.* Falkirk, 15 Dec. 1865; *s.* of late James Wilson, solicitor; *m.* Florence Allen, *e. d.* of late Rt. Hon. and Rev. Thomas Hamilton, D.D., LL.D., *widow* of Professor W. N. Watts, Barrister; one *s.* one *d.* Studied at the Universities of Edinburgh, Marburg, and Freiburg; Demonstrator in Zoology at Edinburgh University, 1891; Acting Professor of Biology at Sydney University, 1898; subsequently Lecturer on Zoology at the Heriot-Watt College and at Surgeons' Hall, and Professor of Biology in the Royal Veterinary College, Edinburgh; Inspector of Fisheries for England and Wales, 1902; Professor of Natural History in Queen's College, Belfast. 1902-9; Professor of Zoology, Queen's University, Belfast, 1909-31; formerly Major in Territorial Force; Commanded Belfast University Contingent O.T.C., 1910-20. After retirement acted as Registrar (Hon.) and Hon. Treasurer of Queen's University; Acting Commissioner St. John Ambulance Brigade, 1941-42. *Publications:* papers, chiefly embryological, in various scientific magazines. *Address:* Transy, Beechlands, Malone Road, Belfast. *T.:* Belfast 65520. [*Died* 28 *March* 1951.

WILSON, Harold William, M.S.; F.R.C.S.; Consulting Surg., St. Bartholomew's Hospital; *b.* Deer Park, Carlisle; *s.* of late John and Mary Wilson; *m.* 1911, Hester Laird Cox; one *d.* *Educ.:* King Edward's School, Chelmsford; St. Bartholomew's Medical College. Late Assistant Surgeon to Victoria Hospital for Children and The Cancer Hospital. *Publications:* Editor of Gask and Wilson's Surgery, etc. *Recreations:* fishing, shooting, sailing, gardening. [*Died* 14 *Nov.* 1959.

WILSON, Colonel Right Hon. Sir Leslie Orme, P.C. 1922; G.C.S.I., *cr.* 1929; G.C.M.G., *cr.* 1937 (C.M.G. 1916); G.C.I.E., *cr.* 1923; D.S.O. 1900; Grand Croix de l'ordre de la Couronne, 1926; *b.* 1 Aug. 1876; *e. s.* of late H. Wilson; *m.* 1909, Winifred, *e. d.* of late Captain Charles Smith of Goderich, Sydney; one *s.* one *d.* *Educ.:* St. Michael's, Westgate; St. Paul's School. Appointed 2nd Lieut. R.M.L.I., 1895; Lieut., 1896; Captain, 1901. Served South Africa, 1899-1901 (severely wounded, despatches, Queen's medal 5 clasps, D.S.O.); A.D.C. to Gov. of N.S.W., 1903-09; contested Poplar Division of Tower Hamlets (U.) 1910, and Reading, 1910. Captain in the Berkshire Royal Horse Artillery (Territorials); promoted Temp. Lt.-Col. R.M., and appointed to command Hawke Batt. R.N.D.; served through operations in Gallipoli, 1914-15 (despatches, C.M.G.); served in France, 1915-16 (severely wounded, Nov. 1916); M.P. (U.) Reading, 1913-22, (C.) Sth. Portsmouth, 1922-23; Parliamentary Assistant Secretary to the War Cabinet, 1918; Chairman National Maritime Board, 1919; Parliamentary Secretary to the Ministry of Shipping, 1919: Parliamentary Secretary to the Treasury and Chief Unionist Whip, 1921-23; Governor of Bombay, 1923-28; Governor of Queensland, 1932-46; LL.D. (Hon.) University of Brisbane, 1935; K.St.J. *Recreations:* golf, shooting. *Address:* Mount House, Wentworth, Surrey. *Club:* Carlton. [*Died* 29 *Sept.* 1955.

WILSON, Sir Mark, Kt., *cr.* 1950; B.A., LL.D. (Dublin); Chief Justice of the Gold Coast since 1948; *b.* 22 Oct. 1896; *y. s.* of William Shore Wilson, Castle Comer, Co. Kilkenny, and Kate, *d.* of Jonathan Smyth; *m.* 1927, Dr. Isabella Kilpatrick McNeilly, M.B., B.Ch., B.A.O., *e. d.* of Robert McNeilly, Pentagon House, Ballymena, Co. Antrim; one *s.* one *d.* (and one *d.* decd.). *Educ.:* Kilkenny College; Mountjoy School; Trinity College, Dublin. Served R.A.F., 1918-19; 1st Schol. Hist. and Polit. Sci.; B.A. (Senior Moderator and Gold Medallist), 1921; LL.B. 1922; ed. University magazine "T.C.D.," 1921-22; Auditor, College Historical Society, 1921-22; called to Irish Bar (1st cl. hons.), 1924. Cadet, Colonial Administrative Service, Tanganyika, 1924; District Magistrate, Uganda, 1926; Sen. Magistrate, 1935; Chancellor, Uganda Diocese, 1934-36; Puisne Judge, Tanganyika, 1936-48. Chairman, Tanganyika War Compensation Claims Tribunal, 1939-46; Member, Makerere College Council, 1940-47; Chairman, Trade Disputes Tribunal, 1943; Commissioner, Arusha-Moshi Lands Commn., 1946-47 (thanks of Secretary of State for Colonies); Chairman, Gold Coast Judicial Service Commission, 1954-; Pres., Gold Coast Branch, Internat. Law Assoc., 1954-; Pres. Gold Coast Magistrates' Assoc., 1955-; LL.D. (*jure dignitatis*) 1949. *Publication:* International Peace and the League of Nations, 1922. *Recreations:* rugby football (captain, Dublin Wanderers F.C.; played in Irish Internat. trial matches, 1920-21); gardening and golf. *Address:* Supreme Court, Accra, Gold Coast; The Manor House, Brede, Sx. *T.:* 297. *Clubs:* Royal Empire Society; Rye Golf (Camber). [*Died* 10 *April* 1956.

WILSON, Lt.-Col. Sir Mathew Richard Henry, 4th Bt., *cr.* 1874; C.S.I. 1911; D.S.O. 1918; *b.* 25 Aug. 1875; *e. s.* of 3rd Bt. and late Georgina Mary, *e. d.* of R. T. Lee, of Grove Hall, Yorks; *S.* father, 1914; *m.* 1905, Hon. Barbara Lister (*d.* 1943; author of Dear Youth, 1937, The House of Memories, edited Lord Ribblesdale's Impressions and Memories), *d.* of 4th Baron Ribblesdale; three *s.* Entered 10th Royal Hussars, 1897; Captain, 1902; Major, 1908; Officer Company of Gentlemen Cadets, R.M.C., 1897-99; served South Africa, 1899-1902 (Queen's medal 3 clasps, King's medal 3 clasps); Instructor at Royal Military College, Sandhurst, 1907; Military Secretary to Commander-in-Chief, India, 1909; retired, 1912; served Egypt, 1915 (D.S.O.); M.P. (U.) Bethnal Green, 1914-22. *Heir:* *s.* Mathew Martin, *b.* 2 July 1906. *Address:* Eshton House, Gargrave, Skipton, Yorks. *Clubs:* St. James', Turf. [*Died* 17 *May* 1958.

WILSON, Sir Maurice; *see* Bromley-Wilson.

WILSON, Mona; *b.* 1872; *e. d.* of late Rev. James Maurice Wilson, D.D. *Educ.:* Clifton High School; St. Leonard's School, St. Andrews; Newnham College, Cambridge. Secretary of the Women's Trade Union League; National Health Insurance Commissioner (England), 1912-19; member of the Industrial Fatigue Research Board, 1919-29; J.P. Wilts. *Publications:* These were Muses; Life of William Blake, 1927; Sir Philip Sidney, 1931; Queen Elizabeth, 1932; Queen Victoria, 1933; Jane Austen and some Contemporaries, 1938; Johnson, 1950. *Address:* The Old Oxyard, Oare, Marlborough, Wilts. [*Died* 26 *Oct.* 1954.

WILSON, Philip Whitwell; author and lecturer; *b.* 1875; *s.* of I. Whitwell Wilson, J.P., Westmorland, and Annie, *d.* of Jonathan Bagster, Bible publisher; *m.* 1st, 1899, Alice S. (*d.* 1939), *o. d.* of Henry Collins, Pawtucket, R.I.-U.S.A.; three *s.* two *d.*; 2nd, 1944, Mary Eliza, beth (*d.* 1951), *e. d.* of George R. Cross, Edgewater, New Jersey. *Educ.:* Kendal Grammar School; Clare College, Cambridge. President of the Cambridge Union Society; editor of the

Granta, Public School Magazine, 1897-99; M.P. (L.) South St. Pancras, 1906-10; contested Appleby Division, Westmorland, 1910; was in Press Gallery, House of Commons, twelve years; later, American correspondent, Daily News; contributes regularly to New York Times; has spoken on British subjects hundreds of times in United States. *Publications:* The Christ we Forget; The Church we Forget; The Vision we Forget; The Irish Case; The Unmaking of Europe; A Layman's Confession of Faith; An Unofficial Statesman: Robert C. Ogden; An Explorer of Changing Horizons: W. E. Geil; William Pitt the Younger, 1930; editor of the Greville Diary, 1927; Is Christ Possible? 1932; The Romance of the Calendar, 1938; Newtopia, 1941; Bride's Castle, 1944; Black Tarn, 194. *Address:* Linden House, 3001 Henry Hudson Parkway, New York City. *Club:* National Liberal; City (New York).
[*Died* 6 *June* 1956.

WILSON, Rt. Rev. Piers Holt. *Educ.:* Oriel College, Oxford; Wells Theological College. B.A. 1905; M.A. 1908; Deacon, 1909; Priest, 1910; Rector of All Saints, St. Andrews, 1930-43; Dean of St. Andrews, Dunkeld, and Dunblane, 1940-43; Bishop of Moray, Ross and Caithness, 1943-52. *Address:* 10 Queen's Gardens, St. Andrews, Fife. [*Died* 3 *Feb.* 1956.

WILSON, Reginald Appleby; Director, Lloyds Bank Ltd., London (Vice-Chm., 1945-1955); Director of Lloyds and National Provincial Foreign Bank Ltd., London; *b.* 1878; 3rd *s.* of late Richard Wilson, J.P., of Westfield, Armley, Leeds; *m.* 1908, Florence, 3rd *d.* of late Alfred Woodall, Oxton, Cheshire; one *s.* one *d.* *Educ.:* Lancing College. Entered private banking firm of William Williams Brown & Co., Leeds, 1898; Amalgamated with Lloyds Bank, 1900; President Institute of Bankers 1937-38, 1938-39. *Recreation:* golf. *Address:* Tyrrells Green, Leatherhead. *T.:* Leatherhead 2365. *Club:* Devonshire. [*Died* 12 *Sept.* 1955.

WILSON, Hon. Sir (Reginald) Victor, K.B.E., *cr* 1926; Chairman National Press, Sydney; Member National Health and Research Council of the Commonwealth; Member North Sydney Hospital Board; Member Research Council of N.S.W.; Member of Board Australian General Assurance; *b.* 30 June 1877; *s.* of late James Wilson of Riverton, S. Australia; *m.* 1901, Lily, *d.* of late M. Suckling, Riverton, S. Australia; one *s.* two *d.* *Educ.:* Whinham Coll., North Adelaide. Senator of the Commonwealth of Australia for S. Australia, 1920-26; Hon. Minister, 1923-25; Minister for Markets and Migration, Commonwealth of Australia, 1925-26. Australian Delegate with Prime Minister to Imperial Economic Conference, 1923; Australian Commissioner, British Empire Exhibition, 1924; Pres. of the Motion Pictures Distributors of Australia, 1926-39. *Address:* 48 Shell Cove Road, Neutral Bay, Sydney, N.S.W. [*Died* 13 *July* 1957.

WILSON, Capt. Robert Amcotts, D.S.O. 1915; R.N. (retd.); *b.* 1882; *s.* of Sir Mathew Wilson, 3rd Bt., and Georgina Mary, *e. d.* of R. T. Lee, Grove Hall, Yorks; *m.* 1st, 1912, Gladys (*d.* 1918), *d.* of William Gillilan, formerly of 6 Palace Gate, Kensington, W.; (one *s.* killed in action, N. Africa, 1942); 2nd, 1928, Marjorie, widow of E. Clarence Jones, New York. Lieut. 1903; Lt.-Comdr. 1911; Comdr. 1915; retired, 1920; Capt. (retd.) 1927. Served European War, 1914-18 (despatches, D.S.O.). War of 1939-45, anti-submarine squadron, 1939-41; Naval Attaché, Brazil and Venezuela, 1941-1945. *Clubs:* White's, St. James', Portland, Royal Yacht Squadron; Racquet and Tennis (New York). [*Died* 26 *June* 1960.

WILSON, Major-General Thomas Arthur Atkinson, C.B. 1938; Indian Army, retired; late 2nd Royal Lancers (G.H.); *b.* 17 June 1882; *s.* of John Wilson, Longford, Ireland; *m.* 1918, Helen Findlay (*d.* 1957), *d.* of James Currie; no *c.* *Educ.:* Campbell College, Belfast; R.M.C., Sandhurst. Entered Indian Army, 1902; Commander 2nd (Sialkot) Cavalry Brigade, 1932-34; Brigadier, General Staff, Southern Command, India, 1934-38; D.A. & Q.M.G., Southern Command, Poona, India, 1938; retired, 1940; re-employed, 1941-1942. European War, 1914-19, France, Belgium, Egypt and Mesopotamia (despatches, 1914 Star, two medals); A.D.C. to the King, 1936. *Recreations:* shooting, golf. *Address:* 2 Stanford Court, Cornwall Gardens, S.W.7. *T.:* Western 0198. *Club:* Naval and Military.
[*Died* 18 *Aug.* 1958.

WILSON, Rev. Thomas Erskine, M.A.; *b.* 1874; *s.* of Rev. James Wilson, Vicar of St. Stephen's, Norwich; *m.* 1914, Ella, *d.* of H. Gibbs, The Hollies, Handcross, Sussex; two *s.* one *d.* *Educ.:* Aldenham School; Gonville and Caius Coll., Cambridge; Clergy Training School, Cambridge. B.A. 1897; M.A. 1904; Assistant Master at Bradfield College, Berks, 1899-1909; Housemaster Junior House, Bradfield College, 1909-14; Headmaster St. Saviour's School, Ardingly, 1915-32; Rector of West Walton, 1933-46; Deacon, 1900; Priest, 1901. *Recreations:* cricket, golf. *Address:* Muttons, Bolney, Haywards Heath, Sussex.
[*Died* 31 *July* 1951.

WILSON, Sir Thomas George, Kt., *cr.* 1950; C.M.G. 1942; M.D., Ch.M. Syd., F.R.C.S. Edin., F.R.A.C.S.; founder F.R.C.O.G. Lond.; Original Representative for Australia on Regional Council, F.A.C.S., 1924; Hon. Cons. Gynæcologist, Adelaide Hosp.; Hon. Cons. Obstetrician and Pres. Board of Management, Queen's Maternity Home, 1935-50; *b.* Armidale, N.S.W., 1876; *s.* of C. G. Wilson; *m.* Elsa May Cuzens, Warnambool, Victoria; two *s.* *Educ.:* New England Grammar School; Sydney University. Studied various London Hospitals, U.S.A., and Vienna; started practice in Adelaide, 1902; on active service with A.I.F 1914-1918; various theatres of the war; rank Lieut.-Col.; consulting practice in Adelaide since 1908; Director of Obstetrics and Gynæcology and Edward Willis Way Lecturer, Univ. of Adelaide, 1920-43; President, B.M.A., South Australian Branch, 1922. *Publications:* numerous papers to medical journals, etc. *Recreations:* tennis, golf. *Address:* 296 Ward Street, North Adelaide, S. Australia. *Clubs:* Oriental (London); Adelaide (Adelaide).
[*Died* 14 *March* 1958.

WILSON, Hon. Sir Victor; *see* Wilson, Hon. Sir R. V.

WILSON, Walter Gordon, C.M.G. 1918; B.A., M.Inst.C.E., Hon. M.Inst.M.E., Hon. M.J.Inst.E.; Hon. Major Tank Corps; late Chief of Design, Mechanical Warfare Department; *b.* 21 April 1874; *s.* of late George Orr Wilson, Dunardagh, Blackrock, Dublin; *m.* Ethel Crommelin, *d.* of late S. O. Gray, Swaines, Rudgwick, Sussex; three *s.* *Educ.:* H.M.S. Britannia; King's College, Cambridge. *Address:* The Elms, Itchen Abbas, Winchester, Hants. *T.:* Itchen Abbas 206. *Clubs:* Royal Automobile, Flyfishers'. [*Died* 30 *June* 1957.

WILSON, Sir Wemyss G.; *see* Grant-Wilson.

WILSON, Engr.-Captain William Anderson, C.M.G. 1918; late R.N.; *b.* 1868; *m.* 1907, Hilda Margaret, *d.* of late Fleet-Paymaster John Bremner, Royal Navy. Entered R.N. Engineering College, 1884; R.N. 1890; served Dardanelles, 1914-15 (C.M.G.); retired, 1918. *Address:* c/o Lloyds Bank Ltd., Hastings.
[*Died* 29 *Dec.* 1957.

WILSON, William James, B.A., D.Sc., M.D., D.P.H.; Emeritus Professor of Public Health, Queen's University, Belfast; Consultant Director of Public Health Laboratory Services, Northern Ireland; *b.* 1879; *s.* of Thomas Wilson and Elizabeth Dundee,

Straid Mills, Co. Antrim; *m.* Maud Welsh, *d.* of Edward Lewis, Bangor, Co. Down; three *s.* one *d.* *Educ.:* Royal Academical Institution, Belfast; Queen's Univ., Belfast; Univ. of Berlin. Late Brevet Major, R.A.M.C. *Publications:* Textbook of Hygiene and papers in Journal of Hygiene. *Address:* 10 Malone Road, Belfast. [*Died* 6 *May* 1954.

WILTON, Sir Ernest Colville Collins, K.C.M.G., *cr.* 1923 (C.M.G. 1904); *b.* 6 Feb. 1870; *m.* 1927, Violet Evelyn, *d.* of late George Brown. Student Interpreter, China, 1890; employed with Mission to Tibet, 1903-4; Consul, Teng-Yueh, 1906; British Commissioner Tibet Trade Regulations, 1908; Special Opium Commissioner, 1912-14, 1914-15; Chinese Secretary, 1914; Consul-General, Canton, 1916; Chengtu, 1917; Hankow, 1918; British Commissioner on the Teschen International Commission, 1919; British Commissioner in Lithuania, 1920; British Minister for Esthonia and Latvia, 1921-22; Foreign Chief Inspector of the Chinese Salt Gabelle, 1923-26; President of the Saar Governing Commission, 1927-1932. *Address:* Ashington, Wild Oak Lane, Taunton. [*Died* 28 *Dec.* 1952.

WILTON, Herbert George; Fellow of the Institute of Actuaries; General Manager and Actuary, Norwich Union Life Insurance Society, 1934-37, Director, 1937-57, retired; Director, Norwich Union Fire Insurance Society Ltd., 1934-57; *b.* 21 May 1882; *s.* of late John Wilton and late Harriet Matilda Husk; *m.* 1912, Ethel Jane, 3rd *d.* of late Thomas Walter Brumwell; one *s.* one *d.* *Educ.:* King Edward VI Middle School, Norwich. Assistant Actuary, Norwich Union Life Insurance Society, 1919, Secretary, 1923. *Address:* East Carleton Lodge, near Norwich. *T.:* Mulbarton 281. [*Died* 9 *May* 1959.

WIMPERIS, Arthur Harold; dramatic author; *b.* 3 Dec. 1874; *s.* of E. M. Wimperis, Vice-President Royal Institute of Painters in Water Colours. *Educ.:* Dulwich College. Trained as black and white artist; joined Daily Graphic staff when eighteen years old; served through South African War with Paget's Horse; started writing, 1903. Films: (in collaboration) Wedding Rehearsal, 1932; Counsel's Opinion, The Private Life of Henry VIII., 1933; Catherine the Great, 1934; The Scarlet Pimpernel, lyrics in Sanders of the River, 1935; Dark Journey, Knight Without Armour, 1936; Mrs. Miniver, Random Harvest, The Paradine Case, 1942. *Publications:* lyrics and burlesques for the Follies; Lyrics of the Dairymaids; The Gay Gordons; The Balkan Princess; The Arcadians; The Mousmé; The Sunshine Girl; part-author The Girl in the Taxi, Within the Law, Love and Laughter, Mam'selle Tralala, By Jingo, Bric-a-Brac, My Lady Frayle, Follow the Crowd, Buzz-Buzz, Princess Charming, Tavern Maid, and Song of the Sea; author of The Passing Show, The Laughing Husband, Vanity Fair, Pamela, As You Were, Just Fancy; London, Paris, and New York; The Trump Card, 1921; The Curate's Egg, The Return, Bluebeard's Eighth Wife, Lovely Lady. *Recreations:* hunting, fishing, golf. *Address:* Yew Tree Cottage, River Road, Taplow, Bucks. *Club:* Arts. [*Died* 14 *Oct.* 1953.

WIMPERIS, Harry Egerton, C.B. 1935; C.B.E. 1928; M.A. (Camb.), D.Eng. (Hon.) Melbourne; F.R.Ae.S.; Hon. Fellow and Crown Governor, Imperial College, London; *b.* 27 Aug. 1876; *m.* 1907, Grace d'Avray, 3rd *d.* of late Sir George Parkin, K.C.M.G., D.C.L.; three *d.* *Educ.:* Gonville and Caius College, Cambridge (Mechanical Sciences Tripos); Royal College of Science (Tyndall Prizeman); Whitworth Scholar. Engineering Experience with Southern Railway (Locomotive Works), Armstrong Whitworth & Co. (Elswick Works), Crown Agents for the Colonies; Inventor of the Wimperis Accelerometer (1909), Gyro-Turn Indicator (1910), Course Setting Sight for Aircraft (1917); Experimental Officer in R.N.A.S. (Lt.-Comdr. R.N.V.R.) and R.A.F., 1915-24; Director of Scientific Research, Air Ministry, 1925-37; President of the Royal Aeronautical Society, 1936-38; Wilbur Wright Lecturer, 1932; Member of Aeronautical Research Cttee.; Hon. Fell. of Amer. Institute of Aeronautical Sciences; Member of Executive Cttee., of National Physical Laboratory, 1931-37; Past Member of Council I.E.E.; visited Australia to advise Commonwealth Government on Aeronautical Research, 1937-38; President of Engineering Section of the British Association, 1939; Thos. Hawksley Lecturer, 1944; Atomic Energy Study Group, Chatham House, 1946-50; Mem. of Council of British Association, 1948-54; *Publications:* The Internal Combustion Engine, 1909; Application of Power to Road Transport, 1913; Air Navigation, 1920; Aviation, 1945; World Power and Atomic Energy, 1946. *Address:* 46A Inverleith Place, Edinburgh 3. *Club:* Athenæum. [*Died* 16 *July* 1960.

WINBY, Lieut.-Col. Lewis Phillips; *b.* 17 Jan. 1874; *s.* of late F. C. Winby, 47 Portland Place, W.1. *Educ.:* Brighton College; Trinity College, Cambridge. (M.A.Mech. Science Tripos). Lieut. Royal Engineers; South African War, 1899-1902 (despatches, 2 medals, 5 clasps); European War, 1914-18; Lt.-Col. Westminster Dragoons (despatches, Croix de Guerre); M.P. (U.) Harborough Division, Leicester, 1924-1929. *Address:* Potters Hatch House, Crondall, Nr. Farnham, Surrey. *T.:* Crondall 415. *Club:* Carlton. [*Died* 27 *Jan.* 1956.

WINCKWORTH, Chauncey P. Tietjens; Yarrow Lecturer in Assyriology, University of Cambridge, since 1926; *b.* 1896; *o. s.* of Arthur and Marie Winckworth; *m.* 1920, Maud Lindsay Charlesworth; two *d.* *Educ.:* University College School; Christ's College, Cambridge. Wright Student in Arabic, Cambridge, 1920-23; Yarrow Student in Assyriology, 1923-26; Member of Council of Royal Asiatic Society, 1924-28; Epigraphist to the Joint Expedition of the British Museum and of the Museum of the University of Pennsylvania to Mesopotamia, 1930; Chairman of Milton (Cambs.) Parish Council, 1934; Rector's Warden, 1933-47. *Publications:* A New Interpretation of the Pahlavi Cross-Inscriptions of Southern India; various articles on Oriental Philology; History of Babylonia and Assyria in Story of the Nations. *Recreations:* fishing, photography, flute, and languages. *Address:* Milton House, Milton, Cambs. *T.:* Waterbeach 251. [*Died* 15 *July* 1954.

WINDAUS, Professor Dr. Adolf Otto Reinhold, Dr.phil.; Emeritus Professor, Göttingen University; Emeritus Director of the Chemical Laboratory, Göttingen; *b.* Berlin, 25 Dec. 1876; *m.* 1915; two *s.* one *d.* *Educ.:* Universities of Freiburg-im-Breisgau and Berlin. Privatdozent, 1903; Professor, Univ. of Göttingen, 1915, Emeritus, 1944. Member, Göttingen Acad. of Sciences, and Berlin Acad. of Sciences; Hon. mem. Chemical Society of London; Foreign mem. Prussian Acad. of Sciences; Corresp. mem. Bavarian Acad. of Sciences, etc. Nobel Prize for Chemistry, 1928; Pasteur Medal, 1938; Goethe Medallist. Dr.rer.nat. (*h.c.*); Dr. med. (*h.c.*); Dr.Ing. (*h.c.*); Dr. med. vet. (*h.c.*), etc. *Address:* Georg August-Universität, Wilhelmsplatz 1, Göttingen, Germany; Rohnsweg 22, Göttingen. [*Died* 9 *June* 1959.

WINDER, Sir Arthur (Benedict), Kt., *cr.* 1943; *b.* 12 Feb. 1875; *s.* of late Rev. John Harrison Winder, B.A.; *m.* 1905, Suzanne Brown; (one *d.* decd.). *Educ.:* Giggleswick School; Sheffield University (Mappin medal and Premium for Honours in Metallurgy and Associateship). In the Steel Works at Thos. Firth & Sons, now Firth Brown's; Manager of Steel Making

Dept. at Jonas & Colver, 1906; Head of Steel Making Dept. at Thomas Firth & Sons, 1918; in 1921 became Works Manager and Director of Industrial Steels, which was purchased by English Steel Corpn. in 1932; Director 1934-44, General Manager, 1932-44, English Steel Corporation, Vickers Works, Sheffield; also Director of Vickers Armstrong, Darlington Forge, and other companies. *Recreations:* golf and deep-sea fishing. *Address:* Brooklands, 406 Fulwood Road, Sheffield 10. *Clubs:* The Club, St. James' (Sheffield). [*Died* 11 *Dec.* 1953.

WINDEYER, John Cadell, M.D., Ch.M. Sydney; M.R.C.S., L.R.C.P. London; F.R.A.C.S.; F.R.C.O.G.; Prof. Emeritus, University of Sydney, since 1941; *b.* Raymond Terrace, N.S.W., 27 Nov. 1875; *s.* of late John Windeyer, Grazier; *m.* Aileen Spencer, *d.* of Herbert A. Evans; one *d.* two *s.* *Educ.:* The King's School, Parramatta; The University of Sydney; M.B., Ch.M. Sydney University, 1899; M.R.C.S. England, L.R.C.P. London, 1901; M.D. Sydney Univ., 1926. Hon. Assist. Surgeon Royal Hospital for Women, Sydney, 1904-19; Hon. Surgeon 1919-41; Hon. Consulting Obstetrician and Gynæcologist since 1941; Professor of Obstetrics, University of Sydney, 1925-1941; Dean of the Faculty of Medicine and Fellow of the Senate of the Univ. of Sydney, 1930-31 and 1939; Member of N.S.W. Medical Board, 1939-46; Nurses' Registration Board, N.S.W., 1926-41; Bancroft Orator (Queensland), 1927; Hon. Consulting Physician, Tressillian Mothercraft Training School, since 1923; Foundation Fellow R.A.C.S. and R.C.O.G.; Member: N.S.W. Post Graduate Cttee. in Medicine, 1935-41; of Editorial Cttee. of Australian and N.Z. Journal of Surgery, 1928-41; Vice-Pres. Section of Obstetrics and Gynæcology Australasian Med. Congress of B.M.A., 2nd session Dunedin, N.Z., 1927, and of B.M.A. Annual Meeting, Melbourne, 1935. *Publications:* Diagnostic Methods used during the later months of Pregnancy and during Labour, 1933, 1934, 1937, 1941 and 1945; articles to Australian Med. Journals, etc. *Recreation:* gardening. *Address:* Wahroonga, N.S.W. *Club:* University (Sydney). [*Died* 15 *Aug.* 1951.

WINDLESHAM, 1st Baron, *cr.* 1937, of Windlesham; **Major George Richard James Hennessy,** 1st Bt., *cr.* 1927; O.B.E. 1918; *b.* 1877; *s.* of Richard Hennessy; *m.* 1898, Ethel M. Wynter (*d.* 1951); two *s.* four *d.* *Educ.:* Eton. Joined Militia, 1896; served South African War; resigned with rank of Major, 1907; joined 9th Batt. K.R.R.C. Dec. 1914; Staff of 8th Division, Feb. 1917-Nov. 1918 (despatches twice, O.B.E.); J.P. Hampshire; High Sheriff of Hants, 1911; Member of Hants County Council, 1910-19; M.P. (U.) Winchester Division, 1918-31; Parliamentary Private Secretary to Minister of Labour, 1920-22; Junior Lord of the Treasury 1922-24; Vice-Chamberlain of H.M.'s Household, 1925-28; Treasurer of Household, 1928-29 and 1931; Civil Commissioner North Western Area, in General Strike, 1926; Vice-Chairman of the Conservative Party, 1931-41. *Recreations:* shooting, golf. *Heir:* *s.* Brig. Hon. James Brian Hennessy, late Gren. Gds. [*b.* 4 Aug. 1903; *m.* 1929, Angela Mary, 2nd *d.* of Julian Duggan, 2 Lowther Gardens, Princes Gate, S.W.; one *s.* three *d.*]. *Address:* Sunning House, Sunningdale, Berks. *Club:* Carlton. [*Died* 8 *Oct.* 1953.

WINDSOR, Lt.-Col. Frank Needham, Indian Medical Service (retired); late Chemical Analyst to Govt. of Bengal; *b.* 2 May 1868; 2nd *s.* of James Windsor, merchant, of Manchester, and Sarah Needham Windsor; *m.* 1898, Amie, (*d.* 1936) *d.* of John Carrick, of Carlisle; no *c.* *Educ.:* The Owens College, Manchester; Emmanuel College, Cambridge (Natural Science Scholar); The Manchester Royal Infirmary. B.Sc. (Victoria) 1887; B.A. (Cantab.) 1890; M.A., 1922; M.B., B.Chir. (Cantab.) 1892; M.R.C.S. (England), L.R.C.P. (London) 1892; House Surgeon, Manchester Royal Infirmary, and Senior House Surgeon, Oldham Infirmary; entered the Indian Medical Service with second place in competitive examination, 1895; on active service with Malakand Field Force, 1897 (North-West Frontier medal and clasp). European War, 1914-19; Military duty, Asiatic theatre, 1915-19 (1914-15 Star, British War and Victory Medals). *Publication:* Indian Toxicology. *Address:* 2 St. Paul's Road, Cambridge. [*Died* 12 *Sept.* 1951.

WINFIELD, Sir Percy Henry, Kt., *cr.* 1949; Q.C. 1943; F.B.A.; LL.D.; F.R.Hist.S.; J.P.; Hon. LL.D. Harvard, Leeds and London; Barrister and Hon. Bencher, Inner Temple; Fellow of St. John's Coll. Cambridge; *b.* Stoke Ferry, Norfolk, 16 Sept. 1878; *y. s.* of Alderman F. C. Winfield; *m.* 1909, Helena, *d.* of W. T. Scruby; two *s.* one *d.* *Educ.:* King Edward VII School, King's Lynn; St. John's College, Cambridge. Senior in both parts of Law Tripos; Whewell Scholar in International Law; MacMahon Law Student; practised on S.E. Circuit, 1902-05; Lieut. in Cambs. Regt. 1915-19; wounded in action near Morlancourt, Aug. 1918; attached to Staff at W.O. 1919; Home Guard, 1940-44; President of Society of Public Teachers of Law, 1929-30; Law Lecturer, St. John's Coll., 1918-28, and at Trinity Coll., Cambridge, 1918-26; Univer. Lecturer in Law, Cambridge, 1926-28; Rouse Ball Prof. of English Law, Cambridge, 1928-43; Reader in Common Law to Council of Legal Education, 1938-49; formerly Deputy County Court Judge, Circuit No. 35; Tagore Law Professor, Calcutta University, 1930; Lecturer on English Legal History in Law School of Harvard University, 1923; Member of Council of Senate, Cambridge University, 1924-32; Member of Lord Chancellor's Law Revision Committee and Law Reporting Committee. *Publications:* History of Abuse of Legal Procedure; Present Law of Abuse of Legal Procedure; Wise and Winfield, Outlines of Jurisprudence; 1923 edition of Lawrence's International Law; Chief Sources of English Legal History; Salmond and Winfield, Law of Contracts; Province of the Law of Tort; Text-book of Law of Tort; Cases on the Law of Tort; Foundations and Future of International Law; 11th, 12th and 13th edn. of Pollock on Contract; joint ed. of Cambridge Legal Essays, and of Maitland's Selected Essays; editor-in-chief of Cambridge Law Journal, 1927-47; editor Law Quarterly Review, 1929; numerous contributions to legal and other encyclopædias and to law magazines and other periodicals. *Recreations:* lawn tennis (Capt. Cambridge County, 1912-14), gardening. *Address:* 13 Cranmer Road, Cambridge. *Club:* Athenæum. [*Died* 7 *July* 1953.

WINGATE, Gen. Sir (Francis) Reginald, 1st Bt., *cr.* 1920, of Dunbar and Port Sudan; G.C.B., *cr.* 1914 (K.C.B., *cr.* 1899; C.B. 1895); G.C.V.O., *cr.* 1912; G.B.E., *cr.* 1918; K.C.M.G., *cr.* 1898; D.S.O. 1889; T.D. 1935; D.L. East Lothian; Colonel Commandant Royal Regt. of Artillery, 1917; *b.* Broadfield, Renfrewshire, 25 June 1861; 7th *s.* of late Andrew Wingate and Bessie, *d.* of Richard Turner; *m.* 1888, Catherine Leslie (D.B.E. 1920, D.G.St.J. and Grand Cordon of Egyptian Order of El Kamal; she died 1946), *o. d.* of Capt. Joseph Sparkhall Rundle, R.N., and Renira Catherine, *d.* of Comdr. Walter Wemyss Leslie, R.N.; one *s.* (and two decd.; 2nd *s.* killed on active service, 1918) one *d.* *Educ.:* R.M.A., Woolwich. Lieut. R.A. 1880; served in India and Aden, 1881-83; joined Egyptian Army, 1883; Comdt. Cholera Hosp., 1883 (4th Osmanieh); acted as A.D.C. and Mil. Sec. to Gen. Sir Evelyn Wood during Nile Expedition and in Bayuda desert, 1884-85 (medal with clasp, bronze star, 4th Medjidie, despatches); A.D.C. to G.O.C. Eastern District,

1886; rejoined Egyptian Army, 1886; promoted Capt. and Bt.-Maj. 1889; Battle of Toski as A.A.G. Intelligence, 1889 (despatches, D.S.O. and clasp); action of Afafit and recapture of Tokar, 1891 (clasp to bronze star and 3rd Medjidie); acted as Governor Red Sea littoral and O.C. troops, Suakim, 1894; Dongola Campaign as Director of Military Intelligence, 1896 (despatches, Bt. Lt.-Col., medal, 2 clasps); member of special mission to The Emperor Menelek of Abyssinia, 1897 (2nd class star of Ethiopia); Nile Expedition, 1897 (A.D.C. to Queen, Bt.-Col., clasp); Battle of the Atbara, 1898 (despatches, clasp); Battle of Khartoum and Expedition to Fashoda (despatches, K.C.M.G., clasp, thanked by both Houses of Parliament); in command of operations resulting in death of Khalifa, near Gedid (K.C.B., 2nd class Osmanieh, 2 clasps); Col., 1899; Maj.-Gen., 1903; Lieut.-Gen., 1908; Gen., 1913; Pasha of Egypt; has Grand Cordons of Osmanie, 1905; Medjidie, 1900; the Nile, 1915, Mohammed Ali, 1916, and El Nahda, 1919; Coronation medals, 1902, 1911, and 1937; Silver Jubilee Medal, 1935; Knight of Grace St. John of Jerusalem; D.C.L. Oxford, 1905; LL.D. Edinburgh, 1919; Sirdar Egyptian Army and Governor-General of Sudan, 1899-1916; High Commissioner, Egypt, 1917-19; organised numerous expeditions for the pacification of the Sudan, including the reconquest of the Province of Darfur, 1916 (despatches, Sudan medal, 1910, and clasp); G.O.C. Hedjaz operations, 1916-19; 1914-15 Bronze Star; Overseas and Victory medals, 1914-19; retired pay, 1922; formerly Hon. Colonel 65th (Manchester Regt.) Anti-Aircraft Regiment, R.A. (T.A.), 37th Medium Scottish Bde., R.A. (T.A.). and 9th Bn. The Manchester Regt. (T.A.). Gold Medal (Royal African Society), 1926; Dir. of Tanganyika Concessions Ltd., and Associated Cos. till April 1945. *Publications:* Mahdism and the Egyptian Sudan, 1889; Ten Years' Captivity in the Mahdi's Camp, 1891; translated and edited Slatin Pasha's Fire and Sword in the Sudan, 1895; The Story of the Gordon College and its Work; Foreword to Colonel Sandes' book The Royal Engineers in Egypt and the Sudan. *Heir:* s. Lt.-Col. R. E. L. Wingate, C.M.G., C.I.E., O.B.E. *Address:* Knockenhair, Dunbar, East Lothian. *T.:* 335. *Clubs:* Athenæum, Army and Navy; New (Edinburgh). [*Died* 28 *Jan.* 1953.

WINGFIELD, Sir Anthony H., Kt., *cr.* 1937; D.L.; *b.* 1857; *e. s.* of George John Wingfield, J.P., of Ampthill House, Beds., and Sophia, *d.* of Philip Pauncefort-Duncombe, of Great Brickhill, Bucks; *m.* 1889, Julia (*d.* 1907), *d.* of Richard Benyon, of Englefield, Berkshire; one *s.* (and one *s.* decd.). *Educ.:* Harrow; Christ Church, Oxford. High Sheriff of Bedfordshire, 1903; Chairman of Quarter Sessions until 1936; late Member of Council of Royal Zoological Society of England. *Recreation:* is owner of a private zoological collection at Ampthill House. *Address:* Ampthill House, Ampthill. *T.A.:* Ampthill. *T.:* Ampthill 10. *Club:* St. James'. [*Died* 20 *Sept.* 1952.

WINGFIELD, Sir Charles John FitzRoy Rhys, K.C.M.G., *cr.* 1933 (C.M.G. 1927); *b.* 18 February 1877; 3rd *s.* of late Edward Rhys Wingfield, D.L., J.P., Barrington Park, Gloucestershire; *m.* 1905, Lucy Evelyn, *e. d.* of late Sir Edmund Fane, K.C.M.G., of Boyton Manor, Wilts; one *d.* *Educ.:* Charterhouse. 2nd Lieut. 7th (Militia) Batt. of the Royal Fusiliers, 1896; Captain, 1898; resigned commission on entering Diplomatic Serviced attaché, 1901; to Paris, 1902; 3rd Secretary, 1903; to Athens, 1903; passed exam. in Public Law, 1903; to Berlin, 1904; Madrid, 1906; 2nd Secretary, 1907; Christiania, 1909 (Chargé d'Affaires in 1909, 1910 and 1911); Lisbon, 1911 (Chargé d'Affaires in 1912 and 1913); Vienna, 1913; 1st Secretary, 1914; Foreign Office, 1914; Tokyo, 1915; Counsellor in Madrid, 1919 (Chargé d'Affaires in 1920, 1921 and 1922); Brussels, 1922 (Chargé d'Affaires in 1923, 1924 and 1925); Rome, 1926 (Chargé d'Affaires in 1926. 1927, and 1928); British Minister at Bangkok, 1928-29; at Oslo, 1929-34; to the Holy See, 1934-35; British Ambassador to Portugal, 1935-37; Adviser on Foreign Affairs to Press Censorship at Ministry of Information, 1939-41. *Recreations:* fishing, shooting, golf. *Address:* 11 Wellington Court, Knightsbridge, S.W.1. *T.:* Kensington 4841. *Club:* Travellers'. [*Died* 26 *March* 1960.

WINGFIELD, Maj.-Gen. Hon. Maurice Anthony, C.M.G. 1918; C.V.O. 1953; D.S.O. 1916; Chairman of A. W. Bain and Sons, Ltd.; *b.* 21 June 1883; 2nd *s.* of 7th Viscount Powerscourt; *m.* 1906, Sybil Frances, *o. d.* of F. D. Leyland, 193 Queen's Gate; one *s.* one *d.* *Educ.:* Charterhouse; Sandhurst. Joined Rifle Bde., 1902; p.s.c. 1910-12; Col. 1922; served European War 1914-18 on Staffs of 3rd Army Corps, 7th Division, 2nd Army and 11th Army Corps (temp. Brig.-Gen.) (despatches seven times, Bt. Major and Lt.-Col., D.S.O., C.M.G., Legion of Honour, Ordre de la Couronne, Belgium, Order of the Crown of Italy, Rising Sun of Japan); Directing Staff, Staff College, 1919-22; Deputy Director Staff Duties, War Office, 1922-25; commanded 143rd (Warwickshire) Infantry Brigade, 1925-26; retired pay, 1926; Director of Quartering, War Office, 1939-41; Harbinger of H.M.'s Body Guard of the Honourable Corps of Gentlemen at Arms, 1949-52, and Standard Bearer, 1952-53. Chm. of Conservative Political Education Committee, E. Midlands Area, 1947-50. President Corporation of Insurance Brokers, 1952-55. *Address:* 79 Albion Gate, W.2. *Clubs:* Carlton, City of London. [*Died* 14 *April* 1956.

WINGFIELD, Mervyn Edward George Rhys; late Lt.-Col. 3rd Batt. Gloucester Regiment; *b.* 1872; *e. s.* of Edward Rhys Wingfield (*d.* 1901), of Barrington Park; *m.* 1919, Florence Marguerite Erle, *d.* of late Lt.-Col. R. E. Benson; three *s.* two *d.* *Educ.:* Eton. D.L., J.P. Oxon and Gloucester; late Lt. 2nd Life Guards and Capt. 4th (Militia) Gloucester Regiment; F.Z.S.; patron four livings; High Sheriff for Oxfordshire, 1934-35. *Address:* Barrington Park, Great-Barrington, Oxford. *T.A.:* Wingfield, Great-Barrington. *Clubs:* Cavalry, Junior Carlton, Guards; Royal Yacht Squadron (Cowes). [*Died* 2 *Jan.* 1952.

WINMILL, Thomas Field; Chairman of British-American Tobacco Company, Ltd., since 1949; ret. 1953; *b.* 13 Sept. 1888; *s.* of Richard and Agnes Frances Winmill, London; *m.* 1913, Lucy Marjorie Andrew, *d.* of Robert Clarke, Worcester; (one *d.* decd.). *Educ.:* Bancroft's School, Essex; London, Oxford and Cambridge Universities. Joined British-American Tobacco Company, Ltd., 1920, Deputy Chairman, 1941. *Address:* Hill House, Earl Soham, Suffolk. *T.:* Earl Soham 277. *Clubs:* Oxford and Cambridge; Royal Wimbledon. [*Died* 20 *Nov.* 1953.

WINTER, Canon Emeritus George Percival Thomas Horden; Canon Treas., Leicester Cathedral, 1950-52; *b.* 15 Sept. 1885; *s.* of George Smith Winter (one time Archdeacon of York, Moosonee) and Emma (*née* Milton); *m.* 1912, Rebecca, *d.* of John Wilkinson, Bristol; two *d.* (and one *d.* decd.). *Educ.:* Rossall School; Bristol School; Emmanuel College and Ridley Hall, Cambridge. Curate of Charles, Plymouth, 1909; Curate of Bolton, 1909; Curate in Charge, Lostock, 1911; Vicar of: Monton, 1914; St. James, Leeds, 1918; St. Saviour, Bolton, 1920; org. sec. Church Missionary Society, 1923. Vicar of St. Philip in Leicester, 1929-1949. Hon. Canon of Leicester, 1938-1944, Canon Residentiary, 1944. Proctor in Convocation, 1941-50; Rural Dean of Christianity, 1945-48. *Recreation:* golf.

Address: 42 Hillview Drive, Hucclecote, Glos. *Club:* Royal Empire Society. [*Died* 23 *Feb.* 1953.

WINTER, Reginald Keble, C.M.G. 1934; *b.* 25 April 1883; *s.* of late Canon E. G. A. Winter and late Horatia, *d.* of Maj. Gen. Alex. McMahon; *m.* 1926, Patricia Marjorie Stabler; one *s.* *Educ.:* Felsted; St. Andrews University; Oriel College, Oxford. Entered Sudan Political Service, 1908; served in Halfa, Red Sea, Blue Nile, and Bahr el Ghazal Provinces; Assistant Civil Secretary, 1926; Secretary for Education and Health, 1932; Governor General's Council, 1932; retired, 1937; Order of the Nile 3rd Class, 1927. *Recreations:* cricket, golf, painting. *Address:* Eastbury Park, Blandford Forum, Dorset. *T.:* Tarrant Hinton 295. [*Died* 25 *Sept.* 1955.

WINTERS, Ellen Dorothea Margaret; *b.* 14 Sept. 1894; *e. c.* of Rev. Charles Thomas Winters and Ellen Elizabeth Woodward. *Educ.:* Bridlington High School; Somerville College, Oxford. Honour School of Modern History Class I., 1919. Ministry of Munitions, 1916-19, work on its History; teaching Malvern Girls College, 1919; Downs School, Seaford, 1920; Maria Grey Training College, 1921; London Teachers' Diploma (distinction Theory and Practice of Teaching), 1922; Senior History Mistress Colchester County High School, 1922-33; Headmistress Farnham Girls' Grammar School, 1933-37; Headmistress City of London School for Girls, 1937-49. *Recreations:* travel, music. *Address:* 7 Broomfield Road, Kew Gardens, Surrey. *Club:* English-Speaking Union. [*Died* 5 *Oct.* 1956.

WINTHROP YOUNG, Geoffrey; *see* Young.

WINTRINGHAM, Margaret, J.P.; *m.* 1903, Thomas Wintringham, M.P. (*d.* 1921). *Educ.:* Girls Grammar School, Keighley; Bedford Training College. M.P. (Ind. Lib., Louth Division of Lincs., 1921-24. *Address:* 21 Minster Yard, Lincoln. [*Died* 10 *March* 1955.

WINWOOD, Lieut.-Col. William Quintyne, C.M.G. 1915; D.S.O. 1900; O.B.E. 1919; 5th Dragoon Guards; *b.* 24 Sept. 1873; *s.* of late Rev. Henry Hoyte Winwood, M.A., F.R.G.S.; *m.* 1909, Gertrude (*d.* 1939), *d.* of Rev. Dolben Paul and *widow* of T. B. Hope. Entered army, 1893; Adjutant, 1899-1903; Captain, 1901; Major, 1904; Lieut.-Colonel commanding Regiment, 1914-18; Commandant, Cavalry Corps School, 1918; Romsey Remount Depôt, 1919 till closing down; D.A.D.R. Aldershot, 1919-28; served South Africa, 1899-1902 (despatches four times, Queen's medal 3 clasps, King's medal 2 clasps, D.S.O.); European War, 1914-18 (despatches twice, wounded, C.M.G., Commander of the Order of Leopold, Belgian Croix de Guerre, 1914 Star with clasp, British War Medal, Victory Medal, O.B.E.). *Address:* c/o Barclays Bank, Cirencester, Glos. *Club:* Cavalry. [*Died* 1 *Dec.* 1954.

WIPPELL, Adm. Sir Henry D. P.; *see* Pridham-Wippell.

WISDOM, George Evan Cameron, C.M.G. 1954; Resident Commissioner, Malacca, 1949-54; *b.* 24 December 1899; *s.* of George Edward Wisdom and Ethel Evans; *m.* 1927, Dorothea Charlotte Rodwell; two *s.* *Educ.:* Prince Edward's, Salisbury, S. Rhodesia; Oxford University (B.A.). Colonial Administrative Service from 1924, Gold Coast and Malaya. Served European War, 1917-19, Royal Air Force; War of 1939-45, North Africa and Far East, 1942-45, Colonel. *Address:* Hazel Hatch, Edenbridge, Kent. [*Died* 25 *May* 1958.

WISEMAN, Robert Arthur, C.M.G. 1937; *b.* Norwich, 8 March 1886; *s.* of Arthur William Wiseman, M.A., Mus.Bac.; *m.* 1919, Penelope Beatrice, *d.* of Arthur Cardew, M.A., Wimbledon; two *s.* one *d.* *Educ.:* Monmouth School; Magdalen College, Oxford (demy). Entered Admiralty, 1910; transferred to Colonial Office, 1911; Assistant Sec., 1927; Dominions Office, 1928; retired 1946. *Address:* Bayfield, East Hill, Braunton, Devon. *T.:* Braunton 2173. [*Died* 23 *July* 1955.

WISHART, Professor George Macfeat, B.Sc., M.D., F.R.F.P.S.G., F.R.S.E.; Dean of the Faculty of Medicine and Director of Post-graduate Medical Education, University of Glasgow, since 1947; *b.* 18 Aug. 1895; *s.* of George Wishart, Grain Merchant, Glasgow; *m.* 1926, Elizabeth Mary, *d.* of Canon F. Bedale, Nuneaton; two *d.* *Educ.:* Uddingston Grammar School; Glasgow University. Graduated Medicine, 1918; R.A.F. Medical Service, 1918-19; Assistant to Regius Professor of Physiology, Glasgow University, 1919-21; Grieve Lecturer in Physiological Chemistry, Glasgow University, 1921-35; Gardiner Professor of Physiological Chemistry, Glasgow University, 1935-47. Member of General Medical Council; Member of General Nursing Council for Scotland. *Publications:* Groundwork of Biophysics, 1931; various contributions to physiological and biochemical literature. *Address:* 5 Hillhead Street, Glasgow, W.2. *T.:* Western 6767. [*Died* 18 *July* 1958.

WISHART, John, M.A. (Edin. and Cantab.), 1922; D.Sc. (Lond.) 1928; F.R.S.E., Fellow Royal Statistical Soc.; Fellow, Cambridge Phil. Soc.; Fellow, Assoc. of Incorporated Statisticians; Fellow, Inst. Math. Statistics and Amer. Statist. Assoc.; Mem. Internat. Inst. of Statistics; Associate Editor, Biometrika; Clare College, Cambridge; Reader in Statistics, University of Cambridge, since 1931; *b.* 28 Nov. 1898; 2nd *s.* of John Wishart, Montrose, Scotland; *m.* 1924, Olive Birdsall, Thorparch, Yorks; two *s.* *Educ.:* Perth Academy; Edinburgh University. 2nd Lt. 7th Black Watch (Royal Highlanders), 1918; Capt. Intelligence Corps, 1940-42; Mathematics Master, West Leeds High School, 1922-24; Research Assistant, Galton Laboratory, University of London, 1924-27; Demonstrator in Mathematics, Imperial College, 1927; Statistician, Rothamsted Experimental Station, Harpenden, 1927-31; Secretary of Mathematical Tables Cttee., British Assoc., 1936-46; Temp. Asst. Secy. Admiralty, 1942-1946. *Publications:* Principles and Practice of Field Experimentation (with H. G. Sanders), 1935; Field Trials; their Lay-out and Statistical Analysis, 1940; "Student's" Collected Papers (with E. S. Pearson), 1943; Analisis de la Varianza y Covarianza, 1949; Field Trials II: The Analysis of Covariance, 1950; Research Papers in Biometrika, Proc. Roy. Soc. Edin., Lond. Math. Soc., Jour. Roy. Stat. Soc., etc. *Address:* 130 Milton Rd., Cambridge. *T.:* 2446. *Club:* Overseas. [*Died* 14 *July* 1956.

WITHERS, Colonel Charles M'Gregor, C.B. 1929; Indian Army (retired); *b.* 1876; *s.* of late Major E. Withers, Auckland, New Zealand; *m.* 1st, 1907, Elaine, *d.* of late M. Curry, Hove; 2nd, 1915, Margery, *d.* of late F. P. Foster, Ealing; two *d.* *Educ.:* Bedford School; Sandhurst. Entered Indian Army, 1897; served in Somaliland, 1902-3; East Africa, 1905-6; European War, 1917-18; N.W.F., India, 1919; retired, 1929. *Recreation:* gardening. *Address:* Manydown, Fitzroy Road, Fleet, Hants. [*Died* 20 *Oct.* 1958.

WITHERS, Captain Edgar Clements, C.I.E. 1917; C.B.E. 1946; R.I.N. (retd.); *b.* 1883; *s.* of late Henry Pearce Withers, Reading; *m.* Lizette Catharine Willemina, *d.* of late William Petrus van Wageningen, Amsterdam; one *s.* one *d.* Served European War, 1914-19; retired, 1925; Served in War of 1939-45. *Address:* c/o Coutts & Co., 440 Strand, W.C.2.
[*Died* 31 *Jan.* 1951.

WITHYCOMBE, Brig.-Gen. William Maunder, C.B. 1921; C.M.G. 1915; D.S.O. 1918; the King's Own (Yorkshire Light Infantry); *b.* 8 May 1869; *s.* of late William Withycombe of Gothelney, Charlinch, Somerset; *m.* 1894, Cecil Mary (*d.* 1948), *d.* of late Rev. F. C. Platts; one *s.* *Educ.:* Malvern College. Entered Army, 1888; Captain, 1895; Bt. Major, 1902; Major, 1904; Lt.-Col. 1914; Col. 1918; served S. African War, 1899-1902 (despatches twice, Bt. Major; Queen's medal 4 clasps, King's medal 2 clasps); European War, 1914-18 (despatches seven times, C.M.G., D.S.O.); retired with rank of Brigadier-General, 1924. *Address:* 6 The Crescent, Thirsk, Yorkshire.
[*Died* 14 *July* 1951.

WITT, Sir Robert Clermont, Kt., *cr.* 1922; C.B.E. 1918; D.Lit., F.S.A.; *s.* of G. A. Witt; *m.* 1899, Mary Helene, *d.* of Charles Marten; one *s.* *Educ.:* Clifton; New College, Oxford (M.A.). Served in Matabele War, 1896; acted as War Correspondent with Cecil Rhodes; one of the founders and President, National Art-Collections Fund; Trustee of National Gallery, 1916-23, 1924-1931 (Chairman, 1930), 1933-40; Trustee of Tate Gallery, 1916-31; Trustee of Watts Gallery, Compton; Vice-President, National Institute of Industrial Psychology; Hon. Fellow, New College, Oxford. *Publications:* How to look at Pictures; 100 Masterpieces of Painting; The Nation and its Art Treasures; Catalogue of Painters and Draughtsmen represented in the Witt Library, 2 vols.; verses, articles, and reviews in various periodicals. *Recreation:* the formation of a library of photographs of pictures and drawings of all western schools at 32 Portman Square, W., open, when possible, for the use of serious students and others interested in art. *Address:* 32 Portman Square, W.1. *T.:* Welbeck 6214; Old Clergy House, Alfriston, Sussex. *Club:* Royal Automobile.
[*Died* 26 *March* 1952.

WITTET, John, C.B.E. 1937; F.R.I.B.A.; F.R.I.A.S.; J.P.; Architect; *b.* 5 Feb. 1868; *s.* of William Wittet, Bridge of Earn, and Mary Shanks; *m.* 1898, E. M. Riddoch; two *s.* one *d.* *Educ.:* Bridge of Earn Public School; Heriot-Watt College, Edinburgh. Apprenticed to David Smart, Architect in Perth, then with Hippolyte J. Blanc in Edinburgh; commenced practice in Elgin, 1892; served for 20 years in the Town Council of the City and Royal Burgh of Elgin, for 6 years Lord Provost; Hon. Sheriff-Substitute of Moray and Nairn since 1928. Director Morayshire Literary and Scientific Association and other societies. *Publications:* various papers on Historical and Architectural subjects in Morayshire. *Recreation:* travelling *Address:* Torr House, Elgin. *T.:* Elgin 2661. *Club:* Elgin.
[*Died* 10 *March* 1952.

WITTGENSTEIN, Ludwig, Ph.D., Professor of Philosophy, Cambridge University, 1939-48; Fellow, Trinity College, Cambridge; *b.* 1889. *Educ.:* Trinity Coll., Cambridge. *Publications:* Tractatus Logico-Philosophicus (English trans.), 1922; (posthumous): Philosophical Investigations (trans. G. E. M. Anscombe), 1953; Remarks on Foundations of Mathematics (ed. G. H. von Wright, trans. Anscombe), 1956; The Blue and Brown Books, 1958. *Relevant publications:* Ludwig Wittgenstein (by N. Malcolm) (a Memoir, with biog. sketch by G. H. von Wright), 1958; An Introduction to Wittgenstein's Tractus (by G. E. M. Anscombe), 1959.
[*Died* 29 *April* 1951.

WODEHOUSE, Philip Peveril John, C.I.E. 1919; *b.* 26 Sept. 1877; *s.* of late Henry Ernest Wodehouse, C.M.G.; *m.* 1920, Laura Gertrude, *widow* of Dr. Harold Macfarlane and *d.* of late Rev. X. Peel Massy. *Educ.:* Elizabeth College, Guernsey. Hong-Kong Civil Service, 1897-1932. *Recreation:* golf. *Address:* Greenaway, Brockenhurst, Hants.
[*Died* 26 *Nov.* 1951.

WOLFF, Eugene; Ophthalmic Surgeon, Royal Northern Hospital, since 1928; Surgeon, Westminster Branch, Moorfields Westminster and Central Eye Hospital since 1936; *b.* 11 March 1896; *s.* of A. Wolff, Oudtshoorn, Cape Province, S. Africa; *m.* 1923, Lydia Abravanel; one *d.* *Educ.:* University College School; University Coll. and Hospital. M.B.B.S. Lond. 1918; F.R.C.S. Eng. 1927. Demonstrator of Anatomy, U.C. London, 1919-30; Ophthalmic Registrar, U.C. Hosp. Lister medal for Clin. Surg., 1918. Capt. South African Med. Corps, 1918-19. Late Vice-Pres. Ophthalmological Soc. of U.K.; late Vice-Pres. Ophthalmic Section Roy. Soc. Med. Hon. mem. Belgian and Greek Ophthalmological socs. *Publications:* Anatomy of Eye and Orbit, 1948, 4th edn. 1953; Pathology of the Eye, 3rd edn., 1951; Diseases of the Eye, 3rd edn., 1948, 4th edn. 1952; Anatomy for Artists, 3rd edn., 1947. *Recreation:* microscopy. *Address:* 46 Wimpole St., W.1. *T.:* Welbeck 9475. [*Died* 25 *Feb.* 1954.

WOLLASTON, Sir Gerald Woods, K.C.B., *cr.* 1937; K.C.V.O. *cr.* 1935 (M.V.O. 1904); Kt., *cr.* 1930; M.A., LL.M.; F.S.A.; Norroy and Ulster King of Arms since 1944; Inspector of Regimental Colours since 1929; *b.* 2 June 1874; *o. c.* of Sir Arthur N. Wollaston, K.C.I.E. (*d.* 1922); *m.* 1908, Olive, D.J.St.J., *e. d.* of late Sir R. A. McCall, K.C.V.O., K.C.; two *s.* two *d.* *Educ.:* Harrow; Trinity College, Cambridge. Head of the 2nd class in the Law Tripos at Cambridge, 1896; called to Bar at Inner Temple, 1899; Fitzalan Pursuivant of Arms Extraordinary, 1902; Bluemantle Pursuivant, 1906; Richmond Herald, 1919-28; Norroy King of Arms, 1928-30; Garter Principal King of Arms, 1930-44; Earl Marshal's Secretary, 1944-54 (retired); Extra Secretary at the British Embassy, Madrid, 1918-19. Hon. Freedom of Deal. K.St.J. *Publication:* Coronation Claims, 2nd edition, 1910; Supplement, 1936. *Recreations:* sailing, music. *Address:* College of Arms, Queen Victoria Street, E.C.; Glen Hill, Walmer. *Club:* Athenæum. [*Died* 4 *March* 1957.

WOLSELEY, Sir Edric Charles Joseph, 10th Bt., *cr.* 1628; J.P. Staffordshire; A.R.S.M.; mining and electrical engineer; *b.* 7 April 1886; *s.* of Sir Charles Michael Wolseley, 9th Bt., and Anita Theresa (*d.* 1937), *d.* of D. T. Murphy, San Francisco; *S.* father, 1931; *m.* 1916, Clare Mary Annette, *d.* of late C. E. de Trafford; two *s.* two *d.* (and *e. s.* killed in action, 1944). *Educ.:* Beaumont College, Old Windsor; King's College, London; Royal School of Mines. 1st Honours Chemistry Intermediate (London University). Lieutenant Staffordshire Yeomanry, and served on staff in Egypt and Palestine during war, 1914-19. *Recreations:* shooting, golf. *Heir:* *g.s.* Charles Garnet [*b.* 16 June 1944; *s.* of late Capt. Stephen Garnet Hubert Francis Wolseley, Royal Artillery, and Pamela Barry Power, *yr. d.* of late Capt. F. Barry, and Mrs. W. N. Power, Old Court, Whitchurch, Herefordshire]. *Address:* Wolseley Hall, Stafford. *T.A.:* Wolseley Bridge. *T.:* Rugeley 81. [*Died* 17 *Sept.* 1954.

WOLSELEY-LEWIS, Mary; *b.* 20 May 1865; *d.* of Rev. T. Wolseley-Lewis, M.A. *Educ.:* Ladies' College, Cheltenham. B.A. London, Class I.; Gilchrist Medallist. Mistress, Ladies' College, Cheltenham, 1886-94; Headmistress of the Francis Holland School for Girls, Eaton Square Branch, in Graham Street, 1894-1908; Principal of North Foreland School for Girls 1909-31. *Publication:* The Sevenfold Gifts, 1906. *Address:* Wynstow, St. Omer Road, Guildford. *T.:* Guildford 61166. [*Died* 31 *May* 1955.

WOLSTENCROFT, Frank, C.B.E. 1947; *b.* 23 Dec. 1882. *Educ.:* Elementary School, Royton. Working joiner until 1920; Royal Commission on Betting, Lotteries and Gaming; Assistant General Secretary, Amalgamated Society of Woodworkers, 1920, General Secretary, 1926-48; Member of British Trades Union Congress General Council, 1928-49; President of the T.U.C., 1941-42. *Recreations:* football and cricket. *Address:* 36 Arnfield Road, Withington, Manchester. *T.:* Didsbury 5367. [*Died* 30 *June* 1952.

WONNACOTT, Ven. Thomas Oswald; Archdeacon of Suffolk, 1938-47, Emeritus since 1947; *b.* 22 July 1869; *s.* of John Wonnacott, formerly of Liskeard, Cornwall; *m.* 1942, Norah Robinson, Woburn Sands. *Educ.:* Private School; King's College, Cambridge. Held Curacies in Gloucester and Exeter Dioceses; Vicar of Lanteglos by Fowey, later Vicar of Great Bricet, Little Finborough, and Wattisham (Suffolk); Rector of Stonham Aspal, 1919; Proctor in Convocation, 1929-38; serves on Diocesan Boards of Finance, Dilapidations, and Education (Secretary since 1922), and on Queen Anne's Bounty Area Committee, No. 9. *Recreations:* music and history. *Address:* The White House, Trimley St. Mary, Ipswich. *T.:* Felixstowe 588. [*Died* 7 *Dec.* 1957.

WONTNER, Arthur; Knight of the Order of the Crown of Italy, 1932; retd. actor manager; *b.* London, 21 Jan. 1875; *m.* 1903, Rosecleer Alice Amelia Blanche Kingwell (*d.* 1943), Moat Hill House, Totnes, Devon; two *s.* one *d.*; *m.* 1947, Florence Eileen Lainchbury. Studied for the stage under Sarah Thorne at the Theatre Royal, Margate; joined Louis Calvert on tour in Shakespeare; appeared in London with Lewis Waller; toured with Edward Compton and Mrs. Lewis Waller; visited Australia and New Zealand in Sir Herbert Tree's Company, 1903-05; reappeared in London, 1906, under Charles Frohman in Raffles; succeeded Matheson Lang in The Christian; appeared in An Englishman's Home and Madame X; played Laertes to H. B. Irving's Hamlet; with Sir Herbert Tree played Bassanio in The Merchant of Venice and other parts; rejoined Frohman in plays with Irene Vanbrugh; appeared with Lillah McCarthy, Mrs. Patrick Campbell, Martin Harvey, and Sir John Hare; was the original Hilary Cutts in The New Sin; played Ben Hur at Drury Lane, 1912; joined Granville Barker in The Voysey Inheritance and Twelfth Night; was Count Orloff in the 1913 revival of Diplomacy and appeared in this part at Windsor Castle, 1914; joined Sir George Alexander at St. James's; later starred in On Trial, The Maid of the Mountains, By Pigeon Post; in 1919 joined Lady Wyndham in management at the Criterion in Our Mr. Hepplewhite; under his own management, 1920-21, produced Gold Fields, The Romantic Age, A Lady Calls on Peter, 1921-26, The Voice from the Minaret, Woman to Woman, The Bat, Our Nell, Tiger Cats, Henry VIII; went to America, 1926; appeared in New York in The Captive, in Mariners, and as Sir John Marlay in Interference; toured the United States; reappeared in London, 1929; Richelieu at Drury Lane, 1930; Fouché in Napoleon, Malvolio in Twelfth Night, 1932; revived The Joker, 1933; in Sally Who, What Happened to George; Pontius Pilate in Good Friday, The Author in Village Wooing, 1934; Justice and the Skin Game, 1935; Duet in Floodlight, The Great Experiment, 1936; The Day is Gone, 1937; The Immortal Garden, 1942; The Desert Song, 1943; toured in Ten Little Niggers, 1944, later playing the Bishop in a revival of Shaw's Getting Married; The Great Adventure, 1945; The Golden Eagle, 1946; The Paragon, 1948; first appeared on the screen, 1915; has since made many films and has portrayed Sherlock Holmes in five; On the Radio since 1925; Television since 1937; Treasurer of the British Actors' Equity Association, 1930-41; a Trustee of the Valentine Memorial Pension Fund; formerly a Member of London Theatre Council; for more than 25 years a Member of the Committee of the Actors' Orphanage. *Recreations:* books, gardening, and fishing. *Address:* 134 Windsor Lane, Burnham, Buckinghamshire. *T.:* Burnham 187. *Club:* Garrick. [*Died* 10 *July* 1960.

WOOD, Sir Alfred, Kt. 1937; F.C.A.; intimately associated (pioneer) with British Beet Sugar Industry from its first introduction into this country; *b.* 1878; *e. s.* of Thomas Wood, Manchester; *m.* 1st, 1906, Sarah Gwendoline (*d.* 1949), *d.* of late William Henry Roberts, Colwyn Bay; one *d.*; 2nd, 1953, Evylin Felton, widow of Sydney de Nyst Clark. *Educ.:* Manchester Gram. School. First Secretary to British Sugar Corporation, 1936-41, a Director, 1941-1949. Senior Warden, Guild of Freemen of City of London, 1957-59. *Publication:* (Jointly) Ministry of Agriculture's Report on the Sugar Beet Industry at Home and Abroad, 1931. *Address:* The Waldorf Hotel, Aldwych, W.C.2. *T.:* Temple Bar 2400; Little Fir Knob, Churt Road, Hindhead, Surrey. *T.:* Hindhead 140. *Clubs:* City Livery, Farmers', United Wards. [*Died* 25 *May* 1960.

WOOD, Capt. Sir Basil S. H. H.; *see* Hill-Wood.

WOOD, Rt. Rev. Cecil John; *b.* 1874; *m.* 1919, Marjorie Allen, *d.* of late Rev. Canon J. Allen Bell; one *s.* one *d.* *Educ.:* St. Peter's College, Cambridge (scholar). Ordained 1897; Curate of High Halden, Kent, 1897-99; St. Marylebone, 1899-1902; St. Andrew, Bethnal Green, 1902-06; Wimbledon, 1906-12; Bishop of Melanesia, 1912-19; Rector of Witnesham, Suffolk, 1919-24; Assistant Bishop in Diocese of Newcastle and Vicar of St. George's, Jesmond, Newcastle on Tyne, 1924-33; Rural Dean of Horsham, 1934-40; Rector of West Grinstead, Sussex, 1933-46. *Address:* 2 St Barnabas Houses, Newland, Malvern. [*Died* 27 *April* 1957.

WOOD, Sir David John Hatherley P.; *see* Page-Wood.

WOOD, Gervase E.; Member of the Court of Common Council; Deputy for the Ward of Cripplegate Within; H.M. Lieut. City of London, 1950; *b.* Hawksworth, Notts, 21 Sept. 1877. Sheriff of City of London, 1943-44. Formerly Member City of London Board of Guardians; ex-Chief Commoner and Chairman City Lands Committee; Past Chairman City of London Freemen's School. *Address:* Holmwood, 34 York Road, Cheam, Sy. [*Died* 27 *Oct.* 1954.

WOOD, Haydn; violinist and composer; *b.* Slaithwaite, Huddersfield, 25 March 1882; *m.* 1909, Dorothy (*d.* 1958), *d.* of Thos. Court, Liverpool; no *c.* *Educ.:* Royal College of Music, London (Open Violin Scholarship); under Cesar Thomson, Brussels; studied violin with Senor Arbos and composition with Sir Chas. Stanford for six years; toured abroad and British Isles with Madame Albani for eight years. *Publications:* Over 200 songs, most popular being Roses of Picardy, A Brown Bird Singing; Love's Garden of Roses, Bird of Love Divine; It is only a Tiny Garden, etc.; several Albums of Songs; also choral works, orchestral suites, Overtures, Rhapsodies, and Suites, in addition to numerous smaller pieces for orchestra; a string Quartette which won a Cobbett Prize, a violin concerto, a piano concerto, a set of Variations for cello and orchestra, choral works, and several violin pieces. *Address:* c/o Barclays Bank, 119 Baker Street, W.1. *Club:* Savage. [*Died* 11 *March* 1959.

WOOD, Hugh McKinnon; *b.* 23 Oct. 1884; *s.* of Rt. Hon. Thomas McKinnon Wood, P.C., M.P., LL.D., D.L., and Isabella Mill Sandison; *m.* 1928, Catherine Prescot Elwood; one *s.* one *d.* *Educ.* Highgate School; Balliol College, Oxford. Scholar, Jenkins Exhibitioner, Craven Exhibition, Greek Essay Prize, 1st class Classical Mods. and Greats, Fellow and Tutor, 1908-12; Barrister-at-law, Inner Temple, 1914; enlisted Inns of Court Regt., but found medically unfit; War Trade Intelligence Dept. and Ministry of Food, 1915-18; Inns of Court O.T.C., 1918; Mem. British Deleg. Peace Conf. and staff of British mem. Rhineland High Commn., 1919; League of Nations, 1920-40; (Counsellor and actg. Legal Adviser) Sec.-Gen. War Crimes Commission, 1943-45; temp. member Foreign Office and member of U.K. delegation to United Nations, 1945-46; Professor of International Law in the University of London, 1947-49. *Publications:* articles on international law in legal journals and periodicals. *Address:* 70 Melton Court, S.W.7. *T.:* Kensington 8801. *Club:* Reform. [*Died* 21 *Feb.* 1955.

WOOD, Sir John, 1st Bt., *cr.* 1918; D.L. Herefordshire (Sheriff, 1900); J.P. Suffolk and Derbyshire; M.P. (C.) Stalybridge, 1910-1918; Stalybridge and Hyde Division of Cheshire, Dec. 1918-22; *b.* 8 Sep. 1857; *o. s.* of late J. H. Wood, J.P., Whitfield, Derbyshire; *m.* 1st, 1883, Estelle, *d.* of Henry Benham; one *s.* one *d.*; 2nd, 1892, Hon. Gertrude Emily (*d.* 1927), 3rd *d.* of 2nd Baron Bateman. *Educ.:* Rugby; Magdalen College, Oxon (M.A.). Barrister, Inner Temple, 1883; Lieut.-Colonel and Hon. Colonel retired 4th Vol. Battalion Cheshire Regiment; V.D. *Heir: s.* John Arthur Haigh, M.C., D.S.C. [*b.* 22 May 1888; *m.* 1919, Hon. Evelyn Saumarez (*d.* 1934), *e. d.* of 4th Baron de Saumarez. Barrister, Inner Temple, 1912; served European War as Capt. in East Surrey Regt., and Lieut. R.N.V.R., 1914-18. *Club:* Carlton]. *Address:* Hengrave Hall, Bury St. Edmunds. *T.:* Culford 46; Forrest Lodge, Dalry, Galloway. *Clubs:* Carlton, United University, Constitutional. [*Died* 28 *Jan.* 1951.

WOOD, John, C.M.G. 1938; M.I.C.E.; *b.* Dec. 1880; *s.* of John Wood, Edinburgh; *m.* 1906, Mabel, *d.* of Frederick Collis, Oamaru; one *s.* four *d.* *Educ.:* State School, Timaru; Timaru Boys' High School. Entered New Zealand Public Works Dept., 1900; Assistant Engineer-in-Chief, 1931; Engineer-in-Chief, 1936-41, and Under-Secretary, Public Works Dept., 1936-41; Chairman, Main Highways Board, 1936-41. *Address:* Raumati Beach, Wellington, New Zealand. [*Died* 12 *July* 1952.

WOOD, Sir John Stuart Page, 6th Bt., *cr.* 1837; Commander late R.N.; *b.* 28 Jan. 1898; *o. s.* of 5th Bt. and Violet Mary Frances Stuart, *d.* of late H. Stuart Johnson, Edinburgh; *S.* father, 1912; *m.* 1919, Barbara (1st Officer W.R.N.S.), *e. d.* of late Major E. J. Arundell Clarke; two *s.* Entered Navy, 1914; took part in operations in Dardanelles and Jutland Battle, 1915 (despatches). *Heir: s.* John Hatherley Page Wood, Lt. R.N.V.R. [*b.* 6 Oct. 1921; *m.* 1947, Evelyn Hazel Rosemary, *d.* of Capt. G. E. Bellville; one *s.* (*b.* 6 Feb. 1951) one *d.* War of 1939-45 (despatches)]. *Address:* 7 Thurloe Square, S.W.7. *T.:* Kensington 1286. [*Died* 2 *April* 1955.

WOOD, John Vincent; Managing Director R. A. Lister & Co. Ltd., Buenos Aires, since 1949; *b.* 21 Mar. 1905; *e. s.* of late John Vincent Wood, Dudley, Worcs.; *m.* 1st (marriage dissolved); 2nd, 1946, Lucy Giels, 2nd *d.* of A. Joly de Lotbinière, County de Lotbinière, Province of Quebec, Canada; one *s.* *Educ.:* Tettenhall College, Staffs. Director J. V. Wood & Sons, Ltd.; Manager Eastern Div. B.O.A.C.; Managing Director B.E.A.C., 1947-49. *Recreations:* flying, golf. *Address:* (Temp.) Hotel Continental, Avda R.S. Peña 725, Buenos Aires; Kingshead House, Beaconsfield, Bucks. *Club:* Royal Automobile. [*Died* 28 *April* 1952.

WOOD, Lawson, F.Z.S.; artist; *b.* Highgate, 1878; *s.* of Pinhorn Wood and *g.s.* of late L. J. Wood, R.I.; *m.* 1903, Charlotte Forge; two *s.* one *d.* *Educ.:* privately. Studied Art at Slade School and at Heatherley's; head artist of staff of C. A. Pearson, Ltd., for six years; works for leading illustrated journals in England, U.S.A., etc.; known chiefly for humorous and animal subjects; served in France as officer in Kite Balloon Wing, R.F.C. *Recreations:* riding, sea-fishing, active worker for animal welfare. *Address:* Downlands, Salcombe Hill, Sidmouth, Devon. [*Died* 26 *Oct.* 1957.

WOOD, Prof. Robert Williams, LL.D. Ph.D.; Professor of Experimental Physics, Johns Hopkins University, 1901; Research Professor, 1937; *b.* Concord, Mass., 2 May 1868; *s.* of Dr. Robert Williams Wood; *m.* 1892, Gertrude Ames, San Francisco; one *s.* two *d.* *Educ.:* Harvard Univ.; University of Berlin. Hon. Fellow in Chemistry, Univ. of Chicago, 1892-94; Graduate Student in Physical Chemistry and Physics, Univ. of Berlin, 1894-96; Instructor of Physics, Univ. of Wisconsin, 1897; Assistant Professor, 1898-1901; originated electrical method of thawing frozen water-pipes; Foreign Member of Royal Society and of other scientific societies; LL.D. University of Birmingham, 1913; Rumford medal from American Academy, 1909, for researches in Light; Gold Medal for Physics, 1918; Soc. Ital. d. Scienze (dei XL.) Rome; Ives Medal, American Optical Soc., 1933; Rumford Medal from Royal Soc., London, 1938; Draper Medal of National Academy of Science for Contributions to Astro-physics, 1940; Hon. LL.D. Edinburgh, 1921; Ph.D. (Hon.) Univ. of Berlin, 1932; Dr. Sci. Hon. Causa, Oxford, 1948. Major U.S.A., 1917-1919; Developed Secret Signalling Devices employing both Visible and Invisible Light. In War of 1939-45 Consultant on Atom bomb, and experimental work on cavity charges and their spectra. *Publications:* Physical Optics, 1905; enlarged and revised, 1933; "How to tell the Birds from the Flowers and other Woodcuts"; The Man who Rocked the Earth (with Arthur Train), 1915; over 250 papers dealing with optics, spectroscopy, atomic and molecular radiation, supersonics, improvements in construction and use of diffraction gratings. *Address:* 1023 St. Paul Street, Baltimore, Md.; East Hampton, Long Island, N.Y. (Summer). [*Died* 11 *Aug.* 1955.

WOOD, Sydney Herbert, C.B. 1943; M.C.; *b.* 3 Mar. 1884; *s.* of James London and Maria Colvin Wood; *m.* 1st, 1911, Frances Chick, O.B.E. (*decd.*); one *d.*; 2nd, 1922, Phyllis Hope Taunton; two *s.* *Educ.:* Univ. Coll. London. Warden, University Coll. Hall, Ealing, 1908-10. Entered Board of Education, 1910; Principal Assistant Secretary, 1939-45; European

War, 1916-19; visited India on invitation of Govt. of India, 1936-37; Lectured on education in Australia, 1946, and in U.S.A., 1947; Chm. of German Educational Reconstruction since its foundation in 1942 until 1952. *Publication:* (with A. Abbott) Report on Vocational and General Education in India (Delhi, the Punjab and the United Provinces), 1937. *Recreation:* walking. *Club:* Reform.

[*Died* 4 *March* 1958.

WOOD, W. H., B.Sc., M.D. (Gold Medallist, Manch.); Emeritus Professor of Anatomy, Liverpool University, since 1949; *b.* 11 April 1888; *m.*; one *d.* *Educ.:* Lymm Grammar School; Victoria University of Manchester. Derby Professor of Anatomy, Liverpool University, 1925-49, retired. Dean of the Faculty of Medicine, The University, Liverpool, 1933-39. *Address:* Tremnant, Aberdaron, Pwllheli, N. Wales.

[*Died* 21 *Jan.* 1954.

WOOD, William L.; Newspaper Proprietor and Publisher; Editor of the Architect and Building News, 1926-46; *b.* 29 Aug. 1879; *s.* of William Browning Wood and M. Martin; *m.* 1st, 1908, Mary L. Bonnor (*d.* 1933); two *s.* one *d.*; 2nd, 1937, Dorothy Clara, *d.* of Herman Guy, Ashtead, Surrey; three *s.* *Educ.:* St. Ann's; Non-Collegiate, Oxford; St. John's College, Cambridge. Editor Vogue, English edition, 1916-23; House and Garden, 1920-23; Architect and Building News, 1925. *Recreations:* farming, shooting. *Address:* West End House, Frensham, Surrey. [*Died* 9 *Oct.* 1958.

WOOD, William Thomas, R.W.S. 1918 (A.R.W.S. 1913); R.O.I. 1927; Vice-President Royal Society of Painters in Water Colours, 1924-27; Member Artists of Chelsea, 1949; Hon. Mem., Chelsea Art Society, 1953. Chairman Association of Students Sketch Clubs, 1934; landscape and flower painter; *b.* Ipswich, 17 June 1877; *s.* of Thomas Wood and Annie Tighe; *m.* Bérénice, *d.* of Davidson Knowles, artist; one *s.* one *d.* *Educ.:* Regent Street Polytechnic School of Art; Italy. Represented in Victoria and Albert Museum; London Museum, and provincial, Australian, and N.Z. galleries. Exhibitor at Paris Salon, the New English Art Club, and the principal provincial exhibitions; during European War an Observer, Kite-Balloons, R.F.C. (despatches); appointed British Official War Artist (Balkans), 1918; Home Guard, 1941; Official Exhibition at the Leicester Galleries of 50 drawings and paintings—The Salonika Front; Exhibitions at the Leicester Galleries of oil paintings of Flowers, 1924 and 1927; Exhibition of English Landscape in Water Colour, Rembrandt Gallery, 1936. *Publication:* The Salonika Front, water-colour drawings and pencil drawings. *Recreations:* painting and fishing. *Address:* 61 Glebe Place, Chelsea, S.W.3. *T.:* Flaxman 8766.

[*Died* 2 *June* 1958.

WOOD, Sir William Valentine, K.B.E., *cr.* 1947; Kt., *cr.* 1937; *b.* 14 February 1883; *s.* of late George Wood, Belfast; *m.* 1912, Dora, *d.* of late Thomas Kernahan, Belfast; one *s.* two *d.* *Educ.:* Methodist College, Belfast. Accountants Department, Midland Railway, Belfast, 1898-1916; Irish Railway Executive Committee, 1917; Director of Transport Accounting, Ministry of Transport, 1919; Assistant Accountant General L.M.S. Railway Co., 1924; Controller of Costs and Statistics, 1927; Vice-President, 1930; President, 1941; President, Institute of Transport, 1943-44; Member, British Transport Commission, 1947-53. Col., Engineer and Railway Staff Corps. C.St.J. U.S.A. Medal of Freedom with Gold Palm. *Publication:* (with late Lord Stamp) Railways (Home University Library). *Address:* The Grey House, Alexandra Road, Watford, Herts. *T.:* Watford 2727.

[*Died* 26 *Aug.* 1959.

WOODALL, Colonel Frederic, C.M.G. 1917; *b.* 15 July 1866; *m.* 1st, Anna Dane (*d.* 1939), *e. d.* of Geo. L. O'Keeffe of Daneville, Bundoran and Mount Keeffe, Co. Cork; two *s.*; 2nd, Annie E. M., *e. d.* of Edwin Maunsel Selfe, Bristol. Was over six years in ranks; Second Lieut. R. Sussex Regt., 1892; Capt., 1898; Major, 1909; Lt.-Col., 1914; Col. 1915; Staff Paymaster, 1909; Chief Paymaster, 1915; served East Africa, 1908-1910 (despatches, medal with clasp); European War, 1914-17 (C.M.G.); Inspector of Army Pay Offices, 1916-18; retired pay, 1923. *Address:* Fairhaven, Graham Avenue, Withdean, Sussex. [*Died* 18 *Nov.* 1956.

WOODALL, Lieut.-Colonel Harold Whiteman, C.I.E. 1918; late Joint M.F.H., S. Dorset; *b.* 1872; *s.* of Sir Corbet Woodall; *m.* 1901, Elizabeth Nora McLean. Served European War, 1914-19. *Address:* Waterston Manor, Dorchester. *Club:* Reform.

[*Died* 28 *Aug.* 1951.

WOODCOCK, His Honour Hubert Bayley Drysdale, Q.C. 1923; F.L.S. 1941; Judge of County Courts on Circuit, No. 14 (Leeds and Wakefield), 1924-35; on No. 43 (Marylebone), 1936-40, when he retired; Barr.-at-law, Middle Temple, 1891; *b.* 1867; *e. surv. s.* of late Thomas Woodcock, of Antigua, W. Indies, sometime Queen's Advocate of the Gold Coast Colony; *m.* 1891, Charlotte Simpson (*d.* 1942), *o. d.* of George Boyce Gwyn, Hampstead; one *s.* two *d.* *Educ.:* Eastbourne College; City of London School. Recorder of Stamford, 1913-24; Acting Chairman Quarter Sessions of the Soke of Peterborough, 1916-42; Member of the Mauritius Royal Commission, 1909; contested (L.) Canterbury, Jan. 1910; Southport, Dec. 1910; Chatham Division of Rochester, 1918. *Publications:* (with John Coutts) Lilies, their Culture and Management, 1935; (with W. T. Stearn) Lilies of the World, 1950. *Address:* Jaynes Court, Bisley, Glos. *T.:* Bisley 255. *Clubs:* National Liberal, Eighty. [*Died* 12 *Feb.* 1957.

WOODCOCK, Brig.-Gen. Wilfrid James, D.S.O. 1918; late Group Commander, Home Guards; *b.* 3 May 1878; *s.* of late Henry Woodcock, J.P., of Bank House Wigan, and Bolnore, Sussex; *m.* 1907, Caroline May, *d.* of late Walter Lawrie; one *d.* *Educ.:* Winchester College; R.M.C., Sandhurst. 2nd Lieut. Lancashire Fusiliers, 1898; Lieut., 1899; Captain, 1901; Major, 1915; Brevet Lieut.-Colonel, 1919; Colonel, 1923; Brigadier-General 101st Brigade, 1918-19; A.M.S., Egypt, 1921-1923; Instructor, Senior Officers School, Sheerness; Commander East Lancashire and Border Brigade, T.A. Carlisle, 1930-34; retired pay, 1934; served South African War, 1900-02 (despatches twice, two medals and clasps); European War (twice wounded, despatches, Brevet Lieut.-Colonel, D.S.O., Legion of Honour 4th and 5th class, French War Cross); Ireland, 1920 (wounded) A.F.S., London, 1939-40; Group Commander, East Herts H.G., 1940-43. *Recreations:* shooting and travelling. *Club:* Army and Navy.

[*Died* 17 *Nov.* 1960.

WOODD, Ven. Henry Alexander; Vicar-General, 1922-49; Archdeacon of Newcastle, Australia, 1921-49; Canon of Christ Church Cathedral, Newcastle, 1910; Examining Chaplain to the Bishop of Newcastle, 1904; Fellow of St. Paul's College, Sydney, 1926; *b.* 6 June 1865; *s.* of Rev. George Napoleon Woodd, B.A., of Wadham College, Oxford, and Caroline, *d.* of William Rust of Fouchers, Good Easter, Essex; *m.* 1902, Dorothy Mabel, *d.* of William Arlington Wilson of Rosedale Murrurundi; three *d.* *Educ.:* St Paul's College, University of Sydney. B.A.; Th. Soc. (A.C.T.), 1934; Deacon, 1888; Priest, 1889; Curate of All Saints', Woollahra, 1888-92; Curate of St. Luke, Scone, 1892-93; Incumbent of Gundy, 1893; Rector of Murrurundi, 1895; Rector of Morpeth, 1901; Archdeacon of Gloucester, Australia, 1909; Rector of Muswell Brook, 1910-19; Archdeacon of Durham, 1910; Archdeacon of Durham and Hunter, 1919; Stanton Chaplain 1919-35. *Address*: Takamuna, Merewether, N.S.W. [*Died* 8 *Nov.* 1954.

WOODHEAD, Arthur Longden, M.A., J.P., Part Proprietor and Chairman of Directors of Joseph Woodhead & Sons, Ltd., proprietors of the Huddersfield Examiner (Daily and Weekly); *b.* 13 Sept. 1862; *s.* of Joseph Woodhead, first Member of Parliament for the Spen Valley Div. of Yorkshire; *m.* Mary Ann Robinson; four *d.* *Educ.*: Huddersfield Coll.; Edinburgh University. Joined the staff of the Huddersfield Examiner on leaving Edinburgh, 1883; Pres. of the Newspaper Soc., 1925; and of the Yorkshire Newspaper Soc., 1926; President Huddersfield Music Club; Pres. and one of the Founders, Central Lads' Brunswick Club; filled many positions in connection with English, Yorkshire and local golf clubs, and acted on many public and semi-public cttees. *Address*: Deveron House, Queen's Road, Huddersfield. *T.*: 1433. *Clubs*: National Liberal, Press; Senior Golfers'; Huddersfield; Huddersfield Golf (Pres.) (Huddersfield); Carnarvonshire Golf (Conway). [*Died* 9 *July* 1957.

WOODHEAD, Henry George Wandesford, C.B.E. 1920; retd.; *b.* Devonport, 1883; *m.* 1908, Florence Louise Hamlin; one *s.* three *d.* *Educ.*: Brighton College. Editor China Year Book, 1912-39; Editor of the Peking and Tientsin Times 1914-30; Lecturer at the University of Chicago (Harris Memorial Foundation), 1925; Editor, Oriental Affairs, 1933-41; Chairman, Shanghai British Residents' Association, 1932; Chairman China Association, Shanghai, 1938-40; imprisoned by the Japanese at Shanghai, March-June 1942; Repatriated, Oct. 1942; Head of Far Eastern Reference Section, Ministry of Information, Dec. 1942; Times, Correspondent, Hong Kong, 1946 - 48. Editor, Far East Trader, 1950-54. Chevalier of Order of Leopold II.; Médaille de la Reconnaissance Française (d'Argent). *Publications*: The Truth about the Chinese Republic; Occidental Interpretations of the Far Eastern Problem; The Yangtsze and its Problems, 1932; A Visit to Manchukuo; A Journalist in China, 1934. *Address*: 50 Leopold Rd., Wimbledon, S.W.19. *Club*: Junior Carlton (London); Overseas Press (New York). [*Died* 29 *Sept.* 1959.

WOODHOUSE, Brigadier Harold Lister, C.B.E. 1940; M.C.; *b.* 30 Jan. 1887; *e. s.* of late Lister Woodhouse, A.C.A., A.I.A.; *m.* 1921, Dorothy Frances, *d.* of Professor S. L. Loney, M.A., J.P.; one *s.* *Educ.*: Cheltenham; R.M.A., Woolwich. 2nd Lieut. R.E. 1906; Colonel, 1933; served European War, 1914-18, East Africa and Palestine and Turkey (M.C., despatches); attached Indian State Railways, 1922; Chief Engineer, 1936; Director of Civil Engineering, Railway Board, Govt. of India, 1934-38; attached A.R.P. Technical Branch, Home Office, 1939; Deputy Director-General, Transportation B.E.F. 1939-40 (C.B.E., wounded); Post Graduate Diploma, Imperial College, London University, 1922; M.I.C.E. Member Surrey County Council. *Recreations*: golf, tennis. *Address*: Danejohn, Woodham Rise, Woking. *T.*: Woking 2642. *Club*: United Service. [*Died* 6 *Jan.* 1960.

WOODHOUSE, Herbert, C.B.E. 1920; J.P.; M.A., LL.D.; F.R.S.A.; *b.* 1 Dec. 1859; *s.* of late James Woodhouse, Manchester, and Dorothy, *d.* of late Thomas Marton of Terrington, Yorks; *m.* 1888, Frances Harriette (*d.* 1954), *d.* of late Wm. J. Halliday, Manchester; one *s.* five *d.* *Educ.*: Manchester Grammar School; Trinity Hall, Cambridge. Clerk of Peace for City and County of Kingston-upon-Hull, 1898-1952; resigned 1952; Cox of Cambridge Boat of 1881; Lord of the Manor of Flambro. *Address*: Newgate House, Cottingham, East Yorks. *T.A.*: Legality, Hull. *T.*: Cottingham 47758. [*Died* 16 *Jan.* 1957.

WOODHOUSE, Rt. Rev. John Walker; *b.* 28 Jan. 1884; *s.* of Robert H. Woodhouse, 1 Hanover Square, W., and Ralsbury, Ealing, W.; *m.* 1921, Kathleen Mary, *d.* of late Canon W. L. Harnett, St. George's Vicarage, Wolverton, Bucks; three *s.* one *d.* *Educ.*: Charterhouse; University College, Oxford; Bishops Hostel, Farnham. B.A. 1907; M.A. 1910; Travelling Secretary Student Christian Movement, 1907-09; Deacon, 1910; Priest, 1911; Curate of St. James, Milton, Portsmouth, 1910-14; Curate of Bermondsey Parish Church, 1914-20; C.F., served in France, 1915-19; Vicar of St. John's, Waterloo Road, S.E., 1921-25; Vicar of Christ Church, Luton, Beds, 1925-34; Rural Dean of Luton, 1928-34; Vicar of St. George's Newcastle upon Tyne, 1934-42; Hon. Chaplain to Bp. of Newcastle, 1937; Hon. Canon of Newcastle Cathedral, 1938; Vicar of Huddersfield, Rural Dean of Huddersfield, Hon. Canon of Wakefield, 1942-45; Suffragan Bishop of Thetford, 1945-53. Select preacher Cambridge University, 1946; Archdeacon of Lynn, 1946-53; Vicar of Stanford and Rector of West Tofts with Buckenham Parva, 1949-1953. *Recreations*: golf, sketching. *Address*: 86 High Street, Blakeney, Norfolk. *T.*: Cley 260. *Club*: Norfolk (Norwich). [*Died* 13 *March* 1955.

WOODING, John Conrad, Q.C. (Leeward Islands), 1950; M.A. (Durham); Attorney General, Leeward Islands, since 1949; Puisne Judge of the Supreme Court of the Windward and Leeward Islands since 1953; *b.* 5 Jan. 1901; *s.* of late Samuel Augustus Clayton Wooding and late Louisa (*née* King), Barbados, B.W.I.; *m.* 1926, Elvira Augustina, *e. d.* of Robert A. Barton, Montserrat, B.W.I.; three *s.* three *d.* *Educ.*: Harrison College and Codrington College, Barbados, B.W.I. Registrar and Provost Marshal, St. Kitts-Nevis, 1935. Called to Bar, Middle Temple, 1938. Magistrate: St. Kitts-Nevis, 1939; Antigua, 1940; Crown Attorney, St. Lucia, 1943; acted Asst. Administrator and Administrator, St. Lucia, various periods during 1946-49; Governor's Deputy: Windward Is. during 1947; Leeward Is. during 1950; Chairman: U.S. Bases Compensation Cttee., Deptl. Reorganization Cttee., and Land Policy Cttee., St. Lucia, 1945; Commn. of Inquiry into sinking of motor vessel Bernadin, St. Lucia, 1944; Actg.: Puisne Judge, Windward and Leeward Is., March-May 1948 and Oct.-Nov. 1949; Judge, Windward and Leeward Is. Court of Appeal, Jan. 1949; Colonial Sec., Leeward Is., June-Sept. 1950. Chm. Constitutional Reform Cttee., Leeward Is., 1950; Chancellor of Diocese of Antigua, 1950. *Recreations*: motoring, swimming, gardening. *Address*: Castriss, St. Lucia, B.W.I. *Club*: New (St. John's, Antigua). [*Died* 17 *Aug.* 1954.

WOODLAND, William Norton Ferrier, D.Sc. (Lond.); retired; late of Helminthology Department, Wellcome Research Institution; *b.* 16 July 1879; *s.* of John Woodland, F.L.S., F.C.S., and Julia Evans Smith; *m.* 1912, Edith Fontaine Wilson; one *s.* *Educ.*: University College, London. Lecturer Zoology, King's College, London, 1905-7; assistant Professor Zoology, University College, London, 1908-12 (Fellow, 1911); Professor Zoology, Allahabad University, India (I.E.S.), 1912-22 (Fellow, 1913). *Publications*: papers to scientific journals. *Recreations*: music, travel. *Address*: Harbour View, Bosham, Sussex. *T.*: Bosham 3144. [*Died* 22 *June* 1952.

WOODROFFE, Paul Vincent; *b.* 1875; *s.* of Francis Henry Woodroffe, Madras Civil Service; *m.* 1907, Dorothy, *d.* of Col. Lynch-Staunton; one *s.* (and one *s.* decd.). *Educ.*: Stonyhurst; Slade School of Art. Designer of books, stained glass, heraldic work. Designed the windows for Lady Chapel, St. Patrick's Cathedral, New York; Member of

Art-Workers' Guild; Ministry of Munitions, 1914-18. *Publications:* several books of Nursery Rhymes and Nursery Songs, and Herrick's Hesperides (with Joseph Moorat); Little Flowers of St. Francis; The Tempest; Froissarts Chronycles. *Address:* Berkeley Cottage, Mayfield, Sussex. *T.:* 3104. [*Died* 7 *May* 1954.

WOODS, Rev. Vice-Adm. Alexander Riall Wadham, D.S.O. 1916; Chaplain of Red Ensign Club and Assistant curate of St. Paul's, Whitechapel since 1933; *b.* 1880. Served at Battle of Jutland, 1916 (despatches, D.S.O. with bar, Orders of St. Stanislas and St. Maurice and St. Lazarus); Captain of the Dockyard, Deputy-Superintendent and King's Harbour Master, Portsmouth, 1926-28; Rear-Admiral and retired list, 1931; Vice-Adm., retired, 1936; ordained deacon 1933; Priest, 1934. *Address:* Red Ensign Club, Dock Street, E.1. [*Died* 1 *Nov.* 1954.

WOODS, Major-Gen. Edward Ambrose, C.B. 1946; C.B.E. 1944; M.C. 1916; *b.* 4 April 1891; *m.* 1917, Dorothy Vyvyan Grace, *yr. d.* of late C. E. Pitman, C.I.E.; one *s.* two *d.* (and one *s.* decd.). *Educ.:* Tonbridge; R.M.A. Woolwich. 2nd Lt. R.A. 1910; served European War, 1914-1918 (wounded twice, despatches, M.C.); Inspector General Armaments, Woolwich, 1942; retired pay, 1946. *Address:* Western Ting Tong, Budleigh Salterton. *T.:* 572. *Club:* United Service. [*Died* 3 *May* 1957.

WOODS, Rt. Rev. Edward Sydney, D.D., Hon. C.F.; Bishop of Lichfield since 1937; High Almoner to the Queen (and to King George VI, 1946-52); *b.* Hereford, 1 Nov. 1877; *s.* of Rev. Frank Woods and Alice Octavia Fry; *m.* 1903, Clemence Rachel Barclay (*d.* 1952); three *s.* three *d.* *Educ.:* Marlborough Coll.; Trinity Coll., Cambridge. Ordained, 1901; priest, 1902; chaplain and lecturer, Ridley Hall, Cambridge, 1901-02; Vice-Principal, 1903-07; Chaplain R.M.C., Sandhurst, 1914-19; Vicar of Holy Trinity, Cambridge, 1918-27; Vicar of Croydon, 1927-37; Rural Dean, 1927-37; Archdeacon of Croydon, 1930-37; Bishop of Croydon, 1930-37; Proctor in Convocation, Ely, 1921-23; Hon. Canon of Ely, 1923-27; Hon. Canon of Canterbury, 1927; Select Preacher, Cambridge University, 1916, 1921, 1927, 1935, 1941; Select Preacher, Oxford Univ., 1936. *Publications:* Everyday Religion; Modern Discipleship; A Faith that works; Theodore, Bishop of Winchester (with Very Rev. F. B. Macnutt), 1933; What is this Christianity?, etc. *Recreations:* lawn tennis, golf, shooting. *Address:* The Palace, Lichfield. [*Died* 11 *Jan.* 1953.

WOODS, Rev. George Saville; M.P. (Lab.) Mossley Division of Lancashire, 1945-50, Droylsden since 1950; Member of Central Board and National Executive of Co-operative Union Limited; Member of National Council of Labour; Director of Co-operative Press Ltd., People's Entertainment Soc. Ltd.; Minister S. Saviourgate Chapel, York, since 1921; *b.* 13 Sept. 1886; *s.* of Thomas William and Alice Antice Woods; *m.* 1914, Edith Alice Mote, L.L.A.; one *d.* *Educ.:* Handsworth College, Birmingham; Manchester College, Oxford. Minister Mary Street Chapel, Taunton, 1914-21; President Yorkshire Unitarian Union, 1932-34; M.P. (Lab.) Finsbury, 1935-45; various service to and posts in the Trade Union, Co-operative and Socialist and Political Labour Movements, including Chairmanship of Taunton Labour Party, York Labour Party and President of York Co-operative Society; served on York Board of Guardians and York City Council. *Publications:* Contributions to Co-operative Press and Pamphlets. *Recreations:* angling, gardening. *Address:* Hopgrove, York. *T.:* York 4468. [*Died* 9 *July* 1951.

WOODS, Colonel Harold, C.B.E. 1937; (O.B.E. 1918); late Reserve of Officers; late Commercial Counsellor British Embassy in Turkey; at present employed as Representative in Turkey of Export Credits Guarantee Dept.; *b.* 1879; *s.* of late Sir Henry Woods, K.C.V.O., retired R.N., a Pasha and Admiral and A.D.C. General under the Sultanate of Turkey. *Educ.:* Royal Naval College, Eltham; private tuition. Inspector in the Ottoman Public Debt, 1900-09; Chief of Staff to late Sir Richard Crawford, G.C.M.G., K.B.E., Financial and Economic Adviser to the Turkish Government, 1909-14; Intelligence Officer Corps, H.Q., Anzac; G.S.O. 3, G.H.Q., Egyptian Expeditionary Force; G.S.O. 2 G.H.Q. Palestine; Allied Food Controller in Turkey for the Armistice; Legion of Honour; despatches thrice, Turkish War Medal, Turco-Greek War, 1897. Order of Medjedieh and Osmanie, Balkan War Red Cross Medal; King's Silver Jubilee Medal; Coronation Medal, 1937. *Clubs:* St. James', Junior United Service; Royal Harwich Yacht. [*Died* 28 *Oct.* 1952.

WOODS, Henry, F.R.S., M.A., F.G.S.; *b.* 18 Dec. 1868; *s.* of Francis Woods; *m.* 1910, Ethel Gertrude (*d.* 1939), *d.* of Prof. W. W. Skeat. *Educ.:* St. John's College, Cambridge (Scholar). First Class Natural Sciences Tripos, Part I., 1889, and Part II., 1890; Harkness Scholar in the University of Cambridge, 1890; Sedgwick Prize, 1895; Demonstrator in Palæontology, 1892-99; University Lecturer in Palæozoology, Cambridge, 1900-34; Examiner in the Natural Sciences Tripos, 1896-97, 1902-3, 1915-16, 1918-1919; awarded the Lyell Medal by the Geological Society, 1918, the Wollaston Medal, 1940; and member of the Council, 1907-11, 1922-25; Hon. Member Royal Society, N.Z. *Publications:* A Monograph of the Cretaceous Lamellibranchia of England, 2 vols., 1899-1913; Catalogue of Type Fossils in the Woodwardian Museum, Cambridge, 1891; Palæontology-Invertebrate (Camb. Biol. Series), 8th ed., 1946; The Cretaceous Fauna of Pondoland, 1906; The Palæontology of the Upper Cretaceous Deposits of Northern Nigeria, 1911; The Cretaceous Fauna of the South Island of New Zealand, 1917; a Monograph of the Fossil Macrurous Crustacea of England, 1925-31; Tertiary Mollusca and Crustacea in T.O. Bosworth, Geol. N. W. Peru, 1922. *Address:* Meldreth, near Royston, Herts. [*Died* 4 *April* 1952.

WOODS, Sir Robert Stanton, Kt., *cr.* 1929; M.D.; F.R.C.P.; retired; Consulting Physician to the London Hospital, Department of Physical Medicine; Consultant Adviser, E.M.S., Ministry of Health; *b.* 10 Feb. 1877; *m.* 1917, Violet Mary, *d.* of Clarence Trelawny, and *widow* of Major B. Liebert, 7th Hussars; one *d.* *Educ.:* University College, London; London Hospital; Stockholm; Vienna. Major, R.A.M.C. (despatches). *Address:* c/o Midland Bank Ltd., High St., Marylebone. [*Died* 18 *Nov.* 1954.

WOODWARD, Sir (Alfred) Chad (Turner), Kt., *cr.* 1944; D.L., J.P.; F.R.C.S. Ed. and Eng.; Chairman Worcestershire C.C.; Chairman Standing Joint Committee; Ex-Chairman: River Severn Catchment Board; Board of Conservators, Severn Fishery District; *b.* 2 March 1880; 2nd *surv. s.* of Robert Woodward, D.L., J.P., Arley Castle, nr. Bewdley; *m.* 1934, Martha Grace, *d.* of Rev. Canon Rowland Wilson, Great Witley, Worcs.; three *d.* *Educ.:* Radley College; Edinburgh Univ. Served European War, 1914-19; late Major R.A.M.C. County Alderman, 1934; Member of Radium Commission, 1939-43. Governor: London School of Tropical Medicine; Birmingham University; Member of Board of Governors of Police College. *Recreations:* fishing, archery. *Address:* Arley Cottage, nr. Bewdley, Worcs. *T.:* Arley 5. *Clubs:* Athenæum; County (Worcester); Union (Birmingham). [*Died* 2 *Feb.* 1957.

WOODWARD, Rt. Rev. Clifford Salisbury, M.C.; D.D.; *b.* 1878; *e. s.* of late Rev. R. S. Woodward; *m.* 1905, Grace

WOODS, Walter Sainsbury, C.M.G., LL.D. See page xxxi.

Stewart (*d.* 1939), *widow* of Col. Charles Stewart, Black Watch; no *c.* *Educ.:* Marlborough; Jesus College, Oxford. Deacon, 1902; Priest, 1903; Curate of Bermondsey, 1902-05; Secretary South London Church Fund, 1905-1909; Chaplain of Wadham College, 1909-13; Examining Chaplain to Bishop of Southwark, 1912-19; Canon and Precentor of Southwark Cathedral, 1913-19; Rector of St. Saviour with St. Peter, Southwark, 1913-19; Vicar of St. Peter's, Cranley Gardens, S.W., 1919-26; Canon of Westminster and Rector of St. John the Evangelist, Westminster, 1926-33; Bishop of Bristol, 1933-46; Bishop of Gloucester, 1946-53; Chaplain to H.M. the King, 1919-33; Hon. Fellow Jesus College, Oxford, 1935; Rural Dean of Kensington, 1925; temp. C.F., France, 1916 (M.C.). *Publications:* Stories told to the Scamps, 1924; Jesus among the Children, 1925; Christ in the Common Ways of Life, 1928; Dreams and Fables, 1929. *Recreation:* none. *Address:* Little Fountains, Dulcote, Wells, Somerset. *T.:* Wells 2120. *Club:* Athenæum. [*Died* 14 *April* 1959.

WOODWARD, Rear-Admiral Sir Henry William, K.C.B., *cr.* 1936 (C.B. 1934); J.P. Kent; *b.* 19 July 1879; *s.* of late Arthur Waller Woodward, Shrub End, Colchester, Essex; *m.* 1947, Christine Rozel Pigot, *widow* of Maj. Mark Gregson, R.A., and *d.* of late Adm. H. P. Williams. Entered R.N. 1907; Paymaster Rear Adm., 1933; Sec. to Naval Commander in Chief at The Cape, 1910-12; China, 1925-27; The Nore, 1927-30; Paymaster Director General Admiralty, 1933-36; retired list, 1936; served European War, 1914-18, in Grand Fleet; Chief Telegraph Censor, 1940-41. *Recreations:* fishing, shooting, golf. *Address:* Old Barn House, Charing, Kent. *T.:* Charing 432. *Club:* Army and Navy. [*Died* 18 *Feb.* 1959.

WOOLDRIDGE, Prof. George Henry, F.R.C.V.S.; M.R.I.A.; F.Z.S. (Hon.); F.R.San.I.; Emeritus Professor of Veterinary Medicine, Royal Veterinary College, London, Vice-Principal, 1936-43; Professor of Medicine, 1908-43; formerly Reader and Examiner in Veterinary Hygiene and Meat Inspection in Univ. of London; President of Royal College of Veterinary Surgeons, 1939-1940, Vice-Pres. 1938, 1940-41-42; Pres. National Veterinary Medical Assoc. of Great Britain and Ireland, 1926-27; Steel Memorial Medallist (R.C.V.S.), 1928; sometime Examiner in Univ. of Cambridge, Manchester, Liverpool, Reading, and Bristol; Examiner for Meat Inspector's Certificate of Royal Sanitary Institute; Member: Royal Irish Academy; Therapeutics Requirements Committee, Medical Research Council; Hon. Consulting Veterinary Surgeon to the Zoological Society; *b.* Stoke-on-Trent; *s.* of L. Wooldridge, Newcastle, N. Staffordshire; *m.* Elsie Maud, *d.* of T. Salusbury Price, of Essex Lodge, Brixton Hill, S.W. *Educ.:* St. Peter's School, Stoke-on-Trent; Orme Boys' School, Newcastle-under-Lyme; Royal Veterinary College, London. 1st Honours, Final Professional Exam., 1899; Centenary Scholarship, 1899; Coleman medallist, 1st; medallist, Surgery, Medicine, Anatomy, Biology, Chemistry, etc.; Junior Assistant E. M. School; Newcastle-under-Lyme, 1892-93; pupil with J. Wilson, M.R.C.V.S. Nantwich, Cheshire, 1893-1897; commenced studies at the R.V.C., London, 1895; tutor Royal Veterinary College, London; Editor of the Veterinary Student, 1899-1900; Professor of Vet. Science and Bacteriology, R.A.C., Cirencester, 1900-1903; Prof. of Medicine at Royal Veterinary College of Ireland, 1903-08; Joint-Editor of the Veterinary Journal, 1906-14; has been Pres. of the Central and Royal Counties Veterinary Societies; Victory Medallist, Central Veterinary Society, 1925; Vice-Pres. R.S.M. and President section of Comparative Medicine, 1930-31. Pres. Clinical Section International Vet. Congress, New York, 1934; Vice-President Research Defense Society; Stephen Paget Memorial Lecturer, 1947. *Publications:* Encyclopædia of Veterinary Medicine, Surgery, and Obstetrics, 2 vols., 2nd ed., 1935; Abortion in Cattle; Hæmoglobinuria in Cattle; The Temperature of Healthy Dairy Cattle; The Temperature of Tubercular Dairy Cattle not showing Clinical Symptoms; Actinomycosis and Botriomycosis; Anæsthesia, Local and General (International Vet. Congress, 1914); Purpura Hæmorrhagica in the Horse; Equine Influenza; articles and papers. *Recreations:* riding and driving, lawn tennis, golf, bowls, curling. *Address:* Royal Veterinary College, Camden Town, N.W.1; 2 Sherwood Road, N.W.4. *T.:* Hendon 2708. [*Died* 30 *Aug.* 1957.

WOOLF, Albert Edward Mortimer, B.A.; M.B., B.Ch. (Cantab.), F.R.C.S. (England); retired; Consulting Surgeon: Queen Mary's Hospital for East End and Forest Hospital, Buckhurst Hill; St. Margaret's Hospital, Epping; Consulting Surgeon Epping and District Cottage Hospital; Surgeon, East End Maternity Hospital, E.1; Emeritus Surgeon, Lord Mayor Treloar's Home, Alton, Hants; *b.* Oct. 1884; *s.* of late Mortimer Woolf, O.B.E., and Miriam Woolf; *m.* Laura Nathan; two *d.* *Educ.:* Clifton College; Emmanuel College, Cambridge. House Physician, Receiving Room Officer and House Surgeon, London Hospital, 1909-11; Surgical Specialist, B.E.F. in France, 1915, subsequently in Mesopotamia and India and Serbia; Past Demonstrator of Anatomy, King's College, London; Past Secretary, Hunterian Society; Pres., Hunterian Soc., 1926-28 and 1945; Hunterian Soc. Orator, 1931; Chm. Yeatman & Co. Ltd., Watford. *Publications:* Indications and contra-indications for Operation in Disease of the Thyroid, 1925; The Early Diagnosis of Gall-Stones, 1925; Pain (Pres. Address Hunterian Society, 1926); Some Personalities of the Hunterian Epoch (Pres. Address Hunterian Society, 1927); The Use of Heroin after Abdominal Operations—a Warning, 1929; Some Affections of the Gall-Bladder, 1930; numerous contributions to medical press. *Recreations:* golf, travel, music. *Address:* Ash Green, Baldwin's Hill, Loughton, Essex. *T.:* Loughton 114. *Club:* Savage. [*Died* 6 *April* 1957.

WOOLF, Rev. Bertram Lee, Ph.D., M.A., B.Sc. B.D. (Edinburgh); Minister, Westbourne, Bournemouth; *m.* 1911, Margaret A. Jones; two *s.* one *d.* *Educ.:* Universities of Edinburgh, Halle, Marburg, and Berlin; United Independent Coll., Bradford. In business till age 20; proceeded to Edinburgh and Continent; served in Y.M.C.A. during European War; Minister, Listerhills, in Bradford, 1911-14; West Bromwich, 1914-19; Toxteth, Liverpool, 1919-27; Acton, 1927-29; King's Weigh House Church, London, 1933-34; Minister-in-Charge, Whitefield Memorial Church, London, 1942-45. Professor and Lecturer, New College, London, 1928-45; Extension Lecturer, Univ. of London, 1932-54; University of Oxford, 1940-52. *Publications:* The Authority of Jesus and its Foundation; The Approach to Religion, in God and the Universe; Ethics of Gambling; Pilgrim's Progress: a Dramatised Version; The Background and Beginnings of the Gospel Story, 1935; Reformation Writings of Martin Luther—a new translation with Introduction and notes, Vol. I. 1952, Vols. II. and III., 1956; A Breath of Fresh Air and other stories for children. Has translated numerous German theological works. *Address:* 80 The Grove, Christchurch, Hants. *T.:* 300. *Club:* Central Y.M.C.A. [*Died* 23 *Jan.* 1956.

WOOLLCOMBE, Admiral Louis Charles Stirling, C.B. 1919; M.V.O.; D.L. Devon, 1936; *b.* 1872; *s.* of Rev. George Woollcombe; *m.* 1905, Constance Perry, *d.* of Rev. R. Perry Circuitt; two *s.* one *d.* *Educ.:* Clifton College; H.M.S. Britannia. Entered Royal Navy, 1885; Commander, 1905; Captain, 1912; Rear-Adm. 1922; Commander in H.M.S. Medina during King and Queen's visit to India, 1911-12; European War, 1914-16, Battle of Jutland Bank (despatches, C.B.); Admiral Superintendent of Devonport Dockyard, 1924-27; retired list, 1927; Adm., retired, 1932. *Address:* Mote House, Abbots Kerswell, S. Devon. [*Died* 26 *Oct.* 1951.

WOOLLEY, Sir (Charles) Leonard, Kt., *cr.* 1935; M.A. Oxon, Hon. D.Litt. Dublin; Hon. LL.D. St. Andrews; Hon. Fellow of New College, Oxford; Hon. Fellow, Türk Tarih Kurumu; Hon. A.R.I.B.A. F.S.A.; *b.* 17 April 1880; *s.* of Rev. George Herbert and Sarah Woolley; *m.* Katharine Elizabeth (*d.* 1945), *widow* of Lt.-Col. Francis Keeling, O.B.E., M.C. *Educ.:* St. John's, Leatherhead; New College, Oxford. Asst. Keeper, Ashmolean Museum, Oxford, 1905-7; Excavations at Corbridge, 1906-7; Excavating in Nubia for the Eckley B. Coxe Jnr. Expedition, 1907-11; Oxford University Expedition to Nubia, 1912; British Museum excavations at Carchemish, 1912-14; Archæological work in Sinai for the Palestine Exploration Fund, 1914; Capt. R.F.A.; Intelligence work on staff in Egypt, 1914-16 (despatches, Croix de Guerre); prisoner in Turkey, 1916-18; Maj. political dept., N. Syria, 1919; Excavations at Carchemish, 1919; Excavations at Tel el Amarna for Egypt Exploration Soc., 1921-22; Excavations at Ur, 1922-34; Excavations at Al Mina, near Antioch, Syria, 1936-37; at Atchana, Hatay, 1937-39. Major G.S. P.R. Directorate, 1939-43; Lt.-Col. G.S. Archæological Adviser to Civil Affairs Directorate, 1943-46; Excavations at Atchana, Hatay, 1946-49. Huxley Memorial Lecturer, 1942. Myres Memorial Lecturer, 1960. Museum of the University of Pennsylvania, Lucy Wharton Drexel Medal, 1955. Univ. of London, Flinders Petrie Medal, 1957. *Publications:* Areika, Karanog, Karanog: the town, Buhen (with D. Randall MacIver: Eckley, B. Coxe, Jnr. Expedition of the University Museum, Philadelphia); The Wilderness of Sin (with T. E. Lawrence, Palestine Exploration Fund); Carchemish (British Museum); The City of the Aten (with T. G. Peet, Egypt Exploration Society); al'Ubaid (with Dr. H. R. Hall); Dead Towns and Living Men; The Sumerians; Ur of the Chaldees; Digging up the Past, 1930; Ur Excavations: The Royal Cemetery, 2 vols., 1934; The Development of Sumerian Art, 1935; Abraham, 1936; Ur Excavations: The Ziggurat and its Surroundings, 1938; The Protection of the Treasures of Art and History in War Areas, 1947; Carchemish, vol. III, 1954; Alalakh, 1955; A Forgotten Kingdom, 1953; Spadework, 1953; Excavations at Ur, 1954; Ur Excavations—The Early Periods, 1955; History Unearthed, 1958; The Bronze Age in U.N.E.S.C.O.'s History of the Scientific and Cultural Development of Mankind, 1958; As I Seem to Remember, 1962 (posth.). *Address:* King's Worthy Court, nr. Winchester. *Club:* Athenæum. [*Died* 20 *Feb.* 1960.

WOOLNOUGH, Walter George, D.Sc., F.G.S.; *b.* Brushgrove, N.S.W., 15 Jan. 1876; *s.* of Rev. James W. and E. P. Woolnough; *m.* 1902, Margaret Ilma, 3rd *d.* of Rev. W. Wilson; one *s.* one *d.* (and one *s.* decd.). *Educ.:* High School, Newington College and University, Sydney; B.Sc. 1898; D.Sc. 1904. Demonstrator in Geology, University of Sydney, 1898-1901; Lecturer in Mineralogy and Petrology, University of Adelaide, 1902-04; Lecturer in Geology, University of Sydney, 1905-10; Assistant Professor, 1911-12; Professor of Geology, University of Western Australia, 1913-19; Geologist to Brunner, Mond & Co. Ltd., Northwich, 1919-27. Geological Adviser to Australian Commonwealth Government 1927-41; Translator and Bibliographica, Officer, Ministry of Post-War Reconstruction, later Ministry of National Development, Melbourne, 1942-51; retired 1951. First Chairman, Commonwealth Government Oil Advisory Committee; Member of Prof. David's Funafuti Expedition, 1897; Leader two expeditions to Fiji, 1901 and 1905; Member Commonwealth Preliminary Scientific Expedition to the Northern Territory, 1911; Chairman Royal Commission on Collie Coal Industry, W.A., 1914-15; Official Tour of Oil Fields of U.S.A. and Argentina on behalf of Commonwealth Government, 1930; extensive geological investigations throughout Australia, Papua and Mandated Territory of New Guinea; Consultant to the Govt. Committee in charge of aerial and geophysical survey of Northern Australia, 1934-40; President, Royal Society of N.S.W., 1926-27; Leader, Commonwealth Aerial Geological Survey Expedition round Australia, 1932. Hon. Mem. Geol. Soc. of Australia, 1958. Medal of Royal Soc. N.S.W., 1956. *Publications:* Direction Finding by Sun, Moon and Stars without Mathematical Calculation, 1943; numerous translations of technical and scientific articles, chiefly from German, Russian, Spanish, Finnish and Swedish; papers on geological subjects, and official reports. *Address:* 28 Calbina Rd., Northbridge, Sydney, N.S.W. [*Died* 28 *Sept.* 1958.

WOOLVERIDGE, Air Commodore Harry Leonard, C.B. 1946; O.B.E. 1938; late Director of Equipment, Air Ministry; *b.* 29 June 1887, British; *m.* 1916, Marie Victoria Buser; one *d.* *Educ.:* Battersea Grammar School. Joined R.F.C. Sept. 1914; France, 1914-16 (B.E.F.); Home Defence Bde., 1916-18; 1st Bde. France, Aug. 1918; Royal Air Force in United Kingdom, Iraq and India, Units, Commands and at Air Ministry; retired 1947. *Address:* Woodside, Vale Close, Lower Bourne, Farnham, Surrey. [*Died* 29 *March* 1960.

WORDSWORTH, Capt. Sir William Henry Laycock, Kt., *cr.* 1937; J.P.; late Yorkshire Regiment; *b.* 6 March 1880; *s.* of John Wordsworth, Blackgates, nr. Wakefield; *m.* 1906, Ethel Marian (*d.* 1952), *d.* of Richard Rudgard, The Hall, Scalby; no *c.* *Educ.:* Worcester College, Oxford. Chairman and Hon. Treasurer of the Scarborough and Whitby Division, Conservative and Unionist Association; Member of Primrose League Grand Council; A Vice-Chairman of Primrose League (Yorkshire Area); County Councillor North Riding, Yorks, 1919-46; Chairman of the Scalby Urban District Council, 1940-46. *Address:* The Glen, Scalby, near Scarborough. *T.A.:* Scalby. *T.:* Scalby 14. *Clubs:* Bath; Yorkshire (York). [*Died* 31 *March* 1960.

WORKMAN, Rev. Herbert Brook, D.Lit. (Lond.); hon. D.D. (Aberdeen); F.R.Hist. Soc.; Hon. Secretary of Education Committee of Methodist Church; *b.* 2 Nov. 1862; *s.* of late Rev. J. S. Workman, Methodist minister; *m.* Ethel Mary, *e. d.* of late A. G. Buller, J.P., of King's Heath, Birmingham; two *s.* one *d.* *Educ.:* Kingswood School, Bath; Owens College, Manchester. Methodist minister since 1885; Principal, Westminster Training College, S.W., 1903-30; Fernley Lecturer, 1906; Cole Lecturer to Nashville (Tenn.), 1916; Fraternal Delegate of British Methodist Conference to Methodist Episcopal Church of America, 1916; Member of the Senate of London University, of the Board of Studies in Theology, and of the London Library Committee for many years; Special Lecturer, Chicago University, 1927; Pres., of Wesleyan Conference, 1930-31; Examiner in Ecclesiastical History for Welsh Univ. *Publications:* The Church of the West in the Middle Ages (2 vols.), 1898; The Dawn of the Reformation (2 vols.), 1900; The Letters of John Hus, 1904; Persecution in the Early Church, 1906; A New History of Methodism (2 vols.), 1909; Development of Christian Thought to the Reformation, 1911; Methodism, 1912; The Evolution of the Monastic Ideal, 1913; Foundations of Modern Religion, 1916; John Wyclif (2 vols.), 1926. *Address:* 29 Vineyard Hill Road, Wimbledon Park, S.W.19. *T.:* Wimbledon 3499. [*Died* 26 *Aug.* 1951.

WORKMAN, William Arthur, F.I.A., F.C.I.I.; Director of Legal and General Assurance Society Ltd., Gresham Life Assurance Society Ltd., and Gresham Fire and Accident Insurance Society Ltd.; *b.* London, 13 Feb. 1877; *s.* of late William Day Workman; *m.* Helen, 2nd *d.* of late Matthew Fraser, J.P., Teignmouth; one *d.* *Educ.:* Sir George Monoux Grammar School; privately. F.I.A. 1902 (sometime Member of Council); served with Imperial Insurance Co. and Equitable Assurance Society prior to appointment as Secretary, Legal and General Assurance Soc., 1909; General Manager, 1921-37; Managing Director, 1937-1942; Chairman, Life Offices Association, 1929 and 1930; President Insurance Institute of London, 1931-32; Chairman British Insurance Association, 1933-34; Pres. Chartered Insurance Institute, 1941-42; Chairman Actuaries Club, 1941-43; President Insurance Clerks Orphanage and Insurance Benevolent Fund, 1942-43; Member of Air Ministry Committee on Control of Private Flying and other Civil Aviation Questions, 1933-34. *Recreation:* motoring. *Address:* 123 Cliffords Inn, E.C.4; The Grey House, Dixwell Road, Folkestone, Kent. *Clubs:* Reform, Actuaries; Radnor (Folkestone). [*Died* 23 *Feb.* 1956.

WORNUM, George Grey, C.B.E., 1957; F.R.I.B.A.; Architect, practising as Wornum and Payne, 19 Queen Anne's Gate, S.W.1, and at 1020 Green St., San Francisco; Hon. Corresponding Member American Institute of Architects; *b.* 17 April 1888; *s.* of George Porter Wornum and Edith Howard; *m.* 1923, Miriam Alice Gerstle, San Francisco; one *s.* two *d.* *Educ.:* Bradfield College; Slade School. Articled to late R. Selden Wornum, F.R.I.B.A. and studied at the Architectural Association, London; commenced practice, 1910; served with the Artists Rifles and Durham Light Infantry, 1914-18; President of Architectural Association, 1930-31; Member of R.I.B.A. Council, 1935; Winner of Competition for New R.I.B.A. premises, 1932; designed New British Girls' College, Alexandria, Egypt, 1935; Decoration Architect for s.s. Queen Elizabeth, 1936; R.I.B.A. Street Architecture Bronze Medal, 1939, for New Highways Depôt, City of Westminster; Municipal Housing Schemes for various London Boroughs, 1945-; New Lay-out, Parliament Square, 1950. Royal Gold Medal for Architecture, 1952. *Publications:* (Joint) Housing, a European Survey by the Building Centre; (with John Gloag) House out of Factory. *Clubs:* Arts, Garrick. [*Died* 11 *June* 1957.

WORRALL, Arthur Hardey, T.D.; M.A.; Head Master of Victoria College, Jersey, 1911-33; *b.* 1868; *m.* 1917, Amabel, *d.* of late Very Rev. S. Falle, Dean of Jersey. *Educ.:* King's School, Grantham; St. John's College, Oxford (Open Scholar, 1st Class Classical Mods., 1888, 2nd Class Lit. Hum. 1890). Sixth Form Master at Loretto, 1890-1892; Lancing, 1892-93; Headmaster's Assistant at Bradfield, 1893-1900; Headmaster King Edward VI. School, Louth, 1901-11; twenty years' service in Volunteer and Territorial Forces; Captain Lincolnshire Regiment (T.F.); war service (wounded). *Address:* 25 Cleveland Road, Jersey, C.I. [*Died* 21 *March* 1960.

WORSLEY-GOUGH, Lt.-Col. H. W.; *see* Gough.

WORSLEY-TAYLOR, Sir Francis (Edward), 4th Bt., *cr.* 1917; *b.* 14 July 1874; *s.* of 1st Bt. and Harriette Sayer (*d.* 1913), *o. d.* of Sir Edward William Watkin, 1st Bt.; *S.* nephew, 1952. *Educ.:* Wellington College; University College, Oxford (M.A.). *Heir:* none. *Address:* Newton Hall, Newton-in-Bowland, nr. Clitheroe, Lancs. *T.:* Slaidburn 231. *Club:* Junior Carlton. [*Died* 13 *Dec.* 1958 (*ext.*).

WORSLEY-TAYLOR, Capt. Sir John Godfrey, 3rd Bt., *cr.* 1917; Scots Guards; *b.* 24 Nov. 1915; *o. s.* of 2nd Bt. and Audrey Frances, *d.* of Sir Frederic S. P. Philipson-Stow, 1st Bt.; *S.* father, 1933; *m.* 1942, Anne (from whom he obtained a divorce, 1950), *o. d.* of late Capt. J. Otho Paget; one *d.* *Educ.:* Eton; Trinity College, Oxford. *Heir:* *u.* Francis Edward, *b.* 14 July 1874. *Recreations:* shooting, rowing. *Address:* Town Head, nr. Clitheroe, Lancs; Goodshaw Farm, nr. Longridge. *Club:* Carlton. [*Died* 15 *July* 1952.

WORTH, Arthur Hovenden; Landowner; *b.* 9 Aug. 1877; 3rd *s.* of Thomas Maudaunt Worth, Sutton Bridge, Lincs; *m.* 1900, Lizzie, *d.* of George Thompson, Long Sutton, Lincs; one *s.* (elder son killed in action in 1941) three *d.* *Educ.:* Bedford. Farming. High Sheriff of Lincolnshire, 1940. Chairman of Holbeach Magistrates, retired 1948. *Recreations:* shooting and fishing. *Address:* Top Hall, Lyndon, Oakham, Rutland. [*Died* 3 *Dec.* 1955.

WORTHAM, Hugh Evelyn; Journalist; since 1934 Peterborough of the Daily Telegraph; *b.* 7 May 1884; *y. s.* of late Rev. B. H. Wortham, Kneesworth, Cambs; *m.* 1913, Sadie (*d.* 1947), *y. d.* of Charles Newkirk, New York; one *s.* (and one *s.* decd.). *Educ.:* King's Coll., Camb., M.A. 1921. Worked as foreign corresp. and editor in Egypt, 1909-19. *Publications:* A Musical Odyssey; Oscar Browning; Three Women; Mustapha Kemal of Turkey; The Delightful Profession; Gordon: an Intimate Portrait; Edward VII; Marcus Aurelius. *Recreations:* anything high brow. *Address:* Mill Stream Cottage, Egerton, Ashford, Kent. *T.:* Egerton 248. *Clubs:* Athenæum, United University. [*Died* 9 *July* 1959.

WORTHAM, Brigadier Philip William Temple Hale, C.B. 1917; *b.* 21 March 1874; *m.*; two *s.* Entered Duke of Wellington's Regiment from Suffolk Militia, 1895; Captain, 1901; transferred A.O.D. 1908; Major, 1911; Bt. Lieut.-Colonel, 1915; Lieut.-Col. 1916; Bt. Colonel, 1919; Col. 1924; employed in Uganda and Somaliland, 1899-1903 (African General Service Medal and two clasps); A.D.E.O.S. War Office, 1927; I.A.O.S. War Office, 1928; Deputy Director of Ordnance Services, with rank of Brig., 1929; retired pay, 1931; employed in Ministry of Supply, Sept. 1939-Apr. 1946. *Address:* Glebe Cottage, West Itchenor, Sussex. *Club:* Army and Navy. [*Died* 16 *June* 1955.

WORTHINGTON, Colonel Sir Edward Scott, K.C.V.O., *cr.* 1918 (M.V.O. 1911); Kt., *cr.* 1913; C.B.1918; C.M.G. 1915; C.I.E. 1921; late K.H.P.; late R.A.M.C.; M.D., C.M., Toronto; late Assistant Director-General War Office; late Physician to Duke of Connaught; *b.* 15 Oct. 1876; *m.* 1914, Winifred Jean (who obtained a divorce, 1931), *o. d.* of late John Wallace, Glassingall, Dunblane, and 9 Grosvenor Street, W.; one *s.* one *d.* *Educ.:* privately; Trinity University, Toronto. M.R.C.S. and L.R.C.P., London, 1897; entered R.A.M.C. 1900; Captain, 1903; Major, 1912; served South Africa, 1899-1902 (Queen's medal 4 clasps, King's medal 2 clasps); European War, 1914-18 (despatches twice, C.B., C.M.G., Bt. Col., Belgian Croix de Guerre, American Distinguished Service Medal, Officer of the Order of Leopold of Belgium, Officer of the Sacred Elephant of Siam); retired pay, 1926; Medical Officer on staff of Duke of Connaught for opening of Union of South Africa Parliament, and when Governor-General of Canada, 1911-14; K.G.St.J.; M.O. on the staff of Duke of Connaught for the opening of the Princes Council, India, 1920-21. *Address:* 16 Cadogan Square, S.W.1. *T.:* Sloane 5294. *Club:* Boodle's. [*Died* 5 *April* 1953.

WORTHINGTON, John Morton, C.V.O. 1954; J.P. Registrar, 1926-55, Cursitor, 1952, Lancashire Palatine Court of Chancery; Deputy of the Chancellor of the Duchy of Lancaster, 1952; *b.* 16 July 1883; *s.* of J. H.

WORLEY, Frederick Palliser. See page xxxi.

Worthington, Oak Lodge, Fulwood; *m.* 1915, Olive Dewhurst Blacklidge; one *d.* *Educ.:* Preston Grammar School. Solicitor, 1905; Barrister, 1921. J.P. Lancs, 1933. *Recreation:* Freemasonry. *Address:* 23 West Cliff, Preston, Lancs. *T.:* 4000. *Club:* Winckley (Preston). [*Died* 5 *June* 1956.

WORTHINGTON, Sir John Vigers, Kt., *cr.* 1935; *b.* 1872; 2nd *s.* of J. C. Worthington, Lowestoft; *m.* 1904, Agnes Janet, *d.* of Elisha John Edwards, Assam; one *s.* one *d.* *Educ.:* Woodbridge; Haileybury; London Hospital. Joined Dunlop Rubber Co., 1901; left as technical superintendent, 1921. M.P. (Nat. Lab.) Forest of Dean Division of Gloucester, 1931-35; Parliamentary Private Secretary to Prime Minister, 1931-35. Late of Moran. Tea Co. Ltd., St. Dunstan's Hill, E.C.3. *Address:* Queen Anne's Lodge, Lyme Regis, Dorset. [*Died* 16 *June* 1951.

WORTLEY, Hon. Mrs. V. S.; *see* Stuart Wortley.

WRAGG, Sir Herbert, Kt., *cr.* 1944; *o. surv. s.* of late Alderman J. D. Wragg, J.P. of Swadlincote, Derbyshire; *m.* 1st, Fanny Greenwood (*d.* 1918), *d.* of Thomas Sutcliffe, of Heptonstall Slack, Yorks; two *s.* one *d.* (and one *s.* decd.); 2nd, 1919, Marion Sutcliffe; one *d.* *Educ.:* Uppingham. Chm. and Managing Director of Thomas Wragg & Sons, Ltd., and James Woodward, Ltd., of Swadlincote; Past Pres. Ceramic Society; Past Pres. National Federation of Clay Industries; M.P. (C.) Belper, 1923-29 and 1931-45. Member of Unofficial Parliamentary Delegation to Poland, 1925; of Parliamentary Commercial Delegation to Brazil, 1927; Lord of the Manor of Swadlincote and Gresley; J.P. Derbyshire. *Recreation:* shooting. *Address:* 37 East Avenue, Bournemouth. *Clubs:* St. Stephen's; County (Derby); Bournemouth (Bournemouth). [*Died* 13 *Feb.* 1956.

WRAXALL, Sir Charles Frederick Lascelles, 7th Bt., *cr.* 1813; *b.* 28 Sept. 1896; *o. s.* of 6th Bt. and Honorine Herminia, *d.* of late John Lanzon, of Alexandria; *S.* father, 1902; *m.* 1921, Marceline, *d.* of O. Cauro, of Cauro, Corsica; one *s.* one *d.* *Heir:* *s.* Morville William Wraxall, *b.* 11 June 1922. [*Died* 7 *July* 1951.

WREN, Maj.-Gen. John, C.B. 1955; C.B.E. 1953; F.D.S.; retired; late Royal Army Dental Corps; *b.* 4 June 1896. Qualified as B.D.S. Served in Royal Air Force. Entered Army Dental Corps; Lieutenant, 1918; Substantive Lieutenant 1921; Captain 1922; Major 1930; Colonel 1947; Major-General 1951. Employed under the Air Ministry, Nov. 1918-July 1925. Formerly Deputy Director of Dental Services, Eastern Command (United Kingdom); formerly Hon. Dental Surgeon to the Queen; Director, Army Dental Service, 1951-55; retired 1955. *Address:* c/o Department of the Adjutant-General to the Forces, War Office, S.W.1. [*Died* 23 *Feb.* 1958.

WRENCH, Lady, C.B.E. 1918; **Hylda Henrietta;** *widow* of Sir Frederick des Voeux, 7th Bart.; *o. surv. d.* of late Sir Victor Brooke, 3rd Bart., Colebrooke, Co. Fermanagh, Northern Ireland; *m.* 2nd, 1937, *cousin,* Sir Evelyn Wrench, C.M.G.; one *d.* by 1st *m.* *Educ.:* abroad. Was born in France at Pau and lived there with her mother till she was married in 1899; Chairman of Overseas League's Soldiers and Sailors Fund, 1914-18; Honorary Controller of the Overseas League, 1918-40. *Address:* The Mill House, Marlow, Bucks. [*Died* 7 *Oct.* 1955.

WRIGHT, Albert Ernest, C.M.G. 1954; O.B.E. 1947; United Nations service since 1957; *b.* 30 June 1902; *s.* of Ernest Sykes Wright and Florence Wright; *m.* 1929, Iris May Rees; one *d.* *Educ.:* King Edward VII School, Sheffield; Queen's College, Oxford; University of Paris. Queen's College: Hastings Schol., 1921; Laming Fell., 1925. Imperial Customs Service (India), 1926; Commissioner Northern India, Central Excises and Salt, 1939; Govt. of Pakistan. Collector, Central Excise and Customs, East Pakistan, Chittagong, 1947; Collector of Customs, Karachi, 1950; Member Central Board of Revenue and Joint Secretary Ministry of Finance, Government of Pakistan, from 1952. Retired, 1957. *Publications:* miscellaneous articles, book reviews, broadcasts. *Recreations:* music, reading, amateur dramatics, travel. *Address:* c/o The Resident Representative, U.N. Technical Assistance Board, P.O. 1555, Teheran, Iran. *Clubs:* East India and Sports; Sind (Karachi). [*Died* 11 *Nov.* 1960.

WRIGHT, Sir Arthur C. C.; *see* Cory-Wright.

WRIGHT, Charles Henry Conrad, M.A.; Emeritus Professor of the French Language and Literature, Harvard University, Cambridge, Mass.; *b.* Chicago, Illinois, 16 Nov. 1869; *o. s.* of Charles H. Wright and Margaret B. Upham; *m.* 1914, Elizabeth Longfellow Woodman; three *s.* *Educ.:* Coll. of Honfleur; Harvard; Trinity College, Oxford. Boyhood spent almost entirely in Europe (England, France, Italy); school education in France with the exception of one year at Bethlehem, Pennsylvania; graduated from Harvard with degree of A.B. *summa cum laude,* 1891; B.A. at Oxford 1895, and M.A. 1899; F.A.A.S. *Publications:* A History of French Literature, 1912; A History of the Third French Republic, 1916; French Classicism, 1920; The Background of Modern French Literature, 1926; many contributions to journalism and reviews, signed and unsigned; editions of French texts for use in schools and colleges. *Address:* 9 Lowell Street, Cambridge, Mass., U.S.A. [*Died* 16 *May* 1957.

WRIGHT, Edward Fitzwalter; Chairman and Managing Director of The Butterley Co., Ltd., Derby; *b.* 1 June 1902; 3rd and *o. surv. s.* of late A. Leslie Wright, Butterley Hall, Derby, and Margaretta, *d.* of John Bridges Plumptre, Goodnestone Park, Kent; *m.* Jane Fairrie Wilson McGuffie, *d.* of late T. C. McGuffie, Abbotswood, St. George's Hill; one *s.* three *d.* *Educ.:* Winchester; Christ Church, Oxford. J.P. Derbyshire; High Sheriff County Derbyshire, 1942. *Address:* Morley Manor, Derbyshire. *T.:* Horsley 247. *Clubs:* Travellers', White's. [*Died* 27 *March* 1957.

WRIGHT, Frank Lloyd; Architect; *b.* 8 June 1869; *s.* of W. R. Cary and A. L. Jones; *m.* 1st, Catherine Lee; four *s.* two *d.*; 2nd, Miriam Noel; 3rd, Olga Lazovich; one *d.* *Educ.:* University of Wisconsin. Practised at Chicago, 1893; Architect of buildings in Japan, Europe, etc. M.A., Wesleyan Univ., 1939; Hon. Dr. of Fine Arts, Princeton, 1947. Hon. Member R.I.B.A., 1941 (awarded Gold Medal for 1941 by King George VI), and similarly honoured in several countries; Gold Medal for 1949, Amer. Institute of Architects; Gold Medal of City of Florence, 1951; Star of Solidarity, Italy, 1951; Hon. Degree, Univ. of Venice, 1951. Founder cultural experiment in the arts, non-profit organization, entitled the Frank Lloyd Wright Foundation at Taliesin, Wisconsin (summer), and Arizona (winter) (*circa* 40 apprentices). Editor of Taliesin Fellowship Magazine and Taliesin Square Papers. *Publications:* An Interpretation of Japanese Prints, 1912; In the Cause of Architecture (essays), 1909-23; Experimenting with Human Lives, 1923; Ausgeführte Bauten und Entwürfe, 1909, Sonderheit, 1910, Wendungen, 1925 (last three pub. in Europe); Modern Architecture (Kahn lectures at Princeton), 1931; The Nature of Materials, 1932; An Autobiography—Frank Lloyd Wright, 1932, later revised, expanded and brought up to date, 1943; The Disappearing City, 1932; (with Baker Brownell) Architecture and Modern Life; Frank Lloyd Wright on Architecture, 1894-1940 (ed.

F. Gutheim); In the Nature of Materials (ed. H. R. Hitchcock), 1941; When Democracy Builds, 1946; Genius and the Mobocracy, 1949; The Future of Architecture, 1955. *Address:* Taliesin, Spring Green, Wis., U.S.A.; Taliesin West, Paradise Valley, Phœnix, Ariz., U.S.A. [*Died* 9 *April* 1959.

WRIGHT, George Maurice, A.C.A.; Director (formerly Chairman and a Managing Director) of Debenhams Ltd., 91 Wimpole St., W.1; Chairman: Debenham and Freebody Ltd.; Harvey Nichols and Co. Ltd.; Kennards Ltd.; Marshall and Snelgrove Ltd.; Swan and Edgar Ltd., and other companies; Director of Woollands Brothers Ltd., and other companies. *Address:* Debenhams Ltd., 91 Wimpole Street, W.1. [*Died* 18 *Oct.* 1956.

WRIGHT, Right Rev. George William; *b.* 17 Dec. 1873; *s.* of G. W. E. Wright, Barnsley, Yks.; *m.* 1910, Anna May, *d.* of Archdeacon Binns, Mombasa, Kenya; three *s.* two *d.* (and two *s.* one *d.* decd.). *Educ.:* Barnsley Grammar School. Civil Servant, 1887-1902; Church Missionary College, Islington, 1902-06; Curate of Christ Church, Derby, 1906; Missionary C.M.S., Mombasa; English Chaplaincy, Mombasa Cathedral; Principal, Buxton High School, Mombasa; Domestic Chaplain, Bishop of Mombasa; Evangelistic Missionary, Digo, Kabare, Muitira, 1906-21; Vicar of Boulton, 1921-23; Bishop of Sierra Leone, 1923-36; Bishop in North Africa, 1936-43; Rector of Templecombe, 1942-51. Assistant Bishop of Bath and Wells. *Address:* 154B Upper Grosvenor Road, Tunbridge Wells, Kent. [*Died* 11 *Aug.* 1956.

WRIGHT, Henry Robert, Ph.D.; Chairman and Managing Director of Siemens Brothers & Co. Ltd. since 1946; *b.* 8 Sept. 1877; *s.* of late Henry Samuel Wright; *m.* 1907, Louise Margaret Leuchs; no *c.* *Educ.:* Polytechnic, Regent Street, London; Technical High Schools, Munich and Karlsruhe; Munich University. Siemens Works: Vienna, 1902; Stafford, Experimental Test House, followed by taking charge of Test House, 1904; Woolwich, 1907. General Manager, Siemens Brothers & Co., Ltd., 1925, Managing Director, 1926; Director: six Siemens Bros. Subsidiaries; The Siemens and General Electric Railway Signal Co. Ltd. Inventions include: train lighting system based on armature reaction, 1904; electro-hydraulic system of ship-steering, 1906; forerunner of predictor, 1916. Initiated prototype of "Hais" Cable through which 172 million gallons of petrol conveyed across Channel for European invasion (Operation Pluto). *Publication:* photometry of the diffuse reflection of light on matt surfaces, Philosophical Magazine, 1900. *Recreation:* in earlier days mountaineering. *Address:* Forest Lodge, Keston, Kent. *T.:* Farnborough (Kent) 422. *Club:* Junior Carlton. [*Died* 13 *Jan.* 1951.

WRIGHT, Sir Johnstone, Kt., *cr.* 1943; M.I.C.E., M.I.E.E.; a Director of British Insulated Callender's Cables Ltd.; *b.* 22 Jan. 1883; *s.* of late Johnstone Wright, Dunning, Perthshire; *m.* 1911, Edith Bertha Barrow; two *d.* *Educ.:* Perth Academy; Royal Technical College, Glasgow. North East Coast Power Companies; Constructional and Mechanical Engineer and Power Stations Operation Engineer, 1906-19; Deputy City Electrical Engineer, Bradford, 1919-22; Chief Electrical Engineer, and General Manager, Belfast Corporation Electricity Undertaking, 1922-27; Deputy Chief Engineer, Central Electricity Board, 1927-33; Chief Engineer, 1933-44; General Manager, 1944-47; Chairman, 1947-48; retired 1948. President, I.E.E., 1939-40; Member of Fuel Research Board, 1944-47. *Recreation:* golf. *Address:* Nurscombe Farm, Bramley, nr. Guildford, Surrey. *T.:* Bramley 2007. *Club:* Athenæum. [*Died* 19 *July* 1953.

WRIGHT, His Honour Judge Percy Malcolm, M.B.E. 1946; Q.C. 1954; Judge of County Courts, Circuit 44, since 1959 (Circuit 56, 1957-59); *b.* 11 February 1906; *s.* of late Rev. Percy Malcolm Wright, B.Sc., Calne, Wilts., and late Mrs. Clara Pattie Wright (*née* Jeffrey); *m.* 1943, Peggy Prince, B.E.M., Dymchurch, Kent; one *s.* one *d.* *Educ.:* Kingswood Sch., Bath; Trinity Hall, Cambridge. Holt Schol. (joint) Lee Prizeman, Gray's Inn; Squire Law Schol., B.A., LL.B., M.A., Cambridge. Called to Bar, 1929; joined Western Circuit and Devon Sessions, 1930; Recorder of Devizes, 1954-57; Member General Council of the Bar, 1946-1947, 1949-53 and 1955-57; Hon. Sec., Devon Sessions Bar Mess, 1946-53; one of Administrative Governors, Kingswood School, 1937-48; Churchwarden of St. Bride's, Fleet Street, since 1954. Served War, 1940-45, in R.A.F.V.R.; Squadron Leader, 1943. *Recreations:* music, cine-photography, shooting. *Address:* 114 Downlands Road, Purley, Surrey. *T.:* Uplands 7287. *Club:* Junior Carlton. [*Died* 13 *Aug.* 1959.

WRIGHT, Professor Samson, M.D., F.R.C.P.; John Astor Professor of Physiology in the University of London at Middlesex Hospital Medical School since 1930. *Educ.:* Middlesex Hospital Medical School. M.R.C.S. Eng. 1920; M.B., B.S. (Hons., Gold Medal) 1922; M.D. (Lond.) 1925; F.R.C.P. 1933. Late Lecturer in Physiology, King's College, London; sometime Examiner in Physiology, R.C.S. of England and of Edinburgh, University of London and other univs.; Oliver-Sharpey Lecturer, Royal College of Physicians; Physiological Editor, British Abstracts, 1938-49. *Publications:* Applied Physiology (9th Edn.), 1952; contrib. on physiological subjects to medical scientific journals. *Address:* 37 Gresham Gardens, N.W.11; Middlesex Hospital Medical School, Mortimer Street, W.1. [*Died* 11 *March* 1956.

WRIGHT, Brig.-Gen. Wallace Duffield, V.C. 1903; C.B. 1926; C.M.G. 1916; D.S.O. 1918; H.M.'s Body Guard of the Hon. Corps of Gentlemen-at-Arms, 1932-50; *m.* 1919, Flora Macdonald Bewick, Georgia, U.S.A.; one *d.* Entered The Queen's Royal Regt., 1896; Capt. 1903; Major, 1915; Bt. Lt.-Col. 1916; Col. 1919; served N.-W. Frontier, India, with Malakand Field Force and Tirah Expeditionary Force, 1897-98 (wounded, medal with two clasps); served with West African Frontier Force in Northern Nigeria under Colonial Office, 1901-4 (wounded, medal with two clasps); European War (Cameroons), 1914-15; France, 1915-19 (despatches, C.M.G., D.S.O., Officer Legion of Honour); Colonel General Staff, Army of Occupation on the Rhine, 1923-26; Brigade Commander 8th Infantry Brigade, Plymouth, 1925-27; retired pay, 1927; Home Guard from 1940. M.P. (C.) for the Tavistock Division of Devonshire, 1928-31. D.L. Surrey, 1947. *Address:* Westways Farm, Chobham, Surrey. *T.:* Chobham 212. *Clubs:* Army and Navy, Royal Automobile. [*Died* 25 *March* 1953.

WRIGHT, Rev. Canon William Joseph, M.B.E.; M.A. (Oxon); retired September 1953; *b.* 4 Aug. 1881; *s.* of G. D. Wright; *m.* 1936, Elizabeth Clidsdale, *d.* of Berkeley Morris Carter; one *s.* one *d.* *Educ.:* Dorchester Grammar School; St. Edmund Hall and Wycliffe Hall, Oxford. B.A. 1908; M.A. 1911; Curate of All Saints, South Lambeth, 1909-16; Vicar of Christ Church, High Wycombe, 1916-20; Priest in charge of All Saints Cathedral, Nairobi, 1920-29; Canon, 1926-29; Dean of Nairobi, 1929-39; Rector of Lambourne with Abridge, 1939-42; Vicar of Nayland and Wissington, Suffolk, 1942-47; Assistant priest St. Peter and St. Paul, St. Leonards on Sea, 1952-53; Priest-in-charge, St. Peter's, North Lowestoft, May-Sept. 1953. *Recreations:* playing, preaching, writing. *Address:* Epworth, Hadleigh Rd., Frinton, Essex. *Clubs:* East India and Sports; Nairobi (Nairobi). [*Died* 29 *March* 1954.

WRIGHT, William Hammond. See page xxxi.

WRIGHT, Sir William Owen, Kt., *cr.* 1934; O.B.E.; V.D.; Chevalier of Order of The Crown of Belgium; *b.* 11 Aug. 1882; *s.* of General Sir William Purvis Wright, K.C.B., The Royal Marines, and Louisa Sparkes Owen; *m.* 1912, Barbara Dorothea Mabel Mullaly (Kaisar-i-Hind Gold Medal, 1935). *Educ.:* St. Paul's School. Partner Parry and Company, Madras, 1919; Director, 1928-38; formerly Chairman Madras Telephone Company Ltd.; President or Vice-President Madras Local Board of the Imperial Bank; Trustee Madras Port Trust; Chairman Madras Chamber of Commerce, 1935; Member Madras Legislative Council representing General European Constituency; Chairman Madras Branch European Association, 1931-33; Member All India Council European Association; Government Nominee at Simla Conference Representatives Sugar Industry, 1933; Associated Chambers of Commerce India Nominee as unofficial adviser to Indian Delegation at the Indo-Japanese Trade Negotiations, Simla, 1933. Steward Madras Race Club. Ministry of Supply R.O.F. (F), 1942-44. *Recreations:* formerly: golf, racing. *Address:* 18 Archery Square, Walmer, Deal. *Club:* Deal and Walmer Union. [*Died* 8 *May* 1951.

WRIGHTSON, Captain Charles Archibald Wise, C.B.E. 1919, late Royal Navy; *b.* 17 July 1874; 2nd *s.* of late Sir Thomas Wrightson, 1st Bart.; unmarried. *Educ.:* Stoke House, Slough; H.M.S. Britannia, Dartmouth. Joined H.M.S. Rodney as Naval Cadet, 1891; Commander, 1909; Capt. 1917; Commanded H.M.S. Dunedin, 1st Light Cruiser Squadron, Mar. 1920-Mar. 1921; during European War commanded H.M.S. Recruit and H.M.S. Ebro, 10th Cruiser Squadron; retired list, 1922. *Recreations:* tennis, shooting, fishing. *Address:* St. Edward's Chantry, Shaftesbury, Dorset. *T.:* 2059. *Club:* Army and Navy. [*Died* 7 *Feb.* 1953.

WRIXON-BECHER, Henry; *see* Becher, H. W.

WROBLEWSKI, Wladyslaw; Dr. Juris; Professor at the High School of Political Science, Warsaw, 1937; *b.* Cracow, Poland, 1875; *s.* of Wincenty and Walerja Bossowska Wroblewski; *m.* Zofja Obtulowicz, Lwow, Poland; two *s.* one *d.* *Educ.:* University of Cracow. Professor of Constitutional Law at the University of Cracow, 1909-18; General Director of the Agricultural Syndicate, Cracow; Under-Secretary of State of the Presidency of Ministerial Council, 1918; Ministry of Foreign Affairs, Warsaw, 1919; President of the Polish Delegation for the taking over of former Prussian Provinces of Poland, 1919; Deputy Chairman Polish Peace Delegation, Minsk, 1920; Polish Minister to the Court of St. James, 1921-22; Polish Minister to United States, 1922-25; President of the Bank of Poland, 1929-36. *Publications:* several in Polish on Constitutional Law, and numerous contributions to the Polish Newspaper Press. *Recreations:* riding, walking. *Address:* c/o Bank of Poland, Warsaw, Poland. [*Died* 1952.

WRONG, Humphry Hume, M.A., B.Litt.; Under-Secretary of State for External Affairs, Ottawa, Canada, since 1953; *b.* Toronto, 10 Sept. 1894; *s.* of late Prof. G. M. Wrong, M.A.; *m.* 1922, Joyce Hutton; one *s.* one *d.* *Educ.:* Upper Canada Coll., Toronto; Ridley College, St. Catharine's, Ont.; Univ. of Toronto; Balliol College, Oxford. European War, 1915-18, with 4 Bn. Oxf. & Bucks, Lieut. Inf., and R.F.C.; Asst. Professor of History, Univ. of Toronto, 1921-27; 1st Sec. Canadian Legation, Washington, 1927; Counsellor, 1930; Permanent Delegate of Canada to League of Nations, 1937; Special Economic Adviser, Canada Ho., London, 1939; Minister Counsellor, Canadian Legation, Washington, 1941; Asst. Under Sec. of State for External Affairs, Ottawa, 1942; Associate Under Sec. of State for External Affairs, 1944; Canadian Ambassador to the United States, 1946-53. *Publications:* The Government of the West Indies, 1922; Sir Alexander Mackenzie, Explorer and Fur Trader, 1927. *Address:* Department of External Affairs, Ottawa, Canada. [*Died* 24 *Jan.* 1954.

WROTTESLEY, Captain Francis Robert, D.S.O.; R.N. (retired); *b.* 1877; *e. s.* of late Rev. F. J. Wrottesley Vicar of Denstone, Staffs; *m.* Leila, *d.* of late General Sir Charles William Dunbar Staveley, G.C.B. H.M.S. Britannia, 1891; Midshipman, 1893; Sub-Lieutenant, 1897; Lieutenant, 1899; served in China as Flag-Lieutenant, H.M.S. Barfleur, 1900; present at taking of Taku Forts (medal, 2 clasps, despatches); Order of St. Anne of Russia, 1908; Commander, 1909; served European War, North Sea, 1914-15, Egypt, 1916, Mesopotamia, 1916-17 (despatches three times, D.S.O.); invalided 1919; Younger Brother Trinity House, 1912. *Recreations:* shooting and fishing. *Address:* Wick Cottage, Downton, Salisbury, Wilts. [*Died* 13 *Nov.* 1954.

WURTZBURG, Charles Edward, M.C. 1918; Managing Director of The Glen Line since 1937; Chairman of McGregor, Gow & Holland Ltd. since 1937; President of Chamber of Shipping of U.K., 1951-52; *b.* 5 June 1891; *s.* of E. A. Wurtzburg, Barrister-at-Law, and Elizabeth Cuffe; *m.* 1924, Rhoda Eleanor Blake; two *s.* two *d.* *Educ.:* Aldenham School; Emmanuel College, Cambridge. Joined Alfred Holt & Co., 1913; served European War, 1914-18, Liverpool Rifles (T.F.), Major; rejoined Alfred Holt & Co., 1919; transferred to Mansfield & Co. Ltd., Singapore, 1920. Chairman: Mansfield & Co. Ltd.; Straits Steamship Co. Ltd. Mission to S. Africa with Sir Robert Tolerton, 1942; chief rep. Ministry of War Transport, S. & E. Africa, Autumn 1942-44. Governor of Pangbourne Nautical College, 1945-; Pres. Assoc. of British Malaya, 1946-48; Dep. Chm. King George's Fund for Sailors, 1949-. *Address:* 78 Marsham Court, Marsham Street, S.W.1; (business) 16 St. Helen's Place, E.C.3. *T.:* London Wall 2333. *Club:* City of London. [*Died* 30 *April* 1952.

WYATT, Brigadier Arthur Geoffrey, C.B.E. 1943; U.S. Legion of Merit (Officer) 1944; late Royal Engineers; *b.* 2 Oct. 1900; *s.* of Geoffrey Allington Wyatt and Rose Janet Henegan; *m.* 1940, Joan Lindsay Eddis; two *s.* *Educ.:* Sherborne School; R.M.A., Woolwich. 2nd Lt. R.E. 1920; Capt. 1931; Major, 1938; Temp. Lt.-Col. 1941; Temp. Col. 1942; Acting Brig. 1944; Lt.-Col. 1946; Col. 1948. Service in India, 1924-38. Campaigns: N.W.F.P. 1934 (Mohmand) (despatches); France, 1939-40 (despatches); Tunis, 1942-43; Sicily, 1943; Italy, 1943-44; S.E.A.C., 1944-45; retired, 1950. Now Registrar Faraday House Electrical Engineering College, W.C.1. *Recreations:* fishing, travel. *Address:* Windy How, Ledborough Lane, Beaconsfield, Bucks. [*Died* 26 *July* 1960.

WYATT, Colonel Ernest Robert Caldwell, C.B.E. 1923; D.S.O. 1917; *b.* 27 April 1880; *e. s.* of late Rev. J. L. Wyatt, *m.* 1908, Barbara Elizabeth, *y. d.* of Rev. A. W. Booker, late Rector of Sutton Veney, near Warminster; two *d.* *Educ.:* Cheltenham; Sandhurst. Passed Staff College; served Somaliland, 1902-04; European War, 1914-17 (D.S.O., Bt. Lt.-Col., despatches thrice); Malabar operations, 1921-22 (despatches, C.B.E.); Waziristan operations, 1923-24 (despatches); A.A. and Q.M.G. Lahore District, 1928-32; retired, 1932. *Address:* The Old Court House, Woodbridge, Suffolk. [*Died* 31 *March* 1957.

WYATT, Horace Matthew, B.A.; Member (Gold Medallist, 1932) of the Institute of Transport; *b.* 1876; *y. s.* of late Robert Wyatt, M.A., Barrister-at-law, of Acton Hill, nr. Stafford; *m.* 1909, Annie Mary (*d.* 1952), *d.* of David Morgan of Cardiff; one

WURTH, Wallace Charles, C.M.G. See page xxxi.

d. *Educ.:* Malvern Coll.; St. Catharine's College, Cambridge (Mathematical Scholar). Studied engineering at Cambridge. Mathematical Tripos, 1897; head of Engineering Department, Seafield Park College, 1901-05; organised deputation to Chancellor of Exchequer to obtain concessions in taxation of industrial motor vehicles, 1909; acted for Lords and Commons Committee (1911) as organiser of Country Tour of Representatives of Dominion Parliaments, and in connection with formation of Empire Parliamentary Association; Organising Hon. Secretary of the Imperial Motor Transport Conferences, 1913 and 1920; Organiser of the World Motor Transport Congress, London, 1927, and Joint Organiser of the Similar Congress in Rome, 1928. *Publications:* The Motor Bus and the Ratepayer, 1912; (joint author) Motor Traction for Business Purposes, 1913; Motor Transport and the Empire, 1913; Motor Transports in War, 1914; Malice in Kulturland, 1915; The Motor Cyclist's A.B.C., 1916; The Motor Industry, 1917; Jersey in Jail, 1945; numerous articles. *Address:* 146 New Bond Street, W.1; 2 Roland Mansions, Old Brompton Road, S.W.7. *Club:* Royal Automobile. [*Died* 2 *Jan.* 1954.

WYATT, James Montagu; Consulting Obstetric Physician to St. Thomas's Hospital; Consulting Surgeon to Grosvenor Hospital for Women; Member of the S.W. Metropolitan Regional Board; *b.* 1883; *s.* of Thomas Henry Wyatt, M.V.O., and Julia Wyatt. *Educ.:* Merchant Taylors' School; St. Thomas's Hospital. M.B., B.S. London; F.R.C.S. England; F.R.C.O.G.; late Examiner to Universities of London, Oxford, Cambridge, and Manchester. *Publications:* contrib. to Modern Trends in Obstetrics and Gynæcology (Puerperal Infection); Toxaemias of Pregnancy; Testosterone Propionate in Inoperable Carcinoma of the Uterus. *Address:* Upton Grey, Basingstoke, Hants. *T.:* Upton Grey 46. [*Died* 31 *July* 1953.

WYATT, Brig.-Gen. Louis John, D.S.O. 1916; *b.* 14 Sept. 1874; *y. s.* of J. Matthew G. Wyatt, Kingston Hill; *m.* Gipsy, *d.* of W. Sloane, Moore, Cheshire; two *d.* *Educ.:* King's College, London. Joined, Prince of Wales' (N. Stafford) Regt., 1895; served Dongola Expedition, 1896 (medals); S. Africa, 1900-02 (despatches, wounded, medals); European War, 1914-18 (despatches, wounded, D.S.O., Chevalier Légion d'Honneur, Grand Officier Ordre di Aviz); Lt.-Col. 1/4 Yorks and Lancs Regt., 1915-17; temp. Brig.-General, 1918; G.O.C. British troops in France and Flanders, 1920; O.C. 2nd North Staffordshire Regt., 1921-24; temp. Col. Commandant 18th Infantry Brigade, 1922; Commanded 164th (North Lancashire) Infantry Brigade, 1924-28; retired as Hon. Brig.-Gen., 1928. Colonel, N. Staffordshire Regt. (The Prince of Wales's) 1936-45. D.L. Westmorland, 1946; High Sheriff of Westmorland, 1948. *Address:* Kirkby Lonsdale, Westmorland. *T.:* Kirkby Lonsdale 252. *Club:* United Service. [*Died* 28 *April* 1955.

WYATT, Travers Carey, O.B.E., A.M.I.C.E., M.A.; University Lecturer in Faculty of Engineering, Cambridge University, 1926; Fellow, Christ's Coll., Camb., 1921, Bursar, 1937, Vice-Master, 1950-52. Chartered Engineer; *b.* 1887; *s.* of Alfred John Wyatt, M.A.; *m.* 1st, Marjorie Eldridge; one *s.*; 2nd, Betty, *y. d.* of Arthur Kingham, J.P., Watford; two *s.* *Educ.:* Leys; Christ's College, Cambridge (Scholar). Proctor, 1927-30; P.Prov.G.Reg., Cambridgeshire; a governor of Leys School, Cambridge, 1936. *Recreations:* fishing, sailing. *Address:* Fen House, Chaucer Road, Cambridge. *T.:* Cambridge 4092. *Club:* C.U. Cruising (Cambridge). [*Died* 11 *Dec.* 1954.

WYATT-SMITH, Stanley; *see* Smith.

WYKES-SNEYD, Vice-Adm. Ralph Stuart, D.S.O. 1916; R.N.; *b.* 1882; *e. s.* of late George Edward Sneyd; *m.* 1920, Harriet Rose Mary, *e. d.* of Edward Sydenham Fursdon; one *s.* one *d.* Served European War, 1914-18 (despatches, D.S.O., promoted, Croix de Guerre, Legion of Honour, Order of Leopold of Belgium); retired list, 1929. *Address:* Moorland House, St. Cleer, Liskeard, Cornwall. *T.:* Liskeard 2197. [*Died* 19 *Dec.* 1951.

WYLDE, Rt. Rev. Arnold Lomas, C.B.E. 1957; M.A. Oxford; Bishop of Bathurst (N.S.W.), since 1937; *b.* 31 March 1880; *s.* of James Lomas Wylde, woollen manufacturer, Leeds, and Sarah Jane Taylor, Leverington, Cambs.; unmarried. *Educ.:* Wakefield Grammar School; Univ. Coll., Oxford (IIIrd Class Mod., IIIrd Class History). Oxford House, 1903-06; Cuddesdon College, 1906; Deacon, 1906; Priest, 1907; Assistant Curate S. Simon Zelotes, Bethnal Green, 1906-12; Vicar, 1912-21; Priest Brother in the Brotherhood of the Good Shepherd and Curate of Gilgandra, 1921-23; Principal of the Brotherhood of the Good Shepherd, 1923-1928; Rector of Gilgandra, 1923-34; Bishop Coadjutor of Bathurst, N.S.W., 1927-36; Bishop Administrator of Bathurst, 1936-1937. *Address:* Bishopscourt, Bathurst, N.S.W., Australia. *T.:* Bathurst 3501. [*Died* 6 *June* 1958.

WYLIE, Sir Francis James, Kt., *cr.* 1929; M.A.; *b.* 1865; *s.* of late Richard Northcote Wylie, S. Petersburg; *m.* 1904, Kathleen, *d.* of late Edmond Kelly, Paris and New York; three *s.* two *d.* (and one *s.* decd.). *Educ.:* S. Edward's School, Oxford; Glasgow University; Balliol College, Oxford. 1st class Classical Mods., 1886, 1st class Lit. Hum., 1888; Assistant Master S. Edward's School, 1888; Tutoring 1889-1891; Lecturer, Fellow, and Tutor Brasenose College, Oxford, 1891-1903, Hon. Fellow, 1931; Junior Proctor, 1903-04; Oxford Sec. to Rhodes Trustees, 1903-July 1931; retired, 1931; LL.D. Union College, Schenectady; LL.D. Swarthmore; L.H.D. Bowdoin; F.R.Emp. Soc. *Address:* Wootton Ridge, Boar's Hill, Oxford. *T.:* Oxford 85173. [*Died* 29 *Oct.* 1952.

WYLIE, Miss I. A. R.; author. *Educ.:* Brussels; Cheltenham Ladies' Coll.; Germany. *Publications:* The Rajah's People, 1910; My German Year, 1910; Rambles in the Black Forest, 1911; In Different Keys, 1911; Dividing Waters, 1911; The Daughter of Brahma, 1912; The Red Mirage, 1913; The Paupers of Portman Square, 1913; Eight Years in Germany, 1914; Happy Endings, 1915; The Temple of Dawn, 1915; Arm-chair Stories, 1916; Tristram Sahib, 1916; The Shining Heights, 1917; The Duchess in Pursuit, 1918; All Sorts, 1919; Towards Morning; Brodie and the Deep Sea, 1920; The Dark House, 1922; Ancient Fires, 1924; Black Harvest, 1925; The Silver Virgin, 1929; Some Other Beauty, 1930; The Things We Do, 1932; To the Vanquished, 1934; Prelude to Richard, 1934; Furious Young Man, 1935; The Young in Heart, 1939; Strangers are Coming, 1943; Keeper of the Flame, 1944; Storm in April, 1945; Ho! The Fair Wind, 1946; Where No Birds Sing, 1948; Candles for Therese, 1952; The Undefeated, 1957; Home are the Hunted, 1959. *Recreations:* riding, motoring, and travelling. *Address:* c/o A. M. Heath & Co., 35 Dover St., W.1.; Trevenna Farm, Orchard Road, Skillman, N.Y., U.S.A. [*Died* 4 *Nov.* 1959.

WYLIE, Lieut.-Colonel Macleod, C.I.E. 1936; Indian Army, retired; *b.* 26 Sept. 1881; *s.* of Major-General H. Wylie, C.S.I.; *m.* 1912, Hilda Russell, *d.* of Rev. Donald Miller, D.D.; one *s.* one *d.* *Educ.:* Haileybury; Royal Military College, Sandhurst. Joined 4th P.W.O. Gurkha Rifles, 1902; 1st K.G.O. Gurkha Rifles, 1923; commanded 2nd Battn. 1st K.G.O. Gurkha Rifles, 1926-30; Recruiting Officer for Gurkhas, 1930-34; served European War, 1914, France and Flanders; N.W. Frontier of India, 1919-20. *Address:* Kingswell, St.

John's Road, Farnham, Surrey. *T.:* Farnham 5041. [*Died* 31 *Aug.* 1952.

WYNCH, Lionel Maling, C.I.E. 1906; C.B.E. 1918; *b.* 21 July 1864; *s.* of William Maling Wynch; *m.* 1918, Violet (*d.* 1950), *d.* of late Sir A. T. Arundel, K.C.S.I., and *widow* of Col. Evelyn Norie. *Educ.:* Bedford Grammar School; Balliol College, Oxford. Entered I.C.S., 1885, Madras Presidency; Dep. Director Land Records, 1892-94; Secretary to the Board of Revenue, 1894-96; Collector and Magistrate, 1897-1901; Private Secretary to H.E. the Governor of Madras, 1901-06; Secretary to the Government of Madras Revenue Department; retired, 1914; European War, Deputy Comr. Br. Red Cross, France (despatches twice, K.G.St.J.) *Address:* Gannicox, London Road, Sunningdale, Ascot, Berks. *T.:* 997. *Clubs:* East India and Sports, English-Speaking Union. [*Died* 20 *Dec.* 1955.

WYNN, Rt. Rev. Harold Edward, D.D., M.A.; Bishop of Ely since 1941; Fellow of Pembroke College, Cambridge, since 1921; Hon. Fellow of Trinity Hall, Cambridge, since 1950; Hon. Chaplain to the Forces, 3rd Class; Visitor of Peterhouse, Jesus College and St. John's College, Cambridge; *b.* 15 Jan. 1889; *y. s.* of John Wynn, Buckhurst Hill, Essex; unmarried. *Educ.:* Mercers' School, London; Trinity Hall, Cambridge; Ely Theological Coll. Hon. S.T.D., Berkeley School of Divinity, U.S.A. Chaplain and Lecturer of Jesus College, Cambridge, 1912-14; Chaplain to the Forces, 1914-19, France, Italy, Army of Rhine (despatches, Croce di Guerra); Vice-Principal of Westcott House, Cambridge, 1919-21; Dean of Pembroke College, Cambridge, 1921-36; Examining Chaplain to the Bishop of Sheffield, 1914-38; Select Preacher, Cambridge University, 1920, 1926, 1935, 1942, 1949; Lady Margaret's Preacher, Cambridge, 1947; Select Preacher, Oxford University, 1935-36-37, 1948-49; Junior Proctor, 1927; Tutor of Pembroke College, 1936-41; Member of the Archbishops' Commission on Training for the Ministry, 1938; Member of the Archbishop's Commission on Divine Healing, 1953; Member of the Historical Manuscripts Commission, 1953. *Address:* Bishop's House, Ely. *T.:* Ely 2749. *Clubs:* Athenæum, Royal Societies. [*Died* 12 *Aug.* 1956.

WYNN, Col. Sir Robert W. H. W.; *see* Williams-Wynn.

WYNN, Rev. Walter; *b.* Cheltenham, 16 Dec. 1865; *m.* Melissa Mortimer, Sandy Lane, Bradford, Yorks; one *d.* *Educ.:* Nottingham University College. Whiteley's, Westbourne Grove, W., from 16 to 19; Nottingham Baptist College, 19 to 23; Minister since then, at Sandy Lane, Bradford, Yorks; Earby, Yorks; Chesham United Free Church, 1906-1933; Editor of The British Man and Woman, 1920; visited America and Canada on preaching and lecturing tour in 1913, and South Africa in 1921. *Publications:* The Secrets of Success in Life; The Bible and the War; Revelation in the Light of the War and Modern Events; Rupert Lives; The Bible and the After-Life; The Gladstone Spirit-photograph; In Defence; What *Will* Come to Pass; The Last and Next War; How I Cured Myself by Fasting; How to be Happy tho' Living; The Sphinx Unveiled; Man and the Universe; Jesus, the Spiritual Astronomer; Christ and a Mad World; Health for Everybody; What Has and What Will Come to Pass; Love's Closed Doors; Alone; The Atomic Bomb Defeated, etc. *Recreations:* reading, walking. *Address:* Darak, Rushmere Lane, Orchard Leigh, Chesham, Bucks. *T.A.:* Wynn, Chesham. [*Died* 5 *May* 1951.

WYNN, William Henry, M.D., B.Sc. (Lond.); M.Sc. (Birm.); F.R.C.P.; Emeritus Professor of Medicine, University of Birmingham, and Director of Graduate Medical Studies; Consulting Physician, Birmingham United Hospital; ex-Censor, Fitzpatrick lecturer, (1948-49), Royal College of Physicians; Regional Adviser in Medicine, Hospital Emergency Service; Consulting Physician to Dudley Road Municipal Hospital, to Birmingham General Dispensary, Municipal Sanatorium, Birmingham, Sutton Coldfield Hospital, Smallwood Hosp., Redditch, Halesowen Hosps.; Midland Counties Institution, and Birmingham Med. Mission, Hereford and Tenbury Hosps.; formerly Examiner in medicine, London Univ., Conjoint Board; *b.* Birmingham, 2 Feb. 1878; *s.* of late H. J. Wynn; *m.* 1907, Florence (*d.* 1935), *d.* of G. B. Ashford; one *s.* two *d.* *Educ.:* King Edward's School, Aston; Birmingham University. Gold medal in Physiology, Inter. M.B. Lond., 1898; Constance Naden Gold Medal, 1897, and Heslop Gold Medal, 1899, Mason University College; House Physician, Queen's Hospital, Birmingham, 1901; Pathologist, General Hospital, 1903; Assistant Physician, 1904; Captain R.A.M.C. (T.), 1st Southern General Hospital; F.R.S.M. *Publications:* numerous contributions to medical press. *Recreations:* foreign travel, archæology, fruit farming. *Address:* 51 Calthorpe Road, Edgbaston, Birmingham; Redmarley, 32 Pritchatts Road, Edgbaston. *T.:* Edgbaston 2330, 0225. *Clubs:* Overseas; Union (Birmingham). [*Died* 11 *June* 1956.

WYNNE, Pamela; *see* Scott, Winifred Mary.

WYNNE-EYTON, A. J. F.; *see* Fairbairn-Wynne-Eyton.

WYNNE WILLSON, Preb. Archdall B.; *see* Willson.

WYNTER, Brig. Henry Walter, D.S.O. 1915; late R.A.; *b.* 14 Apr. 1882; *s.* of late Col. Walter Wynter. *Educ.:* Eton. Entered Army, 1900; Capt. 1912; Major, 1915; Bt. Lt.-Col. 1918; Lt.-Col. 1928; Col. 1929; served European War, 1914-18 (despatches six times, D.S.O., Bt. Lt.-Col.); Brig., R.A., Eastern Command, India, 1932-1936; retired pay, 1936. *Address:* Lloyds Bank, 6 Pall Mall, S.W.1. [*Died* 31 *July* 1959.

WYSE, Henry Taylor; former Lecturer in Art, Provincial Training College, Edinburgh; *b.* 6 Feb. 1870; *s.* of Henry Wyse, banker, Dundee; *m.* 1896, Isobel (*d.* 1938), *d.* of John Lothian, Mains, Dundee; one *s.* two *d.* *Educ.:* West End Academy, Dundee; School of Art, Glasgow; Académies Julian and Colarossi, Paris. Art Master, Coatbridge Technical School, Arbroath High School, George Watson's Ladies' College, Edinburgh, Merchiston Castle School, Edinburgh; is a landscape painter in oil, watercolour and pastel; has exhibited at numerous galleries in London, Edinburgh, and the provinces since 1908; Artist-Potter. *Publications:* Rudiments of Design; Modern Methods of Art Instruction; Embroidery and Stencilling; Fifty Japanese Stencils; Modern Type Display; Formal Writing and Lettering; Geometrical Patterns; Memory and Imaginative Drawing; Blackboard Drawing; Formal Writing; Stencilling; Embroidery Design; Simple Pottery; Art Printing Processes; Twelve Old Masters. *Recreations:* Orchestral Music and the Drama. *Address:* 1 Craigleith Grove, Blackhall, Edinburgh, 4. *T.:* 30557. [*Died* 24 *March* 1951.

Y

YAHUDA, Abraham Shalom Ezekiel, Ph.D. (Strassburg); *b.* Jerusalem, 18 June 1877; *y. s.* of Benjamin Ezekiel Yahuda; a British-born subject; *m.* 1921, Ethel Rachel Judes, Johannesburg. *Educ.:* Universities of Heidelberg and Strassburg. Professor of Biblical Exegesis and Semitic Philology at High School of Hebrew Learning, Berlin, 1905-14; Professor of Hebrew Literature and Language of the Jewish-Spanish period at Madrid University, 1915-22; Professor of Semitic Philology at the Centro de Estudios Históricos, Madrid, 1914-20; Corresponding Member of the Spanish Academy of History, Madrid, of the Academy of History and Art,

Toledo, and of the Society of Geography, Lisbon. *Publications:* Pre-Islamic History of the Arabs (in Hebrew), 1893-4; On Arabic Poetry of the Jews in Spain (Hebrew), 1895; Hebrew translations of Pre-Islamic Arabic Poetry, 1896 and 1903; several essays on Biblical subjects; Hapax Legomena im A.T., 1902; Prolegomena zu einer erstmaligen Herausgabe des Kitāb al-Hidāya, etc., 1904; Die Bibl. Exegese in Ihren Beziehungen zur Semitischen Philologie, 1906; Bagdadische Sprichwörter, 1906; Über die Unechtheit des Samaritanischen Josua, 1908; Al Hidāya ila Farā' id al-Qulūb by Bahya ibn Josef (the Arabic original text of Hobōth Hal-Lebabōth with an introduction), 1912; Jemenische Sprichwörter, 1911; Un Capítulo sobre la poesía Hebráica Religiosa de España, 1915; Contribución al Estudio del Judeo-Español, 1915; Die Sprache des Pentateuch in Ihren Beziehungen zum Ägyptischen, Bd. I., 1929; The Language of the Pentateuch in its Relations to Egyptian. 1933; The Accuracy of the Bible, 1934; Les murailles d'Jéricho et la vérité biblique sur la date de l'Exode, 1935; The Nazi Menace to Liberty of Thought, 1935; Don Isaac Abrabanel, homme d'État et érudit, 1937; The Symbolism and Worship of the Serpent, 1939; Sigmund Freud and his Moses (Hebrew); The Two Synagogues of Toledo (Hebrew); Les Récits Bibliques de Josèph et l'exode; Confirmiés à la Lumière des Monumens Égyptiens, 1940; The Kaiser and his Jewish Friends; Joseph's Rule in Egypt (Hebrew), 1941; On David Yellin's Life and Work; Saadia Gaon and his Arab Surrounding, 1942; When I was taught Rashi's Commentary (Memoirs, Hebrew). The Story of a Forgery and the Mesa Inscription, 1944; The Osiris Cult—in the Bible, 1944; The Name of Balaam's Homeland, 1945; Eber We-Arab, a Collection of Hebrew Studies, 1946; The Meaning of the Name Esther, 1946; Hebrew Words of Egyptian Origin, 1947; Medica and Anatomical Terms in the Pentateuch in the Light of Egyptian Medical Papyri, 1948; A Contribution to Quran and Hadith Interpretation, 1948. *Address:* 162 Bishop St., New Haven, Conn., U.S.A. [*Died* 13 *Aug.* 1951.

YAPP, Sir Frederick Charles, Kt., *cr.* 1942; *b.* 1880; *s.* of William Henry Yapp; *m.* 1905, Katie Vincent (*d.* 1950), *d.* of James Payne; one *s.* one *d.* Formerly a Director of Vickers Ltd. and Chairman of Vickers-Armstrongs Ltd. *Address:* Grange Cottage, George V Avenue, Worthing, Sussex. [*Died* 5 *Sept.* 1958.

YARROW, Eleanor, Lady; Eleanor Cecilia, *d.* of W. Goodwin Barnes, Foxley, Bishop's Stortford; *m.* 1921 (as his 2nd wife), Sir Alfred Yarrow, 1st Bt., F.R.S., LL.D. (*d.* 1932); no *c.* *Publications:* Sir Alfred Yarrow: his Life and Work, 1923; As the Water Flows, record of travels in a canoe. *Recreation:* music (piano). *Address:* 3 Upper Ely Place, Dublin, Eire; Journey's End, Co. Dublin. [*Died* 15 *March* 1953.

YARWORTH-JONES, Sir William, Kt., *cr.* 1919; *b.* 11 Jan. 1870; *s.* of late Wm. Morgan-Jones of Fairfield, Chepstow, Mon., and Elizabeth Pritchard, Coleford, Glos.; *m.* 1909, Francis Flora, *d.* of John Burdett, Melbourne; no *c.* *Educ.:* Monmouth Grammar School; St. John's Wood Art Schools; Kennington Modelling Schools. Articled to Signor Raggi, Sculptor, of Devonshire Street; went to America, and then took up commercial life at the age of twenty-three; retired from business, 1920. *Recreations:* shooting; in younger days amateur boxer, cricketer, and Rugby footballer. *Address:* Glencoe, Queen's Road, Kingston Hill. *T.:* Kingston 4603. *Club:* Oriental. [*Died* 4 *Jan.* 1953.

YATES, Col. Clarence Montague, C.B.E. 1919; M.V.O. 1915; M.C.; *b.* 1881; *s.* of R. P. Yates, J.P.; *m.* 1915, Joyce, *e. d.* of John Mares of Manor House, Basingstoke. Entered Royal Warwickshire Regt., 1899; Capt. The King's (Liverpool Regt.), 1910; Major, 1915; retired with rank of Col. in the Army, 1920; served S. African War, 1900-1 (Queen's medal with three clasps); European War, 1914-18 (despatches, M.V.O., M.C., Legion of Honour). *Address:* Longwater Lodge, Eversley Cross, Hants. *T.:* Eversley 3155. [*Died* 11 *Jan.* 1952.

YATES, Dornford; *see* Mercer, Maj. C. W.

YATES, Rev. Canon William R., M.A.; F.R.S.L.; Vicar of St. Mary, Leigh Woods, Clifton, Bristol, since 1923; *b.* Bury, Lancs, 1870; *s.* of Robert and Anne Yates; *m.*; one *s.* two *d.* *Educ.:* privately; University College, Durham; St. Stephen's House, Oxford; Burgh and Canterbury Missionary Colleges. Missionary in Trinidad, 1896; invalided home same year; Curate Padiham, 1897-9; Precentor Bermuda Cathedral, 1899-1900; Curate St. Peter's, Blackburn, 1901; All Saints, Newcastle-on-Tyne, 1902; St. Mary's, Newcastle-on-Tyne, and Evening Lecturer St. Thomas', Newcastle-on-Tyne, until 1908; Bishop's Commissary in Jerusalem, British Chaplain at Assouan, and Canon, 1908-14; Vicar of St. Saviour's, Weston-super-Mare, 1914-23; Lecturer in Literature to the Oxford University Extension Delegacy since 1917. *Publications:* The Cultural Side of Education; various sermons and articles. *Recreation:* golf. *Address:* Leigh Woods Vicarage, Clifton, Bristol. *T.:* 33337. [*Died* 25 *Dec.* 1951.

YEARSLEY, (Percival) Macleod, F.R.C.S., F.Z.S.; Aural Surgeon to Gerrards Cross Hosp.; late Deputy Head Warden and Divisional Surgeon A.R.P.; late Consulting Aural Surgeon to St. James's Hospital, Balham, and L.C.C.; Senior Surgeon to Royal Ear Hospital; Consulting Aural Surgeon to Royal School for Deaf and Dumb, etc.; *s.* of Stephen Yearsley and Jeanna Bowring Chittenden; *m.* Florence Louise, *d.* of late C. M. Cooper, M.D.; one *s.* *Educ.:* Merchant Taylors' School; the Westminster and London Hospitals; Major National Reserve; Hon. Major; was Major (2nd in Command) London Army Troops Comps., Royal Engineers (Vols.). *Publications:* Nursing in Diseases of the Throat, Nose and Ear; Text-book of Diseases of the Ear, 1908; Throat and Ear Troubles (3rd edition), 1915; Electro-phonoïd Method of Zünd-Burguet, 1927; Otosclerosis, 1933; Translation of Forel's Sensations des Insectes, and Moure's Du Malmenage de la Voix, Zünd-Burguet's Conduction Sonore; The Story of the Bible, 1922; A Fairy Tale of the Sea, 1923; The Folklore of Fairy-Tale, 1924; The Sanity of Hamlet, 1933; Doctors in Elizabethan Drama, 1933; Le Roy est Mort, 1935. *Recreations:* science and archæology. *Address:* Winscombe, Ethorpe Close, Gerrards Cross. *T.:* 3291. [*Died* 4 *May* 1951.

YEATS, Jack Butler, R.H.A.; LL.D. (Hon.) Dublin; D.Litt. (Hon.) National University of Ireland; Officier de la Légion d'Honneur; Irish Painter; Governor and Guardian National Gallery of Ireland; *y. s.* of late J. B. Yeats, R.H.A., and Susan Pollexfen; *m.* Mary Cottenham White (*d.* 1947). *Educ.:* privately in Sligo. Represented in Municipal Gallery, Dublin, Cork, Waterford and Limerick Municipal Galleries, Tate Gallery, City of Birmingham Art Gall., Aberdeen Art Gall.; Museum of Art, Cleveland, O.; Toledo (U.S.A.) Museum of Art; Phillip's Gall., Washington; Mus. of Fine Arts, Boston, U.S.A.; Temple Newsam Gall., Leeds; Aberdeen; Tel-aviv Museum of Art; Contemporary Art Society; Musée National d'Art Moderne, Paris; Loan Exhibition of 34 paintings, National Gallery, 1942; National Loan Exhibition of 179 paintings, Dublin, 1945; Loan Exhibition of 19 paintings, Edinburgh, in Soc. of Scottish Artists' Annual Exhibition, shown with 7 paintings by father, late John Butler Yeats, R.H.A., 1946; Loan Exhibition of 80 paintings, Tate Gallery, 1948; Loan Exhibition of 36 paintings at: Inst. of Contemporary Art, Boston,

Phillips Gallery, Washington, D.C., De Young Memorial Museum, San Francisco, Colorado Springs Fine Art Center, Toronto Art Gallery, all 1951; Detroit Inst. of Fine Arts, National Gallery, New York 1952; Loan Exhibition of 39 Paintings, Galerie Beaux-Arts, Paris, 1954; 22 Paintings, Belfast, 1956. *Publications:* The Broadsheet, monthly, 1902-03; The Broadside, monthly, 1908-15; Life in the West of Ireland, 1912; Sligo, 1930; Sailing, Sailing Swiftly, 1933; Apparitions, 1933; The Amaranthers, 1936; The Charmed Life, 1938; Ah Well, 1942; La, La Noo, 1943; And to You Also, 1944; The Careless Flower, 1947; *plays:* Harlequin's Positions, produced Dublin, 1939; La, La Noo, Dublin, 1942; In Sand, Dublin, 1949, etc. *Address:* 18 Fitzwilliam Square, Dublin. *Clubs:* United Arts, University (Dublin). [*Died* 28 *March* 1957.

YELVERTON, Admiral Bentinck John Davies, C.B. 1916; *y. s.* of Rowland Davies and the Hon. Mrs. Bingham, Redinnick House, Cornwall; *g.s.* of Rev. F. C. Yelverton and Hon. Louisa, *d.* of 1st Baron Clanmorris; assumed name of Yelverton under will of gt.-aunt Hon. Anna Yelverton, Belleisle, Roscrea; *m.* Blanche Ada (*d.* 1953), *d.* of Charles Cole, Devonshire House Southsea. *Educ.:* H.M.S. Britannia. Bronze medal Royal Humane Society, 1886; 2nd Award Testimonial on parchment, 1895; Inspecting Captain of Mechanical Training Establishment, 1910-12; Rear-Adm. 1915; Vice-Adm. (retired), 1919; Adm. (ret.), 1924; served European War, 1914-18 (C.B.); Officer Legion of Honour, 1919. *Address:* Mead House, Great Bookham, Sy. *T.:* Bookham 77. *Club:* United Service. [*Died* 7 *Jan.* 1959.

YEN, W. W.; *b.* Shanghai, 1877. B.A. University of Virginia, 1900; Phi Beta Kappa, 1909; Professor of English, St. John's University, Shanghai; Doctor of Literature, Peking, 1906; Secretary, Chinese Legation, Washington, 1908; Hanlin Scholar, Junior Counsellor, Foreign Office, Peking, 1911; Vice-Minister Foreign Affairs, 1912; Minister to Germany, Sweden, and Denmark, 1913-20; Minister Foreign Affairs, 1920-22; Minister Agriculture and Commerce, Prime Minister, Minister Interior, 1924; ex-President Red Cross of China; President, China Int. Famine Relief Commission; Minister to U.S.A., 1931; 1st Delegate to Ord. and Extraord. Assemblies (Manchurian Conflict), Delegate on Council, Ambassador to Soviet Union, 1932-36; delegate to London Mon. and Econ. Conference; 1st class of all Chinese Orders, also Grand Cross of Dannebrog, Légion d'Honneur, Christ, Le Sol, Polar Star, Pius IX.; Mason. *Address:* 955 Chungcheng Road (Central), Shanghai. [*Died* 25 *May* 1950.
[*But death not notified in time for inclusion in Who Was Who* 1941–1950, *first edn.*

YEO, Rt. Rev. Monsignor Henry D.; Parish Priest, St. Mary's, The Mount, Walsall, since 1918; *b.* Tavistock, Devon, 1872; *s.* of Henry Dovell and Elizabeth Yeo. *Educ.:* Cotton College, North Staffs.; Oscott College, Birmingham. Ordained Priest (R.C.) 1897; Asst. Priest, Leamington, 1898-1909; Parish Priest, St. John's, Tamworth, 1909-18. Canon of St. Chad's Cathedral Chapter, Birmingham, 1934, Provost, 1943; Domestic Prelate to Pope Pius XII., 1947; Tamworth Board of Guardians, 1913-18; Walsall Board of Guardians, 1919-30; Walsall Public Asst. Cttee. (Chm.), 1929-30; Walsall Gen. Hosp. Cttee. (Vice-Chm.), 1922-48; Walsall Borough Council, 1926-30. *Recreations:* social work, especially hospital management; civic service. *Address:* The Mount, Walsall. *T.:* Walsall 2633. [*Died* 6 *Dec.* 1952.

YEOMAN, Rev. Alexander Ross, C.M.G. 1916; M.A.; D.D. (Edin.); *b.* 1874; *y. s.* of late A. R. Yeoman, M.A., late H.M. Inland Revenue; *m.* 1915, Margherita Agnew, 2nd *d.* of Rev. J. Agnew, Abbey Church, Dunbar. *Educ.:* King Edward VIth Grammar School, Louth; George Watson's College, Edinburgh. Studied Arts and Divinity, Edinburgh University, 1891-98; Jeffrey Scholar in Semitic Languages, 1898; Hon. Chaplain St. Giles' Cathedral, 1903; Army Interpreter in High Dutch and Cape Dutch, 1914; served European War, 1914-18 (wounded, despatches twice, C.M.G.); Deputy Assistant Principal Chaplain, 1917; Assistant Chaplain-General, Scottish Command, 1926-32; Deputy Chap.-General to the Forces, 1933-34; K.H.C. 1933-34; retired pay, 1934. *Recreation:* fishing. *Address:* c/o Glyn, Mills and Co., Whitehall, S.W.1. [*Died* 9 *Aug.* 1956.

YERKES, Robert Mearns; Psychobiologist; *b.* Breadysville, Pa., 26 May 1876; *s.* of Silas Marshall Yerkes and Susanna Addis Carrell; *m.* 1905, Ada Watterson, N.Y. City; one *s.* one *d.* *Educ.:* A.B. Ursinus College, 1897, A.B. Harvard, 1898, A.M. 1899, Ph.D. 1902; LL.D. Ursinus, 1923; D.Sc. Wesleyan, 1923; Hon. M.A. Yale, 1931. Began as teacher and investigator at Harvard, 1901; Assistant Professor Comparative Psychology, 1908-17; Psychologist to Psychopathic Hospital, Boston, 1913-17; Prof. Psychology and Director Psychological Laboratory, University of Minnesota, 1917-19 (absent on military duty, Chief of Div. of Psychology, Office of Surgeon-General, U.S. Army, 1917-18); Chairman, Research Information Service, National Research Council, 1919-24; Professor Psychology, Institute of Psychology, Yale University, 1924-29; organised and directed Yale Laboratories of Primate Biology, Orange Park, Fla. 1929-41; Professor, Psychobiology, Yale, 1929-44, emeritus since 1944. Consulting and committee services to War Dept. and National Research Council during War of 1939-45. *Publications:* The Dancing Mouse: A Study in Animal Behaviour, 1907; Introduction to Psychology, 1911; Methods of Studying Vision in Animals (with J. B. Watson), 1911; Outline of a Study of the Self (with D. W. La Rue), 1914; A Point Scale for Measuring Mental Ability (with J. W. Bridges and R. S. Hardwick), 1915; The Mental Life of Monkeys and Apes: A Study of Ideational Behavior, 1916; Psychological Examining in the U.S. Army (with others), 1921; Chimpanzee Intelligence and Its Vocal Expressions (with B. W. Learned), 1925; Almost Human, 1925; The Mind of a Gorilla, 1927-28; The Great Apes (with A. W. Yerkes), 1929; Chimpanzees: A Laboratory Colony, 1943; papers on physiology of the nervous system, etc. *Address:* 4 St. Ronan Ter., New Haven 11, Conn., U.S.A. *Club:* Cosmos (Washington, D.C.). [*Died* 3 *Feb.* 1956.

YETTS, W. Perceval, C.B.E. 1944 (O.B.E. 1919); D.Lit.; M.R.C.S. (Eng.); Prof. of Chinese Art and Archæology, London University, 1932-46, Professor Emeritus, 1946; *b.* 25 April 1878; *s.* of late A. M. Yetts; *m.* 1912, Gwendoline Mary, *d.* of late D. Hughes, F.R.C.S.; no *c.* *Educ.:* Bradfield; Lausanne; London. Entered Royal Naval Medical Service, 1903; Admiralty Gold Medallist for Naval Hygiene, 1904; retired as Staff Surgeon, 1912; Acting Medical Officer, British Legation, Peking, 1913; served in R.A.M.C. 1914-19, Major (temp.) and Deputy Assistant Director of Medical Services Embarkation (O.B.E.); Deputy Comr. of Medical Services, Ministry of Pensions, 1919-20; Medical Officer, Ministry of Health, 1920-27. Member of Executive Committee and Chairman of Selection Committee, International Exhibition of Chinese Art, 1935-36. Chairman of China Society, 1940-45. Hon. Vice-Pres. of Royal Asiatic Society. Hon. Member Oriental Ceramic Society. Triennial Gold Medal, Roy. Asiatic Soc. 1956. Order of Brilliant Star (China), 1947. *Publications:* Chinese Bronzes, 1925; Eumorfopoulos Collection Catalogue of the Chinese and Corean Bronzes, Sculpture, etc., 3 volumes, 1929-32; The Cull Chinese Bronzes, 1939; An-yang: A Retrospect, 1942; The Legend of Confucius, 1943; Memoir of L. C. Hopkins, 1954; The Three Dynasties, 1957; articles in various periodicals. *Recreation:* painting. *Address:* Aubrey Cottage, Long Park, Chesham Bois, Bucks. *T.:* Amersham 14. *Club:* United Service. [*Died* 14 *May* 1957.

YORKE, Brig.-General Ralph Maximilian, C.M.G. 1919; D.S.O. 1917; *y. s.* of late John Reginald Yorke, M.P., and 2nd wife, Sophia Matilda, *d.* of Baron Vincent de Tuyll de Serooskerken; *b.* 22 Oct. 1874; *m.* 1906, Hon. Muriel Fanny Herschell, *d.* of 1st Baron Herschell; two *d.* *Educ.:* Eton; R.M.C. Sandhurst. Late Captain 11th Hussars; Lt.-Col. Gloucestershire Yeomanry; served European War, 1914-18 (D.S.O., C.M.G.); Companion of the Orders of St. Maurice and Lazarre and Crown of Roumania. *Address:* Summerhill, Tenterden, Kent. *T.:* Tenterden 169. *Clubs:* Pratt's, Lansdowne. [*Died* 25 *Feb.* 1951.

YORKE, Robert Langdon; *b.* 2 Feb. 1887; 2nd *s.* of late James Charles Yorke, Langton, Dwrbach, Pembrokeshire; *m.* 1914, Enid Cicely Nugent, *d.* of late C. F. E. Meares of Bedford. *Educ.:* Haileybury Coll.; Lincoln College, Oxford. B.A. Oxford 1910; entered I.C.S., 1910; Judge, Chief Court of Oudh, 1938; Additional Judge, High Court, Allahabad, 1941; Puisne Judge, High Court of Judicature at Allahabad, U.P., India, 1943-1947; retired, 1947. *Recreation:* fishing. *Address:* Roseway, Woolton Hill, nr. Newbury. [*Died* 12 *June* 1954.

YORKE, Vincent Wodehouse, J.P. Glos.; M.A.; *b.* 21 May 1869; *s.* of J. R. Yorke; *m.* 1899, Hon. Maud Evelyn Wyndham, *d.* of 2nd Baron Leconfield; two *s.* *Educ.:* Eton (Newcastle Scholar, 1888); King's College, Cambridge (Scholar and Fellow). Late captain Royal Gloucester Hussars Yeomanry; formerly Chm. National Provident Institution. *Publications:* has contributed to Journal Royal Geographical Society, Journal of Hellenic Studies. *Recreations:* hunting and shooting. *Address:* Forthampton Court, Gloucester. *Club:* Oxford and Cambridge. [*Died* 27 *Nov.* 1957.

YOUNG, Hon. Sir Alexander; *see* Young, Hon. Sir J. A.

YOUNG, Major-General Charles Frederic Gordon; Indian Army; retired; *b.* 1859; *s.* of late Col. G. Gordon Young, I.A.; *m.* 1892, Agnes Hilda (*d.* 1934), *d.* of late G. L. Monck Gibbs; two *s.* two *d.* *Educ.:* St. Andrew's College, Bradfield; R.M.C., Sandhurst. 2nd Lieut. 99th Foot, 1878; Lieut. The Wilts Regiment, 1880; entered Bengal Staff Corps and joined 6th B.L.I. 1880; Capt. 1889; Major, 1898; Lt.-Col. 1904; Brevet Col. 1907; Col. on the Staff, 1911; Maj.-General, 1912; D.A.A.G. Meerut Dist. 1895-1900; Commanded 6th Jat L.I. 1904-11; Jhansi Brigade, 1911-13; Peshawar Infantry Brigade, 1913-15; Rangoon Brigade, 1915-19; served South Africa, 1878-79, with 99th Foot (medal and clasp); China, 1900-01, 6th Jat L.I. (medal). *Address:* St. Berins, Milford-on-Sea, Hants. [*Died* 17 *March* 1956.

YOUNG, Sir Cyril Roe Muston, 4th Bt., *cr.* 1821; *b.* 21 Aug. 1881; *s.* of Sir William Young, 3rd Bt., and Isabella, *d.* of John Leach, Exeter, and Black Torrington, Devon; *S.* father 1934; *m.* 1912, Gertrude Annie, *d.* of John Elliott, Braunton, N. Devon; three *s.* one *d.* Formerly with firm of Butterfield and Swire, merchants, of Shanghai. War of 1939-45, interned at Yangchow, Shanghai; liberated 1945. *Heir:* *s.* John William Roe, *b.* 28 June 1913. *Address:* 545 Middle Gap Rd., The Peak, Hong Kong. [*Died* 15 *June* 1955.

YOUNG, Ernest, B.Sc. (London); F.R.G.S.; late Assistant Secretary for Higher Education, Middlesex Education Committee; contested (independent Liberal) N. Hammersmith, 1918; joined the Middle Temple, 1915; passed the Final, Dec. 1916; formerly Inspector of Anglo-Vernacular Schools, Siam; Headmaster John Lyon School, Harrow, 1899; County School, Harrow, 1911; *b.* 1869; *m.* May Josephine (*d.* 1925), *y. d.* of late Edwin A. Norbury, R.C.A. *Publications:* The Kingdom of the Yellow Robe; A Class Book of Practical Geography; Adventures among Hunters and Trappers; A Peep at Siam; A Peep at Corsica; Finland, the Land of a Thousand Lakes, 1912; The New Era in Education, 1921; From Russia to Siam, 1914; How to Run a Troop, 1916; Kingsway Junior Readers in Geography, 1933; South American Excursion, 1939; North American Excursion, 1948; West of the Rockies, 1949; (with J. Fairgrieve) Human Geographies (Elementary Series), Books i.-vi., 1919; The World, 1921 (Secondary Series), Parts I.-III., 1922; The British Empire, 1924; The Gateways of Commerce, 1920; A Contour Exercise Book; Junior Contour Exercise Book, 1922; Human Geography, Grade by Grade (U.S.A. edition), 1924; The Imperial Commonwealth, 2 vols., 1931; The Human Geography of Pacific Lands, 1935; Real Geography, 1939; (with S. C. Gilmour) Life Overseas, Books I.-VI., 1931-35; (with P. R. Rayner) The Social Geographies, 1936. *Recreations:* photography, entertaining children. *Address:* (Monomark): BM/KPGW., London, W.C.1. *Clubs:* Savage, Royal Automobile. [*Died* 10 *Feb.* 1952.

YOUNG, Brig.-Gen. Ernest Douglas, C.B. 1923; C.M.G. 1918; *b.* 1872; *m.* 1903, Cecil Mary (*d.* 1936), *d.* of Maj.-Gen. E. D. Newbolt; Attached Egyptian Army, 1899-1909 (Order of Osmanieh); served European War, 1914-18 (despatches four times, Bt. Lt.-Col., C.M.G., Legion of Honour, Order of Redeemer of Greece, Greek Medal for Military Merit); Military Mission to Russia, 1919 (Order of St. Vladimir); Bt. Col. 1919; commanding 1st Bn. Devons, 1919-23; Ireland, 1920-21; A.Q.M.G. British Army of the Rhine, 1923-27; Brigadier in charge of Administration, Army of the Rhine, 1927-30; retired pay, 1929. *Address:* Sandhills, Reading Road, Fleet, Hants. [*Died* 20 *Feb.* 1957.

YOUNG, Miss Evelyn Lucy; First Head Mistress, Queen Ethelburga's School, Harrogate, 1911-50, retd.; *b.* 4 Jan. 1879; *d.* of Henry Savill Young and Rebecca Isabella Brewis. *Educ.:* Alice Ottley School, Worcester; Lady Margaret Hall, Oxford (Scholar). Assistant Mistress, Queen Margaret's School, Scarborough, 1906-11. *Address:* 98B Banbury Road, Oxford. *Club:* English-Speaking Union. [*Died* 10 *May* 1960.

YOUNG, Francis Brett, M.B.; (Hon.) D.Litt.; Major, late R.A.M.C.; novelist; *b.* 1884; *e. s.* of T. Brett Young, M.D., Hales Owen, Worcs.; *m.* 1908, Jessie Hankinson. *Educ.:* Epsom College; University of Birmingham (Sands Cox Scholar). *Publications:* Robert Bridges, A Critical Study, 1913; Undergrowth (with E. Brett Young), 1913; Deep Sea, 1914; The Dark Tower, 1914; The Iron Age, 1916; Five Degrees South—Poems, 1917; The Crescent Moon; Marching on Tanga, 1918; The Young Physician; Poems, 1919; The Tragic Bride, 1920; The Black Diamond, The Red Knight, 1921; Pilgrim's Rest, 1922; Woodsmoke, 1924; Cold Harbour, 1924; Sea Horses, 1925; Portrait of Clare, 1927 (awarded James Tait Black Memorial Prize); The Key of Life; My Brother Jonathan, 1928; Black Roses, 1929; Jim Redlake, 1930; Mr. and Mrs. Pennington, 1931; The House under the Water, 1932; The Cage Bird and Other Stories, 1933; This Little World, 1934; White Ladies, 1935; Far Forest, 1936; They Seek a Country; Portrait of a Village, 1937; Dr. Bradley Remembers, 1938; The City of Gold, 1939; Mr. Lucton's Freedom, 1940; Cotswold Honey, 1940; A Man about the House, 1942; The Island, 1944; In South Africa, 1952; *plays:* Captain Swing, 1919; The Furnace, 1928; *music:* Songs of Robert Bridges, 1912. *Address:* Montagu, Cape of Good Hope, S. Africa.

T.A.: Brett Young, Montagu, Cape, S.A. *Club:* Garrick. [*Died* 28 *March* 1954.

YOUNG, Frederick George Charles, C.B.E. 1943; I.S.O. 1936; late Asst. Secretary, Air Ministry; *b.* 1 Feb. 1877; *yr. s.* of Frederick Young; *m.* 1902, Amy Julia, *yr. d.* of Henry Purcell, Norwich; two *s.* one *d.* Admiralty, 1891-1918; Air Ministry, 1918-1944. Chairman, Miscellaneous Trades Joint Council for Government Industrial Establishments, 1939 - 44. *Address:* Bracondale, 8 Homesdale Rd., Orpington, Kent. *T.:* Orpington 24684. [*Died* 12 *March* 1955.

YOUNG, Geoffrey Winthrop, Hon. D.Litt.; F.R.S.L.; Chevalier Legion of Honour, etc.; *b.* 25 Oct. 1876; 2nd *s.* of Sir George Young, 3rd Baronet, of Formosa, and Dame Alice Eacy Young; *m.* 1918, Eleanor, *d.* of W. Cecil Slingsby, of Heversham; one *s.* one *d.* *Educ.:* Marlborough; Trinity College, Cambridge (M.A., Chancellor's Verse Medallist, 1898, 1899); Jena University; Geneva; France. Roy. Soc. Lit. Award for 1952. Assistant Master, Eton College, 1900-1905; one of H.M. Inspectors of Secondary Schools, 1905-13; Consultant for Europe to the Rockefeller Foundation, 1925-33; Reader in Comparative Education, University of London, 1932-41; Special War Correspondent, Belgium and France, July-Sept. 1914; commanding at the Front the Friends' Ambulance Unit, Oct. 1914 - July 1915 (Liaison Officer to the civil population for the VIII. French and the II. British Armies, responsible for the Ypres sector; organiser of Aide Civil Belge, etc.); commanding at the Front, and subsequently commanding the First British Ambulance Unit for Italy, Aug. 1915-Jan. 1919 (severely wounded at the Battle of Monte San Gabriele, despatches, Order of Leopold I. with swords, silver medal For Valour twice, Italian Red Cross silver medal of honour with palm, Legion of Honour, Belgian War Cross, Italian War Cross, Order of the Crown of Italy, Italian Decoration for the disabled, 1914 Star with rose, British Campaign medal with oak leaf, Victory medal, Italian Campaign medal with three stars). *Publications:* Collected Edition (Poems); From the Trenches (Louvain to the Aisne); Bolts from the Blues; Wall and Roof Climbing; Mountain Craft; On High Hills; Mountains with a Difference (W. H. Heinemann Prize, 1952); The Grace of Forgetting, etc.; (jointly) Snowdon Biography. *Recreations:* mountaineering, swimming. *Address:* Grovehurst, Horsmonden, Kent. *Clubs:* United University, Alpine. [*Died* 6 *Sept.* 1958.

YOUNG, Sir George, 4th Bt., *cr.* 1813; M.V.O. 1906; *b.* 25 Oct. 1872; *e. s.* of Sir George Young 3rd Bt., and Alice Eacy (*d.* 1922), *d.* of Evory Kennedy, M.D., Belgard, Co. Dublin; *S.* father, 1930; *m.* 1904, Jessie Helen (*d.* 1946), *d.* of Sir Courtenay Ilbert, G.C.B.; two *s.* two *d.*; *m.* 1948, Joan, *d.* of late Rev. Frank Bullock-Webster, Embassy Chaplain. *Educ.:* Eton, and universities in France, Germany, and Russia. Hon. Attaché, Washington, 1896; Attaché there, 1897; transferred to Athens, 1900; to Constantinople, 1901; to Madrid, 1904; to Belgrade as Chargé d'Affaires, 1906; and to Washington, 1906; Secretary to the North Atlantic Fisheries Arbitration at the Hague, 1910; National Health Insurance Commission, 1912-13; First Secretary at Lisbon, 1914; organised an Intelligence Section in the Admiralty, 1915; enlisted in H.A.C. March 1918, and obtained a commission in the R.M.A.; Daily News Correspondent, Berlin, Jan.-July 1919; Professor of Portuguese, 1919-22, and Examiner in Ottoman Law, London University; Visiting Professor in Political Science and International Law in American Universities; Labour candidate, South Bucks, 1923 and 1924, South Norfolk, 1929; Expert Delegate, Missions to Russia, 1920 and 1924. *Publications:* Corps de Droit Ottoman, 1904; Nationalism and War in the Balkans, 1914; Portugal, 1917; New Germany, 1920; Diplomacy, Old and New, 1921; Constantinople, 1925; Egypt, 1927; Freedom of the Seas, 1928; The Pendulum of Politics, 1930; Tales of Trespass, 1932; The New Spain, 1933; Poor Fred, 1937; Federalism and Freedom, 1942. *Heir: s.* George Peregrine, *q.v.* *Address:* The Grove, Sonning, Berks; Torremolinos, Malaga. [*Died* 26 *Sept.* 1952.

YOUNG, George Malcolm, C.B. 1917; Trustee of National Portrait Gallery since 1937; Member of Standing Commission on Museums and Galleries since 1938; Member of Historical MSS. Commission since 1948; Trustee British Museum, 1947-57; *b.* 1882; *s.* of G. F. Young. *Educ.:* St. Paul's School; Balliol College, Oxford. Fellow of All Souls. Hon. D.Litt. (Cantab., Durham); Hon. Fell. of Balliol. *Publications:* Gibbon, 1932; Origin of the West-Saxon Kingdom, 1934; Early Victorian England (edited), 1934; Charles I and Cromwell, 1932; Victorian England, 1936; Daylight and Champaign, 1937; Mr. Gladstone (Romanes Lecture, 1944); To-day and Yesterday, 1948; Last Essays, 1950; Stanley Baldwin (James Tait Black Memorial Book Prize), 1952. Edited (with W. D. Handcock): English Historical Documents, 1833-1874, 1957. *Club:* Athenæum. [*Died* 18 *Nov.* 1959.

YOUNG, Sir George (Peregrine), 5th Bt., *cr.* 1813; C.M.G. 1951; Minister at the British Embassy in Paris, since Nov. 1956; *b.* 8 Sept. 1908 at H.M. Embassy, U.S.A.; *s.* of Sir George Young, 4th Bart., M.V.O., and Jessie Helen (*d.* 1946), *d.* of Sir Courtenay Ilbert, G.C.B., K.C.S.I.; *S.* father 1952; *m.* 1939, Elisabeth (*d.* 1957), *er. d.* of Sir Hughe Knatchbull-Hugessen, K.C.M.G.; two *s.* one *d.* *Educ.:* Westminster (Schol.); Christ Church, Oxf. (Schol., Fell. of Queen's). Appointed as Third Secretary to Foreign Office, 1931; transferred to Berlin, 1933, and to Pekin, 1935; Second Secretary, 1937; transferred to Foreign Office, 1938; to Madrid, 1940; to F.O., 1941; 1st Sec., 1942; to Beirut, 1944; Counsellor, 1947; to Rio de Janeiro, 1947; to F.O., 1950; Minister, 1951; to Rome, 1952-1953; Assistant Secretary, Cabinet Office, 1953-55; to F.O., 1955; Head of Foreign Office News Department, 1955-56. Commander, Legion of Honour, 1957. *Heir: s.* George Samuel Knatchbull, *b.* 16 July 1941. *Address:* Formosa Fishery, Cookham, Berks. *T.:* Bourne End 1041. *Clubs:* St. James', Leander. [*Died* 17 *March* 1960.

YOUNG, Brig. Henry Ayerst, C.B.E. 1946; D.S.O. 1940; late Comdg. Woolwich Garrison and Comdt. the Royal Artillery Depôt; *b.* 28 Aug. 1895; *s.* of Col. E. W. Young, I.M.S., and Alexandra Jean Beatrice Clark; *m.* 1922, Winifred, *d.* of Lt.-Col. E. F. Villiers, C.M.G., D.S.O.; no *c.* *Educ.:* Cheltenham College; R.M.A., Woolwich. Commissioned, Sept. 1914; served European War, 1914-18, France, Egypt, Macedonia, Serbia, Palestine (despatches); War of 1939-45; retd. pay, 1946. *Recreations:* keen horseman; hunting and polo; paints in oils and water-colours. *Club:* Junior United Service. [*Died* 15 *May* 1952.

YOUNG, Brig.-General Henry George, C.I.E. 1921; D.S.O. 1917; D.L. Co. Antrim; *b.* 7 Mar. 1870; 3rd *s.* of Rt. Hon. John Young, Galgorm Castle, Co. Antrim; *m.* 1908, Adelaide Mary Glencairn, *d.* of Colin Campbell; one *s.* *Educ.:* Harrow; Sandhurst. Served in Royal Fusiliers, 1890-92; 10th Lancers (Hodson's Horse), 1892-1917; 22nd (Sam Browne's Cavalry), 1917-20; Brig.-Gen. 7th Cavalry Brigade, 1919-21; Chitral Campaign, 1895 (medal and clasp); N.W. Frontier Campaign, 1897-8 (clasp); South Africa, 1902 (medal and 2 clasps); Mesopotamia, 1916-21 (despatches five times, 2 medals, D.S.O., Croix de Guerre, C.I.E.); retired, 1921. Serjeant-at-Arms, Parliament of Northern Ireland, 1921-51.

Address: Skeffington Lodge, Antrim. *Club:* Ulster (Belfast). [*Died* 16 *Aug*. 1956.

YOUNG, Hon. Sir (James) Alexander, K.C.V.O., *cr.* 1935; late Supervising Director of Dental Department, Auckland Hospital; *b*. Auckland, 1875; *m.*; one *s*. two *d*. *Educ.:* Wellesley Street Public School, Auckland. Member House of Representatives, N.Z., 1911-35; Minister of Health, 1926-28 and 1931-35; Minister for Immigration, New Zealand, 1931-35; Minister for Internal Affairs, 1933-35; Minister for Employment, 1934-35. *Address:* 11 Valley Road, Auckland, New Zealand. [*Died* 18 *April* 1956.

YOUNG, James Barclay Murdoch, of Greenbank and Rogerton; M.C. and Bar, 1917; Q.C. (Scot.) 1947; Sheriff-Substitute of Renfrew and Argyll at Paisley since 1950; *b*. 9 Dec. 1897; 2nd *s*. of John George Kirkpatrick Young, Glendoune, Ayrshire. *Educ.:* Morrison's Academy; Wadham College, Oxford; University of Edinburgh. Served European War, 1914-18, Royal Berkshire Regiment, 1916-20; B.A. 1923; LL.B. 1925; admitted to the Faculty of Advocates, 1925; Treasurer of Faculty, 1938; Clerk of Faculty, 1938-47. War of 1939-45, Royal Artillery; commanded 104th H.A.A. and 64th L.A.A. Regiments R.A. (despatches). Chairman War Pensions (Special Review) Tribunals, 1948. King's Bodyguard for Scotland, 1946. *Recreations:* field sports. *Address:* Greenbank, Clarkston, Renfrewshire. *T.:* Newton Mearns 1999. *Clubs:* New (Edinburgh); Western (Glasgow); The Club (Paisley). [*Died* 12 *Dec*. 1957.

YOUNG, Patrick Charles, C.B.E. 1919; M.A.; Chevalier of the Legion of Honour; Director of the Chinese Engineering and Mining Company Ltd.; *b*. 22 Jan. 1880; *s*. of Peter Alexander Young, M.D., Edinburgh; *m*. 1908, Elizabeth Harvey, *d*. of Patrick Turnbull, C.A., Edinburgh; one *s*. (and two *s*. decd.) three *d*. *Educ.:* Edinburgh Acad.; Christ's Coll., Cambridge. Assistant Engineer, Caledonian Railway, 1902; Assistant Engineer, Public Works Department, India, 1903; Assistant Secretary, Railway Board, India, 1911; Officiating Secretary, 1914; Engineer-in-Chief, Nushki Extension Railway, with relative rank of Lieut.-Col., 1916; Deputy Chief Railway Construction Engineer, France; Lt.-Col., 1917; Assistant Inspector-General of Transportation, France; Colonel, 1918; General Manager, The Kailan Mining Administration, Tientsin, 1923-31; Chairman, British Municipal Council, Tientsin, 1921-31; Coal Commissioner for India, 1944. *Address:* The Moorings, Woodbridge, East Suffolk. [*Died* 18 *Aug*. 1951.

YOUNG, Sir Robert, Kt., *cr*. 1931; O.B.E. 1917; retired; *b*. 26 Jan. 1872; working-class parents; *m*. 1910, Bessie Laurina (*d*. 1950), *d*. of C. J. Choldcroft, Oxford; two *s*. one *d*. *Educ.:* Elementary Schools; Ruskin College, Oxford. In stationer's shop for 4½ years; worked in locomotive engineer's as apprentice and journeyman, 1888-1902; Ruskin College, 1903-05, as A.S.E. Student and College Lecturer to Trade Unions and Co-op. Societies on Higher Education for Working-men; Assistant General Secretary A.S.E., 1908-1913; General Secretary, 1913-19. M.P. (Lab); Newton, Lancashire, 1918-31, and935-510; Chairman of Ways and Means, and Deputy Speaker, 1924 and 1929-31; Temporary Chairman of Committees, House of Commons, since 1935; Member of Select Committee on National Expenditure; Chairman Select Committee on H. of C. Procedure, 1945-46. Independent Chairman Ophthalmic Benefit Approved Committee, 1937-48; Chairman Nat. Temperance Federation and of the Parliamentary Temperance group since 1935 and President, 1950. *Address:* 213 Barry Road, E. Dulwich, S.E.22. *T.:* Forest Hill 7182. [*Died* 13 *July* 1957.

YOUNG, Major-General Robert, C.B. 1919; C.M.G. 1916; D.S.O. 1915; *b*. Sunderland, 5 Jan. 1877; *s*. of late Rev. Robert Young; *m*. 1899, Florence, *d*. of S. Ward; five *s*. three *d*. *Educ.:* Nelson College, N.Z. Served European War, 1914-1918 (despatches, C.B., C.M.G., D.S.O., Officer Legion of Honour); Officer commanding Canterbury Military District, 1919-21; Col. Commandant New Zealand Staff Corps, and Officer Commanding Southern Command, 1921-25; Major-General, 1925; G.O.C. N.Z. Forces, 1925-31; retired, 1931; Commander New Zealand Home Guard, 1940-42; Director-General with rank of Brigadier, 1941-42; Inspector of Army Aerodrome Defences, 1942. *Address:* Tasman Beach, Otaki, N.Z. [*Died* 25 *Feb*. 1953.

YOUNG, Sir Robert Arthur, Kt., *cr*. 1947; C.B.E. 1922; M.D., B.Sc. Lond.; F.R.C.P. Lond.; F.S.A.; Hon. Freeman, Society of Apothecaries 1957; Consulting Physician Middlesex Hospital and Hospital for Consumption and Diseases of the Chest, Brompton; Physician to the London Life Association; late Hon. General Physician to the City of London Lying-in Hospital; Consulting Physician to St. Saviour's Hospital, and St. Luke's Hostel; Chairman of the Medical Committee of King Edward VII Sanatorium, Midhurst; Vice-Chm. Council Nat. Assoc. for the Prevention of Tuberculosis; late Chairman Board of Management, the Hospitals for Diseases of the Chest; *b*. 6 Nov. 1871; *m*. Fanny Caroline Phoebe (*d*. 1944), *d*. of late R. M. Kennedy, I.C.S.; one *s*. *Educ.:* United Westminster Schools; King's College and Middlesex Hospital, London. University Scholar in Physiology at B.Sc.; qualified for gold medal in M.D.; Entrance Scholar, Murray Scholar and Medallist at Middlesex Hospital Medical School; formerly House Physician to Middlesex Hospital and Brompton Hospital; Lecturer on Physiology and Pharmacology; Pathologist and Curator of Museum, Middlesex Hospital, and Warden of the College; Examiner in Medicine, Physiology, Materia Medica, and Pharmacy to the Conjoint Board of the Royal Colleges of Physicians and Surgeons; Physician City of London Red Cross Hospital; External Examiner in Pharmacology and Materia Medica, University of Birmingham and University of Bristol; Lettsomian Lecturer, Orator and President Medical Society of London; late Senior Censor, Harveian Orator and Lumleian Lecturer, Royal College of Physicians. *Publications:* editor and translator of Brass's Atlas of Histology; part author, Diseases of the Respiratory System in Price's Text Book of Medicine; author of various papers in scientific and medical journals. *Address:* 22 Down Street, W.1. *T.:* Langham 1467. *Club:* Savage. [*Died* 22 *Aug*. 1959.

YOUNG, Robert Fitzgibbon; *e. s*. of late R. M. Young, M.R.I.A., M.A., J.P., of Rathvarna, Belfast, and *g.s*. of late Rt. Hon. Robert Young, P.C.; *m*. 1917, Pauline Ida, *y. d*. of late Benson Clough; one *s*. one *d*. (and *yr. s*. killed on military service, 1946). *Educ.:* Trinity College, Oxford First Class Litt. Hum., 1902; M.A., 1906; Universities of Jena and Berlin, 1903-04. Lecturer on History and Political Science at Leeds University, 1906-07; Examiner under Ministry of Education, 1908; Lieut. R.N.V.R.; Secretary to the British Diplomatic Mission to Czechoslovakia, Dec. 1918-June 1919; Sec. to the Consultative Committee of the Ministry of Education, 1920-39; D.Phil. Masaryk Univ. of Brno (Brünn), 1936; For. Mem. Roy. Bohemian Soc. of Sciences: Corresp. Mem. of Šafárik Soc. of Bratislava. *Publications:* Chapter on the Teschen Question in Vol. IV, of A History of the Peace Conference of Paris, 1921; A Bohemian Philosopher at Oxford in the 17th century, George Ritschel of Deutsch kahn (1616-1683), 1925; A Czech Humanist in

London in the 17th century, Jan Sictor Rokycansky (1583-1652), 1926; A Bohemian Scholar at Heidelberg and Oxford in the 16th century, Jan Bernart of Přerov (1553-1600), 1928; Comenius and the Indians of New England, 1929; Chapter (with K. Veleminsky) on Education in Czechoslovakia in The Education Yearbook, 1932; Comenius in England, 1932; various articles in English and Czech periodicals; Historical Introductions for the following Reports of the Consultative Committee of Ministry of Education; Differentiation of Curriculum for Boys and Girls in Secondary Schools, 1923; The Education of the Adolescent, 1926 (The Hadow Report); Books in Public Elementary Schools, 1928; The Primary School, 1931; Infant and Nursery Schools, 1933; Secondary Education, 1939 (The Spens Report). *Address:* Westwind, Fitzroy Park, Highgate Village, N.6. *Club:* Athenæum. [*Died* 17 *July* 1960.

YOUNG, Sir William, K.B.E., *cr.* 1935; C.B. 1924; *b.* 1875; *s.* of late David Young, of Castlewellan, Ireland; *m.* 1912, Edith Marguerite Matravers; two *s.* one *d.* Asst. Secretary, Customs and Excise, 1911-18; Asst. Secretary, Treasury, 1919-20; Commissioner of Customs and Excise, 1921-36 (Deputy Chairman from 1933); retired 1936. *Address:* 18 St. Margaret's, Rottingdean, Sussex. *T.:* 2933. [*Died* 25 *Aug.* 1957.

YOUNG, William Arthur; journalist; *b.* 26 July 1867; *m.* 1895, Frances Mary Bellairs, Newborough, Northants; two *s.* two *d.* *Educ.:* private schools, Cambridge. Apprenticed in Cambridge to the hardware and engineering trades; turned over to technical and commercial journalism; joined staff of The Ironmonger, 1900; editor, 1925-34; founder member of the Newcomen Society, President, 1938-39. *Publications:* The Silver and Sheffield Plate Collector; papers in the Transactions of the Newcomen Society. *Address:* 61 Colchester Road, Halstead, Essex.
[*Died* 13 *Jan.* 1955.

YOUNG, William Arthur, M.B., B.S., B.Sc., D.T.M.&.H., M.R.C.S., L.R.C.P., F.R.Soc.Med., F.R.IP.H., etc.; *b.* Blackheath, 18 Apr. 1890; 2nd *s.* of Henry Reginald Young, Blackheath, and Fenchurch Street, E.C. *Educ.:* Colfe; University College, London; Guy's Hospital Medical School (Entrance Scholarship in Arts); Golding-Bird Gold Medal in Bacteriology. Served European War, 1914-19; Officer in Charge of Mobile Bacteriological Laboratory, B.E.F.; Director of Pathological Dept., Royal Herbert Hospital, Woolwich; served War of 1939-45, 1941-45, R.W.A.F.F. and R.A.M. College, Millbank, S.W.1; Major, R.A.M.C.; Medical Research Council Student in Tuberculosis; Pathologist to St. John's Hosp. for Diseases of the Skin, the Roy. Chest Hosp., the Grosvenor Hosp., London; late Acting Principal, King Edward VII. Coll. of Medicine; and Sec., S.S. and F.M.S. Medical Council, etc.; Rockefeller Professor of Bacteriology, College of Medicine, Singapore; late Dir. of Med. Laboratories, W. Australia. *Publications:* late Editor, Malayan Medical Journal; various articles in Medical and Scientific Journals. *Recreation:* motoring. *Address:* c/o Glyn, Mills & Co., Whitehall, S.W.1. *Club:* Moor Park Golf.
[*Died* 3 *April* 1955.

YOUNG-JAMIESON, Vice-Adm. (retd.) Douglas, C.B. 1949; *b.* 12 October 1893; *s.* of Lt.-Col. H. J. Young-Jamieson and Mary Rashleigh; *m.* 1922, Joan Bridgman Willyams; one *s.* (and one *s.* decd.). *Educ.:* Royal Naval Colleges Osborne and Dartmouth. Royal Navy. As Capt. commanded: H.M.S. Kent, 1939-41, China and East Indies and Mediterranean: H.M.S. Devonshire, 1942-43, Eastern Fleet. Commodore Levant, 1943-44; Commodore Red Sea and Canal Area, 1944-45; Commodore R.N. Barracks, Devonport, 1946-47. Head of British Naval Mission, Greece, 1948-1949; President Admiralty Selection Board for Officers, 1949; Vice-Adm. retd. 1950. *Recreations:* shooting, fishing. *Address:* Barn Park, Bodmin, Cornwall. *T.:* Bodmin 148. *Club:* United Service.
[*Died* 28 *May* 1955.

YOUNGER, Brigadier Arthur Allan Shakespear, D.S.O. 1918; late Royal Artillery; *b.* 3 June 1881; *m.* 1918, Marjorie Rhoda, *d.* of Mr. and Mrs. Halliley, Burnham, Somerset; two *s.* *Educ.:* Wellington College. Served European War, 1914-18 (despatches, D.S.O.); Commander 27th (London) Air Defence Brigade T.A., 1931-35; Commander 1st Anti-Aircraft Group, 1935-38; retired pay, 1938. War Office and Ministry of Supply (Rocket Experimental), 1938-42; Ministry of Information, 1944-45. *Address:* Little Close, Bradfield, Berks. *Club:* National Book League.
[*Died* 5 *Sept.* 1960.

YOUNGER, Harry George; Chairman of Wm. Younger & Co. Ltd.; *b.* 1866; *s.* of Henry Younger of Benmore; *m.* 1st, 1890, Annette Emily Berkeley Farmar (*d.* 1922); one *s.* one *d.*; 2nd, 1922, Maud (*d.* 1934), *d.* of late John Kirk, W.S. *Educ.:* Winchester. Contested (U.) East Edinburgh, 1895 and 1899. *Address:* Belhaven House, Dunbar. *Clubs:* Bath; University (Edinburgh). [*Died* 29 *June* 1951.

YOUNGER, Rev. William; an Ex-President of Methodist Conference; *b.* Morpeth, 1869; *s.* of William and Isabella Younger; *m.* 1898, Agnes Ruth Dixon; two *s.* *Educ.:* Shankhouse, Northumberland; Hartley Victoria College, Manchester. Began ministry in 1894 in Middlesbrough; later in Bishop Auckland, 5 years; Harrogate, 11 years, Newcastle on Tyne, 13 years; Methodist Minister, Hull, 1930-39; President of ex-Primitive Methodist Conference, 1932; Presided, Albert Hall, 1932 at inaugural Assembly in Union of Wesleyan, Primitive Methodist and United Methodist Churches in what is now the Methodist Church; President of Methodist Church, 1934; Delegate of Methodist Ecumenical Conferences; Preacher and Lecturer in Free Churches of England, Wales, Ireland, Scotland, United States and Canada; travelled extensively. *Publications:* The International Value of Christian Ethics, 1924; numerous articles in magazines and newspapers. *Recreations:* light reading, including sports news and gardening. *Address:* 45 Sea Road, Westgate-on-Sea, Kent. *T.:* Thanet 317641.
[*Died* 15 *Feb.* 1956.

YPRES, 2nd Earl of, *cr.* 1922; Viscount, *cr.* 1916; of Ypres and of High Lake; **John Richard Lowndes French;** Capt. late R.A.; *b.* 6 July 1881; *e. s.* of 1st Earl and Eleanora, *d.* of R. W. Selby-Lowndes of Elmers, Bletchley; *S.* father, 1925; *m.* 1st, 1916, Olivia Mary (*d.* 1934), *d.* of late Maj.-Gen. Thomas John; one *s.* one *d.*; 2nd, 1941, Violet, *o. d.* of late Col. J. L. Irvine, C.B., R.E. Served European War, 1915-17. *Heir:* *s.* Viscount French. *Address:* The Old Court House, Hampton Court. *T.:* Molesey 1310. [*Died* 5 *April* 1958.

YULE, George Udny, C.B.E. 1918; F.R.S. 1921; M.A.; formerly University Lecturer and Reader in Statistics, Cambridge, 1912-31; Fellow of St. John's Coll.; *b.* 1871; *o. s.* of late Sir George Udny Yule, K.C.S.I., C.B. *Educ.:* Winchester; Univ. College, London. Demonstrator, 1894-96, and Assistant-Professor of Applied Mathematics, 1896-99, Fellow, 1926, University College, London; Assistant in Department of Technology, City and Guilds of London Institute, 1899-1912; Newmarch Lecturer in Statistics, University College, 1902-9; Guy (gold) Medallist (1911), and Honorary Vice-President (Past President) of the Royal Statistical Society of London; Fellow and sometime Member of F.R.A.I. and its Council; Pilot's Certificate A, Nov. 1931. *Publications:* An Introduction to the Theory of Statistics, 1911 (14th ed. rewritten, with M. G. Kendall, 1950); The Statistical Study of Literary Vocabulary, 1944; numerous papers on statistics and statistical method. *Address:* St. John's College, Cambridge. *Club:* Savile. [*Died* 26 *June* 1951.

Z

ZACHAREWITSCH, Michael; solo violinist; *b.* Ostrow, Russia, 26 Aug. 1878; naturalised British, 1915. *Educ.:* Petrograd; Moscow. Studied under Sevcik in Prague and under Ysaye in Brussels. Made *début* at age of twelve under the direction of Tschaikowsky; has played in four Continents and almost every big capital in Europe; 1948-49, 1st performance on any London platform of Paganini's 24 caprices in their entirety with piano accompaniment (in three recitals), 1952 (in one recital); evolved The Crowning of the Violin (to glorify great composers, 1685-1950), first performance, London, 1950. Vice-President of the Modern Symphony Orchestra, 1951. *Publications:* many violin solos; The New Art of Violin Playing with a standardised fingering and application of the Chromatic Scale, 1934; The New Century Violin Scale, 1938; A Formula for one finger Formations covering 36 Scale Keys; Violin Concerto, Dunkirk—1940 (Epic of Britain), 1945; The Ladder to Paganini's Profound Mastery, 1951. Secrets of Violin Playing (by Paganini), 1952. *Recreations:* fishing, shooting, and reading. *Address:* 118 Greencroft Gardens, N.W.6. *T.:* Maida Vale 7036. [*Died* 20 *Dec.* 1953.

ZANZIBAR, Sultan of, H.H. Seyyid Khalifa-bin-Harub-bin-Thuwaini bin-Said, Hon. G.C.B. 1956; Hon. G.C.M.G. 1936 (K.C.M.G. 1914); Hon. G.B.E. 1935 (K.B.E. 1919); Coronation Medals, 1911, 1937, 1953; *b.* Muscat, 1879; *S.* 1911; *m.*; one *s.*, Prince Abdullah, Seyyid Abdullah bin Khalifa, Hon. K.B.E. 1959; Hon. C.M.G. 1936. Came to Zanzibar, 1893; pilgrimageto Mecca, 1902; attended King George V's Coronation Ceremony, London, 1911; visited London, 1929, as the guest of His Majesty's Government; attended Coronations of King George VI, 1937, Queen Elizabeth II, 1953. *Recreation:* sailing. *Address:* The Palace, Zanzibar, East Africa. *Club:* (Hon. Mem.) Royal Yacht Squadron. [*Died* 9 *Oct.* 1960.

ZIMMERN, Sir Alfred, Kt., *cr.* 1936; *b.* Surbiton, 1879; *s.* of Adolf and Matilda Zimmern; *m.* 1921, Lucie, *d.* of late Pastor Maurice Hirsch and Olympe Flotron de Coetlogon. *Educ.:* Winchester; New College, Oxford. Lecturer in Ancient History, New College, 1903; Fellow and Tutor, 1904-9; Univ. Sec. of Joint Committee on Oxford and Working-Class Education, 1907-08; Staff Inspector, Board of Education, 1912-15; Political Intelligence Department, Foreign Office, 1918-19; Wilson Professor of International Politics, University College of Wales, Aberystwyth, 1919-21; Acting Professor of Political Science, Cornell University, U.S.A., 1922-23; Deputy Director, League of Nations Institute of Intellectual Co-operation, Paris, 1926-30; Montague Burton Prof. of International Relations, Oxford University, 1930-44; Deputy-Director, Research Dept., Foreign Office, 1943-45; Adviser Information and External Relations, Ministry of Education, 1945; Sec.-Gen. Constituent Conf. of U.N.E.S.C.O., 1945; Exec. Sec., later Adviser, U.N.E.S.C.O. Preparatory Commission, 1946; Director Greater Hartford Council for U.N.E.S.C.O., 1950. Director, Geneva School of International Studies, 1925-1939. Visiting Prof., Trinity Coll., Hartford, Conn., U.S.A., 1947-49. Hon. LL.D. Aberdeen, Hon. D.Litt. Bristol, Hon. Litt.D. Melbourne; D.Litt. Trinity Coll., Hartford, Conn. *Publications:* Henry Grattan, 1902; translator of Ferrero's Greatness and Decline of Rome, vols. i. and ii., 1907; The Greek Commonwealth, 1911; edited and contributed to The War and Democracy, 1914; Nationality and Government, with other War-time Essays, 1918; Europe in Convalescence, 1922; The Third British Empire, 1926; Learning and Leadership, 1926; Solon and Crœsus, and other Greek Essays, 1928; The Prospects of Democracy and other Essays, 1929; The League of Nations, and the Rule of Law, 1918-35, 1936; Spiritual Values and World-Affairs, 1939; ed. Modern Political Doctrines, 1939; The American Road to World Peace, 1953. *Address:* Country Club Road, Avon, Connecticut, U.S.A. *Club:* Athenæum. [*Died* 24 *Nov.* 1957.

ZULUETA, Francis de; Regius Professor of Civil Law, Oxford, 1919-48, Emeritus since 1948; Hon. Doctor (Paris); Hon. LL.D. (Aberdeen); Fellow (for.) Accademia dei Lincei; Fellow All Souls College, 1919-48; Sub-warden, 1934-36; of Lincoln's Inn; Barrister-at-law; *b.* 1878; *s.* of Señor Don Pedro de Zulueta, sometime first Secretary of the Spanish Embassy in London, and Laura Mary, *d.* of Sir Justin Sheil, K.C.B.; *m.* 1915, Marie Louise, 2nd *d.* of late Henry Alexander Lyne Stephens; one *s.* *Educ.:* Beaumont College; the Oratory School; New College, Oxford (Scholar); First classes in Classical Moderations, Lit. Hum. and Jurisprudence; Fellow of Merton College, 1902-7, Hon. Fellow, 1937; Vinerian Scholar, 1903. Called to the Bar, 1904; Fellow and Tutor of New College, 1907; Sub-warden of New College, 1914; Lieut. 12th Batt. Worcestershire Regiment, 1914; Captain, 1916; All Souls Reader in Roman Law, 1912-1917. *Publications:* Patronage in the Later Empire; The Liber Pauperum of Vacarius; The Roman Law of Sale; Institutes of Gaius. *Address:* 85 Cadogan Gdns., S.W.3. *T.:* Kensington 2731. [*Died* 16 *Jan.* 1958.

ZWEMER, Rev. Samuel Marinus, D.D., F.R.G.S., M.R.A.S., LL.D., Litt.D.; Hon. Phi Beta Kappa; Editor-Emeritus The Moslem World; Professor-Emeritus of Missions and the History of Religion at the Theological Seminary, Princeton, New Jersey; *b.* 1867; *s.* of Adrian Zwemer and Katharina Boon, Dutch-French ancestry; *m.* 1st, 1895, Amy E. Wilkes (*d.* 1937), Bagdad; one *s.* three *d.*; 2nd, 1940, Margaret Clarke (*d.* 1950). *Educ.:* Hope Coll., Holland, Mich.; Theological Seminary, New Brunswick, N.J. Missionary in Arabia, 1890-1912; in Egypt, 1913-1929; crossed Oman Peninsula; visited Sana'a in Yaman, 1892 and 1894; visited chief Moslem Centres, China, 1917 and 1933; Organiser and Chairman, 1st and 2nd General Missionary Conferences on Islam, Cairo and Lucknow. *Publications:* Arabia, the Cradle of Islam, 1902; Topsy Turvy Land, 1902; Raymund Lull, 1904; Moslem Doctrine of God, 1906; Islam, a Challenge to Faith; The Moslem World; The Unoccupied Mission Fields, 1910; The Moslem Christ, 1912; Zigzag Journeys in the Camel Country, 1912; Childhood in the Moslem World. 1915; Mohammed or Christ, 1915; Influence of Animism on Islam, 1920; Christianity the Final Religion, 1920; Al Ghazali, a Moslem Mystic, 1920; The Call to Prayer, 1923; The Law of Apostacy in Islam, 1924; Moslem Women, 1926; The Glory of the Cross, 1928; Across the World of Islam, 1928; Thinking Missions with Christ, 1934; Origin of Religion, 1935; Taking Hold of God, 1936; It is hard to be a Christian; The Solitary Throne, 1937; The Golden Milestone, 1938; Dynamic Christianity, 1939; Studies in Popular Islam, 1939; Glory of the Manger, 1940; The Art of Listening to God, 1941; The Cross above the Crescent, 1941; Into All the World, 1943; Evangelism: Message not Method, 1944; Heirs of the Prophets—The Moslem Clergy, 1945; The Glory of the Empty Tomb, 1946; Survey of the Moslem World, 1946; How Rich the Harvest; Sons of Adam, 1950. *Address:* 156 Fifth Avenue, New York City, U.S.A.; 33 Fifth Avenue, New York City. [*Died* 2 *April* 1952.